Harrison's
PRINCIPLES
OF INTERNAL
MEDICINE

EDITORS OF PREVIOUS EDITIONS

T. R. Harrison, Editor-in-Chief, Editions 1, 2, 3, 4, 5

W. R. Resnik, Editor, Editions 1, 2, 3, 4, 5

M. M. Wintrobe, Editor, Editions 1, 2, 3, 4, 5
      Editor-in-Chief, Editions 6, 7

G. W. Thorn, Editor, Editions 1, 2, 3, 4, 5, 6, 7
      Editor-in-Chief, Edition 8

R. D. Adams, Editor, Editions 2, 3, 4, 5, 6, 7, 8, 9, 10

P. B. Beeson, Editor, Editions 1, 2

I. L. Bennett, Jr., Editor, Editions 3, 4, 5, 6

E. Braunwald, Editor, Editions 6, 7, 8, 9, 10

K. J. Isselbacher, Editor, Editions 6, 7, 8, 10
      Editor-in-Chief, Edition 9

R. G. Petersdorf, Editor, Editions 6, 7, 8, 9
      Editor-in-Chief, Edition 10

J. D. Wilson, Editor, Editions 9, 10

J. B. Martin, Editor, Edition 10

Harrison's
PRINCIPLES OF INTERNAL MEDICINE
Eleventh Edition

Editors

EUGENE BRAUNWALD, A.B., M.D., M.A. (Hon.), M.D. (Hon.)   Hersey Professor of the Theory and Practice of Physic and Herrman Ludwig Blumgart Professor of Medicine, Harvard Medical School; Chairman, Department of Medicine, Brigham and Women's and Beth Israel Hospitals, Boston

KURT J. ISSELBACHER, A.B., M.D. Mallinckrodt Professor of Medicine, Harvard Medical School; Physician and Chief, Gastrointestinal Unit, Massachusetts General Hospital, Boston

ROBERT G. PETERSDORF, A.B., M.D., M.A. (Hon.), D.Sc. (Hon.), M.D. (Hon.), L.H.D. (Hon.) Professor of Medicine, Dean and Vice Chancellor, Health Sciences, University of California School of Medicine, San Diego, La Jolla

JEAN D. WILSON, M.D. Professor of Internal Medicine, The University of Texas Southwestern Medical School, Dallas

JOSEPH B. MARTIN, M.D., Ph.D., F.R.C.P.(C), M.A. (Hon.)   Julieanne Dorn Professor of Neurology, Harvard Medical School; Chief, Neurology Service, Massachusetts General Hospital, Boston

ANTHONY S. FAUCI, M.D. Chief, Laboratory of Immunoregulation and Director, National Institute of Allergy and Infectious Diseases, National Institutes of Health, Bethesda

McGRAW-HILL BOOK COMPANY   *New York   St. Louis   San Francisco   Auckland   Bogotá Hamburg   Johannesburg   London   Madrid   Mexico Milan   Montreal   New Delhi   Panama   Paris   São Paulo Singapore   Sydney   Tokyo   Toronto*

Harrison's
Principles of Internal Medicine

1 2 3 4 5 6 7 8 9 0   DOW DOW   8 9 8 7 6

Foreign Editions
FRENCH (Eleventh Edition)—Flammarion, © 1988 (est.)
GERMAN (Tenth Edition)—Schwabe and Company, Ltd., © 1986
GREEK (Tenth Edition)—Parissianos, © 1986
ITALIAN (Eleventh Edition)—McGraw-Hill Libri Italia S.r.l. © 1987 (est.)
JAPANESE (Tenth Edition)—Hirokawa, © 1985
PORTUGUESE (Eleventh Edition)—Editora Guanabara Koogan, S.A., © 1987 (est.)
SPANISH (Tenth Edition)—Libros McGraw-Hill de Mexico, S.A., © 1986

This book was set in Times Roman by Monotype Composition Company.
The editors were J. Dereck Jeffers, Eileen J. Scott, and Mariapaz Ramos-Englis
The indexer was Philip James; the production supervisor was Ave McCracken; the cover was designed by Edward R. Schultheis
R. R. Donnelley & Sons Company was printer and binder.

Library of Congress Cataloging-in-Publication Data

Principles of internal medicine.
  Harrison's principles of internal medicine.

  Also issued in 2 v.
  Includes bibliographies and index.
  1. Internal medicine. I. Harrison, Tinsley Randolph, Date. II. Braunwald, Eugene, Date. III. Title. [DNLM: 1. Internal Medicine. WB 115 P957]
RC46.P895 1987   616   86-14383
ISBN 0-07-007261-2 (1-vol. ed.)
ISBN 0-07-079454-5 (2-vol. ed. : set)

A salute to George W. Thorn by the editors of Harrison's

George W. Thorn, one of the founding editors of *Harrison's* and Editor-in-Chief of the eighth edition, has enjoyed a long association with this book. He has had an enormous impact on the book and thereby on the education of countless thousands of physicians and medical students. His incisiveness, inventiveness, and originality, coupled with his broad knowledge of clinical medicine and medical science and his unswerving dedication to the application of techniques of contemporary science to the advance of clinical medicine, have played a vital role in the basic organization of this textbook. Thorn has always championed the view that students, residents, and practicing physicians require more of a textbook of medicine than discussions of clinical disorders, but that their understanding of and ability to deal with patients is enhanced by a detailed appreciation of how the sciences fundamental to medicine affect the clinical process.

George Thorn began his remarkable career in endocrinologic research as a medical student at the University of Buffalo School of Medicine. Following a stint in general practice, which subsequently served him well as an educator, clinical investigator, and consultant, he obtained research training and held faculty positions at several institutions. He became Harvard's eighth Hersey Professor of Medicine and the Brigham's third Physician-in-Chief at the age of 36. During the three decades in which he filled these positions with distinction he created a model academic medical unit. During the 1950s and 1960s, the halcyon years of post-World War II academic medicine, the education of the physician-scientist, the highest standard of clinical care, and the conduct of exciting clinical research on his service were inextricably intertwined and mutually reinforcing. Thorn's personal investigative interests focused on the adrenal cortex and the kidney. He developed techniques for the diagnosis of adrenal disease which are still in wide use today. He characterized salt-losing nephritis and catalyzed the development of renal dialysis and the work that led to the development of renal transplantation.

George Thorn has played many leadership roles in medicine and medical science. As a member of the governing board of the Massachusetts Institute of Technology (MIT) he was instrumental in the development of the Harvard-MIT program in Health Science and Technology. Under his leadership the Howard Hughes Medical Institute has become a major force in the conduct of the fundamental and clinical research which is certain to improve the care of patients in the twenty-first century.

George Thorn has influenced most profoundly a number of institutions—Harvard, the Brigham, MIT, and the Hughes Institute. To these, and to *Harrison's*, he has brought a unique blend of ebullience, imagination, curiosity, personal leadership, good humor, optimism, warmth, and compassion, which has inspired generations of Harvard medical students, Brigham residents and research fellows, and colleagues. Therefore, the present editors are pleased to express their admiration and affection for this medical giant and beloved friend by dedicating this edition of *Harrison's* to George W. Thorn.

ABBREVIATED CONTENTS

CONTENTS

**PART SEVEN
DISORDERS OF THE GASTROINTESTINAL
SYSTEM**

**Section 1: Disorders of the
alimentary tract**

Section 2: Hepatobiliary disease

**Section 3: Disorders of the
pancreas**

**PART EIGHT
DISORDERS OF THE IMMUNE SYSTEM,
CONNECTIVE TISSUE, AND JOINTS**

**Section 1: Disorders of the
immune system**

LIST OF CONTRIBUTORS

RAYMOND D. ADAMS, B.A., M.A., M.D., M.A. (Hon.), D.Sc. (Hon.), M.D. (Hon.)
Bullard Professor of Neuropathology, Emeritus, Harvard Medical School; Consultant Neurologist and formerly Chief of Neurology Service, Massachusetts General Hospital; Emeritus Director, Eunice K. Shriver Research Center, Boston; Médicin Adjoint, L'Hôpital Cantonale de Lausanne, Lausanne

JOHN W. ADAMSON, M.D.
Professor of Medicine and Head, Division of Hematology, Department of Medicine, University of Washington School of Medicine, Seattle

ELLIOT ALPERT, M.D.
Professor of Medicine and Chief, Division of Gastroenterology, Baylor College of Medicine, Houston

JOSEPH S. ALPERT, M.D.
Professor of Medicine, University of Massachusetts Medical School; Director, Division of Cardiovascular Medicine, University of Massachusetts Medical Center, Worcester

ROBERT J. ANDERSON, M.D.
Associate Professor of Medicine, University of Colorado Health Sciences Center, Denver

JACK P. ANTEL, M.D.
Associate Professor of Neurology, University of Chicago Pritzker School of Medicine, Chicago

BARRY G. W. ARNASON, M.D.
Professor and Chairman, Department of Neurology, University of Chicago Pritzker School of Medicine, Chicago

PAUL M. ARNOW, M.D.
Associate Professor of Medicine, Section of Infectious Disease, University of Chicago Hospital and Clinics, Chicago

ARTHUR K. ASBURY, M.D.
Ruth Wagner Van Meter and J. Ray Van Meter Professor of Neurology, University of Pennsylvania School of Medicine and Hospital of the University of Pennsylvania, Philadelphia

K. FRANK AUSTEN, M.D.
Theodore B. Bayles Professor of Medicine, Harvard Medical School; Physician-in-Chief, Robert B. Brigham Division and Chairman, Department of Rheumatology and Immunology, Brigham and Women's Hospital, Boston

ROBERT AUSTRIAN, M.D., D.Sc. (Hon.)
John Herr Musser Professor and Chairman, Department of Research Medicine, University of Pennsylvania School of Medicine, Philadelphia

BERNARD M. BABIOR, M.D., Ph.D.
Head, Division of Biochemistry, Department of Basic and Clinical Research, Scripps Clinic and Research Foundation, La Jolla

JEFFREY P. BAKER, M.D., F.R.C.P. (C)
Assistant Professor of Medicine, University of Toronto; Consultant Staff Gastroenterologist, Toronto Western Hospital, Toronto

M. FLINT BEAL, M.D.
Assistant Professor, Harvard Medical School; Assistant Neurologist, Massachusetts General Hospital, Boston

HARRY N. BEATY, M.D.
Professor of Medicine and Dean, Northwestern University Medical School, Chicago

ARTHUR L. BEAUDET, M.D.
Investigator, Howard Hughes Medical Institute; Professor of Pediatrics and Cell Biology, Baylor College of Medicine, Houston

JOHN E. BENNETT, M.D.
Head, Clinical Mycology Section, National Institute of Allergy and Infectious Diseases, National Institutes of Health, Bethesda

JEFFREY D. BERNHARD, M.D.
Assistant Professor of Medicine, Director, Division of Dermatology, and Director of Phototherapy Center, Department of Medicine, University of Massachusetts Medical Center, Worcester

EDWIN L. BIERMAN, M.D.
Professor of Medicine and Chief, Division of Metabolism, Endocrinology, and Nutrition, University of Washington School of Medicine, Seattle

ALAN B. BISNO, M.D.
Professor of Medicine and Chief, Division of Infectious Diseases, University of Tennessee Center for the Health Sciences, Memphis

HENRY R. BOURNE, M.D.
Chairman, Department of Pharmacology, School of Medicine, University of California, San Francisco

WALTER G. BRADLEY, D.M., F.R.C.P.
Chairman and Professor of Neurology, University of Vermont College of Medicine; Chairman, Department of Neurology, University Health Center, Burlington

DAVID L. BRAFF, M.D.
Associate Professor, Department of Psychiatry, School of Medicine, University of California at San Diego; Director, Psychiatric Inpatient Services, U.C.S.D. Medical Center, San Diego

EUGENE BRAUNWALD, A.B., M.D., M.A. (Hon.), M.D. (Hon.)
Hersey Professor of the Theory and Practice of Physic and Herrman Ludwig Blumgart Professor of Medicine, Harvard Medical School; Chairman, Department of Medicine, Brigham and Women's and Beth Israel Hospitals, Boston

BARRY M. BRENNER, B.S., M.D., M.A. (Hon.)
Samuel A. Levine Professor of Medicine, Harvard Medical School; Senior Physician and Director, Renal Division, Brigham and Women's Hospital, Boston

KAREN THATCHER BRITTON, M.D., Ph.D.
Assistant Professor of Psychiatry, School of Medicine, University of California at San Diego, La Jolla

SAMUEL BRODER, M.D.
Associate Director, Clinical Oncology Program, Division of Cancer Treatment and Deputy Clinical Director, National Cancer Institute, National Institutes of Health, Bethesda

MICHAEL S. BROWN, M.D.
Paul J. Thomas Professor, Department of Molecular Genetics, The University of Texas Health Science Center, Dallas

H. FRANKLIN BUNN, M.D.
Professor of Medicine, Harvard Medical School; Senior Physician and Director, Hematology Research, Brigham and Women's Hospital; Investigator, Howard Hughes Medical Institute, Boston

JOHN R. BURTON, M.D.
Associate Professor of Medicine, Johns Hopkins University School of Medicine; Deputy Director of Department of Medicine, Director of Division of Geriatric Medicine, Francis Scott Key Medical Center, Baltimore

ALFRED E. BUXTON, M.D.
Assistant Professor of Medicine, University of Pennsylvania School of Medicine; Director, Cardiac Electrophysiology Laboratory, Hospital of the University of Pennsylvania, Philadelphia

CHARLES B. CARPENTER, M.D.
Professor of Medicine, Harvard Medical School; Senior Physician, Brigham and Women's Hospital, Boston

CHARLES C. J. CARPENTER, M.D.
Professor of Medicine, Brown University; Physician-in-Chief, The Miriam Hospital, Providence

BRUCE R. CARR, M.D.
Associate Professor, Department of Obstetrics and Gynecology and Cecil and Ida Green Center for Reproductive Biology Sciences, The University of Texas Health Science Center, Dallas

EDWIN CASSEM, M.D.
Associate Professor of Psychiatry, Harvard Medical School; Chief, Psychiatric Consultation–Liason Service, Massachusetts General Hospital, Boston

RICHARD CHAMPLIN, M.D.
Associate Professor of Medicine and Director, Leukemia/Bone Marrow Transplant Service, School of Medicine, University of California at Los Angeles

KEITH H. CHIAPPA, M.D.
Assistant Professor of Neurology, Harvard Medical School; Director, EEG and Evoked Potentials Unit of the Clinical Neurophysiology Laboratory and Department of Neurology, Massachusetts General Hospital, Boston

WALLACE A. CLYDE, Jr., M.D.
Professor of Pediatrics and Microbiology, University of North Carolina School of Medicine, Chapel Hill

FREDRIC L. COE, M.D.
Professor of Medicine and Physiology and Chief, Nephrology Program, University of Chicago Pritzker School of Medicine, Chicago

ALAN S. COHEN, M.D.
Chief of Medicine and Director, Thorndike Memorial Laboratory, Boston City Hospital; Conrad Wesselhoeft Professor of Medicine, Boston University School of Medicine, Boston

HARVEY R. COLTEN, M.D.
Professor and Chairman, Department of Pediatrics, Washington University School of Medicine, St. Louis

WILSON S. COLUCCI, M.D.
Assistant Professor of Medicine, Harvard Medical School; Associate Physician, Brigham and Women's Hospital, Boston

PATRICIA C. COME, M.D.
Assistant Professor of Medicine, Harvard Medical School; Director,

Noninvasive Cardiovascular Diagnostic Laboratory, Beth Israel Hospital, Boston

MAX D. COOPER, M.D.
Professor of Pediatrics and Microbiology, Cellular Immunobiology Unit, The University of Alabama in Birmingham, Birmingham

RICHARD A. COOPER, M.D.
Dean and Professor of Medicine, Medical College of Wisconsin, Milwaukee

LAWRENCE COREY, M.D.
Professor of Laboratory Medicine and Microbiology and Adjunct Professor of Medicine and Pediatrics, University of Washington School of Medicine, Seattle

RONALD G. CRYSTAL, M.D.
Chief, Pulmonary Branch, National Heart, Lung and Blood Institute, National Institutes of Health, Bethesda

JOHN J. CUSH, M.D.
Fellow in Rheumatology, Department of Internal Medicine, The University of Texas Health Science Center, Dallas

DAVID C. DALE, M.D.
Professor of Medicine and Dean, University of Washington School of Medicine, Seattle

JAMES E. DALEN, M.D.
Professor and Chairman, Department of Medicine, University of Massachusetts Medical School; Physician-in-Chief, University of Massachusetts Hospital, Worcester

THOMAS M. DANIEL, M.D.
Professor of Medicine, Case Western Reserve University School of Medicine; Physician, University Hospitals of Cleveland, Cleveland

GILBERT H. DANIELS, M.D.
Associate Professor of Medicine, Thyroid Unit, Massachusetts General Hospital, Boston

ROBERT B. DAROFF, M.D.
Gilbert W. Humphrey Professor and Chairman, Case Western Reserve University School of Medicine, Director, Department of Neurology, University Hospitals of Cleveland; Neurology Service, Cleveland Veterans Administration Medical Center, Cleveland

JOHN R. DAVID, M.D.
Professor of Medicine, Harvard Medical School; Chief, Division of Tropical Medicine, Robert B. Brigham Division of Brigham and Women's Hospital; John LaPorte Given Professor and Chairman, Department of Tropical Public Health, Harvard School of Public Health, Boston

G. ROBERT DeLONG, M.D.
Assistant Professor of Neurology, Harvard Medical School; Associate Neurologist and Associate Pediatrician, Massachusetts General Hospital, Boston

VINCENT T. DeVITA, Jr., M.D.
Director, National Cancer Institute, National Institutes of Health, Bethesda

MARC A. DICHTER, M.D., Ph.D.
Professor of Neurology, University of Pennsylvania School of Medicine, Philadelphia

JULES L. DIENSTAG, M.D.
Associate Professor of Medicine, Harvard Medical School; Assistant Physician, Massachusetts General Hospital, Boston

ROBERT G. DLUHY, M.D.
Associate Professor of Medicine, Harvard Medical School; Associate Program Director of the Clinical Research Center, Brigham and Women's Hospital, Boston

RAPHAEL DOLIN, M.D.
Professor of Medicine and Head, Infectious Diseases Unit, University of Rochester School of Medicine and Dentistry, Rochester

ANDREW G. ENGEL, M.D.
Professor of Neurology, Mayo Medical School; Department of Neurology, Mayo Clinic, Rochester

KENNETH H. FALCHUK, M.D.
Associate Professor of Medicine, Harvard Medical School; Brigham and Women's Hospital, Boston

ANTHONY S. FAUCI, M.D.
Chief, Laboratory of Immunoregulation and Director, National Institute of Allergy and Infectious Diseases, National Institutes of Health, Bethesda

MURRAY J. FAVUS, M.D.
Associate Professor of Medicine, University of Chicago Pritzker School of Medicine, Chicago

RALPH D. FEIGIN, M.D.
Professor and Chairman, Department of Pediatrics, Baylor College of Medicine; Physician-in-Chief, Texas Children's Hospital, Houston

BERNARD N. FIELDS, M.D.
Adele Lehman Professor and Chairman, Department of Microbiology and Molecular Genetics, Harvard Medical School; Professor of Medicine, Division of Infectious Diseases, Brigham and Women's Hospital, Boston

ALFRED P. FISHMAN, M.D.
William Maul Measey Professor of Medicine, University of Pennsylvania; Director, Cardiovascular-Pulmonary Division, Hospital of the University of Pennsylvania, Philadelphia

THOMAS B. FITZPATRICK, M.D., Ph.D.
Edward Wigglesworth Professor of Dermatology and Chairman, Department of Dermatology, Harvard Medical School; Chief, Dermatology Service, Massachusetts General Hospital, Boston

DANIEL W. FOSTER, M.D.
Professor of Internal Medicine, The University of Texas Health Science Center, Dallas

MICHAEL M. FRANK, M.D.
Chief, Laboratory of Clinical Investigation and Clinical Director, National Institute of Allergy and Infectious Diseases, National Institutes of Health, Bethesda

STANLEY D. FREEDMAN, M.D.
Head, Division of Infectious Diseases, Scripps Clinic and Research Foundation; Associate Clinical Professor of Medicine, University of California at San Diego, La Jolla

LAURENCE S. FRIEDMAN, M.D.
Assistant Professor of Medicine, Jefferson Medical College and Thomas Jefferson University Hospital, Philadelphia

PAUL A. FRIEDMAN, M.D.
Associate Professor of Medicine and Pharmacology, Harvard Medical School; Associate Physician, Beth Israel Hospital, Boston

WILLIAM F. FRIEDMAN, M.D.
J. H. Nicholson Professor of Pediatrics and Executive Chairman, Department of Pediatrics, Los Angeles Medical Center, University of California, Los Angeles

LAWRENCE A. FROHMAN, M.D.
Professor of Medicine, Director of Division of Endocrinology and Metabolism, University of Cincinnati College of Medicine, Cincinnati

JOHN I. GALLIN, M.D.
Scientific Director, National Institute of Allergy and Infectious Diseases, National Institutes of Health, Bethesda

ROBERT C. GALLO, M.D.
Chief, Laboratory of Tumor Cell Biology, Division of Cancer Treatment, National Cancer Institute, National Institutes of Health, Bethesda

PIERCE GARDNER, M.D.
Professor of Medicine and Pediatrics, University of Chicago Pritzker School of Medicine; Director, Infectious Diseases Training Program, University of Chicago Medical Center, Chicago

MARC B. GARNICK M.D.
Associate Professor of Medicine, Dana-Farber Cancer Institute, Harvard Medical School; Associate Physician, Brigham and Women's Hospital, Boston

JAMES L. GERMAN III, M.D.
Professor (Genetics), Department of Pediatrics, Cornell University Medical College; Senior Investigator and Director, Laboratory of Human Genetics, The New York Blood Center, New York

ELOISE R. GIBLETT, M.D.
Research Professor of Medicine, University of Washington School of Medicine; Executive Director, Puget Sound Blood Center, Seattle

BRUCE C. GILLILAND, M.D.
Professor of Medicine and Laboratory Medicine, University of Washington School of Medicine; Chief of Medicine, Pacific Medical Center, Seattle

J. CHRISTIAN GILLIN, M.D.
Professor of Psychiatry, University of California at San Diego, La Jolla

SID GILMAN, M.D.
Professor and Chairman, Department of Neurology, The University of Michigan Medical Center, Ann Arbor

RICHARD J. GLASSOCK, M.D.
Professor of Medicine, School of Medicine, University of California at Los Angeles; Chairman, Department of Medicine, Harbor-UCLA Medical Center, Torrance

ROBERT M. GLICKMAN, M.D.
Samuel Bard Professor of Medicine, Columbia University College of Physicians and Surgeons; Director, Medical Service, Presbyterian Hospital, New York

DAVID W. GOLDE, M.D.
Professor of Medicine and Chief, Division of Hematology/Oncology, School of Medicine, University of California at Los Angeles, Los Angeles

STEPHEN E. GOLDFINGER, M.D.
Associate Professor of Medicine and Associate Dean of Continuing Education, Harvard Medical School; Physician, Gastrointestinal Unit, Massachusetts General Hospital, Boston

PAUL GOLDHABER, D.D.S.
Dean and Professor of Periodontology, Harvard School of Dental Medicine, Boston

LEE GOLDMAN, M.D.
Associate Professor of Medicine, Harvard Medical School; Assistant Physician-in-Chief, Brigham and Women's Hospital, Boston

JOSEPH L. GOLDSTEIN, M.D.
Paul J. Thomas Professor and Chairman, Department of Molecular Genetics, The University of Texas Health Science Center, Dallas

RAJ K. GOYAL, M.D.
Rabb Professor of Medicine, Harvard Medical School; Chief, Division of Gastroenterology, Beth Israel Hospital, Boston

JOHN W. GRAEF, M.D.
Assistant Clinical Professor, Harvard Medical School; Director, The Lead/Toxicology Clinic, The Children's Hospital, Boston

IGOR GRANT, M.D.
Professor of Psychiatry, School of Medicine, University of California at San Diego, La Jolla

HARRY B. GREENBERG, M.D.
Associate Professor of Medicine, Department of Medicine, Stanford University Medical School; Palo Alto Veterans Administration Medical Center, Palo Alto

NORTON J. GREENBERGER, M.D.
Peter T. Bohan Professor and Chairman, Department of Medicine, University of Kansas School of Medicine, Kansas City

JAMES E. GRIFFIN III, M.D.
Associate Professor of Internal Medicine, The University of Texas Health Science Center, Dallas

ROBERT C. GRIGGS, M.D.
Professor of Neurology and Medicine, University of Rochester School of Medicine and Dentistry, University of Rochester Medical Center, Rochester

JOHN H. GROWDON, M.D.
Associate Professor of Neurology, Harvard Medical School; Associate Neurologist, Massachusetts General Hospital, Boston

RICHARD L. GUERRANT, M.D.
Professor of Medicine and Head, Division of Geographic Medicine, University of Virginia School of Medicine, Charlottesville

BEVRA HANNAHS HAHN, M.D.
Professor of Medicine and Chief of Rheumatology, University of California, Los Angeles

ROBERT I. HANDIN, M.D.
Associate Professor of Medicine, Harvard Medical School; Director, Hematology Division, Brigham and Women's Hospital, Boston

H. HUNTER HANDSFIELD, M.D.
Director, Sexually Transmitted Disease Control Program, Seattle-King County Department of Public Health; Associate Professor of Medicine, University of Washington School of Medicine, Seattle

JAMES P. HARNISCH, M.D.
Clinical Associate Professor of Medicine, University of Washington School of Medicine; Chief of Dermatology, Pacific Medical Center, Seattle

DONALD H. HARTER, M.D.
Benjamin and Virginia T. Boshes Professor of Neurology and Chairman, Department of Neurology, Northwestern University Medical School; Chairman, Department of Neurology, Northwestern Memorial Hospital, Chicago

BARTON F. HAYNES, M.D.
Associate Professor of Medicine and Assistant Professor of Microbiology and Immunology, Duke University School of Medicine, Durham

HARLEY A. HAYNES, M.D.
Associate Professor of Dermatology, Harvard Medical School; Director, Dermatology Division, Department of Medicine, Brigham and Women's Hospital; Chief, Dermatology, West Roxbury Veterans Administration Hospital, Boston

WILLIAM R. HAZZARD, M.D.
Professor and Chair, Department of Medicine, Bowman-Gray School of Medicine, Wake Forest University; Chief of Medicine, North Carolina Baptist Hospital, Winston-Salem

STEVEN C. HEBERT, M.D.
Assistant Professor of Medicine, Harvard Medical School; Associate Physician, Brigham and Women's Hospital, Boston

FRED J. HENDLER, M.D., Ph.D.
Assistant Professor of Internal Medicine, Division of Hematology/Oncology, The University of Texas Health Science Center, Dallas

JANE ELLEN HENNEY, M.D.
Associate Vice Chancellor and Associate Professor of Medicine, Division of Clinical Oncology, Department of Medicine, University of Kansas Medical Center, Kansas City

RAYMOND L. HINTZ, M.D.
Professor of Pediatrics and Head, Division of Pediatric Endocrinology, Stanford University School of Medicine, Stanford

MARTIN S. HIRSCH, M.D.
Associate Professor, Harvard Medical School; Associate Physician, Infectious Disease Unit, Massachusetts General Hospital, Boston

JAN V. HIRSCHMANN, M.D.
Assistant Chief, Medical Service, Seattle Veterans Administration Medical Center; Associate Professor of Medicine, University of Washington School of Medicine, Seattle

FRED HOCHBERG, M.D.
Associate Professor of Neurology, Harvard Medical School; Associate Neurologist, Massachusetts General Hospital, Boston

PAUL D. HOEPRICH, M.D.
Professor of Medicine and Chief, Section of Medical Mycology, Department of Internal Medicine, Division of Infectious and Immunologic Diseases, School of Medicine, University of California, Davis

JOHN H. HOLBROOK, M.D.
Associate Professor of Medicine, Division of General Internal Medicine, Department of Medicine, University of Utah Medical Center, Salt Lake City

MICHAEL F. HOLICK, M.D., Ph.D.
Professor of Physiology and Nutrition and Director of Vitamin D and Bone Metabolism Laboratory, U.S. Department of Agriculture/Human Nutrition Research Center, Tufts University, Boston

NORMAN K. HOLLENBERG, M.D.
Professor of Radiology, Harvard Medical School; Physician, Brigham and Women's Hospital, Boston

KING K. HOLMES, M.D., Ph.D.
Professor and Vice Chairman, Department of Medicine, University of Washington School of Medicine; Chief of Medicine, Harborview Medical Center, Seattle

THOMAS M. HOSTETTER, M.D.
Associate Professor of Medicine, University of Minnesota School of Medicine; Director, Division of Renal Diseases, University Hospital, Minneapolis

LEIGHTON Y. HUEY, M.D.
Associate Professor of Psychiatry, University of California at San Diego; Chief of Psychiatry Service, San Diego Veterans Administration Medical Center, San Diego

GARY W. HUNNINGHAKE, M.D.
Professor of Internal Medicine and Director, Pulmonary Division, University of Iowa College of Medicine, Iowa City

SIDNEY H. INGBAR, M.D., D.Sc.
William Bosworth Castle Professor of Medicine, Harvard Medical School; Director, Thorndike Laboratory, Beth Israel Hospital, Boston

ROLAND H. INGRAM, Jr., M.D.
Parker B. Francis Professor of Medicine, Harvard Medical School; Director, Respiratory Division, Brigham and Women's Hospital, Boston

KURT J. ISSELBACHER, A.B., M.D.
Mallinckrodt Professor of Medicine, Harvard Medical School; Physician and Chief, Gastrointestinal Unit, Massachusetts General Hospital, Boston

KHURSHEED N. JEEJEEBHOY, M.B.B.S., Ph.D., F.R.C.P. (Lond.), F.R.C.P. (Edin.), F.R.C.P. (C).
Professor of Medicine, University of Toronto; Director, Division of Gastroenterology, Toronto General Hospital, Toronto

MARK E. JOSEPHSON, M.D.
Professor of Medicine, University of Pennsylvania School of Medicine; Chief, Cardiovascular Section, Hospital of the University of Pennsylvania, Philadelphia

LEWIS L. JUDD, M.D.
Professor and Chairman, Department of Psychiatry, School of Medicine, University of California at San Diego, La Jolla

DENNIS L. KASPER, M.D.
Professor of Medicine, Harvard Medical School; Chief, Division of Infectious Diseases, Beth Israel Hospital; Associate Director, Channing Laboratory, Brigham and Women's Hospital, Boston

SATISH KATHPALIA, M.D.
Assistant Professor of Medicine, University of Chicago Pritzker School of Medicine; Attending Physician, Michael Reese Hospital and Medical Center, Chicago

DONALD KAYE, M.D., F.A.C.P.
Professor and Chairman, Department of Medicine, Medical College of Pennsylvania; Chief of Medicine, Hospital of the Medical College of Pennsylvania, Philadelphia

WILLIAM N. KELLEY, M.D.
John G. Searle Professor and Chairman, Department of Internal Medicine, University of Michigan Medical School, Ann Arbor

PHILIP KIRBY, M.D.
Instructor in Medicine, Division of Dermatology, University of Washington School of Medicine, Seattle

J. PHILLIP KISTLER, M.D.
Associate Professor of Neurology, Harvard Medical School; Associate Neurologist, Massachusetts General Hospital, Boston

RAYMOND S. KOFF, M.D.
Professor of Medicine, Boston University School of Medicine; Chief of Hepatology Section, Boston University Medical Center; Chief of Medicine, Framingham Union Hospital, Framingham

WILLIAM J. KOVACS, M.D.
Assistant Professor of Medicine, Division of Endocrinology, Vanderbilt University School of Medicine, Nashville

STEPHEN M. KRANE, M.D.
Professor of Medicine, Harvard Medical School; Physician and Chief, Arthritis Unit, Massachusetts General Hospital, Boston

J. THOMAS LaMONT, M.D.
Professor of Medicine, Boston University Medical Center; Chief, Gastrointestinal Section, University Hospital, Boston

LEWIS LANDSBERG, M.D.
Professor of Medicine, Harvard Medical School; Director, Division of Endocrinology and Metabolism, Beth Israel Hospital, Boston

H. CLIFFORD LANE, M.D.
Senior Investigator, Laboratory of Immunoregulation and Deputy Clinical Director, National Institute of Allergy and Infectious Diseases, National Institutes of Health, Bethesda

THOMAS J. LAWLEY, M.D.
Senior Investigator, Dermatology Branch, National Cancer Institute, National Institutes of Health, Bethesda

ALEXANDER R. LAWTON, M.D.
Professor of Pediatrics and Microbiology, Division of Pediatric Immunology, Vanderbilt University School of Medicine, Nashville

J. MICHAEL LAZARUS, M.D.
Associate Professor of Medicine, Harvard Medical School; Physician, Brigham and Women's Hospital, Boston

NORMAN G. LEVINSKY, M.D.
Wade Professor and Chairman, Division of Medicine, Boston University School of Medicine; Physician-in-Chief and Director, Evans Memorial Department of Clinical Research, University Hospital, Boston

PETER E. LIPSKY, M.D.
Professor of Internal Medicine and Microbiology and Chief, Division of Immunologic and Rheumatologic Diseases, Department of Internal Medicine; Director, Harold C. Simmons Arthritis Research Center, The University of Texas Health Science Center, Dallas

RICHARD M. LOCKSLEY, M.D.
Assistant Professor of Medicine, University of San Francisco; Chief of Infectious Diseases, University of San Francisco Medical Center, Moffitt-Long Hospital, San Francisco

DAN L. LONGO, M.D.
Associate Director, Biological Response Modifiers Program, Division of Biology and Diagnosis, National Cancer Institute-Frederick Cancer Research Facility, Frederick

FREDERICK H. LOVEJOY, Jr., M.D.
Associate Professor, Harvard Medical School; Associate Physician-in-Chief, The Children's Hospital; Director, Massachusetts Poison Control System, Boston

SHEILA A. LUKEHART, Ph.D.
Research Assistant Professor, Division of Infectious Diseases, University of Washington School of Medicine, Seattle

WALTER C. MacDONALD, M.D.
Chairman, GI Tumor Group, Cancer Control Agency of British Columbia, Vancouver

RAYMOND MACIEWICZ, M.D.
Assistant Professor of Neurology, Harvard Medical School; Assistant Neurologist, Massachusetts General Hospital, Boston

HENRY J. MANKIN, M.D.
Edith M. Ashley Professor of Orthopedic Surgery, Harvard Medical School; Chief, Orthopedic Services, Massachusetts General Hospital, Boston

FRANCIS E. MARCHLINSKI, M.D.
Assistant Professor of Medicine, University of Pennsylvania School of Medicine; Director, Arrhythmia Evaluation Center, Hospital of the University of Pennsylvania, Philadelphia

JOSEPH B. MARTIN, M.D., Ph.D., F.R.C.P. (C), M.A. (Hon.)
Julieanne Dorn Professor of Neurology, Harvard Medical School; Chief, Neurology Service, Massachusetts General Hospital, Boston

HENRY MASUR, M.D.
Deputy Chief, Critical Care Medicine, Clinical Center, National Institutes of Health, Bethesda

ROGER J. MAY, M.D.
Instructor in Medicine, Harvard Medical School; Assistant in Medicine, Beth Israel Hospital, Boston

E.R. McFADDEN, Jr., M.D.
Argyl J. Beams Professor of Medicine and Director, Asthma and Allergic Disease Center, Case Western Reserve University, Cleveland

JAMES E. McGUIGAN, M.D.
Chairman, Department of Medicine, University of Florida College of Medicine, Gainesville

RIMA McLEOD, M.D.
Associate Professor of Medicine, University of Chicago Pritzker School of Medicine; Attending Physician, Michael Reese Hospital and Medical Center, Chicago

MARK S. McPHEE, M.D.
Clinical Associate Professor of Medicine and Director, Gastrointestinal Endoscopy Unit, University of Kansas, Kansas City

NANCY K. MELLO, Ph.D.
Professor of Psychology, Department of Psychiatry, Harvard Medical School; Co-Director, Alcohol and Drug Abuse Research Center, McLean Hospital, Belmont

JERRY R. MENDELL, M.D.
Professor of Neurology, Ohio State University College of Medicine, Columbus

JOHN MENDELSOHN, M.D.
Chairman, Department of Medicine and Head, Division of Medical Oncology, Memorial Sloan-Kettering Cancer Center; Professor of Medicine, Cornell University Medical College, New York

JACK H. MENDELSON, M.D.
Professor of Psychiatry, Harvard Medical School; Co-Director, Alcohol and Drug Abuse Research Center, McLean Hospital, Belmont

URS A. MEYER, M.D.
Professor of Pharmacology and Chairman, Department of Pharmacology, Biocenter of the University of Basel, Basel, Switzerland

MARTIN C. MIHM, Jr., M.D.
Professor of Pathology, Harvard Medical School; Chief, Dermatopathology Unit, Massachusetts General Hospital, Boston

EDGAR L. MILFORD, M.D.
Assistant Professor of Medicine, Harvard Medical School; Associate Physician, Brigham and Women's Hospital, Boston

MYRON MILLER, M.D.
Professor of Medicine, State University of New York Upstate Medical Center; Chief of Gerontology, Veterans Administration Medical Center, Syracuse

RICHARD A. MILLER, M.D.
Assistant Professor of Medicine, University of Washington School of Medicine; Division of Infectious Diseases, Pacific Medical Center, Seattle

JOHN D. MINNA, M.D.
Chief, NCI-Navy Medical Oncology Branch, National Cancer Institute, National Institutes of Health; Professor of Medicine, Uniformed Services University for the Health Sciences, Naval Hospital, Bethesda

JAY P. MOHR, M.D.
Sciarra Professor of Clinical Neurology, College of Physicians and Surgeons of Columbia University Neurological Institute, New York

KENNETH M. MOSER, M.D.
Professor of Medicine, School of Medicine, University of California at San Diego; Director, Pulmonary and Critical Care Division, U.C.S.D. Medical Center, San Diego

ARNOLD M. MOSES, M.D.
Professor of Medicine and Director, Clinical Research Center, State University of New York Upstate Medical Center; Chief, Endocrinology Section, Veterans Administration Medical Center, Syracuse

DAVID B. MOSHER, M.D.
Clinical Instructor in Dermatology, Harvard Medical School; Assistant in Dermatology, Massachusetts General Hospital, Boston

HARALAMPOS M. MOUTSOPOULOS, M.D., F.A.C.P.
Professor and Head of Medicine, Medical School, University of Ioannina, Ioannina, Greece

FREDERICK M. MURPHY, M.D.
Fellow in Neonatology, Baylor School of Medicine, Houston

JOHN F. MURRAY, M.D., D.Sc. (Hon.)
Professor of Medicine, University of California at San Francisco; Chief, Chest Service, San Francisco General Hospital, San Francisco

ROBERT J. MYERBURG, M.D.
Professor of Medicine and Physiology and Director, Division of Cardiology, University of Miami Medical Center, Miami

THEODORE E. NASH, M.D.
Senior Scientist, Laboratory of Parasitic Diseases, National Institute of Allergy and Infectious Diseases, National Institutes of Health, Bethesda

PAUL NEIMAN, M.D.
Professor of Medicine, University of Washington School of Medicine; Member and Associate Director for Basic Sciences, Fred Hutchinson Cancer Research Center, Seattle

HAROLD C. NEU, M.D.
Professor of Medicine and Pharmacology and Chief, Division of Infectious Diseases, College of Physicians and Surgeons, Columbia University, New York

JOHN A. OATES, M.D.
Professor and Chairman, Department of Medicine, Vanderbilt University School of Medicine; Physician-in-Chief, Vanderbilt University Hospital, Nashville

JERROLD M. OLEFSKY, M.D.
Professor of Medicine and Head, Division of Endocrinology and Metabolism, School of Medicine, University of California at San Diego, La Jolla

ROBERT A. O'ROURKE, M.D.
Charles Conrad and Anna Sahm Brown Professor of Medicine, University of Texas; Director, Division of Cardiovascular Diseases, The University of Texas Health Science Center, San Antonio

THOMAS D. PALELLA, M.D.
Assistant Professor of Internal Medicine, Division of Rheumatology, University of Michigan Medical School, Ann Arbor

DARWIN L. PALMER, M.D.
Professor of Medicine and Chief, Division of Infectious Disease, University of New Mexico School of Medicine; Chief, Infectious Disease Section, Veterans Administration Medical Center, Albuquerque

JOHN A. PARRISH, M.D.
Professor of Dermatology, Harvard Medical School; Director, Wellman Research Laboratory, Massachusetts General Hospital, Boston

A. WILLIAM PASCULLE, D.Sc.
Associate Professor of Pathology, University of Pittsburgh School of Medicine; Associate Director of Microbiology, Presbyterian-University Hospital, Pittsburgh

RICHARD C. PASTERNAK, M.D.
Assistant Professor of Medicine, Harvard Medical School; Assistant Physician and Director, Coronary Care Unit, Beth Israel Hospital, Boston

MADHUKAR A. PATHAK, M.S., Ph.D.
Senior Associate in Dermatology, Harvard Medical School; Dermatology Service, Massachusetts General Hospital, Boston

RICHARD D. PEARSON, M.D.
Associate Professor of Medicine and Pathology, Division of Geographic Medicine, University of Virginia School of Medicine, Charlottesville

LAWRENCE L. PELLETIER, Jʀ., M.D.
Professor of Medicine, University of Kansas School of Medicine; Chief, Medical Service, Wichita Veterans Administration Medical Center, Wichita

PETER L. PERINE, M.D., M.P.H.
Professor and Director, Division of Tropical Public Health and Professor of Medicine, Uniformed Services University of the Health Sciences School of Medicine, Bethesda

ROBERT G. PETERSDORF, M.D., M.A. (Hon.), D.Sc. (Hon.), M.D. (Hon.), L.H.D. (Hon.)
Dean and Professor of Medicine and Vice Chancellor, Health Sciences, School of Medicine, University of California at San Diego, La Jolla

KIRK L. PETERSON, M.D.
Professor of Medicine, University of California at San Diego; Director, Cardiology Service, U.C.S.D. Medical Center, San Diego

JAMES J. PLORDE, M.D.
Professor, Departments of Medicine and Laboratory Medicine and Chief, Clinical Microbiology Laboratory, Veterans Administration Medical Center, Seattle

FRANCIS ALLAN PLUMMER, M.D., F.R.C.P. (C)
Assistant Professor, Departments of Medicine and Medical Microbiology and Division of Community Medicine, University of Manitoba, Winnipeg

DANIEL K. PODOLSKY, M.D.
Associate Professor of Medicine, Harvard Medical School; Assistant Physician, Gastrointestinal Unit, Massachusetts General Hospital, Boston

JOHN T. POTTS, Jʀ., M.D.
Jackson Professor of Clinical Medicine, Harvard Medical School; Chief of the General Medical Service, Massachusetts General Hospital, Boston

LAWRIE W. POWELL, M.D.
Professor of Medicine, University of Queensland; Physician, Royal Brisbane Hospital, Brisbane, Australia

DARWIN J. PROCKOP, M.D., Ph.D.
Professor and Chairman, Department of Biochemistry, Jefferson Medical College of Thomas Jefferson University; Director, Department of Biochemistry, Jefferson Institute of Molecular Medicine, Philadelphia

AMY PRUITT, M.D.
Assistant Professor of Neurology, Harvard Medical School; Associate Neurologist, Massachusetts General Hospital, Boston

PAUL G. RAMSEY, M.D.
Associate Professor of Medicine, Department of Medicine, University of Washington School of Medicine, Seattle

JOEL M. RAPPEPORT, M.D.
Associate Professor of Medicine, Harvard Medical School; Physician, Brigham and Women's Hospital, Boston

C. GEORGE RAY, M.D.
Professor of Pathology and Pediatrics and Chief, Clinical Virology-Serology and Pediatrics Infectious Diseases Sections, University of Arizona College of Medicine, Tucson

PETER REICH, M.D.
Professor of Psychiatry, Harvard Medical School; Chief of Psychiatry, Brigham and Women's Hospital, Boston

RICHARD C. REICHMAN, M.D.
Associate Professor of Medicine, Infectious Diseases Unit, University of Rochester School of Medicine and Dentistry, Rochester

JACK S. REMINGTON, M.D.
Chairman, Department of Immunology and Infectious Diseases, Research Institute, Palo Alto Medical Foundation; Professor of Medicine, Division of Infectious Diseases, Stanford University School of Medicine, Palo Alto

EDWARD P. RICHARDSON, JR., M.D.
Bullard Professor of Neuropathology, Harvard Medical School; Neurologist, Massachusetts General Hospital, Boston

HAL B. RICHERSON, M.D.
Professor of Internal Medicine and Director, Allergy-Immunology Division, University of Iowa College of Medicine, Iowa City

JAMES M. RICHTER, M.D.
Assistant Professor of Medicine, Harvard Medical School, Assistant Physician, Gastrointestinal Unit, Massachusetts General Hospital, Boston

CRAIG RISCH, M.D.
Associate Professor of Psychiatry, School of Medicine, University of California at San Diego, La Jolla

L. JACKSON ROBERTS II, M.D.
Associate Professor of Medicine, Pharmacology, and Clinical Pharmacology, Vanderbilt University School of Medicine, Nashville

R. PAUL ROBERTSON, M.D.
Professor of Medicine, Director of Clinical Research Center, and Director, Diabetes Center, University of Minnesota, Minneapolis

ALLAN R. RONALD, M.D.
H.F. Sellers Professor and Chairman, Department of Medicine, University of Manitoba; Physician-in-Chief, Department of Medicine, Health Sciences Centre, Winnipeg

RICHARD K. ROOT, M.D.
Professor and Chairman, Department of Medicine, University of California, San Francisco

ALLAN H. ROPPER, M.D.
Associate Professor of Neurology, Harvard Medical School; Director of Neurological/Neurosurgical Intensive Care Unit and Assistant Neurologist, Massachusetts General Hospital, Boston

LEON E. ROSENBERG, M.D.
Dean and C.N.H. Long Professor of Human Genetics, Medicine, and Pediatrics, Yale University School of Medicine, New Haven

MICHAEL ROSENBLATT, M.D.
Vice President for Biological Research, Merck, Sharp and Dohme Research Laboratories, West Point

JOHN ROSS, JR., M.D.
Professor of Medicine and Head, Division of Cardiology, School of Medicine, University of California at San Diego; Attending Physician, U.C.S.D. Medical Center, San Diego

ARTHUR H. RUBENSTEIN, M.D.
Professor and Chairman, Department of Medicine, University of Chicago Pritzker School of Medicine, Chicago

CYRUS E. RUBIN, M.D.
Professor of Medicine and Adjunct Professor of Pathology, Division of Gastroenterology, University of Washington School of Medicine, Seattle

DANIEL RUDMAN, M.D.
Chief, Geriatric Medicine Division and Chief of Staff, Veterans Administration Medical Center; Professor of Medicine, University Health Science Center, Chicago Medical School, Chicago

ARTHUR I. SAGALOWSKY, M.D.
Associate Professor of Urology and Surgical Director of Renal Transplantation, The University of Texas Health Science Center, Dallas

JAY P. SANFORD, M.D.
Professor of Medicine and Dean, F. Edward Hebert School of Medicine; President, Uniformed Services University of the Health Sciences, Bethesda

DENNIS R. SCHABERG, M.D.
Associate Professor of Medicine, University of Michigan, Ann Arbor

ANDREW I. SCHAFER, M.D.
Assistant Professor of Medicine, Harvard Medical School; Associate Physician, Brigham and Women's Hospital, Boston

I. HERBERT SCHEINBERG, M.D.
Professor of Medicine and Head, Division of Genetic Medicine, Albert Einstein College of Medicine; Attending Physician, Hospital of the Albert Einstein College of Medicine, New York

ALAN L. SCHILLER, M.D.
Associate Professor of Pathology, Harvard Medical School; Associate Pathologist and Chief, Autopsy Pathology and Bone Laboratory, Massachusetts General Hospital, Boston

RUDI SCHMID, M.D.
Professor of Medicine and Dean, School of Medicine, University of California, San Francisco

R. NEIL SCHIMKE, M.D.
Professor of Pediatrics and Internal Medicine and Director, Division of Metabolism, Endocrinology, and Genetics, The University of Kansas College of Health Sciences, Kansas City

ROBERT T. SCHOOLEY, M.D.
Assistant Professor of Medicine, Harvard Medical School; Massachusetts General Hospital, Boston

ROBERT W. SCHRIER, M.D.
Professor and Chairman, Department of Medicine, University of Colorado School of Medicine, Denver

MARC A. SCHUCKIT, M.D.
Professor of Psychiatry, School of Medicine, University of California at San Diego; Director, Alcohol Research Center, San Diego Veterans Administration Medical Center, San Diego

WILLIAM J. SCHWARTZ, M.D.
Assistant Professor of Neurology, Harvard Medical School; Assistant Neurologist, Massachusetts General Hospital, Boston

DAVID S. SEGAL, Ph.D.
Professor of Psychiatry, School of Medicine, University of California at San Diego, La Jolla

JULIAN L. SEIFTER, M.D.
Assistant Professor of Medicine, Harvard Medical School; Associate Physician, Brigham and Women's Hospital, Boston

ANDREW P. SELWYN, M.D.
Associate Professor of Medicine, Harvard Medical School; Director, Cardiac Catheterization Laboratory, Brigham and Women's Hospital, Boston

BHAGWAN T. SHAHANI, M.B., B.S.
Associate Professor of Neurology, Harvard Medical School; Associate Neurologist, Massachusetts General Hospital, Boston

GORDON C. SHARP, M.D.
Professor of Medicine and Pathology and Director, Division of Rheumatology, University of Missouri-Columbia School of Medicine, Columbia

ELIZABETH M. SHORT, M.D.
Director, Division of Biomedical Research and Faculty Development, American Association of Medical Colleges, Washington, DC

WILLIAM SILEN, M.D.
Johnson and Johnson Professor of Surgery, Harvard Medical School; Surgeon-in-Chief, Department of Surgery, Beth Israel Hospital, Boston

FRED E. SILVERSTEIN, M.D.
Associate Professor of Medicine, Division of Gastroenterology, University of Washington School of Medicine, Seattle

JAMES B. SNOW, Jr., M.D.
Professor and Chairman, Department of Otorhinolaryngology and Human Communication, University of Pennsylvania School of Medicine, Philadelphia

BURTON E. SOBEL, M.D.
Lewin Professor of Medicine, Washington University School of Medicine; Director, Cardiovascular Division, Barnes Hospital, St. Louis

ARTHUR J. SOBER, M.D.
Associate Professor of Dermatology, Harvard Medical School; Associate Dermatologist, Massachusetts General Hospital, Boston

FRANK E. SPEIZER, M.D.
Professor of Medicine, Harvard Medical School; Director, Occupational and Environmental Health Center, Brigham and Women's Hospital, Boston

JOHN W. STAKES, M.D.
Instructor in Neurology, Harvard Medical School; Assistant Neurologist, Massachusetts General Hospital, Boston

WALTER E. STAMM, M.D.
Professor of Medicine, University of Washington School of Medicine; Head, Division of Infectious Disease, Harborview Medical Center, Seattle

ALLEN C. STEERE, M.D.
Associate Professor of Medicine, Yale University School of Medicine, New Haven

KARI STEFANSSON, M.D.
Assistant Professor of Neurology and Pathology (Neuropathology), University of Chicago Pritzker School of Medicine, Chicago

GENE H. STOLLERMAN, M.D.
Professor of Medicine, Boston University School of Medicine; Attending Physician, University Hospital, Boston

D. E. STRANDNESS, Jr., M.D.
Professor of Surgery, University of Washington School of Medicine; University Hospital, Seattle

DAVID H. P. STREETEN, M.B., D. Phil, F.R.C.P.
Professor of Medicine and Head, Section of Endocrinology, State University of New York Upstate Medical Center, Syracuse

E. DONNALL THOMAS, M.D.
Professor, Department of Medicine, University of Washington School of Medicine; Associate Director for Clinical Programs, Fred Hutchinson Cancer Research Center, Seattle

GENNARO M. TISI, M.D.
Professor of Medicine, Pulmonary and Critical Care Division, School of Medicine, University of California at San Diego; U.C.S.D. Medical Center, San Diego

PHILLIP P. TOSKES, M.D.
Professor of Medicine and Director, Division of Gastroenterology, Hepatology, and Nutrition, University of Florida College of Medicine; Veterans Administration Medical Center, Gainesville

MARVIN TURCK, M.D.
Professor of Medicine and Associate Dean, University of Washington School of Medicine; Medical Director, Harborview Medical Center, Seattle

KENNETH L. TYLER, M.D.
Assistant Professor of Neurology, Harvard Medical School; Clinical Assistant in Neurology, Massachusetts General Hospital, Boston

JOHN E. ULTMANN, M.D.
Professor of Medicine, Department of Medicine; Director, University of Chicago, Cancer Research Center; Dean for Research and Development, Division of the Biological Sciences, University of Chicago Pritzker School of Medicine, Chicago

MAURICE VICTOR, M.D.
Professor of Neurology, Case Western Reserve University School of Medicine; Director, Neurology Service, Cleveland Metropolitan General Hospital, Cleveland

JAMES F. WALLACE, M.D.
Professor of Medicine, University of Washington School of Medicine; Associate Physician-in-Chief, University Hospital, Seattle

PATRICK C. WALSH, M.D.
David Hall McConnell Professor and Director, Department of Urology, The Johns Hopkins University School of Medicine; Urologist-in-Chief, James Buchanan Brady Urological Institute, The Johns Hopkins Hospital, Baltimore

PETER D. WALZER, M.D.
Associate Professor of Medicine, University of Cincinnati College of Medicine; Chief, Infectious Diseases Section, Cincinnati Veterans Administration Medical Center, Cincinnati

JACK R. WANDS, M.D.
Associate Professor of Medicine, Harvard Medical School; Associate Physician, Gastrointestinal Unit, Massachusetts General Hospital, Boston

LOUIS WEINSTEIN, M.D., Ph.D., Sc.D. (Hon.)
Lecturer in Medicine, Harvard Medical School; Senior Consultant in Medicine, Brigham and Women's Hospital, Boston

JOHN B. WEST, M.D., Ph.D., D.Sc., F.R.C.P., F.R.A.C.P.
Professor of Medicine and Physiology, School of Medicine, University of California at San Diego; Physician, U.C.S.D. Medical Center, San Diego

NICHOLAS J. WHITE, M.D., M.R.C.P
Tropical Medicine Unit, Nuffield Department of Clinical Medicine, Oxford University, England; Faculty of Tropical Medicine, Mahidol University, Bangkok, Thailand

RICHARD J. WHITLEY, M.D.
Professor of Pediatrics and Microbiology, School of Medicine, University of Alabama in Birmingham, Birmingham

GRANT R. WILKINSON, M.D.
Professor of Pharmacology, Vanderbilt University School of Medicine, Nashville

GORDON H. WILLIAMS, M.D.
Professor of Medicine, Harvard Medical School; Chief, Endocrinology-Hypertension Division, Brigham and Women's Hospital, Boston

JEAN D. WILSON, M.D.
Professor of Internal Medicine, The University of Texas Health Science Center, Dallas

SHELDON M. WOLFF, M.D.
Endicott Professor and Chairman, Department of Medicine, Tufts University School of Medicine; Physician-in-Chief, New England Medical Center, Boston

ALASTAIR J. J. WOOD, M.D., M.B., Ch.B., M.R.C.P.
Associate Professor of Medicine and Associate Professor of Pharmacology, Vanderbilt University School of Medicine; Attending Physician, Vanderbilt University Hospital, Nashville

THEODORE E. WOODWARD, B.S., M.D., D.Sc. (Hon.)
Professor of Medicine Emeritus, University of Maryland School of Medicine; Distinguished Physician; Veterans Administration Hospital, Baltimore

SHIRLEY H. WRAY, M.D., Ph.D., F.R.C.P.
Associate Professor of Neurology, Harvard Medical School; Director, Unit for Neurovisual Disorders, Department of Neurology, Massachusetts General Hospital, Boston

JOSHUA WYNNE, M.D.
Professor of Internal Medicine and Chief, Division of Cardiology, Wayne State University School of Medicine; Chief, Section of Cardiology, Harper-Grace Hospitals, Detroit

JAMES B. YOUNG, M.D.
Professor of Medicine, Harvard Medical School; Associate Physician, Beth Israel Hospital, Boston

ROBERT R. YOUNG, M.D.
Professor of Neurology, Harvard Medical School; Neurologist and Director, Clinical Neurophysiology Laboratory, Massachusetts General Hospital, Boston

PREFACE

In this, the eleventh edition of *Harrison's Principles of Internal Medicine,* the editors have attempted to incorporate the latest advances in the biology, pathophysiology, diagnosis, and treatment of disease. The objective has been to provide appropriate bridges between the basic sciences and clinical medicine and to emphasize those advances in biomedical research which are of clinical importance, while retaining those facts which, while not new, remain clinically useful.

In adherence to the principles of those who founded the book, Part One, "Cardinal Manifestations of Disease," remains a mainstay of this edition. Its 54 chapters form a comprehensive introduction to clinical medicine with an emphasis on the pathophysiology of disease and the mechanisms of symptoms. The chapters in Part Two, "Biologic Considerations in the Approach to Clinical Medicine," focus on disorders which usually affect multiple organ systems, including genetic diseases, immune disturbances, disorders of nutrition, neoplasia, and geriatric medicine. In this section the interface between the "new biology" and clinical medicine receives major emphasis. These multisystem disorders are then followed, in Part Three, by a predominantly etiologically oriented section on infections, while the diseases of the major organ systems are discussed in the remaining ten parts of the book.

The eleventh edition also pays close attention to updated and current references. Although space constraints require that references be kept to a modest number, the editors have made particular efforts to include papers that were published in 1984, 1985, and even 1986. Although this has required omission of some important older papers, these almost always appear in the bibliographies of the newer ones. The reverse is, of course, not the case and hence our effort to keep the references up-to-date.

Cognizant of the current requirements for continuing education for licensure and relicensure, as well as the emphasis on certification and recertification, a revision of the *PreTest Self-Assessment and Review* appears in conjunction with this edition. *PreTest Self-Assessment and Review* consists of several hundred questions based upon the textbook, along with answers and explanations for the answers.

The rapid developments in clinical medicine and in the basic sciences on which it rests have mandated more extensive changes in the preparation of this edition of *Harrison's* than of any other edition.

Although we cannot highlight in this short preface all of the new and extensively updated parts of the eleventh edition, we would like to call the reader's attention to several of these:

● A new chapter attempts to demonstrate how rigorous quantitative methods may be applied in clinical reasoning and decision making.

● The genetics section has been reorganized and expanded to emphasize the relevance of molecular genetics to medicine in general and of oncogenes to the understanding of neoplasia.

● The endocrinology and metabolism section contains new comprehensive chapters on neuroendocrine and anterior pituitary disease, on disorders of growth, and on hereditable disorders of connective tissue. The chapter on diabetes mellitus has been extensively revised to take into account advances in the nosology and etiology of the disease. The section on disorders of bone and mineral metabolism has been extensively revised and contains a new chapter on hypercalcemic and hypocalcemic disorders.

● The autonomic nervous system is recognized to play a key role in many disease states, and drugs which affect this system are of increasing importance in many areas of clinical medicine. The normal and abnormal physiology and the pharmacology of this system are discussed in an expanded chapter.

● In the area of infectious diseases, more than a third of the chapters are new. Among these, the following are of particular importance: The chapter on *infections in the compromised host* has been completely revised and includes the most current understanding of the mechanisms of host defenses and their relationship to protection from infectious disease. The significance of *skin rashes* in infections is covered both in the text and in the expanded color atlas. There is an extensive update on *antibiotics,* including agents that are still under investigation, but are likely to become available in the near future; there is a new chapter on *antiviral chemotherapy.* In view of the growing importance of *sexually transmitted diseases,* there is considerable expansion of these chapters. The section on *virology* has been entirely revamped, with particular emphasis on the molecular biology of viral diseases. The chapters on cytomegalovirus infection and Epstein-Barr virus infection include the most current understanding of the relationship of these infections to modulation of the immune system. The chapter on *Pneumocystis carinii pneumonia* has been revised, particularly with regard to the newly appreciated importance of this infection in patients with AIDS. New chapters on *schistosomiasis* and such new parasitic pathogens as *cryptosporidiosis* have been added. An extensive and up-to-date description of Lyme arthritis is provided.

● The major advances in cardiology that are emphasized in new or radically revised chapters include noninvasive methods of cardiac examination, electrophysiologic approaches to the diagnosis and treatment of cardiac arrhythmias, percutaneous transluminal angioplasty, and thrombolytic treatment of acute myocardial infarction.

● There has been considerable progress in understanding the pathogenesis and management of cystic fibrosis, hypersensitivity pneumonitis, and interstitial lung disease. The section on respiratory disease includes new chapters on these important disorders.

● Major revisions have been made in the gastrointestinal section with special emphasis on gastrointestinal endoscopy. New color plates of the appropriate endoscopic findings of various gastrointestinal disorders are included.

● The entire section on liver diseases has undergone major revision with a totally new chapter on viral as well as on drug-induced hepatitis, including the approach to the diagnosis of non-A, non-B hepatitis and the delta agent. Similarly, the important area of cirrhosis has also been revised. There is a new chapter on liver transplantation.

● The sections on disorders of the immune system and disorders of immune-mediated injury have been rewritten almost completely. These chapters now represent the most updated understanding of the relationship between aberrancies of immune function and immune-mediated diseases. Of particular note is the chapter on the acquired immunodeficiency syndrome which provides an in-depth understanding of all aspects of this syndrome. Also of note in this section is the much expanded chapter on the vasculitic syndromes. This chapter provides a coherent organization of these complex diseases and a better understanding of pathogenesis as well as the most modern approaches toward therapy.

● In the section on hematology there are new chapters on the anemias due to bone marrow failure and bone marrow transplantation. The chapters on platelets and blood coagulation are completely new with a new author for this important section. The chapter on enlargement of lymph nodes and spleen has been expanded to include a detailed description of the multiple mechanisms of lymph node and spleen enlargement, while the chapter on disorders of the phagocytic cells includes the most updated understanding of the metabolism of functional capabilities of phagocytic cells.

● The rapid advances in oncology are reflected in new chapters on the basic principles of neoplasia, carcinoma of the ovary and testis, the endocrine manifestations of neoplasia, and neurologic manifestations of neoplastic disorders. The chapter on the human T-lymphotropic virus is a comprehensive and authoritative treatise on the role of these important retroviruses in human diseases, an observation which has only recently been made and which has important potential implications in understanding the role of viruses in neoplastic as well as nonneoplastic diseases. The new chapter on the leukemias includes the modern classification of these important disorders.

• The neurology section, long a key component of *Harrison's*, has undergone substantial change. There are new chapters on acute and chronic pain, on dizziness and vertigo, ataxia and disorders of equilibrium and gait, the peripheral neuropathies, cerebrovascular diseases, and brain trauma. A radically revised chapter on the degenerative diseases of the nervous system with particular focus on Alzheimer's disease and Parkinson's disease brings the latest information about the neurochemistry, neuropathology, and management of these important disorders.

• The entire section on psychiatry has been rewritten and represents a major addition to this edition.

One of the strengths of *Harrison's* has been the close-knit relationships among the editors. Dr. Joseph Martin, the Julieanne Dorn Professor of Neurology at Harvard Medical School and Chief of the Neurological Services of the Massachusetts General Hospital, worked together with his distinguished predecessor, Dr. Raymond D. Adams on the tenth edition. With the latter's retirement from the textbook, Dr. Martin assumed sole editorial responsibility for the sections on neurology, myology, and psychiatry in the eleventh edition. He has been an important addition to the editorial group.

The editors warmly welcome Dr. Anthony S. Fauci, Director of the National Institute of Allergy and Infectious Diseases and Chief of its Laboratory of Immunoregulation, to *Harrison's*. Dr. Fauci is one of the leading clinical immunologists in the world. He has made a profound contribution to this edition with his expertise in this critically important area of biology and his ability to describe its impact on many areas of internal medicine.

We also wish to express our appreciation to our many associates and colleagues who, as experts in their fields, have helped us with constructive and valuable criticisms of the chapters in the eleventh edition. We wish to thank the following for many helpful suggestions: Drs. Stuart Aaronson, Raymond D. Adams, John W. Adamson, John F. Alksne, Ronald J. Anderson, Elliott M. Antman, Gust H. Bardy, Robert C. Bast, John E. Bennett, David Bilheimer, Harry G. Bluestein, Neil Breslau, Oscar L. Bronsther, Michael S. Brown, Robert H. Brown, George P. Canellos, Antonino Catanzaro, Bayard D. Catherwood, Bruce A. Chabner, Robert M. Chanock, Harold A. Chapman, Thomas N. Chase, William W. Chin, Mario Chojkier, Charles G. Cochrane, David I. Cohen, Steven E. Come, Rex William Cowdry, Clyde S. Crumpacker, Gilbert H. Daniels, Charles E. Davis, David M. Dawson, Leonard J. Deftos, Thomas L. Delbanco, Robert O. Dillman, Robert G. Dluhy, William P. Docken, Jeffrey M. Drazen, David M. Eddy, Leonard Ellman, Arthur S. Elstein, Darrell D. Fanestil, Alvan R. Feinstein, Mark Feldman, Joshua Fierer, Brian

G. Firth, Daniel W. Foster, Fred H. Frankel, Lawrence S. Friedman, Paul A. Friedman, Peter Friedman, Theodore Friedmann, Gary R. Fujimoto, Harris H. Funkenstein, Ary L. Goldberger, Joseph L. Goldstein, John L. Gollan, Harvey H. Gralnick, Mark R. Green, James E. Griffin, Robert C. Griggs, Richard H. Haas, Ivan R. Harwood, Fred Hendler, Martin S. Hirsch, Stephen B. Howell, Gary W. Hunninghake, Jon I. Isenberg, Stephen P. James, Kenneth Lee Jones, Lewis L. Judd, Albert Z. Kapikian, Dennis L. Kasper, Barrett Katz, Robert Katzman, Robert S. Kauffman, Martin J. Kelly, Anthony L. Komaroff, Conrad V. Kufta, Randi Y. Leavitt, Mark Leshin, Ronald Levy, Matthew H. Liang, Markku Linnoila, John D. Loeser, Kenneth Luskey, Paula Macrae, John A. Mannick, Lawrence F. Marshall, Henry Masur, J. Allen McCutchan, Henry F. McFarland, Dale E. McFarlin, George R. Merriam, Edgar L. Milford, Brian R. Murphy, James R. Nelson, Anne Nicholson-Weller, Michael R. Oxman, Charles Y. C. Pak, Alan G. Palestine, Sebastian Palmeri, Alfred F. Parisi, Joseph E. Parillo, Stephen G. Pauker, Alan S. Pearlman, James E. Pennington, Candace B. Pert, Marion Peters, Kirk L. Peterson, Willy F. Piessens, Richard Platt, Robert M. Post, William Z. Potter, Joe W. Ramsdell, Samuel I. Rapaport, Peter Reich, Michael Ronthal, Richard K. Root, Allan H. Ropper, Saul W. Rosen, David S. Rosenthal, John F. Rothrock, Daniel Rotrosen, John W. Rowe, John D. Rutherford, John E. Salvaggio, Martin A. Samuels, Stephen Scharfstein, Joseph D. Schmidt, Brian Schmitt, Edward L. Schneider, Lowell E. Schnipper, Peter H. Schur, John D. Schwankhaus, William J. Schwartz, Dennis J. Selkoe, Larry J. Shapiro, Clifford W. Shults, Cecelia M. Smith, Stephen A. Spector, Frank E. Speizer, Stephen E. Straus, Michael R. Swenson, Raymond Taetle, Ira B. Tager, Michael D. Tharp, David E. Trentham, Jerry S. Trier, H. Richard Tyler, Athol J. Ware, Steven E. Weinberger, Michael E. Weinblatt, Michael H. Weisman, Peter F. Weller, Alison Wichman, Robert F. Wilkens, Shirley H. Wray, Neal S. Young, Randall K. Young, Robert C. Young, Robert R. Young, and Elizabeth J. Ziegler.

This book could not have been edited without the dedicated help of our coworkers in the editorial offices of the individual editors. We are especially indebted to Patricia A. Clougherty, Patricia E. DeLosh, Lourdes C. Felix, Hilda Gardner, Brenda Hennis, Mary Jackson, Ann C. London, Lucy Renzi, Darlene Reynolds, Janice Stearns, and Michéle M. Stewart.

Finally, we need to say a word of thanks to our colleagues at McGraw-Hill, Dereck Jeffers, Executive Editor, and Eileen Scott, Development Editor. They formed a most effective team who gave the editors constant encouragement, and were of enormous help in the countless efforts involved in bringing this complex effort to fruition.

THE EDITORS

VOLUME 2

**PART FIVE
THROUGH
PART THIRTEEN**

COLOR ATLASES

Atlas 1   Atlas of common lesions encountered during the physical examination of the skin

The skin and mucous membrane may frequently contain a variety of lesions that are rarely a major complaint (see Fig. 47-1). They are, therefore, incidental findings in the general physical examination. The recognition of "bumps and blemishes" is a necessary first step for physicians inasmuch as they will be required to distinguish the trivial from the serious and important skin changes. For example, such a serious lesion as a malignant melanoma may be incidentally discovered during a routine physical examination (see Figs. A1-30 to A1-32 and the discussion in Chap. 302).

The common disorders of the skin that every physician should be able to recognize are presented in this series of color photographs (Figs. A1-1 to A1-23).

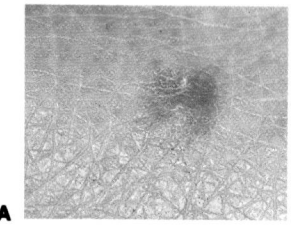 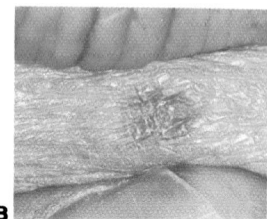

A   **B**

A1-1 **Dermatofibroma** is especially common in middle life and in women. The lesions, when pigmented, are occasionally confused with malignant melanoma. They appear as isolated, slightly elevated, hard, button-like nodules (*A*). In fair-skinned persons, the lesions are not usually skin color, but are pink or dark red, yellowish brown, or gray-black. They are usually less than 1 cm in diameter. A diagnostic sign is that a dermatofibroma dimples or becomes depressed (*B*) when it is laterally compressed; melanocytic nevus and melanoma, however, with which dermatofibroma may be easily confused, become elevated with lateral compression.

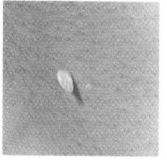

A1-2 **Acrochordon** (skin tag) is very common after middle life and appears on the neck, especially in women, in the axillae, and on the upper part of the trunk. The lesions are small (1 to 5 mm), soft, pedunculated papules, usually of normal skin color.

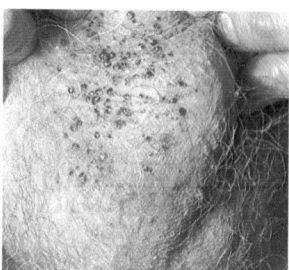

A1-3 **Angiokeratomas** are bizarre vascular dilatations that occur under the tongue and on the scrotum and consist of myriads of 2- to 3-mm purplish red papules. They are of no known significance. When they occur on the trunk and extremities, a biopsy is indicated to rule out glycolipid lipidosis or Fabry's disease.

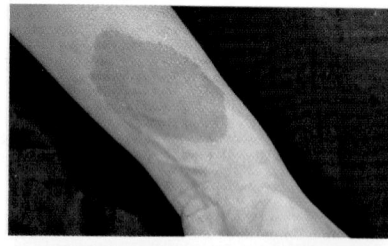

A1-4 **Café au lait macules** are found in about 10 percent of the normal population and, in fair-skinned persons, are light yellowish brown macules, which may also be markers of neurofibromatosis and polyostotic fibrous dysplasia (Albright's syndrome). The presence of six or more café au lait macules with a diameter of 1.5 cm or greater is diagnostic of neurofibromatosis.

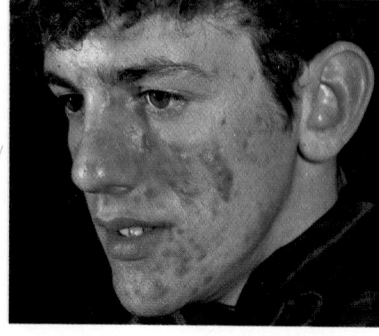

A1-5 **Acne** is a condition in which the most characteristic lesion is the comedo, or "blackhead," that later becomes a conical erythematous papule or pustule. A third type of lesion is the "blind boil," which is a dermal cyst without an orifice. This lesion is often associated with atrophic or hypertrophic scarring. Cystic acne may appear with only a very few comedones; also, comedo-like acne may occur with few cysts or erythematous papules.

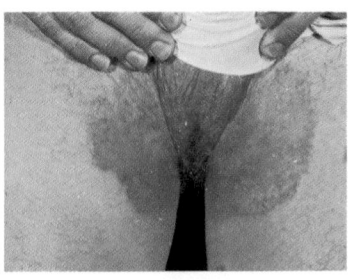

A1-6 **Dermatophytosis** is identified by the striking polycyclic, annular shape of the scaling, especially on the feet and hands, where there is often a scalloped pattern. A positive diagnosis of dermatophytosis is quickly established by direct examination of scales from the advancing border; the mycelia are revealed when the scales are immersed in 10% potassium hydroxide or Swartz stain.

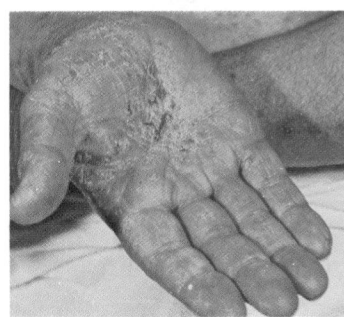

A1-7 **Eczematous dermatitis** is a very common cutaneous reaction that is localized to the hands of housewives, to the legs in patients with chronic venous insufficiency, and behind the ears in patients with seborrheic dermatitis. In subacute eczematous dermatitis, there are mild erythema, dry scales, and often small red papules, many of which are excoriated. In chronic eczematous dermatitis, lichenification is the most prominent feature.

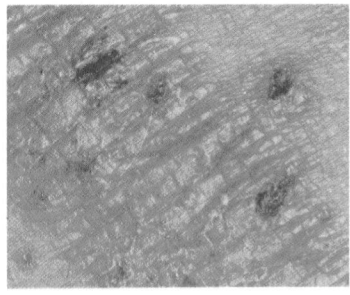

A1-8 **Localized lichenification** results from repeated rubbing of the skin and consists of isolated, circumscribed plaques. These single lesions vary in size from 2 to 10 cm and occur most often on the extensor aspect of the forearm and in the scrotal, nuchal, inguinal, and anogenital areas. The perianal and vulvar areas may become diffusely lichenified. Lichenification is thought to be more frequent in persons with an atopic background.

A1-9 **Melasma (chloasma)** is the so-called "mask" of pregnancy, but it also occurs in men and in women taking progestational agents. The pigmentation is uniform and is limited to the exposed areas of the face. There is no scaling or epidermal change. In fair-skinned persons, the pigment may be any shade from light tan to a very dark brown. It is most often seen on the cheek and upper lip, as here, and on the forehead.

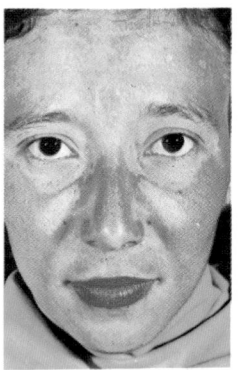

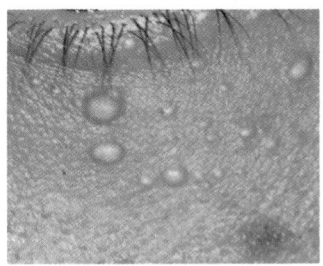

A1-10 **Milia** are a collection of lesions, occurring most commonly on the face, and consist of tiny (1 to 2 mm), white, hard, rounded, superficial papules. There is no orifice, and the keratinous contents are easily expressed by lateral compression after the making of a tiny incision in the dome of the lesion.

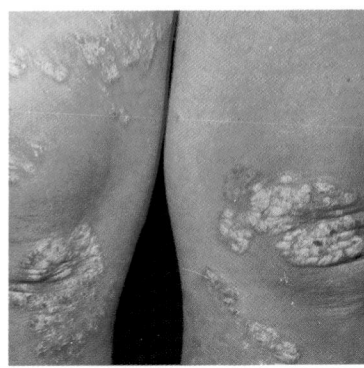

A1-11 **Psoriasis,** affecting more than 2 percent of the population, consists of isolated scaling papules or plaques and is quite commonly observed in the routine physical examination. The lesions occur most frequently on the scalp, elbows, and knees. The color and type of scales are the identifying features of the lesions. The scales are either dense and lamellated with peripherally detached edges or loose and branny. The plaques are pink to deep red, and the borders are distinct.

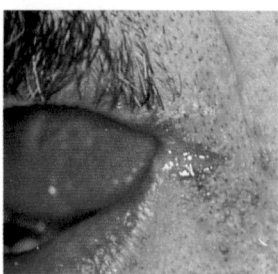

A1-12 **Perlèche** consists of painful small fissures at the angles of the mouth, often covered with yellow crusts. Perlèche most often occurs with poorly fitting dentures and in moniliasis and secondary syphilis.

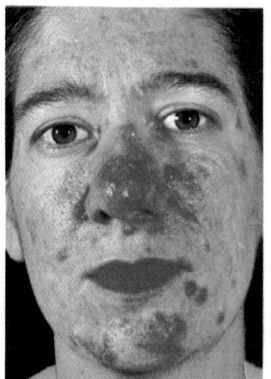

A1-13 **Rosacea,** usually limited to the face, consists of tiny, erythematous papules and pustules 1 to 5 mm in size. The pustules, often tiny and sometimes hardly visible, sit on the dome of the papules. The diffuse redness of the face is due to vasodilatation, as well as to myriad telangiectases. In men, rhinophyma, a disfiguring enlargement of the nose, may occur.

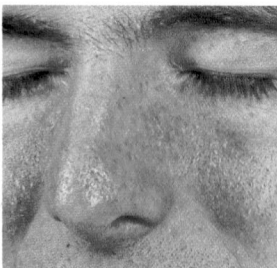

A1-14 **Seborrheic dermatitis,** a common disorder found in all age groups, occurs most frequently on the scalp, eyebrows, and nasolabial folds and behind the ears. Scaling is the prominent feature and is loose and branny; it may be yellow and oily or dry and white. The lesion may become exudative and crusted or eczematous.

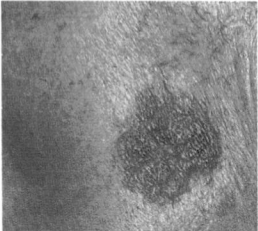

A1-15 **Seborrheic keratosis** appears in middle life and may occur on exposed or unexposed areas but is especially common on the trunk. The lesions are irregularly round or oval flat-topped papules or plaques that seem "stuck" on the skin. The margins are distinct, and the surface is often warty or consists of multiple tiny projections (vegetation). In fair-skinned persons, the lesions are light brown at first but, enlarging, become more heavily pigmented and may be confused with malignant melanoma.

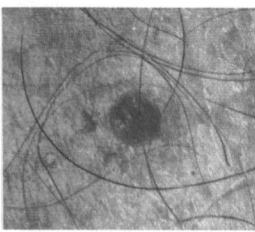

A1-16 **Senile angioma ("cherry red spot")** appears in the third decade. On the lip, the lesion is usually singular and consists of a bluish red round nodule. On the trunk, the lesions are small (2 to 3 mm), bright red, globular papules.

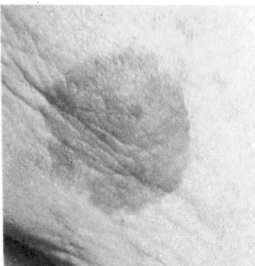

A1-17 **Senile lentigo** occurs as a single macule or as a group of isolated, sharply circumscribed macules on the exposed areas, especially on the dorsal surfaces of the hands and arms and on the forehead and cheeks. The macules are usually light yellowish brown, but may be dark brown; the color is somewhat variegated, rather than uniform as it is in a café au lait macule. Rarely, dark brown *papules* develop in these lesions, and then the condition is called *lentigo maligna,* which may slowly develop, over a period of years, into a melanoma (lentigo maligna melanoma).

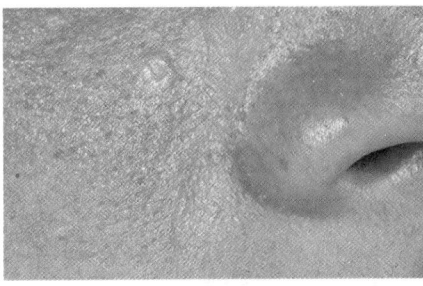

A1-18 **Senile sebaceous adenoma** occurs on the face in patients over 40 and is often diagnosed as basal-cell carcinoma. The lesions are soft, small, flat-topped papules, varying in size from 1 to 8 mm, and are characterized by a minute central depression from which sebaceous material can be exuded by lateral compression.

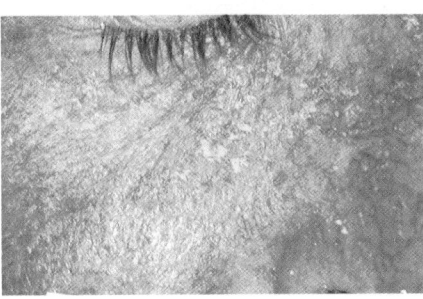

A1-19 **Solar keratosis** (1) occurs usually in persons with light skin prone to sunburn or with darker skin after chronic excessive exposure; (2) is strictly limited to exposed skin, especially on the face and dorsal surfaces of the hands; (3) is more easily felt than seen (gritty and sandpaperish); (4) in fair-skinned persons, consists of skin-colored or light brown macules or slightly raised papules with superficial adherent scales not easily removed; and (5) is associated with marked wrinkling, telangiectasia, and often diffuse, tiny, pale yellow papules indicating solar degeneration of connective tissue ("turkey skin").

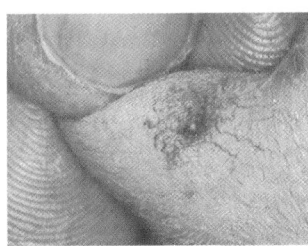

A1-20 **Spider nevus** consists of a central, punctate, bright red macule or papule (the body) from which fine red lines radiate like spider legs. There is often a red flare between the radiating vessels. On diascopy, the central body pulsates.

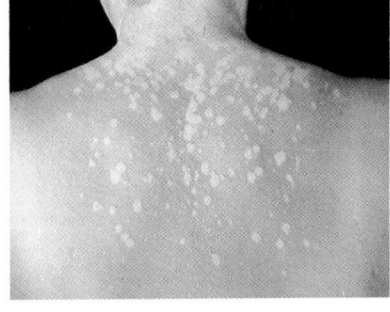

A1-21 **Tinea versicolor** is a relatively common disorder occurring primarily on the trunk and appearing in two forms: as scattered, 3- to 5-mm, very slightly scaling brown macules or as whitish macules that may be confused with vitiligo. The fungal spores and hyphae can be easily demonstrated on direct examination of the scales using Swartz stain.

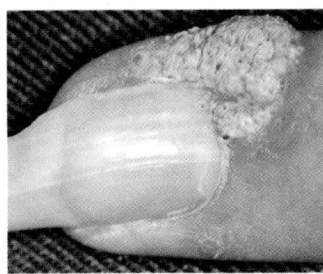

A1-22 **Verruca vulgaris** may occur at any age, but it is most common in children. The lesions, which vary in size from 0.5 to 2.0 cm, are round or oval, firm, skin colored papules with multiple tiny keratotic, rounded or filiform projections covering the surface (vegetation). They occur most frequently on the hands and soles.

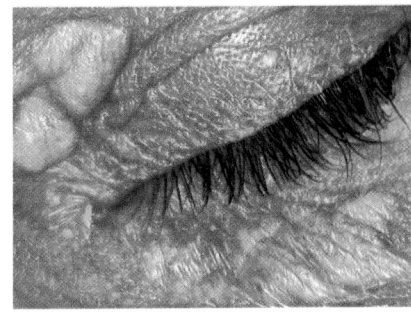

A1-23 **Xanthelasma** consists of one or more bright yellow, sharply marginated plaques with no epidermal change, usually occurring on the eyelids. All patients with xanthelasma should be investigated for evidence of plasma lipid abnormalities.

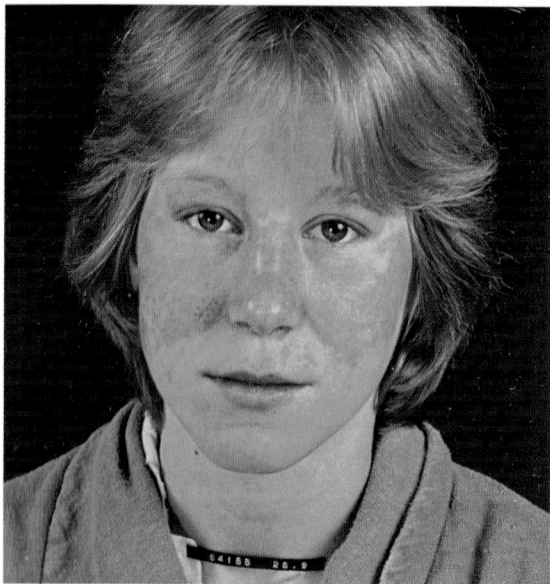

A1-24 **Systemic lupus erythematosus.** Erythematous, confluent, butterfly-like eruption with fine scaling.

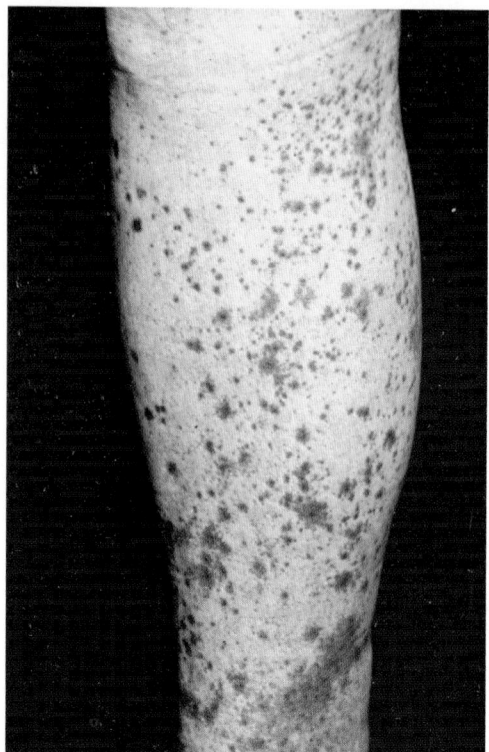

A1-25 **Necrotizing vasculitis syndrome.** Scattered discrete, purpuric eruption on the legs. The purpura is "palpable."

A

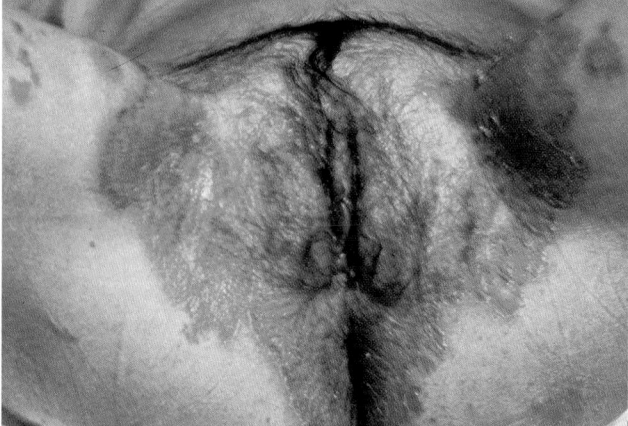

A1-26 **Glucagonoma** (*A*) and **acquired zinc deficiency** (*B*). Circinate and gyrate areas of blistering, erosion, and maceration. The eruption is often mistaken for psoriasis or mucocutaneous moniliasis.

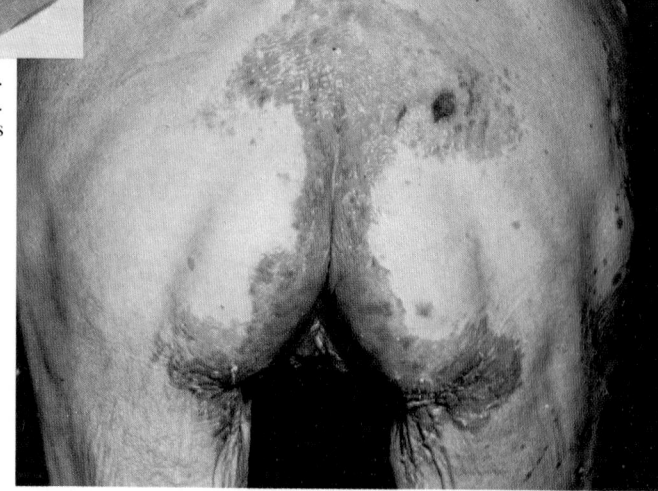

B

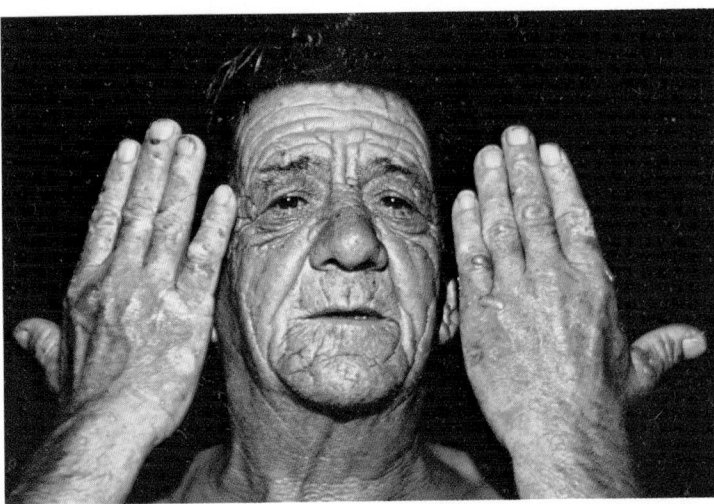

A1-27 **Porphyria cutanea tarda.** Violaceous suffusion in the periorbital skin is evident. There are erosions and pink atrophic scars at sites of previous bullae on the dorsa of the hands.

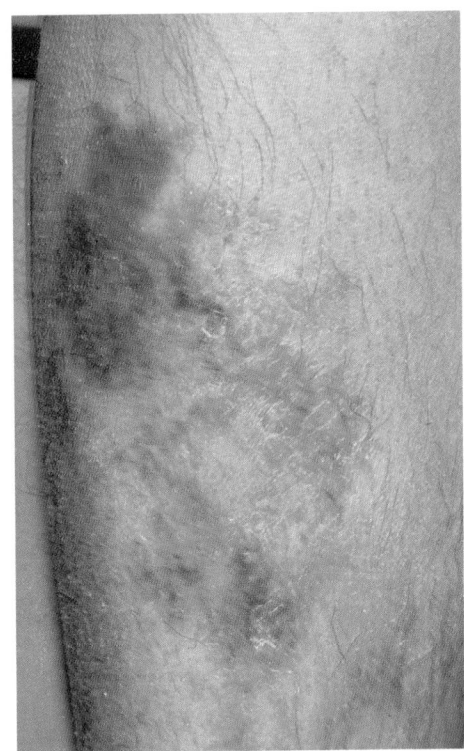

A1-28 **Necrobiosis lipoidica.** The lesion often begins as a small, dusky red, elevated nodule with a sharp border. It slowly enlarges, becomes flattened and eventually depressed as the dermis becomes atrophic. The color becomes brownish yellow except for the border, which may remain reddened. Delicate vessels can be seen through the atrophic epidermis.

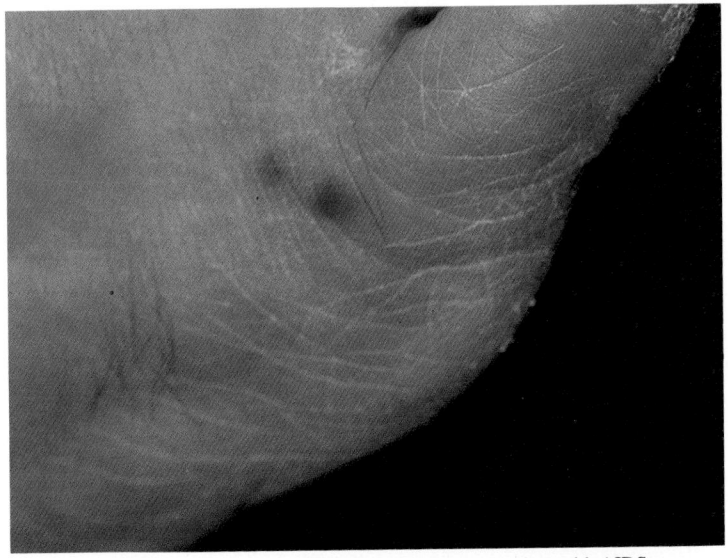

A1-29 Two purplish red nodules of **Kaposi's sarcoma** in a patient with AIDS.

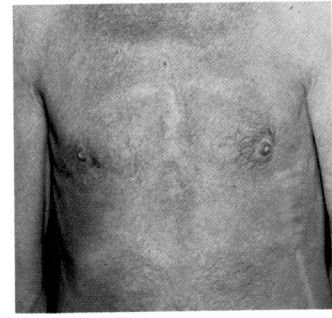

A1-30 **Carcinoid** showing the effect of stroking. In contrast to the flushing that occurs in other disorders, the flush in carcinoid is typically a panorama of colors, ranging from bizarre pinkish orange to bright red to violaceous to blanching white. The flush (which lasts only a few minutes) spreads from the face to the neck, shoulders, chest, and arms.

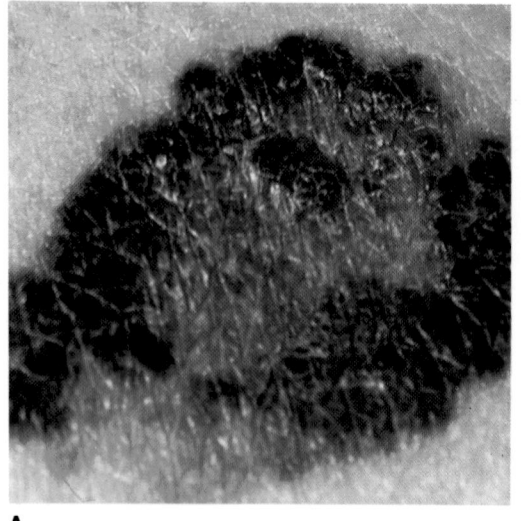

A

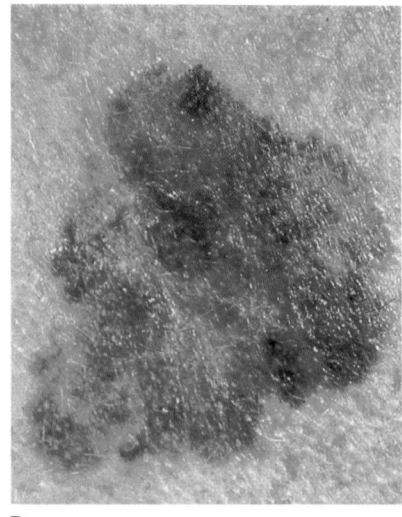

B

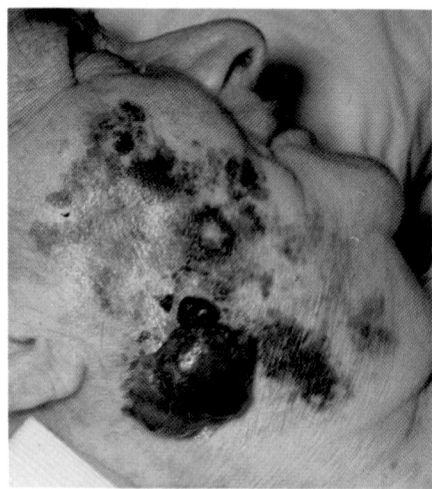

C

D

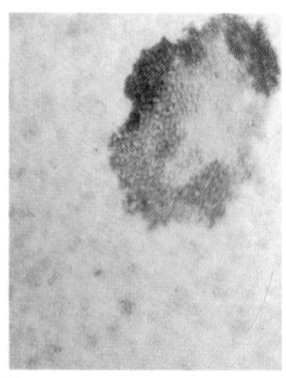

E

F

A1-31 **Malignant melanoma.** On close inspection melanomas shown are characterized by irregular surface (*A*), irregular border and notching (*B*), and nodularity (*C*). Also shown are a reniform melanoma (*D*), an extensive lentigo maligna on face of patient (*E*) and a regressive melanoma characterized by grayish color infiltrated with pink areas (*F*). (From Hospital Practice, January 1982, with permission.)

A

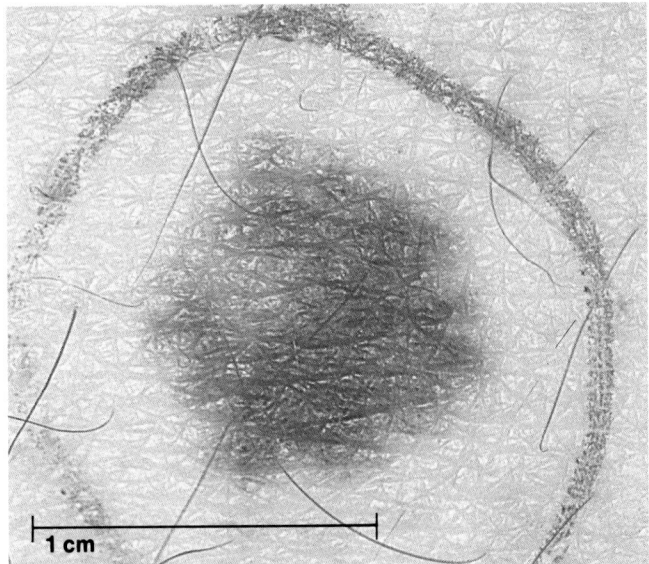

B

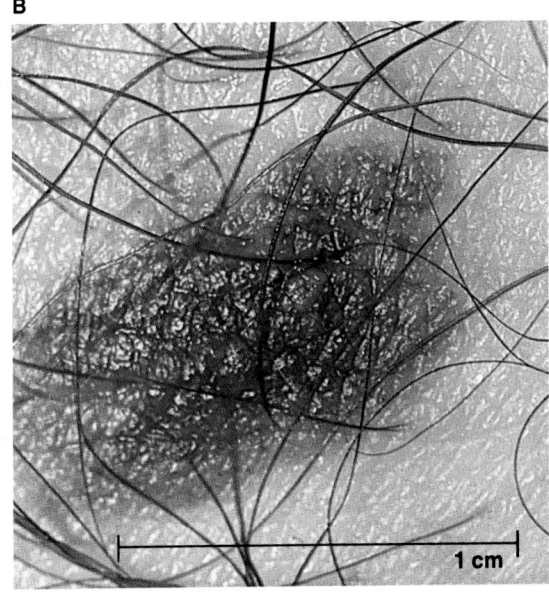

A1-32 **Dysplastic melanocytic nevi.** (*A*) Round, essentially macular lesions in which the slightly elevated area is present at 12:00 o'clock. The elevation is detectable only by oblique lighting. Note striking variegation of color with tan, brown, and pink areas. (*B*) This lesion is more obviously elevated in the central portion. Note "pebbly" surface. Both lesions have indistinct and irregular borders. (From Dermatologic Capsule & Comment 7(4):4, 1985, with permission.)

A1-33 **Malignant melanoma – dysplastic nevus syndrome.** This 28-year-old woman gave a history of a rapidly growing (3 to 6 months), asymptomatic lesion on her right scapular area. Her mother had melanoma and both mother and siblings had many dark "moles." Diagnosis: (1) Superficial spreading melanoma, level IV, 4.75 mm. (2) Regional nodes — of 32 removed, 1 was positive. (3) Dysplastic nevus syndrome with family history of melanoma. Note primary lesion and many dark "moles" on back (*A*) and dysplastic nevi on untanned areas under the bathing suit straps (*B*). (From Dermatologic Capsule & Comment 6(4):3, 1984, with permission.)

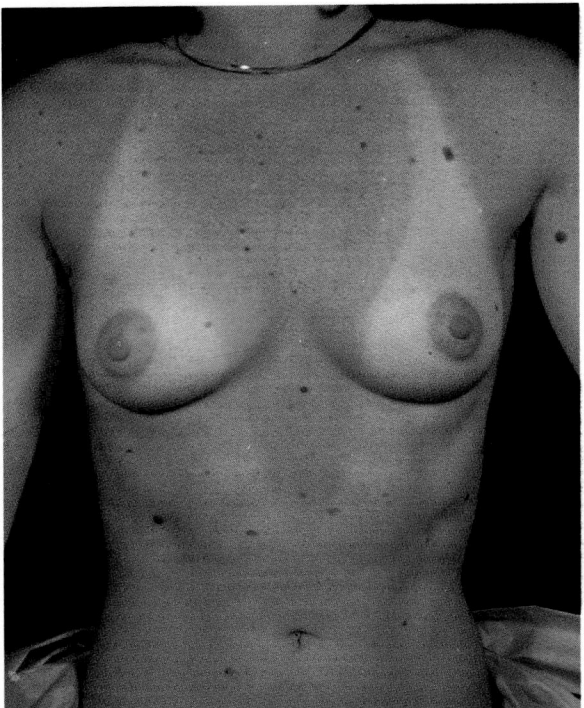

B

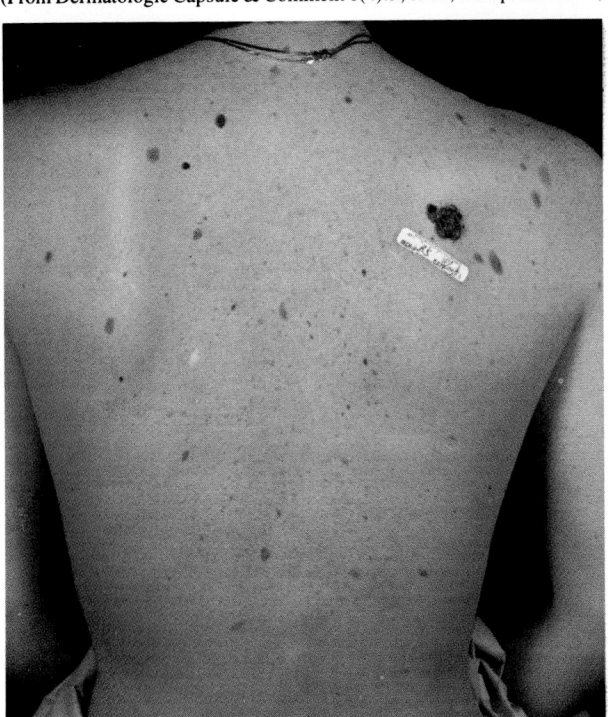

A

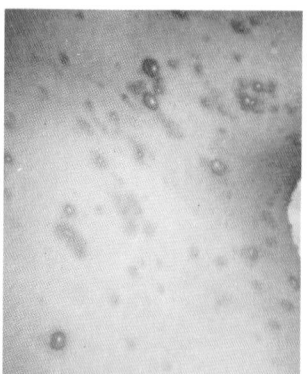

A2-1 **Varicella** (chickenpox).[3]

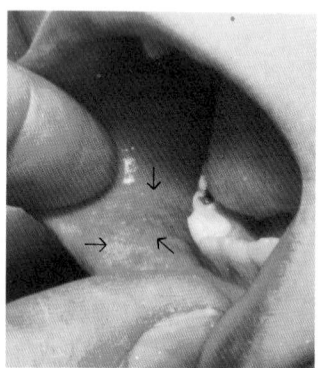

A2-2 **Measles** (rubeola).[3]

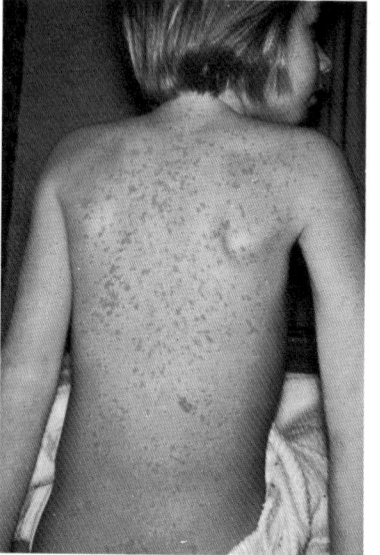

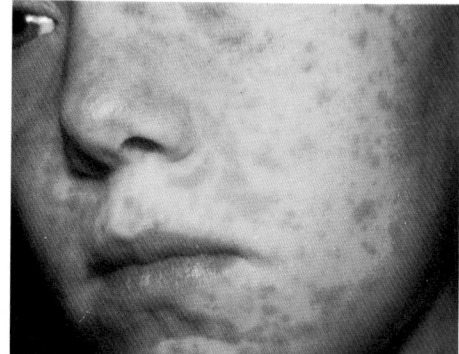

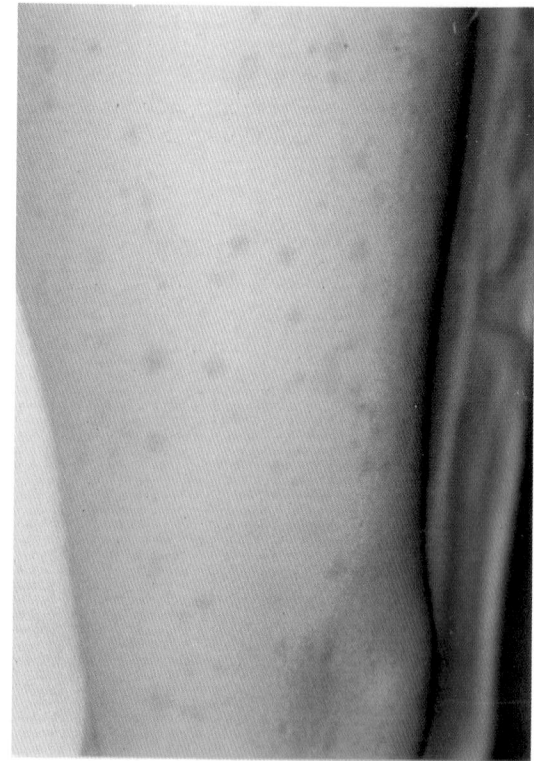

A2-3 **Rocky Mountain spotted fever** — early rash.[2]

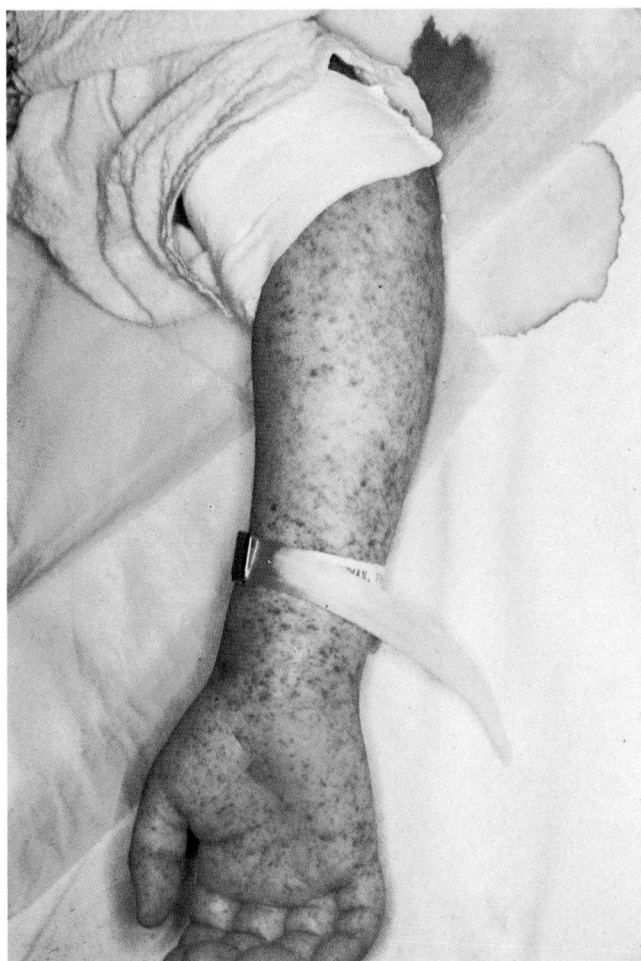

A2-4 **Rocky Mountain spotted fever** — late rash.[2]

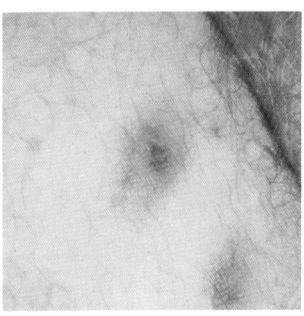

A2-7 **Pseudomonas septicemia**.[3]

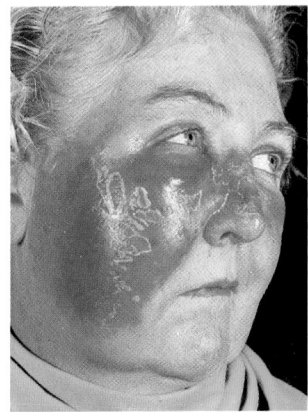

A2-8 **Facial erysipelas**.[3]

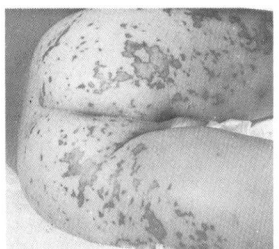

A2-5 **Meningococcemia**.[3]

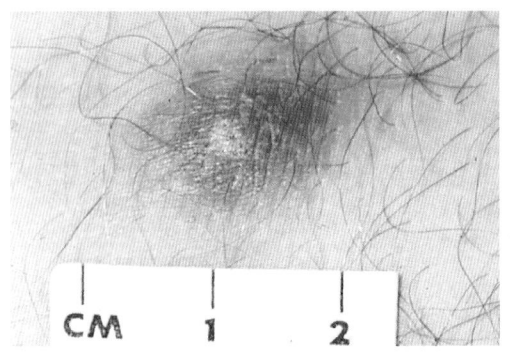

A2-6 **Disseminated gonococcal infection** — skin lesion.[4]

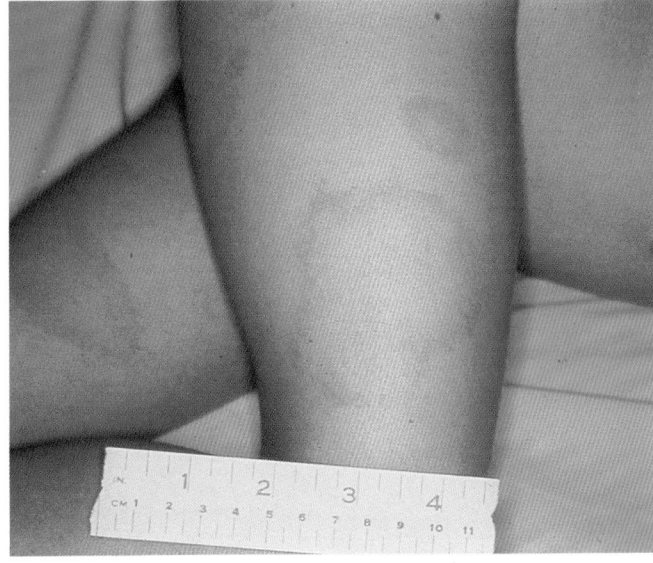

A2-9 **Lyme disease: erythema chronicum migrans** — secondary lesion.[5]

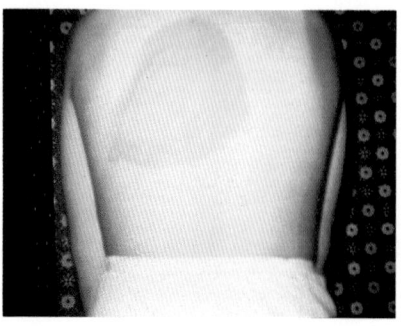

A2-10 **Lyme disease: erythema chronicum migrams** – primary lesion.[5]

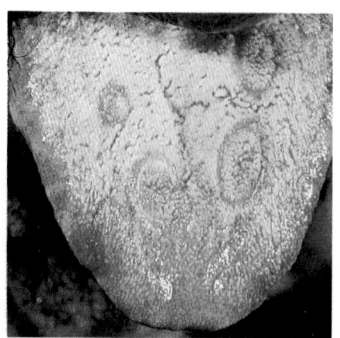

A2-11 Mucous patches involving the tongue in **secondary syphilis**.[4]

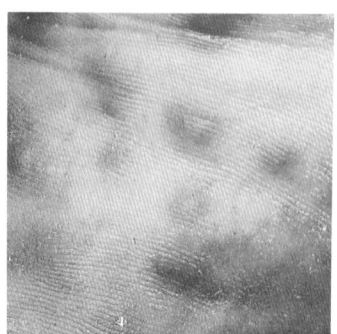

A2-12 **Papulosquamous lesions of secondary syphilis** on the sole of the foot.[4]

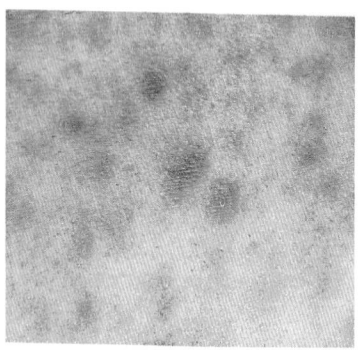

A2-13 **Macular syphilids** in early secondary syphilis.[4]

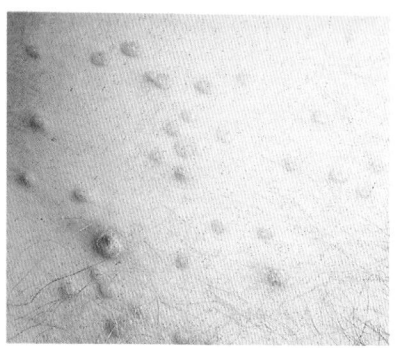

A2-14 **Molluscum contagiosum** of the lower abdomen in a patient with coexisting genital molluscum lesions. Note central umbilication and pale-salmon color.[4]

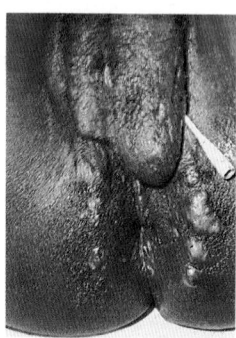

A2-15 **Esthiomene** due to lymphogranuloma venereum.[4]

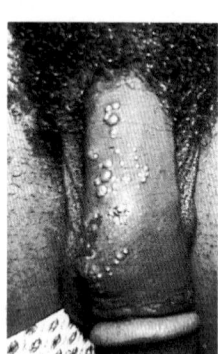

A2-16 **Severe primary HSV* infection** with extensive vesicles, ulcerations, and penile edema.[4]

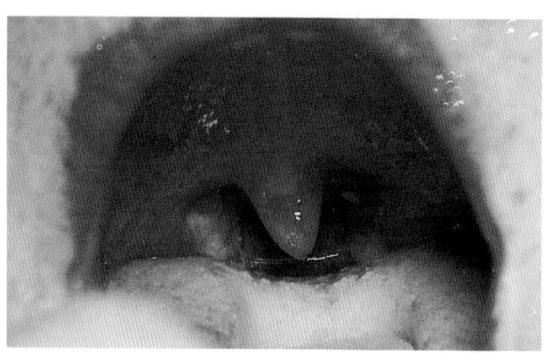

A2-17 **Primary HSV* pharyngitis** showing ulcerative lesions on the uvula and palate together with exudative tonsillitis. HSV-2 was recovered from pharyngeal and genital lesions.[4]

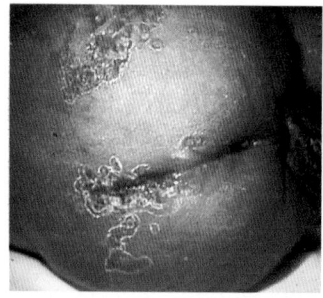

A2-18 **Neonatal HSV* infection.** Ulcers and crusting lesions on the buttocks.[4]

*Herpes Simplex Virus

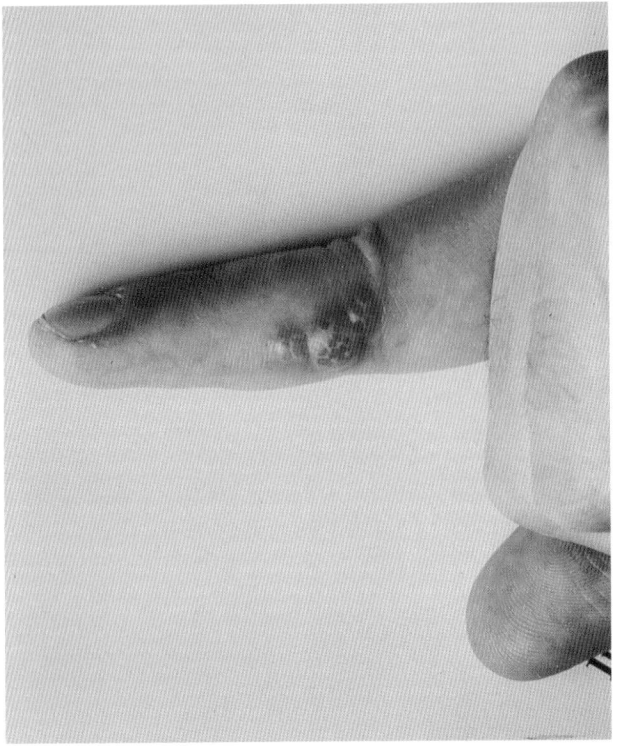

A2-19 **Herpetic whitlow**.[1]

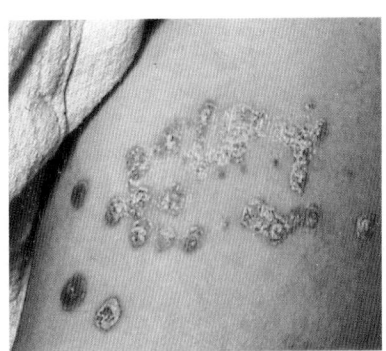

A2-20 **Keratodermia blenorrhagica** in Reiter's syndrome.[4]

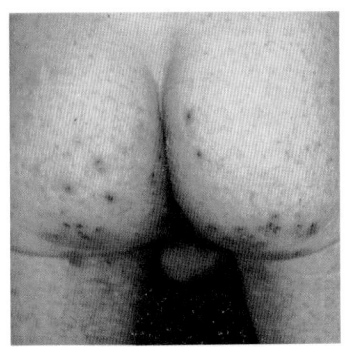

A2-21 Grouped excoriations due to **scabies** on the lower buttocks, simulating dermatitis herpetiformis.[4]

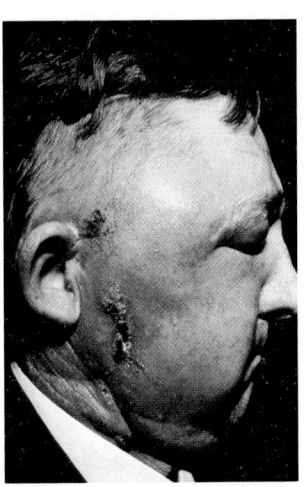

A2-22 **Cervicofacial actinomycosis**.[3]

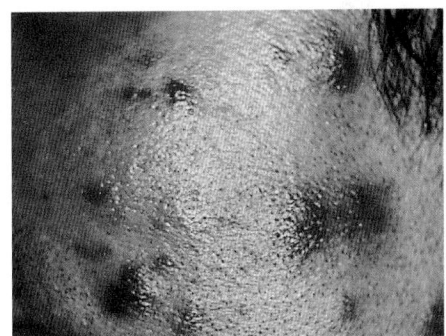

A2-23 Lesions of **Kaposi's sarcoma** on the cheek of a homosexually active man.[4]

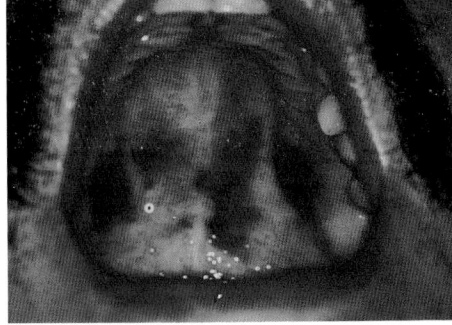

A2-24 **Kaposi's sarcoma** involving the palate of a homosexually active man.[4]

Sources

1 Courtesy of Lawrence Corey, M.D.
2 Courtesy of Theodore E. Woodward, M.D.
3 Fitzpatrick TB et al: *Dermatology in General Medicine*, 2nd ed. New York, McGraw-Hill, 1984
4 Holmes KK et al: *Sexually Transmitted Diseases*. New York, McGraw-Hill, 1984
5 Steere AC et al: Ann Intern Med 86:685, 1977 (reprinted with permission)

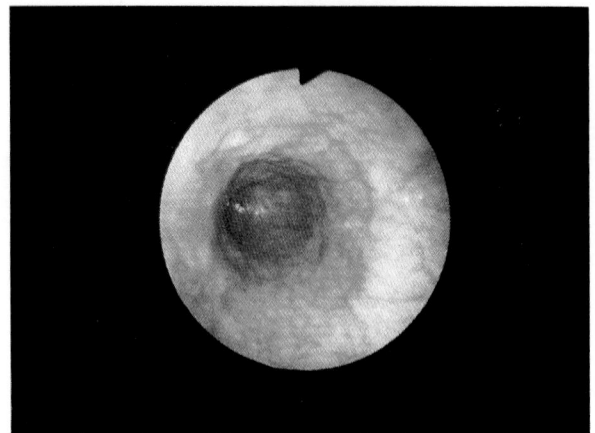

A3-1 **Normal esophagus;** normal fine vasculature can be seen.

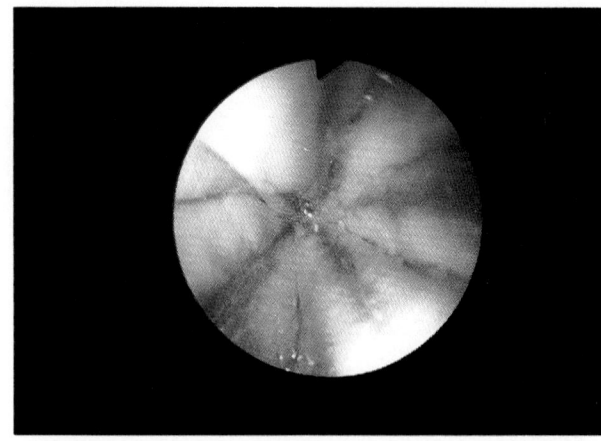

A3-2 **Peptic regurgitant esophagitis;** linear red streaks with a central white streak are noted extending up the esophagus.

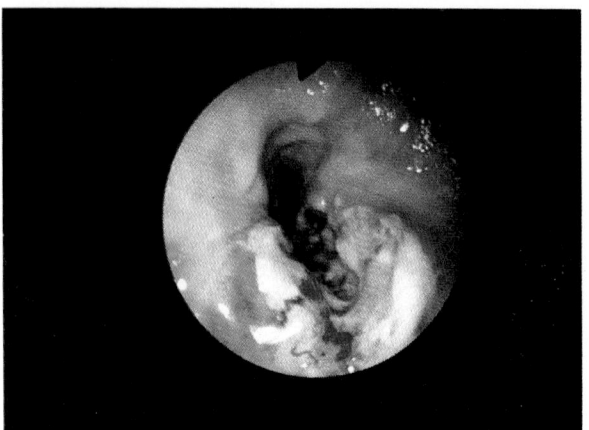

A3-3 **Ulcerated squamous cell carcinoma,** with a depressed center, involving one wall of the esophagus.

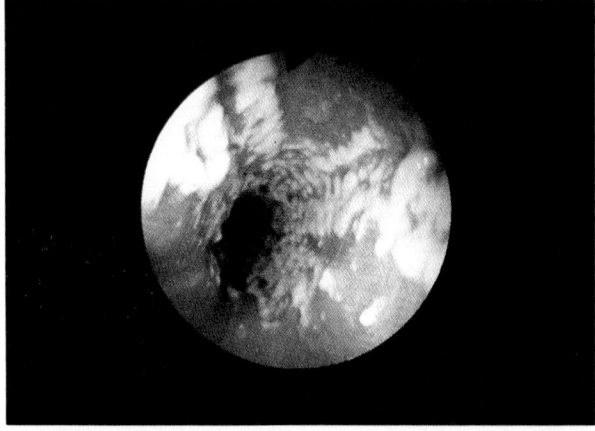

A3-4 **Moniliasis of the esophagus.** A white exudate is seen with underlying erythematous mucosa.

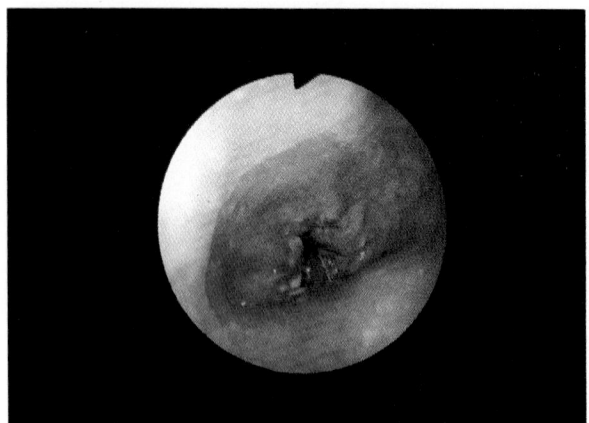

A3-5 **Barrett's metaplasia of the esophagus with an adenocarcinoma.** The squamo-columnar junction is noted in the proximal esophagus. A mucosal irregularity in the center of the photograph was an adenocarcinoma.

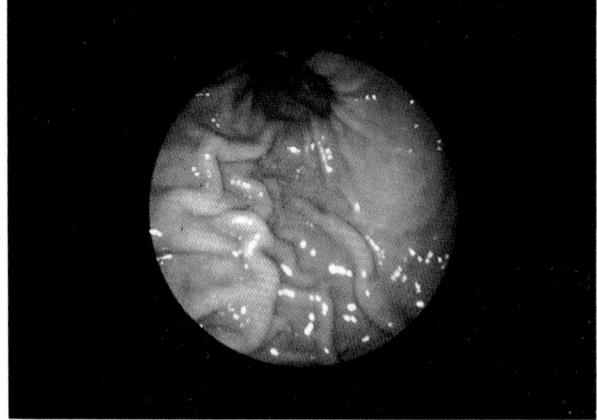

A3-6 **Normal body of the stomach with rugal folds.**

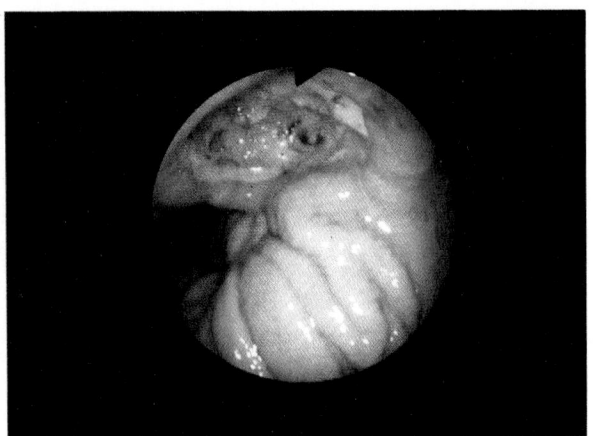

A3-7 **Large, benign, lesser curve, gastric ulcer.** The folds end at the ulcer margin.

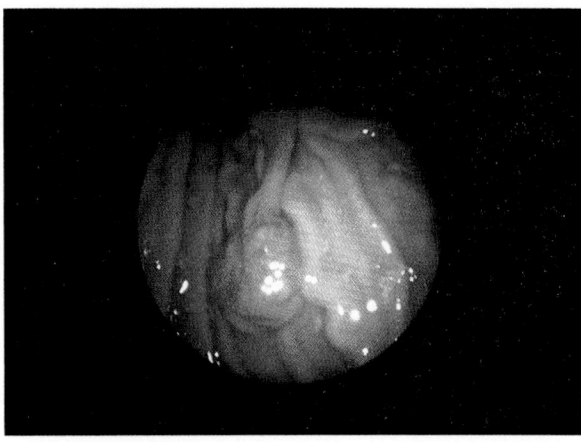

A3-8 **Gastric polyp.** The histologic type must be determined by excision and pathologic examination.

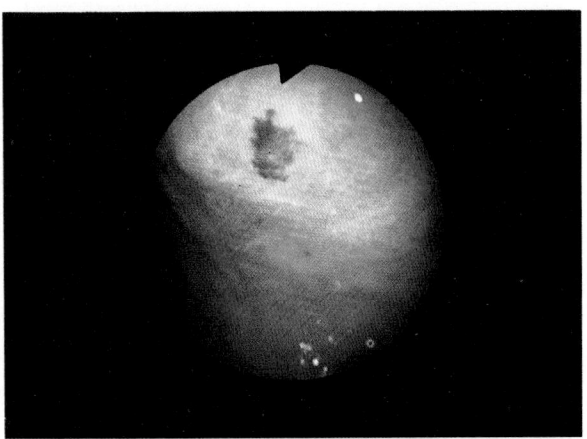

A3-9 **Arteriovenous malformation of the gastric mucosa.**

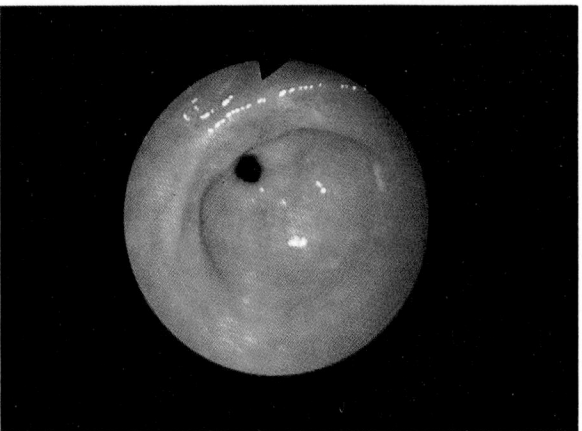

A3-10 **Normal pylorus.** Note the absence of gastric rugal folds in the antrum proximal to the pylorus.

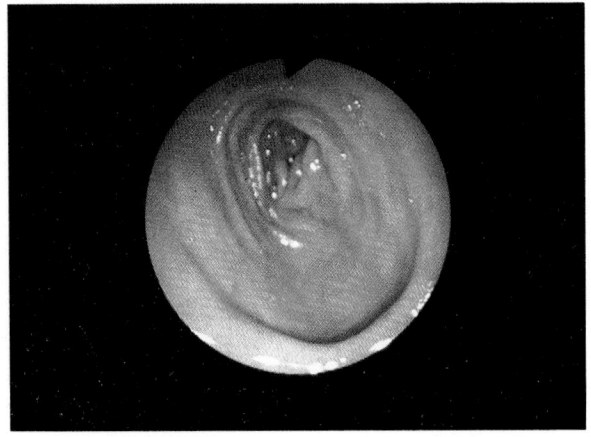

A3-11 **Normal duodenal bulb.**

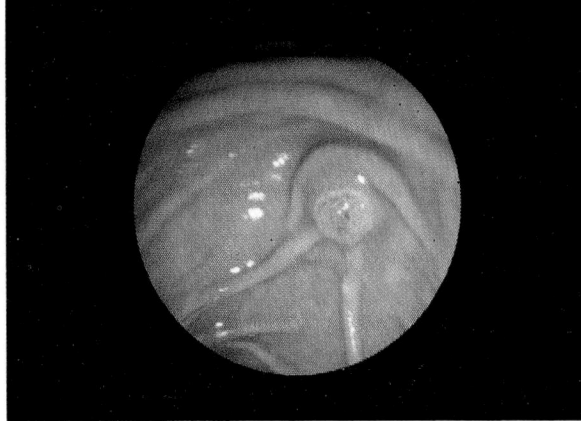

A3-12 **Normal papilla of Vater.** The fold pattern surrounding the papilla is normal; bile is seen adjacent to the papilla.

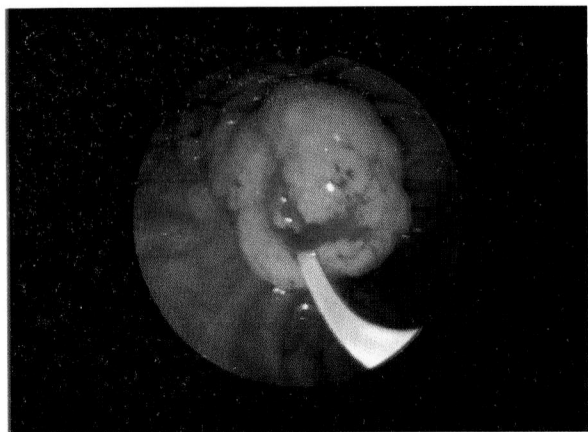

A3-13 **Periampullary carcinoma.** The mass at the papilla of Vater has been catheterized during ERCP.

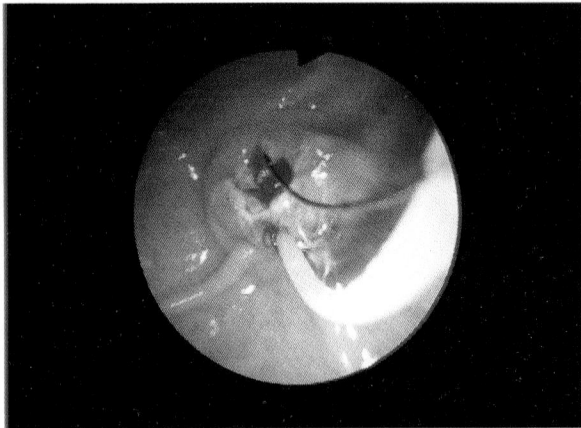

A3-14 **Endoscopic papillotomy.** A papillotome has been passed into the papilla, the wire bowed, and an incision made, with electrosurgical current, in the superior aspect of the papilla.

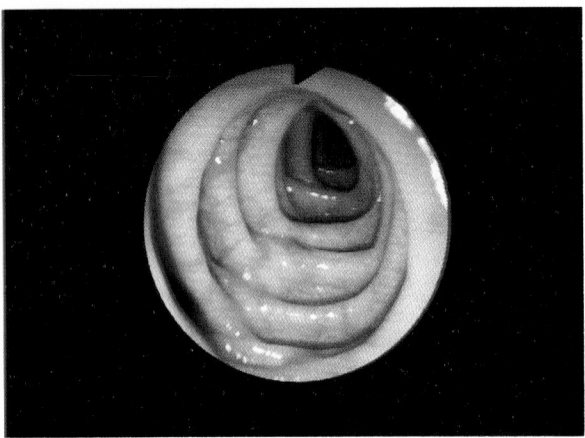

A3-15 **Normal colon;** typical haustral folds and a normal vascular pattern can be seen.

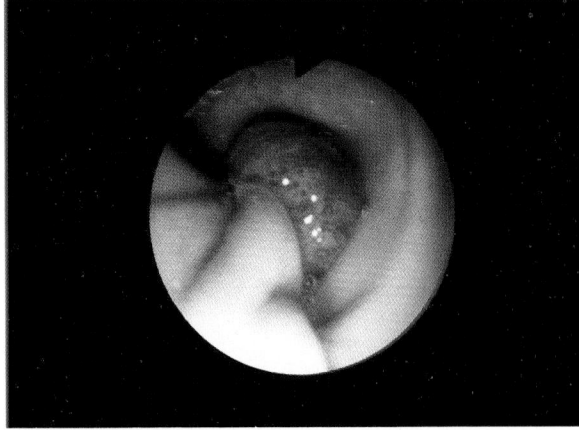

A3-16 **Colonic adenomatous polyp.** The polyp is erythematous; a stalk is seen covered with normal mucosa.

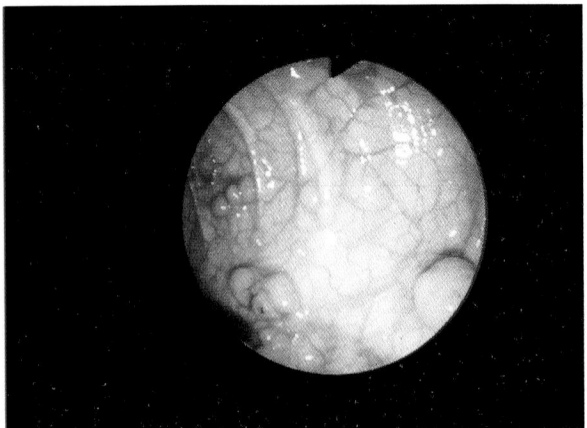

A3-17 **Multiple, small, colonic adenomatous polyps** in a case of familial polyposis coli. This colon must be removed to prevent the development of cancer.

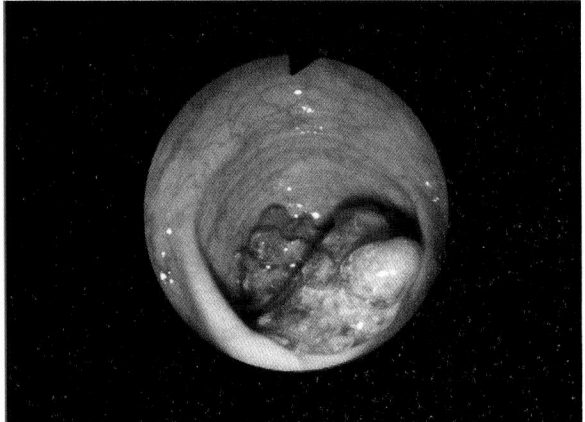

A3-18 **Colon adenocarcinoma.** The cancer is multilobed and growing into the lumen.

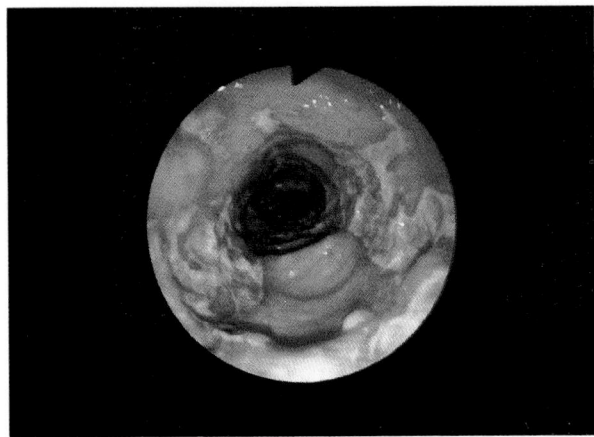

A3-19 **Crohn's colitis** with linear, serpiginous, white-based ulcers surrounded by colonic mucosa which is relatively normal.

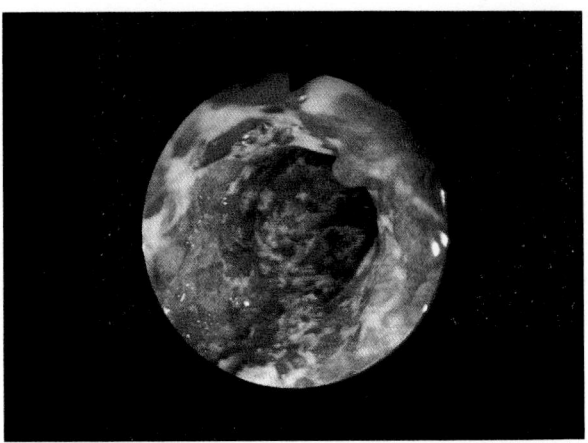

A3-20 **Severe ulcerative colitis** with diffuse ulceration, bleeding, and exudation.

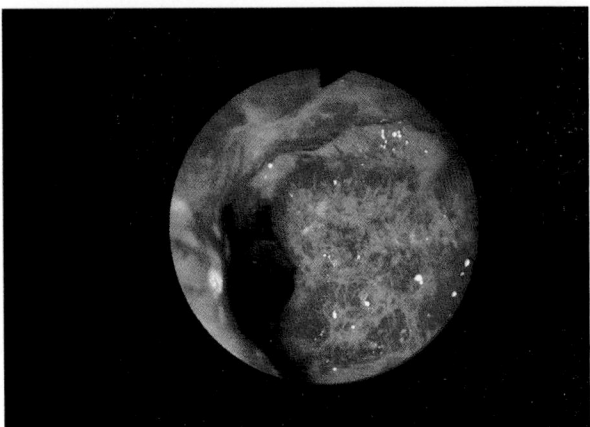

A3-21 **Kaposi's sarcoma involving the colon** in a patient with AIDS. The erythematous lesions involve most of the colonic mucosa in the photograph.

Source: Courtesy of FE Silverstein and GN Tytgat: *Atlas of Gastrointestinal Endoscopy.* Gower Medical Publishing, New York, 1987.

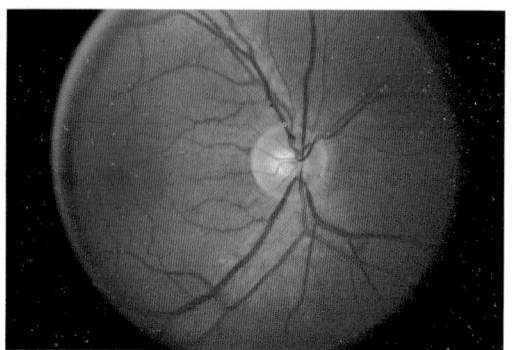

A4-1 **Normal optic nerve and retina.**

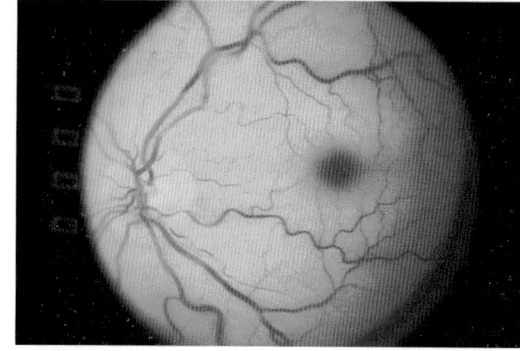

A4-2 **Central retinal artery occlusion.**

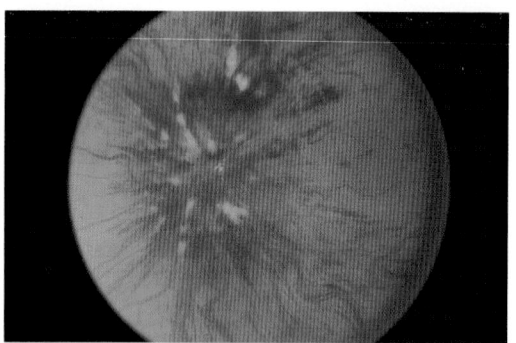

A4-3 **Central retinal vein occlusion.**

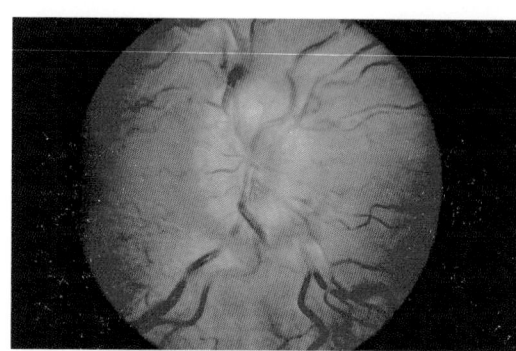

A4-4 **Early papilledema.**

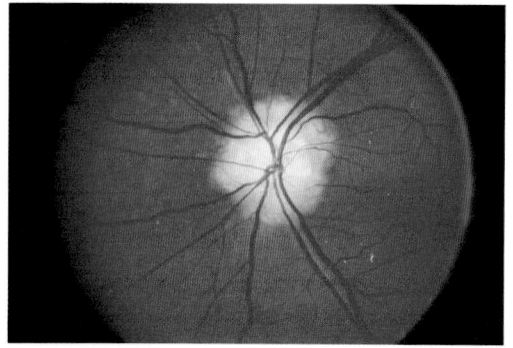

A4-5 **Drusen of the optic nerve head.**

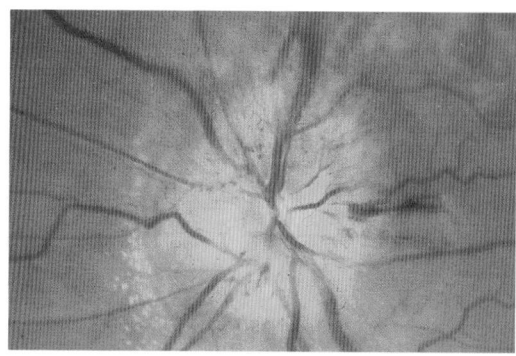

A4-6 **Anterior ischemic optic neuropathy.**

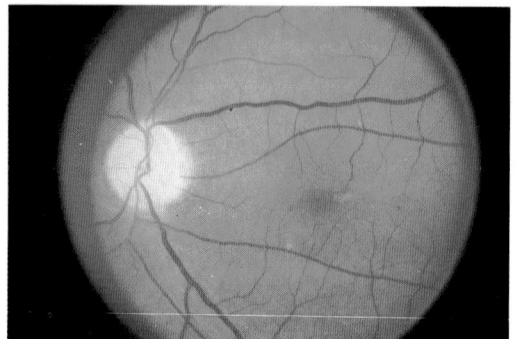

A4-7 **Primary optic atrophy.**

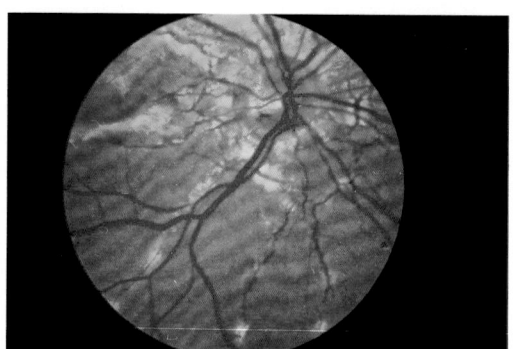

A4-8 **Angioid streaks.**

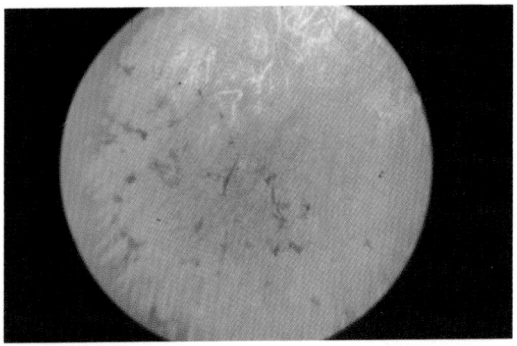

A4-9 **Retinitis pigmentosa.**

A4-10 **Band keratopathy.**

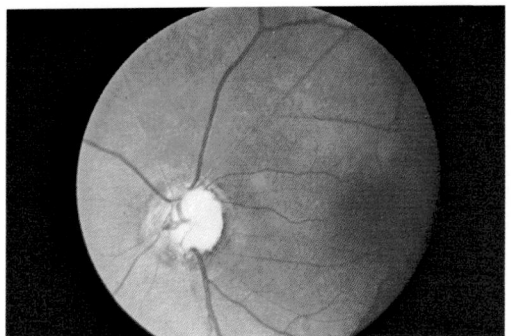

A4-11 **Glaucomatous optic disk with secondary atrophy.**

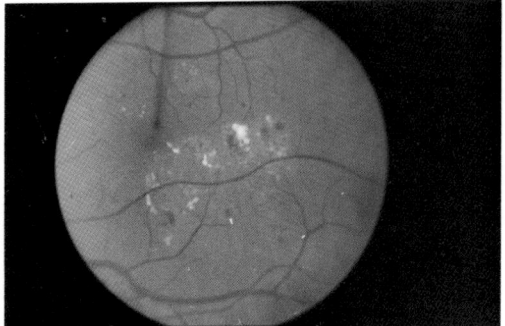

A4-12 **Diabetic retinopathy with microaneurysms.**

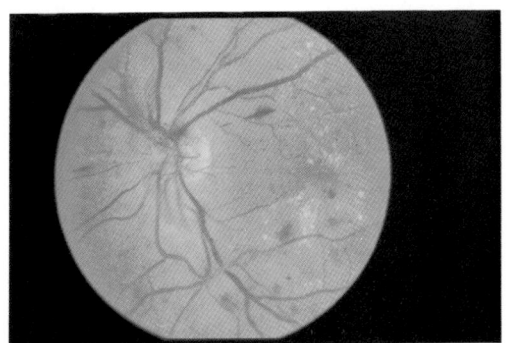

A4-13 **Proliferative diabetic retinopathy.**

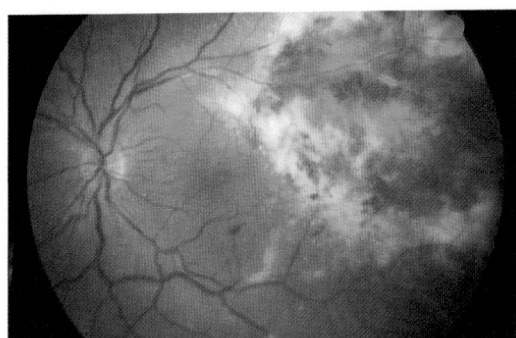

A4-14 **Cytomegalovirus retinitis in AIDS.**
(Courtesy of Donald J. D'Amico, M.D.)

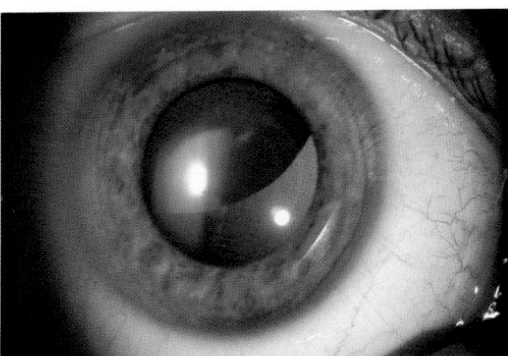

A4-15 **Dislocated lens in Marfan's disease.**
(Courtesy of S. Fourman, M.D.)

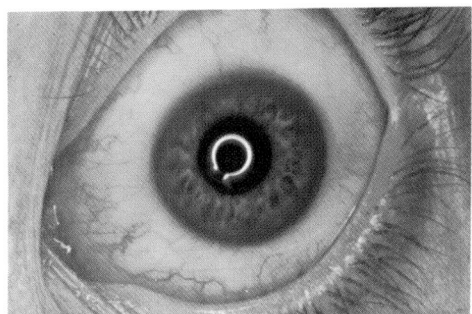

A4-16 **Kayser-Fleischer ring in Wilson's disease.**
(Note: The ring is the golden brown pigment at the periphery of the cornea and is characteristically broader superiorly and inferiorly than it is medially and laterally.)

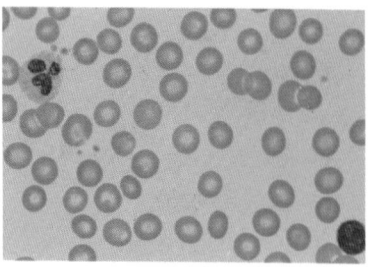

A5-1 **Normal blood smear.** Normal red blood cells are round, possess an area of central pallor, appear slightly smaller than the nucleus of a mature lymphocyte, and vary little in size (anisocytosis) or in shape (poikilocytosis).

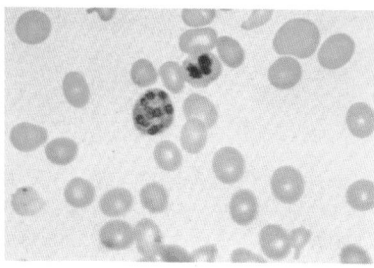

A5-2 **Megaloblastic anemia.** Oval macrocytes, well filled with hemoglobin, are admixed with lesser numbers of small teardrop-shaped red blood cells. Note also hypersegmented granulocyte.

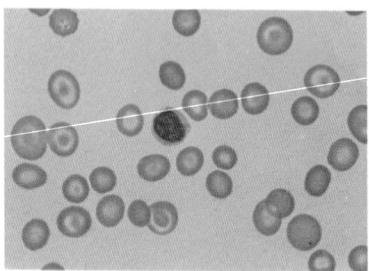

A5-3 **Liver disease.** Round macrocytes of rather uniform size are seen. Many of the macrocytes are also target cells.

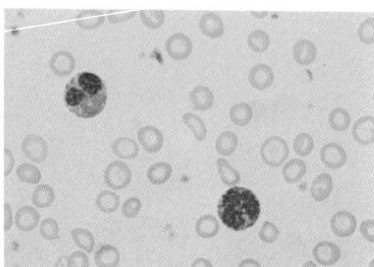

A5-4 **Iron-deficiency anemia.** In severe iron deficiency, the red blood cells are smaller than normal (microcytosis), and their central area of pallor is expanded (hypochromia) so that the cells appear to have only a thin rim of hemoglobin.

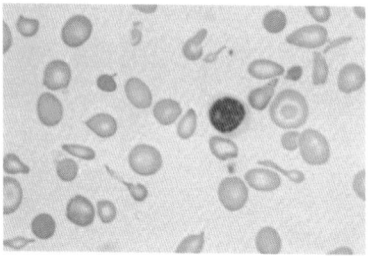

A5-5 **β thalassemia intermedia.** Microcytic and hypochromic red blood cells are seen that resemble the red blood cells of severe iron deficiency anemia shown in Fig. A5-4. Many elliptical and teardrop-shaped red blood cells are noted.

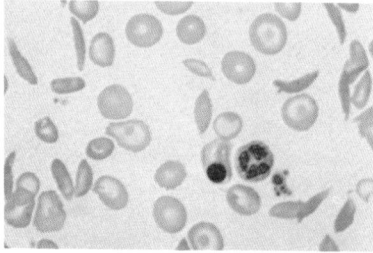

A5-6 **Sickle cell anemia.** The elongated and crescent-shaped red blood cells seen on this smear represent circulating irreversible sickled cells. Target cells and a nucleated red blood cell are also seen.

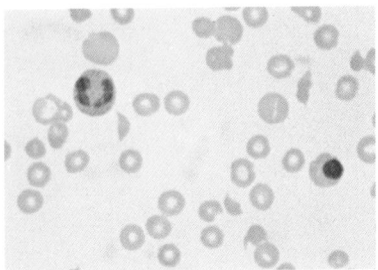

A5-7 **Traumatic hemolysis.** The helmet-shaped red blood cell and the small triangular-shaped red blood cells seen on this smear represent morphologic evidence of mechanical damage to red blood cells within the circulatory tree.

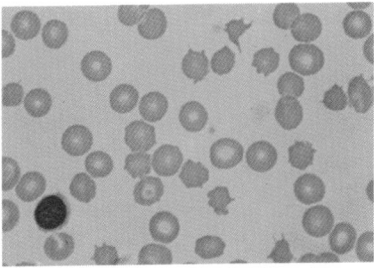

A5-8 **Spur cell anemia.** Spur cells are recognized as distorted red blood cells containing several irregularly distributed thornlike projections. Cells with this morphologic abnormality are also called acanthocytes.

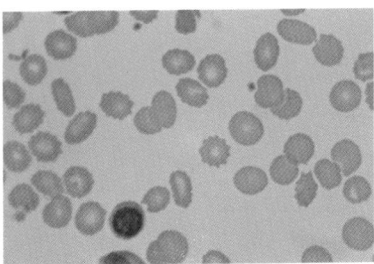

A5-9 **Uremia.** The red blood cells in uremia may acquire numerous, regularly spaced, small spiny projections. Such cells, called burr cells or echinocytes, are readily distinguishable from the irregularly spiculated acanthocytes shown in Fig. A5-8.

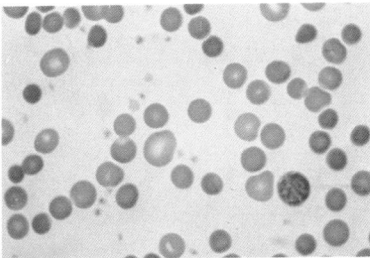

A5-10 **Hereditary spherocytosis.** Small, densely staining red blood cells are seen that have lost their central area of pallor (microspherocytes). Microspherocytes may also be found in other hemolytic disorders (Fig. A5-11).

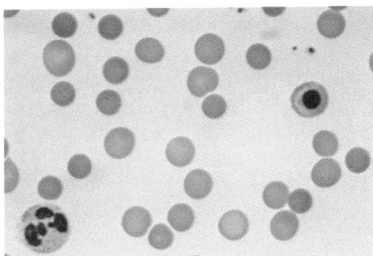

A5-11 **Immunohemolytic anemia.** Microspherocytes are seen on this blood smear along with several macrocytes with a slight purple tinge (polychromasia). The latter represent new red blood cells released early from the bone marrow. The microspherocytes seen in immunohemolytic anemia may be indistinguishable from the microspherocytes seen in hereditary spherocytosis (Fig. A5-10).

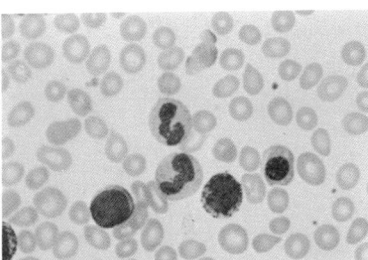

A5-12 **Myeloid metaplasia.** Teardrop-shaped red blood cells, a nucleated red blood cell, and immature myeloid cells are seen on this blood smear.

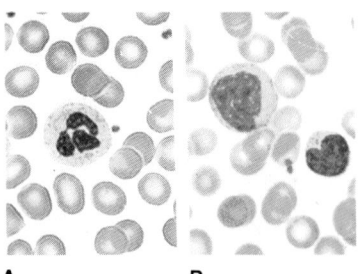

A   **B**

A5-13 A. **Normal granulocyte.** The normal granulocyte has a segmented nucleus with heavy, clumped chromatin; fine neutrophilic granules are dispersed throughout its cytoplasm. *B.* **Normal monocyte and lymphocyte.** The normal monocyte is a large cell with an indented or folded nucleus containing loose, strandlike chromatin; the cytoplasm is a blue-gray color and usually contains fine azurophilic granules. The normal lymphocyte is a smaller cell. Its nucleus is usually round but may be indented, as in the cell shown in this plate. The nuclear chromatin has a smudgy appearance; the cytoplasm is a blue color.

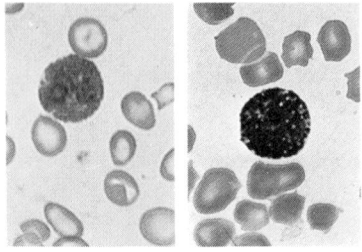

A   **B**

A5-14 A. **Normal eosinophil.** The eosinophil contains large, bright-orange granules; the nucleus is bilobed. *B.* **Basophil.** The basophil contains large purple-black granules which fill the cell and obscure the nucleus.

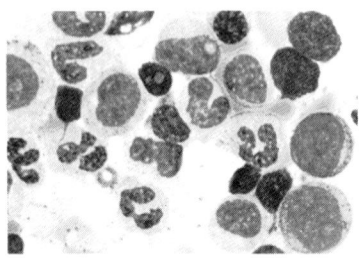

A5-15 **Normal granulocyte precursors in marrow.** The earliest granulocytic precursor (myeloblast) possesses a round nucleus with fine, punctate chromatin and one or more nucleoli; the cytoplasm is blue. As nuclear differentiation proceeds, the nucleoli disappear, the chromatin coarsens, and the nucleus becomes increasingly indented and finally segmented. As cytoplasmic differentiation proceeds, azurophilic granules appear and the cytoplasm changes color from blue to the yellow-pink-gray hue of the mature granulocyte, and as this occurs the azurophilic granules become obscured by fine neutrophilic granules.

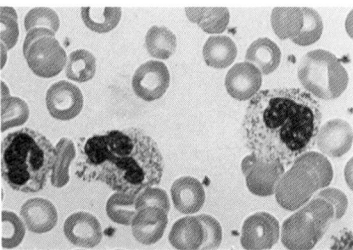

A5-16 **Neutrophils with toxic granulation.** In infection and other toxic states, azurophilic granules may become visible in mature granulocytes as coarse, dark-staining cytoplasmic granules.

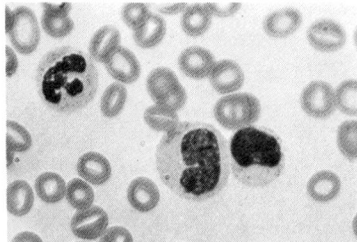

A5-17 **Band with Döhle body** (center). Döhle bodies are discrete, blue-staining, nongranular areas found in the periphery of the cytoplasm of the neutrophil in infections and other toxic states. They represent aggregates of rough endoplasmic reticulum.

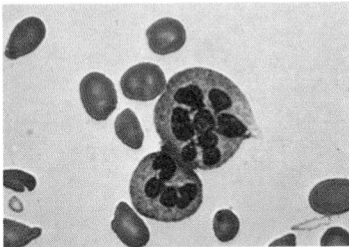

A5-18 **Hypersegmentation.** Frequent five-lobed granulocytes on a blood smear or granulocytes with more than five lobes are evidence of hypersegmentation, an important clue to the diagnosis of megaloblastic anemia.

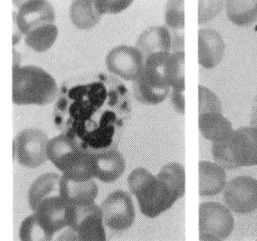

A   **B**

A5-19 *A*. **Chédiak-Higashi anomaly.** In this ultimately fatal disorder, the granulocytes contain huge cytoplasmic granules, formed from aggregation and fusion of azurophilic and specific granules. Large, abnormal granules are found in other granule-containing cells throughout the body. *B*. **Pelger-Hüet anomaly.** In this benign disorder, the majority of granulocytes are bilobed. The nucleus frequently has a spectacle-like or "pince-nez" configuration.

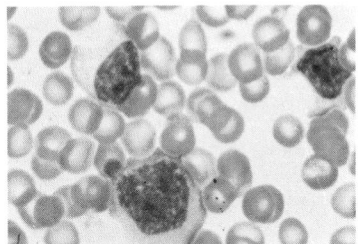

A5-20 **Reactive lymphocytes** (infectious mononucleosis). Reactive lymphocytes are usually large, cytoplasmic lymphocytes. The nucleus may be eccentrically placed and may have irregular borders and indentations (not seen on this plate). The cytoplasm contains areas that stain a darker blue due to their increased content of RNA. The cytoplasm may be indented where it abuts against a red blood cell.

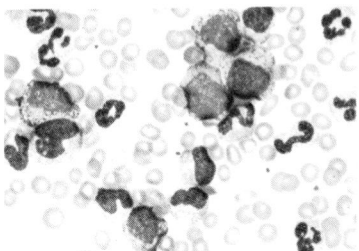

A5-21 **Chronic granulocytic leukemia.** The peripheral blood WBC count is high due to increased numbers of granulocytes and their precursors. The majority of the WBCs are segmented granulocytes or band forms, but as seen on this plate, myelocytes and pro-myeloblasts (not seen on this plate) may also be found on review of the blood smear.

A5-22 **Leukemic cell in acute pro-myelocytic leukemia.** Note multiple Auer rods.

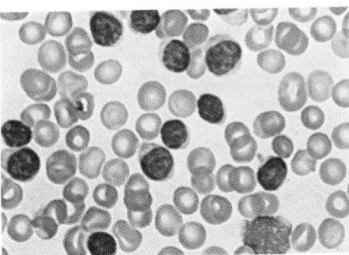

A5-23 **Chronic lymphocytic leukemia.** The peripheral blood WBC count is high due to increased numbers of small, well-differentiated lymphocytes. However, the leukemic lymphocytes are fragile, and substantial numbers of broken, smudged cells are usually also present on the blood smear.

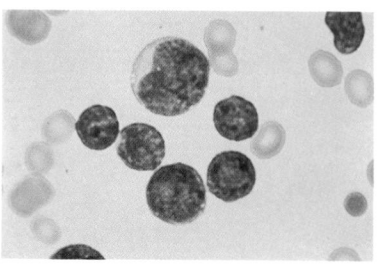

A5-24 **Leukemic cells in acute lympho-blastic leukemia** characterized by round or convoluted nuclei, high nuclear/cytoplasmic ratio and absence of cytoplasmic granules.

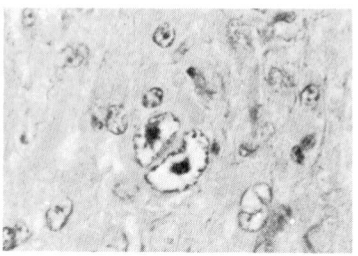

A5-25 **Hodgkin's disease:** Reed-Sternberg cell in marrow (center). The Reed-Sternberg cell is recognized by its bilobed, mirror-image nucleus, which contains in each lobe a giant, inclusion body–like nucleolus. The cytoplasmic borders of the cell cannot be identified on this plate.

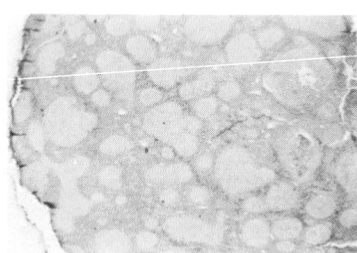

A5-26 **Non-Hodgkin's nodular lymphoma** (lymph node). This low-power view illustrates that a proliferative process has caused the normal architecture of the lymph node to be replaced by multiple nodules of varying size that extend throughout the entire lymph node.

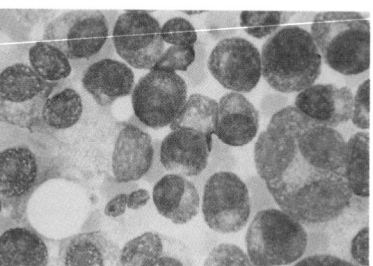

A5-27 **Multiple myeloma** (marrow). The cells bear the characteristic morphologic features of plasma cells, round or oval cells with an eccentric nucleus composed of coarsely clumped chromatin, a densely basophilic cytoplasm, and a perinuclear clear zone (hof) containing the Golgi apparatus. Binucleate and multinucleate malignant plasma cells can also be seen.

PART FIVE DISORDERS OF THE RESPIRATORY SYSTEM

199 APPROACH TO THE PATIENT WITH DISEASE OF THE RESPIRATORY SYSTEM

EUGENE BRAUNWALD

As in other branches of medicine, a careful and detailed history and physical examination are the cornerstones for establishing an accurate diagnosis in patients with disorders of the respiratory system. In addition, the roentgenographic examination occupies a particularly important role in the evaluation of patients with lung disease. Since abnormalities of the respiratory system are frequently a manifestation of a systemic process, attention must be focused not only on the chest but also a comprehensive evaluation of the patient's entire health status is essential. For example, the presence of a pulmonary lesion on x-ray may be due to metastatic disease with the primary disease elsewhere, and hemoptysis may be due to a disorder of hemostasis. Diffuse scleroderma may result in diffuse pulmonary infiltrative disease (Chaps. 209 and 264), and multiple pulmonary cavities may be a manifestation of Wegener's granulomatosis (Chap. 269). All of the so-called collagen vascular diseases may have prominent pulmonary manifestations. Carcinoma of the lung (Chap. 213) may be accompanied by prominent extrathoracic manifestations, which may overshadow the pulmonary lesion. These include myopathy, peripheral neuropathy, hypertrophic pulmonary osteoarthropathy, and a variety of endocrine and metabolic manifestations, including Cushing's syndrome, the carcinoid syndrome, a hyperparathyroid-like picture, inappropriate secretion of antidiuretic hormone, gonadotropin (Chap. 303), and increased frequency of pulmonary infections.

HISTORY In eliciting the history of patients with pulmonary disease, it must be appreciated that an increasing fraction of the population is exposed to materials which are potentially toxic to the lung (Chap. 204). The history must therefore contain a detailed *occupational and personal history* with a description of exposure to hazards such as asbestos, coal, silica, beryllium, bagasse, iron oxide, tin oxide, cotton dust, titanium oxide, silver, nitrogen dioxide, animals, moldy hay, air conditioners, and furnace humidifiers. It is useful to construct a work history, which includes the patient's duties, duration of exposure, use of protective devices, and illness in fellow workers. The occupational history should include information on a job-by-job basis as well as the military service. Contact with both wild and domestic animals may result in pulmonary symptoms, such as bronchospasm in subjects allergic to pets, or, less commonly, acute pneumonitis in patients with psittacosis (Chap. 150), tularemia (Chap. 113), or Q fever. Because it is such an important risk factor for many forms of lung disease, history of tobacco consumption must be sought and should be quantified. The habits of the patient with pulmonary disease must be gone into. Aspiration pneumonia and pneumococcal and *Klebsiella* pneumonia are often seen in alcoholics, lung abscess occurs in intravenous drug abusers, and *Pneumocystis carinii* pneumonia is a frequent complication of the acquired immunodeficiency syndrome. (Chap. 257). A record of the patient's *previous residence* is of considerable importance in the diagnosis of histoplasmosis (the

south and midwestern United States), coccidioidomycosis (the southwestern United States), tropical eosinophilia, and South American blastomycosis. For example, pulmonary mass lesions in patients in the Mediterranean Basin may be due to hydatid cysts, hemoptysis in patients from central China may be caused by paragonimiasis (Chap. 167), and cor pulmonale in Egypt frequently results from schistosomiasis (Chap. 164).

It is vitally important to elicit a history of *drug exposure* since essentially every class of drugs can produce pulmonary toxicity (Chap. 203), and all parts of the respiratory apparatus can be affected, including the alveoli, tracheobronchial tree, mediastinum, pleural cavities, pulmonary vessels, respiratory muscles, and the medullary respiratory center. Examples include the interstitial infiltrative diseases caused by bleomycin, cyclophosphamide, methotrexate, and nitrofurantoin; noncardiogenic pulmonary edema caused by aspirin; bronchospasm caused by beta-adrenergic blockers and nonsteroidal anti-inflammatory drugs; pulmonary vasculitis from intravenous drug abuse; pulmonary thromboembolism in women receiving oral contraceptives; (drug-induced) systemic lupus erythematosus with pleural involvement caused by hydralazine and procainamide; and weakness of the respiratory muscles caused by the aminoglycoside antibiotics.

The *family history* should consider pulmonary diseases which may be genetic, such as cystic disease of the lung, pulmonary emphysema due to alpha₁ antitrypsin deficiency (Chap. 208), cystic fibrosis (Chap. 207), asthma (Chap. 202), hereditary telangiectasia, Kartagener's syndrome, and alveolar microlithiasis, as well as infections due to the tubercle bacilli, fungi, and schistosoma where exposure to involved family members is important.

Dyspnea is a cardinal manifestation of diseases involving the respiratory and cardiovascular systems (Chap. 26). A detailed physical examination of both organ systems is therefore mandatory in every patient with this symptom. Dyspnea secondary to cardiac disease is often recognized by the presence of other evidence of heart failure, such as cardiac enlargement, gallop rhythms, and cardiac murmurs. It may be difficult to differentiate paroxysmal nocturnal dyspnea due to pulmonary edema of cardiac origin from nocturnal attacks of bronchial asthma, but a detailed description of the circumstances in which this symptom occurs is most useful. Dyspnea also is a common functional complaint, and an important clue in the identification of this form is the observation that shortness of breath often occurs at rest and is relieved during exertion; the opposite is the case in patients in whom this symptom is secondary to disease of the lungs or heart. Equally important in the differential diagnosis is a careful elucidation of the relationship of dyspnea to other symptoms such as cough or angina pectoris.

Patients with diseases involving the respiratory system may also present with *chest pain* which is frequently caused by inflammation of the pleura, occurring in pneumonia, pulmonary thromboembolism, tuberculosis, and malignancy (Chap. 4). Pleuritic pain is usually localized to one side of the chest and is related to respiration and to movements of the thorax. Lesions confined to the pulmonary parenchyma do not produce pain, while diseases involving the organs in the mediastinum (Chap. 214) may cause local discomfort with radiation characteristic of the specific organ. Pain may also originate in or be referred to the chest wall; it may be due to intercostal neuritis, as in herpes zoster, or to compression of the intercostal nerves as they leave the spinal cord. Such pain is often superficial in character and may be related to coughing and straining. Thoracic pain may also be due to myositis, costochondral disturbances, myocardial ischemia, pericarditis, esophageal disease, and aortic dissection and aneurysm (Chap. 4).

Cough and *expectoration* are also cardinal features of pulmonary disease (Chap. 25). Few patients can describe the severity of cough or quantity of expectoration reliably, and it is therefore desirable for the physician to inspect a 24-h collection of sputum. Cough is often precipitated by foreign materials irritating nerve endings in airways and is frequently caused by inflammation of the bronchi; the latter may be persistent (as in patients with a cigarette cough and chronic bronchitis) or acute (as in a variety of viral and bacterial infections). The time of occurrence of the cough and the character and quantity of expectorated material may point to the diagnosis. For example, bronchiectasis and lung abscess produce purulent sputum which may have an offensive odor or be streaked with blood (Chaps. 205 and 206). In pulmonary edema, the sputum is pink, frothy, and watery (Chap. 26). Mucoid (translucent, viscid, shiny, white or gray) or mucopurulent (mucoid with flecks of yellow or green pus) sputum is characteristic of acute and chronic bronchitis. Sputum is bloody or rusty in pneumonia; it is thick, gelatinous, brick red, and laced with pus in *Klebsiella* pneumonia. Paroxysmal cough may also be the presenting feature in patients with bronchial asthma, in whom physical examination reveals wheezing respirations and squeaking musical sounds (Chap. 202), as well as in patients with left ventricular failure, in whom it generally occurs at night and in the recumbent position (Chap. 182). Pulmonary tuberculosis (Chap. 119), though less common than previously, remains a common cause of chronic cough, as does primary neoplasm of the lung (Chap. 213). A change in the character of a chronic cough, unaccompanied by an acute infection, should alert the physician to the need of carrying out a detailed examination.

Hemoptysis is often a frightening symptom (Chap. 25). Faint streaking of the sputum with blood may be observed in acute infections of the respiratory tract. However, many patients with bloody sputum have serious disease, such as pulmonary thromboembolism, tuberculosis, critical mitral stenosis, neoplasm of the lung, or bronchiectasis. In all instances it is necessary to exclude sources of blood in the nasopharynx and bleeding of gastric or esophageal origin. The character of the bloody expectorate should be defined, since it may be helpful in identifying the underlying disease process. Sputum which is frankly bloody without mucus or pus may be due to pulmonary thromboembolism (Chap. 211). When pus is present, pneumonia, bronchiectasis, or lung abscess should be considered. Dilute, pink, frothy sputum is observed in acute pulmonary edema (Chap. 26).

PHYSICAL EXAMINATION In addition to a careful examination of the thorax, a meticulous *general physical examination* is mandatory in patients with disorders of the respiratory system. Disturbances of mentation or even coma occur in patients with acute carbon dioxide retention and hypoxemia. Telltale stains on the fingers point to heavy cigarette smoking; infected teeth and gums may occur in patients with aspiration pneumonitis and lung abscess; characteristic cutaneous lesions may point to sarcoidosis (Chap. 270), collagen vascular disease, Wegener's granulomatosis, and berylliosis, all of which may have prominent pulmonary manifestations. Clubbing of the fingers or, when advanced, osteoarthropathy (Chap. 278) may suggest carcinoma (Chap. 213) or suppurative disease (Chap. 205) of the lung; chronic hypoxia, as occurs in patients with chronic bronchitis (Chap. 208); pulmonary arteriovenous fistula; or congenital heart disease with right-to-left shunt (Chap. 185). However, clubbing is also seen in some patients with biliary cirrhosis, regional enteritis, and ulcerative colitis. A careful search for infection in the teeth, gums, tonsils, or sinuses is recommended in patients known to have or to be suspected of having bronchiectasis or lung abscess. Neurologic findings including headache, drowsiness, papilledema, and other evidence of increased intracranial pressure may occur in patients with

pulmonary disease who have hypoxemia and hypercapnia. Vascular collapse is a late complication of carbon dioxide intoxication and is characterized by hypotension, flushed skin, sweating, and tachycardia.

DIAGNOSTIC TESTS The *roentgenographic examination* of the chest represents the cornerstone of the diagnostic workup of the patient with suspected pulmonary disease, and it is the integration of the information obtained from the clinical examination and the roentgenogram which often provides the key to diagnosis. Unfortunately, physical examination of the chest has been deemphasized, largely because of the recognition of the enormous value of radiographic techniques. However, abnormalities such as small or moderate amounts of fluid in the alveoli or in the mediastinum, bronchospasm, and pleural effusions can often be detected more accurately by physical examination than by chest roentgenography. Tracheal deviation can be readily recognized on physical examination and may be observed in obstruction of a major bronchus and in atelectasis.

Chest roentgenograms obtained in the lateral decubitus position frequently reveal small pleural effusions not evident in the upright posture. A number of other abnormalities may be associated with normal roentgenograms. These include solitary lesions less than 6 mm in diameter, acute pulmonary thromboembolism without infarction, early interstitial pneumonia, diffuse granulomatous disease such as miliary tuberculosis, interstitial disease such as scleroderma and systemic lupus erythematosus, bronchiectasis, acute chronic bronchitis, mild to moderate emphysema, endobronchial masses only partially obstructing the airways, and the majority of instances of hypoventilation due to disorders of the central nervous system or neuromuscular disease. On the other hand, gross abnormalities of thoracic structure; pulmonary, mediastinal, and pleural masses; parenchymal consolidation, cysts, cavities, and abnormalities of the pulmonary vascular bed are all detected more reliably by roentgenographic than by physical examination.

An abnormal chest roentgenogram may be the presenting feature in an asymptomatic patient. In such circumstances the physician must make every effort to obtain earlier films in order to determine whether the lesion is new or old. Laminography, computerized tomography, angiocardiography, and pulmonary scintigraphy are additional procedures which may be helpful in establishing a diagnosis in a patient with an abnormality on the plain chest roentgenogram.

A variety of other diagnostic procedures are helpful in the workup of the patient with known or suspected pulmonary disease. These are presented in Chap. 201 and include skin tests for tuberculosis; scratch or intradermal tests to detect atopic reactions; appropriate serum complement fixation tests; and examination and culture of the sputum, pleural fluid, and bronchial washings. Bronchoscopy, bronchial brushings, and bronchoscopic biopsy have been greatly facilitated by the development of the fiberoptic bronchoscope. Mediastinoscopy, scalene node and mediastinal node biopsy, and pleural and lung biopsy may also be instrumental in establishing a diagnosis in an otherwise asymptomatic patient. Particularly important points which must be investigated in the history of the asymptomatic patient with an abnormality discovered on a routine chest roentgenogram include exposure to individuals with tuberculosis; previous tuberculin and fungous skin tests; residence in or visits to areas where fungal disease is endemic; a history of smoking and of exposure to dusts; and symptoms of systemic disease such as fever, sweat, fatigue, and weight loss. Physiologic (lung function) studies (Chap. 200) are of limited value in establishing an etiologic diagnosis in the patient with pulmonary diseases. They are, however, very helpful in assessing the physiologic consequences of disorders of the respiratory system and chest wall, as well as in following the effects of their progression or remission. Simple functional tests, such as observing the patient climbing one or two flights of stairs, are often valuable in determining whether or not the patient is grossly disabled.

In the approach to a patient with pulmonary disease, consideration must be given to the observation that substantial changes in the relative incidence of disease affecting the respiratory system have taken place in the United States during the past three decades. The prevalence of chronic infectious disorders such as tuberculosis, lung abscess, and bronchiectasis have decreased. On the other hand, patients with chronic bronchitis and with emphysema now survive longer and form an increasing fraction of patients with chronic respiratory disease, as do patients with environmental lung disease and with drug-induced disease. Modern intercontinental travel has increased the appearance in the western world of parasitic infestations of the lung. Also, the reduction of immunologic competence which occurs in patients with the acquired immunodeficiency syndrome (Chap. 257) and in diabetics as well as in the treatment of patients with a variety of malignancies and following organ transplantation has led to an increasing incidence of opportunistic infections of the lungs with a variety of microorganisms rarely pathogenic in the past.

REFERENCES

FISHMAN AP (ed): *Pulmonary Diseases and Disorders*, 2d ed. New York, McGraw-Hill, 1987

SNIDER GL (ed): *Clinical Pulmonary Medicine*. Boston, Little, Brown, 1981

200 DISTURBANCES OF RESPIRATORY FUNCTION

JOHN B. WEST

The prime function of the lung is to exchange gas between the inspired air and the venous blood. A convenient starting point, therefore, for a discussion of disturbances of respiratory function is the alveolar membrane across which gas exchange occurs (Fig. 200-1). This blood-gas barrier is less than 1 μm thick and has a surface area of some 100 m². It is therefore ideally suited to its gas exchange function.

Air is pumped to one side of this membrane and blood to the other. The air flows through conducting tubes, the bronchi; these are not lined with blood capillaries, with the result that no gas exchange can occur within them. These conducting airways, therefore, comprise the *anatomic dead space*. Beyond these airways is the *alveolar gas*, which makes up most of the volume of the lung. This gas is in a constant state of agitation because of molecular diffusion, and thus all the alveolar gas has access to the capillary blood via the alveolar membrane.

On the other side of the membrane, blood is pumped from the right side of the heart to the pulmonary capillaries. These delicate vessels have diameters of only about 10 μm, so that the blood is spread out in a thin film, one or two red blood cells thick, around the air sacs.

It is worth emphasizing two features of the basic lung unit shown in Fig. 200-1: (1) its symmetry, i.e., air and blood are equally important in the central process of gas exchange (this simple fact is sometimes forgotten in clinical medicine, where the patient's difficulties in moving air in and out of the lung often dominate the picture); (2) the simplicity of the lung unit compared with, say, the nephron. The structure of the lung is simple because its main role is simple; i.e., it brings together air and blood so that gas exchange can occur by passive diffusion. By contrast, the kidney carries out many functions involving active transport, and its structure is correspondingly complicated (compare Fig. 218-2).

VENTILATION

This is the process of moving inspired air into the alveolar gas compartment, where the gas exchange with the blood occurs. Some typical values for ventilation are shown in Fig. 200-1. A normal breath is about 500 mL, so that with a breathing frequency of 15 per minute some 7 to 8 liters of air enters the lung each minute. This is the *total ventilation*. However, because the volume of the conducting airways (anatomic dead space) is about 150 mL, only 350 of the 500 mL of air inhaled with each breath reaches the alveolar gas compartment. The rest remains behind in the airways and is subsequently exhaled. Thus, the volume of fresh gas entering the alveoli each minute is about 350 mL × 15, or some 5 liters. This is known as the *alveolar ventilation* and is of key importance to gas exchange. Of the 5 liters of fresh air entering the alveoli, some 300 mL of oxygen moves across into the blood each minute to be replaced by about 250 mL of carbon dioxide. Thus less than 5 percent of the gas volume inhaled is exchanged with the blood.

The above figures apply to resting conditions. On exercise, the oxygen uptake may rise as high as 4 to 6 liters per minute and the total ventilation inspired may increase twentyfold. This is accomplished by an increase in both tidal volume and frequency of breathing.

It should be noted that inspired air passes only a limited distance down the airways by ordinary bulk flow. Before it gets to the alveoli, its forward velocity is reduced to something like a millimeter per second, because of the enormous combined cross-sectional area of the small airways. In addition, the volume of gas in the bronchioles is so large that the alveoli and their ducts have completed their expansion before the fresh inspired air reaches them. The last few millimeters of its travel are therefore accomplished by molecular diffusion within the small airways. This process is very rapid for gas molecules but exceedingly slow for dust particles if they are over 0.5 μm in diameter. For this reason most inhaled dusts and aerosols never reach the alveoli, and many are deposited in the region of the terminal bronchioles.

MEASUREMENT OF VENTILATION The total volume of air passing the lips is easily measured by connecting a large bag or spirometer to the patient via a mouthpiece and one-way valve. The resting and exercise ventilations are increased when disease impairs the efficiency of pulmonary gas exchange, but the measurement of ventilation by itself is often unreliable because it is partly under voluntary control and is often changed by the stress of the measurement.

CONTROL OF VENTILATION The rhythmic act of breathing is initiated in the respiratory centers of the pons and medulla. The level of ventilation is controlled by the arterial P_{CO_2}, P_{O_2}, and pH and by reflexes originating in the lung and elsewhere. The chief regulation is carried out by the medullary chemoreceptors which respond to changes in the partial pressure of carbon dioxide, P_{CO_2}, in arterial blood. There is evidence that these chemoreceptors are exquisitely sensitive to a fall in pH of the extracellular fluid around them, which occurs when carbon dioxide diffuses across the blood-brain barrier. This dissolved gas moves easily across the blood-brain barrier,

FIGURE 200-1 *Simplified diagram of the lung showing typical volumes and flows. There is considerable variation around these values. (From West, 1985.)*

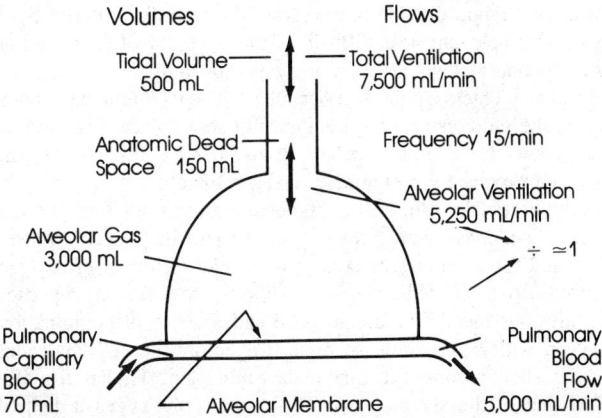

whereas H^+ and HCO_3^- do not. The composition of extracellular fluid is similar to that of cerebrospinal fluid.

Arterial hypoxemia also increases the ventilation through its action on the peripheral chemoreceptors in the carotid bodies. This hypoxic stimulus is normally relatively weak and variable but may dominate during chronic hypoxemia—for example, following ascent to high altitude. This is also often the situation in patients with chronic respiratory failure, with the result that the administration of oxygen may cause hypoventilation and severe carbon dioxide retention.

The pH of the arterial blood has an effect on ventilation which is independent of the P_{CO_2}. This is why ventilation may be increased during metabolic acidosis, thus reducing the arterial P_{CO_2}.

Reflexes from the lung from stretch receptors, irritant receptors, and receptors situated in the alveolar walls (juxtacapillary or J) also influence ventilation under some conditions.

HYPOVENTILATION   When inspired air reaches the alveoli, oxygen is removed from it and carbon dioxide is added. The concentrations, or partial pressures, of these two gases in the alveoli depend on a balance between two processes. On the one hand, the removal of oxygen from (or addition of carbon dioxide to) the alveolar gas is determined by the metabolic demands of the body. On the other hand, the addition of oxygen to (or removal of carbon dioxide from) the alveolar gas depends on the amount of alveolar ventilation. Thus, if the alveolar ventilation is low in relation to oxygen uptake and carbon dioxide output, the partial pressure of oxygen in alveolar gas and arterial blood falls, and the level of carbon dioxide rises. This is hypoventilation.

Hypoventilation is commonly caused by disease outside the respiratory system and often exists in the presence of normal lungs. Causes include depression of the respiratory center by drugs or anesthesia, damage to the medulla by disease, diseases affecting the nerve supply to the muscles of the thorax or the muscles themselves, injury to the chest wall, and obstruction to the airways. Because the lungs themselves are often (though not always) normal, the prognosis may be excellent if the precipitating cause is removed. Note that hypoventilation always causes both hypoxemia and hypercapnia, although the first can be abolished by adding oxygen to the inspired air. The carbon dioxide retention can be relieved only by increasing the ventilation, e.g., by using a ventilator. Disorders leading to hypoventilation are discussed in more detail in Chap. 215.

HYPERVENTILATION   If the alveolar ventilation is abnormally high for the carbon dioxide production of the body, the arterial P_{CO_2} falls. This may occur in metabolic acidosis, e.g., uremia, where the chemoreceptors respond to the low blood pH. Hysterical hyperventilation also occurs. For more information on hyperventilation see Chap. 215. The sensation of respiratory distress, or *dyspnea*, which should be clearly distinguished from *hyperpnea*, is considered in detail in Chap. 26.

DIFFUSION ACROSS THE BLOOD-GAS BARRIER

Oxygen and carbon dioxide move across the blood-gas barrier by a process of simple physical diffusion from a region of high partial pressure to one of low, just as water runs downhill. Consider a red blood cell as it enters a pulmonary capillary. The P_{O_2} in mixed venous blood (in the pulmonary artery) is typically about 40 mmHg, and as the cell enters the capillary the P_{O_2} in alveolar gas less than 1 μm away is approximately 100 mmHg. Oxygen therefore moves rapidly across the barrier into the cell to combine with hemoglobin, and the P_{O_2} rises. As a consequence, the oxygen pressure difference between the cell and the alveolar gas falls, and the rate of inflow of oxygen is reduced. However, under normal conditions, the diffusion properties of the alveolar membrane are so good and the rate of combination of oxygen with hemoglobin so rapid that before the cell has spent more than about a third of its time in the capillary, its P_{O_2} has virtually reached that of the alveolar gas. This transfer of oxygen is helped

by the shape of the oxygen dissociation curve; the nearly flat upper part of the curve (see Fig. 283-4) ensures that the driving pressure difference is maintained until almost all the oxygen has moved across. Thus, under ordinary circumstances, there is no measurable difference between the P_{O_2} of alveolar gas and that of the blood at the end of the pulmonary capillary. Indeed, the normal lung has plenty of reserve diffusion.

Two factors which stress the diffusion ability of the lung are exercise and alveolar hypoxia. During strenuous exercise, the time spent by the red blood cells in the capillaries is greatly reduced, perhaps to a half or a third of that at rest, so that the time available for the diffusion process is curtailed. Even so, the P_{O_2} in the capillary blood almost reaches that of the alveolar gas, except possibly during the most exhausting work. Additional stress occurs if the lung inspires a low oxygen mixture, thus reducing the alveolar P_{O_2}. Because the pressure difference between the oxygen in the gas and that in the red blood cells as they enter the capillary is lowered, the rate of movement of oxygen across the membrane is slowed. There is evidence that heavy work when the inspired P_{O_2} is very low (e.g., at high altitude) causes lowering of the arterial P_{O_2} because of inadequate diffusion into the pulmonary capillary. It is generally argued that carbon dioxide transfer is never limited by diffusion across the alveolar membrane because of the much higher diffusion rate of this gas in tissue, but recent work suggests that this may not always be the case.

MEASUREMENT OF DIFFUSING CAPACITY   This can be done using carbon monoxide. The subject inspires a low concentration (approximately 0.1 percent), and the rate of uptake of the gas by the blood is calculated from the difference between the inspired and expired concentrations. The measurement can be made during the course of a single 10-s breath-holding period or during a minute or so of steady breathing. In both cases, the diffusing capacity is expressed as the milliliters per minute of carbon monoxide taken up by the lung per millimeter of mercury of partial pressure of carbon monoxide in the alveolar gas. Normal values are in the region of 20 (mL/min)/mmHg at rest, rising to 60 (mL/min)/mmHg or more on exercise.

The reason why the uptake of carbon monoxide measures the diffusing capacity is the remarkable avidity of blood for this gas. This means that appreciable amounts of carbon monoxide can be combined with hemoglobin in the blood at an exceedingly low partial pressure. As a result, the rise in partial pressure of carbon monoxide in the red blood cells as they pass along the pulmonary capillaries is negligible, and the amount of the gas which is transferred into the blood is determined only by the diffusion properties of the alveolar membrane and the rate of combination of carbon monoxide with hemoglobin. This rate depends on the P_{O_2} in the alveoli; by measuring the carbon monoxide uptake at various inspired oxygen partial pressures, it is possible to determine separately the diffusing capacity of the alveolar membrane itself and the volume of blood in pulmonary capillaries. In patients who smoke, the level of carboxyhemoglobin in the blood may not be negligible and should be allowed for.

The measurement of carbon monoxide uptake is a relatively simple procedure, and there is no problem in following changes of diffusing capacity in the normal lung under a variety of conditions. Unfortunately, however, it is very difficult to say how far the carbon monoxide uptake reflects the true diffusion characteristics of the alveolar membrane and the capillary blood in the presence of appreciable lung disease. The reason for this is that inequalities of ventilation, diffusion properties of the alveolar membrane, and blood volume within the lung reduce the carbon monoxide in an unpredictable way. For this reason, the term *transfer factor* is sometimes used (especially in Europe), and the test should be looked upon as a general index of the efficiency of gas exchange in the lung rather than as a specific test of diffusion.

IMPAIRMENT OF DIFFUSION   The diffusion properties of the alveolar membrane depend on its thickness and area. Thus, the diffusing capacity is reduced by diseases in which the thickness is increased, including diffuse interstitial fibrosis (Chap. 209), sarcoidosis (Chap.

270), asbestosis (Chap. 204), and alveolar cell carcinomatosis (Chap. 213). The diffusing capacity also falls when the area of the membrane is reduced. This occurs following pneumonectomy and in emphysema. In addition, as we saw above, the diffusing capacity falls when the capillary blood volume or the number of red blood cells in the capillaries is reduced. This is the case in anemia and in diseases such as pulmonary embolism.

The importance of diffusion impairment as a cause of hypoxemia has long been disputed. In those lung diseases such as diffuse interstitial fibrosis in which microscopically the alveolar wall is thickened, it is tempting to attribute all the hypoxemia to defective diffusion. The term *alveolar-capillary block* was coined for this situation, and it is certainly an easy one to remember. However, more recent work indicates that impaired diffusion is not the principal cause of the hypoxemia in these patients. It is probably impossible for normal ventilation and blood flow to occur in an alveolus which has a thickened wall. Studies in which it is possible to assess the extent of ventilation-perfusion inequality in patients with interstitial lung disease using the multiple inert gas technique indicate that, at rest, all the hypoxemia can be attributed to uneven ventilation and blood flow. However, on exercise, a small component of the hypoxemia is apparently caused by diffusion impairment. Thus, most of the hypoxemia in patients with so-called alveolar-capillary block must be attributed to ventilation-perfusion inequality.

BLOOD FLOW

Mixed venous blood is pumped to the pulmonary capillaries directly from the right side of the heart so that the total *pulmonary blood flow* is equal to the cardiac output, say 5 or 6 liters per minute in a normal adult. Figure 200-1 shows that the volume of fresh inspired air entering the alveoli each minute, the *alveolar ventilation,* is some 5 liters. Thus, the overall ratio of ventilation to blood flow, or *ventilation/ perfusion ratio,* is about 1.

Even though the volumes of fresh gas and blood reaching the alveoli each minute are about the same, the volumes involved in exchanging gas at any instant are very different. Thus, while the alveolar gas volume is 2 to 3 liters at the end of a normal expiration, the capillary blood volume is only some 70 mL.

The pressures in the pulmonary circulation have long been considered the domain of the cardiologist, but they have an important bearing on gas exchange in the lung. The normal pulmonary arterial pressure is only just sufficient to raise blood to the top of the upright lung; if the pressure is reduced, as in hemorrhagic shock, the upper part of the lung is unperfused and gas exchange is impaired. Alterations in the pulmonary venous pressure, too, affect the distribution of blood flow in the lung.

VENTILATION-PERFUSION RELATIONSHIPS

Life would be much simpler if all lung units behaved identically. In practice, however, the lung is not homogeneous, and the differences in behavior between the millions of units are responsible for the greater part of the hypoxemia and carbon dioxide retention seen in clinical practice. We shall see that even in the normal lung, there are marked regional differences in blood flow and ventilation which affect gas exchange, while in diseased states, the inhomogeneity becomes so severe that respiratory failure may ultimately develop.

NORMAL DISTRIBUTION OF BLOOD FLOW It is possible to measure the regional distribution of blood flow and ventilation in the lung by using radioactive gases. In one technique, the inert gas xenon 133 is employed. To measure blood flow, the xenon is dissolved in saline and injected into a peripheral vein. On reaching the lung, it is evolved into alveolar gas because of its poor solubility; there it remains during breath holding, and its radiation can be detected by external counters. To measure ventilation, the patient inhales a single breath of the radioactive gas and again its regional distribution is measured. In both instances, a further measurement after a period of rebreathing of xenon allows a correction for lung volume to be made.

In the normal upright lung, blood flow per unit volume decreases rapidly from bottom to top, reaching very low values at the apex. This pattern is affected by change of posture and exercise. When the subject lies supine, the apical and basal blood flows become the same, but the posterior (dependent) part of the lung has a higher blood flow than the anterior region. In the lateral position, the dependent regions are best perfused. On exercise in the upright position, both apical and basal blood flows increase, so that the proportion of the total flow going to the apex rises.

The cause of this uneven distribution of blood flow lies in the hydrostatic pressure differences within the lung. The pulmonary circulation is unique in that air and blood are separated by a very delicate membrane over a vertical distance of some 30 cm in the upright position, and consequently, the hydrostatic effect of this large column of blood determines the caliber of the small vessels. The distribution of blood flow depends on the relative magnitudes of the pulmonary arterial, venous, and alveolar pressures. In particular, if pulmonary arterial pressure falls (as in hemorrhage, shock, and anesthesia) or alveolar pressure is raised (as in positive-pressure ventilation), the distribution of blood flow becomes more uneven. The normal pattern is also commonly affected by both heart and lung disease.

NORMAL DISTRIBUTION OF VENTILATION Ventilation also increases down the upright lung, though the changes are less marked than for blood flow. This distribution of ventilation which is seen under normal resting conditions is altered at low lung volumes. It has been shown that when a normal subject exhales as far as possible (to *residual volume*) and then gradually inhales in small steps, initially very little air goes into the lower zones, but the upper zones are well ventilated. However, before the subject reaches a normal resting lung volume (*functional residual capacity*), this distribution is reversed and the lower zones are better ventilated than the upper. This pattern is then maintained right up to maximal volumes. The poor ventilation of the dependent regions of the lung at low lung volumes is seen in the erect, supine, and lateral situations, and it has important implications in clinical situations in which the lung volume is low, e.g., in obesity or following abdominal surgery. Since the dependent regions are the best perfused, the impairment of gas exchange may then be severe.

The cause of the normal uneven distribution of ventilation has to do with the weight of the lung and the way it is supported inside the chest. It is known that the expanding pressure on the lung is less in the dependent zones, because these regions help to support the lung above them. Thus, the intrapleural pressure is less negative at the bottom of the lung than at the top. The reason for the greater ventilation of the dependent regions at normal volumes is twofold: (1) these alveoli have a smaller resting volume, and (2) their increase in volume is relatively large because, having a smaller volume, they are more distensible. By contrast, these dependent regions are poorly ventilated at low lung volumes because the expanding forces on them are then too weak to inflate them. Indeed, under these conditions, the airways to these alveoli may close and the alveoli become unventilated.

The volume at which the lower zone airways close (the *closing volume*) is considerably less than the functional residual capacity in normal young subjects. However, as the lung ages, and especially in the presence of chronic obstructive lung disease, the closing volume increases until it encroaches on the normal breathing range. Thus elderly normal subjects and patients with chronic bronchitis and emphysema frequently close their lower zone airways during resting breathing; this results in a poorly ventilated region which impairs gas exchange.

The closing volume can be measured from the single-breath nitrogen test (see ''Measurement of Ventilation Inequality'' below). There is some evidence that the measurement of closing volume is a sensitive test of early disease affecting the small airways, though this is disputed.

VENTILATION/PERFUSION RATIO   We have seen that while blood flow increases greatly down the upright lung, the change in ventilation is less. As a result, the ventilation/perfusion ratio varies from a high value at the top of the lung to a low value at the bottom. The ventilation/perfusion ratio is of key importance because it determines the gas exchange which occurs in any part of the lung.

We saw earlier that the partial pressure of oxygen in the alveolar gas (and therefore in the end-capillary blood) is set by a balance between the rate of its removal by the blood flow, on the one hand, and the rate of its replenishment by the ventilation on the other. Thus, if the ventilation is gradually reduced but the blood flow is maintained, the oxygen partial pressure will gradually fall. The limit is reached when the unit is not ventilated, and the P_{O_2} becomes that of venous blood. This is a ventilation/perfusion ratio of zero. By contrast, if perfusion is gradually reduced, the P_{O_2} will rise. The limit now occurs when the unit is unperfused and the P_{O_2} in the alveolus is the same as that of inspired air. This is a ventilation/perfusion ratio of infinity.

Thus, the crucial factor determining the oxygen partial pressure is the ventilation/perfusion ratio; this is also true for the partial pressure of carbon dioxide, and indeed of any other gas that might be present. It can be shown that marked regional differences of gas exchange occur in the normal upright lung as a consequence of the uneven ventilation/perfusion ratios.

OVERALL GAS EXCHANGE   Though such regional differences in gas exchange are of interest, more important is the effect of uneven ventilation/perfusion ratios on overall gas exchange, i.e., the ability of the lung to take up oxygen and put out carbon dioxide. The reason why gas transfer is impaired by uneven ventilation and blood flow is that those lung units which are overperfused in relation to their ventilation, and which therefore have a low P_{O_2}, contribute a disproportionate amount of the blood flow to the systemic arterial system. The net result is that the arterial P_{O_2} is depressed because it is loaded with less well oxygenated blood. In the same way, because these lung units have a relatively high P_{CO_2}, they tend to elevate the arterial P_{CO_2}. It is as if uneven ventilation/perfusion ratios set up a barrier between the gas and the blood, with the result that the arterial P_{O_2} is depressed and the P_{CO_2} is raised. The effects of ventilation/perfusion ratio inequality on arterial P_{O_2} are exaggerated by the nonlinearity of the oxygen dissociation curve.

In the normal lung, the effects of uneven ventilation/perfusion ratios on overall gas exchange are trivial; the arterial P_{O_2} is reduced by only a few millimeters of mercury and the P_{CO_2} is raised by less than 1 mmHg, if all else remains the same. Both these liabilities can be met if the total ventilation of the lung and thus its overall ventilation/perfusion ratio are increased. Indeed, the level of overall ventilation is normally set by the medullary respiratory center via the arterial P_{CO_2}. Thus, if uneven ventilation/perfusion ratios elevate the arterial P_{CO_2}, this is brought back by the increased respiratory drive and the consequently higher overall ventilation.

In the diseased lung, the effects of ventilation/perfusion ratio inequality on gas transfer may be very severe because the degree of uneven ventilation and blood flow is far greater than in the normal lung. The arterial P_{O_2} may be depressed by 50 mmHg or more, and in practice no amount of increased ventilation can return it to its normal level. The P_{CO_2}, however, is often maintained at the normal level by an increase in total ventilation. The reason why an increase in ventilation to diseased lungs can reduce the arterial P_{CO_2} but cannot increase the P_{O_2} to normal levels lies in the different shapes of the two dissociation curves. If the ventilation is not increased, the P_{CO_2} remains elevated. Ventilation/perfusion ratio inequality is much the commonest cause of hypoxia and hypercapnia in generalized lung disease.

MEASUREMENT OF VENTILATION/PERFUSION INEQUALITY   Unfortunately, it is difficult to derive much information about the pattern of uneven ventilation and blood flow in the diseased lung. Because much of the inequality is at the microscopic level, radioactive gas detectors which "see" relatively large regions of lung give little indication of the extent of the unevenness. The simplest way to obtain information about the amount of ventilation/perfusion inequality is by the analysis of expired gas and arterial blood.

One valuable measurement is the *alveolar-arterial P_{O_2} difference*. This is obtained by subtracting the arterial P_{O_2} from the so-called ideal alveolar P_{O_2}. The latter is the P_{O_2} which the lung would have if there were no ventilation/perfusion inequality. It is calculated from the arterial P_{CO_2} and the respiratory exchange ratio; specialized texts should be consulted for details.

An increased alveolar-arterial P_{O_2} difference is caused both by abnormally low and abnormally high ventilation/perfusion ratios within the lung. It is possible to assess separately the approximate contribution of these two groups to the impairment of gas exchange. For the units with low ventilation/perfusion ratios, we can calculate the *physiologic shunt*. To do this we assume that all the hypoxemia is caused by blood passing through unventilated alveoli (although we know this is an oversimplification). The calculation is made using a modified shunt equation.

The effect of lung units with abnormally high ventilation/perfusion ratios is assessed by calculating the *physiologic dead space*. Here we assume that all the reduction of P_{CO_2} in expired gas is caused by unperfused alveoli together with the anatomic dead space. A modified dead space equation is used for the calculation. Again, a specialized text should be consulted for details.

Another method of measuring ventilation/perfusion inequality uses a continuous infusion of six foreign inert gases into the venous blood. After a steady state of gas exchange has been established, the consequent partial pressures in arterial blood and expired gas are then measured. From this information, it is possible to derive an almost continuous distribution of ventilation/perfusion ratios. Young normal subjects have very narrow distributions centered on the normal value of about 1. Patients with chronic obstructive lung disease and asthma, for example, often have bimodal distributions with substantial amounts of blood flow going to lung units with very low ventilation/perfusion ratios.

MEASUREMENT OF VENTILATION INEQUALITY   Because the measurement of ventilation/perfusion ratio inequality is a relatively difficult procedure, the simpler measurement of uneven ventilation is often made. Although it would be theoretically possible for a patient to have ventilatory inequality but no mismatch of ventilation and blood flow, this is not seen in practice.

The simplest method of measuring uneven ventilation is the single-breath nitrogen wash-out test. For this, the patient takes a vital capacity inspiration of pure oxygen and then exhales fully. A rapid nitrogen meter at the lips measures expired nitrogen concentration, and expired volume is recorded simultaneously. After 750 mL has been expired (sufficient to clear the dead space), the rise in nitrogen concentration over the next 500 mL is measured. This is less than 1.5 percent in normal subjects. However, in patients with uneven ventilation, the nitrogen concentration rises more rapidly because the degree of dilution of the nitrogen by the inhaled oxygen varies throughout the lung, and also because the poorly ventilated regions (which receive little oxygen and therefore have the most nitrogen) always empty last. This is a simple, quick, and useful test, and it may also be used to give the closing volume (see earlier under "Normal Distribution of Ventilation").

Uneven ventilation can also be detected by a multibreath nitrogen wash-out test, but this is now usually confined to the research laboratory.

VENTILATION/PERFUSION RATIO INEQUALITY IN DISEASE   Virtually all generalized diseases of the lung, such as emphysema, chronic bronchitis, diffuse interstitial fibrosis, and the pneumoconioses, result in mismatch of ventilation and blood flow. As yet little is known about the pattern of unevenness in these conditions, though it is not difficult to imagine that an area of fibrosis or a bulla, for example, must interfere with both ventilation and blood flow.

There is evidence that, in general, areas of the lung which are poorly ventilated are also poorly perfused. One reason for this is that local pathologic change tends to disturb both processes by its mechanical effects. However, there are other physiologic mechanisms which reduce the mismatch of ventilation and perfusion. One is the reduction in blood flow to a poorly ventilated, hypoxic region of the lung, which has now been demonstrated on many occasions. The precise mechanism is unknown, but the phenomenon appears to be a local response to alveolar hypoxia since it occurs in the isolated denervated lung. Another mechanism is the reduction of ventilation which has been shown to follow obstruction of a branch of the pulmonary artery. This is apparently due to an increase in resistance of the small airways caused by a fall in P_{CO_2} in the region. This mechanism is weak in human beings.

How far these two mechanisms operate in practice is unknown, but it has been shown that the administration of various bronchodilator and vasodilator drugs to patients with generalized lung disease can exaggerate their hypoxemia. For example, isoproterenol (by aerosol) and epinephrine and aminophylline (by injection) have been shown to reduce the arterial P_{O_2} of some patients with chronic obstructive lung disease and bronchial asthma. It is possible that one of the actions of these drugs is to interfere with these active mechanisms which reduce ventilation/perfusion ratio inequality.

MECHANICS OF BREATHING

The bellows function of the lung is one of the easiest to measure and also one of the most informative measurements in practice. Serious malfunction of the lung is almost always accompanied by a reduced ventilatory capacity.

LUNG AND CHEST WALL The lung is elastic and collapses if it is not held expanded. The pressure *inside* the lung (alveolar pressure) is the same as atmospheric pressure at the end of inspiration or expiration if the glottis is open. The pressure *outside* the lung (intrapleural pressure) is less than atmospheric pressure, or "negative." This pressure keeps the lung inflated and is developed because the chest wall, which is also elastic, tends to bow outward, whereas the lung tends to collapse inward. If air is introduced into this space and a pneumothorax is produced, the lung collapses and the chest wall moves outward.

MUSCLES OF RESPIRATION The most important muscle of inspiration is the diaphragm, a thin, dome-shaped sheet of muscle which is inserted into the lower ribs and spine. It is supplied by the phrenic nerves from cervical segments 3, 4, and 5. When the diaphragm contracts, the abdominal contents are forced downward and forward, and the vertical dimension of the chest cavity is increased. In addition, the rib margins are lifted and moved out, causing a widening of the transverse diameter of the thorax.

In normal tidal breathing, the dome of the diaphragm descends about 1 cm, but on forced inspiration and expiration, a total descent of up to 10 cm may occur. If the diaphragm is paralyzed, it moves up rather than down with inspiration because of the fall of intrathoracic pressure. This is known as *paradoxical movement* and can be demonstrated at fluoroscopy by asking the patient to sniff.

The external intercostal muscles connect adjacent ribs and slope downward and forward. When they contract, the ribs are pulled upward and forward, causing an increase in both the lateral and anteroposterior diameters of the thorax. The lateral dimension of the rib cage also increases because of the "bucket-handle" movement of the ribs. The intercostal muscles are supplied by intercostal nerves which come off the spinal cord at the same level. Paralysis of the intercostal muscles alone does not seriously affect breathing because the diaphragm is so effective.

The accessory muscles of inspiration include the scalene muscles, which elevate the first two ribs, and the sternocleidomastoid muscles,

which raise the sternum. There is little if any activity in these muscles during quiet breathing, but during exercise they may contract vigorously. Other muscles which play a minor role include the alae nasi, which cause flaring of the nostrils, and the small muscles in the neck and head.

Expiration is passive during quiet breathing. The lung and chest wall tend to return to their equilibrium positions after being actively expanded during inspiration. During exercise and voluntary hyperventilation, expiration becomes active. The most important muscles of expiration are those of the abdominal wall, including the rectus abdominus, internal and external oblique muscles, and transversus abdominus. When these muscles contract, intraabdominal pressure is raised and the diaphragm is pushed upward. They also contract forcefully during coughing, vomiting, and defecation.

The internal intercostal muscles assist active expiration by pulling the ribs downward and inward (opposite to the action of the external intercostal muscles) thus decreasing the thoracic volume. In addition, they stiffen the intercostal spaces to prevent them from bulging outward during straining.

Disease affects the action of the respiratory muscles. In patients who have a greatly increased work of breathing, the diaphragm may become fatigued; this can result in inadequate ventilation and carbon dioxide retention. There is some evidence that diaphragmatic fatigue plays an important role in the respiratory failure of some patients.

In some newborns, the action of the various respiratory muscles may be poorly coordinated. This may be a factor in the sudden infant death syndrome (Chap. 215).

COMPLIANCE This is a term used to describe the elastic properties of the lung and chest wall. The normal lungs expand by about 200 mL when the expanding pressure (intrapleural pressure) falls by 1 cmH$_2$O. Thus the compliance (or distensibility) of the lungs is said to be 200 mL/cmH$_2$O. In fact, this figure only applies at normal resting lung volumes; at high lung volumes, the lungs are less easy to expand and their compliance falls. A more complete description of the elastic properties of the lungs, therefore, is the pressure-volume curve over the whole range of lung volumes; for this reason, this measurement is preferred in many pulmonary function laboratories. The compliance of the normal chest wall is about the same as that of the lungs, and the compliance of both lung and chest wall together is therefore about half this value, i.e., 100 mL/cmH$_2$O.

The compliance of the lung depends very much on how much tissue is present. A single lobe, for example, will clearly not change its volume as much as a whole lung for the same change in expanding pressure. Compliance is therefore sometimes corrected for lung volume and called *specific compliance*.

The normal elastic behavior of the lungs is partly caused by the elastic tissue within it. The two most important tissue components are elastin and collagen, and fibers of both kinds can be seen in the alveolar walls and around vessels and bronchi. Probably the elastic behavior of the lung has less to do with simple elongation of these fibers than with their geometric arrangement. An analogy is a nylon stocking which is very distensible because of its knitted makeup, although the individual nylon fibers are very difficult to stretch. The changes in elastic recoil that occur in the lung with age and in emphysema are presumably caused by changes in the configuration of these elastic tissue elements.

Another important component of the elastic behavior is the surface tension of the fluid lining the alveoli. The lungs may be regarded as composed of 300 million tiny bubbles which tend to collapse for the same reason that a soap bubble on the end of a bubble pipe does (although this is clearly an oversimplification). The surface forces which tend to reduce the area of the surface thus tend to reduce the volume of the bubble. These surface forces therefore contribute to the elastic force of the lung. Fortunately some of the cells lining the alveoli produce a phospholipid which lowers the surface tension of the lining fluid to extremely low values, especially at low lung volumes. The substance is known as a *surfactant*. This lowering of the surface tension is of great physiologic importance, because it helps to maintain the stability of the alveoli and discourage atelectasis. About half the normal elastic recoil force of the lung is due to these surface forces.

The exact composition of pulmonary surfactant is not known, but dipalmitoyl phosphatidyl choline (DPPC) is an important constituent. This is secreted by type 2 alveolar cells. Electron microscopy shows osmiophilic laminated bodies within the cells which are extruded into the alveoli and transform into surfactant. Some of the surfactant can be washed out of lungs by rinsing them with saline solution. Surfactant is formed relatively late in fetal life, and premature babies born without adequate amounts develop the infant respiratory distress syndrome (hyaline membrane disease).

The normal elastic behavior of the lung is disturbed by many diseases. Diffuse pulmonary fibrosis, pleural thickening, healed tuberculosis with scarring, and atelectasis all reduce the compliance of the lung. Heart disease such as mitral stenosis and left ventricular failure also commonly lowers compliance, although it is often difficult to be certain whether the volume of ventilating lung is reduced by edema in the airways, for example, or whether the elastic behavior of the lung tissue itself is altered. In emphysema and old age, the lungs become more compliant and have an abnormally large volume at normal expanding pressures.

Dynamic compliance refers to a measurement of compliance made at end inspiration and end expiration during breathing. In normal lungs, this is the same as the static compliance referred to above. However, when airway disease is present, dynamic compliance is smaller because some parts of the lung have not completely filled at the end of inspiration as a result of their increased airway resistance. Measurements of dynamic compliance can be used to infer increases in airway resistance.

AIRWAY RESISTANCE   So far we have been looking at the static forces involved in maintaining the expansion of the lung. However, during ventilation, additional forces are required to move air along the airways, because of the resistance offered to flow. This is expressed as the pressure difference between the alveoli and the mouth per unit of airflow rate. The normal value is in the vicinity of 1 to 2 cmH_2O per liter per second of flow at normal flow rates. The resistance rises at higher flow rates.

Until recently it was thought that the chief site of resistance was the small airways. However, it is now known that most of the resistance lies in the medium-sized bronchi and that the bronchioles less than 2 mm in diameter contribute less than 20 percent of the total airway resistance. The reason for this is the prodigious number of small airways and their large collective cross-sectional area. As a consequence, substantial increases in resistance of these bronchioles will not be detected by the usual pulmonary function tests, and they are said to constitute a "silent zone." There are tests designed to detect changes in the small airways. These include the single-breath nitrogen test, the measurement of closing volume referred to above, and the measurement of "frequency-dependent compliance," i.e., the apparent fall in dynamic compliance which occurs at high breathing rates. Whether these tests are better at detecting early airway disease than is the time-honored forced expiratory volume (see below under "Measurements of Mechanics") has not yet been established.

Various factors alter airway resistance. For example, the resistance is higher during expiration than inspiration, and it is greater at small lung volumes because the airways are then not held open so much. A single deep inspiration often reduces the resistance, but the inhalation of cigarette smoke or other irritants increases it through reflex contraction of airway smooth muscle following stimulation of irritant receptors located in the airway wall.

A dramatic increase in airway resistance occurs during forced expiration. The cause of this is collapse of the airways, called *dynamic compression*. The explanation is that the high intrapleural pressure is applied not only to the alveoli in an effort to empty them but also to the outside walls of the airways which lie within the chest. Consequently the airways are compressed, and as a result, the expiratory flow rate is independent of respiratory effort over a large range, since the greater the effort, the more the collapse. In normal subjects, this phenomenon takes place only during forced expirations, but it occurs much more readily in patients with chronic bronchitis and emphysema. This is because the airway walls are diseased and weakened, or because the airways lose their support by radial traction from the surrounding lung. In addition, the pressure difference responsible for expiration during dynamic compression is alveolar pressure minus pleural pressure, and this difference is reduced when compliance is increased, as in emphysema.

Diseases which increase airway resistance during normal breathing include bronchial asthma and chronic bronchitis. The resistance may rise to many times its normal value and even during clinical remissions of the disease can be shown to be abnormally high. Lung volume increases in these conditions, and this has two helpful consequences: the airways are pulled open more, thus limiting the increase in resistance, and the higher passive recoil pressure of the lung assists expiration.

WORK OF BREATHING   To move the lungs and chest wall and force air along the airways, work is required, and the respiratory muscles must consume oxygen. In normal subjects, the work of breathing is very small except during the large ventilation of heavy exercise. In patients with obstructive lung disease, however, the frictional resistance to airflow is high even at rest and the work of breathing is much increased, perhaps to 5 or 10 times its normal value. Under these conditions, the oxygen cost of breathing may become an appreciable fraction of the total oxygen consumption.

Patients with a reduced compliance of the lungs or chest wall have a higher work of breathing, because the stiffer structures are more difficult to move. These patients tend to use rapid shallow breaths, which reduce their oxygen cost of ventilation. However, if breathing becomes too shallow, the volume of air merely moved in and out of the anatomic dead space becomes disproportionately high, and gas exchange is consequently impaired. A compromise is therefore reached.

MEASUREMENTS OF MECHANICS   One of the most useful tests in the armamentarium of the pulmonary function laboratory is the analysis of a single forced expiration. The patient makes a full inspiration and then exhales as hard and as fast as possible into a lightweight spirometer. Typical records are shown in Fig. 200-2. It can be seen that for a normal subject the total volume exhaled is large. This is called the vital capacity or, preferably, the *forced vital capacity* (FVC). (The word *forced* is added because the volume may be less than the vital capacity measured with a slow expiration.) Also, about 80 percent of this volume is exhaled in 1 s. This is called the *forced expiratory volume,* or FEV_1. In *obstructive lung disease,* e.g., chronic bronchitis and emphysema, the forced vital capacity is reduced because the airways close and limit expiration before the patient has breathed out fully. In addition, the FEV_1 is grossly reduced, as is the FEV/FVC percentage. This is because of the high airway resistance which slows the rate of expiration. In *restrictive lung disease,* e.g., sarcoidosis, the FVC is low because of the limited expansion of the lung or chest wall. However, the FEV_1 is often not reduced proportionately, because airway resistance is normal. Thus the FEV/FVC percentage is normal or high. Normal values for lung volumes and spirometric tests are found in the appendix.

Other indexes of ventilatory function can be derived from a forced expiration. One is the maximal midexpiratory flow ($FEF_{25-75\%}$), which is obtained by dividing the volume between 75 percent and 25 percent of the vital capacity by the corresponding elapsed time (Fig. 200-2). This correlates well with the FEV_1 but may be a more sensitive measure of airway obstruction in early chronic obstructive lung disease.

Impaired lung function is frequently associated with a reduced FEV_1, and the test is therefore a valuable screening procedure. It is also useful in assessing the efficacy of bronchodilator therapy and in following the progress of patients with asthma or chronic obstructive lung disease.

Other lung volumes can also be measured at the same time. The *total lung capacity* is the total volume of gas in the lung at full inspiration. The *inspiratory capacity* is the maximum volume that can be inspired from the resting volume of the lungs, which is called the *functional residual capacity*. The maximum volume that can be expired from the resting level is the *expiratory reserve volume*. This leaves the *residual volume* still in the lungs, and this and the functional residual capacity can only be measured indirectly. One technique is to connect the patient to a spirometer circuit containing helium and measure the degree of dilution of this gas which occurs after several minutes of rebreathing. Another is to use a body plethysmograph (see below).

These volumes are often altered by disease. The functional residual capacity and residual volume are typically increased in diseases in which there is an increased airway resistance, for example, in emphysema, chronic bronchitis, and asthma. Indeed, at one time an elevated residual volume was regarded as an essential feature of emphysema, but less emphasis is placed on this test now. A reduced functional residual capacity and residual volume are often seen in patients with a reduced lung compliance, for example, in diffuse interstitial fibrosis. Here the lung is stiff and tends to recoil to a much smaller resting volume.

The measurement of compliance and airway resistance is more difficult. In order to determine lung compliance, i.e., volume change per unit of pressure change, the pressure expanding the lungs must be known. In practice this can be found by passing a small latex balloon connected to a manometer down into the esophagus. Esophageal pressure is then taken as a measure of intrapleural pressure. To measure airway resistance, i.e., the pressure drop along the airways per unit of airflow, alveolar pressure must be known. This can be found by seating the patient in a large airtight box, or plethysmograph. First, the patient is asked to try to breathe against a complete obstruction, and from the change in box pressure, lung volume can be calculated. Next, the patient is asked to pant, and again box pressure is recorded. Alveolar pressure can then be derived and airway resistance calculated. This equipment is available only in specialized centers.

Aging has an important influence on lung function. With increasing age there is a fall in vital capacity and forced expiratory volume and an increase in functional residual capacity, residual volume, and closing volume. In addition, lung elastic recoil decreases. Some inequality of ventilation and ventilation/perfusion ratios develops and the arterial P_{O_2} falls almost linearly with age. It is therefore important to take account of the age of the patient when interpreting many pulmonary function tests.

ACID-BASE DISTURBANCES If pulmonary gas exchange is impaired, the P_{CO_2} in the arterial blood may rise, which tends to depress the pH and causes *respiratory acidosis*. A decrease in P_{CO_2} causes *respiratory alkalosis*. The compensatory mechanisms which are then brought into play are discussed in Chap. 42.

MEASUREMENT OF BLOOD GASES Blood gas measurements play a vital role in the management of respiratory failure. Arterial blood can be obtained by direct puncture, and the oxygen and carbon dioxide partial pressures and the pH can be measured by electrodes. Oxygen saturation can be derived by spectrophotometry.

HYPOXEMIA

The four main causes of a low arterial P_{O_2} are (1) ventilation/perfusion ratio inequality, (2) right-to-left shunt, (3) hypoventilation, and (4) impaired diffusion. In addition, living at high altitude or deliberately inspiring a low oxygen mixture causes hypoxia.

1 *Ventilation/perfusion ratio inequality* is the commonest cause and is responsible for almost all the hypoxemia seen in chronic lung disease. Specific tests of ventilation/perfusion inequality are not generally available, although the multiple inert gas infusion technique referred to earlier can be used in specialized centers. The demonstration of ventilatory inequality (see above) is a useful pointer. Mild degrees of ventilation/perfusion ratio inequality may be present without hypoxemia, and considerable inequality may exist without hypercapnia if overall ventilation is increased. However, carbon dioxide retention almost always develops eventually. The hypoxemia is eventually abolished by the administration of 100% oxygen. However, with severe inequality, the arterial P_{O_2} may take so many minutes to rise to normal values because of very poorly ventilated areas that, in practice, the levels seen in normal subjects may not be attained. Exercise may or may not aggravate the hypoxemia and hypercapnia (see Table 200-1). The response of the arterial P_{O_2} to exercise depends to a large extent on the changes in total ventilation and blood flow.

2 *Shunted blood*, i.e., blood which has bypassed ventilated areas of the lung, causes hypoxemia. Patients with right-to-left shunts through congenital heart defects or a pulmonary arteriovenous fistula belong to this group. Patients with ventilation/perfusion ratio inequality often have some parts of the lung completely unventilated, and the contribution of these regions is indistinguishable from that of a shunt. The hypoxemia due to shunt is not abolished (although it is reduced) by administering 100% oxygen, and this test will distinguish it from the other causes of hypoxemia. The level of the arterial P_{O_2} under these conditions allows the percentage of shunted blood to be measured. The arterial P_{O_2} rises

TABLE 200-1 Features helpful in distinguishing the various causes of hypoxemia and hypercapnia

	Hypox-emia	Hyper-capnia	Hypox-emia on exercise	Hyper-capnia on exercise	Hypox-emia on 100% O_2
Ventilation/per-fusion ratio in-equality	Yes	Yes or no	Yes	Yes or no	No
Shunt	Yes	No	Yes	Possible	Yes
Hypoventilation	Yes	Yes	Often severe	Often severe	No
Impaired diffu-sion	Yes (rarely)	No	Often severe	No	No

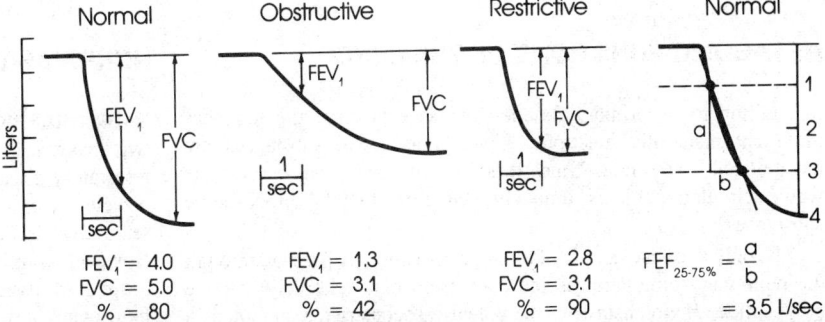

FIGURE 200-2 *Measurement of the forced expiratory volume, FEV_1; forced vital capacity, FVC; and maximum midexpiratory flow, $FEF_{25-75\%}$. The patient makes a full inspiration and then exhales as hard and as fast as possible. As the patient exhales the pen moves down. The FEV_1 is the volume exhaled in 1 s; the FVC is the total volume exhaled. The $FEF_{25-75\%}$ is the mean flow rate measured over the middle half of the FVC. Note the differences between the normal, obstructive, and restrictive patterns.*

Normal
$FEV_1 = 4.0$
$FVC = 5.0$
$\% = 80$

Obstructive
$FEV_1 = 1.3$
$FVC = 3.1$
$\% = 42$

Restrictive
$FEV_1 = 2.8$
$FVC = 3.1$
$\% = 90$

Normal
$FEF_{25-75\%} = \dfrac{a}{b}$
$= 3.5$ L/sec

to some extent because of the addition of dissolved oxygen to the pulmonary blood. The hypoxemia of shunt may be exaggerated by exercise. Hypercapnia does not occur unless the shunt is very gross, because the respiratory center increases the ventilation, thus holding the arterial P_{CO_2} down.

3 *Hypoventilation* always causes both hypoxemia and hypercapnia. Because of the shape of the oxygen dissociation curve, which means that a substantial fall in arterial P_{O_2} can occur with little reduction in oxygen saturation (see Fig. 283-4), considerable carbon dioxide retention may be present without recognizable cyanosis. If the patient is inhaling an enriched oxygen mixture, e.g., in the anesthetic recovery room, hypoxemia is not present but the hypercapnia may be severe.

4 *Impaired diffusion* rarely causes hypoxemia but does not cause hypercapnia. The hypoxemia is accentuated by exercise but abolished if an enriched oxygen mixture is administered. As we have seen, diffusion impairment may occur in normal subjects during work at very high altitude, but its importance as a cause of hypoxemia in disease is minimal.

HYPERCAPNIA

The two chief causes of carbon dioxide retention are ventilation/perfusion ratio inequality and hypoventilation. Ventilation/perfusion ratio inequality is the commonest cause, although many patients have some degree of uneven ventilation and blood flow without hypercapnia. A combination of the two causes can occur.

Why does a patient with chronic lung disease develop hypercapnia? Progressive lung disease (perhaps aggravated by an acute infection) causes increasing mismatch of blood flow and ventilation and greater impairment of carbon dioxide transfer. For a time, the respiratory center is able to hold the arterial P_{CO_2} down to the normal level by increasing the ventilation, but the work of breathing is usually high because of airway obstruction, so that eventually a compromise is reached and the arterial and alveolar partial pressures rise. This has the advantage that more carbon dioxide is put out for the same ventilation, so it may be looked upon as a compensatory mechanism, albeit a hazardous one. As the ventilation/perfusion ratio inequality becomes worse, the tendency is for the arterial P_{CO_2} to rise further.

A particularly dangerous situation may arise if such a patient is given oxygen to breathe. The chief stimulus to ventilation in these patients is often hypoxemia, and when this is suddenly relieved, the ventilation may drop precipitously and the arterial P_{CO_2} climb rapidly. The carbon dioxide retention and acidosis may then cause clouding of consciousness, muscular twitching, and a raised intracranial pressure. Drugs which depress the respiratory center may produce a similar effect. Thus while oxygen administration is indicated in these patients because of their severe hypoxemia, it should be given with caution and the blood gases should be frequently measured.

Another hazardous situation often arises when these patients are taken off oxygen because they are retaining too much carbon dioxide. Since the body stores of carbon dioxide are so large, many minutes elapse before the alveolar P_{CO_2} returns to reasonable levels. During this recovery period, this high alveolar carbon dioxide dilutes the alveolar oxygen and may cause profound hypoxia.

METABOLIC FUNCTIONS OF THE LUNG

In addition to its primary function of gas exchange, the lung has important metabolic functions. Several vasoactive substances are metabolized by the lung. Since it is the only organ that receives the whole circulation, it is uniquely suited to modify blood-borne substances.

The only known example of biologic activation by passage through the pulmonary circulation is the conversion of a relatively inactive polypeptide, angiotensin I, to the potent vasoconstrictor, angiotensin

II. The latter, which is up to 50 times more active than its precursor, is unaffected by passage through the lung. The conversion of angiotensin I is catalyzed by angiotensin-converting enzyme (ACE), which is located in small pits in the surface of the capillary endothelial cells.

Many vasoactive substances are completely or partially inactivated during passage through the lung. Bradykinin is largely inactivated (up to 80 percent); the enzyme responsible is ACE. The lung is also the major site of inactivation of serotonin (5-hydroxytryptamine), but this is not by enzymatic degradation but by an uptake and storage process. Some of the serotonin may be transferred to platelets in the lung or stored in some other way and released during anaphylaxis. The prostaglandins E_1, E_2, and $F_{2\alpha}$ are also inactivated in the lung, which is a rich source of the responsible enzymes. Norepinephrine is also taken up by the lung to some extent. Histamine appears not to be affected by the intact lung but is readily inactivated by lung slices.

Some vasoactive materials pass through the lung without significant gain or loss of activity. These include epinephrine, prostaglandins A_1 and A_2, angiotensin II, and vasopressin (ADH).

Several vasoactive substances are normally synthesized or stored within the lung but may be released into the circulation in pathologic conditions. For example, in anaphylaxis or during an asthma attack, histamine, bradykinin, prostaglandins, and "slow-reacting substances" are discharged into the circulation (see Chap. 202). Other conditions in which the lung may release potent chemicals include pulmonary embolism and alveolar hypoxia.

In disease, the lung has a remarkable potential for hormone production and secretion. For example, neoplasms such as bronchial carcinomas can produce a variety of polypeptide hormones.

REFERENCES

Cotes JF: *Lung Function,* 4th ed. St Louis, Mosby, 1979
West JB: *Pulmonary Pathophysiology—The Essentials,* 2d ed. Baltimore, Williams & Wilkins, 1982
———: *Respiratory Physiology—The Essentials,* 3d ed. Baltimore, Williams & Wilkins, 1985.

201 DIAGNOSTIC PROCEDURES IN RESPIRATORY DISEASES

KENNETH M. MOSER

In seeking a definitive diagnosis in the patient with respiratory disease, a wide choice of diagnostic procedures is available. These procedures vary considerably, not only in diagnostic reliability and specificity, but also in terms of the discomfort and hazard to the patient. Hence, an orderly sequence of test selection is mandatory. This sequence should begin with procedures involving little risk and, only if necessary, move on to those which entail higher morbidity and potential mortality.

NONINVASIVE PROCEDURES

RADIOGRAPHIC PROCEDURES   The *chest roentgenogram* serves two major roles in the search for a diagnosis in the patient with respiratory disease: *detector* and *guide*. Occasionally, in its role as a detector, the routine chest roentgenogram initiates the diagnostic search by disclosing an abnormality in an asymptomatic individual. However, routine chest roentgenography (e.g., as an element of all hospital admissions) is neither necessary nor cost-effective. Therefore, more commonly, it detects pulmonary involvement in someone already ill. Rarely, detection may coincide with diagnosis; e.g., in spontaneous pneumothorax or when a radiopaque foreign body has been aspirated.

Far more frequently, however, the roentgenogram, having detected potential disease, provides a guide to the selection of subsequent diagnostic procedures. Many radiographic findings are quite characteristic of certain diseases. A number of radiographic patterns are sufficiently repetitive to warrant descriptive names, such as bilateral hilar adenopathy, solitary pulmonary nodule, diffuse interstitial infiltrate, alveolar filling pattern, multinodular lesion, and honeycomb lung. Thus, a particular radiographic finding, combined with other pertinent data, often permits establishment of a reasonable list of possible diagnoses. For example, the roentgenographic detection of bilateral hilar adenopathy in an asymptomatic, 26-year-old black male immediately places sarcoidosis at the top of the list. A chest roentgenogram disclosing upper lobe cavities in a febrile male whose brother recently was admitted to a tuberculosis sanitarium would make tuberculosis the most likely entity. Or a ''diffuse interstitial'' infiltrate—for which more than 100 causes exist—may yield a prompt diagnosis of varicella pneumonia when combined with the classical skin lesions. Multinodular lesions, with some cavitating, in a patient with sinusitis and red cell casts on urinalysis makes Wegener's granulomatosis a primary diagnostic possibility. However, no roentgenographic pattern is sufficiently specific to *establish* a diagnosis. Lung cancer (primary and metastatic) can present many roentgenographic patterns, as can both infectious and noninfectious lung disorders. For example, cardiogenic pulmonary edema may present as a perihilar or diffuse alveolar filling pattern, as an interstitial process and, rarely, as a lobar infiltrate or interlobar collection of fluid (''pseudotumor'')—all with or without a pleural effusion.

In some instances, special radiographic techniques may provide valuable diagnostic insights.

Fluoroscopy allows visualization of the thoracic contents in a dynamic rather than static manner and also permits a wide range of special views. It also indicates whether a lesion is pulsatile, what its precise location in the thorax is, whether the hemidiaphragms move normally, i.e., whether they are fixed or move paradoxically, and how various zones of the lung behave during inspiration and expiration. Thus, fluoroscopy can define whether a roentgenographic density is actually in a rib or in the pleura rather than in the parenchyma; and may distinguish between a unilateral hyperlucent lung due to emphysema (mediastinum shifts toward the normal lung on expiration) or to unilateral pulmonary arterial obstruction (no shift).

Tomography (laminography, planigraphy) is a radiographic technique by which a sequence of roentgenograms, each representing a ''slice of the lung'' at a different depth, is obtained. Ordinarily, ''cuts'' are made at 0.5- to 1-cm distances through the area of interest. Tomograms can identify a number of features which were not appreciated on the ''routine'' roentgenogram, including calcium in a solitary nodule (which if diffuse or in concentric rings signifies a benign etiology); distinction between hilar adenopathy and dilated pulmonary arteries; a cavity in a mass lesion; and the contours of masses in the mediastinum.

Thoracic *computerized tomography* (*CT*) *scanning*, also may provide information not available through other techniques. It is particularly useful in the definition of pleural disease (e.g., differentiating fluid from tumor; identifying calcium in asbestos-exposed individuals); in evaluating hilar, paratracheal, and subcarinal node enlargement; with contrast injections, in differentiating tissue masses from vascular structures; and in identifying small parenchymal nodules. However, to some extent, the sensitivity of CT will be a mixed blessing until it is known how many ''normal'' individuals have pleural or parenchymal abnormalities by CT and how these small, benign, hitherto undetected lesions can be distinguished from neoplastic lesions.

Magnetic resonance imaging (MRI) remains, in terms of its potential value in pulmonary diseases, an investigational technique.

SKIN TESTS Having arrived at a tentative list of diagnostic possibilities based on the history, physical examination, and radiographic appearance, the physician should move to other procedures. One of the simplest and most commonly overlooked is the application of *skin tests* with specific antigens. Antigens are now available to assist in the diagnosis of tuberculosis, histoplasmosis, coccidioidomycosis, blastomycosis, trichinosis, toxoplasmosis, and aspergillosis. These tests vary with respect to sensitivity and cross-reactivity, and attention to scrupulous technique in performance and interpretation is vital. Also, some antigens (e.g., histoplasmosis) may confound serologic tests performed subsequently. A positive skin test indicates only that the antigen has been encountered previously by the host; it does not, regardless of reaction intensity, imply active disease. Furthermore, drugs or diseases which depress cell-mediated immunity (e.g., prednisone, cyclophosphamide, lymphomas, sarcoidosis, disseminated tuberculosis, or coccidioidomycosis) may cause skin anergy. Indeed, a negative battery of skin tests, if it incorporates antigens such as mumps, streptokinase-streptodornase, *Trichophyton*, and *Monilia*, suggests that a cause of skin anergy should be sought.

SEROLOGIC TESTS These tests also may be useful in the diagnosis of histoplasmosis, blastomycosis, coccidioidomycosis, toxoplasmosis, *Mycoplasma* pneumonia, Legionnaires' disease, a variety of other infectious diseases involving the lungs, and certain immunologically mediated lung diseases (e.g., lupus erythematosus). Often, more extensive diagnostic procedures can be avoided if appropriate serologic tests are obtained. However, there is substantial interinstitutional variability with respect to the sensitivity, specificity, and types of serologic tests available. Therefore, their appropriate use requires close interaction with the responsible laboratory.

SPUTUM EXAMINATION Another rapid, innocuous diagnostic procedure is *sputum examination*. It is important that the specimen contain sputum, not saliva, the latter being identified by the presence of squamous (mouth) rather than epithelial (bronchial) cells. The gross nature of the sputum—color, odor, and the presence of blood—may provide valuable clues; e.g., foul sputum suggesting anaerobic pulmonary infection and blood, in any amount, indicating an abnormality that mandates further investigation. Carefully stained smears of the sputum should be examined next, for these may disclose the causative organism in many bacterial pneumonias, in tuberculosis, and in some fungous infections. Sputum eosinophilia can suggest the presence of reversible airway disease responsive to corticosteroids; hemosiderin-laden macrophages suggest the possibility of Goodpasture's syndrome. Often valuable time is lost because the sputum smear is not examined and results of culture are awaited instead.

Culture of expectorated sputum (spontaneous or induced) has fallen into disrepute because of uncertain yield and, particularly, because of frequent and unavoidable contamination by the oropharyngeal bacterial flora. Although such cultures are invaluable for identification of organisms responsible for tuberculous and fungous infections, their utility in detection of other bacterial agents responsible for pulmonary infection is often uncertain and can be misleading, particularly in patients who are immunocompromised, intubated, or receiving antimicrobial therapy. Five procedures, described below, are now gaining wide acceptance because they limit oropharyngeal contamination and/or can be used to obtain representative samples of lung secretions from the area of lung involvement: (1) catheter-brush sampling, (2) bronchoalveolar lavage, (3) transtracheal aspiration, (4) transbronchial lung biopsy, and (5) percutaneous needle aspiration of the lung.

Exfoliative cytology of the sputum is helpful in the diagnosis of carcinoma of the lung (Chap. 213). Proper handling of such specimens is essential. Sputum samples often can be obtained in patients who are not coughing by having them inhale a heated mixture of a mildly irritative solution which induces cough.

PULMONARY FUNCTION TESTS (see also Chap. 200) Certain ''patterns'' of derangement in spirometric tests, arterial blood gases, diffusing capacity, and other functional parameters are particularly suggestive of certain pulmonary diseases. For example, diffuse interstitial fibrotic diseases of the lungs (Chap. 209) produce a "restrictive" spirometric defect, reduced pulmonary compliance, a reduced diffusing capacity, and an alveolar-arterial oxygen tension difference which is widened at rest and widens further with exercise. Emphysema (Chap. 208) characteristically causes expiratory obstruction, lung hyperinflation, decreased static elastic recoil (increased compliance), and a reduced diffusing capacity.

PULMONARY SCINTIPHOTOGRAPHY   Scintiphotographs ("scans") of intrathoracic structures are obtained by a variety of "scanning" devices which record the pattern of intrathoracic radioactivity after intravenous injection or inhalation of gamma-emitting radionuclides. Direct photographic or computer-derived images, or digital data, reflecting radionuclide distribution are used for diagnostic purposes. The most commonly used images are those which reflect the distribution of pulmonary blood flow (perfusion) and ventilation. Such scans have multiple diagnostic applications. For example, a normal perfusion scan excludes the diagnosis of acute pulmonary embolism (Chap. 211). When perfusion scans showing defects are combined with ventilation scans, ventilation-perfusion patterns are provided which assist in the diagnosis of parenchymal lung diseases and vascular occlusive disorders, including pulmonary embolism.

Another type of scan involves intravenous injection of radionuclides which have an affinity for intrathoracic inflammatory and neoplastic tissues. Gallium 67 is the most useful of such radionuclides now available. Concentration of such agents, defined by scanning, may permit detection of neoplastic or inflammatory disease in the lungs or mediastinal lymph nodes. Uptake by the lungs may, in some patients, reflect the intensity of inflammatory activity associated with diffuse interstitial pneumonitis, sarcoidosis, and granulomatous infections. Inapparent extrapulmonary foci of granulomatous or neoplastic diseases also may be detected by body scanning.

New radionuclides continue to emerge which, when complexed with such materials as platelets, white blood cells (e.g. indium 111), fibrinogen, and albumin, may allow imaging of intrathoracic vessels, thrombi, inflammation, and neoplasms. Tomographic and other image-processing methods are emerging which may further extend the value of these techniques.

All the above procedures involve minimal risks and discomfort to the patient. Where applicable, these approaches should be considered before the more invasive techniques discussed below are considered, unless the condition of the patient demands immediate diagnosis.

INVASIVE PROCEDURES

BRONCHOSCOPY   The primary objectives of bronchoscopy include direct visualization of the tracheobronchial tree, including abnormalities such as tumors or granulomatous lesions; biopsy of suggestive or obvious endobronchial lesions; and lavage, brushing, or biopsy of lung regions for cultural and cytologic examinations. Both the *diagnostic reach of* and *accessibility to* bronchoscopy have been expanded by the flexible fiberoptic bronchoscope (FOB). This can be understood best by comparing the FOB with the "standard" rigid bronchoscope.

The rigid bronchoscope is a wide-bore metal tube which incorporates a lighted mirror-lens system. The FOB is composed of fiberoptic bundles which provide both illumination and visualization pathways. A small channel with a diameter of 1 to 3 mm traverses the FOB, through which instruments can be passed, fluids delivered, and suction applied. The rigid bronchoscope comes in various external diameters limited only by the feasibility of introducing the rigid device orally and through the larynx. Biopsy and other procedures are carried out through the rather capacious interior of the rigid tube. The FOB also is available in various external diameters, but all are substantially smaller than rigid bronchoscopes (since no "wall" exists in the FOB). The distal tip of the FOB can be *flexed* easily to 90° and usually to 130° or more from the vertical.

Thus, the rigid bronchoscope permits visualization only of lobar bronchi and the orifices of some segmental bronchi. The flexible,

smaller FOB extends the range of *view* to all segmental and subsegmental bronchi and the range for *biopsy and sampling* to the pulmonary parenchyma itself. A biopsy forceps, catheter, or brush passed through the FOB can be directed well beyond the tip of the bronchoscope itself, permitting *transbronchial lung biopsy, brushings,* or *aspiration of secretions* for culture and cytologic examination from the most distal regions of the lung. Indeed, both forceps and brush can reach and perforate the pleura, leading to pneumothorax. Therefore, when the lesion being approached is distal, fluoroscopic guidance is essential. Not only does this permit placement of the FOB, forceps, catheter, or brush directly into the area of interest, but also it ensures that the pleura will not be inadvertently reached and punctured. The FOB also allows *regional* lung lavage to obtain materials for cytologic examination and culture. The use of specially designed catheters (see below) placed through the FOB is quite useful in obtaining representative, noncontaminated secretions for culture, thus avoiding the problems mentioned previously with expectorated sputum.

Thus, the FOB has sharply increased the limited diagnostic reach previously available with rigid bronchoscopy. Equally important, the FOB has made bronchoscopy more available to the physician and more acceptable to the patient. The performance of rigid bronchoscopy requires the supine position for peroral insertion of the device; can be performed safely by a relatively few trained surgeons; and is often carried out under general anesthesia in an operating room. Therefore, it has been a procedure requiring significant preparation and hence delay. Fiberoptic bronchoscopy can be performed in the sitting or supine position, since the FOB is easily inserted transnasally; can be performed by a large number of trained pulmonary specialists as well as surgeons; usually requires only local anesthesia; and can be performed safely on the wards, in diagnostic rooms equipped with a "dentist-type" chair, and in intensive care units. The FOB can be used easily in intubated patients on ventilators with simple "side-arm" adapters attached to the endotracheal tube. Therefore, when bronchoscopy is indicated, it is not surprising that fiberoptic bronchoscopy is now commonly the first choice. The roomier rigid bronchoscope is now usually reserved for situations in which the small biopsy-suction channel in the FOB may be inadequate (e.g., for removal of large foreign bodies, for laser surgery). The FOB also has a widening range of therapeutic applications including aspiration or lavage of secretions in patients with airway obstruction or atelectasis due to retained secretions; obstruction of bleeding areas of the lung, with a wedged FOB itself or with a balloon catheter passed via the FOB, in patients who are poor surgical risks; removal of small foreign bodies; and placement of radionuclides in tumors. Transtracheal needle aspiration of paratracheal and subcarinal nodes also can be performed via the FOB, a procedure which is particularly useful in the staging of carcinoma of the lung.

The hazards of bronchoscopy are modest but should be recognized. In addition to the risk of general anesthesia which rigid bronchoscopy usually requires, they can include hypoxemia, laryngospasm, bronchospasm, pneumothorax, and, of course, bleeding following biopsy. Proper management before, during, and after bronchoscopy should prevent most of these complications. There is no absolute contraindication to FOB. Even in the presence of massive hemoptysis, FOB with appropriate precautions can yield useful information. Patients with bronchospasm (or a history of bronchospasm) are at particular risk of acute enhancement of spasm and should be approached after good preparation and with resources for intubation-ventilation at hand. The primary contraindication to both rigid and fiberoptic bronchoscopy is the same: performance by inexperienced personnel. Lack of experience sharply reduces diagnostic and therapeutic yield while increasing risks.

BRONCHOGRAPHY   In this method, radiopaque material is instilled into the tracheobronchial tree via a catheter or bronchoscope. Positioning of the patient and catheter permits the material to coat all portions of the tracheobronchial tree for a sufficient period so that their outline can be recorded on chest roentgenograms. Bronchography is indicated for the diagnosis of bronchiectasis, for the identification of obstruction in distal bronchi, and for the detection of other types of congenital and acquired forms of tracheobronchial distortion or malformation. Like FOB, bronchography may induce bronchospasm; also, the irritative effects of the contrast medium may persist for some days.

TRANSTRACHEAL, CATHETER-BRUSH, AND PERCUTANEOUS NEEDLE ASPIRATION OF THE LUNG

All three of these procedures are used to obtain material for culture and microscopic examination. In the case of culture, all three techniques bypass the oropharyngeal flora, though transtracheal aspiration is the least certain in this regard.

Transtracheal aspiration involves needle puncture of the crico-thyroid membrane, insertion of a plastic cannula, and instillation of a saline solution, followed by suctioning of a sample. The procedure cannot be performed in intubated patients; contamination rates are high in previously intubated patients or those who have aspirated oropharyngeal contents. Because the procedure entails risks, although these are minimized by meticulous technique and experience, clear indications for its use should exist. These include patients with apparent pulmonary infection who are unable to cough, in whom cough is nonproductive, or in whom there has been a lack of response to therapy based on smears or cultures from expectorated sputum.

In these same contexts, *catheter-brush devices* specially designed with a distal plug to avoid oropharyngeal contamination can be used. These are manipulated (through an FOB or without it) under fluoroscopic guidance into the involved lung area. The distal absorbable plug is then ejected and the inner brush or catheter advanced for sampling. Finally, an alternative procedure is direct percutaneous aspiration, which can be performed using a small (23- or 25-gauge), thin-walled, *noncutting* needle. The needle, connected to a syringe, is introduced percutaneously into the area of the lung of interest; 2 to 3 mL saline is injected and then aspirated into the syringe and the needle withdrawn. Both the catheter-brush and needle approaches are high-yield, low-contamination procedures. In experienced hands, the risks are low, consisting chiefly of pneumothorax and bleeding. Patients should be carefully monitored for both.

The presence of a hemorrhagic diathesis is a relative contraindication to all three of the above procedures.

THORACENTESIS AND PLEURAL BIOPSY

Thoracentesis should be performed to obtain pleural fluid in all pleural effusions of uncertain etiology and may be indicated for relief of symptoms in some patients with effusion of known cause. In effusions of uncertain cause, closed (needle) pleural biopsy should be performed as part of the same procedure.

When pleural fluid is small in amount or when its presence or location is uncertain from routine or lateral decubitus roentgenograms, performance of the thoracentesis and biopsy under fluoroscopic, ultrasound, or CT scan guidance enhances both yield and safety. Pleural fluid obtained should be examined for specific gravity, white blood cell count and differential, protein and glucose concentrations, lactic acid dehydrogenase (LDH), pH, P_{CO_2} (sample collected anaerobically), and amylase. Gram stain, cultures, and exfoliative cytologic specimens should be obtained; and in some instances, rheumatoid factor and complement levels are measured. The gross appearance of the fluid, the quantity obtained, and the precise location of the thoracentesis should be recorded. A combination of a pleural fluid LDH above 200 IU, a pleural fluid/serum protein ratio greater than 0.5, and a pleural fluid/serum LDH ratio greater than 0.6 all indicate that an "exudative" rather than "transudative" process is present. A low pH (<7.20) indicates that an empyema, probably requiring tube drainage, is present (Chap. 214). Specific diagnostic findings in pleural fluid may include the opalescent, pearly fluid characteristic of chylothorax; positive smears or cultures for tuberculosis or other infections; a marked elevation of amylase indicative of effusion secondary to pancreatitis or a ruptured esophagus; and the very low glucose values often seen in effusions associated with rheumatoid arthritis.

As already noted, closed (needle) pleural biopsy should follow thoracentesis whenever the diagnosis is uncertain. It is important to leave some fluid in the pleural space as this makes biopsy easier and safer. Bleeding, pneumothorax, and bronchopleural fistula induced by cutting through the visceral pleura are all more likely in the absence of fluid, and a satisfactory biopsy specimen is less likely to be obtained. Several special needles are available for biopsy of the parietal pleura. All have a cutting edge and some device for retaining the biopsy. The needle is inserted into the pleural effusion, then withdrawn until it is seated on the parietal pleura, from which a biopsy is obtained with the cutting edge. Usually, three biopsies are taken from different sites at the same session. Care should be exercised to place the needle in a position least likely to impinge on the intercostal vessels. All fluid to be used for diagnosis should be removed before biopsy since postbiopsy bleeding may obscure the true character of the fluid.

Pleuroscopy, using a modified FOB inserted through an intercostal trocar, also can be used for both direct inspection and biopsy of the pleura. In the absence of a pleural effusion, two other options exist for obtaining tissue from pleural-based lesions: aspiration needle biopsy and open biopsy. The technique for aspiration biopsy is the same as that described above, although some physicians use "cutting" needles (see "Lung Biopsy" below). Open pleural biopsy involves a limited thoracotomy, requiring anesthesia. A small intercostal incision is made, and the parietal pleura is biopsied under direct visualization. The incision is then closed, often without an intercostal tube. Open biopsy has several advantages because a larger specimen is obtained and the pleura and underlying lung can be seen and palpated. When pleural involvement is "spotty," open biopsy increases the possibility of establishing a diagnosis.

PULMONARY AND BRONCHIAL ANGIOGRAPHY

Radiopaque materials are injected rapidly by vein or via a catheter into the systemic veins, right heart chambers, or the pulmonary artery. Magnification techniques allow visualization of smaller pulmonary vessels. *Digital pulmonary angiography*, providing computer-derived images of digital data, may allow imaging of the larger pulmonary arteries with contrast injected more proximally (into superior or inferior vena cava or peripheral vein) or at lower concentrations; however, motion artifacts limit its sensitivity and specificity. Angiography is frequently used to detect pulmonary emboli and a variety of congenital and acquired lesions of the pulmonary vessels. The procedure is not without risk, particularly in patients with pulmonary hypertension, and clear indication for it must exist as well as personnel experienced in its performance and interpretation.

Angioscopy, an experimental technique for direct visualization of the right cardiac chambers and pulmonary arterial system, can be accomplished by insertion of a fiberoptic device via a peripheral vein. The diagnostic role of this procedure in embolic and other disorders remains to be defined.

Bronchial arteriography is now used in some centers to identify otherwise obscure bleeding sites in the lungs. Transarterial placement of a catheter into the orifices or parent vessels of bronchial arteries can be accomplished by experienced operators. Radiopaque material is then injected so that these arteries can be visualized. If a bleeding site is identified, emboli can be injected via the catheter as a means for halting hemoptysis.

MEDIASTINOSCOPY AND MEDIASTINOTOMY

Another favored site for biopsy is the lymph nodes in the mediastinum. Because they receive lymphatic drainage from the lungs, these nodes often disclose intrathoracic diseases such as carcinoma, granulomatous infections, and sarcoidosis. As noted above, transtracheal needle aspiration of mediastinal nodes via the FOB is one new approach to such nodes. Another is mediastinoscopy, which involves insertion of a lighted mirror-lens system, much like a bronchoscope, through an incision at the base of the neck anteriorly. The instrument is advanced under visual control into the mediastinum, where inspection and biopsy can be carried out. Because of its higher yield of diagnostic lymph nodes, mediastinoscopy has virtually replaced biopsy of the *scalene fat pad* for nodes of interest on the right side of the mediastinum. However, for anatomic reasons, mediastinoscopy on the left is less satisfactory and more hazardous. Nodes in this location are usually approached through a limited left anterior thoracotomy (mediastinotomy) or, occasionally, by scalene fat pad biopsy. Needle aspiration, mediastinoscopy, and mediastinotomy are low-risk, high-yield procedures. They are invaluable in the "staging" of patients with known or suspected pulmonary malignancy.

LUNG BIOPSY   Finally, if the diagnosis still remains unclear, biopsy of the lung may be required. Again, "closed" and "open" approaches are available. Closed biopsies are of three types: transbronchial, aspiration, and "cutting needle." Transbronchial biopsy, carried out through the fiberoptic bronchoscope, is a highly useful procedure, particularly since larger forceps have been introduced and the taking of multiple biopsies during one procedure has become routine.

However, when lesions are small and/or anatomically located beyond the reach of the FOB, direct aspiration needle biopsy is often more rewarding. *Aspiration* biopsy, mentioned previously, provides cytologic material but does not actually obtain a specimen of lung whose architecture can be examined, a feature which may be necessary to establish a diagnosis. Various "cutting" needles are available which do provide a "core" of the involved lung. However, this approach has waned in popularity because of the high incidence of pneumothorax and bleeding, occasional deaths due to air embolism, and the small size of the biopsy specimen, which may limit diagnostic interpretation. Fluoroscopic guidance is essential in all these closed approaches, and they are contraindicated if pulmonary hypertension or a hemorrhagic diathesis is present.

Open lung biopsy, requiring thoracotomy, is the final diagnostic resort. It is, however, a relatively safe procedure even in patients with respiratory failure, hemorrhagic diathesis, or pulmonary hypertension if meticulous surgical and anesthetic techniques are observed. Direct visualization allows selection of an optimum biopsy site, and of course, a specimen of adequate size is obtained. In selecting among these closed and open options, consideration of local expertise in their performance is a key factor.

All specimens obtained by biopsy should be both cultured and processed for pathologic examination.

REFERENCES

BARON RL et al: Computed tomography in the pre-operative evaluation of bronchogenic carcinoma. Radiology 145:727, 1982

BARTLETT JG, FINEGOLD SM: Bacteriology of expectorated sputum with quantitative culture and wash technic compared to transtracheal aspirates. Am Rev Resp Dis 117:1019, 1979

BORDOW RA, MOSER KM: *Manual of Clinical Problems in Pulmonary Medicine.* Boston, Little, Brown, 1985

COLICE GL etal: Comparison of computerized tomography with fiberoptic bronchoscopy in identifying endobronchial abnormalities in patients with known or suspected lung cancer. Am Resp Dis 131:397, 1985

GODWIN D et al: Distinguishing benign from malignant pulmonary nodules by computed tomography. Radiology 144:349, 1982

HAYES DA et al: Evaluation of two bronchofiberoscopic methods of culturing the lower respiratory tract. Am Rev Resp Dis 122:319, 1980

POE RH: Sensitivity and specificity of the non-specific transbronchial lung biopsy. Am Rev Resp Dis 119:25, 1979

SACKNER MA (ed): *Diagnostic Technics in Pulmonary Disease.* New York, Dekker, 1981

SEGELMAN SS et al: *Pulmonary System: Practical Approaches to Pulmonary Diagnosis.* New York, Grune & Stratton, 1980

SHURE D, FEDULLO PF: The role of carinal biopsy via the fiberoptic bronchoscope in the routine staging of lung cancer. Am Rev Resp Dis 119:693, 1984

SNIDER GL (ed): *Clinical Pulmonary Medicine.* Boston, Little, Brown, 1981

WESSELIUS LJ et al: Computer-assisted versus usual lung gallium-67 index in normals and patients with interstitial lung disorders. Am Rev Resp Dis 128:1084, 1983

WILLIFORD ME et al: Computed tomography of pleural disease. Am J Roentgenol 140:909, 1983

202   ASHTMA

E. R. McFADDEN, JR.

DEFINITION   Asthma is a disease of airways that is characterized by increased responsiveness of the tracheobronchial tree to a multiplicity of stimuli. Asthma is manifested physiologically by a widespread narrowing of the air passages which may be relieved spontaneously or as a result of therapy and clinically by paroxysms of dyspnea, cough, and wheezing. It is an episodic disease, acute exacerbations being interspersed with symptom-free periods. Typically, most attacks are short-lived, lasting minutes to hours, and after them the patient seems to recover completely clinically. However, there can be a phase in which the patient experiences some degree of airway obstruction daily. This phase can be mild, with or without superimposed severe episodes, or much more serious, with severe obstruction persisting for days or weeks, a condition known as *status asthmaticus.*

PREVALENCE AND ETIOLOGY   The prevalence and incidence of asthma is difficult to assess with certainty because of the lack of reliable population-based figures which have used uniform diagnostic criteria. However, it has been suggested that approximately 5 percent of adults and 7 to 10 percent of children in the United States and Australia have the disorder. Bronchial asthma occurs at all ages but predominantly in early life. About one-half of the cases develop before age 10 and another third occur before age 40. In childhood, there is a 2:1 male/female preponderance which equalizes by age 30.

From an etiologic standpoint, asthma is a heterogeneous disease, and attempts to define it in etiologic or pathologic terms have proved difficult. It is useful for epidemiologic and clinical purposes to classify the forms of this disease by the principal stimuli that incite or are associated with acute episodes. However, it is important to emphasize that the distinction between various types of asthma may often be artificial, and the response of a given subclassification may be initiated by more than one type of stimulus. With this reservation in mind, one can describe two broad groups: allergic and idiosyncratic.

Allergic asthma is often associated with a personal and/or family history of allergic diseases such as rhinitis, urticaria, and eczema; positive wheal-and-flare skin reactions to intradermal injection of extracts of airborne antigens; increased levels of IgE in the serum; and/or positive response to provocation tests involving the inhalation of specific antigen.

A significant segment of the asthmatic population will present with negative family or personal histories of allergy, negative skin tests, and normal serum levels of IgE, and therefore cannot be classified on the basis of defined immunologic mechanisms. These we term *idiosyncratic.* Many of these will develop a typical symptom complex upon contracting an upper respiratory illness. The initial insult may be little more than a common cold, but after several days the patient begins to develop paroxysms of wheezing and dyspnea that can last for days to months. These individuals should not be confused with the so-called infective asthmatics or with persons in whom the symptoms of bronchospasm are superimposed upon chronic bronchitis (see Chap. 208).

Unfortunately, many patients will not clearly fit into either of the above categories but will fall into a mixed group with features of each. In general, those patients whose onset of disease is in early life will tend to have a strong allergic component to their illness, while those who develop their asthma late tend to be nonallergic or to have mixed etiologies.

PATHOGENESIS OF ASTHMA   The common denominator underlying the asthmatic diathesis is a nonspecific hyperirritability of the tracheobronchial tree. This phenomenon is the cardinal feature of asthma and is thought to be the primary pathogenic event in the disease. The increased airway reactivity can be familial or acquired and is materially worsened by events that promote airway inflammation. Heightened airway responsiveness is also found in first-degree relatives of asthmatics who are free of the disease and in some individuals with allergic rhinitis, cystic fibrosis, and chronic bronchitis. In asthmatics it correlates well with the clinical features of the illness, and it rises with repeated exposures to inciting stimuli and falls with avoidance and therapy. As the disease process becomes more severe, as indicated by increasing symptoms and medication requirements, the airways become more irritable and so respond more to nonspecific stimuli. Pulmonary function then becomes more unstable with greater diurnal variation.

The stimuli that increase airway responsiveness and incite acute episodes of asthma can be grouped into seven major categories: allergenic, pharmacologic, environmental, occupational, infectious, exercise-related, and emotional.

Allergens Allergic asthma is dependent upon an IgE response controlled by T and B lymphocytes and activated by the interaction of antigen with mast cell–bound IgE molecules. Most of the allergens that provoke asthma are airborne, and in order to induce a state of sensitivity, they must be reasonably abundant for considerable periods of time. Once sensitization has occurred, however, the patient can then exhibit exquisite responsivity, so that minute amounts of the offending agent can produce significant exacerbations of the disease. Immunologic mechanisms appear to be causally related to the development of asthma in 25 to 35 percent of all cases, and contributory in perhaps another third. Allergic asthma is frequently seasonal, and it is most often observed in children and young adults. A nonseasonal form may result from allergy to feathers, animal danders, molds, and other antigens present continuously in the environment. Exposure to antigen typically produces an immediate response in which airway obstruction develops in minutes and then resolves. In 30 to 50 percent of patients a second wave of bronchoconstriction, the so-called late reaction, develops 6 to 10 h later. In a minority only a late reaction occurs. In some individuals following a single exposure marked cyclic changes in airway lability may recur daily for a variable period. This phenomenon is frequently associated with an increase in airway responsivity.

The mechanism by which an inhaled antigen can provoke an acute episode of asthma is unknown but seems to depend, in part, upon antigen-antibody interactions on the surface of pulmonary mast cells with the subsequent generation and release of the mediators of immediate hypersensitivity. Current postulates hold that very small antigenic particles penetrate the lung's defenses and come in contact with mast cells that are interdigitating with the epithelium at the luminal surface of the central airways. The subsequent elaboration of mediators produces an immediate direct effect on airway smooth muscle and bronchial capillary permeability, thereby allowing an intense local reaction that is then followed by a more chronic one. The mediators released—histamine; bradykinin; the leukotrienes C, D, and E; prostaglandins PGG_2, $PGF_{2\alpha}$, and PGD_2, and thromboxane A_2—produce an intense inflammatory reaction with bronchoconstriction, vascular congestion, and edema formation. In addition to their ability to produce prolonged contraction of airway smooth muscle and mucosal edema, the leukotrienes also produce some of the other pathophysiologic features of asthma such as increased mucus production and impaired mucociliary transport mechanisms. The chemotactic factors that are elaborated, such as eosinophil and neutrophil chemotactic factors of anaphylaxis and leukotriene B_4, bring eosinophils, platelets, and polymorphonuclear leukocytes to the site of the reaction, and they, plus plasma proteins, immunoglobulins, and complement, provide the essential ingredients for a severe humoral and cellular inflammatory reaction involving both components. Diffusion of mediators through the mucosal edema can disrupt more defenses and spread the reaction along the airways. Further amplification can also occur if the reaction takes place in the vicinity of neural receptors. In this fashion, reflex bronchoconstriction can develop, and so an event which began in a single airway can now extend to involve a large part of the tracheobronchial tree. Whether frequent, persistent, or chronic low-grade mediator release alone is sufficient to establish an acquired state of airway hyperreactivity has not yet been established.

Pharmacologic stimuli The drugs most commonly associated with the induction of acute episodes of asthma are aspirin, coloring agents such as tartrazine, beta-adrenergic antagonists, and sulfiting agents. The typical aspirin-sensitive respiratory syndrome primarily affects adults, although the condition may be seen in childhood. This problem usually begins with perennial vasomotor rhinitis that is followed by a hyperplastic rhinosinusitis with nasal polyps. Progressive asthma then appears. On exposure to even very small quantities of aspirin, affected individuals typically dvelop ocular and nasal congestion and acute, often severe, episodes of airway obstruction. The prevalence of aspirin sensitivity in asthmatic subjects varies from study to study, but many authorities feel that 10 percent is a reasonable figure. There is a great deal of cross-reactivity between aspirin and other nonsteroidal anti-inflammatory compounds. Indomethacin, fenoprofen, naproxen, zomepirac sodium, ibuprofen, mefenamic acid, and phenylbutazone are particularly important in this regard. On the other hand, acetaminophen, sodium salicylate, choline salicylate, salicylamide, and propoxyphene are well tolerated. The exact frequency of cross-reactivity to tartrazine and other dyes in aspirin-sensitive asthmatic subjects is also controversial, and again 10 percent is the commonly accepted figure. This peculiar complication of aspirin-sensitive asthma is particularly insidious, however, in that tartrazine and other potentially troublesome dyes can be present in many of the drugs used to treat airway and nasal diseases and may unknowingly be administered to sensitive patients.

Patients with aspirin sensitivity can be desensitized by daily administration of the drug. Following this form of therapy cross tolerance also develops to other nonsteroidal anti-inflammatory agents. The mechanism by which aspirin and other such drugs produce bronchospasm is unknown; however, immediate hypersensitivity does not seem to be involved.

Beta-adrenergic antagonists regularly produce airway obstruction in asthmatics as well as in others with heightened airway reactivity and should be avoided in such individuals. Even the selective $beta_1$ agents have this propensity, particularly at higher doses. In fact, even the local use of $beta_1$ blockers in the eye for the treatment of glaucoma has been associated with worsening asthma.

Sulfiting agents, such as potassium metabisulfite, potassium and sodium bisulfite, sodium sulfite, and sulfur dioxide, which are widely used in the food and pharmaceutical industry as sanitizing and preservative agents, can also produce wheezing in sensitive individuals. Exposure usually follows ingestion of food or beverages containing these compounds, e.g., salads, fresh fruit, potatoes, shellfish, and wine. Recently, however, exacerbation of asthma has been reported following the use of sulfite-containing topical ophthalmic solutions, intravenous glucocorticoids, and some inhalational bronchodilator solutions. The incidence and mechanism of action of this phenomenon are unknown. When suspected, the diagnosis can be confirmed by either oral or inhalational provocations.

Environment and air pollution (see Chap. 204) Environmental causes of asthma are usually related to climatic conditions that promote the concentration of atmospheric pollutants and antigens. These conditions tend to develop in heavy industrial or densely populated urban areas and are frequently associated with thermal inversions or other situations associated with stagnant air masses. In these circumstances, although the general population can develop respiratory symptoms, patients with asthma and other respiratory diseases tend to be more severely affected.

Occupational factors (see Chap. 204) Occupational-related asthma is a significant health problem, and acute and chronic airway obstruction has been reported to follow exposure to a large number of compounds used in many types of industrial processes: bronchoconstriction can result from working with, or exposure to, *metal salts* (platinum, chrome, and nickel); *wood and vegetable dusts* (oak, western red cedar, grain, flour, castor bean, green coffee bean, mako, gum acacia, karay gum, and tragacanth); *pharmaceutical agents* (antibiotics, piperazine, and cimetidine); *industrial chemicals and plastics* (tidoluene isocyanate, phthalic acid anhydride, trimellitic anhydride, persulfates, ethylenediamine, paraphenylenediamine, and various dyes); *biologic enzymes* (laundry detergents and pancreatic enzymes); and *animal and insect dusts, serums, and secretions*. It is important to recognize that exposure to sensitizing chemicals, particularly those used in paints, solvents, and plastics, can also occur during leisure or non-work-related activities.

The underlying mechanisms for this airway obstruction appear to be three in number: (1) in some cases the offending agent results in the formation of a specific IgE, and the cause seems immunologic (the immunologic reaction can be immediate, late, or dual); (2) materials being employed, in other cases, cause a direct liberation of bronchoconstrictor substances; and (3) work-related irritant substances, in still other cases, directly or reflexly stimulate the airways of either latent or frank asthmatics. With occupational exposures, other than those that give an immediate and dual immunologic reaction, the patients give a characteristic cyclic history. They are well when they arrive at work; symptoms develop toward the end of the shift, progress after leaving the work site, and then regress. Absence from work during weekends or vacation periods brings about a remission. Frequently, there are similar symptoms in fellow employees.

Infections Respiratory infections are the most common of the stimuli that evoke acute exacerbations of asthma. Well-controlled investigations have demonstrated that respiratory viruses and not bacteria are the major etiologic factors, and there is no evidence to support the concept that bacterial infections or allergy play any role in this phenomenon. In young children, the most important infectious agents are respiratory syncytial virus and parainfluenza virus. In older children and adults, rhinovirus and influenza virus predominate as pathogens. Simple colonization of the tracheobronchial tree is insufficient to evoke acute episodes of bronchospasm, and attacks of asthma occur only when symptoms of an ongoing respiratory tract infection are, or have been, present. The mechanism by which viruses induce asthma is unknown, but it is probable that the resulting inflammatory changes in the airway mucosa produce a reduction in the firing thresholds of the subepithelial vagal receptors. Supporting evidence for this concept is derived from the fact that the airway responsiveness of normal nonasthmatic subjects to nonspecific stimuli is transiently increased after a viral infection. Increased airway responsiveness can last from 2 to 8 weeks after the infection in both normals and asthmatics.

Exercise Asthma can also be induced or made worse by physical exertion. Provocation of bronchospasm by exercise is probably operative to some extent in every asthmatic patient, and in some it may be the only trigger mechanism that will produce symptoms. In the latter circumstance, when such patients are followed for sufficient periods of time, they often develop recurring episodes of airway obstruction independent of exercise: thus, the onset of this problem can frequently serve as the first manifestation of the full-blown asthmatic syndrome. Exercise-induced asthma is particularly troublesome in children and young adults because of their usual high level of physical activity. The mechanism by which exercise produces acute exacerbations of asthma is related to the thermal changes that develop in the intrathoracic airways as heat and water are transferred from the mucosa to the inspired air to bring the latter to body conditions before it reaches the alveoli. The higher the ventilation and the colder, hence drier, the inspired air, the more the airway temperature falls, and so there is a significant interaction between the stress of the exercise task, the climatic environment in which it is performed, and the magnitude of the postexertional obstruction. Thus, for the same inspired air conditions, running will produce a more severe attack of asthma than will walking. Conversely, for a given task, the inhalation of cold air during its performance will markedly enhance the response, while warm, humid air will blunt or abolish it. Consequently, activities such as ice hockey, cross-country skiing, or ice skating are more provocative than is swimming in an indoor heated pool. The mechanism by which airway thermal changes evoke obstruction is unknown.

Emotional stress Abundant objective data now exist which demonstrate that psychological factors can interact with the asthmatic diathesis to worsen or ameliorate the disease process. The pathways and nature of the interactions are complex but probably operational to some extent in almost half of the patients studied. Changes in airway caliber seem to be mediated through modification of vagal efferent activity. The most frequently studied variable has been that of suggestion, and the weight of current evidence is that it can be quite an important influence in selected asthmatics. When psychically responsive individuals are given the appropriate suggestion, they can actually decrease or increase the pharmacologic effects of adrenergic and cholinergic stimuli on their airways. The extent to which psychological factors participate in the induction and/or continuation of any given acute exacerbation is unknown but probably varies from patient to patient and in the same patient from episode to episode.

PATHOLOGY In a patient who has died of acute asthma, the most striking feature of the lungs at necropsy is their gross overdistention and failure to collapse when the pleural cavities are opened. When the lungs are cut, numerous gelatinous plugs of exudate are found in the majority of the bronchial branches down to the terminal bronchiole. Histologic examination shows hypertrophy of the bronchial smooth muscle, mucosal edema, denudation of the surface epithelium, pronounced thickening of the basement membrane, and eosinophilic infiltrates in the bronchial wall. In asthmatic patients who die from trauma and causes other than asthma itself, mucous casts, basement membrane thickening, and eosinophilic infiltrates are frequently observed. In both situations there is an absence of any of the well-recognized forms of destructive emphysema.

PATHOPHYSIOLOGY AND CLINICAL CORRELATES The pathophysiologic hallmark of asthma is a reduction in airway diameter brought about by contraction of smooth muscle, edema of the bronchial wall, and thick tenacious secretions. Although the relative contributions of each component to the patient's ventilatory impairment are unknown, the net result is an increase in airway resistance, decreased forced expiratory volumes and flow rates, hyperinflation of the lungs and thorax, increased work of breathing, alterations in respiratory muscle function, changes in elastic recoil, abnormal distribution of both ventilation and pulmonary blood flow, mismatched ratios, and altered arterial blood gases. Thus, although asthma is considered to be primarily a disease of airways, virtually all aspects of pulmonary function are compromised during an acute attack. In addition, in very symptomatic patients there frequently is electrocardiographic evidence of right ventricular hypertrophy, and pulmonary hypertension can be found. Quantification of the changes that develop during an acute episode of asthma demonstrate that when a patient presents for therapy, his or her forced vital capacity tends to be ≤50 percent of normal. The 1-s forced expiratory volume (FEV_1) averages 30 percent of predicted, while the maximum and minimum midexpiratory flow rates are reduced to 20 percent or less of expected. In keeping with the alterations in mechanics, the associated air-trapping is substantial. In acutely ill patients, residual volume (RV) frequently approaches 400 percent of normal, while functional residual capacity doubles. The patients tend to report that their attacks have ended clinically when their RV has fallen to 200 percent of its predicted value and when the FEV_1 rises to 50 percent.

Hypoxia is a universal finding during acute exacerbations, but frank ventilatory failure is relatively uncommon, being observed in 10 to 15 percent of patients presenting for therapy. Most asthmatics have hypocapnia and a respiratory alkalosis. Statistically, the finding of normal arterial carbon dioxide tension tends to be associated with quite severe levels of obstruction and consequently, when found in a symptomatic individual, should be viewed as impending respiratory failure and treated as such. Equally, the presence of metabolic acidosis in the setting of acute asthma heralds severe obstruction. Usually, there are no clinical counterparts to the derangements in blood gases. Cyanosis is a very late sign. Thus, a dangerous level of hypoxia can go undetected. Likewise the signs which are attributable to carbon dioxide retention such as sweating, tachycardia, and wide pulse pressure or to acidosis such as tachypnea do not tend to be of great value in predicting the presence of hypercapnia or hydrogen ion excess in individual patients, for they are too frequently seen in anxious patients with more moderate disease to be of much use. Consequently, trying to judge the state of an acutely ill patient's ventilatory status on clinical grounds alone can be extremely hazardous and should not be relied upon with any confidence. Arterial blood gas tensions, therefore, must be measured.

The symptoms of asthma consist of a triad of dyspnea, cough, and wheezing, the latter often being regarded as the sine qua non. In its most typical form asthma is an episodic disease, and all three symptoms coexist. Attacks often occur at night, for reasons which are not clear but may relate to fluctuations in airway receptor thresholds that may result from circadian variations in the circulating levels of endogenous catecholamines and histamine. Attacks may also abruptly follow exposure to a specific allergen, physical exertion, a viral respiratory infection, or emotional excitement. At the onset the patient experiences a sense of constriction in the chest, often with a nonproductive cough. Respiration becomes audibly harsh, and wheezing in both phases of respiration becomes prominent, expiration becomes prolonged, and patients frequently have tachypnea, tachycardia, and mild systolic hypertension. The lungs rapidly become overinflated, and the anterior-posterior diameter of the thorax increases. If the attack is severe or prolonged, the accessory muscles become visibly active and frequently a paradoxical pulse will develop. These two signs have been found to be extremely valuable in indicating the severity of the obstruction. In the presence of either, pulmonary function tends to be significantly more impaired than in its absence. It is important to note that the development of these signs depends upon the generation of large negative intrathoracic pressures. Thus, if the patient's breathing is shallow, these signs could be absent even though obstruction is quite severe. The other signs and symptoms of asthma imperfectly reflect the physiologic alterations that are present, so much so that if one relies upon the loss of subjective complaints, or even the sign of wheezing, as being the end point at which therapy for an acute attack should be terminated, an enormous reservoir of residual disease is missed.

Termination of the episode is frequently marked by a cough producing thick stringy mucus which often takes the form of casts of the distal airways (Curschmann's spirals), and when examined microscopically often shows eosinophils and Charcot-Leyden crystals. In extreme situations, wheezing may markedly lessen or even disappear completely, cough may become extremely ineffective, and the patient may begin a gasping type of respiratory pattern. These findings imply extensive mucous plugging and impending suffocation. Ventilatory assistance by mechanical means may be required. Atelectasis due to inspissated secretions may occasionally occur with asthmatic attacks. Other complications such as spontaneous pneumothorax and/or pneumomediastinum are rare.

Less typically, a patient with asthma may complain of intermittent episodes of nonproductive cough or dyspnea only on exertion. Unlike other asthmatics when examined during their symptomatic periods, these patients tend to have normal breath sounds but will wheeze after repeated forced exhalations and will show dynamic ventilatory impairments when tested in the laboratory.

The differentiation of asthma from other diseases associated with dyspnea and wheezing is usually not difficult, particularly if the patient is seen during an acute episode. The physical findings and symptoms listed above, and the history of periodic attacks, are quite characteristic. A personal or family history of allergic diseases such as eczema, rhinitis, or urticaria is valuable contributory evidence. *Upper airway obstruction by tumor* or *laryngeal edema* can occa-

sionally be confused with asthma. Typically, such a patient will present with stridor, and the harsh respiratory sounds can be localized to the area of the trachea. Diffuse wheezing throughout both lung fields is usually absent. However, differentiation can sometimes be difficult, and indirect laryngoscopy or bronchoscopy may be required. Recently a group of patients with glottic dysfunction have been described. These individuals close their glottis during inspiration and produce episodic attacks of severe airway obstruction that mimic asthma, yet they do not respond to standard therapy. Frequently they produce enough obstruction to develop carbon dioxide retention. However, unlike asthma the arterial oxygen tension is well preserved, and the alveolar-arterial gradient for oxygen narrows during the episode and does not widen as is the case with lower airway obstruction.

Persistent wheezing localized to one area of the chest in association with paroxysms of cough indicates *endobronchial disease* such as foreign-body aspiration, neoplasms, or bronchial stenosis.

The signs and symptoms of *acute left ventricular failure* can occasionally mimic asthma, but the findings of moist basilar rales, gallop rhythms, blood-tinged sputum, and other signs of heart failure (Chap. 182) allow the appropriate diagnosis to be reached.

Recurrent episodes of bronchospasm can occur with *carcinoid tumors* (Chap. 299), *recurrent pulmonary emboli* (Chap. 211), and *chronic bronchitis* (Chap. 208). In the last there are no true symptom-free periods in that one can usually obtain a history of chronic cough and sputum production as a background upon which acute attacks of wheezing are superimposed. Recurrent emboli, particularly in young women on oral contraceptives, are occasionally very difficult to separate from asthma. Frequently, these patients will present with episodes of breathlessness, particularly on exertion, and they can sometimes wheeze. Pulmonary function studies may show evidence of peripheral airway obstruction (Chap. 200), and when these changes are present, lung scans may also be abnormal. The therapeutic response to bronchodilators, discontinuation of the contraceptives, and institution of anticoagulant therapy may be helpful, but pulmonary angiography may be necessary in order to establish the correct diagnosis.

Eosinophilic pneumonias (Chap. 203) are often associated with asthmatic symptoms as are various chemical pneumonias and exposures to insecticides and cholinergic drugs. Bronchospasm can occasionally be a manifestation of *systemic vasculitis* with pulmonary involvement.

LABORATORY FINDINGS   It is difficult to establish the diagnosis of asthma in the laboratory, for no single test is conclusive. Positive wheal-and-flare reactions to skin tests can be demonstrated to various allergens, but that finding does not necessarily correlate with the intrapulmonary events. Sputum and blood eosinophilia and measurement of serum IgE levels are also helpful but are not specific for asthma. Chest roentgenograms showing hyperinflation are nondiagnostic, as are tests of pulmonary function. The latter, however, are quite useful in that one can measure the degree of obstruction present, document its reversible nature, and, when combined with provocational challenges, demonstrate the airway hyperirritability so characteristic of this disease. Furthermore, the performance of forced vital capacity maneuvers is very helpful in the evaluation of acute asthmatic attacks. A reduction in the FEV_1 to less than 25 percent of that predicted or to less than 750 mL with little or no response following the administration of a bronchodilator indicates that the patient should receive very careful surveillance in conjunction with intensive treatment.

THERAPY   Elimination of the causative agent(s) from the environment of an allergic asthmatic is the most successful means available for treating this condition (for details on avoidance see Chap. 260). Desensitization or immunotherapy with extracts of the suspected allergens has enjoyed widespread favor, but controlled studies are limited and have not proved it to be highly effective.

Drug treatment   The drugs used in the treatment of asthma may be conveniently grouped into five major categories: beta-adrenergic agonists, methylxanthines, glucocorticoids, chromones, and anticholinergics. No one group is effective against all of the pathologic processes producing the disease, and since the degree of relief of airway obstruction is frequently incomplete with the use of a single agent, multiple drug regimens are commonplace.

ADRENERGIC STIMULANTS   The drugs in this category consist of the catecholamines, resorcinols, and saligenins. These agents are analogues and produce airway dilatation through stimulation of beta receptors with the resultant formation of cyclic AMP. The catecholamines in widespread clinical use are epinephrine, isoproterenol, isoetharine, rimiterol, and hexoprenaline. The latter two are not yet available in the United States. As a group these compounds are short-acting and effective only by inhalational or parenteral routes. Epinephrine and isoproterenol are not beta$_2$-selective and have considerable chronotrophic and inotrophic cardiac effects. Epinephrine also has substantial alpha-stimulating effects. The usual dose is 0.3 to 0.5 mL of a 1:1000 solution administered subcutaneously. Isoproterenol is devoid of alpha activity and is the most potent agent of this group. It is usually administered in a 1:200 solution by inhalation. Controlled studies have shown that repetitive doses of epinephrine or isoproterenol are considerably more efficacious than the use of methylxanthines in the therapy of acute exacerbations of asthma. Isoproterenol has been used by the intravenous route in the management of status asthmaticus. In these circumstances, extremely careful monitoring of heart rate, rhythm, and blood pressure is an absolute requirement; and this therapy is not recommended save for very dire emergencies. Isoetharine is the most beta$_2$-selective compound of this class, but is a relatively weak bronchodilator. It is employed as an aerosol and supplied as a 1% solution. The pharmacologies of hexoprenaline and rimiterol are similar to isoetharine.

The commonly used resorcinols are metaproterenol, terbutaline, and fenoterol, and the most widely known saligenin is albuterol, or salbutamol. With the exception of metaproterenol, these drugs are highly selective for the respiratory tract and virtually devoid of significant cardiac effects except in high doses. They are active by all routes of administration, and because their chemical structures allow them to bypass the metabolic processes used to degrade the catecholamines, their effects are long-lasting, exceeding 6 h in many studies.

The method by which beta agonists are administered is of great importance since it influences both the clinical response and the metabolic fate. Inhalation increases the bronchial selectivity of these drugs, allows maximal bronchodilation to occur with fewer side effects than other routes of administration, and is considered by many as the route of choice. Recent data indicate that this is true not just in maintenance therapy but also during the treatment of severe acute obstruction. A frequent side effect of these drugs is tremor.

METHYLXANTHINES   Theophylline, and its various salts, are medium potency bronchodilators. Like the beta agonists, they improve the movement of airway mucus. Although efficacious, the drugs in this class are not as potent as the sympathomimetics, and they have a narrower therapeutic-toxic window. The mechanism responsible for the bronchodilator effect of the methylxanthines is unknown. It was formerly thought that these drugs increased cyclic AMP by the inhibition of phosphodiesterase. However, recent evidence no longer supports this concept. The therapeutic plasma concentrations of theophylline lie between 10 and 20 μg/mL. But the dose required to achieve this level varies widely from patient to patient due to differences in the metabolism of the drug. Theophylline clearance, and thus dosage requirements, is decreased substantially in neonates and the elderly and those with acute and chronic hepatic dysfunction, cardiac decompensation, and cor pulmonale. Clearance is also decreased during febrile illnesses. Clearance is increased in children. In addition a number of important drug interactions can alter theophylline metabolism. Clearance falls with the concurrent use of cigarettes, marijuana, erythromycin and troleandomycin, allopurinol, cimetidine, and propranolol. It rises with phenobarbital and phenytoin or any other drug that has the capability of inducing hepatic microsomal enzymes.

In contrast to the large number of oral compounds, aminophylline is the only compound available for intravenous use. The recommendations for intravenous therapy in children aged 9 to 16 and young adult smokers not currently receiving theophylline products are as follows: a loading dose of 6 mg/kg is given followed by an infusion of 1.0 (mg/kg)/h for the next 12 h and then 0.8 (mg/kg)/h thereafter. In nonsmoking adults, older patients, and those with cor pulmonale, congestive heart failure, and liver disease, the loading dose remains the same but the maintenance dose is reduced to between 0.1 and 0.5 (mg/kg)/h. In those patients already receiving theophylline, the loading dose is frequently withheld or in extreme situations given in a reduced amount at 0.5 mg/kg.

The most common side effects of theophylline are nervousness, nausea, vomiting, anorexia, and headache. At plasma levels greater than 30 μg/mL there is a risk of seizures and cardiac arrhythmias.

GLUCOCORTICOIDS   Glucocorticoids have been used for many years in the treatment of asthma, but controversy still surrounds such basic issues as their specific indication and dose. Glucocorticoids are not bronchodilators, and their major use is in reducing airway inflammation. Although it is difficult to provide precise recommendations because objective data are lacking, there are several situations in the management of acute and chronic asthma in which all would agree that steroids should be employed. In acute illness, that is, when severe airway obstruction is not resolving, or is even worsening despite intense optimal bronchodilator therapy, and in chronic disease, steroids are most helpful when there has been failure of a previously optimal regimen with frequent recurrences of symptoms of progressive severity.

Although many dosage schedules have been proposed, few objective data on pulmonary function are available to support them. Those that are available indicate that plasma cortisol levels above 100 μg/dL may be required to produce an effect. In acute situations, this can be achieved by the intravenous administration of 4 mg per kilogram of body weight of hydrocortisone as a loading dose, followed several hours later by an infusion regulated to deliver 3 mg/kg every 6 h. It should be emphasized that the effects of steroids in acute asthma are not immediate and may not be seen for 6 h or more after their initial administration. Consequently, it is mandatory to continue vigorous bronchodilator therapy during this interval. After 24 to 72 h, depending upon response, the patient can be switched to oral agents. A usual starting point is 40 to 60 mg prednisone as a single daily morning dose. The amount can then be reduced by half every fourth to fifth day. In situations in which it appears that continued steroid therapy will be needed, an alternate-day schedule should be instituted to minimize side effects. This is particularly important in children, since continuous corticosteroid administration interrupts growth. Long-acting preparations such as dexamethasone should not be used in this approach for they defeat the purpose of alternate-day schedules by causing prolonged suppression of the pituitary-adrenal axis.

Several inhaled steroids of high topical potency are available and greatly facilitate the withdrawal of oral agents. They are also useful in reducing airway sensitivity and as an alternative to oral glucocorticoids in situations where asthma symptoms are escalating. Hyperadrenal corticism and adrenal suppression are not major issues, and the most frequent side effect is symptomatic oropharyngeal candidiasis. This can be controlled by the use of a spacing device on the metered-dose inhaler.

CHROMONES   Cromolyn sodium is not a bronchodilator. Its major therapeutic effect is the inhibition of degranulation of mast cells, thereby preventing the release of the chemical mediators of anaphylaxis. The drug does not inhibit the combination of antigen with antibody, nor does it affect the fixation of IgE to mast cells. Cromolyn has been shown to be of use in atopic and nonatopic asthmatics, and it blunts exercise-induced asthma in both children and adults. Numerous trials have shown that about 75 percent of patients derive worthwhile benefits from the drug in terms of reduction of medications and improvement in symptoms. Therapy is best initiated between attacks or in periods of relative remission. If no response is noted by 4 to 6 weeks, the drug can be discontinued.

ANTICHOLINERGICS Anticholinergic drugs, such as atropine sulfate, are known to produce bronchodilatation in patients with asthma, but their use has been limited by systemic side effects. Recently, newer nonabsorbable quaternary ammonium (atropine methylnitrate and ipratropium bromide) aerosol agents have undergone extensive trials and have been found to be both effective and remarkably free of untoward effects. These new agents, when generally available, may be of particular benefit in patients with asthma and coexistent heart disease, in whom use of methylxanthines and beta stimulants may be dangerous. A chief disadvantage of the anticholinergics are their slow onset of action. Sixty to 90 min may be required before peak bronchodilatation is achieved.

MISCELLANEOUS Opiates, sedatives, and tranquilizers should be absolutely avoided in the acutely ill asthmatic because the risk of depressing alveolar ventilation is great and respiratory arrest has been reported to occur shortly after their use. Admittedly most individuals are anxious and frightened, but experience has shown that they can be calmed equally well by the physician's presence and reassurances. Beta-adrenergic blockers and parasympathetic agonists should be avoided, or used with great caution, for they can cause marked deterioration in lung function.

Expectorants and mucolytic agents have enjoyed great vogue in the past, but there is little evidence available to indicate that they add significantly to the treatment of the acute or chronic phases of this disease. Mucolytic agents such as acetylcysteine may actually produce bronchospasm when administered to susceptible asthmatics. This can be overcome by aerosolizing them in solution with a beta-adrenergic agent. The use of intravenous fluids in the treatment of acute asthma has also been advocated. There is little evidence to indicate that this adjunct hastens recovery, but it may prevent dehydration and through that forestall the inspissation of secretions, by replacing the larger insensible water losses that could occur with prolonged hyperventilation.

PROGNOSIS AND CLINICAL COURSE Death from asthma is uncommon. Available mortality statistics for the United States indicate a death rate of approximately 0.3 per 100,000 persons.

The available information on the clinical course of asthma suggests that somewhere between 50 to 80 percent of all patients can expect to have a reasonably good prognosis, particularly those whose disease is mild and develops in childhood. The number of children still having asthma 7 to 10 years after the initial diagnosis varies from 26 to 78 percent with an average of 46 percent; however, the percentage who continue to have severe disease is relatively low (6 to 19 percent). The natural course of asthma in adult life has been little investigated. Some studies suggest that spontaneous remissions occur in approximately 20 percent of those who develop the disease as adults and 40 percent or so can be expected to improve with less frequent and severe attacks as they grow older.

REFERENCES

FANTA CH, MCFADDEN ER JR: Status Asthmaticus, in *Current Therapy in Internal Medicine*, TM Bayless et al (eds). Philadelphia, Decker, 1984, pp 6–10

HENDELES L, WEINBERGER M: Theophylline. Pharmacotherapy 3:2–44, 1983

MCFADDEN ER JR: Beta₂ receptor agonists: metabolism and pharmacology. J Allergy Clin Immunol 68:91–97, 1981

———: Asthma. Airway dynamics, cardiac function, and clinical correlates, in *Allergies: Principles and Practice*, E Middleton et al (eds). St Louis, CV Mosby, 1983, pp 843–862

WASSERMAN SI: Mediators of immediate hypersensitivity. J Allergy Clin Immunol 72:191–115, 1983

203 HYPERSENSITIVITY PNEUMONITIS

GARY W. HUNNINGHAKE / HAL B. RICHERSON

DEFINITION Hypersensitivity pneumonitis (HP), or extrinsic allergic alveolitis, is an immunologically induced inflammation of the lung parenchyma, involving alveolar walls and terminal airways, secondary to repeated inhalation of a variety of organic dusts and other agents by a susceptible host. In contrast to many of the other interstitial lung diseases, the etiology of this interstitial and alveolar filling disease is known. Although a number of etiologic agents have been identified, most are rare, and a few well-documented syndromes are associated with the vast majority of cases. The diagnosis of HP requires a constellation of clinical, radiographic, physiologic, pathologic, and immunologic criteria, each of which by itself is rarely pathognomonic, and the preferred treatment is avoidance of the causative antigen.

ETIOLOGY Agents implicated as causes of HP include those listed in Table 203-1. Many cases of HP occurring in various occupations involve exposure to similar agents, particularly the thermophilic actinomycetes. Except for exotic occupational exposures, the usual sources of causative antigens are "moldy" hay, silage, or grain, pet birds, and heating, cooling, and humidification systems. Simple chemicals, such as isocyanates, may also cause hypersensitivity pneumonitis.

PATHOGENESIS The finding that precipitating antibodies against extracts of moldy hay were demonstrable in most patients with farmer's lung led to the early conclusion that HP was an immune-complex-mediated reaction. Subsequent investigations of HP in human beings and animal models also provided evidence for the importance of cell-mediated hypersensitivity. The early (acute) reaction is likely a result of the formation of immune complexes in the lung, and is characterized by an increase in polymorphonuclear leukocytes in the alveoli and small airways. This early lesion is followed by an influx of mononuclear cells into the lung and the formation of granulomas. The latter lesion appears to be a classic delayed hypersensitivity reaction to repeated inhalation of antigen and adjuvant-active materials.

Bronchoalveolar lavage in patients with HP has consistently demonstrated an increase in T lymphocytes in lavage fluid (a finding which is also observed in patients with other granulomatous lung disorders). Patients with recent or continual exposure to antigen may also have an increase in polymorphonuclear leukocytes in lavage fluid. In most patients examined during recovery from acute disease, the T lymphocytes in lavage fluid are predominantly the suppressor/cytotoxic T-cell subset, which expresses surface antigens detected by OKT8 or Leu 2a monoclonal antibodies. In patients with very recent exposure to antigen, however, the numbers of helper T cells (OKT4⁺ or Leu 3a⁺) may increase in lavage fluid. Similar findings may be present as well in similarly exposed, asymptomatic individuals. These observations suggest that there is an active modulation of granuloma formation in the lung by immunoregulatory T cells in this disorder.

CLINICAL PRESENTATION The *clinical picture* varies from patient to patient and is related to the frequency and intensity of exposure to the causative antigen and perhaps other host factors. The presentation can be *acute*, *subacute*, or *chronic*. In the *acute form*, symptoms such as cough, fever, chills, malaise, and dyspnea may occur 6 to 8 h after exposure to the antigen and usually clear within a few days if there is no further exposure to antigen. The *subacute form* often appears insidiously over a period of weeks marked by cough and dyspnea, and may progress to cyanosis and severe dyspnea requiring hospitalization. In some patients, a subacute form of the disease may persist after an acute presentation of the disorder, especially if there is continued exposure to antigen. In most patients with the acute or subacute form of HP, the symptoms, signs, and other manifestations

TABLE 203-1 Selected examples of hypersensitivity pneumonitis

Disease	Antigen	Source of antigen
Farmer's lung	Thermophilic actinomycetes*	Contaminated hay, grain, silage
Bird fancier's, breeders, or handler's lung	Parakeet, pigeon, dove, chicken, turkey proteins	Avian droppings
Humidifier or air-conditioner lung	Thermophilic actinomycetes, *Aureobasidium pullulans*, amoeba, other	Contaminated water in humidification aerosols, vaporizers, sprays
Woodworker's lung	Wood dust; *Alternaria*	Oak cedar, mahogany dusts; pine and spruce pulp
Sauna taker's lung	*A. pullulans*, other	Contaminated sauna steam
Bagassosis	Thermophilic actinomycetes	Contaminated bagasse (sugar cane)
Malt worker's lung	*Aspergillus fumigatus, A. clavatus*	Moldy barley
Mushroom worker's lung	Thermophilic actinomycetes, other	Mushroom compost
Sequoiosis	*Aureobasidium, Graphium* species	Redwood sawdust
Maple bark stripper's disease	*Cryptostroma corticale*	Maple bark
Coffee worker's lung	Coffee bean dust	Coffee beans
Miller's lung	Infested wheat flour	*Sitophilus granarius* (wheat weevil)
Bathtub refinisher's lung	Toluene diisocyanate (TDI)	Porcelain-surfacing catalyst
Chemical worker's lung	Toluene diisocyanate TDI, methylene diisocyanate (MDI), phthallic anhydride, vinyl chloride, other	Polyurethane foam and insulation, synthetic rubber manufacturing, meat wrapping and labeling, other

* *Thermophilic actinomycetes species include* Micropolyspora faeni, Thermoactinomyces vulgaris, T. saccharrii, T. viridis, *and* T. candidus.

of HP disappear within days, weeks, or months if the causative agent is no longer inhaled. Transformation to a chronic form of the disease may occur in patients with continued antigen exposure, but the frequency of such progression is uncertain. The *chronic form* of the disease may also present as a gradually progressive interstitial disease associated with cough and exertional dyspnea without a prior history consistent with acute or subacute disease. Such a gradual onset of the disease frequently occurs with low-dose exposure to the antigen.

DIAGNOSIS Following acute exposure to antigen, neutrophilia and lymphopenia are frequently present. All forms of the disease may be associated with elevations in erythrocyte sedimentation rate, C-reactive protein, rheumatoid factor, and serum immunoglobulins. Antinuclear antibodies are rarely present.

Examination for *serum precipitins* against suspected antigens, such as those listed in Table 203-1, is an important part of the diagnostic workup. If found, precipitins indicate sufficient exposure to the causative agent for generation of an immunologic response. The diagnosis of HP is not established solely by the presence of precipitins, however, since precipitins merely indicate a significant exposure to an antigen source. Precipitins are found in sera of many individuals exposed to appropriate antigens who demonstrate no other evidence of HP. False-negative results may occur because of poor quality antigens or an inappropriate choice of antigens. Extraction of antigens from the patient's environment may at times be helpful.

No specific or distinctive *chest roentgenogram* occurs in HP. It can be normal even in symptomatic patients. The acute or subacute phase may be associated with poorly defined, patchy or diffuse infiltrates or with discrete, nodular infiltrates. In the chronic phase, the chest x-ray usually shows a diffuse reticulonodular infiltrate. Honeycombing may eventually develop as the condition progresses. Abnormalities rarely seen in hypersensitivity pneumonitis include pleural effusion or thickening, and hilar adenopathy.

Pulmonary function studies in all forms of HP may show a restrictive pattern with loss of lung volumes, impaired diffusion capacity, decreased compliance, and an exercise-induced hypoxemia. Depending on the severity of the disease, a resting hypoxemia may be found. Functional abnormalities may gradually increase in severity or may occur rapidly following acute or subacute exposure to antigen. As the chronic stage progresses, changes consistent with airway obstruction may also become increasingly prominent.

Bronchoalveolar lavage is used in some centers to aid in diagnostic evaluation, and the characteristic features of the lavage fluid are described above.

Lung biopsy may be indicated in patients without sufficient other criteria to make a definitive diagnosis. The initial biopsy procedure is usually a transbronchial biopsy. In some patients, an open-lung biopsy may be necessary since this procedure will provide adequate material for pathologic studies, whereas transbronchial biopsy may not. Although the histopathology is distinctive, it may not be pathognomonic of HP. When the biopsy is taken during the active phase of disease, typical findings include an interstitial alveolar infiltrate consisting of plasma cells, lymphocytes, and occasional eosinophils and neutrophils, usually with accompanying granulomas. Interstitial fibrosis is common but most often mild in earlier stages of the disease. Some degree of bronchiolitis is found in about half the cases, whereas vasculitis is not a feature of the disorder.

The lack of standardized, nonirritating antigens and of proven controlled protocols makes *skin testing* and *inhalational challenge* useful only for experimental purposes. Similarly *in vitro tests of cell-mediated (delayed) hypersensitivity* have not been shown to consistently correlate with clinical HP and cannot be recommended in the routine diagnostic workup.

DIFFERENTIAL DIAGNOSIS The diagnosis of HP should be initially considered in any patient with a history of recurrent "pneumonias" or with interstitial lung disease, as well as in those with typical presentations of acute, subacute, or chronic HP. A condition termed *pulmonary mycotoxicosis* (or "atypical" farmer's lung) occurs in patients massively exposed to moldy silage and is manifested by fever, chills, and cough within a few hours. Precipitins are not present, suggesting this disease may occur in individuals not previously sensitized to the inhaled antigen.

Chronic HP may often be difficult to distinguish from a number of other interstitial lung disorders such as idiopathic pulmonary fibrosis, interstitial lung disease associated with a collagen vascular disorder, and drug-induced lung diseases. A negative history for use of appropriate drugs and no evidence of a systemic disorder usually exclude the presence of drug-induced lung disease or a collagen vascular disorder. In some patients, a lung biopsy may be required to differentiate chronic HP from idiopathic pulmonary fibrosis.

The lung disease associated with acute or subacute HP may resemble other disorders which present with systemic symptoms and recurrent pulmonary infiltrates. These disorders include the collagen vascular disorders, drug-induced lung disease, allergic bronchopulmonary aspergillosis and other eosinophilic pneumonias. Eosinophilic pneumonia is often associated with asthma and is typified by peripheral eosinophilia; neither of these are features of HP. Allergic bronchopulmonary aspergillosis is sometimes confused with HP because of the presence of precipitating antibodies to *Aspergillus fumigatus*.

TREATMENT Because effective treatment depends largely on avoiding the antigen, identification of the causative agent and its source is essential. This is usually possible if the physician takes a careful environmental and occupational history or, if necessary, visits the patient's environment.

The simplest way to avoid the incriminated agent is to remove the patient from the environment, or the source of the agent from the patient's environment. This recommendation cannot be taken lightly when it completely changes the life-style or livelihood of the patient. In many cases, however, the source of exposure (birds, humidifiers) can easily be removed. If occupational exposure is involved, an initial attempt can be made at antigen avoidance maneuvers least disruptive to the patient's livelihood, which usually means avoiding areas associated with heavy exposure, and wearing an appropriate mask. This will not suffice for small-molecular-weight agents such as isocyanates, which require elaborate filtration devices. Pollen masks, personal dust respirators, airstream helmets, and ventilated helmets with a supply of fresh air are increasingly efficient means of purifying inhaled air. If symptoms recur or physiologic abnormalities progress in spite of these measures, then more effective measures to avoid antigen exposure must be pursued.

Compromises with environmental control pertain only to the acute, recurrent, transient clinical form of HP and must be accompanied by careful follow-up. Subacute forms are ordinarily the result of a heavy, sustained exposure. The chronic form typically results from low-grade exposure over many months to years, and the lung disease may already be partially irreversible. These patients should be advised to avoid completely all possible contact with the offending agent.

Patients with the *acute*, recurrent form of HP usually recover without need for corticosteroids. *Subacute* HP may be associated with severe symptoms and marked physiologic impairment, and may continue to progress for several days despite hospitalization. Urgent establishment of the diagnosis and prompt institution of corticosteroid treatment are indicated in such patients. Corticosteroid therapy may also hasten recovery in patients with lesser involvement. Prednisone at a dosage of 1 mg/kg per day or its equivalent is continued for 7 to 14 days, and then tapered over the ensuing 2 to 6 weeks at a rate which depends on the patient's clinical status.

Patients with *chronic* extrinsic allergic alveolitis may gradually recover without therapy following environmental control. In many patients, however, a trial of prednisone may be useful to obtain maximal reversibility of the lung disease. Following initial prednisone therapy (1 mg/kg per day for 4 to 6 weeks), the drug is tapered to the lowest dosage that will maintain the functional status of the patient. Many patients will not require or benefit from long-term therapy if there is no further exposure to antigen.

THE EOSINOPHILIC PNEUMONIAS

The eosinophilic pneumonias are composed of distinct individual syndromes characterized by eosinophilic pulmonary infiltrates and, commonly, peripheral blood eosinophilia. Since Loeffler's initial description of a transient, benign syndrome of migratory pulmonary infiltrates and peripheral blood eosinophilia of unknown cause, this group of disorders has been enlarged to include diseases of known and unknown etiology (Table 203-2). These diseases may be considered as examples of hypersensitivity lung disease but are not to be confused with hypersensitivity pneumonitis (extrinsic allergic alveolitis) in which eosinophilia is not a feature.

When an eosinophilic pneumonia is associated with bronchial asthma, it is important to determine if the patient has extrinsic (allergic, atopic) asthma and has wheal-and-flare skin reactivity to *Aspergillus* allergens. If so, other criteria should be sought for diagnosis of *allergic bronchopulmonary aspergillosis* (ABPA) (Table 203-3). *Aspergillus fumigatus* is the most common etiologic agent although other *Aspergillus* species have also been implicated. The chest roentgenogram in ABPA may show transient, recurrent infiltrates or suggest the presence of central bronchiectasis. The bronchial asthma of ABPA likely involves an IgE-mediated hypersensitivity whereas the bronchiectasis associated with this disorder is thought to result from a deposition of immune complexes in proximal airways. Adequate treatment usually requires the long-term use of systemic corticosteroids.

Tropical eosinophilia is usually caused by filarial infection; however, eosinophilic pneumonias also occur with other parasites such as *Ascaris*, *Ancyclostoma* species, *Toxocara* species, and *Strongyloides stercoralis*. Tropical eosinophilia due to *Wuchereria bancrofti* or *W. malayi* occurs most commonly in southern Asia, Africa, and South America, and is treated successfully with diethylcarbamazine.

TABLE 203-2   The eosinophilic pneumonias

1 Etiology known
a Allergic bronchopulmonary aspergillosis
b Parasitic infestations
c Drug reactions
2 Idiopathic
a Loeffler's syndrome
b Chronic eosinophilic pneumonia
c Allergic granulomatosis of Churg and Strauss
d Hypereosinophilic syndrome

Drug-induced eosinophilic pneumonias are typified by acute reactions to nitrofurantoin which may begin 2 h to 10 days after nitrofurantoin is started, with symptoms of dry cough, fever, chills, and dyspnea; an eosinophilic pleural effusion accompanying patchy or diffuse pulmonary infiltrates may also occur. Other drugs associated with eosinophilic pneumonias include sulfonamides, penicillin, chlorpropamide, thiazides, tricyclic antidepressants, hydralazine, mephenesin, mecamylamine, nickel carbonyl vapor, gold salts, isoniazid, para-aminosalicylic acid, and others. Treatment consists of withdrawal of the incriminated drugs and the use of corticosteroids, if necessary.

The idiopathic eosinophilic pneumonias consist of a group of diseases of varying severity. *Loeffler's syndrome* is a benign, acute eosinophilic pneumonia characterized by migrating pulmonary infiltrates and minimal clinical manifestations. *Chronic eosinophilic pneumonia* presents with significant systemic symptoms including fever, chills, night sweats, cough, anorexia, and weight loss lasting several weeks to months. The chest x-ray frequently shows peripheral infiltrates which have been described as a photographic negative of pulmonary edema. Some patients also have bronchial asthma which is of the intrinsic or nonallergic type. Dramatic clearing of symptoms and chest x-rays is often noted within 48 h after initiation of corticosteroid therapy.

Allergic angiitis and granulomatosis of Churg and Strauss is a multisystem vasculitic disorder which frequently involves the skin, kidney, and nervous system in addition to the lung (Chap. 269). The disorder may occur at any age and favors persons with a history of bronchial asthma. The asthma often is progressive until the onset of fever and exaggerated eosinophilia at which time the symptoms of asthma may ease. The illness may be fulminating and the prognosis grave unless treated aggressively with corticosteroids and immunosuppressive therapy.

The hypereosinophilic syndrome is characterized by a peripheral blood eosinophilia over 1500 eosinophils per cubic millimeter for 6 months or longer; lack of evidence for parasitic, allergic, or other known causes of eosinophilia; and signs or symptoms of multisystem organ dysfunction. Consistent features are blood and bone marrow eosinophilia with tissue infiltration by relatively mature eosinophils. The organs affected typically include the heart, lungs, liver, spleen, skin, and nervous system. Therapy of the disorder consists of corticosteroids and/or hydroxyurea plus therapy as needed for cardiac dysfunction, which is frequently responsible for much of the morbidity and mortality in this syndrome.

TABLE 203-3   Diagnostic features of allergic bronchopulmonary aspergillosis (ABPA)

MAIN DIAGNOSTIC CRITERIA

1 Bronchial asthma
2 Pulmonary infiltrates
3 Peripheral eosinophilia (>1000 per cubic millimeter)
4 Immediate wheal-and-flare response to *Aspergillus fumigatus*
5 Serum precipitins to *A. fumigatus*
6 Elevated serum IgE
7 Central bronchiectasis

OTHER DIAGNOSTIC FEATURES

1 History of brownish plugs in sputum
2 Culture of *A. fumigatus* from sputum
3 Elevated IgE (and IgG) class antibodies specific for *A. fumigatus*

REFERENCES

Hypersensitivity pneumonitis

HUNNINGHAKE GW, BEDELL GN: Interstitial lung disease: Concepts of pathogenesis. Sem Resp Med 6:31, 1984
——— et al: Inflammatory and immune processes in the human lung in health and disease: Evaluation by bronchopulmonary lavage. Am J Pathol 97:149, 1979
LEATHERMAN JW et al: Lung T cells in hypersensitivity pneumonitis. Ann Intern Med 100:390, 1984
RICHERSON HB: Hypersensitivity pneumonitis (extrinsic allergic alveolitis), in AP Fishman (ed), *Pulmonary Diseases and Disorders.* New York, McGraw-Hill, 1980, pp 691–698
———: Hypersensitivity pneumonitis—pathology and pathogenesis. Clin Rev Allergy 1:469, 1983

The eosinophilic pneumonias

MALO JL et al: Studies in chronic allergic bronchopulmonary aspergillosis. 1. Clinical and physiological findings. 2. Radiological findings. 3. Immunological findings. 4. Comparison with a group of asthmatics. Thorax 32:254, 262, 269, 275, 1977
MAYCOCK RL, SALDANA MJ: Eosinophilic pneumonia, in AP Fishman (ed), *Pulmonary Diseases and Disorders,* New York, McGraw-Hill, 1980, pp 926–939
SCHATZ M et al: The eosinophil and the lung. Arch Intern Med 142:1515, 1982
SCHOENBERGER CI, CRYSTAL RG: Drug-induced lung disease, in KJ Isselbacher et al (eds), *Update IV: Harrison's Principles of Internal Medicine.* New York, McGraw-Hill, 1983, pp 49–74
SLAVIN RG: Allergic bronchopulmonary aspergillosis. Clin Rev Allergy 3:167, 1985

204 ENVIRONMENTAL LUNG DISEASES

FRANK E. SPEIZER

This chapter is designed to provide a perspective on the approaches used to assess pulmonary diseases for which environmental causes are suspected. This assessment is important because removal of the patient from a harmful environment is often the only intervention that might prevent further significant deterioration or lead to improvement in a patient's condition. Furthermore, the identification of an environmentally associated disease in a single patient may lead to primary preventive strategies in other similarly exposed people who have not yet developed disease. Unless the physician specifically considers environmental exposures, these diseases and their causes will go undetected.

The exact magnitude of the problem is unknown, but there is no question that large numbers of people are at risk of developing serious respiratory disease as a result of occupational or environmental exposures. For example, even if only 5 percent (a conservative estimate) of workers currently exposed to asbestos, cotton dust, or silica are to suffer from respiratory disease as a result of their exposure, this represents more than 100,000 individuals in the United States. Although industries are required to spend substantial amounts of capital in efforts to protect their workers, occupationally related respiratory diseases continue to occur. These diseases are often attributed to exposures in the distant past at a time when we were not aware of or at least did not consider worker protection to the degree that we do today. We have, as a society, elected to pay compensation to affected individuals, and the physician is often called upon to judge not only the physical condition of such a patient but also the degree to which the illness can be related to, or aggravated by, a particular occupational exposure.

HISTORY AND PHYSICAL EXAMINATION The patient history is of paramount importance in assessing any potential occupational or environmental exposure. Often one is dealing with potential exposures in industries or environmental settings in which the physician has little personal experience. The physician must, therefore, ask the patient to describe a suspected environmental exposure in detail.

Inquiry into specific work practices should include questions about specific contaminants involved, the availability and use of personal respiratory protection devices, the size and ventilation of workspaces, the numbers of other workers potentially at risk of exposure, and whether other coworkers have similar complaints. In addition, the patient must be questioned about alternative sources for potentially toxic exposures, including hobbies or other environmental exposures at home. Short-term exposures to potential toxic agents in the distant past also must be considered. This information can be best elicited by a detailed occupational history which inquires about every job (beginning even with part-time jobs during schooling), about the nature of the work, the materials handled, and the duration and chronologic years of employment.

Many people are aware of the potential hazards in their workplaces, and recent legislation has made it a requirement in many states that employees be informed about potentially hazardous exposures. These requirements include the provision of specific educational materials, personal protective equipment, along with instruction in its use, and information on environmental control procedures. Reminders posted in the workplace may warn workers about hazardous substances. Protective clothing, lockers, and shower facilities may be considered necessary parts of the job. However, even in these ideal settings, the introduction of new processes, particularly when related to the use of new chemical compounds, may change exposure significantly, and often only the employee on the production line is aware of the change. For the physician who regularly sees patients from a particular industry, a visit to the work site can be very instructive.

The physical examination of patients with environmentally related lung diseases may help to determine the nature and severity of the pulmonary condition. Unfortunately, the pulmonary response to most injurious agents is the development of a limited number of nonspecific physical signs. These findings do not point to the specific causative agent, and other types of information must be used to arrive at an etiologic diagnosis.

PULMONARY FUNCTION TESTS AND CHEST RADIOGRAPH The use of pulmonary function tests and radiographic examinations of the chest can provide insight into the nature of the exposures which have led to the current condition of the patient and the level of impairment. Many mineral dusts produce characteristic alterations in the mechanics of breathing and lung volumes which clearly indicate a restrictive pattern (Chaps. 200 and 209). On the other hand, exposures to a number of organic dusts or chemical agents capable of producing occupational asthma result in pronounced obstructive patterns of pulmonary dysfunction that may be reversible (Chap. 202). Standardized approaches for measuring the mechanics of breathing and diffusion across the alveolar membrane (Chap. 200) have been proposed for screening large industrial groups. Measurement of change in forced expiratory volume (FEV_1) before and after a working shift can be used to detect an acute bronchoconstrictive response. An acute decrement of FEV_1 over the Monday work shift is a characteristic feature of cotton textile workers with byssinosis.

For many years the chest radiograph has been used to detect and monitor the pulmonary response to mineral dusts. To provide a standardized way of recording judgments about the kind and severity of radiographic abnormalities, the International Labour Organization (ILO)/International Classification of Radiographs of Pneumoconioses was developed. The ILO scheme involves classifying chest roentgenograms according to the nature and size of opacities seen and the extent of involvement of the parenchyma. Extensive description of the ILO system is beyond the scope of this chapter; however, judgments based only on chest radiographs may over- or underestimate the functional impact of pneumoconiosis. With dusts causing rounded, regular opacities, such as in coal worker's pneumoconiosis, the degree of involvement on the chest radiograph may be quite extensive, while pulmonary function may be only minimally impaired. In contrast, in pneumoconiosis causing linear, irregular opacities, as seen in asbestosis, the radiograph may lead to underestimation of the severity of the impairment. It is possible to have a history of exposure, moderately reduced forced vital capacity (FVC), and a reduced diffusion in asbestosis with a relatively normal chest radiograph. The radiographic findings of irregular or linear opacities are simply more difficult to separate from normal markings until relatively late in the disease. When shadows become large (radiographic lesions greater than 1 cm in diameter), the condition is termed *complicated pneumoconiosis,* sometimes called *progressive massive fibrosis* (PMF).

Other diagnostic procedures of use in identifying environmentally induced lung disease include evaluating heavy metal exposures (arsenic, cadmium in battery plant workers); bacteriologic studies (tuberculosis in medical care personnel, anthrax in wool sorters); fungal studies (coccidioidomycosis in southwestern farm workers, histoplasmosis in poultry or pigeon handlers); or serologic studies (psittacosis in pet shop workers or owners of sick birds, Q fever in tanners or slaughterhouse workers). Ultimately, a lung biopsy may be required both to make a morphologic diagnosis of the underlying pulmonary disease and to attempt to identify the specific etiologic agent.

MEASUREMENT OF EXPOSURE If reliable environmental sampling data are available, these sources of information should be used in assessing a patient's exposure. Since many of the chronic diseases result from exposure over many years, current environmental measurements should be combined with work histories to arrive at estimates of past exposure. However, the dose of any environmental agent is a complex interaction of chemical reaction, both at the emission source and in the ambient atmosphere, and physiologic factors, including ventilation rate and depth, which may affect transport and deposition of aerosols and gases in the lung. Even in acute conditions, when monitoring of exposure may be possible, little may be known about the actual dose received by the lung. Most of the research on health effects of air pollutants (discussed later in this chapter) has relied upon fixed-station monitoring of outdoor air, often at locations somewhat distant from the residences of the people being studied. In addition, most people spend less than 20 percent of their time outdoors. Efforts to determine the penetration rate of outdoor contaminants into the indoors suggest that these penetration rates are highly pollutant specific. Therefore, outdoor measurements can be used only in a relative sense, and they cannot be relied upon to estimate actual dose.

In situations where individual exposure to specific agents has been determined, either in a work setting or for ambient air pollutants, transport of these agents through the airways may be an important factor affecting dose. The upper airways are remarkably effective filters of both particles and gases. For example, virtually 100 percent of sulfur dioxide, a highly soluble gas, is absorbed in the upper airways in concentrations as high as 35 parts per million (ppm) during quiet breathing, and even during exercise sulfur dioxide is unlikely to penetrate beyond the large bronchi. On the other hand, nitrogen dioxide, which is less soluble, may reach the bronchioles and alveoli in sufficient quantities to result in an acute life-threatening disease in farmers exposed even briefly to the gas evolved from moldy hay in silos (silo filler's disease).

Particle size and chemistry of air contaminants also must be considered. Particles above 10 to 15 μm, because of their settling velocities in air, do not penetrate beyond the upper airways. These larger particles are often referred to as "fugitive dusts" and include pollens, other windblown dusts, and dusts resulting from mechanical industrial processes. They have little or no role in chronic respiratory disease except as possibly related to cancer (see below).

Particles below 10 μm in size are created by the burning of fossil fuel or high-temperature industrial processes resulting in condensation products from gases, fumes, or vapors. These particles are divided into two size fractions on the basis of their chemical characteristics. Particles approximately 2.5 to 10 μm (coarse-mode fraction) contain crustal elements, such as silica, aluminum, and iron. These particles mostly deposit relatively high in the tracheobronchial tree. Particles less than approximately 2.5 μm (fine-mode fraction or accumulation mode) contain sulfates, nitrates, and organic compounds. The deposition of the fine-mode particles is more often in the terminal bronchioles and alveoli. The smallest particles, those less than 0.1 μm in size, remain in the airstream and deposit in the lung only on a random basis as they come into contact with the alveolar walls through thermal forces and/or Brownian movement.

Besides the size characteristics of particles and the solubility of gases, the actual chemical composition, mechanical properties, and immunogenicity or infectivity of inhaled material determine in large part the nature of the diseases found among exposed persons.

OCCUPATIONAL EXPOSURES AND PULMONARY DISEASE

INORGANIC DUSTS   Asbestos exposure Except in localized regions with single industrial exposures, such as coal-mining or granite-quarrying regions, the most frequent inorganic dust–related chronic pulmonary diseases are associated with industries using *asbestos fibers.* Asbestos is a generic term for several different mineral silicates, including chrysotile, amosite, anthophyllite, and crocidolite. Approximately 9.1 million workers in the United States who had exposure to the various forms of asbestos fibers were estimated to be alive in 1980 and therefore subsequently at risk of asbestos-related diseases. Besides mining, milling, and manufacturing of asbestos products, exposures occur in the construction trades (pipe fitters, boiler makers) because of the exceptional properties of asbestos fibers for use in thermal and electric insulation. In addition, asbestos is used in the manufacture of fire-smothering blankets and safety garments, as filler for plastic materials, in cement and floor tiles, and in friction materials, such as brake and clutch linings.

Exposure to asbestos is not limited to persons who directly handle the material. Cases of asbestos-related diseases have been encountered in individuals with only moderate exposure, such as the painter or electrician who works alongside the insulation worker in a shipyard, or the housewife who does no more than shake out and wash her husband's work clothes. Community exposure has probably resulted from the use of asbestos-containing material sprayed on steel girders in many large buildings as a safety feature to prevent buckling in case of fire. Clusters of cases of mesothelioma have been noted in the neighborhood of an asbestos plant in London and in the communities near asbestos mines in South Africa.

Asbestos was first used extensively in the 1940s. Starting in 1975 it has been replaced with alternatives, such as fiberglass or slag wool. The major health effects from exposure to asbestos are pulmonary fibrosis (asbestosis) and cancers of the respiratory tract and pleura and, rarely, peritoneum.

Asbestosis is a diffuse interstitial fibrosing disease of the lung which is directly related to the intensity and duration of exposure. Except for a history of exposure to asbestos (generally in a work setting), asbestosis resembles the other forms of diffuse interstitial fibrosis (Chap. 209). Usually at least 10 years of moderate to severe exposure has occurred before the disease becomes manifest.

Physiologic studies reveal a restrictive pattern with a decrease in lung volumes. Flow rates are commonly reduced less than would be predicted on the basis of the volume reduction. An early sign of severe disease may be a reduction in diffusing capacity.

Pulmonary fibrosis occurs following exposure to any of the four common types of asbestos fiber. The fibrotic lesions do not appear to relate to either shape or chemical composition of any of the four, although the prevalence of disease may be influenced by fiber type. Recent studies indicate that during phagocytosis of the asbestos fiber, the membrane of the macrophage is damaged, which results in the release of lysosomes containing enzymes which may act to damage the lung parenchyma. The clinical manifestations are typical of those physical findings in any patient with pulmonary fibrosis (Chap. 209).

The chest radiograph can be used to determine a number of manifestations of asbestos exposure, as well as to identify specific lesions. Past exposure is specifically indicated by pleural plaques, which are characterized by either thickening or calcification along the parietal pleura, particularly along the lower lung fields, the diaphragm, and the cardiac border. Without additional manifestations, pleural plaques imply only exposure, not pulmonary impairment. Benign pleural effusions may occur, particularly in patients with abestosis, but not necessarily restricted to those with overt disease. The fluid is sterile, but may be a serous or blood-stained exudate and may occur bilaterally. Often the effusion may be slowly progressive or may resolve spontaneously.

The radiographic diagnosis of asbestosis depends upon the presence of irregular or linear opacities, usually first noted in the lower lung fields and spreading into the middle and upper lung fields as the disease becomes progressively worse. An indistinct heart border or a "ground glass" appearance in the lung fields is seen in some cases. As the fibrotic changes in the parenchyma begin to coalesce, the patient develops obliteration of entire acinar units with eventual formation of the classical honeycombed lung, which appears on chest radiographs as coarse infiltrates with small (about 7- to 10-μm) air spaces. No specific therapy is available in the management of patients with asbestosis. The supportive care is that of any patient with diffuse interstitial fibrosis from any cause. In general, newly diagnosed cases will have resulted from exposure levels that were present many years before, and in spite of the patients' having left the industry, are attributable to that former exposure. Because of present-day occupational safety and health regulations protecting workers from exposure, in theory, at least, one need not advise currently exposed workers to leave their jobs. In contrast, because the association of smoking and asbestosis increases the risk of developing lung cancer (see below), it is extremely important to advise such patients to stop smoking.

Lung cancer (Chap. 213), either squamous cell or adenocarcinoma, is the most frequent cancer associated with asbestos exposure. The excess frequency of lung cancer in asbestos workers is associated with a minimum lapse of 15 to 19 years between first exposure and development of the disease. Persons with more exposure are at greater risk of disease. In addition, there appears to be a significant multiplicative effect which leads to a far greater risk of lung cancer in persons who are cigarette smokers and have asbestos exposure than would be expected by taking the sum of both risks. Efforts to consider these high-risk individuals for special surveillance studies, including sputum cytologic examinations and repeated chest x-rays as frequently as every 4 to 6 months, suggest that cancers can be detected at an earlier stage and that the survival of these patients is prolonged.

Mesotheliomas (Chap. 214), both pleural and peritoneal, are also associated with asbestos exposure. In contrast to lung cancer there does not appear to be any association with smoking. Relatively short-term exposures of 1 to 2 years or less occurring some 20 to 25 years in the past have been associated with the development of mesotheliomas (which stresses the point of obtaining a complete environmental exposure history). The risk for this type of tumor peaks 30 to 35 years after initial exposure. Although approximately 50 percent of mesotheliomas metastasize, the tumor generally is locally invasive, and death usually results from local extension. Most patients present with effusions that may obscure the underlying pleural tumor. In contrast to other causes of effusion, because of the restriction placed on the chest wall no shift of mediastinal structures toward the opposite chest will be seen. The major diagnostic problem is differentiation from peripherally spreading pulmonary adenocarcinoma or adenocarcinoma metastatic to pleura from an extrathoracic primary site. A needle or even open biopsy is helpful in diagnosis.

One concern in making a definitive diagnosis of a mesothelioma relates to potential compensation to the survivors of a patient with this usually fatal disease. Since epidemiologic studies have shown that up to 80 percent of mesotheliomas may be associated with asbestos exposure, documented mesothelioma in a worker with occupational exposure to asbestos may be compensable in many parts of the United States.

Silicosis   In spite of the technical adequacy of existing protective equipment, *free silica* (SiO_2), or crystalline quartz, is still a major occupational hazard. In the United States estimates of potential numbers of exposed workers range between 1.2 to 3 million people. The major occupational exposures include mining, stone cutting, abrasive industries, blasting, road and building construction, farming, and quarrying, particularly of granite. Most often the progressive pulmonary fibrosis (silicosis) occurs in a dose-response fashion after many years of exposure.

Workers exposed to sandblasting in confined spaces, tunneling through rock with high quartz content (15 to 25 percent), and engaged in the manufacture of abrasive soaps may develop acute silicosis with as little as 10 months' exposure. The disease may be rapidly fatal in less than 2 years in spite of the worker being removed from exposure. A radiographic picture of profuse miliary infiltration or consolidation is characteristic of acute silicosis.

In long-term, relatively less intense exposure, radiographic changes of rounded, small opacities in the upper lobes with retraction and hilar adenopathy classically appear after 15 to 20 years of exposure. Calcification of hilar nodes may occur in as many as 20 percent of cases and produces the characteristic "eggshell" pattern. These changes may be preceded by or be associated with a reticular pattern of irregular densities which are uniformly present throughout the upper lung zones.

The nodular fibrosis may be progressive in the absence of further exposure, with coalescence and formation of nonsegmental conglomerates of irregular masses in excess of 1 cm in diameter. These masses become quite large and are characteristic of progressive massive fibrosis (PMF). Significant functional impairment with both restrictive and obstructive components may be associated with this form of silicosis. In the late stages of the disease ventilatory failure may develop. Patients with silicosis are at greater risk of acquiring *Mycobacterium tuberculosis* infections (silicotuberculosis), although tuberculosis is not always involved in the progression of the disease to PMF. Because the frequency with which tuberculosis has been found at autopsy in patients with PMF exceeds considerably the frequency of premorbid diagnosis, treatment for tuberculosis is indicated in any patient with silicosis and a positive tuberculin test.

Other less hazardous silicates include fuller's earth, kaolin, mica, diatomaceous earths, silica gel, soapstone, carbonate dusts, and cement dusts. The production of fibrosis in workers exposed to these agents is believed to be related to either the free silica content of these dusts or, for substances which contain no free silica, to the potentially large dust loads to which these workers may be exposed.

Other silicates, including *talc dusts,* may be contaminated with asbestos and/or free silica. Accidental exposure to significant quantities of talc may result in an acute syndrome with cough, cyanosis, and labored breathing (acute talcosis). Severe progressive fibrosis with respiratory failure may ensue within a few years. Far more common is the fibrosis and/or pleural or lung cancer associated with chronic exposure in rubber workers who use commercial talc as a lubricant in tire molds. Pure talc does not produce fibrosis; thus, it is difficult to sort out whether the effects are due to the contamination of commercial talc by asbestos or by free silica.

Coal worker's pneumoconiosis (CWP)   *Coal dust* is associated with CWP, which has enormous social, economic, and medical significance in every nation in which coal mining is an important industry. Simple radiographically identified CWP is seen in 12 percent of all miners and in as many as 50 percent of anthracite miners with more than 20 years' work on the coal face. The prevalence of disease is lower in workers in bituminous coal mines. Since much of the western United States coal is bituminous, CWP is less prevalent in that region.

Much of the symptomatology associated with simple CWP appears to be similar and additive to the effects of cigarette smoking on the development of chronic bronchitis and obstructive ventilatory disease (Chap. 208). In the early stages of simple CWP, radiographic abnormalities consist of small, irregular opacities (reticular pattern). With prolonged exposure, one sees small, rounded, regular opacities, 1 to 5 mm in diameter (nodular pattern). Calcification is generally not seen, although approximately 10 percent of older anthracite miners have calcified nodules.

Complicated CWP is manifested by the appearance on the chest radiograph of nodules ranging from 1 cm in diameter to the size of an entire lobe, generally confined to the upper half of the lungs. This condition, considered a form of PMF, is associated with premature mortality and is accompanied by significant reduction in diffusing capacity. In contrast to patients with silicosis, only a relatively small percentage of underground miners with simple CWP (5 to 15 percent, depending on the type of coal) develop PMF.

The mechanism whereby PMF occurs in CWP is not fully understood. Several hypotheses have been proposed, including (1) sufficient free silica is present in the dust; (2) normal clearance mechanisms are unable to clear the excessive dust loads; (3) an interplay occurs between an intrinsic immunologic mechanism and the dust and/or damaged lung tissue; and (4) atypical reactions to *Mycobacterium tuberculosis* occur. As previously described, PMF in silicosis is associated with prolonged duration and high intensity of exposure to free silica. Heavy exposure to carbon particles free of silica occurs in carbon black, graphite, and charcoal workers. The prolonged exposure of these workers may result in sufficient accumulation of carbon in the lung to produce PMF. The mechanism appears to relate to a breakdown of the clearance capacity of the airways.

Caplan's syndrome, which includes seropositive rheumatoid arthritis with characteristic PMF, is consistent with an immunopathologic mechanism. The syndrome was first described in coal miners but subsequently has been found in a number of pneumoconioses. Similarly, the high prevalence of antinuclear antibodies in sandblasting workers with silicosis and the elevation of gamma globulin levels in silicotic individuals suggest an immunologic mechanism. Although mycobacterial infections are found more often in coal miners than PMF is found in silicotic patients, tuberculosis does not appear to be associated with most of the cases of PMF in coal miners.

Berylliosis Beryllium may produce an acute pneumonitis or, far more commonly, a chronic interstitial pneumonitis. Histologically, it may be difficult to differentiate the chronic form of the disease from sarcoidosis (Chap. 270). Nonspecific pulmonary function tests may be normal or may indicate evidence of restrictive disease. Between 2 and 15 years of exposure, depending on its intensity, is required for the disease to become manifest. Unless one inquires specifically about occupational exposures to beryllium in the manufacture of alloys, ceramics, high-technology electronics, and, before the 1950s, in the production of fluorescent lights, one may miss entirely the etiologic relationship to an occupational exposure.

Rarely, other hard metals, including aluminum powders, chromium, cobalt, titanium dioxide, and tungsten, may produce an interstitial pneumonitis.

Other inorganic dusts Other dusts are considered *nuisance dusts* because their major impact seems to be reduction in visibility and irritation of eyes, ears, nasal passages, and other mucous membranes. If they penetrate to the lower airways, they do not affect the architecture of the terminal bronchioles or acinar spaces or destroy collagen. Generally, clinical effects are reversible. Pulmonary function tests are usually normal unless another disease process coexists. If radiodense, macular collections of these dusts may produce striking radiographic pictures which are so characteristic that patients with a history of significant exposure are easily diagnosed as having the condition which bears the name reflecting the nature of the dust. Examples are iron and iron oxides from welding or silver finishing (*siderosis*); tin oxide used in metallurgy, color stabilization, printing, and the manufacture of porcelain, glass, and fabric (*stannosis*); and barium sulfate used as a catalyst for organic reactions, drilling mud components, and electroplating (*baritosis*). Other metal dusts producing similar radiodense pictures include *cerium dioxide* and *antimony salts*.

Most of the inorganic dusts discussed thus far are associated with the production of either dust macules or interstitial fibrotic changes in the lung. Another set of dusts (see Table 204-1), along with some of the dusts previously discussed, is associated with chronic mucous hypersecretion (chronic bronchitis), with or without reduction of expiratory flow rates. These conditions may be caused by cigarette smoking, and any effort to attribute some component of the disease to occupational and environmental exposures must take cigarette smoking into account. In some studies the evidence suggests an additive effect of dust exposure and smoking. Those exposures associated with obstructive syndromes are generally represented by one or two studies of specific occupational groups with a small number of affected nonsmokers. Cigarette smoke is usually the more noxious agent, and dust effects may be discernible only in nonsmokers.

ORGANIC DUSTS Some of the specific diseases associated with organic dusts are discussed in detail in the chapters on asthma (Chap. 202) and on hypersensitivity pneumonitis (Chap. 203). Many of these diseases are named for the specific setting in which the disease is found, e.g., farmer's lung, malt worker's disease, or mushroom worker's disease. Occupational and other environmental exposures must be sought when these conditions are suspected. Often the temporal relation of symptoms to exposure furnishes the best evidence for the diagnosis. Three occupational groups are singled out for discussion because they represent the largest proportion of people affected by the diseases resulting from organic dusts.

Cotton dust (byssinosis) Estimates of the number of exposed persons in the United States vary, but probably over 800,000 are exposed occupationally to cotton, flax, or hemp in the production of yarns for cotton, linen, and rope making. Although this discussion focuses on cotton, the same syndrome to a somewhat lesser degree has been reported in exposure to flax, hemp, and jute.

Although cotton dust–related disease was first described in the seventeenth century, it is only in the last 35 years that the disease has been recognized as a worldwide problem in the textile industry. Exposure occurs throughout the manufacturing process but is most pronounced in those portions of the factory involved with the treatment of the cotton prior to spinning—i.e., blowing, mixing, and carding (straightening of fibers). Cases reported from spinning rooms are believed to be due to secondary contamination from carding rooms. Recent attempts to control dust levels by use of exhaust hoods, general increase in ventilation, and wetting procedures in some settings have been highly successful. However, respiratory protective equipment appears to be required during certain operations to prevent workers from being exposed to levels of dust that exceed the current United States cotton dust standard.

Byssinosis is characterized clinically as occasional (early stage) and then regular (late stage) chest tightness toward the end of the first day of the workweek (Monday chest tightness). In epidemiologic studies, up to 80 percent of carding room employees may show a significant drop in their FEV_1 over the course of a Monday shift, depending on the level of exposure in the carding room air.

Initially the symptoms do not recur on subsequent days of the week. However, in 10 to 25 percent of workers, the disease may be progressive with chest tightness recurring or persisting throughout the workweek. After more than 10 years of exposure, workers with recurrent symptoms are more likely to have an obstructive ventilatory pattern on pulmonary function testing. These higher grades of impairment are seen in workers exposed both to high levels of dust and for greater durations. There is an additive effect of cotton dust exposure plus cigarette smoking. The highest grades of impairment are generally seen in smokers.

Treatment in the early stages of the disease is directed toward reversing the bronchospasm with bronchodilators; however, the chest tightness appears at least in part to relate to histamine release, and antihistamines have been shown to lessen anticipated fall in FEV_1 the first day of the week. Clearly, reduction of dust exposure is of primary importance. All workers with persistent symptoms or significantly reduced levels of pulmonary function should be moved to areas of lower risk of exposure. Regular surveillance of pulmonary function in the industry has made it easier to identify affected persons.

TABLE 204-1 Selected occupational dusts believed to be associated with mucous hypersecretion and/or obstructive airway disease and other respiratory diseases*

Agent	Exposure	Mucus hypersecretion	Obstruction	Other conditions†	Agent	Exposure	Mucus hypersecretion	Obstruction	Other conditions†
INORGANIC DUST					Mica	Insulation, roofing shingles, oil refining, rubber manufacturing	X		P
Antimony	Storage batteries, bearing, solder, ceramics, glass, plastics	X		P	Phosphorus, elemental chlorides, sulfides	Manufacture of fireworks, agricultural chemicals, insecticides, pesticides	X	X	
Arsenic	Manufacture of pesticides, pigments, glass, alloys	X		C	Rock dusts	Miners, tunnelers, quarry workers	X		P
Barium and compounds including BaO, BaSO₄, BaCO₃	Catalyst, drilling mud, electroplating	X		P	Vanadium pentoxide	Welding electrodes, additive to steel, by-product in ash from oil burning	X	X	
Cadmium dust	Electroplating, battery manufacture, welding, smelting, aluminum soldering	X	X	P	**ORGANIC DUST (see Chap. 203)**				
Cement dust	Construction trades, manufacture of cement blocks	X	X		Cotton dust, flax, hemp	Manufacture of yarns for linen, rope, cotton; ginning, cottonseed crushing; waste fiber processing	X	X	
Chromium and CrO₃, CrF₂	Corrosion inhibitor pigment, metallurgy, electroplating	X		C	Grain dusts	Farmers, workers in grain elevators, barge and grain ship crewmembers	X	X	
Coal dust	Mining	X		P	Moldy hay	Farmers, other animal attendants	X		HP
Coke oven emissions	Retort house, coke ovens	X	X	P, C					
Graphite	Steelmaking, lubricants, pencils, paints, stove polish	X	X	P					
Iron dust	Steel and nonferrous foundry workers, welding	X		P					

* *The table excludes agents associated with asthma as the primary disease (see Chap. 202).*
† *Other conditions include hypersensitivity pneumonitis (HP), pneumoconiosis (P), and cancers (C).*
NOTE: *X indicates that mucous hypersecretion or obstruction are associated with exposure.*

Persons with reduced pulmonary function, a personal history of respiratory allergy, and positive history of continued cigarette smoking should be considered at increased risk of developing byssinosis in association with working in the cotton industry.

Grain dust Although the exact number of workers at risk in the United States is not known, at least 500,000 people work in grain elevators, and over 2 million farmers are potentially at risk. The presentation of disease in grain elevator employees or workers in flour or feed mills is virtually identical to the characteristic finding in cigarette smokers, i.e., persistent cough, mucus hypersecretion, wheeze and dyspnea on exertion, and reduced FEV_1 and FEV_1/FVC ratio (Chap. 200).

Dust concentrations in grain elevators vary greatly but appear to be in excess of 10,000 μg/m³ with approximately one-third of the particles by weight being in the respirable range. The effect of grain dust exposure is additive to that of cigarette smoking with approximately 50 percent of workers who smoke having symptoms. Among nonsmoking grain elevator operators, approximately one-quarter have mucous hypersecretion, about five times the number that would be expected in unexposed nonsmokers. However, evidence of obstruction is observed only in workers who smoke. It is not clear if this results from an enhancement of cigarette smoking effect in exposed workers or if smokers are more susceptible to the effects of grain dust.

Farmer's lung This condition results from exposure to moldy hay containing spores of thermophilic actinomycetes that produce a hypersensitivity pneumonitis (Chap. 203). There are few good population-based estimates of the frequency of occurrence of this condition in the United States. However, among farmers in Great Britain the rate of disease ranges from approximately 10 to 50 per 1000. The prevalence of disease varies in association with rainfall, which determines the amount of fungal growth, and with differences in agricultural practices related to turning and stacking hay.

The patient with acute farmer's lung presents 4 to 8 h after exposure with fever, chills, malaise, cough, and dyspnea without wheezing. The history of exposure is obviously essential to separate this disease from similar symptoms that might occur in influenza or pneumonia. In the chronic form of the disease, the history of repeated attacks after similar exposure is important to separate this syndrome from other causes of patchy fibrosis, e.g., sarcoidosis.

A wide variety of other organic dusts are associated with the occurrence of hypersensitivity pneumonitis (Chap. 203). For those patients who present with hypersensitivity pneumonitis, specific and careful inquiry about occupations, hobbies, or other home environmental exposures will, in most cases, reveal the source of the etiologic agent.

ASSESSMENT OF DISABILITY Significant reduction of dust levels in coal mines has resulted from federal legislation, enacted in the

United States in 1969, which requires that respirable dust levels in underground mines be reduced to less than 2000 $\mu g/m^3$. This same legislation authorized payment to coal miners (or their survivors) totally disabled by CWP. The criteria for disability from CWP remain unclear and arbitrary. Much of the difficulty relates to the inability to determine in an individual with simple CWP what proportion of an observed respiratory impairment is related to coal dust and what proportion is due to cigarette smoking. The laws as currently interpreted suggest that to be eligible for payment of a claim, one need only show that an underlying condition (i.e., chronic bronchitis with obstruction, presumably due to cigarette smoking) is aggravated by CWP. Thus, it becomes critical that physicians involved in occupational lung disease claim cases be aware of detailed exposure histories of their patients, both in terms of occupational exposures and other environmental exposures (cigarette smoking). In addition, these physicians must understand that the extent to which the level of physiologic impairment incapacitates an individual may not be the sole criterion for determining disability. To assess disability properly may require input not only from physicians but also from experts in ergonomics and vocational rehabilitation, lawyers, and employer and employee representatives. Similar separate bills have been introduced into Congress to deal with other single occupational diseases, such as asbestosis and byssinosis.

TOXIC CHEMICALS Exposure to toxic chemicals affecting the lung generally occurs in the form of gases and vapors. A common accident is one in which the victim is trapped in a confined space where the chemicals have accumulated to toxic levels. In addition to the specific toxic effects of the chemical, the victim will often sustain considerable anoxia, which can play a dominant role in determining whether the individual recovers.

Table 204-2 lists a variety of toxic agents which can produce acute and sometimes life-threatening reactions in the lung. All of these agents in sufficient concentrations have been demonstrated, at least in animal studies, to affect the lower airways and disrupt alveolar architecture, either acutely or as a result of chronic exposure. Some of these agents may be generated acutely in the environment. For example, when plastics burn, a number of compounds, including hydrogen cyanide and hydrochloric acid, may be formed and released. The effects and treatment of exposure to these toxic gases are discussed elsewhere (Chap. 171).

Fire fighters and fire victims are at risk of *smoke inhalation*, a numerically important cause of acute cardiorespiratory failure. Smoke inhalation kills more fire victims than does thermal injury. Exposed victims may suffer some degree of lower respiratory tract inflammation, similar to that seen with exposure to irritant gases, e.g., chlorine. Severe cases may develop pulmonary edema. Carbon

TABLE 204-2 Selected common toxic chemical agents

Agents	Selected exposures	Acute effects from high or accidental exposure	Chronic effects from relatively low exposure
Acid fumes; H_2SO_4, HNO_3	Manufacture of fertilizers, chlorinated organic compounds, dyes, explosives, rubber products, metal etching, plastics	Mucous membrane irritation, followed by chemical pneumonitis 2–3 days	No data
Ammonia	Refrigeration, petroleum refining, manufacture of fertilizers, explosives, plastics, and other chemicals	Same as for acid fumes	Chronic bronchitis
Cyanides	Electroplating, extraction of gold or silver, manufacture of mirrors, fumigants, photo supplies	Increase in respiratory rate followed by respiratory arrest, lactic acidosis, pulmonary edema, death	No data
Diazomethane	Methylating agent for acid compounds; laboratory workers	Violent coughing, dyspnea, wheezing, pulmonary edema	No data
Formaldehyde	Manufacture of resins, leathers, rubber, metals, & woods; laboratory workers, embalmers; emission from urethane foam insulation	Same as for acid fumes	Cancers in one species of animals; no data on humans
Halides (Cl, Br, F)	Bleaching in pulp, paper, textile industry; manufacture of chemical compounds; synthetic rubber, plastics, disinfectant, rocket fuel, gasoline	Mucous membrane irritation, pulmonary edema; possible reduced FVC 1–2 yrs after exposure	Dryness of mucous membrane, epistaxis, dental fluorosis, tracheobronchitis
Hydrogen sulfide	By-product of many industrial processes, oil, other petroleum processes and storage	Low exposure: conjunctival irritation; higher: respiratory paralysis similar to cyanides	Chronic bronchitis, recurrent pneumonitis
Isocyanates (TDI, HDI, MDI)	Production of polyurethane foams, plastics, adhesives, surface coatings	Mucous membrane irritation, dyspnea, cough, wheeze, pulmonary edema	Upper respiratory tract irritation, cough, asthma, allergic alveolitis
Nitrogen dioxide	Silage, metal etching, explosives, rocket fuels, welding, by-product of burning fossil fuels	Cough, dyspnea, pulmonary edema may be delayed 4–12 h; possible result from acute exposure: bronchiolitis obliterans in 2–6 wks	Emphysema in animals, ? chronic bronchitis
Ozone	Arc welding, flour bleaching, deodorizing, emissions from copying equipment, photochemical air pollutant	Mucous membrane irritant, pulmonary hemorrhage and edema	Chronic eye irritation
Phosgene	Organic compound, metallurgy, volatization of chlorine-containing compounds	Delayed onset of bronchiolitis and pulmonary edema	Chronic bronchitis
Phthalic anhydride	Manufacture of resin esters, polyester resins, thermoactivated adhesives	Nasal irritation, cough	Asthma, chronic bronchitis
Sulfur dioxide	Manufacture of sulfuric acid, bleaches, coating of nonferrous metals, food processing, refrigerant, burning of fossil fuels, wood pulp industry	Mucous membrane irritant, epistaxis	? Chronic bronchitis

monoxide poisoning with resulting significant hypoxemia can be life-threatening (Chap. 171). Fire fighters may inappropriately use the "blackness" of the smoke to indicate the degree to which incomplete combustion and, thus, elevation of carbon monoxide levels are present. The increased use of synthetic materials (plastic, polyurethanes), which, when burned, may release a variety of other toxic agents, must be considered when evaluating smoke inhalation victims.

Fire fighters and victims also may be exposed to large quantities of particulate smoke. Significant long-term effects are not clearly associated with this particulate exposure except as related to the production of irritating effects on the upper airways. Studies attempting to demonstrate either an increased risk of cardiovascular events, presumably from recurrent exposure to carbon monoxide, or excess incidence of chronic respiratory disease from repeated smoke inhalation, are inconclusive, partly because of the difficulties in measuring exposure.

Some agents used in the manufacture of synthetic materials such as plastics, polyurethanes, and other polymers have resulted in some workers being sensitized to extremely low levels of *isocyanates, aromatic amines,* or *aldehydes.* Repeated exposure to these agents causes some workers to develop chronic cough and sputum production, asthma, or episodes of low-grade fever and malaise. Occasionally, as in byssinosis, these symptoms occur early in the workweek, but usually recur without workweek periodicity. In the case of exposure to diisocyanate in the production of polyurethane, chronic and persistent asthma in selected individuals appears to result from exposure to concentrations well below the recognized industrial standard. Methods to identify susceptible individuals are needed. At present, challenge testing is being used to determine if a given patient is sensitive. These challenges can be carried out in special environmental chambers where the physician can simulate the work exposure. Alternatively, nonspecific challenges with either pharmacologic agents, such as methacholine and histamine, or isocapneic cold air breathing are being used to identify patients with hyperreactive airways. The usefulness of this nonspecific approach as a method to screen potential workers has yet to be established.

An unusual route of exposure occurs in *polymer fume fever.* Polymers, notably fluorocarbons, which at normal temperatures produce no reaction, may be transmitted from a worker's hands to his or her cigarettes. Upon burning the cigarette, the polymer is volatilized, and the inhaled agent causes a characteristic syndrome of fever, chills, malaise, and occasionally mild wheezing. The same condition occurs in workers exposed to heated polymers without cigarette use. The syndrome is obviously controlled by proper attention to hygiene in the workplace. A similar self-limited, influenza-like syndrome—*metal fume fever*—results from acute exposure to fumes or smoke of zinc, copper, magnesium, and other volatilized metals. The syndrome may begin several hours after work and resolves within 24 h, only to return on repeated exposure. A proper occupational history should make the diagnosis evident.

ENVIRONMENTAL RESPIRATORY CARCINOGENS   Historically, it has been the astute clinician who has recognized a higher incidence of malignant tumors associated with certain environmental exposures. When these observations are linked to an occupational setting, they must be pursued by epidemiologic studies of relatively large groups of both current and former workers. Often the concentration and/or exact nature of the substances contained in the putative exposures cannot be determined. Rarely, the possibility that a substance can play an etiologic role in cancer is supported by observing that a few cases of a very rare tumor in a particular group represent "an epidemic." Two best examples of this are nasal sinus and lung cancer in nickel workers and angiosarcomas in vinyl chloride workers.

Only in those few cases in which animal studies have been carried out can one confirm that a given suspected agent is really a carcinogen. For example, bis(chloromethyl) ether (BCME) has been shown to produce tumors in animals and oat cell cancer of the lung in humans. In this particular case, BCME, used as a chemical intermediary in the manufacture of a number of organic compounds, was known to produce tumors in animals almost before the substance was introduced into industry. (This case is one of the prime examples of why federal legislation was enacted in the United States in the 1970s to control the release of toxic substances, particularly new chemicals.)

In addition to the asbestos trades, other occupational exposures associated with either proven or suspected respiratory carcinogens include acrylonitrile, arsenic compounds, beryllium (animal studies only), BCME, chromium, coke ovens (exposure to polycyclic hydrocarbons), iron oxide, isopropyl oil (nasal sinuses), mustard gas, the various ores used to produce pure nickel, talc (possible asbestos contamination in both mining and milling), vinyl chloride, welding, wood used in woodworking (nasal cancer only), and uranium. The occurrence of excess cancers in uranium miners raises the possibility that there exists a large number of workers at risk by virtue of exposure to similar radiation hazards. This includes not only workers involved in processing uranium, up to and including its use in nuclear power plants and in military nuclear hardware, but also workers exposed in underground mining operations where radon daughters may be emitted from rock formations. In the latter case, the levels of exposure are generally considered to be relatively low; however, specific consideration must be given to the possibility of excess exposure for any hard rock miner.

GENERAL ENVIRONMENTAL EXPOSURES

AIR POLLUTION   Dramatic and disastrous episodes of air pollution inversion have been documented in many industrialized centers in the world. Each of these episodes has been associated with excess acute mortality in the very old, the very young, and in those with chronic cardiopulmonary diseases. The most dramatic event was the London fog of 1952, in which approximately 4000 excess deaths occurred over a 2-week period following 5 days of severe cold and dense fog. Similar episodes in the United States, although less dramatic in terms of total deaths, occurred in Donora, Pennsylvania, in 1948, and in New York City in the 1960s. In these episodes, generally associated with cold temperature and air stagnation, patients with underlying cardiopulmonary disease were most severely affected.

In addition to significant excess mortality during these episodes, a large number of people required medical care for cardiorespiratory complaints. Subsequent follow-up studies failed to implicate these episodic disasters in the etiology of chronic respiratory disease in adults. On the other hand, many epidemiologic studies of both international and regional differences in the prevalences of chronic respiratory disease suggest that long-term exposures in polluted areas in the early to middle part of the twentieth century were associated with excess chronic respiratory disease.

In 1970, the U.S. federal government established air quality standards for several pollutants believed to be responsible for excess cardiorespiratory diseases. Primary standards regulated by the Environmental Protection Agency (EPA) designed to protect the public health with an adequate margin of safety exist for sulfur dioxide, total suspended particulates, nitrogen dioxide, ozone, lead, and carbon monoxide. These standards vary in their averaging times and levels, in part related to the differences in the known physiologic responses and epidemiologic evidence for each pollutant.

Pollutants are generated from both stationary sources (power plants and industrial complexes) and mobile sources (automobiles), and none of the pollutants occur in isolation. Thus, except for the change in carboxyhemoglobin from carbon monoxide exposure, it becomes extremely difficult to relate any specific health effect to any single pollutant. Furthermore, pollutants may be changed by chemical reactions after being emitted. For example, reducing agents, such as sulfur dioxide and particulate matter from a power plant stack, may react in air to produce acid sulfates and aerosol (acid rain), which can be transported long distances in the atmosphere. Oxidizing substances, such as oxides of nitrogen and oxidants from automobile exhaust, may react with sunlight to produce ozone. Although originally a problem confined to the southwestern part of the United States, in recent years, at least during the summertime, elevated ozone and sulfate levels can occur throughout the United States. Both acute and chronic effects of these exposures are currently under investigation.

The symptoms and diseases associated with air pollution are the same as the nononcogenic conditions commonly associated with cigarette smoking. In addition, respiratory illness in early childhood has been associated with chronic exposure to only modestly elevated levels of SO_2 and total suspended particulates. It is not known whether persistent chronic exposure to a relatively constant level of pollutant(s) and recurrent short-term peak exposures which average to the same mean level have different effects. For a patient with significant cardiopulmonary impairment, one can only advise the individual to stay indoors during periods when pollution exceeds current standards.

INDOOR EXPOSURE Because of increased concern about energy costs, efforts to become energy efficient have led to reduced air exchange rates in indoor environments. The effects of these efforts have been to increase exposures to a variety of air contaminants heretofore not considered important. Two examples of potential health effects from exposure to indoor pollutants are discussed to indicate the magnitude of possible problems.

For many years little attention, beyond its nuisance effect, has been given to the effects of *passive cigarette smoking*. The implication has been that passive smoking exposures were too low to be of any consequence. Recent studies have shown that the respirable particulate load in any household is directly proportional to the number of cigarette smokers living in the home. Increases in prevalence of respiratory illnesses and reduced levels of pulmonary function measured with simple spirometry have been found in children of smoking parents in a number of studies. The long-term consequences of these findings are unknown. Other potential health effects are discussed in Chap. 173.

A novel source of indoor exposure to *formaldehyde* results from the curing process involved in the placement of urea-formaldehyde insulating foam or in several wood products used in modern furniture and the construction of mobile homes. Natural "degassing" of formaldehyde occurs during the first few months after the foam has been blown into the walls, with concentrations of formaldehyde as high as 5 ppm rapidly dropping off to less than 0.1 ppm. Chronic exposure to low levels of urea-formaldehyde (generally less than 1 ppm) may result if the foam is improperly installed. Patients apparently sensitive to concentrations of formaldehyde generally well below 1 ppm will complain of upper airway irritation with occasional epistaxis and sore throats. Lower respiratory complaints, such as chest pain and wheeze, however, are uncommon, and often the most disturbing complaints are mild memory and mood disorders. Formaldehyde is a proven animal carcinogen. Whether it causes cancer in humans is not established.

PORTAL OF ENTRY The lung is a primary source of entry into the body for a number of toxic agents that affect other organ systems. For example, the lung is the route of entry for benzene (bone marrow), carbon disulfide (cardiovascular and nervous systems), cadmium (kidney), and mercury (kidney, central nervous system). Thus, in any disease state of obscure origin, it is important to consider possible inhaled environmental agents. Such consideration can sometimes furnish the clue needed to identify a specific external cause for a disorder that might otherwise be labeled "idiopathic."

REFERENCES

AMERICAN THORACIC SOCIETY: *Update: Health Effects of Air Pollution.* New York, American Lung Association, (in press)

ATTFIELD M et al: The incidence and progression of pneumoconiosis over nine years in U.S. coal miners. Am J Ind Med 6:407, 1984

COCHRANE AL, MOORE FA: A 20-year follow-up of men aged 55–64 including coal-miners and foundry workers in Stavley, Derbyshire. Br J Ind Med 37:226, 1980

CRAIGHEAD JE, MOSSMAN BT: The pathogenesis of asbestos-associated diseases. N Engl J Med 306:1446, 1982

FERRIS BG JR: Epidemiology Standardization Project. Am Rev Respir Dis 118(6)(2):1, 1978

Guidelines for the Use of International Labour Office Classification of Radiographs of Pneumoconiosis. Occupational Safety and Health Sciences 22 (Revised 1980). Geneva, ILO, 1980

KILBURN KH: Byssinosis: Causes and practical control. Ann Intern Med 101:252, 1984

KOSKINEN H: Symptoms and clinical findings in patients with silicosis. Scan J Work Environ Health 11:101, 1985

MUNDIE TG et al: Byssinosis: Serum immunoglobulin and complement concentrations in cotton mill workers. Arch Environ Health 40:326, 1985

PARKES WR: *Occupational Lung Disorders,* 2d ed. London, Butterworth, 1982

PETO R, SCHNEIDERMAN M (eds): *Quantification of Occupational Cancer,* Banbury Report, 9. Cold Spring Harbor, 1981

SCHMIDT JA et al: Silica-stimulated monocytes release fibroblast proliferation factors identical to interleukin. A potential role for interleuken I in the pathogenesis of silicosis. J Clin Invest 73:1462, 1984

WEILL J: Occupational pulmonary diseases and acute and accidental exposures to irritant gases, in *Pulmonary Diseases and Disorders,* 2d ed, A P Fishman (ed). New York, McGraw-Hill, 1987, chap. 54.

---

205 PNEUMONIA AND LUNG ABSCESS

JAN V. HIRSCHMANN / JOHN F. MURRAY

PNEUMONIA

DEFINITION Pneumonia is defined as inflammation in the lung parenchyma, the portion distal to the terminal bronchioles and comprising the respiratory bronchioles, alveolar ducts, alveolar sacs, and alveoli. Although the inflammation may have many different causes and varying durations, the term *pneumonia* most commonly refers to acute infections.

PATHOGENESIS Organisms reach the lung to cause pneumonia by one of four routes: (1) inhalation of microbes present in the air, (2) aspiration of organisms from the naso- or oropharynx, the most common cause of bacterial pneumonia, (3) hematogenous spread from a distant focus of infection, or rarely, (4) direct spread from a contiguous site of infection or penetrating injury.

Lung defense mechanisms Although inhalation of organisms and aspiration of oropharyngeal contents are probably common, even in healthy people, the airway distal to the larynx is normally sterile or possesses a sparse flora because of several protective mechanisms. The glottis reflexly closes when material is aspirated; whatever reaches the trachea and large bronchi usually evokes coughing, which expels the material from the tracheobronchial tree. The airways between the larynx and the terminal bronchioles are further protected by their lining of mucus-covered ciliated epithelium, which propels trapped inhaled matter from the smaller to the larger airways, where it can be eliminated by expectoration or swallowing.

The immunoglobulins constitute another defense mechanism. IgA, present in high concentrations in the upper respiratory tract, protects against viral infection. It is less abundant in the lower respiratory secretions, where it may help agglutinate bacteria, neutralize microbial toxins, and reduce bacterial attachment to mucosal surfaces. IgG in the serum and lower respiratory tract agglutinates and opsonizes bacteria; activates complement, promoting chemotaxis of granulocytes and macrophages; neutralizes bacterial toxins and viruses; and lyses gram-negative bacteria. Also present on the alveolar surface are alveolar macrophages, which ingest and kill organisms, and alveolar lining material, which may enhance phagocytic function. In addition, neutrophils, which ingest and kill organisms, and lymphocytes, providing humoral and cell-mediated immunity, migrate from the bloodstream into the parenchyma to help combat infection.

Predisposing conditions Pneumonia may occur in healthy people but is usually associated with conditions that impair one or more of the defense mechanisms listed above. Altered consciousness from alcoholism, cranial trauma, seizures, general anesthesia, drug overdose, cerebrovascular disease, or other causes, and old age depress the cough and glottic reflexes, allowing the aspiration of oropharyngeal contents. Pain from trauma or thoracic or upper abdominal surgery; weakness from malnutrition or neuromuscular disease; thoracic cage deformities such as serious kyphoscoliosis; or severe obstructive lung disease may prevent the full inspiration and brisk expiration necessary to generate an effective cough. An endotracheal tube or tracheostomy eliminates glottic closure and impedes effective coughing.

Mucociliary transport is impaired by alcohol, cigarette smoke, old age, and preceding viral respiratory infections, which may cause necrosis and desquamation of the tracheobronchial epithelium. Endobronchial obstruction from tumor, foreign body, or other causes compromises effective clearance mechanisms. Thick mucus from cystic fibrosis or chronic bronchitis makes the transport system less effective. Indeed, in chronic bronchitis, the tracheobronchial tree is typically colonized with an abundant flora, especially pneumococci and *Haemophilus influenzae*.

Lymphocyte disorders, including congenital and acquired immunodeficiencies, and granulocyte abnormalities may predispose to pneumonia (see Chaps. 56, 84, and 256). Pulmonary infection may also occur when alveolar macrophage function is impaired by cigarette smoke, hypoxia, starvation, anemia, pulmonary edema, and viral respiratory infections.

Oropharyngeal flora   Most pneumonias arise from the aspiration of oropharyngeal flora, normally a complex assortment of aerobic and anaerobic bacteria. Which of these organisms causes the pneumonia seems to depend upon the identity of the microbes present and the quantity of material aspirated. *Streptococcus pneumoniae, H. influenzae, Staphylococcus aureus,* and even *Neisseria meningitidis,* all potential pathogens, are often found in the oropharynx of healthy adults. Each of these organisms, as single agents, may cause pneumonia when aspirated into alveoli. Anaerobes, however, which outnumber aerobes severalfold in the oral cavity, are weak pathogens individually and usually cause infection by an interaction among several species. These organisms, therefore, are likely to cause pneumonia, usually as a polymicrobial infection, only when aspirated in relatively large quantities.

Coliforms, such as *Escherichia coli, Klebsiella,* and *Proteus,* are uncommon in the oropharynx of healthy adults. Several conditions, especially hospitalization, however, favor their growth. Serious underlying illness, confinement in an intensive care unit, the use of an endotracheal tube or tracheostomy, contaminated respiratory equipment, and antimicrobial therapy, which frequently selects out organisms resistant to the agents used, especially encourage colonization with coliforms present in the hospital environment. Certain illnesses, such as acute granulocytic leukemia, alcoholism, and diabetes mellitus, are associated with an increased frequency of oropharyngeal colonization with aerobic gram-negative bacilli whether or not the patient is hospitalized.

Aspiration pneumonia   Since most bacterial pneumonias originate from the aspiration of oropharyngeal flora into the lung parenchyma, they are, strictly speaking, examples of *aspiration pneumonia.* In common use, however, this term refers to the aspiration of *large* quantities of oropharyngeal contents, primarily in patients with impaired consciousness, altered swallowing, or feeble coughs. In aspirations occurring outside the hospital the organisms causing infections are likely to be pneumococci or a mixture of aerobes and anaerobes. These microbes are also common pathogens in hospitalized or institutionalized patients but because their oropharyngeal flora has often changed, infections with aerobic gram-negative rods are frequent.

The term *aspiration pneumonia,* however, has also been applied to the aspiration of *gastric* contents in patients with altered consciousness, gastric outlet obstruction, esophageal disorders, or vomiting. The initial pulmonary reaction is not an infection, but an inflammatory response to irritating chemicals, chiefly HCl, present in gastric fluid, which is usually sterile or contains only a sparse flora. Antimicrobial therapy is reserved for the uncommon and delayed complication of superinfection, suggested by fever and purulent sputum, with pathogens present on Gram's stain and culture. If the patient is seen to aspirate gastric contents, the major therapy is vigorous chest physiotherapy, nasotracheal suctioning, and maintenance of adequate oxygenation. Corticosteroids are not useful.

CLINICAL MANIFESTATIONS   The major symptoms of pneumonia, occurring in varying combinations, are cough, fever, chest pain, dyspnea, and the production of sputum, which may be mucoid, purulent, or even bloody. In some patients, extrapulmonary features such as confusion or disorientation may predominate, and occasionally, especially in elderly, alcoholic, or neutropenic patients, respiratory symptoms and signs are absent altogether. Important in the history are inquiries about prodromal symptoms, the type of onset (abrupt or gradual), the presence of rigors and pleuritic chest pain, similar illness in family members or acquaintances, animal exposure, and recent travel.

Common physical findings are fever, tachycardia, and tachypnea. Severely hypoxic patients may be cyanotic. On chest examination there may be decreased respiratory excursion on the affected side because of pleuritic pain and dullness to percussion from pneumonic consolidation or an accompanying pleural effusion. Among the earliest auscultatory findings is the presence of high-pitched, end-inspiratory crackles, originating from fluid-filled alveoli, that are often increased by, or heard only after, coughing. Secretions in the airways may cause lower-pitched, early or midinspiratory crackles. Consolidated lung surrounding a patent bronchus often gives rise to bronchial breath sounds, an accentuation of both the inspiratory and expiratory phases of breathing. In some patients, despite impressive roentgenographic abnormalities, physical examination of the chest is entirely normal. In patients whose pneumonia is secondary to hematogenous spread, the primary site of infection may be apparent. Alternatively, bacteremia arising from pneumonia may cause infection in distant sites, such as meningitis, septic arthritis, or pustular skin lesions.

The arterial blood gases commonly reveal hypoxia and, in the absence of other pulmonary disease, hypocarbia and respiratory alkalosis. The hypoxia results from right-to-left shunting of blood, because of the continued perfusion of the nonventilated areas affected by the pneumonia.

ROENTGENOGRAPHIC FINDINGS   The microbial etiology of a pneumonia cannot be accurately predicted by its roentgenographic characteristics. Nevertheless, certain appearances are more typical of some organisms than others. Pneumonias tend to conform to one of three pathologic and roentgenographic patterns (Fig. 205-1): (1) alveolar or air space pneumonia, (2) bronchopneumonia, or (3) interstitial pneumonia. In air space pneumonia the organism causes an inflammatory exudate that spreads from one alveolus to the next via the communicating channels, known as the pores of Kohn, and the canals of Lambert. Segmental boundaries are not preserved, and the bronchi, relatively uninvolved, remain patent. The roentgenographic result is nonsegmental consolidation with air bronchograms, the classic example being pneumococcal pneumonia. Some organisms produce bronchopneumonia, which consists of inflammation in the conducting airways, especially terminal and respiratory bronchioles, and the surrounding alveoli. Because interalveolar spread in the peripheral air spaces is minimal, the pneumonia tends to maintain a distribution corresponding to the involved pulmonary segment. Inflammation affects the bronchi themselves, sometimes causing atelectasis, and air bronchograms are absent. An example is staphylococcal pneumonia. *Mycoplasma pneumoniae* and viruses often cause an interstitial pneumonia, where inflammation is predominantly in the interalveolar septa, producing a reticular radiographic appearance.

DIAGNOSTIC TECHNIQUES   Among the most useful procedures to define a pneumonia's etiology is the microscopic examination of a Gram-stained sputum specimen. Although precise speciation of bacteria is impossible by Gram's stain alone, the appearance of organisms allows reasonable inferences about their identity. An acceptable sputum sample, one genuinely arising from the lower respiratory tract rather than the oropharynx, has more than 25 leukocytes per low-power field (100×). Squamous epithelial cells from the oropharynx are sparse, and alveolar macrophages are often present. Specimens that fail to meet these standards represent mostly saliva and are useless for further examination or culture. Acceptable specimens should be cultured on appropriate media.

Adequate staining of acceptable specimens is crucial for accurate interpretation. If cells, including the nuclei of leukocytes, are not gram-negative (red), the sample is underdecolorized. If gram-positive (blue) organisms are present near the gram-negative leukocytes, the stain is suitable. If the cells and all the organisms are gram-negative, the slide may be overdecolorized and may require restaining. The slide should be examined carefully for the predominant organism; bacteria overlying squamous epithelial cells should be disregarded.

Usually, sputum expectorated after a deep cough is acceptable for stain and culture by the criteria outlined above. When the patient cannot produce a satisfactory specimen, inhalation of ultrasonically nebulized saline or suctioning with a catheter introduced through the nose into the posterior pharynx will often induce coughing and provide an adequate sample. Since sputum that is expectorated or obtained by nasotracheal suction is unavoidably contaminated by oropharyngeal flora, which normally contains anaerobic organisms, it is not appropriate for anaerobic cultures.

Another method of obtaining sputum is transtracheal aspiration with a polyethylene catheter inserted into the trachea through the cricothyroid membrane. This procedure is generally safe but should be accompanied by oxygen administration in those with hypoxia and avoided in uncooperative patients and those with serious clotting disorders or platelet defects. This method avoids contamination with the abundant, complex mouth flora and yields a specimen suitable for anaerobic culture. An alternate way of obtaining lower respiratory secretions is transthoracic aspiration of the lung with a spinal needle attached to a syringe. The major complications are pneumothorax or pulmonary hemorrhage. Lower respiratory secretions may also be obtained by bronchoscopy. Because contamination with oropharyngeal flora is generally unavoidable, even with preceding endotracheal intubation, these specimens are approximately equivalent to good expectorated sputum samples, unless specially designed catheters, which may provide uncontaminated specimens, are used.

Occasionally, lung biopsy may be necessary for accurate diagnosis and treatment, especially in immunocompromised patients. This procedure is discussed later in the chapter under "Treatment, Pneumonia in Compromised Hosts."

Since bacteremia sometimes accompanies pneumonia, blood cultures taken from two separate venipuncture sites may grow the responsible organism. Similarly, the presence of a pleural effusion requires a thoracentesis, which may yield infected fluid. Skin lesions, joint effusions, and cerebrospinal fluid should be cultured if these areas appear infected.

Although viruses, *M. pneumoniae*, *Coxiella burnetti*, *Legionella pneumophila*, and *Francisella tularensis*, may grow from sputum specimens cultured on appropriate media, pneumonias due to these agents are usually diagnosed by serology. Acute and convalescent serum samples should be obtained when these agents are suspected; seroconversion to *L. pneumophila* may take 6 weeks. Legionnaires' disease may also be diagnosed by direct immunofluorescence of respiratory tract secretions (see Chap. 117).

DIFFERENTIAL DIAGNOSIS Community-acquired pneumonias

Pneumococcal pneumonia (see Chap. 93), the most common bacterial pneumonia, in its classic form frequently follows an upper respiratory infection and begins abruptly with a single shaking chill, fever, pleuritic chest pain, and a cough productive of purulent, often bloody sputum. In some patients, especially the elderly and those with serious underlying disorders such as alcoholism or chronic obstructive lung disease, the illness is often considerably less dramatic, with the insidious onset of fever, cough, and dyspnea or extrapulmonary features such as confusion or weakness. The white blood cell count is usually elevated, with increased immature forms, but may be normal or low. The typical sputum Gram's stain shows numerous neutrophils and abundant, gram-positive lancet-shaped diplococci as the predominant organism. The chest roentgenogram characteristically demonstrates a unilateral, homogeneous, nonsegmental air space consolidation, usually abutting against a visceral pleural surface. Unilateral or bilateral multilobar involvement may occur, and in patients with emphysema the consolidation may have an inhomogeneous appearance of multiple "holes" from the radiolucent, unconsolidated bullae. Cavitation rarely occurs, but parapneumonic pleural effusions, usually small but occasionally voluminous, are frequent.

Pneumonia from *S. pyogenes* (see Chap. 95) is very uncommon. It may follow pharyngitis or a viral illness, especially influenza, or occasionally occurs as outbreaks in closed populations, such as military recruits. The onset is typically abrupt, with multiple rigors, fever, a productive cough, and pleuritic chest pain. Pharyngitis is often present. The white blood cell count is commonly elevated, and immature forms increased. The sputum Gram's stain shows multiple neutrophils and gram-positive cocci in chains. The chest roentgenogram usually reveals a large pleural effusion, which develops rapidly after the onset of illness, and which tends to obscure any underlying pneumonia.

Pneumonia from *S. aureus* (see Chap. 94), also quite uncommon, tends to follow an influenza attack. The onset is generally abrupt and the course rapid, with fever, multiple rigors, purulent sputum production, and pleuritic chest pain. The white blood cell count is

FIGURE 205-1 *Roentgenographic appearances of pneumonia. A. Air space pneumonia. There is a dense, homogeneous, nonsegmental consolidation in the right lower lobe with a visible air bronchogram. B. Interstitial pneumonia.* A linear or reticular pattern involves the lower lung fields bilaterally, more on the right. C. Bronchopneumonia. A segmental infiltrate without a visible air bronchogram appears in the left lower lung field.

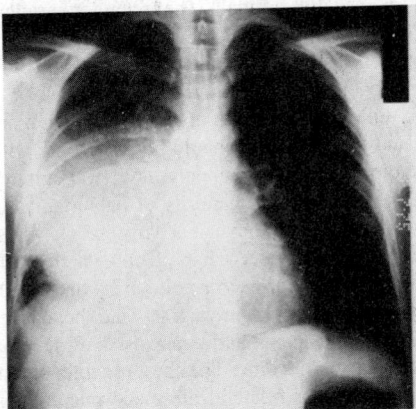
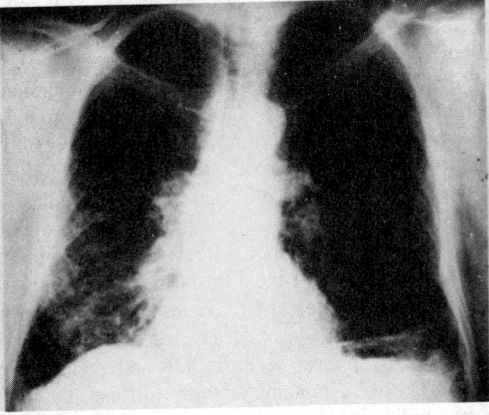
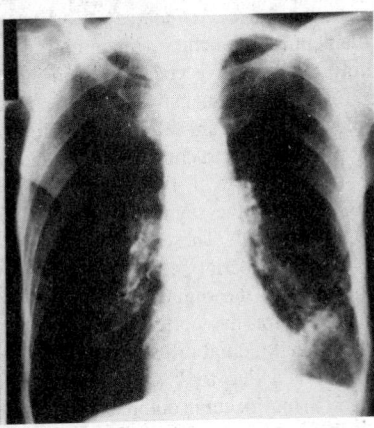

A   B   C

elevated, and immature forms are increased. The sputum smear shows numerous neutrophils and gram-positive cocci in clumps. The chest roentgenogram reveals bronchopneumonia, often bilateral, frequently with cavitation and pleural effusions. Pneumatoceles, thin-walled cystic spaces, may develop, primarily in children.

Pneumonia due to *N. meningitidis* (see Chap. 103) may occur in sporadic cases, following viral respiratory infections, or in closed populations, especially in military recruits. The onset may be abrupt, resembling pneumococcal pneumonia, or more gradual, with cough, fever, sore throat, and chest pain. Meningitis or cutaneous evidence of meningococcemia is uncommon, and blood cultures are typically sterile. Neutrophilic leukocytosis is usual. The sputum smear shows gram-negative diplococci that are often present within the cytoplasm of neutrophils. The chest film most commonly demonstrates patchy alveolar consolidation, predominantly in the lower lobes. Pleural effusions and pulmonary cavitation are rare.

Although *H. influenzae* (see Chap. 109) pneumonia may occur in healthy young adults, the typical patient is over 50 years old and has chronic obstructive lung disease or is an alcoholic. The onset may be abrupt but is more frequently gradual. The major complaints are fever, productive cough, chills, dyspnea, and pleuritic chest pain. Neutrophilic leukocytosis is usual. The sputum smear shows abundant neutrophils and many pleomorphic gram-negative organisms that range from cocci to bacilli of various sizes and are often especially predominant in the cytoplasm of the white blood cells. The bacilli are slender, unlike the typical plump appearance of enteric organisms. The chest film usually discloses diffuse bronchopneumonia, often bilateral, although air space consolidation sometimes occurs. Pleural effusions developing rapidly in the course of disease are common, but lung abscess is rare.

Klebsiella pneumoniae (see Chap. 105) pneumonia is very uncommon. It typically occurs in middle-aged or elderly patients with underlying chronic disease, especially alcoholism or diabetes mellitus. The illness begins abruptly with fever, rigors, productive cough, and dyspnea. Neutrophilic leukocytosis is usual, although neutropenia occasionally occurs. The sputum may be tenacious and bloody. Plump gram-negative bacilli of uniform size are visible on the sputum smear. The chest roentgenogram shows an air space pneumonia usually in one of the upper lobes that is frequently complicated by abscess formation and a pleural effusion. The inflammatory exudate in the lung may be so voluminous that the interlobar fissure bulges, a characteristic, but not pathognomonic, finding.

Pneumonia from *anaerobic organisms* (see Chap. 102) usually occurs in patients with periodontal disease, which increases the number of bacilli in the mouth, and in patients with a propensity to aspirate because of swallowing disorders, altered consciousness, or other causes. The onset may be abrupt but is usually gradual, with several days to weeks of fever, weight loss, and a productive cough. The sputum may be foul smelling, a feature diagnostic of anaerobic infection. The sputum smear typically shows many neutrophils, and a large number of several different organisms, usually both gram-positive and gram-negative. Many anaerobic bacteria have a characteristic appearance. *Actinomyces, Eubacterium,* and Bifidobacterium are filamentous, branching, thin gram-positive rods. Peptostreptococci are tiny gram-positive cocci in chains. *Fusobacterium* appears as a long, fusiform gram-negative rod with pointed ends, while *Bacteroides* are pleomorphic gram-negative bacilli that range from coccoid to long, filamentous structures. Understandably, aerobic cultures typically fail to grow a likely pathogen. Chest films demonstrate consolidation in the segments where gravitation favors the flow of aspirated material. These are the posterior segments of the upper lobes and the superior segments of the lower lobes, when aspiration has occurred in the supine position, and the basilar segments of the lower lobes for the upright position. Single or multiple areas of cavitation and pleural effusions are very common.

Pneumonia due to *L. pneumophila* (Legionnaires' disease, see Chap. 117) may occur in outbreaks or sporadically. The first symptoms of myalgia and headache are followed by fever, chills, and a cough that is nonproductive or yields small amounts of mucoid sputum. Diarrhea, chest pain that is often pleuritic, and confusion or delirium are common. Sputum smears show few leukocytes and rare bacteria. The organism itself is not visible on Gram's stain. The chest film reveals air space consolidation that may develop into unilateral or bilateral, poorly marginated, rounded opacities. Pleural effusions, if present, are usually small, and cavitation rarely occurs.

Pneumonia due to *Francisella tularensis* (see Chap. 113) follows tick bites or exposure to infected animals. A cutaneous ulcer and regional lymphadenopathy may be present but are absent in the typhoidal form. The illness typically begins abruptly with fever, chills, headache, and cough, which is usually nonproductive. The leukocyte count is usually normal but may be elevated. The sputum smear may show neutrophils, but the organism is rarely seen. The chest roentgenogram typically shows a bronchopneumonia, often with hilar adenopathy, a finding seldom seen in other bacterial pneumonias. Sometimes the pneumonia appears as a distinctive, oval, homogeneous consolidation. Pleural effusions are common, but cavitation is rare.

The most frequent cause of community-acquired, nonpyogenic pneumonia is *M. pneumoniae* (see Chap. 149). It occurs most commonly in children or young adults, but may develop in older persons, especially during outbreaks in a family group. It differs from the bacterial pneumonias described above in many respects. It has an insidious, rather than abrupt, onset and a cough that is nonproductive or yields only small amounts of mucoid sputum. Pleuritic chest pain, rigors, and hemoptysis are distinctly uncommon. The temperature is generally less than 38.9°C (102°F), and headache is a prominent symptom. As in other nonpyogenic pneumonias, the sputum smear typically demonstrates mononuclear leukocytes or neutrophils but few organisms, since the agent is not visible on Gram's staining. The white blood cell count is usually normal or only mildly elevated, with a normal differential. The chest roentgenogram demonstrates segmental bronchopneumonia, or sometimes a predominant interstitial pattern, mostly affecting the lower lung fields. Bilateral involvement is common, but, unlike many bacterial pneumonias, substantial pleural effusions or cavitation are rare. The extent of radiographic involvement is often more impressive than the clinical examination would suggest.

Other community-acquired nonpyogenic pneumonias are Q fever, psittacosis, and viral pneumonia. Q fever (see Chap. 148) occurs from the inhalation of aerosolized particles containing *Coxiella burnetti,* the usual sources being placental tissues, amniotic fluid, milk, and feces of infected cattle, sheep, and goats. It is largely an occupational disease of those exposed to livestock. It begins abruptly with headache, fever, chills, and myalgias. Chest pain, often pleuritic, and a nonproductive cough follow. The white blood cell count is usually normal, and the chest film typically shows segmental consolidation that is predominantly in the lower lobes.

Psittacosis (see Chap. 150), also an occupational disease, occurs in those exposed to infected birds. Fever, an excruciating headache, myalgias, and an unproductive cough are the predominant symptoms. Splenomegaly, rare in most pneumonias, is seen occasionally. The white blood cell count is usually normal. The roentgenographic appearance varies from homogeneous to patchy consolidation, which may be segmental or lobar in distribution. Sometimes the chest film shows nodular or miliary opacities.

Viral pneumonias are quite uncommon in civilian adults who are not immunosuppressed, and this diagnosis should be made only with strong clinical or epidemiologic evidence, supported by viral cultures and serologic studies. The overwhelming majority of pneumonias in adults are due to the agents discussed above, not viruses. The most frequent viral pneumonia is *influenza* (see Chap. 130), which tends to occur in patients with underlying cardiac or pulmonary disease. It begins as typical influenza, with fever, myalgias, and headache. Twelve to thirty-six hours later dyspnea and cyanosis may develop rapidly and often proceed to a fatal outcome. The chest roentgenogram shows diffuse, patchy, unilateral or bilateral air space pneumonia. Even with these typical clinical features, a bacterial superinfection, especially with pneumococci or *S. aureus*, may be responsible for the pneumonia, instead of the virus itself.

Varicella (see Chap. 135) can cause pneumonia in adults and typically begins 2 to 3 days after the vesicular eruption appears. Fever, cough, dyspnea, hemoptysis, and pleuritic chest pain are the major symptoms. The chest film demonstrates patchy, diffuse, generally discrete air space consolidations that are coarsely nodular.

Measles (see Chap. 132) pneumonia in adults generally occurs in military recruits and may begin just before, with, or after the skin rash. The chest film shows a diffuse bilateral reticular pattern.

Adenovirus (see Chap. 131) pneumonia also occurs predominantly in military recruits. Fever, cough, rhinitis, and pharyngitis are the major features. The chest film shows patchy consolidation, generally in the lower lung fields.

In endemic areas the fungi *Coccidioides immitis, Blastomyces dermatitidis,* and *Histoplasma capsulatum* (see Chap. 147) must be considered in the differential diagnosis of community-acquired pneumonia.

In chronic pneumonias—those lasting for weeks or months—the primary infectious causes are anaerobic bacteria, mycobacteria, *Nocardia asteroides,* and various fungi. Among the fungi, *Cryptococcus neoformans* and *Sporothrix schenckii* are found worldwide, while *Blastomyces dermatitidis, Coccidioides immitis, Histoplasma capsulatum,* and *Paracoccidioides brasiliensis* have limited geographic distributions. In southeast Asia one form of melioidosis, an infection caused by the bacterium *Pseudomonas pseudomallei,* presents as a chronic pneumonia. Previous travel history is very important in evaluating chronic pulmonary infections.

Hospital-acquired pneumonia Because of changes in oropharyngeal flora with hospitalization, hospital-acquired pneumonias, unlike community-acquired ones, are likely to be due to a wide variety of aerobic gram-negative bacilli with varying antimicrobial susceptibilities and, less frequently, *S. aureus,* pneumococci, or *H. influenzae.* Only rarely is it possible to distinguish among pneumonias caused by different species of gram-negative rods on the basis of the clinical or roentgenographic features. Adequate sputum Gram's stains and cultures, therefore, are especially important in defining the etiologic agent and suggesting the appropriate antibiotic therapy.

Hospitalized patients with endotracheal tubes or tracheostomies receiving mechanical ventilation are an important group in whom the diagnosis of pneumonia is particularly difficult to make. Shortly after intubation, the tracheobronchial tree becomes colonized with organisms, and a purulent tracheobronchitis commonly ensues. Even though there is purulent sputum with plentiful organisms, this tracheobronchitis requires no antimicrobial therapy, which only encourages the growth of drug-resistant organisms, unless pneumonia is present. The diagnosis of pneumonia requires evidence of parenchymal lung involvement and in this setting depends upon the presence of purulent tracheobronchial secretions *plus* fever, leukocytosis, and a new or progressive pulmonary infiltrate on chest films.

TREATMENT Community-acquired pneumonia Patients whose history or physical examination suggests the likelihood of pneumonia should have a chest roentgenogram to confirm the diagnosis and delineate the pattern and extent of pulmonary involvement. Most patients with mild to moderate disease on clinical and radiologic assessment can be treated as outpatients. In them, a white blood cell count may be useful in the differential diagnosis, but routine blood cultures and arterial blood gases are unnecessary. The clinical and radiographic features and the sputum Gram stain should dictate the choice of antimicrobial therapy. If sputum is unobtainable or unhelpful and the other information inconclusive, oral erythromycin, 500 mg qid, is a good choice. It is effective against pneumococci and *M. pneumoniae,* the two most frequent causes of community-acquired pneumonia, but also should be satisfactory to treat Legionnaires' disease and many cases of *H. influenzae* pneumonia and anaerobic pneumonias. Auxiliary measures should include adequate hydration, analgesics to relieve chest pain, if present, and cough suppressants

for those with the harassing, unproductive cough characteristic of *M. pneumoniae.* In patients with good clinical improvement, a repeat chest film after 6 weeks is appropriate to document radiographic resolution. Failure to resolve by then indicates possible endobronchial obstruction and the necessity for bronchoscopy.

Reasons for hospitalization include severe dyspnea or hypoxia; evidence of empyema or extrapulmonary foci of infections, such as meningitis; shock; serious underlying disease, especially cardiac or pulmonary; severe systemic manifestations such as delirium, whose presence warrants a lumbar puncture to exclude concomitant meningitis; or social circumstances making treatment at home unfeasible. These patients should have two blood cultures obtained from separate venipuncture sites; a complete blood count, including white blood cell differential; and arterial blood gas measurements if there is marked tachypnea, severe dyspnea, altered mental status potentially attributable to hypoxia, cyanosis, or serious underlying cardiopulmonary disease. The clinical and radiographic features and, especially, the sputum Gram's stain should indicate the proper antibiotic choice. Since the most common community-acquired pneumonia requiring hospitalization is pneumococcal, the appropriate agent usually is penicillin, 2.4 million units daily, intramuscularly or intravenously. If the sputum smear is unsatisfactory or unobtainable by expectoration or nasotracheal suctioning, transtracheal aspiration may be indicated, particularly if the patient has an underlying illness like alcoholism that makes gram-negative pneumonia more likely.

In patients with unobtainable or uninformative sputum, penicillin remains the drug of choice in most circumstances, including suspected anaerobic infections following the aspiration of large quantities of oropharyngeal contents. Reasonable alternatives include clindamycin, 300 mg intravenously every 6 h, parenteral cefazolin, 500 mg every 8 h, or erythromycin, 1 g intravenously every 6 h, especially in suspected Legionnaires' disease, where it is the drug of choice. In drug addicts and in patients developing pneumonia after an influenza attack, pneumococcus or *S. aureus* are the likely pathogens, and a semisynthetic penicillinase-resistant penicillin like oxacillin or nafcillin, 8 to 12 g daily intravenously, is indicated. Alternatives include vancomycin, 2 g intravenously daily, or cephalothin, 8 to 12 g intravenously daily. In patients with chronic bronchitis complicated by acute pneumonia, pneumococcus and *H. influenzae* are the most common causes, and ampicillin, 2 to 6 g daily intravenously, is a good choice for therapy in the unusual patient whose sputum sample is inadequate for diagnosis. Alternatives include tetracycline, 2 g daily; chloramphenicol, 2 g daily; or cefamandole, 2 g daily, all given intravenously.

Auxiliary measures include adequate hydration, the administration of humidified oxygen, relief of chest pain by adequate analgesics or nonsteroidal anti-inflammatory drugs, and the encouragement of coughing to expectorate sputum. Intermittent positive pressure breathing (IPPB), however, is not helpful, and postural drainage should generally be reserved for those with bronchiectasis or lung abscess. Mechanical ventilation is required when the diffuseness of the pneumonia or the severity of underlying cardiopulmonary disease prevents adequate oxygenation with spontaneous respiration and supplemental oxygen by mask or nasal prongs.

Hospital-acquired pneumonia Since the range of organisms causing hospital-acquired pneumonias is so wide and their antimicrobial susceptibilities so variable, precise bacteriologic diagnosis is crucial. Patients with hospital-acquired pneumonias should have blood cultures, and vigorous attempts must be made to obtain sputum by expectoration, nasotracheal suctioning, or, if these are unsuccessful, transtracheal aspiration. When gram-negative rods are the predominant organism on Gram's stain, an aminoglycoside effective against *Pseudomonas aeruginosa,* like gentamicin, plus an antipseudomonal penicillin like ticarcillin or carbenicillin should be given. If gram-positive cocci resembling *S. aureus* are present, vancomycin or a penicillinase-resistant penicillin is appropriate. If a mixture of these organisms is present or no sputum is obtainable, a combination of an aminoglycoside plus a penicillinase-resistant penicillin or a cephalosporin is a good choice. Determination of the precise agents used should be guided by knowledge of the local hospital flora and its antimicrobial sensitivities. The regimen should be altered later according to the identity and susceptibility of the organisms isolated. If the sputum smear reveals organisms characteristic of pneumococci, anaerobes, or *H. influenzae,* which sometimes cause nosocomial pneumonias, the appropriate therapy for these organisms recommended in Chap. 88 should be given.

Pneumonia in compromised hosts (see also Chap. 84)   Compromised hosts with pneumonia require special consideration. Patients who are severely neutropenic from acute leukemia or from cytotoxic agents generally develop pneumonia from aerobic gram-negative bacilli. Unless the Gram's stains strongly indicate otherwise, these patients should receive an aminoglycoside effective against *P. aeruginosa* and an antipseudomonal penicillin like ticarcillin or carbenicillin until the culture results return.

In severely immunosuppressed patients without neutropenia, the possible causes of fever and a new pulmonary infiltrate are legion. They fall into four categories: (1) the disease itself, such as Hodgkin's disease of the lung; (2) the effects of treatment, such as radiation pneumonitis or pulmonary toxicity from agents like methotrexate; (3) infections; and (4) miscellaneous disorders such as pulmonary emboli and intrapulmonary hemorrhage. Possible infectious causes include not only bacteria but also fungi, like *Candida* or *Aspergillus*; viruses, especially cytomegalovirus; and protozoa, particularly *Pneumocystis carinii* (see Chap. 158). In these patients unless the initial evaluation, including sputum smears, strongly indicates a specific diagnosis, further information obtained by bronchoscopic biopsy and lavage, transthoracic needle aspiration, or open-lung biopsy is necessary for definitive diagnosis.

For safe performance, all these procedures, except lavage, require correction of severe thrombocytopenia and clotting disorders. *Transthoracic needle aspiration* may be useful in peripheral, localized disease, but because it fails to provide tissue specimens, it is not recommended for diffuse infiltrates, where histologic examination rather than stains and cultures of aspirated material is so frequently necessary for specific diagnosis. Pneumothorax occurs in about 20 percent, requiring chest tube placement in about 10 percent; significant pulmonary hemorrhage develops in about 5 percent. Contraindications include uncorrectable hypoxia, lack of patient cooperation, bullous lung disease, and mechanical ventilation. *Fiberoptic bronchoscopy* with washings, sterile brushings, and transbronchial biopsy is appropriate for both localized and diffuse processes, but the quantity of tissue obtained is small and may be unrepresentative, especially in diffuse disease. The procedure yields a specific diagnosis in about 50 percent of cases. Pneumothorax or significant hemorrhage each occurs in about 5 to 10 percent, with about one-half of pneumothoraxes requiring chest tube drainage. Contraindications include uncorrectable

hypoxia or an uncooperative patient. Bleeding complications are considerably greater in uremia, although it is not an absolute contraindication. In patients with acquired immunodeficiency syndrome (AIDS) (see Chap. 257), fiberoptic bronchoscopy demonstrates the cause of diffuse pulmonary infections in almost all cases. *Open-lung biopsy* yields accurately representative tissue in nearly all patients. A specific diagnosis is established in about 70 percent of immunodeficient patients without AIDS; in the remaining 30 percent nonspecific inflammation and fibrosis are found whose cause is unknown and for which there is no effective therapy. Such a finding allows antimicrobial agents to be withheld or discontinued. Open-lung biopsy is remarkably safe, with a mortality rate of less than 1 percent in these very ill patients. It can be performed even in patients requiring mechanical ventilation.

While many clinicians initiate these invasive diagnostic procedures in immunodeficient patients without AIDS as soon as the initial, rapid clinical evaluation and examination of sputum smears prove inconclusive, others reserve them for patients who fail to respond to "empiric" therapy within 48 to 72 h. Empiric treatment is initiated with an aminoglycoside combined with a cephalosporin, carbenicillin, or ticarcillin. With diffuse infiltrates sulfamethoxazole-trimethoprim is added to treat *P. carinii.* For those patients who fail to respond and are unable to undergo invasive diagnostic procedures, amphotericin B is added for focal infiltrates, especially if the patient has recently received prolonged broad-spectrum antibiotic therapy and is leukopenic. This empiric approach is usually less advisable than obtaining a specific diagnosis with invasive techniques. Patients with known or suspected AIDS and pulmonary complications should not be treated empirically but should undergo fiberoptic bronchoscopy.

LUNG ABSCESS

DEFINITION   A lung abscess is a necrotic area of lung parenchyma containing purulent material. An etiologic classification appears in Table 205-1.

PATHOGENESIS   The pathogenesis of infectious lung abscesses is nearly identical to that of pneumonia. Most arise from the aspiration of naso- or oropharyngeal contents. The development of a lung abscess, instead of just pneumonia, depends upon the infecting organism's ability to cause necrosis of lung tissue. Pneumococci, *H. influenzae, M. pneumoniae,* and viruses rarely cause necrosis, but it is common in pulmonary infections due to *K. pneumoniae* and other enteric gram-negative bacilli and *S. aureus.* Anaerobic organisms are the most frequent cause of pyogenic lung abscesses and tend to occur when large quantities of oropharyngeal material are aspirated because of disordered consciousness or impaired swallowing.

Processes that cause mechanical or functional obstruction of the bronchi may predispose to lung abscesses. Mechanical causes include tumor, foreign body, or bronchial stenosis. Lung cancer is particularly important because occult bronchogenic neoplasms may be complicated by a distal abscess, or a cavitating, uninfected carcinoma may mimic a lung abscess.

Less frequently, abscesses arise from hematogenous spread of organisms to the lung. This may occur during bacteremia originating from a distant site of infection or as a result of septic emboli either from right-sided endocarditis or from septic thrombophlebitis associated with infections in the extremities or the abdominal cavity.

Patients with tuberculosis (see Chap. 119), pulmonary fungal infections (see Chap. 147), and pleuropulmonary amebiasis (see Chap. 153) may develop one or more areas of lung necrosis. Although usually labeled "cavities," these lesions are really abscesses. While the clinical course typically distinguishes these conditions from pyogenic lung abscess, there may be many similarities that cause confusion in the differential diagnosis.

CLINICAL MANIFESTATIONS   The clinical features of pulmonary infections due to staphylococci, streptococci, and aerobic gram-negative bacilli are discussed earlier in this chapter and in the chapters

---

TABLE 205-1   Classification of lung abscesses according to cause

1 Necrotizing infections
   a Pyogenic bacteria (*S. aureus, Klebsiella,* group A streptococcus, *Bacteroides, Fusobacterium,* anaerobic and microaerophilic cocci and streptococci, other anaerobes, *Nocardia*)
   b Mycobacteria (*Mycobacterium tuberculosis, M. kansasii, M. intracellularis*)
   c Fungi (*Histoplasma, Coccidioides, Aspergillus*)
   d Parasites (amoebas, lung flukes)
2 Cavitary infarction
   a Bland embolism
   b Septic embolism (various anaerobes, *Staphylococcus, Candida*)
   c Vasculitis (Wegener's granulomatosis, periarteritis)
3 Cavitary malignancy
   a Primary bronchogenic carcinoma
   b Metastatic malignancies (very uncommon)
4 Other
   a Infected cysts
   b Necrotic conglomerate lesions (silicosis, coal miner's pneumoconiosis)

dealing with the specific organisms. These are usually rapidly progressive infections in which single or multiple cavities develop as complications of an acute pneumonia. Persistent fever, profuse sputum production, and hemoptysis are common. Occasionally, an abscess ruptures into the pleural cavity, causing an empyema or, rarely, a pneumothorax.

Anaerobic lung abscess Although the spectrum of illness in anaerobic lung abscess may vary from a mild productive cough to acute disease with severe systemic manifestations, the onset is usually insidious, with the symptoms gradually worsening over several weeks. The most common feature is a cough productive of moderate to large amounts of purulent sputum that is often fetid and bloody. Fever, pleuritic or dull chest pain, dyspnea, weakness, anorexia, and weight loss, which can be considerable, are common. A condition predisposing to aspiration, such as alcoholism or epilepsy, is usually present.

Most patients are febrile. Oral examination usually discloses poor dentition, with caries, gingivitis, and periodontal infection, conditions which increase the number of anaerobes in the oral cavity. The chest examination may be normal or may include signs of consolidation, rales, and, occasionally, amphoric or cavernous breath sounds over the involved area. An empyema, present in about one-third of cases, may cause dullness to percussion and decreased breath sounds. Clubbing, although uncommon, may occur. Neutrophilic leukocytosis with an increase in immature forms is usual, and, if the infection has persisted for several weeks, anemia and hypoalbuminemia may be present. The medical history, physical findings, and routine laboratory results are often nonspecific; foul-smelling sputum, which is present in about half the patients, however, clearly indicates an anaerobic pulmonary infection. Definitive diagnosis rests on the demonstration of an abscess cavity on chest films and the identification of the causative organisms on culture.

The chest roentgenogram reveals an area of consolidation containing a radiolucency. Not all radiolucent areas are abscesses, however, and either a wall or a border completely surrounding the lucent area or a fluid level within it should be present to diagnose an abscess cavity. Even these criteria are not definitive, since infected bullae or cysts or an empyema with a bronchopleural fistula may have an identical appearance. The abscess cavities are located in those segments that are most dependent at the time of aspiration: the posterior segment of the upper or superior segment of the lower lobes, especially on the right, when the patient is supine or the basilar segments of the lower lobes when upright.

Examination of the sputum by both microscopy and culture is essential to establish the correct diagnosis. In staphylococcal and aerobic gram-negative bacillary infections, the single causative organism clearly predominates on smear and culture. Gram's stain of sputum from an anaerobic abscess reveals abundant neutrophils and numerous organisms, including gram-positive cocci and rods and gram-negative rods of varying size and configuration. Since expectorated sputum is unavoidably contaminated by the normal anaerobic oral flora, anaerobic sputum cultures are appropriate only for specimens obtained by transtracheal or transthoracic aspiration. Secretions aspirated through the fiberoptic bronchoscope (unless a special catheter is used) are unsuitable because the instrument is contaminated as it passes through the naso- or oropharynx, even with preceding endotracheal intubation. Appropriately collected and cultured sputum specimens usually grow two or more anaerobic organisms, most commonly *Peptococcus, Peptostreptococcus, Fusobacterium nucleatum,* and *Bacteroides melaninogenicus.* In about 60 percent of cases the infecting flora is exclusively anaerobic; in 40 percent both aerobes and anaerobes are present. The most common aerobic isolates are *S. aureus* and enteric gram-negative bacilli.

Associated pleural effusions should be aspirated and cultured aerobically and anaerobically. Blood cultures are usually sterile.

Septic pulmonary emboli In patients with septic pulmonary emboli, the site of origin is usually tricuspid valve endocarditis, particularly in intravenous drug abusers, or septic thrombophlebitis, which may occur in the arm veins of patients with infected intravenous catheter sites, infected injection sites from intravenous drug abuse, or infected arteriovenous shunts used in hemodialysis. Other areas of septic thrombophlebitis include pelvic veins with postpartum or postoperative pelvic infections, peritonsillar and internal jugular veins with pharyngeal infections, and veins adjacent to undrained suppuration, such as soft tissue infections or osteomyelitis. Rigors, high fever, dyspnea, cough, tachycardia, and tachypnea are the major clinical manifestations in these acutely ill patients. Neutrophilic leukocytosis is usual. The chest film typically discloses multiple, bilateral, round, or wedge-shaped opacities. These frequently and rapidly excavate to form thin-walled cavities, often without fluid levels. Small pleural effusions on one or both sides are common. Blood cultures are usually positive. Patients may not produce sputum, but if they do, it usually reveals the responsible organism, most commonly *S. aureus,* on Gram's stain and culture.

TREATMENT The history, physical examination, chest roentgenograms, and most importantly, Gram's and acid-fast sputum stains usually indicate whether an abscess is caused by aerobic organisms, anaerobes, or tubercle bacilli. Abscesses caused by aerobic organisms usually require prolonged treatment with the antibiotics recommended in the chapters dealing with them.

Where septic pulmonary emboli from septic thrombophlebitis are suspected, it is important not only to institute appropriate antimicrobial therapy but also to identify the source. Removal of catheters, incision and drainage of systemic abscesses or infected veins, or ligation of the inferior vena cava may be necessary to prevent further embolization.

When the clinical findings and the sputum Gram's stain suggest an anaerobic abscess, clindamycin probably is the drug of choice. It is usually given in doses of 600 mg intravenously every 8 h until clinical improvement (return of appetite, defervescence) occurs. Oral clindamycin in doses of about 300 mg four times daily is then given for the duration of therapy. Some clinicians use oral medication from the start. Many physicians prefer penicillin as the initial treatment, reserving clindamycin for fulminant infections or those failing to respond to penicillin after 5 to 7 days. The dose is 10 to 12 million units intravenously daily, followed by oral penicillin V, 750 mg to 1 g four times a day. Because of relapses with shorter courses, antibiotics are usually given for 6 weeks.

Ancillary measures include postural drainage and chest physiotherapy to help drain the abscess cavity. The role of bronchoscopy is unsettled. Some physicians believe that every patient with a lung abscess deserves bronchoscopy; most others reserve its use for patients who fail to respond as anticipated to antibiotic therapy, who have evidence of an obstructing tumor or foreign body, or who have poorly communicating cavities that fail to drain adequately. Features that especially suggest the possibility of lung cancer and the necessity for bronchoscopy include a long history of smoking, lack of a predisposing cause to aspirate, good oral hygiene, evidence of volume loss or mediastinal or hilar lymph node enlargment on chest film, location of the cavity in a nondependent area, and failure to respond to appropriate antibiotic therapy.

Except for the tube thoracostomy drainage of an associated empyema, surgery for lung abscess is rarely necessary. Incomplete roentgenographic resolution is not a sufficient reason for resectional surgery since delayed closure is common. Resection is indicated for massive hemoptysis, malignancy, or associated symptomatic bronchiectasis. Rarely, tube thoracostomy or some other form of surgical drainage may be necessary to manage uncontrolled sepsis arising from a poorly draining abscess.

REFERENCES

Pneumonia

BARTLETT JG: Anaerobic bacterial pneumonitis. Am Rev Resp Dis 119:19, 1979

FRASER RG, PARE JAP: *Diagnosis of Diseases of the Chest.* Philadelphia, Saunders, 1978, vol II, chap 6

GEORGE WL, FINEGOLD SM: Bacterial infections of the lung. Chest 81:502, 1982

GREEN GM et al: Defense mechanisms of the respiratory membrane. Ann Rev Resp Dis 115:479, 1977

PIERCE AK, SANFORD JP: Aerobic gram-negative bacillary pneumonias. Am Rev Resp Dis 110:647, 1974

————: The gram-negative bacillary pneumonias, in *Update IV: Harrison's Principles of Internal Medicine,* KJ Isselbacher et al (eds). New York, McGraw-Hill, 1983, pp 75–86

REYNOLDS HY (ed): Respiratory infections. Clin Chest Med 2:1, 1981

Lung abscess

BARTLETT JG et al: Bacteriology and treatment of primary lung abscess. Am Rev Resp Dis 109:510, 1974

JOHANSON WG et al: Aspiration pneumonia, anaerobic infections, and lung abscess. Med Clin N Am 64:385, 1980

LEVISON ME et al: Clindamycin compared with penicillin for the treatment of anaerobic abscess. Ann Intern Med 98:466, 1983

---

206   BRONCHIECTASIS AND BRONCHOLITHIASIS

JOHN F. MURRAY

These disorders both involve branches of the tracheobronchial system, have numerous, rather than single, underlying causes, and occasionally coexist. However, the pathogenesis, clinical manifestations, treatment, and prognosis of the two conditions are remarkably different.

BRONCHIECTASIS

DEFINITION   Bronchiectasis can be defined as a permanent abnormal dilatation of one or more bronchi, those airways that contain cartilage and bronchial glands, due to destruction of the elastic and muscular components of the bronchial wall. This definition is not completely satisfactory because bronchi are also abnormally dilated in chronic bronchitis. Thus chronic bronchitis merges into bronchiectasis, and the distinction between them depends upon the *degree* of dilatation. The semantic problem is complicated further by the fact that the two conditions frequently coexist.

Classification is therefore difficult and is not useful in indicating the clinical severity of the disease; however, certain descriptive terms are commonly used to describe the appearance of bronchi displayed by bronchography. *Saccular (cystic) bronchiectasis* occurs mainly in the proximal large bronchi; affected airways show marked dilatation ending in large sacs at about the fourth bronchial division. *Cylindrical (fusiform) bronchiectasis* involves airways from the sixth to the tenth generation; the bronchographic appearance shows mild to moderate uneven widening, without a great increase in diameter, of bronchi that often look beaded and end squarely and abruptly. *Varicose bronchiectasis* is intermediate between saccular and cylindrical changes and is used to describe bronchi that resemble varicose veins. Because all three types may be present in the same patient, these terms have little therapeutic or prognostic implication.

Although "true" bronchiectasis is not reversible, the concept of reversibility is important, because abnormalities displayed by bronchography in some patients with reversible lung diseases (atelectasis, tracheobronchitis) may simulate bronchiectasis. Atelectasis causes shortening and tortuosity of airways in the involved region, producing an accordion-like appearance on bronchography. Similarly, ulcerations of the bronchial mucosa, which are common in viral infections of the lower respiratory tract, appear as an irregular pattern on bronchography. Both conditions resemble cylindrical bronchiectasis. Reexpansion of the collapsed lung and/or regeneration of the epithelium results in reversibility of the "pseudobronchiectasis." Thus

bronchography, if indicated, should be delayed for several months after an episode of tracheobronchitis, pneumonia, or atelectasis.

PATHOGENESIS   Since bronchiectasis is defined by the presence of morphologic changes in the caliber of bronchi, its pathogenesis depends on antecedent factors that either cause or lead to necrosis of the bronchial wall and supporting tissues. Necrotizing inflammation, nearly always infectious in origin, seems clearly to be the most important cause of bronchiectasis. Local pressure on the bronchial wall from retained secretions may act as a contributing factor. Hereditary, congenital, or mechanical abnormalities that predispose to bronchopulmonary infection and sputum retention are often also present. The use of vaccines and antibiotic drugs has resulted in a marked decline in the incidence of severe necrotizing pneumonias and their bronchiectatic complications in developed countries, however, bronchiectasis as a complication of underlying systemic disorders appears to be increasing.

Hereditary and congenital factors   Several hereditary and congenital disorders have been identified in which there is a high incidence of secondary bronchiectasis. *Congenital bronchiectasis* occurs at the site of a pre- or postnatal development defect of the bronchial system. The formation of cysts, cul-de-sacs, or bronchomalacia leads to pooling of secretions and bacterial infection. The generalized disorder of exocrine gland secretions in patients with *cystic fibrosis,* discussed in Chap. 207, affects the physical properties of tracheobronchial mucus and/or the adequacy of mucociliary clearance; this causes retention of secretions, with partial or complete plugging of airways, that provides a nidus for implantation and growth of bacteria. Most deaths (95 percent) of patients with cystic fibrosis who survive beyond 1 year of age are now caused by the consequences of bronchiectasis and accompanying chronic bronchopulmonary suppuration. The diffuse bronchiectasis rarely encountered with patients with *atopic bronchial asthma,* in whom there is often a strong familial association (Chap. 202), presumably is related to diffuse obstruction, as described below.

A variety of hereditary *immune-deficiency diseases,* secondary to either cellular or humoral defects, is associated with a high incidence of bacterial infections. Involvement of the sinuses and airways is particularly common, and the tendency for infections to recur in the lower airways often leads to bronchiectasis in patients with impaired immunologic mechanisms.

A group of genetically determined disorders called the *immotile cilia syndrome,* which includes *Kartagener's syndrome* (bronchiectasis, dextrocardia, and sinusitis) is characterized by ultrastructural changes causing immotility of cilia in the respiratory tract epithelium, sperm, and other cells. These abnormalities lead to recurrent sinopulmonary infections, infertility, and presumably disturbances during embryogenesis. This definition has recently been broadened to include patients with chronic sinobronchial disease from impaired mucociliary clearance who had "ciliary dyskinesia," not immotile cilia. The high incidence of unexplained bronchiectasis in Polynesians has been attributed to hereditary abnormalities of respiratory tract ciliary motility.

Obstruction   Postobstructive bronchiectasis was much commoner in preantibiotic years than it is today. The availability of antimicrobial therapy and corrective surgical procedures accounts for the decreased incidence of this form of the disease. It is now recognized that obstruction per se does *not cause* bronchiectasis but *favors its development* by impairing clearance mechanisms, which enhances bacterial infection. Any process that leads to bronchial obstruction, therefore, may be associated with bronchiectasis distal to the site of involvement. Since the disorders causing obstruction are usually confined to one part of the bronchial system, postobstructive bronchiectasis is of the localized rather than the diffuse variety found in most forms of congenital-hereditary bronchiectasis. An exception is the bronchiectasis associated with diffuse obstruction of airways in patients with chronic bronchitis, atopic asthma, and cystic fibrosis. Patients with atopic asthma are liable to have secondary infections with *Aspergillus*, which produces the syndrome of bronchopulmonary aspergillosis characterized by proximal airway bronchiectasis, eosinophilia, and recurrent bouts of mucous plugging (Chap. 203).

Endobronchial tumors or foreign bodies, compression of airways from enlarged hilar lymph nodes or tumor masses, and bronchostenosis from endobronchial inflammatory disease (especially tuberculosis) all cause bronchial obstruction and may predispose to the development of postobstructive bronchiectasis.

Necrotizing inflammation Virtually all forms of bronchiectasis are associated with bacterial infections. If it were not for the presence of infection, the complications of bronchiectasis would be negligible. Although the development of the causative infection(s) is often precipitated by the presence of a hereditary disorder and/or bronchial obstruction that predisposes the patient to secondary bacterial involvement, bronchiectasis can occur as the result of necrotizing infections in a previously healthy individual. This presumably is the mechanism underlying the bronchiectasis that follows tuberculosis and staphylococcal or other suppurative pneumonias; furthermore, the tendency for necrotizing pneumonias occasionally to complicate measles, pertussis, adenovirus infections, and influenza accounts for the occurrence of bronchiectasis as a sequela of these disorders.

In rare instances, bronchiectasis may follow the introduction of corrosive chemical substances, commonly hydrocarbons, into the tracheobronchial tree. Similarly, the repeated aspiration of gastric fluid into the lungs may cause bronchiectasis. Since recurrent ulceration from chemical causes is invariably associated with secondary bacterial infection, it is difficult to dissociate the contributions of these two factors.

CLINICAL MANIFESTATIONS The signs and symptoms of bronchiectasis depend on the extent, severity, and location of the abnormal airways, and the presence of complications, but the hallmarks of the disease are chronic cough with sputum production, hemoptysis, and recurrent pneumonia. Even these vary greatly in frequency and severity and may be absent or intermittent if the disease is mild or involves only the upper lobes of the lung.

The most frequent symptom is a *chronic cough* that produces sputum. The amount of sputum varies considerably but may be voluminous and is apt to be purulent during bouts of intercurrent infections. Streaks of blood in the sputum are common, and frank hemoptysis of large amounts of blood may develop if necrosis of the mucosa is severe. Exacerbation of chronic bronchial infection is frequent and may progress to pneumonia, occasionally with lung abscess or empyema formation. Associated systemic features of bronchiectasis are fever, weight loss, anemia, and weakness; these usually indicate the presence of active sepsis from severe disease or untreated intercurrent bacterial infection.

In what was once the typical patient with bronchiectasis, symptoms developed during infancy or early childhood; the onset was usually acute and followed suppurative pneumonia or pulmonary infection complicating measles or pertussis. However, because of the success of antimicrobials and vaccines in treating or preventing these disorders, acute onset of bronchiectasis at an early age is becoming infrequent, except in those areas of the United States and other countries where, owing to isolation or poverty, good medical care is not available.

Although chronic childhood bronchiectasis is decreasing, another group of patients with a different form of the disease appears to be increasing: these patients have recurrent lower respiratory tract infections that initially respond to treatment, with symptom-free intervals between episodes. The infections usually begin during childhood or young adulthood. As the number of recurrent bouts increases, the time between them tends to shorten and the response to treatment becomes less complete. Finally, chronic symptoms of cough and sputum develop. Patients in this category are likely to have cystic fibrosis, immune-deficiency diseases, immotile cilia, or atopic asthma.

Sinusitis is a common accompaniment of diffuse bronchiectasis and may be an expression of the vulnerability of the entire respiratory tract in these patients. Development of digital clubbing, metastatic abscesses (often brain), and amyloidosis were common complications in the past but are less frequent now. If the disease is widespread, it may resemble other forms of chronic obstructive lung disease, with generalized wheezing and ultimate progression to cor pulmonale; this constellation is particularly apt to occur in patients with underlying systemic abnormalities that lead to diffuse pulmonary involvement.

DIAGNOSIS Bronchiectasis is defined as a morphologic disorder; hence its diagnosis depends on demonstrating the abnormal anatomy of the bronchial system. Ordinarily this is accomplished by roentgenographic techniques, either *bronchography* or *computed tomography*. The diagnosis should be *suspected* in any patient with chronic productive cough, especially if the sputum intermittently becomes more purulent and streaked with blood. The distinction between bronchiectasis and chronic bronchitis, which may cause identical symptoms and which may coexist, is unimportant except when surgery is contemplated. Physical examination seldom reveals the severity and extent of distribution of the disease. Inspiratory rales are often the only evidence of pulmonary involvement. Occasionally, advanced cases of saccular bronchiectasis can be diagnosed by routine (plain) chest roentgenography; in such cases multiple 1- to 2-cm cystic lesions or fluid levels in poorly delineated sacs can be seen. More often, however, plain chest roentgenograms show only streaky infiltrations and loss of volume in involved areas; at times the chest roentgenograms may appear completely normal.

Bronchography (Chap. 201) should not be performed routinely in all patients with suggestive symptoms but is indicated primarily in the evaluation of patients for possible operation, those with recurrent, localized pneumonias or severe hemoptysis. Since the information from bronchography contributes little to the management of patients in whom surgery is contraindicated, such as those with minimal disability, with generalized involvement, or with obstructive airways disease, the procedure should be avoided in these patients because of its hazards. When bronchography is indicated, it should not be performed in patients during exacerbations of their cough and sputum production, but only after the manifestations have been thoroughly treated (see next section) and the volume of secretions is minimal. It is safer and advisable to study one lung at a time, owing to alterations in pulmonary function and to occasional inflammatory reactions induced by the procedure. Filling must be adequate and all segments must be visualized if the study is to be considered satisfactory for diagnostic purposes.

Computed tomography is being increasingly used to diagnose bronchiectasis. At present, the procedure is not a substitute for bronchography in the evaluation of patients for surgery. Computed tomography appears to be a useful, noninvasive—but expensive—way of making the diagnosis in patients who are not candidates for bronchography.

Bronchoscopy does not establish the diagnosis of bronchiectasis but may be useful in identifying the source of secretions in patients with cough and sputum and in determining the site of bleeding in patients with hemoptysis.

All patients with multiple episodes of sinopulmonary infections should have an immunologic survey to detect immune-deficiency diseases. Similarly, patients with suspected cystic fibrosis should have measurements of the concentrations of sodium and chloride in two or more samples of sweat (Chap. 207). Electron photomicrographic studies of sperm or mucosal biopsies from the respiratory tract reveal characteristic abnormalities in patients with the immotile cilia syndrome in whom tracheobronchial clearance is delayed or absent. Patients with asthma and suspected bronchiectasis from bronchopulmonary aspergillosis should have sputum cultures for *Aspergillus*, serologic studies for aspergillin precipitins, and measurement of serum IgE values.

The sputum volume, color, cellular content, and bacterial inhabitants are useful guides to the presence of active infection. Sputum eosinophilia provides a clue to the presence of asthma and/or bronchopulmonary aspergillosis. During exacerbations of the disease, the sputum increases in volume, becomes more purulent, and contains large numbers of polymorphonuclear leukocytes and bacteria that can be identified by Gram's stain. Culture of the sputum often reveals normal nasopharyngeal flora and, less commonly, *Streptococcus pneumoniae* or *Haemophilus influenzae*. Fetid sputum signifies the presence of anaerobic microorganisms. Sputum from patients receiving prolonged or frequent treatment with broad-spectrum antibiotic drugs may grow *Staphylococcus* species or a mucoid strain of *Pseudomonas aeruginosa;* this finding is especially common in patients with cystic fibrosis, and indicates superinfection by an organism refractory to conventional treatment.

The blood count is usually within the normal range but may reveal anemia, reflecting chronic infection, or leukocytosis, signifying active suppuration. The urinalysis is normal except in the rare instances of *amyloidosis*, when proteinuria occurs. The electrocardiogram is normal until the late stages, when *cor pulmonale* may supervene and right ventricular hypertrophy develops. Owing to the wide variations in the extent and severity of the disease, only broad generalizations about pulmonary function abnormalities are possible, although a correlation exists between the overall impairment of lung function and the number of involved segments. Vital capacity and expiratory flow rates tend to be reduced but may be within normal limits if the disease is mild. In the late stages of diffuse bronchiectasis severe airflow obstruction can occur. A mild to moderate reduction in arterial oxygen tension (P_{O_2}) reflects regional abnormalities in the distribution of ventilation with respect to perfusion. Disturbances of ventilation in excess of those of perfusion, as expected in a disorder of the airways, are the physiologic hallmark of bronchiectasis and can now be examined in regions of the lung by the use of radioactive gases, e.g.,^{133}Xe (Chap. 200). Pulmonary function studies are helpful in defining the extent and severity of abnormalities, in assessing the need for and effects of bronchodilator therapy, and in evaluating patients for surgery.

TREATMENT Since bacterial infections are associated with most forms of bronchiectasis initially and are responsible for its exacerbation, antibiotics are the major weapons for its prevention and treatment. The choice of antimicrobial agents should be guided by the results of sputum culture; however, as indicated, these may reveal "normal flora" and no conspicuous pathogen. The drug of choice for patients with this finding is ampicillin or one of its derivatives; patients allergic to the penicillins usually respond to trimethoprim-sulfamethoxazole or one of the tetracyclines. When pneumococci are present, it is best to avoid the tetracycline drugs, as some pneumococcal strains are resistant to these agents. Antibiotics should be given until sputum production becomes minimal and purulence disappears; this desirable therapeutic result is usually achieved swiftly (5 to 7 days) if antibiotics are started early in the course of an exacerbation—as soon as the patient's cough increases and becomes productive of sputum in greater quantity and purulence than customary—but much longer periods are required if the infection is well established. Continuous treatment with antimicrobials or "prophylactic" schedules such as 1 week per month has not been shown to be beneficial and promotes the development of resistant organisms. Antibiotics should be administered either orally or by injection, *not* by nebulization (owing to failure of delivery, inactivation of the antibiotic, and risk of sensitization).

Adjuvant medical measures are useful in diminishing the consequences of bronchiectasis. Postural drainage and physical therapy are recommended for those with thick or tenacious sputum, especially if present in large amounts. Many patients with bronchiectasis have reversible bronchospasm as shown by the results of pulmonary function studies; these patients should be treated with bronchodilators. Expectorants and humidifiers are of questionable value. Adequate hydration is probably just as effective as the administration of expectorants. Fiberoptic bronchoscopy is useful in identifying sites of endobronchial disease (Chap. 201) and sources of secretions and

hemoptysis, and permits removal of secretions by aspiration under direct vision. Repeated bronchoscopies are helpful in the management of the unusual patient with problems of sputum retention. Similarly, bronchial lavage has been tried as a "last resort" in patients with large volumes of inspissated secretions. Oxygen should be given to patients with hypoxia during acute exacerbations; it can be administered outside the hospital to patients who are severely and chronically hypoxic. Inflammation from any cause will aggravate the effects of chronic bronchiectasis; therefore, smoking should be prohibited, exposure to air which is excessively polluted should be avoided, and influenza and pneumococcal vaccines should be administered yearly.

Resectional surgery, once the mainstay of treatment, is used far less often now than previously for two reasons: (1) medical management is very effective in controlling bronchiectasis and preventing disability from it; (2) many patients with bronchiectasis have a generalized disorder that makes their entire tracheobronchial system vulnerable; although their bronchiectasis may appear well localized when evaluated initially, new sites of involvement may appear later. Operation should be considered in patients with localized (i.e., resectable) lesions who do not respond to medical management or who are so disabled by complications that either their livelihood or their emotional life is impaired. Bouts of hemoptysis, especially if massive, and recurrent localized pneumonias are the usual complications that require hospitalization, cause repeated disability, and require that the patient be evaluated for surgery.

PREVENTION The best approach to bronchiectasis is prevention. Patients with heritable diseases that predispose to bronchiectasis and their families should obtain genetic counseling to minimize the incidence of these disorders. Prompt diagnosis and effective antimicrobial treatment of bacterial infections of the lower respiratory tract constitute the best way of avoiding their potential chronic sequelae. The eradication of measles and pertussis by vaccines will eliminate these diseases as harbingers of bronchiectasis.

Prompt removal of foreign bodies, tumors, and other causes of bronchial obstruction should diminish postobstructive bronchiectasis.

BRONCHOLITHIASIS

The term *broncholith* has two meanings: in a general sense it indicates any calcification that impinges on and distorts the wall of a bronchus; in a restricted sense it refers to a calcified tissue fragment that is loose within the lumen of a bronchus. Intraluminal broncholiths can form in three ways: (1) calcification of aspirated food or tissue that was retained in the airway for a long time, (2) protrusion into the lumen and fragmentation of a calcified bronchial cartilage because of necrosis of the bronchial wall in bronchiectasis, and (3) erosion of a contiguous calcified granuloma through the wall. Numerous disorders leave calcified deposits that can be detected by chest roentgenography, but clinically significant broncholithiasis is rare. It is usually a late complication of one of the three common granulomatous infections: tuberculosis, histoplasmosis, and coccidioidomycosis. Of these, histoplasmosis has the greatest tendency to heal with multiple residual calcifications, and coccidioidomycosis has the least; hence broncholithiasis in the United States, especially in the central and eastern regions, is most likely to be related to previous infection with *Histoplasma capsulatum*; in Europe half the cases are caused by tuberculosis.

The clinical consequences of broncholithiasis are related to the movement of stones through the airway wall and their release into the lumen. The process of erosion is often accompanied by paroxysms of cough, intermittent hemoptysis, and bronchopulmonary infection. The overlying inflammatory reaction impairs bronchial clearance and narrows the lumen; these conditions may lead to distal bronchiectasis or, if the obstruction is complete, atelectasis. The hallmark of broncholithiasis is the coughing and expectoration of chalky sediment, sandy (gritty) particles, or stones. Such episodes are usually single but may be multiple.

Broncholithiasis should be suspected in any patient with recurrent cough and hemoptysis whose chest roentgenograms show multiple calcifications in the lung and/or mediastinal lymph nodes. The diagnosis can be established by recovering stones in the sputum, by visualizing broncholiths penetrating the bronchial wall at the time of bronchoscopy, or by establishing that calcified particles have disappeared on serial chest x-ray films. Computed tomography is helpful in determining with greater precision than routine roentgenograms the presence and location of calcifications in and around bronchi.

Treatment depends on the magnitude of the symptoms. The disorder is self-limiting once the stone has eroded into the lumen and is coughed up; however, ulceration by the particle may be slow and attended by significant symptoms. Antimicrobial agents are useful in the treatment of associated bacterial infection. Bronchoscopy should be performed and the stone removed if possible. At times, thoracotomy and lung resection are necessary, usually for obstructive complications or massive hemoptysis.

REFERENCES

Bronchiectasis

BREATNACH ES et al: Preoperative evaluation of bronchiectasis by tomography. J Comput Assist Tomogr 9:949, 1985
DAVIES PB et al: Bronchiectasis and oligospermia: Two families. Thorax 40:376, 1985
LEWISTON NJ: Bronchiectasis in childhood. Pediatr Clin North Am 31:865, 1984
MURPHY MB et al: Atopy, immunological changes, and respiratory function in bronchiectasis. Thorax 39:179, 1984
PROTO AV: Evaluation of the bronchi with CT. Semin Radiol 19:199, 1984
SWARTZ MN: Bronchiectasis, in Pulmonary Diseases and Disorders, 2d ed, AP Fishman (ed). New York, McGraw-Hill, 1987, chap 93

Broncholithiasis

DIXON GF et al: Advances in the diagnosis and treatment of broncholithiasis. Am Rev Respir Dis 129:1028, 1984
TRASTEK VF et al: Surgical management of broncholithiasis. J Thorac Cardiovasc Surg 90:842, 1985

207 CYSTIC FIBROSIS

HARVEY R. COLTEN

Cystic fibrosis (CF) is an inherited multisystem disorder which is characterized by an abnormality in exocrine gland function. Nearly all patients develop chronic progressive disease of the respiratory system. Pulmonary disease is the most common cause of death and morbidity in patients with cystic fibrosis. Pancreatic dysfunction (exocrine or endocrine) occurs in 85 percent of patients; hepatobiliary and genitourinary disease are also frequent. Prior to the 1930s the syndrome was confused with several other disorders with signs and symptoms of intestinal malabsorption.

CF is common in populations of European origin. Estimates of the incidence of the disorder range from about 1/500 in Amish (Ohio) to 1/90,000 in Hawaiian Orientals. For the white American population the disease occurs in 1/1600 to 1/2000 live births. The disease is recognized less frequently in black Americans (about 1/17,000) and rarely, if at all, among black Africans. Hence, although the "CF gene" is undetectable in the heterozygous state, from the apparent autosomal recessive mode of inheritance the gene frequency in white Americans is estimated at 1/20. The inability to detect heterozygous individuals has retarded more extensive genetic studies and limits the value of genetic counseling for relatives of patients with CF. On the other hand, several DNA probes localized to the long arm of chromosome 7 which detect restriction fragment length polymorphisms linked to the "CF gene" have been identified. These markers will be used for carrier detection, antenatal diagnosis, and ultimately determination of the molecular basis of this disorder. Most cases of CF appear to be due to defect(s) at a single locus, but the possibility of genetic heterogeneity has not been excluded.

Currently, the median survival for patients with CF is about 20 years, and many patients survive to the third and fourth decades. A few have survived to age 50 and beyond. Even though survival of CF patients has improved, the mutation is semilethal. More than 98 percent of males with CF are infertile (see below), and fertility is reduced in women with the disease. This, together with the high incidence of the disease suggests a selective advantage for the individual heterozygous for the CF gene, but there is a paucity of basic information about the genetic defect.

CLINICAL MANIFESTATIONS General The majority of CF patients are diagnosed in infancy or childhood, but some escape detection until adulthood. Table 207-1 summarizes the multiple clinical features of this disease. Substantial pancreatic disease is more common in patients diagnosed early in life, because acute intestinal obstruction (meconium ileus at birth) or malnutrition and poor growth or development alerts the pediatrician and family. Patients with minimal or absent gastrointestinal complaints and atypical respiratory symptoms may be diagnosed for the first time when adult. The finding of microorganisms typically isolated from sputum of CF patients (a mucoid form of *Pseudomonas aeruginosa*) or male infertility in association with evidence of obstructive pulmonary disease suggests CF in a previously undiagnosed adult.

Respiratory All levels of the respiratory tract may be affected in CF. Nasal polyposis, sinusitis, and lower respiratory tract disease are common. Abnormalities in water and electrolyte transport across the respiratory epithelium are said to be uniquely abnormal in patients with CF. Primary qualitative or quantitative alterations in mucous

TABLE 207-1 Principal clinical manifestations of cystic fibrosis

I Respiratory/cardiovascular
  A Bronchitis, bronchopneumonia, bronchiectasis, lung abscesses, aspergillosis (allergic)
  B Atelectasis
  C Sinusitis, nasal polyposis
  D Pulmonary hypertension
  E Cor pulmonale and congestive heart failure
  F Hemoptysis
  G Pneumothorax
  H Respiratory failure
II Gastrointestinal
  A Intestinal
    1 Meconium ileus
    2 Volvulus
    3 Ileal atresia
    4 Rectal prolapse
    5 Intussusception
    6 Fecal impaction
    7 Pneumatosis intestinalis
  B Pancreatic
    1 Nutritional deficit and growth failure due to pancreatic insufficiency
    2 Steatorrhea
    3 Diabetes mellitus
    4 Recurrent pancreatitis
  C Hepatobiliary
    1 Atrophic gallbladder, cholelithiasis
    2 Loss of bile salts
    3 Focal biliary cirrhosis
    4 Portal hypertension
      a Esophageal varices
      b Hypersplenism
      c Hemorrhoids
III Reproductive system
  A Males: sterility; absent or defective vas deferens, epididymis, and seminal vesicles in about 99 percent of males
  B Females: decreased fertility; increased viscosity of vaginal secretions
IV Skeletal
  A Retardation of bone age
  B Demineralization
  C Hypertrophic osteoarthropathy
V Other
  A Salt depletion
  B Heat stroke
  C Salivary gland hypertrophy
  D Retinal hemorrhage
  E Hypertrophy of apocrine glands

secretion that are characteristic for CF have been suggested, but most if not all that have been experimentally determined appear similar to findings in patients with chronic bronchitis or bronchiectasis of diverse etiologies. Autopsy studies of infants dying of meconium ileus suggest that the lungs of newborns with CF are normal. The earliest pulmonary changes are hypertrophy of bronchial glands followed by mucous plugging and obstruction of small airways. Subsequent infection leads to a bronchiolitis, and centripetal progression of endobronchial disease results in chronic bronchitis, bronchiectasis, and peribronchial inflammation. The release of toxic oxygen species and proteolytic enzymes by bacterial and inflammatory cells probably contributes to the progression of airway disease. Specific and nonspecific systemic host defenses are normal or increased, though chronic inflammatory disease may lead to mechanical interference with local defense mechanisms.

Three major bacterial organisms chronically colonize or infect the airways of patients with CF. *Staphylococcus aureus* and *Haemophilus influenzae* are recovered from sputum in a minority, and *P. aeruginosa*, especially mucoid forms, are detected in more than 90 percent of CF patients. Once the *P. aeruginosa* is acquired, the organism is rarely if ever eliminated. Other bacteria (mucoid forms of *Escherichia coli, Legionella,* etc.) and other microorganisms, including viruses, mycoplasma, and fungi, may be present in the sputum of patients with CF. Colonization with *Pseudomonas cepacia* may herald a more unfavorable short-term prognosis. The mucoid *Pseudomonas* strains are detected almost exclusively in the CF population. Even family members of patients with CF are not colonized by this organism, so that recovery of a mucoid form of *P. aeruginosa* from patients with chronic pulmonary disease should prompt further diagnostic studies to rule out CF.

Acute and chronic pulmonary parenchymal involvement leads to loss of tissue, extensive fibrosis, and changes in lung and airway mechanics. The inflammatory and structural changes in airways and lung parenchyma lead to airway obstruction, hyperinflation, and ventilation-perfusion imbalance. The upper lobes are generally more involved than lower lobes. Pleural involvement is rare, and extrathoracic infection with respiratory pathogens is virtually absent. Secondary changes in pulmonary and bronchial vasculature in patients with advanced respiratory disease may lead to the substantial hemoptysis often observed in older patients. Pulmonary hypertension develops frequently in CF patients with severe airway obstruction and hypoxemia, resulting in progressive right ventricular failure (cor pulmonale). Clubbing is seen in nearly all patients.

TREATMENT   Treatment of CF pulmonary disease is directed toward increasing mechanical drainage, as in patients with chronic bronchitis (Chap. 208), with the use of chest physiotherapy, exercise programs, etc. Control of bacterial infection or colonization is effected by antibiotic therapy specific for the common bacterial organisms isolated from CF sputum. Antibiotic-resistant strains of *P. aeruginosa* are frequently isolated from patients with advanced disease, but in general intravenously administered aminoglycosides in combination with modified penicillins or cephalosporins are employed for treatment of pulmonary exacerbations. Aerosolized antibiotics have been used as well. Management of the bronchospastic component of the disease involves the use of systemic and aerosolized bronchodilators. Occasionally surgery (e.g., lobectomy) is required when infection or tissue destruction is localized. Prompt attention to and specific therapy of complications of pulmonary disease have been important factors in the improved survival of patients with CF. Small pneumothoraxes can generally be managed expectantly, while many will respond to tube thoracostomy alone. However the best evidence suggests that this approach is associated with high recurrence rates. Therefore most episodes are treated with pleural sclerosis (with agents such as tetracycline or quinacrine), open pleurectomy, or pleurodesis. Massive hemoptysis is treated most safely and effectively by bronchial artery embolization via a percutaneous catheter. Congestive heart failure is managed as described elsewhere (Chaps. 182 and 191).

Gastrointestinal   Pancreatic insufficiency leading to fat and protein malabsorption is a feature in the majority of cases (Chap. 255). Deficiencies of fat-soluble vitamins, caloric deprivation, failure to grow and develop, and other manifestations such as rectal prolapse occur in patients with untreated pancreatic insufficiency. About 5 percent of patients with CF are born with meconium ileus, i.e., intestinal obstruction secondary to inspissated meconium in the terminal ileum. Occasionally perforation and meconium peritonitis can occur. Treatment of pancreatic insufficiency with oral pancreatic enzymes corrects most of the deficits. For instance, it decreases the number and bulk of stools; the amount of flatulence, abdominal pain, and distention; and it largely corrects the malabsorption and hence corrects the nutritional deficiencies.

In patients with intact or partial pancreatic exocrine function, recurrent acute pancreatitis may occur. A minority of patients (2 to 5 percent) develop overt diabetes mellitus requiring exogenous insulin, but subclinical abnormalities in glucose metabolism can be detected in a much larger group of CF patients. The longer survival of patients with CF may allow the development of typical diabetic complications such as retinal and glomerular lesions. These should prompt more aggressive efforts to maintain optimal diabetic control.

Hepatobiliary disease is common in older patients. There is chronic cholestasis, inflammation, fibrosis, and even cirrhosis. All of the features of portal hypertension have been recognized. Extrahepatic disease of the biliary system is common.

Genitourinary   Abnormalities of the genitourinary tract are present in 98 percent of males. These are due to an interruption in wolffian duct structures (atresia of the vas deferens) which results in azoospermia and decreased ejaculate volume (Chap. 330). Sexual development and potency are unaffected by the genitourinary abnormalities. Women have abnormal cervical mucus. Sexual development, the menstrual cycle, and fertility in women are less affected by direct effects of the mutation than by the effects of poor nutrition and/or chronic pulmonary disease. Women with CF can conceive and deliver healthy infants, but the maternal and fetal risks are functions of the extent of pulmonary disease and its complications. Close monitoring and prompt therapy in centers expert in high-risk obstetrical management are indicated.

Sweat glands   The abnormality in the eccrine sweat gland function provides the most reliable diagnostic test for CF at present. Sodium, potassium, and chloride are elevated in sweat of patients with CF. The chloride concentration exceeds 70 meq per liter, and the sodium concentration is greater than 60 meq per liter in sweat of nearly all patients, though some individuals with "borderline values" may have many other manifestations of the disease. The corresponding values for chloride and sodium in normals rarely exceed 50 and 40 meq per liter, respectively. Sweat electrolytes are measured most reliably by the pilocarpine iontophoresis method. Even when qualitative screening methods are used, the diagnosis cannot be made without a quantitative sweat electrolyte measurement. The increased electrolyte content results from a failure of reabsorption in the sweat duct. Electrolyte losses may lead to significant salt depletion, especially in young children.

CONCLUSION   Increasing survival of patients with typical findings of CF as well as patients undiagnosed until adult life requires an increased awareness of this disorder among physicians. The relatively high prevalence of this disorder and the enormous resources required to treat patients with CF has stimulated research activity to define the basic genetic defect responsible for the protean clinical manifestations of CF.

REFERENCES

DAVIS PB: Cystic fibrosis. Semin Resp Med 6:243, 1985

DI SANT'AGNESE PA, DAVIS PB: Cystic fibrosis in adults: 75 cases and a review of 232 cases in the literature. Am J Med 66:121, 1979

FELLOWS KE et al: Bronchial artery embolization in cystic fibrosis: Technique and long-term results. J Pediatr 95:959, 1979

KNOWLES M et al: Increased bioelectrical potential difference across respiratory epithelia in cystic fibrosis. N Engl J Med 305:1489, 1981

MATTHEWS WJ et al: Hypogammaglobulinemia in patients with cystic fibrosis. N Engl J Med 302:245, 1980

PARK RW, GRAND RJ: Gastrointestinal manifestations of cystic fibrosis: A review. Gastroenterol 81:1143, 1981

SCANLIN TF: Cystic fibrosis (including assessment of pulmonary performance), in *Pulmonary Diseases and Disorders*, 2d ed, AP Fishman (ed). New York, McGraw-Hill, 1987, chap 76

SHWACHMAN H et al: The sweat test: Sodium and chloride values. J Pediatr 98:576, 1981

TALAMO RC et al: Cystic fibrosis, in *Metabolic Basis of Inherited Disease*, 5th ed, JB Stanbury et al (eds). New York, McGraw-Hill, 1983

208 CHRONIC BRONCHITIS, EMPHYSEMA, AND AIRWAYS OBSTRUCTION

ROLAND H. INGRAM, JR.

Chronic bronchitis and emphysema are two distinct processes, often present in combination in patients with chronic airways obstruction. The diagnosis of chronic bronchitis is made by history, chronic airways obstruction is assessed physiologically, and emphysema can be diagnosed with certainty only by histologic examination of sections of whole lung fixed at inflation. Although the relationships between clinical characteristics, physiologic derangements, and morphologic changes have been diligently studied for many years, reasonably certain and uniform clinical criteria are still not available. Definitions and classifications have evolved, but these are not universally accepted. Nonetheless, the following definitions along with brief qualifications and descriptions are currently used by most persons involved in the diagnosis, treatment, and epidemiology of the chronic obstructive airways syndromes.

DEFINITIONS *Chronic bronchitis* is a condition associated with excessive tracheobronchial mucus production sufficient to cause cough with expectoration for at least 3 months of the year for more than 2 consecutive years. Several subclassifications have been proposed. *Simple chronic bronchitis* describes a condition characterized by mucoid sputum production. *Chronic mucopurulent bronchitis* is characterized by persistent or recurrent purulence of sputum in the absence of localized suppurative diseases such as bronchiectasis. Since there may or may not be obstruction as assessed by the use of the forced expiratory vital capacity maneuver, *chronic bronchitis with obstruction* deserves a separate classification. There is a further subset of patients with chronic bronchitis and obstruction who experience severe dyspnea and wheezing in association with inhaled irritants or during acute respiratory infections. Such patients are said to have *chronic infective asthma* or *chronic asthmatic bronchitis*. Confusion is possible between patients with this condition and those with asthma (Chap. 202) who may also have *chronic airways obstruction*. The patient with chronic asthmatic bronchitis has a long history of cough and sputum production with a later onset of wheezing, whereas the asthmatic with chronic obstruction gives a long history of wheezing with later onset of chronic productive cough.

Emphysema is defined as distention of the air spaces distal to the terminal bronchiole with destruction of alveolar septa. *Chronic obstructive lung disease* is defined as a condition in which there is chronic obstruction to airflow due to chronic bronchitis and/or emphysema (see below). Although the degree of obstruction may be less when the patient is free from respiratory infection and may improve somewhat with bronchodilator drugs, some obstruction is always present.

PREVALENCE Approximately 20 percent of adult males have chronic bronchitis, yet only a minority of these are clinically disabled. According to all surveys males are more often affected than females. With increased cigarette smoking in women, however, the prevalence of bronchitis in them is increasing. Although cigarette smoking is the single most important etiologic factor, occupational and environmental exposures are now receiving more attention.

Since no criteria have been agreed upon for making the diagnosis of emphysema during life, the incidence data are derived solely from postmortem surveys. It is rare to find adult lungs completely free of emphysema. There is a distinct increase in the extent of emphysema in the fifth decade with further increases through the seventh decade and little increase after that. Approximately two-thirds of adult males and one-fourth of females (most without recognized dysfunction) will have well-defined emphysema, which is often limited in extent. Therefore, the majority of those with emphysema will not have had disability or even symptoms associated with it. The situation is analogous to atherosclerosis in that the morphologic changes are far more frequent than the clinical manifestations attributable to the changes.

PATHOLOGY *Chronic bronchitis* is associated with hyperplasia and hypertrophy of the mucus-producing glands found in the submucosa of large cartilaginous airways. Quantitation of this anatomic change, known as the *Reid index*, is based upon the ratio of the thickness of the submucosal glands to that of the bronchial wall. In persons without a history of chronic bronchitis the mean ratio is 0.44 with a standard deviation ±0.09, whereas in those with such a history the mean ratio is 0.52 ± 0.08. Although a low index is *rarely* associated with symptoms and a high index is commonly associated with symptoms during life, there is a great deal of overlap. Therefore many persons will have morphologic changes in large airways without having had chronic bronchitis.

Perhaps more important than the abnormalities in large airways are the changes often found in the small noncartilaginous airways. Goblet-cell hyperplasia, mucosal and submucosal inflammatory cells, and edema, peribronchial fibrosis, intraluminal mucus plugs, and increased smooth muscle are characteristic findings in small airways. The frequency of these latter findings in relation to premortem clinical and functional status has not been determined. However, in lungs from patients with chronic obstructive lung disease which have been studied at postmortem, the major site of airflow obstruction has been shown to be in the small airways.

Emphysema is classified according to the pattern of involvement of the gas-exchanging units (acini) of the lung distal to the terminal bronchiole. Although several morphologic patterns have been described, the two most important in the context of this discussion are those involving the respiratory bronchioles and alveolar ducts in the center of the acinus (centriacinar emphysema) and those involving the entire acinus (panacinar emphysema). Quite often both morphologic patterns are present in a single lung of a patient dying from chronic obstructive lung disease, although one type may predominate over the other.

With centriacinar emphysema the distention and destruction are mainly limited to the respiratory bronchiole and alveolar ducts, with relatively less change peripherally in the acinus. Because of the large functional reserve in the lung, many units must be involved in order for overall dysfunction to be detectable. The centrally destroyed regions of the acinus have a high ventilation/perfusion ratio because the capillaries are missing yet ventilation continues. This results in increased wasted ventilation (Vd/Vt), while the peripheral portions of the acinus have crowded and small alveoli with intact, perfused capillaries giving a low ventilation/perfusion ratio. This results in wasted blood flow to give a high alveolar-arterial P_{O_2} difference ($PA_{O_2} - Pa_{O_2}$) (Chap. 200). Mild degrees of centriacinar emphysema, often limited to the lung apices, are extremely common in lungs from persons above age 50 and are practically considered a normal finding.

Panacinar emphysema involves both the central and peripheral portions of the acinus which results, if the process is extensive, in a reduction of the alveolar-capillary gas exchange surface and loss of elastic recoil properties. When emphysema is severe, it may be difficult to distinguish between the two types which most often coexist in the same lung.

CONTRIBUTORY FACTORS **Smoking** Cigarette smoking is the most commonly identified correlate with both chronic bronchitis during life and extent of emphysema at postmortem. Experimental studies have shown that prolonged cigarette smoking impairs ciliary movement, inhibits function of alveolar macrophages, and leads to hypertrophy and hyperplasia of mucus-secreting glands; massive exposure in dogs can produce emphysematous changes. In addition to these chronic effects it is probable that smoke causes polymorphonuclear leukocytes to release proteolytic enzymes acutely. Inhaled cigarette smoke can produce an acute increase in airways resistance due to vagally mediated smooth-muscle constriction, presumably by way of stimulating submucosal irritant receptors. The relationship of such recurrent episodes of acute bronchial constriction to the development and progression of chronic airways obstruction is uncertain. Recent studies, however, indicate that increased airways reactivity is associated with more rapid progression in those with chronic airways obstruction.

It is now well established that some young asymptomatic smokers have considerable obstruction in small airways without there being either an increase of airway resistance or a diminution in the forced expiratory volume in 1 s. Since small airways, because of their large total cross-sectional areas, contribute very little to overall airflow resistance, more sensitive tests must be used to detect mild degrees of small-airways obstruction. Some tests, such as a decrease in compliance and resistance at rapid breathing rates, are based upon nonuniform behavior of the lung which is apparent only at increased frequencies. Obstruction of small airways also results in airways closure at higher lung volumes than in persons of the same age with unobstructed airways (Chap. 200). The measurements of closing volume and frequency dependence of resistance and compliance require special equipment not often available to clinicians. However, the simple spirogram is useful since flow rates at or below the midvital capacity range are often diminished in persons with mild small-airways obstruction. It has been shown that obstruction of small airways is the earliest demonstrable mechanical defect in young cigarette smokers and that the obstruction may disappear after cessation of smoking. It is possible, but has not been established with certainty, that those with small-airways obstruction are at greater risk of developing disabling chronic airways obstruction at some future time.

Not only is cigarette smoking the most common single factor leading to chronic airways obstruction, it also interacts with virtually every other contributory factor to be discussed below.

Air pollution The incidence and mortality rates of both chronic bronchitis and emphysema may be higher in heavily industrialized urban areas. Exacerbations of bronchitis are clearly related to periods of heavy pollution with sulfur dioxide (SO_2) and particulate matter. While nitrogen dioxide (NO_2) can produce small-airways obstruction (bronchiolitis) in experimental animals exposed to high concentrations, there are no data convincingly implicating NO_2, at even the highest pollutant levels, in the pathogenesis or worsening of airways obstruction in humans (Chap. 204).

Occupation Chronic bronchitis is more prevalent in workers who engage in occupations exposing them to either inorganic or organic dusts or to noxious gases. Epidemiologic surveys have succeeded in demonstrating an accelerated decline in lung function in many such workers—e.g., workers in plastics plants exposed to toluene diisocyanate and carding room workers in cotton mills (Chap. 204)—suggesting that their occupational exposure contributes to their future disability.

Infection Morbidity, mortality, and frequency of acute respiratory illnesses are higher in patients with chronic bronchitis. Many attempts have been made to relate these illnesses to infection with viruses, mycoplasmas, and bacteria. However, only the rhinovirus is found more often during exacerbations; that is to say, pathogenic bacteria, mycoplasmas, and viruses other than rhinovirus are found just as often between as during exacerbations. It is intuitively appealing to assign some role to respiratory infections in the pathogenesis and progression of chronic obstructive lung disease, and although this question is under study, there has been no conclusion to date. Recent epidemiologic studies, however, implicate acute respiratory illness as one of the major factors associated with the etiology as well as the progression of chronic airways obstruction. It has been shown that cigarette smokers may either transitorily develop or worsen small-airways obstruction in association with even mild viral respiratory infections. There is also some evidence that severe viral pneumonia early in life may lead to chronic obstruction, predominantly in small airways.

Familial and genetic factors Familial aggregation of chronic bronchitis has been well demonstrated in the past. Recent surveys have shown that children of smoking parents may experience more frequent and severe respiratory illnesses and have a higher prevalence of chronic respiratory symptoms. In addition, nonsmokers who remain in the presence of cigarette smokers (passive smokers) have increased blood levels of carbon monoxide which indicate that they are significantly exposed to smoke. Another well-documented form of indoor air pollution relates to the use of natural gas for cooking. The role of such pollution, however, remains controversial. Thus a part of the familial aggregation may be related to home air pollution. However, some studies of monozygotic twins have suggested some genetic predisposition to the development of chronic bronchitis independent of personal or familial smoking habits and other indoor air pollution. The exact genetic mode of transmission, if it exists at all, is uncertain.

The protease inhibitor alpha₁ antitrypsin is an acute-phase reactant, and normally the serum levels rise in association with many inflammatory reactions and with estrogen administration. Either deficient or absent serum levels of alpha₁ antitrypsin are found in some patients with the early onset of emphysema. By use of the techniques of acid starch gel and immunoelectrophoresis, genetic typing of the protease inhibitor (Pi) types has been possible. Most of the normal population have two M genes, designated as Pi type MM, and have serum alpha₁ antitrypsin levels in excess of 250 mg/dL. Several genes are associated with alterations in levels of serum alpha₁ antitrypsin, but the commonest ones associated with emphysema are the Z and S genes. Individuals who are homozygous ZZ or SS have serum levels often near 0 but always less than 50 mg/dL and develop severe panacinar emphysema in the third and fourth decades of life. The panacinar process predominates at the lung bases. Progressive dyspnea with minimal cough characterizes the clinical presentation, although chronic bronchitis is prominent in smokers. Given that alpha₁ protease inhibitors can be chemically synthesized or biologically produced in significant quantities and can be shown with intravenous infusion to restore the protease-antiprotease balance in liquid lavaged from the lungs of ZZ patients, it has been suggested that replacement therapy should be of value in preventing the development of emphysema; limited clinical trials are underway. The MZ and MS heterozygotes have intermediate levels of serum alpha₁ antitrypsin (i.e., between 50 and 250 mg/dL); hence the genetic expression is that of an autosomal codominant allele. It is a matter of some controversy whether the heterozygous state is associated with lung function abnormalities. Published studies are in direct conflict on this point, and further data are needed to be certain. The matter is of some importance, since the heterozygous state is common, with incidence estimates varying between 5 and 14 percent of the general population.

The precise way in which antitrypsin deficiency produces emphysema is unclear. In addition to inhibition of trypsin, alpha₁ antitrypsin is an effective inhibitor of elastase and several other proteolytic enzymes. There is experimental evidence that the structural integrity of lung elastin depends upon this antienzyme, which protects the lung from proteases released from leukocytes. It is tempting to speculate that recurrent inflammatory reactions related to infection and pollutants play some role in pathogenesis by calling forth leukocytes whose released proteases are uninhibited and are free to cause the damage.

The role of proteolytic enzymes in the induction of emphysema is not restricted to patients with alpha$_1$ antitrypsin deficiency. Evidence is accumulating that proteolytic enzymes derived from neutrophilic leukocytes and alveolar macrophages can produce emphysema even in subjects with normal circulating levels of antiproteases. It is possible that local concentrations of proteolytic enzymes may exceed the inhibitory capacity of antiproteases, that some proteases present are not susceptible to the available antiproteases, or that some of the proteolytic enzymes may be physically inaccessible to the antiprotease activity. The ultimate clinical utility of exogenously produced protease inhibitors currently under development will undoubtedly depend upon which of the protease-antiprotease interactions predominates in the production of emphysema.

PATHOPHYSIOLOGY On the basis of the use of flow rates from forced expiratory vital capacity maneuvers and more sophisticated measures of airways resistance and elastic recoil properties of the lung, it has become clear that both chronic bronchitis and emphysema can exist without evidence of obstruction. However, by the time a patient begins to experience dyspnea as a result of these processes, obstruction is always demonstrable. Since chronic bronchitis and emphysema are usually combined, it might appear fruitless to determine the role of each in producing an individual patient's disability. However, one process may dominate over the other, and to the extent that inflammatory airways disease, secretions, and bronchospasm are present, there are therapeutic possibilities with some hope for improvement. Therefore it is of value to understand the mechanisms of airways obstruction in order to guide therapy and anticipate results.

Both chronic bronchitis and emphysema result in airways narrowing. In addition to the primary airways processes of chronic bronchitis, loss of elastic recoil of the lung in emphysema accounts for a decrease in airways caliber through loss of radial traction on airways. Narrowing of airways is often associated with both an increase in airways resistance and a diminution in maximal expiratory flow rates.

There are occasions in which a normal or only slightly elevated airways resistance is accompanied by low maximal expiratory flow rates. Under such circumstances an increase in the dynamic collapsibility of intrathoracic airways during forced exhalation is a possible explanation. Also in this context, the elastic recoil pressure of the lung must be considered in a slightly different way. In addition to providing radial support to airways during quiet breathing, the elastic recoil properties of the lung serve as a major determinant of maximal expiratory flow rates. The static recoil pressure of the lung is the difference between alveolar and intrapleural pressure. During forced exhalations, when alveolar and intrapleural pressures are high, there are points in the airway at which bronchial pressure equals pleural pressure. Flow does not increase with higher pleural pressure after these points become fixed so that the effective driving pressure between alveoli and such points is the elastic recoil pressure of the lung (Fig. 208-1). Hence maximal expiratory flow rates represent a complex and dynamic interplay between airways caliber, elastic recoil pressures, and collapsibility of airways. As a direct consequence of the altered pressure-airflow relationships, the work of breathing is increased in bronchitis and emphysema. Since flow-resistive work is flow rate–dependent, there is a disproportionate increase in the work of breathing with increased ventilation.

The designated subdivisions of the lung volume outlined in Chap. 200 are abnormal to varying degrees in both bronchitis and emphysema. The residual volume (RV) and functional residual capacity (FRC) are almost always higher than normal. Since the normal FRC is the volume at which the inward recoil of the lung is balanced by the outward recoil of the chest wall, loss of elastic recoil of the lung would clearly result in a higher static FRC. In addition, prolongation of expiration in association with obstruction would lead to a dynamic increase in FRC if inspiration is initiated before the respiratory system

reaches its static balance point. Elevations of total lung capacity (TLC) are frequent. The exact cause is uncertain, but increases in TLC are often found in association with decreases in the elastic recoil of the lung. The vital capacity is frequently decreased, yet significant airways obstruction can be present with a normal to near-normal vital capacity.

The consequences of the airways and parenchymal processes are far more extensive than just the mechanical alterations discussed above. Maldistribution of inspired gas and blood flow is always present to some extent. When the mismatching is severe, impairment of gas exchange is reflected in abnormalities of arterial blood gases. There are regions of the lung with ventilation in excess of perfusion which increase the wasted ventilation ratio (that is, Vd/Vt; Chap. 200). At a normal resting CO_2 production, the net effective alveolar ventilation, as reflected by the arterial P_{CO_2}, may be excessive, normal, or insufficient depending upon the relationship of the overall minute volume to the wasted ventilation ratio. The net contribution of regions with perfusion in excess of ventilation can be assessed by either estimating or measuring the alveolar-arterial P_{O_2} difference (that is, $P_{A_{O_2}} - P_{a_{O_2}}$; Chap. 200). Whatever the clinical syndrome associated with chronic bronchitis and emphysema, there are to some degree increases in both wasted ventilation and wasted blood flow.

The clinical manifestations depend, in large part, upon the ventilatory response to the disordered lung function. Some patients, at the cost of extremely high effort of breathing and chronic dyspnea,

FIGURE 208-1 *A. A schematic diagram of the lung and intrathoracic airways with no airflow. The alveolar pressure (Palv) is greater than pleural pressure (Ppl) by an amount equal to the elastic recoil pressure of the lung (Pel)—i.e., Palv is the algebraic sum of Ppl + Pel. With no airflow Palv = P atmospheric, and for all of the intrathoracic airways, pressure outside is less than the pressure inside due to the Pel. B. The same schematic lung during forced exhalation when pleural pressure becomes quite positive. Palv is still greater than Ppl by an amount equal to Pel. However, there is a pressure drop along the airway associated with flow, and at some point Ppl equals local bronchial pressure (so-called equal pressure point, EPP). Mouthward from this point, Ppl exceeds local bronchial pressure and hence acts to compress the airways. C. Pressure within the airways from alveoli to the intrathoracic trachea is shown as a dashed line (---) and Ppl is shown as a constant (———). Therefore, the driving pressure from alveoli to EPP is equal to Pel, and a decrease in Pel (i.e., loss of elastic recoil) would mean a smaller driving pressure and smaller flow rates.*

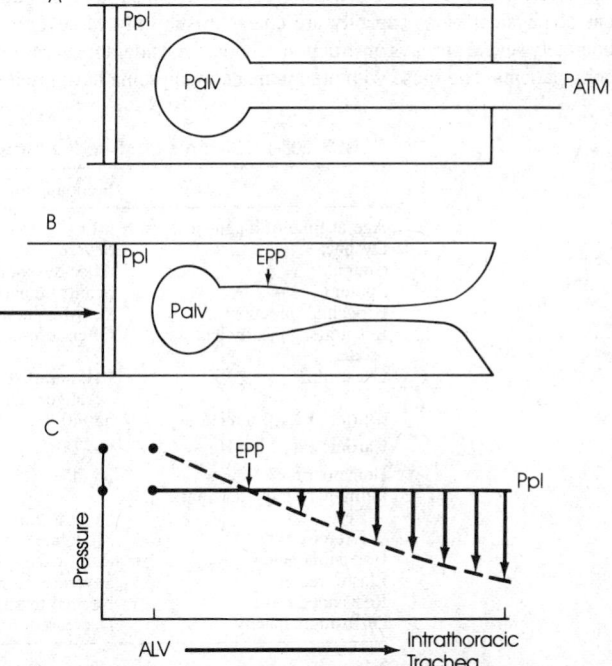

will maintain a strikingly increased minute volume, which results both in a normal to low arterial P_{CO_2}, despite the high Vd/Vt, and a relatively high arterial P_{O_2}, despite the high difference, $PA_{O_2} - Pa_{O_2}$. Other patients with only modest increases in effort of breathing and less dyspnea will maintain a normal to only moderately elevated minute volume at the cost of accepting a high arterial P_{CO_2} and a severely depressed arterial P_{O_2}.

Factors which account for clear differences in ventilatory responses between patients have been studied and debated for years. The bulk of available evidence suggests that those patients who maintain relatively normal or low arterial P_{CO_2} levels are those with an increased ventilatory drive relative to their blood gas values and those who chronically maintain high arterial P_{CO_2} and lower P_{O_2} levels have a diminished ventilatory drive in relation to their more severely deranged blood gas values. It is not at all certain whether individual differences are accounted for by variations in peripheral or central chemoreceptor sensitivity or through other afferent pathways. Perhaps of more immediate value is the fact that patients with predominant emphysema are either normally or excessively responsive both to hypercapnia and to exercise, whereas those with predominant bronchitis are less responsive to both, despite similar degrees of airways obstruction by spirometry.

The pulmonary circulation malfunctions not only in terms of regional distribution of blood flow but in terms of abnormal overall pressure-flow relationships. There is often mild to severe pulmonary hypertension at rest with further increases disproportionate to cardiac output elevations during exercise. A reduction in the total cross-sectional area of the pulmonary vascular bed can be attributed to anatomic changes and constriction of vascular smooth muscle in pulmonary arteries and arterioles as well as destruction of alveolar septa with loss of capillaries. Rarely does loss of capillaries alone lead to severe pulmonary hypertension with cor pulmonale, except as a terminal event. Of more importance is the constriction of pulmonary vessels in response to alveolar hypoxia. The constriction is reversible upon increase in alveolar P_{O_2} with therapy. There is a synergism between hypoxia and acidosis which assumes importance during episodes of acute or chronic respiratory insufficiency. Chronic hypoxia leads not only to pulmonary vascular constriction but also to secondary erythrocytosis. The latter, although not proved to be a significant contributor to pulmonary hypertension, could add an unfavorable rheologic load. As discussed in Chap. 191, the chronic afterload on the right ventricle leads to hypertrophy and, in association with disordered blood gases, ultimately to failure.

CLINICAL-FUNCTIONAL CORRELATIONS   Dyspnea and impairment of physical work capacity are characteristic only of severe to moderately severe airways obstruction. There is considerable variation among patients, and those with predominant emphysema have greater dyspnea and restriction of physical activity with lesser degrees of obstruction than those in whom chronic bronchitis predominates. The majority of patients have functionally mixed disease, will usually experience exertional dyspnea when the forced expiratory volume in 1 s (FEV_1) falls below 50 percent of that predicted, and will have dyspnea at rest when the FEV_1 is less than 25 percent of that predicted. In addition to dyspnea at rest, carbon dioxide retention and cor pulmonale frequently occur when the FEV_1 falls to 25 percent of that predicted. However, those with predominant bronchitis often have carbon dioxide retention and cor pulmonale with FEV_1 values above 25 percent of normal, in contrast to patients with predominant emphysema whose FEV_1 usually falls well below that level before the onset of carbon dioxide retention and cor pulmonale. With a respiratory infection, small changes in the degree of obstruction can make a large difference in symptoms and gas exchange. Thus small therapeutic gains have rewarding results.

In general, the more severe the obstruction, the poorer the prognosis. Despite the general relationship, 20 to 30 percent of patients with severe obstruction and carbon dioxide retention will survive beyond 5 years.

CLINICAL SYNDROMES   It is clear that the clinical presentation can vary in severity from simple chronic bronchitis without disability to the severely disabled state with chronic respiratory failure. From a practical standpoint, it is well to consider that any symptom or any measurable abnormality may foreshadow the development of severe disabling disease; hence cessation of smoking and avoidance of environmental irritants and toxins are to be advised. However, the advice to modify behavior and life patterns is rarely taken, and most physicians are called upon to categorize and treat patients with fully developed, chronic airways obstruction. Thus the approach taken here is to describe two polar opposite types of fully developed, chronic obstructive pulmonary disease with the realization that the majority of patients will have some features of both types. The salient features of each type are outlined in Table 208-1.

Predominant emphysema   These patients often give a long history of exertional dyspnea with minimal cough which is productive of only small amounts of mucoid sputum. Mucopurulent exacerbations in association with infections are not frequent. The body build is asthenic with evidence of weight loss. The patient appears distressed with obvious use of accessory muscles of respiration which serve to lift the sternum in an anterosuperior direction with each inspiration. There is tachypnea with a relatively prolonged expiration through pursed lips, or expiration is begun with a grunting sound. While sitting, these patients often lean forward, extending the arms to brace themselves. The neck veins may be distended during expiration, yet they collapse briskly with inspiration. The lower intercostal spaces

TABLE 208-1   Chronic obstructive lung disease: Salient features of the two types

	Predominant emphysema	Predominant bronchitis
Age at time of diagnosis, yrs	60±	50±
Dyspnea	Severe	Mild
Cough	After dyspnea starts	Before dyspnea starts
Sputum	Scanty, mucoid	Copious, purulent
Bronchial infections	Less frequent	More frequent
Respiratory insufficiency episodes	Often terminal	Repeated
Chest film	"Hyperinflation" ± bullous changes, small heart	Increased bronchovascular markings at bases, large heart
Chronic Pa_{CO_2}, mmHg	35–40	50–60
Chronic Pa_{O_2}, mmHg	65–75	45–60
Hematocrit, %	35–45	50–55
Pulmonary hypertension:		
Rest	None to mild	Moderate to severe
Exercise	Moderate	Worsens
Cor pulmonale	Rare, except terminally	Common
Elastic recoil	Severely decreased	Normal
Resistance	Normal to slight increase	High
Diffusing capacity	Decreased	Normal to slight decrease

retract with each inspiration, and by palpation the lower lateral chest wall can be felt to move inward. The percussion note is hyperresonant, and by auscultation the breath sounds are diminished, with faint, high-pitched rhonchi heard toward the end of expiration. The cardiac impulse, if at all visible, is seen only in the xiphoid and subxiphoid regions, and cardiac dullness is either absent or severely reduced. By palpation there is frequently a sustained forward and downward right ventricular impulse in the subxiphoid region, and a presystolic gallop accentuated during inspiration is commonly heard.

The arterial P_{O_2} is often in the mid-70s (mmHg), and the P_{CO_2} is low to normal. Because of the maintained increase in minute volume and the maintenance of arterial P_{CO_2} sufficient to nearly saturate hemoglobin, these patients have been referred to as "pink puffers."

The TLC and RV are invariably increased, the vital capacity is low, and the maximal expiratory flow rates are diminished. The elastic recoil properties of the lung are severely impaired, and in direct proportion to this impairment, the capacity of the lung to transfer carbon monoxide is lowered.

On radiographic examination the diaphragms are low and flattened, the bronchovascular shadows do not extend to the periphery of the lung, and the cardiac silhouette is lengthened and narrowed. These findings in association with a large retrosternal translucency on lateral chest radiographs are interpreted as hyperinflation, which correlates well with increases in TLC and loss of elastic recoil. Peripheral attenuation of bronchovascular markings and increased retrosternal lucency correlate best with subsequent postmortem demonstration of extensive and severe emphysema which is predominantly of the panacinar type.

It is fortunate that the patient with predominant emphysema is less prone to mucopurulent relapses than is the patient with predominant bronchitis, since such relapses frequently lead to severe respiratory failure and death. That is to say, right-sided heart failure and hypercapnic respiratory failure are often terminal events in those patients with predominant emphysema. In the absence of such relapses, the clinical course is characterized by severe and progressive dyspnea for which little can be done. The physician's role is to seek out and treat any factor that is possibly reversible and strive to avoid pollutants and infections.

Predominant bronchitis The patient with predominant bronchitis usually has an impressive history of cough and sputum production for many years with an immodest history of cigarette smoking. Initially the cough is present only in the winter months, and the patient is apt to seek medical attention, if at all, only during the more severe of the frequent mucopurulent relapses. Over the years the cough progresses from hibernal to perennial, and mucopurulent relapses increase in frequency, duration, and severity. After beginning to experience exertional dyspnea, the patient often seeks medical help and will be found to have a severe degree of obstruction. Occasionally such a patient will seek out a physician only after the onset of peripheral edema secondary to overt right ventricular failure. More rarely the initial medical contact is made by family members who present the physician with a deeply cyanotic, edematous, and stuporous patient with acute respiratory insufficiency.

The patient with predominant bronchitis is often overweight and cyanotic. There is usually no apparent distress at rest, the respiratory rate is normal or only slightly increased, and there is no apparent usage of accessory muscles. The chest percussion note is normally resonant, and by auscultation, one can usually hear coarse rhonchi and wheezes which change in location and intensity after a deep and productive cough. There may be a sustained heave along the lower left sternal border which indicates right ventricular hypertrophy. In the presence of right ventricular failure there are often an early diastolic gallop and occasionally a holosystolic murmur, both of which are accentuated by inspiration. The latter finding is indicative of functional tricuspid regurgitation which is frequently accompanied by neck vein distention characterized by large v waves and brisk y descents. With right ventricular failure the cyanosis deepens and peripheral edema becomes prominent. Clubbing of the digits is unusual.

With or without right ventricular failure, the minute volume is only slightly increased. Failure to increase minute volume greatly in the face of significant proportions of wasted ventilation and blood flow results in severely deranged arterial blood gases, with arterial P_{CO_2} values which are chronically increased to the range of the high 40s to low 50s (mmHg). The lowered P_{O_2} produces desaturation of hemoglobin, serves to stimulate erythropoiesis, and results in hypoxic pulmonary vasoconstriction. Desaturation and erythrocytosis combine to produce the cyanosis, and hypoxic pulmonary vasoconstriction accentuates the right-sided heart failure. Because of cyanosis and edema secondary to heart failure, such patients have been referred to as "blue bloaters." It has been proposed, with some supporting data, that one of the pathophysiologic events in the blue bloaters is the occurrence of repeated episodes of severe nocturnal oxygen desaturation in association with sleep apnea.

The TLC is often normal, and there is a moderate elevation of RV. The vital capacity is mildly diminished, and maximal expiratory flow rates are invariably low. The elastic recoil properties of the lung are normal or only slightly impaired, and the capacity of the lung to transfer carbon monoxide is either normal or minimally decreased.

On radiographic examination the diaphragms are well rounded, the bronchovascular markings are increased in the lower lung fields, and the cardiac silhouette is somewhat enlarged. In association with right ventricular failure the cardiac silhouette enlarges further, pulmonary arteries become more prominent, and an antigravity distribution of perfusion is apparent.

Despite well-planned management (see below) the patient with predominant bronchitis may experience many episodes of respiratory failure from which recovery is frequent with proper therapy (see p. 1093). The ability to recover from such repeated episodes in those patients is in striking contrast to the frequently fatal outcome of such events in those with predominant emphysema. Ultimately, the lungs at postmortem will be found to have severe bronchitic changes in both large and small airways and only moderate emphysema, predominantly of the centriacinar variety.

PRINCIPLES OF MANAGEMENT Intelligent management must be based upon as complete knowledge as possible of the degree of obstruction, the extent of disability, and the relative reversibility of the patient's illness. To the extent that obstructive processes in the airways are contributory, there is a chance for treatment to be effective. Since emphysema is an irreversible process, prevention of progression and avoidance of acute insults constitute the only approach. History, physical examination, and chest radiographs should be supplemented by tests of lung function performed during a symptomatically stable period. Ideally, complete spirometry, plethysmographic lung volumes, airways resistance, transfer of carbon monoxide, arterial blood gases, and lung elastic recoil properties should be measured. Spirometry, lung volumes, and resistance should be remeasured after the administration of bronchodilators in order to assess the degree of acutely reversible airways obstruction. Failure to see an acute change with bronchodilator drugs does not rule out the possibility of improvement with more prolonged administration of these agents. In instances in which the degree of exertional dyspnea appears to be disproportionately greater than the degree of obstruction, measurements of blood gases, minute volume, CO_2 production, and O_2 consumption during exercise are indicated in order to determine whether impaired lung function is sufficient to account for the symptoms. After the initial assessment the physician has some idea of the relative emphasis to be placed upon patient education, preventive measures, and direct therapeutic interventions in management of the patient and the illness.

Cessation of smoking is the only certain means of influencing the progression of the chronic obstructive airways syndromes, and such behavior modification is most effective at early stages of the disease processes. In the instances in which occupational or environmental exposures are thought to play a significant role, change of occupation or relocation of dwelling is advisable. The validity of such advice should be carefully considered since the impact on both the patient and the family is likely to be great. A simpler environmental change is that of eliminating aerosol sprays such as deodorants, hair sprays, and insecticides from the household. Hair sprays have been shown to produce acute airways responses even in normal subjects. Other preventive measures include yearly vaccination against the common or expected influenza virus strains. The patient should be given pneumococcal polysaccharide vaccine only once. Recent evidence of severe Arthus-type immunologic reactions following repeat pneumococcal vaccination has led to this "once-in-a-lifetime" recommendation.

Infections cannot be totally avoided, and the patient should be made aware that increasing purulence, viscosity, or volume of secretions signals the onset of an infection which should be treated early. The commonest pathogenic bacteria found are *Haemophilus influenzae* and *Streptococcus pneumoniae*. As mentioned above, however, the role of such bacteria is in question since they are just as often isolated during periods of relative clinical quiescence. Nonetheless, tetracycline or ampicillin should be given for a 7- to 10-day course. It is practical to have the patient keep a 7- to 10-day supply of antibiotics at home and to begin treatment at the onset of symptoms. In Great Britain it is common practice to give continuous antibiotic therapy during winter months in order to prevent mucopurulent relapses. Although there is evidence that viruses are frequent causes of mucopurulent relapses, clinical studies have shown that the standard antibiotic regimens decrease the duration and severity of infective episodes unrelated to culturable bacterial pathogens. Microscopic examination and culture of sputum are indicated if there are chills, fever, or chest pain or if purulence fails to respond to usually administered antibiotics.

It has been shown repeatedly that exercise programs, although not accompanied by measurable improvement in lung function, result in increased exercise tolerance and an improved sense of well-being. The improvement is usually task-specific, so that most physicians advise walking in preference to the use of special apparatus, such as stationary bicycles or wall gyms.

Bronchodilator drugs are often quite helpful in alleviating symptoms, especially in those patients who respond to them acutely in the laboratory. These drugs form three categories: the methylxanthines, sympathomimetics with strong beta$_2$-adrenergic-stimulating properties, and anticholinergics. Theophylline, the most commonly used methylxanthine, can be given orally, rectally, or parenterally; in addition to bronchodilatation, it stimulates respiration and has cardiotonic and diuretic properties. Selective beta$_2$-stimulating drugs such as albuterol and metaproterenol can be given both orally and by aerosol with fewer cardiac side effects than are experienced with isoproterenol. Anticholinergic agents such as atropine have been avoided in the past because of their tendency to desiccate secretions, but such drugs are effective bronchodilators; new analogues that are given by inhalation with less effect on secretions are now being developed and tested and may be found useful in the future.

The use of glucocorticosteroids is, at our present state of knowledge, based upon very little scientific data from properly controlled clinical trials. Since these agents have time- and dose-related side effects that vary from deleterious to catastrophic, the almost invariable subjective benefit must be supported by objective measurements. There is little room for doubt in the minds of physicians that some patients respond well, even dramatically, to these agents in both objective and subjective terms. The real problem is how to select those most likely to benefit. Eosinophilia in the sputum, rather than in the blood, appears to help identify that subgroup in advance. However, the best guidelines are, first, to try these agents only after maximal bronchodilator and bronchopulmonary drainage measures have been tried without success; second, to begin prednisone 30 mg once per day; third, to confirm the objective change in terms of spirometry and gas exchange, stopping these agents if no objective

benefit is seen; and fourth, to decrease to the smallest dose that will maintain the improved level of function.

Bronchopulmonary drainage should be maintained in patients with hypersecretion. If the coughing mechanism is ineffective or if paroxysms of coughing are exhausting, postural drainage is often a useful adjunct. Although liquefaction of secretions by means of orally administered expectorants or aerosol delivery of mucolytic agents is an appealing idea, it has never been shown by properly designed trials to be more effective than simple maintenance of total-body hydration.

Intermittent positive pressure breathing (IPPB) devices have long been advocated for home management. The various rationales include diminution in the work of breathing, promotion of bronchopulmonary drainage, and more efficient delivery of bronchodilator drugs. The first of the rationales has been shown to have no basis in fact, and the goals of the last two have been shown to be as well accomplished by postural drainage and use of less elaborate aerosol generators. Hence the use of IPPB for home management cannot be justified.

When arterial hypoxia is persistent and severe (Pa$_{O_2}$ <55 mmHg) in association with cor pulmonale (see Chap. 191) and signs of right heart failure, continuous oxygen therapy is indicated. The available data indicate that supplemental oxygen improves both exercise tolerance and neuropsychological function and alleviates pulmonary hypertension and right heart failure. In patients with severe hypoxemia the need for hospitalization occurs less frequently and life span is lengthened by the use of supplemental oxygen. In view of the expense of such therapy and the dangers of uncontrolled oxygen delivery (see below), it should be given only when it can be carefully monitored and its beneficial effects objectively verified.

Since most patients with chronic airways obstruction, especially those with features of predominant bronchitis, can be shown to decrease their Pa$_{O_2}$ values significantly during sleep, most prominently during the REM phase, nocturnal oxygen administration has been suggested. While the rationale is clear and the results quite good, a recent cooperative clinical trial that compared nocturnal with continuous O$_2$ supplementation in severely hypoxic patients found that continuous O$_2$ administration was associated with a significantly lower mortality rate. Patients in both treatment groups experienced neuropsychological and hemodynamic benefits. Thus, supplemental nocturnal oxygen is better than none, but continuous oxygen is better than nocturnal in such severely ill patients.

Secondary erythrocytosis with the hematocrit in excess of 50 percent is most easily viewed as a mechanism allowing greater oxygen delivery to compensate for the chronically lowered arterial Pa$_{O_2}$; hence improvement in oxygenation through improved lung function or by oxygen administration is the most physiologic means to reverse erythrocytosis. Since erythrocytosis results in elevation of blood viscosity at all shear rates, the proposal has been made that pulmonary vascular hypertension is aggravated by its presence. Although no study has demonstrated an objective improvement in hemodynamics, lung mechanics, or gas exchange at rest following phlebotomy, ventilatory and cardiovascular function during exercise improve. Some patients who complain of headaches and a sense of head fullness show a favorable subjective response to periodic phlebotomy when the hematocrit is in excess of 55 percent. In support of this subjective improvement is the demonstration that, following phlebotomy, cerebral blood flow, previously diminished, returns toward normal.

ACUTE RESPIRATORY FAILURE

DIAGNOSIS Although it may be strongly suspected on clinical grounds, the firm diagnosis of acute respiratory failure in chronic airways obstruction is based upon measurements of arterial blood gas (Pa$_{O_2}$, Pa$_{CO_2}$) and pH values that must be interpreted in relation to the patient's chronic status. Since many patients will have chronically lowered Pa$_{O_2}$ levels and increased Pa$_{CO_2}$ values, the diagnosis is based upon the degree of change from the usual state of the individual patient. With regard to oxygenation, an acute decrease in Pa_{O_2} from a usual mid-70-mmHg range to the low 60s (mmHg) is just as indicative of acute respiratory failure as is an acute drop from a chronic mid-50-mmHg range to the mid-40s (mmHg). Thus a drop in Pa_{O_2} equal to or greater than 10 to 15 mmHg indicates acute failure.

Since renal compensation for chronic hypercapnia results in adjustment of arterial pH to near-normal values, the acuteness of the increase in Pa_{CO_2} can often be judged by the pH, unless there is a concomitant metabolic acidemia. As a practical guide, any level of hypercapnia associated with an arterial pH value less than 7.30 should be considered as acute respiratory failure.

PRECIPITATING FACTORS   Increases in volume, viscosity, and/or purulence of secretions, presumably due to infection of the tracheo-bronchial tree, are the most common antecedents of acute respiratory failure in chronic obstructive lung disease. Increasing airways obstruction with airways inflammation and secretion, especially in association with a relatively blunted ventilatory drive, leads to worsening hypoxia and increasing CO_2 retention. Agitation, insomnia, and increasing dyspnea with impending respiratory failure are occasionally treated, mistakenly, with either sedatives or narcotics, and these, too, may precipitate frank respiratory failure. In fact such depressant drugs which impair ventilatory drive should be avoided at all times in patients with severe chronic obstructive lung disease. Major episodes of air pollution can also lead to respiratory failure, and the physicians responsible for patients with severe bronchitis and emphysema should be alert to these environmental events.

Pneumonia, thromboembolism, left ventricular failure, and pneumothorax occasionally precipitate acute respiratory failure and are extremely difficult to detect unless considered and specifically sought. As a minimum, chest radiographs, electrocardiograms, and sputum examinations should be obtained in addition to arterial blood gas measurements in all patients with respiratory failure.

TREATMENT OF RESPIRATORY FAILURE   The treatment of respiratory failure consists of two simultaneous processes: (1) maintaining acceptable levels of oxygenation and ventilation; and (2) treatment of infection, removal of secretions, and reversing any airway constriction present.

With regard to the first, these patients *need* oxygen when they are severely hypoxic, and while fears of respiratory depression due to the removal of the hypoxic respiratory stimulus are realistic, O_2 must be used, yet in the smallest concentration possible, to give a Pa_{O_2} in the mid-50-mmHg range while the patient's Pa_{CO_2}, pH, and clinical status are carefully monitored. It is best to begin with only modest increases in $F_{I_{O_2}}$ to approximately 0.24 (cf. air at 0.21), which can be accomplished using nasal prongs with O_2 flows at 1 to 2 liters per minute or, more precisely, with the use of a 0.24 Venturi mask. These latter masks, based upon Bernoulli's principle, deliver a fixed concentration of O_2 irrespective of the O_2 flow rate by entraining air in direct proportion to O_2 flow rate. They are high-flow masks (oxygen plus air entrained from the room), each designed for a specific $F_{I_{O_2}}$ (0.24, 0.28, 0.35, 0.40). Even small increases in Pa_{O_2} when starting from low levels result in significant increases in arterial oxygen content due to the shape of the oxygen-hemoglobin saturation curve over this range (Chap. 283). With improved oxygenation some patients will concomitantly increase their Pa_{CO_2} values. The standard explanation has been that this increase is due to the removal of the hypoxic drive to ventilation leading to further hypoventilation. While this is the most important mechanism, recent data indicate that worsening ventilation-perfusion relationships (Chap. 200) occur with O_2 treatment. This is attributed to reversal of hypoxic pulmonary arterial constriction in the more initially hypoxic, less well ventilated regions, which in turn leads to decreased perfusion of initially less hypoxic, better ventilated regions. The result is an increase in the wasted ventilation ratio (Vd/Vt, Chap. 200) leading to a smaller effective alveolar ventilation. In either case, the $F_{I_{O_2}}$ should be

increased as little as possible to achieve a Pa_{O_2} in the mid-50-mmHg range. Some increase in Pa_{CO_2} can be expected and should not cause alarm if the patient is alert. The majority of patients can be managed in this conservative way with excellent results. However, occasionally large increases in Pa_{CO_2} occur and lead to stupor and coma. This can be explained by CO_2-induced cerebral vascular dilatation with increased intracranial pressure, including the development of papilledema, combined with the effect of hypercapnia and hypoxia on cerebral function. It must be emphasized that if stupor and coma supervene, stopping the administration of oxygen is the *worst possible* course of action. When CO_2 narcosis is present, respirations are sufficiently depressed from the CO_2 itself so that the patient will no longer respond to the rapidly worsening hypoxia, and fatal arrhythmias, generalized seizures, and death may ensue. The only alternative is to intubate the trachea and provide mechanical ventilatory support. Mechanical ventilators are described in Chap. 216.

Once mechanical ventilation has been instituted, the tidal volume and frequency should be set gradually to decrease the Pa_{CO_2} only down to the chronically elevated level rather than attempt to decrease it to or below a normal value. Since such patients have renal compensation for their chronic hypercapnia, Pa_{CO_2} values at or below the normal level result in significant alkalemia which in turn can lead to severe tachyarrhythmias and generalized seizures.

As mentioned above, maintaining oxygenation and ventilation serves to buy time while secretion removal, bronchial dilatation, and treatment of infection are instituted. Removal of secretions is accomplished by urging the patient to cough or by passing suction catheters into the trachea which, in addition to removing secretions that are present, stimulate cough that brings more secretions up to the region of the catheter tip. The advantage, if any, from the use of mucolytic agents in this process has yet to be demonstrated. However, beta$_2$-adrenergic bronchodilating agents have been shown to increase the rate of transport of particles by the mucociliary blanket, and, thus, in addition to bronchodilatation, such agents should improve the clearance of airway secretions. Postural drainage and chest percussion are other often-used adjuncts that have been shown, especially when secretions are voluminous, to improve tracheobronchial clearance, to increase sputum volume beyond that produced by cough, and to reduce airways obstruction.

Bronchodilatation with aminophylline given orally or by infusion and beta$_2$-adrenergic agonists by inhalation or subcutaneous injection has assumed a prominent role in treatment of acute respiratory failure in chronic airways obstruction. In addition to bronchodilatation these agents improve bronchopulmonary clearance and may help induce diuresis and hemodynamic improvement when there is cor pulmonale with failure (Chap. 191). Unless there is clearly an acute pneumonia, the use of antibiotics is more controversial in the setting of acute respiratory failure than in mucopurulent relapses without failure. Nonetheless, broad-spectrum antibiotics, if no single agent is suspected or isolated, or erythromycin, if legionellae or mycoplasmas are suspected, should be added to the regimen.

Complications arising in the course of treatment for acute respiratory failure are cardiac arrhythmias, most often multifocal supraventricular tachycardias, left ventricular failure, pulmonary emboli, and gastrointestinal hemorrhage from stress ulceration. Cardiac arrhythmias resulting from rapid decreases in oxygenation or increases in pH due to overventilation can be readily avoided. However, when giving multiple drugs having cardiotonic properties, the question always arises as to whether the arrhythmias are related to these. Keeping serum theophylline levels in the 10 to 20 mg per liter range and using relatively selective beta agonists, such as isoetharine by inhalation, can minimize these effects.

Left ventricular failure, usually attributable to coronary atherosclerosis with acute myocardial infarction, systemic hypertension, or aortic valvular disease, is difficult to detect in the presence of cor pulmonale. Fortunately, improving lung function and oxygenation most often reverse the pulmonary hypertension and right ventricular failure (Chap. 191) and induce a brisk diuresis. If signs of congestive failure persist or worsen after providing adequate oxygenation, consideration must be given to left ventricular failure; an assessment in such patients is best made through echocardiography or radioventriculography since the usual physical and radiographic findings are obscured in such patients. Only in the presence of adequate gas exchange and only with either the firm demonstration of, or strong clinical suspicion of, left ventricular failure should digitalis be used. Diuretic agents should also be reserved for left ventricular failure. They almost invariably produce hypokalemic, hypochloremic metabolic alkalemia that results in depression of ventilatory drive and interference with removal from mechanical ventilatory support.

Pulmonary emboli are suspected to be common in the setting of acute respiratory failure and are extremely difficult to detect since the lung scan is totally nonspecific and signs of cor pulmonale fluctuate in concert with the degree of lung dysfunction. Hence low-dose heparin prophylaxis should be used to prevent this complication. Gastrointestinal hemorrhage commonly complicates acute respiratory failure and is thought to be due to stress ulceration of the gastric mucosa. Awareness of this complication enhances the ability to detect it and act quickly. Antacids, nasogastric suction, and/or cimetidine have been used to diminish the frequency.

For those patients who have required mechanical ventilatory support, the process of removal from that support is largely empirical. In general, improving gas exchange and lung mechanics along with alertness and responsiveness of the patient signal that the support can be removed. Data such as maximal voluntary inspiratory mouth pressures greater than 20 cmH_2O, vital capacity greater than 10 mL per kilogram of body weight, and spontaneous tidal volume greater than 5 mL per kilogram of body weight are reassuring. However, many patients can be removed from such support with lesser values than these.

Failure to maintain gas exchange after removal of mechanical ventilatory support can usually be explained. *First* on the list is the continued administration or persistence of sedative and tranquilizing drugs that may have been prescribed earlier for agitation. These should be discontinued and time allowed for their metabolism. *Second* is the possibility that the endotracheal tube is of small bore and imposes a resistive load. If so, it should be replaced by a larger one. *Third* is worsening airways obstruction and accumulation of secretions; continued bronchial dilatation and airway suctioning avoid these. *Fourth* is a metabolic alkalemia, with or without diuretic therapy, that should be treated with potassium chloride. *Fifth* is having maintained a Pa_{O_2} and Pa_{CO_2} while being on mechanical ventilation that are too high and too low, respectively. This can be avoided by using an FI_{O_2} just sufficient to keep the Pa_{O_2} around 60 mmHg and using the assist mode with small enough tidal volumes to keep the Pa_{CO_2} at the expected chronic level (i.e., that associated with a normal or slightly low arterial pH) before discontinuing mechanical support. *Sixth* is poor nutrition, hypokalemia, or neuromuscular disease, making the patient too weak to maintain breathing or resulting in fatigue of the respiratory muscles. Nutrition, of course, is a longer range problem that should be anticipated, while hypokalemia is often handled along with the metabolic alkalemia. Muscle fatigue, especially diaphragmatic, has received a great deal of attention. From a practical standpoint, paradoxical (inward) movement of the upper abdomen with inspiration is the key clinical finding. Experimental evidence suggests that therapeutic levels of aminophylline reverse the manifestations of fatigue but the role of respiratory stimulants continues to be debated and the data to be inconclusive. In those patients with severely blunted ventilatory drive and improving lung function, stimulants may be tried cautiously. If there is severe metabolic alkalemia, acetazolamide can be tried as a stimulant while chloride replacement is being carried out. Medroxyprogesterone, a central stimulant, or almitrine, a peripheral chemoreceptor stimulant, appear to be safe and, in some instances, effective. Hypothyroidism is a metabolic condition with neuromuscular consequences and is difficult to detect in this clinical setting. Thus any prolonged and difficult weaning process should lead to the assessment of thyroid function.

PROGNOSIS   On the average, data collected on large populations demonstrate a slow and relentless diminution in ventilatory function in patients with chronic airways obstruction. Although slow, the decrement in function with time far exceeds the rate of change seen with normal aging. In general, the likelihood of episodes of acute respiratory failure increases when the FEV_1 falls below 25 percent of predicted normal values. Although the in-hospital mortality rate averages 30 percent for a single episode and the 5-year survival rate after the initial episode of respiratory failure averages only 15 to 20 percent, the clinical syndrome is extremely important in determining both the short- and long-range prognosis. As noted above, those patients with predominant emphysema have a poorer prognosis after the onset of respiratory failure than do those with predominant bronchitis. In either case long-term oxygen treatment in those with severe hypoxemia results in prolongation of life and improvement in the quality of life.

BULLOUS EMPHYSEMA   Confluent air spaces with diameters in excess of 1 cm are occasionally congenital but most often are found in association with generalized emphysema or progressive fibrotic processes. Gradual increases in size of such air spaces (or bullae) result from traction applied by regions with better elastic recoil properties, and such regions lose volume as the bullae become enlarged. If disability is severe, if the bulla is extremely large, and if either lobar gas sampling or ventilation and perfusion scans demonstrate that sufficient function remains in the nonbullous regions, surgical excision of the bulla may lead to functional improvement. Usually, however, improvement is relatively transitory because other emphysematous regions gradually enlarge into bullae after surgery.

VARIANTS OF EMPHYSEMA   In addition to the centriacinar and panacinar forms of emphysema described above, other structural patterns have been described but are functionally less important. Often there is overdistention and alveolar septal destruction in lung regions surrounding scar tissue (paracicatricial or scar emphysema) or along the borders of the acinus (paraseptal emphysema). The latter form, when it occurs at the visceral pleural surface, may predispose to episodes of spontaneous pneumothorax (Chap. 214). Infants rarely develop a check valve mechanism in a lobar bronchus which leads to rapid and life-threatening overdistention (congenital lobar emphysema). Unilateral emphysema may be an incidental radiographic finding (Macleod's or Swyer-James's syndromes). Since, in this condition, the airways are normal in number and structure but the alveoli are reduced in number, this form of unilateral emphysema has been attributed to disease occurring before the age of 8 years when alveoli are normally increasing in number. Overdistention and alveolar septal destruction are not present, and so this condition does not fit the definition of true emphysema. Most often the pulmonary artery on the affected side is hypoplastic. Although usually an incidental finding, the affected lung may become repeatedly infected so that surgical excision may be indicated.

MISCELLANEOUS DIFFUSE OBSTRUCTIVE SYNDROMES   *Bronchiolitis obliterans* is a term applied to widespread inflammatory and fibrotic obstruction of small airways. Initially this syndrome was thought to be restricted to those persons who had suffered severe viral infections in childhood, particularly those due to parainfluenza virus. However, recently this syndrome has also been described in adult patients with rheumatoid arthritis. The response to bronchodilator treatment is poor, as would be expected from the histopathologic findings, and fatal respiratory failure often ensues within 2 years. There have been reports suggesting a relationship between penicillamine therapy and the development of bronchiolitis obliterans in patients with rheumatoid arthritis; however, it is clear that this syndrome can develop in patients who have never received penicillamine.

A syndrome with similar histopathology has been described in recipients of autologous bone marrow transplants. Although most often interstitial pneumonitis and fibrosis are sequelae, it has been documented that some patients develop a bronchiolitis obliterans picture. It appears that the development of this process occurs most often in the setting of a chronic graft-versus-host syndrome; however, it is clear that diffuse airways obstruction has developed without evidence of this syndrome in bone marrow recipients.

Lymphangioleiomyomatosis is a rare disease affecting young women. It is characterized by proliferation of smooth muscle in the lymphatics of the abdomen and the thorax. The clinical syndrome is that of an obstructive ventilatory defect in association with disproportionately poor gas exchange and interstitial lung disease by radiography with recurring chylous pleural effusions and/or pneumothoraces. Recent evidence suggests that oophorectomy or progesterone administration halts the progression of this otherwise untreatable disease.

Cystic fibrosis in the adult with chronic airways obstruction is discussed elsewhere (Chap. 207).

REFERENCES

ANTHONISEN NR: Home oxygen therapy, in *Update VI: Principles of Internal Medicine,* RG Petersdorf et al (eds). New York, McGraw-Hill, 1985, p 203

BLOCK ER: Oxygen therapy, in *Update: Pulmonary Diseases and Disorders,* AP Fishman (ed). New York, McGraw-Hill, 1982, p 349

CAMPBELL AH et al: Factors affecting the decline of ventilatory function in chronic bronchitis. Throax 40:741, 1985

CATTERAL JR et al: Mechanism of transient nocturnal hypoxemia in hypoxic chronic bronchitis and emphysema. J Appl Physiol 59:1698, 1985

COHEN AB (ed): Proteases and antiproteases in the lung. Am Rev Resp Dis 127 (Suppl):S1, 1983

CHETTY KG et al: Improved exercise tolerance of the polycythemic lung patient following phlebotomy. Am J Med 74:415, 1983

FISHMAN AP: The spectrum of chronic obstructive disease of the airways, in *Pulmonary Diseases and Disorders,* 2d ed, AP Fishman (ed). New York, McGraw-Hill, 1987, Chap 68

HUGH-JONES P, WAIMSTER W: The etiology and management of disabling emphysema: State of the art. Am Rev Resp Dis 117:343, 1978

LAROS CD et al: Bullectomy for giant bullae in emphysema. J Thorac Cardiovasc Surg 91:63, 1986

PUSA T, TCHERZEWSKI H: Analysis of proteolytic enzymes and their natural inhibitors in serum and bronchial lavage fluid in atopic bronchial asthma, chronic bronchitis and pneumonia. Allerg Immunol 31:169, 1985

THURLBECK WM: A pathologist's approach to clinical bronchitis and emphysema, in *Update: Pulmonary Diseases and Disorders,* AP Fishman (ed). New York, McGraw-Hill, 1982, p 137

209 INTERSTITIAL LUNG DISORDERS

RONALD G. CRYSTAL

The interstitial lung disorders (ILD) are chronic, nonmalignant, noninfectious diseases of the lower respiratory tract characterized by inflammation and derangement of the alveolar walls. The major consequence of ILD is loss of functional alveolar-capillary units and thus a limitation in the transfer of O_2 from air to blood. Affected individuals have dyspnea, particularly with exercise, and are restricted in their activities. If the disease progresses, death usually results from O_2 deprivation of vital organs.

The ILD derive their name from the fact that all are characterized, to a variable extent, by derangements of the alveolar interstitium, the connective tissue matrix that forms the structural backbone of the alveolar walls. Because these derangements usually include the deposition of scar tissue, they are also called the "fibrotic lung diseases." Alternatively, because the widespread inflammation and fibrosis of the alveolar walls are reflected in the chest x-ray as "infiltration" of the lung parenchyma, the ILD are often grouped with the "diffuse infiltrative diseases" of the lung, a term that also includes infectious and neoplastic disorders. Since they are inflammatory disorders of the lower respiratory tract, the interstitial lung diseases are also called the "interstitial pneumonias" or "chronic pneumonitides."

Together, there are approximately 180 different ILD. Conveniently, they are categorized into those of known etiology (Table 209-1) and those of unknown etiology (Table 209-2). Despite this diversity, all are diffuse disorders associated with derangements of the lung parenchyma and loss of functioning alveoli and thus display certain common pathologic, physiologic, and clinical features. This chapter provides an overview of all of the ILD and discusses in detail the ILD of unknown etiology. Information on the specific disorders of known etiology are discussed in the chapters identified in Table 209-1.

NORMAL ANATOMY (See Fig. 209-1) The ILD of unknown etiology are diseases of the lower respiratory tract, structures that include alveoli, terminal bronchioles, alveolar ducts, and the small pulmonary arteries and veins that serve the pulmonary capillaries. Although all of these structures can be involved, it is the loss of functional alveoli that causes the respiratory dysfunction that characterizes these diseases.

The normal adult lung contains 300×10^6 alveoli. Together, they form a beehive-like structure, with each alveolus 200 to 300 μm in diameter, with walls 5- to 10-μm thick. The total surface area of the alveoli is approximately 150 m²; it is through this surface that gas exchange takes place between alveolar air and the approximately 200

TABLE 209-1 Interstitial lung disorders of known etiology

Inhalation of environmental agents (see also Chaps. 203 and 204)
  Inorganic dusts (the "pneumoconioses")
  Organic dusts ("hypersensitivity pneumonitis" or "extrinsic allergic alveolitis")
  Gases
  Fumes
  Vapors
  Aerosols
Drugs (see also Chap. 65)
Secondary to the inflammation associated with lung infections
Radiation
Poisons (see also Chap. 171)
Recovery phase of adult respiratory distress syndrome (see also Chap. 216)

TABLE 209-2 Interstitial lung disorders of unknown etiology

Sarcoidosis (Chap. 270)
Idiopathic pulmonary fibrosis
ILD* associated with the collagen-vascular disorders
  Rheumatoid arthritis (Chap. 263)
  Progressive systemic sclerosis (Chap. 264)
  Systemic lupus erythematosus (Chap. 262)
  Polymyositis-dermatomyositis (Chap. 356)
  Sjögren's syndrome (Chap. 266)
Histiocytosis X
Chronic eosinophilic pneumonia
Idiopathic pulmonary hemosiderosis
Goodpasture's syndrome (Chap. 224)
Hypereosinophilic syndrome
Immunoblastic lymphadenopathy
Undefined lymphocytic infiltrative disorders
  Lymphocytic interstitial pneumonitis
  Pseudolymphoma
Lymphangiomyomatosis
Amyloidosis (Chap. 259)
Alveolar proteinosis
Bronchocentric granulomatosis
Inherited disorders
  Familial pulmonary fibrosis
  Tuberous sclerosis (Chap. 351)
  Neurofibromatosis (Chap. 351)
  Hermansky-Pudlak syndrome
  Niemann-Pick disease (Chap. 316)
  Gaucher's disease (Chap. 316)

ILD associated with liver disease
  Chronic active hepatitis (Chap. 248)
  Primary biliary cirrhosis (Chap. 249)
ILD associated with bowel disease
  Whipple's disease (Chap. 237)
  Ulcerative colitis (Chap. 238)
  Crohn's disease (Chap. 238)
  Weber-Christian disease (Chap. 318)
ILD associated with pulmonary vasculitis
  Wegener's granulomatosis (Chap. 272)
  Lymphomatoid granulomatosis
  Churg-Strauss syndrome (Chap. 269)
  Systemic necrotizing vasculitis (overlap vasculitides) (Chap. 269)
  Hypersensitivity vasculitis (Chap. 269)
ILD associated with chronic cardiac disease
  Left ventricular failure
  Left-to-right shunt
ILD associated with chronic renal disease with uremia
ILD associated with graft-versus-host reaction (Chap. 291)

* *ILD = interstitial lung disease.*

mL of blood present at any one time in the pulmonary capillaries passing through the alveolar walls. In the normal lung, the capillaries are in close proximity to the alveolar air, so the path for gas exchange between air and blood is only 0.6 to 0.8 μm.

The alveolar walls are made up of four basic cell types: the type I and II epithelial cells, endothelial cells, and mesenchymal cells. The type I cells are flat, floppy, ''fried-egg''–shaped cells that cover 95 percent of the alveolar epithelial surface. The type II cells are cuboidal cells responsible for producing surfactant, a lipid-protein aggregate stored in lamellar bodies in the cytoplasm; the surfactant is secreted onto the alveolar surface, where it reduces surface tension and stabilizes air space units. The junctions between the alveolar epithelial cells are tight, providing a barrier that protects the air surface from fluid that might leak from injured pulmonary capillaries. Together, the type I and II cells form a continuous epithelial layer, and both are attached to a continuous basement membrane sheet 0.1 μm thick. The endothelial cells that line the pulmonary capillaries are similar to capillary endothelial cells elsewhere. The endothelial cells also rest on a continuous 0.1-μm basement membrane; at sites where the capillaries and epithelial cells are in close apposition the respective basement membranes fuse. The mesenchymal cells are part of a family of cells that are dominated by fibroblasts, but include myofibroblasts, smooth muscle cells, and pericytes. These cells produce the bulk of the connective tissue matrix of the alveolar walls.

The connective tissue of the alveolar wall is called the ''interstitium'' and is composed of the epithelial and endothelial basement membranes surrounding a connective tissue matrix dominated by type I collagen but including type III collagen, fibronectin, elastic fibers, and proteoglycans. Together, these macromolecules provide the mechanical support that defines the architecture of the alveolar walls and dictate the mechanical properties of the lower respiratory tract.

DISEASE-RELATED CHANGES OF THE LUNG PARENCHYMA (See

Fig. 209-2)   To a variable degree, the morphologic changes of all ILD include an interstitial and/or intraalveolar inflammatory process superimposed upon derangements of the lower respiratory tract that include loss of pulmonary capillaries, alterations of the alveolar

FIGURE 209-1   *Anatomy of the normal lower respiratory tract. A. Schematic low-power view showing a terminal bronchiole opening into the alveoli. B. Schematic high-power view of a cut surface of the alveolar wall. Shown are the flat type I epithelial cells, cuboidal type II epithelial cells, endothelial cells, mesenchymal cells, and interstitial connective tissue.*

epithelial cells, and fibrosis of the alveolar walls. For most ILD, the extent and type of derangements are defined by the character of the injury and the ability, or inability, of the remaining parenchymal cells to reestablish the normal architecture. In some disorders, such as sarcoidosis, where the injury is usually mild, the normal architecture can be completely restored if the disease is suppressed. In contrast, in diseases like idiopathic pulmonary fibrosis, where the injury is more intense, the derangements to the affected alveoli are permanent. If the changes are extensive, the normal architecture is lost, leaving large masses of fibrotic tissue interspersed with cystic air spaces. Such regions of ''end-stage lung'' are not capable of mediating effective gas exchange.

The extent of the epithelial changes depends on the type and severity of the disease. Typically, there are losses in the numbers of type I epithelial cells and replacement with cuboidal epithelial cells, mostly type II cells but also bronchial cells migrating from the terminal brochioles. The loss of capillaries is not accompanied by new capillary growth, and there are changes in the pulmonary arteries secondry to pulmonary hypertension.

The alveolar walls can be thickened several-fold. Depending on the extent of these changes, the consequences include a widening of the distance between the air and blood, a reduction in the amount of air that can be contained in the alveolar air spaces, and an alteration of the mechanical properties of the lung parenchyma. In part, the thickening results from a mild edema of the alveolar walls. Most, however, results from the fibrosis, a process that includes an expansion in the numbers of mesenchymal cells and accumulation of their connective tissue products, particularly type I collagen. In some disorders, the fibrosis is entirely within the alveolar interstitium. In others, breaks in the epithelial basement membrane allow the fibrotic process to expand into the alveolar spaces. Sometimes the mass of this ''intraalveolar fibrosis'' is reincorporated into the alveolar walls, contributing to the thickening of the walls.

PATHOGENESIS   The derangements to the alveoli that characterize most ILD are caused almost entirely by chronic inflammatory processes involving the lower respiratory tract, either exclusively or as part of a more generalized process. In the ILD of known etiology, the chronic inflammation is initiated by the causative agent. In some of these diseases, such as the drug-induced disorders or paraquat poisoning, the causative agent also directly injures the lung parenchyma, usually because it is cytotoxic to the parenchymal cells. For a few of the ILD of unknown etiology, the inflammation plays a minor role and

A

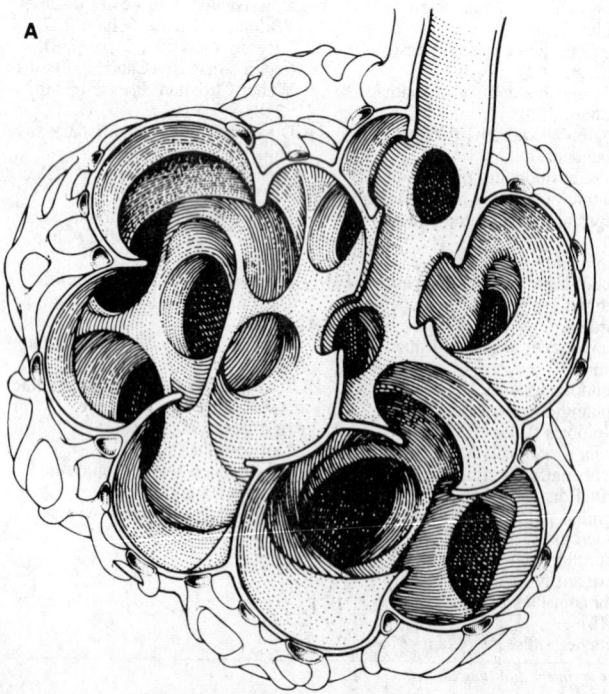

B

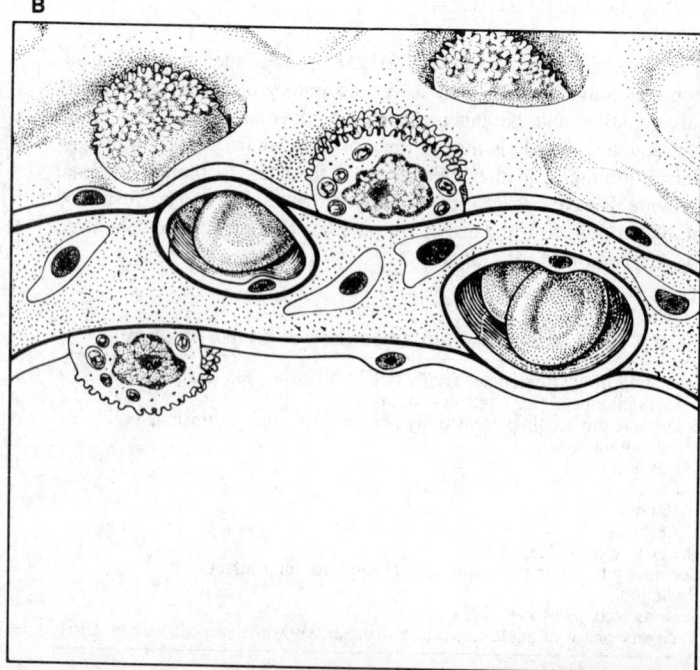

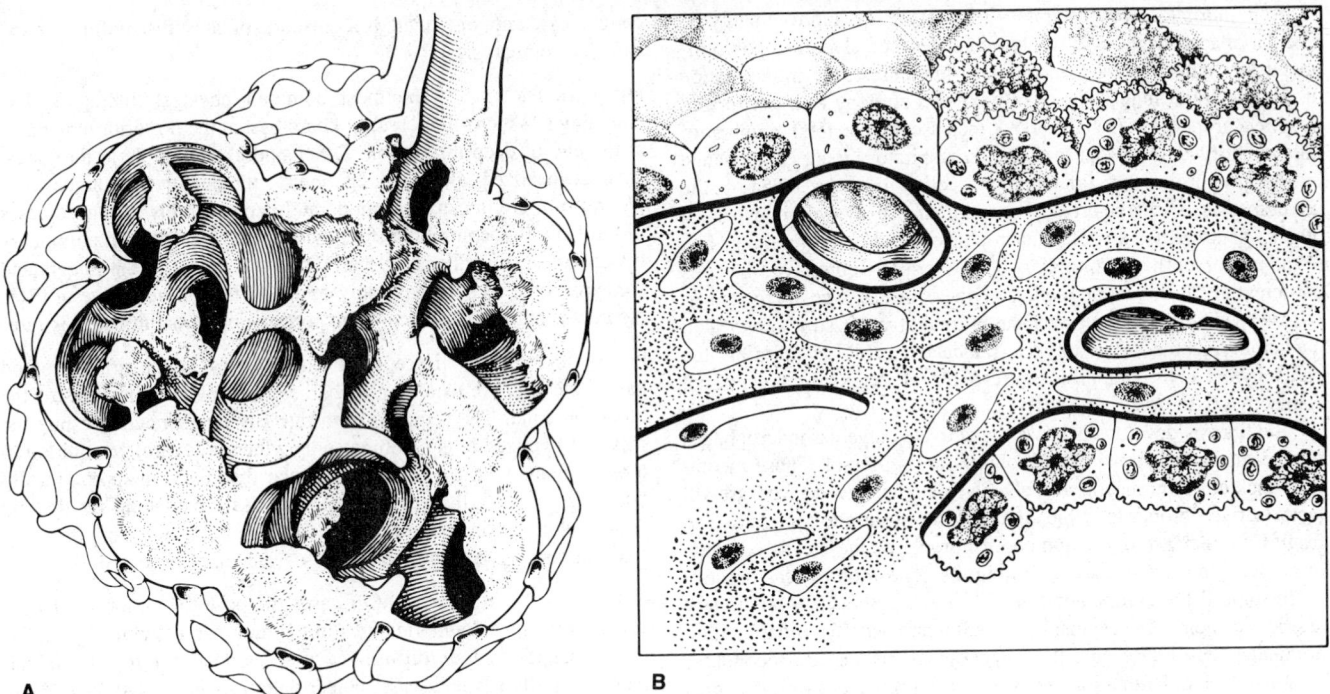

A   **B**

FIGURE 209-2 *Disease-related changes of the lung parenchyma in ILD.*
A. Schematic low-power view showing thickening of the alveolar walls,
intraalveolar fibrosis, and areas where intraalveolar fibrosis has been
incorporated into the alveolar walls. B. Schematic high-power view showing
lost type I epithelial cells replaced by type II epithelial cells (cells with

microvilli) and bronchiolar epithelial cells (smooth cuboidal cells). One
capillary is compromised by the proliferation of fibroblasts and thickening of
the alveolar walls with fibrosis. The basement membranes are thickened, but
at one site the epithelial basement membrane is interrupted, allowing the
interstitial components egress into the alveolar air space.

the derangements of the lung parenchyma result from the abnormal
proliferation of mesenchymal cells (e.g., lymphangioleiomyomatosis)
or the deposition of an extracellular material not normally present in
the lower respiratory tract (e.g., alveolar proteinosis).

 The inflammatory cells derange the alveoli by two general
mechanisms. First, the accumulation of the inflammatory cells in the

confined regions of the alveolar walls distorts the normal architecture,
thus altering the intimate relationship between air and blood. Second,
the inflammatory cells release a battery of mediators that can injure
the parenchymal cells and connective tissue matrix and stimulate
fibroblasts to proliferate, thus promoting the development of fibrosis
(Fig. 209-3).

FIGURE 209-3 *Schematic concept*
of the pathogenesis of idiopathic pul-
monary fibrosis, one of the major ILD
of unknown etiology. Although the
mechanisms shown are specific for
IPF, and not applicable to all ILD,
the concept of local inflammation
causing the derangements and fibro-
sis serves as a paradigm for the
pathogenesis of the ILD. AMDGF =
alveolar macrophage–derived growth
factor.

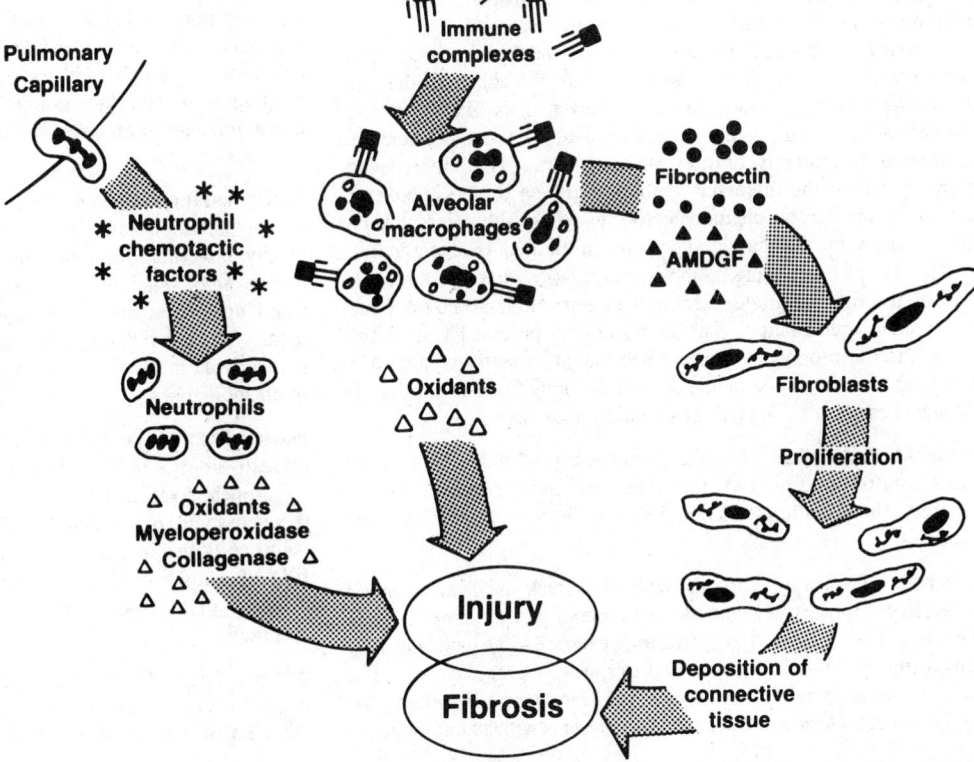

In the normal lower respiratory tract, there are approximately 60 alveolar macrophages and 15 lymphocytes per alveolus; polymorphonuclear leukocytes are uncommon. In contrast, the inflammation of the interstitial lung diseases of unknown etiology is characterized by three properties: (1) a marked increase in the total number of inflammatory cells present in the lower respiratory tract; (2) a change in the proportions of inflammatory cells; in some diseases the inflammation is characterized by a dominance of lymphocytes, in others, neutrophils, alveolar macrophages, and/or eosinophils; and (3) activation of the inflammatory cells. Normally quiescent, the cells participating in the inflammation of these diseases are activated to release mediators that can alter the normal alveolar structures. Such mediators include toxic oxygen radicals capable of injuring the parenchymal cells and proteases capable of deranging the normal connective tissue matrix.

The fibrosis develops because the activated alveolar macrophages release mediators that signal fibroblasts to proliferate. These mediators, including fibronectin and alveolar macrophage–derived growth factor, drive fibroblasts in the damaged interstitium to replicate. The result is an increase in the number of fibroblasts; these cells continue to produce connective tissue, causing the deposition of scar tissue.

In some ILD the inflammation also involves the small pulmonary arteries and veins. Occasionally, the pulmonary vascular inflammation dominates the disease, and the parenchymal changes are secondary. In some, the inflammation includes the terminal bronchioles, thus limiting airflow to the associated alveoli, while in others it includes the visceral pleura, generating a pleuritis and pleural effusion.

PATHOPHYSIOLOGY   The major consequence of the ILD is the inability of the lung to mediate the transfer of the normal amounts of O_2 from air to blood. The hypoxemia occurs by two mechanisms. First, some alveoli have insufficient ventilation to supply the capillary blood with the amount of O_2 necessary to saturate the red blood cells in the local capillaries. Second, there is an increased path for O_2 diffusion due to the thickening of alveolar walls. When this is combined with the fact that because of the loss of capillaries, the output of the right side of the heart can be maintained only by moving the blood through the remaining capillaries more quickly, the time the red blood cells remain in the proximity of the alveolar air is insufficient for the hemoglobin to be saturated with O_2. The hypoxemia resulting from these processes is usually mild at rest, but with exercise the ventilation-perfusion mismatching and diffusion abnormalities worsen and there is a further reduction in the Pa_{O_2}.

In contrast to their effects on O_2 transfer, the derangements in the lower respiratory tract do not usually disturb the ability of the lung to transfer CO_2 from blood to air. However, it is likely that CO_2 transfer is inefficient, and is maintained at the cost of increased ventilation. Despite this, in most patients the Pa_{CO_2} is mildly reduced, probably due to the increased ventilation driven by the hypoxemia sensed by the carotid chemoreceptors together with afferent nerve fibers sensing mechanical derangements in the lung parenchyma.

The loss of functioning pulmonary capillaries increases the workload on the right ventricle, forcing it to generate increased pressure to maintain cardiac output. This compensatory process has its limits; as the disease progresses, the cardiac output cannot increase sufficiently to meet increased demands for total-body O_2 consumption. In advanced cases of ILD, right heart failure may occur.

CLINICAL FEATURES   Despite the diversity of the ILD, they all affect the lower respiratory tract and thus share common clinical features. The specific characteristics of each disorder are discussed separately.

SYMPTOMS   Typically, patients with ILD seek medical attention because of symptoms attributable to an inability of the lungs to meet the demands for increased oxygen during exercise—the patient usually senses this as fatigue, malaise, and dyspnea in everyday activities. Other systemic symptoms, such as fever, anorexia, and weight loss, are infrequent. Occasionally the disease presents with a nonproductive cough; less commonly there is a sensation of chest discomfort, pleural pain, or hemoptysis.

PHYSICAL FINDINGS   The most common physical finding is dry, crackling ("Velcro-like") rales, heard best at the posterior lung bases at the end of deep inspiration. Other findings referable to the lungs, such as localized wheezing, egophony, tubular breath sounds, or a pleural rub, are unusual. In moderately and severely advanced cases of the ILD, it is common to find evidence consistent with pulmonary hypertension (see Chaps. 191 and 210). Clubbing of the fingers and sometimes the toes is commonly observed late in the course of these disorders, but the syndrome of hypertrophic osteoathropathy is rare.

BLOOD AND URINE   Except for the changes in the arterial blood gases, the ILD are usually not characterized by abnormalities of the blood or urine. The sedimentation rate can be elevated. Despite the fact that hypoxemia is common, polycythemia is rare. In addition to those patients with the collagen-vascular disorders, in approximately 5 to 10 percent of all cases of the ILD, the serum contains rheumatoid factor, antinuclear antibodies, and occasionally other autoimmune-like findings. Hyperglobulinemia is occasionally observed.

CHEST X-RAY   In 90 percent of cases the posteroanterior and lateral chest x-rays reveal abnormalities in the lung parenchyma. Typically, these changes include diffuse reticular, nodular, or reticulonodular patterns. Early in the disease, acinar patterns can be observed. These changes are diffuse but in most disorders are most apparent in the lower and midlung zones; occasionally they are localized. Small cystic spaces ("honeycombing") are seen in some disorders and are common features of the late stages of most. Despite these "classic" x-ray features, a normal chest x-ray does not exclude the possibility of significant ILD. Alternatively, an abnormal chest x-ray does not necessarily mean that there is lung dysfunction resulting in abnormalities in gas exchange.

LUNG FUNCTION TESTS   Typically, the ILD are characterized as "restrictive" disorders: there is a reduction in lung volumes (vital capacity, total lung capacity) together with a normal or supranormal ratio of expiratory volume in 1 s to forced vital capacity (FEV_1/ FVC). There is usually a decrease in the diffusing capacity, reflecting a loss of functioning alveolar capillary units. Arterial blood-gas analysis reveals mild hypoxemia which worsens with exercise. The Pa_{CO_2} is mildly reduced and remains so with exercise. The pH is typically normal, but if O_2 delivery is insufficient to meet systemic demands with exercise, the arterial pH drops as metabolic acidosis develops. Although rarely carried out in routine clinical practice, evaluation of static lung compliance shows "stiff" lungs, i.e., high transpulmonary pressures are required to achieve maximum lung volumes.

SCINTIGRAPHIC FINDINGS   The technetium-99m macroaggregated albumin perfusion scan and xenon-133 ventilation scan demonstrate patchy abnormalities reflecting dysfunction of capillary units and narrowing of small airways, respectively. Gallium-67 is not normally taken up by the lung parenchyma, but in circumstances in which there is diffuse inflammation, such as is typically found in the lung parenchyma in the ILD, the gallium-67 lung scan is usually positive in all lung zones.

BRONCHOALVEOLAR LAVAGE   The inflammation that characterizes these disorders is reflected by the types of inflammatory cells recovered by bronchoalveolar lavage. Depending on the disorder, the cells recovered are dominated by alveolar macrophages, lymphocytes, neutrophils, eosinophils, or various mixtures of these cells. In the ILD of known etiology caused by inhalation of inorganic dusts, evidence of the specific dust may frequently be found in the lung washings.

OTHER   The ECG findings are usually nonspecific, but as pulmonary hypertension develops, evidence of right heart abnormalities becomes manifest. It is unusual to perform right heart catheterization in these patients, but the findings typically include pulmonary hypertension, normal wedge pressure, and, late in the disease, a mild elevation of the right ventricular end-diastolic pressure. Despite the fact that there is progressive limitation of available pulmonary capillaries to handle the right ventricular output, frank right ventricular failure is rare.

DIAGNOSTIC EVALUATION   The initial approach includes a history, physical examination, posteroanterior and lateral chest x-rays, and lung function tests, including vital capacity, total lung capacity, diffusing capacity, FEV_1/FVC, and arterial blood gases at rest. Together, the information derived should be sufficient to determine whether a diffuse parenchymal lung disorder is present. The age of the patient plays an important role in considering alternative diagnoses. For example, in the setting of a history of dyspnea and chest x-ray evidence of hilar adenopathy and a reticular nodular infiltrate, a 25-year-old would most likely have sarcoidosis while a 60-year-old is more likely to have a malignant neoplasm. A detailed exposure history with specific reference to inorganic or organic dusts, fumes, gases, aerosols, and drugs may help to identify or eliminate the known causes of ILD. Although routine blood screening occasionally helps to identify systemic disorders, with rare exceptions, blood studies do not help in making a specific diagnosis. The major noninterstitial lung disorders that may be confused with these diseases include congestive heart failure (Chap. 182) and the whole spectrum of malignant (Chap. 213) and infectious disorders of the lung parenchyma (Chaps. 205 and 206). Fiberoptic bronchoscopy is usually carried out to rule out infection and malignancy, and bronchoalveolar lavage helps to characterize the inflammation. Although helpful in judging disease activity, gallium-67 scans usually do not provide useful diagnostic information. For the ILD of known etiology, a lung biopsy is unnecessary if the relationship to the causative agent is "classic." In contrast, with few exceptions (see below), identification of the specific disorders of unknown etiology requires histologic evaluation of the lung parenchyma. If a lung biopsy is to be carried out, with the exception of sarcoidosis in which a transbronchial biopsy is adequate, an open lung biopsy is usually necessary.

Staging   There are two aspects to staging these disorders: staging the extent of the derangements to the lung parenchyma and staging the activity of the disease. The extent of the parenchymal abnormalities is assessed with a combination of history, physical examination, chest x-ray, and routine lung function tests. Since it is the inflammation in the lower respiratory tract that causes these derangements to the lung parenchyma that, in turn, cause the loss of lung function, accurate assessment of disease activity must include an accurate assessment of the inflammation ongoing in the alveolar structures. Chest x-rays and lung function tests do not specifically evaluate the intensity of the inflammation in the lower respiratory tract and hence cannot be used to accurately judge the activity of the disease process. The best method is an open lung biopsy, but this is generally used only once in the course of the disease. Since the inflammation is compartmentalized in the lower respiratory tract, it is not reflected in abnormalities in blood tests. In major centers evaluating these disorders, gallium-67 scans and bronchoalveolar lavage are used to specifically document the extent and character of the inflammation.

THERAPY   The most important therapy for the ILD of known etiology is to remove the individual from exposure to the causative agent. With the exception of the pneumoconioses, which generally are not treated, specific therapy for most of the ILD of known and unknown etiology is directed toward suppressing the inflammatory process in the lower respiratory tract. Typically, oral corticosteroids are used, starting with a high dose (usually 1 mg/kg of prednisone daily) for 4 to 6 weeks and then gradually taping to a low maintenance dose (0.25 mg/kg of prednisone) or, if the disease is suppressed, no therapy. Other anti-inflammatory and anti-immune agents such as cyclophosphamide are used for specific disorders (see below). Nonspecific therapeutic agents such as bronchodilators are used in those disorders accompanied by a component of reversible bronchospasm.

Late in the course of the disease, once the Pa_{O_2} at rest is less than 50 to 55 mmHg, supplemental oxygen is used, first with exercise only and then continuously. Because the hypoxemia results from ventilation-perfusion inequalities and diffusion abnormalities, it is usually possible to reestablish a normal Pa_{O_2}. In most cases O_2 therapy can be given without concern for the complication of CO_2 retention.

Complications   The ILD have a variable course depending on the specific disorder. While some are progressive and invariably fatal, others stabilize, while still others run a fluctuating course. Most complications are related to the inability of the lung to provide sufficient O_2 for systemic demands. As a result, these patients suffer the consequences of O_2 deprivation of vital organs; these consequences include stroke, cardiac arrhythmias, and myocardial infarction. Late in the course of the disease lung infections are common. Despite the fact that most patients are treated with corticosteroids, opportunistic infections are unusual.

INTERSTITIAL LUNG DISORDERS OF KNOWN ETIOLOGY   Overall, the ILD of known etiology represent approximately one-third of all cases of ILD. The most common disorders in this group are those due to inhalation of inorganic dusts, inhalation or organic dusts, or to adverse reactions to pharmacologic agents. All of these disorders are discussed in separate chapters (see Table 209-1).

INTERSTITIAL LUNG DISEASE OF UNKNOWN ETIOLOGY

The ILD of unknown etiology represent two-thirds of all cases of ILD (Table 209-2). The most common disorder in this group, sarcoidosis, is discussed separately (Chap. 270). Among the other frequently encountered ailments are idiopathic pulmonary fibrosis and the ILD associated with the collagen-vascular disorders. Most others are relatively uncommon.

IDIOPATHIC PULMONARY FIBROSIS (IPF)   This is a chronic, usually progressive disorder affecting only the lower respiratory tract. It is the "classic" interstitial lung disease of unknown etiology, with clinical features representative of this group of diseases. It was previously referred to as the "Hamman-Rich syndrome" and in the pathology literature as "desquamative interstitial pneumonitis" (early IPF) and "usual interstitial pneumonitis" (late IPF); in the British literature it is called "cryptogenic fibrosing alveolitis."

The derangements to the lung parenchyma in IPF result from a chronic inflammatory process initiated by immune complexes produced within the lower respiratory tract (Fig. 209-3). The immune complexes are directed against unknown antigens, likely components of the lung parenchyma. The inflammatory process is initiated by the immune complexes interacting with Fc receptors on alveolar macrophages; consequently the alveolar macrophages release mediators that amplify the inflammation, injure lung parenchymal cells, and stimulate fibroblasts to proliferate. Among these mediators are chemotactic factors, including leukotriene B4, that recruit neutrophils, and to a lesser extent, monocytes and eosinophils. Together with the recruited neutrophils and eosinophils, the activated macrophages release oxidants such as superoxide and hydrogen peroxide that injure the normal lung parenchymal cells. The neutrophils release type I collagenase, an enzyme that modifies the major connective tissue component of the alveolar walls, and myeloperoxidase, an enzyme that catalyzes the conversion of hydrogen peroxide to the hypohalide radical, an oxidant very toxic to the lung parenchymal cells. Among the alveolar macrophage mediators released in increased amounts in IPF are fibronectin and alveolar macrophage–derived growth factor, growth factors that together are sufficient to stimulate fibroblasts to proliferate, thus causing an expansion of numbers of fibroblasts in the alveolar walls, resulting in fibrosis. In some alveoli, the inflammation induces breaks in the epithelial basement membranes, allowing the interstital components to protrude into the alveolar air spaces, causing intraalveolar fibrosis.

The *clinical findings* of IPF are those typical for ILD (see above). Males and females are affected equally. IPF most commonly develops in middle age but the disorder can occur in any age group. There is no history of exposure to the known causes of ILD. The chest x-ray, lung function tests, and blood findings are typical for diseases in this category. When the disease is active, the gallium-67 scan is moderately positive and bronchoalveolar lavage usually shows a dominance of alveolar macrophages and, to a lesser extent, neutrophils. Rarely, eosinophils and lymphocytes are major components of the inflammation.

The *diagnosis* of IPF requires an open lung biopsy. The morphology shows diffuse changes typical of ILD (Fig. 209-1) with a superimposed mononuclear phagocyte-neutrophil inflammatory process interspersed with lymphocytes and some eosinophils.

IPF is usually fatal 4 to 5 years after the onset of symptoms despite therapy. Approximately 10 percent die of bronchogenic carcinoma. Therapy for the ILD is directed toward suppressing the alveolitis. Corticosteroids are usually used, but a persistent neutrophil component of the inflammation can be suppressed by cyclophosphamide. Occasionally low-dose oral corticosteroids are supplemented with large doses of intravenous corticosteroids administered weekly.

ILD ASSOCIATED WITH DISORDERS OF IMMUNE-MEDIATED INJURY (COLLAGEN-VASCULAR DISORDERS) In most cases of ILD in association with the collagen-vascular disorders, the collagen-vascular disease is generally evident before the ILD becomes manifest. The ILD associated with the collagen-vascular disorders are usually mild and of little functional significance, but they can become the dominant feature of the disease and can be fatal. The pathogenesis of the ILD is assumed to be part of the systemic process, but the mechanisms causing the specific lung abnormalities are unknown.

The clinical features of these disorders are generally similar to a mild form of IPF in the presence of a systemic collagen-vascular disorder; occasionally other features dominate the clinical picture (see below). The diagnosis is made with the clinical, x-ray, and physiologic evidence of ILD in the presence of a diagnosis of a specific collagen-vascular disorder. Lung biopsy is usually not needed, but if the presentation is unusual, or if the ILD is clearly progressive, an open lung biopsy is often performed to confirm the diagnosis and help in making therapeutic decisions. Bronchoalveolar lavage analysis of inflammatory cells generally is dominated by macrophages, often with a mild neutrophil component, but occasionally lymphocytes are increased in numbers. The gallium-67 scan is usually mildly positive.

If the disease is mild, no therapy is used. If the ILD is progressive, corticosteroids are administered. There is no evidence that any other agents are effective, although there are anecdotal reports of cytotoxic drugs being used.

Rheumatoid arthritis (see Chap. 263) Lung function abnormalities are observed in about 50 percent of patients with rheumatoid arthritis, and 25 percent have x-ray evidence of ILD. The pulmonary abnormalities associated with rheumatoid arthritis are usually similar to IPF. Less commonly, the disease manifests as rheumatoid nodules in the lung parenchyma, pulmonary arterial arteritis with hypertension and secondary interstitial changes, or an acute, patchy inflammation associated with pleuritis and pericarditis. Coal workers with rheumatoid arthritis have an increased incidence of an interstitial lung disease referred to as "rheumatoid pneumoconiosis" or "Caplan's syndrome." In addition to the parenchymal disease, individuals with rheumatoid arthritis commonly develop pleural effusion, thickening, and adhesions. Rarely, rheumatoid arthritis is associated with a marked obstructive functional pattern along with inflammation, fibrosis, and obliteration of small airways, a condition termed *bronchiolitis obliterans*.

Progressive systemic sclerosis (see Chap. 264) Of individuals with progressive systemic sclerosis 30 to 50 percent have some form of ILD. Most commonly, the pulmonary disease is like IPF, but with less intense inflammation. Unique among the sufferers of ILD, these patients have an increased incidence of bronchoalveolar cell carcinoma. Alternatively, the ILD may be secondary to pulmonary arterial disease. If the diagnosis of ILD associated with progressive systemic sclerosis is considered, attention should be paid to the fact that these patients commonly have esophageal problems and therefore can have chronic aspiration. They also frequently develop cardiac disease, sometimes with left ventricular failure. Both of these entities may be mistaken for ILD. In rare cases, scleroderma of the chest wall restricts respiration, mimicking the functional abnormalities of ILD.

Systemic lupus erythematosus (see Chap. 262) ILD is less common in SLE than in the other collagen-vascular disorders. The pulmonary disease can be like IPF, but more commonly is an acute inflammatory process causing patchy infiltrates on the x-ray, sometimes with atelectasis. In the acute disease, concomitant parenchymal lung infections are common as are pleuritis and pleural effusion. Rarely, patients with lupus develop a lymphocytic infiltrative disease, small vessel pulmonary vasculitis, or a disorder similar to idiopathic pulmonary hemosiderosis.

Polymyositis-dermatomyositis (see Chap. 356) ILD is uncommon in this disorder, but when it occurs, it can precede the systemic disease. The ILD is usually like IPF. Since polymyositis can affect the muscles of respiration, the contribution of the ILD is sometimes difficult to separate from the functional abnormalities caused by the loss of intercostal muscle and diaphragm function.

Sjögren's syndrome (see Chap. 266) Patients with Sjögren's syndrome commonly develop a dry cough, usually due to the decreased secretions and resulting mucosal irritation in the airways. ILD is relatively uncommon; when it occurs, it is similar to IPF or characterized by a diffuse lymphocytic infiltrate.

Histiocytosis X This is a disorder of the mononuclear phagocyte system characterized by the accumulation of mononuclear phagocytes (described in the morphologic literature as "tissue histiocytes") in various organs. In the pediatric age group it usually manifests itself as Letterer-Siwe disease and Hand-Shüller-Christian disease. In adults it is usually an ILD referred to as histiocytosis X or eosinophilic granuloma.

The adult disease is characterized by a mixture of fibrotic and destructive changes in the lung parenchyma. The fibrotic changes are typical for ILD and the destruction is characterized by small cystic spaces. There is a focal but massive accumulation of mononuclear phagocytes in the lung parenchyma, often centered about terminal bronchioles. The mononuclear phagocytes are a mixture of alveolar macrophages and Langerhans cells (also called *HX cells*); the HX cell is normally present in skin but rarely in the lung parenchyma. It is characterized by a surface antigen identified by the OKT6 monoclonal antibody and 40- to 45-nm wide pentalamellar cytoplasmic inclusions called X bodies. Although they are known to be a derivative of the mononuclear phagocyte system, it is not known why HX cells accumulate in the lung in this disease or how they contribute to the derangements of the lung parenchyma.

Histiocytosis X usually develops in individuals 20 to 40 years of age. More than 90 percent are former current cigarrette smokers, but the relationship of smoking to the pathogenesis of the disease is unknown. The disease often presents insidiously with a nonproductive cough, dyspnea, and chest pain. Spontaneous pneumothorax occurs in 10 percent of cases and a small portion of individuals develop diabetes insipidus, bone involvement, and/or skin lesions.

The x-ray has a characteristic appearance with a reticulonodular infiltrate with superimposed small cystic spaces in the mid and upper lung zones. Lung function testing reveals a mixed restrictive-obstructive pattern with a decreased diffusing capacity and mild hypoxemia that worsens with exercise. Bronchoalveolar lavage reveals large numbers of mononuclear phagocytes including OKT6-positive HX cells. The gallium-67 scan is usually negative. There is no known treatment. Most individuals stabilize with some lung dysfunction, but the disease can be progressive and fatal.

Chronic eosinophilic pneumonia This disorder is characterized by fever, chills, weight loss, malaise, fatigue, dyspnea, and cough. Unlike most patients with ILD, many have chronic asthma. Females are affected more commonly than males. There is usually a blood eosinophilia and increased levels of immunoglobulins, particularly IgG. The x-ray shows patchy, nonsegmental infiltrates that are poorly defined and typically spare the central lung zones. A lung biopsy shows an eosinophilic inflammatory process in the lower respiratory tract, together with macrophages, lymphocytes, and neutrophils. There can be eosinophilic abscesses, a mild vasculitis, and occasional granulomas. The derangements to the lung parenchyma are usually mild but can be severe and progressive. Therapy with corticosteroids generally results in dramatic resolution, but the disorder often recurs spontaneously.

Hypereosinophilic syndrome This is a poorly understood disorder characterized by a persistent marrow and blood eosinophilia with eosinophilic infiltration of various organs, particularly the heart. A mild ILD occurs in about 20 to 40 percent of patients but is usually not a prominent feature of the disease. The disease has a variable course; therapy is usually with corticosteroids and/or hydroxyurea.

Idiopathic pulmonary hemosiderosis This ILD is characterized by recurrent pulmonary hemorrhage, dyspnea, and iron-deficiency anemia. It usually begins in childhood, but can occur in adults. The recurrent pulmonary hemorrhage may be life-threatening. The pathogenesis of the disease is unknown. There is usually a mild to moderate interstitial disease than can be progressive. The inflammation is dominated by alveolar macrophages containing deposits of hemosiderin, the normal epithelial cells are replaced by cuboidal cells, and a variable degree of fibrosis is seen. The lung function abnormalities are typical for an ILD, but the diffusing capacity can be falsely elevated secondary to the carbon monoxide test gas "artifactually" interacting with hemoglobin deposited in the lung parenchyma. The x-ray shows transient, patchy infiltrates that clear in a few weeks. Diagnosis of this disorder requires an open lung biopsy. Idiopathic pulmonary hemosiderosis is not associated with kidney disease or anti-basement membrane antibodies, thus differentiating it from Goodpasture's syndrome. Treatment includes iron for the anemia and corticosteroids for the lung disease, although there is no evidence that the latter alters the course of the disorder. The disease is often progressive and fatal but can stabilize.

Goodpasture's syndrome Patients with this disorder present with relapsing pulmonary hemorrhage, anemia, and renal disease (see Chap. 224). Adult males are most commonly affected. Renal failure is common and there are circulating antibodies that cross-react with glomerular and alveolar basement membranes. The kidneys show focal or diffuse proliferative or necrotizing glomerulonephritis. The lung disease is identical to idiopathic pulmonary hemosiderosis. While the lung hemorrhage can be life-threatening, the ILD is usually mild. Diagnosis is usually made by demonstrating circulating anti-basement membrane antibodies together with a renal biopsy showing the characteristic pattern of immunoglobulin staining; these findings differentiate this disorder from idiopathic pulmonary hemosiderosis, uremic pneumonitis, Wegener's granulomatosis, and systemic lupus erythematosus. Therapy is usually corticosteroids and cyclophosphamide, often combined with plasmapheresis to remove the circulating antibodies.

Immunoblastic lymphadenopathy Also called angioimmunoblastic lymphadenopathy, this is a disease of older individuals characterized by fever, malaise, generalized lymphadenopathy, hemolytic anemia, and, in some individuals, ILD. It is thought to be a disorder of the control of B lymphocytes. There is usually a polyclonal increase in immunoglobulins. Biopsy of lymph nodes shows a replacement of the normal architecture by pleomorphic lymphocytes in various stages

of differentiation. Hilar and mediastinal lymph nodes are usually increased in size, and the lung parenchyma shows an accumulation of interstitial and intraalveolar lymphocytes, a deposition of intraalveolar eosinophilic material, and mild to moderate changes typical of ILD. Despite therapy with corticosteroids and cytotoxic drugs, most patients die within 1 year, often from lung infections or the development of a T-lymphocyte malignancy.

Lymphocytic infiltrative diseases These are poorly understood and inadequately classified ILD characterized by the accumulation of lymphocytes in the lung parenchyma, often in association with dysproteinemias and the eventual development of lymphoid malignancy. *Lymphocytic interstitial pneumonitis* is a term used to characterize patients with ILD showing a diffuse accumulation of mature lymphocytes in the alveolar walls and airspaces. There is often a coexisting systemic autoimmune disorder such as Sjögren's disease (Chap. 266). Occasionally there is a history of phenytoin usage. If the lymphocytes form germinal centers in the lung parenchyma, the disease is referred to as *pseudolymphoma*. The ILD may be mild but can progress and be fatal. Alternatively, the disease can develop into a lymphocytic malignancy. Therapy is usually with corticosteroids and/or cytotoxic agents.

Lymphangioleiomyomatosis This unusual disorder is found almost exclusively in women of childbearing age. It presents with progressive dyspnea, unilateral or bilateral chylous pleural effusions, pneumothoraxes, and occasional hemoptysis. The lung parenchyma shows an accumulation of smooth muscle cells in the alveolar walls and around bronchioles and venules. Thoracic and abdominal lymphatics and lymph nodes are frequently involved. In addition to the thickening of the alveolar walls, there is some lung destruction. There is a mild inflammation of the lung parenchyma dominated by macrophages. The chest x-ray shows a diffuse reticulonodular infiltrate intermixed with cystic spaces. Lung function testing usually reveals normal total lung capacity, reduced diffusing capacity, and limitation of airflow. Diagnosis requires an open-lung biopsy. There is no proven therapy, but, because the disease occurs in women 20 to 40 years of age, hormonal manipulation with progesterone or oophorectomy has been tried. Surgical intervention is occasionally used for the chylous effusions, but can result in a shifting of the effusion to other spaces. Death is invariable within 10 years of onset.

Amyloidosis (see Chap. 259) Although uncommon, amyloidosis can involve the lung parenchyma and/or airways diffusely or in a nodular fashion. When it occurs, it is usually associated with systemic primary amyloid or multiple myeloma and/or less frequently with secondary amyloid. Diagnosis is made by open-lung biopsy demonstrating deposits of amyloid in the alveolar walls, pulmonary vasculature, and/or airways. There is mild parenchymal inflammation dominated by macrophages. The clinical picture depends on the site of amyloid deposition; nodules are usually asymptomatic, airway deposition causes airflow obstruction, and parenchymal amyloid presents as typical ILD. There is no specific therapy available for the ILD.

Alveolar proteinosis This disorder is more properly conceptualized as an intraalveolar disorder rather than an ILD. It is rare, affects mostly males, and is characterized by diffuse filling of the air spaces with granular eosinophilic PAS-positive protein-lipid material. This intraalveolar material includes lamellated concentric structures similar to the cytoplasmic structures in type II epithelial cells. There is mild inflammation with changes in the alveolar epithelial cells typical of the ILD. There is dyspnea, cough, some sputum production, weight loss, and occasional fever. The chest x-ray shows diffuse, fine nodular infiltrates and can be confused with pulmonary edema. Lung function tests reveal decreased lung volumes associated with moderate to severe hypoxemia usually due to a large right-to-left shunt. Although lipid-laden macrophages recovered by bronchoalveolar lavage may suggest this disorder, diagnosis requires a lung biopsy. Although the disease is recurrent and can be life-threatening, the material can be removed from the lungs with whole-lung lavage under general anesthesia with temporary, and sometimes permanent, improvement in lung function. The pathogenesis of alveolar proteinosis is unknown, but since the intraalveolar material resembles the lipid componenet of surfactant, dysfunction of type II cells has been suggested. Rare cases are associated with massive silica exposure or with lung infections.

Bronchocentric granulomatosis   This disorder is characterized by masses of granulomas centered in the walls of airways and the surrounding tissues, including pulmonary arteries. There is destruction of the bronchiolar walls, and, like the vasculitides involving the lung, there are varying degrees of parenchymal inflammation and derangement typical of the ILD. The disease was originally defined by morphologic criteria without regard for the associated specific clinical features, and it likely represents several different diseases, including a hypersensitivity-type disorder in response to fungi such as aspergilli. Treatment is usually with corticosteroids, but their efficacy and the natural history of this disorder have not been well defined.

Inherited disorders   In addition to family clusters of sarcoidosis, there are some rare inherited disorders associated with ILD. Except for familial IPF, the pathogenesis of the lung derangements have not been defined, and there are no guidelines for their specific management.

FAMILIAL IPF   This autosomal dominant disorder with incomplete penetrance is identical to IPF. The ILD with lung function abnormalities usually manifests itself in the fourth to fifth decades, but younger family members have been identified with evidence of alveolar inflammation but without derangements to the lower respiratory tract, supporting the concept that chronic inflammation plays a critical precursor role in the pathogenesis of the ILD.

TUBEROUS SCLEROSIS (see Chap. 351)   This autosomal dominant disorder with incomplete penetrance is characterized by mental retardation, seizures, adenoma sebaceum, and proliferation of smooth muscle in various tissues including the lung parenchyma. The ILD is similar to lymphangioleiomyomatosis, but chylous effusions are rare.

NEUROFIBROMATOSIS (see Chap. 351)   ILD, often in association with some lung destruction, occurs in 10 to 20 percent of patients with this autosomal dominant disorder characterized by skin and nervous system neurofibromas and cutaneous café au lait spots. There are no neurofibromas in the lung, and the pathogenesis of the ILD is unknown.

HERMANSKY-PUDLAK SYNDROME   This is an autosomal recessive disorder manifesting as oculocutaneous albinism, platelet dysfunction, and the accumulation of a ceroid-like material in various organs including the lung parenchyma. The ILD is a prominent feature of the disease. It usually develops in the third to fourth decades.

NIEMANN-PICK DISEASE (see Chap. 316)   This is an autosomal recessive storage disorder characterized by the accumulation of sphingomyelin in tissue. Although hepatosplenomegaly and central nervous system abnormalities dominate the clinical picture, ILD can be prominent, particularly in type B disease.

GAUCHER'S DISEASE (see Chap. 316)   This is an autosomal recessive disorder associated with an accumulation of glucosylceramide in various tissues. The disease manifests primarily as hepatosplenomegaly and erosion of bones, but ILD can occur and cause respiratory failure.

ILD associated with liver disease   Patients with chronic active hepatitis can have an IPF-like syndrome with systemic autoimmune features suggesting an overlap with the collagen-vascular disorders. Primary biliary cirrhosis also occurs in conjunction with ILD; the lung disease is usually like sarcidosis, but a disorder similar to IPF is occasionally seen.

ILD associated with bowel disease   Whipple's disease (Chap. 237) is classically localized to the small intestine, but similar abnormalities can occur in other organs, including the lower respiratory tract, causing a mild form of ILD. Ulcerative colitis can be associated with a disorder like IPF, and Crohn's disease with a disorder like sarcoidosis. A systemic form of the relapsing panniculitis of Weber-Christian disease (Chap. 318) can involve the lung parenchyma; there are fat globules, necrosis, and changes typical of ILD.

ILD associated with pulmonary vasculitis   Except for polyarteritis nodosa, most of the systemic vasculitides can involve the pulmonary arteries and/or veins. ILD usually plays an important role in the clinical picture of Wegener's granulomatosis, lymphomatoid granulomatosis, and the Churg-Strauss syndrome, but the inflammation and derangements in the alveolar structures are thought to be secondary to the primary vascular disease. The ILD associated with the pulmonary vasculitides are managed like the primary disorders.

ILD associated with chronic cardiac disease or chronic renal disease   Prior to cardiac surgery for congenital cardiac lesions, mitral or aortic valvular disease and high-flow left-to-right shunts were occasionally associated with chronic ILD. Likewise, prior to widespread use of dialysis, chronic uremia was associated with a variety of derangements of the lower respiratory tract. Both categories of disease are rarely seen today.

ILD associated with graft-versus-host reaction   One of the adverse reactions to bone marrow transplantation (Chap. 291) is a graft-versus-host syndrome with airway inflammation and injury, sometimes in association with ILD. Treatment is directed toward suppression of the immune reaction. Care must be taken to exclude infectious complications, which are frequently seen in immunosuppressed transplant recipients.

REFERENCES

CRYSTAL RG et al: Interstitial lung disease of unknown etiology: Disorders characterized by chronic inflammation of the lower respiratory tract. N Engl J Med 310:154, 235, 1984

——— et al: Interstitial lung disease: Current concepts of pathogenesis, staging, and therapy. Am J Med 70:542, 1981

DAVIS WB, CRYSTAL RG: Chronic interstitial lung disease, in *Current Pulmonology*, D Simmons, (ed). New York; Wiley, 1984, vol V, pp 347–473

FISHMAN AP: *Pulmonary Diseases and Disorders* 2d ed. New York, McGraw-Hill, 1987

FRASER RG, PARE JAP: *Diagnosis of Diseases of the Chest*. Philadelphia, Saunders, 1978

KATZENSTEIN A-L A, ASKIN FB: *Surgical Pathology of Non-neoplastic Lung Disease*, Philadelphia, Saunders, 1982

210   PRIMARY PULMONARY HYPERTENSION

JOHN ROSS, JR.

Primary (or idiopathic) pulmonary hypertension is an uncommon disease, the diagnosis of which can be established only after a thorough search for the usual causes of pulmonary hypertension. The patient with primary pulmonary hypertension typically is a young female between the ages of 20 and 40, although older and younger patients of either sex have been described. The clinical and laboratory features of severe pulmonary hypertension are present, but there is no evidence of parenchymal pulmonary disease or of primary heart disease, nor is there evidence for the occurrence of pulmonary emboli. Anatomic verification often has been necessary to distinguish clearly the primary form of pulmonary hypertension from that due to multiple pulmonary emboli, although angiography and radioisotope scanning methods have facilitated this differentiation considerably.

PATHOLOGY The findings on pathologic examination of patients with primary pulmonary hypertension usually are confined to the right side of the heart and lungs. The right atrium often is enlarged and the right ventricle is hypertrophied. Frequently, the large pulmonary arteries exhibit atherosclerotic plaques. The disease process involves the small pulmonary arteries (between 40 and 300 μm in diameter), which exhibit muscular hypertrophy and intimal hyperplasia, sometimes with fibrosis. On occasion, a necrotizing arteritis may be encountered. Other histologic studies have shown a reduced number of small arteries, as well as fewer capillaries in the alveolar wall. Electron-microscopic studies have documented an increase in thickness of the endothelial cells and basement membranes of alveolar capillaries, and some capillaries are blocked by the abnormal epithelial cells. Medial hypertrophy of muscular pulmonary arteries may be the first response to prolonged pulmonary vasoconstriction, but in later stages of the disease concentric laminar intimal fibrosis and plexiform lesions appearing as cellular, intraluminal tufts (so-called plexogenic pulmonary arteriopathy) may develop. Patients with recurrent pulmonary thromboembolism may clinically resemble patients with primary pulmonary hypertension, but histologic sections of the lung exhibit various degrees of organization of pulmonary thromboemboli; some may be recanalized, there may be fibrous septa and eccentric fibrosis in the vessels; secondary medial hypertrophy of muscular arteries may be marked, but plexiform lesions are not present. In infants and young children with pulmonary venoocclusive disease the clinical picture may suggest primary pulmonary hypertension, and the pulmonary wedge pressure may be normal. Organized thrombotic disease is found in the venules and small veins, together with proximal hypertrophy of the muscular venous wall and secondary medial hypertrophy in the pulmonary arterioles.

Rarely, disease of the systemic arterial vascular bed resembling that found in the pulmonary blood vessels has been described. The syncope and sudden death which may occur in this disease have been attributed in some patients to involvement of the coronary arterial branch supplying the sinoatrial node.

ETIOLOGY The cause of primary pulmonary hypertension is unknown, but a number of possible etiologic factors have been suggested. A few patients with primary pulmonary hypertension have been reported in whom minimal changes were found in the pulmonary vessels on pathologic examination, and this observation has raised the possibility that a neurohumoral vasoconstrictor mechanism is involved. Support for this view has been provided by the observation that the pulmonary vascular resistance can be acutely reduced in some patients with this disease by the infusion of vasodilators, or by administering oxygen. A febrile illness may precede the onset of the disease by a variable period and has been implicated in the etiology. In 15 to 20 percent of female patients with this disorder, symptoms begin soon after pregnancy, which has prompted the suggestion that unrecognized thromboemboli or amniotic fluid emboli during pregnancy may play a role. In other patients, it seems quite possible that the disease may represent an end stage of earlier, unrecognized emboli originating from the legs or pelvic veins. An apparent association between an increased occurrence of primary pulmonary hypertension and use of the anorectic agent aminorex fumarate, a drug having structural similarity to ephedrine, was observed in Europe between 1967 and 1970. The alkaloids in many species of crotalaria plants used in herbal brews may cause pulmonary hypertension in human beings, as demonstrated experimentally in rats. The use of oral contraceptives may bear a relation to the occurrence of pulmonary hypertension, particularly in patients with predisposing factors such as systemic lupus erythematosus or a family history of primary pulmonary hypertension.

Raynaud's phenomenon precedes the onset of primary pulmonary hypertensive disease by a number of years in an appreciable number of patients. This association and the occurrence of Raynaud's disease in scleroderma, disseminated lupus erythematosus, rheumatoid arthritis, and dermatomyositis have led to the speculation that primary pulmonary hypertension may represent a form of collagen vascular disease. Moreover, primary pulmonary hypertension and collagen vascular disease, including lupus erythematosus, have been reported to occur simultaneously in a number of patients. It also has been suggested that the disease may be congenital and present from birth; however, the closely packed, parallel elastic fibers in the main pulmonary arteries in patients having Eisenmenger's syndrome from birth, described by some investigators, usually have not been observed in patients with primary pulmonary hypertension. Finally, primary pulmonary hypertension has been reported in a number of families; sometimes more than two members and up to three generations have been affected. A fibrinolytic defect was reported in one family study.

PATHOPHYSIOLOGY Some studies have suggested that the response of the pulmonary vascular bed is labile early in the course of this disease, as evidenced by a response to vasodilating agents and oxygen. It also has been proposed that the disease tends to progress. Thus, serial cardiac catheterizations have shown a tendency for the pulmonary vascular resistance to increase and to become fixed. With the development of severe pulmonary vascular disease, abnormal elevation of the pulmonary arterial pressure occurs, often to a striking degree, and the pulmonary arterial pressure may be equal to that in the systemic arterial bed. The pulmonary arterial wedge pressure is normal in patients with primary pulmonary hypertension, the cardiac output is normal or reduced, and no intracardiac shunts are detected. In many patients the mean right atrial pressure is elevated, and the *a* wave in the right atrium may be markedly elevated, an indication of the forceful atrial contraction necessary to fill the hypertrophied right ventricle. With the long-standing overload on the right side of the heart, right ventricular failure finally develops. In some patients, peripheral cyanosis occurs secondary to reduced cardiac output, and occasionally central cyanosis becomes evident at the end stage of the disease because of right-to-left shunting through a patent foramen ovale. Mild systemic arterial desaturation is quite common, even in the absence of heart failure, and may be due to shunting within the lungs. Pulmonary function in patients with primary pulmonary hypertension generally is normal, although hyperventilation often is present, resulting in hypocapnia and a decreased serum bicarbonate concentration. A low carbon monoxide–diffusing capacity has been described in some patients.

CLINICAL PICTURE The patient, usually a young female, gives a history of relatively recent onset of symptoms. Ordinarily, the natural course of the disease encompasses less than 5 years, but occasionally survival for 25 years or more has been reported. In one large retrospective study, the median time from initial symptoms to diagnosis was about 2 years, and that from diagnosis to death was about 2 years, with over 75 percent of deaths occurring within 5 years after diagnosis. Not uncommonly, patients with primary pulmonary hypertension are classified as neurotic early in the course of their disease because of the hyperventilation, chest discomfort, and the relative paucity of objective findings. Precordial pain on exertion occurs in from 25 to 50 percent of patients, and occasionally severe chest pain has been associated with a dissection of the main pulmonary artery. Other common symptoms are weakness, fatigue, exertional dyspnea, and effort syncope, which usually results from peripheral vasodilatation in the presence of a fixed cardiac output. Hoarseness may be noted because of compression of the left recurrent laryngeal nerve by the enlarged pulmonary artery. Unexplained sudden death occurs relatively often. Sudden death also has occurred during cardiac catheterization or surgical procedures and after the administration of barbiturates or anesthetic agents. The terminal course usually is characterized by right-sided heart failure. Very rarely, spontaneous regression of the disease has been reported.

On physical examination, the jugular venous pulse usually shows a prominent *a* wave, there is a right ventricular heave, and an impulse may be felt over the region of the main pulmonary artery. An ejection click may be audible at the pulmonic area, the second heart sound is narrowly split, and the pulmonic closure sound is markedly accentuated and may be palpable. Often, an atrial gallop sound is heard at the lower left sternal border, and in some patients there is an ejection murmur at the pulmonic area or the early diastolic murmur of pulmonic regurgitation. The chest roentgenogram may show cardiac enlargement with right ventricular and right atrial prominence, and there is marked dilatation of the pulmonary artery segment. Peripherally, the pulmonary arteries taper sharply, and the lung fields may appear oligemic. The electrocardiogram almost always shows some evidence of right ventricular enlargement, with right axis deviation, right ventricular hypertrophy in the precordial leads, and sometimes inverted T waves over the right precordium. Right atrial enlargement also may be evident on the electrocardiogram. Echocardiography is useful for identifying right ventricular enlargement, and in pulmonary hypertension the pulmonic valve usually shows attenuation or absence of the *a* dip and midsystolic notching.

DIFFERENTIAL DIAGNOSIS It is imperative that the diagnosis of primary pulmonary hypertension not be made until potentially treatable causes of elevated pulmonary arterial pressure have been excluded. The presence of pulmonary hypertension and cor pulmonale caused by chronic pulmonary disease can be established readily by finding abnormalities in pulmonary function. In particular, interstitial lung diseases with fibrosis, such as sarcoidosis, and pneumoconioses, such as silicosis, as well as hypoxic pulmonary hypertension associated with impaired ventilation should be excluded. Cardiac catheterization and/or echocardiographic studies are necessary to search for a primary cardiac defect, and angiography or radioactive lung-scanning studies also may be indicated to detect emboli to relatively large pulmonary arteries (Chap. 211). In performing pulmonary arteriography, the use of small amounts of contrast medium, preferentially injected selectively into the branches of the main pulmonary artery, is advisable since sudden death during catheterization has occasionally occurred. Patients having chronic emboli to the lungs are difficult to distinguish from those with primary pulmonary hypertension, but the distinction is important because anticoagulants, inferior vena caval interruption, and pulmonary embolectomy sometimes have been effective in patients with embolic disease. The lung scan and pulmonary arteriogram are typically normal in primary pulmonary hypertension, but with thromboembolic pulmonary hypertension, perfusion defects on lung scan or pulmonary arterial occlusions and filling defects on angiography often are visible. With pulmonary embolism, serial chest x-rays may show evidence of pulmonary infarction. Open lung biopsy has been used occasionally to differentiate primary pulmonary hypertension from the thromboembolic variety. Sometimes a site of origin for emboli cannot be identified in the leg veins, and other possible sources should be considered, such as right atrial thrombus, or ovarian and pelvic vein thromboses. Occasionally, pulmonary hypertension is due to parasitic disease, such as schistosomiasis or filariasis, or to multiple pulmonary artery thromboses consequent to sickle cell disease. Although the importance of accurate diagnosis is emphasized, short of open lung biopsy clinical differentiation may be impossible between the three main pathologic types of pulmonary hypertension (pulmonary venoocclusive, thromboembolic or thrombotic, and plexogenic pulmonary arteriopathic types), and they are frequently categorized by the clinician as primary pulmonary hypertension.

Several congenital cardiac conditions must be considered and excluded by appropriate echocardiographic or cardiac catheterization studies. Valvular pulmonic stenosis usually can be distinguished from pulmonary hypertension by identification of the delayed, soft pulmonic closure sound, but peripheral stenoses of the pulmonary arteries may be associated with an increased second heart sound. A left-to-right shunt at the pulmonary arterial, ventricular, or atrial levels should be sought. The wide, fixed splitting of the second heart sound should be helpful in identifying patients with atrial septal defect. Eisenmenger's syndrome in a patient with ventricular septal defect or patent ductus arteriosus (Chap. 185) may be confused with primary pulmonary hypertension, but usually in Eisenmenger's syndrome cyanosis, polycythemia, and clubbing are present, and at cardiac

catheterization a large right-to-left shunt at the ventricular, atrial, or pulmonary arterial level can be demonstrated.

The murmurs of tricuspid or pulmonic regurgitation and the atrial gallop sounds heard in patients with primary pulmonary hypertension may be mistaken for the murmurs of rheumatic mitral and aortic valve disease, or vice versa. Before making the diagnosis of primary pulmonary hypertension, the presence of left atrial hypertension due to undetected mitral stenosis, or to a more unusual lesion such as left atrial myxoma or cor triatriatum, should be specifically sought and excluded. This can be done by echocardiography, by obtaining pulmonary arterial wedge pressure tracings, or by catheterization of the left side of the heart, with angiography if necessary.

THERAPY In many patients with primary pulmonary hypertension the downhill course is progressive despite treatment, and therapy must be palliative. The use of anticoagulants has been considered of doubtful value, provided chronic pulmonary embolic phenomena can be excluded. However, in a retrospective natural history study of 120 patients, postmortem examinations in 56 patients showed organized thrombus in small arteries (embolic or in situ) to be present in over 50 percent of patients; the only apparent clinical difference between these patients and those with plexiform arteriopathy was a somewhat older average age. Anticoagulation within 12 months of diagnosis was an independent predictor of improved survival rate, and anticoagulant therapy was recommended for all patients. The diagnosis of chronic thrombotic obstruction of major pulmonary arteries is important because surgical thromboendarterectomy in such patients has been successful in a number of patients.

Right-sided heart failure should be treated with a cardiotonic and diuretic regimen (Chap. 182). Since there is no hypercapnia in these patients, the hypoxia which may accompany heart failure can be treated safely with oxygen therapy.

Recent reports have indicated that in some patients pharmacologic therapy can produce clinical and hemodynamic improvement. Although long-term observations concerning prolongation of life are not available, several categories of drugs have been found useful in small groups of patients: (1) direct vascular smooth-muscle relaxants (nitroprusside, diazoxide, nitroglycerine, and hydralazine); (2) beta agonists (sublingual isoproterenol, oral terbutaline); (3) alpha-adrenergic blocking agents (phentolamine and phenoxybenzamine); (4) calcium antagonists (nifedipine and verapamil); and (5) angiotensin converting enzyme inhibitors. Immunosuppressive agents and prostaglandin antagonists (indomethacin) have rarely been used. Prostacyclin (PGI$_2$) has been employed successfully intravenously as a test of vascular reactivity and for short-term therapy.

In some patients, favorable hemodynamic effects from orally administered drugs such as diazoxide or hydralazine have been sustained for many months, with clinical improvement manifested by relief of severe dyspnea and reduction in the number of syncopal episodes. Hydralazine and nifedipine are currently used most commonly. The calcium channel blocker nifedipine has been reported to lower pulmonary artery pressure and pulmonary vascular resistance and to increase cardiac output, as well as to improve exercise tolerance in some patients. Although few long-term studies are available, limited data suggest that the lowered pulmonary vascular resistance may be maintained over many months in some patients. Initial studies suggest that the angiotensin-converting enzyme inhibitor captopril may be effective in a few patients, but it appears to have its main effect on the systemic circulation to lower arterial pressure and increase cardiac output, with a less prominent action on the pulmonary circulation. Prior to instituting long-term therapy with such drugs, measurement of the acute responses of the pulmonary artery pressure, pulmonary vascular resistance, cardiac output, and arterial pressure is usually indicated in order to assess efficacy and to detect unfavorable effects. In some patients hemodynamic deterioration has been reported following the use of vasodilators.

Heart and lung transplantation has now been successful in a number of patients, with survival for several years. Although early mortality was relatively high (about 30 percent), the functional status of survivors has been good, and such treatment represents a possible approach in selected patients if suitable donors can be found.

REFERENCES

FUSTER V et al: Primary pulmonary hypertension: Natural history and the importance of thrombosis. Circulation 70:580, 1984

GROSSMAN W, BRAUNWALD E: Pulmonary hypertension, in *Heart Disease*, 2d ed, E Braunwald (ed). Philadelphia, Saunders, 1984, p 823

HAWORTH SG: Primary pulmonary hypertension. Br Heart J 49:517, 1983

HUGHES JD, RUBIN LJ: Primary pulmonary hypertension: An analysis of 28 cases and a review of the literature. Medicine 65:56, 1986

JAMIESON SW et al: Heart and lung transplantation for pulmonary hypertension. Am J Surg 147(6):740, 1984

McGOON MD, VLIETSTRA RE: Vasodilator therapy for primary pulmonary hypertension. Mayo Clin Proc 59:872, 1984

MOSER KM et al: Chronic thrombotic obstruction of major pulmonary arteries. Results of thromboendarterectomy in 15 patients. Ann Intern Med 99:299, 1983

OLIVARI MT et al: Hemodynamic effects of nifedipine at rest and during exercise in primary pulmonary hypertension. Chest 86(1):14, 1984

PACKER M: Vasodilator therapy for primary pulmonary hypertension. Ann Intern Med 103:258, 1985

REITZ BA: Heart-lung transplantation, in *Pulmonary Diseases and Disorders*, 2d ed, AP Fishman (ed). New York, McGraw-Hill, 1987, Part 18

RICH S, BRUNDAGE BH: Primary pulmonary hypertension: Current update. JAMA 251:2252, 1984

VOELKEL N, REEVES JT: Primary pulmonary hypertension, in *Pulmonary Vascular Diseases*, KM Moser (ed). New York, Marcel Dekker, 1979

WAGENVOORT CA, WAGENVOORT N: *Pathology of Pulmonary Hypertension*. New York, Wiley 1977

211 PULMONARY THROMBOEMBOLISM

KENNETH M. MOSER

Pulmonary thromboembolism (PTE) is a leading cause of morbidity and mortality and can appear in many clinical contexts. Epidemiologic surveys indicate that PTE is responsible for more than 50,000 deaths in the United States annually. However, available data suggest that less than 10 percent of all pulmonary emboli result in death. Thus, the incidence of fatal plus nonfatal emboli in this nation probably exceeds 500,000 annually. This overall incidence seems verified by autopsy statistics. Evidence of recent or old embolism is detected in 25 to 30 percent of routine autopsies; with special techniques, this figure exceeds 60 percent. Even these data underestimate incidence, since many emboli resolve without trace and are not found at postmortem examination. The high incidence of PTE at autopsy contrasts sharply with the incidence of antemortem diagnosis. Available information suggests that an antemortem diagnosis has been made in only 10 to 30 percent of all cases in which old or recent embolism is demonstrated at autopsy.

VENOUS THROMBOSIS

PATHOGENESIS Available data indicate that more than 95 percent of pulmonary emboli arise from thrombi in the deep venous system of the lower extremities. Thrombi occurring in the right cardiac chambers or in other veins account for the remainder. In situ pulmonary arterial thrombosis is rare. Thus, embolism should be viewed as a *complication* of deep venous thrombosis (DVT). Furthermore, it appears that the larger leg veins (those above the knee) are the most common source of those pulmonary emboli which reach clinical attention. These facts have several important implications with respect to PTE: (1) prevention of DVT is the most effective approach to prevention of embolism; (2) prompt treatment of DVT may limit the frequency of embolism; (3) techniques which allow the diagnosis of DVT in the leg veins will allow identification of the vast majority of patients at high risk of embolism.

The three factors which promote DVT (and, therefore, embolic risk), as defined by Virchow in the nineteenth century, are stasis, abnormalities of the vessel wall, and alterations in the blood coagulation system. Coagulation alterations have been studied extensively, but as yet there is no reliable test for a state of "hypercoagulability," i.e., a test which will predict the risk of DVT (except for the infrequent patients with antithrombin III, protein C, or protein S deficiencies or cystinuria). In the absence of such a test, the risk of DVT is best assessed by recognizing the presence of known "clinical" risk factors. Conditions associated with a high risk of venous thromboembolism include the postpartum period, left and right ventricular failure, fractures or other injuries of the lower extremities, chronic deep venous insufficiency of the legs, prolonged bed rest, carcinoma, obesity, and the use of estrogens.

NATURAL HISTORY In the contexts noted above, deep venous thrombi usually develop in the region of a venous valve. Platelets aggregate, forming a nidus (white thrombus), followed by development of a large fibrin (red) thrombus. The process is apparently a rapid one; large, extensive thrombi can develop within minutes. Growth occurs by continued fibrin and platelet accretion. Beyond formation, two processes may contribute to resolution: fibrinolysis and organization. Fibrinolysis may result in complete resolution within hours to several days. Any remaining thrombus undergoes organization, leaving behind a fibrotic zone that becomes reendothelialized. Valves are often rendered incompetent by this process, and modest or extensive luminal narrowing may occur. Once thrombus growth has halted, fibrinolysis/organization reaches a stable state in 7 to 10 days. It is during the first few days after formation, therefore, that embolic risk is highest.

DETECTION The clinical diagnosis of DVT is difficult. DVT is frequently present in the absence of clinical signs (e.g., pain, heat, swelling), and it is absent in 50 percent of patients in whom clinical signs or symptoms suggest its presence. Therefore a number of diagnostic tests have been developed. There are three reliable noninvasive procedures available for the early detection and follow-up of DVT: (1) impedance plethysmography (IPG), which detects venous outflow obstruction, is highly sensitive to above-knee thrombosis, but fails to detect many below-knee thrombi; (2) the Doppler technique, which is highly operator-dependent; (3) the radiofibrinogen method, which is very sensitive to thrombus formation in calf veins and lower thigh veins, but not sensitive to thrombi which form in the upper thigh or above (also, 24 h is required for a definitive answer). The IPG and radiofibrinogen tests correlate well with the definitive (but invasive) standard for the diagnosis of DVT, i.e., *ascending contrast phlebography*. The combination of IPG and radiofibrinogen leg scanning is equal in accuracy to contrast venography. Radiovenography and the use of [111]indium-labeled platelets await validation.

PROPHYLAXIS Application of these noninvasive approaches to the early diagnosis and follow-up of patients at high risk of DVT has led to significant changes in the approach to the prevention of DVT (and therefore of PTE). One validated prophylactic method is the use of small doses of subcutaneous heparin. Multiple studies, utilizing chiefly radiolabeled fibrinogen, have shown the high incidence of DVT in certain groups: patients over the age of 40 years with fractures of the pelvis and/or lower extremities; patients with myocardial infarction and/or severe congestive heart failure; patients undergoing major abdominal, thoracic, or gynecologic surgery. Furthermore, in the last group of patients, investigations have demonstrated a significant reduction in the incidence of DVT, PTE, and lethal PTE when heparin is given subcutaneously, in a dose of 5000 units every 12 h, beginning *before* operation (or on admission to the hospital) and continued until the patient is ambulatory. There is general agreement that this prophylactic approach, which has limited effect on coagulation tests and is associated with little risk of hemorrhage, should also be applied to *medical* patients at high risk of DVT and PTE. In the case of acute myocardial infarction, high risk would be imposed by the development of congestive failure, the presence of severe obesity, chronic venous insufficiency, or a prior history of DVT or PTE. Devices which compress the calf intermittently (usually once a minute) appear an effective alternative for prophylaxis in patients at risk of hemorrhage with low-dose heparin (neurosurgery, spinal cord trauma) or in whom low-dose heparin has proved ineffective (hip surgery, prostate surgery).

NATURAL HISTORY OF EMBOLISM

THE ACUTE EVENTS The immediate result of thromboembolism is complete or partial obstruction of the pulmonary arterial blood flow to the distal lung. This obstruction leads to a series of pathophysiologic events which can be categorized as the "respiratory" and "hemodynamic" consequences of PTE.

Respiratory consequences Embolic obstruction produces a zone of the lung which is ventilated but not perfused—an intrapulmonary "dead space" (Chap. 200). Because it cannot participate in the process of gas exchange, ventilation of this nonperfused area is "wasted," in the functional sense. A potential consequence of embolic obstruction is constriction of the air spaces and airways in the affected lung zone. This pneumoconstriction, which might be viewed as a homeostatic mechanism to reduce wasted ventilation, appears to be due to the marked bronchoalveolar hypocapnia that results from cessation of pulmonary capillary blood flow, because it is abolished by inhalation of carbon dioxide–enriched air. While it occurs in animal experiments in which a double-lumen tube separates the ventilation from each lung, it probably occurs very rarely in patients who inhale dead space air (rich in carbon dioxide) into embolized lung zones.

Another disturbance caused by embolic obstruction—loss of alveolar surfactant—does not occur immediately. This surface-active lipoprotein is required to maintain alveolar stability. In its absence, alveolar collapse occurs. Cessation of pulmonary capillary blood flow leads to reduction in surfactant within 2 or 3 h, which becomes severe at 12 to 15 h. Frank atelectasis—the morphologic expression of alveolar instability—can be detected at 24 to 48 h after interruption of blood flow.

Arterial hypoxemia is a common, though by no means universal, consequence of embolism. Several mechanisms can contribute to hypoxemia: ventilation-perfusion disturbances; cardiac failure with a lowered mixed venous P_{O_2} (widened arteriovenous difference); and obligatory perfusion through hypoventilated lung zones. Such obligatory perfusion develops because elevation of pulmonary arterial pressure due to embolic obstruction can overcome the vasoconstriction normally present in hypoventilated lung zones.

Hemodynamic consequences The primary hemodynamic consequence of thromboembolic obstruction is a reduction in the cross-sectional area of the pulmonary arterial bed. This loss of vascular capacity increases the resistance to pulmonary blood flow, which, if marked, leads to pulmonary hypertension and acute failure of the right ventricle. Tachycardia and often a decline in cardiac output also occur.

The factors which determine the severity of these hemodynamic changes have been the subject of continued debate. There is agreement that the *extent of embolic obstruction* is a key factor. However, the reserve capacity of the pulmonary arteriocapillary bed is so extensive that more than 50 percent of the vascular area must be obstructed before significant elevation in pulmonary arterial pressure results. Because pulmonary hypertension occurs in some patients with occlusion of lesser extent, investigators have searched for reflex or humoral vasoconstrictor mechanisms associated with embolism. Despite long and careful search for such mechanisms, their extent and frequency in human PTE remains unknown. Hence, some workers maintain that the degree of embolic obstruction itself is the only determinant

of hemodynamic impairment. They suggest that instances of apparent disparity between the extent of embolism and clinical response reflect only clinical underestimation of the magnitude of the embolism. Other investigators, however, have presented compelling evidence to support the occurrence of pulmonary vasoconstriction with embolism. Some have demonstrated that constriction is associated with obstruction of the smaller, but not the larger, pulmonary arterial vessels. Another thesis holds that serotonin or thromboxane, known pulmonary vasoconstrictive-bronchoconstrictive substances, are released from platelets, which coat fresh emboli as they lodge in the pulmonary tree. This thesis introduces the attractive concept that an embolus might be regarded, in part, as a packet with pharmacologic, as well as obstructive, potential. A consensus view is that, while the extent of embolism is a key factor, humoral and/or reflex influences probably operate in certain patients and compromise the pulmonary circulation to a greater extent than might be expected on an anatomic basis alone.

The cardiopulmonary status of the patient prior to embolism is also critical in determining the clinical severity of embolism. A small embolus may have limited impact upon an otherwise healthy individual but may have serious consequences in someone with advanced cardiac or pulmonary disease.

Both experimental and clinical studies have established that infarction—death of lung tissue—rarely accompanies embolic occlusion. It is likely that less than 10 percent of emboli in humans lead to infarction. That infarction rarely follows embolism should occasion little surprise. The lung has three avenues for obtaining oxygen: the pulmonary arterial circulation, the bronchial arterial circulation, and the airways. Thus, infarction occurs infrequently, and its appearance usually is associated with compromise of bronchial arterial flow and/or airways to the involved area. Such compromise is promoted by the existence of other cardiac or pulmonary diseases, such as left ventricular failure, mitral stenosis, and chronic obstructive lung disease. Thus, infarction may occur in 30 percent or more of such patients, while it is quite rare in individuals who are free of cardiopulmonary disease.

BEYOND THE ACUTE STATE The vast majority of pulmonary emboli resolve, and resolve rather quickly. Resolution of fresh emboli begins within the first few days and is well advanced in 10 to 14 days. As in DVT, two mechanisms promote restoration of vascular patency: the fibrinolytic system and the process of organization. However, the fibrinolytic system appears capable of more rapid dissolution of emboli than of venous thrombi.

The availability of these two efficient mechanisms raises the question as to why not all emboli resolve. There may be some impairment of the intrinsic fibrinolytic system. The emboli may have been well organized prior to their lodgment in the lung so that they are subject to neither fibrinolytic attack nor further organization. Alternatively, some emboli may be recurrent, so that their failure to resolve is more apparent than real.

Another important element of the natural history of thromboembolism is the development of bronchial arterial collateral circulation. If pulmonary arterial obstruction persists, bronchial arterial flow increases substantially over a period of several weeks, restoring flow to the capillary bed. With the return of flow, surfactant production is restored, so that alveolar stability is regained and atelectasis resolves.

DIAGNOSTIC FEATURES

While sequential studies of patients with venous thrombosis have demonstrated that embolism can occur without causing symptoms, *sudden onset of unexplained dyspnea* is the most common, and often the only symptom of pulmonary embolism. *Pleuritic chest pain and hemoptysis are present only when infarction has occurred* and, because bland embolism rarely leads to infarction, are usually absent.

With extensive embolism, severe substernal oppressive discomfort may be present, probably due to right ventricular ischemia. Patients also may present with syncope, suggesting a neurologic disorder. Other "occult" presentations in which embolism should be considered include repetitive bouts of otherwise unexplained supraventricular tachyarrhythmias; sudden onset or worsening of congestive heart failure (Chap. 182); sudden deterioration in the patient with chronic obstructive lung disease; and as an alternative to the diagnosis of "psychic" (anxiety-associated) hyperventilation. The most reliable symptom, however, is breathlessness. Severe, persistent dyspnea is an ominous sign, for it usually indicates extensive embolic occlusion.

PHYSICAL EXAMINATION Findings on physical examination, like the history, may be deceptively normal. Examination of the lungs may disclose a few atelectatic rales; localized wheezes rarely are heard. A pleural friction rub or evidence of pleural effusion will not be present unless infarction has occurred.

On cardiac examination, the single consistent finding is tachycardia. Only in the rare cases of massive embolism will signs such as a right ventricular gallop, a palpable "lift" over the right ventricle (along the left sternal border), a loud pulmonary closure sound, or prominent a waves in the jugular venous pulse be found. A scratchy systolic ejection-type murmur may be heard in the pulmonic area. Also, a systolic or continuous murmur accentuated by inspiration may be audible over the lung fields. These murmurs appear to be generated by turbulence of flow in vessels partially obstructed by emboli since they disappear after resection or resolution of emboli. They should be carefully sought in any patient suspected of having PTE. Wide splitting of the second heart sound may be present. This indicates extensive embolic obstruction and implies both severe pulmonary hypertension and right ventricular failure. As embolic resolution occurs, this finding disappears. Absence of an accentuated pulmonic closure sound is not a reliable guide to the severity of PTE,

since when embolism is sufficiently massive to reduce cardiac output, pulmonary closure may be normal or diminished.

The detection of *deep venous thrombosis* qualifies as an excellent clue to the diagnosis of embolism, but its absence does not exclude embolism. Even when sought with diligence, *clinical* evidence of thrombophlebitis is found in less than half of patients with PTE. *Fever* in patients with pulmonary embolism is uncommon without complicating infection or infarction. With infarction, fever of 37.8 to 38.3°C (oral) is the rule; but temperature elevations to 39°C or above may occur, making the differentiation between pulmonary infarction and infection difficult.

On clinical grounds alone, then, a firm diagnosis of embolism cannot be made; the clinical *suspicion* of embolism requires confirmation by laboratory studies (Fig. 211-1).

LABORATORY STUDIES Routine laboratory studies contribute little toward the diagnosis. Leukocytosis and elevation of the sedimentation rate are rarely present in the absence of infarction. A variety of other blood tests, such as assay for specific fibrinopeptides, fibrin degradation products, or enzymes, have been proposed; none has been shown to be diagnostically sensitive or specific.

Aside from tachycardia, the *electrocardiogram* is normal in most patients. With extensive embolization, there may be evidence of acute pulmonary hypertension, rightward shift of the QRS axis, a tall, peaked P wave, and ST-T changes indicative of right ventricular strain (Chap. 178). These changes are often transient, lasting minutes to hours, but when persistent, suggest severe pulmonary vascular obstruction.

The *chest roentgenogram* may show a parenchymal infiltrate and evidence of a pleural effusion if *infarction* has occurred. Characteristically, the infiltrates caused by infarction abut against the pleura. However, their shape varies, and they do not usually appear until 12 to 36 h after the embolism has occurred. The effusion, which often

FIGURE 211-1 *Flow chart used in diagnosis of pulmonary embolism (PE). IPG, impedance plethysmogram; V scan, ventilation scan.*

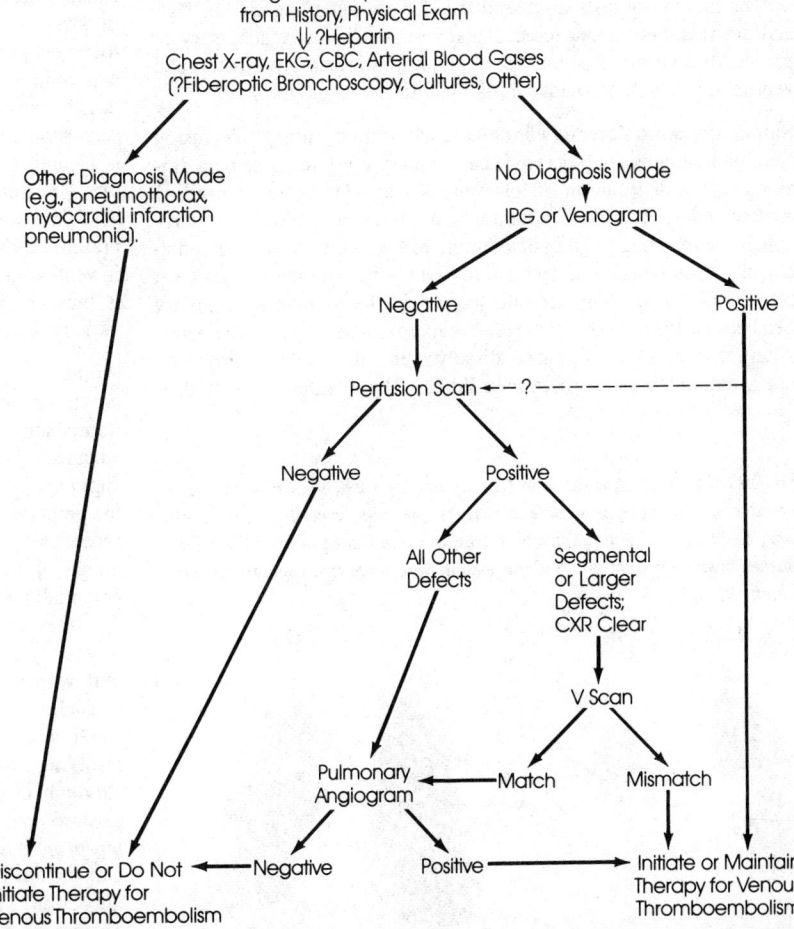

precedes the infiltrate, is characteristically small. Thoracentesis usually, but by no means invariably, yields hemorrhagic fluid, with the characteristics of an exudate.

The radiographic findings with embolism alone are more subtle. *Differences in diameter between vessels which should be of equivalent size* should raise the suspicion of embolism. For example, embolic obstruction of the right main pulmonary artery can lead to dilation of the left main pulmonary artery because that vessel must accept the entire pulmonary flow. There may be *abrupt "cutoff"* of a vessel; i.e., as the vessel is traced distally, it suddenly disappears. Clot has the same radiodensity as blood, accounting for the proximal shadow; the absence of flow beyond the clot explains the sudden radiographic "disappearance" of the vessel.

Organization of a clot within a pulmonary artery may lead to retraction of the vessel's walls and a so-called rattail configuration, in which the vessel is relatively normal proximally and suddenly tapers to a sharp point. Finally, there may be *abnormal radiolucency* in some lung zones due to absent or decreased flow. Such abnormally lucent areas, indicative of proximal arterial obstruction, are best appreciated by examining comparable areas in the two lung fields.

Even in embolization without infarction, the roentgenogram may show small infiltrates, which appear in about 24 h and reflect atelectasis secondary to surfactant depletion. They are not associated with effusion, may fail to touch a pleural surface, and disappear without the linear scarring characteristic of infarction. It should be emphasized that a *normal chest roentgenogram does not exclude the diagnosis of PTE.* Indeed, a *normal* chest roentgenogram is the *most common* finding in embolic disease.

Analysis of arterial blood gases   Massive embolism is commonly associated with arterial hypoxemia, hypocapnia, and respiratory alkalosis. In addition, the difference between alveolar P_{CO_2} and arterial P_{CO_2} ($Pa_{CO_2} - Pa_{CO_2}$) may be widened owing to the increase in alveolar dead space (Chap. 200). However, a normal P_{O_2} does not exclude the diagnosis.

The laboratory tests discussed thus far are often negative in PTE and are relatively nonspecific. Therefore, it is usually necessary to proceed to two more definitive techniques: pulmonary perfusion and ventilation radiophotoscans and the pulmonary angiogram.

Pulmonary perfusion and ventilation scintiphotography   Perfusion scintiphotographs (photoscans) are obtained by gamma camera imaging of the distribution of intravenously injected, gamma-emitting radionuclides. The most commonly used radionuclides are microspheres or macroaggregates of albumin (MAA), labeled with a gamma-emitting isotope such as technetium 99m. The radioactive particles, 50 to 100 μm in diameter, are trapped in the pulmonary capillary bed because the pulmonary capillaries approximate 10 μm in diameter. Alternatively, xenon 133 gas, dissolved in saline solution, may be used, but patients must hold their breath. The distribution of labeled particles entrapped in capillaries, or of xenon 133 evolved from them, accurately depicts the distribution of pulmonary blood flow.

The camera-generated perfusion image can be recorded on radiographic film, on special photographic film, on a television screen, or on videotape. Normal scans exhibit homogeneous distribution of radioactivity, smooth margins, and a configuration which corresponds to the normal anatomy of the lungs. Any deviation from these characteristics requires explanation because it represents an abnormality in blood flow distribution.

The perfusion lung photoscan is quite valuable in the diagnosis of embolism. A properly performed perfusion scan which is *normal* excludes the diagnosis of clinically significant pulmonary embolism. On the other hand, a scan demonstrating zones of absent or sharply decreased radioactivity in the patient whose other findings are compatible with PTE keeps the diagnosis of embolism among the possibilities. Scanning is simple, safe, and rapid. It can be repeated to define the resolution, or recurrence, of obstructive vascular phenomena. Like any laboratory test, however, the photoscan must be applied and interpreted with care. It is important, for example, to obtain multiple scan views because lesions not apparent in one view may be easily detected in others. Furthermore, the lung photoscan demonstrates only abnormalities of the *distribution of blood flow*. It does not provide anatomic information. Many disorders other than PTE are associated with abnormalities in the distribution of pulmonary blood flow. Any disease process, such as pneumonia, atelectasis, or pneumothorax, which reduces the ventilation of a lung zone will decrease its perfusion. Parenchymal diseases, such as emphysema, sarcoidosis, bronchogenic carcinoma, and tuberculosis, can all produce scan defects. Therefore a perfusion defect lacks specificity. One approach to enhancing specificity is the performance of a ventilation scan, best achieved by having patients breathe a radioactive gas such as xenon 127 or xenon 133. To assist in deciding whether a ventilation scan may be useful and when pulmonary angiography is required, two factors should be considered: the size of the perfusion defect(s) and the chest roentgenographic findings. If all defects are subsegmental in size *or* if all defects (of any size) are limited to areas of roentgenographic infiltration, ventilation scanning will not be useful, and pulmonary angiography is required. If defect(s) are segmental or larger in size, and one or more are in areas clear by x-ray, a ventilation scan should be done. If the radioactive gas enters ("washes in") and is cleared ("washes out") from the area(s) of perfusion defect(s), this "mismatch" of ventilation and perfusion is characteristic of vascular obstruction (Fig. 211-2). Pulmonary vascular obstruction is present in 90 percent or more of patients with this pattern. However, if ventilation is also abnormal (i.e., ventilation-perfusion "match" is present), no reliable diagnostic conclusion can be reached; pulmonary angiography is required.

Pulmonary angiography   This is the only established means for providing anatomic information about the pulmonary vasculature. Radiopaque material is injected, preferably through a cardiac catheter advanced into the pulmonary artery. Cardiac catheterization and angiography require specialized personnel, and a reasonable period for preparation and performance, and they entail more risk than the procedures discussed above. However, angiography provides a visual image of the pulmonary vessels, and catheterization can provide potentially important hemodynamic data (pulmonary artery and wedge pressures, cardiac output). Interpretive limitations of angiography are of three types: (1) *Injection artifacts* may occur which suggest absence of flow to a vessel. Injection should be repeated whenever the question of such artifacts exists. (2) The inability to evaluate the patency of small vessels is another limitation. Emboli in vessels below the resolving capability of the method cannot be detected with certainty, although magnification techniques can extend resolving capability. (3) Interpretive errors may also be a consequence of *not looking for the proper type of defect.* There are only two diagnostic findings. One is the *abrupt "cutoff"* of a vessel at the point of embolic impaction. However, complete embolic obstruction is uncommon. Therefore, *filling defects* are the most frequent finding; i.e., the

FIGURE 211-2   *Perfusion scan (left), posterior view, shows multiple segmental and larger perfusion defects in right upper and lower lobes, left lower lobe, and lingula. Ventilation scan (right) is normal at equilibrium. Xenon^{133} washed in and out normally. Multiple emboli were confirmed angiographically. L, left; R, right.*

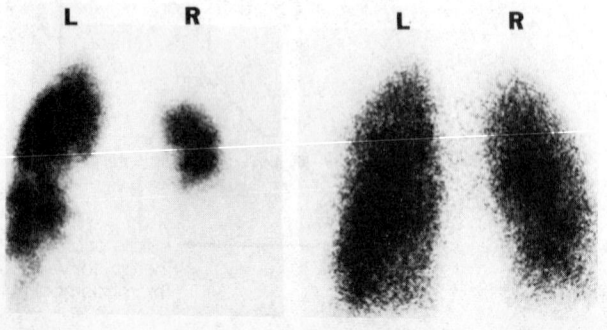

embolus creates a "negative" shadow as the radiopaque material flows around it. The major contraindication to angiography is the absence of personnel who are experienced in both performing the procedure and interpreting the results. Serious diagnostic errors are commonplace if optimal techniques are not used or the complexities of interpretation are not appreciated. However, the risks of angiography are low in experienced hands. Injection of large boluses of contrast medium into the main pulmonary artery should be avoided in favor of small injections into vessels supplying lung regions identified as abnormal on the perfusion scan.

How far one should proceed down the diagnostic pathway outlined above depends on many factors, the major ones being the presence or absence of documented venous thrombosis, the severity of the patient's symptoms, and the hazards of contemplated therapy. In each condition, there is a need for precise diagnosis. If IPG or venography already has documented deep venous thrombosis, one is committed to anticoagulant therapy; thus, proceeding beyond perfusion scanning is rarely necessary. This means that evaluation for venous thrombosis is an integral part of the evaluation of the embolic suspect. Unfortunately, the absence of venous thrombosis cannot be used to exclude the diagnosis of pulmonary embolism. More than 20 percent of patients with embolism have no evidence of venous thrombosis, apparently because the entire venous thrombus has embolized. Therefore, in such patients, if symptoms are severe and/ or the hazards of therapy are substantial, diagnostic precision is mandatory, and there should be no hesitancy in proceeding to angiography. Substantial hazards of therapy which mandate angiography include a high risk of bleeding on, or absolute contraindication to, anticoagulant therapy and consideration of embolectomy, thrombolytic therapy, or vena caval interruption.

TREATMENT

Initial intravenous administration of heparin is the therapy of choice for PTE. With a strong *suspicion* of embolism based on clinical and routine laboratory tests, such therapy should be instituted immediately, without awaiting diagnostic confirmation, unless the initial dose of heparin places the patient at clear risk (i.e., in patients with recent or active bleeding or a known hemostatic defect). Except in such patients, heparin therapy should not await diagnostic confirmation; one can always stop therapy if such confirmation is not forthcoming.

There is consensus regarding the goals of therapy in both DVT and PTE: (1) immediate inhibition of the growth of thromboemboli, (2) promotion of thromboembolic resolution, and (3) prevention of recurrence. Heparin achieves the first goal; it encourages the second by allowing fibrinolytic dissolution to be achieved unopposed by thrombus growth; and it assists in, although it does not ensure, prevention of recurrence. In addition, heparin inhibits platelet aggregation (and therefore potential release of thromboxane and serotonin) at the embolic site, and its anticoagulant action is promptly reversible.

There is *not* consensus, however, regarding (1) heparin regimens which best combine safety and efficacy; (2) the need for, and type of, tests for monitoring coagulation behavior during heparin therapy; (3) how long, and with what agents, antithrombotic therapy should be maintained; or (4) in which patients thrombolytic therapy should antedate antithrombotic therapy.

REGIMENS   In DVT, three methods of heparin administration have been advocated by various investigators: continuous intravenous, intermittent intravenous, intermittent subcutaneous. Continuous intravenous heparin is usually given in a dose of approximately 1000 units per hour. Intermittent intravenous heparin is commonly given in a dose of approximately 5000 units every 4 h or 7500 every 6 h. Subcutaneous heparin has been recommended as a dose of 5000 units every 4 h, 10,000 every 8 h, or 20,000 every 12 h. Studies exist which indicate that each of these regimens is more efficacious, safer, or both. Therefore, at this time, one can conclude only that *each* of these regimens (which approximate 30,000 units per 24 h) represents

an acceptable treatment regimen. At present, the continuous intravenous regimen, delivered by an infusion pump, is the most popular. *Intramuscular* injection of heparin is to be avoided because hematomas will develop.

In PTE, the same options for heparin therapy exist. The only additional question is whether an initial large intravenous bolus (10,000 to 20,000 units) should be given to inhibit the aggregation (and release reaction) of platelets adherent to the embolus. Most workers advocate such a dose, with one of the "standard" regimens being started 2 to 4 h later.

MONITORING   The value of clotting times (CT), partial thromboplastin times (PTT), or other coagulation tests to monitor heparin effect and guide alterations in dose is not clearly established. The risk of hemorrhage (the principal complication of heparin therapy) is not clearly related to coagulation test alterations; rather, it appears related to factors such as the coexistence of other diseases associated with bleeding risk (gastric or duodenal ulcer, coagulopathies, uremia) and advanced age. Likewise, achievement of the desired effect of heparin (cessation of thrombus growth in vivo) has not been related to coagulation tests. Therefore, it is questionable whether monitoring with such tests is superior to empiric use of one of the regimens described above. While animal investigations have disclosed that maintaining the PTT above 1.5 times control does prevent growth of venous thrombi, such data are not available for human patients. If done improperly or poorly timed, the CT or PTT tests are worthless and may be misleading. If used appropriately, the usual objective is to keep the CT or PTT, measured *just prior to the next* intermittent dose, at or above 1.5 times the baseline CT or PTT and at 1.5 to 2.0 times control with continuous infusion.

DURATION OF THERAPY   In DVT, one of the "full-dose" regimens is usually maintained for 7 to 10 days, the rationale being that this is the period required for dissolution and/or organization of the thrombus. In PTE, for the same reasons, a similar duration of therapy is advised. Bed rest is indicated until cardiopulmonary or leg symptoms subside. Carefully applied elastic support hose should be used (to encourage venous flow) as soon as leg pain, if present, subsides.

Beyond the acute phase, there are three therapeutic options available: cessation of heparin, maintenance of low-dose heparin, or initiation of therapy with *prothrombinopenic drugs*. In deciding among these options, it should be recognized that the question being addressed is: Does the patient need continued protection against the risk of *recurrent* DVT (and, therefore, PTE)? If the risk factor(s) that precipitated the acute episode of DVT-PTE is no longer present, the patient is asymptomatic, and the IPG is normal, it is acceptable to reduce heparin to a lower dose starting on day 7, ambulate the patient, and, if no symptoms develop, discontinue heparin on day 9 or 10. If these criteria are not met, prolonged prophylactic therapy is warranted. There is no consensus regarding the optimal duration of such therapy because firm data on this point are lacking. If *reversible* risk factors are present (e.g., immobilization after a leg fracture), therapy should be continued until the risk factors present have resolved. If the risk factors present are nonreversible (e.g., severe left and/or right ventricular failure) or if the IPG remains positive, empiric decisions are made. At a minimum, 3 months of therapy seems wise because recurrence is relatively common during this period. Beyond 3 months, however, continuation depends upon the balance among specific risk factors exhibited by the patient, IPG results, and the risks of continued therapy. In some instances, this balance may warrant lifetime maintenance on anticoagulant drugs.

Prothrombinopenic drugs are not suitable for initial therapy in thromboembolism. Their only role is in maintaining anticoagulant protection for prolonged periods. If prothrombinopenic drugs are to be used, the patient should be "in range" as defined by a prothrombin time 1.5 to 2.0 times the control time for 3 to 5 days before heparin is discontinued. An alternative to the prothrombinopenic agents is the use of self-injected subcutaneous heparin. Current data suggest that a dose of 7500 to 10,000 units every 12 h is adequate for this type of prophylaxis, is well tolerated, and need not be monitored with coagulation tests.

Thrombolytic (fibrinolytic) agents such as streptokinase and urokinase can hasten the resolution of venous thrombi and pulmonary emboli. They do not replace antithrombotic therapy. When used, thrombolytic agents must be followed by a standard course of antithrombotic therapy. Despite extensive study and a clear demonstration that these agents can enhance the speed of resolution, it has not been established that their use alters the short- or long-term morbidity or mortality rates among patients with either DVT or PTE. Both drugs are associated with hemorrhagic risk, particularly in patients who recently have had, or require, any invasive procedure (e.g., venipuncture, arterial puncture, angiography, Swan-Ganz catheterization). If they do offer a therapeutic advantage, it would appear to be (1) in patients with extensive, large-vein DVT (e.g., iliofemoral); and (2) in patients with massive embolism and persistent systemic hypotension in whom embolectomy would otherwise be contemplated. The potential role of new thrombolytic agents (e.g., tissue plasminogen activator), which may pose less hemorrhagic risk and allow the concomitant use of heparin, remains to be determined.

Surgical therapy for DVT (thrombectomy) is now rarely considered because the results have not been encouraging. In PTE, surgical therapy should be reserved for those patients in whom heparin therapy is deemed inadequate or impractical. Anticoagulant therapy may be contraindicated by the presence of a bleeding diathesis, or the patient may be in such critical condition that it is felt unwise to await a response to medical therapy. In such instances *venous interruption* and *pulmonary embolectomy* must be considered.

The objective of venous interruption is to prevent immediate recurrence of embolism. Ligation of the superficial femoral vein offers no protection against embolization from the deep femoral venous system, and ligation of the common femoral vein is unacceptable because of severe obstruction to venous drainage. Furthermore, these procedures must be bilateral to grant protection from a suspected embolic focus in the legs. For these reasons, interruption of the inferior vena cava has replaced more distal ligation procedures. A number of surgical procedures have been applied to the inferior vena cava: simple ligation; plication, in which fine channels are preserved; and the application of totally or partially occlusive clips or filters. Nonsurgical interruption also can be accomplished by introducing "umbrella," balloon, or filter devices, attached to catheters, into the inferior vena cava via neck or upper extremity veins. Each procedure has advantages and disadvantages. For example, total interruption leads to a transient fall in cardiac output and variable degrees of edema of the legs; successful plication does not prevent small emboli from reaching the lungs; devices introduced into the inferior vena cava may migrate upward or be badly placed. Unfortunately, no form of inferior vena caval interruption precludes embolic recurrence. There are several reasons for this: sizable collateral channels develop weeks to months after complete occlusion of the cava, through which embolization may recur; thromboembolism may originate at the site of caval manipulation; caval blockade does not prevent embolization from foci within the right cardiac chambers; small emboli may traverse clips, filters, or plications, and such devices may themselves thrombose. Therefore, because most pulmonary emboli do resolve, caval interruption should be regarded as a *lifesaving procedure* to be restricted to patients who could not tolerate an *immediate* embolic recurrence or those with documented venous thrombosis in whom anticoagulant therapy is contraindicated.

There is one instance, however, in which prompt caval ligation is the therapy of choice: septic thrombophlebitis of pelvic origin with multiple septic pulmonary emboli. If these patients do not respond promptly to a heparin-antibiotic regimen, they may die unless caval (and left ovarian vein) ligation is carried out promptly.

Two criteria should be met before emergency pulmonary embolectomy is performed: (1) there must be evidence of severe hemodynamic compromise due to embolism, particularly sustained systemic hypotension, which is not responsive to supportive measures; and (2) the personnel and equipment required for embolectomy carried out with the aid of cardiopulmonary bypass must be available.

SPECIAL CONSIDERATIONS   Total resolution of emboli does not always occur. If residual vascular obstruction is substantial, the patient may present, months or years after the actual embolic events, with dyspnea and pulmonary hypertension of uncertain cause, often with right ventricular failure. Such patients commonly are misdiagnosed, for months or years, as having "asthma," "chronic lung disease," "primary" pulmonary hypertension (Chap. 210), or cor pulmonale of unclear etiology (Chap. 191).

Such patients should be studied by appropriate techniques, since emboli in the main or lobar arteries can be surgically removed (thromboendarterectomy), allowing cure of this otherwise fatal form of pulmonary hypertensive disease.

PROGNOSIS IN PULMONARY EMBOLISM   The prognosis of the patient with pulmonary embolism *in whom therapy is promptly instituted* is excellent. As stated at the outset of this chapter, less than 1 embolic event in 10 is lethal. The majority of these deaths occur suddenly and can be avoided only by prophylaxis (see above). The remainder appear to be due to embolic extension or recurrence, which therapy can moderate. Thus, for patients who survive long enough to reach medical attention and receive heparin, the outlook is quite good. Morbidity following embolism is uncommon since embolic resolution is the rule, and few patients develop the pulmonary hypertensive problem noted above.

Limited reliable data are available regarding recurrence rates in the months and years after a single embolic event (with or without prolonged postembolic anticoagulant therapy). In the absence of risk factors, or a positive IPG, recurrence appears to be uncommon, but more precise data are needed.

NONTHROMBOTIC EMBOLISM

Because the lung vasculature serves as a filter of the venous circulation, it is the recipient of diverse materials which can gain entry into venous blood, including bone marrow, foreign bodies, parasites, and tumor cells. The most frequently encountered form of nonthrombotic embolism is *fat embolism*. This dramatic and controversial entity follows the introduction of neutral fat into the venous circulation, most commonly after bone trauma or fracture (marrow fat), but occasionally after trauma to adipose tissue or liver infiltrated by fat. The clinical sequence is characteristic. After a latent period of 12 to 36 h or more, during which the patient is asymptomatic, sudden cardiopulmonary and neurologic deterioration appears. Mental aberrations, delirium, and coma develop. Dyspnea, tachypnea, and tachycardia occur, and the chest roentgenographic and physiologic components of the "adult respiratory distress syndrome" appear (see Chap. 216). Anemia and thrombocytopenia are common, as are petechiae on the upper thorax and arms. The pathogenesis of the syndrome is not clear, but it seems likely that two events occur: release of free fatty acids (by action of lipases on the neutral fat), which induces a toxic vasculitis, followed by platelet-fibrin thrombosis; and actual obstruction of small pulmonary arteries by macroaggregates of fat. Several forms of therapy have been proposed (corticosteroids, heparin, ethanol), but none has proved effective; treatment remains supportive and mortality rate high.

Another dramatic form of nonthrombotic embolism is *amniotic fluid embolism*. This occurs during both spontaneous delivery and cesarean section. Sudden and massive obstruction of the pulmonary microvasculature occurs, leading to shock and, often, death. With survival of the initial phase of the disease, the picture of disseminated intravascular coagulation appears. The syndrome is due to the entrance of a significant quantity of amniotic fluid into the venous circulation. This fluid is a potent thromboplastic agent which induces thrombosis in the pulmonary vasculature and elsewhere. The fluid also contains particulates which lodge in the lung. Treatment consists of supportive measures.

Nonembolic pulmonary arterial obstruction due to *vasculitis* has become a common problem among intravenous drug users. This vasculitis, caused by the drugs per se or materials (e.g., talc) mixed with the drugs, can induce thrombosis. This entity may be difficult to distinguish from PTE. Repetitive episodes may lead to irreversible and severe pulmonary hypertension.

REFERENCES

FEDULLO PF et al: [111]-Indium labelled platelets: Effect of heparin on uptake by venous thrombi and relationship to the activated partial thromboplastin time. Circulation 66:632, 1982

FISHMAN AP, KELLEY MA: Pulmonary thromboembolism (including prophylaxis, treatment, sickle cell disease and multiple pulmonary thrombi), in *Pulmonary Diseases and Disorders*, 2d ed, AP Fishman (ed). New York, McGraw-Hill, 1987, Chap 66.

GOLDHABER SZ (ed): *Pulmonary Embolism and Deep Venous Thrombosis*. Philadelphia, Saunders, 1985

HULL R et al: Pulmonary angiography, ventilation lung scanning and venography for clinically suspected pulmonary embolism in the abnormal perfusion scan. Ann Intern Med 98:891, 1983

——— et al: Adjusted subcutaneous heparin versus warfarin sodium in the long-term treatment of venous thrombosis. N Engl J Med 305:189, 1982

——— et al: Combined use of leg scanning and impedance plethysmography in suspected venous thrombosis. N Engl J Med 296:1497, 1977

KAKKAR VV et al: Prevention of post-operative embolism by low-dose heparin: An international multicenter trial. Lancet 2:45, 1975

KIPPER MS et al: Long-term follow-up of patients with suspected pulmonary embolism and a normal lung scan. Chest 82:411, 1982

MERCANDETTI A et al: Influence of perfusion and ventilation scans on therapeutic decision-making and outcome among embolic suspects. West J Med 142:208, 1985

MOSER KM: Pulmonary vascular obstruction due to embolism and thrombosis, in *Pulmonary Vascular Disease*, KM Moser (ed). New York, Dekker, 1979, p 341

——— et al: Chronic thrombotic obstruction of major pulmonary arteries: Results of thromboendarterectomy in 15 patients. Ann Intern Med 99:299, 1983

———, FEDULLO PF: Venous thromboembolism: Three simple decisions. Chest 83:117, 256, 1983

SALZMAN EW et al: Intraoperative external pneumatic calf compression to afford long-term prophylaxis against deep vein thrombosis in urologic patients. Surgery 87:239, 1980

SASAHARA AA, DALEN JE: Controversy: Should fibrinolytic drugs be used to treat acute pulmonary embolism? J Cardiovasc Med 5:793, 1980

212   DISEASES OF THE UPPER RESPIRATORY TRACT

LOUIS WEINSTEIN

Disorders of the upper respiratory tract (nose, nasopharynx, paranasal sinuses, and larynx) are among the commonest forms of human illness. In most instances, they result in discomfort which is more annoying and distracting than disabling, and while they may interfere with the individual's function sufficiently to prevent participation in normal activities, usually they are not life-threatening and do not lead to serious chronic disability.

NOSE

ANOSMIA   Total loss of olfactory sense is most common as a transient manifestation of acute infections of the upper respiratory tract. It may be present with chronic nasal obstruction due to edema of the mucosa or marked swelling of the turbinates and with congenital defects, ozena, tumors (see below), trauma involving the olfactory nerves, and nasal polyps.

RHINITIS AND NASAL OBSTRUCTION   Intermittent or persistent nasal discharge may be caused by a variety of disorders, including hay fever, vasomotor rhinitis and complicating nasal polyposis, acute coryza, and other forms of viral rhinitis, the upper respiratory manifestations of measles, syphilis (the "snuffles" of the congenital

disease), tuberculosis, and nasal diphtheria, intranasal foreign bodies, and chronic use of vasoconstrictor drugs.

Acute and self-limited nasal obstruction is usually associated with acute upper respiratory tract infections, most commonly viral. Hypertrophy and inflammation of the turbinates leading to nasal obstruction, with or without persistent nasal discharge, may be caused by allergic reactions. A common reason for difficulty in breathing through the nose is a *deviated septum*. Menstruation is associated, in some instances, with bogginess of the turbinates to a degree sufficient to produce retardation of airflow through the nose; pregnancy may produce the same phenomenon.

RHINORRHEA   Although unilateral nasal discharge may be caused by intranasal foreign bodies, when it is intermittent or persistent, the possibility that it is due to *cerebrospinal fluid (CSF) rhinorrhea* must be considered. This condition may be diagnosed by injecting a marker such as a dye (fluorescein) or a radioactive tracer into the CSF and following its appearance in nasal secretions.

EPISTAXIS   Probably the commonest cause is nose picking, leading to tearing of the rich network of veins in the anterior nares (Kiesselbach's plexus). Minor epistaxis may also appear in the course of viral infections of the upper respiratory tract. Among the more serious infections in which acute nosebleed may develop are typhoid fever, unilateral nasal diphtheria, pertussis, and malaria. Other causes of intermittent epistaxis are uncontrolled hypertension, vicarious menstruation, bleeding diatheses, polycythemia vera, rhinoliths, acute sinusitis especially involving the ethmoid sinus with thrombosis of the ethmoidal vein, tumors of the nose and paranasal sinuses, and nasal angiomas. Episodes of bleeding or the severity of attacks are frequently increased in patients receiving aspirin. Vitamin C and prothrombin deficiency are *not* associated with isolated epistaxis, although this may occur with bleeding from other sites. In hereditary hemorrhagic telangiectasia (Osler-Rendu-Weber syndrome) the only site of bleeding may be the nose; a family history of repeated hemorrhages from this and other sites should suggest this diagnosis.

NASAL FURUNCULOSIS   Furuncles involving the internal or external surfaces of the nose pose potential threats to life because of the possibility of spread to the cavernous sinus via the draining veins. When seen in their early stage, they respond rapidly to antimicrobial therapy which should be directed primarily against *Staphylococcus aureus* and given in large doses (Chap. 94). Oral treatment may be adequate in the early stages of the disease, but parenteral therapy is necessary when the constitutional reaction is severe and there is marked edema of the intra- or extranasal tissues. *Under no circumstances should these lesions be squeezed* because of the danger of spread of organisms to intracranial venous sinuses. Also, incision for drainage should not be carried out unless pain becomes severe or the lesion has become large.

PHARYNX

ACUTE PHARYNGITIS   The outstanding symptom of acute pharyngitis, regardless of cause, is a sore throat. About two-thirds of all acute illnesses in families are viral infections of the upper respiratory tract, with varying degrees of pharyngeal discomfort present. The acute pharyngitides can be classified into three groups: (1) treatable infections, (2) untreatable infections, and (3) noninfectious disorders (Table 212-1).

Physical examination of the pharyngeal mucosa may reveal changes varying in intensity from mild redness and congestion of blood vessels (many viral infections) to intense red-purple color, patchy yellow exudate, hypertrophy of all the lymphoid tissue, and marked vascular injection (e.g., severe disease due to group A *Streptococcus pyogenes*). Symptoms may be variable and may range from a complaint of "scratchy throat" to pain so severe that swallowing of saliva is difficult. In some cases, the lingual tonsils, situated on the posterolateral surface of the tongue, may be infected in the course of streptococcal pharyngitis. This causes pain on movement of the tongue. The presence of exudate does not establish a specific etiology and may be noted in infections due to *S. pyogenes, Haemophilus influenzae, H. parainfluenzae* (children), *Corynebacterium diphtheriae, and Streptococcus pneumoniae* (rare) as well as in some viral diseases, such as those caused by adenovirus and Epstein-Barr (EB) virus. Ulcerations involving the posterior pharyngeal wall and/or tonsils are characteristically present in fusobacterial infections (Plaut-Vincent's angina), pharyngeal tularemia, syphilis (primary chancre), tuberculosis, following local trauma to the pharynx, and in immunosuppressed and agranulocytic patients in whom invasion by fusobacteria or other members of the indigenous pharyngeal microflora takes place. The presence of limited or extensive pseudomembrane does not always indicate a specific microbial cause. While most characteristic of faucial diphtheria, such lesions may be present in infectious mononucleosis (EB virus), agranulocytosis, staphylococcal pharyngitis, and diffuse injury to the pharyngeal mucosa following direct trauma or chemical or thermal burns.

The tonsils are often involved in the course of viral and bacterial pharyngitis; they may be markedly reddened and swollen and contain exudate in the crypts.

The etiologic diagnosis of acute pharyngitis is difficult to establish on the basis of visual examination of the throat. However, in some instances in which characteristic findings are present, such as the typical pseudomembrane and suggestive odor of diphtheria, severe group A streptococcal infection, the ulceration and anaerobic odor of fusobacterial disease, or the white irregular patches overlying shallow ulcers produced by *Candida*, a specific cause may be suspected.

TABLE 212-1 Etiology of pharyngitis

I Infectious
  A Treatable
    1 Group A *Streptococcus pyogenes*
    2 *Hemophilus influenzae*
    3 *H. parainfluenzae*
    4 *Neisseria gonorrhoeae*
    5 *N. meningitidis*
    6 *Corynebacterium diphtheriae*
    7 *Spirochaeta pallida*
    8 *Fusobacterium*
    9 *F. tularensis*
    10 *Candida*
    11 *Cryptococcus*
    12 *Histoplasma*
    13 *Mycoplasma pneumoniae*
    14 *Streptococcus pneumoniae* (?)
    15 *Staphylococcus aureus* or gram-negative bacilli (usually found in neutropenic patients or those treated with antibiotics)
    16 *Chlamydia trachomatis*
  B Untreatable
    1 Primary
      a Influenza virus
      b Rhinovirus
      c Coxsackievirus A
      d Epstein-Barr virus
      e Echovirus
      f Herpes simplex
      g Reovirus
    2 Manifestation of systemic disease
      a Poliomyelitis
      b Measles
      c Chickenpox
      d Smallpox
      e Viral hepatitis
      f Rubella
      g Pertussis
II Noninfectious
  A Trauma by heat, sharp objects, etc.
  B Inhalation of irritants
  C Dehydration—mouth breathing
  D Glossopharyngeal neuralgia
  E Subacute thyroiditis (tends to be prolonged or frequently recurrent, often associated with low-grade fever)
  F Psychogenic
  G Monomyelocytic leukemia
  H Immunosuppressed state

Cultures of the pharyngeal mucosa, tonsils, or exudate will usually reveal the bacteria responsible for the disease and determine the choice of antimicrobial agent. It should be stressed, however, that these are not always rewarding. For example, only 70 percent of single throat cultures yield *S. pyogenes,* even when pharyngitis due to this organism is severe. Patients suspected of having streptococcal pharyngitis but whose throat cultures fail to yield the organism should be treated if this kind of disease is known to be present in the community. The sore throat of subacute thyroiditis may be relieved occasionally by the administration of thyroid hormone or prednisone. None of the viral pharyngitides is treatable.

Gonococcal pharyngitis is almost always the result of orogenital contact. The incidence of the disease in heterosexual men varies from 0.2 to 1.4 percent. It ranges from 5 to 25 percent in homosexual males; 20 percent of those with genital infection have simultaneous involvement of the throat. From 5 to 18 percent of women with other manifestations of gonorrhea have pharyngitis; in 1 to 3 percent this is the only disease. While mild to severe sore throat is present in about 30 percent of patients, the majority are asymptomatic. Because the clinical features of gonococcal pharyngitis may mimic disease produced by other organisms, the diagnosis is based on isolation and identification of *Neisseria gonorrhoeae*. The isolated organism must be confirmed as the gonococcus by its biologic properties because of the presence of other *Neisseria* in the pharynges of most normal individuals.

PERITONSILLAR CELLULITIS AND ABSCESS (QUINSY) This condition is most often a complication of acute pharyngitis. The organisms commonly involved are *S. pyogenes* and *Staphylococcus aureus*. The first sign of this disease is marked enlargement of the tonsils, which are surrounded by red, edematous pillars. The tonsillar and peritonsillar hypertrophy may progress to a degree threatening occlusion of the upper airway. High-grade fever and leukocytosis are present, and severe rigors may occur. In its early stages, the process is a cellulitis, but, in the absence of therapy, abscess develops as infection progresses and involves one or both tonsils; at this time, soft grayish-white exudate may cover the tonsillar surfaces. The diagnosis is made on the basis of the physical findings. If detected early when only peritonsillar cellulitis is present, administration of a properly selected antimicrobial agent may clear the infection and abort the development of abscess. Antimicrobial therapy alone is inadequate after abscess has developed. The optimal treatment at this stage is incision and drainage of the involved tonsil(s).

PARAPHARYNGEAL SPACE ABSCESS This syndrome is always a complication of acute pharyngitis. Primary or secondary bacterial invasion of one of the tonsils results in the development of an intratonsillar abscess accompanied by considerable edema and inflammatory reaction in the parapharyngeal space. The lesion is usually unilateral and the involved tonsil protrudes toward the midline; there is frequently very little pharyngeal discomfort, but there is marked tenderness at the angle of the jaw on the same side as the tonsillar abscess. The remainder of the throat frequently has a benign appearance. There is usually considerable fever and leukocytosis. If unrecognized and not treated early in its course, the infection spreads through the tonsillar veins to the jugular vein, where it produces thrombophlebitis. Septic emboli from this source may be widely disseminated and cause widespread metastatic thrombosis and infection with single or multiple abscesses of the lungs, a highly fatal syndrome termed *postanginal sepsis*. Early recognition and institution of therapy before spread to the jugular vein results in rapid clearing of the infection.

RETROPHARYNGEAL ABSCESS Although retropharyngeal abscess is most common in children under the age of 4 years because of the presence of lymph nodes in the retropharynx that may become infected in the course of acute pharyngitis, the disease also occurs in adults. The factors that predispose to the development of a retropharyngeal abscess in adults include acute infections of the ears, nose, and throat, dental disease, regional trauma such as ingestion of a foreign body, oroendotracheal intubation, endoscopic procedures, external penetrating injuries, fracture of vertebral bodies, and blunt trauma to the neck. Diabetes mellitus, a poor nutritional state, or immunosuppression may predispose to development of this infection in adults. A very important lesion that may lead to development of a retropharyngeal abscess in adults is cervical or cervicodorsal vertebral osteomyelitis complicated by the development of paravertebral abscess. Among the organisms responsible for the infection of the bone and the related abscess are *Mycobacterium tuberculosis*, pyogenic bacteria, and *Coccidioides immitis*.

TUMORS AND OTHER CAUSES OF CHRONIC SORE THROAT

Although not always associated with pharyngeal pain, some patients with various neoplastic diseases are troubled by a persistent sore throat. The fever which may be present is not always caused by microbial invasion but rather by the pyrogenic activity of the tumor itself. Carcinoma of the tonsil is the second commonest tumor of the upper airway (osteoma is most common, see below). Other neoplasms that involve the pharynx and may cause pain are nasopharyngeal carcinoma, multiple myeloma, myelomonocytic leukemia, and Hodgkin's disease. The solid tumors often involve only one tonsil; leukemia tends to produce diffuse pharyngitis. Treatment of the neoplasms may induce a persistent sore throat not present earlier. Immunosuppression induced by the drugs used to treat the tumors, and may lead to the development of mucositis, or infection by uncommon organisms such as *Aspergillus*, *Mucor*, *Actinomyces*, and *Pseudomonas*.

Among a number of benign causes of chronic sore throat is "mouth breathing." Many elderly persons breathe through an open mouth while asleep, and when they wake experience pharyngeal discomfort which usually disappears with intake of fluids. Another group of "mouth breathers" are patients with severe obstruction of the nasal passages due to marked deviation of the septum. In them, the pharyngeal discomfort is constant and not relieved without surgical correction of the septum. Exposure to irritants like tobacco smoke in those who are heavy smokers of cigars and pipes may induce persistent sore throat. Subacute thyroiditis is often associated with severe pain in the pharynx that may persist for weeks to months. Patients often seek medical attention because of the severe pharyngitis and are unaware that this is a manifestation of inflammation of the thyroid. A helpful diagnostic finding is the normal appearance of the pharyngeal mucosa at the time when the pain is severe. Emotional disorders may occasionally be associated with chronic low-grade discomfort in the pharynx. A rare cause of severe and persistent pain in the throat is glossopharyngeal neuralgia.

SINUSES

ACUTE SINUSITIS The organisms most often responsible for acute sinusitis are *S. pneumoniae*, *S. pyogenes*, and *H. influenzae*. Other bacteria may be involved in patients receiving immunosuppressive therapy, in those who have received antibiotics, or in whom penetrating trauma, local tumors, or vasculitis is a predisposing factor. The etiology of chronic sinusitis may be the same as that of the acute form, but more than one pathogen may be present. In many instances, however, cultures yield only members of the indigenous microflora of the upper respiratory tract.

The commonest predisposing factor of acute purulent sinusitis is viral infection of the upper respiratory tract, which may lead to obstruction of drainage of the paranasal sinuses and the development of localized pain, tenderness, and low-grade fever. These manifestations usually clear as the viral disease subsides. In a number of instances, however, invasion by pyogenic bacteria supervenes and is responsible for the development of purulent sinusitis. Obstruction of meatal drainage of any type or direct introduction of bacteria into the sinuses may lead to the development of acute infection of the paranasal

sinuses. Abscesses of the roots of the upper bicuspid or molar teeth that rupture into the maxillary sinuses, swimming and diving, and direct local injury may be inciting mechanisms. Fractures of the bones encompassing the sinuses, especially the frontals and ethmoids, may be followed by infection. Wegener's granulomatosis and tumors of the meatuses of the turbinates may produce the clinical picture of acute or chronic sinusitis. In some of these patients, bacterial infection is superimposed, and when these patients are studied only after infection develops, the underlying lesion is often overlooked. This underscores the fact that recurrent or prolonged episodes of sinusitis that are refractory to antimicrobial therapy, or that relapse soon after treatment is discontinued, must be investigated thoroughly for the presence of a noninfectious obstructing lesion.

The diagnosis of acute purulent sinusitis is usually made when constitutional manifestations are present, such as fever, chills, pain and tenderness of the involved sinuses, nasal obstruction, and recurrent headaches that change in intensity with position and disappear shortly after getting out of bed. Isolation of a pathogenic organism from the nasal secretions or from material draining into the meatuses of the nasal turbinates may help to solidify the diagnosis. When there is marked swelling of the turbinates, they can be shrunk by the local application of cocaine or other potent vasoconstrictors. This exposes the meatuses and permits the collection of exudate draining directly from the involved sinus. Transillumination of the sinuses is also helpful, while radiologic study is of value in identifying the specific sinus involved.

Effective management of acute sinusitis rests on demonstration of a specific pathogenic organism in the secretion present in the nose or drained from the sinuses, testing of the organism for sensitivity to a variety of antimicrobial agents, and administration of the most active agent in adequate doses (Chap. 88). Vasoconstrictors are of help in producing transient relief of symptoms but must not be used excessively. Surgical drainage may be indicated when infection becomes prolonged or local or intracranial complications develop.

Frontal sinusitis is characterized by pain over the forehead approximately in the area of the underlying sinus. Although the overlying site is usually normal, it may be swollen and reddened over an area outlining the sinuses. Pressure applied over the sinuses and on the lateral edge of the orbital ridges produces pain. Examination of the nasal turbinates shows purulent exudate in the middle or superior meatus if drainage is not prevented by swelling of these structures. Pain, swelling, and tenderness in the anterior portions of the maxillae are the outstanding features of *maxillary sinusitis*. When the infection is severe, pain may be referred to the upper teeth which may become loosened, and hemorrhage may be present in the surrounding tissues. Pus is visible in the middle meatus of the turbinates. The symptoms and signs of *ethmoid sinusitis* are pain in the upper medial areas of the nose, frontal headache, and redness of the skin and tenderness to pressure over the superior areas of the nasal bones adjacent to the inner canthi of the eyes. Pus is visible in the middle meatus when the anterior cells of the sinus are involved, and in the superior meatus if the posterior cells are infected; in most instances, both areas of the sinus are involved and exudate is present in both meatuses. The manifestations of infection of the *sphenoid sinus* are tenderness and pain over the vertex of the skull, the mastoid bones (in the presence of normal tympanic membranes), and the occipital portion of the head. Rarely, streaks of redness may be detectable over both zygomas as a result of irritation of the maxillary branch of the trigeminal nerve that lies in close proximity to the sinus.

Osteomyelitis of the frontal bone is a rare complication of frontal sinusitis. This is characterized by fever, chills, leukocytosis, frontal headache, and the presence of cool, pale edema over the forehead (Pott's puffy tumor). Involvement of the bone in which the ethmoid sinus lies may be manifested by unilateral or bilateral exophthalmos when one or both sinuses are involved. This is usually due to a sterile or pyogenic orbital cellulitis secondary to a "sympathetic" inflammation or perforation of the lamina papyracea, the lateral wall of the sinus, and the medial wall of the orbit. Impairment of venous return from the orbits may lead to the development of retinal hemorrhages. Intracranial spread of infection from the sinuses through the diploic veins may lead to meningitis, infection, and thrombosis of the superficial cerebral veins or cavernous and sagittal venous sinuses, cranial nerve palsies, and extradural abscess.

Bacterial meningitis is also a rare complication of purulent sinusitis, usually involving the frontal sinuses, and associated with cranial osteomyelitis and subdural and brain abscess. Sudden onset of

TABLE 212-2 Differential diagnosis of hoarseness and other manifestations of laryngeal dysfunction

I Intralaryngeal disease
  A Infectious
    1 Common cold
    2 Viral laryngitis
    3 *Hemophilus influenzae*
    4 Membranous laryngitis (*Streptococcus pyogenes, Pseudomonas, Fusobacterium*)
    5 Diphtheria (laryngeal membrane)
    6 Herpes simplex
    7 Actinomycosis
    8 Candidiasis
    9 Blastomycosis
    10 Histoplasmosis
    11 Tuberculosis (ulcers)
    12 Leprosy
    13 Syphilis (secondary stage, chondritis, gumma)
    14 *Mycoplasma pneumoniae*
    15 *Syngamus laryngeus*
  B Noninfectious
    1 Trauma (edema or hematoma)
    2 Vocal cord nodules (singer's nodes)
    3 Papillomas of vocal cords
    4 Pachyderma of vocal cords
    5 Inhalation of smoke, fire, irritating gases, tobacco smoke
    6 Leukoplakia of vocal cords
    7 Rheumatoid arthritis (involvement of cricoarytenoid joint)
    8 Chronic alcoholism
    9 Benign tumors
    10 Cancer
    11 Foreign bodies
II Extralaryngeal disease
  A Lesions in neck [produce hoarseness because of (1) pressure on larynx that interferes with movement of vocal cords, (2) edema secondary to decreased venous and lymphatic drainage, and (3) impingement on laryngeal nerves with paresis or paralysis of cords]
    1 Hemorrhages and/or edema due to trauma, severe traction of neck, thyroidectomy, tracheostomy, and biopsy of scalene node
    2 Tumors of hypopharynx
    3 Tumors of carotid body
    4 Thrombophlebitis of jugular bulb
  B Local and systemic disorders outside neck (produce hoarseness by pressure on laryngeal nerves anywhere along the course outside the neck, or paresis or paralysis of the vocal cords as a manifestation of generalized neurologic dysfunction)
    1 Local lesions
      a Bacterial meningitis
      b Meningovascular syphilis
      c Infectious mononucleosis (enlarged mediastinal nodes)
      d Angioneurotic edema
      e Mitral stenosis (enlarged pulmonary artery)
      f Aneurysms of arch of aorta, carotid or innominate arteries
      g Ligation of patent ductus arteriosus
      h Tumors of mediastinal structures
      i Tumors of parotid gland
      j Relapsing polychondritis
      k Neoplastic disease of meninges
      l Fracture of base of skull
      m Cancer or nodules of thyroid
      n Goiter
    2 Systemic disorders
      a Diphtheria (peripheral neuritis)
      b Poliomyelitis (bulbar)
      c Infectious mononucleosis (nervous system involvement)
      d Herpes zoster
      e Mucoviscidosis
      f Myxedema
      g Acromegaly
      h Wegener's granulomatosis
      i Lupus erythematosus
      j Diabetic neuropathy
      k Poisoning by lead, mercury, arsenic, botulinus toxin

convulsions, hemiplegia, and aphasia in a patient with acute frontal sinusitis should suggest the possibility of subdural abscess with thrombophlebitis of the sagittal sinus or superficial cerebral veins. Infections of the ethmoid sinus may be complicated by paralysis of the third cranial nerve due to invasion of the dural sinuses, or profuse epistaxis as a result of thrombosis of the ethmoidal veins that drain into the cavernous sinus, which may become thrombosed. Chronic or recurrent purulent sinusitis may eventually be responsible for the development of bronchiectasis. An unusual form of chronic sinusitis in association with bronchiectasis and situs inversus is *Kartagener's syndrome*. Patients with this disorder have been noted to have delayed mucociliary transport in the lower airways—the immotile ciliary syndrome; this is accompanied in men by lack of motility of sperm, the numbers of which are normal.

CHRONIC SINUSITIS It is difficult to establish the diagnosis of chronic sinusitis in the absence of documented recurrences of acute purulent infection. Many patients complaining of headaches, often frontal in nature, and troubled by obstruction of the nasal airway, may have some degree of tenderness over any of the paranasal sinuses. X-ray examinations of the sinuses often reveal thickening of the mucous membranes. Cultures of the nose or nasal discharge frequently yield no pathogenic organisms. In many instances, an allergic background is present in individuals with this syndrome; in these cases, relief of symptoms is often produced by the judicious use of nasal vasoconstrictors, and treatment is directed to the specific allergy. The manifestations presented by many patients are not related to chronic infection, but are due to other factors such as irritating dusts or gases or excessive exposure to tobacco smoke.

TUMORS OF THE SINUSES The commonest benign tumor of the paranasal sinuses is osteoma. Fifty percent of cases involve the frontal, 40 percent the ethmoid, and 10 percent the maxillary and sphenoid sinuses. The malignant tumors include carcinoma of the maxilla, sarcoma, Burkitt's lymphoma, myeloma, and adenocarcinoma. Melanoma of the nasal cavity may extend into the paranasal sinuses. Other malignant diseases originating in the sinuses may invade the nasal cavity and, because they produce obstruction, lead to consideration of the nose as the primary site of the lesion. A neoplastic lesion should be ruled out in patients who experience repeated episodes of acute sinusitis or who have chronic symptoms, particularly repeated epistaxis in the absence of an identifiable pathogenic organism.

LARYNX

SYMPTOMS AND SIGNS OF LARYNGEAL DISEASE There are three main causes of laryngeal disease: (1) intralaryngeal lesions, (2) extralaryngeal processes that produce other manifestations by direct pressure on either the larynx or the nerves that supply the vocal cords, and (3) disorders in which either local or diffuse disease of the nervous system leads to dysfunction of the vocal cords. A differential diagnosis of the various disorders of the larynx is presented in Table 212-2.

Hoarseness is the commonest symptom of disorders of the larynx, regardless of etiology. The common denominator of the numerous causes of this symptom is interference with normal phonatory function of the larynx. Both inflammatory and noninflammatory diseases of this organ as well as functional disturbances (hysterical aphonia) may be causative factors. Although hoarseness is usually of short duration with acute self-limited processes such as infections, it may persist for long periods.

Cough is common with any type of laryngeal disease. *Pain* occurs occasionally, while *stridor* and *dyspnea* are uncommon manifestations of laryngeal involvement. However, when present, these are ominous because they indicate the development of airway obstruction which may rapidly become complete. Obstruction to breathing is not only associated with intralaryngeal lesions or those which exert pressure directly on this organ but may also occur as a result of neurologic disorders in which paralysis of both vocal cords develops.

The exact cause of laryngeal obstruction can be detected only by direct or indirect examination of the larynx. *This is usually necessary when manifestations have persisted for longer than 2 or 3 weeks.* However, if serious obstruction of the airway develops rapidly in acute disorders of the larynx, laryngoscopic examination should be carried out promptly and tracheostomy performed if necessary.

The disorders of the larynx described below require specific and early diagnosis because of their life-threatening potential.

EPIGLOTTITIS Although much less common than in children, epiglottitis may occur in adults. Some of the clinical and microbiologic features in the older age group are different from those in youngsters. Men are involved three times more often than women. Predisposing factors include multiple myeloma, Hodgkin's disease, myelomonocytic leukemia, laryngeal blastomycosis, and disorders that lead to immunosuppression. Among the organisms reported to be responsible for the disease are *H. influenzae, H. parainfluenzae, S. pneumoniae, S. pyogenes, Escherichia coli,* and "normal flora"; primary blastomycosis of the larynx may extend to the laryngeal surface of the epiglottis. Bacteremia supervenes in about 50 percent of cases. The symptoms of epiglottitis in adults differ from those in children. Sore throat is present in all patients. Next, in order of decreasing frequency, are fever (80 percent), dyspnea, dysphagia, and hoarseness (about 15 percent). Objective evidence of pharyngitis and tenderness of the neck are relatively uncommon. Abscess of the epiglottis occurs in about 12 percent of cases. Examination discloses a red, swollen epiglottis that may be so large that it protrudes into the lower pharynx. The diagnosis is proved by "cross-table" radiographic study of the neck. Antimicrobial therapy is mandatory, and the choice is based on the nature of the responsible organism. Dyspnea that progresses to the point of threatening complete obstruction of the airway is an indication for tracheostomy.

FUNGAL LARYNGITIS Disease caused by *Candida* species is uncommon but occurs occasionally in patients with mucocutaneous candidiasis and those who have been receiving antibiotics or are immunosuppressed. Because it is almost always associated with candidal esophagitis, it has been suggested that all persons with involvement of the esophagus by *Candida* undergo laryngoscopy. Hoarseness is not common. Scarring of the larynx may develop if antifungal therapy is not administered.

Two true fungi, *Histoplasma capsulatum* and *Blastomyces dermatitidis,* may produce chronic laryngitis. Symptoms common to both include hoarseness, dyspnea, and dysphagia; obstruction of the airway and hemoptysis may occur in some cases. The lesions may appear as large masses. Ulcerations are common and are probably the reason for the bleeding.

TUBERCULOUS LARYNGITIS Although decreasing in incidence over many years, infection of the larynx by *Mycobacterium tuberculosis* is still a problem. Many of the clinical features of this disease have changed over the last 40 years. It is now most common in older patients (50 to 59 years), more frequent in men than in women (3:1), and may be present in the absence of radiographic evidence of pulmonary disease. Hoarseness is present in almost all cases. While multiple ulcers, present primarily on the posterior aspect of the vocal cords, were common in the past, they are now relatively infrequent. The vocal cords are involved in 50 percent of cases; disease of the false cords and ventricles is next most common. In some cases, only hyperemia and edema are present; this may lead to a misdiagnosis of nonspecific laryngitis.

SYNGAMOSIS OF THE LARYNX This disease, caused by the worm *Syngamus laryngeus,* is a problem in the Caribbean islands, Brazil, and the Philippines. The vectors of the parasite are domestic and wild birds and cattle. Infestation is initiated by inhalation of the worm, which attaches to the mucosa of the larynx, pharynx, or trachea. Symptoms include severe, paroxysmal, nonproductive cough,

occasional hemoptysis, and a "crawling" sensation in the larynx. Diagnosis is established by washing out the trachea and demonstrating the characteristic eggs. There is no specific treatment. The disease usually clears when the eggs and worms are coughed out.

FOREIGN BODY Inhalation of a foreign body rapidly produces symptoms. *Pain* is "sticking" in quality and localized to the larynx. *Laryngeal spasm* is usually present. *Dyspnea* may develop as a result of edema and lead to a degree of obstruction sufficient to compromise the airway. There is often a *change in the quality of the voice;* complete *aphonia* may occur. If the inhaled object is sharp, as a chicken bone, there is rapid development of local swelling and progressive obstruction to breathing. Perforation of the larynx may occur and lead to infection that extends from the local site to other areas in the neck and mediastinum. Suspicion of a foreign body makes mirror or laryngoscopic examination an emergency procedure.

CANCER OF THE LARYNX This lesion develops at an average age of 60 years and is 10 times more common in men than in women. Cancers of the larynx are of two types: *intrinsic,* arising on the anterior segment of the vocal cords (70 percent of the cases), and *extrinsic,* extending beyond the vocal cords. Although hoarseness develops early in the course of intrinsic lesions, it is frequently late in onset with extrinsic ones. The treatment of choice for this disease is surgery.

Small lesions of the middle third of the cord often respond to radiation alone. Total or partial laryngectomy is required in the majority of cases. When the cancer involves the epiglottis and/or the false cords, partial supraglottic laryngectomy is the preferred operative procedure because it does not result in loss of normal speech and has a high chance of cure. In some instances, preoperative irradiation of the larynx and surrounding lymph nodes may help in the eradication of the tumor. About 90 percent of cancers of the larynx are cured if detected and treated early.

REFERENCES

BAILEY CM, WINDLE-TAYLOR PC: Tuberculous laryngitis: A series of 37 patients. Laryngology 91:93, 1981
DONEGAN JO, WOOD MD: Histoplasmosis of the larynx. Laryngoscope 94:206, 1984
ELIASSON R et al: The immotile-cilia syndrome: A congenital ciliary abnormality as an etiologic factor in chronic airway infections and male sterility. N Engl J Med 297:1, 1977
KHILANANI U, KHATIB R: Acute epiglottitis in adults. Am J Med Sci 287:65, 1984
KOOPMANN CF JR, COULTHARD SW: Retropharyngeal abscess—a ten-year experience. Laryngoscope 94:455, 1984
LEVENSON MJ et al: Laryngeal tuberculosis: Review of twenty cases. Laryngoscope 94:1094, 1984
MORGAN MA et al: Fungal sinusitis in healthy and immunocompromised individuals. Am J Clin Pathol 82:597, 1984
PAPARELLA MM, SHUMRICK DA: *Otolaryngology.* Philadelphia, Saunders, 1980
PAYNE J, KOOPMANN CF JR: Laryngeal carcinoma—Or is it laryngeal blastomycosis? Laryngoscope 94:608, 1984
WEINSTEIN L, MOLAVI A: *Syngamus laryngeus* infection. Ann Intern Med 74:577, 1971

---

213 NEOPLASMS OF THE LUNG

JOHN D. MINNA

In 1984, primary carcinoma of the lung affected more than 96,000 males and 43,000 females in the United States, most of whom died within 1 year. The peak incidence occurs between ages 55 and 65 years, and lung cancer is the leading cause of cancer death in men and the second leading cause of death in women. The incidence is increasing, causing the age-adjusted lung cancer death rate for both sexes to double every 15 years. At the time of diagnosis, only 20 percent of all lung cancer patients will have local disease, while 25 percent will have disease spread to regional lymph nodes, and 55 percent will have distant metastatic sites. Even in those patients with supposedly localized disease, overall 5-year survival is only 30 percent for males and 50 percent for females, and this survival rate has not changed significantly over the past 20 years. Thus, primary carcinoma of the lung is a major health problem with a generally grim prognosis. However, an orderly approach to diagnosis, staging, and treatment based on knowledge of the clinical behavior of lung cancer, combined with a critical review of clinical treatment trials, allows selection of the best therapy for individual patients for either potential cure or optimal palliation. This approach should be multi-disciplinary, involving the interaction of medical internists or chest physicians, medical, radiation, and surgical oncologists, pathologists, as well as diagnostic and supportive care personnel.

PATHOLOGY

The histologic classification of primary lung neoplasms recommended by the World Health Organization in 1977 should be used (see Table 213-1). Four major cell types make up 95 percent of all primary lung neoplasms. These are squamous or epidermoid carcinoma, small cell (also called "oat cell") carcinoma, adenocarcinoma (including bronchioloalveolar), and large cell (also called large cell anaplastic) carcinoma. The various cell types have different natural histories and responses to therapy, and thus a correct histologic diagnosis by an experienced pathologist is the first step to correct treatment.

Major treatment decisions are made on the basis of whether the tumor is histologically classified as a small cell carcinoma or one of the "non-small cell" varieties (which include epidermoid, adenocarcinoma, large cell carcinoma, bronchioloalveolar carcinoma, and mixed versions of these). Some of these distinctions are summarized in Tables 213-2 and 213-3.

In general, small cell carcinoma has spread beyond the bounds of resectional surgery at the time of presentation and is primarily managed with chemotherapy with or without radiotherapy, while if they are found to be localized at the time of presentation, the non-small cell varieties should be considered for a curative attempt with either surgery or radiotherapy.

Epidermoid cancer is the most common histologic type found in males, while adenocarcinoma is the most common type found in females. Ninety percent of patients with lung cancer of all histologic types are cigarette smokers, while the rare nonsmoking patient who develops lung cancer usually has adenocarcinoma. However, in nonsmokers with adenocarcinoma involving the lung, the possibility of other primary sites, particularly breast cancer, should be considered. Epidermoid and small cell cancers usually present as central masses with endobronchial growth, while adenocarcinomas and large cell cancers tend to present as peripheral nodules or masses with pleural involvement. Epidermoid and large cell cancers cavitate in 20 to 30 percent of cases. Bronchioloalveolar carcinoma can present as a single mass, a diffuse, multinodular lesion, or as a fluffy infiltrate.

TABLE 213-1　World Health Organization (WHO) classification of malignant pleuropulmonary neoplasms

I Epidermoid carcinoma
II Small cell carcinoma (including fusiform, polygonal, lymphocyte-like, and others)
III Adenocarcinoma (including acinar, papillary, and bronchioloalveolar)
IV Large cell carcinoma (including solid tumors with and without mucin and giant cell and clear cell tumors)
V Combined epidermoid and adenocarcinomas
VI Carcinoid tumors
VII Bronchial gland tumors (including cylindromas and mucoepidermoid tumors)
VIII Papillary tumors of the surface epithelium
IX "Mixed" tumors and carcinosarcomas
X Sarcomas
XI Unclassified
XII Mesotheliomas (including localized and diffuse)
XIII Melanomas

ETIOLOGY

The large majority of lung cancers are associated with and probably caused by cigarette smoking; benzo[*a*]pyrene is a major carcinogen in tobacco smoke. There is a dose-response relationship between the lung cancer death rate and the total amount (often expressed in "cigarette pack-years") of cigarettes smoked, such that the risk is increased sixty- to seventyfold for the man smoking two packs a day for 20 years compared to the nonsmoker. Conversely, the chance of developing lung cancer decreases with cessation of smoking but may never return to the nonsmoker level. The increase in lung cancer in women is also associated with a rise in female cigarette smoking. As a preventive measure, efforts to get persons to stop smoking should continue. Probably there is a cocarcinogenic effect of smoking and industrial or environmental pollutants. Also, peripheral adenocarcinomas occur more frequently in areas of chronic scarring caused by chronic inflammatory changes, chronic interstitial fibrosis, or scleroderma. Molecular genetic studies have revealed the presence of activated cellular oncogenes in lung cancer cells. These include point mutations in specific coding regions of *ras* oncogenes (*H*, *K*, and *N-ras* genes), occurring in 15 percent of all types of lung cancer; and amplified *myc* family oncogenes (*c*, *N*, and *L-myc*), occurring primarily in small cell lung cancer. Changes in the expression and function of the products of these genes are likely to account for the malignant behavior of lung cancer and represent targets for future efforts at prevention and treatment.

CLINICAL MANIFESTATIONS AND MODE OF PRESENTATION

The natural history of lung cancer begins with cytologic changes of atypia in bronchial epithelial cells progressing through carcinoma in situ to frank invasion. These changes usually occur before signs or symptoms have developed and are only seen in cytology (e.g., sputum and bronchial washings) or biopsies. Lung cancer gives rise to chest radiograph findings and other signs and symptoms from local tumor growth, invasion or obstruction of adjacent structures, growth in regional nodes via lymphatic spread, growth in distant metastatic sites after hematogenous dissemination, or as a remote effect of the tumor (paraneoplastic syndrome) usually resulting from peptide hormone secretion by the tumor. Appropriate identification of these signs and symptoms as tumor-related will guide further evaluation and therapy and be of prognostic importance.

If mass screening programs are excluded, 5 to 15 percent of patients are detected while asymptomatic, usually on a routine chest radiograph, while the vast majority of patients present with some sign or symptom. Signs and symptoms secondary to central or endobronchial growth of the primary tumor include cough, hemop-

TABLE 213-2　Incidence, frequency of metastases, and surgical resectability of the major lung cancer histologic types

Cell type	Incidence in autopsy series, %	Necropsy frequency of distant metastases when clinically localized, %*	Resectability rate (AJC study), %†	5-year survival after curative resection, %
Non-small cell carcinoma:				
Epidermoid	33	17	60	37
Adenocarcinoma	25	40	38	27
Large cell carcinoma	16	14	38	27
Small cell carcinoma	25	63	11	<1

* *Determined from autopsy studies of patients dying of causes other than cancer within 30 days following an apparent curative surgical resection.*
† *AJC = American Joint Committee Study for Cancer Staging and End Results Reporting, indicating percentage of cases thought to undergo a curative resection.*
SOURCE: *Adapted from Minna et al, 1985.*

tysis, wheeze and stridor, dyspnea, and pneumonitis (fever and productive cough) from obstruction. Signs and symptoms secondary to the peripheral growth of the primary tumor include pain from pleural or chest wall involvement, cough, dyspnea on a restrictive basis, and symptoms of lung abscess resulting from tumor cavitation. Signs and symptoms related to the regional spread of tumor in the thorax by contiguity or by metastasis to regional lymph nodes include tracheal obstruction, esophageal compression with dysphagia, recurrent laryngeal nerve paralysis with hoarseness, phrenic nerve paralysis with elevation of the hemidiaphragm and dyspnea, and sympathetic nerve invasion and paralysis with Horner's syndrome. *Pancoast's, or superior sulcus tumor, syndrome* results from local extension of a tumor (usually epidermoid) growing in the apex of the lung with involvement of the eighth cervical and first and second thoracic nerves, with shoulder pain which characteristically radiates in the ulnar distribution of the arm, and often with radiologic destruction of the first and second ribs. Often Horner's syndrome and Pancoast's syndrome will coexist. Other problems of regional spread include *superior vena cava syndrome* from vascular obstruction; pericardial and cardiac extension with resultant tamponade, arrhythmia, or cardiac failure; lymphatic obstruction with resultant pleural effusion; and lymphangitic spread through the lungs with hypoxemia and dyspnea. In addition, bronchioloalveolar carcinoma can spread transbronchially, producing tumor growing along multiple alveolar surfaces with resultant impairment of oxygen transfer, respiratory insufficiency, dyspnea, hypoxemia, and production of large amounts of sputum.

Extrathoracic metastatic disease is found at autopsy in over 50 percent of patients with epidermoid carcinoma, 80 percent of patients with adeno- and large cell carcinoma, and over 95 percent of patients with small cell cancer. These autopsy studies have found lung cancer metastases in virtually every organ system. Thus, the majority of lung cancer patients eventually need therapy to palliate symptoms. Common clinical problems related to metastatic disease of lung cancer include brain metastases with neurologic deficits; bone metastases with pain and pathologic fractures; bone marrow invasion with cytopenias or leukoerythroblastosis; liver metastases causing biochemical liver dysfunction, anorexia, biliary obstruction, and pain; lymph node metastases in the supraclavicular region and occasionally in the axilla and groin that can be painful and ulcerate; and spinal cord compression syndromes from epidural or bone metastases.

Remote effects of cancer or *paraneoplastic syndromes* are common in lung cancer patients and may be the presenting finding or first sign of recurrence. In addition, paraneoplastic syndromes may mimic metastatic disease and, unless detected, lead to inappropriate palliative rather than curative treatment. Often the paraneoplastic syndrome may be relieved with successful treatment of the tumor, and tumor treatment is the basis for correcting such syndromes. In some cases the pathophysiology of the paraneoplastic syndrome is known, particularly when a hormone with biologic activity is secreted by a tumor (Chap. 303). However, in many cases the pathophysiology is unknown. *Systemic symptoms* of anorexia, cachexia, and weight loss (seen in 30 percent of patients), fever (20 percent), and suppressed immunity are paraneoplastic syndromes of unknown etiology. *Endocrine syndromes* are seen in 12 percent of patients and have the best understood pathophysiology, including hypercalcemia and hypophosphatemia resulting from ectopic parathyroid hormone production by epidermoid cancer; hyponatremia with the syndrome of inappropriate secretion of antidiuretic hormone by small cell cancer; and Cushing's syndrome resulting from ectopic secretion of ACTH by small cell cancer. *Skeletal connective tissues syndromes* include clubbing in 30 percent (usually non-small cell), and hypertrophic pulmonary osteoarthropathy in 1 to 10 percent (usually adenocarcinomas) with periostitis and clubbing giving pain, tenderness, and swelling over the affected bones, and a positive bone scan. *Neurologic-myopathic syndromes* are seen in only 1 percent of patients but are dramatic and include the myasthenic *Eaton-Lambert syndrome* with small cell cancer, peripheral neuropathies, subacute cerebellar degeneration, cortical degeneration, and polymyositis seen with all lung

cancer types. *Coagulation and thrombotic and hematologic manifestations* occur in 1 to 8 percent of patients and include migratory venous thrombophlebitis (*Trousseau's syndrome*); nonbacterial thrombotic (marantic) endocarditis with arterial emboli; disseminated intravascular coagulation with hemorrhage; and anemia, granulocytosis, and leukoerythroblastosis. *Cutaneous manifestations* such as dermatomyositis and acanthosis nigricans are uncommon (1 percent or less) as are the *renal manifestations* of nephrotic syndrome or glomerulonephritis (1 percent or less).

DIAGNOSIS AND STAGING

EARLY DIAGNOSIS Screening persons at high risk (males over 45 years of age smoking 40 or more cigarettes per day) for lung cancer with sputum cytologies and chest radiographs every 4 months has shown a prevalence rate of lung cancer in asymptomatic patients of 4 to 8 cases per 1000 persons. With follow-up screening, 4 new cases of lung cancer are found per 1000 persons followed per year. These lung cancers are detected 72 percent of the time by radiographs alone, 20 percent by cytology alone, while 6 percent are detected by both methods. In contrast to nonscreened patients, 90 percent of these screened patients who develop lung cancer are asymptomatic, 62 percent have resectable lung cancer, and 53 percent of all the new cases are American Joint Commission (AJC) postsurgical stage I (see below) with a 5-year survival probability of 45 percent. These results are being prospectively compared to a randomized control group not

TABLE 213-3 Comparison between small cell and "non-small cell" lung cancers

	Small cell	Non-small cell
HISTOLOGY		
	Scant cytoplasm, indistinct nucleoli, small hyperchromatic nuclei	Abundant cytoplasm, prominent nucleoli, enlarged, pleomorphic nuclei
BIOCHEMICAL		
	L-Dopa decarboxylase, neuron-specific enolase, creatinine kinase BB isoenzyme	Keratin (epidermoid) Mucin (adenocarcinoma)
CELL SURFACE ANTIGENS		
	Absent-low: HLA, B$_2$m Leu-7 expressed	HLA, B$_2$m expressed Leu-7 not expressed
CYTOGENETICS		
	Deletion 3p(14–23)	No known specific defect
HORMONE PRODUCTION		
	ACTH, AVP, calcitonin, bombesin, neurotensin	PTH (epidermoid)
RESPONSE TO RADIOTHERAPY		
	+++ (often complete)	+ (uncommonly complete)
RESPONSE TO COMBINATION CHEMOTHERAPY		
Overall regression rate	90%	30%
Complete regression rate	50%	5%
OVERALL 5-YEAR SURVIVAL RATES		
	5%	8%

receiving this intensive screening. If the lung cancer death rate is reduced significantly in the screened group, screening should be generally practiced in high-risk patients.

ESTABLISHING A TISSUE DIAGNOSIS OF LUNG CANCER   Once signs, symptoms, or screening studies suggest lung cancer, it is necessary to establish a tissue diagnosis of malignancy, determine the histologic cell type, and stage the patient for appropriate treatment. In the initial evaluation of each patient, tumor tissue should be obtained so that a histologic diagnosis of cancer and tumor cell type can be firmly made. Distinction of small cell from non-small cell lung cancer can sometimes be difficult in cytology preparations. Therefore, cytologic diagnoses from washings or needle aspirates should be reserved for very high risk patients or patients relapsing with cancer after initial treatment. Tumor tissue can be obtained at the time of definitive surgical resection, from a bronchial biopsy or transbronchial forceps biopsy at fiberoptic bronchoscopy, from node biopsy at mediastinoscopy, from percutaneous biopsy of an enlarged lymph node, soft tissue mass, lytic bone lesion, bone marrow, or pleural lesion; or from an adequate cell block from a malignant pleural effusion.

STAGING PATIENTS WITH LUNG CANCER   Lung cancer staging consists of two parts: first, a determination of the location of tumor (anatomic staging) and second, an assessment of a patient's ability to withstand various antitumor treatments (physiologic staging). For example, in a patient with non-small cell lung cancer it is crucial to determine if the tumor can be resected by a standard surgical procedure such as a lobectomy or pneumonectomy (determination of "resectability") based on the anatomic stage of the tumor and whether the patient could tolerate such a surgical procedure (determination of "operability") based on the cardiopulmonary condition of the patient.

TABLE 213-4   TNM classification of lung cancer

PRIMARY TUMOR (T)

TX	Occult cancer; only evidence in bronchial washings cytologically
T1	Less than 3 cm, surrounded by lung or visceral pleura, and without bronchoscopic invasion proximal to a lobar bronchus
T2	Tumor more than 3 cm; or tumor with atelectasis or pneumonitis extending to hilum but less than entire lung, within a lobar bronchus, and more than 2 cm distal to carina; no pleural effusion
T3	Tumor of any size with extension into parietal pleura, chest wall, diaphragm, mediastinum; less than 2 cm from carina; or atelectasis, pneumonitis of entire lung; pleural effusion with or without malignant cells

REGIONAL LYMPH NODES (N)(see Note)

N0	Negative hilar and mediastinal nodes
N1	Positive ipsilateral hilar nodes
N2	Positive mediastinal nodes (also scored when vocal cord paralysis, SVC obstruction, and trachea or esophageal compression are present, all of which strongly indicate mediastinal node invasion)

DISTANT METASTASIS (M)

M0	No known distant metastasis
M1	Distant metastasis present with site specified (e.g., brain)

STAGE GROUPING

Occult carcinoma	TX, N0, M0
Stage I	T1, N0, M0; T1, N1, M0; T2, N0, M0
Stage II	T2, N1, M0
Stage III	T3 with any N or M; N2 with any T or M; M1 with any T or N

NOTE: *For planning surgical treatment and assigning postoperative prognosis, the ATS has recommended dropping the terms* hilar *(for N1) and* mediastinal *(for N2) nodal disease. They recommend that N1 include ipsilateral intrapulmonary, lobar, and segmental nodes; ipsilateral paratracheal and peribronchial (on the left) and tracheobronchial (on the right) nodes be assigned an uncertain prognosis (i.e., may be either N1 or N2); while all remaining nodes be scored as N2. In practical terms, the decision to resect N1 or N2 involved nodes will have to be made by the surgeon at the time of thoracotomy.*

Non-small cell lung cancer   The TNM (tumor size, or T factor; regional nodal involvement, or N factor; and presence or absence of distant metastases, M factor) staging system developed by the AJC on End Results Reporting should be used in non-small cell lung cancer, particularly in preparing patients for curative attempts with surgery or radiotherapy (Table 213-4). The various T, N, and M factors are combined to form three different groups (stages I, II, and III) and a fourth group consisting of occult carcinoma detected on screening cytology exams but with no other evidence of tumor (Table 213-4). This stage grouping can be performed at different times.

Small cell lung cancer   A simple two-stage system adapted from the Veterans Administration Lung Cancer Study Group is used. In this two-stage system, *limited stage disease* (about 40 percent of all small cell cancer patients) is defined as disease confined to one hemithorax and regional lymph nodes (including mediastinal, contralateral hilar, and usually ipsilateral supraclavicular nodes), while *extensive stage disease* (about 60 percent of all patients) is defined as disease beyond this. In part, the definition of *limited stage* relates to whether the known tumor can be encompassed within a tolerable radiation therapy port. Thus, contralateral supraclavicular nodes, recurrent laryngeal nerve involvement, and superior vena caval obstruction can all be limited stage disease. However, cardiac tamponade, malignant pleural effusion, and bilateral pulmonary parenchymal involvement are generally scored as extensive stage disease because of the size of the radiation therapy port required to cover all known disease.

GENERAL STAGING PROCEDURES   All lung cancer patients should have a complete history and physical examination, with evaluation of all other medical problems and a determination of performance status and weight loss.

An ear, nose, and throat examination is necessary because of the frequent occurrence of second cancers in this area. Chest roentgenograms are needed to evaluate tumor size and nodal involvement, and it is very useful, if not mandatory, to obtain any old x-ray films for comparison. Tomograms are only used for specific diagnostic problems. Chest computerized tomography (CT) scans are now widely used in the staging and follow-up of lung cancer patients. CT scans are of use in non-small cell lung cancer in preoperative staging to detect mediastinal nodes and pleural extension, and in the planning of curative radiation therapy to allow design of fields to encompass all known tumor volume while avoiding as much normal tissue as possible. However, as recommended by the American Thoracic Society (ATS), definitive characterization of mediastinal nodal involvement should depend upon histologic proof when planning curative treatment. In small cell lung cancer, CT scans are used for chest radiation treatment planning and assessing the response to chemotherapy and radiation therapy. In following patients after surgery or radiotherapy, procedures which can make interpretation of conventional chest x-rays difficult, CT scans can provide good evidence of tumor recurrence.

A complete blood count with platelet determination, routine blood chemistries, skin test for tuberculosis, electrocardiogram, and pulmonary function studies are obtained. Arterial blood gas measurements are obtained if any signs or symptoms of respiratory insufficiency are present. If signs or symptoms suggest organ involvement by tumor, appropriate radionuclide scans (e.g., brain, liver, or bone) are performed, as well as radiographs of any suspicious bony lesions. Routine radionuclide scans are not obtained in the asymptomatic patient because of the high frequency of false-positive and false-negative studies. Any accessible lesions suspicious for cancer should be biopsied if a histologic diagnosis has not already been made, or if treatment or staging decisions would be based on whether or not the lesion contained cancer. In candidates for curative surgery or radiotherapy, a barium swallow is performed, if esophageal symptoms are present, followed by esophagoscopy if abnormalities are found.

In patients presenting with a mass lesion on chest x-ray and no obvious contraindications to a curative approach with surgery or radiotherapy after the initial evaluation and fiberoptic bronchoscopy (see below), the mediastinum must be investigated. This varies between different centers and includes (1) chest CT scan, and if this is positive, mediastinoscopy; (2) proceeding directly to mediastinoscopy (right-sided tumors) or lateral mediastinotomy (left-sided lesions) on all patients; (3) proceeding directly to thoracotomy with staging of the mediastinum at this time. In patients presenting with disease confined to the chest but not resectable, thus making them candidates for curative radiotherapy, other tests are only done as indicated to evaluate specific symptoms.

Pretreatment staging for patients with histologically documented small cell lung cancer includes the initial general lung cancer evaluation as well as fiberoptic bronchoscopy with washings and biopsies to determine the tumor extent before therapy; brain CT scan; bone marrow biopsy and aspiration since 20 to 30 percent of patients have tumor in the bone marrow; and radionuclide scans of liver and bone if symptoms or other findings are suggestive of disease involvement in these areas. Percutaneous or peritoneoscopy-directed liver biopsy may be performed if other findings are suggestive but not diagnostic of the presence of tumor in the liver, particularly if this would alter the planned therapy.

If signs or symptoms of spinal cord compression or leptomeningitis develop at any time in lung cancer patients of any histologic type, a myelogram and examination of the cerebrospinal fluid cytology are performed to determine the need for local therapy to the site of compression (usually with radiotherapy), and intrathecal chemotherapy (usually with methotrexate) if malignant cells are detected. In addition, a brain CT scan is performed to search for brain metastases that are often associated with compression or leptomeningitis.

STAGING OF NON-SMALL CELL CANCER WITH METASTATIC DISEASE In patients presenting with disease that is not curable by either surgery, radiotherapy, or their combination, all of the general procedures are done plus fiberoptic bronchoscopy as indicated to evaluate hemoptysis, obstruction, or pneumonitis; and pleurocentesis and cytologic examination if fluid is present.

A variety of other staging procedures including gallium 67 citrate scanning, computed tomography (outside the chest), tomograms, angiograms, venograms, scintiscans, sonography, and blind nodal biopsies at present should not be part of the routine staging evaluation of the lung cancer patient.

DETERMINATION OF RESECTABILITY AND OPERABILITY In patients with non-small cell lung cancer, the following are major contraindications to curative attempts by surgery or radiotherapy alone using standard treatment methods: extrathoracic distant metastases; superior vena cava syndrome; vocal cord and, in most cases, phrenic nerve paralysis; malignant pleural effusion; cardiac tamponade; tumor within 2 cm of the carina (not curable by surgery but potentially curable by radiotherapy); metastasis to the contralateral lung; bilateral endobronchial tumor (potentially curable by radiotherapy); metastasis to the supraclavicular lymph nodes; lymph node metastasis in the contralateral mediastinum (potentially curable by radiotherapy); involvement of the main stem pulmonary artery; and a histologic diagnosis of small cell lung cancer.

PHYSIOLOGIC STAGING Patients with lung cancer often have cardiopulmonary and other medical problems related to chronic obstructive pulmonary disease as well as other medical problems. Since it is not always possible to predict whether a lobectomy or pneumonectomy will be required until the time of operation, a conservative approach is to restrict resectional surgery to patients who could potentially tolerate a pneumonectomy. In addition to nonambulatory performance status, a myocardial infarction within the past 3 months is a contraindication to thoracic surgery because 20 percent of patients will die of reinfarction alone, while an infarction in the past 6 months is a relative contraindication. Other major contraindications include uncontrolled major arrhythmias; maximum breathing capacities of less than 40 percent predicted; an FEV_1 less

than 1 liter, though an FEV_1 over 2.5 liters allows pneumonectomy (recommending surgery when the FEV_1 is 1.1. to 2.4 liters requires careful judgment); CO_2 retention (which is more serious than hypoxemia); and severe pulmonary hypertension. In patients with borderline pulmonary status or a question of pulmonary hypertension, split pulmonary function testing by ventilation-perfusion lung scans or bronchospirometry and right heart catheterization study with temporary unilateral pulmonary artery occlusion can define physiologic operability.

TREATMENT

After a histologic diagnosis is obtained and appropriate anatomic and physiologic staging studies are completed, the overall treatment approach to patients with lung cancer may be formulated (Table 213-5).

NON-SMALL CELL LUNG CANCER: LOCALIZED DISEASE In patients with non-small cell lung cancer of AJC clinical stages I and II (Table 213-4) who can tolerate operation, the treatment of choice is pulmonary resection. In some stage III cases with favorable age, cardiopulmonary function, and anatomy resection should also be considered. Currently, there is interest in carrying out resectional therapy followed by postoperative radiotherapy in some patients with positive ipsilateral N2 nodes that do not exhibit extracapsular tumor extension. If a complete resection is possible, the 5-year survival rate for N1 disease is about 50 percent, while it is about 30 percent for N2 disease. However, only 20 percent of all patients who have N2 disease are technically resectable, and in most cases these resectable patients are only discovered to have N2 disease at thoracotomy. Patients with contralateral or bilateral N2 nodes, extracapsular nodal involvement, or fixed nodes are not currently considered resectable. The extent of resection is a matter of surgical judgment based on findings at exploration. In general, conservative resection that encompasses all known tumor gives survival equal to that obtained with more extensive procedures. Thus, lobectomy is preferred to pneumonectomy, while wedge resections and segmentectomies are reserved for patients with poor pulmonary reserve and small peripheral lesions.

TABLE 213-5 Summary of treatment approach to lung cancer patients

NON-SMALL CELL LUNG CANCER

Resectable (AJC stage I, II, and selected T3, N2 lesions)
  Surgery
  Radiotherapy for "nonoperable" patients
  Postoperative radiotherapy for N2 disease
Nonresectable (N2 and M1)
  Confined to chest: high-dose chest radiotherapy (RT) if possible
  Extrathoracic: RT to symptomatic local sites; chemotherapy (CT) (for
  good-performance-status patients, with evaluable lesions)

SMALL CELL LUNG CANCER

Limited stage (good performance status)
  High-dose combination chemotherapy ± chest RT
Extensive stage (good performance status)
  High-dose combination chemotherapy
Complete tumor responders all stages
  Prophylactic cranial RT
Poor-performance-status patients (all stages)
  Modified dose combination chemotherapy
  Palliative RT

ALL PATIENTS

Radiotherapy for brain metastases, spinal cord compression, weight-bearing lytic bony lesions, symptomatic local lesions (nerve paralyses, obstructed airway, hemoptysis in non-small cell lung cancer and in small cell cancer not responding to chemotherapy)
Appropriate diagnosis and treatment of other medical problems and supportive care during chemotherapy
Encouragement to stop smoking

Approximately 43 percent of all lung cancer patients will undergo thoracotomy. Of these, 76 percent will have a definitive resection, 12 percent will only be explored for disease extent, and 12 percent will have a palliative procedure with known disease left behind. The fraction of long-term survivors following definitive surgical therapy is remarkably consistent throughout major centers performing lung cancer surgery in the United States. Approximately 30 percent of all patients resected for cure survive 5 years, and 15 percent survive 10 years. The 30-day hospital mortality following pulmonary resection at major centers is also very consistent, 3 percent for lobectomy and 6 percent for pneumonectomy. The 5-year survivals following resection for the different histologic types are epidermoid, 33 percent; adenocarcinoma, 26 percent; large cell carcinoma, 28 percent; bronchioloalveolar carcinoma, 51 percent; and small cell carcinoma, less than 1 percent. As a function of postsurgical treatment stage the AJC 5-year survival data are epidermoid: stage I, 54 percent, stage II, 35 percent, stage III N0–N1, 19 percent, stage III N2, 13 percent; adenocarcinoma and large cell carcinoma: stage I, 51 percent, stage II, 18 percent, stage III N0–N1, 10 percent, stage III N2, 2 percent. Thus, the majority of patients who were initially thought to have a "curative" resection ultimately died of metastatic disease (usually within 2 years of surgery), indicating the need for some form of adjuvant treatment.

MANAGEMENT OF OCCULT CARCINOMA   When sputum cytology screening indicates malignant cells but a normal chest radiograph is found (TX tumor stage), the lesion must be localized. Over 90 percent can be localized by meticulous examination of the bronchial tree with a fiberoptic bronchoscope under general anesthesia and collection of a series of differential brushings and biopsies.

Often carcinoma in situ or multicentric lesions are found. Thus, current recommendations are for the most conservative surgical resection, allowing removal of the cancer and conservation of lung parenchyma even if the bronchial margins are positive for carcinoma in situ. The 5-year overall survival for these occult cancers is approximately 60 percent. Close follow-up of these patients is indicated because of the high incidence of second primary lung cancers (approximately 5 percent per patient per year).

SOLITARY PULMONARY NODULE   When a patient presents with an asymptomatic, solitary pulmonary nodule (defined as an x-ray density completely surrounded by normal aerated lung, with circumscribed margins, of any shape, usually 1 to 6 cm in greatest diameter) a decision to resect or follow the nodule must be made. Approximately 35 percent of all such lesions in adults will be malignant, the majority being primary lung cancer, while less than 1 percent are malignant in nonsmoking patients under 35 years of age. A complete history, including a smoking history, physical examination, routine laboratory tests, fiberoptic bronchoscopy, and old chest x-rays are obtained. If no diagnosis is immediately apparent, the following risk factors would all argue strongly in favor of proceeding with resection to establish a histologic diagnosis: history of cigarette smoking; age 35 years or older; a relatively large-sized lesion; lack of calcification; chest symptoms; associated atelectasis, pneumonitis, or adenopathy; and growth of the lesion compared to old x-rays. At present, only two radiographic criteria are strongly reliable for benignity of a solitary pulmonary nodule: lack of growth over a period greater than 2 years and certain characteristic patterns of calcification. Calcification alone does not exclude malignancy. However, a dense central nidus, multiple punctate foci, "bull's eye" (granuloma), and "popcorn ball" (hamartoma) calcifications are all highly suggestive of a benign lesion.

When old x-rays are not available and the characteristic calcification patterns are absent, the following approach is reasonable: nonsmoking patients under 35 years can be followed with serial chest x-rays every 3 months for 1 year and then yearly. If any significant growth is found, a histologic diagnosis is needed. For patients over 35 and all patients with a smoking history, a histologic diagnosis must be made. This can either occur at the time of nodule resection or, if the patient

is a poor operative risk, via transthoracic fine-needle biopsy. Some institutions would use preoperative fine-needle aspiration on all such lesions; however, all positive lesions will have to proceed to resection, and negative cytologic findings will in most cases have to be confirmed by histology on a resected specimen. While much has been made of sparing patients an operation, the high probability of finding a malignancy (particularly in smokers over 35) and the excellent chance for surgical cure when the tumor is small, all suggest an aggressive approach to these lesions.

RADIOTHERAPY   Those patients who are AJC stage III M0, as well as those with AJC stages I and II disease who refuse surgery or appear not to be candidates for pulmonary resection for medical reasons, should be considered for radiation therapy with curative intent. The decision to administer high-dose and potentially curative radiotherapy is based upon the extent of disease and the volume of the chest that requires irradiation. Patients with distant metastases, positive supraclavicular nodes, pleural effusion, or cardiac involvement are generally not considered for such curative radiation treatment. The median survival for unresectable patients with non-small cell lung cancer localized to the chest undergoing primary radiotherapy with curative intent is less than 1 year. However, 5-year survival data show up to 6 percent of patients alive when treated with radiotherapy alone. In addition to potential cure, radiotherapy, by controlling the primary tumor, may increase the quality and length of life of noncured patients, although there are few data to support this latter consideration directly. Treatment usually involves midplane doses of 55,000 to 60,000 mGy (5500 to 6000 rad), and the major concern is the amount of lung parenchyma and other organs in the thorax included within the treatment plan, including the spinal cord, heart, and esophagus. Patients with a major degree of underlying pulmonary disease may have to have the treatment plan compromised because of the deleterious effect of radiation on pulmonary function. Either split course or continuous fraction radiotherapy can be given with similar survival results. The development of radiation pneumonitis is proportional to the dose of radiation and volume of lung incorporated within the radiation field. The full clinical syndrome (dyspnea, fever, and radiographic infiltrate corresponding to the treatment port) occurs in 5 percent of cases. Acute radiation esophagitis occurs during treatment but usually is self-limited, while spinal cord injury should be avoided by careful treatment planning.

COMBINED MODALITY THERAPY   At present there appears to be no consensus for the routine use of pre- or postoperative radiation therapy, debulking surgery, or adjuvant chemotherapy. Currently, these forms of combined modality therapy should only be administered as part of approved clinical trials. However, many centers give high-dose, postoperative radiation if postsurgical staging documents N2 nodal disease. Another exception to this is the management of carcinomas of the superior pulmonary sulcus producing *Pancoast's syndrome*. These patients should have the usual preoperative staging procedures, including mediastinoscopy as well as CT scans to determine tumor extent and neurologic examination with electromyography to document neurologic findings. Often a histologic diagnosis is not made, and with the constellation of tumor location and pain distribution the diagnostic accuracy for cancer is better than 90 percent. If mediastinoscopy is negative, two curative approaches may be used in treating a Pancoast's syndrome tumor. The first preoperative irradiation [30,000 mGy (3000 rad) in 10 treatments] is given to the area followed by an en bloc resection of the tumor and involved chest wall 3 to 6 weeks later. At 3 years, survival figures of 42 percent for epidermoid and 21 percent for adeno- and large cell carcinomas have been reported. The second approach involves radiotherapy alone in curative doses and standard fractionation with similar survival to combined modality therapy reported. Data have now appeared suggesting a high frequency of brain metastases as isolated sites of relapse in patients with adenocarcinoma of the lung otherwise cured by surgery or radiotherapy. While there is no proven role for "prophylactic" cranial irradition, it is not unreasonable to follow potentially cured, asymptomatic adenocarcinoma patients with frequent brain CT scans to detect such recurrence at the earliest possible time.

DISSEMINATED NON-SMALL CELL LUNG CANCER

The 70 percent of patients who turn out to have unresectable non-small cell cancer have a poor prognosis. For example, median survivals of 34, 25, 17, 8, and 4 weeks are seen for patients with performance status scores of 0 (asymptomatic), 1 (symptomatic, fully ambulatory), 2 (in bed < 50 percent of the time), 3 (in bed > 50 percent of the time), and 4 (bedridden), respectively. Standard medical management, the judicious use of pain medications, and the appropriate use of radiotherapy form the cornerstone of management. Patients whose primary tumors are causing symptoms such as bronchial obstruction with pneumonitis, hemoptysis, or upper airway or superior vena caval (SVC) obstruction should, in general, have radiotherapy to the primary tumor. The case for prophylactic treatment of the asymptomatic patient is to prevent major symptoms from occurring within the thorax, if follow-up is uncertain. However, if the patient can be followed closely, deferring treatment until the development of symptoms is appropriate. Usually a course of 30,000 to 40,000 mGy (3000 to 4000 rad) over 2 to 4 weeks is given to the tumor. The frequencies of relief by radiation therapy of intrathoracic symptoms are hemoptysis, 84 percent; SVC syndrome, 80 percent; dyspnea, 60 percent; cough, 60 percent; atelectasis, 23 percent; and vocal cord paralysis, 6 percent. Other symptoms of metastatic disease treated with radiotherapy include cardiac tamponade (treated with pericardiocentesis and radiation therapy to the entire cardiac silhouette); painful bony metastases (with relief in 66 percent of cases); and brain, spinal cord compression, or brachial plexus involvement. Usually, with brain and cord compression, dexamethasone (25 to 100 mg total per day in four divided doses) is also given and then rapidly tapered to the lowest dosage which relieves neurologic symptoms. In all cases, the key to effective palliation is to detect the complication and begin radiotherapy at the earliest possible time. Pleural effusions are common and are usually treated with thoracentesis as needed, but without radiotherapy. If they recur and are symptomatic, chest tube drainage with a sclerosing agent such as intrapleural tetracycline is used. The chest is first completely drained. Then 1000 mg of tetracycline is dissolved in 100 mL of normal saline, and 50 mL of 1% xylocaine added, and this is injected via the chest tube. The chest tube is clamped and the patient rotated onto different sides to distribute the sclerosing agent. Then 24 to 48 h later the chest tube is pulled when there is little drainage (usually less than 100 mL per 12 h).

Anticancer chemotherapy is not yet standard therapy for non-small cell lung cancer and, in general, should only be given as part of clinical trials approved by the local institutions. Approximately 10 to 20 percent of patients will have objective tumor shrinkage with the most active single agents, and 30 to 40 percent of patients will respond to combination chemotherapy. However, a complete clinical regression of tumor occurs (a "complete response") in less than 5 percent of cases. Those patients whose tumors respond to chemotherapy have significantly longer survivals (around 30 to 40 weeks median survival) compared to those patients who do not respond to therapy (10 to 20 weeks median). The problem is that the responding patients also have better prognostic features (such as good performance status), and it is difficult to separate the effect of these on survival from that of chemotherapy. However, in patients with good performance status, response to chemotherapy is also associated with prolonged survival, and in some cases, relief of symptoms. Nevertheless, such combination chemotherapy can have severe side effects including treatment-related mortality. Thus, in those patients with non-small cell lung cancer who desire nonprotocol chemotherapy, it is reasonable to give chemotherapy if the patient is fully ambulatory, has an evaluable tumor mass (to follow response to therapy), has not received prior chemotherapy, and is able to understand and accept the potential benefits and toxicities from such therapy. The chemotherapy should be delivered by an experienced physician or medical oncologist, and one of the published standard regimens such as "CAP" [cyclophosphamide, doxorubicin (Adriamycin), *cis*-platin] or vindesine (an experimental drug) or vinblastin plus *cis*-platin should be used.

SMALL CELL LUNG CANCER

The goal of initial treatment is to obtain a complete clinical regression of tumor documented by repeating the initial positive staging procedures, particularly fiberoptic bronchoscopy with washings and biopsy. This initial response, determined 6 to 12 weeks after the start of therapy, predicts both median and long-term survival and potential cure. Patients obtaining a complete clinical regression of tumor survive longer than patients with an objective but only partial regression (tumor shrinkage of more than 50 percent of visible disease with no sign of tumor progression elsewhere), who in turn survive longer than patients with no response. In addition, all long-term (over 3 years) survivors come from the complete response group. Untreated patients with small cell lung cancer have median survivals of only 6 to 17 weeks, and randomized trials have shown that radiotherapy alone is superior to surgery alone, that chemotherapy is superior to radiotherapy, and that chemotherapy plus radiotherapy is superior to radiotherapy alone. Randomized trials comparing chemotherapy plus radiotherapy to chemotherapy alone are currently underway. Thus, the correct integration of chemotherapy with or without radiotherapy or surgery is the cornerstone of the treatment of small cell cancer.

Following initial staging, patients are grouped into the limited or extensive disease stages and classified as being physiologically able or not able to tolerate intensive combination chemotherapy or combined modality chemoradiotherapy. Such intensive therapy should be reserved for ambulatory patients, with no prior chemotherapy or radiotherapy, no other major medical problems, and adequate heart, liver, renal, and bone marrow function. The arterial P_{O_2} on room air should be above 50 mmHg, and there should be no CO_2 retention. All patients with some or more of these limitations must have their initial chemoradio- or chemotherapy modified to prevent undue toxicity. The overall mortality rate from initial high-dose combination chemotherapy even in these selected patients is about 5 percent at major centers. This figure is comparable to the operative mortality rate for pulmonary resection and indicates the need for physiologic staging of patients before chemotherapy.

In appropriate patients, high-dose combination chemotherapy with or without radiotherapy should be given ("induction therapy"). This must be coupled with supportive care for infectious, hemorrhagic, and other medical complications. Meticulous attention to the details of therapy and the day to day management of the patient through the initial 6 to 12 weeks of treatment is essential if therapy-related mortality is to be kept low. Because of this the induction period should be supervised by a medical oncologist.

Chemotherapy The current principles of primary chemotherapy may be summarized as follows: first, combination chemotherapy using three or four of the known active agents concurrently should be used. A variety of combination chemotherapies have been reported, including CMC (cyclophosphamide + methotrexate + CCNU), alternating with VAP (vincristine + doxorubicin + procarbazine); CAV (cyclophosphamide + doxorubicin + vincristine); CCMV (cyclophosphamide + CCNU + methotrexate + vincristine); CAVP-16 (cyclophosphamide + doxorubicin + VP-16); and VP-16 (etoposide) + *cis*-platin. At present there is no evidence that any one regimen is better than another if adequate drug dose and schedules are given. Second, the initial combination chemotherapy is given in high doses during the first 6 to 8 weeks such that severe granulocytopenia (e.g., granulocyte counts less than 500 per microliter) and moderate to severe thrombocytopenia (platelets less than 50,000 per microliter) are to be expected. Following the initial intense (or "induction") therapy, patients should be restaged to determine if they have entered a "complete clinical remission," including complete disappearance of all clinically evident lesions and paraneoplastic syndromes, or a "partial remission"; or have "no response" or tumor progression (seen in 10 percent of patients or less). Following this, "maintenance" chemotherapy is given to responding patients for periods of 6 to 12 months in 3-, 4-, or 6-week cycles, depending on the combination of chemotherapy used. Appropriate drug dose modifications are made to keep the white blood count above 2000 per microliter and the platelet count above 50,000 per microliter. The patients are restaged between 6 and 12 months, depending on the individual regimens; if they are still in a complete remission, chemotherapy is stopped. The value of more prolonged chemotherapy is not documented. Patients with a partial tumor regression are generally kept on chemotherapy until the time of objective tumor progression and then switched to new chemotherapy (either with known activity or on an experimental protocol). Patients not responding or with objective tumor progression should be switched to new chemotherapy, preferably with a non-cross-resistant combination in an attempt to get an objective tumor response. High-dose [40,000 mGy (4000 rad)] radiotherapy to the whole brain should be given to patients with documented brain metastases. Prophylactic cranial radiotherapy may be given to patients with complete responses, as this will significantly decrease the development of brain metastases (occurring in 60 to 80 percent of patients living 2 or more years who do not receive such prophylactic radiotherapy), but such prophylactic therapy has not been shown to prolong survival. In the case of symptomatic progressive lesions in the chest or at other critical sites, if radiotherapy has not yet been given to these areas, it may be administered in full doses (e.g., 40,000 mGy to the chest tumor mass). Occasionally, a "recall" phenomenon will be seen in the radiation field (manifested by esophagitis, or erythema) if the patient has received prior doxorubicin chemotherapy. The management of other metastatic disease is similar to that for non-small cell lung cancer.

There are definite toxicities of both an acute and chronic nature that should be expected with combined modality chemoradiotherapy, particularly if chemo- and radiotherapy are given concurrently. Thus, the role of radiotherapy in the primary treatment of small cell lung cancer is still undergoing clinical investigation. However, retrospective analysis of long-term survivors, and analysis of local failures in the chest following chemotherapy alone, are suggestive that chest radiotherapy is of benefit. If radiotherapy is to be given to the primary lesion, patients should be selected (limited stage disease with PS 0–1 and initial good pulmonary function) such that radiotherapy can be given in full doses, by conventional fractionation, and in a manner that will not compromise the needed combination chemotherapy or sacrifice too much lung. The radiation oncologist must be prepared to deliver tailored radiotherapy with shaping of fields during treatment, much the same as is done for Hodgkin's disease. In extensive stage disease, the routine use of chest radiotherapy is to be avoided. However, if chemotherapy is inadequate to relieve local tumor symptoms, a course of radiotherapy can be added.

Applying these principles, several centers around the world have reported potential cure rates of 15 to 25 percent for limited stage disease and 1 to 5 percent for extensive stage disease. Overall, approximately 50 percent of patients with limited stage and 30 percent with extensive stage disease will enter a complete remission, and 90 to 95 percent of all patients will have some objective tumor shrinkage (complete or partial response). These responses increase the median survival from 2 to 4 months for untreated patients to 10 to 12 months for extensive stage and 14 to 18 months for limited stage patients. In addition, most patients have relief of their tumor-related symptoms and improvement of performance status. However, the maintenance of good performance status by the patient while receiving outpatient chemotherapy requires judgment and skill on the part of the medical oncologist delivering the chemotherapy so as to avoid undue therapeutic toxicity. A variety of new drug treatments are being tried (such as new drug combinations, alternating combinations of drugs, very intensive initial or "reinduction" therapy with autologous bone marrow infusion), as well as novel forms of combining chemo- and radiotherapy and surgery, but these should all be reserved for approved clinical protocols.

While surgical resection is not routinely recommended for small cell lung cancer, occasional small cell cancer patients will either meet the usual AJC requirements for resectability (stage I or II with negative mediastinal nodes) or only have a histologic diagnosis made on review of the resected surgical specimen. Such patients have been reported to have high cure rates (above 25 percent) if adjuvant combination chemotherapy is used. Thus, such uncommon, resectable small cell lung cancer patients are candidates for combined modality surgery and chemotherapy.

CLINICAL TRIALS AND BIOLOGIC STUDIES

The current poor prognosis for most lung cancer patients requires the continued performance of well-designed clinical trials to test new forms of therapy. Such trials have shown that there is no survival benefit from currently available immunotherapies such as BCG or levamisole. In addition, the development of methods to culture tumor cells directly from patients will allow (1) the prospective testing of tumor sensitivity in vitro to drugs, radiation therapy, and biologic response modifiers such as monoclonal antibodies; (2) the analysis of tumor cell growth factors, hormone and other nutritional requirements including "autocrine" growth factors such as bombesin (gastrin-releasing peptide); and (3) the biochemical and genetic study of lung cancer cells, including the characterization of oncogenes and paraneoplastic syndromes. All of these should provide a more rational basis for treatment.

BENIGN LUNG NEOPLASMS

The benign neoplasms of the lung, representing less than 5 percent of all primary tumors, include bronchial adenomas and hamartomas (90 percent of such lesions) and a group of very uncommon neoplasms (chondromas, fibromas, lipomas, hemangiomas, leiomyomas, teratomas, pseudolymphomas, and endometriosis). The diagnostic and primary treatment approach is basically the same for all of these neoplasms. They can present as central masses causing airway obstruction, cough, hemoptysis, and pneumonitis with or without x-ray findings but be accessible to fiberoptic bronchoscopy. Alternatively, they can present without symptoms as solitary pulmonary nodules and thus will be evaluated as part of a solitary pulmonary nodule workup. In all cases, the extent of surgery must be determined at operation, and a conservative procedure with appropriate reconstructions is usually performed.

BRONCHIAL ADENOMAS   Bronchial adenomas (80 percent of which are central) are slowly growing intrabronchial lesions which represent 50 percent of all benign pulmonary neoplasms. Eighty to ninety percent are carcinoids, 10 to 15 percent are adenocystic tumors (or cylindromas), and 2 to 3 percent are mucoepidermoid tumors. Adenomas present in patients 15 to 60 years old (average age 45) as intrabronchial lesions and are often symptomatic for several years. Patients may have chronic cough, recurrent hemoptysis, or obstruction with atelectasis, lobar collapse, or pneumonitis and abscess formation. Bronchial carcinoids, which usually follow a benign course, and small cell lung cancers, which are highly malignant, are both derived from the same normal bronchial epithelial component, the Kulchitsky cell. This cell is part of the amine precursor uptake and decarboxylation (APUD) system. Carcinoids, like small cell lung cancers, may secrete other hormones such as ACTH or arginine vasopressin and thus cause paraneoplastic syndromes which resolve with resection. In addition, bronchial carcinoids when metastatic (usually to the liver) may produce the carcinoid syndrome, with cutaneous flush, bronchoconstriction, diarrhea, and cardiac valvular lesions (see Chap. 299), which small cell lung cancer does not. Occasionally pathologists may have difficulty in distinguishing carcinoids from small cell lung cancers, and carcinoid tumors appearing more aggressive histologically (referred to as "atypical carcinoids") metastasize in 70 percent of cases to regional nodes, liver, or bone, compared to only a 5 percent metastasis rate of carcinoids with typical histology.

Bronchial adenomas of all types, because of their endobronchial and often central location, are usually visible via fiberoptic bronchoscopy, and tissue for histologic diagnosis is obtained in this manner. Because they are hypervascular, they can bleed profusely after bronchoscopic biopsy, and this should be anticipated. Bronchial adenomas must be dealt with as potentially malignant and thus require removal not only for symptom relief but also because they can be locally invasive or recurrent, potentially can metastasize, or because they produce paraneoplastic syndromes. Surgical excision is the primary treatment for all types of bronchial adenomas. The extent of surgery is determined at operation and should be as conservative as possible. Often bronchotomy with local excision, sleeve rejection, segmental resection, or lobectomy is sufficient. Five-year survival rates following surgical resection are 95 percent, decreasing to 70 percent if regional nodes are involved. The treatment of metastatic pulmonary carcinoids is currently unclear because they can either be indolent, growing slowly over several years, or behave more like small cell lung carcinoma. Assessment of the tempo and the histology of the disease in the individual patient is necessary to determine if and when chemotherapy or radiotherapy is indicated.

HAMARTOMAS Pulmonary hamartomas have a peak incidence at age 60 and are more frequent in men than women. Histologically, they contain normal pulmonary tissue components (smooth muscle and collagen) in a disorganized fashion. They are usually peripheral, clinically silent, and benign in their behavior. While it would be advantageous to avoid thoracotomy in these older patients, unless the radiographic findings are pathognomonic of hamartoma with "popcorn" calcification, the lesions will usually have to be resected for diagnosis, particularly if the patient is a smoker.

METASTATIC PULMONARY TUMORS

The lung is frequently the site of metastatic disease from primary cancers outside the lung. Usually such metastatic disease is considered incurable. However, two special situations may arise. First is the development of a solitary pulmonary shadow on chest x-ray in a patient known to have an extrathoracic neoplasm. This may represent a metastasis or a new primary lung cancer. Because the natural history of lung cancer is worse than for most other primary tumors, it is wise to approach the single pulmonary nodule in a patient with a known extrathoracic tumor as though the nodule were a primary lung cancer, particularly if the patient is over 35 years of age and a smoker. This means a vigorous evaluation looking for other sites of active cancer and, if none are found, surgical resection of the nodule. Second, multiple pulmonary nodules may be resected for cure as well. This is usually recommended if, after careful staging, (1) the patient can tolerate the contemplated pulmonary resection; (2) the primary tumor has been definitively and successfully treated; and (3) all known metastatic disease can be encompassed by the projected pulmonary resection. The key is selection and screening of patients to exclude patients with uncontrolled primary tumors and extrapulmonary metastases. Primary tumors whose pulmonary metastases have been successfully resected for cure include osteogenic and soft tissue sarcomas; colon, rectal, uterine, cervix, and corpus tumors; head and neck, breast, testis, and salivary gland cancer; melanoma; and bladder and kidney tumors. Five-year survival rates of 20 to 30 percent have been found in carefully selected patients, and the most dramatic results have been seen in osteogenic sarcomas, where resection of pulmonary metastases (sometimes requiring several thoracotomies) is becoming a standard curative treatment approach.

REFERENCES

ATTAR S et al: Bronchial adenoma: A review of 51 patients. Ann Thorac Surg 40:126, 1985

BUNN PA JR, MINNA JD: Paraneoplastic syndromes, in *The Principles and Practice of Oncology*, 2d ed, VT DeVita et al (eds). Philadelphia, Lippincott, 1985, p 1798

CARNEY et al: Cancer of the lungs, in *Pulmonary Diseases and Disorders*, 2d ed, AP Fishman (ed). New York, McGraw-Hill, 1987, Section 14

DEDRICK CG: The solitary pulmonary nodule and staging of lung cancer. Clin Chest Med 5:345, 1984

GAZDAR AF: The biology of endocrine tumors of the lung, in *The Endocrine Lung in Health and Disease*, KL Becker, AF Gazdar (eds). Philadelphia, Saunders, 1984

GOLUMB H: Non-small cell lung cancer. Semin Oncol 10:1, 1983

HAMPER UM et al: Pulmonary hamartoma: Diagnosis by transthoracic needle-aspiration biopsy. Radiology 155:15, 1985

LUKE WP et al: Prospective evaluation of mediastinoscopy for assessment of carcinoma of the lung. J Thorac Cardiovasc Surg 91:53, 1986

MARTINI N et al: Results of resection in non-oat cell carcinoma of the lung with mediastinal lymph node metastases. Ann Surg 198:386, 1983

MINNA JD et al: Lung cancer, in *The Principles and Practice of Oncology*, 2d ed. VT DeVita et al (eds). Philadelphia, Lippincott, 1985, p 507

RADFORD EP et al: Lung cancer in Swedish iron miners exposed to low doses of radon daughters. N Engl J Med 310:1485 1984

SAMET JM et al: Uranium mining and lung cancer in Navajo men. N Engl J Med 310:1481, 1984

TISI GM et al: Clinical staging of primary lung cancer. Am Rev Resp Dis 127:1, 1983

WEISS ST: Passive smoking and lung cancer. What is the risk? Am Rev Respir Dis 133:1, 1986

---

214 DISEASES OF THE PLEURA, MEDIASTINUM, AND DIAPHRAGM

ROLAND H. INGRAM, JR.

THE PLEURA

The visceral and parietal pleurae form a continuous membrane that encloses a potential space which normally contains only a small amount of liquid. This liquid is dynamic, and, as with all movements of liquid between the vascular and extravascular compartments, the principles of the Starling equation (Chap. 26) apply. Under normal circumstances, the liquid is filtered out of the parietal pleura, which is supplied by systemic capillaries at a mean pressure of 30 cmH$_2$O, and most is taken up at the visceral pleura, supplied by the pulmonary circulation that has a mean capillary pressure of 11 cmH$_2$O. For the removal of macromolecules plus some liquid there are, in addition, lymphatic stomata in the diaphragmatic and basilar portions of the parietal pleura. Abnormal accumulations of liquid, designated as pleural effusions, occur with changes in hydrostatic and oncotic forces (transudation) or with alterations in membrane permeability (exudation) such as occurs with inflammation or neoplastic involvement.

The parietal pleura is supplied by segmental nerves and when inflamed gives rise to pain which is referred to superficial regions supplied by the intercostal nerves and the thoracic segments. This pain is sharp and superficial, and is aggravated during inspiration (Chap. 4). Since the location of the pain is determined by the distribution of the somatic afferents, pain may be referred to the shoulder if the diaphragmatic pleura (C3 to C5) is involved or to the upper abdomen if the lower thoracic intercostals are affected. The visceral pleura is supplied by visceral afferents that do not produce sharp and localizable pain.

The patient with pleuritic chest pain frequently has shallow, rapid breathing, and there may be lesser excursion of the affected hemithorax than the unaffected side (splinting). Inflammation of the pleural surfaces may also cause a pleural friction rub which may be localized or may be best heard at the lower thorax posteriorly, the region where there is greatest respiratory excursion. A pleural friction rub has a harsh, scratchy quality and is heard throughout the respiratory cycle; it is maximal toward the end of inspiration and early in expiration.

PLEURITIS Inflammation of the pleura can occur with or without apparent underlying pulmonary disease and has many causes, including pneumonia, tuberculosis, pulmonary infarction, and neoplasm. Pleural pain in the *absence of physical and roentgenographic findings* suggests the diagnosis of epidemic pleurodynia (Bornholm's disease, Chap. 139), other viral infections of the pleura, or connective tissue disorders such as systemic lupus erythematosus. The *presence of parenchymal disease on the chest roentgenogram* in a patient with pleuritic chest pain and fever suggests an infectious process such as acute bacterial pneumonia (Chap. 205). Pulmonary infarction secondary to pulmonary embolism (Chap. 211) may also cause inflammation of the pleural surface. Under these circumstances, hemoptysis is a common presenting feature. The finding of a *pleural effusion in the absence of parenchymal disease* suggests postprimary tuberculosis, subdiaphragmatic abscess, mesothelioma, or primary bacterial infection of the pleural space.

Treatment of pleuritis is directed toward the underlying disease and relief of pain. Analgesics frequently suppress pain, but generally they do not completely eradicate the pain associated with deep breaths and coughing. If pain prevents the patient from coughing up secretions, regional anesthesia by blockade of the appropriate intercostal nerves with a medium-duration local anesthetic is helpful. Occasionally, acute pleuritis leads to chronic adhesive pleuritis as a sequela of tuberculosis, empyema, or hemothorax. Adhesive pleuritis is characterized by marked thickening of the pleura, which may interfere with pulmonary function. Under these circumstances, the thickened pleura encases the lung and "traps" it, so that the lung behaves as if it were small and stiff, despite having intrinsically normal mechanical properties. If symptoms such as dyspnea are severe, surgical removal of the thickened pleura (decortication) may be indicated.

PLEURAL EFFUSION Pleural effusions may or may not be associated with disease of the pleura. In general, effusions due to pleural disease more nearly resemble plasma (exudates), while those occurring with a normal pleura are ultrafiltrates of the plasma (transudates). Effusions in association with pleuritis are due to increased permeability of the parietal pleura secondary to inflammatory or neoplastic involvement. A good example of pleural effusion with a normal pleura is that associated with congestive heart failure. Both increased liquid formation from the parietal pleura due to systemic capillary hypertension and decreased reabsorption from the visceral pleura secondary to elevations in pulmonary capillary pressure account for the abnormal collection of pleural liquid in this condition. Hypoalbuminemia, as occurs in nephrosis or cirrhosis, also leads to increased formation and decreased resorption of pleural liquid on the basis of decreased intravascular oncotic pressures. An additional mechanism, lymphatic obstruction, also leads to effusions in the absence of pleural disease. In this case the sharp distinction between exudates and transudates may become fuzzy. Since the lymphatic channels provide the only route for reabsorption of protein from the pleural space, protein concentrations in the effusion are often high, even though the pleura is not abnormally permeable.

The extent to which a pleural effusion compromises lung volume will depend in part on the relative stiffness of the lung and chest wall. At lung volumes in the normal breathing range, the chest wall tends to recoil outward while the lung tends to recoil inward. Many pleural effusions are asymptomatic, but patients may complain of shortness of breath. Whatever the underlying cause, dyspnea that accompanies large pleural effusions is often relieved by the removal of 1 liter of liquid. The mechanism for this relief is not totally clear since the increase in gas volume of the lungs is usually less than half the amount of liquid removed; decrease in the volume of hemithorax by inward movement of the chest wall accounts for more than half the volume change. It is possible that the inward movement of the chest wall, which puts the muscles of inspiration at a better mechanical advantage, may account for the relief of dyspnea. Pleuritic chest pain or a dull sensation in the chest may also be present. The physical signs include deviation of the trachea away from the affected side,

dullness to percussion, and diminished breath sounds over the affected side. Egophony may be heard at the upper border of the effusion.

The most common appearance of a pleural effusion on chest roentgenogram is obliteration of the sharp angle between the diaphragm and rib cage (costophrenic angle) with an upward concavity of the liquid level. Occasionally, effusions lie underneath the lung (*subpulmonic effusion*) and give the appearance of an elevated hemidiaphragm. A chest roentgenogram in the lateral decubitus position (affected side down) will show the pleural liquid layering out along the lateral chest wall, provided the liquid is not loculated. A clue to the presence of a subpulmonic effusion in the left hemithorax from the chest roentgenograph taken in the upright posture is a wide density between the gastric air bubble and the apparent upper border of the diaphragm. Another clue to the presence of a subpulmonic effusion in the upright position on either side is a lateral displacement and slight flattening of the apparent dome of the diaphragm as liquid moves laterally. Pleural effusions may be missed on anteroposterior roentgenograms taken in the supine posture since the liquid layers out posteriorly. In this case it produces a generally hazy shadow that is difficult to detect when unilateral and impossible to detect when bilateral. Occasionally, effusions may form between lobes of the lungs and produce a rounded opacity on the chest roentgenogram that resembles a solitary nodule. Since these often disappear with resolution of the effusion, they are referred to as *phantom tumors*.

Aspiration of the pleural effusion under local anesthesia should always be performed if the etiology of the effusion is in doubt, or if the effusion is causing dyspnea. If the diagnosis of neoplasm or tuberculosis is seriously considered, closed pleural biopsy with an Abrams or Cope needle should be performed at the time of the initial thoracentesis. Biopsy under direct visualization via a fiberoptic thorascope should be considered if liquid analysis and blind needle biopsy fail to provide a diagnosis and if someone experienced in the procedure is available.

Characteristics of pleural fluid Pleural fluid that is bloodstained is suggestive of neoplasm or pulmonary infarction; however, blood may also be present in effusions due to infection, congestive heart failure, and trauma. The differentiation of pleural effusions into *transudates* and *exudates* is of considerable diagnostic importance. Many different tests on the pleural liquid have been advocated (Table 214-1); however, no single test is diagnostic. Effusions which have a high protein content, high pleural liquid-to-serum lactic dehydrogenase (LDH) activity ratios, and many white blood cells are indicative of exudates. However, transudates secondary to congestive heart failure may have high protein contents after the volume of the effusion decreases with diuresis; any effusion that contains cellular debris may have a high pleural fluid-to-serum LDH ratio; and there is no absolute leukocyte count that clearly differentiates transudates from exudates. Clearly the diagnosis depends on interpretation of the test results in the context of the patient's illness. In addition to chemical tests, exudative pleural liquid should receive complete cytologic and microbiologic examinations. Figure 214-1 presents an approach to the evaluation of pleural effusions. Despite an orderly and complete approach, no cause will be found for the pleural effusion in up to 25 percent of patients.

Postprimary tuberculous effusions present as isolated pleural effusions in the absence of radiologically demonstrable parenchymal disease and occur within months of primary subclinical infection. The patient may be asymptomatic or, more commonly, presents with fever, malaise, and weight loss. Occasionally, high fever and pleuritic chest pain are present. More than 90 percent of patients have a positive tuberculin skin test. Thoracentesis reveals an *exudative* effusion, with predominant lymphocytosis. Acid-fast bacilli are rarely seen on direct smear, and cultures are positive in fewer than 20 percent of pleural effusions due to tuberculosis. The diagnostic yield is higher with closed pleural biopsy, which will reveal noncaseating granulomas and/or positive culture material in more than 50 percent of the cases.

TABLE 214-1   Constituents of pleural effusions

	Transudate	Exudate
ROUTINE TESTS		
Protein	<3.0 g/100 mL	>3.0 g/100 mL
Lactic dehydrogenase	Low	High
Pleural fluid/serum LDH ratio	<0.6	>0.6
SPECIAL TESTS		
RBC	<10,000/mm³	>100,000/mm³ suggests neoplasm, infarction, trauma; >10,000, <100,000/mm³ indeterminate
WBC	<1000/mm³	Usually >1000/mm³
Differential WBC	Usually >50% lymphocytes or mononuclear cells	>50% lymphocytes (tuberculosis, neoplasm) >50% polymorphonuclear (acute inflammation)
pH	>7.3	<7.3 (inflammatory)
Glucose	Same as blood (±)	Low (infection) Extremely low (rheumatoid arthritis, occasionally neoplasm)
Amylase		>500 units/mL (pancreatitis; occasionally neoplasm, infection)
Specific proteins		Low C3, C4 components of complement (SLE, rheumatoid arthritis) Rheumatoid factor Antinuclear factor

Neoplastic pleural effusions are common; they are usually exudative. *Bronchogenic carcinoma* is the commonest malignancy causing pleural effusions and may do so by direct extension to the pleural surface, obstruction to lymphatic drainage (secondary to mediastinal spread), or by pleural inflammation secondary to pneumonia behind an obstructed bronchus. Patients usually present with symptoms referable to the primary lesion (Chap. 213) but may present with dyspnea or pleuritic chest pain. The effusion is invariably an exudate with or without blood. Pleural liquid cytology and pleural biopsy will confirm the diagnosis in up to 60 percent of cases. *Metastatic carcinoma,* most commonly from the breast, may also cause pleural effusions and is a more frequent cause of bilateral pleural effusions than bronchogenic carcinoma. *Lymphoma* may directly involve the pleura or may obstruct lymphatic drainage leading to a pleural effusion. Malignant effusions reaccumulate rapidly after aspiration, and repeated aspirations are not warranted. Instillation of sclerosing compounds such as tetracycline or cytotoxic agents may succeed in producing adhesions between parietal and visceral pleural surfaces and decrease the rate of liquid accumulation.

Rheumatoid arthritis (Chap. 263) may cause exudative pleural effusions with or without nodular changes in the pulmonary parenchyma or on the pleural surface. Patients are most often males, and subcutaneous nodules are usually associated with the arthritis. The pleural liquid is characteristically turbid and greenish yellow and has a very low glucose concentration (less than 20 mg/dL) due to impaired glucose transport into the pleural liquid. These effusions are usually asymptomatic and do not require specific therapy. However, on occasion pleuritic chest pain and fever herald the onset of rheumatoid effusions, and, because of the acute presentation along with low glucose levels in the liquid, infectious empyema must be ruled out. Mononuclear pleocytosis and negative Gram stains and cultures aid in eliminating empyema.

Symptoms and signs referable to the chest very frequently accompany *subphrenic (subdiaphragmatic) abscess.* Fever, pleuritic chest pain, and an exudative pleural effusion are common. The chest roentgenogram usually reveals elevation of the hemidiaphragm, a small pleural effusion, and basal atelectasis, but is rarely diagnostic. Thoracentesis usually reveals sterile liquid, but an empyema due to direct extension of the infection may be present. It should be emphasized that pleural effusions following abdominal surgery are very common and should not be taken as a sign of a subdiaphragmatic abscess in the absence of other clinical features.

In *pancreatitis,* a left-sided pleural effusion may be present in up to 15 percent of patients with acute pancreatitis or pancreatic pseudocysts. Effusions are typically exudative and have a high amylase concentration. A high pleural fluid amylase concentration has occasionally been reported in neoplasm and infection, and may also be found in cases of esophageal rupture where the amylase is of salivary origin. No specific therapy of pleural effusion secondary to pancreatitis is indicated. An exception is the occurrence of a chronic effusion due to a fistula connecting a pancreatic pseudocyst to the pleural space. Surgical management of the primary pancreatic problem is indicated.

Pleural effusion and ascites in association with nonmetastatic pelvic tumors in women has been designated as *Meigs's syndrome.* The pleural effusion is most commonly right-sided, may be an exudate or transudate, and is thought to develop from movement of ascitic liquid across the diaphragm. Both the ascites and pleural liquid dramatically resolve following removal of the pelvic tumor.

Eosinophilic pleural effusion is defined as the finding of eosinophils in excess of 10 percent in the pleural liquid; this attention-getting yet nonspecific finding may be present in effusions due to acute bacterial pneumonia, viral pleuritis, pancreatitis, and trauma. Eosinophilic effusions, however, are uncommon with neoplasms and quite rare with tuberculosis.

Patients have been described with the triad of *yellow nails, lymphedema of the extremities, and pleural effusions.* The effusions have a high protein concentration and are thought to be due to impaired lymphatic drainage of the pleural space rather than to pleural disease.

CHYLOTHORAX Leakage of thoracic duct lymph into the pleural space may be due to trauma to the thoracic duct or obstruction of the duct by a malignant process (lymphoma, mediastinal spread of bronchogenic carcinoma) or mediastinal fibrosis. A rare disorder, *lymphangiomyomatosis,* is frequently accompanied by chylothorax. Thoracentesis reveals a milky white liquid which is characteristically an exudate. Fat globules may be seen microscopically on staining with Sudan III dye. Total fat content ranges from 1 to 4 g/dL. In cases of traumatic rupture of the thoracic duct, conservative man-

FIGURE 214-1 *Approach to the diagnosis of pleural effusions.*

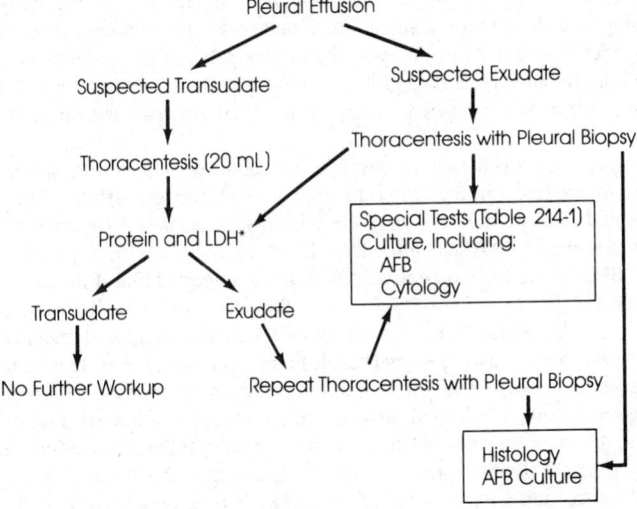

*Draw Blood Sample Simultaneously to Compare with Pleural Fluid Values

agement by repeated aspiration or thoracostomy-tube drainage and by cessation of oral feedings is tried initially. If this fails, lymphangiography followed by surgical ligation of the thoracic duct may be indicated. A chylothorax secondary to malignancy should not be repeatedly aspirated, since it reaccumulates rapidly.

Pseudochylous effusions do not contain fat globules but have a cloudy, milky appearance due to high concentrations of cholesterol in the pleural liquid. Cholesterol crystals may give a metallic sheen to the pleural liquid. This condition most frequently occurs in long-standing pleural effusions, and the most frequent underlying diagnoses are tuberculosis and rheumatoid lung disease.

HEMOTHORAX Hemothorax due to frank bleeding into the pleural space most commonly follows blunt or penetrating trauma to the chest. A small amount of bleeding may complicate a spontaneous pneumothorax, producing a hemopneumothorax when preexisting adhesions are disrupted as air separates the parietal and visceral pleurae. Patients with hematologic disorders or who are taking anticoagulants may bleed into the pleural space following procedures such as closed pleural biopsy; therefore, a pleural biopsy should never be performed without first ensuring that the patient's coagulation status is adequate. Treatment of hemothorax is directed toward adequate drainage of the pleural space. Continued bleeding, inadequate drainage, or shock unresponsive to blood replacement require thoracotomy. Inadequate drainage of a hemothorax may lead to an intense, fibrous reaction (fibrothorax) where the thickened pleura encases the lung (trapped lung); early decortication is indicated.

EMPYEMA The presence of infected liquid or frank pus in the pleural space is termed an empyema. In the majority of cases it is the result of spread of infection from a contiguous structure and may complicate the course of bacterial pneumonia, subdiaphragmatic abscess, lung abscess, or esophageal perforation. Up to 20 percent of empyemas follow thoracic surgery or instrumentation of the pleural space (thoracentesis, inadvertent entry of the pleural space during puncture of the subclavian vein). Direct infection of the pleural space without involvement of the underlying lung by hematogenous spread of organisms from a distant site accounts for the remaining cases and is more common in children than adults. Bacteria implicated in the etiology of empyema include *Staphylococcus aureus* (most common in all ages), *Pseudomonas aeruginosa, Klebsiella pneumoniae, Escherichia coli, Pneumococcus* spp., and anaerobic bacteria.

Chest pain, fever and night sweats, cough, and weight loss are common complaints. These symptoms may be mild if an empyema develops during the course of antibiotic treatment for bacterial pneumonia; hence the empyema may go unrecognized. Signs of a pleural effusion will be present, and the chest roentgenogram will reveal pleural liquid and usually underlying parenchymal disease. Thoracentesis may reveal thick, purulent liquid, but in the early stages of the disease, thin, serous liquid with a high leukocyte count (>5000 per cubic millimeter; polymorphonuclear cells predominate), high protein content (>3 g/dL), and low glucose concentration (<20 mg/dL) may be obtained. Gram's stain usually reveals the causative organism.

Treatment is directed at providing adequate drainage of the pleural space in addition to appropriate antimicrobial therapy. If the pleural liquid is thin, drainage may occasionally be achieved by repeated thoracenteses. Most commonly, closed thoracostomy-tube drainage will be required. Prospective studies have suggested that if the initial pleural liquid pH is <7.0, tube thoracostomy will be needed irrespective of the other characteristics of the liquid. If closed drainage of the pleural space does not result in the disappearance of fever and general improvement of the patient within 4 to 5 days, a limited thoracotomy is indicated, at which time resection of a small portion of the overlying rib and manual breakdown of pleural adhesions is performed. If this approach fails, or if treatment has been delayed, decortication with removal of the thick, fibrous tissue covering the lung (pleural peel) may be necessary to obtain lung expansion and obliteration of the empyema cavity. Rarely, an unrecognized empyema

may rupture through the chest wall and spontaneously drain onto the body surface (*empyema necessitans*).

Occasionally a loculated empyema and an edematous, inflamed pulmonary lobe or segment may resemble each other on routine radiographic examination. In such instances ultrasonography or computer-assisted tomography aid in making the differential diagnosis. In the case of a loculated empyema, drainage under guidance of such detection techniques is often successful.

The mortality rate of empyema is high among patients who are elderly, who have serious underlying disease, or in whom treatment is delayed.

PNEUMOTHORAX A pneumothorax is a collection of gas in the pleural space that results in complete or partial collapse of the lung. Normally, the pressure in the pleural space at the end of a quiet breath is subatmospheric due to a balance between the tendency of the lung to recoil inward and the tendency of the chest wall to recoil outward (Chap. 200). The lung may therefore be thought to be held in an expanded position by the surrounding negative pleural pressure much as a balloon would be held inflated when surrounded by a vacuum. When air enters the pleural space, pleural pressure in the affected hemithorax tends toward atmospheric pressure; the less negative the pleural pressure, the greater the degree of lung collapse. The mediastinum shifts toward the unaffected side as a result of the normal elastic recoil of the unaffected lung. If pressure inside the pneumothorax becomes above atmospheric, as may occur with a one-way leak into the pleural space ("ball-valve" leak) or when a pneumothorax occurs as a complication of positive pressure ventilation, a *tension pneumothorax* is present. Under these circumstances the affected lung is compressed, the mediastinum is further shifted toward the unaffected side, and cardiac output may be severely compromised due to the positive intrathoracic pressure decreasing venous return to the heart. Tension pneumothorax is a medical emergency.

A pneumothorax may occur spontaneously or may be secondary to underlying lung disease, chest trauma, mechanical ventilation, or perforated esophagus.

Spontaneous pneumothorax Spontaneous pneumothorax most commonly occurs in previously healthy adults between 20 and 40 years of age. In such patients there is a strong tendency toward recurrence of the pneumothorax. Air leaks into the pleural space due to rupture of small blebs on the surface of the visceral pleura; the etiology of these blebs is unclear. They tend to be at the apex of the lung, perhaps due to the more negative pleural pressure around the lung apex. Some patients have been found to have small pleural nodules consisting of histiocytes, giant cells, and other inflammatory cells (*reactive eosinophilic pleuritis*). These lesions should be differentiated from pulmonary eosinophilic granuloma.

Pleuritic chest pain and dyspnea are the commonest complaints in patients with pneumothorax. Physical examination reveals tachypnea, asymmetric expansion of the chest on the affected side (due to outward recoil of the chest wall as the lung collapses), mediastinal shift with deviation of the trachea and apex beat away from the pneumothorax, and hyperresonance to percussion and diminished breath sounds over the affected side. The chest roentgenogram reveals a visible visceral pleural edge with no lung markings between this edge and the chest wall. Chest roentgenograms should be taken in the upright position before a pneumothorax can be excluded, since in the supine posture upward movement of air with approximation of visceral and parietal pleurae laterally may obscure its presence. Small pneumothoraxes may be more easily seen if the chest roentgenogram is taken at the end of a maximal expiration. If pneumothorax is associated with tearing of adhesions in the pleural space, *hemopneumothorax* may develop, with a gas-liquid level visible in the pleural space.

Treatment depends on the size of the pneumothorax. A small pneumothorax needs only close observation, since the air leak has usually sealed by the time the patient presents. The air in the pleural space will be reabsorbed spontaneously, since the sum of the partial pressures of the gases in the pleural space (i.e., air = 760 mmHg at sea level) is greater than the sum of the partial pressures of gases in the end-capillary blood due to the low end-capillary P_{O_2}. Modestly sized pneumothoraxes can be easily evacuated using commercially available catheters prepackaged with insertion needles and one-way flutter valves that allow escape but not reentry of air. Larger pneumothoraxes should be aspirated or treated with closed thoracostomy-tube drainage. Failure of the lung to reexpand, despite application of suction to the chest tube, indicates that the lung is "trapped," that a major bronchus is occluded, or that there is a large continuing air leak through a major communication between the pleural space and lung (*bronchopleural fistula*). A bronchopleural fistula rarely occurs spontaneously unless there is underlying lung disease such as rupture of a lung abscess into the pleural space or necrotizing pneumonia, but may occur following lung resection or chest trauma or during mechanical ventilation (barotrauma). Spontaneous *tension* pneumothorax is unusual, but if present, it should be treated by immediate aspiration through a wide-bore needle placed in the pleural space at the level of the second intercostal space anteriorly at the midclavicular line. If there is circulatory collapse and severe dyspnea, tension pneumothorax should be suspected and treated without waiting for roentgenographic confirmation.

Approximately 50 percent of patients with spontaneous pneumothorax have a recurrence, and the incidence of further recurrence is even higher following the second episode. Repeated spontaneous pneumothorax should be treated surgically by application of irritants to the pleural surfaces so that they adhere to each other (*pleurodesis*) or by performing a *parietal pleurectomy*. Because of the tendency of pneumothorax to recur, if both sides are ever involved, even at different times, surgical intervention is indicated.

Patients with pneumothorax should not be moved in unpressurized aircraft because the decrease in atmospheric pressure may result in enlargement of the pneumothorax to an extent that it may seriously compromise ventilatory and cardiac function. Similarly, patients with a history of spontaneous pneumothorax should not pilot aircraft or undertake scuba diving. Should a pneumothorax occur underwater, enlargement of the pneumothorax on ascent may be catastrophic.

Pneumothorax may occur spontaneously in patients with a wide variety of lung diseases, such as asthma, emphysema, lung abscess, neoplasm, eosinophilic granuloma, and the adult respiratory distress syndrome. In the presence of underlying lung disease closed thoracotomy-tube drainage will almost always be needed. *Catamenial pneumothorax* is a rare disorder characterized by spontaneous pneumothorax at the time of the menstrual period. The right side is more frequently, but not invariably, affected. The pathogenesis of this disorder is not understood but may be related to intrathoracic endometriosis. Hormonal therapy with suppression of ovulation is usually successful.

PLEURAL TUMORS Two types of *mesothelioma*, a rare tumor of the visceral and parietal pleurae, are recognized. The *localized form* is a solitary growth on the pleural surface that only occasionally causes a pleural effusion and may be cured by surgical resection. Patients are often asymptomatic or may complain of chest pain and cough. The *diffuse mesothelioma* is a highly malignant tumor that is usually associated with a serous or blood-stained pleural effusion. There is no effective therapy for this tumor. Clubbing of the digits and hypertrophic pulmonary osteoarthropathy are associated with pleural-based tumors. The diagnosis of mesothelioma may be obtained from cytologic examination of the pleural liquid or closed pleural biopsy, but difficulty may be encountered distinguishing this tumor histologically from adenocarcinoma. There is an increased incidence of pleural and peritoneal mesotheliomas among persons exposed to asbestos; a higher incidence is found among those engaged in the processing and use of asbestos products than those in the mining industry. The interval between exposure and tumor development often exceeds 20 years; continuous exposure to asbestos is not necessary.

In addition to primary tumors, the pleura is a common site for *metastases* from neoplasms of the bronchus, breast, ovary, and gastrointestinal tract.

MEDIASTINUM

The mediastinum occupies the central portion of the chest and is anatomically defined by the thoracic inlet above, the diaphragm below, the mediastinal pleura laterally, the paravertebral gutter and ribs posteriorly, and the sternum anteriorly. The mediastinum is divided into four compartments for descriptive purposes (Fig. 214-2). The *superior mediastinum* is bounded above by the plane of the first rib and below by an imaginary line drawn anteroposteriorly from the sternal angle to the lower edge of the fourth thoracic vertebra. It contains the trachea, upper esophagus, thymus gland, thoracic duct, great veins, arch of the aorta and its branches, and the phrenic, vagus, and left recurrent laryngeal nerves. Below the superior mediastinum lie three further compartments. The *anterior mediastinum* contains fibroareolar tissue and lymph nodes, but no major structures. The *middle mediastinum* contains the heart, ascending aorta, great veins, pulmonary artery, and phrenic nerves. The *posterior mediastinum* contains the esophagus, thoracic duct, descending aorta, sympathetic chain, and intercostal and vagal nerves.

TUMORS AND CYSTS The commonest mediastinal masses in adults are metastatic carcinomas (most commonly bronchogenic carcinoma) and lymphomas. These masses may represent enlargement of lymph nodes and the possibility of sarcoidosis, infectious mononucleosis, and the diffuse lymphadenopathy syndrome in association with the acquired immunodeficiency syndrome must be considered in addition to lymphoma and carcinoma. Neurogenic tumors, teratodermoids, thymomas, and bronchogenic cysts account for approximately two-thirds of the remaining mediastinal masses.

One-third of patients are asymptomatic, with the mediastinal mass detected on a routine chest roentgenogram. In the remainder, chest pain, cough, dyspnea, and symptoms due to compression or invasion of structures in the mediastinum may be present (e.g., dysphagia, hoarseness due to recurrent laryngeal nerve involvement, superior vena caval obstruction). Symptoms are more common with malignant tumors.

Investigation of a mediastinal mass begins with posteroanterior and lateral chest roentgenograms to which are added oblique views, a contrast study of the esophagus, and tomography, if needed, to define more clearly the anatomic location and borders of the mass. The anatomic site of the lesion is of diagnostic importance, and may determine the next step in the diagnostic workup (Fig. 214-2). Computerized tomography of the chest with injection of contrast material into a peripheral vein, or angiography of the pulmonary circulation or aorta may be needed to distinguish vascular from nonvascular lesions, a differentiation of particular importance if biopsy of the mass is considered. A further value of computerized tomography is the detection of the cystic nature of a lesion, a finding

FIGURE 214-2 *Common sites for mediastinal masses.*

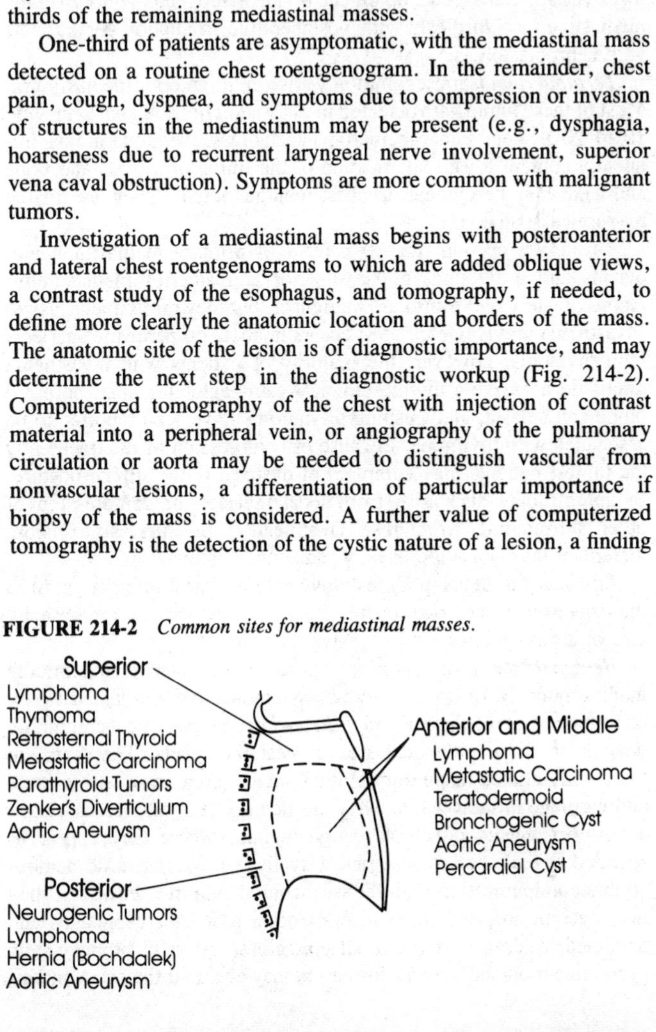

Superior
Lymphoma
Thymoma
Retrosternal Thyroid
Metastatic Carcinoma
Parathyroid Tumors
Zenker's Diverticulum
Aortic Aneurysm

Anterior and Middle
Lymphoma
Metastatic Carcinoma
Teratodermoid
Bronchogenic Cyst
Aortic Aneurysm
Percardial Cyst

Posterior
Neurogenic Tumors
Lymphoma
Hernia (Bochdalek)
Aortic Aneurysm

that strongly indicates that it is benign. Mediastinoscopy and biopsy are useful in the diagnosis of mediastinal masses if metastatic carcinoma, lymphoma, or sarcoidosis are considered likely. Lymph nodes behind the trachea and below the aortic arch on the left side are not accessible for biopsy using this approach. Scalene lymph node biopsy in the absence of palpable nodes may provide the diagnosis if lymphoma or metastatic carcinoma is suspected. Bronchoscopy is unlikely to be helpful in the diagnostic workup unless there are symptoms suggestive of an endobronchial lesion (e.g., hemoptysis) or unless there is evidence of lobar collapse, consolidation, or a mass lesion in the lung parenchyma on chest roentgenograph. Special tests such as radionuclide scanning with ^{131}I to detect an active retrosternal goiter may also be helpful.

Neurogenic tumors are the most common primary mediastinal neoplasms and are found almost exclusively in the posterior mediastinum near the paravertebral gutter. The majority of these neoplasms are benign; neurofibromas, schwannomas, and ganglioneuromas are the commonest tumors seen. Vague chest pain and cough may be present, but "root" pain is an infrequent complaint. *Paravertebral abscesses* also appear in the posterior mediastinum, and the clinical picture of infection often gives the major clue. Neurofibromas may occur singly or in association with von Recklinghausen's disease (Chap. 351). Occasionally these are accompanied by hypertrophic pulmonary osteoarthropathy. *Ganglioneuromas* arise from the sympathetic chain and, together with *neuroblastomas*, may secrete hormones which lead to diarrhea, flushing, and hypertension. Vanillylmandelic acid (VMA) may be found in the urine. Mediastinal *neuroblastoma* usually occurs in children, is particularly responsive to irradiation, and has a better prognosis than neuroblastomas of the abdomen or retroperitoneal space. *Pheochromocytoma* is a rare mediastinal tumor which may secrete catecholamines and present the same clinical picture as the more common (but still rare) abdominal form (Chap. 326). The treatment of all neurogenic tumors of the mediastinum is surgical, with postoperative irradiation for patients with neuroblastomas.

Teratodermoids most commonly arise in the anterior mediastinum. Most of these tumors are detected in early adult life and approximately 10 to 20 percent undergo malignant changes. Teratodermoids frequently contain linear calcification of the lining of a cyst, and bone and teeth may be evident on chest roentgenogram. They are treated by surgical excision.

Thymomas account for 10 percent of primary mediastinal neoplasms and are found in the superior and anterior mediastinum. Approximately one-fourth are malignant, but they rarely metastasize. Myasthenia gravis (Chap. 358) occurs in about 50 percent of patients with thymoma; however, the majority of patients with myasthenia gravis do not have a thymic tumor. Agammaglobulinemia, pure red blood cell aplasia, and Cushing's syndrome have been reported to be associated with thymoma. Because of compression of the trachea by the tumor, patients may complain of dyspnea in the supine posture. Symptoms may also arise from local invasion or compression of other surrounding structures. Treatment is by surgical excision; malignant thymomas are usually radiation-sensitive.

Lipomas can develop almost anywhere but most often are seen in the superior or anterior mediastinum. Computerized tomography almost always allows a noninvasive diagnosis.

Benign cysts most commonly arise in the anterior and middle mediastinum. Most do not produce symptoms and are detected only on routine chest roentgenography. *Bronchogenic cysts* most commonly develop in the paratracheal area or near the carina. The cysts are lined with ciliated respiratory epithelium and contain smooth muscle and cartilage in their walls. They are liquid-filled and therefore have a uniform density on chest roentgenogram, where they appear as rounded or tear-shaped opacities. Usually the cysts have no demonstrable communication with the tracheobronchial tree; however, they may become infected. *Enteric cysts* occur along the esophagus and are lined by gastric or intestinal epithelium. As with bronchogenic cysts, infection and abscess formation may occur. If the cyst contains

acid-secreting cells, ulcer formation, perforation, and hemorrhage may occur. The *pericardial cyst* is a developmental anomaly and is attached to the pericardium but only rarely communicates with the pericardial cavity.

Hernias through the diaphragm produce mediastinal masses that may or may not contain intestinal gas. The commonest is through the esophageal hiatus as discussed below. More rarely a defect in the posterolateral portion (so-called foramen of Bochdalek) of the diaphragm allows herniation of intestine into the left side of the chest. More often presenting as a mediastinal mass is a retrosternal herniation through the foramen of Morgagni.

SUPERIOR VENA CAVAL SYNDROME Obstruction of the superior vena cava (SVC) secondary to compression or infiltration by superior mediastinal tumors results in a characteristic constellation of physical findings with dilatation of collateral veins of the upper thorax and neck, plethora and edema of the face and neck, conjunctival edema, and headache. Visual disturbances and alterations in the state of consciousness may occur. Compression of the adjacent esophagus and trachea may cause dysphagia, wheeze, and shortness of breath.

Obstruction of the SVC is most often due to malignant disease, approximately 75 percent of the cases being due to *bronchogenic carcinoma*. *Lymphoma* accounts for almost all the remaining cases. Right-sided tumors much more frequently produce the syndrome as would be expected on an anatomic basis. Rarely, this syndrome occurs with *fibrosing mediastinitis* that is either idiopathic or secondary to histoplasmosis or occurs in association with methylsergide ingestion. *Retrosternal thyroid* and *aortic aneurysms* are among the other benign causes of SVC obstruction. Using invasive diagnostic procedures such as bronchoscopy, esophagoscopy, and mediastinoscopy in an attempt to obtain a tissue diagnosis is contraindicated due to the risk of bleeding during the procedure. Unless clinical examination and noninvasive investigations suggest a benign cause for the obstruction, or unless there is tissue elsewhere to biopsy (e.g., lymphadenopathy, skin lesions), the patient should receive irradiation or chemotherapy before attempts are made to obtain a tissue diagnosis. Corticosteroids are sometimes given during the initial stages of management in an effort to decrease edema at the site of obstruction.

PNEUMOMEDIASTINUM (MEDIASTINAL EMPHYSEMA) Air within the planes of the mediastinum may appear spontaneously or may be secondary to chest trauma, perforation of the trachea, bronchus, or esophagus, spread of air from the fascial planes of the neck or pharynx, or from dissection of air from the retroperitoneal space. When pneumomediastinum occurs with no apparent cause, it is referred to as a *spontaneous pneumomediastinum*. In contrast to spontaneous pneumothorax, as discussed above, there is no tendency for recurrence. Air is thought to dissect from alveoli to the interstitial space and into the vascular adventitia to the hilum. From there it moves into the mediastinum, neck, or retroperitoneal space. Occasionally mediastinal air ruptures into the pleural space, giving a small pneumothorax, most often on the left side. Predisposing factors include raised intrathoracic pressure, as with coughing, vomiting, and Valsalva maneuvers. Rapid decompression such as occurs with sudden ascent during diving has also been implicated. Pneumomediastinum may also occur spontaneously during an attack of asthma. The patient with pneumomediastinum may be asymptomatic but usually complains of retrosternal pain and dyspnea; less commonly there is sore throat due to dissection of air into the retropharyngeal space. Examination may reveal subcutaneous crepitus in the upper body, and a crunching sound synchronous with the heart beat may be heard over the precordium (Hamman's sign). Fever and mild leukocytosis are common with uncomplicated pneumomediastinum. Occasionally, cardiac function is compromised with physical signs of cardiac tamponade (Chap. 194). A lateral chest roentgenogram should always be obtained if pneumomediastinum is suspected since abnormalities may be seen only on this view. Air is seen outlining the pulmonary artery trunk and root of aorta and may be seen tracking into the neck.

Pneumomediastinum secondary to *esophageal perforation* may follow endoscopy or may occur with vomiting (Boerhaave's syndrome). Esophageal perforation is a surgical emergency and should be suspected if there is increasing pain aggravated by swallowing or fever and when signs of increasing mediastinal width and left pleural effusion occur on chest roentgenogram. Acute and fulminant mediastinitis is a frequent sequela and should be treated with immediate surgical drainage, closure of the perforation site, and broad-spectrum antibiotic therapy.

THE DIAPHRAGM

The diaphragm is the major muscle of inspiration and is derived embryonically from the septum transversum and the pleuroperitoneal membranes. Its motor nerve supply is from the phrenic nerves (C3 to C5); the afferent supply is derived both from the phrenic and lower intercostal nerves. When the diaphragm contracts, intrathoracic pressure is lowered and intraabdominal pressure is increased. Thus, the diaphragm acts as if it were "pulling" on the lung (by lowering intrathoracic pressure) and "pushing" on the rib cage (by raising abdominal pressure), resulting in an increase in lung volume and outward movement of both rib cage and abdomen as it descends on inspiration.

DIAPHRAGMATIC PARALYSIS *Unilateral diaphragmatic paralysis* is often the result of injury to a phrenic nerve secondary to trauma or tumor in the mediastinum. However, slightly more than half the cases remain unexplained even after intensive investigation and several years of follow-up; some patients spontaneously recover function. The lesion is usually asymptomatic, but the patient may complain of dyspnea in the supine posture when the diaphragm, weakened by unilateral paralysis, must work against the added load of the abdominal contents. Unilateral paralysis results in only a small decrease in vital capacity. The diagnosis is suggested by the finding of an elevated hemidiaphragm on chest roentgenogram and can be confirmed by fluoroscopy. Paradoxical (i.e., upward) motion of the affected hemidiaphragm occurs when the patient is asked to sniff, a maneuver that suddenly lowers intrathoracic and raises intraabdominal pressure.

Bilateral diaphragmatic paralysis is less common than unilateral paralysis, but it has far greater consequences on respiration. Bilateral paralysis may be due to high cervical cord injury, motor neuron disease, poliomyelitis, polyneuropathies, or bilateral involvement of the phrenic nerve by mediastinal lesions. Recently the use of ice slush in the pericardium for cardioplegia during cardiac surgery has been associated with bilateral paralysis due to cold injury of the phrenic nerves. The patient with bilateral diaphragmatic paralysis usually has severe shortness of breath, particularly in the supine position, and often hypercapnic respiratory failure is present. In most of these patients there is paradoxical (i.e., inward) motion of the abdomen on inspiration, a finding easily observed at the bedside, particularly with the patient supine. This is due to passive ascent of the diaphragm as intrathoracic pressure is lowered by the intercostal and accessory muscles. In a few patients paradoxical abdominal motion may not be obvious with the patient erect due to use of the abdominal muscles during expiration. Here, abdominal motion will appear normal as contraction of the abdominal muscles causes inward abdominal motion on expiration and relaxation results in outward abdominal motion on inspiration. Under these circumstances the diaphragm may appear to move normally at fluoroscopy, and the diagnosis of diaphragmatic paralysis will be missed.

The vital capacity which is reduced in the upright posture is even more severely reduced when the patient is supine because the paralyzed diaphragm is sucked upward during a maximal inspiration with displacement of abdominal contents into the thorax. The diagnosis of bilateral diaphragmatic paralysis is established by assessment of transdiaphragmatic pressure obtained by comparison of simultaneous measurements of esophageal and gastric pressures. Treatment of this disorder may be conservative, using a rocking bed at night; in patients with intact phrenic nerves, electrical pacing of those nerves has been successful.

ELEVATION OF THE HEMIDIAPHRAGM ON CHEST ROENTGENO-GRAPH Normally, the right side of the diaphragm is approximately 4 cm higher than the left due to displacement by the liver. *Apparent elevation* of one hemidiaphragm is due to a subpulmonic pleural effusion, and a lateral decubitus chest roentgenogram will establish this diagnosis. *True elevation* of one hemidiaphragm is most commonly due to upward displacement secondary to intraabdominal masses or ascites, or it may be due to loss of lung volume on the affected side secondary to pulmonary collapse or fibrosis. *Eventration of the diaphragm* is a rare congenital disorder more common on the left side. The anterior two-thirds of the diaphragm is replaced by a thin membrane, resulting in upward movement of abdominal contents into the thoracic cage. Patients are usually asymptomatic, and the diagnosis is made following a routine chest roentgenogram. No treatment is necessary. Rarely, eventration of the diaphragm may seriously compromise ventilatory function in the newborn. Plication of the hemidiaphragm is then performed. Eventration must be distinguished from *diaphragmatic hernias* through which abdominal contents are displaced into the chest. The most common location is at the esophageal hiatus with displacement of part of the stomach into the posterior mediastinum (Chap. 234).

MISCELLANEOUS DISEASES OF THE DIAPHRAGM Neoplasms of the diaphragm are rare; they include lipomas, fibromas, neurofibromas, and cysts. These benign tumors are approximately 1 to $1\frac{1}{2}$ times more frequent than the malignant fibrosarcoma. The diaphragm may be involved by direct extension of primary lung or abdominal tumors and may be the site of metastases from distant tumors.

REFERENCES

AHMAN FR: A reassessment of the clinical implications of the superior vena caval syndrome. J Clin Oncol 2:961, 1984

CAMFFERMAN F et al: Idiopathic bilateral diaphragmatic paralysis. Eur J Respir Dis 67:65, 1985

HAUSHEER FH, YARBRO JW: Diagnosis and treatment of malignant pleural effusion. Semin Oncol 12:54, 1985

KOPECKY SL: Pneumomediastinum: Pitfalls in diagnosis and management. Minn Med 67:683, 1984

LIGHT RW et al: Parapneumonic effusions. Am J Med 69:507, 1980

MARVASTA MA et al: Misleading density of mediastinal cysts on computed tomography. Ann Thorac Surg 31:167, 1981

NEWSOM DJ et al: Diaphragm function and alveolar hypoventilation. Q J Med 177:87, 1976

SABISTON DC: Primary neoplasms and cysts of the mediastinum, in *Pulmonary Diseases and Disorders*, AP Fishman (ed). New York, McGraw-Hill, 1987, chap 130

SILVERMAN NA, SABISTON DC: Mediastinal masses. Surg Clin North Am 60:757, 1980

---

215 DISORDERS OF VENTILATION

JOHN B. WEST

The principles governing pulmonary ventilation and its regulation are discussed in Chap. 200. The fine control of ventilation is normally carried out by the central chemoreceptors near the central surface of the medulla which respond to changes in pH of the extracellular fluid around them. The composition of this fluid is mainly determined by the cerebrospinal fluid. For example, a fall in pH caused by diffusion of carbon dioxide across the blood-brain barrier increases respiratory drive, thus holding the arterial P_{CO_2}[1] within close limits (Fig. 215-1). The response of the central chemoreceptors is augmented by the effects of P_{CO_2} on the peripheral chemoreceptors. The extreme sensitivity of these feedback controls is seen when a normal subject

[1] *Unless otherwise stated, the partial pressures refer to arterial blood.*

inhales air containing carbon dioxide. Typically the ventilation may double for a rise in P_{CO_2} of only 2 to 3 mmHg.

Arterial hypoxemia constitutes a coarse control through its action on the peripheral chemoreceptors in the carotid bodies. Although this control is minor under normal conditions, it becomes very important during chronic hypoxia, as in people living at high altitude, or in patients with chronic lung disease. Under these conditions the increased ventilation lowers the P_{CO_2} of the arterial blood and cerebrospinal fluid, but the pH of the cerebrospinal fluid is reset to near its normal level of about 7.32 by outward movement of bicarbonate.

Additional control is afforded by changes in pH of the arterial blood irrespective of its P_{CO_2}. This relatively weak regulation apparently occurs through stimulation of the peripheral chemoreceptors, and although it is seldom seen under normal conditions, it may dominate in the control of ventilation in metabolic acidosis. Reflexes originating in the lung and elsewhere also affect ventilation under some circumstances.

Disorders of the regulation of respiration include hypoventilation, hyperventilation, and abnormal patterns of breathing. A cardinal feature of hypoventilation is carbon dioxide retention (Table 215-1), and indeed these terms are often used virtually interchangeably. This can be misleading, but following common usage, the various types of carbon dioxide retention are grouped here under the heading of hypoventilation.

FIGURE 215-1 *Scheme to illustrate the various causes of carbon dioxide retention. These include (1) disorders of the respiratory center, (2) disorders of the supplying nerves, (3) disorders of muscles of ventilation, or (4) some mechanical problem in lung or chest wall, including obstruction to the upper airways. All these conditions result in hypoventilation. However, chronic obstructive pulmonary disease (5) in effect diverts blood from the ventilated regions, so that carbon dioxide retention occurs in spite of a normal (or high) ventilation. In addition, the ventilatory response is inappropriate for the level of carbon dioxide in these patients because of the increased work of breathing and sometimes also because of a reduced sensitivity of the respiratory center.*

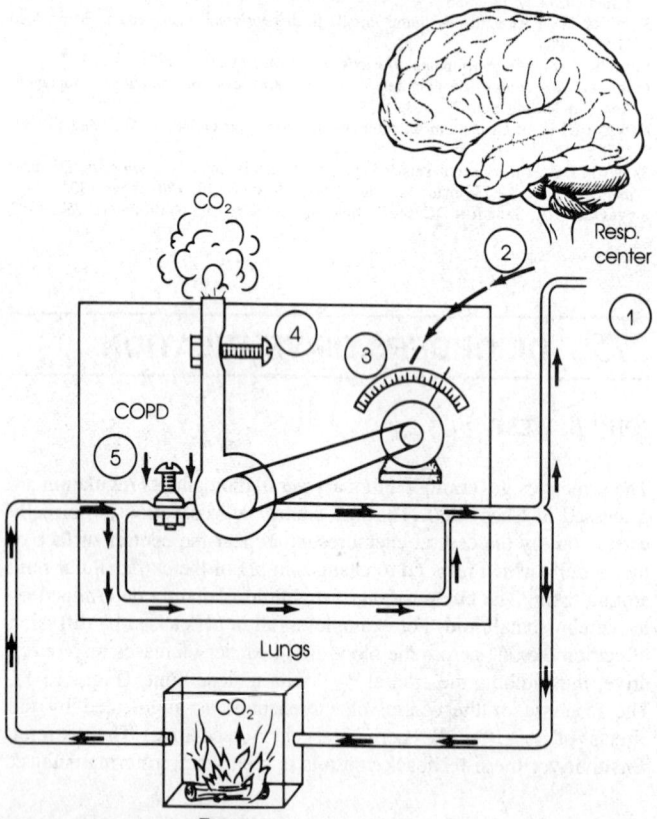

HYPOVENTILATION

CARBON DIOXIDE RETENTION CAUSED BY PURE HYPOVENTILATION (NORMAL LUNGS)
In this group of diseases, the amount of air going into the lungs each minute is reduced. Strictly, it is the volume of air entering the alveoli, or *alveolar ventilation*, which is crucial (Chap. 200). However, in practice, the volume of the conducting airways remains fairly constant so that if the amount of air passing the lips is abnormally low, hypoventilation is said to be present.

The alveolar ventilation and alveolar P_{CO_2} are related by the following equation:

$$\text{Alveolar } P_{CO_2} = \frac{CO_2 \text{ output}}{\text{alveolar ventilation}}$$

In normal lungs, the P_{CO_2} of arterial blood is virtually the same as that in alveolar gas, and the carbon dioxide output at rest remains fairly constant. Thus the expression implies that if the alveolar ventilation is halved, the arterial P_{CO_2} is doubled.

The level of alveolar ventilation also influences the P_{O_2}. As the ventilation falls and the P_{CO_2} rises, the P_{O_2} falls. An important practical point is that if the P_{CO_2} is considerably increased by pure hypoventilation, say to 70 mmHg, the P_{O_2} may still be well above the level at which cyanosis can be detected clinically. Thus a patient may have serious carbon dioxide retention and yet appear a "healthy" pink color. Note also that if a patient is given an oxygen-enriched mixture to breathe, the hypoxia will be abolished, but the hypercapnia remains (Chap. 208).

Conditions affecting the respiratory center During normal *sleep*, the P_{CO_2} rises by 3 or 4 mmHg. Patients with idiopathic hypoventilation or with the Pickwickian syndrome (see below) are particularly likely to develop depressed breathing when they are asleep. One of the commonest causes of hypoventilation is depression of the respiratory center by *drugs*. These include many anesthetics, the barbiturates, and morphine and its derivatives. Respiratory center depression is often seen in the recovery room, before the effects of anesthesia and preoperative sedatives have worn off, and also in the emergency room in patients who have taken an overdose of barbiturate. In these circumstances, the arterial P_{CO_2} should be measured, and assisted ventilation following endotracheal intubation or tracheostomy may be lifesaving. Depression of the respiratory center is often accompanied by impairment of the cough reflex and difficulties with swallowing, so that aspiration of fluid into the lungs may occur and lead to pneumonia. An additional advantage of intubation is that it allows the airways to be sucked free of secretions and inhaled material (Chap. 216).

Brainstem abnormalities Conditions which may cause hypoventilation include inflammation, hemorrhage, trauma, and rarely neo-

TABLE 215-1 Causes of carbon dioxide retention

1 Pure hypoventilation (normal lungs)
  a Respiratory center depression—morphine derivatives, barbiturates, some general anesthetics
  b Diseases of the brainstem—encephalitis, hemorrhage, trauma, neoplasm (rare)
  c Abnormalities of spinal cord conducting pathways—high cervical dislocation
  d Anterior horn cell disease—poliomyelitis
  e Diseases of nerves to respiratory muscles—Guillain-Barré syndrome, diphtheria
  f Diseases of the myoneural junction—myasthenia gravis, anticholinesterase poisoning
  g Diseases of the respiratory muscles—progressive muscular dystrophy
  h Thoracic cage abnormalities—crushed chest, kyphoscoliosis (lungs may be abnormal)
  i Upper airway obstruction—thymoma, aortic aneurysm
  j Hypoventilation associated with extreme obesity (Pickwickian syndrome)
  k Idiopathic hypoventilation
  l Other causes—metabolic alkalosis
2 CO$_2$ retention associated with chronic lung disease

plasms. Encephalitis and acute bulbar poliomyelitis (even in the absence of involvement of the respiratory muscles) may cause slowing and shallowness of respiration. Irregularities of rhythm and periods of apnea may develop. The first signs of these abnormalities often appear during sleep. The ventilatory response to inhaled CO_2 mixtures is depressed. These patients can return their blood gases to normal by voluntarily increasing their ventilation, and indeed they can sometimes be managed by being reminded to breathe when periods of apnea develop. However, they may die because of apnea during sleep. Respiratory depression may be associated with loss of the cough and swallowing reflexes and consequent accumulation of secretions.

Neuromuscular disorders Neuromuscular disorders affecting the spinal conducting pathways, the anterior horn cells, the nerves to the respiratory muscles, and the respiratory muscles themselves are important causes of hypoventilation (Table 215-1). Examples include compression of the cervical cord, poliomyelitis, the Guillain-Barré syndrome, and myasthenia gravis. The most important muscle of respiration is the diaphragm, and patients with progressive disease often do not complain of dyspnea until the diaphragm is involved. By then their ventilatory reserve is severely compromised, and they must be carefully observed. The converse also occurs. Patients with neurologic disease such as amyotrophic lateral sclerosis may complain of dyspnea as their initial symptom at a time when their neurologic findings may be extremely subtle. The progress of the disease can be monitored by measuring the vital capacity and the arterial blood gases. Again, the treatment of hypoventilation in these conditions is assisted ventilation either by oropharyngeal intubation in acute states, or with a tracheostomy for long-term management (Chap. 208). Patients with chronic paresis of their respiratory muscles are likely to develop chest infections because of their difficulty in getting rid of secretions.

Thoracic cage abnormalities CRUSHED CHEST An increasingly common cause of hypoventilation is trauma to the thoracic cage resulting from automobile accidents. Frequently this is caused by impact of the steering wheel with the sternum, or the chest is crushed when a wheel of a car runs over it. Usually there are multiple injuries. There may be dissociation of movement of the chest wall, so that one region is sucked in while the remainder of the chest wall moves out during inspiration ("flail chest"). Prompt intubation and assisted ventilation is often required, and careful monitoring of the arterial blood gases is mandatory.

SCOLIOSIS Bony deformity of the chest can lead to respiratory failure with a raised arterial P_{CO_2}. *Scoliosis* refers to lateral curvature of the spine, and *kyphosis* to posterior curvature. The effects of scoliosis on cardiopulmonary function are the more serious, especially if the angulation is situated high in the vertebral column. Scoliosis is frequently associated with rotation of the spine and backward protuberance of the ribs, giving the appearance of an added kyphosis. In fact, the term *kyphoscoliosis* is often used for this condition, although true kyphoscoliosis is rare. Some 80 percent of cases of scoliosis are idiopathic in origin. The rest are caused by neuromuscular disorders such as poliomyelitis or are congenital in origin.

The initial complaint is dyspnea on exertion. Later hypoxemia develops; eventually carbon dioxide retention and signs of failure of the right side of the heart may supervene. Sometimes bronchitis may complicate the picture, especially in smokers. The chief cause of the CO_2 retention is the deformity of the chest wall which leads to an inefficient action of the respiratory muscles and a great increase in the work of breathing. The compliance of the chest wall is reduced (it is stiffer), especially in older patients, and this results in rapid, shallow breathing, so that an increasingly large fraction of the tidal volume is wasted in the dead space of the bronchi. The hypoventilation causes not only hypercapnia but also hypoxemia. Pulmonary vasoconstriction results, pulmonary artery pressure rises, and the work of the right side of the heart increases. This is exaggerated by the polycythemia which develops (Chap. 191).

It should be noted, however, that these patients also have abnormal lungs. These tend to be remarkably small, and the restricted pulmonary vascular bed probably also plays a role in the development of pulmonary hypertension. Areas of atelectasis are common, presumably because the volume of the thoracic cage is greatly reduced. Uneven ventilation of the lungs has been demonstrated in many cases, so that ventilation-perfusion inequality contributes to the hypoxemia.

Pulmonary function tests show a reduction in all lung volumes; indeed the total lung capacity may be reduced to half the predicted normal value. Some of the inequality of ventilation can be explained by airway closure in dependent regions of the lung as a result of the gross reduction of lung volume. Airway resistance in relation to lung volume is approximately normal, but the maximum breathing capacity is reduced because of the restricted vital capacity. The diffusing capacity of the lung for carbon monoxide is not markedly abnormal when related to lung volume. In advanced disease, a reduced ventilatory response to inhaled carbon dioxide can be demonstrated. This is probably related to the large increase in the work of breathing caused by the deformity of the chest wall. Not only is the chest wall stiff, but the respiratory muscles operate inefficiently.

Little specific therapy is available. Just as the cause of most cases of the disease is unknown, so are the factors determining its progression poorly understood. Some help can be obtained from orthopedic braces such as the Milwaukee brace, in the early stages of the disease. Corrective surgery such as the Harrington procedure during adolescence improves the appearance and may relieve back pain. However, the long-term effects on cardiopulmonary function are unknown. Any pulmonary infection should be promptly and vigorously treated with appropriate antibiotics. If hypoxemia is severe and O_2 therapy is required (Chap. 216), the patient should be carefully watched for evidence of increasing hypoventilation. Cor pulmonale and right-sided heart failure should be treated with diuretics, digitalis, and perhaps phlebotomy if the polycythemia is severe.

OTHER CONDITIONS Also associated with an abnormal chest wall are ankylosing spondylitis and pectus excavatum. In *ankylosing spondylitis* (Chap. 267) there is immobility of the vertebral joints and fixation of the ribs, so that movement of the chest wall may be grossly reduced. There is a reduction of vital capacity and total lung capacity, but good movement of the diaphragm is preserved so that the ventilatory capacity is unimpaired. Some fall in the compliance of the chest wall has been reported and also some uneven ventilation, the latter possibly caused by the reduced lung volume. In general, however, the lungs are virtually normal and do not show the pathologic changes seen in kyphoscoliosis. Hypoventilation is not a feature, and secondary heart failure does not occur.

Pectus excavatum is a congenital abnormality in which the lower part of the sternum is depressed toward the spine. In spite of the bizarre appearance of the chest, little interference with pulmonary function is the rule. There may be a slight reduction in vital capacity, total lung capacity, and maximum breathing capacity, but gas exchange is virtually normal, and hypoventilation does not occur. Surgical correction for cosmetic reasons may be considered.

Obstruction to the upper airways Tracheal stenosis can be caused by neoplasms such as thymoma in structures adjacent to the trachea, by scarring following injury, by aortic aneurysm, or by a congenital abnormality. Tumors originating in the upper airways and foreign bodies may also be responsible for airways obstruction. Hypoventilation with CO_2 retention may occur, and this may be of long standing. It is possible to distinguish tracheal obstruction from the airway obstruction of chronic obstructive lung disease by the stridor and by the reduced flow rates during both forced inspiration and expiration. In addition, pulmonary function tests show no inequality of ventilation. Intermittent upper airway obstruction may occur in obese and other people during sleep (see "Sleep Apnea" below).

Hypoventilation associated with extreme obesity (Pickwickian syndrome) Some extremely obese patients hypoventilate, and the association of obesity, somnolence, polycythemia, and excessive appetite has been dubbed the *Pickwickian syndrome*, after the fat boy, Joe, in Charles Dickens's *Pickwick Papers*. Apart from the obesity, the clinical features are similar to those in patients with idiopathic hypoventilation (see below). In the fully developed form they include marked obesity (body weight typically over 130 kg), somnolence, twitching, cyanosis, periodic respiration, secondary polycythemia, right ventricular hypertrophy, and right-sided heart failure.

The obesity may have been present for years, but in some cases a recent rapid gain in weight has been described. The somnolence may be a striking feature, the patient sometimes dozing off halfway through a sentence. The cyanosis and periodic breathing are particularly marked during sleep. Sleep apnea may occur (see below), and in some patients this is caused by upper airway obstruction as a result of collapse of the pharyngeal walls. Ankle edema is a common symptom, and an enlarged liver and engorged neck veins are seen.

Blood gas measurements show an elevated P_{CO_2} and depressed P_{O_2}; the former may be as high as 70 mmHg. Lung function tests show a reduction in lung volumes, particularly in the expiratory reserve volume (the volume which can be forcibly exhaled from normal end expiration). The vital capacity is also reduced, as is the compliance of the chest wall. The abdominal pressure is raised, especially when the patient is supine, thus forcing the diaphragm into the chest. There are no indications of airway obstruction and little inequality of ventilation, but the energy cost of moving the chest wall is abnormally high. The ventilatory response to inhaled CO_2 is therefore generally greatly decreased. In these respects the syndrome is similar to kyphoscoliosis. However, in addition, some patients have a diminished sensitivity of the respiratory center to CO_2. The reduction of lung volume causes airway closure in the dependent regions of the lung, and this contributes to the hypoxemia. There is an increase in the resting O_2 consumption of these patients which aggravates the effects of their impaired ventilation.

A striking feature of this syndrome is the dramatic improvement that takes place in all symptoms when the patient loses weight. Objective indices of improvement include a fall in arterial P_{CO_2}, a rise in P_{O_2}, increases in vital capacity, total lung capacity, and total ventilation, and an enhanced ventilatory response to inhaled CO_2. In addition, signs of heart failure often disappear. Even a loss of 15 to 20 kg is often sufficient to bring about a remarkable improvement in well-being. Treatment by caloric restriction is indicated. In addition, recent work shows that some patients respond well to progesterone, which stimulates ventilation. If upper airway obstruction causes sleep apnea, tracheostomy is often very beneficial.

It is important to note that not all extremely obese patients develop hypoventilation. Some investigators have suggested that the Pickwickian individual is simply a patient with idiopathic hypoventilation who happens to be obese. The term *Pickwickian syndrome* is often used rather loosely. It should be reserved for very obese patients who have an increased P_{CO_2} without evidence of lung disease. The cause of the hypoventilation is not clear but presumably is related to the high energy cost of moving the chest wall. In addition the reduction in lung volumes caused by elevation of the diaphragm causes shallow, inefficient breathing. However the association of marked somnolence and voracious appetite suggests that, in some patients at least, there is an abnormality in the central nervous system.

Idiopathic hypoventilation   Idiopathic, or primary, hypoventilation is a rare disease of unknown cause occurring in patients whose lungs and chest wall are normal. A colorful name sometimes given to this condition is *Ondine's curse*, after the fairy whose human lover lost the ability to breathe automatically and had to will himself to do so. Most of the reported patients have been between 20 and 60 years of age, and there has been a preponderance of males. Typical symptoms include lack of energy, somnolence, headache, and some breathlessness on exertion. Cyanosis, especially when the patient is asleep, is a common observation, this being caused by a combination of the hypoxemia and polycythemia. Periodic breathing is often noted at night. Occasionally unusual sensitivity to sedatives or hypnotic drugs

given preoperatively has been a feature. In some cases, an acute respiratory infection has prompted awareness of the condition. Several patients have had a past history of encephalitis, neurosyphilis, or schizophrenia. Signs of heart failure including engorged neck veins, enlarged heart, palpable liver, and peripheral edema have been described in severe cases.

The P_{CO_2} is elevated, generally in the range of 55 to 80 mmHg, and the P_{O_2} is depressed; these can rapidly be restored to near normal by asking the patient to increase ventilation voluntarily. Indeed some observers have found considerable variability in the P_{CO_2}, because when the patients are tested and become aware of their breathing, they tend to breathe more. For this reason the finding of a raised plasma bicarbonate indicating metabolic compensation of the chronic respiratory acidosis may be a useful diagnostic pointer. The hematocrit is typically between 50 and 70 percent. The ventilatory response to inhaled CO_2 is greatly impaired, though the work of breathing is not increased. Tests of pulmonary function are generally normal with no indication of airway obstruction. The pulmonary arterial pressure is typically increased because of the alveolar hypoxemia.

No specific pathologic changes have been found in the central nervous system of these patients. Congestive heart failure and respiratory infections should be treated vigorously.

Metabolic alkalosis   A few patients with metabolic alkalosis hypoventilate, although this causes no symptoms and is difficult to detect clinically. The commonest causes include severe vomiting and potassium and chloride loss such as that caused by diuretics or steroid therapy. The arterial pH is always raised, indicating only partial respiratory compensation. Many patients with metabolic alkalosis do not hypoventilate at all.

Sleep apnea   Over the last 15 years a number of patients have been described in whom breathing periodically stops during sleep. Sleep apnea is defined as cessation of airflow at the nostrils and mouth for at least 10 s. This can occur in normal subjects up to 10 times a night and then only during rapid eye movement (REM) sleep. But in the patients with sleep apnea syndrome there are usually over 10 apneic periods per hour of sleep.

Sleep apnea is of two types: obstructive and central. In *obstructive sleep apnea,* airflow (as measured by thermistors at the nose and mouth) ceases despite persistent respiratory efforts as shown by abdominal and thoracic inspiratory movements. These movements can be recorded by transducers around the abdomen and chest. Sometimes the patient seeks medical advice because of loud snoring and daytime somnolence. The airway obstruction can be caused by backward movement of the tongue, narrowing of upper airway by obesity, collapse of the pharyngeal walls due to failure of the genioglossus muscle, or greatly enlarged tonsils or adenoids. Arterial oxygen saturation (measured by ear oximeter) falls during the apneic periods, cardiac arrhythmias may develop, and acute elevations in systemic and pulmonary artery pressures can occur. There is often chronic sleep deprivation, and the patient may exhibit daytime somnolence, chronic fatigue, and morning headaches. Personality disturbances such as paranoia, hostility, and agitated depression may develop. Long-term tracheostomy has been shown to be beneficial in some of these patients. Weight loss is valuable if the patient is obese. Methoxyprogesterone has been used as a respiratory stimulant, but its value is uncertain.

Central sleep apnea is caused by a transient cessation of inspiratory muscle activity. It is recognized by the absence of both airflow and respiratory movements. Patients who tend to hypoventilate (see Table 215-1) may develop apneic episodes during sleep when respiratory drive is depressed. It is now known that during REM sleep breathing is often irregular and unresponsive to chemical and vagal drives. The exception is hypoxemia, which remains a powerful stimulus to breathe. Even during hypoxemia, irregular breathing and periods of apnea may develop if normal respiratory drive is altered by sleep. This is seen to a striking degree in the Cheyne-Stokes breathing of normal subjects at high altitude.

Sudden infant death syndrome This is sometimes known as "crib death." Typically the infant is found dead in the crib with no apparent cause. The etiology of this is still obscure, but some investigators believe that this is a special case of the sleep apnea syndrome described above. In addition it is known that the rib cage collapses easily in some young infants and there may be paradoxical movement of the chest wall; that is, the rib cage moves in rather than out during inspiration. This may be accentuated by poor coordination of the respiratory muscles as a result of immaturity of the nervous system. It has also been shown that infants do not respond to transient airway obstruction by increasing their respiratory efforts, as occurs in the normal adult. This would make them abnormally vulnerable to upper respiratory tract infections. Finally, it is possible that some deaths are caused by cardiac arrhythmias during an apneic period.

CARBON DIOXIDE RETENTION ASSOCIATED WITH CHRONIC LUNG DISEASE The commonest clinical situation in which CO_2 retention is seen is chronic lung disease. Patients with this condition are often said to be "hypoventilating," but the cause of their hypercapnia is clearly very different from that in patients with normal lungs whom we have considered so far. Historically it is easy to see how the term *hypoventilation* came to be applied so indiscriminately. When in the late 1950s it became possible to measure the P_{CO_2} of arterial blood in the clinical setting, CO_2 retention was found to be a common and serious complication of chronic lung disease which could always be abolished by artificially increasing the ventilation. Thus it was natural to say that these patients had a reduced ventilation, and this term had the advantage of keeping an important therapeutic option in the forefront.

It is important to understand the factors leading to CO_2 retention in these patients if their disease is to be managed most effectively. Figure 215-1 shows a scheme of the factors determining CO_2 elimination in patients with lung disease. CO_2 is produced in the tissues at a rate which depends on the level of metabolic activity; at rest there is little variation. It is transported to the lungs in the venous blood and pumped out by the ventilation. The speed of the pump is normally set by the level of the P_{CO_2} via the medullary chemoreceptors. In the presence of lung disease, the efficiency of the pump is impaired. Thus, for the same level of ventilation, less CO_2 is eliminated. This is principally because ventilation and blood flow are unevenly matched within the lung (see Chap. 200). In any event the result is that for a normal level of ventilation, inadequate amounts of CO_2 are excreted, and CO_2 retention occurs.

When the increased arterial P_{CO_2} causes a fall in the cerebrospinal fluid pH which is sensed by the medullary chemoreceptors, the ventilation is increased. The peripheral chemoreceptors also respond to the increased P_{CO_2}. The result is that the P_{CO_2} returns to normal, because fortunately even lungs with grossly mismatched ventilation and blood flow can greatly increase their elimination of CO_2 when their ventilation is raised. (Contrast this with the behavior of O_2 where uneven ventilation and blood flow invariably result in low P_{O_2}; this follows from the shape of the O_2 dissociation curve as discussed in Chap. 200.) Thus a common end result is a normal P_{CO_2}, but at the expense of increased ventilation. However, in the presence of severe disease, the ventilation may not be increased enough to restore the P_{CO_2} to normal, and CO_2 retention therefore occurs.

The ventilatory response to CO_2 in these patients can be reduced for two reasons. One is an increased work of breathing. It has been shown that if normal subjects breathe through a resistance, their ventilatory response to inhaled CO_2 is depressed. Indeed, the relationship between increase in ventilation and inspired CO_2 concentration may become indistinguishable from that observed in patients with chronic airway obstruction. In most cases of chronic obstructive lung disease, the resistance to airflow is high so that the increase in ventilation for a given rise in arterial P_{CO_2} is depressed. Such patients may have a normal neural output of the respiratory center in response to an increased P_{CO_2}, but nevertheless the ventilatory response is impaired.

However, some patients also have a reduced neural output of the respiratory center in response to an increased arterial P_{CO_2}. This can be established by specialized tests such as measurement of the mechanical work performed during inspiration or the inspiratory pressure developed during a brief period of airway occlusion. The reason for the diminished sensitivity of the respiratory center in these patients is not understood, though in some cases it may be congenital. There is evidence that the sensitivity of the respiratory center to CO_2 (and hypoxemia) varies considerably among normal subjects. It may be that those patients who have good respiratory center sensitivity are more distressed by dyspnea, while those who respond weakly may succumb to CO_2 retention and respiratory failure.

When CO_2 retention becomes established, the respiratory center becomes reset at a higher arterial P_{CO_2}. This can be explained by an increase in bicarbonate concentration in the cerebrospinal fluid because of transport of bicarbonate across the blood-gas barrier. As a result the pH of the cerebrospinal fluid is returned to near its normal value of 7.32 in spite of its increased P_{CO_2}. Since this pH apparently chiefly determines the response of the medullary chemoreceptors, respiratory drive may then not be much increased despite the raised P_{CO_2}.

Further CO_2 retention occurs in some patients with chronic lung disease following the administration of oxygen. These patients have chronic hypercapnia and hypoxemia but a near normal pH in their arterial blood (compensated respiratory acidosis) and in their cerebrospinal fluid. Their main stimulus to ventilation may be the arterial hypoxemia via the peripheral chemoreceptors, so that when this is relieved, ventilation almost ceases. The ensuing rise in P_{CO_2} may further depress ventilation because of the narcotic effect of high levels of CO_2. This extremely dangerous situation should be avoided by giving carefully controlled O_2 concentrations, for example, 24 to 28%, assiduously watching the patient, and measuring the arterial P_{O_2}, P_{CO_2}, and pH frequently. CO_2 retention in chronic obstructive lung disease is considered in Chap. 208, and the treatment of acute and chronic respiratory failure in Chap. 216.

MEASUREMENT OF CONTROL OF VENTILATION The cause of disorders of ventilation can sometimes be elucidated by studying the control of ventilation. The ventilatory response to CO_2 can be measured by means of a rebreathing technique. A bag is filled with a mixture of about 6% CO_2 in O_2, and the patient rebreathes from this over a period of several minutes. The P_{CO_2} in the bag increases at the rate of 4 to 6 mmHg per minute, and thus the change in ventilation per mmHg rise in P_{CO_2} can easily be determined. A similar technique can be employed to measure the ventilatory response to hypoxia. In this instance the bag is filled with 24% O_2, 7% CO_2, and the balance N_2. The P_{CO_2} in the bag is monitored and held constant. Rebreathing can be continued until the inspired P_{O_2} falls to about 40 mmHg.

Another method of assessing the output of the respiratory center is to measure the inspiratory pressure during a brief period of airway occlusion. The patient breathes through a valve box, the inspiratory port of which is provided with a shutter. This is closed during an expiration (the patient being unaware), so that the first part of the next inspiration is against an occluded airway. The shutter is opened after about 0.5 s. The pressure generated during the first 0.1 s of attempted inspiration ($P_{0.1}$) is taken as a measure of respiratory center output.

HYPERVENTILATION

Hyperventilation is most commonly caused by lesions of the central nervous system, metabolic acidosis, and anxiety states. In addition, hyperventilation may be seen in salicylate poisoning, acute or chronic hypoxemia (as at high altitude), severe hypoglycemia, and hepatic coma. A patient with severe cerebral hemorrhage causing coma may exhibit deep, regular respirations of a mechanical nature. This causes a reduced P_{CO_2} in the arterial blood, which initially shows a high pH and a normal base excess. Irregularities of breathing such as Cheyne-Stokes respiration may also occur. In metabolic acidosis caused, for example, by uncontrolled diabetes mellitus or by chronic renal insufficiency, deep regular respiration known as *Kussmaul breathing* is frequently seen. Active rather than passive expiratory movements are a feature of this pattern. Here the low P_{CO_2} is accompanied by reduction in base excess and a low pH (see Chap. 42).

In the hyperventilation of anxiety states, the patient may be very apprehensive and complain of shortness of breath, difficulty in taking a deep breath, a feeling of chest tightness, or a sense of suffocation. The patient is often a nervous, anxious woman who has other functional disturbances due to tension. There are often accompanying symptoms such as numbness in the limbs, palpitations, and epigastric discomfort. The fall in P_{CO_2} and the consequent alkalosis may be severe and may cause tetany with carpopedal spasm. The reduced plasma bicarbonate level and relatively normal arterial pH (compensated respiratory alkalosis) distinguish chronic hyperventilation from the acute hyperventilation with fall in P_{CO_2} which frequently accompanies an arterial puncture. The patient may complain of fainting spells and blurring of vision; these are probably related to the reduction in cerebral blood flow caused by low P_{CO_2}. The finding of slow waves of high voltage in the EEG suggests that these changes may be the result of hypoxemia. The changes can be reversed by hyperbaric oxygenation. The serum calcium level remains normal. It is likely that some of the cardiovascular symptoms are related to the release of epinephrine.

These patients are usually not aware of the overbreathing, although they may admit to periods of sighing. It is often possible to reproduce many of the symptoms of an attack by encouraging them to overbreathe spontaneously. It is also useful to demonstrate to these patients that they can hold a breath for a considerable period even during an attack. An attack can sometimes be terminated by having the patient breathe in and out of a plastic bag, or inhale a 5% CO_2 mixture. However, attention to the underlying anxiety state is indicated.

Hyperventilation also occurs in some types of lung disease, including interstitial lung disease and pulmonary edema. The hyperventilation of interstitial disease is particularly marked on exercise where the breathing is typically rapid and shallow, and the arterial P_{CO_2} may fall to the 20s. The cause of the hyperventilation is uncertain, but stimulation of the juxtacapillary (J) receptors in the alveolar wall by the process involving the lung has been suggested as a possible cause. Part of the hyperventilation may also be explained by the stimulation of the peripheral chemoreceptors by the severe arterial hypoxemia which may occur in these conditions.

ABNORMAL PATTERNS OF VENTILATION

CHEYNE-STOKES BREATHING   This is a form of periodic breathing characterized by alternating periods of apnea and hyperpnea. The patient often lies motionless for 10 to 20 s and then begins to breathe shallowly at first, then with increasing amplitude, and finally shallowly again. The respirations during this period of breathing are regular in time.

The cause of this disturbance presumably lies in some abnormality in the control process which results in "hunting" for the equilibrium condition. Periodic breathing can be produced in experimental animals by lengthening the distance over which blood travels from the thorax to the brain. As a result, the response of the chemoreceptors lags behind the blood gas changes produced by the lungs, and a cyclic chain of events is created. Any increase in chemoreceptor gain also tends to make the system unstable. Conditions in which Cheyne-Stokes breathing is seen include congestive heart failure when the circulation time is prolonged (Chap. 182), brain damage caused by trauma or cerebral hemorrhage, and chronic hypoxia. It occurs in normal subjects living at high altitude, especially during sleep.

BIOT'S BREATHING   This is another form of periodic breathing in which periods of apnea are punctuated by a few deep breaths which may be irregular and which do not have the waxing and waning pattern of Cheyne-Stokes respiration. It is most frequently associated with brain damage.

OTHER TYPES   Brain injury can result in bizarre patterns of ventilation. These include apneustic breathing, which is characterized by a postinspiratory pause (rather than the usual postexpiratory), and ataxic breathing, which is irregular in timing and depth.

REFERENCES

CHOLLET S et al: Contribution of nocturnal polygraphy to the diagnosis of Pickwickian syndrome. Respiration 46:272, 1984

HORNBEIN TF: *Regulation of Breathing*, Part II. New York, Marcel Dekker, 1981

LISBOA C et al: Inspiratory muscle function in patients with severe kyphoscoliosis. Am Rev Respir Dis 132:48, 1985

MILLMAN RP, FISHMAN AP: Sleep apnea syndrome, in *Pulmonary Diseases and Disorders*, AP Fishman (ed). New York, McGraw-Hill, 1987, Section 17, Part III, chap 6

ROUSSOS C, MACKLEM PT: Disorders of the respiratory muscle function, in *Update III: Harrison's Principles of Internal Medicine*, KJ Isselbacher et al (eds). New York, McGraw-Hill, 1982, p 83

SAUNDERS NA, SULLIVAN CE: *Sleep and Breathing*. New York, Marcel Dekker, 1984

WEST JB: *Pulmonary Pathophysiology—The Essentials*, 2d ed. Baltimore, Williams & Wilkins, 1982

216   ADULT RESPIRATORY DISTRESS SYNDROME

ROLAND H. INGRAM, JR.

Adult respiratory distress syndrome is a descriptive term that has been applied to many acute, diffuse infiltrative lung lesions of diverse etiologies when they are accompanied by severe arterial hypoxemia. The term was chosen because of several clinical and pathologic similarities between such acute illnesses in adults and the neonatal respiratory distress syndrome. However, in the neonatal form, immaturity of alveolar surfactant production and a highly compliant chest wall are primarily involved in the pathophysiology, whereas in the adult, alveolar surfactant changes are secondary to the primary process, and the chest wall is not compliant. Despite the large number of causes (Table 216-1), the clinical characteristics, respiratory pathophysiologic derangement, and current techniques for management of these acute abnormalities are remarkably similar. It has been argued that the "lumping" of such processes of different etiologies obscures the unique features of each in terms of pathogenesis, prevention, and specificity of treatment. It is clear that the conditions listed do not always lead to respiratory failure and that specific treatment of the underlying processes will often be different. Therefore, the reader is urged to refer to the appropriate sections of this text for the unique characteristics of each condition and to recognize that only the common features at the onset of respiratory failure will be focused upon in this chapter. It should be further emphasized that many of the listed conditions are often present in combination and may come into play at different times in the clinical course of the adult respiratory distress syndrome.

PATHOPHYSIOLOGY   Regardless of the initiating process, the adult respiratory distress syndrome is invariably associated with increased liquid in the lungs. Thus it is a form of pulmonary edema, yet it is distinct from cardiogenic pulmonary edema because pulmonary capillary hydrostatic pressures are not elevated (Chap. 26). Since hydrostatic pressures are not elevated, there is increased permeability of the alveolocapillary membranes that occurs via direct chemical injury in the case of inhaled toxic gases or aspirated acid or indirectly through activation and aggregation of formed elements of the blood within pulmonary capillaries in the case of septicemia and/or endotoxemia. Although platelet aggregation occurs, the major offenders appear to be the neutrophilic leukocytes that adhere to endothelial surfaces. These leukocytes undergo a respiratory burst to inflict oxidant injury and release mediators of inflammation such as leukotrienes, thromboxanes, and prostaglandins. Initially the injury to the alveolocapillary membrane results in leakage of liquid, macromolecules, and cellular components from the blood vessels into the

TABLE 216-1 Conditions which may lead to the adult respiratory distress syndrome

1 Diffuse pulmonary infections (e.g., viral, bacterial, fungal, *Pneumocystis*)
2 Aspiration (e.g., gastric contents with Mendelson's syndrome, water with near drowning)
3 Inhalation of toxins and irritants (e.g., chlorine gas, NO_2, smoke, ozone, high concentrations of oxygen)
4 Narcotic overdose pulmonary edema (e.g., heroin, methadone, morphine, dextropropoxyphene)
5 Nonnarcotic drug effects (e.g., nitrofurantoin)
6 Immunologic response to host antigens (e.g., Goodpasture's syndrome, systemic lupus erythematosus)
7 Effects of nonthoracic trauma with hypotension ("shock lung")
8 In association with systemic reactions to processes initiated outside the lung (e.g., gram-negative septicemia, hemorrhagic pancreatitis, amniotic fluid embolism, fat embolism)
9 Postcardiopulmonary bypass ("pump lung," "postperfusion lung")

interstitial space and, with increasing severity, into the alveoli. The increasing vascular permeability to proteins (decreased reflection coefficient, σ, discussed in Chap. 26) leaves the hydrostatic gradient unopposed so that even mild elevations in capillary pressures greatly increase interstitial and alveolar edema. Alveolar collapse occurs secondary to the effect of the alveolar liquid, especially its fibrinogen, that interferes with normal surfactant activity and because of possible impairment of further surfactant production by injury to the granular pneumocytes. Though radiographically diffuse, the regional dysfunction is nonhomogeneous; it leads to severe ventilation-perfusion imbalance and the shunting of blood through regions in which alveoli are collapsed or filled with liquid. The lungs become less compliant—i.e., stiffen because of interstitial edema, alveolar collapse, and increase in surface forces. Because of the decreased compliance, large inspiratory pressures must be generated by the respiratory muscles so that the work of breathing is elevated. The large mechanical loads lead to fatigue of the muscles of breathing with resulting diminution in tidal volumes and worsening gas exchange. Both hypoxemia and the stimulation of receptors in the stiff lung parenchyma cause an increase in respiratory frequency, decrease in tidal volume, and deterioration in gas exchange.

PATHOLOGY In the absence of specific demonstrable pathogens, the pathology is remarkably similar among the various conditions leading to the adult respiratory distress syndrome, since the lung has a limited number of ways in which it reacts to an almost limitless number of injuries. Grossly, the lungs are heavy, edematous, and almost airless with regions of hemorrhage, atelectasis, and consolidation. By light microscopy there is edema and cellular infiltration of interalveolar septa and interstitial spaces surrounding airways and blood vessels, atelectasis and hyaline membranes in many regions, engorgement of vessels with red blood cells, and aggregates of platelets and neutrophilic leukocytes along with interstitial and alveolar hemorrhage. In addition, both hyperplasia and dysplasia of the granular pneumocytes are often present.

If the illness has been prolonged beyond 10 days, there is often a surprising amount of fibrosis in addition to the acute changes. In instances of recovery and subsequent death from another cause, significant interstitial fibrosis and emphysematous changes may be found in the lung. A significant number of patients, however, will recover completely and have normal pulmonary function with no respiratory symptoms. Hence aggressive clinical management is both indicated and often rewarding.

CLINICAL CHARACTERISTICS At the time of initial injury and for several hours thereafter the patient may be free of respiratory symptoms or signs. The earliest sign often is an increase in respiratory frequency followed shortly by dyspnea. Arterial blood gas measurement in the earlier period will disclose a depressed P_{O_2} despite a decreased P_{CO_2} so that the alveolar-arterial difference for oxygen (Chap. 200) is increased. At this early stage, administration of oxygen by mask or nasal prongs results in a significant increase in the arterial P_{O_2}. The brisk rise in P_{O_2} indicates that ventilation-perfusion mismatching and, possibly, diffusion impairment account for the widened alveolar-

arterial P_{O_2} difference ($PA_{O_2} - Pa_{O_2}$) initially. Physical examination may be unremarkable, although a few fine inspiratory rales may be audible. Radiographically the lung fields may be clear or demonstrate only minimal and scattered interstitial infiltrates. With progression, the patient becomes cyanotic and increasingly dyspneic and tachypneic. Rales are more prominent and are easily heard throughout both lung fields along with regions of tubular breath sounds; the chest radiograph demonstrates diffuse, extensive bilateral interstitial and alveolar infiltrates (Fig. 216-1). At this point hypoxemia cannot be corrected by the simple expedient of increasing the oxygen concentration of the inspired gas, and mechanical ventilatory support must be started. Right-to-left shunting of blood through collapsed or filled alveoli becomes the major mechanism for arterial hypoxemia at this more advanced stage. In contrast to ventilation-perfusion mismatching and diffusion impairment, with right-to-left shunts, $PA_{O_2} - Pa_{O_2}$ remains high with breathing of pure oxygen. Positive end-expiratory pressure (PEEP) serves to increase lung volume, which in turn opens collapsed alveoli and decreases shunting. With further progression, and if mechanical ventilator and PEEP therapy are delayed, the combination of increasing tachypnea and decreasing tidal volumes results in alveolar hypoventilation, a rising P_{CO_2}, and worsening hypoxemia; these represent a near-terminal constellation of findings.

MANAGEMENT OF HYPOXEMIC RESPIRATORY FAILURE The brief description given above contains the salient principles of management, integrated with the clinical events that lead to escalation of therapeutic interventions. Implicit in that description is that the simplest method and the lowest inspired fraction of oxygen (FI_{O_2}) should be used to give the desired result. The oxyhemoglobin dissociation curve gives some guide as to the Pa_{O_2} for which to aim. At a P_{O_2} of 60 mmHg, hemoglobin is approximately 90 percent saturated. Therefore, a reasonable objective is to achieve a Pa_{O_2} of 60, since higher levels add little to oxygenation and introduce the risk of oxygen toxicity to the lung. In contrast to respiratory failure complicating chronic airways obstruction (Chap. 208), depression of ventilation is not an issue in hypoxemic respiratory failure.

There are multiple means to deliver O_2, in order of increasing

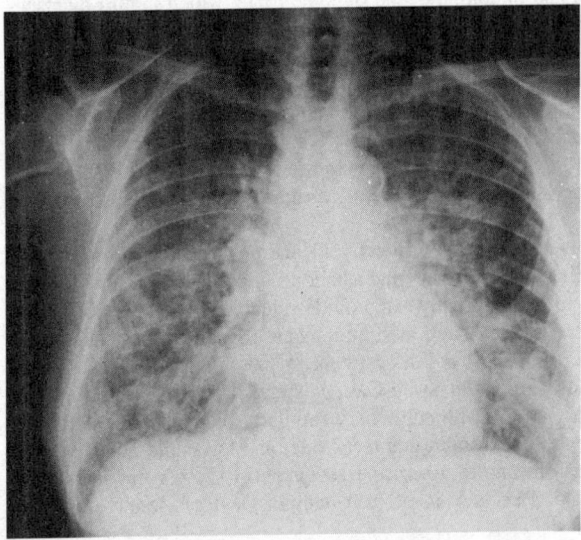

FIGURE 216-1 *A standard posteroanterior chest radiograph from a patient with the adult respiratory distress syndrome secondary to a severe viral pneumonitis. Such a diffuse radiographic change is typical of all conditions listed in Table 216-1 when they are severe enough to cause acute hypoxemic respiratory failure. A similar radiographic picture is also seen in pulmonary edema due to left ventricular failure (Chap. 26). Often in such acutely ill patients, the radiograph must be taken with a portable unit and the film exposed from the anterior direction. Both the anteroposterior exposure and the failure to take a deep inspiration result in an apparent enlargement of the cardiac silhouette which further obscures the reliable detection of left ventricular failure.*

effectiveness: soft nasal prongs, simple face masks, and face masks with inspiratory reservoir bags. The effective F_{IO_2} (that is actually entering the trachea) will be determined by the concentration of O_2 delivered from the tank or wall device, its flow rate, and the minute ventilation of the patient. In the hypoxemic form of respiratory failure, it is reasonable to start with moderate flow rates (5 to 10 liters per minute of 100% O_2) and monitor arterial blood gases, adjusting flow rates and O_2 concentrations depending upon results.

If adequate oxygenation cannot be maintained with these less invasive measures, endotracheal intubation should be carried out and mechanical ventilatory support should be instituted. The rationale behind mechanical ventilatory support in a patient who is hyperventilating is *not* to increase ventilation but to increase mean lung volume, thereby opening previously closed airways and improving oxygenation. This is done by using large tidal volumes (approximately 15 mL per kilogram of lean body weight) at a slower breathing rate (12 to 15 breaths per minute) than the spontaneous one of the patient. Most often, at this juncture, the respiratory system is sufficiently stiff that high inflation pressures are required and a volume-cycled ventilator (in contrast to the pressure-cycled ones) is needed. If the patient makes expiratory efforts during the inflation cycle, peak inspiratory pressures will increase, possibly enough to activate the high-pressure pop-off valve, which results in delivery to the patient of a smaller tidal volume than selected. Under these circumstances consideration is often given to sedation and/or neuromuscular paralysis. However, a much more logical way to proceed is to institute synchronized intermittent mandatory ventilation (SIMV). In the SIMV mode, the patient is allowed to breathe spontaneously with periodic delivery of mandatory breaths that are synchronized with spontaneous inspiratory efforts. If the spontaneous breathing rate is so rapid that expiratory efforts occur before the mandatory breath is fully delivered, only then should sedation and/or paralysis be used.

Should the Pa_{O_2} be greater than 60 mmHg, the next step is to lower the F_{IO_2}. If the F_{IO_2} can be lowered to 0.6 or less with a Pa_{O_2} equal to or greater than 60 mmHg, the mechanical ventilation should proceed at that F_{IO_2} as long as necessary. There are two basic indications for the addition of PEEP, the basic rationale for which is to increase lung volume further, thereby opening previously closed alveoli. First, if the F_{IO_2} cannot be lowered to or below 0.6, then PEEP should be added to allow a decrease of the F_{IO_2} below the toxic range. Second, if the Pa_{O_2} cannot be increased to or above 60 mmHg with an F_{IO_2} of 1.0, PEEP should be added. The optimal magnitude of the PEEP is determined by the response of the Pa_{O_2} and the extent of the cardiovascular alterations resulting from the higher pressure. The major alteration is a decrease in cardiac output due to two mechanisms. First, increased intrapleural pressures serve to impede venous return directly, an effect which is, to a variable extent, offset by peripheral venoconstriction. Second, increases in lung volume may increase pulmonary vascular resistance, leading to increased pressure and dilatation of the right ventricle, which in turn displaces the interventricular septum toward the left. This displacement, in effect, decreases left ventricular diastolic compliance; hence less filling leads to smaller stroke volumes. An additional mechanism for decreased diastolic filling of the ventricles is direct compression of the heart by the stiffened lung. In a physiologic sense optimal levels of PEEP are those associated with the greatest delivery of O_2 to the body; the latter is the product of cardiac output and arterial oxygen content.

In patients who are critically ill and/or unstable, insertion of a catheter into a radial artery and a balloon-tipped (Swan-Ganz) catheter into the pulmonary artery can provide valuable information in guiding supportive therapy such as requirements for intravenous fluids, the need for diuresis, and assessment of the effects of mechanical ventilation. From the Swan-Ganz catheter it is possible to measure pulmonary arterial and pulmonary capillary wedge pressures, cardiac output by the thermodilution technique, and to sample mixed venous blood as a means to assess the adequacy of O_2 delivery in relation to demand. Recognition of over-damping and accelerative artifacts

in the pulmonary arterial pressure signal and learning the criteria for true wedging are essential if serious misinterpretations are to be avoided. Even with accurate pressure measurements, there is an additional precaution that must be taken with regard to interpretation of intrathoracic vascular pressures referenced to atmosphere when PEEP is being used. If pleural pressure is greater than atmospheric, as is most often the case with PEEP, the true effective (i.e., intravascular minus pleural) pressure will be overestimated and could lead to errors in both assessment and management. A reasonable estimate of the true value is gained by examining vascular pressures just before inflation and subtracting from these pressures an amount equal to one-half the value of PEEP. In view of the leaky alveolo-capillary membrane it is best to keep the pulmonary capillary wedge pressure as low as is compatible with a reasonable cardiac output, arterial pressure, and urinary output. Recently, inotropic and selective vasoactive agents (e.g., dopamine, page 911) have been used with some success to achieve this, but require careful monitoring to assess effects and adjust doses.

Mixed venous blood P_{O_2} values have long been considered to indicate the adequacy of oxygen delivery relative to demand. A low value (e.g., <20 mmHg) surely indicates that there is tissue hypoxemia irrespective of measured cardiac output and Pa_{O_2}. However, a high value does not exclude serious hypoxemia of the tissues, especially in gram-negative bacillary septicemia, in which systemic low-resistance shunts can develop and leave several capillary beds underperfused.

Body position may also affect the degree of arterial oxygenation. Although patients with the adult respiratory distress syndrome have diffuse lung disease, there may be some regional variation in the extent of disease such that one side is more severely involved than the other. In this instance the less involved lung should be the more dependent one when the patient is in a lateral position. Since the distribution of pulmonary blood flow is so heavily determined by gravity (Chap. 200), having the more involved lung, with its minimal ventilation, in the more dependent position results in a measurable increase in intrapulmonary shunt, manifested as a striking fall in Pa_{O_2}. The possible contribution of a positional effect on arterial oxygenation should always be considered before escalating therapeutic interventions.

Occasionally PEEP must be gradually increased to levels in excess of 20 cmH$_2$O in an attempt to maintain arterial oxygenation. At these high levels of PEEP there may be a paradoxic decrease in Pa_{O_2}. The explanation for this paradox is as follows: high levels of PEEP may not open some of the closed airways but will overdistend those units already open. Overdistension of units increases the vascular resistance in these regions and results in more blood perfusing regions with closed airways, thereby increasing the degree of shunt. The only alternative is to decrease PEEP back to that level associated with the greatest delivery of oxygen to the body (product of cardiac output and arterial oxygen content).

In the situations where maximal PEEP with F_{IO_2} of 1.0 does not supply sufficient oxygen, the possibility of utilizing extracorporeal membrane oxygenators (ECMO) has been both considered and tried. Despite the logical appeal of this form of supportive therapy, a randomized, large prospective study of ECMO therapy has demonstrated that, while it can support gas exchange, there is no effect on survival in acute hypoxemic respiratory failure.

Complications Increasing severity of the clinical illness and continued radiographic progressions in association with the primary process often obscure complications that arise during the course of acute hypoxemic respiratory failure. The development of *left ventricular failure* is a good example of a common, easily missed complication. This is because all patients are likely to have diffuse rales and rhonchi, even without left ventricular failure, and these sounds also serve to make it difficult to detect gallop rhythms. An additional difficulty is that portable chest films are taken in the anteroposterior direction, often at less than full lung inflation, so that the cardiac silhouette appears enlarged. Thus the ordinary physical and radiographic assessments are difficult to rely on. With deterioration, therefore, left ventricular failure should be suspected; it is helpful to insert a Swan-Ganz (see above) catheter which can be used to monitor pulmonary arterial pressure continuously and intermittently to assess pulmonary capillary wedge pressure and oxygen content of mixed venous blood.

With a diffuse radiographic pattern, a secondary bacterial infection is easily overlooked; therefore, frequent sputum smears and cultures should be obtained, especially when there is fever. With many conditions—e.g., gram-negative septicemia, acute hemorrhagic pancreatitis, and "shock lung"—there may be associated *disseminated intravascular coagulation,* which leads to gastrointestinal and intrapulmonary hemorrhage (Chap. 281). Frequent monitoring of platelet count, fibrinogen level, and partial thromboplastin and prothrombin times is helpful in the early detection of this complication and in guiding treatment.

Bronchial obstruction by endotracheal or tracheostomy tubes often occurs. These tubes, when too long or poorly anchored, slide into one main bronchus, usually the right one because of its less angulated origin from the trachea. The tube then blocks ventilation of the other main bronchus, and atelectasis may ensue. Such an event usually causes abrupt deterioration in the patient with respiratory failure. It is detected readily by physical examination, which reveals the absence of breath sounds over the occluded lung. The tube should immediately be pulled back slowly if this complication is suspected. Finally, in the course of treating the illness with mechanical ventilators and high inflation pressures, *pneumothorax* or *pneumomediastinum* may develop and may be impossible to detect except radiologically. Occasionally the presence of subcutaneous emphysema provides a clinical clue. Any deterioration should lead the physician to suspect this complication, repeat the chest radiograph, and institute immediate treatment should pneumothorax be present. If deterioration is sudden, *tension pneumothorax* should be suspected; if physical signs are present, a pleural catheter should be inserted immediately without radiographic confirmation. It is important to realize that high oxygen concentrations (>0.60) for prolonged periods can produce both the lesions and the clinical picture of the adult respiratory distress syndrome. Therefore, as discussed under clinical management above, the *minimal* oxygen concentration associated with acceptable arterial oxygenation should always be used.

Discontinuation of mechanical ventilatory support   The ability of the patient to maintain adequate gas exchange without the support of a mechanical ventilator is most often heralded by a decreasing $F_{I_{O_2}}$ requirement, smaller inflation pressures for mandatory or assisted breaths, and a spontaneous respiratory rate below 30 per minute. Other useful guidelines are a spontaneous tidal volume ≥ 5 mL per kilogram of lean body weight, a vital capacity ≥ 15 mL/kg, and the ability to generate a static inspiratory pressure ≥ 20 cmH$_2$O. Despite these indicators and guidelines, some patients are unable to support themselves for long periods of time so that multiple weaning "trials" guided by mechanical and gas exchange data are carried out in a semiempirical way. Synchronized intermittent mandatory ventilation (SIMV) as described above has been advocated as a logical transitional mode whereby the frequency of the mandatory breaths is gradually decreased. There is a great deal of intuitive appeal to this approach, but it has not been appropriately tested and compared with more abrupt, intermittent withdrawal trials. As in patients with hypercapnic respiratory failure, the six mechanisms for failure to wean should be considered in these patients as well (p. 1094).

Prognosis   Given the diversity of the etiologies and the frequency of associated diseases, it is difficult, if not impossible, to give meaningful prognostic figures for the adult respiratory distress syndrome. If all recently published series are taken together, the mortality rate runs between 50 and 60 percent. This represents an improved survival rate over the virtual 100 percent mortality rate of a few years ago and is a result of the application of modern treatment techniques described above. If the syndrome is due to drug overdose, the mortality rate is low; if associated with shock, the chances of a fatal outcome are much greater. Recently, it has become apparent that multiple organ system failure (e.g., renal, hepatic) supervenes when there is an extrapulmonic source of sepsis in need of surgical drainage and that almost all such patients succumb despite maximal support of the respiratory and cardiovascular systems. Other etiologies and associated diseases are between these two extremes. The following factors appear to be associated with a poor outcome: an increase in $PA_{O_2} - Pa_{O_2}$, requiring increasing inspired O$_2$ concentrations and PEEP; decreasing compliance, requiring greater inflation pressures; either low or falling colloid osmotic pressures; and the onset of systemic arterial hypotension not responding to intravascular volume replacement.

In survivors with previously normal lung function, the long-term prognosis for recovery appears to be remarkably good. Lung volumes and arterial blood gases have been shown to return to normal levels within 4 to 6 months after respiratory failure. There are instances, however, when the fibrotic residua are sufficiently great that complete recovery is unlikely.

REFERENCES

Bell RC et al: Multiple organ system failure and infection in the adult respiratory distress syndrome. Ann Intern Med 99:293, 1983

Fanta CH: Pathophysiology and clinical recognition of the adult respiratory distress syndrome. Med Grand Rounds 2:284, 1983

Hall JB, Wood LDH: Acute hypoxemic respiratory failure. Med Grand Rounds 3:183, 1984

Hanley ME, Bone RC: Acute respiratory failure. Pathophysiology, causes, and clinical manifestations. Postgrad Med 79:166, 172, 1986

Hyers TM, Fowler AA: Adult respiratory distress syndrome: Causes, morbidity and mortality. Fed Proc 45:25, 1986

Molloy WD et al: Effects of dopamine on cardiopulmonary function and left ventricular volumes in patients with acute respiratory failure. Am Rev Resp Dis 130:396, 1984

Schuster DP et al: Prospective evaluation of the risk of upper gastrointestinal bleeding after admission to a medical intensive care unit. Am J Med 76:623, 1984

Tate RM, Repine JE: Neutrophils and the respiratory distress syndrome. State of the art. Am Rev Resp Dis 128:552, 1983

Viires N et al: Effects of aminophylline on diaphragmatic fatigue during acute respiratory failure. Am Rev Resp Dis 129:396, 1984

217 APPROACH TO THE PATIENT WITH DISEASES OF THE KIDNEYS AND URINARY TRACT

FREDRIC L. COE / BARRY M. BRENNER

Specific diseases of the kidneys and urinary tract frequently give rise to consistent arrays, or clusters, of clinical signs, symptoms, and laboratory findings called *syndromes*. Syndromes are useful diagnostically because each has fewer causes than the individual clinical signs and symptoms it contains. For example, any injured capillary bed from glomerulus to the urethral meatus can cause hematuria, but only glomerular injury can also cause heavy albuminuria and erythrocyte casts (Chap. 40), and only a few of the diseases that injure the glomerular capillaries enough to cause hematuria and proteinuria also cause a rapid fall in glomerular filtration rate. Routine clinical evaluation is often sufficient to suggest that a particular syndrome may be present (Table 217-1), but additional laboratory measurements beyond the routine, as well as radiologic and/or urologic evaluation and sequential clinical observations, are usually required to establish the diagnosis. This chapter presents the general features of the syndromes, the clinical and laboratory data base required for their recognition, and outlines the diseases that cause them. Succeeding chapters in this section describe the diseases and their treatment in detail.

ACUTE (ARF) AND RAPIDLY PROGRESSIVE RENAL FAILURE (RPRF)

Whether the glomerular filtration rate falls over a period of days (acute renal failure) or weeks (rapidly progressive renal failure) is a useful distinction, because the causes of these two syndromes are somewhat different (Tables to 217-1 and 217-2). For example, acute tubular necrosis, from sepsis, nephrotoxic materials, shock, or other cause (see Chap. 219), presents itself as, and is the usual cause of, acute renal failure, whereas extracapillary proliferative (crescentic) glomerulonephritis, due to immunologic injury or to vasculitis, is an important cause of rapidly progressive, but not acute, renal failure (Chap. 223).

Proof for the existence of either syndrome requires serial determination of the glomerular filtration rate (GFR), or blood urea nitrogen or serum creatinine level. Anuria or oliguria (Chap. 40) strongly suggest acute renal failure, as life cannot be sustained for very long with such inadequate renal function. Symptoms and signs of uremia of recent onset suggest rapidly progressive or acute renal failure, but could also result from chronic renal failure that has only recently become life-threatening. Although edema, hypertension, and abnormalities of electrolytes and the urine sediment (Table 217-1) are frequent in acute and rapidly progressive renal failure, they occur in other syndromes as well and are not specific.

The causes of these two important syndromes number about 36, but only 18 (indicated by T, Table 217-2) typically cause acute renal failure and 8, rapidly progressive renal failure. Urinary obstruction, acute tubular necrosis, some forms of vasculitis, major renal vascular accidents, and endogenous and exogenous nephrotoxins are the usual causes of acute renal failure. Vasculitis and crescentic forms of glomerulonephritis are the main causes of rapidly progressive renal failure. Hemolytic-uremic syndrome, malignant nephrosclerosis, and essential mixed cryoimmunoglobulinemia occasionally present as rapidly progressive renal failure. Idiopathic rapidly progressive glomerulonephritis—the prototype of a disease that produces rapidly progressive renal failure—sometimes causes acute renal failure. Chronic renal failure may occur in some patients with diseases that typically cause acute renal failure. Nevertheless, despite some variability of disease presentations, the finding of acute or rapidly progressive renal failure narrows the range of causes.

ACUTE NEPHRITIS (AN)

A number of diseases involve the glomeruli and, to a generally lesser extent, the tubules in an acute but transient inflammatory process, manifested clinically by acute reduction in GFR, rapidly progressive renal failure, and salt and water retention. Expansion of the extracellular volume, if marked, causes hypertension, pulmonary vascular congestion, and facial and peripheral edema (Chap. 223). Since the causes of this syndrome all can damage the glomerular wall enough to permit red blood cells and plasma proteins to enter the urinary space and appear in the urine, gross or microscopic hematuria, red blood cell casts, and proteinuria are necessary for the diagnosis of acute nephritis, and their absence should suggest other diagnostic possibilities. Acute nephritis itself is a transient inflammatory process, so its clinical and laboratory manifestations wax and wane in synchrony over days to a few weeks. Many of the diseases that cause acute nephritis also cause acute or rapidly progressive renal failure (Table 217-2).

The fact that many diseases produce both acute nephritis and acute or rapidly progressive renal failure, some produce only acute nephritis, and some produce acute or chronic renal failure without acute nephritis is useful in diagnosis. Only two diseases, poststreptococcal glomerulonephritis and nonstreptococcal postinfectious glomerulonephritis, typically cause acute nephritis alone (Table 217-2), and only three of the diseases that typically cause acute renal failure, idiopathic rapidly progressive glomerulonephritis, Goodpasture's syndrome, and non-Goodpasture's antiglomerular basement membrane (anti-GBM) disease, also cause acute nephritis (Table 217-2). On the other hand, most of the diseases that cause acute nephritis also cause rapidly progressive renal failure.

Acute glomerulonephritis following infection with group A streptococci is the prototype of a disease that causes acute nephritis alone (Chap. 223). Immune complexes deposit in the subepithelial region of the glomerular capillary wall, between the basement membrane and the visceral epithelial cells that separate the membrane from the urinary space, and provoke an intense but transient inflammatory process. GFR falls, but returns to normal within weeks to months in the vast majority of affected patients. Deposition of immune complexes is also believed to be the cause of acute nephritis following other bacterial and viral infections, and of lupus nephritis, membranoproliferative glomerulonephritis, Henoch-Schönlein purpura, and Berger's disease, i.e., IgA nephropathy. That the typical presentations of the last four diseases are chronic renal failure, nephrotic syndrome, and asymptomatic urinary abnormalities (Table 217-2) illustrate the weakness of relationships between pathogenesis and final clinical manifestations.

TABLE 217-1 Initial clinical and laboratory data base for defining major syndromes in nephrology

Syndromes	Important clues to diagnosis	Findings which are common but not of diagnostic value	Location of discussion of diseases causing syndrome
Acute or rapidly progressive renal failure	Anuria Oliguria Documented recent decline in GFR	Hypertension, hematuria Proteinuria, pyuria Casts, edema	Chaps. 219, 223, 226, 227, 230
Acute nephritis	Hematuria, RBC casts Azotemia, oliguria Edema, hypertension	Proteinuria Pyuria Circulatory congestion	Chaps. 222 to 224
Chronic renal failure	Azotemia for > 3 months Prolonged symptoms or signs of uremia Symptoms or signs of renal osteodystrophy Kidneys reduced in size bilaterally Broad casts in urinary sediment	Hematuria, proteinuria Casts, oliguria Polyuria, nocturia Edema, hypertension Electrolyte disorders	Chaps. 218, 220
Nephrotic syndrome	Proteinuria > 3.5 g per 1.73 m² per 24 h Hypoalbuminemia Hyperlipidemia Lipiduria	Casts Edema	Chaps. 223, 224
Asymptomatic urinary abnormalities	Hematuria Proteinuria (below nephrotic range) Sterile pyuria, casts		Chap. 223
Urinary tract infection	Bacteriuria > 10⁵ colonies per milliliter Other infectious agent documented in urine Pyuria, leukocyte casts Frequency, urgency Bladder tenderness, flank tenderness	Hematuria Mild azotemia Mild proteinuria Fever	Chap. 225
Renal tubule defects	Electrolyte disorders Polyuria, nocturia Symptoms or signs of renal osteodystrophy Large kidneys Renal transport defects	Hematuria "Tubular" proteinuria Enuresis	Chaps. 226, 228
Hypertension	Systolic/diastolic hypertension	Proteinuria Casts Azotemia	Chaps. 29, 196, 227
Nephrolithiasis	Previous history of stone passage or removal Previous history of stone seen by x-ray Renal colic	Hematuria Pyuria Frequency, urgency	Chap. 229
Urinary tract obstruction	Azotemia, oliguria, anuria Polyuria, nocturia, urinary retention Slowing of urinary stream Large prostate, large kidneys Flank tenderness, full bladder after voiding	Hematuria Pyuria Enuresis, dysuria	Chap. 230

Renal biopsy is usually required for the evaluation of patients with acute nephritis, whether or not acute or rapidly progressive renal failure is also present. The usual histologic picture is proliferative glomerulonephritis, often with extracapillary crescent formation, but prognosis and treatment are influenced strongly by the precise histologic and ultrastructural pattern, as well as the types of immune complexes and immunoglobulins deposited in the renal tissues.

CHRONIC RENAL FAILURE (CRF) Chronic renal failure is a syndrome which results from progressive and irreversible destruction of nephrons, regardless of cause (Chap. 220). This syndrome may be considered to exist when GFR is found to be reduced and is known to have been reduced for at least 3 to 6 months (Table 217-1). Often, in fact, a gradual decline in GFR can be documented over a period of years. Proof of chronicity is also provided by the demonstration by abdominal scout film, ultrasonography, intravenous pyelography, or tomography of bilateral reduction of kidney size. Other findings consistent with long-standing renal failure, such as renal osteodystrophy or signs and symptoms of uremia, also help to establish this syndrome (Table 217-1). Several laboratory abnormalities are often regarded as reliable indicators of chronicity of renal disease, such as anemia, hyperphosphatemia, or hypocalcemia, but these are not specific and may be misleading (Chap. 218). In contrast, the finding of broad casts in the urinary sediment (Chap. 40) is quite specific for chronic renal failure, the wide diameters of these casts reflecting the compensatory dilatation and hypertrophy of surviving nephrons. Proteinuria is a frequent but nonspecific finding, as is hematuria. Chronic obstructive uropathy, polycystic and medullary cystic diseases, analgesic nephropathy, and the inactive end stage of any chronic tubulointerstitial nephropathy are excellent examples of conditions in which the urine often contains little or no protein, cells, or casts even though nephron destruction has progressed to the stage of chronic renal failure.

When ARF occurs and there is also clear evidence of CRF, the acute component must be evaluated as if CRF were not present, largely because the acute component is potentially reversible. In most instances, depletion of extracellular fluid volume accounts for the acute deterioration of renal function, but other factors such as urinary tract obstruction, drug-induced nephrotoxicity, or exacerbation of the underlying renal disease may also be responsible (Chap. 220).

NEPHROTIC SYNDROME (NS) This syndrome is generally held to be present when a patient excretes more than 3.5 g protein per 1.73 m² per 24 h that consists mainly of albumin (massive proteinuria) and has reduced serum albumin concentration, edema, and hyperlipidemia (Table 217-1). Massive proteinuria alone has come to define the syndrome since this finding connotes serious renal disease whether or not the protein losses lead to hypoalbuminemia, lipid disturbances, or edema (Chap. 40). Provided the proteins appearing in the urine are not abnormal paraproteins readily excreted by the normal kidney (e.g., light chains in multiple myeloma), massive proteinuria is invariably a sign of injury to the glomeruli.

Common causes of the nephrotic syndrome include minimal change disease, idiopathic membranous glomerulopathy, focal glomerulosclerosis, and diabetic glomerulosclerosis (Chaps. 223 and 224). Because these diseases typically cause less inflammation than those that cause acute nephritis, the urine contains fewer cellular elements, and acute changes in GFR and urine volume are uncommon. Hematuria may be a frequent manifestation of some forms of nephrotic syndrome, however, especially chronic membranoproliferative glomerulonephritis (Chap. 223). The presence of many cellular or granular casts should suggest lupus nephritis (Chap. 224) or one of the other causes

TABLE 217-2 Syndromes produced by diseases of the kidneys and urinary tract

Diseases (Chap.)	ARF	RPRF	AN	CRF	NS	AUA
Bilateral arterial occlusion (227)	T					
Acute tubular necrosis (219)	T					
Bilateral acute renal vein thrombosis (227)	T					
Acute uric acid nephropathy (226)	T					
Hypovolemia (219)	T					
Cardiovascular collapse (219)	T					
Acute bilateral upper tract obstruction (230)	T			O		
Hypercalcemic nephropathy (226)	T					
Hemolytic uremic syndrome (227)	T	O	O			
Malignant nephrosclerosis (227)	T	O				
Essential mixed cyroimmunoglobulinemia (224)	T	O	O	O	O	
Nephrotoxic drugs and chemicals (226)	T			O		
Oxalate nephropathy (226)	T			O		
Cortical necrosis (219)	T			O		
Postpartum glomerulosclerosis (219)	T			O		
Hypersensitivity nephropathy (226)	T		O			P,H,L
Scleroderma (227)	T					P
Idiopathic rapidly progressive GN (223)	O	T	T		R	
Goodpasture's syndrome (223)	O	T	T	O		P,H
Non-Goodpasture's anti-GBM disease (223)	O	T	T	O		P,H
Acute bacterial endocarditis or visceral sepsis (223)		T	T	O	O	
Microscopic polyarteritis nodosa (224, 227)		T	T			
Wegener's granulomatosis (224, 227)		T	T			
Allergic granulomatosis (269)		T	T			
Acute radiation nephritis (226)		T	T			P
Poststreptococcal glomerulonephritis (223)		R	T	O	R	P,H
Nonstreptococcal postinfectious GN (223)		R	T	R	R	P,H
Macroscopic polyarteritis nodosa (269, 224, 227)				T		P,H
Diffuse proliferative lupus nephritis (224)	R	O	R	T	O	P,H,L
Chronic radiation nephritis (226)				T	O	
Balkan nephropathy (226)				T		P*,H
Analgesic nephropathy (226)				T		L,H
Heavy metals (lead, cadmium, mercury) (226)				T		P*
Cystinosis (226)				T		P*
Chronic obstructive uropathy (230)				T		H
Adult polycystic renal disease (228)				T		H,P
Medullary cystic renal disease (228)				T		
Gouty nephropathy (226)				T		
Minimal change disease (223)					T	
Idiopathic membranous nephropathy (223)				O	T	P,H
Membranoproliferative glomerulonephritis (223)		R	O	O	T	P,H
Renal amyloidosis (224)				O	T	P
Membranous lupus nephropathy (224)				O	T	P
Chronic renal vein thrombosis	O			O	T	
Rheumatoid arthritis (224)				O	T	
Congenital nephrotic syndrome (224)					T	
Dermatomyositis (223)				O	T	P
Dermatitis herpetiformis (223)						T:H
Medullary sponge kidney (228)						T:H
Nephrolithiasis (229)						T:H
Neoplasms (226)						T:P
Arteriolar nephrosclerosis (227)				O		T:P
Waldenström's macroglobulinemia (224)	O					T:P
Multiple myeloma (224)	O	O		O	O	T:P
Reflux nephropathy (225, 227)				O	O	T:P
Diabetic nephropathy (224)				O	O	T:P
Toxemia of pregnancy (227)						T:P
Orthostatic proteinuria (223)						T:P
Sarcoid nephropathy (224)						T:P
Hypokalemic nephropathy (226)						T:P
Berger's (IgA) nephropathy (223)	R	R	O	O	O	T:H,P
Henoch-Schönlein purpura (224)			O	R	O	T:H,P
Fabry's disease (224)				O		T:H,P
Alport's syndrome (224)				O		T:H,P
Sickle cell nephropathy (224)				O	R	T:H,P
Subacute bacterial endocarditis (188)						T:H,P
Minimal and mesangial lupus nephritis (224)						T:P,H
Mesangial proliferative GN (223)				R	O	T:P,H
Mixed connective tissue disease (224)					R	T:P,H
Chronic glomerulonephritis (224)				O		T:P,H
Nail patella syndrome (224)				R		T:P,H
Focal glomerulosclerosis (223)		R	O	O	O	T:P,H,L
Focal and segmental lupus nephritis (224)				O	O	T:P,H,L
Sjögren's syndrome (224)						T:L,P
Urinary and renal infection (225)						T:L,H

NOTE: *T, typical presentation; O, occurs frequently, but not invariably; R, occurs rarely; P*, tubular proteinuria; P, proteinuria; H, hematuria; L, leukocyturia; ARF, acute renal failure; RPRF, rapidly progressive renal failure; AN, acute nephritis; CRF, chronic renal failure; NS, nephrotic syndrome; AUA, asymptomatic urinary abnormality.*

of acute nephritis associated with massive proteinuria such as essential mixed cryoimmunoglobulinemia, acute bacterial endocarditis, visceral sepsis, and Henoch-Schönlein purpura (Table 217-2).

ASYMPTOMATIC URINARY ABNORMALITIES (AUA) As indicated in Table 217-2, mild degrees of microscopic hematuria, pyuria, casts, or less than 3.5 g protein per 1.73 m^2 per 24 h may be present in the urine of a patient lacking concurrent evidence of other nephrologic syndromes. By exclusion, these patients are best considered to belong to the syndrome of asymptomatic urinary abnormalities. Isolated hematuria or proteinuria, or unexplained pyuria, are the most frequent abnormalities that occur in this syndrome.

Isolated hematuria, without proteinuria or casts, may be the sole clue to the presence of neoplasm, stone, or infection (e.g., tuberculosis) in any part of the urinary tract (Chaps. 40, 225, 229, and 231). Isolated hematuria may also arise from renal papillae in analgesic and sickle cell nephropathies (Chaps. 226 and 227). Persistent isolated hematuria often requires intravenous pyelography, cystoscopy, and, occasionally, renal arteriography to identify the source of bleeding. *Nephronal hematuria,* in which red blood cells or hemoglobin pigment is present in casts, indicates damage to the nephron (Chap. 40). It occurs without proteinuria, mainly in benign recurrent hematuria and Berger's disease (Chap. 223). *Nephronal hematuria and proteinuria* occur together in many specific renal diseases that may eventually lead to chronic renal failure (Chap. 220). In general, the combination of nephronal hematuria and proteinuria suggests a worse prognosis than either one alone.

Isolated proteinuria, without red blood cells or other formed elements in the urinary sediment, is characteristic of many renal diseases which manifest little or no inflammatory reaction within the glomeruli (e.g., diabetes mellitus, amyloidosis). Less than nephrotic-range proteinuria is common in mild forms of all the diseases that can cause overt nephrotic syndrome (Chaps. 223 and 224). "Tubular" proteinuria (Chap. 40) is the rule in cystinosis; in heavy metal intoxication from cadmium, lead, or mercury, and in the peculiar Balkan nephropathy localized to only a small region along the Danube River (Chap. 226).

Pyuria (leukocyturia) may also be a sole urinary abnormality and frequently reflects infection or inflammation of the lower urinary tract, rather than intrinsic parenchymal renal disease. Nevertheless, prominent pyuria can occur in any inflammatory disease of the kidneys, especially tubulointerstitial nephritis, lupus nephritis, pyelonephritis, and renal transplant rejection, but usually in association with mild proteinuria or hematuria. The finding of leukocyte casts (Chap. 40) establishes the kidney as the site of the inflammatory reaction.

Pyuria associated with urine that is sterile on routine bacteriologic culture presents a special problem. Certain causes of "sterile pyuria" that are clinically obvious include (1) recent bacterial urinary infection being treated with antibiotics, (2) adrenocortical steroid therapy, (3) acute febrile episodes, (4) cyclophosphamide administration, (5) pregnancy, (6) renal transplant rejection, (7) recent genitourinary trauma, and (8) prostatitis and cystourethritis. Leukocytes from vaginal secretions may contaminate the urine, so a midstream, clean-catch urine sample should be collected to substantiate a urinary origin. Pyuria associated with proteinuria, nephronal hematuria (Chap. 40), or casts probably signifies inflammatory disease of the renal glomeruli, tubules, interstitium, or microcirculation, and evaluation should focus not upon the pyuria but upon identifying the nature of the renal disease.

Persistent sterile pyuria that cannot be ascribed to any of the foregoing causes has a narrow differential diagnosis. Unusual infections, such as tuberculosis, fungi, atypical mycobacteria, *Haemophilus influenzae,* anaerobic bacteria, fastidious bacteria that grow only on enriched media, and L forms, all must be sought. Intravenous pyelography is needed to detect causes such as urinary tract calculi, papillary necrosis, and renal infiltration by lymphoma or myeloma cells. The latter is usually suspected because of other evidence of myeloma or lymphoma, for both rarely involve only the kidneys. If all tests are negative, cystoscopy may reveal cystitis or trigone inflammation.

URINARY TRACT INFECTION (UTI) This syndrome is defined by the demonstration in urine of pathogenic organisms, either bacteria, tubercle bacilli, or fungi (Chap. 225). When urine specimens are obtained for culture, the condition under which the urine is collected must minimize contamination from external genitourinary surfaces. Women should void into a wide-mouthed sterile container after preliminary cleansing of the vulva with a moist, sterile gauze pledget. In men, midstream collection is usually adequate. Bacterial colony counts of 10^5 organisms per milliliter or greater in urine generally indicate urinary tract colonization and infection. Levels above 10^2 colonies per milliliter are sufficient to indicate infection in symptomatic patients (Table 217-1) and in urine samples obtained by suprapubic aspiration or bladder catheter (Chap. 226). When the urinary tract is anatomically normal, *Escherichia coli* is the usual bacterial pathogen. After prolonged antibiotic treatment of persistent infections, particularly when urinary drainage is impaired or stones are present, *Klebsiella, Enterobacter,* and *Proteus* species predominate.

As discussed in Chap. 225, the presence of a positive urine culture need not imply that an organism is producing tissue inflammation or injury. In some patients, tissue effects may be trivial; in others, injury may be occurring even though symptoms or urinary abnormalities are not present at the time of evaluation. When bacteriuria is associated with tissue inflammation or injury, clinical manifestations usually depend upon the site(s) involved. Dysuria, frequency, urgency, and suprapubic tenderness are common symptoms of bladder and urethral inflammation (Chap. 40 and Table 217-1). Prostatitis also leads to frequency, dysuria, and urgency, and the prostate may be boggy and tender on rectal examination. Flank pain, chills, fever, nausea and vomiting, hypotension from sepsis, and leukocyte casts all suggest true renal parenchymal infection, i.e., pyelonephritis (Chap. 225); their absence, however, does not exclude pyelonephritis.

RENAL TUBULE DEFECTS (RTD) This syndrome encompasses a large number of acquired and hereditary disorders, all of which tend to affect tubules more than glomeruli. Hereditary anatomic defects, including such entities as polycystic renal disease, medullary cystic disease, and medullary sponge kidney, are readily detected by intravenous pyelography, which is usually performed because of hematuria, bacteriuria, flank pain, or unexplained azotemia (Chap. 228).

Defects in tubule transport functions, on the other hand, tend not to be associated with prominent renal anatomic defects and arise either as inherited traits (Chap. 228) or during the course of acquired renal disease (Chap. 226). In general, these functional defects impair secretion and/or reabsorption of electrolytes and organic solutes, or limit urinary concentrating and diluting ability (Table 217-1). Typical manifestations of such functional disturbances include polyuria and nocturia (Chap. 40), metabolic acidosis (Chap. 42), and various disorders of fluid and electrolyte balance (Chap. 41). Such defects are defined by direct physiologic measurements; their elucidation requires a sound understanding of normal renal physiology.

HYPERTENSION (H) The syndrome of hypertension is considered to exist when the average of a series of reliable blood pressure measurements exceeds 140 mmHg systolic or 90 mmHg diastolic (Table 217-1). The pathogenetic mechanisms, clinical and laboratory manifestations, and therapeutic approaches are discussed in detail elsewhere (Chaps. 29 and 196). In addition, a number of renal complications of hypertension are reviewed in Chap. 227, as is the entity of renal artery stenosis, an infrequent but potentially curable cause of hypertension.

NEPHROLITHIASIS (N) This syndrome is established with certainty when a stone is passed, visualized by x-ray, or removed at surgery or cystoscopy (Table 217-1 and Chap. 229). Less certain, but highly suggestive, evidence of nephrolithiasis exists in the patient with renal colic, painful hematuria, or unexplained pyuria, dysuria, and urinary frequency (Chap. 40). Colic varies in its symptomatology but usually begins suddenly in one flank, radiates downward toward the groin, and is excruciatingly painful.

Most renal stones are composed of calcium, uric acid, cystine, or struvite (magnesium ammonium phosphate). All are radiopaque except for those composed solely of uric acid and are, therefore, visible by routine abdominal radiography. Uric acid stones appear as radiolucent filling defects and can be mistaken for tumor or blood clot. The causes of stones are diverse; the approach to their detection, treatment, and prevention is discussed in Chap. 229.

URINARY TRACT OBSTRUCTION (UTO) Documentation of the various structural or functional causes of urinary tract obstruction usually requires radiologic or surgical visualization. The manifestations of obstruction, which initiate the search for its causes, are numerous (Table 217-1) and are reviewed in Chap. 230. Anuria in an adult is almost always due to obstruction of bladder outflow. Less commonly, blockage of upper urinary drainage from both kidneys, or from a solitary functioning kidney, accounts for total or near-total cessation of urine flow. A large bladder after voiding is a sign of outflow obstruction, usually due to urethral stricture, tumor, stone, neurogenic causes, or prostatic hypertrophy. Nocturia, frequency and overflow incontinence, and slowing or hesitancy of micturition are also suggestive of outflow obstruction (Chap. 40). Upper tract obstruction often produces few clinical manifestations. When it is incomplete or unilateral, urine volume may be normal, or even elevated because of a loss of renal concentrating ability (Chap. 40). Urinary stasis secondary to obstruction commonly predisposes to recurrent urinary tract infection, chronic obstruction to progressive loss of renal function (Table 217-2).

REFERENCES

BLACK DAK: Diagnosis and renal disease, in *Renal Disease*, 4th ed, DAK Black (ed). St. Louis, Blackwell, 1980

CAMERON JS: The natural history of glomerulonephritis, in *Renal Disease*, 4th ed, DAK Black (ed). St. Louis, Blackwell, 1980, p. 329

COE FL: The clinical and laboratory assessment of the patient with renal disease, in *The Kidney*, 3d ed, BM Brenner, FC Rector Jr (eds). Philadelphia, Saunders, 1986, p 703

218 DISTURBANCES OF RENAL FUNCTION

BARRY M. BRENNER / THOMAS H. HOSTETTER / STEVEN C. HEBERT

Near constancy of the composition of the internal environment, including the volume, tonicity, and compartmental distribution of the body fluids, is a state essential to human survival. With day-to-day variations in amount as well as composition of food and fluids, preservation of the internal environment requires the continuous excretion of these substances (and/or their by-products) in amounts that balance precisely the quantities acquired by ingestion and metabolic transformation. Although losses from skin, lungs, and intestine normally contribute to this excretory capacity, by far the greatest responsibility for solute and water excretion is borne by the kidneys.

The kidneys operate primarily to maintain the composition and volume of the *extracellular* fluid compartment. The continuous exchange of water and solutes that takes place across all cell membranes during life, however, permits the kidneys to contribute significantly to the regulation of the volume, composition, and tonicity of the *intracellular* fluids as well. To accomplish these tasks, the human kidney has evolved a number of physiologic mechanisms that enable the individual to excrete any excesses of water and nonmetabolized solute contained in the diet, as well as the nonvolatile end products of nitrogen metabolism, such as urea and creatinine. By contrast, when faced with deficits of water and/or any of the other major constituents of the body fluids, renal excretion of these substances can be curtailed, reducing the likelihood of severe volume or solute depletion. The purpose of this chapter is to review the major excretory functions of the normal kidney and to examine the way these functions are affected by disorders that impair the operations of this organ in humans.

MECHANISMS OF RENAL EXCRETORY FUNCTION WITH NORMAL AND REDUCED NEPHRON MASS

The volume of urine excreted per day (about 1.5 liters, or roughly 1 mL/min) is the small residuum of two very large, and in many ways opposing, processes—namely, *ultrafiltration* of 180 liters or more fluid per day (approximately 125 mL/min) across glomerular capillaries on the one hand and, on the other, *reclamation* (or *reabsorption*) of more than 99 percent of this ultrafiltrate by transport processes operating in the renal tubules. The enormity of the initial step in this process in humans is underscored by the fact that, under resting conditions, about 20 percent of the cardiac output passes through the kidneys, which together comprise less than 1 percent of body weight. Hence, per unit weight of tissue, the rate of blood flow to the kidneys is much greater than that to other solid organs generally considered to be well perfused, including the heart, brain, and liver.

GLOMERULAR ULTRAFILTRATION Urine formation begins with the elaboration of a protein-free ultrafiltrate of plasma across the walls of the glomerular capillaries. The rate of ultrafiltration (glomerular filtration rate, GFR) is determined by three factors: (1) the balance of pressures acting across the capillary wall (the glomerular capillary hydrostatic and Bowman's space oncotic pressures tend to favor filtration, while glomerular capillary oncotic and Bowman's space hydrostatic pressures tend to retard it), (2) the rate at which plasma flows through the glomeruli, and (3) the permeability and the total surface area of the filtering capillaries. A decrease in GFR can be expected when (1) glomerular hydrostatic pressure is reduced (as in hypotensive shock), (2) tubule (hence, Bowman's space) hydrostatic pressure is increased (ureteral or bladder neck obstruction), (3) plasma oncotic pressure rises to unusually high levels (hemoconcentration due to dehydration; multiple myeloma or other dysproteinemias), (4) renal (hence, glomerular) blood and plasma flow are decreased (circulatory collapse, profound heart failure), and (5) permeability and/or total filtering surface area is reduced (acute or chronic glomerulonephritis).

Despite the extraordinarily high rate of water movement across the glomerular capillary wall, all but the smallest of the circulating plasma proteins are normally excluded from passage through this barrier. Molecules the size of inulin (approximately 5200 mol wt), or smaller, normally appear in glomerular urine in the same concentrations as in plasma water, whereas the transport of substances of increasingly greater size diminishes progressively, normally approaching very low values as the size of serum albumin is approached. The *glomerular capillary basement membrane* and the *slitlike diaphragms* that connect adjacent epithelial cell foot processes on the urinary aspect of the glomerular capillary wall (Fig. 40-1, page 193) are believed to serve as major barriers to protein filtration. In addition to these mechanical gates, *electrostatic factors* also serve to retard the filtration of plasma proteins, especially albumin. The albumin molecule behaves as a polyanion in physiologic solution, and is therefore retarded by the highly anionic glycoproteins contained in the various component layers of the glomerular wall. With disruption of these mechanical and electrostatic barriers, as seen in many forms of glomerular injury (see Chaps. 222 to 224); abnormally large quantities of plasma proteins gain access to the urine.

BIOLOGIC CONSEQUENCES OF SUSTAINED REDUCTIONS IN GFR

Measurement of total GFR of both kidneys provides a sensitive and commonly employed index of overall renal excretory function. When renal excretory function is impaired, either acutely or chronically, one or more of the determinants of GFR in affected nephrons is altered unfavorably so that total GFR declines. The magnitude of the decline is determined by the sum of the impairments of function of individual glomeruli. Initially, the effect of such impairments in single-nephron GFR (SNGFR), no matter how small, is to reduce the total rate of excretion of water and those solutes normally contained in the glomerular ultrafiltrate. In the steady state, these reduced rates of filtration, when accompanied by comparably reduced rates of excretion, lead to *retention* and *accumulation* of the unexcreted substances in the body fluids. Further reduction in GFR augments the degree to which these substances are retained.

Figure 218-1 depicts the major patterns of response to these impairments in filtration. The degree of reduction in total GFR is plotted on the abscissa, expressed as a percentage of normal (100 percent). For the various solutes normally contained in glomerular filtrate, three general types of response are common, depicted by curves A, B, and C. Curve A describes the pattern seen with substances, such as creatinine and urea, which normally depend largely on glomerular filtration for their excretion into the urine; i.e., secretion fails to influence urinary excretion appreciably. Therefore, as GFR falls, plasma levels of creatinine, urea, and other substances normally excreted largely by filtration rise progressively, albeit in the nonlinear manner illustrated.

The clinical course of chronic renal failure (CRF) usually also conforms to the pattern described by *curve A*. Patients with CRF usually pass from a long asymptomatic period of "compensation" to a more accelerated and clinically symptomatic terminal phase. In other words, chronic forms of renal injury which lead to slow but inexorable destruction of nephron mass usually lead to progressive but modest elevations in creatinine and urea levels in plasma, but not to levels beyond the range of normal, despite loss of as much as 50 percent of total GFR. With further loss of nephron mass, and further reduction in GFR, however (even though the rate of nephron destruction may not be accelerated), the limits of renal reserve are exceeded, and continued accumulation of *curve A–type solutes* leads

to plasma concentrations clearly beyond the range of normal (Fig. 218-1). Because these retained solutes are believed to exert "toxic" effects on virtually all organ systems, manifestations of CRF now become overt. As a result, for patients with reduced renal mass, even small additional decrements in total GFR may spell the difference between "compensation" and overt uremia.

The accumulation of *curve A–type solutes* with progressive renal failure continues until external balance for these solutes is achieved, that is, until acquisition and/or production rates and excretion rates are exactly matched. In the case of creatinine, for example, assuming a constant rate of creatinine production, a 50 percent reduction in GFR results in an approximate doubling of the plasma creatinine concentration. The latter restores the filtered load of creatinine (that is, GFR × plasma creatinine concentration) to the preillness level, and urinary excretion rate again becomes equivalent to the rate of creatinine production. Unfortunately, since no mechanism exists in human beings for augmenting creatinine excretion beyond this level, elimination of retained creatinine is not possible, and plasma concentration remains twice normal. With progressive reduction in GFR, plasma creatinine levels continue to rise, due both to the most recent loss of nephron excretory function and to the retention associated with earlier nephron destruction (Fig. 218-1). *In practice, so long as the net rates of acquisition and production remain reasonably constant, the inverse relationship between plasma concentrations of solutes such as creatinine and urea and GFR is sufficiently reliable and predictable to allow plasma levels of such solutes to serve as useful clinical indexes of GFR.*

In contrast to solutes of the *curve A type*, plasma levels of substances such as phosphate, urate, and potassium (K^+) and hydrogen (H^+) ions usually fail to rise above the normal range until GFR falls to a small percentage of normal. With progressive renal failure this pattern of response, depicted by *curve B* in Fig. 218-1, reflects the participation of tubule transport mechanisms that contribute to the excretion of these substances. In other words, *as GFR declines, the tubules facilitate the excretion of progressively greater fractions of the filtered load of these solutes, either by enhancing their net secretion and/or by diminishing their net reabsorption.* Plasma levels of *curve B–type solutes*, therefore, rise much less than do those of *curve A* because, with progressive reduction in GFR, *excretion rate per nephron* and, therefore, *fractional excretion* both increase. Eventually, however, enhanced fractional excretion can no longer offset the reduction in the filtered load of these solutes caused by a markedly diminished GFR, and plasma levels rise above the normal range (Fig. 218-1). For urate, phosphate, and K^+ at least, increased fractional excretion usually serves to maintain normal plasma levels until GFR falls to less than one-fourth of normal.

Finally, for certain solutes, such as sodium chloride (NaCl), concentrations in plasma remain virtually constant, and at normal levels, throughout the entire course of CRF, despite continued ingestion of these substances in normal amounts. Such solutes conform to the pattern described by *curve C* in Fig. 218-1. The extent of compensation is nearly complete and represents a fundamental adaptation to renal injury. To illustrate the magnitude of the adaptation involved, it is useful to compare the excretion of Na^+ in an individual with normal renal excretory function (GFR of 125 mL/min) with that in an individual with advanced renal insufficiency (GFR of 2 mL/min). Both subjects are allowed to ingest a diet containing 7 g salt per day (120 meq Na^+). With a normal serum Na^+ concentration of 140 meq per liter, external Na^+ balance is achieved in the normal individual by excreting approximately 0.5 percent of the filtered load of Na^+. By contrast, for external balance to be maintained in the patient with CRF, fractional excretion of Na^+ must rise to 30 percent. *In other words, external balance for Na^+ demands that the same quantity of Na^+ (120 meq) be excreted into the urine each day in the subject with CRF as in the normal subject.* Given the drastic reduction in GFR faced by the patient with CRF, external balance can be achieved only by a progressive transformation of the Na^+ reabsorptive processes in surviving tubules, so that a progressively

FIGURE 218-1 *Representative patterns of adaptation for different types of solutes in body fluids in chronic renal failure. (After NS Bricker et al, in Brenner and Rector, 2d ed.)*

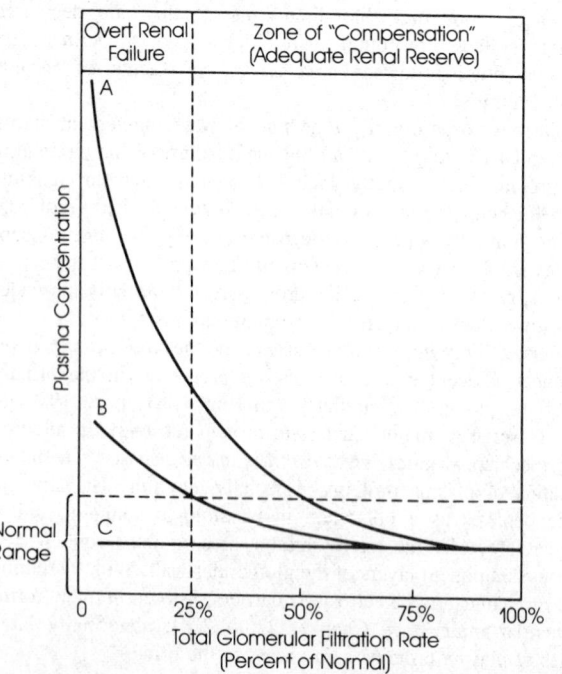

larger fraction of the filtered load of Na^+ escapes reabsorption and appears in final urine. In short, *the rate of excretion of Na^+ per surviving nephron increases in inverse proportion to the composite GFR of surviving nephrons.*

MECHANISMS OF TUBULE TRANSPORT WITH NORMAL AND REDUCED NEPHRON MASS

Loss of renal function with nearly all forms of progressive renal disease is usually attended by a progressive distortion of renal morphology and architecture. Despite this structural disarray, glomerular and tubule functions often remain as closely integrated (i.e., *glomerulotubular balance*) in the diseased kidney as they do in the normal organ, at least until the final stages of CRF. A fundamental feature of this *intact nephron hypothesis* is that following loss of nephron mass, residual renal function derives primarily from the operation of surviving healthy nephrons, while the diseased nephrons are believed to cease functioning. Despite progressive nephron destruction, there is considerable evidence to suggest that many of the mechanisms that contribute to the maintenance of solute and water balance differ only quantitatively, and not qualitatively, from those believed to govern fluid and solute homeostasis under normal physiologic conditions. The most important of these are considered below.

Tubule transport of sodium chloride and water in health Most of the filtered water and Na^+ salts are reabsorbed by the tubules, leaving small and variable amounts, equivalent on a day-to-day basis to the quantities ingested, to reach the final urine. About two-thirds of the glomerular ultrafiltrate is reabsorbed in the *proximal tubule* with little change in the osmolality or Na^+ concentration of the unreabsorbed fraction (Fig. 218-2). In other words, fluid reabsorption in the proximal tubule is nearly *isosmotic* and is coupled to the active transport of Na^+. Since Cl^- and HCO_3^- are the primary anions in the extracellular fluid, most of the filtered Na^+ is reabsorbed with these anions. In the early convoluted portion of the proximal tubule, bicarbonate is the principal anion accompanying the reabsorption of sodium. This process occurs via a Na^+/H^+ exchange mechanism at the luminal brush border and is dependent upon both cystolic and brush border carbonic anhydrase. Glucose, amino acids, and other organic solutes (e.g., lactate) are also extensively reabsorbed in the proximal convoluted tubule by a cotransport process that links the cellular entry of these organic substrates with Na^+. Three processes appear to operate in parallel to couple water (i.e., volume) absorption with solute absorption in the proximal tubule. First, given the remarkably high water permeability of this nephron segment, very small transepithelial osmolality differences, that is, *luminal hypotonicity* on the order of 2 to 3 mosmol, produced by solute absorption, could drive volume absorption. Second, due to the *preferential absorption of HCO_3^- and organic solutes in the early portions of the proximal tubule, the concentrations of these substances decrease while that of Cl^- increases along the length of the proximal tubule. Volume absorption would occur if the rate of Na^+ and Cl^- diffusion down their respective electrochemical gradients were more rapid than the back diffusion of sodium bicarbonate into the lumen. Finally, an *effective osmotic gradient* would be established (despite equal macroscopic osmolalities of luminal and peritubular fluids) if the effective osmolality produced by Cl^- in the lumen were greater than that for bicarbonate in the peritubular fluid.

The rate of reabsorption of fluid from proximal convoluted tubules and peritubular interstitium is sensitive to the effects of *physical factors*, i.e., the hydrostatic and colloid osmotic (or oncotic) pressures acting across the walls of the peritubular capillaries. Because the plasma proteins in glomerular capillaries are concentrated by ultrafiltration, there is a marked rise in the oncotic pressure as plasma flows along the glomerular capillary network. This step-up in plasma oncotic pressure is transmitted largely unchanged to the peritubular capillaries, via the efferent arterioles. These resistance vessels cause a substantial drop in hydrostatic pressure, however, so that when the plasma reaches the peritubular capillaries, oncotic pressure greatly

exceeds hydrostatic pressure. These *Starling forces* are therefore oriented in an *uptake mode*, in contrast to the *filtration mode* at the glomerulus, where hydrostatic pressure exceeds oncotic. The extent to which oncotic pressure exceeds hydrostatic pressure in the peritubular capillary network is thought to modulate the overall rate of reabsorption of fluid by the proximal tubules. Therefore, when peritubular oncotic pressure falls, or hydrostatic pressure rises, uptake of fluid by these capillaries is reduced. As a result, fluid is retained in the interstitial space, altering the hydrostatic pressure in the space, and ultimately retarding the egress of fluid from the lateral intercellular channels. Without an adequate route of drainage, fluid in the channels leaks back into the tubule lumen and diminishes *net fluid reabsorption* by this tubule segment. The opposite occurs in states in which peritubular oncotic pressure increases (increased filtration fraction), or hydrostatic pressure decreases (enhanced efferent arteriolar tone). Under these circumstances, peritubular capillary uptake of reabsorbate is augmented, leading ultimately to *enhanced net fluid reabsorption* by the proximal tubule.

In contrast to the proximal tubule, active outward transport of NaCl from tubule lumen to peritubular blood has not been established for the *thin limbs of Henle's loop*. However, passive outward salt transport does occur, as indicated in Fig. 218-2. In the next segment of the nephron, the *medullary thick ascending limb of Henle*, the concentration of NaCl is reduced below the level that prevails at the beginning of this segment. Here Cl^- absorption occurs by an active process involving a furosemide-sensitive $Na^+:K^+:2Cl^-$ cotransport mechanism in the luminal membrane, with one-half of Na^+ absorption proceeding passively, driven by the lumen-positive transepithelial voltage. Since the ascending limb of Henle is always impermeable to water, net NaCl reabsorption not only generates hypotonic tubule fluid, but also gives rise to the high NaCl concentration in the outer medullary interstitium (Fig. 218-2). In certain animals the antidiuretic hormone (ADH) enhances NaCl absorption but not water permeability in the medullary portion of the thick ascending limb, but an effect of this hormone on this segment in human beings is uncertain.

The fluid leaving the thick ascending limb of Henle is normally low in NaCl concentration, a condition largely independent of the organism's diet or state of hydration. In the *distal convoluted tubule,* water reabsorption is variable, depending on the state of hydration or, more specifically, on the presence or absence of the ADH in plasma. In the absence of ADH, this and more distal nephron segments are impermeable to water, so that the hypotonic fluid entering this segment is excreted as *dilute urine*. Indeed, continued salt reabsorption along the distal convoluted tubule results in further dilution of the urine. In the presence of ADH, the permeability of the late portion of this segment to water increases, and as a result, the osmolality of the late distal tubule fluid rises to a value close to that of plasma. NaCl continues to be reabsorbed from the tubule lumen, against moderately steep chemical and electrical gradients. The reabsorptive process for NaCl at this site is enhanced by *aldosterone*.

The *cortical collecting tubule* possesses an extremely low permeability to water in the absence of ADH, whereas this permeability increases greatly in the presence of the hormone. The sensitivity of this segment to ADH appears to be more pronounced than that of the distal convoluted tubule. As with the distal convoluted tubule, the cortical collecting tubule is capable of further active reabsorption of NaCl.

The terminal segment of the distal nephron is the highly branched *papillary collecting duct.* Continued electrolyte transport in this segment results in the large ion concentration differences that normally exist between urine and plasma. As in the cortical collecting tubule, Na^+ transport appears to be active since reabsorption proceeds against sizable electrochemical gradients. The rate of Na^+ transport in this segment depends on the diet and on the load of Na^+ delivered from more proximal segments, and is affected by aldosterone. The permeability of this segment to water also increases markedly in the presence of ADH.

Effects of reduced nephron mass on sodium chloride transport in surviving nephrons With progressive destruction of nephrons, *maintenance of external balance for NaCl requires that fractional salt excretion increase as GFR decreases.* Very likely several mechanisms contribute to this adaptive increase in fractional salt excretion. With losses of functioning nephron units, peritubular capillary hydrostatic and oncotic pressures are probably altered in directions that serve to suppress proximal tubule reabsorption of NaCl and water. For example, a rise in peritubular capillary hydrostatic pressure, which tends to inhibit net proximal fluid reabsorption, might

be anticipated with arterial hypertension, a common feature of renal insufficiency. Similarly, peritubular oncotic pressure might be expected to decline with renal injury, owing both to reductions in filtration fraction and to hypoalbuminemia. While such alterations in peritubular factors clearly account for diminution in proximal fluid reabsorption in response to falling levels of GFR in animals, such alterations have not been established with certainty in humans. Aldosterone, normally an important determinant of Na^+ reabsorption in distal portions of the nephron, is probably not a major factor responsible for reducing fractional Na^+ reabsorption, since aldosterone

FIGURE 218-2 *Transport functions of the various anatomic segments of the mammalian nephron. Fluid reabsorption across the proximal tubule is isosmotic and accounts for reabsorption of approximately two-thirds of the filtered Na^+ and H_2O. The major portions of the filtered HCO_3^-, amino acids, and glucose are reabsorbed in the early proximal convoluted tubule. Reabsorption of glucose and amino acids is coupled to Na^+ transport and thereby generates a negative potential difference within the tubule lumen. At the same time, HCO_3^- is reabsorbed by a nonelectrogenic mechanism, via H^+ secretion. The active transport of these solutes results in transepithelial concentration and effective osmotic pressure gradients promoting H_2O flow across the proximal tubule, into the peritubular capillaries. The rise in tubule fluid Cl^- concentration is a necessary reciprocal consequence of the decreased luminal HCO_3^- concentration. The resultant high concentration of Cl^- becomes an important force for the outward passive transport of Cl^- down its concentration gradient, resulting in a lumen positive potential difference in the late proximal convoluted tubule. The pars recta of the proximal tubule is capable of active electrogenic transport of Na^+ independent of organic solute transport. Under normal conditions, approximately one-third of the glomerular filtrate enters the descending limb of Henle's loop. Because the thin descending limb is incapable of active outward NaCl transport and is characterized by low permeability to Na^+ but high H_2O permeability, H_2O is abstracted passively as the fluid approaches the bend of Henle's loop.*

Hypertonic fluid with a greater NaCl concentration but lower urea concentration than the surrounding medullary interstitium thus enters the thin ascending limb of Henle. This segment differs from the descending limb in that it is largely impermeable to H_2O and urea but highly permeable to NaCl. These characteristics allow for passive diffusion of NaCl out of the ascending limb. Active electrogenic NaCl transport across the water-impermeable thick ascending limb of Henle allows for separation of solute and water. In consequence tubule fluid becomes dilute, and the medullary interstitium hypertonic. Irrespective of the final osmolality of the urine, the fluid that enters the distal convoluted tubule is always hypoosmotic. This segment exhibits active Na^+ reabsorption. All but the terminal portion of the distal convoluted tubule is water impermeable, even in the presence of ADH. Aldosterone exerts its effect in this segment by enhancing Na^+ reabsorption, which is variably coupled to K^+ and H^+ secretion. The cortical and papillary portions of the collecting duct are sites where ADH exerts its principal effect. The permeability of these segments to H_2O in the absence of ADH is very low but can be greatly enhanced in the presence of ADH. These segments are also characterized by active Na^+ reabsorption, which appears to depend on the presence of mineralocorticoid. In the absence of ADH, the collecting tubule is water impermeable so that hypotonic tubule fluid courses through it. However, in the presence of ADH, water is avidly reabsorbed here, resulting in hypertonic final urine.

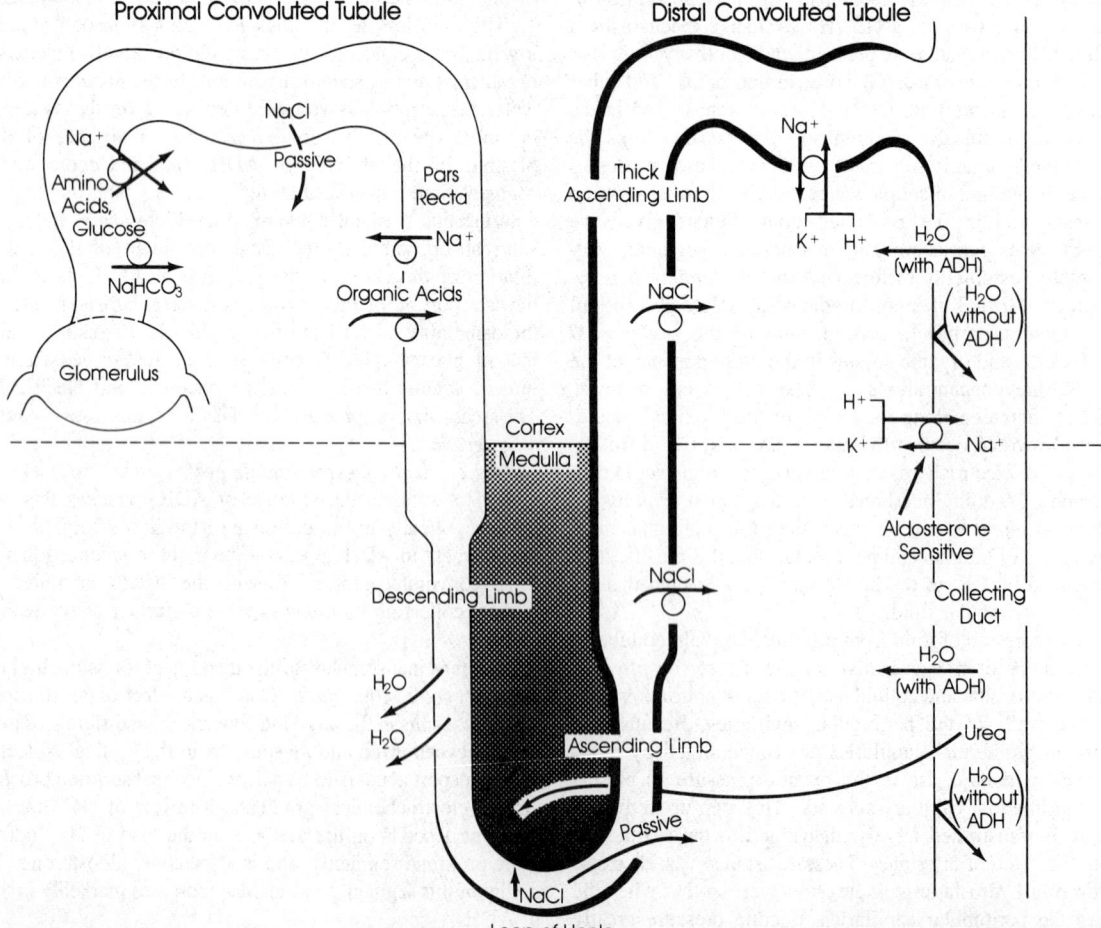

levels in plasma are rarely reduced in CRF. Furthermore, external Na^+ balance has been shown to be preserved in bilaterally adrenal-ectomized uremic dogs maintained on fixed doses of mineralocorticoid hormones. Yet another factor that has received attention in contributing to the suppression of fractional NaCl reabsorption in CRF relates to the retention of solutes as GFR declines. In addition to urea and creatinine, a host of *organic acids* (including *hippurates*) also accumulate. These substances are normally excreted by both filtration and tubule secretion; the latter process involves a carrier-mediated organic acid transport system in proximal tubule epithelia. When GFR is reduced and plasma levels of these organic acids increase, sufficient fluid may accompany the secretion of these organic anions into the proximal tubule lumen (by osmosis) to diminish net fluid reabsorption, and even favor net fluid secretion. Evidence in support of this intriguing mechanism derives from studies in which uremic serums were capable of inducing net fluid secretion in isolated proximal tubules of rabbits studied in vitro.

It has also been suggested that NaCl transport across the mammalian renal tubule may be governed, at least in part, by a *natriuretic hormone.* In support of this possibility, serums and urine from patients and dogs with uremia have been reported to contain factors capable of inhibiting NaCl transport across frog skin, toad bladder, and rat renal tubule. However, accumulation of natriuretic factors in uremia may not be without cost; the "trade-off" for maintenance of external Na^+ balance is the possibility of abnormalities occurring in Na^+ transport across cell membranes, which often occurs in advanced renal insufficiency. This possibility is discussed in greater detail in Chap. 220.

The obligatorily high rate of solute excretion per surviving nephron (so-called osmotic diuresis due to urea and other retained solutes) may also contribute to enhancing fractional NaCl excretion, much as occurs in normal subjects following administration of nonreabsorbable solutes such as mannitol. Finally, certain forms of CRF tend to be associated with unusually pronounced salt losses in urine. These *salt-wasting nephropathies* include chronic pyelonephritis and other tubulointerstitial diseases (see Chap. 226) as well as polycystic and medullary cystic diseases. These disorders have in common greater destruction of medullary and interstitial, than cortical and glomerular, portions of the renal parenchyma. Preferential impairment of tubule reabsorptive function, rather than a primary reduction in GFR, may, therefore, underlie the salt-losing tendency in these disorders. A number of clinical derangements associated with the altered renal handling of NaCl in CRF (including hypo- and hypervolemia, hypertension, etc.) are considered in Chap. 220.

Effects of reduced nephron mass on water reabsorption in surviving nephrons

As with NaCl, there is a progressive increase in the fractional excretion of water with advancing renal insufficiency, so that even the patient with a total GFR of 5 mL/min or less can usually maintain external water balance. The adaptations in the handling of water by the tubules of the diseased kidney are of importance in the pathogenesis of the urinary concentrating defect and, hence, of the polyuria and nocturia seen commonly in CRF (see Chap. 40). To appreciate the mechanisms involved, the responses of a normal and a uremic subject in maintaining external water balance need to be compared. Assuming that both subjects ingest the same diet and also the same amount of fluid, total solute and volume excretion in each subject should be identical as well. If the *obligatory solute load* to be excreted in each is assumed to be 600 mosmol per day, and urine osmolality is 300 mosmol/kg, a urine volume of 2 liters per day will be required to excrete the total solute load in each subject. If GFR in normal and uremic subjects is 180 and 4 liters per day, respectively, urinary volume excretion of 2 liters per day represents excretion of slightly more than 1 percent of the filtered water in the normal individual, compared with a much larger value, 50 percent, in the uremic subject. Since the range of urine osmolalities that the diseased kidney can achieve (250 to 350 mosmol/kg) is much narrower than in the normal (40 to 1200 mosmol/kg), the individual with normal function is able to excrete the obligatory daily solute load of 600

mosmol in as little as 500 mL urine per day or as much as 15 liters per day, compared with the much narrower range in the patient with renal insufficiency, from about 1.7 to 2.4 liters per day.

In CRF, the limited ability to concentrate the urine usually correlates closely with other measures of impaired renal function. Isosthenuria is, therefore, a nearly universal finding when GFR falls below 25 mL/min. At this level of GFR and below, urine osmolality does not rise even with supramaximal parenteral doses of ADH, suggesting that the concentrating defect is related not only to loss of diseased nephrons but also to impaired concentrating ability in surviving nephrons. As has been discussed, with diminution in functioning nephron mass, there is a concurrent increase in fractional excretion of a number of solutes. As a consequence, solute diuresis per nephron obligates a nearly isosmotic amount of water and prevents the elaboration of either hypotonic or hypertonic urine. Disease-induced abnormalities of the architecture of the renal medulla (loops of Henle, vasa rectae), aberrations in renal medullary blood flow, and defective transport of NaCl in the ascending limb of Henle undoubtedly also contribute to this defect in urine concentration. Finally, there is suggestive evidence that uremia per se may impair the responsiveness of terminal nephron segments to ADH.

Since patients with renal insufficiency are usually unable to excrete concentrated urine, they must have access to adequate amounts of water in order to ensure the excretion of total daily solute loads. For this reason, restriction of fluid intake may prove extremely hazardous in patients with CRF. Likewise, impairment of diluting capacity may prevent many patients from excreting large amounts of ingested fluids. The consequences of the abnormal water excretion patterns in CRF, including the tendencies to development of hypo- and hyper-natremia, are considered in Chaps. 41 and 220.

Tubule transport of phosphate with normal and reduced nephron mass

Under normal physiologic conditions, about 80 to 90 percent of the filtered load of phosphate is reabsorbed, mainly in the proximal tubule. *Parathyroid hormone (PTH)*, by augmenting phosphate excretion via inhibition of this proximal reabsorptive process (Chap. 335), plays a key role in phosphate homeostasis. In normal humans, when dietary phosphate intake increases, a *transient* rise in plasma phosphate concentration is usually observed. This results in a similarly transient reduction in the plasma ionized calcium concentration (due largely to calcium-phosphate deposition in bone), which, in turn, stimulates PTH secretion. By enhancing fractional phosphate excretion, PTH restores external phosphate balance and normophosphatemia. This then enables plasma ionized calcium levels to return to normal, thereby removing the stimulus to PTH release, and restoring all elements of the phosphate control system to the original steady state.

With advancing renal disease, and constant dietary intake of phosphate, external phosphate balance is achieved by progressive reduction in fractional phosphate reabsorption. Enhanced PTH secretion is an important determinant of this phosphaturic response to reduced nephron mass. With each succeeding decrement in GFR, the total amount of phosphate filtered by surviving glomeruli is reduced, leading to transient retention of phosphate and, therefore, a rise (albeit small) in the phosphate concentration in extracellular fluid, including plasma. This rise in plasma phosphate concentration leads to a reciprocal small decline in plasma ionized calcium concentration and a corresponding increase in PTH secretion. Although the phosphaturic response of surviving tubules to this elevation in circulating PTH is thought to restore plasma phosphate and, therefore, calcium levels to normal (at least in the "compensated" stage of CRF described by the relatively flat portion of curve B in Fig. 218-1), the biologic cost of this return to normophosphatemia and normocalcemia is a *persistent elevation in the plasma PTH level.* With successive decrements in GFR, each stage in this overall process is repeated, but at an ever-increasing cost, namely, *progressive elevation in the circulating level of PTH.* At least two additional processes are thought to contribute to elevated PTH levels in renal failure. One relates to the skeletal resistance to the calcemic effect of PTH seen in uremia. This resistance necessitates a greater than normal level of circulating PTH to effect an increment in serum calcium concentration. The other derives from the finding that reductions in renal mass impair the ability of the kidneys to degrade circulating PTH. The fact that phosphate conforms more to a curve B– than curve C–type solute in Fig. 218-1 indicates that these forms of adaptation are limited; ultimately phosphate retention occurs when GFR falls below about 25 mL/min.

Since PTH exerts major biologic effects on bone, as well as renal tubules, the external balance of phosphate in CRF is achieved at the expense of elevated PTH levels, which, in turn, account for many of the bone changes of renal osteodystrophy (i.e., *secondary hyperparathyroidism*, Fig. 220-1). In support of this ingenious *trade-off hypothesis*, studies in animals with CRF suggest that when dietary phosphate intake is reduced in proportion to the reduction in GFR, external balance of phosphate no longer requires augmentation of fractional phosphate excretion in surviving nephrons. Accordingly, circulating PTH levels no longer rise, and the typical bone changes of secondary hyperparathyroidism are diminished, if not prevented.

Destruction of renal mass also impairs phosphate, calcium, and skeletal metabolism by mechanisms largely independent of impaired excretory function. The kidneys are normally the major site of *metabolic conversion of vitamin D to its active metabolites*. Whereas the tendency to secondary hyperparathyroidism begins, at least theoretically, when a single nephron unit is destroyed, impaired vitamin D biotransformation is not usually apparent until GFR falls to below 25 percent of normal. As discussed in Chap. 336, precursors of the active form of vitamin D, synthesized in skin or acquired from foods, undergo initial hydroxylation in the liver to form 25-hydroxy-vitamin D_3 [25(OH)D_3]. The kidney is the site of a second important hydroxylation step, to form 1,25-dihydroxyvitamin D_3 [1,25(OH)$_2D_3$]. This activated form of vitamin D operates to enhance intestinal calcium and phosphate absorption, as well as to promote resorption of these ions from bone. In addition, 1,25(OH)$_2D_3$ probably opposes the phosphaturic action of PTH at the level of the renal tubule by augmenting, rather than diminishing, phosphate reabsorption. With advancing renal disease, reduction in renal mass causes vitamin D hydroxylation to be impaired; phosphate retention has also been shown to suppress this important hydroxylation reaction. Reduction in circulating 1,25(OH)$_2D_3$ levels, by suppressing calcium absorption from gut, contributes further to the development of the hypocalcemia and PTH excess of CRF, the consequences of which are considered in Chap. 220.

Hydrogen and bicarbonate transport with normal and reduced nephron mass

As discussed in Chap. 42, the pH of extracellular fluid in humans is normally maintained within a narrow range, 7.36 to 7.44, despite day-to-day variations in the quantity of acids entering the body fluids from dietary and metabolic sources (approximately 1 meq H^+ per kg per day). These acids consume both intracellular and extracellular buffers, of which bicarbonate (HCO_3^-) is the most important in the intracellular compartment. Such buffering minimizes the changes in pH that would otherwise occur. The HCO_3^- buffer system would be of little long-term benefit were it not for homeostatic mechanisms, however, since with unrelenting acquisition of nonvolatile acids from dietary and metabolic sources, buffering capacity would ultimately be exhausted, eventually culminating in fatal acidosis. The kidneys normally function to prevent this possibility by *regenerating* HCO_3^- and, thereby, maintaining the concentration of HCO_3^- in the plasma. In addition to generating HCO_3^-, the kidneys also *reclaim* essentially all the HCO_3^- present in the glomerular ultrafiltrate. This reabsorptive process takes place largely in the proximal tubule and is virtually complete below a critical serum HCO_3^- concentration—the threshold concentration—which in humans is normally about 26 meq per liter, identical to the concentration of HCO_3^- in plasma. As a consequence, urinary wastage of HCO_3^- is prevented. Alternatively, when plasma HCO_3^- concentration rises above this threshold level, reabsorption of HCO_3^- becomes less complete, and the excess HCO_3^- escapes into the final urine,

returning the plasma HCO_3^- concentration to the threshold level. Despite reabsorption of all the filtered HCO_3^-, metabolic acidosis would still ensue if HCO_3^- consumed in buffering nonvolatile strong acids were not constantly regenerated.

The *reabsorption* of filtered HCO_3^- in the proximal tubule occurs by the following mechanism. In proximal tubule cells, H^+, formed by the splitting of water into H^+ and OH^-, is secreted into the tubule lumen, very likely in exchange for Na^+. The OH^- ion, under the influence of *carbonic anhydrase*, combines with CO_2 to form HCO_3^-, which diffuses across the peritubular cell membrane to enter the extracellular HCO_3^- pool. The H^+ secreted into the tubule lumen combines with a filtered HCO_3^-, forming H_2CO_3. Dehydration of the latter in the proximal tubule lumen leads to the formation of CO_2 which also diffuses from lumen to peritubular blood. As a result, *a filtered HCO_3^- ion is reclaimed*. Secreted H^+ ions are also free to combine with non-HCO_3^- buffers (e.g., phosphate or ammonia) in the tubule fluid and are excreted in these forms in the final urine. HCO_3^-, the other original product of the breakdown of H_2CO_3, formed within the tubule cell, enters the peritubular blood, and *a HCO_3^- ion is regenerated*.

Hydrogen ions in the urine are bound primarily to filtered buffers (e.g., phosphate) in an amount (the so-called titratable acid) equivalent to the amount of alkali required to titrate the pH of the urine to the pH of blood. It is usually not possible, however, to excrete all the daily acid load as titratable acid alone. To serve as an additional buffer, the cells of the renal tubules generate ammonia (NH_3), largely from the hydrolysis of glutamine. NH_3 diffuses from these cells into the tubule lumen, where it combines with H^+ to form NH_4^+. As noted above, each mole of NH_4^+ excreted into the urine is associated with the regeneration of 1 mol of HCO_3^-. *Ammoniagenesis*, a process which occurs within proximal tubule cells, is responsive to the acid-base needs of the individual. When faced with an acute acid burden and an increased need for HCO_3^- regeneration, the rate of renal ammonia synthesis increases sharply.

The quantity of hydrogen ions excreted as titratable acid and NH_4^+ is equal to the quantity of HCO_3^- regenerated in tubule cells and added to the plasma. Under steady-state conditions, the quantity of net acid excreted into the urine (the sum of titratable acid and NH_4^+ minus HCO_3^-) must equal the quantity of acid gained by the extracellular fluid from all sources. Metabolic acidosis and alkalosis result when this delicate balance is perturbed, the former the result of *insufficient* net acid excretion, the latter due to *excessive* acid excretion.

Progressive loss of renal function usually causes little or no change in arterial pH, plasma bicarbonate concentration, or arterial carbon dioxide tension (P_{CO_2}) until GFR falls below 50 percent of normal. Thereafter, all three quantities tend to decline as *metabolic acidosis* ensues. In general, the metabolic acidosis of CRF is not due to overproduction of endogenous acids, but is largely a reflection of the reduction in renal mass, which limits the amount of NH_3 (and therefore HCO_3^-) that can be generated. Although surviving nephrons are probably capable of generating supernormal quantities of NH_3 *per nephron*, the diminished nephron population causes overall NH_3 production to be reduced to an extent inadequate to permit sufficient buffering of H^+ in urine. Though patients with CRF may acidify the urine normally (i.e., urine pH as low as 4.5), the defect in NH_3 production limits total daily acid excretion to 30 to 40 meq, or half to two-thirds the quantity of nonvolatile acid formed in the same time period. Metabolic acidosis is the inevitable consequence of this positive balance for H^+, which in most patients with stable CRF is relatively mild and nonprogressive (arterial pH of approximately 7.33 to 7.37).

Given this substantial daily accumulation of H^+, and the typically stable and nonprogressive nature of the resulting acidosis, including the observed relative constancy of the plasma HCO_3^- concentration (albeit at reduced levels of 14 to 20 meq per liter), it follows that some large tissue source of buffering must account for the stability of the acidosis in CRF. Bone is the most likely candidate, particularly in view of its large reservoir of alkaline salts (calcium phosphate and calcium carbonate). Dissolution of this buffer source probably contributes to the osteodystrophy of CRF (see Fig. 220-1).

Although the acidosis of CRF is a consequence of the reduction in total renal mass and is therefore tubule in origin, it nevertheless depends to a large extent on the level of GFR. When GFR is reduced to only a moderate extent (i.e., to about 50 percent of normal), retention of anions, principally sulfates and phosphates, is not pronounced, so that as the plasma HCO_3^- level falls owing to tubule dysfunction, retention of Cl^- by the kidneys leads to the development of *hyperchloremic acidosis*. At this stage, therefore, *the anion gap is normal*. With further reduction in GFR and more pronounced azotemia, however, retention of phosphates, sulfates, and other *unmeasured* anions is the rule, and plasma Cl^- concentration falls to normal levels despite the reduction in plasma HCO_3^- concentration. *A moderate to large anion gap therefore develops.*

Tubule potassium transport with normal and reduced nephron mass As with H^+, the concentration of K^+ in extracellular fluid is normally maintained within a relatively narrow range, 4 to 5 meq per liter. Ninety-five percent or more of total body K^+ is in the intracellular fluid compartment, where the intracellular concentration is approximately 160 meq per liter. Normal individuals maintain external K^+ balance by excreting into the urine an amount of K^+ per day equivalent to the amount ingested, minus the relatively small amounts lost in stool and sweat. K^+ is freely filtered at the glomerulus, although the amount excreted usually represents no more than about 20 percent of the quantity filtered. The great bulk of the filtered K^+ is *reabsorbed* in the early portions of the nephron, about two-thirds in the proximal tubule, and an additional 20 to 25 percent in the loop of Henle. A K^+ *secretory process* operates in the distal tubule and terminal nephron segments. This process is largely dependent on exchange of K^+ for Na^+, the reabsorbed Na^+ creating an electrical gradient across the tubule wall, lumen negative. K^+ therefore diffuses from the cell interior into the lumens of distal tubules and collecting ducts, down this electrochemical gradient.

The ability to maintain external K^+ balance and normal plasma K^+ concentration as well, until relatively late in the course of CRF, is a consequence primarily of a progressive increase in fractional excretion of K^+. Greatly enhanced rates of K^+ secretion in distal portions of surviving tubules appear to underlie this adaptation. The augmented secretion rate of aldosterone is believed to contribute to enhanced tubule secretion of K^+, as do the increased distal tubule flow rates in residual functioning nephrons due to the osmotic diuresis and the enhanced luminal electronegativity created by the increased concentration of highly impermeable anions such as phosphate and sulfate. Aldosterone also stimulates net entry of K^+ into the lumen of the colon, a mechanism known to be enhanced in CRF. More detailed discussions of the abnormalities in K^+ homeostasis in acute and chronic forms of renal failure are given in Chaps. 219 and 220.

REFERENCES

BRENNER BM, RECTOR FC JR (eds): *The Kidney*, 3d ed. Philadelphia, Saunders, 1986

BRICKER NS: On the pathogenesis of the uremic state: An exposition of the "trade-off" hypothesis. N Engl J Med 286:1093, 1972

HAYSLETT JP: Functional adaptation to reduction in renal mass. Physiol Rev 59:137, 1979

HOSTETTER TH, BRENNER BM: Glomerular adaptations to renal injury, in *Contemporary Issues in Nephrology*, vol 8: *Chronic Renal Failure*. New York, Churchill Livingstone, 1981

MAXWELL MH et al: *Clinical Disorders of Fluid and Electrolyte Metabolism*, 4th ed. New York, McGraw-Hill, 1987

ROSE BD: *Clinical Physiology of Acid-Base and Electrolyte Disorders*, 2d ed. New York, McGraw-Hill, 1984

219 ACUTE RENAL FAILURE

ROBERT J. ANDERSON / ROBERT W. SCHRIER

Acute renal failure is broadly defined as a rapid deterioration in renal function sufficient to result in accumulation of nitrogenous wastes in the body. Approximately 5 percent of all hospitalized patients develop acute renal failure. The causes of such deterioration include renal hypoperfusion, obstructive uropathy, and intrinsic renal disease such as disease of renal vasculature, glomeruli, and interstitium. After exclusion of these entities, there remains a group of patients with acute renal failure commonly referred to as acute tubular necrosis. However, the histologic findings of tubular necrosis are not present in all of these patients. Many clinicians use the terms acute renal failure and acute tubular necrosis interchangeably to denote the clinical syndrome of reversible intrinsic acute renal failure in the absence of renal vascular, glomerular, and interstitial disease.

ETIOLOGY Sixty percent of all cases of acute renal failure are related to surgery or trauma. Forty percent occur in a medical setting, and 1 to 2 percent are related to pregnancy. The most common general cause of acute renal failure is *renal ischemia*. Clinical conditions associated with renal ischemia include severe hemorrhage, profound volume depletion, intraoperative hypotension, cardiogenic shock, and operative procedures associated with interruption of renal circulation. The duration of the renal ischemia is very important in the occurrence of acute renal failure. If ischemia is brief, then correction of the course of ischemia can restore renal function (i.e., prerenal azotemia). With longer duration of renal hypoperfusion, acute tubular necrosis may supervene. Recent studies suggest that removal of the vasodilating influence of renal prostaglandins with nonsteroidal anti-inflammatory agents can enhance renal ischemia. Thus, use of these agents in patients with diminished basal renal blood flow (cardiac failure, hepatic cirrhosis, nephrotic syndrome, glomerulonephritis, hypoalbuminemia, old age) may precipitate acute renal failure.

Nephrotoxic agents are a frequent cause of acute renal failure. In the past, heavy metals, organic solvents, and glycols were common inducers of acute renal failure. Although these toxins are less frequently encountered currently, their occasional occurrence serves to illustrate the importance of seeking a history of occupational and environmental toxin exposure in each patient with acute renal failure. More recent studies suggest that *aminoglycoside antibiotics* and radiographic contrast agents are now the leading nephrotoxic cause of acute renal failure. Acute renal failure occurs in 10 to 20 percent of patients receiving a course of an aminoglycoside. The acute renal failure associated with these drugs is enhanced by depletion of intravascular volume, advancing age, the presence of underlying renal disease, potassium depletion, and the concomitant use of other nephrotoxic agents or potent diuretics. Radiographic contrast agents have little nephrotoxicity in healthy individuals. However, in patients with underlying renal disease, particularly patients with diabetic nephropathy, contrast exposure is associated with a 10 to 40 percent frequency of acute renal failure. Some anesthetic agents (methoxyflurane and enflurane) also may induce acute renal failure.

Release of large amounts of *myoglobin* into the circulation is now recognized with increasing frequency as a cause of acute renal failure. Rhabdomyolysis and myoglobinuria are often due to extensive trauma with crush injuries. However, nontraumatic rhabdomyolysis associated with increased muscle oxygen consumption (heat stroke, severe exercise, and seizures), decreased muscle energy production (hypokalemia, hypophosphatemia, and genetic enzymatic deficiencies), muscle ischemia (arterial insufficiency, drug overdosage with resultant coma and muscle compression), infections (influenza, Legionnaires' disease), and direct toxins (alcohol) also can produce rhabdomyolysis resulting in acute renal failure. Careful questioning of patients with acute renal failure for muscular symptoms as well as examination for tender, swollen muscles is therefore important, although many of these patients may have muscle necrosis without muscle symptoms. The exact mechanism whereby myoglobinuria results in acute renal failure is uncertain. There is substantial evidence that myoglobin is not directly nephrotoxic. However, direct nephrotoxicity of other muscle breakdown products, as well as tubular obstruction due to myoglobin precipitation and cast formation, has been proposed. Most patients with rhabdomyolysis-associated acute renal failure also have concomitant depletion of intravascular volume and renal hypoperfusion.

Intravascular hemolysis may also cause acute renal failure. Although pure hemoglobin per se is not a potent nephrotoxin, toxic substances from red blood cell stroma and concomitant renal hypoperfusion may act synergistically to induce acute renal failure. Lastly, in spite of intensive investigation, experienced clinicians are often unable to establish a definite etiology for some cases of acute renal failure. In other cases, multiple etiologies are likely, as in patients with shock who are volume-depleted, have received blood transfusions, are septic, and have received nephrotoxic antibiotics.

PATHOPHYSIOLOGY (Fig. 219-1)   Current pathogenic theories of acute renal failure have been developed largely in animal models. These theories can be divided into those suggesting either a tubular or a vascular basis for acute renal failure. One tubular theory suggests that casts and cellular debris obstruct tubular lumina with resultant increases in intratubular pressure sufficient to decrease net filtration pressure. Alternatively, some investigators feel that "back-leak" of glomerular filtrate across damaged renal tubular epithelium is responsible for azotemia in acute renal failure. Proponents of a vascular basis for acute renal failure suggest that marked decreases in renal perfusion pressure, severe afferent arteriolar constriction, or efferent arteriolar dilatation reduce glomerular plasma flow and hydrostatic pressure sufficiently to diminish glomerular filtration. This vascular theory has led some proponents to suggest that *vasomotor nephropathy* might be the preferred term for many cases of acute renal failure. Another theory of acute renal failure suggests that alterations in the permeability properties of the glomerular capillary wall are responsible for acute renal failure. While a precise pathogenic schema of acute renal failure is not available at present, it seems likely that both tubular and vascular events interact to cause acute renal failure. For example, ischemia may cause a lower glomerular capillary pressure, which then predisposes to slow tubular flow. Ischemic cellular necrosis with release of apical membrane into the tubular lumen results in sludging debris, and ultimately secondary tubular obstruction. Additional studies are required to define the relative importance of each factor and to differentiate between mechanisms that are involved in

the initiation (early) and maintenance (late) phases of acute renal failure.

PATHOLOGY   The histopathologic alterations observed in kidneys of patients with acute renal failure are variable. Frequently, no, or minimal, overt abnormalities are observed on light microscopy. However, varying degrees of tubular necrosis with disrupted, necrotic, or regenerating tubular epithelium, intratubular casts, interstitial edema, and interstitial cellular infiltration can be seen. Tubular collapse and dilated tubules both can be observed. Unless either disseminated intravascular coagulation or severe, prolonged ischemic insults are present, intrarenal blood vessels and glomeruli are normal by light and electron microscopy. Microdissection studies demonstrate two general types of renal lesions. Following direct nephrotoxic injury, a uniform, diffuse necrosis of proximal tubular cells, especially of proximal convoluted and straight tubules, is observed. The tubular basement membrane is unaltered. In contrast, following renal ischemia, mild, patchy necrosis occurs throughout the nephron, which tends to be most marked in tubular segments at the corticomedullary junction. The juxtamedullary proximal straight tubule and medullary thick ascending limb of Henle appear particularly vulnerable. Disruption of tubular basement membrane is also observed. Despite these histologic differences, the clinical courses of nephrotoxic and ischemic acute renal failure are similar. A striking lack of correlation between renal histopathologic changes and renal functional parameters is often noted in acute renal failure. Renal biopsies performed after recovery from acute renal failure either demonstrate minor abnormalities or are normal.

DIFFERENTIAL DIAGNOSIS (See Table 219-1)   The diagnosis of acute renal failure is one of exclusion since prerenal (renal hypoperfusion), postrenal (obstruction of urine flow), and other intrarenal disorders (glomerulonephritis, renal interstitial and vascular diseases) may all lead to an identical clinical syndrome of deteriorating renal function. In contrast to acute renal failure, however, prerenal, postrenal, and other intrarenal glomerular or vascular disorders may be specifically treatable.

Impaired renal perfusion from extrarenal causes may result in sufficient reduction in glomerular filtration that the daily endogenous load of nitrogenous wastes cannot be excreted. The azotemia can be reversed if the cause of the renal ischemia is corrected. This may require expansion of extracellular fluid volume, improvement in cardiac output, or restoration of normal renal perfusion pressure. A careful history with regard to weight and volume loss or sequestration and symptoms of impaired cardiac output then is necessary in patients with declining renal function. In addition, physical examination with specific attention to orthostatic hypotension and tachycardia, jugular

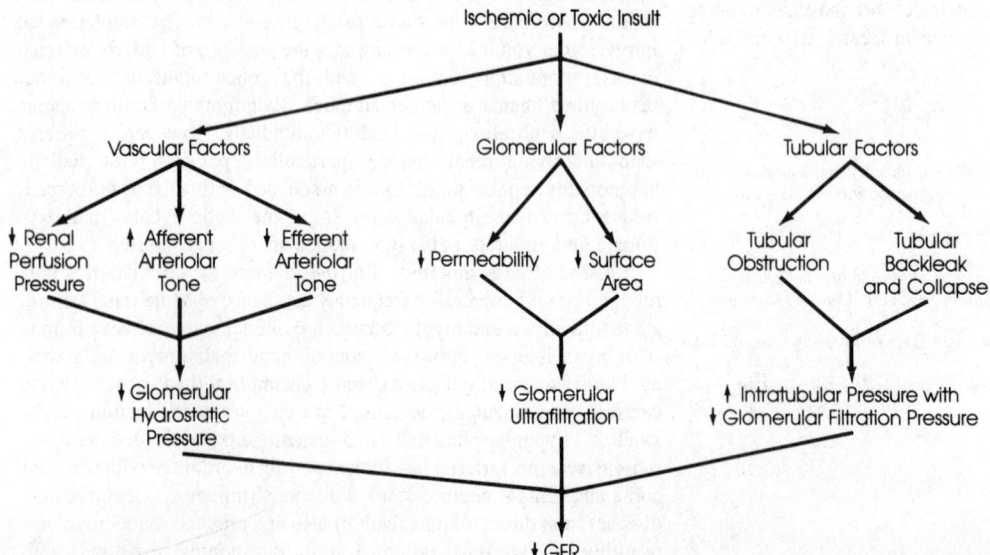

FIGURE 219-1 *Potential pathogenic schema in acute renal failure.*

venous pressure, cardiac function, skin turgor, and mucous membranes should be an initial undertaking in any patient with renal deterioration.

Obstruction to urine flow at any level of the urinary tract must be considered in every patient with renal failure. This form of acute deterioration in renal function is often reversible and will be encountered in 1 to 10 percent of patients with decreasing renal function. Urinary retention secondary to anatomic (prostatic disease) or functional (organic or drug-induced neuropathy) bladder neck obstruction is a relatively common cause of renal failure and can be evaluated by suprapubic palpation and percussion as well as by a single bladder catheterization to measure postvoiding residual volume. Obstruction of the upper urinary tract is a less common cause of renal failure since it requires simultaneous obstruction of both ureters or unilateral ureteric obstruction with absence of, or severe disease in, the contralateral kidney. Causes of bilateral urinary tract obstruction include retroperitoneal fibrosis and space-occupying processes such as tumor or abscess, surgical accident, and bilateral intraureteric occlusion (stones, papillary tissue, blood clots, or pus). A careful rectal and pelvic examination is essential in evaluation for postobstruction renal failure. A plain film of the abdomen may help detect retroperitoneal disease or radiopaque calculi. If obstruction of the upper urinary tract cannot be excluded by ultrasound, infusion pyelography, computerized tomography (CT scanning), or investigation of the patency of the ureter(s) by retrograde pyelography may be required. Obstruction to urine flow can also occur within the kidney. Such intrarenal obstruction is usually due to intratubular precipitation of poorly soluble material such as uric acid (tumor chemotherapy), oxalic acid (ethylene glycol overdose, methoxyflurane anesthesia, small bowel bypass), methotrexate (insoluble metabolites), sulfonamides (outdated, long-acting insoluble compounds), and perhaps myeloma proteins.

Once pre- and postrenal disorders have been excluded, it is appropriate to consider specific renal disorders such as renal vascular disorders, glomerulonephritis, and interstitial nephritis (Table 219-1). The frequency with which these specific renal disorders will be encountered as a cause of deteriorating renal function depends on the patient's age. In adults, only 5 to 10 percent of all cases of decreasing renal function can be attributed to these specific disorders, while this figure may be as high as 40 to 60 percent in the pediatric population. Although these disorders are less frequent than acute tubular necrosis, they are often amenable to specific therapy and should be considered in each case of deterioration in renal function.

The initial presentation of the patient with end-stage renal failure may be confused with acute renal failure when there is no information about renal function prior to presentation. Under these circumstances, the presence of uremic osteodystrophy, uremic neuropathy, small kidney size on abdominal films, and unexplained anemia suggests chronic renal failure. However, some end-stage renal diseases, such as amyloidosis, polycystic disease, diabetic glomerulosclerosis, scleroderma, and rapidly progressive glomerulonephritis, may present with normal-sized or enlarged kidneys, necessitating time for continued observation and rarely renal biopsy to distinguish between potentially reversible forms of acute renal failure and end-stage chronic renal failure.

Observation of the pattern of urine flow may provide a diagnostic clue as to the cause of declining renal function. Complete anuria (no urine by catheterization) is rare in acute tubular necrosis. Potential causes of total anuria include complete bilateral ureteric obstruction, diffuse cortical necrosis, rapidly progressive glomerulonephritis, and bilateral renal artery occlusion. Wide fluctuations in daily urine output suggest intermittent obstructive uropathy. Polyuria (>3 liters per day) can be a hallmark of partial urinary tract obstruction. This occurs secondary to the accompanying defect in renal concentrating ability. Although oliguria (<400 mL per day) has been considered to be a cardinal feature of acute renal failure, many patients have urine volumes of greater than 1 liter per day. This situation has been termed nonoliguric acute renal failure.

Examination of the urinary sediment is of great value in the differential diagnosis of acute impairment of renal function. Sediment containing few formed elements or only hyaline casts strongly suggests prerenal azotemia or obstructive uropathy. With acute tubular necrosis, brownish pigmented cellular casts and many renal tubular epithelial cells are observed in over 75 percent of patients. Red blood cell casts suggest the presence of glomerular or vascular inflammatory diseases of the kidney and rarely, if ever, occur with acute tubular necrosis. The presence of large numbers of polymorphonuclear leukocytes, singly or in clumps, suggests acute diffuse interstitial nephritis or papillary necrosis. Eosinophilic casts on Hansel's stain of urine sediment support a diagnosis of acute allergic interstitial nephritis. The combination of brownish pigmented granular casts and positive occult blood tests on urine in the absence of hematuria indicates either hemoglobinuria or myoglobinuria. In acute renal failure, the finding in fresh, warm urine of large numbers of uric acid crystals may suggest a diagnosis of acute uric acid nephropathy, while the finding of large numbers of oxalic acid or hippuric acid crystals suggests ethylene glycol toxicity. The presence of large numbers of broad casts (greater than two to three white blood cells in diameter) suggests chronic renal disease. Chemical analysis of urine composition is also helpful in differentiating acute tubular necrosis from prerenal azotemia in the oliguric patient and is depicted in Table 219-2. It is important to recall that other disorders associated with abrupt deterioration in renal function and intact renal tubular integrity, such as glomerulonephritis and early (few hours) obstructive uropathy, have urine chemical values similar to those encountered in prerenal azotemia. Prior administration of diuretic agents, osmotic diuresis due to glycosuria, bicarbonaturia, and ketonuria may interfere with avid renal tubular reabsorption of sodium and water and thus alter urinary chemical indexes. A urinary uric acid/creatinine concentration

TABLE 219-1 Major causes of acute renal failure

Disorder	Example
PRERENAL FAILURE	
Hypovolemia	Skin, gastrointestinal, or renal volume loss; hemorrhage; sequestration of extracellular fluid (burns, pancreatitis, peritonitis)
Cardiovascular failure	Impaired cardiac output (infarction, tamponade); vascular pooling (anaphylaxis, sepsis, drugs)
POSTRENAL FAILURE	
Extrarenal obstruction	Urethral occlusion; bladder, pelvic, prostatic, or retroperitoneal neoplasms; prostatism; surgical accident; medications; calculi; pus; blood clots
Intrarenal obstruction	Crystals (uric acid, oxalic acid, sulfonamides, methotrexate)
Bladder rupture	Trauma
SPECIFIC RENAL DISEASES	
Vascular diseases	Vasculitis; malignant hypertension; thrombotic thrombocytopenic purpura; scleroderma; arterial and/or venous occlusion
Glomerulonephritis	Immune-complex disease; antiglomerular basement membrane disease
Interstitial nephritis	Drugs; hypercalcemia; infections, idiopathic
ACUTE TUBULAR NECROSIS	
Postischemic	All conditions listed above for prerenal failure
Pigment-induced	Hemolysis (transfusion reaction, malaria); rhabdomyolysis (trauma, muscle disease, coma, heat stroke, severe exercise, potassium or phosphate depletion)
Toxin-induced	Antibiotics; contrast material; anesthetic agents; heavy metals; organic solvents
Pregnancy-related	Septic abortion; uterine hemorrhage; eclampsia

ratio of greater than 1 is compatible with acute uric acid nephropathy as a cause of the acute renal failure.

Rarely, the cause of declining renal function will not be readily apparent. In other cases, features considered atypical for acute tubular necrosis (gradual onset of renal failure; anuria in the absence of obstructive uropathy; the presence of marked hypertension, heavy proteinuria, significant hematuria, underlying systemic disease, and prolonged oliguria) will be present. Since such atypical features may indicate the presence of a potentially treatable form of renal parenchymal disease, e.g., secondary Wegener's disease, systemic lupus erythematosus, Goodpasture's syndrome, or rapidly progressive glomerulonephritis, a diagnostic renal biopsy may be indicated when the cause of renal failure is not apparent or such atypical features are present.

CLINICAL COURSE The clinical course in acute tubular necrosis can be divided into an initiating phase, a maintenance phase, and a recovery phase. The initiating phase is the period of time between the precipitating event and the appearance of acute renal failure which is no longer reversible by alteration in extrarenal factors. Recognition of the initiating phase of acute renal failure is extremely important since early correction of the underlying cause of renal failure may theoretically prevent the development of the maintenance phase. However, the initiating phase of acute renal failure may be evident to the clinician only in retrospect because it lacks characteristic signs and symptoms.

Oliguria has been considered the cardinal feature of the initiating and maintenance phases of acute renal failure. However, recent studies suggest that 40 to 50 percent of all patients with acute renal failure are nonoliguric (urine volume >400 mL per day). Although progressive acute renal failure without oliguria can result from any type of renal insult, including both ischemic and toxic insults, this form of renal failure appears to be particularly frequent following nephrotoxic (e.g., aminoglycoside) drug administration. Progressive azotemia occurs in nonoliguric patients owing to the marked impairment in glomerular filtration rate and renal concentrating capacity. For example, maximal urine osmolality of the nonoliguric patient averages only 350 mosmol per kilogram of water. Therefore, with a urine output of 1000 mL per day, a maximum of 350 mosmol solute can be excreted daily. In acute renal failure, daily solute loads may be increased from normal values of 600 mosmol to values as high as 1000 mosmol. Thus, a positive solute (predominately urea and creatinine) balance and azotemia would occur despite a daily urine output of 1 liter.

Oliguria characterizes the maintenance phase of acute renal failure in more than 50 percent of cases. When oliguria occurs, it starts shortly following the inciting event and lasts an average of 10 to 14 days. However, the oliguric phase may be as short as a few hours or as long as 6 to 8 weeks. Prolonged oliguria is common in the elderly patient with underlying vascular disease. If oliguria persists for longer than 4 weeks, the diagnosis of acute tubular necrosis should be reconsidered, and entities such as diffuse cortical necrosis,

rapidly progressive glomerulonephritis, renal artery occlusion, renal vasculitis, and superimposed volume depletion are possible. Anuria is not characteristic of acute tubular necrosis. However, several days of severe oliguria with urine volume less than 100 mL per day may be encountered with acute tubular necrosis.

Urinary elimination of nitrogenous wastes, water, electrolytes, and acid is impaired in the initiating and maintenance phases of acute renal failure. The magnitude of resultant abnormalities in blood chemistry depends on whether the patient is oliguric or nonoliguric and on the catabolic state of the patient. Nonoliguric patients have higher levels of glomerular filtration than do oliguric patients and thus excrete more nitrogenous waste, water, and electrolytes in their urine. Hence, abnormalities in blood chemistry are generally milder in nonoliguric than oliguric patients with acute renal failure.

In the afebrile, noncatabolic, oliguric patient with acute renal failure, the daily increments in blood urea nitrogen (BUN) and serum creatinine average 10 to 20 and 0.5 to 1.0 mg/dL, respectively. In catabolic patients with fever, sepsis, or extensive trauma, daily increments in BUN and serum creatinine may be as high as 40 to 100 and 2 to 5 mg/dL, respectively. In patients with acute renal failure due to rhabdomyolysis, the daily increment in serum creatinine may be disproportionately higher compared with the BUN. This is due to the release from muscle of creatine, which is converted by nonenzymatic hydrolysis to creatinine.

Salt and water overload with resultant hyponatremia, edema, and pulmonary congestion are ever-present dangers in patients with acute renal failure, particularly oliguric patients. Hyponatremia results from excessive water intake, and edema from excessive sodium and water intake. If urinary losses are not replaced, the nonoliguric patient with a relatively high rate of urine flow and high concentration of urine sodium will develop intravascular volume depletion which may retard recovery of renal function.

Hyperkalemia due to decreased renal elimination of potassium occurring with continued tissue potassium release is a frequent accompaniment of acute renal failure. The usual rate of increase in serum potassium in the noncatabolic, oliguric patient is 0.3 to 0.5 meq per day. Higher rates of rise in serum potassium concentration should suggest the possibility of an endogenous (tissue destruction, hemolysis) or exogenous (medication, diet, blood transfusion) potassium load or of cellular shift of potassium due to acidemia. Generally, hyperkalemia is asymptomatic until serum potassium increases to values greater than 6.0 to 6.5 meq per liter. Above that level, electrocardiographic abnormalities (bradycardia, recent appearance of left axis deviation, peaked T waves, prolonged QRS complexes, prolonged PR interval, and decreased amplitude of the P waves) and ultimately cardiac arrest can occur. Hyperkalemia can also result in muscle weakness and flaccid quadriparesis.

Hyperphosphatemia, hypocalcemia, and mild *hypermagnesemia* are usually present in acute renal failure. Hyperphosphatemia results from decreased renal phosphorus elimination in the presence of continued release of phosphorus from tissues. The serum phosphorus is usually in the range of 6 to 8 mg/dL, but much higher values may be encountered in the traumatized, catabolic patient as well as the patient with rhabdomyolysis. Hypocalcemia in the range of 6 to 9 mg/dL often develops during acute renal failure. The reason for this decrease in serum calcium concentration is not clear. Asymptomatic increases in serum magnesium to levels of 2 to 3 mg/dL are often observed in acute renal failure. The serum magnesium elevation is mild unless magnesium-containing compounds such as antacids are ingested.

Metabolic acidosis is a regular accompaniment of acute renal failure. The daily production of approximately 1 meq per kilogram of body weight of nonvolatile acid from endogenous metabolic sources can no longer be eliminated by the damaged kidney. A retention of organic acids results, which is sufficient to produce a daily decrease of 1 to 2 meq in plasma bicarbonate and metabolic acidosis with an anion gap.

Hyperuricemia in the range of 9 to 12 mg/dL due to decreased

TABLE 219-2 Urine findings in prerenal azotemia and acute renal failure

Laboratory test	Prerenal azotemia	Acute renal failure
Urine osmolality (mosmol/kg)	>500	<400
Urine sodium (meq/liter)	<20	>40
Urine/plasma creatinine	>40	<20
Fractional excretion* of filtered sodium	<1	2
Urine sediment	Normal or occasional hyaline and granular casts	Brown granular casts, cellular debris

$$*\frac{Urine\ Na/serum\ Na}{Urine\ creatinine/serum\ creatinine} \times 100$$

renal uric acid excretion is usually present in acute renal failure. In catabolic patients with extensive tissue damage, much higher values of serum uric acid may be observed. Elevation of serum amylase due to impaired renal amylase excretion may be observed in the absence of clinical evidence of pancreatitis. The elevations of amylase are mild and are usually less than twice the upper limit of normal.

Abnormalities in the hematologic examination are usually present in acute renal failure. A normocytic normochromic anemia occurs shortly following the onset of significant azotemia, and the hematocrit usually stabilizes between values of 20 to 30 volume percent. This anemia is due to impaired erythropoiesis as well as to a mild and variable degree of shortened red blood cell survival. Additional factors that often contribute to anemia include hemodilution, gastrointestinal blood loss, and suppressed erythropoiesis due to infections or drug administration. White blood cell production is not severely disturbed in acute renal failure. However, since acute renal failure usually occurs in the setting of stress and tissue damage, mild leukocytosis is usually present. Leukocytosis persisting after the initial week of acute renal failure should suggest the possibility of infection. Mild degress of thrombocytopenia due to reduction of bone marrow platelet production may be observed early in the course of acute renal failure. Qualitative defects in platelet function occur and, in association with additional poorly defined coagulation disturbances, contribute to the bleeding tendency of acute renal failure. Acute renal failure may follow intravascular hemolysis and may also be a complication of several primary hematologic or vascular disorders that have major hematologic manifestations such as disseminated intravascular coagulation, thrombotic thrombocytopenic purpura, hemolytic uremic syndrome, and systemic lupus erythematosus.

Infections complicate 30 to 70 percent of all cases of acute renal failure and are a leading cause of morbidity and mortality. The sites of infection include the respiratory tract, operative sites, and urinary tract. Resultant septicemia is frequent, and both gram-positive and gram-negative organisms are encountered. Operative site abscesses (especially intraabdominal) are associated with a poor prognosis if not recognized and treated promptly. Although the exact factors responsible for the high rate of infection remain to be determined, disruption of normal anatomic barriers with intravenous infusions and indwelling catheters may play a role. There is also evidence of impaired host defenses including leukocyte dysfunction in the setting of uremia. Minimization of use of catheters and intravenous lines, careful daily examination, and prompt thorough evaluation of fever is particularly important in patients with acute renal failure. It is also important to emphasize that uremia may obscure the fever associated with infections.

Cardiovascular complications of acute renal failure involve circulatory congestion, hypertension, arrhythmias, and pericarditis. Circulatory congestion is usually due to excessive sodium and water administration. Mild hypertension is seen in 15 to 25 percent of cases and usually appears in the second week of oliguria. This hypertension is usually a manifestation of extracellular fluid volume overload; however, the increased activity of the renin-angiotensin system may also be involved in some instances. Supraventricular arrhythmias may complicate 20 to 30 percent of cases of acute renal failure. Known causes for these arrhythmias include congestive heart failure, electrolyte abnormalities, digitalis intoxication, pericarditis, and anemia. Pericarditis currently occurs infrequently, probably because of the early institution of dialytic therapy.

Neurologic abnormalities are common in acute renal failure. In undialyzed patients, lethargy, somnolence, confusion, disorientation, asterixis, agitation, myoclonic muscle twitching, and generalized seizures may be observed. These neurologic abnormalities are most often encountered in the elderly patient and generally respond well to dialytic therapy. In addition to uremia per se, drug administration, metabolic and electrolyte abnormalities, and primary neurologic disease should be considered as potential causes of neurologic disturbances in the patient with acute renal failure.

Gastrointestinal complications of acute renal failure are common and include anorexia, nausea, vomiting, ileus, and poorly defined abdominal complaints. The combination of stress of acute illness and hemostatic abnormalities can lead to gastrointestinal hemorrhage in 10 to 30 percent of patients. Fortunately, the gastrointestinal hemorrhage is usually mild in nature and easily controlled with conservative therapy. Intravenous 1-deamino-8-arginine-vasopressin (DDAVP, 0.4 μg/kg intravenously) has been shown to lower the bleeding time and improve hemostasis in some patients with acute renal failure. Cryoprecipitate can also be used especially in cases refractory to DDAVP.

The recovery phase of acute renal failure commences when the glomerular filtration rate increases so that the BUN and serum creatinine concentrations no longer continue to increase. In oliguric acute renal failure, the recovery phase is heralded by a progressive increase in urine volume. Generally, in the first days the urine volume may double daily, and in some cases a daily urine volume of greater than 2 liters may be observed for a few days. In nonoliguric patients, a marked diuretic phase is usually not observed. The duration of the recovery phase in patients with BUN and serum creatinine concentrations greater than 50 and 5 mg/dL, respectively, averages 15 to 25 days in oliguric patients and 5 to 10 days in nonoliguric patients. The major complications of acute renal failure, such as infections, gastrointestinal hemorrhage, fluid and electrolyte disturbances, and cardiovascular dysfunction, may persist or first appear during the recovery phase of acute renal failure. In addition, during the recovery phase, persistent abnormalities in glomerular and tubular function can lead to over- or underhydration or electrolyte disturbances unless careful daily weight, intake and output, biochemical, and clinical monitoring are continued during the recovery phase of acute renal failure. Hypercalcemia may occur during the recovery phase, especially in patients with rhabdomyolysis. The cause of this complication remains obscure.

Although the major improvement in renal function occurs within the first 1 to 2 weeks of the recovery phase, renal function continues to improve for up to a year following acute renal failure. Sensitive tests of glomerular and tubular function also suggest that some mild defects in renal function may persist indefinitely following acute tubular necrosis. However, the vast majority of patients achieve clinically normal renal function, and there is no evidence of later progression of renal dysfunction or of complications such as hypertension.

The mortality rates in large series of patients with acute renal failure vary from 30 to 60 percent. The mortality rates are highest in postoperative or traumatized patients (50 to 70 percent), intermediate in patients with acute renal failure encountered in a medical setting (30 to 50 percent), and lowest in acute renal failure observed in an obstetrical setting (10 to 20 percent). Advanced age, the presence of serious underlying illness, and the development of multiple medical complications during the course of acute renal failure are associated with higher mortality rates. Nonoliguric acute renal failure is associated with a lower morbidity and mortality rate than oliguric acute renal failure. Infections, complications resulting from fluid and electrolyte disturbances, gastrointestinal hemorrhage, and progression of the primary underlying disease are the major causes of mortality in acute renal failure.

MANAGEMENT (Table 219-3) The first principle of therapy in acute renal failure is to exclude causes of deterioration in renal function which are potentially remedial. A search for prenal factors, obstructive uropathy, glomerulonephritis, renal vascular and interstitial disease, and intrarenal crystal precipitation should be performed. Once the diagnosis of acute tubular necrosis is made by exclusion, little specific therapy is available. Dialysis for the removal of nephrotoxins, such as carbon tetrachloride, ethylene glycol, and heavy metals following chelation therapy, may be indicated. Even in the presence of acute tubular necrosis, any prenal factors should be corrected both to improve the circulation and to avoid delay in the onset of the recovery phase. In the oliguric patient in whom prenal factors have been corrected, it has become common clinical practice to administer either a potent loop diuretic or mannitol in an attempt to enhance urine flow. In patients who remain oliguric despite potent diuretics, low dose intravenous infusions of dopamine [1 to 3 (µg/kg)/min] may increase renal blood flow and allow a diuretic response to potent diuretics. The rationale for such therapy is based on the thought that there is an early phase of renal failure during which the correction of prerenal factors and establishment of urine flow can lead to a nonoliguric state. Prospective studies have demonstrated lower morbidity and mortality rates in nonoliguric as compared with oliguric acute renal failure. However, a prospective controlled study of the utility of potent diuretics and dopamine in early acute renal failure to convert oliguric to nonoliguric renal failure with attendant decrease in morbidity and mortality rates is needed.

Conservative therapy is capable of controlling many of the manifestations of acute renal failure. After any defects in intravascular volume have been corrected, fluid intake should equal measured output plus estimated insensible losses. Sodium and potassium administration should not exceed measured losses. Daily monitoring of fluid balance and body weight allow assessment of the patient's volume status. A daily weight loss of 0.2 to 0.3 kg occurs in the well-managed patient with acute renal failure. Greater weight loss suggests hypercatabolism or volume depletion, and lesser weight loss suggests excessive salt and water administration. Since most pharmacologic agents are eliminated at least in part by the kidney, careful attention to medication usage and dosage adjustment is needed. The serum sodium concentration provides a guideline for water administration. A decrease in serum sodium concentration indicates that an excess of total body water is present, while an abnormally high serum sodium concentration indicates a deficiency of body water.

In an effort to minimize catabolism, daily intake should include at least 100 g of carbohydrate. Recently some studies suggest that central intravenous administration of a mixture of amino acids and hypertonic glucose improves morbidity and mortality in patients with acute renal failure following surgical procedures or trauma. Since parenteral hyperalimentation may be associated with significant complications, this form of nutrition should be reserved for catabolic patients in whom the enteral routine of alimentation does not prove to be satisfactory. In the past, anabolic androgens have been utilized in an effort to decrease protein catabolism and diminish the rate of rise of BUN. Such therapy is not generally utilized at present. Additional means of minimizing catabolism include early removal or debridement of necrotic tissue, control of pyrexia, and early, specific antimicrobial therapy.

The mild metabolic acidosis associated with acute renal failure is generally not treated unless serum bicarbonate falls to below 10 meq per liter. Rapid correction of acidemia by acute alkali administration may decrease ionized calcium concentrations and precipitate tetany. Hypocalcemia is usually asymptomatic and rarely requires specific therapy. Hyperphosphatemia should be controlled with 30 to 60 mL aluminum hydroxide administered orally four to six times per day, since a high calcium-phosphorus product (>70) may cause soft tissue

calcification. For the occasional patient with profound hyperphosphatemia, early dialysis therapy and alimentation may help control elevated serum phosphate concentration. Unless acute uric acid nephropathy is a diagnostic consideration, the secondary hyperuricemia of acute renal failure is usually not treated with allopurinol. Because of the decreased glomerular filtration rate, the filtered load of uric acid, and thus intratubular deposition, is low. Also, for unknown reasons, clinical gout rarely complicates acute renal failure, despite hyperuricemia. Careful observation of the hematocrit and stool for occult blood is important in the early detection of gastrointestinal blood loss. If a rapid decrease in hematocrit occurs which appears to be out of proportion to the degree of renal failure, alternative causes of anemia should be sought.

Congestive heart failure and hypertension indicate the presence of volume overload and should be treated accordingly, recognizing, of course, that many drugs such as digoxin are largely excreted by the kidneys. As suggested earlier, hypertension occasionally may persist in the absence of volume overload; thus factors such as hyperreninemia may contribute to the hypertension. Selective histamine-2 receptor blockade (cimetidine, ranitidine) therapy has been of benefit in preventing gastrointestinal bleeding in some seriously ill patients but has not yet been studied in acute renal failure. Avoidance and early detection of infection require minimization of interruption of normal anatomic barriers, including avoidance of long-term catheterization of the urinary bladder, provision of mouth and skin care, promotion of early mobilization, utilization of aseptic techniques for intravenous and tracheostomy sites, and close clinical monitoring. Fever and suspected infection should be promptly evaluated with careful inspection of lung, wounds, urinary tract, and intravenous sites.

Hyperkalemia is an ever-present threat in acute renal failure. Mild elevations of serum potassium (<6.0 meq per liter) can best be treated by withdrawal of all sources of potassium and by continued close laboratory observation. If serum potassium increases to values greater than 6.5 meq per liter and particularly if any electrocardiographic changes appear, active therapy should be instituted. Therapy of such hyperkalemia can be divided into emergent and nonemergent forms. Emergent therapy includes intravenous administration of calcium (5 to 10 mL of 10% calcium chloride solution intravenously over 2 min with electrocardiographic monitoring), bicarbonate (44 meq intravenously over 5 min), and insulin and glucose (200 to 300 mL of 20% glucose with 20 to 30 units regular insulin given intravenously over 30 min). Nonemergent therapy includes administration of potassium-binding ion exchange resins such as sodium polystyrene sulfonate. This can be administered orally every 3 to 4 h in 25- to 50-g doses with 100 mL 20% sorbitol to avoid constipation. Alternatively, in the patient who cannot take oral medications, 50 g sodium polystyrene sulfonate and 50 g sorbitol in 200 mL water can be given as a retention enema at 1- to 2-h intervals. With refractory hyperkalemia, hemodialysis may be necessary.

Some patients with acute renal failure, particularly those who are nonoliguric and noncatabolic, can be successfully managed with minimal or no dialytic therapy. There has been an increasing tendency to use dialysis therapy early in acute renal failure in an attempt to minimize the development of complications. Early (prophylactic) use of dialysis frequently simplifies management, allowing more liberal fluid and potassium intake and improvement of the general well-being of the patient. Absolute indications for dialysis include symptomatic uremia (usually manifested by central nervous system and/or gastrointestinal symptomatology), development of resistant hyperkalemia, severe acidemia or fluid overload not responsive to medical therapy, and pericarditis. In addition, many centers attempt to keep predialysis levels of BUN and serum creatinine less than 100 and 8 mg/dL, respectively. Adequate prevention of uremic symptoms may require infrequent dialysis in the noncatabolic, nonoliguric patient or daily dialysis in the catabolic, traumatized patient. Often, peritoneal dialysis is an acceptable alternative to hemodialysis. Peritoneal dialysis may be especially useful in the patient with noncatabolic acute renal failure when the need for infrequent dialysis is anticipated. Slow,

TABLE 219-3 General therapeutic approach to patient with acute renal failure

1 Exclude all specifically treatable causes of decreasing renal function including correction of prerenal and postrenal factors.
2 Attempt to establish a urine output.
3 Conservative therapy:
  a Decrease intake of nitrogen, water, and electrolytes to match output.
  b Provide adequate nutrition.
  c Alter medication therapy.
  d Maintain clinical monitoring (frequency of vital signs determined by patient status; intake and output, body weight, inspection of wound and intravenous sites, and physical examination required daily).
  e Maintain biochemical monitoring (frequency of BUN, creatinine, electrolytes, and blood counts will be dictated by patient status; in catabolic oliguric patients, daily determination will be needed; calcium, phosphorus, magnesium, and uric acid can often be determined less often).
4 Provide dialytic therapy.

continuous arteriovenous filtration using highly permeable filters has been advocated as a means of controlling extracellular volume in patients with acute renal failure. Currently available filters connected to the patient via an arteriovenous shunt allow for removal of 5 to 12 liters of plasma ultrafiltrate per day without use of a pump. Thus, these devices appear particularly useful in the oliguric volume-overloaded patient with hemodynamic instability.

PREVENTION Because of the high mortality and morbidity of acute renal failure, prophylactic therapy deserves special mention. A fivefold reduction in deaths secondary to acute renal failure occurred from the Korean war to the Vietnamese conflict. This reduction in the acute renal failure mortality rate paralleled earlier evacuation from the field and early expansion of intravascular volume. Thus, identification of patients at high risk for the development of acute renal failure is important. Such high-risk patients include those with multiple trauma, burns, rhabdomyolysis, and intravascular hemolysis; those receiving potential nephrotoxins; and those undergoing operative procedures necessitating interruption of renal blood flow. In these patients, particular attention should be given to maintaining optimal intravascular volume, cardiac output, and urine flow rates. Care in the use of potential nephrotoxic drugs, early therapy of cardiogenic shock, sepsis, and eclampsia of pregnancy may also reduce the occurrence of acute renal failure.

ACUTE RENAL FAILURE IN PREGNANCY When acute renal failure occurs during pregnancy, it is usually in either the earlier or later stages of gestation. During the first trimester of pregnancy, acute renal failure usually occurs in the setting of nontherapeutic, nonsterile abortion. In these cases, volume depletion, sepsis, and nephrotoxins contribute to the acute renal failure. This form of acute renal failure has markedly declined with the current widespread availability of sterile abortion.

Acute renal failure can also occur because of either excessive postpartum hemorrhage or preeclampsia in the later stages of pregnancy. The majority of patients with this type of acute renal failure generally recover total renal function. A small number of pregnant patients with acute renal failure, however, have not recovered renal function, and in these cases histologic evidence of diffuse cortical necrosis is found. This entity usually complicates the severe hemorrhage of abruptio placentae and is associated with clinical and laboratory evidence of intravascular coagulation.

A rare form of acute renal failure occurring 1 to 12 weeks following uncomplicated pregnancy has been described and termed postpartum glomerulosclerosis. This form of renal failure is usually characterized by irreversible, rapidly progressive renal failure, although milder cases have been described. All of these patients have an associated microangiopathic hemolytic anemia. The renal histopathologic changes are indistinguishable from malignant hypertension or scleroderma. The pathophysiology of this disorder has not been defined. No therapeutic modality is consistently successful, although heparin therapy has been advocated.

HEPATORENAL SYNDROME The hepatorenal syndrome is a serious complication of advanced liver disease in which renal failure occurs in the absence of clinical, laboratory, or anatomic evidence of other causes of renal dysfunction. The renal failure is usually associated with oliguria, an unremarkable urinary sediment, and low urinary sodium concentrations (<10 meq per liter). Generally, the renal failure occurs in the setting of advanced hepatic cirrhosis complicated by jaundice, ascites, and hepatic encephalopathy. Occasionally, this syndrome may complicate fulminant hepatitis. The mechanism of the renal failure is not known. The lack of consistent histopathologic alterations in kidneys of patients with this syndrome and the restoration of normal renal function when kidneys from donors with hepatorenal syndrome are transplanted into recipients without liver disease suggest a functional defect.

Treatment of the hepatorenal syndrome is usually unsuccessful. Care should be taken in the cirrhotic patient not to induce major changes in intravascular volume by large paracentesis or aggressive diuresis, maneuvers which may precipitate hepatorenal syndrome. Since this syndrome mimics prerenal azotemia, a cautious trial of expansion of intravascular volume is warranted. In a few cases, recovery has followed portacaval shunting, insertion of an abdominal-venous (Leveen) shunt, or prolonged hemodialysis. These treatment modalities have not been subjected to controlled trials. The abdominal-venous shunt may be associated with peritonitis, intravascular coagulation, and pulmonary congestion. Improvement in hepatic function often results in parallel improvement in renal function. Every effort should be made to ensure that more specifically treatable causes of concomitant liver and renal dysfunction, such as infections (leptospirosis, hepatitis with immune-complex disease), toxins (aminoglycosides, carbon tetrachloride), and circulatory disorders (severe heart failure, shock), are not present. It should also be recalled that jaundiced patients with liver disease may be particularly susceptible to acute tubular necrosis.

REFERENCES

BENNETT WM et al: Drug prescribing in renal failure: Dose guidelines for adults. Am J Kid Dis 3:155, 1983

BRENNER BM, LAZARUS JM (eds): *Acute Renal Failure*. Philadelphia, Saunders, 1983

BREZIS M et al: Renal ischemia: A new perspective. Kid Int 26:375, 1984

CONGER JD, SCHRIER RW: Acute renal failure: Pathogenesis, diagnosis and management, in *Renal and Electrolyte Disorders*, RW Schrier (ed). Boston, Little, Brown, 1985

CRONIN RE: The patient with acute azotemia, in *Manual of Nephrology, Diagnosis and Therapy*, RW Schrier (ed). Boston, Little, Brown, 1985, p 135

GROSS PA, ANDERSON RJ: Acute renal failure and toxic nephropathy. Contemp Nephrol, 1986

HOU SH et al: Hospital-acquired renal insufficiency: A prospective study. Am J Med 74:243, 1983

220 CHRONIC RENAL FAILURE: PATHOPHYSIOLOGIC AND CLINICAL CONSIDERATIONS

BARRY M. BRENNER / J. MICHAEL LAZARUS

In contrast to the remarkable capacity of the kidney to regain function following the various forms of acute renal injury discussed in the preceding chapter, renal injury of a more sustained nature is often not reversible but leads instead to progressive destruction of nephron mass. Despite successful treatment of hypertension, urinary tract obstruction and infection, and systemic disease, many forms of renal injury associated with permanent nephron loss progress inexorably to chronic renal failure (CRF). Reduction of renal mass has been shown to cause structural and functional hypertrophy of remaining nephrons. Recent experimental evidence in animals suggests that this "compensatory" hypertrophy is due to adaptive hyperfiltration mediated by increases in glomerular capillary pressures and flows. Eventually these adaptations prove "maladaptive" in that they predispose to glomerular sclerosis, an enhanced functional burden on less affected glomeruli, leading in turn to their ultimate destruction.

Glomerulonephritis, in one of its several forms, is the most common initiating cause of CRF. The other major etiologies of chronic renal failure are listed in Table 220-1. These and other progressive forms of renal disease are considered in detail in the remaining chapters of this section. Irrespective of cause, the eventual impact of severe reduction in nephron mass is an alteration in function of virtually every organ system in the body. *Uremia* is the term generally applied to the clinical syndrome observed in patients suffering from profound loss of renal function. Although the cause(s) of the syndrome remain unknown, the term uremia was adopted originally because of

TABLE 220-1 Causes of chronic renal failure*

Diagnosis	Percent
Glomerulonephritis	24
Glomerulosclerosis	2
Diabetes mellitus	15
Polycystic kidney disease	9
Nephrosclerosis	8
Hypertension	9
Pyelonephritis	3
Other interstitial nephritis	5
Unknown etiology	6
Other	19

* *Patients presenting for treatment of end-stage renal disease in New England as of December 1982.*

the presumption that the abnormalities seen in patients with chronic renal failure (CRF) resulted from *retention* in the blood of urea and the other end products of metabolism normally excreted into the urine. It is clear that the uremic state represents more than failure of renal excretory function alone, because a host of metabolic and endocrine functions normally subserved by the intact kidney are also impaired in CRF. Furthermore, the inexorably progressive course to renal failure is often accompanied by severe malnutrition, impaired metabolism of carbohydrates, fats, and proteins, and defective utilization of energy. Because CRF involves more than just retention of normal urinary constituents in blood, the term *uremia* in current usage is devoid of any pathophysiologic connotation, but is employed instead to refer, in a general sense, to the constellation of signs and symptoms associated with CRF, regardless of etiology.

The presentation and severity of signs and symptoms of uremia often vary greatly from patient to patient, depending, at least in part, on the magnitude of the reduction in functioning renal mass as well as the rapidity with which renal function is lost. As discussed in Chap. 218, in the relatively early stage of CRF [i.e., when total glomerular filtration rate (GFR) is reduced but not to levels below about 35 to 50 percent of normal], overall renal function is sufficient to maintain the patient symptom-free, although renal reserve may be diminished. At this stage of renal impairment baseline excretory, biosynthetic, and other regulatory functions of the kidney are generally well maintained. At a somewhat later stage in the course of CRF (GFR about 20 to 35 percent of normal), *azotemia* occurs, and initial manifestations of renal insufficiency usually appear. Although patients are relatively asymptomatic at this stage, renal reserve is diminished sufficiently that any sudden stress, such as intercurrent infection, urinary tract obstruction, dehydration, or administration of a nephrotoxic drug, may compromise renal function still further, often leading to signs and symptoms of overt uremia. With further loss of nephron mass (GFR below 20 to 25 percent of normal), the patient develops *overt renal failure*. Uremia may be viewed as the final stage in this inexorable process, when many of or all the untoward manifestations of CRF become evident clinically. In this chapter the causes and clinical characteristics of the disturbances of the various organ systems seen in patients with CRF will be considered.

PATHOPHYSIOLOGY AND BIOCHEMISTRY OF UREMIA

ROLE OF RETAINED TOXIC METABOLITES The finding that serums from patients with uremia exert toxic effects in a variety of biologic test systems has motivated a diligent search to identify the responsible toxin(s). The most likely candidates thought to qualify as toxins in uremia are the *by-products of protein and amino acid metabolism*. Unlike fats and carbohydrates, which are eventually metabolized to carbon dioxide and water, substances which are easily excreted even in uremic subjects via lungs and skin, the products of protein and amino acid metabolism depend largely on the kidneys for excretion. A vast number of such products have been identified, with urea being quantitatively the most important. *Urea* represents some 80 percent or more of the total nitrogen excreted into the urine in patients with CRF maintained on diets containing 40 or more

grams of protein per day. The *guanidino compounds* are the next most abundant of the nitrogenous end products of protein metabolism and include substances such as guanidine, methyl- and dimethylguanidine, creatinine, creatine, and guanidinosuccinic acid. As with urea, guanidines are derived, at least in part, from urea cycle amino acids. Other metabolic products of amino acid and protein catabolism that have been implicated as possible uremic toxins include *urates and other end products of nucleic acid metabolism, aliphatic amines,* a variety of *peptides,* and, finally, several *derivatives of the aromatic amino acids tryptophan, tyrosine, and phenylalanine.* The role of these substances in the pathogenesis of the clinical and biochemical abnormalities seen in CRF is unclear. It is generally believed that uremic symptoms correlate only in a rough and inconsistent way with concentrations of urea in blood. Nevertheless, although urea is probably not a major cause of overt uremic toxicity, it may account for some of the less serious clinical abnormalities, including anorexia, malaise, vomiting, and headache. On the other hand, elevated levels of plasma *guanidinosuccinic acid,* by interfering with activation of platelet factor III by adenosine diphosphate (ADP), have been shown to contribute to the impaired platelet function seen in CRF. *Creatinine,* generally regarded as a nontoxic substance, may cause adverse effects in uremic subjects following conversion to more toxic metabolites such as sarcosine and methylguanidine. Whether these substances, as well as *creatine,* a metabolic precursor of creatinine, and the other compounds cited above, are of clinical importance in the pathogenesis of uremic toxicity remains to be established.

Nitrogenous compounds of larger molecular weight are also retained in CRF. A toxic role for these substances has been suggested, on the impression that patients treated with intermittent peritoneal dialysis are less troubled with neuropathy than patients maintained on chronic hemodialysis, despite higher levels of urea and creatinine in blood in the former group. Since the clearance of small molecules depends mainly upon blood and dialysate flow rates, which are higher with hemodialysis, whereas clearance of larger molecules depends more on membrane surface area and time, which are greater with peritoneal dialysis, this latter form of therapy may be a more effective means of removing these substances of larger molecular weight. Using a variety of chemical separation procedures, several groups of workers have obtained evidence in support of this "middle-molecule hypothesis" by observing differences in composition between normal and uremic plasmas, with prominent abnormal "uremic peaks" in the molecular weight range of about 300 to 3500. Evidence from amino acid analysis suggests that these substances of larger molecular weight are polypeptides. Despite the foregoing, proof that efficient removal of middle molecules is associated with objective evidence of clinical well-being, and improvement in neuropathy in particular, remains to be provided. On the other hand, when there is insufficient removal of substances of smaller molecular weight (e.g., urea), symptoms of uremia are frequently aggravated.

Not all these middle-sized molecules accumulate in uremic plasma because of decreased renal excretion alone. The kidney normally *catabolizes* a number of circulating plasma proteins and polypeptides; with reduced renal mass, this capacity may be impaired greatly. Furthermore, plasma levels of many polypeptide hormones [including parathyroid hormone (PTH), insulin, glucagon, growth hormone, luteinizing hormone, and prolactin] rise with advancing renal failure, often markedly so, not only because of impaired renal catabolism but also because of enhanced endocrine secretion. The consequences of high circulating levels of many of these hormones in CRF are considered below and in Chap. 218.

EFFECTS OF UREMIA ON CELLULAR FUNCTIONS

Alterations in the composition of intracellular and extracellular fluids in CRF have long been recognized. Such abnormalities are believed to be a consequence, at least in part, of *defective ion transport* across cell membranes generally, with retained uremic toxins possibly mediating these alterations in transmembrane ion transport. Integrity of cellular volume and composition depends to a large extent on the active outward transport of Na^+ from cell interior to exterior, the resulting intracellular fluid being relatively low in Na^+ and high in K^+, whereas the reverse is true for extracellular fluid. Active Na^+ transport is a metabolically costly process, accounting for a major fraction of basal energy utilization and oxygen consumption. The consequences of this efflux of Na^+ from cells are many and include, most notably, (1) the generation of a resting electrical potential difference across the cell membrane (with this transcellular voltage oriented so that cell interior is electronegative to cell exterior), and (2) a mechanism for enhancing the influx of K^+ into cells.

In experimental animals, partial inhibition of this active efflux mechanism for Na^+ across cell membranes leads to alterations in body composition and cell functions similar to those demonstrable in erythrocytes, leukocytes, skeletal muscle, and other tissues obtained from uremic subjects. These include increased and decreased intracellular concentrations of Na^+ and K^+, respectively, and reduction in magnitude of the transcellular voltage. These alterations have been shown to be largely reversed by efficient hemodialysis and, for erythrocytes at least, to be recreated when cells from normal subjects are incubated in uremic serums. Other derangements in cellular function have also been implicated as causes for altered body composition in uremia. For example, *Na^+- and K^+-stimulated ATPase activity* has been shown to be decreased in erythrocytes and brain tissue derived from uremic patients and animals, respectively. Whether the "uremic toxins" which account for these derangements in cellular function represent abnormally retained products of metabolism which fail to be excreted, or normal substances present in increased quantities in response to reduced renal mass, remains unknown. *Parathyroid and natriuretic hormones*, examples of this category of substances, are discussed in this context in Chap. 218.

EFFECTS OF UREMIA ON WHOLE-BODY COMPOSITION

What is the impact of these disturbances in active transcellular Na^+ transport on the uremic organism as a whole? From the pathophysiologic considerations already discussed, CRF is likely to lead to abnormally high intracellular Na^+ concentrations, and hence to osmotically induced overhydration of cells generally, whereas these same cells are thought to be relatively deficient in K^+. With the inevitable onset of malaise, anorexia, nausea, vomiting, and diarrhea, patients with CRF may eventually develop classic protein-calorie malnutrition and negative nitrogen balance, often with profound losses of lean body mass and fat deposits. Owing to the concomitant tendency for salt and water retention, these losses often go unnoticed until the late stages of CRF. Whereas a large fraction of the increase in total body water in uremia is the result of expansion of intracellular volume, extracellular volume expansion also is observed commonly. With initiation of intermittent hemodialysis or renal transplantation, there is often an immediate and substantial loss of body weight, due primarily to correction of this overhydration. With successful transplantation, the initial diuresis is followed by a period of impressive weight gain, due to restoration of lean body mass and fat deposits to preillness levels. For patients on chronic dialysis, the anabolic response is less dramatic, even when therapy is regarded as optimal, involving mainly reaccumulation of fat deposits. The failure to restore lean body mass to normal with chronic dialysis may reflect insufficient intake of protein, which, in adequately dialyzed patients, should be maintained at levels of 0.8 to 1.4 g/kg per day.

The occurrence of deficits in intracellular K^+ concentration in CRF has already been mentioned and may result from inadequate intake (poor diet or overzealous K^+ restriction by the physician), excessive losses (vomiting, diarrhea, diuretics), reduction of Na^+- and K^+-stimulated ATPase, or a combination of these. In addition to promoting losses of K^+ into urine (which may be substantial if urine volume remains relatively normal in uremic subjects), the high levels of plasma aldosterone often seen in CRF may also augment net secretion of K^+ into the colon, thereby contributing to marked K^+ losses in stool or diarrheal fluids. Despite deficits in intracellular K^+ concentration, serum K^+ is usually normal or high in CRF, owing most often to metabolic acidosis, which induces an efflux of K^+ from cells. Additionally, uremic patients are relatively resistant to the action of insulin (see below), a hormone which normally enhances K^+ uptake by skeletal muscle.

EFFECTS OF UREMIA ON METABOLISM

HYPOTHERMIA   In experimental animals injections of urine, urea, or other retained toxic metabolites can induce hypothermia, and basal heat production diminishes soon after nephrectomy. Since active Na^+ transport across cell membranes accounts for a major proportion of basal energy production, it is generally believed that the inverse relationship between body temperature and degree of azotemia is due, in part, to inhibition of the sodium pump by some retained toxin(s). Dialysis usually returns body temperature to normal.

CARBOHYDRATE METABOLISM   The ability to metabolize an exogenous glucose load is impaired in most patients with CRF. The defect largely involves a slowing of the rate at which blood glucose concentration declines to the normal range after administration of a glucose load. Fasting blood sugar levels are usually normal or only slightly elevated; severe hyperglycemia and/or ketosis is uncommon. Consequently, the *glucose intolerance of CRF* usually does not require specific therapy (hence the term *azotemic pseudodiabetes*). Because insulin depends to a large extent on the kidney for its removal from plasma and eventual degradation, circulating insulin levels tend to be increased in uremia. Whereas insulin levels in plasma are only slightly to moderately increased in most fasting uremic subjects, levels considerably in excess of normal are usually found in response to a glucose load. The response to intravenous insulin in patients with CRF is also abnormal, and the rate of utilization of glucose by peripheral tissues often is diminished substantially. The glucose intolerance of uremia is thought to result largely from this peripheral resistance to the action of insulin. Other possible factors contributing to the glucose intolerance include intracellular deficits of potassium, metabolic acidosis, increased levels of glucagon and other hormones including catecholamines, growth hormone, and prolactin, as well as the myriad of potentially toxic metabolites retained in CRF. In true insulin-dependent diabetics, there is often a decrease in insulin requirement with progressive azotemia, a phenomenon not related solely to decreased caloric intake.

NITROGEN AND LIPID METABOLISM   Given that the capacity to eliminate the nitrogenous end products of protein catabolism is reduced drastically, CRF may be regarded as a state of *protein intolerance*. As discussed above, retention of these end products of nitrogen metabolism is thought to represent a dominant cause of the signs and symptoms of uremic toxicity.

Hypertriglyceridemia and decreased high-density lipoprotein cholesterol are common in uremia, whereas cholesterol levels in plasma are usually normal. Whether uremia accelerates triglyceride production by the liver and intestine is unknown. The well-known lipogenic effect of hyperinsulinism may contribute to increased triglyceride synthesis. The rate of removal of triglycerides from the circulation, which depends in large part on the enzyme *lipoprotein lipase*, has been shown to be depressed in uremia, an effect not corrected appreciably by hemodialysis. The high incidence of premature atherosclerosis seen in patients on chronic dialysis (see "Cardiovascular and Pulmonary Abnormalities" below) may be related, at least in part, to these abnormalities in lipid metabolism.

CLINICAL SPECTRUM OF ABNORMALITIES IN UREMIA

The diagnosis of chronic renal failure is based on recognition of a constellation of signs and symptoms with or without reduced urine

TABLE 220-2   Clinical spectrum of abnormalities in uremia*

FLUID AND ELECTROLYTE DISTURBANCES

Volume expansion and contraction (I)
Hypernatremia and hyponatremia (I)
Hyperkalemia and hypokalemia (I)
Metabolic acidosis (I)
Hyperphosphatemia and hypophosphatemia (I)
Hypocalcemia (I)

ENDOCRINE-METABOLIC DISTURBANCES

Renal osteodystrophy (I or P)
Osteomalacia (D)
Secondary hyperparathyroidism (I or P)
Carbohydrate intolerance (I)
Hyperuricemia (I or P)
Hypothermia (I)
Hypertriglyceridemia (P)
Protein-calorie malnutrition (I or P)
Impaired growth and development (P)
Infertility and sexual dysfunction (P)
Amenorrhea (P)

NEUROMUSCULAR DISTURBANCES

Fatigue (I)
Sleep disorders (P)
Headache (I or P)
Impaired mentation (I)
Lethargy (I)
Asterixis (I)
Muscular irritability (I)
Peripheral neuropathy (I or P)
Restless legs syndrome (I or P)
Paralysis (I or P)
Myoclonus (I)
Seizures (I or P)
Coma (I)
Muscle cramps (D)
Dialysis disequilibrium syndrome (D)
Dialysis dementia (D)
Myopathy (P or D)

CARDIOVASCULAR AND PULMONARY DISTURBANCES

Arterial hypertension (I or P)
Congestive heart failure or pulmonary edema (I)
Pericarditis (I)
Cardiomyopathy (I or P)
Uremic lung (I)
Accelerated atherosclerosis (P or D)
Hypotension and arrhythmias (D)

DERMATOLOGIC DISTURBANCES

Pallor (I or P)
Hyperpigmentation (I, P, or D)
Pruritus (P)
Ecchymoses (I or P)
Uremic frost (I)

GASTROINTESTINAL DISTURBANCES

Anorexia (I)
Nausea and vomiting (I)
Uremic fetor (I)
Gastroenteritis (I)
Peptic ulcer (I or P)
Gastrointestinal bleeding (I, P, or D)
Hepatitis (D)
Refractory ascites on hemodialysis (D)
Peritonitis (D)

HEMATOLOGIC AND IMMUNOLOGIC DISTURBANCES

Normocytic, normochromic anemia (P)
Lymphocytopenia (P)
Bleeding diathesis (I or D)
Increased susceptibility to infection (I or P)
Splenomegaly and hypersplenism (P)
Leukopenia (D)
Hypocomplementemia (D)

---

* *Virtually all the abnormalities contained in this table are completely reversed in time by successful renal transplantation. The response of these abnormalities to hemo- or peritoneal dialysis therapy is more variable. (I) denotes an abnormality which usually improves with an optimal program of dialysis and related therapy. (P) denotes an abnormality which tends to persist or even progress, despite an optimal program. (D) denotes an abnormality which develops only after initiation of dialysis therapy.*

output but always with elevation in serum urea nitrogen and creatinine concentrations. Differentiation between acute and chronic renal failure can be difficult. The history is often most helpful, particularly if normal renal function existed prior to a sudden recent insult. The laboratory findings and physical examination may not be helpful in the differentiation. The hallmark of chronic renal failure is the presence of reduced kidney size on either ultrasound, abdominal scout film, or pyelogram. In the absence of small kidneys, renal biopsy may be necessary for diagnosis.

As noted earlier, CRF leads ultimately to disturbances in function of every organ system in the body. With the advent and increasingly greater application of chronic dialysis in the past two decades, the incidence and severity of these disturbances have been modified enormously, so that virtually everywhere that modern medicine is practiced, the overt and florid manifestations of uremia have largely disappeared. Unfortunately, however, even optimal dialysis therapy is not a panacea for the patient with CRF, because, as indicated in Table 220-2, some disturbances resulting from impaired renal function fail to respond fully, while others may even progress despite dialysis treatment. Furthermore, as with many modern and complex therapeutic modalities, intermittent dialysis may be responsible for the appearance of unique abnormalities not seen prior to initiation of therapy; these abnormalities should be viewed as complications of dialysis.

FLUID, ELECTROLYTE, AND ACID-BASE DISORDERS (See also Chaps. 41 and 42)   **Sodium and volume homeostasis**   In most patients with stable CRF, modest increases in total body Na^+ and water content can be documented, although objective signs of extracellular fluid (ECF) volume expansion may not be apparent clinically. With ingestion of excessive amounts of salt and water, however, control of excess volume becomes an important clinical and therapeutic consideration. In general, excessive *salt* ingestion contributes to, or aggravates, congestive heart failure, hypertension, ascites, and edema formation. On the other hand, hyponatremia and weight gain are the typical consequences of excessive ingestion of *water,* abnormalities which in most patients are relatively mild and asymptomatic. In the majority of patients, daily intake of fluid equal in volume to urine volume per day plus about 500 mL usually will maintain the serum Na^+ concentration at normal levels. Hypernatremia is encountered relatively infrequently in CRF. In the edematous patient with CRF not maintained on dialysis, diuretics and modest restriction of salt and water intake are the mainstays of therapy. In volume-expanded dialysis patients, management should include ultrafiltration and restriction of salt and water intake between dialyses.

Patients with CRF have grossly impaired renal mechanisms for conserving Na^+ and water (discussed in detail in Chap. 218). When confronted with an *extrarenal* cause for increased fluid loss (e.g., vomiting, diarrhea, fever), these patients are prone to develop ECF volume depletion, with signs and symptoms of dry mouth and other mucous membranes, dizziness, syncope, tachycardia, decreased filling of jugular veins, orthostatic hypotension, and even vascular collapse. Depletion of extracellular fluid volume typically results in deterioration of residual renal function and, in the previously stable and asymptomatic patient with mild CRF, signs and symptoms of overt uremia. Cautious fluid repletion usually restores extracellular and intravascular volumes to normal and often, but not always, returns renal function to previously stable levels.

Potassium homeostasis   Derangements in K^+ balance (see also Chaps. 41 and 218) are occasionally documented by laboratory analysis in patients with CRF, but are rarely responsible for clinical symptoms unless GFR is below 5 mL/min or an endogenous (hemolysis, trauma, infection) or exogenous (stored blood, K^+-containing medications) K^+ load is administered. Despite progression of renal failure, most patients maintain normal serum K^+ concentrations until the final stages of uremia. As discussed in Chap. 218, this ability to sustain K^+ balance with advancing renal failure is due to adaptations in the renal distal tubules and colon, sites where aldosterone and other factors serve to enhance K^+ secretion. Not surprisingly, oliguria, or disruption of key adaptive mechanisms, can lead to *hyperkalemia* and its potentially ominous effects on cardiac function. Antikaliuretic drugs, such as spironolactone or triamterene, should be used with extreme caution in CRF. Hyperkalemia in CRF may also be induced by abrupt lowering of arterial blood pH, since acidosis is associated with efflux of K^+ from intracellular to extracellular fluids. A clinically useful index of the magnitude of this hydrogen-potassium exchange is that for every 0.1-unit change in blood pH, there will be a reciprocal change in serum K^+ concentration of approximately 0.6 meq per liter. Correction of acidosis-induced hyperkalemia with sodium bicarbonate is the treatment of choice. Intravenous insulin and dextrose are useful in lowering serum potassium acutely, while the ion exchange resin sodium polystyrene sulfonate (Kayexalate) is useful in longer-term control of hyperkalemia. Patients in whom hyperkalemia persists in the absence of excessive K^+ intake, oliguria, or acute acidosis should be evaluated for the possibility of *hyporeninemic hypoaldosteronism*. Patients with this syndrome have reduced circulating levels of renin and aldosterone in the plasma and often also have diabetes mellitus.

Hypokalemia due to diminished ability of the kidneys to conserve K^+ is uncommon in most forms of CRF. When hypokalemia occurs in these patients, poor dietary K^+ intake, usually in association with excessive diuretic therapy or gastrointestinal losses, is likely to be the underlying cause. When hypokalemia occurs as a result of primary K^+ wasting in urine, it may represent a solitary renal reabsorptive defect or, more commonly, be associated with other solute transport abnormalities, as in Fanconi's syndrome, renal tubular acidosis, or other forms of hereditary or acquired tubulointerstitial diseases (see Chaps. 226 and 228). A detailed discussion of the clinical consequences and management of hypokalemia and hyperkalemia is given in Chap. 41.

Metabolic acidosis   With advancing renal failure, total daily acid excretion and buffer production fall below the level needed to maintain external balance of hydrogen ions. Metabolic acidosis is the inevitable result, and the mechanisms involved are considered in Chap. 218. In most patients with stable renal insufficiency, administration of 20 to 30 meq sodium bicarbonate or sodium citrate per day will usually correct the acidosis. In response to a sudden acid challenge (whether from an endogenous or exogenous source), however, patients with CRF are particularly susceptible to profound acidosis, which requires more substantial quantities of alkali for correction. Administration of sodium must be carried out with careful attention to the patient's volume status.

Phosphate, calcium, and bone   As discussed in detail in Chap. 218, serum phosphate concentration begins to rise when GFR falls below about 25 percent of normal. Calcium deposition in bone is critically dependent upon the availability of phosphate; retention of phosphate in plasma, therefore, facilitates calcium entry into bone and thereby contributes to the *hypocalcemia* and *elevations in plasma PTH* levels seen in CRF. Hypocalcemia in CRF also results from the impaired ability of the diseased kidney to synthesize *1,25-dihydroxy-vitamin D_3* [*$1,25(OH)_2D_3$*], the active metabolite of vitamin D (Fig. 220-1). Reabsorption of calcium in the gut is impaired when circulating levels of this active metabolite are low. Finally, in patients with advanced CRF, the ability of PTH to mobilize calcium salts from bone may be altered. Despite these various causes of hypocalcemia, symptoms such as tetany are rare unless patients are treated with large amounts of alkali.

Overproduction of parathyroid hormone, disordered vitamin D metabolism, chronic metabolic acidosis, and excessive fecal losses of calcium all contribute to the occurrence of bone diseases in uremia (Fig. 220-1). *Renal* or *metabolic osteodystrophy* are broad and imprecise terms that encompass a number of distinct skeletal abnormalities, including osteomalacia, osteitis fibrosa cystica, osteosclerosis, and, in children especially, impaired bone growth. Although clinical symptoms of bone disease are uncommon, occurring in less than 10 percent of predialysis patients with advanced renal failure, radiologic and histologic abnormalities are observed in about 35 and 90 percent, respectively. In patients who have been treated by means of dialysis for several years, symptoms from bone disease are a major cause of morbidity. Renal osteodystrophy is seen more often in growing children than in adults, and especially in patients with congenital renal anomalies associated with very slowly progressive renal insufficiency. On radiologic examination, three types of lesions can be identified: (1) changes analogous to those described in children with nutritional rickets, namely, widened osteoid seams at the growth margin of bones (so-called renal rickets); (2) the bone changes of *secondary hyperparathyroidism* (*osteitis fibrosa cystica*), character-

FIGURE 220-1   *Pathogenesis of bone diseases in chronic renal failure.*

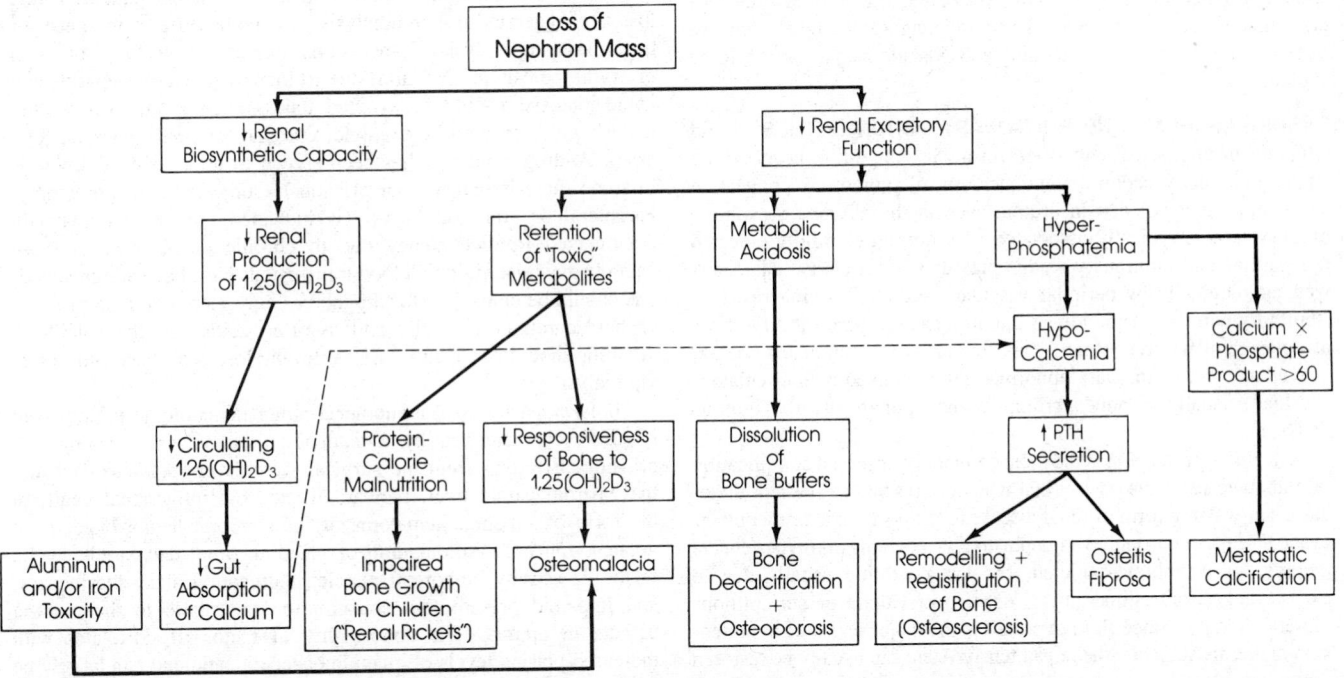

ized by osteoclastic bone resorption and manifested by subperiosteal erosions, especially of the phalanges, long bones, and distal ends of the clavicles; and (3) *osteosclerosis,* often best noted by enhanced bone density in the upper and lower margins of vertebrae, producing the so-called rugger jersey spine.

With renal osteodystrophy there is a tendency to *spontaneous fractures,* which are often slow to heal. The ribs are most commonly involved. Painful joints may occur in association with renal osteodystrophy due to calcium deposition in bursas and other periarticular structures. Bone pain is due to osteitis fibrosa cystica as well as to osteomalacia. Osteomalacia was initially thought to be secondary to decreased availability of 1,25-dihydroxycholecalciferol. There is now evidence that at least a component of osteomalacia is due to deposition of aluminum and/or iron at the calcification fronts. The aluminum is thought to be derived from increased aluminum in the dialysis fluid, as well as aluminum-containing phosphate-binding gels. Iron excess is usually secondary to frequent transfusions. When bone pain is severe, a proximal *myopathy* often coexists, giving rise to gait abnormalities and even leading to cessation of ambulation. The incidence of *aseptic necrosis of the hip* is increased in renal transplant recipients, probably related to such factors as chronic corticosteroid therapy, secondary hyperparathyroidism, and altered vitamin D metabolism. In CRF there is often a tendency to *extraosseous,* or *metastatic, calcification,* especially when the calcium-phosphate product exceeds 60. Medium-sized blood vessels; subcutaneous, articular, and periarticular tissues; myocardium; eyes; and lungs are common sites of metastatic calcification.

Management of patients with renal osteodystrophy includes reduction in dietary phosphate available for absorption through the use of restricted, 1 g phosphate, diet as well as phosphate-binding agents. Supplementation of calcium, primarily by judicious increase in the calcium ion concentration of the dialysate, but also by oral calcium intake (1 to 1.5 g per day) and efforts to enhance intestinal calcium absorption with 1,25-dihydroxycholecalciferol or dihydrotachysterol, may improve osteitis fibrosa cystica, osteomalacia, and myopathy. Treatment with phosphate binders, calcium, and vitamin D should be initiated early in chronic renal failure so that hyperparathyroidism and bone disease may be prevented. Serum phosphorus must be maintained below 4.5 mg/dL before administering calcium and/or vitamin D analogues, in order to avoid metastatic calcification.

Other solutes   Other inorganic solute derangements in CRF include *hyperuricemia* and *hypermagnesemia.* Uric acid retention is a common feature of CRF but rarely leads to symptomatic gout. Hypophosphatemia is usually a consequence of overzealous oral administration of phosphate-binding gels. Because serum magnesium levels tend to rise in CRF, magnesium-containing antacids and cathartics should be avoided.

CARDIOVASCULAR AND PULMONARY ABNORMALITIES   Fluid retention in uremic patients often results in congestive heart failure and/or pulmonary edema. A unique form of pulmonary congestion and edema may be seen in uremia even in the absence of volume overload and is typically associated with normal or mildly elevated intracardiac and pulmonary wedge pressures. This entity, characterized radiologically by perihilar vascular congestion giving rise to a "butterfly wing" distribution, is due to increased permeability of the alveolar capillary membrane. This low-pressure pulmonary edema, as well as cardiopulmonary abnormalities associated with circulatory overload, usually responds promptly and dramatically to vigorous dialysis.

Arterial hypertension is the most commonly observed complication of end-stage renal disease. When it is not present, the patient either has a salt-wasting form of renal disease (e.g., polycystic or medullary cystic disease or chronic pyelonephritis), is receiving antihypertensive therapy, or is volume-depleted, the last condition usually due to excessive gastrointestinal fluid losses, overzealous or surreptitious diuretic therapy. Since fluid overload is the major cause of hypertension in uremic subjects, the normotensive state can usually be restored

by dialysis. Nevertheless, some patients remain hypertensive, despite rigorous salt and water restriction and ultrafiltration, because of hyperreninemia. In most cases, routine antihypertensive drug therapy is effective. A small minority of these patients develop *accelerated or malignant hypertension,* manifested by markedly elevated systolic and diastolic pressures, severe hyperreninemia, encephalopathy, seizures, retinal changes, and papilledema. Use of more potent drugs such as diazoxide, minoxidil, captopril, and nitroprusside, along with control of extracellular volume, will generally control such hypertension and has obviated the need for bilateral nephrectomy.

Pericarditis, once a common complication of CRF, is now seen infrequently because of early initiation of dialysis. Retained metabolic toxins are thought to be the cause of *pericarditis* in patients with CRF. The very unusual finding of pericarditis in the well-dialyzed patient is usually due to viral infection or systemic disease.

The clinical presentation of pericarditis in uremic subjects is generally similar to that of other etiologies (Chap. 194), except that pericardiocentesis for effusions usually yields hemorrhagic fluid. Treatment with intensive dialysis is recommended, and systemic anticoagulation should be avoided to minimize the possible occurrence of hemorrhagic tamponade. Oral indomethacin may be useful for relief of pain in pericarditis. In some patients, pericardiocentesis with intrapericardial instillation of air or steroids is effective for pericardial tamponade. Pericardiectomy should be considered only after more conservative treatment has failed.

Clinical experience with chronically dialyzed patients followed for the past decade or more has revealed the disturbingly high incidence of *accelerated atherosclerosis,* leading to development of significant coronary, cerebral, and peripheral vascular disease. There are seemingly ample causes for these complications, including long-term hypertension, hyperlipidemia, glucose intolerance, chronic high cardiac output, and metastatic vascular and myocardial calcification.

HEMATOLOGIC ABNORMALITIES   *Normochromic, normocytic anemia* occurs regularly in CRF and contributes to fatigability and listlessness in these patients. Erythropoiesis is depressed in CRF, due both to the effects of retained toxins on bone marrow and to diminished biosynthesis of erythropoietin by the diseased kidney or to the presence of erythropoietin inhibitors. *Hemolysis* also occurs and involves an extracorpuscular defect since survival of erythrocytes from normal subjects is reduced when these cells are transfused into uremic patients, and erythrocytes from patients with CRF have relatively normal survival times when transfused into normal individuals. Gastrointestinal and chronic dialyzer *blood loss* contributes to anemia, as does *hypersplenism* in the occasional patient. Blood loss is exaggerated in hemodialysis patients because of the need for heparin during dialysis. Transfusions may contribute to suppression of erythropoiesis in CRF and, due to increased risk of hepatitis and hemosiderosis, should be avoided unless anemia aggravates other underlying disorders (for example, coronary or cerebrovascular disease). Androgen therapy has been shown to improve erythropoiesis in some dialysis patients not previously subjected to nephrectomy. Parenteral or oral iron therapy is indicated only in patients with documented iron deficiency due to chronic blood loss. In those patients in whom multiple blood transfusions have been administered, one should be concerned for the increasingly more common problem of hemachromatosis. Folic and ascorbic acids and the soluble B vitamins should be given to offset chronic losses of these substances via dialysis.

Abnormal hemostasis is another common hematologic derangement in CRF, characterized by a tendency to abnormal bleeding and bruising. Bleeding from the surgical wounds or spontaneously into the gastrointestinal tract, pericardial sac, and intracranial vault, in the form of subdural hematoma or intracerebral hemorrhage, is of greatest concern. Prolongation of bleeding time, decreased platelet factor III activity, abnormal platelet aggregation and adhesiveness, and impaired prothrombin consumption contribute to the clotting defects in uremia. The abnormality in factor III correlates with increased plasma levels of guanidinosuccinic acid and can largely be corrected by dialysis. Prolongation of the bleeding time continues to be a common finding even in the well-dialyzed patient.

A wide variety of changes in leukocyte formation and function also occur in uremia leading to *enhanced susceptibility to infection.* Lymphocytopenia and atrophy of lymphoid structures occur in CRF, whereas neutrophil production is relatively unimpaired. Nevertheless, there is evidence to suggest that all leukocyte cell types are affected adversely by uremic serum. Decreased chemotaxis is among the best documented of the defects occurring in uremic leukocytes, with resulting impairment of acute inflammatory response and decreased delayed hypersensitivity. There is a tendency for uremic patients to have less fever in response to infection. For these reasons, infections may be more difficult to recognize in uremia. Leukocyte function may also be impaired in patients with CRF because of such coexisting factors as acidosis, hyperglycemia, protein-calorie malnutrition, and serum and tissue hyperosmolarity (due to azotemia). Mucosal barriers to infection may also be defective, and, in dialysis patients, vascular access devices also serve as common portals of entry for pathogens, particularly staphylococci. Anti-inflammatory steroids and immunosuppressive drugs add further to the risk of serious infection in many of these patients. Leukopenia is a common transient finding in patients exposed to cellophane-derived membranes during dialysis (Chap. 221).

NEUROMUSCULAR ABNORMALITIES Subtle disturbances of central nervous system function, including inability to concentrate, drowsiness, and insomnia, are among the earliest symptoms of uremia. Mild behavioral changes, loss of memory, and errors in judgment soon follow and often are associated with signs of neuromuscular irritability, including hiccups, cramps, and fasciculations and twitching of large muscle groups. Asterixis, myoclonus, and chorea are common in terminal uremia, as are stupor, seizures, and coma. Many of these neuromuscular complications of severe uremia resolve with dialysis, although nonspecific EEG abnormalities may persist.

Peripheral neuropathy is a relatively common complication of advanced CRF. Initially, sensory nerve involvement exceeds motor, lower extremities are involved more than the upper, and the distal portions of the extremities more than proximal. The "restless legs syndrome," characterized by ill-defined sensations of discomfort in the feet and lower legs and frequent leg movement, is a disturbing complication in some uremic patients. If dialysis is not instituted soon after onset of sensory abnormalities, motor involvement follows, often leading to loss of deep tendon reflexes, weakness, peroneal nerve palsy (foot drop), and, eventually, flaccid quadriplegia. Accordingly, early evidence of peripheral neuropathy is generally taken as a firm indication to initiate dialysis or transplantation.

Two types of neurologic disturbances appear to be unique to patients on chronic dialysis. One is the syndrome of *dialysis dementia,* seen in patients who have been on dialysis for a number of years. This syndrome is characterized by speech dyspraxia, myoclonus, dementia, and eventually seizures and death. The possibility of aluminum intoxication has been suggested. Other factors are also likely to play a role in such patients since a very small percentage of the patients with increased aluminum exposure develop the syndrome. The other disturbance, dialysis disequilibrium, occurs during the first few dialyses, in association with rapid reduction of blood urea levels. Nausea, vomiting, drowsiness, headache, and even grand mal seizures have been attributed to the more rapid (dialysis-induced) pH change and reduction in osmolality of extracellular than intracellular fluids within the cranium, leading to cerebral edema and raised intracranial pressure.

GASTROINTESTINAL ABNORMALITIES Anorexia, hiccups, nausea, and vomiting are common and early manifestations of uremia. The use of carefully monitored protein restriction in the diet may be useful to slow progression of renal insufficiency if initiated early. Protein restriction is also useful in diminishing the frequent symptoms of nausea and vomiting late in the course. Protein restriction should

not, of course, be implemented in those patients with severe protein-calorie malnutrition. *Uremic fetor,* a uriniferous odor to the breath, derives from the breakdown of urea in saliva to ammonia and is often associated with unpleasant taste sensation. Mucosal ulcerations leading to blood loss can occur at any level of the gastrointestinal tract in very late stages of CRF—so-called uremic gastroenteritis. Peptic ulcer disease is particularly common, occurring in as many as one-fourth of uremic subjects. Whether this high incidence is related to increased gastric acidity, hypersecretion of gastrin, or secondary hyperparathyroidism is unknown. Most of the gastrointestinal symptoms, except those related to peptic ulcer disease, usually improve with dialysis. A syndrome of idiopathic ascites is seen rarely in patients on chronic dialysis, presumably secondary to fluid overload and/or chronic passive hepatic congestion. Patients with chronic renal failure, particularly those with polycystic kidney disease, have an increased incidence of diverticulosis. Viral hepatitis is more commonly seen in patients on chronic dialysis and is discussed in detail in Chap. 221.

ENDOCRINE-METABOLIC DISTURBANCES The common disturbances in parathyroid function, glucose, and insulin metabolism, as well as the lipid, protein-calorie, and other nutritional abnormalities of uremia have already been considered. In general, pituitary, thyroid, and adrenal gland functions are relatively normal, often despite measurable abnormalities in circulating thyroxine, growth hormone, aldosterone, and cortisol levels. In women, estrogen levels are low and amenorrhea and inability to carry pregnancies to term are early manifestations of uremia. While menses frequently reappear after chronic dialysis is initiated, successful pregnancies remain rare. In men with CRF, including those on chronic dialysis, impotence, oligospermia, and germinal cell dysplasia are common, as are reduced plasma testosterone levels. As with growth, sexual maturation is often impaired in adolescent children, even among those on chronic dialysis.

DERMATOLOGIC ABNORMALITIES The skin shows many abnormalities. This is not surprising in view of anemia (pallor), defective hemostasis (ecchymoses and hematomas), calcium deposition and secondary hyperparathyroidism (pruritus, excoriations), dehydration (poor skin turgor, dry mucous membranes), and the general cutaneous consequences of protein-calorie malnutrition. A sallow, yellow cast may reflect the combined influences of anemia and retention of a variety of pigmented metabolites, or *urochromes.* In advanced uremia urea concentrations in sweat may reach sufficiently high levels that, after evaporation, a fine white powder can be found on the skin surface—so-called uremic (urea) frost. Although many of these cutaneous abnormalities improve with dialysis, *uremic pruritus* may persist and is usually resistant to most systemic and topical therapies. Hemochromatosis causes a slate-gray–bronze discoloration of the skin and is common in the dialysis patient who has received multiple transfusions.

REFERENCES

ACCHIARDO SR et al: Malnutrition as the main factor in morbidity and mortality of hemodialysis patients. Kidney Int 24:S199, 1983

ANDRASSY K, RITZ E: Uremia as a cause of bleeding. Am J Nephrol 5:313, 1985

BRENNER BM et al: Dietary protein intake and the progressive nature of kidney disease: The role of hemodynamically mediated glomerular injury in the pathogenesis of progressive glomerular sclerosis in aging, renal ablation, and intrinsic renal disease. N Engl J Med 307:652, 1982

DEYKIN D: Uremic bleeding. Kidney Int 24:698, 1983

DUMBAULD S et al: Carbohydrate metabolism during fasting in chronic hemodialysis patients. Kidney Int 24:222 1983

GOKAL R et al: Iron metabolism in hemodialysis patients: A study of the management of iron therapy and overload. Q J Med 48:369, 1979

GOLDBLUM SE, REED WP: Host defenses and immunologic alterations associated with chronic hemodialysis. Ann Intern Med 93:597, 1980

KOPPLE JD, MASSRY SG: Uremic toxins: What are they? How are they identified? Semin Nephrol 3:263, 1983

MAHONEY C et al: Central and peripheral nervous system effects of chronic renal failure. Kidney Int 24:170, 1983

MASSRY SG et al: Current status of the use of 1,25-(OH)$_2$D3 in the management of renal osteodystrophy. Kidney Int 18:409, 1980

MITCH WE et al: A simple method of estimating progression of chronic renal failure. Lancet 2:1326, 1976

PARKINSON IS et al: Dialysis encephalopathy, bone disease and anemia: The aluminum intoxication syndrome during regular hemodialysis. J Clin Pathol 34:1285, 1981

ROSTAND SG et al: Dialysis-associated ischemic heart disease: Insights from coronary angiography. Kidney Int 25:653, 1984

221 DIALYSIS AND TRANSPLANTATION IN THE TREATMENT OF RENAL FAILURE

CHARLES B. CARPENTER / J. MICHAEL LAZARUS

Over the past three and one-half decades, dialysis and transplantation have become effective treatment modalities in prolonging the life of patients with renal insufficiency. The approach to treatment in acute renal failure is different than in chronic renal failure because of the irreversible nature of the latter. Conservative medical management or dialysis are the mainstays of therapy for acute renal failure. Obviously, transplantation is not a treatment modality for this group of patients. Options for treatment of patients with *chronic* or *irreversible* renal failure are outlined in Fig. 221-1.

Initially patients are managed with conservative therapy, but eventually they require hemodialysis, peritoneal dialysis, or cadaver or related donor transplantation. Because of limited success with each of these treatment modalities, chronic renal failure should be approached with the concept of moving from one form of therapy to another as indicated by the degree of success and incidence of complications with each form of treatment.

Therapy for renal failure should be initiated at a time in the disease process when complications will be moderate, but not when the patient is completely asymptomatic. The advanced complications of uremia, as noted in Chap. 220, should be avoided by early treatment. Early dialysis is especially applicable to patients with acute renal failure in whom resumption of renal function can be expected and to patients with chronic renal failure who have a good immunologic match with a related donor in whom transplantation can be carried out promptly and will very likely lead to resumption of normal renal function. In the remainder of patients, the clinical judgment to move from conservative treatment to dialysis or transplantation is determined by the patient's quality of life and whether or not the benefits of treatment outweigh the risks. Treatment with protein restriction as described in Chap. 220 may prolong the time before dialysis and transplantation are required but should be carried out only if complications of such therapy do not negatively impact on long-term morbidity and mortality.

Selection of patients to receive dialysis and/or transplantation is a matter of some debate. Because of the reversible nature of acute renal failure, *all* patients with this diagnosis should be supported with dialysis, at least for some period of time, to allow return of renal function. In patients with irreversible or chronic renal failure, criteria for selection for transplantation are generally more stringent than those for dialysis and are guided by the possibility of complications related to immunosuppressive therapy. Table 221-1 lists practical considerations in the selection of a recipient for a human renal allograft. Such a procedure should be undertaken only when conservative treatment has failed, when there are no reversible elements in the patient's renal failure, and when the patient is too ill to be maintained comfortably with the usual methods of treatment. However, morbidity is less if transplantation is performed before the patient is critically ill. Transplantation should not be utilized in an attempt to salvage patients from failure to thrive on dialysis.

The recipient should be free of life-threatening extrarenal complications such as cancer, severe coronary artery disease, and cerebrovascular disease. Provided that diffuse vascular involvement is not present, diabetes itself is not a contraindication. Oxalosis may recur in relatively short order in a transplanted kidney and is generally a contraindication for this procedure. Although age may be a limiting factor, it is advanced "physiologic" rather than chronologic age which contraindicates transplantation. In general, patients reach a "physiologic" limit at approximately age 60 to 65 years when the incidence of complications due to prednisone become much higher than in younger patients. Although abnormalities of the bladder and urethra present additional hazards, successful renal allografts have been placed in individuals with these abnormalities by prior constitution of an artificial bladder (i.e., ileal conduit) into which the donor ureter is placed. Patients with any disease process which may be aggravated by prednisone, cyclosporine, azathioprine, or other immunosuppressive agents, or any patient with medical complications so severe that the risks of operation and drug therapy are high, should obviously not be offered transplantation. In evaluating potential exclusionary diseases, it should be kept in mind that quality of life and long-term results are superior in the *successful* renal transplantation.

Criteria for treatment with hemodialysis or peritoneal dialysis are more liberal since dialysis has less morbidity than transplantation in older patients and those with the aforementioned medical complications. Because of the cost of these programs, some have suggested restricted entry. These decisions, based on moral and social issues, continue to generate debate. In most areas of the world today, the cost of medical care for chronic renal failure is borne by government. With economic support from the government for dialysis and transplant programs, rules and regulations have been and will continue to be generated which will affect the selection and the type of treatment employed.

CONSERVATIVE TREATMENT As discussed in Chap. 220, conservative (nondialytic, nontransplant) therapy should be instituted early to control symptoms, minimize complications, prevent long-term sequelae of uremia, and slow the progression of renal insufficiency. Every effort should be made to correct any of the numerous reversible components which aggravate renal impairment. In patients with acute renal failure, prerenal factors, such as volume depletion, decreased cardiac output, or renal artery stenosis, or postrenal components, such as urethral or ureteral obstruction, must be sought and corrected. Such pre- and postrenal components may exacerbate

FIGURE 221-1

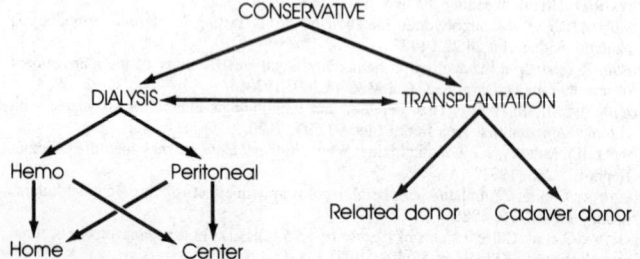

TABLE 221-1 Contraindications to kidney transplantation

1 Absolute contraindications
  a Reversible renal involvement
  b Ability of conservative measures to maintain useful life
  c Advanced forms of major extrarenal complications (cerebrovascular or coronary disease, neoplasia)
  d Active infection
  e Active glomerulonephritis
  f Previous sensitization to donor tissue
2 Relative contraindications (see text)
  a Age
  b Presence of vesical or urethral abnormalities
  c Iliofemoral occlusive disease
  d Diabetes mellitus
  e Psychiatric problems
  f oxalosis

underlying parenchymal disease in patients with chronic renal insufficiency and must be treated in this group as well. Most important is treatment of the underlying disease or complications of renal insufficiency which further hasten the loss of nephrons. Hypertension, urinary tract infections, nephrolithiasis, structural abnormalities of the urinary tract, or those forms of glomerulonephritis which may respond to therapy should be treated aggressively. Preventive aspects include avoidance of nephrotoxic drugs and large doses of radiopaque agents in the patient with already compromised renal insufficiency.

Modification of diet is an important aspect of conservative therapy. Early restriction of sodium and fluid may be important in the treatment of hypertension. As renal insufficiency progresses, restriction of foods high in phosphate and potassium is necessary. Reduction of protein content reduces anorexia, nausea, and vomiting and, if initiated early, may retard progression of the disease. Adult patients should receive no less than 0.6 g of protein per kilogram per day to avoid negative nitrogen balance. Supplementation of low-protein diets with essential ketoamino acid therapy may be useful in prolonging the period of conservative therapy by allowing utilization of urea as a source of nonessential nitrogen. Correction of electrolyte imbalance, e.g., use of sodium bicarbonate or calcium carbonate to correct mild acidosis, or bicarbonate, dextrose and insulin, and potassium exchange resins for treatment of hyperkalemia, will be necessary in more advanced states of uremia. Some chemical abnormalities occurring with renal failure do not require or are not amenable to treatment; hypermagnesemia, hyperamylasemia, hypertriglyceridemia, or mild carbohydrate intolerance generally do not require therapy. Treatment of hyperuricemia may be in order if the patient suffers from gout. However, hyperuricemia alone has not been shown to be detrimental. It has been suggested that secondary hyperparathyroidism may accentuate progression of renal failure. Whether this is due to hyperphosphatemia, an elevated calcium-phosphorus product, or parathyroid hormone itself is not clear. Nonetheless, vigorous efforts using phosphate-binding agents and calcium supplements and vitamin D products (dihydrotachysterol or 1,25-dihydroxycholecalciferol) to maintain the serum calcium are effective in suppressing parathyroid stimulation, perhaps in slowing renal insufficiency, and likely avoiding severe bone disease later (see Chap. 336). To avoid visceral and vascular calcification it is important to maintain the calcium-phosphorus product below 60. Fluid, sodium, potassium, phosphate, and protein restriction offer the patient a very restricted and often unacceptable diet. This, coupled with the administration of multiple medications, often occurs at a time when the complications of uremia appear and consideration for dialysis and/or transplantation is in order.

While conservative measures are being carried out, it is necessary to prepare the patient with an intensive educational program to explain the possibilities of eventual renal failure and the various forms of therapy available. The more knowledgeable patients are concerning hemodialysis, peritoneal dialysis, and transplantation, the easier and more appropriate will be their decisions at a later time. With hemodialysis, the major method of obtaining blood for treatment is from an arteriovenous fistula. Since these devices often take several months to develop, prophylactic placement of a fistula in a patient planning for hemodialysis is important in minimizing future complications of circulatory access. For those patients who select peritoneal dialysis (continuous ambulatory peritoneal dialysis—CAPD; or continuous cyclic peritoneal dialysis—CCPD), placement of the peritoneal catheter does not require preparation, and therapy can be instituted as soon as uremic signs and symptoms develop. In those patients who may perform home dialysis or undergo transplantation, early education of family members for selection and preparation as a home dialysis helper or a related donor for transplantation should occur well before the onset of symptomatic renal failure. In those patients who may have a good antigenic match with a willing donor, transplantation without intervening hemodialysis or peritoneal dialysis should be considered. In considering related donor transplantation, the risk of unilateral nephrectomy, including development of pro-

teinuria and hypertension, should be considered. As discussed below, the success rate of cadaver donor transplantation has improved sufficiently that this form of therapy should be carefully considered both with the patient and with family members who are potential donors.

HEMODIALYSIS Hemodialysis employs the process of diffusion across a semipermeable membrane (cellophane, cellulose acetate, polyacrylnitrile, or polymethylmethacrylate) to remove unwanted substances from the blood while adding desirable components. A constant flow of blood on one side of the membrane and a cleansing solution–dialysate on the other allows removal of waste products in a fashion grossly similar to that of glomerular filtration. By altering the composition of the dialysate, the method of exposure of blood and dialysate (geometry of the dialyzer), the type and surface area of dialysis membrane, and the frequency and duration of exposure, patients without renal function can be maintained in a relatively healthy state. Hemodialysis equipment consists of three components—the blood delivery system, the composition and delivery system of the dialysate, and the dialyzer itself. Blood is pumped to the dialyzer by a roller pump through lines with appropriate equipment to measure flow and pressures within the system; blood flow should be approximately 250 to 300 mL/min. Hydrostatic pressure within the system can be manipulated to achieve desirable fluid removal, so-called ultrafiltration. The dialysate is delivered to the dialyzer from a storage tank or proportioning system which manufactures dialysate on line. In most systems dialysate passes once across the membrane, countercurrent to blood flow at a rate of 500 mL/min, or it may be recirculated multiple times at higher flow rates. The composition of the dialysate is similar to plasma water, but may be altered depending upon the patient's needs. There are two principal types of dialyzers—the flat plate dialyzer, in which flat sheets of membrane are layered one on another with intervening plastic templates; and the hollow fiber or capillary dialyzer, in which membrane material is spun into fine capillaries, thousands of which are packed into bundles with blood flowing through the capillaries while dialysate is circulated on the outside of the fiber bundle (Fig. 221-2).

Most patients require between 10 and 15 h of dialysis per week, equally divided into several sessions. The time depends upon body size, residual renal function, dietary intake, complicating illnesses, and the degree of anabolism or catabolism. The time, frequency of treatments, type and size of dialyzer, and dialysate composition, blood, or dialysate flow may all be altered to accomplish specific

FIGURE 221-2 *Hollow fiber or capillary dialyzer; the most commonly used artificial kidney.*

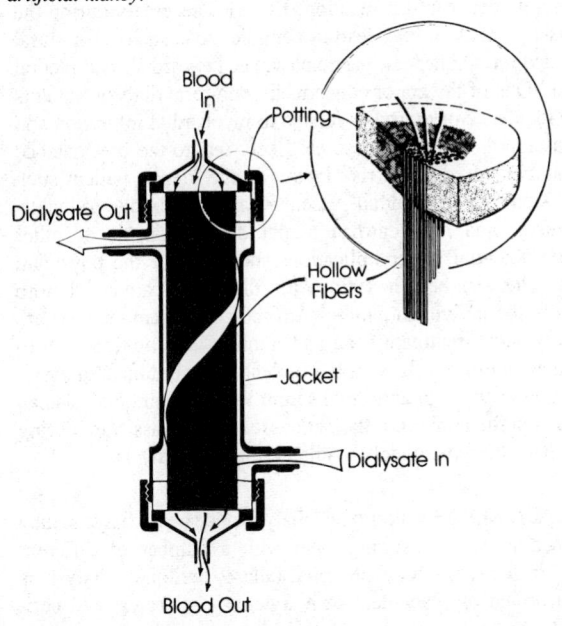

Blood In

Potting

Dialysate Out

Hollow Fibers

Jacket

Dialysate In

Blood Out

needs. In recent years, kinetic modeling, utilizing urea generation and protein catabolic rates, has lead to a more definite dialysis prescription.

Many complications in the chronic dialysis patient are related to underlying disease or those uremic conditions not reversed by dialytic therapy. These and other related problems of hemodialysis are discussed in Chap. 220. The Achilles' heel of hemodialysis is access to the circulation. In the early 1960s, development of the arteriovenous shunt made chronic dialysis possible. This device has had a high failure rate because of infection and thrombosis and led in 1966 to the development of the arteriovenous (AV) fistula. The fistula is preferably created from a native vein, but if not available, a prosthetic conduit (Dacron, extended polytetrafluoroethylene, bovine carotid arteries, human umbilical cord artery) subcutaneously placed between an artery and a nearby vein may be utilized. Cannulation of arteriovenous fistulas with 15- to 16-gauge needles allows blood flow sufficient to carry out hemodialysis. Unfortunately, infection, thrombosis, and aneurysm formation also occur in the arteriovenous fistula, particularly in prosthetic devices. There is a relatively high incidence of septicemia and septic embolization associated with shunt and fistula infection; the most common infecting agent is *Staphylococcus aureus*.

In addition, a significant psychological impact is related to the failure of the AV fistula. Depression and altered self-image are other common psychiatric problems. The rapid flux in osmolality may cause a disequilibrium syndrome, while rapid changes in electrolytes (particularly potassium) may lead to arrhythmia during dialysis. Hypotension is a common phenomenon during hemodialysis and is due to many factors—the size of the extracorporeal circulation, degree of ultrafiltration, change in serum osmolality, presence of autonomic neuropathy, concomitant use of antihypertensive agents, removal of catecholamines, or infusion of acetate (used as the dialysate buffer) which is a cardiac depressant and vasodilator. Syndromes of dialysis dementia and osteomalacia may be secondary to aluminum contamination of dialysate water or from oral intake of aluminum hydroxide. An increased incidence of HB-S (hepatitis B–surface) antigenemia is related to decreased immunologic integrity. Patients with chronic antigenemia are usually asymptomatic and have little derangement of liver function. There is a higher rate of non-A, non-B hepatitis and cytomegalovirus infection, but these, too, are usually of mild degree. Mechanical and/or iatrogenic complications such as hemolysis, air embolus, blood leaks, and contaminated dialysate have become less common with improved equipment. Device-induced adverse reactions may occur, as exemplified by complement-mediated leukopenia and hypoxemia due to exposure of blood to cellophane. More prominent symptoms such as back and chest pain, bronchospasm, and anaphylaxis may rarely occur in this reaction. Heparin, necessary during the hemodialysis procedure, may lead to complications such as subdural hematoma and retroperitoneal, gastrointestinal, pericardial, and pleural hemorrhage. One of the major concerns in long-term dialysis patients is the high incidence of mortality related to myocardial infarction and cerebral vascular accidents. These are likely due to the preexistence and continuation of common risk factors in the uremic patient such as hypertension, hyperlipidemia, vascular calcification due to hyperparathyroidism, and high cardiac output due to anemia or other factors. The potential for complications should cause the physician to evaluate the risk/benefit ratio with dialysis treatment before proceeding in the individual patient. Advantages of hemodialysis are the relatively short treatment time and minimal interruption of lifestyle between treatments. It is more efficient than peritoneal dialysis, allowing rapid changes in abnormal serum values. Hemodialysis can be performed in the home, but the patient requires an assistant during treatment. It is the most widely available form of dialysis.

PERITONEAL DIALYSIS Peritoneal dialysis, like hemodialysis, may be performed in various settings and with a number of different techniques. In patients with acute renal failure, peritoneal dialysis is usually performed by placement of a stylet-type catheter, and peritoneal lavage is constantly performed for 24 to 72 h. One- to two-liter exchanges every 20 to 60 min can be carried out until the desired clinical and/or chemical improvements are achieved. The catheter is then removed and the patient observed until symptoms or laboratory results dictate the need for a further 1 to 3 days of peritoneal dialysis. Chronic peritoneal dialysis has been attempted since the late 1940s but was relatively unsuccessful until development of a permanent peritoneal catheter in 1968—the Tenckhoff catheter. Use of this indwelling catheter and closed continuous-cycle dialysate delivery equipment led to treatment protocols with which patients were treated 2 to 3 times per week for a total of 30 to 40 h (intermittent peritoneal dialysis—IPD) to achieve clearances and fluid removal similar to those of hemodialysis. In 1978, the concept of constant peritoneal lavage with prolonged dwell times led to the development of CAPD, which differs from intermittent peritoneal dialysis in that patients instill fluid into the peritoneal cavity, seal the catheter, continue in an ambulatory mode, and every 4 to 6 h empty the peritoneal cavity and replace the dialysate. This technique utilizes 2-liter containers of dialysate and obviates the need for dialysis equipment. Modification of the technique using a cyclic dialysate delivery device to exchange dialysate during the night with chronic dwelling of fluid during the waking hours (CCPD) may be more acceptable to some patients.

Twenty-four– to seventy-two–hour acute peritoneal dialysis using a stylet-catheter is usually performed in a hospital setting. IPD or CCPD may be performed in a center or at home (usually overnight), while CAPD can be performed anywhere. As with hemodialysis, the composition of the dialysate can be modified to accommodate ultrafiltration and clearance needs. The major difference in peritoneal dialysate formulas is the larger quantity of dextrose used as an osmotic agent to achieve fluid removal. Advantages of peritoneal dialysis are avoidance of heparinization and vascular surgery and a slower clearance rate which may be advantageous in some patients with cardiovascular instability. It is more amenable to total self-treatment. Disadvantages include the longer treatment time—either longer periods intermittently or continuous involvement. It should not be used in patients with recent abdominal surgery or pulmonary compromise. Inadequate clearance may occur in some patients, e.g., those with scleroderma, vasculitis, malignant hypertension, or any disease involving the peritoneum. Complications include catheter tunnel infection, peritonitis, moderate protein loss, hypertriglyceridemia, hypercholesterolemia, obesity, and inguinal and abdominal hernias. CAPD requires a higher degree of patient compliance and has a higher rate of peritonitis than intermittent peritoneal dialysis because of multiple entries into the system, but is the predominant form of peritoneal dialysis.

RESULTS At the end of 1983, approximately 72,000 patients were on chronic dialysis, while over the past 15 years, nearly 55,000 patients have undergone renal transplantation in the United States. Approximately 85 to 90 percent of patients are on hemodialysis, while 15 percent perform some type of peritoneal dialysis. Of all new patients with end-stage renal disease, approximately 35 to 50 percent are physically and psychologically suitable for renal transplantation. Many of these patients are sensitized with high antibody titers and are on hemodialysis and peritoneal dialysis awaiting availability of a cadaver kidney. An acutely ill or medically complicated patient will likely undergo dialysis in a hospital dialysis unit or intensive care unit, while stable patients may be dialyzed as outpatients in the hospital dialysis unit, in an out-of-hospital dialysis center, or at home. Most centers attempt to have patients participate in their own care, so-called self-dialysis. Approximatley 14,000 patients were performing home dialysis at the end of 1983, this number representing 12 to 40 percent of all patients on dialysis, depending upon the area of the country and factors such as population density, economics, and social issues. Home dialysis (either hemodialysis or peritoneal) is preferable for many because of self-reliance and freedom from hospital or center dialysis schedules. Patient motivation is the primary factor in selection of home or in-center self-dialysis. Dialysis performed in the hospital setting is most expensive, while home dialysis with a nonpaid family assistant or alone (peritoneal dialysis only) is somewhat less expensive than in-center dialysis. Despite absence of equipment, peritoneal dialysis remains equally as expensive as home hemodialysis because of the cost of dialysate and hospitalization related to an increased incidence of peritonitis.

The mean age for patients on dialysis is the late fifties, partly because nephrosclerosis and eventual renal failure from other parenchymal diseases occur in older patients, but more likely because the selection process favors transplantation in younger patients.

Approximately 10 to 20 percent of patients with chronic renal failure are totally rehabilitated by dialysis, and another 30 to 40 percent of nondiabetic patients may be expected to be rehabilitated to a functional status even if not employed. Twenty percent of patients will be returned to a level of function not considered rehabilitated but able to care for themselves. The remainder (approximately 20 percent) are fully dependent on support from others. Diabetics, who have a rehabilitation rate and survival rate significantly lower than that of nondiabetic patients, make up much of the latter two groups. Determination of mortality rates is variable because of age and the disease process; however, most chronic dialysis programs have annual mortality rates of approximately 5 to 10 percent per year.

TRANSPLANTATION

Transplantation of the human kidney has become a justified procedure for the treatment of advanced chronic renal failure. Worldwide, tens of thousands of such procedures have been performed and occur at the rate of 50 to more than 100 per year in some medical centers. When azathioprine (Imuran) and prednisone are used as immunosuppresive drugs, the results with properly matched familial donors are superior to those obtained with organs from cadaveric donors, with 75 to 90 percent compared to 50 to 60 percent graft survival rates at 1 year, respectively. When antilymphocyte globulins (ALG) have been added to the treatment regimens in some centers, the results with cadaveric donors have approached those with living related donors, at least for the initial 1 to 2 years after transplantation. Most recently, the new fungal endecapeptide cyclosporine has significantly improved 1-year cadaveric survival rates to the 80 percent range, when used along with prednisone in place of azathioprine and ALG. With all therapies, the rate of graft loss from rejection is much slower after the first year, although occasionally an acute irreversible rejection episode may occur after many months of good function. This is especially likely if the patient neglects to take the immunosuppressive drugs. There has been a most striking improvement in clinical renal transplant results in recent years in patient morbidity and mortality rates, the latter declining to less than 5 percent in a number of centers. These findings represent an increasing tendency on the part of transplant teams to decrease immunosuppressive therapy so that in the case of severe rejection the kidney rather than the patient is lost. The beneficial effects of blood transfusions in the preconditioning of potential recipients are clearly established. Nontransfused recipients are at highest risk for rejecting their grafts, while multiple random transfusions or transfusions from specific donors can greatly improve chances for graft survival. An increasing number of second and even third transplants are being performed, and the overall results show only a 10 to 20 percent reduction in expected survival compared to first transplants; in other words, rejection of a graft does not necessarily prejudice the results of another transplant attempt.

DONOR SELECTION Donor sources are cadavers or volunteer blood-related living donors. Living volunteer donors should be normal on physical examination and of the same major ABO blood group, because there is good evidence that crossing major blood group barriers prejudices survival of the allograft. It is, however, possible to transplant a kidney of a type O donor into an A, B, or AB recipient. Selective renal arteriography should be performed on volunteer donors to rule out the presence of multiple or abnormal renal arteries, because the surgical procedure is inordinately difficult and the ischemic time of the transplanted kidney prohibitively long when vascular abnormalities exist. Cadaveric donors should be free of malignant neoplastic disease because of the possible transmission of cancer to the recipient.

A coordinated regional or national system of computerized information sharing and logistical support for the transportation of cadaver kidneys to suitable recipients is under development. It is now possible to remove cadaver kidneys and to maintain them for over 48 h on cold pulsatile perfusion or simple flushing and cooling. This permits adequate time for various typing, cross matching, transportation, and selection problems to be solved.

TISSUE TYPING AND CLINICAL IMMUNOGENETICS Matching for antigens of the HLA major histocompatibility gene complex (Chap. 63) has long been accepted as an ideal criterion for selection of donors for renal allografts. Each mammalian species studied has shown evidence for a single chromosomal region which encodes the strong, or major, transplantation antigens, and the analogous sixth chromosomal region is called *HLA* in human beings. Other antigens, called "minor," may nevertheless play crucial roles, especially the ABH(O) blood groups and an endothelial antigen which is shared with blood monocytes, but not lymphocytes. Evidence for designation of HLA as the genetic region encoding strong transplantation antigens comes from the success rate in living related donor renal and bone marrow transplantation, with superior results in HLA-identical sibling pairs. Nevertheless, 10 to 15 percent of HLA-identical renal allografts are rejected, often within the first weeks after transplantation. It is likely, though not proved, that these failures represent states of prior sensitization to non-HLA antigens. Non-HLA antigens are relatively weak and therefore suppressible by conventional immunosuppressive therapy. Once priming has occurred, however, secondary responses are much more refractory to treatment. In fact, ABH incompatibilities are hazardous because of the presence of natural anti-A and anti-B antibodies.

Living related donors For more than two decades, during which time azathioprine was the mainstay immunosuppressive drug, living related donors provided superior graft survivals. Among first-degree relatives, the general level of expected graft success was in direct proportion to matching for 2,1, or no HLA haplotypes, as defined by HLA serologic typing and the presence or absence of a proliferative response in the mixed lymphocyte response (MLR) (Chap. 63). HLA-incompatible siblings did barely better than the overall average with cadaveric donors (50 to 60 percent at 1 year), while HLA semi-identicals (haploidentical) were in the 70 to 75 percent range. Intrafamilial MLRs among haploidenticals were found to be a measure of responsiveness. Low responder donor-recipient pairs had a 1-year graft survival rate of 90 percent, while vigorous responders were at the level of 55 percent unless donor-specific blood transfusions were given to eliminate this disadvantage. The MLR is a relatively imprecise technique, but it has been repeatedly shown that for both living related and cadaveric donors, MLR reactivity with a specific donor is more predictive of graft outcome than serologic typing for HLA-A, -B, -C, or -DR antigens. Cyclosporine is having a major impact upon the assumption that living related donors are generally superior to cadaveric donors, because in most recent series the improvement in cadaveric results rivals the 80 percent 1-year result previously attained only with haploidentical relatives. One must now weigh the choices in light of the availability of organs and waiting times on dialysis, rather than on the initial rate of graft success. It must be pointed out that long-term survival rates, comparing the various donor types and treatment protocols, have yet to be discerned. With azathioprine, the half-life of graft function after the first year is 34 years with HLA-identical donors, 11½ years with haploidentical donors, and 7 years with cadaveric donors. Long-term use of cyclosporine, assuming that cumulative nephrotoxicity is not a problem, may or may not sustain a high rate of survival.

Cadaveric donors   For first transplants receiving cyclosporine overall success rate for unrelated donors is 80 percent of grafts functioning at 1 year. It has been extremely difficult to assess the role of HLA matching in cadaveric donor grafting because of considerable variation in overall results from center to center, including, until recently, relatively high mortality rates. The so-called full-house match of two HLA-A and two HLA-B antigens between unrelated individuals does not ensure matching for other loci adjacent to HLA-A and -B, in contrast to first-degree relatives where the HLA-A and -B antigens are excellent markers for the other linked loci. The degree to which two-A and two-B antigen matching improves cadaveric renal graft survival is in the range of 10 percent and is most likely attributable to the fact that some of these matches will also include compatibility for HLA-D because of the nonrandomness of the association of linked alleles (linkage disequilibrium) in the population (Chap. 63). The more racially homogeneous the population, the greater the chances that any given marker will be in linkage disequilibrium with another.

Rapid assessment of MLR (e.g., within 24 h) is not possible; therefore, serologic techniques are used to approximate degrees of compatibility. Of the class II HLA molecules, DP, DQ, and DR, the last plays the major role in the MLR; indeed, matching for DR provides the most significant improvement in cadaveric renal transplantation. Pooled data from all over the world from over 5000 cadaveric transplants show a 20 percent improvement when the two DR antigens are matched compared to cases when both are mismatched. In addition, when HLA-B antigens are also matched, there is further improvement. The likelihood of obtaining a DR match depends upon the size of the waiting pool, and also on the willingness of transplant centers to share organs on this basis. A 20-percent DR match rate has been readily achieved in some transplant programs. Data on the impact of cyclosporine on the role of HLA matching show that it is additive to HLA-B and -DR matching. As results are improved by multiple approaches (therapy, matching, blood transfusions), it becomes more difficult to discern which factors may or may not be additive. A greater than 90 percent success rate for cadaveric grafts has not as yet been claimed, however.

Presensitization   A positive cross match of recipient serum with donor T lymphocytes representing anti-HLA class I is usually predictive of an acute vasculitic event termed *hyperacute* rejection. A few years ago it was thought that patients making such antibodies against a surrogate panel of normal lymphocytes were at high risk for accelerated, if not hyperacute, rejection, even when the donor-specific cross match was negative. That this is no longer so can be attributed to the greater efforts being made in monitoring patients on dialysis, defining not only the presence or absence of antibodies but also the HLA antigens to which they are directed. Patients with anti-HLA antibodies can be safely transplanted if careful cross matching is performed. Patients sustained by hemodialysis often show fluctuating antibody titers and specificity patterns, sometimes, but not always, temporally related to receipt of blood transfusions. At the time of assignment of a cadaveric kidney, cross matches are performed with more than one highly reactive serum, and the previously analyzed antibody specificities are also taken into account. It has recently been found that anti-HLA antibody responses do not necessarily recur

several months later when the incompatible antigen is given in a blood product transfusion. Indeed, it seems relatively safe to ignore positive cross matches with sera kept in storage for several months as long as recent sera are negative. The loss of anamnesis to HLA by chronic dialysis patients may result from development of specific unresponsiveness due to suppressor cell activation, or from anti-idiotypic immunity. Presensitization to antigens expressed on B lymphocytes, but not T lymphocytes, is not a contraindication to transplantation. Some of these antibodies are anti-DR, while others are non-HLA IgM antibodies active in the cold and at room temperature, but apparently not relevant to graft survival.

Endothelial-monocyte system   In some cases of unexpected accelerated rejection, antibodies with reactivity to renal endothelium and blood monocytes have been found, both in the circulation and in eluates from rejected grafts. Practical aspects of typing and cross matching for this non-HLA system are difficult. Second transplants following rapid loss of the first graft seem to be particularly at risk.

Overview of transplantation immunogenetics   In addition to the ABH(O) blood groups, the important histocompatibility antigens presently known are HLA-A, -B, -C, -DR, and the endothelial-monocyte system (Table 221-2). The best current data suggest that major immunogenicity lies in the DR antigens, while A, B, C, and endothelial-monocyte antigens provide the major targets for effector IgG, and in the case of A, B, and C, at least, for killer T lymphocytes. Hence the current emphasis is on A, B, and C cross matching and DR matching.

Blood transfusions   At a time when it appeared that transfusion-induced sensitization against a random lymphocyte panel was predictive of a high graft failure rate, a number of transplantation units undertook a policy of withholding blood from as many dialysis patients as possible. The clinical need for blood was found to be less than originally thought, especially in nonnephrectomized patients, and avoidance of possible exposure to hepatitis was also a consideration. The overall experience with the nontransfused patients has been a dramatic one, confirmed many times over: such patients are at the *highest risk* for graft failure. Still at issue is the number of transfused units needed for optimal graft survival, with the bulk of the evidence showing that more than 5 units is optimal, although some studies claim an effect with 1 or 2 units, given in advance or at the time of transplantation. Data are presently lacking on the question of using fresh vs. frozen vs. washed cells, as well as the precise methods of storage employed. As in many areas of clinical transplantation, there are not a sufficient number of cases and/or carefully randomized trials. Nevertheless, the large number of cases included in prospective studies has already provided impressive overall evidence that avoidance of blood exposure reduces graft success rate by 20 to 30 percent.

The mechanisms of the transfusion effect are unknown but may involve a selection process of screening out responders to certain HLA antigens, or, alternatively, transfusions may induce states of specific suppression. Assessment of the combined effects of transfusions and DR matching shows that they are not additive. If there is a good match for HLA-DR antigens, prior priming to induce low responsiveness appears to be unnecessary. Alternatively, if the recipient is exposed to multiple units of blood, HLA-DR matching adds no further benefit. Living donor haploidentical grafts also benefit from blood transfusions. In particular, the use of blood from the intended donor on three occasions prior to transplantation results in superior graft survival in those 70 percent of recipients who do not become sensitized to HLA. Part of the effect is one of selection of antibody nonresponders; in addition, it is likely that specific suppression is induced. The preliminary data with donor-specific transfusions show a success rate of greater than 90 percent at 1 year, in the range attained by HLA identical grafts. Again, experience with cyclosporine may alter the impact of blood transfusion policies, but firm data are currently unavailable.

TABLE 221-2   Histocompatibility in renal transplantation

RELATIVE IMPORTANCE OF TYPING AND CROSS MATCHING FOR SEROLOGICALLY DEFINED ANTIGENS

Antigens	Typing (antigen matching)	Cross matching
Class I (HLA-A, -B, -C)	+	+ + +
Class II (HLA-DR)	+ + +	−
Endothelial-monocyte (non-HLA)	? −	+ + +

IMMUNOLOGY OF REJECTION Knowledge of the immunology of tissue transplantation stems largely from animal experimentation. However, enough evidence has accumulated in humans, particularly in kidney transplantation, to indicate that the evidence is similar though not identical for the different species. The immunologic mechanisms are not qualitatively different from those found in other areas of immunology (Chap. 62). The evidence is that early rejection is associated with T lymphocytes having direct specificity against donor antigens. These may be cytotoxic cells (T8 + or T4 +) or cells which mediate DTH (T4 +); however, significant numbers of B lymphocytes, null cells, natural killer (NK) cells, and macrophages appear in the early infiltrate, and cells capable of mediating antibody-dependent cell-mediated cytotoxicity (ADCC) are also present (Fig. 221-3). Many of the B lymphocytes produce immunoglobulins. The spectrum of cellular and humoral response and graft injury is quite varied, depending upon specific genetic differences between donor and recipient and states of presensitization. The greater the degree of presensitization, the more likely it is that one will find antibody-mediated vascular lesions. All of the processes shown in Fig. 221-3 are possible, but their relative contribution varies from case to case. Further dissection of the heterogeneity of the human allograft response, utilizing newer techniques for identification of lymphocyte subsets, is adding to the value of graft biopsy as a guide to therapy and prognosis. Monitoring of peripheral blood lymphocyte subsets, utilizing monoclonal antibodies (Chap. 62) to functionally related surface molecules, such as T4 (T-helper cells) and T8 (T-suppressor cells), has been related to the degree of rejection activity in some surveys, but the T4/T8 ratio has not always been clinically meaningful. Part of the problem may lie in the fact that these subsets are not as uniquely related to function as originally believed. Finally, the cytokine mediators of the cellular immune response (IL 1, IL 2, IL 3, IFNγ) (Chap. 62) have been shown to be importantly involved in the control and expression of the alloimmune rejection response. For example, T-cell production of IFNγ causes increased expression of HLA antigens upon endothelial cells. In normal immunobiology this effect may be to promote more efficient presentation of foreign antigen, while in the transplantation it enhances the immunogenicity of the vascularized transplant.

The failure of transplanted kidneys after 2 or even 3 years of adequate function is due to a form of "chronic rejection." In such kidneys the development of nephrosclerosis, with proliferation of the vascular intima of renal vessels, and intimal fibrosis, with marked decrease in the lumen of the vessels, takes place (Fig. 221-4). The result is renal ischemia, hypertension, widespread tubular atrophy, interstitial fibrosis, and glomerular atrophy with eventual renal failure.

IMMUNOSUPPRESSIVE TREATMENT When histocompatibility differences exist between donor and recipient, it is necessary to modify or suppress the immune response in order to enable the recipient to accept a graft. Immunosuppressive therapy, in general, suppresses all immune responses, including those to bacteria, fungi, and even malignant tumors. In the 1950s when clinical renal transplantation began, sublethal total-body irradiation was employed. Currently, immunosuppression is more safely induced pharmacologically. Agents used in humans to suppress the immune response are discussed in the following paragraphs.

Drugs *Azathioprine* (Imuran), an analogue of mercaptopurine, is the keystone to immunosuppressive therapy in humans. This agent can inhibit synthesis of deoxyribonucleic acid (DNA), ribonucleic acid (RNA), or both. Because cell division and proliferation are a necessary part of the immune response to antigenic stimulation, suppression by this agent may be mediated by the inhibition of mitosis of immunologically competent lymphoid cells, interfering with synthesis of DNA. Alternatively, immunosuppression may be brought about by blocking the synthesis of RNA (possibly messenger RNA), to inhibit processing of antigens prior to lymphocyte stimulation. Azathioprine metabolites block the formation of rosettes by T cells with sheep red blood cells. This latter phenomenon is produced by

receptors on the T11 molecule, which is part of a system for activating T cells. This drug has little effect in suppressing a secondary immune response, however. Therapy with azathioprine is generally instituted 2 days prior to transplantation in the recipient of a living donor kidney and on the day of transplantation in the case of a cadaveric donor kidney recipient at a level of 4 mg/kg per day. The drug is later tapered to levels of 1.5 to 3 mg/kg per day, as long as the allograft functions. Because the drug is rapidly metabolized by the liver, its dosage need not be varied directly in relation to renal function, even though renal failure results in retention of the metabolites of azathioprine. Some patients are unusually sensitive to this drug, particularly when renal function is compromised, and reduction in dosage is required because of leukopenia and occasionally thrombocytopenia. Excessive amounts of azathioprine may also cause jaundice, anemia, and alopecia. If it is essential to administer allopurinol concurrently, the azathioprine dose must be drastically reduced, since inhibition of xanthine oxidase delays degradation. This combination is best avoided.

The *glucocorticosteroids* are important adjuncts to immunosuppressive therapy. Of all the agents employed, prednisone has effects that are easiest to assess, and in large doses it is unquestionably the most effective agent for the reversal of rejection. In general, 30 to 40 mg prednisone is given immediately prior to or at the time of

FIGURE 221-3 *Overall scheme of the development of effector mechanisms in graft rejection. Bone marrow stem cells differentiate under the influence of the thymus gland into mature thymus-derived (T) lymphocytes, or under the influence of an equivalent to the avian bursa of Fabricius into mature bone marrow–derived (B) lymphocytes. Exposure to antigen (Δ) results in an interaction between T cells and B cells, and often involves macrophages. The sensitized B cells, after mitoses, develop into immunoglobulin-secreting cells (e.g., plasma cells), illustrated here by IgG and IgM. Such immunoglobulins may form immune complexes with antigen in the circulation which activate the complement sequence, or they may react directly with antigens on the blood vessel surface. Elaboration of secondary mediators, including the products of complement activation, results in vascular damage as illustrated. Sensitized T lymphocytes are the primary effector cells in cell-mediated immunity (CMI) and may react directly with antigens in the graft to exert a cytotoxic effect. In addition, T cells release factors, such as macrophage migration inhibition factor (MIF), which may accelerate the rate of mononuclear cell infiltration. This process is similar to delayed-type hypersensitivity (DTH). It has also been shown that unsensitized non-T cells (K cells) can be activated to exert cytotoxic effects by the fixation of IgG to target cells, followed by interaction of the IgG (Fc portion) with a receptor on the K cell. Finally, platelet aggregation and thrombosis can occur following the endothelial damage induced by any of these mechanisms.*

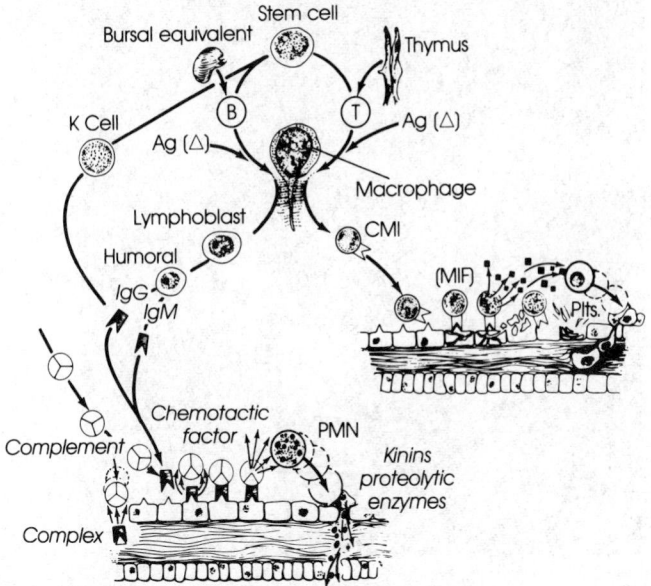

transplantation, and the dosage is gradually reduced. The well-known side effects of the glucocorticosteroids, particularly impairment of wound healing and predisposition to infection, make it desirable to taper the dose as rapidly as possible in the immediate postoperative period. Customarily methylprednisolone, 1 to 2 g intravenously, is administered immediately upon diagnosis of beginning rejection and continued once daily for 3 days. When the drug is effective, the results are usually apparent within 48 to 96 h. Such "pulse" doses are less effective in the slow rejection process, which may not become apparent until 2 to 3 years after transplantation. Most patients whose renal function is stable after 6 months or a year do not require large doses of prednisone; maintenance doses of 15 or 20 mg per day are the rule. Many patients tolerate an alternate-day course of steroids better than daily doses without an increased risk of rejection.

A major effect of steroids is upon the monocyte/macrophage system, preventing the release of IL 1. Although lymphopenia results from large doses of corticosteroids, this is primarily due to sequestration of recirculating blood lymphocytes to lymphoid tissue.

When jaundice or nephritis appears in patients maintained on azathioprine, *cyclophosphamide* may be substituted. It appears to be as effective in the maintenance of renal allografts as azathioprine and somewhat more effective in hepatic allografts. Leukopenia, alopecia, cystitis, ovarian fibrosis, and aspermia may result if the dosage is not carefully regulated. Prospective cadaveric *donors* have been treated with massive doses of cyclophosphamide and methylprednisolone in an attempt to decrease the antigenicity of the graft by

FIGURE 221-4 *Biopsy of the renal cadaveric allograft illustrating obliterative endarteritis. Loss of the media is associated with intimal thickening. The elastic tissue shows dissolution of the elastica. The evidence for arteritis with subsequent thrombosis is typically the gaps in the elastica and media. The intimal thickening probably represents organization of a thrombus formed in response to the arteritis. [From GJ Dammin, JP Merrill, in Structural Basis for Renal Disease, EL Becker (ed), New York, Hoeber-Harper, 1968.]*

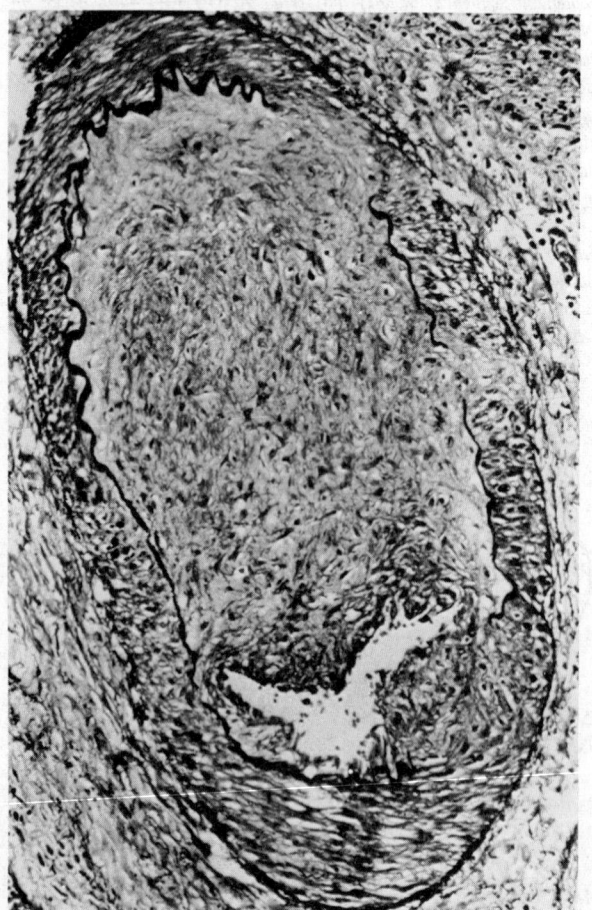

eliminating "passenger leukocytes." The results of this technique are somewhat uncertain.

Cyclosporine A is a fungal peptide having potent immunosuppressive activity in animals and in in vitro systems. It appears to have a preferential effect upon early activation of helper-inducer T lymphocytes, thereby augmenting suppressor T-cell responses. Assessment of this agent in human renal transplantation has generally shown that it works well only in conjunction with corticosteroids. Since cyclosporine blocks production of IL 2 by helper-inducer (T4 +) T cells, its combination with steroids is expected to produce a double block in the macrophage → IL 1 → T cell → IL 2 sequence. As noted, clinical results with several hundreds of renal transplants have been impressive. Of all its toxic effects (nephrotoxicity, hepatotoxicity, hirsutism, tremor, gingival hyperplasia), only nephrotoxicity presents a serious management problem, and is discussed further below.

Antilymphocyte globulin (ALG)   When serum from animals made immune to host lymphocytes is injected into the recipient, a marked suppression of cellular immunity to the tissue graft results. The action upon cell-mediated immunity is considerably greater than upon humoral immunity. A globulin fraction of the serum is the agent generally employed. For use in humans, peripheral human lymphocytes, thymocytes, or lymphocytes from spleens or thoracic duct fistulas have been injected into horses, rabbits, or goats to produce antilymphocyte serum, from which the globulin fraction is then separated. Although ALG, or ATG (antithymocyte globulin), is unquestionably effective in prolonging grafts in experimental animals, its efficacy in the transplantation of human tissue is somewhat less clear, as it varies from source to source. Heterologous antibody against defined T-lymphocyte subsets, in the form of mouse antihuman monoclonal IgG, may offer a more precise approach to this form of therapy. Two such antibodies, OKT3 and anti-T12, directed against molecules expressed on virtually all mature T lymphocytes, have undergone initial trials in reversal of established rejection episodes. OKT3, while somewhat toxic initially, is generally effective, while anti-T12 does not work in all circumstances. These are considered prototypes of reagents having improved selectivity for immunologic manipulation in the future.

Other techniques   Among other techniques of immunosuppression, thymectomy and splenectomy have not been widely accepted. Local irradiation of the transplanted kidney in two or three doses of 3500 mGy (350 rads) has also been utilized. This technique may result in fewer early rejection episodes in cadaveric transplants than in nonirradiated controls. Fractional total-lymph-node irradiation (TLI), as employed in the therapy of Hodgkin's disease, is an interesting new modality currently under investigation.

CLINICAL COURSE AND MANAGEMENT OF THE RECIPIENT

Bilateral nephrectomy at some point prior to transplantation is performed for a specific cause but not as a routine. Hypertension which is difficult to control or infection involving the end-stage kidneys are the two most common indications. Nephrectomized patients maintain a much lower hematocrit level, but this is no longer considered a disadvantage per se, because blood transfusions need not be avoided in preparation for transplantation. Difficulties do arise when these multiply transfused patients become sensitized and must remain on dialysis. Nephrectomy per se does not appear to affect the survival of subsequent renal allografts.

Adequate hemodialysis should be performed within 48 h of surgery, and care should be taken that the serum potassium level is not markedly elevated so that intraoperative cardiac arrhythmias can be averted. The diuresis that commonly occurs postoperatively must be carefully monitored; in many instances it may be massive, reflecting the inability of ischemic tubules to regulate sodium and water excretion. Massive potassium losses may occur and occasionally result in cardiac arrhythmias. Most chronically uremic patients have some excess of extracellular fluid, and some degree of negative balance should be accomplished, provided circulatory hemodynamics remain stable. Acute tubular necrosis (ATN) may cause immediate oliguria or may follow an initial short period of graft function. ATN is most likely to occur when cadaveric donors have been hypotensive, or if the interval between cessation of blood flow and organ harvest (warm ischemic time) has been more than a few minutes. Recovery usually occurs within 3 weeks, although periods as long as 6 weeks have been reported. Superimposition of rejection upon ATN is common, and the differential diagnosis may be difficult. Cyclosporine therapy aggravates ATN, and some patients do not diurese until they are converted to azathioprine.

The rejection episode Early diagnosis of rejection allows prompt institution of therapy to preserve renal function and prevent irreversible damage due to fibrosis. Clinical evidence of rejection may be characterized by fever, swelling, and tenderness over the allograft, and by significant reduction in urine volume. In patients whose renal function is good initially, oliguria may be accompanied by decreased urinary sodium concentration and increased osmolarity. These changes may not be present in the more chronic stages of rejection or when renal function is impaired at the onset of rejection.

Arteriography and radioactive iodohippurate sodium (Hippuran) renograms of the transplanted kidney may be useful in ascertaining changes in the renal vasculature and in renal blood flow, even in the absence of urinary flow. Diagnostic ultrasound has become the procedure of choice to rule out urinary obstruction or to confirm the presence of perirenal collections of urine, blood, or lymph. When renal function has been good initially, a rise in the serum creatinine level and a decrease in the creatinine clearance is the most sensitive and reliable indicator of rejection.

Cyclosporine may cause deterioration in renal function in a manner similar to a rejection episode. In fact, rejection processes tend to be more indolent with cyclosporine, and the only way to make a diagnosis may be by renal biopsy. There is no universally accepted lesion(s) which makes a diagnosis of cyclosporine toxicity, although interstitial fibrosis and thickening of arteriolar walls have been noted by some pathologists. Basically, if the biopsy does not reveal moderate and active cellular rejection activity, the serum creatinine will most likely respond to a reduction in cyclosporine dose. Blood levels of drug can be useful if very high or very low, but precise correlation with renal function does not exist. If rejection activity is present in the biopsy, appropriate therapy is indicated.

Management problems Modification of the usual clinical manifestations of infection by immunosuppressive therapy is a major problem in the posttransplant period. The signs and symptoms of infection may be masked and distorted, and fever without obvious cause is common. Only after days or weeks will it become apparent that it has a viral or fungal origin. The importance of blood cultures in such patients cannot be overemphasized, because systemic infection without obvious foci is frequent, although wound infections with or without urinary fistulas are most common. Particularly important are rapidly occurring pulmonary lesions, which may result in death within 5 days of onset. When these become apparent, immunosuppressive agents should be discontinued except for maintenance doses of prednisone. The major toxic effect of azathioprine is bone marrow suppression, while cyclosporine has no marrow effects. They both may predispose to unusual opportunistic infections, however. In the case of *Pneumocystis carinii* (Chap. 158) trimethoprim-sulfamethoxazole is the treatment of choice; amphotericin B has been used effectively in systemic fungal infections. Involvement of the oropharynx with *Candida* (Chap. 147) may be treated with local nystatin. Small doses (a total of 300 mg) of amphotericin given over a period of 2 weeks may be effective in refractory oral candidiasis. *Aspergillus* (Chap. 147), *Nocardia* (Chap. 146), and cytomegalovirus (CMV) (Chap. 137) infections also occur. The latter are particularly common

in transplant recipients, and active CMV infection is frequently associated with rejection episodes. The complications of corticosteroid therapy are well known and include gastrointestinal bleeding, impairment of wound healing, osteoporosis, diabetes, cataract formation, and hemorrhagic pancreatitis. The treatment of jaundice in transplant patients should include cessation of azathioprine or cyclosporine therapy. It is surprising that total cessation of azathioprine therapy often does not result in rejection of a graft. In some instances of jaundice, cyclophosphamide may be substituted for azathioprine. Antiplatelet agents and anticoagulants, although effective in theory, have not been successful in the prevention of the chronic vascular lesion. Persistent elevations of serum creatinine levels above 2.5 mg/dL in patients maintained on cyclosporine may be an indication for conversion to azathioprine, particularly if reduction in dose provokes either rejection activity or toxicity. Another indication for conversion would be in the patient recovering from a series of infections developing while cyclosporine is being administered. Our own experience with such conversions between 4 and 8 months after transplantation has been quite satisfactory; however, 30 percent of patients had temporally related rejection episodes requiring additional steroid therapy. Subsequent follow-up showed improved renal function in most cases. Hence, if the nephrotoxic potential of cyclosporine should indeed grow with each passing year, conversion to azathioprine remains an option.

In spite of the potential teratogenic effects of immunosuppressive agents, both women and men have become parents after transplantation. The incidence of congenital abnormalities in the offspring is not unusual.

Glomerular lesions Even identical twins who do not require immunosuppression may develop glomerular lesions after transplantation. These represent recurrence of a glomerulonephritic process. Glomerular lesions may occur in 10 to 15 percent of allografts, even when the original disease was accidental removal of a solitary kidney. The pathogenesis is related to a chronic rejection process. In other cases the lesions resemble those of the patient's own original disease. The recurrence of the nephrotic syndrome with "nil disease" in transplanted kidneys whose recipient's original nil disease had progressed to renal failure with focal sclerosis, and the recurrence in renal allografts of the classic lesions of IgA nephropathy and of membranoproliferative glomerulonephritis with electron-dense deposit disease are classic examples. In the last of these, the incidence of recurrence has been reported to be as high as 30 to 40 percent. In most instances, however, the recurrence of the original renal lesions represents no threat to the patient's immediate prognosis, and a primary diagnosis of glomerulonephritis is rarely taken as a contraindication to transplantation.

Malignancy The incidence of tumors arising in patients on immunosuppressive therapy is 5 to 6 percent, or approximately 100 times greater than that observed in the general population in the same age range. The most common lesions are cancer of the skin and lips and carcinoma in situ of the cervix, as well as lymphomas, particularly reticulum cell sarcoma in the central nervous system and gastrointestinal tract.

Other complications *Hypercalcemia* after transplantation may indicate failure of hyperplastic parathyroid glands to regress. Aseptic necrosis of the head of the femur is probably due to preexisting hyperparathyroidism. With improved management of calcium and phosphorus metabolism during chronic dialysis the incidence of parathyroid-related complications has fallen dramatically.

Both chronic dialysis and renal transplant patients have a higher incidence of death from myocardial infarction and stroke than in the population at large, and this is particularly true in diabetics. Contributing factors are hypertension and hypertriglyceridemia. Depressed high-density lipoprotein cholesterol (HDL) concentrations in dialysis patients may persist after transplantation.

REFERENCES

CARPENTER CB, MILFORD EL: Renal transplantation: Immunobiology, in *The Kidney*, 3d ed, B Brenner, F Rector (eds). Philadelphia, Saunders, 1986, p 1907

COHEN DJ, LOERTSCHER R et al: Cyclosporine: A new immunosuppressive agent for organ transplantation. Ann Intern Med 101:667, 1984

HAKIM RM, LAZARUS JM: Medical aspects of hemodialysis, in *The Kidney*, 3d ed, B Brenner, F Rector (eds). Philadelphia, Saunders, 1986, p 1791

————: Hemodialysis in acute renal failure, in *Acute Renal Failure*, B Brenner, JM Lazarus (eds). Philadelphia, Saunders, 1983, p 643

LAZARUS JM: Complications in hemodialysis: An overview. Kidney Intern 18:783, 1980

————: Hemodialysis, in *Chronic Renal Failure, Contemporary Issues in Nephrology*, vol 7: B Brenner, J Stein (eds). New York, Churchill-Livingstone, 1981, p 153

MORRIS PJ (ed): *Kidney Transplantation. Principles and Practice*, 2d ed. New York, Grune & Stratton, 1983

NOLPH KD et al: Continuous ambulatory peritoneal dialysis: Three-year experience at one center. Ann Intern Med 92:609, 1980

OPELZ G: Correlation of HLA matching with kidney graft survival in patients with or without cyclosporine treatment. Transplantation 40:240, 1985

STROM TB, TILNEY NL: Renal transplantation: Clinical aspects, in *The Kidney*, 3d ed, B Brenner, FC Rector (eds). Philadelphia, Saunders, 1986, p 1941

222   IMMUNOPATHOGENIC MECHANISMS OF RENAL INJURY

RICHARD J. GLASSOCK / BARRY M. BRENNER

Recognition of the important role played by aberrant immunologic processes in many forms of renal injury, especially those involving the glomerular circulation, constitutes one of the most significant conceptual advances made in the understanding of renal diseases during the last quarter century. Although the fine details of these abnormal processes have been elucidated for many disease entities, large gaps in knowledge still exist concerning both the initiating events and the etiologic factors involved in renal disease.

In its broadest conceptual framework the immunopathogenesis of renal injury can be simplified to a few fundamental mechanisms, which are presented in Chap. 62. One involves the reaction of a circulating antibody with its respective renal antigen in situ. The antigen may be either an intrinsic constituent of the kidney or one which has been bound to the tissue by a particular biochemical or immunologic reaction. Antigens in basement membranes of glomerular capillaries or renal tubules and antibodies to these basement membranes are prime components of this mechanism. A variety of antigenic components of the glomerular capillary walls and renal tubules are now recognized. Binding of circulating antibody to these tissue antigens gives rise to several distinctive structural alterations and immunohistochemical appearances, as will be discussed below. This category of immune processes is often referred to as the *antitissue antibody–mediated diseases*.

Another pathogenic category, by far the most prevalent in human renal disease, involves the localization of circulating macromolecular aggregates composed of antigens and antibodies (i.e., circulating immune complexes) within renal structures, principally glomeruli. This mechanism is referred to as *immune-complex–mediated disease*. The immune complexes need not bear any special immunochemical relationships to renal structures; thus the kidney can be viewed as a passive participant or an innocent party, damaged by processes originating elsewhere. The source of the antigen may be either *endogenous* (*autologous*) or *exogenous* (*environmental*). Further, exogenous antigens may be biologically inert or derived from an organism capable of self-replication (e.g., bacteria, viruses, etc.). Under special circumstances environmental agents may also combine with autologous substances to result in new antigenic compounds (hapten-protein conjugates), which may act in concert with antibodies to form immune complexes. In contrast to the above mechanisms, *cell-mediated* immune processes are far less well established as possible mechanisms in glomerular and vascular diseases of the

kidney. Finally, certain human glomerular diseases are prominently associated with abnormal activation of the *alternative pathway of the complement cascade*.

IMMUNOPATHOGENIC MECHANISMS   Once initiated, immune injury is mediated by the interaction of a number of humoral and cellular factors. Activation of the complement (C) cascade may lead to the direct cytolysis of the cellular constituents of the glomerulus or may lead to the production of biologically active fragments capable of enhancing vascular permeability or attracting polymorphonuclear leukocytes and other cellular constituents. Coagulation may be directly initiated by alterations in the endothelial surface and exposure of collagen matrix, followed by localized platelet aggregation. Interactions between the complement cascade and the coagulation process are numerous and complex. Complement activation may trigger coagulation and vice versa. Activation of the Hageman factor may initiate the kallikrein-kinin system. Potent vasoactive peptides, prostaglandins, and leukotrienes may thus be released and may play a role in alterations in local and systemic hemodynamics observed in conjunction with immunologically induced renal diseases. Polymorphonuclear leukocytes, eosinophils, and monocytes (macrophages) and platelets all may be called forth to participate in immune-mediated injury to varying degrees. Polymorphonuclear leukocytes and monocytes appear to participate in glomerular injury by virtue of their ability to release factors locally which are capable of degrading basement membrane glycoproteins enzymatically and by facilitating the local production of toxic oxygen species (hydroxyl radical and superoxide anion). Activated monocytes may also express a membrane-bound procoagulant, thus fostering local fibrin deposition. Platelet deposition may be involved in the proliferation of glomerular cells via the release of a platelet-derived growth factor or may alter the anionic charge of the capillary wall by local release of cationic proteins, thus facilitating altered glomerular permselectivity. The composite result of these events is to alter the structural and functional integrity of the glomerular capillary and/or peritubular capillary wall, and lead to reduced filtration capacity, enhanced permeability to plasma proteins, and migration of cellular elements (i.e., erythrocytes and leukocytes) outside the intravascular compartment.

ANTITISSUE ANTIBODY–MEDIATED RENAL INJURY   Anti-basement membrane antibody disease   This form of renal injury is relatively rare in humans, accounting for less than 5 percent of all immunologically mediated glomerulonephritides. By mechanisms which remain obscure, autoantibodies (usually of the IgG isotype) which are directed to epitopes on noncollagenous domains of type IV (basement membrane) collagen arise in the circulation. These autoantibodies deposit in basement membranes of the kidney (glomerular basement membrane, GBM, and/or tubular basement membrane, TBM) and on occasion elsewhere (alveolar basement membrane, choroid plexus basement membrane). Since the epitope is a part of a repeating subunit uniformly expressed in basement membrane, the deposits of IgG will appear *linear* when studied by immunofluorescence microscopy (Fig. 222-1A). Electron-dense lattices of antigen and antibody complexes are not seen by electron microscopy. The local interaction of the autoantibody with the fixed and native basement membrane antigen leads to local activation of mediator systems as described above.

Although the activation of the complement cascade facilitates injury by virtue of chemotactic and cytolytic effects, glomerular injury may occur independent of complement activation. Proteinuria results from loss of glomerular anionic residues (see Chap. 40) and by structural defects in the capillary wall. Glomerular filtration rate may decline if the loss of filtering surface area is sufficient to overcome adaptive increases in capillary flows and pressures in remaining nephron units. Leakage of macromolecules and cells such as fibrinogen and monocytes into Bowman's space through gaps in the capillary wall may provoke extracapillary proliferation (crescents) as fibrinogen is polymerized to fibrin and monocytes divide, proliferate, and release monokines locally.

Renal disease due to anti-basement membrane autoantibody production is seen primarily in three circumstances: in connection with glomerulonephritis and pulmonary hemorrhage due to anti-GBM autoantibodies (Goodpasture's syndrome), in idiopathic crescentic glomerulonephritis due to anti-GBM antibodies (without pulmonary hemorrhage), and in idiopathic tubulointerstitial nephritis due to anti-TBM antibody production. In all instances, characteristic findings are present which serve to identify the pathogenic mechanism underlying the disease: (1) circulating autoantibodies reactive with basement membrane antigens in vitro are present; (2) linear deposits of IgG are found in the involved tissue; and (3) eluates of diseased tissue will contain Ig reactive with normal, native basement membrane antigens both in vivo and in vitro.

Other nonglomerular basement membrane–related antitissue antibody diseases   It now seems clear that the glomerular capillary wall and mesangium are composed of a number of potentially immunogenic glycoproteins other than the classic GBM glycoprotein mentioned above. These antigens are distributed in various patterns along the glomerular capillary wall and/or within the mesangium and are probably biochemically distinct structural components of the glomerulus. Binding in situ of passively administered heterologous antibody or the actively induced autoantibody to these antigens will therefore produce differing patterns of immunoglobulin localization and functional and structural alterations of the capillary wall. If the antigen is localized in clusters in relation to the capillary wall the reaction with antibody in situ may give rise to discontinuous deposits of Ig detected by immunofluorescence and to electron-dense deposits noted on electron microscopy. While the number of possible antigen-antibody interactions in this category is quite large, very few have in fact been documented to be responsible for human glomerular or tubulointerstitial disease. Thus far, animal experimentation has proceeded at a greater pace than understanding of human analogues of this mechanism. The best-studied animal model is Heymann's nephritis, which is induced in rats by passive administration of a heterologous antibody to a particular glomerular capillary wall antigen or by active immunization with the antigen in complete Freund's adjuvant. The antigen-antibody interaction occurs in the subepithelial space of the glomerulus and at the brush border of the proximal tubule, where the antigen is synthesized as a component of endocytotic, clathrin-coated pits on the surface of the glomerular visceral and proximal tubular epithelial cells. A granular pattern of IgG deposits and subepithelial dense deposits are seen by immunofluorescence and electron microscopy, respectively. A similar mechanism might account for some instances of idiopathic membranous glomerulonephritis in man.

Finally, it is also now well recognized that circulating endogenous or environmental substances having special biologic or biochemical affinity for glomerular structures, including the glomerular capillary wall or mesangium, may deposit in these structures in a nonimmunologic fashion and thus act as a "planted" antigen. An antibody or cellular response to these planted nonglomerular antigens could result in disease upon the formation of antigen-antibody complexes in situ. The pattern of disease produced would depend upon the sites of deposition of the planted antigen and the nature of the immune response. Examples of such planted antigens thus far described include certain drugs, plant lectins, cationized plasma proteins, aggregated immunoglobulins, and deoxyribonucleic acid. Several experimental models of this pathogenic sequence have been described, but there is little definitive information concerning the prevalence of this mechanism in human renal disease.

IMMUNE-COMPLEX–MEDIATED RENAL INJURY (See Chap. 261)   **Circulating immune-complex disease**   The deposition in the kidney of immune complexes formed in the circulation accounts for the majority of diseases of the kidney for which there is clear evidence of participation of some immunologic process. In this category an immunogenic replicating or nonreplicating substance arises in the circulation either from an endogenous (autologous) or exogenous

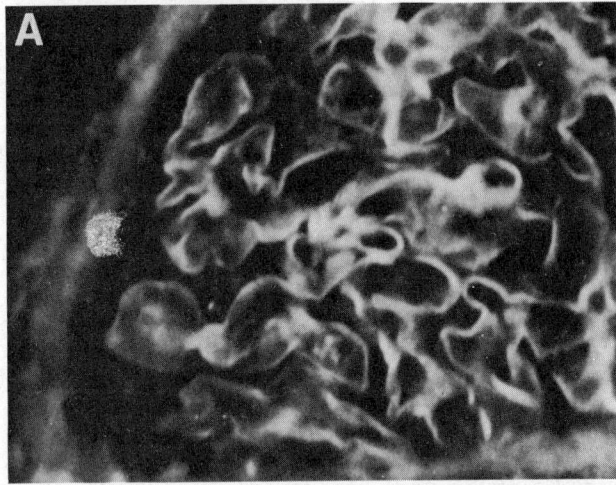

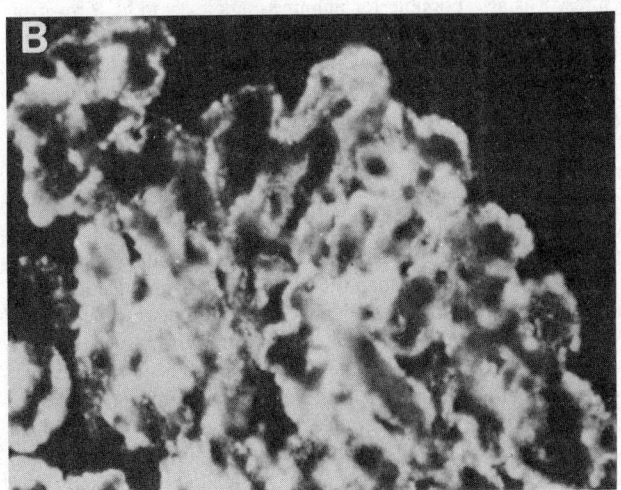

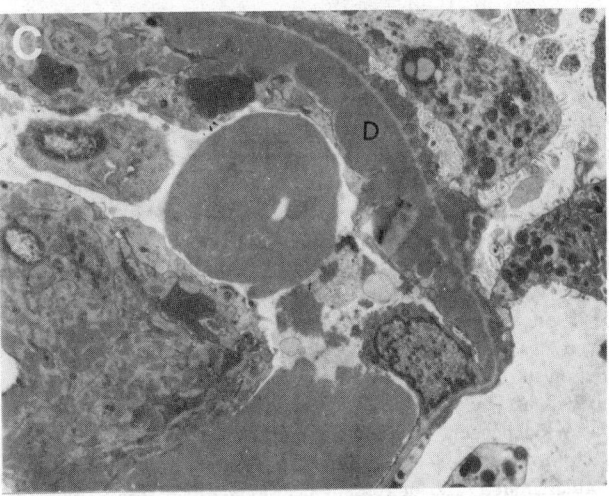

FIGURE 222-1   A. *Immunofluorescence photomicrograph of a portion of a glomerulus from a patient with antiglomerular basement membrane antibody–mediated glomerular injury. Note the linear deposits (fluorescein-labeled antihuman IgG). B. Immunofluorescence photomicrograph of a portion of a glomerulus from a patient with immune-complex–mediated glomerular injury. Note the irregular, granular deposits (fluorescein-labeled antihuman IgG). C. Electron micrograph of a portion of a glomerular capillary from a patient with immune-complex–mediated glomerular injury. Note the electron-dense deposits (D).*

(environmental) source. Antibody response to the antigen occurring while the antigen remains in the circulation leads to the formation of an aggregate of antigen and antibody known as a *circulating immune complex*. A small fraction of circulating immune complexes may escape removal by the mononuclear phagocyte system and instead be trapped by vascular structures including the glomeruli. Circulating immune complexes trapped in these sites have the capability of evoking inflammation utilizing many of the mediator systems described above. One of the best-studied examples of this circulating immune-complex disease involving a nonreplicating antigen is serum sickness, which results from the acute or chronic administration of an immunogenic, soluble, heterologous, foreign serum protein (see Fig. 261-1). A small portion of the immune complexes will then localize within the glomerular mesangium; in the walls of peripheral capillaries; and in joints, heart valves, choroid plexus, splenic sinusoids, and larger blood vessels, particularly at sites of turbulent flow. Once deposited, these complexes possess unique properties which evoke an inflammatory response at the site of deposition.

Although this formulation presupposes that immune complexes form within the circulation and then are deposited in vascular structures, it is also possible for immune complexes to be formed in the extravascular (interstitial) compartment by virtue of diffusion into this fluid compartment of cell-derived antigens and circulating antibody. Such a phenomenon may explain the deposition of immune complexes in the interstitial areas of the kidney, with relative sparing of the glomerular circulation. Regardless of the nature of the antibody or antigen or the particular circumstances surrounding the immunologic events, a valuable clue to the presence of immune-complex deposition is the morphologic pattern found when tissues are examined by immunofluorescence or electron microscopic techniques. Granular, discontinuous, and irregular deposits of Ig, often in conjunction with complement components, are found by immunofluorescence (Fig. 222-1*B*), whereas electron-dense deposits are seen by electron microscopy (Fig. 222-1*C*). Sometimes these deposits acquire a definite substructure, but for the most part they are rather homogeneous. The deposits may develop in several locations within the glomerulus: beneath the epithelial cells (subepithelial), within the basement membrane (intramembranous), beneath the endothelium (subendothelial), and within the mesangial matrix. Immune complexes may also localize in the peritubular capillary network. The precise reason for localization at these differing sites is not well understood but may involve factors such as size or charge of the complexes, receptors for the Fc or complement components within glomerular structures, or local hemodynamic events. The deposits appear to increase in size by aggregation, and there is some evidence that glomerular cells may participate in their removal. The persistence of deposits is related to the rate of formation balanced by the activity of removal systems. Ig itself in a circulating immune complex trapped in the glomerular circulation may behave as a planted antigen, either via the idiotypic determinants present in the antigen-binding sites of antibody or via the Fc portions evoking an anti-immunoglobulin (rheumatoid factor) response. The roles played by anti-idiotype antibody or rheumatoid factor in the evolution of glomerular lesions in immune-complex–mediated disease is not yet clear. Once deposited in glomeruli, circulating immune complexes evoke local inflammatory and functional changes, which at least for the glomerular circulation may be relatively independent of complement or polymorphonuclear leukocytes. Infiltrating monocytes may play a critical role in mediating glomerular injury. The morphologic lesions which result from immune-complex deposition may vary considerably, from diffuse proliferative to nonproliferative membranous or sclerosing lesions. Coagulation, platelet aggregation, activation of the complement cascade, and release of vasoactive amines may participate in determining the pattern of morphologic response.

The *exogenous* antigens involved in circulating immune-complex–mediated disease are derived chiefly from infectious agents such as bacteria, viruses, or parasites. Replication of the organism provides a continuing source of antigen. The best-studied examples of these in humans are *infective endocarditis, leprosy, syphilis, hepatitis B,* and *malaria*. The *endogenous* antigens involved in human disease vary considerably and include *DNA, thyroglobulin, autologous immunoglobulins, erythrocyte stroma, renal tubule antigens,* and *tumor-specific* or *tumor-associated* antigens.

COMPLEMENT-ASSOCIATED GLOMERULAR INJURY Although there is little evidence that complement activation, independent of antitissue antibody or circulating immune complexes, can bring about glomerular injury, there are certain associations between complement and renal disease in humans. The clinicopathologic entity known as *idiopathic mesangiocapillary glomerulonephritis* (see also Chap. 223) may be associated with patterns of serum complement component deposition within glomeruli suggestive of involvement of the alternative pathway of complement activation, perhaps independent of immune-complex deposition. These patterns are not, however, necessarily unique to this group of disorders since they may also be observed in a wide variety of postinfectious glomerulonephritides and in certain collagen-vascular diseases.

As discussed in greater detail in Chap. 62, the alternative pathway mechanism of complement activation depends upon the interaction of aggregated or immune-complex IgA, polysaccharides, or lipopolysaccharides with factors B, D of the alternative pathway system and C3 of the classical complement cascade. Subsequently, an enzyme capable of cleaving native C3 is assembled, composed of a fragment of C3 (C3b) and an altered form of factor B (Bb). This alternative pathway C3 convertase is analogous to the C3 convertase generated in the classic pathway of complement activation. The alternative pathway C3 convertase is stabilized by binding to properdin and degraded by several inactivators (C3b inactivator, β1H). Alternative pathway C3 convertase cleaves C3 into C3a (anaphylatoxin I) and C3b, which is further cleaved by C3 inactivator into C3c and C3d, biologically inactive fragments. The C3b formed in this manner can also autocatalytically form additional alternative pathway C3 convertase in the presence of factors B, D, and of Mg^{2+}. The hallmarks of activation of the alternative pathway are depressed serum levels of native C3, circulating fragments of C3 (C3c, C3d), low levels of factor B, and circulating fragments of B (Bb), all occurring in the absence of perturbations in the early classic components C1q, C4, and C2. The terminal complement components C5 through C9 may also be activated and even result in lysis of cells in the absence of antibody. Depression of the synthesis of C3 may also contribute to diminished serum levels, since circulating fragments of C3 may reduce cellular production.

In *idiopathic mesangiocapillary glomerulonephritis,* particularly the subset known as *dense deposit disease,* serum C3 levels are depressed; C4, C1, and C2 levels tend to be normal; and C3 may be deposited in glomeruli without Ig (see also Chap. 223). In addition, an oligoclonal autoantibody (an immunoconglutinin) to alternative pathway C3 convertase is frequently found in the circulation. This autoantibody reacts with a conformational neoantigen of the alternative pathway C3 convertase and acts to stabilize this enzyme from the influence of C3b inactivator and β1H in a fashion similar to properdin. As a result serums containing this autoantibody are capable of inducing C3 cleavage in vitro by permitting the assembly of a stable fluid phase C3 convertase. This antibody is also known as C3 nephritic factor (C3NeF) and was first described in the serums of patients with glomerulonephritis and persistent depression of C3 levels.

The relationship between these aberrations in the complement pathway and glomerular injury is uncertain. No experimental models of persistent activation of the alternative pathway have been associated with glomerulonephritis; thus, glomerular injury may be a closely associated but pathogenically unrelated phenomenon, perhaps genetically determined. The recognition that certain structural genes for complement components (C2, C4) are closely associated with the major histocompatibility complex provides a potential explanation for the association of disease susceptibility with defects in biosynthesis of complement proteins. On the other hand, some have suggested that persistent hypocomplementemia may interfere with the normal removal processes for environmental antigens such as viruses. Such a defect might favor the persistence of these antigens in the circulation and enhance the likelihood of formation of circulating immune complexes. The discovery that C3 and its degradation product (primarily C3b) are able to solubilize aggregates of antigen and antibody may provide an additional explanation for the occurrence of immune-complex disease in association with defects of complement synthesis or activation.

CELL-MEDIATED IMMUNITY IN GLOMERULAR AND TUBULOIN- TERSTITIAL DISEASES The roles of specifically sensitized cells acting independently of antibody (T cytotoxic cells), "armed" macrophages, and antibody-dependent cell-mediated cytotoxicity in the pathogenesis of glomerular and tubulointerstitial diseases have been difficult to establish firmly. The glomerulus and more than likely the cortical interstitium possess all of the necessary elements to support a cell-mediated response to an autologous or heterologous antigen. Mononuclear cells capable of processing antigen and activating T-helper inducer cells in a major histocompatibility complex– restricted fashion are present in the glomerular mesangium and interstitium. A number of experimental diseases of the kidney, most notably tubulointerstitial nephritis, have been developed which are uniquely the consequence of a cell-mediated immune response. However, at the present time, relatively few human diseases can be ascribed with certainty to cell-mediated immune processes exclusively. The rejection of renal allografts in nonsensitized recipients is clearly a cell-mediated process. This subject is dealt with in greater detail in Chap. 221.

It is true that by utilizing a variety of in vitro techniques cell-mediated hypersensitivity to both environmental and endogenous antigens may be demonstrable in several diseases of the kidney, including glomerulonephritis. The precise role such "sensitized" cells play in the actual tissue injury is unclear, especially in human glomerular disease. No doubt the burgeoning knowledge in the field of cell-cell interactions will eventually clarify these uncertainties. It is very likely that some diseases which do not fit into an antibody- or immune-complex–mediated category will find an explanation in reactions of the cell-mediated variety. One likely candidate for this category is so-called minimal change disease, one of the morphologic subsets of idiopathic nephrotic syndrome. Furthermore, because of the prominence of lymphoid cell infiltration, various forms of chronic tubulointerstitial nephritis have also been suggested as examples of cell-mediated reactions (see Chap. 226).

REFERENCES

BRENTJENS JR, et al: Immunologically mediated lesions of kidney tubules and interstitium of laboratory animals and man. Springer Semin Immunopathol 5:357, 1982

CUMMINGS NB et al: *Immune Mechanisms in Renal Disease.* New York, Plenum Medical Book Co., 1983

GLASSOCK RJ, COHEN AH: Immunologically mediated renal disease, in *Contemporary Nephrology*, S Klahr and S Massry (eds). New York, Plenum Medical Book Co., 1985, vol 3

NEALE TJ, WILSON CB: Glomerular antigens in glomerulonephritis. Springer Semin Immunopathol 5:221, 1982

WILLIAMS DG, PETERS DK: The immunology of nephritis, in *Clinical Aspects of Immunology*, 4th ed, PJ Lachmann and DK Peters (eds). Oxford, Blackwell, 1982, p 853

WILSON CB, DIXON FJ: Renal response to immunological injury, in *The Kidney*, 3d ed, BM Brenner and FC Rector Jr (eds). Philadelphia, Saunders, 1986, p 800

223   THE MAJOR GLOMERULOPATHIES

RICHARD J. GLASSOCK / BARRY M. BRENNER

Disease-induced alterations of the structural and functional integrity of the glomerular capillary circulation are often associated with the findings, either singly or in combination, of hematuria, proteinuria, reduced glomerular filtration rate (GFR), and hypertension. Five major glomerulopathic syndromes are recognized: *acute glomerulonephritis, rapidly progressive glomerulonephritis, chronic glomerulonephritis*, the *nephrotic syndrome*, and *asymptomatic urinary abnormalities*. This chapter deals with each of these syndromes in some detail, describing diseases in which the kidney is either the sole or predominant organ involved (i.e., the primary glomerulopathies) or is involved as a complication of infection or drug exposure. Glomerular injury associated with multisystem disorders or heredofamilial conditions is discussed in Chap. 224.

ACUTE GLOMERULONEPHRITIS (AGN)

The causes of AGN are given in Table 223-1. The "acute nephritic syndrome" consists of the abrupt onset of *hematuria* and *proteinuria*, accompanied by evidence of *azotemia* (i.e., reduced GFR) and renal *salt and water retention*. If GFR is reduced markedly, oligoanuria may be present (see also Chap. 219). Salt and water retention leads to circulatory congestion, hypertension, and edema. Hematuria is most likely the consequence of migration of erythrocytes across damaged glomerular and/or peritubular capillary walls leading to the addition of erythrocytes to tubule fluid in the early part of the nephron. Proteinuria is the consequence of either a loss of anionic charges of the capillary wall (charge-selective defect) or the appearance of a population of glomerular capillaries with larger-than-normal pore radius, permitting large plasma protein molecules to traverse the glomerular filter. Glomerular filtration rate is reduced presumably because of infiltration of the capillaries by inflammatory cells, which thereby reduce filtering surface area. Extensive crescentic disease may obliterate Bowman's space, further impeding filtration. Fluid retention is due in part to decreased glomerular filtration rate but also to persistence of avid distal nephron salt and water reabsorption. Extracellular and intravascular fluid volumes are expanded by primary renal salt and fluid retention.

The edema of acute glomerulonephritis tends to appear initially in areas of low tissue pressure, such as the *periorbital* areas, but may subsequently progress to involve dependent portions of the body and lead to *ascites* and/or *pleural effusions*. *Circulatory congestion* is manifested by an increase in systemic and pulmonary vascular pressures, normal or increased cardiac output, and a shortened circulation time. In the absence of underlying valvular, myocardial, or coronary artery disease or severe diastolic hypertension there is little likelihood that true left ventricular congestive heart failure will

TABLE 223-1   Causes of acute glomerulonephritis

I Infectious diseases
  A Poststreptococcal glomerulonephritis
  B Nonpoststreptococcal glomerulonephritis
    1 Bacterial: infective endocarditis, "shunt nephritis," sepsis, pneumococcal pneumonia, typhoid fever, secondary syphilis, meningococcemia
    2 Viral: hepatitis B, infectious mononucleosis, mumps, measles, varicella, vaccinia, echovirus, and coxsackievirus
    3 Parasitic: malaria, toxoplasmosis
II Multisystem diseases: systemic lupus erythematosus, vasculitis, Henoch-Schönlein purpura, Goodpasture's syndrome
III Primary glomerular diseases: mesangiocapillary glomerulonephritis, Berger's disease, "pure" mesangial proliferative glomerulonephritis
IV Miscellaneous: Guillain-Barré syndrome, irradiation of Wilms's tumor, self-administered diphtheria-pertussis-tetanus vaccine, serum sickness

develop. If pulmonary capillary pressure rises above the opposing plasma oncotic pressure, however, pulmonary edema may ensue. *Arterial diastolic hypertension* is the consequence of several factors, including extracellular fluid volume expansion, enhanced cardiac output, and modest increases in peripheral vascular resistance. Plasma renin activity, aldosterone, and the sympathetic nervous system are relatively suppressed. Hypertension may at times be accompanied by encephalopathy, particularly in young children.

The extent and severity of urinary abnormalities in AGN vary considerably. Gross (macroscopic) *hematuria* is the most common, and is often described by the patient as smoky-, coffee-, or cola-colored urine. Lesser degrees of hematuria may go unrecognized by the patient or parent; for this reason, the features of fluid retention and hypertension may be ascribed erroneously to other illnesses if a careful examination of the urine sediment is omitted from the initial laboratory evaluation. Hematuria is often, but not invariably, accompanied by the excretion of *red cell casts*. The erythrocytes in the urinary sediment are characteristically distorted, fragmented, and hypochromic (dysmorphic hematuria). Leukocyturia and leukocyte casts may also occur, indicating the presence of inflammation in the glomerulus and interstitium. The degree of *proteinuria* varies according to the nature and severity of the underlying glomerular lesions. Rarely, protein excretion rates may fall within the normal range, but generally are between 0.2 and 3 g per day. If proteinuria is marked and sustained, features of the nephrotic syndrome may appear (see below).

The short-term evolution of acute nephritis generally depends upon the nature of the underlying glomerular lesion; however, within a week or so of onset most patients with postinfectious AGN will begin to experience spontaneous resolution of fluid retention and hypertension. Urinary abnormalities often take longer to resolve. A few patients with the acute nephritic syndrome will go on in the ensuing weeks or months to develop a rapidly progressive form of renal failure (i.e., rapidly progressive glomerulonephritis, discussed below). The long-term outlook for patients with AGN is considered below in the context of treatment of specific lesions. Renal biopsy is useful in characterizing the nature of the underlying lesion but need not be done in every case (see below).

ACUTE POSTSTREPTOCOCCAL GLOMERULONEPHRITIS (PSGN)

Clinical features and diagnosis   This disorder can be viewed as the archetype of AGN. PSGN follows in the wake of *pharyngeal or cutaneous infection* with one of a limited number of strains of *group A β-hemolytic streptococci*. These potentially "nephritogenic" streptococci may be identified by serotyping of a cell wall antigen (M protein). Among outbreaks of infection with proved "nephritogenic" strains of streptococci the PSGN attack rate is relatively uniform, but because of variation in the nephritogenicity among group A streptococci, attack rates with outbreaks of infection may vary considerably. Among families, asymptomatic episodes of PSGN exceed symptomatic episodes by a factor of 3 or 4 to 1. Immunity to M protein is type-specific, long-lasting, and protective. Repeated episodes of PSGN are therefore unusual. Outbreaks of pharyngeal infection–associated PSGN are commonest in children aged 6 to 10. AGN following cutaneous streptococcal infection is more commonly associated with factors such as poor personal hygiene, overcrowding, and concomitant cutaneous disease, such as scabies infestation. Seasonal and geographic variations in prevalence of PSGN are more marked for pharyngeal- than for cutaneous-associated disease.

An important feature of PSGN is the existence of a *latent period* between the earliest manifestations of infection and the onset of recognizable signs and symptoms of nephritis. The latent period is more apparent following pharyngeal infections, where it usually is 6 to 10 days in duration. Cutaneous infections are associated with longer latent periods, averaging about 2 weeks. Definitive signs of glomerular inflammation occurring at the same time as, or shortly after, infection usually indicate an *exacerbation* of a preexisting

chronic glomerular disease such as Berger's disease (IgA nephropathy) (see below).

The diagnosis of PSGN rests upon the demonstration of at least two of the following features: (1) The presence of a group A β-hemolytic streptococcus of a potentially nephritogenic M-protein type in a throat or skin lesion. (2) The demonstration of an immune response to one or more of the streptococcal *exoenzymes,* including anti-streptolysin O (ASO), antistreptokinase (ASK), anti-deoxyribonuclease B (ADNAase B), anti-nicotinyl adenine dinucleotidase (ANADase), or antihyaluronidase (AH). ASO responses are typically brisk in pharyngeal infections, but often absent in cutaneous infection; whereas AH, ADNAase, and ANADase responses occur after the latter. Testing for multiple antibody responses and serial determinations is necessary to achieve a diagnostic accuracy of 90 percent. Early antimicrobial therapy may prevent the antibody response to exoenzymes and render throat cultures negative, but may not interfere with the development of PSGN; this makes accurate serologic diagnosis difficult or impossible. (3) The demonstration of a transient decline in the serum concentration of the C3 component of complement, with a return to normal within 8 weeks after the first signs of renal disease. Other complement components (i.e., C1q and C4) are frequently less depressed. In addition to these laboratory features it is desirable to document a latent period appropriate to the nature of the infection. Furthermore, the patient should not have any known preexisting renal disease.

Other laboratory features commonly observed in PSGN include transient cryoimmunoglobulinemia, positive tests for circulating immune complexes, and circulating high-molecular-weight fibrinogen complexes. The erythrocyte sedimentation rate is usually elevated, while C-reactive protein and rheumatoid factor are generally normal or absent. Mild anemia and hypoalbuminemia, both largely dilutional in origin, may be present. Severe hypoalbuminemia may be encountered if heavy proteinuria is present and prolonged. Excretion rates of urinary protein in excess of 3.5 g per day occur in less than 20 percent of hospitalized patients. Proteinuria is usually of a nonselective character and frequently contains high concentrations of fibrin-degradation products (FDP) and C3 protein, particularly during the diuretic phase. Hyponatremia, hyperchloremia, hyperkalemia, and metabolic acidosis may be seen in azotemic or oliguric patients, especially those having free access to water or potassium. Urinary sodium concentration is usually low, reflecting avid salt reabsorption in the distal nephron. Abdominal films reveal normal or enlarged kidneys. The chest x-ray may be normal or reveal a slightly enlarged heart, often accompanied by signs of pulmonary congestion. The electrocardiogram may reveal nonspecific T-wave abnormalities. Rheumatic fever rarely coexists with acute PSGN.

The differential diagnosis of PSGN includes other infectious or primary renal diseases which may produce an identical acute nephritic syndrome (Table 223-1). Multisystem diseases such as SLE, Henoch-Schönlein purpura, and vasculitis may present initially as acute nephritis (Chap. 224). Predominantly nonglomerular diseases, including thrombotic thrombocytopenic purpura, hemolytic-uremic syndrome, atheroembolic renal disease, and acute hypersensitivity interstitial nephritis may also present the features of the acute nephritic syndrome (Chaps. 226 and 227).

Pathology and pathogenesis   Renal biopsies performed early in the course of PSGN reveal *diffuse, endocapillary proliferative glomerulonephritis*. Infiltration of glomeruli with polymorphonuclear leukocytes and monocytes is also common. The glomerular capillary walls are usually thin and delicate and free of necrosis. Occasional discrete proteinaceous deposits projecting from the outer aspects of the capillary wall toward the urinary space (humps) may be recognized by light microscopy and coincide with the electron-dense deposits seen by electron microscopy. Segmental extracapillary proliferation (crescents) may involve a few glomeruli, but diffuse crescent formation is uncommon except among a subset of patients presenting with severe and rapidly progressive acute renal failure (see section below on rapidly progressive glomerulonephritis). Extraglomerular vessels and tubulointerstitial areas are usually normal. Red blood cells are frequently seen in the lumens of distal tubules, where they form red blood cell casts and dysmorphic erythrocytes.

By immunofluorescence microscopy, granular deposits of IgG are seen in peripheral capillary loops and mesangium, nearly always accompanied by C3 and properdin, but less commonly by C1q and C4 (Chap. 222). A variety of patterns of Ig and/or C3 deposition has been described. Extensive involvement of the peripheral capillary loops with deposits may be associated with a poorer prognosis, while deposits exclusively involving the mesangium usually indicate a more benign outcome. The precise nature of the antigen-antibody systems involved remains unknown. Most likely the antigen is derived from the streptococcal organism itself, but this has been difficult to verify. The profile of altered serum complement components described above, and the prominent C3 and properdin deposition in glomeruli, are suggestive of involvement of the alternative pathway of complement activation (Chap. 222).

Course and treatment   The ultimate *prognosis* for PSGN appears to differ between sporadic and epidemic forms and between adults and children. *Epidemic* forms of the disease in *children* have a uniformly favorable short- and long-term prognosis. Few patients die of complications of renal failure (fewer than 1 percent), and nearly all experience a spontaneous resolution of abnormal clinical signs within a week after the onset of illness. Abnormalities in the urinary sediment and protein excretion subside slowly in the ensuing months; in a few cases, several years elapse before the urinary sediment becomes consistently normal. Among children with PSGN during epidemics of streptococcal infection, and in whom some form of preexisting chronic glomerular disease was absent, long-term follow-up has revealed little or no evidence of progression to chronic renal disease. A very small percentage may develop extensive crescentic glomerulonephritis with its relentlessly progressive course. The site of the streptococcal infection, the type of M protein, the severity in abnormalities of complement components or urinary sediment, or the extent of the rise in antibody response to exoenzymes have little or no bearing on the ultimate prognosis of PSGN. Prolonged and persistent heavy proteinuria and/or abnormal GFR imply a more unfavorable outcome. *Sporadic* cases of PSGN among *children* may have more serious long-term consequences, although this remains controversial. After the subsidence of the acute disease, some children subsequently develop slowly progressive glomerular capillary obliteration (glomerulosclerosis), reduced GFR, and hypertension; after several decades, end-stage renal failure from chronic glomerulonephritis may result. The persistence of abnormal proteinuria is the rule in such cases.

The prognosis for *adults* with PSGN seems to be less favorable than for children. The reason for this apparent age difference is poorly understood. Although the overall prognosis for PSGN in *epidemics* seems good, *sporadic* PSGN in adults appears to be associated with lasting and/or progressive deterioration in renal function in as many as one-third to one-half of all cases. This may take the form of persistent proteinuria and/or hematuria, or of slowly progressive glomerulosclerosis and renal failure, often accompanied by hypertension. This evolution seems more likely to occur when the initial disease has been unusually severe. Whether milder forms of sporadic PSGN can lead to chronic disease is an important but unresolved issue (see "Chronic Glomerulonephritis" below).

The *treatment* of acute PSGN is supportive. It seems reasonable to recommend bed rest until the signs of glomerular inflammation and circulatory congestion (primarily hypertension) subside, but prolonged forced periods of inactivity are of no demonstrable benefit in the healing process. Fluid retention, circulatory congestion, and edema may be treated with sodium and fluid restriction, or loop diuretics. Diuresis alone will often ameliorate mild to moderate hypertension. If severe hypertension is present, vasodilator drugs such as nitroprusside, nifedipine, hydralazine, or diazoxide may be

useful. Encephalopathy and pulmonary congestion will generally improve with lowering of blood pressure and the relief of circulatory overload. Digitalis preparations should be avoided except in instances of well-documented organic heart disease with congestive failure. Treatment with ion exchange resins and/or dialysis may be required for cases of severe oliguria, fluid overload, and hyperkalemia. Mild protein restriction is desirable for azotemic patients. A 7- to 10-day course of antimicrobials (e.g., penicillin or erythromycin) should be given if streptococcal infection is documented. Long-term chemoprophylaxis is not indicated. Steroids and cytotoxic drugs have not been shown to be of value.

NONSTREPTOCOCCAL ACUTE GLOMERULONEPHRITIS   Clinical features and diagnosis   A variety of infectious illnesses other than those caused by group A β-hemolytic streptococci may also be associated with AGN (Table 223-1). These include *bacteremic states* and various *viral* and *parasitic* diseases. Ordinarily these diseases can be diagnosed by the presence of typical extrarenal clinical features or by bacteriologic or serologic findings. Infective endocarditis, visceral sepsis, typhoid fever, infectious mononucleosis, acute viral hepatitis (hepatitis B), falciparum malaria, and toxoplasmosis represent examples of infectious diseases capable of evoking AGN. A substantial body of evidence indicates that circulating immune complexes play an important role in the pathogenesis of AGN in these diseases. Bacteremic states are frequently associated with persistent depression of serum concentrations of complement components C1q, C4, and C3, elevated levels of rheumatoid factor, circulating cryoimmunoglobulins, and strongly positive tests for circulating immune complexes. Control of infection usually results in the resolution of the signs of glomerular inflammation, although, in occasional instances, rapidly progressive or chronic glomerulonephritis may ensue.

RAPIDLY PROGRESSIVE GLOMERULONEPHRITIS (RPGN)

Transient azotemia, often associated with a brief period of oliguria, is commonly observed in AGN. A diuresis usually follows within days or a few weeks and GFR returns to normal. On the other hand, some cases of AGN are characterized by a *rapidly progressive* form of renal failure, which often develops abruptly and displays little tendency for spontaneous or complete recovery. The clinical term *rapidly progressive glomerulonephritis* (RPGN) is often applied to this group to connote the development of renal failure in a period of weeks to months, rather than years or decades, as is typical of chronic glomerulonephritis (see below). Usually, but not invariably, extensive *extracapillary (crescentic) glomerulonephritis* is found as the pathologic lesion underlying the syndrome of RPGN, and the two terms are often used interchangeably.

RPGN can arise in three clinical settings (Table 223-2): (1) as a renal complication of an acute or subacute infectious disease, (2) as a renal complication of many multisystem diseases, and (3) as a

TABLE 223-2   Causes of rapidly progressive glomerulonephritis

I Infectious diseases
A Poststreptococcal glomerulonephritis
B Infective endocarditis
C Occult visceral sepsis
II Multisystem diseases
A Systemic lupus erythematosus
B Henoch-Schönlein purpura
C Vasculitis (including Wegener's granulomatosis)
D Goodpasture's syndrome
E Essential cryoimmunoglobulinemia
F Malignancy (rare)
III Primary glomerular diseases
A Idiopathic crescentic glomerulonephritis
B Mesangiocapillary glomerulonephritis
C Berger's disease (rare)
D Membranous glomerulonephritis complicated by anti-glomerular basement membrane antibody formation (rare)

primary or idiopathic glomerular disease. The first category is discussed in Chap. 222, the second in Chap. 224, and the third will be considered here.

IDIOPATHIC RAPIDLY PROGRESSIVE GLOMERULONEPHRITIS

Clinical features and diagnosis This disorder affects individuals in a broad age distribution and has a predilection for males. Wide geographic differences in the prevalence of the disease have been noted, and outbreaks ("miniepidemics") may occur. Some patients have had recent heavy exposure to volatile hydrocarbons, but there is little evidence to support a cause-and-effect relationship. While a flulike or viral prodrome may occur, frank arthritis, sinusitis, otitis, skin rash, neuritis, or encephalopathy are uncommon and are more in keeping with a multisystem disease. Symptoms of weakness, nausea, and vomiting (indicative of azotemia) usually dominate the clinical picture. Oliguria, abdominal or flank pain, and hemoptysis may also be present (see "Goodpasture's Syndrome," Chap. 224). The blood pressure is usually normal or only modestly elevated. Urinalysis typically reveals dysmorphic hematuria and red cell casts, but exceptional cases with relatively benign urine sediments have been observed. Proteinuria is always present and may occasionally be massive. Other biochemical features of the nephrotic syndrome are uncommon, probably because of the concomitant reduction in GFR. Proteinuria is typically nonselective, and high concentrations of FDP are found in urine. Azotemia develops early and tends to progress at a rapid rate. Other clinical and laboratory features relate to the underlying pathology and pathogenesis.

Pathology and pathogenesis It is clear that idiopathic RPGN is far from a homogeneous disease. By light microscopy the characteristic abnormality found in the kidneys is *extensive extracapillary proliferation,* i.e., *crescents.* The extent and degree of glomerular involvement varies considerably; however, among patients with rapid deterioration of renal function it is usual for more than 70 percent of glomeruli to be involved with circumferential crescents. Endocapillary proliferation may also be seen but, if very prominent, suggests the presence of antigen-antibody complexes. Fibrin-related antigens are nearly always demonstrable within the crescents by special stains or by immunofluorescence. Gaps or focal discontinuities in the glomerular basement membrane (GBM) and/or Bowman's capsule are observed in association with crescents.

Variations in the underlying pathogenetic mechanisms responsible for RPGN are revealed by immunofluorescence studies of renal biopsies (Chap. 222). In approximately one-third of cases, *linear deposits* of IgG, often accompanied by C3, indicate involvement of *anti-GBM antibodies.* Circulating anti-GBM antibodies are found in this group by indirect immunofluorescence, hemagglutination, or radioimmunoassay techniques. Patients falling into this pathogenetic subgroup tend to have normal serum complement levels and a marked tendency to develop hemoptysis (see also "Goodpasture's Syndrome," Chap. 224). About one-third of cases will have findings indicative of *immune-complex–mediated disease,* namely, *granular deposits* of immunoglobulin by immunofluorescence microscopy and electron-dense deposits by electron microscopy. This mechanism of RPGN tends to occur in older individuals, to produce more constitutional symptoms, and to result in more disturbances of the complement pathways than does anti-GBM antibody–mediated disease. Hemoptysis may also occur, but circulating anti-GBM antibodies are absent. The remainder of cases of RPGN reveal scanty or no immunoglobulins or complement by immunofluorescence; their pathogenesis is unknown. This group also tends to include older individuals, in whom serum complement concentrations are normal and anti-GBM antibodies are absent. Occasionally, mild hemoptysis may occur.

It is obvious from the foregoing discussion that lung hemorrhage may be observed in a variety of circumstances associated with RPGN. This subject is covered in greater detail in the section on Goodpasture's syndrome in Chap. 224. As noted in Table 223-2, other idiopathic (primary) renal diseases may, from time to time, be accompanied by a prominent tendency for crescent formation and a rapidly progressive course.

Course and treatment In general, the prognosis for preservation of renal function in RPGN is poor. Patients with crescent formation in 70 percent or more of glomeruli, oliguria or severe reduction in GFR (less than 5 mL/min) at the time of presentation, or an anti-GBM antibody–mediated process have the worst prognosis. Although advances in treatment are changing the outlook for patients with RPGN, at least one-half to two-thirds of patients currently require maintenance hemodialysis within 6 months of discovery of the illness. Exceptional patients with crescentic glomerulonephritis will have a more protracted illness. Spontaneous resolution is very uncommon, except among patients with infection as the basis for formation of antigen-antibody complexes, where removal of antigen can take place.

The treatment of RPGN is currently undergoing reevaluation. *Corticosteroids,* in the form of "pulses" of parenteral methylprednisolone in high doses, or continuous oral prednisone daily, often combined with *cytotoxic agents* (azathioprine or cyclophosphamide), have yielded varying degrees of success, particularly in the patients revealing granular or minimal Ig deposits in glomeruli. Since no controlled studies have yet been conducted, however, it is difficult to verify the exact value of these approaches. Nonetheless, more than two-thirds of patients treated with several "pulses" of intravenous methylprednisolone have experienced improvement in renal function often sufficient to avoid the necessity of dialysis for renal failure. The addition of *anticoagulants* (heparin or warfarin sodium) and antithrombotic agents (cyproheptadine, dipyridamole, sulfinpyrazone) seems rational on the basis of evidence suggesting involvement of the coagulation process in the genesis of crescent formation. However, objective evidence of benefit from such therapies in animals afflicted with experimentally induced crescentic glomerulonephritis has been inconsistent, in part because of variations in the severity of the disease models, the timing of treatment, and the nature of the anticoagulant or antithrombotic agent used. Anticoagulants may be hazardous in patients with advanced renal failure. *Ancrod,* a fibrinogenolytic agent not yet released in the United States, may also prove to be an effective agent. *Intensive plasma exchange* (plasmapheresis—2 to 4 liters of plasma daily or three times weekly), combined with steroids and cytotoxic agents, has been employed in patients with RPGN with very encouraging preliminary results, especially in patients revealing linear Ig deposits in glomeruli (anti-GBM antibody–mediated disease). Beneficial effects appear to be greatest when such combined therapy is instituted early in the course of disease, before glomerular abnormalities are advanced. Therefore, renal biopsy assessment of the nature, severity, and potential reversibility of disease is a vital aspect of evaluation of patients suspected of having rapidly progressive glomerulonephritis. Such renal biopsies should be performed early rather than late in the course of disease. Despite aggressive therapy, patients with oliguria continue to do poorly. Clearly, treatment must be individualized, and because regular dialysis therapy and/or transplantation are available to virtually all patients with RPGN, one should probably err on the side of a conservative approach, unless compelling evidence in support of potential reversibility is present.

RPGN may recur in the renal transplant. It is difficult to be certain of the precise risk in individual cases. At present it seems prudent to recommend that, after initiating dialysis, a period of 3 to 6 months be allowed to elapse before undertaking renal transplantation in patients who have circulating anti-GBM antibodies. There is no convincing evidence that bilateral nephrectomy in advance of transplantation reduces the risk of recurrent disease in the transplant.

THE NEPHROTIC SYNDROME (NS)

In its overt form, NS is characterized by *albuminuria, hypoalbuminemia, hyperlipidemia,* and *edema.* These abnormalities are direct or indirect consequences of excessive glomerular leakage of plasma proteins into the urine (see also Chaps. 28 and 40). The defects in the charge- or size-selective barriers of the glomerular capillary wall which underline the excessive filtration of plasma proteins can arise as a consequence of a wide variety of disease processes, including immunologic disorders, toxic injuries, metabolic abnormalities, biochemical defects, and vascular disorders. Thus, nephrotic syndrome should be viewed as a common end point of a variety of disease processes damaging the permeability properties of the glomerular capillary wall. *Heavy proteinuria* is the hallmark of the nephrotic state. Arbitrarily, protein excretion rates in excess of 3.5 g per 1.73 m² per day (or urinary protein concentration of greater than 3.5 mg/dL creatinine) are considered to be in the nephrotic range, primarily because proteinuria of this magnitude is seldom observed in tubulointerstitial and vascular diseases of the kidney. Sustained heavy proteinuria is often, but not invariably, accompanied by *hypoalbuminemia*. Excessive urinary losses, increased renal catabolism, and inadequate hepatic synthesis of albumin all contribute to this depression of plasma albumin. The resulting decrease in plasma oncotic pressure leads to a disturbance in the Starling forces acting across peripheral capillaries. Intravascular fluid migrates into the interstitial tissue (i.e., *edema*), particularly in areas of low tissue pressure. These disturbances initiate a series of homeostatic adjustments designed to correct the resulting deficit in effective plasma volume. These include activation of the renin-angiotensin-aldosterone system, enhanced antidiuretic hormone secretion, stimulation of the sympathetic nervous system, and perhaps a reduction in the secretion of a postulated "natriuretic hormone." These and other poorly understood adjustments lead to renal sodium and water retention, primarily because of avid reabsorption in distal nephron segments, resulting in unrelenting edema. The severity of edema correlates with the level of serum albumin and with the extent of urinary protein losses. The extent and severity of edema is significantly conditioned by the presence of other factors such as heart disease or peripheral vascular disease. Profound hypoalbuminemia may occasionally be associated with severe plasma volume reduction, postural hypotension, syncope, and shock. Very occasionally acute renal failure may occur. Although this formulation would indicate that nephrotic syndrome is invariably accompanied by a significant deficit in intravascular volume and homeostatically appropriate renal salt and water retention, this pattern is not always observed. In fact, measurements of plasma volume, renin, and aldosterone, and determination of the events underlying renal salt and water reabsorption have uncovered considerable heterogeneity in the pathophysiology of fluid volume homeostasis in the nephrotic syndrome. Some cases demonstrate expanded intravascular fluid volume and suppressed renin-aldosterone axis, presumably mediated by primary, non-aldosterone-dependent renal salt and fluid retention, resembling the pathophysiology of acute nephritis (see above). These patients often, but not invariably, have some decrease in GFR and structural glomerular lesions. At the other end of the spectrum are patients with overt hypovolemia, hyperreninemia, and avid, secondary renal salt retention. Serum albumin levels are low, extracellular fluid volume is expanded, and edema is usually present in both groups.

The diminished plasma oncotic pressure also appears to stimulate hepatic lipoprotein synthesis, and *hyperlipidemia* is a frequent accompaniment of the nephrotic state. Low-density lipoproteins and cholesterol are elevated most frequently, but as the plasma oncotic pressure falls to very low levels, very low density lipoproteins and triglycerides also increase. Excessive urinary losses of plasma protein factors regulating lipoprotein synthesis or disposal may also contribute to the hyperlipidemic state. Whether these lipid abnormalities contribute to accelerated atherosclerosis remains controversial. Lipid bodies (fatty casts, oval fat bodies) commonly appear in the urine.

Urine losses of plasma proteins other than albumin are also of importance in NS. Loss of thyroxine-binding globulin may produce abnormalities in thyroid function tests, including a low T4 and an enhanced resin T3 uptake. Loss of cholecalciferol-binding protein may lead to a vitamin D deficiency state, secondary hyperparathy-

roidism, and bone disease, and also may contribute to the hypocalcemia and hypocalciuria seen commonly in NS. Enhanced urinary excretion of transferrin may produce an iron-resistant microcytic, hypochromic anemia. Zinc and copper deficiency may result from urinary losses of metal-binding proteins. Loss of antithrombin III (heparin cofactor) in the urine may be associated with increased coagulability, which may or may not be balanced by losses of procoagulant factors in the urine. If it is not, it may produce a hypercoagulable state, and the increased tendency to thrombosis may lead to renal vein thrombosis.

Some patients with NS develop severe IgG deficiency, in part due to urinary losses and hypercatabolism. Low-molecular-weight complement components may also be lost in the urine and contribute to defects in the opsonization of bacteria. Various drug-binding proteins (chiefly albumin) may be decreased, altering the pharmacokinetic and toxicity properties of many drugs. Cellulose acetate electrophoresis of serum reveals, in addition to diminished albumin levels, increases of alpha and beta globulins.

COMPLICATIONS AND MANAGEMENT OF THE NEPHROTIC SYNDROME   *Edema* should be managed cautiously and conservatively. Overly vigorous diuresis with potent loop diuretics (furosemide or ethacrynic acid) may result in an abrupt decline in effective plasma volume as the deficit in plasma oncotic pressure may preclude mobilization of the extracellular fluid into the intravascular compartment. This is more likely to occur if plasma volume is already diminished and may lead to further reduction in GFR, worsening azotemia, and postural hypotension. Severe extracellular volume depletion may predispose to the development of acute renal failure. The temptation to administer concentrated salt-poor albumin should be resisted, as nearly all the administered protein will be excreted in 24 to 48 h, so that any beneficial effect on plasma oncotic pressure will be transient. However, such treatment may be necessary in severely hypoalbuminemic patients suffering from profound postural symptoms or very refractory anasarca.

The treatment of *hyperlipidemia* is difficult at best and its influence on morbidity and mortality uncertain. Most agents effective in reducing cholesterol and/or triglyceride levels are either too toxic (e.g., clofibrate) or poorly tolerated (e.g., cholestyramine) for chronic use. The value of newer agents in the management of hyperlipidemia in NS is not well established.

The *thromboembolic complications* of NS are reasonably common and have a broad range of clinical manifestations, including spontaneous peripheral venous and/or arterial thromboses, as well as pulmonary arterial and renal venous occlusions. *Renal vein thrombosis* (RVT), either unilateral or bilateral, is a particularly distressing complication of NS. In the past, this was regarded as a cause rather than a consequence of NS, a conclusion no longer held to be true. Certain glomerular lesions are more likely than others to be associated with RVT. These include membranous glomerulonephritis, mesangiocapillary glomerulonephritis, and amyloidosis. Features which are suggestive of acute RVT include unilateral or bilateral flank or loin pain, gross hematuria, left-sided varicocele, widely fluctuating GFR and urinary protein excretion rates, and asymmetry of renal size and/or function. Scalloping of the ureters (due to collateral circulation) and evidence of pulmonary emboli and/or infarction (Chap. 227) may occur in chronic RVT.

Chronic forms of RVT are commonly asymptomatic. The approach to the patient with *chronic* RVT is widely debated. Some advocate an aggressive approach in patients with nephrotic syndrome due to lesions associated with inherently high prevalence of RVT (e.g., membranous glomerulonephritis), routinely employing selective renal venous angiography. If RVT is detected, long-term (optimal duration unknown) anticoagulants are prescribed. Such an approach might prevent later development of serious embolic complications, but since the true risk of pulmonary embolism in this group of patients is not known, but is probably low, the benefits/risk relationship of this approach cannot be determined. Long-term anticoagulation of nephrotic patients is not without risk, and the benefits for renal functional preservation are uncertain. A more conservative approach has also been advocated in which renal venous angiography is performed only in those patients who have a documented pulmonary embolism (e.g., symptoms, compatible laboratory findings, and a high-probability ventilation-perfusion scan or pulmonary angiogram) and who have negative noninvasive studies directed at detecting deep venous thrombosis in the lower extremities. Since such patients would receive anticoagulant therapy in any case, the value of localizing the site of thrombosis is not well established. Positive ventilation-perfusion scans in asymptomatic nephrotic patients are likely to have limited value, since subsegmental defects in perfusion may be observed even in the absence of renal vein or lower extremity deep venous thrombosis in nephrotic patients. These changes could conceivably be due to in situ pulmonary arterial thrombosis. The risk of renal vein thrombosis or deep venous thrombosis is increased primarily in patients with nephrotic syndrome and a very low serum albumin level (e.g., less than 2 g/dL). The presence of a documented thromboembolic complication of NS is usually regarded as a clear indication for long-term oral anticoagulation. The effectiveness of heparin may be impaired by concomitant antithrombin III deficiency, a plasma factor required for the full expression of the heparin-induced antithrombin effect.

High-protein diets are frequently prescribed; however, the beneficial effect of this approach can be challenged since the main effect of increasing dietary protein is to increase urinary protein excretion rate and the effect on serum albumin levels is very modest. Furthermore, such diets are difficult to manage with concomitant salt restriction, and at least theoretically, could aggravate the rate of progression of an underlying structural glomerular lesion. An alternative approach would be to prescribe modest protein restriction (e.g., 0.6 g/kg per day), particularly in azotemic patients; some also advocate adding a supplementary amount of dietary protein equal to urinary protein losses. Dietary protein should be of high biologic value and can be supplemented with amino acids. Plasma albumin and transferrin concentrations as well as urinary protein excretion rates should be monitored to evaluate the effect of dietary regimens on overall nutritional status. Correction of transport protein deficiencies is not feasible. Supplemental vitamin D might be desirable if overt deficiency is present, but this has not been fully evaluated

TABLE 223-3   Causes of the nephrotic syndrome

I Primary glomerular diseases
  A Minimal change disease
  B Mesangial proliferative glomerulonephritis*
  C Focal and segmental glomerulosclerosis
  D Membranous glomerulonephritis
  E Mesangiocapillary glomerulonephritis
    1 Type I
    2 Type II
    3 Other variants
  F Other uncommon lesions
    1 Crescentic glomerulonephritis
    2 Focal and segmental proliferative glomerulonephritis*
    3 Unclassifiable lesions
II Secondary to other diseases
  A Infections: poststreptococcal glomerulonephritis, endocarditis, "shunt nephritis," secondary syphilis, leprosy, hepatitis B, HTLV-III, infectious mononucleosis, malaria, schistosomiasis, filariasis
  B Drugs: organic gold; inorganic, organic, and elemental mercury; penicillamine; "street" heroin; probenecid; captopril; Tridione; mesantoin; perchlorate; antivenom; antitoxins; contrast media
  C Neoplasia: Hodgkin's disease, lymphomas, leukemia, carcinomas, melanoma, Wilms's tumor
  D Multisystem: systemic lupus erythematosus, Henoch-Schönlein purpura, vasculitis, Goodpasture's syndrome, dermatomyositis, dermatitis herpetiformis, amyloidosis, sarcoidosis, Sjögren's syndrome, rheumatoid arthritis
  E Heredofamilial: diabetes mellitus, Alport's syndrome, sickle cell disease, Fabry's disease, nail-patella syndrome, lipodystrophy, congenital nephrotic syndrome
  F Miscellaneous: preeclamptic toxemia, thyroiditis, myxedema, malignant obesity, renovascular hypertension, chronic interstitial nephritis with vesicoureteric reflux, chronic allograft rejection, beestings

* *Includes Berger's disease (IgA nephropathy).*

clinically. In rare circumstances, profound protein malnutrition or other complications of massive proteinuria may justify ablation of renal function by medical or surgical means.

A classification of the causes of NS is provided in Table 223-3. The multisystemic, heredofamilial, neoplastic, and metabolic causes are discussed in Chap. 224. The primary (idiopathic) glomerular diseases associated with NS, as well as the diseases secondary to infectious or drug etiologies, are considered below.

IDIOPATHIC NEPHROTIC SYNDROME   This diagnosis is arrived at by exclusion of known causes of NS, such as infections, drug exposure, malignancy, multisystem disease, or hereditary disorders. The idiopathic forms of NS are further classified according to the morphologic features found on renal biopsy (Table 223-4). Performance of a renal biopsy, at least among adults, is required for the accurate diagnosis of idiopathic NS and for the formulation of a rational plan of treatment. Children need not always be subjected to renal biopsy since careful clinical study can often lead to accurate diagnosis.

Minimal change disease   This is often referred to as *lipoid nephrosis, nil lesion,* or *foot process disease.* In this form of idiopathic NS, although little or no alterations of the glomerular capillaries are demonstrable by light microscopy (hence the designation "minimal change"), *diffuse epithelial foot process effacement*[1] is evident by electron microscopy. Immunofluorescence microscopy reveals absent or irregular and nonspecific deposits of immunoglobulin and complement components. Minimal change disease is the most frequently encountered form of idiopathic NS in children, accounting for more than 70 to 80 percent of cases diagnosed before the age of 8. This lesion is not rare in adults, representing 15 to 20 percent of cases of idiopathic NS in patients over the age of 16. There is a slight predilection for males. Typically patients present with overt NS, normal blood pressure, normal or slightly reduced GFR, and a "benign" urinary sediment. Varying degrees of microscopic hematuria are found in up to 20 percent of cases. Urinary protein is typically highly selective in children (e.g., it contains principally albumin and minimal amounts of high-molecular-weight plasma proteins such as IgG, alpha$_2$ macroglobulin, or C3) but is variable in adults. The pattern of protein excretion indicates a major "charge-selective" defect in permselectivity. Fibrin split products and C3 are absent in the urine. Serum levels of complement components are normal, except for a slight reduction in C1q. IgG concentrations are often quite depressed during relapse, whereas IgM levels are modestly increased, both during remission and relapse. Some cases may have associated allergic diathesis (e.g., to milk, pollens, etc.), a history of recent immunization, or upper respiratory infection. Circulating immune complexes may be found in some patients using certain assays. The histocompatibility antigen HLA-B12 is more prevalent when minimal change disease is associated with atopy, indicating a possible genetically based predisposition to this disease. Thromboembolic manifestations occur, but renal vein thrombosis is uncommon.

Spontaneous remissions and relapses of heavy proteinuria may occur, usually for reasons which are unexplained. Interestingly, an identical lesion is encountered in patients with Hodgkin's disease in whom NS develops, suggesting a role for lymphocytes in its pathogenesis. Except for patients who develop focal and segmental sclerosing lesions (see below), a progressive decline in GFR does not occur. Acute renal failure is rare. In the preantibiotic era infection with encapsulated organisms (e.g., pneumococci) was a leading cause of death, but now the mortality rate is exceedingly low and most deaths are associated with complications of treatment rather than the disease itself. Rarely, acute renal failure may occur even in the absence of profound hypovolemia. The mechanism of this phenomenon is obscure but could relate to tubular obstruction from heavy proteinuria or severe glomerular epithelial cell effacement. The renal failure is responsive to steroids and diuretics.

[1] *The term "fusion" is often used to describe these changes in foot processes, although true fusion of cell membranes does not occur.*

Since the etiology and pathogenesis are unknown, treatment is empirical and symptomatic. A large body of evidence indicates that corticosteroids markedly enhance the natural tendency for this disease to undergo spontaneous remission. Daily or alternate-day oral steroid therapy seem to be equally effective, the latter associated with fewer steroid-related complications. Daily prednisone (60 mg/m² in children, 1 to 1.5 mg/kg in adults) for 4 weeks, followed by alternate-day prednisone (35 to 40 mg/m² in children, 1 mg/kg in adults) for 4 additional weeks is a regimen often recommended for initial treatment of this disorder. The vast majority of patients who respond do so within the first 4 weeks of treatment, but occasionally a favorable response requires more prolonged therapy. The absence of a response within 8 weeks is usually indicative of an error in diagnosis and should provoke a review of the renal biopsy. In many patients who respond, withdrawal of steroid treatment is often accompanied by relapse; this usually occurs within the first year after cessation of treatment. Such relapses may be re-treated with the initial regimen as described above, but with gradual withdrawal of prednisone and low-maintenance doses of 5 to 10 mg daily or on alternate days for 3 to 6 months. A steroid-dependent patient or one with multiple relapses may be benefited by a brief course of cyclophosphamide (2 to 3 mg/kg per day) or chlorambucil (0.1 to 0.2 mg/kg per day) for 8 to 10 weeks. When given with steroids to patients to induce remissions, either of these agents reduces the likelihood of a subsequent relapse. However, these agents have serious adverse effects on bone marrow and, in the case of cyclophosphamide, the gonads and urinary bladder. Careful monitoring of hematologic and urinary findings is mandatory. They may also be oncogenic. Azathioprine has been demonstrated to be ineffective in inducing prolonged remissions. The use of cytotoxic agents should be reserved for patients who develop serious or life-threatening complications of multiple courses of steroid therapy. The long-term prognosis of patients with the minimal change lesion is excellent; a 10-year survival in excess of 90 percent can be expected, but a few develop renal failure usually as a consequence of development of focal sclerosing glomerular lesions (see below).

Mesangial proliferative glomerulonephritis The lesion is characterized by a mild to moderate diffuse, but distinct, increase in the cellularity of the glomerular capillary bed. The peripheral glomerular capillary walls are thin and delicate, and extracapillary proliferation is not seen. The precise nature of the proliferating cells is not clearly understood but may represent combinations of proliferating mesangial cells, endothelial cells, and infiltrating mononuclear cells. Glomerular involvement is usually reasonably uniform, although there may be some segmental accentuation of hypercellularity. Necrosis of glomerular tufts is absent. Deposits of proteinaceous material, if seen, are confined to the mesangial areas. Interposition of mesangial cells and cytoplasm into the periphery of the glomerular capillary wall is not seen. By immunofluorescence, a variety of patterns are observed. If granular IgA deposits in the mesangium predominate, accompanied by C3 and fibrin-reactive antigens but not the early acting components of the complement cascade, then the lesion is categorized as IgA nephropathy, or Berger's disease (see below). Other patterns of immunofluorescence may be observed, including a predominance of IgM deposits in a granular pattern diffusely throughout the mesangium, isolated mesangial C3 deposits, scattered mesangial IgG deposits, and no immunoglobulin or complement deposits. Thus, the light-microscopic appearance of mesangial proliferative glomerulonephritis represents an extremely heterogeneous category of glomerular diseases with respect to underlying pathogenesis and undoubtedly to etiology. Some patients presenting with this morphologic lesion may in fact represent instances of resolving postinfectious glomerulonephritis, hereditary nephritis, or other multisystem diseases such as Henoch-

TABLE 223-4 Idiopathic nephrotic syndrome

SELECTED FEATURES OF UNDERLYING PRIMARY GLOMERULAR LESIONS

Lesion	Morphology* LM	IFM	EM	Approximate prevalence in children/adults, %	Common clinical/lab features	Response to therapy†	Likelihood of maintaining renal function‡
Minimal change	Normal or very mild proliferation	Negative–trace IgM	Foot process fusion, no deposits	70+/15–20	Highly selective proteinuria,§ *normal* C3, decreased IgG, increased IgM	Steroids + + Cytotoxic drugs + (cyclophosphamide, chlorambucil) Frequent relapses	95 +
Mesangial proliferative	Diffuse proliferation	Negative or variable mesangial IgM, IgG, C3	Mesangial deposits	15–20/5–10	Hematuria, *normal* C3	Steroids ± Cytotoxic drugs (?)	80 (?)
Focal sclerosis	Focal and segmental sclerosis	Focal and segmental IgM, C3	Foot process fusion, sclerosis, hyaline	10/10–20	Hematuria, leukocyturia, poorly selective proteinuria, *normal* C3	Steroids ± Cytotoxic drugs − Anticoagulants (?)	45–50
Membranous glomerulonephritis	Thick capillary wall, spikes of BM material	Diffuse granular capillary wall IgG	Subepithelial deposits	<5/30–40	Variable protein selectivity, *normal* C3, renal vein thrombosis	Steroids + Cytotoxic drugs (?)	50–70
Mesangial proliferative glomerulonephritis							
Type I	Mesangial interposition, lobular change	Diffuse C3; variable IgG, IgM	Subendothelial deposits	8/<5	Hematuria, *reduced* C3 (intermittent)	Steroids (?) Anticoagulants (?) Cytotoxic drugs (?) Antithrombotics +	60
Type II	Mesangial interposition	C3 capillary wall and mesangial nodules	Intramembranous deposits	3/<5	Hematuria, *reduced* C3 (persistent), +C3NF	Steroids − Cytotoxic drugs −	45

* LM = light microscopy, IFM = immunofluorescence microscopy, EM = electron microscopy, BM = basement membrane.
† Response to therapy: + + = highly responsive, + = variably responsive, ± = occasionally responsive, − = unresponsive.
‡ Percent of patients maintaining sufficient renal function to obviate need for chronic dialysis or transplantation within 5 years.

Schönlein purpura, vasculitis, or systemic lupus erythematosus. Electron-microscopic findings are nonspecific. Occasionally small electron-dense paramesangial deposits may be observed. The findings of large electron-dense deposits in the mesangium in association with the morphologic appearance of mesangial proliferative glomerulonephritis should heighten the suspicion of a multisystem disease or Berger's IgA nephropathy.

This lesion accounts for approximately 10 percent of instances of idiopathic nephrotic syndrome in adults and 15 percent in children. It tends to be more common in older children and young adults. Males tend to be affected slightly more often than females. Hematuria, either gross or microscopic, is commonly observed. Loin pain, bilateral or unilateral, may be seen in the idiopathic disorder but is more frequently observed in patients who have underlying IgA nephropathy. Laboratory features are not distinctive. Renal function may be modestly decreased at the time of diagnosis but is most often normal. Complement component levels are most often normal. IgG levels may be modestly reduced. IgA levels may be increased in IgA nephropathy. Circulating immune complexes may be found in some patients. Anti-streptolysin O titers are usually normal. Proteinuria is most often nonselective. No association with HLA antigens has yet been described for that category of patients who do not display predominant IgA mesangial deposits. The pathogenesis of this lesion is unknown and almost certainly the result of diverse pathogenetic processes. The presence of mesangial immunoglobulin deposits and circulating immune complexes in some, but not all, patients suggests an immune-complex pathogenesis, although the antigen(s) is unknown.

Among patients with well-developed nephrotic syndrome and moderate to severe diffuse mesangial proliferation, there is a tendency for persistence of proteinuria and progression to renal insufficiency. This is particularly true if areas of focal and segmental glomerular sclerosis are noted to be superimposed on the mesangial proliferative lesion at the time of the initial renal biopsy. Patients with milder forms of mesangial proliferative glomerulonephritis, particularly when unassociated with mesangial immunoglobulin deposition, may follow a more benign course. Some patients behave in a fashion quite similar to those with the minimal change lesion. Since renal biopsies from patients with the minimal change lesion may display mild degrees of glomerular hypercellularity, the apparently benign course followed by this subset of patients may indicate that they should be categorized as examples of minimal change lesion with more prominent mesangial proliferation rather than separately categorized under the heading of mesangial proliferative glomerulonephritis. Well-developed mesangial proliferative lesions, particularly in association with mesangial IgM deposits, tend to be unresponsive to corticosteroid therapy and to evolve with time into those of focal and segmental glomerular sclerosis. Indeed, the lesion of mesangial proliferative glomerulonephritis may be a predecessor of the lesion of focal and segmental glomerulosclerosis. Patients with mesangial proliferative glomerulonephritis who have complete remissions of proteinuria following treatment with corticosteroids in a fashion similar to that described for the minimal change lesion tend to do well with little inclination toward progressive renal insufficiency. Exacerbations and remissions of proteinuria may occur. Steroid-unresponsive patients with persistent nephrotic syndrome have a tendency to progress to renal insufficiency at variable rates. The role of adjunctive cytotoxic therapy (cyclophosphamide, chlorambucil, or azathioprine) has not yet been established in this category of lesions. Some studies have indicated that long-term therapy with indomethacin may be of benefit in this category of lesions, but no suitably controlled long-term studies have yet been performed.

Because of the highly variable pathogenesis in mesangial proliferative glomerulonephritis and its relative rarity, long-term prospective studies of natural history and therapy have not yet been conducted. Many patients, particularly those with mild degrees of proliferation and a remitting course following corticosteroid therapy, will have a very benign prognosis. Other patients, particularly those with steroid unresponsiveness and focal and segmental glomerulosclerosing lesions on the initial biopsy, will have a poor prognosis, often developing end-stage renal failure in 5 to 10 years following the initial diagnosis.

Focal and segmental glomerulosclerosis (focal sclerosis) This lesion is characterized by sclerosis and hyalinization of some, but not all, glomeruli (hence the term *focal*). Among affected glomeruli, only a portion of the glomerular tuft is abnormal (hence, *segmental*). There is a predilection for these lesions initially to affect the *juxtamedullary glomeruli* and to be associated with progressive tubulointerstitial damage. By immunofluorescence, granular and nodular deposits of IgM and C3 are found in the segmental sclerosing lesion. By electron microscopy, focal basement membrane collapse and denudation of epithelial surfaces are noted. All glomeruli reveal diffuse epithelial foot process effacement. This lesion accounts for 10 to 15 percent of cases of idiopathic NS seen among children and adults. Males tend to be affected slightly more often than females. Many investigators believe that focal sclerosis represents a stage in the evolution of a subgroup of patients with minimal change disease or "pure" mesangial proliferative glomerulonephritis (see above). In more than two-thirds of cases of focal sclerosis overt NS will be present at the time of diagnosis; in the remainder only isolated proteinuria in the nonnephrotic range is present. Hypertension, reduced GFR, abnormal tubule function, and abnormal urinary sediment occur commonly. It is important to emphasize that focal sclerosis may have clinical features indistinguishable from either minimal change disease, mesangial proliferative glomerulonephritis, or membranous glomerulopathy (see below). Proteinuria is nearly always nonselective or becomes so on follow-up. FDP and C3 may be present in the urine. Serum levels of C3 are normal and IgG levels are reduced, but not as severely as in minimal change disease. Similar lesions may be seen in association with "street" heroin abuse, vesicoureteral reflux, acquired immunodeficiency syndrome, solitary kidney, and renal allograft rejection and may complicate a variety of other primary glomerular diseases in the late stages. The occurrence of focal and segmental glomerulosclerosis in remnant glomeruli after extensive renal ablation has led to the suggestion that hyperfiltration (or some hemodynamic determinant thereof) may play a causative role in pathogenesis. Abnormalities in the prevalence of HLA antigens have not been consistently described. Renal vein thrombosis is uncommon.

There is little tendency for spontaneous remission, except among children. A progressive decline in GFR is the rule, albeit at variable rates. A subset of patients with focal sclerosis, who have extremely heavy proteinuria (i.e., greater than 15 to 20 g per day) and profound hypoalbuminemia, progress quite rapidly to end-stage renal failure, occasionally in a period of only a few months. Rarely, acute renal failure without recovery occurs.

The etiology and pathogenesis of focal sclerosis are unknown. Immune-complex–mediated disease has been postulated, primarily on the basis of immunofluorescence findings, and circulating immune complexes have been found in a small minority of cases.

Although very few prospective clinical trials have been conducted, a decline in the level of proteinuria concomitant with corticosteroid therapy and a lowered risk of progressive renal failure among patients experiencing a complete or partial remission of proteinuria suggest that corticosteroids may exert a beneficial effect on the natural history of the disorder. The effect of cytotoxic drugs and anticoagulants requires further study. At least 50 percent of patients with persistent heavy proteinuria develop end-stage renal failure or die of intercurrent illnesses within 10 years of diagnosis. The prognosis is much poorer for those patients with persistent NS in whom azotemia or hypertension is evident at time of diagnosis. This lesion has been found to recur in renal allografts, occasionally within a few hours of transplantation, suggesting the possibility of a circulating glomerular permeability "toxin" in its pathogenesis.

Membranous glomerulonephritis This lesion is characterized by the presence of irregular, discontinuous proteinaceous deposits along the outer (or subepithelial) aspect of the glomerular capillary wall.

These deposits contain IgG and appear dense by electron microscopy. Unlike focal sclerosis, *all glomeruli are involved uniformly.* At an early stage all glomeruli may appear normal by light microscopy, but as the disease progresses, immune deposits coalesce, causing the capillary wall to thicken. Eventually, increased amounts of basement membrane material project outward between deposits toward the urinary space, giving the appearance of "spikes." There is little proliferation of capillary endothelial or mesangial cells, although mesangial sclerosis may occur in advanced cases. Tubulointerstitial atrophy and vascular lesions are other late manifestations.

This disorder accounts for 30 to 40 percent of cases of idiopathic NS in adults but is quite rare in children. In over 80 percent of cases overt NS is present. In the remainder only isolated proteinuria is found. Males tend to be affected more often than females. Blood pressure, GFR, and urinary sediment tend to be normal early in the course, making it extremely difficult to distinguish membranous glomerulopathy from minimal change disease on clinical grounds alone. Urinary protein selectivity is quite variable. Serum complement components are normal, but IgG levels are usually modestly depressed. Membranous glomerulonephritis may develop in association with systemic lupus erythematosus (Chap. 224), certain chronic infections (e.g., malaria, hepatitis B), solid tumors (e.g., melanoma and cancer of the lung and colon), or after exposure to heavy metals (gold, mercury) or drugs (penicillamine, captopril). A careful search for these causes is warranted in every case of idiopathic NS due to membranous glomerulonephritis. There appears to be a high frequency of renal vein thrombosis in affected patients (see above).

Spontaneous complete remissions of NS are quite common in children but take place in only 20 to 25 percent of adults. Steroid treatment does not greatly influence the development of lasting complete remissions, but may induce a reduction of proteinuria to nonnephrotic levels. A beneficial effect of steroids is still a source of controversy, since spontaneous partial remissions also occur, although somewhat less frequently than in steroid-treated patients. There is presently no agreement about optimal dosage and duration of therapy; however, alternate-day steroid therapy seems to be the safest approach and may be associated with a lower risk of progressive renal failure. Regimens involving combinations of corticosteroids and alkylating agents have variable effects, but may be associated with a higher remission rate and a slower rate of progression of renal failure.

Slowly progressive renal functional impairment occurs almost exclusively among those patients with persistent proteinuria in the nephrotic range. Partial or complete spontaneous or treatment-associated remissions provide nearly complete protection from renal failure. Complete or partial remissions occur at variable times after the discovery of the disease, but renal failure is unlikely to develop in the first few years. Within 10 years of the time of the diagnosis, however, 35 to 50 percent of patients will die of intercurrent illness or develop end-stage renal failure. The vast majority of survivors will have had complete or partial remission of proteinuria. Rare cases have recurred in renal transplants. A few patients are known to have developed superimposed anti-GBM antibody–mediated disease and RPGN.

Mesangiocapillary glomerulonephritis This group of disorders is characterized by proliferation of mesangial cells, often with segmental or diffuse interposition of these cells or their cytoplasm into peripheral capillary loops. There is evidence of increased synthesis of mesangial matrix as well. The glomerular capillary wall is irregularly thickened, by virtue of the mesangial extensions and the attendant synthesis of basement membrane–like material. This group of disorders is also known as *membranoproliferative* or *lobular glomerulonephritis.* Several immunofluorescence and electron-microscopic patterns are present and are believed to reflect heterogeneous mechanisms of pathogenesis. In the ultrastructural *type I* lesion, subendothelial electron-dense deposits are present. C3 is deposited in a granular pattern indicative of immune-complex pathogenesis, but IgG and the early components of complement are present inconsistently. In the ultrastructural *type*

II lesion the lamina densa of the GBM is transformed into an extremely electron-dense character, giving rise to the term *dense deposit disease.* Basement membranes in Bowman's capsules and in tubules are similarly affected. C3 is found irregularly in the GBM and in granules or rings in the mesangium. Small amounts of Ig (typically IgM) are present, but the early acting complement components are absent from the deposits. Properdin deposition is variable. Additional ultrastructural variants, based upon location of deposit and basement membrane changes, have also been described.

Mesangiocapillary glomerulonephritis, types I and II, is found in 5 to 10 percent of cases of idiopathic NS in children, particularly between the ages of 8 to 16 years, and somewhat less commonly in adults. Type I accounts for at least two-thirds of cases. Sexes are affected equally. In 50 to 75 percent of patients, a full-blown NS is present, often with features of AGN. In the remainder, proteinuria is in the nonnephrotic range and is nearly always accompanied by microscopic hematuria. Blood pressure and GFR are frequently abnormal, and the urinary sediment is typically active. Functional abnormalities of the renal tubules are common. Urinary protein selectivity is usually poor; FDP and C3 are found in the urine. Serum C3 levels are reduced in 70 to 80 percent of cases of type I and in over 90 percent of type II disease. The early acting complement components C1q, C4, and C2 are often normal, however, especially in type II disease. This pattern may be indicative of activation of the alternate complement pathway (see Chap. 222). C3 nephritic factor (C3NF) is often found in the serum of patients with type II, especially if the C3 level is quite low. Circulating immune complexes are found in type I. Lesions similar to type I membranoproliferative glomerulonephritis may also be found in SLE, hemolytic-uremic syndrome, transplant rejection, chronic hepatitis B antigenemia, and "shunt" nephritis. Renal vein thrombosis may occur. Type II nephritis may be associated with partial lipodystrophy.

Spontaneous remissions are uncommon. Long-term, alternate-day steroid therapy (0.3 to 0.5 mg/kg every other day) may delay the progression of the disease. Treatment regimens which combine steroids and cytotoxic agents are not of proven value. Recently, evidence suggesting a beneficial effect of anticoagulants and inhibitors of platelet aggregation (acetylsalicylic acid plus dipyridamole) has appeared. The course is usually relentlessly progressive, and approximately one-half of patients die or develop end-stage renal failure within 10 years of the diagnosis. The prognosis for type II lesions seems somewhat worse than for type I. Type II disease almost invariably recurs in the transplanted kidney but does not always result in the premature loss of the allograft.

Other forms of idiopathic nephrotic syndrome In a small percentage of adults and children with idiopathic NS (i.e., 5 to 10 percent) other lesions are encountered on renal biopsy. These include *crescentic glomerulonephritis* and *focal* and *segmental proliferative glomerulonephritis.* The pathogenetic mechanisms responsible for these lesions vary. For example, some of the cases of focal and segmental glomerulonephritis may have extensive mesangial IgA deposits and fit into the category of Berger's disease (see below). Serum C3 levels are usually normal. The clinical characteristics, natural history, and response to treatment of these lesions are not well defined. Hematuria is common and may be recurrent. Proteinuria tends to be nonselective. Spontaneous remissions of NS are uncommon. Since no controlled studies have been conducted, it is not possible to evaluate the effectiveness of treatment. Crescentic glomerulonephritis is likely to have a poor prognosis, whereas mesangial and focal and segmental proliferative glomerulonephritis have a more favorable long-term outlook.

NEPHROTIC SYNDROME CAUSED BY INFECTIOUS AGENTS, DRUGS, OR CHEMICALS Table 223-3 lists the common infectious and drug-related etiologies of NS. In many instances, NS will abate following cure of the infection or withdrawal of the offending medication. In patients receiving organic gold therapy for rheumatoid arthritis, or in those exposed to inorganic, organic, or elemental mercury or to penicillamine therapy, membranous glomerulonephritis is usually the lesion responsible for NS. NS is known to follow immunization and antiserum treatment of tetanus or snakebite and to occur in situations associated with atopy.

ASYMPTOMATIC URINARY ABNORMALITIES

This group of patients is identified principally by the findings of *proteinuria in the nonnephrotic range and/or hematuria*, unaccompanied by edema, reduced GFR, or hypertension. Abnormalities are often discovered incidentally and may be persistent or recurrent. This syndrome may, of course, be but a phase in the natural history of other glomerulopathic syndromes, especially nephrotic syndrome or chronic glomerulonephritis. Common glomerular disorders which present as asymptomatic proteinuria and/or hematuria at some point in their natural history are listed in Table 223-5. The heredofamilial and multisystem diseases are discussed in Chap. 224. The presence of dysmorphic erythrocytes and/or red cell casts is a very useful finding indicative of an underlying glomerular cause for the hematuria.

IDIOPATHIC RENAL HEMATURIA (See also Chap. 40) **Berger's disease (IgA nephropathy)** This disorder was first described by Berger and Hinglais in 1968 and is characterized by recurrent episodes of gross or microscopic hematuria. The diagnosis depends on the finding of prominent IgA deposits in the mesangium by immunofluorescence microscopy. Berger's disease is the most common cause of recurrent hematuria of glomerular origin. It most commonly affects young adults, mostly males. Typically, episodes of macroscopic hematuria are associated with minor flulike illnesses or vigorous exercise. Patients frequently complain of vague constitutional symptoms, but skin rash, arthritis, and abdominal pain are absent. Urine protein excretion rates are usually less than 3.5 g per day; not uncommonly protein excretion is normal or only mildly increased. The nephrotic syndrome develops occasionally. Blood pressure, GFR, and serum albumin are normal, at least early in the disease. Serum IgA levels are increased in about 50 percent of cases, while serum complement component levels remain normal. Biopsy of the skin of the volar surface of the forearm will often reveal dermal capillary deposits of IgA, C3, and fibrin, but not early acting complement components or IgA secretory fragments. Similar skin biopsy findings may be encountered in Henoch-Schönlein purpura (Chap. 224). Indeed, Berger's disease may be a monosymptomatic form of Henoch-Schönlein purpura.

Renal biopsy reveals a spectrum of changes by light microscopy, but diffuse mesangial proliferative or focal and segmental proliferative

TABLE 223-5 Glomerular causes of asymptomatic urinary abnormalities

I Hematuria with or without proteinuria
  A Primary glomerular diseases
    1 Berger's disease (IgA nephropathy)
    2 Mesangiocapillary glomerulonephritis
    3 Other primary glomerular hematurias accompanied by "pure" mesangial proliferation, focal and segmental proliferative glomerulonephritis, or other lesions
  B Associated with multisystem or heredofamilial diseases
    1 Alport's syndrome and other "benign" familial hematurias
    2 Fabry's disease
    3 Sickle cell disease
  C Associated with infections
    1 Resolving poststreptococcal glomerulonephritis
    2 Other postinfectious glomerulonephritides
II Isolated nonnephrotic proteinuria
  A Primary glomerular diseases
    1 "Orthostatic" proteinuria
    2 Focal and segmental glomerulosclerosis
    3 Membranous glomerulonephritis
  B Associated with multisystem or heredofamilial diseases
    1 Diabetes mellitus
    2 Amyloidosis
    3 Nail-patella syndrome

glomerulonephritis is found most often. In some cases glomerular morphology may be normal by light microscopy; rarely, crescents may be found. The distinguishing feature is the finding by immunofluorescence microscopy of *diffuse mesangial deposition of IgA*, often accompanied by lesser amounts of IgG and nearly always by C3 and properdin, but not by C1q or C4. Fibrin reactive antigens are also commonly demonstrable in the mesangium or in association with crescents if the latter are present. The pathogenesis of IgA nephropathy is unknown, but the systemic character of the IgA deposits (skin and glomerular capillaries), the presence of circulating IgG and IgA complexes in the majority of cases, and its similarity to Henoch-Schönlein purpura suggest that it is an immune-complex–mediated disease. The nature and source of the antigen are unknown.

The prognosis is variable, but, in general, the disease tends to progress slowly. It has been estimated that approximately 50 percent of patients can be expected to develop end-stage renal failure within 25 years of the time of diagnosis. Azotemia, hypertension, or proteinuria in the nephrotic range at the time of diagnosis are associated with a poor prognosis. At present, there is no evidence to suggest that any form of therapy greatly influences the natural history. Some have suggested that intermittent steroid therapy may reduce the frequency of episodes of gross hematuria. Corticosteroids may also result in remissions of proteinuria in those patients with nephrotic syndrome and mild glomerular abnormalities by light microscopy.

Other primary renal hematurias Some cases of recurrent hematuria do not reveal the typical immunofluorescence findings seen in Berger's disease. This group of patients is poorly defined, and in them the etiology and pathogenesis is varied. Some may represent resolving episodes of acute glomerulonephritis or early examples of mesangiocapillary or hereditary glomerulonephritis (Alport's syndrome, see Chap. 224). The morphologic lesions most commonly encountered are focal and segmental or diffuse mesangial proliferative glomerulonephritis, although mild and nonspecific glomerular changes may also be observed. Immunofluorescence studies reveal varying degrees of immunoglobulin and/or complement component deposition (principally IgM and/or C3) in the mesangium. Some cases show linear deposits of IgG, suggesting a possible anti-GBM antibody pathogenesis. Electron microscopy may reveal dense deposits in the mesangium or thin and attenuated glomerular basement membranes. Overall, this group of patients is believed to have an excellent prognosis, with spontaneous permanent remissions of recurrent hematuria. Progressive renal insufficiency is unusual. Because of the benign prognosis no treatment is indicated.

ISOLATED NONNEPHROTIC PROTEINURIA OF GLOMERULAR ORIGIN (See also Chap. 40) The discovery of mild to moderate degrees of proteinuria (i.e., greater than 150 mg but less than 2.0 g per day), unaccompanied by abnormalities in the urinary sediment or evidence of hypertension or reduced renal function, is a common problem in internal medicine. Such patients may display other features of heredofamilial or multisystem diseases, including diabetes mellitus, amyloidosis, rheumatoid arthritis, or cancer. Among cases of isolated proteinuria consequent to primary glomerular disease the abnormality may either be persistent or evanescent. Proteinuria may occur primarily in the upright posture (*orthostatic proteinuria*) or be present both in recumbent and erect positions (*constant proteinuria*). Fixed and reproducible orthostatic proteinuria is regarded as having a benign prognosis and frequently disappears on long-term follow-up. Renal biopsies will most often reveal normal glomeruli or trivial alterations of dubious significance. On the other hand, persistent and constant proteinuria may be indicative of a more serious disease, and renal biopsies will more often reveal definite evidence of a structural lesion. Some of the lesions which might be encountered have been discussed in the context of idiopathic nephrotic syndrome. Other patients may prove to have a clinically unsuspected disease such as amyloidosis or diabetes mellitus. In the remainder, the lesions are usually trivial and nonspecific and their long-term significance is quite uncertain. In the case of primary glomerular diseases, so long as urinary protein excretion remains modest, the prognosis is excellent and deterioration of renal function is uncommon. Renal biopsy is not commonly undertaken in patients with persistent and isolated nonnephrotic proteinuria, as determining underlying morphology seldom leads to specific therapy and adds information chiefly of a prognostic nature. Since patients having proteinuria over 2.0 g per day are more likely to have lesions which will later progress, many experienced nephrologists limit renal biopsies to this latter group of patients.

CHRONIC GLOMERULONEPHRITIS (CGN)

The syndrome of CGN is characterized chiefly by *persistent urinary abnormalities* (e.g., proteinuria and/or hematuria) and by *slowly progressive impairment of renal function,* eventuating in hypertension, contracted granular kidneys, and end-stage renal failure. With the possible exception of the minimal change lesion associated with idiopathic nephrotic syndrome (see above) all the disorders described in this chapter and in Chap. 224 can lead eventually to CGN. The pathophysiology of the syndrome of CGN as it appears in the context of renal failure is described in Chaps. 218 and 220.

The glomerular structural alterations that underlie this syndrome may be categorized as *proliferative* (including mesangial, endo- and/or extracapillary proliferative glomerulonephritis, and focal and segmental proliferative glomerulonephritis), *sclerosing* (including focal and diffuse glomerular sclerosis), and *membranous.* Such lesions are found in the vast majority of patients with CGN. In the small remainder, the underlying lesions are not readily categorized morphologically. These are often referred to as *chronic "nonspecific" glomerulonephritis.*

The clinical characteristics of the specific lesions are described in other sections of this chapter. The etiologic and pathogenetic origins of chronic nonspecific glomerulonephritis are unknown but are undoubtedly heterogeneous. Complicating vascular disease contributes to the glomerular obliteration seen in this group of disorders. It is quite reasonable to suspect that some of the patients categorized as having chronic nonspecific glomerulonephritis may have had an earlier unrecognized or undiagnosed episode of acute PSGN. However, such patients usually fail to recall a specific episode of acute nephritis.

The detection of CGN usually occurs in one of several ways: (1) by the incidental finding of abnormal urine, impaired renal function, or hypertension during multiphasic screening of asymptomatic individuals or during evaluation of such individuals for an unrelated illness; (2) as the result of the insidious onset of progressive symptoms or signs of advanced renal disease, especially anemia and hypertension; or (3) after an exacerbation of glomerulonephritis, usually during the course of a nonspecific viral or bacterial illness. In advanced stages of the syndrome, the clinical separation of CGN from other causes of renal failure may be difficult; however, the presence of symmetrically contracted kidneys, moderate to heavy proteinuria, abnormal urinary sediment (especially red blood cell casts), and x-ray evidence of normal pyelocalyceal systems are all suggestive of CGN.

The evolution of CGN varies considerably, depending upon the nature of the underlying disease and the presence or absence of complications, especially hypertension. Ten, fifteen, twenty, or more years may elapse from the first discovery of an abnormal urine sediment until the development of end-stage renal failure. Renal biopsy is necessary to define the precise nature of the underlying glomerular lesion. The principal advantage of a morphologic evaluation among patients presenting with the syndrome of CGN is to determine prognosis rather than therapy.

Treatment of patients with CGN is supportive and symptomatic. Despite many years of controlled and uncontrolled trials, unequivocal evidence of a favorable effect of treatment with steroids, cytotoxic agents, nonsteroidal anti-inflammatory agents, and anticoagulants has yet to be provided. The management of specific lesions is discussed in greater detail in the relevant sections of this chapter. Hypertension

and symptomatic urinary tract infections should be treated vigorously, taking care to avoid nephrotoxic agents. Diuretics should generally be employed only as adjuncts to antihypertensive management or to deal with debilitating degrees of edema. Fluid and sodium should be provided according to the dictates of blood pressure control. Rigorous salt restriction is usually unnecessary and may be hazardous. In the absence of congestive heart failure or marked hypoalbuminemia, severe edema rarely occurs in CGN until the terminal phases of the illness. Potassium restriction is usually unnecessary. Protein and phosphate restriction may slow the rate of progression of renal failure.

REFERENCES

BRENNER BM, STEIN JH (eds): Nephrotic syndrome, in *Contemporary Issues in Nephrology,* vol 9. New York, Churchill Livingstone, 1982

COUSER WG: Idiopathic rapidly progressive glomerulonephritis. Am J Nephrol 2:57, 1982

D'AMICO G et al (eds): IgA mesangial nephropathy. Contrib Nephrol 40:1, 1984

GLASSOCK RJ (ed): Primary glomerular diseases. Semin Nephrol 2:190, 1982

——— et al: Primary glomerular diseases, in *The Kidney,* 3d ed, BM Brenner, FC Rector Jr (eds). Philadelphia, Saunders, 1986, p 929

MADAIO MP, HARRINGTON JT: The diagnosis of acute glomerulonephritis. N Engl J Med 309:1299, 1983

MALLICK NP et al: Clinical membranous nephropathy. Nephron 34:209, 1983

---

224 GLOMERULOPATHIES ASSOCIATED WITH MULTISYSTEM DISEASES

RICHARD J. GLASSOCK / BARRY M. BRENNER

Glomerular injury may be a prominent feature of diseases which affect multiple organs and systems. By and large the etiologies of these diseases are unknown, but aberrant immunologic processes, neoplasia, metabolic disturbances, and genetically based biochemical abnormalities are believed to be dominant factors in their pathogenesis. These processes lead to a variety of alterations in glomerular structure and function. Some of the glomerular lesions are specific for the underlying disease entity (e.g., amyloidosis, nodular diabetic glomerulosclerosis); however, the majority are nonspecific. Proteinuria results from defects in the charge- and/or size-selective glomerular permeability barriers. Reductions in glomerular filtration rate develop because of progressive loss of filtration surface area. Although the extrarenal manifestations of these diseases are useful in establishing a diagnosis, some may present with predominant or exclusive renal involvement and only covert extrarenal manifestations.

IMMUNOLOGICALLY MEDIATED MULTISYSTEM DISEASES

SYSTEMIC LUPUS ERYTHEMATOSUS (See also Chap. 262)   Systemic lupus erythematosus (SLE) is the archetype of an immunologically mediated multisystem disease (see Chap. 222) and is representative of the multisystem diseases in which renal involvement is common. The etiology of SLE is unknown; however, viral infection, genetic factors, and abnormal immune responsiveness probably interact to produce the disease. The principal mechanism for tissue injury in SLE appears to be the deposition of circulating immune complexes, although other mechanisms may also play a role, including antitissue antibody and in situ immune-complex formation (see Chap. 222). The circulating immune complexes may be composed of a wide variety of endogenous antigens combined with autoantibodies. DNA (single-stranded and double-stranded) is a major antigenic component of immune complexes. The prevalence of clinically evident renal involvement in SLE ranges from as low as 35 percent to more than 90 percent in different series. Manifestations of renal disease range from mild abnormalities of the urinary sediment (predominantly hematuria) to massive proteinuria and from chronic indolent glomerulonephritis to a fulminant inflammatory process leading to rapidly progressive renal failure.

The diagnosis and extrarenal manifestations of SLE are described in Chap. 262. This section will deal with the renal involvement. Although extrarenal features often dominate the clinical picture, SLE may present initially solely with renal manifestations. Morphologic evidence of renal involvement may exist with or without clinical manifestations. If immunofluorescence and electron-microscopic studies of renal tissue are performed, abnormalities are present in virtually every patient with SLE. The abnormal glomerular morphologic lesions in SLE form a spectrum based upon such correlative light- and electron-microscopic and immunofluorescence studies of renal biopsies.

Minimal lupus glomerular lesion   This pattern is characterized by few or no changes by light microscopy. Immunofluorescence studies reveal moderate immunoglobulin (Ig) and complement deposits exclusively in mesangium. Scattered electron-dense deposits are found in mesangium by electron microscopy. Clinical renal manifestations may include mild proteinuria and microscopic hematuria. Nephrotic syndrome is uncommon. Glomerular filtration rate (GFR) is almost always normal. Serologic manifestations vary depending upon the activity of extrarenal disease. Antibodies to DNA are usually present in low titer, and levels of C3 and C4 may be decreased, especially if dermatitis is severe. Circulating immune complexes may also be detected in patients with skin lesions.

Mesangial lupus glomerulonephritis   This pattern is characterized by mild to moderate diffuse mesangial cell proliferation and/or mesangial sclerosis. Immunofluorescence studies reveal immunoglobulins (IgG, IgM, and IgA) and complement components (C1q, C4, and C3) deposited in a granular pattern principally in the mesangium. By electron microscopy, electron-dense deposits are also found to be confined to the mesangium. This morphologic appearance may be present in the absence of clinical renal disease or may be associated with minor abnormalities in the urinary sediment and modest proteinuria. Nephrotic syndrome and hypertension may occasionally be present. GFR is almost always normal. Mesangial lupus glomerulonephritis may be the initial renal involvement in SLE, from which other patterns evolve. Associated serologic abnormalities depend upon the degree of extrarenal activity. These include increased levels of antibody to denatured, single-stranded DNA (ssDNA) or native, double-stranded DNA (dsDNA); depressed serum levels of C3, C4, and C1q; and detectable levels of circulating immune complexes (CIC) (Table 224-1).

Focal and segmental lupus glomerulonephritis   This pattern is characterized by focal and segmental cellular proliferation, often

associated with necrosis, superimposed on diffuse mesangial hypercellularity. Granular deposits of immunoglobulins and complement components are more extensive than in the mesangial form and involve both the mesangium and occasional glomerular capillary loops. By electron microscopy, dense subendothelial deposits are found in the mesangium and in a few peripheral capillary loops. Clinical and laboratory evidence of renal injury is more common than in mesangial lupus glomerulonephritis. Nephrotic syndrome may occur in 10 to 20 percent of patients, but in general GFR is well preserved. This lesion may persist, resolve, or progress to diffuse proliferative lupus glomerulonephritis. Serologic features of active disease are often present in untreated patients.

Diffuse proliferative lupus glomerulonephritis   This pattern is characterized by diffuse mesangial and endothelial cell proliferation which may include extensive peripheral capillary wall interposition of mesangial cells. In addition focal cellular necrosis, hematoxylinophilic bodies, fibrinoid necrosis, and "wire loops" (capillaries whose basement membranes are thickened markedly owing to subendothelial deposits) may be present. Extensive extracapillary proliferative (crescentic) glomerulonephritis, vasculitis, and interstitial nephritis may also be found. Granular deposits of immunoglobulins and complement components are extensive and involve the mesangium and nearly every capillary loop. Electron microscopy reveals extensive subendothelial and mesangial electron-dense deposits as well as occasional intramembranous or subepithelial deposits. Most patients have an active urinary sediment, heavy proteinuria, and progressive impairment of renal function; occasionally, clinical evidence of renal involvement is lacking. In the untreated patient evidence of serologic activity is usually present, including depressed serum C3 and C4 concentrations, high levels of precipitating and nonprecipitating complement-fixing antibody to dsDNA, cryoimmunoglobulinemia, and circulating immune complexes. This lesion is associated with an ominous prognosis, although vigorous treatment may modify the course (see below).

Membranous lupus glomerulonephritis   This pattern is nearly identical with that described for idiopathic membranous glomerulonephritis (Chap. 223), except that mesangial deposits and mesangial proliferation are more frequent. There is thickening of the glomerular capillary wall due to the presence of immunoglobulin and complement-containing electron-dense deposits in the subepithelial space, often associated with a spike-like basement membrane reaction. Nearly all patients have heavy proteinuria and the nephrotic syndrome. Although GFR may be normal initially, most patients ultimately develop progressive renal failure. A proliferative lesion may occasionally evolve, and the prognosis then assumes that of diffuse proliferative glomerulonephritis. Serologic features of SLE may or may not be present at the time of diagnosis of this nephropathy. Antibody to dsDNA tends to be nonprecipitating. Some patients with membranous lupus glomerulonephritis may be erroneously categorized as having

TABLE 224-1   Serologic findings in selected multisystem diseases

Disease	C3	Ig	FANA	Anti-dsDNA	Anti-GBM	Cryo-Ig	CIC
Systemic lupus erythematosus	↓↓	↑ IgG	+++	++	−	++	+++
Goodpasture's syndrome	−	−	−	−	+++	−	±
Henoch-Schönlein purpura	−	↑ IgA	−	−	−	±	++
Polyarteritis	↓	↑ IgG	+	±	−	++	+++
Wegener's granulomatosis	↓↑	↑ IgA, IgE	−	−	−	±	++
Cryoimmunoglobulinemia	↓	±	−	−	−	+++	++
Multiple myeloma	−	↓↑IgG, IgA, IgD, IgE	−	−	−	+	±
Waldenström's macroglobulinemia	−	↑ IgM	−	−	−	−	−
Amyloidosis	−	± Ig	−	−	−	−	−

NOTE: *C3 = C3 component of complement; Ig = immunoglobulin levels; FANA = fluorescent antinuclear antibody assay; anti-dsDNA = antibody to double-stranded (native) DNA; anti-GBM = antibody to glomerular basement membrane antigens; cryo-Ig = cryoimmunoglobulin; CIC = circulating immune complexes; − = normal; + = occasionally slightly abnormal; ++ = often abnormal; +++ = severely abnormal.*

idiopathic membranous glomerulopathy (see Chap. 223). Measurements of the level of antibody to dsDNA or ssDNA and circulating immune complexes and biopsies of skin for dermal-epidermal deposits of Ig ("lupus band test") may be helpful for diagnosis in such cases.

Sclerosing or end-stage lupus glomerulonephritis This pattern is characterized by obliterative and sclerosing lesions of the glomeruli and probably represents a late stage of proliferative lesions. Immunofluorescence studies may be only weakly positive for immunoglobulins; subendothelial deposits are infrequent. Hypertension and impaired renal function are common. Serologic parameters of activity of SLE may or may not be present.

Prognosis and treatment The prognosis and treatment of SLE with renal involvement depends upon the nature of the underlying renal lesion especially with regard to the class and the activity of the morphologic disease and to the extent and severity of associated glomerulosclerosis and interstitial fibrosis. Patients with milder forms of renal disease (e.g., minimal, mesangial, or focal lupus glomerulonephritis) tend to do well if treatment is directed to control of the extrarenal manifestations of the disease. Corticosteroids in modest doses, salicylates, or antimalarials are usually sufficient. Potent nonsteroidal, anti-inflammatory agents may cause functional depression of GFR and should be used with caution in patients with known renal involvement. Serologic parameters, including anti-dsDNA and complement components (C3, C4), should be followed serially. Fluorescent antinuclear antibody tests have little value in prognosis or in following the effectiveness of treatment. A return to normal values for antibody to dsDNA and/or complement components is a favorable sign; however, persistently abnormal serologic features do not necessarily indicate worsening or progressive renal involvement, especially in patients with active extrarenal manifestations. For patients with mild lesions, 85 percent or more can be expected to survive at least 10 years. Patients with membranous lupus glomerulonephritis who receive treatment directed primarily at the extrarenal features also have favorable long-term prognosis. On the other hand, patients with diffuse proliferative lupus glomerulonephritis do less well and, therefore, warrant a more aggressive approach toward ameliorating the renal disease. High-dose, long-term oral glucocorticoid therapy, although capable of improving extrarenal signs of active disease and reducing the acute inflammatory component of the renal lesions, is not an altogether satisfactory regimen for lupus nephritis. Such treatment is associated with a high prevalence of side effects and may not prevent progression of chronic lesions. High-dose, short-term intravenous methylprednisolone is effective in reducing signs of systemic activity of the disease, especially in patients with recent deterioration. Adjunctive use of cytotoxic agents (azathioprine, cyclophosphamide, or chlorambucil) exerts a steroid-sparing effect and may prevent progression of chronic lesions, particularly among those with mild chronic lesions prior to therapy. The optimal regimen has not yet been established; however, intermittent intravenous cyclophosphamide plus low-dose oral prednisone (0.5 mg/kg per day) and combinations of azathioprine, cyclophosphamide, and low-dose oral prednisone appear to be more effective than azathioprine or cyclophosphamide combined with low-dose prednisone. Because prospective randomized trials have involved only small numbers of patients, it is premature to adopt any particular regimen as the treatment of choice. Even combinations of azathioprine and low-dose prednisone may exert a benefical effect in certain subsets of patients. Little is gained by using a combined steroid-cytotoxic approach in patients with advanced renal failure due to progressive glomerular capillary obliteration and sclerosis. These patients are best treated with dialysis and/or transplantation. Plasma exchange accompanied by immunosuppressive therapy for fulminating disease appears promising. Serologic studies, especially serial measurements of antibody to dsDNA, complement components, and circulating immune complexes, are useful parameters to follow in patients under therapy. Return of these parameters to normal usually

indicates satisfactory control of disease and indicates that drug dosage can be safely diminished. These measurements also need to be monitored to guide more aggressive therapy when appropriate.

Overall, long-term prognosis for patients with SLE and renal involvement has improved. Whether improvements in methods of diagnosis, serologic monitoring, or treatment are responsible is unknown. Progression to end-stage renal disease is now relatively uncommon even for patients with diffuse proliferative glomerulonephritis. Cerebral involvement and infectious complications of therapy are now major causes of morbidity and mortality in SLE. Patients with SLE seem to do well on regular chronic dialysis; moreover, as uremia develops, some patients experience remissions of extrarenal activity. In transplanted patients, recurrence of SLE in the renal allograft is uncommon. Thus, patients with SLE and nephritis are satisfactory candidates for both dialysis and transplantation.

GOODPASTURE'S SYNDROME This disorder consists of *pulmonary hemorrhage, glomerulonephritis,* and *antibody to basement membrane antigens*. Its etiology is unknown. Goodpasture's syndrome may appear at any age and typically affects young men. However, an increasing number of affected women are being recognized.

Pulmonary hemorrhage may be mild and easily overlooked or severe and life-threatening. The initial manifestations of pulmonary involvement are cough, mild shortness of breath, and hemoptysis. Hilar pulmonary infiltrates may be seen by chest x-ray, and hypoxia is frequent. With marked intraalveolar hemorrhage pulmonary carbon monoxide uptake is increased, and the pulmonary clearance of radioactive carbon monoxide is depressed. Pulmonary iron sequestration may be documented by scanning of the lungs with ^{59}Fe. Hemosiderin-laden macrophages may be seen in the sputum, but this is a nonspecific finding. Iron-deficiency anemia may result if pulmonary bleeding is prolonged and severe. A history of recent inhalation of volatile hydrocarbons or of viral influenza may be obtained. Fever, arthralgias, and other systemic symptoms are mild or absent at the time of presentation. Pulmonary hemorrhage may also be associated with renal failure in SLE, polyarteritis, Wegener's granulomatosis, cryoimmunoglobulinemia, Henoch-Schönlein purpura, pulmonary embolism consequent to renal vein thrombosis, Legionnaires' disease, and congestive heart failure in patients with end-stage renal disease. These disorders can ordinarily be differentiated from Goodpasture's syndrome by their extrarenal features and by typical serologic findings (Table 224-1).

The glomeruli in Goodpasture's syndrome range from normal or nearly normal to focal proliferative and necrotizing glomerulonephritis; most often there is extensive extracapillary proliferation (crescents). Rapidly progressive renal failure is the common feature, although patients may initially have normal renal function and mild microscopic abnormalities in the urinary sediment. Immunofluorescence studies of renal biopsy material reveal the typical *linear deposits* of anti-basement membrane antibody, often but not necessarily always accompanied by C3 deposition. Electron-microscopic studies do not reveal electron-dense deposits.

Circulating antibody to glycopeptide antigens related to the noncollagenous domains on type IV (basement membrane) collagen are found in over 90 percent of cases if serums are examined early in the course by immunofluorescence or radioimmunoassay (Table 224-1). The level of circulating antibody does not correlate well with the severity of the renal or pulmonary manifestations. Measurements of circulating antibody are of diagnostic value and have no prognostic significance. Serum complement components are nearly always normal, and circulating immune complexes and cryoimmunoglobulins are absent.

The course is variable. Patients surviving an initial bout of severe hemoptysis may undergo long-term remissions or may have repeated bouts of pulmonary hemorrhage. Mild forms of glomerular injury may not progress, and the principal clinical problems may be related to recurrent hemoptysis. The diagnosis in such patients may be confused with idiopathic pulmonary hemosiderosis. More commonly the renal disease is progressive, sometimes fulminant, leading to oliguric renal failure in a matter of a few weeks or months (i.e., rapidly progressive glomerulonephritis).

Life-threatening degrees of pulmonary hemorrhage may respond temporarily to high doses of parenteral methylprednisolone (10 to 15 mg/kg) given over short periods. The effectiveness of such therapy in reversing extensive crescentic glomerular lesions is not established. Anticoagulants are contraindicated in the face of active pulmonary hemorrhage. Intensive plasma exchange (2 to 4 liters of plasma per day), in combination with cytotoxic drugs and modest doses of corticosteroids, has been associated with dramatic remissions of pulmonary hemorrhage and improvement of the glomerular lesions. This is particularly true if treatment is initiated early in patients with relatively acute disease in whom oliguria has not yet developed. The duration and frequency of plasma exchanges depend upon the response of the patient and the results of monitoring levels of circulating antibody to glomerular basement membrane antigens. Renal biopsy is helpful in guiding the management, but even in the presence of extensive crescent formation responses may be satisfactory. If irreversible glomerular obliteration, extensive interstitial fibrosis, and tubular atrophy are found, especially in the oliguric patient with long-standing disease, plasma exchange offers little hope for improving the renal lesion. Such patients are best managed by regular hemodialysis and/or transplantation. Although recurrences may occasionally develop, the diagnosis is not a contraindication to transplantation so long as the procedure is delayed until levels of circulating anti-basement membrane antibody decrease to undetectable levels.

HENOCH-SCHÖNLEIN PURPURA (See also Chap. 280)

This disorder is characterized by nonthrombocytopenic purpura, arthralgias, abdominal pain, and glomerulonephritis. Renal involvement is common and is manifested chiefly by hematuria and proteinuria. In some instances renal involvement is severe, leading to rapidly progressive glomerulonephritis or nephrotic syndrome. The onset of the disease may resemble acute postinfectious glomerulonephritis. Serum complement component levels are usually normal. Serum IgA levels are increased in about half the patients (Table 224-1). Renal biopsy reveals a spectrum of abnormalities. Mild diffuse mesangial cell proliferation and/or focal and segmental proliferative glomerulonephritis is most common when bouts of macroscopic hematuria and proteinuria are present. More severe and diffuse proliferative glomerulonephritis, sometimes accompanied by extracapillary proliferation (crescents), arises in patients with heavy proteinuria and/or rapidly diminishing GFR. Characteristically, immunofluorescence studies reveal mesangial and peripheral capillary granular deposits of IgA, IgG, C3, and fibrinogen but not C1q, C4, or IgA secretory piece. Similar immunofluorescence findings are present in the dermal capillaries of biopsies of involved and uninvolved skin. Electron microscopy reveals electron-dense deposits principally in the mesangium. These findings suggest that Henoch-Schönlein purpura is due to circulating IgA-containing immune complexes. Circulating cryoimmunoglobulins and immune complexes may be present, but the nature of the antigen and the antibody reactivity of the IgA are unknown. Although food allergies and upper respiratory infections may be present, there is no clear-cut etiologic relationship. *Berger's disease* (IgA nephropathy, Chap. 223) may represent a form of Henoch-Schönlein purpura.

The diagnosis is ordinarily not difficult when the typical clinical features are present. The differential diagnosis includes SLE, polyarteritis, infective endocarditis, postinfectious glomerulonephritis, and essential cryoimmunoglobulinemia.

The course is usually benign; however, progressive renal failure may occur. Renal biopsy is a useful prognostic tool. Patients with persistent urinary abnormalities may experience deterioration of renal function several years after diagnosis. Treatment is symptomatic. There is no convincing evidence that corticosteroid or immunosuppressive therapy is beneficial for the renal lesion, although these treatments may ameliorate extrarenal features. Patients with rapidly progressive (crescentic) glomerulonephritis benefit from intensive plasma exchange or immunosuppressive drugs combined with anticoagulant and antithrombotic agents (see Chap. 223).

SYSTEMIC NECROTIZING VASCULITIS (See also Chap. 269)

Glomerular involvement is common in the heterogeneous group of disorders which result from widespread inflammatory and necrotizing lesions of blood vessels. Several variations are recognized, including microscopic polyarteritis (hypersensitivity angiitis), macroscopic polyarteritis (periarteritis nodosa), Wegener's granulomatosis, allergic angiitis and granulomatosis, rheumatoid vasculitis, temporal arteritis, and Takayasu's arteritis. Henoch-Schönlein purpura and SLE can also be considered as examples of vasculitis.

MISCELLANEOUS IMMUNOLOGICALLY MEDIATED MULTISYSTEM DISEASES Mixed connective tissue disease (MCTD)

In this disorder, which is described in Chap. 265, renal disease is uncommon and, if present, is usually mild. Clinical manifestations include hematuria and proteinuria and occasionally nephrotic syndrome. Pathologically, membranous glomerulonephritis or mesangiocapillary glomerulonephritis is seen. The prognosis is generally favorable, and treatment is directed at extrarenal manifestations. Corticosteroid therapy often results in improvement of the glomerular lesions.

Rheumatoid arthritis Several forms of glomerular injury may occur in rheumatoid arthritis (Chap. 263). Secondary amyloidosis is present in 5 to 10 percent of patients with long-standing arthritis. Nephrotic syndrome may arise as a complication of either gold or penicillamine therapy (see Chap. 223). In addition, the kidney may share in the vasculitis seen occasionally in severe rheumatoid arthritis. Finally, patients with rheumatoid arthritis (untreated with gold or penicillamine) may develop a mild proliferative glomerulitis or membranous glomerulonephritis which resembles lesions seen in SLE. Proteinuria, sometimes with nephrotic syndrome, is the principal clinical feature of such lesions. Prolonged and excessive use of analgesics may lead to renal papillary necrosis.

Other disorders *Sjögren's syndrome* (Chap. 266) may be associated with nephrotic syndrome due to membranous or mesangiocapillary glomerulonephritis (type I) or, more frequently, interstitial nephritis. *Sarcoidosis* is rarely complicated by membranous glomerulonephritis. *Partial or total lipodystrophy* may be associated with mesangiocapillary glomerulonephritis (type II, dense deposit disease) (see Chaps. 223 and 318). Complement abnormalities are found, consisting of depressed C3 levels, normal C1q and C4 levels, and circulating C3 nephritic factor.

Chronic liver disease may be complicated by glomerular disease. The nephrotic syndrome may appear in the course of *chronic active hepatitis* associated with persistent hepatitis B surface antigenemia. Glomerular lesions include membranous glomerulonephritis or mesangiocapillary (type I) glomerulonephritis. Immunofluorescence studies in such patients reveal granular deposits of immunoglobulins, complement components, and hepatitis B viral antigens, indicating an immune-complex disease. Serum C3 levels are often reduced, and tests for CIC and cryoimmunoglobulins are frequently positive. Occasionally patients with little clinical evidence of liver disease develop distinct glomerular lesions secondary to chronic hepatitis B infection. *Acute viral hepatitis* may be associated with transient hematuria or proteinuria and may resemble other postinfectious glomerulonephritides (see Chap. 223). Severe *chronic liver disease* (cirrhosis) may be associated with diffuse glomerulosclerosis. Few clinical manifestations of glomerular disease are found. Prominent mesangial IgA deposits, of unknown pathogenic significance, have been noted in patients with cirrhosis.

MULTISYSTEM DISEASES ASSOCIATED WITH PARAPROTEINEMIA AND NEOPLASIA

ESSENTIAL (MIXED) CRYOIMMUNOGLOBULINEMIA

This disorder is associated with circulating cold precipitable immunoglobulins (cryoimmunoglobulins), usually consisting of IgG and IgM; the latter possesses rheumatoid factor activity. Purpura, necrotizing skin lesions in cold-exposed areas, arthralgias, fever, and hepatosplenomegaly are common. Hepatitis B infection and other occult fungal, bacterial, or viral infections may be the cause of this syndrome. Circulating cryoimmunoglobulins are also found in chronic infections and probably represent circulating immune complexes with unusual physical properties. Glomerular disease results from the precipitation of the cryoimmunoglobulin in the glomerular capillaries and may result in acute renal failure, rapidly progressive (crescentic) glomerulonephritis, or the nephrotic syndrome. Serum complement components are depressed, and circulating immune complexes are present (Table 224-1). Pathologically, a diffuse proliferative glomerulonephritis may be seen with findings consistent with the deposition of the circulating cryoimmunoglobulin. Eradication of the underlying infection, if possible, is of value in treatment. Intensive plasma exchange, accompanied by the administration of corticosteroids and cytotoxic agents, has been of some success in severe cases.

MONOCLONAL GAMMOPATHIES *Multiple myeloma* (Chap. 258) may be associated with at least three types of glomerular injury. Amyloidosis (Chap. 259) (see below) occurs in 10 to 15 percent of patients with multiple myeloma. Lesions may resemble nodular diabetic glomerular sclerosis, and monoclonal cryoimmunoglobulins may be deposited in glomeruli. Proteinuria and the nephrotic syndrome are common. In addition, a tubulointerstitial lesion (myeloma kidney) consisting of large, laminated intratubular casts, tubule cell atrophy, interstitial fibrosis, and inflammation is common in patients with multiple myeloma and acute or chronic renal failure. *Waldenström's macroglobulinemia* may cause acute renal failure when the IgM paraprotein precipitates in glomerular capillaries as "thrombi." Intensive plasma exchange and therapy with alkylating agents may be beneficial. Hyperviscosity may cause functional alterations in GFR. Renal amyloidosis is uncommon. *Benign monoclonal gammopathies* are seldom associated with glomerular complications, except for mild asymptomatic proteinuria and, rarely, nephrotic syndrome. Excessive production of *light chains of Ig* (especially kappa type) may evoke glomerular alterations (nodular glomerulosclerosis, focal sclerosis) due to deposition of the protein in mesangium or along the subendothelial aspect of the glomerular capillary wall.

AMYLOIDOSIS (See also Chap. 259) This disorder may occur in the absence of systemic disease (primary amyloidosis), may be secondary to chronic inflammatory processes (e.g., rheumatoid arthritis, osteomyelitis, paraplegia), multiple myeloma or other neoplastic diseases, or may occur in a heredofamilial form (e.g., familial Mediterranean fever). All forms may affect the glomeruli.

Primary amyloidosis commonly affects the kidneys and usually occurs in older age groups. Proteinuria, often of nephrotic proportions, is the most common manifestation of renal involvement. The urine sediment tends to be benign. The degree of proteinuria is not necessarily related to the extent of glomerular deposition of amyloid. Enlarged kidneys may be present in patients with well-preserved renal function, but this is a nonspecific finding. The blood pressure is normal unless advanced uremia is present. Typical pathologic features include hypocellular glomeruli infiltrated with amorphous deposits that stain with Congo red and exhibit green birefringence under polarized light. The fibrillar nature of the amyloid deposits can be demonstrated by electron microscopy. The fibrils in primary amyloidosis and in multiple myeloma are related immunologically to the immunoglobulin light chain. Immunofluorescence studies reveal amorphous deposits of immunoglobulin and complement in glomeruli. Renal vein thrombosis may complicate the course of amyloidosis.

Renal amyloidosis is a progressive disease for which there is no established treatment. Remissions may occur in secondary amyloidosis if the cause can be eliminated. Remissions in primary amyloidosis are exceedingly rare; a few reports describe remissions following the use of cytotoxic agents. Overall the 5-year survival for patients with primary amyloidosis is less than 20 percent. Azotemia, persistent

nephrotic syndrome, and myocardial involvement confer an even more ominous prognosis.

NEOPLASTIC DISEASE Glomerular alterations may develop with a variety of neoplastic diseases. *Carcinomas,* especially adenocarcinoma of lung, colon, stomach, and breast, may be accompanied by glomerular lesions resembling idiopathic membranous glomerulonephritis, although, on occasion, crescentic or focal and segmental proliferative glomerulonephritis or amyloidosis may be present. Nephrotic syndrome is the most common clinical renal manifestation, and approximately 6 to 10 percent of patients with idiopathic nephrotic syndrome associated with membranous glomerulonephritis harbor an underlying malignancy. Successful treatment of the tumor, especially by surgical means, may lead to a remission of the renal manifestation. Presumably the glomerular lesions arise because of the deposition of circulating immune complexes that are composed of tumor antigen and antitumor antibody. Amyloidosis may occasionally occur.

Lymphomas and leukemias may also give rise to glomerular abnormalities. Hodgkin's disease is commonly associated with the findings of idiopathic nephrotic syndrome (minimal change disease). Other glomerular lesions may include membranous glomerulonephritis, focal proliferative and sclerosing glomerulonephritis, and amyloidosis. The mechanism of the association of Hodgkin's disease with minimal change disease may involve an underlying T-cell abnormality. Proteinuria may wax and wane with fluctuations in the clinical activity of the Hodgkin's disease. Remissions may be produced by local irradiation of involved lymph nodes or by systemic chemotherapy.

METABOLIC, BIOCHEMICAL, AND HEREDITARY DISORDERS

DIABETIC NEPHROPATHY (See also Chap. 327) Diabetes mellitus affects the structure and function of the kidney in many ways. The term *diabetic nephropathy* encompasses all the lesions occurring in the kidneys of patients with diabetes mellitus. These lesions include *glomerulosclerosis* (diffuse or nodular), *arterionephrosclerosis, chronic interstitial nephritis, papillary necrosis,* and various tubular lesions. Diabetic nephropathy is associated with a variety of clinical syndromes, including mild asymptomatic proteinuria, nephrotic syndrome, progressive renal failure (acute, rapidly progressive, or chronic), and hypertension. Glomerular lesions are particularly common and account for the majority of abnormal clinical findings referable to the kidney. *Diffuse diabetic glomerulosclerosis* (diffuse intercapillary glomerulosclerosis) is the most common lesion and can be identified in the vast majority of diabetic patients regardless of the presence of abnormal clinical findings referable to the kidney. This lesion consists of a mild diffuse increase in mesangial matrix accompanied by an increased width of the glomerular basement membrane. Various exudative lesions, such as capsular drops and fibrin caps, may also be present. Hyaline arteriosclerosis, particularly of the efferent arteriole, is also common. Taken together, these lesions suggest the diagnosis of diabetes mellitus, but individually they are not specific. *Nodular glomerulosclerosis* (Kimmelstiel-Wilson lesion), on the other hand, is reasonably specific for juvenile onset (type I) diabetes mellitus. This lesion consists of PAS-positive, laminated, intercapillary nodules on a background of an increase in mesangial matrix. At the periphery of the nodules open glomerular capillary loops are found. The nodules are relatively acellular, in contrast to the cellular lesions of membranoproliferative glomerulonephritis (often referred to as *lobular glomerulonephritis*). A variable percentage of glomeruli may be affected.

The pathogenesis of diffuse or nodular diabetic glomerulosclerosis is poorly understood. Evidence supporting a role for both the abnormal diabetic milieu (e.g., insulinopenia, hyperglycemia, glycosuria) and genetic factors is reviewed in Chap. 327.

The principal clinical manifestation of diabetic glomerular disease is proteinuria. Initially, only small amounts of albumin (20 to 40 μg/

min) are excreted, particularly following exercise (microalbuminuria). This amount of albumin excretion is undetectable by routine screening methods. Under ordinary circumstances, microalbuminuria develops within 10 to 15 years from the onset of hyperglycemia and usually progresses within 3 to 5 years to overt proteinuria and clinical diabetic nephropathy. With "tight" control of hyperglycemia, the development of microalbuminuria may be prevented or reversed. With time, the quantity of protein excreted usually increases and may progress to an overt nephrotic syndrome. Glomerular filtration rate is initially elevated and subsequently falls towards normal coincident with the onset of overt proteinuria. The urinary sediment is typically benign, although microhematuria and/or pyuria may also be present if a complicating urinary tract infection or papillary necrosis is present. Hypertension develops if GFR falls but is seldom of malignant proportions. When hypertension is severe or abrupt in onset, one should suspect a complicating atherosclerotic renal arterial stenosis. Typically, plasma renin activity is normal or decreased. Acquired hyporeninemic hypoaldosteronism with persistent hyperkalemia and mild hyperchloremic metabolic acidosis is common. Once azotemia develops, the disease progresses at variable rates. End-stage renal failure usually develops within 5 years of the onset of overt proteinuria and clinical nephropathy. Despite poor control of hyperglycemia, only about 50 to 60 percent of type I (insulin-dependent) diabetic patients develop clinical nephropathy. The factors that protect the remaining patients from renal failure are unknown. Patients with type II (non-insulin-dependent) diabetes mellitus may also develop clinical nephropathy.

Until the cause of diabetes mellitus is established, prevention of the glomerulopathy will not be feasible. If the abnormal diabetic milieu is responsible for the vascular complications (including glomerular disease), as some have suggested, then very precise regulation of blood sugar (e.g., meticulous attention to diet, exercise, and insulin dosage and servofeedback devices for insulin administration) may be effective in reducing the development of nephropathy. Once the nephropathy has reached a clinically recognizable stage, aggressive management of hypertension may slow the rate of loss of renal function, but strict control of blood sugar does not seem to retard the rate of progression. Patients with end-stage renal failure due to diabetic nephropathy are not ideal candidates for long-term dialysis because of concomitant multiple organ dysfunction secondary to widespread arteriovascular disease. Mortality rates among diabetics on chronic dialysis are about three times higher than among similarly treated nondiabetics of comparable age. Renal transplantation may be successful in the younger diabetic, especially if a living related donor is available. The success rate is somewhat less than in the nondiabetic population, but transplantation is a viable alternative to dialysis in selected patients. Recurrence of typical diabetic glomerular lesions has been documented in renal allografts, but thus far, progressive loss of GFR secondary to recurrent disease has not been noted.

ALPORT'S SYNDROME This disorder consists of sensorineural deafness associated with hereditary nephritis. Renal disease manifests itself at an early age, principally as recurrent hematuria. Men are more frequently and severely affected than women. Slowly progressive renal insufficiency in men commonly terminates in end-stage renal disease in the second to third decade. There is no clear-cut relationship between the onset or severity of the hearing abnormality and the extent of renal disease. Other associated abnormalities include two related ophthalmologic complications, spherophakia and lenticonus, as well as thrombocytopathia, hyperprolinemia, and cerebral dysfunction. Family studies have indicated autosomal dominant or X-linked modes of inheritance with variable expressivity. The pathogenesis may be due to defective synthesis of glycopeptide (noncollagenous) components of glomerular and tubular basement membranes.

The pathologic features detected by light microscopy are nonspecific, and a diagnosis cannot be established by optical microscopy alone. Both glomerular and interstitial lesions are present. Focal and diffuse glomerular proliferation, with segmental sclerosis, is common. Interstitial foam cells are nonspecific findings. Electron microscopy reveals thinning, splitting, and delamination of both glomerular and tubular basement membranes, thought by some to be specific for the syndrome. Immunofluorescence studies fail to reveal deposits of immunoglobulins or complement components. The autoantibody to basement membrane antigens found in patients with Goodpasture's syndrome does not react with the glomeruli of some patients with Alport's syndrome. Treatment is supportive; corticosteroids and cytotoxic agents are ineffective. The disease is not known to recur following transplantation.

FABRY'S DISEASE (See also Chap. 316) This disorder, angiokeratoma corporus diffusum, is an X-linked inborn error of glycosphingolipid metabolism that leads to the accumulation of neutral glycosphingolipids in many tissues including the kidney. A milder disease may develop in heterozygous females. Manifestations include angiokerotomas involving the lower trunk, scrotum, and buttocks; acroparesthesia; corneal opacities; tortuous retinal veins; and premature coronary and cerebral ischemic disease. Renal manifestations include hematuria and modest proteinuria, often associated with slowly progressive renal failure. Light-microscopic findings include foamy alterations of the epithelial cells of the glomerulus due to the accumulation of lipid. Electron microscopy reveals intracellular rounded laminated bodies ("myelin figures"). The disorder is untreatable unless replacement of the deficient enzyme can be ensured; successful renal transplantation may correct the enzyme deficiency. Perhaps transplantation of other tissues (e.g., bone marrow) may ultimately become the treatment of choice.

NAIL-PATELLA SYNDROME This autosomal dominant disease is characterized by dystrophic nails, absence of one or both patellae, iliac horns, and renal disease. The renal manifestations include isolated proteinuria and hematuria and occasionally the nephrotic syndrome. Progressive renal failure is uncommon. Glomerular lesions are nonspecific by light microscopy, but electron microscopy reveals a characteristic moth-eaten appearance of the glomerular basement membrane associated with intramembranous collagen fibrils. The prognosis is generally favorable. No treatment is known.

CONGENITAL NEPHROTIC SYNDROME This autosomal recessive trait is characterized by the development of nephrotic syndrome at the time of or shortly after birth. It occurs with highest frequency in families of Finnish origin. Affected individuals have very large placentas, low birth weight, anasarca, polycythemia, and initially normal GFRs. Levels of α-fetoprotein are increased in amniotic fluid and maternal serum. Proteinuria is marked and nonselective. Nephrotic syndrome appearing several months after birth is usually due to other causes, especially minimal change disease or focal glomerular sclerosis (Chap. 223). Congenital syphilis and congenital toxoplasmosis may produce similar syndromes and must be excluded. Pathologically, microcystic transformation of the cortical nephrons results in proximal tubular dilatation. Glomerular changes are nonspecific. Extensive effacement of the foot processes and sclerosis of the glomerular tufts are seen by electron microscopy. Immunofluorescence findings are nonspecific. The course is progressive, and few patients survive the first year of life. Treatment is ineffective. Death is usually due to inanition, infection, or renal failure. A few patients may survive long enough to be considered for renal transplantation.

SICKLE CELL DISEASE (See also Chap. 288) This disorder is an autosomal trait characterized by an abnormal hemoglobin (hemoglobin S). Glomerular lesions occur occasionally in homozygous disease. The medulla is affected, leading to impairment of concentrating ability and acid excretion and, occasionally, to papillary necrosis. Rarely, patients develop mainly glomerular lesions, either membranous or mesangiocapillary glomerulonephritis and are accompanied by proteinuria and a nephrotic syndrome. Immunofluorescence studies demonstrate renal deposition of immunoglobulin and complement in a granular pattern suggesting immune-complex–mediated disease. In a few instances, renal tubuloepithelial antigens are localized in these

TABLE 224-2 Drugs associated with glomerular lesions

Elemental, inorganic, or organic mercury compounds
Organic gold compounds
Penicillamine
Captopril
Heroin
Amphetamines
Probenecid
Oxazoladinedione derivatives (e.g., Trimethadione)
Antivenoms and antitoxins
Sulfonamides
Vaccinations

deposits, suggesting that ischemic damage of the kidney may release autologous antigens to provoke the immune-complex disease. The course in patients with the glomerulopathy of sickle cell disease is often relentless, leading to end-stage renal disease. No treatment is known to be effective. Transplantation has been successful occasionally.

LECITHIN: CHOLESTEROL ACYLTRANSFERASE DEFICIENCY (See also Chap. 315) This autosomal recessive trait leads to absence in plasma of the enzyme that catalyzes the conversion of lecithin and cholesterol to lysolecithin and cholesteryl ester. Multiple lipoprotein abnormalities develop, including absence of α and pre-β lipoproteins, hypertriglyceridemia, accumulation of abnormal lipoproteins, and increased plasma-esterified cholesterol. Corneal opacities, anemia, hyperuricemia, proteinuria and progressive renal failure are characteristic. Foam cells are present in bone marrow and glomeruli, and a picture resembling focal and segmental glomerulosclerosis may evolve. Treatment is generally ineffective, but plasma or blood transfusions may transiently correct the disorder. Renal failure has been corrected by renal transplantation, but recurrence of disease in allografts may occur.

DRUG-INDUCED GLOMERULAR DISEASE Many drugs have been associated with the development of glomerular disease; however, it is usually difficult to establish a direct cause and effect relationship. In a few situations the association is clear-cut, and reexposure has led to recurrence of disease. A partial listing of these drugs is provided in Table 224-2. Certain *heavy metals* (Hg, Au) and their inorganic salts or organic compounds may produce membranous glomerulonephritis and nephrotic syndrome. Removal of the drug is not invariably associated with resolution. *Sulfhydryl compounds* (penicillamine, captopril) may also cause membranous or proliferative glomerulonephritis. The risk of developing a renal complication following penicillamine or gold therapy for rheumatoid arthritis is influenced by genes in the major histocompatibility complex. *Nonsteroidal anti-inflammatory agents* may produce nephrotic syndrome (minimal change disease), interstitial nephritis, and acute renal failure. *Probenecid, trimethadione,* or *paramethadione* may be associated with nephrotic syndrome and a variety of glomerular lesions, including minimal change disease and membranous glomerulonephritis. *Heroin* abuse may be associated with focal and segmental glomerulosclerosis that may progress to nephrotic syndrome and progressive renal failure. *Intravenous amphetamine abuse* may be associated with systemic necrotizing vasculitis. Chronic hepatitis B infection may also participate in the development of glomerular lesions in association with intravenous drug abuse.

REFERENCES

CAMERON JS: Henoch-Schönlein purpura, in *Textbook of Nephrology*, SG Massry and RJ Glassock (eds). Baltimore, Williams & Wilkins, 1983, p. 6.104
FAUCI AS et al: Wegener's granulomatosis: Prospective clinical and therapeutic experience with 85 patients for 21 years. Ann Intern Med 98:76, 1983
GLASSOCK RJ et al: Secondary glomerular diseases, in *The Kidney*, 3d ed. BM Brenner and FC Rector Jr (eds). Philadelphia, Saunders, 1986, p 1014
HILL GS et al: Renal lesions in multiple myeloma: Their relationship to associated protein abnormalities. Am J Kidney Dis 2:423, 1983
HUGHES GRV (ed): Systemic lupus erythematosus. Clin Rheum Dis 8:1, 1982
SPEAR GS: Hereditary nephritis (Alport's syndrome), 1983. Clin Nephrol 21:3, 1983
WETZELS JF et al: The changing natural history of nephropathy in type I diabetes. Am J Med 80: A63, 1986

225 URINARY TRACT INFECTION, PYELONEPHRITIS, AND RELATED CONDITIONS

WALTER E. STAMM / MARVIN TURCK

DEFINITIONS Acute infections of the urinary tract can be subdivided into two general anatomic categories: lower tract infection (urethritis, cystitis, and prostatitis) and upper tract infection (acute pyelonephritis). Infections at these various sites may occur together or independently, and may be asymptomatic or present as the clinical syndromes outlined below.

Recurrent infections can be classified as relapses (a recurrence with the same strain, as judged by species identification, serotype, and antibiogram, that occurs within 1 to 2 weeks of stopping antibiotic therapy) or reinfections (a recurrence with a new strain). Most relapses are thought to result from unresolved renal or prostatic infection.

Symptoms of dysuria, urgency, and frequency unaccompanied by significant bacteriuria have been termed the acute urethral syndrome. Although widely used, this term lacks anatomic precision because many cases of urethral syndrome are in actuality bladder infections. Moreover, since the causative agent can usually be identified in these patients, the term *syndrome,* implying unknown causation, is inappropriate.

Chronic pyelonephritis refers to chronic interstitial nephritis believed to result from bacterial infection of the kidney (see Chap. 226). Many noninfectious diseases also cause an interstitial nephritis indistinguishable pathologically from chronic pyelonephritis.

Microbiologically, urinary tract infection exists when pathogenic microorganisms are detected in the urine, urethra, kidney, or prostate. In most instances, growth of more than 10^5 organisms per milliliter from a properly collected midstream "clean catch" urine sample indicates infection. However, significant bacteriuria may be absent in some circumstances when true urinary infection exists. Especially in symptomatic patients, a smaller number of bacteria (10^2 to 10^4 per milliliter of midstream urine) may accompany infection. In urine specimens obtained by suprapubic aspiration or "in and out" catheterization, or from a patient with an indwelling catheter, colony counts of 10^2 to 10^4 per milliliter generally indicate infection. Conversely, colony counts in excess of 10^5 per milliliter of midstream urine are occasionally due to specimen contamination.

ACUTE INFECTIONS OF THE URINARY TRACT: URETHRITIS, CYSTITIS, AND PYELONEPHRITIS

EPIDEMIOLOGY Epidemiologically, urinary tract infections should be subdivided into catheter-associated (or nosocomial) infections and noncatheter-associated (or community-acquired) infections. In either category, infections may be symptomatic or asymptomatic. Acute infections in noncatheterized patients occur very commonly, especially in women, and account for over 6 million office visits annually in the United States. These infections occur in 1 to 3 percent of schoolgirls, and then increase markedly in incidence with the onset of sexual activity in adolescence. The vast majority of acute symptomatic infections occur in young women. Acute symptomatic urinary infections are rare in men under the age of 50. The occurrence of asymptomatic bacteriuria parallels that of symptomatic infection and is rare in men under 50, but is common in women between the ages of 20 and 50.

ETIOLOGY Many different microorganisms can infect the urinary tract, but by far the most common agents are the gram-negative bacilli. *Escherichia coli* causes approximately 80 percent of acute infections in patients without urologic abnormalities or calculi. Other gram-negative rods, including *Proteus, Klebsiella, Enterobacter,*

Serratia, and *Pseudomonas,* account for a smaller proportion of uncomplicated infections. These organisms assume increasing importance in recurrent infections and infections associated with urologic manipulation, calculi, or obstruction. They play a major role in nosocomial, catheter-associated infections (see below). *Proteus* species, by virtue of urease production, and *Klebsiella* species, through production of extracellular slime and polysaccharides, predispose to stone formation and are isolated more frequently from patients with calculi.

Gram-positive cocci play a lesser role in urinary tract infections. However, *Staphylococcus saprophyticus,* a novobiocin-resistant, coagulase-negative staphylococcus, accounts for 10 to 15 percent of acute symptomatic urinary tract infections in young females. Enterococci and *Staphylococcus aureus* cause infections in patients with renal stones or previous instrumentation. Isolation of *S. aureus* should arouse suspicion of bacteremic infection of the kidney.

About one-third of women with dysuria and frequency have either a nonsignificant number of bacteria in midstream urine cultures or completely sterile cultures, and have been previously defined as having the urethral syndrome. About three-quarters of these women have significant pyuria, while one-quarter have no pyuria and little objective evidence of infection. In the women with pyuria, two groups of pathogens account for the majority of infections. Low quantities (10^2 to 10^4 bacteria per milliliter) of typical bacterial uropathogens such as *E. coli, S. saprophyticus, Klebsiella,* or *Proteus* in midstream urine specimens are found in the majority of these women, are probably the causative agents because they can usually be isolated from a suprapubic aspirate, are usually associated with pyuria, and respond to appropriate antimicrobial therapy. In other women with acute urinary symptoms, pyuria, and sterile urine (even on suprapubic aspiration), sexually transmitted urethritis-producing agents such as *Chlamydia trachomatis, Neisseria gonorrhoeae,* and herpes simplex virus are important etiologic agents. These sexually transmitted agents are more frequently found in young, sexually active women with new sexual partners.

Viruses can produce pyelonephritis in animals and may increase the kidney's susceptibility to infection with gram-negative bacteria. In humans, viruses (cytomegalovirus, for example) are most commonly recovered from the urine without evidence of acute urinary disease, although some adenoviruses cause acute hemorrhagic cystitis. Similarly, *Candida* and other fungi may colonize the urine of catheterized patients or diabetics, and rarely cause acute symptomatic infection.

PATHOGENESIS AND SOURCES OF INFECTION
The urinary tract should be viewed as a single anatomic unit connected by a continuous column of urine that extends from the urethra to the kidney. In the vast majority of infections, bacteria gain access to the bladder via the urethra. Ascent of bacteria from the bladder may then follow and is probably the usual pathway for most renal parenchymal infections.

The distal urethra is normally colonized with diphtheroids, streptococcal species, and staphylococcal species but not with the enteric gram-negative bacilli that commonly cause urinary tract infections. In females prone to development of cystitis, however, enteric gram-negative organisms residing in the bowel colonize the introitus, the periurethral skin, and the distal urethra prior to and during episodes of bacteriuria. Factors predisposing to periurethral colonization with gram-negative bacilli remain poorly understood but may involve alteration of the normal perineal flora by antibiotics or by other genital infections, absence of local antibody, and/or enhanced attachment of organisms to the epithelial cells of infection-prone women. Small numbers of periurethral bacteria probably gain entry to the bladder frequently, facilitated in some women by urethral massage during intercourse. Whether bladder infection ensues then depends upon interaction between the pathogenicity of the strain, the inoculum size, and local and systemic host defense mechanisms.

Under normal circumstances, bacteria placed in the bladder are rapidly cleared in humans or experimental animals. This results partly from the flushing and dilutional effects of voiding, but also from direct antibacterial properties of urine and the bladder mucosa. Due mostly to high urea concentration and high osmolarity, the bladder urine of many normal persons inhibits or kills bacteria. Prostatic secretions possess antibacterial properties as well. Polymorphonuclear leukocytes in the bladder wall also appear to play a role in clearing bacteriuria. The role of locally produced antibody remains unclear. Hematogenous pyelonephritis occurs most often in debilitated patients who either have chronic illnesses or who are receiving immunosuppressive therapy. Staphylococcal pyelonephritis may follow bacteremia from distant foci of infection in the bone, skin, endothelium, or elsewhere.

CONDITIONS AFFECTING PATHOGENESIS **Gender and sexual activity** The female urethra appears particularly prone to colonization with colonic gram-negative bacilli, owing to its proximity to the anus, its short length (about 4 cm), and its termination beneath the labia. Urethral massage, as occurs during sexual intercourse, causes introduction of bacteria into the bladder, and appears to be very important in the pathogenesis of urinary infections in younger women. In addition, diaphragm use has been associated with a twofold increase in risk of urinary infection. In males, prostatitis or urethral obstruction due to prostatic hypertrophy are important factors predisposing to bacteriuria.

Pregnancy Depending on socioeconomic status, urinary infections are detected in 2 to 8 percent of pregnant women. In particular, symptomatic upper tract infections occur more commonly during pregnancy; fully 20 to 30 percent of pregnant women with asymptomatic bacteriuria subsequently develop pyelonephritis. This predisposition to upper tract infection during pregnancy results from the decreased ureteral tone, decreased ureteral peristalsis, and temporary incompetence of the vesicoureteral valves seen in pregnancy. Bladder catheterization during or after delivery causes additional infections. Cystitis and pyelonephritis are no more common in women with toxemia of pregnancy than in other pregnant women. An increased prevalence of prematurity and newborn mortality may result from urinary infections during pregnancy.

Obstruction Any impediment to the free flow of urine—tumor, stricture, stone, or prostatic hypertrophy—results in hydronephrosis and greatly increased frequency of urinary tract infection. Infection superimposed on urinary tract obstruction may lead to rapid destruction of renal tissue. It is of utmost importance, therefore, when infection is present, to repair obstructive lesions. On the other hand, with minor degrees of obstruction that are not progressive or associated with infection, great caution must be exercised in attempting surgical correction. The introduction of infection in such patients may be more damaging than uncorrected minor obstructions which do not significantly impair renal function.

Neurogenic bladder dysfunction Interference with the nerve supply to the bladder, as in spinal cord injury, tabes dorsalis, multiple sclerosis, diabetes, or other diseases, may be associated with urinary tract infection. The infection may be initiated by the use of catheters for bladder drainage and is favored by the prolonged standing of urine in the bladder. An additional factor often present in these patients is bone demineralization due to immobilization, which causes hypercalciuria, calculus formation, and obstructive uropathy.

Vesicoureteral reflux This condition is defined as reflux of urine from the bladder cavity up into the ureters and sometimes into the renal pelvis. It occurs during voiding or with elevation of pressure in the bladder. In practice, vesicoureteral reflux exists when retrograde movement of radiopaque or radioactive material can be demonstrated. However, since a fluid connection between the bladder and kidney always exists in the patent urinary system, during infections some retrograde movement of bacteria probably occurs normally but is not detected by radiologic techniques. An anatomically impaired ureterovesical junction facilitates reflux of bacteria.

Vesicoureteral reflux is common in children with anatomic abnormalities of the urinary tract and in children with anatomically normal but infected urinary tracts. In the latter group, reflux disappears with advancing age and probably results from rather than causes urinary infection. Follow-up of children with urinary tract infection who were found to have reflux establishes that renal damage correlates with massive reflux, not with infection.

The routine search for reflux would be aided by development of noninvasive tests applicable to young children, where the need is greatest. In the meantime, it appears reasonable to search for massive reflux in anyone with unexplained failure of renal growth or renal scarring, because urinary tract infection per se is an insufficient explanation for these abnormalities. On the other hand, it is doubtful that all children with recurrent urinary tract infections but normal urinary tracts on pyelography should be subjected to voiding cystoureterography merely to detect the rare patient with massive reflux that did not reveal itself on the intravenous pyelogram.

Bacterial virulence factors Bacterial virulence factors influence the likelihood that a given strain, once introduced into the bladder, will cause urinary tract infection. The majority of strains that cause symptomatic urinary tract infections in noncatheterized patients belong to a small number of serogroups, produce hemolysin, and share certain other properties. Adherence of bacteria to uroepithelial cells is a critical first step in the initiation of infection. For both *E. coli* and *Proteus*, fimbriae (hairlike surface appendages) mediate bacterial attachment to specific receptors on epithelial cells. Nearly all strains of *E. coli* that cause pyelonephritis in patients with anatomically normal urinary tracts possess a particular pilus (the P pilus or gal-gal pilus) that mediates attachment to a digalactoside portion of glycosphingolipids present on uroepithelium. Strains that produce pyelonephritis are also usually hemolysin producers and are resistant to the bactericidal action of human serum.

LOCALIZATION OF INFECTION Infections involving the upper urinary tract usually cause a significant rise in serum antibodies directed against the O antigen of the infecting strain. They also produce a temporary defect in renal concentrating ability in many patients, and may be associated with formation of leukocyte casts. Lower tract infections rarely result in increased antibody titers, concentrating defects, or white cell casts. Unfortunately, these methods of distinguishing renal parenchymal infection from cystitis are neither reliable nor convenient enough for routine clinical use. More sensitive tests for distinguishing pyelonephritis from cystitis (bilateral ureteral catheterization and the bladder wash-out technique originated by Fairley) are inherently invasive and too complex for clinical practice. The development of a simpler and clinically applicable test to separate upper and lower tract infections based upon antibody coating of bacteria in the urine has been studied. In this test, bacteria from patients with pyelonephritis demonstrate antibody coating on their surface when they have been exposed to a fluorescein-labeled antihuman globulin and are viewed under a fluorescence microscope. No surface antibodies can be seen on bacteria from patients with cystitis. This antibody response consists mainly of IgG and can be reproduced in an experimental pyelonephritis model in animals. However, false-negative results occur in 15 to 20 percent of patients who have upper tract infection as judged by direct localization procedures. These false-negatives probably occur because antibody production, particularly in first infections, requires 10 to 15 days, and most patients are treated before this length of time elapses. False-positive results occur in males with prostatitis and women with hemorrhagic cystitis, heavy proteinuria, and vaginal or fecal contamination of midstream urine. Infections with yeast or *Pseudomonas* cause false-positives due to autofluorescence, and staphylococci with protein A nonspecifically bind human immunoglobulin, also causing false-positives. The antibody-coated bacteria test does not have sufficient sensitivity and specificity to be of value in the routine clinical management of patients. An elevated C-reactive protein often accompanies acute pyelonephritis and rarely is seen in cystitis, but this acute phase reactant is nonspecific and occurs in infections other than pyelonephritis as well.

CLINICAL PRESENTATION Clinical signs and symptoms cannot be relied upon to diagnose urinary tract infection correctly or to localize the site of infection. Many patients with significant bacteriuria (including some with upper tract infection) have no symptoms at all. Of those with significant bacteriuria and symptoms of cystitis, about one-half have lower tract infection and about one-half have clinically silent upper tract infection that is evident only upon performing localization studies. Clinical symptoms and signs of pyelonephritis, though often suggestive, do not always indicate upper tract infection. Finally, among women presenting with acute dysuria and frequency, only 60 to 70 percent have significant bacteriuria, but the majority of those without significant bacteriuria also have urinary tract or urethral infections.

Enumeration of the number of bacteria in the urine is an extremely important diagnostic procedure. In symptomatic infections of the urinary tract, bacteria are usually demonstrable in the urine in large numbers. Quantitative estimation of the number of bacteria in voided urine specimens as a rule makes it possible to distinguish contaminants from true bacteriuria, and 10^5 or more bacteria per milliliter has been the criterion traditionally used for this purpose. However, in symptomatic women with pyuria, counts of 10^2 to 10^4 *E. coli*, *Klebsiella*, *Proteus*, or *S. saprophyticus* per milliliter of midstream urine usually indicate infection, not contamination, and should not be disregarded. In asymptomatic patients, two or three consecutive urine specimens should be examined bacteriologically before instituting therapy, and 10^5 or more per milliliter of a single species should be demonstrable in the repeated specimens. A quantitative estimate of the degree of bacteriuria can be made by direct microscopic examination of a Gram's stain of uncentrifuged, freshly voided urine. If bacteria can be found by this method, it may be assumed that the number present approximates 100,000 per milliliter. Since the large number of bacteria in the bladder urine is due in part to bacterial multiplication during residence in the bladder cavity, samples of urine from the ureters or renal pelvis might contain fewer than 10^5 bacteria per milliliter and yet indicate infection. Similarly, the presence of bacteriuria of any degree in suprapubic aspirates or of 10^2 or more bacteria per milliliter of urine obtained by catheterization usually indicates infection. In some circumstances (antibiotics, high urea concentration, high osmolarity, low pH), urine will inhibit bacterial multiplication, resulting in a lower number of bacteria in the presence of infection. For this reason, antiseptic solutions should not be used in washing the periurethral area prior to collection of the urine specimen. Water diuresis or recent voiding also reduces the bacterial counts in urine.

Cystitis Patients with dysuria, frequency, urgency, and suprapubic pain usually have cystitis. The urine often becomes grossly cloudy, malodorous, and, in about 30 percent of cases, bloody. Pyuria without leukocyte casts and bacteria should be present on examination of the unspun urine in most patients. However, some women with cystitis have only 10^2 to 10^4 bacteria per milliliter of urine, which cannot be seen on Gram's stain of unspun urine. Physical examination generally reveals only a tender urethra or suprapubic tenderness. If a genital lesion or a vaginal discharge is present, especially with fewer than 10^5 bacteria per milliliter on culture, causes of urethritis, vaginitis, or cervicitis such as *C. trachomatis*, gonorrhea, *Trichomonas*, *Candida*, and *Herpesvirus hominis* should be ruled out. Prominent systemic manifestations like fever over 101°F, nausea, vomiting, and costovertebral angle tenderness usually indicate concomitant renal infection. However, the absence of these findings does not ensure that infection is limited to the bladder and urethra.

Acute pyelonephritis Symptoms generally develop rapidly over a few hours or a day and include fever which is often 103°F or greater, shaking chills, nausea, vomiting, and diarrhea. Symptoms of cystitis may or may not be present. Besides fever, tachycardia, and generalized muscle tenderness, physical examination reveals marked tenderness on deep pressure in one or both costovertebral areas or on deep abdominal palpation. In some patients, signs and symptoms of gram-negative sepsis predominate. Most patients have significant leukocytosis, pyuria with leukocyte casts in the urine, and bacteria on a Gram's stain of unspun urine. Hematuria may be present during the acute phase of the disease, but if it persists after acute manifestations of infection have subsided, a stone, tumor, or tuberculosis should be considered.

Except in individuals with papillary necrosis or urinary obstruction, the manifestations of acute pyelonephritis usually subside within a few days, even without specific antibacterial therapy. However, despite the absence of symptoms, bacteriuria or pyuria may persist. With severe pyelonephritis, fever subsides more slowly and may not disappear for several days, even after appropriate antibiotic treatment has been instituted.

Urethritis Approximately 30 percent of women with acute dysuria, frequency, and pyuria have midstream urine cultures that show either no growth or nonsignificant bacterial growth. Clinically, these women cannot be readily distinguished from those with cystitis. In these women distinction should be made between those having sexually transmitted pathogens such as *C. trachomatis, Neisseria gonorrhoeae,* or herpes simplex virus, and those having low-count *E. coli* or staphylococcal infection. Women with a gradual onset of illness, no hematuria, no suprapubic pain, and a history of more than 7 days of symptoms should be suspected of having chlamydial infection. The additional history of a recent sex partner change, especially if the patient's partner has recently had chlamydial or gonococcal urethritis, should heighten the suspicion of a sexually transmitted infection, as would the finding of mucopurulent cervicitis. Gross hematuria, suprapubic pain, abrupt onset of illness, a duration of illness of less than 3 days, and a history of previous urinary tract infections favor *E. coli* or staphylococcal infection.

Catheter-associated urinary tract infections Bacteriuria occurs in at least 25 percent of hospitalized patients with indwelling urethral catheters. The risk of infection is about 5 percent per day of catheterization. *Proteus, Pseudomonas, Klebsiella,* and *Serratia,* in addition to *E. coli,* usually cause these infections. Many infecting strains show marked antimicrobial resistance compared with organisms that cause community-acquired urinary infections. Factors associated with an increased risk of infection include female sex, lengthy period of catheterization, severe underlying illness, faulty catheter care, and poorly trained nursing personnel.

Infection occurs when bacteria reach the bladder by one of two routes: by migrating through the column of urine in the catheter lumen (intraluminal route); or by moving up the mucous sheath outside the catheter (periurethral route). Hospital-acquired pathogens reach the patient's catheter or urine-collecting system on the hands of hospital personnel, in contaminated solutions or irrigants, and via contaminated instruments or disinfectants. Entry of bacteria into the catheter system usually occurs at the catheter–collecting tube junction or at the drainage bag portal. Bacteria then ascend intraluminally into the bladder. More often, the patient's own bowel flora migrate to the perineal skin and periurethral area and reach the bladder via the external surface of the catheter. This route is particularly common in women.

Most catheter-associated infections appear to be benign. They cause minimal symptoms, no fever, and often resolve after withdrawal of the catheter. The frequency of upper tract infection associated with catheter-induced bacteriuria is unknown. Gram-negative bacteremia, which follows 1 to 2 percent of cases of catheter-associated bacteriuria, is the most significantly recognized complication of catheter-induced urinary infections. The catheterized urinary tract has repeatedly been demonstrated to be the most common source of gram-negative bacteremia in hospitalized patients. It has also been suggested that bacteriuria in catheterized patients is associated with an adjusted increased relative risk of death of approximately threefold compared with similar patients without bacteriuria.

Catheter-associated urinary tract infections can be partially prevented in patients catheterized less than 2 weeks by use of a sterile closed collecting system, attention to aseptic technique during insertion and care of the catheter, use of meatal antiseptic ointments, and by measures to minimize cross infection. Despite these precautions, the majority of patients catheterized longer than 2 weeks develop bacteriuria. The optimal treatment for such patients has not been established. Removal of the catheter and a short course of antibiotics to which the organism is susceptible is probably the best course of action and nearly always eradicates the bacteriuria. If the catheter cannot be removed, antibiotic therapy usually proves to be unsuccessful and may result in infection with a more resistant strain. In this situation, the bacteriuria should be ignored unless the patient develops symptoms or is at high risk of developing bacteremia. In these cases, systemic antibiotics or urinary bladder antiseptics may reduce the degree of bacteriuria and the likelihood of bacteremia. In patients who require long-term catheterization, sterile intermittent in-and-out catheterization performed by a nurse or by the patient results in fewer infections than does continuous indwelling catheterization.

TREATMENT Several therapeutic principles should underlie treatment of urinary tract infections:

1 A quantitative urine culture, a positive Gram stain, or an alternative rapid diagnostic test should be obtained to confirm infection before starting treatment, and antimicrobial sensitivity testing should be used to direct therapy in these patients.

2 Factors predisposing to infection, such as obstruction, neurogenic bladder, calculi, etc., should be identified and corrected if possible.

3 Relief of clinical symptoms does not always indicate bacteriologic cure.

4 After completion of therapy, each treatment episode should be classified as a failure (bacteriuria not eradicated during therapy or upon the immediate posttreatment culture) or a cure (resolution of symptoms and elimination of bacteriuria). Recurrent infections should be classified as relapses or reinfections.

5 In general, uncomplicated infections confined to the lower urinary tract respond to low doses and short courses of therapy, while upper tract infections require longer periods of treatment. Relapses usually indicate an upper tract focus of infection while reinfection more often indicates lower tract infection.

6 Community-acquired infections, especially initial infections, are nearly always due to antibiotic-sensitive strains.

7 Patients with repeated infections, instrumentation, or recent hospitalization should be suspected of harboring resistant strains.

The anatomic location of a urinary tract infection greatly influences success or failure of a therapeutic agent. Bladder bacteriuria (cystitis) can usually be eliminated with nearly any antimicrobial to which the infecting strain is sensitive; as little as a single dose of 500-mg intramuscular kanamycin eliminates bladder bacteriuria in most patients. A 7-day course of therapy with oral drugs appears more than adequate. With upper tract infections, however, single-dose therapy fails in the majority of cases and even a 7-day course will be unsuccessful in many patients. Longer periods of treatment (2 to 6 weeks) aimed at eradicating a persistent focus of infection may be necessary in cases of relapse.

In *acute uncomplicated cystitis,* more than 90 percent of infections are due to *E. coli,* and although resistance patterns vary geographically, most strains are sensitive to many antibiotics. Single-dose amoxicillin (3.0 g), trimethoprim-sulfamethoxazole (4 to 6 single-strength tablets), trimethoprim (400 mg), and sulfa alone (2.0 g) have been successfully used to treat acute uncomplicated episodes of cystitis. Amoxicillin appears to result in a lower cure rate than the other three agents. The advantages of single-dose therapy include less expense, ensured compliance, fewer side effects, and perhaps less intense selective pressure for emergence of resistant organisms in the gut, vaginal, or perineal flora. Although some studies suggest more relapses occur after single-dose therapy than after longer treatment, it does appear safe and efficacious for women presenting with acute uncomplicated cystitis. Single-dose therapy should be used only in reliable patients in whom posttreatment follow-up can be ensured, and in patients in whom symptoms have been present for less than 10 days. It should not be used in women with symptoms or signs of pyelonephritis or in women with urologic abnormalities or stones. In women with previous infections due to antibiotic-resistant organisms, single-dose therapy may be less appropriate. Further evaluation of single-dose therapy in children and pregnant women with bacteriuria is needed before it can be recommended in these populations. In these populations, 7 days of therapy with the antimicrobials listed above should be given. Males with urinary tract infection often have urologic abnormalities or prostatic involvement and positive antibody-coated-bacterial bacteriuria, and hence are not candidates for single-dose therapy.

Treatment of the acute urethritis in women depends upon the etiologic agent involved. In chlamydial infection, tetracycline (500 mg orally qid for 7 days) should be used. Women with acute dysuria and frequency, negative urine cultures, and no pyuria do not usually respond to antimicrobial agents.

Acute pyelonephritis without accompanying clinical evidence of calculi or urologic disease is due to *E. coli* in most cases. Although the optimal route and duration of therapy have not been established, a 10- to 14-day course of trimethoprim-sulfamethoxazole, trimethoprim alone, an aminoglycoside, or a cephalosporin usually provides adequate therapy. Ampicillin should not be used as initial therapy since 20 to 30 percent of *E. coli* are now resistant in vitro. Intravenous antibiotics, at least for the first several days of treatment, should probably be given to all but minimally symptomatic patients. Some patients relapse following therapy and should be investigated to determine whether unrecognized calculi or urologic disease is present. If not, treatment should be extended to 2 to 6 weeks to eliminate a presumed upper tract focus causing recurrent bacteriuria.

When suspected *gram-negative sepsis* complicates acute pyelonephritis, hospitalization, prompt parenteral therapy with an aminoglycoside, and ancillary measures to treat sepsis should be provided (see Chap. 86). When the antibiotic sensitivities of the infecting strain are available, therapy can be changed to a less toxic agent. Similar therapy should be used for infected patients with calculi or urologic abnormalities who have suspected sepsis.

In *pregnancy*, acute cystitis can be managed with 7 days of amoxicillin, nitrofurantoin, or a cephalosporin. After treatment, a culture should be obtained to ensure cure and repeated monthly thereafter. Acute pyelonephritis in pregnancy should be managed by hospitalization and parenteral antibiotics, generally a cephalosporin or an extended-spectrum penicillin. Continuous low-dose prophylaxis with nitrofurantoin should be given to women who have recurrent infections during pregnancy.

Asymptomatic bacteriuria should be documented with at least two positive cultures before treatment is given. Seven days of an oral agent to which the organism is sensitive should be given initially. If bacteriuria persists, it can be followed without further treatment in most patients. In patients who may be at high risk because of neutropenia, compromised host defenses, renal transplant, or previous development of pyelonephritis or bacteremia, further treatment with either 6 weeks of oral therapy or 4 to 6 weeks of combined parenteral and oral therapy should be given.

Optimal treatment regimens for patients with *catheter-associated urinary tract infections* have not been well established. These infections often remit spontaneously or with short-term antibiotic therapy if the catheter can be removed. If the catheter cannot be removed, systemic antibiotics or urinary antiseptics may reduce bacteriuria, but do not usually eliminate it. Asymptomatic bacteriuria in catheterized patients can probably be left untreated in most patients who are not immunosuppressed or who are not at high risk for sepsis because of old age, severe underlying disease, diabetes, or pregnancy.

UROLOGIC EVALUATION Very few women with recurrent urinary tract infections have correctable lesions discovered at cystoscopy or upon intravenous pyelography, and these procedures should not be routinely performed in such patients. In selected women, namely those with relapsing infection, those with a history of childhood infections, those with stones or painless hematuria, and those with recurrent pyelonephritis, urologic evaluation should be performed. All males with urinary infection should be evaluated urologically. Men or women presenting with acute infection and signs or symptoms suggestive of an obstruction or stones should undergo urologic evaluation, generally ultrasound.

PROGNOSIS In patients with uncomplicated cystitis or pyelonephritis, treatment ordinarily results in complete resolution of symptoms. In fact, symptoms usually remit even without specific therapy. Lower tract infections in adult women are of concern mainly because they cause discomfort, minor morbidity, and time lost from work. Cystitis may also result in upper tract infection or in bacteremia (especially during instrumentation), but there is little evidence to suggest that renal impairment follows. When repeated episodes of cystitis occur, they are nearly always reinfections, not relapses. Why a significant subpopulation of adult women develops a predisposition to multiple recurrent infections remains poorly understood. In some cases, residual urine, urethral stenosis, or other anatomic explanations exist, but most women with recurrent infections have no such demonstrable abnormality. Their uroepithelial cells appear highly prone to persistent colonization with *E. coli;* the explanation for this phenomenon is not clear.

Uncomplicated acute pyelonephritis in adults rarely progresses to functional impairment and chronic renal disease. Repeated upper tract infections often indicate relapse rather than reinfection, and a vigorous search for renal calculi or an underlying urologic abnormality should be undertaken. If neither is found, 6 weeks of chemotherapy may be useful in eradicating an unresolved focus of infection.

Repeated symptomatic urinary tract infections in children, and in adults with obstructive uropathy, neurogenic bladder, structural renal disease, or diabetes more often progress to chronic renal disease. Asymptomatic bacteriuria in these groups, as well as in adults without urologic disease or obstruction, predisposes to increased episodes of symptomatic infection but does not result in renal impairment in most instances.

PREVENTION Patients with frequent symptomatic infections may benefit from long-term low-dose antibiotics directed at preventing recurrences. A single dose of trimethoprim-sulfamethoxazole (80 mg trimethoprim and 400 mg sulfamethoxazole daily), trimethoprim alone (100 mg daily), or nitrofurantoin (50 mg daily) have been particularly effective. Suppressive therapy should be initiated only after bacteriuria has been eradicated with a full-dose treatment regimen. Women having more than two infections every 6 months should be considered for preventive antibiotics. Low-dose antibiotics (nitrofurantoin 50 to 100 mg) after sexual intercourse may also be of benefit in preventing episodes of symptomatic infections. Other situations in which prophylaxis appears to have some merit include men with chronic prostatitis; patients undergoing prostatectomy, both during the operation and postoperative periods; and pregnant women with asymptomatic bacteriuria. All pregnant women should be screened for bacteriuria in the first trimester, and should be treated if bacteriuria is found.

CHRONIC PYELONEPHRITIS

Chronic interstitial nephritis thought to result from bacterial infection of the kidney has been termed *chronic pyelonephritis*. It may occur in patients with predisposing urologic abnormalities (obstruction, vesicoureteral reflux, or neurogenic bladder) or in patients with apparently normal urinary tracts. Unlike acute urinary tract infections, for which simple diagnostic criteria and characteristic clinical syndromes exist, no pathognomonic clinical, laboratory, or pathologic criteria can be used to identify cases of chronic pyelonephritis, and few reliable data on the incidence or prevalence of this condition have been collected. Many patients with renal lesions that fulfill the pathologic criteria for chronic pyelonephritis at autopsy have sterile urine cultures and were not known to have had clinical episodes of bacterial urinary tract infection or urinary obstruction during life. Such cases suggest that other forms of renal injury result in morphologic changes indistinguishable from those produced by bacterial infection. Conversely, relatively few individuals with acute urinary infection develop chronic infection or progressive renal impairment. Most often, this occurs in patients with anatomic obstruction, neurogenic bladder, or vesicoureteral reflux.

Patients with many episodes of urinary tract infection; impaired renal function; pyuria with white cell casts; bacteriuria; an intravenous pyelogram showing an irregularly outlined renal pelvis with caliectasis and cortical scars; and typical pathologic changes can be diagnosed as having chronic pyelonephritis. In less typical patients, the relationship of infection to renal damage is uncertain and the diagnosis often remains unclear.

PATHOLOGY Characteristically, the kidneys are asymmetric in size, scarred, and irregularly pitted on the surface. Pathologic changes usually begin in the interstitial tissue of the medulla and papillae, with connective tissue, lymphocytes, and plasma cells completely replacing interstitium and tubules. Foci of active interstitial inflammation may be seen throughout the medulla, and leukocyte casts are found in some tubules. Other tubules contain large amounts of eosinophilic material and colloid casts, and may be dilated. Early in the disease, most glomeruli appear relatively normal. A proliferative endarteritis may be present. With progression, involvement of glomeruli and vessels becomes more pronounced and uniform, eventually resulting in an ''end-stage'' kidney.

None of the foregoing changes is pathognomonic for chronic pyelonephritis. Similar morphologic features may result from the nephropathy of chronic hypokalemia, nephrocalcinosis, chronic analgesic abuse, primary vascular disease of the kidneys, obstruction, diabetes mellitus, and Balkan nephropathy (see Chap. 226).

CLINICAL FEATURES Early signs and symptoms are minimal and nonspecific and often include hypertension. Later, as glomerular filtration and renal blood flow decline, the characteristic clinical and laboratory features of uremia appear (see Chap. 220).

The appearance of white blood cell casts in the urine suggests the diagnosis of chronic pyelonephritis. However, bacteria, leukocytes, and leukocyte casts may appear only intermittently and often are not present during the chronic stage of the disease. Intravenous pyelography is often normal early in the course of the disease but subsequently shows bilateral small kidneys with irregular outlines, calyceal blunting or dilatation, and cortical scarring. Renal biopsy may be normal owing to the focal nature of the disease early in its course.

PROGNOSIS The course of chronic pyelonephritis may be prolonged and compatible with a comfortable life even after considerable impairment of renal function. Associated hypertension generally worsens the prognosis. In perhaps no other renal disease can fluctuations in renal function be so marked or frequent. During acute infections or episodes of dehydration, renal decompensation may progress to the stage of advanced uremia; yet the patient may recover and regain adequate renal function for years. Correction of obstructing lesions may prevent progression of the disease.

TREATMENT Surgically approachable obstructive lesions should be promptly corrected. Antibiotic therapy for proven infections should be given and should be based on antimicrobial sensitivity tests. Hypertension should be controlled to reduce renal vascular complications. The treatment of chronic renal failure is discussed in Chap. 220.

PAPILLARY NECROSIS

The renal papilla is of major importance in the pathogenesis of chronic interstitial nephritis and, when complicated by bacterial infection, pyelonephritis. It has become evident that a variety of underlying conditions cause primary renal papillary damage, resulting eventually in the renal lesions of chronic interstitial nephritis. When urinary infection does not supervene, the resulting renal disease may progress slowly and silently to the point of renal insufficiency. The pathology of this renal injury may be indistinguishable from that of pyelonephritis. In addition to common diseases such as gout and diabetes mellitus, which cause renal papillary damage, many medications, which achieve enormous concentrations in the urine traversing the renal papilla, may be toxic for that zone of the kidney. The best known of these are phenacetin-containing analgesic mixtures. This problem is much more common than generally recognized, and diagnosis requires a careful history.

It is not known how many other substances may be important in the pathogenesis of primary renal papillary disease. However, in view of the benignity of urinary infection in persons without underlying renal papillary damage, it is reasonable to assume the presence of primary underlying renal papillary damage in any patient with urinary infection who shows the development or progression of renal damage.

When severe infection of the renal pyramids is present in association with vascular diseases of the kidney or with urinary tract obstruction, renal papillary necrosis is likely to result. Patients with diabetes, sickle cell disease, chronic alcoholism, and vascular disease seem peculiarly susceptible to this complication. Hematuria, pain in the flank or abdomen, and chills and fever are the most common presenting symptoms. Acute renal failure with oliguria or anuria sometimes occurs. Rarely, sloughing of a pyramid may take place without symptoms in a patient with chronic urinary infection, and the diagnosis is made when the necrotic tissue is passed in the urine or identified as a ''ring shadow'' on pyelography. If renal function deteriorates suddenly in a diabetic or a patient with chronic obstruction, the diagnosis of renal papillary necrosis should be entertained, even in the absence of fever or pain. Although renal papillary necrosis is often bilateral, when it is unilateral, nephrectomy may be lifesaving in the management of overwhelming infection.

RENAL AND PERINEPHRIC ABSCESS

See Chap. 87.

PROSTATITIS

The term *prostatitis* has been used for various inflammatory conditions affecting the prostate, including acute and chronic infections with specific bacteria and, more commonly, instances in which signs and symptoms of prostatic inflammation are present but no specific organisms can be detected. To classify patients with suspected prostatitis correctly, each patient should be evaluated using first-void and midstream urine specimens, a prostatic expressate, and a post-massage urine specimen. All specimens should be quantitatively cultured and evaluated for numbers of leukocytes. Based on the results of these studies, patients can be classified as having acute bacterial prostatitis, nonbacterial prostatitis, or prostatodynia. Patients with suspected prostatitis usually have low back pain, perineal or testicular discomfort, mild dysuria, and lower urinary obstructive symptoms. Microscopic pyuria may be the only objective manifestation of prostatic disease.

ACUTE BACTERIAL PROSTATITIS This disease generally affects young male adults when it occurs spontaneously, but it may also be associated with an indwelling urethral catheter. It is characterized by fever, chills, dysuria, and a tense or boggy, extremely tender, prostate on examination. Although prostatic massage usually produces purulent secretions with a large number of bacteria on culture, bacteremia may result from manipulation of the inflamed gland. For this reason, and because the etiologic agent can usually be identified on urine

Gram stain and culture, vigorous prostatic massage should be avoided. In noncatheter-associated cases, the infection is generally due to one of the common gram-negative urinary tract pathogens or *Staphylococcus aureus*. Initially, intravenous trimethoprim-sulfamethoxazole, a cephalosporin or an aminoglycoside can be utilized if gram-negative rods are seen in the urine Gram stain, and a cephalosporin or nafcillin if gram-positive cocci are seen. Although these drugs do not readily diffuse into the noninflamed prostate gland, the response to antibiotics is usually prompt, perhaps because drugs penetrate more readily into the acutely inflamed prostate. In catheter-associated cases, a broader spectrum of etiologic agents is seen, including hospital-acquired gram-negative rods and enterococci. In such cases, an aminoglygoside or a third-generation cephalosporin should be used for initial therapy until the organism has been isolated and susceptibilities determined. The long-term prognosis is good, although in some instances acute infection may result in abscess formation, epididymoorchitis, seminal vesiculitis, septicemia, and residual chronic bacterial prostatitis. Since the advent of antibiotics, the frequency of acute bacterial prostatitis has diminished markedly. Many so-called cases of acute prostatitis are probably posterior urethritis.

CHRONIC BACTERIAL PROSTATITIS This entity is a major cause of recurrent bacteriuria in males but may be difficult to diagnose. Symptoms are usually absent, the prostate feels normal on palpation, and although many white blood cells may be seen in the urinary sediment, results of conventional bacteriologic studies are often negative. Bacteria may be cultured from the expressed prostatic secretion or postmassage urine. The presence of these bacteria can be determined only by careful quantitative bacteriologic techniques when the bladder urine is sterile, employing the method used by Stamey and colleagues. Intermittently, symptoms of frequency, urgency, and dysuria occur when infection spreads to the bladder urine. The pattern of recurrent bladder infection in the male with chronic bacterial prostatitis is clinically not very different from that seen in the recurrent cystourethritis of the female. Antibiotics are of limited value in eradicating the focus of chronic infection in the prostate, but they do relieve the symptoms of the acute exacerbations promptly. The relative ineffectiveness of antimicrobials in part results from the poor penetration of most antibiotics into the prostate because the low pH which prevails in this organ precludes solubility of most drugs. The macrolide group of drugs (erythromycin) do enter the prostatic secretions, but these agents are generally ineffective against gram-negative organisms. Sulfonamide-trimethoprim has been employed successfully in some of these infections. Patients with frequent episodes of acute cystitis should be treated with prolonged courses of antimicrobials (usually sulfonamide, trimethoprim, or nitrofurantoin), with a view toward suppressing symptoms and keeping the bladder urine sterile. Total prostatectomy produces cure of chronic prostatitis but is associated with considerable morbidity. Transurethral prostatectomy is safer but cures only one-third of patients.

NONBACTERIAL PROSTATITIS Patients who present with symptoms and signs of prostatitis, increased leukocytes in their expressed prostatic secretions and postmassage urine, and no bacterial growth in cultures are classified as having nonbacterial prostatitis. Prostatic inflammation can be considered present when the expressed prostatic secretion and postmassage urine contain at least tenfold more leukocytes than the first-void and midstream specimens, or when the expressed prostatic secretion contains ≥ 1000 leukocytes per cubic millimeter. The presumed infectious etiology of this condition remains unidentified. Evidence for the causative role of both *Ureaplasma urealyticum* and *Chlamydia trachomatis* has been presented, but is not conclusive. Since most cases of nonbacterial prostatitis occur in young, sexually active men, and since many cases arise following an episode of nonspecific urethritis, the causative agent may well be sexually transmitted. The effectiveness of antimicrobial agents in this condition remains uncertain. Some patients benefit from a 4- to 6-week course of erythromycin, doxycycline, or trimethoprim-sulfamethoxazole.

PROSTATODYNIA Patients who have symptoms and signs of prostatitis but no evidence of prostatic inflammation (normal leukocyte counts) and negative urine cultures should be classified as having prostatodynia. Despite their symptoms, these patients most likely do not have prostatic infection and should not be given antimicrobial agents.

REFERENCES

BAILEY RR: Single-dose therapy for uncomplicated urinary tract infections. NZ Med J 98:327, 1985

BRUMFITT W, ASSCHER AW: *Urinary Tract Infection*. New York, Oxford University Press, 1973

FRANCOIS B, PERRIN P: *Urinary Infection: Insights and Prospects*. London, Butterworth, 1983

JONES SR et al: Localization of urinary tract infection by detection of antibody-coated bacteria in urine sediment. N Engl J Med 290:591, 1975

KOMAROFF AL: Acute dysuria in women. N Engl J Med 310:368, 1984

KRIEGER JN: Prostatitis syndromes: Pathophysiology, differential diagnosis, and treatment. Sex Transm Dis 11:100, 1984

KUNIN CM: *Detection, Prevention and Management of Urinary Tract Infections*, 3d ed. Philadelphia, Lea & Febiger, 1979

MEARES EM: Prostatitis syndromes: New perspectives about old woes. J Urol 123:141, 1980

PLATT R et al: Mortality associated with nosocomial urinary tract infection. N Engl J Med 307:637, 1982

RONALD AR: Current concepts in the management of urinary tract infections in adults. Med Clin N Am 68:335, 1984

———, HARDING GKM: Urinary prophylaxis in women. Ann Intern Med 94:268, 1981

———: Current concepts in the management of urinary tract infections in adults. Med Clin North Am 68:335, 1984

STAMEY TA: *Urinary Infections*. Baltimore, Williams & Wilkins, 1972

STAMM WE et al: Causes of the acute urethral syndrome in women. N Engl J Med 303:409, 1980

——— et al: Diagnosis of coliform infection in acutely dysuric women. N Engl J Med 307:463, 1982

WONG ES, HOOTON TM: Guidelines for prevention of catheter-associated urinary tract infections. Infect Control 2:125, 1980

226 TUBULOINTERSTITIAL DISEASES OF THE KIDNEY

BARRY M. BRENNER / THOMAS H. HOSTETTER

A large and etiologically diverse group of bilateral renal diseases can be distinguished from those considered in Chaps. 223 and 224 because the histologic and functional abnormalities involve the tubules and interstitium to a greater degree than the glomeruli and renal vasculature (see Table 226-1). Morphologically, acute forms of these tubulointerstitial disorders are characterized predominantly by interstitial edema, often associated with cortical and medullary infiltration by polymorphonuclear leukocytes and patchy areas of tubule cell necrosis. In more chronic forms, interstitial fibrosis predominates, inflammatory cells are typically mononuclear, and abnormalities of the tubules tend to be more widespread, as evidenced by atrophy, luminal dilatation, and thickening of tubule basement membranes. In the past, the diagnosis of chronic pyelonephritis was almost universally applied when these chronic tubulointerstitial abnormalities were found. It is now apparent that only a small proportion of these lesions results from infection. Nonbacterial factors, including exogenous toxins and metabolic and immunologic derangements, constitute the major pathogenic mechanisms thought to be involved. Because of the nonspecific nature of the histology, particularly in chronic tubulointerstitial diseases, biopsy specimens rarely provide a specific diagnosis. The urine sediment is also unlikely to be diagnostic, except in allergic forms of acute tubulointerstitial disease in which eosinophils may predominate in the urinary sediment (see below).

Defects in tubule function often accompany these alterations of tubule and interstitial structure. Proximal tubule dysfunction may be manifested as selective reabsorptive defects leading to hypokalemia, aminoaciduria, glycosuria, phosphaturia, uricosuria, or bicarbonaturia (proximal or type II renal tubular acidosis, see Chap. 228). In combination these defects constitute the *Fanconi syndrome*. Protein excretion is usually modest, rarely exceeding 2 g per 24 h. The excreted proteins are typically of low molecular weight and include beta$_2$ microglobulin, lysozyme, and immunoglobulin light chains. Defective proximal tubule reabsorption of these readily filtered small-molecular-weight proteins accounts for their augmented excretion in these disorders. Tubule sodium reabsorption may also be deranged in patients with advanced tubulointerstitial diseases, predisposing them to the tendency to salt wasting and the threat of overt hypovolemia. One or more of these reabsorptive defects are commonly encountered with heavy metal poisoning, multiple myeloma, and other tubulointerstitial processes affecting the renal cortex diffusely.

Defects in urinary acidification and concentrating ability often represent the most troublesome of the tubule dysfunctions encountered in patients with tubulointerstitial disease. Metabolic acidosis of the hyperchloremic type often develops at a relatively early stage in the course of the renal insufficiency. Patients with this finding generally elaborate urine of maximal acidity (pH of 5.3 or less). In such patients the defect in acid excretion usually proves to be caused by a reduced capacity to generate and excrete ammonia due to the reduction in renal mass. Preferential damage to the collecting ducts, as in amyloidosis or chronic obstructive uropathy, may also predispose to distal or type I renal tubular acidosis, characterized by abnormally high urine pH (>5.5) during spontaneous or NH_4Cl-induced metabolic acidosis. Patients with tubulointerstitial diseases affecting medullary and papillary structures predominantly may also evidence substantial concentrating defects, with resultant nocturia and polyuria. The impairment in maximal concentration is typically unresponsive to the administration of antidiuretic hormone, hence a form of nephrogenic

diabetes insipidus. Analgesic nephropathy and sickle cell disease are prototypes of this form of injury.

Although the major structural defects originate in the tubules and interstitium, progressive reduction in glomerular filtration rate (GFR) is a common functional accompaniment of most, if not all, forms of tubulointerstitial damage, reflecting secondary injury to glomeruli and other elements of the renal microcirculation. Indeed oliguric, acute renal failure may be caused by acute forms of tubulointerstitial disease, and as many as one-third of patients with chronic renal insufficiency suffer from a primary chronic tubulointerstitial disease.

TOXINS

A number of factors make the renal tubules and interstitium particularly prone to toxic injury. Although the kidneys constitute less than 1 percent of total body mass, they receive approximately 20 percent of the cardiac output, and 90 percent or more of this very large renal blood flow is distributed to the renal cortex. Exposure of tubules and interstitium of the renal cortex to circulating toxins is, therefore, quantitatively greater than is that of most other tissues. Transport processes operating in renal tubules contribute further to the intrarenal accumulation of toxins, thereby enhancing local concentrations of noxious agents. Furthermore, the urinary concentrating mechanism can establish high levels of toxins within medullary and papillary portions of the kidney, predisposing these regions to chemical injury. Finally, the relatively acid pH of the fluid within most nephron segments may affect the ionization characteristics of potentially toxic compounds and thereby influence local concentration and solubility. Although these normal physiologic processes render the kidney particularly vulnerable to toxic injury, the role of nephrotoxins in the causation of renal damage often goes unrecognized, largely because the manifestations of such injury are usually nonspecific in nature and insidious in onset. Diagnosis largely depends upon obtaining a history of exposure to a certain toxin, a difficult matter since exposure may be occult. Particular attention should, therefore, be paid to the patient's occupational history, as well as to an assessment of exposure, current as well as remote, to pharmaceutical agents, especially antibiotics and analgesics. The clinical recognition of a potential association between a patient's renal disease and exposure to a nephrotoxin is of crucial importance because, unlike many other forms of renal disease, progression of the functional and morphologic abnormalities associated with toxin-induced nephropathies may be prevented, and even reversed, simply by eliminating additional exposure.

EXOGENOUS TOXINS   **Analgesic nephropathy**   Over the past three decades, numerous studies have established that individuals who ingest large quantities of analgesic drugs are particularly prone to develop tubulointerstitial damage and papillary necrosis. Indeed, in Australia, Switzerland, and Sweden, analgesic abuse ranks as one of the most common causes of chronic renal failure, and it is now recognized as an important cause of renal insufficiency in the United States as well. Studies in animals have demonstrated that *phenacetin* and *aspirin* can induce papillary necrosis when either of these drugs is given in quantities far in excess of usual therapeutic doses. However, these chemicals are most likely to cause renal damage, and clinically apparent renal disease, when ingested in combination. Epidemiologic studies leave no doubt that the chronic ingestion of mixtures of these analgesics produces permanent and irreversible renal injury in humans.

Morphologically, analgesic nephropathy is characterized by papillary necrosis and tubulointerstitial inflammation. At an early stage prior to overt papillary necrosis, damage to the vascular supply of the inner medulla (vasa recta) leads to a local interstitial inflammatory reaction and, eventually, to papillary ischemia, necrosis, fibrosis, and calcification. Destruction of papillae usually precedes extension of the tubulointerstitial abnormalities to the renal cortex and, therefore, occurs before renal size and GFR are reduced significantly. It is

TABLE 226-1   Principal causes of tubulointerstitial disease of the kidney

I Toxins
   A Exogenous toxins
      1 Analgesic nephropathy
      2 Lead nephropathy (see Chap. 172)
      3 Miscellaneous nephrotoxins (e.g., antibiotics, radiographic contrast media, heavy metals)
   B Metabolic toxins
      1 Acute uric acid nephropathy (see Chap. 309)
      2 Gouty nephropathy (see Chap. 309)
      3 Hypercalcemic nephropathy (see Chap. 336)
      4 Hypokalemic nephropathy (see Chap. 41)
      5 Miscellaneous metabolic toxins (e.g., hyperoxaluria, cystinosis, Fabry's disease)
II Neoplasia
   A Lymphoma (see Chap. 294)
   B Leukemia (see Chap. 292)
   C Multiple myeloma (see Chap. 258)
III Immune disorders
   A Hypersensitivity nephropathy
   B Sjögren's syndrome (see Chap. 266)
   C Amyloidosis (see Chap. 259)
   D Transplant rejection (see Chap. 221)
   E Tubulointerstitial abnormalities associated with glomerulonephritis (see Chaps. 223 and 224)
IV Vascular disorders (see Chaps. 219 and 227)
   A Arteriolar nephrosclerosis
   B Atheroembolic disease
   C Sickle cell nephropathy
   D Acute tubular necrosis
V Hereditary renal diseases
   A Hereditary nephritis (Alport's syndrome) (see Chap. 224)
   B Medullary cystic disease (see Chap. 228)
   C Medullary sponge kidney (see Chap. 228)
VI Infectious injury (see Chap. 225)
   A Acute pyelonephritis
   B Chronic pyelonephritis
VII Miscellaneous disorders
   A Chronic urinary tract obstruction (see Chap. 230)
   B Vesicoureteral reflux
   C Radiation nephritis
   D Balkan nephropathy

important to recognize that although papillary necrosis is a common finding in patients with the nephropathy of analgesic abuse, necrosis of papillae may also be seen in patients with chronic pyelonephritis, diabetes mellitus, sickle cell disease, and obstructive uropathy. The susceptibility of the renal papillae to damage by analgesic compounds which contain phenacetin is believed to be related to the establishment of a renal corticomedullary gradient for the phenacetin metabolite *acetaminophen,* resulting in papillary tip concentrations which are more than tenfold higher than those present in renal cortex. Hydration serves to dissipate this gradient and may explain the protective effect of this maneuver in preventing phenacetin-induced papillary necrosis in animals. The aspirin in these analgesic compounds is also believed to contribute to renal injury, by uncoupling oxidative phosphorylation in renal mitochondria and by inhibiting the synthesis of renal prostaglandins, which are potent endogenous renal vasodilator hormones. Both effects of aspirin favor hypoxia in renal tissues and, therefore, enhance the susceptibility of the inner medulla to nephrotoxic injury.

Clinically, analgesic nephropathy occurs some three to five times more commonly in women than men. A direct relationship exists between the total amount of analgesic compounds ingested and the degree of renal impairment. An intake of 1.0 g phenacetin per day for 1 to 3 years, or total ingestion of 2 kg phenacetin in combination with other analgesics, appears to represent minimum requirements for the development of analgesic nephropathy. In such patients, renal function usually declines gradually, in association with chronic necrosis of papillae and diffuse tubulointerstitial damage to the renal cortex. Occasionally, papillary necrosis may be associated with gross hematuria, and even renal colic, due to obstruction of a ureter by a fragment of necrotic tissue. More than half of patients with analgesic nephropathy have pyuria, which, if persistently associated with sterile urine, provides an important clue to the diagnosis. Nonetheless, active pyelonephritis may coexist in patients with analgesic nephropathy. Proteinuria, if present, is typically mild (less than 1 g per 24 h). Patients with analgesic nephropathy are usually unable to generate maximally concentrated urine, reflecting the underlying medullary and papillary damage. An acquired form of distal renal tubular acidosis has been described and may contribute to the development of *nephrocalcinosis.* The occurrence of anemia out of proportion to the degree of azotemia may also provide a useful clue to the diagnosis of analgesic nephropathy. Occult gastrointestinal bleeding (usually secondary to analgesic-induced gastritis) and, in an occasional patient, hemolysis (particularly in those with glucose 6-phosphate dehydrogenase deficiency) are believed to contribute to the severity of the anemia. Vague abdominal complaints, as well as nonspecific headaches and arthralgias, are common in these patients. Moderate hypertension is also a common finding, which progresses to a malignant phase in only a small minority of patients. When analgesic nephropathy has progressed to the stage of moderate to severe renal insufficiency, the kidneys usually appear bilaterally shrunken on intravenous pyelography, and the calyces are deformed. A "ring sign" on the pyelogram is pathognomonic of papillary necrosis and represents the radiolucent sloughed papilla surrounded by the radiodense contrast material which fills the calyx. Also, transitional cell carcinoma may develop in the urinary pelvis or ureters as a late complication of analgesic abuse.

Every effort must be made to convince the patient who ingests excessive quantities of analgesics to discontinue this hazardous practice. When renal damage is at an early stage, cessation of drug abuse will usually arrest the progression of the nephrotoxic process; not infrequently, overall renal function will improve with time. With continued abuse of these drugs, however, progressive renal damage leads invariably to chronic renal failure.

Lead nephropathy (see also Chap. 172)   Children and adults suffering from lead intoxication often develop a chronic form of tubulointerstitial renal disease. In children, lead poisoning usually results from ingestion of lead-based paints (pica). The oxide of lead liberated from paint, or present in the vapor arising from the welding of metals covered with lead-based paint, may be inhaled in substantial quantities, thereby constituting an industrial form of exposure in adults. Alcohol, illegally distilled in an apparatus constructed from automobile radiators (so-called moonshine), is yet another source of lead poisoning. Tubule transport processes enhance the accumulation of lead within renal cells, particularly of the proximal convoluted tubule, leading to cell degeneration, mitochondrial swelling, and eosinophilic intranuclear inclusion bodies rich in lead. In addition to tubule degeneration and atrophy, lead nephropathy is associated with ischemic changes in the glomeruli, fibrosis of the adventitia of small renal arterioles, and focal areas of cortical scarring. Eventually, the kidneys become grossly atrophic. In addition to progressive azotemia, abnormalities of tubule function may occur, particularly *renal glycosuria* and *aminoaciduria.* Urinary excretion of lead, bile pigments, and porphyrin precursors, particularly δ-aminolevulinic acid, coproporphyrin, and urobilinogen, may be increased. Patients with chronic lead nephropathy are characteristically *hyperuricemic,* a consequence of enhanced reabsorption of filtered urate. Acute gouty arthritis (so-called saturnine gout) occurs in about 50 percent of patients with lead nephropathy, in striking contrast to other forms of chronic renal failure in which gout is rare. Hypertension is also a frequent complication of this disorder. Therefore, in any patient with slowly progressive renal failure, atrophic kidneys, gout, and hypertension, the diagnosis of lead intoxication should be seriously considered. In addition to these manifestations, patients with chronic lead poisoning often complain of frequent episodes of abdominal colic and have evidence of anemia, peripheral neuropathy, and encephalopathy. The diagnosis may be suspected by finding elevated serum levels of lead. However, because blood levels may not be elevated even in the presence of a toxic total-body burden of lead, the quantitation of lead excretion following a standardized infusion of the chelating agent calcium disodium ethylenediaminetetraacetic acid (EDTA) is a more reliable indicator of serious lead exposure. Urinary excretion of more than 0.6 mg of lead per day is indicative of overt or potential toxicity. Treatment includes removing the patient from the source of exposure and augmenting lead excretion with a chelating agent such as calcium disodium EDTA.

Miscellaneous nephrotoxins   Therapeutic use of lithium salts for manic-depressive illness has been associated with evidence of tubulointerstitial disease. The most frequent clinical finding is a mild to moderate form of nephrogenic diabetes insipidus resulting in polyuria and polydipsia. It is more controversial whether long-term lithium therapy produces irreversible chronic tubulointerstitial lesions and impairment of glomerular filtration rate. Though present evidence suggests that some patients develop histologic evidence of such injury, there are only rare reports of chronic renal insufficiency attributable to this agent. In any case, renal function should be followed in patients taking this drug, and extreme caution should be exercised if lithium is employed in patients with underlying renal disease.

Many agents which commonly lead to acute renal failure are also capable of producing tubulointerstitial injury (see Chap. 219). These include antibiotics (e.g., aminoglycosides, amphotericin B), radiographic contrast agents, various hydrocarbons (e.g., carbon tetrachloride), and heavy metals (e.g., mercury, cadmium, and bismuth).

METABOLIC TOXINS   Acute uric acid nephropathy (see also Chap. 309)   Disorders characterized by acute overproduction of uric acid and extreme hyperuricemia often lead to a rapidly progressive form of renal insufficiency, so-called acute uric acid nephropathy. This tubulointerstitial disease is usually seen in patients given cytotoxic drugs for the treatment of lymphoproliferative or myeloproliferative disorders, but may also occur in these patients even before such treatment is begun. The pathologic changes associated with acute uric acid nephropathy are largely the result of deposition of uric acid crystals in the kidneys and their collecting systems leading to partial or complete obstruction of collecting ducts, renal pelvis, or ureter. Since obstruction is often bilateral, patients typically show the clinical course of acute renal failure, characterized by oliguria and rapidly rising serum creatinine concentration. In the early phase of this disorder, uric acid crystals can often be found in urine, usually in association with microscopic or gross hematuria. Peak serum uric acid levels vary but are almost always above 20 mg/dL and may even exceed 60 mg/dL.

Prevention of hyperuricemia in patients at risk, by treatment with allopurinol in doses of 200 to 800 mg per day prior to cytotoxic therapy, greatly reduces the danger of acute uric acid nephropathy. Once hyperuricemia develops, however, efforts should be directed to preventing deposition of uric acid within the urinary tract. Increasing urine volume with potent diuretics (furosemide or mannitol) effectively lowers intratubular uric acid concentrations, and alkalinization of the urine to pH 7 or greater with sodium bicarbonate and/or a carbonic anhydrase inhibitor (acetazolamide) enhances uric acid solubility. If these efforts, together with allopurinol therapy, are ineffective in preventing acute renal failure, dialysis should be instituted to lower the serum uric acid concentration as well as to treat the acute manifestations of uremia. The combination of conservative therapy and hemodialysis allows most patients with acute uric acid nephropathy to survive this form of acute renal failure and ultimately recover renal function essentially completely.

Gouty nephropathy (see also Chap. 309)   Patients with less severe but more prolonged forms of hyperuricemia are predisposed to a more chronic tubulointerstitial disorder, often referred to as *gouty nephropathy*. Since other conditions associated with hyperuricemia, such as hypertension, nephrolithiasis, pyelonephritis, and even lead poisoning, may contribute to renal damage, the effect of chronic hyperuricemia per se on renal function is unclear. Nevertheless, the severity of renal involvement in this disorder correlates well with the duration and magnitude of the elevation of the serum uric acid concentration. Histologically, the distinctive feature of gouty nephropathy is the presence of crystalline deposits of uric acid and monosodium urate salts in kidney parenchyma. These deposits are believed to represent the primary pathogenic process in gouty nephropathy, with intraluminal crystallization of uric acid taking place in distal tubules and collecting ducts where urine pH is generally quite low and where uric acid concentrations are considerably in excess of levels in plasma. These deposits not only cause intrarenal obstruction, but also incite an inflammatory response, leading to lymphocytic infiltration, foreign-body giant cell reaction, and eventual fibrosis, especially of medullary and papillary regions of the kidney. Bacteriuria and pyelonephritis occur in about one-fourth of cases, presumably as complications of intrarenal urinary stasis. Since patients with gout frequently suffer from hypertension and hyperlipidemia, degenerative changes of the renal arterioles may constitute a striking feature of the histologic abnormality, often out of proportion to other morphologic defects. Clinically, gouty nephropathy is an insidious cause of renal insufficiency. Early in its course, GFR may be near normal, often despite focal morphologic changes in medullary and cortical interstitium, proteinuria, and diminished urinary concentrating ability. Whether reducing serum uric acid levels with allopurinol exerts a beneficial effect on the kidney remains to be demonstrated. Although such undesirable consequences of hyperuricemia as gout and uric acid stones respond well to allopurinol, use of this drug in asymptomatic hyperuricemia has not been shown to improve renal function consistently. On the other hand, uricosuric agents such as probenecid, which may increase uric acid stone production, clearly have no role in the treatment of renal disease associated with hyperuricemia.

Hypercalcemic nephropathy (see also Chap. 336)   Chronic hypercalcemia, as occurs in primary hyperparathyroidism, sarcoidosis, multiple myeloma, vitamin D intoxication, or metastatic bone disease, is a well known cause of tubulointerstitial damage and progressive renal insufficiency. Pathologically, the earliest renal lesion induced by hypercalcemia is a focal degenerative change in renal epithelia, primarily in collecting ducts, distal convoluted tubules, and loops of Henle. Tubule cell necrosis leads to nephron obstruction and stasis

of intrarenal urine, favoring local precipitation of calcium salts and infection. Dilatation and atrophy of tubules eventually occur, as do interstitial fibrosis, mononuclear leukocyte infiltration, and interstitial calcium deposition (nephrocalcinosis). Calcium deposition may also occur in glomeruli and the walls of renal arterioles. Clinically, the most striking defect is an inability to concentrate the urine maximally, resulting in polyuria and nocturia. Defective transport of chloride in the ascending limb of Henle's loop is believed to be responsible, at least in part, for this concentrating defect. Additionally, reduced collecting duct responsiveness to ADH may contribute to this abnormality. Reductions in GFR and renal blood flow also occur, both in states of acute severe hypercalcemia as well as with prolonged hypercalcemia of lesser severity. Distal renal tubular acidosis and sodium and potassium wasting have also been described in these chronic states. Eventually, uncontrolled hypercalcemia leads to severe tubulointerstitial damage and overt renal failure. Urinalysis is rarely a clue to the presence of hypercalcemic renal failure, but abdominal x-rays may demonstrate nephrocalcinosis as well as nephrolithiasis, the latter due to the hypercalciuria which often accompanies hypercalcemia. Treatment for hypercalcemic nephropathy consists of reducing the serum calcium concentration toward normal and correcting the primary abnormality of calcium metabolism. The management of hypercalcemia is discussed in Chap. 336. Prognosis for recovery of renal function depends upon the severity of the renal lesion at the time hypercalcemia is corrected. Renal dysfunction of recent onset secondary to acute hypercalcemia may be completely reversible. Gradual, progressive renal insufficiency related to chronic hypercalcemia, however, may not improve with correction of the calcium disorder. Nonetheless, every effort should be made to return serum calcium concentration to normal in order to minimize further loss of renal function.

Hypokalemic nephropathy (see also Chap. 41)   Disturbances of renal structure and function are observed commonly in patients with moderate to severe potassium depletion of at least several weeks' duration. Histologically, renal epithelial cells are often seen to contain numerous vacuoles, most marked in proximal, and to a lesser extent, distal convoluted tubules. These findings usually disappear with potassium repletion. Glomeruli are reduced in size and may become sclerotic while larger blood vessels are usually uninvolved. Whether prolonged or recurrent potassium deficiency results in irreversible tubulointerstitial fibrosis, scarring, and atrophy is still a controversial issue. Loss of urinary concentrating ability is the most commonly encountered functional defect. Experimental studies in animals have shown that this urinary concentrating abnormality is preceded by a period of primary polydipsia. The reduced concentrating capacity which eventually develops is due, at least in part, to defective operation of the countercurrent multiplier system. Elevated rates of intrarenal prostaglandin synthesis may also contribute to this concentrating defect, since prostaglandins are known to antagonize the hydroosmotic action of antidiuretic hormone on collecting-duct epithelium. Symptoms of nocturia, polyuria, and polydipsia are frequently encountered in patients with chronic potassium depletion, although, occasionally, patients with severe hypokalemia have no complaints referable to the urinary tract. It has been suggested that patients with hypokalemic nephropathy have an enhanced susceptibility to pyelonephritis, but this issue remains unresolved. The polydipsia is probably due to both the impaired renal concentrating ability and a primary disorder of the thirst mechanism, which is believed to be a common feature of most chronic potassium depletion states. Urinalysis often reveals no abnormalities except for mild proteinuria. Serum creatinine and urea nitrogen concentrations usually remain within normal limits. Treatment should be directed at repleting body potassium stores and correcting the primary process responsible for potassium loss. With correction of body potassium stores, functional and histologic abnormalities of the kidneys usually disappear, although maximal urinary concentrating ability may not return to normal for several months.

Miscellaneous metabolic toxins Urinary oxalate, derived from the metabolism of glycine and, to a variable extent, from ingested oxalate, may deposit as insoluble intratubular calcium oxalate crystals and result in chronic tubulointerstitial damage in patients with hereditary or acquired forms of *hyperoxaluria*. *Cystinosis* and *Fabry's disease* are other hereditary depositional disorders affecting the renal tubules and interstitium. The reader is referred to Chaps. 224, 228, and 229 for more detailed discussions of these and other uncommon metabolic causes of tubulointerstitial injury.

RENAL PARENCHYMAL DISEASE ASSOCIATED WITH EXTRARENAL NEOPLASM

In addition to being the site of origin of several benign and malignant neoplasms (see Chap. 231), the kidneys are frequently affected by neoplasms arising outside the urinary tract. Except for the glomerulopathies associated with lymphomas and several solid tumors (see Chap. 224), the renal manifestations of primary extrarenal neoplastic processes are confined mainly to the interstitium and tubules. Although metastatic renal involvement by solid tumors is unusual, the kidneys are often invaded by neoplastic cells in various lymphomas and leukemias and in multiple myeloma. In postmortem studies of patients with *lymphoma*, renal involvement is found in approximately one-half of cases. The involvement may be focal, in the form of multiple discrete nodules, or diffuse, with lymphomatous infiltration throughout the renal parenchyma. Diffuse infiltration is seen most commonly in lymphomas other than Hodgkin's disease. There may be flank pain related to massive renal infiltration, and x-rays may show enlargement of one or both kidneys. Renal insufficiency occurs in a distinct minority of cases, and overt uremia is rare. Treatment of the primary disease may improve renal function in these cases.

The kidneys are also commonly involved in various forms of *leukemia*. At postmortem examination, bilateral renal involvement can be demonstrated in approximately 50 percent of cases. As with lymphoma, uremia is rarely, if ever, a consequence of leukemic infiltration of the kidneys. The kidneys can also be involved in leukemias because of the associated high incidence of hyperuricemia, hypercalcemia, and lysozymuria. The myelogenous leukemias, particularly of the monocytic type, may be complicated by tubule defects involving potassium and magnesium wasting.

In contrast, infiltration of the kidneys with *myeloma* cells is infrequent (see also Chap. 258). When it occurs, the process is usually focal, so that renal insufficiency from this cause is also uncommon. The more usual lesion is *myeloma kidney*, which is characterized histologically by atrophic tubules, many with eosinophilic intraluminal casts, and numerous multinucleated giant cells within tubule walls as well as in the interstitium. The frequent occurrence of myeloma kidney in patients with Bence-Jones proteinuria has suggested a causal relation. Bence-Jones proteins are thought to cause myeloma kidney through direct toxicity to renal tubule cells. In addition, Bence-Jones proteins may precipitate within the distal nephron where the high concentrations of these proteins and the acid composition of the tubule fluid favor intraluminal cast formation and intrarenal obstruction. Indeed, positive immunofluorescence staining for light chains can often be demonstrated in casts found in myeloma kidneys. Occasionally, acute renal failure occurs after intravenous pyelography in patients with multiple myeloma and is believed to result from the further precipitation of Bence-Jones proteins induced by dehydration prior to radiographic study. Routine dehydration of the patient with myeloma in preparation for intravenous pyelography should, therefore, be avoided. Multiple myeloma may also affect the kidneys indirectly. Hypercalcemia or hyperuricemia may occur and lead to the nephropathies described above. Proximal tubule disorders are also seen occasionally in patients with myeloma, including type II proximal renal tubular acidosis and the Fanconi syndrome. Additionally, intrarenal deposits of *amyloid* (see below) may contribute to impaired excretory function in patients with multiple myeloma.

IMMUNE DISORDERS

HYPERSENSITIVITY NEPHROPATHY An acute diffuse tubulointerstitial reaction may result from hypersensitivity to a number of drugs. First reported after the use of sulfonamides, acute tubulointerstitial damage is now seen most often with the antibiotic *methicillin*, although other drugs, including *ampicillin, penicillin, cephalothin, phenindione, thiazides, furosemide,* and nonsteroidal anti-inflammatory drugs have also been implicated. Of note, the tubulointerstitial nephropathy which develops in some patients taking nonsteroidal anti-inflammatory drugs may be associated with nephrotic-range proteinuria and histologic evidence of minimal change glomerulopathy. Grossly, the kidneys are usually enlarged. Histologically, the glomeruli appear normal. The principal pathologic abnormalities are in the interstitium of the kidney, which reveals pronounced edema and infiltration with polymorphonuclear leukocytes, lymphocytes, plasma cells, and, in some cases, large numbers of eosinophils. If the process is severe, tubule cell necrosis and regeneration may also be apparent. Immunofluorescence studies in a number of cases either have been unrevealing or have demonstrated a linear pattern of immunoglobin and complement deposition along tubule basement membranes. In a few cases of methicillin-induced acute tubulointerstitial disease, circulating antitubule basement membrane antibodies have also been found, suggesting that autoantibody formation may have been induced by the penicilloyl hapten of methicillin (by conjugation of hapten with tubule basement membrane proteins, thereby altering the native antigenicity of the basement membrane). In cases associated with nonsteroidal, anti-inflammatory drugs a role for cell-mediated immunity has been proposed, since renal infiltration by both T and B lymphocytes has been observed with a relative predominance of cytotoxic T cells. Evidence for an immunologic basis for these various drug-related nephropathies also derives from the facts that the onset of nephropathy does not appear to be dose-related, often follows a second exposure to the drug presumed to be responsible for the renal injury, and often is associated with increased levels of serum IgE. In the case of methicillin, the patients usually develop evidence of renal injury after about 2 weeks of drug administration. Hematuria, fever, skin rash, and eosinophilia are prominent. Many patients develop azotemia which typically resolves after withdrawal of the offending drug. Proteinuria and pyuria often accompany the hematuria, and occasionally eosinophils are found in the urine sediment. The clinical picture may be confused with acute glomerulonephritis, but when acute azotemia and hematuria are accompanied by eosinophilia, skin rash, and a history of drug exposure, a hypersensitivity reaction leading to acute tubulointerstitial nephritis should be regarded as the leading diagnostic possibility. Discontinuation of the drug usually results in complete reversal of the renal injury; rarely, renal damage may be irreversible. Corticosteroids have been used, but their value in this disorder has not been established with certainty.

SJÖGREN'S SYNDROME (See also Chap. 266) Keratoconjunctivitis sicca, or Sjögren's syndrome, is an immunologic disorder characterized by dryness of mucous membranes and mononuclear cell infiltration of salivary and lacrimal glands; it is often seen in patients with rheumatoid arthritis. When the kidneys are involved in Sjögren's syndrome, the predominant histologic findings are those of chronic tubulointerstitial disease. Interstitial infiltrates are composed primarily of lymphocytes, causing the histology of the renal parenchyma in these patients to resemble that of the salivary and lacrimal glands. Renal functional defects associated with this disorder include diminished urinary concentrating ability and distal (type I) renal tubular acidosis. Urinalysis may show pyuria (predominantly lymphocyturia) and mild proteinuria.

AMYLOIDOSIS (See also Chaps. 224 and 259) Glomerular pathology usually predominates and leads to heavy proteinuria and azotemia. However, tubule function may also be deranged, giving rise to a nephrogenic form of diabetes insipidus and to distal (type I) renal tubular acidosis. In several cases these functional abnormalities have been correlated with peritubular deposition of amyloid, particularly in areas surrounding vasa rectae, loops of Henle, and collecting ducts. Bilateral enlargement of the kidneys, especially in a patient with massive proteinuria and evidence for tubule dysfunction, should raise the possibility of amyloid renal disease.

TUBULOINTERSTITIAL ABNORMALITIES ASSOCIATED WITH GLOMERULONEPHRITIS

A number of primary glomerulopathies may also be associated with damage to tubules and interstitium. Pathogenetically, the extraglomerular component in these renal disorders often involves the same mechanisms that are responsible for the more pronounced glomerular injury. For example, in more than half of patients with the nephropathy associated with systemic lupus erythematosus, deposits of immune complexes can be identified in tubule basement membranes, usually accompanied by an interstitial mononuclear inflammatory reaction. Similarly, in many patients with glomerulonephritis associated with antiglomerular basement membrane antibody, the same antibody can be shown to be reactive against tubule basement membranes as well.

MISCELLANEOUS DISORDERS

VESICOURETERAL REFLUX

(See also Chaps. 225 and 230) Normally, the junction of the terminal ureter with the urinary bladder provides a competent sphincter so that during micturition urine leaves the bladder only via the urethra. However, when the function of the ureterovesical junction is impaired, urine may reflux into the ureters due to the high intravesical pressure that develops during voiding. Clinically, reflux is often detected on the voiding and postvoiding films obtained during intravenous pyelography, although voiding cystourethrography may be required for definitive diagnosis. Bladder infection may ascend the urinary tract to the kidneys through incompetent ureterovesical sphincters. Not surprisingly, therefore, reflux is often discovered in patients with acute and/or chronic urinary tract infections. In children particularly, reflux of minor degree may disappear with time and standard therapy of intercurrent urinary infection. With more severe degrees of reflux, characterized by marked dilatation of ureters and renal pelves, progressive renal damage often appears, and although active infection may also be present, uncertainty exists as to the necessity of infection in producing the scarred kidney of reflux nephropathy. In contrast to those with other forms of chronic tubulointerstitial disease, patients with renal insufficiency and scarring due to reflux often demonstrate substantial proteinuria. Indeed, in such cases glomerular lesions similar to those of idiopathic focal glomerulosclerosis (Chap. 223) are often present in addition to the more usual changes of chronic tubulointerstitial disease. Surgical correction of reflux is usually necessary only with the more severe degrees of reflux since renal damage appears to best correlate with the extent of reflux. Obviously, if extensive glomerulosclerosis already exists, urologic repair may no longer be warranted.

RADIATION NEPHRITIS

Clinical renal dysfunction can be expected to occur if 2300 R or more of x-ray irradiation is administered to both kidneys during a period of 5 weeks or less. Histologic examination of the affected kidneys reveals hyalinized glomeruli, atrophic tubules, extensive interstitial fibrosis, and hyalinization of the media of renal arterioles. Radiation-induced renal ischemia is believed to be the main pathogenic factor responsible for the widespread tubulointerstitial damage, which may not become evident clinically for weeks to months after completion of irradiation. The clinical presentation of acute radiation nephritis includes rapidly progressive azotemia, moderate to malignant hypertension, anemia, and proteinuria which may reach the nephrotic range. More than 50 percent of these cases progress to chronic renal failure. A more insidious form of radiation nephritis may also occur; it is characterized by slower development of azotemia, anemia, and nephrotic syndrome. Malignant hypertension has also been known to follow unilateral renal irradiation and to

resolve with ipsilateral nephrectomy. Radiation nephritis in recent years has all but vanished because of heightened awareness of its pathogenesis by radiotherapists.

BALKAN NEPHROPATHY

Balkan nephropathy is an acquired, endemic disorder restricted to the small geographic region where Yugoslavia, Romania, and Bulgaria meet to form the Danubian basin. The renal lesions seen in affected patients from this region progress from focal tubular atrophy, interstitial edema, and mononuclear cell infiltration to diffuse interstitial fibrosis, leading eventually to bilaterally shrunken, atrophic kidneys. Epidemiologic studies point to an environmental toxin as the cause, but the offending agent has not yet been identified. Defects in urinary concentrating ability, low-molecular-weight ("tubular") proteinuria, and renal tubular acidosis are common. In most cases, the disease is progressive, leading eventually to chronic renal failure. A high incidence of papillary transitional carcinoma of the renal pelvis and upper ureter appears to be a late complication in patients with this endemic nephropathy.

REFERENCES

BATUMEN V et al: The role of lead in gout nephropathy. N Engl J Med 304:520, 1981

BUCKALEW VM JR, SCHEY HM: Analgesic nephropathy: A significant cause of morbidity in the United States. Am J Kidney Dis 7:164, 1986

COTRAN RS: Glomerulosclerosis in reflux nephropathy. Kidney Int 21:528, 1982

—— et al: Tubulointerstitial diseases, in *The Kidney*, 3d ed, BM Brenner, FC Rector Jr (eds). Philadelphia, Saunders, 1986, p 1143

CUSHNER HM et al: Acute interstitial nephritis associated with mezlocillin, nafcillin, and gentamicin treatment for *Pseudomonas* infection. Arch Intern Med 145:1204, 1985

DITLOVE J et al: Methicillin nephritis. Medicine 56:483, 1977

HALL PW, DAMMIN GJ: Balkan nephropathy. Nephron 22:281, 1978

HUMES HD, WEINBERG J: Toxic nephropathies, in *The Kidney*, 3d ed, BM Brenner, FC Rector Jr (eds). Philadelphia, Saunders, 1986, p 1491

KINCAID-SMITH P: Analgesic abuse and the kidney. Kidney Int 17:250, 1980

MURRAY T, GOLDBERG M: Chronic interstitial nephritis: Etiologic factors. Ann Intern Med 82:453, 1975

RUBIN RH et al: Urinary tract infection, pyelonephritis, and reflux nephropathy, in *The Kidney*, 3d ed, BM Brenner, FC Rector Jr (eds). Philadelphia, Saunders, 1986, p 1085

SINGER I: Lithium and the kidney. Kidney Int 19:374, 1981

TORRES VE et al: The progression of vesicoureteral reflux nephropathy. Ann Intern Med 92:776, 1980

WILSON CB, DIXON FJ: Renal response to immunological injury, in *The Kidney*, 3d ed, BM Brenner, FC Rector Jr (eds). Philadelphia, Saunders, 1986, p 800

227   VASCULAR INJURY TO THE KIDNEY

NORMAN K. HOLLENBERG

Processes ranging from renal artery stenosis and occlusion to arteriolar nephrosclerosis, polyarteritis nodosa, the hemolytic uremic syndromes, scleroderma, and preeclampsia share a sufficient number of clinical features, morphologic characteristics, and pathogenetic consequences to justify their consideration together. The clinical, functional, and morphologic expressions of interrupting the renal blood supply depend on the degree of obstruction to flow, the rate at which the occlusion occurs, the level of vessel involved, and the total mass of ischemic parenchyma. Because the intrarenal arterial tree is made up of end arteries, sudden occlusion results in infarction with clinical manifestations that vary with the level at which the occlusion occurs. More gradual partial occlusion, on the other hand, results in ischemic atrophy and a different functional and clinical picture.

Renal blood flow, averaging 4.0 (mL/g)/min, exceeds by three- to fivefold the flow in such metabolically active organs as the heart, liver, and brain. Renal blood flow is not adjusted to satisfy metabolic need, but rather to provide the plasma flow and pressure to the glomerular capillary bed required to sustain glomerular filtration. Renal perfusion is also an important determinant of sodium handling by the kidney. For these reasons, a reduction in renal blood flow too small to result in cell death has important consequences including a reduction in filtration rate, increased sodium reabsorption, increased renin release, and hypertension. To a varying extent all are features common to the syndromes resulting from abnormalities in the renal circulation.

ACUTE ARTERIAL OCCLUSION Acute, complete occlusion of the main renal artery or a major intrarenal arterial branch may follow blunt trauma to the abdomen or back or embolism in patients with mitral stenosis and atrial fibrillation, infective endocarditis, mural thrombi overlying myocardial infarcts, or ulcerating atherosclerotic disease of the aorta. The kidneys receive about one-fifth of the cardiac output, making embolic occlusion of the small intrarenal arteries relatively common. Acute occlusion results in coagulation necrosis in the region supplied by the obstructed artery, the size of the wedge-shaped infarct varying with the level of the occlusion.

The clinical features also depend on the size of the infarct. Small infarcts, involving a portion of the renal cortex, are often clinically silent. Larger infarcts may induce a sudden, sharp unremitting pain in the flank or upper abdomen associated with fever, leukocytosis, and gross or microscopic hematuria. The impact on renal function also varies. Even total occlusion of one main renal artery may leave the blood urea nitrogen (BUN) and serum creatinine in the normal range in the presence of a healthy contralateral kidney which can undergo hypertrophy. When the patient has only a solitary functioning kidney, arterial occlusion enters the differential diagnosis of acute oliguric renal failure. Although total destruction of the kidney will generally occur within hours of occlusion, at least a dozen case reports of restoration of renal function after days to weeks of total occlusion have appeared, generally in a setting in which prior partial occlusion has led to a rich collateral arterial blood supply sufficient for nutrition although inadequate to maintain renal function. Angiography is necessary to establish the diagnosis. Evidence of collateral filling of the intrarenal arterial tree suggests that operation may restore renal function.

RENAL ARTERY STENOSIS (See also Chap. 196) Partial occlusion of the renal artery or its major branches by atherosclerotic narrowing or by fibromuscular dysplasia is responsible for about 1 to 2 percent of cases of hypertension; its importance lies in the fact that it represents the most common curable form of hypertension. *Renal arterial atherosclerosis*, as with atherosclerosis elsewhere, is more frequent in males, and its incidence increases with advancing age, previous hypertension, or diabetes mellitus. The *fibromuscular dysplasias* of the renal artery are a heterogeneous group of lesions in which fibrous or fibromuscular thickening may involve the intima, the media, or the subadventitial region. The process is frequently bilateral and may extend into the intrarenal tree. The fibrous dysplasias are 10 times more common in females, appear most often in the third and fourth decades, and, presumably because the individuals are younger, are associated with a lower surgical morbidity and a higher cure rate than are atherosclerotic renal arterial lesions.

The clinical features which may be helpful in detecting renal artery stenosis include a history of the onset of hypertension at an age which is unusual for essential hypertension, i.e., under 30 or over 50 years of age, a poor response to medical therapy, and a bruit in the flank or upper abdominal region. Routine laboratory evaluation often reveals evidence of secondary hyperaldosteronism including hypokalemia and metabolic alkalosis. As in primary aldosteronism, hypokalemia may be masked by a restricted sodium intake.

The intravenous pyelogram (IVP) and the radionuclide Hippuran renogram are still the most widely used screening tests for renovascular hypertension. Characteristics in the pyelogram suggesting renal artery stenosis include a reduction in renal size of at least 1.5 cm compared with the opposite kidney, a delay in the appearance of contrast in the involved kidney when films are obtained at 1, 2, and 3 min after injection of the contrast agent, hyperconcentration of contrast on the involved side in the late films, and filling defects in the renal pelvis and ureter reflecting the local effects of dilated collateral arteries. In the Cooperative Study on Renovascular Hypertension, the character-

istic features of the late appearance of contrast medium in a small kidney which showed late hyperconcentration of contrast in the renal pelvis was never seen in patients with essential hypertension. Unfortunately, only 22 percent of patients with renovascular hypertension had this triad, and so it was relatively insensitive. The presence of any single abnormality was found in 78 percent of patients with renovascular hypertension, but with a sharp reduction in specificity since 11 percent of patients with essential hypertension had at least one of these manifestations, most commonly a significant difference in renal size. The characteristics of a radiohippuran renogram which suggest renal artery stenosis include a delay in the rate of rise of the tracer in the kidney, a delay in the time to reach the peak, and a reduced rate of disappearance from the kidney. The renogram identified 75 percent of patients with renovascular hypertension, with a false-positive rate of 24 percent. Because both the IVP and the renogram compare the two kidneys, they are less often positive when stenosis is bilateral. Digital subtraction angiography is finding increased use, but it is still more invasive and expensive than the IVP, and its specificity and sensitivity have not yet been defined clearly.

Because of the prevalence of hypertension and the low yield of renovascular hypertension when a detailed evaluation is undertaken, the clinical indications for laboratory investigations in search of renovascular hypertension are gradually undergoing modification. No more than 1 to 2 percent of patients with hypertension have a curable renal arterial lesion. The evaluation is costly. Finally, operation, especially in patients with atherosclerosis, carries considerable risk. For these reasons a detailed evaluation for renal artery stenosis is currently recommended only when the yield is likely to be high, including patients in whom the onset of hypertension has occurred before the age of 30 years, in the presence of a bruit, or when hypertension is severe and responds poorly to medical therapy.

If the screening test is positive, identification of renal artery stenosis is accomplished only by arteriography. Because all arterial lesions are not hemodynamically significant, ancillary tests are used to assess the hemodynamic significance of the stenosis. The most widely used test involves the measurement of renin activity in blood samples obtained from both renal veins and either the lower inferior vena cava or the aorta. A positive test, strongly suggestive of curable renovascular hypertension, reveals a plasma renin activity from the involved renal veins which exceeds the contralateral renal vein concentration by at least 50 percent, and evidence of suppression of renin-release from the intact contralateral kidney, i.e., identical renin activity in the arterial and contralateral renal venous plasma. With these criteria the false-positive rate is only 7 percent, but there is a quantitatively important false-negative rate. At present we employ renal arteriography and renal vein renin determinations in patients in whom the history, physical examination, and screening tests make renovascular hypertension likely.

The Cooperative Study on Renovascular Disease has provided a clear picture of the current results of operation. When renal artery stenosis was due to fibromuscular disease, the cure rate exceeded 90 percent with a mortality of no more than 3 percent—probably reflecting the youth of the population, which was largely free of additional systemic disease. In patients with atherosclerotic disease, on the other hand, the mortality was 9 percent and the failure rate exceeded 25 percent. For these reasons evaluation for renal artery surgery in older patients who are likely to have atherosclerotic disease is restricted in many centers to patients in whom medical management fails.

If medical therapy is selected because of surgical risk, the converting enzyme inhibitor captopril is particularly effective in renovascular hypertension and is recommended for the patient with hypertension which is resistant to a standard regimen. Medical therapy, while it may control the hypertension, will not prevent the progress of the renal arterial lesion. The agent should be used cautiously or avoided in the patient with advanced bilateral renal artery disease or with stenosis of the artery to a single kidney as it may precipitate functional renal failure. Percutaneous transluminal angioplasty, in which a balloon-tipped catheter is employed to dilate the stenotic area during renal arteriography, has been most successful in renal vascular hypertension due to fibromuscular dysplasia. When atherosclerosis has been at the origin of the renal artery, i.e., is ostial, the results of angioplasty have been much poorer.

ARTERIOLAR NEPHROSCLEROSIS Small-vessel changes in the kidney are so intimately associated with both long-standing hypertension and the normal aging process that it is difficult to define the boundary between normal and disease and to discuss the vascular lesion without discussing hypertension. At least some degree of small-vessel lesion is found in about 70 percent of normotensive individuals who die after the age of 60 years. The frequency and severity is increased in younger age groups with predisposing factors, hypertension and diabetes. Large and medium-sized arteries at the interlobar and arcuate levels show intimal thickening of variable degree. Typically, more widespread and more severe abnormalities are seen in the small arteries and arterioles where, in addition, there is an eosinophilic hyalin thickening which results in a variable degree of vascular narrowing. As a consequence there is patchy ischemic atrophy which parallels that of the vascular change.

The vascular changes presumably account for most of the loss of renal function which accompanies normal aging and which is accentuated in the patient with hypertension. The reductions in renal plasma flow and glomerular filtration rate account for the loss of an element of functional reserve, making older individuals more prone to develop azotemia when faced with volume depletion or surgical stress. The increased incidence of drug-induced complications in the elderly presumably reflects the important role played by glomerular filtration in the excretion of drugs and metabolites. Some examples are the propensity of the elderly to suffer toxicity with streptomycin and digoxin. Other features of arteriolar nephrosclerosis include a moderate loss of concentrating power and often mild proteinuria. Occasionally more profound renal functional abnormalities occur, but marked renal insufficiency is uncommon.

On the other hand, "accelerated nephrosclerosis" associated with malignant hypertension is a dramatic complication of all forms of hypertension in which an abrupt change in course, renal insufficiency, and a uremic death were common before effective therapy became available (Chap. 196). The onset of the malignant phase is characterized by a sharp increase in blood pressure, with diastolic pressures typically exceeding 130 mmHg. In essential hypertension, the malignant phase is usually preceded by a benign period of variable duration, but occasionally occurs de novo. This process also occurs as a complication of all forms of secondary hypertension. Until recently it was suggested that accelerated nephrosclerosis does not complicate the course of primary aldosteronism, but several well-documented cases now exist. In pheochromocytoma accelerated hypertension is typically associated with preserved renal function.

The renal lesions of malignant hypertension include petechial hemorrhages of the cortical surface, responsible for the characteristic "flea-bitten" appearance; fibrinoid necrosis of afferent arterioles; a hyperplastic endarteritis of the interlobular and arcuate arteries; and severe ischemic atrophy or infarction distal to the abnormal vessels. Immunofluorescent and electron-microscopic studies have shown that the amorphous material in the arteriolar wall consists of fibrin. Severe hypertension, per se, is probably responsible for the vascular necrosis resulting from endothelial injury and leakage of fibrin and other plasma constituents into the arteriolar wall.

The clinical features include severe hypertension, neuroretinopathy with blurring of vision, retinal hemorrhages, exudates, and papilledema. Hypertensive encephalopathy is evidenced by severe headache, changes in the sensorium, and seizures. Congestive heart failure and rapidly progressive uremia are common. The renal manifestations include gross or microscopic hematuria, marked proteinuria, and a rapid rise in BUN and creatinine. As in renal artery stenosis, evidence of secondary aldosteronism is common with hypokalemia and a metabolic alkalosis, until the metabolic acidosis of renal failure supervenes.

Prior to the availability of effective therapy for the hypertension, the mortality in patients with this syndrome approximated 50 percent in 3 months and 90 percent within 1 year. In the past two decades, the availability of effective antihypertensive therapy (Chap. 196) has greatly improved the prognosis of accelerated nephrosclerosis. In the early 1950s a BUN which exceeded 30 mg/dL at the time the diagnosis was made guaranteed a rapid demise. Today a patient with a BUN which exceeds this level by three- or fourfold may have a stable course with effective therapy.

SCLERODERMA RENAL CRISIS (PROGRESSIVE SYSTEMIC SCLEROSIS) (See also Chap. 264) The renal aspects of scleroderma are considered in some detail here because renal involvement is second only to that of heart and lungs as a cause of death, and the characteristic morphologic lesions and clinical course closely resemble those associated with accelerated nephrosclerosis.

As in accelerated nephrosclerosis, the morphologic features include kidneys which are only slightly reduced in size even in patients who have died with renal failure. Petechial hemorrhages and wedge-shaped cortical infarcts are common. The most striking and distinctive abnormality is seen in the intralobular arteries, which are markedly narrowed or occluded as a result of fibrinoid change and deposition of fibrin and acid mucopolysaccharides. The afferent arterioles in some patients also show fibrinoid necrosis and occasional occlusion by fibrin thrombi. Distal to the occlusion, ischemic atrophy and infarction are evident. Although the renal vascular lesions may be secondary to the hypertension, they have been documented at necropsy in patients with scleroderma who have never been hypertensive.

Renal involvement is rarely the presenting feature. In one study renal involvement was found at presentation in only 3 percent of patients with scleroderma. However, in a 20-year longitudinal survey, 47 percent of patients ultimately developed a clinically important renal lesion. Renal failure contributes to or is primarily responsible for 40 to 50 percent of all deaths. Most patients with clinically evident renal disease die in less than 1 year and often within 3 months. Indeed, in the aforementioned longitudinal study only 10 percent of patients without renal involvement died, whereas 60 percent of patients with proteinuria, azotemia, or hypertension succumbed.

Renal involvement in scleroderma is usually characterized clinically by an abrupt onset and an explosive course; accelerated hypertension is followed by oliguria and a uremic death within months. Clinical evidence of major renal involvement is typically noted 3 to 5 years after the onset of manifestations in the skin and other systems. Occasionally, however, renal disease antedates obvious skin involvement.

A second, less distinct clinical expression of renal involvement is also being recognized. Isolated proteinuria unaccompanied by either hypertension or azotemia adversely affects prognosis but less strikingly than does the syndrome of malignant hypertension. Mild hypertension, without proteinuria or azotemia, occurs with greater frequency in scleroderma than would be anticipated from known prevalence of essential hypertension. Mild hypertension without proteinuria or azotemia occurs later than the malignant form and has a much less grave prognosis.

No specific therapy exists for scleroderma. A series of reports have indicated that very aggressive antihypertensive therapy sometimes makes renal failure avoidable. Presumably because the hypertension is renin-mediated, the converting enzyme inhibitor, captopril, has been especially effective. Furthermore, renal transplantation has been successful in a limited number of patients with scleroderma.

SICKLE CELL NEPHROPATHY (See also Chaps. 224 and 288) Patients with sickle cell disease, sickle cell trait, sickle thalassemia, and other combinations of hemoglobin S with abnormal hemoglobins often have clinically important disorders of renal structure and function. The most dramatic of the renal manifestations is gross painless hematuria. The bleeding arises from miliary gross and microscopic infarcts in the papillae, renal pelvis, and renal cortex. For unknown reasons the bleeding occurs from the left side in 80 percent of cases and, despite the systemic nature of the primary process, is bilateral in only 11 percent. Abnormalities in the IVP, most commonly a pelvic filling defect reflecting blood clot, are frequent and have led to unnecessary surgical intervention. Most cases remit spontaneously. Because causes other than sickle cell anemia may be responsible for hematuria in these patients, a complete urologic assessment is generally performed (Chap. 40). When filling defects are found, serial studies are recommended; surgical exploration should be considered only if they persist. Operation may also be required in rare instances of life-threatening hemorrhage.

Failure of urinary concentration is the most consistent feature of sickle cell nephropathy. In very young children with sickle cell anemia the concentrating defect can be reversed by multiple transfusions, but the capacity for improvement is lost with age, becoming negligible in patients after 15 years of age. In older adults the maximal concentration of the urine rarely exceeds 400 mosmol per liter. The failure of urinary concentration is typically attributed to a disorder of perfusion of the renal medulla, perhaps due to the sickling process per se. Both hypoxia and an increased osmolality precipitate the sickling phenomenon and sickle cells increase blood viscosity significantly, so this condition may impede the normal circulation through the vasa recta, which normally have a very high resistance to flow. Microangiographic studies have revealed obliteration and distortion of the remaining vasa recta.

Appreciable proteinuria is common in sickle cell disease and occurred in 31 percent of patients in one series. On occasion proteinuria is sufficiently severe that the nephrotic syndrome develops. Distal renal tubular acidosis has also been reported as an uncommon complication.

With increasing age, the growing number and size of cortical infarcts result in a progressive reduction in glomerular filtration rate and renal plasma flow, which are typically higher than normal in the young patients with sickle cell disease. Deterioration of renal function caused by sickle cell anemia to the point at which dialysis becomes necessary has not been described. However, it has been shown that patients with sickle cell disease can be maintained on chronic hemodialysis without encountering undue complications.

HEMOLYTIC-UREMIC SYNDROMES (See also Chap. 287) The coincidence of acute renal failure, hemolytic anemia, and thrombocytopenia has emerged as a clearly defined, relatively common entity in which infants or children develop acute anemia, signs of renal and central nervous system injury, and gastrointestinal bleeding after a prodrome of digestive, respiratory, and systemic symptoms. The hallmarks of the syndrome are hemolysis due to red blood cell fragmentation, a reduction in platelet count, and biochemical and pathologic evidence of intravascular coagulation. The differential diagnosis includes thrombotic thrombocytopenic purpura (TTP), renal cortical necrosis as part of the Shwartzman reaction in gram-negative sepsis, and severe vasculitis. Differentiation among these entities may be extremely difficult, even at necropsy. TTP, which has a worse prognosis, is more likely if the patient is a young adult, if there is a continuing fever, and if the central nervous system involvement is more severe than the renal failure.

Initially only severe, generally fatal cases were recognized, but with increasing familiarity patients with mild or moderate lesions have been identified. The immediate prognosis is related to the degree of renal failure and the severity of involvement of the central nervous system. If the patient survives, the hematologic abnormality is short-lived and does not recur. In some patients the extent of renal destruction precludes prolonged survival without dialysis. In a few others severe neurologic sequelae have been permanently disabling. In many patients the renal lesions heal completely, but on occasion slowly progressive renal failure occurs after the initial insult.

Although primarily a disease of children, there has been increasing recognition of this syndrome in adults. In adults the prodrome, which resembles a nondescript viral illness, is less striking, but associations have been found with pregnancy and the postpartum period, use of oral contraceptive agents, and infection, including typhoid fever, gram-negative bacteremia, mumps, and infectious mononucleosis. The clinical manifestations are similar to those in children, and the prognosis appears to be poorer, although that may reflect confusion with TTP.

Because evidence of coagulation disturbances and fibrin deposition in small arteries and arterioles is common and because the syndrome is accompanied by a microangiopathic hemolytic anemia, there is widespread belief that intravascular coagulation plays a major role. The commonly observed coagulation disturbances include thrombocytopenia, a prolonged prothrombin time, and accumulation of fibrin degradation products in the serum. For unknown reasons the kidney is the most extensively involved organ in the hemolytic-uremic syndrome. Because in adults pregnancy and oral contraceptive agents appear to predispose to cortical necrosis and pregnancy also predisposes to the Shwartzman reaction induced by endotoxin in animals, it has been suggested that the Shwartzman reaction and the hemolytic-uremic syndrome share a common mechanism. The morphologic lesions are also strikingly similar; immunofluorescent studies have revealed intense staining with antibody to fibrin in both conditions.

The treatment is largely supportive. There is controversy as to whether heparin therapy modifies the natural history. Controlled studies have been disappointing, but in individual patients heparin therapy has been temporally associated with improvement in renal function. Other forms of therapy including corticosteroids, immunosuppressive agents, antiplatelet agents, exchange transfusions, and dextran have met with equivocal results.

RENAL VEIN THROMBOSIS Thrombosis of one or both of the renal veins is an uncommon cause of the nephrotic syndrome. Occlusion of both renal veins usually, but not necessarily, implies thrombosis of the inferior vena cava as well. Renal vein thrombosis is most commonly associated with membranous glomerulonephritis. It is not clear whether the glomerulonephritis predisposes to renal vein thrombosis or vice versa, but the weight of evidence favors the former (Chap. 223). Other causes of renal vein thrombosis include local trauma, invasion of the renal vein by hypernephroma, and severe dehydration, especially in children.

Clinical and morphologic features depend on the availability of an adequate collateral venous drainage. Sudden complete thrombosis of a renal vein, without adequate collateral drainage, causes severe lumbar pain, hematuria, and loss of function of the involved kidney. The kidney is enlarged and suffers hemorrhagic infarction. When the process is bilateral or involves a solitary kidney, this sequence leads to oliguria and renal failure. If the occlusion is more gradual, especially if adequate collateral venous channels develop, renal function is preserved, and massive proteinuria results in the nephrotic syndrome. Hypertension is uncommon, and the urinary sediment may be entirely normal or contain only a few red blood cells.

The diagnosis is suggested by a history of trauma, pain, or a predisposing factor such as prolonged travel in a cramped position. A history of pulmonary embolism should also lead to suspicion of this diagnosis. Physical examination may reveal a venous collateral map on the anterior abdominal wall if the inferior vena cava is involved. The intravenous pyelogram may show filling defects in the renal pelvis and ureter reflecting collateral draining veins. The diagnosis is established by inferior vena caval and selective renal venography. Diagnostic ultrasound is playing an increasing role in diagnosis.

Surgical removal of a clot from the renal venous system has been successful in a small number of patients, especially in children in whom the onset is often in association with dehydration and occurs acutely. In most circumstances, however, medical management with anticoagulants has been used. Recanalization of the renal veins has led to amelioration of the nephrotic syndrome in occasional patients. Typically, however, anticoagulants are employed to prevent pulmonary embolism and extension of the thrombus into the open collateral veins.

PREECLAMPSIA AND ECLAMPSIA: TOXEMIAS OF PREGNANCY

Toxemia of pregnancy is characterized by the appearance, during gestation or within 7 days of delivery, of a constellation of abnormalities which includes hypertension, edema, and proteinuria (preeclampsia). When hypertension is more severe, convulsions and coma may occur (eclampsia). Preeclampsia usually begins after the thirty-second week of pregnancy but may begin earlier, particularly in women with preexisting renal disease or hypertension. Preeclampsia in the first trimester occurs in hydatidiform mole. Toxemia has a bimodal frequency with peak incidence in the young primipara and in multiparous women over 35 years of age. In the United States toxemia occurs in approximately 7 percent of pregnancies. There is an increased prevalence in the economically underprivileged. Most series include many patients in whom preexisting renal disease or hypertension either begins during or is exacerbated by pregnancy. In addition, there is a specific process affecting the kidney and the vascular system which in most patients improves dramatically when, or soon after, pregnancy is terminated.

The morphologic features in the kidney include reversible generalized swelling of the glomerular tufts and apparent thickening of the glomerular basement membrane due to an increase of the cytoplasm of the endothelial cells with narrowing of the capillary lumina, a finding termed *glomerular endotheliosis*, and sub- or interendothelial fibrinoid deposition. In patients who die of acute toxemia of pregnancy, necrosis of renal tubules and of liver cells is frequent, along with evidence of disseminated intravascular coagulation and petechial hemorrhage in the brain.

The pathogenesis is not clearly understood. Sodium retention and an increase in blood volume are normal concomitants of pregnancy. Considerable evidence suggests that plasma volume is *lower* in the toxemic than in the normal pregnancy, and from this observation debate about the role of too little or too much sodium intake has emerged. Whether the reduced plasma volume is a cause or consequence of the process is unclear. Uteroplacental ischemia occurs with toxemia. The uterus, like the kidney, synthesizes both vasoconstrictors (renin) and vasodilators (prostaglandins of the E series). One current hypothesis is that an imbalance in their action is responsible for the severe hypertension. Recent studies have also demonstrated production of a sodium-potassium ATPase inhibitor in such patients that could lead to hypertension by enhancing vascular responsiveness to constrictor stimuli.

The onset is typically insidious but may be abrupt. Because arterial blood pressure normally falls during pregnancy, pressures which exceed 125/75 mmHg should be considered abnormal, especially if they are rising. Headache, visual disturbances, epigastric distress, and apprehension are frequently associated with toxemias. Edema usually appears coincident with hypertension; it is typically generalized, being particularly evident in the face and hands. Proteinuria generally follows the onset of the syndrome within several days but occasionally precedes the hypertension and edema. Examination of the optic fundi reveals segmental arteriolar narrowing and a glistening retinal sheen indicative of edema. Hemorrhages and exudates occur late and only in severe cases.

The urine contains trace to 10 g protein per 24 h, as well as granular and hyalin casts, but red blood cells and cellular casts are infrequent. Because of the physiologic increase of glomerular filtration rate and reduction in serum urea and creatinine concentration which occurs in a normal pregnancy, a blood urea nitrogen of 20 mg/dL is usually indicative of a sharp diminution in filtration rate. A more striking increase in blood uric acid is common, reflecting a reduction in urate clearance.

Treatment varies with the severity of the process. In patients with mild hypertension and minimal proteinuria, bed rest and mild sedation are routinely used: whether restriction of sodium intake, which may be required to control edema, is a precipitating factor in preeclampsia is debated. Diuretics are generally avoided. If the process is more severe, patients are admitted to the hospital for sustained bed rest and closer control of sodium intake and blood pressure. Antihypertensive agents employed include hydralazine, methyldopa, and beta blockers. Marked hypertension and involvement of the central nervous system with convulsions are unequivocal indications for termination of pregnancy, which is usually followed by prompt improvement of the mother. At this stage parenteral magnesium sulfate is widely used for its central nervous system and antihypertensive effects. Emptying of the uterus is the most effective treatment. Proteinuria and hypertension usually disappear within weeks but on occasion may persist for as long as 6 months. A substantial fraction of multiparous patients over the age of 35 years with preeclampsia are left with a process that is undistinguishable from essential hypertension. Whether such patients were candidates for development of essential hypertension which became apparent during, or was precipitated by, pregnancy is not yet clear.

VASCULITIS (See also Chaps. 224 and 269)

Because renal involvement occurs in at least 80 percent of patients with vasculitis and contributes to death in a substantial number, they are considered here, although some vasculitides such as rheumatic arteritis and temporal arteritis rarely involve the kidney. An expanded classification for the vasculitides with a discussion of the distinctions and overlaps among various syndromes is contained in Chap. 269. They are generally thought to be a form of immune complex disease, and the rate, site, and size of the vessel involved may reflect the physiochemical properties of the complex and events in the vessel such as flow turbulence.

Polyarteritis nodosa (PAN) is a recurrent or progressive, necrotizing inflammatory disease of the medium and small-sized muscular arteries. The kidney is the most common organ involved, with estimates ranging upward of 70 percent, and renal failure is one of the major causes of death. Hypertension occurs in at least 50 percent of patients and often terminates in a malignant phase with hypertensive encephalopathy or heart failure. Renal involvement may be manifested by proteinuria, microscopic or gross hematuria, urinary casts, azotemia, and edema.

In classic PAN (see Chap. 269), the lesions involve only the medium and small muscular arteries, especially at sites of branching. Classically there are subendothelial and medial edema and fibrinoid necrosis; infiltration of all vessel coats with an inflammatory exudate including polymorphonuclear leukocytes, eosinophils, lymphocytes, and plasma cells; destruction of the media and internal elastica; proliferation of fibroblasts, which generally starts in the adventitia and progresses during a stage of granulation through the vessel wall with healing, and a reduction in the acute inflammatory process; and healed lesions in which the vessel wall is replaced by fibrous tissue and the lumen is generally narrowed or occluded. Glomerular lesions are common. Any or all of these stages may be present at any time in the kidney. Renal insufficiency and hypertension characteristically develop during the healing stages. Because larger vessels are involved, a renal biopsy of the cortex may miss the characteristic lesion.

The pathogenetic factors responsible for polyarteritis are becoming clearer. Multiple lines of evidence have implicated an immunologic mechanism involving immune complexes and hepatitis B as the responsible antigen in as many as 30 percent of patients with necrotizing vasculitis and the PAN syndrome. A vasculitis indistinguishable from PAN is also recognized in intravenous drug abusers. Because of the multiplicity of the chemical agents injected, and the high probability of contamination, the exact etiologic agent has not been unequivocally defined, but methamphetamine appears to be a common denominator.

Hypersensitivity angiitis includes many identifiable groups such as drug-related, Henoch-Schönlein purpura, that associated with serum sickness, or that underlying primary disease such as systemic lupus erythematosus. It is often an acute illness characterized by an acute necrotizing inflammatory process involving small vessels, particularly postcapillary venules; however, small arteries, arterioles, and capillaries may also be involved. Proteinuria and hematuria are present in many patients, but hypertension is generally absent and azotemia substantially less common than in the polyarteritis group.

Therapy of the vasculitides is discussed in Chap. 269. General supportive measures include control of hypertension, which is required in most patients with renal involvement. The pathogenesis of the hypertension is similar to that in scleroderma renal crisis, as is the therapy. Corticosteroids are widely employed and with immunosuppressive agents are the only presently available therapy of any potential value. In patients with renal involvement, steroids may have an initial adverse effect on the clinical course because vascular healing is frequently associated with obliteration of arteries, resulting in focal renal infarction, increasing hypertension, and azotemia. The addition of cyclophosphamide has been shown to be useful in the patient in whom steroids are ineffective, especially when there is renal involvement.

REFERENCES

ALLEYNE GAQ et al: The kidney in sickle cell anemia. Kidney Int 7:371, 1975

BECKETT VL et al: Use of captopril as early therapy for renal scleroderma: A prospective study. Mayo Clin Proc 60:763, 1985

FAUCI AJ: Systemic vasculitis, in Current Therapy in Allergy and Immunology, LM Lichtenstein, AS Fauci (eds). Decker, Philadelphia, 1983, p 130

FERRIS TF: Toxemia and hypertension, in Medical Complications During Pregnancy, GN Burrow, TF Ferris (eds). Philadelphia, Saunders, 1975

GIANANTONIO CA et al: The hemolytic-uremic syndrome. Nephron 11:174, 1973

HUMPHREYS MH, ALFREY AC: Vascular diseases of the kidney, in The Kidney, 3d ed, BM Brenner, FC Rector Jr (eds). Philadelphia, Saunders, 1986, p 1175

KEATING MA, ALTHAUSEN AF: The clinical spectrum of renal vein thrombosis. J Urol 133:938, 1985

MAXWELL MH: Cooperative study of renovascular hypertension: Current status. Kidney Int 8:S153, 1975

MILLAN VG et al: Percutaneous transluminal renal angioplasty in nonatherosclerotic renovascular hypertension. Long-term results. Hypertension 7:668, 1985

OLIVER JA, CANNON PJ: The kidney in scleroderma. Nephron 18:141, 1977

RATLIFF NB: Renal vascular disease: Pathology of large blood vessel disease. Am J Kidney Dis 5:A93, 1985

STIMPEL M et al: The spectrum of renovascular hypertension. Am J Med 79:14, 1985

THIND GS: Role of renal venous renins in the diagnosis and management of renovascular hypertension. J Urol 134:2, 1985

228 HEREDITARY TUBULAR DISORDERS

FREDRIC L. COE / SATISH KATHPALIA

POLYCYSTIC RENAL DISEASE IN ADULTS

ETIOLOGY AND PATHOLOGY This disease is found in 1 in 500 autopsies and 1 in 3000 hospital admissions and accounts for approximately 5 percent of end-stage renal failure. Inheritance is autosomal dominant. The cortex and medulla of both kidneys are usually filled with thin-walled, spherical cysts, ranging from millimeters to centimeters in diameter, that enlarge the organs and interfere with their functioning, presumably by compressing the nephrons and causing localized obstruction. The cysts, which are lined by a low cuboidal epithelium, contain straw-colored fluid that becomes hemorrhagic with trauma or infection. The intervening renal parenchyma may be normal or show changes of nephrosclerosis or interstitial nephritis.

CLINICAL FEATURES Symptoms usually begin in the third or fourth decades. Flank pain is frequent. Other common symptoms include gross and microscopic hematuria, especially after trauma, and nocturia due to impaired concentrating ability. Ten percent of patients pass renal calculi whose composition and pathogenesis have not been well studied. Stones and blood clots both cause renal colic. Usually the kidneys are palpable and asymmetric and have a knobby surface. Hypertension develops in 75 percent of patients, and progression to chronic renal failure usually occurs (Table 228-1).

Proteinuria is common, but rarely exceeds 2 g per day. Urinary infection ultimately occurs in most patients, especially as a conse-

quence of instrumentation and renal calculi. Erythrocytosis may occur because of high erythropoietin levels; in other patients blood loss anemia may result from the hematuria.

Acute renal failure can result from infection, ureteral obstruction due to clots or stone, or sudden angulation of a ureter by a nearby cyst. Azotemia progresses slowly in the absence of these complications. Patients with end-stage chronic renal failure tend to have higher hematocrits than their counterparts with other renal diseases. Fluid overload is infrequent because of a tendency for renal salt wasting.

Hepatic cysts are present in about 30 percent of patients. Hepatic function is usually normal, and the liver cysts can be asymptomatic or cause epigastric discomfort or biliary colic or become infected. Cysts also may occur in the spleen, pancreas, lungs, ovaries, testes, epididymis, thyroid, uterus, broad ligament, and bladder. Subarachnoid hemorrhage from intracranial aneurysm is the cause of death in about one-tenth of patients.

DIAGNOSIS Palpable kidneys, hypertension, or asymptomatic abnormalities of urine are often the only manifestations. Excretory or retrograde urography typically shows large kidneys with elongated pelvises and flat calyces indented by cysts. Ultrasonography and radioisotopic renal scanning can both demonstrate the cysts quite well. Gray scale sonography may be an alternative to intravenous pyelography for screening individuals at risk, especially when genetic counseling is desired. Computerized tomography may be useful.

TREATMENT Superimposed renal damage such as is produced by analgesics, obstruction, urinary infection, nephrotoxic antibiotics, and hypertension must be guarded against. Dehydration and inadequate intake of sodium chloride (less than 100 mmol per day) should be avoided. The management of chronic renal failure is simplified because fluid overload is not a usual problem and the hypertension is usually amenable to treatment, but the cysts can cause special problems, such as pain, bleeding, infection, or ureteral obstruction. Puncture of cysts, and in some instances even nephrectomy, may be necessary.

POLYCYSTIC RENAL DISEASE IN INFANTS AND CHILDREN

CLINICAL FEATURES The *infantile form* manifests itself at birth by diffusely enlarged kidneys, renal failure, and maldevelopment of intrahepatic bile ducts. The *childhood form* consists of medullary ductal ectasia which is usually asymptomatic, in association with congenital hepatic fibrosis and portal hypertension. Inheritance of both the infantile and childhood forms is autosomal recessive. Renal failure develops frequently in both forms, but death in the childhood form usually results as a consequence of hepatic disease.

MORPHOLOGY In the infantile form, the distal tubules and collecting ducts are dilated into elongated cysts that are arranged in a radial fashion, particularly in the cortex, and make the kidneys large and spongy. In the childhood form, cysts are fewer in number, cortical collecting ducts are less involved, and the kidneys are not as large. Small intrahepatic bile ducts are irregularly dilated, and large interconnecting spaces, lined by hyperplastic epithelium, fill the portal areas. There is portal fibrosis rather than dilatation and proliferation of small bile ducts, and portal hypertension is the rule by late childhood.

DIAGNOSIS AND TREATMENT Infantile polycystic kidneys may be large enough to cause dystocia. At birth they do not function and cause oliguric renal failure, respiratory distress, hypertension, and congestive heart failure. Intravenous pyelography may reveal a mottled nephrogram with variable retention of contrast material in cysts that correspond to dilated cortical and medullary collecting ducts. On retrograde urography the calyces are blunted, and pyelotubular reflux may be seen. In the childhood type the intravenous pyelogram may suggest medullary sponge kidney, because medullary tubular ectasia is prominent. Renal failure and chronic infection are common.

TABLE 228-1 Renal tubule defects

Disease	Renal morphologic abnormalities	Functional abnormalities	Mode*	Associated abnormalities and system consequences
Adult polycystic disease	Cortical and medullary cysts	Chronic renal failure	AD	Hepatic cysts, intracranial aneurysms
Infantile polycystic disease	Distal tubule and collecting duct cysts	Renal failure in the newborn	AR	Intrahepatic bile duct abnormalities
Childhood polycystic disease	Medullary ductal ectasia	Variable chronic renal failure	AR	Hepatic fibrosis and portal hypertension
Medullary sponge kidneys	Ectatic ducts of Bellini	Nephrocalcinosis	AD + S	None
Medullary cystic disease, recessive	Distal tubule and collecting duct cysts	Chronic renal failure, <20 yr salt wasting polyuria	AR	Variable retinal degeneration (renal retinal dysplasia)
Medullary cystic disease, dominant	Same	Chronic renal failure, >20 yr salt wasting, polyuria	AD	None
Bartter's syndrome	Hyperplasia of juxtaglomerular and medullary interstitial cells	Hypokalemia, high renin and aldosterone levels, polyuria	AR	None
Liddle's syndrome	None	Hypokalemia, low aldosterone levels	AR	None
Familial nephrogenic diabetes insipidus	None	Vasopressin-resistant renal concentrating defect	XLR	None
Renal tubular acidosis, type 1	Papillary nephrocalcinosis	Inability to lower urine pH normally, reduced acid excretion	AD	Periodic paralysis, hypokalemia, non-anion-gap metabolic acidosis, growth retardation, rickets
Renal tubular acidosis, type 2	None	Reduced bicarbonate reabsorption	AR AD XLR	Non-anion-gap metabolic acidosis, growth retardation rickets, Fanconi syndrome
Renal tubular acidosis, type 4	Underlying renal disease (HTN, DM, OBST)	Reduced proton and potassium secretion	ACQ	Azotemia
X-linked vitamin D–resistant rickets	None	Reduced phosphate reabsorption, hypophosphatemia	XLR	Rickets, osteomalacia, normal serum 1,25-D
Vitamin D–dependent rickets, type 1	None	Defective renal 1,25-D production	AR	Rickets, osteomalacia, low serum 1,25-D
Vitamin D–dependent rickets, type 2	None	Defective cell, 1,25-D receptors	AR	Rickets, osteomalacia, high serum 1,25-D, variable alopecia
Oncogenic osteomalacia	None	Reduced phosphate reabsorptions, hypophosphatemia	ACQ	Osteomalacia; mesenchymal tumors; cancer of the prostate or lung
Renal glucosuria	None	Reduced glucose reabsorption	AD	None
Isolated hypouricemia	None	Reduced urate reabsorption	AR	Variable hypercalciuria, bone demineralization
Cystinuria	Cystine stones	Reduced reabsorption of dibasic amino acids	AR	Short stature
Hartnup's disease	None	Reduced reabsorption of mono-amino and carboxylic amino acids	AR	Pellagra-like rash, ataxia, delirium
Iminoglycinuria	None	Reduced reabsorption of proline, hydroxyproline, and glycine	AR	None
Adult Fanconi syndrome	Swan neck deformity of the proximal tubule	Reduced proximal tubule reabsorption of bicarbonate, glucose, uric acid, phosphate, and amino acids	AR	Rickets, osteomalacia, acidosis, dwarfism, low serum potassium
Lowe's syndrome (oculocerebrorenal syndrome)	Same	Same	XLR	Ocular and cerebral malformations

* *AR, autosomal recessive; AD, autosomal dominant; XLR, X-linked recessive; ACQ, acquired; HTN, hypertension; DM, diabetes mellitus; OBST urinary tract obstruction; S, sporadic.*

MEDULLARY SPONGE KIDNEY

PATHOLOGY In this condition the ducts of Bellini, i.e., the terminal collecting ducts that reach to the ends of the papillae and drain the urine into the renal pelvis, are dilated to cystic proportions and frequently contain calcium oxalate calculi. The kidneys are asymmetric, and the more abnormal kidney is usually the larger. One or more medullary cysts are found near the tip of each involved papilla, and calculi form in the terminal collecting ducts in, or proximal to, the cysts (Fig. 228-1). Parenchymal alterations are secondary to intrarenal obstruction. The cysts are lined by cuboidal and, sometimes, pseudostratified and stratified squamous epithelium.

CLINICAL DIAGNOSIS AND TREATMENT Medullary sponge kidney is present in 1 of 200 unselected intravenous pyelograms. Although most cases are sporadic, autosomal dominant inheritance has been described. The disease has a bimodal pattern of appearance, the first in adolescence and the second during the third and fourth decades. Calculi, infection, and hematuria occur in 60, 35, and 30 percent of patients, respectively. Papillary nephrocalcinosis due to clusters of stones in cysts is common. Hypercalciuria occurs in nearly half of stone-forming patients but is equally common in other forms of calcium stone disease (Chap. 229). Hypertension is no more common than in the general population. Renal failure is rare, unless nephrolithiasis and/or renal infections are severe.

The diagnosis of medullary sponge kidney is made by intravenous urography. The magnitude of pyelotubular backflow may vary from a simple papillary blush to frank tubular ectasia at the tips of the papillae. Small pyramidal cysts and nephrocalcinosis are frequent, and papillary concretions are obscured by the urographic contrast medium. Ectatic collecting ducts are difficult to fill during retrograde pyelography, and so the contrast material remains separate from papillary concretions in the cysts.

Asymptomatic patients require no treatment except advice to avoid dehydration and thereby reduce the risk of stone formation. The metabolic etiology of stones should be sought and treated conventionally, while infection and urologic consequences of stones should be treated as described in Chap. 229. Medullary sponge kidneys are vulnerable to infection, and urologic instrumentation should, therefore, be minimized.

MEDULLARY CYSTIC DISEASE (NEPHRONOPHTHISIS COMPLEX)

ETIOLOGY Several hereditary medullary cystic diseases have similar morphology but differing patterns of inheritance. The recessive form is associated with renal failure before 20 years of age (early-onset type), whereas the dominant form causes renal failure only after the second decade (adult-onset type). When renal disease is associated with retinal degenerative changes (renal retinal dysplasia), inheritance is always recessive, but renal failure occurs during adult life.

PATHOLOGY In both forms, most of the cysts are in the medulla and the corticomedullary region and have been localized to collecting ducts and distal convoluted tubules. Cysts have a low, frequently atrophic, epithelium and range in size from microscopic dimensions to millimeters. The kidneys usually are asymmetrically scarred and shrunken. Both tubular atrophy and periglomerular fibrosis are present, but the former is more severe. In advanced cases, glomeruli become sclerotic and hyalinized, cortical fibrosis and cellular interstitial infiltration appear, and the histology is difficult to differentiate from that of chronic interstitial nephritis.

DIAGNOSIS AND TREATMENT Concentrating ability, acid excretion, and sodium conservation are defective as might be expected from a lesion that damages distal segments of the nephron. The disease is marked by polyuria, progressive renal failure, stunted growth, severe anemia, hyperchloremic metabolic acidosis, and poor sodium conservation. In adults, the inability to conserve sodium may cause a salt-wasting syndrome that resembles adrenal insufficiency but is unresponsive to mineralocorticoids. Hypertension usually is a terminal event. The urinalysis is normal at first, but proteinuria may develop. On intravenous pyelography, the kidneys are small, scarred, and without calcification. The calyces are distorted by numerous cysts in the corticomedullary area.

High sodium and water intake, and alkali replacement for acidosis, are needed. Treatment of infections, anemia, hypertension, and other aspects of end-stage renal failure are as discussed in Chap. 220. Genetic counseling may be helpful in family planning and in selection of an unaffected related donor for renal transplantation.

FIGURE 228-1 *A. Radiographic appearance of medullary sponge kidney. Abdominal flat plate reveals multiple bilateral calcifications. B. Radiographic contrast material accumulates in the dilated and cystic terminal collecting ducts and obscures the calcifications.*

BARTTER'S SYNDROME

Bartter's syndrome consists of hypokalemia due to renal potassium wasting, elevated plasma renin activity and aldosterone secretion, normal blood pressure, hyporesponsiveness of blood pressure to infused angiotensin II, and hyperplasia of the granular cells of the juxtaglomerular apparatus of the kidney. Weakness or periodic paralysis and polyuria occur because of chronic potassium depletion. Hyperplasia of renal medullary interstitial cells, which produce prostaglandins PGE and PGF, has been described, along with elevated PGE_2 production. Inheritance is autosomal recessive, and manifestations commonly begin in childhood.

PATHOGENESIS While the pathogenetic sequence is not understood with certainty, there is some evidence for a defect of tubular chloride or potassium transport. Either may produce hypokalemia, which stimulates release of prostaglandins E_2 and I_2, which in turn results in increased secretion of renin, leading to enhanced concentration of circulating angiotensin II and thus aldosterone. Both angiotensin II and aldosterone increase renal kallikrein, which increases plasma bradykinin, while aldosterone further enhances renal potassium loss. The normality of blood pressure results from the vasodepressor actions of PGE_2 and bradykinin, despite increased production of renin, angiotensin, and aldosterone.

Excessive production of PGE_2 resulting from hypokalemia, a known stimulator of PGE_2 synthesis, may therefore be a secondary consequence of the syndrome. In some cases blockade of PGE_2 production with indomethacin lowers renin levels and restores vascular response to angiotensin II infusion, but does not reduce potassium wasting.

TREATMENT The dietary intake of sodium chloride and potassium should be liberal; potassium supplements may be required. Pharmacologic blockade of aldosterone effects on distal tubules with spironolactone can prevent potassium wasting, though sodium intake must be increased. Inhibition of prostaglandin synthesis with indomethacin, ibuprofen, or aspirin has met with varying success, as indicated above. Beta-adrenergic blockade may lower renin production.

LIDDLE'S SYNDROME (PSEUDOHYPERALDOSTERONISM)

This rare inherited disorder is characterized by hypertension, hypokalemic alkalosis, and negligible aldosterone secretion. It appears to be due to an unusual tendency of distal tubules or collecting ducts to conserve sodium and excrete potassium despite the virtual absence of aldosterone. No other biochemical abnormalities have been described. However, transport rates of sodium in red blood cells are

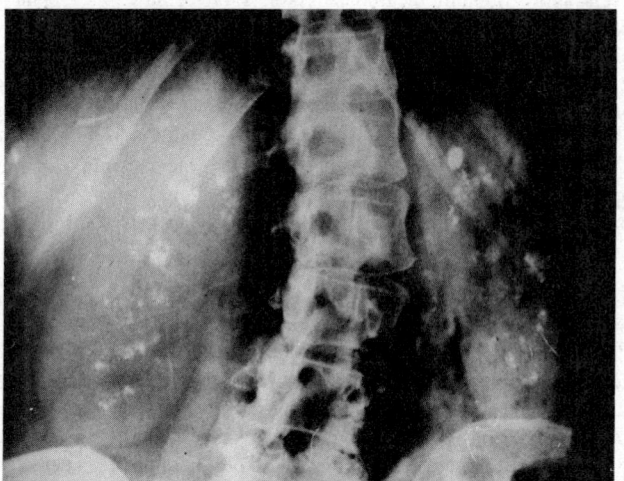

A

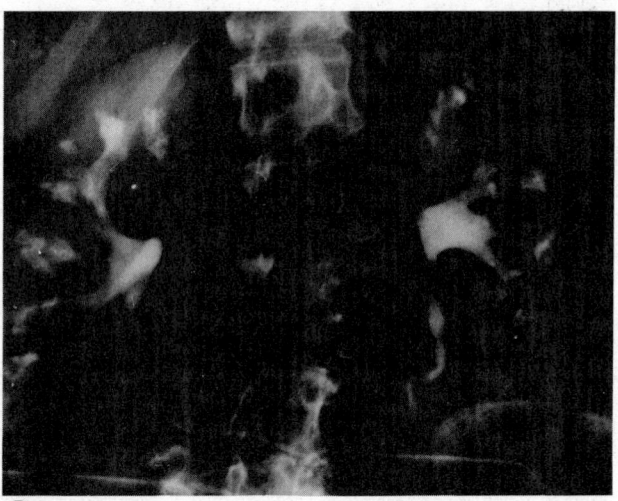

B

altered. These patients respond to 100 mg per day of triamterene (Chap. 182), a diuretic agent that blocks sodium and potassium exchange in the distal tubule.

FAMILIAL NEPHROGENIC DIABETES (DI)

In this disease the distal tubules and collecting ducts are unresponsive to vasopressin because of an X-linked recessive disease, with variable expressivity in heterozygous females. Affected individuals excrete large volumes of hypotonic urine even when plasma osmolality and vasopressin concentration are both high. Polyuria, polydipsia, and hypertonic dehydration following restriction of fluid intake all result from renal tubular insensitivity to antidiuretic hormone (ADH) (also see Chap. 323). Unresponsiveness to vasopressin may be secondary to reduced production of cyclic adenosine 5'-monophosphate (cyclic AMP) in the epithelium of the collecting ducts, to the inability of cyclic AMP to increase the permeability of collecting duct luminal cell membranes to water, or to a combination of the two. Other hereditary tubular defects such as juvenile nephronophthisis, medullary cystic and polycystic diseases, cystinosis, and congenital or acquired chronic urinary tract obstruction can also cause vasopressin-resistant (nephrogenic) DI, but in these syndromes the characteristic features of the underlying disorder are present.

Affected infants easily become dehydrated, hypernatremic, and hyperthermic, and damage of the central nervous system, including mental retardation, may result. In the absence of dehydration, overall renal function is normal. On intravenous pyelography the renal pelvis, ureters, and bladder are dilated, as in any form of DI, because of massive diuresis.

Oral hydration usually is adequate treatment except during early infancy, when hypotonic parenteral fluids may be required. Vasopressin and its synthetic analogues are ineffective, but diuretic agents such as chlorothiazide reduce polyuria. This drug inhibits NaCl reabsorption in the cortical portions of the thick ascending limb of the loop of Henle, thereby reducing production of free water. In addition, chlorothiazide produces a diuresis that causes contraction of extracellular fluid volume which, in turn, stimulates reabsorption of NaCl and water in the proximal tubule and limits their delivery to the thick ascending limb. Sodium restriction enhances its effect.

RENAL TUBULAR ACIDOSIS (RTA)

In this group of disorders renal excretion of acid is reduced out of proportion to any reduction of glomerular filtration rate. Metabolic acidosis results, but in contrast to renal failure the anions that accompany surplus hydrogen ions in the blood, such as sulfate and phosphate, are excreted normally and are unavailable to balance the fall in serum bicarbonate. Therefore, the kidneys reabsorb chloride in unusually large amounts, and serum chloride rises to preserve electroneutrality in the extracellular fluid. The result is *hyperchloremic acidosis*, and the unmeasured anion gap is normal. There is general

agreement that four types of RTA exist (Table 228-2). Types 1 and 2 are often hereditary. Type 3 is a rare mixture of types 1 and 2. Type 4 is acquired and is associated with either hyporeninemic hypoaldosteronism or tubular hyporesponsiveness to circulating mineralocorticoids.

TYPE 1 (DISTAL) RTA Sporadic cases occur, but autosomal dominant inheritance is usual. The kidney does not lower urine pH normally, either because the collecting ducts permit excessive back-diffusion of hydrogen ions from lumen to blood or fail to transport hydrogen ions against a steep pH gradient. Since titration of urine buffers and diffusion trapping of NH_4^+ in the tubules both depend upon a low intraluminal pH, excretion of acid is deficient. However, urine ammonium excretion is as high or higher than in normal people whose urine is equally alkaline. Urinary osmotic concentration and potassium conservation also tend to be impaired.

Chronic acidosis lowers tubule reabsorption of calcium, causing renal hypercalciuria and mild secondary hyperparathyroidism. The hypercalciuria, alkaline urine, and low levels of urine citrate—which normally serves to complex about 40 percent of urine calcium—cause calcium phosphate stones and papillary nephrocalcinosis. Growth is stunted in children because of rickets; this growth defect responds to amelioration of the acidosis with sodium bicarbonate or other alkali. In the adult, bone disease takes the form of osteomalacia. In both children and adults, bone disease may result, in part, from acidosis-induced loss of bone mineral and from inadequate production of 1,25-dihydroxyvitamin D_3 [1,25($OH)_2D_3$]. Since the kidney does not conserve potassium or concentrate the urine normally, polyuria and hypokalemia occur. Given the stress of an intercurrent illness, acidosis and hypokalemia can become life-threatening.

The diagnosis is suggested by osteomalacia or rickets, hyperchloremic acidosis associated with alkaline urine, and calcium phosphate stones or nephrocalcinosis. To prove that the urine pH cannot be lowered normally, the oral ammonium chloride (NH_4Cl) loading test should be carried out: 0.1 g (1.9 mmol) NH_4Cl per kilogram is administered, and the blood and urine pH are followed with time. Although systemic acidosis worsens, urine pH does not fall below 5.5. Urinary infection must not be present during this test because bacteria may possess urease, which hydrolyzes urea to ammonia and produces a very alkaline urine. When hyperchloremic acidosis is severe and the urine is grossly alkaline, the test is unnecessary.

A confusing situation may occur when type 1 RTA results from nephrocalcinosis due to hereditary idiopathic hypercalciuria. In this circumstance, stones usually are composed of calcium oxalate, and hypokalemia is absent. Other hereditary diseases that cause RTA, such as medullary sponge kidney, galactosemia, Ehler-Danlos syndrome, Fabry's disease, and hereditary elliptocytosis, can be excluded by clinical findings. The relatives of patients with type 1 RTA should be screened for this treatable cause of renal damage.

Treatment Sodium bicarbonate tablets (10 grains = 7.2 mmol base) and Shohl's solution (1 mmol base per milliliter, as Na and K citrate) are both convenient for treatment; the dose should be 0.5 to 2.0 mmol/kg in four or five divided doses daily. The total dose of alkali should be raised until acidosis and hypercalciuria are both eliminated, and the patients should be followed by measurements of serum chloride and CO_2 content and of urine calcium excretion approximately twice yearly. Potassium supplementation usually is not required. Requirements for alkali usually increase during intercurrent illnesses but are usually below 4 mmol/kg per day.

TYPE 2 (PROXIMAL) RTA Proximal RTA usually occurs as part of a generalized disorder of proximal tubule function. It can be a transient disorder of infancy which usually disappears in childhood. An isolated form, i.e., without accompanying phosphaturia, aminoaciduria, and uricosuria, has been described in one family. The pathophysiology of proximal RTA is the same whether isolated or part of a generalized disorder. Bicarbonate reabsorption in the proximal tubule is defective, and renal bicarbonate wasting occurs at a normal concentration of

TABLE 228-2   Comparison of three types of renal tubular acidosis*

Finding	Type 1	Type 2	Type 4
Non-anion-gap acidosis	Yes	Yes	Yes
Minimum urine pH	>5.5	<5.5	<5.5
% filtered HCO_3 excreted	<10	>15	<10
Serum potassium	Low	Low	High
Fanconi syndrome	No	Yes	No
Stones/nephrocalcinosis	Yes	No	No
Daily acid excretion	Low	Normal	Low
Ammonium excretion	High for pH	Normal	Low for pH
Daily HCO_3 replacement needs	<4 mmol/kg	>4 mmol/kg	<4 mmol/kg

* HCO_3, bicarbonate. Type 3 renal tubular acidosis is a rare form of a mixture of types 1 and 2.

plasma bicarbonate. As plasma bicarbonate falls, the filtered load drops to a level that the defective tubule can reabsorb. Then the urine is free of bicarbonate and has a low pH. Potassium wasting and hypokalemia occur, especially when supplementary alkali is given, because bicarbonate is excreted in the urine partly as the potassium salt. Hypercalciuria is moderate, and stone formation is rare. During the NH_4Cl loading test, urine pH falls below 5.5.

Treatment is often not required. When acidosis is severe, bicarbonate must be given in large amounts daily, often above 4 mmol/kg, and even up to 10 mmol/kg per day, because bicarbonate is rapidly excreted in the urine. Another approach is to use a thiazide diuretic and a low-salt diet, which induce mild volume depletion and enhance proximal bicarbonate reabsorption, thereby reducing the required dose. Potassium supplements are needed during treatment because excessive sodium bicarbonate reaches the distal nephron, where much of the sodium is exchanged for potassium, which is then lost in the urine.

TYPE 4 RTA Some patients have a form of renal tubular acidosis that differs from types 1 and 2 and has been called type 4. They have metabolic acidosis without an elevation of the anion gap but differ from type 1 patients in having an acid urine during periods of severe acidosis (Table 228-2), and from type 2 patients in having low urine excretion of bicarbonate and a daily replacement alkali requirement of <4 mmol per kilogram of body weight. They differ from both types 1 and 2 in having a high serum potassium level and a low urine ammonia excretion rate. They have neither Fanconi syndrome nor stone disease. Because potassium and hydrogen excretion are abnormal, they are considered to have generalized distal nephron dysfunction that is due either to intrinsic renal disease or to abnormal aldosterone levels. Hyperkalemia worsens acidosis by suppressing renal production of ammonia, which is the most important urinary buffer, and thereby limiting acid excretion.

The most common patients with type 4 renal tubular acidosis have hyporeninemic hypoaldosteronism; plasma levels of renin and aldosterone are subnormal, even during extracellular volume depletion. Diabetic nephropathy, nephrosclerosis from hypertension, and chronic tubulointerstitial nephropathies are the usual causes. Hyperkalemia and acidosis can be treated with replacement doses of a mineralocorticoid hormone such as fludrocortisone, 0.1 to 0.2 mg per day; some patients may require 0.3 to 0.5 mg per day, suggesting tubule unresponsiveness to the hormone. Furosemide can also improve the hyperkalemia and acidosis, provided salt intake is sufficient to prevent extracellular volume contraction.

A less common condition is *mineralocorticoid-resistant hyperkalemia;* hyperkalemia and acidosis do not improve despite mineralocorticoid hormone treatment. This occurs in occasional patients with underlying renal disease who also have severe salt wasting, as a consequence of distal nephron damage. Plasma renin and aldosterone levels are elevated, and patients are prone to extracellular fluid volume depletion. Treatment requires salt supplements and alkali, but mineralocorticoid hormones are not necessary. Other patients with mild acidosis have no evidence of renal disease and do not waste salt in their urine. Plasma renin and aldosterone levels are low, but hyperkalemia and acidosis do not respond to mineralocorticoid hormone treatment. The cause is thought to be abnormally high distal tubule permeability to chloride ion; sodium chloride reabsorption is elevated, the potential across the distal tubule epithelium is presumed to be below normal, potassium secretion is reduced because it is driven by the transepithelial voltage, hyperkalemia causes acidosis by suppressing ammonia production, and extracellular volume expansion from sodium chloride absorption suppresses renin and aldosterone levels and causes hypertension. The main evidence for this formulation is that infusion of sodium with anions such as bicarbonate or sulfate raises potassium excretion to normal or supranormal levels. Treatment of this rare condition is with thiazide diuretic agents or low-sodium diet.

Primary mineralocorticoid deficiency from diseases of the adrenals

also causes hyperkalemia and acidosis. Evaluation and treatment of adrenal disorders is discussed in Chap. 325.

VITAMIN D DISORDERS

FAMILIAL X-LINKED HYPOPHOSPHATEMIC VITAMIN D–REFRACTORY RICKETS (See also Chap. 337)   Reduced tubular reabsorption of phosphate by the proximal tubule and hypophosphatemia occur in this X-linked dominant disease, which can also be termed *renal phosphate leak*. Patients may be asymptomatic but are usually short and have rachitic bones; their legs are particularly short and deformed, and they develop osteomalacia in adult life. Bone age and dentition are retarded, and the teeth are poorly developed. The skull becomes deformed, and the maxillofacial region may be abnormal. Overgrowth of bone at sites of muscular attachment can limit movement or compress nerves. Bony abnormalities are less common in women. Serum alkaline phosphatase levels are elevated, serum parathyroid levels are normal or high, serum calcium concentration is usually normal, and urinary calcium excretion rate is normal or low.

The hypophosphatemia arises in part from decreased tubular reabsorption of phosphate and increased fractional excretion of phosphate. Intestinal absorption of calcium and phosphate may be decreased in untreated patients but increased during treatment with vitamin D. Although glycinuria and mild glucosuria may occur, most patients exhibit only a defect in excretion of phosphate. Absence of hyperchloremic acidosis and a normal serum calcium concentration help to exclude RTA, malabsorption syndrome, and nutritional rickets.

Treatment requires oral neutral phosphate, 1 to 4 g daily, in divided doses, and 10,000 to 50,000 units of vitamin D; one must watch for hypercalcemia. Combination of oral phosphate with calcitriol $[1,25(OH)_2D_3]$ may be more beneficial. Bony deformities require orthopedic management, but corrective surgery, except for genu valgum, should be postponed until active growth is completed.

VITAMIN D–DEPENDENT RICKETS TYPE 1 (See also Chap. 337)   Also known as hereditary pseudovitamin D–deficiency rickets, this disease is inherited as an autosomal recessive trait. Defective production of $1,25(OH)_2D_3$ by the kidneys, perhaps because of a genetic defect in 25-hydroxycholecalciferol 1α-hydroxylase, has been proposed as the basis for the disease. But the dose of calcitriol required to heal rickets is higher than that for vitamin D–deficiency rickets, suggesting an attenuated response to, or excessive degradation of, $1,25(OH)_2D_3$.

Rickets usually appears before 2 years of age. Serum calcium is low, parathyroid hormone concentration and alkaline phosphatase are high, and plasma phosphorus is variable. Urinary calcium is decreased, fecal calcium is increased, and tubular phosphate reabsorption is reduced. Serum levels of $1,25(OH)_2D_3$ are undetectable. Aminoaciduria and hyperchloremic acidosis can occur, but urinary cyclic AMP increases normally in response to PTH infusion.

The 1α-hydroxylated metabolites of vitamin D bypass the enzyme defect and produce a dramatic healing of rickets. Vitamin D_2, 10,000 to 40,000 units per day, is also effective, but oral calcium, 0.5 to 2.0 g per day, is needed as well. The need for vitamin D persists throughout life. Calcitriol, an ideal replacement therapy, is the drug of choice, but one must watch for hypercalcemia.

VITAMIN D–DEPENDENT RICKETS TYPE 2   Like type 1, this disease causes rickets, hypocalcemia, hypophosphatemia, and secondary hyperparathyroidism, but serum levels of $1,25(OH)_2D_3$ are elevated, and treatment with additional $1,25(OH)_2D_3$ does not increase the serum calcium level or heal the bone disease even though it can reduce serum levels of parathyroid hormone. Generalized alopecia is often present and may be either a linked defect or the result of the mineral disorder. The cause appears to be an autosomal recessive defect of the $1,25(OH)_2D_3$ receptor. Treatment with a high dose of calcitriol and mineral supplements may achieve healing of bone, but relapse may occur despite continued treatment.

ONCOGENIC OSTEOMALACIA   Mesenchymal tumors, usually benign, can cause renal phosphate wasting similiar to that of X-linked hypophosphatemic rickets, with resulting osteomalacia. Carcinoma of the prostate and oat cell carcinoma of the lung also have caused this syndrome. The disease almost always occurs in adults and develops gradually, over years. The tumors occur mainly in the extremities, scalp, nose, and mandible, in close association with bone. Their removal cures the phosphate wasting and leads to healing of the osteomalacia.

RENAL GLUCOSURIA

See Chap. 308.

ISOLATED HYPOURICEMIA (See also Chap. 308)

This disorder, in which there is a defect in proximal tubular reabsorption of sodium urate, appears to be inherited as an autosomal recessive trait. Hypouricemia can occur in the Fanconi syndrome, Hartnup's disease, and Wilson's disease. Uric acid clearance is high, and urine oxypurine levels are normal, excluding hereditary xanthinuria. Patients are asymptomatic except for occasional uric acid nephrolithiasis. No specific treatment is needed except the avoidance of dehydration. Coexistent hypercalciuria and decreased bone density have been described in a few patients, who may have a related disease.

SELECTIVE DISORDERS OF AMINO ACID TRANSPORT

HARTNUP'S DISEASE (See also Chap. 308)   In this rare autosomal recessive disorder, renal and intestinal transport of monoamino–monocarboxylic amino acids is defective. An erythematous, scaly, pellagra-like rash appears after exposure to sunlight, and episodic cerebellar ataxia, emotional instability, delirium, and aminoaciduria all occur. The prevalence is 1 in 15,000 newborns and is higher in the offspring of consanguineous marriages.

Dietary monoamino–monocarboxylic amino acids remain in the intestinal lumen where they undergo bacterial degradation. At the same time, they are lost in the urine. Inadequate tryptophan availability limits nicotinamide synthesis and leads to pellagra. Decreased absorption and urine loss of the other monoamino–monocarboxylic amino acids can cause generalized malnutrition.

The diagnosis is based upon demonstration of massive urine losses of alanine, serine, threonine, asparagine, glutamine, valine, leucine, isoleucine, phenylalanine, tyrosine, tryptophan, histidine, glycine, and citrulline. Hypouricemia may occur. Renal function is otherwise normal. Most patients respond to treatment with oral nicotinamide, 40 to 200 mg per day, and a high-protein diet to compensate for amino acid malabsorption and loss. The ultimate prognosis is good, and the disease often improves with age.

FAMILIAL IMINOGLYCINURIA (See also Chap. 308)   This autosomal recessive trait is characterized by excessive urinary excretion of proline, hydroxyproline, and glycine despite normal plasma levels of these amino acids, probably because of deletion or alteration of a membrane transport protein of the renal tubule cells. The patients are well. Iminoglycinuria can occur in normal newborn infants for up to 3 months.

FANCONI SYNDROME

Fanconi syndrome is a constellation of transport defects in the proximal tubule involving amino acids, monosaccharides, sodium, potassium, calcium, phosphate, bicarbonate, uric acid, and proteins. Generalized aminoaciduria, glucosuria, salt wasting, hypercalciuria, hypophosphatemia, proximal renal tubular acidosis, hypouricemia, and tubular proteinuria (Chap. 40) may result. Fanconi syndrome can be acquired secondary to diseases such as cystinosis, tyrosinemia, galactosemia, fructose intolerance, glycogen storage disease (type 1), Wilson's disease, familial nephrosis, and hereditary amyloidosis. Lowe's (or oculocerebrorenal) syndrome is an X-linked recessive form of the Fanconi syndrome associated with ocular and cerebral abnormalities.

An autosomal recessive disease, *adult Fanconi syndrome*, occurs in the absence of any systemic disorder. The term *adult* is misleading since cases are recognized in childhood, but no abnormalities are apparent at birth. Dwarfism and hypophosphatemic rickets occur along with the laboratory abnormalities of Fanconi syndrome. Renal failure is rare, and the prognosis is good when the systemic manifestations are treated. Typically, there is a "swan neck" deformity of the initial portion of the proximal tubule which is probably the anatomic basis of this tubular disorder. There is cellular atrophy in the deformed tubular segment. The consequences of the defects in the transport of water, sodium, potassium, acid, and phosphate excretion often require treatment. Water, sodium, and potassium intake must be liberal, and phosphate supplements may be needed. Metabolic acidosis can be corrected by the administration of alkali. Vitamin D helps promote bone healing. Glucosuria, uricosuria, and tubular proteinuria do not require treatment.

CYSTINURIA

See Chap. 308.

REFERENCES

AVIOLI LV: Vitamin D–resistant rickets, in *Diseases of the Kidney*, 3d ed, LE Earley, CW Gottschalk (eds). Boston, Little, Brown, 1979, p 1055

BATTLE DC, ARRUDA JAL: Renal tubular acidosis syndromes. Miner Electrolyte Metab 5:83, 1981

BERNSTEIN J, KISSANE JM: Hereditary disorders of the kidney. Part 1: Parenchymal defects and malformations. Perspect Pediatr Pathol 1:117, 1973

BRENES LG et al: Familial proximal renal tubular acidosis. Am J Med 52:244, 1977

CANTANI A et al: Familial juvenile nephronophthisis: A review and differential diagnosis. Clin Pediatr 25:90, 1986

CULPEPPER RM et al: Nephrogenic diabetes insipidus, in *The Metabolic Basis of Inherited Disease*, 5th ed, JB Stanbury et al (eds). New York, McGraw-Hill, 1983, p 1867

DANOVITCH GM: Clinical features and pathophysiology of polycystic disease in man, in *Cystic Diseases of the Kidney*, KD Gardner (ed). New York, Wiley, 1976, p 123

DEFRONZO FA, THIER SO: Inherited disorders of renal tubule function, in *The Kidney*, 3d ed, BM Brenner, FC Rector Jr (eds). Philadelphia, Saunders, 1986, p 1297

GAMBLIN GT et al: Vitamin D–dependent rickets type 2. J Clin Invest 75:954, 1985

GARRICK R et al: Bartter's syndrome: A unifying hypothesis. Am J Nephrol 5:379, 1985

HALPERIN EC, THIER SO: Cystinuria, in *Contemporary Issues in Nephrology*, BM Brenner, JH Stein (eds), FL Coe (guest ed). New York, Churchill Livingstone, 1980, vol 5, p 208

——— et al: Distal renal tubular acidosis syndromes: A pathophysiological approach. Am J Nephrol 5:1, 1985

JEPSON JB: Hartnup disease, in *The Metabolic Basis of Inherited Disease*, 5th ed, JB Stanbury et al (eds). New York, McGraw-Hill, 1983, p 1804

KUPIER JJ: Medullary sponge kidney, in *Cystic Diseases of the Kidney*, KD Gardner Jr (ed). New York, Wiley, 1976, p 151

LIBBER S et al: Treatment of nephrogenic diabetes insipidus with prostaglandin synthesis inhibitors. J Pediatr 108:35, 1986

LIDDLE GW et al: A familial renal disorder simulating primary aldosteronism but with negligible aldosterone secretion. Trans Assoc Am Phys 76:199, 1963

RASMUSSEN H, ANAST C: Familial hypophosphatemic rickets and vitamin D–dependent rickets, in *The Metabolic Basis of Inherited Disease*, 5th ed, JB Stanbury et al (eds). New York, McGraw-Hill, 1983, p 1743

RYAN EA, REISS E et al: Oncogenous osteomalacia. Am J Med 77:501, 1984

SCRIVER CR: Familial iminoglycinuria, in *The Metabolic Basis of Inherited Disease*, 5th ed, JB Stanbury et al (eds). New York, McGraw-Hill, 1983, p 1792

——— et al: Genetic aspects of renal tubular transport: Diversity and topology of carriers. Kidney Int 9:149, 1976

SEGAL S: Disorders of renal amino acid transport. N Engl J Med 294:1044, 1976

TOFUKU Y et al: Hypouricemia due to renal urate wasting: Two types of tubular transport defects. Nephron 30:39, 1982

229 NEPHROLITHIASIS

FREDRIC L. COE / MURRAY J. FAVUS

TYPES OF STONES

Calcium salts, uric acid, cystine, and struvite ($MgNH_4PO_4$) are the basis of virtually all kidney stones formed by patients residing in the western hemisphere. Calcium oxalate and calcium phosphate stones make up 75 to 85 percent of the total (Table 229-1) and may be admixed in the same stone. Calcium phosphates in stones are usually hydroxyapatite [$Ca_5(PO_4)_3OH$] or, less commonly, brushite ($CaHPO_4 \cdot H_2O$).

Calcium stones are formed mainly by men; the average age of onset is the third decade. Most persons who form a single calcium stone will eventually form another, and the intervals between successive stones shorten or remain constant, suggesting that stone-forming activity usually does not wane with time. The average rate of new stone formation in patients who have previously formed a stone is about one stone every 2 or 3 years. Calcium stone disease is strongly familial.

In the urine, calcium oxalate monohydrate crystals (whewellite) usually grow as biconcave ovals that resemble red blood cells in shape and size, but also occur in a larger, "dumbbell" form. In polarized light the crystals appear bright against a dark background with an intensity dependent upon orientation, a property known as *birefringence*. Calcium oxalate dihydrate crystals (weddellite) are bipyramidal and only weakly birefringent. Apatite crystals do not exhibit birefringence and appear amorphous, because the actual crystals are too small to be resolved by light microscopy. Brushite produces elongated lathlike (narrow, long, rectangular) crystals.

Uric acid stones are radiolucent, account for 5 to 8 percent of all stones (Table 229-1), and are also formed mainly by men. Half of the patients who form uric acid stones have gout; whether or not gout is present, uric acid lithiasis is usually familial. In urine, uric acid crystals become red-orange in color because they adsorb the pigment uricine. Anhydrous uric acid produces very small crystals that appear amorphous by light microscopy. They are indistinguishable from apatite crystals, except for their birefringence. Uric acid dihydrate tends to form teardrop-shaped crystals as well as flat, square plates; both are strongly birefringent. Uric acid gravel appears like red dust, and the stones are also orange or red on some occasions. *Cystine stones* are very uncommon (less than 1 percent of all stones), are lemon yellow, and sparkle; they are radiopaque because they contain sulfur. Cystine crystals appear in the urine as flat, hexagonal plates.

Struvite ($MgNH_4PO_4$) *stones* are common (Table 229-1) and potentially dangerous. These stones, formed mainly by women, result from urinary tract infection with bacteria that produce urease, usually *Proteus* species. The stones can grow to a large size and fill the renal pelvis and calyces to produce a "staghorn" appearance. They are radiopaque and have a variable internal density. In urine, struvite crystals are rectangular prisms that have been likened to coffin lids.

MANIFESTATIONS OF STONES

As stones grow upon the surfaces of the renal papillae or within the urinary collecting system, they need not produce symptoms. Accordingly, asymptomatic stones are often discovered during the course of abdominal radiographic studies undertaken for unrelated reasons. Sometimes stones cause only gross or microscopic hematuria. In fact, stones rank, along with benign and malignant neoplasms, renal cysts, and genitourinary tuberculosis, as among the most common causes of isolated hematuria. Much of the time, however, stones break loose

TABLE 229-1 **Major causes of renal stones**

Stone type and causes	Percent of all stones*	Percent occurrence of specific causes*	Ratio of men to women	Etiology	Diagnosis	Treatment
Calcium stones	75–85		2:1 to 3:1			
Idiopathic hypercalciuria		50–55	2:1	Hereditary (?)	Normocalcemia, unexplained hypercalciuria†	Thiazide diuretic agents
Hyperuricosuria		20	4:1	Diet	Urine uric acid >750 mg per 24 h (women), >800 mg per 24 h (men)	Allopurinol or diet
Primary hyperparathyroidism		5	3:10	Neoplasia	Unexplained hypercalcemia	Surgery
Distal renal tubular acidosis		Rare	1:1	Hereditary	Hyperchloremic acidosis, minimum urine pH >5.5	Alkali replacement
Intestinal hyperoxaluria		~1–2	1:1	Bowel surgery	Urine oxalate >50 mg per 24 h	Cholestyramine or oral calcium loading
Hereditary hyperoxaluria		Rare	1:1	Hereditary	Urine oxalate and glycolic or L-glyceric acid increased	Fluids and pyridoxine
Idiopathic stone disease		20	2:1	Unknown	None of the above present	Oral phosphate, fluids
Uric acid stones	5–8					
Gout		~50	3:1 to 4:1	Hereditary	Clinical diagnosis	Alkali to raise urine pH
Idiopathic		~50	1:1	Hereditary (?)	Uric acid stones, no gout	Allopurinol if daily urine uric acid above 1000 mg
Dehydration		?	1:1	Intestinal, habit	History, intestinal fluid loss	Alkali, fluids, reversal of cause
Lesch-Nyhan syndrome		Rare	Men	Hereditary	Reduced hypoxanthine-guanine phosphoribosyltransferase level	Allopurinol
Malignant tumors		Rare	1:1	Neoplasia	Clinical diagnosis	Allopurinol
Cystine stones	1		1:1	Hereditary	Stone type; elevated cystine excretion	Massive fluids, alkali, D-penicillamine if needed
Struvite stones	10–15		2:10	Infection	Stone type	Antimicrobial agents and judicious surgery

* Values are percent of patients who form a particular type of stone and who display each specific cause of stones.
† Urine calcium above 300 mg per 24 h (men), 250 mg per 24 h (women), or 4 mg/kg per 24 h either sex. Hyperthyroidism, Cushing syndrome, sarcoidosis, malignant tumors, immobilization, vitamin D intoxication, rapidly progressive bone disease, and Paget's disease all cause hypercalciuria and must be excluded in diagnosis of idiopathic hypercalciuria.

and enter the ureter, or occlude the ureteropelvic junction, causing pain and obstruction.

STONE PASSAGE A stone can traverse the ureter without symptoms, but most of the time passage produces pain and bleeding. The pain begins gradually, usually in the flank, but increases over the next 20 to 60 min to become so severe that narcotic drugs are often needed for its control. The pain may remain in the flank or spread downward and anteriorly toward the ipsilateral loin, testicle, or vulva. Pain that migrates downward always indicates that the stone has passed to the lower third of the ureter, but if the pain does not migrate, the position of the stone cannot be predicted. A stone in the portion of the ureter within the bladder wall causes frequency, urgency, and dysuria that may be confused with urinary tract infection. Hematuria is the rule with passage of a stone.

OTHER SYNDROMES Staghorn calculi Struvite, cystine, and uric acid stones often grow too large to enter the ureter. They gradually fill the renal pelvis and may extend outward through the infundibula to the calyces themselves.

Nephrocalcinosis Calcium stones grow on the renal papillae. Most break loose and cause colic, but sometimes they remain in place so that multiple papillary calcifications are found by x-ray, a condition termed *nephrocalcinosis*. Papillary nephrocalcinosis is very common in hereditary distal renal tubular acidosis and in other states characterized by severe hypercalciuria. In medullary sponge kidney disease (Chap. 228) calcification may occur in dilated distal collecting ducts.

Sludge There can be enough uric acid or cystine in the urine to plug both ureters with precipitate. Calcium oxalate crystals do not do this because usually less than 100 mg oxalate is excreted daily in the urine in even severe hyperoxaluric states, compared with 1000 mg uric acid in patients with ordinary hyperuricosuria and 400 to 800 mg cystine in patients with homozygous cystinuria. Calcium phosphate crystals can render the urine milky but do not plug the urinary tract.

INFECTION Although urinary tract infection is not a direct consequence of stone disease, it is a frequent complication that arises from instrumentation and surgery of the urinary tract, which are frequently required in the treatment of stone disease. Stone disease and urinary infection can enhance the seriousness of one another and interfere with treatment. Obstruction of an infected kidney by a stone may lead to sepsis and extensive damage of renal tissue, since it converts the urinary tract proximal to the obstruction into a closed, or partially closed, space that can become an abscess. On the other hand, some forms of infection, those due to bacteria that possess the enzyme urease, can produce stones composed of struvite.

ACTIVITY OF STONE DISEASE *Active disease* means that new stones are forming or that preformed stones are growing. Sequential radiographs of the renal areas are needed to document the growth or appearance of new stones and to ensure that stones which pass are actually newly formed, not preexistent ones.

PATHOGENESIS OF STONES

Urinary stones usually arise because of the breakdown of a delicate balance. On the one hand the kidneys must conserve water, but they must also excrete materials that have a low solubility. These two opposing requirements must be balanced against one another during adaptation to a particular combination of diet, climate, and activity. The problem is mitigated to some extent by the fact that urine contains some substances that inhibit crystallization of calcium salts and others that bind calcium in soluble complexes. But these protective mechanisms are less than perfect. When the urine becomes supersaturated with insoluble materials, because their excretion rates are excessive, and/or because water conservation is extreme, crystals form and may grow and aggregate with one another to form a stone.

SUPERSATURATION Consider a solution that is in equilibrium with crystals of calcium oxalate. The product of the chemical activities of the calcium and oxalate ions in the solution is termed the *equilibrium solubility product*, because it is the activity product that is unique to the equilibrium condition. If the crystals are removed, and if either calcium or oxalate is added to the solution, the activity product will rise, but the solution will remain clear; no new crystals form. Such a solution is considered to be *metastably supersaturated*. If new calcium oxalate seed crystals are now added, they will grow in size. Ultimately, the activity product will reach a critical value at which a solid phase begins to develop spontaneously. This value is called the *upper limit of metastability*, or the *formation product*. Stone growth in the urinary tract requires a urine that, on the average, is above the equilibrium solubility product. Persistence of a stone requires an average activity product at least equal to the solubility product. In general there is agreement that excessive supersaturation is a factor common to the formation of most stones.

Calcium, oxalate, and phosphate form many stable soluble complexes among themselves and with other substances in urine, such as citrate. As a result, their free ion activities are considerably below their chemical concentrations and can be measured only by indirect techniques. Reduction in ligand such as citrate can increase ion activity without changing measurably total urinary calcium. Urine supersaturation can be increased by dehydration or by overexcretion of calcium, oxalate, or phosphate. Supersaturation of the urine with cystine or uric acid also occurs when overexcretion or low urine volume is present. Urine pH can also be an important factor; phosphate and uric acid are weak acids that dissociate readily over the physiologic range of urine pH. Alkaline urine contains more urate and dissociated phosphate, favoring deposits of sodium hydrogen urate, octocalcium phosphate, and apatite. Below a urine pH of 5.5, uric acid crystals (pK 5.47) predominate, whereas phosphate crystals are rare. The solubility of calcium oxalate, on the other hand, is not influenced by changes in urine pH. Measurements of supersaturation in a 24-h urine sample are averages that probably underestimate the risk of precipitation. Transient dehydration or postprandial bursts of overexcretion may cause values that are considerably above the average.

NUCLEATION Homogeneous nucleation In urine that is supersaturated with respect to calcium oxalate, these two ions come together and form clusters. The higher the supersaturation, the larger and more numerous the clusters become. Most small clusters eventually disperse because the internal forces between ions that hold them together are too weak to overcome the random tendency of ions to move away. Clusters of over 100 ions can remain stable because attractive forces balance surface losses. Once they are stable, nuclei can grow at a supersaturation far below that needed for their creation. The formation product marks the point at which stable nuclei become frequent enough to create a permanent solid phase.

Heterogeneous nucleation If a supersaturated urine is seeded with preformed nuclei of a crystal that is similar in structure to calcium oxalate, calcium and oxalate ions in solution will bind to the crystal's surface as they would upon a seed crystal of calcium oxalate itself. The organized growth of one crystal on the surface of another is called *epitaxial growth*, and the seeding of a supersaturated solution by foreign nuclei is called *heterogeneous nucleation*. Sodium hydrogen urate, uric acid, and hydroxyapatite crystals can serve as heterogeneous nuclei that permit calcium oxalate stones to form even though urine calcium oxalate supersaturation never exceeds the metastable limit.

INHIBITORS OF CRYSTAL GROWTH AND AGGREGATION Stable nuclei must grow and aggregate to produce a stone of clinical significance. Urine contains potent inhibitors of both of these processes for calcium oxalate and calcium phosphate, but not for uric acid, cystine, or struvite crystals. Inorganic pyrophosphate is a potent inhibitor which appears to affect calcium phosphate more than calcium oxalate crystals. Other urine inhibitors that appear to be glycoproteins strongly inhibit the growth of calcium oxalate crystals. Slowing of crystal growth must raise the apparent upper limit of metastability, because the critical growth of ion clusters into stable nuclei is hindered. As a consequence of the presence of these inhibitors, crystal growth in urine is very slow compared with simple salt solutions, and the upper limit of metastability is higher. Urine citrate may also inhibit crystal growth or nucleation.

EVALUATION AND TREATMENT OF PATIENTS WITH NEPHROLITHIASIS

A majority of patients with nephrolithiasis harbor remediable metabolic disorders that cause stones and can be detected by chemical analysis of the serum and urine. A practical outpatient evaluation consists of three 24-h urine collections, each with a corresponding blood sample. Serum and urine calcium, uric acid and creatinine, urine oxalate and citrate, and serum electrolyte measurements should be made. Whenever possible, the composition of kidney stones should be determined because treatment depends on stone type (Table 229-1). No matter what disorders are found, every patient should be counseled to avoid dehydration and to drink six to eight glasses of water daily. Since treatment is prolonged, the use of medications must be justified by the activity and severity of stone disease and the desire the patient may have for protection against new stones.

The management of stones that are already present in the kidneys or urinary tract requires a combined medical and surgical approach. The specific treatment for any individual patient depends upon the details of the location of the stone, the extent of obstruction, the function of the affected and unaffected kidneys, the presence or absence of urinary tract infection, the progress of stone passage, and the risk of operation or anesthesia, given the overall clinical state of the patient. In general, severe obstruction, infection, intractable pain, or serious bleeding are indications for removal of a stone.

In the past, stones could be removed only by operation upon the kidney, renal pelvis, or ureter or by passing a flexible basket retrograde up the ureter from the bladder during cystoscopy. However, there now are three new alternatives. Stones can be fragmented in situ by exposing them to extracorporeal shock waves. The patient is submerged in a water tank, the kidney with the stone is centered at the focal point of parabolic reflectors, and high-intensity shock waves are created by high-voltage discharge. The waves are focused by the reflectors so that they pass through the patient. The rigid stone fractures as the shock wave passes by. After many discharges, most stones are reduced to powder that passes through the ureter into the bladder. Larger fragments are removed by cystoscopy. Extracorporeal lithotripsy is used for stones in the kidney, renal pelvis, or proximal ureter. A second method is percutaneous ultrasonic lithotripsy, in which a rigid cystoscope-like instrument is passed into the renal pelvis through a small incision in the flank. Stones can be disrupted by a small ultrasound transducer, and fragments removed directly. The last method is endoscopic passage of an ultrasonic transducer into the ureter via a cystoscope; ureteral stones that are inaccessible to extracorporeal or percutaneous lithotripsy can be fragmented and removed. Extracorporeal, percutaneous, and endoscopic lithotripsy seem to be replacing pyelolithotomy and ureterolithotomy.

CALCIUM STONES Idiopathic hypercalciuria (see also Chap. 336) This condition appears to be hereditary, and its diagnosis is straightforward (Table 229-1). In some patients, primary intestinal hyperabsorption of calcium causes transient postprandial hypercalcemia that suppresses secretion of parathyroid hormone. The renal tubules are deprived of their most potent normal stimulus to reabsorb calcium at the same time that the filtered load of calcium is increased. In other patients, reabsorption of calcium by the renal tubules appears to be defective, and secondary hyperparathyroidism is evoked by urinary losses of calcium. Renal activation of 1,25-dihydroxyvitamin D is increased, producing intestinal hyperabsorption of calcium. In the past, the separation of "absorptive" and "renal" forms of

hypercalciuria has been used to guide treatment. However, these may not be separate entities but the extremes of a continuum of behavior. Hypercalciuria contributes to stone formation by raising urine saturation with respect to calcium oxalate and calcium phosphate.

Thiazide diuretics lower urine calcium in both types of hypercalciuria and are very effective in preventing the formation of stones. The drug effect requires slight contraction of the extracellular fluid volume, and massive use of NaCl will reduce its therapeutic effect. Potassium citrate is useful to prevent hypokalemia and raise urine citrate; the latter lowers urine calcium ion levels.

Hyperuricosuria About 20 percent of calcium oxalate stone formers are hyperuricosuric, primarily because of an excessive intake of purine from meat, fish, and poultry. The mechanism of stone formation probably is heterogeneous nucleation of calcium oxalate by crystals of sodium hydrogen urate or uric acid that lodge in the terminal ends of the collecting ducts and produce an anchored site on which calcium oxalate can deposit. A change in diet is ideal treatment but difficult for many patients to achieve. The alternative is allopurinol, usually 100 mg bid. Some patients eventually alter their diets so that allopurinol can be withdrawn.

Primary hyperparathyroidism (see also Chap. 336) The diagnosis of this condition, which is more common in women than men, is established by documenting hypercalcemia that cannot be otherwise explained accompanied by inappropriately elevated serum concentrations of parathyroid hormone. Hypercalciuria, which is usually present, raises the urine supersaturation of calcium phosphate and/or calcium oxalate (Table 229-1). It is important to establish the diagnosis since parathyroidectomy is effective treatment and should be carried out before renal damage has occurred.

Distal renal tubular acidosis (see also Chap. 228) The defect in this condition seems to reside in the distal nephron, which cannot establish a normal pH gradient between urine and blood, leading to hyperchloremic acidosis. The minimum urine pH in response to an oral challenge with NH_4Cl, 1.9 mmol/kg, is above 5.5. Hypercalciuria, an alkaline urine, and a low urine citrate excretion cause supersaturation with respect to calcium phosphate. Calcium phosphate stones are formed, nephrocalcinosis is common, and osteomalacia or rickets may occur. Renal damage is frequent, and a gradual fall in glomerular filtration rate usually occurs. Treatment with supplemental alkali reverses hypercalciuria and limits the production of new stones. The usual dose of sodium bicarbonate is 0.5 to 2.0 meq/kg, in four to six divided doses. An alternative is Shohl's solution, which contains citrate and citric acid. Incomplete renal tubular acidosis (RTA) refers to a disease in which systemic acidosis is absent, but the kidneys cannot lower urine pH below 5.5 when patients are given an exogenous acid load such as ammonium chloride. Incomplete RTA may be acquired by some patients who form calcium oxalate stones because of idiopathic hypercalciuria; the importance of the RTA in producing stones is uncertain, and thiazide treatment is a reasonable alternative. Some patients with incomplete RTA form calcium phosphate stones because of low urine citrate and an abnormally alkaline urine, and are best treated as if RTA were complete: with alkali.

Hyperoxaluria Overabsorption of dietary oxalate and consequent oxaluria, i.e., so-called intestinal oxaluria, has been ascribed to fat malabsorption (Chap. 237). The latter can be caused by a variety of conditions, including bacterial overgrowth syndromes, chronic disease of the pancreas and biliary tract, jejunoileal bypass in treatment of obesity, or ileal resection greater than 22 cm for inflammatory bowel disease. With fat malabsorption, calcium in the bowel lumen is bound by fatty acids instead of precipitating with oxalate, which is left free for excessive absorption in the colon. Delivery of unabsorbed fatty acids and bile salts to the colon may injure the colonic mucosa and permit excessive oxalate absorption. Dietary excess of oxalate, ascorbic acid loading, and hereditary hyperoxaluric states due to overproduction of oxalate are much less common causes of hyperoxaluria. Ethylene glycol intoxication and methoxyflurane, an anesthetic agent, can also cause oxalate overproduction and hyperoxaluria. Hyperoxaluria from any cause can produce tubulointerstitial nephropathy (Chap. 226) and lead to stone formation.

Cholestyramine, a resin that can bind oxalate, at a dose of 8 to 16 g per day, correction of fat malabsorption, and a low-fat diet are effective treatments for oxaluria secondary to intestinal absorption. Calcium lactate, 8 to 14 g per day, which acts by precipitating oxalate in the gut lumen is an alternative form of therapy. Both treatments require additional study to assess their effectiveness. There is no effective treatment for hereditary hyperoxaluria, a disorder characterized by an enzymatic defect involving the metabolism of the precursor of oxalate and transmitted as an autosomal recessive. A high fluid intake, phosphate, and pyridoxine (200 mg per day) are recommended, but irreversible renal failure secondary to recurrent stone formation usually occurs before the age of 20 years.

Idiopathic calcium lithiasis   At least 20 percent of patients have no obvious cause for stones (Table 229-1). The best treatment for them appears to be a high fluid intake, so that the urine specific gravity remains below approximately 1.005 throughout the day and night. Oral phosphate at a dose of 2 g phosphorus daily may lower urine calcium and increases urine pyrophosphate excretion, and thereby may bring about a reduction in the rate of recurrence of stones. Orthophosphate causes mild nausea and diarrhea initially, but tolerance may improve with continued intake. Thiazide treatment to reduce calcium excretion and allopurinol to diminish uric acid output may also be helpful. There are no adequate studies to support the use of supplemental magnesium, pyridoxine, or methylene blue, commonly mentioned remedies.

URIC ACID STONES   These stones form because the urine becomes supersaturated with undissociated uric acid, uric acid that is protonated at its N-9 position. This proton has a pK of 5.35 in urine. In gout, idiopathic uric acid lithiasis, and dehydration, the average pH is abnormally low, usually below 5.4, and often below 5.0. Undissociated uric acid therefore predominates, and can dissolve in urine in concentrations of only 100 mg per liter. Concentrations above this level represent supersaturation that causes crystals and stones to form. Hyperuricosuria, when present, increases supersaturation; but urine of low pH can be excessively supersaturated with undissociated uric acid even though the daily excretion rate is normal. Myeloproliferative syndromes, chemotherapeutic treatment of malignant tumors, and the Lesch-Nyhan syndrome cause such massive production of uric acid and consequent hyperuricosuria that stones and uric acid sludge occur even at a normal urine pH. The renal collecting tubules can be plugged by uric acid crystals with consequent acute renal failure.

The two goals of treatment are to raise urine pH and to lower urine uric acid excretion when it is very high, i.e., above 1000 mg per day. Supplemental alkali, 1 to 3 meq/kg per day, should be given in three or four evenly spaced divided doses, one of which should be reserved for bedtime. The form of the alkali may be important. Potassium citrate may reduce the risk of calcium salts crystallizing when urine pH is increased, whereas sodium citrate or sodium bicarbonate may increase the risk. If the overnight urine pH is below 5.5, the evening dose of bicarbonate may be raised, or 250 mg acetazolamide added at bedtime. With massive overexcretion of uric acid, high doses of allopurinol, exceeding 300 mg daily, may be needed. Treatment with allopurinol should be instituted before chemotherapy of highly cellular tumors, since massive hyperuricosuria can be expected. Alkali treatment must be avoided if hypercalciuria is also present.

CYSTINURIA AND CYSTINE STONES (See also Chap. 308)   Proximal tubular and jejunal transport of cystine and the other dibasic amino acids, lysine, arginine, and ornithine, are defective, and excessive amounts are lost in the urine. Clinical disease is due solely to the insolubility of cystine, which forms stones. Patients are short, probably because of a linked inherited tendency rather than amino acid losses. Cystinuria is transmitted as an autosomal recessive trait whose prevalence in newborns is 1 in 7000.

Pathogenesis   The weight of available evidence indicates that cystinuria occurs because of defective transport of amino acids by the brush borders of renal tubule and intestinal epithelial cells. Cystine, lysine, arginine, and ornithine appear to share a common renal transport pathway, because infusion of lysine decreases tubular reabsorption of the other three. But cystine also seems to be transported by a separate transport mechanism, because cystinuria and dibasic aminoaciduria can each occur independently. The inheritance of the brush border transport defects is complex. The intestinal defects are not similar in all patients who are homozygous for cystinuria, and the extent of aminoaciduria in those relatives of cystinuric patients who are heterozygous carriers of the defect, for example, their siblings, varies from family to family. Thus far three types of inheritance have been described (Table 229-2).

Diagnosis and treatment   Cystine stones are formed only by patients with cystinuria, but 10 percent of stones formed by cystinuric patients do not contain cystine; therefore, every stone former should be screened for the disease. The sediment from a first morning urine specimen in many patients with homozygous cystinuria reveals typical flat hexagonal platelike cystine crystals. Cystinuria can also be detected using the sodium nitroprusside test on a urine sample. The test gives a positive response to 75 to 125 mg cystine per gram of creatinine, a concentration lower than that found in the urine of patients with homozygous cystinuria but well above the levels encountered in normal urine. Because the test is sensitive, it will be positive in many individuals who are heterozygous for cystinuria, most of whom do not form cystine stones (Table 229-2). A positive nitroprusside test or the finding of cystine crystals in the urine sediment should be evaluated by measurement of daily cystine excretion. Normal adults excrete 40 to 60 mg per gram of creatinine; heterozygotes usually excrete less than 300 mg/g; and patients with homozygous cystinuria almost always excrete above 250 mg/g.

Treatment consists of a high fluid intake, even at night. Daily urine volume should exceed 3 liters. Raising urine pH with alkali is helpful, provided the resulting daily urine pH exceeds 7.5. Because drug side effects are frequent, D-penicillamine, which forms the soluble mixed disulfide cysteine-penicillamine, should be used only when fluid loading and alkali therapy have been ineffective. *N*-Acetyl-D-penicillamine has a similar mode of action and may have fewer side effects, but is not available for routine use. Mercaptopropinylglycine has been used to dissolve renal calculi by perfusion of the renal pelvis and has been given by mouth to prevent stones, but also is experimental. Low-methionine diets have not proved to be practical for clinical use.

STRUVITE STONES   These stones are always a result of urinary infection with bacteria, usually *Proteus* species, which possess urease, an enzyme that degrades urea to NH_3 and CO_2. The NH_3 hydrolyzes to NH_4^+ and raises pH, usually to 8 or 9. The CO_2 hydrates to H_2CO_3 and then dissociates to CO_3^{2-} which precipitates with calcium as $CaCO_3$. The NH_4^+ precipitates PO_4^{3-} and Mg^{2+} to form the triple salt $MgNH_4PO_4$. The result is a stone of calcium carbonate admixed with struvite. It is impossible to form struvite in urine without infection, because NH_4^+ concentration is very low in urine that is

TABLE 229-2   Classification of cystinuria

	Type I	Type II	Type III
Intestinal transport:			
Cystine	0	↓↓	N—↓
Lysine	0	0	↓
Arginine	0	–	–
Urine excretion in heterozygotes:			
Cystine	N	↑	↓
Lysine	N	↑	↑

NOTE: ↑ = *increased;* ↓ = *reduced;* ↓↓ = *very reduced;* 0 = *absent transport;* N = *normal urinary excretion rates;* – = *not known.*

alkaline in response to physiologic stimuli. Chronic *Proteus* infection can occur because of impaired urinary drainage, infection of retained stones of any type, urologic instrumentation or surgery, and especially chronic antibiotic treatment, which can favor the emergence of *Proteus* as the predominant urinary tract flora.

Treatment Mandelamine, which lowers urine pH and liberates formaldehyde, is used for chronic suppression of infection when a stone is present. More extreme lowering of urine pH with chronic administration of NH_4Cl may retard stone growth but may also raise urine calcium level and promote the formation of calcium oxalate stones. Antimicrobial treatment is best reserved for dealing with acute exacerbation of infection and for maintenance of a sterile urine after surgery, in the hope of preventing recurrence or minimizing stone growth. Surgery should be reserved for severe obstruction, intractable pain, bleeding, or serious manifestations of urinary infection. Since stones can regrow from any infected fragment which is left behind, recurrences following operation are quite common. In some centers, it is possible to irrigate the renal pelvis and calyces with Renacidin, a solution that dissolves struvite, using a catheter passed through a cutaneous flank incision into the kidney.

REFERENCES

COE FL: Nephrolithiasis: Pathogenesis and treatment. Chicago, Year Book, 1978
——— et al: Effect of low calcium diet on urine calcium excretion, parathyroid function, and serum 1,25(OH)$_2$D$_3$ levels in patients with idiopathic hypercalciuria and in normal subjects. Am J Med 72:25, 1982
FLEISCH H et al (eds): *Urolithiasis Research.* New York, Plenum, 1976
———, FAVUS MJ: Disorders of stone formation, in *The Kidney,* 3d ed, BM Brenner, FC Rector Jr (eds). Philadelphia, Saunders, 1986, p 1403
GRANTHAM JR et al: Renal stone disease treated with extracorporeal shock wave lithotripsy: Short-term observations in 100 patients. Radiology 158:203, 1986
NAKAGAWA Y et al: Purification and characterization of the principal inhibitors of calcium oxalate monohydrate crystal growth in human urine. J Biol Chem 258:12594, 1983
PAK CYC (ed): Urolithiasis. Kidney Int 13:341, 1978
———: Kidney stones, in *Williams' Textbook of Endocrinology,* 7th ed, JD Wilson, DW Foster (eds). Philadelphia, Saunders, 1985, p 1256
STRAUSS AL et al: Factors that predict relapse of calcium nephrolithiasis during treatment. Am J Med 72:25, 1982
WEBB DR et al: Extracorporeal shockwave lithotripsy, endourology and open surgery: The management and follow-up of 200 patients with urinary calculi. Ann R Coll Surg Engl 67:337, 1985

230 URINARY TRACT OBSTRUCTION

BARRY M. BRENNER / EDGAR L. MILFORD / JULIAN L. SEIFTER

Obstruction to the flow of urine, with attendant stasis and elevation in urinary tract pressure, impairs renal and urinary conduit functions and represents a common cause of acute and chronic renal failure. With early relief of obstruction, these defects in function usually disappear completely. However, chronic obstruction may produce profound and permanent loss of renal mass (renal atrophy) and excretory capability, as well as enhanced susceptibility to local infection and stone formation. Early and accurate diagnosis and prompt and appropriate therapy are, therefore, essential to minimize the otherwise devastating effects of obstruction on urinary tract structure and function.

ETIOLOGY Obstruction to urine flow can result from *intrinsic* or *extrinsic mechanical blockade* as well as from *functional defects* not associated with fixed occlusion of the urinary drainage system. Lesions causing mechanical obstruction can occur at any level of the urinary tract, from the renal calyces to the external urethral meatus. Normal points of narrowing, such as the ureteropelvic and uretero-vesical junctions, bladder neck, and urethral meatus, are common sites of obstruction. When blockage is above the level of the bladder, unilateral dilatation of the ureter (*hydroureter*) and renal pyelocalyceal

system (*hydronephrosis*) occur; when the lesion is at or below the level of the bladder, bilateral involvement is the rule.

Common forms of obstruction are listed in Table 230-1. In childhood, *congenital malformations,* including marked narrowing of the ureteropelvic junction, anomalous (retrocaval) location of the ureter, and posterior urethral valves predominate. The latter defect is the most common cause of bilateral hydronephrosis in the male child. Children may also have bladder dysfunction secondary to congenital urethral stricture, urethral meatal stenosis, or bladder neck obstruction. In adults, urinary tract obstruction is due mainly to *acquired defects.* Pelvic tumors, calculi, and urethral stricture predominate. Ligation of, or injury to, the ureter during pelvic or colonic surgery can lead to hydronephrosis which, if unilateral, may remain relatively silent and undetected. Obstructive uropathy may also result from extrinsic neoplastic (carcinoma of cervix or colon, retroperitoneal lymphoma) or inflammatory disorders. One such inflammatory disorder is retroperitoneal fibrosis, a process of unknown cause seen most commonly in middle-aged males, which occasionally leads to bilateral ureteral obstruction. Occurring in some patients taking methysergide for relief of migraine, retroperitoneal fibrosis must be distinguished from other retroperitoneal causes of ureteral obstruction, particularly lymphomas and pelvic neoplasms.

Functional impairment of urine flow usually results from disorders which involve both the ureter and bladder. Common functional lesions include neurogenic bladder, often with adynamic ureter, and vesicoureteral reflux. Reflux of urine from bladder to ureter(s) is more common in children than adults and may result in severe unilateral or bilateral hydroureter and hydronephrosis. Abnormal insertion of the ureter into the bladder is the most common cause of vesicoureteral reflux in children. Reflux occurring in the absence of urinary tract infection or bladder neck obstruction usually does not lead to renal parenchymal damage and often resolves spontaneously as the child matures. Surgical reinsertion of the ureter into the bladder is indicated if reflux is severe and unlikely to improve spontaneously, if renal function deteriorates, or if urinary tract infections recur despite chronic antimicrobial therapy.

TABLE 230-1 Common mechanical causes of urinary tract obstruction

Ureter	Bladder outlet	Urethra
CONGENITAL		
Ureteropelvic junction narrowing or obstruction	Bladder neck obstruction	Posterior urethral valves
Ureterovesical junction narrowing or obstruction	Ureterocele	Anterior urethral valves
Ureterocele		Stricture
Retrocaval ureter		Meatal stenosis
		Phimosis
ACQUIRED INTRINSIC DEFECTS		
Calculi	Benign prostatic hypertrophy	Stricture
Inflammation	Cancer of prostate	Tumor
Trauma	Cancer of bladder	Calculi
Sloughed papillae	Calculi	Trauma
Tumor	Diabetic neuropathy	Phimosis
Blood clots	Spinal cord disease	
Uric acid crystals		
ACQUIRED EXTRINSIC DEFECTS		
Pregnant uterus	Carcinoma of cervix, colon	Trauma
Retroperitoneal fibrosis	Trauma	
Aortic aneurysm		
Uterine leiomyomata		
Carcinoma of uterus, prostate, bladder, colon, rectum		
Retroperitoneal lymphoma		
Accidental surgical ligation		

CLINICAL FEATURES   The pathophysiology and clinical features of urinary tract obstruction are summarized in Table 230-2. Pain is the symptom which most commonly provokes the need for medical attention. The pain of urinary tract obstruction is due to distention of the collecting system or renal capsule. The severity of the pain is influenced more by the rate at which distention develops than the degree of distention. Acute supravesical obstruction, as from a stone lodged in a ureter (Chap. 229), is associated with excruciatingly severe pain, usually called *renal colic*. This pain is relatively steady and continuous, with little fluctuation in intensity, and often radiates to the lower abdomen, testes, or labia. By contrast, more insidious causes of obstruction, such as chronic narrowing of the ureteropelvic junction, may produce little or no pain, yet result in total destruction of the affected kidney. Flank pain which comes on only with micturition is pathognomonic of vesicoureteral reflux.

Azotemia develops in urinary tract obstruction when overall excretory function is impaired. This may occur in the setting of bladder outlet obstruction, bilateral renal pelvic or ureteric obstruction, or unilateral disease in a patient with a solitary functioning kidney. Complete bilateral obstruction should be suspected when acute renal failure is accompanied by anuria. Any patient with renal failure otherwise unexplained or with a history of nephrolithiasis, hematuria, prostatic enlargement, pelvic surgery, trauma, or tumor should be evaluated for urinary tract obstruction.

Symptoms of *polyuria* and *nocturia* commonly accompany chronic partial urinary tract obstruction and result from impaired renal concentrating ability. This defect usually does not improve with administration of exogenous vasopressin and is therefore a form of acquired nephrogenic diabetes insipidus. Disturbances in sodium chloride transport in the ascending limb of Henle and, in azotemic patients, the osmotic (urea) diuresis per nephron lead to decreased medullary hypertonicity and, hence, a concentrating defect. Partial obstruction, therefore, may be associated with increased rather than decreased urine output. Indeed, wide fluctuations in urinary output in a patient with azotemia should always raise the possibility of intermittent or partial urinary tract obstruction. If fluid intake becomes inadequate in these patients, severe dehydration and hypernatremia may develop. Hesitancy and straining to initiate the urinary stream, postvoid dribbling, urinary frequency, and (overflow) incontinence are complaints common to patients with obstruction at or below the level of the bladder (see Chap. 40).

TABLE 230-2   Pathophysiology of bilateral ureteral obstruction

Hemodynamic effects	Tubule effects	Clinical features
ACUTE		
↑ Renal blood flow ↓ GFR ↓ Medullary blood flow ↑ Vasodilator prostaglandins	↑ Ureteral and tubule pressures ↑ Reabsorption of Na⁺, urea, water	Pain (capsule distention) Azotemia Oliguria
CHRONIC		
↓ Renal blood flow ↓ ↓ GFR ↑ Vasoconstrictor prostaglandins ↑ Renin-angiotensin production	↓ Medullary osmolarity ↓ Concentrating ability Structural damage ↓ Transport functions for Na⁺, K⁺, H⁺	Azotemia Hypertension ADH-insensitive polyuria Natriuresis Hyperkalemic, hyperchloremic acidosis
RELEASE OF OBSTRUCTION		
Slow ↑ in GFR (variable)	↓ Tubule pressure ↑ Solute load per nephron (urea, NaCl) Natriuretic factors present	Postobstructive diuresis Potential for volume depletion and electrolyte imbalance (Na⁺, K⁺, PO₄²⁻, Mg²⁺)

In addition to loss of urinary concentrating ability and azotemia, partial bilateral urinary tract obstruction often results in other derangements of renal function, including *acquired distal renal tubular acidosis, hyperkalemia,* and *renal salt wasting.* These defects in tubule function are often accompanied by histologic evidence of widespread renal tubulointerstitial damage. Morphologic abnormalities appear early in the course of obstruction; initially the interstitium becomes edematous and infiltrated with mononuclear inflammatory cells. With continued obstruction, the interstitium becomes fibrotic; scarring and atrophy of the papillae and medulla occur and precede these processes in the cortex.

The possibility of urinary tract obstruction must always be considered in patients with urinary tract infections or urolithiasis. Urinary stasis encourages the growth of organisms as well as the formation of crystals, especially magnesium ammonium phosphate (struvite). *Hypertension* is seen frequently in acute and subacute forms of unilateral obstruction and is usually a consequence of increased release of renin by the involved kidney. Chronic unilateral or bilateral hydronephrosis, in the presence of extracellular volume expansion or other forms of renal disease, may result in significant hypertension. *Polycythemia,* an infrequent complication of obstructive uropathy, is probably secondary to increased erythropoietin production by the obstructed kidney.

DIAGNOSIS   A history of difficulty in voiding, pain, infection, or changes in urinary volume is common. Evidence for distention of the kidney or urinary bladder often can be obtained by palpation and percussion of the abdomen. A careful rectal examination may reveal enlargement or nodularity of the prostate, abnormal rectal sphincter tone, or a rectal or pelvic mass. The penis should be inspected for evidence of meatal stenosis or phimosis. In the female, vaginal, uterine, and rectal lesions responsible for urinary tract obstruction are usually revealed by inspection and palpation.

Urinalysis and examination of the urine sediment may reveal hematuria, pyuria, and bacteriuria. Often, however, the urine sediment is devoid of abnormal elements, even when obstruction leads to marked azotemia and extensive structural damage. An abdominal scout film should be obtained to evaluate the possibility of nephrocalcinosis or a radiopaque stone at any level of the urinary collecting system. As indicated in Fig. 230-1 if urinary tract obstruction is suspected, abdominal ultrasonography should be performed to evaluate renal and bladder size, as well as pyelocalyceal and ureteral contours. If distention of these structures is absent, functionally significant urinary tract obstruction can safely be excluded in differential diagnosis. Abdominal ultrasound may also detect an obstructing pelvic mass.

Intravenous pyelography is frequently employed if an obstructive abnormality is revealed by ultrasound. If the patient is not azotemic, a standard dose of contrast medium usually provides adequate information. With renal insufficiency, however, high-dose (drip-infusion) pyelography with nephrotomography is usually required for adequate visualization. In the presence of obstruction, the appearance time of the nephrogram is often delayed but eventually becomes more dense than normal because of slow tubular fluid flow rate which results in enhanced water reabsorption by the nephrons and greater concentration of contrast medium within tubules. The kidney involved by an acute obstructive process is usually slightly enlarged, and there is dilatation of the calyces, renal pelvis, and ureter above the obstruction. The ureter, however, is not tortuous, as is the case when the obstruction is chronic. In comparison with the nephrogram, the pyelogram may be extremely faint, especially if the dilated renal pelvis is voluminous, causing dilution of the contrast medium. The radiographic study should be continued until the site of obstruction is determined or the contrast medium is excreted. Delayed films taken as long as 48 h after contrast administration may be necessary to determine the exact site of obstruction.

Patients suspected of having intermittent ureteropelvic obstruction (whether functional or mechanical) should have radiologic evaluation while they are in pain, since a normal pyelogram is commonly seen during asymptomatic periods. Hydration or mannitol infusion often helps to provoke a symptomatic attack. Voiding cystourethrography is of great value in the diagnosis of vesicoureteral reflux and bladder neck and urethral obstructions. Patients with obstruction at or below the level of the bladder exhibit thickening, trabeculation, and diverticula of the bladder wall. Postvoiding films reveal residual urine. If these radiographic studies fail to provide adequate information for diagnosis, endoscopic visualization by the urologist often permits precise identification of lesions involving the urethra, prostate, bladder, and ureteral orifices. To facilitate visualization of a suspected lesion in a ureter or renal pelvis, *retrograde* or *antegrade pyelography* should be attempted. These diagnostic studies may be preferable to the intravenous pyelogram in the azotemic patient in whom poor excretory function precludes adequate visualization of the collecting system. Furthermore, intravenous pyelography carries the risk of contrast-induced renal failure in some patients with renal insufficiency, diabetes mellitus, and multiple myeloma, particularly when performed under conditions of dehydration. For these reasons retrograde and antegrade pyelography may offer advantages over the intravenous approach in the diagnostic evaluation of the azotemic patient. The retrograde approach involves catheterization of the involved ureter under cystoscopic control, while the antegrade technique necessitates placement of a catheter into the renal pelvis via a needle inserted percutaneously under ultrasonic or fluoroscopic guidance. While the antegrade approach carries the added advantage of providing immediate and certain decompression of a unilateral obstructing lesion, many urologists initially attempt the retrograde approach and resort to the antegrade method only when attempts at retrograde catheterization have been unsuccessful or when cystoscopy or general anesthesia is contraindicated.

TREATMENT AND PROGNOSIS An individual with any form of urinary tract obstruction complicated by infection requires relief of obstruction as soon as possible to prevent development of generalized sepsis and progressive renal damage. On a temporary basis, depending on the site of obstruction, drainage is often satisfactorily achieved by nephrostomy, ureterostomy, or ureteral, urethral, or suprapubic catheterization. When infection is not present, immediate surgery often is not required, even in the presence of complete obstruction and anuria (because of the availability of dialysis), at least until acid-base, fluid and electrolyte, and cardiovascular status have been restored to normal. Nevertheless, the site of obstruction should be ascertained as soon as feasible, in part because of the possibility that sepsis may occur and necessitate prompt urologic intervention. Elective relief of obstruction is usually recommended in patients with urinary retention, recurrent urinary tract infections, persistent pain, or progressive loss of renal function. Infrequently, mechanical obstruction can be alleviated by nonsurgical means, as with radiation therapy for retroperitoneal lymphoma. Likewise, functional obstruction secondary to neurogenic bladder may be decreased with the combination of frequent voiding and cholinergic drugs. The approach to obstruction secondary to renal stones is discussed in Chap. 229.

FIGURE 230-1 *Diagnostic approach for urinary tract obstruction in unexplained renal failure. Circles represent diagnostic procedures and squares indicate clinical decisions based on available data (CT, computerized tomography; IVP, intravenous pyelogram).*

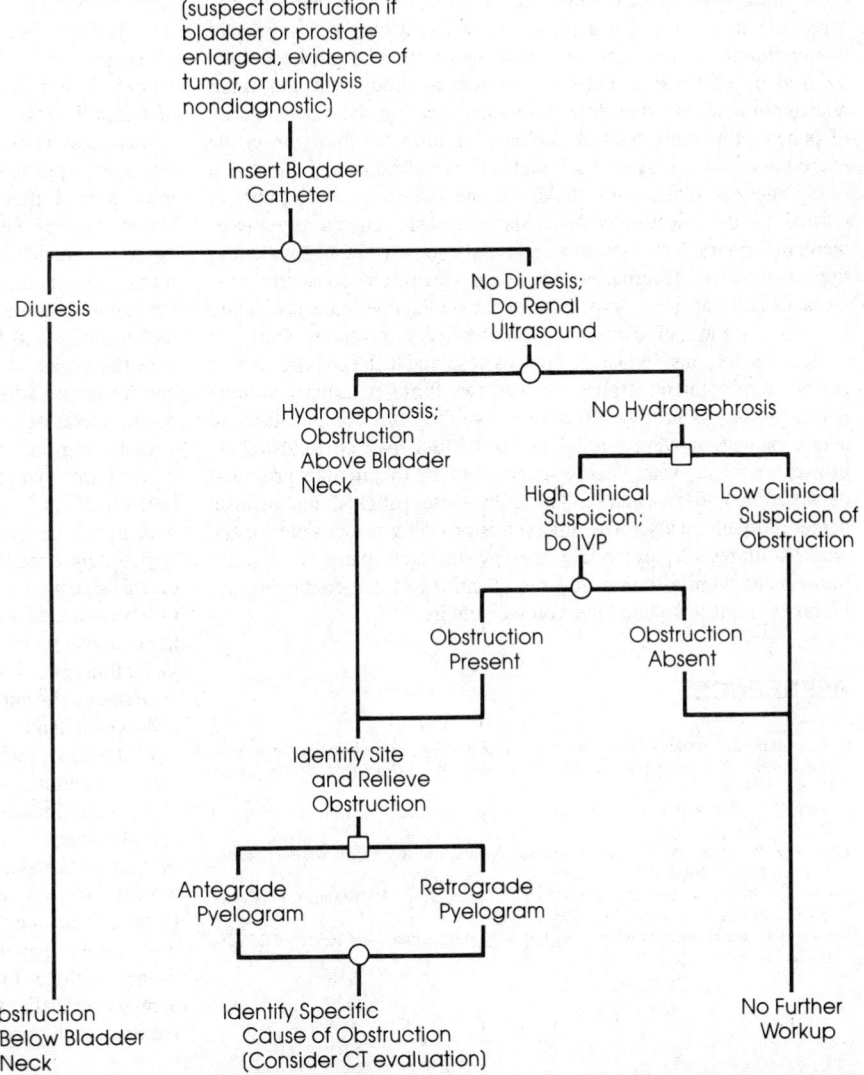

With relief of obstruction, the *prognosis* regarding return of renal function depends largely upon whether irreversible renal damage has occurred. When obstruction is not relieved, the patient's course will depend mainly on whether the obstruction is complete or incomplete, bilateral or unilateral, and whether urinary tract infection is also present. Complete obstruction with infection can lead to total destruction of the kidney within days. Experimental studies in dogs suggest that relief of complete obstruction of 1 and 2 weeks' duration restores glomerular filtration rate to 60 and 30 percent of normal, respectively; after 8 weeks, recovery does not occur. Nevertheless, in the absence of definitive evidence of irreversibility, every effort should be made to facilitate decompression in the hope of restoring renal function at least partially.

In patients undergoing cystectomy for bladder cancer, the ileal conduit is the currently preferred urinary diversionary procedure. In benign disease a sigmoid conduit may result in less ureteral reflux and secondary chronic renal insufficiency. These approaches are preferable to ureterosigmoidostomy, a procedure complicated by a high incidence of ureteral obstruction, reflux, hypokalemic metabolic acidosis, pyelonephritis, and neoplasms developing at the ureteral anastomotic site.

POSTOBSTRUCTIVE DIURESIS Relief of bilateral, but not unilateral, complete urinary tract obstruction commonly leads to a postobstructive diuresis, characterized by polyuria, which may be massive. The urine is usually hypotonic and may contain a large amount of sodium chloride. The natriuresis is due, at least in part, to the excretion of retained urea, which acts as a poorly reabsorbable solute and diminishes salt and water reabsorption in the tubules (osmotic diuresis). The increase in intratubular pressure very likely also contributes to the impairment in net sodium chloride reabsorption, especially in the terminal nephron segments. It has been suggested that natriuretic factors (other than urea) also accumulate during uremia induced by obstruction and serve to depress tubule salt and water reabsorption when urine flow is reestablished. In the vast majority of patients this diuresis is physiologic, resulting in the *appropriate* excretion of the excesses of salt and water retained during the period of obstruction. When extracellular volume and composition return to normal, the diuresis usually abates spontaneously. Therefore, replacement of urinary losses should serve only to prevent hypovolemia, hypotension, or disturbances in serum electrolyte concentrations. Occasionally, iatrogenic expansion of extracellular volume, secondary to administration of excessive quantities of intravenous fluids, is responsible for, or sustains, the diuresis observed in the postobstructive period. Replacement of no more than two-thirds of urinary volume losses per day is usually effective in avoiding this complication. In a rare patient, however, relief of obstruction may be followed by urinary salt and water losses severe enough to provoke profound dehydration and vascular collapse. In these patients, an intrinsic defect in tubule reabsorptive function is probably responsible for the marked diuresis. Appropriate therapy in such patients includes intravenous administration of large quantities of salt-containing solutions to replace sodium and volume deficits.

REFERENCES

GUGGENHEIM SJ, SCHRIER RW: Obstructive nephropathy: Pathophysiology and management, in *Renal and Electrolyte Disorders*, 2d ed, RW Schrier (ed). Boston, Little, Brown, 1980

HARRIS RH, YARGER WE: The pathogenesis of post-obstructive diuresis. J Clin Invest 56:880, 1975

KAYE AD, POLLACK HM: Diagnostic imaging approach to the patient with obstructive uropathy. Semin Nephrol 2:55, 1982

KLAHR S et al: Urinary tract obstruction, in *The Kidney*, 3d ed, BM Brenner, FC Rector Jr (eds). Philadelphia, Saunders, 1986, p 1443

WILSON DR: Renal function during and following obstruction. Ann Rev Med 28:329, 1977

231 TUMORS OF THE URINARY TRACT

MARC B. GARNICK / BARRY M. BRENNER

TUMORS OF THE KIDNEY

RENAL CELL CARCINOMA Renal cell carcinoma (renal adenocarcinoma—formerly "hypernephroma") accounts for 85 percent of all primary renal neoplasms. Approximately 18,000 new cases are diagnosed annually with 8000 deaths in the United States. The peak age incidence is between 55 and 60 years; the male-to-female ratio is 2:1. Environmental risk factors include exposure to cigarette smoke and cadmium. Genetically transmitted forms of renal cell carcinoma, which are commonly multifocal and bilateral, occur in a high proportion of patients with von Hippel–Lindau disease (retinal and central nervous system hemangiomas, autosomal dominant transmission). Marker chromosomal translocations between chromosomes 3 and 8 and 3 and 11 have been found in several kindreds with familial renal cancer. Patients with end-stage renal disease on chronic dialysis may develop renal cystic disease and associated renal carcinomas. Using electron-microscopic and immunologic techniques, renal cell carcinoma has been shown to arise from the proximal convoluted tubular epithelium. The term "hypernephroma" for renal cell carcinoma (reflecting the previously held notion of cellular origin from adrenal "rests") should be abandoned.

Clinical features Renal cell carcinoma has been called the "internist's tumor" because the lesion is often diagnosed, even in the absence of metastases, by its *systemic* rather than urologic manifestations. The triad of *gross hematuria, flank pain*, and a *palpable abdominal mass*, although considered as classic evidence for the clinical diagnosis, is encountered in less than 10 percent of cases; however, approximately one-third of patients will demonstrate at least one of these manifestations. The most common presenting abnormality is *hematuria*, which occurs in 60 percent of cases. Although microscopic hematuria is a consistent abnormality of the urinary sediment, bleeding is not usually evident grossly, allowing the tumor to grow to a large size before clinical manifestations such as flank pain and fullness appear. Contiguous extension to the renal capsule, perirenal fat, lymph nodes, renal vein, inferior vena cava, and ipsilateral adrenal gland is common. The most common sites of distant metastases include lung, mediastinum, bone, central nervous system, thyroid, and liver.

Systemic symptoms of fatigability, weight loss, and cachexia are found in about 50 percent of patients. Intermittent fever, unassociated with infection, occurs occasionally and may be the only presenting sign. Anemia may be present at the onset in approximately 50 percent of cases. Erythrocytosis is seen in about 5 percent of patients and has been linked to elaboration of erythropoietin. Eosinophilia, leukemoid reactions, thrombocytosis, and increased erythrocyte sedimentation rate also occur. Renal cell carcinomas may produce hormones or hormone-like substances, including parathyroid hormone and prostaglandins (which may lead to hypercalcemia), prolactin (galactorrhea), renin (hypertension), gonadotropins (feminization and masculinization), and glucocorticoids (Cushing's syndrome). In vascular tumors, intrarenal arteriovenous fistulas may predispose to high-output congestive heart failure. Tumor invasion of the renal vein and inferior vena cava may result in the development of abrupt, symptomatic left varicocele and lower extremity edema, respectively. Hepatic vein occlusion by tumor, with or without vena caval obstruction, may lead to hepatosplenomegaly and ascites. Disturbances in liver function are sometimes found in patients without demonstrable liver metastases and are often reversed following removal of the primary tumor.

Diagnosis (see Fig. 231-1) Although intrarenal calcifications and/or alterations in renal contours seen on the abdominal scout film may suggest the presence of a renal cell carcinoma, *intravenous pyelography* (IVP) with *nephrotomography* is the primary examination by which most renal masses are detected and evaluated. The major task is to differentiate cystic lesions from renal neoplasms. Splaying, distortion or nonvisualization of the collecting system, and distorted renal outlines suggest cancer. Nephrotomography provides clear delineation of renal borders and further aids in distinguishing cystic from solid lesions. *Ultrasonography* has greatly improved the ability to distinguish simple sonographic cysts from renal neoplasms. When combined with nephrotomography, the accuracy of ultrasonography in diagnosing a benign cyst approaches 97 percent. If a cystic lesion on IVP, combined with a benign-appearing sonolucent cystic lesion on ultrasound, is found in an asymptomatic patient without hematuria, cyst puncture is probably unnecessary. Repeat IVP or ultrasound should then be performed periodically.

If diagnostic accuracy beyond 97 percent is required or if there are changes on repeat IVP or ultrasound, needle aspiration with evaluation of the aspirated fluid for cytology can be performed. A renal cystogram following aspiration can provide additional valuable information. Although renal cell carcinoma may coexist within a simple cyst, this is a rare occurrence.

If the IVP or ultrasound examination demonstrates a lesion which does not satisfy the criteria for a benign, simple cyst, *computerized tomography* (CT) is the next modality employed. CT is comparable and possibly superior to selective renal arteriography in both diagnosing and staging renal cell carcinoma. In addition, CT is equivalent to selective renal arteriography in the determination of renal vein

involvement and superior to arteriography in determining whether regional nodes are enlarged (representing either tumor or hyperplasia) and/or the liver is involved. CT is the preferred modality for the diagnosis and staging of renal cell carcinoma. If, however, the findings on CT are equivocal or additional definition of vascular anatomy is required, renal arteriography should complement CT studies.

OTHER STUDIES Evaluation of urinary cytology is not useful in the diagnosis of renal adenocarcinomas. Retrograde pyelography may be a useful adjunct for opacifying the collecting systems that are not filled by standard IVP and may suggest the diagnosis of transitional cell carcinoma of the renal pelvis. In patients who present with hematuria and a renal mass, cystoscopy is an important adjunct to exclude the coexistence of an unsuspected urothelial tumor, such as carcinoma of the bladder.

If the diagnosis of renal cell carcinoma is considered likely, the patient should then undergo routine chest x-ray, bone scan, and liver function studies, in addition to the abdominal CT, to evaluate other potential sites of tumor spread.

Staging, primary treatment, and prognosis If there is no evidence of metastatic disease following the preoperative evaluation, the treatment of choice for renal cell carcinoma is radical nephrectomy. In addition to en bloc removal of the kidney with the surrounding Gerota's fascia, many urologic surgeons advocate regional lymphadenectomy to help determine prognosis. Preoperative arterial embolization of the main renal artery with a variety of agents may help to simplify the operative approach for large lesions. There is no role for localized pre- or postoperative radiation therapy.

Following surgical and pathologic evaluation, renal cell cancers are staged as follows: stage I, tumor confined within the kidney

FIGURE 231-1 *Diagnostic evaluation for renal mass.*

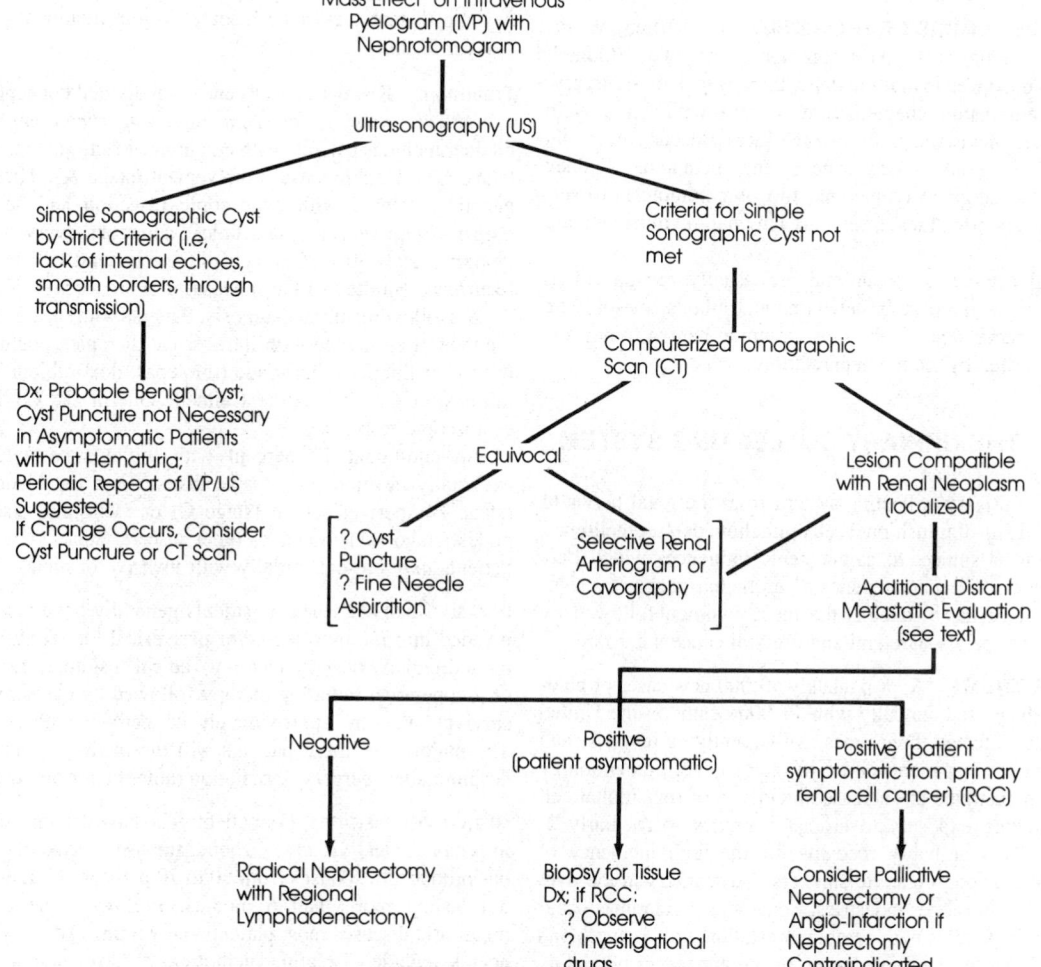

capsule; stage II, invasion through the renal capsule but confined within Gerota's fascia; stage III, involvement of regional lymph nodes, ipsilateral renal vein, or vena cava; stage IV, distant metastases. Five-year survival rates for stage I range from 60 to 75 percent; for stage II, 47 to 65 percent; for stage III without regional lymph node involvement, 25 to 50 percent; with regional lymph node involvement, 5 to 15 percent; for stage IV, less than 5 percent.

Systemic therapy for metastatic disease   There is no standard chemotherapeutic, hormonal, or immunologic program for patients with metastatic renal cancer. Although early reports demonstrated a favorable effect using progestational or androgenic agents, there seems to be very little role for hormonal therapy of renal cell carcinoma. Commonly employed chemotherapy programs include the use of vinblastine sulfate, with or without the use of nitrosoureas. Interferons have been used with limited success. The systemic management of patients with renal adenocarcinoma remains investigational, and entry of patients into phase II clinical trials is encouraged.

Selected surgical management of patients with metastatic disease   There is little wisdom in hoping for spontaneous regression of metastases by removing the kidney of a patient who presents with stage IV renal cell carcinoma who is otherwise asymptomatic. If, however, the primary lesion is associated with pain, bleeding, or other paraneoplastic phenomena, it is sometimes useful to remove the primary tumor or consider angioinfarction for local therapy despite the presence of metastatic disease. In patients who have had renal cell cancer in the past who then present with an isolated pulmonary or central nervous system metastasis, it is often useful to surgically resect these metastases. Generally, patients selected for surgical nodulectomy have been disease-free for at least 1 year from the original diagnosis to the time of metastatic development and have tumors which demonstrate a slow doubling time.

MISCELLANEOUS TUMORS OF THE KIDNEY   In children, Wilms tumor (nephroblastoma) is the most common cancer of the kidney. These tumors respond well to multimodality therapy including surgery, radiation, and combination chemotherapy, usually with actinomycin D and vincristine. Metastatic lesions to the kidney occur commonly in patients with lung and breast cancer, and melanoma. Kidney involvement with malignant lymphoma, too, is common; however, functional renal abnormalities from parenchymal involvement are unusual.

Benign renal tumors do occur and are usually recognized as incidental findings at autopsy. In newborns and infants, mesoblastic nephroma (fetal hamartoma) is the most common benign tumor and is successfully treated by simple nephrectomy.

TUMORS OF THE URINARY COLLECTING SYSTEM

The lining of the urinary collecting system from the renal pelvis to the urethra is made up of transitional cell epithelium or "urothelium." This entire lining is subject to carcinogenic influences which may explain the multicentric characteristics of urothelial neoplasms. Numerically, cancer of the bladder is the most common followed by tumors of the renal pelvis. Ureteral and urethral cancers are rare.

BLADDER CARCINOMA   Approximately 40,000 new cases of bladder cancer are diagnosed annually with 11,000 deaths in the United States. Males are affected three times as frequently as females, and the disease is unusual in patients under 40 years of age. Epidemiology studies have demonstrated an increased incidence of transitional cell carcinoma following exposure to aromatic amines, particularly 2-naphthylamine. This probably accounts for the high incidence of urothelial cancers among cigarette smokers and workers in the dye, chemical, and certain rubber industries. Squamous carcinomas occur more frequently in patients with chronic infestation with *Schistosoma haematobium*. Long-term administration of the anticancer alkylating agent cyclophosphamide, which is metabolized to the active com-

pounds acrolein and phosphoramide mustard, has been associated with the development of urothelial neoplasms.

Clinical features   While gross and microscopic hematuria are the most common presenting complaints, other features include dysuria, urinary frequency, or urgency, which may be the only manifestations of bladder carcinoma, and the persistence of these symptoms in a previously asymptomatic patient deserves careful attention. Other manifestations, such as ureteral obstruction, pelvic pain, or symptoms from visceral or osseous metastases, occur in a minority of patients at presentation.

Diagnosis and staging   Urinary cytology, obtained by bladder washing, catheterized or voided urine, IVP, and cystoscopic evaluation with tumor biopsies and selected mucosal biopsies, as well as bimanual examination under anesthesia, have been the mainstays for diagnosis of bladder cancer. Findings on IVP which suggest a bladder carcinoma include unilateral or bilateral ureteral obstruction with hydronephrosis, filling defect, or lack of distensibility of the bladder. Additional staging information may be obtained with abdominal or pelvic CT scanning. Following endoscopic resection of a bladder neoplasm, the depth of penetration into the bladder wall is assessed. If additional staging workup, including physical examination, chest x-ray, and routine serum chemistries, are within normal limits, the patient is clinically staged, based upon the cystoscopic biopsy, as having either *superficial* or *invasive* disease. Additional information about perivesical extension or nodal metastases can be obtained at the time of cystectomy and indicates the true pathologic stage of disease. A substantial number of patients who are clinically staged endoscopically as having muscle-invasive disease will have occult lymphatic or distant metastases if pathologically staged at the time of cystectomy. Such occult micrometastatic disease indicates systemic involvement and accounts for the high percentage of patients who eventually develop distant metastatic disease despite treatment of the primary bladder lesion.

Treatment   Bladder cancer can be subdivided conceptually as being *superficial, invasive,* or *metastatic. Superficial carcinoma* of the bladder includes patients with carcinoma in situ, mucosal involvement (stage O), or submucosal involvement (stage A). These patients are generally treated with endoscopic resection and selected bladder biopsies with repeat cystoscopic evaluations every 3 to 6 months. Approximately 50 to 70 percent of these patients will have a superficial recurrence (limited to the mucosa or submucosa) within a period of 3 years following initial diagnosis. Patients with superficial recurrences are then often treated with intravesical therapies, including N,N',N''-triethylenethiophosphoramide (thiotepa), doxorubicin hydrochloride, mitomycin C, or bacillus Calmette-Guérin (BCG) in addition to cystoscopic resection.

An additional 12 percent with initial superficial disease will eventually develop progressive disease into the bladder muscularis (stage B), perivesical fat (stage C) or metastatic disease to lymph nodes (stage D1), bone, or other viscera (stage D2). Alternatively, patients may present initially with invasive or metastatic disease.

INVASIVE DISEASE   These patients generally have disease which has invaded into the muscle and/or perivesical fat. Traditional treatment modalities have been cystectomy (radical or simple), radiation therapy, or preoperative radiation therapy followed by cystectomy. Five-year survival rates are approximately 45 percent with such treatments. The majority of these patients will die of distant metastatic disease despite radical surgery or radiation rather than from local recurrences.

METASTATIC DISEASE   For patients who have distant metastatic disease in lymph nodes, viscera, or bone, the use of systemic chemotherapy has produced responses from 30 to 70 percent of patients, but usually not lasting more than 6 months. Following the development of metastatic disease, most patients die within 2 years. The most active agents include cisplatin, methotrexate, doxorubicin hydrochloride, cyclophosphamide, and vinblastine, and combinations of these agents have recently produced meaningful and durable remissions. One current therapeutic strategy for patients with invasive disease consists of initiating chemotherapy followed by definitive local treatment to the bladder (surgery or radiation). The goal of such programs is to eradicate micrometastases which are commonly present in patients with invasive disease.

TRANSITIONAL CELL CANCER OF THE RENAL PELVIS Renal pelvic tumors account for approximately 10 percent of all primary renal cancer. Nearly 90 percent are transitional cell carcinomas. In addition to the etiologic associations implicated for bladder carcinoma, renal pelvic tumors occur with analgesic abuse nephropathy. These patients are usually middle-aged women with a psychiatric history or chronic headaches who ingest >3 kg of analgesics over years. The exact amount and type of analgesic which induces transitional cell cancer of the renal pelvis is unknown, although aspirin and/or phenacetin can induce the disease experimentally. Balkan nephropathy (see also Chap. 226) is associated with a high incidence of renal pelvic and ureteral tumors, especially in women.

Most patients present with painless, gross hematuria. Ureteral obstruction and pain secondary to clots are unusual. The diagnosis is suggested by IVP, which may demonstrate an obstructed, poorly functioning, or nonvisualized kidney or filling defects in a visualized kidney, and a positive urinary cytology. Cystoscopy and retrograde pyelography with brush biopsy generally will establish the nature and location of the renal pelvic or ureteral tumor. For low-grade, low-stage tumors, conservative treatment with local excision and preservation of the kidney parenchyma has been associated with very favorable 5-year survival rates. For high-stage, high-grade lesions, the treatment of choice is radical nephroureterectomy and removal of the cuff of the bladder containing the ipsilateral ureteral orifice. This latter operative approach has been dictated by the high likelihood of recurrence in the ureteral stump and orifice if the ureter or orifice are not removed. In addition, routine follow-up with cystoscopies and urinary cytologies are mandatory to help detect the subsequent development of metachronous bladder carcinomas and/or contralateral ureteral and renal pelvic tumors. Five-year survival rates range from 10 to 50 percent. Although chemotherapy programs employed for bladder cancer have been used for patients with metastatic transitional cell carcinoma of the renal pelvis, the overall results are not as successful.

REFERENCES

CHISHOLM GD, ROY RR: The systemic effects of malignant renal tumors. Br J Urol 43:687, 1971

CRONIN RE et al: Renal cell carcinoma: Unusual systemic manifestations. Medicine 55:291, 1976

GARNICK MB (ed): *Genitourinary Cancer. Contemporary Issues in Clinical Oncology,* vol 5. New York, Churchill Livingstone, 1985

————, RICHIE JP: Renal neoplasia, in *The Kidney,* 3d ed, BM Brenner, FC Rector Jr (eds). Philadelphia, Saunders, 1986, p 1533

HENEY NM et al: Superficial bladder cancer: Progression and recurrence. J Urol 130:1083, 1983

PATHAK S et al: Familial renal cell carcinoma with a 3;11 chromosome translocation limited to tumor cells. Science 217:939, 1982

RICHIE JP et al: Computed tomography scan for diagnosis and staging of renal cell carcinoma. J Urol 129:1114, 1983

RIESELBACH RE, GARNICK MB (eds): *Cancer and the Kidney.* Philadelphia, Lea & Febiger, 1982

SKINNER DG et al: Diagnosis and management of renal cell carcinoma. A clinical and pathologic study of 309 cases. Cancer 28:1165, 1971

WHITMORE WF JR (ed): Urothelial tumors. Semin Oncol 1:1, 1983

section 1 Disorders of the alimentary tract

232 APPROACH TO THE PATIENT WITH GASTROINTESTINAL DISEASE

KURT J. ISSELBACHER / ROGER J. MAY

GENERAL CONSIDERATIONS Gastrointestinal symptoms occur not only with primary gastrointestinal tract disease but frequently as manifestations of other organic and functional disorders. Thus anorexia, nausea, and vomiting may be seen in patients with anxiety or depression, congestive failure, and uremia; diarrhea or constipation may be seen as a consequence of metabolic derangements such as electrolyte changes or alterations in thyroid function. With advances in medical technology, all too often physicians are willing to diagnose (or misdiagnose) gastrointestinal disease simply by relying on routine procedures such as x-ray studies of the upper and lower parts of the gastrointestinal tract. Such an overwhelming dependence on technical procedures often leads to great pitfalls. It cannot be overemphasized that the proper initial approach still demands a carefully obtained history and thorough physical examination before proceeding with any diagnostic tests.

IMPORTANCE OF THE HISTORY To evaluate gastrointestinal symptoms, a careful history is crucial. Pain or indigestion is the most common intestinal complaint. Correlation between pain and gastrointestinal function must of necessity be chronologic. There should be a meticulous inquiry as to the frequency and specificity of the complaint. The questioning should include the location of the pain and whether it is circumscribed or diffuse. It is important to determine what factors aggravate or relieve the discomfort. *Does eating produce the symptom?* If so, determine whether the discomfort occurs *while eating* (as in esophageal disorders and abdominal angina), shortly *after the meal* (as often occurs in biliary tract disease), or *30 to 90 min later* (as typically seen with peptic ulcer). *Does eating relieve the symptom,* and if so, for how long? Temporary relief of epigastric pain is characteristic of gastritis and peptic ulceration. Many patients have tried or taken antacids by the time they come to the physician, and a history indicating relief of epigastric pain by antacids is suggestive of peptic disease of the upper part of the intestine. *What is the relation of pain to bowel movements?* The patient with ulcerative colitis often obtains temporary relief from lower abdominal cramps by defecation.

Attention should be paid to *anorexia* and *weight loss;* their combined occurrence should make one suspicious of an underlying depression as well as of an occult malignancy. If *weight* loss is accompanied by an increased appetite, one must consider the diagnosis of malabsorption or maldigestion as well as of a hypermetabolic state, such as thyrotoxicosis. If *diarrhea* is present, one should determine the average number of the stools, their consistency, and their timing.

To some patients, diarrhea means an increased number of stools, even though they are relatively normal in consistency; to others, diarrhea means watery stools. The occurrence of nocturnal diarrhea is suggestive of organic rather than functional bowel disease. In a patient with diarrhea one should ask about stool *odor* (malodorous stools being typical of pancreatic insufficiency and sprue), change in stool *color* (light-colored stools are seen with steatorrhea or cholestasis), and whether blood or mucus has been noted (blood is characteristic of inflammatory bowel disease or infectious dysentery but is hardly ever noted in functional bowel disease).

In the evaluation of male patients, especially those with diarrhea, a tactful inquiry into sexual activity is essential. Homosexual males are at increased risk for a large variety of gastrointestinal infections as well as the acquired immunodeficiency syndrome, which may present with gastrointestinal symptoms. Finally, careful attention must be given to a "drug history." Unless asked, patients may forget to mention that they take aspirin almost daily for headache, and this may indeed account for occult blood in the stool. Many patients take daily laxatives, which may explain chronic diarrhea and colonic changes on x-ray. Still others may be taking illicit drugs, and this history may be difficult to obtain.

PHYSICAL EXAMINATION, ENDOSCOPY, AND RADIOLOGY A vague history of abdominal distress may be brought into focus by a thorough physical examination. Upper abdominal distress together with tenderness in the right upper quadrant suggests that cholecystitis or hepatitis may be present. In a young patient, a history of intermittent abdominal pain together with a palpable mass or tender loop of bowel in the right lower quadrant should make one suspicious of regional enteritis. All too often, however, in gastrointestinal diseases the routine physical examination is negative, and other techniques for examining the intestine are needed. Among the techniques which should almost be routine as an extension of the physical examination is *sigmoidoscopy.* This procedure may be performed with the customary rigid instrument or with the flexible fiberoptic sigmoidoscope. Sigmoidoscopy is important in the diagnosis of colonic cancer because (1) 50 percent or more of large-intestine malignancies are within the reach of the sigmoidoscope; and (2) small rectosigmoid tumors may be missed on barium enema examination because of the tortuosity and redundancy of the intestine in this area. Sigmoidoscopy also permits inspection of the mucosa for edema, erythema, friability, or ulceration. In a patient with diarrhea due to nonspecific causes, the mucosa may be normal; with dysentery due to agents such as *Shigella,* the mucosa may be friable, edematous, and hyperemic; if the latter findings are combined with extensive ulcerations, ulcerative or amebic colitis may be present. In almost all patients with diarrhea, sigmoidoscopy should be done before barium studies.

As discussed in Chap. 233, the use of fiberoptic instruments has assumed increasing importance in the assessment of patients with gastrointestinal disorders. Routine upper gastrointestinal endoscopy permits evaluation of the esophagus, stomach, and duodenum, while the colonoscope permits direct inspection of the entire large bowel and frequently the terminal ileum. The appropriate use of these techniques with respect to the more limited examination obtained via a rigid or flexible sigmoidoscope remains to be fully clarified. Specialized fiberoptic instruments may be used to identify the ampulla of Vater, permitting peroral opacification of pancreatic and/or biliary ducts (ERCP). These techniques and their related merits are discussed in detail in Chap. 233. Increasingly, fiberoptic examination is supplementing conventional radiologic studies, permitting direct visual inspection and the opportunity to obtain samples for microbiologic and histologic studies.

The roles of endoscopic versus radiologic examination remains an area of debate. While routine barium studies remain the most effective way to assess mucosal and other structural lesions in the small intestine, increasingly, proximal and distal portions of the GI tract are more efficiently studied for the presence of anatomic disease using fiberoptic instruments. However, these tools are not useful in assessing GI tract motility, which can be more effectively appreciated fluoroscopically or by using manometric techniques. With the decreasing use of conventional x-ray studies, other modalities have become increasingly important. These newer techniques include most notably ultrasound (US), computed tomography (CT), and radionuclide scanning. Both US and CT are useful in the delineation of abdominal mass lesions. While the latter is more expensive, it may be more effective in evaluation of the lower abdomen. Both are useful in the assessment of the structure and function of the gallbladder and bile ducts, but lower cost and lack of ionizing radiation tends to make US preferable.

While the use of barium studies has diminished, these x-rays continue to play a role in GI tract evaluation. In preparing a patient for *barium enema,* preparation or prior cleansing is important for a proper examination, but the physician must keep in mind that with obstructing lesions of the colon or small intestine or in the presence of active ulcerative colitis, the use of strong cathartics may be hazardous and even life-threatening. *No x-ray preparation should be considered routine.* In fact, the barium examination itself may aggravate an acute ulcerative colitis or precipitate colonic perforation or the onset of toxic megacolon. Similarly, if partial obstruction of the intestine is detected by plain x-ray of the abdomen, the physician must be wary of introducing barium from above for fear of producing further or complete intestinal obstruction. In patients with active GI bleeding, barium studies should be avoided lest they preclude subsequent angiographic evaluation.

Consultation with the radiologist   Finally, one cannot overemphasize the importance of providing the radiologist with as much information as possible about the nature of the disease process under investigation. This will focus the attention of the radiologist on the appropriate region of the GI tract and optimize the information gained from the study.

All too often the busy physician allows a negative x-ray report to be the decisive factor in the diagnosis. It is essential to recognize the limitations of any diagnostic modality. With regard to routine radiologic studies, a negative barium enema may simply reflect that too much fecal material has been retained in the colon or that the area of concern was never well visualized. Similarly, if the patient has typical symptoms of biliary colic, the physician should not discard the diagnosis merely because of a negative x-ray report.

On the other hand the physician must be able to determine whether the abnormal finding is causally related to the symptoms. This is especially true in older patients where the presence of a hiatus hernia, gallstones, or diverticulosis is not unusual and hence may be coincidental.

DIAGNOSTIC APPROACHES   Problems of swallowing   The approach should be as follows:

1 *Careful visual and neurologic examination* of the pharynx, with tests for myasthenia gravis if indicated.

2 *Routine esophageal x-rays* in the upright and lateral or Trendelenburg position. The horizontal views are essential for demonstration of the swallowing mechanism, unaided by gravity, and of the esophagogastric junction. For details of the pharyngoesophageal area cineradiography is necessary because of the rapidity with which the contrast media passes through. Hiatus hernia is extremely common (in 15 to 35 percent of persons over 50) and often asymptomatic unless spontaneous reflux of gastric contents can be demonstrated to occur repeatedly.

3 *Esophagoscopy.* This procedure is desirable to describe lesions suggested by x-ray or, if the lesion is unsuspected, to obtain biopsies from masses or abnormal mucosa and to obtain washings for exfoliative cytologic study. The diagnosis of peptic esophagitis is best made endoscopically. Esophageal varices can be identified by this approach when they are too small to be seen radiologically, although the latter technique will pick up 70 percent of large varices.

4 *Manometric studies* of the upper esophagus, particularly in conjunction with cineradiography. At present, this procedure offers the best differential between disorders primary in the central nervous system, primary pharyngeal muscular disease, and cricopharyngeal dystonia. Manometry of the lower esophagus is useful in the diagnosis of diffuse esophageal spasm, achalasia, and infiltrative diseases which can alter esophageal motility.

Peptic or digestive disorders   The approaches to these disorders include:

1 *Insertion of a nasogastric tube.* This is used to establish whether significant gastric retention (more than 75 mL of gastric contents in the fasting state) exists, and whether there is acid, bile, blood, or other material in these contents. If pyloric obstruction or gastric atony is present, the tube is used to maintain suction while the patient's electrolyte and fluid balance is restored to normal; the stomach is kept as clean as possible so that reliable diagnostic investigation may be carried out.

2 *Upper intestinal endoscopy.* This procedure is most helpful in identifying the diffuseness of the mucosal response in gastritis or, together with biopsy and brushings for cytology, in differentiating between peptic and neoplastic ulcerating lesions. Gastroscopy may permit the diagnosis of superficial erosive gastritis and the Mallory-Weiss syndrome as a cause of bleeding when the x-ray examination is negative. It may identify a specific bleeding site in clinical situations where several potential bleeding sites could exist, such as in the patient with portal hypertension. Gastroscopy is also particularly helpful in inspecting the postoperative stomach, especially in detecting stomal ulceration or alkaline reflux gastritis. The first and second portions of the duodenum can also be examined with the fiberoptic gastroscope, and important information about ulcers and other lesions can be obtained by this procedure. Radiologic studies may be useful when endoscopy is not readily available or in the assessment of suspected motility disorders (e.g. gastroparesis). In addition, radiologic examination may be preferred when there are contraindications to safe endoscopy.

3 *Gastric acid secretory studies.* These are useful in the diagnosis of the Zollinger-Ellison syndrome or atrophic gastritis and for determination of completeness of vagotomy. Suspected gastric carcinoma is better diagnosed directly through gastroscopy and biopsy than indirectly through acid secretory studies (achlorhydria). They should not be obtained for the routine diagnosis of uncomplicated duodenal ulcer. There is no convincing evidence that acid studies are useful in determining the type of surgery for duodenal ulcer.

Obstructive and vascular disorders of the small intestine   When intestinal problems present as obstructive syndromes, the plain x-ray of the abdomen is the most important diagnostic adjunct to careful physical examination. Patterns of dilatation of individual loops of intestine may be characteristic, as in volvulus or acute pancreatitis; erect and decubitus views will often show fluid levels in the affected segments. Motility disorders of the small intestine (pseudo obstruction) may also present with obstructive symptoms and similar x-ray findings but must be managed medically without surgical intervention. Air under the diaphragm is diagnostic of a perforated viscus; air in the portal vein usually results from intestinal necrosis secondary to mesenteric vascular occlusion. The diagnostic accuracy of the plain x-ray in all types of intestinal obstruction is about 75 percent. In patients with symptoms of incomplete obstruction, the radiographic small-bowel series will often be diagnostic in defining the site and degree of obstruction. Infrequently, in this setting, all conventional x-ray studies are unremarkable. In such cases, the radiologist may perform a small-bowel enteroclysis study by passing a special tube into the proximal jejunum; the rapid instillation of barium through the tube will distend the intestine and often reveal subtle lesions missed by other tests.

Vascular diseases of the small intestine are among the most difficult diseases to diagnose. In chronic mesenteric ischemia, radiographic, endoscopic, and laboratory tests are usually normal. Early in the course of acute mesenteric ischemia, the plain film of the abdomen may be unremarkable despite complaints of severe abdominal pain. In these settings, prompt mesenteric angiography is essential in confirming the diagnosis of vascular disease.

Inflammatory and neoplastic diseases of small and large intestine Patients with these conditions are usually identified by history, physical examination, and careful examination of the stools for exudate and blood. Sigmoidoscopy is valuable in identifying mucosal and neoplastic lesions of the lower 25 cm of the colon. The mucosal surface of the entire colon and terminal ileum can be examined directly and biopsied through the fiberoptic sigmoidoscope or colonoscope. The radiologic examination of the small intestine is highly reliable in identifying the prestenotic and stenotic lesions of Crohn's disease. In the colon a single examination in a well-prepared patient has a diagnostic accuracy of 80 to 85 percent; the addition of air-contrast technique brings the accuracy up over 90 percent, but none of these figures is meaningful if the patient is poorly prepared for the examination. In the demonstration of small polyps the degree of accuracy is understandably not so high, but for polyps larger than 1 cm, which are of greater clinical importance, it is satisfactory. The cecal area is the hardest to examine adequately because of its anatomy; colonoscopy may be preferable. The immunologic assay for the carcinoembryonic antigen has not proved to be specific for colonic cancer; nevertheless, it does contribute to the evaluation of the extent of tumor and to the detection of residual or recurrent disease in postoperative patients.

Peroral biopsy of the small intestine and forceps biopsy of the rectosigmoid are of considerable importance in revealing mucosal disease. Rectal biopsy is an excellent means of demonstrating amyloidosis, schistosomiasis, and amebiasis. Submucosal disease is not seen in these superficial biopsies. Hirschsprung's disease is histologically diagnosed by a deep surgical biopsy of the lower part of the rectum.

Malabsorption syndromes Malabsorption may be suspected on the basis of history and physical examination and is confirmed by examination of the stools. Radiologic examination is of general help in ruling out local lesions and suggesting motor and secretory dysfunction, but it is rarely diagnostic unless an abnormal small-bowel mucosa or fistulas between intestine and stomach are demonstrated.

The tests useful in the diagnosis of malabsorption are discussed in Chap. 237. A simple screening test for excessive fat in the stools can be accomplished by the microscopic examination of a stool specimen stained with Sudan. Chemical analysis of 3-day stool collection for fat, with the patient on a standard diet, is used to establish the diagnosis of steatorrhea. The D-xylose absorption test is about 90 percent accurate in separating mucosal disease from pancreatic insufficiency. Peroral biopsy of the small intestine is of value in the diagnosis of celiac disease, and it may show the less

common infiltrations of the mucosa by amyloid or bacterial mucoproteins (Whipple's disease). Leakage of protein into the intestinal lumen may cause hypoproteinemia and can be demonstrated by the recovery in stools of intravenously administered markers such as albumin labeled with iodine or chromium isotopes.

Pancreas The pancreas is difficult to study directly because of its anatomic location and relative inaccessibility. Calcification of the pancreas on a plain abdominal film is highly suggestive of chronic pancreatitis and may be associated with fat malabsorption. Pancreatic exocrine insufficiency can be documented by intubation of the duodenum and collection of pancreatic juice after stimulation with secretin or a test meal. Abdominal ultrasound and CT are the best radiographic means of searching for pancreatic enlargement (see Chaps. 254 and 255). Both techniques may also be used to guide needle biopsies of the pancreas and may provide sufficient diagnostic information to obviate the need for exploratory surgery. The pancreatic duct can be cannulated via the fiberoptic duodenoscope and visualized by the injection of radiographic dye. Visualization of the duct may be helpful in the diagnosis of pancreatic pseudocysts, carcinoma, or chronic pancreatitis.

233 GASTROINTESTINAL ENDOSCOPY

FRED E. SILVERSTEIN

Fiberendoscopes have revolutionized the examination of the gastrointestinal tract. Because of the flexibility of the fiberoptic bundles and because of controllability of the instrument tip, the operator can steer the instrument around multiple bends under visual control. A side channel permits passage of a variety of endoscopic tools such as biopsy forceps, foreign-body forceps, cytology brushes, wash tubes, and electrocautery snares. The viewing window and the light at the instrument's distal end can be washed free of obscuring material. Fluid can be aspirated from hollow organs, and air can be insufflated as needed to improve visualization. A new development is the video endoscope in which a miniature TV camera transmits the image which appears on a TV screen. This system permits storage, analysis, and transmission of the endoscopic images.

The usefulness of fiberendoscopy in diagnosing gastrointestinal disease is well established. Shallow lesions such as erosions or healing ulcers are missed by single-contrast x-ray but not by endoscopy. The brilliant success of polypectomy via the colonoscope has led to the development of other endoscopic techniques which are beginning to replace some invasive surgical techniques; the most significant advances in the future will probably be in this area.

Although esophagogastroduodenoscopy (EGD) is not a procedure for the occasional operator, it should be available in every general hospital. It is a relatively easy procedure to perform technically, but training and continued experience are necessary for optimal diagnostic accuracy. Complications are most frequent when the operator is inexperienced. Before the procedure the competent endoscopist always takes a history and examines the patient. Prior evaluation of cardiac status and clotting mechanisms is also essential.

The more complex procedures such as colonoscopy and endoscopic retrograde cholangiopancreatography (ERCP) require special dexterity, a substantial investment of time for learning, and constant practice to maintain adequate skill; they are probably best accomplished by subspecialists. Colonoscopy, one hopes, will be simplified so that it can be as widely available as esophagogastroduodenoscopy.

UPPER GASTROINTESTINAL ENDOSCOPY Forward-viewing, oblique, and side-viewing instruments may be used for EGD. After a careful explanation of the procedure to the patient, pharyngeal topical anesthesia with viscous lidocaine is followed by intravenous diazepam to the point of mild sedation. With the newer, small-caliber instruments less or no diazepam is needed. The tip of the endoscope is placed at the upper cricopharyngeal sphincter of the esophagus and the patient is encouraged to swallow while gentle pressure is exerted. Small amounts of air are passed through the endoscope to visualize the esophageal lumen. The endoscope is then passed under direct vision into the stomach. The gastric body and antrum are carefully examined. The instrument tip is retroflexed to view the gastric cardia, the fundus, and the whole lesser curvature. The pylorus is traversed, and the first and second portions of the duodenum are visualized. The whole examination is repeated as the instrument is withdrawn. Visualized lesions can be recorded on still photographs, movies, or videotape. Biopsies and brush cytologic examinations can be obtained from suspicious areas.

EGD is a relatively safe procedure in experienced hands. Several large surveys suggest a risk of serious complications during diagnostic EGD of approximately 1 in 800 and a risk of death of approximately 1 in 5000. The risks are higher in emergency procedures and in the elderly or seriously ill. In a survey of patients examined by endoscopy during bleeding, 1 in 200 had serious complications and 1 in 700 died from the procedure. A nationwide survey revealed a morbidity of 0.13 percent and a mortality of 0.004 percent. The main causes of mortality were cardiopulmonary complications and perforations by the instrument. Upper endoscopy is usually substituted for x-ray in the urgent diagnosis of gastrointestinal illness in women who might be pregnant.

Peptic regurgitant esophagitis   Esophagitis is one of the commonest benign diseases of the upper gastrointestinal tract (see Chap. 234). Esophageal pain may be confused with cardiac disease, or esophagitis may present as painless blood loss. Because esophagitis usually involves only the superficial mucosa, it cannot be diagnosed by routine single-contrast x-ray. At endoscopy, the diffuse bleeding, linear erosions, friability, and ulcerations of erosive esophagitis are clearly visible. Not every patient with heartburn requires esophagoscopy, but the procedure is indicated if the patient complains of dysphagia, if an x-ray shows a stricture, a mass, or an ulcer, if symptoms persist despite therapy, or if antireflux surgery is contemplated.

The squamous mucosa of the esophagus is far more vulnerable to peptic digestion than is the columnar epithelium of the stomach. Thus, bleeding esophagitis is located on the squamous side of the esophagogastric junction and is most severe in the distal esophagus where the squamous mucosa is most exposed to regurgitated acid and pepsin from the stomach. Discrete peptic ulceration of the esophagus is uncommon.

A short area of esophagitis or a stricture can be seen at levels as high as the arch of the aorta. This is explained by progressive replacement of distal eroded squamous mucosa with metaplastic epithelium, which is more resistant to peptic digestion (Barrett's epithelium). This finding can be documented by biopsy. Such epithelium is more prone to malignant transformation and, therefore, may merit regular surveillance with esophagoscopy and biopsy and/or exfoliative cytology every 12 to 24 months.

Esophagitis may progress to scarring and stricture formation. The endoscopic appearance of a benign stricture is characteristic but not diagnostic because a malignancy can be missed; this should be ruled out before medical treatment is undertaken with dilation and antacids. The whole length of the stricture should therefore be sampled by biopsy and cytologic brushing to rule out cancer, if necessary, at repeat endoscopy after dilation. Endoscopy is often indicated in an esophageal ulcer, with biopsy of the rim of the ulcer to rule out cancer.

Dilations of difficult strictures are best initiated by passing a flexible-tipped guide wire via the side channel of the endoscope through the stricture under direct vision. The endoscope can then be withdrawn over the wire, which serves as a guide for passage of progressively larger metal olives or other dilators through the stricture

under fluoroscopic control. A new technique utilizes balloon catheters passed via the endoscope channel or over a guide wire through the stricture. The balloon is inflated under endoscopic and/or fluoroscopic guidance to dilate the stricture.

Peptic ulcer   Esophagogastroduodenoscopy is more accurate than upper gastrointestinal x-ray in detecting ulcers. It has been suggested that x-ray be abandoned entirely in favor of endoscopy for detecting ulcers. This makes sense when the source of acute upper gastrointestinal bleeding is sought if urgent surgical intervention is being considered; in such situations, obscuring barium would make endoscopy impossible. However, in the workup of the patient with less pressing ulcer complaints, an upper gastrointestinal x-ray is still often used as the initial diagnostic test. As more radiologists routinely use air contrast to obtain better mucosal detail, diagnostic sensitivity for superficial lesions will increase. The greater expense and discomfort of endoscopy are justified if the x-ray is equivocal, if the ulcer is possibly malignant, if the x-ray is negative but the clinical picture is suggestive of peptic ulceration, or if the patient is about to be operated on for ulcer and there is a need to be sure that an ulcer is present and that other lesions have not been missed. Patients with duodenal ulcers shown by x-ray or with classic ulcer deformities of the duodenal bulb do not require endoscopy for diagnosis if the presenting symptoms are characteristic and if the symptomatic response to strict antiulcer treatment is good. Some feel that screening endoscopy using the new small-diameter endoscopes may be the preferable initial diagnostic approach to the symptomatic patient. These instruments can be passed easily, often without sedation, for rapid and complete upper gastrointestinal examinations. When used in this manner the cost of the endoscopy should be reduced.

There are some situations in which x-ray reveals ulcers missed by endoscopy, e.g., ulcers in hourglass constrictions of the stomach or in small duodenal bulbs incompletely visualized by currently available instruments. Fiberendoscopy is especially useful in visualizing postbulbar ulcers, giant duodenal ulcers, and stomal ulceration after partial gastrectomy, all of which can be missed by x-ray. Endoscopy may be of use in determining the cause of gastric outlet obstruction. In most circumstances, patients with duodenal ulcers do not need follow-up endoscopy to see if the ulcer has healed.

In the enthusiasm for fiberendoscopy one must not forget that visual interpretation of gross pathology is subjective—one observer's ulcer is another's erosion. An erosion is confined to the mucosa and heals without a trace, whereas an ulcer is deeper and usually implies a chronic recurrent disease. Endoscopically, erosions are superficial, small, and multiple; ulcers are deeper and larger and tend to be solitary. In the future it is likely that lesions seen endoscopically will be easily recorded for review on videotape or disk, just as currently all lesions seen fluoroscopically are demonstrated in spot films.

Cancer   The endoscopic appearance of upper gastrointestinal cancer may seem obvious, especially if there is a mass growing into the lumen. On the other hand, malignant ulcers, infiltrative carcinomas, or small early carcinomas are frequently impossible to diagnose by their gross appearance. The biopsies obtained with currently available forceps are very small, and deeper lesions can be missed. Only one of multiple biopsies may reveal the cancer. Therefore, it is recommended that six to eight biopsies be taken from the rim of a gastric ulcer. A larger particle of tissue may be removed from a suspicious elevated mucosal lesion with an electrocautery snare or with a large biopsy forceps passed via the large channel of an endoscope, and this may facilitate diagnosis. Experience and skill in choosing the biopsy site improve the accuracy. A cytologic examination of the lavage or brush specimen adds to the diagnostic accuracy in all areas of the upper gastrointestinal tract (see Chap. 236).

It may be impossible to differentiate severe esophagitis from infiltrative cancer by the gross appearance at esophagoscopy. Biopsies from patients with cancer may show only the associated inflammation. Thus, all such lesions should have careful cytologic examination, either by lavage or by brushing. Because chronic inflammation may predispose to esophageal cancer, patients with lye stricture or the stasis esophagitis of achalasia merit esophagoscopy and cytologic examination when they are first seen and when periodically rescreened, or whenever their symptom patterns change.

Radiologic demonstration of healing of a benign-appearing gastric ulcer is very reassuring but not infallible in excluding cancer. A history of ingesting ulcerogenic drugs increases the likelihood of benignancy. Ulcers in such patients are followed to complete healing radiologically or endoscopically after treating the ulcer. Diagnostic accuracy in differentiating benign from malignant gastric ulcer by exfoliative cytologic lavage, endoscopic biopsy, or brush cytology depends on the combined skills of endoscopists, cytologists, and pathologists. Among North American communities accuracy in diagnosing cancer may vary from 70 to 90 percent. Physicians must individually decide which patients should be examined by methods that have proved accurate in their own community, and which patients should be referred to centers with greater resources.

Primary gastric lymphoma can mimic benign gastric ulcer or adenocarcinoma on gastroscopy or x-ray. It can be diagnosed by biopsy or cytology, although the accuracy is not as high as in adenocarcinoma. The 5-year survival for lymphoma is higher than for adenocarcinoma.

If a polypoid lesion of the stomach is covered by mucosa that appears normal by gastroscopy, the likelihood of malignancy is very small. Such lesions are often intramural, extramucosal benign tumors such as leiomyomas or pancreatic rests. Polyps covered by abnormal-appearing mucosa can be benign or malignant. Random biopsy can miss carcinoma within a polyp. If technically feasible, polyps should, therefore, be removed in their entirety by snare cautery for histologic examination. If over 2 cm in diameter, they are more likely to contain cancer (see Chap. 236). Large polyps may require surgical excision.

Ampullary carcinoma may be diagnosed by biopsy and brush cytology during duodenoscopy. Other primary duodenal malignancies are very rare. Extensions from pancreatic or biliary tract cancer are difficult to diagnose because the tumor may not have extended into the mucosa and may therefore not be accessible for endoscopic biopsy or cytologic examination. In these secondary tumors, diagnosis must depend upon some combination of echography, hypotonic duodenography, selective pancreatic angiography, and endoscopic retrograde cholangiopancreatography, with cytologic examination of ductal contents.

Upper gastrointestinal bleeding (see also Chap. 37) Endoscopy within the first 12 to 24 h of an upper gastrointestinal hemorrhage can be very helpful in planning rational therapy by visualizing the bleeding source. Shallow lesions not visible by x-ray may be seen (esophagitis, Mallory-Weiss tear, erosive gastritis, shallow stress ulcer, and telangiectasia). Lesions which are visible by x-ray may not be the source of bleeding. Only endoscopy can determine the actual bleeding site. For example, visualization of a spurting artery which is flooding the stomach indicates massive ongoing bleeding requiring prompt therapeutic intervention. Several studies have shown that the demonstration at endoscopy of any bleeding whatsoever or a nonbleeding vessel in the ulcer base makes rebleeding more likely.

A conservative estimate of the diagnostic accuracy of emergency endoscopy in upper gastrointestinal bleeding is 80 to 85 percent, which is far superior to emergency x-ray examination. Endoscopic diagnosis of bleeding erosive gastritis may be made too frequently when blood from another unsuspected source spreads over the gastric mucosa or when trauma from overly vigorous antecedent lavage creates submucosal ecchymoses. To avoid overdiagnosis of erosive gastritis, portions of the gastric wall should be washed free of blood to determine the true appearance of the underlying gastric mucosa.

Every patient having endoscopy for upper gastrointestinal bleeding merits a complete endoscopic examination of the esophagus, stomach, and duodenum. Finding a potential bleeding lesion is not proof that this is the source of hemorrhage unless active bleeding is seen. Approximately one-half of patients with esophageal varices can be shown endoscopically to be bleeding from another source such as erosive gastritis, duodenal ulcer, or gastric ulcer. Occasionally it is not possible to diagnose the exact lesion which is bleeding, but localizing the area of bleeding can be very helpful; for example, bright red arterial blood may be seen pouring into the stomach from the duodenum when the esophagus and stomach are relatively free of blood.

There are three controversial areas. First, *do all bleeders need endoscopy?* The author feels that endoscopy is indicated in all patients who may require surgery because of continual bleeding or rebleeding. Although 85 percent of upper gastrointestinal bleeders stop spontaneously, it is impossible to predict which ones will; therefore, endoscopy is recommended for most bleeders. Second, *how early should endoscopy be performed in the acutely bleeding patient?* Most studies suggest that the diagnostic accuracy of esophagogastroduodenoscopy remains high for the first 12 to 24 h after the bleeding episode. All would agree that it is desirable to delay endoscopy until vital signs have been stabilized after adequate blood replacement. Upper endoscopy is usually performed during waking hours at a time during the first day of bleeding when the patient's vital signs are stable and when the full endoscopic team is available. Emergency endoscopy at night should be reserved for those patients with continued massive bleeding or rebleeding requiring an immediate decision regarding surgery or other treatment. If the patient is exsanguinating, endoscopy can follow induction of anesthesia just preceding surgery. Thus, the patient's airway is protected by an endotracheal tube. Finally, *does endoscopy affect the clinical outcome?* Current studies suggest that it does not. This may be more a reflection on the inadequacies of medical therapy and the dangers of nonelective surgical treatment of bleeding patients who are severely ill than on the usefulness of more accurate endoscopic detection of the bleeding source. If endoscopic or pharmacologic methods of stopping bleeding prove to be safe and effective in controlled trials, more accurate endoscopic diagnosis may indeed affect the outcome favorably. Endoscopic treatment of bleeding lesions with heater probes, bipolar probes, or lasers (Nd:YAG) is now being studied. The data suggest that these methods are effective and safe and may improve outcome in the bleeding patient.

Emergency endoscopy is not for the inexperienced. It requires considerable technical skill and interpretative experience and the best available instruments.

Other indications Upper endoscopy is usually substituted for x-ray in the urgent diagnosis of gastrointestinal illness in *pregnancy.* Patients with *dysphagia* merit esophagoscopy because the cause is frequently organic and may be missed by x-ray. Dysphagia caused by esophageal spasm or dysrhythmia is best diagnosed by manometry or cineradiography in addition to endoscopy. *Painful swallowing* (odynophagia), especially in immunosuppressed or diabetic patients, may merit esophagoscopy because biopsy and brushings of the involved esophageal wall may reveal monilial, herpetic, or cytomegalic virus infections. Soon after ingestion of a corrosive agent, if there is no indication of wall necrosis, limited and gentle esophagoscopy is useful in evaluating the severity of injury. Many impacted foreign bodies can be removed from the esophagus or stomach with a snare or forceps; sharp foreign bodies are usually best removed by pulling them into the lumen of a rigid tubular esophagoscope or by pulling them into a protective overtube around a fiberoptic endoscope. Careful esophagoscopy after removal of an esophageal foreign body is important to determine whether there is an underlying lesion which caused the impaction (e.g., cancer, benign stricture, peptic esophagitis).

In the postoperative stomach, gastroscopy is especially useful in detecting carcinoma, recurrent ulceration, retrograde intussusception, and stomal stricture. Several European studies indicate a definite threat of carcinoma developing in the gastric stump 10 to 20 years after a Billroth II gastrectomy. The diagnosis of such postoperative carcinomas may require many biopsies of seemingly normal mucosa near the anastomosis. Studies of the natural history of this condition in the United States do not suggest a similar high incidence of postoperative carcinoma.

When the duodenal bulb shows reddening or nodularity, many endoscopists diagnose *duodenitis*. There is little evidence to suggest that this picture is of significance. On the other hand, diffuse and bleeding erosions of the duodenal bulb merit a diagnosis of *erosive duodenitis*, especially after ingestion of gastric irritants such as aspirin; such erosions may also be a precursor of frank ulcerations. A nodular or narrow duodenum will occasionally yield granulomas on biopsy, indicative of Crohn's disease.

ENDOSCOPIC RETROGRADE CHOLANGIOPANCREATOGRAPHY (ERCP)

This endoscopic technique involves placing a side-viewing instrument in the descending duodenum. The papilla of Vater is cannulated, contrast medium is injected, and the pancreatic ducts and hepatobiliary tree are visualized radiologically. Skilled operators can visualize 90 to 95 percent of pancreatic ducts and 80 to 85 percent of biliary ducts.

ERCP is performed on an x-ray table. The oropharynx is usually anesthetized with topical lidocaine, and most endoscopists sedate the patient with intravenous diazepam. Atropine and glucagon are given intravenously to induce duodenal hypotonia. The pancreatic duct is usually visualized first and gently filled throughout its entire length with 2 to 5 mL contrast material with constant fluoroscopic monitoring (Fig. 233-1*A*). Injection is continued until the first side branches are seen or until the patient complains of pain. Overfilling is avoided. By insertion of the cannula at a more acute cephalad angle, the common bile duct and the whole biliary tract including the gallbladder are visualized (Fig. 233-1*B*).

At present not all indications for ERCP are clearly established. Those for the hepatobiliary tree are clearer than those for the pancreatic duct. Because ERCP is not without risk, it is justified only to seek an operable lesion or to prevent an unnecessary operation. As therapeutic procedures such as endoscopic papillotomy are being utilized increasingly, the diagnostic ERCP may be performed to determine if endoscopic treatment is indicated. This may be especially relevant in a patient with common duct stones and cholangitis. Asymptomatic amylase elevations occur in 30 to 40 percent of patients after the procedure and are rarely of clinical significance. Pancreatitis occurs in only 1 percent of patients but is usually benign and self-limited. By monitoring the pancreas during injection using a high-resolution TV screen, the force of injection can be limited to avoid filling of pancreatic acini. This probably minimizes the complication of pancreatitis. In a nationwide survey of complications, the morbidity rate was 3 percent and mortality rate 0.2 percent. It is significant that the complication rate was highest for the inexperienced operator (7 percent). The morbidity and mortality rates are substantially lower from large centers with great experience. The main serious complication is retention of nonsterile contrast material proximal to an obstructed duct, causing cholangitis or pancreatic sepsis. Patients suspected of having bile duct obstruction are started on systemic antibiotics prior to the ERCP. Furthermore, if bile duct or pancreatic duct obstruction is first revealed by ERCP, antibiotic coverage is indicated to reduce the incidence of bacteremia; such patients should be drained if possible either with endoscopic therapy (papillotomy, stents, nasobiliary drains, etc.) or surgically within 36 h. No patient should have ERCP unless advance arrangements for possible operation have been made with the patient and a surgical consultant.

Retrograde cholangiography This procedure is especially useful in patients with persistent jaundice the cause of which cannot be established by conventional diagnostic methods. The important differential diagnosis is between "surgical" and "medical" jaundice. When the cause of jaundice is unclear, approximately 15 percent of patients thought to have "medical" jaundice prove to have extrahepatic biliary obstruction requiring surgery, and, conversely, the same percentage of patients thought to have "surgical" jaundice prove to have an open ductal system by ERCP and can be spared unnecessary surgery.

Remediable causes of obstructive jaundice which can be diagnosed by retrograde cholangiography include common duct stones (Fig. 233-1*C*), gallbladder stones, benign strictures, and, occasionally, resectable ductal carcinomas. In jaundiced patients with suspected primary liver disease, such as primary biliary cirrhosis, ERCP can relieve the worry that an operable obstruction is being missed.

In addition to ERCP, there are four other methods of visualizing the biliary tree in the jaundiced patient. Which test to use first depends on the clinical situation, the availability of equipment, and the experience of the specialists using the techniques. The first method is *percutaneous transhepatic cholangiography* (PTC), in which contrast material is injected from the exterior via a "skinny" needle into the intrahepatic bile ducts under fluoroscopic control; success in visualizing the ducts is 90 to 100 percent if the ducts are dilated, but only approximately 66 percent if they are not dilated. PTC is generally safe, but complications do occur (sepsis, bleeding, bile leak, etc.). The morbidity for this procedure is approximately 10 percent; the reported mortality varies from 0.1 to 0.9 percent. The three other methods, which are noninvasive, use *ultrasound*, *computerized tomography* (CT scan), and *PIPIDA scans* (^{99m}Tc-labeled paraisopropyliminodiacetic acid). The first two techniques employ sound waves or x-rays to visualize organs and any stones, cysts, or solid masses within them. They can also be used to determine whether the biliary ducts or gallbladder are enlarged. The PIPIDA scans are used to determine patency of the cystic and common ducts and to study gallbladder emptying after administration of cholecystokinin (CCK).

The relative usefulness of these five tests is not established. Many physicians first try ultrasound or CT scan to see whether the biliary ducts are dilated and to seek the cause of the patient's jaundice (stones, pancreatic mass, etc.). The PIPIDA scan will determine if the cystic duct and bile ducts are patent. Direct visualization is undertaken if the diagnosis is not established, PTC first if the hepatic ducts are dilated, and ERCP if not. Advantages of the endoscopic approach are that the papilla and the pancreatic duct are seen (in addition to the biliary ducts) and that therapy can be performed with papillotomy or drainage when appropriate. In the event of a technical failure or incomplete information resulting from either ERCP or PTC, the other technique is tried. This approach detects most lesions requiring surgical intervention.

ERCP or PTC can also be useful in patients with biliary pain, cholangitis, or impaired liver function after previous biliary surgery. Remediable postoperative lesions such as strictures can be discovered, and their precise anatomy outlined so that reoperation is less difficult.

Retrograde pancreatography Patients with recurrent or chronic pancreatitis may merit retrograde pancreatography to seek a lesion which can be approached surgically, such as localized pancreatitis in the tail or ductal pathology amenable to drainage.

Patients with symptoms, signs, or laboratory findings suggesting pancreatic carcinoma may have pancreatograms suggesting malignancy with a narrowed, encased, or sharply "cutoff" pancreatic duct (Fig. 233-1*D*). Differentiation of such pancreatic ductal findings from benign inflammatory disease can be difficult. Cytologic examination of pancreatic duct contents obtained during ERCP may prove helpful. Unfortunately, most patients with symptomatic pancreatic cancer diagnosed by ERCP are inoperable.

Patients presenting with painless steatorrhea of pancreatic origin may be shown to have a ductal pattern suggesting chronic pancreatitis or pancreatic carcinoma. Pancreatography has not been useful in the study of obscure upper abdominal pain. Pancreatic cysts can be better diagnosed by noninvasive techniques such as ultrasound, and pancreatography should be reserved for those cases where it is desirable to outline the anatomy immediately prior to surgery. Pancreatography alone does not seem promising as a method of screening for early pancreatic carcinoma, although cytologic examination of ductal fluid may prove useful.

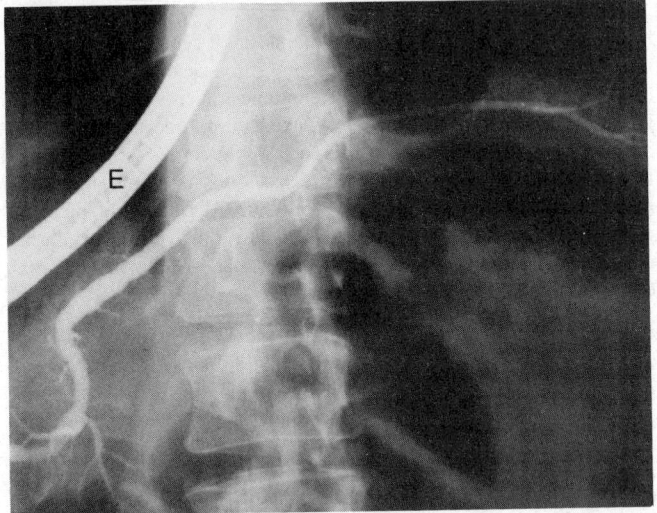

A

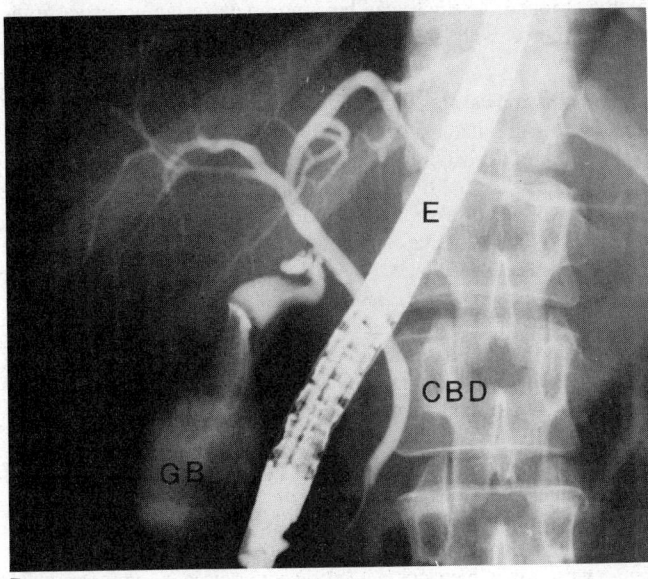

B

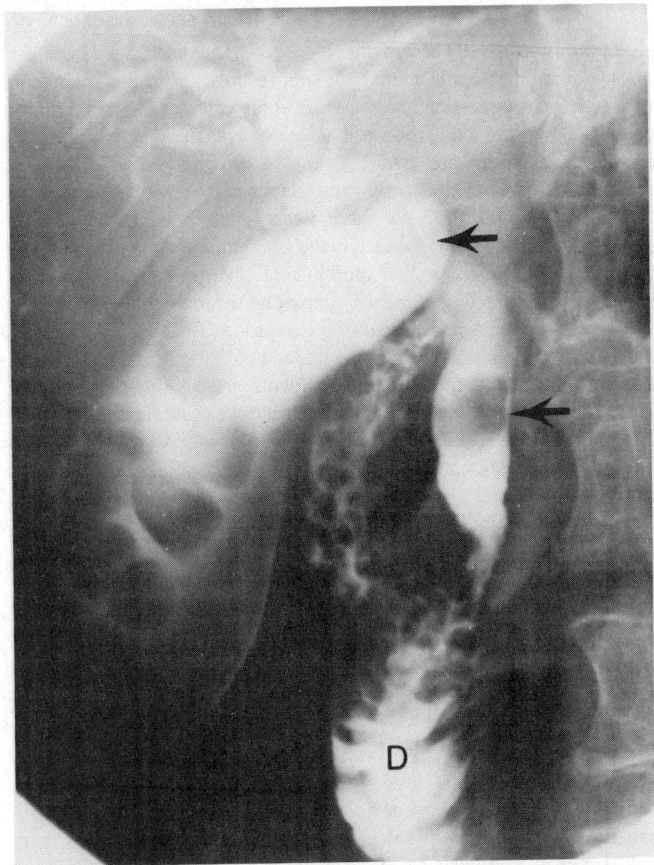

C

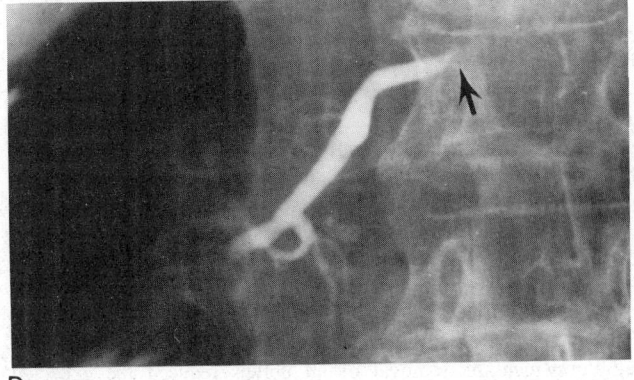

D

FIGURE 233-1 *A. A tapering pancreatic duct of normal caliber is seen and may be compared to the endoscope (E) 1 cm in diameter. B. Normal cholangiogram. The diameter of the common duct (CBD) is normal. The intrahepatic ducts branch normally, and the gallbladder (GB) can be seen. The endoscope (E) is seen in the duodenum. C. Several stones (arrows) can be seen in an obstructed, dilated common duct. The gallbladder also contains several stones. Regurgitated contrast material is seen in the duodenum (D). D. The sharp cutoff (arrow) of the pancreatic duct is caused by a carcinoma of the body of the pancreas. (Courtesy of Dr. Charles Rohrmann.)*

Therapeutic ERCP   Successful endoscopic papillotomy of the sphincter of Vater with extraction of retained stones is possible. An electro-surgical wire attached to the ERCP catheter can be used to cut the sphincter of Vater. Balloon catheters can be used to extract stones which do not pass spontaneously. New devices which mechanically crush or ultrasonically shatter large stones which will not pass spontaneously or with a balloon are being investigated. Certainly this approach is being used increasingly in patients who are poor operative risks. The overall success rate is approximately 90 percent, with a mortality rate of about 0.8 percent and a complication rate of about 7 percent. Complications include bleeding, perforation, pancreatitis, cholangitis, and stone impaction. These results compare favorably with surgery, especially in the high-risk patient with previous biliary surgery. Endoscopic papillotomy may also permit nonoperative biliary drainage via transnasal tubes or stents placed into the common bile duct. Manometry of the sphincter presents certain technical difficulties,

but it may yet prove invaluable in the diagnosis of periampullary stenosis.

Other diagnostic techniques   Critical comparative studies are needed of the various approaches to biliary tree disorders and to pancreatic diseases (ERCP, PTC, angiography, CT scanning, and ultrasound). The role of magnetic resonance imaging in diseases of the pancreas and biliary tree is yet to be defined. Endoscopic ultrasound may also prove to be a valuable technique to image the intestinal wall and adjacent organs.

COLONOSCOPY   The interior of the entire length of the colon from anus to cecum can be visualized by the experienced colonoscopist. This method may prove to be the most significant diagnostic and therapeutic application of fiberoptic endoscopy because it can diagnose potentially curable colonic cancers missed by other techniques and remove potentially precancerous adenomatous polyps.

Approximately 40 percent of colonoscopies are performed because of an abnormal barium enema showing a polyp or a narrowing or filling defect suggesting carcinoma. Approximately 40 percent of colonoscopies are done because of gastrointestinal bleeding. The ability to examine the whole colon is proving valuable in the management of some patients with inflammatory bowel disease.

Patients are prepared for colonoscopy with a liquid diet for 2 days, magnesium citrate laxation the evening before examination, and tap water enemas the morning of the procedure. Another increasingly utilized method of preparing the colon is a total-gut lavage with a nonabsorbable electrolyte solution. This method prepares the patient without laxatives or enemas and only requires a few hours. Immediately before the procedure patients are lightly sedated with intravenous diazepam and meperidine. Intravenous anticholinergics and glucagon are used when needed to relax local spasm. Vasovagal bradycardial reactions can be reversed quickly by intravenous anticholinergics.

The main complications of colonoscopy are hemorrhage and perforation (morbidity rate is 0.5 to 1.3 percent; mortality rate is 0.02 percent). The complication rate for polypectomy is 1 to 2 percent. Diverticular or ischemic disease and prior irradiation make the procedure more difficult and hazardous. The risk of perforation is also increased in the patient with very active colitis, and colonoscopy should be avoided during the acute phase.

Polyps (see also Chap. 239)   A polyp seen on barium enema merits colonoscopy for several reasons: It may be an artifact or a cancer, and a second polyp or cancer may have been missed. The polyp can usually be excised, with lower morbidity and mortality rates than with surgery. The best way to rule out cancer within a polyp is to remove it completely for histologic examination. Hyperplastic polyps do not become malignant; colonic polyps which show benign neoplasia histologically may become malignant (tubular and villous adenomas). The risk of neoplastic polyps being cancerous increases with their size. The risk is also higher in villous adenomas. Pedunculated polyps with cancer confined to the mucosa and with an uninvolved stalk can be cured by removal with an electrocautery snare during colonoscopy. Thus, most colonoscopists will remove all polyps more than 0.5 cm in diameter. It is more difficult to know what to do with polyps smaller than 0.5 cm in diameter because more than 50 percent may be adenomatous. A coagulating biopsy technique can be used to both biopsy and destroy even the smallest adenomatous polyp in the hope that the subsequent risk of developing colonic cancer will be reduced. The wisdom of this course of action is suggested by a sigmoidoscopic study in which the removal of all polyps reduced the expected incidence and invasiveness of subsequently developing cancers in the anatomic area screened. Most agree that the patient with adenomatous polyps is more likely to develop another polyp or cancer and therefore merits a regular screening program. The optimal frequency of follow-up examinations after polypectomy is not yet established. The current recommendation is a digital examination and stool test for occult blood yearly. When a polyp is discovered, the entire colon should be examined for synchronous polyps or cancer. This should probably be repeated at 1 year and, if negative, every 3 years thereafter. If stools are positive for occult blood or symptoms develop, immediate evaluation is indicated.

Cancer screening by x-ray   All filling defects on barium enema merit evaluation by colonoscopy. If the lesion is a pedunculated polyp, it can be removed for histologic examination; if its appearance suggests a cancer, it can be biopsied and brushed for histologic and cytologic confirmation. When a polyp or a carcinoma is found, the remainder of the colon should be screened for additional polyps and synchronous carcinoma. This avoids multiple colotomies to search for a second lesion and reduces surgical morbidity. Approximately 40 percent of lesions diagnosed as a mass by x-ray are not present on colonoscopy or are found to be due to lesions such as a polyp rather than a cancer.

Narrowing by x-ray   An etiologic diagnosis of segmental narrowing may be difficult by x-ray. Colonoscopy often determines the cause of segmental narrowing and differentiates adenocarcinoma from inflammation secondary to ischemia, irradiation, diverticular disease, or Crohn's colitis. Even the most classic "apple-core" lesion indicated by x-ray may be covered by normal mucosa at colonoscopy, suggesting an extrinsic inflammatory lesion. In 10 to 30 percent of patients, narrowed segments present on x-ray are not visualized during colonoscopy, probably because they are areas of temporary spasm. Such findings avoid unnecessary operations.

Chronic bleeding (x-ray and sigmoidoscopy negative)   This condition leads to approximately 40 percent of colonoscopies. The x-ray is more likely to miss a lesion when single contrast is used rather than air contrast. The cause of bleeding is found in approximately 40 percent of such patients. The common bleeding sources are adenomatous polyp (20 percent), adenocarcinoma (10 percent), and Crohn's disease (7 percent). Many of these carcinomas are resectable, and this group may benefit most from colonoscopy. If no bleeding source is found, a search may be appropriate for an upper gastrointestinal source with an upper gastrointestinal x-ray and/or upper endoscopy.

Inflammatory bowel disease   Colonoscopy is not routinely indicated in patients with inflammatory bowel disease. Colonoscopy may help in the initial diagnosis, especially in differentiating Crohn's colitis from ulcerative colitis. It can aid the surgeon in assessing the activity and extent of the disease before surgery. Colonoscopy can evaluate radiographic abnormalities suggesting cancer, such as strictures, polyps, or masses. Colonoscopy may be indicated in patients with ulcerative colitis of more than 10 years' duration because of the increased risk of carcinoma; it is hoped that repeated colonoscopies will serve to detect these malignancies earlier than x-ray and while the lesions are still curable. The frequency of colonoscopy and/or double-contrast barium enema examination in such patients is not yet established. If an expert pathologist finds "precancer" or "dysplastic" changes in colonic biopsies in a patient with long-standing ulcerative colitis, many consider this to be an indication for colectomy. Preparation for colonoscopy must often be modified for patients with inflammatory bowel disease. Colonoscopy is contraindicated in patients with toxic megacolon, very active disease, or a possible intestinal perforation.

Other indications   The flexible sigmoidoscope may replace the rigid 25-cm sigmoidoscope for routine screening because it can be passed to 40 to 60 cm with minimal preparation, less discomfort, and a higher diagnostic yield. After segmental colonic resection for carcinoma, colonoscopy may detect early mucosal recurrence and differentiate it from benign anastomotic strictures or bleeding suture granulomas. These patients must also be periodically screened for the development of polyps or additional carcinomas. Colonoscopy is occasionally used during laparotomy to assist the surgeon in ruling out other lesions. The colonoscope can be advanced to the cecum rapidly with the surgeon's assistance, and additional polyps removed without colotomy. The author believes that the best diagnostic approach to acute lower intestinal bleeding is a labeled RBC scan to determine if bleeding is active and to localize the general anatomic area of the source, followed (if active) by selective angiography; this may be useful not only for finding lesions such as angiodysplasia and bleeding diverticula but also for permitting treatment with vasoconstrictors. Endoscopic hemostatic therapy may be useful in some types of bleeding colonic lesions such as angiodysplasia. However, visualizing a bleeding site by colonoscopy may be difficult when there is massive bleeding.

Colonoscopy detects some carriers of the dominant familial polyposis gene before diagnosis by barium enema and sigmoidoscopy. Carcinoma is a great threat in those familial polyposis syndromes which produce many adenomatous polyps (familial polyposis and Gardner's syndrome); in these conditions, polypectomy is useful for diagnosis, but colectomy is the only treatment which prevents development of carcinoma. These patients are also at risk of developing duodenal and periampullary cancer and should probably undergo periodic surveillance with a side-viewing duodenoscope. Peutz-Jeghers syndrome and generalized juvenile polyposis produce mostly hamartomatous polyps and, therefore, have a very much lower incidence of gastrointestinal carcinoma; the cancers that develop in these patients may be related to occasional polyps undergoing adenomatous change or may occur in adjacent colonic mucosa.

Malignant tumors develop in 2 to 3 percent of patients with Peutz-Jeghers syndrome, and they are mostly located in the stomach, duodenum, and the rest of the small intestine. Thus these patients may merit regular upper endoscopy and prophylactic polypectomy.

CONTRAINDICATIONS All types of fiberoptic endoscopy are contraindicated in certain clinical situations, including patients who are uncooperative or combative, who have had an acute myocardial infarction, or who have perforation of the intestine.

CONSCIOUS LAPAROSCOPY The potentials for laparoscopy in conscious patients have not been as fully appreciated in North America as they have been in other countries, where it has been used widely for over 20 years. This procedure has extremely low mortality and morbidity rates in experienced hands. The instrument used for laparoscopy is a stiff tube with a lens system that provides a superb view. Under local anesthesia pneumoperitoneum is gradually induced with air or nitrous oxide.

Much of the exterior of the liver, gallbladder, spleen, peritoneum, diaphragm, and pelvic organs can be clearly visualized. Portions of the colon and small bowel can also be seen. Lesions can be biopsied under direct vision and any resultant bleeding controlled by electrocoagulation. Furthermore, in centers with extensive experience contrast material can be injected into the liver to visualize vascular, lymphatic, and biliary systems.

Laparoscopy may permit one to make a difficult diagnosis without resorting to laparotomy by biopsying localized hepatic disease under direct vision. Laparoscopy can often help differentiate "medical" from "surgical" jaundice and may also enable staging of malignant disease without laparotomy.

REFERENCES

BLACKSTONE MO: *Endoscopic Interpretation.* New York, Raven Press, 1984

COTTON PB, BEALES JSM: Endoscopic pancreatography in management of relapsing acute pancreatitis. Br Med J 1:608, 1974

———, WILLIAMS CB: *Practical Gastrointestinal Endoscopy.* Oxford, Blackwell, 1982

FLEISCHER D: Endoscopic therapy of upper gastrointestinal bleeding in humans. Gastroenterology 90:217, 1986

GILBERT DA et al: The national ASGE colonoscopy survey—Analysis of colonoscopic practices and yield. Gastrointest Endosc 30:143, 1984(A)

HAGGITT RC et al: Prognostic factors in colorectal carcinomas arising in adenomas: Implications for lesions removed by endoscopic polypectomy. Gastroenterology 89:328, 1985

KOCH H: Operative endoscopy. Gastrointest Endosc 24:65, 1977

PETERSON WL et al: Routine early endoscopy in upper gastrointestinal tract bleeding: A randomized, controlled trial. N Engl J Med 304:925, 1981

The role of endoscopy in upper gastrointestinal bleeding: Proceedings of the NIH consensus workshop. Dig Dis Sci 26:1s, 1981

SAFRANY L: Duodenoscopic sphincterotomy and gallstone removal. Gastroenterology 72:330, 1977

SIVAK MV (ed): *Gastroenterology Series: Endoscopic Sclerotherapy of Esophageal Varices.* New York, Praeger, 1984

TEAGUE RH et al: Colonoscopy for investigation of unexplained rectal bleeding. Lancet 1:1350, 1978

234 DISEASES OF THE ESOPHAGUS

RAJ K. GOYAL

The two major functions of the esophagus are the transport of the food bolus from the mouth to the stomach and the prevention of retrograde flow of gastrointestinal contents. The transport function is achieved by peristaltic contractions (see Chap. 32). Retrograde flow is prevented by the two esophageal sphincters, which remain closed between swallows and which are functional rather than distinct anatomic entities. The upper esophageal sphincter remains closed by the elastic properties of its wall and by contraction of the cricopharyngeus and inferior pharyngeal constrictor muscles due to continuous neural excitation of the lower motor neurons which innervate these muscles via motor end plates. Many neuromuscular disorders involving these muscles result in reduction in resting sphincter pressure and consequent esophagopharyngeal reflux. In contrast, the lower esophageal sphincter remains closed because of its intrinsic myogenic tone, and a neural pathway, consisting of preganglionic parasympathetic fibers in the vagus nerve and postganglionic myenteric inhibitory neurons, causes its relaxation. The neurotransmitter of preganglionic neurons is acetylcholine and that of postganglionic neurons is vasoactive intestinal peptide (VIP). A reflex increase in the lower sphincter pressure occurs with an increase in intraabdominal pressure and ingestion of a protein meal. Fatty meals, smoking, and beverages with a high xanthine content (tea, coffee, cola) cause a reduction in sphincter pressure. Many hormones and neurotransmitters can modify lower sphincter pressure. Cholinergic muscarinic (M-2 receptor) agonists, alpha-adrenergic agonists, gastrin, pancreatic polypeptide, substance P, and prostaglandin $F_{2\alpha}$ cause contraction; in contrast, ganglionic stimulants, beta-adrenergic agonists, dopamine, cholecystokinin, secretin, VIP, ATP, and adenosine cause relaxation of the sphincter. These effects are mediated by actions on the inhibitory intramural neurons or on the sphincter muscle directly. Effects of many of these agents are pharmacologic rather than physiologic.

SYMPTOMS

DYSPHAGIA See Chap. 32.

ESOPHAGEAL PAIN *Heartburn,* or pyrosis, is characterized by burning retrosternal discomfort that may move up and down the chest like a wave. When severe, it may radiate to the sides of the chest, neck, and angles of the jaw. Heartburn is a characteristic symptom of reflux esophagitis and may be associated with regurgitation or a feeling of warm fluid climbing up the throat. It is aggravated by bending forward, straining, or lying recumbent and is worse after meals. It is relieved by upright posture, by swallowing of saliva or water, or, more reliably, by antacids. Heartburn appears to be produced by heightened mucosal sensitivity and can be reproduced by infusion of dilute (0.1 N) hydrochloric acid (Bernstein test) or neutral hyperosmolar solutions into the esophagus.

Odynophagia, or painful swallowing, is characteristic of nonreflux esophagitis, particularly monilial and herpes esophagitis. Odynophagia may also occur with peptic ulcer of the esophagus (Barrett's ulcer), carcinoma with periesophageal involvement, caustic damage of the esophagus, and esophageal perforation. Odynophagia is unusual in uncomplicated reflux esophagitis. Crampy chest pain associated with impaction of the small bowel should be distinguished from odynophagia.

Chest pain other than heartburn and odynophagia occurs when the esophageal muscle contracts with excessive force, for a long duration, and repetitively, as in diffuse esophageal spasm. This may occur spontaneously or during a meal. Chest pain due to periesophageal involvement caused by carcinoma or peptic ulcer may be constant and agonizing. Sometimes different types of esophageal pains exist together in the same patient, and frequently patients are not able to describe the pain accurately enough to allow its classification.

REGURGITATION Regurgitation is the effortless appearance of gastric or esophageal contents in the mouth. In distal esophageal obstruction and stasis, as in achalasia or a large diverticulum, the regurgitated material consists of tasteless mucoid fluid or undigested food. Regurgitation of sour or bitter-tasting material occurs in severe gastroesophageal reflux and is associated with incompetence of both the upper and lower esophageal sphincters. Regurgitation may result in laryngeal aspiration, with spells of coughing and choking that awaken the patient from sleep, and aspiration pneumonia. Water brash is reflex salivary hypersecretion which occurs in response to peptic esophagitis; it should not be confused with regurgitation.

DIAGNOSTIC TESTS

RADIOLOGIC STUDIES Barium swallow with fluoroscopy and esophogram is the most widely used test for diagnosis of esophageal disease and can be used to evaluate both structural and motor disorders. The pharynx is examined to detect stasis of barium in the valleculae and pyriform sinuses and regurgitation of barium into the nose and tracheobronchial tree. Since the pharyngeal phase of swallowing lasts no more than a second, cineradiography may be necessary to permit detection and analysis of abnormalities of pharyngeal function. Spontaneous reflux of barium from the stomach into the esophagus should be sought in patients with suspected reflux esophagitis. Esophageal peristalsis is best studied in the recumbent position since in the upright position the passage of most of the barium occurs by gravity alone. A double-contrast esophagram, obtained by coating the esophageal mucosa with barium and distending the esophageal lumen with air using effervescent granules, is particularly useful in demonstrating mucosal ulcers and early cancers. Figures 234-1 and 234-2 illustrate the radiographic appearance of some esophageal lesions.

ESOPHAGOSCOPY Fiberoptic esophagogastroduodenoscopy is described in Chap. 233. Esophagoscopy is the direct method of establishing the cause of mechanical dysphagia and of identifying mucosal lesions, such as superficial ulcers and esophagitis, which may not be identified by the usual barium swallow. In the presence of marked luminal narrowing, examination can be achieved by using a smaller caliber endoscope, although on occasion a stricture must be dilated prior to a complete endoscopic examination. Transendoscopic biopsies are useful in diagnosing carcinoma, reflux esophagitis, or other mucosal diseases. Obtaining cells by scraping the mucosa with a Teflon brush during endoscopy may enable the cytologist to detect carcinoma missed by mucosal biopsies.

ESOPHAGEAL MOTILITY The study of esophageal motility entails simultaneous recording of pressures from different sites in the esophageal lumen. This is usually done with a train of 3 to 4 water-filled catheters connected to pressure transducers. The assembly is passed by mouth or nose through the esophagus into the stomach and then gradually withdrawn 1 cm at a time until pressures from each centimeter of the esophagus and pharynx are recorded in between and during swallows. The upper and lower esophageal sphincters appear as zones of high pressure which relax on swallowing. The pharynx and esophageal body show peristaltic waves with each swallow.

Esophageal motility studies are very helpful in the diagnosis of achalasia, diffuse esophageal spasm and its variants, scleroderma, and other motor disorders of the esophagus, as well as neuromuscular disorders of the upper esophagus and pharynx (Fig. 234-3) but are of no value in the diagnosis of mechanical dysphagia. In patients with reflux esophagitis, esophageal manometry is useful in quantitating lower esophageal competence and providing information on the status of the esophageal body motor activity. The information obtained by manometry is quantitative and cannot be obtained by barium swallow or endoscopy.

Special tests for the evaluation of reflux esophagitis are described later.

MOTOR DISORDERS

STRIATED MUSCLE Pharyngeal paralysis Pharyngeal paralysis is characterized by dysphagia, nasal regurgitation, and tracheobron-

FIGURE 234-1 *Radiographic appearance of some motor disorders of the pharynx and esophagus. (1) Pharyngeal paralysis with tracheal aspiration (arrow). (2) Cricopharyngeal achalasia. Note the prominent cricopharyngeus which is recognized by its smoothness and location in the posterior wall. (3) Diffuse esophageal spasm. Note typical corkscrew appearance of the lower part of the esophagus. (4) Achalasia showing dilation of esophageal body* *with air fluid level and closed lower esophageal sphincter. (5) Muscular (contractile) lower esophageal ring. Note a nice symmetric contraction in 5A that has disappeared in 5B obtained during the same examination. (6) Scleroderma esophagus showing dilated esophagus with a stricture in 6A and reflux of barium from the stomach into the esophagus in 6B. (Courtesy of Dr. Harvey Goldstein.)*

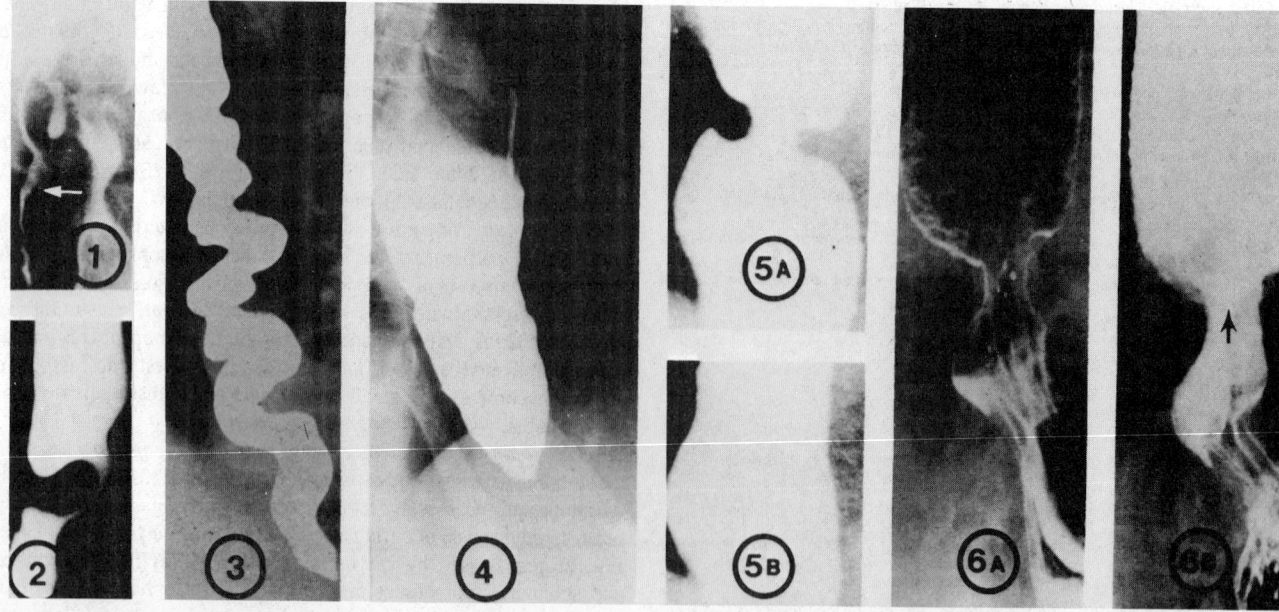

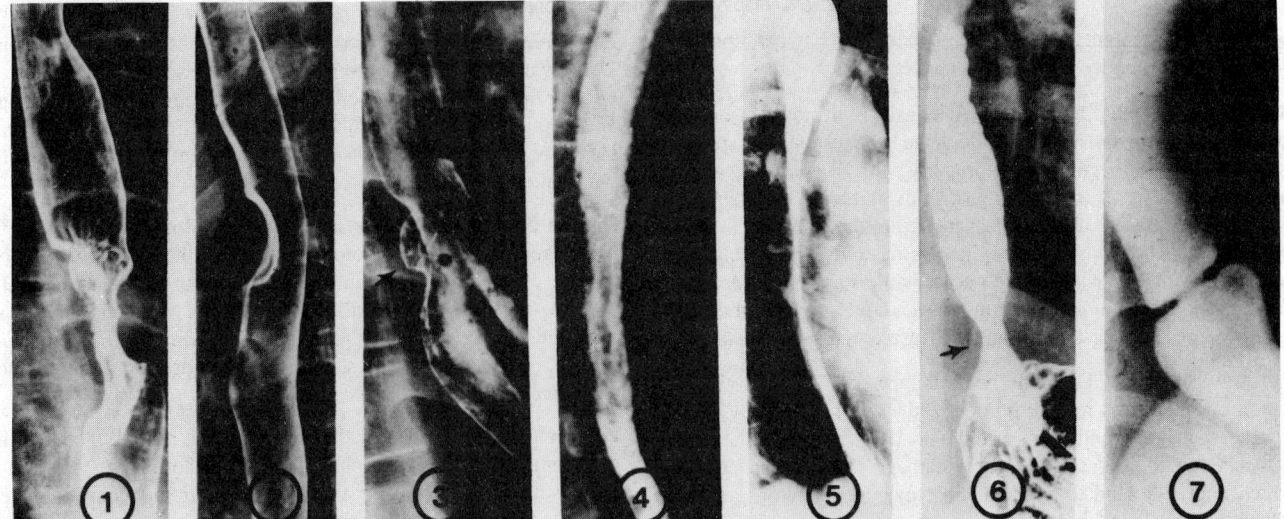

FIGURE 234-2 *Radiographic appearance of selected structural lesions of the esophagus. (1) Carcinoma of the esophagus. Note the typical annular narrowing with overhanging margins and destruction of the mucosa. (2) Leiomyoma of the esophagus. Note the smooth filling defect and right angles of origin from the esophageal wall. (3) Esophageal ulcer in columnar-cell-lined esophagus (Barrett's esophagus). (4) Monilial esophagitis. Note irregular plaquelike filling defects. (5) Long stricture secondary to lye ingestion. (6) Peptic stricture which is short and tubular. Note the associated hiatus hernia. (7) Mucosal lower esophageal mucosal (Schatzki) ring. Note a thin weblike annular constriction at the esophagogastric junction. It is associated with a small hiatal hernia. (Courtesy of Dr. Harvey Goldstein.)*

chial aspiration during swallowing. It occurs in a variety of neuromuscular disorders (see Table 32-2). Some of these disorders may also involve laryngeal and orofacial muscles. When the suprahyoid muscles are also paralyzed, the opening of the upper sphincter with swallowing is also impaired, causing severe dysphagia.

Barium swallow and cineradiography reveal stasis of barium in the valleculae and pyriform sinuses, nasal and tracheobronchial aspiration, and closed upper sphincter (Fig. 234-1). Pharyngeal motility studies demonstrate reduced amplitude of pharyngeal and upper esophageal contractions and reduced basal upper esophageal sphincter pressure without further relaxation on swallowing (Fig. 234-3). Patients with myasthenia gravis and polymyositis respond to treatment for these diseases (see Chap. 358). Dysphagia in patients with cerebrovascular accident improves with time, although not completely. Treatment in most instances is mainly supportive, consisting of nasogastric tube feeding and physiotherapy. Cricopharyngeal myotomy is sometimes performed but its usefulness is unproved.

Extensive operative procedures to prevent aspiration are rarely needed. Death is often due to pulmonary complications.

Cricopharyngeal achalasia   Failure of the cricopharyngeus to relax on swallowing leads to a contracted cricopharyngeus, which appears as a prominent bar on the posterior wall of the pharynx on barium swallow (Fig. 234-1). A transient cricopharyngeal bar is seen in up to 5 percent of subjects without dysphagia undergoing upper gastrointestinal studies; it can be produced in normal subjects during a Valsalva maneuver. When contraction is persistent, patients may complain of food sticking in their throats. Cricopharyngeal myotomy may be helpful, but it is contraindicated in the presence of gastroesophageal reflux because in such patients this procedure may lead to pharyngeal and pulmonary aspiration.

Globus hystericus   A sensation of a constant lump in the throat but with no difficulty during swallowing occurs especially in subjects with emotional disorders, particularly in women. Barium studies are

FIGURE 234-3 *Motility patterns in selected esophageal and pharyngeal disorders. In normal subjects, the upper and lower esophageal sphincters appear as zones of high pressure. With a swallow (indicated by ↑), pressure in the sphincters falls and a contraction wave starts in the pharynx and progresses down the esophagus. In scleroderma, the lower part of the esophagus (smooth muscle) shows reduced amplitude of contractions, which may be peristaltic or simultaneous in onset, and hypotension of the lower sphincter. In achalasia, the lower part of the esophagus shows reduced amplitude of contractions that are simultaneous in onset. In contrast to scleroderma, the lower esophageal sphincter in achalasia is hypertensive and fails to relax in response to a swallow. In diffuse esophageal spasm, the lower part of the esophagus shows simultaneous onset, large amplitude, long duration, repetitive contractions. In polymyositis, the smooth-muscle part of the esophagus is normal. The skeletal muscle part shows reduced amplitude of contractions. The upper esophageal sphincter is hypotensive and may not relax normally on swallowing due to associated weakness of the suprahyoid muscles.*

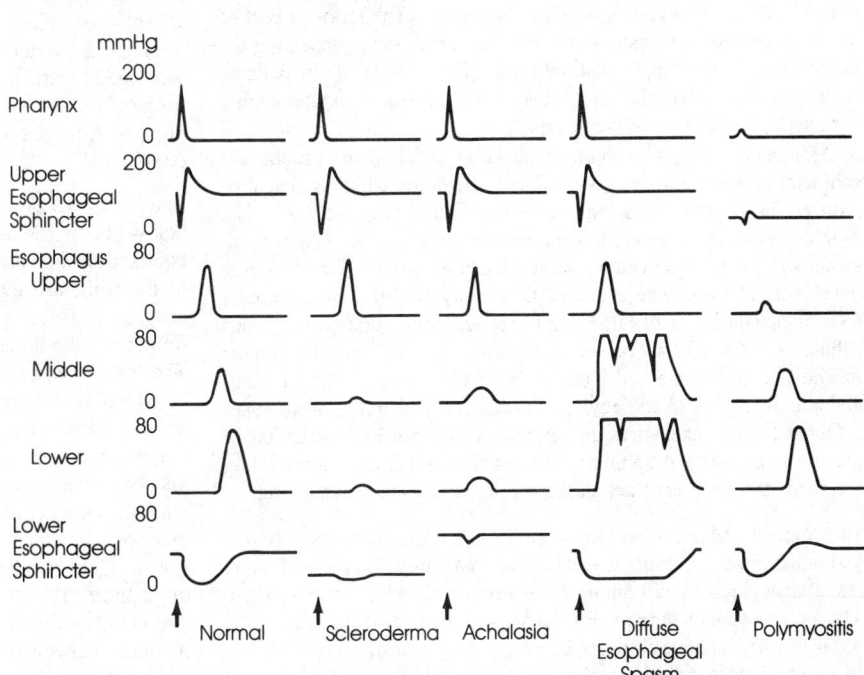

normal, but manometry shows a hypertensive upper sphincter. Treatment is primarily one of reassurance.

SMOOTH MUSCLE Achalasia Achalasia is a motor disorder of the esophageal smooth muscle in which the lower esophageal sphincter is hypertensive, does not relax properly with swallowing, and the normal peristalsis of the esophageal body is replaced by abnormal contractions. Based upon the changes in the esophageal body, achalasia can be of two types: in *classic achalasia* simultaneous contractions of small amplitude occur, while in *vigorous achalasia* contractions are simultaneous in onset, large in amplitude, and repetitive, resembling those seen in diffuse esophageal spasm.

PATHOPHYSIOLOGY The underlying abnormality is defective innervation of the smooth-muscle portion of the esophageal body and the lower esophageal sphincter. Pathologically, vigorous achalasia is associated with less severe neural damage than classic achalasia which shows a marked reduction in myenteric neurons. Primary idiopathic achalasia accounts for most of the patients seen in the United States. Secondary achalasia may be caused by gastric carcinoma infiltrating the esophagus, lymphoma, Chagas' disease, neuropathic chronic intestinal pseudoobstruction syndrome, irradiation, and certain toxins and drugs. Hypertensive or hypercontracting lower esophageal sphincter may be considered as variants of achalasia.

CLINICAL FEATURES Achalasia affects patients of all ages and both sexes. Dysphagia, chest pain, and regurgitation are the main symptoms. Dysphagia occurs early with both liquids and solids and is worsened by emotional stress and hurried eating. Various maneuvers designed to increase intraesophageal pressure, including the Valsalva, may help passage of the bolus into the stomach. Chest pain is more pronounced in vigorous achalasia than in classic achalasia. Regurgitation and pulmonary aspiration occur because of retention of large volumes of saliva and ingested food in the esophagus. The presence of gastroesophageal reflux argues against achalasia, although some of these patients may describe their chest pain as heartburn. The overall course is usually chronic with progressive dysphagia and weight loss over months to years.

DIAGNOSIS Chest x-ray shows absence of the gastric air bubble and sometimes a tubular mediastinal mass beside the aorta. The presence of an air-fluid level in the mediastinum in the upright position represents unpassed food in the esophagus and is characteristic. Barium swallow shows esophageal dilatation, and in advanced cases the esophagus may become sigmoid. On fluoroscopy normal peristalsis is lost in the lower two-thirds of the esophagus. The terminal part of the esophagus shows a persistent beaklike narrowing representing the nonrelaxing lower esophageal sphincter [Fig. 234-1(2)]. In patients with vigorous achalasia, there may be pronounced nonperistaltic contractions without a dilated esophagus.

Manometry shows normal or elevated basal lower esophageal sphincter pressure and swallow-induced relaxation which is absent or reduced in degree, duration, and consistency (Fig. 234-3). The esophageal body shows elevated resting pressure. In response to swallows, primary peristaltic waves are replaced by simultaneous-onset contractions. These contractions may be of poor amplitude (classic achalasia) or of large amplitude and long duration (vigorous achalasia). Administration of the cholinergic muscarinic agonist mecholyl causes a marked increase in baseline esophageal pressure, and administration of cholecystokinin (CCK), which normally causes a fall in the sphincter pressure, paradoxically causes contraction of the lower esophageal sphincter. Endoscopy is helpful in excluding the secondary causes of achalasia, particularly gastric carcinoma.

TREATMENT Medical treatment using soft foods, sedatives, nitrates, and anticholinergic drugs is usually unsatisfactory. Calcium channel antagonists such as nifedipine have been used with some success. The best available therapy involves balloon dilation to reduce the basal lower esophageal sphincter pressure by tearing muscle fibers. In experienced hands this technique is effective in about 85 percent

of patients. Perforation and bleeding are potential complications. Heller's extramucosal myotomy of the lower sphincter, in which the circular muscle layer is incised, is equally effective. Reflux esophagitis and peptic stricture may follow successful treatment of achalasia. However, this complication is more frequent with myotomy than with balloon dilation.

Diffuse esophageal spasm and related motor disorders Diffuse esophageal spasm is a motor disorder of the esophageal smooth muscle characterized by multiple spontaneous contractions and by swallow-induced contractions that are of simultaneous onset, large amplitude, long duration, and repetitive occurrence. Variants of diffuse esophageal spasm show some but not all of these motor abnormalities.

PATHOPHYSIOLOGY The pathogenesis of the various abnormalities of peristalsis in diffuse esophageal spasm is not known. Histopathologic studies show patchy neural degeneration localized to nerve processes rather than the prominent degeneration of nerve cell bodies seen in achalasia.

Variants of diffuse esophageal spasm, such as large amplitude but peristaltic contractions (sometimes called nutcracker esophagus) or normal amplitude but simultaneous contractions, frequently occur as a primary disease or in association with a variety of diseases as well as emotional stress and aging. Collagen vascular disease, diabetic neuropathy, reflux esophagitis, irradiation esophagitis, esophageal obstruction, and cholinergic and anticholinergic drugs can cause esophageal motor abnormalities. The relationship between reflux esophagitis and motor abnormalities is controversial. Overlapping features of diffuse esophageal spasm and achalasia occur in vigorous achalasia. The variant syndromes are more frequent in clinical practice than classic diffuse esophageal spasm.

CLINICAL FEATURES The symptomatic patient with diffuse spasm or its variants presents with chest pain, dysphagia, or both. Chest pain is particularly marked in patients with esophageal contractions of large amplitude and of long duration. Chest pain usually occurs at rest but may be brought on by swallowing or by emotional stress. The pain is retrosternal; it may radiate to the back, sides of the chest, both arms, or the sides of the jaw and may last for a few seconds to several minutes. It may be acute and severe, mimicking the pain of myocardial ischemia. Dysphagia for solids and liquids may occur with or without chest pain.

Diffuse esophageal spasm must be differentiated from other causes of chest pain, particularly ischemic heart disease with atypical angina. Often a complete cardiac workup is done before the esophageal etiology is seriously considered. The presence of dysphagia in association with pain should point to the esophagus as the site of disease. Symptoms of esophageal spasm should be carefully distinguished from those of reflux esophagitis; sometimes the two may coexist.

DIAGNOSIS Barium swallow shows that normal sequential peristalsis below the aortic arch is replaced by uncoordinated simultaneous contractions that produce the appearance of curling or multiple ripples in the wall, sacculations, and pseudodiverticula—the "corkscrew" esophagus [Fig. 234-1(3)]. Sometimes an esophageal contraction obliterates the lumen and barium is pushed away in both directions. The lower esophageal sphincter opens normally.

Manometry reveals the characteristic prolonged large amplitude and repetitive contractions of simultaneous onset in the lower part of the esophagus (Fig. 234-3). Only one or two of these abnormalities may be present in variants of diffuse spasm. Because the abnormalities may be episodic, manometry may be normal at the time of the study; therefore, several techniques are used in attempt to provoke esophageal spasm. Cold swallows produce chest pain but do not produce spasm on manometric studies. Solid boluses and pharmacologic agents, particularly edrophonium, induce both chest pain and motor abnormalities. However, there is a poor correlation between induction of pain and motility changes. Ergonovine may cause coronary artery spasm and should not be used. Overall, the usefulness of pharmacologic provocative tests is limited.

TREATMENT Anticholinergics are usually of limited value because the main nerves that mediate esophageal contractions are noncholinergic. Agents which relax smooth muscle such as sublingual nitroglycerin (0.3 to 0.6 mg) or longer acting agents such as isosorbide dinitrate (2.5 to 10 mg sublingually before meals) and nifedipine (10 to 20 mg before meals) may be helpful in some cases. Esophageal dilation with mercury-filled rubber dilators may produce symptomatic relief as a result of distention of the lower esophagus, but this is largely a placebo effect. Reassurance and tranquilizers are helpful in allaying patients' apprehension. Balloon dilation is sometimes attempted but can be hazardous in inexperienced hands. In severe cases resistant to all therapy, a longitudinal myotomy of esophageal circular muscle is performed; it relieves pain in up to two-thirds of patients.

Scleroderma involving the esophagus The esophageal lesions in systemic sclerosis consist of muscular atrophy of the smooth-muscle portion, with weakness of contraction in the lower two-thirds of the esophageal body and incompetence of the lower esophageal sphincter. The esophageal wall is thin and atrophic with or without areas of patchy fibrosis. Patients present with dysphagia to solids and to liquids in the recumbent position. They may also present with heartburn and regurgitation due to gastroesophageal reflux and esophagitis, which in turn may lead to stricture formation and more pronounced dysphagia. Barium swallow shows dilation and loss of peristaltic contractions in the middle and distal portions of the esophagus. The lower esophageal sphincter is patulous, and gastroesophageal reflux may occur freely (Fig. 234-1). Mucosal changes from esophageal ulceration may be detected, and esophageal stricture may be present. Motility studies show marked reduction in the amplitude of smooth-muscle contractions, which may be peristaltic or nonperistaltic. Lower esophageal sphincter resting pressure is subnormal, but relaxation is normal (Fig. 234-3). Currently, there is no effective treatment for the motor difficulty. Reflux esophagitis and its complications should be treated aggressively as described under reflux esophagitis.

INFLAMMATORY DISORDERS

GASTROESOPHAGEAL REFLUX AND ESOPHAGITIS Reflux esophagitis consists of esophageal mucosal damage resulting from reflux of gastric or intestinal contents into the esophagus. Depending on the causative agent, it is referred to as peptic, bile, or alkaline esophagitis.

Pathophysiology Three considerations involved in the pathophysiology of reflux esophagitis are (1) the pathogenesis of the esophageal reflux episode, (2) the cumulative, or net, esophageal reflux, and (3) the pathogenesis of esophagitis.

Two conditions must be met for a *reflux episode* to occur: the gastrointestinal contents must be "ready" to reflux, and the antireflux mechanism at the lower end of the esophagus must be compromised. Gastrointestinal contents are most likely to reflux (1) when gastric volume is increased (after meals, with pyloric obstruction or gastric stasis syndrome, and in acid hypersecretory states), (2) when the gastric contents are located near the gastroesophageal junction (due to recumbency or bending), and (3) when gastric pressure is increased (with obesity, pregnancy, ascites, or tight binders or girdles).

The normal antireflux mechanisms consist of the lower esophageal sphincter (LES) and the anatomic configuration of the gastroesophageal junction. Reflux occurs only when the LES–gastric pressure gradient is lost. It can be caused by increased intragastric pressure or a transient or sustained decrease in the sphincter tone itself. Most patients with reflux have lower than normal LES pressures. The incompetence of the LES may be primary or secondary. The secondary causes include scleroderma-like diseases, a myopathic type of chronic intestinal pseudoobstruction syndrome, pregnancy, female sex hormones, smoking, smooth-muscle relaxants (such as beta-adrenergics, aminophylline, nitrates, and calcium channel blockers), destruction of the sphincter by surgical resection, myotomy or balloon dilation, and esophagitis. Some patients have normal lower esophageal sphincter pressures but their sphincter relaxes inappropriately, allowing reflux to occur. The importance of the anatomic configuration of the esophagogastric junction is not fully known at present. However, the role of a sliding hiatal hernia in the impairment of the reflux barrier is not felt to be so important as was once thought.

The net or *cumulative esophageal reflux,* i.e., the amount and duration of refluxed material remaining in the esophagus, is dependent on (1) the amount of refluxed material per episode and frequency of episodes, (2) the clearing of the esophagus by gravity and peristaltic contraction, and (3) neutralization by salivary secretion.

Esophagitis is a complication of reflux, and it develops when the mucosal defenses that normally counteract the effect of injurious agents on the esophageal mucosa succumb to the onslaught of the refluxed acid pepsin or bile. *Histologic esophagitis* shows microscopic changes of mucosal infiltration with granulocytes or eosinophils, hyperplasia of basal cells, and elongation of dermal pegs. It can occur with or without endoscopic abnormalities. *Erosive esophagitis* shows endoscopically visible damage to the mucosa in the form of marked redness, friability, bleeding, superficial linear ulcers, and exudates. *Peptic stricture* results from fibrosis that causes constriction of the esophageal lumen. The fibrosis is predominantly submucosal, but it may involve the whole wall. Peptic strictures occur in about 10 percent of patients with reflux esophagitis. Short peptic strictures caused by spontaneous reflux are usually 1 to 3 cm long and are present in the distal esophagus near the squamocolumnar junction (Fig. 234-2). Long and tubular peptic strictures are the result of persistent vomiting or prolonged nasogastric intubation. Replacement of the squamous epithelium of the esophagus by columnar epithelium *(Barrett's esophagus)* may also result from reflux esophagitis. Columnar-cell-lined esophagus may be further complicated by peptic ulcer or peptic stricture high up in the lower or midesophagus, and adenocarcinoma in 2 to 5 percent.

Clinical features Heartburn is the characteristic symptom and is produced by the contact of refluxed material with the inflamed esophageal mucosa. However, this symptom may be absent in some patients. Dysphagia suggests development of peptic stricture. In peptic strictures, the usual history is of several years of heartburn preceding dysphagia. However, in one-third of patients dysphagia may be the presenting symptom. Progressive dysphagia and weight loss may indicate development of adenocarcinoma in Barrett's esophagus. Bleeding occurs due to mucosal erosions or Barrett's ulcer. Reflux in the absence of esophagitis is usually asymptomatic. Severe reflux may reach the pharynx and mouth and result in laryngitis, morning hoarseness, and pulmonary aspiration. Recurrent pulmonary aspiration can cause aspiration pneumonia, pulmonary fibrosis, or chronic asthma.

Diagnosis Evaluation of reflux esophagitis is designed to assess the presence and severity of reflux, nature of refluxant, presence and severity of esophagitis, and pathophysiology of reflux. History, barium swallow, esophagoscopy, mucosal biopsy, esophageal motility, and a variety of special tests are utilized.

The *presence of reflux* is suggested by history. Spontaneous reflux from the stomach into the esophagus on barium examination suggests advanced reflux. Reflux of barium induced by stressful maneuvers is not very helpful, however, because of a high incidence of false-positive and false-negative results. Recently, scintiscan using radio-labeled technetium 99m sulfur colloid has been used to quantitate gastroesophageal reflux. Several tests that utilize the recording of esophageal luminal pH with a small pH electrode have been proposed to detect and quantitate reflux of gastric acid. In these tests the pH electrode is swallowed, positioned in the stomach, gradually withdrawn across the LES, and then fixed at 5 cm above the sphincter. In the standard acid reflux test, a diagnosis of reflux can be made by failure of the pH to rise as the electrode enters the esophagus and by a decrease in esophageal pH with straining maneuvers. Quantitative information on the acid reflux is obtained by long-term (24-h) esophageal pH recording. The pH recordings are helpful only in the evaluation of acid reflux. The presence of bile or alkaline reflux is suggested by the occurrence of reflux symptoms in the absence of gastric acid and by the demonstration of bile in the aspirate of esophageal reflux.

The *presence and complications of reflux esophagitis* are assessed by barium swallow, esophagoscopy, mucosal biopsy, and the Bernstein test. Barium swallow is usually normal in uncomplicated esophagitis but may reveal the complication of stricture or ulcer formation. A high esophageal peptic stricture, deep ulcer, and adenocarcinoma suggest complications of Barrett's esophagus. Uncomplicated Barrett's esophagus is not diagnosed by barium studies. Esophagoscopy may reveal the presence of erosive esophagitis, distal peptic stricture, or columnar-cell-lined lower esophagus with or without a proximally located peptic stricture, ulcer, or adenocarcinoma. Esophagoscopy may be normal in many patients with esophagitis; in such patients mucosal biopsies and Bernstein tests are helpful. The mucosal biopsies should be obtained 5 cm above the LES because in the distal esophagus mucosal changes are quite frequent in normal subjects. False-positive and false-negative results occur in approximately 10 percent of biopsies. Patients with Barrett's esophagus will show columnar mucosa lining the esophagus which may be of gastric fundic, cardiac, or specialized type. The Bernstein test consists of an infusion of solutions of 0.1 N HCl and normal saline into the esophagus. It is useful in diagnosing reflux esophagitis which is not endoscopically obvious. In patients with reflux esophagitis, infusion of acid, but not of saline, reproduces the symptoms of heartburn. Infusion of acid in normal subjects produces no symptoms. Reflux esophagitis should be included in the differential diagnosis of chest pain, esophagitis, upper gastrointestinal bleeding, and dysphagia.

The *causative and predisposing factors* are assessed by history, esophageal motility, and esophageal clearance studies. Esophageal motility studies may provide useful quantitative information on the competence of the LES and of esophageal motor function. Barium swallow and scintiscans can be used to study esophageal clearance. An esophageal acid clearance test using a pH electrode quantifies the number of swallows necessary to clear the esophagus of 10 mL of instilled dilute 0.1 N HCl.

Full diagnostic evaluation is not necessary in every patient with reflux esophagitis. In transient and mild cases with a clear-cut history of reflux esophagitis, a therapeutic trial may be sufficient. In persistent cases, and in those in whom the diagnosis is not clear, barium swallow, esophagoscopy, and esophageal motility with pH monitoring are indicated.

Treatment The main principle of treatment is neutralization of the offending material (by antacids and H_2-receptor antagonists in peptic esophagitis, and by cholestyramine and aluminum hydroxide in bile esophagitis). In general, management of uncomplicated cases includes weight reduction, sleeping on a bed with elevation of the head of the bed, antacids (80 meq 1 and 3 h after meals), cimetidine (300 mg at bedtime), elimination of factors that increase abdominal pressure, and avoidance of smoking and harmful medications. Patients should avoid fatty foods, coffee, chocolate, alcohol, mint, orange juice, and any other foods they find that exacerbate their symptoms. Anticholinergic drugs should not be used since they may reduce LES pressure and impair esophageal clearance.

In moderate to severe cases, the above measures are more strictly enforced, particularly elevation of the head end of the bed usually by 6 to 8 in. Cimetidine, 300 mg qid, may be added. Long-acting H_2-receptor antagonists, such as ranitidine, may be more convenient to use. In the case of bile esophagitis, cholestyramine or aluminum

hydroxide antacid is used. If the patient does not fully respond, metoclopramide (10 mg qid) or bethanecol (25 mg qid) can be prescribed to raise sphincter pressure, hasten gastric emptying, and improve esophageal clearance. Their usefulness, however, is limited. Coating agents such as sucralfate are useful in some cases. Patients with reflux esophagitis with complications such as Barrett's esophagus with or without deep ulcer should be vigorously treated. Patients who have an associated peptic stricture are treated with dilators to relieve dysphagia in addition to vigorous treatment for reflux.

Antireflux surgery (Belsey repair, Nisson's fundoplication, and Hill repair), in which the gastric fundus is wrapped around the esophagus, increases the lower sphincter pressure and should be considered in resistant and complicated cases of reflux esophagitis that do not fully respond to medical therapy and in which there is persistently inadequate lower sphincter pressure but normal peristaltic contractions in the esophageal body.

Close follow-up is indicated in patients with complications of Barrett's esophagus because some of them may develop adenocarcinoma.

VIRAL ESOPHAGITIS (See also Chap. 136) *Herpes simplex virus* may be normally present in saliva and may cause esophagitis in patients who are debilitated and immunosuppressed. These patients complain of the acute onset of odynophagia and dysphagia. Bleeding may occur in severe cases, and systemic manifestations such as fever, chills, and mild leukocytosis may be present. Herpes blisters on the lips provide a clue to the diagnosis. Endoscopy shows vesicles and small, discrete, punched-out superficial ulcerations with or without fibrinous exudate. In later stages of the disease there is diffuse erosive esophagitis caused by enlargement and coalescence of the ulcers. Mucosal cells from biopsy of the edge of an ulcer show ballooning degeneration, ground-glass change in the nuclei with eosinophilic intranuclear inclusions (Cowdry type A), and giant-cell formation. These changes may also be detected in cytologic specimens. Culture of the tissue for herpes simplex virus is required for definitive diagnosis. Examination of serial serum specimens for rising titers of complement-fixing antibodies to herpes simplex type I is helpful in diagnosis. Acyclovir (200 mg qid orally or 5 mg every 8 h intravenously) is the treatment of choice. *Cytomegalovirus* (CMV) can also cause ulcerative esophagitis in immunosuppressed patients. The CMV ulcers usually occur within normal-appearing mucosa. The CMV inclusions have a deeper submucosal location and are best diagnosed on a large biopsy. There is no good treatment for CMV infection.

CANDIDA (MONILIAL) ESOPHAGITIS Many *Candida* species are normal inhabitants of the throat but become pathogenic and produce esophagitis in the setting of malignant neoplasms (particularly lymphoma and leukemia); treatment with immunosuppressive agents, steroids, and broad-spectrum antibiotics; diabetes mellitus; hypoparathyroidism; systemic lupus erythematosus; hemoglobinopathy; and corrosive esophageal injury. Occasionally, monilial esophagitis occurs in the absence of any of the above predisposing factors. Patients may be asymptomatic or complain of odynophagia and dysphagia. Oral thrush or other evidence of mucocutaneous moniliasis may be absent. Systemic invasion with *Monilia* may occur.

Barium swallow may be normal or may show multiple nodular filling defects of various sizes (Fig. 234-2). Large nodular defects may resemble clusters of grapes. Endoscopy shows small yellow-white raised plaques with surrounding erythema in mild disease. In extensive disease, confluent linear and nodular plaques are seen. Diagnosis is made by demonstration of yeast or hyphal forms in the plaques using 10% KOH. Biopsies are not always positive. Culture is helpful in confirming the species and, if needed, the drug sensitivities of the yeast (see Chap. 147).

Nystatin oral suspension (100,000 units per milliliter) in doses of 4 to 6 mL every 4 h) has been used. The current treatment of choice is ketoconazole (200 to 400 mg in a single oral daily dose). In poorly responsive patients, treatment is amphotericin B (10 to 15 mg as intravenous infusion over 6 h, daily for a total dose of 300 to 500 mg).

OTHER TYPES OF ESOPHAGITIS *Irradiation esophagitis* is a common occurrence during radiation treatment for lung, mediastinal, or esophageal carcinoma. The frequency of esophagitis increases with the amount of radiation to the area. Dysphagia and odynophagia are the main symptoms and may last several weeks to several months after the conclusion of therapy. The esophageal mucosa becomes erythematous, edematous, and friable. Superficial erosions coalesce to form larger superficial ulcers. Submucosal fibrosis and degenerative changes in the blood vessels, muscles, and myenteric neurons may be present. The treatment is relief of pain with viscous lidocaine. Esophageal stricture may develop, causing severe dysphagia. Strictures are treated by dilation with rubber dilators. *Corrosive esophagitis* occurs following ingestion of caustic agents, such as strong alkalis, or acids. When severe, corrosive injury may lead to esophageal perforation, bleeding, and death. Healing is usually associated with stricture formation. Caustic strictures are usually long and rigid (Fig. 234-2). They can be dilated by passing a metal dilator of increasing diameter over a guide-wire through the stricture. *Pill-induced esophagitis* is associated with the ingestion of certain pills and now accounts for many cases of errosive esophagitis. Antibiotics account for over half of the patients with pill-induced esophageal injury; the most commonly incriminated has been doxycycline. Other commonly prescribed pills which cause esophageal injury include potassium chloride, ferrous sulfate, quinidine, and various steroidal and non-steroidal anti-inflammatory agents. *Esophagitis associated with mucocutaneous disease* occurs in epidermolysis bullosa, pemphigoid, Behçet's syndrome, and Stevens-Johnson syndrome. Esophageal involvement in these disorders is indicated by development of odynophagia and dysphagia. Esophageal involvement responds to treatment of primary conditions.

TUMORS OF THE ESOPHAGUS

BENIGN TUMORS Benign tumors of the esophagus account for less than 10 percent of all esophageal tumors. The majority of benign esophageal tumors present as intramural lesions. Among them, leiomyoma accounts for 80 percent, esophageal cysts 10 percent, and all others 10 percent. Benign tumors presenting as an intraluminal mass are rare; almost 80 percent of them are fibrovascular polyps, 10 percent are papillomas, and the rest include all other types. These tumors are frequently asymptomatic, although dysphagia occurs in a few patients when the esophageal lumen is severely compromised. Benign tumors must be distinguished from malignant tumors, although often this distinction cannot be made with certainty prior to surgical removal. Endoscopic mucosal biopsies are not helpful in the diagnosis of submucosal tumors.

MALIGNANT TUMORS The primary malignant tumors of the esophagus are squamous-cell carcinoma (90 percent) and adenocarcinoma (less than 10 percent). Adenocarcinomas usually arise from metaplastic columnar epithelium (Barrett's esophagus) but may rarely arise from esophageal glands. Other uncommon tumors include carcinosarcoma, pseudosarcoma, melanoma, and verrucous squamous-cell carcinoma. In addition, adenocarcinoma of the stomach may spread to the esophagus by direct extension. Local spread from carcinoma of the lung or thyroid is unusual. Metastatic lesions from malignancies of remote organs are rare. Esophageal involvement may occur in up to 25 percent of patients with lymphoma, although symptomatic esophageal involvement occurs in less than 5 percent of these patients.

Squamous-cell carcinoma Squamous-cell carcinoma of the esophagus is the fifth most common cancer in adult males. A unique feature of this tumor is a marked geographic variation with a very high incidence (greater than 35 per 100,000 people per year) in certain regions of China, Iran, and Russia. In the United States the white population is at lower risk than blacks. Throughout the world the incidence increases with age, with males at greater risk than females.

Alcohol and smoking are important predisposing factors in the United States. Esophageal tumors may occur with higher frequency in association with carcinoma of the head and neck, lye strictures, ionizing radiation exposure, achalasia, Plummer-Vinson syndrome, and tylosis, a rare genetic disease in which the skin of the hands and feet is thickened.

CLINICAL FEATURES Progressive dysphagia and weight loss of short duration are characteristic. Dysphagia begins with solid foods and gradually progresses to include semisolids and liquids. In eccentric tumors and those arising from the stomach, dysphagia may be mild and may not occur until late in the disease. Dysphagia is rarely present for more than 1 year. Chest pain occurs as the tumor spreads to periesophageal tissues. Weight loss is usually profound because of anorexia and dysphagia. Bleeding from the tumor is usually slow, but brisk bleeding may occur. Rarely, invasion of the tumor into the aorta causes rapid exsanguination. Pulmonary aspiration, pneumonia, and, rarely, lung abscess can result from esophageal obstruction and aspiration or from tracheoesophageal fistula. Hoarseness may result from recurrent laryngeal nerve involvement. Physical examination is usually not striking except for evidence of recent weight loss. Supraclavicular nodes and an enlarged liver may be found when the tumor has spread to these sites. Signs of pulmonary aspiration may be present. Hypercalcemia may result from tumor production of a parathyroid hormone-like substance.

DIAGNOSIS The disease is usually advanced when the diagnosis is first made, and early detection is unusual. Carcinoma must be excluded by careful workup in all patients with persistent dysphagia and/or weight loss of short duration. Patients with gastric carcinoma involving the terminal esophagus may present with symptoms suggestive of reflux esophagitis, while others may have what appears to be achalasia or diffuse esophageal spasm. Recent development of any such symptoms in subjects over 40 years old should be carefully investigated.

The esophogram is the mainstay of diagnosis. Adequate esophageal distention and multiple views may be needed to diagnose early lesions. Double-contrast studies may also be helpful. An ulcerating lesion should be distinguished from a peptic ulcer in the columnar-cell-lined esophagus. Any esophageal ulcer that occurs without associated columnar-cell-lined esophagus should be considered carcinoma until proved otherwise. An infiltrating lesion may resemble a peptic stricture or may produce a picture resembling achalasia. Polypoid lesions should be distinguished from various benign neoplasms and from other types of carcinoma.

Endoscopy should be performed in all patients to detect suspected cases that may be missed on barium studies and to obtain tissue confirmation of cases that have been diagnosed on x-ray. Multiple biopsies and brush cytologies should be obtained. A thorough examination of the fundus of the stomach by turning the endoscope back on itself is imperative in all cases.

Computerized tomography has been helpful in determining extraesophageal spread to mediastinal structures and paraaortic abdominal lymph nodes.

TREATMENT The prognosis of esophageal carcinoma is poor; the 5-year survival rate is less than 5 percent, regardless of therapy. Curative surgical resection and anastomosis using gastric tube reconstruction and colonic or jejunal interposition is possible particularly in those with disease of the lower third of the esophagus. This is usually combined with radiation therapy [40 to 60 Gy (4000 to 6000 rad)] and/or chemotherapy. In over 60 percent of the patients palliative therapy alone is possible. This may include a surgical bypass procedure or more conservative methods to maintain esophageal luminal patency such as laser curettage, dilation, and sometimes insertion of a prosthesis. These measures are combined with palliative radiation and/or chemotherapy to shrink the tumor.

OTHER ESOPHAGEAL DISORDERS

PHARYNGEAL AND ESOPHAGEAL DIVERTICULA   Diverticula are outpouchings of the wall of the esophagus. *Zenker's diverticula* appear in the natural weakness in the posterior hypopharyngeal wall and cause halitosis and regurgitation of saliva and food particles consumed several days previously. When they become large and filled with food, they may compress the esophagus and cause dysphagia or complete obstruction. *Midesophageal diverticula* may be caused by traction from old adhesions or by propulsion associated with esophageal motor abnormalities. *Epiphrenic diverticula* may be associated with achalasia. Small- or medium-sized diverticula and midesophageal and epiphrenic diverticula are usually asymptomatic. *Diffuse intramural diverticulosis* of the esophagus is due to dilation of the deep esophageal glands. This may lead to chronic candidiasis or a stricture high up in the esophagus. These patients may present with dysphagia.

Symptomatic Zenker's diverticula are treated by cricopharyngeal myotomy with or without diverticulectomy. Very large symptomatic esophageal diverticula are removed surgically. When they are associated with motor abnormalities, distal myotomy is performed. Stricture associated with diffuse intramural diverticulosis is treated with rubber dilators.

ESOPHAGEAL WEBS   Weblike constrictions of the esophagus are usually congenital but may be acquired. Asymptomatic hypopharyngeal webs are demonstrated in up to 10 percent of normal individuals. When concentric, they cause intermittent dysphagia to solids. Symptomatic hypopharyngeal webs with iron-deficiency anemia in middle-aged women constitute Plummer-Vinson syndrome. The clinical importance of this syndrome is uncertain. Midesophageal webs are rare. Symptomatic webs are treated by rupture of the web with a rubber dilator.

LOWER ESOPHAGEAL RINGS   Lower esophageal *mucosal ring* (Schatzki ring) is a thin weblike constriction located at the squamocolumnar mucosal junction at or near the border of the lower esophageal sphincter (Fig. 234-2). It invariably produces dysphagia when the diameter is less than 1.3 cm. The dysphagia to solids is the only symptom and it is usually episodic. Asymptomatic rings may be present in about 10 percent of normal individuals. Lower esophageal ring is one of the common causes of dysphagia. Treatment is simple rupture of the ring with a large-diameter rubber dilator.

Lower esophageal *muscular ring* (contractile ring) is located proximal to the site of mucosal rings and may represent the abnormal uppermost segment of the lower esophageal sphincter. These rings are characterized by a change in size and shape from one time to another (Fig. 234-1). They may also cause dysphagia and should be differentiated from peptic strictures, achalasia, and lower esophageal mucosal rings. They are treated with rubber dilators.

HIATAL HERNIA   Hiatal hernia is a herniation of a part of the stomach into the thoracic cavity through the esophageal hiatus in the diaphragm. A *sliding hiatal hernia* is one in which the gastroesophageal junction and fundus of the stomach slide upward. A sliding hernia may result from weakening of the anchors of the gastroesophageal junction to the diaphragm, longitudinal contraction of the esophagus, or increased intraabdominal pressure. Small sliding hernias can be demonstrated commonly during barium studies if intraabdominal pressure is increased. Their incidence increases with age; in the sixth decade of life the prevalence of such hernias is around 60 percent. It is unlikely that a small sliding hiatal hernia by itself produces any clinical symptoms, and its role in the pathogenesis of reflux esophagitis is uncertain.

A *paraesophageal* hernia is one in which the esophagogastric junction remains fixed in its normal location and a pouch of stomach herniates beside the gastroesophageal junction through the esophageal hiatus. A paraesophageal or mixed paraesophageal and sliding hernia may become incarcerated and strangulate. This situation is manifested by acute chest pain, dysphagia, and a mediastinal mass, and requires prompt operative treatment. A herniated gastric pouch may cause dysphagia and may be the site of gastritis and ulceration causing chronic blood loss. A large paraesophageal hernia should be repaired because of a high rate of complications.

ESOPHAGEAL RUPTURE   Perforation of the esophagus may be caused by (1) iatrogenic damage from instrumentation of the esophagus or external trauma; (2) increased intraesophageal pressure associated with forceful vomiting or retching (this is also called spontaneous rupture or Boerhaave's syndrome); or (3) diseases of the esophagus such as corrosive ingestion, peptic ulcer, neoplasm, and, rarely, esophagomalacia. The site of perforation is variable and depends on the cause. Instrumental perforation usually occurs in the pharynx or in the lower esophagus. The esophageal perforation often occurs just above the diaphragm in the posterolateral wall.

Esophageal perforation causes severe retrosternal chest pain which may be worsened by swallowing. Free air enters the mediastinum and spreads to neighboring structures and causes palpable subcutaneous emphysema in the neck, mediastinal crackling sounds on auscultation, and pneumothorax. Pleural effusion and hydropneumothorax may ensue, and severe cases are associated with shock. With time, secondary infection supervenes, and mediastinal abscess and pleuropulmonary suppurative complications may develop. Esophageal perforation associated with vomiting usually deposits gastric contents in the mediastinum and causes severe mediastinal complications. On the other hand, instrumental perforation may be mild and free of severe complications.

Spontaneous rupture of the esophagus may mimic myocardial infarction, pancreatitis, or ruptured abdominal viscus. Symptoms of chest pain may be mild, particularly in the elderly. Mediastinal emphysema may develop late. X-ray of the chest shows abnormalities in the majority of patients, and diagnosis is confirmed by swallow of radiopaque contrast material.

Treatment includes esophageal and gastric suction and parenteral broad-spectrum antibiotics. Surgical drainage and repair of the laceration should be performed as soon as possible. In patients with terminal carcinoma, surgical repair may not be feasible, and those with minor instrumental perforations can be treated conservatively. Extensive corrosive damage may require esophageal diversion and subsequent excision of the damaged portion of the esophagus.

MALLORY-WEISS SYNDROME   Vomiting and retching may cause a tear that involves only the mucosa and is not transmural. The tear usually involves the gastric mucosa near the squamocolumnar mucosal junction, but it may also involve the esophageal mucosa. Patients present with upper gastrointestinal bleeding which may be severe. Most patients recover with only conservative management, but those with severe arterial bleeding require surgery.

FOREIGN BODIES   Foreign bodies may lodge in the cervical esophagus just beyond the upper esophageal sphincter, around the aortic arch, or above the lower esophageal sphincter. Impaction of a bolus of food, particularly a piece of meat or bread, may occur when the esophageal lumen is narrowed due to stricture, carcinoma, or a lower esophageal ring. Acute impaction causes complete inability to swallow and severe chest pain. Both foreign bodies and food boluses may be removed endoscopically. Use of meat tenderizer to facilitate passage of an obstructed meat bolus is to be discouraged because of potential esophageal perforation and aspiration pneumonia.

REFERENCES

CAMERON AJ et al: The incidence of adenocarcinoma in columnar lined (Barrett's) esophagus. N Engl J Med 313:857, 1985

CASTELL DO: Gastroesophageal reflux: Pathogenesis, diagnosis, therapy. Ann Intern Med 97:93, 1982

DEMEESTER TR et al: Esophageal function in patients with angina-like chest pain and normal coronary angiograms. Ann Surg 196:488, 1982

DODDS WJH et al: Mechanism of gastroesophageal reflux in patients with reflux esophagitis. N Engl J Med 307:1547, 1982

FLEISER D, KESSLER F: Endoscopic YAG laser therapy for carcinoma of the esophagus: A new form of palliative treatment. Gastroenterology 85:600, 1983

GELFORD M et al: Isosorbide dinitrate and nifedipine treatment of achalasia: A chemical, manometric and radionuclide evaluation. Gastroenterology 83:963, 1982

GOYAL RK: Disorders of the circopharyngeus muscle. Otolaryngol Clin North Am 17:115, 1984

KELSEN D: Chemotherapy of esophageal cancer. Semin Oncol 11:159, 1984

KIKENDALL JW et al: Pill-induced esophageal injury—case reports and review of the medical literature. Dig Dis Sci 28:174, 1983

LEICHMAN L et al: Properative chemotherapy and radiation therapy for patients with cancer of the esophagus: A potentially curative approach. J Clin Oncol 2:75, 1984

McDONALD GB et al: Esophageal infections in immunosuppressed patients after marrow transplantation. Gastroenterology 88:1111, 1985

SPECHLER SJ, GOYAL RK: *Barrett's Esophagus: Pathophysiology, Diagnosis and Treatment.* New York, Elsevier, 1985

TRIER JS, BJORKMAN DJ: Esophageal, gastric and intestinal candidiasis. Am J Med 77:39, 1984

VANTRAPPEN G, HELLEMANS J: Treatment of achalasia and related motor disorders. Gastroenterology 79:144, 1980

235 PEPTIC ULCER

JAMES E. McGUIGAN

The term *peptic ulcer* is used to refer to a group of ulcerative disorders of the upper gastrointestinal tract which appear to have in common the participation of acid-pepsin in their pathogenesis. The major forms of peptic ulcer are chronic duodenal and gastric ulcer. The Zollinger-Ellison syndrome, which is caused by gastrin-releasing tumors (gastrinomas), may also be considered a form of peptic ulcer.

Although our present knowledge of the etiology of peptic ulcer is incomplete, information from studies in humans and in experimental animals indicates that acid-pepsin is crucial for development of peptic ulcer. The presence or absence of peptic ulcer is determined by the delicate interplay between aggressive factors (secreted gastric acid and pepsin) and defensive factors (mucosal resistance). Peptic ulcer is produced when the aggressive effects of acid-pepsin dominate the protective effects of gastric or duodenal mucosal resistance. Why do not all humans develop peptic ulcer? The normal capacity of gastric and proximal duodenal mucosa to resist the corrosive effects of acid-pepsin is extraordinary and unique. This resistance to acid-pepsin is not shared by other tissues—hence the susceptibility of the esophageal mucosa to injury when exposed to refluxed gastric juice and the frequent ulceration of the small intestine at the site of surgical attachment to actively secreting gastric mucosa.

Much has been learned concerning the mechanisms regulating gastric secretion and about a variety of factors which appear important in the development of peptic ulcer. Consideration of gastric physiology provides an understanding of some elements responsible for producing peptic ulcer as well as a rational basis for its treatment.

GASTRIC PHYSIOLOGY RELATED TO PEPTIC ULCER

The gastric mucosa possesses an extraordinary capacity to secrete acid. Parietal (oxyntic) cells secrete hydrochloric acid by a process involving oxidative phosphorylation. Parietal cells, located in mucosal glands in the body and fundus of the stomach, can secrete hydrogen ions at a concentration 3 million times that found in blood. Hydrogen ions are secreted into the gastric lumen by a proton pump mechanism involving a specific hydrogen–potassium adenosine triphosphatase (H^+,K^+-ATPase) located on the microvilli of the secretory canaliculi of the parietal cells. The estimated concentration of HCl secreted directly by parietal cells is approximately 160 mM. Each secreted hydrogen ion (H^+) is accompanied by a chloride ion (Cl^-). With increased gastric hydrogen ion secretion, there is a reciprocal decrease in sodium ion secretion. For each hydrogen ion secreted into the gastric lumen, one bicarbonate ion (HCO_3^-) is returned via the gastric venous circulation, accounting for the *alkaline tide,* which reflects directly the magnitude of gastric H^+ secretion. Bicarbonate is released from carbonic acid; the latter is generated from carbon dioxide by parietal cell carbonic anhydrase. The two-component hypothesis for secretion of gastric juice proposes that parietal cells secrete pure HCl, which is mixed (in various proportions) with nonparietal cell alkaline secretions, similar in ionic composition to extracellular fluid.

Multiple *chemical, neural,* and *hormonal* factors participate in regulation of gastric acid secretion. Acid secretion is stimulated by gastrin and by cholinergic postganglionic vagal fibers via muscarinic receptors on parietal cells. Gastrin, the most potent known stimulant of gastric acid secretion, is present in cytoplasmic secretory granules in gastrin cells (or G cells) which are interspersed singly or in small clusters among other epithelial cells principally in the mid and deeper portions of the antral pyloric glands. Gastrin, as most, if not all, the gastrointestinal regulatory peptides, is present in multiple molecular forms (Fig. 235-1). The major form of tissue gastrin is heptadecapeptide gastrin (G-17) which contains 17 amino acid residues. Gastrin II is the form of gastrin in which the tyrosyl residue at position 12 is sulfated, and gastrin I is the nonsulfated form. Approximately two-thirds of circulating serum gastrin consists of a larger molecular species of gastrin, namely, "big gastrin," or G-34. This species of gastrin contains 34 amino acids, the carboxyl-terminal 17 of which are identical with heptadecapeptide gastrin and may also be present in sulfated (G-34 II) or nonsulfated (G-34 I) forms. Although G-17 has a shorter half-life than G-34, on a molar basis circulating G-17 is approximately as potent as G-34 in stimulating gastric acid secretion.

More than 90 percent of antral mucosal gastrin is in the form of G-17. Gastrin is also present in duodenal mucosa, the highest concentration being in the most proximal duodenum (approximately 10 percent of the antral concentration). The mucosal concentration of gastrin and the proportion as G-17 decrease with progression down the duodenum. The effects of gastrin and the vagus on gastric acid secretion are intimately related. Vagal stimulation increases gastric acid secretion by (1) directly stimulating parietal cells, (2) stimulating release of gastrin into the circulation, and (3) lowering the parietal cell threshold for response to circulating gastrin concentrations. There is also evidence that certain vagal branches or fibers inhibit gastrin release.

Histamine is present in large concentrations in mast cells in the lamina propria of the parietal cell–containing regions of the gastric mucosa. Histamine-containing mast cells are located in close proximity to parietal cells, with a ratio of one mast cell to every two or three parietal cells. For many years views have differed on the importance of histamine in stimulating gastric acid secretion; some suggested that histamine is the "final common pathway" for cholinergic and

FIGURE 235-1 *Amino acid sequences of selected gastrin peptides, all of which contain the common C-terminal pentapeptide amide. (*Tyrosyl is sulfated in gastrin II and nonsulfated in gastrin I molecules.)*

Big Gastrin (G34)

⌐Glu-Leu-Gly-Pro-Gln-Gly-Pro-Pro-His-Leu-Val-Ala-Asp-Pro-Ser-Lys-Lys-
-Gln-Gly-Pro-Trp-Leu-Glu-Glu-Glu-Glu-Glu-Ala-Tyr*-Gly-Trp-Met-Asp-Phe-NH₂

Heptadecapeptide Gastrin (G 17)

⌐Glu-Gly-Pro-Trp-Leu-Glu-Glu-Glu-Glu-Glu-Ala-Tyr*-Gly-Trp-Met-Asp-Phe-NH₂

Minigastrin (G 14)

Trp-Leu-Glu-Glu-Glu-Glu-Glu-Ala-Tyr*-Gly-Trp-Met-Asp-Phe-NH₂

C-Terminal Pentapeptide

Gly-Trp-Met-Asp-Phe-NH₂

gastrin stimulation of parietal cell acid secretion, while others were skeptical about any role for histamine in the acid secretory process.

Interest in the role of histamine in acid secretion was renewed by the discovery of H-2-receptor antagonists which competitively inhibit the action of histamine on H-2 receptors (located on gastric parietal, cardiac atrial, and uterine smooth-muscle cells). These drugs exert negligible effect on H-1 receptors, which are readily inhibited by conventional antihistamines. H-2-receptor antagonists (e.g., cimetidine and ranitidine) inhibit both basal acid secretion and secretory responses to feeding, gastrin, histamine, hypoglycemia, and vagal stimulation. Most data support the conclusions that (1) histamine plays an important role in stimulating gastric acid secretion, and that (2) histamine acts in concert with gastrin and cholinergic activity on parietal cells, which bear receptors for histamine, gastrin, and acetylcholine, but that (3) there is still uncertainty as to whether histamine is the final common effector molecule in the stimulation of parietal cell secretion.

Food ingestion is the major physiologic stimulus of gastric acid secretion. Traditionally, gastric acid secretion has been classified into three phases—cephalic, gastric, and intestinal. This classification is of some value in examining the multiple factors which regulate gastric acid secretion. The *cephalic phase* represents the gastric acid secretory response to the sight, smell, taste, and anticipation of food. The *gastric phase* is induced by the presence of food in the stomach. The *intestinal phase* is due to the entry or presence of food within the lumen of the small intestine. Although these three phases are convenient for considering the diverse contributions to gastric acid secretion, each phase is complex and not necessarily due to a single stimulatory control mechanism.

The cephalic phase appears to be mediated primarily by the vagus, which increases gastric acid secretion by stimulation of parietal cells directly and to a lesser extent by stimulating the release of gastrin into the circulation. The gastric phase results from stimulation of chemical and mechanical receptors in the gastric wall by luminal contents. Mechanical distention of the stomach stimulates gastric acid secretion but results in little, if any, gastrin release; this mechanical effect is inhibited by atropine and appears to be mediated by vagal reflexes. Food in the stomach promotes gastric acid secretion by increasing gastrin release, principally due to the *protein* content and the *products* of *protein digestion* contained in the meal; oral glucose and fat cause slight increases in serum gastrin but do not stimulate gastric acid secretion. Food in the proximal small intestine stimulates the intestinal phase of gastric acid secretion. A peptone meal (which contains partially hydrolyzed meat protein) introduced into the small intestine stimulates gastric acid secretion but not gastrin release. It has been proposed that food in the small intestine induces release of an intestinal hormone, presumably a polypeptide, which stimulates gastric acid secretion. This substance is believed to be distinct from gastrin and, unlike gastrin, appears to be degraded substantially during its portal transit through the liver.

Ingestion of both caffeine-containing and caffeine-free *coffee* stimulates gastric acid secretion: both forms of coffee stimulate gastrin release. Ingestion of *ethanol* and ethanol-containing beverages stimulates gastric acid secretion. Specifically, ingestion of 5 and 10% ethanol solutions and 10% bourbon whiskey results in prompt stimulation of gastric acid secretion without increasing gastrin release; however, white wine stimulates both gastric acid secretion and gastrin release. Furthermore, intravenous ethanol stimulates gastric acid secretion, suggesting that both systemic and local mechanisms are involved. Intravenous *calcium* stimulates acid secretion and produces minimal increases in serum gastrin levels. Oral calcium has been reported to stimulate gastric acid secretion directly, i.e., without an increase in serum calcium or gastrin concentrations. Except in patients with gastrinoma, hypercalcemia is usually not associated with acid hypersecretion or increases in serum gastrin.

Inhibition of gastric acid secretion can be produced by several mechanisms. Acid secretion may be inhibited by acid in the stomach or duodenum, by hyperglycemia, or by hypertonic fluids or fat in the duodenum. Reduction of the intragastric pH to 3.0 produces partial inhibition of gastrin release; further reduction to pH 1.5 or below blocks the release of gastrin to almost all stimuli. There is evidence that *somatostatin* is involved in the inhibition of gastrin release produced by acid in the gastric lumen. Somatostatin is present in high concentrations in antral mucosal endocrine cells (D cells) which possess cytoplasmic processes that extend to neighboring gastrin cells. The action of somatostatin in inhibiting gastrin release appears to be mediated by its local (paracrine) effects on gastrin cells. The cytoplasmic processes of somatostatin cells also extend to intimate contact with parietal and other cells in the acid-secreting portions of the stomach. Somatostatin is believed to reduce gastric acid secretion by inhibiting gastrin release and by directly inhibiting parietal cell secretion. Acid in the duodenum also inhibits gastric acid secretion; this may be secondary to stimulating the release of secretin and/or other peptides capable of inhibiting gastric acid secretion. *Secretin* is a linear polypeptide containing 27 amino acids bearing structural similarities to glucagon. Secretin is released from endocrine cells (S cells) in the mucosa of the small intestine in response to mucosal acidification. Fat in the duodenum also inhibits gastric acid secretion; gastric inhibitory peptide (GIP) has been proposed as a candidate for this enterogastrone action; however, this effect for GIP remains to be proved. The mechanisms by which hyperglycemia or intraduodenal hyperosmolality inhibit gastric acid secretion are not known. Additional peptides identified in the mucosa of the gastrointestinal tract which have the capacity to inhibit gastric acid secretion include glucagon-like peptides (e.g., glicentin), vasoactive intestinal peptide (VIP), and urogastrone; the latter appears to be structurally and functionally identical with epidermal growth factor. Vasoactive intestinal peptide, which is located in neurons, is unlikely to inhibit gastric acid secretion as a circulating hormone, since it is inactivated during its portal passage through the liver. The extent to which these peptides contribute to the regulation of gastric acid secretion is not clear.

The proteolytic effects of *pepsins* and the corrosive effects of acid appear to be integral components in the tissue injury which leads to peptic ulceration. Acid catalyzes the cleavage of inactive pepsinogen molecules to active pepsins and also provides the appropriate pH required for pepsin activity. Pepsin activity is substantially reduced above pH 4.0, and these enzymes are irreversibly inactivated at neutral or alkaline pH. There are a variety of pepsinogens and pepsins in gastric juice. Pepsinogens (and their corresponding active pepsins) have been classified by immunochemical techniques as either PG I (pepsinogens 1 through 5) or PG II (pepsinogens 6 and 7). Pepsinogen I is present in chief and mucous cells in the body and fundus of the stomach. Pepsinogen II is located in cells of the pyloric glands, Brunner's glands of the duodenum, mucous cells of the gastric cardiac glands, and the same cells in which PG I is found. Both PG I and PG II are present in plasma, while only PG I can be detected in urine. A high degree of correlation exists between serum concentrations of PG I and maximal gastric acid secretion. In general, agents which stimulate gastric acid secretion also stimulate pepsinogen secretion. Cholinergic action is particularly potent in promoting pepsinogen secretion. Secretin, although it inhibits gastric acid secretion, stimulates pepsinogen secretion.

Parietal cells also secrete *intrinsic factor*. Agents which stimulate gastric acid secretion also lead to secretion of intrinsic factor.

The precise mechanisms whereby the normal stomach and duodenum resist the corrosive effects of acid-pepsin (i.e., *mucosal resistance*) have not been defined. A variety of factors have been proposed as potential contributors to mucosal resistance. Gastric mucus, secreted by gastric mucous cells, is present in solution in gastric juice and as an insoluble mucus gel layer which coats the mucosal surface of the stomach. It has been suggested that *gastric mucus* may play a role in mucosal defense against injury, and thus in preventing peptic ulceration. Mucus secretion is enhanced by mechanical or chemical irritation and by cholinergic stimulation. Gastric mucus is a large polymeric glycoprotein (2×10^6 mol wt) containing four subunits connected by disulfide bridges. Depolymerization of the glycoprotein subunits of mucus, which may be produced by peptic digestion or disruption of disulfide bonds, renders the glycoprotein incapable of forming a viscous gel. When intact, this mucus gel serves as an unstirred layer which permits ionic diffusion but is impermeable to penetration by macromolecules such as pepsin (34,000 mol wt). Bicarbonate ions are secreted by gastric surface epithelial cells (nonparietal cells) and enter the unstirred layer of mucus gel; this mechanism facilitates the development of a microenvironment with a substantial hydrogen ion gradient between the gel opposing the gastrin luminal contents (more acid) and the gel surface facing and in intimate contact with the apical surfaces of gastric mucosal cells (more alkaline). Pepsin secreted into the gastrin lumen is denied reentry by the impermeable mucus gel, thereby potentially protecting the mucosal cells from proteolytic injury. Gastric mucus also contains glycoprotein blood group substances. Approximately three-fourths of the population secrete gastric juice containing these AB(H) substances and those individuals are referred to as *secretors.*

Normally the gastric luminal epithelial cell surfaces and intercellular tight junctions provide an almost completely impermeable barrier to back-diffusion of hydrogen ions from the lumen. This *gastric mucosal barrier* may participate in mucosal resistance to acid-peptic ulceration. This barrier may be interrupted by various agents including bile acids, salicylates, alcohol, and weak organic acids, thus permitting *back-diffusion of hydrogen ions* from the lumen to intra- and intercellular sites. Such back-diffusion may result in cellular injury, release of histamine from mast cells, further stimulation of acid secretion, damage to small blood vessels, mucosal hemorrhage, and superficial ulceration. Interruption of the gastric mucosal barrier may be responsible (at least in part) for the hemorrhagic erosive gastritis associated with salicylate and ethanol ingestion and may also contribute to other forms of gastric mucosal injury.

However, the relationship between the gastric mucosal barrier and mucosal resistance to chronic peptic ulcer has not been completely elucidated. *Decreased mucosal blood flow,* accompanied by back-diffusion of available hydrogen ions, also appears to contribute to gastric mucosal damage. Maintenance of normal mucosal blood flow is an essential component of mucosal resistance to injury. *Prostaglandins* are present in abundant quantities in the gastric mucosa. Various prostaglandins, particularly those of the E series, have been shown to inhibit gastric mucosal injury due to a wide variety of agents. It is possible that endogenous prostaglandins contribute to mucosal resistance and may thereby have a "cytoprotective" function. Mild mucosal injury or irritation may induce prostaglandin synthesis, thereby potentially enhancing mucosal resistance to injury, a concept referred to as *adaptive cytoprotection.*

Other mucosal factors, some of which are genetic, but which have not been clearly defined, apparently contribute to the ability of the gastric mucosa to resist or permit the development of peptic ulceration.

MEASUREMENT OF GASTRIC ACID SECRETION

Since HCl secretion by the stomach appears to be an important factor in the production of peptic ulcer disease, measurement of basal and stimulated gastric acid secretion may be of value in the assessment of peptic ulcer patients. In general, basal and stimulated acid outputs in females are approximately two-thirds to three-fourths those found in males. The range of values for normal subjects is extremely broad and overlaps substantially with those found in patients with duodenal ulcer, gastric ulcer, and even the Zollinger-Ellison syndrome. Mean basal acid output (BAO) in normal males without known ulcer disease is about 1.5 to 2.0 meq/h. In duodenal ulcer patients mean basal acid output averages from 4 to 6 meq/h, again with a wide degree of variation. Patients with gastric ulcer tend to have gastric acid secretory rates which are normal or even slightly less than those of normal subjects.

Measurement of gastric acid output is not helpful in either diagnosing peptic ulcer or excluding it. Thus measuring gastric acid secretion is clearly not necessary in all patients with duodenal ulcer. However, detection of gastric acid hypersecretion is of value when the Zollinger-Ellison syndrome is suspected. Measurement of gastric acid output is useful to detect achlorhydria, as found in patients with pernicious anemia. Since patients with benign gastric ulcer virtually always secrete some acid, pentagastrin-fast achlorhydria in a patient with a gastric ulcer almost always indicates malignancy. Measurement of gastric acid secretion is indicated in the search for the cause of ulcer recurrence after surgery for peptic ulcer.

In order to measure gastric acid output, a radiopaque gastric tube is passed so that its tip is located in the most dependent portion of the stomach. With the patient in a reclining or semirecumbent position on the left side, the position of the tube is verified by fluoroscopy. Gastric contents are aspirated and discarded. Basal gastric acid secretions are then collected in four consecutive 15-min intervals to determine the 1-h basal acid output. Secretion volume and acid concentration (titrated with 0.1 N sodium hydroxide to pH 7.0 or calculated by formula from the pH of the aspirated gastric juice) are measured, and acid output is expressed as milliequivalents per hour.

A variety of substances have been used to stimulate maximal acid output (MAO) by the stomach. These have included *histamine, betazole* (Histalog)—a structural analogue of histamine—and *pentagastrin* (Peptavlon). Histamine, the first standard stimulant to be used for gastric acid secretory testing, requires the simultaneous administration of an antihistaminic agent (H-1-receptor antagonist) to inhibit untoward systemic side effects. Betazole possesses fewer undesired side effects of histamine and does not require the concomitant administration of an antihistamine. Pentagastrin (*N-tert*-butyloxycarbonyl-β-Ala-Try-Met-Asp-Phe-NH$_2$) contains the biologically active carboxyl-terminal tetrapeptide amide portion of the gastrin molecule and is currently the preferred and most commonly used agent to induce maximal acid secretion. Following collection of basal acid secretion gastric juice is collected for four additional consecutive 15-min periods after the subcutaneous injection of pentagastrin (6 μg/kg). The MAO is the expression of the milliequivalents of acid aspirated during the 1 h after pentagastrin administration. Peak acid output (PAO) is calculated by combining the two highest consecutive 15-min acid outputs following pentagastrin injection and multiplying by 2.

DUODENAL ULCER

GENERAL CONSIDERATIONS Duodenal ulcer is a chronic and recurrent disease. The ulcer is usually deep and sharply demarcated. It tends to penetrate through the submucosa and often into the muscularis propria. The ulcer floor contains no intact epithelium and usually consists of a zone of eosinophilic necrosis resting on a base of granulation tissue surrounded by variable amounts of fibrosis. The ulcer bed may be clear or contain either blood or a proteinaceous exudate with entrapped erythrocytes and acute and chronic inflammatory cells. More than 95 percent of duodenal ulcers occur in the first portion of the duodenum, and approximately 90 percent of these are located within 3 cm of the junction of the pyloric and duodenal mucosa. Duodenal ulcers are usually round or oval, but they may be irregular or elliptic. They are usually less than 1 cm in diameter. Rarely, duodenal ulcers may be extremely large (3 to 6 cm in diameter) and may be mistaken radiographically for the entire duodenal bulb. These giant ulcers often escape radiologic detection and are usually identified directly by endoscopy or at surgery or postmortem examination.

The absolute prevalence of duodenal ulcer in the population is not known. Estimates have ranged from 6 to 15 percent. This variation may be related to the populations examined, differences in study design and diagnostic methods (e.g., endoscopy vs. radiological examination), and perhaps to actual changes or differences in frequency of duodenal ulcer disease. The best current estimates suggest that approximately 10 percent of the population has clinical evidence of duodenal ulcer at some time in their lifetime. Duodenal ulcer is slightly more common in males than in females and is three times as frequent as clinically recognized gastric ulcer. During the past 35 years the frequency of duodenal ulcer (and its complications) has been decreasing in the United States and England especially in males. The reason or reasons for this reduction are not known.

Approximately 60 percent of healed duodenal ulcers recur within 1 year and from 80 to 90 percent within 2 years. Although much is now known concerning factors which contribute to the development of duodenal ulcer, we do not completely understand its pathogenesis. Acid secretion by the stomach is required for production of a duodenal ulcer, but the factors which render the acid-secreting subject susceptible to duodenal ulceration are not completely understood. As a group, duodenal ulcer patients secrete more acid than normal; however, from one-half to two-thirds of duodenal ulcer patients have gastric acid secretory rates, both BAO and MAO, within the normal range. Duodenal ulcer patients have been shown to have approximately 1.9 billion parietal cells, with a maximum capacity to secrete approximately 42 meq of gastric acid per hour; this is in contrast to 1.0 billion parietal cells and 22 meq/h for nonduodenal ulcer subjects (mean values). However, variations in both groups are so large that most duodenal ulcer patients fall within the normal range. As a group, duodenal ulcer patients also have comparable increases in gastric secretion of pepsin and in serum pepsinogen I levels. Peptic ulcer is believed to develop when there is an unfavorable balance between gastric acid-pepsin secretion and gastric or duodenal mucosal resistance. In duodenal ulcer disease, the evidence favors the etiologic importance of absolute or, in most instances, relative gastric acid hypersecretion. However, in patients with gastric ulcer, defective mucosal resistance appears to be the major permissive factor.

Fasting *serum gastrin* concentrations are normal in duodenal ulcer patients. However, most studies have shown that in response to a protein-containing meal, more gastrin is released into the circulation in duodenal ulcer patients than in normal subjects. Duodenal ulcer patients also have a greater gastric acid secretory response to gastrin than normal persons. Thus, a given dose of pentagastrin or gastrin produces more acid secretion, and smaller doses of pentagastrin or gastrin are required to achieve the same fraction (50 percent) of the maximal acid secretory response in duodenal ulcer patients than in normal subjects. In addition, in duodenal ulcer patients intragastric acid is less effective in inhibiting both gastrin release and gastric acid secretion. Therefore, although fasting serum gastrin levels are normal in duodenal ulcer patients, gastrin may still play an important role in their often observed acid hypersecretion. Duodenal ulcer patients tend to empty their stomachs more rapidly than nonduodenal ulcer patients. This phenomenon, together with acid hypersecretion, may contribute to greater hydrogen ion concentrations in the first part of the duodenum (the primary location of ulceration) in patients with duodenal ulcer.

Genetic factors appear to be important. Duodenal ulcers are approximately three times as common in first-degree relatives of duodenal ulcer patients when compared with the population at large. Patients with duodenal ulcers have an increased frequency of blood group O and of the nonsecretory status [those who do not secrete AB(H) antigens in their gastric juice], but these associations are weak. An increased incidence of HLA-B5 antigen in white male subjects with duodenal ulcer has also been shown. Elevated serum pepsinogen I (PG I) levels have been found in approximately 50 percent of patients with duodenal ulcer. Increases in serum pepsinogen appear to be inherited as an autosomal dominant trait. Individuals with this trait have a frequency of duodenal ulcer eight times greater than the general population. Thus an elevated PG I level may prove to be a valuable subclinical marker of the duodenal ulcer diathesis in families with this autosomal dominant form of peptic ulcer disease.

Cigarette smoking has been associated with increased duodenal ulcer frequency, decreased responses to therapy, and an increased mortality (from duodenal ulcer). Cigarette smoking does not increase gastric acid secretion. It has been suggested that the increased incidence of duodenal ulcer among cigarette smokers may be secondary to the effects of nicotine or cigarette smoking in inhibiting pancreatic bicarbonate secretion (an endogenous neutralizer of secreted gastric acid) and/or by acceleration of gastric emptying of acid into the duodenum. The incidence of duodenal ulcer has also been reported to be increased in patients with chronic renal failure, alcoholic cirrhosis, renal transplantation, hyperparathyroidism, systemic mastocytosis, and chronic obstructive pulmonary disease. Antibodies to herpes simplex have been reported to be higher in titer and more frequent in serums of patients with duodenal ulcer than in normals.

The importance of *psychological factors* in the pathogenesis of duodenal ulcer remains controversial. Contrary to earlier views, there is no single characteristic duodenal ulcer personality. There is no identifiable difference in frequency of duodenal ulcer among different socioeconomic classes or occupation groups. Chronic anxiety and psychological stress may, however, be factors in exacerbation of ulcer activity.

CLINICAL FEATURES Epigastric pain is the most frequent symptom of duodenal ulcer. The pain is often described as burning or gnawing. Just as frequently, however, the pain may be ill-defined, boring, or aching, or is perceived as abdominal pressure or fullness, or as a sensation of hunger. In approximately 10 percent of patients the pain is located to the right of the midepigastrium. The pain characteristically occurs from 90 min to 3 h after eating. It frequently awakens the patient at night. Pain on awakening before breakfast is sufficiently rare in patients with duodenal ulcer as to challenge the diagnosis. The pain is usually relieved within a few minutes by food or antacids. The severity of pain varies substantially from patient to patient, and symptoms tend to be recurrent and episodic. Duodenal ulcer may recur in the absence of pain. Episodes of pain may persist for periods of several days to weeks or months. Periods of remission may last from weeks to years and are almost always longer than the episodes of pain. In some patients the disease is more aggressive, with frequent persistent symptoms and development of complications. Pain relief (whether with antacids or food) is believed to result from acid neutralization. Ingestion of food leads to a transient partial neutralization of gastric acid, which is followed by gastrin release and resultant stimulation of acid secretion. With subsequent gastric emptying and increasing gastric acid secretion, a sufficiently low pH is achieved that pain results. Acid-induced pain in patients with duodenal ulcer is believed due to (1) acid stimulation of chemical receptors and/or (2) alterations in gastric motility.

Changes in the character of the pain may signal the development of complications. For example, ulcer pain which becomes constant, is no longer relieved by food or antacids, or radiates to the back or either upper quadrant may herald *penetration* of the ulcer (often into the pancreas). Ulcer pain which is accentuated rather than relieved by food, and/or is accompanied by vomiting, often indicates *gastric outlet obstruction*. Abrupt, severe, or generalized abdominal pain is characteristic of free *perforation* into the peritoneal cavity. Weight loss, in the absence of some degree of gastric outlet obstruction, is unusual. Duodenal ulcer may cause acute gastrointestinal *hemorrhage*, with vomiting of blood or coffee-grounds material, or with melena, and the passage of black tarry stools or even frank red blood, if the bleeding is massive.

It is important to emphasize that *many patients with active disease have no ulcer symptoms*. This leads to a significant, although not quantifiable, underestimation of duodenal ulcer frequency and recurrence in the population. Recent studies, especially those using duodenoscopy, indicate that there is poor correlation between ulcer activity, resolution of symptoms, and ulcer healing. Since many duodenal ulcer patients are asymptomatic, the absence of ulcer-type pain does not exclude duodenal ulcer as a potential cause for gastrointestinal hemorrhage or symptoms due to gastric outlet obstruction or abrupt ulcer perforation.

On *physical examination* epigastric tenderness is by far the most frequent abnormal finding. The area of tenderness is usually in the midline, often midway between the umbilicus and the xiphoid process. In 20 to 30 percent of patients the tender area is to the right of the midline. Acute free perforation of the ulcer into the peritoneal cavity often produces a rigid, boardlike abdomen, usually with generalized rebound tenderness. In patients with gastric outlet obstruction caused by a duodenal or pyloric channel ulcer one may find a "succussion splash" due to fluid and air in the distended stomach. Tachycardia or hypotension, in some instances demonstrable only by orthostatic maneuvers, may reflect acute hemorrhage from duodenal ulcer. Cutaneous and mucosal pallor may result from anemia from acute or chronic blood loss.

Only about 5 percent of duodenal ulcers are located distal to the duodenal bulb, and most of these are in the immediate postbulbar portion of the first part of the duodenum. Most postbulbar ulcers are of the common duodenal ulcer variety. However, postbulbar ulceration, when located in or beyond the second portion of the duodenum, suggests the Zollinger-Ellison syndrome. Postbulbar ulcer pain may be located in the right upper quadrant or radiate through to the back. Obstruction and hemorrhage are more frequent with postbulbar ulcers than with those in the duodenal bulb.

The pyloric channel, which is 1 to 2 cm in length, is the narrowest portion of the gastric outlet. Because of their gastric acid secretory characteristics and clinical features, pyloric channel ulcers are classified with duodenal rather than gastric ulcer. Ulcers in this location often produce symptoms similar to those of a duodenal ulcer; however, symptoms due to these tend to be less responsive to food and antacids. In patients with pyloric channel ulcers, food may accentuate rather than relieve ulcer pain and may result in vomiting secondary to partial gastric outlet obstruction. In general, surgery is required more frequently with pyloric channel ulcers than with those in the duodenal bulb.

DIAGNOSIS Epigastric pain readily relieved by food or antacids strongly suggests duodenal ulcer. However, many patients with ulcerlike symptoms may have no evidence of an ulcer even after careful radiographic and endoscopic examination. Barium examination of the upper gastrointestinal tract is of value in identifying duodenal ulcer and is the usual method used to establish the diagnosis. The proportion of ulcers identified radiographically depends on the skill, persistence, enthusiasm, and diagnostic criteria of the radiologist. Using conventional barium contrast techniques, 70 to 80 percent of duodenal ulcers visualized by endoscopy can be identified by x-ray examination. With newer double-contrast barium examinations, it is possible to detect approximately 90 percent of duodenal ulcers. On x-ray the typical duodenal ulcer appears as a discrete crater in the proximal portion of the duodenal bulb. Marked deformity of the duodenal bulb, common in patients with chronic recurrent duodenal ulcer, may make radiographic identification of the ulcer difficult or impossible (Figs. 235-2 and 235-3).

Use of fiberoptic endoscopic examination of the upper gastrointestinal tract has facilitated accurate diagnosis of duodenal ulcer disease. Duodenoscopy is not required for diagnosis of duodenal ulcer when it has been established by barium radiographic examination. Endoscopy may be of great value, however, (1) in detecting suspected duodenal ulcer in the absence of radiographically demonstrable ulcer and in patients with radiographic deformity and uncertainty regarding ulcer activity, (2) in identifying ulcers too small or too superficial to be recognized by x-ray, and (3) in identifying an ulcer as the source of active gastrointestinal hemorrhage. Duodenoscopy also permits direct visualization and photographic documentation of the character of the ulcer, its size, shape, and location, and it may provide a reference basis for the assessment of healing. Endoscopic studies have shown that 85 percent of duodenal ulcers are less than 1 cm in diameter, with approximately 70 percent having a diameter between 0.5 and 1 cm.

Measurement of gastric acid secretion is not necessary in most patients with clinical features of a typical duodenal ulcer. Determi-

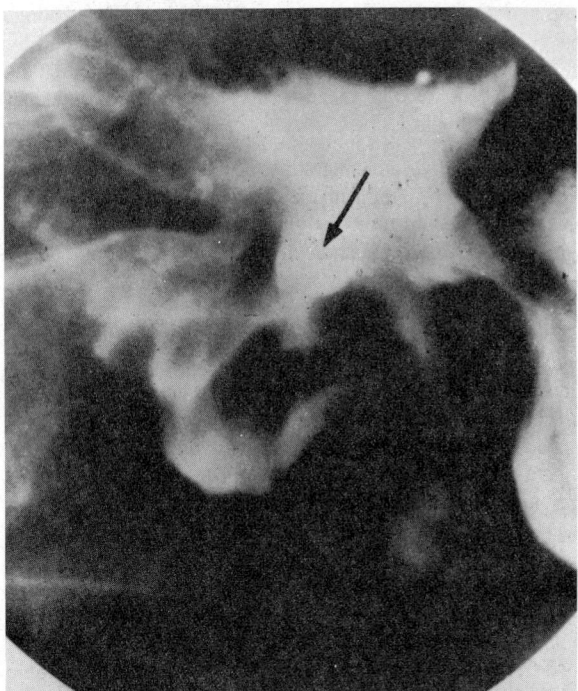

FIGURE 235-2 *Deformed duodenal bulb with ulcer crater.*

nation of serum gastrin is recommended in those patients in whom surgery is planned or gastrinoma is suspected.

MEDICAL TREATMENT Major objectives of therapy are relief of pain and ulcer healing. Prevention of ulcer recurrence and complications are additional objectives. In the past enthusiasm has been expressed for virtually every mode of treatment which has ever been tried for this disease. In many instances conclusions regarding the

FIGURE 235-3 *Distortion of the duodenal bulb with "cloverleaf" deformity.*

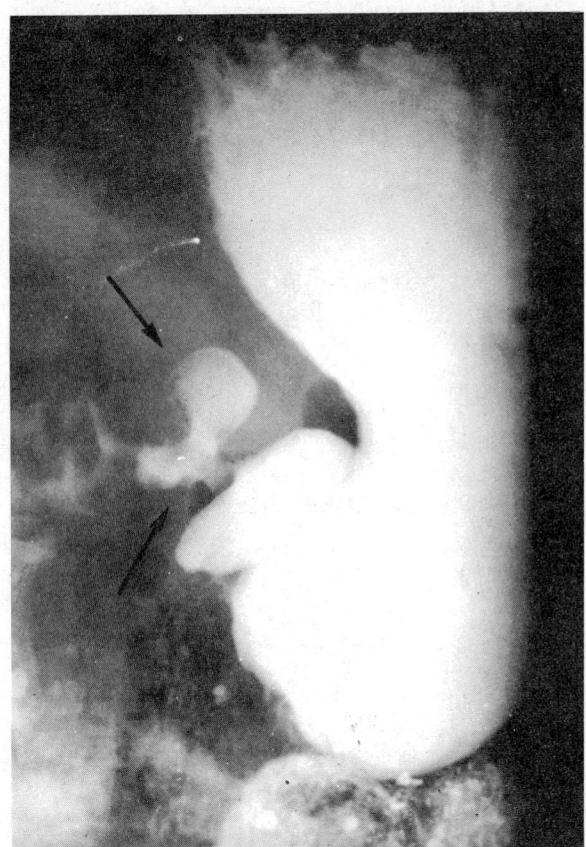

effectiveness of therapy have been obscured by spontaneous healing, an intrinsic component of the natural history of the disease, and by imprecise methods used to assess ulcer activity. Specific agents currently available and recommended for use in treatment of duodenal ulcer are considered below.

Antacids Traditionally, administration of antacids has been the major accepted form of treatment for duodenal ulcer. Studies with endoscopic verification of ulcer activity have established the effectiveness of antacids in accelerating duodenal ulcer healing. Many types of antacids are available and have been used in the treatment of duodenal ulcer. The ideal antacid should be potent in neutralizing acid, inexpensive, not absorbed from the gastrointestinal tract, and contain negligible amounts of sodium. The ideal antacid should be sufficiently palatable to be readily tolerated with repeated dosage and should be free from side effects. Although the ideal antacid is yet to be developed, a number of preparations are available which can be used in treatment of patients with duodenal ulcer. Individual antacids differ substantially in their capacities to neutralize acid, their sodium contents, their absorption properties, and their potential adverse effects.

Calcium carbonate is a potent and inexpensive antacid. In neutralizing acid, it is converted to calcium chloride in the stomach. Approximately 10 percent of calcium ingested as calcium carbonate is absorbed from the proximal small intestine. Unfortunately, chronic calcium carbonate administration may be associated with the milk-alkali syndrome, producing elevations of serum calcium, phosphate, blood urea nitrogen, creatinine, and bicarbonate. These patients may develop renal calcinosis and progressive renal insufficiency. Calcium carbonate is unique among antacids in that its ingestion is followed by stimulation of gastric acid secretion (a genuine "acid rebound" phenomenon). This is due to the direct action of calcium in stimulating parietal cell acid secretion and, perhaps to a lesser extent, to calcium-mediated stimulation of gastrin release. Because of its potential adverse effects, calcium carbonate is not recommended for use as an antacid for treatment of patients with peptic ulcer.

FIGURE 235-4 *Chemical structures of histamine and the H-2-receptor antagonists cimetidine, ranitidine, and famotidine. Note the imidazole ring shared by histamine and cimetidine but absent in ranitidine and famotidine.*

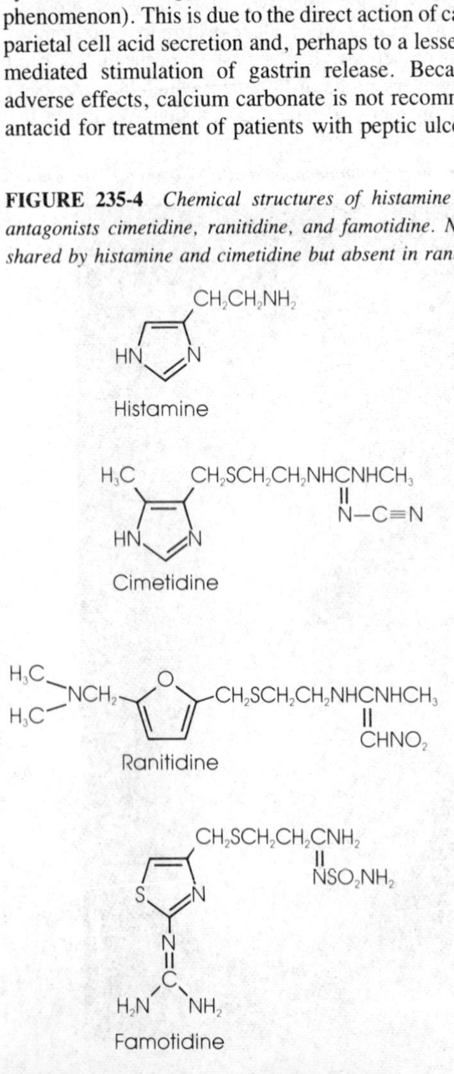

Sodium bicarbonate is a potent, rapidly acting, inexpensive antacid. However, because of its tendency to induce systemic alkalosis and its high sodium content, it should not be used as an antacid in treatment of peptic ulcer.

The most widely used antacid preparations are mixtures of aluminum hydroxide and magnesium hydroxide, in some instances with additional agents. *Aluminum hydroxide* neutralizes hydrochloric acid with the production of aluminum chloride and water. Use of aluminum hydroxide tends to produce constipation. Aluminum binds phosphate within the gut lumen, thereby facilitating its excretion. As a consequence, prolonged and regular use of aluminum hydroxide may induce systemic phosphate depletion with resultant weakness, malaise, and anorexia. This complication is probably restricted to, and must be considered in, patients with a phosphate-deficient diet, e.g., dietary deficiency associated with chronic alcoholism or other states of reduced dietary protein intake.

Magnesium hydroxide is a potent antacid which neutralizes hydrochloric acid to produce magnesium chloride and water. Magnesium hydroxide may produce loosening of the stools. This laxative effect and the constipating effects of aluminum hydroxide can be overcome by using these agents in combination, or by alternating their use. Antacid combinations vary enormously in their capacities to neutralize hydrochloric acid. *Magnesium trisilicate*, which is frequently included in various antacid mixtures, is a slow-acting weak antacid. In general, tablet preparations of magnesium hydroxide–aluminum hydroxide are less potent than their liquid forms.

Acceptance of the crucial role of acid in the pathogenesis of duodenal ulcer provides a rational basis for the use of antacids in treatment of patients with duodenal ulcer. There have been controlled studies on the effects of antacids on duodenal ulcer healing, in which vigorous antacid therapy has been compared with placebo, and ulcer response has been verified by endoscopy. Four weeks of treatment with a potent magnesium and aluminum hydroxide antacid mixture has been shown to increase duodenal ulcer healing. Ulcer healing occurred in 45 percent of patients receiving placebo and in 78 percent of those treated with 30 mL antacid (144 meq) given 1 and 3 h after meals and at bedtime.

H-2-receptor antagonists It has been known for decades that conventional antihistamines, which readily block the actions of histamine on smooth muscle of the gut or bronchi, do not inhibit histamine-stimulated gastric acid secretion. The parietal cell receptor for histamine has been classified as the H-2 receptor and that blocked by classic antihistamines as the H-1 receptor. H-2-receptor antagonists, which are potent inhibitors of basal (unstimulated) and stimulated gastric acid secretion, are the agents which at the present time are most frequently used in the treatment of duodenal ulcer.

The H-2-receptor antagonist *cimetidine* was the first of the agents to be developed and made available for clinical use and is used widely in the treatment of duodenal ulcer. Cimetidine is related structurally to histamine (Fig. 235-4), sharing the same imidazole ring, but bearing an extended side chain which contains a cyanoguanidine group. Cimetidine, at a dose of 300 mg, inhibits basal acid secretion by more than 80 percent and meal-stimulated acid secretion by approximately 70 percent. It strikingly reduces acid secretory responses to histamine, caffeine, insulin, hypoglycemia, and gastrin. Cimetidine has been shown to be more effective than placebo in promoting endoscopically verified duodenal ulcer healing. Its effectiveness in promoting duodenal ulcer healing appears to be comparable to that of vigorous antacid therapy. The oral dose of cimetidine used most commonly for treatment of patients with duodenal ulcer is 300 mg four times daily, with meals and at bedtime. Treatment with 400 mg cimetidine twice each day has also been shown to be effective in treatment of duodenal ulcer. Treatment of active duodenal ulcer with cimetidine is continued for periods from 4 to 8 weeks. Chronic administration of cimetidine, in doses of 400 mg at bedtime or 400 mg twice each day, has been shown to reduce substantially the frequency of duodenal ulcer recurrence during the 12-month period of treatment. Considering the enormous numbers of patients who have been treated with cimetidine, few serious adverse effects have been experienced. Cimetidine administration has been associated with slight and reversible increases in serum transaminase and creatinine levels. Instances of diarrhea, fatigue, and skin rash have also been described. Central nervous system abnormalities (confusion, agitation, coma, disorientation, and seizures) may occur, especially in elderly patients, in those receiving large doses or when there is substantial hepatic/renal functional impairment. Tender gynecomastia may occur especially in patients with the Zollinger-Ellison syndrome, treated with large doses for prolonged periods of time; this is believed to be caused by the weak antiandrogenic effects of cimetidine. Brief increases in serum prolactin have been shown to follow intravenous and oral cimetidine. Cimetidine has been shown to bind to and inhibit the P_{450} cytochrome-mixed oxygenase hepatic enzyme system. As a result, cimetidine may increase blood levels and the duration of action and pharmacologic effects of drugs whose metabolism depends upon this system. These drugs include, among others, phenytoin, chlordiazepoxide, diazepam, warfarin, carbamazepine, and antipyrine. Cimetidine does not interfere with the elimination of benzodiazepines which are eliminated utilizing glucuronide conjugation, for example, lorazepam and oxazepam. Cimetidine also reduces the rate of elimination of lidocaine due to reduced oxidative biotransformation and, perhaps, to reduced hepatic blood flow. Cimetidine may also increase blood levels of theophylline, presumably by inhibition of the terminal oxidase step in its hepatic metabolism.

Ranitidine is a more recently introduced H-2-receptor antagonist which is also commonly used in the treatment of patients with duodenal ulcer. It is a substituted aminomethlyfuran and is structurally unrelated to histamine or cimetidine (Fig. 235-4). On a molar basis, ranitidine is about six times as potent as cimetidine in inhibiting gastric acid secretion. Both cimetidine and ranitidine have similar half-lives of disappearance, approximately 120 min. Ranitidine and cimetidine appear to be comparably effective in accelerating healing of duodenal ulcer. The recommended dose of ranitidine is 150 mg twice each day. It appears to have no antiandrogen properties and exhibits little, if any, inhibitory effect on the cytochrome P_{450} mixed oxygenase enzyme system.

A variety of other H-2-receptor antagonists are under development and evaluation. Among these is *famotidine*, which contains a thiazole ring and is not related structurally to cimetidine or ranitidine (Fig. 235-4). It is not yet available in the United States. Famotidine is an extraordinarily potent H-2-receptor antagonist, being approximately 8 to 10 times as potent as ranitidine in inhibiting gastric acid secretion.

Anticholinergic agents Anticholinergic agents, such as atropine, act by inhibiting the effects of acetylcholine on muscarinic receptors. These agents decrease gastric acid secretion, but not as effectively as H-2-receptor antagonists. Anticholinergics reduce basal gastric acid secretion by approximately 50 percent, histamine- or gastrin-stimulated acid secretion by 40 percent, and postprandial acid secretion by 30 percent. They also delay gastric emptying. Most studies have *not* shown that anticholinergic agents hasten healing or improve symptoms of duodenal ulcer; therefore, they are not recommended as primary therapy for duodenal ulcer. However, anticholinergic agents may prove to be useful when combined in a program of treatment with antacids or H-2-receptor antagonists. Side effects of anticholinergic agents include dryness of mouth, blurring of vision, cardiac arrhythmias, and urinary retention. They should not be used in patients with glaucoma, impaired gastric emptying, or history or symptoms of urinary retention.

There is recent evidence for the existence of two classes of muscarinic cholinergic receptors (M-1 and M-2). *Pirenzepine* appears to be a selective anticholinergic agent in that it is more specific for M-2 receptors. It exhibits greater specificity in inhibiting gastric acid secretion, with fewer side effects than other anticholinergic agents. Pirenzepine, not yet available for use in the United States, has been shown to be effective in the treatment of duodenal ulcer. It may prove to be useful not only as primary therapy but as adjunctive therapy in duodenal ulcer patients.

Coating agents There are several drugs which act neither by neutralization nor by inhibition of gastric acid secretion. Among these is *sucralfate*, a complex polyaluminum hydroxide salt of sucrose sulfate. Its actions are principally local, and it may act in a "cytoprotective" manner. Sucralfate becomes highly polar at acid pH and binds to ulcer tissue for up to 12 h, while relatively little binds to intact gastric or duodenal mucosa. It is believed that adherence of sucralfate to granulation tissue prevents diffusion of hydrochloric acid to the base of the ulcer, thereby potentially protecting it. In addition, sucralfate binds bile acids and pepsin and may therefore reduce their injurious effects on the mucosa. Sucralfate appears to be similar to antacids and H-2-receptor antagonists in its effectiveness in the treatment of duodenal ulcer and in the prevention of duodenal ulcer recurrence. The recommended dose of sucralfate is 1 g 1 h before each meal and at bedtime. It is only minimally absorbed, with less than 5 percent appearing in the urine. *Colloidal bismuth* compounds also aid ulcer healing by forming (in an acid medium) a bismuth-protein coagulant which protects the ulcer from acid-peptic digestion.

Prostaglandins A variety of *prostaglandins*, particularly those of the E series (PGE_1 and PGE_2), are effective in the treatment of duodenal ulcer, with healing rates comparable to those achieved with vigorous antacid therapy and H-2-receptor antagonists. Their action is believed to be twofold: (1) they reduce basal and stimulated gastric acid secretion, and (2) they enhance mucosal resistance to tissue injury (i.e., they are "cytoprotective"). The mechanism, or mechanisms, by which prostaglandins enhance mucosal defense have not been clarified. In addition to their capacity to reduce gastric acid secretion, PGEs (1) stimulate gastric mucus secretion, (2) stimulate gastric and duodenal bicarbonate secretion, (3) maintain gastric mucosal blood flow, (4) maintain the electronegative potential difference of the gastric lumen (compared with the serosa), and (5) stimulate mucosal cellular renewal and regeneration. At present, PGE preparations are not yet available for use in the treatment of duodenal ulcer in the United States.

Diet Many different dietary programs have been recommended and used for treatment of patients with duodenal ulcer. There is no evidence that bland diets reduce gastric acid secretion, promote healing, or relieve symptoms in patients with duodenal ulcer. Similarly soft diets or diets free of spices or fruit juices have not been proved to be of benefit. Traditionally, milk and cream have been prescribed in the treatment of ulcer patients. However, there is no evidence that ulcer healing is benefited by milk and cream diets; in fact, they may contribute to the development of the milk-alkali syndrome.

What dietary measures, if any, should be recommended? Clearly, strict diet control is not necessary. Milk should not be used as a component of treatment for patients with duodenal ulcer. It is reasonable to suggest that if patients experience symptoms after ingestion of certain foods, these should be avoided. A regular diet can be combined with antacids as described below. Because of their effects on gastric secretion it is probably wise for duodenal ulcer patients to avoid coffee, with or without caffeine, as well as other caffeine-containing beverages. It is desirable also to restrict alcohol intake in these patients.

Possible drugs for the future A number of other drugs have been shown in some studies to promote healing of duodenal or gastric ulcer. *Omeprazole*, a specific inhibitor of hydrogen-potassium ATPase of the parietal cells has been shown to be extraordinarily potent in decreasing gastric acid secretion. This drug, which is currently being evaluated clinically, appears to be effective in treatment of patients with common duodenal ulcers and in patients with ulcers associated with gastrinoma (see below). *Sulpiride* is an orthopramide, which is structurally related to metoclopramide, possesses antiemetic and antidepressant properties, and has been used in the treatment of duodenal ulcer patients. *Proglumide*, a derivative of isoglutamic acid, is believed to block gastrin receptors, reduce acid secretion, and increase mucosal resistance.

General therapeutic considerations   How does one integrate available information concerning treatment of duodenal ulcer to construct a reasonable therapeutic formulation? Clinical studies have verified the effectiveness of a variety of drugs in the promotion of duodenal ulcer healing. On the basis of present knowledge, there appear to be several alternative effective approaches for the medical treatment of duodenal ulcer—based on the neutralization of gastric acid by frequent use of potent antacids, the inhibition of gastric acid secretion by H-2-receptor antagonists, or the local "protective" actions of some of the available agents.

Antacid treatment of duodenal ulcer, when selected, should consist of frequent doses of a potent liquid antacid. However, the minimal or optimal doses of antacids required for duodenal ulcer healing are not precisely known. On the basis of an antacid program which has been shown to be effective, it is recommended that the antacid (100 to 140 meq of neutralizing activity; for most antacids this equals 30 to 60 mL) be given 1 and 3 h after each meal and at bedtime. Such a regimen should be continued for approximately 6 weeks. Symptom recurrence may be treated by shorter periods of therapy, at similar dose levels. When *H-2-receptor antagonist* treatment is selected and when *cimetidine* is used, a 300-mg tablet is recommended with each meal and at bedtime or 400 mg twice daily for 6 to 8 weeks. When *ranitidine* is used, the dose is 150 mg twice daily. The locally acting agent *sucralfate* should be given (1 g) 1 h before each meal and on retiring at night for 6 to 8 weeks. Sucralfate should not be given within 30 min of antacids (before or after) because acid is needed to induce adherence of sucralfate to the ulcer. When anticholinergics are used in conjunction with other drugs, they are administered either once a day at bedtime or four times a day (i.e., before meals and at bedtime).

GASTRIC ULCER

INCIDENCE AND ANATOMIC LOCATION   The peak incidence for gastric ulcer is in the sixth decade, approximately 10 years later than for duodenal ulcer. Approximately 55 percent of gastric ulcers occur in males. They are also similar histologically to duodenal ulcers. Characteristically, gastric ulcers are deep and extend beyond the mucosa of the stomach. Almost all benign gastric ulcers are located in the *antrum,* in a zone immediately distal to the junction of the antral mucosa with the acid-secreting mucosa of the body of the stomach. The location of this junction is variable, especially on the lesser gastric curvature. In general, the antrum extends approximately two-thirds of the way up the lesser curvature and one-third of the way up the greater curvature of the stomach. Benign gastric ulcers are rare in the fundus of the stomach. Benign gastric ulcers are almost always accompanied by gastritis and variable amounts of mucosal atrophy involving the antrum. Gastritis may be present or absent with aspirin-associated gastric ulcers; ulcers associated with salicylate ingestion are usually located in the antrum, but they are not confined to the junction of the antral and parietal cell mucosa, as are common gastric ulcers.

ETIOLOGY AND PATHOGENESIS   Acid-pepsin appears to be important in the pathogenesis of gastric ulcer. In contrast to duodenal ulcer, however, gastric ulcer patients generally have acid secretory rates which are normal, or even reduced, when compared with nonulcer subjects. Although many patients with gastric ulcer have reduced rates of acid secretion, *true achlorhydria* in response to stimulation *almost never occurs* in patients with *benign* gastric ulcer. Ten to twenty percent of patients with gastric ulcer also have duodenal ulcer disease. Patients with both duodenal and gastric ulcers tend to have acid secretory patterns which parallel those of duodenal ulcer. Patients with pyloric channel ulcers have acid secretory rates and clinical patterns similar to those found with common duodenal ulcer.

Various factors are involved in the pathogenesis of gastric ulcer. Most evidence supports the importance of primary defects in gastric mucosal resistance and/or direct gastric mucosal injury as the most important elements. Serum gastrin levels are increased in some gastric ulcer patients, but these increases are limited to those with gastric acid hyposecretion. Gastric emptying has also been shown to be delayed. It has been suggested that regurgitation of duodenal contents, especially those containing bile, may induce gastric mucosal injury and subsequent gastric ulceration. Gastric ulcer patients have been shown to have increased duodenal-gastric reflux of bile and greater concentrations of bile in their stomachs when compared with nonulcer subjects or duodenal ulcer patients. It has been proposed that bile acids injure the gastric mucosa by interruption of the gastric mucosal barrier with resultant back-diffusion of secreted hydrogen ions. The factors producing duodenal-gastric reflux in gastric ulcer patients have not been clearly established; a defect in pyloric sphincter function has been proposed.

CLINICAL FEATURES   As with duodenal ulcer, epigastric pain is the most common symptom. However, this symptom is much less typical and predictable than those in patients with duodenal ulcer. While the pain may be similar to that noted with duodenal ulcers, some gastric ulcer patients experience no relief of pain with eating, and pain may actually be precipitated or accentuated by food. Relief of symptoms with antacids is also less consistent with gastric than with duodenal ulcers. Gastric ulcers tend to heal, but then recur, often in the same location. Recognizable episodes of recurrent gastric ulcer activity are usually less frequent than with duodenal ulcer. The precise incidence of gastric ulcer is not known, since many gastric ulcer patients are asymptomatic. Although duodenal ulcer is identified clinically as more frequent than gastric ulcer, most autopsy studies show an equal or greater proportion of gastric ulcers when compared with duodenal ulcers. This may be due in part to more acute preterminal events but also may reflect the often asymptomatic clinical course of gastric ulcer. While nausea and vomiting almost always indicate gastric outlet obstruction in duodenal ulcer patients, these symptoms may occur in patients with gastric ulcer in the absence of mechanical obstruction. Weight loss occurs in about 40 percent of patients due to anorexia or to food aversion from discomfort produced by eating.

Hemorrhage is a common complication, occurring in approximately 25 percent. Gastric ulcer perforation is less frequent than hemorrhage. Mortality with perforation of gastric ulcers is approximately three times that which occurs with duodenal ulcers. This increased mortality is due only in part to the increased age of gastric ulcer patients. The greater mortality may also be due to uncertainty and delay in diagnosis, as well as to greater soilage of the peritoneum with gastric ulcer perforation. Mortality is also greater in patients with hemorrhage due to gastric ulcer than when associated with duodenal ulcer. Gastric outlet obstruction may develop when ulcers are in the pyloric channel or in the most distal antrum, but it is not a common complication in other parts of the stomach.

DIAGNOSIS   The history may be of value in suspecting gastric ulcer, but it is not as characteristic as in duodenal ulcer. The two major methods for diagnosis are barium examination and endoscopy. Gastric ulcer can usually be identified by the standard barium examination with an accuracy that approaches 90 percent. Superficial ulcerations and erosions, however, may escape radiographic identification. Approximately 4 percent of gastric ulcers which appear benign radiographically prove to be malignant (by endoscopic biopsy or at surgery). Both benign and malignant gastric ulcers are more common on the lesser than on the greater curvature (Fig. 235-5). Radiation of gastric mucosal folds from the margin of the ulcer crater suggests a benign lesion. Large gastric ulcers, i.e., those greater than 3 cm in diameter, are more often malignant than smaller ones. An ulcer within a mass, as defined radiographically, also suggests malignancy. Because of false-positive and false-negative errors, radiographic appearance cannot be used as the sole criterion for the benign or malignant nature of a gastric ulcer.

Endoscopic visualization of the ulcer allows one to define its size, location, and, by biopsy, its histologic characteristics. At gastroscopy a total of at least six biopsies should be obtained from the inner

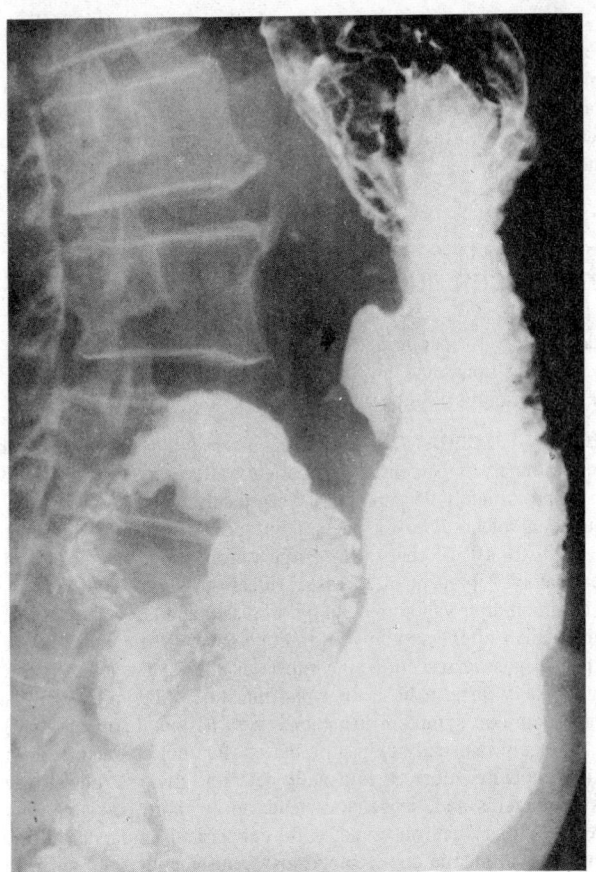

FIGURE 235-5 *Benign lesser curvature gastric ulcer. Note ulceration beyond the projected margins of the stomach and the collar of edema.*

margin of the ulcer and from the ulcer bed. If accurate cytology is available, brushings of the ulcer should be obtained prior to biopsy. By application of combined radiographic, endoscopic, and histologic techniques, distinguishing a malignant from a benign gastric ulcer should be possible with greater than 95 percent confidence.

Gastric ulcer in association with histamine- or pentagastrin-fast achlorhydria, is rare. When it occurs, it almost always indicates that one is dealing with a gastric carcinoma. However, most patients with gastric carcinoma (about two-thirds to three-fourths) are capable of secreting some gastric acid, although it is usually less than normal.

MEDICAL TREATMENT *Antacids* are effective in gastric ulcer treatment. However, since acid hypersecretion is not characteristic of the disease, smaller doses of antacid may be required than for treatment of duodenal ulcer. It is suggested that 15 to 30 mL of a potent liquid antacid be taken 1 and 3 h after meals and at bedtime. *H-2-receptor antagonists* and *sucralfate* are approximately as effective as antacid therapy in the treatment of gastric ulcer. The recommended dosage schedules for these drugs are similar to those in patients with duodenal ulcer. In general, a gastric ulcer tends to heal more slowly than a duodenal ulcer, and the healing response rates are somewhat less than those for a duodenal ulcer.

Anticholinergic agents have been recommended by some physicians. However, because of substantial side effects of anticholinergic drugs, their tendency to reduce gastric emptying, which is already impaired in these patients, the fact that gastric ulcer patients are often older and, therefore, more susceptible to the complications of these agents, and the lack of evidence for their benefit, the use of anticholinergic drugs in gastric ulcer treatment does not appear justified. Some studies suggest that hospitalization and/or cessation of smoking are of benefit in gastric ulcer healing.

Since salicylate ingestion has been associated with the development of gastric ulcers, patients with gastric ulcer should not ingest salicylates. Alcohol, because of its injurious effects on the gastric mucosa, should also be avoided. Milk and cream, as well as bland or homogenized diets, have not been shown to be of value in treatment. In general, it is probably sufficient to recommend that patients take a diet of their own choice. Since coffee (caffeine-containing or caffeine-free) and other caffeine-containing liquids stimulate gastric acid secretion, it may be desirable to omit these beverages.

Carbenoxolone has been used in many countries (but not in the United States) in the treatment of gastric ulcer. This drug is a hydrolytic product of glycyrrhizic acid (derived from licorice) and has been shown to decrease symptoms and increase the rate of gastric ulcer healing. Carbenoxolone does not decrease gastric acid secretion but increases the life span of gastric mucosal epithelial cells and increases the secretion and viscosity of gastric mucus. Carbenoxolone possesses aldosterone-like effects, and thus sodium and water retention tend to occur. It is possible to inhibit the aldosterone-like effects of carbenoxolone by use of aldosterone antagonists; however, the latter also abolish the healing effects of carbenoxolone. Problems with sodium and water retention and the availability of alternative drugs have led to its decreased use.

The failure of gastric ulcer to decrease satisfactorily in size and to heal with medical treatment has been used to suggest gastric malignancy. Benign gastric ulcers should heal completely after 3 months of vigorous therapy. Upper gastrointestinal barium examination or gastroscopy should be performed after 4 weeks of treatment, at which time definite healing should be demonstrable in benign gastric ulcers—the diameter of most ulcers should be reduced by more than 50 percent. If at 4 weeks the ulcer is not reduced in size, malignancy must be suspected and sought for by appropriate biopsies of the ulcer and exfoliative cytology. If the ulcer has not healed completely at 8 weeks, endoscopic examination should be repeated in another month, at which time most benign gastric ulcers should have healed. In general, large gastric ulcers heal more slowly than smaller ones. It is important to continue treatment to endoscopically verify complete ulcer healing. One must be alert, however, to the occasional "healing" of an ulcerating gastric carcinoma with treatment. Apparent complete healing does not assure the benign nature of a gastric ulcer since approximately 70 percent of gastric ulcers eventually found to be malignant will undergo significant healing (albeit usually incomplete) with medical treatment.

COMPLICATIONS AND SURGERY FOR PEPTIC ULCER

Surgery is reserved for patients with complications of peptic ulcer and for those who do not respond to vigorous and attentive medical treatment. Complications include hemorrhage, obstruction, and perforation.

Hemorrhage occurs in approximately 15 to 20 percent of patients with duodenal ulcers; there may be a recurrence of bleeding in about 40 percent of patients with an initial hemorrhage. In most patients hemorrhage from peptic ulcer responds satisfactorily to medical management—including gastric suction and antacid or H-2-receptor antagonist administration.

Free *perforation* into the peritoneal cavity occurs in approximately 6 percent of patients with duodenal ulcer. Five to ten percent of these patients will have had no recognizable ulcer symptoms prior to perforation. Simultaneous hemorrhage occurs in approximately 10 percent of patients with duodenal ulcer perforation; mortality is greatly increased in this group. Duodenal ulcers, especially those located posteriorly, may penetrate into adjacent structures, most often the pancreas—frequently resulting in increased serum amylase levels. Less commonly, duodenal ulcers may penetrate into the liver, biliary tract, or colon.

Gastric outlet *obstruction* occurs in 2 to 4 percent of patients admitted to the hospital with duodenal or pyloric channel ulcers.

Symptoms include abdominal bloating, nausea, vomiting, and weight loss. These patients usually have had ulcer symptoms for many years and often obstructive symptoms for several months.

Failure to respond satisfactorily to medical treatment requires consideration of surgery. The true incidence of lack of ulcer healing with vigorous medical programs is not known; it is clear, however, that most patients with peptic ulcer can be treated successfully without surgery.

Decisions regarding surgery for patients with complications of peptic ulcer must be individualized. Risks of surgery must be balanced with risks of the disease. The patient's discomfort, costs of medical care and hospitalization, and time lost from work must be weighed in relation to the morbidity and possible mortality associated with surgery and anesthesia, risks of recurrent ulcer, and long-term postoperative sequelae. The skill and experience of the surgeon must be weighed as major factors in considering operation.

SURGERY FOR DUODENAL ULCER   No single surgical procedure has been accepted universally as the most satisfactory duodenal ulcer operation. At present the most commonly performed surgical procedures are *vagotomy with antrectomy, vagotomy with pyloroplasty, and parietal cell vagotomy* (also referred to as *proximal gastric or superselective vagotomy*) without a gastric drainage procedure. With conventional (truncal) vagotomy and antrectomy, the vagal trunks are transected, the antrum is removed, and gastrointestinal continuity is reestablished by anastomosis of the remaining stomach with the proximal duodenum (Billroth I anastomosis) or with a loop of the jejunum (Billroth II anastomosis). Vagotomy and antrectomy is an effective procedure with a low recurrence rate (approximately 1 percent). Morbidity and mortality with vagotomy and antrectomy are variable, depend upon patient selection and the skill of the surgeon, but are probably slightly greater than with vagotomy and pyloroplasty.

When the procedure of vagotomy and pyloroplasty is selected, pyloroplasty is performed to facilitate gastric drainage after truncal or selective vagotomy. Vagotomy is performed to inhibit vagal stimulation of gastric acid secretion. Vagotomy does not inhibit gastrin release; in fact, release of gastrin is enhanced after vagal interruption. As indicated above, three types of vagotomy are now used in the surgical treatment of duodenal ulcer and pyloric channel ulcer, namely, *truncal vagotomy, selective vagotomy*, and *parietal cell vagotomy*. Pyloroplasty with truncal vagotomy, which is still the most commonly performed method of vagal transection in the United States, is associated with approximately 1 percent mortality. Ulcer recurrence during the 5 years after surgery is about 5 to 8 percent. With selective vagotomy only the branches of the vagus which supply the stomach are transected, preserving the vagal innervation of the other abdominal viscera. Selective vagotomy has been found by some surgeons to result in a more complete vagotomy, less ulcer recurrence, and fewer postvagotomy complications than truncal vagotomy. Parietal cell vagotomy denervates only the acid-secreting portion of the stomach, sparing the branches of the vagus which innervate the antrum, and a gastric drainage procedure is unnecessary. Both immediate and late postoperative complications are less common with parietal cell vagotomy than with truncal vagotomy, and reductions in acid secretion with parietal cell vagotomy are generally comparable with those achieved with truncal or selective vagotomy. Mortality with parietal cell vagotomy is less than 1 percent. Most studies indicate that with experience in the performance of parietal cell vagotomy, recurrence is comparable to that with other forms of vagotomy with pyloroplasty. This procedure, which is being used with increasing frequency, appears to be an effective and safe surgical therapy for duodenal ulcer.

SURGERY FOR GASTRIC ULCER   Surgical treatment is required for gastric ulcer patients who do not respond satisfactorily to medical therapy or who develop complications similar to those described for duodenal ulcer. With the available diagnostic accuracy of careful radiographic examination, endoscopy, biopsy of the ulcer margins, and exfoliative cytology, it should rarely be necessary to operate

because of a remaining uncertainty regarding the malignant or benign nature of the ulcer. The recommended surgical procedure for the treatment of gastric ulcer is antrectomy with gastroduodenal (Billroth I) anastomosis. It is not necessary to perform a vagotomy when antrectomy is performed for gastric ulcer (not located in the pyloric channel).

CONSEQUENCES AND SYNDROMES AFTER PEPTIC ULCER SURGERY

Modern surgery for peptic ulcer is effective in both the treatment of ulcer complications and in the prevention of ulcer recurrence. However, numerous postoperative sequelae and syndromes may occur.

RECURRENT ULCERATION   Recurrent ulceration has been reported in approximately 5 percent of all patients after surgery for peptic ulcer. Approximately 95 percent of these recurrences follow surgery for duodenal ulcer disease. The risk of development of recurrent ulcer is 3 to 10 percent after surgery for duodenal ulcer and approximately 2 percent after gastric ulcer surgery. Recurrence is more common after vagotomy and pyloroplasty and after parietal cell vagotomy than after vagotomy and antrectomy. When ulcers occur after partial gastric resection, the site is usually at the anastomosis or immediately distal to it in the small intestine. Abdominal pain is the most common symptom in patients with a stomal (or marginal) ulcer. The pain is usually epigastric but is often not characteristic of common duodenal ulcer. It is usually, but not always, relieved by meals or antacids and, in general, tends to be more persistent and progressive than that observed with unoperated duodenal ulcer. Hemorrhage or anemia due to blood loss, nausea and vomiting from obstruction, weight loss, or symptoms from perforation may occur. The development of a stomal ulcer after duodenal ulcer surgery usually indicates that an incomplete vagotomy was performed. Inadequate gastric resection, when performed without vagotomy, may also result in stomal ulceration. Additional causes for the development of recurrent ulcer include an excessively long jejunal afferent loop, an inadvertently performed gastroileal or gastrocolic anastomosis, poor gastric drainage, and ingestion of ulcerogenic drugs. Less commonly, a marginal ulcer may be caused by gastrinoma or by acid hypersecretion secondary to retained antrum. If patients with gastrinomas are treated by gastroenterostomy, stomal ulceration is almost inevitable.

Radiographic examination with barium is of limited diagnostic value and identifies only from 50 to 65 percent of stomal ulcerations. Surgical deformity at the anastomotic site may often mimic stomal ulcer in its absence, or conceal it when present. When suspected, endoscopic examination is required to identify stomal ulceration. Medical treatment with antacids is almost always unsatisfactory in patients with stomal ulcer. Cimetidine has been used successfully in inducing healing of recurrent ulcer. The long-term effects of cimetidine on recurrent ulcers and the prevention of their further recurrence remain to be established. Surgery is usually necessary for treatment of ulcer recurrence and it is usually, but not invariably, successful. In patients with recurrent ulcer provocative testing should be performed and measurements made of serum gastrin to identify or exclude gastrinoma (see below).

RECURRENT ULCER DUE TO RETAINED ANTRUM   Recurrent ulcers have been described in a small number of patients after antrectomy with gastrojejunostomy (Billroth II anastomosis) in which the antral resection was not complete. In these patients the distal antrum, inadvertently not resected, remains in continuity with the duodenum after surgery. These patients usually develop or continue to have gastric acid hypersecretion due to gastrin release by the residual antral mucosa which is no longer in contact with gastric acid, the normal inhibitor of gastrin release. In these patients fasting serum gastrin levels may be normal to moderately increased. Patients with retained antrum can be distinguished from those with gastrinoma by intravenous injection of secretin with measurements of serum gastrin. Gastrinoma patients exhibit paradoxical increases in serum gastrin, whereas in those with retained antrum, serum gastrin levels decrease after secretin administration (see Table 235-1). These patients can be treated successfully by surgical removal of the remaining antrum.

AFFERENT LOOP SYNDROMES Patients with partial gastric resection with gastrojejunostomy (Billroth II anastomosis) may experience abdominal bloating and pain 20 min to 1 h after eating, frequently followed by nausea and vomiting. The vomitus often contains large amounts of bile. Characteristically, the bloating and abdominal discomfort are relieved by vomiting. This type of afferent loop syndrome, which is uncommon, is believed to be caused by distention of an incompletely draining afferent intestinal loop by pancreatic and biliary secretions which are stimulated by eating. Serum amylase levels may be mildly or moderately increased. Because of partial obstruction it is often difficult to demonstrate the afferent loop by barium meal examination. Treatment is surgical correction of the incomplete afferent loop obstruction, and, in some instances, revision to a gastroduodenal anastomosis.

A second form of afferent loop dysfunction is that due to stasis with bacterial overgrowth within the afferent loop. These patients may exhibit the same characteristics as are found with other forms of small intestinal bacterial overgrowth or blind loop syndromes (see Chap. 237). These include malabsorption, especially of fat and vitamin B_{12}. Correction of the afferent loop bacterial overgrowth syndrome can be accomplished by surgical revision of the afferent loop.

BILE REFLUX GASTRITIS After peptic ulcer surgery a small proportion of patients experience early satiety, abdominal discomfort, and vomiting, which is believed due to reflux of duodenal contents into the stomach. Endoscopic examination usually reveals regurgitated bile in the stomach and diffuse gastritis, often involving the entire gastric remnant. Various terms assigned to this entity include *alkaline reflux gastritis, bile reflux gastritis, duodenogastric reflux,* and *bilious vomiting.* The mechanisms or materials contained in the refluxed intestinal contents accounting for these symptoms have not been defined. Although the term bile reflux gastritis has been used, there is no certainty that regurgitated bile is responsible for the syndrome. Administration of cholestyramine, intended to bind bile acids and facilitate their excretion, has not been of benefit in this disorder. Some surgeons have reported successful treatment of bile reflux gastritis by diversion of duodenal contents from proximity to the stomach with a Roux en Y anastomosis.

DUMPING SYNDROME Following peptic ulcer surgery some patients experience an assortment of vasomotor symptoms after eating. These include palpitation, tachycardia, lightheadedness, diaphoresis, and, less frequently, postural hypotension. Abdominal discomfort and vomiting may also occur. The vasomotor symptoms, referred to as the *early dumping syndrome,* are usually experienced within 30 min after eating and are believed to result from rapid emptying of hyperosmolar gastric contents into the proximal small intestine. This leads to a shift of fluid into the gut lumen and produces intestinal distention and contraction of plasma volume. Additional proposed mechanisms for these symptoms include stimulation of autonomic reflexes secondary to small intestinal distention and/or release of hormones from the gut in response to rapid entry of gastric contents into the duodenum or jejunum.

The *late dumping syndrome* refers to a symptom complex comprising dizziness, lightheadedness, palpitation, diaphoresis, confusion, and, in rare instances, syncope, occurring 90 min to 3 h after eating. The symptoms can often be precipitated by meals rich in simple carbohydrates, especially sucrose. The syndrome appears to be caused by hypoglycemia due to insulin release stimulated by abrupt increases in blood glucose secondary to rapid emptying of sugar-containing meals into the proximal small intestine.

Both forms of the dumping syndrome are treated by dietary measures. These include limitation of simple sugar-containing liquids and solids (sweets), elimination of liquids at mealtime, and frequent small meals. Most patients have not been benefited by surgical procedures such as insertion of reversed jejunal loops and isoperistaltic jejunal interposition.

POSTVAGOTOMY DIARRHEA A significant number of patients experience diarrhea after peptic ulcer surgery, especially with a procedure including truncal vagotomy. Diarrhea usually occurs within 2 h of eating. Although the mechanism is not clear, interruption of vagal fibers to the abdominal viscera appears to play an important role in the production of the diarrhea. The surgical drainage procedure, pyloroplasty or antrectomy, which removes the pyloric regulatory emptying mechanism, may also contribute to the diarrhea. Diarrhea has been estimated to occur in 20 to 30 percent of patients after truncal vagotomy with drainage, in 4 to 20 percent with selective vagotomy and drainage, and in only 1 to 8 percent of those with parietal cell vagotomy (without drainage). Rapid emptying of gastric contents into the small intestine, resulting in increased fluid volume within the intestinal lumen, due to the osmotic action of the meal, may also contribute to the diarrhea.

HEMATOLOGIC COMPLICATIONS Intrinsic factor secreted by gastric parietal cells is necessary for active absorption of vitamin B_{12} by the distal ileum. Patients who have had total gastrectomy invariably will develop malabsorption of vitamin B_{12} and should receive monthly intramuscular injections of vitamin B_{12} (50 to 100 μg indefinitely). Megaloblastic anemia due to vitamin B_{12} deficiency is rare after partial gastric resection; however, reduced serum vitamin B_{12} levels have been observed in about 14 percent of these patients. Even more rarely vitamin B_{12} deficiency may be produced by bacterial overgrowth in a stagnant afferent loop following Billroth II anastomosis. Gastritis in the remaining stomach develops in more than 60 percent of duodenal ulcer patients after vagotomy and antrectomy or vagotomy and pyloroplasty. This may result in decreased vitamin B_{12} absorption. Inasmuch as the stomach secretes intrinsic factor in excess of need by approximately 100 times, peptic ulcer patients treated with partial gastric resection do not develop vitamin B_{12} deficiency secondary to the amount of stomach resected. (In addition, the resected portion of the stomach is almost always principally antrum, which contains few parietal cells.) However, after peptic ulcer surgery patients may develop decreased serum vitamin B_{12} levels due to reduced absorption of food-bound vitamin B_{12}; these patients will often have normal absorption of free vitamin B_{12}, as used in the Schilling test. The precise mechanism for the malabsorption of food-bound vitamin B_{12} is not known. It may be due in part to rapid emptying of gastric contents, with reduced efficiency of intrinsic factor binding of vitamin B_{12}. Anemia after peptic ulcer surgery may also result from deficiency produced by malabsorption of iron or folate. A combined deficiency of vitamin B_{12}, iron, and folate is common in patients with anemia following partial or subtotal gastric resection. Iron deficiency is the

TABLE 235-1 Provocative gastrin tests

Disorder	Serum gastrin response (change from basal levels)	
	After IV secretin injection	After test meal
Zollinger-Ellison (gastrinoma)	Increase (greater than 200 pg/mL)	Little or no increase (increases less than 50%)
Common duodenal ulcer	No change (or slight decrease or slight increase)	Moderate increase (may be slightly more than normal, but less than in gastrin cell hyperplasia)
Antral gastrin cell hyperplasia	Decrease	Striking increase (greater than 200%)
Achlorhydria (e.g., pernicious anemia, chronic gastritis)	Decrease	Moderate increase

most common single hematologic defect after peptic ulcer surgery and may result from either blood loss (e.g., with persistent or recurrent ulcer) or from iron malabsorption. Patients with gastric resection malabsorb dietary iron but have normal absorption of iron salts; therefore they will respond favorably to treatment with therapeutic oral iron preparations. Folate deficiency may result from either reduced dietary intake or impaired folate absorption. Except for the anemia produced by blood loss in association with early recurrent ulcer disease, the development of anemia after peptic ulcer surgery is gradual, usually occurring several years postoperatively.

The nature of the anemia after ulcer surgery should be clarified by determination of the red blood cell morphology and by measurements of serum iron, folate, and vitamin B_{12}. Iron or folate deficiency may be treated by oral replacement. Vitamin B_{12} deficiency should be treated with monthly intramuscular injections of the vitamin.

OSTEOMALACIA AND OSTEOPOROSIS   Osteoporosis and osteomalacia may develop after partial or complete gastrectomy but occur rarely after vagotomy and pyloroplasty. Osteomalacia is extremely frequent following gastrojejunostomy or Billroth II anastomosis. These bone changes are believed to result from malabsorption of calcium and vitamin D. Patients may develop bone pain and have pathologic fractures. The incidence of bone fractures in men following gastric resection has been estimated to be almost twice that of control subjects of similar age. Reduced bone density requires years to develop and can be identified by x-ray. Patients with osteomalacia usually have increased levels of serum alkaline phosphatase and may have reduced serum calcium concentrations. These patients should be treated by supplemental oral vitamin D and calcium. In fact, the frequency of osteoporosis and osteomalacia after partial or complete gastrectomy is sufficiently great that treatment with vitamin D and calcium should probably be instituted and continued indefinitely in these patients, especially females, following gastric resection.

GENERAL MALABSORPTION (See Chap. 237)   Mild, chemically demonstrable steatorrhea is common in patients after ulcer surgery. Weight loss is more common after partial gastric resection than with vagotomy without resection and occurs in approximately 60 percent of patients in whom a portion of the stomach has been removed. The major cause of weight loss after peptic ulcer surgery is reduced food intake. On a 100-g fat diet, loss of stool fat seldom exceeds 15 g per day (normal individuals, less than 7 g per day). The causes of maldigestion and malabsorption after peptic ulcer surgery include rapid gastric emptying, reduced dispersion of food in the stomach, reduced bile concentrations in the gut lumen, increased rate of transit of the meal through the small intestine, and reduced or delayed pancreatic secretory responses to feeding. Steatorrhea and weight loss, sometimes accompanied by vitamin B_{12} malabsorption, may develop as a result of bacterial overgrowth, especially in patients with afferent loop bacterial stasis. Overt symptoms and other manifestations of malabsorption appearing after surgery for peptic ulcer may also be due to other preexisting conditions, including latent celiac sprue and chronic pancreatitis.

CARCINOMA AFTER PARTIAL GASTRECTOMY   Several studies have documented an increased incidence of adenocarcinoma of the stomach in duodenal ulcer patients following partial gastric resection and after vagotomy and drainage without resection. This usually develops 10 or more years after ulcer surgery. The possibility of carcinoma of the stomach should be considered when abdominal symptoms, which may be similar to or distinct from those due to the original ulcer, appear many years after apparently successful surgery.

ZOLLINGER-ELLISON SYNDROME (GASTRINOMA)

In 1955 Zollinger and Ellison described the syndrome which bears their names, i.e., ulcer disease of the upper gastrointestinal tract, marked increases in gastric acid secretion, and nonbeta islet-cell tumors of the pancreas.

ETIOLOGY AND PATHOGENESIS   Zollinger and Ellison, in their original description of the syndrome, suggested that the ulcer disease in these patients resulted from liberation of a secretagogue from the islet-cell tumors which accounted for the often enormously increased rates of gastric acid secretion. Their proposal was proved correct when in 1960 extracts of Zollinger-Ellison (Z-E) tumors were shown to stimulate gastric acid secretion. Subsequently, it was found that the pancreatic tumors contained gastrin and that large amounts of this hormone were released into the circulation, producing the pathophysiologic characteristics of the syndrome. These gastrin-containing tumors are, therefore, now referred to as *gastrinomas*. Gastrin has been demonstrated in these tumors by chemical isolation of polypeptides with amino acid compositions and peptide mapping patterns identical with those of human gastrin molecules. In addition, large amounts of gastrin have been demonstrated by radioimmunoassay in gastrinomas and in serums of patients with the Z-E syndrome.

Most gastrinomas are found within the pancreas. Multiple, apparently primary, tumors are common. Pancreatic gastrinomas may be single or multiple and may vary in size from 2 mm to more than 20 cm in diameter. In from one-half to two-thirds of patients multiple gastrinomas are present within the pancreas; however, more than half of these are not identified at surgery. Pancreatic gastrinomas are most common in the body or tail of the pancreas. Approximately 13 percent of patients with this syndrome have tumors in the wall of the proximal duodenum. Gastrinomas have also been located less commonly in other sites, including the hilum of the spleen and very rarely in the stomach. Primary gastrinomas, surrounded by lymphoid tissue, have been found in proximity to the pancreas, proximal duodenum, and spleen. These may be confused with, but are distinct from, metastasis to regional lymph nodes. In rare instances, the Z-E syndrome has resulted from ectopic gastrin-containing tumors, e.g., parathyroid and ovarian adenomas. Many, and when sought for, most, gastrin-secreting islet-cell tumors have been found to contain multiple hormones, which may or may not be released, but are usually clinically silent. These have included adrenocorticotropic hormone, glucagon, insulin, pancreatic polypeptide, and vasoactive intestinal peptide. The absolute frequency of multiple hormones contained in or released by these tumors is not known. Approximately one-third of patients with gastrinomas have increases in serum concentrations of *pancreatic polypeptide*. About two-thirds are histologically or biologically malignant, and about half have spread to the liver when the tumor is identified. Malignant gastrinomas usually grow slowly. From one-half to two-thirds of patients with gastrinomas have metastases, most commonly to regional lymph nodes and liver; spread may also be to peritoneal surfaces, spleen, bone, skin, or mediastinum. Gastrinomas have light-microscopic similarities to carcinoid tumors and may be mistaken for carcinoid tumors, especially when arising from the mucosa of the small intestine or stomach. Pancreatic islet-cell hyperplasia occurs in approximately 10 percent of patients with the Z-E syndrome. Hyperplasia of the islets, accompanying recognizable or unidentified gastrinoma, appears to be an association or a consequence rather than a cause of excess gastrin release, since gastrin is not present in the hyperplastic tissue.

In most gastrinomas approximately 90 to 95 percent of gastrin is in the form of heptadecapeptide gastrin (G-17 or little gastrin), with most of the remainder being big gastrin (G-34). In contrast, approximately two-thirds of circulating gastrin in gastrinoma patients is G-34; most of the remainder of circulating gastrin is G-17. However, smaller amounts of even larger forms of gastrin and smaller gastrin fragments can be detected in the serum. The parietal cell mass is substantially expanded to from three to six times normal, secondary to the trophic effects of gastrin on parietal cells.

In from 20 to 25 percent of patients with the Z-E syndrome, the gastrinoma is a component of the multiple endocrine neoplasia type I (MEN-I) syndrome, an autosomal dominant disorder with a high degree of penetrance and great variability in expressivity. Patients with MEN-I may have hyperplasia, adenomas, or carcinoma involving the parathyroid glands, pancreatic islets, and pituitary: the organs involved are in that order of frequency. Hyperparathyroidism is present in 87 percent of patients with the MEN-I syndrome, and gastrinoma is present in approximately half of these patients (see Chap. 334).

While the true incidence of the Z-E syndrome is not known, estimates are that it accounts for 0.1 to 1 percent of peptic ulcers. The Z-E syndrome may occur at any age, but initial manifestations are most common between ages 30 and 60.

CLINICAL FEATURES From 90 to 95 percent of patients with gastrinomas develop ulceration of the gastrointestinal tract at some point during the course of their disease. Profound gastric hypersecretion is found in most, but not all, patients. Symptoms are often similar to those seen in patients with typical peptic ulcer disease. However, the ulcer symptoms may be more fulminant, progressive, and persistent, and usually respond poorly to usual medical and surgical peptic ulcer treatment programs. The anatomic site of the ulcers in patients with gastrinoma is similar, but not identical, to that of patients with common types of peptic ulcer. About 75 percent of gastrinoma patients have ulcers in the first portion of the duodenum or in the stomach; these are usually single, but may be multiple. When multiple ulcers occur, they are frequently located not only in the first portion of the duodenum, but also in the remainder of the duodenum or even the jejunum. In one large series, 14 percent of the ulcers were found in the duodenum beyond its first portion, and 11 percent in the jejunum. Prompt recurrence of ulcer, often with hemorrhage or perforation, after peptic ulcer surgery without total gastrectomy (in which the Z-E syndrome had not been recognized) is characteristic of gastrinoma.

Diarrhea occurs in about 40 percent of patients, and about 7 percent of patients with gastrinoma may have diarrhea in the absence of ulcer disease. The diarrhea is due to the outpouring of large amounts of hydrochloric acid into the proximal duodenum and can be reduced or eliminated by aspiration of gastric juice. The excessive acid has been shown to reduce the pH within the lumen of the proximal and distal jejunum to as low as 1 and 3.6, respectively. Inflammatory changes may develop in the mucosa of the small intestine, presumably secondary to the injurious effect of the increased amounts of acid and pepsin. Steatorrhea, which is less common than diarrhea, appears to result from inactivation of pancreatic lipase by the large concentration of acid in the proximal small intestine and from decreases in luminal bile acids. The decrease in bile acid concentration of the intraluminal contents is caused by precipitation of the major bile acids at low pH. This leads to impaired micelle formation which, in turn, reduces the intestinal absorption of fatty acids and monoglycerides (see Chap. 237). Vitamin B_{12} malabsorption, not correctable by addition of intrinsic factor, has been detected in some patients with the Z-E syndrome. Although the secretion of intrinsic factor appears normal, the reduced pH within the gut interferes with intrinsic factor mediation of vitamin B_{12} absorption. This can be corrected by neutralization of the intestinal contents. The mechanism by which low pH in the gut interferes with intrinsic factor action is not known.

Diarrhea in patients with gastrinoma is invariably accompanied by gastric acid *hypersecretion.* (This does not occur in patients with common duodenal ulcer with similar rates of hypersecretion of gastric acid; the reason for this difference is not known.) Severe diarrhea is also seen with other nonbeta islet-cell tumors of the pancreas, which are usually associated with *hyposecretion* of gastric acid or even achlorhydria [pancreatic cholera or WDHA (watery diarrhea, hypokalemia, and achlorhydria) syndrome]. In most cases, the pancreatic cholera syndrome appears to be due to tumor release of VIP (see Chaps. 334 and 255).

DIAGNOSIS The presence of a gastrinoma should be suspected in patients with a compatible clinical history, especially in those with evidence of marked acid hypersecretion. Two-thirds of gastrinoma patients have basal gastric acid outputs (BAO) which exceed 15 meq/h. In some instances the basal output may be greater than 100 meq/h.

However, as stated earlier, there is substantial overlap in the rates of gastric acid secretion among patients with gastrinoma, duodenal ulcer, and normal subjects. Gastrinoma patients often have basal acid output rates which are greater than 60 percent of those induced by maximal stimulation (MAO). In most normal subjects and duodenal ulcer patients basal acid secretory rates are less than 60 percent of maximal secretion. However, because of frequent patient variations, with exceptions to these guidelines by patients with gastrinomas and common duodenal ulcers, the use of the BAO/MAO ratio is of no value in the certain identification of gastrinoma patients.

Some radiographic features may suggest and support the diagnosis of the Z-E syndrome. Large mucosal folds may be demonstrated in the stomach, duodenum, and, in some instances, the jejunum. The lumen of the stomach and small intestine often contains large amounts of fluid. Radiographic features of most ulcers in these patients, except when they are multiple or distal in location, are similar to the common peptic ulcer. Arteriography is of limited value in identifying patients with gastrinoma; primary tumors or hepatic metastases demonstrated at surgery have been identified in only from 20 to 30 percent of gastrinoma patients. Some reports suggest that computerized axial tomography may be of slightly greater value in identifying primary or metastatic gastrinoma. Endoscopic retrograde pancreaticoduodenography (ERCP) has not proved to be of assistance in the diagnosis or exclusion of pancreatic gastrinomas. A small number of duodenal wall gastrinomas have been identified and confirmed histologically by duodenoscopy.

The diagnosis in a patient with clinical features consistent with the Z-E syndrome depends upon the demonstration of *increased serum gastrin levels* by radioimmunoassay. Fasting serum gastrin levels in normal subjects and patients with typical duodenal ulcer average approximately 40 to 50 pg/mL and usually do not exceed 150 pg/mL. Patients with gastrinoma almost always have fasting serum gastrin levels which are greater than 200 pg/mL and have been reported as high as 450,000 pg/mL. Approximately half of these patients have fasting serum gastrin levels which are less than 1000 pg/mL.

Several provocative tests have been used to evaluate patients with possible gastrinoma, especially in those who do not exhibit pronounced hypergastrinemia (i.e., serum gastrin greater than 1000 pg/mL). These tests utilize the measurement of serum gastrin levels in response to intravenous calcium infusion, secretin injection, or ingestion of a standard test meal (see Table 235-1).

In the *secretin injection test,* secretin (Kabi secretin, 2 units per kilogram) is given intravenously over 30 to 60 s. (Boots secretin is approximately one-sixth as potent as Kabi secretin prepared by the Karolinska Institute, Stockholm. Boots secretin should not be used, since it contains large amounts of gastrin-like material which is immunoreactive with antibodies to gastrin and, therefore, can spuriously increase serum gastrin concentrations.) Gastrin is measured in serum samples obtained before injection of secretin and at 5-min intervals thereafter for 30 min. In normal individuals and patients with common duodenal ulcer, secretin produces either no change or small reductions or small increases in serum gastrin levels. In contrast, in gastrinoma patients intravenous secretin induces substantial increases in serum gastrin. The gastrin levels increase promptly, usually at 5 min, (and virtually always by 10 min), by at least 200 pg/mL. The *calcium infusion test* involves constant 3-h intravenous infusion of calcium gluconate (5 mg calcium per kilogram per hour). Serum samples for gastrin measurements are obtained before and at 30-min intervals for 4 h after initiation of infusion. In gastrinoma patients serum gastrin concentrations usually increase above the basal serum gastrin by at least 50 percent or by more than 400 pg/mL. The third provocative test involves the *feeding of a standard meal;* gastrin is measured in serum samples obtained before the meal and at 15-min intervals for 90 min. In gastrinoma patients peak serum gastrin levels do not increase (or increase minimally) and do not reach values 50 percent greater than fasting levels (see Table 235-1).

The secretin injection test is the provocative test of greatest value in identifying gastrinoma patients. Positive serum gastrin responses to intravenous secretin are detected in more than 95 percent of patients with gastrinoma. Using the criteria suggested, substantial increases in serum gastrin following secretin injection have not been detected in nongastrinoma patients. Exaggerated release of gastrin in response to calcium infusion has been found in more than 80 percent of gastrinoma patients; however, this exaggerated response to calcium infusion has been observed in some nongastrinoma patients with hypergastrinemia (e.g., achlorhydria with or without pernicious anemia). In gastrinoma patients enhanced gastrin release with calcium infusion is not observed in the absence of paradoxical gastrin release in response to secretin. Since the calcium infusion test does not add to the sensitivity or specificity of the secretin injection test and since calcium infusion is potentially more hazardous, it is not recommended as a provocative test in evaluating patients in whom the diagnosis of gastrinoma is considered.

In a very small proportion of duodenal ulcer patients (less than 1 percent), gastric acid hypersecretion may be accompanied by increased serum gastrin levels due to hyperfunction and/or hyperplasia of antral gastrin cells (G cells). These can be distinguished from gastrinoma patients by the secretin and meal stimulation tests. In patients with this antral gastrin cell abnormality, intravenous secretin reduces serum gastrin and ingestion of the test meal leads to striking increases in serum gastrin levels, exceeding the fasting serum gastrin concentration by more than 200 percent.

TREATMENT   In general, these patients are resistant to medical treatment regimens and surgical procedures designed for and usually effective in common peptic ulcer. Antacids may produce transient symptomatic relief but seldom induce ulcer healing or sustained relief of symptoms. Incomplete gastric resection (with or without vagotomy or pyloroplasty with vagotomy) is frequently followed by prompt and often fulminant ulcer recurrence. Many patients with gastrinoma have had multiple surgical procedures, particularly when the diagnosis was not established initially. Mortality has been lowest when gastrectomy was performed as the initial surgical procedure. For this reason, when gastric surgery is required in gastrinoma patients, total gastrectomy has been considered the surgical procedure of choice; subtotal gastric resections should not be performed.

The recent development of more effective drugs and more precise diagnostic techniques has substantially altered the therapeutic options available for gastrinoma patients. Patients with the Z-E syndrome due to gastrinoma are highly heterogeneous in respect to their clinical manifestations and extent of disease. The key to management is individualization of treatment.

The *H-2-receptor antagonists* are effective in reducing gastric acid secretion, producing symptom relief and inducing ulcer healing in patients with the Z-E syndrome. *Cimetidine* has been widely and successfully used. Improvement in clinical symptoms, decreases in gastric acid output, and ulcer healing occur in 80 to 85 percent of patients so treated. Administration of cimetidine has been required at 4- to 6-h intervals, with total daily doses usually 2 to 5 times those used in the treatment of common duodenal ulcer. More recently, *ranitidine* has also been effectively used. The increased potency of ranitidine compared with cimetidine has provided a therapeutic advantage because of the large doses required. A further advantage of ranitidine is that it does not produce gynecomastia, a common consequence of large and prolonged doses of cimetidine in male patients with gastrinoma. When instituted, H-2-receptor antagonist therapy must be continued indefinitely, since even its temporary discontinuance is usually followed by ulcer recurrence. The effectiveness of the H-2-receptor antagonist therapy in reducing gastric acid secretion can be assessed by measuring unstimulated gastric acid output for 1 h immediately prior to the next anticipated dose of the drug; the goal is to reduce gastric acid output to less than 10 meq/h. H-2-receptor antagonists are indicated as initial treatment of gastrinoma patients, for prolonged treatment of those patients who are poor candidates for tumor reaction, and in those in whom total gastrectomy is not anticipated.

Clinical trials have also demonstrated even more effective reduction in acid secretion and ulcer healing with omeprazole, a potent hydrogen-potassium ATPase inhibitor. A small number of Z-E patients have been treated effectively with parietal cell vagotomy combined with indefinitely continued treatment with reduced doses of H-2-receptor antagonists.

In selecting the best therapy for the individual patient, the biologic behavior of these turmors and the clinical manifestations in each patient must be taken into consideration. Complete surgical resection of the tumors, when possible, represents optimal treatment in patients with gastrinoma. Successful tumor resection is seldon achieved in gastrinoma patients with MEN-I, because of the overwhelming likelihood of multifocal tumors, frequently with metastasis, at the time of diagnosis. Therapeutic doses of H-2-receptor antagonists are indicated in the period during which the diagnosis is being established, while the location and extent of the tumor are being determined and also as treatment prior to anticipated surgery. At present, H-2-receptor antagonists are certainly indicated for patients who are poor operative candidates, for those who refuse surgery, and for those in whom surgery is not possible. When metastatic or otherwise nonresectable gastrinoma is present, control of the ulcer disease may be achieved in most instances by treatment with H-2-receptor antagonists or by total gastric resection. There is no convincing evidence that tumor progression is influenced by gastrectomy. Patients with progressive invasive gastrinoma may be benefited by streptozotocin and 5-fluorouracil, which may reduce tumor bulk and partially reduce serum gastrin levels.

The most difficult treatment decisions are in those patients in whom the location and extent of the tumor have not been defined. With more general use of gastrin radioimmunoassay, patients with gastrinomas are being detected earlier in the course of their disease. Prior studies indicated that the morbidity and mortality in patients with the Z-E syndrome were largely due to the complications of the severe ulcer disease. However, with earlier diagnosis, effective antiulcer treatment and longer follow-up, more frequent consequences of the invasive properties of malignant gastrinoma are being recognized. Complete surgical removal of gastrinoma, with cure, has been achieved in less than 25 percent of patients with the Z-E syndrome. However, earlier detection, careful examination for tumor in and outside of the pancreas, and use of transhepatic portal venous sampling techniques for gastrin measurement and tumor localization may make it possible to improve upon these results.

STRESS ULCERS AND EROSIONS

A variety of acute ulcerative lesions of the gastrointestinal tract are distinct clinically from chronic peptic ulcer. Among these are the acute upper gastrointestinal erosions and ulcerations which are often observed in patients with shock, burns, sepsis, and severe trauma. These are often referred to as *stress erosions* and *ulcers*. These lesions, which are frequently multiple, are most common in the acid-secreting portion of the stomach, but they may also occur in the antrum and duodenum. Acute stress erosions and ulcerations are usually superficial, with necrosis limited to the mucosa.

These erosions and superficial ulcers are extremely frequent and occur in about 90 percent of patients with massive injuries and burns. The most common clinical finding in patients with acute erosions or ulcerations is painless gastrointestinal hemorrhage. Blood loss is usually minimal but may be substantial. Erosions develop most frequently approximately 24 h after trauma. Small amounts of blood loss may be detected in the first 24 to 48 h after trauma. However, when massive hemorrhage occurs, it is usually more than 2 or 3 days after the acute insult. The diagnosis is best established by upper gastrointestinal endoscopy. The erosive lesions are frequently too superficial to be recognized by barium examination of the upper gastrointestinal tract. Acute ulcerations and erosions should be suspected when there is evidence of upper gastrointestinal bleeding in patients with severe injuries, burns, infections, and shock.

Many theories have been proposed to explain stress-associated acute mucosal ulceration, but the mechanism for the mucosal injury is still not clear. Gastric acid appears to be involved in the production of these acute stress erosions and ulcers, although there is usually no evidence of acid hypersecretion. The lesions cannot be produced in experimental animals in the absence of acid. The two major mechanisms which have been proposed are mucosal ischemia and enhanced back-diffusion of hydrogen ions. Investigation of the gastric mucosal barrier indicates that it is intact after severe burns and injuries. Most evidence supports the conclusion that mucosal ischemia is the most important element in the production of stress erosions and ulceration.

The treatment of acute stress ulcerations and erosions is principally preventive. In high-risk patients the frequency of stress ulcerations can be diminished by the vigorous use of antacids to neutralize gastric contents. While anticholinergics are of no value, there is evidence that inhibition of acid secretion by H-2-receptor antagonists may be effective in prevention of stress ulceration; however, they do not appear as effective as vigorous (every 30 to 60 min) therapy with antacids. When medical therapy fails to arrest bleeding, surgical approaches have varied from pyloroplasty and vagotomy to total gastrectomy.

The term *Cushing's ulcer* has been applied to acute ulceration of the upper gastrointestinal tract associated with intracranial injury or increases in intracranial pressure, e.g., with brain tumors. These ulcers may involve the stomach, proximal duodenum, or esophagus, and frequently lead to hemorrhage or perforation. They do not differ histologically from acute stress ulceration. Treatment includes correction of increased intracranial pressure, when possible, and the usual measures for treatment of acute erosions and ulcerations.

DRUG-ASSOCIATED ULCERS AND EROSIONS

Gastric and duodenal ulcers have been described following administration of many drugs. Salicylate ingestion (specifically aspirin) has been shown to be associated with an increased incidence of gastric ulcer and is a frequent cause of hemorrhagic gastric erosions and gastritis. There is no evidence of an increased frequency of duodenal ulcer among patients treated with salicylates. The specific mechanism by which salicylates induce, or are associated with, gastric ulcer has not been established. However, at least two mechanisms have been proposed. It has been suggested that salicylates contribute to the development of gastric ulcer by mucosal injury induced by interruption of the gastric mucosal barrier, permitting back-diffusion of hydrogen ions and consequent erosive gastritis. An additional mechanism by which salicylates may injure the gastric mucosa is by their capacity to inhibit prostaglandin synthesis, since various prostaglandins have been shown to have cytoprotective properties, by which they prevent damage to the gastric mucosa in response to a variety of agents, including salicylates. Patients with gastric ulcer should avoid salicylates, and many physicians also withhold recommending salicylates in patients with duodenal ulcer. Gastric mucosal injury, similar to that produced by aspirin, has also been observed in patients treated with a variety of nonsteroidal anti-inflammatory agents (e.g., indomethacin, ibuprofen, naproxen, tolmetin, sulindac, piroxicam, diflunisal, fenoprofen). The concerns about aspirin use also apply to these agents.

Administration of corticosteroids has been reported to be associated with development of ulcer disease of the upper gastrointestinal tract. Although for the most part this proposal has been widely accepted, there are no firm data conclusively establishing the association between corticosteroids and gastric or duodenal ulcers. Most controlled studies have failed to demonstrate an increased incidence of ulcers in patients treated with corticosteroids. Most studies have supported an increased incidence of ulcer disease in patients with rheumatoid arthritis: these patients may often be receiving other potentially ulcerogenic drugs, which may account for the apparent increase in ulcer frequency when these patients are treated with corticosteroids. At present a direct association between treatment with corticosteroids and an increased incidence of duodenal or gastric ulcer has not been firmly established.

REFERENCES

BARDHAN KD et al: Double blind comparison of cimetidine and placebo in the maintenance and healing of chronic duodenal ulceration. Gut 20:158, 1979

ELASHOFF JD, GROSSMAN MI: Trends in hospital admissions and death rates for peptic ulcer in the United States from 1970 to 1978. Gastroenterology 78:280, 1980

HOWARD JM et al: Famotidine, a new potent, long-acting histamine H₂-receptor antagonist: Comparison with cimetidine and ranitidine in the treatment of Zollinger-Ellison syndrome. Gastroenterology 88:1026, 1985

ISENBERG JI et al: Increased sensitivity to stimulation of acid secretion by pentagastrin in duodenal ulcer. J Clin Invest 55:330, 1975

KURATA JH et al: Sex differences in peptic ulcer disease. Gastroenterology 88:96, 1985

LAMERS BHW et al: Omeprazole in Zollinger-Ellison syndrome: Effects of a single dose and a long-term treatment in patients resistant to histamine H₂-receptor antagonists. N Engl J Med 310:758, 1984

McGUIGAN JE, TRUDEAU WL: Differences in rates of gastrin release in normal persons and patients with duodenal ulcer. N Engl J Med 288:64, 1973

———, WOLFE MM: The secretin injection test in the diagnosis of gastrinoma. Gastroenterology 79:1324, 1980

MAN WK et al: Histamine and duodenal ulcer: effect of omeprazole on gastric histamine in patients with duodenal ulcer. Gut 27:418, 1986

MARTIN F et al: Comparison of the healing capacities of sucralfate and cimetidine in the short-term treatment of duodenal ulcer: A double blind randomized study. Gastroenterology 82:401, 1982

NYREN O et al: Absence of therapeutic benefit from antacids or cimetidine in non ulcer dyspepsia. N Engl J Med 314:339, 1986

PEURA DA, JOHNSON LF: Cimetidine for prevention and treatment of gastroduodenal lesions in patients in an intensive care unit. Ann Int Med 103:173, 1985

PRIEBE HJ et al: Antacid versus cimetidine in preventing acute gastrointestinal bleeding. N Engl J Med 302:426, 1980

RICHARDSON CT: Sucralfate. Ann Int Med 97:269, 1982

ROBERT A: Cytoprotection by prostaglandins. Gastroenterology 77:761, 1979

TAKEUCHI KD: Role of pH gradient of mucus in protection of gastric mucosa. Gastroenterology 84:331, 1983

WOLFE MM et al: Zollinger-Ellison syndrome associated with persistently normal serum gastrin concentrations. Ann Int Med 103:215, 1985

---

236 GASTRIC TUMORS, GASTRITIS, AND OTHER GASTRIC DISEASES

WALTER C. MacDONALD / CYRUS E. RUBIN

CANCER

CARCINOMA Throughout the world gastric cancer is one of the most common lethal malignancies. Although its frequency is decreasing in the United States, it still causes about 15,000 deaths each year. Because symptoms in the early, potentially curable phase are often minimal or nonexistent, patients usually seek medical advice too late. Thus, less than 15 percent of patients survive 5 years, despite improved diagnostic and surgical techniques.

Epidemiology Gastric cancer is very common in Japan, in the Central and South American Andes, and in parts of eastern Europe. The children of Japanese who migrated to the United States have a much lower incidence of gastric cancer, suggesting environmental influences on pathogenesis. Gastric cancer has become far less common in the United States, where in the past 50 years its annual mortality has fallen from 25 to 6 per 100,000. A lesser decline is apparent in western Europe and, more recently, even in Japan. When the reasons for this remarkable decline have been elucidated, a giant step will have been made in understanding the pathogenesis of gastric cancer. While the frequency of carcinoma of gastric body and antrum in the United States has declined, carcinoma of the proximal stomach (cardia) has increased from 10 to almost 30 percent of cases. It is uncertain whether this represents a real increase in gastric cardia carcinoma or reflects a change in the incidence of carcinomas extending into the stomach from a primary adenocarcinoma complicating Barrett's columnar-lined esophagus.

Throughout the world, gastric cancer is twice as common in men as in women; it occurs in North America at a mean age of 60 years, with less than 5 percent under 40.

Etiology The cause of gastric cancer is unknown, but diet has been implicated. Gastric cancer can be readily induced in some animals by the oral administration of N-methyl-N'-nitrosoguanidine. It has been suggested that gastric cancer may be related to the formation of N-nitroso compounds by the conversion of ingested nitrates to nitrites, which then interact in the stomach with secondary or tertiary amines. Interestingly, this reaction is inhibited by ascorbic acid. There is also speculation that hypertonic salted, pickled, or smoked foods may be promoting factors in gastric carcinogenesis.

Predisposing factors Gastric cancer is two to four times more common in first-degree relatives of patients with the disease and the concordance rate is greater for identical than dizygotic twins, suggesting a small genetic element in pathogenesis.

Atrophic gastric mucosa, especially when associated with intestinal metaplasia, probably increases the risk of gastric cancer. Such mucosal changes are invariably seen in pernicious anemia, and about 5 percent of these patients develop stomach cancer. Comparison of Japanese and American autopsy results shows that the high-risk Japanese have more extensive atrophic gastritis and intestinal metaplasia than the low-risk Americans. Serial biopsy studies also suggest that persons with atrophic gastritis are more likely to develop gastric cancer than those with normal mucosa. However, atrophic gastritis is common in older people without cancer, and some patients with gastric cancers have no gastritis in the uninvolved portions of the stomach.

Adenomatous gastric polyps either contain adenocarcinoma or are associated with carcinoma elsewhere in the stomach in as many as 30 percent of cases. It is not known whether these uncommon adenomatous polyps contain cancer from the onset or whether they were originally benign. Certainly most gastric cancers do not begin as polyps. Patients with hyperplastic gastric polyps are predisposed to cancer elsewhere in the stomach to a far lesser degree. This predisposition is possibly related to the atrophic gastritis which is regularly seen surrounding both kinds of polyps.

Benign gastric ulcer has not been shown to be a precursor of gastric cancer. Some, but not all, European studies have shown that there is an increased risk of gastric cancer 10 to 20 years after partial gastrectomy for peptic ulcer. In the United States no such risk has been shown.

Pathology Gastric cancers are almost always adenocarcinomas. Gross and microscopic classification of these carcinomas is frequently impossible because many are of mixed pattern. In general, there are five macroscopic types: polypoid, ulcerative, combined ulcerative and infiltrative, diffuse infiltrative (linitis plastica), and superficial spreading. Microscopic classification is particularly difficult and has no prognostic value. Polypoid, ulcerative, and superficial spreading cancers are often less malignant than the infiltrative types. The most important factors in prognosis are the depth of invasion through the gastric wall, the spread to lymph nodes, and the presence of distant metastases.

Gastric cancer spreads by direct extension through the gastric wall to the perigastric tissues. Sometimes direct extension involves the pancreas, colon, or liver. Proximal gastric tumors often involve the esophagus, but distal ones less commonly cross the pylorus into the duodenum. Spread to perigastric nodes is common; nodes in the preaortic area, porta hepatis, and hilum of the spleen are often involved as well. Spread via the thoracic duct can involve the left supraclavicular (Virchow's) lymph nodes. Peritoneal metastases are evident in about 20 percent of patients, but intraabdominal metastases may be confined to the ovary (Krukenberg's tumor) or prerectal pouch (Blumer's shelf). Blood-borne metastases to the liver are apparent in about 30 percent of patients. The lungs, brain, or other organs are involved less often.

Clinical features The history is of little help in distinguishing benign from malignant gastric ulcer because many of the varied symptoms may be seen in both diseases. Approximately 25 percent of patients with cancer have classic ulcer symptoms. The most common presenting complaint, however, is upper abdominal discomfort of insidious onset. This is often mild but varies greatly in severity from a vague, postprandial fullness to a severe, steady pain. Anorexia, often with slight nausea, is very common but is not the usual presenting complaint. Weight loss is observed in at least 50 percent of patients. Nausea and vomiting are particularly prominent with tumors of the pylorus but can occur with advanced disease elsewhere in the stomach. Dysphagia is the major symptom of cardia tumors. Weakness, hematemesis, melena, and alteration in bowel habits are other presenting complaints. Some patients suffer from the symptoms of anemia, or their anemia may be discovered on routine examination. Occasionally an ulcerating carcinoma perforates, and rarely a gastrocolic fistula develops.

The initial symptoms may be related to metastases. These include abdominal distention by malignant ascites; jaundice from biliary tract obstruction by porta hepatis nodes or by intrahepatic metastases; pain from bone involvement; neurologic symptoms secondary to brain or meningeal metastases; and shortness of breath from lung spread. Mechanical bowel obstruction can be secondary to peritoneal metastases, and pelvic symptoms can result from ovarian spread.

The duration of symptoms before patients see a physician is remarkably variable but averages 6 months. Symptoms of several years' duration are not uncommon. Some patients with long-standing functional gastrointestinal complaints may notice a change in their pain pattern. In North America, less than 10 percent of patients with symptoms have early gastric cancer, i.e., disease confined to the mucosa or submucosa. Screening studies in Japan confirm that most patients with early curable gastric cancer are asymptomatic, although some have mild epigastric distress or ulcer symptoms.

An epigastric mass is palpable in only a minority of patients; it is a sign of poor prognosis but does not exclude the possibility of cure. Abdominal tenderness is found in about one-third of patients. Pallor or cachexia may be observed, and occasionally a gastric succussion splash is demonstrable. Physical signs suggesting metastases should be carefully sought because distant metastases that are proved by biopsy or aspiration cytology exclude curative surgery. These include hepatomegaly, jaundice, enlargement of left supraclavicular or scalene nodes, a shelf-like mass anteriorly in the prerectal pouch above the prostate or cervix on rectal examination, an ovarian mass on vaginal or abdominal examination, ascites, an umbilical mass, and skin nodules. A low-grade fever may occur with advanced disease, particularly with liver metastases. Rarely gastric cancer is associated with dermatomyositis, acanthosis nigricans, neuromyopathy, hypoglycemia, or multiple seborrheic keratoses.

Laboratory findings Iron-deficiency anemia because of occult bleeding is found in about two-thirds of patients. Occasionally the cancer is associated with pernicious anemia. Rarely a pancytopenia is caused by bone marrow replacement. A "leukemoid" reaction and disseminated intravascular coagulation are other rare findings. Occult blood is demonstrable in the stools in up to 80 percent of patients if repeated tests are done. Elevation of 5'-nucleotidase suggests the presence of liver metastases, which can be confirmed by liver scan. The serum albumin may be low because of protein leakage from the involved gastric mucosa. Measurement of gastric acid secretion is considered less helpful than in the past. Achlorhydria after stimulation with pentagastrin usually excludes a benign peptic ulcer, but the test is of limited value because most patients with a malignant ulcer secrete some acid. A rise in the carcinoembryonic antigen (CEA) after treatment suggests recurrence of carcinoma, but this test is of little initial diagnostic value.

Diagnosis In North America x-ray of the stomach is still the initial method used for detecting gastric carcinoma. In more than 90 percent of symptomatic patients, skillfully performed, double-contrast x-ray detects gastric abnormalities. In practice, the radiologic differentiation of benign from malignant gastric lesions is accurate in approximately 75 percent of cases. Thus, gastroscopy with biopsy or brush cytology must be used to confirm or exclude a diagnosis of cancer (see Chap. 233). It may be more important to the patient to exclude gastric cancer than to diagnose it because unnecessary emotional trauma and surgical morbidity or mortality can be avoided by definitive diagnosis of benign disease.

The diagnostic accuracy of x-ray is greatest when it is used wisely. Equivocal examinations should always be repeated. The use of double-contrast techniques helps to detect small lesions by improving mucosal detail. The stomach should be distended at some time during every x-ray examination because decreased distensibility may be the only indication of a diffuse infiltrative carcinoma. Although gastric ulcers can be detected fairly easily, it may be impossible to distinguish the benign from the malignant ones. Differential x-ray diagnosis is also difficult when the antrum is narrowed or when mucosal folds are enlarged. Cancer of the proximal stomach invading the neural plexuses of the esophagus may mimic achalasia by x-ray. In cancer of the cardia the x-ray appearance may be considered normal or may be confused with benign mucosal distortion secondary to a hiatus hernia. It is impossible to differentiate adenocarcinoma from lymphoma radiologically. Cancer of the pancreas or colon invading the stomach may be confused with primary gastric neoplasm.

Fiberoptic gastroscopy with biopsy and brush cytology is especially useful for confirming the diagnosis of cancer suspected by x-ray, differentiating cancer from lymphoma, clarifying equivocal radiologic findings, and checking suspicious clinical findings despite negative x-rays. At least six biopsies should be taken from representative areas of a suspected neoplasm; if the tissue is serially sectioned and thoroughly examined by an expert, accuracy in the diagnosis of cancer approaching 95 percent can be achieved. The addition of brush cytology raises the accuracy in detecting cancer even higher but slightly raises the risk of a false diagnosis of cancer. Diffuse infiltrative tumors and recurrent cancers can be impossible to diagnose even by these methods because malignant cells may not be present in the biopsied mucosal layer. Despite improved diagnostic techniques, laparoscopy or laparotomy may be required for diagnosis.

The x-ray demonstration of a benign-appearing gastric ulcer presents special problems. Some physicians feel that gastroscopy is not mandatory if the x-ray features are typically benign, if healing at 6 weeks is complete by x-ray, and if a follow-up x-ray examination several months later is negative. However, many feel that gastroscopic biopsy and brush cytology are required for all patients with a gastric ulcer in order to exclude malignancy, particularly an early, curable gastric cancer. The marked drop in the incidence of malignant gastric ulcers in North America has raised the question whether it is cost-effective to endoscope all patients with gastric ulcer rather than to confine endoscopy to those with a suspicious x-ray or clinical course.

Using x-ray and intragastric photography for mass screening, the Japanese have detected many early, curable cancers of the stomach. In North America, such screening methods are probably not cost-effective because the disease is relatively uncommon. However, special attention must be paid to patients over 40 years of age who are predisposed to gastric cancer because of pernicious anemia, the presence or history of an adenomatous gastric polyp, a family history of gastric cancer, or birth in countries where gastric cancer is common. In addition, one must be certain that all gastric ulcers treated medically are indeed benign.

Treatment Surgical removal of the tumor offers the only chance for cure. A careful evaluation for evidence of distant metastases will avoid unnecessary surgery. Physical examination is supplemented by chest x-ray, liver function tests, and abdominal ultrasound. The use of computerized tomography (CT scan) has increased the accuracy of preoperative staging. Suspected areas of metastasis should be sampled, for example, lymph nodes or liver and pleural or peritoneal effusions. If metastases are suspected but unproved, laparoscopy

under local anesthesia with direct biopsy of suspected areas of metastasis is particularly helpful in assessing operability. Cancer of the distal and midstomach is usually treated by subtotal gastrectomy; removal of the regional lymph nodes requires resection of the greater and lesser omentum and sometimes the spleen. Tumors of the proximal stomach are usually treated by distal esophagectomy and proximal gastrectomy. Total gastrectomy is indicated only occasionally. If obstruction is present or if bleeding is a problem, palliative resection may be worthwhile even though the disease is known to be incurable. The operative mortality rate for gastric cancer is still as high as 10 percent in many hospitals.

It is often difficult to assess the reported results of surgical treatment. Careful and standardized descriptions by surgeon and pathologist would facilitate comparison of different series. These should include depth of tumor penetration, extent of lymph node involvement, and presence of distant metastases. More than 80 percent of cancers confined to the mucosa or submucosa are curable, compared with 10 to 20 percent when the tumor extends through the gastric wall. Up to 50 percent survive 5 years after curative resection if the lymph nodes are not involved. Tumor diameter of less than 2 cm and a long history of symptoms are good prognostic signs. However, in North America only 10 to 15 percent survive 5 years after diagnosis. Rarely, patients live for 5 years without treatment or for many years after a palliative resection.

Chemotherapy with 5-fluorouracil (5-FU) causes some tumor regression in about 10 percent of patients. Combination chemotherapy (e.g., 5-FU, doxorubicin, and mitomycin C) induces a response in a higher percentage of patients, but the median survival is still less than 1 year. The effectiveness of adjuvant radiotherapy, or chemotherapy, remains to be proved. Palliative radiotherapy may be useful to control bleeding, to relieve obstruction at the cardia, or to alleviate pain from bone metastases. Other palliative measures include replacement of iron and vitamin B_{12}, dilation of obstructing cardia tumors with or without placement of plastic tubular stents, relief of cardia obstruction by laser therapy, treatment of postgastrectomy problems, and the judicious use of analgesics and antiemetics.

LYMPHOMA Primary gastric lymphomas account for about 5 percent of gastric malignancies although the percentage is higher in referral centers. Most are diffuse large cell (histiocytic) lymphomas or mixed small cell (lymphocytic) and large cell lymphomas; Hodgkin's disease is relatively uncommon, and plasmacytoma is rare. Some gastric lymphomas present a varied histologic picture that defies classification. Gastric involvement secondary to disseminated lymphoma is more common than the primary form. In one large series, one-third of histiocytic lymphomas and one-sixth of lymphosarcomas spread to the stomach. The sexes are affected equally, and the mean age is about 55 years.

The symptoms are indistinguishable from those of gastric ulcer or cancer. Hematemesis and perforation occur more often than with carcinoma. An abdominal mass is palpable in approximately one-third of patients. Approximately half of patients have iron-deficiency anemia, usually with occult blood in the stool.

X-ray studies usually show an abnormality difficult to distinguish from adenocarcinoma. Large rigid folds, multiple ulcers, or duodenal involvement suggest the possibility of lymphoma. The x-ray appearance may also be confused with that of Ménétrier's disease or benign peptic ulcer. The tumor is usually obvious at gastroscopy, but its gross appearance is seldom diagnostic. A preoperative diagnosis can often be made by the combination of endoscopic biopsy and cytologic examination, but even these methods may fail and surgical excision may be required for diagnosis.

A careful search for evidence of disseminated disease should precede treatment and should include chest x-ray, lymphangiography, CT scan, and bone marrow biopsy. Primary gastric lymphoma has most often been treated by a combination of surgical excision and radiotherapy. Usually surgery precedes radiotherapy, but it may be advantageous to shrink large tumor with radiation before attempting to excise them. About 50 percent of patients so treated survive 5 years. Survival is particularly good if the tumor does not penetrate the serosa or involve the perigastric nodes. The role of chemotherapy for primary gastric lymphoma is still not well defined. The tendency of the disease to recur outside the abdomen and the sensitivity of the tumor to available agents have led several groups to recommend adding combination chemotherapy to the initial management. Unresectable gastric lymphoma has a 5-year survival of 25 percent or less. It is now often treated with combination chemotherapy with or without radiotherapy. Newer drug regimens promise to substantially improve the results. The treatment of disseminated lymphoma is discussed in Chap. 79.

LEIOMYOSARCOMA   These tumors account for 1 to 3 percent of gastric malignancies. The mean age is about 60 years, and the sexes are affected equally. The tumors are usually large, spherical, and in the upper half of the stomach; they tend to ulcerate and become necrotic in the center. The tumor may spread to the peritoneum or liver but rarely to lymph nodes. Most patients complain of pain. The majority are anemic, and massive bleeding occurs in about one-third. A mass is palpable in more than 50 percent. X-rays show a large, smooth tumor, often with central ulceration and sometimes with a sinus tract to the center of the neoplasm. It is impossible to differentiate leiomyosarcoma by x-ray from benign leiomyoma except that leiomyosarcomas tend to be larger. Though endoscopic biopsy rarely provides a correct preoperative diagnosis, brush cytology of the ulceration may on occasion provide additional information. Treatment is by wide surgical excision if feasible; about 25 to 40 percent of patients are cured. Doxorubicin in combination with various other agents has been used to achieve modest palliation in a minority of patients with advanced disease. Radiotherapy is ineffective.

CARCINOID TUMORS AND OTHER MALIGNANCIES   Gastric carcinoids are uncommon. Like carcinoids elsewhere, they may be multiple. As many as 3 percent of patients with pernicious anemia may have gastric carcinoids. Carcinoids are often symptomless but can cause bleeding or epigastric pain. The x-ray appearance is that of a smooth, rounded, sessile filling defect, sometimes with ulceration. About 25 percent are malignant, but only a minority cause the malignant carcinoid syndrome. Small carcinoids can be excised locally; those larger than 2 cm and those that are malignant require partial gastrectomy. The chemotherapy of malignant carcinoids and the treatment of the carcinoid syndrome are described in Chap. 299.

Rare primary gastric malignancies include carcinosarcoma, hemangiopericytoma, neurogenic sarcoma, fibrosarcoma, and liposarcoma. Metastases to the stomach most often originate from generalized lymphoma, lung cancer, breast cancer, or malignant melanoma. Kaposi's sarcoma may involve the stomach, especially in patients with acquired immunodeficiency syndrome (AIDS).

BENIGN TUMORS

EPITHELIAL POLYPS   After cancer, benign epithelial polyps are the most common tumors of the stomach (5 to 10 percent). While there is considerable confusion regarding their nomenclature, it is important to remember that 80 to 90 percent of them are not neoplastic and probably never become malignant. The most common nonneoplastic polyp is called *hyperplastic;* it is composed almost completely of normal surface mucous cells and at times of mucus-secreting pyloric glands. The glands are intermingled with smooth-muscle fibers and may be cystic. More than 90 percent of such polyps are less than 1.5 cm in diameter. They may be single or multiple, pedunculated or sessile and can occur in any part of the stomach. They are covered with normal-appearing mucosa and frequently have a superficial ulceration. The mucosa surrounding them often shows nonerosive gastritis or atrophy. Although hyperplastic polyps probably never become malignant, carcinoma elsewhere in the same stomach is somewhat more common than in the general population.

Of epithelial polyps, 10 to 20 percent are composed of benign neoplastic epithelium and are called *adenomas*. In general, they resemble adenomatous polyps of the colon. They are usually larger than 2 cm in diameter and enlarge with time. As many as 40 percent of all adenomatous gastric polyps already contain cancer when first diagnosed and the rest may become malignant. They can be pedunculated but are more often sessile. They are solitary in two-thirds of cases and are covered with abnormal reddened velvety mucosa which may be lobulated or mammillated. Most are located in the antrum. The mucosa surrounding them is usually atrophic, and carcinoma elsewhere in the stomach is common (30 percent or more in various series).

Both hyperplastic and adenomatous polyps occur more frequently in patients over 50 years of age, and 80 percent or more of these patients are achlorhydric. From 6 to 20 percent of patients with pernicious anemia have epithelial polyps. Most are asymptomatic. Occult bleeding is the most frequent symptom and may be associated with vague epigastric distress. Rarely vomiting results from prolapse of a large, pedunculated antral polyp into the duodenum. Radiologically the polyps appear as smooth, rounded, or lobulated filling defects, with or without a stalk. Although those greater than 2 cm in diameter are more likely to be adenomas or polypoid carcinomas, exceptions are not uncommon.

Hyperplastic polyps may have a different gross appearance from adenomas at endoscopy, but one cannot differentiate between the two with certainty even after sampling them by forceps biopsy. To determine the histologic nature of a polyp and to exclude malignancy, the whole lesion is best examined. Most pedunculated or small sessile polyps can be removed with an electrocautery snare during gastroscopy by an experienced endoscopist. Endoscopic removal of larger sessile polyps or those with a broad pedicle may cause severe bleeding. Such lesions can be biopsied endoscopically by removing a sizable superficial portion of the polyp with a coagulating cautery snare. If the lesion is adenomatous, it should be removed surgically because of its malignant potential. Such patients must also be followed regularly with endoscopic and cytologic examinations because of the high risk of cancer in the surrounding mucosa. Partial or even total gastrectomy may eventually be needed.

Diffuse gastric polyposis is a rare and poorly defined condition in which the gastric mucosa is covered with numerous sessile or pedunculated epithelial polyps, most of which are hyperplastic. It is neither practical nor necessary to remove all hyperplastic polyps, but the patient should be endoscoped regularly to detect development of carcinoma in the surrounding epithelium. Multiple gastric adenomas are very rare but may be seen in familial polyposis or Gardner's syndrome and may require gastrectomy. Most of the multiple gastric polyps seen in familial polyposis are made up of benign fundal glands and require no treatment.

Rare hamartomatous gastric polyps are made up of the various benign epithelial cells normally present in the gastric mucosa. They are usually part of two familial polyposis syndromes: Peutz-Jeghers and juvenile polyposis. Twenty-five percent of Peutz-Jeghers cases involve the stomach or duodenum and 2 to 3 percent develop gastric or duodenal carcinoma. Malignant change in gastric juvenile polyposis is either very rare or absent. Cronkhite-Canada syndrome is a rare cause of benign gastric retention polyps composed of dilated cystic glands with markedly edematous stroma.

LEIOMYOMAS AND RARE BENIGN TUMORS   Most leiomyomas are tiny and of no clinical significance. Larger ones, usually 3 cm or more in diameter, may cause massive or occult bleeding or epigastric pain. The x-ray appearance is that of a smooth, rounded, sessile filling defect, often with a central ulcer. The gastroscopic appearance is highly suggestive but not diagnostic. Mucosal biopsies are usually too superficial for diagnosis, but brush cytology of the ulcerated area may help rule out leiomyosarcoma. Small symptomatic lesions may be treated by local surgical excision, and larger ones by partial gastrectomy. Other rare benign gastric tumors include lipomas, schwannomas, hemangiomas, lymphangiomas, adenomyomas, and fibromas.

PSEUDOTUMORS A number of gastric conditions other than peptic ulcer simulate neoplasms by x-ray. These include hypertrophic pyloric stenosis; antral gastritis; Ménétrier's disease and other gastric hyperplasias; pseudolymphoma; heterotopic pancreas; gastric eosinophilic granuloma; Crohn's disease; gastric varices; hematoma; deformity after fundoplication (Nissen repair); extrinsic pressure by the liver, pancreas, or spleen; and bezoars or retained food. Often endoscopic evaluation and consideration of the total clinical picture solve these problems, but in rare cases surgical exploration is necessary to exclude malignancy.

GASTRITIS

EROSIVE GASTRITIS Erosive gastritis (also known as hemorrhagic gastritis or multiple gastric erosions) is a frequent cause of upper gastrointestinal bleeding, but it is rarely severe. Erosions may be completely asymptomatic. As detected by endoscopy, multiple bleeding erosions are distributed diffusely throughout the gastric mucosa or are localized to the fundus, body, or antrum. The intervening mucosa may appear reddened and friable, or it may appear normal.

Histologically, the mucosal destruction by erosions does not extend below the muscularis mucosae to involve the more vascular submucosa; characteristically, the mucosal lesions heal completely. At any one time, different erosions can be observed in various stages of evolution and regression. Erosions may occur in flat mucosa or on the crests of small mucosal mounds which may stud the crests of folds. Between erosions there may be areas of surface epithelium depleted of mucus and focal or diffuse extravasation of blood into the lamina propria. Erosions may develop in mucosa that is histologically normal or that shows changes of any histologic type of gastritis. If the process persists, erosions may extend into the submucosa to form acute ulcers (Chap. 235); then bleeding may become severe.

Erosive gastritis can occur for no apparent reason. Many cases, however, are associated with the ingestion of aspirin or nonsteroidal anti-inflammatory drugs (NSAIDs). Because aspirin is not ionized in the acid milieu of the gastric lumen, it is absorbed readily by passive nonionic diffusion. At the neutral intracellular pH within the gastric surface epithelium, aspirin becomes an ionized acid which can destroy the cells and provide an entry point for acid-peptic digestion. When aspirin is given with sodium bicarbonate it does not injure the gastric mucosa because it is ionized and poorly absorbed gastrically. When aspirin is covered with an enteric coating it passes through the stomach and is absorbed in the small bowel. Aspirin and most NSAIDs interfere with prostaglandin synthesis, thus impairing mucosal resistance to injury. NSAIDs such as phenylbutazone or indomethacin are especially associated with erosive gastritis. Acute alcohol ingestion is an important cause of gastric erosions, and portal hypertension is a predisposing factor.

Severe stress secondary to burns, sepsis, trauma, surgery, shock, or respiratory, renal, or liver failure often causes gastric erosions or acute ulcers. Their pathogenesis is poorly understood and probably varies with different predisposing conditions. Alterations in mucosal blood flow may lead to areas of microinfarction with further evolution of the lesion dependent upon acid-peptic digestion. With better intensive care, hyperalimentation, and a strict antacid regimen, erosions in severely stressed patients infrequently progress to ulcers with resultant severe hemorrhage or perforation.

Patients may present with hematemesis and/or melena. Chronic blood loss may occur. Many have no symptoms, but some notice mild epigastric discomfort or nausea. The diagnosis is best made by gastroscopy on the same day as the bleeding episode, because otherwise the lesions may have healed and disappeared. The newer small-caliber screening endoscopes are just slightly bigger than a nasogastric tube and may be passed easily in very sick patients after only pharyngeal anesthesia. Only expert double-contrast x-ray may demonstrate some of these superficial erosions. Presumptive clinical diagnoses of erosive gastritis in patients with upper gastrointestinal bleeding and negative x-rays are often wrong. The source of upper gastrointestinal bleeding is best determined by early esophagogastroduodenoscopy.

The usual measures for restoring circulating blood volume should be undertaken promptly (Chap. 37). Not uncommonly, the bleeding has stopped by the time a tube is passed. If not, lavage of the stomach with iced isotonic saline solution is used, although its efficacy is unproved in all types of upper gastrointestinal bleeding, especially in erosive gastritis. In any event, lavage with noniced saline solution via an Ewald tube may facilitate diagnostic endoscopy by removing some of the obscuring blood. Gravity drainage, *not suction*, should be used for emptying the saline solution from the stomach, lest suction artifacts be produced which are indistinguishable from acute erosions endoscopically.

If bleeding stops, a regimen of hourly antacids and cimetidine or ranitidine is instituted. If bleeding continues, selective infusion of vasopressin into the left gastric artery or embolization may be warranted. In the rare case in which bleeding continues and is life-threatening, one of the erosions may have progressed to a deeper acute ulcer. If this ulcer can be visualized endoscopically, it may be treatable by electrocoagulation or with a heater probe via the endoscope. If this fails, vagotomy and pyloroplasty with oversewing of the bleeding ulcers is the preferred surgical treatment, but it also may not be successful. Very rarely persistent severe bleeding requires total gastrectomy.

NONEROSIVE GASTRITIS This is a *histologic* diagnosis and not a clinically recognizable entity because it probably does not cause symptoms. In fact, histologic evidence of gastritis is frequent in asymptomatic individuals, especially as they get older. Thus, the usual clinical assumption that most nonulcer dyspepsia is caused by "gastritis" is not justified. Similarly, gross endoscopic mucosal appearances of erythema, ecchymoses, petechiae, nodularity, or thickened folds do not necessarily indicate histologic changes. Nonerosive gastritis can *only* be diagnosed by biopsy, and it may or may not be of clinical significance.

The gastric mucosa is divided into two layers: (1) the superficial, nonglandular surface (foveolar) epithelium facing the lumen which is normally replaced every 5 days; and (2) the deeper, glandular layer which is a more stable population of epithelial cells which are replaced very slowly and which have specific functions. These cells include the *parietal cells*, which make HCl and intrinsic factor, the *chief cells* in the fundal glands, which make pepsin, the *pylorocardiac glandular* cells, which make mucus, and the endocrine G cells in the pyloric glands, which make gastrin. The patterns of gastritis involve both superficial and glandular areas, and the sequence is one of chronic and/or acute inflammation which may cause glandular destruction and may be followed by regeneration, metaplasia, or loss of glands (atrophy). To the pathologist chronic inflammation means the presence of increased plasma cells and lymphocytes in the lamina propria and acute inflammation means the presence of polymorphonuclear leukocytes. This does not necessarily indicate that the process is clinically chronic or acute, and thus morphologic interpretation may be confusing to clinicians. The probable morphologic sequence is that the superficial layer is first inflamed (superficial gastritis) and that epithelial destruction and inflammation within the surrounding lamina propria then penetrates to the deeper glandular areas (atrophic gastritis) leading finally to loss of glands (gastric atrophy) or replacement by metaplastic glands (intestinal metaplasia or pyloric gland metaplasia of fundal glands).

If one cannot ascribe symptoms to these histologic changes, what indeed is their clinical significance? It is known that chronic atrophic gastritis, gastric atrophy, and intestinal metaplasia occur at a younger age, are more widely distributed in the stomach, and are more frequent in populations with a higher incidence of carcinoma of the body and antrum of the stomach. Perhaps this is the "soil" in which this type of cancer develops more easily. But even in the United States, where this type of gastric cancer is decreasing, such gastric changes with aging are common. What is clinically significant in the United States is a completely normal fundal gland area, free of gastritis, in patients 70 years of age or older. These usually are patients with peptic ulcer disease of the hypersecretory, perhaps hereditary, type who commonly have duodenal ulcers and severe reflux esophagitis. The fundal glands of these patients do not undergo the "normal" gastric changes of aging. Interestingly, such patients often have antral (pyloric gland) gastritis.

What about the patient with a chronic benign gastric ulcer? These patients have chronic gastritis at the edge of their peptic ulcers and secrete normal or less than normal amounts of HCl. Thus, if endoscopic biopsies of the edge of a gastric ulcer show no gastritis, there is a strong likelihood that the ulcer is not a typical peptic ulcer; rather, it is probably associated with aspirin or NSAID ingestion, and discontinuance of the offending drugs will be curative. Atrophic fundal gland gastritis and/or atrophy is often seen in patients with thyroid disease or idiopathic iron deficiency anemia and is regularly seen in pernicious anemia. Perhaps a common denominator in all of these conditions is an autoimmune destruction of the gastric mucosa, but this hypothesis remains unproven.

Severe fundal gland atrophy is invariably present in pernicious anemia where parietal cells secreting intrinsic factor and HCl are virtually absent. As a result, vitamin B_{12} in food is not absorbed. Serum gastrin levels are high because the uninvolved antrum secretes gastrin continuously in the absence of acid. The pyloric glands are preserved and relatively free of gastritis. Serum antibodies to parietal cells are present in the serum of about 60 percent of persons with atrophic fundal gastritis and in 80 to 90 percent of those with pernicious anemia. Antibodies to intrinsic factor are present in the serum or gastric juice of most patients with pernicious anemia; they are not found in patients with superficial or atrophic gastritis. The relationship between these immunologic findings and the fundal gland atrophy of pernicious anemia is uncertain.

Antral (pyloric gland) gastritis is common in asymptomatic persons. With age, this type of gastritis probably tends to extend proximally and to replace some fundal glands. If peptic ulcer is located in the upper stomach, pyloric gland gastritis may extend far more proximally. Unlike fundal gastritis, in antral gastritis serum gastrin levels tend to be low and there may be antibodies to gastrin-producing cells rather than to parietal cells. It has been postulated that regurgitation of duodenal contents, particularly bile salts, into the stomach causes pyloric gland gastritis. Spiral bacilli have been isolated from some patients, but their significance is uncertain. Occasionally, pyloric gland gastritis is associated with narrowing of the antrum suggestive of malignancy by x-ray; such patients often complain of ulcer-like pain and may, indeed, prove to have ulcers subsequently. At gastroscopy, normal antral motility suggests pliability, and malignancy can usually be excluded. The symptoms often respond to antacids and inhibitors of H-2 receptors.

Ordinarily, nonerosive gastritis requires no treatment, but it is essential to rule out vitamin B_{12} malabsorption in persons who are found to be achlorhydric. If pernicious anemia is proved, it is treated as discussed in Chap. 285. Iron-deficiency anemia should not be attributed to atrophic fundal gland gastritis unless other causes are excluded; it responds to oral iron.

GASTRIC HYPERPLASIAS ("HYPERTROPHIC" GASTRITIS) Hypertrophic gastritis is a histologic misnomer. The individual mucosal epithelial cells are not enlarged (hypertrophic), but there are more of them (hyperplasia), and thus the mucosa is thickened. There are three causes for gastric mucosal hyperplasia: Ménétrier's disease, hypersecretory gastropathy, and Zollinger-Ellison syndrome (gastrinoma; see Chap. 235). Most hyperplastic mucosal conditions produce enlarged gastric folds which may be indistinguishable by x-ray or endoscopy from infiltrative cancer, lymphoma, or a functional abnormality.

Ménétrier's disease The cause of this uncommon type of gastric mucosal hyperplasia is unknown. It is characterized grossly by tortuous enlargement of the gastric mucosal folds resembling cerebral convolutions, and histologically by a thickened mucosa with hyperplasia of mucous cells and loss of most parietal and chief cells. The gastric pits are markedly elongated and tortuous and often exhibit cystic dilatation; these cysts may penetrate through the muscularis mucosae into the submucosa. The lamina propria often contains increased numbers of lymphocytes. Intestinal metaplasia may be present. The mucosal involvement may be localized or diffuse and tends to be most prominent on the greater curvature. The antrum is uninvolved in more than 50 percent of patients. Occasionally the gross appearance suggests diffuse polyposis.

Epigastric pain is the most common complaint. Anorexia, nausea, vomiting, weight loss, or diarrhea are other symptoms. Bleeding is not uncommon because of superficial erosions. Some patients develop a gastric ulcer. Carcinoma may develop rarely. Loss of protein through the mucosa often causes hypoalbuminemia, and sometimes peripheral edema. Widening of tight junctions between surface epithelial cells revealed by electron microscopy may explain the protein loss. The gastric juice contains little or no hydrochloric acid but often excessive mucus. X-ray shows very large folds and sometimes hypomotility. The diagnosis can usually be made from clinical, radiologic, and laboratory data supplemented by gastroscopy (preferably using one of the newer, larger biopsy forceps to get the deeper biopsy needed for diagnosis), and brush cytology to rule out cancer. Occasionally, laparotomy with full-thickness biopsy of the stomach is necessary to establish the diagnosis and to exclude malignancy.

There is no specific treatment, but frequent small meals may give some symptomatic relief. Those with gastric ulcers should receive antacids or H-2 receptor antagonists. A high-protein diet should be given to patients with hypoalbuminemia, but diuretics or intravenous albumin may be necessary for those with severe edema. Treatment with anticholinergic drugs or cimetidine reduces protein loss in some patients. Partial gastrectomy may be helpful for intractable symptoms if the disease is sufficiently well localized. Rarely, total gastrectomy may be necessary. The latter should be deferred as long as possible because spontaneous improvement or complete reversal of chronic disease has been documented.

Hypersecretory gastropathy Patients with this rare syndrome differ from those with classical Ménétrier's disease because the thickened mucosa secretes gastric acid normally or excessively but not at the high rate seen in gastrinoma; furthermore, blood gastrin levels are normal. The mucosa is histologically indistinguishable from that seen in Zollinger's syndrome with an excess of parietal and chief cells. Many of these patients may represent the upper end of the spectrum of increased fundal gland mass seen in patients with duodenal ulcer. Some have a protein-losing gastropathy. Ulcer symptoms may improve after antacids or H-2 receptor inhibitors, but some patients may require surgery. Protein loss, when present, may be difficult to control unless the disease remits spontaneously.

Gastrinoma (Zollinger-Ellison syndrome) This is a fundal gland hyperplasia caused by excessive gastrin secretion by a gastrinoma, usually located in the pancreas. The pathogenesis, clinical features, and treatment are described in the previous chapter on peptic ulcer.

CORROSIVE GASTRITIS The accidental or suicidal ingestion of strong alkali, such as lye, or of acids, such as hydrochloric or carbolic acid, can cause necrosis of the gastric wall, particularly in the prepyloric region. Alkali usually injures the esophagus more severely than the stomach, whereas the reverse tends to occur with acid. The degree of gastric injury varies with the quantity and concentration of irritant ingested and the amount of food present in the stomach. Patients complain of burning of the mouth, throat, and retrosternal area. With gastric injury, there is severe epigastric pain and often vomiting. Perforation, peritonitis, or massive hemorrhage may occur shortly after ingestion of a corrosive agent or may be delayed. Later, scarring may cause esophageal or pyloric stenosis.

If the patient is seen shortly after ingesting a corrosive agent, some clinicians suggest emptying the stomach gently via a small, soft rubber tube. Acid neutralization is not recommended for alkali ingestion because the heat of the ensuing reaction may aggravate the injury. Antacids may be given for acid ingestion after preliminary dilution with milk or water. Intravenous therapy, sedation, analgesia, airway maintenance, and careful observation are instituted. The use of corticosteroids and antibiotics is controversial, but corticosteroids may be helpful if edema threatens the airway and antibiotics may help treat aspiration pneumonia. Visible mouth and pharyngeal burns are not necessarily accompanied by esophageal or gastric injury. Therefore, early, gentle endoscopy with a small-caliber screening endoscope may establish the extent of injury. However, early in the course of acid injury the damage may be missed even endoscopically. If perforation or peritonitis is suspected, laparotomy should be performed and a partial gastrectomy done if full-thickness injury to the wall is found. Surgical treatment may be necessary also for acute massive bleeding or for late obstruction caused by scarring. Parenteral nutrition may be required.

PHLEGMONOUS GASTRITIS This rare condition should be considered when a patient presents with acute upper abdominal pain, signs of peritonitis, fever, purulent ascitic fluid, nausea or vomiting, and a normal serum amylase. It is a bacterial infection of the gastric wall, most often caused by streptococci, although staphylococci, pneumococci, *Escherichia coli,* or gas-forming bacteria can be responsible. Alcoholism, upper respiratory or other infection, peptic ulcer, endoscopic polypectomy, and gastric surgery are predisposing conditions. Vigorous antibiotic therapy should be followed immediately by laparotomy which is both diagnostic and therapeutic. Depending upon the operative findings, drainage or partial gastrectomy should be performed. Without surgery the mortality is nearly 100 percent; with surgery it is approximately 20 percent.

OTHER GASTRIC DISORDERS

ACUTE GASTRIC DILATATION This is an uncommon but serious condition. The use of nasogastric suction has greatly reduced its frequency in the postoperative period. Gastric dilatation may also occur after trauma, the use of body casts, pneumonia, diabetic acidosis, or large doses of anticholinergic drugs. It is a rare complication of many diseases and also may occur for no apparent reason. The patient complains of anorexia and epigastric fullness and often vomits small amounts of fluid. Increasing abdominal distention with tympany, especially in the left hypochondrium, and a succussion splash are demonstrable. Untreated, large volumes of fluid are sequestered in a gastric "third space" with resultant sodium and potassium depletion. The patient becomes restless and listless; hypovolemia, tachycardia, reduced urine output, and, finally, shock develop. Aspiration pneumonia may occur. X-ray of the abdomen shows massive gastric distention with an air-fluid level. Continuous nasogastric suction and restoration of fluid and electrolyte balance result in rapid improvement.

ADULT HYPERTROPHIC PYLORIC STENOSIS In this uncommon condition, the pyloric muscle is enlarged because of hypertrophy and possibly hyperplasia of the fibers of the circular layer. Many cases are associated with a peptic ulcer near the pylorus. In others, the pyloric muscle hypertrophy has been attributed to associated antral gastritis or neoplasm. A minority of cases without other gastric disease may be due to unrecognized infantile hypertrophic pyloric stenosis. Most often symptoms of pyloric obstruction such as nausea, vomiting, and epigastric fullness develop in mid-adult life, although occasionally mild symptoms are lifelong. An epigastric mass is not palpable in adults as it is in infants. Barium x-ray studies show a long, narrowed pyloric canal, often with triangular outpouchings within the canal. Gastroscopy shows a narrowed pylorus that is fixed in the open position. Although the diagnosis often appears highly likely from the above studies, an infiltrating cancer may be difficult to exclude without operation. A limited gastric resection is said to give better symptomatic relief than a pyloromyotomy, and in addition it provides an exact histologic diagnosis. The frequently associated juxtapyloric ulcers merit vagotomy.

BEZOARS AND FOREIGN BODIES Conglomerates of food and mucus or phytobezoars composed of vegetable matter sometimes form in the gastric remnant after partial gastrectomy, especially if a vagotomy was also performed. They occur less often after vagotomy and pyloroplasty. Autonomic neuropathy associated with diabetes mellitus is another predisposing condition. Rarely yeast bezoars have been found. Patients complain of anorexia, epigastric fullness, nausea, or vomiting. The diagnosis is often apparent from the barium x-ray examination, but endoscopy may be needed to distinguish the food mass from a neoplasm. The food conglomerate or bezoar can often be removed by vigorous and repeated gastric lavage. Fragmenting the lesion at gastroscopy may facilitate removal by lavage. Some phytobezoars can be partially digested with cellulase and then broken up successfully by lavage. Occasionally surgical removal is necessary. If the mass passes into the small bowel, it can cause obstruction requiring surgery. Treatment with metoclopramide and a low-fiber diet may be tried to prevent recurrence.

Bezoars in the intact stomach are rare. Phytobezoars are most common, a well-known type being the persimmon ball. Trichobezoars are composed of hair. Concretions of inorganic substances such as shellac, asphalt, or calcium carbonate are occasionally seen. Bezoars of the intact stomach often require surgical removal, although nonoperative methods may be successful for phytobezoars. Persimmon balls have responded to treatment with papain and sodium bicarbonate.

Small foreign bodies such as coins, marbles, or even closed safety pins usually pass through the stomach and bowel without difficulty. Elongated, sharp objects such as needles, toothpicks, or open safety pins may hold up at some point and cause obstruction, ulceration, bleeding, abscess, or peritonitis. Occasionally, large objects such as forks or knives are swallowed by emotionally disturbed persons. Patients who have swallowed dangerous objects should be promptly referred to an experienced endoscopist who may elect endoscopic removal, observation, or surgical treatment.

GASTRIC DIVERTICULA These uncommon lesions usually occur just below the cardia on the posterior wall near the lesser curvature. Almost all are asymptomatic and require no treatment. Pain, bleeding, and perforation are rare complications. Surgery should not be undertaken except for severe intractable symptoms that cannot be attributed to another cause. The x-ray appearance is usually diagnostic, but occasionally gastroscopy is needed to distinguish the lesion from a peptic ulcer.

GASTRIC VOLVULUS OR TORSION Rarely the stomach can twist about its longitudinal axis, thus turning itself upside down and obstructing the lower esophagus. The volvulus may be acute but is more often chronic. It tends to be associated with a paraesophageal hernia or eventration of the diaphragm. The stomach can also twist about the vertical axis of the gastrohepatic omentum to produce a torsion rather than a true volvulus. Acute volvulus is associated with severe upper abdominal pain and retching which produces saliva rather than gastric or duodenal contents. Passage of a nasogastric tube beyond the cardia is usually impossible. Plain x-ray films of the abdomen show distention of the stomach; the finding of two separate fluid levels is diagnostic. Acute volvulus may be of short duration and may subside spontaneously or may be associated with strangulation and require emergency surgical treatment. Those with chronic volvulus may be asymptomatic or have intermittent pain, often associated with eating. Severe symptoms may require surgical correction of the volvulus, including repair of an associated paraesophageal hernia, if present.

RARE GASTRIC DISEASES Pseudolymphoma This is a localized benign lymphoid hyperplasia of the stomach. Its etiology is unknown, but in some instances it is a reaction to a benign gastric ulcer. Grossly the lesion is usually single and ulcerated. Some lesions are nodular;

others may present as enlarged folds. The x-ray and endoscopic findings may suggest either malignancy or peptic ulcer. There is marked lymphocytic infiltration of the gastric wall which may be transmural. Partial gastrectomy is usually required for diagnosis and treatment. The lesion may be distinguished from true lymphoma by the polyclonal nature of the infiltrate shown by immunohistochemical staining.

Eosinophilic gastroenteritis   The antrum may be involved in this condition, which is associated with marked peripheral eosinophilia. The diagnosis can be made by mucosal biopsy, and chronic treatment with small doses of corticosteroids is usually effective.

Inflammatory fibroid polyp   This is usually a circumscribed lesion of the antrum and is not associated with peripheral eosinophilia. In the past it has been called *eosinophilic granuloma* but this is a misnomer. It does not respond to corticosteroid treatment and may require excision because of pyloric obstruction or other symptoms.

Gastric granulomas   Epithelioid granulomas of the stomach are most commonly caused by Crohn's disease and only rarely are a manifestation of sarcoid or tuberculosis. Some granulomas adjacent to peptic ulcers are foreign-body reactions. Idiopathic isolated granulomas often prove to be due to Crohn's disease or may be a manifestation of immunoglobulin deficiency or of chronic granulomatous disease.

Other specific gastritides   Tuberculosis and tertiary syphilis rarely affect the stomach. The diagnosis can sometimes be made from the clinical picture and endoscopic biopsy, but more often operation is needed to exclude malignancy. Appropriate antibiotic therapy is effective. Gastric infections, particularly candidiasis but also cytomegalovirus, herpes simplex, and histoplasmosis, are occasionally seen in immunosuppressed patients. Gastric anisakiasis is a nematode infection of the stomach acquired by eating raw fish. Previously, it was largely confined to Japan, where sashimi (raw fish) is a delicacy. It is now seen occasionally in the United States, where sashimi has become popular.

REFERENCES

Antonioli DA et al: Changes in the location and type of gastric adenocarcinoma. Cancer 50:775, 1982

Diehl JT et al: Gastric carcinoma—A ten year review. Ann Surg 198:9, 1983

Domschke S et al Gastroduodenal damage due to drugs, alcohol and smoking. Clin Gastroenterol 13:405, 1984

Dworken B et al: Primary gastric lymphoma. Dig Dis Sci 27:986, 1982

Graham DY, Smith JL: Aspirin and the stomach. Ann Int Med 104:390, 1986

Kreuning J et al: Gastric and duodenal mucosa in "healthy" individuals, an endoscopic and histopathological study of 50 volunteers. J Clin Pathol 31:69, 1978

Shafer LW et al: The risk of gastric carcinoma after surgical treatment for benign disease. N Engl J Med 309:1210, 1983

Weinstein WM: Gastritis, in *Gastrointestinal Disease*, 3d ed, J Sleisinger and JS Fordtran (eds). Philadelphia, Saunders, 1983

237   DISORDERS OF ABSORPTION

NORTON J. GREENBERGER / KURT J. ISSELBACHER

MECHANISMS OF ABSORPTION

Diseases of the small intestine are frequently accompanied by alterations in intestinal function, and clinically this impaired function is seen as the malabsorption syndrome. In order to obtain a better appreciation of the derangements which occur in the many disorders of intestinal function, the processes of normal absorption will first be reviewed.

It is important to distinguish between digestion and absorption, since an increased loss of nutrients in the stool may be a reflection of a derangement of either process. Digestion involves the breakdown or hydrolysis of nutrients to smaller molecules in order to prepare the ingested substances for absorption, or transport across the intestinal cell. It will be recalled that most of the digestive process is initiated in the stomach by acid and pepsin and is continued in the upper small intestine primarily by the action of pancreatic enzymes such as lipase, amylase, and trypsin. As a result of these digestive actions carbohydrates are broken down to monosaccharides and disaccharides, proteins to peptides and amino acids, and fats to monoglycerides and fatty acids. In the adult it is in this form that nutrients are, to a large extent, transported across the epithelial surface of the intestinal cell.

ANATOMIC AND PHYSIOLOGIC FACTORS   The intestine has an enormous surface area. This can be attributed in large part to its length, which in the adult is more than 12 ft, and to the foldings of the surface plicae. At the light microscopic level, the villi of the small intestine provide additional surface area, which is further augmented by the presence of microvilli (approximately 2×10^8 per square centimeter) on the outer, or brush border, region of epithelial cells. Thus the total absorptive area of the small intestine is enormous.

Motility (contractility) of the bowel is an important process which permits nutrients to remain in intimate contact with the intestinal cells and possibly influences the continued movement of the nutrients *into* and along the absorbing channels, such as the lymphatics. Two types of motility aid in this process: the gross motility of the intestine itself and the motility of individual villi. Entrance of the nutrients into the general circulation is achieved via the capillaries into the portal system or via the lacteals into the intestinal lymphatics.

TYPES OF ABSORPTION   Four mechanisms have been considered to be important in the transport of substances across the intestinal cell membrane, namely, active transport, passive diffusion, facilitated diffusion, and endocytosis.

Active transport involves the transport of a substance across the cell against an electric or chemical gradient; this process requires energy, is carrier-mediated, and is subject to competitive inhibition. *Passive diffusion* is the opposite of this process; energy is not required, transport is with (rather than against) the electric or chemical gradient, the process is not carrier-mediated, and it does not show properties of competitive inhibition. Thus active transport may be viewed as "uphill" transport, whereas passive diffusion is equivalent to "downhill" transport. *Facilitated diffusion* is similar to passive diffusion except that such a process shows evidence of being carrier-mediated and frequently subject to competitive inhibition.

Endocytosis is a process akin to phagocytosis. By this mechanism nutrients (soluble or particulate) upon entering the cell are surrounded by the components of the outer plasma cell membrane. In the intestinal tract endocytosis occurs in the neonatal period and, contrary to earlier belief, also occurs to a limited extent in the adult organism. While quantitatively limited, it appears to account, for example, for uptake of antigens.

SITES OF ABSORPTION   While many substances are absorbed throughout the length of the small intestine, certain nutrients tend to be absorbed more in one region than in others. The proximal intestine is a major area for the absorption of iron, calcium, water-soluble vitamins, and fat (monoglycerides and fatty acids). Sugars are absorbed in the proximal intestine and also the midintestine. While the amino acids appear to be absorbed primarily in the middle of the small intestine, or jejunum, some absorption also occurs in the upper and lower areas. The distal small intestine appears to be the *major* absorptive area for bile salts and vitamin B_{12}. As is emphasized below, this factor is of clinical significance in circumstances where there has been removal or disease of the ileum.

The colon is important for the absorption of water and electrolytes, a process which occurs predominantly in the cecum. Although the rectum is not a usual site for absorption of ingested foodstuffs, drugs introduced by rectum may be absorbed there. Thus drugs introduced by this route, such as salicylates or steroids, may have systemic as well as local effects.

ABSORPTION OF SPECIFIC NUTRIENTS Carbohydrate absorption

Much of the carbohydrate we ingest is in the form of starch, a complex polysaccharide consisting of many hexose units (attached either in a 1,4 or 1,6 linkage). By the action of salivary and pancreatic amylase, starch is hydrolyzed to oligosaccharides and then to disaccharides (mostly maltose). While monosaccharides such as glucose are readily absorbed, disaccharides are not. Disaccharides are split enzymatically into their component sugars by disaccharidases (or oligosaccharidases) located on or within the microvilli of intestinal epithelial cells. The two types of disaccharidases are β-galactosidases (lactase) and α-glucosidases (sucrase, maltase). By the action of these enzymes, lactose is split into glucose and galactose, sucrose into glucose and fructose, and maltose into two molecules of glucose. The resultant monosaccharides are then transported through the cell into the portal circulation. Most disaccharides are hydrolyzed so rapidly by brush border enzymes that the capacity of the transport mechanism is exceeded and some monosaccharides diffuse back into the intestinal lumen. Lactose, however, is hydrolyzed at a slower rate, and thus lactose hydrolysis is the rate-limiting step in lactose absorption.

Sugars such as glucose and galactose are absorbed by an active transport mechanism. The transport rate of sugars can be related to the substrate concentration by the expression K_t, where K_t stands for the monosaccharide substrate concentration that produces half the maximal transport rate. Published K_t values for glucose transport have varied widely, partly because of failure to consider the unstirred water layer, which constitutes a diffusion barrier for solutes.

Glucose (and galactose) entry into the cell is largely coupled to sodium ions (so-called symport); both sodium and glucose appear to bind to the hexose carrier in the microvillus membrane. Energy is required for the movement of glucose into the cell, which seems largely to come from the sodium pump and the Na^+,K^+-ATPase of the basolateral membrane (see below).

Protein and amino acid absorption

Dietary proteins are initially subject to degradation in the stomach by pepsin. However, complete hydrolysis is largely achieved by the action of the pancreatic enzymes trypsin and chymotrypsin as well as by other endopeptidases and exopeptidases such as carboxypeptidase. By these enzymatic processes oligopeptides, dipeptides, and amino acids are formed. Just as there are disaccharidases in mucosal cells to digest disaccharides, there are also oligopeptidases to split small peptides. Dipeptidases are located in the cytoplasm as well as on the microvilli. Dipeptides are absorbed more rapidly than amino acids, and presumably their uptake involves a separate mechanism. Thus, digestion of proteins to amino acids occurs in three locations: intestinal lumen, brush border, and cytoplasm of mucosal cells. As indicated above, contrary to earlier beliefs proteins can also be absorbed by the adult intestine. Although quantitatively limited, protein absorption probably is immunologically significant.

Most naturally occurring amino acids are L-amino acids, and these are subject to a number of different transport processes. *Neutral* amino acids seem to share a common carrier mechanism; thus amino acids such as tryptophan and alanine show competitive inhibition. Among the *dibasic* amino acids which appear to have a distinct transport mechanism are arginine, ornithine, and lysine. The neutral amino acid cystine shares this mechanism. There is also a separate transport system for *glycine* and the *imino acids* proline and hydroxyproline. There is also a transport system for *dicarboxylic* acids such as glutamic and aspartic acids. Therefore, in genetic disorders, such as cystinuria, one will find impaired absorption not only of cystine but also of arginine, ornithine, and lysine. Similarly in Hartnup disease, a defect in the transport of neutral amino acids (especially of tryptophan, phenylalanine, histidine) is found. In these genetic disorders uptake and absorption of dipeptides is normal.

Absorption of amino acids is rapid in the duodenum and jejunum but slow in the ileum. The actual mechanism of the absorption of amino acids by the intestine has not been elucidated. As in the case of carbohydrates, sodium ions appear to be required for the entry of these acids and the energy needed for their concentration within the cell. Some amino acids have affinity for more than one mechanism. For example, glycine may be transported by both the neutral and imino acid transport systems.

Fat absorption (Fig. 237-1)

Most of the ingested dietary fats are in the form of long-chain triglycerides. These triglycerides contain both saturated fatty acids (such as palmitic and stearic) and unsaturated fatty acids (such as oleic and linoleic). The particle size of the fat is decreased largely by the churning action of the stomach. The entry of fat into the duodenum plus the presence of acid causes release of secretin and pancreozymin-cholecystokinin, which in turn leads to a stimulation of the flow of bile and pancreatic juice.

ROLE OF PANCREATIC LIPASE The hydrolysis of triglycerides by pancreatic lipase is a complex process involving lipase, colipase, and bile salts. Pancreatic lipase is an enzyme that binds to the oil-water interface of an emulsified triglyceride substrate. The detergent properties of bile salts permit pancreatic lipase to gain access to water-insoluble lipids. One of the important functions of bile salts is to clear the oil-water interface of dietary fat from proteins of exogenous and endogenous origin, thus making it available for pancreatic lipolysis. Colipase, a protein present in pancreatic juice, is also essential for the action of lipase; its function is to anchor the lipase close to the surface of the triglyceride droplet. All three components, i.e., pancreatic lipase, colipase, and bile salts, form a *ternary complex*, which generates lipolytic products that diffuse away from the complex and are absorbed. With colipase present, lipase remains at the interface and forms 2-monoglycerides and fatty acids, which are the major end products of triglyceride hydrolysis. Less than 5 percent of ingested

FIGURE 237-1 *Scheme of intestinal digestion, absorption, esterification, and transport of dietary triglycerides. TG = triglycerides; FA = fatty acids; MG = monoglycerides; BS = bile salts.*

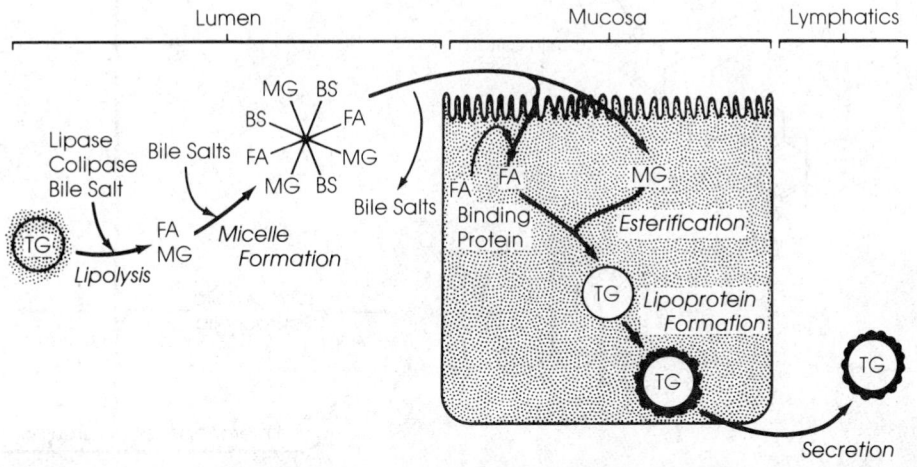

fat remains in the form of diglycerides and triglycerides. Without colipase, bile acids would actually wash pancreatic lipase away from the interface, and the hydrolytic rate of triglycerides would be reduced.

ROLE OF BILE SALTS (Fig. 237-2)   Bile salts play an important role in the digestion and absorption of fat. They are synthesized in the liver (approximately 200 to 600 mg daily) from cholesterol and excreted in the bile in the form of their glycine or taurine conjugates. In humans the principal bile acids excreted are conjugates of cholic and chenodeoxycholic acid. Bile salts are good detergents, because they have both polar (hydrophilic) and nonpolar (hydrophobic) groups. During digestion the concentration of conjugated bile salts in the lumen is in the range of 5 to 15 μmol/mL, and at these concentrations the bile salts aggregate to form *micelles*. Fatty acids and monoglycerides enter these micelles, forming mixed micelles. An emulsion of triglyceride is turbid; mixed micelles containing bile salts, fatty acids, and monoglycerides are clear solutions. The formation of *mixed micelles* and hence the solubilization of fatty acids and monoglycerides is much more effectively achieved with *conjugated bile salts* at the pH which normally exists in the intestinal lumen (Fig. 237-2).

Most conjugated bile salts are absorbed in the ileum and after entering the portal vein are subject to an enterohepatic circulation. By this process about 90 percent of the conjugated bile salts reaching the ileum is reabsorbed. As a consequence only about 200 to 600 mg bile salts is excreted in the feces per day, while, as part of the enterohepatic circulation, as much as 20 to 30 g bile salts recirculates daily between the liver and intestine. When the enterohepatic circulation is intact, the size of the bile salt pool is largely determined by the frequency of the enterohepatic circulation, i.e., the number of cycles per day (see also Chap. 253). If the ileum is diseased or removed, absorption of bile salts is impaired, and a significant fecal loss of bile salts will occur. As a consequence of this bile salt depletion, the concentration of bile salts in the intestinal lumen will also decrease, leading to further impairment of fat absorption. A similar result will occur if bile salt reabsorption is prevented by chelating agents, such as cholestyramine (see ''Regional Enteritis'' below).

INTRAMUCOSAL ASPECTS OF FAT ABSORPTION (Fig. 237-1)   After the hydrolysis of fatty acids to monoglycerides and their interaction with bile salts to form mixed micelles, the lipids pass through an ''unstirred'' water layer covering the cell surface. The mixed micelles apparently do not enter the cell, but instead the component fatty acids and monoglycerides are released from the micellar phase and then enter the cell by diffusion. In aqueous duodenal contents, large bile salt mixed micelles saturated with products of lipolysis coexist with larger liquid crystal liposomes of the same lipids saturated with free fatty acids and mixed bile salts. These phases are interconvertible and both may be important in fat digestion and absorption. Upon entry into the mucosal cell, fatty acids may interact with specific binding proteins. The subsequent fate of the intracellular lipid is strongly influenced by the fatty acid chain length. Fatty acids and monoglycerides derived from long-chain triglycerides (i.e., containing C-16 to C-18 fatty acids) are promptly *reesterified to triglycerides* by enzymes of the endoplasmic reticulum. These triglycerides then interact with specific apolipoproteins plus cholesterol and phospholipid to form chylomicrons and very low density lipoproteins. These initially accumulate in the Golgi region of the cell and then are secreted into the lacteals and the intestinal lymph. There are thus four major steps in the absorption of long-chain fatty acids and monoglycerides: (1) mucosal uptake and interaction with binding proteins, (2) reesterification to triglycerides, (3) lipoprotein formation, and (4) secretion into lymph.

By contrast, fatty acids derived from medium-chain triglycerides (i.e., containing C-8 and C-12 fatty acids) are *not reesterified* to any significant extent within the cell and are not incorporated into lipoproteins. Instead, they rapidly enter the portal venous system, where they are transported as fatty acids bound to albumin. The major aspects of fat absorption are summarized in Fig. 237-1.

Absorption of cholesterol and fat-soluble vitamins (A, D, E, K)   In addition to contributing significantly to the total-body synthesis of cholesterol, the intestine also plays an active role in the absorption of cholesterol and its esters. Within the lumen, cholesterol esters from the bile and diet are hydrolyzed by a pancreatic esterase. There

FIGURE 237-2 *Scheme of hepatic and intestinal metabolism of bile salts and the enterohepatic circulation (from ileum to liver). Note that bacteria lead to the formation of secondary bile acids; of the latter, only deoxycholic acid is absorbed to any appreciable extent.*

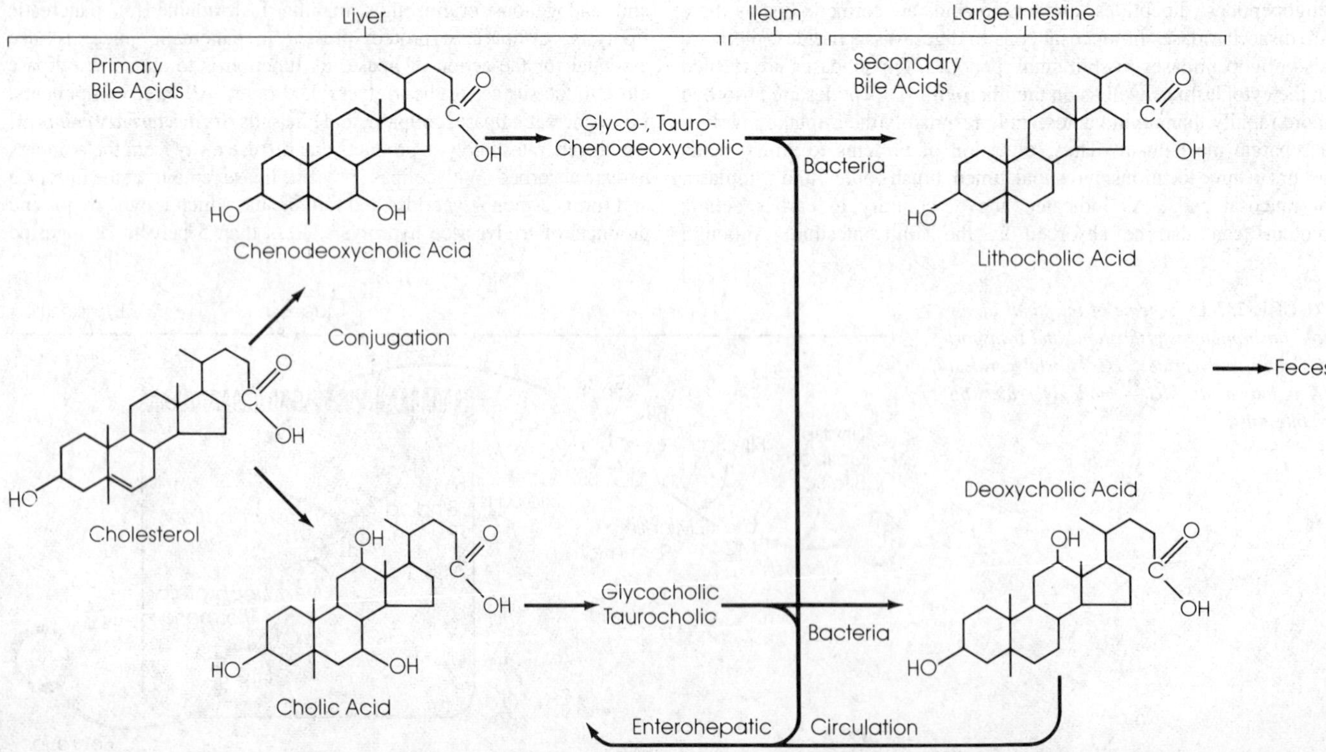

is also a separate cholesterol esterase in the intestinal microvilli, which completes this hydrolysis. As a result, only free cholesterol appears to enter the intestinal cell. However, just as in the case of long-chain fatty acids, much of the cholesterol is reesterified and is then secreted primarily into lymph.

The absorption mechanisms of the fat-soluble vitamins A, D, E, and K are not well understood. The intestine is able to convert β-carotene into vitamin A. The vitamin A thus formed or absorbed from the lumen is esterified in the mucosa primarily with palmitic acid, transported in the chylomicrons of the lymph, and stored as retinol palmitate in the liver. The other lipid-soluble vitamins also appear in lymph chylomicrons, but esterification with fatty acids does not appear to be necessary for their transport.

Water and sodium absorption In spite of extensive investigations the main mechanisms of water and electrolyte transport are not well understood. The mechanisms responsible for fluid absorption differ in the jejunum, ileum, and colon. There are two pathways by which water and ions cross the intestinal mucosa: the paracellular and transcellular pathways. Individual intestinal mucosa cells are joined near their apex by a "tight junction," and ions and water traverse this *paracellular* pathway during absorption and secretion. It is believed that the tight junction pathway contains aqueous-filled channels or pores. Such intercellular spaces are closed in the resting state and dilated during absorption. Considerable evidence has accumulated indicating that pumps and carriers are involved in intestinal water and solute transport. For example, in the ileum, Na^+ enters in exchange for H^+, and Cl^- enters in exchange for HCO_3^-. Sodium entry into the cell also occurs coupled with glucose via the glucose-sodium carrier in the microvillus membrane. Inside the cell, the Na^+ pump located in the basolateral membrane actively transports Na^+ out of the mucosal cell and into the intercellular space. *Transcellular* transport requires passage of ions through two membrane barriers, i.e., the apical brush border plasma membrane and the basolateral membrane. After Na^+ and Cl^- are transported across the brush border membrane into the cell, Na^+ is pumped across the basolateral membrane and Cl^- either follows passively or is also pumped into the intercellular space. The Na^+,K^+-ATPase is present in the basolateral but not in the brush border membrane and is the biochemical mediator of this pump. Bulk water movement obviously influences the movement of Na^+, K^+, and Cl^-. This "solvent drag" effect is explained by two mechanisms: (1) solutes may be caught in a moving stream of water and transported across a membrane, and (2) water movement results in increased concentration of solute on the side of the membrane from which water was transported, which causes solute to diffuse through the direction of flow. Diarrhea can be simply defined as impaired net absorption of water and electrolytes by the small intestine or colon. Some mechanisms producing diarrhea are listed in Table 237-1.

Calcium absorption Calcium is actively transported by the small intestine, and this process is intimately linked to the active form of vitamin D_3, namely, 1,25-dihydroxycholecalciferol. The role of two other intestinal cell proteins, calcium-binding protein and calmodulin, in the absorption of calcium remains unclear.

Iron absorption The formation of soluble iron complexes is important for maintaining intraluminal iron in an absorbable form. Gastric acid facilitates the chelation of inorganic iron with substances such as ascorbic acid, sugars, amino acids, and bile; these macromolecular complexes then remain soluble in the more alkaline duodenum and jejunum. With the average western diet luminal content of the iron intake averages 15 to 25 mg per day; iron absorption averages 0.5 to 1.0 mg per day in men and 1.0 to 2.0 mg per day in women during their reproductive years. A regulatory mechanism for the absorption of inorganic iron appears to exist within the small-intestinal mucosal cells. Iron is actively transported by the small intestine, and the duodenum is the principal site of iron absorption. The absorption of elemental iron in humans and animals involves at least two distinct steps: (1) mucosal uptake of iron from the lumen and (2) mucosal transfer of iron to the plasma. Much of the iron entering the mucosal cell is not transferred to the plasma but remains trapped within the cell and is excreted into the lumen when the cell is shed. Iron lost by this mechanism seems to vary inversely with body iron stores. However, this mucosal regulatory mechanism can be overcome when pharmacologic doses of iron are ingested. Hemoglobin iron is also absorbed by human subjects, depending upon body requirements for iron; the heme is split from globin in the lumen and absorbed as an intact metalloporphyrin. Organic iron in the form of hemoglobin is absorbed more effectively than iron from cereals and vegetables. The absorption of inorganic iron is increased by ascorbic acid. Similarly, the presence of anemia, liver injury, pregnancy, idiopathic hemochromatosis, or a portacaval shunt may result in increased iron absorption. Conversely, the prior ingestion of large doses of iron and the presence in the lumen of phosphates, carbonates, and phytates may lead to decreased absorption of inorganic iron. Impaired absorption of iron is frequent in disorders (such as nontropical sprue) which involve the duodenal mucosa.

Water-soluble vitamins *Vitamin B_{12} absorption* is discussed in Chap. 285. In the case of *folic acid absorption*, it should be emphasized that folates exist in food conjugated with glutamyl peptides. These *polyglutamates* must be deconjugated (by folic deconjugase) to monoglutamates for absorption to occur. Certain drugs (such as oral contraceptives, sulfasalazine, diphenylhydantoin, trimethoprim, and pyrimethamine) inhibit the absorption of dietary folate and hence can cause folate deficiency. Sulfasalazine, for example, competitively inhibits three enzymes important in the intestinal metabolism of folate, i.e., dihydrofolate reductase, methylene tetrahydrofolate reductase, and serine transhydroxymethylase. Thiamine and riboflavin appear to be absorbed by passive diffusion.

TABLE 237-1 Some mechanisms in the production of diarrhea

I Secretory diarrhea
  A Secretory agents associated with adenylate cyclase system
    1 Enterotoxin-producing bacteria *(Vibrio cholerae, Escherichia coli)*
    2 Methylxanthines (caffeine, theophylline)
    3 Prostaglandins
    4 Vasoactive intestinal peptide (VIP)
    5 Dihydroxy bile acids (affect colon primarily; effects seen after ileal resection)
  B Secretory agents *not associated* with adenylate cyclase system
    1 Glucagon, secretin, cholecystokinin-pancreozymin, serotonin, calcitonin, gastrin inhibitory polypeptide (GIP)
    2 Some laxatives* (ricinoleic acid, bisacodyl, phenolphthalein, dioctyl sodium sulfosuccinate)
    3 Bacterial enterotoxins *(Shigella, Staphylococcus aureus, Clostridium perfringens)*
  C Mucosal injury, altered cell permeability
    1 *Salmonella, Shigella,* invasive *E. coli,* gastroenteritis viruses
    2 Celiac sprue
    3 Inflammatory bowel disease (ulcerative colitis, regional enteritis)
  D Neoplasms with or without hormone production
    1 Gastrinoma (gastrin)
    2 Carcinoid syndrome (serotonin, prostaglandins)
    3 Medullary carcinoma of thyroid (calcitonin, prostaglandins)
    4 Pancreatic cholera syndrome (? VIP)
    5 Villous adenoma
II Osmotic diarrhea
  A Impaired carbohydrate absorption
    1 Disaccharidase deficiency (lactose or sucrose-isomaltose intolerance)
    2 Glucose-galactose malabsorption
  B Laxative ingestion or abuse
    1 Nonabsorbable osmotically active agents (lactulose, sorbitol, mannitol)
    2 Saline purgatives (magnesium phosphate, magnesium hydroxide–containing antacids)
  C Postsurgical disorders
    1 Vagotomy and pyloroplasty*
    2 Gastrojejunostomy* (Billroth I and II)
III Motility disorders
  A Laxative abuse*
  B Irritable bowel syndrome
  C Diverticular disease of the colon
  D Diabetic diarrhea with visceral neuropathy

* Multiple mechanisms involved in production of diarrhea.

TABLE 237-2 Tests useful in the diagnosis of malabsorptive disorders

Test	Normal values	Typical findings — Malabsorption (nontropical sprue)	Maldigestion (pancreatic insufficiency)	Comment
I Stool studies				
A Quantitative determination of stool fat	<6 g per 24 h; >95% coefficient of fat absorption	>6 g per 24 h	>6 g per 24 h	Best test for establishing presence of steatorrhea
B Fat in stool, %	<6	often <9.5	>9.5	Increased stool fat concentration strongly suggests that steatorrhea is due to pancreatic insufficiency
II Carbohydrate absorption				
A D-Xylose absorption (25-g oral dose)	5-h urinary excretion >4.5 g; peak blood level >30 mg/dL	↓	Normal	A good screening test for carbohydrate absorption
III Small-intestine x-rays		Malabsorption pattern	Normal or minimal malabsorption pattern; occasionally pancreatic calcification	Moulage sign and other abnormalities may be present in several disorders (see text)
IV Blood tests				
A Serum calcium	9–11 mg/dL	Frequently ↓	Usually normal	
B Serum albumin	3.5–5.5 g/dL	Frequently ↓	Usually normal	Decreased levels of both serum albumin and globulins should raise the question of protein-losing enteropathy
C Serum cholesterol	150–250 mg/dL	↓	Frequently ↓	Usually decreased in disorders associated with significant steatorrhea
D Serum iron	80–150 μg/dL	Frequently ↓	Normal	Low values may reflect decreased body iron stores
E Serum magnesium	1.2–2.0 meq/liter	Frequently ↓	Usually normal	
F Serum zinc	12–20 μmol/liter	Frequently ↓	Usually normal	Decreased levels common in malnutrition, cirrhosis, and malabsorption
G Serum carotenes	>100 IU/dL	↓	Usually ↓	Fairly satisfactory screening tests for malabsorption
H Serum vitamin A	>100 IU/dL	↓		
I Prothrombin time	70–100%; 12–15 s	Frequently ↓	Frequently ↓	
V Small intestinal mucosal biopsy		Abnormal	Abnormal	A specific diagnosis can be established in a small number of disorders (see text)
VI Urine tests				
A Vitamin B_{12} absorption	>8% urinary excretion in 48 h	Frequently ↓	Frequently ↓	Useful in determining whether vitamin B_{12} malabsorption is due to gastric or small-intestinal disorders
B Urine 5-hydroxyindoleacetic acid (5-HIAA)	2–9 mg per 24 h	↑	Normal	Slightly increased level (12–16 mg per 24 h) characteristically found in nontropical sprue
VII Breath tests				
A Breath H_2 (after 50 g lactose)	Minimal breath H_2	May be ↑	Normal	Secondary to lactase deficiency (see text)
B Breath H_2 (after 10 g lactulose)	Minimal breath H_2	May be normal or ↓	Normal	Early peak in bacterial overgrowth; can be used to determine intestinal transit time
C Breath $^{14}CO_2$ (after ^{14}C xylose)	Minute amounts $^{14}CO_2$	May be ↓	Usually normal	Increased in bacterial overgrowth
D Glycocholic acid metabolism (oral glycine-1-[^{14}C]glycocholate)	<1% of dose excreted $^{14}CO_2$ in 4 h	Normal	Normal	Increased $^{14}CO_2$ excretion with bacterial overgrowth or bile acid malabsorption (due to ileal resection or inflammatory disease)
	<4% of dose excreted in stools	Normal	Normal	Increased fecal excretion of ^{14}C in bile acid malabsorption
E [^{14}C]Triolein absorption (breath test)	>3.5% of dose as breath $^{14}CO_2$ per hour	Decreased	Decreased	Correlates well with chemical stool fat; recently introduced test
VIII Miscellaneous				
A Bacteria (culture)	<10^3 organisms per milliliter	Normal	Normal	>10^5 organisms per milliliter indicates bacterial overgrowth
B Secretin test	Volume >1.8 (mL/kg)/h Bicarbonate concentration >80 meq/liter	Normal	Abnormal	See discussion of pancreatic insufficiency in Chaps. 254 and 255
C Bentiromide test	Urine excretion arylamines ≥50%	May be abnormal	Abnormal	See discussion of pancreatic disease in Chaps. 254 and 255

TESTS USEFUL IN THE DIAGNOSIS OF MALABSORPTION

Most of the tests useful in the diagnosis of malabsorption indicate the presence of abnormal absorptive or digestive function, and only a few tests may suggest a specific diagnosis. Accordingly, it is frequently necessary to employ a combination of tests to establish a diagnosis. To illustrate the use of various tests, the characteristic findings in nontropical sprue, an example of a primary malabsorptive disorder, and pancreatic insufficiency, an example of impaired digestion, are compared in Table 237-2.

Stool fat The qualitative examination of the stool for undigested muscle fibers, neutral fat, and split fat is a simple and reliable screening test for steatorrhea. The finding of an increased number of muscle fibers indicates impaired intraluminal digestion. Properly performed, the qualitative microscopic examination of a stool specimen with the Sudan III stain is of value and correlates well with the quantitative determination of fecal fat by the Van de Kamer method. The latter remains the most reliable measurement of steatorrhea. A normal fecal fat excretion is less than 6 g for 24 h, or greater than 94 percent coefficient of fat absorption. A fecal fat concentration greater than or equal to 9.5 percent suggests that steatorrhea is due to pancreatic exocrine insufficiency.

Oral [^{14}C]triolein can also be used as an effective test for fat absorption. During the digestive process the triolein is hydrolyzed, and the labeled glycerol is absorbed and metabolized by the liver. The $^{14}CO_2$ produced is exhaled and can then be measured hourly (for 6 h) in the expired air. Normally more than 3.5 percent of the administered label [0.185 MBq (5 μCi)] appears in the breath per hour.

Xylose absorption In the most commonly employed test of carbohydrate absorption, the patient ingests 25 g D-xylose. A 5-h urine xylose excretion of 4.5 g or greater is considered normal. There is some decreased renal excretion with age, and over age sixty-five 3.5 g is the normal value. Low values may be obtained in patients with ascites, intestinal bacterial overgrowth, or renal insufficiency, after administration of certain drugs (e.g., aspirin, indomethacin), and most commonly if the urine collection is incomplete. To obviate difficulties in interpreting the test, it is advisable to determine the blood xylose level 2 h after ingestion of xylose. A blood xylose level of 30 mg/dL or greater indicates normal absorption of D-xylose. An abnormal D-xylose absorption test is found most frequently in disorders affecting the mucosa of the proximal small intestine, such as nontropical and tropical sprue.

Gastrointestinal x-ray studies All patients with malabsorption should have radiographic examinations of the small intestine and, in many cases, of the esophagus, stomach, and colon as well. Occasionally, the latter two examinations may provide important clues to the presence of such disorders as gastroileostomy, scleroderma, Zollinger-Ellison syndrome, ulcerative colitis, and intestinal fistulas. The typical small-bowel radiographic abnormalities in patients with a malabsorption syndrome are a breaking up of the barium column with segmentation, clumping, and coarsening of the mucosal folds. Segmentation or clumping of the barium in a small-bowel loop is often termed a *moulage sign*. Less frequently there is dilatation of the proximal small bowel and loss of a normal mucosal pattern. Collectively, these changes have been referred to as a *malabsorption pattern*. These findings are nonspecific and may be found in several of the disorders listed in Table 237-3. Some representative examples of abnormal small-bowel radiographs are shown in Fig. 237-3.

Small-intestinal biopsy The most commonly used instruments for obtaining peroral biopsy specimens from the small intestine include the Rubin tube, the Crosby, Carey, and Ross-Moore capsules, and the upper gastrointestinal endoscope. Examination of small-bowel biopsy specimens has proved to be of considerable value in the differential diagnosis of malabsorptive disorders. Table 237-3 lists disorders associated with abnormalities in intestinal biopsies, and Fig. 237-4 depicts some illustrative lesions.

Schilling test for vitamin B$_{12}$ absorption The Schilling test is valuable in the differential diagnosis of malabsorption and is frequently carried out in three stages: (1) without intrinsic factor, (2) with intrinsic factor, and (3) after a course of treatment with antibiotics. Since vitamin B$_{12}$ is absorbed primarily in the distal ileum, an abnormal Schilling test may indicate a pathologic condition of the distal small bowel. In disorders affecting the terminal ileum, such as regional enteritis and lymphomas, the first-stage Schilling test is frequently abnormal. The ileal receptor site appears to be damaged in these disorders, and the impaired absorption of B$_{12}$ is not corrected by the addition of intrinsic factor or the use of antibiotics. The Schilling test may also be useful in establishing a diagnosis of abnormal bacterial overgrowth of the small bowel, which may be present in disorders such as blind loop syndrome, scleroderma, and multiple small-bowel diverticula (see below). In the blind loop syndrome, for example, the bacteria can actually take up vitamin B$_{12}$ with resultant impaired absorption of B$_{12}$. Under these conditions the first-stage Schilling test is frequently abnormal, as is the second stage. After appropriate antibiotic treatment the Schilling test usually returns to normal. Vitamin B$_{12}$ absorption is frequently abnormal in patients with exocrine pancreatic insufficiency (see Chap. 255).

Secretin test The secretin test, secretin pancreozymin test, and intraduodenal perfusion with essential amino acids, which may be useful in establishing a diagnosis of pancreatic insufficiency, are discussed in detail in Chap. 254.

Serum calcium, albumin, cholesterol, magnesium, and iron Abnormal serum calcium, albumin, cholesterol, magnesium, and iron values may be found in several malabsorptive disorders. The primary value of such tests is to suggest that abnormal intestinal absorptive function may be present. These tests are usually of limited value in the *differential diagnosis* of malabsorption, but if abnormal, may be helpful in supporting this diagnosis.

Serum carotenes, vitamin A, and prothrombin time Absorption of the fat-soluble vitamins A, D, K, and E is frequently impaired in patients with steatorrhea. Measurements of serum carotene and vitamin A levels are useful as screening tests for malabsorption. However,

---

TABLE 237-3 Disorders associated with abnormalities in small-bowel biopsy specimens

I Disorders in which biopsy is of diagnostic value (diffuse lesions)

  A Whipple's disease: Lamina propria infiltrated with macrophages containing PAS-positive glycoproteins

  B Abetalipoproteinemia: Villus structure normal; epithelial cells vacuolated due to excess fat

  C Agammaglobulinemia: Flattened or absent villi; increased lymphocyte infiltration; absence of plasma cells

II Disorders in which biopsy may be of diagnostic value (patchy lesions)

  A Intestinal lymphoma: Infiltration of lamina propria and submucosa with malignant cells

  B Intestinal lymphangiectasia: Dilated lacteals and lymphatics in lamina propria; clubbed villi

  C Eosinophilic enteritis: Diffuse or patchy eosinophilic infiltration in lamina propria and mucosa

  D Amyloidosis: Presence of amyloid confirmed by special stains

  E Regional enteritis: Noncaseating granulomas

  F Parasitic infestations: Parasitic invasion of mucosa; adherence of trophozoites to mucosal surface, as in giardiasis

  G Systemic mastocytosis: Mast cell infiltration of lamina propria

III Disorders in which biopsy is abnormal but not diagnostic

  A Celiac sprue: Shortened or absent villi; hypertrophied crypts; damaged surface epithelium; mononuclear infiltrate

  B "Collagenous" sprue: Indistinguishable from celiac sprue; extensive subepithelial collagen deposition

  C Tropical sprue: Lesion similar to celiac sprue with shortened or absent villi; lymphocyte infiltration

  D Folate deficiency: Shortened villi; megalocytosis; decreased mitoses in crypts

  E Vitamin B$_{12}$ deficiency: Similar to folate deficiency

  F Acute radiation enteritis: Similar to folate deficiency

  G Systemic scleroderma: Fibrosis around Brunner's glands

  H Bacterial overgrowth syndromes: Patchy damage to villi and increased lymphocyte infiltration

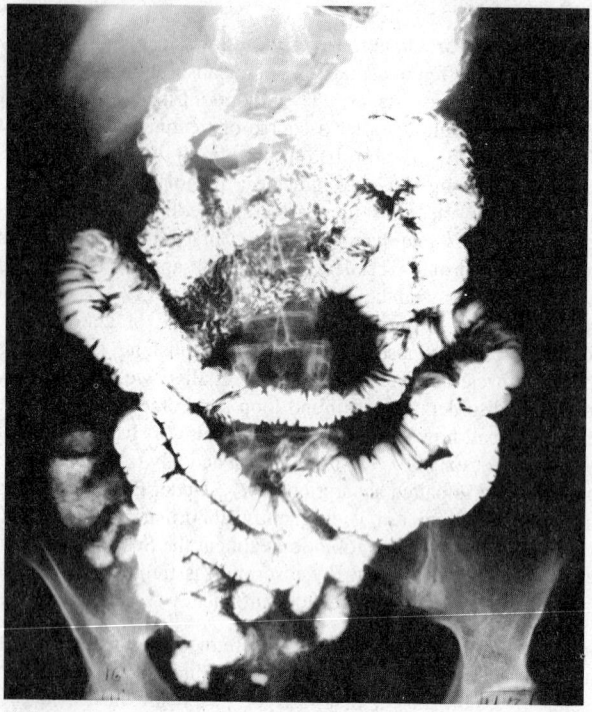

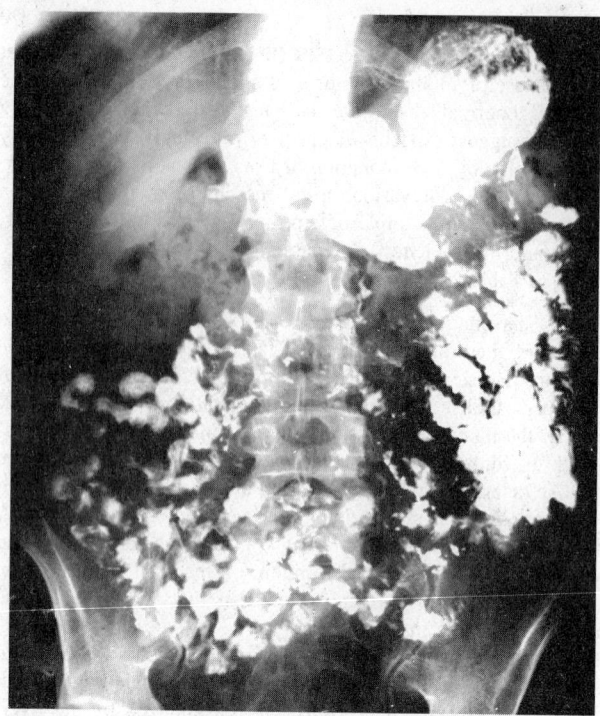

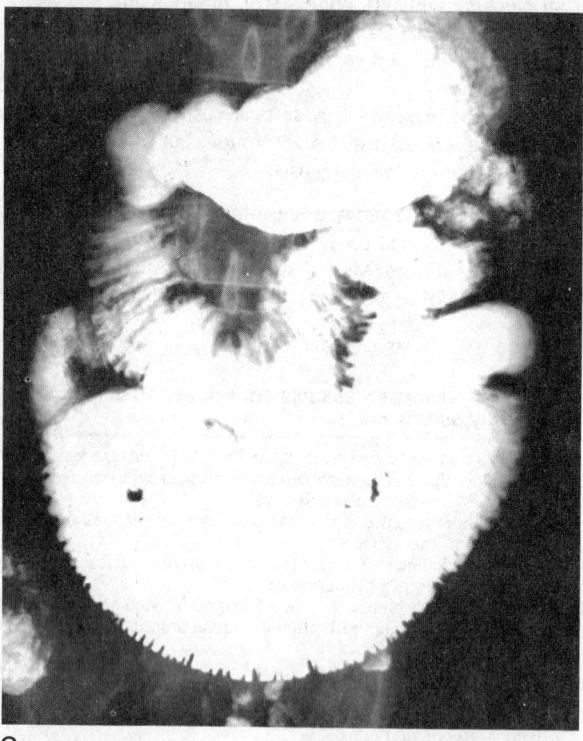

FIGURE 237-3 *A. X-ray of a normal small intestine showing good mucosal pattern. B. Intestinal x-ray of a patient with nontropical sprue. Note dilatation of small bowel, lack of mucosal markings, and segmentation and clumping of barium. C. Intestinal x-ray of patient with obstructed lymphatics due to Köhlmeier-Degos disease. Note "accordion-pleated" pattern at lower edge of film.*

other tests not only are more sensitive but often give more specific information than the serum carotene and vitamin A levels. The blood prothrombin time is an important test, since patients with malabsorption may present with abnormal bleeding due to vitamin K deficiency. If the decreased prothrombin activity is due to malabsorption, it should be readily correctable with parenteral vitamin K.

Breath tests The bile acid breath test utilizing [^{14}C]cholylglycine is a reasonably reliable screening test for bacterial overgrowth syndromes. Approximately two-thirds of patients with a positive small-bowel culture will have an abnormal bile acid breath test. However, in patients with suspected malabsorption of bile acids the test is rather insensitive without the additional determination of fecal bile acid excretion. The excretion of breath hydrogen after ingestion of lactose is a sensitive, specific, and noninvasive test for detecting lactase deficiency. Lactulose and [^{14}C]xylose breath tests for bacterial overgrowth have also been found helpful.

PATHOPHYSIOLOGIC BASIS FOR SYMPTOMS AND SIGNS IN MALABSORPTIVE DISORDERS The common symptoms and signs found in malabsorptive disorders are listed in Table 237-4. The most frequent symptoms are those of malnutrition, weight loss, and diarrhea. However, in each of the clinical settings listed in Table 237-4, it is important to consider the cause of the malabsorption.

DISORDERS ASSOCIATED WITH MALABSORPTION
(See Table 237-5)

INADEQUATE DIGESTION Liver and biliary tract disease It is not generally appreciated that patients with acute or chronic liver disease may develop malabsorption due to impaired intraluminal digestion. Steatorrhea has been described in acute viral hepatitis, chronic extrahepatic biliary tract obstruction, primary biliary cirrhosis, and postnecrotic and nutritional cirrhosis. Absorption of D-xylose and vitamin B$_{12}$ are usually normal, and small-intestinal mucosal biopsy specimens are generally unremarkable. The steatorrhea associated with liver and biliary tract disease is thought to be due to impaired hepatic synthesis or excretion of conjugated bile salts, resulting in impaired formation of micellar lipid. In addition to steatorrhea, patients with liver disease may have impaired absorption of vitamin D and calcium, resulting in severe metabolic bone disease. This is particularly common in patients with primary biliary cirrhosis. Skeletal roentgenograms may show increased porosity of bone, cortical thinning, vertebral compression, and spontaneous pathologic fractures. Patients with alcohol-induced liver disease may also have exocrine pancreatic insufficiency. Accordingly, pancreatic function should be evaluated in patients with liver disease and malabsorption.

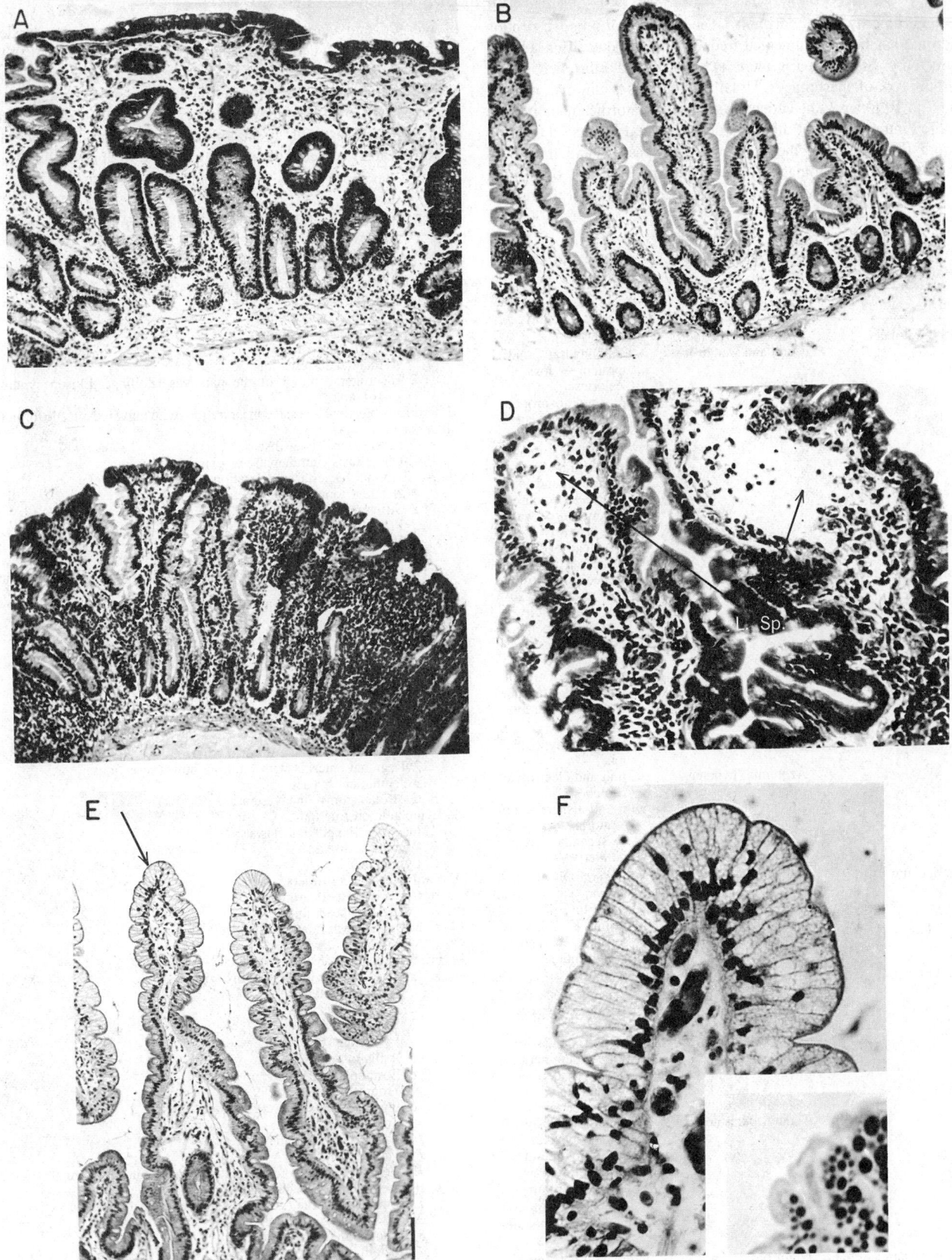

FIGURE 237-4 *Typical peroral intestinal biopsies. A. Jejunal mucosa of patient with nontropical sprue. Note virtual absence of villi, elongated crypts (some are cut in cross section), mononuclear infiltrate, cuboidal instead of columnar epithelium on top of villi (300×). B. Biopsy from the same patient as in A, after 9 months on a gluten-free diet. Note the reappearance of villi with normal-appearing columnar cells and reduction in infiltrate and crypt height (300×). C. Biopsy from patient with agammaglobulinemia. The features bear a striking resemblance to those of nontropical sprue. There is a marked mononuclear infiltration, some of it in aggregates (200×). D. Close-up of* *villi of patient with protein-losing enteropathy. Tips of villi are broadened and dilated. Lymphatic spaces are present (arrows) (450×). E. Intestinal biopsy from patient with abetalipoproteinemia. The villus tips have a ''lacy'' appearance (arrow) due to retained fat (300×). (This is more apparent at the higher magnification shown in F.) F. High-power micrograph of villus from patient with abetalipoproteinemia. The vacuoles are filled with lipid (750×). Insert shows dark-staining (osmium) lipid droplets in mucosal cells (osmium counterstained with Giemsa; 800×).*

Postgastrectomy malabsorption The presence of a malabsorption syndrome has been documented frequently in patients after subtotal gastrectomy. Steatorrhea is more common with a Billroth II than a Billroth I type of anastomosis. Usually the fat loss is minimal, ranging from 7 to 10 g per 24 h. Patients with gross steatorrhea usually have impaired intraluminal fat digestion due to several factors: (1) With a Billroth II anastomosis the duodenum is bypassed, and there is a decreased entry of stomach contents into the proximal duodenum (i.e., afferent loop). This leads to a decreased stimulus for the release of *secretin* and *cholecystokinin-pancreozymin* from the duodenum and may result in a depressed pancreatic enzyme response. (2) There may be *inadequate mixing* of the pancreatic enzymes and bile salts secreted into the proximal duodenum with the gastric contents entering the jejunum. (3) There may be *stasis* of intestinal contents in the afferent loop, resulting in abnormal bacterial proliferation in the proximal small bowel. This in turn may lead to abnormalities in bile

TABLE 237-4 Pathophysiologic basis for symptoms and signs in malabsorptive disorders

Organ system	Symptom or sign	Pathophysiology
Gastrointestinal	Generalized malnutrition and weight loss	Malabsorption of fat, carbohydrate, and protein → loss of calories
	Diarrhea	Impaired absorption or increased secretion of water and electrolytes; unabsorbed dihydroxy bile acids and fatty acids → decreased absorption of water and electrolytes; excess load of fluid and electrolytes presented to the colon may exceed its absorptive capacity
	Flatus	Bacterial fermentation of unabsorbed carbohydrate
	Glossitis, cheilosis, stomatitis	Deficiency of iron, vitamin B₁₂, folate, and other vitamins
Genitourinary	Nocturia	Delayed absorption of water, hypokalemia
	Azotemia, hypotension	Fluid and electrolyte depletion
	Amenorrhea, ↓ libido	Protein depletion and "caloric starvation" → secondary hypopituitarism
Hematopoietic	Anemia	Impaired absorption of iron, vitamin B₁₂, and folic acid
	Hemorrhagic phenomena	Vitamin K malabsorption → hypoprothrombinemia
Musculoskeletal	Bone pain	Protein depletion → impaired bone formation → osteoporosis; Calcium malabsorption → demineralization of bone → osteomalacia
	Osteoarthropathy	Cause uncertain
	Tetany, paresthesias	Calcium malabsorption → hypocalcemia; magnesium malabsorption → hypomagnesemia
	Weakness	Anemia; electrolyte depletion (hypokalemia)
Nervous system	Night blindness	Impaired absorption vitamin A → vitamin A deficiency
	Xerophthalmia	Vitamin A deficiency
	Peripheral neuropathy	Vitamin B₁₂, thiamine deficiency
Skin	Eczema	Cause uncertain
	Purpura	Vitamin K deficiency
	Follicular hyperkeratosis and dermatitis	Deficiency of vitamin A, zinc, essential fatty acids, and other vitamins

TABLE 237-5 Classification of the malabsorption syndromes

I Inadequate digestion
  A Postgastrectomy steatorrhea*
  B Deficiency or inactivation of pancreatic lipase
    1 Exocrine pancreatic insufficiency
      a Chronic pancreatitis
      b Pancreatic carcinoma
      c Cystic fibrosis
      d Pancreatic resection
    2 Ulcerogenic tumor of the pancreas (Zollinger-Ellison syndrome, gastrinoma)*
II Reduced intestinal bile salt concentration (with impaired micelle formation)
  A Liver disease
    1 Parenchymal liver disease
    2 Cholestasis (intrahepatic or extrahepatic)
  B Abnormal bacterial proliferation in the small bowel
    1 Afferent loop stasis
    2 Strictures
    3 Fistulas
    4 Blind loops
    5 Multiple diverticula of the small bowel
    6 Hypomotility states (diabetes, scleroderma, intestinal pseudoobstruction)
  C Interrupted enterohepatic circulation of bile salts
    1 Ileal resection
    2 Ileal inflammatory disease (regional ileitis)
  D Drugs (by sequestration or precipitation of bile salts)
    1 Neomycin
    2 Calcium carbonate
    3 Cholestyramine
III Inadequate absorptive surface
  A Intestinal resection or bypass
    1 Mesenteric vascular disease with massive intestinal resection
    2 Regional enteritis with multiple bowel resections
    3 Jejunoileal bypass
  B Gastroileostomy (inadvertent)
IV Lymphatic obstruction
  A Intestinal lymphangiectasia
  B Whipple's disease*
  C Lymphoma
V Cardiovascular disorders
  A Constrictive pericarditis
  B Congestive heart failure
  C Mesenteric vascular insufficiency
  D Vasculitis
VI Primary mucosal absorptive defects
  A Inflammatory or infiltrative disorders
    1 Regional enteritis*
    2 Amyloidosis
    3 Scleroderma*
    4 Lymphoma*
    5 Radiation enteritis
    6 Eosinophilic enteritis
    7 Tropical sprue
    8 Infectious enteritis (e.g., salmonellosis)
    9 Collagenous sprue
    10 Nonspecific ulcerative jejunitis
    11 Mastocytosis
    12 Dermatologic disorders (e.g., dermatitis herpetiformis)
  B Biochemical or genetic abnormalities
    1 Nontropical sprue (gluten-induced enteropathy); celiac sprue
    2 Disaccharidase deficiency
    3 Hypogammaglobulinemia
    4 Abetalipoproteinemia
    5 Hartnup disease
    6 Cystinuria
    7 Monosaccharide malabsorption
VII Endocrine and metabolic disorders
  A Diabetes mellitus*
  B Hypoparathyroidism
  C Adrenal insufficiency
  D Hyperthyroidism
  E Ulcerogenic tumor of the pancreas (Zollinger-Ellison syndrome, gastrinoma)*
  F Carcinoid syndrome

* *Malabsorption caused by multiple defects.*

salt metabolism (see "Malabsorption Due to Bacterial Overgrowth of the Small Bowel, Pathophysiology" below). (4) The presence of maldigestion may lead to *protein depletion,* which in turn may produce further impairment in pancreatic function. (5) The *loss of the reservoir function of the stomach* may result in decreased intestinal transit time. Perhaps the most important factor is rapid gastric emptying, which results in low luminal concentrations of digestive secretions for the first 60 to 80 min after a meal. Such a disorder has been described in patients with subtotal gastrectomy and duodenostomy (Billroth I), gastrojejunostomy (Billroth II), and truncal vagotomy and pyloroplasty (V&P). That gastric emptying rates are somewhat slower in patients with V&P may account for the overall less severe nutritional deficiencies in such patients. In some patients treatment with pancreatic enzymes may lead to significant improvement. Specimens of duodenal or jejunal fluid should be obtained for culture of both aerobic and anaerobic organisms and appropriate antibiotic therapy instituted if there is evidence of abnormal bacterial overgrowth (colony count of greater than 10^7 per milliliter of jejunal fluid). Because the duodenum is the principal site of absorption of iron and calcium, in patients with a Billroth II anastomosis impaired absorption of calcium and iron may also develop. Occult metabolic bone disease occurs frequently in this setting.

INADEQUATE ABSORPTIVE SURFACE (SHORT BOWEL SYNDROME)

Extensive intestinal resection often results in the short bowel syndrome. The most common disorders resulting in short bowel syndrome are (1) massive intestinal resection following a vascular insult to the small intestine, (2) regional enteritis with multiple bowel resections, and (3) jejunoileal bypass for morbid obesity. In general, the absorption of nutrients will be influenced by the extent and site of small bowel resected, the presence of the ileocecal valve, and adaptation of the remaining small bowel. Resection of 40 to 50 percent of the small bowel is usually well tolerated, provided the proximal duodenum, the distal half of the ileum, and the ileocecal valve are spared. By contrast, resection of the ileum and the ileocecal valve alone may induce severe diarrhea and malabsorption, even though less than 30 percent of the small intestine is resected.

Several measures are important in the management of short bowel syndrome: (1) The diet should contain at least 2500 kcal and consist primarily of carbohydrate and protein with fat restricted to less than 40 g per day. A fat-restricted diet is effective in reducing diarrhea, presumably because there is decreased production of hydroxy fatty acids from long-chain fats. Such hydroxy fatty acids, in essence, are cathartics and increase net secretion of water and electrolytes by the colon as well as the small bowel. (2) It is often necessary to provide vitamin and mineral supplements, which usually include K^+, Cl^-, Mg^{2+}, Ca^{2+}, trace metals (Zn, Cd, Mn), iron, folate, vitamin B_{12}, other vitamins (A, D, E, K, B_1, B_2, B_6, biotin), and essential fatty acids. (3) Specific drugs (for example, belladonna alkaloids, diphenoxylate, loperamide, and codeine), which decrease intestinal motility and prolong mucosal contact time, are helpful in controlling diarrhea. These agents also decrease ileostomy outputs. (4) A bile salt–sequestering agent such as cholestyramine blunts the effects of bile salts, which stimulate net secretion of water and electrolytes by the colon. (5) Patients with short bowel syndrome may have gastric acid hypersecretion, which is often transient, and which results in dilution of pancreatic secretions as well as inactivation of pancreatic enzymes. Under these conditions, the histamine H-2 receptor antagonist, cimetidine, is useful because it will suppress gastric acid secretion and decrease the volume of fluid entering the proximal small bowel, thus leading to an increased concentration of pancreatic enzymes. In addition, supplemental pancreatic enzyme therapy may be required. (6) A bypassed colon can be used to receive infusions of fluid and electrolytes since a portion of the colon can still absorb 1000 to 1500 mL fluid per day. Finally, (7) total parenteral nutrition is frequently required during the first 6 months after massive intestinal resection until some degree of adaptation has occurred. Such patients may also require long-term parenteral hyperalimentation with a silicone rubber catheter in the superior vena cava, and this can be done at home.

For a discussion of regional enteritis see Chap. 238.

MALABSORPTION DUE TO BACTERIAL OVERGROWTH OF THE SMALL BOWEL

The proximal small intestine is usually bacteriologically sterile because of three factors: (1) the acid milieu of the stomach; (2) intestinal peristalsis, which sweeps bacteria to the distal small bowel; and (3) secretion into the lumen of the intestine of immunoglobulins, which may serve as coproantibodies. When bacteria are isolated from the upper small bowel, they are frequently contaminants transported from the mouth and upper respiratory tract, and the colony count rarely exceeds 10^4 per milliliter of jejunal fluid. The major mechanism limiting the growth of bacteria in the small intestine is normal peristalsis. Any disorder leading to impaired intestinal motility may result in abnormal stasis of intestinal contents with ineffective mechanical cleansing of bacteria. This in turn may lead to abnormal bacterial proliferation and malabsorption. Several malabsorptive disorders have been associated with bacterial overgrowth of the small bowel, and these are listed in Table 237-6.

Pathophysiology Bacterial overgrowth may result in changes in bile salt metabolism, and these are believed directly and indirectly to account for the steatorrhea. First, bacteria (especially anaerobic gram-positive bacteria) may lead to the intraluminal deconjugation of bile salts with a consequent production of free bile acids. In contrast to conjugated bile salts, unconjugated bile salts may be absorbed in the proximal small bowel by nonionic diffusion, resulting in decreased intraluminal concentrations of bile salts in the jejunum. Second, the decreased bile salt concentrations, the increase of unconjugated bile salts, and the decrease of the conjugated salts all serve to contribute to impaired intraluminal micelle formation and hence fat malabsorption. In addition to abnormalities in bile salt metabolism, intestinal mucosal lesions have been demonstrated in patients with intestinal stasis. Such lesions are often patchy in distribution, and the histologic appearance ranges in severity from minimal changes in villous architecture to severe lesions with virtual absence of villi. The etiology of these lesions is unclear; possible causes include damage caused by bacterial invasion, bacterial toxins, or metabolic products such as unconjugated bile salts. In this regard, certain bacteria such as *Bacteroides* elaborate proteases which solubilize brush border proteins and destroy disaccharidases such as sucrase and maltase. The impaired absorption of vitamin B_{12} is not related to the disturbed bile salt metabolism but appears to be due to uptake of vitamin B_{12} by microorganisms.

Many of the above abnormalities in bile salt metabolism may be

TABLE 237-6 Causes of intestinal bacterial overgrowth (intestinal colonization)

I Structural abnormalities producing stasis of intestinal contents
  A Multiple small-bowel diverticula
  B Strictures
    1 Regional enteritis*
    2 Radiation enteritis*
    3 Occlusive vascular disease; vasculitis
  C Billroth II subtotal gastrectomy with afferent loop stasis*
  D Multiple laparotomies resulting in adhesions and partial small-bowel obstruction
II Fistulas
  A Gastrocolic, gastroileal, jejunoileal, jejunocolic
III Motor abnormalities resulting in intestinal hypomotility
  A Scleroderma*
  B Amyloidosis*
  C Diabetes mellitus*
  D Hypothyroidism
  E Vagotomy
  F Intestinal pseudoobstruction (see Table 237-7)
IV Miscellaneous
  A Hypogammaglobulinemia*
  B Nodular lymphoid hyperplasia
  C Pernicious anemia
  D Pancreatic insufficiency
V No underlying disorder detected

* *Multiple mechanisms may contribute to malabsorption in these disorders*

reversed by appropriate antibiotic therapy. When such treatment is instituted, unconjugated bile salts in the jejunal fluid decrease, an increase in the micellar lipid phase will occur, and steatorrhea diminishes or disappears. In addition, significant improvement in the absorption of vitamin B_{12} will occur with broad-spectrum antibiotics such as tetracycline.

Clinical manifestations   Breath tests, i.e., tests with [^{14}C]-labeled bile acid, [^{14}C]xylose, and lactulose, are useful screening tests for malabsorption syndrome due to abnormal bacterial overgrowth of the small intestine. A definitive diagnosis is established by demonstrating larger numbers of microorganisms (greater than 10^5 per milliliter) and a polymicrobial flora in cultures of duodenal or jejunal fluid. Other clinical features include the following: (1) steatorrhea of a moderate degree, usually in the range of 15 to 30 g fecal fat per 24 h; (2) macrocytic anemia with a megaloblastic bone marrow; (3) impaired absorption of vitamin B_{12} which is not corrected by intrinsic factor; and (4) correction of steatorrhea and impaired vitamin B_{12} absorption by antibiotic therapy. Absorption of D-xylose, peroral small-intestinal biopsy specimens, and other tests of absorptive function (Table 237-2) may be normal in these patients. A single course or intermittent courses (2 to 3 weeks per month) of therapy with antibiotics such as tetracycline, ampicillin, or trimethoprim-sulfamethoxazole are usually given.

Chronic intestinal pseudoobstruction (see also Chap. 239)   Chronic intestinal pseudoobstruction is a heterogeneous syndrome with a variety of causes (Table 237-7). Primary or idiopathic intestinal pseudoobstruction is a chronic illness characterized by recurrent episodes of intestinal obstruction in which all known causes of mechanical obstruction and other illnesses known to produce intestinal pseudoobstruction have been excluded. In addition to abnormalities in small-bowel motility, derangements in esophageal, gastric, and colonic motility have also been described. Malabsorption, secondary to stasis of intestinal contents with resultant abnormal bacterial proliferation in the small bowel, is frequently present.

Tropical sprue   Tropical sprue is a malabsorptive disorder of unknown cause affecting residents of or visitors to tropical regions. Both epidemic and endemic forms of the disease have been recognized. Tropical sprue may have its onset months or even years after a patient has returned from the tropics. The etiology of the disorder has not been elucidated, but it might well result from one or more of the following: (1) a nutritional deficiency, (2) a transmissible infectious microorganism, and (3) a toxin elaborated by a microorganism or contained in the diet. It is of interest that coliform organisms, shown to produce an enterotoxin causing fluid secretion, have been isolated from the jejunum of tropical sprue patients but not from other patients with bacterial overgrowth of the proximal small bowel. Anorexia, diarrhea, weight loss, symptoms of anemia, sequelae of nutritional deficiency (Table 237-4), and abdominal distention are common findings. Patients are frequently deficient in iron as well as vitamin B_{12} and folate. Laboratory studies usually reveal anemia (megaloblastic

TABLE 237-7   Causes of chronic intestinal pseudoobstruction

I Primary: Idiopathic
II Secondary
   A Collagen vascular disease
      1 Scleroderma
      2 Dermatomyositis/polymyositis
      3 Systemic lupus erythematosus
   B Amyloidosis
   C Endocrine disorders
      1 Myxedema
      2 Diabetes mellitus
   D Neurologic diseases
      1 Chagas' disease
   E Others
      1 Jejunoileal bypass
      2 Jejunal diverticulosis
      3 Drugs (tricyclic antidepressants, clonidine, etc.)

in 60 percent of cases) and impaired absorption of fat, xylose, and vitamin B_{12}. Malabsorption of at least two nutrients is considered essential for the diagnosis. Jejunal biopsy classically reveals shortened and thickened villi, increased crypt depth, and increased infiltration of mononuclear cells in the lamina propria and epithelium (Table 237-3). However, these biopsy findings are not specific, and the lesion may be patchy; in addition, interpretation is difficult because "control" biopsies from asymptomatic residents in the same tropical region are often considered abnormal when compared with normal biopsies from patients in temperate zones. Such histologic findings have been termed *tropical jejunitis*. Treatment with vitamin B_{12}, folate, and antibiotics have all been effective in inducing a remission. A short course, i.e., 2 to 4 weeks, of therapy with a sulfonamide or tetracycline is usually given. Occasional patients require more prolonged antibiotic therapy.

Scleroderma   Although there are numerous reports of small-intestinal involvement in scleroderma, frank malabsorption has been reported infrequently. It has been suggested that malabsorption may be due to several factors: (1) lymphatic obstruction; (2) reduced arterial blood supply to the gut; (3) impaired intestinal motility leading to relative stasis of intestinal contents and hence bacterial overgrowth; and (4) involvement of the intestinal wall by the disease. At present there is little evidence to support the first two postulated mechanisms. In some cases abnormal bacterial proliferation in the upper small bowel has been documented, and in these patients antibiotic therapy has resulted in decrease in steatorrhea, gain in weight, and increased absorption of vitamin B_{12}. In the intestinal wall there may also be extensive deposition of collagen, especially in the muscular mucosa, submucosa, and muscularis externa, with significant muscle atrophy. Studies of duodenal myoelectric activity in scleroderma revealed normal slow-wave frequency and propagation velocity but decreased excitability of the bowel to mechanical stimuli such as distention and humoral stimuli such as pentagastrin and secretin. This motor dysfunction may be an important factor in the dilatation, atony, and stasis of intestinal contents in scleroderma.

Malabsorption in the acquired immunodeficiency syndrome   Diarrhea and weight loss occur frequently in patients with the acquired immunodeficiency syndrome (AIDS). These symptoms are often due to enteric infections or small-intestinal Kaposi's sarcoma. However, such symptoms can be due to malabsorption, which has been well-documented in patients with AIDS in whom identifiable enteric infections and intestinal involvement with Kaposi's sarcoma have been excluded. The presence of malabsorption in these patients has been documented by steatorrhea and abnormal D-xylose absorption tests. Serum zinc levels may be decreased. In addition, small-bowel biopsy specimens have revealed dense infiltration of mononuclear cells and histiocytes. Microorganisms have also been identified in the mucosa.

DISORDERS ASSOCIATED WITH LYMPHATIC OBSTRUCTION
Whipple's disease   This is a rare disorder characterized clinically by arthralgia, abdominal pain, diarrhea, progressive weight loss, dilated lacteals in the bowel wall, and impaired intestinal absorption. Wasting, low-grade fever, increased skin pigmentation, and peripheral lymphadenopathy are frequently present. In addition, central nervous system manifestations including confusion, memory loss, focal cranial nerve signs, nystagmus, and ophthalmoplegia may be present. Laboratory examination usually reveals the presence of steatorrhea, impaired xylose absorption, abnormal small-bowel x-rays, hypoalbuminemia, and anemia. Hypoalbuminemia is due to excessive loss of serum albumin into the gastrointestinal tract as well as impaired synthesis of albumin.

The diagnosis is established by demonstrating the presence in the mucosa of macrophages containing large cytoplasmic granules which give a brilliant magenta stain with the periodic acid Schiff reagent (PAS). Such macrophages may also be seen in other tissues such as lymph nodes, spleen, or liver. The finding of PAS-positive macrophages in the lamina propria is not specific for Whipple's disease, but virtual replacement of most cellular elements in the lamina propria by these macrophages has been seen only in this disorder. In addition to the PAS-positive macrophages, jejunal biopsies frequently show dilated lymphatics and some degree of blunting of the intestinal mucosal villi.

Electron-microscopic studies have revealed the presence of rod-shaped structures (or bacilliform bodies) 0.3 by 1.5 to 2.5 μm within and adjacent to the macrophages in the lamina propria as well as within epithelial cells and polymorphonuclear leukocytes. The ultra-structural features of these bacilliform bodies suggest that they are microorganisms. It is of particular interest that after treatment of the patient with antibiotics the bacilliform bodies decrease or disappear together with a decrease in the number of PAS-positive macrophages. In addition, the reappearance of the bacteria often heralds the onset of a clinical relapse after antibiotics have been withdrawn.

Whipple's disease at one time was thought to be invariably fatal. However, it is now clear that therapy with antibiotics will usually induce a clinical remission. In a few cases there has been complete reversal of the histologic abnormalities in the jejunal mucosa, and some of these cases have been followed for 10 years. Patients with Whipple's disease should be treated with antibiotics such as trimethoprim-sulfamethoxazole for at least 1 year. Treatment with tetracycline alone or penicillin alone is not adequate initial therapy; relapse rates with these drugs are approximately 40 percent. The most important parameter for following the disease and predicting its course is the presence or absence of bacilli in sections of small-bowel biopsies.

Intestinal lymphoma Steatorrhea is a manifestation of *primary* intestinal lymphoma. The disease occurs predominantly in men, and the mean age of onset of symptoms is about 50 years. The diagnosis should be suspected in patients with malabsorption with the following findings: (1) a malabsorption syndrome in which clinical and biopsy features resemble those of nontropical sprue but in which there is an incomplete response to a gluten-free diet, (2) the presence of *abdominal pain* and *fever,* and (3) signs and symptoms of intestinal obstruction. The usual stigmata of generalized lymphoma are frequently absent. Hepatomegaly, splenomegaly, palpable abdominal masses, and peripheral adenopathy are usually not found. Lymphangiography and CT scanning may reveal abnormal intraabdominal nodes. The diagnosis can be established by laparotomy and often may be made by thorough examination of multiple mucosal biopsy specimens obtained perorally. There may be a total absence of villi or lesser degrees of blunting and shortening of the villi. In contrast to nontropical sprue, the lamina propria is usually massively infiltrated with lymphoid cells. Malignancy may be diagnosed by demonstrating lymphoid cells with the cytologic features of malignancy, the presence of reticulum cells outside germinal centers, and infiltration and destruction of crypts by pleomorphic lymphoid cells. Some patients elaborate or secrete a fragment of the heavy chain of IgA immunoglobulins (α-*chain disease*). The latter is probably a variant of intestinal lymphoma.

The mechanism of malabsorption in intestinal lymphoma may be related to several factors: (1) diffuse involvement of the small-intestinal mucosa; (2) involvement of the bowel wall with lymphatic obstruction; and (3) localized stenosis with stasis of intestinal contents and bacterial overgrowth. It should be emphasized that it is often difficult, by clinical and morphologic features alone, to distinguish nontropical sprue from intestinal lymphoma. Indeed, there is evidence to suggest that lymphoma may develop as a late complication of nontropical sprue.

The course of intestinal lymphoma has ranged from 4 months to 4 years from the onset of symptoms. Perforation, bleeding, and intestinal obstruction are common terminal complications. There is insufficient evidence to determine whether radiation therapy, chemotherapy, or localized surgical resection modify the natural course of the disease.

CARDIOVASCULAR DISORDERS Steatorrhea has been described in patients with chronic congestive heart failure, superior mesenteric artery insufficiency, and constrictive pericarditis. Abnormal dilated mucosal lymphatics and excessive enteric loss of protein have been demonstrated in patients with constrictive pericarditis. The mechanism of steatorrhea in patients with chronic heart failure remains uncertain. It might be due to congestion and edema of the mucosa, mucosal hypoxia, or abnormalities in pancreatic function. Although pronounced steatorrhea is uncommon in congestive heart failure, these patients are frequently anorectic, and a low fat intake could mask a latent steatorrhea. Steatorrhea is quite infrequent in patients with vasculitis and is thought to be due to segmental infarction of the small bowel in addition to intestinal ischemia.

DEFECTS IN MUCOSAL FUNCTION

INFLAMMATORY OR INFILTRATIVE DISORDERS Regional enteritis The clinical features of regional enteritis are described in Chap. 238. Malabsorption in regional enteritis may result from several factors: (1) interruption of the enterohepatic circulation of bile salts by ileal disease or resection; (2) deconjugation of bile salts due to bacterial overgrowth, in turn related to strictures and/or fistulas; (3) active inflammatory bowel disease causing impaired mucosal cell function; (4) inadequate absorptive surface resulting from intestinal resection or fistulas; and (5) severe protein depletion producing impaired exocrine pancreatic function. Active ileal disease and/or ileal resection resulting in an interrupted enterohepatic circulation of and deficiency of conjugated bile salts appears to be the major factor responsible for steatorrhea as well as impaired absorption of vitamin B_{12}. Small-bowel absorptive function has been correlated with the extent of ileal disease or resection. When the length of ileal dysfunction exceeds 90 to 100 cm, virtually all patients will have steatorrhea and vitamin B_{12} malabsorption. After intestinal resection, the functional capacity of the remaining small bowel will depend on the site and extent of resection as well as the presence of residual inflammatory disease. Massive intestinal resection usually results in impaired absorption of all food constituents. When the malabsorption is due to strictures and blind loops as a result of previous surgical therapy, antibiotic therapy may be helpful, but surgical removal of these areas is usually necessary for long-term improvement. With diffuse inflammatory disease a florid malabsorption syndrome may occur with steatorrhea, hypocalcemia, impaired vitamin B_{12} absorption, and hypoalbuminemia due to increased enteric protein loss. Treatment with sulfasalazine and corticosteroid drugs may be beneficial (see Chap. 238).

After *ileal resection,* patients frequently have bothersome diarrhea. This appears to be due to *interruption of the enterohepatic circulation* whereby increased amounts of bile salts reach the colon, where they interfere with water and electrolyte absorption and thus have a cathartic effect. The *bile salt–induced diarrhea* after ileal resection may respond to treatment with cholestyramine, an exchange resin which binds bile salts and causes them to lose their biochemical effect on the bowel. Patients with ileal resection of less than 100 cm and fecal fat excretion less than 20 g per day show the best symptomatic response to cholestyramine.

Chronic nongranulomatous ulcerative jejunoileitis This disorder is characterized by abdominal pain, weight loss, fever, diarrhea, steatorrhea, hypoalbuminemia, and protein-losing enteropathy. Clinical features mimic those found in both regional enteritis and celiac sprue. Indeed, the intestinal lesion may be indistinguishable from celiac sprue. However, exclusion of gluten from the diet does not result in any benefit. Corticosteroid treatment has resulted in transient improvement, but long-term effects are unpredictable.

Amyloidosis This disorder is discussed in detail in Chap. 259.

Radiation injury to the small bowel Extensive morphologic damage of the small-intestinal mucosa often follows normal or excessive abdominal irradiation. These changes include a decrease in crypt mitoses, marked shortening of the villi, megalocytosis of epithelial cells, and inflammatory cell infiltration of the lamina propria. This may be associated with transient diarrhea and impaired intestinal absorption. However, restoration of normal intestinal architecture is usually complete within 2 weeks after cessation of therapy. Persistent diarrhea and malabsorption may develop shortly after x-ray therapy, or there may be a latent period of several years before the onset of diarrhea. Steatorrhea, ranging from 10 to 40 g per day, has been frequently observed, but impaired absorption of calcium, iron, D-xylose, or vitamin B_{12} is less common. In some patients intestinal strictures due to vasculopathy and ischemia may develop following irradiation, and thus stasis of intestinal contents and abnormal bacterial proliferation may occur. In others, intestinal lymphangiectasia, presumably due to lymphatic obstruction, has been documented. Diarrhea and malabsorption may be refractory to all methods of management. Treatment with antibiotics, pancreatic enzymes, gluten-free diet, adrenal corticosteroids, and opiates has met with but limited success.

Eosinophilic enteritis Eosinophilic gastroenteritis is a disorder of the stomach, small bowel, and colon of unknown etiology characterized by peripheral blood eosinophilia and eosinophilic infiltration of the gut wall but without evidence of vasculitis. The clinical manifestations, usually recurrent, are protean and relate to the site of gastrointestinal tract involvement. Three main patterns have been identified: (1) Predominant mucosal disease manifested by iron-deficiency anemia, hypoalbuminemia due to protein-losing enteropathy, and mild steatorrhea. Patients in this group often present with a malabsorption syndrome and a history of intolerance to specific foods. (2) Predominant muscle layer disease characterized by marked thickening and rigidity of the stomach and proximal small bowel with obstructive symptoms and radiologic features of pyloric narrowing and obstruction. The obstructive form of eosinophilic gastroenteritis accounts for half of the cases reported since 1970. Accordingly, eosinophilic enteritis should be considered in the differential diagnosis of gastric outlet obstruction, diffuse small-bowel disease, and ileocolitis. Indeed, eosinophilic enteritis often mimics regional enteritis. (3) Predominant subserosal disease in which the cardinal manifestation is ascites with marked eosinophilia in the ascitic fluid. Although the above classification based on tissue layer of major involvement is useful in understanding the principal manifestations, it should be emphasized that multiple clinical forms, e.g., ascites (serosal involvement) and obstruction (muscular involvement), also occur.

Previous reports have emphasized food allergy and mucosal features of this disease. However, food sensitivity is related to symptoms in less than 20 percent of patients. In such patients fasting serum IgE levels are often elevated, and challenge with offending foods frequently evokes symptoms of abdominal pain and diarrhea in addition to a marked increase in serum IgE levels. In most patients with eosinophilic enteritis, however, immunologic studies including serum immunoglobulins, serum complement, lymphocyte quantitation, and lymphocyte response to nonspecific mitogens reveal no abnormalities. Thus, both IgE-mediated and IgE-dependent mechanisms may be operative in different patients with eosinophilic gastroenteritis. Several nonreaginic factors influence peripheral blood and tissue eosinophilia. It seems clear that evidence of allergy or food sensitivity is often absent and is not required for the diagnosis of eosinophilic enteritis. In addition, even in patients with food allergies, elimination diets are frequently ineffective and such patients may require prolonged corticosteroid therapy to remain well. Surgical treatment for relief of obstructive symptoms and corticosteroids are the mainstays of therapy.

Dermatitis and malabsorption A malabsorption syndrome, usually mild, has been reported in patients with a variety of dermatologic disorders, including psoriasis, eczematoid dermatitis, and dermatitis herpetiformis. Proximal intestinal mucosal abnormalities are almost invariably found in patients with dermatitis herpetiformis. In one study 21 of 22 patients had lesions ranging in severity from a completely "flat" to an almost normal intestinal mucosa. The mucosal lesions were often patchy in distribution. Clinical and laboratory evidence of significant malabsorption was infrequent, possibly due to the limited length of small intestine involved in this skin disorder. While the skin lesions of dermatitis herpetiformis respond to sulfone, the gut lesions do not. By contrast, in some patients with blunted and flattened intestinal mucosal lesions, and steatorrhea, there may be a striking improvement in villous architecture and regression of steatorrhea after withdrawal of gluten from the diet without improvement in the skin lesions. Further, in patients with dermatitis herpetiformis and a morphologically normal small-intestinal mucosa, administration of a high-gluten diet may result in blunted and flattened mucosal lesions indistinguishable from those of nontropical sprue. As in the latter disease, an increased frequency of HLA-A1 and HLA-B8 are also seen. These observations raise the interesting question as to whether certain patients with dermatitis herpetiformis and a malabsorption syndrome have latent nontropical sprue.

BIOCHEMICAL OR GENETIC ABNORMALITIES Nontropical sprue Nontropical sprue is a disorder characterized by malabsorption, abnormal small-bowel structure, and intolerance to gluten, a protein found in wheat and wheat products. It has been appropriately referred to as *gluten-induced enteropathy*. Celiac disease in children and nontropical sprue of the adult are probably one and the same disorder with the same pathogenesis.

There are insufficient data to provide an accurate estimation of the incidence of nontropical sprue in any population. This is largely because the severity of the disease varies greatly and individuals may have typical mucosal change and yet have no overt symptoms. Seventy percent of the cases in most reported series are women. The incidence in siblings appears to be many times higher than that in the general population, and it has been suggested that sprue may be inherited through a dominant gene of incomplete penetrance. Celiac sprue patients have an increased frequency of serum histocompatibility antigens, particularly of the HLA-B8 and HLA-Dw3 types. The HLA-B8 phenotype has been found in 85 to 90 percent of sprue patients as compared with 20 to 25 percent in normal subjects. The HLA-B8 antigen may be linked to immune response genes which may determine the immunologic recognition of certain substances. It has been suggested that such genetic factors may predispose to immunologic tolerance of dietary proteins such as the peptides in gluten or to the production of pathogenic antigluten antibodies which could result in binding of gluten to epithelial cells with subsequent tissue damage.

PATHOPHYSIOLOGY Gluten and the related substance gliadin are high-molecular-weight proteins found especially in wheat. These proteins, as well as the larger peptide hydrolysis products (containing glutamine), are toxic when administered to patients with sprue in remission. The exact mechanism for this effect is not clear, but two theories have been proposed, namely, a "toxic" and an immunologic theory. One possible mechanism is that patients with sprue lack a specific mucosal peptidase, so that gluten or its larger glutamine-containing peptides are not effectively hydrolyzed to smaller peptides (i.e., dipeptides or amino acids). As a consequence "toxic" peptides might accumulate in the mucosa. It has been demonstrated that patients with sprue in remission will develop steatorrhea and typical mucosal changes when they are given gluten. Similar results will occur with the administration of peptide hydrolysates containing at least eight amino acids with a terminal glutamine residue. It has been shown that when gluten is instilled into the *ileum* of sprue patients, histologic changes begin to occur within hours. This does not occur in the *upper jejunum*, suggesting that the effect is immediate and local rather than systemic. After noxious gluten fractions damage surface absorptive cells, the damaged cells are sloughed rapidly from the mucosal surface into the gut lumen. To compensate for this, cell proliferation increases, crypts hypertrophy, and cell migration is accelerated to replace the damaged and sloughed epithelial cells. This more rapid than normal epithelial cell renewal can be reversed by a gluten-free diet. The intestinal mucosa of patients with sprue shows many enzyme alterations, including decreased levels of disaccharidases, alkaline phosphatase, and peptide hydrolases, as well as impaired ability to digest gluten peptides. However, these abnormalities usually revert toward normal after successful treatment with a gluten-free diet. There is additional evidence supporting the concept of toxicity of gluten and gluten breakdown products in sprue. First, gliadin is toxic to sprue mucosa maintained in organ culture, causing ultrastructural changes and depression of disaccharidase activity. Second, sprue mucosa hydrolyzes a specific fraction of a gliadin digest (i.e., fraction 9) in a defective manner, and fraction 9 is selectively toxic to sprue mucosa. Third, specific fractions of gluten fed to sprue patients cause transient alterations in mucosal histology and depression of disaccharidase activity, but full recovery is observed in 72 h. The rapid onset of these changes and prompt recovery are consistent with a direct toxic effect. Despite intensive study, however, no persistent, specific, or selective peptidase deficiency has been demonstrated.

It has also been suggested that gluten or gluten metabolites may initiate an *immunologic reaction* in the intestinal mucosa. The presence of a mononuclear inflammatory cell infiltrate in the lamina propria of the mucosa, the beneficial response to corticosteroid drugs, the finding of abnormal antibodies to gliadin in the serum of sprue patients, the synthesis of increased amounts of antigliadin antibody by sprue mucosa maintained in organ culture, and the elaboration of lymphokines such as migration inhibitory factor (MIF) by sprue mucosa incubated with gliadin have all been cited as evidence in support of this hypothesis. However, the evidence indicating that an abnormal (immune) mechanism is important in initiating or perpetuating this disease process remains to be determined.

Jejunal biopsy specimens from patients with nontropical sprue usually show a characteristic lesion. There is blunting and flattening of the mucosal surface, with villi either absent or broad and short. The crypts are elongated, and there is generally a dense infiltration of inflammatory cells in the lamina propria. The surface epithelium is altered with a sparse brush border, cuboidal rather than the normal columnar cells, and infiltration of inflammatory cells in the epithelial layer. These changes are usually most severe in the proximal small bowel, presumably because this area of the bowel is exposed to the highest gluten concentration. The typical morphologic changes illustrated in Fig. 237-4 are characteristic of nontropical sprue but are not specific. Similar changes have been described in other conditions, including lymphoma, tropical sprue, and hypogammaglobulinemia associated with malabsorption. Many biochemical abnormalities have been demonstrated in mucosal biopsy specimens from nontropical sprue patients. Impaired esterification of fatty acids to triglycerides, decreased uptake of amino acids, and decreased activity of intestinal disaccharidases (especially lactase) have been well documented. The latter observation may account for the high incidence of milk intolerance in untreated sprue patients or those in relapse. However, the greater abundance of undifferentiated crypt cells may be important, since crypt cells normally have a lower capacity for nutrient uptake than do villus cells.

Since the mucosa is damaged and altered in patients with nontropical sprue, there may be *decreased release of pancreato-tropic hormones* (secretin and cholecystokinin-pancreozymin). This results in decreased stimulation of the pancreas with lower than normal intraluminal levels of pancreatic enzymes in response to a meal. In addition, the gallbladder appears to be resistant to the action of cholecystokinin, resulting in absent or minimal contractions of the gallbladder, in turn leading to sequestration of bile salts in an inert gallbladder. These two defects may result in impaired intraluminal digestion of fat and protein, which will be superimposed on the defect in intestinal transport caused by a damaged mucosa.

Diarrhea is common in sprue patients and is due to a number of factors, including *impaired absorption* of salt and water by duodenum and jejunum, net *secretion* of water and electrolytes by an abnormally permeable jejunal mucosa, and net colonic secretion of water and electrolytes induced by unabsorbed fatty acids and hydroxy fatty acids. However, the distal small intestine in sprue has the ability to adapt to the damage and loss of absorptive capacity in the proximal small intestine. Indeed, increased ileal absorption of sodium, chloride, and water has been demonstrated in sprue patients.

CLINICAL FEATURES   Most patients with nontropical sprue will have a typical malabsorption syndrome characterized by weight loss, abdominal distention and bloating, diarrhea, steatorrhea, and abnormal tests of absorptive function. The characteristic alterations in tests of intestinal absorption are outlined in Table 237-2. It should be emphasized, however, that some sprue patients may present with isolated abnormalities which initially do not suggest the diagnosis of nontropical sprue. Thus, a patient may be admitted for investigation of iron-deficiency anemia without apparent blood loss or of abnormal bleeding due to hypoprothrombinemia but may not have diarrhea or overt steatorrhea. Likewise, sprue patients may present with puzzling metabolic bone disease without diarrhea or steatorrhea. Such patients usually complain of bone pain and tenderness and frequently are found to have extensive demineralization of bone, compression deformities, kyphoscoliosis, and Milkman's fractures. Emotional disturbances are common in these patients, and many individuals with a diagnosis of weight loss initially considered related to severe anxiety and depression are subsequently found to have nontropical sprue. In each of the above clinical settings, the diagnosis of sprue should be considered in the differential diagnosis.

Since there is no specific diagnostic test, three criteria should be met in order to establish a definite diagnosis of nontropical sprue: (1) evidence of malabsorption; (2) an abnormal small-bowel (jejunal) biopsy showing blunting and flattening of the villi along with changes in the surface epithelium; and (3) clinical, biochemical, and histologic improvement after institution of a gluten-free diet. In equivocal cases, the patient can be challenged with 30 to 50 g gluten orally, and if this promptly results in increased diarrhea and steatorrhea, the diagnosis of gluten-induced enteropathy is established. It should be emphasized that tests of intestinal absorption may reveal abnormalities which range from very minimal alterations to severe changes. Abnormalities in absorption tests have been shown to correlate reasonably well with the length of small-bowel involvement and to a lesser extent with the severity of the proximal lesion. A possible variant of celiac sprue is *collagenous* sprue. In this disorder small-bowel biopsy specimens characteristically reveal a blunted and flattened mucosa and large masses of eosinophilic hyalin material in the lamina propria. In one study of 349 jejunal biopsy specimens from 145 patients with celiac sprue, 45 (31 percent) showed basement membrane thickening often associated with collagen deposition, but dense collagen deposition was found in only 11 patients. Fatal, unremitting malabsorption developed in four of the latter patients. These observations suggest that collagenous membrane thickening is a fairly frequent finding in jejunal biopsies from patients with sprue but that dense collagen deposits are an unusual feature and may indicate a poor prognosis.

TREATMENT   Despite the uncertainties concerned with the diagnosis of nontropical sprue, approximately 80 percent of the patients improve after institution of a *gluten-free diet*. Symptomatic improvement usually occurs within a few weeks, but improvement in tests of absorptive function and small-bowel histologic characteristics may not occur for months. It has been repeatedly demonstrated that strict adherence to a gluten-free diet more consistently results in improvement than does suboptimal gluten restriction. Nevertheless, even with strict diet adherence some cases show little improvement in intestinal histologic features. Patients with nontropical sprue treated with corticosteroids but continuing a normal gluten-containing diet have shown symptomatic improvement as well as improvement in intestinal histology and tests of intestinal absorptive function. The mechanism by which corticosteroids protect the mucosa from the effects of gluten is not clear.

If a patient with nontropical sprue does not respond to a gluten-free diet, other possibilities or complicative factors must be considered:

(1) the diagnosis is incorrect; (2) the patient is not adhering strictly to the diet; (3) there may be another concurrent disease, such as pancreatic insufficiency; (4) the patient may have ulceration of the jejunum or ileum; (5) lactase deficiency may be present with resultant milk intolerance; (6) the patient may have collagenous sprue; or (7) he or she may have developed intestinal lymphoma, a disease which appears to occur more frequently in patients with sprue than in the general population. Finally, it should be emphasized that a small number of patients show a markedly delayed response to a gluten-free diet, with significant improvement occurring only after 24 to 36 months of therapy. Approximately 50 percent of patients with refractory sprue respond to corticosteroids; such patients may also require parenteral hyperalimentation.

Disaccharidase deficiency syndromes   As indicated above, the hydrolysis of disaccharides occurs on or within the brush border (microvilli) of intestinal epithelial cells by specific disaccharidases located there. As would be anticipated, both primary (genetic or familial) and secondary (acquired) deficiencies of these disaccharidases have been observed.

LACTASE DEFICIENCY IN THE ADULT   Instances of isolated deficiency of mucosal lactase occur; they are associated with symptoms of lactose intolerance. Since lactose is the principal carbohydrate of milk, such individuals show milk intolerance with symptoms of abdominal cramps, bloating or distention, and diarrhea. Similar symptoms will occur following the ingestion of lactose. The symptoms are due to the fact that lactose when not hydrolyzed is not absorbed, and its osmotic effect in the lumen leads to shifts of fluid into the intestinal tract. The pH of the stool will also decrease because of the production of lactic acid and short-chain fatty acids from the fermentation of lactose by colonic bacteria. Although primary intestinal lactase deficiency seems to be hereditary, lactose or milk intolerance may not become clinically evident until puberty or late adolescence. There are significant racial differences in the incidence of this entity. It would appear that about 5 to 15 percent of the adult white population shows intestinal lactase deficiency, but in black Americans, Bantus, and Orientals, the incidence has been reported as high as 80 to 90 percent.

The diagnosis may be suspected when one obtains a history of gastrointestinal symptoms following milk ingestion. It should be emphasized that the ingestion of only moderate amounts of lactose, e.g., 5 to 12 g or the amount contained in 100 to 240 mL milk, often results in symptoms. Bloating, cramps, and flatulence, but not diarrhea, are usually produced with ingestion of small to moderate amounts of lactose. The vast majority of lactose-intolerant patients are aware that they are milk-intolerant and avoid milk. That these symptoms are not due to allergic reactions to the proteins in milk (i.e., milk allergy or hypersensitivity) can be demonstrated by performing a lactose tolerance test. This test consists of administering an oral dose of lactose (usually from 0.75 to 1.5 g per kilogram of body weight) and obtaining serial blood samples for measurements of blood glucose. In a positive test, intestinal symptoms occur, and the blood glucose increases less than 20 mg/dL above the fasting level. However, false-positive and false-negative tests occur in 20 percent of normal subjects because the test is influenced by gastric emptying and glucose metabolism. Measurement of breath hydrogen after ingestion of 50 g lactose is a more sensitive and specific test. The rationale for this test is that hydrogen is released from unabsorbed lactose by colonic bacteria and breath hydrogen excretion subsequently rises. The test is noninvasive and is not influenced by gastric emptying or metabolic factors.

Acquired lactase deficiency is often seen in association with a variety of gastrointestinal diseases, in many of which there is histologic evidence of mucosal damage. The disorders in which lactose intolerance and lactase deficiency may occur include nontropical and tropical sprue, regional enteritis, viral and bacterial infections of the intestinal tract, giardiasis, abetalipoproteinemia, cystic fibrosis, and ulcerative colitis.

DEFICIENCY OF OTHER DISACCHARIDASES   Damage to the intestinal mucosa may produce decreased levels of other disaccharidases, such as sucrase-isomaltase, but usually these are not as depressed as lactase, and symptoms of specific intolerance, such as sucrose intolerance, are uncommon. There are instances of primary and apparently hereditary sucrose intolerance, but these always occur in association with sucrase-isomaltase deficiency.

Hypogammaglobulinemia   Malabsorption may be associated with hypogammaglobulinemia or agammaglobulinemia. The hypogammaglobulinemia may be of the congenital or the acquired type, with the onset either in childhood or adulthood. When malabsorption has been noted, it has included impaired absorption of fat, D-xylose, and vitamin B_{12}. Peroral intestinal biopsy may reveal changes comparable to those seen in nontropical sprue, but often one finds a more striking mononuclear infiltrate giving a nodular appearance to the mucosa both microscopically and macroscopically. Diarrhea and steatorrhea may precede or follow the development of hypogammaglobulinemia, and these may worsen during infections and subside after the infection is controlled with antibiotics. Intestinal infestation with *Giardia lamblia* is common in hypogammaglobulinemic patients. Meticulous collection and culture of intestinal fluids have revealed excessive numbers of anaerobic bacteria in the small bowel of some patients with hypogammaglobulinemia. However, the relationship between such overgrowth with anaerobes and diarrhea and steatorrhea remains to be clarified. Arthritis, resembling rheumatoid arthritis, and thymoma have also been described in patients with this syndrome. In some patients improvement in diarrhea and malabsorption may occur spontaneously, whereas in others improvement may follow treatment with a gluten-free diet, corticosteroids, antibiotics, injections of gammaglobulin, and cholestyramine. These forms of therapy have not been uniformly successful. Although transient improvement is common, complete cessation of symptoms is distinctly unusual.

The relationship between hypogammaglobulinemia and malabsorption remains obscure. There is no evidence to date indicating that excessive enteric loss of gammaglobulin or alteration of the intestinal microflora occurs, but abnormalities in IgA metabolism may be important in this syndrome. This immunoglobulin is the predominant one in the intestinal mucosa and is found in many exocrine secretions, including tears, saliva, gastric juice, and intestinal juice. A few patients have been described with malabsorption and selective deficiency of IgA.

Abetalipoproteinemia   See Chap. 315.

Hartnup disease, cystinuria   See Chap. 308.

ENDOCRINE AND METABOLIC DISORDERS   Diabetes mellitus The occurrence of diarrhea and steatorrhea in patients with diabetes mellitus has been well documented. When steatorrhea accompanies diabetes, it may be due to the presence of (1) exocrine pancreatic insufficiency, (2) coexistent nontropical sprue, (3) abnormal bacterial proliferation in the proximal small bowel, or (4) severe and uncontrolled diabetes per se (e.g., so-called diabetic diarrhea). Patients falling into the first three categories will usually respond in a satisfactory manner to treatment with pancreatic extracts, a gluten-free diet, and antibiotics, respectively. The pathogenesis of diarrhea and steatorrhea in patients in the fourth category remains poorly understood, and the response to various forms of therapy has been quite variable. It has been demonstrated that patients with diabetic diarrhea and steatorrhea may have involvement of the autonomic nervous system with degenerative changes in the sympathetic and parasympathetic nerves and ganglia. In some patients bacterial overgrowth in the stomach and proximal small bowel may occur and contribute to the diarrhea and steatorrhea.

The clinical features in patients with diarrhea and steatorrhea due to diabetes per se seem to be fairly uniform. Diabetes usually develops at a young age and is often severe and difficult to control. There is a distinct predominance of males. Several signs of autonomic neuropathy are usually present, including postural hypotension, anhydrosis, impotence, and bladder irregularities. Peripheral vascular disease and peripheral neuropathy are also common. Gastrointestinal x-rays may show delayed gastric emptying and disordered transit through the small bowel. Peroral small-bowel biopsy specimens are normal. Tests of intestinal absorptive function are normal except for steatorrhea and azotorrhea. There has been no consistent response to therapy with pancreatic extracts, gluten-free diet, or corticosteroids. When bacterial overgrowth is present, broad-spectrum antibiotics may be helpful.

Hypoparathyroidism   Steatorrhea has been documented in several patients with idiopathic hypoparathyroidism. In addition to hypocalcemia, impaired absorption of D-xylose and vitamin B_{12}, decreased serum iron values, and abnormal small-intestinal roentgenograms have been demonstrated in some cases. In such patients the serum phosphorus level is elevated (due to the hypoparathyroidism) rather than low (as in primary malabsorption). The cause of malabsorption in this disorder is unclear.

Adrenal insufficiency   Although there are few studies on fat excretion in adrenal insufficiency in human beings, malabsorption, especially of fat, appears to occur more frequently than has been generally appreciated. Patients with adrenal insufficiency have been found to have steatorrhea which is corrected by therapy with adrenal corticosteroids.

Hyperthyroidism   There are few detailed studies on intestinal absorptive function in patients with hyperthyroidism. Mild to moderate steatorrhea and hypoalbuminemia have been reported, but absorption of D-xylose and vitamin B_{12} is frequently normal. Steatorrhea usually remits after successful treatment of hyperthyroidism. Clinical studies suggest that steatorrhea in hyperthyroidism is not due to any defect of pancreatic, biliary, or small-intestinal mucosal function but is a result of hyperphagia with ingestion of unusually large amounts of fat occurring in association with rapid gastric emptying and intestinal transit.

Ulcerogenic tumor of the pancreas (Zollinger-Ellison syndrome)   The clinical features of ulcerogenic tumor of the pancreas are described in Chap. 235. Malabsorption is frequently found in this disease. The acidification and dilution of intestinal contents caused by gastric acid hypersecretion leads to major disturbances in fat digestion and absorption. Impaired formation of micellar lipid due to inactivation of pancreatic lipase is probably the major factor in the production of steatorrhea. Other factors contributing to fat malabsorption in this disorder include (1) precipitation of glycine-conjugated bile salts due to low intraluminal pH, (2) alteration of the intestinal mucosa with ulceration and metaplasia, and (3) impaired fatty acid esterification and chylomicron formation.

Carcinoid syndrome (see Chap. 299)   Although diarrhea is common in the carcinoid syndrome, malabsorption with significant steatorrhea is unusual. In many of the cases of carcinoid syndrome with steatorrhea there has been a prior intestinal resection (usually ileal), and in these cases the resection is the important factor in the causation of steatorrhea. However, direct involvement of the bowel wall and mesentery by the carcinoid tumor have been well documented. That abnormalities in serotonin metabolism may also be important is suggested from the decrease in the steatorrhea observed in some of these patients when treated with the antiserotonin drug methysergide. Although side effects may occur, for control of diarrhea and steatorrhea patients may be given a trial of 8 to 12 mg methysergide per day.

PROTEIN-LOSING ENTEROPATHY   The gastrointestinal tract has been shown to play a significant role in the metabolism and physiologic degradation of plasma proteins. The exact magnitude of the normal gastrointestinal protein loss in human beings has remained unclear, but studies with labeled albumin have suggested that between 10 and 20 percent of the normal turnover of albumin may be accounted for by enteric protein loss. However, under certain pathologic conditions, excessive gastrointestinal protein loss may develop. An extensive number of disorders have been found to be associated with intestinal protein loss. Some of these are listed in Table 237-8.

Pathophysiology   Several mechanisms have been proposed for the passage of plasma proteins across the gastrointestinal mucosa, both normally and in certain disease states. First, plasma proteins may pass into the gastrointestinal tract through an inflamed or ulcerated mucosa and account for the protein loss occasionally seen in regional enteritis and ulcerative colitis. Second, plasma protein loss may occur as a result of disordered mucosal cell structure. For example, patients with nontropical sprue have abnormal villous structure and surface epithelium, and these changes could facilitate the diffusion of plasma protein between the cells. Third, in the presence of increased lymphatic pressure, there may be increased passage of plasma proteins into the lumen via the intercellular spaces of the mucosal epithelium. This might be expected to occur in disorders in which there is granulomatous or neoplastic involvement of lymphatics. Fourth, dilated lymph vessels in the mucosa may rupture through the surface epithelium, discharging their contents into the intestinal lumen. This is thought to be important in the pathogenesis of steatorrhea and hypoproteinemia in patients with idiopathic intestinal lymphangiectasia (see "Intestinal Lymphangiectasia" below).

Several techniques have been developed for the detection and quantitation of gastrointestinal protein loss. In the past these have primarily involved the use of intravenously administered radiolabeled macromolecules such as ^{125}I-labeled serum albumin, ^{51}CrCl$_3$, ^{51}Cr-labeled albumin, and indium 111. ^{111}In-labeled transferrin and ^{51}CrCl$_3$ (which rapidly become attached to circulating transferrin) are the compounds available commercially for clinical use. After the intravenous administration of 0.93 to 1.11 MBq (25 to 30 μCi) of the labeled compound to normal subjects, between 0.1 and 0.7 percent of the administered radioactivity is recovered in the stool over a 4-day period. Patients with excessive enteric protein loss may excrete from 2 to 40 percent of the injected radioactive label. False-positive results may be obtained if the stool specimen is contaminated with urine. There is also a reliable and sensitive nonisotopic method to measure intestinal protein loss which involves the measurement of α_1-antitrypsin (AT). This serum enzyme, which has the same molecular weight as albumin (50,000), is resistant to proteolysis and when leaked into the intestinal lumen is not degraded. One can easily

TABLE 237-8   Disorders associated with protein-losing enteropathy

I Stomach
   A Gastric carcinoma
   B Giant hypertrophy of the gastric mucosa
   C Atrophic gastritis
   D Postgastrectomy syndrome
II Small intestine
   A Intestinal lymphangiectasia
   B Nontropical sprue
   C Tropical sprue
   D Regional enteritis
   E Whipple's disease
   F Lymphoma
   G Intestinal tuberculosis
   H Acute infectious enteritis
   I Scleroderma
   J Jejunal diverticulosis
   K Allergic gastroenteropathy
III Colon
   A Colonic neoplasm
   B Ulcerative colitis
   C Granulomatous colitis
   D Megacolon
IV Heart
   A Congestive heart failure
   B Constrictive pericarditis
   C Interatrial septal defect
   D Primary cardiomyopathy
V Miscellaneous
   A Esophageal carcinoma
   B Gastrocolic fistula
   C Agammaglobulinemia
   D Nephrosis

measure AT in serum and stool by radial immunodiffusion in order to obtain AT loss in stool (normal loss is less than 2.6 mg per gram of stool) or intestinal clearance of AT (normal is less than 13 mL/day). Results using AT as a marker of intestinal protein loss correlate well with the more cumbersome and costly isotopic methods. Random fecal AT assays can also be used as a simple screening method for enteric protein loss.

The rate of albumin synthesis and degradation can be determined using intravenously administered radioiodinated albumin and measuring the decline in radioactivity in the serum. Such studies carried out in patients with protein-losing enteropathies have demonstrated a reduced circulating (intravascular) and total-body pool of albumin, a normal or increased rate of albumin synthesis, markedly shortened albumin survival, and increased fecal protein loss. Whereas normal subjects catabolize 5 to 10 percent of their intravascular albumin pool each day (the fractional catabolic rate), patients with excessive enteric protein loss may have fractional catabolic rates of 50 to 60 percent.

Studies utilizing radioiodinated immunoglobulins have demonstrated a decreased intravascular globulin pool and increased fractional catabolic rate. However, the synthesis of IgG is usually normal, suggesting that a decreased level of IgG and increased enteric protein loss is not a potent stimulus for IgG synthesis. The increase in fractional catabolic rate is comparable for albumin, IgG, and IgM immunoglobulins, further suggesting that there is bulk loss of plasma proteins into the intestinal tract and not a selective loss of certain proteins. The finding of decreased globulins often is an ancillary aid in excluding renal, cardiac, and hepatic cases of hypoalbuminemia.

Abnormalities in albumin and globulin metabolism in patients with a protein-losing enteropathy may be reversed or diminished within a few months after the institution of appropriate therapy. It is obviously important that a specific etiologic diagnosis should be established in all patients with treatable disorders, who may be expected to have a remission induced by the appropriate therapy for the underlying disease. The intestinal protein loss in patients with nontropical sprue, Whipple's disease, constrictive pericarditis, regional enteritis, ulcerative colitis, and Ménétrier's disease has been ameliorated by therapy appropriate to the underlying disorder.

Intestinal lymphangiectasia PATHOPHYSIOLOGY The disorder intestinal lymphangiectasia is characterized by increased enteric loss of protein, hypoproteinemia, edema, lymphocytopenia, malabsorption, and abnormal dilated lymphatic channels in the small intestine. The high incidence of chylous effusions and abnormal peripheral, retroperitoneal, and thoracic lymphatics indicates that intestinal lymphangiectasia is part of a generalized congenital disorder of the lymphatic system. It has been suggested that the hypoplastic visceral lymphatic channels result in obstruction to lymph flow, with the subsequent development of increased intestinal lymphatic pressure. This in turn may lead to dilated lymphatic vessels throughout the small-bowel wall and mesentery. Hypoproteinemia and steatorrhea are thought to be due to rupture of the dilated lymphatic vessels with discharge of lymph into the bowel lumen. In adults approximately 1500 mL lymph, containing 70 g fat and 50 g albumin, passes through the thoracic duct each day. The leakage of a small amount of this lymph might be expected to result in considerable loss of protein and fat into the intestinal lumen. In addition, absorption of dietary long-chain triglycerides stimulates lymph flow, and this may increase further the retrograde leakage of intestinal lymph into the lumen. Three lines of evidence support the concept of intestinal leakage of lymph in intestinal lymphangiectasia: (1) chylous fluid has been recovered from the duodenum in these patients; (2) retrograde passage of contrast material from retroperitoneal lymphatics into the duodenum and jejunum has been documented; and (3) significant steatorrhea may persist in patients after institution of a completely fat-free diet, suggesting an increased enteric loss of endogenous fat present in lymph.

CLINICAL FEATURES The disease affects primarily children and young adults. All patients have edema, which may be asymmetric because

of hypoplastic peripheral lymphatics. Chylous effusions and diarrhea are common symptoms. The primary laboratory finding is hypoproteinemia with decreased serum levels of albumin, immunoglobulins IgG, IgA, and IgM, transferrin, and ceruloplasmin. Despite moderate to severe hypogammaglobulinemia there does not appear to be an increased incidence of pyogenic bacterial infections. In addition, circulating antibody response to challenge with *Brucella* and typhoid antigens is normal. Steatorrhea is usually mild, although in some instances fat loss may be as much as 40 g per day. Some patients have hypocalcemia and impaired absorption of vitamin B$_{12}$. Lymphocytopenia (due to the loss of lymphocytes in lymph) is common, with lymphocyte counts ranging from 400 to 1000 per milliliter (normal: 1500 to 4000 per milliliter). This is associated with abnormal delayed hypersensitivity, as evidenced by prolonged homograft survival and impaired cutaneous responsiveness to antigens such as mumps and monilia.

Small-bowel roentgenograms are frequently abnormal, showing changes of mucosal edema and a malabsorption pattern. Lymphangiograms may demonstrate hypoplastic peripheral and visceral lymphatics with the absence of groups of retroperitoneal lymph nodes. Specimens of jejunal mucosa characteristically reveal dilated and telangiectatic lymphatic vessels in the lamina propria and submucosa. The villi may be club-shaped because of distortion from grossly dilated lymphatics (Fig. 237-4). Such changes in the intestinal mucosa may be reversed after appropriate therapy. The diagnosis of intestinal lymphangiectasia is therefore established by (1) small-intestinal biopsy and (2) demonstration of increased enteric protein loss using radioactive macromolecules.

TREATMENT A low-fat diet, by decreasing lymph flow, usually results in significant improvement with decreased fecal fat excretion, decreased enteric protein loss, increased serum calcium and albumin levels, and an increased half-life of injected ^{125}I-labeled albumin. Similar results may be obtained by the substitution of medium-chain triglycerides (MCT) for dietary long-chain triglycerides, since MCT are transported as medium-chain fatty acids by the portal vein rather than via the lymph.

REFERENCES

AMENT ME et al: Structure and function of the gastrointestinal tract in primary immunodeficiency syndromes. Medicine (Baltimore) 52:227, 1973

BO-LINN GW et al: Fecal fat concentration in patients with steatorrhea. Gastroenterology 87: 319, 1984

BOND JH, LEVITT MD: Use of breath hydrogen (H$_2$) in the study of carbohydrate absorption. Am J Dig Dis 22:379, 1977

CALDWELL JH et al: Eosinophilic gastroenteritis with obstruction. Immunological studies of seven patients. Gastroenterology 74:825, 1978

CHUNG YC et al: Protein digestion and absorption in human small intestine. Gastroenterology 76:1415, 1979

COOPER BT et al: Celiac disease and malignancy. Medicine (Baltimore) 59:249, 1980

FLORENT C et al: Intestinal clearance of α$_1$-antitrypsin: A sensitive method for the detection of protein-losing enteropathy. Gastroenterology 81:777, 1981

GASKIN KJ et al: Colipase and maximally activated pancreatic lipase in normal subjects and patients with steatorrhea. J Clin Invest 69:368, 1982

GRAY GM: Carbohydrate digestion and malabsorption, in *Physiology of the Gastrointestinal Tract*, LR Johnson et al (eds). New York, Raven, 1981

GILLIN JS et al: Malabsorption and mucosal abnormalities of the small intestine in the acquired immunodeficiency syndrome. Ann Intern Med 102:619, 1985

HOWDLE PD et al: Cell-mediated immunity to gluten within the small intestinal mucosa in coeliac disease. Gut 23:115, 1982

KEINATH RD et al: Antibiotic treatment and relapse in Whipple's disease. Long term followup of 88 patients. Gastroenterology 88:1867, 1985

KLIPSTEIN FA: Tropical sprue in travelers and expatriates living abroad. Gastroenterology 80:590, 1981

LOUGHRAN TP et al: T-cell intestinal lymphoma associated with celiac sprue. Ann Int Med 104:44, 1986

MACGREGOR I et al: Gastric emptying of liquid meals and pancreatic and biliary secretion after subtotal gastrectomy or truncal vagotomy and pyloroplasty in man. Gastroenterology 72:195, 1977

NEWCOMER AD et al: Triolein breath test. A sensitive and specific test for fat malabsorption. Gastroenterology 76:6, 1979

PETERS TJ, BJARNASON I: Coeliac syndrome: Biochemical mechanisms and the missing peptidase hypothesis revisited. Gut 25:913, 1984

WESER E et al: Short bowel syndrome. Gastroenterology 77:572, 1979

238   INFLAMMATORY BOWEL DISEASE
Ulcerative colitis and Crohn's disease

ROBERT M. GLICKMAN

DEFINITION *Inflammatory bowel disease* (IBD) is a general term for a group of chronic inflammatory disorders of unknown etiology involving the gastrointestinal tract. Since there are no pathognomonic features or specific diagnostic tests, in a strict sense, these disorders remain diagnoses of exclusion. Their features are sufficiently characteristic, however, to permit accurate diagnosis in the majority of cases. Chronic IBD may be divided into two major groups, chronic nonspecific *ulcerative colitis* and *Crohn's disease.* The original description of the disease by Crohn, Ginzberg, and Oppenheimer in 1932 localized the disease to segments of ileum. However, the same process may involve the buccal mucosa, esophagus, stomach, and duodenum as well as the jejunum and ileum. Crohn's disease of the small bowel is also known as *regional enteritis.* In addition, a similar inflammatory picture may occur in the colon, either alone or with accompanying small-intestinal involvement. In most instances, this form of colitis can be distinguished clinically and pathologically from ulcerative colitis and is also referred to as *Crohn's disease of the colon.* Granulomatous colitis is a less accurate term since only a portion of cases exhibit granulomas. Clinically these disorders are characterized by recurrent inflammatory involvement of intestinal segments with diverse clinical manifestations often resulting in a chronic, unpredictable course.

EPIDEMIOLOGY The epidemiologic and etiologic considerations in ulcerative colitis and Crohn's disease share many features in common and will be discussed together. These diseases are more common in whites than in blacks and orientals with an increased incidence (three- to sixfold) in Jews compared to non-Jews. Both sexes are equally affected.

The incidence and prevalence of the two diseases differ slightly with most studies showing ulcerative colitis to be more common. When analyzed in western Europe and the United States, ulcerative colitis (including ulcerative proctitis) has an incidence of approximately 6 to 8 cases per 100,000 population and an estimated prevalence of approximately 70 to 150 cases per 100,000 population. Estimates of the incidence of Crohn's disease (colonic plus small bowel) are approximately 2 cases per 100,000 population; the prevalence is estimated at 20 to 40 per 100,000 population. Although there is no firm documentation, many believe the incidence of Crohn's disease (especially colonic) to be increasing.

While peak occurrence of both diseases is between ages 15 and 35, it has been reported in every decade of life. A familial incidence of IBD has been recorded with estimates that 2 to 5 percent of persons with Crohn's disease or ulcerative colitis will have one or more relatives affected. There is no specificity, however, for a given form of IBD within a given family. Such epidemiologic clustering of cases could argue for either genetic or common environmental influences on the development of these diseases (see below). It has been suggested that there is a probable hereditary basis for these disorders plus a strong environmental component.

ETIOLOGY AND PATHOGENESIS While the cause of ulcerative colitis and Crohn's disease remains unknown, certain features of these diseases have suggested several areas of possible etiologic importance. These include familial or genetic, infectious, immunologic, and psychological factors.

Inflammatory bowel disease is more common in whites, occurs with an increased frequency in Jews, and exhibits some familial clustering. This suggests that there may be a *genetic* predisposition to the development of the disease. In addition, the disease has been described in monozygotic twins. A search for genetic markers which might be of value in identifying susceptible individuals has not identified any single marker (i.e., histocompatibility antigen) in patients with inflammatory bowel disease.

The chronic inflammatory nature of these diseases has prompted a continuing search for a possible *infectious etiology.* In spite of numerous attempts to find known bacterial, fungal, or viral agents, no etiologic agent has thus far been isolated. Preliminary reports of isolates of cell wall variants of *Pseudomonas* or of transmissible agents producing cytopathic effects in tissue culture have yet to be confirmed. Efforts to produce specific granulomatous tissue reactions with filtrates from Crohn's disease tissue have yielded conflicting and nonreproducible results. As discussed below, many infectious agents can produce *acute* colitis or ileitis; however, there is no evidence that these agents are involved in *chronic* inflammatory bowel disease.

The theory that an *immune* mechanism may be involved is based on the concept that the extraintestinal manifestations which may accompany these disorders (e.g., arthritis, pericholangitis) may represent autoimmune phenomena and that therapeutic agents, such as corticosteroids and azathioprine, may exert their effects via immunosuppressive mechanisms. Patients with inflammatory bowel disease may have *humoral antibodies* to colon cells, bacterial antigens such as *Escherichia coli,* lipopolysaccharide, and foreign proteins such as cow milk protein. In general, the presence and titer of these antibodies does not correlate with disease activity. It is likely that these antigens gain access to immunocompetent cells secondary to epithelial damage. In addition, IBD has been described in association with agammaglobulinemia as well as IgA deficiency, casting further doubt on the pathogenetic role of humoral antibodies. *Immune complexes* have also been invoked to explain extraintestinal manifestations of IBD. While there are well-defined examples of tissue injury resulting from immune complexes, studies utilizing specific detection techniques have failed to demonstrate an increased frequency of immune complexes in patients with IBD.

Associated abnormalities of *cell-mediated immunity* include cutaneous anergy, diminished responsiveness to various mitogenic stimuli, and decreases in the number of peripheral T cells. Since many of these changes may revert to normal when the disease is quiescent, it is likely that they are secondary phenomena. Experimental colitis has been produced in laboratory animals by prior sensitization with dinitrochlorobenzene, suggesting a T-cell–dependent mechanism of tissue injury. It remains to be determined whether the regulation of immune function (e.g., suppressor T cells) is of pathogenic importance in the etiology of IBD. Thus far, none of the altered immunologic findings have been specific for either ulcerative colitis or Crohn's disease.

The *psychological* features of patients with inflammatory bowel disease have also been stressed. It is not uncommon for these diseases to present initially or to flare in association with major psychological stresses such as the loss of a family member. It has been suggested that patients with IBD have a characteristic personality which renders them susceptible to emotional stresses which in turn may precipitate or exacerbate their symptoms. While there is little evidence directly relating possible emotional factors to the etiology of inflammatory bowel disease, there is little doubt that a chronic disease of unknown etiology affecting individuals in the prime of their life often results in feelings of anger, anxiety, and some degree of depression. These reactions are undoubtedly important factors in modifying the course of these diseases and in the response to therapy.

PATHOLOGY In ulcerative colitis there is an inflammatory reaction primarily involving the colonic mucosa. Grossly, the colon appears ulcerated, hyperemic, and usually hemorrhagic (Fig. 238-1). A striking feature of the inflammation is that it is *uniform* and *continuous* with no intervening areas of normal mucosa. The rectum is usually involved (95 percent of cases) and the inflammation extends proximally in a continuous fashion but for a variable distance. When there is involvement of the entire colon, there may be minimal involvement of a few centimeters of the terminal ileum, referred to as "backwash ileitis." This involvement never leads to the thickening and narrowing

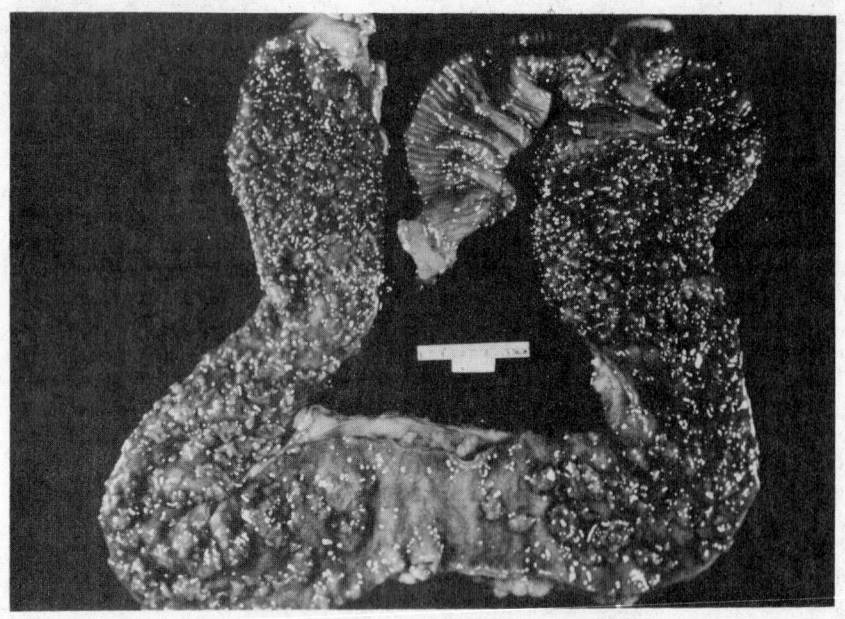

FIGURE 238-1 *Ulcerative colitis. Resected colon with portion of terminal ileum. The specimen showed uniform inflammation, erythema, and hemorrhage and a normal terminal ileum.*

characteristic of Crohn's disease. The surface mucosal cells as well as the crypt epithelium and submucosa are involved in an inflammatory reaction with neutrophilic infiltration (Fig. 238-2A). This progresses to epithelial damage with loss of surface epithelial cells resulting in multiple ulcerations. Infiltration of the crypts with neutrophils results in characteristic (but not specific) small crypt abscesses and their eventual destruction. There may also be loss of crypt epithelium with a loss of goblet (mucus-producing) cells and submucosal edema. With repetitive cycles of inflammation, mild submucosal fibrosis develops. Regenerative activity is evidenced by irregular crypt epithelium often showing bifurcation at the base of the crypts. It is important to stress that, unlike Crohn's disease, deeper layers of the bowel beneath the submucosa usually are not involved. In severe ulcerative colitis, as seen with toxic megacolon, the bowel wall may become extremely thin, the mucosa denuded with inflammation extending to the serosa leading to dilatation and subsequent perforation.

Recurrent inflammation may lead to characteristic features of chronicity. Fibrosis and longitudinal retraction result in shortening of the colon. Loss of the normal haustral pattern leads radiologically to a smooth, "lead-pipe" appearance of the colon. Regenerating islands of mucosa surrounded by areas of ulceration and denuded mucosa appear as "polyps" protruding into the lumen of the colon. However, these protrusions are inflammatory in nature and not neoplastic and are therefore called pseudopolyps (Fig. 238-2B).

With long-standing ulcerative colitis, the surface epithelium may show features of *dysplasia*. Changes of nuclear and cellular atypia are thought to represent a premalignant change occurring in the setting of long-standing ulcerative colitis. Marked dysplasia in colonic biopsies in the setting of long-standing colitis is associated with a significant risk of a coexistent carcinoma elsewhere in the colon and may influence the decision to advise colectomy.

Crohn's disease, in contrast to ulcerative colitis, is characterized by chronic inflammation extending through *all layers of the intestinal wall* and involving the mesentery as well as regional lymph nodes. Whether or not the small bowel or colon is involved, the basic pathologic process is the same.

The earliest pathologic changes in Crohn's disease are poorly defined since surgery is usually not electively undertaken early in the course of the disease. At laparotomy, the terminal ileum appears hyperemic and boggy, with mesentery and mesenteric lymph nodes swollen and reddened. At this early stage, the bowel wall, although edematous, is usually pliable. While some patients with this initial presentation will subsequently develop typical regional enteritis, a significant number will recover completely. This acute form of ileitis will undoubtedly be shown to have diverse etiologies. Indeed,

approximately 80 percent of patients with this presentation have been shown to be infected with *Yersinia enterocolitica,* an organism capable of producing a self-limited, acute inflammatory ileitis.

As the disease progresses, the gross appearance assumes a characteristic picture. The bowel appears greatly thickened and leathery with the lumen narrowed (Fig. 238-3). This characteristic stenosis can occur in any portion of the intestine and may be associated with varying degrees of intestinal obstruction. The mesentery appears greatly thickened, fatty, and often extends over the serosal surface of the bowel in characteristic fingerlike projections. The appearance of the mucosa is variable, depending on the severity and stage of the disease, but may appear relatively normal in sharp contrast to ulcerative colitis. In more advanced cases, the mucosa has a nodular, "cobblestoned" look. This is the result of submucosal thickening and mucosal ulceration, often linear in the long axis of the bowel at the base of mucosal folds. These ulcerations may penetrate into the submucosa and muscularis and coalesce to form intramural channels which become manifested as fistulas and fissures.

There are other morphologic features distinguishing Crohn's disease from ulcerative colitis. In Crohn's disease, the disease is often *discontinuous;* severely involved segments of bowel are separated from each other with intervening segments of apparently normal bowel, producing "skip areas." In approximately 50 percent of Crohn's disease of the colon, the rectum may be spared. In sharp contrast, in ulcerative colitis the involvement is contiguous and the rectum is almost always involved. In addition, in Crohn's disease the transmural inflammatory process, involving serosa and mesentery, also accounts for the characteristic fistula and abscess formation. As a result of serosal inflammation, adjacent loops of small intestine may become adherent and matted together by a fibrinous peritoneal reaction, leading to palpable mass, most often in the right lower quadrant. Fistula formation may occur between adherent loops of intestine, colon, or other adjacent organs such as the bladder or vagina. Fistulous tracts may also lead to the skin or end blindly within the peritoneum or retroperitoneum, surrounded by adherent

FIGURE 238-2 *Colonic biopsies in inflammatory bowel disease. A. Ulcerative colitis. The surface mucosa is destroyed and the submucosa is diffusely infiltrated with polymorphonuclear leukocytes. Crypt abscesses are also present. B. Pseudopolyp. Regenerating island of mucosa with adjacent area of ulceration. C. Ulcerative colitis. Severe dysplasia occurring in long-standing chronic ulcerative colitis. Note atypical changes in the nuclei and marked palisading of nuclei of the crypt epithelium. D. Crohn's disease of the colon. Note the relatively intact mucosa with a solitary granuloma in the lamina propria.*

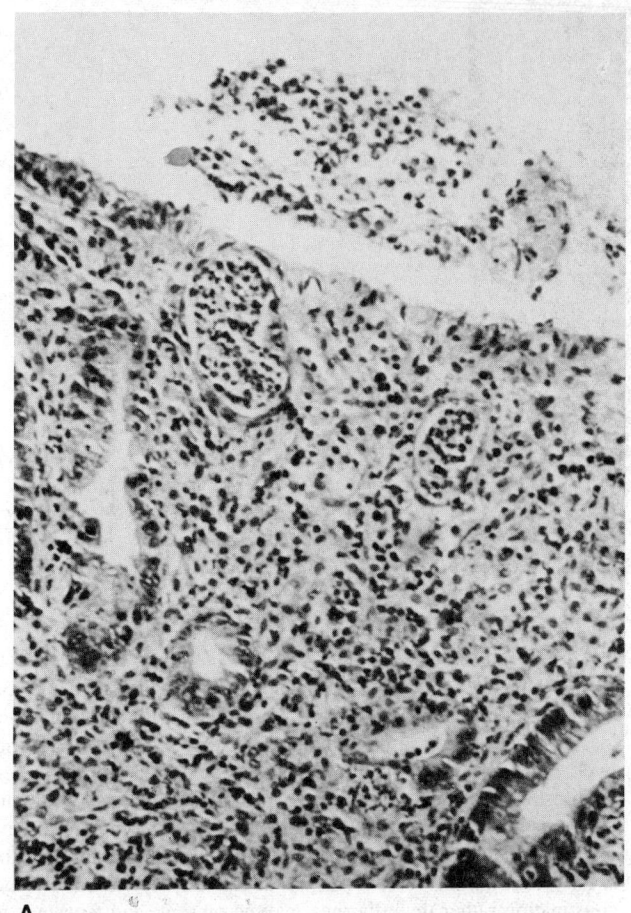

A

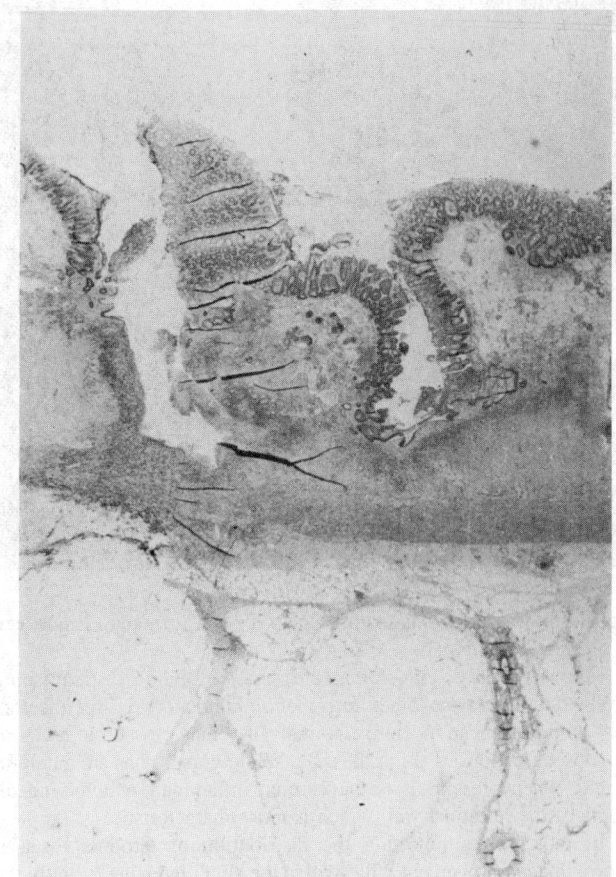

B

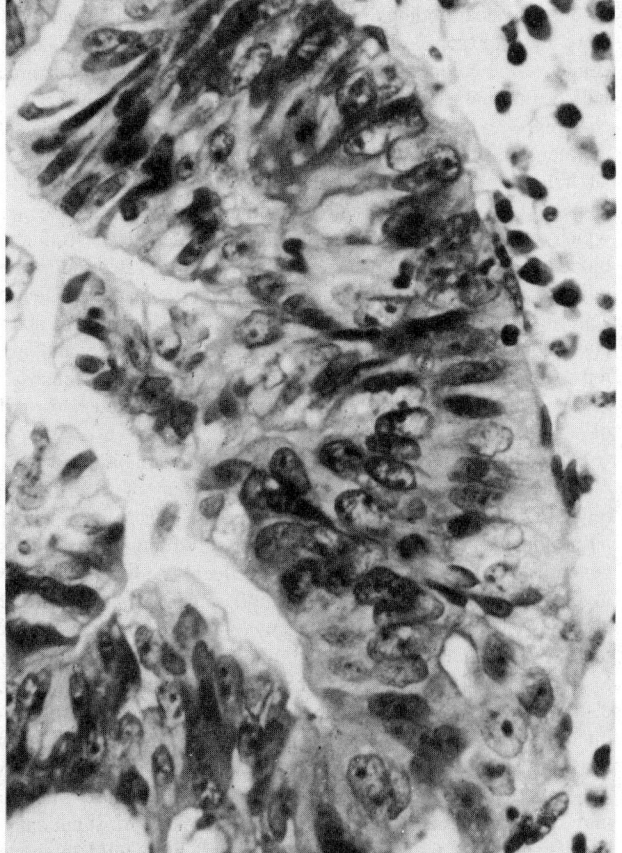

C

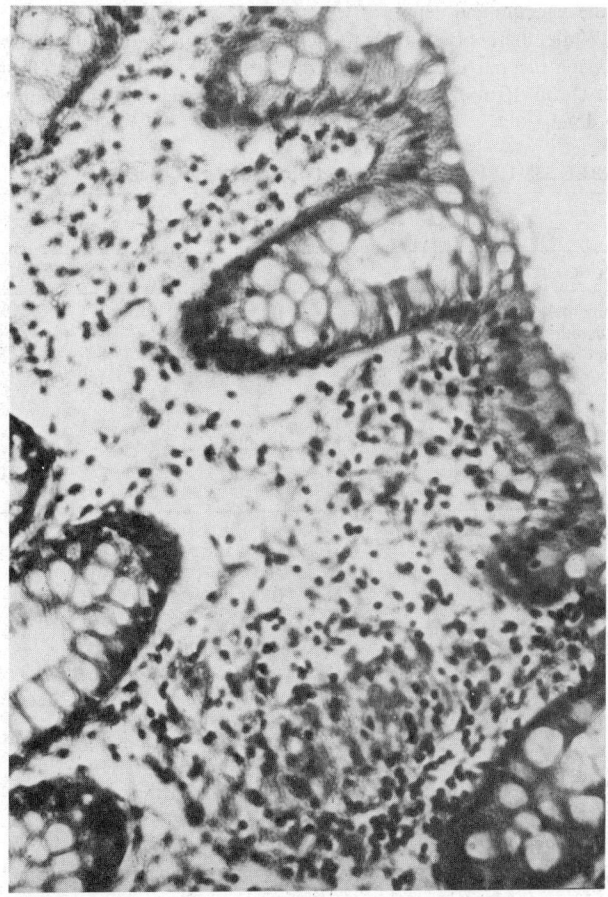

D

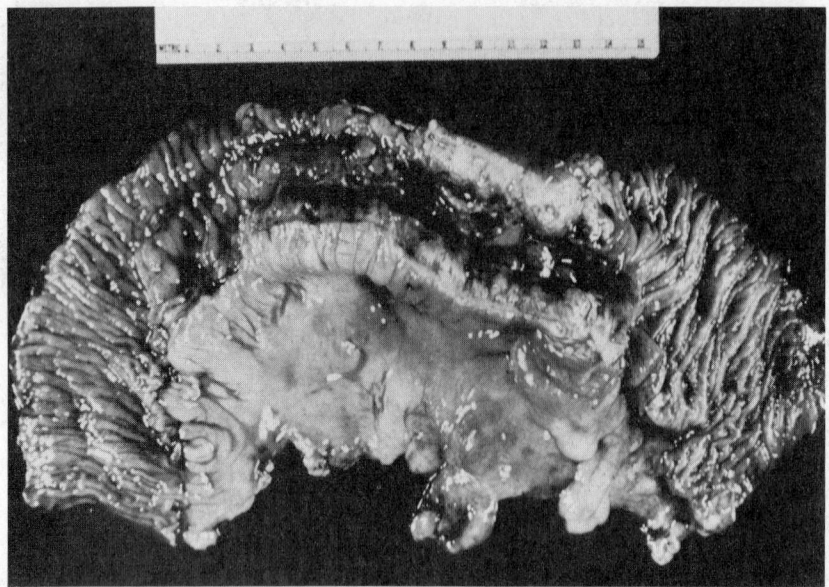

FIGURE 238-3 *Regional enteritis. Resected specimen of terminal ileum demonstrates thickened bowel wall and chronically inflamed mucosa. Note the relatively sharp demarcation of the diseased segment with grossly normal mucosa on either side.*

loops of bowel and inflammatory tissue. Fistula formation is not seen in ulcerative colitis.

Microscopically, granulomas are most helpful in distinguishing Crohn's disease from other forms of inflammatory bowel disease; they do not occur in ulcerative colitis. They may be seen in rectal or colonoscopic biopsies (Fig. 238-2*D*). While granulomas are a helpful finding when present, it is the chronic inflammation involving all layers of the intestinal wall which is most characteristic.

In most series reporting the distribution of Crohn's disease, approximately 30 percent will involve the small intestine (usually the terminal ileum) without colonic disease, 30 percent with only colonic involvement, and 40 percent with ileocolic involvement usually of the ileum and right colon. In a small number of patients (mostly children and adolescents) there may be diffuse and extensive ulceration of the jejunum and ileum.

While there often are sufficient features to permit distinction between ulcerative colitis and Crohn's disease of the colon (Table 238-1), in 10 to 20 percent of cases this distinction may not be possible.

TABLE 238-1   Pathologic and clinical features of IBD

	Ulcerative colitis	Crohn's disease
PATHOLOGIC		
Segmental	0	+ +
Transmural involvement	+ / −	+ +
Granulomas	0	+ / + + (50%)
Fibrosis	+	+ +
Fissuring, fistulas	+ / −	+ +
Mesenteric fat, lymph node involvement	0	+ +
CLINICAL		
Diarrhea	+ +	+ +
Rectal bleeding	+ +	+
Abdominal pain	+	+ +
Palpable mass	0	+ +
Fistulas	+ / −	+ +
Strictures	+	+ +
Small bowel involvement	+ / − ("backwash ileitis")	+ +
Rectal involvement	+ + (95%)	+ / + + (50%)
Extracolonic disease	+	+
Toxic megacolon	+	+ / −
Recurrence after colectomy	0	+
Malignancy (with long-standing disease)	+	+ / −

NOTE: *0 = never; +/− = rare; + = occasional; + + = Frequent, common.*

CLINICAL FEATURES

ULCERATIVE COLITIS   The major symptoms of ulcerative colitis are bloody diarrhea and abdominal pain, often with fever and weight loss in more severe cases. With mild disease, there may be one or two semiformed stools containing little blood and with no systemic manifestations. In contrast, the patient with severe disease may have frequent liquid stools containing blood and pus, complain of severe cramps, and demonstrate symptoms and signs of dehydration, anemia, fever, and weight loss. With predominantly rectal involvement, constipation rather than diarrhea may be present, and tenesmus may be a major complaint. On occasion, intestinal symptoms may be overshadowed by fever, weight loss, or one of the extracolonic manifestations of the disease (see below).

The physical findings in ulcerative colitis are usually nonspecific; there may be some abdominal distention or tenderness along the course of the colon. In mild cases, the general physical examination will be normal. Extracolonic manifestations include arthritis, skin changes, or evidence of liver disease. Fever, tachycardia, and postural hypotension are usually associated with more severe disease. The laboratory findings are often nonspecific and usually reflect the degree and severity of bleeding and inflammation. There may be anemia which reflects chronic disease as well as iron deficiency from chronic blood loss. Leukocytosis with a left shift and an elevated sedimentation rate are often seen in the severely ill, febrile patient. Electrolyte abnormalities, especially hypokalemia, reflect the degree of diarrhea. Hypoalbuminemia is common with extensive disease and usually represents luminal protein loss through an ulcerated mucosa. An elevated alkaline phosphatase may indicate associated hepatobiliary disease (see below).

The clinical course of ulcerative colitis is variable. The majority of patients will suffer a relapse within 1 year of the first attack, reflecting the recurrent nature of the disease. There may, however, be prolonged periods of remission with only minimal symptoms. In general, the severity of symptoms reflects the extent of colonic involvement and the intensity of the inflammation. At one end of the spectrum are patients who present with limited involvement of the rectum (ulcerative proctitis) or rectum and sigmoid (ulcerative proctosigmoiditis). Consistent with this limited colonic involvement, the disease is usually mild, with minimal systemic or extracolonic manifestations. The major symptoms are rectal bleeding and tenesmus. Most of these patients, especially those with only rectal involvement, will not develop more extensive disease. In the remainder, the disease may extend proximally with variable involvement. Most patients with ulcerative colitis (perhaps 85 percent) will have mild to moderate disease of an intermittent nature and can be managed without hospitalization. In approximately 15 percent of patients, the disease assumes a more fulminant course, involves the entire colon, and presents with severe bloody diarrhea and systemic signs and symptoms. The patients are at risk to develop toxic dilatation and perforation of the colon (described below) and represent a medical emergency.

CROHN'S DISEASE As discussed above, the basic pathologic features of Crohn's disease are the same whether the disease involves the small bowel or colon. The clinical presentation, however, will largely reflect the anatomic location of the disease and to some degree will predict which complications of the disease may develop. The clinical features of ulcerative colitis and Crohn's disease are compared in Table 238-1.

The major clinical features of Crohn's disease are fever, abdominal pain, diarrhea often without blood, and generalized fatigability. There may be associated weight loss. With *colonic involvement* diarrhea and pain are the most frequent symptoms. Rectal bleeding is distinctly less common than with ulcerative colitis and reflects (1) sparing of the rectum in many patients, and (2) the transmural nature of the disease with only irregular mucosal involvement. There may be associated severe anorectal complications such as fistulas, fissures, and perirectal abscess. Such features may antedate the clinical onset of colitis and should always raise the suspicion of associated Crohn's disease. With recurrent perirectal inflammation the anal canal may be thickened, and perianal fistulas or scarring may be present. With extensive colonic involvement, dilatation of the colon may occur. However, since Crohn's disease often results in a thickened colonic wall, this is less common with Crohn's disease than with ulcerative colitis. Extracolonic manifestations (discussed below), particularly arthritis, are seen more commonly with colonic than with small bowel Crohn's disease (regional enteritis).

With involvement of the *small bowel* there may be additional presenting signs and symptoms. Typically, the disease has its onset in a young adult with a history of fatigue, variable weight loss, right lower quadrant discomfort or pain, and diarrhea. Low-grade fever, anorexia, nausea, and vomiting may also be present. The abdominal pain may be steady and localized to the right lower quadrant or may assume a colicky or crampy pattern, reflecting variable degrees of intestinal stenosis. The diarrhea is often moderate, usually without gross blood; if there is no rectal involvement, tenesmus is absent. Physical examination at this time often reveals right lower quadrant tenderness with an associated fullness or mass reflecting adherent loops of bowel. At this time the patient may have mild anemia, mild to moderate leukocytosis, and an elevated sedimentation rate.

Since acute ileitis may have an abrupt onset with fever, leukocytosis, and right lower quadrant pain, the clinical picture may be indistinguishable from acute appendicitis. The diagnosis can be made only at laparotomy, when the characteristic beefy red terminal ileum, boggy mesenteric fat, and succulent mesenteric lymph nodes indicate that appendicitis alone could not produce this picture.

While the symptoms of diarrhea and abdominal pain will usually alert the clinician to the possibility of regional enteritis, other symptoms may dominate the clinical presentation. In children, and the aged, fever of undetermined origin and unexplained weight loss may be prominent and initially may cause one to suspect underlying malignancy. In some patients, the first manifestation of the disease may be intestinal obstruction; in others the disease may present with fistula formation in the form of perianal sepsis or urinary tract infection resulting from an enterovesical fistula. Similarly, right ureteral obstruction and hydronephrosis may occur due to external compression of the ureter by a right lower quadrant inflammatory mass. On occasion, often in the setting of extensive small-bowel involvement, features of malabsorption may be prominent. These features, along with anorexia and the catabolic effects of the chronic inflammatory process, may combine to produce striking degrees of weight loss.

The complications of the disease are often local, resulting from intestinal inflammation and involvement of adjacent structures.

Intestinal obstruction is a frequent complication, occurring in 20 to 30 percent of patients during the course of the disease. In the initial stages, the obstruction usually is due to the acute inflammation and edema of the involved intestinal segment, usually the terminal ileum. However, as the disease progresses and fibrosis develops, obstruction may be due to a fixed narrowing of the bowel.

Fistula formation is a frequent complication of chronic regional enteritis as well as Crohn's disease of the colon. Fistulas may occur between contiguous segments of intestine; they may also burrow into the retroperitoneal spaces and present as cutaneous fistulas or indolent abscesses. In a significant number of patients, the first indication of the disease may be the presence of persistent rectal fissures, a perirectal abscess, or a rectal fistula. Although uncommon, pneumaturia should raise the suspicion of enterovesical fistula and is often associated with a persistent urinary tract infection.

Since Crohn's disease is a transmural disease with the bowel wall greatly thickened, free *intestinal perforation* is uncommon. In a small number of cases, however, it may be the presenting feature, and the disease is first discovered at the time of laparotomy for a perforated viscus. The passage per rectum of bright red blood should alert one to the possible coexistence of rectal involvement (i.e., ileocolitis). Crohn's disease may also involve the *stomach* and *duodenum*. The involvement is usually of the antrum and/or the first and second portions of the duodenum. Symptoms may include pain mimicking peptic ulcer disease. Later in the course of the disease, chronic scarring may produce gastric outlet or duodenal obstruction.

There are increasing reports of *small-bowel* and *colonic malignancy* developing in the setting of long-standing Crohn's disease. Although the risk of developing malignancy is statistically increased, the complication is uncommon when compared with the frequency of malignancy in ulcerative colitis (see below). As in other chronic inflammatory diseases, patients with long-standing Crohn's disease may rarely develop secondary *amyloidosis*, which may manifest itself with hepatosplenomegaly or significant proteinuria. The presence of extensive ileal disease, resulting in *bile salt malabsorption*, is associated with a decreased bile salt pool and an increased lithogenicity of bile (see Chap. 237). Up to 30 percent of patients with extensive ileal disease will develop gallstones. Also, in the setting of ileal disease and an intact colon there is increased colonic absorption of dietary oxalate with resultant hyperoxaluria and the development of *urinary oxalate stones*. Dehydration due to diarrhea is an additional predisposing factor in renal stone formation.

DIAGNOSIS

The diagnosis of IBD should be entertained in all patients presenting with diarrhea or bloody diarrhea, persistent perianal sepsis, and abdominal pain. There may be atypical presentations such as fever of unexplained origin in the absence of bowel symptoms or with extracolonic manifestations such as arthritis or liver disease antedating or overshadowing the bowel involvement. Since Crohn's disease may also involve the small intestine, it should be considered in the differential diagnosis of all types of malabsorption syndromes, intermittent intestinal obstruction, and abdominal fistulas.

The laboratory examination is usually nonspecific and reflects the extent and severity of the inflammatory reaction. In addition, when Crohn's disease involves the small bowel, laboratory features of malabsorption may be present. There may be a variable degree of anemia, from occult blood loss or the effect of chronic inflammation on the bone marrow. Folate or vitamin B_{12} malabsorption may also contribute to the anemia. While the Schilling test may be abnormal in patients with extensive ileal disease, frank macrocytic anemia due to vitamin B_{12} malabsorption alone is unusual, attesting to the marked efficiency of ileal absorption of the vitamin. When there is significant diarrhea, electrolyte abnormalities (hypokalemia, hypomagnesemia) may be prominent. Hypocalcemia may reflect extensive mucosal involvement and malabsorption of vitamin D. Hypoalbuminemia may result from amino acid malabsorption as well as from protein-losing enteropathy. Variable degrees of steatorrhea may result from bile salt depletion and mucosal damage. Mild abnormalities of liver function (especially an increased serum alkaline phosphatase) may reflect the development of a fatty liver in the malnourished patient or a coexisting pericholangitis. Significant jaundice is unusual. Proteinuria may reflect secondary amyloidosis, a rare complication.

Sigmoidoscopy and *radiologic* studies of the bowel are most important in establishing the diagnosis of inflammatory bowel disease. Sigmoidoscopy must be performed in all patients presenting with chronic diarrhea and in all instances of rectal bleeding. While meticulous air-contrast barium enema examination of the perfectly prepared colon may disclose the earliest mucosal changes in either ulcerative colitis or Crohn's disease (see below), a conventional barium enema examination is often "normal" in early disease. Direct visualization of the colonic mucosa combined with biopsy is the most sensitive way of determining whether rectal inflammation is present. It can often be performed without prior enema preparation in the patient actively having diarrhea. The goal of sigmoidoscopy is to establish *whether* mucosal inflammation is present and not necessarily to determine its full *extent* at the initial examination. Thus, if sigmoidoscopic changes are encountered within the first 8 to 10 cm, it is not necessary to pass the instrument to its full length which may cause discomfort when the bowel is acutely inflamed. In ulcerative colitis, findings include a loss of mucosal vascularity, diffuse erythema, friability of the mucosa, and often an exudate consisting of mucus, blood, and pus. The most characteristic feature is mucosal friability, best demonstrated by lightly wiping the surface of the mucosa with a cotton swab and observing the mucosa for the appearance of diffuse, small bleeding points. Equally characteristic is the uniformity of involvement. Once diseased mucosa is encountered (usually in the rectum), there are no areas of intervening normal mucosa before the proximal extent of the disease is reached. Ulceration is shallow, may be small or confluent, but invariably occurs in segments of active colitis. Rectal biopsy may corroborate mucosal inflammation. With more chronic disease, the mucosa may show a granular appearance and pseudopolyps may be present.

Endoscopic examination of the colon is also of value in the diagnosis of colonic Crohn's disease. The findings are of ulcerations which may be tiny, aphthous erosions or deep, longitudinal fissures. They usually occur in segments of otherwise normal mucosa. Since the mucosa is not uniformly involved, friability and diffuse granularity, which are hallmarks of ulcerative colitis, are not characteristic of Crohn's colitis. Rather a cobblestone appearance, which is a coarse irregularity of the mucosal surface, reflects submucosal inflammation and is characteristic of Crohn's disease. Pseudopolyps, edema, and strictures may be seen in Crohn's colitis as well as in ulcerative colitis. Colonic mucosal biopsy reveals granulomas in 30 to 50 percent of specimens taken from involved areas. Features such as crypt abscesses, infiltration with inflammatory cells, or ulcerations are nonspecific but compatible features. Since skip areas and rectal sparing are characteristic of Crohn's disease, colonoscopy may be superior to sigmoidoscopy in the evaluation of Crohn's disease. Colonoscopic examination is also indicated when Crohn's disease appears only to involve the small bowel. Ileal biopsy may be feasible, and coexisting colonic involvement occurs in a significant number of cases. Perianal inflammatory lesions as well as areas of rectal disease seen at endoscopy will often show granulomatous inflammation. Rectal biopsy of seemingly "uninvolved" areas may also show microscopic evidence of granulomatous inflammation in only 15 percent of patients.

The *radiologic evaluation* of the bowel provides essential information in the diagnosis of IBD. Barium enema, in ulcerative colitis, may reveal the extent of the disease and help define associated features such as stricture, pseudopolyposis, or carcinoma. The earliest features seen in ulcerative colitis are irritability and incomplete filling due to associated inflammation. Fine ulcerations may be seen at this time as serrations along the contour of the bowel producing a hazy

FIGURE 238-4 *Acute ulcerative colitis, air-contrast study. Note the diffuse fine ulceration involving the entire colon producing a fine serration along the contour of the bowel. (Courtesy of Dr R Gold, Columbia Presbyterian Medical Center.)*

FIGURE 238-5 *Chronic ulcerative colitis. Note the loss of haustrations and the fusiform stricture in the transverse colon. (Courtesy of Dr R Gold, Columbia Presbyterian Medical Center.)*

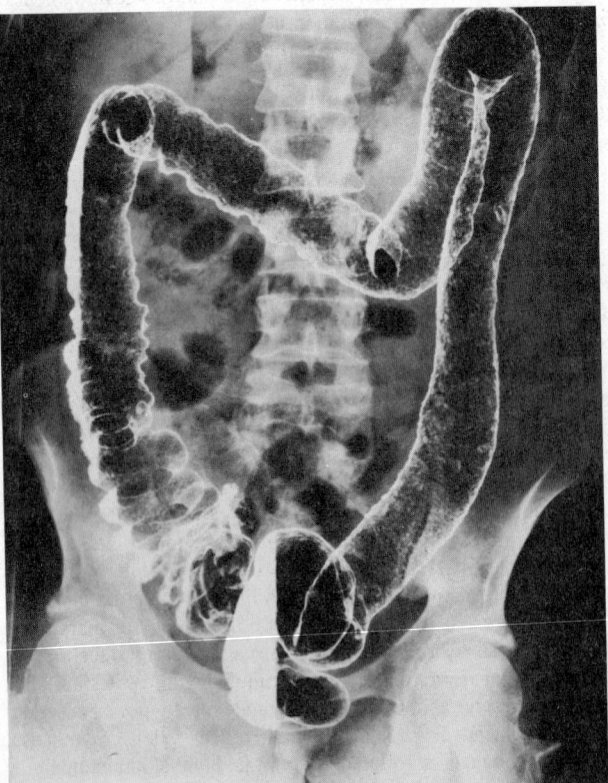

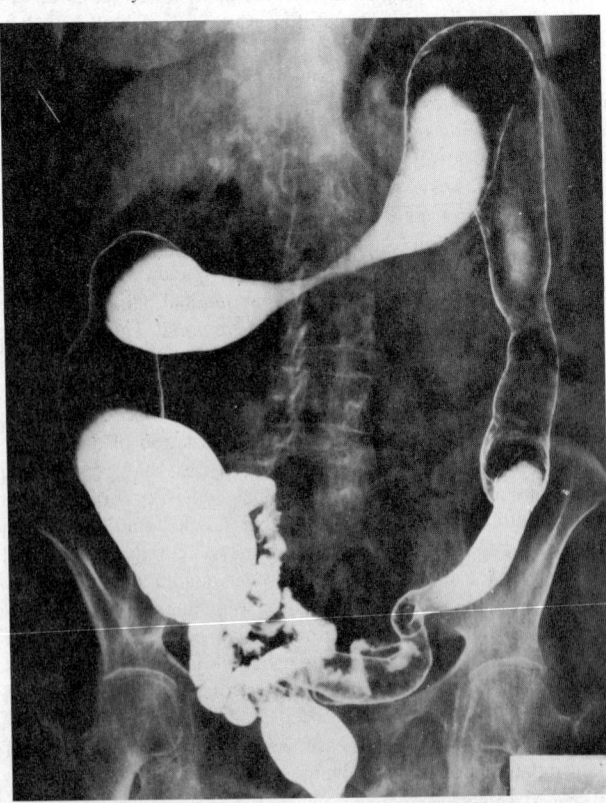

margin (Fig. 238-4). The ulcerations may become deeper and with more fulminant disease produce a grossly ragged and irregular contour. Polypoid defects appear as a result of edematous mucosa between ulcerations. The diffuse pattern of ulceration is best seen on the evacuation film or on air-contrast barium enema. In the chronic stage of the disease (Fig. 238-5), the characteristic features are shortening of the bowel, depression of the flexures, narrowing of the bowel lumen, and rigidity. The bowel has a symmetric, ahaustral, tubular appearance with a decreased mucosal pattern. Although strictures are uncommon, when they occur they have a concentric lumen with fusiform tapering margins. Eccentricity should raise the suspicion of an associated carcinoma.

Barium enema examination in Crohn's disease of the colon has features which usually distinguish it from ulcerative colitis. Features characteristic of Crohn's disease include rectal sparing, the presence of skip lesions, and the finding of small ulcerations occurring on small irregular nodules. The small ulcerations often extend to produce longitudinal ulcers (Fig. 238-6) and transverse fissures which in reality are limited sinus tracts. These may extend into adjacent tissues to produce fistulas. Irregular thickening and fibrosis may lead to stricture formation which may be multiple. In 10 to 15 percent of cases the disease may uniformly involve the entire colon, making differentiation from ulcerative colitis more difficult. Reflux of barium into the terminal ileum during barium enema may reveal characteristic ileal changes of regional enteritis.

When Crohn's disease involves the small intestine, the terminal ileum is most characteristically involved with features similar to colonic involvement. Careful x-ray examination of the small bowel may demonstrate loss of mucosal detail and rigidity of involved segments resulting from submucosal edema or stenosis. The submucosal inflammation may lead to the characteristic radiologic cobblestoned appearance of the mucosa (Fig. 238-7), and fistulous tracts may be seen, especially in the ileocecal area (Fig. 238-8). Involvement of the stomach and duodenum usually appears radiologically as stiffening and infiltration of the mucosa and can mimic an infiltrative tumor. If such an appearance is due to regional enteritis, there is almost always coexistent involvement of either the jejunum or ileum.

While barium studies often provide information on the pattern and extent of inflammatory bowel disease, caution must be exercised in obtaining these studies in the acutely ill patient with severe colitis in whom barium study and the bowel cleansing which precedes it may result in a worsening of the disease and can precipitate toxic dilatation of the colon.

Fiberoptic colonoscopy has added greatly to the diagnosis of colonic inflammatory bowel disease. Areas formerly beyond the reach of the sigmoidoscope can now be directly visualized and biopsy material obtained. Early in the course of colonic inflammation, endoscopic examination and biopsy are the most sensitive techniques to demonstrate mucosal involvement. Polypoid lesions, strictures, and unclear x-ray features can usually be fully defined. Periodic colonoscopic examination and biopsy are being increasingly used in cancer surveillance in patients with long-standing inflammatory bowel disease (see below).

DIFFERENTIAL DIAGNOSIS

Many entities must be considered in the differential diagnosis in IBD. The focus of the differential diagnosis will in large measure be determined by the presenting features of the disease. When *rectal bleeding* is the presenting complaint, a colonic source should be considered. While *hemorrhoids* are commonly found, they must be considered a tentative source of bleeding until sigmoidoscopy and barium enema have eliminated other colonic lesions. Colonic *neoplasms* (carcinoma, adenomatous polyps) may also present with rectal bleeding and can usually be diagnosed by barium enema with subsequent sigmoidoscopic or colonoscopic biopsy. It should be

remembered that carcinoma may complicate long-standing colitis. Rectal bleeding from *colonic diverticula* or *arteriovenous malformations* usually present no problem in differential diagnosis since radiologic and endoscopic features of inflammatory bowel disease are absent. *Radiation proctitis,* which may present as a localized area of colitis, is usually found in the setting of pelvic irradiation. The onset may, however, occur at variable (months to years) periods of time after irradiation. Characteristic features on sigmoidoscopy include mucosal atrophy and telangiectasia along with friability and small ulcerations. A colitis sometimes indistinguishable from ulcerative colitis may occur in Behçet's syndrome and is associated with aphthous oral ulceration, uveitis, and urethritis.

Acute colitis may be caused by a variety of *infectious* agents (Chap. 89). Often presenting with bloody diarrhea, infectious colitis may be difficult to distinguish from IBD at initial presentation. A listing of these agents is given in Table 238-2.

Amebiasis may present with bloody diarrhea and at sigmoidoscopy be indistinguishable from idiopathic ulcerative colitis. A history of recent foreign travel or homosexual exposure should always be

FIGURE 238-6 *Crohn's colitis. Air-contrast study.*

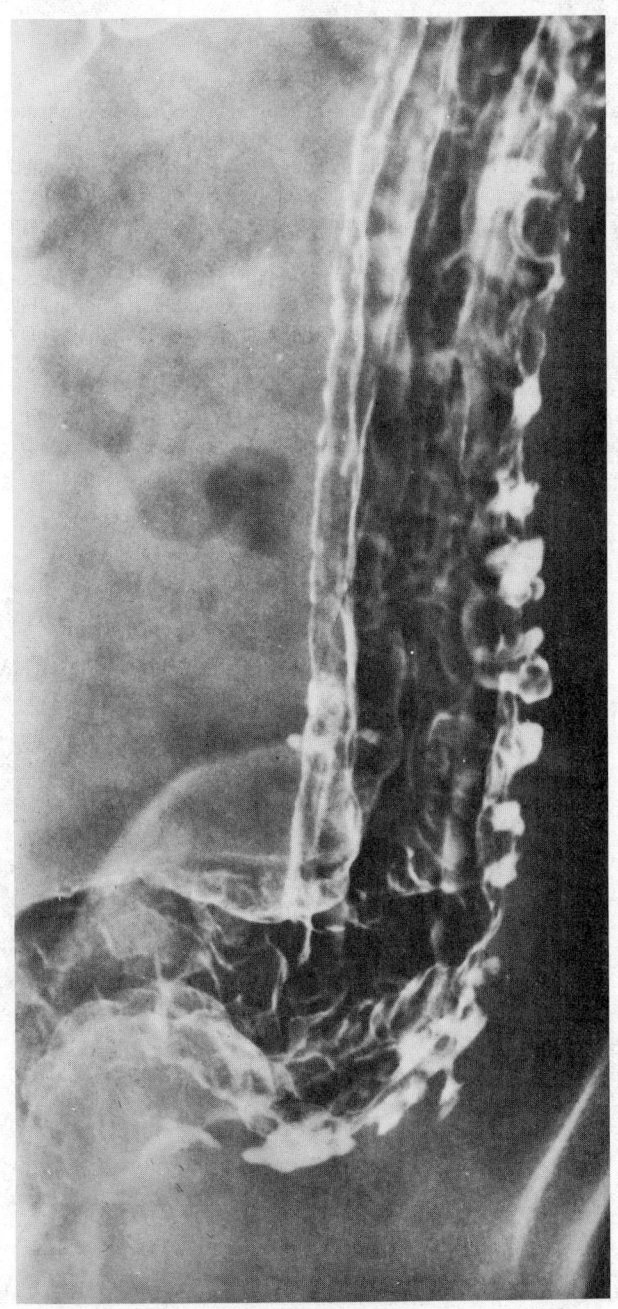

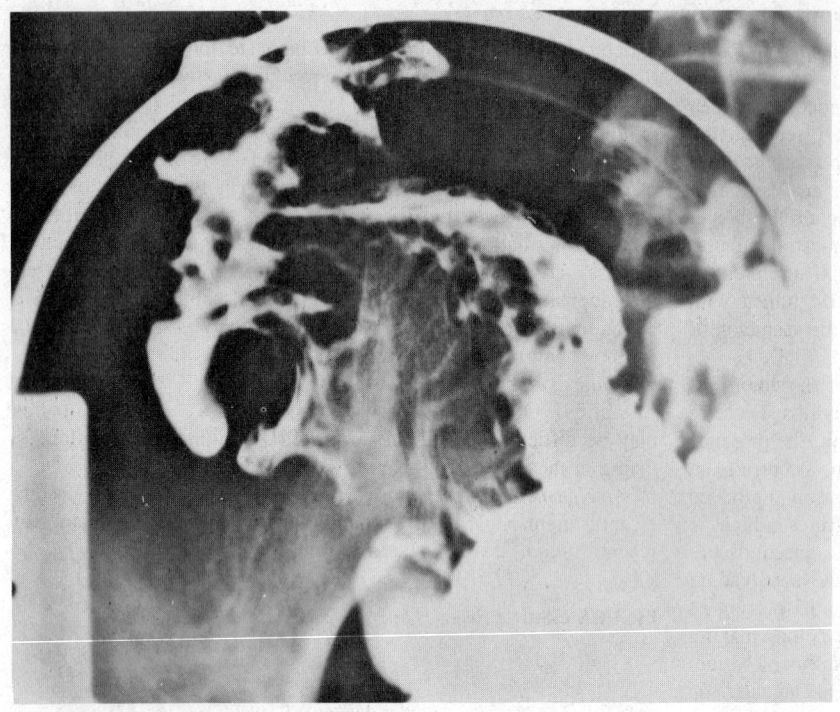

FIGURE 238-7 *Crohn's ileocolitis. Note the nodularity and ulceration of the terminal ileum and the deformity of the cecum.*

sought. Since specific amebicidal therapy is necessary to eradicate this infection and corticosteroids may be detrimental, every effort should be made to exclude this diagnosis in appropriate individuals. Acute *bacillary dysentery* may be caused by *Shigella* and *Salmonella* or *Campylobacter,* all easily diagnosed by stool culture. *Yersinia enterocolitis,* which often presents as acute ileitis, can also produce a self-limited colitis, sometimes with granulomatous reaction. Infectious agents may cause acute proctitis indistinguishable from idiopathic ulcerative proctitis. Such infections, often seen in homosexuals, may be due to *gonorrhea* or *lymphogranuloma venereum* (LGV) as well as *amebiasis.* Recently, in homosexual men, non-LGV strains of *Chlamydia* have been shown to produce a granulomatous proctitis closely resembling Crohn's disease of the rectum.

Pseudomembranous colitis (antibiotic-associated colitis) is caused by a necrolytic toxin elaborated by *Clostridium difficile,* which under certain circumstances proliferates within the bowel. Most often the disease is a result of antibiotic therapy which presumably upsets the normal ecologic balance of the bowel flora permitting *C. difficile* to proliferate. Almost every antibiotic has been implicated, although cases related to the use of vancomycin or aminoglycosides are rare. Most often diarrhea is profuse and watery, although bloody diarrhea occurs in 5 percent of cases. Characteristic lesions are seen on sigmoidoscopy and appear as multiple, discrete yellowish plaques which on biopsy show features of acute inflammation and ulceration with a pseudomembrane of fibrin and necrotic material. On occasion lesions may be beyond reach of the sigmoidoscope and require

FIGURE 238-8 *Regional enteritis. X-ray showing fistulas between loops of bowel. Insert is a compression film of this area; note fistulas between adjacent loops of bowel.*

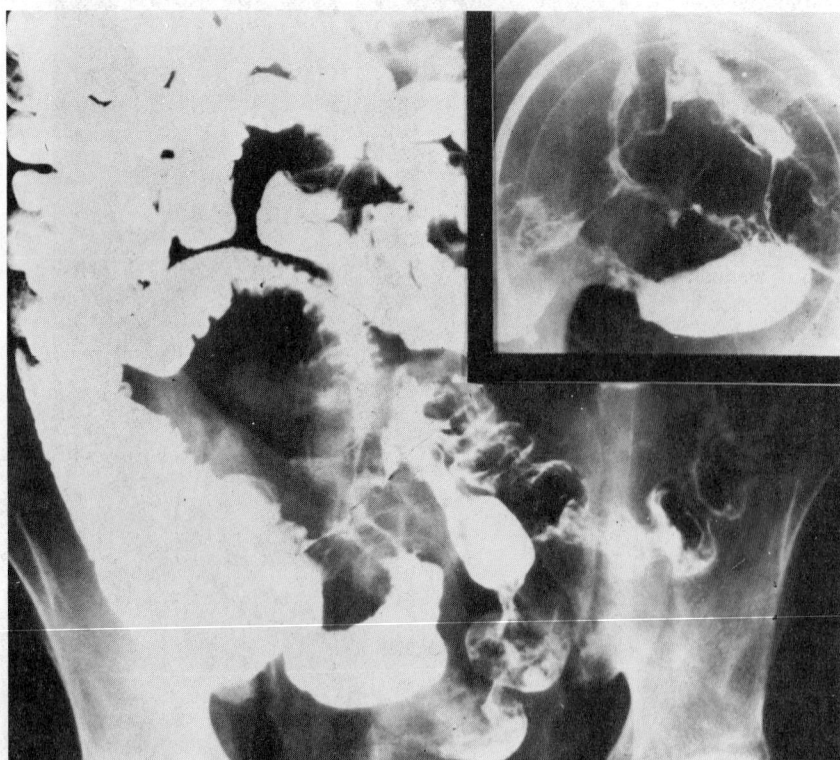

TABLE 238-2 Microbiologic causes of colitis

Shigella
Salmonella
Amebiasis
Yersinia
Campylobacter
Lymphogranuloma venereum (LGV)
"Non-LGV" *Chlamydia*
Gonorrhea
Pseudomembranous colitis (*Clostridium difficile* toxin)
Tuberculosis

colonoscopy. Diagnosis is best made by detecting *C. difficile* toxin in the stool. Treatment is either directed at binding the toxin or at eradicating the *C. difficile* organisms. Anion exchange resins such as cholestyramine (4 g PO qid for 5 days) will bind the toxin and may be used in mild cases. Vancomycin (250 mg PO qid for 7 to 14 days) is the treatment of choice for more severely ill patients and should produce clinical improvement within 5 days. Since vancomycin therapy is expensive, alternative therapies have been proposed. Metronidazole (500 mg PO tid) or bacitracin (25,000 units PO qid) have been suggested as alternative therapies. With all forms of therapy, relapse rates (15 to 30 percent) have been observed and may require a subsequent course of therapy to eradicate the organism. On occasion, infectious causes of colitis will be superimposed on ulcerative colitis or Crohn's disease. In this case, once the acute infection has subsided, symptoms and inflammatory mucosal changes may persist, raising the possibility of associated idiopathic IBD. Similar considerations apply to the patient with IBD who uncommonly may develop associated *pseudomembranous* colitis. The finding of *C. difficile* toxin in the stool and subsequent treatment will serve to clarify this presentation.

Abdominal pain in association with rectal bleeding, especially in the older age group, may be due to *ischemic colitis*. Because of an excellent collateral circulation, the rectum is usually spared. Radiologic features are often characteristic.

Inflammatory bowel disease may be difficult to distinguish from functional diarrhea early in the course of disease. The presence of constitutional symptoms such as fatigue, fever, and weight loss, coupled with laboratory features of anemia, elevated erythrocyte sedimentation rate, or occult blood in the stool should alert the clinician to the possibility of IBD. Similarly, finding leukocytes in a stained stool specimen points to an inflammatory basis for the diarrhea. In all cases, stool cultures and parasitologic examination of the stool are required to rule out enteric bacterial pathogens or amebiasis. In the *irritable bowel syndrome* sigmoidoscopy, rectal biopsy, and barium enema examination are all normal.

Once the diagnosis of idiopathic IBD has been established, the distinction between ulcerative colitis and Crohn's disease of the colon is usually possible. Differential diagnostic features are shown in Table 238-1.

With small-intestinal involvement (regional enteritis) the differential diagnosis should include disorders presenting with intraabdominal abscesses, fistulas, intestinal obstruction, and malabsorption. The finding of associated colonic involvement in patients with ileal disease will often serve to distinguish Crohn's disease from other ileal disorders. With diffuse involvement of the jejunum and ileum, regional enteritis must be distinguished from *nongranulomatous ulcerative jejunoileitis*. Abdominal pain and diarrhea are prominent features of this disorder, and weight loss, malabsorption, and hypoproteinemia tend to be more prominent than in regional enteritis. Small-bowel biopsy shows a more diffuse lesion with flattened villi (similar to celiac sprue), infiltration of the lamina propria, and mucosal ulceration. *Abdominal lymphoma* may likewise present with clinical and radiologic features difficult to distinguish from regional enteritis. Hepatosplenomegaly and peripheral adenopathy, when present, are helpful clues, but often disease is confined to the intestine. In such cases, laparotomy is usually required to make the definitive histologic diagnosis.

The advanced presentation of regional enteritis with areas of stenosis and draining fistulas may also be confused with *chronic fungal infection of the bowel*, including actinomycosis, aspergillosis, and blastomycosis. These infections often are seen in debilitated patients with impaired host defenses. Fungal skin tests and examination of fistula drainage and biopsy material for characteristic granules and fungi are helpful in making the diagnosis.

Intestinal tuberculosis characteristically produces stenotic lesions, usually in the terminal ileum, also often involving the contiguous cecum and ascending colon. Unlike regional enteritis, "skip areas" are unusual. Histologically, the granulomatous inflammation seen with *Mycobacterium* tuberculosis may be indistinguishable from regional enteritis; acid-fast stains and cultures are required. Fortunately in western countries primary intestinal tuberculosis is now rare; when intestinal involvement does occur, it invariably is associated with pulmonary tuberculosis.

COMPLICATIONS OF INFLAMMATORY BOWEL DISEASE

The complications of IBD may be classified as local, which are a direct reflection of mucosal inflammation and its extension, or systemic complications (Table 238-3). Local complications of IBD such as fistulas, abscesses, and strictures have been described above. In addition, perforation, toxic dilatation, and the development of carcinoma may complicate both ulcerative colitis and Crohn's disease.

PERFORATION Intestinal perforation can occur in severe ulcerative colitis since with extensive ulceration the bowel wall may become extremely thin. The clinical features are those of acute peritonitis with signs of peritoneal inflammation and the demonstration of free air under the diaphragm on upright film of the abdomen. These are an indication for immediate colectomy.

Toxic dilatation of the colon may occur in Crohn's colitis but is more common in ulcerative colitis. This complication can best be considered as a severe form of ulcerative colitis with the additional feature of colonic dilatation. It is thought that the neuromuscular tone of the bowel is affected by the severe inflammation resulting in dilatation. Injudicious use of hypomotility agents (codeine, diphenoxylate, loperamide, paregoric, anticholinergic agents) to treat diarrhea in the setting of acute colitis can precipitate this complication.

TABLE 238-3 Some systemic complications of inflammatory bowel disease

1 Nutritional and metabolic
   a Weight loss, ↓ muscle mass, growth retardation (children)
   b Electrolyte deficiency (K$^+$, Ca^{2+}, Mg^{2+})
   c Hypoalbuminemia (↓ nutrition, protein-losing enteropathy)
   d Anemia (chronic disease, iron deficiency; rarely folate or vitamin B$_{12}$ deficiency in Crohn's disease)
   e Bile salt deficiency with ileal disease (steatorrhea and fat-soluble vitamin deficiency; ↑ colonic oxalate absorption → renal stones; ↑ lithogenicity of bile → gallstones)
2 Musculoskeletal
   a Peripheral arthralgia, arthritis
   b Ankylosing spondylitis, sacroileitis
   c Granulomatous myositis (rare)
3 Hepatobiliary disease
   a Fatty liver
   b Cholelithiasis
   c Pericholangitis, biliary cirrhosis (rare)
   d Sclerosing cholangitis
   e Bile duct carcinoma
   f Chronic active hepatitis and cirrhosis
4 Skin and mucous membrane
   a Erythema nodosum
   b Pyoderma gangrenosum
   c Aphthous stomatitis
   d Crohn's disease of buccal mucosa, gingiva, vagina
5 Eye
   Iritis, uveitis, episcleritis
6 Venous thrombosis and thromboembolism (hypercoagulability, dehydration, stasis)

Similarly, cathartic preparation and barium enema examination as well as superimposed hypokalemia may be contributing factors. Clinically, features of severe colitis are present with high fever, tachycardia, volume depletion, electrolyte imbalance, and abdominal pain. On examination, the patient appears toxic, and colonic dilatation may be evident. There is abdominal tenderness and if perforation has already occurred, peritoneal signs are present. Diarrhea may actually decrease markedly due to colonic atony, creating the false impression that the colitis is clinically improved. Plain film of the abdomen will show colonic dilatation with the colonic diameter more than 6 cm. There may be air in the wall of the colon, and irregular, ulcerated islands of mucosa may be silhouetted against the air shadow. While the transverse colon is the most common site of dilatation, this is probably largely positional, since with the patient supine, this is the highest portion of the colon. This presentation of colitis represents a true medical emergency and is associated with a mortality of greater than 30 percent if perforation has occurred. Appropriate therapy is discussed below.

CARCINOMA AND INFLAMMATORY BOWEL DISEASE   There is an increased incidence of carcinoma in patients with chronic IBD when compared to the general population, especially in patients who have more extensive mucosal involvement (i.e., pancolitis) and those who have had their disease for extended periods of time. Cumulative risk of cancer rises steadily with the duration of disease. It has been estimated that with pancolitis there is a risk of cancer of 12 percent at 15 years, 23 percent at 20 years, and 42 percent at 24 years. In children, the risk of cancer appears to rise more sharply after the first 10 years of disease, perhaps reflecting the higher incidence of pancolitis in children. Limited involvement of the colon (i.e., proctitis) has a low risk of malignant degeneration. Malignancy developing in Crohn's disease of the colon or small bowel is less well documented, but the incidences of both small- and large-bowel malignancies are increased compared to the general population. The incidence, however, is less than in ulcerative colitis.

The development of colon carcinoma arising in the setting of IBD demonstrates important differences when compared to carcinoma arising in a noncolitic population. Clinically, many of the earlier warning signs of a colonic neoplasm (i.e., rectal bleeding, change in bowel habits) will be difficult to interpret in the setting of colitis. In colitic patients the distribution of carcinomas is more uniform throughout the colon than in noncolitic patients; in the latter the majority of carcinomas are in the rectosigmoid within reach of the sigmoidoscope. In colitis patients the tumors are more often multiple, flat, and infiltrating and appear to have a higher grade of malignancy. There is some evidence to suggest that these features may reflect the younger age at which they occur rather than the associated colitis. Further adding to the difficulty in diagnosis is the frequent occurrence of mucosal irregularities, ulcerations, and pseudopolyps, making a small carcinoma difficult to diagnose radiologically or endoscopically.

Efforts have been directed to devise effective screening procedures to detect carcinoma developing in the setting of IBD. Carcinoembryonic antigen (CEA) may be elevated nonspecifically in ulcerative colitis and therefore is of limited value. Periodic barium enemas and/or sigmoidoscopy or colonoscopy have been suggested, but interpretation is sometimes hampered by abnormalities related to the colitis itself. The addition of colonic mucosal biopsy may add a significant dimension. It was originally suggested that a generalized precancerous lesion may be present in high-risk patients with colitis who either harbor an occult malignancy or who will develop cancer. Subsequent studies of rectal biopsies in patients with long-standing colitis showed that if dysplasia was present, there was approximately a 50 percent chance that an associated malignancy was present in those patients who subsequently came to colectomy. Complicating these findings was the fact that dysplastic changes were only found in rectal biopsies 60 percent of the time, making colonoscopy with multiple biopsies desirable. In addition, in some patients not undergoing colectomy, dysplasia was not a consistent finding on subsequent biopsies. While

more information is needed on the prognostic significance and reproducibility of finding dysplastic changes on mucosal biopsy, it seems prudent to examine patients with colonic IBD of greater than 8 to 10 years' duration with colonoscopy and multiple mucosal biopsies at regular intervals. The frequency of such examinations has not been established, with recommendations varying from 6 months to 2 years. If severe dysplasia is found, then confirmation at less than 6-month intervals seems prudent. While most authorities would not advise "prophylactic" colectomy in the patient with long-standing colitis, the finding of severe dysplasia may well identify a subgroup who already harbor an occult carcinoma or who are at high risk of its development. There can be no uniform recommendation for this small group of patients, but many physicians will advise colectomy in this setting.

EXTRAINTESTINAL MANIFESTATIONS OF INFLAMMATORY BOWEL DISEASE

There are a variety of nonintestinal symptoms and signs which may be associated with IBD and occur in both ulcerative colitis and Crohn's disease (Table 238-3). Since some of these manifestations may not coincide with, or may overshadow, the underlying bowel disease, they may on occasion pose difficult diagnostic problems. Their etiology is currently unknown.

Joint manifestations are common in patients with IBD (~25 percent incidence). These may range from arthralgia only to an acute arthritis with painful, swollen joints.

The nondeforming arthritis is mono- or polyarticular and often migratory. Knees, ankles, and wrists are most commonly involved, but any joint may be affected. Joint fluid, if aspirated, reveals findings of an acute arthritis without crystals or evidence of infection. Tests for specific forms of arthritis (rheumatoid factor, antinuclear antibody, and LE factor) are negative. Typically, the arthritis correlates with activity of the underlying bowel disease. Rarely, peripheral arthritis may truly antecede clinical bowel symptoms. Arthritis is more commonly found in patients with colonic than with small-bowel involvement alone (regional enteritis).

In contrast, the central arthritis or ankylosing spondylitis associated with IBD is unrelated to the activity of the underlying bowel disease. It may antedate the bowel disease by years and persist after surgical or medical remission of the disease has been achieved. Symptoms are of low backache and stiffness with eventual limitation of motion. This may be associated with sacroileitis as well. X-rays usually reveal characteristic changes. In contrast to the peripheral arthritis, there is a strong association of HLA-B27 with ankylosing spondylitis, whether or not IBD is present.

Like the peripheral arthritis *skin manifestations* are more common with colonic disease. They occur in about 15 percent of patients, and when present the severity correlates with activity of the bowel disease. *Erythema nodosum* may be seen and heals without scarring. *Pyoderma gangrenosum,* an ulcerating lesion often occurring on the trunk, is relatively painless and may heal with scarring. In the rare patient, the lesion may persist even after colectomy for ulcerative colitis. *Aphthous ulcers* resemble "canker sores" of the mouth, and in approximately 5 to 10 percent of patients they are present during periods of active disease and then resolve. Their etiology is unknown and they are treated symptomatically. *Ocular manifestations* such as episcleritis, recurrent iritis, and uveitis occur in approximately 5 percent of patients and may represent a severe manifestation of the disease. In general, their activity parallels the course of the bowel disease, and the lesions may respond dramatically when colectomy is done for other indications.

Abnormalities of *liver function* are common in IBD. In the severely ill, malnourished patient, mild abnormalities of serum aminotransferases and alkaline phosphatase are often seen and represent nonspecific focal hepatitis or fatty infiltration. Factors favoring fatty infiltration of the liver in the severely ill patient are poor nutrition and often concomitant steroid therapy. The lesion is not progressive and resolves with disease remission. *Pericholangitis* is characterized histologically by portal tract inflammation, some bile ductular proliferation, and concentric fibrosis around bile ductules. Most often, the lesion is clinically insignificant, and its sole manifestation is an elevated serum alkaline phosphatase. It is usually nonprogressive and requires no therapy. Rarely, there may be an apparent progression to cirrhosis of either the postnecrotic or biliary type. Uncommonly, patients with IBD may develop *sclerosing cholangitis* (Chap. 253), a chronic inflammation of unknown etiology involving the extrahepatic and intrahepatic bile ducts which may produce varying degrees of extrahepatic biliary obstruction. Corticosteroids and immunosuppressive therapy are not beneficial. Reversal of the disease after colectomy is an inconsistent result and should not form the sole indication for colectomy. Cholangiocarcinoma, arising in the extrahepatic biliary tree, has an increased incidence in patients with chronic ulcerative colitis. Such patients will present with extrahepatic biliary obstruction which must be distinguished from sclerosing cholangitis. Finally, *chronic active hepatitis* which may progress to *cirrhosis* may be seen in IBD, although the exact relationship between these disorders is unknown. The evaluation and therapy are similar to the disease occurring in noncolitic patients. There is no clear evidence that colectomy influences the course of this form of liver disease.

TREATMENT

In general, the treatment of ulcerative colitis and Crohn's disease shares certain common principles. Initial treatment of all forms of uncomplicated IBD is primarily medical, and the principles of medical therapy are similar. Surgery is reserved for (1) specific complications and (2) intractability of disease. There are certain important differences, however, between ulcerative colitis and Crohn's disease; namely, the response to drug therapy may differ, complications often differ, and the prognosis after surgical therapy is not the same.

ULCERATIVE COLITIS Medical therapy Once the diagnosis is established, the severity of the disease must be assessed. Mild ulcerative colitis, including ulcerative proctitis, can usually be treated on an ambulatory basis. More severe disease, especially at initial presentation, is best treated in a hospital setting. The disease can rapidly worsen, and the course of a given attack cannot be predicted at the outset. The aims of therapy are to control the inflammatory process and replace nutritional losses. A certain degree of improvement usually follows intravenous correction of fluid and electrolyte disturbances. Blood transfusions may be required in severe anemia, especially when there is continued active bleeding. Agents to control diarrhea (diphenoxylate, loperamide, codeine, anticholinergics) should be used with extreme caution for fear of precipitating colonic dilatation and toxic megacolon. The decision to institute specific nutritional replacement therapy will be determined by the nutritional status of the patient and whether a protracted clinical course can be anticipated. In the severely ill patient, even clear liquids orally may stimulate colonic activity, and it is often wise to give the patients nothing by mouth. In this setting, intravenous alimentation, either peripheral or central, has been used as interim nutritional replacement therapy (see Chap. 75). While there is no evidence that intravenous alimentation is effective as primary therapy, it is an important component of a treatment program. In the less severely ill patients able to tolerate fluids by mouth, the use of elemental oral diets may be beneficial providing supplemental nutrition with low fecal volume. While milk is not contraindicated in ulcerative colitis, diarrhea will be exacerbated if there is an associated lactase deficiency.

The principal drugs used in the therapy of ulcerative colitis are the *anti-inflammatory agents, sulfasalazine* (Azulfidine) and *adrenal corticosteroids* or ACTH. Sulfasalazine consists of a sulfonamide (sulfapyridine) moiety chemically bound to a salicylate (5-aminosalicylate); it undergoes bacterial cleavage in the colon. The liberated

sulfapyridine is efficiently absorbed and largely excreted in the urine; the liberated 5-aminosalicylate believed to be the active component remains largely in the colon and is excreted in the stool. The salicylate moiety is thought to exert its action through inhibition of prostaglandin synthesis. While most physicians are familiar with the use of sulfasalazine to prevent recurrences of ulcerative colitis, it is less well appreciated that this agent is effective in the therapy of acute ulcerative colitis of mild to moderate severity. Therapeutic doses of 4 to 6 g daily are required. The drug is usually started at a dose of 500 mg bid and then increased daily or every other day by 1 g until the therapeutic dose is achieved.

In the severely ill patient who may not tolerate oral medication and for whom a more rapid time frame of therapy is often desired, initial therapy is begun with corticosteroids or ACTH. While some physicians still prefer ACTH to corticosteroids, these agents appear equally effective when given in equivalent dosages and by comparable routes of administration. The choice is one of individual preference; however, oral prednisone (45 to 60 mg daily) is often employed initially. Alternatively, intravenous ACTH may be given (40 to 60 units) over an 8-h drip infusion. In the severely ill patient, parenteral administration of corticosteroids is preferable to avoid the uncertainty of adequate oral absorption. Improvement is usually noted after 7 to 10 days of such therapy by a reduction in fever, decreased bloody diarrhea, and an improvement in appetite.

After initial improvement low-roughage oral feedings can be resumed. At this point the dose of steroids can be tapered, or if ACTH was used initially, oral prednisone at reduced dosage can be started. There is no specific schedule for tapering corticosteroids. The guiding principle, however, is that once clinical remission is achieved, there is no evidence that chronic steroid administration favorably influences the long-term outlook of the disease or that recurrences can be prevented by chronic steroid therapy. In practice, steroid therapy can be tapered and discontinued over a 2- to 3-month period after discharge. In some patients (10 to 15 percent) efforts to completely eliminate steroids may be associated with a flare of the disease, and low to moderate steroids (10 to 15 mg of prednisone daily) may be required to suppress disease activity. This should not be confused with the prophylactic administration of steroids to patients in remission, but rather represents incompletely responsive disease. Once the acutely ill patient is taking oral feedings, sulfasalazine should be added as described above in a daily dose of 2 g. Controlled trials have shown that this dose of sulfasalazine, when administered chronically to patients with ulcerative colitis, is effective in decreasing the frequency of relapses and should be continued chronically after corticosteroids have been discontinued. Patients with glucose phosphate dehydrogenase deficiency or those exhibiting severe allergic reactions to the drug unfortunately cannot be maintained on it. Patients who exhibit intolerance for the drug (headache, nausea) or mild skin allergic reactions can be "desensitized" by gradually reintroducing the drug in small doses. Sulfasalazine is discontinued for 1 to 2 weeks and then is restarted at a dose of 0.125 to 0.25 g per day for 1 week with a gradual increase by 0.125 g per week to a maintenance dose of 2 g per day.

The use of immunosuppressive therapy with drugs such as azathioprine is less well established in ulcerative colitis. As a single agent in the therapy of acute ulcerative colitis, the drug is ineffective. However, the drug may be added to the regimen at a dose of 1.5 to 2.0 mg/kg when corticosteroids fail or when the steroid dose needed to reduce inflammation is too high. It is desirable to monitor the blood count and observe the patient carefully for infection. Azathioprine may also have a limited role as a "steroid-sparing agent" in the patient with chronic ulcerative colitis who must be maintained on corticosteroids to control disease activity.

Toxic megacolon is a major complication of severe ulcerative colitis which requires rapid, intensive management best carried out jointly by the internist or gastroenterologist and surgeon. Once the diagnosis is established, prompt and vigorous use of intravenous fluids, electrolyte replacement therapy, and blood transfusions are indicated. Because of the fear of perforation and high likelihood that bacteremia and occult perforation have occurred, many physicians will institute broad-spectrum antibiotic coverage after appropriate cultures have been obtained. The patient is given nothing by mouth, and nasogastric suction is often instituted. Full intravenous corticosteroid therapy is also begun. Majority opinion favors an initial period of medical stabilization for the first 24 to 48 h. If significant objective improvement has not occurred and if perforation seems imminent, emergency colectomy should be carried out. While it is certainly true that some patients, under maximal medical therapy, may slowly improve and thus avoid colectomy, the risk of this course of action must be carefully considered. If perforation occurs, mortality rates rise sharply, approaching 50 percent in those who subsequently go on to colectomy.

At the other end of the spectrum is the patient with mild ulcerative colitis, limited to the rectum or rectosigmoid, who is managed on an ambulatory basis. Therapy is initiated with sulfasalazine, 0.5 to 1.0 g four times a day with meals. If rectal symptoms such as tenesmus are prominent, topical steroids in the form of small enemas may produce marked improvement. The equivalent of 100 mg hydrocortisone (20 mg prednisone) in 60 to 100 mL saline is used as a bedtime enema. On occasion the use of steroid foam preparations may be better tolerated in the patient with severe tenesmus. Retention enemas have been shown to deliver medication as far as the descending colon, and absorption of steroid is small ($\sim$ 10 to 20 percent). If large doses of rectal steroids are required for control, it is preferable to use oral prednisone at a moderate dosage (20 mg daily).

Psychotherapy   The elements of trust and mutual understanding combined with the compassion and expertise of the physician are essential in the therapy of any chronic disease and are particularly important in the long-term management of patients with inflammatory bowel disease. Often these patients are intelligent young adults who are frequently resentful of a disease affecting them during the most productive years. Through the vigorous participation of the physician many patients are able to lead reasonably stable and productive lives. More formal psychiatric assistance may be required in the chronically ill patient, in particular children or adolescents, or in the elderly where severe depressive reactions are common. This is particularly true when colectomy is being advised and in the emotional adjustment which must be made after colectomy.

Pregnancy and ulcerative colitis   While many physicians are apprehensive about the management and prognosis of ulcerative colitis in the pregnant patient, the outcome for the patient and the fetus is excellent. In general, the pregnancy is not threatened by coexistent colitis, with no increase in stillbirths or premature deliveries when compared to the general population. When patients with inactive colitis become pregnant, approximately 50 percent may have an exacerbation of their disease with some clustering of these flares during the first trimester and in the postpartum period. The therapy of ulcerative colitis during pregnancy is largely the same as in the nonpregnant patient. Sulfasalazine is used to treat mild to moderate disease since there is no evidence that the drug is harmful to the fetus or leads to increased incidence of fetal malformations. Women with inactive colitis who enter a pregnancy on maintenance sulfasalazine should be continued on the drug. Since sulfapyridine appears in breast milk, in the newborn with unconjugated hyperbilirubinemia from other causes, breast feeding should be discontinued or the drug stopped if the colitis is inactive. In most situations, however, the drug should be continued to protect the mother during the postpartum period from a relapse of disease. Corticosteroids should be used in the same dosage and for the same indications as in the nonpregnant patient.

Thus, it is clear that the patient with colitis can realistically plan to have a family. It is prudent, however, to bring active disease under control before pregnancy is undertaken to ensure the most optimal physical and emotional setting for the pregnancy. Similar conclusions apply to the management of Crohn's disease during pregnancy.

Surgical therapy   Approximately 20 to 25 percent of patients with ulcerative colitis will require colectomy during the course of their disease. A major indication for colectomy is failure to respond to intensive medical management. Such patients, although not showing colonic dilatation, may fail to improve after 7 to 10 days of optimal medical therapy. Fever, persistent bloody diarrhea, and severe fatigue may persist, and consideration should be given to semielective colectomy. Elective colectomy may be performed in patients whose disease remains chronically active and who require continuous corticosteroid administration. Such patients are at risk of developing the complications of chronic steroid therapy. After colectomy these patients often feel more energetic and usually gain back weight to their preillness level. As discussed above the patient with longstanding colitis is at high risk for colonic cancer. While most authorities do not advise "prophylactic" colectomy in the patient with quiescent disease, the finding of marked dysplasia on colonoscopic biopsies done as a part of a surveillance program should make the physician think seriously about advising colectomy.

The decision to advise colectomy in other than emergency circumstances is difficult for both patient and physician. Many patients have an understandable reluctance to undergo colectomy and have difficulty in conceptualizing life with an ileostomy. In most metropolitan centers there are ileostomy groups who visit patients preoperatively and can provide answers to many practical questions. It is also desirable for the patient to be visited by a nurse familiar with stoma care to instruct the patient on the practical aspects of handling the ileostomy.

While total proctocolectomy with permanent ileostomy is the procedure of choice for almost all patients undergoing colectomy, several alternative approaches have been suggested. The *continent ileostomy* is an ileal loop reservoir fashioned under the skin with a nipple valve to prevent spilling of ileal contents. Ileal effluent collects in this reservoir which must be emptied with a soft rubber catheter. Only a small stoma is externally visible, thus eliminating an external ileostomy appliance. Problems with this procedure include a failure of continence, irritation of the mucosa of the ileal reservoir from stasis ("pouchitis"), and bacterial overgrowth which may lead to mild malabsorption. Repeat operations are common, and this procedure should only be done by skilled surgeons familiar with the technique. *Ileorectal anastomosis* with *mucosal stripping* of the rectal segment is sometimes done in children who require colectomy. Newer forms of surgical therapy include ileoanal anastomosis with internal reservoirs thus preserving sphincteric function. These approaches are recent and not generally available.

CROHN'S DISEASE   The medical management of colonic Crohn's disease is similar in most respects to that of ulcerative colitis. In a multicenter study (National Cooperative Crohn's Disease Study) sulfasalazine was shown to be effective in the therapy of active colonic disease. Corticosteroids also were efficacious but less so than with small-bowel involvement. The indications and dosages of these medications are similar to those for ulcerative colitis. Since in Crohn's disease, intraabdominal sepsis can result from fistula or abscess formation, corticosteroids must be used with caution and constant attention is required to detect evidence of sepsis, which can be masked by these agents. In general, the disease is less explosive in onset, and although toxic dilatation and perforation can occur, they are less common than in ulcerative colitis. The principles of management are the same. Because of the indolent nature of the disease, the response to therapy is often less complete than in ulcerative colitis, and the disease tends to progress despite apparent clinical inactivity. It may be more difficult to achieve a clinical remission and to withdraw steroids completely. As in ulcerative colitis, controlled studies have shown no benefit to continuing steroids after remission since the frequency of recurrence is not altered by prophylactic steroid therapy. Disappointingly, sulfasalazine did not decrease recurrence rates in Crohn's disease.

While response to therapy of the initial attack of Crohn's colitis may be satisfactory, many patients continue to have persistently active disease. This may express itself as progressive weight loss, diarrhea, and deterioration of general health. Perianal disease with predominantly left-sided colonic involvement (fistula formation and perirectal abscesses) may constitute a recurrent problem. In one controlled study, *metronidazole* (20 mg/kg per day in divided dosage) resulted in marked improvement in 10 of 18 patients with chronic perineal fistulas associated with Crohn's disease. It is not clear whether the drug is active because of its antibacterial properties or through another mechanism. It is possible that this drug may prove to be of value in the therapy of the perineal complications of Crohn's disease before surgical therapy is attempted. The role of immunosuppressive therapy such as azathioprine has been controversial in Crohn's disease. The multicenter United States study (National Cooperative Study) found azathioprine to be ineffective as a single agent in the therapy of active Crohn's disease. Yet there have been reports of dramatic improvement in a small percentage of patients when azathioprine (1.5 to 2 mg/kg) is added to a maximal program in the nonresponding patient. Some investigators have found 6-mercaptopurine (the active metabolite of azathioprine) effective in controlling disease activity when added to corticosteroids and sulfa-salazine. However, a beneficial response may take 6 to 8 months in some patients.

The management of Crohn's disease of the small intestine (regional enteritis) is similar to that for colonic Crohn's disease, and as noted many patients have concomitant small and large bowel disease. Several additional considerations are pertinent, however. *Intestinal obstruction* is not uncommonly a presenting feature with ileal involvement. Initially, this may be secondary to acute inflammation and will respond to corticosteroids. With recurrent involvement and the development of fibrosis, steroid therapy is less effective and surgical decompression is required. *Nutritional problems* often are more severe with involvement of the small intestine than with colonic involvement alone. Added to the general catabolic nature of the disease may be loss of absorptive surface which may result from progressive involvement or because of surgical resection. Refinements in the technique of parenteral alimentation have made it possible to provide a patient's total daily caloric intake intravenously for a period of weeks or even months (see Chap. 75). Parenteral alimentation has been employed with increasing frequency in the severely ill patient as a means of placing the gastrointestinal tract "at rest" and in preparing the malnourished patient for surgery. With this approach the disease may become quiescent, and the drainage from fistulas may decrease. However, disease activity frequently recurs when oral feedings are resumed. On occasion, prolonged intravenous alimentation, administered at home, may be required when oral feedings are not effective or in children exhibiting severe growth failure associated with Crohn's disease. Most often it is possible to design a dietary program of oral supplementation to nourish the patient adequately.

In patients with extensive small-bowel involvement or in those with a short bowel resulting from extensive intestinal resection, supplementation of electrolytes, minerals, and vitamins will be required. Extensive ileal disease or resection often results in diarrhea induced by bile salts and in malabsorption; cholestyramine may be needed to control the diarrhea and medium-chain triglycerides added to reduce fat malabsorption (see Chap. 237). In patients with stenotic segments of intestine, a low-residue (low-fiber) diet should be recommended. A lactose-free diet should be instituted if there is an associated lactase deficiency. Other dietary modifications have not been shown to have any beneficial effect on the primary disease process. Patients should be encouraged to eat a nutritious, appealing diet of their own choosing. *Surgical therapy* is generally reserved for the complications of Crohn's disease rather than as a primary form of therapy. In contrast to ulcerative colitis, more patients with Crohn's disease will require surgery in the chronic management of the disease. Approximately 70 percent of patients will require at least one operation during the course of their disease. Although each case and situation

must be individualized, in general, surgery may be required (1) for persistent or fixed bowel narrowing or obstruction; (2) for symptomatic fistula formation to the bladder, vagina, or skin; (3) for persistent anal fistulas or abscesses; and (4) for intraabdominal abscesses, toxic dilatation of the colon, or perforation. In contrast to ulcerative colitis, where colectomy is curative, in Crohn's disease surgical resection of the small or large intestine is followed by a high rate of recurrence. With resection of segments of small bowel or ileum and reanastomosis a recurrence rate of 50 to 75 percent over a 5-year period is not unusual. Recurrence of disease is invariably proximal to the created anastomosis. When total colectomy and ileostomy are performed for Crohn's disease of the colon without significant small-intestinal involvement, recurrence rates are lower, varying from 10 to 30 percent. Despite these recurrences, most patients do not develop a short bowel syndrome and usually can expect significant improvement. Faced with the possibility of recurrent disease many physicians are reluctant to advise surgery in Crohn's disease, except for the type of clear-cut complications described above. Alternatively, patients with persistently active disease may require chronic maintenance on unacceptably high levels of corticosteroids and with the appreciable risk of steroid side effects. Just as a failure of medical therapy should lead to colectomy in ulcerative colitis, it should be the conclusion in the patient with Crohn's colitis without major small-bowel involvement. While in this setting there is also a definite rate of recurrence, such recurrences are often not disabling. When extensive small-bowel disease is present, surgical therapy is often not feasible and should only be reserved for specific disease complications.

The therapy of Crohn's disease in children presents special problems since normal growth and development may be retarded in the presence of active disease. In addition to conventional drug therapy, intensive nutritional therapy or the judicious use of surgery may be required.

PROGNOSIS

The overall prognosis of IBD has been favorably affected by the use of corticosteroids and sulfasalazine, as well as by supportive techniques such as intravenous alimentation. In *acute* ulcerative colitis these therapeutic modalities can result in a remission in almost 90 percent of patients. The mortality of an initial acute attack is approximately 5 percent. Poor prognostic factors and an increased mortality rate are likely when there is total colonic involvement, when the onset occurs over age 60, and when toxic megacolon develops.

The long-term prognosis of *chronic* ulcerative colitis is more difficult to assess due to the variable and intermittent nature of the disease and improvements in therapy. Left-sided colitis and ulcerative proctitis have a very favorable prognosis and probably no increase in mortality; similarly the long-term prognosis for extensive colitis has improved greatly. Older studies suggested a poor prognosis for extensive colitis, with less than 50 percent of patients surviving 15 years after onset. More recent observations (longest follow-up 11 years) show a 10-year mortality rate of between 5 and 10 percent for severe first attacks (excluding toxic megacolon). Approximately 75 percent of patients will experience relapses, and 20 to 25 percent will require colectomy. The problem of carcinoma developing in the setting of long-standing chronic ulcerative colitis is an important factor in determining the long-term prognosis of ulcerative colitis. As discussed above, periodic surveillance with colonoscopy and multiple biopsies to detect dysplastic changes is indicated to detect a high-risk group for which to advise colectomy.

The prognosis for Crohn's disease is not as favorable as for ulcerative colitis. An exception is *acute regional enteritis*, often discovered during laparotomy for suspected appendicitis; this has an excellent prognosis. More than two-thirds of such patients may show no subsequent evidence of regional enteritis, and this form of acute ileitis may well be due to yersinia infection (see above). Prevailing surgical opinion favors a conservative approach in this situation, and in most instances operative resection is not advised.

In the majority of patients with Crohn's disease the course is chronic and intermittent regardless of the site of involvement. The disease responds less well to medical therapy with time, and over two-thirds of patients develop complications requiring surgery at some point in their disease. In contrast to ulcerative colitis, where mortality appears greatest early in the disease, in Crohn's disease the mortality rate increases with the duration of the disease, and probably ranges from 5 to 10 percent. Most deaths occur from peritonitis and sepsis. As indicated above, following surgery patients with Crohn's disease often have recurrence and relapses. Nevertheless, the therapy of Crohn's disease will result in reasonably stable and productive lives for most Crohn's disease patients.

REFERENCES

General

KIRSNER JB, SHORTER RG (eds): *Inflammatory Bowel Disease*, 2d ed. Philadelphia, Lea & Febiger, 1980

————, ————: Recent developments in "nonspecific" inflammatory bowel disease. N Engl J Med 306:775, 837, 1982

SLEISENGER MH, FORDTRAN JS (eds): *Gastrointestinal Diseases*, 2d ed. Philadelphia, Saunders, 1978

Etiology and diagnostic aspects

BEEKEN WL: Transmissible agents in inflammatory bowel disease. Med Clin North Am 64:1031, 1980

BLASER MJ, RELLER LB: *Campylobacter* enteritis. N Engl J Med 305:1444, 1981

CHAPMAN RW et al: Serum antibodies, ulcerative colitis, and sclerosing cholangitis. Gut 27:86, 1986

GOODMAN MJ et al: The usefulness of rectal biopsy in inflammatory bowel disease. Gastroenterology 72:952, 1977

GREENSTEIN AJ et al: The extraintestinal complications of ulcerative colitis and Crohn's disease: A study of 700 patients. Medicine 55:401, 1976

JESS P: Acute terminal ileitis: A review of recent literature on the relationship to Crohn's disease. Scand J Gastroenterol 16:321, 1981

QUINN TC et al: *Chlamydia trachomatis* proctitis. N Engl J Med 305:195, 1981

TRNKA YM, LAMONT JT: Association of *Clostridium difficile* toxin with symptomatic relapse of chronic inflammatory bowel disease. Gastroenterology 80:693, 1981

VAN TRAPPEN G et al: *Yersinia enteritis* and enterocolitis: Gastroenterological aspects. Gastroenterology 72:220, 1977

Therapy of inflammatory bowel disease

AZAD KHAN AK et al: Optimum dose of sulphasalazine for maintenance treatment in ulcerative colitis. Gut 12:232, 1980

BERNSTEIN LH et al: Healing of perineal Crohn's disease with metronidazole. Gastroenterology 79:357, 1980

FARMER RG et al: Long-term follow-up of patients with Crohn's disease. Relationship between clinical pattern and prognosis. Gastroenterology 88:1818, 1985

GREENSTEEN AJ et al: Reoperation and recurrence in Crohn's colitis and ileocolitis. N Engl J Med 293:658, 1975

GYDE SN et al: Malignancy in Crohn's disease. Gut 21:1024, 1980

KELTS DG et al: Nutritional basis of growth failure in children and adolescents with Crohn's disease. Gastroenterology 76:720, 1979

LENNARD JONES JE et al: Cancer in colitis: Assessment of the individual risk by clinical and histological criteria. Gastroenterology 73:1280, 1977

LOCK MR et al: Recurrence and reoperation for Crohn's disease. N Engl J Med 304:1586, 1981

PEPPERCORN MA: Sulfasalazine. Ann Intern Med 3:377, 1984

PRESENT DH et al: Treatment of Crohn's disease with 6-mercaptopurine. N Engl J Med 302:981, 1980

RIDDELL RH et al: Dysplasia in inflammatory bowel disease. Hum Pathol 14:931, 1983

SUMMERS RW et al: National cooperative Crohn's disease study: Results of drug treatment. Gastroenterology 77:849, 1979

URSING B et al: A comparative study of metronidazole and sulfasalazine for active Crohn's disease. The Cooperative Crohn's Disease Study in Sweden. Gastroenterology 83:550, 1982

239 DISEASES OF THE SMALL AND LARGE INTESTINE

J. THOMAS LaMONT / KURT J. ISSELBACHER

SYMPTOMS OF INTESTINAL DISEASE

SYMPTOMS OF DISEASES OF THE SMALL INTESTINE The major clinical manifestations of small-bowel disease are *motility disturbances*, abdominal *pain* and *distention*, gastrointestinal *bleeding*, and *malabsorption*.

An alteration in the normal propulsive activity of the small intestine is a common manifestation of a variety of diseases. The presentation may be one of decreased motility, such as paralytic ileus resulting from metabolic disturbance or peritonitis, or intestinal obstruction caused by tumors, adhesions, volvulus, or intussusception (Chap. 240). Diarrhea frequently accompanies small-bowel disease (Chap. 36) resulting from direct involvement of the mucosa by inflammatory or infiltrative lesions (sprue, regional enteritis). The associated malabsorption of fat and bile salts is an important factor in the pathogenesis of diarrhea in these conditions (Chaps. 36 and 237).

Abdominal pain due to small-intestinal disease is usually periumbilical or supraumbilical and often poorly localized. With obstruction, pain is classically described as intermittent or colicky. Visceral pain arises from distention or stretching of the intestinal wall, or from inflammation of the overlying parietal peritoneum. As the intestine becomes progressively dilated with loss of muscular tone, the colicky nature of the pain may become less apparent. Acute inflammation of the small intestine which involves the visceral or parietal peritoneum is associated with steady, aching pain, usually located directly over the inflamed area, and may be accompanied by guarding and rebound tenderness if the parietal peritoneum is involved. *Gastrointestinal bleeding* due to small-bowel disease may be detected as occult bleeding or, less commonly, brisk hemorrhage. In general, bleeding from the stomach or small intestine causes black or tarry stool (melena), while bleeding from the colon causes passage of red blood or clots. Obviously, the appearance of blood in the stool depends not only on site of bleeding but also on the rate of the hemorrhage and the rapidity of transit; thus localization of the bleeding site by stool appearance alone may be misleading.

An important clue to the presence of small-bowel disease is the demonstration of malabsorption of fat. With extensive mucosal damage or lymphatic obstruction, the presenting symptoms may relate to any of the features of a malabsorption syndrome or protein-losing enteropathy (Chap. 237) and should direct attention to the small intestine.

SYMPTOMS OF COLONIC DISEASE The major symptoms of colonic disease are *alteration in bowel habit, rectal bleeding*, and *pain*. Alteration in bowel habit implies a change from previous patterns of defecation; hence a detailed history is important. Most normal individuals have one to three movements of well-formed stools each day. *Diarrhea* means the passage of watery or loose stools usually with increased frequency, while *constipation* implies infrequent passage of hard, dry stools; *obstipation* is the absence of spontaneous bowel movements. A persistent change in bowel habit, particularly in older individuals with no previous irregularity, is usually an important early symptom of organic disease of the colon and should never be labeled *functional* unless a thorough diagnostic evaluation is negative. The appearance of the stool may also provide important diagnostic clues. Blood coating the exterior of a formed stool implies a lesion in the anal canal or rectum, while blood admixed with the feces indicates a bleeding source higher in the colon. Brisk hemorrhage from the colon or distal small intestine results in passage of fresh blood, called *hematochezia*. This may appear as fresh blood and clots if the lesion is in the left colon, or darker maroon-colored blood if the bleeding source is in the right colon.

Pain resulting from colonic disease is usually localized to either of the lower abdominal quadrants, as opposed to pain of small-intestinal origin, which is localized to the periumbilical area or higher. Rectal pain is often felt deep in the pelvis, while pain in the anal canal is accurately localized to the perineum. The mechanisms of colonic pain are similar to those in other intestinal viscera (see Chap. 5). Distention from gas or fluid causes crampy or colicky pain from stretching of the muscle layers and resulting contraction or spasm. Pain of this type is often relieved by passage of flatus or stool. Pain may also result if the colonic wall is inflamed or infiltrated by tumor. Acute colonic inflammation which involves the visceral or parietal peritoneum produces sharply localized pain, which may be accompanied by abdominal guarding and rebound tenderness. An important symptom of rectal disease is *tenesmus,* or painful straining at stool, with a sensation of incomplete emptying after defecation. This symptom can be caused by retention of stool in the rectum, by tumors of the rectum which simulate retained stools, or by colonic inflammation.

DIAGNOSTIC PROCEDURES

PHYSICAL EXAMINATION Careful *examination* of the abdomen may disclose a mass or fistula associated with inflammatory or neoplastic disease, localized tenderness, or abdominal distention resulting from ileus or intestinal obstruction. The physical examination and findings in the patient with acute abdominal pain are discussed in Chap. 5.

Thorough examination may also reveal extraintestinal findings associated with small-intestinal diseases. Thus buccal pigmentation or telangiectasia may indicate coexistent small-bowel polyposis or telangiectasia and may clarify episodes of abdominal pain or chronic bleeding. Similarly, evidence of iritis, arthritis, or erythema nodosum may suggest the presence of inflammatory bowel disease.

Perhaps the most important part of the physical examination in the diagnosis of colonic diseases is the *digital rectal examination.* This procedure should never be omitted for reasons of modesty or fear of embarrassment because it is essential in the diagnosis of perianal, sphincteric, and ampullary lesions; prostatic and uterine abnormalities; and even small rectal masses. A metastatic tumor may be felt in the perirectal tissues as a shelf-like deformity (Blumer's shelf), especially anteriorly above the prostate. The fecal material on the glove should be immediately tested with guaiac-impregnated cards for occult blood. Approximately one-half of all rectal carcinomas lie within reach of the index finger, and omission of the rectal examination may delay diagnosis and worsen the prognosis.

STOOL EXAMINATION Abnormal stools constitute important objective evidence of colonic disease. Stools should be examined by the physician as soon as possible after defecation for the presence of visible blood on the surface or within the specimen. A small sample should be tested for occult blood. Microscopic examination of fresh stool is important in the diagnosis of parasitic diseases, particularly in amoebic colitis when motile trophozoites can be seen in fresh, warm stool suspensions. Stool suspensions can also be stained with a drop of methylene blue for polymorphonuclear leukocytes, which indicate the presence of an acute inflammatory exudate characteristic of ulcerative colitis, amoebic colitis, and bacillary dysentery. Fixed and stained slides of stool may also reveal amoebas and other parasites, while stool culture is essential for the diagnosis of bacillary dysentery. Sudan III stain of stool is a useful screening test for steatorrhea.

BARIUM STUDIES The considerable length of the small intestine (some 12 to 22 ft in the adult) makes *radiologic studies* of the small bowel of prime importance and usually forms the basis for the diagnosis of small-bowel diseases. *Small-bowel x-rays* are not usually part of a routine upper gastrointestinal series and must be specifically requested. In view of the length of the small bowel and wide variations in transit time, it is essential to provide the radiologist with as much information as possible, since the precise nature of the problem may determine various technical aspects of the examination. Enteroclysis is a specialized small-bowel barium study during which barium is infused rapidly via a nasogastric tube into the jejunum. This technique allows distention of bowel loops and rapid filling of the entire small intestine, thus avoiding the problems of inadequate distention and poor transit sometimes encountered in routine small-bowel barium studies. Enteroclysis is indicated in patients with suspected small-bowel lesions not visualized by ordinary barium studies.

Barium enema is an extremely accurate diagnostic tool for the identification of structural abnormalities of the colon. A careful study in a well-prepared patient can demonstrate mucosal lesions as small as 0.5 cm. For high-quality resolution of subtle lesions, such as small polyps or early changes of ulcerative colitis, an air-contrast barium enema is useful. In this study the mucosa is outlined by a thin coat of barium, after which air is injected to enhance contrast and outline small lesions. The combined use of the digital examination, stool guaiac test, proctosigmoidoscopy, and barium enema will identify most colonic lesions. However, barium enema does occasionally miss significant tumors or mucosal inflammation. Colonoscopy is often used to complement barium studies or to follow up suspected lesions seen by barium enema. Colonoscopy provides the additional opportunity to biopsy suspicious lesions and to remove smaller polyps.

SIGMOIDOSCOPY Contrary to the general impression, the technique of sigmoidoscopy is not difficult to master, and with practice the discomfort to the patient is minimal. The availability of flexible fiberoptic sigmoidoscopes now makes it possible to examine the lower 40 to 60 cm of the colon, compared to the 25-cm limit of the rigid sigmoidoscope. Flexible sigmoidoscopy is generally less painful than rigid sigmoidoscopy. Because approximately half of all colorectal neoplasms lie in the distal 50 cm of the bowel, sigmoidoscopy is an important diagnostic tool. It should be stressed that a rectal carcinoma can be missed on routine barium enema yet easily visualized and biopsied through the sigmoidoscope. Furthermore, the earliest changes of ulcerative colitis may not be demonstrated radiographically but may be obvious through the sigmoidoscope. Rectal biopsy is easily and painlessly accomplished through the instrument and is associated with minimal morbidity except in the presence of bleeding disorders.

COLONOSCOPY See Chap. 233.

MESENTERIC ANGIOGRAPHY Angiography is helpful in the diagnosis of two conditions: intestinal ischemia and gastrointestinal hemorrhage. Patients suspected of having acute intestinal ischemia from arterial embolus as well as chronic ischemia (intestinal angina) should undergo angiography to locate the site of blockage. Angiography is also very helpful in some patients with acute gastrointestinal blood loss. The success of this technique is related to the rate of blood loss, being most successful when bleeding exceeds 0.5 mL/min.

RADIONUCLIDE BLEEDING SCAN Bleeding from the small or large bowel can be localized in certain circumstances by radionuclide scanning of the abdomen after intravenous injection of technetium 99m sulfur colloid or autologous red cells labeled with the same agent (Fig. 239-1). If the patient is bleeding at a rate of 0.1 to 0.5 mL/min or greater, the location of radioactivity in the abdomen may indicate the source of bleeding. This diagnostic approach usually requires confirmation by another diagnostic modality such as angiography or endoscopy. The radionuclide bleeding scan is noninvasive, a particular advantage in older patients with bleeding from the small bowel or colon. The bleeding scan is not recommended in patients with suspected bleeding from the esophagus, stomach, or duodenum, who are best studied by upper endoscopy.

DISORDERS OF INTESTINAL MOTILITY

A major function of the intestinal tract is to propel the intestinal contents (food, secretions, chyme, feces) from stomach toward anus. Abnormalities of motility comprise the most common intestinal diseases: diverticulosis, megacolon, constipation, and irritable bowel syndrome. Although these conditions share a common abnormality, i.e., dysmotility, their clinical features are quite diverse.

DIVERTICULOSIS   Diverticula may be either congenital or acquired and may affect either the small or large intestine. Congenital diverticula are herniations of the entire thickness of intestinal wall, while the more common acquired diverticula consist of herniations of the mucosa through the muscularis, generally at the site of a nutrient artery.

Small-intestinal diverticula   Diverticula may occur in any portion of the small intestine; however, with the exception of Meckel's diverticulum, the most common locations are in the duodenum and jejunum. Most often diverticula are asymptomatic and discovered incidentally on upper gastrointestinal x-rays. On occasion, however, they may cause symptoms either because of their anatomic proximity to other structures or rarely from inflammation or bleeding.

Duodenal diverticula arise singly from the medial surface of the second portion of the duodenum. In most patients, they cause no symptoms. Rarely, they may present as acute diverticulitis with abdominal pain, fever, gastrointestinal bleeding or, most rarely, perforation. Adjacent structures, such as the bile or pancreatic ducts, may become involved; cases of common-duct obstruction and pancreatitis have been reported. Jejunal diverticula, while less common, may also be the site of acute inflammation, bleeding, or perforation with resulting abscess or peritonitis.

Multiple jejunal diverticula may be associated with a malabsorption syndrome related to bacterial overgrowth within the diverticula, similar to other situations where intestinal stasis (i.e., blind loops) permits bacterial proliferation. The consequences of bacterial proliferation with resultant mucosal damage, deconjugation of bile salts, and vitamin B_{12} malabsorption are discussed in Chap. 237.

Meckel's diverticulum, a persistent omphalomesenteric duct, is the most frequent congenital anomaly of the digestive tract, occurring in approximately 2 percent of autopsied adults. The diverticulum is wide-mouthed, about 5 cm long, and arises from the antimesenteric border of the ileum, usually within 100 cm of the ileocecal valve.

FIGURE 239-1   *Radionuclide bleeding scan using intravenous injection of technetium-labeled autologous red cells. Ten minutes after injection, a blush appears in the right abdomen over the cecum (arrow). Thirty minutes after injection, the blush has increased in intensity. The cardiac blood pool is noted at the top. Surgery revealed a bleeding diverticulum in the cecum.*

The sac may be lined with normal ileal mucosa (approximately 50 percent) or contain gastric, duodenal, pancreatic, or colonic mucosa. While rarely symptomatic after age 5, Meckel's diverticulum may produce hemorrhage, inflammation, and obstruction in children and teenagers.

Hemorrhage occurs almost exclusively before age 10 and invariably results from peptic ulceration of ileal mucosa adjacent to a Meckel's diverticulum lined with gastric mucosa. The diagnosis may be established by isotope scanning of the abdomen after injection of technetium, which is taken up by the ectopic gastric mucosa in the diverticulum. False-negative and false-positive Meckel's scans are not uncommon; thus other clinical and laboratory features must be carefully assessed before recommending surgery. In older children and young adults inflammation of the diverticulum may mimic acute appendicitis. Mechanical obstruction may also occur if the diverticulum intussuscepts into the lumen of the bowel or twists on a fibrous remnant of the omphalomesenteric duct which extends from the diverticulum to the abdominal wall. The treatment of any of these complications of Meckel's diverticulum is surgical excision.

Colonic diverticula   Diverticula of the colon are herniations or saclike protrusions of the mucosa through the muscularis, at the point where a nutrient artery penetrates the muscularis. Diverticula occur most commonly in the sigmoid colon and decrease in frequency in the proximal colon. They increase with age, and the incidence ranges between 20 and 50 percent in western populations over age 50. The exact mechanism for their formation is unknown but may be related to an increase in intraluminal pressure. Thickening of the muscle coat of the colon in most patients with diverticula suggests that herniations of mucosa are caused by increased pressure produced by colonic muscle contractions. The rarity of colonic diverticula in underdeveloped nations in contrast to their frequent occurrence in western countries has led to the speculation that diverticula result from the highly refined western diet, which is deficient in dietary fiber or roughage. It is proposed that such diets result in decreased fecal bulk, narrowing of the colon, and an increase in intraluminal pressure in order to move the smaller fecal mass. The role of dietary fiber in the etiology and treatment of diverticular disease remains to be determined.

Colonic diverticula are usually asymptomatic and are an incidental finding on barium enema performed for other reasons. The major complications of inflammation, both acute and chronic, and hemorrhage occur in only a small percentage of individuals with diverticulosis. Since diverticulosis is quite common in older patients, one must avoid the temptation of attributing symptoms to the diverticula unless other conditions, especially colonic neoplasm, have been excluded.

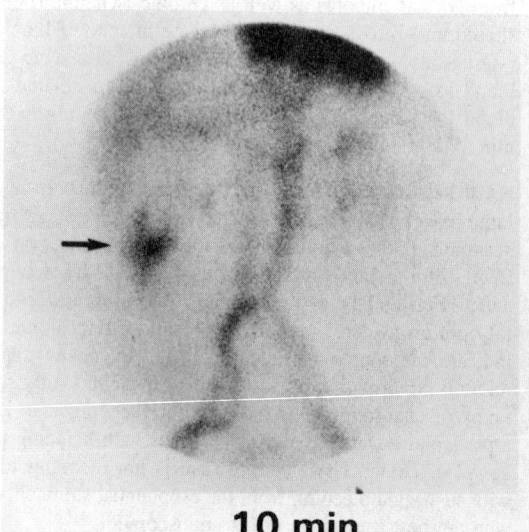
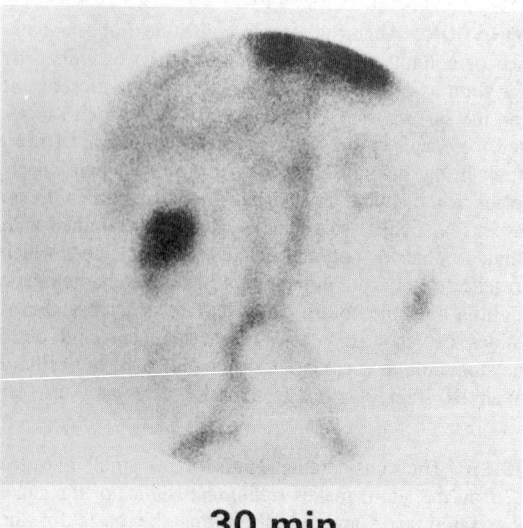

10 min   **30 min**

Diverticulitis Inflammation can occur in or around the diverticular sac. The cause of diverticulitis is probably mechanical, related to retention in the diverticula of undigested food residues and bacteria, which may form a hard mass called a *fecalith*. This compromises the blood supply to the thin-walled sac (made up solely of mucosa and serosa) and renders it susceptible to invasion by colonic bacteria. The inflammatory process may vary from a small intramural or pericolic abscess to generalized peritonitis. Some attacks are accompanied by minimal symptoms and seem to heal spontaneously. Studies of resected specimens indicate that most perforations of the diverticular sac are small and result in inflammation of the sac itself and the adjacent serosal surface. Diverticulitis occurs more often in men than women, and three times as often in the left as in the right colon. This suggests that diverticulitis may be related to the higher intraluminal pressures and the more solid fecal material in the sigmoid and descending colon.

Acute diverticulitis is a disease of variable severity characterized by fever, lower abdominal pain, made worse by defecation, and signs of peritoneal irritation—muscle spasm, guarding, rebound tenderness. Rectal examination may reveal a tender mass if the area of inflammation is close to the rectum. Although constipation may not have been noted prior to the onset of the illness, the inflammation around the colon often results in some degree of constipation. Rectal bleeding, usually microscopic, is noted in 25 percent of cases; it is rarely massive. Polymorphonuclear leukocytosis is common. Complications include free perforation, which results in acute peritonitis, sepsis, and shock, particularly in the elderly. The perforation may be walled off by adherent omentum or neighboring structures such as the bladder or small bowel. Abscess formation or fistulas then occur as the inflammatory mass burrows into other organs. Severe pericolitis may cause a dense, fibrous reaction or stricture around the bowel which can be associated with colonic obstruction.

DIFFERENTIAL DIAGNOSIS In the less acute situation differential diagnosis is principally that of a neoplasm in the area of the diverticulosis. Sigmoidoscopy or colonoscopy may show an acutely inflamed mucosa over an apparent extrinsic mass; passing the instrument through the contracted lumen is usually impossible. During the acute phase of diverticulitis, barium enema may be hazardous, since contrast material under pressure may lead to rupture of an inflamed diverticulum and convert a walled-off inflammatory lesion to a free perforation. The examination is usually safe after adequate treatment and healing of the diverticulitis. The radiologic findings on barium enema suggestive of diverticulitis are leakage of barium from a diverticular sac, stricture formation, and the presence of a pericolic inflammatory mass. In many patients, the distortion caused by inflammation prevents a clear distinction between cancer and diverticulitis; surgical excision may be required for accurate diagnosis.

TREATMENT For the mild case without signs of perforation, treatment consists of bed rest, stool softeners, liquid diet, and a wide-spectrum antibiotic such as tetracycline or ampicillin. Repeated attacks of diverticulitis in the same area generally require surgical resection. Severe attacks with acute peritoneal signs, suspected abscess, or perforation require intravenous antibiotics directed against gramnegative anaerobic bacteria, followed by surgical drainage or resection. The usual procedure is a diverting colostomy with resection of the involved colon; reanastomosis is then performed at a second operation.

Painful diverticular disease without diverticulitis Some patients with diverticulosis develop recurrent left lower quadrant colicky pain without clinical or pathologic evidence of acute diverticulitis. They often have bouts of alternating constipation and diarrhea, and the pain may be relieved by defecation or passage of flatus. These features suggest the coexistence of the irritable bowel syndrome (see below). Examination during a bout of pain reveals tenderness of the sigmoid colon, but signs of peritoneal inflammation such as rebound tenderness, muscle guarding, fever, and leukocytosis are absent. Barium enema shows typical diverticula without evidence of inflammation and stricture, plus a "sawtooth" irregularity of the lumen reflecting muscle hypertrophy and spasm. In some patients the pain is severe enough to warrant observation in a hospital and restriction of food since feeding aggravates the pain by causing colonic contraction. Anticholinergics, which reduce sigmoid contractions, and mild sedation are usually all that is required. After recovery the patient should be started on a high-residue diet or given a bulk laxative such as hemicellulose, unprocessed bran, or psyllium extract. Surgical excision is usually not indicated unless acute diverticulitis or its complications occur.

Hemorrhage from diverticula Massive hemorrhage from colonic diverticula is one of the commonest causes of hematochezia in patients over age 60. This complication of diverticulosis is caused by erosion of a vessel by a fecalith within the diverticular sac. The bleeding is painless and not accompanied by signs or symptoms of diverticulitis. Most cases of mild or moderate hemorrhage stop spontaneously with bed rest and blood transfusion. Localization of bleeding can be obtained by bleeding scan or angiography. In patients with severe hemorrhage mesenteric angiography can be both diagnostic in localizing the bleeding site and therapeutic since vasoconstrictive drugs or artificial blood clot infused intraarterially can effectively control hemorrhage. The angiographer can direct the surgeon to the area of bleeding if surgery is required for continued or recurrent bleeding. The location of bleeding diverticula demonstrated at angiography on several series has been more commonly in the right colon, particularly the ascending colon, in contrast to the sigmoid colon, where diverticula are more numerous.

MEGACOLON Megacolon, or giant colon, is characterized by massive distention of the colon usually accompanied by severe constipation or obstipation. This condition can be either congenital or acquired and is seen in all age groups. Acute toxic megacolon is a severe complication of chronic ulcerative colitis (see Chap. 238).

Aganglionic megacolon (Hirschsprung's disease) This is a congenital disorder which becomes manifest in early infancy, occurring more frequently in males, and is often familial. These infants have massive abdominal distention, absent bowel movements, and impaired nutrition due to chronic obstruction of the colon. In some individuals with less severe symptoms the disease may not be diagnosed until adolescence or early adulthood. The inability to defecate is caused by the absence of ganglion cells (Meissner's and Auerbach's plexuses) in a small segment of the distal colon, usually near the anus. This aganglionic segment is unable to relax to permit passage of stool, causing the normal colon proximal to it to become greatly dilated. On rectal examination the ampulla is empty of feces and the anal sphincter is normal. Barium enema reveals a narrowed segment in the rectosigmoid area, with massive dilatation above. Diagnosis is made by full-thickness surgical biopsy under anesthesia and demonstration of absent ganglion cells in the diseased segment. In most patients the aganglionic segment is in the rectosigmoid colon; in rare instances the lesion may involve more proximal bowel or even the entire colon. The treatment of choice is surgery which restores normal defecation. The most effective operation is a pull-through procedure in which normally innervated colon is anastomosed to the distal rectum just above the internal sphincter, thus bypassing the contracted aganglionic segment.

Chronic idiopathic megacolon This condition, also called *psychogenic megacolon*, has its onset later in childhood, usually at the time toilet training begins. It is characterized by severe chronic constipation and distention, and in contrast to Hirschsprung's disease, digital examination reveals the rectal ampulla to be invariably distended with feces. Barium enema shows the entire colon to be distended with stools, no narrowed segment is seen, and rectal biopsy discloses the normal complement of ganglion cells in Auerbach's plexus. Treatment is based on education in normal bowel habits, but a long course of enemas or large doses of mineral oil may be required until the patient acquires more normal bowel movements.

Acquired megacolon In Central and South America infection with *Trypanosoma cruzi* (Chagas' disease) can result in destruction of the ganglion cells of the colon, producing a clinical picture similar to congenital megacolon, except that the onset is in adult life rather than childhood. A number of other diseases are associated with megacolon in adults. Patients with schizophrenia or depression, particularly institutionalized patients, may have obstipation and massive colonic dilatation. Severe neurologic disorders including cerebral atrophy, spinal cord injury, and parkinsonism may also cause megacolon. Myxedema, infiltrative diseases such as amyloidosis, and scleroderma can also reduce colonic motility and produce marked colonic distention. Narcotic drugs, particularly morphine and codeine, can cause severe constipation, especially when administered to bedridden patients. Digital rectal examination of adults with acquired megacolon reveals a rectum distended with feces, as opposed to the empty rectum in aganglionic megacolon. Treatment is aimed at the underlying disease as well as the careful use of enemas and cathartics.

INTESTINAL PSEUDOOBSTRUCTION Intestinal pseudoobstruction is an acute or chronic motility disorder characterized by distention or dilatation of the small and large intestine. Abdominal pain, nausea, and vomiting may lead to diagnostic confusion with mechanical obstruction, but as the name of this condition implies, the underlying cause is not obstruction but rather a severe dysmotility resulting in distention. Pseudoobstruction may be primary or secondary and acute or chronic. In primary or idiopathic pseudoobstruction no other contributing condition can be identified, and the motility disorder is attributed to abnormalities of sympathetic innervation or of the muscle layers of the intestine. Secondary pseudoobstruction may result from scleroderma, diabetes, amyloidosis, neurologic diseases, drugs, or sepsis.

Chronic or intermittent secondary pseudoobstruction Numerous medical conditions can cause chronic dilatation of the large and small bowel. Some of these may involve the intestinal smooth muscle such as scleroderma, dermatomyositis, amyloidosis, or muscular dystrophy. Endocrine disorders, including myxedema and diabetes mellitus, may result in chronic distention which in the diabetic results from autonomic visceral neuropathy. Chronic neurologic diseases including Parkinson's disease and stroke may be complicated by chronic pseudoobstruction; in these patients drugs and relative immobility are contributing features. Finally, psychotic patients, (especially those who are institutionalized) may suffer from prolonged megacolon.

The symptoms of chronic secondary pseudoobstruction are chronic or intermittent constipation, crampy abdominal pain, anorexia, and bloating. Gastric distention and disordered swallowing may be present. Abdominal x-rays reveal gaseous distention of the large and small bowel, and occasionally of the stomach. Air fluid levels are unusual and should raise the possibility of mechanical obstruction. Upper gastrointestinal series and barium enema do not reveal specific abnormalities of the intestine such as tumor, stricture, or volvulus. The presence of an autoimmune disorder or endocrinopathy may require confirmation by serologic or blood tests; biopsy may be needed as in amyloidosis or muscular dystrophy.

The treatment of chronic intestinal pseudoobstruction is made difficult due to the complexity and chronicity of the underlying systemic disease. Patients with scleroderma may respond to broad-spectrum antibiotics if intestinal bacterial overgrowth is suspected. Metoclopramide may benefit gastric dysmotility in the diabetic. Discontinuation of psychotropic or anti-Parkinson drugs may occasionally result in improvement. Cathartics and enemas may be required to relieve fecal impaction, and the regular use of stool softeners and a high-fiber diet may help prevent recurrences.

Idiopathic intestinal pseudoobstruction This term encompasses patients with signs and symptoms of pseudoobstruction in whom no systemic disease can be identified. The typical patient has recurrent attacks of abdominal pain and distention with nausea and vomiting. The small intestine is primarily involved, and chronic constipation is much less frequent than in secondary pseudoobstruction. Steatorrhea secondary to bacterial overgrowth of the small intestine is common and may lead to chronic diarrhea and malnutrition. Many patients exhibit abnormalities of motility in the esophagus and urinary bladder, in addition to the small and large intestine. Various defects have been described in patients with this syndrome, including abnormalities of the mesenteric plexus and myopathy of the intestinal and urinary bladder smooth muscle (so-called hollow visceral myopathy). Elevated prostaglandin E levels have been reported in some patients. Treatment of idiopathic pseudoobstruction is unsatisfactory. Surgery to relieve "obstruction" is to be avoided, since the condition is often worsened by abdominal surgery. Medical therapy with metoclopramide and cholinergic agents has been unsuccessful. Nutritional support in the form of low-residue elemental diets or parenteral hyperalimentation may be helpful. Unfortunately the lack of effective therapy and the progressive nature of the illness make the prognosis of idiopathic pseudoobstruction rather unfavorable. Death from malnutrition and steatorrhea are common. The long-term impact of total parenteral nutrition on this disease is not yet clear.

Acute intestinal pseudoobstruction This entity, sometimes referred to as Ogilvie's syndrome, is characterized by acute intestinal dilatation, involving primarily the colon but occasionally also the small intestine. As in other forms of pseudoobstruction, the clinical features are difficult to distinguish from mechanical obstruction. The patient may complain of colicky lower abdominal pain and acute constipation. Examination reveals a distended, tympanitic abdomen, with reduced or absent bowel sounds. Localized tenderness over the distended colon is common, but diffuse abdominal tenderness, rigidity, or rebound tenderness are unusual. Abdominal films reveal massive dilatation of the colon and small intestine, occasionally with the presence of air fluid levels. The cecum, being the most capacious part of the colon, is often massively dilated and tender. The onset of these symptoms usually occurs in patients who have recently undergone severe surgical or medical stress such as major surgery, myocardial infarction, sepsis, or respiratory failure. Patients with acute pseudoobstruction are frequently on a respirator, have received narcotics or sedatives, and have metabolic and electrolyte disturbances.

Management of acute pseudoobstruction requires careful correction of fluid and electrolyte abnormalities, intubation of the stomach or small intestine for decompression, and avoidance of drugs which depress intestinal motility. Barium enema may be hazardous because of the risk of perforating the already dilated bowel. Some authorities recommend cecostomy when the diameter of the colon exceeds 8 cm to avoid ischemic necrosis and perforation. Decompressive colonoscopy is beneficial in some patients. The outcome depends in large part on the prognosis of the associated medical or surgical conditions. Patients who recover from the underlying medical or surgical conditions usually have a return of normal colonic function.

IRRITABLE BOWEL SYNDROME The irritable bowel syndrome (IBS) is the most common gastrointestinal disease in clinical practice, and although not a life-threatening illness, it causes great distress to those afflicted and a feeling of helplessness and frustration for the physician attempting to treat it. The patient with irritable bowel syndrome may present with one of *three clinical variants*. Patients with so-called spastic colitis complain primarily of chronic abdominal pain and constipation. A second group has chronic intermittent watery diarrhea, often without pain. Some patients have both features and complain of alternating constipation and diarrhea.

The basic pathophysiologic abnormality in the irritable bowel syndrome is an alteration of intestinal motility. Patients with the spastic colon variant (pain and constipation) have *increased* resting colonic motility; in contrast, those presenting primarily with diarrhea have *decreased* resting colonic motility. Both groups have an increase in colonic motility after injection of cholinergic drugs or cholecystokinin; motility may also be increased in association with psychological stress. It has been suggested that cholecystokinin may be a normal stimulus of intestinal motility and that the spastic colon may result from an exaggerated response to the normal release of chole-cystokinin after eating.

Patients with the irritable bowel syndrome also exhibit an abnormal basic electrical rhythm in the colon, characterized by an increase in 3-cycle-per-minute (cpm) slow-wave activity. It is not certain, however, whether these abnormalities of smooth-muscle contraction are primary or secondary to another underlying abnormality of intestinal neuromuscular function.

Evidence of significant psychological disturbances may be seen in some patients with irritable bowel syndrome. Depression, hysteria, and obsessive-compulsive traits are common, and psychological stress frequently triggers an exacerbation of symptoms. It should be noted, however, that in normal individuals colonic motility is altered by stress. For example, increased intracolonic pressure has been observed in normal volunteers during a stressful interview. This suggests that psychological stress may be a nonspecific trigger of symptoms in the irritable bowel syndrome, as is the case in many other illnesses of diverse etiology.

Clinical features The irritable bowel syndrome is a disease of young or middle-aged adults; female/male ratio is 2:1. The predominant feature is a history of chronic constipation, diarrhea, or both. The typical patient describes watery diarrhea occurring *intermittently* for months or years. The diarrhea is usually worse in the morning upon arising or after breakfast. After the passage of three or four loose stools with excessive mucus the patient may feel well for the remainder of the day. Diarrhea throughout the day or especially nocturnal diarrhea is most unusual. The diarrhea may last for weeks or months and then disappear spontaneously for variable periods of time. Some patients describe "pencil-like" pasty stools rather than diarrhea.

Another typical presentation is that of chronic abdominal pain with constipation, or with alternating constipation and diarrhea. These patients describe intermittent crampy lower abdominal pain, often over the sigmoid colon, which is usually relieved by passage of flatus or stool. The patient may describe excessive bloating which is not discernible to the physician. A variety of other complaints, such as heartburn, excessive bloating, back pain, weakness, faintness, and palpitations, are frequent in patients with irritable bowel syndrome. The pain may occasionally be in the right upper quadrant or midepigastrium, leading to diagnostic confusion with biliary tract or peptic ulcer disease.

Physical examination reveals these patients to be anxious but otherwise normal. During intense pain, the abdomen may be distended, but no visible peristalsis is noted; the abdominal musculature is relaxed, and a tender sigmoid full of feces may be palpated in the left lower quadrant. Characteristically, the rectal ampulla is empty of feces. Sigmoidoscopic examination is usually normal or at most shows a prominent vascular pattern. There may be difficulty in negotiating the rectosigmoid curve at 13 to 15 cm from the anus because of spasm. Large amounts of clear mucus are frequently encountered during the examination.

The *diagnosis* of the irritable colon syndrome is suggested by the chronic intermittent nature of symptoms without obvious signs of physical deterioration, the relation of symptoms to environment or emotional stress, and the exclusion of other conditions. The evaluation should include a careful history, complete physical examination including sigmoidoscopy, stool examination (for occult blood, parasites, and pathogenic bacteria), and in older patients a barium enema. The latter study serves to rule out other lesions since there are no diagnostic x-ray findings for this syndrome, although spasticity of the sigmoid, accentuated haustra, and a tubular appearance to the descending colon may be observed when the patient is symptomatic. Lactase deficiency may masquerade as irritable colon syndrome and should be excluded by a trial of milk restriction, a lactose tolerance test, or a lactose breath hydrogen test (see Chap. 237). Thyrotoxicosis is easily confused with irritable bowel syndrome and should be excluded by appropriate laboratory studies.

Treatment of the irritable colon syndrome requires both skill and patience. It is important that the patient be reassured that this condition normally does not lead to the development of inflammatory bowel disease (i.e., ulcerative colitis) or colonic malignancy. It is also important for both the patient and the physician to realize that the condition is chronic, and while it may be alleviated, it cannot be cured. The patient should be encouraged to adapt to the symptoms so as to minimize their impact on life-style. The physician should not imply that the symptoms are largely emotional or psychological in origin, since this is usually rejected by the patient. It is appropriate, however, to emphasize the relationship between psychological stress and the onset of severity of symptoms, as this may allow the patient to better deal with the disease. After the diagnosis is established, frequent x-rays and endoscopies are not necessary; general physical examinations, hemograms, and stool examinations, however, should be carried out at regular intervals.

Drug treatment is aimed at altering the abnormal colonic motility in this disease. Patients with constipation may respond to an increase in dietary bulk in the form of unprocessed bran or other nonabsorbed bulk laxatives. Mild sedation with phenobarbital or tranquilizers may be indicated, and anticholinergic drugs are useful in some patients. Troublesome diarrhea may respond to diphenoxylate (Lomotil) or paregoric. Unfortunately, no specific drug or dietary regimen affords good relief in all patients, and thus a number of therapeutic maneuvers need to be tried.

CHRONIC CONSTIPATION In Chap. 36 the mechanism of defecation is discussed. Disorders involving the sensory or motor components of this mechanism may arise from destruction of the nerves subserving these functions, from invasion or inflammation of the rectosigmoid itself, or from central nervous system lesions. Most cases of chronic constipation arise from habitual neglect of afferent impulses, failure to initiate defecation, and accumulation of large, dry fecal masses in the rectum. This voluntary suppression of the call to stool may arise during the period of toilet training in childhood, or later in life because of a sense of social impropriety, unaccustomed surroundings, uncomfortable toilet facilities, or illnesses which require confinement to bed. Chronic constipation is much more common in women, with onset typically in late adolescence or early adulthood. As constant distention of the rectum with feces becomes chronic, the patient grows less aware of rectal fullness. Bowel movements become progressively more difficult, and painful hemorrhoids or anal fissures reinforce suppression of the urge to defecate. To avoid these problems, the patient begins the chronic use of laxatives or enemas, without which defecation becomes impossible.

Treatment The physician should make every attempt to educate the patient about the chain of events which has led to chronic constipation. Attempts should be made to alter patterns of many years' duration, and the patient must recognize the importance of responding to, rather than suppressing, the urge to defecate. It is helpful to initiate a routine whereby defecation is attempted at a given time each day. In most individuals the call to stool occurs in the morning after breakfast. Physical exercise such as a brisk walk just before attempts at defecation may be helpful. Patients are instructed to increase dietary bulk with foods rich in fiber, such as green vegetables and unprocessed cereal grains, or by the regular use of bulk laxatives, such as hemicellulose, psyllium extract, and powdered unprocessed bran. The success of such a regimen depends to some extent on the duration of symptoms. Elderly patients with long-standing constipation and reliance on enemas or laxatives are more resistant to these measures than younger patients whose bowel patterns are less established. Moreover, poor muscle tone, reduced physical activity, and increased incidence of other medical conditions make the problem more difficult in the older age group. Bedridden elderly patients often develop severe constipation and even fecal impaction unless preventive measures are taken. This applies not only to patients with previous constipation but also to those with regular bowel movements prior to their confining illness. Regular administration of stool softeners, bulk laxatives, or mild cathartics is necessary until full ambulation and a normal diet are resumed. The onset of fecal impaction in bedridden patients is heralded by a feeling of rectal distention, urgency of defecation, or tenesmus. Occasionally the fecal impaction will result in low-grade chronic obstruction with dilatation and increased fluid content proximal to the impaction; "paradoxical diarrhea" may thus occur as fluid moves past the obstructing fecal mass. This situation will be aggravated if antidiarrheal drugs are given because the underlying constipation will be worsened. The appropriate maneuver is to disimpact the rectum manually or to administer gentle enemas if the impaction is beyond the reach of the finger.

VASCULAR DISORDERS OF THE INTESTINE

Ischemia is the end result of interruption or reduction of the blood supply of the intestine. However the clinical manifestations of intestinal ischemia range from mild chronic symptoms to catastrophic episodes, depending on the segment involved, the degree of involvement, and the rapidity of the process. Thus, the clinician should be aware of a spectrum of intestinal ischemia ranging from mild chronic symptoms to catastrophic episodes. The gut derives its arterial blood supply from the celiac axis and the superior and inferior mesenteric arteries. The small intestine is supplied by the celiac and superior mesenteric arteries; the colon is supplied by branches of the superior and inferior mesenteric arteries. A rich network of anastomotic vessels and the possible development of collateral circulation determine the clinical picture of acute or chronic intestinal arterial insufficiency.

MESENTERIC ISCHEMIA AND INFARCTION Acute small-intestinal ischemia may be classified as *occlusive* or *nonocclusive*. Occlusion may result from arterial thrombus or embolus of the celiac or superior mesenteric arteries, or from venous occlusion in the same distribution. Arterial embolus occurs most commonly in patients with chronic or recurrent atrial fibrillation, artificial heart valves, or valvular heart disease, while arterial thrombosis is associated with extensive atherosclerosis or low cardiac output. Venous occlusion is quite rare and is occasionally seen in women taking oral contraceptives. Approximately two-thirds of patients with mesenteric ischemia do not have a definite occlusion of a major vessel, a condition referred to as *nonocclusive* ischemia. The exact cause of nonocclusive disease is obscure; systemic arterial hypotension, cardiac arrhythmias, prolonged heart failure, digitalis therapy, dehydration, and endotoxemia have been suggested as contributing factors.

The outstanding clinical feature of acute mesenteric ischemia is severe abdominal pain, often colicky and periumbilical at the onset, later becoming diffuse and constant. Vomiting, anorexia, diarrhea, and constipation are also frequent but of little diagnostic help.

Examination of the abdomen may reveal tenderness and distention. Bowel sounds are often normal even in the face of severe infarction. Some patients have a surprisingly normal abdominal examination in spite of severe pain. Mild gastrointestinal bleeding is often detected by guaiac examination of stool, but gross hemorrhage is unusual except in ischemic colitis (see below). A typical laboratory finding is a pronounced polymorphonuclear leukocytosis. Late in the course of the disease (24 to 72 h) gangrene of the bowel occurs with diffuse peritonitis, sepsis, and shock. Abdominal plain films in patients with mesenteric ischemia may reveal air fluid levels and distention. Barium study of the small intestine reveals nonspecific dilatation, poor motility, and evidence of thick mucosal folds ("thumbprinting") (Fig. 239-2).

Acute mesenteric ischemia is a grave condition with a high morbidity and mortality. Patients suspected of having acute arterial embolus should undergo immediate celiac and mesenteric angiography to localize the embolus, followed by embolectomy. Restoration of normal circulation may allow complete recovery if performed before irreversible necrosis or gangrene has occurred. Unfortunately infarction and transmural necrosis are frequently found at surgery, necessitating resection. Arterial or venous thrombosis is not generally amenable to surgical removal of the thrombus, and resection of the affected bowel is required. Similarly, patients with nonocclusive ischemia are not candidates for corrective vascular surgery (as major vessels are patent). These individuals often have extensive necrosis of the small or large intestine because of the widespread nature of the ischemic event. The decision to operate on patients with suspected mesenteric ischemia is a difficult one as the typical patient is a poor surgical risk owing to advanced age, dehydration, sepsis, and other serious medical conditions.

Chronic arterial insufficiency may precede acute vascular insufficiency, producing so-called abdominal angina. As in angina pectoris, the pain of chronic mesenteric insufficiency occurs under conditions of increased demand for splanchnic blood flow. The patient complains of intermittent dull or cramping midabdominal pain 15 to 30 min after a meal, lasting for several hours postprandially. Significant weight loss is primarily due to a decreased food intake; however, chronic intestinal ischemia may also produce mucosal damage and malabsorption, which in turn aggravates the weight loss. Since abdominal angina may progress to bowel infarction, serious consideration should be given to performing arteriographic studies to confirm the diagnosis in those patients who are candidates for abdominal vascular surgery. The only definitive treatment is surgical removal of the arterial obstruction or the construction of bypass arterial grafts to the ischemic bowel.

A variety of systemic conditions are associated with *vasculitis* of the large and small arteries supplying the intestine. Most often, these

FIGURE 239-2 *Barium enema showing "thumbprinting" or submucosal edema of the inferior margin of the transverse colon, in a patient with acute ischemic colitis.*

disorders can be recognized by the associated extraintestinal manifestations as in polyarteritis nodosa, lupus erythematosus, dermatomyositis, Henoch-Schönlein purpura (allergic vasculitis), and rheumatoid vasculitis. When larger arteries are involved, as in polyarteritis nodosa, the picture of acute intestinal infarction is similar to embolic or atherosclerotic vascular occlusion. Often the involvement of smaller vessels leads to areas of intramural hemorrhage and edema leading to abdominal pain, variable degrees of intestinal obstruction, and bleeding. Barium enema may show "thumbprinting" and "spiculation" due to localized edema, hemorrhage, and ulceration. In many instances, treatment of the underlying disorder may lead to regression of symptoms. If signs of an acute abdomen develop, surgical exploration is usually indicated.

Intramural small-intestinal hemorrhage may occur with vasculitis, trauma, or impaired coagulation, especially in patients receiving anticoagulants. The clinical and radiologic features resemble those seen with vasculitis and local mucosal hemorrhage.

ISCHEMIC COLITIS Ischemia of the colon most often affects the elderly population because of the greater frequency of vascular disease in that group. Ischemic colitis is almost always a nonocclusive disease, that is, obstruction of major arteries is not seen. Shunting of blood away from the mucosa may contribute to this condition, but the mechanism of ischemia is not known.

The clinical picture depends upon the degree of ischemia and the rate of its development. In *acute fulminant ischemic* colitis the major manifestations are severe lower abdominal pain, rectal bleeding, and hypotension. Dilatation of the colon and physical signs of peritonitis are seen in severe cases. Plain abdominal films may reveal thumbprinting from submucosal hemorrhage and edema. Barium enema is hazardous in the acute situation because of the risk of perforation. Sigmoidoscopy or colonoscopy may detect ulcerations, friability, and bulging folds from submucosal hemorrhage. Angiography is not helpful in the management of patients with presumed ischemic colitis since a remedial occlusive lesion is very rarely found. Surgical resection may be required in some patients with fulminant ischemic colitis to remove gangrenous bowel; others with lesser degrees of ischemia may respond to conservative medical management.

Subacute ischemic colitis, the most common clinical variant of ischemic colonic disease, produces lesser degrees of pain and bleeding, often occurring over several days or weeks. The left colon may be involved, but the rectum is usually spared because of collateral blood flow, a distinguishing feature from acute ulcerative colitis. Barium enema reveals edema, cobblestoning, thumbprinting, and occasionally superficial ulceration. Angiography is not indicated as almost all cases are nonocclusive. Occasionally *stricture formation* may follow a bout of ischemic colitis or may present de novo without a history of antecedent pain or bloody diarrhea. Most cases of nonocclusive ischemic colitis resolve in 2 to 4 weeks and do not recur. Surgery is not required except for obstruction secondary to postischemic stricture.

ANGIODYSPLASIA OF THE COLON These are vascular ectasias (not neoplasms) which occur in the right colon of many older individuals and may cause bleeding (see Chap. 37). Angiodysplasia is a degenerative lesion consisting of dilated, distorted, thin-walled vessels lined by vascular endothelium. Grossly these ectasias look similar to spider angiomas of the skin and appear as star-shaped branching vessels in the submucosa measuring from 2 mm to 1 cm in diameter. The lesions are usually multiple and are found primarily in the cecum and ascending colon. Angiodysplasia may result from partial obstruction of the submucosal venous plexus by the tension generated in the cecal wall during muscular contraction.

Cecal angiodysplasia is important because of the likelihood of bleeding, either massively or chronically. In patients over 60 approximately one-quarter of colonic bleeding episodes are secondary to angiodysplasia. The diagnosis requires careful angiography with a demonstration of extravasation of contrast material into the lumen, or by direct visualization of bleeding lesions at colonoscopy. Hemorrhage from angiodysplasia may be controlled by embolization during arteriography or by electrocautery through the colonoscope. Some patients with massive uncontrolled bleeding or multiple sites of angiodysplasia may require right hemicolectomy.

PRIMARY NONSPECIFIC ULCERATION OF THE SMALL INTESTINE

Although the existence of rare solitary and unexplained ulcers of the small intestine has been recognized for many years, a recent increased incidence has suggested vascular factors producing ischemic necrosis of the mucosa in one or more areas of the small bowel. Most of these ulcers occur in patients receiving enteric-coated drugs known to be irritating to the mucosa; the most commonly implicated agent is potassium chloride, given to patients on chronic diuretic therapy. The symptoms are those of abdominal pain and obstruction, rarely with peritonitis and perforation. Surgical excision of the ulcerated or stenotic intestinal segment is generally required.

TUMORS OF THE SMALL INTESTINE

Small-bowel tumors comprise only 3 to 6 percent of gastrointestinal neoplasms. Because of their rarity correct diagnosis is often delayed. Abdominal symptoms are usually vague and poorly defined, and conventional x-ray studies of the upper and lower intestinal tract are usually normal. Small-bowel tumors should be considered in the following situations: (1) recurrent, unexplained episodes of crampy abdominal pain; (2) intermittent bouts of intestinal obstruction, especially in the absence of inflammatory bowel disease or prior abdominal surgery; (3) intussusception in the adult; and (4) evidence of chronic intestinal bleeding in the face of negative conventional x-rays. A careful small-bowel barium study is the diagnostic procedure of choice. The diagnostic accuracy is improved by infusing barium through a nasogastric tube placed in the duodenum (enteroclysis).

BENIGN TUMORS In general, the histology of benign small-bowel tumors is difficult to predict on clinical and radiologic grounds alone. The symptomatology of benign tumors is not distinctive, with pain, obstruction, and hemorrhage being the most frequent symptoms. These tumors are usually discovered in the fifth and sixth decades of life, more often in the distal rather than the proximal small intestine. The most common benign tumors are adenomas, leiomyomas, lipomas, and angiomas.

Adenomas These tumors include those of the islet cells and Brunner's glands as well as polypoid adenomas. *Islet cell adenomas* are occasionally located outside the pancreas, and the associated syndromes are discussed in Chap. 329. *Brunner's gland adenomas* are not truly neoplastic but represent a hypertrophy or hyperplasia of submucosal duodenal glands. These appear as small nodules in the duodenal mucosa. Most often this is an incidental finding on x-ray not associated with any clinical disorder.

Polypoid adenomas Approximately 25 percent of benign small-bowel tumors are polypoid adenomas. They may present as single polypoid lesions or less commonly as papillary villous adenomas. As in the colon, the sessile or papillary form of the tumor is sometimes associated with coexistent carcinoma. Multiple polypoid tumors may occur throughout the small bowel in the Peutz-Jeghers syndrome (Chap. 51) and are usually hamartomas. The malignant potential of these lesions is low.

Leiomyomas These arise from smooth-muscle components of the intestine and are usually intramural lesions affecting the overlying mucosa. Ulceration of the mucosa may cause gastrointestinal hemorrhage of varying severity.

Lipomas These tumors occur with greatest frequency in the distal ileum and at the ileocecal valve. Their radiolucent appearance on x-ray is characteristic. They are usually intramural and asymptomatic but may on occasion be associated with bleeding.

Angiomas   While not true neoplasms, these lesions are important because they frequently cause intestinal bleeding. They may take the form of telangiectasia or hemangiomas. Multiple intestinal telangiectasia occurs in a nonhereditary form confined to the gastrointestinal tract or as a part of the hereditary Osler-Rendu-Weber syndrome (Chap. 280). Vascular tumors may also take the form of isolated hemangiomas, most commonly in the jejunum. Angiography, especially during a bout of bleeding, is the procedure of choice in evaluating these lesions.

MALIGNANT TUMORS   While not too common, small-bowel malignancies occur in patients with long-standing regional enteritis and celiac sprue with greater frequency than in the general population. In contrast to benign tumors, malignant tumors of the small bowel are frequently associated with fever, weight loss, anorexia, bleeding, and an abdominal mass on physical examination. After ampullary carcinomas [many of which arise from the bile or pancreatic duct (see Chap. 255)], the most frequent small-bowel malignancies are adenocarcinomas, lymphomas, leiomyosarcomas, and carcinoid tumors.

Adenocarcinomas   These occur with highest frequency in the distal duodenum and proximal jejunum, where they tend to ulcerate and cause hemorrhage or obstruction. Radiologically, they may be confused with chronic duodenal ulcer disease or Crohn's disease if the patient has long-standing regional enteritis. The diagnosis is best made by endoscopy and biopsy under direct vision.

Leiomyosarcomas   Large, bulky tumors, leiomyosarcomas often are greater than 5 cm in diameter and may be palpable on abdominal examination. Bleeding, obstruction, and perforation are the most common manifestations.

LYMPHOMAS   Lymphoma of the small bowel is usually of the diffuse non-Hodgkin's type (Chap. 294), with diffuse histiocytic lymphoma comprising the largest group. Lymphoma of the intestine may be primary or secondary; primary intestinal lymphoma indicates that the initial symptoms arise from the intestine even though bone marrow, lymph nodes, and liver may also be involved. Intestinal lymphoma usually involves the jejunum or ileum in the form of localized or nodular mass lesions which narrow the lumen. This results in periumbilical abdominal pain, made worse by eating. Anorexia, weight loss, nausea, and vomiting are common. Intestinal bleeding and abdominal mass lesions are also common in patients with intestinal lymphoma.

Some patients with intestinal lymphoma have diffuse rather than localized or nodular involvement of the small bowel. This type of lymphoma was first described in oriental Jews and Arabs and is referred to as Mediterranean lymphoma. The typical presentation includes chronic diarrhea, malabsorption, and abdominal pain; the clinical findings may be confused initially with infectious diarrhea, Crohn's disease, or sprue. A curious feature in many patients with Mediterranean lymphoma is the presence in the blood and intestinal secretions of an abnormal IgA which contains only alpha-heavy chains and is devoid of light chains. It is suspected that the abnormal alpha chains are produced by plasma cells infiltrating the intestine.

The diagnosis of intestinal lymphoma is often delayed because the patient may initially be suspected of having another disorder, such as peptic ulcer, pancreatitis, Crohn's disease or infectious diarrhea. The diagnosis is suggested by barium studies of the small intestine showing nodular filling defects, irregular strictures, or infiltrated folds. The diagnosis can be confirmed by surgical exploration and resection of involved segments. Intestinal lymphoma may occasionally be diagnosed by peroral intestinal biopsy, but the disease mainly involves the lamina propria and usually requires full-thickness surgical biopsies.

Many authorities recommend staging of the lymphoma by means of bone marrow biopsy, and laparotomy with splenectomy and biopsies of the liver and regional lymph nodes. In patients with localized lymphoma (stage I), surgical excision followed by whole abdominal radiation therapy is recommended. Patients with more advanced lymphoma with lymph node and other organ involvement are best treated with combination chemotherapy, and with radiotherapy for localized recurrences or bulky tumors. The probability of sustained remission or cure is approximately 75 percent in localized disease, but 25 percent or less in patients with widespread lymphoma.

Carcinoid tumors   Among the most common epithelial tumors of the small intestine are carcinoid tumors. They arise from argentaffin cells of the crypts of Lieberkühn and are most commonly found from the midduodenum to the transverse colon, areas embryologically derived from the midgut. The appendix is the most common location for gastrointestinal carcinoid, where the tumor is found incidentally at the time of appendectomy. Most intestinal carcinoids are asymptomatic and of low malignant potential, but invasion and metastases may occur and lead to the carcinoid syndrome (see Chap. 299).

TUMORS OF THE LARGE INTESTINE

Neoplasms of the colon, both benign and malignant, are very common in western society. Benign polypoid adenomas of the colon are found at autopsy in about 50 percent of older Americans. While these lesions are generally harmless, it is now recognized that most colon cancers arise in adenomas. Furthermore, recent advances in colonoscopy have made polypectomy a relatively simple procedure. For these reasons, it is important to be familiar with the clinical presentation and management of benign polyps as well as colonic cancers.

COLONIC POLYPS   A polyp is defined as a structure arising from the mucosa and projecting into the lumen and is either *neoplastic* or *nonneoplastic*. Neoplastic polyps in turn may be benign (adenomatous polyp) or malignant (polypoid carcinoma). Nonneoplastic polyps include hyperplastic polyps, inflammatory polyps, juvenile polyps, and hamartomas. Although nonneoplastic polyps are more common, most morbidity and mortality are attributed to neoplastic polyps.

Adenomas   Single adenomatous polyps are common and increase with age so that about two-thirds of individuals above age 60 will harbor at least one adenoma. Adenomatous polyps occur more commonly in the rectosigmoid colon (80 percent) than in the rest of the colon (20 percent). Adenomas may be pedunculated or sessile. Most of them are silent and are discovered by routine barium enema or screening endoscopy. A few may bleed or cause obstructive symptoms, especially when they are greater than 2 cm in diameter. The major clinical significance of adenomas is that approximately 1 percent become malignant. The size of adenomas correlates with the risk of becoming malignant. Approximately 1 percent of polyps smaller than 1 cm in diameter contain foci of malignant cells, compared to about 50 percent for polyps greater than 2 cm. About 25 percent of patients with polyps will have more than one polyp. The number and size tend to increase with age, as does the risk of malignancy.

Adenomatous polyps of the colon are classified into three histologic types: tubular, tubulovillous, and villous. *Tubular adenomas* are the most common and are generally less than 1 cm in diameter. *Villous adenomas* are less common and are generally larger with approximately 50 to 60 percent over 2 cm in diameter. *Tubulovillous adenomas* are intermediate in size between the smaller tubular and larger villous types, suggesting that some tubular adenomas evolve into villous adenomas.

Villous adenomas tend to be sessile and are much more likely to become malignant; approximately 40 to 60 percent contain foci of carcinoma in situ or frankly invasive carcinoma extending through the lamina propria. Some villous adenomas in the rectosigmoid area may produce rectal bleeding or passage of large amounts of mucus.

Adenomatous polyps are usually diagnosed by detection of occult fecal blood loss in asymptomatic patients being screened for colon cancer. Polyps may also be detected by barium enema examination (Fig. 239-3) or by proctosigmoidoscopy and colonoscopy. Because of their malignant potential *all* colonic adenomatous polyps, but especially those larger than 1 cm in diameter, should be removed in toto via the colonoscope and carefully examined for evidence of malignancy. Removal of all adenomas, even those without malignant change, will reduce the incidence of subsequent colon cancer. Colonoscopic polypectomy is curative if the adenoma removed shows evidence of carcinoma in situ, since metastases from this lesion do not occur. If the carcinoma invades the submucosa of the head of a pedunculated polyp (polyp on a stalk), polypectomy alone is still probably curative. However, if the carcinoma invades the stalk, if the polyp is sessile, or if the carcinoma is undifferentiated, the patient should undergo a standard cancer resection to remove tumor which may have spread beyond the polyp into the wall of the colon or local lymph nodes.

Nonneoplastic colonic polyps Nonneoplastic polyps are a heterogenous group of lesions which occasionally cause rectal bleeding or pain. In contrast to adenomas, which are true neoplasms, these polyps do not undergo malignant change. Therefore, removal of nonneoplastic polyps is required only if they cause bleeding, obstruction, or other symptoms. The most common colonic polyp is the *hyperplastic* polyp, a sessile excrescence usually less than 0.5 cm. These tiny polyps are of no pathologic or clinical significance. Hyperplastic polyps larger than 1 cm in diameter may contain foci of adenoma; thus these larger polyps should be removed colonoscopically. *Juvenile polyps* are hamartomas composed of an excess of lamina propria and dilated cystic glands. They arise during childhood and may bleed or prolapse through the rectum during defecation. They generally do not recur after polypectomy. *Inflammatory polyps* are thought to result from regeneration following injury or inflammation. Histologically these lesions resemble juvenile polyps, but they may occur in other individuals. Sometimes multiple inflammatory polyps may mimic one of the hereditary polyp syndromes.

HEREDITARY POLYP SYNDROMES *Familial colonic polyposis* is a rarer autosomal dominant disorder characterized by the appearance of numerous (often 1000 or more) adenomatous polyps involving the entire colon. Occasional cases with no family history presumably result from a spontaneous mutation. The polyps are not present at birth but appear in childhood and adolescence, giving rise to rectal bleeding or diarrhea. Once this disease is diagnosed, it is imperative that the entire family be screened by sigmoidoscopy and barium enema. The probability of cancer of the colon occurring in affected individuals approaches 100 percent by age 40. Hence, prophylactic colectomy is indicated, usually in late adolescence or early adulthood. Most surgeons prefer total colectomy and ileostomy, while others leave the rectum, which allows the patient to have normal bowel movements. These patients require careful follow-up sigmoidoscopy and removal of all polyps in the rectal stump. However, the rate of carcinoma in the rectal stump is so high that total colectomy is recommended.

Gardner's syndrome refers to the coexistence of multiple colonic and duodenal adenomatous polyps together with benign soft tissue tumors (lipomas, fibromas, sebaceous cysts) and osteomas (particularly of the jaw and skull). In this syndrome the colonic polyps develop later than in multiple colonic polyposis, but the malignant potential is the same and thus colectomy is also recommended. Many patients with Gardner's syndrome have gastric and especially duodenal polyps, and cancer of the duodenum has been reported in some of these individuals.

An entity confused with multiple colonic (adenomatous) polyposis is *juvenile polyposis,* in which multiple hamartomatous polyps occur in the colon or in both large and small bowels. Juvenile colonic polyposis also occurs in kindreds and can cause rectal bleeding or diarrhea, rectal prolapse of the polyp, abdominal pain, and intussusception. Juvenile polyps have no malignant potential and colectomy is not recommended.

The *Peutz-Jeghers syndrome* is characterized by multiple hamartomatous polyps of the entire gastrointestinal tract, associated with melanotic spots on the skin, lips, and buccal mucosa. Although the polyps in this syndrome are most prevalent in the small intestine, colonic polyps may also occur. Several cases of malignant degeneration of duodenal polyps have been reported. Clinical features alone do not allow accurate differentiation of the various hereditary polyp syndromes (see Table 239-1). For this reason, a careful histologic examination of polyps from several areas should always be obtained prior to colectomy in patients with suspected adenomatous polyposis coli.

FIGURE 239-3 *Barium enema revealing a 2-cm polyp of the sigmoid colon. Pathologic examination revealed a benign adenoma.*

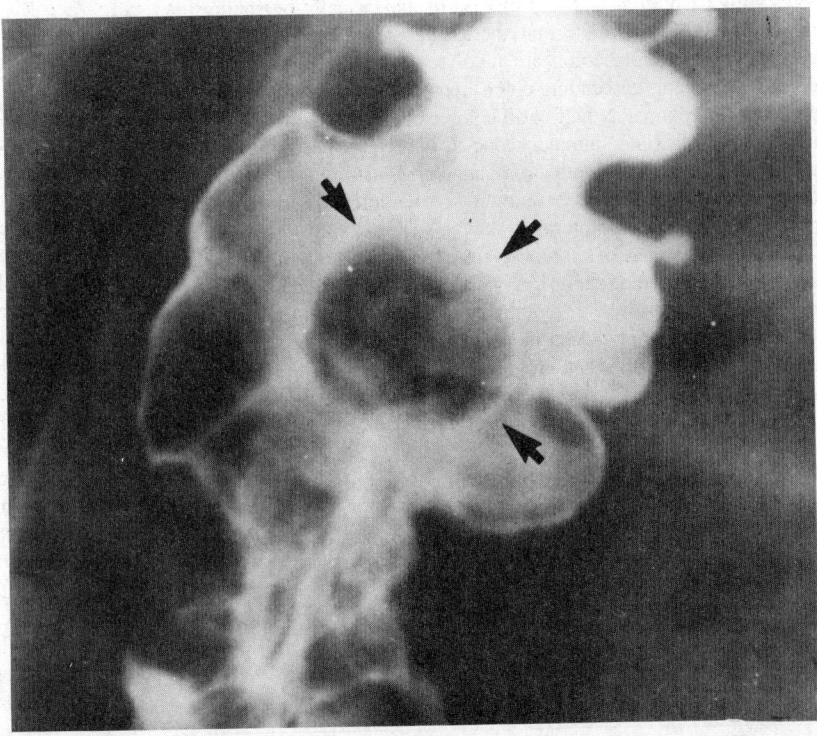

TABLE 239-1   Hereditable gastrointestinal polyp syndromes

Syndrome	Distribution of polyps	Histologic type	Malignant degeneration	Associated lesions
Familial colonic polyposis	Large intestine	Adenoma	Common	None
Gardner's syndrome	Large intestine and duodenum	Adenoma	Common	Osteomas, fibromas, lipomas, epidermoid cysts
Peutz-Jeghers syndrome	Small and large intestine	Hamartoma	Rare	Mucocutaneous pigmentation
Juvenile polyposis	Small and large intestine	Hamartoma, inflammatory	Absent	None

COLORECTAL CANCER   Cancer of the colon and rectum is one of the commonest carcinomas in both males and females, and accounts for about 20 percent of deaths due to malignant disease in the United States. Unfortunately, the death rate for this disease has not changed for the past 40 years and will undoubtedly remain the same until methods for earlier detection and improved treatment are available.

Etiology and risk factors   Although the specific cause(s) of colon cancer is unknown, epidemiologic studies suggest that dietary factors may be important. The incidence of colon cancer is much higher in Europe and North America than in the Far East, Africa, and developing nations. Furthermore, migrants from low-incidence areas such as Japan to high-incidence areas such as the United States acquire the higher incidence of the adopted country. It has been suggested that the higher intake of dietary animal fat in western society compared to other countries may account for the excess of colon cancer.

Certain diseases and conditions increase the risk of colon cancer. As noted previously adenomatous polyps of the colon, whether single or multiple, increase the risk of colon cancer. Patients with previous colon polyp or cancer are at higher risk for subsequent development of cancer. It also appears that some women with a history of uterine or breast cancer are at higher risk of developing colon cancer. Ulcerative colitis and to a lesser extent Crohn's colitis are also associated with a higher incidence of colon cancer. The risk in ulcerative colitis is increased in patients with active pancolitis for more than 10 years. Certain families appear to have a much higher incidence of colon cancer, which may affect up to 50 percent or more of family members. However, patients from these high-risk groups account for only 1 percent or less of all colon cancers in the United States. The remainder have no discernible risk factor except age and residence in a high-incidence area.

Pathology   Colon cancer is a disease of age, usually beginning in the fourth or fifth decade and increasing steadily thereafter. The cecum and ascending colon are involved in 15 percent; transverse colon, 10 percent; descending colon, rectosigmoid, and rectum in 75 percent. Approximately half of all colorectal cancers are within reach of the 60-cm flexible sigmoidoscope. Colorectal cancers may occur as fungating sessile tumors or as annular constricting lesions; the latter are somewhat more common on the left side, where they produce obstructive symptoms.

Adenocarcinomas of the colon are classified histologically based on degree of differentiation; in general, undifferentiated cancers are more invasive than well-differentiated ones. The presence of mucin-secreting "signet ring" cells indicates a higher likelihood of metastases. The most important prognostic information is the extent of spread of the cancer at the time of diagnosis or surgical removal.

Colorectal cancers are staged clinically according to the Duke's classification (Table 239-2). When the tumor is confined to the mucosa and submucosa (stage A) or to the colonic wall (stage B), the chance for surgical cure is excellent; spread beyond the wall of the bowel to regional lymph nodes (stage C) or to other organs (stage D) lowers the 5-year survival considerably. Since surgical removal is the only curative therapy currently available, the impact of early diagnosis on survival is obvious.

Clinical features   The major symptoms of colon cancer are rectal bleeding, abdominal pain, and change in bowel habit. The clinical presentation in the given patient is related to the size and location of the tumor. Cancers in the cecum and ascending colon are often flat and sessile (Fig. 239-4) and thus remain "silent" because they do not obstruct the lumen. Patients with cecal cancer often present with iron-deficiency anemia and guaiac-positive stool; gross hematochezia is rare. Cancers in the transverse and left colon may grow in an annular fashion (Fig. 239-5), producing symptoms of partial obstruction. The patient typically complains of intermittent crampy pain, often worsened by eating and relieved by passage of gas or feces. Cancer of the rectum or distal sigmoid colon also causes pain which may be confused with diverticulitis. These tumors may also interfere with the normal pattern of defecation, and they can produce diarrhea, constipation, or tenesmus. Rectal bleeding in patients over age 40 should always raise the suspicion of malignancy and should never be attributed to hemorrhoids without further examination. Similarly, unexplained iron-deficiency anemia in older individuals always requires a thorough evaluation for intestinal cancer.

Diagnosis   The diagnosis of colon cancer may be suspected by symptoms, such as rectal bleeding, pain, change in bowel habit, weight loss, or anemia. Since colorectal cancer is surgically curable before it has metastasized, delay in diagnosis, on the part of either physician or patient, may seriously lessen the chance of finding a curable lesion.

Evaluation of a patient for colon cancer should include a careful abdominal examination to search for mass lesions or hepatomegaly.

Complications   Since it is characteristic for tumors to invade, many tumors of the colon are first diagnosed because of a complication of the original lesion. The tumor may perforate the bowel wall, giving rise to acute peritonitis; may perforate slowly and wall itself off, giving rise to a local inflammatory mass and localized peritonitis; or may invade blood vessels to produce an episode of brisk rectal bleeding. More often, the tumor partially obstructs the bowel lumen for a long period of time, during which the colon proximal to the tumor dilates slowly without dramatic change in symptoms until frank obstruction occurs. This happens most often when the tumor is in the sigmoid, where the stool is driest. Tumors also weaken the colonic wall in such a way that an intussusception may occur, the tumor leading the intussusception. Similarly, fixation of the bowel wall by a tumor may produce a volvulus, which is most frequently seen in the sigmoid colon. Very large and slowly growing tumors may produce symptoms by pressure on neighboring organs such as uterus, bladder, or ureters. Inguinal hernias may become apparent as the first sign of such increased pressure. Fistulas between the colon and pelvic organs should lead to a thorough search for an underlying neoplastic infiltration. Abscesses inside the peritoneal cavity and cellulitis of the abdominal wall secondary to tumor infiltration are occasionally seen.

TABLE 239-2   Duke's classification of colorectal cancer

Stage	Pathologic description	Approximate 5-year survival, %
A	Cancer limited to mucosa and submucosa	90
B	Cancer extends into muscularis or serosa	60–75
C	Cancer involves regional lymph nodes	30–40
D	Metastases to liver, bone, lung	5

Treatment   The current approach to treatment of colon cancer is primarily surgical. Some surgeons prefer preoperative radiation therapy to prevent metastases, but it has not been convincingly demonstrated that this improves survival. Surgeons generally prefer abdominoperineal resection and colostomy for tumors located below the peritoneal reflection; above this area there is considerably more freedom of choice, depending primarily on the size and extent of the lesion. Even patients with obvious metastases usually benefit from a limited palliative resection, since this will relieve or prevent painful obstruction and hemorrhage. The overall operative mortality for colectomy is about 5 percent, except for emergency resections for perforation or obstruction. The operative mortality is somewhat higher for lesions in the left colon and for tumors which have perforated. Discussion of the complications of surgical therapy and the management of colostomies can be found in surgical texts.

The overall 5-year survival rate for all patients undergoing resection for colonic malignancy is approximately 50 percent. As already noted, surgical cure is possible only when the tumor is confined to the bowel wall. Palliative surgical attempts should not be discouraged because the symptomatic relief they produce may allow the patient to live in comfort for the remaining months of life. Chemotherapy with 5-fluorouracil or other agents is used in patients with metastases to the liver, but temporary improvement is obtained only in 25 percent or less of cases, and overall survival is not significantly affected. Localized radiation therapy for painful liver or bone metastases is occasionally palliative.

ANORECTAL PROBLEMS

HEMORRHOIDS   The internal hemorrhoidal plexus of veins is located in the submucosal space above the valves of Morgagni. The anal canal separates it from the external hemorrhoidal venous plexus, but the two spaces communicate under the anal canal, the submucosa of which is attached to underlying tissue to form the interhemorrhoidal depression. Whenever the internal hemorrhoidal plexus is enlarged, there is associated increase in supporting tissue mass, and the resultant

venous swelling is called an *internal hemorrhoid*. When veins in the external hemorrhoidal plexus become enlarged or thrombosed, the resultant bluish mass is called an *external hemorrhoid*.

Both types of hemorrhoids are very common and are associated with increased hydrostatic pressure in the portal venous system, such as during pregnancy, straining at stool, or with cirrhosis. When internal hemorrhoids enlarge, pain is not a usual feature until the situation is complicated by thrombosis, infection, or erosion of the overlying mucosal surface. Most persons complain of bright red blood on the toilet tissue or coating the stool, with a feeling of vague anal discomfort. The discomfort is increased when the hemorrhoid enlarges or prolapses through the anus; prolapse is often accompanied by edema and sphincteric spasm. Prolapse, if not treated, usually becomes chronic as the muscularis stays stretched, and the patient complains of constant soiling of underclothing with very little pain. Prolapsed hemorrhoids may become infected or thrombosed; the overlying mucous membrane may bleed profusely as the result of the trauma of defecation.

External hemorrhoids, because they lie under the skin, are quite often painful, particularly if there is a sudden increase in their mass. These episodes result in a tender blue swelling at the anal verge due to thrombosis of a vein in the external plexus and need not be associated with enlargement of the internal veins. Since the thrombus usually lies at the level of the sphincteric muscles, anal spasm often occurs.

The diagnosis of internal and external hemorrhoids is made by inspection, digital examination, and direct vision through the anoscope and proctoscope. Since such lesions are very common, they must not

FIGURE 239-5   *Annular, constricting adenocarcinoma of the descending colon. This radiographic appearance is referred to as an "apple-core" lesion and is always highly suspicious of malignancy.*

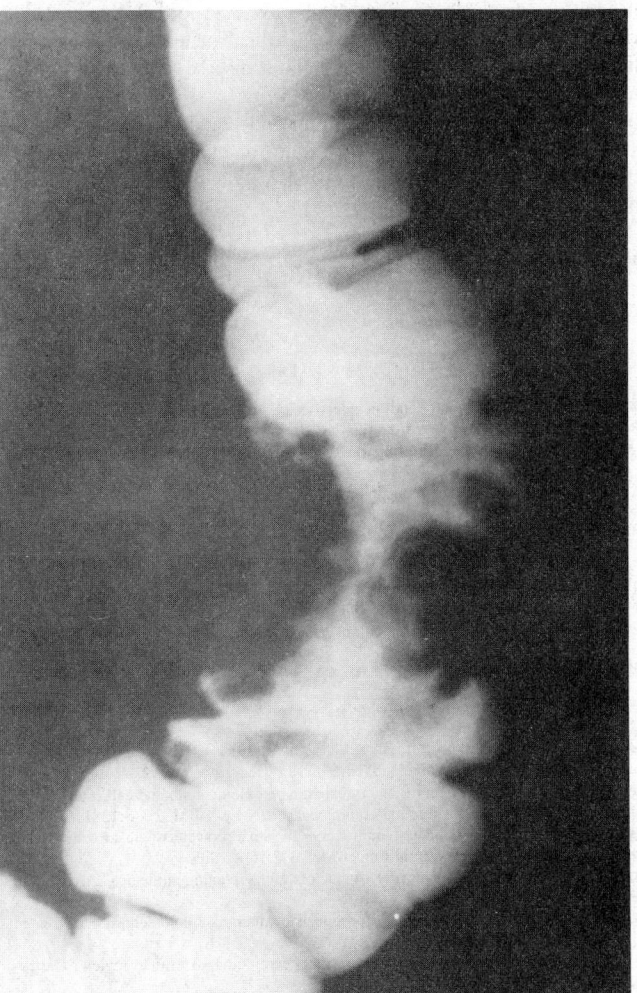

FIGURE 239-4   *Double-contrast air-barium enema revealing a sessile tumor of the cecum in a patient with iron-deficiency anemia and guaiac-positive stool. The lesion at surgery was a stage B adenocarcinoma.*

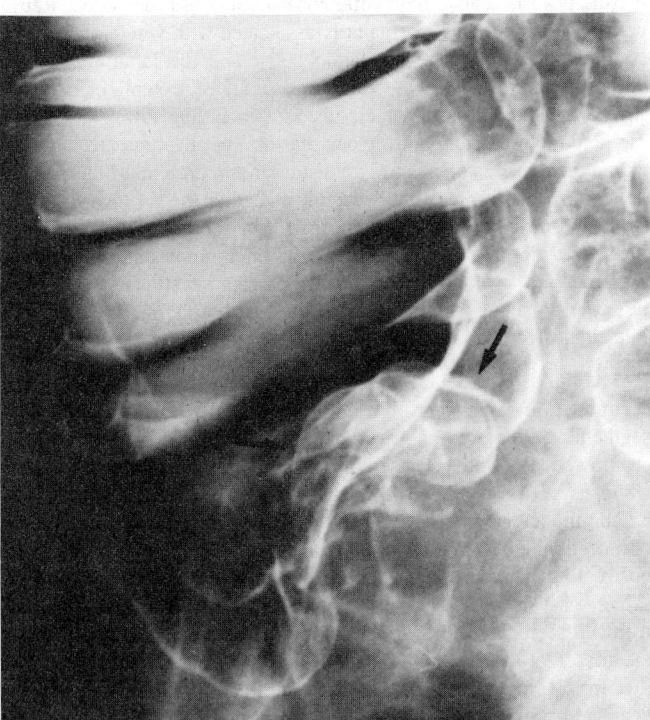

be regarded as the cause of rectal bleeding or chronic hypochromic anemia until a thorough investigation has been made of the more proximal gastrointestinal tract. Acute blood loss can occasionally be attributed to internal hemorrhoids. Chronic anemia in the presence of large but not definitely bleeding hemorrhoids should provoke a search for a polyp, cancer, or ulcer.

Most hemorrhoids respond to conservative therapy such as sitz baths or other forms of moist heat, suppositories, stool softeners, and bed rest. Internal hemorrhoids which remain permanently prolapsed are best treated surgically; milder degrees of prolapse or enlargement with pruritus ani or intermittent bleeding can be successfully handled by banding or injection of sclerosing solutions. External hemorrhoids which become acutely thrombosed are treated by incision, extraction of the clot, and compression of the incised area following clot removal. No surgical procedure should be carried out in the presence of acute inflammation of the anus, ulcerative proctitis, or ulcerative colitis. Both proctoscopy and barium enema should always be performed before a patient is subjected to hemorrhoidectomy.

ANAL INFLAMMATION Perianal inflammatory lesions may be primary or may be associated with inflammatory bowel disease or diverticular disease as mentioned above. Anal *fissures* are superficial erosions of the anal canal which usually heal rapidly with conservative therapy. Anal *ulcers* are more chronic and deep and give symptoms largely as the result of painful spasm of the external anal sphincter during and after defecation. Bleeding may occur with either fissure or ulcer; healing of the ulcer often is associated with a hypertrophied anal papilla and some degrees of anal contracture. *Fistula in ano,* a tract leading from the rectal lumen to the perianal skin, usually results from local crypt abscesses; fewer than 5 percent of such lesions found in medical practice in the United States are due to tuberculosis or cancer. The fistula is a chronically inflamed canal made up of fibrous tissue surrounding granulation tissue, the lumen of which may be difficult to demonstrate. Perirectal *abscesses* often represent the tracking down into the anal area of purulent material escaping from the rectosigmoid; diverticulitis, Crohn's disease, ulcerative colitis, or previous surgery may be the underlying cause. Fistulas between the rectum and vagina or the rectum and bladder represent serious complications of granulomatous, septic, or malignant disorders and require the patient to be hospitalized for definitive diagnostic and therapeutic procedures.

REFERENCES

Disorders of motility

BODE WE et al: Colonoscopic decompression for acute decompression of the colon. Am J Surg 147:243, 1984
LATIMER P et al: Colonic motor and myoelectric activity. Gastroenterology 80:893, 1981
PRESTON DM et al: Positive correlation between symptoms and circulating motilin, pancreatic polypeptide and gastrin concentrations in functional bowel disorders. Gut 26:1059, 1985
SCHUFFLER MD et al: Chronic intestinal pseudo-obstruction. Medicine 60:173, 1981

Intestinal ischemia

ABEL M et al: Ischemic colitis: Comparison of surgical and nonoperative management. Dis Colon Rectum 26:113, 1983
LEVINE D: Intestinal vascular ectasia. Am J Med 76:1151, 1984
MARSHAK RH et al: Ischemia of the colon. Mount Sinai J Med 48:108, 1981

Intestinal neoplasia

BURT RW et al: Upper gastrointestinal polyps in Gardner's syndrome. Gastroenterology 86:295, 1984
DECOSSE JJ: Malignant colorectal polyp. Gut 25:433, 1984
FLETCHER RH: Carcinoembryonic antigen. Ann Int Med 104:66, 1986
LIPKIN M, NEWMARK H: Effect of dietary calcium on colonic epithelial-cell proliferation in subjects at high risk for familial colonic cancer. N Engl J Med 313:1381, 1985
MATUCHANSKY C et al: Malignant lymphoma of the small bowel associated with diffuse nodular lymphoid hyperplasia. N Engl J Med 313:166, 1985
MOORE JR et al: Colorectal cancer: Risk factors and screening strategies. Arch Intern Med 144:1819, 1984
MORSON BC et al: Histopathology and prognosis of malignant colorectal polyps treated by endoscopic polypectomy. Gut 25:437, 1984
SIMON JB: Occult blood screening for colorectal carcinoma. A critical review. Gastroenterology 88:820, 1985

WEINGRAD DN et al: Primary gastrointestinal lymphoma. A 30 year review. Cancer 49:1258, 1982
WELLER IVD: The gay bowel. Gut 26:869, 1985

Other

GILINSKY NH et al: Plasma cell infiltration of the small bowel: Lack of evidence for a non-secretory form of alpha-heavy chain disease. Gut 26:928, 1985

---

240 ACUTE INTESTINAL OBSTRUCTION

WILLIAM SILEN

ETIOLOGY AND CLASSIFICATION Intestinal obstruction may be *mechanical* or *nonmechanical* (resulting from neuromuscular disturbances which produce either *adynamic* or *dynamic ileus*). The causes of mechanical obstruction of the lumen are conveniently divided into (1) lesions *extrinsic* to the intestine, e.g., adhesive bands, internal and external hernias; (2) lesions *intrinsic* to the wall of the intestine, e.g., diverticulitis, carcinoma, regional enteritis; and (3) obturation of the lumen, e.g., gallstone obstruction, intussusception. From the clinical standpoint, however, it is most useful to consider whether the obstructive mechanism involves the small or large intestine, because the causes, symptoms, and treatment are different (see below). Adhesions and external hernias are the most common causes of obstruction of the small intestine, constituting 70 to 75 percent of cases of this type. Adhesions, however, almost never produce obstruction of the colon, while carcinoma, sigmoid diverticulitis, and volvulus, in that order, are the most common etiologies and together account for about 90 percent of the cases.

Adynamic ileus is probably the most common overall cause of obstruction. Recent studies indicate that the development of this condition is mediated via the hormonal component of the sympathoadrenal system. Adynamic ileus will occur after any peritoneal insult, and its severity and duration will be dependent to some degree on the type of peritoneal injury. Hydrochloric acid, colonic contents, and pancreatic enzymes are among the most irritating substances, whereas blood and urine are less so. Adynamic ileus occurs to some degree after any abdominal operation, and its severity varies directly with the amount of intestinal handling and the length of the operation; it usually lasts 2 to 3 days after most operative procedures. Retroperitoneal hematomas, particularly associated with vertebral fracture, commonly cause severe adynamic ileus, and the latter may occur with other retroperitoneal conditions such as ureteral calculus or severe pyelonephritis. Thoracic diseases including lower-lobe pneumonia, fractured ribs, and myocardial infarction frequently produce adynamic ileus, as do electrolyte disturbances, particularly potassium depletion. Finally intestinal ischemia, whether the result of vascular occlusion or intestinal distention itself, may perpetuate an adynamic ileus. Spastic or dynamic ileus is very uncommon and results from extreme and prolonged contraction of the intestine. It has been observed in heavy metal poisoning, uremia, porphyria, and extensive intestinal ulcerations.

PATHOPHYSIOLOGY Distention of the intestine is caused by the accumulation of gas and fluid proximal to and within the obstructed segment. Seventy to eighty percent of intestinal gas consists of swallowed air, and because this is composed mainly of nitrogen, which is poorly absorbed from the intestinal lumen, removal of air by continuous gastric suction is an important adjunct in the treatment of intestinal distention. The accumulation of fluid proximal to the obstructing mechanism results not only from ingested fluid, swallowed saliva, gastric juice, and biliary and pancreatic secretions but also from interference with normal sodium and water transport. During the first 12 to 24 h of obstruction there is a marked depression of flux from lumen to blood of sodium and consequently water in the distended proximal intestine. After 24 h, there is also movement of sodium and water into the lumen, contributing further to the distention and fluid losses. Intraluminal pressure rises from a normal of 2 to 4 cmH_2O to 8 to 10 cmH_2O. During peristalsis, when simple obstruction or a ''closed loop'' is present, pressures reach 30 to 60 cmH_2O. Closed-loop obstruction of the small intestine results when the lumen is occluded at two points by a single mechanism such as a hernial ring or adhesive band, thus producing a closed loop whose blood supply is often obstructed at the same time. Strangulation of the loop itself is thus common in association with marked distention proximal to the involved loop. A form of closed-loop obstruction is encountered when complete obstruction of the colon exists in the presence of a competent ileocecal valve (85 percent of individuals). Although the blood supply of the colon is not entrapped within the obstructing mechanism, distention of the cecum is extreme because of its greater diameter (LaPlace's law), and impairment of the intramural blood supply is considerable with consequent gangrene of the cecal wall, usually anteriorly. Necrosis of the small intestine may occur by the same mechanism of interference with intramural blood flow when distention is extreme, but this sequence is uncommon in the small intestine. Once impairment of blood supply occurs, bacterial invasion supervenes and subsequent peritonitis develops. The systemic effects of extreme distention include elevation of the diaphragms with restricted ventilation and subsequent atelectasis. Venous return via the inferior vena cava may also be impaired.

The loss of fluids and electrolytes may be extreme, and unless replacement is prompt, leads to hemoconcentration, hypovolemia, renal insufficiency, shock, and death. Vomiting, accumulation of fluids within the lumen by the mechanisms described above, and the sequestration of fluid into the edematous intestinal wall and peritoneal cavity as a result of impairment of venous return from the intestine all contribute to massive loss of fluid and electrolytes. As soon as significant impedance to venous return is present, the intestine becomes severely congested, and blood begins to seep into the intestinal lumen. Blood loss may reach significant levels when long segments of intestine are involved.

SYMPTOMS *Mechanical small-intestinal obstruction* is characterized by cramping midabdominal pain which tends to be more severe the higher the obstruction. The pain occurs in paroxysms, and the patient is relatively comfortable in the intervals between the pains. Audible borborygmi are often noted by the patient simultaneously with the paroxysms of pain. The pain may become less severe as distention progresses, probably because motility is impaired in the edematous intestine. When strangulation is present, the pain is usually more localized and may be steady and severe without a colicky component, a fact which often causes delay in diagnosis of obstruction. Vomiting is almost invariable, and it is earlier and more profuse the higher the obstruction. The vomitus initially contains bile and mucus and remains as such if the obstruction is high in the intestine. With low ileal obstruction, the vomitus becomes feculent, i.e., orange-brown in color with a foul odor, which results from the overgrowth of bacteria proximal to the obstruction. Singultus is common. Obstipation and failure to pass gas by rectum are invariably present when the obstruction is complete, although some stool and gas may be passed spontaneously or after an enema shortly after onset of the complete obstruction. Diarrhea is occasionally observed in partial obstruction. Blood in the stool is rare, even in the completely obstructed patient, but does occur in cases of intussusception. Other than some minor but inconsistent differences in pain patterns noted above, the symptoms of strangulating obstructions cannot be distinguished from those of nonstrangulating obstructions.

Mechanical colonic obstruction produces colicky abdominal pain similar in quality to that of small-intestinal obstruction but of much lower intensity. Complaints of pain are occasionally absent in stoic elderly patients. Vomiting occurs late, if at all, particularly if the ileocecal valve is competent. Paradoxically, feculent vomitus is very rare. A history of recent alterations in bowel habits and blood in the stool is common because carcinoma and diverticulitis are the most frequent causes. Constipation becomes progressive, and obstipation with failure to pass gas ensues. Acute symptoms may develop over a period of a week.

In *adynamic ileus*, colicky pain is absent, and only discomfort from distention is evident. Vomiting may be frequent but is rarely profuse. It usually consists of gastric contents and bile and is almost never feculent. Complete obstipation may or may not occur. Singultus is very common.

PHYSICAL FINDINGS *Abdominal distention* is the hallmark of all forms of intestinal obstruction. It is least marked in cases of obstruction high in the small intestine and most marked in colonic obstruction. Early in the course of the disease, especially in closed-loop strangulating small-bowel obstruction, distention may be barely perceptible or absent. Tenderness and rigidity are usually minimal; the temperature is rarely above 100°F in nonstrangulating obstruction of the small and large intestine. Contrary to popular belief the same is true of strangulating obstruction until very late in the course of the disease, a fact which has often resulted in unfortunate delay in treatment. Signs and symptoms of shock also occur *very late* in strangulating obstruction. The appearance of shock, tenderness, rigidity, and fever often means that there has been contamination of the peritoneum with infected intestinal content. The presence of a palpable abdominal mass usually signifies a closed-loop strangulating small-bowel obstruction because the tense fluid-filled loop is the palpable lesion. Auscultation may reveal loud high-pitched borborygmi coincident with the colicky pain, but this classic finding is often not present late in strangulating or nonstrangulating obstruction. A quiet abdomen does not eliminate the possibility of obstruction, nor does it necessarily establish the diagnosis of adynamic ileus.

LABORATORY AND X-RAY FINDINGS Leukocytosis, with shift to the left, usually occurs when strangulation is present, but a normal white blood cell count does not exclude strangulation. Elevation of the serum amylase is encountered occasionally in all forms of intestinal obstruction, especially the strangulating variety.

The x-ray is extremely valuable but under certain circumstances may also be misleading. In nonstrangulating complete small-bowel obstruction, x-rays are almost completely reliable. Distention of fluid- and gas-filled loops of small intestine usually arranged in a ''step-ladder'' pattern with air-fluid levels and an absence or paucity of colonic gas are pathognomonic (Fig. 240-1). These findings, however, are absent in slightly over half the cases of strangulating small-bowel obstruction, especially early in the disease. A general haze due to peritoneal fluid and sometimes a ''coffee-bean''-shaped mass are seen in strangulating obstruction. Occasionally the films are normal, but when symptoms are consistent with obstruction of the small intestine, a normal film should suggest strangulation. Roentgenographic differentiation of partial mechanical small-bowel obstruction from adynamic ileus may be impossible since gas is present in both small and large intestine; however, colonic distention is usually more prominent in adynamic ileus. A radiopaque dye given by mouth is useful in making this distinction.

Colonic obstruction with a competent ileocecal valve is easily recognized because distention with gas is mainly confined to the colon. Barium enema, sigmoidoscopy, or colonoscopy, depending upon the suspected site of obstruction, are usually advisable to determine the nature of the lesion except when concomitant perforation is suspected, a rare occurrence. Sigmoidoscopy may be therapeutic in cases of sigmoid volvulus. When the ileocecal valve is incompetent, the films resemble those of partial small-bowel obstruction or adynamic ileus, and barium enema or colonoscopy is necessary to establish the correct diagnosis. Barium given by mouth is perfectly safe when obstruction is in the small intestine since the barium sulfate does not become inspissated in this location. *Barium should never be given by mouth to a patient with possible colonic obstruction* until that possibility has been excluded by barium enema.

PROGNOSIS AND TREATMENT **Small-intestinal obstruction** The overall mortality rate for obstruction of the small intestine is about

10 percent, even under the most optimal conditions. While the mortality rate for nonstrangulating obstruction is as low as 5 to 8 percent, that for strangulating obstruction has been reported to be between 20 and 75 percent. Well over half of the deaths from small-bowel obstruction occur in those with strangulation; however, the latter constitute only one-fourth to one-third of the cases. Careful studies indicate that the clinical, laboratory, and x-ray findings are not reliable in distinguishing strangulating from nonstrangulating obstruction when obstruction is complete. Complete obstruction is suggested when there has been a total cessation in the passage of gas or stool per rectum and when gas is absent in the distal intestine by x-ray. Since strangulating small-bowel obstruction is always complete, operation should always be undertaken in such patients after suitable preparation. Prior to operation, fluid and electrolyte balance should be restored, and decompression instituted by means of a nasogastric tube. Six to eight hours of preparation may be necessary. During this period broad-spectrum antibiotics are indicated if strangulation is felt to be likely, but operation should not be delayed unless there is unequivocal clinical and roentgenographic evidence of resolution of the obstruction during the period of preparation. Attempts to pass a long tube into the small intestine usually fail while putting the patient through uncomfortable unproductive manipulations which delay appropriate fluid replacement and decompression. *There are probably few if any indications for the use of a long intestinal tube.* Procrastination of operation because of improvement in well-being of the patient during resuscitation and gastric decompression usually leads to unnecessary and hazardous delay in proper treatment. Purely nonoperative therapy is safe only in the presence of incomplete obstruction and is best utilized in patients with (1) repeated episodes of partial obstruction, (2) recent postoperative partial obstruction, and (3) partial obstruction following a recent episode of diffuse peritonitis.

Colonic obstruction   The mortality rate for colonic obstruction is about 20 percent. As in small-bowel obstruction, nonoperative treatment is contraindicated unless the obstruction is incomplete. Occasionally, but not always, when the obstruction is incomplete,

FIGURE 240-1 *Acute mechanical obstruction of small intestine (upright film). Note air-fluid levels, marked distention of bowel loops, and absence of colonic gas.*

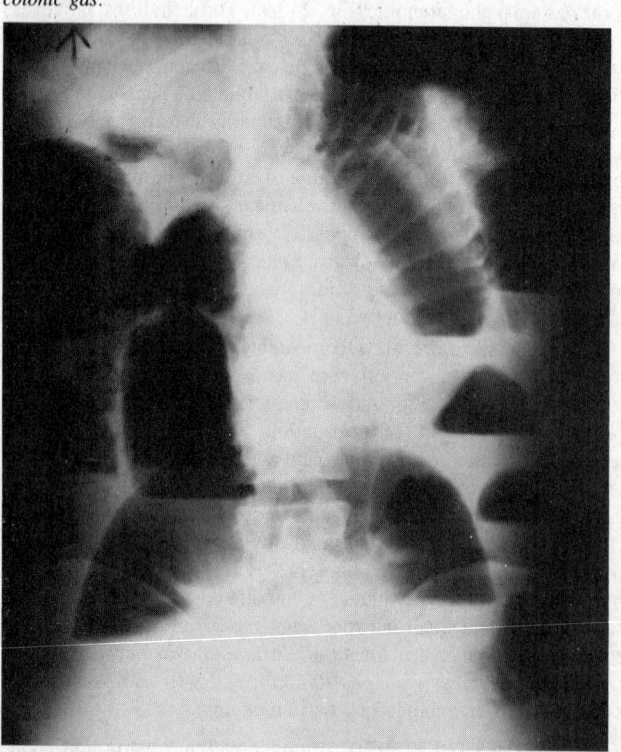

nonoperative therapy may result in sufficient decompression that a definitive operative procedure can be undertaken at a later date. This can usually be accomplished by discontinuation of all oral intake and perhaps by nasogastric suction, although attempts to decompress a *completely* obstructed colon by intubation are almost invariably futile. A long intestinal tube will not decompress an obstructed colon with a competent ileocecal valve. When obstruction is complete, early operation is mandatory, especially when the ileocecal valve is competent; cecal gangrene is likely if the cecal diameter exceeds 10 cm on plain abdominal film. For obstruction on the left side of the colon, the most common site, preliminary operative decompression by cecostomy or transverse colostomy followed by definitive resection of the primary lesion is the treatment of choice. For a lesion of the right or transverse colon, primary resection and anastomosis can safely be performed because distention of the ileum with consequent discrepancy in size and hazard in suture are not present.

Adynamic ileus   This type of ileus usually responds to nonoperative continuous decompression and adequate treatment of the primary disease. The prognosis is usually good. Rarely, adynamic colonic distention may become so great that cecostomy is required if cecal gangrene is feared. Spastic ileus usually responds to treatment of the primary disease.

REFERENCES

BECKER WF: Acute adhesive ileus: A study of 412 cases with particular reference to the abuse of tube decompression in treatment. Surg Gynecol Obstet 95:472, 1952
BULKLEY GB et al: Intraoperative determination of small intestinal viability following ischemic injury: Prospective controlled trial of two adjuvant methods (Doppler and fluorescein) compared with standard clinical judgement. Ann Surg 193:628, 1981
COHN I, ATIK M: Strangulation obstruction: Closed loop studies. Ann Surg 153:94, 1961
DUBOIS A et al: Postoperative ileus: Physiopathology, etiology and treatment. Ann Surg 178:781, 1973
GOUGH IR: Strangulating adhesive small bowel radiographs. Br J Surg 65:431, 1978
HOFSETTER SR: Acute adhesive obstruction of the small intestine. Surg Gynec Obstet 152:141, 1981
JACKSON BR: The diagnosis of colonic obstruction. Dis Colon Rectum 25:603, 1982
NOLAN DJ: Barium examination of the small intestine. Gut 22:682, 1981
SHIELDS R: The absorption and secretion of fluid and electrolytes by the obstructed bowel. Br J Surg 52:774, 1965
SILEN W: *Cope's Early Diagnosis of the Acute Abdomen*, 16th ed. London, Oxford, 1983

---

241   ACUTE APPENDICITIS

WILLIAM SILEN

INCIDENCE AND EPIDEMIOLOGY   The maximum incidence of acute appendicitis occurs in the second and third decades of life. While the disease may be encountered at any time of life, it is relatively rare at the extremes of age. Males and females are equally affected except between puberty and age 25, when males predominate in a 3:2 ratio. Perforation is relatively much more common in infancy and in the aged, during which periods mortality rates are highest. The mortality rate has decreased steadily in Europe and the United States from 8.1 per 100,000 of the population in 1941 to less than 1 per 100,000 in 1970. The absolute incidence of the disease also decreased by about 40 percent between 1940 and 1960 but since then has remained unchanged. Although various factors such as changing dietary habits, altered intestinal flora, and better nutrition and intake of vitamins have been suggested to explain the reduced incidence, the exact reasons have not been elucidated. Of interest is that the overall incidence of appendicitis is much lower in underdeveloped countries, especially parts of Africa, and in lower socioeconomic groups.

PATHOGENESIS The primary pathogenetic hallmark has always been thought to be luminal obstruction. While obstruction can be identified by careful examination in 30 to 40 percent of cases, recent studies have shown that ulceration of the mucosa is the initial event in the majority. The causation of the ulceration is unknown, although a viral etiology has been postulated. Whether the inflammatory reaction attendant with ulceration is sufficient to obstruct the tiny appendiceal lumen even transiently is also not clear. Obstruction, when present, is most commonly caused by a fecalith, which results from accumulation and inspissation of fecal matter around vegetable fibers. Enlarged lymphoid follicles associated with viral infections (e.g., measles), inspissated barium, worms (e.g., pinworms, *Ascaris,* and *Taenia*), and tumors (e.g., carcinoid or carcinoma) may also obstruct the lumen. Secretion of mucus distends the organ, which has a capacity of only 0.1 to 0.2 mL, and luminal pressures rise as high as 60 cmH$_2$O. Luminal bacteria multiply and invade the appendiceal wall as venous engorgement and subsequent arterial compromise result from the high intraluminal pressures. Finally, gangrene and perforation occur. If the process evolves slowly, adjacent organs such as the terminal ileum, cecum, and omentum may wall off the appendiceal area so that a localized abscess will develop, whereas rapid progression of vascular impairment may cause perforation with free access to the peritoneal cavity. Subsequent rupture of primary appendiceal abscesses may produce fistulas between the appendix and bladder, small intestine, sigmoid, or cecum. Occasionally, acute appendicitis may be the first manifestation of Crohn's disease. While chronic infection of the appendix with tuberculosis, amebiasis, and actinomycosis may occur, a useful clinical aphorism states that *chronic appendiceal inflammation is not usually the cause of prolonged abdominal pain of weeks' or months' duration.* In contrast, it is clear that recurrent acute appendicitis does occur, often with complete resolution of inflammation and symptoms between attacks. Recurrent acute appendicitis may become more frequent as antibiotics are dispensed more freely.

CLINICAL MANIFESTATIONS The history and sequence of symptoms are among the most important diagnostic features of appendicitis. The initial symptom is almost invariably *abdominal pain* of the visceral type, resulting from appendiceal contractions or distention of the lumen. It is usually poorly localized in the periumbilical or epigastric regions. There is often an accompanying urge to defecate or pass flatus, neither of which relieves the distress. This visceral pain is mild, often cramping, and rarely catastrophic in nature, usually lasting 4 to 6 h, but may not be noted by stoic individuals or by some patients during sleep. As inflammation spreads to the parietal peritoneal surfaces, the pain becomes somatic, steady, and more severe, aggravated by motion or cough and usually located in the *right lower quadrant. Anorexia* is so frequent that the presence of hunger should arouse serious suspicion of the diagnosis of acute appendicitis. *Nausea* and *vomiting* occur in 50 to 60 percent of cases, but vomiting is rarely profuse and protracted. The development of nausea and vomiting before the onset of pain is extremely rare. Change in bowel habit is of little diagnostic value since any or no alteration may be observed, although the presence of diarrhea caused by an inflamed appendix in juxtaposition to the sigmoid may cause serious diagnostic difficulties. Urinary frequency and dysuria occur if the appendix lies adjacent to the bladder. The typical sequence of symptoms (poorly localized periumbilical pain followed by nausea and vomiting with subsequent shift of pain to the right lower quadrant) occurs in only 50 to 60 percent of patients, and some variations are considered below.

Physical findings vary with time after onset of the illness and according to the location of the appendix, which may be situated deep in the pelvic cul-de-sac, in the right lower quadrant in any relation to the peritoneum, cecum, and small intestine, in the right upper quadrant, or even in the left lower quadrant. *The diagnosis cannot be established unless tenderness can be elicited.* While tenderness is sometimes absent in the early visceral stage of the disease, it ultimately always develops and is found in any location corresponding to the position of the appendix. Abdominal tenderness may be completely absent if a retrocecal or pelvic appendix is present, in which case the sole physical finding may be tenderness in the flank or on rectal or pelvic examination. Percussion, rebound tenderness, and referred rebound tenderness are often, but not invariably, present; they are most likely to be absent early in the illness. Flexion of the right hip and guarded movement by the patient are due to parietal peritoneal involvement. Hyperesthesia of the skin of the right lower quadrant and a positive psoas or obturator sign are often late findings and are rarely of diagnostic value. When the inflamed appendix is in close proximity to the anterior parietal peritoneum, muscular rigidity is present, yet is often minimal early. The temperature is usually normal or slightly elevated (99 to 100.5°F), but a temperature above 101°F should always suggest the presence of perforation. Tachycardia is commensurate with the elevation of the temperature. Rigidity and tenderness become more marked as the disease progresses to perforation and localized or diffuse peritonitis. Distention is rare unless severe diffuse peritonitis has developed. The alleged disappearance of pain and tenderness just prior to perforation is extremely unusual. A mass may develop if localized perforation has occurred but usually will not be detectable before 3 days after onset of the disease. Earlier presence of a mass suggests carcinoma of the cecum or Crohn's disease. Perforation is rare before 24 h after onset of symptoms, but the rate may be as high as 80 percent after 48 h.

Laboratory examination does not establish the diagnosis since the latter is based primarily on clinical grounds. Although moderate leukocytosis of 10,000 to 18,000 cells per cubic millimeter is frequent (with a concomitant shift to immature cells), the absence of leukocytosis does not eliminate the possibility of acute appendicitis. Leukocytosis of greater than 20,000 cells per cubic millimeter should alert the clinician to the probability of perforation. Anemia and blood in the stool suggest a primary diagnosis of carcinoma of the cecum, especially in elderly individuals. The urine may contain a few white or red blood cells without bacteria if the appendix lies close to the right ureter or bladder.

Urinalysis is most useful, however, in excluding genitourinary conditions which may mimic acute appendicitis. X-rays are rarely of value except when an opaque fecalith (5 percent of patients) is observed in the right lower quadrant (especially in children) together with other clinical findings consistent with appendicitis. Consequently there is no routine need to obtain films of the abdomen unless there is a possibility of other conditions such as intestinal obstruction or ureteral calculus. In some cases in which symptoms are either recurrent or more prolonged, a careful barium enema may disclose an extrinsic defect on the medial wall of the cecum or a calcified fecalith.

While the typical historical sequence and physical findings are present in 50 to 60 percent of cases, it is obvious that a wide variety of atypical patterns of disease are encountered, especially at the age extremes and during pregnancy. The 70 to 80 percent incidence of perforation and generalized peritonitis in infants under 2 years of age is dramatic testimony to the importance of the history in the early detection of the disease. Any infant or child with diarrhea, vomiting, and abdominal pain is highly suspect. Fever is much more common in this age group, and abdominal distention is often the only physical finding. In the elderly, pain and tenderness are often obtunded, and thus the diagnosis is frequently delayed. A 30 percent incidence of perforation in patients over 70 attests to the importance of this delay. Elderly patients often present themselves initially with a slightly painful mass (a primary appendiceal abscess), or sometimes appear with adhesive intestinal obstruction 5 or 6 days after a previously undetected perforated appendix. Appendicitis occurs about once in every 1000 pregnancies and is the most common extrauterine condition requiring abdominal operation. The diagnosis may be missed or delayed because of the frequent occurrence of mild abdominal discomfort and nausea and vomiting during pregnancy. During the last trimester when the mortality rate from appendicitis is highest, uterine displacement of the appendix to the right upper quadrant and laterally leads to confusion in diagnosis.

DIFFERENTIAL DIAGNOSIS   A listing of the differential diagnoses of acute appendicitis would produce an encyclopedic compendium of all conditions which cause abdominal pain since appendicitis may simulate any of these diseases. Diagnostic accuracy is about 75 to 80 percent for experienced clinicians and must be based solely on the clinical criteria outlined above. It is probably better to err slightly in the direction of overdiagnosis since delay is associated with perforation and increased morbidity and mortality. In unperforated appendicitis the mortality rate is 0.1 percent, little more than that associated with general anesthesia; for perforated appendicitis there is an overall mortality of 3 percent, a figure which increases to 15 percent in the elderly. In doubtful cases 4 to 6 h of observation is always more beneficial than harmful, however. The most common conditions discovered at operation when acute appendicitis is erroneously diagnosed are, in rough order of frequency, mesenteric lymphadenitis, no organic disease, acute pelvic inflammatory disease, ruptured graafian follicle or corpus luteum cyst, and acute gastroenteritis. In addition, acute cholecystitis, perforated ulcer, acute pancreatitis, acute diverticulitis, strangulating intestinal obstruction, ureteral calculus, and pyelonephritis frequently present diagnostic difficulties.

It is useful to consider separately some of the more common and difficult diagnostic possibilities, especially in the female. Differentiation of *pelvic inflammatory disease* from acute appendicitis may be virtually impossible. Gram-negative intracellular diplococci on cervical smear are not pathognomonic unless *Neisseria gonorrhea* can be cultured. Pain on movement of the cervix is not specific and may occur in appendicitis if perforation has occurred or if the appendix lies adjacent to the uterus or adnexa. *Rupture of a graafian follicle* (mittelschmerz) occurs at midcycle with spill of blood and fluid to produce pain and tenderness more diffuse and usually of a less severe degree than in appendicitis. Fever and leukocytosis are usually absent. *Rupture of a corpus luteum cyst* is identical clinically to rupture of a graafian follicle but develops about the time of menstruation. The presence of an adnexal mass and evidence of blood loss help differentiate *ruptured tubal pregnancy. Twisted ovarian cyst* and *endometriosis* occasionally are difficult to distinguish from appendicitis.

Acute mesenteric lymphadenitis is the appellation usually given when enlarged, slightly reddened lymph nodes at the root of the mesentery and a normal appendix are encountered at operation in a patient who usually has right lower quadrant tenderness and a somewhat higher temperature than most patients with acute appendicitis. Whether this is a single, discrete entity is unclear since the causative factor is not known. It has been recognized recently that some of these patients have infection with *Yersinia pseudotuberculosis* or *Y. enterocolytica* in which case the diagnosis can be established by culture of the mesenteric nodes or by serologic titers (Chap. 114). The diagnosis is essentially impossible clinically, although retrospectively there often appears to have been more diffuse pain and tenderness. Children seem to be affected more frequently than adults. Operation should be undertaken unless there is rapid resolution of all symptoms and findings. *Acute gastroenteritis* usually causes profuse watery diarrhea, often with nausea and vomiting but without localized findings. Between cramps, the abdomen is completely relaxed. In salmonella gastroenteritis the abdominal findings are similar, although the pain may be more severe and more localized, and fever and chills are common. The occurrence of similar symptoms among other members of the family may be helpful. When the diagnosis of acute pelvic appendicitis with perforation has been missed, gastroenteritis is the most common previous working diagnosis. Persistent abdominal or rectal tenderness should eliminate the diagnosis of gastroenteritis. *Regional enteritis* (Crohn's disease) is usually associated with a more prolonged history, often with previous exacerbations regarded by the patient or physician as episodes of gastroenteritis unless the diagnosis

has been established previously. *Meckel's diverticulitis* usually cannot be distinguished from acute appendicitis but is very rare.

TREATMENT   Cathartics and frequent enemas should be avoided if appendicitis is under consideration, and antibiotics should not be administered when the diagnosis is in question, as they will only mask the presence or development of perforation. The treatment is early operation and appendectomy as soon as the patient can be prepared. Preparation rarely takes more than 1 to 2 h in early appendicitis but may require 6 to 8 h in cases of severe sepsis and dehydration associated with late perforation. The *only* circumstance in which operation is *not* indicated is the presence of a palpable mass 3 to 5 days after the onset of symptoms. Should operation be undertaken at that time, a phlegmon rather than a definitive abscess will be found, and complications from dissection of such a phlegmon are frequent. Such patients treated with broad-spectrum antibiotics, parenteral fluids, and rest usually show resolution of the mass and symptoms within 1 week. *Interval appendectomy* can and should be done safely 3 months later. Should the mass enlarge or the patient become more toxic, drainage of the abscess is necessary. The complications of subphrenic, pelvic, or other intraabdominal abscesses usually follow perforation with generalized peritonitis and can be avoided by early diagnosis of the disease.

REFERENCES

BOLTON JP: Assessment of the value of the white cell count in management of suspected acute appendicitis. Br J Surg 62:906, 1975

BUSUTTIL RW et al: Effect of prophylactic antibiotics in acute nonperforated appendicitis: A prospective, randomized double-blind clinical study. Ann Surg 194:502, 1981

BUTLER C: Surgical pathology of acute appendicitis. Hum Pathol 12:870, 1981

KOEPSELL TD et al: Factors affecting perforation in acute appendicitis. Surg Gynecol Obstet 153:508, 1981

OWENS BJ III, HAMIT HF: Appendicitis in the elderly. Ann Surg 187:392, 1978

SAKOVER RP, DEL FAVA RL: Frequency of visualization of normal appendix with barium enema examination. Am J Roentgenol Rad Therap Nucl Med 121:312, 1974

THOMAS DR: Conservative management of appendix mass. Surgery 73:677, 1973

VANTRAPPEN G et al.: *Yersinia* enteritis and enterocolitis: Gastroenterological aspects. Gastroenterology 72:220, 1977

242   DISEASES OF THE PERITONEUM AND MESENTERY

KURT J. ISSELBACHER / J. THOMAS LaMONT

ACUTE PERITONITIS   Peritonitis is a localized or generalized inflammatory process of the peritoneum that may appear in both acute and chronic forms. In the acute form the motor activity of the intestine is decreased, and the intestinal lumen becomes distended with gas and fluid. Fluid accumulates as a result of failure to reabsorb the 7 or 8 liters normally secreted daily into the lumen and absorbed from the distal small bowel and colon. There is also accumulation of fluid in the peritoneal cavity as well as decreased oral intake. These combined losses can lead to rapid depletion of the plasma volume with impaired cardiac and renal function.

Etiology   Peritonitis may be due to entry of bacteria into the peritoneal cavity from a perforation in the gastrointestinal tract or from an external penetrating wound. It may be secondary to severe chemical reactions from the release of pancreatic enzymes, the digestive juices of the upper gastrointestinal tract, or bile as a result of injury or perforation of the intestine or biliary tract. Patients with systemic lupus erythematosus may have bouts of peritonitis during attacks of their disease.

The most common causes of bacterial peritonitis are appendicitis, perforations associated with diverticulitis, peptic ulcer, gangrenous gallbladder, and gangrenous obstruction of the small bowel from adhesive bands, incarcerated hernia, or volvulus. Any lesion leading to the escape of intestinal bacteria may be a source, including a perforating carcinoma, foreign body, and ulcerative colitis. The peritoneal cavity is remarkably resistant to contamination, and unless continuing contamination occurs, the disease process becomes localized. Patients with alcoholic cirrhosis and ascites have an increased susceptibility to spontaneous bacterial peritonitis, usually from enteric pathogens. This complication occurs in the absence of recognizable perforation of a viscus, and may be due to leakage of bacteria through the intestinal wall.

Clinical features These usually consist of increasing abdominal pain, distention, nausea and vomiting, inability to pass feces or flatus, fever, hypotension, tachycardia, thirst, and oliguria. On physical examination the patient appears acutely ill and febrile and has a variable degree of abdominal distention. The abdomen is usually acutely tender and tympanitic, often with rebound tenderness. The location of the pain and tenderness depends on the underlying cause and whether the inflammation is localized or generalized. In *localized* peritonitis, as seen in uncomplicated appendicitis or diverticulitis, the physical findings are limited to the area of inflammation. With widespread peritoneal inflammation there is *generalized* peritonitis with diffuse abdominal tenderness and rebound. Rigidity of the abdominal wall is a common finding in peritonitis and may be localized or generalized.

Peristalsis may be present initially but usually disappears as the illness progresses. Hypotension is common, as is leukocytosis, which often is greater than 20,000 cells per cubic millimeter. Plain abdominal films may reveal dilatation of the large and small bowel with edema of the small-bowel wall as evidenced by the distance between adjacent loops of gas-filled small intestine. Diagnostic paracentesis is sometimes valuable in determining the nature of the exudate as well as whether bacteria can be demonstrated or cultured. Diabetic ketoacidosis, lead colic, gastric crises of syphilis, and acute porphyria may cause severe abdominal symptoms that resemble the picture of acute peritonitis.

GONOCOCCAL PERITONITIS This usually involves an extension of gonococcal infection from a primary focus in the female reproductive tract. The signs of inflammation usually are limited to the pelvis, but there may be findings of a mild generalized peritonitis. Occasionally the patient has right upper quadrant pain and tenderness caused by gonococcal perihepatitis involving the liver capsule and adjacent peritoneum (Fitz-Hugh–Curtis syndrome; see also Chap. 104).

STARCH PERITONITIS An acute granulomatous peritonitis can develop in some patients as a foreign-body reaction to cornstarch used to powder surgical gloves. The clinical picture is that of acute abdominal pain and fever 10 to 30 days after an abdominal operation. The diagnosis can be made by paracentesis and demonstration of starch granules in monocytes. However, most patients are reexplored because of the fear of abscess or bacterial peritonitis, with the finding of foreign-body granuloma studding the peritoneum.

PSEUDOMYXOMA PERITONEI This is a rare condition resulting from rupture of a mucocele of the appendix or of a mucinous ovarian cyst. The abdomen becomes filled with masses of jelly-like material. Occasionally, with removal of the mucocele or the ovarian cyst and most of the myxomatous material, a cure may ensue. In other cases, however, the mucoid material recurs, leading to progressive wasting and eventual death. Colloid carcinoma arising from the stomach or colon with peritoneal implants may resemble pseudomyxoma at laparotomy. The course of this type of highly malignant tumor is one of rapid cachexia and early death. The diagnosis can usually be made by the appearance of many highly malignant cells in the peritoneal implants.

CANCER OF THE PERITONEUM Aside from mesothelioma, which in most patients is caused by previous exposure to asbestos, cancer of the peritoneum is usually secondary to a neoplasm within the abdomen, most commonly of the stomach and ovary. This type of metastatic malignancy is invariably associated with progressive ascites with a high specific gravity and high protein content, often with large numbers of red blood cells or even gross blood. The diagnosis is established by demonstrating malignant cells in the fluid. The clinical progress of this malignant spread can sometimes be arrested by installations of radioactive gold, nitrogen mustard, or chloroquine.

FAMILIAL MEDITERRANEAN FEVER See Chap. 271.

PNEUMATOSIS CYSTOIDES INTESTINALIS This is a condition in which multiple gas-filled blebs or cysts accumulate in the intestinal wall beneath the serosal surface of the bowel. The exact source of the gas has not been explained satisfactorily. In some instances, this disease is associated with specific ulceration of the intestinal mucosa, in particular peptic ulcer with outlet obstruction. Cysts in the wall of the small bowel are seen as an occasional complication of mesenteric vascular occlusion. In the large bowel, these cysts are usually benign, may be seen with a variety of other disorders, and usually disappear in time.

There are no specific physical findings secondary to the pneumatosis, and the diagnosis is made either by x-ray or at laparotomy. Occasionally the subserosal cysts may rupture, resulting in pneumoperitoneum.

CHYLOUS ASCITES This term refers to the accumulation of chyle (intestinal lymph) in the peritoneal cavity. The condition is sometimes associated with chylothorax. The fluid in the peritoneal cavity appears milky or creamy because of the presence of chylomicrons. This fat may be demonstrated microscopically by staining with Sudan III and may be removed by acidification of the fluid followed by extraction with ether. The chyle (lipid) will then go into the ether phase. Many conditions may be associated with the cloudy or milky-appearing peritoneal fluid, so-called pseudochylous ascites. The milky or turbid appearance is usually due to the presence of protein and desquamated cells. The turbidity of this fluid will not be removed with the ether but will clear with addition of alkali.

The causes of chylous ascites include (1) penetrating or nonpenetrating trauma that damages the main duct in the lymphatic system within the abdomen, (2) intestinal obstruction if it is associated with rupture of a major lymphatic channel, (3) congenital lymphangiectasia, (4) malignant disease or tuberculous infection that obstructs the intestinal lymphatics, (5) filariasis, or (6) cirrhosis.

The sudden accumulation of chyle in the peritoneal cavity often results in abdominal pain, signs of peritoneal irritation, and leukocytosis. These symptoms gradually subside, leaving the patient with a distended but nontender, fluid-filled abdomen. Lymphangiography is of value in determining the location of the leak or site of obstruction to the lymphatic channels. The course depends upon the underlying etiologic factors.

MESENTERIC LIPODYSTROPHY This is a rare disorder usually affecting middle-aged women and characterized pathologically by infiltration of the mesentery with lipid-laden macrophages and fibrous tissue. These patients present with ill-defined abdominal pain and occasionally an abdominal mass. The diagnosis is made at laparotomy by demonstration of thick fibrofatty masses at the root of the mesentery with retraction and distortion of the bowel loops.

REFERENCES

HOEFS JC et al: Spontaneous bacterial peritonitis. Hepatology 2:1054, 1982

KIPFER RE et al: Mesenteric lipodystrophy. Ann Intern Med 80:582, 1974

LIMBER GK et al: Pseudomyxoma peritonei. Ann Surg 1978:587, 1973

PRESS OW et al: Evaluation and management of chylous ascites. Ann Intern Med 96:358, 1982

SCHWARTZ SI et al: *Principles of Surgery*, 3d ed. New York, McGraw-Hill, 1979

WARSHAW AL: Diagnosis of starch peritonitis by paracentesis. Lancet 2:1054, 1972

243 APPROACH TO THE PATIENT WITH LIVER DISEASE

KURT J. ISSELBACHER

GENERAL CONSIDERATIONS While disease of the liver or biliary tract may be directly responsible for the symptoms that bring the patient to the physician, examination for nonhepatic complaints may occasionally provide the clues to otherwise asymptomatic or occult hepatobiliary disease. Liver function studies and other diagnostic procedures such as biopsy (as discussed in Chap. 245) are crucial, but much valuable information as to the possible nature and extent of liver disease can be obtained by a carefully elicited history and thorough physical examination.

Importance of clinical history Since laboratory tests often do not establish the specific cause of liver disease, the history is of the greatest significance. *Family history* is important with respect to jaundice, anemia, splenectomy, or cholecystectomy; a positive history may be helpful in diagnosing hemolytic anemia, congenital or familial hyperbilirubinemia, or gallstones. In Wilson's disease (hepatolenticular degeneration), there may be a family history of tremor or neurologic abnormalities. *Occupation* should be reviewed in detail, and *environmental factors* need to be examined. Note should be made of any contact with rats or other animals possibly carrying Weil's disease and of exposure to toxins such as carbon tetrachloride, beryllium, or vinyl chloride. The patient should be asked about travel to other countries, especially to areas where hepatitis may be endemic. Careful questioning regarding alcohol intake is important in most cases. Since the alcoholic often denies or understates the amounts consumed, it is desirable to check the validity of the history with close friends or relatives of the patient.

Contact with jaundiced patients (including intimate or sexual relations) should be noted. If the patient has had any *injections* in the previous 6 months, hepatitis B or non-A, non-B infection may be the underlying disease. Injections include blood tests, blood or plasma transfusions, tattooing, and dental treatment. The patient should be asked about narcotics, hallucinogens, or stimulant *drugs* taken parenterally, as well as about agents taken orally, such as chlorpromazine or estrogen-containing drugs known to affect liver function.

A previous history of indigestion and right upper quadrant pain suggests cholelithiasis or choledocholithiasis. Jaundice following shortly after operation on the biliary tract suggests residual stone, that which occurs within 6 months suggests hepatitis B or posttransfusion hepatitis, and that occurring after 1 or more years may be due to stricture of the common bile duct. Postoperative jaundice may be due to the anesthetic, especially after multiple uses of halothane, or to the impaired hepatic excretory function resulting from relative hypoxemia of liver cells during the operative or postoperative period.

The *onset of the illness* should be noted. The relatively abrupt onset of nausea, anorexia, and aversion to smoking followed by progressive jaundice suggests viral hepatitis. A gradual development of jaundice associated with pruritus suggests cholestasis. Intermittent right upper quadrant abdominal pain followed by cholestatic jaundice points to gallstone disease, while the gradual onset of painless jaundice with weight loss is suggestive of tumor, such as carcinoma of the head of the pancreas. Jaundice associated with fever and chills makes cholangitis and extrahepatic biliary obstruction likely possibilities.

The patient with hepatitis generally feels ill, and dark urine and light stools occur before the appearance of scleral or skin icterus. In cholestatic hepatitis, the patient may feel relatively well and complain only of symptoms due to the obstruction, such as pruritus.

Physical examination Jaundice is looked for in the sclera as well as the skin. Pallor indicative of anemia may be a reflection of hemolysis, cirrhosis, or neoplasm. Significant cachexia, especially of the extremities, may be associated with cancer or active cirrhosis. In the alcoholic, one should look for stigmas of cirrhosis such as parotid gland enlargement, Dupuytren's contracture, gynecomastia, testicular atrophy, and diminished axillary or pubic hair.

The *skin examination* may reveal ecchymoses due to prothrombin deficiency, or purpura due to thrombocytopenia. *Palmar erythema* or *spider angiomas* may reflect acute or chronic liver disease. Spider angiomas are usually found above the umbilicus and especially on the face, neck, shoulders, forearms, and dorsum of the hands. The presence of a few spider angiomas is not abnormal in women, especially during pregnancy. However, their appearance in men is always abnormal and should be carefully searched for. In chronic cholestasis, *scratch marks, finger clubbing,* and *xanthoma* of the eyelids and extensor surfaces of the tendons of the wrists and ankles may be found. A *slate color* to the skin due to increased melanin should suggest the presence of hemochromatosis.

Evaluation of the *mental state* and *neurologic function* is important. Slight deterioration of the intellect and minimal personality changes may suggest hepatocellular disease or the presence of portal-systemic venous shunts, but care must be taken to exclude other causes such as neurologic disease. The presence of flapping tremor of the hands (asterixis) may be found in association with portal-systemic encephalopathy or impending hepatic coma.

Abdominal examination may reveal ascites, which, together with dilatated periumbilical veins, suggests cirrhosis and extensive portal collateral circulation. A very large nodular and rock-hard liver suggests the presence of hepatoma or hepatic metastases. Careful percussion is necessary to evaluate the size of a nonpalpable liver. A small liver may indicate cirrhosis (especially postnecrotic); a small liver which diminishes in size suggests severe hepatitis or massive hepatic necrosis. In the alcoholic, fatty infiltration and cirrhosis often produce a uniform enlargement of the liver. The liver edge is tender in hepatitis, in congestive heart failure, and occasionally in malignant disease and with alcoholism (especially "alcoholic hepatitis").

A palpable and sometimes visibly enlarged gallbladder (Courvoisier's sign) suggests extrahepatic biliary obstruction often due to pancreatic cancer. A tender gallbladder and positive Murphy's sign suggests cholelithiasis or choledocholithiasis. A palpable spleen may indicate hepatitis or cirrhosis; significant splenomegaly may be a reflection of portal hypertension.

Abdominal auscultation may reveal the presence of a venous hum over dilatated collateral veins radiating from the umbilicus, the so-called caput medusae. In advanced cirrhosis this venous hum is virtually diagnostic of significant portal hypertension. A bruit may sometimes be heard over large regenerating nodules in cirrhosis and occasionally over hepatomas and metastatic nodules in the liver. The presence of a friction rub strongly suggests neoplastic disease or a hepatic abscess. A friction rub may occasionally be heard over hepatomas and metastatic liver nodules.

Liver function tests Serum assays for biochemical markers of liver disease are an integral part of the proper evaluation of liver and biliary tract disease. In general, the serum bilirubin is measured to confirm the presence and severity of the jaundice and determine the degree of bilirubin conjugation. Aminotransferase (transaminase) elevations reflect the severity of active hepatocellular damage, and the alkaline phosphatase elevations are found with cholestasis and hepatic infiltrates. Serum albumin and the prothrombin time are determined as indexes of hepatic synthetic function. These and other tests are reviewed in Chaps. 38 and 245.

Diagnostic procedures (see Chap. 245) The further evaluation of patients with hepatobiliary disease should be individualized depending on the history, physical findings, and initial screening laboratory tests. Hepatocellular disease such as hepatitis is often sufficiently clear so that no additional tests are needed. However in severe, chronic, or ambiguous cases, computerized tomography (CT), ultrasound, scintiscans, or liver biopsy may be needed to determine the nature of the liver disease. When hepatic tumors are suspected, CT, ultrasound, or scintiscan may be performed followed by liver biopsy, angiography, or laparoscopy for a more specific diagnosis. When biliary obstruction is suspected, the first examination is usually an ultrasound study to determine the size of the bile ducts, whether gallstones are present, or whether there is the suggestion of a mass in the head of the pancreas. Frequently more information is needed and thus a percutaneous endoscopic cholangiogram or exploratory laparotomy may be performed.

CLASSIFICATION OF LIVER DISEASE The classification of the various types of liver disease has been difficult because in many instances the etiology and pathogenetic mechanism are obscure. As a consequence, one finds an abundance of labels and names applied to hepatic disorders. Some individuals use the term *hepatitis* to imply viral infection, others simply to connote evidence of hepatic inflammation. One finds ambiguity in the use of the words *acute, subacute,* and *chronic. Chronicity* should refer to continuing or recurrent disease (i.e., duration). *Activity* should refer to evidence of the presence of perpetuation of liver cell injury; this is most readily identified on

TABLE 243-1 Classification of liver disease

I Parenchymal
  A Hepatitis (viral, drug-induced, toxic)
    1 Acute
    2 Chronic (persistent or active)
  B Cirrhosis
    1 Alcoholic (portal, nutritional, Laennec's cirrhosis)
    2 Postnecrotic
    3 Biliary
    4 Hemochromatosis
    5 Rare types (e.g., Wilson's disease, galactosemia, cystic fibrosis of pancreas, alpha$_1$-antitrypsin deficiency)
  C Infiltrations
    1 Glycogen
    2 Fat (neutral fat, cholesterol, gangliosides, cerebrosides)
    3 Amyloid
    4 Lymphoma, leukemia
    5 Granuloma (e.g., sarcoidosis, tuberculosis, idiopathic)
  D Space-occupying lesions
    1 Hepatoma, metastatic tumor
    2 Abscess (pyogenic, amoebic)
    3 Cysts (polycystic disease, *Echinococcus*)
    4 Gummas
  E Functional disorders associated with jaundice
    1 Gilbert's syndrome
    2 Crigler-Najjar syndrome
    3 Dubin-Johnson and Rotor syndromes
    4 Cholestasis of pregnancy and benign recurrent cholestasis
II Hepatobiliary
  A Extrahepatic biliary obstruction (by stone, stricture, or tumor)
  B Cholangitis
III Vascular
  A Chronic passive congestion and cardiac cirrhosis
  B Hepatic vein thrombosis (Budd-Chiari syndrome)
  C Portal vein thrombosis
  D Pylephlebitis
  E Arteriovenous malformations

biopsy by the degree of hepatocellular necrosis and by serum transaminase elevations.

Because of the difficulties involved in defining the etiology of many types of liver disease, in most instances the process is best defined and described by an examination of the morphologic character of the lesion. Therefore, a *morphologic classification* of liver disease, as outlined in Table 243-1, appears at present more practical than one based on etiology.

REFERENCES

SCHIFF L: *Diseases of the Liver,* 5th ed. Philadelphia, Lippincott, 1982
SHERLOCK S: *Diseases of the Liver and Biliary System,* 7th ed. Philadelphia, Davis, 1985
WRIGHT R et al: *Liver and Biliary Disease,* 2d ed. Philadelphia, Saunders, 1985

244 DERANGEMENTS OF HEPATIC METABOLISM

DANIEL K. PODOLSKY / KURT J. ISSELBACHER

The liver plays a central role in the maintenance of metabolic homeostasis. It is therefore not surprising that the development of clinically important liver disease is accompanied by diverse systemic manifestations of disordered metabolism. The liver has considerable reserve capacity, so minimal or even moderate cell injury may not be reflected by measurable changes in its metabolic function. However, some functions of the liver are more sensitive than others, and a variety of defects may be seen, depending on the nature and extent of the initial insult.

The biochemical functions in which the liver plays a major role include (1) the intermediate metabolism of amino acids and carbohydrates, (2) synthesis and degradation of proteins and glycoproteins, (3) metabolism and degradation of drugs and hormones, and (4) regulation of lipid and cholesterol metabolism. The derangements of these functions are discussed in connection with their occurrence in various forms of parenchymal liver disease. Alterations of bilirubin, bile salt, and porphyrin metabolism are discussed elsewhere (Chaps. 37, 237, 312).

Metabolic derangements are most evident in the patient with advanced liver disease, and the manifestations are similar regardless of the initial etiologic insult. To a varying degree similar abnormalities are observed in patients with severe chronic hepatitis, micronodular cirrhosis, and postnecrotic cirrhosis. Since the many functions of the liver may be affected to varying degrees in individual patients, no single test effectively measures the overall state of liver function. The proper interpretation of liver function tests is discussed in Chap. 245.

CARBOHYDRATE METABOLISM The liver functions to maintain normal levels of blood sugar by a combination of glycogenesis, glycogenolysis, glycolysis, and gluconeogenesis. These pathways are regulated by a number of hormones including insulin, glucagon, growth hormone, and certain catecholamines. Although it has been presumed that exquisite sensitivity of the hepatocytes to insulin is responsible for the uptake of an oral glucose load by the liver, there are also data that have challenged the importance of insulin-mediated glucose uptake by the hepatocyte. In the fasting state, the liver contributes to glucose homeostasis by glycogenolysis and gluconeogenesis in response to hypoinsulinemia and hyperglucagonemia. Maintenance of normal blood glucose levels through gluconeogenesis is ultimately related to catabolism of muscle protein, which provides the necessary amino acid precursors, especially alanine. In a complementary fashion, in the postprandial state, the liver directs alanine and branched-chain amino acids to the peripheral tissues, where they are then incorporated into muscle protein. These reciprocal pathways form a glucose-alanine shuttle which is modulated by ambient changes in the hormones mentioned above (Fig. 244-1). While it has been presumed that synthesis of glycogen and fatty acid in the postprandial state arises from direct conversion of glucose, there are data to suggest that, in fact, these pathways are *indirect* with products deriving from 3-carbon metabolites of glucose or other gluconeogenic compounds such as lactate, fructose, and alanine.

Abnormalities of glucose homeostasis are common in cirrhosis (Table 244-1). Most frequently hyperglycemia and glucose intolerance are observed. Glucose intolerance is associated with normal or increased levels of plasma insulin (except in patients with hemochromatosis), suggesting that insulin resistance rather than insulin deficiency may be responsible. One of the factors that may play a role in the apparent insulin resistance is an absolute decrease in the liver's ability to metabolize a glucose load because of a decrease in functioning hepatocellular mass. There is also evidence that response to insulin is diminished due to both receptor and postreceptor defects in hepatocytes of patients with cirrhosis. In addition, both hyperinsulinemia and hyperglucagonemia may be present due to decreased hepatic clearance of this hormone resulting from portal-systemic shunting. In patients with hemochromatosis, insulin levels, however, may indeed be low due to pancreatic iron deposition and sometimes concomitant genetic diabetes mellitus. Patients with cirrhosis may also have elevated serum lactate levels reflecting the decreased capacity of the liver to utilize lactate for gluconeogenesis.

Hypoglycemia, although more common in acute fulminant hepatitis, may also be seen with end-stage cirrhosis. Glycogen in the liver accounts for 5 to 7 percent of the normal tissue weight. Because the capacity of the liver to store glycogen is limited (approximately 70 g) and glucose consumption continues at a constant rate (approximately 150 g per day), hepatic glycogen stores are depleted after 1 day of fasting. Hypoglycemia in end-stage cirrhosis may be due to decreased hepatic glycogen stores, diminished glucagon responsiveness, or decreased capacity to synthesize glycogen due to extensive parenchymal destruction.

AMINO ACID AND AMMONIA METABOLISM   Through a variety of anabolic and catabolic processes, the liver is the major site of amino acid interconversion. Amino acids utilized for hepatic protein synthesis are derived from dietary protein, metabolic turnover of endogenous protein (primarily from muscle), and direct synthesis in the liver. Most of the amino acids entering the liver via the portal vein are catabolized to urea (except for the branched-chain amino acids leucine, isoleucine, and valine). A lesser amount is released into the general circulation as free amino acids, and these may play an important role in the glucose-alanine cycle mentioned above. In addition, amino acids are utilized for the synthesis of liver intracellular proteins, plasma proteins, and special compounds such as glutathione, glutamine, taurine, carnosine, and creatine. Disruption of normal amino acid metabolism may be reflected in altered plasma amino acid concentrations. In general, levels of aromatic amino acids normally metabolized by the liver (as well as methionine) are elevated, while those of the branched-chain amino acids, largely utilized by skeletal muscle, tend to be normal or depressed. It has been suggested that an alteration in the ratio of these two types of amino acids plays a role in the development of hepatic encephalopathy (see below), but there is not agreement on this concept.

Hepatic catabolism or degradation of amino acids involves two major reactions: transamination and oxidative deamination. Transamination, the process by which the amino group of an amino acid is transferred to a keto acid, is catalyzed by aminotransferases. These enzymes are found in very high amounts in liver but are also present in other tissues, such as kidney, muscle, heart, lung, and brain. Glutamic-oxaloacetic acid transaminase (aspartate aminotransferase, AST) has been studied most extensively, and increased levels are found in the serum secondary to various types of liver injury (e.g., acute viral and drug-induced hepatitis). As a result of transamination, amino acids can enter the citric acid cycle and then function in the intermediary metabolism of carbohydrates and lipids. Most of the nonessential amino acids are also synthesized in the liver by transamination. Oxidative deamination, which results in conversion of amino acids to keto acids (and ammonia), is catalyzed by L-amino-acid oxidase with two exceptions: glycine oxidation is catalyzed by glycine oxidase, and glutamic oxidation is catalyzed by glutamic dehydrogenase. With severe liver damage (e.g., massive hepatic necrosis), utilization of amino acids is impaired, free amino acids in the bloodstream increase, and an "overflow" type of aminoaciduria may occur.

Urea production is intimately related to the metabolic pathways outlined above, providing a means for disposal of ammonia, the toxic product of nitrogen metabolism. Disruption of this process is of particular clinical importance in the patient with severe acute and

FIGURE 244-1 *Carbohydrate-protein exchange between muscle and liver. After an overnight fast there is net release of amino acids by muscle (predominantly alanine and glutamine). These are derived from transamination of pyruvate, degraded amino acids, and glucose. Branched-chain amino acids (BCAA) are particularly important as a source of nitrogen for alanine synthesis. Alanine is utilized for gluconeogenesis by the liver, and urea is formed as a by-product. The main sites of glutamine uptake are the kidney and gut, where it is used for ammonia production and as a possible source of energy, respectively. Following ingestion of dietary protein, skeletal muscle goes into an anabolic phase; there is selective hepatic escape and muscle uptake of dietary BCAA, reduced muscle output of alanine and glutamine, and a reduced rate of hepatic gluconeogenesis. Hepatic tissue protein also goes into an anabolic phase following protein ingestion.*

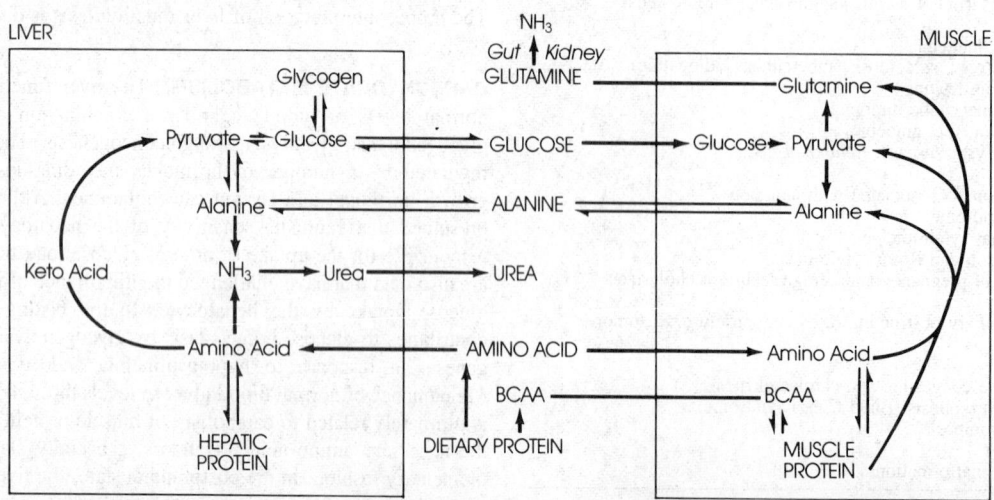

chronic liver disease. The fixation of amino acid–derived NH_3 in the form of urea is carried out via the Krebs-Henseleit cycle. The final step of this cycle, the formation of urea by arginase, is irreversible. In advanced liver disease urea synthesis is often depressed, leading to an accumulation of NH_3, usually with a significant reduction in blood urea nitrogen (BUN), an ominous sign of liver failure. This finding may be obscured by superimposed renal impairment, which often develops in patients with severe hepatic failure. Urea is mostly excreted by the kidney, but approximately 25 percent will diffuse into the intestine where it is converted to NH_3 by bacterial urease. The intestinal production of ammonia also occurs from the bacterial deamination of unabsorbed amino acids and of protein derived from the diet, exfoliated cells, or blood in the gastrointestinal tract.

Gut NH_3 is absorbed and transported to the liver via the portal vein, where it is again converted to urea. The kidney also produces varying amounts of NH_3, largely by the deamination of glutamine. The contributions of the gut and kidney to ammonia synthesis have important implications for the management of the hyperammonemic state frequently seen in patients with advanced liver disease usually in association with portal-systemic shunting of blood.

While the exact chemical mediators of hepatic encephalopathy remain unknown, elevated levels of blood NH_3 generally correlate with the degree of encephalopathy, although approximately 10 percent of such patients have normal levels of blood ammonia. In addition, therapeutic measures that reduce serum NH_3 levels also usually lead to clinical improvement. The several mechanisms known to lead to increased blood NH_3 levels in patients with cirrhosis are illustrated in Fig. 244-2 and include the following: (1) If there is excessive nitrogenous material in the intestine (from bleeding or dietary protein), excessive amounts of NH_3 will be formed by bacterial deamination of amino acids. (2) If renal function declines (as in the hepatorenal syndrome), blood urea nitrogen rises, leading to increased diffusion of urea into the intestinal lumen, where bacterial urease converts it to NH_3. (3) If hepatic function is significantly depressed, diminished urea synthesis may occur with a resultant decrease in the removal of NH_3. (4) If alkalosis (often due to central hyperventilation) and hypokalemia accompany hepatic decompensation, there may be a decrease in the renal availability of H^+ ions; as a result, the NH_3 produced from glutamine by the action of renal glutaminase is permitted to enter the renal vein (rather than being excreted as NH_4^+) leading to increased peripheral blood NH_3 levels. In addition hypokalemia itself leads to increased NH_3 production. (5) If portal hypertension is present and anastomoses exist between the portal vein and systemic venous channels, these portal-systemic shunts will allow NH_3 from the gut to bypass hepatic detoxification, leading to elevated blood NH_3 levels. Thus, with portal-systemic shunting of blood, elevated NH_3 levels may develop even with relatively little hepatocellular dysfunction.

An additional factor important in determining whether a given NH_3 level in the blood will be detrimental to the central nervous system is the blood pH. The more alkaline the pH, the more toxic a given level of NH_3 is likely to be. At 37°C the pK of NH_3 is 8.9;

this is close enough to the pH of blood so that minor changes in pH can affect the NH_4^+/NH_3 ratio. Because un-ionized NH_3 crosses membranes more readily than NH_4^+ ions, alkalosis favors the entry of ammonia into the brain (with subsequent changes in cell metabolism) by shifting the equilibrium of the following reaction to the right

$$NH_4^+ + OH^- \rightleftharpoons NH_3 + HOH$$

As a result, alkalosis not only increases peripheral blood NH_3 levels by renal mechanisms but also increases tissue levels by influencing the diffusion of NH_3 across membranes.

PROTEIN SYNTHESIS AND DEGRADATION The liver is an important site of protein synthesis and degradation. Although the body muscle mass produces the greatest total amount of protein, the liver has the highest rate of synthesis per gram of tissue. The liver synthesizes not only the proteins it needs, but also and perhaps more importantly it produces numerous export proteins. Among the latter, albumin is the most important; *it is produced at a rate of approximately 12 g per day,* representing 25 percent of total hepatic protein synthesis and half of all exported protein. The average normal half-life of serum albumin is 17 to 20 days. The proportion of hepatocytes carrying out active albumin synthesis varies from 10 to 60 percent depending on the body's requirements. Approximately 60 percent of albumin is found in the extravascular spaces, but plasma albumin is still the most abundant circulating protein. Although albumin secreted by the hepatocytes lacks significant carbohydrate, it may undergo nonenzymatic glycosylation in the circulation as a reflection of ambient serum glucose concentrations.

Albumin contributes significantly to the plasma oncotic pressure. In addition, it is the principal binding and transport protein for numerous substances including some hormones, fatty acids, trace metals, tryptophan, bilirubin, and other organic anions of both endogenous and exogenous origin. Despite the many important functions of albumin, rare individuals with congenital analbuminemia appear to have no major physiologic derangements other than the excessive accumulation of extravascular fluid. While many of the less hydrophobic ligands may be transported in the unbound form, this suggests that other serum proteins may also play a role in binding and transport.

FIGURE 244-2 *Major factors (steps 1 to 4) influencing the level of blood ammonia. In cirrhosis with portal hypertension, venous collaterals allow ammonia to bypass the liver (step 5), permitting the entry of ammonia into the systemic circulation (portal-systemic shunting).*

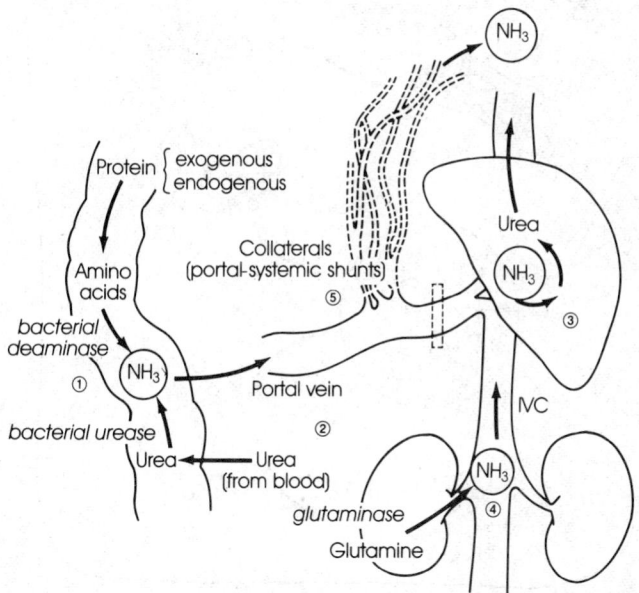

TABLE 244-1 Alteration of glucose metabolism in cirrhosis

Factors leading to hyperglycemia:
  Decreased hepatic glucose uptake
  Decreased hepatic glycogen synthesis
  Hepatic resistance to insulin
  Portal-systemic glucose shunting
  Peripheral insulin resistance
  Hormonal abnormalities (serum)
    ↑ Glucagon
    ↓ Cortisol
    ↑ Insulin (↓ in hemochromatosis)
Factors leading to hypoglycemia:
  Decreased gluconeogenesis
  Decreased hepatic glycogen content
  Hepatic resistance to glucagon
  Poor oral intake
  Hyperinsulinemia secondary to portal-systemic shunting

Much has been learned about the mechanisms involved in the synthesis of secretory proteins, especially of albumin (see Fig. 244-3). Polyribosomes bound to the rough endoplasmic reticulum (RER) of the hepatocyte are the principal site of translation of messenger ribonucleic acid (mRNA) coding for export proteins; in contrast proteins destined for intracellular use, such as ferritin, are synthesized on free rather than bound polyribosomes in the cytoplasm. After a short-term fast, there is a decrease in the amount of albumin mRNA associated with the RER; instead more mRNA is found in the cytosol and in a state dissociated from polyribosomes. Albumin, like secretory proteins produced by other organs, appears to be synthesized initially as a larger precursor, preproalbumin. This precursor molecule contains an additional 24 extra amino acid residues on the N terminus, referred to as a "signal peptide," which undergoes two sequential cleavages (or "processing"); the molecule is then transported to the Golgi apparatus prior to secretion. The "pre" portion of preproalbumin is cleaved within the RER even before protein synthesis is completed; the "pro" segment is removed within the lumen of the ER. Once synthesis and processing are completed, albumin is transported from the Golgi vesicles to the hepatocyte surface by mechanisms which are unclear but almost certainly involve the microfilaments and microtubule apparatus of the cell. Although the hepatic lymph space of Disse provides a potential avenue for the newly released albumin, most secreted proteins enter the plasma.

Albumin synthesis is subject to a number of regulatory influences. These include the rate of transcription of specific mRNAs and the availability of the substrate tRNA (transfer RNA). At the translational level, the integrity of polyribosomes and their synthetic abilities is modified by factors affecting initiation, elongation, and release of peptides and proteins as well as by the availability of ATP, GTP, and magnesium ions. The rate of albumin synthesis is also influenced by the availability of amino acid precursors, especially tryptophan, the scarcest of the essential amino acids. Indeed in patients with large carcinoid tumors albumin synthesis may decrease precipitously when tryptophan is shunted from albumin production into the pathway leading to 5-hydroxytryptophan (serotonin) synthesis (see Chap. 306). The rate of albumin synthesis is also affected by colloid oncotic pressure with increased production occurring in response to falling oncotic pressure. Finally, hormonal influences on hepatic protein metabolism such as insulin and glucagon are closely integrated with the nutritional factors discussed above.

The liver also produces a wide variety of other secretory proteins, most of which have a synthetic pathway and processing procedure similar to albumin (Fig. 244-3). The presence of a *signal peptide*, such as the "prepro" segment of albumin, which is subsequently removed during protein maturation appears to be a general mechanism for orienting proteins in the membranes of the ER and directing them for export rather than for intracellular use or degradation. Most proteins undergo even further modification in the form of sequential *glycosylation* in the RER and Golgi apparatus. The carbohydrate moieties of these glycoproteins appear to be important in determining their site of action and their rate of tissue uptake after secretion. Some of the clinically important secretory glycoproteins include ceruloplasmin, alpha$_1$ antitrypsin, and most other alpha and beta globulins. While the site of albumin catabolism is uncertain, the removal of terminal sialic acid residues after secretion and the resultant exposure of penultimate galactose or N-acetylglucosamine residues appears to result in receptor-mediated uptake of "aged" proteins by hepatocytes and Kupffer cells, followed by their subsequent degradation. Reduced amounts of the hepatic receptor for asialoglycoproteins appear to result in elevated serum concentrations of these glycoproteins in patients with severe and chronic liver disease.

One of the clinically most important derangements in protein metabolism is the development of hypoalbuminemia, which results largely from reduced synthetic activity. Decreased synthesis may be caused by a decrease in the number as well as the function of hepatocytes. A decrease in the dietary supply of amino acids can also contribute to deficient synthesis. To some extent the body attempts to compensate for decreased albumin synthesis by reducing the rate of degradation. Attempts to raise the serum albumin level by intravenous infusions are often futile because this compensatory mechanism can be blunted and the decrease in albumin degradation may not occur. The reduced degradation of albumin is not a general phenomenon in chronic liver disease because other proteins such as fibrinogen are degraded more rapidly than normal. The degree of hypoalbuminemia is also augmented in the patient with ascites, in which large amounts of the body's albumin are present in the ascitic fluid. When there is increased hepatic venous pressure (as in postsinusoidal or hepatic vein outflow block), there may be increased hepatic lymph production with extravasation into the peritoneal cavity. In contrast to intestinal lymph, the protein content of hepatic lymph appears to be relatively uninfluenced by ascitic oncotic pressure, most likely reflecting the lack of tight junctions between sinusoidal endothelial cells.

Other proteins produced by the liver include many of the blood-clotting factors: fibrinogen (factor I), prothrombin (factor II), and factors V, VII, IX, and X as well as inhibitors of both coagulation and fibrinolysis. Factors II, VII, IX, and X are vitamin K–responsive and are dependent upon normal intestinal fat absorption. Vitamin K activates an enzyme system in liver endoplasmic reticulum which catalyzes the γ carboxylation of selected glutamyl residues in clotting factor precursors. The γ carboxylation enhances the Ca^{2+} and phospholipid binding capacity of prothrombin and permits its rapid

FIGURE 244-3 *Schematic diagram illustrating major steps in synthesis, processing, and secretion of proteins and glycoproteins by the liver. Ribosomal subunits and mRNA form polysome complexes to initiate protein synthesis. Polyribosomes synthesizing proteins destined for export (e.g., albumin) associate with membranes to form membrane-bound polysomes [i.e., the rough endoplasmic reticulum (RER)]. Synthesis of precursor molecule (e.g., "preproalbumin") occurs and is followed by stepwise proteolytic cleavage and secretion from the cell. Other export proteins (e.g., alpha$_1$ antitrypsin) are first glycosylated in the RER and Golgi prior to secretion. Proteins produced for intracellular use (e.g., ferritin) are synthesized on non-membrane-bound cytosolic polyribosomes and processed by stepwise proteolytic cleavage and secretion from the cell.*

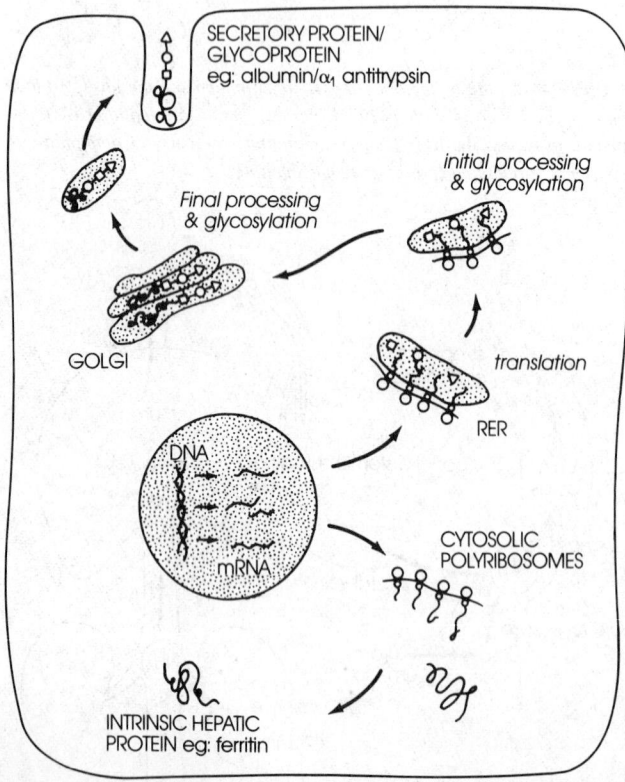

SECRETORY PROTEIN/
GLYCOPROTEIN
eg: albumin/α$_1$ antitrypsin

Final processing & glycosylation

initial processing & glycosylation

GOLGI

translation

RER

DNA

mRNA

CYTOSOLIC POLYRIBOSOMES

INTRINSIC HEPATIC PROTEIN eg: ferritin

conversion to thrombin in the presence of factors V and X (Chap. 281).

The liver is involved in the process of hemostasis by virtue of both anabolic and catabolic functions. As expected, severe liver disease leads to reduced synthesis of prothrombin, a vitamin K–dependent clotting factor. The presence of malnutrition, the use of broad-spectrum antibiotics, or concomitant impairment of fat absorption due to reduction in intestinal bile salt concentration (e.g., cholestasis) may accentuate hypoprothrombinemia by decreasing the amount of vitamin K that can be absorbed from the intestine. In these situations, prothrombin levels may be at least partially corrected by parenteral vitamin K administration. However, when the coagulopathy results from impaired hepatocellular function and not cholestasis or intestinal factors, exogenous vitamin K is unlikely to correct or improve prothrombin synthesis. The vitamin K–dependent clotting proteins have a substantially shorter serum half-life than albumin; therefore, hypoprothrombinemia usually precedes the development of hypoalbuminemia, especially in the patient with acute hepatocellular disease. In cirrhosis, coagulopathy may be further aggravated by the thrombocytopenia resulting from hypersplenism.

Since the liver is also the site of production of non-vitamin K–dependent clotting factors, severe liver disease injury may lead to decreased plasma concentrations of factor V in addition to factors II, VII, IX, and X. It is unusual for fibrinogen to be reduced significantly, unless there is an associated disseminated intravascular coagulation (DIC). For unclear reasons, the damaged liver may actually produce increased amounts of fibrinogen as well as other proteins collectively designated acute-phase reactants (C-reactive proteins, haptoglobin, ceruloplasmin, and transferrin). The latter are produced both in response to liver injury (e.g., severe chronic active hepatitis) and in association with systemic illnesses such as cancer, rheumatoid arthritis, bacterial infections, burns, and myocardial infarctions. However, while the diseased liver may produce normal or increased amounts of fibrinogen, the molecules themselves may be qualitatively abnormal (i.e., structurally and functionally), reflecting more subtle derangements in protein synthesis. These functionally abnormal fibrinogen molecules may contribute to the altered hemostasis frequently found in patients with chronic liver disease.

DETOXIFICATION MECHANISMS Water-soluble drugs and endogenous substances usually are excreted unchanged in the urine or bile. However, lipid-soluble compounds tend to accumulate in the body and affect cellular processes, unless they are converted to less active compounds or to more water-soluble metabolites which are more easily excreted. Hepatic blood flow, protein binding, and the intrinsic capacity of the liver to eliminate a drug are all primary determinants of hepatic drug clearance. The liver has an important role in the metabolism of many exogenous drugs and endogenous hormones by virtue of several enzyme systems involved in biochemical transformation. The relative importance of these various factors differs depending on how well a drug is extracted by the liver. There are two major types of reactions. The first, *phase I reactions*, result in chemical modification of reactive groups by oxidation, reduction, hydroxylation, sulfoxidation, deamination, dealkylation, or methylation. Such modifications usually involve one of several enzymatic systems, including the mixed function oxidases, cytochromes b_5 and P_{450} (microsomal), and the glutathione S-acyltransferases (cytoplasmic). These biochemical reactions usually lead to *inactivation* of drugs such as barbiturates and benzodiazepines. However, *activation* may also occur. For example, cortisone is activated to cortisol and prednisone to prednisolone (both products being more potent than the parent compounds); imipramine, a depressant, is converted to desmethylimipramine, an antidepressant. On the other hand, phase I reactions may convert a nontoxic compound to a toxic one as in the metabolism of isoniazid and acetaminophen. Similarly, some carcinogens may be activated by formation of highly reactive epoxide intermediates in the liver, while other carcinogens may be detoxified.

The enzymes responsible for phase I reactions, especially those involving the cytochrome P_{450} system, can be induced by drugs such as ethanol, barbiturates, haloperidol, and glutethimide. Conversely, hepatic microsomal enzymes may be inhibited by agents such as chloramphenicol, cimetidine, disulfiram, dextropropoxyphene, allopurinol, and, paradoxically, by ethanol. The concomitant administration of two drugs metabolized by the same microsomal enzyme may result in modification, potentiation, or diminution of the pharmacologic efficacy of either or both drugs. Activity of phase I reactions may also change with aging.

Phase II reactions may follow phase I reactions or proceed independently; these involve the conversion of substances to their glucuronide, sulfate, acetyl, taurine, or glycine derivatives, thereby converting lipophilic substances to water-soluble derivatives and permitting their excretion in bile or urine. Conjugation catalyzed by microsomal UDP (uridine diphosphate)-glucuronyltransferases to form glucuronide derivatives is one of the most common phase II reactions. In general, the conjugates are more soluble than the parent compound and are pharmacologically inactive.

An awareness that there may be varying degrees of impairment in the hepatic uptake, detoxification, and excretion of certain drugs is important in the clinical management of patients with chronic liver disease. Portal-systemic shunting of blood may decrease the "first-pass effect" of drugs absorbed from the gut. In cirrhosis, altered intrahepatic hemodynamics due to a disordered liver architecture may also reduce the rates of hepatic drug clearance. Hypoalbuminemia will permit drugs usually bound to albumin to be present in increased concentrations of their unbound form in the circulation and extracellular spaces; this may result in an increased activity of such drugs. Most importantly, a decrease in the amount of function of microsomal enzymes responsible for phase I and phase II reactions will result in slower rates of drug inactivation and elimination. Drugs for which there may be a decreased clearance in patients with liver disease include anticonvulsants (e.g., phenytoin, phenobarbital), anti-inflammatory agents (e.g., acetaminophen, phenylbutazone, corticosteroids), minor tranquilizers, cardioactive drugs (e.g., lidocaine, quinidine, propranolol), and antibiotics (e.g., nafcillin, chloramphenicol, tetracyclines, clindamycin, trimethoprim, rifampin, pyrazinamide). This will lead to decreased dosage requirements and a narrowing of the range between therapeutic and toxic drug levels. In the future, the aminopyrine clearance test may permit an assessment of the degree of impairment of detoxification mechanisms in individual patients. In this test, orally administered [^{14}C]aminopyrine is absorbed from the gut and metabolized by the hepatic cytochrome P_{450} system releasing [^{14}C]O_2, which is excreted and easily measured in the breath. In hepatocellular disease, the rate of [^{14}C]O_2 production will be reduced. Finally, the patient with chronic liver disease may demonstrate alterations in the pharmacologic effects of drugs in addition to or independent of changes in their pharmacokinetics such as an increased central nervous system sensitivity to opiates and other sedatives.

The difficulties in safely administering pharmacologic agents to patients with both acute and chronic liver disease are underscored by the frequency with which administration of benzodiazepines is cited as precipitating hepatic coma. It may be very difficult clinically to determine whether agitation, confusion, and irrational behavior are due to early hepatic encephalopathy or related to the concurrent use of benzodiazepines, opiates, barbiturates, and other depressants. It should be recognized that there is great variation of drug clearance in patients with liver disease; although data on average clearances may provide a reasonable estimate for initial dosages, subsequent adjustments in dose need to be individualized in order to attain the desired plasma drug concentration.

The mechanism by which some agents exert a hepatotoxic effect may involve the same metabolic pathways responsible for normal drug detoxification. The mechanism of acetaminophen toxicity is particularly illustrative. Acetaminophen is metabolized and detoxified by the hepatic mixed-function oxygenase system, but one of the intermediate products is a potent free radical (postulated metabolite

N-acetylimidoquinone) which can inactivate many enzymes and proteins by binding irreversibly to their sulfhydryl groups. Normally this interaction can be prevented by reduced glutathione. In the presence of excessive amounts of the acetaminophen free radical (e.g., from overdosage or underlying liver disease), the glutathione levels of the hepatocytes are readily exhausted and the excess free radicals can lead to inactivation of cellular proteins and produce widespread hepatocellular necrosis. In the case of acetaminophen overdosage, the very early administration of sulfhydryl groups in the form of *N*-acetylcysteine can often prevent this drug-induced liver injury.

HORMONE METABOLISM   In addition to its role in the metabolism of diverse pharmacologic agents, the liver is also responsible for inactivation or modification of several endogenous hormones; therefore, chronic liver disease may be accompanied by signs of apparent hormonal imbalance. Some hormones (e.g., insulin and glucagon) are inactivated in the liver by proteolysis or deamination. Thyroxine and triiodothyronine are metabolized in the liver by reactions involving deiodination. Steroid hormones, such as corticosteroids and aldosterone, are first inactivated to their tetrahydro derivative (by reduction of the Δ^4 double bond and the 3-keto group), followed by conjugation, mostly with glucuronic acid. Testosterone is metabolized to the isomeric 17-ketosteroids androsterone and etiocholanolone and excreted in the urine mostly as sulfate conjugates. Estrogens, such as estradiol, may be converted to estriol and estrone and then conjugated with glucuronic acid or sulfate. Abnormalities in estrogen (and testosterone) metabolism are believed to be involved in the development of the spider angiomas, loss of axillary or pubic hair, and testicular atrophy frequently seen in patients with chronic liver disease. In addition, increased portal-systemic shunting of testosterone and androstenedione secondary to portal hypertension may lead to the development of gynecomastia in cirrhotic males due to increased peripheral conversion to estradiol and estrone especially in patients with alcoholic cirrhosis. In patients with alcoholic liver disease, feminization may also be related to the direct toxic effects of alcohol on the gonadal-pituitary-hypothalamic axis which lead to the overall reduction in serum testosterone found in patients with cirrhosis. Similar effects are also seen in patients with hemochromatosis due to deposition of iron in these sites. However, gynecomastia is often lacking in the latter, apparently due to a coincident reduction in

plasma concentration of androstenedione a major precursor for estrogen synthesis.

Estrogens also act directly on the liver to impair hepatic secretory activity. Estradiol and related estrogens, such as those present in contraceptive pills, interfere with sodium sulfobromophthalein and bile salt excretion and worsen the preexisting defect in secretion of conjugated bilirubin in patients with Dubin-Johnson syndrome; they may also elevate plasma alkaline phosphatase levels (see Chap. 245). Related steroids such as etiocholanolone and pregnanediol have been shown to stimulate δ-aminolevulinic acid (ALA) synthetase activity leading to increased porphobilinogen excretion. Since these steroids exert these effects only in their unconjugated form, the increased hepatic levels of δ-aminolevulinic acid synthetase in patients with alcoholic cirrhosis may be secondary to the action of gonadal steroids.

LIPID METABOLISM: FATTY ACIDS AND TRIGLYCERIDES   Under normal conditions, most of the fatty acids taken up by the liver and esterified to triglyceride are derived from adipose tissue or the diet. Some fatty acids (especially saturated ones) are synthesized in the liver from acetate. The fatty acids may then be converted enzymatically to triglyceride, esterified with cholesterol, incorporated into phospholipids, or oxidized to CO_2 or ketone bodies. Most of the triglyceride is produced for export, but in order to be secreted it must be converted to lipoproteins by combining with relatively specific apoprotein moieties. This emphasizes the importance of protein synthesis for the release and secretion of triglyceride from the liver. It should be noted that the liver plays a major role in regulating lipoprotein levels by virtue of both its degradative and synthetic functions. Thus, the liver is quantitatively the major site of low-density lipoprotein (LDL) catabolism with dual high- and low-affinity receptor-mediated pathways playing a role. In addition chylomicron remnants are removed and degraded by the liver, where their constituents have a number of metabolic effects. The liver is not only the primary site of very low density lipoprotein (VLDL) secretion but also accounts for a major portion of its subsequent degradation by mechanisms similar to that of chylomicron remnant degradation and conversion to LDL via the action of hepatic lipase. The liver may also play a role in high-density lipoprotein (HDL) catabolism. It is noteworthy that with the exception of cholestatic disease (see below), clinically significant alterations in lipoprotein and cholesterol metabolism are usually not found in patients with chronic liver disease.

Studies on the production of fatty liver have shown that singly or in combination, one or more of the steps depicted in Fig. 244-4 may be involved. An increased influx of fatty acids mobilized from adipose tissue due to drugs (e.g., ethanol or corticosteroids) or secondary to diabetic ketosis may lead to a fatty liver. Similarly, increased levels of fatty acids in the liver, either from enhanced fatty acid synthesis or from decreased fatty acid oxidation may lead to increased triglyceride formation. In some instances (e.g., ethanol excess) there may also be increases in the carbohydrate backbone, α-glycerophosphate, involved in fatty acid esterification to triglyceride. Since release of triglyceride involves the formation of lipoproteins, lipid accumulation may occur because of decreased apoprotein synthesis. This appears to be the case in fatty livers seen in patients with protein-calorie malnutrition (kwashiorkor) and due to toxins such as carbon tetrachloride, phosphorus, or ethionine, as well as following excessive doses of antibiotics like tetracycline that can inhibit protein synthesis. Finally, there may be impaired lipoprotein secretion from the liver. Alcohol is perhaps the most common agent leading to a fatty liver, but the mechanism(s) whereby alcohol leads to increased liver triglyceride is not clear. Depending on factors such as dose or duration, alcohol ingestion may affect any of the seven steps shown in Fig. 244-4; however, the primary factor for the production of the alcohol-induced fatty liver remains to be determined. The alterations in the redox state due to excessive accumulation of NADH resulting from oxidation of alcohol may also contribute.

In addition to the changes leading to fatty liver, there are many metabolic alterations which may be found in the blood of patients

FIGURE 244-4 *Factors in the uptake and esterification of fatty acids to triglyceride by the liver, including the formation and release of triglyceride as lipoprotein. The numbers refer to steps, which, if altered, may result in increased liver triglyceride (i.e., fatty liver).*

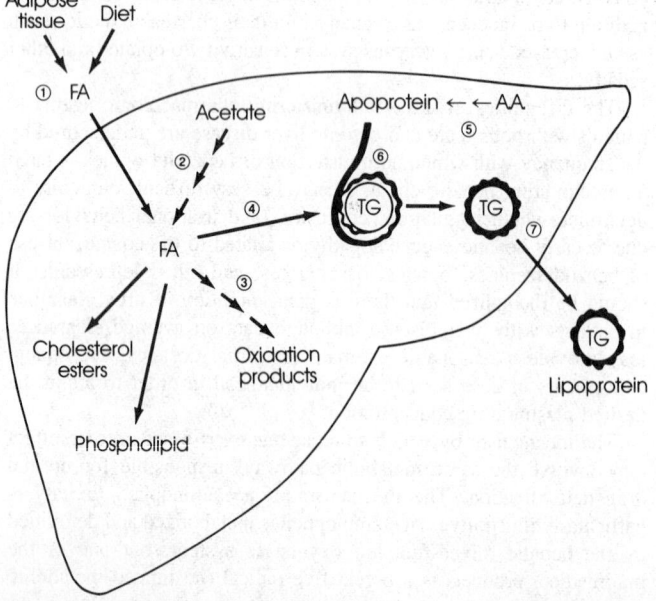

following the ingestion of large amounts of alcohol. These include, among others, *increased* plasma levels of lactate, proline, urate, and triglycerides and *decreased* plasma levels of glucose, magnesium, phosphate, and triiodothyronine (T_3).

CHOLESTEROL Cholesterol and bile acid synthesis is carried out primarily by the liver. Cholesterol synthesis is subject to a number of metabolic controls, most of them mediated via the rate-limiting biosynthetic enzyme 3-hydroxy-3-methylglutaryl coenzyme A reductase (HMG-CoA reductase). Cholesterol exists either free or combined with fatty acids in the form of cholesterol esters; in the plasma both are found primarily in association with β-lipoproteins. The plasma and liver also contain lecithin–cholesterol acyltransferase (LCAT), an enzyme involved in the conversion of free cholesterol to its esterified form. Since there is exchange of free cholesterol between tissues, changes in plasma cholesterol levels reflect changes in total body cholesterol. However, decreases in plasma cholesterol esters may reflect hepatic damage and impaired hepatic cholesterol esterification.

Severe liver injury often leads to a decrease in *total* serum cholesterol levels, including both free and esterified fractions. This may be due to decreased synthesis of cholesterol and cholesterol esters, decreased apoprotein synthesis, or both. In cholestasis (either intra- or extrahepatic) total serum cholesterol often increases strikingly. Disorders of cholestasis are associated with marked abnormalities of lipoprotein metabolism. In primary biliary cirrhosis there are pronounced elevations in serum free cholesterol and LDL; conversely, serum HDL is reduced and may disappear from the serum in patients with long-standing disease. Similar but less marked changes are seen in other cholestatic conditions.

The increase in serum free cholesterol (and phospholipid) and the concomitant decrease in esterified cholesterol in cholestasis may be related to a decrease in the hepatic production of LCAT. Reduced levels of LCAT are also correlated with the appearance of an abnormal LDL, referred to as lipoprotein X (LP-X). Although LP-X, which has a high content of free cholesterol and triglyceride, was originally thought to be a specific indicator of biliary tract obstruction, it is evident that it appears in any cholestatic condition. While the depressed hepatic production of LCAT may be responsible for altered lipid content and composition of lipoproteins, the factors leading to the overall increase in total serum cholesterol are not clear. In experimental animals, bile duct ligation results in a net increase in hepatic cholesterol synthesis, and in ''regurgitation'' of bile salts, cholesterol, and LP-X into venous radicals. However, it is difficult to translate these experimental findings to the patient with primary biliary cirrhosis unless any insult to cells lining the biliary canaliculi and ductules can impair the delicate balance of lipid synthesis and removal.

Most of the derangements of hepatic metabolism discussed above are evident only in patients with severe or long-standing liver disease. Indeed, in all but the most severe cases of acute viral hepatitis, hepatic metabolic functions are remarkably well preserved, and in most cases of mild to moderate acute viral hepatitis, it is uncommon to observe clinically important alterations in carbohydrate, protein, and lipid metabolism. However, in the patients with severe or fulminant hepatitis, whether from a viral or toxic agent, the metabolic derangements may be similar to those seen in more chronic disease. For example, in fulminant hepatitis there may be pronounced hypoprothrombinemia and impaired coagulation, hypoalbuminemia, and the relatively acute development of ascites, as well as hyperammonemia and encephalopathy. However, in contrast to patients with cirrhosis, abnormalities in carbohydrate metabolism are more likely to lead to profound hypoglycemia rather than to hyperglycemia. This hypoglycemia appears to reflect both a marked decrease in hepatic glycogen stores as well as diminished glucagon responsiveness. There may also be poor oral intake due to nausea and anorexia together with increased glucose utilization secondary to hyperinsulinemia (due to portal-systemic shunting and decreased insulin degradation).

REFERENCES

CAVALLO-PERIN P et al: Mechanism of insulin resistance in human liver cirrhosis. Evidence of a combined receptor and post-receptor defect. J Clin Invest 75:1659, 1985

COOPER AD: Role of the liver in the degradation of lipoproteins. Gastroenterology 88:192, 1984

FLANNERY DB et al: Current status of hyperammonemic syndromes. Hepatology 2:495, 1982

HOYUMPA AM et al: Hepatic encephalopathy. Gastroenterology 77:803, 1979

KLEG HK et al: Conversion of androgens to estrogens in idiopathic hemochromatosis: Comparison with alcoholic liver disease. J Clin Endocrin Metab 61:1, 1985

ONSTAD GR, ZIEVE L: What determines blood ammonia? Gastroenterology 77:803, 1979

OWEN OE et al: Hepatic, gut and renal substrate flux rates in patients with hepatic cirrhosis. J Clin Invest 68:240, 1981

SHERLOCK S: *Diseases of the Liver and Biliary System*, 7th ed. London, Blackwell, 1985

SMITH AR et al: Alteration in plasma and CSF amino acids, amines and metabolites in hepatic coma. Ann Surg 187:343, 1978

WILLIAMS RC: Drug administration in hepatic disease. N Engl J Med 309:1616, 1983

WRIGHT R et al: *Liver and Biliary Disease*. 2d ed. Philadelphia, Saunders, 1985

245 DIAGNOSTIC PROCEDURES IN LIVER DISEASE

DANIEL K. PODOLSKY / KURT J. ISSELBACHER

The diversity of normal liver functions and their variable disruption by the spectrum of disorders which may affect the liver precludes the use of any single test as a reliable measure of overall liver function. Many disease processes may lead to severe impairment of some liver functions while others remain entirely unaffected. Since no battery of tests is universally applicable, those most appropriate to a given clinical problem must be selected, their potential value and risks considered, and the results interpreted in relation to the clinical findings.

In assessing the severity and course of liver disease, the physician should be guided by several practical principles. The tests selected should (1) assess different parameters of liver function, (2) be used *serially* in order to evaluate the evolution or course of the disease, and (3) be interpreted within the total clinical context, with recognition that any single laboratory test may be fallible.

BLOOD TESTS OF LIVER FUNCTION (See Table 245-1)

Bilirubin Bilirubin metabolism and its assessment are discussed in detail in Chaps. 38 and 246. Spectrophotometric determinations of serum bilirubin in the clinical laboratory measure two pigment fractions: (1) the water-soluble conjugated fraction that gives a *direct reaction* with the diazo reagent and consists largely of conjugated bilirubin (as the mono- and diglucuronide), and (2) the lipid-soluble *indirect-reaction* fraction (total minus direct) that represents primarily

TABLE 245-1 Abnormalities shown by tests of liver function

Test	Type of liver disease	
	Obstructive	Parenchymal
AST and ALT (SGOT and SGPT)	↑	↑ – ↑↑↑
Alkaline phosphatase	↑↑↑	↑
Albumin	N	↓ – ↓↓↓
Prothrombin time	N – ↑ *	↑ – ↑↑↑
Bilirubin	N – ↑↑↑	N – ↑↑↑
γ-Glutamyl transpeptidase (GGT)	↑↑↑	N – ↑↑↑
5′-Nucleotidase	↑ – ↑↑↑	N – ↑

* *Correctable with parenteral vitamin K if elevated.*
NOTE: *N, normal:* ↑, *elevated;* ↓, *decreased.*

unconjugated bilirubin. The serum of normal adults (when measured by the van den Bergh reaction) contains less than 0.25 mg direct-reacting bilirubin per deciliter and 1 mg or less of total bilirubin per deciliter. Studies with high-performance liquid chromatography (HPLC) suggest that even these levels may be artifactually high in normal persons (see Chap. 38).

Conjugated hyperbilirubinemia with elevated direct- and indirect-reacting material indicates impairment of secretion into the bile, while unconjugated hyperbilirubinemia reflects impaired conjugation. The latter is found in a limited number of processes including such nonhepatic conditions as hemolytic anemia and ineffective erythropoiesis (increased pigment load) and a few hepatic disorders, principally Gilbert's syndrome or the relatively rare Crigler-Najjar syndrome. Although measurement of both the direct and total serum bilirubin will determine whether the patient has predominantly unconjugated or conjugated hyperbilirubinemia, this distinction is of limited usefulness since the majority of hepatobiliary disorders lead to conjugated hyperbilirubinemia. Fractionation of serum bilirubin does not distinguish cholestasis due to parenchymal disease from that arising from biliary tract processes.

Bilirubin appears in the urine only after it is converted to a water-soluble form; generally this involves conjugation with polar glucuronide groups which enhance water solubility. Rapid assessment of bilirubinuria is possible using commercially available dipsticks and may be helpful as an initial screening measure. Bilirubinuria occurs with even minimal degrees of jaundice and may be detected before jaundice is evident. Its usefulness is otherwise quite limited. Urobilinogen, a product of lumenal bacterial metabolism of bilirubin, is reabsorbed from the bowel and secreted in the urine. Complete bile duct obstruction blocks excretion of bilirubin into the gut and results in disappearance of urobilinogen from the urine. Assessment of urobilinogen in a freshly collected 2-h urine specimen by the Watson method (normal values 0.2 to 1.2 units) may distinguish biliary tract obstruction from parenchymal dysfunction, but this test has been largely superseded by newer methods.

Serum enzyme assays   A number of serum enzymes have been used to distinguish and assess hepatocellular injury and biliary tract dysfunction or obstruction. All have inherent limitations in sensitivity and specificity, and none truly distinguish these processes definitively. Elevations in enzyme activities may also be seen in association with nonhepatic disorders. Nevertheless, with proper and careful interpretation, a number of serum enzymes provide important clinical tools.

AMINOTRANSFERASES (TRANSAMINASES)   Assays of many serum enzymes have been proposed as indicators of hepatocellular damage. Of these, aspartate aminotransferase (AST,SGOT) and alanine aminotransferase (ALT,SGPT) activities have proven most useful. These enzymes catalyze the transfer of the γ-amino groups of aspartate and alanine, respectively, to the γ-keto group of ketoglutarate, leading to the formation of oxaloacetic acid and pyruvic acid. In contrast to ALT, which is found primarily in the liver, AST is present in many tissues including heart, skeletal muscle, kidney, and brain and is thus somewhat less specific as an indicator of liver function. The source of serum AST and ALT in the normal person (less than 40 IU) is unclear, and the mechanism responsible for clearance of these enzymes is uncertain. In the hepatocyte, ALT is found exclusively in the cytosol, while different isoenzymes of AST exist in mitochondria and the cytosol. Although elevated serum levels of AST or ALT may be observed in a variety of nonhepatic diseases, notably in myocardial infarction and skeletal muscle disorders, these disorders can usually be clinically distinguished from liver disease. Conversely, uremia may lead to spuriously low aminotransferase values.

Serum AST and ALT are elevated to some extent in nearly all liver disorders. Highest levels are found in association with conditions causing extensive hepatic necrosis, such as severe viral hepatitis, toxin-induced liver injury, or prolonged circulatory collapse. Lesser elevations are encountered in mild acute viral hepatitis as well as in both diffuse and focal chronic liver diseases (e.g., chronic active hepatitis, cirrhosis, and hepatic metastases). However, the absolute levels of aminotransferases correlate poorly with severity of liver injury or prognosis, and serial determinations are usually most helpful. Thus in the patient with massive hepatic necrosis, there may be marked elevations in the early phase (i.e., 24 to 48 h), but by the time the patient is tested 3 to 5 days later the levels may be in the range of 200 to 400 IU. It is noteworthy that in severe alcoholic hepatitis one commonly finds only modest increases in these enzymes (generally less than 300 IU). Minimal elevations of AST and ALT (less than 100 IU) may also be found in association with biliary tract obstruction; higher levels suggest the development of cholangitis with resultant hepatic cell necrosis.

In general AST and ALT levels parallel each other, with one exception. In alcoholic hepatitis the AST/ALT ratio may be greater than 2; this appears to result from a reduction in hepatic ALT content due to a deficiency in the cofactor pyridoxine-5-phosphate.

ALKALINE PHOSPHATASE   Human serum contains several forms of alkaline phosphatase, a plasma membrane–derived enzyme of uncertain physiologic function which hydrolyzes synthetic phosphate esters at pH 9. These activities arise from bone, intestine, liver, and placenta. A number of different assays have been developed which utilize different substrates. The most widely used methods are expressed in international units (IU) (normal: 25 to 85 units), Bodansky units (normal: 1.4 to 4.5 units) or King-Armstrong units (normal: 1.5 to 4.5 units).

In the absence of bone disease or pregnancy, elevated levels of alkaline phosphatase activity usually reflect impaired biliary tract function. The increased levels reflect increased synthesis of the enzyme by hepatocytes and biliary tract epithelium rather than regurgitation of enzyme due to obstruction. Bile acids may play a role both by inducing synthesis and by promoting solubilization of the membrane-associated enzyme activity.

Slight to moderate increases in alkaline phosphatase (1 to 2 times normal) occur in many patients with parenchymal liver disorders such as hepatitis and cirrhosis; transient increases may occur in all types of liver disease. However, the most striking increases in alkaline phosphatase (3 to 10 times normal) occur with extrahepatic biliary tract (mechanical) obstruction or with intrahepatic (functional) cholestasis, as in drug-induced cholestasis or primary biliary cirrhosis. Conversely, it is unusual for the serum alkaline phosphatase to remain normal when there is obstructive jaundice, and a normal enzyme level argues strongly against the presence of cholestasis. The alkaline phosphatase is almost always mildly elevated in metastatic or infiltrative liver disease (e.g., leukemia, lymphoma, and sarcoid). The enzyme may be elevated in the presence of incomplete biliary obstruction or when there is obstruction of only one hepatic duct, conditions in which the serum bilirubin is often normal or only slightly elevated. Serum alkaline phosphatase is also elevated in nonhepatic disorders, most notably in some bone disorders (e.g., Paget's disease, osteomalacia, and metastases to bone) and sometimes with malignancy. Occasionally tumors produce an alkaline phosphatase which is identical or similar to the placental form, the so-called Regan isoenzyme.

Although one can usually make a reasonable assessment as to whether an elevation of the alkaline phosphatase is of hepatic or nonhepatic origin, several methods can distinguish the different isoenzymes facilitating resolution of any uncertainty. In contrast to that derived from bone, the hepatic isozyme is stable to treatment with heat (56°C for 15 min) or urea. These enzymes can also be separated by electrophoresis, but this is usually impractical. Parallel determination of serum 5'-nucleotidase activity is also helpful; an increase of both 5'-nucleotidase and alkaline phosphatase is consistent with an hepatobiliary source of the enzyme elevation. Even after correction for age and sex (higher levels being found in the young and in older women), isolated elevations in alkaline phosphatase may occasionally be encountered in adults with no apparent disease.

5′-NUCLEOTIDASE, LEUCINE AMINOPEPTIDASE, AND γ-GLUTAMYL-TRANSPEPTIDASE 5′-*Nucleotidase* catalyzes the hydrolysis of phosphate from the 5′ position of the pentose component of the nucleotide. Although tissue distribution is widespread, elevations are generally associated with hepatobiliary disease. The principal value of the 5′-nucleotidase measurement is to confirm the hepatic origin of an elevated alkaline phosphatase level in children, pregnant women, or in those settings where coincident bone disease may be present. However, 5′-nucleotidase levels do not always parallel alkaline phosphatase in liver disease, and lack of elevation does not exclude an hepatic source of elevated serum alkaline phosphatase.

Despite a widespread tissue distribution, *leucine aminopeptidase,* a protease which cleaves amino-terminal amino acids from peptides, is significantly elevated only in diseases of the pancreas and hepatobiliary system. There is considerable overlap in values of the peptidase levels found in patients with hepatocellular disease and in those with cholestatic jaundice; thus, in general, its measurement is of little clinical value.

γ-GLUTAMYLTRANSPEPTIDASE (GGT) catalyzes the transfer of the γ-glutamyl group from peptides such as glutathione to other amino acids and may play a role in amino acid transport. It is found throughout the hepatobiliary system as well as in other tissues. In liver disease, GGT correlates with alkaline phosphatase levels and is the most sensitive indicator of biliary tract disease. However, elevations of GGT are nonspecific and may be associated with pancreatic, cardiac, renal, and pulmonary disorders as well as with diabetes and alcoholism. This enzyme may be increased by agents which induce microsomal enzymes, and it has been suggested as a potential marker of alcoholism. However, overall lack of specificity has limited its clinical usefulness.

OTHER ENZYMES Measurement of total serum lactic dehydrogenase (LDH) or its isoenzymes is usually not helpful in diagnosis of liver disease because of this enzyme's nearly ubiquitous body distribution. Moderate LDH elevations are common in acute viral hepatitis, cirrhosis, and metastatic carcinoma to the liver. Biliary tract disease may also produce slight elevations. Numerous other dehydrogenases (e.g., isocitrate dehydrogenase, sorbitol dehydrogenase, and glutamate dehydrogenase) have been used or proposed as markers of liver disease, but none appear to offer significant diagnostic improvement over standard aminotransferase determinations. Elevation of serum ornithine carbamyl transferase (OCT), a urea cycle enzyme present only in liver and intestine, occurs primarily in liver disease, but its lack of association with any specific type of liver disease has limited its diagnostic usefulness also.

Serum proteins Extensive liver injury may lead to *decreased* blood levels of albumin, prothrombin, fibrinogen, and other proteins synthesized exclusively by hepatocytes. In contrast to measurements of serum enzymes, serum protein levels reflect liver synthetic function rather than just cell injury. Three important caveats should be remembered regarding interpretation of serum protein levels: (1) they are neither early nor sensitive indicators of liver disease (because of the extent of hepatic reserve and their half-life, see below), (2) they are of little value in the differential diagnosis of liver disease, and (3) decreases in their serum levels are not specific for liver disease.

ALBUMIN AND GLOBULIN Albumin is quantitatively the most important serum protein synthesized by the liver; the normal serum value ranges from 3.5 to 5 g/dL (see Chap. 244). Albumin has a fairly long half-life (14 to 20 days) with less than 5 percent turnover daily; it is therefore not a good indicator of acute or mild liver injury. Furthermore, there is a substantial reserve of hepatic albumin synthesis; thus, adequate synthesis may continue until there is extensive hepatocellular injury. Serum levels are influenced by a variety of nonhepatic factors, most notably nutritional status, hormonal factors, and plasma oncotic pressure. Routes of degradation in health remain undefined, but nonhepatic conditions may lead to depressed serum

albumin levels mainly due to excessive loss despite adequate synthetic function (e.g., nephrotic syndrome or protein-losing enteropathy). Nonetheless, reduction in the serum albumin levels provides an excellent indication of the severity of chronic liver disease. In the patient with ascites, an increased volume of distribution as well as an absolute reduction in protein synthesis may contribute to hypoalbuminemia.

Serum globulins are a heterogeneous group of proteins whose production in a variety of tissues is influenced by a number of factors. Serum globulins (normal: 2 to 3.5 g/dL) include alpha and beta globulins as well as serum immunoglobulins, the latter largely accounting for the gamma fraction. Serum globulins are often diffusely elevated in association with chronic liver disease and in other nonhepatic disorders. In cirrhosis varying degrees of hyperglobulinemia may occur; this may reflect increased stimulation of the peripheral reticuloendothelial compartment due to shunting of antigens past the liver and impaired clearance by hepatic Kupffer cells. Although some have suggested that elevations in different globulin fractions as assessed by electrophoretic or other means may have a differential diagnostic value, this remains a largely unfulfilled promise. Similarly, the albumin/globulin ratio has no physiologic significance.

CLOTTING FACTORS The liver synthesizes six coagulation factors: fibrinogen (factor I), prothrombin (factor II), and factors V, VII, IX, and X. With the exception of factor V, production of functional proteins requires the presence of the cofactor, vitamin K. Because most of these factors are normally present in excess, impaired coagulation is usually seen only in severe liver disease. Abnormalities of these factors can be most efficiently determined by the one-stage *prothrombin time,* which measures the rate of prothrombin conversion to thrombin in the presence of thromboplastin and calcium and requires the integrity of most of the vitamin K–dependent clotting factors (see Chap. 54). Factor VII is the rate-limiting factor in this pathway and thus has the greatest influence on the prothrombin levels. The prothrombin time is dependent on normal hepatic synthesis of clotting factors and sufficient intestinal uptake of vitamin K. Absorption of this fat-soluble vitamin itself requires adequate dietary intake and normal function of intestinal mucosa and biliary secretion. Severe acute or chronic parenchymal liver injury may lead to prolongation of the prothrombin time due to impaired synthesis of the clotting proteins. Because these proteins have a shorter half-life than that of albumin, the prothrombin time may be an earlier indicator than serum albumin of severe liver injury. In both acute and chronic hepatocellular injury, an increase in the prothrombin time serves as an ominous prognostic sign. Because it is a fat-soluble vitamin, prolongation of the prothrombin time may result from vitamin K malabsorption and may occur with cholestasis due either to biliary tract disease or to fat malabsorption (steatorrhea) of any cause (e.g., pancreatic insufficiency). Poor dietary intake, antibiotic therapy, or use of warfarin-type anticoagulants are additional causes of a prolonged prothrombin time, owing to deficiencies of active vitamin K. These processes can be distinguished from hepatic synthetic failure by demonstrating normalization of the prothrombin time (within 24 to 48 h) after parenteral injections of vitamin K. The *partial thromboplastin time,* which reflects the activities of fibrinogen, prothrombin, and factors V, VIII, IX, X, XI, and XII, may also be prolonged in severe liver disease. Clotting functions should be assessed in all patients with liver disease prior to any surgical procedure, including liver biopsy (see Chaps. 54 and 280).

Blood ammonia Ammonia is elevated in the blood of some patients with either acute or chronic liver disease. Although influenced by a number of factors (summarized in Chap. 244), elevations in blood ammonia reflect disruption of the pathways of urea synthesis by which the liver detoxifies amine groups. A markedly elevated blood ammonia usually reflects severe hepatocellular necrosis. Cirrhotic patients, especially those with endogenous or surgically created portal-systemic shunting, often have varying degrees of hyperammonemia and hepatic encephalopathy. However, there is only a rough correlation between blood ammonia levels and the degree of hepatic encephalopathy; some patients will function normally with a twofold elevation, while others will be stuporous at the same concentration. Ammonia levels may increase before the onset of coma; similarly they may return to normal some 48 to 72 h before improvement of the neurologic status.

Serum lipids and lipoproteins and bile acids   Abnormalities in serum lipids and lipoproteins are sensitive but nonspecific indicators of liver diseases. Acute parenchymal liver disease is commonly associated with increased plasma triglycerides, decreased cholesterol esters, and abnormal lipoproteins. The absence of alpha and prebeta bands with a concomitant increase in the beta fraction is typical of acute viral hepatitis. Less marked but more persistent abnormalities are found in patients with chronic parenchymal disease reflecting deficiencies in lecithin:cholesterol acyltransferase (LCAT) and hepatic triglyceride lipase. Either intra- or extrahepatic cholestasis may lead to an increase in unesterified cholesterol and in serum phospholipids. Lipoprotein X, a distinctive lipoprotein encountered in cholestasis, consists of equimolar amounts of unesterified cholesterol and lecithin which is regurgitated from the biliary tract. Although characteristically seen in patients with extrahepatic biliary obstruction, lipoprotein X may be found in any cholestatic condition.

Removal of bile acids from portal blood is impaired in liver disease because of parenchymal damage and portal-systemic shunts; there may also be reentry of bile acids into blood from injured hepatocytes or an obstructed biliary tract. Although there are a variety of techniques for measuring serum bile acids, these determinations are not yet of proven value for routine clinical use.

IMMUNOLOGIC AND OTHER TESTS

A number of immunologic derangements may be seen in liver disease. Antimitochondrial antibodies are found in 85 to 90 percent of patients with primary biliary cirrhosis. In this test, serum is incubated with rabbit hepatocytes. The presence of antimitochondrial antibodies can then be assessed after subsequent staining with a fluorescein-tagged second antibody. However, this marker is not entirely specific and is occasionally found in patients with chronic active hepatitis and drug-induced hepatitis. Its primary value is in helping to distinguish primary biliary cirrhosis from extrahepatic biliary obstruction. In chronic active hepatitis the *lupus erythematosus–cell test* (LE-cell test) may be positive, and *antinuclear antibodies* as well as *anti-smooth-muscle antibodies* may be present (see Chap. 262). Alpha-fetoprotein is of value in the diagnosis of hepatoma (see Chap. 250). Measurements of serum alpha$_1$-antitrypsin and ceruloplasmin should be performed in infants with cirrhosis or hepatitis since they may reflect alpha$_1$-antitrypsin deficiency or Wilson's disease, respectively (see Chaps 251 and 311).

RADIOLOGIC AND OTHER IMAGING PROCEDURES

Plain abdominal x-ray and barium studies of the gastrointestinal tract   Standard plain films of the upper abdomen and barium studies provide little diagnostic information. The former may permit some estimation of hepatic size and the presence of splenic enlargement or ascites but is of limited value except for the demonstration of calcified lesions (e.g., echinococcal cysts or benign hemangiomas) and the now increasingly uncommon presence of previously administered thorotrast. Barium swallow will demonstrate esophageal varices with reasonable accuracy in patients with portal hypertension, although varices may be better demonstrated endoscopically.

Cholecystography and cholangiography   A number of imaging techniques may be used to examine gallbladder function and biliary tract anatomy. *Oral cholecystography* involves assessment of gallbladder opacification following overnight oral administration of the dye iopanoic acid, which is normally concentrated in the gallbladder if both intestinal absorption and hepatocellular excretory function are intact. This test may be confounded by a variety of factors (e.g., diarrhea), and as many as 15 percent of normal patients will require a second dose of dye for good visualization. Consequently, the specificity and sensitivity of this test are substantially limited and it has been largely superseded by ultrasonography. *Intravenous cholangiography* requires the administration of dye as an intravenous bolus to visualize the bile ducts and gallbladder. Even mild impairment of liver excretory functions may prevent adequate visualization by this technique, thus limiting its application to the evaluation of patients with serum bilirubin levels below 2.5 to 3 mg/dL. In view of these limitations and a high rate of serious reactions to the contrast dye, this test should no longer be employed.

Ultrasonography has provided an important advance in the non-invasive evaluation of the biliary tree and gallbladder. It is not dependent on liver function and therefore can be used in patients with jaundice. It permits expeditious evaluation of the gallbladder, intra- and extrahepatic bile ducts, and hepatic parenchyma. It is also highly sensitive and specific for the detection of cholelithiasis (>95 percent) or signs of biliary tract obstruction. In the patient with obstructive jaundice, ultrasonography may indicate whether the site of obstruction is in the intra- or extrahepatic ducts. Mass lesions in the head of the pancreas or porta hepatis as well as gallstones may be associated findings that provide clues to the nature of the obstructing lesion. However, successful imaging of the biliary tree and the terminal portion of the common bile duct is confounded by the effects of gas in the overlying intestine in as many as 20 percent of patients. Ultrasonography is discussed in greater detail later in this chapter.

Visualization of the biliary tree by direct injection of radiopaque dye may be accomplished by *percutaneous transhepatic cholangiography (THC)* or by cannulation of the ampulla of Vater during endoscopic retrograde cholangiopancreatography (ERCP). THC involves puncture of the liver with a "skinny" needle which is then advanced under fluoroscopic guidance until ductal opacification is verified by injection of contrast material. With experience and proper precautions, dilated major ducts proximal to an obstructing lesion can be cannulated and visualized in up to 90 percent of cases; normal or small ducts associated with intrahepatic cholestasis are more difficult to demonstrate, but with modern techniques they can be opacified in up to 75 percent of cases.

ERCP with the fiberoptic duodenoscope is another method of demonstrating the bile and pancreatic ducts radiographically. (This is discussed in detail in Chap. 233.) The papilla of Vater is cannulated under direct vision, and contrast material is injected into the biliary and pancreatic ducts. ERCP is particularly useful in jaundiced patients with suspected lesions in the head of the pancreas or ampulla of Vater, since one may also obtain cytologic and histologic evaluation of mass lesions. ERCP does not rely upon dilatation of the bile ducts for success, and since the liver itself is not punctured, there is no risk of bile peritonitis when there is high-grade biliary obstruction. However, acute pancreatitis may result from injection of contrast material into the pancreatic duct, and successful cannulation may not be accomplished in 10 to 15 percent of patients. In most clinical settings THC and ERCP offer equivalent visualization of the biliary tract although particular features of an individual patient may favor one approach. Both techniques also offer the opportunity for therapeutic intervention in the patient with obstructive jaundice following diagnostic evaluation. Decompression of the biliary tree via external drainage or placement of an internal stent may be accomplished following THC. Endoscopic papillotomy may permit passage of common bile duct stones and in some circumstances obviate the need for surgical intervention.

Angiography   Improvement in contrast agents and techniques of vascular catheterization has led to increased sophistication in the use of selective angiography in the evaluation of patients with liver disease. Selected cannulation of the hepatic artery or one of its branches is particularly helpful in the assessment of patients with suspected vascular abnormalities (e.g., arteriovenous malformation) and some mass lesions. In some circumstances angiographic features may be nearly diagnostic, as in hemangioma and focal nodular hyperplasia. The technique is especially useful in the preoperative evaluation of patients with isolated mass lesions in whom resection is contemplated. Visualization of the portal venous circulation following arterial injection provides important anatomic information regarding the patency of the portal vein and the direction of portal blood flow and should be a part of the preoperative evaluation prior to elective shunt surgery.

Radioisotope liver scans (scintiscans) Hepatic scintiscans are performed by external scanning of the upper abdomen after intravenous injection of gamma-emitting isotopes selectively extracted by the liver. These techniques have limited spatial resolution but are relatively noninvasive and offer particular advantages in some clinical settings. There are basically three types: (1) colloidal scans which depend on uptake of labeled colloid by Kupffer cells, permitting assessment of the liver parenchyma (e.g., ^{99m}Tc-labeled sulfur colloid), (2) the HIDA or PIPIDA scans (^{99m}Tc-labeled, N-substituted iminoacetic acids), in which dye is taken up and excreted by hepatocytes into the biliary tree allowing evaluation of biliary tract processes, and (3) the gallium scan in which the radionuclide ^{67}Ga is concentrated in neoplastic and inflammatory cells to a greater extent than in hepatocytes. Because these reagents are concentrated by different cellular components of the liver, they may yield complementary images in various conditions. Hence, a hepatoma or liver abscess will lead to reduced uptake or a "cold spot" on colloid or PIPIDA scans, but to increased uptake or a "hot spot" with gallium.

Colloidal scans with ^{198}Au-labeled gold or ^{99m}Tc-labeled sulfur are the scans most commonly used to assess hepatic parenchyma. Metastatic cancer deposits greater than 2 to 3 cm in diameter may be reliably demonstrated as filling defects. Colloid scans are nearly equivalent to ultrasound in this setting and are most effectively used in conjunction with other liver function tests. However, a distorted lobular architecture, as in cirrhosis, can also result in irregular uptake and produce apparent filling defects.

The HIDA or PIPIDA scans are most useful for assessing patency of the biliary tract since these radionuclides are secreted by hepatocytes into the bile canaliculi. These scans have been used to differentiate intrahepatic from extrahepatic obstruction; in complete biliary obstruction there is failure of the isotope to enter the duodenum, while in intrahepatic cholestasis some isotope will be seen in the lumen of the small bowel. However, clear-cut distinctions may be difficult. These scans are most helpful in the diagnosis of acute cholecystitis, where failure of the nuclide to enter the gallbladder indicates the presence of cystic duct or common bile duct obstruction. Adequate visualization may be accomplished even with moderate hyperbilirubinemia.

Ultrasonography The usefulness of *ultrasound* evaluation of structures in the right upper quadrant continues to increase. Sound waves are generated by a piezoelectric crystal which also serves as a sensitive detector of those waves reflected back from the tissue. This noninvasive technique depends upon the differential reflection of sound waves at tissue interfaces resulting from differences in acoustical impedance. The limits of instrumental resolution continue to improve with gray-scale scanning, while real-time ultrasonography now permits evaluation of some dynamic processes. As mentioned above, ultrasound is the preferred method for imaging the biliary tree and gallbladder. In addition, ultrasound is useful for evaluation of suspected hepatic mass lesions and may resolve deposits as small as 1 to 2 cm. Ultrasound is particularly useful in distinguishing abscesses or cystic structures from solid lesions. However, distinction among solid masses may be difficult, and ultrasound may not reliably differentiate neoplastic (primary hepatocellular or metastatic) from regenerative nodules. In those few patients in whom physical findings are uncertain, particularly in the obese patient, the presence of ascites

may be effectively assessed with this modality. This tool may also yield important information about other abdominal structures (e.g., mass in the head of the pancreas). In addition, this imaging technique may be used to facilitate guided "skinny" needle biopsy of isolated hepatic lesions.

Computed tomography and magnetic resonance imaging Computed tomography (CT scan) utilizes a computer to synthesize differences in absorption of a large number of x-rays into a coherent cross-sectional image. Images may be taken with or without prior injection or ingestion of contrast material to highlight vascular or luminal digestive structures. CT scanning is particularly useful in differentiating among intrahepatic fluid collections such as cysts, abscesses, and hematomas, since the fluid density can be determined with relative accuracy. Using the CT scan, the gallbladder, extrahepatic bile ducts, and portal vein as well as a number of solid intraabdominal organs such as pancreas, liver, and spleen may be examined noninvasively with only modest radiation. In contrast to its effect on ultrasound, intestinal gas does not interfere with CT, although paucity of fat sometimes limits resolution in thin patients. CT scanning and ultrasound are often equivalent in their diagnostic yield of mass lesions, gallstones, or obstructive jaundice; in those conditions ultrasound is usually the procedure of choice since it is less expensive and involves no radiation.

Magnetic resonance imaging (MRI) is a technique which depends upon differences in the magnetic properties of molecules within different cell and tissue types based on their effect on the field of a large magnet. This technology offers the opportunity for spatial scanning comparable to that of ultrasound and CT scanning. In particular, it may be helpful in assessing blood flow and portal vein patency. It may also be effective in delineating focal disease processes, e.g., metastases (see Fig. 245-1). The range of applications of MRI is in a state of rapid development and its role relative to other imaging modalities is still evolving.

OTHER DIAGNOSTIC PROCEDURES

Percutaneous needle biopsy of the liver Percutaneous needle biopsy is a safe, simple, and valuable method for the diagnostic evaluation of liver disease. *Diffuse parenchymal disorders* such as cirrhosis, hepatitis, and drug reactions may be diagnosed with remarkable accuracy. In *disseminated focal diseases* (such as granulomas or tumor infiltrates) serial sections may demonstrate characteristic lesions.

Biopsy is performed under local anesthesia, usually with the Menghini (aspiration), Klatskin, or Vim-Silverman (cutting) needle, by either a transpleural or subcostal approach. If the operator is skillful and patients carefully selected, morbidity should be quite low and limited to occasional postbiopsy pain or vasovagal reactions.

Some of the most frequent indications for needle biopsy are (1) unexplained hepatomegaly or hepatosplenomegaly; (2) cholestasis of uncertain cause; (3) persistently abnormal liver function tests; (4) suspected systemic or infiltrative diseases such as sarcoidosis, miliary tuberculosis, or fever of unknown origin; and (5) suspected primary or metastatic liver tumor. Percutaneous liver biopsy may be performed either for diagnostic purposes or to evaluate the extent and severity of a known disease process. However, other new and improved noninvasive diagnostic methods have obviated the need for biopsy in many circumstances, and thus biopsy should be performed only when information from these other techniques is inadequate.

Needle biopsy should not be performed if (1) the patient is unable to cooperate; (2) clinical or laboratory evidence indicates impaired hemostasis (prothrombin time prolonged by 3 s or more over control, thrombocytopenia less than 80,000 to 100,000 platelets per cubic millimeter, or partial thromboplastin time or bleeding time prolonged); (3) there is infection of the right pleural space or septic cholangitis; (4) tense ascites is present, with risk of continued leakage of ascitic

Normal Human   Iron 0.15 mg/g

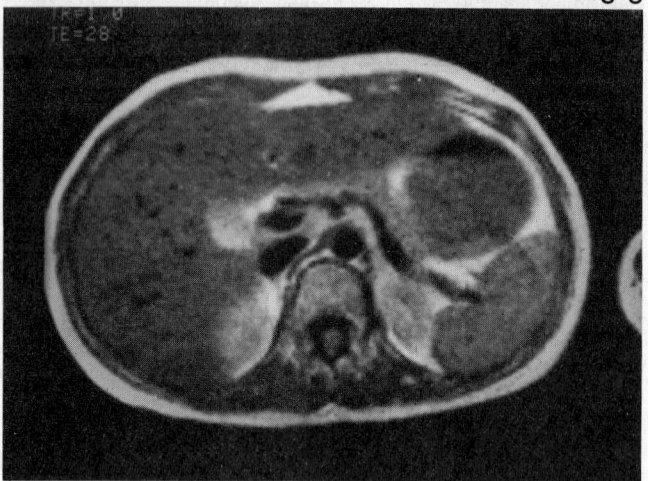

Hemochromatosis   Iron 12.5 mg/g

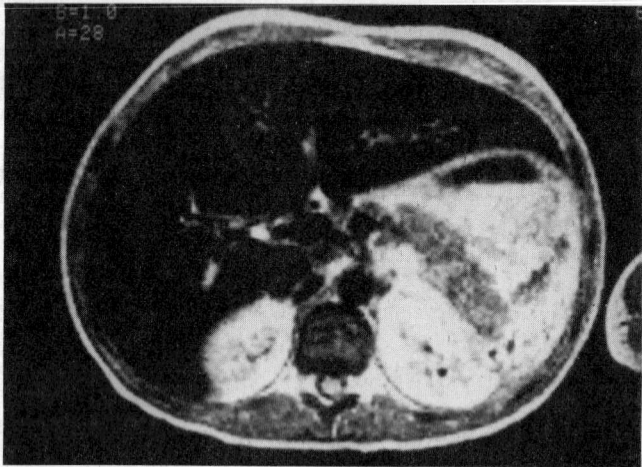

FIGURE 245-1 *Magnetic resonance imaging (MRI) of human liver using spin-echo technique. Upper panel, appearance of normal hepatic parenchyma. Lower panel, alteration in signal in proportion to hepatic iron content. (Courtesy of Dr. David Stark.)*

fluid; (5) compatible blood is not available for transfusion in case of hemorrhage or (6) high-grade biliary obstruction is suspected and there is an increased risk of bile peritonitis. With the increasing use of CT scan and ultrasonography, it is possible to perform "directed" aspiration biopsies of isolated lesions with very thin needles. Aspirated material can be used for cytology (tumors) and culture (abscesses) but is often inadequate for assessment of liver architecture.

Laparoscopy and laparotomy (peritoneoscopy) (see Chap. 233)

REFERENCES

BERK RN JR et al (eds): *Radiology of the Gallbladder and Bile Ducts.* Philadelphia, Saunders, 1983

BRENSILVER HL, KAPLAN MM: Significance of elevated liver alkaline phosphatase in serum. Gastroenterology 68:1556, 1975

FERRUCCI JT JR et al (eds): *Interventional Radiology of the Abdomen,* 2d ed. Baltimore, Williams and Wilkins, 1985

KEMENY MM et al: A projected analysis of laboratory tests and imaging studies to detect hepatitic lesions. Ann Surg 195:163, 1982

MAURO MA et al: Hepatobiliary scanning with 99mTc-PIPIDA in acute cholecystitis. Radiology 142:193, 1982

MOSS, AA et al Hepatic tumors: Magnetic resonance and CT appearance. Radiology 150:191, 1984

ROSALI SB: Enzyme tests in diseases of the liver and hepatobiliary tract, in *The Principles and Practice of Diagnostic Enzymology,* JH Wilkinon (ed). Chicago, Year Book, 1976, pp 303–360

SABESIN SM: Cholestatic lipoproteins—Their pathogenesis and significance. Gastroenterology 83:704, 1982

246 DISTURBANCES OF BILIRUBIN METABOLISM

KURT J. ISSELBACHER

The normal metabolism of bilirubin and the approach to the patient with jaundice have been presented in Chap. 38. With a consideration of these pathways, the disorders of bilirubin metabolism can be divided into four major categories, namely, those due to (1) increased pigment production, (2) reduced hepatic uptake of bilirubin, (3) impaired hepatic conjugation, and (4) decreased excretion of the conjugated pigment from the liver into bile. The first three of these disorders are associated with predominantly unconjugated hyperbilirubinemia. The fourth group, defective excretion, is associated with predominantly conjugated hyperbilirubinemia and bilirubinuria.

DISORDERS CAUSING PREDOMINANTLY UNCONJUGATED HYPERBILIRUBINEMIA

The plasma concentration of unconjugated bilirubin is determined by (1) the rate at which newly synthesized bilirubin enters the plasma (bilirubin turnover) and (2) the rate of removal of bilirubin by the liver (hepatic bilirubin clearance). The latter can result from derangements of hepatic bilirubin uptake, conjugation, or both. Measurements of these variables, although not routinely available, permit a classification of patients into those with *increased bilirubin turnover* (e.g., hemolysis), those with *decreased bilirubin clearance* (e.g., Gilbert's syndrome), and those in whom both mechanisms operate.

OVERPRODUCTION OF BILIRUBIN (INCREASED TURNOVER)
Increased destruction of circulating erythrocytes (intravascular and extravascular hemolysis) In disorders associated with hemolysis, most commonly the hemolytic anemias, the rate of bilirubin production is increased and may even exceed the amount that can be removed by a normal liver. The resulting jaundice is primarily an unconjugated hyperbilirubinemia. There is often also a small increase in the serum conjugated bilirubin (see Chap. 38). If significant anemia or other adverse factors are present (e.g., fever, sepsis, hypoxemia, or vascular collapse), the ability of the liver to handle the pigment load will be compromised, and the degree of jaundice will be greater.

The clinical and diagnostic features of the various hemolytic anemias are described in Chap. 287. The presence of reticulocytosis, shortened red blood cell survival, and increased fecal urobilinogen, in the absence of clinical and laboratory evidence of liver disease, strongly suggest hemolysis and overproduction of bilirubin as the cause of the jaundice. It is obvious, however, that in some cases (e.g., cirrhosis, tumors, and sepsis), hemolysis *plus* deranged liver function may be present. In most cases of uncomplicated hemolytic states, the mean serum bilirubin level will be in the range of 3 to 5 mg/dL; rarely, levels up to 10 mg/dL may be seen.

Jaundice due to increased pigment production may also be seen as a consequence of *tissue infarction* (e.g., pulmonary infarcts) and large *collections of blood in tissues* (e.g., leakage from blood vessels after catheterization studies, rupture of an aortic aneurysm). If hypotension and hypoxemia also supervene, jaundice is usually more pronounced, and the resulting impairment of liver function may also lead to a significant increase in the serum conjugated bilirubin level (see "Postoperative Jaundice" below).

Except in early infancy, elevations of serum unconjugated bilirubin levels are not generally harmful per se, and the prognosis is that of the hemolytic process itself. However, in the neonatal state and infancy, unconjugated bilirubin levels above 20 mg/dL may lead to *kernicterus* due to bilirubin deposition in the lipid-rich basal ganglia (see Chap. 351). Chronic overproduction of bilirubin may result in the formation of gallstones composed predominantly of bilirubin ("pigment stones"). In this situation, all the potential complications of calculus disease of the biliary tract (Chap. 253) may be superimposed on the chronic hemolytic state which produced it.

Increased production of bilirubin from sources other than circulating erythrocytes

As indicated in Chap. 38, about 15 to 20 percent of the circulating bilirubin is normally derived from sources other than the destruction of circulating red blood cells. This represents the so-called early-labeled fraction; it includes the synthesis of bilirubin from nonhemoglobin heme in the liver and from hemoglobin heme in the marrow.

In some conditions, jaundice results from an increased destruction of red blood cells or their precursors in the marrow—a process referred to as *ineffective erythropoiesis* (see Chaps. 38 and 53). In patients with thalassemia, pernicious anemia, and congenital erythropoietic porphyria, such an increased rate of formation of the early-labeled bilirubin fraction has been demonstrated. It is possible that some cases of unexplained unconjugated hyperbilirubinemia may be caused by an increased hepatic production of bilirubin from nonhemoglobin heme, but this phenomenon has not yet been demonstrated clinically.

IMPAIRED HEPATIC UPTAKE OF BILIRUBIN

Drugs Only a few drugs have been definitely shown to influence the uptake of bilirubin by the liver. Flavaspidic acid, used in the treatment of tapeworm infestation, may cause unconjugated hyperbilirubinemia, as well as impairment of sodium sulfobromophthalein (BSP) clearance, during its administration. The jaundice readily subsides following treatment. Flavaspidic acid competes with bilirubin for binding to ligandin, leading thereby to unconjugated hyperbilirubinemia. The jaundice which may occur with novobiocin and some cholecystographic dyes is also apparently due to an interference in bilirubin uptake.

Gilbert's syndrome Some cases of this syndrome of chronic unconjugated hyperbilirubinemia may be due to a defect in hepatic uptake (as reflected by alteration in BSP kinetics). In most cases, however, a deficiency of bilirubin glucuronyl transferase can be demonstrated. Hence this syndrome is best considered as a defect in bilirubin conjugation (see below).

IMPAIRED BILIRUBIN CONJUGATION (DECREASED ACTIVITY OF BILIRUBIN GLUCURONYL TRANSFERASE)

Neonatal jaundice (physiologic jaundice of the newborn) Almost every infant exhibits some transient unconjugated hyperbilirubinemia between the second and fifth days of life. While during gestation the placenta serves to clear bilirubin from the fetus, after birth infants must detoxify the pigments themselves. However, at this stage the hepatic enzyme glucuronyl transferase is still "immature" and inadequate for the task. As a result, unconjugated bilirubinemia develops, usually not exceeding 5 mg/dL. The activity of glucuronyl transferase increases within several days to 2 weeks after birth, and concomitantly the serum bilirubin returns to normal. In the premature infant the glucuronyl transferase activity is less, and the neonatal jaundice may be more pronounced. The "maturation" of the fetal and neonatal liver may be enhanced by treatment of the pregnant mother or the newborn infant with phenobarbital or related drugs. This results in a clear-cut reduction of the degree and duration of unconjugated hyperbilirubinemia in the newborn. In infants with a superimposed hemolytic process (e.g., erythroblastosis), the excessive pigment load leads to more pronounced jaundice, and bilirubin levels may exceed 20 mg/dL. It should be emphasized that neonatal jaundice is not present at the time of delivery; if jaundice is present at birth, other causes must be considered.

The cytoplasmic liver cell protein ligandin binds bilirubin in the hepatocyte and may assist in the transfer of bilirubin to the endoplasmic reticulum for conjugation (Chap. 38). It has been proposed that deficiency of ligandin may contribute to neonatal jaundice.

An additional facet of the "immature" liver is a concomitant defect in the excretion of *conjugated* bilirubin. Rarely this defect persists beyond the time needed for the development of adequate

glucuronide conjugation and may explain the occasional presence of conjugated hyperbilirubinemia in infants with erythroblastosis (*inspissated bile syndrome*).

When in the neonatal state unconjugated bilirubin levels approach or exceed 20 mg/dL, the infants may develop and die of *kernicterus* (bilirubin encephalopathy). This condition results from unconjugated bilirubin deposition in the lipid-rich basal ganglia. In the past treatment consisted of exchange transfusions, and albumin infusions were used to increase binding of bilirubin in the circulation and diminish its entry into the brain. The current approach is *phototherapy;* intense illumination of these patients with strong white or blue light leads to the photoisomerization of bilirubin to water-soluble isomers that are rapidly excreted in the bile without the prior need of conjugation.

Hereditary glucuronyl transferase deficiency There are currently three syndromes that fall into this category. As indicated in Table 246-1, they reflect progressive decreases in the activity of glucuronyl transferase and thus may be part of a spectrum, i.e., from minimal deficiency to complete absence of bilirubin glucuronyl transferase.

GILBERT'S SYNDROME Since the original report by Gilbert in 1907, there has been an increased recognition of this benign but chronic disorder characterized by mild, persistent, unconjugated hyperbilirubinemia. The patient usually does not manifest this disorder until after the second decade and is often unaware of the jaundice until it is detected by physical examination or routine laboratory testing. The total serum bilirubin level usually ranges and fluctuates from 1.2 to 3 mg/dL and rarely exceeds 5 mg/dL. With the van den Bergh diazo reaction, less than 20 percent of the bilirubin gives a direct reaction; however, studies using more accurate methods (such as high-pressure liquid chromatography) show that the serum bilirubin in patients with Gilbert's syndrome is almost all unconjugated. Typically the jaundice fluctuates and is exacerbated following prolonged fasting (see below), surgery, fever or infection, and excessive exertion or alcohol ingestion. Liver function tests are normal, and the liver cells usually appear normal by light microscopy.

With the exception of hemolytic anemias, this disorder is probably the most common cause of mild unconjugated hyperbilirubinemia. Detailed studies show these patients to have a partial deficiency of bilirubin glucuronyl transferase. Some patients also manifest decreased bilirubin uptake and increased hemolysis. Decreased glucuronyl transferase alone or together with a decrease in bilirubin uptake appears to account for the observed *decrease in hepatic bilirubin clearance*. A decreased clearance and hepatic uptake of bile salts has also been shown.

Previously Gilbert's syndrome was traditionally defined as mild, chronic, unconjugated hyperbilirubinemia occurring in the absence of hemolysis. However, with the use of radiobilirubin kinetics and erythrocyte half-life studies, at least two forms of Gilbert's syndrome

TABLE 246-1 Hereditary unconjugated hyperbilirubinemias with deficiency of glucuronyl transferase

Features	Mild (Gilbert's syndrome)	Moderate (Crigler-Najjar syndrome type II)	Severe (Crigler-Najjar syndrome type I)
Inheritance	Unclear*	Dominant†	Recessive
Serum bilirubin, mg/dL	1–6	6–20	20–45
Kernicterus	No	Rare	Yes
Conjugated bilirubin in bile	Yes (↑ monoconjugates)	Yes (↑↑ monoconjugates)	No
Response to phenobarbital	Yes	Yes	No
Bilirubin conjugation	↓ ‡	↓ ↓	Absent

* *Many cases are without familial incidence.*
† *Variable expressivity.*
‡ *Other defects such as occult hemolysis and ↓ bilirubin uptake may coexist.*

have been described. One group includes patients with decreased bilirubin clearance and *no hemolysis*. A second group includes those who also have *evidence of hemolysis* (often occult) and hence increased bilirubin turnover. The simultaneous presence of both derangements appears to be a chance occurrence of two not uncommon disorders in the same patient and does not imply a causal relationship. There is additional evidence of the heterogeneity of patients with Gilbert's syndrome. Some patients have an increase in hepatocyte lipofuscin and an increase in the smooth endoplasmic reticulum (SER); others show an increase in hepatic lysosomal enzymes.

A feature of Gilbert's syndrome which can be useful diagnostically is the increase in serum bilirubin following prolonged fasting or calorie deprivation. Patients with this disorder, when placed on 300 cal per day for 2 days, will increase their serum bilirubin by 1.5 mg/dL or more, the major increase being in the unconjugated fraction. It appears that a decrease in glucuronyl transferase activity is needed in order to obtain this effect. Patients with hemolysis do not show an increase in serum bilirubin with fasting. As a reflection of the mild decrease in glucuronyl transferase in Gilbert's syndrome (1) serum bilirubin levels will decrease when the enzyme activity is enhanced following phenobarbital administration, and (2) the bile shows a modest increase in monoconjugates of bilirubin (see Table 246-1).

In general, the diagnosis of this benign but not uncommon disorder is made by exclusion. The syndrome is suspected in a patient with low-grade unconjugated hyperbilirubinemia with (1) no systemic symptoms, (2) *no overt* or clinically recognizable hemolysis, (3) normal tests of routine liver function, and (4) a liver biopsy (although usually not necessary) that is normal by light microscopy.

CRIGLER-NAJJAR SYNDROME (TYPES I AND II)   This disorder is known to exist in two forms. Type I is the clinically *severe* form (originally described by Crigler and Najjar) and is due to *absence of glucuronyl transferase*. Type II has more *moderate* clinical findings due to *partial deficiency of glucuronyl transferase*. The major differences between the two variants are summarized in Table 246-1.

Type I (Crigler-Najjar) is a rare disorder. Infants develop high unconjugated bilirubin levels in the serum (20 to 45 mg/dL). Absence of the enzyme can be demonstrated in the liver. Routine liver function tests are normal, as is liver histology. Because of the absence of glucuronyl transferase no conjugated bilirubin is formed by the liver; hence no bilirubin is secreted by the liver, and the bile is colorless.

Phototherapy may temporarily and transiently reduce the unconjugated bilirubin level. Phenobarbital has no effect since the enzyme defect is complete and no drug "induction" is therefore possible. Affected infants usually die within the first year of life, although some patients have survived to the second or third decade of life. Death is usually from kernicterus. A strain of rats (Gunn rat) with the type I defect exists and is widely used as an animal model of the Crigler-Najjar syndrome (type I).

Type II patients have a *partial deficiency* of glucuronyl transferase, and their disorder is less severe. Serum unconjugated bilirubin levels are lower (6 to 20 mg/dL), jaundice may not appear until adolescence, and neurologic complications are uncommon. The bile contains variable amounts of conjugated bilirubin with a significant increase in monoconjugates. Phenobarbital is effective in lowering the serum bilirubin level in type II patients. However, the disorder is relatively benign in those patients whose bilirubin is less than 18 to 20 mg/dL.

Acquired deficiency of glucuronyl transferase   As with any enzyme, glucuronyl transferase is susceptible to inhibition by a variety of agents, and because of the decreased activity of the enzyme in the neonatal state, such inhibition may be more evident at that time. Neonatal jaundice may be aggravated or prolonged in infants treated with *drugs* such as chloramphenicol or novobiocin, or with *vitamin K*. In some breast-fed infants jaundice has been ascribed to the presence in *breast milk* of pregnane-3β,20α-diol, an inhibitor of glucuronyl transferase. When the infant is removed from the breast, the "breast-milk jaundice" subsides.

Hypothyroidism delays the normal "maturation" of glucuronyl transferase. In cretins, neonatal jaundice may be prolonged for weeks or months. In fact, the presence of prolonged unconjugated hyperbilirubinemia after birth may be a clue to an underlying hypothyroidism.

In the infant, as well as in the adult, *liver cell damage* leads to impairment in glucuronide conjugation as a result of decreased transferase activity. However, since excretion is probably the rate-limiting step in bilirubin metabolism and since this step is always interfered with to a greater extent than conjugation in parenchymal liver disease, the pigment which accumulates in the blood is predominantly conjugated bilirubin.

DISORDERS CAUSING COMBINED CONJUGATED AND UNCONJUGATED HYPERBILIRUBINEMIA

In jaundice due to primary liver disease, the plasma usually exhibits elevated levels of both conjugated and unconjugated bilirubin, and *urine contains bilirubin*. The relative proportions of the two pigments are highly variable. In many familial hepatic abnormalities (described below) and in some forms of liver injury, the jaundice is largely due to increases in conjugated bilirubin. Such a serum pigment pattern is also seen with extrahepatic biliary obstruction. One *cannot differentiate* intrahepatic and extrahepatic causes of jaundice from either the levels or proportions of unconjugated and conjugated bilirubin in serum. Thus the main purpose of the initial fractionation of the serum bilirubin is to distinguish hepatic parenchymal and biliary obstructive disease from the disorders associated with predominantly unconjugated hyperbilirubinemia.

FAMILIAL DEFECTS IN HEPATIC EXCRETORY FUNCTION   Dubin-Johnson syndrome   This disorder, also called *chronic idiopathic jaundice,* is a benign, autosomally inherited hyperbilirubinemia characterized by the presence of a dark pigment in the centrilobular region of the liver cells. Functionally there exists a *defect in biliary excretion* of bilirubin, cholephilic dyes, and porphyrins. Using the diazo method for measuring bilirubin, the serum pigment in these patients typically has been observed to be in the range of 3 to 15 mg/dL and predominantly of the conjugated type. However, with the newer and more accurate method (alkaline methanolysis and high-pressure liquid chromatography), homozygous patients with the Dubin-Johnson syndrome have been shown to have significant levels of serum *unconjugated bilirubin*. This finding may in part reflect pigment which, after conjugation by the liver, is deconjugated in the hepatobiliary system and refluxed into the plasma. Moreover, the serum contains more diconjugated than monoconjugated bilirubin, just the reverse of what is seen in acquired hepatobiliary disease and Rotor syndrome. This reversed ratio is believed to be characteristic and diagnostic for homozygous patients.

Patients with Dubin-Johnson syndrome may be asymptomatic or have vague constitutional or gastrointestinal symptoms. Not infrequently the liver is slightly enlarged; in about one-fourth of the cases there is mild hepatic tenderness. Oral and intravenous cholangiography fails to visualize the biliary tract. There is typically and characteristically a late rise in the plasma BSP elimination curve at *90 min*. This is caused by the reflux from the liver of the conjugated dye and reflects the defect in the hepatic excretory transport maximum (T_m). It is noteworthy that there is no such secondary rise in plasma when dyes which are not conjugated by the liver are given, such as indocyanine green. When bile salts such as ursodeoxycholic acid are given, these patients show a decreased hepatic uptake and clearance. In the liver the striking feature is the presence of a brown or black pigment in the hepatocytes. Some findings suggest that this unique pigment is "melanin-like"; others indicate it to be a polymer of epinephrin metabolites.

These patients also show an abnormality in coproporphyrin excretion. Normal urine contains mostly coproporphyrin III and small amounts of coproporphyrin I; Dubin-Johnson patients show a reversal of this pattern, i.e., they excrete predominantly coproporphyrin I. Heterozygotes show an intermediate excretory pattern.

There is impaired excretion of many metabolites, including conjugated bilirubin, BSP, and iodinated dyes. Excretion of bile acids, however, is normal. Oral contraceptive agents may accentuate hyperbilirubinemia or may produce jaundice for the first time. Features of cholestasis such as pruritus or steatorrhea are usually lacking, and, specifically, serum alkaline phosphatase levels are *not* elevated. The overall prognosis of the disorder is excellent.

Rotor syndrome This is similar in many respects to the Dubin-Johnson syndrome. However, *there is no pigment in the liver cells,* and the serum conjugated bilirubin has more monoconjugates than diglucuronide conjugates. The gallbladder is usually visualized on cholecystography, and there is an increase in the *total* urinary coproporphyrins but *not* an increased percentage in excretion of coproporphyrin I. The BSP excretion pattern does *not* show a secondary rise at 90 min. The impairment in excretion which is typical of Dubin-Johnson syndrome is not present; instead in most cases of the Rotor syndrome there is impairment of *hepatic storage capacity (S).* This rare syndrome is inherited as an autosomal recessive trait and is genetically distinct from Dubin-Johnson syndrome.

Benign familial recurrent cholestasis This is a relatively rare syndrome characterized by recurrent attacks of pruritus and jaundice. During an attack the serum alkaline phosphatase and bile acid levels are markedly elevated, and liver biopsy shows the morphologic features of cholestasis. However, there is no mechanical biliary obstruction, with cholangiography revealing a patent biliary tree. Remissions are the rule, and at such times hepatic function tests and liver morphologic features are usually normal. The cause of the disorder is unknown; cirrhosis does not develop, and the disorder is benign. A congenital origin has been postulated on the basis of the early age of onset and familial incidence.

Recurrent jaundice of pregnancy This form of jaundice is also known as *intrahepatic cholestasis of pregnancy.* During a normal pregnancy some derangements in liver function occur, especially during the last trimester. Usually these consist of slight increases in BSP retention and in serum alkaline phosphatase. This mild increase in alkaline phosphatase during pregnancy is normally of placental rather than of hepatic origin. With a normal pregnancy elevations of serum bilirubin either do not occur or are less than 2 mg/dL.

In a small number of pregnant women an intrahepatic cholestasis may appear. This usually occurs in the third trimester but may develop any time after the seventh week of gestation. The clinical features consist primarily of pruritus and jaundice. Serum bilirubin levels are usually less than 6 mg/dL. The serum alkaline phosphatase and cholesterol levels are elevated significantly, while other liver function tests are only mildly deranged. Histologically the liver shows varying degrees of cholestasis but only a few parenchymal cell changes. The clinical and laboratory abnormalities subside promptly after delivery and are usually normal within 7 to 14 days.

This condition has been seen more frequently in Scandinavia and Europe than in the United States. Since steroid hormones and specifically estrogens can induce changes in hepatic excretory function in normal individuals (see Chap. 244), these patients probably have an increased susceptibility or sensitivity to the hepatic effects of estrogenic and progestational hormones. The intrahepatic cholestasis is usually termed *recurrent,* since the syndrome often (but not always) reappears in subsequent pregnancies. The process is benign and self-limited, and treatment is usually not needed, but cholestyramine administration will diminish the pruritus. This disorder must be distinguished from the many other causes of jaundice not unique to pregnancy, such as viral hepatitis. It must also be distinguished from the idiopathic *acute fatty liver of pregnancy* and the *tetracycline-induced* fatty liver. The latter two conditions are rare, occur in the last trimester, and have a high fatality rate; however, in these disorders there is evidence of diffuse parenchymal damage and not just cholestasis.

ACQUIRED DEFECTS OF HEPATIC EXCRETORY FUNCTION

Drug-induced cholestasis A condition entirely analogous to the intrahepatic cholestasis of pregnancy may occur in some women following the use of oral contraceptive agents. A significant number of individuals using these drugs show mild increases in BSP retention, and even more have decreased BSP excretory capacity as measured by infusion tests. In some, mild cholestatic jaundice may occur, liver function returns to normal when the drugs are withdrawn, and chronic liver disease does not appear to result. It is relevant that one-third of the reported patients with jaundice due to oral contraceptives also have a history of recurrent intrahepatic cholestasis of pregnancy.

The nature of these changes produced by the natural and synthetic female sex hormones is very similar to those resulting from the administration of certain testosterone analogues, especially those with α substitutions at the 17 position of the steroid nucleus. These agents (such as methyltestosterone and norethandrolone) commonly cause BSP retention and less commonly cause jaundice or significant changes in other liver functions. However, unlike the female hormones, these agents have been implicated as a cause of chronic liver disease, especially biliary cirrhosis.

Because of these phenomena, synthetic steroid sex hormones should not be used in patients with liver disease. Conversely, in individuals using these agents the appearance of jaundice or elevations in serum aminotransferase (transaminase) levels or alkaline phosphatase contraindicates their further use. However, mild to moderate increases in BSP retention alone are probably not of clinical significance, although liver function tests should be carried out periodically.

As is discussed in detail in Chap. 247, there are many drugs which may produce not only cholestasis but liver injury resembling acute hepatitis or cholestatic hepatitis. In contrast to the jaundice produced by the steroid hormones, the clinical features are those of fever, rash, arthralgia, and eosinophilia, with the liver showing a pronounced inflammatory reaction. These features suggest that such reactions are *allergic* or *toxic* in nature and therefore differ from the effects caused by the steroid hormones, which probably represent an exaggerated response by the liver to the normal action of these hormones.

Postoperative jaundice The occurrence of postoperative jaundice is a problem of increasing importance. It is perhaps seen more frequently now than in earlier years, because patients are able to undergo more major surgical procedures (i.e., cardiac surgery, repair of ruptured aneurysms) and survive. In approaching this problem the possible pathogenic mechanisms listed in Table 246-2 need to be considered. The patient may have *pigment overload,* especially from blood transfusions (with hemolysis of stored blood), from resorption of blood in extravascular spaces, and less commonly from hemolytic anemia. *Hepatocellular damage* and decreased liver cell function may occur due to concurrent use of hepatotoxic drugs (Chap. 247) or anesthetics such as halothane. Hepatocellular necrosis may follow profound shock; with lesser degrees of hypotension or hypoxemia, morphologic damage may be slight, but significant impairment of

TABLE 246-2 Conditions causing or contributing to postoperative jaundice

I Increased pigment load
  A Hemolytic anemia
  B Transfusions (especially of stored blood)
  C Resorption of hematomas, blood in extravascular spaces
II Impaired hepatocellular function
  A Hepatitis-like picture
    1 Halothane anesthesia
    2 Drugs
    3 Shock
    4 Infection with hepatitis viruses
  B Cholestatic picture
    1 Hypotension, hypoxemia
    2 Drugs
    3 Sepsis
III Extrahepatic obstruction
  A Bile duct injury
  B Choledocholithiasis

TABLE 246-3 Laboratory features in icteric states

Bilirubin disorder	Serum bilirubin Unconjugated	Serum bilirubin Conjugated	Urine bilirubin	Comments
I Overproduction				
A Hemolysis (intra- and extravascular)	↑	N	0	↑ Bilirubin turnover; serum bilirubin rarely exceeds 4 mg/dL
B Ineffective erythropoiesis	↑	N	0	Splenomegaly; normal RBC survival; normoblasts in marrow
II Defective hepatic uptake				
A Some drugs (e.g., flavaspidic acid, novobiocin)	↑	N	0	Normal liver biopsy
B Gilbert's syndrome (some cases)				
III Defective conjugation				
A Neonatal jaundice	↑	Low	0	↓ Glucuronyl transferase; ? ↓ ligandin
B Gilbert's syndrome	↑	Low	0	↓ Glucuronyl transferase and ↓ bilirubin uptake; some may have ↑ hemolysis; bile contains ↑ monoconjugates
C Crigler-Najjar syndrome (types I and II)	↑	Low	0	Type I = absence of transferase Type II = deficiency of transferase; bile contains ↑↑ monoconjugates
IV Defective excretion				
A Intrahepatic obstruction				
1 Familial syndromes				
a Dubin-Johnson	↑	↑	+	Abnormal BSP curve, hepatic lipochrome pigment; ↑ urinary coproporphyrin type I
b Rotor	↑	↑	+	No liver pigment; ↑ total urinary coproporphyrin
2 Drugs (e.g., chloramphenicol, methyltestosterone)	↑	↑	+	↑ Alkaline phosphatase but other function tests usually normal
3 Benign recurrent cholestasis	↑	↑	+	↑ Alkaline phosphatase
4 Recurrent jaundice of pregnancy (third trimester)	↑	↑	+	↑ Alkaline phosphatase; may be reproduced in afflicted subjects by estrogens or progesterone
B Extrahepatic obstruction (tumors, stone, stricture of bile duct)				↑↑ Alkaline phosphatase (often > fourfold)
1 Partial	↑	↑	+	
2 Complete	↑	↑	+	
V Hepatocellular disease*				
A Hepatitis	↑	↑	+	Conjugated/total serum bilirubin >50–70%; liver biopsy important for diagnosis
B Cirrhosis: Same as hepatitis	↑	↑		

* *Note that in hepatocellular disease there is generally an interference in all pathways of bilirubin metabolism (i.e., impaired uptake, conjugation, and excretion).*

function may occur. Hence, prior shock or hypotension plus pigment overload may produce significant jaundice. Extensive sepsis can also produce jaundice, often of a cholestatic type. Concurrent renal impairment due to hypotension and hypoxemia may enhance the degree of jaundice because the renal excretion of conjugated bilirubin is decreased. *Extrahepatic obstruction* due to surgical damage or stones needs to be considered, and may be excluded by ultrasound studies.

A form of jaundice referred to as *benign postoperative intrahepatic cholestasis* may be seen. In the typical case the patient has had major and prolonged surgery for a catastrophic event such as a ruptured aortic aneurysm complicated by hypotension and hypoxemia, extensive blood loss into tissues, and massive blood replacement. Jaundice may be noted on the second or third postoperative day, and the serum bilirubin, predominantly conjugated, may reach 20 to 40 mg/dL by the eighth to tenth day. Serum alkaline phosphatase levels may be elevated three- to tenfold. Typically the serum aspartate aminotransferase (AST, SGOT) is only mildly elevated. The liver morphology is striking in that necrosis is not seen, only cholestasis and erythrophagocytosis.

The cause of this type of postoperative cholestatic jaundice is uncertain. However, it probably reflects (1) increased pigment load, (2) decreased liver function due to hypoxemia and hypotension, and (3) decreased renal bilirubin excretion due to varying degrees of tubular necrosis as a result of shock. This diagnostic possibility must be considered in the postoperative patient with marked cholestatic jaundice. The course of the jaundice is self-limited and will subside if the other systemic complications do not predominate and lead to death.

Hepatitis and cirrhosis These disorders, discussed in detail in Chaps. 247 to 249, constitute the *most common disorders associated* with jaundice. As has been stated previously, when the liver cell is damaged, as in viral hepatitis, there is often impairment in all three major hepatic phases of bilirubin metabolism, namely, uptake, conjugation, and excretion. Since the excretory step is the one which is rate-limiting and most readily affected by injury, significant amounts of conjugated bilirubin reenter the systemic circulation. There are also usually lesser increases in the serum unconjugated bilirubin. This phenomenon is probably a reflection of the impaired uptake and conjugation, and is due in part to the shortened life span of red blood cells often found in liver disease. In most patients with hepatitis and cirrhosis, the total serum bilirubin levels tend not to exceed 50 mg/dL, but on rare occasions levels of up to 90 or 95 mg/dL have been described. (For a summary of laboratory features in icteric states, see Table 246-3.)

EXTRAHEPATIC BILIARY OBSTRUCTION Anatomic or mechanical obstruction of the bile ducts is most commonly due to stones, tumors, or strictures. The clinical picture is quite similar to that of intrahepatic cholestasis with pronounced elevations of the serum conjugated bilirubin and alkaline phosphatase levels. Usually, but not always, fever, pain, and chills may be present. In contrast to hepatitis and cirrhosis, the serum bilirubin level often tends to plateau and rarely exceeds levels of 35 mg/dL. The reason for this plateau is not clear but may be related to renal excretion of conjugated bilirubin or alternative pathways of bilirubin catabolism in obstructive jaundice.

REFERENCES

Benign familial recurrent cholestasis

DePagter AGF et al: Familial benign intrahepatic cholestasis. Gastroenterology 71:202, 1976

ENDO T et al: Bile acid metabolism in benign recurrent intrahepatic cholestasis. Gastroenterology 76:1002, 1979

Dubin-Johnson and Rotor syndromes

BERK PD et al: Inborn errors of bilirubin metabolism. Med Clin North Am 59:803, 1975

ROSENTHAL P et al: Homozygous Dubin-Johnson syndrome exhibits a characteristic serum bilirubin pattern. Hepatology 1:540, 1981

SWARTZ HM et al: On the nature and excretion of the hepatic pigment in the Dubin-Johnson syndrome. Gastroenterology 76:958, 1979

WOLKOFF AW et al: Hereditary jaundice and disorders of bilirubin metabolism, in *The Metabolic Basis of Inherited Disease*, 5th ed, JB Stanbury et al (eds). New York, McGraw-Hill, 1983, pp 1385–1420

WOLPERT E et al: Abnormal sulfobromophthalein metabolism in Rotor's syndrome and obligate heterozygotes. N Engl J Med 206:1099, 1977

Glucuronyl transferase deficiency states

BERTHELOT P, DHUMEAUS D: New insights into the classification and mechanisms of hereditary, chronic, non-hemolytic hyperbilirubinemia. Gut 19:474, 1978

DAWSON J et al: Gilbert's syndrome: Evidence of morphologic heterogeneity. Gut 20:848, 1979

FELSHER BF, CARPIO NM: Caloric intake and unconjugated hyperbilirubinemia. Gastroenterology 69:42, 1975

FEVERY J et al: Unconjugated bilirubin and an increased proportion of bilirubin monoconjugates in the bile of patients with Gilbert's syndrome and Crigler-Najjar disease. J Clin Invest 60:970, 1977

OHKUBO H et al: Ursodeoxycholic acid oral tolerance test in patients with constitutional hyperbilirubinemias and effect of phenobarbital. Gastroenterology 81:126, 1981

—— et al: Effects of corticosteroids on bilirubin metabolism in patients with Gilbert's syndrome. Hepatology 1:168, 1981

Postoperative jaundice

KOFF RS: Postoperative jaundice. Med Clin North Am 59:823, 1975

LAMONT JT, ISSELBACHER KJ: Postoperative jaundice, in *Liver and Biliary Disease*, 2d ed, R Wright et al (eds). Philadelphia, Saunders, 1985

247 ACUTE HEPATITIS

JULES L. DIENSTAG / JACK R. WANDS / RAYMOND S. KOFF

ACUTE VIRAL HEPATITIS

Acute viral hepatitis is a systemic infection affecting the liver predominantly. Four categories of viral agents have been implicated: hepatitis A virus (HAV), hepatitis B virus (HBV), non-A, non-B hepatitis agents, and the recently described HBV-associated delta agent. Among these, HAV, HBV, and the delta agent can be distinguished by their antigenic properties, but all four types produce clinically similar illnesses. These range from asymptomatic and inapparent to fulminant and fatal acute infections, on the one hand, and from subclinical persistent infections to rapidly progressive chronic liver disease with cirrhosis and even hepatocellular carcinoma, on the other.

Virology and etiology HEPATITIS A Hepatitis A virus (HAV) is a nonenveloped 27-nm, heat-, acid-, and ether-resistant RNA virus that

has been classified as enterovirus type 72 (Fig. 247-1). Its virion is composed of four polypeptides designated VP1 to VP4. Inactivation of viral activity can be achieved by boiling for 1 min, by contact with formaldehyde and chlorine, or by ultraviolet irradiation. All strains of this virus identified to date are immunologically indistinguishable and belong to one serotype. The virus is present in the liver, bile, stools, and blood during the late incubation period and acute preicteric phase of illness. Despite persistence of virus in the liver, viral shedding in feces, viremia, and infectivity diminish rapidly once jaundice becomes apparent. Unlike other hepatitis viruses, hepatitis A virus has been grown in tissue culture. In addition, its genome has been cloned and characterized.

Antibodies to HAV (anti-HAV) can be detected during acute illness when serum aminotransferase activity is elevated and fecal HAV shedding is still occurring. This early antibody response is predominantly of the IgM class and persists for several months. During convalescence, however, anti-HAV of the IgG class becomes the predominant antibody (Fig. 247-2). Therefore, the diagnosis of hepatitis A is made during acute illness by demonstrating high-titer anti-HAV of the IgM class. Following acute illness, anti-HAV of the IgG class remains detectable indefinitely, and patients with serum anti-HAV are immune to reinfection. Indeed, the IgG anti-HAV present in immune globulin preparations accounts for the protection it affords against HAV infection.

HEPATITIS B This viral infection is unique in that concentrations of viral antigen and viral particles in the blood may reach 500 µg/mL and 10 trillion particles per milliliter, respectively. Electron microscopic studies of serum have demonstrated the morphologic appearance of three types of particles (Table 247-1) related to hepatitis B infection (see Fig. 247-1). The most numerous are the 22-nm particles which appear as spherical or long filamentous forms; these are antigenically identical with the outer surface or coat of hepatitis B virus (HBV), and they are thought to represent excess viral coat protein. Outnumbered in serum by a factor of 100 or 1000 to 1 compared to the spheres and tubules are large 42-nm spherical particles, which represent the intact hepatitis B virion. These large particles consist of an outer coat and an inner icosahedral nucleocapsid core measuring 27 nm in diameter. Previous studies have shown that antiserum obtained from hemophiliacs, who had presumably been repeatedly exposed to hepatitis viruses through multiple blood transfusions, would form a precipitin line by diffusion in agar gel with an antigen present in hepatitis serum. This antigen was originally called Australia antigen or hepatitis-associated antigen and is now referred to as hepatitis B surface antigen (HBsAg). The discovery of this antigen provided the first serologic test to distinguish hepatitis B from other types of hepatitis. HBsAg consists primarily of two major polypeptides, one of 24,000 mol wt and its glycosylated counterpart of 28,000 mol wt. A number of different HBsAg subdeterminants have been identified. There is a common group-reactive antigen, *a*, shared by all HBsAg isolates. In addition, HBsAg may contain one of several subtype-specific antigens, namely, *d* or *y*, *w* or *r*, as well as other more recently characterized specificities. These HBsAg subtypes provide additional epidemiologic markers in evaluating the

FIGURE 247-1 *A. Electron micrograph of 27-nm hepatitis A virus particles purified from stool of a patient with acute hepatitis A virus infection and aggregated by hepatitis A antibody. B. Electron micrograph of concentrated serum from a patient with acute hepatitis B infection, demonstrating the 42-nm virion, tubular forms, and spherical 22-nm particles of hepatitis B surface antigen (132,000×).*

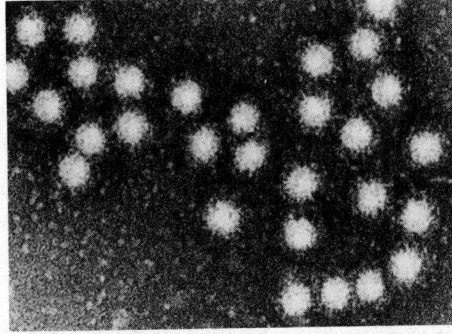

A

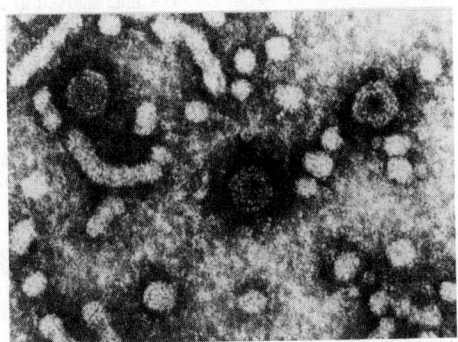

B

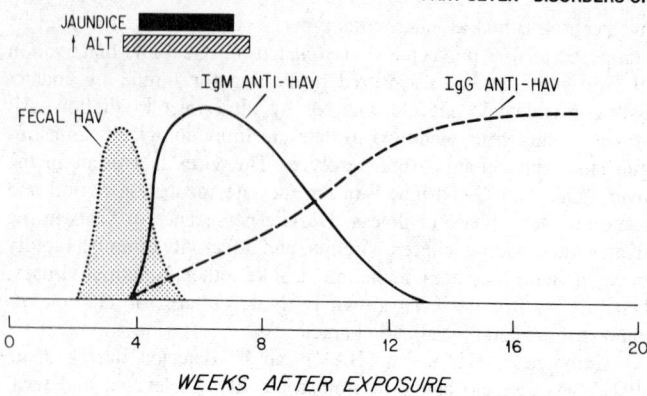

FIGURE 247-2 *Scheme of typical clinical and laboratory features of viral hepatitis type A.*

transmission of hepatitis B infection in that subtypes "breed true." For example, studies of hepatitis outbreaks have shown that index cases and their contacts have identical HBsAg subtypes. Clinical course and outcome, however, are independent of subtype.

The intact 42-nm virion can be disrupted by mild detergents and the 27-nm nucleocapsid core particle isolated. Naked core particles do not circulate in serum. The antigen expressed on the surface of the nucleocapsid core is referred to as hepatitis B core antigen (HBcAg), and the corresponding antibody is anti-HBc. HBcAg does not cross react with HBsAg. A third antigen associated with hepatitis B is hepatitis B e antigen (HBeAg). HBeAg is a soluble, nonparticulate antigen which is found only in HBsAg-positive serum and is immunologically and biochemically distinct from HBsAg and intact HBcAg but appears to be an internal component or degradation product of the core of HBV. HBsAg-positive serum containing HBeAg is more likely to be highly infectious and to be associated with the presence of hepatitis B virions (and DNA polymerase and HBV DNA, see below) than HBeAg-negative or anti-HBe-positive serum. For example, HBsAg carrier mothers who are HBeAg-positive almost invariably transmit hepatitis B infection to their offspring, while HBsAg carrier mothers with anti-HBe rarely infect their offspring.

In every individual with acute hepatitis B infection, HBeAg develops transiently, early in the course of illness, but persistent HBeAg positivity correlates with ongoing viral replication and may be associated with continuing disease actvity in chronic hepatitis; its disappearance may be a harbinger of biochemical improvement and potential resolution of infection. Unfortunately HBeAg is not a sufficiently discriminating marker to support prognostic predictions or to substitute for morphologic evaluation of severity in patients with chronic hepatitis.

Within the nucleocapsid core, in addition to HBeAg, is a predominantly double-stranded, but partially single-stranded, DNA genome measuring 3200 base pairs as well as a DNA polymerase, which directs replication and repair of HBV DNA. In vitro, the polymerase can repair the single-stranded gap and render it double-stranded. Once thought to be unique among viruses, HBV is now recognized as one of a family of animal viruses, hepadnaviruses (hepatotropic DNA viruses), and is classified as hepadnavirus type 1. Viruses similar to HBV infect certain species of woodchucks, ground squirrels, and Pekin ducks, to mention the most carefully characterized. Like HBV, all have the same distinctive three morphologic forms, have counterparts to the virus antigens of HBV, replicate within the liver, contain their own, endogenous DNA polymerase, have partially double-stranded, partially single-stranded genomes, and, for the most part, are associated with acute and chronic hepatitis and hepatocellular carcinoma. Recent evidence suggests that hepadnaviruses rely on replicative strategies typical of retroviruses. Although HBV has not been cultivated in vitro, its genome has been cloned in bacterial, yeast, and mammalian cell vectors and has been completely characterized. Four segments of the genome have been characterized: (1) the pre-S and S gene, which code for HBsAg and several other poorly characterized gene products, including receptors on the HBV surface for polymerized human serum albumin; (2) the C gene, which codes for HBcAg and HBeAg; (3) the P gene, which codes for DNA polymerase; and (4) the X gene, which codes for a recently identified

TABLE 247-1 Nomenclature and features of hepatitis antigens and antibodies

Hepatitis type*	Particle diameter, nm	Description	Antigen	Corresponding antibody	Remarks
A	27	Icosahedral virus particle	Hepatitis A virus (HAV)	Hepatitis A antibody (anti-HAV)	RNA virus; present in stool and serum early in course of hepatitis A
B	42	Intact virion (surface and core); spherical	Hepatitis B surface antigen (HBsAg) Hepatitis B core antigen (HBcAg)	Hepatitis B surface antibody (anti-HBs) Hepatitis B core antibody (anti-HBc)	DNA virus; found in serum
	27	Nucleocapsid core of virion, icosahedral	HBcAg	Anti-HBc	Core contains DNA and DNA polymerase; present in hepatocyte nuclei but not in serum Anti-HBc detected in serum during and after acute infection
	22	Appear as spherical and filamentous forms; both have same antigenic properties as surface of virion; represent excess viral coat material	HBsAg	Anti-HBs	HBsAg detectable in > 90% of patients with acute hepatitis B; found in serum, body fluids, and hepatocyte cytoplasm Anti-HBs appears following B infection; protective antibody
	Nonparticulate	Soluble protein, internal component of nucleocapsid	Hepatitis B e antigen (HBeAg)	Hepatitis B e antibody (Anti-HBe)	HBeAg found in HBsAg-positive serum only, correlates with infectivity and presence of intact virus particles
D	35–37	Hybrid particle with HBsAg coat and delta nucleocapsid core	Hepatitis delta virus (HDV) Hepatitis delta antigen (HDAg)	Hepatitis delta antibody (Anti-HD)	Defective RNA virus, requires helper function of HBV

Non-A, non-B hepatitis viruses are transmissible hepatitis agents, but no immunologic marker or virus particle has yet been satisfactorily demonstrated.

protein seen more frequently in patients with hepatocellular carcinoma but which remains to be further characterized. Not only has the HBV genome been cloned but its gene products have been expressed by recombinant vectors. In addition, the delineation of the gene and amino acid maps of HBV has led to the production in the laboratory of synthetic HBsAg polypeptides.

After infection with HBV, the first virologic marker detectable in serum is HBsAg (Fig. 247-3). Circulating HBsAg precedes elevations of serum aminotransferase activity and clinical symptoms and remains detectable during the entire icteric or symptomatic phase of acute hepatitis B and beyond. In typical cases, HBsAg becomes undetectable 1 to 2 months following the onset of jaundice and rarely persists beyond 6 months. After HBsAg disappears, antibody to HBsAg (anti-HBs) becomes detectable in serum and remains detectable indefinitely thereafter. Because HBcAg is sequestered within an HBsAg coat, HBcAg is not detectable routinely in the serum of patients with HBV infection. On the other hand, antibody to HBcAg (anti-HBc) is readily demonstrable in serum, beginning within the first 1 to 2 weeks after the appearance of HBsAg and preceding detectable levels of anti-HBs by weeks to months. Because variability exists in the time of appearance of anti-HBs following HBV infection, occasionally a gap of several weeks or longer may separate the disappearance of HBsAg and the appearance of anti-HBs. During this ''gap'' or ''window'' period, anti-HBc may represent serologic evidence of current or recent HBV infection, and blood containing anti-HBc in the absence of HBsAg and anti-HBs has been implicated in the development of transfusion-associated hepatitis B. In part because the sensitivity of immunoassays for HBsAg and anti-HBs has increased, however, this window period is rarely encountered. In some persons, years after HBV infection, anti-HBc may persist in the circulation longer than anti-HBs. Therefore, isolated anti-HBc does not necessarily indicate active virus replication; most instances of isolated anti-HBc represent hepatitis B infection in the remote past. Distinction between recent and remote HBV infection can be accomplished by determination of the immunoglobulin class of anti-HBc. Anti-HBc of the IgM class (IgM anti-HBc) predominates during the first approximately 6 months after acute infection, whereas IgG anti-HBc is the predominant class of anti-HBc beyond 6 months. Therefore, patients with current or recent acute hepatitis B, including those in the anti-HBc window, have IgM anti-HBc in their serum. In patients who have recovered from hepatitis B in the remote past as well as those with chronic HBV infection, anti-HBc is of the IgG class. Infrequently, in no more than 1 to 5 percent of patients with acute HBV infection, levels of HBsAg are too low to be detected; in such cases, the presence of IgM anti-HBc establishes the diagnosis of acute hepatitis B. Similarly, isolated anti-HBc may occur in the rare patient with chronic hepatitis B whose HBsAg level is below the sensitivity threshold of contemporary immunoassays (a low-level carrier); in such cases, the anti-HBc is of the IgG class. In persons who have recovered from hepatitis B, anti-HBs and anti-HBc persist indefinitely.

The temporal association between the appearance of anti-HBs and resolution of HBV infection as well as the observation that persons with anti-HBs in serum are protected against reinfection with HBV suggest that *anti-HBs is the protective antibody*. Therefore, strategies for prevention of HBV infection are based on providing susceptible persons with circulating anti-HBs (see below).

The other readily detectable hepatitis B virologic marker, HBeAg, appears concurrently with or shortly after HBsAg. Its appearance coincides temporally with high levels of virus replication and reflects the presence of circulating intact virions, DNA polymerase, and HBV DNA, which are not detected routinely in clinical laboratories; in the hepatocyte nucleus, HBV DNA can be detected in free or episomal form. This *replicative* stage of HBV infection is the time of maximal infectivity. In self-limited HBV infections, HBeAg becomes undetectable shortly after peak elevations in aminotransferase activity, before the disappearance of HBsAg, and anti-HBe then becomes detectable, coinciding with a period of relatively lower infectivity (Fig. 247-3). In protracted HBV infection, HBeAg may remain detectable, indicating persistent replicative infection. When HBeAg is absent and anti-HBe present in chronic hepatitis B, infection is usually *nonreplicative*. In this phase of chronic infection, when HBV DNA is demonstrable in hepatocyte nuclei, it tends to be integrated into the host genome.

DELTA HEPATITIS The most recently recognized hepatitis agent, the delta agent hepatitis D virus (HDV), is a defective RNA virus which coinfects with and requires the helper function of HBV for its replication and expression. Slightly smaller than HBV, delta is a 35 to 37 nm virus with a hybrid structure. Its nucleocapsid expresses delta antigen, which bears no antigenic homology with any of the HBV antigens, and contains a small RNA genome that is nonhomologous with HBV DNA. This delta core is ''encapsidated'' by an outer coat of HBsAg. Thus, delta can only either infect a person simultaneously with HBV or superinfect a person already infected with HBV; when delta infection is transmitted from a donor with one HBsAg subtype to an HBsAg-positive recipient with a different subtype, the delta agent assumes the HBsAg subtype of the recipient, rather than the donor. Because delta relies absolutely on HBV, the duration of delta infection is determined by the duration of and cannot outlast HBV infection. Delta antigen is expressed primarily in hepatocyte nuclei and is occasionally detectable in serum. During acute delta infection, anti-delta of the IgM class predominates; in self-limited infection, anti-delta is low-titer and transient, rarely remaining detectable beyond the clearance of HBsAg and delta antigen. In chronic delta infection, anti-delta circulates in high titer, and both IgM and IgG anti-delta can be detected.

NON-A, NON-B HEPATITIS Sensitive serologic tests for identifying both types A and B hepatitis have led to the identification of hepatitis cases with incubation periods and modes of transmission consistent with an infectious disease but without serologic evidence of hepatitis

FIGURE 247-3 *Scheme of typical clinical and laboratory features of acute viral hepatitis type B.*

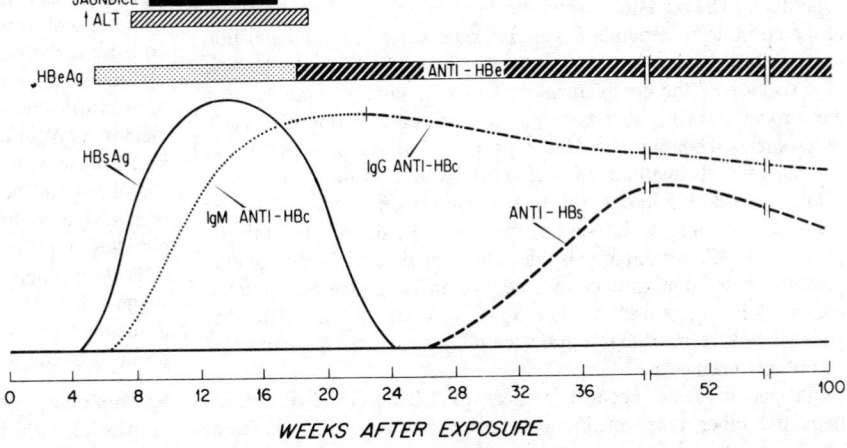

A or B infection. Identified initially among recipients of transfused blood, these cases of so-called non-A, non-B hepatitis have not been associated serologically with Epstein-Barr virus or cytomegalovirus (except in rare instances) or with other viruses known to involve the liver. Although the virus(es) or virus antigens have not been identified definitively, cross-challenge studies in chimpanzees have shown that there are at least two different bloodborne non-A, non-B hepatitis agents. One has been isolated from clotting factor VIII concentrates, is chloroform-sensitive, and induces ultrastructural cytoplasmic tubular changes in hepatocytes. The other has been isolated from clotting factor IX concentrates, is chloroform-resistant, and does not induce cytoplasmic tubular changes in hepatocytes. The latter type appears to be the most frequently encountered after blood transfusion.

In addition, a distinct type of waterborne non-A, non-B hepatitis has been identified in India and Asia (so-called epidemic non-A, non-B hepatitis), which, because of its epidemiologic resemblance to hepatitis A, has been labeled by some "non-A hepatitis." A preliminary report has appeared in which a 27-nm HAV-like virus was detected in stools from patients with epidemic non-A, non-B hepatitis; however, this finding remains to be confirmed.

Acceptable serologic tests to identify antigens and antibodies associated with non-A, non-B hepatitis virus(es) have not been developed. Details of virologic events and humoral immune responses remain to be described.

Pathogenesis   While data on the pathogenesis of hepatitis A, non-A, non-B hepatitis, and delta hepatitis are very limited, evidence suggests that the clinical manifestations of and outcomes following acute liver injury associated with HBV infection are determined by the immunologic responses of the host. The existence of asymptomatic hepatitis B carriers with normal liver histology and function suggests that the virus is not directly cytopathic. The facts that lymphoid cells are juxtaposed with necrotic hepatocytes in the livers of patients with liver injury and that patients with defects in cellular immune competence are more likely to remain chronically infected rather than to clear the virus are cited to support the role of cellular immune responses in the pathogenesis of hepatitis B–related liver injury. To date, however, because adequate animal and laboratory models are lacking, support for this hypothesis remains circumstantial. Still, the model that has the most experimental support involves cytolytic T cells sensitized specifically to recognize host and hepatitis B viral antigens on the liver cell surface. Although HBsAg was initially thought to be the most likely viral target antigen on the hepatocyte surface, recent laboratory observations suggest that HBcAg, present on the cell membrane in minute quantities, is the viral target antigen that, with host antigens, invites cytolytic T cells to destroy HBV-infected hepatocytes. Debate does continue, however, over the relative importance of viral and host factors in the pathogenesis of liver injury associated with hepatitis B and its outcome.

Although the mechanism of HBV-induced liver injury remains uncertain, immune complex–mediated tissue damage appears to play a major pathogenetic role in the extrahepatic manifestations of acute hepatitis B. The occasional prodromal serum sickness–like syndrome observed in acute hepatitis B appears to be related to the deposition in tissue blood vessel walls of circulating immune complexes leading to activation of the complement system. The clinical consequences are urticarial rash, angioedema, and arthritis. During the early prodrome of hepatitis B in these patients, HBsAg in high titer in association with small amounts of anti-HBs leads to the formation of soluble, circulating immune complexes (in antigen excess). Complement components in the serum are depressed during the arthritic phase of the illness and are also detectable in the circulating immune complexes. In addition to complement components, these complexes contain HBsAg, anti-HBs, IgG, IgM, IgA, and fibrin. After the patient recovers from the serum sickness–like syndrome, these immune complexes disappear.

In patients who become carriers of HBsAg following acute hepatitis, other types of immune-complex disease may be seen.

Glomerulonephritis with the nephrotic syndrome is occasionally observed; HBsAg, immunoglobulin, and C3 deposition has been found in the glomerular basement membrane. While polyarteritis nodosa develops in considerably fewer than 1 percent of patients with hepatitis B, 20 to 30 percent of patients with polyarteritis nodosa have HBsAg in serum. In these patients, the affected small and medium-sized arterioles have been shown to contain HBsAg, immunoglobulins, and complement components.

Pathology   The typical morphologic lesions of hepatitis A, B, delta, and non-A, non-B are often similar and consist of panlobular infiltration with mononuclear cells, hepatic cell necrosis, hyperplasia of Kupffer cells, and variable degrees of cholestasis. Hepatic cell regeneration is present, as evidenced by numerous mitotic figures, multinucleated cells, and "rosette" or "pseudoacinar" formation. The mononuclear infiltration consists primarily of small lymphocytes, although plasma cells and eosinophils are occasionally seen. Liver cell damage consists of hepatic cell degeneration and necrosis, cell dropout, ballooning of cells, and acidophilic degeneration of hepatocytes (forming so-called Councilman-like bodies). Large hepatocytes with a ground-glass appearance of the cytoplasm may be seen in chronic but not in acute hepatitis B; these cells have been shown to contain HBsAg and can be identified histochemically with orcein or aldehyde fuchsin. In uncomplicated viral hepatitis, the reticulin framework is preserved.

A more severe histologic lesion, *bridging hepatic necrosis*, also termed *subacute* or *confluent necrosis*, is occasionally observed in some patients with acute hepatitis. "Bridging" between lobules results from large areas of hepatic cell dropout, with collapse of the reticulin framework. Characteristically, the bridge consists of condensed reticulum, inflammatory debris, and degenerating liver cells that span adjacent portal areas, portal to central veins, or central vein to central vein. This lesion has been thought to have prognostic significance; in many of the originally described patients with this lesion, a subacute course terminated in death within several weeks to months, or chronic active hepatitis and postnecrotic cirrhosis developed. More recent investigations have failed to uphold the association between bridging necrosis and such a poor prognosis in patients with acute hepatitis. Although the frequency of bridging may be higher among hospitalized patients with severe acute hepatitis, and although cirrhosis, chronic hepatitis, and even death have been observed in this group, the frequency of bridging necrosis in uncomplicated acute viral hepatitis is probably on the order of 1 to 5 percent. Prospective studies have failed to demonstrate a difference in prognosis between patients with acute hepatitis who have bridging necrosis and those who do not. Therefore, although demonstration of this lesion in patients with chronic hepatitis has prognostic significance (see Chap. 248), its demonstration during acute hepatitis is less meaningful, and liver biopsies to identify this lesion are no longer undertaken routinely in patients with acute hepatitis. In *massive hepatic necrosis* (fulminant hepatitis, acute yellow atrophy), the striking feature at postmortem examination is the finding of a small, shrunken, and soft liver. Histologic examination reveals massive necrosis and dropout of liver cells of most lobules with extensive collapse and condensation of the reticulin framework.

Immunofluorescence and immunoperoxidase antibody studies have been instrumental in localizing HBsAg to the cytoplasm and plasma membrane of infected liver cells. In contrast, HBcAg predominates in the nucleus, but, occasionally, scant amounts are also seen in the cytoplasm and on the cell membrane. Electron-microscopic studies of liver biopsy material have demonstrated the presence of HBsAg particles in the cytoplasm and HBcAg particles in the nucleus of liver cells during hepatitis B infection. These morphologic observations suggest that DNA is synthesized and packaged within core particles in the nucleus, while the surface coat is assembled in the cytoplasm, resulting in the formation of intact hepatitis B virus.

Epidemiology   Prior to the availability of serologic tests for hepatitis viruses, all viral hepatitis cases were labeled either as "infectious" or "serum" hepatitis. Modes of transmission overlap, however, and *a clear distinction among the different types of viral hepatitis cannot be made solely on the basis of clinical or epidemiologic features* (Table 247-2). The most accurate means to distinguish the various types of viral hepatitis involves specific serologic testing.

HEPATITIS A   *This agent is transmitted almost exclusively by the fecal-oral route.* Spread of HAV is enhanced by poor personal hygiene and overcrowding, and large outbreaks as well as sporadic cases have been traced to contaminated food, water, milk, and shellfish. Intrafamily and intrainstitutional spread are also common. Early epidemiologic observations suggested that there is a predilection for hepatitis A to occur in late fall and early winter. In temperate zones, epidemic waves have been recorded every 5 to 20 years as new segments of nonimmune population appeared; however, in developed countries, the incidence of type A hepatitis has been declining, presumably as a function of improved sanitation, and these cyclic patterns are no longer being observed. No HAV carrier state has been identified after acute type A hepatitis; perpetuation of the virus in nature depends presumably on nonepidemic, inapparent subclinical infection.

In the general population, anti-HAV, an excellent marker for previous HAV infection, increases in prevalence as a function of increasing age and of decreasing socioeconomic status. Serologic evidence of prior hepatitis A infection occurs in about 40 percent of urban populations in the United States, fewer than 5 percent of whom recall having had a symptomatic case of hepatitis. In developing countries, exposure, infection, and subsequent immunity are almost universal in childhood.

HEPATITIS B   It has long been recognized that a major route of hepatitis B transmission is percutaneous, but the outmoded designation "serum hepatitis" is an inaccurate label for the epidemiologic spectrum of HBV infection recognized today. As detailed below, most of the hepatitis transmitted by blood transfusion is not caused by HBV; moreover, in approximately half of patients with acute type B hepatitis, there is no history of an identifiable percutaneous exposure. We now recognize that many cases of type B hepatitis result from less obvious modes of nonpercutaneous or covert percutaneous transmission. HBsAg has been identified in almost every body fluid from infected persons—saliva, tears, seminal fluid, cerebrospinal fluid, ascites, breast milk, synovial fluid, gastric juice, pleural fluid and urine and even rarely in feces. Although there is abundant evidence to suggest that feces are not infectious, at least some of these body fluids—most notably semen and saliva—have been shown to be infectious, albeit less so than serum, when administered percutaneously or nonpercutaneously to experimental animals. Among the nonpercutaneous modes of HBV transmission, oral ingestion has been documented as a potential route of exposure but one whose efficiency is quite low. On the other hand, the two nonpercutaneous routes considered to have the greatest impact are intimate (especially sexual) contact and perinatal transmission.

In sub-Saharan Africa, intimate contact among toddlers is considered instrumental in contributing to the maintenance of the high frequency of HBsAg in the population. Perinatal transmission occurs primarily in infants born to HBsAg carrier mothers or mothers with acute hepatitis B during the third trimester of pregnancy or during the early postpartum period. Perinatal transmission is uncommon in North America and western Europe but occurs with great frequency and is the most important mode of HBV perpetuation in the far east and developing countries. Although the precise mode of perinatal transmission is unknown, and although approximately 10 percent of infections may be acquired in utero, epidemiologic evidence suggests that most infections occur approximately at the time of delivery and are not related to breast feeding. Likelihood of perinatal transmission of HBV correlates with the presence of HBeAg; 90 percent of HBeAg-positive mothers but only 10 to 15 percent of anti-HBe-positive mothers transmit HBV infection to their offspring. In most cases, acute infection in the neonate is clinically asymptomatic, but the child is very likely to become an HBsAg carrier.

The more than 200 million HBsAg carriers in the world constitute the main reservoir of hepatitis B in human beings. Serum HBsAg is infrequent (0.1 to 0.5 percent) in normal populations in the United States and western Europe; however, a prevalence of up to 5 to 20 percent has been found in the far east and in some tropical countries, and as high as 30 percent in persons with Down's syndrome, lepromatous leprosy, leukemia, Hodgkin's disease, polyarteritis nodosa, patients with chronic renal disease on hemodialysis, and needle-using drug addicts.

Other groups with high rates of HBV infection include spouses of acutely infected persons, sexually promiscuous persons (especially promiscuous homosexual men), health care workers exposed to blood, persons who require repeated transfusions especially with pooled blood product concentrates (e.g., hemophiliacs), residents and staff of custodial institutions for the mentally retarded, prisoners, and, to a lesser extent, family members of chronically infected patients. In volunteer blood donors, the prevalence of anti-HBs, a reflection of previous HBV infection, ranges from 5 to 10 percent, but the prevalence is higher in lower socioeconomic strata, older age groups, and persons—including those mentioned above—exposed to blood products.

DELTA HEPATITIS   Infection with the delta agent has a worldwide distribution, but two epidemiologic patterns exist. In Mediterranean countries (northern Africa, southern Europe, the middle east), delta infection is endemic among those with hepatitis B, and the disease is transmitted predominantly by nonpercutaneous means, especially close personal contact. In nonendemic areas, such as the United States and northern Europe, delta infection is confined to persons exposed frequently to blood and blood products, primarily drug addicts and hemophiliacs. Delta hepatitis can be introduced into a population through drug addicts or by migration of persons from endemic to nonendemic areas. Thus, patterns of population migration

TABLE 247-2   Comparisons of type A, type B, and non-A, non-B hepatitis

Feature	Hepatitis A	Hepatitis B	Non-A, non-B hepatitis
Incubation	15–45 days (mean 30)	30–180 days (mean 60–90)	15–160 (mean 50)
Onset	Acute	Often insidious	Insidious
Age preference	Children, young adults	Any age	Any age but more common in adults
Transmission route:			
Fecal-oral	+++	−	Unknown
Other nonpercutaneous*	+/−	++	++
Percutaneous	+/−	+++	+++
Severity	Mild	Often severe	Moderate
Prognosis	Generally good	Worse with age, debility	Moderate
Progression to chronicity	None	Occasional (5–10%)	Occasional (10–50%)
Prophylaxis	IG	Standard IG (not documented)	?
		HBIG, hepatitis B vaccine	
Carrier	None	0.1–30%†	Exists but prevalence unknown

* *For example, sexual or maternal-neonatal contact*
† *Varies considerably throughout the world, see text*

and human behavior facilitating percutaneous conttact play important roles in the introduction and amplification of delta infection. Occasionally, the migrating epidemiology of delta hepatitis is expressed in explosive outbreaks of severe hepatitis, such as those that have occurred in remote South American villages as well as in urban centers in the United States.

NON-A, NON-B HEPATITIS   Routine screening of blood donors for HBsAg and the elimination of commercial blood sources has markedly decreased the incidence of hepatitis B after transfusion, but posttransfusion hepatitis still remains a significant medical problem. The incidence of posttransfusion hepatitis has been reported to be from 0.3 to 9 cases per 1000 units transfused, and the risk of anicteric hepatitis following transfusion is much greater than that of clinical hepatitis with jaundice. The risk of viral hepatitis after transfusion of blood derivatives is dependent on the methods by which these products are processed. The *greatest risk* follows the use of multiple pooled donor products such as concentrates of factors II, VII, VIII, IX, and X. Hepatitis has developed in 20 to 30 percent of individuals receiving these pooled products for the first time. Blood products associated with an *average risk* include whole blood, packed red blood cells, single donor platelets, and plasma. Products such as albumin and immune and hyperimmune globulin, because of prior treatment of these substances by heating to 60°C or by cold ethanol extraction, involve *no risk*. It had been suggested that frozen, glycerol-treated, washed red blood cells may carry a reduced risk of hepatitis, but this has been disproved.

Currently, hepatitis B accounts for only 5 to 10 percent of posttransfusion hepatitis. More of a problem is the occurrence of non-A, non-B hepatitis, which accounts for approximately 90 percent of posttransfusion hepatitis cases following transfusion of voluntarily donated blood prescreened for HBsAg. The fact that non-A, non-B hepatitis is transmitted by transfused blood from asymptomatic donors (Table 247-2) and that it can be transmitted to chimpanzees by blood from patients with chronic hepatitis suggests that there is a carrier state for non-A, non-B hepatitis. Currently, the frequency of posttransfusion non-A, non-B hepatitis approaches 7 to 10 percent of blood recipients, especially recipients of multiple units of blood products. Unfortunately, there is no acceptable serologic screening test to identify non-A, non-B hepatitis agents in blood, and elimination of transfusion-associated non-A, non-B hepatitis will remain an elusive goal until a sensitive, specific test is developed.

In addition to being transmitted by transfusion, non-A, non-B hepatitis cases have been observed in other settings of percutaneous and nonpercutaneous exposure, e.g., intrafamily contact, intravenous drug abuse, occupational contact, nosocomial infection, use of hemodialysis units, and intrainstitutional contact. Special attention is merited by non-A, non-B hepatitis in hemophiliacs, in whom the incubation period may be as brief as 1 to 4 weeks, and in renal transplant recipients, up to 20 percent of whom have chronic liver disease. In the early years after transplantation, the death rate in patients with hepatitis is higher, as a result not of liver failure but of severe infections outside the hepatobiliary tree. However, 5 to 10 years after transplantation complications of chronic liver disease account for increased morbidity and mortality.

The *epidemic form* of non-A, non-B hepatitis identified in India and Asia resembles hepatitis A in its modes of spread. Its distribution has not yet been defined. In western countries, non-A, non-B hepatitis accounts for approximately 15 to 30 percent of sporadic cases of viral hepatitis presenting for medical evaluation. Occurrence of multiple bouts of non-A, non-B hepatitis among drug abusers and hemophiliacs reinforces cross-challenge studies in chimpanzees which suggest that there is more than one non-A, non-B hepatitis agent.

Clinical and laboratory features   SYMPTOMS AND SIGNS   The *prodromal symptoms* of acute viral hepatitis are systemic and quite variable. Constitutional symptoms of anorexia, nausea and vomiting, fatigue, malaise, arthralgias, myalgias, headache, photophobia, pharyngitis, cough, and coryza may precede the onset of jaundice by 1

to 2 weeks. The nausea, vomiting, and anorexia are frequently associated with alterations in olfaction and taste. A low-grade fever between 100 and 102°F is more often present in hepatitis A than in non-A, non-B or B, except when hepatitis B is heralded by a serum sickness–like syndrome; rarely, a fever of 103 to 104°F may accompany the constitutional symptoms. Dark urine and clay-colored stools may be noticed by the patient from 1 to 5 days prior to the onset of clinical jaundice.

With the onset of *clinical jaundice* the constitutional prodromal symptoms usually diminish, but in some patients mild weight loss (2.5 to 5 kg) is common and may continue during the entire icteric phase. The liver becomes enlarged and tender and may be associated with right upper quadrant pain and discomfort. Infrequently, patients present with a cholestatic picture, suggesting extrahepatic biliary obstruction. Splenomegaly and cervical adenopathy are present in 10 to 20 percent of patients with acute hepatitis. Rarely, a few spider angiomas appear during the icteric phase and disappear during convalescence. During the *recovery phase*, constitutional symptoms disappear, but usually some liver enlargement and abnormalities in biochemical tests of hepatic function are still evident. The duration of the posticteric phase is variable, ranging from 2 to 12 weeks, and usually is more prolonged in acute hepatitis B and in non-A, non-B hepatitis. Complete clinical and biochemical recovery is to be expected 1 to 2 months after all cases of hepatitis A and 3 to 4 months after the onset of jaundice in three-quarters of uncomplicated cases of hepatitis B and non-A, non-B hepatitis. In the remainder biochemical recovery may be delayed. A substantial proportion of patients with viral hepatitis never become icteric.

Infection with the delta agent (HDV) can occur in the presence of acute or chronic HBV infection; the duration of HBV infection determines the duration of delta infection. When acute delta and HBV infection occur simultaneously, clinical and biochemical features may be indistinguishable from those of HBV infection alone. As opposed to patients with *acute* HBV infection, patients with *chronic* HBV infection can support HDV replication indefinitely. This can happen when acute HDV infection occurs in the presence of a nonresolving acute HBV infection. More commonly, acute HDV infection becomes chronic when it is superimposed on an underlying chronic HBV infection. In such cases, the delta superinfection appears as a clinical exacerbation or an episode resembling acute viral hepatitis in someone already chronically infected with HBV. In the past, events resembling acute hepatitis in a HBV carrier or a patient with chronic hepatitis B were attributed to superimposed non-A, non-B hepatitis or to the natural history of the disease. A proportion of such episodes, however, represent acute superinfection with HDV. Delta superinfection in a patient with chronic hepatitis B often leads to clinical deterioration (see below).

LABORATORY FEATURES   The serum aminotransferases, AST and ALT (previously designated SGOT and SGPT) show a variable increase during the prodromal phase of acute viral hepatitis and precede the rise in bilirubin level (see Figs. 247-2 and 247-3). The acute level of these enzymes, however, does not correlate well with the degree of liver cell damage. Peak levels vary from 400 to 4000 IU or more; these levels are usually reached at the time the patient is clinically icteric and progressively diminish during the recovery phase of acute hepatitis. The diagnosis of anicteric hepatitis is difficult and requires a high index of suspicion; it is based on clinical features and on aminotransferase elevations, although mild increases in conjugated bilirubin may also be found.

Jaundice is usually visible in the sclera or skin when the serum bilirubin value exceeds 2.5 mg/dL. When jaundice appears, the serum bilirubin typically rises to levels ranging from 5 to 20 mg/dL. The serum bilirubin may continue to rise despite falling serum aminotransferase levels. In most instances the total bilirubin is equally divided between the conjugated and unconjugated fractions. Bilirubin levels above 20 mg/dL extending and persisting late into the course of viral hepatitis are more likely to be associated with severe disease.

In certain patients with underlying hemolytic anemia, however, such as glucose 6-phosphate dehydrogenase deficiency and sickle cell anemia, high serum bilirubin is common, resulting from superimposed hemolysis. In such patients bilirubin levels greater than 30 mg/dL have been observed and are not necessarily associated with a poor prognosis.

Neutropenia and lymphopenia are transient and are followed by a relative lymphocytosis. Atypical lymphocytes (varying between 2 and 20 percent) are common during the acute phase. These atypical lymphocytes are indistinguishable from those seen in infectious mononucleosis. Measurement of the prothrombin time (PT) is important in patients with acute viral hepatitis, for a prolonged value may reflect a severe synthetic defect, signify extensive hepatocellular necrosis, and indicate a worse prognosis. Occasionally a prolonged PT may occur with only mild increases in the serum bilirubin and aminotransferase levels. Prolonged nausea and vomiting, inadequate carbohydrate intake, and poor hepatic glycogen reserves may contribute to hypoglycemia noted occasionally in patients with severe viral hepatitis. Serum alkaline phosphatase may be normal or only mildly elevated to levels of 80 to 240 IU, while a fall in serum albumin is uncommon in uncomplicated acute viral hepatitis. In some patients mild and transient steatorrhea has been noted as well as slight microscopic hematuria and minimal proteinuria.

A diffuse but mild elevation of the gamma globulin fraction is common during acute viral hepatitis. Serum IgG and IgM are elevated in about one-third of patients during the acute phase of viral hepatitis, but serum IgM elevation is seen more characteristically during acute hepatitis A. During the acute phase of viral hepatitis, antibodies to smooth muscle and other cell constituents may be present, and low titers of rheumatoid factor, antinuclear antibody, and heterophil antibody can also be found occasionally. These antibodies are nonspecific and can also be associated with other viral and systemic diseases. In contrast, virus-specific antibodies, which appear during and after hepatitis virus infection, are serologic markers of diagnostic importance.

As described above, serologic tests are available with which to establish a diagnosis of hepatitis A and B. Tests for fecal or serum HAV are not routinely available. Therefore, a diagnosis of type A hepatitis is based on detection of IgM anti-HAV during acute illness (Fig. 247-2). Rheumatoid factor can give rise to false-positive results in this test.

A diagnosis of HBV infection can usually be made by detection of HBsAg in serum. Infrequently, levels of HBsAg are too low to be detected during acute HBV infection even with the current generation of highly sensitive immunoassays. In such cases, the diagnosis can be established by the presence of IgM anti-HBc. Alternatively, de novo appearance of anti-HBc and anti-HBs during illness and convalescence may support the diagnostic impression.

The titer of HBsAg bears little relation to the severity of clinical disease. Indeed, there is an inverse correlation between the serum concentration of HBsAg and the degree of liver cell damage. Titers are highest in immunosuppressed patients and in normal carriers, lower in chronic liver disease (but higher in chronic persistent than in chronic active hepatitis), and very low in acute fulminant hepatitis. These observations suggest that in hepatitis B the degree of liver cell damage and the clinical course are probably related to variations in the patient's immune response to HBV rather than to the amount of circulating HBsAg.

Another serologic marker which may be of value in patients with hepatitis B is HBeAg. Its principal clinical usefulness is as an indicator of relative infectivity. Because HBeAg is invariably present during early acute hepatitis B, HBeAg testing is indicated primarily during follow-up of chronic infection.

In patients with hepatitis B surface antigenemia of unknown duration, e.g., blood donors whose blood is found to be HBsAg-positive and who are referred to a physician for evaluation, testing for IgM anti-HBc may be useful to distinguish between acute or recent infection (IgM anti-HBc-positive) and chronic HBV infection (IgM anti-HBc-negative, IgG anti-HBc-positive). A false-positive test for IgM anti-HBc may be encountered in patients with high-titer rheumatoid factor.

Anti-HBs is rarely detectable in the presence of HBsAg in patients with *acute* hepatitis B, but 10 to 20 percent of persons with *chronic* HBV infection may harbor low-level anti-HBs. This antibody is directed not against the common group determinant, *a*, but against the heterotypic subtype determinant (e.g., HBsAg of subtype *ad* with anti-HBs of subtype *y*). In most cases, this serologic pattern cannot be attributed to infection with two different HBV subtypes, and the presence of this antibody is not a harbinger of imminent HBsAg clearance. When such antibody is detected, its presence is of no known clinical significance.

After immunization with hepatitis B vaccine, which consists of HBsAg alone, anti-HBs is the only serologic marker to appear. A summary of the commonly encountered serologic patterns of hepatitis B and their interpretations appears in Table 247-3. Tests for the detection of HBV DNA in liver and serum or DNA polymerase in serum are available in a limited number of research laboratories. Like HBeAg, serum HBV DNA and DNA polymerase are indicators of HBV replication, but they are more sensitive. These markers are useful in following the course of HBV replication in patients with chronic hepatitis B receiving experimental antiviral chemotherapy, with interferon for example.

Because there are no reliable serologic tests for non-A, non-B hepatitis, a diagnosis of non-A, non-B hepatitis is made by serologic exclusion of HAV and HBV infection in the setting of a compatible history. A helpful clue is the episodic pattern of aminotransferase elevation seen frequently in non-A, non-B hepatitis. A diagnosis of acute non-A, non-B hepatitis can be made if tests for HBsAg, IgM

TABLE 247-3 Commonly encountered serologic patterns of hepatitis B infection

HBsAg	Anti-HBs	Anti-HBc	HBeAg	Anti-HBe	Interpretation
+	−	IgM	+	−	Acute HBV infection, high infectivity
+	−	IgG	+	−	Chronic HBV infection, high infectivity
+	−	IgG	−	+	Late-acute or chronic HBV infection, low infectivity
+	+	+	+/−	+/−	1 HBsAg of one subtype and heterotypic anti-HBs (common) 2 Process of seroconversion from HBsAg to anti-HBs (rare)
−	−	IgM	+/−	+/−	1 Acute HBV infection 2 Anti-HBc window
−	−	IgG	−	+/−	1 Low-level HBsAg carrier 2 Remote past infection
−	+	IgG	−	+/−	Recovery from HBV infection
−	+	−	−	−	1 Immunization with HBsAg (after vaccination) 2 Remote past infection (?) 3 False-positive

anti-HBc, and IgM anti-HAV are negative. A diagnosis of non-A, non-B hepatitis may be more difficult to establish in patients with chronic hepatitis who have anti-HBc in their blood. The anti-HBc in such cases will almost invariably be of the IgG class; it represents either HBV infection in the remote past or current HBV infection with low-level virus carriage.

The presence of HDV infection can be identified by demonstrating intrahepatic delta antigen or, more practically, an antidelta seroconversion (a rise in titer of anti-HD or de novo appearance of IgM anti-HD). Circulating HDAg, also diagnostic of acute infection, is detectable only briefly, if at all. Because IgM anti-HD is transient and IgG anti-HD is often undetectable once HBsAg disappears, retrospective serodiagnosis of acute self-limited, simultaneous HBV and HDV infection is difficult.

When a patient presents with acute hepatitis and has HBsAg and anti-HD is the serum, determination of the class of anti-HBc is helpful in establishing the relationship between infection with HBV and HDV. Although IgM anti-HBc does not distinguish *absolutely* between acute and chronic HBV infection, its presence is a reliable indicator of recent infection and its absence a reliable indicator of infection in the remote past. In simultaneous acute HBV and HDV infections, IgM anti-HBc will be detectable, while in acute HDV infection superimposed upon chronic HBV infection, anti-HBc will be of the IgG class.

In the future, tests for the presence of HDV-associated RNA will be useful for determining the presence of ongoing HDV replication and relative infectivity. Currently, probes for this marker are restricted to a limited number of research laboratories.

Liver biopsy is rarely necessary or indicated in acute viral hepatitis, except when there is a question about the diagnosis or when there is clinical evidence suggesting a diagnosis of chronic active hepatitis.

Little agreement exists over routine diagnostic algorithms to be applied in the evaluation of cases of acute viral hepatitis. One potential approach is to test every patient with three serological tests, HBsAg, IgM anti-HAV, and IgM anti-HBc (Table 247-4). The presence of HBsAg, with or without IgM anti-HBc, represents HBV infection. If IgM anti-HBc is present, the HBV infection is considered acute; if IgM anti-HBc is absent, the HBV infection is considered chronic. A diagnosis of acute hepatitis B can be made in the absence of HBsAg when IgM anti-HBc is detectable. A diagnosis of acute hepatitis A is based on the presence of IgM anti-HAV. If IgM anti-HAV coexists with HBsAg, a diagnosis of simultaneous HAV and HBV infections can be made; if IgM anti-HBc (with or without HBsAg) is detectable, the patient has simultaneous acute hepatitis A and B, and if IgM anti-HBc is undetectable, the patient has acute hepatitis A superimposed on chronic HBV infection. Absence of all serologic markers is consistent with a diagnosis of non-A, non-B hepatitis.

TABLE 247-4   Simplified diagnostic approach in patients presenting with acute hepatitis

Test patient's serum for

HBsAg	IgM anti-HAV	IgM anti-HBc	Diagnostic conclusion
+	−	+	Acute hepatitis B
+	−	−	Chronic hepatitis B
+	+	−	Acute hepatitis A superimposed on chronic hepatitis B
+	+	+	Acute hepatitis A and B
−	+	−	Acute hepatitis A
−	+	+	Acute hepatitis A and B (HBsAg below detectable level)
−	−	+	Acute hepatitis B (HBsAg below detectable level)
−	−	−	Compatible with NANB hepatitis

If a serologic diagnosis of chronic hepatitis B is made, testing for HBeAg and anti-HBe is indicated to evaluate relative infectivity. In patients with hepatitis B, testing for anti-HD is useful under the following circumstances: severe and fulminant cases, severe chronic cases, cases of acute hepatitis-like exacerbations in patients with chronic hepatitis B, persons with frequent percutaneous exposures, and persons from areas where delta infection is endemic.

Prognosis   Virtually all previously healthy patients with hepatitis A recover completely from their illness with no clinical sequelae. Similarly in acute hepatitis B, 90 percent of patients have a favorable course and recover completely. There are, however, certain clinical and laboratory features which suggest a more complicated and protracted course. Patients of advanced age and with serious underlying medical disorders such as congestive heart failure, severe anemia, and diabetes mellitus may have a prolonged course and are more likely to experience severe hepatitis. Initial presenting features such as ascites, peripheral edema, and symptoms of hepatic encephalopathy suggest a poorer prognosis. In addition, a prolonged prothrombin time, low serum albumin, hypoglycemia, and very high serum bilirubin values suggest severe hepatocellular disease. Patients with these clinical and laboratory features deserve prompt hospital admission. The case fatality rate in hepatitis A and B is very low (approximately 0.1 percent) but is increased by advanced age and underlying debilitating disorders. Among patients ill enough to be hospitalized for acute hepatitis B, the fatality rate is 1 percent. Non-A, non-B hepatitis occurring after transfusion is less severe during the acute phase than type B hepatitis and is more likely to be anicteric; fatalities are rare, but the precise case fatality rate is not known. In outbreaks of the waterborne type of non-A, non-B hepatitis in India and Asia, the case fatality rate is 10 percent, and pregnant women are at especially high risk. In general, patients with simultaneous acute hepatitis B and delta hepatitis do not experience a higher mortality rate than do patients with acute hepatitis B alone; however, in several recent outbreaks of acute simultaneous HBV and HDV infection among drug addicts, the case fatality rate has approximated 5 percent. In the case of delta superinfection of a person with chronic hepatitis B, the likelihood of fulminant hepatitis and death is increased substantially. Although the case fatality rate for delta hepatitis has not been defined adequately, in outbreaks of severe delta superinfection in isolated populations with a high hepatitis B carrier rate, the mortality rate has been recorded as in excess of 20 percent.

Complications and sequelae   During the prodromal phase of acute hepatitis B, a serum sickness–like syndrome characterized by arthralgia or arthritis, rash, angioedema, and rarely hematuria and proteinuria may develop in some patients. This syndrome occurs prior to the onset of clinical jaundice, and these patients are often erroneously diagnosed as having rheumatoid arthritis or other rheumatologic diseases such as systemic lupus erythematosus. This syndrome occurs in about 5 to 10 percent of patients with acute hepatitis B. The diagnosis can be established by measuring serum aminotransferase levels, which are almost invariably elevated, and serum HBsAg.

The most feared complication of viral hepatitis is *fulminant hepatitis* (massive hepatic necrosis); fortunately this is a rare event. This is primarily seen in hepatitis B and delta hepatitis. Hepatitis B accounts for more than 50 percent of fulminant hepatitis cases, a sizeable proportion of which are associated with delta infection. Fulminant hepatitis is seen less frequently in non-A, non-B hepatitis, and only occasionally in hepatitis A. Patients usually present with signs and symptoms of encephalopathy and, in fact, many progress to deep coma. The liver is usually small, and the prothrombin time excessively prolonged. The combination of rapidly shrinking liver size, rapidly rising bilirubin level, and marked prolongation of the prothrombin time, together with clinical signs of confusion, disorientation, somnolence, ascites, and edema, indicates that the patient has hepatic failure with encephalopathy. Cerebral edema is common; brainstem compression, gastrointestinal bleeding, sepsis, respiratory failure, cardiovascular collapse, and renal failure are terminal events.

The mortality is exceedingly high (greater than 80 percent in patients with deep coma), but patients who survive may have a complete biochemical and histologic recovery.

It is particularly important to document the disappearance of HBsAg following apparent clinical recovery from acute hepatitis B. After clinically apparent acute type B hepatitis, approximately 10 percent of patients remain HBsAg-positive for more than 6 months. Half of these individuals may clear the antigen from their circulation during the next several years, but the other 5 percent remain chronically HBsAg-positive. In their serum, anti-HBc is present in high titer; anti-HBs is either undetected or detected at low titer against the opposite subtype specificity of the antigen (see "Laboratory Features" above). These patients may (1) be asymptomatic carriers, (2) have low-grade chronic persistent hepatitis, or (3) have chronic active hepatitis with or without cirrhosis. The likelihood of becoming an HBsAg carrier after acute HBV infection is especially high among neonates, persons with Down's syndrome, chronically hemodialyzed patients, and immunosuppressed patients.

Chronic active hepatitis is a major late complication of acute hepatitis B occurring in approximately 1 to 3 percent of cases (see Chap. 248). Certain clinical and laboratory features suggest progression of acute hepatitis to chronic active hepatitis: (1) lack of complete resolution of clinical symptoms of anorexia, weight loss, and fatigue and the persistence of hepatomegaly; (2) the presence of bridging or multilobular hepatic necrosis on liver biopsy during protracted, severe acute viral hepatitis, (3) failure of the serum aminotransferase, bilirubin, and globulin levels to return to normal within 6 to 12 months following the acute illness; and (4) the continued presence of HBsAg 6 months or more after acute hepatitis, suggesting chronic viral infection of the liver.

Although acute delta hepatitis infection does not increase the likelihood of chronicity of simultaneous acute hepatitis B, delta hepatitis has the potential for contributing to the severity of chronic hepatitis B. Delta hepatitis superinfection can transform asymptomatic or mild chronic hepatitis B into severe, progressive chronic active hepatitis and cirrhosis; it can also accelerate the course of chronic active hepatitis B. Some delta superinfections in patients with chronic hepatitis B lead to fulminant hepatitis. After transfusion-associated acute non-A, non-B hepatitis, as many as 50 percent of patients have abnormal biochemical liver tests for more than a year. In a majority of such patients, liver histology is consistent with chronic active hepatitis. Although many of these patients have no symptoms and a nonprogressive course, ultimately, cirrhosis develops in as many as 20 percent of those with chronic posttransfusion non-A, non-B hepatitis within 10 years of acute illness. The likelihood of chronic hepatitis is only approximately 10 percent after sporadic non-A, non-B hepatitis occurring in the absence of identifiable percutaneous inoculation with blood products or contaminated needles. In contrast, HAV infection does not cause chronic liver disease.

Rare complications of viral hepatitis include pancreatitis, myocarditis, atypical pneumonia, aplastic anemia, transverse myelitis, and peripheral neuropathy. *Carriers* of HBsAg, particularly those infected in infancy or early childhood, appear to have an enhanced risk of hepatocellular carcinoma (see Chap. 250). In children, hepatitis B may rarely present with anicteric hepatitis, a nonpruritic papular rash of the face, buttocks, and limbs, and lymphadenopathy (papular acrodermatitis of childhood or Gianotti-Crosti syndrome).

Differential diagnosis Viral diseases such as infectious mononucleosis; those due to cytomegalovirus, herpes simplex, and coxsackieviruses; and toxoplasmosis may share certain clinical features with viral hepatitis and cause elevation in serum aminotransferase and less commonly in serum bilirubin levels. Tests such as the differential heterophil and serologic tests for these agents may be helpful in the differential diagnosis, if HBsAg, anti-HBc, and IgM anti-HAV determinations are negative. A complete drug history is particularly important, for many drugs can produce a picture of either acute hepatitis or cholestasis (see below). Equally important is a past history of unexplained "repeated episodes" of acute hepatitis. This should

alert the physician to the possibility that the underlying disorder is chronic active hepatitis. Alcoholic hepatitis must also be considered, but usually the serum aminotransferase levels are not as markedly elevated and other stigmata of alcoholism may be present. The finding on liver biopsy of fatty infiltration, a neutrophilic inflammatory reaction, and "alcoholic hyalin" would be consistent with alcohol-induced rather than viral liver injury. Because acute hepatitis may present with right upper quadrant abdominal pain, nausea and vomiting, fever, and icterus, it is often confused with acute cholecystitis, common duct stone, or ascending cholangitis. Patients with acute viral hepatitis may tolerate surgery poorly; therefore, it is important to exclude this diagnosis, and a percutaneous liver biopsy may be necessary prior to laparotomy. Viral hepatitis in the elderly is often misdiagnosed as obstructive jaundice resulting from a common duct stone or carcinoma of the pancreas. Because acute hepatitis in the elderly may be quite severe and the operative mortality high, a thorough evaluation including biochemical tests, radiographic studies of the biliary tree, and even liver biopsy may be necessary to exclude primary parenchymal liver disease. Another clinical constellation that may mimic acute hepatitis is right ventricular failure with passive hepatic congestion or hypoperfusion syndromes, such as those associated with shock, severe hypotension, and severe left ventricular failure. Clinical features are usually sufficient to distinguish between the two entities.

Management TREATMENT OF ACUTE ATTACK There is no specific treatment for *typical acute viral hepatitis.* Although hospitalization may be required for clinically severe illness, most patients do not require hospital care. Forced and prolonged bed rest is not essential for full recovery, but many patients will feel better with restricted physical activity. A high-calorie diet is desirable, and because many patients may experience nausea late in the day, the major caloric intake is best tolerated in the morning. Intravenous feeding is necessary in the acute stage if the patient has persistent vomiting and cannot maintain oral intake. Drugs capable of producing adverse reactions such as cholestasis and drugs metabolized by the liver should be avoided. If severe pruritus is present, the use of the bile salt–sequestering resin cholestyramine will usually alleviate this symptom. Corticosteroid therapy has no value in acute viral hepatitis. Even in severe cases associated with *bridging necrosis,* controlled trials have failed to demonstrate the efficacy of steroids. In fact, such therapy may be hazardous.

Physical isolation of patients with hepatitis to a single room and bathroom is rarely necessary except in the case of fecal incontinence for hepatitis A or uncontrolled, voluminous bleeding for hepatitis types B and non-A, non-B. Because most patients hospitalized with hepatitis A excrete little if any HAV, the likelihood of HAV transmission from these patients during their hospitalization is low. Therefore, burdensome enteric precautions are no longer recommended. Although gloves should be worn when the bedpans or fecal material of patients with hepatitis A are handled, these precautions do not represent a departure from sensible procedure for all hospitalized patients. For patients with types B and non-A, non-B hepatitis, emphasis should be placed on blood precautions, i.e., avoiding direct, ungloved hand contact with blood and other body fluids. Enteric precautions for these agents are unnecessary. The importance of simple hygienic precautions, such as hand washing, cannot be overemphasized.

Hospitalized patients may be discharged when there is substantial symptomatic improvement, a significant downward trend in the serum aminotransferase and bilirubin values, and a return to normal of the prothrombin time. Mild aminotransferase elevations should not be considered contraindications to the gradual resumption of normal activity.

In *fulminant hepatitis,* the goal of therapy is to support the patient by maintenance of fluid balance, support of circulation and respiration, control of bleeding, correction of hypoglycemia, and treatment of other complications of the comatose state in anticipation of liver regeneration and repair. Protein intake should be restricted and oral lactulose or neomycin administered. Massive doses of corticosteroids have been administered, but such therapy has been shown in controlled trials to be ineffective. Likewise, exchange transfusion, plasmapheresis, human cross-circulation, porcine liver cross-perfusion, and hemoperfusion have not been proven to enhance survival.

Hazards to medical and paramedical personnel Health care workers exposed frequently to blood, body tissues, and fluids have an increased risk of viral hepatitis, primarily hepatitis B. Approximately 15 percent of health workers have one or more serologic markers of HBV infection, and 1 percent are HBsAg-positive. The risk is higher in surgeons, pathologists, laboratory techologists who process blood specimens, technologists who draw blood and insert intravenous cannulas, hemodialysis staff, and others who perform invasive procedures. Transmission of HBV infection in health care settings, however, appears to be unidirectional, from patients to staff. With rare exceptions, HBsAg-positive health personnel do not increase the risk of HBV infection for their patients. Asymptomatic HBsAg carriers represent the greater risk to health personnel, because there are no readily identifiable clinical features that allow their recognition. Approximately 1 percent of all patients admitted to large metropolitan hospitals are HBsAg-positive, but 90 percent of these are not identified routinely. Patients with a past history of hepatitis or multiple transfusions, patients from countries where hepatitis B is endemic, sexually active homosexual men, intravenous drug abusers, and patients with chronic liver disease, chronic renal failure, polyarteritis nodosa, and Down's syndrome should have routine HBsAg determinations because of the high frequency of the HBsAg carrier state in these groups. If positive, they are potentially infectious, and appropriate precautions should be taken during operative or other acute care procedures. In hemodialysis units, introduction of patient and staff education, routine periodic screening for HBsAg and aminotransferase elevations, and segregation of HBsAg-positive patients from susceptible patients have reduced dramatically the incidence of new HBV infections in both patients and medical personnel.

Prophylaxis Because therapy for viral hepatitis is limited, emphasis is placed on prevention through immunization. The prophylactic approach differs for each of the types of viral hepatitis. In the past, immunoprophylaxis relied exclusively on passive immunization with antibody-containing globulin preparations purified by cold ethanol fractionation from the plasma of hundreds of normal donors. Currently, for hepatitis B, active immunization with a vaccine is available as well.

HEPATITIS A   All preparations of immune globulin (IG) contain anti-HAV. Although the titers may vary, all IG preparations appear to have a sufficient antibody concentration to be protective. When administered before exposure or during the early incubation period, IG is effective in preventing clinically apparent type A hepatitis. In some cases, IG does not abort infection but, by attenuating it, renders it inapparent. As a result long-lasting ''passive-active'' immunity occurs; however, this is now considered to be the exception rather than the rule. For intimate contacts (household, institutional) of persons with hepatitis A, administration of 0.02 mL/kg is recommended as early after exposure as possible; it may be effective even when administered as late as 2 weeks after exposure. Prophylaxis is not necessary for casual contacts (office, factory, school, or hospital) for most elderly persons, who are very likely to be immune, or for those known to have anti-HAV in their serum. In day-care centers for young children, recognition of cases of hepatitis A in children or staff should provide a stimulus for immunoprophylaxis. By the time most common-source outbreaks of type A hepatitis are recognized, however, it is usually too late in the incubation period for IG to be effective; however, prophylaxis may limit the frequency of secondary cases. For travelers to tropical countries, developing countries, and other areas outside of standard tourist routes, IG prophylaxis is recommended. When such travel lasts less than 3 months, 0.02 mL/kg is given; for longer travel or residence in these areas, a dose of 0.06 mL/kg every 4 to 6 months is recommended. Administration of

plasma-derived globulin is safe; it has not been associated with transmission of AIDS to recipients, and the AIDS virus, HTLV III, is inactivated by 25 percent alcohol, to which plasma is subjected during the cold ethanol fractionation process. Both live attenuated and genetically engineered hepatitis A vaccines are being developed.

HEPATITIS B   Until recently, prevention of hepatitis B was based on *passive* immunoprophylaxis either with standard IG, containing modest levels of anti-HBs, or hepatitis B immune globulin (HBIG), containing high-titer anti-HBs. The efficacy of standard IG has never been established and remains questionable; even the efficacy of HBIG, demonstrated in several clinical trials, has been challenged, and its contribution appears to be in reducing the frequency of clinical *illness*, not in preventing *infection*. Although HBV cannot be cultivated in vitro, a vaccine for *active* immunization has been prepared from purified, noninfectious 22-nm spherical forms of HBsAg derived from the plasma of healthy HBsAg carriers. The vaccine is subjected to three different chemical inactivation steps which, cumulatively, destroy the infectivity of every known virus, including HTLV III. In controlled clinical trials among high-risk persons, this plasma-derived vaccine has been shown to be immunogenic, highly effective in preventing HBV infection, and, despite its unconventional source, very safe. Current recommendations can be divided into those for preexposure and postexposure prophylaxis.

For *preexposure* prophylaxis against hepatitis B in settings of frequent exposure (health workers exposed to blood, hemodialysis patients and staff, residents and staff of custodial institutions for the developmentally handicapped, intravenous drug abusers, promiscuous homosexual men as well as promiscuous heterosexuals, persons such as hemophiliacs who require long-term, high-volume therapy with blood derivatives, household and sexual contacts of HBsAg carriers, and persons living in or traveling extensively in endemic areas), three intramuscular (deltoid, not gluteal) injections of hepatitis B vaccine are recommended at 0, 1, and 6 months. The recommended dose for each injection is 20 µg for immunocompetent adults, 40 µg for immunosuppressed patients (hemodialysis patients, transplant recipients, and oncology patients receiving chemotherapy), and 10 µg for infants and children under the age of 10.

For unvaccinated persons sustaining an exposure to HBV, *postexposure* prophylaxis with a combination of HBIG (for rapid achievement of high-titer circulating anti-HBs) and hepatitis B vaccine (for achievement of long-lasting immunity as well as its apparent efficacy in attenuating clinical illness after exposure) is recommended. For *perinatal* exposure of infants born to HBsAg-positive mothers, a single dose of HBIG, 0.5 mL, should be administered intramuscularly *immediately after birth*, followed by a complete course of three 10 µg injections of hepatitis B vaccine to be started within the first 12 h to 1 week of life. For those experiencing a direct percutaneous inoculation or transmucosal exposure to HBsAg-positive blood or body fluids (e.g., accidental *needle stick* or ingestion), a single intramuscular dose of HBIG, 0.06 mL/kg, administered as soon after exposure as possible, is followed by a complete course of hepatitis B vaccine to begin within the first week. For those exposed by *sexual* contact to a patient with acute hepatitis B, the Immunization Practices Advisory Committee of the United States Public Health Service recommends a single intramuscular dose of HBIG, 0.06 mL/kg, within 14 days of exposure, to be followed by a second HBIG injection or a complete course of hepatitis B vaccine only when HBsAg positivity in the index case persists beyond 3 months. Other authorities, however, recommend a combination of HBIG followed by a complete course of hepatitis B vaccine injections for all sexual contacts of patients with acute hepatitis B, regardless of the duration of HBsAg positivity in the index case. When both HBIG and hepatitis B vaccine are recommended, they may be given at the same time but at separate sites.

DELTA HEPATITIS   Infection with the delta hepatitis agent can be prevented by vaccinating susceptible persons with hepatitis B vaccine. No product is available for immunoprophylaxis to prevent delta superinfection in HBsAg carriers; for them, avoidance of percutaneous exposures and limitation of intimate contact with persons who have delta infection are recommended.

NON-A, NON-B HEPATITIS For transfusion-associated non-A, non-B hepatitis, the effectiveness or IG prophylaxis has not been demonstrated consistently and is not recommended. The only effective measure for reducing the frequency of posttransfusion non-A, non-B hepatitis is the elimination of commercially obtained donor blood and reliance exclusively on volunteer blood donors. Studies to test the efficacy of standard IG after needle stick, sexual, or perinatal exposure to non-A, non-B hepatitis have not been done. Because the inoculum is considerably smaller in these settings than that associated with transfusion, and because of its safety and low cost, some authorities do recommend postexposure prophylaxis with a single dose of IG, 0.6 mL/kg (or 0.5 mg for neonatal exposure), in these situations.

TOXIC AND DRUG-INDUCED HEPATITIS

Liver injury may follow the inhalation, ingestion, or parenteral administration of a number of pharmacologic and chemical agents. These include industrial toxins (e.g., carbon tetrachloride, trichloroethylene, and yellow phosphorus), the heat-stable toxic bicyclic octapeptides of certain species of *Amanita* and *Galerina* (hepatotoxic mushroom poisoning), and more commonly, pharmocologic agents used in medical therapy. It is essential that any patient presenting with jaundice or impaired liver function be questioned carefully about exposure to chemicals used in work or at home and drugs taken by prescription or bought "over the counter." In general, two major types of chemical hepatotoxicity have been recognized: (1) direct toxic type and (2) idiosyncratic type.

As shown in Table 247-5, direct toxic hepatitis occurs with predictable regularity in individuals exposed to the offending agent and is dose-dependent. The latent period between exposure and liver injury is usually short (often several hours), although clinical manifestations may be delayed for 24 to 48 h. Agents producing toxic hepatitis are generally systemic poisons or are converted in the liver to toxic metabolites. The direct hepatotoxins result in morphologic abnormalities which are reasonably characteristic and reproducible for each toxin. For example, carbon tetrachloride and trichloroethylene characteristically produce a centrilobular zonal necrosis, whereas yellow phosphorus poisoning typically results in periportal injury. The hepatotoxic octapeptides of *Amanita phalloides* usually produce massive hepatic necrosis. The lethal dose of the toxin is about 10 mg, the amount found in a single deathcap mushroom. Tetracycline, when administered in intravenous doses greater than 1.5 g daily, leads to microvesicular fat deposits in the liver. Liver injury, which is often only one facet of the toxicity produced by the direct hepatotoxins, may go unrecognized until jaundice appears.

In idiosyncratic drug reactions the occurrence of hepatitis is usually infrequent and unpredictable, the response is not dose-dependent, and it may occur at any time during or shortly after exposure to the drug. Extrahepatic manifestations of hypersensitivity, such as rash, arthralgias, fever, leukocytosis, and eosinophilia occur in about one-quarter of patients with idiosyncratic hepatotoxic drug reactions; this observation and the unpredictability of idiosyncratic drug hepatotoxicity contributed to the hypothesis that this category of drug reactions is immunologically mediated. More recent evidence, however, suggests that even idiosyncratic reactions represent direct hepatotoxity but are caused by drug metabolites rather than by the intact compound. Even the prototype of idiosyncratic hepatoxicity reactions, halothane hepatitis, and isoniazid hepatotoxicity, associated frequently with hypersensitivity manifestations, are now recognized to be mediated by toxic metabolites which damage liver cells directly. Currently, idiosyncratic reactions are thought to result from differences in metabolic reactivity to specific agents; host susceptibility is mediated by the kinetics of toxic metabolite generation, which differs among individuals. Idiosyncratic reactions lead to a morphologic pattern that is more variable than those produced by direct toxins; a single agent is often capable of causing a variety of lesions, although certain patterns tend to predominate. Depending on the agent involved, idiosyncratic hepatitis may result in a clinical and morphologic picture indistinguishable from viral hepatitis (e.g., halothane) or may simulate extrahepatic bile duct obstruction clinically with morphologic evidence of cholestasis and minimal hepatocellular damage (e.g., chlorpromazine). Morphologic alterations may also include bridging hepatic necrosis (e.g., methyldopa), or, infrequently, hepatic granulomas (e.g., sulfonamides).

Not all adverse hepatic drug reactions can be classified as either toxic or idiosyncratic in type. For example, oral contraceptives, which combine estrogenic and progestational compounds, may result in impairment of hepatic function and occasionally in jaundice. However, they do not produce necrosis or fatty change, manifestations of hypersensitivity are generally absent, and susceptibility to the development of oral contraceptive–induced cholestasis appears to be genetically determined.

Because drug-induced hepatitis is often a presumptive diagnosis and many other disorders produce a similar clinicopathologic picture, evidence of a causal relationship between the use of a drug and subsequent liver injury may be difficult to establish. The relationship is most convincing for the direct hepatotoxins, which lead to a high frequency of hepatic impairment after a short latent period. Idiosyncratic reactions may be reproduced, in some instances, when rechallenge, after an asymptomatic period, results in a recurrence of signs, symptoms, and morphologic and biochemical abnormalities. Rechallenge, however, is often ethically unfeasible, because severe reactions may occur.

Treatment of toxic and drug-induced hepatic disease is largely supportive, as in acute viral hepatitis. Withdrawal of the suspected agent is indicated at the first sign of an adverse reaction. In the case of the direct toxins, liver involvement should not divert attention from renal or other organ involvement which may also threaten survival.

In Table 247-6, several classes of chemical agents are listed, together with examples of the pattern of liver injury produced by them. Certain drugs appear to be responsible for the development of chronic as well as acute hepatic injury. For example, oxphenisatin, alpha methyldopa, and isoniazid have been associated with chronic active hepatitis, and halothane and methotrexate have been implicated

TABLE 247-5 Some features of toxic and drug-induced hepatic injury

Features	Direct toxic effect		Idiosyncratic			Other
	(Carbon tetrachloride, e.g.)	(Acetaminophen, e.g.)	(Halothane, e.g.)	(Isoniazid, e.g.)	(Chlorpromazine, e.g.)	(Oral contraceptive agents, e.g.)
Predictable and dose-related toxicity	+	+	0	0	0	+
Latent period	Short	Short	Variable	Variable	Variable	Variable
Arthralgia, fever, rash, eosinophilia	0	0	+	0	+	0
Liver morphology	Necrosis, fatty infiltration	Centrilobular necrosis	Similar to viral hepatitis	Similar to viral hepatitis	Cholestasis *with* portal inflammation	Cholestasis *without* portal inflammation

in the development of cirrhosis. A syndrome resembling primary biliary cirrhosis has been described following treatment with chlorpromazine, methyl testosterone, tolbutamide, and other drugs. Portal hypertension in the absence of cirrhosis may result from alterations in hepatic architecture produced by vitamin A or arsenic intoxication, industrial exposure to vinyl chloride, or administration of thorium dioxide. The latter three agents have also been associated with angiosarcoma of the liver. Oral contraceptives have been implicated in the development of hepatic adenoma and, rarely, hepatocellular carcinoma and occlusion of the hepatic vein (Budd-Chiari syndrome). Another unusual lesion, peliosis hepatis (blood cysts of the liver), has been observed in some patients treated with oral contraceptives or anabolic steroids. The existence of these hepatic disorders expands the spectrum of liver injury induced by chemical agents and emphasizes the need for a thorough drug history in all patients with liver dysfunction.

The following are the patterns of adverse hepatic reactions for some prototypic agents.

Acetaminophen hepatotoxicity (direct toxin) Acetaminophen, an analgesic and antipyretic that is available without a prescription, has caused severe centrolobular hepatic necrosis when ingested in large amounts in suicide attempts or accidentally by children. A single dose of 10 to 15 g, occasionally less, may produce clinical evidence of liver injury. Fatal fulminant disease is usually (although not invariably) associated with ingestion of 25 g or more. Blood levels of acetaminophen correlate with the severity of hepatic injury (levels above 300 μg/mL 4 h after ingestion are predictive of the development of severe damage, while levels below 150 μg/mL suggest that hepatic injury is highly unlikely). Nausea, vomiting, diarrhea, abdominal pain, and shock are early manifestations occurring 4 to 12 h after ingestion. Then 24 to 48 h later, when these features are abating, hepatic injury becomes apparent. Maximal abnormalities and hepatic failure may not be evident until 4 to 6 days after ingestion. Renal failure and myocardial injury may be present.

Acetaminophen hepatotoxicity is mediated by a toxic reactive metabolite formed from the parent compound by the cytochrome P450 mixed-function oxidase system of the hepatocyte. This metabolite is detoxified by binding to glutathione. When excessive amounts of the metabolite are formed, glutathione levels in liver fall, and the metabolite is covalently bound to nucleophilic hepatocyte macro-

molecules. This process is believed to lead to hepatocyte necrosis; the precise sequence and mechanism are unknown. Hepatic injury may be potentiated by prior administration of alcohol or other drugs, by conditions which stimulate the mixed-function oxidase system, or by conditions such as starvation which reduce hepatic glutathione levels.

Treatment of acetaminophen overdosage includes gastric lavage, supportive measures, and oral administration of activated charcoal or cholestyramine to prevent absorption of residual drug. Neither of the latter agents appears to be effective if given more than 30 min after acetaminophen ingestion; if they are used, the stomach lavage should be done before other agents are administered orally. In patients with high acetaminophen blood levels (>200 μg/mL measured at 4 h or >100 μg/mL at 8 h after ingestion) the administration of sulfhydryl compounds (e.g., cysteamine, cysteine, or N-acetylcysteine) within 12 h of ingestion appears to reduce the severity of hepatic necrosis. These agents appear to act by providing a reservoir of sulfhydryl groups to bind the toxic metabolites or by stimulating synthesis and repletion of hepatic glutathione. Late administration of sulfhydryl compounds is of uncertain value.

Survivors of acute acetaminophen overdose usually have no evidence of hepatic sequelae. In a few patients prolonged or repeated administration of acetaminophen in therapeutic doses appears to have led to the development of chronic active hepatitis and cirrhosis.

Halothane hepatotoxicity (idiosyncratic reaction) Halothane, a nonexplosive fluorinated hydrocarbon anesthetic agent that is structurally similar to chloroform, has been reported to result in severe hepatic necrosis in a small number of individuals, many of whom have previously been exposed to this agent. The failure to produce similar hepatic lesions in animals, the rarity of hepatic impairment in human beings, and the delayed appearance of hepatic injury suggest that halothane is not a direct hepatotoxin but may be a sensitizing agent. However, manifestations of hypersensitivity are seen in fewer than 25 percent of cases. A genetic predisposition leading to an idiosyncratic metabolic reactivity has been postulated and appears to be the most likely mechanism of halothane hepatotoxicity. Adults (rather than children), obese people, and women appear to be particularly susceptible. Fever, moderate leukocytosis, and eosinophilia may occur in the first week following halothane administration. Jaundice usually is noted 7 to 10 days after exposure but may occur earlier in previously exposed patients. Nausea and vomiting may precede the onset of jaundice. Hepatomegaly is often mild, but liver tenderness is common. The serum aminotransferase levels are elevated. The pathologic changes at autopsy are indistinguishable from massive hepatic necrosis resulting from viral hepatitis. The case fatality rate of halothane hepatitis is not known but may vary from 20 to 40 percent in cases with severe liver involvement. In rare instances cirrhosis has been observed following repeated bouts of halothane hepatitis; however, in most patients who recover, the liver returns to normal. It is strongly suggested that patients in whom unexplained spiking fever, especially delayed fever, or jaundice develops after halothane anesthesia not receive this agent again. Because cross-reactions between halothane and methoxyfluorane have been reported, the latter agent should not be used after halothane reactions.

Methyldopa hepatotoxicity (toxic and idiosyncratic reaction) Minor alterations in liver tests are reported in about 5 percent of patients treated with this antihypertensive agent. These trivial abnormalities typically resolve despite continued drug administration. In less than 1 percent of patients, acute liver injury resembling viral hepatitis, or chronic active hepatitis, or rarely a cholestatic reaction is seen 1 to 20 weeks after methyldopa is started. In 50 percent of cases the interval is shorter than 4 weeks. A prodrome of fever, anorexia, and malaise may be noted for a few days before the onset of jaundice. Rash, lymphadenopathy, arthralgia, and eosinophilia are rare. Serologic markers of autoimmunity are infrequently detected, and fewer than 5 percent of patients have a Coombs-positive hemolytic

TABLE 247-6 Principal alterations of hepatic morphology produced by some commonly used drugs and chemicals

Principal morphologic change	Class of agent	Example
Cholestasis	Anabolic steroid	Methyl testosterone*
	Antithyroid	Methimazole
	Chemotherapeutic	Erythromycin estolate
	Oral contraceptive	Norethynodrel with mestranol
	Oral hypoglycemic	Chlorpropamide
	Tranquilizer	Chlorpromazine*
Fatty liver	Chemotherapeutic	Tetracycline
	Anticonvulsant	Valproic acid (sodium valproate)
Hepatitis	Anesthetic	Halothane†
	Anticonvulsant	Phenytoin
	Antihypertensive	Methyldopa†
	Chemotherapeutic	Isoniazid†
	Diuretic	Chlorothiazide
	Laxative	Oxyphenisatin†
Toxic (necrosis)	Hydrocarbon	Carbon tetrachloride
	Metal	Yellow phosphorus
	Mushroom	Amanita phalloides
	Analgesic	Acetaminophen
Granulomas	Anti-inflammatory	Phenylbutazone
	Chemotherapeutic	Sulfonamides
	Xanthine oxidase inhibitor	Allopurinol

* Rarely associated with primary biliary cirrhosis-like lesion.
† Occasionally associated with chronic active hepatitis or bridging hepatic necrosis and cirrhosis.

anemia. In about 15 percent of patients with methyldopa hepatotoxicity the clinical, biochemical, and histologic features are those of chronic active hepatitis with or without bridging necrosis and macronodular cirrhosis. With discontinuation of the drug, the disorder usually resolves, although progression has been seen in a few patients.

Isoniazid hepatotoxicity (toxic and idiosyncratic reaction) In approximately 10 percent of adults treated with the antituberculosis agent isoniazid, elevated serum aminotransferase levels develop during the first few weeks of therapy; this appears to represent an adaptive response to a toxic metabolite of the drug. Whether or not isoniazid is continued, these values (usually below 200 units) return to normal in a few weeks. In about 1 percent of treated patients, an illness develops which is indistinguishable from viral hepatitis; approximately half of these cases occur within the first 2 months of treatment, while in the remainder, clinical disease may be delayed for many months. Liver biopsy reveals morphologic changes similar to those of viral hepatitis or bridging hepatic necrosis. The disease may be severe, with a case fatality rate of 10 percent. Important liver injury appears to be age-related, increasing substantially in frequency after age 35; the highest frequency is in patients over age 50, the lowest under the age of 20. Fever, rash, eosinophilia, and other manifestations of drug allergy are distinctly unusual. A reactive metabolite of acetylhydrazine, a metabolite of isoniazid, may be responsible for liver injury. A picture resembling chronic active hepatitis has been observed in a few patients.

Sodium valproate hepatotoxicity (toxic and idiosyncratic reaction) Sodium valproate, an anticonvulsant useful in the treatment of petit mal and other seizure disorders, has been associated with the development of severe hepatic toxicity and, rarely, fatalities in both children and adults. Asymptomatic elevations of serum aminotransferase levels have been recognized in as many as 45 percent of treated patients. These ''adaptive'' changes, however, appear to have no clinical importance, for major hepatotoxicity is not seen in the majority of patients despite continuation of drug therapy. In those rare patients in whom jaundice, encephalopathy, and evidence of hepatic failure are found, examination of liver tissue reveals microvesicular fat and bridging hepatic necrosis predominantly in the centrolobular zone. Bile duct injury may also be apparent. It seems likely that sodium valproate is not directly hepatotoxic but that its metabolite, 4-pentenoic acid, may be responsible for hepatic injury.

Phenytoin hepatotoxicity (idiosyncratic reaction) Phenytoin, diphenylhydantoin, a mainstay in the treatment of seizure disorders, has been associated in rare instances with the development of severe hepatitis-like liver injury leading to fulminant hepatic failure in some instances. In many patients the hepatitis is associated with striking fever, lymphadenopathy, rash (Stevens-Johnson syndrome or exfoliative dermatitis), leukocytosis, and eosinophilia, suggesting an immunologically mediated hypersensitivity mechanism. Despite these observations, there is also evidence that metabolic idiosyncrasy may be responsible for hepatic injury. In the liver, phenytoin is converted by the cytochrome P450 system to metabolites which include the highly reactive electrophilic arene oxides. These metabolites are normally metabolized further by epoxide hydrolases. A defect (genetic or acquired) in epoxide hydrolase activity would permit covalent binding of arene oxides to hepatic macromolecules, thereby leading to hepatic injury. Regardless of the mechanism, hepatic injury is usually manifest within the first 2 months after beginning phenytoin therapy. With the exception of an abundance of eosinophils in the liver, the clinical, biochemical, and histologic picture resembles that of viral hepatitis. In rare instances, bile duct injury may be the salient feature of phenytoin hepatotoxicity with striking features of intrahepatic cholestasis.

Chlorpromazine hepatotoxicity (cholestatic idiosyncratic reaction) In about 1 percent of patients receiving chlorpromazine, intrahepatic cholestasis with jaundice develops after 1 to 4 weeks of treatment. In rare instances, jaundice has been reported after a single exposure. Anicteric reactions are frequent. The onset may be abrupt with fever, rash, arthralgias, lymphadenopathy, nausea, vomiting, and epigastric or right upper quadrant pain. Pruritus may precede the appearance of jaundice, dark urine, and light stools. Eosinophilia with or without mild leukocytosis may be present, and conjugated hyperbilirubinemia, moderately elevated serum alkaline phosphatase, and mildly elevated serum aminotransferase levels (100 to 200 units) are noted. Liver biopsy reveals cholestasis, bile plugs in dilated bile canaliculi, and a dense portal infiltrate of polymorphonuclear, eosinophilic, and mononuclear leukocytes. Occasionally, scattered foci of hepatic parenchymal necrosis may be evident. Jaundice and pruritus usually subside within 4 to 8 weeks following cessation of therapy, without sequelae, and fatalities are rare. Cholestyramine may be of value in relieving severe pruritus. In a small number of patients, jaundice is prolonged for several months to years; rarely, a disorder resembling but distinct from primary biliary cirrhosis may develop.

Erythromycin hepatotoxicity (cholestatic idiosyncratic reaction) The most important adverse effect associated with erythromycin is the infrequent occurrence of a cholestatic reaction. Although most of these reactions have been associated with erythromycin estolate, other erythromycins may also be responsible. The reaction usually begins during the first 2 or 3 weeks of therapy and includes nausea, vomiting, fever, right upper quadrant abdominal pain, jaundice, leukocytosis, and moderately elevated aminotransferase levels. The clinical picture can resemble acute cholecystitis or bacterial cholangitis. Liver biopsy reveals variable cholestasis, portal inflammation comprising lymphocytes, polymorphonuclear leukocytes, and eosinophils, and scattered foci of hepatocyte necrosis. Symptoms and laboratory findings usually subside within a few days of drug withdrawal, and evidence of chronic liver disease has not been found on followup. The precise mechanism remains ill-defined.

Oral contraceptive hepatotoxicity (cholestatic reaction) The administration of oral contraceptive combinations of estrogenic and progestational steroids results in significant bromsulphthalein (BSP) retention in a high proportion of patients, and, to a far lesser extent, elevation of serum alkaline phosphatase. Weeks to months after taking these agents, intrahepatic cholestasis with pruritus and jaundice is noted in a small number of patients. Especially susceptible seem to be patients with recurrent idiopathic jaundice of pregnancy, severe pruritus of pregnancy, or a family history of these disorders. Laboratory studies, with the exception of liver biochemical tests, are normal, and extrahepatic manifestations of hypersensitivity are absent. Liver biopsy reveals cholestasis with bile plugs in dilated canaliculi and striking bilirubin staining of liver cells. In contrast to chlorpromazine-induced cholestasis, portal inflammation is absent. The lesion is reversible on withdrawal of the agent, and sequelae have not been reported. The two steroid components appear to act synergistically on hepatic function, although the estrogen may be primarily responsible. Oral contraceptives are contraindicated in patients with a history of recurrent jaundice of pregnancy. As indicated above, neoplasms of the liver and hepatic vein occlusion have also been associated with oral contraceptive therapy.

17,α-Alkyl-substituted anabolic steroids (cholestatic reaction) In the majority of patients receiving these agents, used mainly in the treatment of bone marrow failure, mild hepatic dysfunction develops. Impaired excretory function is the predominant defect, but the precise mechanism is uncertain. Jaundice, which appears to be dose-related, develops in only a minority of patients and may be the sole clinical manifestation of hepatotoxicity, although anorexia, nausea, and malaise are described in some patients. Pruritus is not a prominent feature. Serum aminotransferase levels are usually under 100 units, and serum alkaline phosphatase levels are normal, mildly elevated, or, in less than 5 percent of patients, three or more times the upper limit of normal. Examination of liver tissue reveals cholestasis without inflammation or necrosis. Hepatic sinusoidal dilatation and peliosis hepatis have been found in a few patients. The cholestatic disorder is usually reversible on cessation of treatment, although fatalities have been linked to peliosis. An association with hepatic adenoma and hepatocellular carcinoma has been reported.

REFERENCES

Viral hepatitis

ALTER HJ (ed): Hepatitis B. Semin Liver Dis 1:1, 1981

———— (ed): Viral hepatitis. Semin Liver Dis 6:1, 1986

DIENSTAG JL, ISSELBACHER KJ: Therapy of acute and chronic hepatitis. Arch Intern Med 141:1419, 1981

————: Non-A, non-B hepatitis. I. Recognition, epidemiology, and clinical features. II. Experimental transmission, putative virus agents and markers, and prevention. Gastroenterology 85:439 and 743, 1983

FAVERO MS et al: Guidelines for the care of patients hospitalized with viral hepatitis. Ann Intern Med 91:872, 1979

GERETY RJ (ed): *Non-A, Non-B Hepatitis.* New York, Academic 1981

———— (ed): *Hepatitis A.* Orlando, Academic, 1984

———— (ed): *Hepatitis B.* Orlando, Academic, 1985

IMMUNIZATION PRACTICES ADVISORY COMMITTEE: Recommendations for protection against viral hepatitis. Ann Intern Med 103:391, 1985

JACOBSON IM, DIENSTAG JL: Viral hepatitis vaccines. Annu Rev Med 36:241, 1985

KOFF RS: Viral hepatitis. New York, Wiley, 1978

LEMON SM: Type A viral hepatitis: New developments in an old disease. N Engl J Med 313:1059, 1985

RIZZETTO M: The delta agent. Hepatology 3:729, 1983

SEEFF LB, HOOFNAGLE JH: Immunoprophylaxis of viral hepatitis. Gastroenterology 77:161, 1979

SEEFF LB, KOFF R: Passive and active immunoprophylaxis of hepatitis B. Gastroenterology 86:958, 1984

SHAFRITZ DA, LIBERMAN HM: The molecular biology of hepatitis B virus. Annu Rev Med 35:219, 1984

SZMUNESS W et al: Hepatitis B vaccine: Demonstration of efficacy in a controlled clinical trial in a high-risk population in the United States. N Engl J Med 303:833, 1980

———— et al (eds): Viral Hepatitis: 1981 International Symposium. Philadelphia, Franklin Institute Press, 1982

THEILMANN L et al: Detection of pre-SI proteins in serum and liver of HBsAg-positive patients: A new marker for hepatitis B virus infection, Hepatology 6:186, 1986

VERME G et al (eds): *Viral Hepatitis and Delta Infection.* New York, Alan R. Liss, 1983

VYAS GN et al (eds): *Viral Hepatitis and Liver Disease.* Orlando, Grune & Stratton, 1984

Drug-induced hepatitis

BLACK M et al: Isoniazid-associated hepatitis in 114 patients. Gastroenterology 69:389, 1975

ISHAK KG, IREY NS: Hepatic injury associated with the phenothiazines: Clinicopathologic and follow-up study of 36 patients. Arch Pathol 93:283, 1972

LUDWIG J, AXELSEN R: Drug effects on the liver: An updated tabular compilation of drugs and drug-related hepatic diseases. Dig Dis Sci 28:651, 1983

MITCHELL JR, JOLLOW DJ: Metabolic activation of drugs to toxic substances. Gastroenterology 68:392, 1975

SHERLOCK S: Hepatic reactions to drugs. Gut 20:634, 1979

ZAFRANI ES et al: Cholestatic and hepatocellular injury associated with erythromycin esters: Report of nine cases. Am J Dig Dis 24:38, 1979

ZIMMERMAN HJ: Hepatotoxicity. New York, Appleton-Century-Crofts, 1978

———— (ed): Drug-induced liver disease. Semin Liver Dis 1:91, 1981

————, ISAK KG: Valproate-induced hepatic injury: Analysis of 23 fatal cases. Hepatology 2:591, 1982

248   CHRONIC HEPATITIS

JACK R. WANDS / RAYMOND S. KOFF / KURT J. ISSELBACHER

Chronic hepatitis refers to three related disorders—chronic persistent hepatitis, chronic lobular hepatitis, and chronic active hepatitis. These are characterized by a combination of hepatocyte necrosis and inflammation of varying severity persisting for more than 6 months. The clinically most important disorder, chronic active hepatitis, may lead to hepatic failure and death or result in the development of cirrhosis and its sequelae. While all three forms of chronic hepatitis share some histopathologic features and appear to be incited by similar etiologic factors, their pathogeneses, clinical presentations, natural histories, prognoses, and therapies are different.

CHRONIC PERSISTENT AND CHRONIC LOBULAR HEPATITIS

Definition and etiology   Chronic persistent and chronic lobular hepatitis result from infections with hepatitis B virus (HBV) and non-A, non-B hepatitis virus. Other etiologies may exist but are poorly defined. In general, these are both nonprogressive disorders; hepatic failure is not seen and evolution into cirrhosis is exceedingly rare. Occasionally, however, patients with chronic active hepatitis may be misdiagnosed if they are seen during remission, at which time the histopathologic findings may suggest chronic persistent or chronic lobular hepatitis. Under these circumstances relapses and progression to the more serious underlying chronic active hepatitis may be anticipated. Another exception to the nonprogression of chronic persistent and lobular hepatitis occurs in patients positive to hepatitis B surface antigen (HBsAg), in whom superinfection with delta agent (HDV) may lead to the development of chronic active hepatitis (see Chap. 247).

Pathology   In typical chronic persistent hepatitis there is infiltration of the portal areas with mononuclear cells, but there is no erosion of the limiting plate (so-called piecemeal necrosis) or extension of the inflammation into the liver lobule. A "cobblestone" arrangement of liver cells, indicative of hepatic regenerative activity, is a common feature. Minimal fibrosis may be observed, but *cirrhosis is characteristically absent.* In chronic lobular hepatitis, in addition to the portal inflammatory changes, lobular inflammation and focal hepatocellular necrosis are prominent features during clinically active phases. The morphologic features of chronic persistent, lobular, and active hepatitis are compared in Table 248-1.

Clinical and laboratory features   Most patients with chronic persistent and/or lobular hepatitis are asymptomatic, although some may complain of anorexia, fatigue, and occasionally of nausea and vomiting. Physical findings are usually normal, but the liver may be slightly enlarged and tender. Laboratory data show mild elevations of aminotransferase and alkaline phosphatase levels and these abnormalities may persist for months to years. During active phases of chronic lobular hepatitis, aminotransferase levels may resemble those seen in acute viral hepatitis.

Management   Once the diagnosis of chronic persistent or lobular hepatitis has been established by liver biopsy, no specific therapy is required since such patients generally do not develop fibrosis and cirrhosis. Follow-up examination is recommended every 6 to 12 months until aminotransferase values have returned to normal and to identify the rare patient who may progress to chronic active hepatitis.

CHRONIC ACTIVE HEPATITIS

Definition   Chronic active hepatitis is a disorder of diverse etiologies characterized by continuing hepatic necrosis, active inflammation, and fibrosis which may lead to or be accompanied by liver failure, cirrhosis, and death. The prominence of extrahepatic features and seroimmunologic abnormalities has led to the use of a variety of terms to describe this disorder. These terms include autoimmune hepatitis, lupoid hepatitis, subacute hepatitis, and chronic active liver disease. *Chronic active hepatitis* seems to be the most appropriate designation for this clinicopathologic entity, regardless of the etiology and the clinical variations.

Pathology   Although chronic active hepatitis may be suspected from the clinical history and the physical findings, *liver biopsy is necessary to establish the diagnosis.* The cardinal histopathologic features observed in the liver include (1) a dense mononuclear and plasma cell infiltration of the portal zones which greatly expands these areas with extension of the inflammatory infiltrate into the liver lobule; (2) destruction of the hepatocytes at the periphery of the lobule (piecemeal necrosis) with erosion of the limiting plate surrounding the portal triads; (3) connective tissue septa extending from the portal zones into the lobule, isolating parenchymal cells into clusters and envel-

TABLE 248-1 Some distinguishing features of chronic persistent, chronic lobular, and chronic active hepatitis

Features	Chronic persistent hepatitis	Chronic lobular hepatitis	Chronic active hepatitis
CLINICAL			
Onset like acute hepatitis	≈70%	≈90%	≈30%
Recurrent acute episodes	Infrequent	Common	Common
Extrahepatic involvement	Rare	Rare	Common
Prognosis	Good	Good	Variable
LIVER HISTOLOGY			
Piecemeal necrosis	Inconstant	Inconstant	Typical
Site of inflammation	Portal	Portal/lobular in active phase	Portal, extending into lobule
Lobular architecture	Preserved	Preserved	Distorted
Fibrosis	Slight	Slight	Common
Progression to cirrhosis	Rare	Rare	Common

oping bile ducts; and (4) evidence of hepatic regeneration with "rosette" formation, thickened liver-cell plates, and regenerative "pseudolobules." This process may be patchy, and individual liver lobules may remain uninvolved. Councilman-like bodies, which represent necrosis of single liver cells, may be seen in the periportal areas. The lesion of bridging hepatic necrosis may be seen in some patients with chronic active hepatitis. This lesion or its more extensive variant, multilobular bridging hepatic necrosis, suggests the presence of severe disease.

There is substantial morphologic evidence that in some instances chronic active hepatitis will progress to or is accompanied by the development of cirrhosis. On liver biopsy, cirrhosis can be demonstrated in 20 to 50 percent of patients, even early in the course of the disease, and at autopsy postnecrotic cirrhosis may be found. It is also possible that many cases of so-called cryptogenic cirrhosis are the result of chronic active hepatitis after inflammation and necrosis have subsided. In other patients fibrosis is not progressive and morphologic evidence of cirrhosis cannot be found.

Etiology Multiple etiologic agents may initiate chronic active hepatitis. Probably the most important and common triggering factors are infection with hepatitis B virus or the non-A, non-B hepatitis viruses. In about one-third of patients the disease begins abruptly following an illness typical of acute viral hepatitis. Persistence of HBsAg in the serum is found in 20 to 30 percent of patients with chronic active hepatitis, suggesting that persistent hepatitis B virus infection may be related to the development of chronic active hepatitis. Many of these HBsAg-positive patients also have positive tests for the hepatitis B e antigen (HBeAg) (see Chap. 247). Superinfection with delta hepatitis agent (HDV) in HBsAg-positive individuals may lead to the development of chronic active hepatitis. Similarly, persistent non-A, non-B hepatitis virus infections may be responsible for cases of chronic active hepatitis following transfusion-associated and sporadic non-A, non-B hepatitis. Drugs are involved in the pathogenesis of some cases. For example, features typical of chronic active hepatitis have been found in some patients in association with the administration of methyldopa. In these patients challenge with methyldopa has led to increased activity of the disease, while discontinuance has resulted in clinical, biochemical, and histologic improvement. Oxyphenisatin, isoniazid, nitrofurantoin, and other drugs have also been incriminated as etiologic agents in patients with chronic active hepatitis. Thus, chemical as well as viral agents may play a role in the production of chronic active hepatitis. The existence

of other triggering factors seems likely, but their nature and mechanisms of action remain to be determined.

Immunopathogenesis There is increasing evidence that the progressive parenchymal cell destruction in patients with chronic active hepatitis involves an interaction with the immune system conditioned or controlled by genetic factors. Evidence to support this concept includes the following facts: (1) In the liver the histopathologic lesions are composed predominantly of thymus-derived or T lymphocytes and plasma cells in association with progressive liver cell destruction and replacement by fibrous tissue. (2) A variety of circulating "autoantibodies" are frequently detected, such as anti-smooth-muscle, antimitochondrial, and antithyroid antibodies. (3) The persistence of HBsAg in the serum and the hepatitis B core antigen (HBcAg) in the liver cell following an attack of acute hepatitis B is frequently associated with the development of chronic active or chronic persistent hepatitis. (4) Other "autoimmune" diseases such as thyroiditis, diabetes mellitus, ulcerative colitis, Coombs-positive hemolytic anemia, proliferative glomerulonephritis, and Sjögren's syndrome may be associated with chronic active hepatitis or may occur in relatives of affected patients. (5) Histocompatibility antigens HLA-B1 or -B8 and DRw3 and DRw4 are more prevalent than expected in patients with chronic active hepatitis without HBsAg. (6) Finally, the use of corticosteroids, believed to be effective in a variety of immunologic and autoimmune disorders, is often beneficial in the treatment of severe chronic active hepatitis.

There is increasing evidence that cellular immune reactions may be important in the pathogenesis of chronic active hepatitis. It has been suggested that lymphocytes become sensitized to altered or new antigens present on the surface membranes of hepatocytes. This hypothesis is supported in part by studies demonstrating that circulating and liver-derived lymphocytes may have the capability of causing liver cell damage in vitro.

Humoral immune mechanisms may be responsible for some of the clinical manifestations of chronic active hepatitis. In particular, extrahepatic features such as arthralgias, arthritis, rash, and glomerulonephritis appear to be mediated by the deposition of circulating immune complexes. Furthermore, complement activation, as demonstrated by low serum complement levels, and the presence of complement components in immune complexes suggest that circulating immune complexes may be involved in mediating extrahepatic inflammation and tissue damage.

Clinical features The clinical spectrum of chronic active hepatitis extends from asymptomatic illness at one end to fatal hepatic failure at the other. All age groups are affected. In approximately two-thirds of patients the disease has an *insidious onset* over a period of several weeks to months, or the disease is discovered incidentally, and the duration of the illness is uncertain. In the remainder an abrupt onset similar to that in acute viral hepatitis is seen, but features of chronic active hepatitis usually develop during the ensuing 12 to 24 months. The clinical and laboratory features suggesting progression from acute hepatitis to chronic active hepatitis are discussed in Chap. 247. *Fatigue* is a common symptom. Persistent or recurrent *jaundice* is a common feature in severe disease. Intermittent deepening of jaundice and recurrent symptoms of *malaise, anorexia,* and *low-grade fever,* suggestive of a superimposed acute hepatitis, are common throughout the course of the illness. In some patients complications of cirrhosis, such as ascites, variceal bleeding, encephalopathy, coagulopathy, or hypersplenism, may first bring the patient to medical attention. In others the extrahepatic features dominate the clinical picture, and liver disease is entirely unsuspected. Extrahepatic presenting features may include amenorrhea, bloody diarrhea (due to associated ulcerative colitis), abdominal pain, arthralgia or arthritis, macular or papular eruptions, acne, erythema nodosum, pleurisy, pericarditis, anemia, azotemia, and sicca syndrome (of keratoconjunctivitis and xerostomia). These extrahepatic features and abnormal serologic reactions tend to be more frequent in women than men and in patients without serologic evidence of preceding hepatitis B.

The *course* of chronic active hepatitis is variable, and the disease may persist for long periods without clinically overt liver disease. This appears to be particularly true of chronic active hepatitis associated with hepatitis B or non-A, non-B hepatitis. The condition may occasionally remit into a clinically inactive phase, although continuing hepatocellular necrosis or progression to cirrhosis may also occur. The histologic lesion may reverse itself completely before the development of cirrhosis in some HBsAg-positive patients after their antigenemia has spontaneously cleared or following the loss of HBeAg and the development of anti-HBe. If untreated, the case fatality rate may be high during the first few years of illness, especially in patients with clinically and histologically severe disease. Death usually occurs as a result of liver failure and hepatic coma. Later death is often due to a complication of cirrhosis—variceal hemorrhage or intercurrent infection. Primary hepatocellular carcinoma is an uncommon complication of HBsAg-negative chronic active hepatitis even when the disease has progressed to postnecrotic cirrhosis. This finding is in contrast to long-term HBsAg carriers with chronic active hepatitis and/or cirrhosis in whom the incidence of liver carcinoma is increased (see Chap. 247).

Laboratory findings   Liver function tests are invariably abnormal but may not correlate with the clinical severity or histopathologic findings in the individual case. Many patients have normal serum bilirubin, alkaline phosphatase, and globulin levels with only minimial aminotransferase elevations or HBsAg positivity and yet have a liver biopsy consistent with severe chronic active hepatitis. Serum aspartate aminotransferase (SGOT) and alanine aminotransferase (SGPT) levels are increased and fluctuate in the range of 100 to 1000 units in most cases. In severe cases the serum bilirubin is moderately elevated (3 to 10 mg/dL). Mild hypoalbuminemia occurs in patients with active disease or in those with advanced cirrhosis. Serum alkaline phosphatase levels may be moderately elevated or near normal. The prothrombin time is often prolonged, particularly late in the disease or during active phases.

Hypergammaglobulinemia (greater than 2.5 g/dL) is common, particularly in patients with extensive plasma cell infiltration of the liver. A variety of abnormal serologic reactions and circulating autoantibodies are found in chronic active hepatitis. Some of these serologic reactions are nonspecific and may be seen in other viral diseases. Circulating autoantibodies against DNA, IgG, smooth muscle, and mitochrondria support the concept that chronic active hepatitis is indeed a systemic disease. HBsAg may be found in 20 to 30 percent of patients with chronic active hepatitis, more commonly in men than women.

Differential diagnosis   Early in the course of chronic active hepatitis the disease may resemble typical *acute viral hepatitis*. However, the persistence of symptoms, including biochemical abnormalities such as elevated serum aminotransferase and bilirubin levels or circulating HBsAg over the ensuing months indicates that a chronic liver disorder is present. The major entities which must be distinguished from chronic active hepatitis are *chronic persistent and lobular hepatitis*. As indicated in Table 248-1, in chronic persistent and lobular hepatitis the onset of the illness frequently resembles acute hepatitis. The aminotransferase enzyme values are variably elevated, and HBsAg may be present in serum. Fatigue, anorexia, malaise, right upper quadrant discomfort, and hepatomegaly may be associated with all three forms of chronic hepatitis. Thus, a definitive diagnosis can only be established by liver biopsy since a *differentiation between chronic active, chronic persistent, and lobular hepatitis cannot be made by clinical and biochemical criteria*. This distinction is important because chronic persistent and lobular hepatitis are not progressive disorders, rarely if ever result in cirrhosis, and require no therapy.

The presence of extrahepatic manifestations in chronic active hepatitis such as pleuritis, arthritis, and arthralgias may cause confusion with *connective tissue disorders* such as rheumatoid arthritis and systemic lupus erythematosus. The existence of clinical and biochemical features suggestive of progressive liver disease clearly distinguishes chronic active hepatitis from these disorders. In adolescence, *Wilson's disease* may present with features of chronic active hepatitis before the neurologic manifestations become apparent; serum ceruloplasmin, serum and urinary copper determination, and measurement of the liver copper levels will establish the diagnosis. Late in the course of chronic active hepatitis some patients may present with *postnecrotic cirrhosis* without evidence of active hepatitis. This lesion, termed cryptogenic cirrhosis, may also represent an end stage of other destructive liver diseases (e.g., primary biliary cirrhosis). *Primary biliary cirrhosis* may share histologic similarities with chronic active hepatitis, particularly early in the disease. However, in primary biliary cirrhosis the prominence of pruritus plus markedly elevated serum alkaline phosphatase and cholesterol levels, the presence of high titers of antimitochondrial antibodies (in contrast to the low levels seen in chronic active hepatitis), and the pattern of histologic progression will usually permit differentiation from chronic active hepatitis.

Management   Corticosteroid therapy is the treatment of choice in symptomatic HBsAg-negative and severe chronic active hepatitis. Corticosteroids have been shown to be effective in prolonging survival of these patients during the first few years of illness when the mortality rate is high. A therapeutic response characterized by a complete clinical, biochemical, and histologic remission is to be expected in 60 to 80 percent of patients. Either prednisone or prednisolone therapy should be initiated at a dose of 20 to 40 mg daily. This dose can usually be gradually tapered within 2 to 3 months to 10 to 20 mg daily. The beneficial effects of corticosteroid treatment on the course and prognosis of patients with mild or asymptomatic chronic active hepatitis has not been established.

Improvement of fatigue and anorexia is usually noted within days to several weeks. Biochemical improvement is to be expected over several weeks to months, with a fall in serum bilirubin and globulin levels and a rise in serum albumin. The serum aminotransferase level usually drops promptly, but the absolute value of the aminotransferase *alone* does not appear to be a useful marker of recovery in the individual patient. Histologic improvement, characterized by a decrease in mononuclear infiltration and subsequent improvement in the extent of hepatocellular necrosis, may be delayed for 6 to 24 months. After a favorable clinical and biochemical response, repeat liver biopsy may show features consistent with chronic persistent hepatitis. Despite this histologic improvement, relapses are common when corticosteroids are discontinued.

Reduction of the suppressive corticosteroid doses should be performed cautiously, particularly at lower prednisone levels, since even small decrements in therapy may be associated with clinical worsening, and increasing dosage may be needed for control of spontaneous exacerbation. Unless major complications require discontinuation of corticosteroids, they should be prescribed for at least 12 months or longer in order to reduce the risk of relapse.

Other therapeutic approaches have been used in the treatment of severe chronic active hepatitis, particularly in the elderly and in patients with major side effects from corticosteroids. An initial prednisone dosage of 30 mg, tapered down to 10 to 20 mg, in combination with 50 to 75 mg azathioprine has been demonstrated to be effective; this treatment avoids the adverse effects of high dosage of corticosteroids. However, *azathioprine alone is not effective in the treatment of chronic active hepatitis*. Alternate-day prednisone therapy diminishes steroid side effects but usually does not provide adequate therapy.

Corticosteroids have little if any beneficial effect on the natural course of HBsAg-positive chronic active hepatitis. Treatment of *asymptomatic* HBsAg carriers who only have evidence of chronic active hepatitis on liver biopsy is not justified. In *symptomatic* HBsAg-positive patients with severe chronic active hepatitis, corticosteroids have not been shown to be of value either in short- or long-term therapy. Treatment with interferon and other antiviral agents has been studied, but mixed results have been obtained with respect to a favorable clinical response. Use of such drugs is still experimental.

REFERENCES

BERMAN M et al: The chronic sequelae of non-A, non-B hepatitis. Ann Intern Med 91:1, 1979

CZAJA AJ et al: Laboratory assessment of severe chronic active liver disease during and after corticosteroid therapy. Correlation of serum transaminase and gamma globulin levels with histologic features. Gastroenterology 80:667, 1981

HODGES JR et al: Chronic active hepatitis: The spectrum of disease. Lancet 1:550, 1982

LAM KC et al: Deleterious effect of prednisolone in HBsAg-positive chronic active hepatitis. N Engl J Med 304:380, 1981

MACKAY IR, TAIT BD: HLA associations with autoimmune-type chronic active hepatitis: Identification of B8-DRw3 haplotypes by family studies. Gastroenterology 79:95, 1980

SEEF LB, KOFF RS: Therapy for chronic active hepatitis. Adv Intern Med 29:109, 1984

WEISSBERG JI et al: Survival in chronic hepatitis B. An analysis of 379 patients. Ann Intern Med 101:613, 1984

WELLER IVD et al: Effects of prednisone/azathioprine in chronic hepatitis B viral infection. Gut 23:650, 1982

249 CIRRHOSIS

DANIEL K. PODOLSKY / KURT J. ISSELBACHER

Cirrhosis is a pathologically defined entity which is associated with a spectrum of characteristic clinical manifestations. The cardinal pathologic features reflect irreversible chronic injury of the hepatic parenchyma and include extensive fibrosis in association with the formation of regenerative nodules. These features result from hepatocyte necrosis, collapse of the supporting reticulin network with subsequent connective tissue deposition, distortion of the vascular bed, and nodular regeneration of remaining liver parenchyma. The pathologic process should be viewed as a final common pathway of many types of chronic liver injury. Clinical features of cirrhosis derive from the morphologic alterations and often reflect the severity of hepatic damage rather than the etiology of the underlying liver disease. Loss of functioning hepatocellular mass may lead to jaundice, edema, coagulopathy, and a variety of metabolic abnormalities; fibrosis and distorted vasculature lead to portal hypertension and its sequelae, including gastroesophageal varices and splenomegaly. Ascites and hepatic encephalopathy result from both hepatocellular insufficiency and portal hypertension.

Classification of the various types of cirrhosis based solely on etiology or morphology is unsatisfactory. A single pathologic pattern may result from a variety of insults, while the same insult may produce several morphologic patterns. Nevertheless most types of cirrhosis may be usefully classified by a mixture of etiologically and morphologically defined entities as follows: (1) alcoholic; (2) cryptogenic and postnecrotic; (3) biliary; (4) cardiac; (5) metabolic, inherited, and drug-related; and (6) miscellaneous. This chapter considers first the various types of cirrhosis and then the major clinical complications of chronic liver disease and cirrhosis.

ALCOHOLIC LIVER DISEASE AND CIRRHOSIS

Definition Alcoholic cirrhosis, historically referred to as Laennec's cirrhosis, is the most common type of cirrhosis encountered in North America and many parts of western Europe and South America. It is usually characterized by diffuse fine scarring, fairly uniform loss of liver cells, and small regenerative nodules, and therefore, it is sometimes referred to as micronodular cirrhosis. However, micronodular cirrhosis may also result from other types of liver injury (e.g., following jejunoileal bypass), and thus alcoholic cirrhosis and micronodular cirrhosis are not necessarily synonymous. Conversely alcoholic cirrhosis may progress to macronodular cirrhosis with time.

Alcoholic cirrhosis is only one of many consequences resulting from chronic alcoholic ingestion, and it often accompanies other forms of alcohol-induced liver injury. The three principal alcohol-induced hepatic lesions are designated: (1) alcoholic fatty liver, (2) alcoholic hepatitis, and (3) alcoholic cirrhosis. These morphologic categories are rarely found in a pure form, and features of each may be present to varying degrees in an individual patient.

Etiology Although chronic alcoholism is clearly the major cause of alcoholic cirrhosis, the quantity and duration of drinking necessary to cause cirrhosis remain unclear. The typical alcoholic patient with cirrhosis has had a daily consumption of a pint or more of whiskey, several quarts of wine, or an equivalent amount of beer for at least 10 years. The amount and duration of ethanol ingestion, rather than the type of alcoholic beverage or the pattern of ingestion, appear to be the important determinants of liver injury. In general, the latent period preceding the development of cirrhosis is inversely related to the level of daily alcohol intake. Although rates of ethanol metabolism are under genetic control, no metabolic defect has been identified in cirrhotic patients or their families to suggest a unique "susceptibility" to ethanol or its toxic effects. Although malnutrition per se does not appear to lead to cirrhosis, it is possible that nutritional factors may augment the detrimental effects of chronic alcohol ingestion on the liver. The finding that only 10 to 15 percent of alcoholics develop cirrhosis suggests that other factors may affect the impact of alcohol on the liver. Women appear to be more susceptible to alcohol-induced liver injury, suggesting that hormonal factors may play a role.

Alcoholic fatty liver occurs in most heavy drinkers but is reversible on cessation of alcohol consumption and is not thought to be an inevitable precursor of alcoholic hepatitis or cirrhosis. In contrast, alcoholic hepatitis, an inflammatory lesion characterized by infiltration of the liver with leukocytes, liver cell necrosis, and alcoholic hyaline, is thought to be the major precursor of cirrhosis. Subsequent healing accompanied by fibrosis distorts the normal lobular architecture. Indeed, *deposition of collagen in perivenular spaces* may be the earliest manifestation of the process which ultimately leads to cirrhosis.

Pathology and pathogenesis ALCOHOLIC FATTY LIVER The liver is enlarged, yellow, greasy, and firm. Hepatocytes are distended by large cytoplasmic fat vacuoles which push the hepatocyte nucleus against the cell membrane. Accumulation of fat in the liver of the alcoholic results from the combination of impaired fatty acid oxidation, increased uptake and esterification of fatty acids to form triglycerides, and diminished lipoprotein biosynthesis and secretion.

ALCOHOLIC HEPATITIS Morphologic features include hepatocyte degeneration and necrosis, often with ballooned cells, and an infiltrate of polymorphonuclear leukocytes and lymphocytes. The polymorphonuclear cells may encircle damaged hepatocytes which contain *Mallory bodies,* or *alcoholic hyaline.* These are clumps of perinuclear, deeply eosinophilic material believed to represent aggregated intermediate filaments. Mallory bodies are highly suggestive of, but *not specific* for, alcoholic hepatitis, since morphologically similar material has been seen in association with morbid obesity, jejunoileal bypass surgery, poorly controlled diabetes mellitus, and a variety of other disorders including Wilson's disease and Indian childhood cirrhosis. Deposition of collagen around the central vein and in perisinusoidal areas, often termed central hyaline sclerosis, may be associated with an increased likelihood of progression to cirrhosis.

ALCOHOLIC CIRRHOSIS With continued alcohol intake and destruction of hepatocytes, fibroblasts (including myofibroblasts with contractile properties) appear at the site of injury and stimulate collagen formation. Weblike septa of connective tissue appear in periportal and pericentral zones and eventually connect portal triads and central veins. This fine connective tissue network surrounds small masses of remaining liver cells which regenerate and form nodules. Although regeneration occurs within the small remnants of parenchyma, cell loss generally exceeds replacement. With continuing hepatocyte destruction and collagen deposition, the liver shrinks in size, acquires a nodular appearance, and becomes hard as "end-stage" cirrhosis develops. Although alcoholic cirrhosis is usually a progressive disease, appropriate therapy and strict avoidance of alcohol may arrest the disease at most stages and permit functional improvement.

Clinical features SIGNS AND SYMPTOMS Clinical manifestations of *alcoholic fatty liver* are often minimal or entirely absent, and the disorder may not be recognized unless another illness (frequently alcohol-related) brings the patient to medical attention. Hepatomegaly, at times accompanied by tenderness, may be the only finding. Jaundice, ascites, and edema are only seen with more serious liver injury.

The clinical severity of *alcoholic hepatitis* varies enormously, ranging from asymptomatic or mild illness to fatal hepatic insufficiency. Typically, the clinical features of alcoholic hepatitis resemble those of viral or toxic liver injury. Patients often experience anorexia, nausea and vomiting, malaise, weight loss, abdominal distress, and jaundice. Fever as high as 103°F may be seen in about half of cases. On physical examination, tender hepatomegaly is common, and splenomegaly is found in about one-third of patients. The patient may have cutaneous arterial "spider" angiomas and jaundice. More severe cases may be complicated by ascites, edema, bleeding, and encephalopathy. At the time of initial presentation, the central nervous system findings may be difficult to distinguish from manifestations of concurrent alcohol intoxication or withdrawal (see below).

Although jaundice, ascites, and encephalopathy may subside with abstinence, continued alcohol excess and poor dietary habits usually lead to repeated acute episodes of hepatic decompensation. Some patients die during these acute exacerbations, but most recover after several weeks or months. Even after complete abstinence, clinical recovery may be protracted, and histologic abnormalities can persist up to 6 months or longer. Cholestatic jaundice mimicking biliary tract obstruction may also develop in some cases of acute alcoholic hepatitis.

Alcoholic cirrhosis may also be clinically silent; in fact 10 percent of cases are discovered incidentally at laparotomy or autopsy. In many cases symptoms are insidious in onset, occurring usually after 10 or more years of excessive alcohol use and progressing slowly over subsequent weeks and months. Anorexia and malnutrition lead to weight loss and a reduction in skeletal muscle mass. The patient may experience easy bruising, increasing weakness, and fatigue. Eventually the clinical manifestations of hepatocellular dysfunction and portal hypertension ensue, including progressive jaundice, bleeding from gastroesophageal varices, ascites, and encephalopathy. The abrupt onset of one of these complications may be the first event prompting the patient to seek medical attention. In other cases, cirrhosis first becomes evident when the patient requires treatment of symptoms related to alcoholic hepatitis.

A firm, nodular liver may be an early sign of disease; the liver may be either enlarged, normal, or decreased in size. Other frequent findings include jaundice, palmar erythema, spider angiomas, parotid and lacrimal gland enlargement, clubbing of fingers, splenomegaly, muscle wasting, and ascites with or without peripheral edema. Men may have decreased body hair and/or gynecomastia and testicular atrophy, which, like the cutaneous findings, result from disturbances in hormonal metabolism, including increased peripheral formation of estrogen due to diminished hepatic clearance of the precursor androstenedione. Testicular atrophy may reflect hormonal abnormalities or the toxic effect of alcohol on the testes. In women, signs of virilization or menstrual irregularities may occasionally be encountered. Dupuytren's contractures resulting from fibrosis of the palmar fascia with resulting flexion contracture of the digits are associated with alcoholism but are not specifically related to cirrhosis.

Over a period of 3 to 5 years, the cirrhotic patient typically becomes emaciated, weak, and chronically jaundiced. Ascites and other signs of portal hypertension become increasingly prominent. Most patients with advanced cirrhosis die in hepatic coma, commonly precipitated by hemorrhage from esophageal varices or intercurrent infection. Progressive renal dysfunction often complicates the terminal phase of the illness.

LABORATORY FINDINGS Routine hematologic and biochemical blood tests are usually normal in patients with alcoholic fatty liver, except for minimal elevations of the serum AST [aspartate aminotransferase; serum glutamic oxaloacetic transaminase (SGOT)] level; occasionally alkaline phosphatase and bilirubin levels are also elevated. In more advanced alcoholic liver disease, abnormalities of laboratory tests are more common. Anemia may result from acute and chronic gastrointestinal blood loss, coexistent nutritional deficiency (notably of folic acid and vitamin B_{12}), hypersplenism, and a direct suppressive effect of alcohol on the bone marrow. Hemolytic anemia presumably due to effects of hypercholesterolemia on erythrocyte membranes resulting in unusual spurlike projections (acanthocytosis) has been described in some alcoholics with cirrhosis. Leukocytosis is often present in severe alcoholic hepatitis; however, some patients with this disorder may have leukopenia and thrombocytopenia due to hypersplenism or an inhibitory effect of alcohol on the bone marrow. Mild or pronounced hyperbilirubinemia may be found, usually in association with varying elevations of serum alkaline phosphatase levels. The serum ALT [alanine aminotransferase; serum glutamic pyruric transaminase (SGPT)] is frequently elevated, but levels greater than 300 units are unusual and should prompt one to look for other coincident or complicating factors. In contrast to viral hepatitis, the serum AST is usually disproportionately elevated relative to ALT (AST/ALT ratio > 2). This discrepancy may result from the proportionally greater inhibition of ALT synthesis by ethanol, which may be partially reversed by pyridoxal phosphate.

The serum prothrombin time is frequently prolonged, reflecting reduced synthesis of clotting proteins, most notably the vitamin K–dependent factors (see "Coagulopathy" below). The serum albumin level is usually depressed, while serum globulins are increased. Hypoalbuminemia reflects in part overall impairment in hepatic protein synthesis, while hyperglobulinemia is thought to result from nonspecific stimulation of the reticuloendothelial system. Elevated blood ammonia levels in patients with hepatic encephalopathy reflect diminished hepatic clearance because of impaired liver function and shunting of portal venous blood around the cirrhotic liver into the systemic circulation (see below and Chap. 244).

A variety of metabolic disturbances may be detected. Glucose intolerance due to endogenous insulin resistance may be present; however, clinical diabetes is uncommon. Central hyperventilation may lead to respiratory alkalosis in patients with cirrhosis. *Dietary deficiency* and *increased urinary losses* lead to hypomagnesemia and *hypophosphatemia*. In patients with ascites and dilutional hyponatremia, hypokalemia may occur from increased urinary postassium losses due in part to hyperaldosteronism. Prerenal azotemia is also observed in such patients.

Diagnosis *Alcoholic fatty liver* should be suspected in alcoholic patients with hepatomegaly and normal or minimally deranged liver function tests. Alcoholic fatty liver may be seen in combination with alcoholic hepatitis or established cirrhosis. *Alcoholic hepatitis* should be considered in an alcoholic who has been drinking heavily and demonstrates jaundice, fever, an enlarged, tender liver, or ascites. The clinical impression is often supported by the deranged results of tests of liver function and other laboratory abnormalities described above. Alcoholic hepatitis or fatty liver may be present in association with alcoholic cirrhosis.

Alcoholic cirrhosis should be strongly suspected in patients with a history of prolonged or excessive alcohol intake and physical signs of chronic liver disease. The clinical features and laboratory findings are usually sufficient to provide reasonable indication of the presence and extent of hepatic injury. Although a percutaneous needle biopsy of the liver is not usually necessary to confirm the typical findings of alcoholic hepatitis or cirrhosis, it may be helpful in distinguishing patients with less advanced liver disease from those with cirrhosis and in excluding other forms of liver injury such as viral hepatitis.

Biopsy may also be helpful as a diagnostic tool in evaluating patients with clinical findings suggestive of alcoholic liver disease who deny alcohol intake. In patients with features of cholestasis, ultrasonography may be appropriate to exclude the presence of extrahepatic biliary obstruction. When the clinical status of an otherwise stable cirrhotic patient deteriorates without an obvious explanation, complicating conditions, such as infection, portal vein thrombosis, and hepatocellular carcinoma, should be sought.

Prognosis The patient with an alcoholic fatty liver and no complications has a good prognosis; rapid and complete resolution usually follows cessation of alcohol intake. In patients with alcoholic hepatitis, the presence of marked hyperbilirubinemia (>20 mg/dL), rising serum creatinine, marked prolongation of the prothrombin time (> 1.5 times control), ascites, and encephalopathy are associated with a poor short-term prognosis; the in-hospital mortality in these patients may exceed 50 percent. In milder cases, clinical recovery may be complete, but repeated bouts of alcoholic hepatitis usually lead to irreversible and progressive chronic liver injury. Abstinence from alcohol as well as early and appropriate medical care can decrease long-term morbidity and mortality, and delay or prevent the appearance of further complications. Patients who have had a major complication of cirrhosis and who continue to drink, have a 5-year survival of less than 50 percent. However, those patients who remain abstinent have a substantially better prognosis. In general, overall outlook in patients with advanced liver disease remains poor; most of these patients eventually die as a result of massive variceal hemorrhage and/or profound hepatic encephalopathy.

Treatment Alcoholic hepatitis and cirrhosis are serious illnesses that require long-term medical supervision and careful management. Therapy of the underlying liver disease is largely supportive. Specific treatment is directed at particular complications such as variceal bleeding, ascites, etc. (see below). Some studies suggest that administration of prednisone or prednisolone in moderately large doses may be helpful in patients with severe alcoholic hepatitis and encephalopathy. However, the use of corticosteroids in acute alcoholic hepatitis remains controversial and is not recommended. Other agents, such as propylthiouracil, penicillamine, colchicine, and intravenous infusion of insulin and glucagon have been used experimentally, but their therapeutic efficacy and safety remain to be demonstrated.

In the absence of signs of impending hepatic coma, the patient should be placed on a diet containing at least 1 g protein per kilogram of body weight and 2000 to 3000 kcal per day. Use of diets enriched in branched-chain amino acids has been advocated in patients predisposed to hepatic encephalopathy, but the value of these diets in patients with compensated cirrhosis is unproven. Daily multivitamin supplements should be prescribed, with the addition of large parenteral doses of thiamine in patients with Wernicke-Korsakoff disease (see Chap. 349). The patient should be made to realize that there is no medication that will protect the liver against the effects of further alcohol ingestion. Therefore, alcohol should be absolutely forbidden. An important component of the complete care of such patients is encouragement to become involved in an appropriate alcohol counseling program.

All medicines must be administered with caution in the patient with cirrhosis, especially those eliminated or modified through hepatic metabolism or biliary pathways. In particular, care must be taken to avoid overzealous use of drugs that may directly or indirectly precipitate complications of cirrhosis. For example, vigorous treatment of ascites with diuretics may result in electrolyte abnormalities or hypovolemia which can lead to coma. Similarly, even modest doses of sedative can lead to deepening encephalopathy.

POSTNECROTIC CIRRHOSIS, POSTVIRAL CIRRHOSIS

Definition Postnecrotic cirrhosis represents the final common pathway of many types of advanced liver injury. *Coarsely nodular,* *posthepatitic,* and *multilobular cirrhosis* are terms synonymous with postnecrotic cirrhosis. The term *cryptogenic cirrhosis* has been used interchangeably with postnecrotic cirrhosis, but this designation should be reserved for those cases in which the etiology of cirrhosis is unknown (approximately 10 percent of all patients with cirrhosis).

Postnecrotic cirrhosis is characterized morphologically by (1) extensive confluent loss of liver cells, (2) stromal collapse and fibrosis resulting in broad bands of connective tissue containing the remains of many portal triads, and (3) irregular nodules of regenerating hepatocytes, varying in size from microscopic to several centimeters in diameter.

Etiology Postnecrotic cirrhosis is a morphologic term referring to a defined stage of advanced chronic liver injury of both specific and unknown (cryptogenic) causes. Epidemiologic and serologic evidence suggests that viral hepatitis (hepatitis B or non-A, non-B) may be an antecedent factor in at least one-fourth of cases of apparently cryptogenic postnecrotic cirrhosis. In areas where hepatitis B virus infection is endemic (e.g., southeast Asia, sub-Saharan Africa), up to 15 percent of the population may acquire the infection in early childhood, and cirrhosis may ultimately develop in one-fourth of these chronic carriers. Although hepatitis B infection is much less prevalent in the United States, it is relatively common among certain high-risk groups (e.g., promiscuous homosexual men, intravenous drug abusers), and contributes to an increased incidence of cirrhosis. In the United States non-A, non-B hepatitis agents appear to account for many cases of cirrhosis following blood transfusions. It is estimated that non-A, non-B hepatitis occurs in up to 10 percent of blood recipients, of whom as many as 5 to 10 percent may ultimately develop postnecrotic cirrhosis. Because reliable serologic markers for non-A, non-B hepatitis are not yet available, the number of cases of postnecrotic cirrhosis attributable to this agent (or agents) is difficult to determine but may be substantial (see Chap. 247). Postnecrotic cirrhosis may also develop in patients with chronic active hepatitis of the autoimmune type (see Chaps. 247 and 248).

Other probable causes of postnecrotic cirrhosis, including drugs and toxins, are listed in Table 249-1. In some instances, advanced alcoholic liver disease and primary biliary cirrhosis may lead to postnecrotic cirrhosis.

TABLE 249-1   Cirrhosis and/or liver disease associated with infectious, metabolic, hereditary, drug-related, and other types of disorders

1 Infectious diseases
 a Viral hepatitis [hepatitis B, non-A, non-B, hepatitis D, cytomegalovirus (Chaps. 137, 315, and 319)]
 b Toxoplasmosis (Chap 157)
 c Schistosomiasis (Chap. 164)
 d Ecchinococcus (Chap. 168)
 e Brucellosis (Chap. 112)
2 Inherited and metabolic disorders (see also Chap. 251)
 a Hemochromatosis (Chap. 310)
 b Wilson's disease (Chap. 311)
 c Alpha$_1$-antitrypsin deficiency (Chap. 208)
 d Galactosemia (Chap. 314)
 e Glycogen storage disease (Chap. 313)
 f Gaucher's disease (Chap. 316)
 g Hereditary fructose intolerance (Chap. 314)
 h Hereditary tyrosinemia (Chap. 306)
 i Fanconi's syndrome (Chap. 316)
3 Drugs and toxins (Chap. 247)
 a Methyldopa
 b Methotrexate
 c Isoniazid
 d Perhexilene maleate
 e Oxyphenisatin
 f Arsenicals
 g Pyrrolidizine alkaloids (venocclusive disease)
 h Oral contraceptives (Budd-Chiari)
4 Other or unproven causes
 a Sarcoidosis (Chap. 247)
 b Graft-versus-host disease
 c Chronic inflammatory bowel disease (Chap. 238)
 d Cystic fibrosis (Chap. 207)
 e Jejunoileal bypass (Chap. 35)
 f Diabetes mellitus (Chap. 327)

Pathology The postnecrotic liver is typically shrunken in size, distorted in shape, and composed of nodules of liver cells separated by dense and broad bands of fibrosis. The microscopic picture is consistent with the gross impression: nodules are highly variable in size with large amounts of connective tissue separating the disorganized islands of regenerating parenchyma.

Clinical features In patients with cirrhosis of known etiology in whom there is progression to a postnecrotic stage, the clinical manifestations are an extension of those resulting from the initial disease process. Usually clinical symptoms are related to portal hypertension and its sequelae, such as ascites, splenomegaly, hypersplenism, encephalopathy, and bleeding esophageal varices. The hematologic and liver function abnormalities resemble those seen with other types of cirrhosis. In a few patients with postnecrotic cirrhosis the diagnosis may be made incidentally at operation, at postmortem, or by a needle biopsy of the liver performed to investigate asymptomatic hepatosplenomegaly.

Diagnosis and prognosis Postnecrotic cirrhosis should be suspected in patients with signs and symptoms of cirrhosis or portal hypertension. Needle or operative liver biopsies confirm the diagnosis, although nonuniformity of the pathologic process may result in sampling errors. The diagnosis of cryptogenic cirrhosis is reserved for those patients in whom no known etiology can be demonstrated. About 75 percent of patients have progressive disease despite supportive therapy and die within 1 to 5 years from complications including exsanguinating variceal hemorrhage, hepatic encephalopathy, or superimposed hepatocellular carcinoma.

Treatment Management is usually limited to treatment of the complications of portal hypertension, including control of ascites, avoidance of drugs or excessive protein intake that may induce hepatic coma, and prompt treatment of infections (see below). In patients with asymptomatic cirrhosis, expectant management alone is appropriate. In those patients in whom postnecrotic cirrhosis has developed as a result of a treatable condition, therapy directed at the primary disorder may limit further progression (e.g., Wilson's disease, hemochromatosis).

BILIARY CIRRHOSIS

Biliary cirrhosis results from injury to or prolonged obstruction of either the intrahepatic or extrahepatic biliary system. It is associated with impaired biliary excretion, destruction of hepatic parenchyma, and progressive fibrosis. Primary biliary cirrhosis is characterized by chronic inflammation and fibrous obliteration of intrahepatic bile ductules. Secondary biliary cirrhosis is the result of long-standing obstruction of the larger extrahepatic ducts. Although primary and secondary biliary cirrhosis are separate pathophysiologic entities with respect to the initial insult, many clinical features are similar.

PRIMARY BILIARY CIRRHOSIS **Etiology and pathogenesis** The cause of primary biliary cirrhosis remains unknown. Several observations suggest that a disordered immune response may be involved. Primary biliary cirrhosis is frequently associated with a variety of disorders presumed to be autoimmune in nature, such as the CRST syndrome (calcinosis, Raynaud's phenomenon; sclerodactyly, telangiectasia), the sicca syndrome (dry eyes and dry mouth), autoimmune thyroiditis, and renal tubular acidosis. Most importantly, a circulating IgG antimitochondrial antibody is detected in more than 95 percent of patients with primary biliary cirrhosis and only rarely in other forms of liver disease. In addition, elevated serum levels of IgM and cryoproteins consisting of immune complexes capable of activating the alternate complement pathway are found in 80 to 90 percent of patients. Lymphocytes are prominent in the portal regions and surround damaged bile ducts. These histologic findings resemble those noted in graft-versus-host disease following liver and bone marrow transplantation and suggest that damage to bile ducts may be immunolog-

ically mediated, perhaps reflecting a defect in a suppressor cell population.

Pathology Primary biliary cirrhosis is often divided into four stages based on morphologic findings. The earliest recognizable lesion (stage I), termed *chronic nonsuppurative destructive cholangitis*, is a necrotizing inflammatory process of the portal triads. It is characterized by destruction of medium and small bile ducts, a dense infiltrate of acute and chronic inflammatory cells, mild fibrosis, and occasionally bile stasis. At times, periductal granulomas and lymph follicles are found adjacent to affected bile ducts. Subsequently, the inflammatory infiltrate becomes less prominent, the number of bile ducts is reduced, and smaller bile ductules proliferate (stage II). Progression over a period of months to years leads to a decrease in interlobular ducts, loss of liver cells, and expansion of periportal fibrosis into a network of connective tissue scars (stage III). Ultimately, cirrhosis, which may be micronodular or macronodular develops (stage IV).

Clinical features SIGNS AND SYMPTOMS Many patients with primary biliary cirrhosis are asymptomatic, and the disease is initially detected on the basis of elevated serum alkaline phosphatase levels during routine screening. The majority of such patients remain asymptomatic and do not develop progressive liver injury.

Among patients with symptomatic disease 90 percent are women ages 35 to 60. The earliest symptom is usually pruritus, which may be either generalized or limited initially to the palms and soles. After several months or years, jaundice and gradual darkening of the exposed areas of the skin (melanosis) may ensue. Other early clinical manifestations of primary biliary cirrhosis reflect impaired bile excretion. These include steatorrhea and the malabsorption of lipid-soluble vitamins often resulting in easy bruising (vitamin K deficiency), bone pain due to osteomalacia (vitamin D deficiency), occasionally night blindness (vitamin A deficiency), and dermatitis (possibly vitamin E and/or essential fatty acid deficiency). Protracted elevation of serum lipids, especially cholesterol, leads to subcutaneous lipid deposition around the eyes (xanthelasmas) and over joints and tendons (xanthomas). Over a period of months to years, the itching, jaundice, and hyperpigmentation slowly worsen. Eventually signs of hepatocellular failure and portal hypertension develop and ascites appears. Death due to hepatic insufficiency usually occurs within 5 to 10 years after the first signs of the illness and is often precipitated by uncontrolled variceal hemorrhage or infection.

Physical examination may be entirely normal in the early phase of the disease, when patients are asymptomatic or pruritus is the sole complaint. Later there may be jaundice of varying intensity, hyperpigmentation of the exposed skin areas, xanthelasmas and tendinous and planar xanthomas, moderate to striking hepatomegaly, splenomegaly, and clubbing of the fingers. Bone tenderness, signs of vertebral compression, ecchymoses, glossitis, and dermatitis may all be noted. Clinical evidence of the sicca syndrome can be found in as many as 75 percent of patients, and serologic evidence of autoimmune thyroid disease in 25 percent. Other conditions encountered with increased frequency include rheumatoid arthritis, CRST syndrome, scleroderma, pernicious anemia, and renal tubular acidosis.

LABORATORY FINDINGS Primary biliary cirrhosis is increasingly diagnosed at a presymptomatic stage, prompted by the finding of a two- to fivefold elevation of the serum alkaline phosphatase during routine screening. Serum 5'-nucleotidase activity is also elevated. In this setting, serum bilirubin and aminotransferase levels are usually normal, but the diagnosis is supported by a positive antimitochondrial antibody test (titer > 1:40). The latter is both *relatively* specific and sensitive; a positive test is found in over 90 percent of symptomatic patients. As the disease evolves, the serum bilirubin level rises progressively and may reach 30 mg/dL or more in the final stages. Serum aminotransferase values rarely exceed 150 to 200 units. Hyperlipidemia is common, and a striking increase of the serum unesterified cholesterol is often noted. An abnormal serum lipoprotein (lipoprotein X) may be present in primary biliary cirrhosis but is not specific and appears in other cholestatic conditions. A deficiency of bile salts in the intestine leads to moderate steatorrhea and impaired absorption of the fat-soluble vitamins and hypoprothrombinemia. Patients with primary biliary cirrhosis have elevated liver copper levels, but this finding is not specific and is found in all disorders in which there is prolonged cholestasis.

Diagnosis Primary biliary cirrhosis should be considered in middle-aged women with unexplained pruritus or an elevated serum alkaline phosphatase and in whom there may be other clinical or laboratory features of protracted impairment in biliary excretion. Although a positive serum antimitochondrial antibody determination provides important diagnostic evidence, false-positive results do occur, and therefore liver biopsy should be performed to confirm the diagnosis. In most cases the biliary tract should be evaluated to exclude remediable extrahepatic biliary tract obstruction especially in view of the frequent presence of coexisting cholelithiasis.

Treatment There is no specific therapy for primary biliary cirrhosis. Corticosteroids are ineffective and may actually worsen the bone disease. D-Penicillamine has been tried because of its ability to chelate copper and because of its possible antifibrotic and immunomodulating activities. However, the drug appears to be ineffective and has a high incidence of unacceptable side effects. Some have suggested that azathioprine may be helpful in slowing the progression of disease.

Treatment is generally directed toward the relief of symptoms. Although the mechanism of the protracted pruritus is not entirely clear, cholestyramine, an oral bile salt–sequestering resin, may be helpful in doses of 8 to 12 g per day to decrease both the pruritus and the hypercholesterolemia. Steatorrhea can be reduced by a low-fat diet and substituting medium-chain triglycerides for dietary long-chain triglycerides. Fat-soluble vitamins A and K should be given by parenteral injection at regular intervals to prevent or correct night blindness and hypoprothrombinemia, respectively. Zinc supplementation may be necessary if night blindness is refractory to vitamin A therapy. Osteomalacia may be ameliorated by dietary calcium supplements in conjunction with oral vitamin D. In advanced disease, $25(OH)D_3$ or $1,25(OH_2)D_3$ may be preferred to vitamin D since poor hepatic function may limit conversion of vitamin D to the active metabolites. The management of ascites, variceal hemorrhage, and encephalopathy is described below. The role of hepatic transplantation for patients with primary biliary cirrhosis is under study; this may offer the best, and only, hope for survival in patients with end-stage disease.

SECONDARY BILIARY CIRRHOSIS Etiology Secondary biliary cirrhosis results from prolonged partial or total obstruction of the common bile duct or its major branches. In adults, obstruction is most frequently caused by postoperative strictures or gallstones, usually with superimposed infectious cholangitis. Chronic pancreatitis may lead to biliary stricture and secondary cirrhosis. Secondary biliary cirrhosis may also develop in patients with pericholangitis or idiopathic sclerosing cholangitis. Patients with malignant tumors of the common bile duct or pancreas rarely survive long enough to develop secondary biliary cirrhosis. In children, congenital biliary atresia and cystic fibrosis are common causes of secondary biliary cirrhosis. Choledochal cysts if unrecognized may also be a rare cause of secondary biliary cirrhosis.

Pathology and pathogenesis Unrelieved obstruction of the extrahepatic bile ducts leads to (1) bile stasis and focal areas of centrilobular necrosis followed by periportal necrosis, (2) proliferation and dilatation of the portal bile ducts and ductules, (3) sterile or infected cholangitis with accumulation of polymorphonuclear infiltrates around bile ducts, and (4) progressive expansion of portal tracts by edema and fibrosis. Extravasation of bile from ruptured interlobular bile ducts into areas of periportal necrosis leads to the formation of "bile lakes" surrounded by cholesterol-rich pseudoxanthomatous cells. As in other forms of cirrhosis injury is accompanied by regeneration in residual parenchyma. These changes gradually lead to a finely nodular

cirrhosis. In general, at least 3 to 12 months is required for biliary obstruction to result in cirrhosis. Relief of the obstruction is frequently accompanied by biochemical and morphologic improvement.

Clinical features SIGNS AND SYMPTOMS The signs and symptoms of secondary biliary cirrhosis are similar to those of primary biliary cirrhosis. Jaundice and pruritus are usually the most prominent features. In addition, fever and/or right upper quadrant pain, reflecting bouts of cholangitis or biliary colic, are typical. The manifestations of portal hypertension are found only in advanced cases.

LABORATORY TESTS Elevation in serum alkaline phosphatase and conjugated hyperbilirubinemia are nearly always present. There is a moderate increase in serum aminotransferases. When the disease is complicated by cholangitis, elevations in aminotransferase levels and leukocytosis are more pronounced. As in primary biliary cirrhosis, there are abnormalities in serum lipids (including the presence of lipoprotein X) and laboratory findings consistent with steatorrhea. However, the antimitochondrial antibody test is usually negative.

Diagnosis Secondary biliary cirrhosis should be considered in any patient with clinical and laboratory evidence of prolonged obstruction to bile flow, especially when there is a history of previous biliary tract surgery or gallstones, bouts of ascending cholangitis, or right upper quadrant pain. Cholangiography (either percutaneous or endoscopic) usually demonstrates the underlying pathologic process. Liver biopsy, although not always necessary from a clinical standpoint, can document the development of cirrhosis.

Treatment Relief of obstruction to bile flow, by either surgical or endoscopic means, is the most important step in the prevention and therapy of secondary biliary cirrhosis. Effective decompression of the biliary tract results in a significant improvement in both symptoms and survival, even in patients with established cirrhosis. When obstruction cannot be relieved, as in sclerosing cholangitis, antibiotics may be helpful acutely in controlling superimposed infection or, when administered on a chronic basis, as prophylactic therapy in suppressing recurring episodes of ascending cholangitis. Without relief of obstruction, there is a steady progression to end-stage cirrhosis and its terminal manifestations.

CARDIAC CIRRHOSIS

Definition Prolonged, severe right-sided congestive heart failure may lead to chronic liver injury and cardiac cirrhosis. The characteristic pathologic features of fibrosis and regenerative nodules distinguish cardiac cirrhosis from both reversible passive congestion of the liver due to acute heart failure and acute hepatocellular necrosis ("ischemic hepatitis" or "shock liver") resulting from systemic hypotension and hypoperfusion of the liver.

Etiology and pathology In right-sided heart failure, retrograde transmission of elevated venous pressure via the inferior vena cava and hepatic veins leads to congestion of the liver. Hepatic sinusoids become dilated and engorged with blood, and the liver becomes tensely swollen. With prolonged passive congestion and ischemia from poor perfusion secondary to reduced cardiac output, necrosis of centrilobular hepatocytes ensues and leads to fibrosis in these central areas. Ultimately centrilobular fibrosis develops with collagen extending outward in a characteristic stellate pattern from the central vein. Gross examination of the liver shows alternating red (congested) and pale (fibrotic) areas, a pattern often referred to as "nutmeg liver." Improvement in management of cardiac disorders, particularly advances in surgical treatment, has reduced the frequency of cardiac cirrhosis.

Clinical features In acute passive congestion, the liver becomes enlarged and tender, and the patient may complain of severe right upper quadrant pain due to stretching of Glisson's capsule. The serum bilirubin is usually only mildly increased and may be predominantly either conjugated or unconjugated. The AST level is mildly elevated but may be transiently very high following a period of marked systemic hypotension (shock liver), when the clinical picture can mimic acute viral or drug-induced hepatitis. The serum albumin and prothrombin are usually normal, but may become abnormal in shock liver or with the development of cirrhosis. In cases of tricuspid insufficiency the liver may be pulsatile, but this finding disappears as cirrhosis develops. With prolonged right-sided heart failure the liver is enlarged, firm, and usually nontender. The signs and symptoms of heart failure usually overshadow the liver disease. Bleeding from esophageal varices is rare, but chronic encephalopathy may be prominent with a waxing and waning course reflecting variations in the severity of right-sided heart failure. Ascites and peripheral edema, often primarily related to the underlying cardiac dysfunction, may be worsened by the superimposed liver disease.

Diagnosis The presence of a firm, enlarged liver with signs of chronic liver disease in a patient with valvular heart disease, constrictive pericarditis, or cor pulmonale of long duration (>10 years) should suggest cardiac cirrhosis. Liver biopsy can confirm the diagnosis but is usually contraindicated because of coagulopathy or ascites. Coexistent chronic heart and liver disease should also raise the possibility of hemochromatosis, amyloidosis, or other infiltrative diseases.

Budd-Chiari syndrome resulting from the occlusion of the hepatic veins or inferior vena cava may be confused with acute congestive hepatomegaly. In this condition the liver is grossly enlarged and tender, and severe intractable ascites is present. However, signs and symptoms of heart failure are notably absent. The most common cause is thrombosis of the hepatic veins, often in the setting of polycythemia rubra vera, myeloproliferative syndromes, paroxysmal nocturnal hemoglobinuria, or other hypercoagulable states; it may also result from invasion of the inferior vena cava by tumor, such as renal cell or primary hepatocellular carcinoma. Idiopathic membranous obstruction of the inferior vena cava is the most common cause of this syndrome in Japan. Hepatic venography or liver biopsy showing centrilobular congestion and sinusoidal dilatation in the absence of right-sided heart failure establishes the diagnosis of Budd-Chiari syndrome. Venocclusive disease affecting the sublobular branches of the hepatic veins and the hepatic venules may result from hepatic irradiation, treatment with some antineoplastic agents, use of oral contraceptives, or ingestion of pyrrolidizine alkaloids present in some herbal teas ("bush tea disease") and can mimic congestive hepatomegaly.

Treatment Prevention or treatment of cardiac cirrhosis depends on the diagnosis and therapy of the underlying cardiovascular disorder. Improvement in cardiac function frequently results in improvement of liver function and stabilization of the liver disease.

METABOLIC, HEREDITARY, DRUG-RELATED, AND OTHER TYPES OF CIRRHOSIS (See Table 249-1). Cirrhosis or hepatitis may result from a wide variety of other processes encompassing the spectrum of etiologic factors listed in Table 249-2. Although some of these disorders have distinctive clinical or morphologic features, the manifestations of cirrhosis are largely independent of the underlying pathogenic mechanism.

TABLE 249-2 Some causes of noncirrhotic hepatic fibrosis

1 Idiopathic portal hypertension (noncirrhotic portal fibrosis, Banti's syndrome); three variants:
  a Intrahepatic phlebosclerosis and fibrosis
  b Portal and splenic vein sclerosis
  c Portal and splenic vein thrombosis
2 Schistosomiasis ("pipe-stem" fibrosis with presinusoidal portal hypertension)
3 Congenital hepatic fibrosis (may be associated with polycystic disease of liver and kidneys)

NONCIRRHOTIC FIBROSIS OF THE LIVER Several diseases, either congenital or acquired, may be associated with localized or generalized hepatic fibrosis. They are distinguished from cirrhosis by the absence of hepatocellular damage and the lack of nodular regenerative activity. The clinical manifestations in such cases are largely secondary to portal hypertension. The different types of these disorders are indicated in Table 294-2; with the exception of schistosomiasis, all these conditions are relatively rare.

MAJOR SEQUELAE OF CIRRHOSIS

The clinical course of patients with advanced cirrhosis is usually complicated by a number of important sequelae which are independent of the etiology of the underlying liver disease. These include portal hypertension and its consequences (i.e., gastroesophageal varices and splenomegaly), ascites, hepatic encephalopathy, spontaneous bacterial peritonitis, hepatorenal syndrome, and hepatocellular carcinoma.

PORTAL HYPERTENSION Definition and pathogenesis Normal pressure in the portal vein is low (10 and 15 cm saline; 7 to 10 mmHg) because vascular resistance in the hepatic sinusoids is minimal. Portal hypertension (>30 cm saline) most commonly results from increased resistance to portal blood flow. Because the portal venous system lacks valves, resistance at any level between the heart and splanchnic vessels results in retrograde transmission of an elevated pressure. Increased resistance can occur at three levels relative to the hepatic sinusoids: (1) presinusoidal, (2) sinusoidal, and (3) postsinusoidal. Obstruction in the *presinusoidal* venous compartment may be anatomically outside of the liver (e.g., portal vein thrombosis) or within the liver itself but at a functional level proximal to the hepatic sinusoids so that the liver parenchyma is not exposed to the elevated venous pressure (e.g., schistosomiasis). *Postsinusoidal* obstruction may also occur outside the liver at the level of the hepatic veins (e.g., Budd-Chiari syndrome), the inferior vena cava, or, less commonly, within the liver (e.g., venocclusive disease in which the central hepatic venules are the primary site of injury). When cirrhosis is complicated by portal hypertension, the increased resistance is usually sinusoidal. While distinctions between pre-, post-, and sinusoidal processes are conceptually appealing, functional resistance to portal flow in a given patient may occur at more than one level. Portal hypertension may also arise from increased blood flow (e.g., massive splenomegaly or arteriovenous fistulas), but the low-outflow resistance of the normal liver makes this a rare clinical problem.

Cirrhosis is the most common cause of portal hypertension in the United States. Clinically significant portal hypertension is present in greater than 60 percent of patients with cirrhosis. *Portal vein obstruction* is the second most common cause; it may be idiopathic or occur in association with cirrhosis, infection, pancreatitis, or abdominal trauma. *Hepatic vein thrombosis* (Budd-Chiari syndrome) and hepatic venocclusive disease are relatively infrequent causes of portal hypertension (see above). Portal vein occlusion may result in massive hematemesis from gastroesophageal varices, but ascites is usually found only when cirrhosis is also present. Noncirrhotic portal fibrosis accounts for only a small number of patients with portal hypertension.

Clinical features The major clinical manifestations of portal hypertension include hemorrhage from gastroesophageal varices, splenomegaly with hypersplenism, ascites, and acute and chronic hepatic encephalopathy. All of these features are related, at least in part, to the development of portal-systemic collateral channels. The absence of valves in the portal venous system facilitates retrograde (hepatofugal) blood flow from the high-pressure portal venous system to the lower-pressure systemic venous circulation. Major sites of collateral flow involve the veins around the rectum (hemorrhoids), cardioesophageal junction (esophagogastric varices), retroperitoneal space, and the falciform ligament of the liver (periumbilical or abdominal wall collaterals). Abdominal wall collaterals appear as tortuous epigastric vessels that radiate from the umbilicus toward the xiphoid and rib margins (caput medusae).

Diagnosis In patients with known liver disease, the development of portal hypertension usually becomes evident by the appearance of splenomegaly, ascites, encephalopathy, and/or esophageal varices. Conversely, the finding of any of these features should lead one to evaluate the patient for the presence of underlying portal hypertension and liver disease. Varices may be documented by either barium swallow or fiberoptic esophagoscopy and lend indirect support to the diagnosis of portal hypertension. Although rarely necessary, portal venous pressure may be measured directly by percutaneous transhepatic "skinny needle" catheterization or indirectly through transjugular cannulation of the hepatic veins. Both free and wedged hepatic vein pressure (WHVP) should be measured. While WHVP is elevated in sinusoidal and postsinusoidal portal hypertension including cirrhosis, this measurement is usually normal in presinusoidal portal hypertension. In patients in whom additional information is necessary (e.g., preoperative evaluation before portal-systemic shunt surgery) or percutaneous catheterization is not feasible, mesenteric and hepatic angiography may be helpful. Particular attention should be directed to the venous phase to assess the patency of the portal vein and the direction of portal blood flow.

Treatment Although treatment is usually directed toward a specific complication of portal hypertension, attempts are sometimes made to reduce the pressure in the portal venous system. Surgical decompression procedures have been used for many years to lower portal pressure in patients with bleeding esophageal varices (see below). However, portal-systemic shunt surgery does not result in improved survival rates in patients with cirrhosis. There are also reports that beta-adrenergic receptor blockers, such as propranolol, may reduce portal venous pressure. The efficacy of pharmacologic agents in this setting, however, remains controversial and unproven.

Vigorous treatment of patients with alcoholic hepatitis and cirrhosis, chronic active hepatitis, and other liver diseases may lead to a fall in portal pressure and to a reduction in variceal size. In general, however, portal hypertension due to cirrhosis is not reversible. In selected patients hepatic transplantation may be beneficial (e.g., end-stage primary biliary cirrhosis).

VARICEAL BLEEDING Pathogenesis While vigorous hemorrhage may arise from any portal-systemic venous collaterals, bleeding is most common from varices in the region of the gastroesophageal junction. The factors contributing to bleeding from gastroesophageal varices are not entirely understood but include the degree of portal hypertension and the size of the varices. Esophagitis with erosion of underlying varices does not appear to play an important role.

Clinical features and diagnosis Variceal bleeding often occurs without obvious precipitating factors and usually presents with painless but massive hematemesis with or without melena. Associated signs range from mild postural tachycardia to profound shock, depending on the extent of blood loss and degree of hypovolemia. Because patients with varices may bleed from other gastrointestinal lesions (e.g., peptic ulcer, gastritis), in most cases exclusion of other bleeding sources is important even in patients with prior variceal hemorrhage. Fiberoptic endoscopy is the procedure of choice in evaluating upper gastrointestinal hemorrhage in patients with known or suspected portal hypertension.

Treatment Variceal bleeding is a life-threatening emergency. Prompt estimation and vigorous replacement of blood losses to maintain intravascular volume are essential and take precedence over diagnostic studies and more specific intervention to stop the bleeding. Replacement of clotting factors with fresh frozen plasma is important in patients with coagulopathy. Patients are best managed in an intensive care unit and often require close monitoring of central venous or pulmonary capillary wedge pressures, urine output, and mental status. Only when the patient is hemodynamically stable should attention be directed toward specific diagnostic studies (especially endoscopy) and other therapeutic modalities to prevent further or recurrent bleeding.

About half of all episodes of variceal hemorrhage cease without intervention, although the risk of rebleeding is very high. The medical management of acute variceal hemorrhage includes the use of vasoconstrictors (vasopressin), balloon tamponade, and endoscopic sclerosis of varices (sclerotherapy). Intravenous infusion of *vasopressin* at a rate of 0.1 to 0.9 units per minute results in generalized vasoconstriction leading to diminished blood flow in the portal venous system. Intravenous infusion of vasopressin has been shown to be as effective as selective intraarterial administration. Control of bleeding can be achieved in up to 80 percent of cases, but bleeding recurs in more than half after the vasopressin is tapered and discontinued. Furthermore, a number of serious side effects, including cardiac and gastrointestinal tract ischemia, acute renal failure, and hyponatremia, may be associated with vasopressin therapy. *Balloon tamponade* of the bleeding varices may be accomplished with a triple-lumen (Sengstaken-Blakemore) or four-lumen (Minnesota) tube with esophageal and gastric balloons. After the tube is introduced into the stomach, the gastric balloon is inflated and pulled back into the cardia of the stomach. If bleeding does not stop, the esophageal balloon is inflated for additional tamponade. Careful monitoring for complications such as esophageal rupture is essential. *Endoscopic sclerosis* of esophageal varices may be employed if the above measures are ineffective in controlling bleeding. In this procedure, the varices are injected with one of several sclerosing agents (e.g., sodium morrhuate) via a needle-tipped catheter passed through the endoscope. After initial endoscopic identification of varices as the presumed source of bleeding, such "sclerotherapy" controls acute bleeding in up to 90 percent of cases. In addition, repeated sclerotherapy until obliteration of all varices is accomplished should be performed in an effort to prevent recurrent bleeding. While available data support the efficacy of sclerotherapy in controlling bleeding acutely, further studies are needed to define the technique and the overall role of sclerotherapy in the management of variceal bleeding. Transhepatic sclerosis via "skinny needle" puncture has also been used in a limited number of centers although its reported efficacy has varied widely. The role of beta-adrenergic blocking agents in reducing the risk of recurrent hemorrhage remains uncertain.

Surgical therapy of portal hypertension and variceal bleeding involves the creation of a portal-systemic shunt to permit decompression of the portal system. Two types of portal systemic shunts have been used: *nonselective shunts* to decompress the entire portal system and *selective shunts* intended to decompress only the varices while maintaining blood flow to the liver itself. Nonselective shunts include end-to-side or side-to-side portacaval and proximal splenorenal anastomoses; selective shunts include the distal splenorenal shunt. Nonselective shunts are more likely to be complicated by encephalopathy than selective shunts. Emergency portal-systemic nonselective shunts may control acute hemorrhage, but such surgery is usually used only as a last resort because early operative mortality is greater than 30 percent. The role of portal-systemic shunt surgery after initial control of bleeding by nonoperative means is also uncertain. Surgically created shunts effectively reduce the risk of recurrent hemorrhage, but the overall mortality of patients undergoing such surgery is comparable to that of unoperated patients. Although patients who have undergone portal-system surgery succumb to recurrent bleeding less commonly than unoperated patients, this improvement is counterbalanced by increased morbidity from encephalopathy and death from progressive liver failure. Prophylactic shunt surgery should not be performed in patients with nonbleeding varices. The relative merits of therapeutic portal-systemic shunt surgery and serial endoscopic sclerotherapy in cirrhotics who have bled from varices remain to be determined. Other surgical procedures (e.g., esophageal transection) have also been advocated for the management of acute variceal bleeding although their efficacy remains unproven.

SPLENOMEGALY Definition and pathogenesis Congestive splenomegaly is common in patients with severe portal hypertension. In rare instances, massive splenomegaly from nonhepatic disease may lead to portal hypertension due to increased blood flow in the splenic vein.

Clinical features　Although usually asymptomatic, splenomegaly may be massive and contribute to the thrombocytopenia or pancytopenia of cirrhosis. In the absence of cirrhosis, splenomegaly in association with variceal hemorrhage should suggest the possibility of splenic vein thrombosis.

Treatment　Splenomegaly usually requires no specific treatment, although massive enlargement of the spleen may occasionally necessitate splenectomy at the time of shunt surgery. Splenectomy may also be indicated if splenomegaly is the cause rather than the result of portal hypertension. Thrombocytopenia alone is rarely severe enough to necessitate removal of the spleen.

ASCITES　**Definition**　Ascites is the accumulation of excess fluid within the peritoneal cavity. It is most frequently encountered in patients with cirrhosis and other forms of severe liver disease, but a number of other disorders may lead to either transudative or exudative ascites (see Chap. 39).

Pathogenesis　The accumulation of ascitic fluid represents a state of total-body sodium and water excess, but the event that initiates this imbalance is unclear. Two theories have been proposed (see Fig. 249-1). The "underfilling" theory suggests that the primary abnormality is inappropriate sequestration of fluid within the splanchnic vascular bed due to portal hypertension and a consequent decrease in effective circulating blood volume. According to this theory, an apparent decrease in intravascular volume (underfilling) is sensed by the kidney, which responds by retaining salt and water. The "over-flow" theory suggests that the primary abnormality is inappropriate renal retention of salt and water in the absence of volume depletion.

Regardless of the initiating event, a number of factors contribute to accumulation of fluid in the abdominal cavity (see Fig. 249-1). *Portal hypertension* plays an important role in the formation of ascites by raising hydrostatic pressure within the splanchnic capillary bed. *Hypoalbuminemia* and *reduced plasma oncotic pressure* also favor the extravasation of fluid from plasma to peritoneal cavity, and thus ascites is infrequent in patients with cirrhosis unless both portal hypertension and hypoalbuminemia are present. *Hepatic lymph* may weep freely from the surface of the cirrhotic liver due to distortion and obstruction of hepatic sinusoids and lymphatics and contribute to ascites formation. In contrast to the contribution of transudative fluid from the portal vascular bed, hepatic lymph may weep into the peritoneal cavity even in the absence of marked hypoproteinemia because the endothelial lining of the hepatic sinusoids is discontinuous. This mechanism may account for the high protein concentration present in the ascitic fluid of some patients with the Budd-Chiari syndrome.

Renal factors also play an important role in perpetuating ascites. Patients with ascites fail to excrete a water load in a normal fashion. They have increased renal sodium reabsorption by both proximal and distal tubules, the latter due largely to secondary hyperaldosteronism and increased plasma renin activity. Renal vasoconstriction, perhaps resulting from increased serum prostaglandin or catecholamine levels, may also contribute to sodium retention.

Clinical features and diagnosis　Usually ascites is first noticed by the patient because of increasing abdominal girth. More pronounced accumulation of fluid may cause shortness of breath because of elevation of the diaphragm. When peritoneal fluid accumulation exceeds 500 mL, ascites may be demonstrated on physical examination by the presence of shifting dullness, a fluid wave, or bulging flanks. Ultrasound examination can detect smaller quantities of ascites and should be performed when physical examination is equivocal. Paracentesis should usually be performed with a small-gauge needle at the time of initial evaluation or at the time of any clinical deterioration of a cirrhotic patient. A small amount of fluid (less than 200 mL) should be obtained and examined for evidence of infection, tumor, or other possible causes and complications of ascites.

Treatment　When ascites develops in the setting of severe, acute liver disease, resolution of ascites is likely to follow improvement in liver function. More commonly, ascites develops in patients with stable or steadily worsening liver function. Therapeutic intervention is indicated both to prevent potential complications and to control progressive increase in ascites, which may become pronounced enough to cause physical discomfort. However, overzealous attempts to reduce ascites may deplete the intravascular volume faster than fluid can be mobilized from the ascitic compartment and may precipitate renal failure. Thus, therapy aimed at reducing ascites should be gentle and incremental (see below). The goal is the loss of no more than 1.0 kg daily if both ascites and peripheral edema are present and no more than 0.5 kg daily in patients with ascites alone. To initiate therapy it may be desirable to hospitalize the patient so that daily weights and frequent serum electrolyte levels can be monitored and compliance ensured. Although abdominal girth measurements are frequently used as an index of fluid loss, they tend to be unreliable.

Strict bed rest is often recommended because of improved renal clearance in the supine position. However, salt restriction is the most important cornerstone of therapy. A diet containing 800 mg sodium (2 g NaCl) is often adequate to induce a negative sodium balance and permit diuresis. Response to salt restriction and bed rest alone is more likely to occur if the ascites is of recent onset, the underlying liver disease is reversible, a precipitating factor can be corrected, or the patient has a high urinary sodium excretion (~25 meq per day) and normal renal function. Fluid restriction of approximately 1500 mL per day does little to enhance diuresis but may be necessary to prevent or correct hyponatremia. If sodium restriction alone fails to

FIGURE 249-1　*Multiple factors involved in development of ascites. Current concepts suggest that initiating factor may be either primary sodium retention ("overflow") or diminished effective intravascular volume ("underfilling").*

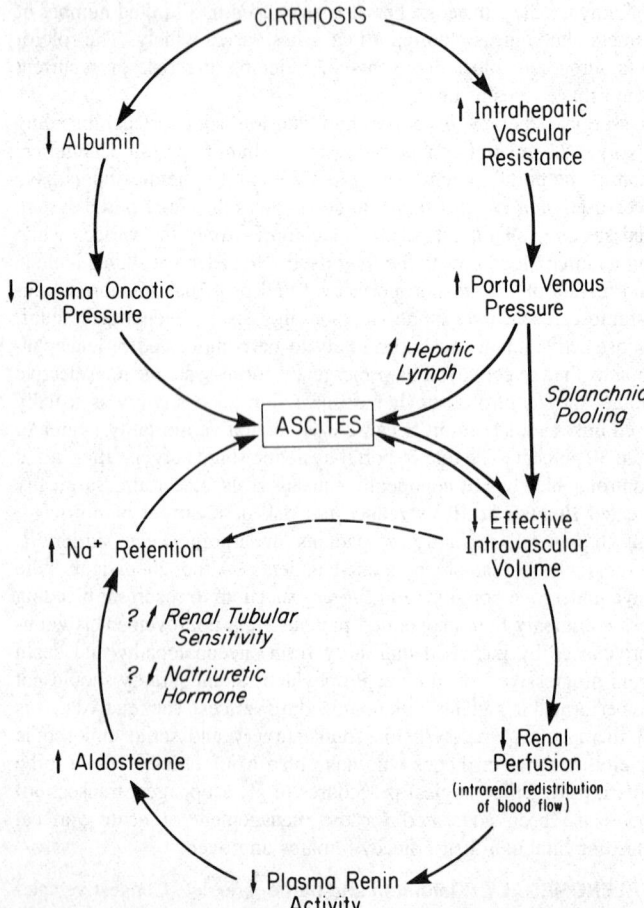

result in diuresis and weight loss, diuretic therapy should be instituted. Because of the role of hyperaldosteronism in sustaining salt retention, spironolactone or other distal tubular–acting diuretics (triamterene, amiloride) are the drugs of choice. These agents are also preferred because of their gentle action and specific potassium-sparing properties. Spironolactone is initially given in a dose of 25 mg four times a day and increased as needed by 100 mg per day every several days up to a maximum dose of 400 mg daily. An indication of the minimum effective dose of spironolactone may be obtained by monitoring urinary electrolyte concentrations for a rise in sodium and fall in potassium levels reflecting effective competitive inhibition of aldosterone. In some patients, diuresis cannot be initiated despite maximal doses of distal tubule–acting agents (e.g., 400 mg spironolactone) because of avid proximal tubular sodium absorption. When this occurs, more potent and proximally acting diuretics (furosemide, thiazide, or ethacrynic acid) may be added cautiously to the regimen. Spironolactone plus furosemide, 40 or 80 mg daily, is usually sufficient to initiate a diuresis in most patients. However, such aggressive therapy must be used with great caution to avoid plasma volume depletion, azotemia, and hypokalemia which may lead to encephalopathy.

A minority of patients with advanced cirrhosis have "refractory ascites" and fail to respond, despite intensive medical therapy. When this occurs in patients with marked hypoalbuminemia, diuresis may be initiated following cautious intravenous infusion of *salt-poor albumin*. Because of the short half-life of infused albumin, this approach is of short-term benefit and may, in fact, precipitate variceal hemorrhage due to expansion of the intravascular volume. In some patients a side-to-side *portacaval shunt* may result in improvement in ascites although generally these patients are extremely poor surgical risks. Intractable ascites can also be treated with the surgical implantation of a plastic *peritoneovenous shunt* which has a pressure-sensitive, one-way valve allowing ascitic fluid to flow from the abdominal cavity to the superior vena cava. However, the usefulness of this technique is limited by a high rate of complications such as infection, disseminated intravascular coagulation, and thrombosis of the shunt. Although removal of large volumes of ascitic fluid is hazardous, occasionally therapeutic paracentesis of 1 to 2 liters may be needed in patients with massive ascites and pronounced respiratory embarrassment or impending rupture of an umbilical hernia.

SPONTANEOUS BACTERIAL PERITONITIS Patients with ascites and cirrhosis may develop acute bacterial peritonitis without an obvious primary source of infection. Typical features include abrupt onset of fever, chills, generalized abdominal pain, and rebound abdominal tenderness accompanied by cloudy ascitic fluid with a high white cell count and usually positive bacterial cultures. However, the clinical symptoms *may be minimal*, and some patients manifest only worsening jaundice or encephalopathy in the absence of localizing abdominal complaints. The diagnosis is based on careful examination of the ascitic fluid. An ascitic fluid leukocyte count of greater than 500 cells per cubic millimeter or more than 250 polymorphonuclear leukocytes should suggest the possibility of bacterial peritonitis while results of bacterial cultures of ascitic fluid are pending. Empiric therapy with ampicillin and an aminoglycoside or cefotaximene should be initiated when the diagnosis is first suspected because enteric gram-negative bacilli are found in the majority of cases; less frequently the infection is caused by pneumococci and other gram-positive bacteria. Specific antibiotic therapy can be selected once the specific organism is identified. Therapy is usually administered for 10 to 14 days.

HEPATORENAL SYNDROME   Definition and pathogenesis Hepatorenal syndrome is a serious complication in the patient with cirrhosis and ascites, and is characterized by worsening azotemia with avid sodium retention and oliguria in the absence of identifiable specific causes of renal dysfunction. The exact basis for this syndrome is not clear, but altered renal hemodynamics appear to be involved. The kidneys are structurally intact; urinalysis and pyelography are usually normal. Renal biopsy although rarely needed is also normal, and in fact kidneys from such patients have been successfully used for renal transplantation. There are indications that an imbalance in certain metabolites of arachidonic acid (prostaglandins and thromboxane) may play a pathogenetic role.

Clinical features and diagnosis Worsening azotemia, hyponatremia, progressive oliguria, and hypotension are the hallmarks of the hepatorenal syndrome. This syndrome, which is distinct from prerenal azotemia, may be precipitated by severe gastrointestinal bleeding, sepsis, or overly vigorous attempts at diuresis or paracentesis; it may also occur without an obvious cause. The diagnosis is supported by the demonstration of avid urinary sodium retention. Typically the urine sodium concentration is less than 5 meq per liter, a concentration lower than that generally found in uncomplicated prerenal azotemia. The urinary sediment is unremarkable.

Treatment Treatment is usually unsuccessful. Although some patients with hypotension and decreased plasma volume may respond to infusions of salt-poor albumin, volume expansion must be undertaken with caution to avoid precipitating variceal bleeding. Vasodilator therapy, including intravenous infusion of dopamine, is not effective.

HEPATIC ENCEPHALOPATHY   Definition Hepatic (portal-systemic) encephalopathy is a complex neuropsychiatric syndrome characterized by disturbances in consciousness and behavior, personality changes, fluctuating neurologic signs, asterixis or "flapping tremor," and distinctive electroencephalographic changes. Encephalopathy may be *acute* and reversible or *chronic* and progressive. In severe cases, irreversible coma and death may occur. Acute episodes may recur with variable frequency.

Pathogenesis The specific cause of hepatic encephalopathy is unknown. The most important factors in the pathogenesis are severe hepatocellular dysfunction and/or intrahepatic and extrahepatic shunting of portal venous blood into the systemic circulation, so that the liver is largely bypassed. As a result of these processes, various toxic substances absorbed from the intestine are not detoxified by the liver and lead to metabolic abnormalities in the central nervous system. Ammonia is the substance most often incriminated in the pathogenesis of encephalopathy. Many, but not all, patients with hepatic encephalopathy have elevated blood ammonia levels, and recovery from encephalopathy is often accompanied by declining blood ammonia levels. Other compounds and metabolites which may contribute to the development of encephalopathy include mercaptans (derived from intestinal metabolism of methionine), short-chain fatty acids, phenol, and gamma-aminobutyric acid (GABA), an inhibitory neurotransmitter. False neurochemical transmitters (e.g., octopamine), resulting in part from alterations in plasma levels of aromatic and branched-chain amino acids, may also play a role. An increase in the permeability of the blood-brain barrier to some of these substances may be an additional factor involved in the pathogenesis of hepatic encephalopathy.

In the patient with otherwise stable cirrhosis, hepatic encephalopathy often follows a clearly identifiable precipitating event (see Table 249-3). Perhaps the most common predisposing factor is *gastrointestinal bleeding*, which leads to an increase in the production of ammonia and other nitrogenous substances which are then absorbed. Similarly, *increased dietary protein* may precipitate encephalopathy as a result of increased production of nitrogenous substances by colonic bacteria. *Electrolyte disturbances*, particularly hypokalemic alkalosis secondary to overzealous use of diuretics, vigorous paracentesis, or vomiting, may precipitate hepatic encephalopathy. Systemic alkalosis causes an increase in the amount of nonionic ammonia (NH_3) relative to ammonium ions (NH_4^+). Only nonionic (uncharged) ammonia readily crosses the blood-brain barrier and accumulates in the central nervous system. Hypokalemia also directly stimulates renal ammonia production. Hypoxia, injudicious use of central nervous system–depressing drugs (e.g., barbiturates, benzodiazepines), and acute infection may trigger or aggravate hepatic encephalopathy, although the mechanisms involved are not clear. Other potential precipitating factors include superimposed acute viral hepatitis, alcoholic hepatitis, extrahepatic bile duct obstruction, surgery, and other coincidental medical complications.

Clinical features and diagnosis   Hepatic encephalopathy has protean manifestations, and any neurologic abnormality, including focal deficits, may be encountered. In patients with acute encephalopathy, neurologic deficits are completely reversible upon correction of underlying precipitating factors and/or improvement in liver function, but in patients with chronic encephalopathy the deficits may be irreversible and progressive. Cerebral edema is frequently present and contributes to the clinical picture and overall mortality in patients with both acute and chronic encephalopathy.

The diagnosis of hepatic encephalopathy should be considered when four major factors are present: (1) acute or chronic hepatocellular disease and/or extensive portal-systemic collateral shunts (the latter may be either spontaneous, e.g., secondary to portal hypertension, or surgically created, e.g., portacaval anastomosis); (2) disturbances of awareness and mentation which may progress from forgetfulness and confusion to stupor and finally coma; (3) shifting combinations of neurologic signs, including asterixis, rigidity, hyperreflexia, extensor plantar signs, and rarely, seizures; and (4) a characteristic (but nonspecific) symmetric, high-voltage, slow-wave (2 to 5 per second) pattern on the electroencephalogram. Asterixis ("liver flap," "flapping tremor") is a nonrhythmic asymmetric lapse in voluntary sustained position of the extremities, head, and trunk. It is best demonstrated by having the patient extend the arms and dorsiflex the hands. Because elicitation of asterixis depends on sustained voluntary muscle contraction, it is not present in the comatose patient. Asterixis is nonspecific and also occurs in patients with other forms of metabolic brain disease. Alterations in personality, mood disturbances, confusion, deterioration in self-care and handwriting, and daytime somnolence are additional clinical features of encephalopathy. *Fetor hepaticus*, a unique musty odor of the breath and urine believed to be due to mercaptans, may be noted in patients with varying stages of hepatic encephalopathy. Some patients may develop spastic paraparesis or *chronic progressive hepatocerebral degeneration*, the latter a clinical variant of hepatic encephalopathy characterized by a slow decline in intellectual function, tremor, cerebellar ataxia, choreoathetosis, and psychiatric symptoms.

Grading or classifying the stages of hepatic encephalopathy is often helpful in following the course of the illness and assessing response to therapy. One useful classification is shown in Table 249-4.

The diagnosis of hepatic encephalopathy is usually one of exclusion. There are no diagnostic liver function test abnormalities, although an elevated serum ammonia level in the appropriate clinical setting is highly suggestive of the diagnosis. Examination of the cerebrospinal fluid is unremarkable, and computerized tomography of the brain shows no characteristic abnormalities. A number of conditions, particularly disorders related to acute and chronic alcoholism, can mimic the clinical features of hepatic encephalopathy. These include acute alcohol intoxication, sedative overdose, delirium tremens, Wernicke's encephalopathy, and Korsakoff's psychosis (see Chap. 349). Subdural hematoma, meningitis, and hypoglycemia or other metabolic encephalopathies must also be considered, especially in patients with alcoholic cirrhosis. In young patients with liver disease and neurologic abnormalities, Wilson's disease should be excluded.

Treatment   Early recognition and prompt treatment of hepatic encephalopathy are essential. Patients with acute, severe hepatic encephalopathy (stage IV) require the usual supportive measures for the comatose patient. Specific treatment of hepatic encephalopathy is aimed at (1) elimination or treatment of precipitating factors and (2) lowering of blood ammonia (and other toxin) levels by decreasing the absorption of protein and nitrogenous products from the intestine. In the setting of acute gastrointestinal bleeding, blood in the bowel should be promptly evacuated with enemas and laxatives in order to reduce the nitrogen load. Protein should be excluded from the diet, and constipation should be avoided. Ammonia absorption can be decreased by the administration of lactulose, a nonabsorbable disaccharide that acts as an osmotic laxative. Metabolism of lactulose by colonic bacteria may also result in an acid pH that favors conversion of ammonia to the poorly absorbed ammonium ion. In addition lactulose may actually diminish ammonia production through its direct effects on bacterial metabolism. Lactulose syrup can be administered in a dose of 30 to 50 mL every hour until diarrhea occurs; thereafter the dose is adjusted (usually 15 to 30 mL three times daily) so that the patient has two to four soft stools daily. Intestinal ammonia production by bacteria can also be decreased by oral administration of the antibiotic neomycin, at a dose of 0.5 to 1.0 g every 6 h. Although poorly absorbed, neomycin may reach sufficient concentrations in the bloodstream to cause renal toxicity. The use of agents such as levodopa, bromocriptine, keto-analogues of essential amino acids, and intravenous amino acid formulations rich in branched-chain amino acids in the treatment of acute hepatic encephalopathy remain of unproven benefit. Hemoperfusion to remove toxic substances and therapy directed primarily toward coincident cerebral edema in acute encephalopathy are also of unproven value.

Chronic encephalopathy may be effectively controlled by administration of lactulose. Management of patients with chronic encephalopathy should include dietary protein restriction, sometimes to levels as low as 40 g daily, in combination with low doses of lactulose or neomycin. Nephrotoxicity or ototoxicity may be limiting in prolonged usage of neomycin. There are suggestions that vegetable protein may be preferable to animal protein.

OTHER SEQUELAE OF CIRRHOSIS   Coagulopathy   Patients with cirrhosis often demonstrate a variety of abnormalities in both cellular and humoral clotting function. Thrombocytopenia may result from hypersplenism. In the alcoholic patient, there may be direct bone marrow suppression by ethanol. Diminished protein synthesis may lead to reduced production of fibrinogen (factor I), prothrombin (factor II), and factors V, VII, IX, and X. Reduction in levels of all

TABLE 249-3   Common precipitants of hepatic encephalopathy

1 Increased nitrogen load
  a Gastrointestinal bleeding
  b Excess dietary protein
  c Azotemia
  d Constipation
2 Electrolyte imbalance
  a Hypokalemia
  b Alkalosis
  c Hypoxia
  d Hypovolemia
3 Drugs
  a Narcotics, tranquilizers, sedatives
  b Diuretics (see 2)
4 Miscellaneous
  a Infection
  b Surgery
  c Superimposed acute liver disease
  d Progressive liver disease

TABLE 294-4   Clinical stages of hepatic encephalopathy

Stage	Mental status	Asterixis	EEG
I	Euphoria or depression, mild confusion, slurred speech, disordered sleep	+/−	Usually normal
II	Lethargy, moderate confusion	+	Abnormal
III	Marked confusion, incoherent speech, sleeping but arousable	+	Abnormal
IV	Coma; initially responsive to noxious stimuli, later unresponsive	−	Abnormal

factors except factor V may be worsened by the coincident malabsorption of the fat-soluble cofactor vitamin K due to cholestasis (see Chap. 237). Recent reports have documented the appearance of normal factor VIII levels following liver transplantation in patients with classical hemophilia probably as a result of production by nonhepatocellular components of the donor organ.

Hepatocellular carcinoma   (See Chap. 250.)

REFERENCES

Alcoholic and postnecrotic cirrhosis

BARRY RE, MCGIVAN JD: Acetaldehyde alone may initiate hepatocellular damage in acute alcoholic liver disease. Gut 26:1065, 1985

BOROWSKY SA et al: Continued heavy drinking and survival in alcoholic cirrhotics. Gastroenterology 80:1405, 1981

POWELL WJ, KLATSKIN G: Duration of survival in patients with Laennec's cirrhosis. Am J Med 44:406, 1968

SØRENSEN TIA et al: Prospective evaluation of alcohol abuse and alcoholic liver injury in man as predictors of development of cirrhosis. Lancet 2:241, 1984

THEODOSSI A et al: Controlled trial of methylprednisolone therapy in severe acute alcoholic hepatitis. Gut 23:75, 1982

VAN THIEL DH et al: Gastrointestinal and hepatic manifestations of chronic alcoholism. Gastroenterology 81:594, 1981

ZETTERMAN RK, SORRELL MF: Immunologic aspects of alcoholic liver disease. Gastroenterology 81:616, 1981

Biliary cirrhosis

BESWICK DR et al: Asymptomatic primary biliary cirrhosis: A progress report on long-term follow-up and natural history. Gastroenterology 89:267, 1985

CHRISTENSEN E et al: Beneficial effects of azathioprine and predictor of prognosis in primary biliary cirrhosis: Final results of an international trial. Gastroenterology 89:1084, 1985

JAMES O et al: Primary biliary cirrhosis—a revised clinical spectrum. Lancet 1:1278, 1981

NEUBERGER J et al: Double-blind controlled trial of D-penicillamine in patients with primary biliary cirrhosis. Gut 26:114, 1985

Hepatic encephalopathy

ATTERBURY CE et al: Neomycin-sorbitol and lactulose in the treatment of acute portal-systemic encephalopathy. Am J Digest Dis 23:398, 1978

CONN HO et al: Comparison of lactulose and neomycin in the treatment of chronic portal-systemic encephalopathy: A double-blind controlled trial. Gastroenterology 72:573, 1977

DUDLEY FJ et al: Hepatorenal syndrome without avid sodium retention. Hepatology 6:248, 1986

FRASER CL, ARIEFF AI: Hepatic encephalopathy. N Engl J Med 313:865, 1985

JONES EA et al: The neurobiology of hepatic encephalopathy. Hepatology 4:1235, 1984

Portal hypertension and ascites

CELLO JP et al: Endoscopic sclerotherapy versus portacaval shunt in patients with severe cirrhosis and variceal hemorrhage. N Engl J Med 311:1589, 1984

CROSSLEY JR, WILLIAMS R: Spontaneous bacterial peritonitis. Gut 26:325, 1985

EPSTEIN FM: Underfilling versus overflow in hepatic ascites. N Engl J Med 307:1577, 1982

EPSTEIN M: The sodium retention of cirrhosis: A reappraisal. Hepatology 6:312, 1986

LEBREC D et al: The effect of propranolol on portal hypertension in patients with cirrhosis. Hepatology 2:523, 1982

MACDOUGALL BRD et al: Increased long-term survival in variceal haemorrhage using injection sclerotherapy: Results of a controlled trial. Lancet 1:124, 1982

MILLIKAN WJ et al: The Emory prospective randomized trial: Selective versus nonselective shunt to control variceal bleeding. Ann Surg 201:712, 1985

NICHOLLS KM et al: Sodium excretion in advanced cirrhosis: Effect of expansion of central blood volume and suppression of plasma aldosterone. Hepatology 6:235, 1986

250   TUMORS OF THE LIVER

ELLIOT ALPERT / KURT J. ISSELBACHER

PRIMARY CARCINOMA   Carcinomas arising within the liver may be of liver cell (*hepatocellular*), bile duct cell (*cholangiocellular*), or mixed origin. Hepatocellular carcinoma (primary liver cell carcinoma) accounts for 80 to 90 percent of liver carcinomas. There is, however, little practical purpose in distinguishing between the two types, since both may be found in different parts of the same tumor and the clinical courses are similar.

Epidemiology and etiology   Primary liver cancers account for only 1 to 2 percent of malignant tumors found at autopsy in North and South America and Europe. However, in parts of Africa and Asia they may account for up to 20 to 30 percent of all types of malignancy. Liver cell carcinoma occurs two to four times more frequently in men than in women. The peak incidence occurs in the fifth and sixth decades of life in the United States, but one to two decades earlier in areas with a high prevalence of liver carcinoma. Cirrhosis, usually macronodular or postnecrotic, is found in 60 to 75 percent of autopsied patients with primary liver cell carcinoma in all parts of the world.

There is wide variation in the incidence of hepatocellular carcinoma in different parts of the world, and a number of etiologic factors may be important.

1 *Chronic liver disease* of any etiology appears to predispose to the development of carcinoma. A variety of metabolic, alcoholic, viral, or idiopathic chronic liver diseases can lead to liver cell carcinoma. Alpha$_1$-antitrypsin deficiency and hereditary tyrosinosis, with active liver disease since birth, have a high incidence of developing into carcinoma. In the adult age group, *hemochromatosis* has the highest risk of malignant degeneration, presumably owing to the long duration of the chronic liver inflammation. However, alcoholic and postnecrotic cirrhosis are the most common forms of underlying liver disease in patients with liver carcinoma in the United States.

2 *Viral hepatitis* is endemic in many areas of Africa and Asia. The prevalence of hepatitis B antigenemia in the normal population is 1 to 10 percent in some parts of Africa. In these areas, most patients with hepatocellular carcinoma superimposed on chronic liver disease will have serologic evidence of hepatitis B infection. There is also evidence of the integration of the hepatitis B virus DNA (HBV-DNA) into the genome of liver cells in some patients with prior HB infection, and most patients with long-standing HBV infection including those who have developed a superimposed carcinoma. Therefore, hepatitis B virus infection is an important cause of chronic liver disease and subsequent liver carcinoma in many parts of the world.

3 *Mycotoxins*, metabolites of saprophytic fungi, including certain known hepatic carcinogens (e.g., aflatoxins), are continuously ingested in foodstuffs in small amounts and are found in high concentrations in foods in parts of Africa and Asia, where liver cell carcinoma is found more frequently. Ingested mycotoxins and viral inflammation can act synergistically to increase the risk of malignant hepatocellular transformation.

4 The male predominance in liver cancer and the effect of sex hormones on experimental carcinogenesis suggest that *hormonal factors* may be important. Significantly, hepatocellular carcinoma has been reported in some patients on long-term androgenic therapy.

5 *Iatrogenic factors* include thorium dioxide, an agent widely used for radiologic images for about 20 years until the mid-1950s. Since there is lifelong hepatic storage and virtually no decay of this radioisotope, the liver is exposed to continuous low-level radiation. After a 15- to 20-year latent period, angiosarcoma or chronic liver disease with carcinoma can develop. Long-term use of oral contraceptives rarely leads to development of hepatic cell adenoma, a benign neoplasm, but malignant transformation into carcinoma has been reported.

Clinical features   Hepatic cancers may escape clinical recognition during life because they often occur in patients with underlying cirrhosis, and the symptoms and signs may initially suggest a progression of the underlying liver disease. *Hepatomegaly*, with *pain* or *tenderness*, usually moderate in degree and localized to the upper abdomen or the right upper quadrant, is a major complaint in more than half the cases. Other clinical features which should alert the clinician to the diagnosis include a *mass* in the liver, particularly if tender; the presence of a *friction rub* or *bruit* over the liver; and *blood-tinged ascites* (hemoperitoneum) which occurs in about 20 percent of cases. On rare occasions one may find metabolic disturbances such as polycythemia, hypoglycemia, acquired porphyria, hypercalcemia, and dysglobulinemia. Jaundice is characteristic of cholangiocarcinoma but is relatively uncommon in hepatocellular carcinoma in the absence of active liver disease.

Anemia and elevated alkaline phosphatase levels are common laboratory findings. In a patient with cirrhosis, a disproportionately high serum alkaline phosphatase in relation to other abnormal liver function tests is often a clue to an infiltrating or partially obstructing liver carcinoma.

Diagnosis   The clinical features outlined above should suggest the possibility of primary liver carcinoma. Liver scintiscans may indicate the presence of one or more hepatic masses but frequently cannot distinguish between regenerating nodules in a cirrhotic liver and primary or metastatic liver tumors. Gallium 67 scans showing hepatocellular uptake in the abnormal area may be more helpful than ^{99m}Tc scans. Ultrasound or CT scans can clearly demonstrate lesions with a density different from normal liver tissue. These two noninvasive techniques also help in directing percutaneous biopsy for definitive diagnosis. Hepatic artery *angiography* may reveal distortion or obstructions of vessels or "tumor blushes" characteristic of neovascularization and usually can define the extent of the tumor and its resectability. Angiography cannot, however, distinguish between types of tumor and may not be able to differentiate benign from malignant solitary tumors.

A unique fetal alpha$_1$ globulin, *alpha fetoprotein* (AFP), is found in the serum of almost all patients with hepatocellular carcinoma. Very high levels, between 500 ng/mL and 5 mg/mL, occur in 70 to 90 percent of patients. The serum AFP may be slightly elevated in about 5 to 10 percent of patients with large hepatic metastases from gastrointestinal tumors, and in about one-third of patients with acute or chronic viral hepatitis, but only rarely to levels over 500 ng/mL in these conditions. Minimally elevated levels of AFP may persist in some patients with chronic hepatitis. AFP is also elevated up to 500 ng/mL in maternal serums during normal pregnancy. Higher levels can occur in maternal serums with fetal distress or death. The detection and persistence of *high levels* of serum AFP (over 500 or 1000 ng/mL) in an adult with liver disease and without an obvious gastrointestinal tract tumor strongly suggest the presence of primary liver carcinoma. Ectopic hormones, such as chorionic gonadotropin, are rarely found. Several variant isoenzymes (including aldolase, alkaline phosphatase, and 5'-nucleotide phosphodiesterase) have been reported in some liver cancer patients and also may be helpful diagnostically when present.

Percutaneous *liver biopsy* can be diagnostic, especially if the biopsy is taken in the area of a palpable nodule or mass localized by ultrasound or CT scans. False negatives may occur in as many as one-fourth of patients if the biopsy is performed in a routine, blind manner with the intercostal approach, and well-differentiated hepatocellular carcinoma may be difficult to diagnose by aspiration cytology or even needle biopsy. Cytologic examination of ascitic fluid is invariably negative for tumor cells. *Laparoscopy* or *laparotomy* with open liver biopsy is often required for diagnosis. This direct approach has the additional advantage of identifying the occasional patient with localized resectable tumor who may be suitable for partial hepatectomy.

Course and management   The course of the disease is fatal and usually rapid. Most patients die within 3 to 6 months from gastrointestinal hemorrhage, progressive cachexia, or hepatic failure.

If the patient is young, in good general health, and has no obvious extrahepatic involvement, solitary hepatic lesions may be excised with *partial hepatectomy*, but the 5-year survival rate is low. Persistently high or rising levels of AFP after excision of the tumor are indicative of residual or recurrent tumor. Hepatocellular carcinoma may respond for brief periods to systemic or intraarterial chemother-

apy. However, the results are still poor, and further trials of combined drug therapy are in progress. Liver transplantation can now be considered a therapeutic option, but recurrence of tumor and frequent appearance of metastases after transplantation have limited the usefulness of this procedure (see Chap. 252). Aggressive surgery or transplantation may prove to be of value in the treatment of small, localized tumors if diagnosed early or in the slower-growing fibrolamellar type of liver cell carcinoma.

OTHER BENIGN AND MALIGNANT TUMORS   These tumors are very rare. Hepatoblastomas are histologically distinct primary malignant tumors of the liver occurring only in infancy and early childhood and characteristically have very high levels of serum AFP. Since they are usually solitary masses, they are more usually resectable and have a higher 5-year survival rate than hepatocellular carcinoma. *Hemangiomas,* the most common of the benign tumors, are usually single and small, but may present as a large hepatic nodule. Percutaneous needle liver biopsy is contraindicated if the diagnosis is suspected because of the danger of hemorrhage. The diagnosis can be made by angiography. Surgical excision is usually not indicated unless the tumors are large and symptomatic or a malignant lesion cannot be excluded. *Hemangioendotheliomas* or *angiosarcomas* are rare malignant vascular tumors. They can be caused by chronic *vinyl chloride* exposure. These rare tumors may also appear 15 to 20 years after the administration of thorium dioxide.

Hepatic adenomas, although quite rare, have been reported with increasing frequency, particularly in women taking oral contraceptives for long periods. These benign neoplasms may regress when the pill is discontinued. Focal nodular hyperplasia, a nonneoplastic hamartoma, may also become more vascular with long-term use of oral contraceptives leading to increased risk of pain or hemorrhage. Other rare tumors include benign cholangiomas, rhabdomyomas, rhabdomyosarcomas, and a number of other benign and malignant tumors arising from various mesenchymal elements. These tumors usually present as a palpable mass in the liver or with intraabdominal hemorrhage. They can be visualized and their extent defined by angiography. Surgical exploration and open biopsy or resection are usually required for definitive diagnosis.

METASTATIC TUMORS   Metastatic malignant tumors of the liver are common in clinical practice, ranking second only to cirrhosis as a cause of fatal liver disease. In the United States the incidence of clinically significant metastatic carcinoma is at least 20 times greater than that of primary carcinoma. Hepatic metastases have been reported at autopsy in 30 to 50 percent of patients dying from malignant disease.

Pathogenesis   The liver is uniquely vulnerable to invasion by tumor cells. Its size, high rate of blood flow, and double perfusion by hepatic artery and portal vein combine to make it the most common site of metastases except for the lymph nodes. In addition, local tissue factors or endothelial membrane characteristics appear to enhance metastatic implants. Virtually all types of neoplasms except those primary in the brain may metastasize to the liver. The most common primary tumors are those of the gastrointestinal tract, lung, breast, and melanomas. Less common are metastases from tumors of the thyroid, prostate, and skin.

Clinical features   Most patients with metastatic malignancy of the liver present with (1) symptoms referable only to the primary tumor, with asymptomatic hepatic involvement discovered in the course of clinical evaluation; (2) nonspecific symptoms of weakness, weight loss, fever, sweating, and loss of appetite; or rarely, with (3) features indicating active hepatic disease, especially abdominal pain, hepatomegaly, or ascites.

Patients with widespread metastatic liver involvement usually have suggestive clinical signs of cancer and hepatic enlargement. Some have localized induration or tenderness, and occasionally a friction rub may be found over tender areas of the liver.

Abnormal liver function tests are frequent but often mild and nonspecific. They reflect the effects of fever and wasting, as well as the infiltrating neoplastic process itself. An increase in serum alkaline phosphatase is the most common and frequently the only abnormality noted. Hypoalbuminemia, anemia, and occasional mild elevation of transaminase levels may also be found with more widespread disease. Greatly elevated serum levels of carcinoembryonic antigen (CEA) are usually found when the metastases are from primary malignancies in the gastrointestinal tract, breast, or lung.

Diagnosis Evidence of metastatic invasion of the liver should be sought actively in any patient with a primary malignancy, especially of the lung, gastrointestinal tract, or breast, before resection of the primary lesion is undertaken. Abnormal liver function tests, particularly an elevated alkaline phosphatase, or demonstration of a mass by liver scintiscan, ultrasound, or CT may provide a presumptive diagnosis. Blind percutaneous needle biopsy of the liver will result in a positive diagnosis in only 60 to 80 percent of cases with established metastases. Serial sectioning of specimens, two or three repeat biopsies, or cytologic examination of biopsy smears may increase the diagnostic yield by 10 to 15 percent. The yield is greatly increased when biopsies are directed by ultrasound or CT or obtained by laparoscopy.

Treatment Most metastatic carcinomas respond poorly to all forms of treatment, which is usually only palliative. Surgical removal of a single large metastasis is rarely feasible. Systemic chemotherapy with combinations of different chemotherapeutic agents briefly may slow tumor growth and reduce symptoms in some patients but does not significantly alter the prognosis. It remains to be determined whether newer drugs or combination chemotherapy eventually will prove to be more effective.

REFERENCES

ALPERT E: Alpha-fetoprotein: Developmental biology and clinical significance, in *Progress in Liver Disease,* vol 5, H Popper, F Schaffner (eds). New York, Grune& Stratton, 1975

BEASLEY RP et al: Hepatocellular carcinoma and hepatitis B virus. Lancet 2:1129, 1981

BRECHOT C et al: Evidence that hepatitis B virus has a role in liver cell carcinoma in alcoholic liver disease. N Engl J Med 306:1384, 1982

LIAW Y-F et al: Early detection of hepatocellular carcinoma in patients with chronic type B hepatitis. A prospective study. Gastroenterology 90:263, 1986

MALT RA: Surgery for hepatic neoplasms. N Engl J Med 313:1591, 1985

MARGOLIS S, HOWEY C: Systemic manifestations of hepatoma. Medicine 51:381, 1972

OKUDA K et al: Prognosis of primary hepatocellular carcinoma. Hepatology 4:13S, 1984

OMATA M et al: Hepatocellular carcinoma in the USA: Etiologic considerations. Localization of hepatitis B antigens. Gastroenterology 76:279, 1979

SHAFRITZ DA et al: Integration of hepatitis B virus DNA into the genome of liver cells in chronic liver disease and hepatocellular carcinoma. N Engl J Med 305:1067, 1981

STARZL T et al: Analysis of liver transplantation. Hepatology 4:47S, 1984

ZAMAN SN et al: Risk factors in development of carcinoma in cirrhosis: Prospective study of 613 patients. Lancet 1:1357, 1985

251 INFILTRATIVE AND METABOLIC DISEASES AFFECTING THE LIVER

KURT J. ISSELBACHER / DANIEL K. PODOLSKY

Many disseminated, systemic, or metabolic diseases involve the liver in a diffuse manner by the infiltration of abnormal cells or the accumulation of chemical substances or metabolites. Chemical accumulation may be extracellular or intracellular and may involve hepatocytes, Kupffer cells, or other elements of the reticuloendothelial system. Although infiltrative diseases may vary widely in their etiology and extrahepatic manifestations, the findings in the liver may be quite similar. Generalized enlargement and firmness of the liver, gradual and nonspecific deterioration of liver function, and, less often, signs of portal hypertension or ascites are typical features of this group of diseases. Differential diagnosis by clinical means may be difficult on occasion, but in patients in whom ancillary clinical findings do not establish the diagnosis, the diffusely infiltrated liver provides an excellent source of tissue for diagnostic purposes.

As discussed in Chap. 58, the tools of molecular biology, especially recombinant DNA probes and restriction fragment length polymorphism will undoubtedly play a significant role in arriving at the molecular basis for many of these disorders. Some diseases will reflect the manifestation of mutant structural genes causing absent or reduced amounts of a gene product (e.g. phenylalanine hydroxylase deficiency leading to classic phenylketonuria), or a structurally *altered* gene which is functionally inactive (e.g., α_1-antitrypsin). In other instances the mutation may affect *gene regulation* as in Menke's syndrome, a rare disorder of zinc metabolism that affects the liver, which appears to result from faulty regulation of metallothionein gene expression.

LIPID INFILTRATIONS

FATTY LIVER Slight to moderate enlargement of the liver due to diffuse infiltration of liver cells by neutral fat (triglyceride) is a common clinical and pathologic finding. Although minimal fatty changes are often transient and have no clinical significance, persistent or extensive fatty infiltration may produce dysfunction and symptoms that require careful evaluation.

Etiology The major causes of fatty liver encountered in clinical practice depend on the age, geographic location, and metabolic-nutritional status of the patient population. *Chronic alcoholism* is the most common cause of fatty liver in this country and in other countries with a high alcohol intake. The severity of fatty involvement is roughly proportional to the duration and degree of alcoholic excess. *Protein malnutrition,* especially in infancy and early childhood, accounts for most cases of severe fatty liver in the tropical zones of Africa, South America, and Asia. The hepatic changes may be associated with other clinical and pathologic features of kwashiorkor. Patients with adult-onset *diabetes mellitus,* especially those who are overweight and are poorly controlled, often have fatty livers. *Obesity* is commonly associated with fatty infiltration of the liver; this recedes as weight reduction occurs. However, *jejunoileal bypass* for surgical treatment of morbid obesity is sometimes associated with severe fatty liver and hepatic failure which may be fatal. In patients with Cushing's syndrome and in those receiving large doses of corticosteroids, fatty infiltration of the liver may occur. In many *chronic illnesses,* especially those complicated by impaired nutrition or malabsorption, increased fat is found in liver cells. For example, patients with ulcerative colitis, chronic pancreatitis, or protracted heart failure frequently have moderately fatty livers at the time of death. Patients maintained on prolonged *intravenous hyperalimentation* may also develop fatty livers.

Acute fatty liver is caused by a number of hepatotoxins and is frequently accompanied by signs and symptoms of liver failure. Carbon tetrachloride intoxication, DDT poisoning, and ingestion of substances containing yellow phosphorus result in severe fatty liver. Acute and prolonged alcohol ingestion may also be considered in this category and may be associated with a rapidly enlarging and fat-laden liver. *Acute fatty liver of pregnancy* is a rare but often fatal condition seen during the third trimester of pregnancy which is characterized by nausea, vomiting, abdominal pain, renal failure, and coma. It should be distinguished from the benign cholestasis more frequently encountered during the third trimester of pregnancy. *Massive tetracycline therapy,* in amounts of 3 to 12 g intravenous, is a rare cause of acute fatty liver and fatal hepatic coma. Other drugs (e.g., valproic acid) have also been associated with the development of a fatty liver.

Pathogenesis The hepatic lipid deposits, which consist largely of triglycerides and lesser amounts of phospholipid and cholesterol, appear as vacuoles of varying size within the cytoplasm of liver cells. In extreme cases, every liver cell is involved, and lipids comprise up to 30 to 40 percent of the total liver weight.

The biochemical mechanisms leading to hepatic triglyceride accumulation are described in Chap. 244. Fatty infiltration has been produced in experimental animals by a variety of toxic agents and drugs, such as alcohol, carbon tetrachloride, and orotic acid. Deficiencies, such as choline deficiency, readily lead to increased fat in the liver in the rat. Many of these factors appear to disrupt synthesis of proteins, including the apoproteins needed for transport of triglycerides out of the liver as lipoproteins. However, with few exceptions experimental studies do not explain the pathogenesis of fatty liver in clinical disease. Moderate doses of ethanol may produce both acute and chronic fatty changes in human subjects, probably by its direct effects on hepatic triglyceride and fatty acid metabolism (Chap. 244). Protein deficiency seems to account for the fatty liver of kwashiorkor, and impaired protein synthesis for the fat accumulation following tetracycline and carbon tetrachloride administration. In diabetes mellitus and in starvation, increased mobilization of fatty acids from adipose tissue may be involved. Fatty infiltration during hyperalimentation appears to be derived from the high concentration of dextrose rather than from any lipid infusions.

Clinical features   The signs and symptoms of fatty liver are related to the degree of fat infiltration, the time course of its accumulation, and the underlying cause. The obese or diabetic patient with chronic fatty liver is usually asymptomatic and has only mild tenderness over the enlarged liver. The liver function tests are normal or show mild elevations of alkaline phosphatase, transaminases, or aminotransferases. In contrast, the rapid accumulation of fat seen in the setting of hyperalimentation may lead to marked tenderness, presumably resulting from stretching of Glisson's capsule. Similarly, alcoholic patients with acute fatty liver following a bout of heavy drinking may have right upper quadrant pain and tenderness often with laboratory evidence of cholestasis. The clinical presentation of acute fatty liver of pregnancy or fatty liver from hepatotoxins is similar to that of fulminant hepatic failure arising from any cause, with evidence of hepatic encephalopathy, marked elevations of prothrombin time and transaminases, and variable degrees of jaundice.

Diagnosis   The findings of a firm, nontender, and generally enlarged liver with minimal hepatic dysfunction in a patient with chronic alcoholism, malnutrition, poorly controlled diabetes mellitus, or obesity should suggest a fatty liver. When diagnostic uncertainty exists, needle biopsy of the liver will demonstrate the increased fatty content and possibly the underlying primary disorder. In acute fatty liver of pregnancy and in most cases of Reye's syndrome (see below), fat accumulates in small vacuoles (microvesicular fat) rather than in the large cytoplasmic droplets encountered in other disorders. The reason for the morphologic appearance of the fat in these two disorders is unclear.

Treatment   Adequate nutritional intake, removal of alcohol or offending toxins, and correction of any associated metabolic disorders usually result in recovery. There is no clinical rationale for the use of lipotropic agents such as choline. When indicated, attention should be directed to abstinence from alcohol, careful control of diabetes, weight loss, or correction of intestinal absorptive defects. In the alcoholic fatty liver there is gradual disappearance of fat from the liver after 4 to 8 weeks of adequate diet and abstinence from alcohol. Similarly, fatty infiltration usually resolves within 2 weeks after discontinuation of parenteral hyperalimentation. However, restitution of intestinal continuity may not prevent progression of disease in patients who have had extensive intestinal bypass surgery.

REYE'S SYNDROME (FATTY LIVER WITH ENCEPHALOPATHY)
This acute illness is encountered exclusively in children below 15 years of age. It is characterized clinically by vomiting, and signs of progressive central nervous system damage, signs of hepatic injury, and hypoglycemia. Morphologically there is extensive fatty vacuolization of the liver and renal tubules. The cause is unknown, although viral and toxic agents, especially salicylates, have been implicated. Increased aspirin use and much higher serum salicylate levels in children with this illness than in the general population have been described during outbreaks of Reye's syndrome. However, it seems clear that this illness may also occur in the absence of exposure to salicylates. In fatal cases, the liver is enlarged and yellow with striking diffuse fatty microvacuolization of cells. Peripheral zonal hepatic necrosis has also been present in some cases. Fatty changes of the renal tubular cells, cerebral edema, and neuronal degeneration of the brain are the major extrahepatic changes. Electron microscope studies show structural alterations of mitochondria in liver, brain, and muscle.

The onset usually follows an upper respiratory tract infection, especially influenza or chicken pox. Within 1 to 3 days persistent vomiting occurs, together with stupor, which usually progresses rapidly to generalized convulsions and coma. The liver is enlarged, but *jaundice is characteristically absent or minimal*. Elevations in serum aminotransferases and prothrombin time, hypoglycemia, metabolic acidosis, and elevated serum ammonia levels are the major laboratory findings. The mortality rate in Reye's syndrome is approximately 50 percent. Therapy consists of infusions of glucose and fresh frozen plasma, as well as intravenous mannitol to reduce the cerebral edema. Chronic liver disease has not been reported in survivors.

NIEMANN-PICK DISEASE (See Chap. 316)   This rare heritable disorder, of which there are five types, is found mainly in Jewish infants and is characterized by the accumulation of sphingomyelin and cholesterol in reticuloendothelial cells of the liver, spleen, bone marrow, and brain due to deficiency of sphingomyelinase. Hepatomegaly and splenomegaly are present, together with elevations in serum aminotransferase and alkaline phosphatase levels, but jaundice and other evidence of hepatic dysfunction are rare. The liver, which is typically large, yellow, and fatty, shows clusters of lipid-filled, foamy Kupffer cells. Diagnosis is made by lipid analysis of the tissue obtained from bone marrow aspiration.

GAUCHER'S DISEASE (See Chap. 316)   Accumulations of large reticuloendothelial cells containing the cerebroside glucosylceramide (Gaucher's cells) in the liver and spleen account for the characteristic moderate to massive hepatosplenomegaly found in patients with the juvenile and adult forms of this disorder. Rarely, ascites or portal hypertension is produced by compression of the intrahepatic vasculature. The diagnosis may be made readily by liver biopsy and demonstration of the Gaucher's cells but should be confirmed by demonstration of a deficiency of the enzyme glucosylceramide β-glucosidase in peripheral leukocytes.

WOLMAN'S AND CHOLESTEROL ESTER STORAGE DISEASES
Wolman's disease is a rare and fatal familial lipidosis of infancy producing hepatosplenomegaly and stippled calcification of the adrenal glands. Liver biopsy shows clusters of foam cells (reticuloendothelial cells filled with cholesterol ester and triglycerides), hepatocytes containing fat, and patchy fibrosis. A related but less severe genetic disorder is cholesterol ester storage disease. In this condition there is hypercholesterolemia and accumulation of both cholesterol esters and triglycerides in hepatic lysosomes. Both of these storage disorders are associated with hepatic deficiencies of cholesterol ester hydrolase and triglyceride lipase.

Other rare lipid disorders associated with hepatomegaly and increased fat in the liver include abetalipoproteinemia, Tangier disease, Fabry's disease, and types I and V hyperlipoproteinemia. (See Chap. 315 for details.)

HEPATIC GLYCOGEN ACCUMULATION

DIABETIC GLYCOGENOSIS   Hepatic enlargement caused by distention of liver cells with glycogen is present in some poorly controlled diabetic patients and often in juvenile diabetic patients (see Chap 327). More often, however, hepatomegaly is related to fatty infiltration (see above). Ketoacidosis and vigorous insulin therapy may further enhance hepatic enlargement and glycogen deposition. In the absence of cirrhosis, hepatomegaly usually decreases with careful control of the diabetes.

GLYCOGEN STORAGE DISEASE (See Chap. 313) The normal liver contains 1 to 5 percent glycogen (by weight). Except for types V and VII, the liver is involved in all genetically determined glycogen storage diseases. There is disruption of glucose homeostasis due to an inability to mobilize hepatic glycogen stores. In types I, II, and VI hereditary glycogen storage diseases, increased amounts of glycogen (and fat) are found. Types III and IV are associated with derangements of glycogen structure, and cirrhosis may be present. Fasting hypoglycemia is present in all these diseases. Enzymatic and chemical analysis of liver tissue is usually needed for diagnosis.

GALACTOSEMIA

Hepatic changes are common in patients with unrecognized or untreated galactosemia. In early weeks of life fatty infiltration and cholestasis may be noted in acutely ill infants. If the disease goes unrecognized for months or years, cirrhosis may develop. (See also Chap. 314.)

HEPATIC MINERAL ACCUMULATION

WILSON'S DISEASE (See Chap. 311) This rare disease, predominantly of young people, is characterized by cirrhosis, softening and degeneration of the basal ganglia, and pigmentation of the cornea (Kayser-Fleischer rings). Increased copper deposition in the tissues seems to be responsible for the liver and basal ganglia changes. Liver cells are ballooned and show increased glycogen with glycogen vacuolization in the nuclei. The liver shows all grades of changes, from minimal to severe periportal or macronodular cirrhosis.

HEMOCHROMATOSIS (See Chap. 310) This relatively common genetically determined disorder involves accumulation of abnormal amounts of iron due to inappropriate absorption in the intestine. The liver, as a primary site of iron storage, is most directly affected. There is diffuse deposition of excess iron in hepatocytes, in contrast to the characteristic accumulation of iron in the reticuloendothelial compartment typical of secondary iron overload and hemosiderosis. Hepatic iron overload commonly results in hepatomegaly. Although liver function is initially well preserved, if the disease is untreated, progressive impairment is followed by the development of cirrhosis.

OTHER INFILTRATIVE DISEASES

HURLER'S SYNDROME (See Chap. 319) This is an uncommon hereditary disease that is characterized by the widespread tissue deposition of mucopolysaccharide (chondroitin sulfate B and heparin sulfate) in many tissues. The liver is frequently enlarged and firm. Microscopically, Kupffer cells and other macrophages are enlarged and filled with metachromatic granular material. Cirrhosis may be a late complication.

ALPHA₁ ANTITRYPSIN DEFICIENCY (See also Chap. 208) Patients with homozygous deficiency of serum alpha₁ antitrypsin (α_1-AT) are prone to develop emphysema in adult life. The disease is suggested by the absence of alpha₁ globulin on serum electrophoresis (α_1-AT makes up 90 percent of this fraction normally) and confirmed by direct measurement of α_1-AT. The exact phenotype can then be determined by starch electrophoresis. Although there are 16 recognized alleles, only PiZ and PiS are associated with clinical disease. The molecular bases of these altered products have been related to single nucleic acid substitutions, e.g., PiZ is caused by a G (guanine) to A (adenine) transposition which results in a substitution of a glutamic acid for lysine at residue 292 in the α_1-AT protein. Hepatocytes of some patients with this deficiency contain globules positive to the periodic acid Schiff (PAS) reaction. Approximately 10 percent of children with homozygous deficiency (PiZZ phenotype) of α_1-AT will develop significant liver disease including neonatal hepatitis and progressive cirrhosis. It has been suggested that 15 to 20 percent of all chronic liver disease in infancy may be attributed to α_1-AT deficiency. In adults, the most common manifestation of α_1-AT deficiency is asymptomatic cirrhosis, which may progress from a micronodular to a macronodular state and may be complicated by the development of hepatocellular carcinoma. The occurrence of liver disease in these patients is not dependent upon the development of lung disease.

RETICULOENDOTHELIAL DISORDERS (See also Chaps. 55 and 294)

Moderate to massive hepatomegaly and splenomegaly occur frequently in the various types of leukemia and lymphoma. Jaundice, when present, is usually slight and results from hemolysis. Deep and protracted jaundice is distinctly rare and is caused by obstruction of the intrahepatic or extrahepatic bile ducts by tumor. Liver biopsy specimens reveal portal and sinusoidal infiltrates in most cases of leukemia, but the cellular pattern may be mixed and nonspecific. Liver biopsy is diagnostic in only 5 percent of patients with Hodgkin's disease. This percentage is increased in those with advanced disease or splenomegaly. Directed biopsy at laparoscopy or laparotomy is more likely to be positive than "blind" needle biopsy. Nonspecific histologic changes in the liver have been described in patients with lymphoma and may contribute to the abnormal liver function tests.

Myeloid metaplasia and other myeloproliferative disorders associated with extramedullary hematopoiesis produce hepatomegaly which may reach huge proportions, especially following splenectomy. Serum alkaline phosphatase elevations are often found. Ascites and portal hypertension, resulting from diffuse involvement of portal venules and lymphatics, are rare complications.

GRANULOMATOUS INFILTRATIONS

Perhaps as a result of the large population of mononuclear phagocytes, a number of systemic granulomatous diseases involve the liver, including sarcoidosis, miliary tuberculosis, histoplasmosis, brucellosis, schistosomiasis, berylliosis, and drug reactions. In addition, isolated granulomas of no diagnostic importance may be found occasionally in patients with various forms of cirrhosis and hepatitis. The liver infiltrated by granulomas may be slightly enlarged and firm, but hepatic dysfunction is usually limited and manifested only by mild increases in serum alkaline phosphatase and occasionally aminotransferase levels. In a few patients with sarcoidosis or brucellosis, portal hypertension may develop, and extensive postnecrotic scarring or postnecrotic cirrhosis may follow healing of the granulomatous lesions as in schistosomiasis.

Needle biopsy of the liver reveals granulomas and often provides the first definite evidence of a systemic or disseminated granulomatous disease. In patients with sarcoidosis who have neither clinical nor laboratory evidence of hepatic involvement, needle biopsy is positive in about 80 percent of cases. In cases of suspected miliary tuberculosis a portion of the biopsy should be cultured and stained for mycobacteria. The organism can be detected in the majority of cases, particularly when caseating granulomas are present. Serial sections of the biopsy specimen should be examined if granulomas are not apparent. Individual granulomas are rarely specific in their microscopic appearance, and final diagnosis usually requires other clinical, laboratory, or histologic data.

In approximately 20 percent of patients it is not possible to identify a cause for the granulomatous infiltration. When these infiltrates are accompanied by fever of unknown etiology, the diagnosis of granulomatous hepatitis should be considered. This is an uncommon disorder of unknown etiology and is diagnosed by exclusion. While granulomatous hepatitis invariably responds to moderate doses of corticosteroids, relapses are frequent, and such therapy should never be undertaken unless tuberculous disease or other causes of granulomatous infiltration have been excluded. This may include an initial empiric trial of antituberculous therapy.

AMYLOIDOSIS (See also Chap. 259)

Systemic amyloidosis, whether primary and idiopathic, familial, or secondary to chronic inflammatory or neoplastic diseases, often involves the liver. Grossly, the liver infiltrated with amyloid is enlarged and pale and rubbery in consistency. Microscopically, the birefringent amyloid deposits appear as homogeneous waxy material within the space of Disse, often being concentrated in the periportal areas and associated with atrophy of adjacent liver cell plates. Selective involvement of the walls of blood vessels, especially of the hepatic arterioles, may be a striking feature of primary amyloidosis. With this possible exception, however, the hepatic lesions are the same in all forms of amyloidosis and are present in 60 to 90 percent of cases.

An enlarged and firm liver is found in about 60 percent of patients, and ascites occurs in advanced stages of the disease in about 20 percent. Jaundice, portal hypertension, and other signs of chronic liver disease are usually absent. Liver function changes, although frequent, correlate poorly with the extent of liver infiltration. Hypoalbuminemia and elevated serum alkaline phosphatase are common. Hypoalbuminemia, however, may be related to the nephrotic syndrome owing to renal involvement; the prothrombin time is usually normal. The diagnosis is established by biopsy of rectum, skin, liver, or other involved organs and demonstration of the characteristic Congo red–staining deposits by polarizing microscopy.

REFERENCES

Bove KE: Reye's syndrome, in Hepatology, A Textbook of Liver Disease, D Zakim, TD Boyer (eds). Philadelphia, Saunders, 1982, pp 1212–1220
Glenner GG: Amyloid deposits and amyloidosis. The β-fibrilloses. N Engl J Med 302:1283, 1980
Heubi JE et al: Grade I Reye's syndrome: Outcome and predictors of progression to deeper coma grades. N Engl J Med 311:1539, 1984
Hurwitz ES et al: Public Health Service Study on Reye's syndrome and medications. N Engl J Med 313:842, 1985
Kidd VJ, Woo SLC: Recombinant DNA probes used to detail genetic disorders of the liver. Hepatology 4:731, 1984
Pockros PJ et al: Idiopathic fatty liver of pregnancy. Medicine 44:1, 1984
Reynolds TB et al: Hepatic granulomas, in Hepatology, A Textbook of Liver Disease, D Zakim, TD Boyer (eds). Philadelphia, Saunders, 1982, pp 995–1009
Spechler SJ, Koff RS: Wilson's disease: Diagnostic difficulties in the patient with chronic hepatitis and hyperceruloplasminemia. Gastroenterology 78:103, 1980
Stanbury JB et al: The Metabolic Basis of Inherited Disease, 5th ed, New York, McGraw-Hill, 1983
Sveger T: Liver disease in α₁-antitrypsin deficiency. N Engl J Med 294:1316, 1976

252   LIVER TRANSPLANTATION

RUDI SCHMID

Orthotopic liver transplantation, i.e., replacement of a diseased liver by a healthy organ recovered from a recently brain-dead individual, is surgically difficult, requires a full array of supporting services usually available only in large tertiary medical centers, and carries a considerable operative and postoperative mortality. However, the risk-versus-benefit ratio has improved to an extent where liver transplantation has become a promising approach for selected patients whose liver disease is progressive, life-threatening, and beyond the reach of traditional therapy.

The first orthotopic liver transplantation in a human was performed by Starzl and associates in 1963 at the University of Colorado in Denver, but the survival of this patient and several subsequently transplanted patients was less than 1 month. The following years brought refinements in both surgical technique and postoperative management that improved survival rates, but by 1976 only 24 percent of adults and 33 percent of children who underwent liver transplantation survived for more than 1 year. Until the 1970s, performance of the operation remained almost entirely limited to the Denver center and to another liver transplantation facility established by Calne in 1968 in Cambridge, England. Since 1980, however, the prospect for prolonged survival with good quality of life has improved owing largely to development of better techniques for organ preservation, improvements in surgical techniques including the development of a pump-driven venovenous bypass system, and advances in immunosuppression, particularly the use of cyclosporine in combination with steroids. As a result, a number of transplant centers have been established, and the total number of successful liver transplants exceeded 1000 by mid-1985.

INDICATIONS FOR LIVER TRANSPLANTATION   In the absence of absolute or relative contraindications (see below), potential candidates for liver transplantation are children and adults up to age 50 who suffer from severe, irreversible liver disease for which alternative medical or surgical treatments have been exhausted. Timing of the operation is of critical importance; the disease should be in a late enough stage to allow the patient all opportunity for spontaneous stabilization or recovery but early enough to give the surgical procedure a fair chance of success. As a general rule, transplantation should be considered in patients with end-stage liver disease who are experiencing or have experienced life-threatening complications of hepatic failure, whose quality of life has deteriorated to unacceptable levels, or whose liver disease predictably will result in irreversible damage to the central nervous system. The decision to transplant requires the combined judgment of an experienced team of hepatologists, transplant surgeons, anesthesiologists, and specialists in supporting services; the well-informed consent of the patient or the patient's family or authorized representative must also be obtained.

TRANSPLANTATION IN CHILDREN Biliary atresia   The most common indication for transplantation in children is biliary atresia. Although hepatoportoenterostomy (Kasai procedure) performed in the first 2 months of life may provide substantial albeit transient improvement, the distortion of intrahepatic bile ducts and cirrhosis always are progressive, resulting in eventual hepatic insufficiency and death. It seems advantageous, however, to delay transplantation especially in the first year of life as long as possible to permit the child optimal development.

Metabolic disorders   Genetically transmitted diseases associated with progressive liver failure constitute another major indication in children and adolescents. In progressive cirrhosis due to alpha₁-antitrypsin deficiency, transplantation results in appearance of the donor alpha₁-antitrypsin phenotype and return of the plasma enzyme level toward normal. In Wilson's disease presenting with acute hepatic failure or with progressive neurologic deficiency that is unresponsive to chelation therapy, liver transplantation is the treatment of choice. Improvement in neurologic function and return of plasma ceruloplasmin concentration to normal have been reported. Liver failure in Byler's, Alagille's, and Wolman's disease and in protoporphyria, tyrosinemia, and some types of glycogenosis have been indications for transplantation. In Crigler-Najjar disease type I and in certain hereditary disorders of the urea cycle and of amino acid or lactate-pyruvate metabolism, transplantation may be the only way to prevent impending deterioration of central nervous system function, despite the fact that the replaced liver is structurally normal. Combined heart and liver transplantation yielded dramatic improvement in cardiac function and plasma cholesterol level in a child with homozygous familial hypercholesterolemia. In hereditary oxalosis, improvement has been reported after combined liver and kidney transplantation.

TRANSPLANTATION IN ADULTS **Nonalcoholic cirrhosis** Chronic active hepatitis due to presumed autoimmunity and cirrhosis of nonviral etiology with liver failure are important indications for transplantation. From the mid-1970s to 1985, the actuarial 1-year survival of 275 patients transplanted for these conditions progressively rose from 31 percent to approximately 70 percent.

Primary biliary cirrhosis Because primary biliary cirrhosis has an indolent and often fluctuating course, liver transplantation is indicated only in patients who have progressed to an end stage of the disease or whose quality of life has deteriorated to an unacceptable level. Survival is similar to that in nonalcoholic cirrhosis. In the posttransplantation period, it is often difficult to distinguish between homograft rejection and the recurrence of the original disease because the clinical, laboratory, and histologic features of the two conditions are similar.

Sclerosing cholangitis Transplantation has been successful in patients with primary sclerosing cholangitis or with Caroli's disease in whom surgical drainage procedures failed to prevent progressive deterioration of hepatic function.

Hepatic vein thrombosis Transplantation has been reported in 17 patients with Budd-Chiari syndrome with an actuarial 3-year survival of 60 percent. Because spontaneous recannulization of the obstructed hepatic veins occasionally occurs, the operation should be reserved for patients with progressive hepatic decompensation or irreversible hepatorenal syndrome. It is controversial whether transplantation is indicated for hepatic vein thrombosis associated with polycythemia vera or myeloproliferative disorders.

Hepatobiliary cancer Overall survival of patients who undergo transplantation for primary hepatocellular carcinoma or cholangiocarcinoma is significantly less than that for other categories of liver disease because the majority of patients succumb to disseminated carcinomatosis. Moreover, because the results have improved only slightly in recent years, the proportion of transplanted patients who received homografts for primary liver cancer has progressively decreased since 1980. The most promising approach to primary liver cancer clearly is early detection when the tumor is small and amenable to total resection.

CONTRAINDICATIONS FOR TRANSPLANTATION Absolute contraindications for transplantation include life-threatening systemic diseases; infections; preexisting cardiovascular, pulmonary, or renal disease; metastatic malignancies; portal vein thrombosis; and therapy-resistant arterial hypotension. In alcohol-related liver disease, the outcome of transplantation generally has been disappointing; only 27 out of 819 patients reported up to August 1984 were transplanted for this condition. In patients with advanced alcohol-related cirrhosis who, despite abstinence for at least 6 months and adequate nutritional state, develop hepatic decompensation, transplantation may be contemplated when all other means of therapy have failed; relatively few patients, however, fulfill these qualifications. Patients with chronic viral hepatitis B, particularly those positive for HBsAg and HBeAg, are poor risks for transplantation because the immunosuppression tends to promote recurrence of the infection in the homograft. Information is inadequate to determine whether this also is true in chronic hepatitis B without evidence of active viral replication. In fulminant hepatitis of all etiologies associated with encephalopathy and/or hepatorenal syndrome, results of transplantation generally have been discouraging; this in part may be due to the rapid progression of the disease rendering optimal timing of the operation difficult.

RESULTS OF TRANSPLANTATION **Survival** Since 1983, the survival rate of patients undergoing liver transplantation has steadily improved. In 1985, the overall prospect for 1-year survival was about 70 percent, with children faring slightly better than adults. Of 152 patients who underwent liver transplantation at various centers between January 1980 and April 1983 and who survived the initial three postoperative months, the 3-year survival rate was 79 percent in adults with nonalcoholic cirrhosis and 92 percent in children with biliary atresia; in 102 patients transplanted after April 1983 who survived the initial three postoperative months, 1-year survival rates reached 89 percent in adults and 96 percent in children.

Posttransplantation quality of life In patients who have undergone transplantation for life-threatening chronic liver disease, objective evaluation of the quality of life after surgery inherently is difficult, and reliable information is sparse. Nonetheless, full rehabilitation seems to have been achieved in the majority of those who survived the first three postoperative months and escaped chronic rejection or unmanageable infection. Immunosuppressive medication in reduced doses usually is continued indefinitely. Several women who underwent transplantation and received immunosuppressive therapy have conceived and carried the pregnancy to term without demonstrable damage to the infants.

TECHNICAL AND MANAGEMENT ASPECTS **Surgical techniques** Liver donors commonly are procured from accident victims 2 months to 45 years of age who are brain-dead and without detectable hepatic dysfunction. Cardiovascular and respiratory functions are sustained artificially until the liver can be removed. Prolonged periods of hypotension or hypoxia preclude donation, and compatibility of ABO blood type and organ size are important considerations in donor selection. Multiple-organ procurement (including the liver, heart, and kidneys, but not the pancreas) is technically feasible. Following perfusion with cold electrolyte solution and packing in ice, the donor liver can be preserved for up to 8 h without significant impairment of graft viability.

Removal of the recipient's liver is technically difficult, particularly in the presence of varices or scarring from previous abdominal operations. After the portal vein and inferior vena cava are dissected, a pump-driven bypass system is applied that reroutes blood from the portal vein and inferior vena cava to the superior vena cava, thereby preventing congestion of visceral organs. In implanting the new liver, meticulous attention must be directed to reestablishment of the portal venous and hepatic arterial circulations and to reconstruction of biliary drainage. The latter usually is achieved by anastomosis of the common bile ducts or by choledochojejunostomy to a Roux en Y limb, if the common bile duct of the recipient cannot be used for reconstruction.

A transplant operation requires 8 to 12 h. Because of excessive bleeding associated with portal hypertension and liver failure, large volumes of blood, blood products, and volume expanders may be required during surgery.

POSTOPERATIVE COURSE AND MANAGEMENT **Postoperative complications** Patients who undergo liver transplantation are frequently malnourished, so that attention to multiple organ failure is of primary importance. Because of the fluids administered during surgery, patients may become overloaded during the immediate postoperative period, necessitating continuous monitoring of cardiovascular and pulmonary function. Postoperative jaundice is almost invariable and reflects the large administered pigment load and variable degrees of ischemic or mechanical injury sustained by the liver during harvesting and implantation. Prerenal azotemia, acute kidney injury due to hypotension, or renal toxicity caused by antibiotics or cyclosporine are frequently encountered in the postoperative period and sometimes require dialysis. Other postoperative complications related to technical difficulties include stenosis or leakage of the anastomosed common bile duct, intraperiotoneal hemorrhage, and thrombosis of the reconstructed hepatic artery or of the portal or hepatic vein. Acute upper gastrointestinal hemorrhage or unexplained transient hemolytic anemia, with or without thrombocytopenia, may occur.

Bacterial, viral, or fungal infections related to the required immunosuppressive therapy may be life-threatening in the later postoperative period. These infections may involve the biliary tree, liver, upper gastrointestinal tract, or lungs, and they demand early recognition and prompt management. *Candida, Nocardia, Pneumocystis carinii*, and cytomegalovirus are frequent infective agents, but viruses of the herpes group, other mycoses, or gram-negative bacteria may also be pathogens. In most transplant centers, patients routinely are given antibiotic therapy prophylactically.

Immunosuppression The introduction in 1980 of cyclosporine as an immunosuppressive agent contributed substantially to the improvement in transplant survival. The drug depresses both humoral and cell-mediated immunity without affecting rapidly dividing cells in the bone marrow, which may account for the reduced incidence of systemic posttransplantation infection. Unfortunately, cyclosporine causes dose-related renal tubular injury, which usually can be managed by reducing the dose. Other adverse effects of long-term cyclosporine use are hypertension, hyperkalemia, tremor, hirsutism, and hyperplasia of the gums. Because of these side effects, combinations of cyclosporine and prednisone are a preferable regimen for immunosuppressive treatment during the initial postoperative months. For long-term management, renal toxicity may make it necessary to reduce cyclosporine to very low doses, which can be accomplished by adding azathioprine as supplemental immunosuppressive medication. In many centers, cyclosporine treatment is initiated prior to or on the day of surgery and is continued by intravenous route through the operation and the immediate postoperative period until oral administration can be resumed.

Transplant rejection Despite the use of cyclosporine alone or in combination with steroids, homograft rejection still occurs in the majority of patients 1 to 6 weeks after surgery. There appears to be no hepatic counterpart to the "hyperacute" rejection observed after renal transplantation. Early signs suggesting liver rejection are leukocytosis, increase in serum bilirubin level, and rise in aminotransferase activity; these may be followed by fever, tenderness in the right upper abdomen, diarrhea, ascites, and progressive deterioration of hepatic function. Because of the lack of specificity of these manifestations, differential diagnosis between homograft rejection, biliary obstruction, viral hepatitis, and recurrence of the original liver disease frequently is difficult. Radiographic visualization of the biliary tree and/or percutaneous liver biopsy often are helpful in establishing the correct diagnosis. Early morphologic features of rejection characteristically include portal infiltration with small lymphocytes and variable numbers of polymorphonuclear leukocytes, centrolobular bile stasis, selective destruction of small bile ducts associated with polymorphonuclear infiltration, and, at times, endothelial inflammation of portal or central veins and occasionally of hepatic arterioles. These finding are similar to those in graft-versus-host disease and may be indistinguishable from those of primary biliary cirrhosis. As soon as transplant rejection is suspected, it should be treated with intravenous methylprednisolone in repeated boluses; this usually reverses the rejection process. Some centers are also using antilymphocyte antibodies.

Chronic rejection is a relatively rare event that appears to be unrelated to the occurrence of preceding acute rejection episodes. It is associated with progressive cholestasis, bile duct proliferation, focal parenchymal necrosis, mononuclear infiltration, and fibrosis. These morphologic findings may be so similar to those of chronic viral hepatitis that differentiation between the two may be difficult. In some patients with therapy-resistant chronic rejection, retransplantation has yielded encouraging results.

REFERENCES

Busuttil RW, Moderator: Liver transplantation today. Ann Intrn Med 104:377, 1986

NIH Consensus Development Conference on Liver Transplantation: Hepatology 4(suppl):15, 1984

Progress in Liver Transplantation, CH Gips, RAF Krom (eds). Amsterdam, Martinus Nijhoff, 1985.

Scharschmidt BF: Human liver transplantation: An analysis of 819 patients from 8 centers, in *Recent Advances in Hepatology,* HC Thomas, EA Jones (eds). London, Churchill-Livingstone, 1985, vol 2

---

253 DISEASES OF THE GALLBLADDER AND BILE DUCTS

MARK S. McPHEE / NORTON J. GREENBERGER

PHYSIOLOGY OF BILE PRODUCTION AND FLOW Bile secretion and composition Bile formed in the hepatic lobules is secreted into a complex network of canaliculi, small bile ductules, and larger bile ducts which run with lymphatics and branches of the portal vein and hepatic artery in portal tracts situated between hepatic lobules. These interlobular bile ducts coalesce to form larger septal bile ducts that join to form the right and left hepatic ducts, which in turn unite to form the common hepatic duct. The common hepatic duct is joined by the cystic duct of the gallbladder to form the common bile duct which enters the duodenum (often after joining the main pancreatic duct) through the ampulla of Vater.

Hepatic bile is a pigmented isotonic fluid with an electrolyte composition resembling blood plasma. The electrolyte composition of gallbladder bile differs from that of hepatic bile since most of the inorganic anions, chloride and bicarbonate, have been removed by reabsorption across the basement membrane.

Major components of bile by weight include water (82 percent), bile acids (12 percent), lecithin and other phospholipids (4 percent), and unesterified cholesterol (0.7 percent). Other constituents include conjugated bilirubin, proteins (IgA, by-products of hormones, and other proteins metabolized in the liver), electrolytes, mucus, and, often, drugs and their metabolic by-products.

The total daily basal secretion of hepatic bile is approximately 500 to 600 mL. The metabolic products of hepatocyte uptake and synthesis are secreted into the bile canaliculi, which are lined by microvillus membrane components associated with microfilaments of actin, microtubules, and other contractile elements. Within the hepatocyte, conjugation of many of the bile constituents may occur, while other components of bile such as primary bile acids, lecithin, and some cholesterol are synthesized de novo. Three mechanisms are important in regulating bile flow: (1) active transport of bile acids from hepatocytes into the canaliculi, (2) bile acid–independent ATPase-mediated transport of sodium, and (3) ductular secretion. The last is a secretin-mediated and cyclic AMP–dependent phenomenon which appears to result from the active transport of sodium and bicarbonate into the ductule with resulting passive movement of water across the cell membrane.

The bile acids The primary bile acids, cholic and chenodeoxycholic acids, are synthesized from cholesterol in the liver, conjugated with glycine or taurine, and excreted into the bile. Secondary bile acids, including deoxycholate and lithocholate, are formed in the colon as bacterial metabolites of the primary bile acids. However, lithocholic acid is much less efficiently absorbed from the colon than deoxycholic acid. Other secondary bile acids, found in trace amounts, which include ursodeoxycholic acid (a stereoisomer of chenodeoxycholate) and a variety of other unusual or "aberrant" bile acids, may be produced in increased amounts in patients with chronic cholestatic syndromes. In normal bile, the ratio of glycine to taurine conjugates is about 3:1, while in patients with cholestasis, increased concentrations of sulfate and glucuronide conjugates of bile acids are often found.

Bile acids are detergents which in aqueous solutions and above a critical concentration of about 2 mM form molecular aggregates called micelles. Cholesterol alone is poorly soluble in aqueous environments, and its solubility in bile depends upon both the lipid concentration and the relative molar percentages of bile acids and lecithin. Normal ratios of these constituents favor the formation of solubilizing "mixed micelles," while abnormal ratios promote the precipitation of cholesterol crystals in bile.

In addition to facilitating the biliary excretion of cholesterol, bile acids are necessary for the normal intestinal absorption of dietary fats via a micellar transport mechanism (see Chap. 237). Bile acids also serve as a major physiologic driving force for hepatic bile flow and aid in water and electrolyte transport in the small bowel and colon.

Enterohepatic circulation Bile acids are efficiently conserved under normal conditions. Conjugated and unconjugated bile acids are absorbed by *passive diffusion* along the entire gut. Quantitatively much more important for bile salt recirculation, however, is the *active transport* mechanism for conjugated bile acids in the distal ileum (see Chap. 237). The reabsorbed bile acids enter the portal bloodstream and are taken up rapidly by hepatocytes, reconjugated, and resecreted into bile (enterohepatic circulation).

The normal bile acid pool size is approximately 2 to 4 g. During digestion of a meal, the bile acid pool undergoes at least one or more enterohepatic cycles depending upon the size and composition of the meal. Normally the bile acid pool circulates approximately 5 to 10 times daily. Intestinal absorption of the pool is about 95 percent efficient, so that fecal loss of bile acids is in the range of 0.3 to 0.6 g per day. This fecal loss is compensated by an equal daily synthesis of bile acids by the liver, and thus the size of the bile salt pool is maintained. Bile acids returning to the liver suppress de novo hepatic synthesis of primary bile acids from cholesterol by inhibiting the rate-limiting enzyme 7α-hydroxylase. While the loss of bile salts in stool is usually matched by increased hepatic synthesis, the maximum rate of synthesis is approximately 5 g per day, which may be insufficient to replete the bile acid pool size when there is pronounced impairment of intestinal bile salt reabsorption.

Gallbladder and sphincteric functions In the fasting state, the sphincter of Oddi offers a high-pressure zone of resistance to bile flow from the common bile duct into the duodenum. This tonic contraction serves to (1) prevent reflux of duodenal contents into the pancreatic and bile ducts, and (2) promote bile filling of the gallbladder. The major factor controlling the evacuation of the gallbladder is the peptide hormone cholecystokinin, which is released from the duodenal mucosa in response to the ingestion of fats and amino acids. Cholecystokinin produces (1) powerful contraction of the gallbladder, (2) decreased resistance of the sphincter of Oddi, (3) increased hepatic secretion of bile, and thus (4) enhanced flow of biliary contents into the duodenum.

Hepatic bile is "concentrated" within the gallbladder by energy-dependent transmucosal absorption of water and electrolytes. Almost the entire bile acid pool may be sequestered in the gallbladder following an overnight fast for delivery into the duodenum with the first meal of the day. The normal capacity of the gallbladder is 30 to 75 mL of bile.

DISEASES OF THE GALLBLADDER

CONGENITAL ANOMALIES Anomalies of the biliary tract may be found in 10 to 20 percent of the population, including abnormalities in number, size, and shape (e.g., agenesis of the gallbladder, duplications, rudimentary or oversized "giant" gallbladders, and diverticula). Phrygian cap is a clinically innocuous entity in which a partial or complete septum (or fold) separates the fundus from the body. Anomalies of position or suspension are not uncommon and include left-sided gallbladder, intrahepatic gallbladder, retrodisplacement of the gallbladder, and "floating" gallbladder. The latter condition predisposes to acute torsion, volvulus, or herniation of the gallbladder.

GALLSTONES Pathogenesis of gallstones Gallstones are quite prevalent in most western countries. In the United States, autopsy series have shown gallstones in at least 20 percent of women and in 8 percent of men over the age of 40. It is estimated that 16 to 20 million persons in the United States have gallstones and that approximately 1 million new cases of cholelithiasis develop each year.

Gallstones are crystalline structures formed by concretion or accretion of normal or abnormal bile constituents. These stones are divided into three major types; cholesterol and mixed stones account for 80 percent of the total, with pigment stones comprising the remaining 20 percent. Mixed and cholesterol gallstones usually contain more than 70 percent cholesterol monohydrate plus an admixture of calcium salts, bile acids and bile pigments, proteins, fatty acids, and phospholipids. Pigment stones are primarily composed of calcium bilirubinate; they contain less than 10 percent cholesterol.

CHOLESTEROL AND MIXED STONES The solubility of cholesterol in bile depends upon the relative molar concentrations of cholesterol, bile acids, and lecithin. These concentrations may be expressed on triangular coordinates as a phase diagram of bile composition (Fig. 253-1). As noted above, cholesterol is relatively water insoluble and normally is kept in solution (in the form of mixed micelles) by bile salts and phospholipids.

The most important mechanism in the formation of lithogenic (stone-forming) bile is increased biliary secretion of cholesterol. This may occur in association with obesity, high-caloric diets, or drugs (e.g., clofibrate) and may result from increased activity of hydroxymethylglutaryl-coenzyme A (HMG-CoA) reductase, the rate-limiting enzyme of hepatic cholesterol synthesis. In some patients, impaired hepatic conversion of cholesterol to bile acids may also occur, resulting in a decrease of the lithogenic cholesterol/bile acid ratio. Lithogenic bile also results from decreased hepatic secretion of bile salts and phospholipids which may follow impaired hepatic synthesis

FIGURE 253-1 *Phase diagram of bile composition. The relative concentrations of cholesterol, bile acids, and lecithin are expressed on triangular coordinates as mole percentages totaling 100 percent. The equilibrium limit of solubility for cholesterol is denoted by the solid line. Hatchmarks indicate the metastable zone, where slow precipitation of cholesterol from supersaturated bile may occur. Point A represents a micellar solution in which cholesterol is solubilized in mixed micelles. Point B, on the equilibrium limit of solubility line, indicates bile saturated with cholesterol. Point C depicts cholesterol supersaturated bile, a composition leading to the precipitation of cholesterol crystals.*

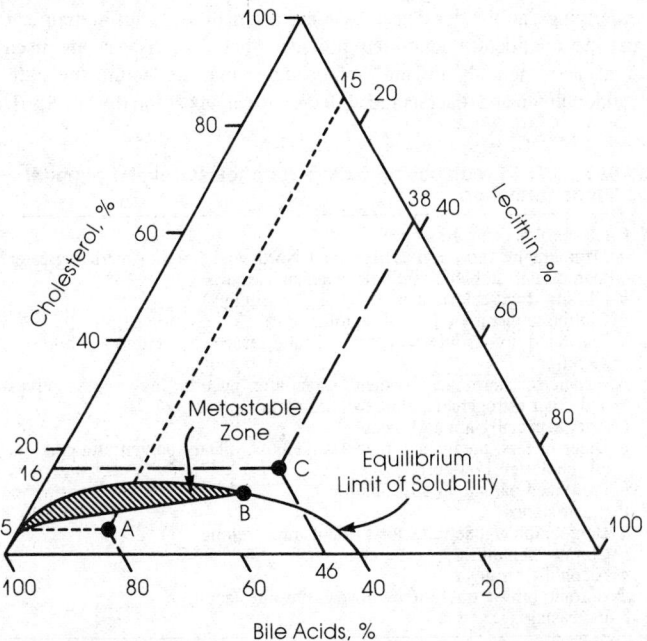

(e.g., rare inborn errors of metabolism such as cerebrotendinous xanthomatosis) or conditions affecting the enterohepatic circulation of these constituents (e.g., prolonged parenteral alimentation or ileal disease or resection). In addition, most patients with gallstones appear to have reduced activity of hepatic cholesterol 7α-hydroxylase, the rate-limiting enzyme for primary bile acid synthesis.

Stone formation in bile supersaturated with cholesterol requires both nucleation and the production of cholesterol monohydrate crystals, which may grow by accretion or concretion to form macroscopic aggregates. In fact, the major difference in supersaturated bile with respect to ability to form cholesterol crystals probably involves the nucleation rather than the crystal growth stage. Gallbladder mucin probably accelerates the nucleation of cholesterol monohydrate crystals and thus may contribute to cholesterol stone formation. Other biliary proteins appear to inhibit cholesterol crystal nucleation in normal human gallbladder bile. The major known predisposing factors to cholesterol stone formation are summarized in Table 253-1.

PIGMENT STONES Gallstones composed largely of calcium bilirubinate are much more common in the orient than in western countries. The presence of increased amounts of unconjugated, insoluble bilirubin in bile results in the precipitation of bilirubin which may aggregate to form pigment stones or may fuse to form the nidus for growth of mixed cholesterol gallstones. In western countries, chronic hemolytic states (with increased conjugated bilirubin in bile) or alcoholic liver disease are associated with an increased incidence of pigment stones. Deconjugation of soluble bilirubin mono- and diglucuronide may be mediated by the enzyme β-glucuronidase, which is sometimes produced when bile is chronically infected by bacteria. Pigment stone formation is especially prominent in Asians and is often associated with infections in the biliary tree (see Table 253-1).

Diagnosis of gallstones Procedures of potential use in the diagnosis of cholelithiasis and other diseases of the gallbladder are detailed in Table 253-2. The plain abdominal film may detect gallstones containing sufficient calcium to be radiopaque (10 to 15 percent of cholesterol and mixed stones and approximately 50 percent of pigment stones). Plain radiography may also be of use in the diagnosis of emphysematous cholecystitis, porcelain gallbladder, limey bile, and gallstone ileus.

Ultrasonography of the gallbladder is very accurate in the identification of cholelithiasis and has several advantages over oral cholecystography (see Fig. 253-2A). The gallbladder is easily visualized with the technique, and, in fact, failure to image the gallbladder successfully in a fasting patient correlates well with the presence of underlying gallbladder disease. Stones as small as 2 mm in diameter may be confidently identified provided that firm criteria are used [e.g., acoustic "shadowing" of opacities that are within the gallbladder lumen and that change with the patient's position (by gravity)].

TABLE 253-1 Predisposing factors for cholesterol and pigment gallstone formation

1 Cholesterol and mixed stones
  a Demography: northern Europe and North and South America greater than orient; probable familial, hereditary aspects
  b Obesity, high-calorie diet (↑ cholesterol output)
  c Clofibrate therapy (↑ cholesterol output)
  d Malabsorption of bile acids (e.g., ileal disease or resection) (↓ bile salt secretion)
  e Female sex hormones: women > men after puberty; oral contraceptives and other estrogens (↓ bile salt secretion)
  f Age, especially among males
  g Other factors: pregnancy, diabetes mellitus, dietary polyunsaturated fats (↑ cholesterol output)
  h Prolonged parenteral alimentation
2 Pigment stones
  a Demographic/genetic factors: orient, rural setting
  b Chronic hemolysis
  c Alcoholic cirrhosis
  d Chronic biliary tract infection, parasite infestation
  e Increasing age

In major medical centers the false-negative and false-positive rates for ultrasound in gallstone patients are about 2 to 4 percent.

Oral cholecystography (OCG) is a useful procedure for the diagnosis of gallstones but has been largely replaced by ultrasound. False-positive results are rare, but the oral cholecystogram may be falsely negative (when good opacification is achieved) in approximately 5 to 10 percent of patients with gallstones. Factors which may produce nonvisualization of the OCG are summarized in Table 253-2. When these can be excluded, nonvisualization of the gallbladder following a second dose of oral contrast agent is highly correlated with underlying cystic duct obstruction or chronic inflammation of the gallbladder.

Radiopharmaceuticals such as ^{99m}Tc-labeled *N*-substituted iminodiacetic acids (HIDA, DIDA, DISIDA, etc.) are rapidly extracted from the blood and are excreted into the biliary tree in high concentration even in the presence of mild to moderate serum bilirubin elevations. Failure to image the gallbladder in the presence of biliary ductal visualization may indicate cystic duct obstruction, acute or chronic cholecystitis, or surgical absence of the organ. Such scans have their greatest application in the diagnosis of acute cholecystitis.

Symptoms of gallstone disease Gallstones usually produce symptoms by causing inflammation or obstruction following their migration into the cystic duct or common bile duct. The most specific and characteristic symptom of gallstone disease is biliary colic. Obstruction of the cystic duct or common bile duct by a stone produces increased intraluminal pressure and distention of the viscus which cannot be relieved by repetitive biliary contractions. The resultant visceral pain is characteristically a severe, steady aching or pressure in the epigastrium or right upper quadrant of the abdomen with frequent radiation to the interscapular area, right scapula, or shoulder.

Biliary colic begins quite suddenly and may persist with severe intensity for 1 to 4 h, subsiding gradually or rapidly. An episode of biliary pain is sometimes followed by a residual mild ache or soreness in the right upper quadrant which may persist for 24 h or so. Nausea and vomiting frequently accompany episodes of biliary colic, and mild elevations of serum bilirubin (not exceeding 5 mg/dL) occur in 25 percent of patients. Persistence of a high serum bilirubin level suggests common duct stones. Fever or chills (rigors) with biliary colic usually imply an underlying complication, i.e., cholecystitis, pancreatitis, or cholangitis. Complaints of vague epigastric fullness, dyspepsia, eructation, or flatulence, especially following a fatty meal, should not be confused with biliary colic. Such symptoms are frequently elicited from patients with gallstone disease but are not specific for biliary calculi. Biliary colic may be precipitated by eating a fatty meal, by consumption of a large meal following a period of prolonged fasting, or by eating a normal meal.

Natural history of gallstones Gallstone disease discovered in an asymptomatic patient or in a patient whose symptoms are not referable to cholelithiasis is a common clinical problem. The natural history of "silent" or asymptomatic gallstones has occasioned much debate. In contrast to previous reports, a study of predominantly male silent gallstone patients suggests that the cumulative risk for the development of symptoms or complications requiring surgery is relatively low—10 percent at 5 years, 15 percent at 10 years, and 18 percent at 15 years. Patients remaining asymptomatic for 15 years were found to be unlikely to develop symptoms during further follow-up, and most patients who did develop complications from their gallstones experienced *prior* warning symptoms.

Complications requiring cholecystectomy appear to be much more common in gallstone patients who have developed symptoms of biliary colic. Patients found to have gallstones at a young age are more likely to develop symptoms from cholelithiasis than are patients older than 60 years at the time of initial diagnosis. Patients with diabetes mellitus and gallstones may be somewhat more susceptible to septic complications, but the magnitude of risk of septic biliary complications in diabetic patients is incompletely defined. In addition, asymptomatic gallstone patients with nonvisualization of the gall-

TABLE 253-2 Diagnostic evaluation of the gallbladder

Procedure	Diagnostic advantages	Diagnostic limitations	Comment

Plain abdominal x-ray	Low cost
	Readily available
		Relatively low yield
		?Contraindicated in pregnancy
			Pathognomonic findings in:
			  Calcified gallstones
			  Limey bile, porcelain GB
			  Emphysematous cholecystitis
			  Gallstone ileus

Oral cholecystogram (OCG)	Low cost
	Readily available
	Accurate identification of gallstones (90–95%)
	Identification of GB anomalies, hyperplastic cholecystoses
	Identification of chronic GB disease after nonvisualization on double dose
		?Contraindicated in pregnancy
		?Contraindicated with history of reaction to iodinated contrast
		Nonvisualization with:
		  Serum bilirubin >2–4 mg/dL
		  Failure to ingest or absorb tablets
		  Impaired hepatic excretion
		Very small stones may be undetected
		More time consuming than GBUS
			Procedure of choice in identification of gallstones if diagnostic limitations prevent GBUS

Gallbladder ultrasound (GBUS)	Rapid Accurate identification of gallstones (>95%) Simultaneous scanning of GB, liver, bile ducts, pancreas "Real-time" scanning allows assessment of GB volume, contractility Not limited by jaundice, pregnancy May detect very small stones	Bowel gas Massive obesity Ascites Recent barium study	Procedure of choice for detection of stones
Radioisotope scans (HIDA, DISIDA, etc.)	Accurate identification of cystic duct obstruction Simultaneous assessment of bile ducts	?Contraindicated in pregnancy Serum bilirubin >6–12 mg/dL Cholecystogram of low resolution	Indicated for confirmation of suspected cholecystitis

bladder on OCG appear to have an increased tendency to develop symptoms and complications.

Treatment of gallstones SURGICAL THERAPY   Although the management of "silent" gallstones remains controversial, the risk of developing symptoms or complications requiring surgery is quite small (in the range of 1 to 2 percent per year) in most asymptomatic gallstone patients. Thus, a recommendation for prophylactic cholecystectomy in a patient with gallstones should probably be based on assessment of three factors: (1) the presence of symptoms which are frequent enough or severe enough to interfere with the patient's general routine; (2) the presence of a prior complication of gallstone disease, i.e., history of acute cholecystitis, pancreatitis, gallstone fistula, etc.; or (3) the presence of an underlying condition predisposing the patient to increased risk of gallstone complications (e.g., calcified or porcelain gallbladder, cholesterolosis, adenomyomatosis, nonvisualizing gallbladder on oral cholecystography, and/or a previous attack of acute cholecystitis regardless of current symptomatic status). Patients with very large gallstones (over 2 cm in diameter) and patients having gallstones in a congenitally anomalous gallbladder might also be considered for prophylactic cholecystectomy. Although age under 50 years is a worrisome factor in asymptomatic gallstone patients, few authorities would now recommend routine cholecystectomy in all young patients with silent stones.

MEDICAL THERAPY—GALLSTONE DISSOLUTION   Treatment with oral chenodeoxycholic acid (CDCA, chenic acid) or its 7β-epimer, ursodeoxycholic acid (UDCA), to dissolve cholesterol or mixed

FIGURE 253-2 *Examples of ultrasound and radiologic studies of the biliary tract. A. An ultrasound study showing a distended gallbladder containing a single large stone (arrow) which casts an acoustic shadow. B. Endoscopic retrograde cholangiopancreatogram (ERCP) showing normal biliary tract anatomy. In addition to the endoscope and large vertical gallbladder filled with contrast dye, the common hepatic duct (chd), common bile duct (cbd), and pancreatic duct (pd) are shown. The arrow points to the ampulla of Vater. C. Percutaneous transhepatic cholangiogram (PTHC) showing choledocholithiasis. The biliary tract is dilatated and contains multiple radiolucent calculi (small arrows). The dilatation is due to obstruction by a large stone in the distal portion of the duct (large arrow). D. ERCP showing sclerosing cholangitis. The common bile duct is to the right of the endoscope. Following retrograde cholangiography, the common bile duct shows thickening of the wall with a narrow, beaded lumen typical of sclerosing cholangitis.*

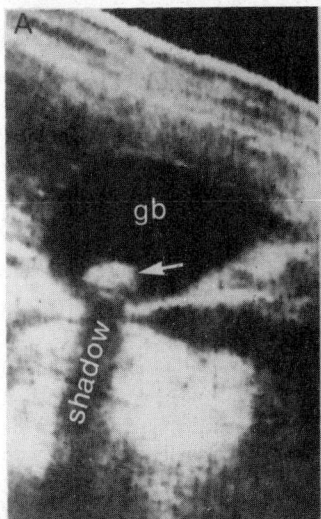
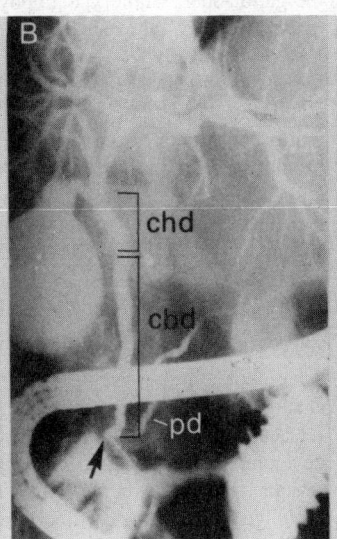
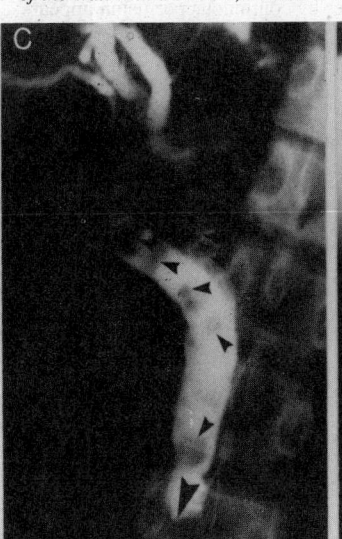
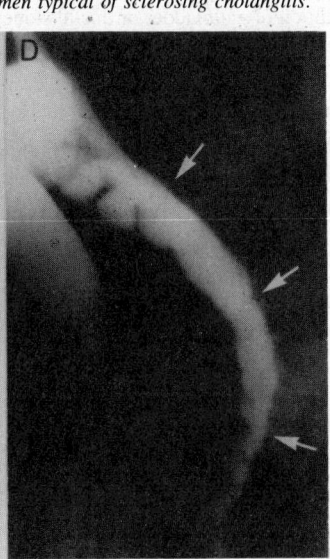

gallstones has resulted in complete or partial dissolution of such stones in approximately 50 to 60 percent of patients with radiolucent gallstones. Biliary secretion of these agents following oral bile acid administration alters the bile acid/cholesterol/lecithin ratio in bile (the lithogenic index). The major therapeutic effect of CDCA, however, is thought to be secondary to a decrease in HMG-CoA reductase activity, which in turn results in decreased hepatic cholesterol synthesis. UDCA administration appears to produce a lamellar liquid crystalline phase in bile which allows dispersion of cholesterol from stones by physical-chemical means.

Oral bile acid therapy is essentially ineffective in dissolving (1) pigment gallstones, which represent approximately 20 percent of radiolucent stones; (2) radiopaque or calcified gallstones; (3) gallstones greater than approximately 1.5 cm in diameter; and (4) gallstones in gallbladders poorly opacified following oral cholecystography. In patients with multiple, small, radiolucent gallstones in a functioning gallbladder, success rates for CDCA therapy of up to 80 percent have been reported if daily doses of 10 to 15 mg/kg of CDCA are used over a 1- to 3-year treatment period. However, lower daily doses of CDCA, i.e., 5 to 10 mg/kg, have resulted in much lower complete dissolution (5 to 15 percent) as well as lower partial dissolution rates (40 percent). Further, some massively obese patients may require doses as high as 20 to 25 mg/kg per day of CDCA to achieve cholesterol desaturation of bile. After successful dissolution of stones and withdrawal of CDCA treatment, *recurrence* of cholelithiasis is likely unless factors initially producing lithogenesis have been altered in the interim. Ultrasound appears to be more sensitive than oral cholecystography in following patients during and after stone dissolution therapy. The results of the U.S. National Cooperative Gallstone Study are summarized in Table 253-3.

Chenodeoxycholic acid therapy is usually associated with self-limited diarrhea in most patients given an optimal therapeutic dose. In addition, approximately 25 percent of patients treated with CDCA acid develop mild (two- to threefold) and transient (less than 6 months) elevations of serum aminotransferase levels. Although hepatic injury has been described, biopsy and liver function studies in humans have shown serious CDCA-related hepatotoxicity in less than 1 to 2 percent of patients.

Ursodeoxycholic acid is therapeutically effective at lower doses (5 to 10 mg/kg per day) than chenodeoxycholic acid and has not been associated with the relatively high incidence of diarrhea and serum aminotransferase elevations seen in CDCA-treated patients. On the other hand, UDCA treatment has been associated with calcification of previously uncalcified gallstones in more than 10 percent of patients.

Direct dissolution of gallstones within a period of hours using methyl tertiary butyl ether or other solvents through percutaneously placed biliary catheters has also been reported. Such solvent dissolution of gallbladder or ductal stones by continuous perfusion appears promising.

TABLE 253-3   Chenodeoxycholic acid (CDCA) and gallstone dissolution

RESULTS OF U.S. NATIONAL COOPERATIVE GALLSTONE STUDY

1 Patients—916 with radiolucent stones, treated 24 months
  a Placebo
  b Low-dose CDCA; 375 mg per day
  c High-dose CDCA; 750 mg per day
2 Results—best with high dose
  a Complete dissolution, 13.5%
  b Partial dissolution, 27.3%; complete plus partial, 40.8%
  c Best results—women, thin patients, small stones
3 Side effects
  a Mild diarrhea
  b Changes in hepatic structure, function; 3% clinically significant liver damage
  c Elevation (10%) of serum LDL cholesterol
4 Recurrence—likely when CDCA stopped

SOURCE: *Schoenfield et al.*

ACUTE AND CHRONIC CHOLECYSTITIS   Acute cholecystitis

Acute inflammation of the gallbladder wall usually follows obstruction of the cystic duct by a stone. Inflammatory response can be evoked by three factors: (1) *mechanical inflammation* produced by increased intraluminal pressure and distention with resulting ischemia of the gallbladder mucosa and wall; (2) *chemical inflammation* caused by the release of lysolecithin (due to the action of phospholipase on lecithin in bile) and other local tissue factors; and (3) *bacterial inflammation,* which may play a role in 50 to 85 percent of patients with acute cholecystitis. The organisms most frequently isolated by culture of gallbladder bile in these patients include *Escherichia coli, Klebsiella* species, group D *Streptococcus, Staphylococcus* species, and *Clostridium* species.

Acute cholecystitis often begins as an attack of biliary colic which progressively worsens. Approximately 60 to 70 percent of patients report having experienced prior attacks which resolved spontaneously. As the episode progresses, however, the pain of acute cholecystitis becomes more generalized in the right upper abdomen. As with biliary colic, the pain of cholecystitis may radiate to the interscapular area, right scapula, or shoulder. Peritoneal signs of inflammation such as increased pain with jarring or on deep respiration may be apparent. The patient is anorectic and often nauseated. Vomiting is relatively common and may produce symptoms and signs of vascular and extracellular volume depletion. Jaundice is unusual early in the course of acute cholecystitis but may occur when edematous inflammatory changes involve the bile ducts and surrounding lymph nodes.

A low-grade fever is characteristically present, but shaking chills or rigors are not uncommon. The right upper quadrant of the abdomen is almost invariably tender to palpation. An enlarged, tense gallbladder is palpable in one-quarter to one-half of patients. Deep inspiration or cough during subcostal palpation of the right upper quadrant usually produces increased pain and inspiratory arrest (Murphy's sign). A light blow delivered to the right subcostal area may elicit a marked increase in pain. Localized rebound tenderness in the right upper quadrant is common, as are abdominal distention and hypoactive bowel sounds from paralytic ileus, but generalized peritoneal signs and abdominal rigidity are usually absent unless perforation has occurred.

The diagnosis of acute cholecystitis is usually made on the basis of a characteristic history and physical examination. The triad of sudden onset of right upper quadrant tenderness, fever, and leukocytosis is highly suggestive. Typically, leukocytosis in the range of 10,000 to 15,000 cells per cubic millimeter with a left shift on differential count is found. The serum bilirubin is mildly elevated (less than 5 mg/dL) in 45 percent of patients, while 25 percent have modest elevations in serum aminotransferases (usually less than a fivefold elevation). The radionuclide (e.g., HIDA) biliary scan may be confirmatory if bile duct imaging is seen without visualization of the gallbladder. Cholecystography by oral or intravenous technique is almost always nonvisualizing.

Approximately 75 percent of patients treated medically have remission of acute symptoms within 2 to 7 days following hospitalization. In 25 percent, however, a complication of acute cholecystitis will occur despite conservative treatment (see below). In this setting, prompt surgical intervention is required. Of the 75 percent of patients with acute cholecystitis who undergo remission of symptoms, approximately one-quarter will experience a recurrence of cholecystitis within 1 year, and 60 percent will have at least one recurrent bout within 6 years. In view of the natural history of the disease, acute cholecystitis is best treated by early surgery whenever possible.

ACALCULOUS CHOLECYSTITIS   In 5 to 10 percent of patients with acute cholecystitis, calculi obstructing the cystic duct are not found at surgery. In over 50 percent of such cases an underlying explanation for acalculous inflammation is not found. An increased risk for the development of acalculous cholecystitis is especially associated with serious trauma or burns, with the postpartum period following prolonged labor, and with orthopedic and other nonbiliary major surgical operations in the postoperative period. Other precipitating factors include vasculitis, obstructing adenocarcinoma of the gallbladder, diabetes mellitus, torsion of the gallbladder, "unusual" bacterial infections of the gallbladder (e.g., *Leptospira, Streptococcus, Salmonella,* or *Vibrio cholerae*), and parasitic infestation of the gallbladder. Acalculous cholecystitis may also be seen with a variety of other systemic disease processes (sarcoidosis, cardiovascular disease, tuberculosis, syphilis, actinomycosis, etc.) and may possibly complicate periods of prolonged parenteral hyperalimentation.

Although the clinical manifestations of acalculous cholecystitis are indistinguishable from those of calculous cholecystitis, the setting of acute gallbladder inflammation complicating severe underlying illness is characteristic of acalculous disease. Ultrasound, CT scanning, or radionuclide examinations demonstrating a large, tense, static gallbladder without stones and with evidence of poor emptying over a prolonged period may be diagnostically useful in some cases. The complication rate for acalculous cholecystitis exceeds that for calculous cholecystitis. Successful management of acute acalculous cholecystitis appears to depend primarily upon early diagnosis and surgical intervention with meticulous attention to postoperative care.

EMPHYSEMATOUS CHOLECYSTITIS   So-called emphysematous cholecystitis is thought to begin with acute cholecystitis (calculous or acalculous) followed by ischemia or gangrene of the gallbladder wall and infection by gas-producing organisms. Bacteria most frequently cultured in this setting include anaerobes such as *Clostridium welchii,* or *perfringens,* and aerobes such as *E. coli.* This condition occurs most frequently in elderly men and in patients with diabetes mellitus. The clinical manifestations are essentially indistinguishable from those of nongaseous cholecystitis. The diagnosis is usually made on plain abdominal film by the finding of gas within the gallbladder lumen, dissecting within the gallbladder wall to form a gaseous ring, or in the pericholecystic tissues. The morbidity and mortality rates with emphysematous cholecystitis are considerable. Prompt surgical intervention coupled with appropriate antibiotics is mandatory.

Chronic cholecystitis   Chronic inflammation of the gallbladder wall is almost always associated with the presence of gallstones and is thought to result from repeated bouts of subacute or acute cholecystitis or from persistent mechanical irritation of the gallbladder wall. The presence of bacteria in the bile occurs in more than one-quarter of patients with chronic cholecystitis. Although the presence of infected bile in a patient with *chronic* cholecystitis undergoing elective cholecystectomy probably adds little to the operative risk, intraoperative Gram's staining and routine culturing of bile has been advocated to identify those patients whose gallbladder is colonized with *Clostridium* species. Appropriate antibiotics intra- and postoperatively are recommended in such patients because colonization with these organisms may be associated with devastating septic complications following surgery. Chronic cholecystitis may remain asymptomatic for years, may progress to symptomatic gallbladder disease or to acute cholecystitis, or may present with one of the complications detailed below.

Complications of cholecystitis   EMPYEMA AND HYDROPS   Empyema of the gallbladder usually results from progression of acute cholecystitis with persistent cystic duct obstruction to superinfection of the stagnant bile with a pus-forming bacterial organism. The clinical picture resembles that of cholangitis with high fever, severe right upper quadrant pain, marked leukocytosis, and, often, prostration. Empyema of the gallbladder carries a high risk of gram-negative sepsis and/or perforation. Emergency surgical intervention with proper antibiotic coverage is required as soon as the diagnosis is suspected.

Hydrops or mucocele of the gallbladder may also result from prolonged obstruction of the cystic duct, usually by a large solitary calculus. In this instance, the obstructed gallbladder lumen is progressively distended, over a period of time, by mucus (mucocele) or by a clear transudate (hydrops) produced by mucosal epithelial cells. A visible, easily palpable, nontender mass often extending from the right upper quadrant into the right iliac fossa may be found on physical examination. The patient with hydrops of the gallbladder

frequently remains asymptomatic, although chronic right upper quadrant pain also may occur. Cholecystectomy is indicated since empyema, perforation, or gangrene may complicate the condition.

GANGRENE AND PERFORATION   Gangrene of the gallbladder results from ischemia of the wall and patchy or complete tissue necrosis. Underlying conditions often include marked distention of the gallbladder, vasculitis, diabetes mellitus, empyema, or torsion resulting in arterial occlusion. Gangrene usually predisposes to perforation of the gallbladder, but perforation may also occur in chronic cholecystitis without premonitory warning symptoms. *Localized perforations* are usually contained by the omentum or by adhesions produced by recurrent inflammation of the gallbladder. Bacterial superinfection of the walled-off gallbladder contents results in abscess formation. Most patients are best treated with cholecystectomy, but some seriously ill patients may be managed with cholecystostomy and drainage of the abscess. *Free perforation* is less common but is associated with a mortality rate of approximately 30 percent. Such patients may experience a sudden transient relief of right upper quadrant pain as the distended gallbladder decompresses; this is followed by signs of generalized peritonitis.

FISTULA FORMATION AND GALLSTONE ILEUS   *Fistulization* into an adjacent organ adherent to the gallbladder wall may result from inflammation and adhesion formation. Fistulas into the duodenum are most common, followed in frequency by those involving the hepatic flexure of the colon, stomach or jejunum, abdominal wall, and renal pelvis. Clinically "silent" biliary-enteric fistulas occurring as a complication of chronic cholecystitis have been found in up to 5 percent of patients undergoing cholecystectomy. Asymptomatic cholecystoenteric fistulas may sometimes be diagnosed by finding gas in the biliary tree on plain abdominal films. Barium contrast studies or endoscopy of the upper gastrointestinal tract or colon may demonstrate the fistula, but oral cholecystography will almost never result in opacification of either the gallbladder or the fistulous tract. Treatment in the symptomatic patient usually consists of cholecystectomy, common bile duct exploration, and closure of the fistulous tract.

Gallstone ileus refers to mechanical intestinal obstruction resulting from the passage of a large gallstone into the bowel lumen. The stone customarily enters the duodenum through a cholecystoenteric fistula at that level. The site of obstruction by the impacted gallstone is usually at the ileocecal valve, provided that the more proximal small bowel is of normal caliber. The majority of patients do not give a history of either prior biliary tract symptoms or complaints suggestive of acute cholecystitis or fistulization. Large stones over 2.5 cm in diameter are thought to predispose to fistula formation by gradual erosion through the gallbladder fundus. Diagnostic confirmation may occasionally be found on the plain abdominal film (e.g., small-intestinal obstruction with gas in the biliary tree and a calcified, ectopic gallstone) or following an upper gastrointestinal series (cholecystoduodenal fistula with small-bowel obstruction at the ileocecal valve). Early laparotomy is indicated with enterolithotomy and careful palpation of the more proximal small bowel and gallbladder to exclude other stones.

LIMEY (MILK OF CALCIUM) BILE AND PORCELAIN GALLBLADDER   Calcium salts may be secreted into the lumen of the gallbladder in sufficient concentration to produce calcium precipitation and diffuse, hazy opacification of bile or a layering effect on plain abdominal roentgenography. This so-called limey bile or milk of calcium bile is usually clinically innocuous, but cholecystectomy is recommended since limey bile most often occurs in an hydropic gallbladder. In the entity called porcelain gallbladder, calcium salt deposition within the wall of a chronically inflamed gallbladder may be detected on the plain abdominal film. Cholecystectomy is advised in all patients with porcelain gallbladder since in a high percentage of cases this finding appears to be associated with the development of carcinoma of the gallbladder.

Treatment of cholecystitis MEDICAL THERAPY   Although surgical intervention remains the mainstay of therapy for acute cholecystitis and its complications, a period of in-hospital stabilization may be required before cholecystectomy. Oral intake is eliminated, nasogastric suction is initiated, and extracellular volume depletion and electrolyte abnormalities are repaired. Meperidine or pentazocine are usually employed for analgesia since they may produce less spasm of the sphincter of Oddi than drugs such as morphine. Intravenous antibiotic therapy is usually indicated in patients with severe acute cholecystitis even though bacterial superinfection of bile may not have occurred in the early stages of the inflammatory process. Postoperative complications of wound infection, abscess formation, or sepsis are reduced in antibiotic-treated patients. Effective single-agent antibiotics include ampicillin, cephalosporins, chloramphenicol, or aminoglycosides, but in diabetic or debilitated patients and in those with signs of gram-negative sepsis, combination antibiotic treatment may be preferable (see also Chap. 92).

SURGICAL THERAPY   The optimal timing of surgical intervention in patients with acute cholecystitis remains controversial. Urgent (emergency) cholecystectomy or cholecystostomy is probably appropriate in most patients in whom a complication of acute cholecystitis such as empyema, emphysematous cholecystitis, or perforation is suspected or confirmed. In uncomplicated cases of acute cholecystitis up to 30 percent of patients fail to resolve their symptoms on appropriate medical therapy, and progression of the attack or a supervening complication leads to the performance of early operation (within 24 to 72 h). The technical complications of surgery are not increased in patients undergoing early as opposed to delayed cholecystectomy. Delayed surgical intervention is probably best reserved for (1) patients in whom the overall medical condition imposes an unacceptable risk for early surgery, and (2) cases in which the diagnosis of acute cholecystitis is in doubt. Early cholecystectomy is the treatment of choice for most patients with acute cholecystitis. Mortality figures for emergency cholecystectomy in most centers approach 3 percent, while the mortality risk for elective or early cholecystectomy approximates 0.5 percent in patients under age 60. Of course, the operative risks increase with age-related diseases of other organ systems and with the presence of long-term or short-term complications of gallbladder disease. Seriously ill or debilitated patients with cholecystitis may be managed with cholecystostomy and tube drainage of the gallbladder. Elective cholecystectomy may then be done at a later date.

Postcholecystectomy complications   Early complications following cholecystectomy include atelectasis and other pulmonary disorders, abscess formation (often subphrenic), external or internal hemorrhage, biliary-enteric fistula, and bile leaks. Jaundice may indicate absorption of bile from an intraabdominal collection following a biliary leak, or mechanical obstruction of the common bile duct by retained calculi, intraductal blood clots, or extrinsic compression. Routine performance of intraoperative cholangiography during cholecystectomy has helped to reduce the incidence of these early complications.

Overall, cholecystectomy is a very successful operation which provides total or near-total relief of presurgical symptoms in 75 to 90 percent of patients. The most common cause of persistent postcholecystectomy symptoms is an overlooked extrabiliary disorder (e.g., reflux esophagitis, peptic ulceration, postgastrectomy syndrome, pancreatitis, or irritable bowel syndrome). In a small percentage of patients, however, a disorder of the extrahepatic bile ducts may result in persistent symptomatology. These so-called postcholecystectomy syndromes may be due to (1) biliary strictures, (2) retained biliary calculi, (3) cystic duct stump syndrome, (4) stenosis or dyskinesia of the sphincter of Oddi, or (5) bile salt–induced diarrhea or gastritis.

CYSTIC DUCT STUMP SYNDROME   In the absence of cholangiographically demonstrable retained stones, symptoms resembling biliary colic or cholecystitis in the postcholecystectomy patient have frequently been attributed to disease in a long (> 1 cm) cystic duct remnant (cystic duct stump syndrome). Careful analysis, however, reveals that postcholecystectomy complaints are attributable to other causes in almost all patients in whom the symptom complex was originally thought to result from the existence of a long cystic duct stump. Accordingly, considerable care should be taken to investigate the possible role of other factors in the production of postcholecystectomy symptoms before attributing them to cystic duct stump syndrome.

BILE SALT–INDUCED CATHARSIS AND GASTRITIS   Postcholecystectomy patients may develop symptoms and signs of gastritis which has been attributed to duodenogastric reflux of bile. However, firm data linking an increased incidence of bile gastritis with surgical removal of the gallbladder are lacking. Similarly, the occurrence of cholestyramine-responsive diarrhea in a small number of patients following cholecystectomy has been attributed to an alteration of the enterohepatic circulation of bile acids induced or unmasked by removal of the gallbladder.

THE HYPERPLASTIC CHOLECYSTOSES   The term *hyperplastic cholecystoses* is used to denote a group of disorders of the gallbladder characterized by excessive proliferation of normal tissue components.

Adenomyomatosis is characterized by a benign proliferation of gallbladder surface epithelium with gland-like formations, extramural sinuses, transverse strictures, and/or fundal nodule (''adenoma'' or ''adenomyoma'') formation. Outpouchings of mucosa termed Rokitansky-Aschoff sinuses may be seen on oral cholecystography in conjunction with hyperconcentration of contrast medium. Characteristic dimpled filling defects may also be seen.

Cholesterolosis is characterized by abnormal deposition of lipid, especially cholesterol esters, in the lamina propria of the gallbladder wall. In its diffuse form (''strawberry gallbladder''), the gallbladder mucosa is brick red and speckled with bright yellow flecks of lipid. The localized form shows solitary or multiple ''cholesterol polyps'' studding the gallbladder wall. Cholesterol stones of the gallbladder are found in nearly half the cases. Cholecystectomy is indicated in both adenomyomatosis and cholesterolosis when symptomatic or when cholelithiasis is present.

CANCER OF THE GALLBLADDER   Most cancers of the gallbladder develop in conjunction with stones rather than polyps. Necropsy series show a prevalence of gallbladder cancer of 0.43 percent, rising to approximately 1 percent in patients with gallstones. In the United States, adenocarcinomas comprise the vast majority of the estimated 6500 new cases of gallbladder cancer diagnosed each year. The female/male ratio is 4:1 and the mean age at diagnosis is approximately 70 years. The clinical presentation is most often one of unremitting right upper quadrant pain associated with weight loss, jaundice, and a palpable right upper quadrant mass. Cholangitis may supervene. The gallbladder is rarely visualized on OCG, and preoperative diagnosis of the condition is rare. Once symptoms have appeared, spread of the tumor outside the gallbladder by direct extension or by lymphatic or hematogenous routes is almost invariable. Over 75 percent of gallbladder carcinomas are unresectable at the time of surgery, the exceptions being tumors discovered incidentally at laparotomy. The 1-year mortality rate for unresectable disease is approximately 95 percent, and only 5 percent of patients survive 5 years or more from the time of diagnosis. Radical operative resection does not appear to improve survival. Results of trials with radiation and chemotherapy of primary gallbladder cancer have also been disappointing (see Chap. 88).

DISEASES OF THE BILE DUCTS

CONGENITAL ANOMALIES   **Biliary atresia and hypoplasia**   Atretic and hypoplastic lesions of the extrahepatic and major intrahepatic bile ducts are the most common biliary anomalies of clinical relevance encountered in infancy. The clinical picture is one of severe obstructive jaundice during the first month of life, with pale stools. The diagnosis is confirmed by surgical exploration with operative cholangiography. Approximately 10 percent of cases of biliary atresia are treatable with Roux en Y choledochojejunostomy, with the Kasai procedure (hepatic portoenterostomy) being attempted in the remainder in an effort to restore some bile flow. Most patients, even those having successful biliary-enteric anastomoses, eventually develop chronic cholangitis, extensive hepatic fibrosis, and portal hypertension.

Choledochal cysts Cystic dilatation may involve the free portion of the common bile duct, i.e., choledochal cyst, or may present as diverticulum formation in the intraduodenal segment. In the latter situation chronic reflux of pancreatic juice into the biliary tree can produce inflammation and stenosis of the extrahepatic bile ducts leading to cholangitis or biliary obstruction. Because the process may be gradual, approximately 50 percent of patients present with onset of symptoms after age 10. The diagnosis may be made by ultrasound, abdominal computed tomography (CT), or cholangiography. Surgical treatment involves excision of the ''cyst'' and biliary-enteric anastomosis. Patients with choledochal cysts are at increased risk for the subsequent development of cholangiocarcinoma.

Congenital biliary ectasia Cystic dilatation of the intrahepatic bile ducts may involve either the major intrahepatic radicles (Caroli's disease) or the inter- and intralobular ducts (congenital hepatic fibrosis) or both. In Caroli's disease, clinical manifestations include recurrent cholangitis, abscess formation in and around the affected ducts, and, sometimes, gallstone formation within portions of ectatic intrahepatic biliary radicles. The CT scan and cholangiographic patterns are usually diagnostic, and treatment with ongoing antibiotic therapy is usually undertaken in an effort to limit the frequency and severity of recurrent bouts of cholangitis. Progression to secondary biliary cirrhosis with portal hypertension, amyloidosis, extrahepatic biliary obstruction, cholangiocarcinoma, or recurrent episodes of sepsis with hepatic abscess formation is common.

CHOLEDOCHOLITHIASIS Pathophysiology and clinical manifestations Passage of gallstones into the common bile duct occurs in approximately 10 to 15 percent of patients with cholelithiasis. The incidence of common duct stones increases with increasing age of the patient, so that up to 25 percent of elderly patients may have calculi in the common duct at the time of cholecystectomy. Undetected duct stones are left behind in approximately 1 to 5 percent of cholecystectomy patients. The overwhelming majority of bile duct stones are cholesterol or mixed stones formed in the gallbladder which then migrate into the extrahepatic biliary tree through the cystic duct. Primary calculi arising de novo in the ducts are usually pigment stones developing in patients with (1) chronic hemolytic diseases; (2) hepatobiliary parasitism or chronic, recurrent cholangitis; (3) congenital anomalies of the bile ducts (especially Caroli's disease); or (4) dilated, sclerosed, or strictured ducts. Common duct stones may remain asymptomatic for years, may pass spontaneously into the duodenum, or (most often) may present with biliary colic or a complication.

Complications CHOLANGITIS Cholangitis may be acute or chronic, and symptoms result from inflammation which usually requires at least partial obstruction to the flow of bile. Bacteria are present on bile culture in approximately 75 percent of patients with acute cholangitis early in the symptomatic course. The characteristic presentation of acute cholangitis involves biliary colic, jaundice, and spiking fevers with chills (Charcot's triad). Blood cultures are frequently positive and leukocytosis is typical. *Nonsuppurative* acute cholangitis is most common and may respond relatively rapidly to supportive measures and to treatment with antibiotics (see Chap. 92). In *suppurative* acute cholangitis, however, the presence of pus under pressure in a completely obstructed ductal system leads to symptoms of severe toxicity—mental confusion, bacteremia, and septic shock.

Response to antibiotics alone in this setting is relatively poor, multiple hepatic abscesses are often present, and the mortality rate approaches 100 percent unless prompt surgical correction of the obstructing lesion and drainage of infected bile is carried out.

OBSTRUCTIVE JAUNDICE Gradual obstruction of the common bile duct over a period of weeks or months usually leads to initial manifestations of jaundice or pruritus without associated symptoms of biliary colic or cholangitis. Painless jaundice may occur in patients with choledocholithiasis, but this manifestation is much more characteristic of biliary obstruction secondary to malignancy of the head of pancreas, bile ducts, or ampulla of Vater.

In patients whose obstruction is secondary to choledocholithiasis, associated chronic calculous cholecystitis is very common and the gallbladder in this setting may be relatively indistensible. The absence of a palpable gallbladder in most patients with biliary obstruction from duct stones is the basis for *Courvoisier's law*, i.e., that the presence of a palpably enlarged gallbladder suggests that the biliary obstruction is secondary to an underlying malignancy rather than to calculous disease. Biliary obstruction causes progressive dilatation of the intrahepatic bile ducts as intrabiliary pressures rise. Hepatic bile flow is suppressed, and regurgitation of conjugated bilirubin into the bloodstream leads to jaundice accompanied by dark urine (bilirubinuria) and light-colored (acholic) stools.

Common bile duct stones should be suspected in any patient with cholecystitis whose serum bilirubin level exceeds 5 mg/dL. The maximum bilirubin level is seldom over 15.0 mg/dL in patients with choledocholithiasis unless concomitant hepatic disease or another factor leading to marked hyperbilirubinemia exists. Serum bilirubin levels of 20mg/dL or more should suggest the possibility of neoplastic obstruction. The serum alkaline phosphatase level is almost always elevated in biliary obstruction. A rise in alkaline phosphatase often precedes clinical jaundice and may be the only abnormality in routine liver function tests. There may be a two- to tenfold elevation of serum aminotransferases, especially in association with acute obstruction. Following relief of the obstructing process, serum aminotransferase elevations usually return rapidly to normal, while the serum bilirubin level may take 1 to 2 weeks to return to normal. The alkaline phosphatase usually falls slowly, lagging behind the decrease in serum bilirubin.

PANCREATITIS The most common associated entity discovered in patients with nonalcoholic acute pancreatitis is biliary tract disease. Biochemical evidence of pancreatic inflammation complicates acute cholecystitis in 15 percent of cases and choledocholithiasis in over 30 percent, and the common factor appears to be the passage of gallstones through the common duct. Coexisting pancreatitis should be suspected in patients with symptoms of cholecystitis who develop (1) back pain or pain to the left of the abdominal midline, (2) prolonged vomiting with paralytic ileus, or (3) a pleural effusion, especially on the left side. Surgical treatment of gallstone disease is usually associated with resolution of the pancreatitis.

SECONDARY BILIARY CIRRHOSIS Secondary biliary cirrhosis may complicate prolonged or intermittent duct obstruction with or without recurrent cholangitis. Although this complication may be seen in patients with choledocholithiasis, it is more common in cases of prolonged obstruction from stricture or neoplasm. Once established, secondary biliary cirrhosis may be progressive even after correction of the obstructing process, and increasingly severe hepatic cirrhosis may lead to portal hypertension or to hepatic failure and death. Prolonged biliary obstruction may also be associated with clinically relevant deficiencies of the fat-soluble vitamins A, D, and K.

Diagnosis and treatment The diagnosis of choledocholithiasis is usually made by cholangiography (see Table 253-4), either preoperatively or intraoperatively at the time of cholecystectomy (see Fig. 255-2C). The incidence of coexisting common duct stones in patients with cholelithiasis is relatively high. Operative cholangiography should be performed routinely during surgical procedures on the

TABLE 253-4 Diagnostic evaluation of the bile ducts

Procedure	Diagnostic advantages	Diagnostic limitations	Contraindications	Complications	Comment
Hepatobiliary ultra-sound (HBUS)	Rapid Simultaneous scanning of GB, liver, bile ducts, pancreas Accurate identification of dilated bile ducts Not limited by jaundice, pregnancy Guidance for fine-needle biopsy	Bowel gas Massive obesity Ascites Barium Partial bile duct obstruction Poor visualization of distal CBD	None	None	Initial procedure of choice in investigating possible biliary obstruction
Computerized body tomography (CT)	Simultaneous scanning of GB, liver, bile ducts, pancreas Accurate identification of dilated bile ducts, masses Not limited by jaundice, gas, obesity, ascites High-resolution image Guidance for fine-needle biopsy	Extreme cachexia Movement artifact Ileus Partial bile duct obstruction High cost May not be readily available	Pregnancy	Reaction to iodinated contrast, if used	Indicated for evaluation of hepatic or pancreatic masses Procedure of choice in investigating possible biliary obstruction if diagnostic limitations prevent HBUS
Intravenous cholangiogram (IVC)	Noninvasive Readily available	Serum bilirubin >3 mg/dL Misses 40% of common duct stones Poor resolution even with tomography	Pregnancy History of reaction to iodinated contrast	Reaction to iodinated contrast	Few indications unless other cholangiography techniques not available or have failed
Percutaneous transhepatic cholangiogram (PTHC)	Extremely successful when bile ducts dilated Best visualization of proximal biliary tract Possible separate visualization of obstructed left ductal system Bile cytology/culture Percutaneous transhepatic drainage	Nondilated or sclerosed ducts	Pregnancy Uncorrectable coagulopathy Massive ascites ? Hepatic abscess	Bleeding Hemobilia Bile peritonitis Bacteremia, sepsis	Usually, initial cholangiogram of choice when bile ducts are dilated
Endoscopic retrograde cholangiopancreatogram (ERCP)	Simultaneous pancreatography Visualization/biopsy of ampulla and duodenum Best visualization of distal biliary tract Bile or pancreatic cytology Endoscopic sphincterotomy and stone removal ? Biliary manometry Not limited by ascites, coagulopathy, abscess	Gastroduodenal obstruction ? Roux en Y biliary-enteric anastomosis	Pregnancy ? Acute pancreatitis ? Severe cardiopulmonary disease	Pancreatitis Cholangitis, sepsis Infected pancreatic pseudocyst Perforation (rare) Hypoxemia, aspiration	Cholangiogram of choice in: Absence of dilated ducts ? Pancreatic, ampullary or gastroduodenal disease Prior biliary surgery PTHC contraindicated or failed Endoscopic sphincterotomy a treatment possibility

biliary tract. Preoperative indications for common duct exploration include (1) cholangiographic demonstration of ductal stones, (2) jaundice or cholangitis preceding operation, (3) a history of gallstone-related pancreatitis, and (4) cholangiographic evidence of a markedly enlarged common bile duct. Operative indications for exploration of the duct include (1) manual palpation of stones in the common bile duct, (2) positive intraoperative cholangiogram, (3) enlargement of the common bile duct or cystic duct at operation, (4) multiple small stones or "sand" in the gallbladder, and (5) a gallbladder empty of stones at surgery in a patient with previously documented gallstones.

In most cases of choledocholithiasis, the treatment of choice is cholecystectomy with choledocholithotomy and T-tube drainage of the bile ducts. A T-tube cholangiogram is usually performed prior to T-tube removal on or before the tenth postoperative day. Retained calculi seen on T-tube cholangiography may be removed percutaneously by placement of a steerable basket catheter under radiographic guidance through the matured T-tube sinus tract. Endoscopic sphincterotomy followed by spontaneous or basket stone extraction is an additional nonsurgical alternative in the management of patients with common duct stones, especially in elderly or poor-risk patients.

TRAUMA, STRICTURES, AND HEMOBILIA Benign strictures of the extrahepatic bile ducts result from surgical trauma in approximately 95 percent of cases and occur in about 1 in 500 cholecystectomies. Strictures may present with bile leak or abscess formation in the immediate postoperative period or with biliary obstruction or cholan-

gitis as long as 2 years or more following the inciting trauma. The diagnosis is established by percutaneous or endoscopic cholangiography. Successful operative correction by a skillful surgeon with duct-to-bowel anastomosis is usually possible, although mortality rates from surgical complications, recurrent cholangitis, or secondary biliary cirrhosis are high.

Hemobilia may follow traumatic or operative injury to the liver or bile ducts, intraductal rupture of a hepatic abscess or aneurysm of the hepatic artery, biliary or hepatic tumor hemorrhage, or mechanical complications of choledocholithiasis or hepatobiliary parasitism. Diagnostic procedures such as liver biopsy, percutaneous transhepatic cholangiography (PTHC), and transhepatic biliary drainage catheter placement may also be complicated by hemobilia. Patients often present with a classic triad of biliary colic, obstructive jaundice, and melena or occult blood in the stools. The diagnosis is sometimes made by cholangiographic evidence of blood clot in the biliary tree, but selective angiographic verification may be required. Although minor episodes of hemobilia may resolve without operative intervention, surgical ligation of the bleeding vessel is frequently required.

EXTRINSIC COMPRESSION OF THE BILE DUCTS Partial or complete biliary obstruction may sometimes be produced by extrinsic compression of the ducts. The most common cause of this form of obstructive jaundice is carcinoma of the head of the pancreas. Biliary obstruction may also occur as a complication of either acute or chronic pancreatitis or involvement of lymph nodes in the porta hepatis by lymphoma or metastatic carcinoma. The latter should be distinguished from cholestasis resulting from massive replacement of the liver by tumor.

HEPATOBILIARY PARASITISM Infestation of the biliary tract by adult helminths or their ova may produce a chronic, recurrent pyogenic cholangitis with or without multiple hepatic abscesses, ductal stones, or biliary obstruction. This condition is relatively rare but does occur in inhabitants of southern China and elsewhere in southeast Asia. The organisms most commonly involved are trematodes or flukes, including *Clonorchis sinensis, Opisthorchis viverrini* or *felineus,* and *Fasciola hepatica.* The biliary tract may also be involved by intraductal migration of adult *Ascaris lumbricoides* from the duodenum or by intrabiliary rupture of hydatid cysts of the liver produced by *Echinococcus* species. The diagnosis is made by cholangiography and the presence of characteristic ova on stool examination. When obstruction is present, the treatment of choice is laparotomy under antibiotic coverage, with common duct exploration and a biliary drainage procedure. It should be emphasized that in the orient, one also sees cholangiohepatitis associated with pigment lithiasis, which may, in fact, be more common than cholangitis due to parasites.

SCLEROSING CHOLANGITIS Primary or idiopathic sclerosing cholangitis is a disorder characterized by a progressive, inflammatory, sclerosing and obliterative process affecting the extrahepatic and, often, the intrahepatic bile ducts. The lesion may appear as an isolated entity or may occur in association with inflammatory bowel disease, especially ulcerative colitis, or with multifocal fibrosclerosis syndromes such as retroperitoneal, mediastinal, and/or periureteral fibrosis, Riedel's struma, or pseudotumor of the orbit. Secondary sclerosing cholangitis may occur as a long-term complication of choledocholithiasis, cholangiocarcinoma, operative or traumatic biliary injury, or contiguous inflammatory processes.

Patients with sclerosing cholangitis often present with signs and symptoms of chronic or intermittent biliary obstruction: jaundice, pruritus, right upper quadrant abdominal pain, or acute cholangitis. Late in the course, complete biliary obstruction, secondary biliary cirrhosis, hepatic failure, or portal hypertension with bleeding varices may occur. The diagnosis is usually established by finding thickened ducts with narrow, beaded lumina on cholangiography (see Fig. 253-2D). Endoscopic retrograde cholangiopancreatogram (ERCP) is probably the cholangiographic technique of choice in suspected cases since intrahepatic ductal involvement may make PTHC difficult or impossible. When a diagnosis of sclerosing cholangitis has been established, a search for associated diseases, especially for chronic inflammatory bowel disease, should be carried out.

Therapy with cholestyramine may help control symptoms of pruritus, and antibiotics are useful when cholangitis complicates the clinical picture. Vitamin D and calcium supplementation may help prevent the loss of bone mass frequently seen in patients with chronic cholestasis. Corticosteroids have not been shown to be efficacious. In cases where complete or high-grade biliary obstruction has occurred, surgical intervention may be appropriate. Efforts at biliary-enteric anastomosis or stent placement may, however, be complicated by recurrent cholangitis and further progression of the stenosing process. The role of colectomy in patients with sclerosing cholangitis complicating chronic ulcerative colitis is uncertain. The prognosis is unfavorable, with a mean survival of 4 to 10 years following the diagnosis, regardless of therapy.

CHOLANGIOCARCINOMA Benign tumors of the extrahepatic bile ducts are extremely rare causes of mechanical biliary obstruction. The majority of these are papillomas, adenomas, or cystadenomas which present with obstructive jaundice or hemobilia. Adenocarcinoma of the extrahepatic ducts is relatively more common. There is a slight male preponderance (60 percent), and the peak age incidence is in the fifth to seventh decades. Apparent predisposing factors include (1) some chronic hepatobiliary parasitic infestations, (2) congenital anomalies with ectatic ducts, (3) sclerosing cholangitis

and chronic ulcerative colitis, and (4) occupational exposure to possible biliary tract carcinogens (workers in rubber or automotive plants). Cholelithiasis is not clearly associated with cholangiocarcinoma as a predisposing factor. The lesions may be diffuse or nodular; the latter often arise at the confluence of the hepatic ducts (Klatskin tumors).

Patients with cholangiocarcinoma usually present with biliary obstruction, painless jaundice, pruritus, weight loss, and acholic stools. A deep-seated, vaguely localized right upper quadrant pain may be an associated complaint. Hepatomegaly and a palpable, distended gallbladder are frequent accompanying signs. Fever is unusual unless associated with ascending cholangitis. Because the obstructing process is gradual, the cholangiocarcinoma is often far advanced by the time it presents clinically. The diagnosis is most frequently made by cholangiography following ultrasound demonstration of dilated intrahepatic bile ducts. Any focal strictures of the bile ducts should probably be considered malignant until proved otherwise. Long-term palliation of the tumor is possible in some cases when radiation and/or chemotherapy are combined with palliative drainage of the biliary tree.

PAPILLARY STENOSIS AND BILIARY DYSKINESIA Symptoms of biliary colic accompanied by signs of recurrent, intermittent biliary obstruction may occasionally be produced by dysfunction of the sphincter of Oddi. Papillary stenosis is thought to result from acute or chronic inflammation of the papilla of Vater or from glandular hyperplasia of the papillary segment. Criteria for the diagnosis of papillary stenosis are highly debatable, and preoperative identification of the lesion may be extremely difficult except by ERCP with manometric assessment of the sphincter of Oddi. Endoscopic, cholangiographic, and manometric findings during ERCP may suggest the diagnosis. Intraoperative palpation of the ampulla with operative cholangiography, probing of the sphincter, and/or operative manometry may be required for attempted confirmation in strongly suspected cases. Treatment consists of endoscopic or surgical sphincteroplasty to ensure wide patency of the distal portions of both the bile and pancreatic ducts.

Criteria for diagnosing dyskinesia of the sphincter of Oddi are even more controversial than those of papillary stenosis. Proposed mechanisms include spasm of the sphincter, denervation sensitivity resulting in hypertonicity, and abnormalities of the sequencing or frequency rates of sphincteric contraction waves. When thorough evaluation has failed to demonstrate another cause for the pain, and when cholangiographic and manometric criteria suggest a diagnosis of biliary dyskinesia, medical treatment with nitrites or anticholinergics to attempt pharmacologic relaxation of the sphincter has been proposed. Endoscopic sphincterotomy or surgical sphincteroplasty may be indicated in patients who fail to respond to a 2- to 3-week trial of medical therapy.

CARCINOMA OF THE PAPILLA OF VATER The ampulla of Vater may be involved by extension of tumor arising elsewhere in the duodenum or may itself be the primary site of origin of sarcomas, carcinoid tumors, or adenocarcinomas. Papillary adenocarcinomas are associated with slow growth and a more favorable clinical prognosis than diffuse, infiltrative cancers of the ampulla, which are more frequently widely invasive. The presenting clinical manifestation is usually obstructive jaundice. ERCP is probably the preferred diagnostic technique when ampullary carcinoma is suspected, because it allows for direct endoscopic inspection and biopsy of the ampulla as well as for performance of pancreatography to exclude a diagnosis of pancreatic malignancy. Cancer of the papilla is usually treated by wide, often radical, surgical excision. Lymph node or other metastases are present at the time of surgery in approximately 20 percent of cases, and the 5-year survival rate following surgical therapy in this group is only 5 to 10 percent. In the absence of metastases, however, radical pancreaticoduodenectomy (Whipple procedure) is associated with 5-year survival rates as high as 40 percent, and several long-term survivors have been reported.

REFERENCES

BACHRACH WH, HOFMANN AF: Ursodeoxycholic acid in the treatment of cholesterol cholelithiasis. Dig Dis Sci 27:737, 1982

BENNION LJ, GRUNDY SM: Risk factors for the development of cholelithiasis in man. N Engl J Med 299:1161, 1978

BISMUTH H, MALT RA: Carcinoma of the biliary tract. N Engl J Med 301:704, 1979

FERRUCCI JT JR, MUELLER PR: Interventional radiology of the biliary tract. Gastroenterology 82:974, 1982

GRACIE WA, RANSOHOFF DF: The natural history of silent gallstones. The innocent gallstone is not a myth. N Engl J Med 307:798, 1982

HOLZBACH RT et al: Biliary proteins: Unique inhibitors of cholesterol crystal nucleation in human gallbladder bile. J Clin Invest 72:35, 1984

LEVY PF et al: Human gallbladder mucin accelerates nucleation of cholesterol in artifical bile. Gastroenterology 87:270, 1984

MCPHEE MS, SCHAPIRO RH: Biliary obstruction: Current approaches to diagnosis and treatment, in Update I: Harrison's Principles of Internal Medicine, KJ Isselbacher et al (eds). New York, McGraw-Hill, 1981, pp 1–22

MESSIN B et al: Does total parenteral nutrition induce gallbladder sludge formation and lithiasis? Gastroenterology 84:1012, 1983

PALME KR, HOFMANN AF: Intraductal monooctanoin for the direct dissolution of bile duct stones: Experience in 343 patients. Gut 27:196, 1986

PARK YH et al: Dissolution of human cholesterol gallstones in simulated chenodeoxycholate-rich and ursodeoxycholate-rich bile: An in vitro study of dissolution rates and mechanisms. Gastroenterology 87:150, 1984

SCHOENFIELD LS et al: Chenodiol (chenodeoxycholic acid) for dissolution of gallstones: The National Cooperative Gallstone Study. A controlled trial of efficacy and safety. Ann Intern Med 95:257, 1981

SHAPERO TF: Discrepancy between ultrasound and oral cholecystography in assessment of gallstone dissolution. Hepalology 2:587, 1982

SOLOWAY RD et al: Pigment gallstones. Gastroenterology 72:167, 1977

WIESNER RH et al: Comparison of clinicopathologic features of primary sclerosing cholangitis and primary biliary cirrhosis. Gastroenterology 88:108, 1985

section 3   Disorders of the pancreas

254   APPROACH TO THE PATIENT WITH PANCREATIC DISEASE

NORTON J. GREENBERGER / PHILLIP P. TOSKES

GENERAL CONSIDERATIONS

Inflammatory disease of the pancreas may be acute or chronic. Although good data exist concerning the frequency of acute pancreatitis (about 5000 new cases per year in the United States with a mortality rate of about 10 percent), the number of patients who suffer with relapsing pancreatitis or chronic pancreatitis is largely undefined. The relative inaccessibility of the pancreas to direct examination and the nonspecificity of the abdominal pain associated with pancreatitis make the diagnosis of pancreatitis difficult and usually dependent on elevation of blood amylase levels. Many patients with chronic pancreatitis do not have elevated blood amylase levels. Some patients with chronic pancreatitis develop signs and symptoms of pancreatic exocrine insufficiency, and thus objective evidence for pancreatic disease can be demonstrated. However, greater than 90 percent of the pancreas must be damaged before maldigestion of fat and protein is manifested. Obviously there is a very large reservoir of pancreatic exocrine function, and the signs and symptoms usually associated with exocrine insufficiency are late manifestations, depending on virtually complete destruction of the gland. Even the secretin stimulation test, which is the most sensitive method of assessing pancreatic exocrine function, is probably abnormal only when greater than 70 percent of exocrine function has been lost. Thus, the number of patients who have subclinical exocrine dysfunction (i.e., less than 90 percent loss of function) is unknown.

The clinical manifestations of acute and chronic pancreatitis and pancreatic insufficiency are protean. Thus, patients may present with hyperlipidemia, vitamin B_{12} malabsorption, hypercalcemia, hypocalcemia, hyperglycemia, ascites, pleural effusions, and chronic abdominal pain with normal amylase levels. Indeed, if the clinician considers pancreatitis as a possible diagnosis only when presented with a patient having classic symptoms (i.e., severe, constant epigastric pain that radiates through to the back, along with an elevated blood amylase level), only a minority of the patients with pancreatitis will be correctly diagnosed.

As emphasized in Chap. 255, the etiologies as well as the clinical manifestations are quite varied. Although it is well appreciated that pancreatitis is frequently secondary to alcohol abuse and biliary tract disease, pancreatitis is also caused by drugs, trauma, and viral infections, and is associated with metabolic and connective tissue disorders. In addition, in approximately 25 percent of patients with chronic pancreatitis, the etiology is obscure.

The incidence of pancreatic cancer in the United States has increased threefold since 1930. Associations have been made with cigarette smoking, exposure to some industrial carcinogens, and diabetes. The outlook for early diagnosis and effective treatment remains dismal.

Cystic fibrosis is usually considered a disease of childhood. However, an appreciable number of children with this disease reach adulthood because of more effective therapy for pulmonary complications. Eighty-five percent of patients with cystic fibrosis have pancreatic exocrine insufficiency; in some, pancreatic impairment may represent the primary clinical defect. This disease, in which the metabolic defect appears to be related to defective anion permeability, affects many organ systems in addition to the gastrointestinal tract.

TESTS USEFUL IN THE DIAGNOSIS OF PANCREATIC DISEASE

Several tests have proved of value in the evaluation of pancreatic exocrine function. Examples of specific tests and usefulness in the diagnosis of acute and chronic pancreatitis are summarized in Table 254-1.

PANCREATIC ENZYMES IN BODY FLUIDS   The serum amylase is widely used as a screening test for acute pancreatitis in the patient with acute abdominal or back pain. A value greater than 150 Somogyi units per deciliter should raise the question of acute pancreatitis. Levels greater than 300 units make the diagnosis more likely, and values greater than three times normal virtually clinch the diagnosis if gut perforation or infarction is excluded. In acute pancreatitis the serum amylase is usually elevated within 24 h and remains so for 1 to 3 days. Levels return to normal within 3 to 5 days unless there is extensive pancreatic necrosis, incomplete ductal obstruction, or pseudocyst formation. Approximately 70 to 75 percent of patients with acute pancreatitis will have an elevated serum amylase. Normal values, however, may occur if (1) there is a delay (2 to 5 days) in obtaining blood samples, (2) the underlying disorder is chronic pancreatitis rather than acute pancreatitis, and (3) hypertriglyceridemia is present. Patients with hypertriglyceridemia and proven pancreatitis

TABLE 254-1 Tests useful in the diagnosis of acute and chronic pancreatitis and pancreatic tumors

Test	Principle	Comment
I Pancreatic enzymes in body fluids		
A Amylase		
1 Serum	Pancreatic inflammation leads to increased enzyme levels	Simple; 20–40% false-negatives and -positives; reliable if test results are two to three times the upper limit of normal
2 Urine	Renal clearance of amylase is increased in acute pancreatitis	May be abnormal when serum levels normal; false-negatives and -positives
3 Amylase/creatinine clearance ratio (C_{am}/C_{cr})	Renal clearance of amylase greater than clearance of creatinine	No more sensitive than the serum amylase; many false-positives
4 Ascitic fluid	Disruption of gland or main pancreatic duct leads to increased amylase concentration	Can establish diagnosis of pancreatitis; false-positives with intestinal obstruction and perforated ulcer
5 Pleural fluid	Exudative pleural effusion with pancreatitis	False-positives with carcinoma of the lung and esophageal perforation
6 Isoenzymes	P isoamylases arise from the pancreas; S isoamylases are from other sources	More sensitive than total serum amylase in diagnosis of acute pancreatitis; useful in identifying nonpancreatic causes of hyperamylasemia
B Serum lipase	Pancreatic inflammation leads to increased enzyme levels	New methods of determination greatly simplified; positive in 70–85% of cases; excellent specificity; normal in nonpancreatic hyperamylasemic conditions
C Serum trypsin-like immunoreactivity (TLI)	Pancreatic inflammation leads to increased levels	*Elevated* in acute pancreatitis and renal failure; *decreased* in chronic pancreatitis *with* steatorrhea; normal in chronic pancreatitis *without* steatorrhea and steatorrhea with normal pancreatic function
D Pancreatic polypeptide (PP)	PP confined almost totally to the pancreas; release stimulated by nutrients and hormones; such release parallels pancreatic enzyme secretion	Basal, meal-simulated, and hormone-(secretin CCK-PZ) stimulated PP levels *decreased* in chronic pancreatitis; fasting PP levels >125 pg/mL argues against chronic pancreatitis and pancreatic cancer
II Studies pertaining to pancreatic structure		
A Radiologic and radionuclide tests		
1 Plain film of the abdomen	Abnormal in acute and chronic pancreatitis	Simple; normal in >50% of both acute and chronic pancreatitis
2 Upper gastrointestinal x-rays	Abnormally thickened duodenal folds; displacement of stomach or widening of duodenal loop suggests a pancreatic mass (inflammatory, neoplastic, cystic)	Simple; frequently normal; largely superseded by US and CT scanning
3 Ultrasonography (US)	Can provide information on edema, inflammation, calcification, pseudocysts, and mass lesions	Simple, noninvasive; sequential studies quite feasible; procedure of choice for diagnosis of pseudocyst
4 Computerized tomography (CT scan)	Permits detailed visualization of pancreas and surrounding structures	Useful in the diagnosis of pancreatic calcification, dilated pancreatic ducts, and pancreatic tumors; may not be able to distinguish between inflammatory and neoplastic mass lesions
5 Selective angiography	Can identify pancreatic neoplasms (1) by sheathing of celiac or superior mesenteric branches by tumor or (2) by tumor staining; displacement of vessels by tumor	Indicated (1) in suspected islet-cell tumors and (2) prior to pancreatic or duodenal resection; most reliable features reflect nonresectable pancreatic cancer
6 Endoscopic retrograde cholangiopancreatography (ERCP)	Cannulation of pancreatic and common bile duct permits visualization of pancreatic-biliary ductal system	Provides diagnostic data in 60–85% of cases; differentiation of chronic pancreatitis from pancreatic carcinoma may be difficult
B Pancreatic biopsy with US or CT guidance	Percutaneous biopsy with skinny needle and localization of lesion by US	High diagnostic yield; laparotomy avoided; requires special technical skills
III Tests of exocrine pancreatic function		
A Direct stimulation of the pancreas with analysis of duodenal contents		
1 Secretin-pancreozymin (CCK-PZ) test	Secretin leads to increased output of pancreatic juice and HCO_3^-; CCK-PZ leads to increased output of pancreatic enzymes; pancreatic secretory response related to functional mass of pancreatic tissue	Sensitive enough to detect occult disease; involves duodenal intubation and fluoroscopy; poorly defined normal enzyme response; overlap in chronic pancreatitis; large secretory reserve capacity of the pancreas
B Indirect stimulation of pancreas with measurement of pancreatic enzymes		
1 Lundh test meal	Test meal (fat, carbohydrate, and protein) causes increased release of CCK-PZ, which causes increased enzyme output; trypsin concentration measured	Useful in pancreatic exocrine insufficiency; false-negatives with delayed gastric emptying; false-positives in primary mucosal disease of the gut and choledocholithiasis; does not measure secretory capacity
2 Benzoyl-tyrosyl-*p*-aminobenzoic (Bz-Ty-PABA, bentiromide) test	Synthetic peptide (Bz-Ty-PABA) specifically cleaved by chymotrypsin, liberating PABA which is absorbed and PABA metabolite excreted in the urine	Simple and reliable test of pancreatic exocrine function
C Measurement of intraluminal digestion products		
1 Microscopic examination of stool for undigested meat fibers and fat	Lack of proteolytic and lipolytic enzymes causes decreased digestion of meat fibers and triglycerides	Simple, reliable; not sensitive enough to detect milder cases of pancreatic insufficiency
2 Quantitative stool fat determination	Lack of lipolytic enzymes brings about impaired fat digestion	Reliable, reference standard for defining severity of malabsorption; does not distinguish between maldigestion and malabsorption
3 Fecal fat concentration	Patients with pancreatic exocrine insufficiency have less severe diarrhea than patients with gastrointestinal disease	Values ≥9.5% in a patient with steatorrhea ≥20 g/day suggest pancreatic insufficiency as the cause of fat malabsorption

TABLE 254-1 Tests useful in the diagnosis of acute and chronic pancreatitis and pancreatic tumors (continued)

Test	Principle	Comment
4 Fecal nitrogen	Lack of proteolytic enzymes leads to imparied protein digestion, causing increase in stool nitrogen	Does not distinguish between maldigestion and malabsorption; low sensitivity
D Measurement of pancreatic enzymes in feces		
1 Chymotrypsin	Pancreatic secretion of proteolytic enzymes	May be useful in cystic fibrosis; tedious; 10% false-positives and false-negatives

have been found to have spuriously low levels of amylase activity presumably because of a circulating amylase inhibitor; serial dilutions of plasma will frequently correct this abnormality and permit identification of hyperamylasemia. Importantly, serum lipase and urinary amylase levels are usually abnormal in this setting, thus facilitating the diagnosis of acute pancreatitis.

The serum amylase is often elevated in other conditions (Table 254-2), in part because the enzyme is found in many organs in addition to the pancreas (salivary glands, liver, small intestine, kidney, fallopian tube) and can be produced by various tumors (carcinoma of the lung, esophagus, and ovary). Isoenzymes of amylase fall into two general categories, those arising from the pancreas (P isoamylases) and those from nonpancreatic sources (S isoamylases). The measurement of serum isoamylases is of clinical importance. Isoamylase analysis of normal serum shows that about 35 to 45 percent of the amylase is of pancreatic origin. For example, in patients with acute pancreatitis, the total serum amylase returns to normal more rapidly than pancreatic isoamylase. Thus, in patients seen after the first day, the pancreatic isoamylase is a more sensitive indicator of pancreatitis than the total serum amylase. In addition, in certain conditions, such as the postoperative state, acute alcohol intoxication, and diabetic ketoacidosis, it had been assumed that elevations in serum amylase indicated acute pancreatitis. However, the elevation of serum amylase in such conditions has been shown

TABLE 254-2 Causes of hyperamylasemia and hyperamylasuria

I Pancreatic disease
  A Pancreatitis
    1 Acute
    2 Chronic: ductal obstruction
    3 Complications of pancreatitis
      a Pancreatic pseudocyst
      b Pancreatogenous ascites
      c Pancreatic abscess
  B Pancreatic trauma
  C Pancreatic carcinoma
II Nonpancreatic disorders
  A Renal insufficiency
  B Salivary gland lesions
    1 Mumps
    2 Calculus
    3 Irradiation sialadenitis
    4 Maxillofacial surgery
  C "Tumor" hyperamylasemia
    1 Carcinoma of the lung
    2 Carcinoma of the esophagus
    3 Ovarian carcinoma
  D Macroamylasemia
  E Burns
  F Diabetic ketoacidosis
  G Pregnancy
  H Renal transplantation
  I Cerebral trauma
  J Drugs: morphine
III Other abdominal disorders
  A Biliary tract disease: cholecystitis, choledocholithiasis
  B Intraabdominal disease
    1 Perforated or penetrating peptic ulcer
    2 Intestinal obstruction or infarction
    3 Ruptured ectopic pregnancy
    4 Peritonitis
    5 Aortic aneurysm
    6 Chronic liver disease
    7 Postoperative hyperamylasemia

SOURCE: After WB Salt II, S Schenker, Medicine 55:269, 1976.

to actually be of the S type. The general availability of a simple assay that employs a protein which selectively inhibits nonpancreatic amylase has led to more widespread use of isoamylase determinations.

Urine amylase is increased in acute pancreatitis and may be elevated for 7 to 10 days after serum values have returned to normal. The finding that the renal clearance of amylase is increased in acute pancreatitis has led to the suggestion that the amylase/creatinine clearance ratio (C_{am}/C_{cr}) may be a more sensitive and specific test for the diagnosis of acute pancreatitis.

However, experience with the C_{am}/C_{cr} has demonstrated that it is no more sensitive than the serum amylase. In addition, the specificity of the C_{am}/C_{cr} has been seriously questioned because the ratio is also increased in a number of other disorders, e.g., diabetic ketoacidosis, burns, pancreatic neoplasms, renal failure, and the postoperative state. The mechanism of increased renal amylase clearance in acute pancreatitis is secondary to a reversible renal tubular defect which results in decreased amylase reabsorption.

Elevation of ascitic fluid amylase occurs in acute pancreatitis as well as (1) in pancreatogenous ascites due to disruption of the main pancreatic duct of a leaking pseudocyst and (2) in other abdominal disorders which simulate pancreatitis (e.g., intestinal obstruction, intestinal infarction, and perforated peptic ulcer). Elevation of pleural fluid amylase occurs in acute pancreatitis, chronic pancreatitis, carcinoma of the lung, and esophageal perforation.

In the past, serum lipase levels were not frequently performed because of methodological problems. However, newer methods are now available and development of automated lipase assays should lead to their routine use and obviate present reliance on total amylase measurements in the diagnosis of acute pancreatitis. In two representative studies, lipase determinations exhibited good *sensitivity* and excellent *specificity;* lipase levels were elevated in 70 to 85 percent of patients with acute pancreatitis and the specificity was 99 percent. An obvious advantage of the lipase assay is that this enzyme is normal in several disorders associated with hyperamylasemia (e.g., macroamylasemia, diabetic ketoacidosis, renal failure, salivary gland lesions).

Assay for trypsinogen (or trypsin-like immunoreactivity) has a theoretical advantage over amylase and lipase determinations in that the pancreas is the only organ that contains this enzyme. The test appears to be useful in the diagnosis of both acute and chronic pancreatitis. Sensitivity and specificity are comparable to amylase and lipase determinations. Since trypsinogen is also excreted by the kidney, elevated values are found in renal failure.

A recent study evaluated the sensitivity and specificity of five assays used to diagnose acute pancreatitis: two amylase assays, one lipase, one trypsinlike immunoreactivity (TLI), and one pancreatic isoamylase. The data obtained show that (1) if the best cutoff level is used, all assays have similar specificities and suggest that (2) total serum amylase is as good an indicator of acute pancreatitis as any of the others. However, inherent in many such studies is the problem that the recognition and diagnosis of acute pancreatitis hinges upon the finding of an elevated serum amylase. The question arises as to whether any diagnostic test result can be proved superior to the total serum amylase level if hyperamylasemia is required for the diagnosis. In other studies, when "objective" confirmation of the clinical diagnosis of pancreatitis was required (ultrasonography, CT, laparotomy), the sensitivity of the serum amylase has been as low as 68 percent. With these limitations in mind, the recommended screening tests for acute pancreatitis are *total serum amylase and serum lipase activities.* Serum amylase values greater than two to three times normal are highly specific.

STUDIES PERTAINING TO PANCREATIC STRUCTURE **Radiologic tests** Plain films of the abdomen provide useful information in 30 to 50 percent of patients with acute pancreatitis. The most frequent abnormalities include (1) a localized ileus usually involving the jejunum (''sentinel loop''); (2) a generalized ileus with air-fluid levels; (3) the ''colon cutoff sign,'' which results from isolated distention of the transverse colon; (4) duodenal distention with air-fluid levels; and (5) a mass, which is frequently a pseudocyst. In chronic pancreatitis, an important radiographic finding is pancreatic calcification, which characteristically is localized adjacent to and superimposed on the second lumbar vertebra (see Fig. 255-1).

Upper gastrointestinal x-rays may reveal displacement of the stomach by the retroperitoneal mass (see Fig. 255-2A) or widening and effacement of the duodenal C loop, which also suggests the presence of a pancreatic mass that could be an inflammatory, cystic, or neoplastic process. The use of hypotonic duodenography or good-quality air-contrast studies increases the diagnostic yield of upper gastrointestinal x-rays in patients with carcinoma of the head of the pancreas.

Ultrasonography (echography) can provide important information in patients with acute pancreatitis, chronic pancreatitis, pancreatic calcification, pseudocyst, and pancreatic carcinoma. It is the procedure of choice in the evaluation of the patient with acute pancreatitis. Echographic appearances can indicate the presence of edema, inflammation, and calcification (not obvious on plain films of the abdomen), as well as pseudocysts, mass lesions, and gallstones (see Figs. 255-1 to 255-3). In acute pancreatitis the pancreas is characteristically enlarged. In pancreatic pseudocyst the usual appearance is that of an echo-free, smooth, round fluid collection. Pancreatic carcinoma distorts the usual landmarks, and mass lesions greater than 3.0 cm are usually detected as localized, echo-free solid lesions. Ultrasound is often the initial investigation for most patients with suspected pancreatic disease. However, obesity, excess small- and large-bowel gas, and recently performed barium-contrast examinations can interfere with ultrasound studies, which are often technically unsatisfactory.

Computerized tomography (CT scan) is the best imaging study for initial evaluation of a suspected chronic pancreatic disorder. It is especially useful in the detection of pancreatic tumors, fluid-containing lesions such as pseudocysts and abscesses, and calcium deposits. Most lesions are characterized by (1) enlargement of the pancreatic outline, (2) distortion of the pancreatic contour, or (3) fluid-containing lesions that have different attenuation coefficients than normal pancreas. However, it is occasionally difficult to distinguish between inflammatory and neoplastic lesions. Oral water-soluble contrast agents may be used to opacify the stomach and duodenum during CT scans; this permits more precise delineation of various organs as well as mass lesions.

Selective catheterization of the celiac and superior mesenteric arteries combined with superselective catheterization of others such as the hepatic, splenic, and gastroduodenal arteries permits visualization of the pancreas and detection of pancreatic neoplasms and pseudocysts. Pancreatic neoplasms can be identified by the sheathing of blood vessels by a mass lesion (see Fig. 255-3). Hormone-producing pancreatic tumors are especially likely to exhibit increased vascularity and tumor staining. Angiographic abnormalities are noted in many patients with pancreatic carcinoma but are uncommon in patients without pancreatic disease. Angiography complements ultrasonography and endoscopic retrograde cholangiopancreatography (ERCP) in the study of a patient with a suspected pancreatic lesion and may be carried out if ERCP is either unsuccessful or nondiagnostic.

Endoscopic retrograde cholangiopancreatography ERCP may provide useful information on the status of the pancreatic ductal system and thus aid in the differential diagnosis of pancreatic disease (see Figs. 255-2 and 255-3). Pancreatic carcinoma is characterized by stenosis or obstruction of either the pancreatic duct or common bile duct; both ductal systems are often abnormal. In chronic pancreatitis ERCP abnormalities include (1) luminal narrowing; (2) irregularities in the ductal system with stenosis, dilatation, sacculation, and ectasia; and (3) blockage of the pancreatic duct by calcium deposits. Differentiation from carcinoma may be difficult because of similar overlapping features, i.e., ductal stenosis and irregularity. Elevated serum amylase levels following ERCP have been reported in 25 to 75 percent of patients, but clinical pancreatitis is uncommon. In a series of 300 patients pancreatitis occurred in only five patients following ERCP.

Pancreatic biopsy with radiologic guidance Percutaneous aspiration biopsy of the pancreas under ultrasound or CT guidance can provide a definitive diagnosis of pancreatic neoplasms.

TESTS OF EXOCRINE PANCREATIC FUNCTION (See Table 254-1)

Pancreatic function tests can be divided into the following categories:

1 *Direct stimulation of the pancreas* by intravenous infusion of secretin or secretin plus cholecystokinin (CCK) followed by collection and measurement of duodenal contents
2 *Indirect stimulation of the pancreas* utilizing nutrients or amino acids, fatty acids, and synthetic peptides followed by assay of proteolytic, lipolytic, and amylolytic enzymes
3 Study of *intraluminal digestion products* such as undigested meat fibers, stool fat, and fecal nitrogen
4 *Measurement of fecal pancreatic enzymes* such as chymotrypsin

The secretin test, used to detect diffuse pancreatic disease, is based on the physiologic principle that the pancreatic secretory response is directly related to the functional mass of pancreatic tissue. In the standard assay, secretin is given intravenously in a dose of 1 clinical unit (CU) per kilogram, either as a bolus or continuous infusion. Obviously, results will vary with the secretin preparation used, dose, mode of administration, and completeness of collection of duodenal contents. Normal values for the standard secretin test are (1) volume output >2.0 mL/kg, (2) bicarbonate (HCO_3^-) concentration >80 meq per liter, and (3) HCO_3^- output >10 meq in 30 min. The most reproducible measurement having the highest level of discrimination between normal subjects and patients with chronic pancreatitis appears to be the maximal bicarbonate concentration.

The *combined secretin-CCK test* permits measurement of pancreatic amylase, lipase, trypsin, and chymotrypsin. Although there is overlap in the distribution of enzyme output in normal subjects and patients with pancreatitis, markedly decreased enzyme outputs suggest advanced damage and destruction of acinar cells. With frank exocrine pancreatic insufficiency there is usually an overall reduction in both HCO_3^- concentration and output of several enzymes. However, with lesser degrees of pancreatic damage there may be a dissociation between HCO_3^- concentration and enzyme output. There may also be a dissociation between the results of the secretin test and other tests of absorptive function. For example, patients with chronic pancreatitis often have abnormally low outputs of HCO_3^- after secretin but have normal fecal fat excretion. Thus, the secretin test measures the secretory capacity of ductular epithelium, while fecal fat excretion indirectly reflects intraluminal lipolytic activity. Steatorrhea does not occur until intraluminal levels of lipase are markedly reduced, underscoring the fact that only small amounts of enzymes are necessary for intraluminal digestive activities. An abnormal secretin test should suggest only that chronic pancreatic damage is present; it will not consistently distinguish between chronic pancreatitis and pancreatic carcinoma.

Another test of exocrine pancreatic function, which indirectly reflects intraluminal chymotrypsin activity, has been evaluated in patients with pancreatic disease. This test (the *tripeptide hydrolysis test*) utilizes a synthetic peptide, *N*-benzoyl-L-tyrosyl-*p*-aminobenzoic acid (Bz-Ty-PABA), that is specifically cleaved by chymotrypsin to Bz-Ty and PABA. Normally, after oral administration, the peptide reaches the small intestine, where it is hydrolyzed by chymotrypsin with the liberation of PABA, which is rapidly absorbed and excreted in the urine. Results in several hundred patients with chronic pancreatitis and other disorders indicate that PABA excretion is significantly lower in chronic pancreatitis compared with controls. The overall sensitivity and specificity of the test remains to be determined.

Measurement of *intraluminal digestion products,* i.e., undigested muscle fibers, stool fat, and fecal nitrogen, is discussed in Chap. 237. Measurement of chymotrypsin in stool reflects pancreatic output of this proteolytic enzyme. Decreased chymotrypsin activity in stool has been reported in patients with chronic pancreatitis and cystic fibrosis. However, normal values may occur in patients with pancreatic insufficiency, and false-positive results have been reported in up to 10 percent of normal individuals.

Tests useful in the diagnosis of exocrine pancreatic insufficiency and the differential diagnosis of malabsorption are also discussed in Chaps. 237 and 255.

255   DISEASES OF THE PANCREAS

NORTON J. GREENBERGER / PHILLIP P. TOSKES / KURT J. ISSELBACHER

BIOCHEMISTRY AND PHYSIOLOGY OF PANCREATIC EXOCRINE SECRETION

GENERAL CONSIDERATIONS   The pancreas secretes 1500 to 3000 mL isosmotic alkaline (pH > 8.0) fluid per day containing about 20 enzymes and zymogens. The pancreatic secretions provide the enzymes needed to effect the major digestive activity of the gastrointestinal tract and provide an optimum pH for the function of these enzymes.

REGULATION OF PANCREATIC SECRETION   Hormonal and neural mechanisms   The exocrine pancreas is under both hormonal and neural control, with hormonal control being of primary importance. *Gastric acid* is the stimulus for the release of secretin, a peptide with 27 amino acids. Sensitive radioimmunoassay studies for secretin suggest that the pH threshold for the release of secretin from the duodenum and jejunum is 4.5. Secretin stimulates the secretion of pancreatic juice rich in *water and electrolytes.* Release of cholecystokinin-pancreozymin (CCK-PZ) from duodenum and jejunum is largely produced by long-chain fatty acids, certain essential amino acids (tryptophan, phenylalanine, valine, methionine), and acid itself. CCK-PZ (a peptide with 33 amino acids) evokes an *enzyme-rich secretion from the pancreas.* Gastrin, although it shares an identical terminal tetrapeptide with CCK-PZ, is a weak stimulus for pancreatic enzyme output. The *parasympathetic nervous system* (via the vagus) exerts some control over pancreatic secretion. Part of this is mediated by the release of gastrin, and part is secondary to a direct effect of acetylcholine on the pancreatic acinar cell. In addition, vagal stimulation effects release of vasoactive intestinal peptide (VIP), a secretin agonist. Vagal control of pancreatic secretion seems to be most important following a truncal vagotomy, but even in such patients severe maldigestion does not ensue. Bile salts also stimulate pancreatic secretion, thereby integrating the functions of the biliary tract, pancreas, and small intestine.

Pancreatic secretion at the cellular level   There appear to be two functionally distinct pathways by which secretagogues can stimulate pancreatic secretion. Studies with isolated pancreatic acinar cells indicate that secretin, VIP, and cholera toxin interact with receptors on the acinar cell, leading to an increase in cellular cyclic adenosine monophosphate (cyclic AMP). CCK-PZ, acetylcholine, gastrin, and various other peptides (e.g., bombesin, caerulein) react with other receptors on the acinar cell to cause an increased turnover of phosphatidylinositol and the release of membrane calcium and induce changes in the electrical properties of the pancreatic acinar cell surface and junctional membranes. When a secretagogue that increases cyclic AMP is added to a secretagogue that increases calcium outflux, potentiation of enzyme secretion occurs.

WATER AND ELECTROLYTE SECRETION   Although sodium, potassium, chloride, calcium, zinc, phosphate, and sulfate are found within pancreatic secretion, *bicarbonate is the ion of primary physiologic importance.* In the acini and in the ducts, secretin causes the cells to add water and bicarbonate to the fluid. In the ducts an exchange occurs between bicarbonate and chloride. There is a good correlation between the maximal bicarbonate output after stimulation with secretin and the pancreatic mass. The bicarbonate output of 120 to 300 meq per day helps neutralize gastric acid production and creates the appropriate pH for the activity of the pancreatic enzymes.

ENZYME SECRETION   The pancreas secretes amylolytic, lipolytic, and proteolytic enzymes. Amylolytic enzymes such as amylase hydrolyze starch to oligosaccharides and to the disaccharide maltose. The *lipolytic enzymes* include lipase, phospholipase A, and cholesterol esterase. Bile salts *inhibit* lipase, but colipase, another constituent of pancreatic secretion, binds to lipase and prevents this inhibition. Bile salts *activate* phospholipase A and cholesterol esterase. *Proteolytic enzymes* include *endopeptidases* (trypsin, chymotrypsin), which act on the internal peptide bonds of proteins and polypeptides; *exopeptidases* (carboxypeptidases, aminopeptidases), which act on the free carboxyl terminal end and free amino terminal end of peptides, respectively; and elastase. The proteolytic enzymes are secreted as inactive precursors (zymogens). Ribonucleases (deoxyribonucleases, ribonuclease) are also secreted. *Enterokinase,* an enzyme found within the duodenal mucosa, cleaves the lysine-isoleucine bond of trypsinogen to form trypsin. Trypsin then activates the other proteolytic zymogens in a cascade phenomenon. All pancreatic enzymes have pH optima in the alkaline range.

AUTOPROTECTION OF THE PANCREAS   Autodigestion of the pancreas is prevented by the packaging of proteases in precursor form and by the synthesis of protease inhibitors. These protease inhibitors are found within the acinar cell, the pancreatic secretions, and the alpha$_1$- and alpha$_2$-globulin fractions of plasma.

EXOCRINE-ENDOCRINE RELATIONSHIPS   Pancreatic glucagon (29 amino acid residues) has a high degree of structural similarity to secretin. It decreases volume and enzyme secretion by the pancreas but not bicarbonate secretion. Glucose, in large concentrations, may also inhibit pancreatic exocrine secretion. The choleretic and insulinotropic effects of secretin are shared by glucagon.

ACUTE PANCREATITIS

GENERAL CONSIDERATIONS   Pancreatic inflammatory disease may be classified as follows: (1) acute pancreatitis, and (2) chronic pancreatitis. This classification is based primarily on clinical criteria with the obvious difference between the acute and chronic varieties; restoration of normal function occurs in the former and permanent residual damage occurs in the latter. The pathologic spectrum of acute pancreatitis varies from *edematous pancreatitis,* which is usually a mild and self-limited disorder, to *necrotizing pancreatitis,* in which the degree of pancreatic necrosis correlates with the severity of the attack and its systemic manifestations. The term *hemorrhagic pancreatitis* is less meaningful in a clinical sense because variable amounts of interstitial hemorrhage can be found in pancreatitis as well as in other disorders such as pancreatic trauma, pancreatic carcinoma, and severe congestive heart failure.

The incidence of pancreatitis varies in different countries and depends upon etiologic factors, e.g., alcohol, gallstones, metabolic factors, and drugs (Table 255-1). In the United States, for example, acute pancreatitis is related to alcohol ingestion more commonly than to gallstones; in England the opposite obtains. Epidemiologic data based on autopsy data indicate that in the United States the overall prevalence of acute pancreatitis is approximately 0.5 percent. An upward trend has been noted in the crude death rate from 1.0 per 100,000 in 1955 to 1.3 in 1965.

ETIOLOGY AND PATHOGENESIS There are many causative factors in the pathogenesis of acute pancreatitis (Table 255-1), but the mechanisms by which these conditions trigger pancreatic inflammation have not been identified. Alcoholic patients with pancreatitis may represent a special subset, since most alcoholics do not develop pancreatitis. The list of identifiable causes is growing, and it is likely that pancreatitis related to viral infections and drugs is more common than heretofore recognized.

Autodigestion is one pathogenetic theory which proposes that proteolytic enzymes (e.g., trypsinogen, chymotrypsinogen, proelastase, and phospholipase A) are activated within the pancreas rather than in the intestinal lumen. A variety of factors (such as endotoxins, exotoxins, viral infections, ischemia, anoxia, and direct trauma) are believed to activate these proenzymes. Activated proteolytic enzymes, especially trypsin, not only digest pancreatic and peripancreatic tissues but also can activate other enzymes such as elastase and phospholipase. The active enzymes then digest cellular membranes and cause proteolysis, edema, interstitial hemorrhage, vascular damage, coagulation necrosis, fat necrosis, and parenchymal cell necrosis. Cellular injury and death result in the liberation of activated enzymes. In addition, activation and release of bradykinin peptides and vasoactive substances (e.g., histamine) are believed to produce vasodilatation, increased vascular permeability, and edema. There is thus a cascade of events culminating in the development of acute necrotizing pancreatitis.

The autodigestion theory has largely eclipsed two older theories. The "common channel" theory holds that such an anatomic arrangement facilitates reflux of bile into the pancreatic duct, and this results in activation of pancreatic enzymes. (Actually, a common channel with free communication between the common bile duct and main pancreatic duct is infrequently encountered.) The second theory is that obstruction and hypersecretion are pivotal in the development of pancreatitis. Obstruction of the main pancreatic duct, however, produces pancreatic edema but not pancreatitis.

A third hypothesis to explain the intrapancreatic activation of zymogens is that they become activated by *lysosomal hydrolases* within the pancreatic acinar cell itself. In two different types of experimental pancreatitis, it has been demonstrated that digestive enzymes and lysosomal hydrolases become admixed; as a result the former can be activated within the acinar cell by the latter. Importantly, lysosomal enzymes such as cathepsin B can activate trypsinogen, and trypsin can activate the other protease precursors.

CLINICAL FEATURES *Abdominal pain* is the major symptom of acute pancreatitis. Pain may vary from a mild and tolerable discomfort to severe, constant, and incapacitating distress. Characteristically, the pain which is steady and boring in character is located in the epigastrium and periumbilical region and often radiates to the back as well as to the chest, flanks, and lower abdomen. The pain is frequently more intense when the patient is supine, and patients often obtain relief by sitting with the trunk flexed and knees drawn up. Nausea, vomiting, and abdominal distention due to gastric and intestinal hypomotility and chemical peritonitis are also frequent complaints.

Physical examination frequently reveals a distressed and anxious patient. Low-grade fever, tachycardia, and hypotension are fairly common. Shock is not unusual and may result from (1) hypovolemia

secondary to exudation of blood and plasma proteins into the retroperitoneal space, i.e., a "retroperitoneal burn"; (2) increased formation and release of kinin peptides which cause vasodilatation and increased vascular permeability; (3) systemic effects of proteolytic and lipolytic enzymes released into the circulation; and (4) impairment of myocardial contractility by kinins and other poorly characterized peptides. Jaundice occurs infrequently; when present it usually is due to edema of the head of the pancreas with compression of the intrapancreatic portion of the common bile duct. Erythematous skin nodules due to subcutaneous fat necrosis may occur. In 10 to 20 percent of patients there are pulmonary findings, including basilar rales, atelectasis, and pleural effusion, the latter most frequently left-sided. Abdominal tenderness and muscle rigidity are present to a variable degree, but compared with the intense pain, these signs may be unimpressive. Bowel sounds are usually diminished or absent. A pancreatic pseudocyst may be palpable in the upper abdomen. A faint blue discoloration around the umbilicus (Cullen's sign) may occur as the result of hemoperitoneum, and a blue-red-purple or green-brown discoloration of the flanks (Turner's sign) reflects tissue catabolism of hemoglobin. The latter two findings, which are uncommon, indicate the presence of a severe necrotizing pancreatitis.

LABORATORY DATA The diagnosis of acute pancreatitis is usually established by the presence of an increased serum amylase. Values

TABLE 255-1 Causes of acute pancreatitis

I Alcohol ingestion (acute and chronic alcoholism)
II Biliary tract disease (gallstones)
III Postoperative (abdominal, nonabdominal)
IV Post-endoscopic retrograde cholangiopancreatography (ERCP)
V Trauma (especially blunt abdominal type)
VI Metabolic
   A Hypertriglyceridemia
   B Hypercalcemia, e.g., hyperparathyroidism
   C Renal failure
   D After renal transplantation*
   E Acute fatty liver of pregnancy†
VII Hereditary pancreatitis
VIII Infections
   A Mumps
   B Viral hepatitis
   C Other viral infections (coxsackievirus, echovirus)
   D Ascariasis
   E Mycoplasma
IX Drug-associated
   A Definite association
     1 Azathioprine
     2 Sulfonamides
     3 Thiazide diuretics
     4 Furosemide
     5 Estrogens (oral contraceptives)
     6 Tetracycline
     7 Valproic acid
   B Probable association
     1 Chlorthalidone
     2 Ethacrynic acid
     3 Procainamide
     4 Iatrogenic hypercalcemia
     5 ʟ-Asparaginase
X Connective tissue disorders with vasculitis
   A Systemic lupus erythematosus
   B Necrotizing angiitis
   C Thrombotic thrombocytopenic purpura
XI Penetrating peptic ulcer
XII Obstruction of the ampulla of Vater
   A Regional enteritis
   B Duodenal diverticulum
XIII Pancreas divisum
XIV Recurrent bouts of acute pancreatitis without obvious cause
   A Consider
     1 Occult disease of the biliary tree or pancreatic ducts
     2 Drugs
     3 Hypertriglyceridemia
     4 Pancreas divisum
XV Other

* *Pancreatitis occurs in 3 percent of renal transplant patients and is due to many factors including surgery, hypercalcemia, drugs (corticosteroids, azathioprine, ʟ-asparaginase, diuretics), and viral infections.*
† *Pancreatitis also occurs in otherwise uncomplicated pregnancy and is most often associated with cholelithiasis.*

elevated two- to threefold above normal virtually clinch the diagnosis if overt salivary gland disease and gut perforation or infarction are excluded. However, there appears to be no definite correlation between the severity of pancreatitis and the degree of serum amylase elevation. After 48 to 72 h, even with continuing evidence of pancreatitis, total serum amylase values tend to return to normal. Importantly, pancreatic isoamylase and lipase levels may remain elevated for 7 to 14 days. It will be recalled that amylase elevations in serum and urine occur in many conditions other than pancreatitis (see Table 254-2). The urine amylase C_{am}/C_{cr} ratio is usually elevated in patients with severe pancreatitis; this ratio usually is not increased in patients with normal serum. Serum lipase activity increases in parallel with amylase activity, and measurement of both enzymes increases the diagnostic yield. An elevated serum lipase is virtually diagnostic of acute pancreatitis; the test is especially helpful in patients with nonpancreatic causes of hyperamylasemia (see Table 254-4). Markedly increased levels of peritoneal or pleural fluid amylase (>5000 units per deciliter) are also helpful, if present, in establishing the diagnosis.

Leukocytosis (15,000 to 20,000 leukocytes per cubic millimeter) occurs frequently. More severe cases may show hemoconcentration with hematocrit values exceeding 50 percent because of loss of plasma into the retroperitoneal space and peritoneal cavity. *Hyperglycemia* is common and is due to multiple factors that include decreased insulin release, increased glucagon release, and increased output of adrenal glucocorticoids and catecholamines. *Hypocalcemia* occurs in approximately 25 percent of cases and its pathogenesis is incompletely understood. While earlier studies suggested that the parathyroid gland response to a decrease in serum calcium is impaired, subsequent observations have failed to confirm this. Intraperitoneal saponification of calcium by fatty acids in areas of fat necrosis occurs as well as increased plasma levels of glucagon and calcitonin, but it is felt that these abnormalities do not adequately explain the hypocalcemia. *Hyperbilirubinemia* (serum bilirubin > 4.0 mg/dL) occurs in approximately 10 percent of patients. However, jaundice is transient and serum bilirubin levels return to normal in 4 to 7 days. Serum alkaline phosphatase and aspartate aminotransferase (SGOT) levels are also transiently elevated and parallel serum bilirubin values. When markedly elevated (i.e., >500 units), serum lactic dehydrogenase (LDH) levels suggest a poor prognosis. Serum albumin is decreased to ≤3.0 g/dL in about 10 percent of cases and is associated with more severe pancreatitis and an increased mortality rate (Table 255-2). Methemalbumin, a circulating heme metabolite attached to albumin, has been considered as a useful index of severe necrotizing pancreatitis. Its usefulness, however, has been limited by its nonspecificity for pancreatitis (it occurs, for example, in abdominal trauma, bone fractures, soft-tissue trauma, and retroperitoneal hematoma) and its absence in the majority of cases of severe necrotizing pancreatitis. *Hypertriglyceridemia* occurs in 15 to 20 percent of cases, and serum amylase levels in such patients are often spuriously normal (see Chap.

TABLE 255-2 Factors adversely influencing survival in acute pancreatitis*

I Risk factors identifiable upon admission to hospital
  A Increasing age
  B Hypotension
  C Abnormal pulmonary findings
  D Abdominal mass
  E Hemorrhagic or discolored peritoneal fluid
  F Increased serum LDH levels
  G Leukocytosis
  H Hyperglycemia
  I First attack of pancreatitis
II Risk factors identifiable during initial 48 h of hospitalization
  A Fall in hematocrit > 10 percent with hydration and/or hematocrit < 30 percent
  B Necessity for massive fluid and colloid replacement
  C Hypocalcemia
  D Hypoxemia with or without adult respiratory distress syndrome
  E Hypoalbuminemia
  F Azotemia

* *Increased mortality with three or more risk factors.*

254). Most patients with hypertriglyceridemia and pancreatitis, when subsequently examined, show evidence of an underlying derangement in lipid metabolism which probably antedated the pancreatitis. Approximately 25 percent of patients have *hypoxemia* (arterial P_{O_2} ≤ 60 mmHg), which may herald the onset of adult respiratory distress syndrome. Finally, the electrocardiogram is occasionally abnormal in acute pancreatitis with ST-segment and T-wave abnormalities simulating myocardial ischemia.

Radiologic studies useful in the diagnosis of acute pancreatitis are listed in Table 254-1 and discussed in Chap. 254. Although one or more of the abnormalities are found in over 50 percent of patients, the findings are inconstant and nonspecific. The chief value of conventional x-rays [chest; kidney, ureter, and bladder (KUB)] in acute pancreatitis is to help exclude other diagnoses, especially a perforated viscus. Upper gastrointestinal tract x-rays have been superseded by ultrasonography and CT scanning. A computerized tomography (CT) scan may confirm the clinical impression of acute pancreatitis even in the face of normal serum amylase levels. Sonography and radionuclide scanning (PIPIDA, HIDA) are useful in acute pancreatitis to evaluate the gallbladder and biliary tree.

DIAGNOSIS Any severe acute pain in the abdomen or back should suggest acute pancreatitis. The diagnosis is usually entertained when a patient with a possible predisposition to pancreatitis presents with severe and constant abdominal pain, nausea, emesis, fever, tachycardia, and abnormal findings on abdominal examination. Laboratory studies frequently reveal leukocytosis, abnormal x-rays of the abdomen and chest, hypocalcemia, and hyperglycemia. The diagnosis is usually confirmed by finding an elevated serum amylase and/or lipase. Obviously, not all the above features have to be present for the diagnosis to be established.

The *differential diagnosis* should include consideration of the following disorders: (1) perforated viscus, especially peptic ulcer; (2) acute cholecystitis and biliary colic; (3) acute intestinal obstruction; (4) mesenteric vascular occlusion; (5) renal colic; (6) myocardial infarction; (7) dissecting aortic aneurysm; (8) connective tissue disorders with vasculitis; (9) pneumonia; and (10) diabetic ketoacidosis. A penetrating duodenal ulcer can usually be identified by upper gastrointestinal x-rays and/or endoscopy. A perforated duodenal ulcer is readily diagnosed by the presence of free intraperitoneal air. It may be difficult to differentiate acute cholecystitis from acute pancreatitis since an elevated serum amylase may be found in both disorders. Pain of biliary tract origin is more right-sided and gradual in onset, and ileus is usually absent; sonography and radionuclide scanning are helpful in establishing the diagnosis of cholelithiasis and cholecystitis. Intestinal obstruction due to mechanical factors can be differentiated from pancreatitis by the history of colicky pain, findings on abdominal examination, and x-rays of the abdomen showing characteristic changes of mechanical obstruction. Acute mesenteric vascular occlusion is usually evident in elderly debilitated patients with brisk leukocytosis, abdominal distention, and bloody diarrhea, in whom paracentesis shows sanguinous fluid and arteriography shows vascular occlusion. Serum as well as peritoneal fluid amylase levels are increased, however, in patients with intestinal infarction. Systemic lupus erythematosus and polyarteritis nodosa may be confused with pancreatitis, especially since pancreatitis may develop as a complication of those diseases. Diabetic ketoacidosis is often accompanied by abdominal pain and elevated total serum amylase levels, thus closely mimicking acute pancreatitis. However, the serum lipase and pancreatic isoamylase are not elevated in diabetic ketoacidosis.

COURSE OF THE DISEASE AND COMPLICATIONS There is an increased mortality rate with three or more risk factors identifiable either at the time of admission to hospital or during the initial 48 h of hospitalization (see Table 255-2). It is important to identify the patient with acute pancreatitis with an increased risk of dying. In one large series such a subgroup was characterized by at least three of the following features: (1) respiratory failure requiring intubation, (2) shock, (3) massive colloid replacement, and (4) serum calcium < 8.0 mg/dL. The survival rate was only 29 percent in the patients treated with medical measures but increased to 64 percent with operative treatment. In another series the mortality rate was 0.9 percent in patients with zero to two factors, 16 percent in patients with three to four factors, and 40 percent with five to six factors present. The high mortality of such severely ill patients, despite maximal medical treatment, suggests that alternative therapeutic approaches such as peritoneal lavage or early surgical intervention merit broader consideration.

The local and systemic complications of acute pancreatitis are listed in Table 255-3. Patients frequently develop an inflammatory mass in the first 2 to 3 weeks after pancreatitis. These may be phlegmons, abscesses, or pseudocysts (see below). Systemic complications include pulmonary, cardiovascular, hematologic, renal, metabolic, and central nervous system abnormalities. Pancreatitis, hypertriglyceridemia, and alcoholism constitute a triad in which cause and effect remain incompletely understood. However, several reasonable conclusions can be drawn. First, hypertriglyceridemia can precede and apparently cause the development of pancreatitis. Second, the vast majority (>80 percent) of patients with acute pancreatitis do not have hypertriglyceridemia. Third, almost all patients with pancreatitis and hypertriglyceridemia are *either* alcoholics who have been drinking shortly before the onset of pancreatitis *or* patients with preexistent hypertriglyceridemia. Fourth, many of the patients with this triad have persistent hypertriglyceridemia after recovery from pancreatitis and abstention from alcohol. Finally, patients with a deficiency of apolipoprotein CII have an increased incidence of pancreatitis; apolipoprotein CII activates lipoprotein lipase, which is important in clearing chylomicrons from the bloodstream.

Purtscher's retinopathy, a relatively unusual complication, refers to the sudden and severe loss of vision in patients with acute pancreatitis. It is characterized by a peculiar funduscopic appearance with cotton-wool spots and hemorrhages confined to an area limited by the optic disk and macula; it is believed to be due to posterior retinal artery occlusion with aggregated granulocytes.

TREATMENT In most patients (approximately 85 to 90 percent) with acute pancreatitis, the disease is self-limited and subsides spontaneously, usually within 3 to 7 days after treatment is instituted. Medical therapy is aimed at reducing pancreatic secretion and, in essence, "putting the pancreas at rest." Conventional measures include (1) analgesics for pain, (2) intravenous fluids and colloids to maintain normal intravascular volume, (3) no oral alimentation, and (4) nasogastric suction to decrease gastrin release from the stomach and prevent gastric contents from entering the duodenum. Recent controlled trials, however, have shown that nasogastric suction offers no clear-cut advantages in the treatment of mild to moderately severe acute pancreatitis. Its use, therefore, must be considered elective rather than mandatory.

Anticholinergic drugs have previously been considered standard therapy in patients with acute pancreatitis, the rationale being to blunt stimulation of the pancreas. However, there are no controlled trials demonstrating that anticholinergic drugs are superior to placebo. Moreover, anticholinergics may make it difficult to determine whether tachycardia, decreased urine output, bowel hypomotility, need for additional fluid replacement, and signs of toxicity are due to the drugs or to a worsening of the pancreatitis. Accordingly, their use is not recommended. Although antibiotics have been used in the treatment of acute pancreatitis, three recent randomized prospective trials have shown no benefit from the use of antibiotics in acute pancreatitis of mild to moderate severity. However, because secondary infection of necrotic pancreatic tissue (phlegmon, abscess, pseudocyst) or obstructed biliary passages (ascending cholangitis, complicating choledocholithiasis) contributes to much of the late mortality, appropriate *antibiotic therapy of established infection* is obviously quite important. Previous reports suggested that glucagon was useful in acute pancreatitis, but controlled trials have not provided convincing

evidence of effectiveness. Similarly, aprotinin (Trasylol) and cimetidine have not proved effective.

The patient with mild to moderate pancreatitis usually requires treatment with intravenous fluids, fasting, and possibly nasogastric suction for 2 to 4 days. A clear liquid diet is frequently started on the third to sixth day and a regular diet by the fifth to seventh day. The patient with unremitting *fulminant pancreatitis* usually requires inordinate amounts of fluid and close attention to complications such as cardiovascular collapse and respiratory insufficiency. Removal of toxic pancreatic exudate from the peritoneal cavity may alter the course of this lethal situation. This can be accomplished by either *peritoneal lavage* via a percutaneous dialysis catheter or *laparotomy* with wide sump drainage. One study has suggested that a 3-day regimen of therapeutic lavage with a conventional peritoneal dialysis solution does not influence the outcome of an attack of severe idiopathic acute pancreatitis. However, occasionally a dramatic response occurs if lavage is accomplished early in an attack of alcohol-induced pancreatitis. If peritoneal lavage does not halt the patient's deterioration, laparotomy should be considered. The use of parenteral nutrition makes it possible to give nutritional support to patients with severe, acute, or protracted pancreatitis who are unable

TABLE 255-3 Complications of acute pancreatitis

I Local
  A Pancreatic phlegmon
  B Pancreatic abscess
  C Pancreatic pseudocyst
    1 Pain
    2 Rupture
    3 Hemorrhage
    4 Infection
    5 Obstruction of gastrointestinal tract (stomach, duodenum, colon)
  D Pancreatic ascites
    1 Disruption of main pancreatic duct
    2 Leaking pseudocyst
  E Involvement of contiguous organs by necrotizing pancreatitis
    1 Massive intraperitoneal hemorrhage
    2 Thrombosis of blood vessels
    3 Bowel infarction
  F Obstructive jaundice
II Systemic
  A Pulmonary
    1 Pleural effusion
    2 Atelectasis
    3 Mediastinal abscess
    4 Pneumonitis
    5 Adult respiratory distress syndrome
  B Cardiovascular
    1 Hypotension
      a Hypovolemia
      b Hypoalbuminemia
    2 Sudden death
    3 Nonspecific ST-T changes in electrocardiogram simulating myocardial infarction
    4 Pericardial effusion
  C Hematologic
    1 Disseminated intravascular coagulation (DIC)
  D Gastrointestinal hemorrhage*
    1 Peptic ulcer disease
    2 Erosive gastritis
    3 Hemorrhagic pancreatic necrosis with erosion into major blood vessels
    4 Portal vein thrombosis, variceal hemorrhage
  E Renal
    1 Oliguria
    2 Azotemia
    3 Renal artery and/or renal vein thrombosis
  F Metabolic
    1 Hyperglycemia
    2 Hypertriglyceridemia
    3 Hypocalcemia
    4 Encephalopathy
    5 Sudden blindness (Purtscher's retinopathy)
  G Central nervous system
    1 Psychosis
    2 Fat emboli
  H Fat necrosis
    1 Subcutaneous tissues (erythematous nodules)
    2 Bone
    3 Miscellaneous (mediastinum, pleura, nervous system)

* *Aggravated by coagulation abnormalities (DIC).*

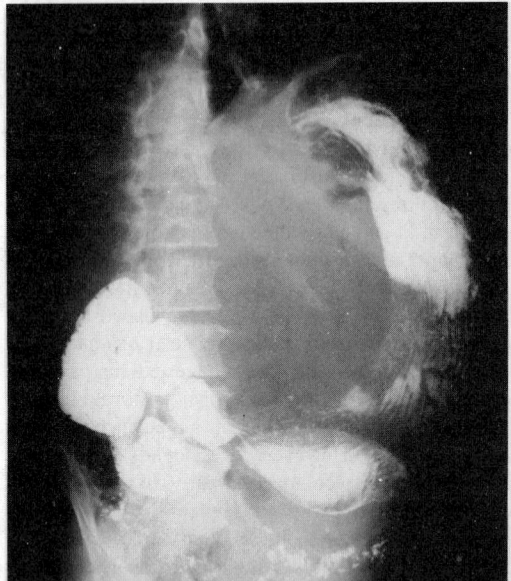

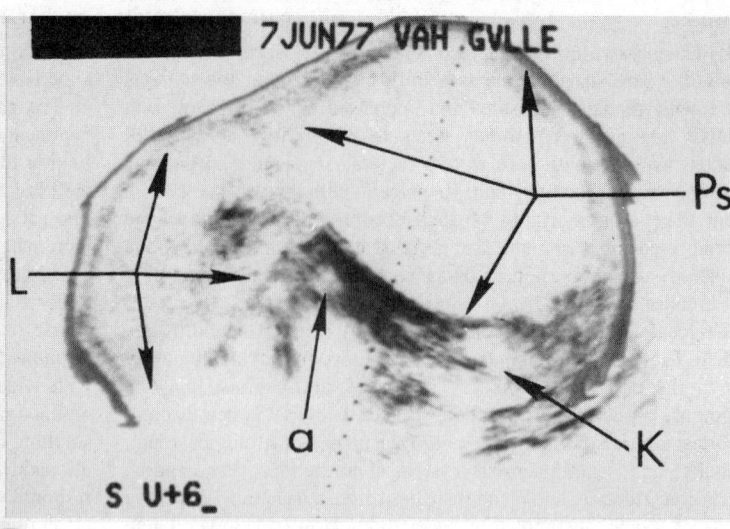

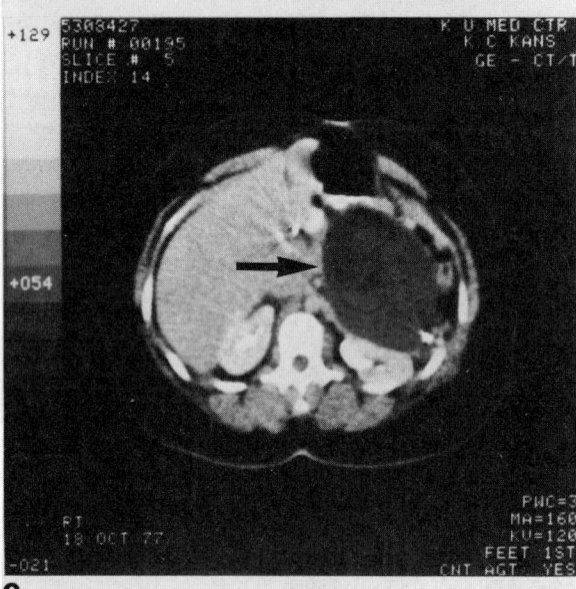

FIGURE 255-1 *Pseudocyst of the pancreas. A. Upper gastrointestinal x-ray showing displacement of stomach by pseudocyst. B. Sonogram showing pseudocyst (Ps), K = kidney, a = aorta, L = liver. C. CT scan showing pseudocyst (arrow) compressing left kidney.*

guidance, has been only moderately successful (resolution in 50 to 60 percent of patients). Accordingly, laparotomy with radical sump drainage and possibly resection of necrotic tissue is usually required because the mortality rate for undrained pancreatic abscess approaches 100 percent. Multiple abscesses are common and reoperation is frequently required.

Pseudocysts of the pancreas are collections of tissue, fluid, debris, pancreatic enzymes, and blood, which develop over a period of 1 to 4 weeks after the onset of acute pancreatitis. In contrast to true cysts, pseudocysts do not have epithelial lining and the walls consist of necrotic tissue, granulation tissue, and fibrous tissue. Disruption of the pancreatic ductal system is common. However, the subsequent course of this disruption varies widely, namely, from spontaneous healing to continuous leakage of pancreatic juice causing tense ascites. Pseudocysts are preceded by pancreatitis in 90 percent of cases and by trauma in 10 percent. Approximately 85 percent are located in the body or tail of the pancreas and 15 percent in the head. Some patients have two or more pseudocysts. Abdominal pain, with or without radiation to the back, is the usual presenting complaint. A palpable, tender mass may be found in the middle or left upper abdomen. The serum amylase is elevated in 75 percent of patients some time during their illness and may fluctuate markedly.

Pseudocysts often displace some portion of the gastrointestinal tract on x-ray examination in 75 percent of cases (Fig. 255-1). Sonography, however, is reliable in detecting pseudocysts and should be the initial diagnostic procedure in a patient suspected of having a pseudocyst (Fig. 255-1). Sonography also permits differentiation between an edematous and an inflamed pancreas (pancreatic phlegmon), which can give rise to a palpable mass and an actual pseudocyst. Furthermore, serial ultrasound studies will indicate whether a pseudocyst has resolved. CT scanning complements the use of ultrasound in the diagnosis of pancreatic pseudocyst (Fig. 255-2), especially when it is infected.

The management of pseudocysts is compromised by incomplete knowledge of the natural history of this disorder. In earlier studies utilizing sonography, pseudocysts resolved in 20 to 30 percent of patients; however, the time frequency of this is not clear. In others, serious complications may occur such as (1) pain caused by expansion of the lesion and pressure on other viscera, (2) rupture, (3) hemorrhage, and (4) abscess. Rupture of a pancreatic pseudocyst is a particularly serious complication. Shock almost always supervenes and mortality rates range from 14 percent if the rupture is not associated with hemorrhage to over 60 percent if hemorrhage has occurred. Rupture

to eat normally. Finally, patients with gallstone-induced pancreatitis may improve dramatically if papillotomy is carried out within the first 36 h of the attack.

PANCREATIC PHLEGMON, ABSCESS, AND PSEUDOCYST The *phlegmon* is a solid mass of swollen, inflamed pancreas often containing patchy areas of necrosis; it may be present for 1 to 2 weeks. This prolonged inflammatory process should not be confused with a pseudocyst, a differentiation which is usually accomplished by sonography. Occasionally, extensive areas of pancreatic necrosis develop in phlegmons and require incision and drainage. Phlegmons may also be secondarily infected, resulting in abscess formation. The latter occurs in 5 to 10 percent of patients with acute pancreatitis. Severe pancreatitis with the presence of three or more risk factors, postoperative pancreatitis, early oral feeding, early laparotomy, and perhaps injudicious use of antibiotics predispose to the development of pancreatic abscess. Pancreatic abscess may also develop because of communication of a pseudocyst with the colon, after inadequate surgical drainage of a pseudocyst, or after needling of a pseudocyst. The characteristic signs of abscess are fever, leukocytosis, ileus, and rapid deterioration in a patient initially recovering from pancreatitis. However, the only manifestations may be persistent fever and signs of continuing pancreatic inflammation. Drainage of pancreatic abscesses by nonsurgical percutaneous catheter techniques, using CT

and hemorrhage are the prime causes of mortality in pancreatic pseudocyst. A triad of findings, e.g., increase in size of the mass, localized bruit over the mass, and a sudden decrease in hemoglobin and hematocrit levels without obvious signs of external blood loss should alert one to the diagnosis of hemorrhage from a pseudocyst. Thus, in pseudocyst patients who are stable and uncomplicated, and in whom serial ultrasound studies show a decreasing pseudocyst, conservative therapy is indicated. Conversely, patients with a pseudocyst which is expanding and which is complicated by rupture, hemorrhage, and abscess should be operated on. Needle aspiration of pseudocysts present for longer than 6 months results in permanent resolution in approximately 25 percent of patients; the remainder require surgical therapy. Therapy consists of internal or external drainage of the cyst. Prolonged observation of a nonresolving pancreatic pseudocyst exposes the patient to increased risks which exceed those of elective surgery.

PANCREATIC ASCITES AND PANCREATIC PLEURAL EFFUSIONS

Pancreatic ascites is usually due to disruption of the main pancreatic duct, often associated with an internal fistula between the duct and the peritoneal cavity or a leaking pseudocyst (see also Chap. 39). The diagnosis of pancreatic ascites is suggested in a patient with an elevated serum amylase who also has increased levels of albumin

(>3.0 g/dL) and amylase in the ascitic fluid. In addition, endoscopic retrograde cholangiopancreatography (ERCP) will often demonstrate passage of contrast material from a major pancreatic duct or a pseudocyst into the peritoneal cavity. As many as 15 percent of patients with pseudocysts have concurrent pancreatic ascites. The differential diagnosis should include intraperitoneal carcinomatosis, tuberculous peritonitis, constrictive pericarditis, and Budd-Chiari syndrome.

If the pancreatic duct disruption is posterior, an internal fistula may develop between the pancreatic duct and pleural space producing a pleural effusion, which is usually left-sided and often massive. This often requires thoracentesis or chest tube drainage.

Treatment usually involves placing the patient on nasogastric solution and parenteral alimentation to decrease pancreatic secretion. In addition, paracentesis is performed to keep the peritoneal cavity free of fluid and, it is hoped, effect sealing of the leak. If ascites continues to recur after 2 to 3 weeks of medical management, the

FIGURE 255-2 *Carcinoma of the pancreas. A. Sonogram showing pancreatic carcinoma (P), dilated intrahepatic bile ducts (d), dilated portal vein (pv), and inferior vena cava (IVC). B. CT scan showing pancreatic carcinoma (arrow). C. ERCP showing abrupt cut off of the duct of Wirsung (arrow). D. Arteriogram showing sheathing of splenic artery by tumor encasement (arrow).*

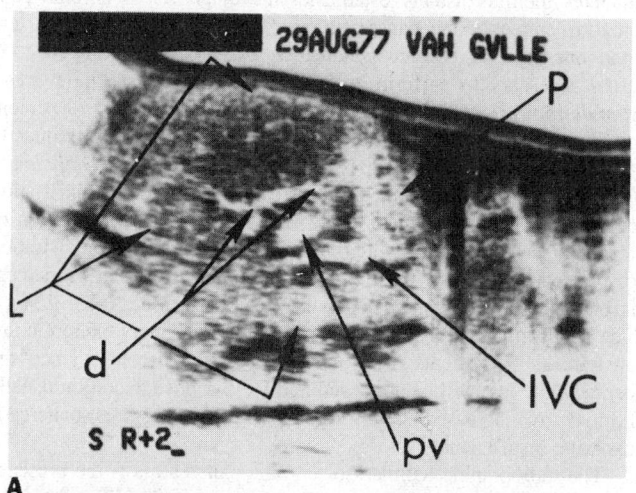

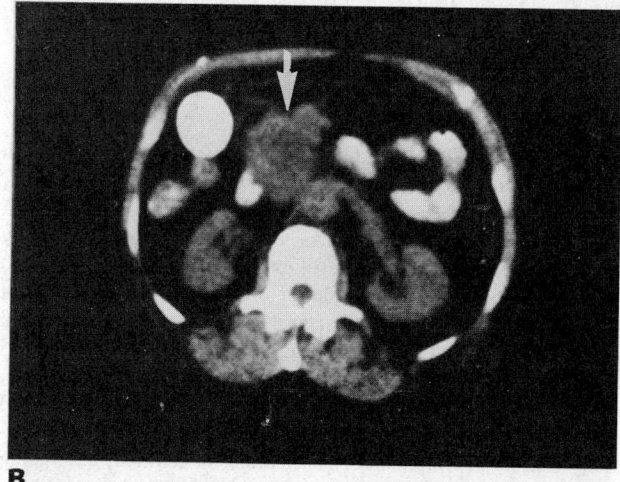

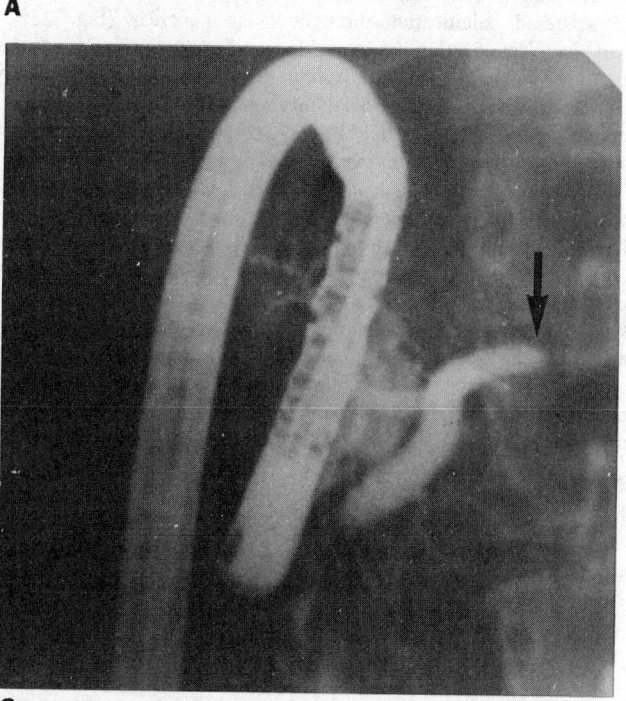

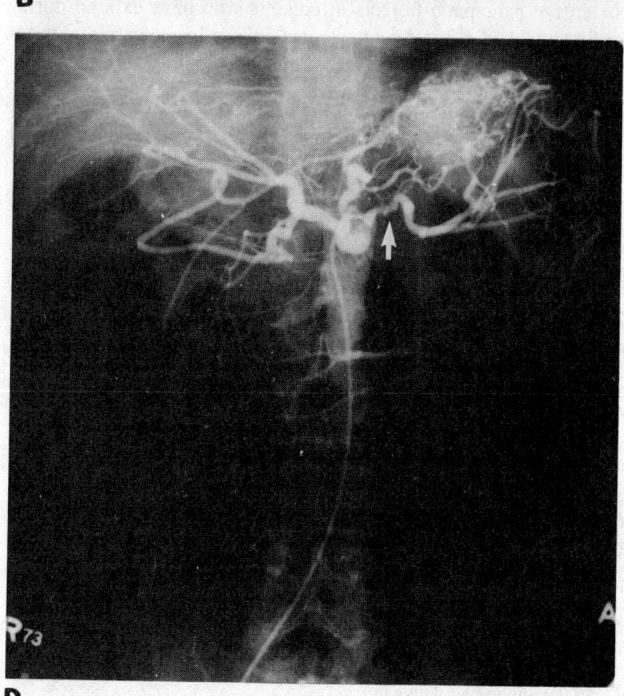

patient should be operated on following pancreatography to define the anatomy of the abnormal duct.

CHRONIC PANCREATITIS AND PANCREATIC EXOCRINE INSUFFICIENCY

GENERAL AND ETIOLOGIC CONSIDERATIONS   Chronic inflammatory disease of the pancreas may present as episodes of acute inflammation superimposed upon a previously injured pancreas or as chronic damage with persistent pain or malabsorption. The causes of relapsing chronic pancreatitis are similar to those of acute pancreatitis (Table 255-2), except that frequently the cause is an appreciable incidence of cases of undetermined origin. In addition, the pancreatitis associated with gallstones is predominantly acute or relapsing acute in nature. A cholecystectomy is almost always performed in patients after the first or second attack of gallstone-associated pancreatitis. Patients with chronic pancreatitis may present with persistent abdominal pain, with or without steatorrhea, and some may present with steatorrhea and no pain.

Patients with chronic pancreatitis who develop extensive destruction of the pancreas (i.e., less than 10 percent of exocrine function remaining) will demonstrate steatorrhea and azotorrhea. In the adult in the United States, alcoholism is the most common cause of clinically apparent pancreatic exocrine insufficiency, while cystic fibrosis is the most frequent cause in children. In other parts of the world, severe protein calorie malnutrition is a common etiology. Table 255-4 lists other causes of pancreatic exocrine insufficiency, but they are relatively uncommon.

PATHOPHYSIOLOGY   Unfortunately, the events that initiate an inflammatory process within the pancreas are still not well understood, and the many hypotheses will not be reviewed. In the case of alcohol-induced pancreatitis, however, it has been suggested that the primary defect may be the precipitation of protein (inspissated enzymes) within the ducts. The resulting ductal obstruction can lead to duct dilatation, diffuse atrophy of the acinar cells, fibrosis, and eventual calcification of some of the protein plugs. While patients with alcohol-induced pancreatitis generally consume large amounts of alcohol, some consume very little (i.e., 50 g or less per day). Thus, prolonged consumption of "socially acceptable" amounts of alcohol is compatible with the development of pancreatitis. In addition, the finding of extensive pancreatic fibrosis in patients who have expired during their first attack of clinical acute alcohol-induced pancreatitis supports the concept that such patients already have chronic pancreatitis.

CLINICAL FEATURES   Patients with relapsing chronic pancreatitis may present with symptoms identical with those found in acute pancreatitis, but their pain may be continuous or intermittent, or pain may be absent. The pathogenesis of this pain is poorly understood.

Although the classic description is that of epigastric pain radiating through the back, the pain pattern is often atypical. The pain may be maximal in the right or left upper quadrants in the back or diffuse throughout the upper abdomen; it may even be referred to the anterior chest or flank. Characteristically, the pain is persistent, deep-seated, and unresponsive to antacids. It often is increased by alcohol and ingestion of heavy meals (especially foods rich in fat). Often the pain is so severe as to require the frequent use of narcotics.

Weight loss, abnormal stools, and other signs of symptoms suggestive of malabsorption (see Table 237-5) are common in chronic pancreatitis. However, clinically apparent deficiencies of fat-soluble vitamins are surprisingly rare. The physical findings in these patients are usually not impressive such that there is a disparity between the severity of the abdominal pain and the paucity of physical signs (save some abdominal tenderness and mild temperature elevation).

DIAGNOSTIC EVALUATION (See Chap. 254)   In contrast to patients with relapsing acute pancreatitis, the serum amylase and lipase levels are usually not elevated. Elevations of the serum bilirubin and alkaline phosphatase may indicate cholestasis secondary to chronic inflammation around the common bile duct (Fig. 255-3). Many patients demonstrate impaired glucose tolerance, and some may have an elevated fasting blood glucose level.

The classic triad of pancreatic calcification, steatorrhea, and diabetes mellitus usually establishes the diagnosis of chronic pancreatitis and exocrine pancreatic insufficiency but is found in less than one-third of chronic pancreatitis patients. Accordingly, it is often necessary to perform an intubation test such as the *secretin stimulation test,* which usually becomes abnormal when 70 percent or more of pancreatic exocrine function has been lost. Approximately 40 percent of patients with chronic pancreatitis have *cobalamin (vitamin B_{12}) malabsorption* which is corrected by the administration of oral pancreatic enzymes. There is usually a marked excretion of fecal fat (see Chap. 237), which can be reduced with the administration of oral pancreatic enzymes. A fecal fat concentration ≥ 9.5 percent is characteristic of pancreatogenous steatorrhea (see Table 254-1). The bentiromide test (Chap. 254) and D-xylose urinary excretion test are useful in patients with "pancreatic steatorrhea," since the bentiromide test will be abnormal and the D-xylose excretion usually normal. A decreased serum trypsin strongly suggests pancreatic exocrine insufficiency.

The radiographic hallmark of chronic pancreatitis is the presence of scattered calcification throughout the pancreas (Fig. 255-3). Pancreatic calcification indicates that significant damage has occurred and obviates the need for the secretin test. Alcohol by far is the most common cause of pancreatic calcification, but it may also be seen in severe protein calorie malnutrition, hyperparathyroidism, hereditary pancreatitis, posttraumatic pancreatitis, and islet-cell tumors.

Special techniques such as sonography, CT scanning, and ERCP have added new dimensions to the diagnosis of pancreatic disease. In addition to excluding pseudocysts and pancreatic cancer, sonography may show calcification or dilated ducts associated with chronic pancreatitis (Fig. 255-3). Similar benefits can be derived from CT scans, but the availability and lower cost make sonography preferable at present. ERCP is the only nonoperative technique which provides a direct view of the pancreatic duct. In patients with alcohol-induced pancreatitis, ERCP may reveal a pseudocyst missed by sonography or CT scan.

COMPLICATIONS OF CHRONIC PANCREATITIS   The complications of chronic pancreatitis are protean. *Cobalamin (vitamin B_{12}) malabsorption* occurs in 40 percent of patients with alcohol-induced chronic pancreatitis and in virtually all with cystic fibrosis. The cobalamin malabsorption is consistently corrected by the administration of pancreatic enzymes (containing proteases). The cobalamin malabsorption may be due to excessive binding of cobalamin by nonintrinsic factor cobalamin-binding proteins. The latter are ordinarily destroyed by pancreatic proteases, but with pancreatic insufficiency the nonspecific binding proteins escape degradation and

---

TABLE 255-4   Causes of pancreatic exocrine insufficiency

 I Alcohol, chronic alcoholism
 II Cystic fibrosis
 III Severe protein calorie malnutrition with hypoalbuminemia
 IV Pancreatic and duodenal neoplasms
 V Pancreatic resection
 VI Gastric surgery
   A Subtotal gastrectomy with Billroth II anastomosis
   B Subtotal gastrectomy with Billroth I anastomosis
   C Truncal vagotomy and pyloroplasty
 VII Gastrinoma (Zollinger-Ellison syndrome)
 VIII Hereditary pancreatitis
 IX Traumatic pancreatitis
 X Hemochromatosis
 XI Shwachman's syndrome (pancreatic insufficiency and bone marrow dysfunction)
 XII Trypsinogen deficiency
 XIII Enterokinase deficiency
 XIV Isolated deficiencies of amylase, lipase, or proteases
 XV Alpha$_1$-antitrypsin deficiency
 XVI Idiopathic pancreatitis

compete with intrinsic factor for cobalamin binding. Although the majority of patients show *impaired glucose tolerance,* the development of diabetic ketoacidosis and coma is uncommon. Similarly, end organ damage (retinopathy, neuropathy, nephropathy) is also uncommon, and the appearance of these complications should raise the question of concomitant genetic diabetes mellitus. A nondiabetic retinopathy, peripheral in location and secondary to vitamin A and/or zinc deficiency, is common in these patients. High amylase-containing *effusions* occur within the pleura, pericardium, or peritoneum. *Gastrointestinal bleeding* may occur from a peptic ulcer, gastritis, a pseudocyst eroding into the duodenum, or from ruptured varices secondary to splenic vein thrombosis due to inflammation of the tail of the pancreas. *Icterus* may occur, owing to either edema of the head of the pancreas compressing the common bile duct or chronic cholestasis secondary to chronic inflammatory reaction around the intrapancreatic portion of the common bile duct (Fig. 255-3). This chronic obstruction may lead to cholangitis and ultimately biliary cirrhosis. *Subcutaneous fat necrosis* may appear as tender red nodules on the lower extremities. *Bone pain* may be secondary to intramedullary fat necrosis. Inflammation of the large and small joints of the upper and lower extremities may occur. The incidence of pancreatic carcinoma is probably increased. Perhaps the most common and troublesome complication is addiction to narcotics.

TREATMENT AND APPROACH TO MANAGEMENT   Therapy for patients with chronic pancreatitis is directed to two major problems, namely, pain and malabsorption. Patients with intermittent attacks of pain are essentially treated like those with acute pancreatitis (see above). Patients with severe and persistent pain should avoid alcohol completely and avoid large meals rich in fat. Since the pain is often severe enough to require frequent use of narcotics (and hence addiction), a number of surgical procedures have been developed for pain relief. ERCP allows the surgeon to plan the operative approach. If there is a stricture of the pancreatic duct, then a *local resection* may ameliorate the pain. Unfortunately isolated localized strictures are not common. In most patients with alcohol-induced disease, the pancreas is diffusely involved and surgically correctible localized ductal disease is rare. When there is primary ductal obstruction, side-to-side pancreaticojejunostomy may provide effective pain palliation. In some of these patients, however, pain relief can be achieved only by resecting 50 to 95 percent of the gland. Although pain relief is achieved in three-quarters of these patients, they tend to develop

FIGURE 255-3   *Radiologic abnormalities in chronic pancreatitis. A. Pancreatic calcification (arrows) and stenosis (tapering) of the intrapancreatic portion of the common bile duct demonstrated by percutaneous transhepatic cholangiography. B. Pancreatic calcification (Ca) demonstrated by sonog-raphy. gb = gallbladder; K = kidney; a = aorta. C. Pancreatic calcification (vertical arrows) and dilated pancreatic duct (horizontal arrow) demonstrated by CT scan. D. Endoscopic retrograde cholangiopancreatogram shows grossly dilated pancreatic ducts (arrows) in a patient with long-standing pancreatitis.*

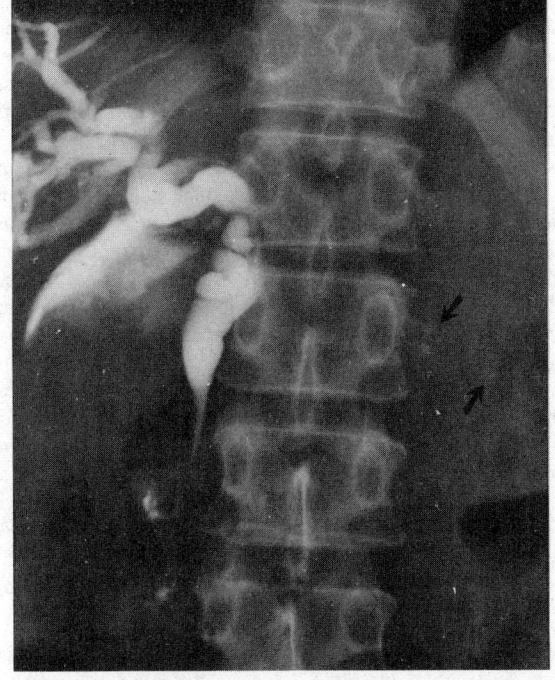

A

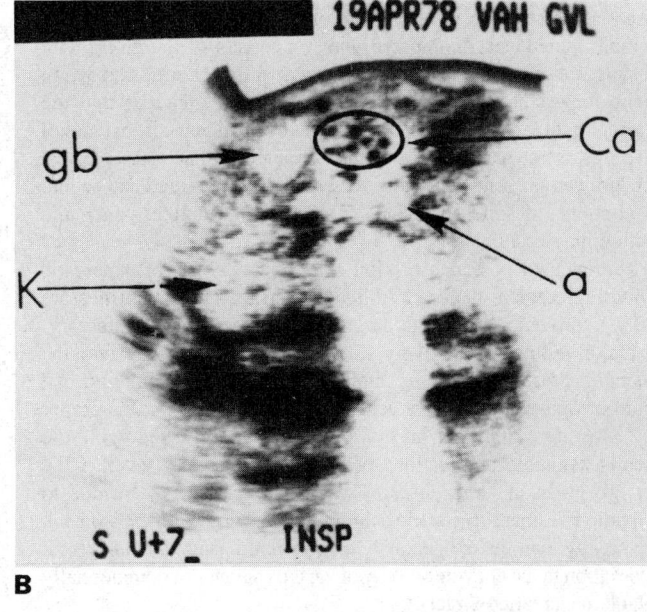

B

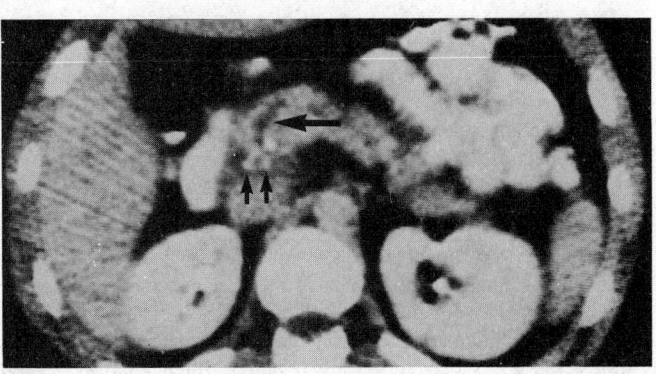

C

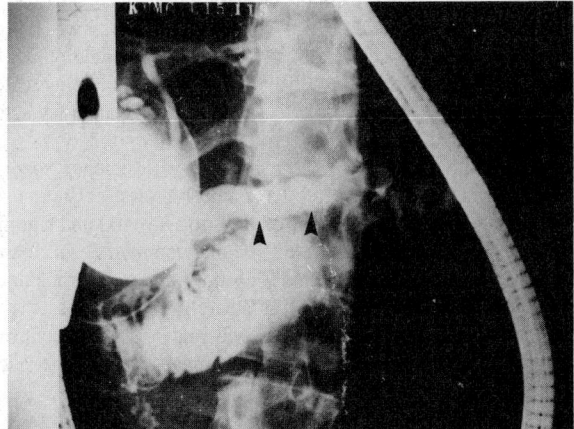

D

pancreatic endocrine and exocrine insufficiency. It is important to screen the patients carefully, for such radical surgery is contraindicated in those who are severely depressed or suicidal or continue to drink. Procedures such as sphincteroplasty, splanchnicectomy and celiac ganglionectomy, and nerve blocks usually bring only temporary relief and are not recommended.

Large doses of pancreatic extract (see below) seem to ameliorate and even abort the pain in some patients with chronic pancreatitis. These clinical observations seem to fit in with data in experimental animals which demonstrate a negative feedback regulation for pancreatic exocrine secretion controlled by the amount of proteases within the lumen of the proximal small intestine. It seems reasonable to approach the patient with severe persistent or continuous abdominal pain thought to be secondary to chronic pancreatitis in the following manner. After other causes of abdominal pain (peptic ulcer, gallstones, etc.) have been appropriately excluded, a pancreatic *sonogram* should be done. If no mass is found, a *secretin test* may be performed, since with chronic pancreatitis and pain this test usually will be abnormal. If the secretin test is abnormal (i.e., decreased bicarbonate concentration or volume output), a 3- to 4-week *trial of pancreatic enzymes* is appropriate. Three to eight capsules or tablets are taken at meals and at bedtime. If no relief is obtained, and especially if the volume secreted during the secretin test is very low, ERCP should be performed. If a pseudocyst or a localized ductal obstruction is found, appropriate surgery should be considered. A provocative study from South Africa questions the significance of the relationship of dilated ducts and/or strictures to pain. The finding of an appreciable obstruction or stricture in 65 percent of the patients who were pain-free more than 1 year, compared with 79 percent of the group with pain, suggests that factors other than duct obstruction or narrowing may be important in the pathogenesis of pain. It may be that the most important factors in the relief of pain are abstinence from alcohol and progressive pancreatic dysfunction rather than the surgical procedure per se. If no surgically remedial lesion is found and severe pain continues despite abstinence from alcohol, subtotal pancreatic resection may be necessary.

The treatment of malabsorption rests upon the use of pancreatic enzyme replacement therapy. Although diarrhea and steatorrhea are usually improved, the results are frequently less than satisfactory. The major problem is delivery of enough active enzyme into the duodenum. Steatorrhea can be abolished if 10 percent of the normal amount of lipase could be delivered into the duodenum at the proper time. This concentration of lipase cannot be achieved with the presently available preparations of pancreatic enzymes, even if the latter are given in large doses. These poor results may be due to inactivation of lipase by gastric acid, food emptying from the stomach more rapidly than the exogenously administered pancreatic enzymes, and variation in the enzyme activity of various batches of commercially available pancreatic extracts.

For the usual patient three to eight tablets or capsules of a potent enzyme preparation should be administered with meals. Some patients require adjuvant therapy to improve enzyme replacement treatment. Although initially cimetidine was considered an effective adjuvant, studies have failed to confirm this. Sodium bicarbonate (1.3 g with meals) is effective and inexpensive. Antacids containing calcium carbonate or magnesium hydroxide are not effective and may actually result in increased steatorrhea.

Patients with severe exocrine pancreatic insufficiency secondary to alcohol who continue to drink have a high mortality (in one series 50 percent were dead when followed for 5 to 12 years) and significant morbidity (weight loss, lassitude, vitamin deficiency, and narcotic addiction). Those with pain usually do not have steatorrhea and are approached as described above. If steatorrhea develops, the pain usually abates. If abstinence is pursued and vigorous replacement therapy is utilized for the maldigestion-malabsorption, the patients do reasonably well.

HEREDITARY PANCREATITIS   Hereditary pancreatitis is a rare disease similar to chronic pancreatitis except for an early age of onset

and evidence of hereditary factors (involving an autosomal dominant gene with incomplete penetrance). These patients have recurring attacks of severe abdominal pain which may last from a few days to a few weeks. The serum amylase and lipase levels may be elevated during acute attacks. Patients frequently develop pancreatic calcification, diabetes mellitus, and steatorrhea, and in addition, they have an increased incidence of pancreatic carcinoma. Abdominal complaints in relatives of patients with hereditary pancreatitis should raise the question of pancreatic disease.

CYSTIC FIBROSIS (See also Chap. 207)

GENERAL CONSIDERATIONS   Cystic fibrosis is the most common hereditary lethal disease in white children. It is transmitted as an autosomal recessive trait, with a prevalence of 1 per 1500 to 2500 births and with approximately 1 in 20 whites being heterozygous for the condition. Patients with cystic fibrosis have defective anion permeability of the mucus-producing exocrine glands in the bronchi, pancreas, liver, and intestine. The decrease in bicarbonate output when pancreatic secretion is stimulated leads to defective water flow and hyperconcentration of protein. However, the basic metabolic defect is unknown. This disease is no longer one of childhood and adolescence. With improvement in the therapy of patients with cystic fibrosis, an increasing number reach adulthood. Twenty-five years ago the mean survival was only 1 year; now, 50 percent of patients may survive to at least 25 years of age.

CLINICAL FEATURES   Although the triad of recurrent pulmonary infections, maldigestion-malabsorption, and an abnormal sweat test are characteristic, patients are frequently seen without these classic manifestations. Approximately 85 percent of patients with cystic fibrosis have impairment of pancreatic exocrine function. Steatorrhea is often marked and accompanied by deficiencies of fat-soluble vitamins (e.g., low prothrombin levels). A small number of patients may have recurrent pancreatitis with abdominal pain and elevated amylase levels. Biliary cirrhosis develops in 5 to 10 percent. Approximately 15 percent of patients may develop intestinal obstruction at birth because of the thick, tenacious intestinal secretions. Similarly, children or adults may develop small- or large-bowel obstruction, ileocolic intussusception, cecal or sigmoid volvulus, rectal impaction, and rectal prolapse. Cobalamin and bile acid malabsorption are common but correctable by oral pancreatic extract. Cobalamin deficiency is rare, perhaps due to the almost universal administration of pancreatic extract to these patients beginning at an early age. The incidence of gallstones is increased. Although frank diabetes is uncommon, glucose intolerance may be present in 40 percent of patients. Nearly all males have aspermia because of a failure in development of the vas deferens, epididymis, and seminal vesicles.

DIAGNOSIS   A properly performed and interpreted sweat test (quantitative pilocarpine iontophoresis) is essential for the diagnosis of cystic fibrosis. In almost all patients the sweat chloride is greater than 60 meq per liter. Secretin or CCK-PZ tests will usually demonstrate severe impairment of bicarbonate output and pancreatic enzymes, respectively. The bentiromide test (Chap. 254) is usually abnormal, and, in addition, may be used to assess the effectiveness of pancreatic enzyme replacement therapy. Recent studies indicate that elevation of serum trypsin levels within the first few weeks of life is diagnostic of cystic fibrosis and thus may serve as an effective screening test. However, as the disease progresses and frank pancreatic insufficiency develops, serum trypsin levels will be decreased.

THERAPY   Treatment includes antibiotics for recurrent pulmonary infections, inhalation and physical therapy, pancreatic extracts, and vitamin supplementation, as well as psychological and emotional support. Although complete correction of fat malabsorption is usually not achieved, satisfactory weight gain is often attained. Elevated blood and urine uric acid levels may occur in children taking excessive doses of pancreatic enzymes, but this is reversible with reduction in dosage and has not been observed with the newer enteric-coated preparations.

CANCER OF THE PANCREAS

GENERAL CONSIDERATIONS Carcinoma of the pancreas is now the fourth commonest cancer causing death in the United States; only cancer of the lung, colon, and breast occur more frequently. It accounts for 10 percent of all tumors of digestive organs and over 20,000 deaths per year. The incidence has increased 300 percent since 1930 to approximately 11 per 100,000 population. The disease is more common in males than females (1.5:1), and the peak incidence is between the ages of 60 to 70. Although the etiologic factors in most cases are not known, incidence of carcinoma of the pancreas is 2.0 to 2.5 times greater in *smokers* than in nonsmokers, and about 2 times greater in patients with *diabetes mellitus*. Epidemiologic evidence suggests that a high-fat diet and certain occupational chemical exposures (e.g., β-naphthylamine) increase the risk of pancreatic cancer. Some reports have also suggested an association between heavy coffee intake and increased risk of pancreatic cancer, but whether a true causal relationship exists is questionable. The tumors are usually adenocarcinomas arising from ductal epithelium. The head of the pancreas is involved in about 65 percent, the body and tail in 30 percent, and the tail alone in 5 percent. At the time of diagnosis the tumor is confined to the pancreas in only 15 percent of patients; 25 percent demonstrate local invasion or regional lymph node spread, and the remaining 60 percent exhibit distinct metastases.

CLINICAL FEATURES Weight loss, abdominal pain, anorexia, and jaundice are the classic symptoms. Nausea, weakness and fatigue, vomiting, diarrhea, dyspepsia, and back pain are also fairly common. The weight loss in carcinoma is extensive (average total loss about 25 lb) and is not fully explained by anorexia and maldigestion. The weight loss in patients with lesions in the body and tail, in whom malabsorption should be minimal, is often as pronounced as when the carcinoma is in the head of the pancreas.

Pain occurs at some time in the course of the disease in 75 to 90 percent of patients. With tumors of the head of the pancreas, the pain is likely to be in the epigastrium and right upper quadrant; with lesions in the body of the pancreas, pain often localizes in the midline, whereas with lesions in the tail, pain may be referred to the left upper quadrant. Abdominal pain may be vague or may be a steady dull, aching, or boring pain often radiating through to the back. Severe and unrelenting pain suggests extension into the retroperitoneal area with invasion of the neural plexus around the celiac axis ganglion.

Jaundice occurs some time in the course of the disease in 80 to 90 percent of patients with carcinoma of the head, and in 10 to 40 percent in patients with tumors of the body and tail. When it occurs it is progressive and accompanied by pruritus. Both constipation and diarrhea have been cited as the predominant alteration of bowel habits. Emotional disturbances frequently occur in cancer of the pancreas and may take the form of insomnia, restlessness, rage, anxiety, depression, suicidal tendencies, and a sense of impending doom.

Physical examination frequently reveals evidence of weight loss, jaundice, and enlarged liver and abdominal tenderness. Although the gallbladder is usually enlarged, it is palpable in only 15 to 40 percent of cases (Courvoisier's sign). The finding of an enlarged gallbladder in a jaundiced patient without biliary colic should suggest malignant obstruction of the extrahepatic biliary tree. Splenomegaly may result from compression, invasion, and thrombosis of the portal venous system, especially the splenic vein. Erosion of the duodenal mucosa may cause occult or frank gastrointestinal bleeding. In carcinoma of the body and tail, an abdominal mass can be felt in 40 to 50 percent of patients; hepatomegaly is less common than in tumors of the head of the pancreas, and obvious hepatic enlargement should suggest hepatic metastasis. An important physical finding is an abdominal

bruit which is usually heard in the periumbilical area and left upper quadrant, and this is due to invasion and/or compression of the splenic artery by tumor. Thrombophlebitis occurs in approximately 10 percent of patients and is more common with the tumors of the body or tail of the pancreas. In acinar-cell carcinomas, which are uncommon, tender subcutaneous nodules due to subcutaneous fat necrosis and polyarthralgia occur.

The diagnosis of pancreatic carcinoma should be suspected in patients past the age of 50 who present with any of the following findings: (1) unexplained weight loss greater than 10 percent of normal body weight; (2) unexplained upper abdominal pain, especially with a negative upper gastrointestinal tract workup; (3) unexplained back pain; (4) an attack of pancreatitis without an obvious cause; (5) stigmata of exocrine pancreatic insufficiency without an obvious cause; (6) sudden onset of diabetes mellitus without a predisposing cause such as obesity or family history; and (7) jaundice with obstructive features. Carcinoma of the hepatic duct bifurcation, of the ampulla of Vater, and of the duodenum also need to be considered in the differential diagnosis, but these all occur quite infrequently.

LABORATORY FINDINGS Laboratory data are only occasionally helpful in suggesting the diagnosis of pancreatic carcinoma. The serum amylase and lipase values are abnormal in only 10 percent of cases. About 20 percent of patients have fasting hyperglycemia or glycosuria. Anemia, which occurs in one-third of patients, and occult blood in the stool, which occurs in one-half of patients, are usually due to erosion of the duodenal mucosa by tumor. Although the stools may have a greasy or pultaceous consistency, frank steatorrhea occurs in only about 10 percent of patients. Carcinoma of the head of the pancreas with bile duct obstruction is accompanied by hyperbilirubinemia and clay-colored stools. By contrast, the blood, urine, and feces in patients with carcinoma of the body and tail of the pancreas are often normal. The serum alkaline phosphatase is usually elevated in patients with jaundice (and may antedate the hyperbilirubinemia). It is elevated in about 35 percent of cases without jaundice.

DIAGNOSTIC PROCEDURES Although standard gastrointestinal x-rays may suggest the presence of carcinoma of the head of the pancreas, the tumor is usually of considerable size before it distorts the duodenal mucosa and the configuration of the duodenal loop. Thus, only 50 percent of patients with carcinoma of the head of the pancreas have an abnormal examination. The frequency of abnormal exams is even lower with lesions in the body and tail of the pancreas.

Ultrasound is valuable in the diagnosis of pancreatic carcinoma, especially as an initial screening procedure; abnormalities are found in 70 to 90 percent of patients with pancreatic carcinoma. Sonography is most likely to be positive if the tumor is over 2 cm in diameter and lies in the head or body of the pancreas; lesions in the body and tail of the pancreas are more difficult to recognize.

CT scanning is frequently abnormal in pancreatic carcinoma; in most series of proved cases, CT scans detected the lesion in over 80 percent. In 5 to 15 percent of patients with proven pancreatic carcinoma the CT scan shows only generalized pancreatic enlargement suggestive of pancreatitis rather than malignancy. False-positive results have also been reported in about 5 to 10 percent of cases where no tumor was found at laparotomy. CT scanning has some advantages over ultrasound, such as better definition of the body and tail of the pancreas as well as contiguous organs, but the cost is greater. Selective and superselective angiography is of definite value in some patients. Advantages of angiography include (1) detection of carcinoma in the body and tail of the pancreas by observing vessel sheathing (Fig. 255-2), vessel displacement, and vascular occlusion; (2) detection of metastatic spread to the liver; and (3) assessment of the degree of involvement of huge pancreatic vessels which may be an important consideration preoperatively. When the arteriogram is positive, about 85 percent of patients can be expected to have pancreatic cancer; however, false-negatives occur in about 15 percent of patients.

ERCP may be diagnostic in 75 to 85 percent of cases. The

characteristic findings are stenosis or obstruction of either the pancreatic or the common bile duct; both duct systems are abnormal in over half the cases. The differentiation, however, between carcinoma and chronic pancreatitis by ERCP can be quite difficult if both diseases are present. False-negative results with ERCP are quite low (less than 5 percent) and usually occur with acinar-cell rather than ductal carcinoma. Finally, *percutaneous aspiration biopsy of the pancreas* under ultrasonic or CT guidance is a procedure which can provide a definitive diagnosis and may obviate surgical exploration.

Tests of exocrine pancreatic function with duodenal intubation and analysis of duodenal contents are abnormal in approximately 80 percent of cases. However, pancreatic function tests do not permit discrimination between pancreatic carcinoma and chronic pancreatitis. Cytologic examination of pancreatic fluid obtained after secretin-cholecystokinin stimulation has not been found reliable enough to diagnose pancreatic cancer. Of the many serologic markers available, none have proved useful in detecting asymptomatic patients with pancreatic cancer.

To summarize, if pancreatic carcinoma is suspected, the first test should be either ultrasound or CT scan. If an abnormality is noted, the next test should be ERCP. If ERCP is nondiagnostic or unsuccessful, selective angiography should be considered. At present, pancreatic function tests, radionuclide pancreatic scintigraphy, and measurement of tumor markers are of limited value in the workup of a patient with suspected pancreatic cancer.

It should be emphasized that patients with carcinoma of the pancreas are frequently investigated for several months before a diagnosis is established. Even laparotomy may not provide a definitive diagnosis because chronic pancreatitis may produce a hard mass in the head of the pancreas indistinguishable from carcinoma by palpation. Furthermore, biopsy of such a mass may not show neoplastic tissue and reveal only evidence of pancreatitis because the carcinoma is often surrounded by edematous, inflamed, and fibrotic tissue, e.g., changes of chronic pancreatitis.

TREATMENT AND COURSE When the diagnosis is confirmed at laparotomy, the tumor is usually inoperable. The resectability rate in most series is only about 15 to 20 percent. If the tumor is localized and has not spread to portal lymph nodes, and is not fixed to other structures (e.g., portal vein, superior mesenteric vein, and common bile duct), the lesion should be considered resectable. Resection under these circumstances offers an opportunity for palliation, although survival does not appear to be prolonged. In many patients, just palliative bypass of biliary tract obstruction should be performed. Importantly, the mortality rate with a Whipple procedure (pancreatoduodenal resection) is about 20 percent in most series. The median survival is 6 months from the time of diagnosis. Approximately 10 percent of patients survive 1 year, and in most reported series, the 5-year survival rate is a dismal 1 to 2 percent. Multicenter studies on patients with inoperable pancreatic cancer suggest that either high-dose small-volume radiation therapy or multidrug chemotherapy (fluorouracil, cyclophosphamide, methotrexate, and vincristine followed by fluorouracil and mitomycin for maintenance) prolong survival in 15 to 30 percent of patients.

PANCREATIC ENDOCRINE TUMORS

Pancreatic endocrine tumors are summarized in Table 255-5 and discussed in Chap. 329.

OTHER CONDITIONS

ANNULAR PANCREAS When there is a failure in communication of the ventral and dorsal anlage of the pancreas, a ring of pancreatic tissue encircles the duodenum. Such an annular pancreas may cause intestinal obstruction in the neonate or the adult. Symptoms of postprandial fullness, epigastric pain, nausea, and vomiting may be present for years before the diagnosis is entertained. The radiographic findings are symmetric dilatation of the proximal duodenum with bulging of the recesses on either side of the annular band, effacement of the duodenal mucosa without destruction of the mucosa, accentuation of the findings in the right anterior oblique position, and the lack of change on repeated examinations. The differential diagnosis should include duodenal webs, tumors of the pancreas or duodenum, postbulbar peptic ulcer, regional enteritis, and adhesions. Patients

TABLE 255-5 Pancreatic endocrine tumors

Syndrome	Hormone(s) produced	Primary hormone effects	Pathologic features	Clinical features
Zollinger-Ellison	Gastrin	Gastric acid hypersecretion with basal acid outputs usually >15 meq/h	Delta-cell islet tumors; 10% aberrant (duodenal); 60% malignant	Severe peptic ulcer disease often refractory to therapy; ectopic ulcers; diarrhea; multiple endocrine adenomas (parathyroid, pituitary, adrenal, thyroid)
Insulinoma	Insulin	Hypoglycemia with inappropriately increased serum insulin levels	Beta-cell islet tumors; 80–90% benign	Hypoglycemic symptoms
Glucagonoma	Glucagon; pancreatic polypeptide	Hyperglucagonemia →glucose intolerance	Alpha-cell islet tumors; 60% malignant	Slow-growing pancreatic tumor; hyperglycemia; bullous and eczematoid dermatitis, weight loss; anemia; gastric and intestinal motor abnormalities
Somatostatinoma	Somatostatin; pancreatic polypeptide	Somatostatin inhibits insulin, gastrin and pancreatic enzyme secretion; decreased bile flow	Delta-cell islet tumor	Pancreatic tumor; diarrhea; steatorrhea; gallstones; diabetes mellitus; anemia
Pancreatic cholera	Vasoactive intestinal peptide (VIP) ? Gastric inhibitory polypeptide ? Prostaglandin E ? Pancreatic peptide	Net secretion of salt and water by gut	? Delta-cell tumor; >50% malignant	Pancreatic tumor with severe watery diarrhea; flushing; weight loss; hypokalemia; hypercalcemia; hypochlorhydria; hyperglycemia; inordinate fecal water and electrolyte losses
Carcinoid	Serotonin; prostaglandins	Altered gut motility; diarrhea	Enterochromaffin cells; non-beta-cell islet tumors	Carcinoid syndrome with flushing; wheezing; diarrhea; alcohol intolerance; hepatomegaly

with annular pancreas have an increased incidence of pancreatitis and peptic ulcer. Because of these and other potential complications, the treatment is surgical even though the condition has been present for years. Retrocolic duodenojejunostomy is the procedure of choice, although some surgeons advocate Billroth II gastrectomy, gastroenterostomy, and vagotomy.

PANCREAS DIVISUM Pancreas divisum occurs when the embryologic ventral and dorsal parts of the pancreas fail to fuse so that pancreatic drainage is accomplished mainly through the accessory papilla (Fig. 255-4). This condition should be thought of not only in patients with recurrent pancreatitis without obvious cause, but also in patients who develop pancreatitis after ingesting small amounts of alcohol, and in patients having ERCP who complain of abdominal pain immediately following the injection of small amounts of contrast material (due to overdistention of the small duct of Wirsung). Since the accessory papilla in the duct of Santorini is too small to accept total pancreatic secretion, obstructive pain and pancreatitis may result. Up to 25 percent of patients with unexplained attacks of acute pancreatitis are associated with pancreas divisum. Accordingly, patients with pancreas divisum and symptoms or signs of pancreatic disease usually have some stenosis of the orifice of the duct of Santorini. The appropriate therapy for this condition is still being defined.

MACROAMYLASEMIA Macroamylasemia is a condition whereby amylase is circulating in the blood in a polymer form too large to be easily excreted by the kidney. The patient with this condition will demonstrate an elevated serum amylase value, a low urinary amylase, and a C_{am}/C_{cr} of less than 1 percent. The presence of macroamylase can be documented by chromatography of the serum. The prevalence of macroamylasemia is 1.5 percent of the nonalcoholic general adult hospital population. Usually macroamylasemia is an incidental finding and is not related to disease of the pancreas or other organs. It is important to be aware of this condition so that patients with macroamylasemia will not be needlessly evaluated and treated for pancreatic disease.

REFERENCES

BRADLEY EL et al: The natural history of pancreatic pseudocysts: A unified concept of management. Am J Surg 137:135, 1979

COTTON PB: Cogenital anomaly of pancreas divisum as a cause of obstructive pain and pancreatitis. Gut 21:105, 1980

FRIESEN SR: Tumors of the endocrine pancreas. N Engl J Med 306:580, 1982

GARDNER JD, JENSEN RT: Gastrointestinal peptides: The basis of action at the cellular level, in *Recent Progress in Hormone Research,* vol 39. New York, Academic, 1983

JACOBSON DG et al: Trypsin-like immunoreactivity as a test for pancreatic insufficiency. N Engl J Med 310:1307, 1984

KOLARS JC et al: Comparison of serum amylase, pancreatic isoamylase and lipase in patients with hyperamylasemia. Dig Dis Sci 29:289, 1984

KOPELMAN H et al: Pancreatic fluid secretion and protein hyperconcentration in cystic fibrosis. N Engl J Med 312:329, 1985

MALLORY A, KERN F: Drug-induced pancreatitis. A critical review. Gastroenterology 78:813, 1980

MALT RA: Treatment of pancreatic cancer. JAMA 250:1433, 1983

FIGURE 255-4 *Illustration of the pancreatic ducts and typical ERCP of pancreas divisum. A. Diagram of the ventral and dorsal structures of the pancreas: (1) duct of Santorini; (2) pancreatic duct from the dorsal analogue; (3) pancreatic duct from the ventral analogue; (4) duct of Wirsung; and (5) common bile duct. B. ERCP showing filling only of the ventral component of the pancreatic duct and the common bile duct (CBD) from cannulization of the duct of Wirsung. Failure to fill the pancreatic duct of the body and tail of the pancreas is diagnostic of ventral pancreas or pancreas divisum. E = endoscope.*

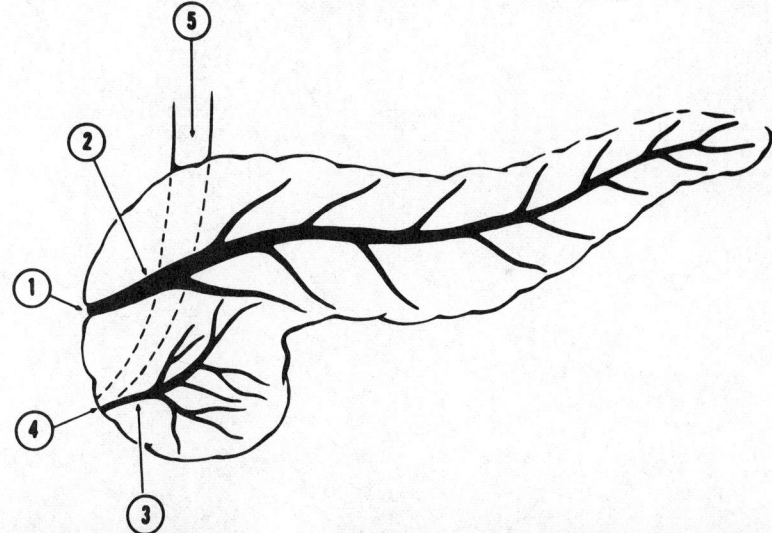

A

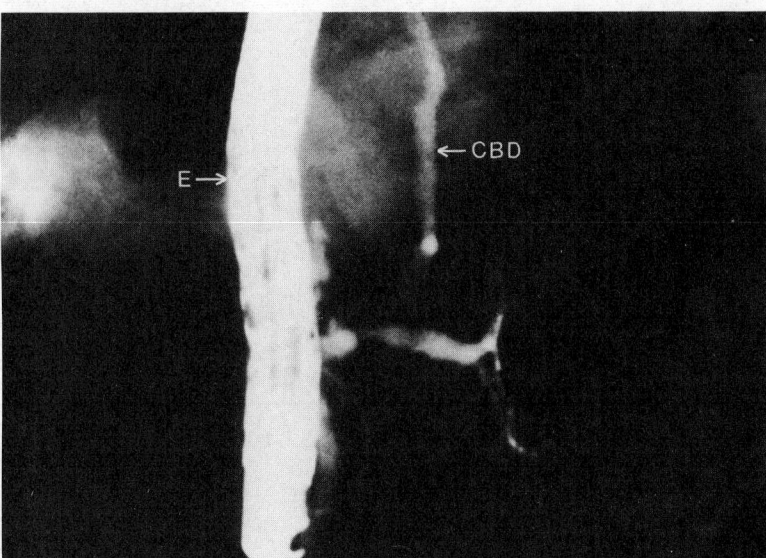

B

MAYER DA et al: Controlled clinical trial of peritoneal lavage for the treatment of severe acute pancreatitis. N Engl J Med 312:399, 1985

NIEDERAU C, GRENDELL JH: Diagnosis of chronic pancreatitis. Gastroenterology 88:1973, 1985

RANSON JH-C: Risk factors in acute pancreatitis. Hosp Pract 20:69, 1985

SCHWACHMAN H et al: Cystic fibrosis: A new outlook: 70 patients above 25 years of age. Medicine 56:129, 1977

SLAFF J et al: Protease specific suppression of pancreatic exocrine secretion. Gastroenterology 87:44, 1984

SOLOMON TE: Regulation of pancreatic secretion. Clin Gastroenterol 13:657, 1984

STEER ML et al: Pancreatitis. The role of lysosomes. Dig Dis Sci 29:934, 1984

STEINBERG WM et al: Comparison of sensitivity and specificity of CA19-9 and carcinoembryonic antigen assays in detecting cancer of the pancreas. Gastroenterology 90:343, 1986

———— et al: Diagnostic assays in acute pancreatitis. Ann Int Med 102:576. 1985

TOSKES PP, GREENBERGER NJ: Acute and chronic pancreatitis. DM vol 24, 1983

VAN DYKE JA et al: Pancreatic imaging. Ann Intern Med 102:212, 1985

PART EIGHT

DISORDERS OF THE IMMUNE SYSTEM, CONNECTIVE TISSUE, AND JOINTS

section 1 Disorders of the immune system

256 IMMUNE DEFICIENCY DISEASES

MAX D. COOPER / ALEXANDER R. LAWTON III

INTRODUCTION Immunologic functions are mediated by two developmentally independent, but functionally interacting, families of lymphocytes. The activities of B and T lymphocytes, and their products, in host defense are closely integrated with the functions of other cells of the reticuloendothelial system. Macrophages, dendritic cells, and the Langerhans' cells in the skin play an important role in the trapping and presentation of antigens to T and B cells to initiate the immune response. Macrophages also become effector cells, especially when activated by products of lymphocytes. The scavenger activity of polymorphonuclear leukocytes is directed and made specific by antibodies in concert with products of the complement system (see Chap. 62). Natural killer (NK) cells, a recently recognized population of granular lymphocytes, may spontaneously kill tumor and virus-infected cells, activities that are enhanced by the interferon products of immune and inflammatory cells. Killing by NK cells can also be targeted by IgG antibodies for which NK cells have cell-surface receptors. The interaction of basophils and tissue mast cells with IgE antibodies in causation of immediate hypersensitivity is discussed in Chap. 260. Consideration of these interrelationships is an important part of the analysis of patients with suspected immune deficiency.

CLINICAL DISEASE FEATURES COMMON TO IMMUNE DEFICIENCY Immunodeficiency syndromes, whether congenital, spontaneously acquired, or iatrogenic, are characterized by unusual susceptibility to infection and, sometimes, to autoimmune disease and lymphoreticular malignancies. The types of infection often provide the first clue to the nature of the immunologic defect.

Patients with defects in humoral immunity have recurrent or chronic sinopulmonary infection, meningitis, and bacteremia, most commonly caused by pyogenic bacteria such as *Haemophilus influenzae, Streptococcus pneumoniae,* and staphylococci. The same pathogens tend to infect patients with normal immune responses, but with either neutropenia or a deficiency of the pivotal third component of complement (C3), suggesting that a tripartite collaboration involving antibody, complement, and phagocytes exists as the chief mechanism of host defense against pyogenic organisms. Binding of antibody to the bacterial surface causes activation of the complement system. One cleavage product of activated C3 serves as a chemotactic factor for polymorphonuclear leukocytes. Activated C3b fixed to bacterial surfaces facilitates phagocytosis by interaction with C3b receptors on neutrophils.

Agammaglobulinemic patients in whom cell-mediated immunity is intact have an interesting response to viral infections. The clinical course of primary infection with viruses such as varicella zoster or rubeola, unless complicated by bacterial infection, does not differ significantly from that of the normal host. However, long-lasting immunity may not develop, and as a result multiple bouts of chickenpox and measles may occur. Such observations suggest that intact T cells may be sufficient for control of established viral infections, while antibodies play an important role in limiting the initial dissemination of virus and in providing long-lasting protection. Exceptions to this generalization are becoming more widely recognized. Agammaglobulinemic patients fail to clear hepatitis B virus from their circulation and have a progressive, and often fatal, course. Poliomyelitis has occurred following live-virus vaccination in some patients. Chronic encephalitis, which may progress over a period of months to years, is being observed with apparently increasing frequency. Echoviruses and adenoviruses have been isolated from brain, spinal fluid, or other sites in such patients; in others no agent has been detected. Immunologic injury resulting from a partial and ineffective immune response may contribute as much to the pathogenesis of these diseases as the direct effects of the viruses.

The occurrence of unusual serious infection, for example, *H. influenzae* meningitis in an older child or adult, warrants consideration of humoral immune deficiency. Bacterial infections in certain sites may also suggest this possibility. Chronic otitis media occurs frequently in patients with hypogammaglobulinemia, and is significant because of its relative rarity in normal adults. Pansinusitis, although almost invariably present in immunoglobulin deficiency, is a less helpful finding because it is not rare in apparently normal people. Bacterial infections of the skin or urinary tract are less frequent problems in hypogammaglobulinemic patients.

Infestation with the intestinal parasite *Giardia lamblia* is a frequent enough cause of diarrhea in antibody-deficient patients to warrant diagnostic duodenal aspiration and intestinal biopsy when the organism cannot be demonstrated in the stool.

Abnormalities of cell-mediated immunity predispose to *disseminated virus infections,* particularly with latent viruses such as herpes simplex (see Chap. 136), varicella zoster (see Chap. 135), and cytomegalovirus (see Chap. 137). In addition, patients so affected almost invariably develop mucocutaneous candidiasis and frequently acquire widely disseminated fungal infections. Pneumonia caused by the protozoan *Pneumocystis carinii* is also common (see Chap. 158).

T-cell deficiency is probably always accompanied by some abnormality of antibody responses (see Fig. 256-1), although this may not be reflected by hypogammaglobulinemia. This may explain in part why patients with primary T-cell defects are also subject to overwhelming bacterial infection.

The most severe form of immune deficiency occurs in individuals, often infants, who lack both cell-mediated and humoral immune functions. They are susceptible to the whole range of infectious agents including organisms not ordinarily considered pathogenic. Multiple infections with viruses, bacteria, and fungi occur, often simultaneously. Because donor lymphocytes cannot be rejected by the recipients, blood transfusions can produce fatal graft-versus-host disease.

DIFFERENTIATION OF T AND B CELLS The functional deficits which occur in both congenital and acquired immunodeficiencies are usefully viewed as being caused by defects at various points along the differentiation pathways of immunocompetent cells. For this reason certain features of the development and differentiation of T and B cells that are especially relevant to the analysis of immunodeficiency are briefly presented here; Chap. 62 provides a general account of their roles in cellular and humoral immunity.

A subpopulation of hematopoietic stem cells may become restricted to lymphoid differentiation prior to migration to the thymus, where T cells are generated, or to the fetal liver and adult bone marrow, where B-cell development begins (Fig. 256-1). A major function of central lymphoid tissues is to generate the clonal diversity character-

istic of the immune system. Each T or B lymphocyte is induced to express surface receptor molecules of a unique specificity for antigen. The receptors of B lymphocytes are immunoglobulin molecules which are formed by paired heavy and light chains of either κ or λ type. The heavy chain gene loci are on the long arm of chromosome 14; the 5'-3' order of these is V_H (variable), D (diversity), and J_H (joining) minigene families followed by the C_H (constant region) genes, C_μ, C_δ, $C_{\gamma3}$, $C_{\gamma1}$, $C_{\alpha1}$, $C_{\gamma2}$, $C_{\gamma4}$, C_ϵ, and $C_{\alpha2}$. The κ gene family, consisting of V_κ, J_κ, and C_κ genes, is located on chromosome 2, and the homologous λ gene loci on chromosome 22.

The T-cell receptors are related cell surface molecules with antigen-binding specificity. The T-cell receptor is composed of two polypeptide chains, presently called α and β. The β-chain family is located on chromosome 7, and consists of V_β, D_β, J_β, and C_β minigene loci. The α-chain family on chromosome 14 similarly consists of a series of V_α, D_α, J_α, and C_α genes.

The genetic strategy for creating functional gene complexes encoding antigen receptors is similar for T and B cells. For example,

FIGURE 256-1 *Differentiation of lymphoid cells is accompanied by acquisition and loss of specific cell-surface antigens as well as morphologic and functional changes. Some antigens are expressed as stem cells, differentiate within the thymus, and are shared by all mature T cells; commercially available monoclonal antibodies to such pan-T-cell antigens include T3 and Leu 4. T6, the human counterpart to the mouse thymic leukemia (TL) antigen, is expressed only by thymocytes. Within the thymus, cells acquiring helper-inducer functions selectively lose the T8 (Leu 2) antigen, while T4 (Leu 3) antigen is lost by cells destined to serve cytotoxic and suppressor functions. HLA-DR antigens are expressed by all cells of the B lineage, up to and including some plasma cells. T cells, in contrast, express HLA-DR only when they have been activated. These differentiation antigens serve as useful markers for evaluation of disorders of development and function of T and B cells. Failure to develop T and B cells may result from defective stem cells* or from inborn metabolic errors affecting both cell types. Rarely, other hematopoietic cell lines are also absent. Absence of either T or B cells suggests malfunction of central lymphoid tissues, including the thymus and the fetal liver–bone marrow complex. B-cell deficiency may result from failure to generate pre-B cells from their stem cell precursors or from failure of pre-B cells to give rise to their B-lymphocyte progeny. Similarly, differentiation may be arrested at several levels within the T-cell lineage; arrests at the thymocyte level and failure to develop the helper-inducer subset have been observed in immunodeficient patients. Agammaglobulinemia and deficiencies of some T-cell functions may occur despite the presence of normal numbers of B or T cells in the circulation. Failure of B lymphocytes to differentiate to plasma cells can be due to intrinsic cellular abnormalities or to faulty T-cell regulation.

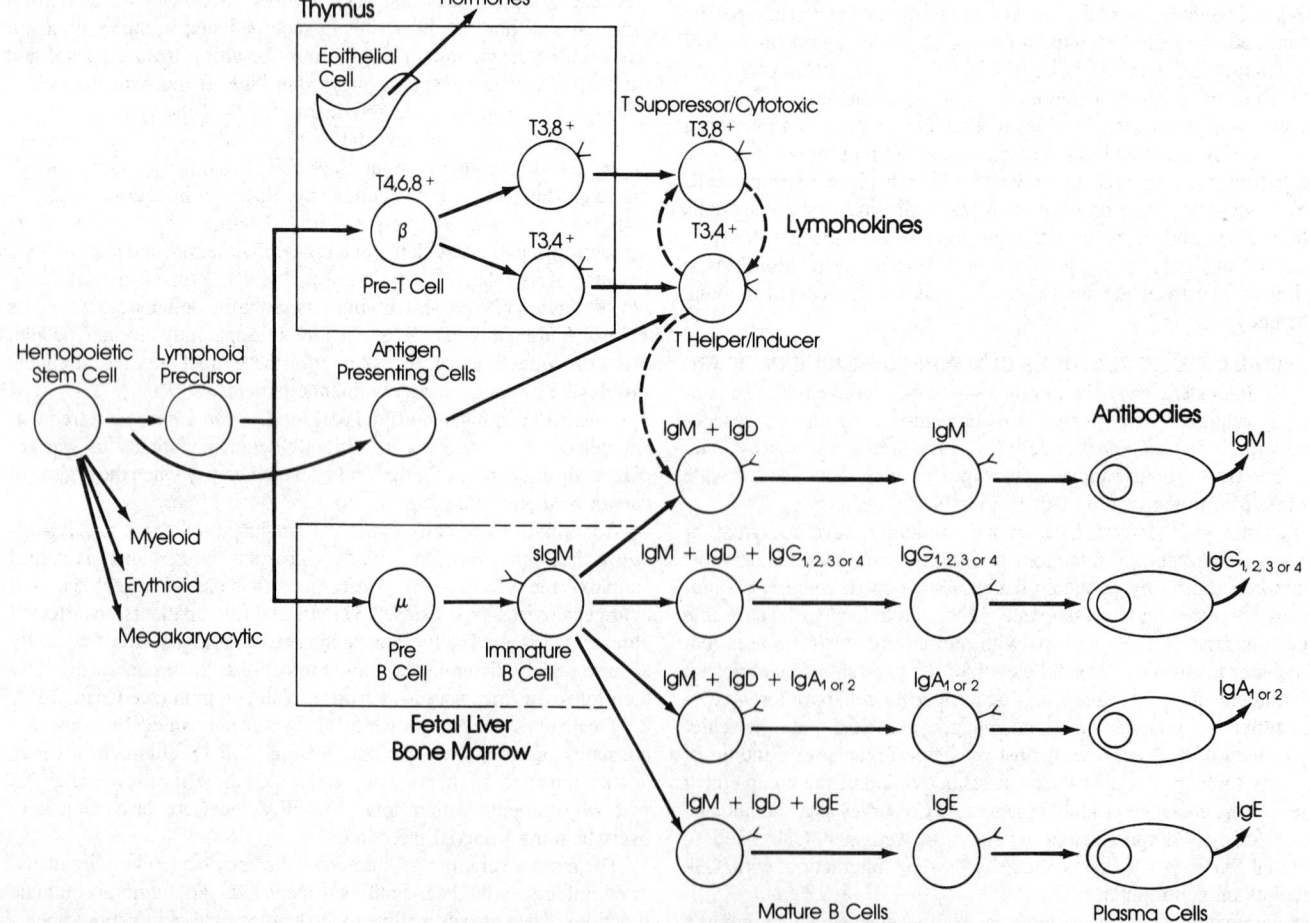

a productive V region gene of the immunoglobulin heavy chain is formed by rearrangement of one each of the V_H, D, and J_H genes and deletion of the intervening DNA to generate a contiguous coding structure which is then transcribed together with the nearest C_H gene. Functional light chain genes are formed by a V-J rearrangement in either the κ or λ gene loci. The V_β gene is similarly composed of a rearranged set of V_β, D_β, and J_β genes to form a contiguous coding structure, which the T cell then transcribes along with the nearest C_β gene. Because there are many different V, D, and J genes, they can be put together in various combinations to encode a large number of receptor molecules having different antigen-binding specificities.

Generation of clonal diversity requires cellular proliferation, such that each of the different receptor specificities encoded in the genome comes to be uniquely expressed by individual cells. A clone consists of all cells that express the identical antigen-binding receptors. Estimates for the total number of B-cell clones usually vary between 10 and 100 million. T-cell clonal diversity is also extensive, but may be less than that of the B-cell population. The process of clonal development is independent of antigen and reflects a genetically programmed sequence of differentiation analogous to that of primary erythropoiesis or myelopoiesis. This phase, termed *primary differentiation,* begins early in human fetal development but probably continues into adult life.

The most primitive morphologically identifiable cell in the B lineage is called a pre-B cell. These cells have undergone a productive V_HDJ_H rearrangement and express cytoplasmic μ chains (the heavy chain of IgM). Since light chain gene rearrangements have not yet occurred at this stage, pre-B cells lack the membrane-bound immunoglobulin receptors which characterize B lymphocytes. Pre-B cells are first generated in fetal liver and are produced exclusively in bone marrow of adults. Pre-B cells proliferate rapidly and, after undergoing a productive rearrangement of light chain VJ genes, spawn immature B lymphocytes which express surface IgM receptors and divide rarely. Young B lymphocytes differ from their more mature counterparts in an important physiologic characteristic; they are highly susceptible to inactivation when their receptors bind antigen. This phenomenon almost certainly is one important mechanism for the development of tolerance to self-antigens.

The developmental sequence for expression of diverse immunoglobulin classes by human B lymphocytes begins with expression of IgM. The expression of IgD on IgM-bearing cells occurs later. Lymphocytes committed to synthesis of IgG, IgA, and IgE are all derived from IgM-bearing precursors through a genetic switch mechanism. Each of the heavy chain constant region genes except C_δ is preceded by a switch region composed of repetitive nucleotide sequences. The heavy chain class switch is accomplished by splicing of the switch region of μ with the switch region in front of the downstream heavy chain gene to be expressed next.

T cells also appear to undergo sequential rearrangements of the minigene families encoding their antigen receptors. Initially, pre-T cells beginning development along this differentiation pathway in the thymus rearrange one each of the V_β, D_β, and J_β genes prior to the expression of a complete β chain. At a later differentiation stage, similar rearrangements occur in the α-chain gene family, and then the completed antigen receptor molecule of one α chain and one β chain is expressed on the cell surface of an immature T cell.

The expression of a group of differentiation antigens, defined by their reactivity with monoclonal antibodies, has become a powerful tool in elucidating developmental relationships of both T and B lymphocytes (Fig. 256-1). All immunocompetent T cells express T3 or Leu 4 molecules, which form a functional complex with the antigen receptor molecules on the cell surface. Of major clinical importance is the demarcation of two independent sets of T lymphocytes. T cells bearing the T4 or Leu 3 markers constitute approximately 70 percent of total T cells and function as helper-inducer cells, necessary for expression of effector functions of both T and B cells. T8$^+$ (or Leu 2$^+$) lymphocytes, constituting 20 to 30 percent of circulating T cells, are responsible for suppression of immune responses and mediate

cytotoxic reactions. Developmental arrests or failure of function of one or the other of these T-cell subsets may be responsible for immunodeficiency or autoimmune diseases.

In addition to generating T cells, the thymus apparently secretes hormonal products which regulate cellular maturation in peripheral lymphoid tissues. These hormones have been called *thymosin* or *thymopoietin;* deficiencies of these factors have been implicated in some immunodeficiencies.

The events designated *secondary differentiation* follow stimulation of specific clones of lymphocytes by antigen. These processes are synonymous with the immune response (see Chap. 62). Particularly important in consideration of immunodeficiencies are the collaborative interactions among macrophages, T cells, and B cells. B lymphocytes can proliferate in response to thymus-dependent antigens without the help of T cells, and may differentiate to IgM-secreting plasma cells when stimulated by thymus-independent antigens such as polysaccharides. However, production of normal quantities of antibodies, particularly those of the IgA and IgG classes, requires the collaboration of T cells.

Differentiation of T or B cells may be arrested at either the primary or secondary stages. Reflecting the complex cellular interactions involved in immune responses and the pivotal role played by T lymphocytes, immune deficiencies primarily involving T cells are usually also associated with abnormal B-cell function. Conversely, immunodeficiencies manifested primarily by inability to produce antibodies may be caused by T-cell defects not associated with abnormal cell-mediated immunity.

EVALUATION OF IMMUNODEFICIENT PATIENTS Many of the laboratory assays used for precise evaluation of immunologic functions in humans are available only in specialized centers; nevertheless, most immunodeficiencies may be diagnosed by thoughtful use of tests available in most clinical laboratories. Table 256-1 presents a résumé of laboratory investigations roughly in order of increasing complexity.

A careful history will usually indicate whether the major problem involves the antibody-complement-phagocyte system or cell-mediated immunity. A history of a normal response to smallpox vaccination or of contact dermatitis due to poison ivy suggests intact cellular immunity. Lymphopenia and the absence of palpable lymph nodes may be important findings. However, patients with profound immunodeficiency may have diffuse lymphoid hyperplasia.

Humoral immunity With rare exceptions, deficiency of humoral immunity is accompanied by diminished serum concentration of one or more classes of immunoglobulin. Normal values vary with age, and adult concentrations of IgM (100 mg/dL) are reached at about 1 year, of IgG (1000 mg/dL) at 5 to 6 years, and of IgA (200 mg/dL) at puberty (see Chap. 62). Also, the wide range of values among normal adults creates difficulty in defining the lower limits of normal. Reasonable estimates for low normal values are 40 mg/dL for IgM, 500 mg/dL for IgG, and 50 mg/dL for IgA. In the presence of borderline hypogammaglobulinemia, assessing the patient's capacity to produce specific antibodies becomes particularly important. Most hospital laboratories can measure isohemagglutinins, anti-streptolysin O, and "febrile agglutinins." Typhoid H and O agglutinins can be measured before and after immunization with standard typhoid vaccine. Many state public health laboratories can perform titrations for antibodies to common viral agents.

Since antibody deficiency may be mimicked clinically by deficiency of complement components, measurement of total hemolytic complement (CH_{50}) should be a part of the evaluation of host defense. Measurement of C3 alone is inadequate for screening, since deficiencies of both early and late complement components may predispose to bacterial infection (see Chap. 62). Estimation of numbers of circulating B lymphocytes has been of great value in determining the pathogenesis of certain types of immune deficiency. B lymphocytes are identified by the presence of membrane-bound immunoglobulins; additional markers include HLA-DR antigens, receptors for aggregated

IgG (Fc receptor), receptors for the third component of complement (C3 receptor), and receptors which specifically bind the Epstein-Barr virus. Following activation, B cells also express receptors for soluble growth and differentiation-promoting factors that are made by T cells. Most of these molecules on the B-cell surface can be identified and enumerated by specific monoclonal antibodies.

Pokeweed mitogen (PWM), an extract of the plant *Phytolacca americana*, has the capacity to induce B lymphocytes in culture to proliferate and differentiate to plasma cells. This activity requires the presence of T lymphocytes, which also proliferate in response to PWM. Thus, this assay can measure not only the capacity of B lymphocytes to differentiate but also the "helper" or "suppressor" function of patients' T lymphocytes.

TABLE 256-1 Laboratory evaluation of host defense defects

I Preliminary screen*
  A Complete blood count with differential smear
  B Quantitative immunoglobulin levels
II Readily available studies†
  A B-cell function
    1 Natural or commonly acquired antibodies: isohemagglutinins, "febrile" agglutinins, antibodies to common viruses (rubella, rubeola, influenza) and toxins (diphtheria, tetanus)
    2 Response to immunization (typhoid, polio, diphtheria-tetanus vaccines)
  B T-cell function
    1 Skin tests (PPD, *Candida, Trichophyton,* histoplasmin), tetanus toxoid (1:100 dilution)
    2 Chest x-ray (thymus shadow in infants, thymoma in adults)
  C Complement
    1 C3
    2 CH_{50} (total hemolytic complement)
  D Phagocyte function
    1 Reduction of nitroblue tetrazolium
    2 Inflammatory skin window (Rebuck)
    3 Bacteria phagocytic and bactericidal indexes
III In-depth investigation
  A B cell
    1 Pre-B cell examination in bone marrow samples
    2 B-lymphocyte membrane markers: IgM, IgD, IgG, IgA; receptors for aggregated IgG (Fc receptor), C3, Epstein-Barr virus; antigens detected by anti-B antibodies
    3 Induction of B-lymphocyte differentiation in vitro stimulated by pokeweed mitogen, Epstein-Barr virus, or other polyclonal B-cell activators
    4 Kinetics and immunoglobulin class of antibody produced in response to specific primary and secondary immunization
    5 Measurement of IgG subclasses and κ/λ ratio
    6 Histologic and immunofluorescent examination of biopsy specimens (intestinal mucosa, lymph node, bone marrow)
  B T cell
    1 Surface markers: binding of sheep erythrocytes (E rosettes), reactivity with monoclonal antibodies recognizing all T cells and the helper and suppressor subsets
    2 In vitro correlates of delayed hypersensitivity
      a Proliferative response to mitogens: phytohemagglutinin, concanavalin A–specific antigens (PPD, *Candida*); allogeneic cells (one-way mixed lymphocyte response)
      b Quantification of lymphokines (migration inhibitory factor, etc.)
      c Induction of killer cells by stimulation with allogeneic lymphocytes
    3 Measurement of thymus hormones
    4 Assays for T-cell "helper" function using supernatants of antigen-activated T cells or T cells plus PWM or antigens to trigger B-lymphocyte differentiation
    5 Skin graft rejection
  C Phagocytes and complement
    1 Chemotactic response in vitro
    2 Bactericidal function
    3 Classic and alternative complement components
  D Natural killer cells
    1 Enumeration with monoclonal antibodies
    2 Functional assay using appropriate target cells
  E Miscellaneous
    1 Lymphocytotoxic antibodies
    2 Measurement of adenosine deaminase and purine nucleoside phosphorylase enzyme activities

* *Together with a history and physical examination, these tests will identify more than 95 percent of patients with primary immunodeficiencies.*
† *These assays are generally available in either hospitals or state public health laboratories. With rare exceptions, information gained from tests in categories I and II is sufficient to diagnose and treat those immunodeficiencies amenable to conventional treatment with gamma globulin or plasma.*

Cellular immunity Human T lymphocytes may be enumerated by their expression of surface molecules which can bind sheep erythrocytes, forming what are called *E rosettes*. The normal function of these receptors is unknown, but they are not related to the antigen-specificity of T cells. The monoclonal antibodies T11 and Leu 5 recognize the sheep erythrocyte sites on human T cells and may soon supplant the E-rosette test. Other monoclonal antibodies which recognize all peripheral T cells (T3 and Leu 4) and distinguish the helper-inducer subset (T4⁺, Leu 3⁺) from cytotoxic-suppressor T cells (T8⁺, Leu 2⁺) are also commercially available.

T-lymphocyte function can be measured in vivo by delayed hypersensitivity skin testing, using a variety of antigens to which the majority of older children and adults have been sensitized. The most generally useful skin test antigen is a 1:100 dilution of tetanus toxoid injected intradermally, since almost all individuals will have been sensitized. Purified protein derivative (PPD), histoplasmin, mumps antigen, and extracts of *Candida* or *Trichophyton* may also be used.

T-lymphocyte function may be estimated in vitro by the capacity of cells to proliferate in response to antigens to which the patient has been sensitized, to lymphocytes from an unrelated donor, or to the T-cell mitogens, which include phytohemagglutinin, concanavalin A, and pokeweed mitogen. The response is usually quantified by measurement of incorporation of radioactive thymidine into newly synthesized DNA. It is also possible to measure the production of lymphokines by activated T cells. Finally, the ability of T cells activated in mixed lymphocyte culture to lyse target cells can be measured.

The capacity of T lymphocytes from immunologically normal persons to be activated in vitro with antigens or mitogens may be markedly diminished by acute febrile illness, treatment with corticosteroids, or stress. Caution should be exercised in interpreting abnormal results in these circumstances.

CLASSIFICATION Primary immunodeficiencies may be either congenital or acquired, and are currently classified according to mode of inheritance and whether the defect involves T cells, B cells, or both. Unfortunately, the best current classification, established by an expert committee of the World Health Organization, still places the majority of immunodeficiency diseases in an ill-defined category called *common varied immunodeficiency*. In general, this classification will be followed in the following discussion, which emphasizes three related concepts; first, that immunodeficiencies are most logically viewed as defects of cellular differentiation; second, that these defects may involve either primary development of T or B cells or the antigen-dependent phase of their differentiation; and third, that defects of secondary B-cell differentiation may in some instances reflect T-cell abnormalities resulting from faulty T-B collaboration.

Secondary immunodeficiencies are those not caused by intrinsic abnormalities in development or function of T and B cells. The best known of these is the acquired immunodeficiency disease (AIDS) which may follow infection with the human lymphotropic virus HTLV III (see Chap. 257). Other examples are immune deficiency associated with malnutrition, protein-losing enteropathy, and intestinal lymphangiectasia. Also considered secondary are immunodeficiencies resulting from hypercatabolic states such as occur in myotonic dystrophy, immunodeficiency associated with lymphoreticular malignancy, and immunodeficiency resulting from treatment with x-rays, antilymphocyte serum, or cytotoxic drugs.

Incidence As a group, the immunodeficiency syndromes discussed in this chapter are relatively common. Isolated IgA deficiency occurs in approximately 1 in 600 individuals; no other specific category approaches this frequency, but the cumulative total is not insignificant. The incidence of diagnosed immunodeficiency diseases is clearly a function of the awareness of physicians in a community. An epidemic of immunodeficiency diseases commonly follows the addition of a clinical immunologist to a medical center staff.

The more severe forms of primary immunodeficiency have their onset early in life and all too frequently result in death during childhood. Immunodeficiencies may be acquired at any age, however, and a substantial number of patients with congenital hypogammaglobulinemia survive to middle age or beyond. In a referral center for patients with immunodeficiency diseases, approximately two-thirds of the immunodeficient patients under care are adults. Improved methods of diagnosis and treatment can be expected to increase this ratio in the future.

Severe combined immunodeficiency (SCID) This syndrome is characterized by gross functional impairment of both humoral and cell-mediated immunity. It is usually congenital, may be inherited either as an X-linked or autosomal recessive defect, or may occur sporadically. Affected infants rarely survive beyond 1 year without treatment. This syndrome has been associated with a diversity of defects in development of immunocompetent cells, some of which may be related to specific enzymatic abnormalities.

The classic example of SCID, *Swiss-type agammaglobulinemia,* is characterized by severe lymphopenia involving both T and B cells, and is inherited with an autosomal recessive pattern. Rarely, other hematopoietic cell lines fail to develop in a variant form of SCID called *reticular dysgenesis.* The cellular defect in these forms of SCID logically rests with the precursor common to both T and B cells. The immunologic defects in a few of these patients have been repaired following transplantation of fetal liver as a source of stem cells, confirming the hypothesis that they have a thymus and bursa equivalent capable of supporting T- and B-cell differentiation of normal stem cells. About half of patients with autosomal recessive SCID are deficient in an enzyme involved in purine metabolism, adenosine deaminase (ADA). These patients have varying degrees of lymphopenia, T cells usually being more deficient than B cells. Studies of the pathophysiologic relationship of ADA deficiency to abortive lymphoid differentiation suggest that intracellular accumulation of adenosine and deoxyadenosine triphosphate, by inhibiting ribonucleotide reductase enzymes, interferes with DNA synthesis. Improvement of both clinical status and immunologic function has occurred in some but not all patients treated with a source of exogenous ADA.

SCID may also occur with an X-linked inheritance pattern. Affected boys may not have severe lymphopenia; some have had normal numbers of B lymphocytes with few or no circulating T lymphocytes. This developmental pattern (which may also occur with autosomal recessive inheritance) suggests the possibility of a faulty thymus epithelium. Mononuclear cells from bone marrow of such patients have been induced to express T-cell characteristics by coculture on normal thymus epithelium or by treatment with thymus hormones.

The SCID syndrome may occur as a consequence of more subtle defects of T-cell maturation. In one patient, circulating T cells present in normal numbers had the phenotypic markers of cortical thymocytes (Fig. 256-1) and lacked functions of mature T cells. Other patients have a selective deficiency of T4$^+$, Leu 3$^+$ helper T cells.

Patients with SCID with and without ADA deficiency have been successfully treated by transplantation of histocompatible bone marrow from sibling donors. The same treatment has been used in children and adults with leukemia or aplastic anemia (see Chap. 291) following purposeful destruction of the immune system by irradiation and cytotoxic drugs. Other modes of treatment, including fetal liver and thymus transplants, have been successful in restoring immunocompetence, but as yet there are only short-term survivors. Treatment of these patients should probably be attempted only in centers with a strong research interest in this problem. It is crucial that these patients be recognized early and not be given blood transfusions which may cause fatal graft-versus-host disease.

T-cell immunodeficiency Reflecting the diversity of T-cell functions, abnormalities of T-cell development may be responsible for a wide spectrum of immune deficiencies including severe combined immunodeficiency, apparently isolated defects in cell-mediated immunity, and syndromes presenting as antibody deficiency with apparently normal cell-mediated immunity. These defects may be acquired (see Chap. 257) as well as congenital. Until recently, laboratory assays of T-lymphocyte function were limited to correlates of cell-mediated immunity; no means were available for studying T-cell regulatory functions. Quantification of T-cell subsets and of their growth factor receptors using monoclonal antibodies, accompanied by functional measurements of helper, suppressor, and cytotoxic activity, are expanding the spectrum of immunodeficiencies primarily related to T-cell abnormalities. The recent identification of the T-cell receptor genes and the availability of these DNA probes for studies of immunodeficient patients will also allow more precise definition of T-cell disorders, the numbers of which will increase with the use of more sophisticated tools for T-cell analysis.

DI GEORGE'S SYNDROME This is the classic example of isolated T-cell deficiency and results from maldevelopment of organs derived embryologically from the interaction between neural crest mesenchyme and epithelial elements of the third and fourth pharyngeal pouches. Affected infants usually present with congenital cardiac defects, particularly those involving the great vessels, hypocalcemic tetany due to failure of parathyroid development, and absence of a normal thymus. Associated abnormalities may include abnormal ears, shortened philtrum, and hypertelorism. Serum immunoglobulin concentrations are frequently normal, but antibody responses, particularly of IgG and IgA isotypes, are usually impaired. Lymphocyte counts may be near normal, but virtually all the lymphocytes are B cells. Carefully performed autopsies have often revealed a tiny, histologically normal thymus, usually in an ectopic location. With time, a few patients developed functional T cells. Several patients with Di George's syndrome transplanted with fetal thymus have developed immunocompetent T cells of host origin. However, it is difficult to be certain whether long-term improvement is the result of a small thymus gland in an ectopic location or due to grafted thymus epithelium.

Children lacking the congenital anomalies associated with Di George's syndrome may present with severe impairment of cell-mediated immunity. Some have normal or even increased immunoglobulin levels, while others have selective deficiencies of one or more immunoglobulin classes. Specific antibody responses are usually impaired even in patients with normal concentrations of immunoglobulins. This ill-defined entity has been called the *Nezelof's syndrome.*

Inherited deficiency of the enzyme purine nucleoside phosphorylase (PNP) is associated with an often severe and selective deficiency of T-lymphocyte function. This enzyme functions in the same purine salvage pathway as ADA; toxic effects of its deficiency may be related to intracellular accumulation of deoxyguanosine triphosphate (GTP).

A few patients with isolated T-cell deficiency have been treated with fetal thymus grafts or thymic humoral factors. Some have shown improvement in numbers of circulating T cells, in vitro reactivity to mitogens, and clinical condition, while others have had no change in status.

ATAXIA-TELANGIECTASIA This is an autosomal recessive genetic disorder characterized by cerebellar ataxia, oculocutaneous telangiectasia, and immunodeficiency. Onset of truncal ataxia usually occurs in infancy and is progressive. Immunodeficiency is clinically manifest by recurrent and chronic sinopulmonary infection leading to bronchiectasis. However, not all patients have immunodeficiency. The two most frequent causes of death are chronic pulmonary disease and malignancy. Lymphomas are most common, although carcinomas have also occurred.

The immunologic abnormalities seem to be related to maldevelopment of the thymus. If found at all, the thymus in autopsied patients has been markedly hypoplastic and similar in appearance to an embryonic thymus. Patients' lymphocytes frequently respond poorly to T-cell mitogens in vitro. Cutaneous anergy and delayed rejection of skin grafts are common. Although the number and class distribution of B lymphocytes are usually normal, most patients are deficient in serum IgE and IgA, and a smaller number have reduced serum levels of IgG, particularly of the IgG2, IgG4 subclasses. IgM and IgD are usually normal.

There is circumstantial evidence that ataxia-telangiectasia may involve a generalized defect in cellular differentiation related to the defects in DNA repair mechanisms which have been identified in these patients. Cultured cells from these patients are highly susceptible to radiation-induced chromosomal damage. Defective DNA repair mechanisms may account for the high incidence of malignancies in these patients. Ovarian agenesis also occurs frequently. Persistence of very high serum levels of oncofetal proteins, including alpha-fetoprotein and carcinoembryonic antigen, may be of diagnostic value.

Only symptomatic treatment is available. Unless a severe IgG deficiency is present, therapy with gamma globulin is not indicated. Unusual sensitivity to x-irradiation should be kept in mind in planning therapy for patients who develop cancer.

Immunoglobulin deficiency syndromes X-LINKED AGAMMA-GLOBULINEMIA This syndrome was long thought to represent a central failure of development of all elements of the B-cell lineage. Recent evidence has modified this concept. Affected males have very few immunoglobulin-bearing B lymphocytes in their circulation and lack primary and secondary lymphoid follicles. However, pre-B cells are found in normal frequency in their bone marrow. This developmental block contrasts with earlier and later arrests in B-cell differentiation characterizing other immunodeficiencies (see below and Fig. 256-1). Patients usually have a substantial number of small mononuclear cells bearing receptors for aggregated immunoglobulin and C3. Although resembling B lymphocytes, these cells have been shown to have markers characteristic of the monocyte line and to lack the B-lymphocyte specific surface antigen(s) and receptors for Epstein-Barr virus. A few patients with well-documented X-linked agammaglobulinemia have had a normal number of B lymphocytes, suggesting that there may be two distinct forms of this disease.

Agammaglobulinemia is a misnomer, as most patients with this and other forms of severe panhypogammaglobulinemia synthesize some immunoglobulins. Within the same family some affected males have had substantial levels of IgM, IgG, and IgA, while others have been nearly agammaglobulinemic. All these patients were markedly deficient in circulating B lymphocytes. This observation suggests that the few B lymphocytes which are generated are fully capable of differentiating to plasma cells and secreting immunoglobulins. A form of arthritis with some of the features of rheumatoid disease occurs in some of these patients and may remit following treatment with gamma globulin. Mycoplasma organisms are sometimes the cause of arthritis in hypogammaglobulinemic patients. Chronic encephalitis, of proven or presumed viral etiology, appears to be an increasingly frequent terminal complication. Some of these patients have also had an associated dermatomyositis.

TRANSIENT HYPOGAMMAGLOBULINEMIA OF INFANCY This is a reversible syndrome in which normal physiologic hypogammaglobulinemia of infancy is unusually prolonged and severe. IgG levels of normal-term infants commonly drop to levels of 300 to 400 mg/dL between 3 and 6 months of age as maternally derived IgG is catabolized; levels subsequently rise reflecting the infants' increased synthetic capacity. In transient hypogammaglobulinemia, the rate of synthesis of IgM, IgG, and IgA remains low for long periods. Reduced numbers of T4$^+$ helper T cells have recently been reported in infants with this condition.

ISOLATED DEFICIENCY OF IgA This is by far the most commonly encountered immunodeficiency, occurring with a frequency of approximately 1 in 600 individuals of European origin. With rare exceptions, IgA1 and IgA2 subclasses are deficient in both serum and mucous secretions. Many adults with isolated IgA deficiency do not seem to have unusual problems with infection. Nevertheless, this condition is not benign. A substantial proportion of IgA-deficient individuals develop precipitating antibodies to IgA. These patients may have severe anaphylactic reactions when transfused with normal blood from a blood bank.

As a group, individuals with IgA deficiency have an increased number of respiratory infections of varying severity, and a few have had severe pulmonary disease such as bronchiectasis. Chronic diarrheal disease also occurs. The incidence of asthma and other atopic diseases among IgA-deficient patients is high, and, conversely, the incidence of IgA deficiency among atopic children has been found to be 20 to 40 times that in the normal population. In one study it was found that combined deficiency of IgE and IgA (or IgE deficiency alone) did not predispose to recurrent respiratory infections, while IgA-deficient patients with normal or elevated IgE had recurrent sinopulmonary disease. Selective reductions in the IgG2 and IgG4 subclasses have also been associated with increased infections in IgA-deficient individuals. IgA deficiency is also significantly associated with autoimmune diseases such as rheumatoid arthritis and systemic lupus erythematosus.

IgA deficiency may be familial, but no single pattern of inheritance has been encountered consistently. It has occurred in association with congenital intrauterine infections, such as toxoplasmosis, rubella, and cytomegalovirus infection. Several patients with abnormalities of chromosome 18 have had isolated IgA deficiency. Most commonly, the syndrome appears as a sporadic defect. It may be transient or acquired late in life.

The pathogenesis of IgA deficiency, whether genetic or caused by environmental insult, involves a block in terminal differentiation of B lymphocytes. Virtually all patients have detectable IgA-bearing B lymphocytes, although their numbers may be reduced. In normal children and adults, B lymphocytes bearing IgA have only that immunoglobulin class on their surface, while in IgA-deficient patients and normal neonates, IgA-bearing lymphocytes also bear surface IgM. This immature phenotype is associated in most patients with failure of their cultured lymphocytes to secrete IgA when stimulated by pokeweed mitogen. Selective T-cell suppression of IgA responses has been described in some patients, and a variety of other, usually mild, defects of T-cell function in others. While there is as yet no generally accepted pathogenic mechanism, suspicion remains high that many of these patients have a primary defect in regulatory T-cell function.

Treatment of IgA deficiency is symptomatic. IgA cannot be effectively replaced by exogenous gamma globulin or plasma, and use of either would increase the risk of development of antibodies to IgA. IgA-deficient patients in need of transfusion should be screened for the presence of antibodies to IgA, and ideally should be given blood only from IgA-deficient donors. All patients known to be IgA-deficient should be warned of the risk of severe transfusion reactions which may occur following infusion of only a few milliliters of blood.

X-LINKED IMMUNODEFICIENCY WITH INCREASED LEVELS OF IgM This is a specific syndrome only because of its inheritance pattern. IgG levels are usually very low, and IgA low or undetectable, while IgD levels may be high. The clinical patterns of infection are similar to those occurring with other hypogammaglobulinemic states. The number and distribution of B lymphocytes bearing IgM, IgG, and IgA have been normal, suggesting that this type of immunodeficiency may also involve a block in terminal differentiation of B lymphocytes. Neutropenia often occurs in affected males and can increase their vulnerability to infections.

ISOLATED DEFICIENCY OF IgM This syndrome has been reported rarely in this country but was detected frequently in a British population. Approximately 20 percent of these patients were asymptomatic while 60 percent had severe recurrent infections, often with bacteremia. Pneumococcal pneumonia and meningitis have often been noted in IgM-deficient patients. Other associated conditions included gastrointestinal disease, atopy, splenomegaly, and development of malignancy. The condition was frequently familial, and was four times more common in males than females. The number of circulating B lymphocytes has varied from very low to normal.

COMMON VARIED IMMUNODEFICIENCY This represents a heterogeneous group of syndromes which may be congenital or acquired, sporadic or familial, and which occur in both males and females. These patients have in common the clinical manifestations of antibody deficiency associated with panhypogammaglobulinemia, with deficiency of IgG and IgA, or rarely, with selective IgG deficiency.

A small subpopulation of these patients have reduced numbers of circulating B lymphocytes, suggesting a central failure of development of this cell line. The remainder have normal numbers of B lymphocytes, although these may have an immature phenotype. In the few patients studied, B lymphocytes capable of binding specific antigens were present, and these increased in frequency following immunization. Consistent with the evidence that B lymphocytes in these patients are able to recognize antigens and proliferate but fail to differentiate to plasma cells is the fairly common finding of lymphoid hyperplasia, including splenomegaly and nodular lymphoid hyperplasia of the gut.

In agammaglobulinemic patients having B lymphocytes, the pathogenesis of immune deficiency must involve the failure of these cells to differentiate to plasma cells. By use of assays capable of measuring B-lymphocyte differentiation to plasma cells in vitro, four major types of defect have been tentatively identified. First, and most common, is an intrinsic abnormality of B lymphocytes. B lymphocytes from these patients can be activated via their immunoglobulin receptors to express functional receptors for T cell–derived growth factors, but they fail to differentiate into immunoglobulin-secreting plasma cells even when provided with differentiation factors from normal T cells. Second, there is evidence that in some patients the T cells, or their products, may actively suppress terminal differentiation of autologous or normal B lymphocytes. The increase in suppressor activity could be either a primary or secondary abnormality; the latter could explain the increase in T-cell suppressor activity in patients with abnormal B lymphocytes and others in whom B lymphocytes are congenitally absent. Third, quantitative deficiency of helper T-cell function has been observed in some patients, usually also in association with defective B-cell function. This functional defect may or may not be associated with reduced numbers of T4$^+$ cells. Finally, in rare instances, plasma cells may produce abnormal immunoglobulins which are degraded in the cytoplasm.

Patients with common varied immunodeficiency may present with signs and symptoms highly suggestive of lymphoid malignancy, including fever, weight loss, splenomegaly, generalized lymphadenopathy, and lymphocytosis. Routine histologic examination of lymphoid tissues usually reveals germinal center hyperplasia which may be difficult to distinguish from nodular lymphoma (see Chap. 294). Demonstration of a normal distribution of immunoglobulin isotypes and light chain classes on circulating and tissue B lymphocytes can serve to distinguish these patients from those having a monoclonal B-cell malignancy with secondary hypogammaglobulinemia. Treatment of several patients with gamma globulin has resulted in relief of symptoms and reversal of lymphoid hyperplasia.

IMMUNODEFICIENCY WITH THYMOMA Recognition of the association of hypogammaglobulinemia with spindle cell thymoma provided one of the early clues as to the role of the thymus in immunobiology. Although T-cell numbers and cell-mediated immunity are frequently intact, several abnormalities have been identified. Patients' lymphoid cells suppress differentiation of normal B lymphocytes in the pokeweed mitogen assay and may also suppress development of erythroid precursors. The suppressor activity is mediated by the subset of lymphocytes bearing receptors for IgG, which are found in increased numbers. It is presently uncertain as to whether the suppressor cells are T cells or NK cells. These patients are very deficient in circulating B lymphocytes, frequently have eosinopenia, and may develop erythroid aplasia. Failure to produce B lymphocytes has been traced to the stem-cell level, since pre-B cells could not be found in their bone marrow. The relationship between the thymoma, T-cell, or NK dysfunction, and apparent abnormalities of hematopoietic stem cells remains conjectural.

WISKOTT-ALDRICH SYNDROME This is an X-linked genetic disease characterized by eczema, thrombocytopenia, and repeated infections. Affected boys often present with bleeding in infancy. Most do not survive childhood, dying of complications of bleeding, infection, or lymphoreticular malignancy. The immunologic defects in this disease are well characterized but poorly understood. Serum concentrations of IgM are usually decreased, while IgA and IgG are normal and IgE is frequently increased. However, synthetic rates for all three classes may be elevated, indicating a significant element of hypercatabolism. The number and class distribution of B lymphocytes usually have been normal. Functionally, these boys are consistently unable to make antibodies to polysaccharide antigens normally; responses to protein antigens are often not impaired. While most patients acquire a diminished number of T cells, serial appraisal of affected males suggests that the T-cell defects are secondary. They frequently become anergic, and their T cells do not respond normally to challenge with ubiquitous antigens. The nature of the primary defect is still unknown.

Transplantation of histocompatible bone marrow from a sibling donor has corrected both hematologic and immunologic abnormalities in several patients. In patients lacking a suitable donor, splenectomy may improve platelet counts and reduce the risk of serious hemorrhage. Because of the increased risk of pneumococcal bacteremia, splenectomized patients should probably receive prophylactic penicillin.

Miscellaneous immunodeficiency syndromes Infection with *Candida albicans* is the almost universal accompaniment of severe deficiencies in cell-mediated immunity. The syndrome of *chronic mucocutaneous candidiasis* is different because superficial candidiasis is usually the only major manifestation of immunodeficiency. These patients rarely develop systemic infection with *Candida* or other fungal agents and are not unusually susceptible to virus or bacterial disease. The syndrome is often congenital and may be associated with single or multiple endocrinopathies as well as iron deficiency. Treatment of associated conditions may lead to improvement or even cure of *Candida* infection.

No uniformity of immunologic defects has been identified in these patients, although defects of antibody formation have been detected occasionally. Humoral immunity, including ability to make specific anti-*Candida* antibodies, is usually normal. Many patients are anergic, some to a variety of antigens and some only to *Candida;* anergy in some patients has been related to inability of their lymphocytes to produce migration inhibition factor.

Results of treatment with antifungal agents, such as amphotericin B, have been variable but generally not encouraging. In some patients, intensive treatment with amphotericin B coupled with surgical removal of infected nails has led to sustained improvement. Ketoconazole, an oral antifungal agent, is reported to be quite effective.

IMMUNODEFICIENCY ASSOCIATED WITH SERUM LYMPHOCYTOTOXINS This syndrome has been reported in a few patients with recurrent bacterial and fungal infections. Most have had fluctuating lymphopenia. Both cellular immunity and specific antibody responses were impaired, although immunoglobulin levels were usually normal. Antibodies specific for B-cell antigens have also been reported as a cause of selective elimination of B cells and resultant hypogammaglobulinemia.

IMBALANCES OF IgG SUBCLASSES Some patients with repeated infections and only moderately decreased serum IgG levels may have a selective deficiency of one or more of the four IgG subclasses. A few such patients appeared to benefit from administration of gamma globulin; others do well without antibody replacement therapy. K *light chain deficiency* has also been reported in association with recurrent infections, and doubtless many more subtle gaps in antibody diversity, which may be clinically significant, will be elucidated.

X-LINKED LYMPHOPROLIFERATIVE SYNDROME This is an X-linked recessive disease in which there appears to be a selective impairment in immune elimination of Epstein-Barr virus (EBV). Infectious mononucleosis in affected males may have a fulminant and fatal outcome, may be associated with development of B-cell malignancies, or may result in acquired hypogammaglobulinemia, aplastic anemia, or agranulocytosis. Antibodies to EBV have been detected in some patients but are often absent in the face of infection. Generation of cytotoxic T cells appears to be the primary mechanism of control of EBV infection in normal persons, and natural killer cells may also play a role in eliminating EBV-infected B cells. While a reduction of natural-killer-cell activity has been noted, the nature of the defect which prevents a normal response to EBV in patients with the X-linked lymphoproliferative syndrome has not been defined.

Metabolic abnormalities associated with immunodeficiency   The relation of deficiencies of the purine salvage enzymes, adenosine deaminase and purine nucleoside phosphorylase, to immunodeficiency was discussed earlier. Other inherited metabolic defects should be briefly mentioned because of their potential importance in understanding the molecular basis of immunologic function. Inherited *deficiency of transcobalamin II*, the serum carrier molecule responsible for transport of vitamin B$_{12}$ to tissues, was associated with failure of immunoglobulin production as well as megaloblastic anemia, leukopenia, thrombocytopenia, and severe malabsorption. All abnormalities were reversed by administration of pharmacologic doses of vitamin B$_{12}$. The syndrome of *acrodermatitis enteropathica* includes severe desquamating skin lesions, intractable diarrhea, bizarre neurologic symptoms, variable combined immunodeficiency, and an often fatal outcome. This disease is apparently caused by an inborn error of metabolism resulting in malabsorption of dietary zinc, and can be effectively treated by parenteral or large oral doses of zinc. Similar disease manifestations have occurred in mice and cattle with different inherited defects leading to zinc malabsorption. Zinc deficiency might in part account for the immunodeficiency which accompanies severe malnutrition.

TREATMENT OF IMMUNODEFICIENCIES   Treatment of immunodeficiency diseases involving severe abnormalities of T-cell function, with or without hypogammaglobulinemia, is currently limited in effectiveness and extremely complicated. Experimental approaches, including transplantation of bone marrow, fetal liver, and thymus, were mentioned in preceding sections. Also under investigation is the use of thymic hormones and of pharmacologic agents which may correct defects in lymphoid function caused by inherited metabolic disorders. The increasing availability of purified gamma interferon, T-cell growth factors, and other biologically active mediators promises to be important in the therapy of certain immunologic disorders. Genetic engineering also holds promise for future therapy of certain genetic defects of the immune system.

Replacement therapy with human gamma globulin should be used in patients who have recurrent bacterial infections and are deficient in IgG. Maintenance of serum IgG levels between 100 and 300 mg/dL is sufficient to prevent most overwhelming infections, although chronic sinusitis, otitis media, and bronchitis often persist. These serum levels usually can be achieved by intramuscular injection of IgG, 100 mg/kg, at monthly intervals, following a loading dose of twice this amount given over a period of several days. Forty milliliters of 16% gamma globulin, given in two or more sites at one time, is about the maximum tolerable in adults. Immunoglobulin preparations suitable for intravenous administration are now available, and provide a needed alternative mode of antibody replacement therapy. The primary advantage of intravenous gamma globulin is that higher amounts of antibodies can be given with less discomfort. In patients with mild to moderate IgG deficiency (300 to 400 mg/dL), the decision to treat must be based on clinical symptoms and on failure to respond to antigenic challenge, because injection of gamma globulin at the recommended doses will not significantly elevate serum IgG levels. Gamma globulin treatment is of no value in patients with deficiencies of immunoglobulins other than IgG. This form of treatment is not benign. Some patients may develop symptoms of diaphoresis, tachycardia, and hypotension immediately following

injections. This reaction is thought to be mediated by aggregates of IgG in the gamma globulin preparation, but why it develops after years of treatment in some patients, and never in others has not been adequately explained. Most patients intolerant of intramuscular gamma globulin injections can be treated successfully with intravenous preparations of gamma globulin or plasma.

Infusion of fresh plasma, 10 to 20 mL/kg at intervals of 3 to 4 weeks, has the advantages of being less painful and of replacing IgM and IgA as well as IgG; however, both IgM and IgA have a half-life of only a few days. The major disadvantage of plasma is the risk of transmitting hepatitis, which is particularly devastating in immunodeficient patients. This risk can be minimized by use of selected donors, usually family members, carefully screened for the absence of HTLV and hepatitis virus infections.

Use of plasma or gamma globulin selected on the basis of a high titer of antibodies to a particular agent may be indicated in certain situations. For example, antibodies to the causative echovirus may dramatically improve encephalitis in immunodeficient patients.

Therapy with exogenous IgG usually does not prevent chronic sinopulmonary infection and its all too frequent progression to pulmonary fibrosis and bronchiectasis. Therefore, maintenance of good pulmonary toilet with regular postural drainage is an especially important part of patient management. The principles of antibiotic therapy are not different in these than other patients, except that the index of suspicion of bacterial infection should remain very high.

REFERENCES

CHANDRA RK et al: Immunodeficiency: Report of a WHO scientific group. WHO Tech Rep 630, 1978
MEISCHER PA, MÜLLER-EBERHARD HJ (eds): *Seminars in Immunopathology*, vol 1: *Immunodeficiency Diseases.* Berlin, Springer-Verlag, 1978
MÖLLER G (ed): T-cell receptors and genes. Immunol Rev 81:1, 1984
REINHERZ EL et al: Abnormalities of T cell maturation and regulation in human beings with immunodeficiency disorders. J Clin Invest 68:699, 1981
ROSEN FS et al: The primary immunodeficiencies. N Engl J Med 311:235, 300, 1984
STIEHM ER, FULGINITI VA (eds): *Immunologic Disorders in Infants and Children*, 2d ed. Philadelphia, Saunders, 1979
STITES DP et al: *Basic and Clinical Immunology*, 5th ed. Los Gatos, Calif, Lange, 1984
WEDGWOOD RJ et al (eds): *Primary Immunodeficiency Diseases, Birth Defects*, Original Article Series, vol XIX. Sunderland, Mass, The National Foundation–March of Dimes, Sinauer Associations, 1983

257   THE ACQUIRED IMMUNODEFICIENCY SYNDROME (AIDS)

ANTHONY S. FAUCI / H. CLIFFORD LANE

DEFINITION   The acquired immunodeficiency syndrome (AIDS) was originally defined empirically by the Centers for Disease Control (CDC) as the presence of a reliably diagnosed disease that is at least moderately indicative of an underlying defect in cell-mediated immunity. Typical examples of such diseases are Kaposi's sarcoma in an individual less than 60 years old or a life-threatening opportunistic infection such as *Pneumocystis carinii* pneumonia. These disorders must occur in the absence of known causes of underlying immune defects, such as iatrogenic immunosuppression or malignant neoplasms. This surveillance definition was used for national reporting and was formulated prior to the recognition of human T lymphotropic virus type III (HTLV III) or lymphadenopathy-associated virus (LAV) as the etiologic agent of the disease. Since tests for HTLV III/LAV antibody and virus are now available, the CDC has refined the case definition. The diagnosis is now excluded if tests for serum antibody to HTLV III/LAV are negative, all other types of HTLV III/LAV tests are negative, and the number of thymus-derived (T) helper lymphocytes is normal. Furthermore, in the absence of a classic opportunistic disease required by the original case definition, in the presence of a positive serologic or virologic test for HTLV III/LAV, any of the following diseases are considered indicative of AIDS: disseminated histoplasmosis; isosporosis causing chronic diarrhea; bronchial or pulmonary candidiasis; non-Hodgkin's (lymphocytic) lymphoma of high-grade pathologic type and of B-cell or unknown immunologic phenotype; and Kaposi's sarcoma diagnosed by biopsy in patients who are 60 years old or older when diagnosed. In addition, in the absence of opportunistic diseases required by the original case definition, a histologically confirmed diagnosis of chronic lymphoid interstitial pneumonitis in a child under 13 years of age is considered indicative of AIDS unless tests for HTLV III/LAV are negative. Finally, patients who have a lymphoreticular malignancy diagnosed more than 3 months after the diagnosis of an opportunistic disease used as a marker for AIDS were previously excluded as AIDS cases based on the presumption that the malignancy could have accounted for the immunosuppression which led to the opportunistic disease. Such patients are now included as having AIDS if they are seropositive for HTLV III/LAV.

ETIOLOGY AIDS is caused by the human retrovirus HTLV III/LAV (see Chap. 293). This is truly a novel virus which has never before been identified. The virus is a human retrovirus which is lymphocytotropic and selectively infects human T lymphocytes of the helper/inducer subset which is designated by the T4 or Leu 3 phenotypic markers. This tropism is similar to that of HTLV I, which is the cause of adult T-cell leukemia/lymphoma (see Chaps. 293 and 294). However, HTLV I causes malignant proliferation of the T4 subset of lymphocytes, while HTLV III causes a cytopathic effect on these cells. The nucleotide sequence of HTLV III differs from that of HTLV I or HTLV II, which has been implicated in hairy-cell leukemia (see Chap. 292). It is, however, quite similar to the lentivirus group of retroviruses, particularly the visna virus which causes a demyelinating disease in sheep.

INCIDENCE AND PREVALENCE AIDS did not exist in the United States until the late 1970s. In the summer of 1981 the CDC announced the unexplained occurrence of *Pneumocystis carinii* pneumonia in previously healthy male homosexuals in Los Angeles and Kaposi's sarcoma in 26 previously healthy male homosexuals in New York and Los Angeles. Since that time, the number of cases has increased geometrically. By mid-1986, approximately 22,000 cases had been reported in the United States. The incidence of the disease has doubled approximately every 12 months. By 1990 over 100,000 cases are anticipated in the United States. The disease will almost certainly evolve into a global epidemic. It is occurring with an increased frequency in several countries in Europe as well as in other continents, particularly Africa, where at least several thousand cases have occurred in central Africa.

Sexual contact is the major mode of transmission of the AIDS retrovirus. Transmission can also occur via blood or blood products as in individuals who share contaminated needles for intravenous drug abuse or individuals who receive blood transfusions or blood products for replacement therapy. Mothers may transmit the virus perinatally to their infants.

Among the adult cases reported in the United States, 73 percent have occurred among homosexual or bisexual men. The highest numbers of cases have been reported from New York City, San Francisco, and Los Angeles, which reflects the high concentration of male homosexuals in these cities. However, the number of cases in other areas of the United States is increasing, and the disease is seen in virtually every state. The next largest number of cases in the United States is found among intravenous drug abusers, who constitute approximately 17 percent of the total cases. Approximately 1 percent of cases occur in hemophiliacs with no history of other risk factors. These individuals are exposed to the AIDS retrovirus by virtue of the large amounts of factor VIII concentrates which they receive intravenously as replacement for deficient clotting factors. An addi-

tional 2 percent of cases occur among nonhemophiliacs who have received blood or blood products usually associated with surgery. Approximately 1 percent of cases have occurred in the heterosexual partners of individuals with AIDS or at risk for AIDS. Approximately 7 percent of adult patients fall into none of the above risk categories. For a significant proportion of these patients, there was not sufficient information to allow classification, usually because the patients died before they could be interviewed. Also included among these 7 percent of patients are Haitian immigrants to the United States who have no history of homosexuality or intravenous drug abuse. It is very likely that the disease has been transmitted among these individuals by heterosexual contact, similar to the situation in Zaire, where the male-to-female ratio for AIDS is approximately equal. In this regard, there are cases reported in the United States among men who have no apparent risk factor except heterosexual promiscuity, usually involving contacts with prostitutes who may also be intravenous drug abusers and hence be at risk for exposure to the AIDS retrovirus. This observation coupled with the reported infection of their sexual partners by male intravenous drug abusers and hemophiliacs raises the possibility of further heterosexual spread of AIDS in the United States among individuals not in the established risk groups. However, while the number of cases of AIDS apparently transmitted by heterosexual contact has increased over the years since AIDS was recognized, the relative proportion of these cases compared to the total number of cases has remained constant. It is possible that cofactors which contribute to the establishment of infection and/or disease in the risk groups are not usually present in the general population in the United States, and for this reason, an increase in the proportion of cases among heterosexuals has not occurred in the United States as in Zaire. There is no indication that the virus can be spread by insects, such as the bite of a mosquito.

There are at least 200 cases of pediatric AIDS (children less than 13 years old) reported in the United States and probably hundreds more who have been infected with the AIDS retrovirus but have not developed the full-blown disease. The vast majority of these children were born of parents with AIDS or at increased risk for AIDS. It is highly likely that these children were infected with the AIDS retrovirus in utero or perinatally. Most of the remainder were hemophiliacs or transfusion recipients.

All epidemiologic data strongly indicate that the AIDS retrovirus is not spread via casual contact. Large seroepidemiologic studies in the United States have shown that thousands of health care workers who are in close daily contact with AIDS patients have not developed AIDS or immunologic abnormalities, or seroconverted to anti-HTLV III antibody positivity. However, a few of the hundreds of health care workers who have been exposed to the virus by penetrating injuries and who are not in an established risk group have been found to have antibodies to HTLV III/LAV. Except for sexual transmission, there is no evidence that the virus is spread among family members living in the same household with AIDS patients. In contrast, the prevalence of infection with the AIDS retrovirus in the established risk groups is extraordinarily high. At least 65 percent of male homosexuals attending a clinic in San Francisco for sexually transmitted diseases were antibody-positive; 87 percent of intravenous drug abusers in New York City and 72 percent of asymptomatic persons with hemophilia A were antibody-positive. In contrast, less than 0.1 percent of the general blood donor pool has been confirmed as antibody-positive. It is estimated that at least 10 percent of asymptomatic individuals and up to 25 percent of symptomatic individuals (see definition of AIDS-related complex below) who are antibody-positive will develop full-blown AIDS within 3 years.

PATHOPHYSIOLOGY AND IMMUNOPATHOGENESIS The hallmark of AIDS is a profound defect in cell-mediated immunity which leads to severe opportunistic infections and Kaposi's sarcoma as well as certain lymphoid malignancies. The underlying cause of the immune defect is quite specific. HTLV III/LAV selectively infects the helper/inducer (T4 or Leu 3) subset of T lymphocytes resulting in a cytopathic effect; lymphopenia ensues, predominantly at the expense of the T4 cell. The suppressor/cytotoxic T lymphocyte defined by the T8 or Leu 2 phenotypic marker is either normal in number or slightly increased or decreased, generally resulting in a marked decrease in the T4/T8 ratio within the peripheral blood T-cell compartment. In addition to the quantitative deficiency in the T4 subset, there is also a qualitative or functional defect in this subset. This is particularly evident in the subset of T4 cells which are responsible for antigen recognition and responsiveness; this particular T4 subset is selectively defective early in the course of the disease.

Since the T4 subset of lymphocytes is responsible for the induction or orchestration of virtually the entire immune response, the selective defect in this subset results in global defects in a number of components of immunity which depend at least in part on inductive signals from the T4 cell. These include defects in natural killer cells, virus-specific cytotoxic T cells, B cells, and monocytes. In addition to defects in chemotaxis, secretion of interleukin 1 (IL-1), and certain cytotoxic functions, monocytes also show a defect in ability to present antigen to T cells. The mechanisms of these defects are unclear at present; however, they may relate to the fact that under certain circumstances both B cells and monocytes may be susceptible to infection with HTLV III/LAV in vitro. It has also been demonstrated that HTLV III/LAV can directly activate B cells without infecting them. This may explain in part the observation that B cells from patients with AIDS are polyclonally activated in vivo. There is a gradation of degree of immunologic dysfunction among the various subsets of AIDS patients. Those patients with Kaposi's sarcoma alone tend to have more competent immune systems compared to those who present with opportunistic infections.

It is unclear what mechanisms are responsible for the development of Kaposi's sarcoma in certain patients with AIDS. Kaposi's sarcoma occurs with a much greater frequency in homosexuals with AIDS than in AIDS patients in the other risk groups. In addition, certain opportunistic infections such as Pneumocystis carinii pneumonia and Mycobacterium avium-intracellulare occur with a much greater frequency in AIDS patients than in individuals who are immunosuppressed for other reasons. On the other hand, certain infections such as nocardiosis and listeriosis are very rare in AIDS patients despite their relatively frequent occurrence in other immunosuppressed patients. The reasons for these discrepancies are unclear, but likely reflect the selectivity and specificity of the immune defect in AIDS.

HTLV III/LAV has been demonstrated in the brain, which might explain the neuropsychiatric abnormalities which have been noted in many infected patients (see below). Virus has also been isolated from semen, saliva, plasma, tears, and cerebrospinal fluid.

CLINICAL MANIFESTATIONS   Infection with HTLV III/LAV results in a spectrum of clinical illnesses. On the one hand, patients may have one or more of the secondary complications of the immune defect thereby fulfilling the criteria for the surveillance definition of AIDS as indicated above. On the other hand, there are a larger number of individuals who have been infected with HTLV III/LAV who are symptomatic, but who do not fulfill the empiric criteria for the full-blown disease. These patients may have fever, weight loss, diarrhea, fatigue, night sweats, lymphadenopathy, and immunologic abnormalities. This constellation of signs and symptoms in the context of HTLV III/LAV infection has been termed the *AIDS-related complex (ARC)*. It is estimated that approximately 25 percent of patients with ARC will develop full-blown disease within 3 years. Nonetheless ARC itself may be a very serious disease. A substantial number of patients have died from the wasting syndrome of ARC without it ever evolving to full-blown AIDS according to the surveillance definition.

An acute illness occurring 3 to 6 weeks after primary infection with HTLV III/LAV infection has been documented in a few patients. It is characterized by fevers, rigors, arthralgias, myalgias, maculopapular rash, urticaria, abdominal cramps, and diarrhea. The symptoms lasted 2 to 3 weeks and resolved spontaneously. Seroversion occurred 8 to 12 weeks after presumed exposure.

Patients with the full-blown syndrome demonstrate one of a number of patterns of disease. Approximately 50 percent of patients develop *Pneumocystis carinii* pneumonia in the absence of Kaposi's sarcoma, and approximately 27 percent develop Kaposi's sarcoma without *Pneumocystis carinii* pneumonia. Less than 10 percent develop both *Pneumocystis carinii* pneumonia and Kaposi's sarcoma. Not infrequently, an individual patient will have more than one opportunistic infection simultaneously. An increasing number of patients are being recognized with lymphoid neoplasms, which are felt to be secondary to the underlying immune defect. The clinical manifestations in any given patient usually reflect closely the type and location of the opportunistic infection or the anatomic distribution of the neoplastic process.

Patients with *Pneumocystis carinii* pneumonia may present with typical findings of the disease such as fever, dyspnea, and hypoxia. However, in contrast to the more classic presentation of *Pneumocystis carinii* pneumonia in non-AIDS immunosuppressed patients in whom the onset is usually abrupt and explosive, patients with AIDS often have a more indolent presentation with symptoms gradually accelerating over weeks prior to establishment of the diagnosis. Because of the usual copiousness of microorganisms, the diagnosis can generally be made by bronchoscopy with histochemical staining of material from transbronchial biopsy or bronchial lavage. This is in contrast to *Pneumocystis carinii* pneumonia in non-AIDS patients in whom thoracotomy and lung biopsy are often required to establish the diagnosis.

Cytomegalovirus (CMV) infections are extremely common in AIDS patients and appear as fever and disseminated organ system involvement. Of particular note is CMV chorioretinitis, which results in serious visual impairment and may eventuate in complete blindness. CMV enteritis may result in intractable diarrhea. Herpes simplex virus may cause serious mucocutaneous disease in AIDS patients, with perianal involvement being typical. Candida albicans is an extremely common infection in AIDS patients and is usually manifest as oral thrush or esophagitis. *Mycobacterium avium-intracellulare* infections generally occur in AIDS patients as smoldering infections and rarely are primarily responsible for the death of the patient despite the fact that there is no effective treatment. *Mycobacterium tuberculosis* is a common opportunistic infection associated with AIDS in Haiti, in Haitians in the United States, and in Zaire, but is rarely seen in the general AIDS patient population in the United States. This discrepancy is likely due to the prevalence of this infection in these populations in general. *Cryptococcus neoformans* infection occurs as meningitis or as disseminated disease. *Toxoplasma gondii* infections may occur as chorioretinitis or more commonly as intracerebral mass lesions. Pediatric patients with AIDS have a much higher incidence of bacterial infections than do adults with the syndrome. In adults, common bacterial infections are not considered part of the spectrum of opportunistic infections.

Persistent diarrhea is extremely common in AIDS as well as in ARC. Diarrheal syndromes have been demonstrated to occur as a result of CMV enteritis, secondary to infection with the coccidial protozoon cryptosporidium (Chap. 161), secondary to Kaposi's sarcoma in the gastrointestinal tract, or secondary to other intestinal parasites. However, a substantial number of patients with AIDS develop intractable diarrhea and malabsorption for which no underlying cause can be identified.

Severe neuropsychiatric disease characterized by a wide range of neurologic findings, including acute or chronic meningitis and progressive dementia in the presence or absence of localizing signs, occurs in approximately one-third of patients with AIDS. In certain patients, this can be attributed to infections of the central nervous system with organisms such Cryptococcus neoformans, Toxoplasma gondii, or CMV. In others, neoplasms such as primary lymphoma of the brain or Kaposi's sarcoma have been identified. However, in many patients no underlying cause of the central nervous system syndrome can be ascertained, and on histopathologic examination, multifocal leukoencephalopathy may or may not be present. Since it has been shown that HTLV III/LAV can infect brain tissue and since

HTLV III nucleic acid has been identified in the brain tissue of AIDS patients, it is likely that neuropsychiatric syndromes directly related to HTLV III/LAV infection of the brain are occurring in at least a portion of AIDS patients. A small number of patients who are HTLV III/LAV antibody–positive have developed neuropsychiatric disease in the absence of other manifestations of full-blown AIDS, indicating that the virus can infect and cause disease in the brain early on prior to the development of other clinical manifestations of infection.

Many patients with AIDS develop a hypercatabolic wasting syndrome that does not appear to be related to the other manifestations of their disease such as opportunistic infections or Kaposi's sarcoma. In the majority of patients, no underlying cause of the syndrome is identified; however, in others the findings may be explained by unrecognized disseminated CMV or *Mycobacterium avium-intracellulare* infections.

Kaposi's sarcoma is a neoplasm manifested primarily by multiple vascular nodules in the skin and other organs. The disease is multifocal with a course ranging from indolent, with only skin manifestations, to fulminating, with extensive visceral involvement. The pattern of Kaposi's sarcoma in AIDS patients differs significantly from that of patients in nonepidemic groups such as elderly men in the United States and Europe and organ transplant recipients who are iatrogenically immunosuppressed. In the latter groups, the disease is generally indolent, and extracutaneous involvement occurs in only 10 percent of patients. In children and young adults with Kaposi's sarcoma in central Africa, there is a 20 percent incidence of extracutaneous spread of disease. In contrast, extracutaneous involvement of Kaposi's sarcoma is seen in over 70 percent of AIDS patients with this neoplasm. Although any organ system can be involved in the disseminated form of the disease, lymph nodes, gastrointestinal tract, and lungs are most commonly involved. Pulmonary involvement often leads to severe diffusing capacity abnormalities and may result in massive pulmonary hemorrhage. Patients with Kaposi's sarcoma of the oral mucous membranes may have extensive, but clinically undetectable, involvement of the remainder of the gastrointestinal tract.

In addition to AIDS, ARC, and neurologic abnormalities, there is increasing evidence that infection with HTLV III/LAV can be associated with a number of other disorders such as lymphomas, certain carcinomas, lymphoid interstitial pneumonitis, and immune-mediated thrombocytopenia (Chap. 293).

DIAGNOSIS   The diagnosis of full-blown AIDS relies on the presence of the empirically defined secondary complications of the underlying immune defect as described above. A highly sensitive and readily available enzyme-linked immunosorbent assay (ELISA) exists for detection of antibodies against HTLV III/LAV. Western blot analysis, which establishes the specificity of the immunologic reaction between the antibodies and the viral encoded proteins, can be used to confirm the ELISA findings, when necessary. Presence of antibodies to the retrovirus does not indicate that an individual has AIDS or even will develop AIDS. It merely indicates that the individual has been exposed to and/or infected with the AIDS retrovirus. Infection can be documented further by isolation of the virus from peripheral blood lymphocytes or other body materials. Here again, isolation of the virus does not indicate that the patient has AIDS unless the other clinical criteria are present. Given the fact that the virus can be isolated from the lymphocytes of a high percentage of patients who are antibody-positive and who do not have AIDS, it must be presumed that such individuals are capable of transmitting the virus.

The common denominator of AIDS is the immunologic profile described above. The presence of lymphopenia with a selective deficiency of the T4 subset of lymphocytes further substantiates the diagnosis in an individual with the characteristic clinical features. However, immunologic abnormalities may be seen in certain individuals within the high-risk groups, particularly male homosexuals, and this does not mean that the person has AIDS or is even infected with HTLV III/LAV. For example, certain viral infections such as CMV and Epstein-Barr virus (EBV) cause reversal of the T4/T8

lymphocyte ratio. However, this is usually due to a relative increase in number of the T8 subset and not to a decrease in the T4 subset as is the case in AIDS.

TREATMENT AND PROGNOSIS   Treatment of AIDS takes three forms: treatment of the secondary complications of the disease, i.e., the opportunistic infections and neoplasms; treatment of the HTLV III/LAV infection; and enhancement or reconstitution of the defective immune system.

Radiation therapy has been successful in the transient palliation of localized Kaposi's sarcoma. Extensive extremity or truncal disease and visceral disease have not shown substantial clinical responses to radiation. However, the use of alpha interferon or single-agent chemotherapy or combination chemotherapy has met with some success in the treatment of advanced disease and some clinical improvement has occurred. Nonetheless, it has not been demonstrated that successful treatment and remission of Kaposi's sarcoma significantly affects survival of patients with AIDS. A major difficulty with the use of chemotherapy is the resulting compounding of an already markedly immunosuppressed state and the increase in risk of opportunistic infections.

Several of the opportunistic infections in AIDS such as *Pneumocystis carinii* pneumonia (Chap. 158), toxoplasmosis (Chap. 157), candidiasis (Chap. 146), cryptococcosis (Chap. 146), herpes simplex (Chap. 136), and *Mycobacterium tuberculosis* (Chap. 119) can be treated with available antimicrobial agents; however, all have a high rate of recurrence. Of note is the fact that although *Pneumocystis carinii* pneumonia in AIDS generally responds to trimethoprim-sulfamethoxasole or pentamidine isethionate, therapy beyond the standard 2 weeks may often be required to eradicate the organisms. Because of the high rate of recurrence of disease, *Toxoplasma gondii* in AIDS patients may need to be treated for life with pyrimethamine-sulfadiazine. In addition, continuous treatment or prophylaxis for other infections may be required.

Substantial but transient success in the treatment of CMV disease in AIDS, particularly the retinitis, has been observed with the use of 9-(1,3-dihydroxy-2-propoxymethyl) guanine (DHPG) (Chap. 137). There is no effective treatment for *Mycobacterium avium-intracellulare* and EBV infections or for cryptosporidiosis.

A number of agents have been demonstrated to have activity in vitro against HTLV III/LAV, predominantly by inhibiting reverse transcriptase activity of the virus. One of these is suramin, which has been used successfully as an antiparasitic agent for the treatment of onchocerciasis and trypanosomiasis (Chaps. 156 and 163). HPA-23, ribavirin, and 3′-azido-3′-deoxythymidine are also agents with demonstrated anti-HTLV III/LAV activity. Phase I clinical trials have demonstrated that several of these agents also inhibit the AIDS retrovirus in vivo in that the virus cannot be isolated from the patient during and immediately after treatment with these agents. However, a clinical effect on the syndrome has not been demonstrated, perhaps because of persistence of undetected virus and/or the irreversibility of the immune defect, or inadequate duration of treatment.

A number of attempts at immune reconstitution have been undertaken. These have included bone marrow transplantation, especially between identical twins when one of the pair has AIDS; infusion of histocompatible lymphocytes; and the administration of soluble immune mediators such as IL-2 and the interferons. Although partial reconstitution of the immune response has been noted in some cases, it has been invariably temporary. Clearly, the virus must be suppressed if immune reconstitution is to be successful or else the reconstituted immune response will also succumb to the cytopathic effect of the causative retrovirus. The greatest hope for cure of the disease lies in the combination of antiretroviral therapy and immunologic reconstitution.

Since the causative virus has been isolated and cloned, vaccine development is being actively pursued.

There have been no reports of spontaneous reversal of the immune defect in AIDS. The typical clinical pattern is one of recurrent bouts of opportunistic infections with or without progressive Kaposi's sarcoma leading ultimately to the death of the patient. The overall mortality of AIDS is approximately 50 percent. However, the long-range mortality of patients with the full-blown disease is likely to approach 100 percent since there are few long-term (5-year) survivors of the disease.

REFERENCES

BARRÉ-SINOUSSI E et al: Isolation of a T-lymphotropic retrovirus from a patient at risk for acquired immune deficiency syndrome. Science 220:868, 1983

CURRAN JW et al: The epidemiology of AIDS: Current status and future prospects. Science 229:1352, 1985

FAUCI AS et al: Acquired immunodeficiency syndrome: Epidemiologic, clinical, immunologic, and therapeutic considerations. Ann Intern Med 100:92, 1984

—— et al: The acquired immunodeficiency syndrome: An update. Ann Intern Med 102:800, 1985

GALLIN JI, FAUCI AS (eds): Advances in Host Defense Mechanisms, Vol V: Acquired Immunodeficiency Syndrome (AIDS). New York, Raven, 1985

GALLO RC et al: Frequent detection and isolation of cytopathic retrovirus (HTLV III) from patients with AIDS and at risk for AIDS. Science 224:500, 1984

GOTTLIEB MS et al: The acquired immunodeficiency syndrome. Ann Intern Med 99:208, 1983

HO DD et al: Primary human T-lymphotropic virus type III infection. Ann Intern Med 103:880, 1985

JAFFE HW et al: The acquired immunodeficiency syndrome in a cohort of homosexual men: A six year follow-up study. Ann Intern Med 103:210, 1985

LANE HC et al: Abnormalities of B-cell activation and immunoregulation in patients with the acquired immunodeficiency syndrome. N Engl J Med 309:453, 1983

—— et al: Qualitative analysis of immune function in patients with the acquired immunodeficiency syndrome. N Engl J Med 313:79, 1985

SELIK RM et al: Acquired immune deficiency syndrome (AIDS) trends in the United States, 1978–1982. Am J Med 76:493, 1984

258   PLASMA CELL DISORDERS

DAN L. LONGO / SAMUEL BRODER

GENERAL PRINCIPLES   The plasma cell disorders are monoclonal neoplasms related to each other by virtue of their development from common progenitors in the B-lymphocyte lineage. Multiple myeloma, Waldenström's macroglobulinemia, primary amyloidosis, and the heavy chain diseases comprise this group and may be designated by a variety of synonyms such as monoclonal gammopathies, paraproteinemias, plasma cell dyscrasias, and dysproteinemias. A schema for the normal development of B lymphocytes is depicted in Fig. 258-1. Mature B lymphocytes bear surface immunoglobulin molecules of both M and G heavy chain isotypes with both isotypes having identical idiotypes (variable regions). Under normal circumstances, maturation to antibody-secreting plasma cells is stimulated by exposure to the antigen for which the surface immunoglobulin is specific; however, in the plasma cell disorders the control over this process is lost. The clinical manifestations of all the plasma cell disorders relate to the expansion of the neoplastic cells, to the secretion of cell products (immunoglobulin molecules or subunits, lymphokines), and to some extent to the host's response to the tumor.

There are three categories of structural variations among immunoglobulin molecules that form antigenic determinants, and these are used to classify immunoglobulins (Chap. 62). *Isotypes* are those determinants that distinguish among the main classes of antibodies of a given species and are the same in all normal individuals of that species. Therefore, isotypic determinants are by definition recognized by antibodies from a distinct species (heterologous serums) but not by antibodies from the same species (homologous serums). There are five chain isotypes (M, G, A, D, E) and two light chain isotypes (kappa, lambda). *Allotypes* are distinct determinants that reflect regular small differences between individuals of the same species in the amino acid sequences of otherwise similar immunoglobulins. These differences are determined by allelic genes, and by definition they are detected by antibodies made in the same species. *Idiotypes* are the third category of antigenic determinants. They are unique to the molecules produced by a given clone of antibody-producing cells. Idiotypes are formed by the unique structure of the antigen binding portion of the molecule.

Antibody molecules (see Fig. 258-2) are composed of two heavy (mol wt ~ 50,000) and two light (mol wt ~ 25,000) chains (Chap. 62). Each chain has a constant portion (limited amino acid sequence variability) and a variable region (extensive sequence variability). The light and heavy chains are linked by disulfide bonds and are aligned so their variable regions are adjacent to one another. This

FIGURE 258-1 *Schematic representation of the pathway of differentiation of normal B cells. CALLA, B1, B2, B4, Ia, PC-1, and sIg (surface immunoglobulin) are cell markers used to distinguish discrete stages of development. Terminal transferase (TdT) is a cellular enzyme. The stage of differentiation arrest for each lymphoproliferative disorder is shown. The following abbreviations are used: ALL, acute lymphoblastic leukemia; DWDL, diffuse well-differentiated lymphocytic lymphoma; CLL, chronic lymphocytic leukemia; NPDL, nodular poorly differentiated lymphocytic lymphoma; DPDL, diffuse poorly differentiated lymphocytic lymphoma; DHL, diffuse histiocytic or large-cell lymphoma.*

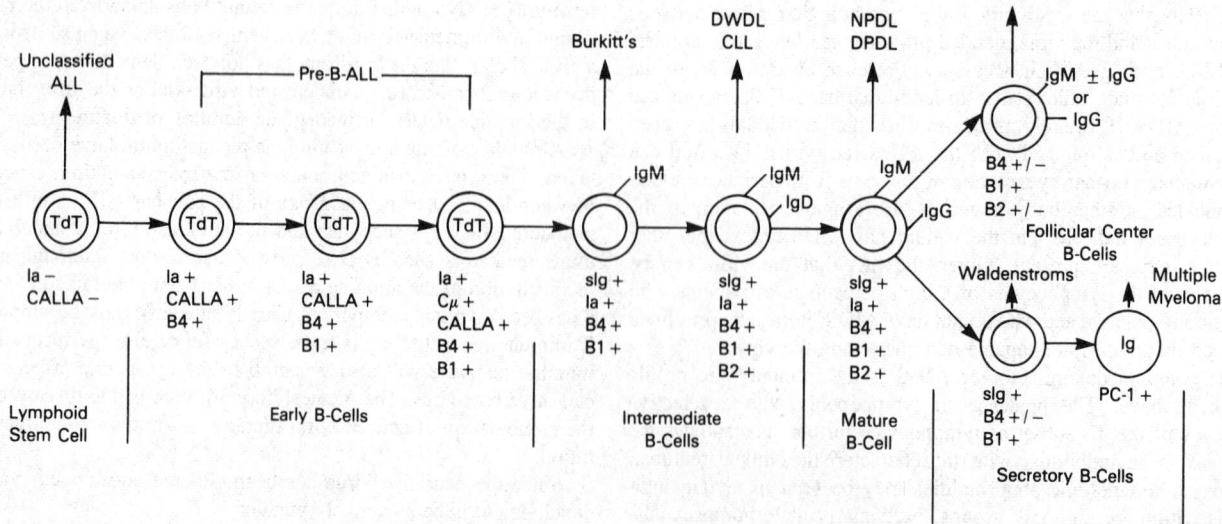

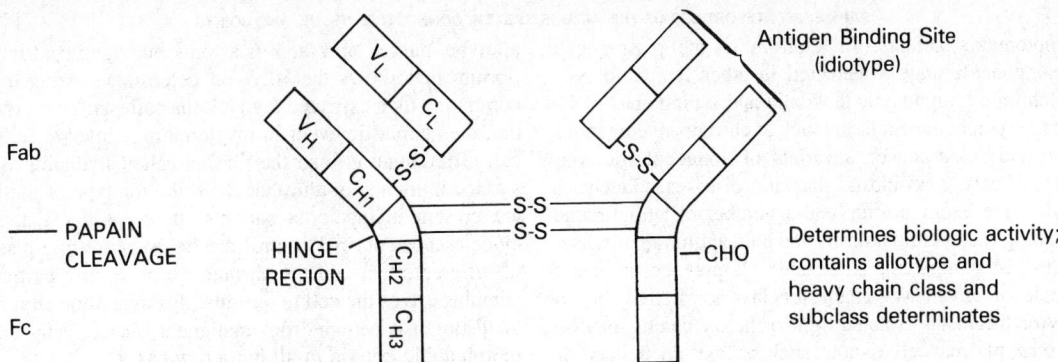

FIGURE 258-2 *Schematic depiction of an IgG molecule. Each molecule consists of two heavy and two light chains linked by disulfide bonds. There are two types of light chains, kappa (genes on chromosome 2) and lambda (chromosome 22), each containing two domains. There are 10 types of heavy chains: 4 types of G (G_1 to G_4), 2 of A (A_1, A_2), 2 of M (M_1, M_2), and 1 each of D and E (all on chromosome 14), each with four domains. A domain is 100 to 110 amino acids in length. Within each domain is an intrachain disulfide bond that produces a loop. V_H (variable domain of the heavy chain) and V_L (variable domain of the light chain) form an antigen binding site whose unique determinants form an idiotype. Immunoglobulins of the same isotype (e.g., $IgG_1\kappa$) differ between individuals. The determinants that distinguish them are called allotypic determinants and are located on C_L (constant domain of the light chain) and C_{H2} (second constant domain of the heavy chain). C_{H2} is also the main site of glycosylation (CHO) and complement binding. Papain cleaves the molecule into antigen-binding (Fab) and crystallizable (Fc) components. The portion of the heavy chain in an Fab fragment is called the Fd piece. Fc receptors on cells bind to the C_{H3} domain. IgM and IgA occur as polymers and each unit of two heavy and two light chains is connected by a J (joining) chain. The heavy chain isotypes determine the function of the antibody.*

variable region forms the antigen recognition site of the antibody molecule; its unique structural features form a particular set of determinants called idiotypes that are reliable markers for a particular clone of cells because each antibody is formed and secreted by a single clone. Each chain is specified by distinct genes, synthesized separately, and assembled into an intact antibody molecule after translation (see Fig. 258-3). Because of the mechanics of the gene rearrangements necessary to specify the immunoglobulin variable regions (VDJ joining for the heavy chain, VJ joining for the light chain; see Fig. 258-3), a particular clone rearranges only one of the two chromosomes to produce an immunoglobulin molecule of only one light chain isotype and only one allotype (allelic exclusion). After exposure to antigen, the variable region may become associated with a new heavy chain isotype (class switch). Each clone of cells performs these sequential gene arrangements in a unique way. This results in each clone producing a unique immunoglobulin molecule. In most cells, light chains are synthesized in slight excess, are secreted as free light chains by plasma cells, and are cleared by the kidney, but less than 10 mg of such light chains is excreted per day.

Electrophoretic analysis of components of the serum proteins permits determination of the amount of antibody in the serum (Fig. 258-4). The variety of immunoglobulins move heterogeneously in an electric field and form a broad peak in the gamma region. The gamma globulin region of the electrophoretic pattern is increased in the serum of patients and animals with plasma cell tumors. There is a sharp spike in this region called an M component (M for monoclonal). The antibody must be present at a concentration of at least 0.5 g/dL to be detectable. This corresponds to approximately 10^9 cells producing the antibody. Confirmation that such an M component is truly monoclonal relies on the use of immunoelectrophoresis that shows a single light and heavy chain type. Hence, immunoelectrophoresis and electrophoresis provide qualitative and quantitative assessment of the M component, respectively. Once the presence of an M component has been confirmed, electrophoresis provides the more practical information for managing patients with monoclonal gammopathies. In a given patient, the amount of M component in the serum is a reliable measure of the tumor burden. This makes the M component an excellent tumor marker; yet it is not specific enough to be used

FIGURE 258-3 *Schematic diagram of the organization and translocation of immunoglobulin genes. Immunoglobulin heavy chains are encoded by four distinct genetic elements, variable (Igh-V), diversity (Igh-D), joining (Igh-J), and constant (Igh-C) genes. The variable region of the immunoglobulin heavy chain is encoded by the V, D, and J genes. The same variable region may be associated with any of the 10 heavy chain constant region genes. In the germline genome (all cells except B cells) the V, D, and J genes are widely separated and there are numerous forms of each. Once a cell becomes committed to B-cell differentiation, a single V gene and a single D gene translocate to a single J gene, and the intervening genetic material is excised. This is called VDJ joining. The newly formed VDJ gene is transcribed into a single message along with either an M or D isotype C gene. Upon exposure to antigen, another rearrangement may occur so that the VDJ gene may be associated with a G, A or E isotype C gene. In light chain genes, there appear to be no D genes, and thus, light chain variable regions are formed by VJ joining.*

CELL TYPES   GENE ORDER   GENE PRODUCT

NONLYMPHOID CELLS
UNCOMMITTED B CELL PRECURSORS

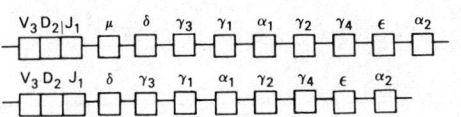

Rearrangements juxtapose $V_3 D_2 J_1$ μ and $V_3 D_2 J_1$ δ genes

B lymphocytes prior to antigen exposure $V_3 D_2 J_1$ μ / $V_3 D_2 J_1$ δ Surface Ig

Class switch rearrangement brings $V_3 D_2 J_1$ next to another heavy chain gene

B lymphocytes after antigen exposure   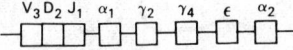 $V_3 D_2 J_1$ α_1 Secreted Ig

None

to screen asymptomatic patients. In addition to the plasma cell disorders, M components may be detected in other lymphoid neoplasms such as chronic lymphocytic leukemia and lymphomas of B- or T-cell origin; nonlymphoid neoplasms such as chronic myelogenous leukemia, breast and colon cancer; a variety of nonneoplastic conditions such as cirrhosis, sarcoidosis, parasitic diseases, Gaucher's disease, and pyoderma gangrenosum; and a number of autoimmune conditions, including rheumatoid arthritis and cold agglutinin disease. The nature of the M component is variable. It may be an intact antibody molecule of any heavy chain subclass, or it may be an altered antibody or fragment. Isolated light or heavy chains may be produced. In some plasma cell tumors such as extramedullary or solitary bone plasmacytomas, less than a third of patients will have an M component. In about 20 percent of myelomas, only light chains are produced. The frequency of myelomas of a particular heavy chain class is roughly proportional to the serum concentration, so that IgG myelomas are more common than IgA and IgD myelomas. In some cases, the antigen specificity of the monoclonal antibody is known.

MULTIPLE MYELOMA Definition

Multiple myeloma represents a malignant proliferation of plasma cells. The terms multiple myeloma and myeloma may be used interchangeably. The disease results from the uncontrolled proliferation of plasma cells derived from a single clone. The tumor, its products, and the host response to it result in a number of organ dysfunctions and symptoms of bone pain or fracture, renal failure, susceptibility to infection, anemia, hypercalcemia, and occasionally clotting abnormalities, neurologic symptoms, and vascular manifestations of hyperviscosity.

Etiology The etiology of myeloma is not known. Myeloma was found to occur with increased frequency in those exposed to the radiation of nuclear warheads in World War II after a 20-year latency. Although there is no direct evidence implicating oncogenes in human myeloma, the observations on c-*myc* and b-*lym* oncogenes in Burkitt's lymphoma, the high incidence of chromosomal translocations in human B-cell tumors, and the role of type C RNA viruses in murine plasmacytoma formation suggest that cells of the B-cell lineage may be susceptible to growth deregulation by such stimuli. The murine plasmacytoma models are particularly interesting in that there is evidence that the induction of plasmacytomas may require exposure to foreign antigens as well as a cellular event. This suggests that chronic antigenic stimulation may play a role in the transformation of a particular B-cell clone. There is also some evidence for a genetic predisposition to myeloma in humans. Patients with myeloma have a significantly higher incidence of expressing the Glm(x) heavy chain

allotype marker, and there is a weak but significant linkage dysequilibrium that shows the HLA-B5 determinant being expressed more commonly than expected in myeloma patients. There is the possibility that the neoplastic event in myeloma may involve cells earlier in B-cell differentiation than the plasma cell. Circulating B cells bearing surface immunoglobulin that share the idiotype of the M component are present in myeloma patients. It is possible that the malignant clone escapes normal control mechanisms at a pre-plasma cell stage of differentiation and the chronic exposure to a particular antigenic stimulus drives the cell to terminal differentiation. It remains difficult to distinguish benign from malignant plasma cells on the basis of morphologic criteria in all but a few cases.

Incidence and prevalence Myeloma is primarily a disease of the elderly and increases in incidence with age. The median age at diagnosis is 64 years. The disease is rare under age 40. The yearly incidence is around 3 per 100,000 and remarkably similar in a variety of countries throughout the world. Males are slightly more commonly affected than females and blacks have nearly twice the incidence of whites. In the age group over 25 years of age the incidence is 30 per 100,000.

Pathogenesis and clinical manifestations (Table 258-1) Bone pain is the most common symptom in myeloma and is present in nearly 70 percent of patients. The pain usually involves the back and ribs, and unlike the pain of metastatic carcinoma which often is worse at night, the pain of myeloma is precipitated by movement. Persistent localized pain in a patient with myeloma usually signifies a pathologic fracture. The bone lesions of myeloma are caused by the proliferation of the tumor cells and the activation of osteoclasts which destroy the bone. The osteoclasts respond to osteoclast activating factor (OAF) made by the myeloma cells; however, production of this factor stops following administration of corticosteroids. The bone lesions are lytic in nature and are rarely associated with osteoblastic new bone formation; therefore, radioisotopic bone scanning is less useful in diagnosis than plain radiography. The bony lysis results in substantial mobilization of calcium from bone, and serious acute and chronic complications of hypercalcemia may dominate the clinical picture (see below). Localized bone lesions may expand to the point that mass lesions may be palpated, especially on the skull (Fig. 258-5), clavicles, and sternum, and the collapse of vertebrae may lead to symptoms of spinal cord compression.

The next most common clinical problem in patients with myeloma is susceptibility to bacterial infections. The most common infections are pneumonias and pyelonephritis, and the most frequent pathogens

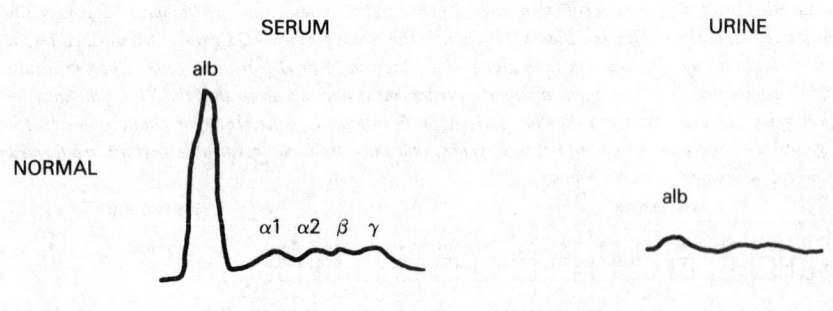

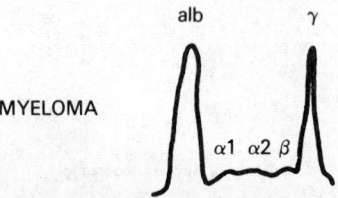

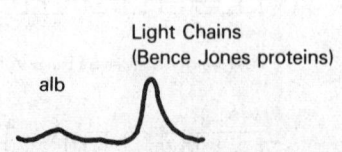

SERUM   URINE

FIGURE 258-4 *Representative electrophoretic patterns of serum and urine. The upper panel illustrates the normal pattern of serum and urine protein on electrophoresis. Since there are many different immunoglobulins in the serum, their differing mobilities in an electric field produce a broad peak. The lower panel illustrates the patterns of serum and urine proteins in a patient with myeloma. The predominance of a product of a single cell is reflected by a "church spire" sharp peak. The presence of free light chains in the urine is reflected in a peak, as well.*

are *Streptococcus pneumoniae, Staphylococcus aureus,* and *Klebsiella pneumoniae* in the lungs and *Escherichia coli* and other gram-negative organisms in the urinary tract (Chap. 84). In about 25 percent of patients recurrent infections are the presenting features, and over 75 percent of patients will have a serious infection at some time in their course. The susceptibility to infection has several contributing causes. First, patients with myeloma have diffuse hypogammaglobulinemia if the M component is excluded. The hypogammaglobulinemia is related to both decreased production and increased destruction of normal antibodies. Moreover, some patients generate a population of circulating regulatory cells in response to their myeloma that can suppress normal antibody synthesis. In the case of IgG myeloma, normal IgG antibodies are broken down more rapidly than normal because the catabolic rate for IgG antibodies varies directly with the serum concentration. The large M component results in fractional catabolic rates of 8 to 16 percent instead of the normal 2 percent. These patients have very poor antibody responses, especially to polysaccharide antigens such as those on bacterial cell walls. Such responses are normally T-cell-independent. Most measures of T-cell function in myeloma are normal. Granulocyte migration is not as rapid as normal in patients with myeloma, probably the result of a product of the tumor. All of these factors contribute to the immune deficiency of these patients.

Renal failure occurs in nearly 25 percent of myeloma patients, and some renal pathology is noted in over half. There are many contributing factors. Hypercalcemia is the most common cause of renal failure. Glomerular deposits of amyloid, hyperuricemia, recurrent infections, and occasional infiltration of the kidney by myeloma cells all may contribute to renal dysfunction. However, tubular damage associated with the excretion of light chains is almost always present. Normally, light chains are filtered, reabsorbed in the tubules and catabolized. With the increase in amount of light chains presented to the tubule, the tubular cells become overloaded with these proteins, and tubular damage results either directly from light chain toxic effects or indirectly from the release of intracellular lysosomal enzymes. The earliest manifestation of this tubular damage is the

adult Fanconi syndrome with increased loss of glucose, amino acids, and defects in the ability of the kidney to acidify and concentrate the urine. The proteinuria is not accompanied by hypertension, and the protein is nearly all light chains. Generally, there is very little albumin in the urine because glomerular function is usually normal. When the glomeruli are involved, the proteinuria is nonselective. Patients with myeloma also have a decreased anion gap [i.e., sodium minus (chloride plus bicarbonate)] because the M component is cationic, resulting in retention of chloride. This is often accompanied by hyponatremia that is felt to be artificial (pseudohyponatremia) because each volume of serum has less water as a result of the increased protein.

Anemia occurs in about 80 percent of myeloma patients. It is usually normocytic and normochromic and related both to the replacement of normal marrow by expanding tumor cells and to the inhibition of hematopoiesis by factors made by the tumor. In addition, mild hemolysis may contribute to the anemia. A larger than expected fraction of patients may have megaloblastic anemia due to either folate or vitamin B_{12} deficiency. Granulocytopenia and thrombocytopenia are very rare. Clotting abnormalities may be seen due to the failure of antibody-coated platelets to function properly or to the interaction of the M component with clotting factors I, II, V, VII, or VIII. Raynaud's phenomenon and impaired circulation may result if the M component forms cryoglobulins, and hyperviscosity syndromes may develop depending on the physical properties of the M component (most common with IgM, IgG3, and IgA paraproteins).

Although neurologic symptoms occur in a minority of patients, they may have many causes. Hypercalcemia may produce lethargy, weakness, depression, and confusion. Hyperviscosity may lead to headache, fatigue, visual disturbances, and retinopathy. Bony damage and collapse may lead to cord compression, radicular pain, and loss of bowel and bladder control. Infiltration of peripheral nerves by amyloid can be a cause of carpal tunnel syndrome and other sensorimotor mono- and polyneuropathies.

Diagnosis and staging The classic triad of myeloma is marrow plasmacytosis (>10 percent), lytic bone lesions, and a serum and/or urine M component. The diagnosis may be made in the absence of bone lesions if the plasmacytosis is associated with a progressive increase in the M component over time or if extramedullary mass lesions develop. There are two important variants of myeloma,

TABLE 258-1 Pathogenesis and clinical manifestations of multiple myeloma

Clinical finding	Underlying cause	Pathogenic mechanism
Hypercalcemia, pathologic fractures, cord compression, lytic bone lesions, osteoporosis, bone pain	Skeletal destruction	Tumor expansion; production of osteoclast activating factor (OAF) by tumor cells
Renal failure	Light chain proteinuria, hypercalcemia, urate nephropathy, amyloid glomerulopathy (rare) Pyelonephritis	Toxic effects of tumor products; light chains, OAF, DNA breakdown products: Hypogammaglobulinemia
Anemia	Myelophthisis, decreased production, increased destruction	Tumor expansion; production of inhibitory factors and autoantibodies by tumor cells
Infection	Hypogammaglobulinemia, decreased neutrophil migration	Decreased production due to tumor-induced suppression; increased IgG catabolism
Neurologic symptoms	Hyperviscosity, cryoglobulins, amyloid deposits Hypercalcemia, cord compression	Products of tumor; properties of M component; light chains; OAF
Bleeding	Interference with clotting factors, amyloid damage of endothelium, platelet dysfunction	Products of tumor; antibodies to clotting factors; light chains; antibody coating of platelets
Mass lesions		Tumor expansion

FIGURE 258-5 *Bony lesions in multiple myeloma. The skull demonstrates the typical "punched out" lesions characteristic of multiple myeloma. The lesion represents a purely osteolytic lesion with little or no osteoblastic activity. (Courtesy of Dr. Geraldine Schechter.)*

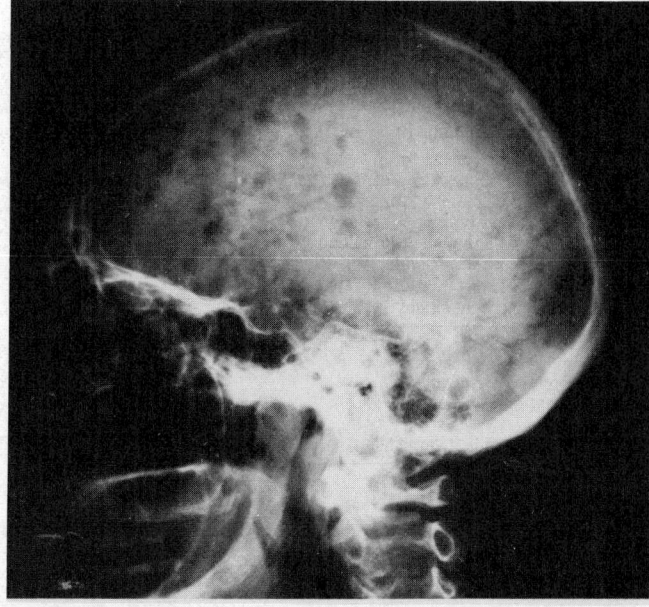

solitary bone plasmacytoma and extramedullary plasmacytoma. These lesions are associated with an M component in less than 30 percent of the cases, they may affect younger individuals, and both are associated with median survivals of 10 or more years. Solitary bone plasmacytoma is a single lytic bone lesion without marrow plasmacytosis. Extramedullary plasmacytomas usually involve the submucosal lymphoid tissue of the nasopharynx or paranasal sinuses without marrow plasmacytosis. Both tumors are highly responsive to local radiation therapy. If an M component is present, it should disappear after treatment. Solitary bone plasmacytomas may recur in other bony sites or evolve into myeloma. Extramedullary plasmacytomas rarely recur or progress.

The most difficult differential diagnosis in patients with myeloma involves their separation from people with benign monoclonal gammopathies or monoclonal gammopathies of uncertain significance (MGUS). MGUS is vastly more common than myeloma, occurring in 1 percent of the population over age 50 and in 3 percent over age 70. Patients with MGUS usually have M components less than 2 g/dL, no urinary Bence Jones protein, less than 5 percent marrow plasmacytosis, and no anemia, renal failure, lytic bone lesions, or hypercalcemia. When bone marrow cells are exposed to radioactive thymidine in order to quantitate dividing cells, patients with MGUS always have a labeling index less than 1 percent and patients with myeloma always have a labeling index greater than 1 percent. Other discriminators include plasma cell acid phosphatase and β-glucuronidase, both of which are low in MGUS patients, and the salmon calcitonin stimulation test, which is positive only in patients with active ongoing bone destruction. Only about 11 percent of patients with MGUS go on to develop myeloma.

Typically, patients with MGUS require no therapy. A number of other diseases may produce M components, including other B-cell neoplasms (especially chronic lymphocytic leukemia and malignant lymphomas), other types of cancer (Hodgkin's disease, chronic myelogenous leukemia, breast and colon cancer), Gaucher's disease, biliary tract diseases like hepatitis and cirrhosis, collagen vascular diseases, chronic infections, and myasthenia gravis. A very rare skin disease known as lichen myxedematosus or papular mucinosis is associated with a monoclonal gammopathy. Highly cationic IgGλ is deposited in the dermis of patients with this disease. It is unclear whether this organ specificity reflects the specificity of the antibody for some antigenic component of the dermis.

The clinical evaluation of patients with myeloma includes a careful physical examination searching for tender bones and masses. It is paradoxic that only a small minority of patients have an enlargement of the spleen and lymph nodes, the physiologic sites of antibody production. Chest and bone radiographs may reveal lytic lesions. A complete blood count with differential may reveal anemia. Very rare patients may have plasma cell leukemia with more than 2000 plasma cells per cubic millimeter. This may be seen in disproportionate frequency (~12 percent) in IgD myelomas. Serum calcium, urea nitrogen, creatinine, and uric acid may be elevated. Protein electrophoresis and measurement of serum immunoglobulins are useful for detecting and characterizing M spikes. Electrophoresis of a 24-h urine specimen with immunologic typing of any M component is necessary. Serum alkaline phosphatase is usually normal even with extensive bone involvement because of the absence of osteoblastic activity. It is also important to quantitate serum beta$_2$ microglobulin (see below).

The serum M component will be IgG in 53 percent of patients, IgA in 25 percent, IgD in 1 percent, and 20 percent of patients will have only light chains in serum and urine. Dipsticks for detecting proteinuria are not reliable at identifying light chains, and the heat test for detecting Bence Jones protein is falsely negative in about 50 percent of patients with light chain myeloma. Fewer than 1 percent of patients have no identifiable M component, and these are usually light chain myelomas in which renal catabolism has made them undetectable in the urine. About two-thirds of patients with serum M components also have urinary light chains. The light chain isotype may have an impact on survival. Patients secreting lambda light chains have a significantly shorter overall survival than those secreting kappa light chains. It is not clear whether this is due to some genetically important determinant of cell proliferation or because lambda light chains are more likely to cause renal damage and form amyloid than are kappa light chains. The heavy chain isotype may have an impact on patient management as well. About half of patients with IgM paraproteins develop hyperviscosity compared to only 2 to 4 percent of patients with IgA and IgG M components. Among IgG myelomas, it is the IgG3 subclass that has the highest tendency to form both concentration- and temperature-dependent aggregates, leading to hyperviscosity and cold agglutination at lower serum concentrations.

The staging system for patients with myeloma is a functional system for predicting survival and is based on a variety of clinical and laboratory tests, unlike the anatomic staging systems for solid tumors. Details of the staging system are given in Table 258-2. Based upon the hemoglobin, calcium, M component, and degree of skeletal involvement, the total-body tumor burden is estimated to be low (stage I, $<0.6 \times 10^{12}$ cells per square meter), intermediate (stage II, 0.6 to 1.2×10^{12} cells per square meter), or high (stage III, $>1.2 \times 10^{12}$ cells per square meter), and the stages are further subdivided on the basis of renal function (A if serum creatinine <2 mg/dL, B if >2). Patients in stage IA have a median survival of more than 5 years and those in stage IIIB about 15 months. Serum beta$_2$ microglobulin [an 11,000-mol wt protein with homologies with the constant region of immunoglobulins that occurs together with the class I major histocompatibility antigens (HLA-A, -B, -C) on the surface of every cell] is the single most powerful predictor of survival and can substitute for staging. Patients with beta$_2$ microglobulin levels less than 6 μg/mL have a median survival of 52 months and those with levels higher than 6 μg/mL only 26 months. It is also felt that once the diagnosis of myeloma is firm, histologic features of atypia may also exert an influence on prognosis.

Treatment and course   About 10 percent of patients with myeloma will have an indolent course demonstrating only very slow progression of disease over many years. Such patients rarely require antitumor

TABLE 258-2 Myeloma staging system

Stage	Criteria	Estimated tumor burden ($\times 10^{12}$ cells/m^2)

I	All of the following:
	1 Hemoglobin >10g/dL
	2 Serum calcium <12 mg/dL
	3 Normal bone x-ray or solitary lesion
	4 Low M-component production
	  a IgG level <5 g/dL
	  b IgA level <3 g/dL
	  c Urine light chain <4 g/24 h
		<0.6 (low)

II	Fitting neither I nor III	0.6–1.20 (intermediate)

III	One or more of the following:
	1 Hemoglobin <8.5 g/dL
	2 Serum calcium >12 mg/dL
	3 Advanced lytic bone lesions
	4 High M-component production
	  a IgG level >7 g/dL
	  b IgA level >5 g/dL
	  c Urine light chains >12 g/24 h
		>1.20 (high)

Subclassification

A Serum creatinine <2 mg/dL
B Serum creatinine >2 mg/dL

Stage	Median survival, months
IA	61
IIA,B	55
IIIA	30
IIIB	15

therapy. Patients with solitary bone plasmacytomas and extramedullary plasmacytomas may be expected to enjoy prolonged, disease-free survival after local radiation therapy to a dose of around 40 Gy. There is a low incidence of occult marrow involvement in patients with solitary bone plasmacytoma. Such patients are usually detected because their serum M component falls slowly or disappears initially only to return after a few months. These patients respond well to systemic chemotherapy.

The vast majority of patients with myeloma require therapeutic intervention. In general, such therapy is of two sorts: systemic chemotherapy to control the progression of myeloma and symptomatic supportive care to prevent serious morbidity from the complications of the disease. All patients with stage II or III disease and stage I patients exhibiting Bence Jones proteinuria, progressive lytic bone lesions, vertebral compression fractures, recurrent infections, or rising serum M component should be treated with systemic combination chemotherapy. Although there are no reported cases of long-term disease-free survival (i.e., cured patients), there is no doubt that therapy can prolong and improve the quality of life in myeloma.

The standard treatment has consisted of intermittent pulses of an alkylating agent [L-phenylalanine mustard (L-PAM, melphalan), cyclophosphamide, or chlorambucil] and prednisone administered for 4 to 7 days every 4 to 6 weeks. The alkylating agents appear to be roughly equally active, but resistance to one agent is often accompanied by resistance to the others. The usual doses are as follows: melphalan, 8 mg/m^2 per day; cyclophosphamide, 200 mg/m^2 per day; chlorambucil, 8 mg/m^2 per day; prednisone, 25 to 60 mg/m^2 per day. Because of their near equivalence in antitumor efficacy, we favor cyclophosphamide because it is less toxic to the marrow stem cell compartment and results in a lower incidence of acute myelodysplastic syndromes than do the other alkylating agents. Doses may need adjustment based on marrow tolerance. Patients responding to therapy generally have a prompt and gratifying reduction in bone pain, hypercalcemia, and anemia, and often have fewer infections. The serum M component lags substantially behind the symptomatic improvement, often taking 4 to 6 weeks to fall. This fall depends upon the rate of tumor kill and the fractional catabolic rate of immunoglobulin, which in turn depends upon the serum concentration (for IgG). Light chain excretion, with a functional half-life of approximately 6 h, may fall within the first week of treatment. However, since urine light chain levels may relate to renal tubular function, they are not a reliable measure of tumor cell kill. Calculations of tumor cell kill are made by extrapolation of the serum M-component level and rely heavily on the assumption that every tumor cell produces immunoglobulin at a constant rate. The data on which this assumption is based are reasonable, but recently it has been possible to alter the rate of immunoglobulin production of a myeloma in vitro with calcium channel blockers, a finding that may have clinical utility, for example, in patients with hyperviscosity. Thus, it is possible that a treatment might affect immunoglobulin production without killing the tumor cell, a situation that would result in an overestimation of the antitumor effects of the treatment if current criteria for response were applied. About 60 percent of patients will achieve at least a 75 percent reduction in serum M-component level and tumor cell mass in response to an alkylating agent and prednisone. Although this is a tumor reduction of less than one log, clinical responses may last many months. Efforts to improve the fraction of patients responding and the degree of response have involved adding other active chemotherapeutic agents to the treatment program. Patients with more advanced disease may benefit most from such approach, but such therapy is experimental at this time.

The ideal duration of therapy has not been determined. Most physicians treat every 4 to 6 weeks for 1 or 2 years. Cessation of therapy is followed by relapse, usually within a year. Retreatment may be associated with a second response in up to 80 percent of patients. Maintenance therapy may prolong the duration of response, but no study has demonstrated this to result in prolonged survival.

The regrowth rate of the tumor during relapse accelerates with each relapse. Patients primarily resistant to initial therapy have a median survival of less than a year.

About 15 percent of patients die within the first 3 months after diagnosis, and subsequently the death rate is about 15 percent per year. The disease usually follows a chronic course for 2 to 5 years before developing an acute terminal phase usually marked by the development of pancytopenia with a cellular marrow that is refractory to treatment. Widespread organ infiltration by myeloma cells occurs and survival is less than 6 months. About 46 percent of patients die in the chronic phase of disease from progressive myeloma (16 percent) and renal failure (10 percent), sepsis (14 percent), or both (6 percent). Death in the acute terminal phase (26 percent) is chiefly from progressive myeloma (13 percent) and sepsis (9 percent). Five percent of patients die of acute leukemia, myeloblastic or monocytic, and although it has been debated that this is related to the primary disease, it appears more likely to be the result of chronic therapy with alkylating agents. Nearly 23 percent of patients die of myocardial infarction, chronic lung disease, diabetes, or strokes, all intercurrent illnesses related more to the age of the patient group than the tumor.

Supportive care directed at the anticipated complications of the disease may be as important as primary antitumor therapy. The hypercalcemia generally responds well to corticosteroid therapy, hydration, and natriuresis. Dichloromethane diphosphonate has also been shown to reduce osteoclastic bone resorption. Treatments aimed at strengthening the skeleton, like fluorides, calcium, and vitamin D with or without androgens, have been suggested but are not of proven efficacy. Iatrogenic worsening of renal function may be prevented by the use of allopurinol during chemotherapy to avoid urate nephropathy and by maintaining a high fluid intake to help excrete light chains and calcium. In the event of acute renal failure, plasmapheresis is approximately 10 times more effective at clearing light chains than peritoneal dialysis, and acutely reducing the protein load may result in functional improvement. Urinary tract infections should be watched for and treated early. Chronic dialysis probably should not be initiated in patients who have failed to respond to antitumor therapy. Plasmapheresis may be the treatment of choice for hyperviscosity syndromes. Although the pneumococcus is a dreaded pathogen in myeloma patients, they do not respond to pneumococcal polysaccharide vaccines. The advent of intravenous gamma globulin preparations raises some hope that prophylactic administration may prevent some serious infections, but this has not been tested. Chronic oral antibiotic prophylaxis is probably not warranted. Patients developing neurologic symptoms in the lower extremities, severe localized back pain, or problems with bowel and bladder control may need emergency myelography and radiation therapy for palliation. Most bone lesions respond to analgesics and chemotherapy, but certain painful lesions may respond most promptly to localized radiation. The chronic anemia may respond to hematinics (iron, folate, cobalamin) and some have responded to androgens. The pathogenesis of the anemia should be established and specific therapy instituted, where possible.

WALDENSTRÖM'S MACROGLOBULINEMIA In 1948, Waldenström described a malignancy of lymphoplasmacytoid cells that secreted IgM. In contrast to myeloma, the disease was associated with lymphadenopathy and hepatosplenomegaly, but the major clinical manifestation was the hyperviscosity syndrome. The disease resembles the related diseases chronic lymphocytic leukemia, myeloma, and lymphocytic lymphoma. Waldenström's macroglobulinemia and IgM myeloma both follow a similar clinical course. The diagnosis of IgM myeloma is usually reserved for patients with lytic bone lesions and is important only because of the hazard of pathologic fractures.

The etiology of macroglobulinemia is unknown. The disease is similar to myeloma in being slightly more common in men and occurring with increased incidence with age (median, 64 years). There have been reports that the IgM in some patients with macroglobulinemia may have specificity for myelin-associated glycoprotein

(MAG), a protein that has been associated with demyelinating disease of the peripheral nervous system and may be lost earlier and to a greater extent than the better known myelin basic protein in patients with multiple sclerosis. There is a surface antigen on natural killer cells that is cross-reactive with the MAG, and coincidentally, natural killer cells are decreased in multiple sclerosis. Sometimes patients with macroglobulinemia develop a peripheral neuropathy before the appearance of the neoplasm. There is speculation that the whole process begins with a viral infection that may elicit an antibody response that cross-reacts with a normal tissue component.

Like myeloma, the disease involves the bone marrow, but unlike myeloma, it does not cause bone lesions or hypercalcemia. Like myeloma, a serum M component is present in the serum in excess of 3 g/dL, but unlike myeloma, the size of the IgM paraprotein results in little renal excretion and only around 20 percent of patients excrete light chains. Therefore, renal disease is not common. The light chain isotype is kappa in 80 percent of the cases. Patients present with weakness, fatigue, and recurrent infections, similar to myeloma patients, but epistaxis, visual disturbances, and neurologic symptoms like peripheral neuropathy, dizziness, headache, and transient paresis are much more common in macroglobulinemia. Physical examination reveals adenopathy and hepatosplenomegaly, and ophthalmoscopic examination may reveal vascular segmentation and dilatation of the retinal veins characteristic of hyperviscosity states. Patients may have a normocytic, normochromic anemia, but rouleaux formation and a positive Coombs' test are much more common than in myeloma. Malignant lymphocytes are usually present in the peripheral blood. About 10 percent of macroglobulins are cryoglobulins. These are pure M components and are not the mixed cryoglobulins seen in rheumatoid arthritis and other autoimmune diseases. Mixed cryoglobulins are composed of IgM or IgA complexed with IgG, for which they are specific. In both cases, Raynaud's phenomenon and serious vascular symptoms precipitated by the cold may occur, but mixed cryoglobulins are not associated with malignancy. Patients suspected of having a cryoglobulin based on history and physical examination should have their blood drawn into a warm syringe to avoid errors in quantitating the cryoglobulin.

Control of serious hyperviscosity symptoms like an altered state of consciousness or paresis can be achieved acutely by plasmapheresis because 80 percent of the IgM paraprotein is intravascular. Aside from this, management is identical to that of myeloma. About 80 percent of patients respond to chemotherapy and their median survival is over 3 years. The absence of other serious organ toxicities results in a longer life span of patients with macroglobulinemia compared to those with myeloma.

HEAVY CHAIN DISEASES

The heavy chain diseases are rare lymphoplasmacytic malignancies. Their clinical manifestations vary with the heavy chain isotype. They secrete a defective heavy chain that usually has an intact Fc fragment and a deletion in the Fd region. Gamma, alpha, and mu heavy chain diseases have been described, but no reports of delta or epsilon heavy chain diseases have appeared. Molecular biologic analysis of these tumors has revealed structural genetic defects that may account for the aberrant chain secreted.

Gamma heavy chain disease (Franklin's disease)   This disease affects people of widely different age groups and countries of origin. It is characterized by lymphadenopathy, fever, anemia, malaise, hepatosplenomegaly, and weakness. Its most distinctive symptom is palatal edema, resulting from node involvement of Waldeyer's ring, and this may progress to produce respiratory compromise. The diagnosis depends upon the demonstration of an anomalous serum M component (often <2 g/dL) that reacts with anti-IgG but not anti-light chain reagents. Most of the paraproteins have been of the gamma$_1$ subclass, but other subclasses have been seen. The patients may have thrombocytopenia, eosinophilia, and nondiagnostic bone marrow. Patients usually have a rapid downhill course and die of infection; however, some patients have survived 5 years with chemotherapy.

Alpha heavy chain disease (Seligmann's disease)   This is the commonest of the heavy chain diseases. It is closely related to a malignancy known as Mediterranean lymphoma, a disease that affects young people in parts of the world such as the Mediterranean, Asia, and South America in which intestinal parasites are common. The disease is characterized by an infiltration of the lamina propria of the small intestine with lymphoplasmacytoid cells that secrete truncated alpha chains. Demonstrating alpha heavy chains is difficult because the alpha chains tend to polymerize and appear as a smear instead of a sharp peak on electrophoretic profiles. Light chains are absent from serum and urine. The patients present with chronic diarrhea, weight loss, and malabsorption and have extensive mesenteric and paraaortic adenopathy. Respiratory tract involvement occurs rarely. Patients may vary widely in their clinical course. Some may develop diffuse aggressive histologies of malignant lymphoma. Chemotherapy may produce long-term remissions. Rare patients appear to have responded to antibiotic therapy, raising the question of the etiologic role of antigenic stimulation perhaps by some chronic intestinal infection.

Mu heavy chain disease   The secretion of isolated mu heavy chains into the serum appears to occur in a very rare subset of patients with chronic lymphocytic leukemia. The only features that may distinguish patients with mu heavy chain disease are the presence of vacuoles in the malignant lymphocytes and the excretion of kappa light chains in the urine. The diagnosis requires ultracentrifugation or gel filtration to confirm the nonreactivity of the paraprotein with the light chain reagents because some intact macroglobulins fail to interact with these serums. The tumor cells seem to have a defect in the assembly of light and heavy chains because they appear to contain both in their cytoplasm. There is no evidence that such patients should be treated differently from other patients with chronic lymphocytic leukemia.

PRIMARY AMYLOIDOSIS

Amyloidosis is a systemic illness resulting from the deposition of polymerized immunoglobulin light chain fragments in organs and tissues. The light chains are arranged in a beta pleated-sheet configuration, appear as homogeneous pink-staining material on light microscopy of hematoxylin-eosin–stained tissue sections, and are identified specifically by their green birefringence under polarized light when tissue secretions are stained with Congo red. The amyloid fibrils are labeled AL in immunocytic amyloidosis because they are composed of light chains. The fibrils of secondary or reactive amyloidosis, which is seen in chronic or acute recurrent infections, and chronic inflammatory diseases like rheumatoid arthritis, are called AA or amyloid A protein. This protein is unrelated to immunoglobulin and is thought to be a fragment of a larger protein called serum amyloid A (SAA) protein.

Immunocytic amyloidosis occurs in about 15 to 20 percent of patients with myeloma and is related to lambda light chains twice as frequently as kappa light chains. About 20 percent of amyloidosis patients have myeloma, and the remainder have monoclonal gammopathies of another origin or even agammaglobulinemia (such patients may produce light chains but not intact immunoglobulins). Even when no underlying diagnosis is apparent, the patient will be found to have a light chain in the urine, a serum M component, or marrow plasmacytosis. Not all light chains are capable of forming amyloid, but the structural features that are prerequisite are not known.

The pathophysiology of amyloidosis is that of organ infiltration. It produces stiffness where there should be flexibility, creates barriers where there should be free flow, and distorts size where there should be fit. The stiffness is particularly damaging to the heart, lungs, blood vessels, and both smooth and skeletal muscle. The barrier effect results in malabsorption in the gastrointestinal tract, renal glomerular dysfunction, cardiac and peripheral nerve conduction defects, and limitation of joint range of motion. The enlarged tongue and narrowed carpal tunnel result in functional compromise. The patient with amyloidosis may have congestive heart failure resistant to the usual therapeutic measures, nephrotic syndrome and nonselective proteinuria from glomerular damage, a bleeding tendency in the skin and gastrointestinal tract from vascular endothelial damage, diarrhea and malabsorption from alterations in the coordinated contraction of intestinal smooth muscle and mucosal infiltration, and orthostatic hypotension and peripheral neuropathies from nerve infiltration. Patients may present with peripheral edema, weakness, paresthesias, light-headedness, and shortness of breath. In addition to the findings of myeloma, they may have hepatomegaly, the "shoulder pad" sign from shoulder muscle infiltration, and the "raccoon sign," i.e. periorbital hemorrhage. The diagnosis depends upon demonstrating amyloid on tissue biopsy. The safest reliable biopsy site is the rectal mucosa, which is diagnostic in about 75 percent of cases. Skin, tongue, or gingival biopsy may yield a diagnosis in most of the remaining cases. Endomyocardial biopsies have been advocated by those experienced in this approach. Biopsies and surgical procedures are generally associated with a greater than normal risk of significant bleeding. Renal and heart failure are the leading causes of death, and the median survival is about a year. Treating amyloidosis patients with therapy which is effective in myeloma has been disappointing. Colchicine and penicillamine have not been found to be effective. Once deposited, it is rare for amyloid to regress.

REFERENCES

BERGSAGEL DE et al: The chemotherapy of plasma cell myeloma and the incidence of acute leukemia. N Engl J Med 301:743, 1979

BRODER SB et al: Impaired synthesis of polyclonal (non-paraprotein) immunoglobulins by circulating lymphocytes from patients with multiple myeloma. N Engl J Med 293:887, 1975

DURIE BGM et al: Pretreatment tumor mass, cell kinetics and prognosis in multiple myeloma. Blood 55:364, 1980

FRANGIONE B, FRANKLIN EC: Heavy-chain diseases: Clinical features and molecular significance of the disordered immunoglobulin structure. Semin Hematol 10:53, 1973

KYLE RA: Monoclonal gammopathy of undetermined significance. Natural history in 241 cases. Am J Med 64:814, 1978

——, GREIPP PR: Amyloidosis (AL), clinical and laboratory features in 229 cases. Mayo Clin Proc 58:665, 1983

MACKENZIE MR, FUDENBERG HH: Macroglobulinemia: An analysis of 40 patients. Blood 39:874, 1972

ROSNER F, GRUNWALD HW: Simultaneous occurrence of multiple myeloma and acute myeloblastic leukemia: Fact or myth? Am J Med 76:891, 1984

SALMON SE et al: Alternating combination chemotherapy and levamisole improves survival in multiple myeloma: A Southwest Oncology Group study. J Clin Oncol 1:453, 1983

SELIGMANN M: Alpha chain disease: Immunoglobulin abnormalities, pathogenesis and current concepts. Br J Cancer 31:356, 1975

259 AMYLOIDOSIS

ALAN S. COHEN

DEFINITION AND CLASSIFICATION Amyloidosis may be defined as the extracellular deposition of the fibrous protein amyloid in one or more sites of the body. This protein has unique ultrastructural, x-ray diffraction, and biochemical characteristics. It can be deposited locally where it has no clinical consequences or may involve virtually any organ system of the body leading to severe pathophysiologic changes, or the disease may fall between these two extremes. The natural history of amyloidosis is poorly understood, and the clinical diagnosis is often not made until the disease is far advanced. The following classification is clinically the most useful: (1) primary (AL type) amyloidosis (no evidence for preexisting or coexisting disease); (2) amyloid associated with multiple myeloma; (also AL type); (3) secondary or reactive (AA type) amyloidosis associated with chronic infectious diseases (e.g., osteomyelitis, tuberculosis, leprosy) or chronic inflammatory diseases (e.g., rheumatoid arthritis and ankylosing spondylitis); (4) heredofamilial amyloidosis, the amyloidosis associated with familial Mediterranean fever (AA type) and a variety of neuropathic (AF prealbumin type), renal, cardiovascular, and other syndromes; (5) local amyloidosis (local, often tumorlike, deposits

which occur in isolated organs without evidence of systemic involvement); and (6) amyloidosis associated with aging, especially in the heart and in the brain.

PATHOLOGY AND STRUCTURE Amyloid is amorphous, eosinophilic, hyaline, extracellular, and ubiquitous in distribution. The involved organs may have a rubbery, firm consistency and a waxy, pink or gray appearance. Organ enlargement, especially of the liver, kidney, spleen, and heart, may be prominent.

Microscopically, amyloid stains pink with the hematoxylin-eosin stain and shows metachromasia with crystal violet. The Congo red stain imparts a unique green birefringence when sections are viewed in the polarizing microscope. This is the single most useful procedure for establishing the presence of amyloid. Amyloid deposits may be focal in almost any area of the body but are most often perivascular.

The heart may show focal or diffuse interstitial deposits in the myocardium, endocardium, or pericardium. In the aged heart, the atrium is usually focally involved or there may occur more diffuse lesions of the atria and ventricles. In the kidney, the glomerulus is primarily affected, although interstitial, peritubular, and vascular amyloid occur. In early lesions, small nodular or diffuse deposits appear near the basement membrane and, as the disease progresses, the glomerulus may be massively laden with amyloid, and its capillary bed will be occluded. In the gastrointestinal tract, there may be perivascular deposits only, or irregular or diffuse deposits may be found in the submucosa, in the muscularis mucosa, or subserosa. The amyloid may appear at any level or portion of the gastrointestinal tract including the gallbladder and pancreas. In the nervous system, amyloid has been described along peripheral nerves, in autonomic ganglia, and in senile plaques, in neurofibrillary tangles, as well as blood vessels ("congophilic angiopathy") of the central nervous system. It may be found in any portion of the orbit including the vitreous humor and cornea. In summary, there is virtually no area of the body that is spared. This ubiquitous distribution elicits a wide variety of clinical symptoms and signs.

All types of human amyloid consist of fine, nonbranching rigid fibrils that in tissue sections measure approximately 100 Å in diameter. The amyloid fibrils are usually seen earliest in the mesangial cell in the kidney and Kupffer cell in the liver. Isolated amyloid fibrils have a delicate, thin, nonbranching fibrous character. The individual fibril (or filament) has a diameter of about 70 Å and tends to aggregate laterally. Each fibril (filament) has subunit protofibrils of 30 to 35 Å diameter.

A second component, the plasma component or pentagonal unit (P component) with a different ultrastructure, x-ray diffraction pattern, and chemical characteristics, has also been isolated from amyloid and is identical with a serum alpha globulin. It has many similarities to C-reactive protein, but it does not behave as a classic acute phase protein. It is not responsible for the characteristic tinctorial properties or ultrastructure of amyloid.

BIOCHEMISTRY OF AMYLOID FIBRILS The bulk of amyloid deposits consists of fibrils. Purified amyloid derived from the fibril is a protein. The chemical composition of the different clinical forms of amyloid are distinct and allow for more precise diagnosis (Table 259-1). The homology of the fibril of primary and myeloma amyloid to the N-terminal region of the variable fragment of an immunoglobulin light chain and subsequently, in a limited number of cases, to a homogeneous light polypeptide chain, has been demonstrated. These light chain–related proteins range in size from about 5000 to 25,000 daltons and are now termed amyloid light chain (AL) or AL_κ or AL_λ (Table 259-1). Amino acid sequence analysis indicates that most primary amyloid proteins contain the N-terminal amino acid residue identical to the variable regions of the light chain (Asp-Ile-Gln-Ser-Pro-Ser-Ser-Leu- . . .).

Another protein that is unrelated to any known immunoglobulin has been described in the secondary amyloid deposits. This protein, amyloid A (AA) protein, can be isolated from the amyloid of patients with secondary amyloidosis and from that associated with familial

TABLE 259-1   Classification of amyloid

Biochemical type	Clinical form	Comment
AL	1 Primary amyloid 2 Multiple myeloma–associated amyloid	Homologous to *N*-terminal residue of variable region of κ or λ light chain (or rarely whole chain). Varied molecular weight.
AA	1 Secondary (reactive) amyloid 2 Amyloid of familial Meditarranean fever	Serum protein SAA is putative precursor; Arg-Ser-Phe-Phe-Ser sequence to 76 amino acids.
$AF_{prealbumin}$	1 Familial amyloid polyneuropathy (Japanese, Swedish, Portuguese)	Most with single amino acid subsitution of methionine for valine at position 30; probably other variants exist.
AE_{mct}	1 Amyloid-associated medullary carcinoma of thyroid	Probable calcitonin precursor; may be true of other endocrine-related forms of amyloid.
AS_c	1 Senile cardiac	May be prealbumin.
AP	1 P component	Distinct from amyloid fibril; found in all systemic forms. Serum SAP is the precursor.

Mediterranean fever. It is a unique protein with a molecular weight of about 8500 daltons made up of 76 amino acid residues arranged in a single chain, and an amino acid sequence beginning with Arg-Ser-Phe. . . . Some heterogeneity has been demonstrated (i.e., AAs of different molecular weights).

Antiserums to alkali-degraded amyloid fibrils of the AA protein have detected an antigenically related serum component, SAA. Amino acid analysis, peptide maps, and sequence studies suggest that AA protein is an amino terminal fragment of SAA and is derived from it by proteolysis. SAA behaves as an acute phase reactant and is elevated in infection and inflammation. In addition, SAA is elevated in amyloid-resistant animals suggesting that the appearance of amyloid is not solely determined by the level of SAA. SAA associates with the HDL_3 subclass of serum lipoproteins and is often referred to as apoSAA. In human beings there are two major isotypes of SAA, and four minor variants have been described. An SAA inducing factor (now known to be interleukin 1) has been shown to be released from stimulated macrophages and to cause the release of SAA from hepatocytes, the site of SAA synthesis. SAA appears to suppress antibody response, suggesting that it might act as an immune regulator. Heterogeneity of SAAs has also been recognized.

Familial amyloid polyneuropathy (FAP) is a dominant hereditary disease affecting kinships originating in Portugal, Japan, Sweden, and elsewhere. A 14,000-dalton protein has been isolated from the tissues of patients from each of the above-noted geographically distributed kinships. Immunologic and amino acid sequence analysis has identified it as prealbumin, the first association of this molecule with a disease. It has also been shown that there is a single amino acid substitution, methionine for valine at position 30 in the prealbumin isolated from the amyloid. Data suggest that other variants may also exist.

In addition, a prothyrocalcitonin has been isolated from the amyloid of medullary carcinoma of the thyroid. It has been suggested that the amyloid associated with other endocrine organs is also made up of a prehormone or preprohormone precursor.

P component of amyloid   In addition to the characteristic fibrils described above, a second component, the P component, has been noted in most amyloid deposits. P component (AP) has been recognized by electron microscopy as a pentagonal-shaped structured unit having an outside diameter of about 90 Å and an inside diameter of about 40 Å. On immunoelectrophoresis it migrates as an alpha

globulin, and it possesses antigenic identity with a constituent of normal human plasma (SAP). The amino acid sequence is distinct from that of the amyloid fibrils. Its pentagonal ultrastructure is similar to C-reactive protein (CRP), but the latter is one-half the molecular weight of AP and has other well-defined differences despite a 50 to 60 percent homology on amino acid sequence. AP binds to amyloid fibrils in a calcium-dependent fashion.

IMMUNOBIOLOGY OF AMYLOID   The etiology and pathogenesis of amyloidosis are unknown. Electron-microscopic autoradiographic studies have revealed high concentrations of fibrils adjacent to reticuloendothelial cells.

Endotoxin stimulation of macrophages has been shown to produce a mediator (interleukin 1) that stimulates hepatic cells, now recognized as a major source of SAA synthesis, to produce SAA. Other studies suggest that SAA is partially degraded by monocyte or leukocyte surface enzymes to form tissue AA. The other form of amyloid (AL) is probably produced by the partial degradation of immunoglobulins by macrophages.

An excess antigenic stimulus has been shown to induce amyloid in animals. However, the basic conditions for the experimental induction of amyloidosis have not been clearly defined. Marked depression of T cells with maintenance of normal or hyperactive B-cell function has been described. These findings suggest that disturbances in immunoregulatory mechanisms may be an important step in the pathogenesis of amyloid disease. A transferable amyloid enhancing factor (AEF) that can be isolated from the spleens of experimental animals has also been identified.

CLINICAL MANIFESTATIONS   The clinical manifestations of amyloidosis are varied and depend entirely on the area of the body which is involved.

Kidney   Renal involvement may consist of mild proteinuria or frank nephrosis. In some cases, the urinary sediment may show only a few red blood cells. The renal lesion is usually not reversible and in time leads to progressive azotemia and death. The prognosis does not appear to be related to the degree of the proteinuria; when azotemia finally develops, the prognosis is grave. In one series the mean survival of patients with renal amyloid from the time of biopsy was 29 months, but in a few cases there was presumptive evidence of regression of the renal amyloid. Hypertension is rare except in long-standing amyloidosis. Renal tubular acidosis or renal vein thrombosis may occur. Localized accumulation of amyloid may be noted in the ureter, bladder, or other parts of the genitourinary tract.

Liver   While hepatic involvement is common, liver function abnormalities are minimal and occur late in the disease. The two tests most useful in indicating hepatic amyloid are the Bromsulphalein (BSP) extraction and serum alkaline phosphatase activity. Liver scans produce variable and nonspecific results. Portal hypertension occurs but is uncommon. Intrahepatic cholestasis has been noted in about 5 percent of patients with AL (primary) amyloidosis. In a series of 38 patients in whom liver tissue was available for examination, all 38 had some amyloid present, irrespective of the type of amyloidosis (primary or secondary), and contrary to previous notions, parenchymal amyloid was more extensive in the AL cases. Amyloidosis of the spleen characteristically is not associated with leukopenia and anemia.

Heart   Cardiac manifestations consist primarily of congestive failure and cardiomegaly (with or without murmurs) and a variety of arrhythmias. Although the cardiac manifestations reflect predominantly diffuse myocardial amyloid, the endocardium, valves, and pericardium may be involved as well. Pericarditis with effusion is rare, although the differential diagnosis of constrictive pericarditis versus restrictive cardiomyopathy frequently arises. Echocardiography has demonstrated symmetric thickening of the left ventricular wall, hypokinesia and decreased systolic thickening of the interventricular septum and left ventricular posterior wall, and left ventricular cavities of small to normal size. Two-dimensional echocardiography is said to produce the characteristic findings of thickened right and left ventricles, a normal left ventricular cavity, and especially a diffuse hyperrefractile "granular sparkling" appearance. Hearts which are heavily infiltrated with amyloid may or may not show an enlarged silhouette. Fluoroscopy usually shows decreased mobility of the ventricular wall; angiographic studies usually demonstrate thickened ventricular wall, decreased ventricular mobility, and absence of rapid ventricular filling in early diastole. Cardiac amyloidosis can present as intractable heart failure. Electrocardiographic abnormalities include a low-voltage QRS complex and abnormalities in atrioventricular and intraventricular conduction, often resulting in varying degrees of heart block. Owing to their propensity to develop conduction defects and arrhythmias, patients with cardiac amyloidosis appear to be especially sensitive to digitalis, and this drug should be used with caution.

Skin Involvement of the skin is one of the most characteristic manifestations of so-called primary amyloidosis. The lesions may consist of slightly raised, waxy papules or plaques which usually are clustered in the folds of the axillae, anal, or inguinal regions, the face and neck, or mucosal areas such as ear or tongue. The lesions are seldom pruritic. Involvement of the skin or mucosa may not be apparent clinically but may be disclosed by biopsy. Gentle rubbing of the skin may induce bleeding into the skin, leading to purpura. Cutaneous involvement also can occur in secondary amyloidosis; in one series it was found in 42 percent of such patients, in 55 percent of a group of patients with primary disease, and in all 11 patients with hereditary amyloid neuropathy.

Gastrointestinal tract Gastrointestinal symptoms are common in amyloidosis. They may result from direct involvement of the gastrointestinal tract at any level or from infiltration of the autonomic nervous system with amyloid. The symptoms include those of obstruction, ulceration, malabsorption, hemorrhage, protein loss, and diarrhea. Infiltration of the tongue occasionally leads to macroglossia. When not enlarged, the tongue may become stiffened and firm to palpation. While infiltration of the tongue is characteristic of primary amyloidosis or amyloidosis accompanying multiple myeloma, it is occasionally seen in the secondary form of the disease.

Gastrointestinal bleeding may occur from any of a number of sites, notably the esophagus, stomach, or large intestine, and may be severe. Amyloid infiltration of the esophagus may lead to an incompetent or nonrelaxing lower esophageal sphincter, nonspecific motility disorders of the esophageal body, or rarely achalasia. Small-bowel lesions may lead to clinical and x-ray changes of obstruction. A malabsorption syndrome is seen at times. Amyloidosis may develop in association with other entities involving the gastrointestinal tract, especially tuberculosis, granulomatous enteritis, lymphoma, and Whipple's disease; differentiation of these conditions, which give rise to secondary amyloidosis, from diffuse primary amyloidosis of the small bowel may be difficult. Similarly, amyloidosis of the stomach may closely mimic gastric carcinoma, with obstruction, achlorhydria, and the radiologic appearance of tumor masses.

Nervous system Neurologic manifestations may include peripheral neuropathy, postural hypotension, inability to sweat, Adie's pupil, hoarseness, and sphincter incompetence. These manifestations are especially prominent in the heredofamilial amyloidoses. The cranial nerves are generally spared except for those involving the pupillary reflexes. Amyloid occurs in the central nervous system as a component of senile plaques, neurofibrillary tangles, and in blood vessels ("congophilic angiopathy"). The protein concentration in the cerebral spinal fluid may be increased. Infiltrates of the cornea or vitreous body may be present in hereditary amyloid syndromes. Certain of these syndromes are characterized by a bilateral scalloping appearance of the pupil. Amyloid may infiltrate the thyroid or other endocrine glands but rarely causes endocrine dysfunction. Local amyloid deposits almost invariably accompany medullary carcinoma of the thyroid. Amyloid infiltration of muscle may lead to a pseudomyopathy.

Joints Amyloid can directly involve articular structures by its presence in the synovial membrane and synovial fluid or in the articular cartilage. Amyloid arthritis can mimic a number of rheumatic diseases because it can present as a symmetric arthritis of small joints with nodules, morning stiffness, and fatigue. Most patients with amyloid arthropathy eventually are found to have multiple myeloma. The synovial fluid usually has a low white blood cell count, a good to fair mucin clot, a predominance of mononuclear cells, and no crystals. Studies of surgical specimens suggest a significant incidence of amyloid in cartilage, capsule, and synovium in osteoarthritis.

Respiratory system The nasal sinuses, larynx, and trachea may be involved by accumulations of amyloid which block the ducts, in the case of the sinuses, or the air passages. Amyloidosis of the lung involves the bronchi and alveolar septa diffusely. The lower respiratory tract is affected most frequently in primary amyloidosis and in the disease associated with dysproteinemia. Pulmonary symptoms attributable to amyloid are present in about 30 percent of these patients and in some are the most serious manifestations of the disease. In secondary amyloidosis, pulmonary disease is a frequent histopathologic accompaniment but seldom gives rise to clinically significant symptoms. Amyloid may also be localized in the bronchi or pulmonary parenchyma and may resemble a neoplasm. In these cases, local excision should be attempted and, when successful, may be followed by prolonged remissions.

Hematopoietic system Hematologic changes may include fibrinogenopenia, increased fibrinolysis, and selective deficiency of clotting factors. Deficient factor X seems to be due to nonspecific calcium-dependent binding to the polyanionic amyloid fibrils. Splenectomy in the patient with such a factor-X deficiency can relieve the deficiency and the associated bleeding disorder.

HEREDOFAMILIAL AMYLOIDOSIS There is no generally accepted nosology for the heredofamilial amyloid syndromes. Some reports emphasize the site of predominant organ involvement as neuropathic, nephropathic, or cardiopathic amyloidosis, while others stress the genetic aspects. To date, virtually all analyses of pedigrees have shown that, with one major exception, the mode of inheritance is autosomal dominant. The exception is amyloidosis of familial Mediterranean fever, which is inherited as an autosomal recessive disorder and is an AA type of amyloid. The recognizable clinical patterns still form the basis for classification, although serum abnormalities (decreased serum prealbumin in several types of familial amyloid polyneuropathy) have been reported. Table 259-2 proposes a tentative

TABLE 259-2 Familial amyloid

Types	Forms
Familial amyloid polyneuropathy	
Type I Portuguese (Andrade)	*1* Portuguese
	2 Swedish
	3 Japanese
	4 Greek
	5 English
	6 German
Type II Indiana (Rukavina)	*1* Swiss
	2 German
Type III Iowa (Van Allen)	*1* Scottish-English-Irish
(possibly same as type I)	*2* Spanish
Type IV Cranial neuropathy and corneal	*1* Finnish
lattice dystrophy	*2* Danish
(Meretoja)	*3* Dutch
Familial oculoleptomeningeal amyloid	*1* German
	2 Dutch
	3 Japanese
Hereditary cerebral amyloid with hemorrhage	*1* Icelandic
Familial nephropathy	
Type I Familial Mediterranean fever	*1* Sephardic Jewish
(Heller)(recessive)	*2* Armenian
	3 Turkish
	4 Arab
Type II Fever and abdominal pain	*1* Swedish
	2 Sicilian
Type III Urticaria, deafness, renal disease	
Familial cardiopathy	
Type I Progressive heart failure	*1* Danish
Type II Hereditary atrial standstill	*1* Mexican-American

classification and is based largely on the major site of organ involvement, in addition to genetic data and ethnic background.

The heredofamilial amyloidoses include a group primarily involving the nervous system. Among these are lower limb neuropathy [familial amyloid polyneuropathy (FAP)], first described in Portugal, which has a poor prognosis and is characterized by progressively severe neuropathy including marked autonomic nervous system involvement. This variety also has been described in Japan, Sweden, and in families of Greek and of Swedish origin in the United States. In some of these individuals, bilateral "scalloped" pupils are pathognomonic of the disease. The second type of neuropathy has been found in families of Swiss origin in Indiana and of German origin in Maryland. It is a milder disease and is often associated with a carpal tunnel syndrome and vitreous opacities. A more severe variety of generalized neuropathy associated with renal amyloidosis has been described in Iowa in a family of English-Irish-Scottish ancestry.

Several types of severe familial renal disease in association with amyloid have been described. Possibly the most remarkable is familial Mediterranean fever (FMF), a disorder subdivided into phenotype I, with irregularly occurring fever and abdominal, chest, or joint pain, preceding or accompanying renal amyloid, and phenotype II, in which amyloidosis is the first or only manifestation of the disease (Chap. 271). Colchicine treatment prevents attacks of FMF and appears to prevent subsequent deposition of amyloid as well. Sporadically, other hereditary forms of renal amyloidosis have been described, including the curious association of urticaria, deafness, and renal amyloid.

Severe familial amyloid heart disease has been described in a Danish family, and familial persistent atrial standstill with amyloid in a family of Mexican-American origin. Hereditary cerebral amyloid with hemorrhage in an Icelandic family appears to be due to gamma trace protein deposits and is associated with decreased gamma trace proteins in the cerebrospinal fluid. Miscellaneous hereditary amyloid syndromes include hereditary multiple endocrine neoplasms type II (including medullary carcinoma of the thyroid with amyloid) as well as others listed in Table 259-2.

DIAGNOSIS The specific diagnosis of amyloidosis depends upon obtaining a tissue specimen by biopsy and the demonstration of amyloid with appropriate stains. First, of course, the disease must be suspected. When a patient with a chronic disorder predisposing to amyloid such as rheumatoid arthritis, tuberculosis, paraplegia, multiple myeloma, bronchiectasis, or leprosy develops hepatomegaly, splenomegaly, malabsorption, cardiac disease, or, most importantly, proteinuria, amyloid should come to mind. In addition, in any heredofamilial syndromes, especially those which have a dominant autosomal mode of inheritance and are characterized by peripheral neuropathy, nephropathy, or cardiopathy, the diagnosis of amyloid should be considered. Finally, primary systemic amyloid should be considered in any individual with a diffuse noninflammatory infiltrative disease involving either mesenchymal tissues—blood vessels, heart, gastrointestinal tract—or parenchymal tissues—kidney, liver, spleen, adrenal.

When the diagnosis is suspected, it is good practice to perform an abdominal subcutaneous fat pad aspirate or a rectal biopsy. If there is a specific reason for not carrying out these procedures, other sites including skin, gums, or the suspected organ—kidney, liver—may be biopsied. All tissues obtained must be stained with Congo red and examined in the polarizing microscope for green birefringence. A modified potassium permanganate stain will allow reasonably accurate differentiation of the AA type from AL amyloid. In the former, pretreatment with permanganate, followed by the standard Congo red stain, abolishes the green birefringence (i.e., the tissue is permanganate-sensitive). The AL and AF prealbumin types are permanganate-resistant.

In order to establish the relationship of immunoglobulin-related amyloid to multiple myeloma, electrophoretic and immunoelectro-phoretic studies on serum or urine should be performed when the biopsy reveals amyloid deposition. Most of these patients will have only relatively small paraprotein components and only a few will have frank multiple myeloma. The therapeutic implications of these findings are discussed in greater detail in Chap. 258.

PROGNOSIS AND TREATMENT The course of amyloidosis is difficult to document since dating the time of origin of the disease is rarely possible. When amyloidosis develops in patients with rheumatoid arthritis, it seldom becomes evident when the arthritis is less than 2 years in duration. The mean duration of arthritis before amyloidosis was detected was 16 years in one series. When amyloidosis develops in patients with multiple myeloma, manifestations leading to initial hospitalization are more apt to be related to amyloid disease than to myeloma. In these cases prognosis is very poor, and life expectancy is usually less than 6 months.

Instances have been reported of amyloidosis accompanying treatable infections, such as osteomyelitis, in which at least partial remission has occurred following treatment of the primary disease. There have been similar experiences following successful treatment of tuberculosis or drainage of chronic empyema. However, many such reports are not substantiated by biopsy proof of resorption.

Generalized amyloidosis is usually a slowly progressive disease and leads to death in several years, but it may have a better prognosis than was suspected in the past. The average survival in most large series is 1 to 4 years, but a number of individuals with amyloid have been followed 5 to 10 years and longer.

The major cause of death is renal failure. Sudden death, presumably due to arrhythmias, is also quite common. Occasionally, gastrointestinal hemorrhage, respiratory failure, intractable heart failure, and superimposed infections are the terminal events.

There is no specific therapy for any variety of amyloidosis. Rational therapy should be directed at (1) decreasing chronic antigenic stimuli that produce amyloid, (2) inhibition of the synthesis and extracellular deposition of amyloid fibrils, and (3) promoting lysis or mobilization of existing amyloid deposits.

A variety of agents have been used to treat amyloidosis. Proof of their efficacy is not available. The finding that a portion of the immunoglobulin light chain is incorporated in the amyloid of patients with primary amyloidosis and its presumed synthesis by plasma cells has led to the use of alkylating agents. However, these agents cause bone marrow depression, and there are reports of acute leukemia developing in amyloidosis patients receiving melphalan. Moreover, there is experimental evidence that immunosuppressive agents may enhance the deposition of preexisting amyloid. Hence, conservative and supportive measures provide the mainstay of management. It is important to provide these patients with a more optimistic outlook.

Two patients with severe renal amyloidosis and azotemia were subjected to bilateral nephrectomy and renal transplantation followed by immune therapy. One patient died of infection 5 months after surgery. The donor kidney showed no evidence of amyloidosis. The second patient achieved a 10-year clinical remission after receiving a transplanted kidney. Notwithstanding the hazards of operating upon patients with systemic amyloidosis who may have cardiac involvement, carefully selected azotemic patients could benefit from transplantation.

Colchicine has been shown to be effective in preventing acute attacks in patients with FMF, and two groups of investigators independently have reported the inhibition of amyloid deposition in the mouse model by colchicine. It is conceivable, therefore, that colchicine is effective in blocking amyloid deposition. One large preliminary study has shown it to be effective in prolonging life in primary (AL) amyloidosis using a life-table survivorship analysis. However, the exact mechanism of its action is unknown, and no controlled human clinical study has been reported. The role of dimethylsulfoxide (DMSO) in the treatment of amyloid is also under investigation.

REFERENCES

COHEN AS: Amyloidosis. N Engl J Med 277:522, 1967
———, SKINNER M: Diagnosis of amyloidosis, in *Laboratory Diagnostic Procedures in the Rheumatic Diseases,* 3d ed, AS Cohen (ed). Orlando, Fla, Grune & Stratton, 1985

——— et al: Amyloid proteins, precursors, mediator, and enhancer, Lab Invest 48:1, 1983
GLENNER GG et al: Amyloid fibril proteins: Proof of homology with immunoglobulin light chains. Science 172:1150, 1971
——— et al: *Amyloid and Amyloidosis.* New York, Excerpta Medica, 1980
KYLE RA, GREIPP PR: Amyloidosis (AL): Clinical and laboratory features in 229 cases. Mayo Clin Proc 58:665, 1983

section 2 Disorders of immune-mediated injury

260 DISEASES OF IMMEDIATE TYPE HYPERSENSITIVITY

K. FRANK AUSTEN

The term *atopic allergy* implies a familial tendency to manifest alone or in combination such conditions as asthma, rhinitis, urticaria, and eczematous dermatitis (atopic dermatitis). However, individuals without an atopic background may also develop hypersensitivity reactions, particularly urticaria and anaphylaxis, associated with the same class of antibody, IgE, found in atopic individuals. The designation *diseases of immediate type hypersensitivity* presents a more suitable framework than the broad term *allergy* or the restrictive definition of atopy.

The fixation of IgE to human basophils has been demonstrated by radioautography and electron microscopy and to intraepithelial and perivenular mast cells in tonsils, adenoids, and nasal polyps of humans by immunofluorescence. IgE-dependent mediator generation and release also occur in the mast cells of human lung slices, nasal polyps, or skin and have been observed in those tissues most involved in diseases of immediate type hypersensitivity.

Studies with purified rat peritoneal mast cells have indicated that the IgE receptor is transmembrane-linked to adenylate cyclase and that stereospecific receptor perturbation generates second messenger cyclic 3′,5′-adenosine monophosphate (cyclic AMP). Cyclic AMP then activates cytoplasmic cyclic AMP–dependent protein kinase, which presumably acts to phosphorylate cell proteins, thereby continuing the biochemical sequence of the coupled activation-secretion response. A parallel membrane response to stereospecific IgE receptor perturbation involves the formation of calcium ion channels with augmented ion influx and the activation of phospholipases. Phospholipases then cleave membrane phospholipids to generate lysophospholipids or diacylglycerol which, being fusogenic, may facilitate the fusion of the secretory granule perigranular membrane with the cell membrane, a step which releases the membrane-free granule containing the preformed or primary mediators of mast cell effects. The arachidonic acid, generated simultaneously by phospholipase action, is processed oxidatively into secondary mediators of the prostaglandin (Fig. 260-1) and leukotriene (Fig. 260-2) classes. The secretory granule of the human mast cell has a crystalline structure, unlike mast cells of lower species, and IgE-dependent cell activation can be characterized morphologically by solubilization and swelling

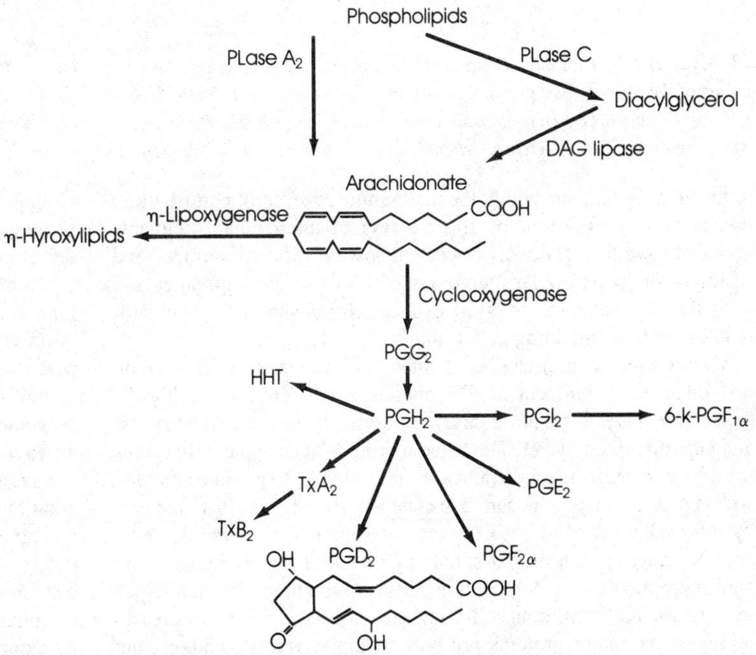

FIGURE 260-1 *Metabolism of phospholipids to arachidonic acid and cyclooxygenase-derived products. Cleavage of arachidonic acid from membrane phospholipids during cellular activation proceeds either by the action of phospholipase A_2 (PLase A_2) or by the sequential action of phospholipase C (PLase C) and diacylglycerol lipase (DAG lipase). Biosynthesis of prostaglandins is depicted with the structure of PGD_2, which is the predominant product from mast cells via the terminal action of a PGD_2 synthetase. η-Lipoxygenase, family of monolipoxygenases; PGG_2, PGH_2, PGI_2, PGE_2, $PGF_{2\alpha}$, PGD_2, prostaglandins G_2, H_2, I_2, E_2, $F_{2\alpha}$, and D_2, respectively; TxA_2, TxB_2, thromboxane A_2 and B_2, respectively; $6-k-PGF_{1\alpha}$, 6-keto-prostaglandin $F_{1\alpha}$; HHT, 12-hydroxy-heptadecatrienoic acid. [Modified from Schwartz and Austen,* Immunological Diseases, *4th ed (in press).]*

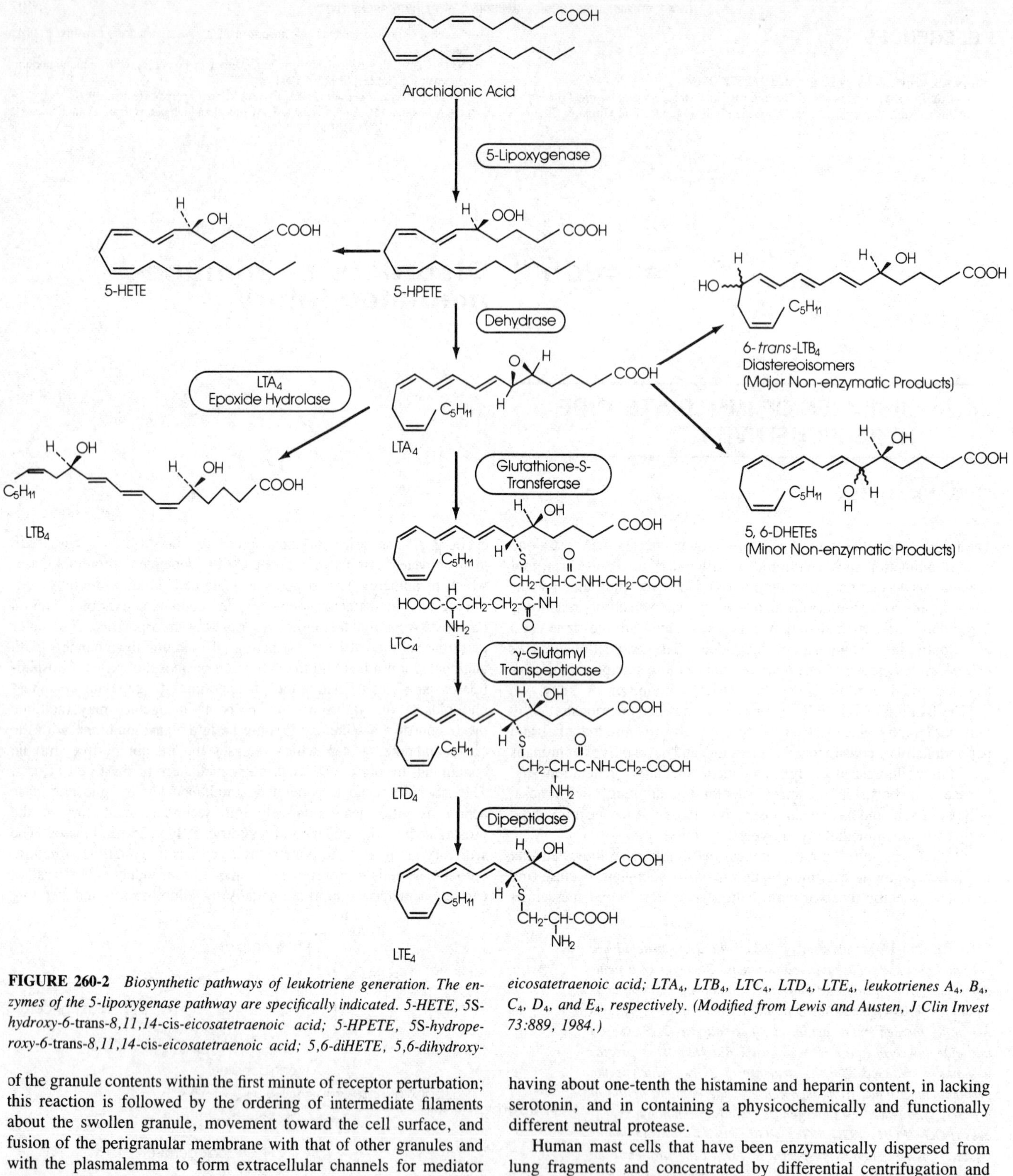

FIGURE 260-2 *Biosynthetic pathways of leukotriene generation. The enzymes of the 5-lipoxygenase pathway are specifically indicated. 5-HETE, 5S-hydroxy-6-trans-8,11,14-cis-eicosatetraenoic acid; 5-HPETE, 5S-hydroperoxy-6-trans-8,11,14-cis-eicosatetraenoic acid; 5,6-diHETE, 5,6-dihydroxy-eicosatetraenoic acid; LTA₄, LTB₄, LTC₄, LTD₄, LTE₄, leukotrienes A₄, B₄, C₄, D₄, and E₄, respectively. (Modified from Lewis and Austen, J Clin Invest 73:889, 1984.)*

of the granule contents within the first minute of receptor perturbation; this reaction is followed by the ordering of intermediate filaments about the swollen granule, movement toward the cell surface, and fusion of the perigranular membrane with that of other granules and with the plasmalemma to form extracellular channels for mediator release while maintaining cell viability.

The secretory granules of human and rat mast cells contain histamine; eosinophilactic acidic peptides; acid hydrolases such as β-hexosaminidase, β-glucuronidase, and arylsulfatase; neutral protease; and heparin proteoglycan. The heparin proteoglycan apparently serves to store, concentrate, and "transport" the solubilized granule complex so that primary mediators can dissociate into the extracellular channels by ion exchange. Mast cells appear to be the major source of tissue neutral protease with the rat supplying about 45 μg of chymase and carboxypeptidase A per 1 million cells and the human about 15 μg of tryptase per 1 million cells; in both cases the neutral proteases represent the major proteins not only of the secretory granules, but of the entire cell. The human mast cell differs from the rat's in

having about one-tenth the histamine and heparin content, in lacking serotonin, and in containing a physicochemically and functionally different neutral protease.

Human mast cells that have been enzymatically dispersed from lung fragments and concentrated by differential centrifugation and purified rat and murine peritoneal mast cells respond to receptor perturbation by generation of prostaglandin D₂ (PGD₂) in preference to the leukotrienes. However, the remarkable vasoactive and spasmogenic potency of the leukotriene products in human skin and airways in vivo, compared to histamine, prostaglandins, and other mediators, indicates that this class of compounds represents an additional important group of mediators in immediate hypersensitivity reactions. Leukotrienes C₄ and D₄ (LTC₄, LTD₄) are 10³ times more potent and leukotriene E₄ (LTE₄) is ten times more potent than histamine in impairing airflow in normal subjects when administered by inhalation and assessed in terms of effects on peripheral airways by expiratory flow initiated at 30 percent of vital capacity.

Two subclasses of mast cells have been recognized in terms of histochemical staining characteristics, a connective tissue mast cell distributed to perivenular sites and serosal surfaces and a mucosal mast cell localized primarily to gastrointestinal and bronchial intraepithelial sites. At present the connective tissue mast cell is defined chemically by the presence of heparin proteoglycan in the secretory granule and the mucosal mast cell by a nonheparin (oversulfated chondroitin sulfate) proteoglycan and by a dependence on a T lymphocyte–derived interleukin for proliferation in vivo or in vitro. In addition there is evidence from studies of rodent mast cells that the heparin mast cell subclass preferentially metabolizes arachidonic acid to PGD_2, whereas the non-heparin-containing mast cell yields predominantly LTC_4 and comparable amounts of LTB_4 and PGD_2. Thus, the mast cells, bearing specific recognition units in the form of IgE Fc receptors and positioned at mucosal surfaces and in tissues about venules, are redistributed to portals of entry for foreign substances and can respond in the sensitized host directly and in sequence to alter the microenvironment. A local increase in venular permeability would represent the action of preformed mediators such as histamine and newly generated mediators such as PGD_2 and the sulfidopeptide leukotrienes and would introduce plasma proteins such as those of the complement system and specific antibody. Phagocytic cells would be attracted by chemotactic peptides released from the secretory granule and by the newly generated lipid chemotactic mediator, LTB_4. Local and subclinical regulation of the tissue microenvironment would represent an initial and homeostatic physiologic response, while an intense or continuous stimulus would result in inflammation and tissue injury which could be either beneficial or detrimental (hypersensitivity) depending upon the appropriateness of the immunologic specificity (Fig. 260-3).

Consideration of the mechanism of immediate type hypersensitivity diseases in the human has focused largely on the IgE-dependent recognition of otherwise nontoxic substances. Support for this thesis has come from the finding that clinical atopic allergy is associated with elevated total levels of IgE and in some instances with an immune response that is specifically linked to the histocompatibility locus. Populations of allergic whites have a significantly higher total serum level of IgE than nonallergic individuals, and highly atopic persons with asthma have significantly higher serum levels of IgE than those with fewer allergic manifestations. IgE distribution in families is consistent with the dominant inheritance of the low IgE phenotype. As a result of the action of a single IgE regulator gene the majority of family members would have elevated IgE levels as a

possible basis for their atopic state. The association between HLA histocompatibility type and the immediate hypersensitivity response has been noted in persons of the low IgE phenotype who were studied with highly purified allergens, generally of small size. Such presumptive evidence of immune response (Ir) genes by linkage disequilibrium, that is, the association of the hypersensitivity response with a particular histocompatibility haplotype, represents an additional element in the polygenic atopic allergic state. Nonetheless, all the studies taken together, both of families and of populations, seem to indicate that the genetically determined elevated IgE levels found in about three-fourths of atopic allergic subjects exert the predominant influence on most specific IgE responses. It is also likely that diseases of immediate type hypersensitivity may occur because of deficient intracellular controls of mediator generation or release, or both, or that the extracellular controls directed against mediator inactivation may be impaired.

ANAPHYLAXIS Definition The life-threatening anaphylactic response of a sensitized human appears within minutes after administration of specific antigen and is manifested by respiratory distress often followed by vascular collapse, or shock without antecedent respiratory difficulty. Cutaneous manifestations exemplified by pruritus and urticaria with or without angioedema are characteristic of such systemic anaphylactic reactions. Gastrointestinal manifestations include nausea, vomiting, crampy abdominal pain, and diarrhea.

Predisposing factors and etiology There is no convincing evidence that age, sex, race, occupation, or geographic location predisposes a human to anaphylaxis except through exposure to some immunogen. According to most studies, atopy does not predispose individuals to penicillin anaphylaxis.

The materials capable of eliciting the systemic anaphylactic reaction in the human include the following: heterologous proteins in the form of antiserum, hormones, enzymes, Hymenoptera venom, pollen extracts, and foods; polysaccharides such as iron dextran; and most commonly diagnostic agents and drugs such as antibiotics and even vitamins. The diagnostic and therapeutic agents are generally of low molecular weight and are considered to function as haptens which form immunogenic conjugates with host proteins. The conjugating hapten may be the parent compound, a nonenzymatically derived storage product, or a metabolite formed in the host.

Pathophysiology and manifestations Individuals differ in the time of appearance of perception of symptoms and signs, but the hallmark

FIGURE 260-3 *Schematic role for mediators in IgE-dependent reactions.*

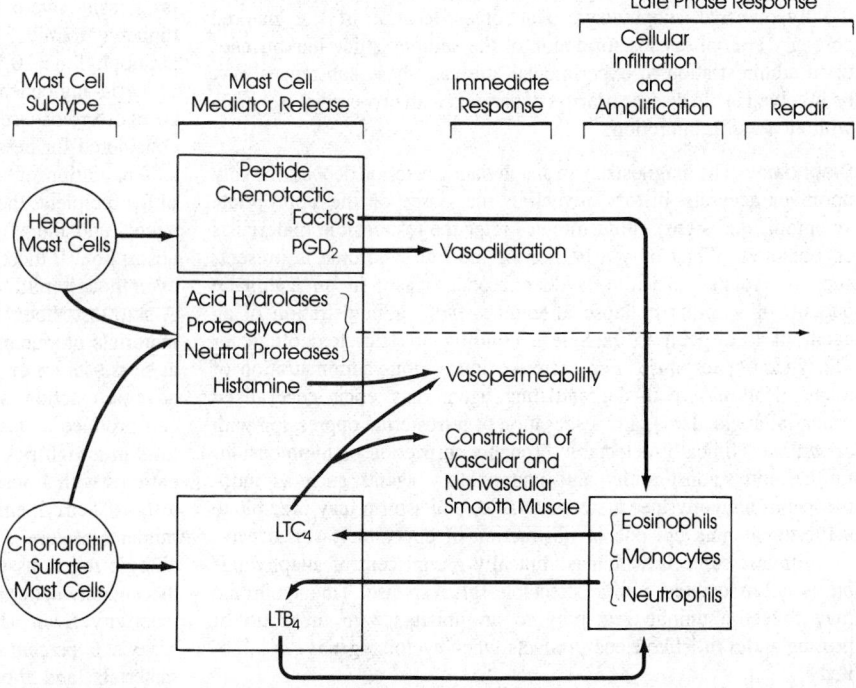

of the anaphylactic reaction is the onset of some manifestation within seconds to minutes after introduction of the antigen, generally by injection or less commonly by ingestion. There may be upper or lower airway obstruction or both. Laryngeal edema may be experienced as a "lump" in the throat, hoarseness, or stridor, while bronchial obstruction is associated with a feeling of tightness in the chest or audible wheezing. A particularly characteristic feature is the eruption of well-circumscribed, discrete cutaneous wheals with erythematous, raised, serpiginous borders and blanched centers. These urticarial eruptions are intensely pruritic and may be localized or distributed. They may coalesce to form giant hives, and seldom persist beyond 48 h. A localized, nonpitting, deeper edematous cutaneous process, angioedema, may also be present. It may be asymptomatic or cause a burning or stinging sensation.

In fatal cases with clinical bronchial obstruction, the lungs show marked hyperinflation on gross and microscopic examination. The microscopic findings in the bronchi, however, are limited to luminal secretions, peribronchial congestion, submucosal edema, and eosinophilic infiltration, and the acute emphysema is attributed to intractable bronchospasm which subsides with death. The angioedema resulting in death by mechanical obstruction occurs in the epiglottis and larynx, but the process is also evident in the hypopharynx and to some extent the trachea; on microscopic examination there is wide separation of the collagen fibers and the glandular elements; vascular congestion and eosinophilic infiltration are also present. Patients dying of vascular collapse without antecedent hypoxia from respiratory insufficiency have visceral congestion but no major shift in the distribution of blood volume. The associated electrocardiographic abnormalities, with or without infarction, noted in some patients could reflect a primary cardiac event or be secondary to a critical reduction in plasma volume.

The angioedematous and urticarial manifestations of the anaphylactic syndrome have been attributed to release of endogenous histamine. A role for the sulfidopeptide leukotrienes in altering pulmonary mechanics by causing marked bronchiolar constriction seems likely. Vascular collapse without respiratory distress in response to experimental challenge with the sting of a hymenopteran was associated not only with marked and prolonged elevations in blood histamine but also with evidence of intravascular coagulation and kinin generation. Based upon the findings that patients with systemic mastocytosis and episodic hypotension proceeding to vascular collapse excrete large amounts of PGD_2 in addition to histamine and are controlled by administration of a nonsteroidal agent but not by antihistamines alone, it may be that PGD_2 is also of importance in the hypotensive anaphylactic reactions. Because of the marked coronary arterial constrictor action of the sulfidopeptide leukotrienes upon administration to experimental animals, these substances may be involved in the disease process of patients with myocardial ischemia without or with infarction.

Diagnosis The diagnosis of an anaphylactic reaction depends largely upon an accurate history revealing the onset of the appropriate symptoms and signs within minutes after the responsible material is encountered. When only a portion of the full syndrome is present, such as isolated urticaria, sudden bronchospasm in an asthmatic patient, or vascular collapse after intravenous administration of an agent, it is difficult to exclude a nonimmunologic, toxicologic or idiosyncratic, response. For example, intravenous administration of a chemical mast cell–degranulating agent may elicit generalized urticaria, angioedema, and a sensation of retrosternal oppression with or without clinically detectable bronchoconstriction or hypotension. Furthermore, nonsteroidal anti-inflammatory agents such as indomethacin, aminopyrine, mefenamic acid, and aspirin may precipitate a life-threatening episode of obstruction of upper or lower airways in asthmatic subjects which is clinically reminiscent of anaphylaxis but is not associated with a detectable IgE response. This syndrome may reflect a unique reactivity to an imbalance in the ratio of prostaglandin to leukotriene products when cyclooxygenase is inhibited.

The presence of a labile reagin (IgE) in the heart blood of a patient dying of systemic anaphylaxis has been demonstrated at postmortem by passive transfer of the serum intradermally into a normal recipient, followed in 24 h by antigen challenge into the same site, with subsequent development of a wheal and flare, the Prausnitz-Küstner reaction. Indeed, such a reagin can be transiently identified in the serum of most patients who develop systemic anaphylaxis to a variety of different agents. In order to avoid the hazards of transferring hepatitis to the recipient in the Prausnitz-Küstner reaction, it is preferable to employ the less sensitive monkey recipient or a human leukocyte suspension enriched with basophils for subsequent antigen challenge. It is presumed that the activity responsible for most cases of systemic anaphylaxis resides with the IgE class, since the Prausnitz-Küstner activity in the serums of patients with systemic reactions to Hymenoptera venom or human seminal plasma protein can be removed by IgE immunosorbent columns. Furthermore, radioimmunoassays have demonstrated specific IgE antibodies in patients with anaphylactic reactions to insulin and to parathormone, but such approaches require purified antigens. In the transfusion anaphylactic reaction which occurs in patients with IgA deficiency, the responsible specificity resides in IgG anti-IgA rather than in IgE; the mechanism of the reaction is presumed to be complement activation with secondary mast cell participation.

Treatment and prevention Early recognition of an anaphylactic reaction is mandatory, since death occurs within minutes to hours after the first symptoms. Mild symptoms such as pruritus and urticaria can be controlled by administration of 0.2 to 0.5 mL of 1:1000 epinephrine subcutaneously, with repeated doses as required at 3-min intervals for a severe reaction. If the antigenic material was injected into an extremity, the rate of absorption may be reduced by prompt application of a tourniquet proximal to the reaction site, administration of 0.2 mL of 1:1000 epinephrine into the site, and removal without compression of an insect stinger, if present. An intravenous infusion should be initiated to provide a route for administration of epinephrine, diluted 1:50,000, volume expanders, and vasopressor agents if intractable hypotension occurs. Epinephrine most likely acts to reverse the action of mediators on target tissues, and its early administration appears critical. When epinephrine fails to control the situation, hypoxia due to airway obstruction or related to a cardiac arrhythmia, or both, must be considered. Oxygen via a nasal catheter or intermittent positive pressure breathing of oxygen with 0.5 mL isoproterenol diluted 1:200 in saline may be helpful, but either endotracheal intubation or a tracheostomy is mandatory if progressive hypoxia exists. Ancillary agents such as the antihistamine diphenhydramine, 50 to 80 mg intramuscularly or intravenously, and aminophylline, 0.25 to 0.5 g intravenously, are appropriate for urticaria-angioedema and bronchospasm, respectively. Intravenous corticosteroids are not effective for the acute event but may be considered for persistent bronchospasm and hypotension.

Prevention of anaphylaxis must take into account the sensitivity of the recipient, the dose and character of the diagnostic or therapeutic agent, and the effect of the route of administration on the rate of absorption. If there is a definite history of a past anaphylactic reaction, even though mild, it is advisable to select another agent or procedure. A skin test should be performed before the administration of certain materials producing a high incidence of anaphylactic reactions, such as horse serum or allergenic extracts, or when the nature of the past adverse reaction is unknown. Since even a skin or conjunctival test can produce a serious reaction, a scratch test should precede these tests in a high-risk situation. With regard to penicillin, two-thirds of patients with a positive reaction history and positive intradermal skin tests to benzylpenicilloyl-polylysine (BPL) and/or the minor determinant mixture (MDM) of benzylpenicillin products experience allergic reactions with treatment, and these are almost uniformly of the anaphylactic type in those patients with minor determinant reactivity. Even patients without a history of previous clinical reactions have a 6 percent incidence of positive skin tests to the two test materials, and about 3 per 1000 with a negative history experience anaphylaxis with therapy with a mortality of about 1 per 100,000. The value of skin testing is both to permit therapy with the agent in question when the risk does not exist and to emphasize the hazards where the sensitivity is confirmed. In the event that an agent must be used despite a positive history, a positive skin test, or both, the following precautionary measures should be taken. An intravenous infusion should be started, with intubation equipment and a tracheostomy set at hand; the material should be given intradermally, then subcutaneously, and then intramuscularly in increasing doses at 20- to 30-min intervals so that the initial dose by the next route does not exceed the final dose by the previous route. It is difficult to be certain that the mediator-containing cells have been exhausted, and therapeutic use of the agent may be accompanied by untoward consequences. It may be critical to give the therapeutic agent at regular intervals to prevent the reestablishment of a sensitized cell pool of large size. A different form of protection involves the development of blocking antibody of the IgG class which is protective against Hymenoptera venom–induced anaphylaxis by interacting with antigen so that less reaches the sensitized tissue mast cells; to be effective this immunotherapy requires the use of specific or cross-reacting Hymenoptera venom rather than whole-insect-body extracts.

URTICARIA AND ANGIOEDEMA **Definition** Urticaria and angioedema may appear separately or together as cutaneous manifestations of localized nonpitting edema; a similar process may occur at mucosal surfaces of the upper respiratory or gastrointestinal tract. *Urticaria* involves only the superficial portion of the dermis presenting as well-circumscribed wheals with erythematous raised serpiginous borders with blanched centers which may coalesce to become giant wheals. *Angioedema* is a well-demarcated localized edema involving the deeper layers of the skin including the subcutaneous tissue. Recurrent episodes of urticaria and/or angioedema of less than 6 weeks' duration are considered acute, while attacks persisting beyond this period are designated chronic.

Predisposing factors and etiology The occurrence of urticaria and angioedema is probably more frequent than usually described because of the evanescent, self-limited nature of such eruptions, which seldom require medical attention when limited to the skin. Although persons in any age group may experience acute or chronic urticaria and/or angioedema, these lesions increase in frequency after adolescence, with the highest incidence occurring in persons in the third decade of life; indeed, one survey of college students indicated that some 15 to 20 percent had experienced a pruritic wheal reaction.

The classification of urticaria/angioedema presented in Table 260-1 focuses on the different mechanisms for eliciting clinical disease. Only the IgE-dependent and the IgG-mediated reactions in IgA-deficient persons should be considered immediate hypersensitivity. However, the other mechanisms are important for differential diagnosis, and most cases of chronic urticaria are idiopathic. The appearance of urticaria and angioedema in atopic persons in the absence of a specific exposure is attributed to the atopic diathesis and implies an IgE mechanism. Urticaria and/or angioedema occurring during the appropriate season in patients with seasonal respiratory allergy or as a result of exposure to animals or molds is attributed to inhalation of pollens, animal dander, and mold spores, respectively. However, urticaria and angioedema secondary to inhalation are relatively uncommon compared with ingestion of fresh fruits, shellfish, chocolate, nuts, tomatoes, and various drugs, including penicillin-contaminated milk products, which may elicit not only the anaphylactic syndrome with prominent gastrointestinal complaints but also chronic urticaria. Additional etiologies include physical stimuli such as cold, solar rays, exercise, and mechanical irritation (dermographism). Angioedema without urticaria occurs with $C\overline{1}$ inhibitor ($C\overline{1}$INH) deficiency that can be inborn as an autosomal dominant characteristic or can be acquired in association with lymphoproliferative disorders. The urticaria and angioedema associated with classical serum sickness or with idiopathic cutaneous necrotizing angiitis is believed to be an immune-complex disease when hypocomplementemia is a concomi-

tant. The idiosyncratic drug reactions to mast cell granule-releasing agents and to nonsteroidal anti-inflammatory drugs can be systemic, resembling anaphylaxis, or limited to cutaneous sites.

Pathophysiology and manifestations Urticarial eruptions are distinctly pruritic, involve any area of the body from the scalp to the soles of the feet, and appear in crops of 24- to 72-h duration with old lesions fading as new ones appear. The most common sites are the extremities, external genitalia, and face, particularly the region of the eyes and lips. Although self-limited in duration, angioedema of the upper respiratory tract may be life-threatening due to laryngeal obstruction, while gastrointestinal involvement may present with abdominal colic, with or without nausea and vomiting, and may precipitate unnecessary surgical intervention. No residual discoloration occurs with either urticaria or angioedema unless there is an underlying process leading to superimposed extravasation of erythrocytes.

The pathology of urticaria and angioedema is usually characterized by massive edema of the dermis in urticaria, and the subcutaneous tissue as well as dermis in angioedema. Collagen bundles in affected areas are widely separated, and the venules are sometimes dilated. The perivenular infiltrate may consist of lymphocytes, eosinophils, and neutrophils that are present in varying combination and number throughout the dermis. Allergen-induced wheal and flare reactions are characterized by mast cell degranulation and an accumulation of eosinophils over hours to days. The elicitation of a wheal and flare response upon injection of the relevant allergen into a patient with urticaria and/or angioedema, or into a site in a normal recipient prepared with serum from the patient, the Prausnitz-Küstner reaction, indicates an IgE-dependent, mast cell–mediated reaction.

Perhaps the best-studied example of mast cell–mediated urticaria and angioedema is *cold urticaria*. Acquired cold urticaria is a disorder in which patients exposed to cold experience an urticarial eruption that may evolve into angioedema and be associated with syncope. Cryoglobulins, cryofibrinogens, cold agglutinins, or hemolysins may be recognized, but not in the majority of patients. The finding in a number of patients of a serum factor, characterized as being of the IgE class, that is capable of transferring the cold urticaria reaction to a skin site of a normal recipient has focused attention upon the mast cell in this condition. Immersion of an extremity in an ice bath precipitates angioedema of the distal portion with urticaria at the air interface within minutes of the challenge. Histologic studies reveal marked mast cell degranulation with associated edema of the dermis and subcutaneous tissues. The venous effluent of the cold-challenged and angioedematous extremity reveals a marked rise in plasma content of histamine, low-molecular-weight eosinophilotactic activity, and high-molecular-weight neutrophil chemotactic activity which are presumably of mast cell origin, whereas the venous effluent of the contralateral normal extremity contains none of these mediators. Elevations of plasma histamine with biopsy-proven mast cell degranulation have also been demonstrated with systemic attacks of *cholin-*

TABLE 260-1 Classification of urticaria with angioedema

1 IgE-dependent
  a Atopic diathesis
  b Specific antigen sensitivity (pollens, foods, drugs, fungi, molds, Hymenoptera venom, helminths)
  c Physical: dermographism; cold; light; cholinergic; vibratory; exercise-related
2 Complement-mediated urticaria
  a Hereditary angioedema
  b Acquired angioedema with lymphoproliferative disorders
  c Necrotizing vasculitis
  d Serum sickness
  e Reactions to blood products
3 Nonimmunologic urticaria
  a Direct mast cell–releasing agents: opiates; antibiotics; curare, D-tubocurarine; radiocontrast media
  b Agents which presumably alter arachidonic acid metabolism: aspirin and nonsteroidal anti-inflammatory agents; azo dyes and benzoates
4 Idiopathic urticaria

ergic urticaria and *exercise-induced erythema-angioedema* precipitated experimentally by exercise on a treadmill while wearing a wet suit.

Diagnosis   The rapid onset and self-limited nature of urticarial and angioedematous eruptions are distinguishing features. Additional characteristics are the occurrence of the urticarial crops in various stages of evolution and the asymmetric distribution of the angioedema. Urticaria and/or angioedema involving IgE-dependent mechanisms are often appreciated by historical considerations implicating specific allergens, by seasonal incidence, by exposure to certain environments, or by physical stimuli such as cold, exercise, sunlight (solar urticaria), or trauma (dermographism). Direct reproduction of the lesion with physical stimuli is particularly valuable because it so often establishes the cause of the lesion. The diagnosis can be confirmed by careful testing with the putative foreign substance to determine if a local wheal and flare results, and by passive transfer of such a reaction with serum of the patient to a skin site in a normal recipient, the Prausnitz-Küstner phenomenon. Passive transfer to the skin of a nonhuman primate or in vitro to human basophils may also be attempted. IgE-mediated urticaria and/or angioedema may or may not be associated with an elevation of total IgE or with peripheral eosinophilia. Fever, leukocytosis, or an elevated sedimentation rate are characteristically absent.

The classification of urticarial and angioedematous states noted in Table 260-1 in terms of possible mechanisms necessarily includes some differential diagnostic points. Hypocomplementemia is not observed in IgE-mediated mast cell disease and can reflect either an acquired abnormality generally attributed to the formation of immune complexes or a genetic deficiency of $C\bar{1}INH$. Chronic recurrent urticaria, generally in females, associated with arthralgias, an elevated sedimentation rate, and normo- or hypocomplementemia suggests an underlying cutaneous necrotizing angiitis. Confirmation depends upon a biopsy which reveals cellular infiltration, nuclear debris, and fibrinoid necrosis of the venules.

Hereditary angioedema is an autosomal dominant state associated with the absence of functional $C\bar{1}INH$. The diagnosis is suggested not only by family history but also by the lack of urticarial lesions, the prominence of recurrent gastrointestinal attacks of colic, and episodes of laryngeal edema. Laboratory diagnosis depends upon demonstrating the antigenic lack of $C\bar{1}INH$ in most kindreds, but some kindreds have an antigenically intact nonfunctional protein and require a functional assay to establish the diagnosis. The natural substrates of uninhibited $C\bar{1}$, C4, and C2 are chronically depleted but fall further during attacks due to the activation of additional C1 to $C\bar{1}$. An acquired form of $C\bar{1}INH$ deficiency, associated with lymphoproliferative disorders, has the same clinical manifestations and differs in the lack of a familial element; in the reduction of $C1/C\bar{1}$ as well as $C\bar{1}INH$, C4, and C2; and in the presence of an anti-idiotypic antibody to the monoclonal immunoglobulin expressed on the B cells.

Urticaria and angioedema must be differentiated from contact sensitivity, an acute vesicular eruption that progresses to chronic thickening of the skin with continued allergenic exposure. They must also be differentiated from atopic dermatitis, a condition that may present as erythema, edema, papules, vesiculation, and oozing proceeding to a subacute and chronic stage in which vesiculation is less marked or absent, and in which scaling, fissuring, and lichenification predominate in a distribution that characteristically involves the flexor surfaces. In cutaneous mastocytosis the reddish-brown macules and papules, characteristic of urticaria pigmentosa, urticate with pruritus upon trauma, and in systemic mastocytosis, without or with urticaria pigmentosa, there is an episodic systemic flushing with or without urticaria but no angioedema.

Prevention and treatment   Identification of the etiologic factor(s) and their elimination provide the most satisfactory therapeutic program; this approach is feasible to varying degrees with IgE-mediated reactions to allergens or physical stimuli. Topically applied steroids

are of no benefit in the management of urticaria and/or angioedema, and while systemic steroids have no general value, they are helpful in an occasional patient with necrotizing cutaneous angiitis, pressure urticaria, or even ordinary urticaria and angioedema. Antihistamines of the H1 class and sympathomimetic agents often provide symptomatic relief; cyproheptadine, hydroxyzine, and a combination of H1 and H2 antihistamines are held to be even more beneficial. The therapy of inborn $C\bar{1}INH$ deficiency has been simplified by the finding that attenuated androgens correct the biochemical defect and afford prophylactic protection. Since the affected individuals are heterozygous, with the depletion of $C\bar{1}INH$ being due to a combination of deficient synthesis and excessive utilization of the normal gene product, the efficacy of the attenuated androgens is attributed to production by the normal gene of an amount of functional $C\bar{1}INH$ sufficient to contain the spontaneous activation of C1 to $C\bar{1}$. Since the use of such agents for children and pregnant women is not yet accepted, the antifibrinolytic agent ϵ-aminocaproic acid may be used occasionally to control spontaneous attacks or for preoperative prophylaxis in some patients.

ALLERGIC RHINITIS   Definition   Allergic rhinitis is characterized by sneezing, rhinorrhea, obstruction of the nasal passages, conjunctival and pharyngeal itching, and lacrimation. Although commonly seasonal because of its relation to airborne pollens, other patterns and etiologies occur. The use of the term "hay fever" to describe seasonal allergic rhinitis is a common convention but is literally inappropriate because the symptom complex is neither produced by hay nor associated with fever.

Predisposing factors and etiology   Allergic rhinitis generally presents in atopic individuals, that is, in persons with a family history of a similar or related symptom complex and a personal history of collateral allergy expressed as eczematous dermatitis, urticaria, and/or asthma (see Chap. 202). Symptoms generally appear before the fourth decade of life and tend to diminish gradually with aging, although complete spontaneous remissions are uncommon. A relatively small number of weeds which depend upon wind rather than insects for cross-pollination, as well as certain grasses and trees, produce sufficient quantities of pollen suitable for wide distribution by air currents to elicit seasonal allergic rhinitis. The dates of pollination of these species generally vary little from year to year in a particular locale but may be quite different in another climate. Molds, which are widespread in nature because they occur in soil or decaying organic matter, may propagate spores in a pattern dependent upon climatic conditions. Perennial allergic rhinitis occurs in response to allergens that are present throughout the year such as in desquamating epithelium in animal dander, the processed materials or chemicals utilized in an industrial setting, or the dust accumulating at work or at home. Dust has a diverse content including mites, and many patients with perennial rhinitis are sensitive only to house dust. Moreover, in many patients with perennial rhinitis, no clear-cut allergen can be demonstrated. The ability of allergens to cause rhinitis rather than lower respiratory symptoms may be attributed to their size, 10 to 100 μm, and retention within the nose. However, even when the allergen penetrates to the lower respiratory tract, whether it elicits a bronchoconstrictor response resulting from mediator release depends on the presence of chronically hyperirritable airways.

Pathophysiology and manifestations   Episodic rhinorrhea, sneezing, and obstruction of the nasal passages with lacrimation and pruritus of the conjunctiva, nasal mucosa, and oropharynx are the hallmarks of allergic rhinitis. The nasal mucosa is pale and boggy, but the nares are not reddened or excoriated. The conjunctiva may be congested and edematous; the pharynx is generally unremarkable but may appear injected. Swelling of the turbinates and mucous membranes with obstruction of the sinus ostia and eustachian tubes precipitates secondary infections of the sinuses and middle ear, respectively, commonly in perennial but rarely in seasonal disease. Nasal polyps often arise concurrently with edema and/or infection within the sinuses and increase obstructive symptoms.

The nose presents a large mucosal surface area through the folds of the turbinates and serves to adjust the temperature and moisture content of inhaled air and to filter out particulate materials. The convoluted nasal passages readily filter out particles above 10 μm in size by impingement in a mucous blanket at bends in their course; ciliary action then moves the entrapped particles toward the pharynx. Entrapment of pollen and digestion of the outer coat by mucosal enzymes such as lysozymes release protein allergens generally of 10,000 to 40,000 molecular weight. Although the initial interaction occurs between the allergen and intraepithelial mast cells sensitized with specific IgE, the bulk of the mast cells are located beneath the mucosal surface and are recruited secondarily. During the symptomatic season when the mucosa are already swollen and hyperemic, there is enhanced adverse reactivity to the seasonal pollen as well as to antigenically unrelated pollens for which there is underlying hypersensitivity. This priming effect is attributed to improved penetration of the allergens to the deeper perivenular mast cells. Biopsy specimens of nasal mucosa during an episodic allergic reaction show profound submucosal edema with infiltration predominantly by eosinophils, although some neutrophil polymorphonuclear leukocytes are present. Polyps, a feature in perennial rhinitis, are mucosal protrusions containing chiefly edema fluid with variable degrees of eosinophilic infiltration.

The mucosal surface fluid contains not only IgA that is present preferentially because of its secretory piece, but also IgE, which apparently arrives by diffusion from plasma cells distributed in proximity to mucosal surfaces. IgE fixes to mucosal and submucosal mast cells, and the intensity of the clinical response to inhaled allergens is quantitatively related to the naturally occurring or experimentally defined pollen dose. Specific IgE is distributed not only to tissue mast cells but also to circulating basophilic leukocytes; patients with more severe clinical disease have basophils which release histamine in response to lesser concentrations of allergen in vitro than do cells from patients with milder disease. Human nasal polyps from ragweed-sensitive patients release histamine, eosinophilotactic peptides, and spasmogenic leukotrienes upon challenge with ragweed allergen in vitro. In sensitive individuals, the introduction of allergen into the nose is associated with sneezing, "stuffiness," and discharge, and the fluid contains histamine, PGD_2, and leukotrienes. Thus, the mast cells of nasal polyp tissue, and of the nasal mucosa and submucosa, generate and release mediators through IgE-dependent reactions which are capable of producing tissue edema and eosinophilic infiltration.

Diagnosis The diagnosis of seasonal allergic rhinitis depends largely upon an accurate history of occurrence coincident with the pollination of the offending weeds, grasses, or trees. The continuous character of perennial allergic rhinitis due to contamination of the home or place of work makes historical analysis difficult, but there may be a variability in symptoms that can be related to animal exposure or work habits. Patients with perennial rhinitis commonly develop the problem in adult life, are more often women than men, and manifest nasal polyps and thickening of the sinus membranes by x-ray. The term *vasomotor rhinitis* designates a symptom complex resembling perennial allergic rhinitis without an established allergic basis. Other entities to be excluded are exposure to irritants, upper respiratory infection, pregnancy with prominent nasal mucosal edema, prolonged topical use of alpha-adrenergic agents in the form of nose drops, and the use of certain therapeutic agents such as rauwolfia. Nasal polyps are a characteristic of perennial allergic rhinitis and are often associated with sinus infection.

The nasal secretions of allergic patients are rich in eosinophils, and peripheral eosinophilia with elevations in relation to clinical exacerbations is a common feature. Local or systemic neutrophilia implies infection. Total serum IgE is frequently elevated, but the demonstration of immunologic specificity for IgE is critical to an etiologic diagnosis. Some normal individuals will exhibit a wheal and flare skin response to intracutaneous inoculation of high concentrations of common airborne allergens. The diagnosis rests not only on the skin test alone, but also on the correlation of the clinical history with skin reactivity to concentrations of allergen selected by controlled testing. This provides the best balance of selectivity with specificity. Scratch tests with food allergens are unreliable, while intracutaneous testing may be dangerous, and elimination diets are the best approach to the diagnosis. Regardless of method of testing, food allergy is uncommon as a significant cause of allergic rhinitis.

Although standard radioimmunodiffusion techniques can be used to screen for patients with markedly elevated levels of IgE, their sensitivity of less than 1000 ng/mL is insufficient to detect the elevations in most atopic allergic patients. A commonly employed technique, sensitive to about 50 ng/mL, is known as the competitive radioimmunosorbent test (RIST). In this procedure, the IgE of the serum competes with radiolabeled IgE for solid-phase-bound anti-IgE; the displacement of radiolabeled IgE is compared to a standard curve to yield the IgE concentration of the serum. Other assays, such as the noncompetitive RIST, in which the anti-IgE immunosorbent is exposed to a series of standard IgE preparations before introducing the unknown, and double antibody radioimmunoprecipitin test (RIP), have greater sensitivity and reproducibility, respectively, and, like the competitive RIST, establish a normal geometric mean serum IgE for nonallergic whites of less than 120 ng/mL. Even more useful is the measurement of specific anti-IgE in serum by its binding to a solid-phase allergen and quantitation by the subsequent uptake of radiolabeled anti-IgE. This radioallergosorbent technique (RAST) correlates satisfactorily with the bioassay of specific IgE by skin test or histamine release from peripheral blood leukocytes and is convenient for the patients; however, it requires defined allergens and full standardization. Further, neither the immunochemical nor bioassay detection of a previous immune response to a foreign material mandates a therapeutic intervention, unless there is relevant concomitant evidence of a significant clinical problem.

Prevention and treatment Avoidance of exposure to the offending allergen is the most effective means of controlling allergic diseases; removal of pets from the home to avoid animal danders, utilization of air filtration devices to minimize the concentrations of airborne pollens, travel to nonpollinating areas during the critical periods, and even a change of domicile to eliminate a mold spore problem may be necessary. *Immunotherapy*, often termed *hyposensitization*, consists of repeated subcutaneous injections of gradually increasing concentrations of the allergen(s) considered to be specifically responsible for the symptom complex. Controlled studies in ragweed and grass allergic rhinitis have established that patients are partially relieved of their symptoms by such treatments applied over a period of years. Improvement appears to be dose-related, and the end point is based either on severe adverse local or systemic reactions to the allergen injection or on satisfactory relief of symptoms. The immunologic characteristics of a response include a rise in antibodies of the IgG class, a small increase in specific IgE early in the treatment course followed by a plateau or decline, and a decline in the percentage of histamine released from peripheral blood basophilic leukocytes challenged with a fixed concentration of the allergen. The antibodies of the IgG class might well reduce or neutralize the quantity of allergen available for interaction with the tissue mast cells but, more importantly, could modify the seasonal booster response in specific IgE synthesis. None of the individual parameters of the response to immunotherapy correlates well with the assessments of clinical efficacy, suggesting that benefit is derived from a complex of effects. Immunotherapy should be reserved for clearly documented seasonal diseases that cannot be managed with drugs because of their side effects.

Management with pharmacologic agents offers a diverse approach. Antihistamines are the only specific end-organ antagonists available for control of a mast cell–derived reaction and are limited to competition with but one mediator. Nonetheless, antihistamines are very effective for some patients, and the side effects such as drowsiness and gastrointestinal distress, which limit the dosage of a particular preparation, can sometimes be circumvented by use of an agent of different structure. An orally active agent with alpha-adrenergic activity is often employed for its decongestant effects and to partially counteract the drowsiness produced by antihistamines. Topical administration of alpha-adrenergic agents may be helpful but has the immediate disadvantage of rebound vasodilatation, and prolonged usage may produce a chronic rhinitis. The topically active steroids of the beclomethasone class ameliorate symptoms of both seasonal and perennial rhinitis without detectable adrenal suppression and represent a major advance in therapy. Cromolyn sodium inhaled nasally has also given encouraging prophylactic results and is of particular merit because it acts to prevent mast-cell activation.

REFERENCES

AUSTEN KF: Biologic implications of the structural and functional characteristics of the chemical mediators of immediate-type hypersensitivity. The Harvey Lectures, Series 73, 1977–1978, p 93

CAULFIELD JP et al: Secretion in dissociated human pulmonary mast cells. Evidence for solubilization of granule contents before discharge. J Cell Biol 85:299, 1980

CRETICOS PS et al: Peptide leukotriene release after antigen challenge in patients sensitive to ragweed. N Engl J Med 310:1626, 1984

GREEN GR et al: Evaluation of penicillin hypersensitivity: Value of clinical history and skin testing with penicilloyl-polylysine and penicillin G. J Allerg Clin Immunol 60:339, 1977

KALINER M et al: Immunologic release of chemical mediators from human nasal polyps. N Engl J Med 289:277, 1973

LEWIS RA, AUSTEN KF: The biologically active leukotrienes: Biosynthesis, metabolism, receptors, functions, and pharmacology. J Clin Invest 73:889, 1984

MARSH DG et al: Genetics of the human immune response to allergens. J Allerg Clin Immunol 65:322, 1980

SCHWARTZ LB, AUSTEN KF: The mast cells and mediators of immediate hypersensitivity, in *Immunological Diseases*, 4th ed, M Samter et al (eds). Boston, Little, Brown (in press)

SOTER NA et al: Urticaria and arthralgias as manifestations of necrotizing angiitis (vasculitis). J Invest Dermatol 63:485, 1974

———: Release of mast cell mediators and alterations in lung function in patients with cholinergic urticaria. N Engl J Med 302:604, 1980

261   IMMUNE-COMPLEX DISEASES

THOMAS J. LAWLEY / MICHAEL M. FRANK

DEFINITION   The term immune-complex disease refers to a group of diseases thought to be mediated by the deposition of immune complexes in specific organ or tissue sites including the glomerulus of the kidney and blood vessel walls. In general these immune deposits are thought to arise from antigen-antibody complexes formed in the circulation. Once deposited in tissues the complexes activate a variety of potent soluble mediators of inflammation, such as the complement proteins, causing an influx of polymorphonuclear neutrophils and monocytes. These activated cells release toxic products of oxygen metabolism as well as various proteases and other enzymes, ultimately causing tissue damage. While the specific etiology of these diseases is variable, they share a common pathophysiology. The clinical features of these diseases are quite diverse, ranging from mild cutaneous eruptions to severe organ involvement with pericarditis, glomerulonephritis, and vasculitis.

PATHOPHYSIOLOGY   The introduction of foreign or noxious materials into an individual is often followed by an immune response. Specific antibody produced in the course of this response binds to antigen, forming immune complexes. In general, these complexes are phagocytosed and destroyed by macrophages of the reticuloendothelial system. However, at times these complexes are deposited in tissues, causing inflammation and tissue damage. In recent years, there has been a concerted effort to understand the mechanisms underlying this damage.

The biologic activity of the complexes has been studied in detail. It has been shown that the isotype of antibody affects biologic activity. Thus IgG- and IgM-containing complexes activate the classic complement pathway, and IgA-containing complexes may activate the alternative complement pathway. In contrast, IgE complexes are capable of mediating the degranulation of mast cells by a noncytotoxic, complement-independent mechanism.

The size of the circulating immune complexes is an important parameter of toxicity. In general the larger (>19 S) complexes cause more tissue damage than do smaller complexes. The size is related to the concentration and molar ratio of antibody and antigen, as well as to the avidity of the antibody for the antigen. The ratio of antigen to antibody may range from antibody excess through antigen-antibody equivalence to antigen excess. In antibody excess, antigen valences are saturated and in general the complexes are small. Under conditions of antigen excess, antibody-combining sites are saturated, chances for lattice formation are limited, and again the complexes are small. At equivalence or mild antigen excess, lattice formation is facilitated and large complexes can form. Immune complexes formed at moderate antigen excess are thought to be most pathogenic, perhaps because they are most efficient at activating the various mediator systems like the complement cascade.

Net charge of antigen and antibody also appears to be important in determining the pathophysiologic effect of the complexes. It has been shown that positively charged immune complexes tend to deposit in renal glomeruli, while complexes containing similar antigen with neutral charge tend to penetrate glomeruli slowly. This is presumably due to the fact that the glomerulus presents a negatively charged surface to the circulation. Similarly, there is a relationship between the degree of binding of immune complexes to the basement membrane of skin which is also negatively charged and the degree of positive charge of the complexes.

The first human disease in which circulating immune complexes were thought to play a pathogenic role was serum sickness. In their classic monograph ''Die Serumkrankheit,'' Clemens von Pirquet and Bela Schick described in great detail their experiences with the use of horse antidiphtheria toxin in children. They found that a reproducible reaction pattern occurred 8 to 13 days following the subcutaneous injection of horse serum protein. The patients developed fever, malaise, cutaneous eruptions, arthralgias, leukopenia, lymphadenopathy, and albuminuria. The authors suggested that this reaction pattern was caused by the interaction of host antibody, formed in the 8 days following the injection of the horse serum, with horse serum protein. They believed that this interaction led to the deposition of antigen-antibody complexes in tissue with resulting tissue damage, but the technology necessary to pursue this hypothesis was not available.

Numerous large retrospective studies of human serum sickness confirmed the observations of von Pirquet and Schick, but it was not until the studies of Germuth and Dixon that evidence for the role of circulating immune complexes in serum sickness was obtained. These investigators utilized rabbit models of serum sickness.

In the acute serum sickness model, the injection of antigen is followed by a period of intravascular equilibration and then by intravascular-extravascular equilibration lasting several days. The equilibration period is followed by a progressive decline in the level of antigen in the circulation, representing the normal degradation of the injected serum protein. Following this period of decay, there is a sudden acceleration in the clearance of the antigen from the circulation, usually beginning at about 7 to 8 days. The period of rapid decline in the level of antigen in the circulation is due to the development of an immune response in the recipient animal. This results in the formation of antigen-antibody complexes and subsequent clearance of the complexes from the circulation by the cells of the reticuloendothelial system (RES) (Fig. 261-1). During the period in which the complexes are being formed in the circulation, there is a fall in the animal's serum complement levels. At this time pathologic changes occur in large arteries, renal glomeruli, joints, and cardiac vessels. The glomerulonephritis noted during this period has been studied extensively. It is characterized by swelling of the endothelial cells and marked proteinuria with little hematuria; an infiltrate of monocytes but very few granulocytes is found in the renal glomeruli. Immunofluorescence studies have shown that antigen, host immunoglobulin, and C3 are deposited along the glomerular basement membrane in a typical granular pattern. On electron-microscopic examination of kidney sections, few abnormalities are seen except swelling of endothelial cells. Late in the reaction subepithelial deposits of electron-dense material are noted in some animals; however, at this time fluorescent antibody examination is negative for immuglobulin and complement in the glomeruli. The deposits may represent immunologically altered immunoglobulin or complement.

There is also a very high incidence of arteritis in the coronary artery outflow tract and at branching points of the aorta in the acute serum sickness model. The arteritis is characterized by marked intimal proliferation of endothelium. Polymorphonuclear neutrophils enter the site of intimal proliferation. This is followed by degradation of the internal elastic lamina and adventitia with resulting fibrinoid necrosis of the vessel. On immunofluorescence microscopy, host immunoglobulin, antigen, and C3 are found roughly in the region of the internal elastic lamina, but these immunoreactive materials are rapidly removed and are gone in several days. It has been suggested that the polymorphonuclear neutrophils present in the lesions phagocytize these complexes. In contrast to the findings in glomerulonephritis, materials which decrease complement activity or inhibit the polymorphonuclear response diminish or block the development of arteritis.

At the time of the development of serum sickness in this animal model, there are high-molecular-weight immune complexes in the circulation; the animals that become sick regularly have complexes that are greater than 19 S in their sedimentation characteristics. Acute serum sickness is present only as long as these circulating immune complexes persist and resolves rapidly once the antigen is cleared from the circulation and the immune complexes are gone.

It is possible to induce chronic glomerulonephritis in animals by the repeated intravenous injection of antigen. The dose of antigen injected is critical to the development of the disease. Antigen excess must be produced after each antigen administration, and immune complexes must circulate in the animals. These animals develop glomerulonephritis but not the arteritis characteristic of acute serum sickness.

Other animal models of immune-complex disease closely resemble systemic lupus erythematosus. The most widely studied and best characterized is the disease which occurs spontaneously in the F_1 hybrid of New Zealand black (NZB) and New Zealand white (NZW) mice. These animals develop antibodies to nucleic acids including double-stranded DNA and have decreased numbers of suppressor T cells. They also develop circulating immune complexes and an immune-complex–mediated glomerulonephritis which eventuates in renal insufficiency and death. Direct immunofluorescence microscopy of the kidneys in these animals reveals deposits of DNA, antibodies to DNA, and C3 in the glomerular basement membrane. The female NZB-NZW mice develop these changes before the males, and this sex difference may be related to a switch in the class of antibodies to DNA from IgM to IgG that occurs much earlier in the females than in the males.

Over the years a great deal of attention has been paid to the fate of immune complexes in animal models. Injection of antigens into immunized animals is followed by the deposition of the antigen in the liver, spleen, and lung, all elements of the RES. Detailed studies have examined the fate of preformed immune complexes of carefully determined size in a variety of animals. In general, the findings of these studies have paralleled those reported in the animal models of serum sickness. The larger complexes are rapidly removed from the circulation, and complexes which are greater than 19 S in their sedimentation characteristics are removed so rapidly by the liver that they persist in the circulation for only a matter of minutes. The major

factor appearing to govern the rate of clearance of these large preformed complexes from the circulation is the rate of hepatic blood flow. In some studies complement activation by complexes is also important in their metabolism, and injected complexes go through a complex series of processing steps. Large lattice-size complexes appear to be dissociated by complement into smaller entities. Following injection, complexes containing complement components become associated with cells with complement receptors. Human erythrocytes have complement receptors, and these cells appear to be particularly important in the processing of complexes. It is believed that complement-coated complexes associate with complement receptors on red cell surfaces and the complexes are stripped from these cells as they course through the sinusoids of the liver. They are then metabolized. Fc receptors for IgG also play a prominent role in the removal of IgG-containing immune complexes from the circulation, and any manipulation that affects the interaction of Fc receptors and the Fc fragment of IgG in the complexes predisposes to failure to clear the complexes and to tissue deposition. It is possible to measure RES Fc receptor functional activity in patients and normal individuals by intravenously injecting IgG-sensitized autologous radiolabeled erythrocytes and then monitoring the rate of disappearance of these immune particles from the bloodstream. In those diseases with tissue deposition of immune complexes there tends to be an associated RES Fc receptor defect and delayed clearance of the antibody sensitized cells from the circulation.

DETECTION OF CIRCULATING IMMUNE COMPLEXES Many different assays are available for the detection of soluble immune complexes in various biologic fluids. Although these assays vary in their sensitivity and reproducibility, they have expanded our understanding of circulating immune complexes and their role in various disease states. In general, early tests for the detection of circulating

FIGURE 261-1 *The rabbit model of acute serum sickness. Radiolabeled antigen is injected at day 0. After a period of equilibration of antigen between the intravascular and extravascular space, there is progressive elimination of antigen from the circulation. With the onset of the animal's immune response there is rapid elimination of antigen from the circulation. Coincident with the phase of rapid elimination is the appearance of antigen-antibody complexes in the circulation and a fall in serum complement. Complete antigen clearance is associated with the appearance of free antibody in the circulation. At the time when antigen-antibody complexes are seen in the circulation, immunopathologic findings are maximal.*

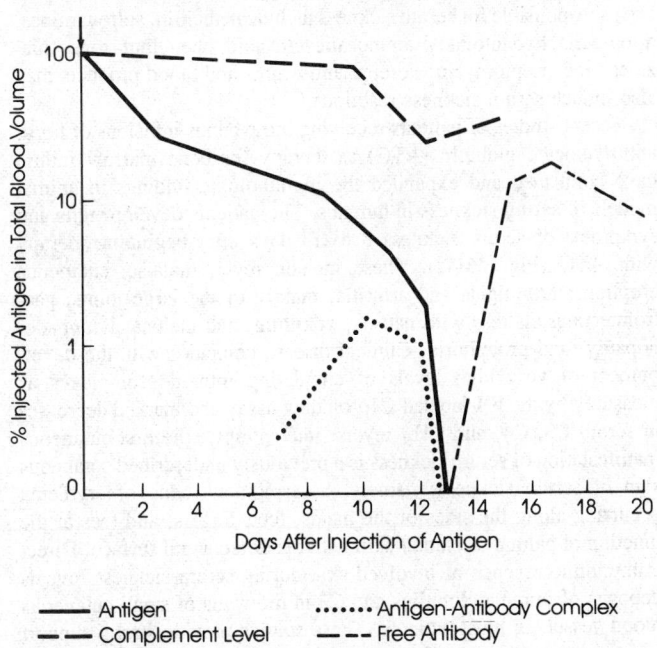

immune complexes relied on physical characteristics of the immune complexes, such as their high molecular weight or cold insolubility. These rather insensitive techniques have been replaced by assays for immunologic components or biologic activities of immune complexes. Although there are now sensitive radioimmunoassays for the detection of circulating immune complexes containing IgG, IgM, and IgA, these tests are not antigen-specific. In fact, in most cases in which circulating immune complexes are demonstrable, the component antigen(s) is (are) unknown. As with most laboratory tests, immune-complex assays may be influenced by other factors. Anticoagulants, endotoxin, and free DNA as well as immunoglobulin aggregates formed after the sample is obtained may result in false-positive results. The impact of these factors can be reduced by the selection of immune-complex assays that are unaffected by these variables and the use of two or more different assays in situations in which critical evaluation of circulating immune complexes is desired. Several of the most sensitive and commonly used immune-complex assays will be described briefly: (1) C1q binding or solid-phase radioassays. C1q is a subcomponent of the first component of complement and will bind to immune complexes containing IgG subclasses 1 to 3 or IgM via noncovalent attachment to a specific site on the Fc portion of immunoglobulin. (2) Raji cell assays. Raji cells are a lymphoblastoid cell line with cell surface receptors for complement, especially C3. The assays are based on the ability of circulating immune complexes which contain bound complement components in their lattices to bind to the surface of the Raji cells via the complement receptors. The bound complexes are easily detected. (3) Conglutinin assays. Conglutinin is a 750,000-dalton nonimmunoglobulin protein found in certain bovine serums that will bind to a cleavage fragment of human C3 known as iC3b. Immune complexes containing iC3b will bind to conglutinin attached to a solid-phase substrate and can be detected.

SERUM SICKNESS Drug hypersensitivity reactions are the most common cause of serum sickness today. Commonly occurring signs and symptoms of serum sickness include fever, cutaneous eruptions (morbilliform and/or urticarial), arthralgias, lymphadenopathy, and albuminuria. Less common manifestations are arthritis, nephritis, neuropathy, and vasculitis. The time required for primary sensitization to an offending agent is approximately 1 to 3 weeks. However, clinical manifestations may develop within 12 to 36 h if there is a history of a previous immunizing exposure. Drug-induced serum sickness usually abates within days after withdrawal of the causative agent. Reactions may persist for longer intervals, particularly if repository or long-acting agents are responsible for the problem. Drugs responsible for serum sickness include penicillin, sulfonamides, thiouracils, hydantoins, p-aminosalicyclic acid, phenylbutazone, thiazides, and streptomycin. Foreign antiserums and blood products may also induce serum sickness reactions.

Recent studies of patients receiving intravenous infusions of horse antithymocyte globulin (ATG) as therapy for bone marrow failure have confirmed and expanded the immunologic findings in animal models of serum sickness in humans. The patients develop signs and symptoms of serum sickness 8 to 13 days after beginning therapy with ATG (Fig. 261-2). These include fever; malaise; cutaneous eruptions; arthralgias and arthritis, mainly of the large joints; gastrointestinal distress with nausea, vomiting, and melena; lymphadenopathy, and proteinuria. Clinical disease coincides with the development of very high levels of circulating immune complexes as measured by the ^{125}I-labeled C1q binding assay and marked decreases in serum C3, C4, and CH_{50} levels. Interestingly, the first cutaneous manifestation of serum sickness is a previously undescribed cutaneous sign of serum sickness, namely, a serpiginous band of erythema occurring along the sides of the hands, feet, fingers, and toes at the junction of palmar or plantar skin with the dorsolateral surface. Direct immunofluorescence of involved skin during serum sickness reveals deposits of immunoglobulins and C3 in the walls of small cutaneous blood vessels in most patients. These studies provide strong support for a pathogenic role for circulating immune complexes in the pathophysiology of human serum sickness.

SYSTEMIC LUPUS ERYTHEMATOSUS Systemic lupus erythematosus (SLE) is a multisystem disease associated with a number of immunologic abnormalities including the production of autoantibodies, hypergammaglobulinemia, suppressor T-cell abnormalities, decreased levels of serum complement, and increased levels of circulating immune complexes. Immune complexes are thought to play a critical role in the pathophysiology of SLE. Early evidence for the role of circulating immune complexes in SLE included the finding by direct immunofluorescence of glomerular deposits of immunoglobulin, complement, and DNA in kidney biopsies. Mixed IgM-IgG cryoglobulins were found in the serums of a substantial number of SLE patients, and when the antibody specificity of these cryoprecipitates was examined, reactivity was found against single- and double-stranded DNA as well as ribonucleoprotein. Utilizing the newer, more sensitive assays, circulating immune complexes have been found in a high percentage of patients with SLE. An explanation for the continued circulation of immune complexes in patients with SLE has been provided by the demonstration of defective function of the reticuloendothelial system (RES) in these patients. Patients with SLE have been shown to have delayed clearance of autologous red blood cells coated with IgG from the circulation, suggesting an impaired function of RES Fc-IgG receptors. The prolonged RES clearance in these patients was found to be correlated with increased levels of circulating immune complexes as measured by the C1q binding assay and with clinical disease activity. Studies in these same patients after their disease improved with treatment revealed a significant correlation between clinical improvement, improvement of Fc-mediated clearance, and decreased levels of circulating immune complexes. Individuals with SLE also have decreased numbers of C3b receptors on their erythrocytes. Whether the decreased number of receptors is primary or secondary remains to be established. Nonetheless, abnormalities of both Fc-IgG and C3b receptors which are responsible for phagocytosis of circulating immune complexes are present in patients with SLE.

VASCULITIS There is strong circumstantial evidence for the role of circulating immune complexes in the various forms of hypersensitivity or necrotizing vasculitis. Features of the classic "palpable purpura" of cutaneous necrotizing vasculitis closely resemble the clinical, histopathologic and immunopathologic features of the Arthus reaction. The Arthus reaction is a model for immune-complex–mediated vascular damage in which antigen is injected intradermally into an animal which possesses circulating antibody against that antigen. In both vasculitis and the Arthus reaction, deposits of immunoglobulin and complement are found in the walls of blood vessels in early lesions. The histopathology of both consists of infiltrates of polymorphonuclear neutrophils, leukocytoclasis, endothelial cell damage and necrosis, hemorrhage, and perivascular deposits of fibrin. Electron microscopy of lesions of cutaneous necrotizing vasculitis reveals subendothelial electron-dense deposits compatible with immune complexes. The available evidence indicates the presence of immune complexes at the site of tissue damage in necrotizing vasculitis. In accord with these findings is the demonstration of circulating immune complexes in a high percentage of patients with this disease.

LABORATORY FINDINGS In theory the essential feature of immune-complex disease would be the finding of circulating immune complexes. In practice there is great variability from disease to disease in the frequency of positive immune-complex assays. In some diseases such as SLE there is a high frequency of positive immune-complex assays. In others like membranoproliferative glomerulonephritis the frequency of positive assays is much lower. Part of the reason for this has to do with the stage of disease under study. In some cases immunologic phenomena are responsible for the initiation of the disease and the initial tissue insult. However, subsequent injury is caused by scarring, inflammation, and repair mechanisms that result in more extensive tissue damage. Thus, disease progression may occur at a time when immunologic injury is no longer occurring. A second reason for the failure to detect circulating immune complexes in diseases thought to be mediated by them has to do with technical difficulties in the measurement of such complexes. There are many types of assays for immune complexes. Most are indirect and rely on a biologic or biochemical property of the complexes such as the binding of complement components. The pattern of positive reaction clearly varies from disease to disease. Clearly each assay recognizes a different type of complex with maximal efficiency. Since multiple assays are rarely performed on one specimen, complexes, although present, may not be detected. Finally, although a disease is classified as immune-complex–related because of the finding of immune deposits in affected tissues or because of the similarity of pathologic findings to animal models, the disease may not be actually caused by circulating immune complexes. For example, antibody may be formed to a tissue component, bind to it in a tissue site, and induce damage. Such is thought to be the case in Goodpasture's disease. For all of these reasons assays for the detection of circulating immune complexes are generally used only for research purposes and are rarely critical for diagnosis or patient management.

Examination of tissues using immunofluorescent techniques to detect immune deposits is also of great interest in establishing the diagnosis of immune-complex disease. Immune complexes deposited in tissues may be evanescent. For example, in cutaneous vasculitis,

lesions must be biopsied within 12 h of their appearance. Although helpful in diagnosis and in establishing pathogenesis, testing for immune deposits in tissue is rarely required for diagnosis.

Another test commonly used to infer the presence of immune complexes is the measurement of serum complement. Decreased levels are taken to indicate the presence of complexes. In fact, it has been suggested that the levels of serum C4 and C3 are the most sensitive indexes of disease activity in SLE. However, the correlation between disease activity and complement levels is rough at best, and some patients with active SLE may have relatively normal complement levels for several reasons. The normal range of complement component levels is wide, and a given patient may have depressed levels with serum concentrations falling from high normal levels to low normal levels. In general complement components act as acute phase reactants, and the lowering of serum complement may be masked by increased synthesis. Moreover, under many circumstances activation of complement may mediate profound pathophysiologic effects, although few molecules of complement are actually involved. For example, complement binding to red cells may be responsible for much of the red cell destruction that occurs with ABO mismatched transfusions; yet serum complement levels may be unchanged because too few molecules are used in erythrocyte destruction to detect a fall in titer. Finally, all types of complexes do not activate complement in the

FIGURE 261-2 *Serum sickness in human beings. Horse antithymocyte globulin was injected into patients with aplastic anemia daily for 10 days. After the fifth day of injection, C1q binding activity begins to rise (A). At the same time there is a dramatic fall in plasma levels of C3 and C4 and onset of clinical symptoms (B).*

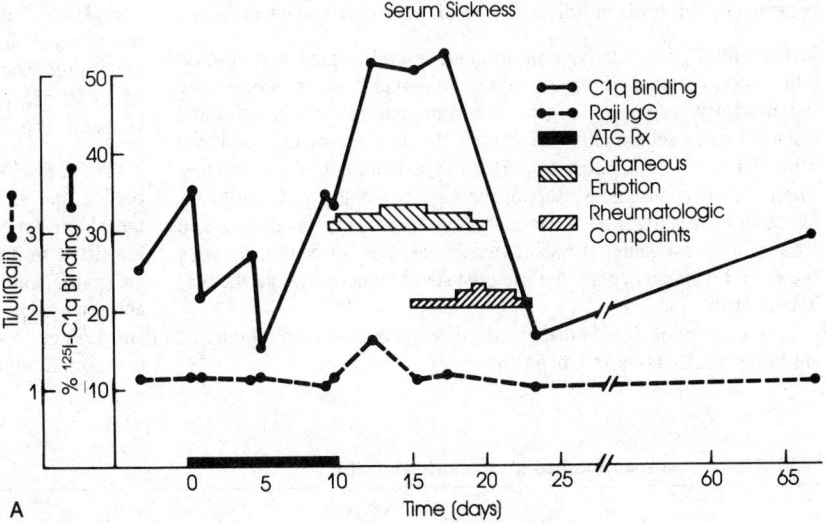

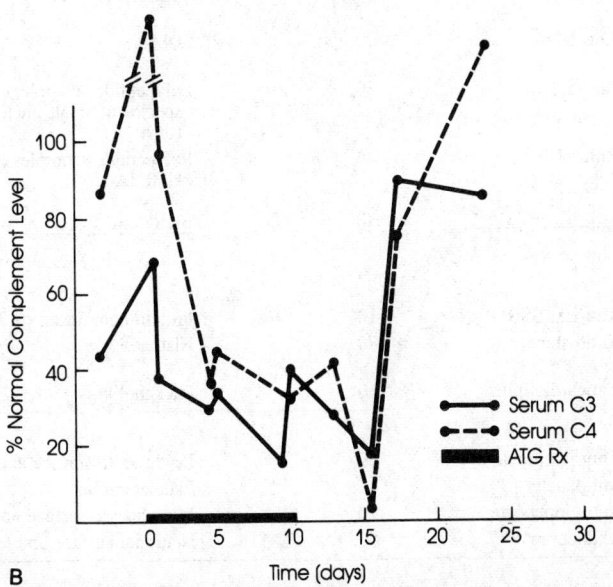

same way. Massive antigen release from red cells occurring during the course of vivax malaria infection leads to the rapid formation of antigen-antibody complexes in the circulation. For unknown reasons these complexes only interact with the early components of the classic complement pathway, while C3 and the later complement components are not recruited. Thus, if one measures levels of C3, no fall in titer is noted, although complexes are present and massive complement activation has taken place. The complexes formed in SLE activate optimally the classic pathway; presumably those involved in IgA glomerulonephritis activate the alternative pathway. Therefore, the complement test chosen for examination may be important.

Other tests may suggest indirectly the presence of immune-complex disease. For example, a finding of mixed IgG-IgM cryoprecipitates suggests the presence of immune complexes. The presence of antinuclear antibodies suggests autoimmunity, as does the presence of a number of tissue-component-specific antibodies. Similarly the presence of specific antigen such as hepatitis B surface antigen in the circulation together with appropriate clinical symptoms may suggest an immune-complex disease. Most patients with active immune-complex–mediated disease have an elevated erythrocyte sedimentation rate, although this is not invariably the case. Patients with Takayasu's arteritis may have a normal erythrocyte sedimentation rate during the later phases of the evolution of lesions where most pathology is caused by scarring, fibrosis, and repair within vessel walls. Finally, specific laboratory tests such as red cell casts in the urine in glomerulonephritis or mild cerebrospinal fluid pleocytosis in the presence of cerebritis are discussed in the respective chapters.

TREATMENT The therapy of immune-complex–mediated disease relies upon removal of the offending antigen and interruption of the inflammatory response. In general serum sickness is a self-limited disease that is seldom life-threatening. In the case of drug-induced serum sickness it is most important to discontinue the offending agent. In many instances, supportive care combined with antihistamines for urticaria and acetaminophen for fever, myalgias, and arthralgias is adequate. If serious renal, vascular, or central nervous sytem involvement occurs, the use of systemic glucocorticoid therapy is indicated.

The therapy of SLE is discussed in Chap. 262 and the therapy of vasculitis is discussed in Chap. 269.

REFERENCES

COCHRANE CB, KOFFLER D: Immune complex disease in experimental animals and man. Adv Immunol 16:185, 1963

DIXON F: The role of antigen-antibody complexes in disease. Harvey Lect 52:21, 1963

FRANK MM et al: Immunoglobulin G Fc receptor mediated clearance in autoimmune diseases. Ann Intern Med 98:206, 1983

GERMUTH FC JR.: A comparative histologic and immunologic study in rabbits of induced hypersensitivity of the serum sickness type. J Exp Med 97:257, 1953

LAWLEY TJ et al: A prospective clinical and immunologic analysis of patients with serum sickness. N Engl J Med 311:1407, 1984

MANNIK M, AREND WP: Fate of preformed immune complexes in rabbits and rhesus monkeys. J Exp Med 134:19s, 1971

VON PIRQUET C, SCHICK B: Serum sickness. Baltimore, Williams & Wilkins, 1951

THEOFILOPOULOS AN, DIXON FJ: The biology and detection of immune complexes. Adv Immunol 28:89, 1979

262 SYSTEMIC LUPUS ERYTHEMATOSUS

BEVRA HANNAHS HAHN

DEFINITION AND PREVALENCE Systemic lupus erythematosus (SLE) is a disease of unknown etiology in which tissues and cells are damaged by deposition of pathogenic autoantibodies and immune complexes. Ninety percent of cases occur in women, usually of child-bearing age, but children, men, and the elderly can be affected. In the United States, the prevalence of SLE in urban areas varies from 15 to 50 per 100,000; it is more common in blacks than in whites. Hispanic and Asian populations also are susceptible.

PATHOGENESIS AND ETIOLOGY Production of pathogenic antibodies and immune complexes, coupled with failure to suppress them, are the basic abnormalities underlying SLE. These antibodies are listed in Table 262-1. Not all antibodies or immune complexes are pathogenic. Some antibodies cause disease because of their antigen specificity. Examples are antibodies to erythrocyte surface antigens or to coagulation factors. Others cause disease because of their immunoglobulin (Ig) isotype, ability to fix complement (C'),

TABLE 262-1 Autoantibodies in patients with SLE

	Incidence, %	Antigen detected	Clinical importance
Antinuclear antibodies	95	Multiple nuclear and cyto-plasmic antigens	Human cell line substrates are more sensitive than standard murine tissues. A repeatedly negative test on both makes SLE diagnosis unlikely. Multiple antibodies are detected.
Anti-DNA	70	DNA	Anti-dsDNA is relatively disease-specific; anti-ssDNA is not. Associated with nephritis and clinical activity.
Anti-Sm	30	Polypeptides complexed to 6 species of small nuclear RNA	Specific for SLE.
Anti-RNP	40	Polypeptides complexed to U1RNA	High titer seen in syndromes with features of polymyositis, scleroderma, lupus and mixed connective tissue disease. If present in SLE without anti-DNA, risk for nephritis is low.
Anti-Ro (SSA)	30	RNA polymerase	Associated with Sjögren's syndrome, DR3 haplotype, subacute cutaneous lupus, complement deficiencies, ANA-negative lupus, lupus in the elderly, neonatal lupus, congenital heart block in infants. Can cause nephritis.
Anti-La (SSB)	10	Protein complexed to RNAs	When associated with anti-Ro, risk for nephritis is low.
Antihistone	70	Histones	More frequent in drug-induced LE (95 percent) than in spontaneous SLE.
Anticardiolipin	50	Phospholipid	Increases risk for venous or arterial thrombosis and for spontaneous abortion. Associated with prolonged PTT (lupus anticoagulant) and false-positive VDRL.
Antierythrocyte	60	Erythrocyte surface antigens	A small proportion of these patients develop overt hemolysis.
Antiplatelet	–	Platelet surface	Associated with thrombocytopenia.
Antilymphocyte	70	Lymphocyte surface antigens	Probably associated with leukopenia and abnormal T-cell function.
Antineuronal	60	Neuronal surface antigens	In CSF, high IgG titers correlate with diffuse but not focal CNS lupus.

tissue avidity, and/or electric charge. For example, complement-fixing cationic antibodies fix to the polyanions in glomerular basement membrane, bind antigen, and cause tissue damage.

The pathogenesis of SLE includes genetic, environmental, and sex hormonal factors; abnormal humoral and cellular immune responses; and inadequate clearing of antibodies and immune complexes. Genetic predisposition is indicated by high concordance for clinical disease in monozygotic but not dizygotic twins, a 10 percent frequency of patients with more than one affected individual in the family, a significantly increased frequency of the MB1/MT1 HLA haplotype (and of HLA-DR2 and -DR3 in some studies), and the fact that 6 percent of SLE patients have inherited deficiencies of complement components, especially C2. Viruses have been suspected as etiologic agents but this is not proven. Phospholipids in cell walls of enteric bacteria may act as polyclonal B-cell activators or antigens to elicit antibodies cross-reactive with the ribose phosphate backbone in DNA. In some patients, exposure to ultraviolet light causes disease flare-ups, probably by altering the antigenicity of DNA or the composition of dermal-epidermal junctions. Sex hormonal influences contribute to the pathogenesis of SLE. In general, estrogen enhances and testosterone reduces antibody responses. Men and women with SLE have increased hydroxylation of estrogen and estrone to 16α-hydroxy-estrone, producing prolonged estrogenic stimulation. The ultimate outcome of all these factors is B-cell hyperactivity, accompanied by multiple abnormalities in immunoregulation. For example, quantities of T helper/inducer and T suppressor/cytotoxic cells are diminished during periods of disease activity, and many functions are abnormal, including their ability to suppress anti-DNA synthesis or to participate in direct and antibody-mediated cytotoxicity. Ability of T cells to secrete interleukins is suppressed, and abnormal interferon is produced by macrophages. Failure to suppress antibodies also results from abnormalities in the humoral idiotype–anti-idiotype network. Finally, immune complexes are cleared more slowly than normal, related in part to both inherited and acquired deficiencies of complement receptors (CR1) on cell surfaces.

Clinical manifestations of the disease are determined by which antibody subpopulations and immune complexes are present in the patients' repertoire, which organs, cells, or cell products are their targets, and which patients have the ability to correct these abnormalities.

CLINICAL MANIFESTATIONS At its onset, SLE may involve only one organ system, with additional manifestations occurring later, or may be multisystemic. Clinical manifestations are listed in Table 262-2. Autoantibodies are usually (but not always) detectable on the patient's initial visit. Disease severity varies from mild and intermittent to persistent and ultimately fatal. Most patients experience exacerbations interspersed with periods of relative quiescence. Fewer than 10 percent have long-lasting symptom-free remissions. *Systemic symptoms* are usually prominent and include fatigue, malaise, fever, anorexia, weight loss, and nausea.

Musculoskeletal Almost all SLE patients experience arthralgias and myalgias; most develop arthritis. Pain is often out of proportion to physical findings, which include symmetric fusiform swelling of joints [most frequently proximal interphalangeal (PIP) and meta-carpophalangeal (MCP) joints of the hands, wrists, and knees], diffuse puffiness of hands and feet, and tenosynovitis. Joint deformities are unusual, although 10 percent of patients develop swan neck deformities and ulnar drift at the MCP joints. Erosions are rare, but subcutaneous nodules over the elbows and fingers occur. Myopathy can be inflammatory and related to active disease, or iatrogenic, secondary to hypokalemia or direct damage caused by glucocorticoids or hydroxychloroquine. Ischemic necrosis of bone also causes "joint" pain and is a common cause of hip and shoulder pain in these patients.

Cutaneous The *malar ("butterfly") rash* is a fixed erythematous rash, flat or raised, over the cheeks and bridge of the nose, often involving the chin and ears. It is usually exacerbated by ultraviolet light. Scarring is absent, but telangiectasias may develop. A more diffuse maculopapular rash, predominant in sun-exposed areas, is also common. Its presence usually indicates disease flare-up. Loss of scalp hair (which often heralds a flare-up) is usually patchy but can be extensive; the hair will regrow, except in discoid lupus erythematosus (DLE). *Vasculitic skin lesions* include subcutaneous nodules, ulcers (usually on the legs), purpura, and infarcts of skin or digits. *DLE lesions* occur in some patients with SLE and can be disfiguring. They are circular with an erythematous rim, raised, and scaly with follicular plugging and telangiectasia. Central scarring produces depigmentation and permanent loss of appendages. They

TABLE 262-2 Clinical manifestations of SLE

	Percent of patients positive during course of disease
Systemic	95
Fatigue, malaise, fever, anorexia, nausea, weight loss	95
Musculoskeletal	95
Arthralgias/myalgias	95
Nonerosive polyarthritis*	60
Hand deformities	10
Myopathy/myositis	40/5
Ischemic necrosis of bone	15
Cutaneous	80
Malar rash*	50
Discoid rash*	15
Photosensitivity*	40
Oral ulcers*	40
Other rashes—maculopapular, urticarial, bullous, subacute cutaneous lupus	40
Alopecia	40
Vasculitis	20
Panniculitis	5
Hematologic	85
Anemia (of chronic disease)	70
Hemolytic anemia	10
Leukopenia (<4000/mm³)	65
Lymphopenia (<1500/mm³) } *	50
Thrombocytopenia (<100,000/mm³)	15
Circulating anticoagulant	10–20
Splenomegaly	15
Lymphadenopathy	20
Neurologic	60
Organic brain syndromes	35
Psychosis } *	10
Seizures	20
Other CNS (see text)	15
Peripheral neuropathy	15
Cardiopulmonary	60
Pleurisy } *	50
Pericarditis	30
Myocarditis	10
Endocarditis (Libman-Sacks)	10
Pleural effusions	30
Lupus pneumonitis	10
Interstitial fibrosis	5
Pulmonary hypertension	<5
ARDS/hemorrhage	<5
Renal	50
Proteinuria >500 mg/24 h } *	50
Cellular casts	50
Nephrotic syndrome	25
Renal failure	5–10
Gastrointestinal	45
Nonspecific (anorexia, nausea, mild pain, diarrhea)	30
Vasculitis—with bleeding or perforation	5
Ascites	<5
Abnormal liver enzymes	40
	15
Thrombosis	15
Venous	10
Arterial	5
Ocular	15
Retina vasculitis	5
Conjunctivitis/episcleritis	10
Sicca syndrome	15

* *In addition to two positive laboratory tests [positive ANA plus one or more of (1) positive LE cells, (2) anti-dsDNA, (3) anti-Sm, or (4) false-positive VDRL], a combination of these clinical and laboratory manifestations totalling four meet American Rheumatism Association criteria for classifying patients in SLE. Bracketed features count as one, even if more than one are present, e.g., leukopenia plus thrombocytopenia = one criterion.*

occur over the scalp, external ears, face, and sun exposed areas of the arms, back, and chest. Only 5 percent of individuals with DLE progress to SLE; however 20 percent of SLE patients have DLE lesions. Less frequent SLE skin lesions include urticaria, periorbital edema, bullae, erythema multiforme, lichen-planus–like lesions, and panniculitis ("lupus profundus").

Patients with *subacute cutaneous lupus* (SCLE) are a distinct subset with recurring extensive skin lesions. Arthritis and fatigue are frequent; central nervous system and renal involvement are not. Some patients are antinuclear antibody (ANA)–negative. The majority hve antibodies to Ro (SS-A) or to single-stranded (ss) DNA and carry the HLA-DR3 phenotype. The skin lesions are photosensitive polycyclic annular or papulosquamous psoriasiform over the arms, trunk, and face; they become hypopigmented but not scarred.

Mucous membrane lesions are usually small, shallow, painless ulcers in the mouth (usually over the palate) and nose.

Renal manifestations   Although almost all patients with SLE have deposits of immunoglobulin in glomeruli, only one-half have clinical nephritis, defined by persistent proteinuria. At presentation, most patients are asymptomatic (unless already uremic) except for those with edema of the nephrotic syndrome. Urinalysis shows hematuria, cylindruria, and proteinuria. As discussed under "Pathology" (see below), most patients with mesangial or mild focal glomerulonephritis do not develop deterioration of renal function. In patients with more severe, active, or chronic lesions, renal failure is a major cause of death. Since mild lesions may not require aggressive therapy with glucocorticoids and/or cytotoxic drugs, whereas severe lesions do, renal biopsy may provide information that will affect therapeutic decisions over the subsequent several months. Patients with deteriorating renal function and active urine sediment also require prompt, aggressive therapy; biopsy is not necessary unless they fail to respond. However, patients with a high proportion of sclerotic glomeruli on biopsy (usually with a serum creatinine >3 mg/100 mL) are unlikely to respond to immunosuppressive therapy. In these cases, dialysis or transplantation should be planned. Patients with persistently abnormal urinalyses associated with high titers of antibodies to double-stranded (ds) DNA and hypocomplementemia are also at risk for severe nephritis; kidney biopsy is useful in these cases if the results are likely to have an impact on therapeutic decisions.

Nervous system   Any region of the brain can be involved in SLE, as can the meninges, spinal cord, and cranial and peripheral nerves. Central nervous system (CNS) events may be isolated, single, or multiple, but usually occur in the setting of active disease in other systems. Mild mental dysfunction is the most frequent manifestation. Seizures are frequent and may be grand mal, petit mal, or focal. Other manifestations include psychosis, organic brain syndromes, headache (including migraine), focal infarcts with resultant deficits,

TABLE 262-3   Laboratory manifestations of SLE

Tests which help *confirm the clinical diagnosis and predict severity*	Tests which may be helpful in *following the clinical course**
Relatively specific for SLE: 　Anti-dsDNA 　Anti-Sm Not specific: 　ANA (most sensitive) 　CH$_{50}$, C3, C4 　Anti-Ro 　Direct Coombs' test 　VDRL 　PTT 　Anticardiolipin 　Hematocrit 　Leukocyte count 　Platelet count 　Urinalysis 　Serum creatinine	Titer of anti-dsDNA Serum complement levels Westergren erythrocyte sedimentation rate Hematocrit Leukocyte count Platelet count Urinalysis Serum creatinine

* *For each patient, the pattern of laboratory abnormalities (if any) associated with a disease flare-up should be established and only those tests used as adjunct to clinical assessments.*

extrapyramidal disorders, cerebellar dysfunction, hypothalamic dysfunction with inappropriate ADH secretion, pseudotumor cerebri, subarachnoid hemmorrhage, aseptic meningitis, transverse myelitis with paraplegia or quadriplegia, optic neuritis, cranial nerve palsies, and peripheral sensorimotor neuropathy resulting either in mononeuritis multiplex or glove-and-stocking deficit. Depression and anxiety are frequent.

The laboratory diagnosis of CNS disease can be difficult. Abnormal electroencephalograms are found in about 70 percent of patients and usually show diffuse slowing or focal abnormalities. The cerebrospinal fluid (CSF) shows elevated protein levels in 50 percent and an elevated number of mononuclear cells in 30 percent of patients. Lumbar puncture should be performed whenever CNS symptoms could result from infection, especially in patients receiving immunosuppressive therapy. Brain scans (including CAT), nuclear magnetic resonance imaging, and angiograms are most likely to be positive when focal neurologic deficits are present, and are less helpful in cases with diffuse, nonfocal manifestations. Standard laboratory measures of disease activity (Table 262-3) often do not correlate with neurologic manifestations. Neurologic problems usually improve (with the exception of deficits related to infarcts) with therapy and/or time; recurrences are common.

Vascular   Thrombosis in capillaries, in small vessels, and in medium-sized veins and arteries can be a major problem. Although vasculitis may play a role, there is increasing evidence that antibodies against phospholipids (anticardiolipin) may initiate clotting. These antibodies may be the "lupus anticoagulant." In addition, degenerative vascular changes associated with years of immune-complex deposition in vessel walls may predispose to symptomatic coronary artery disease in relatively young individuals with SLE. Anticoagulation with warfarin sodium is usually effective in reducing recurrences of venous clots; it is unclear whether any therapies reduce the incidence of arterial clotting.

Hematologic abnormalities   The lupus anticoagulant usually binds to phospholipids in the prothrombin activator complex. It prolongs the partial thromboplastin time; an abnormality not corrected by addition of normal plasma. Three clinical sequelae may be associated with it. First, some patients experience repeated episodes of either venous or arterial clotting; these are often serious, especially if associated with pulmonary emboli, strokes, or occlusion of major arteries. Second, if the anticoagulant is associated with thrombocytopenia or hypoprothrombinemia, significant bleeding can occur. Third, in the absence of clotting or bleeding disorders, it may be a benign laboratory abnormality; biopsies and surgery can be performed without increased risk of bleeding. Antibodies to clotting factors (VIII, IX) are also associated with bleeding. Bleeding syndromes usually respond to glucocorticoids.

Anemia of chronic disease occurs in most patients during periods of disease activity. Frank hemolysis occurs in a small proportion of those with positive Coombs' tests; that syndrome is usually responsive to high-dose glucocorticoids. Splenectomy is sometimes effective in steroid-resistant patients.

Leukopenia is common and usually reflects lymphopenia. In general, it is not associated with recurrent infections and does not require treatment.

Mild thrombocytopenia is common. Severe thrombocytopenia with bleeding and purpura occurs in 5 percent of patients and should be treated with high-dose glucocorticoids. If the platelet count has not risen to a safe range in 5 to 14 days, splenectomy should be considered.

Cardiopulmonary   Pericardial pain is the most frequent symptom of cardiac lupus; pericardial effusions also occur. Tamponade has been reported and constrictive pericarditis occurs, but is rare. Myocarditis can cause arrhythmias and/or cardiac failure. Endocarditis of the Libman-Sacks verrucous type, a diagnosis made at autopsy, is usually not clinically significant; however, it can cause aortic or mitral regurgitation. Rarely, myocardial infarcts result from vasculitis of the coronary arteries; more often they are associated with degenerative arterial disease.

Pleurisy and pleural effusions are common manifestations of SLE. Lupus pneumonitis causes recurrent episodes of fever, dyspnea, and cough; x-rays show infiltrates which come and go over a period of days or weeks, and/or areas of platelike atelectasis; this syndrome responds to glucocorticoids. However, *the most common cause of pulmonary infiltrates in patients with SLE is infection.* Interstitial pneumonitis leading to fibrosis occurs in a small proportion of patients; the inflammatory phase may respond to treatment, while the fibrosis does not. Occasionally, patients develop pulmonary hypertension. Infrequent but often fatal pulmonary manifestations include adult respiratory distress syndrome (ARDS) and massive intraalveolar hemorrhage.

Gastrointestinal   Nonspecific gastrointestinal symptoms are common, but vasculitis of the intestine is the most dangerous manifestation. It causes acute or subacute crampy pain, vomiting, and diarrhea and leads to intestinal perforation and death in almost one-half of the affected patients. Vasculitis is usually present simultaneously in other systems. Another gastrointestinal manifestation of SLE is a pseudoobstruction picture in which patients present with acute crampy abdominal pain; x-rays show dilated loops of small bowel which may be edematous. Surgery should be avoided unless true obstruction is present. Patients generally respond to glucocorticoid therapy. Acute pancreatitis occurs and can be severe; it may result from glucocorticoid therapy or from active SLE. Elevated serum levels of liver enzymes, especially transaminases, are common in patients with active SLE, but are not associated with significant hepatic damage; they return to normal as the disease is treated.

Ocular   The most important ocular manifestation of SLE is retinal vasculitis with infarcts; blindness can develop over a period of days. Examination of the retina shows areas of sheathed, narrow arterioles, and cytoid bodies (white exudates) adjacent to vessels. Other ocular abnormalities include conjunctivitis, episcleritis, and optic neuritis. The sicca syndrome is frequent.

PATHOLOGY   Cutaneous lesions   Acute systemic, discoid (DLE) and subacute cutaneous LE skin lesions show similar histopathology. Characteristic changes include degeneration of the basal layer of the epidermis with disruption of the dermal-epidermal junction (DEJ), and scattered mononuclear cell infiltrates around vessels and appendages in the upper dermis. In DLE follicular plugging and hyperkeratosis are prominent. Deposits of Ig and C' are seen in the DEJ in 80 to 100 percent of lesional and 50 percent of nonlesional skin in patients with active disease; the proportions are lower during remissions. Active subacute cutaneous lesions are positive for deposits of Ig and C' only 50 percent of the time. Ig deposition in the DEJ *is not specific* for *LE.* Vasculitic lesions usually show leucocytoclastic angiitis.

Renal lesions   Most renal lesions are caused by in situ immune-complex formation or by deposition of circulating immune complexes. In mild nephritis, histology shows either no changes or proliferation confined to the mesangium. Ig deposits are found solely in the mesangium; in this setting the prognosis is good and renal failure is rare. If Ig and C' extend outside the mesangium into capillary loops, the prognosis worsens. Associated glomerular histologic changes in ascending order of severity are (1) focal proliferative, (2) membranoproliferative, or (3) diffuse proliferative (see Chap. 224). Membranous changes without proliferation occur but are not common. In addition to those histologic categories, *active disease* and *increased risk of progression to renal failure* are associated with glomerular necrosis, epithelial crescents, hyaline thrombi, or leukocyte infiltrates and with mononuclear cell infiltrates in the tubular interstitium or necrotizing vasculitis. In addition, measures of *chronicity* are important, as they are associated with a *high incidence of renal failure.* They include glomerular sclerosis, fibrous crescents, interstitial fibrosis, and tubular

atrophy. Focal proliferative and membranous changes are associated with an 85 percent 5-year survival; diffuse proliferative glomerulonephritis is associated with 70 percent 5-year survival. Progression from focal to diffuse lesions can occur.

Laboratory manifestations   The presence of characteristic antibodies (Table 262-1) confirms the diagnosis of SLE. Antinuclear antibodies (ANA) are the best screening test. If the test substrate is living human nuclei as in WIL-2 or HEP-2 cells from tissue culture, more than 95 percent of lupus patients will have positive tests. The more frequently used rodent liver or kidney does not detect as wide a range of ANA or anticytoplasmic antibodies; approximately 85 percent of SLE serums are positive on those substrates. A positive ANA is not specific for SLE; ANA occur (usually in low titer) in some normal individuals; the frequency increases with aging. Furthermore, other autoimmune diseases, acute viral infections, and chronic inflammatory processes may cause ANA positivity. Therefore, a positive ANA supports a diagnosis of SLE but *is not specific;* a negative ANA makes the diagnosis unlikely, but not impossible. Antibodies to dsDNA and to Sm are relatively specific for SLE; other autoantibodies listed in Table 262-1 are not. High serum levels of ANA and anti-DNA and low levels of complement usually reflect disease activity, especially in patients with nephritis. Serum levels of cryoglobulins or other immune complexes occasionally correlate with disease activity. Total functional hemolytic complement (CH_{50}) levels are the most sensitive measure of complement activation but also are the most subject to laboratory error. Quantitative levels of C3 and C4 are widely available. Very low levels of CH_{50} with normal levels of C3 suggest inherited deficiency of a complement component.

Hematologic abnormalities are common and include anemia (usually normochromic, normocytic, but occasionally hemolytic), leukopenia, lymphopenia, and thrombocytopenia. In some patients elevation of the Westergren erythrocyte sedimentation rate correlates with disease activity.

Urinalysis and serum creatinine should be measured periodically in patients with SLE. When active nephritis is present, the urinalysis usually shows proteinuria, microscopic hematuria, and cellular or granular casts. Renal biopsy is indicated when results would influence therapeutic decisions (see discussion under "Clinical Manifestations").

Other tests which may be abnormal in SLE include false-positive tests for syphilis and abnormal coagulation tests, especially a prolonged partial thromboplastin time. Both are related to antibodies to cardiolipin, discussed under "Clinical Manifestations." Rheumatoid factors are present in 30 to 50 percent of patients.

The tests which are useful for diagnosis and for following the clinical course of patients with SLE are listed in Table 262-3.

Pregnancy   Since SLE is predominantly a disease of young women, pregnancy is a frequent occurrence. Fertility rates are normal in patients with SLE, but the rate of spontaneous abortion and stillbirths is high (30 to 50 percent), especially in women with lupus anticoagulant and/or antibodies to cardiolipin. There may be increased flare-ups of SLE during the first trimester (SLE may begin during pregnancy) and especially during the first 6 weeks postpartum. If severe renal or cardiac disease are absent and SLE is controlled, many patients complete pregnancy safely and deliver normal infants. Glucocorticoids are inactivated by placental enzymes and do not cause fetal abnormalities except for low birth weights. Neonatal lupus (related to the presence of anti-Ro in maternal serum) occurs in infants but is rare; two syndromes are seen—a transient DLE-like rash and congenital heart block.

DIFFERENTIAL DIAGNOSIS   The American Rheumatism Association has developed diagnostic criteria for SLE. Manifestations which are included are indicated by asterisks in Table 262-2. Any four of those in addition to two characteristic autoantibodies establish the diagnosis of definite SLE. Disease confined to one or two systems may be more difficult to classify. The disorders with which SLE can be confused include rheumatoid arthritis; skin disorders such as urticaria, erythema multiforme, rosacea, lichen planus; neurologic disorders such as idiopathic epilepsy or multiple sclerosis; hematologic disorders such as idiopathic thrombocytopenic purpura; and psychiatric disorders. In these cases, the physician may wish to delay a diagnosis of SLE until additional manifestations appear. It may also be difficult to distinguish SLE from other autoimmune disorders such as dermatomyositis and overlap syndromes. Some authorities classify patients with features of SLE, rheumatoid arthritis, polymyositis, and scleroderma, accompanied by high titers of anti-RNP, as "mixed connective tissue disease" (Chap. 265) and report a low incidence of nephritis and CNS disease and a high incidence of pulmonary disease and evolution into scleroderma. It is impossible to classify some patients into a definite category; therapy should be directed toward the dominant manifestations. The possibility of drug-induced lupus should always be ruled out.

Drug-induced lupus   Several drugs can cause a syndrome resembling SLE in individuals without any obvious predisposition to the disease. The most common offender is procainamide, which induces ANA in 50 to 75 percent of individuals within a few months; 20 percent of patients receiving the drug develop clinical drug-induced LE. Hydralazine induces ANA in 25 to 30 percent of individuals, and lupus-like symptoms in 10 percent. Both procainamide and hydralazine-induced lupus occur more commonly in women, are uncommon in blacks, and are more likely to occur in individuals who acetylate the drug slowly; this is especially true for hydralazine. The clinical syndrome consists of polyarthralgias and systemic symptoms in most patients. Polyarthritis occurs in 25 to 50 percent, and pleuropericarditis in 30 percent, of patients with hydralazine and 50 percent of patients with procainamide-induced lupus. Other manifestations typical of idiopathic SLE are unusual, including nephritis and CNS involvement. All patients with drug-induced lupus are ANA-positive; most have antibodies to histones. Antibodies to dsDNA and hypocomplementemia are rarely present—a helpful point in distinguishing drug-induced from idiopathic lupus. Anemia, leukopenia, lupus anticoagulant, thrombocytopenia, cryoglobulins, rheumatoid factors, false-positive VDRL, and positive direct Coombs' tests can occur. The initial therapeutic approach should be discontinuance of the suspect drug; most patients improve in days or a few weeks. In patients with severe symptoms, a short course (2 to 10 weeks) of glucocorticoids is indicated. Clinical symptoms rarely persist more than 6 months; ANA may remain positive for years. Other drugs which infrequently induce lupus-like illnesses include isoniazid, chlorpromazine, *d*-penicillamine, practolol, methyldopa, oral contraceptives, and possibly hydantoins and ethosuximide. Most lupus-inducing drugs can be used safely in patients with idiopathic lupus if there are no suitable alternatives.

Prognosis   The overall survival in patients with SLE is approximately 71 percent over 10 years. Patients with severe involvement of the brain, lungs, heart, or kidney have the worst outcomes in terms of survival and disability. Infections and renal failure are the leading causes of death.

TREATMENT   There is no cure for SLE. Complete remissions occur but are rare, so patient and physician should plan to control acute, severe flare-ups and to develop maintenance therapies in which symptoms are suppressed to an acceptable level, usually at the cost of some drug side effects. From 20 to 30 percent of SLE patients have mild disease with no life-threatening manifestations. However, their disease may be disabling because of pain and fatigue. These patients should be managed without glucocorticoids. Arthralgias, arthritis, myalgias, fever, and mild serositis may improve on non-steroidal anti-inflammatory drugs (NSAID) including salicylates. However, some NSAID toxicities are especially frequent in SLE patients (hepatitis, aseptic meningitis, and renal impairment). The dermatitides of SLE (including DLE), and occasionally lupus arthritis,

may respond to antimalarials. Doses of 400 mg of hydroxychloroquine daily are associated with improvement of skin lesions in a few weeks in patients destined to respond. Side effects include retinal toxicity, rash, myopathy, and neuropathy. Regular ophthalmologic examinations should be performed at least every 6-months, since retinal toxicity is related to cumulative dose. Other therapies for skin rash include use of sunscreens (an SPF rating of 15 or higher is recommended) to prevent rashes, and of topical or intralesional glucocorticoids if rashes develop. Systemic glucocorticoids should be reserved for patients with disabling, severe lesions.

Life-threatening and severely disabling manifestations of SLE are treated with high doses of *glucocorticoids* (1 to 2 mg/kg per day). When the disease is active, glucocorticoids should be given in divided doses every 8 to 12 h. After the disease has been controlled for several days, doses should be consolidated to one morning dose; thereafter, the daily dose should be tapered as rapidly as clinical disease permits. Ideally, patients should be slowly converted to alternate-day therapy with a single morning dose of a short-acting glucocorticoid (prednisone, prednisolone, methylprednisolone) to minimize side effects. However, the disease may flare-up on alternate days, in which case the lowest single daily dose which suppresses symptoms and major organ damage should be used. Undesirable side effects of chronic glucocorticoid therapy include cushingoid habitus, weight gain, hypertension, infection, capillary fragility, acne, hirsutism, accelerated osteoporosis, ischemic necrosis of bone, cataracts, glaucoma, diabetes mellitus, myopathy, hypokalemia, irregular menses, irritability, insomnia, and psychosis. Prednisone doses of 15 mg daily (or less) given before the hour of noon usually do not suppress the hypothalamic pituitary axis. Side effects can be partially minimized by being alert for them; hyperglycemia, hypertension, edema, and hypokalemia should be treated. Infections should be identified early and treated promptly. Immunizations with influenza and pneumococcal vaccines are safe and generally effective in patients with stable disease. Supplemental calcium (1000 to 1500 mg daily) with vitamin D (50,000 units weekly) in carefully selected patients (normal 24-h urine calcium, normal serum calcium, ambulatory) receiving stable doses of glucocorticoids may help maintain bone mass. Some acutely ill lupus patients, including those with diffuse nephritis, have been treated with 3 to 5 days of 1000-mg intravenous "pulses" of methylprednisolone, followed by maintenance daily or alternate-day glucocorticoids. It is unclear whether there are any special advantages or toxicities to this regimen.

The use of *cytotoxic agents* (azathioprine, chlorambucil, cyclophosphamide) in SLE is somewhat controversial. Their use in lupus nephritis is probably associated with a lower rate of renal failure and fewer disease flare-ups, and permits faster tapering to low maintenance doses of glucocorticoids. Undesirable side effects include bone marrow suppression, irreversible gonadal failure (in approximately 30 percent of patients), hepatotoxicity (azathioprine), bladder toxicity (cyclophosphamide), and an increased risk for malignancies. If a lupus patient has life-threatening disease unresponsive to glucocorticoids, or requires an unacceptably high maintenance dose of glucocorticoids, it is appropriate to consider cytotoxic drugs. Azathioprine is the least toxic; it may be given in a dose of 2 to 3 mg/kg per day orally. Cyclophosphamide is the most effective and the most toxic. Intravenous pulse doses (10 to 15 mg/kg) given once every 4 weeks have less urinary bladder toxicity and more rapid onset of action (5 to 15 days) than daily oral doses, but bone marrow suppression can be severe. Cyclophosphamide can also be used in daily oral doses (1.5 to 2.5 mg/kg per day), or in combination with low doses of azathioprine (0.5 to 1 mg/kg per day of each). After disease activity has been controlled for several months, tapering of cytotoxic agents and attempts to discontinue them are appropriate.

Several experimental therapies for SLE are being studied, including plasmapheresis, total-lymph node irradiation, cyclosporine, and sex hormone therapy.

Patients with nephrotic syndrome often maintain stable renal function in spite of persistent edema and hypoalbuminemia; hypertension is usually a concomitant problem. Such patients should be treated with 3 to 6 months of high-dose glucocorticoid therapy; if proteinuria does not diminish, the drug should be tapered and discontinued and treatment directed toward control of hypertension and hyperlipidemia.

It is appropriate in patients with end-stage nephritis to plan for dialysis or transplantation; their survival is similar to that of patients with other immune nephritides.

In the subsets of patients with SLE who do not have progressive, severe disease, patients should be informed that although SLE is a chronic, potentially serious disease, some patients can lead relatively normal lives if their disease is appropriately managed.

REFERENCES

AUSTIN HA III et al: Prognostic factors in lupus nephritis. Am J Med 75:382, 1983

CARETTE S et al: Controlled studies of oral immunosuppressive drugs in lupus nephritis. Ann Intern Med 99:1, 1983

GINZLER E et al: A multi-center study of outcome in systemic lupus erythematosus. I. Entry variables as predictors of prognosis. Arthritis Rheum 25:601, 1982

ROTHFIELD N: Systemic lupus erythematosus: Clinical aspects and treatment, in *Arthritis and Allied Conditions*, 10th ed, DJ McCarty (ed), Philadelphia, Lea & Febiger, 1985, chap 61, pp 911–935

STEINBERG AD et al: Systemic lupus erythematosus: Insights from animal models. Ann Intern Med 100:714, 1984

STEVENS MB, HAHN BH: Therapy of systemic lupus erythematosus. Bull Rheum Dis 32:35, 1982

Systemic lupus erythematosus, GRV Hughes (ed). Clin Rheum Dis 8:1, 1982

TAN EM: Systemic lupus erythematosus: Immunological aspects, in *Arthritis and Allied Conditions*, 10th ed, DJ McCarty (ed), Philadelphia, Lea & Febiger, 1985, chap 62, pp 936–941

——— et al: The 1982 revised criteria for the classification of systemic lupus erythematosus. Arthritis Rheum 25:1271, 1982

TSOKAS GC, BALOW JE: Cellular immune responses in systemic lupus erythematosus. Prog Allergy 35:93, 1984

263 RHEUMATOID ARTHRITIS

PETER E. LIPSKY

Rheumatoid arthritis (RA) is a chronic, multisystem disease of unknown etiology. Although there are a variety of systemic manifestations, the characteristic feature of RA is persistent inflammatory synovitis, usually involving peripheral joints in a symmetric distribution. The potential of the synovial inflammation to cause cartilage destruction and bone erosions and subsequently joint deformities is the hallmark of the disease. Despite its destructive potential, the course of RA can be quite variable. Some patients may experience only a mild oligoarticular illness of brief duration with minimal joint damage, while others will have a relentless progressive polyarthritis with marked joint deformity. Most patients will experience an intermediate course.

EPIDEMIOLOGY The prevalence of definite RA is approximately 1 percent of the population (range 0.3 to 2.1 percent); women are affected approximately three times more often than men. The prevalence increases with age, and sex differences diminish in the older age group. RA is seen throughout the world and affects all races. The onset is most frequent during the fourth and fifth decade of life, with 80 percent of all patients developing the disease between the ages of 35 and 50.

Family studies indicate a genetic predisposition. For example, severe RA is found at approximately four times the expected rate in first-degree relatives of individuals with seropositive disease. Moreover, 30 percent of monozygous twins are concordant for RA, whereas only 5 percent of dizygous twins are concordant. The role of genetic influences in the etiology of RA was established by the demonstration of an association with the class II major histocompatibility gene complex antigen, HLA-DR4. As many as 70 percent of whites or Japanese with classic or definite RA express HLA-DR4 compared with 28 percent of control individuals. An association with HLA-DR4 has also been noted in blacks, Latin Americans, and Chippewa Indians, although the incidence of HLA-DR4 positivity in individuals with RA in these groups is not as great as in whites. In a number of groups, including Ashkenazi Jews, non-Ashkenazi Jews, Asian Indians, and Yakima Indians, there is no association between the development of RA and HLA-DR4. It was thought initially that HLA-DR4 was associated with seropositive RA, but not with the development of rheumatoid factor in normal people. Recent studies however, have suggested that HLA-DR4 may be associated with severe erosive disease especially in younger women rather than with seropositive disease. No association with HLA-DR4 has been found in individuals with nonerosive RA independent of the occurrence of rheumatoid factor. The explanation for the association of HLA-DR4 and RA remains obscure, although the relationship of the class II histocompatibility gene complex products to immune response genes has suggested that these determinants may play a role in controlling the immunopathogenesis of RA.

There appears to be a genetic predisposition for the development of certain toxic reactions induced by drugs used to treat RA. For example, the presence of the HLA-DR3 allele is highly associated with the development of side effects to gold therapy, including proteinuria, thrombocytopenia, and perhaps skin rash. Similarly, the presence of this allele appears to predispose to the development of proteinuria following therapy with D-penicillamine.

CLINICAL MANIFESTATIONS **Onset** Characteristically, RA is a chronic polyarthritis. In approximately two-thirds of patients, it begins insidiously with fatigue, anorexia, generalized weakness, and vague musculoskeletal symptoms until the appearance of synovitis becomes apparent. This prodrome may persist for weeks or months and defy diagnosis. Specific symptoms usually appear gradually as several joints, especially those of the hands, wrists, knees, and feet, become affected in a symmetric fashion. In approximately 10 percent of individuals, the onset is more acute with a rapid development of polyarthritis often accompanied by constitutional symptoms including fever, lymphadenopathy, and splenomegaly. In approximately one-third of patients, symptoms may initially be confined to one or a few joints. Although the pattern of joint involvement may remain asymmetric in a few patients, a symmetric pattern is more typical.

Signs and symptoms of articular disease Pain, swelling, and tenderness may initially be poorly localized to the joints. Pain in affected joints, aggravated by movement, is the most common manifestation of established RA. It corresponds in pattern to the joint involvement but does not always correlate with the degree of apparent inflammation. Generalized stiffness is frequent and is usually greatest after periods of inactivity. Morning stiffness of greater than 1-h duration is an almost invariable feature of inflammatory arthritis and serves to distinguish it from various noninflammatory joint disorders. The length and intensity of the stiffness can be used as a crude assessment of disease activity. The majority of patients will experience constitutional symptoms such as weakness, easy fatigability, anorexia, and weight loss. Although fever to 40°C occurs on occasion, temperature elevation in excess of 38°C is unusual and suggests the presence of an intercurrent problem such as infection.

Clinically, synovial inflammation causes swelling, tenderness, and limitation of motion. Warmth is usually evident on examination, especially of large joints such as the knee, but erythema is infrequent. Pain originates predominantly from the joint capsule, which is abundantly supplied with pain fibers and is markedly sensitive to stretching or distention. Joint swelling results from accumulation of synovial fluid, hypertrophy of the synovium, and thickening of the joint capsule. Initially, motion is limited by pain. The inflamed joint is usually held in flexion to maximize joint volume and minimize distention of the capsule. Later, fibrous, bony ankylosis, or soft tissue contractures lead to fixed deformities.

Although inflammation can affect any diarthrodial joint, RA most often causes symmetric arthritis with characteristic involvement of certain specific joints such as the proximal interphalangeal and metacarpophalangeal joints. The distal interphalangeal joints are rarely involved. Synovitis of the wrist joints is a nearly uniform feature of RA and may lead to limitation of motion, deformity, and median nerve entrapment (carpal tunnel syndrome). Synovitis of the elbow joint often leads to flexion contractures that may develop early in the disease. The knee joint is commonly involved with synovial hypertrophy, chronic effusion, and frequently ligamentous laxity. Pain and swelling behind the knee may be caused by extension of inflamed synovium into the popliteal space (Baker's cyst). Arthritis in the forefoot, ankles, and subtalar joints can produce severe pain with ambulation as well as a number of deformities. Axial involvement is usually limited to the upper cervical spine. Involvement of the lumbar spine is not seen, and lower back pain cannot be ascribed to rheumatoid inflammation. On occasion, inflammation from the synovial joints and bursae of the upper cervical spine leads to atlantoaxial subluxation. This usually presents as pain in the occiput but on rare occasions may lead to compression of the spinal cord.

With persistent inflammation, a variety of characteristic deformities develop. These can be attributed to a number of pathologic events including laxity of supporting soft tissue structures from destruction or weakening of ligaments, tendons, and the joint capsule; cartilage destruction; muscle imbalance; and unopposed physical forces associated with the use of affected joints. Characteristic deformities of the hand include (1) radial deviation at the wrist with ulnar deviation of the digits often with palmar subluxation of the proximal phalanges ("Z" deformity); (2) hyperextension of the proximal interphalangeal joints, with compensatory flexion of the distal interphalangeal joints (swan neck deformity); (3) flexion deformity of the proximal interphalangeal joints and extension of the distal interphalangeal joints (boutonnière deformity); and (4) hyperextension of the first interphalangeal joint and flexion of the first metacarpophalangeal joint with a consequent loss of thumb mobility and pinch. Typical deformities may also develop in the feet, including eversion at the hindfoot (subtalar joint), plantar subluxation of the metatarsal heads, widening of the forefoot, hallux valgus, and lateral deviation and dorsal subluxation of the toes.

Extraarticular manifestations RA is a systemic disease with a variety of extraarticular manifestations. Although these occur frequently, not all of them have clinical significance. However, on occasion, they may be the major evidence of disease activity and source of morbidity and require management per se. As a rule, these manifestations take place in individuals with high titers of rheumatoid factors.

Rheumatoid nodules develop in 20 to 30 percent of persons with RA. They are usually found on periarticular structures, extensor surfaces, or other areas subjected to mechanical pressure, but they can develop elsewhere including the pleura and meninges. Common locations include the olecranon bursa, the proximal ulna, the Achilles tendon, and the occiput. Nodules vary in size and consistency and are rarely symptomatic, but on occasion they break down as a result of trauma or become infected. They are found almost invariably in individuals with circulating rheumatoid factor.

Clinical weakness and atrophy of skeletal muscle are common. Muscle atrophy may be evident within weeks of the onset of RA and usually is most apparent in musculature approximating affected joints. Muscle biopsy may show type II fiber atrophy and muscle fiber necrosis with or without a mononuclear cell infiltrate.

Rheumatoid vasculitis which can affect nearly any organ system is seen in patients with severe RA and high titers of circulating rheumatoid factor. In its most aggressive form, rheumatoid vasculitis can cause polyneuropathy and mononeuritis multiplex, cutaneous ulceration and dermal necrosis, digital gangrene, and visceral infarction. While such widespread vasculitis is very rare, more limited forms are not uncommon, especially in white patients with high titers

of rheumatoid factor. Neurovascular disease presenting either as a mild distal sensory neuropathy or as mononeuritis multiplex may be the only signs of vasculitis. Cutaneous vasculitis usually presents as crops of small brown spots in the nail beds, nail folds, and digital pulp. Larger ischemic ulcers, especially in the lower extremity, may also develop. Myocardial infarction secondary to rheumatoid vasculitis has been reported as has vasculitic involvement of lungs, bowel, liver, spleen, pancreas, lymph nodes, and testes. Renal vasculitis is rare.

Pleuropulmonary manifestations, which are more commonly observed in men, include pleural disease, interstitial fibrosis, pleuropulmonary nodules, pneumonitis, and arteritis. Evidence of pleuritis is found commonly at autopsy, but symptomatic disease during life is infrequent. Typically, the pleural fluid contains very low levels of glucose in the absence of infection. Pleural fluid complement is also low compared with the serum level when these are related to the total protein concentration. Pulmonary fibrosis can produce impairment of the diffusing capacity of the lung. Pulmonary nodules may appear singly or in clusters. When they appear in individuals with pneumoconiosis, a diffuse nodular fibrotic process (Caplan's syndrome) may develop. On occasion, pulmonary nodules may cavitate and produce a pneumothorax or bronchopleural fistula. Rarely pulmonary hypertension secondary to obliteration of the pulmonary vasculature occurs. In addition to pleuropulmonary disease, upper airway obstruction from cricoarytenoid arthritis or laryngeal nodules may develop.

Clinically apparent heart disease attributed to the rheumatoid process is rare, but evidence of asymptomatic pericarditis is found at autopsy in 50 percent of cases. Pericardial fluid has a low glucose level and is frequently associated with the occurrence of pleural effusion. Although pericarditis is usually asymptomatic, on rare occasions death has occurred from tamponade. Chronic constrictive pericarditis may also occur.

RA tends to spare the central nervous system directly, although vasculitis can cause peripheral neuropathy. *Neurologic manifestations* may also result from atlantoaxial or midcervical spine subluxations. Nerve entrapment secondary to proliferative synovitis or joint deformities may produce neuropathies of median, ulnar, radial (interosseus branch), or anterior tibial nerves.

The rheumatoid process involves the *eye* in less than 1 percent of patients. Affected individuals usually have long-standing disease and nodules. The two principal manifestations are episcleritis, which is usually mild and transient, and scleritis, which involves the deeper coats of the eye and is a more serious inflammatory condition. Histologically, the lesion is similar to a rheumatoid nodule and may result in thinning and perforation of the globe (scleromalacia perforans). Fifteen to twenty percent of persons with RA may develop Sjögren's syndrome with attendant keratoconjunctivitis sicca.

Felty's syndrome consists of chronic RA, splenomegaly, neutropenia, and on occasion anemia and thrombocytopenia. It is most common in individuals with long-standing disease. These patients frequently have high titers of rheumatoid factor, subcutaneous nodules, and other manifestations of systemic rheumatoid disease. Circulating immune complexes are often present, and evidence of complement consumption may be seen. Felty's syndrome may develop after joint inflammation has regressed. The leukopenia is a selective neutropenia with polymorphonuclear leukocyte counts of less than 1500 per cubic millimeter, and sometimes less than 1000 per cubic millimeter. Bone marrow examination usually reveals moderate hypercellularity with a paucity of mature neutrophils. However, the bone marrow may be normal, hyperactive, or hypoactive; maturation arrest may be seen. Hypersplenism has been proposed as one of the causes of leukopenia, but splenomegaly is not invariably found and splenectomy does not always correct the abnormality. Excessive margination of granulocytes caused by antibodies to these cells, complement activation, or binding of immune complexes may contribute to granulocytopenia. Patients with Felty's syndrome have increased frequency of infections usually associated with neutropenia. The cause of the increased susceptibility to infection is related to the defective function of polymorphonuclear leukocytes as well as the decreased number of cells.

Osteoporosis secondary to rheumatoid involvement is common and may be aggravated by corticosteroid therapy and immobilization. Osteopenia involves both juxtaarticular bone and long bones distant from involved joints.

LABORATORY FINDINGS No tests are specific for diagnosing RA. However, rheumatoid factors, which are autoantibodies reactive with IgG, are found in more than two-thirds of adults with the disease. Widely utilized tests largely detect IgM rheumatoid factors. Although rheumatoid factors are found in less than 5 percent of healthy persons, they are not specific for RA. The frequency of rheumatoid factor in the general population increases with age, and 10 to 20 percent of individuals over 65 years old have a positive test. In addition, a number of conditions besides RA are associated with the presence of rheumatoid factor. These include systemic lupus erythematosus, Sjögren's syndrome, chronic liver disease, sarcoidosis, interstitial pulmonary fibrosis, infectious mononucleosis, hepatitis B, tuberculosis, leprosy, syphilis, subacute bacterial endocarditis, visceral leishmaniasis, schistosomiasis, and malaria. In addition, rheumatoid factor may appear transiently in normal individuals after vaccination or transfusion and may also be found in relatives of individuals with RA.

The presence of rheumatoid factor does not establish the diagnosis of RA but can be of prognostic significance because patients with high titers tend to have more severe and progressive disease with extraarticular manifestations. Rheumatoid factor is uniformly found in patients with nodules or vasculitis. Less than one-third of unselected patients with a positive test for rheumatoid factor will be found to have RA. The test is not useful as a screening procedure but can be employed to confirm a diagnosis in individuals with a suggestive clinical presentation and, if present in high titer, to designate patients at risk for severe systemic disease.

Normochromic, normocytic anemia is frequently present in active RA. It is thought to reflect ineffective erythropoiesis; large stores of iron are found in the bone marrow. In general, anemia and thrombocytosis correlate with disease activity. The white blood cell count is usually normal, but a mild leukocytosis may be present. Leukopenia may also exist without the full-blown picture of Felty's syndrome. Eosinophilia, when present, usually reflects severe systemic disease.

The erythrocyte sedimentation rate is increased in nearly all patients with active RA. A variety of other acute phase reactants including ceruloplasmin and C-reactive protein are also elevated, and generally such elevations correlate with disease activity and the likelihood of progressive joint damage.

Synovial fluid analysis confirms the presence of inflammatory arthritis, although none of the findings is specific. The fluid is usually turbid, with reduced viscosity, increased protein content, and a slightly decreased or normal glucose concentration. The white cell count varies between 5 and 50,000 per cubic millimeter; polymorphonuclear leukocytes predominate. Total hemolytic complement, C3, and C4 are markedly diminished in synovial fluid relative to total protein concentration as a result of activation of the classic complement pathway by locally produced immune complexes.

When monoclonal antibodies specific for T-lymphocyte subsets are used to examine peripheral blood mononuclear cells of patients with RA, those with active disease are found to have an increased ratio of T4:T8 (helper-inducer/suppressor-cytotoxic) cells. In addition, an increased number of circulating T cells express class II major histocompatibility gene complex products (HLA-DR), an indication of T-cell activation. This finding is most frequent in patients with active joint disease.

RADIOGRAPHIC EVALUATION Early in the disease, roentgenograms of the affected joints are usually not helpful in establishing a diagnosis. They reveal only that which is apparent from physical examination, namely evidence of soft tissue swelling and joint effusion. As the disease progresses, abnormalities become more pronounced, but none of the radiographic findings are diagnostic of RA. The diagnosis, however, is supported by a characteristic pattern of abnormalities including the tendency toward symmetric involvement. Juxtaarticular osteopenia may become apparent within weeks of onset. Loss of articular cartilage and bone erosions develop after months of sustained activity. The primary value of radiography is to determine the extent of cartilage destruction and bone erosion produced by the disease, particularly when one is considering therapy with disease-modifying drugs or surgical intervention.

CLINICAL COURSE AND PROGNOSIS The course of RA is quite variable and difficult to predict in an individual patient. Five years after the onset of RA, evidence of disease activity may be found in as few as one-third of all patients. However, RA can cause significant social and financial disadvantages in those patients with persistently active disease. Most patients experience persistent but fluctuating disease activity, accompanied by a variable degree of joint deformity. Approximately 15 percent have a short-lived inflammatory process that remits without major deformity, whereas 10 percent experience relentlessly progressive disease leading to marked deformity and disability.

Several features of patients with RA appear to have prognostic significance. Remissions of disease activity are most likely to occur during the first year. White females tend to have more persistent synovitis and progressively erosive disease than males. Persons who present with high titers of rheumatoid factor, C-reactive protein, and haptoglobin also have a worse prognosis, as do individuals with subcutaneous nodules or radiographic evidence of erosions at the time of initial evaluation. Although sustained disease activity of more than 1 year's duration portends a poor outcome, the rate of progression of joint abnormalities is not constant; the greatest progression takes place during the first 6 years of disease and at a much slower rate thereafter.

The median life expectancy of persons with RA is shortened by 3 to 7 years. Of the 2.5-fold increase in mortality rate, RA itself is a contributing feature in 15 to 25 percent. The increased mortality rate seems to be limited to patients with more severe articular disease and can be attributed largely to infection and gastrointestinal bleeding. Drug therapy may also play a role in the increased mortality rate seen in these individuals.

DIAGNOSIS The diagnosis of RA is easily made in persons with typical established disease. In a majority of patients, the disease assumes its characteristic clinical features within 1 to 2 years of onset. The typical picture of bilateral symmetric inflammatory polyarthritis involving small and large joints in both the upper and lower extremities with sparing of the axial skeleton except the cervical spine suggests the diagnosis. Constitutional features indicative of the inflammatory nature of the disease, such as morning stiffness, support the diagnosis. Demonstration of subcutaneous nodules is a helpful diagnostic feature. Additionally, the presence of rheumatoid factor, inflammatory synovial fluid with increased numbers of polymorphonuclear leukocytes, and radiographic findings of juxtaarticular bone demineralization and erosions of the affected joints substantiate the diagnosis.

The diagnosis is somewhat more difficult early in the course when only constitutional symptoms or intermittent arthralgias or arthritis in an asymmetric distribution may be present. A period of observation may be necessary before the diagnosis can be established. A definitive diagnosis of RA depends predominantly on characteristic clinical features and the exclusion of other inflammatory processes. The isolated finding of a positive test for rheumatoid factor or an elevated erythrocyte sedimentation rate, especially in an older person with joint pains, should not itself be used as evidence of RA.

The American Rheumatism Association has developed criteria for the diagnosis of RA (Table 263-1). The presence of seven of these criteria establishes the diagnosis of classic RA, whereas five criteria indicate definite RA, and three, probable RA. Although these criteria were developed as a means of disease classification for epidemiologic purposes, they are useful as guidelines for establishing the diagnosis. Failure to meet these criteria, however, especially during the early stages of the disease, does not exclude the diagnosis.

PATHOLOGY AND PATHOGENESIS Microvascular injury and an increase in the number of synovial lining cells appear to be the earliest lesions of RA. The nature of the insult causing this response is not known. Subsequently, an increased number of synovial lining cells is seen along with perivascular infiltration with mononuclear cells. As the process continues, the synovium becomes edematous and protrudes into the joint cavity as villus projections.

Light-microscopic examination discloses a characteristic constellation of features which include hyperplasia and hypertrophy of the synovial lining cells, focal or segmental vascular changes, and infiltration with mononuclear cells often collected into aggregates or follicles around small blood vessels. The mononuclear cell collections are variable in composition and size. The predominant infiltrating cell is the T lymphocyte. T4 (helper-inducer) cells predominate over T8 (suppressor-cytotoxic) cells and are frequently found in close proximity to HLA-DR–positive macrophages. Although this pathologic picture is typical of RA, it can also be seen in a variety of other chronic inflammatory arthritides.

Although the etiologic stimuli have not been identified, established rheumatoid synovitis is characterized by persistent immunologic activity. The infiltrating T cells express activation antigens such as HLA-DR and produce a variety of lymphokines such as interleukin 2, γ-interferon, macrophage migration inhibition factor, monocyte chemotactic factor, and leukocyte migration inhibition factor which have been isolated from rheumatoid synovial fluid. Evidence of B-cell activation can also be found in the inflamed synovium, and plasma cells producing immunoglobulin and rheumatoid factor are characteristic features of rheumatoid synovitis. Large numbers of macrophages are also found in rheumatoid synovium. In addition, the macrophage-derived cytokine interleukin 1 can be found in rheumatoid synovial fluid. This factor has a wide spectrum of activities both within and outside the immune system and may explain some of the local and systemic manifestations of RA.

These findings have suggested that the propagation of RA is an immunologically mediated event, although the original initiating stimulus has not been characterized. One view is that the inflammatory process in the tissue is driven by the T4 helper-inducer cells infiltrating the synovium. Evidence for this includes (1) the predominance of T4 cells in the synovium; (2) the local production of lymphokines by these infiltrating T cells; and (3) amelioration of the disease by removal of T cells by thoracic duct drainage or suppression of their function by total lymphoid irradiation. Since T lymphocytes produce a variety of cytokines that promote B-cell proliferation and differentiation into antibody-forming cells, T-cell activation may also promote local B-cell stimulation. The resultant production of immunoglobulin and rheumatoid factor can lead to immune-complex formation with consequent complement activation and exacerbation of the inflammatory process by the production of anaphylatoxins and chemotactic factors. The tissue inflammation is reminiscent of delayed-type hypersensitivity reactions occurring in response to soluble antigens or microorganisms. It is, however, unclear whether this represents a response to a persistent exogenous antigen or to altered autoantigens such as collagen, or immunoglobulin. Alternatively, it could represent persistent responsiveness to activated autologous cells such as might occur as a result of Epstein-Barr virus infection. Also, the persistent inflammation could result from deranged immunoregulatory mechanisms.

Overriding the chronic inflammation in the synovial tissue is an acute inflammatory process in the synovial fluid. The exudative synovial fluid contains a large number of polymorphonuclear leukocytes and relatively few mononuclear cells. A number of mechanisms play a role in stimulating the exudation of synovial fluid. Locally produced immune complexes can activate complement and generate anaphylatoxins and chemotactic factors. Local production by mononuclear phagocytes of factors such as interleukin 1 and leukotriene B4, which can act as powerful chemotactic attractants, may also play a role in the emigration of polymorphonuclear leukocytes. In addition, vasoactive mediators such as histamine produced by mast cells may also facilitate the exudation of inflammatory cells into the synovial fluid. Once in the synovial fluid, the polymorphonuclear leukocytes can ingest immune complexes with the resultant production of reactive oxygen metabolites and other inflammatory mediators, further adding to the inflammatory milieu. The production of large amounts of cyclooxygenase and lipoxygenase pathway products of arachidonic acid metabolism by cells in the synovial fluid and tissue further accentuate the signs and symptoms of inflammation.

The precise mechanism by which bone and cartilage destruction occurs has not been completely resolved. The majority of destruction occurs in juxtaposition to the inflamed synovium or pannus that spreads to cover the articular cartilage. This vascular granulation tissue is composed of proliferating fibroblasts, small blood vessels, and a variable number of mononuclear cells. The macrophage-derived cytokine interleukin 1 may play an important role by stimulating the cells of the pannus to release collagenase and other neutral proteases. Cytokines such as interleukin 1 or catabolin may also activate chondrocytes in situ, stimulating them to produce proteolytic enzymes that can degrade cartilage locally. In addition, other mechanisms may contribute to the local demineralization of bone, including the production of osteoclast activating factor by activated T cells and prostaglandin E_2 by fibroblasts and macrophages.

TREATMENT General principles Since the etiology of RA is unknown and the pathogenesis speculative, therapy remains empirical. None of the therapeutic interventions are curative, and, therefore, all must be viewed as palliative, aimed at relieving the signs and symptoms of the disease. The various therapies employed are directed at nonspecific suppression of the inflammatory process in the hope of ameliorating symptoms and preventing progressive damage to articular structures.

Management of patients with RA involves an interdisciplinary approach which attempts to deal with the various problems that these individuals have with functional as well as psychosocial interactions. A variety of physical therapies may be useful in decreasing the symptoms of RA. Rest ameliorates symptoms and can be an important component of the total therapeutic program. In addition, splinting to reduce unwanted motion of inflamed joints may be useful. Exercise directed at maintaining muscle strength and joint mobility without exacerbating joint inflammation is also an important aspect of the therapeutic regimen. A variety of orthotic devices can be helpful in supporting and aligning deformed joints to reduce pain and improve function.

Medical management of RA involves two general approaches. The first is the use of aspirin and other nonsteroidal anti-inflammatory drugs, simple analgesics, and if necessary, low-dose glucocorticoids to control the symptoms and signs of the local inflammatory process. These agents are rapidly effective at mitigating signs and symptoms, but they appear to exert little effect on the progression of the disease. A second group of drugs includes a variety of agents that have been

TABLE 263-1 American Rheumatism Association criteria for the diagnosis of rheumatoid arthritis*

1 Morning stiffness
2 Pain on motion or tenderness in at least one joint
3 Swelling (soft tissue thickening or fluid) in at least one joint
4 Swelling of at least one other joint
5 Symmetric joint swelling
6 Subcutaneous nodules
7 Radiologic changes typical of RA
8 Demonstration of ''rheumatoid factor'' in serum
9 Poor mucin precipitate from synovial fluid
10 Characteristic histologic changes in synovium
11 Characteristic histologic changes in nodules

* *Criteria 1 to 5 must be continuous for at least 6 weeks. Criteria 2 to 6 must be observed by a physician. The presence of seven or more criteria indicates classic disease; five to six criteria indicate definite disease; three to four criteria indicate probable disease.*

classified as the disease-modifying drugs and the cytotoxic immunosuppressive drugs. These agents appear to have the capacity to modify the course of the disease and to slow its progress in some patients.

A number of experimental approaches such as total lymphoid irradiation or lymphoplasmapheresis have also been used to treat RA. Although some show potential for ameliorating disease, none has been shown to be a safe and cost-effective way to treat patients on a long-term basis. A variety of nontraditional approaches have also been claimed to be effective in treating RA, including diets, plant and animal extracts, vaccines, hormones, and topical preparations of various sorts. Many of these are costly and none has been shown to be effective. However, belief in their efficacy ensures their continued use by some patients.

Nonsteroidal anti-inflammatory drugs Besides aspirin, there are now several additional nonsteroidal anti-inflammatory drugs available to treat RA. These include fenoprofen, ibuprofen, indomethacin, naproxen, meclofenamate, piroxicam, sulindac, and tolmetin. As a result of the capacity of these agents to block the activity of the enzyme cyclooxygenase and therefore the production of prostaglandins, prostacycline, and thromboxanes, they have analgesic, anti-inflammatory, and antipyretic properties. These agents are all associated with a wide spectrum of toxic side effects. Some, such as gastric irritation, azotemia, platelet dysfunction, and exacerbation of allergic rhinitis and asthma, are related to the inhibition of cyclooxygenase activity, while a variety of others such as rash, liver function abnormalities, and bone marrow depression may not be. Elderly patients on diuretics may be at higher risk for certain toxic effects. None of the nonsteroidal anti-inflammatory drugs has been shown to be more effective than aspirin in the treatment of RA. However, these nonaspirin drugs are associated with a lower incidence of gastrointestinal intolerance. None of the newer nonsteroidal anti-inflammatory drugs appears to show significant therapeutic advantages over the other available agents. In addition, there is no consistent advantage of any of these newer agents over the others with respect to the incidence or severity of toxic manifestations.

Disease-modifying drugs Clinical experience has delineated a number of agents that appear to have the capacity to alter the course of RA. This group of agents includes gold compounds, D-penicillamine, and the antimalarials. In practice, these agents share a number of characteristics. They exert minimal direct nonspecific anti-inflammatory or analgesic effects, and therefore nonsteroidal anti-inflammatory drugs must be continued during their administration, except in a few cases when true remissions are induced with them. The appearance of benefit from disease-modifying drug therapy is usually delayed for weeks or months. As many as two-thirds of patients develop some clinical improvement as a result of therapy with any of these agents, although the induction of true remissions is unusual. In addition to clinical improvement, there is frequently an improvement in serologic evidence of disease activity, and titers of rheumatoid factor and the erythrocyte sedimentation rate frequently decline as a result of therapy. Despite this, there is only a small body of evidence to support the conclusion that disease-modifying drugs actually retard the development of bone erosions or facilitate their healing.

Each of these drugs is associated with considerable toxicity, and therefore, careful patient monitoring is necessary. Which disease-modifying drug should be the drug of first choice remains controversial, and trials have failed to demonstrate a consistent advantage of one over the other. Toxicity of the various agents thus becomes important in determining the drug of first choice. Failure to respond or development of toxicity to one agent does not preclude responsiveness to another. For example, a similar percentage of RA patients who have failed to respond to gold will respond to D-penicillamine when this agent is administered as the initial disease-modifying drug. No characteristic features of patients have emerged that predict responsiveness to a disease-modifying drug. Guidelines for the use of these drugs are given in Table 263-2.

Glucocorticoid therapy Although systemic glucocorticoid therapy can provide effective symptomatic therapy in patients with RA, these drugs should be avoided if possible because they do not alter the course of the disease and the potential toxicity of long-term therapy is substantial. Low-dose (less than 7.5 mg per day) prednisone has been advocated as useful additive therapy to control symptoms, but trials have not confirmed its efficacy and even low-dose therapy may promote osteoporosis.

Cytotoxic immunosuppressive therapy The cytotoxic immunosuppressive drugs azathioprine and cyclophosphamide have been shown to be effective in the treatment of RA and to exert therapeutic effects that are similar to the disease-modifying drugs. However, these agents are no more effective than the disease-modifying drugs. Moreover, they cause a variety of toxic side effects, and cyclophosphamide appears to predispose the patient to the development of malignant neoplasms. Therefore, these drugs have been reserved for patients who have clearly failed therapy with disease-modifying drugs. On occasion, extraarticular disease such as rheumatoid vasculitis may require cytotoxic immunosuppressive therapy.

Intermittent low-dose methotrexate, a folic acid antagonist, also may be useful in the treatment of RA. Although methotrexate appears to be effective, as many as 20 percent of treated patients develop liver function abnormalities. The long-term significance of these abnormalities has not been elucidated.

Surgery Surgery plays a role in the management of patients with severely damaged joints. Although arthroplasties and total joint replacements can be done on a number of joints, the most successful procedures are carried out on hips and knees. Realistic goals of these procedures are relief of pain, correction of deformity, and modest functional improvement. Reconstructive hand surgery may lead to cosmetic improvement, although functional benefit is marginal. Open or arthroscopic synovectomy may be useful in some patients with persistent monarthritis, especially of the knee. In addition, early tenosynovectomy of the wrist may prevent tendon rupture.

TABLE 263-2 Major disease-modifying drugs: Guide to therapy

	Hydroxychloroquine	Auranofin (oral gold)	Gold sodium thiomalate and gold thioglucose (intramuscular gold)	D-Penicillamine
Administration	<6.5 mg/kg per day	3 mg twice daily	50 mg per week loading → 1 g total; then taper to 50 mg per month	250 mg per day on empty stomach; increase daily dose by 250 mg every 3 months; maximum, 1 g per day
Major toxicity	Retinopathy	Rash, diarrhea; thrombocytopenia, granulocytopenia, and proteinuria rarely seen	Rash, thrombocytopenia, granulocytopenia, proteinuria	Rash, gastrointestinal intolerance, proteinuria, thrombocytopenia, granulocytopenia
Precautions	Ophthalmologic examination every 6 months	CBC, platelet count, urinalysis monthly, prescriptions should be nonrenewable	CBC, platelet count, urinalysis before each injection	CBC, platelet count, urinalysis every 2 weeks × 6 months, then every month

Approach to the patient with RA   At the onset of disease it is difficult to predict the natural history of an individual patient's illness. Therefore, the usual approach is to attempt to alleviate the patient's symptoms with nonsteroidal anti-inflammatory drugs. The major reason to delay more definitive therapy is the possibility that a spontaneous remission will occur. Moreover, since the disease-modifying drugs are potentially toxic and not universally effective, enthusiasm for their use is muted when a natural remission is still a possibility.

At some time during most patient's course, the possibility of initiating disease-modifying drug therapy is entertained. With aggressive disease this might occur sooner, often within 3 to 6 months of disease onset, while in patients with more indolent disease, smoldering activity may not require such therapy for many years. The development of bone erosions or radiographic evidence of cartilage loss is clear-cut evidence of the destructive potential of the inflammatory process and indicates the need for disease-modifying drug therapy. The other indications such as persistent pain, joint swelling, or functional impairment are much more subjective, however. The decision to begin use of a disease-modifying drug requires careful monitoring of joint swelling and functional activity, as well as an understanding of the patient's pain tolerance and expectation of therapy. In this setting, the fully informed patient must play an active role in the decision to begin disease-modifying drug therapy, after careful review of the therapeutic and toxic potential of the various drugs.

If a patient responds to a disease-modifying drug, therapy is continued with careful monitoring to avoid toxicity. All disease-modifying drugs provide a suppressive effect and therefore require prolonged administration. Even with successful therapy, local injection of glucocorticoids may be necessary to diminish inflammation that may persist in a limited number of joints. In addition, nonsteroidal anti-inflammatory drugs may be necessary to mitigate symptoms. Even after inflammation has totally resolved, symptoms from loss of cartilage and supervening degenerative joint disease or deformities may require additional treatment. Surgery may also be necessary to relieve pain or diminish the functional impairment secondary to deformity. Only when patients have persistent inflammatory disease or severe extraarticular manifestations is the use of cytotoxic immunosuppressive drugs or experimental procedures justified.

REFERENCES

BURMESTER GR et al: Identification of three major synovial lining cell populations by monoclonal antibodies directed to Ia antigens and antigens associated with monocytes/macrophages and fibroblasts. Scand J Immunol 17:69, 1983

DECKER JL et al: Rheumatoid arthritis: Evolving concepts of pathogenesis and treatment. Ann Intern Med 101:810, 1984

FEIGENBAUM SL et al: Prognosis in rheumatoid arthritis: A longitudinal study of newly diagnosed younger adult patients. Am J Med 66:377, 1979

HARRIS JR ED: Rheumatoid arthritis: The clinical spectrum, in *Textbook of Rheumatology*, WN Kelley et al (eds). Philadelphia, Saunders, 1981, pp 928–963

HOCHBERG MC: Adult and juvenile rheumatoid arthritis: Current epidemiologic concepts. Epidemiol Rev 3:27, 1981

HURD ER: Extra-articular manifestations of rheumatoid arthritis. Semin Arthritis Rheum 8:151, 1979

KURASAKA M, ZIFF M: Immunoelectron microscopic study of the distribution of T-cell subsets in rheumatoid synovium. J Exp Med 158:1191, 1983

LEGRAND L et al: HLA-DR genotype risks in seropositive rheumatoid arthritis. Am J Hum Genet 36:690, 1984

LIANG MH et al: Costs and outcomes in rheumatoid arthritis and osteoarthritis. Arthritis Rheum 27:522, 1984

LINDBLAD S et al: Phenotypic characterization of synovial tissue cells in situ in different types of synovitis. Arthritis Rheum 26:1321, 1983

LIPSKY PE: Remission-inducing therapy in rheumatoid arthritis. Am J Med 74(4B):40, 1983

MITCHELL DM, FRIES JF: An analysis of the American Rheumatism Association criteria for rheumatoid arthritis. Arthritis Rheum 25:481, 1982

POULTER LW et al: The involvement of interdigitating (antigen-presenting) cells in the pathogenesis of rheumatoid arthritis. Clin Exp Immunol 51:247, 1983

ROTHSCHILD B, MASI AT: Pathogenesis of rheumatoid arthritis: A vascular hypothesis. Semin Arthritis Rheum 12:11, 1982

UTSINGER PD et al (eds): *Rheumatoid Arthritis*. Philadelphia, Lippincott, 1985

VANDENBROUCKE JP et al: Survival and cause of death in rheumatoid arthritis: A 25 year prospective follow-up. J Rheum 11:158, 1984

YOUNG A et al: Association of HLA-DR4/DW4 and DR2/DW2 with radiologic changes in a prospective study of patients with rheumatoid arthritis. Preferential relationship with HLA-DW rather than HLA-DR specificities. Arthritis Rheum 27:20, 1984

ZVAIFLER NJ: The immunopathology of joint inflammation in rheumatoid arthritis. Adv Immunol 16:265, 1973

264   PROGRESSIVE SYSTEMIC SCLEROSIS (DIFFUSE SCLERODERMA)

BRUCE C. GILLILAND

Progressive systemic sclerosis (PSS) is a multisystem disorder characterized by inflammatory, vascular, and fibrotic changes of the skin (scleroderma) and a variety of internal organs, most notably the gastrointestinal tract, lungs, heart, and kidney. The course, extent of involvement, and severity of disease varies greatly among patients. In some patients, skin changes restricted to the distal extremities may be present for many years before visceral involvement becomes apparent, while in others widespread skin changes and visceral disease develop rapidly over a few years. Visceral disease may also occur in the absence of skin involvement. The disease is not always progressive, and skin changes may actually return to near normal after many years. Survival is determined by the severity of visceral disease involving especially the heart, lungs, and/or kidneys.

ETIOLOGY AND PATHOGENESIS   This disease has a worldwide distribution but is apparently rare in Asia, especially among the Chinese, Indians, and Malaysians. The onset of disease is usually in the third to fifth decades, and women are affected four times as often as men. The etiology and pathogenesis of PSS are not known, and the role of heredity has not been clarified. Several examples of familial PSS have been reported. The increased fibrosis in the skin and other organ systems is considered to be due to overproduction of normal collagen. The amount of collagen synthesized by individual fibroblasts is increased compared to appropriate controls. Studies have suggested an abnormal regulation of connective tissue synthesis, degradation, or both.

The primary event in systemic sclerosis is postulated to be endothelial cell injury in blood vessels ranging from small arteries to capillaries. The cause of this endothelial damage is not known, but a serum cytotoxic factor, a serine protease, has been identified in some patients with systemic sclerosis. In small arteries, disruption of endothelial cells leads to platelet aggregation, myointimal cell proliferation, and fibrosis resulting in narrowing, decreased distensibility, and obliteration of the vessels. Elevated plasma levels of von Willebrand factor and antigen in PSS patients reflect endothelial cell damage. The binding of von Willebrand factor to the exposed subendothelium permits adhesion and subsequent aggregation of platelets. Activated platelets release vascular permeability factors and procoagulant factors. Increased vascular permeability from endothelial cell damage produces interstitial edema, fibroblast stimulation, and eventually fibrosis in the surrounding tissue. Thus, the early phase of systemic sclerosis is characterized by target organ edema followed later by fibrosis. The number of capillaries in the skin is reduced by this fibrotic process; the remaining capillaries dilate and proliferate to become visible telangiectatic lesions.

Both humoral and cell-mediated immune phenomena are present in patients with PSS. Hypergammaglobulinemia and antinuclear antibodies are frequent findings. Antibodies have also been demonstrated to the cell membrane of fibroblasts as well as to type I and type IV collagen. The pathogenic role of these various autoantibodies is not known. Perivascular cell infiltrates are found in early skin lesions of PSS. These infiltrates contain T cells, plasma cells, and macrophages. In chronic lesions, fibroblasts and histiocytes predominate. Evaluation of the T-cell population in involved skin utilizing monoclonal antibodies shows an increased T4/T8 ratio due to decreased number of T8 cells. A similar T4/T8 ratio is found in the peripheral blood of some patients with PSS. Soluble extracts from normal and scleroderma skin stimulate lymphocytes from PSS patients as measured by the macrophage migration inhibition test. Peripheral blood lymphocytes from PSS patients have also been shown to be cytotoxic to fibroblasts in cell cultures. It is speculated that T cells sensitized to altered endothelial antigens or other skin tissue antigens elaborate lymphokines which attract and activate monocytes-macrophages. Monokines from stimulated monocytes-macrophages damage endothelium and diffuse into the interstitium to stimulate fibroblasts. In support of cell-mediated immunity playing a role in the pathogenesis of PSS is the appearance of scleroderma-like lesions in patients with graft-versus-host disease following marrow transplantation, a condition known to be mediated by cell-mediated events.

Chromosomal abnormalities have been noted in greater than 90 percent of PSS patients. These acquired abnormalities include chromatid breaks, acentric fragments, and ring chromosomes, and are found in approximately 30 percent of mitotic cells. A chromosomal breakage factor has been found in the serum of PSS patients. The significance of these chromosomal abnormalities is unknown.

Occupational hazards have been associated with the development of PSS. The occurrence of PSS in coal and gold miners appears to be more common than in nonminers, suggesting that silica dust may be a predisposing factor. Workers exposed to polyvinyl chloride may develop Raynaud's phenomenon, acroosteolysis, and scleroderma-like skin lesions. Nail-fold capillary abnormalities similar to those observed in PSS are also present. In addition, these workers also developed hepatic fibrosis and angiosarcoma. Extensive sclerosis of the dermis and subcutaneous tissue has been noted in patients receiving pentazocine, a nonnarcotic analgesic agent. Bleomycin, an anticancer agent, produces fibrotic skin nodules, linear hyperpigmentation, alopecia, gangrene of fingers, and pulmonary fibrosis affecting mainly the lower lobes. Absence of Raynaud's phenomenon and sparing of the face and distal extremities distinguish this entity from PSS.

PATHOLOGY In the skin, a thin epidermis overlies compact bundles of collagen which lie parallel to the epidermis. Fingerlike projections of collagen extend from the dermis into the subcutaneous tissue and bind the skin to the underlying tissue. Dermal appendages are atrophied, and rete pegs are lost. Increased numbers of lymphocytes identified as mostly T cells may be present at the border of skin lesions.

In the lower two-thirds of the esophagus, the histologic findings consist of a thin mucosa and increased collagen in the lamina propria, submucosa, and serosa. The degree of fibrosis is less than in the skin. Atrophy of the muscularis in the esophagus and throughout the involved portions of the gastrointestinal tract is more prominent than the amount of fibrotic replacement of muscle. Ulceration of the mucosa is often present and may be due to either PSS or superimposed peptic esophagitis. Striated muscles in the upper one-third of the esophagus are relatively spared. Similar changes may be found throughout the gastrointestinal tract, especially in the second and third portions of the duodenum, jejunum, and large intestine. Atrophy of the muscularis of the large intestine may lead to the development of large-mouth diverticula. In the later stages of the disease, the involved portions of the gastrointestinal tract become dilated. Infiltration of lymphocytes and plasma cells in the lamina propria is also present.

With pulmonary involvement, diffuse interstitial fibrosis, thickening of the alveolar membrane, and peribronchial fibrosis are observed. Bronchiolar epithelial proliferation accompanies the pulmonary fibrosis. Rupture of septa produces small cysts and areas of bullous emphysema. Small pulmonary arteries and arterioles show intimal thickening, fragmentation of the elastica, and muscular hypertrophy; this may occur without interstitial pulmonary fibrosis and produce pulmonary hypertension.

The synovium in patients with PSS and arthritis is similar to that seen in early rheumatoid arthritis and shows edema with infiltration of lymphocytes and plasma cells. A characteristic finding is a thick layer of fibrin overlying and within the synovium. Later in the disease the synovium may become fibrotic. Fibrinous deposits appear on the surfaces of tendon sheaths and in the overlying fascia, and may lead to audible creaking over moving tendons.

Histologic features of muscle involvement consist of interstitial and perivascular lymphocytic infiltrations, degeneration of muscle fibers, and interstitial fibrosis. Arterioles may be thickened, and capillaries may be decreased in number.

In the heart, myocardial interstitial fibrosis replaces myocardial fibers. Fibrosis also involves the conduction system, leading to atrioventricular conduction defects and arrhythmias. The wall of smaller coronary arteries may be thickened, and lymphocytic infiltration is seen. Fibrinous pericarditis and pericardial effusions are found in some patients.

Renal involvement is found in over half the patients and consists of intimal hyperplasia of the interlobular arteries, fibrinoid necrosis of the afferent arterioles, including the glomerular tuft, and thickening of the glomerular basement membrane. These lesions result in cortical infarctions and glomerulosclerosis. The renal pathologic change is often indistinguishable from that observed in malignant hypertension. Renal vascular lesions, however, may be present in the absence of hypertension. Angiographic renal studies in patients with PSS may show constriction of the intralobular arteries, a finding that simulates the vasospasm of the digital arteries observed in Raynaud's phenomenon. Along with Raynaud's phenomenon, induced by cooling, a decrease in renal blood flow has been observed. These studies are of interest because three-quarters of the deaths from renal involvement in PSS have been shown to occur in the fall and winter.

Primary liver involvement is not common, but diffuse cirrhosis, intrahepatic cholestasis, and chronic passive congestion occur occasionally. Fibrosis of the thyroid may develop. Thickening of the periodontal membrane with replacement of the lamina dura is demonstrated radiographically as widening of the periodontal space and rarely causes loosening of the teeth.

Small arterial and arteriolar lesions are found in many tissues; they consist of concentric acellular thickening of the intima with narrowing or occlusion of the lumen. These lesions are found in the digital arteries and arterioles in patients with PSS and Raynaud's phenomenon. Vascular abnormalities have been described in the lung, skin, kidney, muscle, gastrointestinal tract, pancreas, synovium, vasa vasorum, and the central nervous system. Arteritis with fibrinoid necrosis and infiltration by mononuclear cells of all three layers is occasionally observed.

CLINICAL MANIFESTATIONS PSS usually begins insidiously; the first symptom is frequently Raynaud's phenomenon. Raynaud's phenomenon is defined as episodic vasoconstriction of arteries and arterioles of the fingers, toes, and sometimes the face which is brought on by cold or emotional stimuli. Patients may experience triphasic color changes consisting of pallor, cyanosis, and rubor, occurring usually in this order. Raynaud's phenomenon should be considered when the patient experiences any one or combinations of these changes. Pallor and cyanosis are most often associated with numbness and coldness of the fingers, and rubor with pain and tingling. Raynaud's phenomenon may precede the skin changes by months or even years. Raynaud's phenomenon occurs in 90 percent of patients with the skin changes of scleroderma. The fingers and hands in the early stages are swollen. Subsequently the skin becomes firm, thickened, and leathery in appearance, and tightly bound to the underlying subcutaneous tissue. The skin changes spread to involve the arms, face, chest, abdomen, and back. The lower extremities are relatively spared. The taut skin over the fingers gradually limits full extension, and may lead to fixed flexion contractures. Ulcers may appear on the fingertips and over bony prominences and may become infected. The soft tissue of the fingertips is lost, and in some instances the bone of terminal phalanges is resorbed. The skin may become darkly pigmented even without exposure to the sun; areas of depigmentation and numerous telangiectatic mats often appear on the skin. The skin becomes dry and coarse, and hair is lost. Examination of nail folds with a wide-angle microscope or an ophthalmoscope shows initially disorganization of the capillary bed followed later by a decrease in the number of capillary loops and dilatation of the remaining loops. In some patients, calcific deposits develop in the subcutaneous and periarticular tissue. The overlying skin may break down, with draining of calcific material. Involvement of the face results in the loss of normal skin wrinkles, loss of facial expression, and inability to open the mouth fully. In disease of many years' duration, the hidebound skin may soften and become pliable, but will usually remain atrophic.

The coexistence of calcinosis, Raynaud's phenomenon, esophageal hypomotility, sclerodactyly, and telangiectasia has been termed the CREST syndrome and initially was considered a benign form of PSS. Patients may have skin changes of PSS limited to the distal extremities for many years. However, some of these patients have subsequently developed visceral and more extensive cutaneous lesions of PSS. Pulmonary hypertension may occur any time during the course.

More than half the patients with PSS complain of pain, swelling, and stiffness of the fingers and knees. A symmetric polyarthritis, resembling rheumatoid arthritis, may be seen. In more advanced stages of the disease, leathery crepitation can be palpated over moving joints, especially the knee. Extensive fibrotic thickening of the tendon sheaths in the wrist can produce a carpal tunnel syndrome. Acute myositis with proximal muscle weakness and enzyme elevation occurs in PSS and is indistinguishable from polymyositis. Patients also develop a distinctive indolent myopathy characterized by mild muscle weakness with few laboratory abnormalities.

Symptoms attributable to esophageal involvement, which are present in more than 50 percent of patients, include epigastric fullness, burning pain in the epigastric or retrosternal regions, and regurgitation of gastric contents. These symptoms, most noticeable when the patient is lying flat or bending over, are due to the reduced tone of the gastroesophageal sphincter and to dilatation of the distal esophagus. Peptic esophagitis frequently occurs and may lead to strictures and narrowing of the lower esophagus. However, it seldom results in bleeding. Dysphagia, particularly of solid foods, may occur independent of other esophageal symptoms and is caused by the loss of esophageal motility due to neuromuscular dysfunction. Manometry or cineradiography reveals decreased amplitude or disappearance of peristaltic waves in the lower two-thirds of the esophagus. A closer correlation exists between this finding and Raynaud's phenomenon than with cutaneous manifestations of PSS. Later in the course of the illness, dilatation and atony of the lower portion of the esophagus as well as reflux are seen. With gastric involvement, barium studies show dilatation, atony, and delayed gastric emptying.

Symptoms referable to involvement of the small intestine by PSS include bloating and abdominal pain and may suggest intestinal obstruction or paralytic ileus. Malabsorption syndrome with weight loss, steatorrhea, and anemia also occurs secondary to obliteration of the lymphatics by fibrosis or in some patients due to bacterial overgrowth in the atonic intestine. Involvement of the large intestine may cause chronic constipation and fecal impaction with episodes of bowel obstruction. Roentgenographic features of the second and third portions of the duodenum and of the jejunum include dilatation, loss of the usual feathery pattern, and delayed disappearance of barium. Pneumatosis intestinalis, which occasionally occurs in PSS, is seen as radiolucent cysts or linear streaks within the wall of the small intestine. Benign pneumoperitoneum may result from the rupture of these cysts. Barium studies of the large intestine may show dilatation, atony, and large-mouth diverticula. Some patients may have gastrointestinal PSS with little or no cutaneous or other organ involvement. Hypothyroidism occurs in a few patients with PSS, particularly in those with long-standing cutaneous disease. Fibrosis of the thyroid gland was found in 14 percent of PSS patients at autopsy.

Patients with pulmonary fibrosis often complain of a dry cough and exertional dyspnea; however, shortness of breath as a presenting complaint is unusual. Bilateral basilar rales may be present. Though pleural involvement is not infrequent at postmortem, symptoms of pleurisy are unusual. Restriction of chest movement may rarely occur with extensive skin involvement of the thorax. Additional pulmonary problems result from aspiration pneumonia secondary to esophageal malfunction. Superimposed bacterial or viral pneumonia may be a serious complication in patients with pulmonary fibrosis. Malignant alveolar or bronchiolar cell neoplasms have been reported in some patients with PSS and pulmonary fibrosis. However, no other association of PSS with malignancy has been shown. Pulmonary function test results are abnormal even in early disease and show a low diffusion capacity and a low P_{O_2} on exercise. Roentgenograms of the chest may show a pattern of linear densities, mottling, and honeycombing. These changes are more evident in the lower two-thirds of the lungs. Patients may develop pulmonary arterial hypertension without significant interstitial fibrosis, presumably secondary to the proliferative vascular lesion of PSS involving pulmonary arteries and arterioles. These patients complain of shortness of breath, and on physical examination they have an accentuated pulmonic second heart sound, a fixed split second heart sound, and the systolic murmur of pulmonary artery dilatation. Electrocardiographic evidence of pulmonary hypertension may also be present.

Cardiac involvement by PSS often goes clinically unrecognized; however, varying degrees of heart block and arrhythmias may be seen. Cardiomyopathy attributable to diffuse myocardial fibrosis may also occur. Other cardiac manifestations may be secondary to pulmonary disease and hypertension. Left ventricular failure develops more frequently than cor pulmonale, even with the presence of pulmonary fibrosis. Acute and chronic pericarditis may develop and occasionally produce tamponade. Cardiac involvement is the cause of death in 15 percent of PSS patients.

Renal failure is the leading cause of death in PSS, accounting for almost half of the deaths. The onset of renal involvement is frequently within 3 years of the diagnosis of PSS. Renal failure, however, can present abruptly at any time in an apparently stable patient and is fatal unless treated. Acute renal failure can develop in association with malignant hypertension or in a setting of mild chronic hypertension. Proteinuria, an abnormal urine sediment, hypertension, azotemia, and microangiopathic hemolytic anemia are clinical features associated with progressive renal disease. It is difficult to predict the patient who will develop renal failure. One indicator of impending renal failure is microangiopathic anemia, which may appear several weeks before renal failure. The presence of chronic pericardial effusion may also be associated with subsequent renal failure.

LABORATORY FINDINGS The erythrocyte sedimentation rate may be elevated. Hypoproliferative anemia related to chronic inflammation is the most common cause of anemia in PSS. Anemia may also be caused by iron deficiency secondary to gastrointestinal bleeding. Bacterial overgrowth due to atony of the small bowel may lead to vitamin B_{12} and/or folic acid–deficiency anemia. Microangiopathic hemolytic anemia is most often associated with renal involvement and is caused by the presence of fibrin deposition in the renal arterioles. Hypergammaglobulinemia, with elevated levels mainly of IgG, is found in approximately half the patients. Rheumatoid factor, in low titer, is present in 25 percent of patients. Antinuclear antibodies (ANA) are reported in 33 to 96 percent depending on the tissue substrate used in the test. Utilizing a cultured human laryngeal carcinoma cell line (HEp-2), 96 percent of PSS patients are found to be ANA-positive. Specific antinuclear antibodies include antibodies to nucleolar antigens, nuclear ribonucleoprotein (RNP), centromere, and Scl-70 (an extractable nonhistone nuclear protein, 70,000 daltons). Anti-Scl-70 is relatively specific for PSS but is found in only 20 percent of patients. Antibodies reacting with the centromeric region of metaphase chromosomes are found in most patients meeting the criteria for CREST syndrome, less often in patients with diffuse PSS, and in a few patients with only Raynaud's phenomenon. Anticentromere antibodies rarely occur in other connective tissue disorders.

DIAGNOSIS The diagnosis of PSS presents no difficulty in the presence of Raynaud's phenomenon, with typical skin lesions and visceral involvement. PSS should always be included in the differential diagnosis of patients with Raynaud's phenomenon. Other causes of Raynaud's phenomenon include thoracic outlet (scalenus anticus and cervical rib) syndromes, shoulder-hand syndrome, trauma (jackhammer or vibratory machine operators), previous cold injury, vinyl chloride exposure, and circulating cryoglobulins or cold agglutinins. Linear scleroderma and morphea are localized forms of PSS and may be associated with Raynaud's phenomenon and hypergammaglobulinemia. PSS may initially be confused with rheumatoid arthritis, systemic lupus erythematosus, or polymyositis when articular or muscle involvement is prominent early in the disease. PSS without cutaneous involvement should be considered in patients with unexplained pulmonary fibrosis, pulmonary hypertension, cardiomyopathies, heart block, dysphagia, or malabsorption syndrome. Several conditions have scleroderma-like features but lack the visceral involvement. Scleredema (scleredema adultorum of Buschke) occurs predominantly in children and is characterized by painless edematous induration involving the face, scalp, neck, trunk, and proximal portions of the extremities. Involvement of the hands and feet usually does not occur. Scleredema may be associated with previous streptococcal infection and is usually self-limited, resolving in 6 to 12 months. Histology reveals accumulation of mucopolysaccharides in the dermis and skeletal muscle. A rare entity, scleromyxedema (lichen myxedematosus), is manifested by yellowish or pale-red papules in association with diffuse skin thickening which may involve the face and hands. Acid mucopolysaccharide deposits are found in the dermis. Monoclonal IgG may be detected in some of these patients. Primary amyloidosis may involve the skin of the extremities and face diffusely to give the appearance of scleroderma. Biopsy will clearly differentiate these entities.

Diffuse fasciitis with eosinophilia A scleroderma-like syndrome consisting of fasciitis, myositis, eosinophilia, and hypergammaglobulinemia has been recognized. Patients usually do not have Raynaud's phenomenon or develop sclerodactyly. Systemic involvement seldom occurs. Several patients with eosinophilic fasciitis have been reported to have aplastic anemia; however, the significance of the association is not understood. Patients develop tenderness and swelling of the extremities with the onset of symptoms often related to strenuous physical exertion. The trunk and neck can also be involved. In affected areas, the skin is thickened with a cobblestone or puckered appearance. Full-thickness biopsy consisting of skin, fascia, and superficial muscle shows perivascular infiltration of histiocytes, eosinophils, lymphocytes, and plasma cells in the dermis, subcutaneous fat and fascia, and underlying muscle. Improvement has been noted with administration of glucocorticoids, but spontaneous improvement has also been recorded.

PROGNOSIS In the majority of patients PSS is characterized by a prolonged, relentless course of progressive skin and/or visceral involvement. In some patients remissions occur, including partial improvement of the skin, and the disease progresses slowly; 80 percent of one group of patients were alive 2 years after onset of symptoms, and 20 percent were alive 10 years after onset. Patients with mainly skin involvement have a more gradual and favorable course than those with visceral disease, involving especially the heart, kidneys, and lungs. Among whites the prognosis is worse in males than in females, and worse in patients whose onset of disease occurs after 45 years of age. The disease tends to be more severe in black females. Death occurs most often from cardiac, renal, and pulmonary involvement.

TREATMENT Effectiveness of drug therapy in PSS is difficult to evaluate because of the variable course and severity of the disease. Many drugs have been used in the treatment of PSS without any consistent or prolonged benefit. In uncontrolled studies D-penicillamine has been reported to reduce skin thickening and prevent development of significant organ involvement. Antiplatelet therapy may play a role in the treatment of PSS since the biologic products of platelets affect blood vessels. Low doses of aspirin block the formation of thromboxane A_2, a powerful vasoconstrictor and platelet aggregator. In addition, dipyridamole 200 to 400 mg in divided daily doses also decreases platelet adhesion to damaged vessel walls. Reports of beneficial effects of colchicine or chlorambucil have not been documented in controlled studies. Even though no drug or combination of drugs has been proved to stop this disease, management directed at the involved organ systems may prolong life and improve the quality of life.

The management of Raynaud's phenomenon is directed at control of vasospasm. It is important to prevent periods of vasospasm since the resulting ischemia may be a further stimulant for vascular fibrosis and eventual obliteration. Patients should be advised to dress warmly and wear mittens and socks, not to smoke, to remove causes of external stress, and to avoid drugs such as amphetamine and ergotamine. Warmth of the central body induces peripheral vasodilation. Drugs that block sympathetic vasoconstriction, such as reserpine, guanethidine, α-methyldopa, phenoxybenzamine, and prazosin may be useful in the treatment of Raynaud's phenomenon, but their side effects often curtail extended use. Nifedipine and other calcium channel blockers are sometimes effective in alleviating Raynaud's phenomenon. The dose of nifedipine is 10 to 20 mg tid. Techniques of biofeedback have also been used with variable success for teaching patients to control the temperature of their hands. Surgical sympathectomy usually provides only temporary improvement, and it, along with other forms of therapy, does not prevent progression of the vascular lesion. The response to any therapy for Raynaud's phenomenon is limited by the degree of existing structural narrowing of digital arteries.

Numerous drugs have been claimed to soften the hidebound skin, but documentation in controlled studies is lacking. These drugs include D-penicillamine, colchicine, p-aminobenzoic acid, vitamin E, and dimethyl sulfoxide (DMSO). Dryness of the skin may be reduced by avoiding frequent use of detergent soaps and by applying regularly hydrophilic ointments and bath oils. Regular exercise helps to maintain flexibility of extremities and pliability of skin. Massaging the skin several times a day may also be beneficial. Skin ulcers should be kept clean by soaking or by surgical or chemical debridement. Sympatholytic drugs or local nitroglycerine paste may be beneficial in promoting healing. Infected ulcers can usually be treated with topical antibiotics.

Patients with reflux esophagitis are treated with small frequent meals, antacids between meals, and elevation of the head of the bed. Patients should be advised not to lie down for a few hours after a meal, and to avoid coffee, tea, and chocolate, which reduce the pressure of the lower esophageal sphincter. Cimetidine or ranitidine may be beneficial in some patients. Patients with dysphagia should be instructed to chew their food thoroughly and wash it down with fluids. Malabsorption syndrome due to duodenal hypomotility and bacterial overgrowth may improve with intermittent use of appropriate antibiotics. Stool softeners and mild laxatives are usually adequate for the constipation due to involvement of the colon.

Acute myositis is usually responsive to glucocorticoids; these drugs should not be used for the indolent form of muscle disease of PSS. Articular symptoms are treated with aspirin or other nonsteroidal anti-inflammatory agents.

The pulmonary fibrosis of PSS is not reversible, and therefore the treatment is directed at symptoms or complications. Pulmonary infection requires prompt treatment with antibiotics. Hypoxia necessitates giving low concentrations of oxygen. The role of glucocorticoids in preventing progression of interstitial lung disease is not clear.

Recognition of early renal failure is important in order to preserve remaining function. Renal involvement is usually accompanied by hypertension, but occasional patients may be normotensive. Since most patients have increased renin, drugs that block the renin-angiotensin pathway may be effective in stabilizing or reversing renal failure, as well as lowering the blood pressure. These drugs include propranolol, clonidine, and minoxidil. Another effective drug in treating the renal failure of PSS is captopril, which is an inhibitor of angiotensin converting enzyme. Dialysis may be required in patients with progressive renal failure.

Patients with cardiac failure require careful monitoring of digitalis and diuretic administration. Pericardial effusions may also improve with diuretics. Care should be taken to avoid overdiuresis which may lead to decreased effective plasma volume, decreased cardiac output, and renal failure.

REFERENCES

LeRoy EC: Scleroderma (systemic sclerosis), in *Textbook of Rheumatology*, 2d ed, WN Kelley et al (eds). Philadelphia, Saunders, 1985, pp 1183–1205

Maricq HR et al: Diagnostic potential of in vivo capillary microscopy in scleroderma and related disorders. Arthritis Rheum 23:183, 1980

Shulman LE: Diffuse fasciitis with eosinophilia: A new syndrome. Arthritis Rheum 20:S205, 1977

Whiteside TL et al: Suppressor cell function and T lymphocyte subpopulations in peripheral blood of patients with progressive systemic sclerosis. Arthritis Rheum 26:841, 1983

265 MIXED CONNECTIVE TISSUE DISEASE

GORDON C. SHARP

DEFINITION Mixed connective tissue disease (MCTD) is a syndrome characterized by a combination of clinical features similar to those of systemic lupus erythematosus (SLE), scleroderma, polymyositis, and rheumatoid arthritis and unusually high titers of circulating antibody to a nuclear ribonucleoprotein (RNP) antigen.

ETIOLOGY, PATHOGENESIS, AND PATHOLOGY The etiologic and pathogenic mechanisms of MCTD remain unknown, but a number of clues point to the involvement of immune aberrations: (1) persistence of extremely high titers of antibody to nuclear RNP and a marked polyclonal hypergammaglobulinemia indicative of B-cell hyperactivity; (2) a suppressor T-cell defect; (3) circulating immune complexes during active disease; (4) deposition of IgG, IgM, and complement within vascular walls and along sarcolemmal and glomerular basement membranes; and (5) widespread lymphocytic and plasma cell infiltration of numerous tissues. One of the chief underlying pathologic findings in some adults and children with MCTD is a proliferative intimal and/or medial vascular lesion resulting in narrowing of the lumen of large vessels (e.g., pulmonary, renal, and coronary vessels and aorta) and of small arterioles of many organs. Such lesions in the lungs may contribute to pulmonary hypertension and abnormalities of pulmonary function.

CLINICAL MANIFESTATIONS The age range in published reports of MCTD is from 4 to 80 years, with a mean of 37 years. Approximately 80 percent of patients have been female. Typical clinical features include Raynaud's phenomenon, polyarthritis, swollen hands or sclerodactyly, esophageal dysfunction, pulmonary involvement, and inflammatory myopathy. Malar rash, alopecia, lymphadenopathy, and cardiac and renal disease are less frequent manifestations.

Cutaneous manifestations of MCTD include the swollen, sausage-like appearance of the fingers, nonscarring alopecia, lupus-like rashes, heliotrope eyelids, erythematous patches over the knuckles, periungual telangiectasia, and "squared" telangiectasia over the hands and face. Scleroderma-like changes may be present but only occasionally become extensive.

Musculoskeletal abnormalities occur in most patients. Arthritis is usually nondeforming but may resemble rheumatoid arthritis. Proximal muscle weakness is frequent and may be severe. Serum levels of creatine phosphokinase and aldolase are often markedly elevated, electromyograms are typical of inflammatory myopathy, and biopsies show degeneration of muscle fibers and interstitial and perivascular infiltrates of lymphocytes and plasma cells.

Esophageal dysfunction has been demonstrated in 80 percent of all patients, including 70 percent of asymptomatic patients. Characteristic abnormalities include reduced upper and lower esophageal sphincter pressures and decreased amplitude of peristalsis in the distal two-thirds of the esophagus.

Pulmonary involvement occurs in 85 percent of patients with MCTD but may be clinically silent until far advanced. The most common clinical finding is exertional dyspnea, followed by pleuritic pain and bibasilar rales. Reduced diffusing capacity for carbon monoxide is the most frequent functional abnormality.

Cardiac disease is less common than pulmonary involvement in adults with MCTD but may be more frequent in children. Pericarditis is the most common cardiac finding; other findings have included mitral valve prolapse, myocarditis, congestive heart failure, and aortic insufficiency.

Renal disease in children and adults with MCTD has a combined prevalence of about 28 percent. Progressive renal failure is uncommon, and clinical and histologic findings suggest that vascular lesions may represent a more serious problem than immune complex nephritis in MCTD.

Other less frequent clinical manifestations include fever, lymphadenopathy, neurologic abnormalities, Sjögren's syndrome, hepatosplenomegaly, and intestinal involvement similar to that seen in scleroderma.

LABORATORY FINDINGS Almost all patients have positive fluorescent antinuclear antibody tests at high titers (usually greater than 1:1000) with a speckled pattern and very high titers of antibodies directed against the ribonuclease-sensitive nuclear RNP component of extractable nuclear antigen (ENA). Elevated anti–native DNA antibody titers and antibodies to the ribonuclease-resistant Sm component of ENA are uncommon in MCTD; their presence is usually associated with a severe flare-up of lupus-like features. Rheumatoid factor is found, often at very high titers, in over half of the patients. Diffuse hypergammaglobulinemia is frequently noted and may be elevated to a level of 5 g/dL. A mild to moderate reduction in serum complement levels occurs in about 30 percent of patients. Other less frequent laboratory findings include leukopenia, anemia, and thrombocytopenia (mainly in children).

DIAGNOSIS The diagnosis of MCTD is based on a combination of typical overlapping clinical findings and high titers of circulating antibody to nuclear RNP antigen. In some patients, all the clinical manifestations may be present on initial evaluation. However, as clinicians have become more aware of the syndrome and tests for RNP antibody are being performed more frequently, MCTD is being recognized in an earlier phase in patients presenting with minimal symptoms (e.g., Raynaud's phenomenon, arthralgias, myalgias, and swollen hands). In some this mild "undifferentiated connective tissue disease" syndrome may persist for years, but a recent prospective, long-term study showed that the majority of patients with high titers of RNP antibodies and limited clinical manifestations ultimately developed signs and symptoms consistent with a diagnosis of MCTD.

TREATMENT AND PROGNOSIS Lacking controlled studies, specific treatment recommendations for MCTD are based on anecdotal information. Salicylates, other nonsteroidal anti-inflammatory agents, hydroxychloroquine, vasodilators, and/or low doses of corticosteroids are used to treat mild disease. In general, mild disease is quite responsive to low-dose corticosteroids. If the disease is more severe and significantly involves major organ systems, higher doses of corticosteroids (e.g., 1 mg/kg per day of prednisone) are usually required. As with SLE, a cytotoxic agent may be added in steroid-resistant or -dependent cases. However, the efficacy of this latter therapeutic regimen has not been substantiated by controlled clinical trials. The prognosis for MCTD is generally similar to that of SLE and somewhat better than for scleroderma.

REFERENCES

GRANT KC et al: Mixed connective tissue disease—a subset with sequential clinical and laboratory features. J Rheumatol 8:587, 1981

SHARP GC, SINGSEN BH: Mixed connective tissue disease, in *Arthritis and Allied Conditions*, 10th ed., DJ McCarty (ed). Philadelphia, Lea & Febiger, 1985, chap 64

SULLIVAN WD et al: A prospective evaluation emphasizing pulmonary involvement in patients with mixed connective tissue disease. Medicine 63:92, 1984

266 SJÖGREN'S SYNDROME

H. CLIFFORD LANE / ANTHONY S. FAUCI

DEFINITION Sjögren's syndrome is an immunologic disorder characterized by progressive destruction of the exocrine glands leading to mucosal and conjunctival dryness (sicca syndrome) accompanied by a variety of autoimmune phenomena. The disease can occur either by itself, in which case it is referred to as primary Sjögren's syndrome, or in association with other autoimmune diseases (see Chaps. 262 and 263), in which case it is referred to as secondary Sjögren's syndrome. In addition, some authors have divided the disease into two forms: glandular, when the only clinical manifestations are within the exocrine system, and extraglandular, when other tissues are involved as well.

INCIDENCE AND PREVALENCE The disease predominantly affects women in the third or fourth decades of life. Although precise incidence figures are not known, it has been suggested that Sjögren's syndrome is the second most common rheumatologic disease in the United States. Up to 30 percent of patients with rheumatoid arthritis, 10 percent of patients with systemic lupus erythematosus, and 1 percent of patients with scleroderma have been reported as having secondary Sjögren's syndrome. Immunogenetic predisposition appears to play an important role in the incidence of Sjögren's syndrome. The frequency of the HLA-B8, the HLA-DRw3, and the MT-2 histocompatibility antigens is significantly increased in patients with primary Sjögren's syndrome.

PATHOPHYSIOLOGY AND IMMUNOPATHOGENESIS The two main mechanisms of tissue destruction in Sjögren's syndrome are lymphocytic infiltration and immune-complex deposition. In addition, approximately 10 percent of these patients develop a lymphoproliferative process known as *pseudolymphoma*. This disorder has many histologic features of lymphoma but is associated clinically with a benign course.

Virtually any organ system of the body may be affected in the patient with Sjögren's syndrome. The disease process is most striking in the salivary glands, where there is a progressive mononuclear cell infiltrate which generally leads to complete scarring. Renal disease may result from a lymphocytic interstitial nephritis or an immune-complex glomerulonephritis. Pulmonary involvement is most frequently due to interstitial pneumonitis caused by an infiltration of mononuclear cells, although discrete mass lesions due to pseudolymphoma may occur. Patients with Sjögren's syndrome may also develop an immune-complex vasculitis, at times associated with cryoglobulinemia. Thromboangitis obliterans has also been seen, usually in patients with preexisting Raynaud's phenomena. Both the peripheral and the central nervous system manifestations of this disease are felt to be due to blood vessel inflammation.

Patients with Sjögren's syndrome exhibit two main types of immunoregulatory defects. The first of these is an abnormally active cellular immune system. This is evident by the intense inflammatory mononuclear cell infiltrates seen in the salivary glands of these patients. These infiltrates are made up predominantly of activated T cells; however, activated B lymphocytes can be detected as well. These mononuclear cell infiltrates are responsible for many of the clinical manifestations of Sjögren's syndrome, including the profound dryness of conjunctival and mucosal surfaces, interstitial nephritis, interstitial pneumonitis, and meningoencephalitis. The second immunoregulatory defect seen in patients with Sjögren's syndrome is oligoclonal B-cell activation. This results in hypergammaglobulinemia, oligoclonal spikes on protein electrophoresis, elevated levels of circulating immune complexes, and the production of autoantibodies. Among the autoantibodies seen are rheumatoid factor, SSA (anti-Ro), and SSB (anti-La). While the precise clinical significance of these and other serologic markers is unclear, it does appear that most patients with the more serious systemic manifestations of Sjögren's syndrome are SSA-positive.

CLINICAL MANIFESTATIONS AND LABORATORY ABNORMALITIES The most common clinical manifestations of Sjögren's syndrome are keratoconjunctivitis sicca and xerostomia. Patients often complain initially of a gritty sensation in the eyes or severe dryness of the mouth. Mucosal dryness may extend into the upper airway, in which case patients may complain of a persistent cough or hoarseness which is worse in cold weather. Corneal dryness may be so severe as to result in corneal ulcerations.

Renal involvement is seen in approximately 40 percent of patients with primary Sjögren's syndrome. This generally presents clinically as a mild interstitial nephritis which may result in renal tubular acidosis. This form of kidney disease rarely leads to chronic renal failure; however, it may be associated with a 50 percent reduction in creatinine clearance. A minority of patients with renal disease demonstrate an immune-complex glomerulonephritis. This is seen usually in the context of systemic vasculitis.

Twenty-five percent of patients with primary Sjögren's syndrome develop vasculitis (Chap. 269). This usually takes the form of a cutaneous palpable purpura or hypersensitivity vasculitis of the lower extremities. Patients with Sjögren's syndrome may also develop a severe, systemic vasculitis. This is often seen in the setting of cryoglobulinemia and may result in fever, skin rash, and bowel infarction. The vasculitic syndromes seen in patients with Sjögren's syndrome are generally episodic rather than chronic.

A variety of neurologic conditions have been described in patients with Sjögren's syndrome. The most common nervous system presentation is that of a sensory polyneuropathy and/or mononeuritis multiplex. Central nervous system involvement has been reported in this illness and may be focal or diffuse in its presentation. Patients have also been noted to develop a diffuse proximal myositis.

Pulmonary involvement generally takes the form of an interstitial pneumonitis which is usually of little clinical significance. Pulmonary mass lesions may occur which may be infectious, inflammatory, or neoplastic.

Approximately 10 percent of patients with Sjögren's syndrome develop pseudolymphoma. This unusual lymphoproliferative disorder may present as lymphadenopathy, parotid gland enlargement, or pulmonary nodules. Approximately 10 percent of the Sjögren's syndrome patients with pseudolymphoma may go on to develop a lymphocytic (non-Hodgkin's) lymphoma.

Autoimmune thyroid disease resembling Hashimoto's thyroiditis is a common accompaniment of Sjögren's syndrome. Approximately 50 percent of patients with Sjögren's syndrome have some evidence of biochemical hypothyroidism, and 10 percent of patients require thyroid supplement.

Pregnant women with anti-Ro (SSA) antibodies are at an increased risk of delivering infants with cardiac conduction defects. Thus, pregnancies need to be carefully monitored in this group of patients.

A variety of laboratory abnormalities may be seen in patients with Sjögren's syndrome. Among the serologic and hematologic abnormalities are elevated levels of circulating immune complexes, autoantibodies, leukopenia, thrombocytosis, and an elevation in the erythrocyte sedimentation rate. In addition, patients often have a high urine pH.

While the presence of these abnormalities may increase one's level of suspicion of a diagnosis of Sjögren's syndrome, they are not diagnostic by themselves.

DIAGNOSIS   A diagnosis of Sjögren's syndrome is made when the triad of keratoconjunctivitis sicca, xerostomia, and mononuclear cell infiltration of the salivary gland is noted. This latter finding is made by a lower lip biopsy. The differential diagnosis of Sjögren's syndrome includes sarcoidosis, lymphoma, primary amyloidosis, and graft-versus-host disease.

TREATMENT AND PROGNOSIS   Treatment is geared toward symptomatic relief of mucosal dryness, and includes artificial tears, ophthalmologic lubricating ointments, nasal sprays of normal saline, moisturizing skin lotions, and frequent sips of water. There is currently no effective treatment for the ongoing exocrine gland destruction. Corticosteroids have been used with varying degrees of success in the management of glomerulonephritis, interstitial pneumonitis, and pseudolymphoma. They have not proved to be effective in the management of the cutaneous vasculitis. Patients with systemic vasculitis associated with cryoglobulinemia may benefit from brief courses of immunosupressive therapy (Chap. 269). It should be stressed that this form of systemic vasculitis is episodic, and therefore, in contrast to most forms of systemic necrotizing vasculitis, does not require chronic immunosuppressive therapy. Therapy of pseudolymphoma should be reserved for those cases in which vital organ function is threatened. Due to the fact that there is some suggestion that cytotoxic therapy may predispose to the transition from pseudolymphoma to true lymphoma, this form of immunosuppressive therapy should be reserved for potentially life-threatening situations.

The overall prognosis for patients with Sjögren's syndrome is quite good. Patients with secondary Sjögren's syndrome generally have less severe manifestations of Sjögren's than those with the primary form. Patients with primary disease are best managed with ocular and mucosal lubricants, attention to oral hygiene, frequent monitoring of thyroid function, and the reassurance that their disease, while a substantial source of morbidity, generally does not shorten life.

REFERENCES

ALEXANDER EL et al: Neurologic complications of primary Sjögren's syndrome. Medicine 61:247, 1982

FOX RI et al: Primary Sjögren's syndrome: Clinical and immunopathologic features. Semin Arthritis Rheum 14:77, 1984

MOUTSOPOULOS HM et al: Sjögren's syndrome: Current issues. Ann Intern Med 92:212, 1980

PAVLIDIS NA et al: The clinical picture of primary Sjögren's syndrome: A retrospective study. J Rheumatol 9:685, 1982

267   ANKYLOSING SPONDYLITIS

BRUCE C. GILLILAND

Ankylosing spondylitis, a disease that has been called by many names, including rheumatoid spondylitis and Marie-Strümpell disease, is a chronic and usually progressive inflammatory disease involving the articulations of the spine and adjacent soft tissues. The sacroiliac joints are always affected. Involvement of the hip and shoulder joints commonly occurs; peripheral joints are affected less frequently. The disease predominantly affects young men and begins most often in the third decade. A high association has been found between this disorder and the histocompatibility antigen HLA-B27. The clinical features of this disease are distinctly different from those of rheumatoid arthritis. The etiology is not known.

EPIDEMIOLOGY   Ankylosing spondylitis is found throughout the world. In the white population, the prevalence in men is 0.5 to 4 per 1000 and in women 0.05 to 0.5 per 1000, depending on the criteria employed.

Hereditary factors play an important role in the development of ankylosing spondylitis. Histocompatibility typing has revealed the presence of HLA-B27 antigen in 88 to 96 percent of spondylitic patients, while in the normal white population 7 percent have this antigen. In blacks, HLA-B27 occurs less frequently, which may account for the lower prevalence of this disease among them.

HLA-B27 is inherited in a mendelian fashion, and HLA-B27 is found in 50 percent of first-degree relatives of those spondylitic patients who are positive for HLA-B27. Within the group of relatives, 20 percent have either symptomatic or asymptomatic spondylitis. Ankylosing spondylitis is seen occasionally in patients who are negative for HLA-B27, indicating that other genetic or environmental factors are necessary for the development of the disease.

Several diseases that possess clinical features in common with ankylosing spondylitis also occur more frequently in patients with the HLA-B27 antigen. These disorders include Reiter's syndrome, psoriatic spondyloarthritis, *Yersinia* arthritis, spondyloarthritis of inflammatory bowel disease, and acute anterior uveitis. The role of HLA-B27 antigen in the pathogenesis of these disorders is not known. The currently favored hypothesis is that the HLA-B27 antigen, because of a close association with the immune response genes, is only a marker distinguishing a group of individuals whose immune response to an as yet undefined infectious agent leads to one of the HLA-B27–associated forms of arthritis.

PATHOLOGY   The earliest histopathologic changes usually occur in the sacroiliac joints but may start anywhere in the spine. The disease usually progresses up the spine, and occasionally segments will be skipped.

Synovitis of the involved diarthrodial joints of the spine (apophyseal and costovertebral joints) and of the sacroiliac, hip, shoulder, and peripheral joints resembles that of rheumatoid arthritis. Synovial hyperplasia and focal accumulation of lymphoid and plasma cells are seen histologically. Bony erosions and cartilage destruction ensue, followed later by fibrosis and bony ankylosis. In cartilaginous joints (intervertebral disks, manubriosternal, and symphysis pubis), granulation tissue invades the fibrocartilage, and adjacent bone is replaced later by fibrosis and ossification.

Occasionally, fibrous tissue invades the vertebral body to produce a radiolucent cyst which may be confused with an infectious process. Erosions at the anterior corners of the vertebral bodies destroy their normal anterior concavity and give the vertebrae a square appearance on lateral radiographs. Ossification of the outer layers of the annulus fibrosus at its lateral margins produces the syndesmophytes and "bamboo spine" observed radiographically. Ossification also involves the anterior portion of the annulus fibrosus and occasionally the inner aspect of the anterior longitudinal ligament. The radiographic appearance of the ossification at the anterior disk margins has led to the misconception that only the anterior longitudinal ligament is involved. In ankylosing spondylitis, a common site of inflammation is at the insertion of ligaments, tendons, and capsules into bone. Inflammation at these sites is termed *enthesitis*. The site where a ligament or tendon inserts into bone is the enthesis. The disease process is referred to as enthesopathy, which is common to the spondylarthropathies (ankylosing spondylitis, Reiter's disease, psoriatic arthritis). Bony erosions and new bone formation follow at these sites, most notably at the spinous processes, greater trochanters, pelvic bones, and heels.

Focal medial necrosis at the root of the aorta causes dilatation of the aortic ring. The aortic cusps may be shortened and thickened but are not fused. These processes lead to aortic valve incompetence. Fibrous tissue may enter the membranous septum and invade the atrioventricular bundle, resulting in conduction defects.

MANIFESTATIONS   The disease occurs most commonly between the ages of 15 and 40 years and rarely after age 50. The initial symptoms are low back pain and stiffness, often worse in the early morning. Stiffness of the low back may last for several hours after the patient gets out of bed in the morning and also occurs after periods of inactivity during the day. Pain in the hips, buttocks, and shoulders is often present. Nocturnal back pain may force the patient to walk around in an attempt to gain relief. In approximately 10 percent of patients, early symptoms resemble sciatica, with pain in the buttocks and in back of the thighs. The pain may alternate from side to side and seldom radiates below the knee. Abnormal findings on neurologic examination are unusual. Patients may have the simultaneous onset of peripheral arthritis and back pain; however, peripheral arthritis uncommonly precedes back symptoms in adults. Peripheral arthritis, other than in the hips or shoulders, is relatively infrequent, and residual damage of these joints occurs infrequently. Hip disease occurs in approximately 30 percent of patients and may be a major cause of disability. Severe involvement early in the disease may result in ankylosis of the hip. Hip involvement, on the other hand, may lead to arthritis indistinguishable from osteoarthritis of the hip. Occasionally, patients may experience anterior chest pain from thoracic skeletal involvement which may mimic angina pectoris. Pleuritic chest pain may occur on deep breathing due to inflammation at the insertion of the costosternal and costovertebral muscles. Other causes of chest pain are involvement of the manubriosternal and sternoclavicular joints. Radicular pain from the spine may radiate to the abdomen, suggesting visceral disease. Atlantoaxial subluxation and spinal cord compression occur less commonly than in rheumatoid arthritis. Patients with fused cervical spines are especially susceptible to fractures of the neck on falling.

Aortic valve incompetence is present in 3 percent of patients and may result in severe aortic regurgitation, requiring surgical repair. Conduction abnormalities include varying degrees of heart block and left bundle branch block. The conduction defects are more apt to appear in patients with aortic valve incompetence, but they may exist alone. Some patients require implantation of a pacemaker.

Acute anterior uveitis is observed in 20 to 30 percent of patients and may be recurrent. Occasionally, this may be the presenting symptom, calling attention to the diagnosis of ankylosing spondylitis. Amyloidosis is found in a small number of patients at autopsy and is a cause of uremia in this disease. Bilateral upper lobe fibrosis is a recognized late manifestation of ankylosing spondylitis and may mimic tuberculosis. Patients develop chronic productive cough and dyspnea. The disease may progress to dense fibrosis, and death can result from massive hemoptysis.

The constitutional symptoms are usually mild at the onset and throughout the disease, but in a few patients with severe disease, fatigue, anemia, fever, and weight loss may be present.

Symptoms may be persistent or intermittent for months or years with the typical deformities usually evolving after 10 years or more of disease. In some patients ankylosis of the spine may progress with little or no pain. The degree of spinal involvement varies among patients, ranging from only sacroiliac joint involvement to complete ankylosis of the spine. Once ankylosis of joints occurs, pain usually disappears.

The *cauda equina syndrome* is a rare complication appearing usually in patients with long-standing and apparently inactive disease. The cause of this syndrome is unclear but may be the result of previous arachnoiditis or ischemia. Symptoms result from the involvement of the lumbosacral nerve roots and include buttock or leg pain, lower extremity weakness, and loss of bladder and rectal sphincter control. Loss of sensation occurs in the saddle area, posterior thighs, and lateral aspects of the feet. The deep tendon reflexes are diminished. Myelography shows posterior diverticula along the lumbar nerve root sheets or throughout the entire dural sac, when the study is done with the patient in the supine position. Neurologic manifestations are usually slowly progressive. Adequate treatment is not available.

Physical findings early in the disease may be minimal. Tenderness over the sacroiliac joints can be elicited by direct palpation or percussion, or by maneuvers that stress the joint. Tenderness may also be present over the costosternal joints, spinous processes, iliac crests, ischial tuberosities, greater trochanters, and heels. The lumbar spine will show loss of the normal lordosis and paraspinal muscle spasm. The anterior flexion of the lumbar spine is measured by the Schober test. With the patient standing erect, the skin is marked over the fifth lumbar vertebra and two additional points, 10 cm above and 5 cm below the first mark. The patient is instructed to bend over as far as possible, and the distance between the upper and lower mark is measured. The difference between the original measurement of 15 cm and the measurement with full flexion is calculated and should be 5.0 cm or more in patients below the age of 50 years. Serial measurements in a given patient will reflect the progression of spine involvement. No distraction of such skin marks is seen in a patient with an ankylosed spine. Costovertebral involvement is best measured by chest expansion. The more advanced changes of spondylitis are easily recognized by the rigid spine, often fused in varying degrees of flexion, which may be quite pronounced in the thoracic region of the spine.

LABORATORY FINDINGS   The erythrocyte sedimentation rate (ESR) is elevated in the majority of cases, but its level poorly reflects fluctuations of disease activity, and the ESR is normal in 20 percent of patients with mild disease. A mild hypoproliferative anemia may be present during severe active disease. Tests for rheumatoid factor are negative even when peripheral joint disease is present. Mild to moderate elevations of the spinal fluid protein level may be present in active spondylitis. Synovial fluid from peripheral joints usually shows a moderate neutrophilic leukocytosis.

At the onset of symptoms the radiographs of the sacroiliac joints and the spine are often normal and may remain so for variable periods of time, depending on the rate of progression of the disease. Radiographs of the sacroiliac joints in early disease show blurring of the margins, irregular subchondral erosions, and patchy sclerosis. These changes are initially more pronounced in the lower third of the joint. Both sacroiliac joints are characteristically involved, but findings may first appear on one side. With progression, sclerosis becomes more marked, the joint space is lost, and later osteoporosis appears. Similar changes are observed in other articulations of the axial skeleton, including the symphysis pubis and apophyseal joints. At points of tendon insertions (e.g., pelvis, os calcis) the adjacent bone shows erosions, sclerosis, and fluffy new bone formation. Lateral films of the os calcis may show bony spurs at the site of attachment for the Achilles tendon and for the plantar fascia.

Radiographs of the spine in early phases of the disease may show straightening of the lumbar spine and squaring of the lumbar and lower thoracic vertebrae. With progression, syndesmophytes appear along the lateral and anterior surfaces of the intervertebral disks and bridge adjacent vertebrae. They are characteristically present on both lateral sides of the intervertebral disk at any given level and usually arise from the margin of the vertebral body. The widespread distribution of syndesmophytes in advanced disease produces the picture of the "bamboo spine." Syndesmophytes must be differentiated from the osteophytes observed in degenerative joint disease. The syndesmophyte extends vertically from the adjacent vertebral margins along the outer aspect of the intervertebral disk, while the osteophyte projects horizontally before curving to form an intervertebral bridge.

DIAGNOSIS   A patient with ankylosing spondylitis in the advanced stage is easily recognized by the characteristic bent-over posture, rigid spine, exaggerated dorsal kyphosis, and waddling gait. When peripheral arthritis is present in the early stages of ankylosing spondylitis, confusion with rheumatoid arthritis may occur. Ankylosing spondylitis is predominantly a disease of young men, but the disease also exists in women in a milder form. HLA-B27 antigen is usually present, rheumatoid factor tests are negative, and rheumatoid nodules are not found. Radiographs of the spine show bilateral sacroiliitis and syndesmophytes, which are features not seen in adult rheumatoid arthritis. Ankylosing spondylitis in children often presents as a peripheral arthritis and, therefore, may be initially diagnosed as juvenile rheumatoid arthritis. Hip, sacroiliac, and spine involvement along with attacks of acute anterior uveitis eventually point to the diagnosis of spondylitis. Older boys are most often affected. HLA-B27 is usually present in these children in contrast to juvenile rheumatoid arthritis in which the prevalence of this antigen does not differ from normal persons.

Differentiation from other diseases with spondylitis early in the course may be difficult. Since the spondylitis is indistinguishable from that associated with ulcerative colitis and regional enteritis and may antedate the bowel disease by months or years, symptoms and signs of intestinal disease should always be sought. The spondylitis with Reiter's syndrome and psoriatic arthritis have common radiographic features, but differ from ankylosing spondylitis in having a greater tendency for syndesmophytes to appear at only one lateral margin of the intervertebral disk at any given level and to arise beyond the margin of the vertebral body. The distribution of syndesmophytes is more random, and the degree of spinal involvement is usually less than in ankylosing spondylitis. Other clinical features of Reiter's syndrome and psoriatic arthritis allow for easy separation of these diseases from ankylosing spondylitis. Diffuse idiopathic skeletal hyperostosis (DISH, or Forestier's disease with extra spinal involvement) is distinguished from ankylosing spondylitis by the lack of apophyseal and sacroiliac joint involvement and by its more frequent occurrence in men over 50. Laminated new bone formation involves the anterior and lateral spinal ligaments most prominently in the middle to lower thoracic regions, particularly on the right side, and resembles the dripping of candle wax. The radiologic findings of sacroiliitis are distinguished from osteitis condensans ilii by the finding of sclerosis on only the ilial side of the joint and the preservation of the joint space in the latter. Sciatica of ankylosing spondylitis can be differentiated from that of disk disease, since it may alternate from side to side, the pain seldom radiates below the knee, and neurologic signs are usually absent. Malignancies should be considered in both youngsters and older patients with symptoms of back pain.

TREATMENT   The goal of therapy is to prevent or minimize the deformities of the spine inherent in this disease. With minimal spine deformity, patients may be able to continue working and living in a reasonably normal fashion if hip disease is not severe. Patients should be instructed to maintain an erect posture whether walking, standing, or sitting. They should be encouraged to sleep in a prone position or, if this is not possible, in a supine position on a flat firm mattress using a small pillow or none at all. Breathing exercises should be encouraged.

Drugs will not halt the progression of the disease, but they provide adequate relief to permit maintenance of posture. Indomethacin is effective in maintenance doses of 75 to 150 mg per day. Salicylates or other nonsteroidal anti-inflammatory drugs may be effective. Phenylbutazone in a dose of 200 to 300 mg per day is also effective but because of its potential to cause aplastic anemia, its use is recommended only after all other nonsteroidal anti-inflammatory drugs have failed. Therapy should be discontinued when symptoms abate. Gold and chloroquine have not been beneficial. Any benefit from glucocorticoids is outweighed by their side effects. Iritis can usually be treated with intraocular steroids. No effective therapy is available for the lung fibrosis occurring in patients with ankylosing spondylitis.

Surgical correction of extreme flexion deformities of the spine by wedge resection and refusion in an improved position may be helpful

in selected patients. The potential danger of spinal cord damage and the long convalescent period should be carefully considered before advising surgery. Patients with crippling hip disease may benefit from total hip replacement.

REFERENCES

CALIN A: Ankylosing spondylitis, in *Textbook of Rheumatology*, 2d ed, WN Kelley et al (eds). Philadelphia, Saunders, 1985, pp 993–1007
——— et al: Genetic differences between B27-positive patients with ankylosing spondylitis and B27-positive health controls. Arthritis Rheum Dec:1460, 1983
RESNICK D, NIWAYAMA G: Diffuse idiopathic skeletal hyperostosis (DISH), in *Diagnosis of Bone and Joint Disorders*, D Resnick, G Niwayama (eds). Philadelphia, Saunders, 1981, pp 1416–1452
———, ———: Ankylosing spondylitis, in *Diagnosis of Bone and Joint Disorders*, D Resnick, G Niwayama (eds). Philadelphia, Saunders, 1981, pp 1040–1102

268   REITER'S SYNDROME AND BEHÇET'S SYNDROME

HARALAMPOS M. MOUTSOPOULOS

REITER'S SYNDROME   Reiter's syndrome was originally described as a triad of arthritis, conjunctivitis, and urethritis. Today, the presence of seronegative, oligoarticular, asymmetric arthritis with urethritis and/or cervicitis has been proposed as sufficient manifestations for the diagnosis of the syndrome.

Prevalence, pathogenesis, and pathology   Two clinical forms of Reiter's syndrome are recognized: the postvenereal and the postdysenteric (epidemic). The latter is also called "reactive arthritis." Postvenereal Reiter's syndrome prevails in North America and western Europe, whereas in developing countries, the postdysenteric form appears to be more common.

The exact prevalence of the syndrome is not known. Reiter's syndrome is the most common cause of arthritis in young men, and there is a striking correlation between the disease prevalence and the frequency of the HLA-B27 alloantigen in a given population. The syndrome develops in 1 to 3 percent of males with nongonococcal urethritis, in 2 to 3 percent of patients with bacillary dysentery, and in 20 percent of individuals with the HLA-B27 antigen. In contrast to 10 percent of normal controls, up to 90 percent of Reiter's syndrome patients are HLA-B27–positive. The postvenereal disease is less common in females. The postdysenteric form affects both sexes equally. In children and in the elderly, the syndrome almost always follows dysentery.

The cause and pathogenesis of Reiter's syndrome remain speculative. It is recognized, however, that an infectious process of the urogenital tract or the gut coupled with a specific genetic background in some patients can trigger the development of Reiter's syndrome. Through epidemiologic and serologic studies, *Chlamydia trachomatis* and a *Mycoplasma (Ureoplasma urealyticum)* have been implicated as the most common agents associated with the postvenereal Reiter's syndrome, while *Shigella dysenteriae* and *S. flexneri*, *Salmonella enteritidis*, *Yersinia enterocolitica*, and *Campylobacter jejuni* have been proposed as the responsible microorganisms for the postdysenteric Reiter's syndrome.

This syndrome lacks a specific histopathologic lesion. The histologic changes of an affected synovial membrane vary with the clinical activity and duration of the process. In acute arthritis of a few weeks' duration, the synovial membrane shows hyperemia with an infiltrate consisting primarily of polymorphonuclear leukocytes. In patients with long-standing arthritis, the histologic lesion is indistinguishable from that seen in rheumatoid arthritis. The histology of the skin lesion, which is termed keratoderma blenorrhagica, is similar to pustular psoriasis.

Clinical features The syndrome usually begins with urethritis followed by conjunctivitis and rheumatologic findings. Urethritis can be observed in both forms of the syndrome.

The urethral discharge is intermittent and, in most cases, moderate in amount, serous, and asymptomatic. Infrequently, it is profuse, purulent, and blood-stained. Other rare urologic problems include prostatitis, urethral strictures, seminal vasculitis, cystitis, and urethral stenosis.

The conjunctivitis is usually minimal and lasts for only a few days or weeks. Infrequently, the conjunctivitis is symptomatic, presenting with "red eyes," burning, itching, and profuse purulent discharge. Rarely, nongranulomatous anterior uveitis, symptomatic superficial keratitis, posterior uveitis, and optic neuritis are present.

Rheumatologic manifestations include arthritis, tenosynovitis, dactylitis, and plantar fasciitis. Arthritis is usually acute, asymmetric, oligoarticular, involving predominantly the joints of the lower extremities; knees, ankles, metatarsophalangeal, and toe interphalangeal joints are affected in both types of Reiter's syndrome. The acute arthritis is accompanied by malaise and fever. The joints are warm, erythematous, and painful. Plantar fasciitis and Achilles tendonitis are common. The duration of the acute episode ranges from a few days to several months. Relapses are frequent and may be precipitated by sexual exposure followed by urethritis. Permanent foot abnormalities include calcaneal spurs, pes cavus or planus and dorsiflexion, and tibular deviation of the toes at the metatarsophalangeal joints. Sacroiliitis occurs in Reiter's patients. However, the precise frequency of spondylitis in these patients has not been estimated.

Mucocutaneous lesions are common and appear in the mouth, on the glans penis, the palms, and the soles. Superficial oral mucosal and glans penile lesions are painless and found in approximately one-third of the patients. Keratoderma blenorrhagica, which consists of crusted scaling papules, occurs in up to 30 percent of postvenereal Reiter's syndrome patients, but not in the postdysenteric syndrome patients. These papules appear mainly on the palms, soles, and glans penis, but occasionally may be found on the limbs, trunk, scalp, and scrotum. Accumulation of subungual cornified material occurs in patients with or without keratoderma blenorrhagica. This material lifts the nail plate. Pitting of the nails does not occur, distinguishing this lesion from psoriatic arthritis.

Uncommon manifestations of Reiter's syndrome include pleuropericarditis, aortic regurgitation, neurologic manifestations, and secondary amyloidosis.

Long-term follow-up studies have shown that one-third of patients with Reiter's syndrome have recurrent or sustained disease, while about 15 to 25 percent develop permanent disability. Chronic heel involvement appears to be an early sign of poor prognosis.

Laboratory manifestations There are no specific tests for the syndrome. Mild anemia of chronic disease, leukocytosis, elevated erythrocyte sedimentation rate, and C-reactive protein levels are common. Synovial fluid analysis is also nondiagnostic. The fluid is inflammatory with polymorphonuclear leukocytosis and high complement levels. Rheumatoid factors and antinuclear antibodies are negative.

Roentgenograms in the acute phase are not helpful, revealing only soft tissue edema. In chronic cases, bony erosions and joint space narrowing can be seen. Periosteal bone apposition along the shaft adjacent to the involved joint is frequently seen and is suggestive of Reiter's syndrome. Calcaneal spurs appear late in the disease. In case of ileosacral joint involvement, one or both joints may show irregularity, sclerosis, and fusion.

Diagnosis and differential diagnosis According to the preliminary criteria introduced by the American Rheumatism Association, the presence of asymmetric, seronegative oligoarthritis of 1 month's duration in combination with nonspecific urethritis or cervicitis is sufficient for the diagnosis of Reiter's syndrome with a specificity of around 80 percent. The bases for the differential diagnosis from gonococcal and psoriatic arthritis are presented in Table 268-1.

Treatment Treatment of Reiter's syndrome is empirical and aimed at relieving symptoms. Patient education, reassurance, and physical therapy are of paramount importance.

Acute arthritis is treated with analgesics and nonsteroidal anti-inflammatory drugs such as indomethacin (100 to 150 mg per day).

Systemic corticosteroids must be avoided because they can aggravate the cutaneous manifestations. However, local administration can be helpful for persistent monarthritis, fasciitis, and tendonitis. In cases of chronic destructive arthritis, cytotoxic drugs like methotrexate or azathioprine may be beneficial. The use of antibiotics remains controversial. It is clear that they do not have any direct effects on arthritis. Conjunctivitis and oral lesions usually do not require any treatment. Uveitis is treated with corticosteroids, either topical, periocular, or systemic, depending on the severity of the inflammation.

BEHÇET'S SYNDROME Behçet's syndrome is a multisystem disorder presenting with recurrent oral and genital ulcerations as well as uveitis often leading to blindness.

Prevalence, pathogenesis, and pathology The disease has a worldwide distribution. The prevalence of Behçet's syndrome ranges from 1:1000 in Japan to 1:500,000 in North America and Europe. In the Mediterranean countries the prevalence might be higher. It affects mainly young adults.

The etiology and pathogenesis of this syndrome remain obscure. Bacteria and viruses have been suggested as the causative agents but without convincing proof. Today, Behçet's syndrome is considered an autoimmune disease because of the common denominator of vasculitis in most patients. Circulating autoantibodies to human oral mucous membrane and immune complexes are found in approximately 50 percent of the cases. Familial occurrence has been reported, and in patients from eastern Mediterranean countries and Japan, the disease appears to be linked to HLA-B5 and HLA-DR5 alloantigens.

Clinical features The recurrent aphthous ulcerations are a sine qua non for the diagnosis. The ulcers are usually painful with a diameter ranging from 2 to 10 mm. They can be shallow or deep with a central yellowish necrotic base, appear singly or in crops, and are located on the lips, gums, buccal mucosa, tongue, tonsils, and larynx. The ulcers persist for 1 to 2 weeks and subside without leaving scars. The genital ulcers resemble the oral ones in both appearance and course. Vaginal ulcers are usually painless and may be detected during routine pelvic examination. Painful genital ulcers may occur on the external genitalia.

Skin involvement includes folliculitis, erythema nodosum, and an acnelike exanthem. Severe dermal vasculitis is an infrequent event. Nonspecific skin inflammatory reactivity to any scratches, needle pricks, and intradermal saline injection (pathergy test) is a common and specific manifestation in Japanese and eastern Mediterranean patients.

Eye involvement is the most dreaded complication in that it can occasionally progress rapidly to blindness. The eye disease is usually

TABLE 268-1 Differences between Reiter's syndrome (RS), gonococcal arthritis (GA), and psoriatic arthritis (PA)

	RS	GA	PA
Conjunctivitis	+	−	+
Uveitis	+	+	−
Gonococcus culture	±	±	−
Sacroiliitis	±	−	±
Stomatitis	+	−	−
Balanitis	+	−	−
Keratoderma blenorrhagica	+	−	±
Arthritis	Lower extremities	Upper extremities	Upper extremities
Response to penicillin	−	+	−
HLA-B27	80%	10%	20–50%
Course	Recurrent	Acute	Chronic

present at the onset but also may develop within the first few years. In addition to iritis, posterior uveitis, retinal vessel occlusions, and optic neuritis can be seen in some cases of the syndrome. Hypopyon uveitis, which is considered the hallmark of Behçet's syndrome, is in fact a rare manifestation.

The arthritis of Behçet's syndrome is not deforming and affects the knees and ankles.

Superficial or deep peripheral vein thrombosis is seen in one-fourth of the patients. Pulmonary emboli, however, appear to be an exceptionally rare complication. The superior vena cava is obstructed occasionally, producing a dramatic clinical picture. Arterial involvement occurs infrequently and presents with aortitis or peripheral arterial aneurysm and arterial thrombosis.

The prevalence of central nervous system involvement differs geographically. High figures are quoted from northern Europe and the United States. The most common lesions are benign intracranial hypertension, a multiple sclerosis–like picture, and pyramidal involvement. Psychiatric disturbances are frequent.

Gastrointestinal involvement is reported in patients from Japan and include mucosal ulcerations of the gut.

Laboratory findings are nonspecific indexes of inflammation such as leukocytosis, elevated erythrocyte sedimentation rate as well as C-reactive protein levels, and antibodies to human oral mucosa.

Prognosis and treatment   The severity of the syndrome usually abates with time; male sex and younger age at onset seem to predispose for severe illness. Apart from the cases with neurologic complications, the life expectancy seems to be normal and the only serious complication is blindness.

Treatment of Behçet's syndrome is symptomatic and empirical. Mucous membrane involvement may respond to topical corticosteroids, while the serious manifestations of Behçet's syndrome, i.e., uveitis and central nervous system involvement, require systemic corticosteroid therapy (prednisone, 1 mg/kg per day) and/or cytotoxic agents (chlorambucil, 0.1 mg/kg per day; azathioprine, 1 to 2 mg/kg per day; or cyclophosphamide, 1 to 2 mg/kg per day). There are early reports of the beneficial use of cyclosporin A in the uveitis of Behçet's syndrome. The arthritis responds to rest and analgesics. Thrombophlebitis is treated with aspirin, 500 mg per day, and dipyridamol, 250 mg per day.

REFERENCES

CALIN A, FRIES JF: An "experimental" epidemic of Reiter's syndrome revisited: Follow-up evidence of genetic and environmental factors. Arthritis Rheum 84:564, 1976

KEAT A: Reiter's syndrome and reactive arthritis in perspective. N Engl J Med 309:1606, 1983

MARTIN DH et al: *Chlamydia trachomatis* infections in men with Reiter's syndrome. Ann Intern Med 100:207, 1984

O'DUFFY JD et al: Behçet's disease: Report of 10 cases, 3 with new manifestations. Ann Intern Med 75:561, 1971

SHIMIZU T et al: Behçet's disease (Behçet's syndrome). Semin Arthritis Rheum 8:223, 1979

WILLKENS RF et al: Reiter's syndrome. Evaluation of preliminary criteria for definite disease. Arthritis Rheum 24:844, 1981

YAZICI H, MOUTSOPOULOS HM: Behçet's disease, in *Current Therapy in Allergy and Immunology*, LM Lichtenstein, AS Fauci (eds). Philadelphia, Decker, 1985

269   THE VASCULITIS SYNDROMES

ANTHONY S. FAUCI

DEFINITION   Vasculitis is a clinicopathologic process characterized by inflammation of and damage to blood vessels. The vessel lumen is usually compromised, and this is associated with ischemia of the tissues supplied by the involved vessel. A broad and heterogeneous group of syndromes may result from this process since any type,

size, and location of blood vessel may be involved. Vasculitis and its consequences may be the primary or sole manifestation of a disease; alternatively, vasculitis may be a secondary component of another primary disease. Vasculitis may be confined to a single organ such as the skin, or it may simultaneously involve several organ systems.

PATHOPHYSIOLOGY AND PATHOGENESIS   Generally, most of the vasculitic syndromes are assumed to be mediated at least in part by immunopathogenic mechanisms. However, evidence to this effect is for the most part indirect. Deposition of immune complexes in tissues (see Chap. 261) is the most widely accepted pathogenic mechanism of vasculitis. Nonetheless, the causal role of immune complexes has not been clearly established in most of the vasculitic syndromes. Circulating immune complexes need not result in deposition of the complexes in blood vessels with ensuing vasculitis, and many patients with active vasculitis do not have demonstrable circulating or deposited immune complexes. This situation may result from an inadequacy of the techniques for detecting certain types of immune complexes or from the rapidity with which complexes may be cleared from the circulation. The actual antigen contained in the immune complex has only rarely been identified in vasculitic syndromes. In this regard, hepatitis B antigen has been identified in both the circulating and deposited immune complexes in a subset of patients with systemic vasculitis, most notably within the polyarteritis nodosa group (see below).

The mechanisms of tissue damage in immune-complex–mediated vasculitis resemble those described for serum sickness (Chap. 261). In this model, antigen-antibody complexes are formed in antigen excess and are deposited in vessel walls whose permeability has been increased by vasoactive amines from platelets or from mast cells which have released their intracellular contents as a result of IgE-triggered mechanisms. The deposition of complexes results in activation of complement components, particularly C5a which is strongly chemotactic for neutrophils. These cells then infiltrate the vessel wall, phagocytose the immune complexes, and regurgitate their intracytoplasmic enzymes which damage the vessel wall. As the process becomes subacute or chronic, mononuclear cells infiltrate the vessel wall. The common denominator of the resulting syndrome is compromise of the vessel lumen with ischemic changes in the tissues supplied by the involved vessel.

In addition to the classic immune-complex–mediated mechanisms of vasculitis, other immunopathogenic mechanisms may be involved in damage to vessels. The most prominent of these is cell-mediated immune injury as reflected in the histopathologic feature of granulomatous vasculitis. However, immune complexes themselves may induce granulomatous responses, and the presence of granulomas in or around blood vessels may be indicative of immune-complex mechanisms, delayed hypersensitivity or cell-mediated immune responses, or both. Other mechanisms such as direct cellular cytotoxicity or antibody directed against vessel components or antibody-dependent cellular cytotoxicity have been suggested in certain types of vessel damage. However, there is no convincing evidence to support their contribution to the pathogenesis of any of the recognized vasculitic syndromes.

It is unclear why certain individuals develop vasculitis in response to certain antigenic stimuli whereas others do not. However, it is likely that a number of factors are involved in the ultimate expression of a vasculitic syndrome. These include the genetic predisposition, the regulatory mechanisms associated with immune response to certain antigens, and the ability of the reticuloendothelial system to clear circulating complexes from the blood. The size and physicochemical properties of immune complexes, the relative degree of turbulence of blood flow, the intravascular hydrostatic pressure in different vessels, and the preexisting integrity of the vessel endothelium likely explain why only certain types of immune complexes cause vasculitis and why the vasculitic process is selective for only certain vessels in individual patients.

CLASSIFICATION OF VASCULITIC SYNDROMES A major feature of the vasculitic syndromes as a group is the fact that there is a great deal of heterogeneity at the same time as there is considerable overlap among them. This has led to both difficulty and confusion with regard to the categorization of these diseases. The classification scheme listed in Table 269-1 takes into account this heterogeneity and overlap, and will serve as a matrix to emphasize the fact that certain syndromes are predominantly systemic in nature and almost invariably lead to irreversible organ system dysfunction and even death if untreated, while others are usually localized to the skin and rarely result in irreversible dysfunction of vital organs. The distinguishing and overlapping features of the diseases listed in Table 269-1, which justify this classification scheme, will be discussed below.

SYSTEMIC NECROTIZING VASCULITIS

CLASSIC POLYARTERITIS NODOSA **Definition** Polyarteritis nodosa (PAN) in its classic form was described in 1866 by Kussmaul and Maier. It is a multisystem, necrotizing vasculitis of small- and medium-sized muscular arteries in which involvement of the renal and visceral arteries is characteristic. Classic PAN does not involve pulmonary arteries, although bronchial vessels may be involved; granulomas, significant eosinophilia, and an allergic diathesis are not part of the classic syndrome.

Incidence and prevalence It is difficult to establish an accurate incidence of this disease because of the fact that many reports of PAN actually have included diseases other than the classic syndrome. It is clearly an uncommon, but not a rare, disease. The mean age at onset is 45 years and the male to female ratio is 2.5:1.

Pathophysiology and pathogenesis The vascular lesion in classic PAN is a necrotizing inflammation of small- and medium-sized muscular arteries. The lesions are segmental and tend to involve bifurcations and branchings of arteries. They may spread circumferentially to involve adjacent veins. However, involvement of venules is not seen in classic PAN, and if present, suggest the polyangiitis overlap syndrome (see below). In the acute stages of disease, polymorphonuclear neutrophils infiltrate all layers of the vessel wall and perivascular areas, which results in intimal proliferation and degeneration of the vessel wall. Mononuclear cells infiltrate the area as the lesions progress to the subacute and chronic stages. Fibrinoid necrosis of the vessels ensues with compromise of the lumen, thrombosis, infarction of the tissues supplied by the involved vessel, and, in some cases, hemorrhage. As the lesions heal, there is collagen deposition, which may lead to further occlusion of the vessel lumen. Aneurysmal dilatations up to 1 cm in size along the involved arteries are characteristic of classic PAN. Granulomas and substantial eosinophilia with eosinophilic tissue infiltrations are not characteristically found and suggest allergic angiitis and granulomatosis (see below).

Multiple organ systems are involved, and the clinicopathologic findings reflect the degree and location of vessel involvement and the resulting ischemic changes (Table 269-2). As mentioned above, pulmonary arteries are not involved in classic PAN, and bronchial artery involvement is uncommon. The pathology in the kidney is predominantly that of arteritis; however, glomerulitis occurs in up to 30 percent of patients. In patients with significant hypertension, typical pathologic features of glomerulosclerosis may be seen alone or superimposed on lesions of glomerulonephritis. In addition, pathologic sequelae of hypertension may be found elsewhere in the body.

The presence of hepatitis B antigenemia in approximately 30 percent of patients with systemic vasculitis, particularly of the classic PAN type, together with the isolation of circulating immune complexes composed of hepatitis B antigen and immunoglobulin, as well as the demonstration by immunofluorescence of hepatitis B antigen, IgM, and complement in the blood vessel walls, strongly suggest the role of immunologic phenomena in the pathogenesis of this disease.

Clinical and laboratory manifestations Nonspecific signs and symptoms are the hallmarks of classic PAN. Fever, weight loss, and malaise are present in over one-half of cases. Patients usually present with vague symptoms such as weakness, malaise, headache, abdominal pain, and myalgias. Specific complaints related to the vascular involvement within a particular organ system may also dominate the presenting clinical picture as well as the entire course of the illness (Table 269-3). Renal involvement most commonly manifests as ischemic changes in the glomeruli; however, glomerulonephritis is seen in approximately 30 percent of patients. Hypertension may be related to both the renal polyarteritis as well as the glomerulitis and may dominate the clinical picture. Classic PAN may involve any organ system; the clinical manifestations related to specific organ system involvement are listed in Table 269-3.

There are no diagnostic serologic tests for classic PAN. In over 75 percent of patients the leukocyte count is elevated with a predominance of neutrophils. Eosinophilia is only rarely seen and, when present at high levels, suggests the diagnosis of allergic angiitis and granulomatosis. The anemia of chronic disease may be seen, and an elevated erythrocyte sedimentation rate (ESR) is invariably present. Other common laboratory findings reflect the particular organ involved. Hypergammaglobulinemia may be present, and up to 30 percent of patients have a positive test for hepatitis B surface antigen. Arteriograms may demonstrate characteristic abnormalities such as

TABLE 269-1 Classification of the vasculitic syndromes

Systemic necrotizing vasculitis
  Classic polyarteritis nodosa
  Allergic angiitis and granulomatosis of Churg-Strauss
  Polyangiitis overlap syndrome
Hypersensitivity vasculitis
  Exogenous stimuli proved or suspected
    Henoch-Schönlein purpura
    Serum sickness and serum sickness–like reactions
    Other drug-induced vasculitides
    Vasculitis associated with infectious diseases
  Endogenous antigens likely involved
    Vasculitis associated with neoplasms
    Vasculitis associated with connective tissue diseases
    Vasculitis associated with other underlying diseases
    Vasculitis associated with congenital deficiencies of the complement system
Wegener's granulomatosis
Giant cell arteritis
  Temporal arteritis
  Takayasu's arteritis
Other vasculitic syndromes
  Mucocutanous lymph node syndrome (Kawasaki's disease)
  Isolated central nervous system vasculitis
  Thromboangiitis obliterans (Buerger's disease)
  Miscellaneous vasculitides

TABLE 269-2 Organ system involvement at autopsy in classic PAN

Organ system	Percent
Kidney	85
Heart	76
Liver	62
Gastrointestinal tract:	51
Jejunum	37
Ileum	27
Mesentery	24
Colon	20
Duodenum	10
Gallbladder	10
Rectosigmoid	10
Appendix	7
Muscle	39
Pancreas	35
Testes	33
Peripheral nerves	32
Central nervous system	27
Skin	20

SOURCE: *Cupps and Fauci, 1981, p 32.*

aneurysms in the small- and medium-sized muscular arteries of the kidneys and abdominal viscera.

Diagnosis The diagnosis of classic PAN is based on the demonstration of characteristic findings of vasculitis on biopsy material of involved organs. In the absence of easily accessible tissue for biopsy, the angiographic demonstration of involved vessels, particularly in the form of aneurysms of small- and medium-sized arteries in the renal, hepatic, and visceral vasculature, is sufficient to make the diagnosis. Aneurysms of vessels are not pathognomonic of classic PAN; furthermore, aneurysms need not always be present, and angiographic findings may be limited to stenotic segments and obliteration of vessels. Biopsy of symptomatic organs such as nodular skin lesions, painful testes, and muscle groups provides the highest diagnostic yields, while blind biopsy of asymptomatic organs is frequently negative. In cases associated with hepatitis B antigenemia, the demonstration of circulating hepatitis B antigen serves as important circumstantial evidence in support of the diagnosis.

Treatment and prognosis The prognosis of untreated classic PAN is extremely poor. The usual clinical course is characterized either by fulminant deterioration or by relentless progression associated with intermittent acute flare-ups. Death usually results from renal failure; from gastrointestinal complications, particularly bowel infarcts and perforation; and from cardiovascular causes. Intractable hypertension often compounds dysfunction in other organ systems such as the kidneys, heart, and central nervous system leading to additional late morbidity and mortality. The 5-year survival rate of untreated patients has been reported to be 13 percent, while corticosteroid treatment may increase this figure to over 40 percent. Extremely favorable therapeutic results have been reported in classic PAN with the combination of prednisone, 1 mg/kg per day, and cyclophosphamide, 2 mg/kg per day (see section of Wegener's granulomatosis for a detailed description of this therapeutic regimen). This regimen has been reported to result in up to a 90 percent long-term remission rate even following the discontinuation of therapy. Isolated reports have indicated favorable therapeutic responses in classic PAN using plasmapheresis together with corticosteroids and cytotoxic agents.

ALLERGIC ANGIITIS AND GRANULOMATOSIS (CHURG-STRAUSS DISEASE) Definition Allergic angiitis and granulomatosis was described in 1951 by Churg and Strauss and is a disease characterized by granulomatous vasculitis of multiple organ systems, particularly the lung. It is similar in many respects to classic PAN except that the former has a high frequency of lung involvement, vasculitis of blood vessels of various types or sizes including veins and venules, intra- and extravascular granuloma formation together with eosinophilic tissue infiltration, and a strong association with severe asthma and peripheral eosinophilia.

TABLE 269-3 Clinical manifestations related to organ system involvement in classic PAN

Organ system	Percent incidence	Clinical manifestations
Renal	60	Renal failure, hypertension
Musculoskeletal	64	Arthritis, arthralgia, myalgia
Peripheral nervous system	51	Peripheral neuropathy, mononeuritis multiplex
Gastrointestinal tract	44	Abdominal pain, nausea and vomiting, bleeding, bowel infarction and perforation, cholecystitis, hepatic infarction, pancreatic infarction
Skin	43	Rash, purpura, nodules, cutaneous infarcts, livedo reticularis
Cardiac	36	Congestive heart failure, myocardial infarction, pericarditis
Genitourinary	25	Testicular, ovarian, or epididymal pain
Central nervous system	23	Cerebral vascular accident, altered mental status, seizure

SOURCE: *Cupps and Fauci, 1981, p 29.*

Incidence and prevalence Allergic angiitis and granulomatosis is an uncommon disease whose exact incidence, similar to classic PAN, is difficult to determine due to the grouping of multiple types of vasculitic syndromes in many reported series. The disease can occur at any age with the possible exception of infants. The mean age of onset is 44 years with a male to female ratio of 1.3:1.

Pathophysiology and pathogenesis The vasculitis which is characteristic of allergic angiitis and granulomatosis is similar to that of classic PAN (see above) with certain notable exceptions. In addition to small- and medium-sized muscular arteries, capillaries, veins, and venules can be involved in the former disease. The characteristic histopathologic features of allergic angiitis and granulomatosis are granulomatous reactions that may be present in the tissues or even within the walls of the vessels themselves. These are usually associated with infiltration of the tissues with eosinophils. This process can occur in any organ in the body; however, in sharp contrast to classic PAN, lung involvement is predominant, with skin, cardiovascular system, kidney, peripheral nervous system, and gastrointestinal tract also commonly involved. Although the precise pathogenesis of this disease is uncertain, its strong association with asthma, its clinicopathologic manifestations which strongly suggest hypersensitivity phenomena, and its close similarity to classic PAN point to aberrant immunologic phenomena.

Clinical and laboratory manifestations Patients with allergic angiitis and granulomatosis exhibit nonspecific manifestations such as fever, malaise, anorexia, and weight loss similar to patients with classic PAN. In contrast to the latter disease, the pulmonary findings in allergic angiitis and granulomatosis clearly dominate the clinical picture with severe asthmatic attacks and the presence of pulmonary infiltrates. Skin lesions occur in approximately 70 percent of patients and include nonthrombocytopenic purpura in addition to cutaneous and subcutaneous nodules. Apart from the characteristic pulmonary findings, the multisystem involvement in this disease is quite similar to that of classic PAN (see above); an important exception is the fact that the renal disease in allergic angiitis and granulomatosis is less common and generally less severe than that of classic PAN.

The characteristic laboratory finding in virtually all patients with allergic angiitis and granulomatosis is a striking eosinophilia which reaches levels greater than 1000 cells per cubic millimeter in more than 80 percent of patients. The other laboratory findings are similar to those of classic PAN and reflect the organ systems involved.

Diagnosis Similar to classic PAN, the diagnosis of allergic angiitis and granulomatosis is made by biopsy, demonstrating vasculitis in a patient with the characteristic clinical manifestations. The biopsy findings are distinctive in the latter disease in that granulomatous vasculitis with eosinophilic tissue involvement together with peripheral eosinophilia are typical. Furthermore, pulmonary involvement is extremely common and is usually manifested by severe asthma associated with pulmonary infiltrates that may be fleeting in nature.

Treatment and prognosis The prognosis of untreated allergic angiitis and granulomatosis is poor with a reported 5-year survival of 25 percent. Unlike classic PAN, the cause of death is more likely to be related to pulmonary and cardiac disease as opposed to renal or gastrointestinal involvement. Corticosteroid therapy has been reported to increase the 5-year survival to more than 50 percent. In corticosteroid failures or in patients who present with fulminant multisystem disease, the treatment of choice is a combined regimen of cyclophosphamide and alternate-day prednisone which has resulted in a high rate of complete remission similar to the experience with classic PAN (see above).

POLYANGIITIS OVERLAP SYNDROME Many patients with systemic necrotizing vasculitis manifest clinicopathologic characteristics which overlap both classic PAN and allergic angiitis and granulomatosis and also show features of the hypersensitivity small vessel group of vasculitides (see below). This subgroup has been referred to as the "polyangiitis overlap syndrome" and is part of the major grouping of systemic necrotizing vasculitis. It is clear that this entity does exist, and it has been designated with a distinct classification in order to avoid confusion in attempting to fit such overlap syndromes into one or other of the more classic vasculitic syndromes. This subgroup is truly a systemic vasculitis with the same potential for resulting in irreversible organ system dysfunction as the other systemic necrotizing vasculitides. The diagnostic and therapeutic considerations as well as the prognosis for this subgroup are the same as those for classic PAN and allergic angiitis and granulomatosis.

HYPERSENSITIVITY VASCULITIS

DEFINITION The term hypersensitivity vasculitis has been used to designate a heterogeneous group of disorders which are characterized by a vasculitic syndrome presumed to be associated with a hypersensitivity reaction following exposure to an antigen such as an infectious agent, a drug, or other foreign or endogenous substances. The common denominator of this group of diseases is the involvement of small vessels. Although any organ can be involved with this type of vasculitis, skin involvement generally dominates the clinical picture and the extracutaneous involvement is usually much less severe than that of the systemic vasculitides. There are multiple subgroups within the larger category of hypersensitivity vasculitis.

INCIDENCE AND PREVALENCE Although the exact incidence of this group of vasculitic syndromes is uncertain, it is clearly more common than the systemic necrotizing vasculitis group. The disease can occur at any age and in both sexes; however, different subgroups have a higher incidence in certain age groups and some are more common in males than females, or vice versa.

PATHOPHYSIOLOGY AND PATHOGENESIS The typical histopathologic feature of the hypersensitivity vasculitides is the presence of vasculitis of small vessels. Postcapillary venules are the most commonly involved vessels; capillaries and arterioles may be involved less frequently. This vasculitis is characterized by a leukocytoclasis which refers to the nuclear debris remaining from the neutrophils which have infiltrated in and around the vessels during the acute stages. In the subacute or chronic stages, mononuclear cells predominate; in certain subgroups, eosinophilic infiltration is seen. Erythrocytes often extravasate from the involved vessels, leading to palpable purpura.

Immune-complex deposition is generally considered to be the immunopathogenic mechanism of this type of vasculitis; however, formal proof that this is the case has not been established for all subgroups (see above). The hypersensitivity vasculitides can be broken down into two major categories depending on the type of putative antigen involved in the hypersensitivity reaction. In the originally described group, the antigen was foreign to the host, i.e., a drug, microbe, or foreign protein. In the second category, the antigen is felt to be endogenous to the host. Examples of these are the "self" proteins such as DNA or immunoglobulin which form immune complexes with their respective antibodies and lead to vasculitic complications in systemic lupus erythematosus and rheumatoid arthritis, respectively; other examples are the tumor antigens which form immune complexes with antibody and lead to vasculitis associated with certain neoplasms.

CLINICAL AND LABORATORY MANIFESTATIONS The hallmark of the broad group of hypersensitivity vasculitides is the predominance of skin involvement. Skin lesions may appear typically as palpable purpura; however, other cutaneous manifestations of the vasculitis may occur, including macules, papules, vesicles, bullae, subcutaneous nodules, ulcers, as well as recurrent or chronic urticaria. Despite the fact that skin lesions predominate, other organ systems may be involved to varying degrees and the extent to which this occurs may define a relatively distinct subgroup. Even in patients with isolated

cutaneous involvement, the disease may be characterized by systemic signs and symptoms such as fever, malaise, myalgia, and anorexia. The skin lesions may be pruritic or even quite painful with a burning or stinging sensation. Lesions most commonly occur in the lower extremities in ambulatory patients or in the sacral area in bedridden patients due to the effects of hydrostatic forces on the postcapillary venules. Edema may accompany certain lesions, and hyperpigmentation often occurs in areas of recurrent or chronic lesions.

There are no specific laboratory tests which are diagnostic of hypersensitivity vasculitis. A mild leukocytosis with or without eosinophilia is characteristic as is an elevated ESR. Cryoglobulins and rheumatoid factor may be seen in certain cases, and serum complement levels follow no definite pattern. Laboratory abnormalities related to specific organ dysfunction reflect the involvement of these organs in the particular syndrome in question.

Henoch-Schönlein purpura The most distinctive subgroup of the hypersensitivity vasculitides is Henoch-Schönlein purpura, also referred to as anaphylactoid purpura, which is characterized by palpable purpura, most commonly distributed over the buttocks and lower extremities; arthralgias; gastrointestinal signs and symptoms; and glomerulonephritis. The disease is usually seen in children; however, individuals of any age may be affected. It has a remarkable tendency to resolve and recur several times over a period of weeks or months, usually ending in spontaneous resolution. A small percentage of patients progress to chronic disease. A number of antigens have been implicated in the immunopathogenesis of this disease, including infectious agents, drugs, certain foods, insect bites, and immunizations. IgA is the antibody class most often seen in the immune complexes of these patients. The typical palpable purpura is seen in virtually all patients; most patients develop polyarthralgias in the absence of frank arthritis. Gastrointestinal involvement, which is seen in almost 70 percent of pediatric patients, is characterized by colicky abdominal pain usually associated with nausea, vomiting, diarrhea, or constipation, which is frequently accompanied by the passage of blood and mucus per rectum; bowel intussusception may occur rarely. The renal involvement is usually characterized by a mild glomerulitis leading to hematuria with red blood cell casts (see also Chap. 224). Most patients recover completely and some do not require therapy. When corticosteroid therapy is required, it is usually administered as 1 mg/kg per day of prednisone and tapered according to the clinical response.

Serum sickness and serum sickness–like reactions These reactions are characterized by the occurrence of fever, urticaria, polyarthralgias, and lymphadenopathy 7 to 10 days after primary exposure and 2 to 4 days after secondary exposure to a heterologous protein (classic serum sickness) or a nonprotein drug such as penicillin or sulfa (serum sickness–like reaction). Most of the manifestations are not due to a vasculitis; however, occasional patients will have typical cutaneous venulitis which may progress rarely to a systemic vasculitis. This disorder is discussed in detail in Chap. 261.

Vasculitis associated with other underlying primary diseases A number of diseases have vasculitis as a secondary manifestation of the underlying primary process. Foremost among these are the connective tissue diseases, particularly systemic lupus erythematosus (Chap. 262), rheumatoid arthritis (Chap. 263), and Sjörgen's syndrome (Chap. 266). The most common form of vasculitis in these conditions is the small vessel venulitis isolated to the skin and clinically indistinguishable from the hypersensitivity vasculitides noted in response to an exogenous antigen. However, certain patients may develop a fulminant systemic necrotizing vasculitis indistinguishable from the polyarteritis nodosa group. Cryoglobulinemia may be seen in a number of the diverse vasculitic syndromes. Essential mixed cryoglobulinemia may present as a typical hypersensitivity vasculitis confined to the skin. However, typically it is associated with glomerulonephritis, arthralgias, hepatosplenomegaly, and lymphadenopathy in addition to skin involvement. The cryoglobulins usually consist of cryoprecipitable IgM rheumatoid factor directed against normal endogenous IgG.

Vasculitis can be associated with certain malignancies, particularly lymphoid or reticuloendothelial neoplasms. Leukocytoclastic venulitis confined to the skin is the most common finding; however, widespread systemic vasculitis may occur. Of particular note is the association of hairy-cell leukemia (Chap. 292) with classic PAN.

A leukocytoclastic vasculitis predominantly involving the skin with occasional involvement of other organ systems may be a minor component of many other diseases. These include subacute bacterial endocarditis, chronic Epstein-Barr virus infection, chronic active hepatitis, ulcerative colitis, congenital deficiencies of various complement components, retroperitoneal fibrosis, and primary biliary cirrhosis. Association of hypersensitivity vasculitis with alpha$_1$ antitrypsin deficiency, intestinal bypass surgery, and relapsing polychondritis have been reported.

DIAGNOSIS The diagnosis of hypersensitivity vasculitis is made by the demonstration of vasculitis on biopsy. Given the predominance of cutaneous involvement, biopsy material is generally readily available. Patients who present with what appears to be isolated cutaneous vasculitis should undergo a systemic (usually noninvasive) workup of other organ systems since skin involvement is often the presenting feature of systemic vasculitis.

TREATMENT AND PROGNOSIS Most cases of hypersensitivity vasculitis resolve spontaneously, and others, such as Henoch-Schönlein purpura, remit and relapse before finally remitting completely. In those patients in whom persistent cutaneous disease evolves or in whom extracutaneous organ system involvement occurs, a variety of therapeutic regimens have been tried with variable results. In general, the treatment of this type of vasculitis has not been satisfactory. This is in contrast to the systemic necrotizing vasculitis group (see above) and Wegener's granulomatosis (see below) which generally are much more serious diseases than hypersensitivity vasculitis, but usually respond dramatically to the combination of prednisone and cyclophosphamide. Fortunately, since the disease is generally limited to the skin, this lack of consistent response to therapy usually does not lead to a life-threatening situation. When an antigenic stimulus is recognized as the precipitating factor in the vasculitis, it should be removed; if this is a microbe, appropriate antimicrobial therapy should be instituted. If the vasculitis is associated with another underlying disease, treatment of the latter often results in resolution of the former. In situations where disease is apparently self-limited, no therapy, except possibly symptomatic therapy, is indicated. When disease persists or results in progressive organ system dysfunction such as renal failure in Henoch-Schönlein purpura, corticosteroid therapy should be instituted, usually as prednisone, 1 mg/kg per day, in a regimen aimed at rapid tapering where possible, either directly to discontinuation or by conversion to an alternate-day regimen followed by ultimate discontinuation. In cases that prove refractory to corticosteroids in which irreversible organ system dysfunction is likely, a trial of a cytotoxic agent such as cyclophosphamide in the regimen described above for systemic vasculitis is warranted. Patients with chronic vasculitis isolated to cutaneous venules rarely respond dramatically to any therapeutic regimen, and cytotoxic agents should be used only as a last resort in these patients. Plasmapheresis has been used with some success in fulminant cases.

WEGENER'S GRANULOMATOSIS

DEFINITION Wegener's granulomatosis is a distinct clinicopathologic entity characterized by granulomatous vasculitis of the upper and lower respiratory tracts together with glomerulonephritis. In addition, variable degrees of disseminated vasculitis involving both small arteries and veins may occur.

INCIDENCE AND PREVALENCE Wegener's granulomatosis is an uncommon disease whose true incidence is difficult to determine. It is extremely rare in blacks compared to whites; the male to female ratio is 1.3:1. The disease can be seen at any age but is infrequent among preadolescents; the mean age of onset is approximately 40 years. The disease has been reported to be associated with an increased prevalence of HLA-B8 and HLA-DR2.

PATHOPHYSIOLOGY AND PATHOGENESIS The histopathologic hallmarks of Wegener's granulomatosis are necrotizing vasculitis of small arteries and veins together with granuloma formation which may be either intravascular or extravascular. Lung involvement typically appears as multiple, bilateral, nodular cavity infiltrates which on biopsy almost invariably reveal the typical necrotizing granulomatous vasculitis. Endobronchial disease either in its active form or as a result of fibrous scarring may lead to obstruction with atelectasis. Upper airway lesions, particularly those in the sinuses and nasopharynx, typically reveal inflammation, necrosis, and granuloma formation with or without vasculitis.

It its earliest form, renal involvement is characterized by a focal and segmental glomerulitis which may evolve into a rapidly progressive crescentic glomerulonephritis. Granuloma formation is only rarely seen on renal biopsy. In addition to the classic triad of upper and lower respiratory tracts and kidney disease, virtually any organ can be involved with vasculitis, granuloma, or both.

The immunopathogenesis of this disease is unclear, although the involvement of upper airways and lung suggests an aberrant hypersensitivity response to an exogenous or even endogenous antigen that enters through or resides in the upper airway. The demonstration of circulating and deposited immune complexes in certain patients together with granulomatous reactivity suggests either an overlap of delayed hypersensitivity and immune-complex–mediated mechanisms or a granulomatous response to the immune complexes themselves.

CLINICAL AND LABORATORY MANIFESTATIONS A typical patient presents with severe upper respiratory tract findings such as paranasal sinus pain and drainage, and purulent or bloody nasal discharge with or without nasal mucosal ulceration. Nasal septal perforation may follow, leading to saddle nose deformity. Serous otitis media may occur as a result of eustachian tube blockage.

Pulmonary involvement may be manifested as asymptomatic infiltrates or may be clinically expressed as cough, hemoptysis, dyspnea, and chest discomfort. It is present in approximately 95 percent of patients.

Eye involvement (60 percent of patients) may range from a mild conjunctivitis to episcleritis, scleritis, granulomatous sclerouveitis, ciliary vessel vasculitis, and retroorbital mass lesions leading to proptosis.

Skin lesions (45 percent of patients) appear as papules, vesicles, palpable purpura, ulcers, or subcutaneous nodules; biopsy reveals vasculitis, granuloma, or both. Cardiac involvement (12 percent of patients) manifests as pericarditis, coronary vasculitis, or, rarely, cardiomyopathy. Nervous system manifestations (22 percent of patients) include cranial neuritis, mononeuritis multiplex, or, rarely, cerebral vasculitis and/or granuloma.

Renal disease (85 percent of patients) generally dominates the clinical picture and, if left untreated, accounts directly or indirectly for most of the mortality in this disease. Although it may smolder in some cases as a mild glomerulitis with proteinuria, hematuria, and red blood cell casts, it is clear that once clinically detectable renal functional impairment occurs, rapidly progressive renal failure usually ensues unless appropriate treatment is instituted.

While the disease is active, most patients have nonspecific symptoms and signs such as malaise, weakness, arthralgias, anorexia, and weight loss. Fever may indicate activity of the underlying disease, but more often reflects secondary infection, usually of the upper airway.

Characteristic laboratory findings include a markedly elevated ESR, mild anemia and leukocytosis, mild hypergammaglobulinemia, particularly of the IgA class, and mildly elevated rheumatoid factor. Thrombocytosis may be seen as an acute phase reactant; hypocomplementemia is not seen despite the presence of circulating immune complexes.

DIAGNOSIS The diagnosis of Wegener's granulomatosis is a clinicopathologic one made by the demonstration of necrotizing granulomatous vasculitis on biopsy of appropriate tissue in a patient with the clinical findings of upper and lower respiratory tract disease together with evidence of glomerulonephritis. Pulmonary tissue, preferably obtained by open thoracotomy, offers the highest diagnostic yield, almost invariably revealing granulomatous vasculitis. Biopsy of upper airway tissue usually reveals granulomatous inflammation with necrosis but may not show vasculitis. Renal biopsy confirms the presence of glomerulonephritis.

In its typical presentation, the classic clinicopathologic complex of Wegener's granulomatosis usually provides ready differentiation from other disorders. However, if all of the typical features are not present at once, it needs to be differentiated from the other vasculitides, particularly allergic angiitis and granulomatosis, Goodpasture's syndrome (Chap. 224), tumors of the upper airway or lung, and infectious or noninfectious granulomatous diseases. Of particular note is the differentiation from idiopathic midline granuloma (see Chap. 272) which frequently erodes through the skin of the face, a feature never seen in Wegener's granulomatosis.

Of particular importance in the differential diagnosis is a disease called *lymphomatoid granulomatosis*. It is characterized by lung, skin, central nervous system, and kidney involvement in which atypical lymphocytoid and plasmacytoid cells infiltrate tissue in an angioinvasive manner. In this regard, it clearly differs from Wegener's granulomatosis in that it is not an inflammatory vasculitis in the classic sense, but an infiltration of vessels with atypical mononuclear cells; granuloma may be present in involved tissues. Approximately 50 percent of patients develop a true malignant lymphoma.

TREATMENT AND PROGNOSIS Wegener's granulomatosis was formerly universally fatal, usually within a few months after the onset of clinically apparent renal disease. Corticosteroids alone led to some symptomatic improvement with little effect on the ultimate course of the disease. It has been well established that the treatment of choice in this disease is cyclophosphamide given in doses of 2 mg/kg per day orally. The leukocyte count should be closely monitored during therapy and the dosage adjusted in order to maintain the count above 3000 per cubic millimeter, which generally maintains the neutrophil count at approximately 1500 per cubic millimeter. With this approach, clinical remission can usually be induced and maintained without causing severe leukopenia with its associated risk of infection. Cyclophosphamide should be continued for 1 year following the induction of complete remission and gradually tapered and discontinued thereafter. Patients who cannot tolerate cyclophosphamide or who develop serious toxicity such as severe cystitis may be treated with azathioprine in similar doses.

At the initiation of therapy, corticosteroids should be administered together with cyclophosphamide. This can be given as prednisone, 1 mg/kg per day initially (for the first month of therapy) as a daily regimen with gradual conversion to an alternate-day schedule followed by tapering and discontinuation after approximately 6 months.

Using the above regimen, the prognosis of this disease is excellent and long-term remission is achieved in over 90 percent of patients. A number of patients who developed irreversible renal failure, but who achieved subsequent remission on appropriate therapy, have undergone successful renal transplantation.

TEMPORAL ARTERITIS

DEFINITION Temporal arteritis, also referred to as cranial or giant cell arteritis, is an inflammation of medium- and large-sized arteries. It characteristically involves one or more branches of the carotid artery, particularly the temporal artery, hence the name cranial or temporal arteritis. However, it is a systemic disease and can involve arteries in multiple locations.

INCIDENCE AND PREVALENCE Temporal arteritis is an uncommon disease estimated to occur in 24 per 100,000 people. It is a disease of the elderly, occurring almost exclusively in individuals older than 55 years; however, well-documented cases have occurred in patients 40 years old or younger. It is more common in women than in men and is rare in blacks. Familial aggregation of this disease has been reported as has an increased prevalence of HLA-DR4.

PATHOPHYSIOLOGY AND PATHOGENESIS Although the temporal artery is most frequently involved in this disease, patients often have a systemic vasculitis of multiple medium- and large-sized arteries which may go undetected. Histopathologically, the disease is a panarteritis with inflammatory mononuclear cell infiltrates within the vessel wall with frequent giant cell formation. There is proliferation of the intima and fragmentation of the internal elastic lamina. Pathophysiologic findings in organs result from the ischemia related to the involved vessels. Immunopathogenic mechanisms, particularly cell-mediated immunity, are felt to be involved in this disease, although the etiology is entirely unknown.

CLINICAL AND LABORATORY MANIFESTATIONS The disease is characterized clinically by the classic complex of fever, anemia, high ESR, and headaches in an elderly patient. Other manifestations include malaise, fatigue, anorexia, weight loss, sweats, and arthralgias. Temporal arteritis is closely associated with the polymyalgia rheumatica syndrome, which is characterized by stiffness, aching, and pain in the muscles of the neck, shoulders, lower back, hips, and thighs.

In patients with involvement of the temporal artery, headache is the predominant symptom and may be associated with a tender, thickened, or nodular artery which may pulsate early in the disease but may become occluded later. Scalp pain and claudication of the jaw and tongue may occur. A well-recognized and dreaded complication of temporal arteritis, particularly in untreated patients, is ocular involvement due primarily to ischemic optic neuritis, which may lead to serious visual symptoms, even sudden blindness in some patients. However, most patients have complaints relating to the head or eyes for months before objective eye involvement. Claudication of the extremities, strokes, myocardial infarctions, aortic aneurysms and dissections, and infarctions of visceral organs have been reported.

Characteristic laboratory findings in addition to the elevated ESR include a normochromic or slightly hypochromic anemia. Liver function abnormalities are common, particularly increased alkaline phosphatase levels. Increased levels of IgG and complement have been reported as have increased levels of circulating immune complexes.

DIAGNOSIS The diagnosis of temporal arteritis and its associated clinicopathologic syndrome can often be made clinically by the demonstration of the classic picture of fever, anemia, and high ESR with or without symptoms of polymyalgia rheumatica in an elderly patient. The diagnosis is confirmed by biopsy of the temporal artery. Since involvement of the vessel may be segmental, the diagnosis may be missed on routine biopsy. Dramatic response to a trial of corticosteroid therapy can confirm the diagnosis.

TREATMENT AND PROGNOSIS Temporal arteritis and its associated symptoms are exquisitely sensitive to corticosteroid therapy. Treatment should begin with prednisone, 40 to 60 mg per day followed by a gradual tapering to a maintenance dose of 7.5 to 10 mg per day. When ocular signs and symptoms occur, it is important that therapy be initiated or adjusted to control them. Because of the possibility of relapse, therapy should be continued for at least 1 to 2 years. The prognosis is generally good, and most patients achieve complete remission that is often maintained after withdrawal of therapy.

TAKAYASU'S ARTERITIS

DEFINITION Takayasu's arteritis is an inflammatory and stenotic disease of medium- and large-sized arteries characterized by a strong predilection for the aortic arch and its branches. For this reason, it is often referred to as the aortic arch syndrome.

INCIDENCE AND PREVALENCE Takayasu's arteritis is an uncommon disease, much less common than temporal arteritis. It is most prevalent in adolescent girls and young women. Although it is more common in the Orient, it is neither racially nor geographically restricted. An association of the disease has been described with HLA-DR2, MB1 in Japan and HLA-DR4, MB3 in the United States.

PATHOPHYSIOLOGY AND PATHOGENESIS The disease involves medium- and large-sized arteries with a strong predilection for the aortic arch and its branches; the pulmonary artery may also be involved. The most commonly affected arteries seen by angiography are the subclavians, followed by the aortic arch, ascending aorta, carotids, and femorals. The involvement of the major branches of the aorta is much more marked at their origin than distally. Partial renal artery occlusion with resulting hypertension is common. The disease is a panarteritis with inflammatory mononuclear cell infiltrates and occasionally giant cells. There is marked intimal proliferation and fibrosis, scarring and vascularization of the media, and disruption and degeneration of the elastic lamina. Narrowing of the lumen occurs with or without thrombosis. The vasa vasorum are frequently involved. Pathologic changes in various organs reflect the compromise of blood flow through the involved vessels.

Immunopathogenic mechanisms, the precise nature of which is uncertain, are suspected in this disease.

CLINICAL AND LABORATORY MANIFESTATIONS Takayasu's arteritis is a systemic disease with generalized as well as local symptoms. The generalized symptoms include malaise, fever, night sweats, arthralgias, anorexia, and weight loss which may occur months before vessel involvement is apparent. These symptoms may merge into those related to pain over the involved vessels followed by symptoms of ischemia in organs supplied by the compromised vessels. Pulses are commonly absent in the involved vessels, particularly the subclavian artery. Aortic regurgitation may occur; hypertension is seen in almost 50 percent of cases. Cardiomegaly and cardiac failure secondary to aortic or pulmonary hypertension occur commonly; the coronary arteries themselves are rarely involved. Carotid artery involvement leads to a variety of central nervous system signs and symptoms with over one-half of patients experiencing syncopal episodes; ocular signs and symptoms are present in 60 percent of patients.

The clinical course may be fulminant, may progress gradually, or may stabilize. Complications are related to the distribution of the involved vessels. Death usually occurs from congestive heart failure or cerebrovascular accidents.

Characteristic laboratory findings include an elevated ESR, mild anemia, leukocytosis, and elevated immunoglobulin levels. Angiography of involved vessels reveals the characteristic stenotic or occluded vessels.

DIAGNOSIS The diagnosis of Takayasu's arteritis should be suspected strongly in a young woman who develops a decrease or absence of peripheral pulses, discrepancies in blood pressure, and arterial bruits. The diagnosis is confirmed by the characteristic pattern on arteriography which includes irregular vessel walls, stenosis, poststenotic dilatation, aneurysm formation, occlusion, and evidence of increased collateral circulation. Histopathologic demonstration of inflamed vessels adds confirmatory data; however, tissue is rarely readily available for examination.

TREATMENT AND PROGNOSIS The course of the disease is variable, and spontaneous remissions may occur. However, it is generally considered to be progressive and fatal within a few years. Although corticosteroid therapy in doses of 40 to 60 mg prednisone per day alleviates symptoms, there are no convincing studies which indicate that they alone increase survival. However, recent studies suggest that corticosteroid therapy can induce remissions in a high percentage of individuals and when combined with reconstructive surgery on severely involved vessels, can remarkably improve survival. A few patients who were refractory to corticosteroid therapy responded favorably to cyclophosphamide, 2 mg/kg per day. However, long-term studies will be needed to confirm this.

MUCOCUTANEOUS LYMPH NODE SYNDROME (KAWASAKI'S DISEASE)

Mucocutaneous lymph node syndrome is an acute, febrile, multisystem disease of children. Patients show characteristic findings in the mucous membranes and skin together with lymphadenopathy (see also Chap. 49). Although the disease is generally benign and self-limited, it is associated with coronary artery aneurysms in 17 to 31 percent of cases, with an overall case fatality rate of 0.5 to 2.8 percent. These complications usually occur between the third and fourth week of illness during the convalescent stage. Vasculitis of the coronary arteries is seen in almost all of the fatal cases which have been autopsied. There is typical intimal proliferation and infiltration of the vessel wall with mononuclear cells. Beadlike aneurysms and thromboses may be seen along the artery. Most investigators agree that many of the cases of PAN formerly reported in children were actually arteritic complications of unrecognized mucocutaneous lymph node syndrome. Other manifestations include pericarditis, myocarditis, myocardial ischemia and infarction, and cardiomegaly.

Apart from the up to 2.8 percent of patients who develop fatal complications, the prognosis of this disease for uneventful recovery is excellent. The treatment of choice is aspirin during the acute and convalescent phases of the disease; this has been reported to result in a decrease in the incidence of cardiac complications.

ISOLATED VASCULITIS OF THE CENTRAL NERVOUS SYSTEM

Isolated vasculitis of the central nervous system is an uncommon clinicopathologic entity characterized by vasculitis restricted to the vessels of the central nervous system without other apparent systemic vasculitis. Although the arteriole is most commonly affected, vessels of any size can be involved. The inflammatory process is usually composed of mononuclear cell infiltrates with or without granuloma formation. Cases have been associated with Hodgkin's disease and varicella-zoster infections; however, in several cases no underlying disease process has been identified.

Patients may present with severe headaches, altered mental function, and focal neurologic defects. Systemic symptoms are generally absent. Devastating neurologic abnormalities may occur depending on the extent of vessel involvement. The diagnosis is generally made by demonstration of characteristic vessel abnormalities on arteriography and confirmed by biopsy of the brain parenchyma and leptomeninges. The prognosis of this disease is poor; however, some reports indicate that corticosteroid therapy alone or together with cyclophosphamide in steroid-resistant patients administered as described above for the systemic vasculitides has induced sustained clinical remissions in a small number of patients.

THROMBOANGIITIS OBLITERANS (BUERGER'S DISEASE)

Thromboangiitis obliterans is an inflammatory occlusive peripheral vascular disease of unknown etiology which affects arteries and veins. Thrombosis of the vessels is likely the primary event, and so this disease is not a classic vasculitis. However, it is considered among the vasculitides because of the intense inflammatory response within the thrombus and the fact that there is often a vasculitis of the vasa vasorum in the arterial wall. The disease is discussed in detail in Chap. 198.

MISCELLANEOUS VASCULITIDES

A variety of disorders, many of which are uncommon, are characterized by varying degrees of inflammatory responses involving blood vessels. *Behçet's syndrome* is a clinicopathologic entity characterized by recurrent episodes of oral and genital ulcers, iritis, and cutaneous lesions. The underlying pathologic lesion is a leukocytoclastic venulitis, although vessels of any size and in any organ can be involved. This disorder is described in detail in Chap. 268.

Cogan's syndrome is a disease characterized by nonsyphilitic interstitial keratitis together with vestibuloauditory symptoms. It may be associated with a systemic vasculitis involving vessels of different sizes as well as the aortic valve.

Erythema nodosum is a common disease which is recognized as a hypersensitivity manifestation of a number of other disorders. It is a painful nodular process of the dermis and subcutaneous tissues. However, histopathologically, there is a vasculitis of small venules (see Chap. 48).

Erythema elevatum diutinum is a rare, chronic skin disorder of unknown etiology characterized by persistent red, purple, and yellowish papules, plaques, and nodules usually distributed symmetrically over the extensor surface of the limbs which on biopsy demonstrate a leukocytoclastic venulitis together with a marked dermal inflammatory infiltrate. The disease responds dramatically to dapsone therapy.

Eales' disease is a retinal vasculitis which predominantly affects males in the second and third decade of life and which produces a syndrome of recurrent hemorrhages into the retina and vitreous.

REFERENCES

ALARCON-SEGOVIA D: The necrotizing vasculitides. Med Clin North Am 61:240, 1977

CHRISTIAN CL, SERGENT JS; Vasculitic syndromes: Clinical and experimental models. Am J Med 61:385, 1976

CUPPS TR, FAUCI AS: *The Vasculitides*. Philadelphia, Saunders, 1981

———— et al: Chronic, recurrent small-vessel cutaneous vasculitis. Clinical experience in 13 patients. JAMA 247:1994, 1982

———— et al: Isolated angiitis of the central nervous system. Prospective diagnostic and therapeutic experience. Am J Med 74:97, 1983

FAUCI AS: Vasculitis, in *Clinical Immunology*, CW Parker (ed). Philadelphia, Saunders, 1980, pp 475–519

————: Vasculitis. J Allergy Clin Immunol 72:211, 1983

———— et al: The spectrum of vasculitis. Clinical, pathologic, immunologic, and therapeutic considerations. Ann Intern Med 89:660, 1978

———— et al: Wegener's granulomatosis: Prospective clinical and therapeutic experience with 85 patients for 21 years. Ann Intern Med 98:76, 1983

LEAVITT RY, FAUCI AS: Polyangiitis overlap syndrome. Am J Med, 1986

SHELHAMER JH et al: Takayasu's arteritis and its therapy. Ann Intern Med 103:121, 1985

ZEEK PM: Periarteritis nodosa and other forms of necrotizing angiitis. N Engl J Med 148:764, 1953

---

270 SARCOIDOSIS

RONALD G. CRYSTAL

DEFINITION Sarcoidosis is a chronic, multisystem disorder of unknown etiology characterized in affected organs by an accumulation of lymphocytes and mononuclear phagocytes, noncaseating epithelioid granulomas, and derangements of the normal tissue architecture. Although there are usually skin anergy and depressed cellular immune processes in the blood, sarcoidosis is characterized at the sites of disease by exaggerated helper T-lymphocyte immune processes. All parts of the body can be affected, but the organ most frequently affected is the lung. Involvement of the skin, eye, and lymph nodes is also common. The disease can be acute and self-limiting, but in many individuals it is chronic, waxing and waning over many years.

ETIOLOGY The etiology of sarcoidosis is unknown. A variety of infectious and noninfectious agents have been implicated, but there is no proof that any one agent is responsible. It is likely that there is no specific etiologic agent but that the disease results from an abnormal immune response (acquired, inherited, or both) to many different antigens.

INCIDENCE AND PREVALENCE Sarcoidois is a relatively common disease affecting individuals of both sexes and almost all ages, races, and geographic locations. Females appear to be slightly more susceptible than males. Cases of sarcoid have been described in all of the major races and the disease is found throughout the world. It has been suggested that sarcoid is more common in certain geographic areas such as the southeastern part of the United States but when case-matched controls have been used, these geographic differences are less convincing. The prevalence of sarcoidosis is from 10 to 40 per 100,000 in the United States and Europe. In the United States, the majority of patients are black, with a ratio of blacks to whites ranging from 10:1 to 17:1. In Europe, however, the disease affects mostly whites. There is a remarkable diversity of the prevalence of sarcoidosis among certain ethnic and racial groups. For example, in Irish females living in London it is 200 per 100,000. In contrast, the disease is very rare among Canadian Indians, New Zealand Maoris, and Southeast Asians.

Most patients present with sarcoidosis between the ages of 20 and 40, but it can occur in children and in the elderly. Several hundred kindred groups with familial sarcoidosis have been described, and the disease has been observed in twins, more commonly in monozygotic than in dizygotic pairs. There have also been several instances of husband-wife pairs identified, arguing for some environmental factors in the pathogenesis of the disease. Although the histocompatibility locus HLA-B8 has been suggested to confer certain responses to sarcoidosis, no clear patterns in any HLA locus have emerged. Unlike many diseases in which the lung is involved, sarcoidosis is less common in smokers than in nonsmokers.

PATHOPHYSIOLOGY AND IMMUNOPATHOGENESIS The first manifestation of the disease is an accumulation of mononuclear inflammatory cells, mostly T-helper lymphocytes and mononuclear phagocytes, in affected organs. This inflammatory process is followed by the formation of granulomas, aggregates of macrophages and their progeny, epithelioid cells, and multinucleated giant cells. The typical sarcoid granuloma is a compact structure composed of an aggregate of mononuclear phagocytes surrounded by a rim of T-helper lymphocytes and, sometimes, B lymphocytes. The overall structure is relatively discrete and is interspersed with fine collagen fibrils, presumably remnants of the underlying connective tissue matrix. The giant cells within the granuloma can be of the Langhans' or foreign-body variety and often contain inclusions such as Schaumann bodies (conch-like structures), asteroid bodies (stellate-like structures), and residual bodies (refractile calcium-containing inclusions).

Together, the accumulated T cells, mononuclear phagocytes, and granulomas represent the active disease. Other than the fact that they take up space and thus modify the local architecture, there is no evidence that the mononuclear inflammatory cells either alone or in the granuloma injure the affected organ by releasing mediators that damage the normal parenchymal cells or the extracellular matrix. Rather, organ dysfunction in sarcoid results from the fact that the accumulated inflammatory cells distort the architecture of the affected tissue; if a sufficient number of structures vital to the function of the tissue are involved, the disease becomes clinically apparent in that organ. Thus, while autopsy series show that, to some extent, sarcoidosis involves most organs in the majority of patients, the disease manifests clinically only in organs where it affects function (such as the lung and eye) or in organs where it is readily observed (such as the skin or, by x-ray, the hilar nodes). For example, in the lung the inflammatory cells and granulomas distort the walls of the alveoli, bronchi, and blood vessels (Fig. 270-1A), thus altering the intimate relationships between air and blood necessary for normal gas exchange; this is sensed by the individual as dyspnea. In contrast, most individuals with sarcoidosis have granulomatous mononuclear cell inflammation in the liver but usually do not have symptoms or functional derangements referable to that organ, likely because the disease process does not modify the local structures sufficiently to affect function.

If the disease is suppressed, either spontaneously or with therapy, the mononuclear inflammation is reduced in intensity and the number of granulomas is reduced. The granulomas resolve either by dispersion of the cells or by centripetal proliferation of fibroblasts from the periphery of the granuloma inward, to form a scar which eventually disappears. In chronic cases, the mononuclear cell inflammation persists for years. If the intensity of the inflammation is sufficiently high for a sufficiently long period, the derangements to the affected tissues result in extensive damage, the development of fibrosis, and permanent loss of organ function.

All available evidence suggests that active sarcoidosis results from an aberrant immune response to a variety of antigens, in which the process of T-lymphocyte triggering, proliferation, and activation is skewed in the direction of helper T-lymphocyte processes (Fig. 270-1B). The result is an undamped helper T-cell response, and thus the accumulation of large numbers of activated T cells in the affected organs. Since the activated helper T lymphocyte releases mediators that attract and activate mononuclear phagocytes, it is likely that the process of granuloma formation is a secondary phenomen which is a consequence of the exaggerated T-helper cell process. In this context, the current hypotheses of the cause of sarcoidosis, not mutually exclusive, include: (1) the disease is caused by a class of antigens, nonself or self, that trigger only the helper T-cell arm of the immune response; (2) the disease results from an inadequate suppressor arm of the immune response, such that helper T-cell processes cannot be shut down in a normal fashion; or (3) the disease results from inherited (and/or acquired) differences in immune response genes, such that the response to a variety of antigens is an uncontrolled, helper T-cell process.

Independent of the inciting agent(s) or the reason why there is an undamped helper T-cell response, there is a general understanding of the processes responsible for the maintenance of the inflammation and the development of the granuloma. The T-helper lymphocytes

FIGURE 270-1 *Pathogenesis of sarcoidosis. A. Histologic abnormalities. The normal alveolar wall (left) and the alveolar wall in active sarcoidosis (right), which is distorted by the accumulated T-helper lymphocytes, alveolar macrophages, and macrophages aggregated into granulomas, are illustrated. There is mild damage to alveolar epithelial and endothelial cells. B. The exaggerated T-helper lymphocyte processes in affected organs result in the accumulation of T-helper cells, macrophages, and macrophages aggregated* into granulomas. The triggering signal for the T-helper cells is unknown; it is assumed to be a variety of antigens. The immune response is skewed to produce activated T-helper cells that release interleukin 2, which drives the accumulation of more T-helper cells. The activated T-helper cells also release monocyte chemotactic factor and interferon-gamma, mediators that contribute to the recruitment and activation of monocytes and hence to granuloma formation.

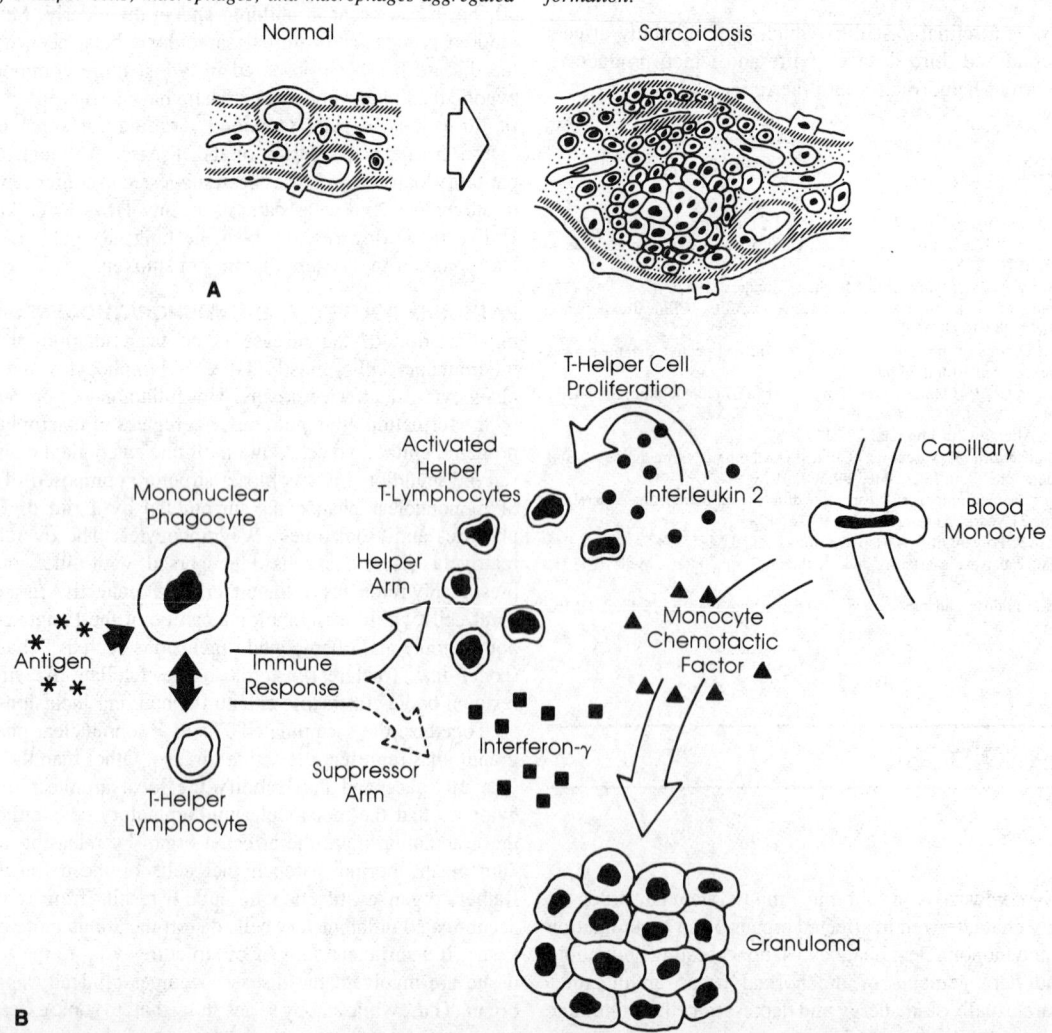

accumulate at the sites of disease because they proliferate in these sites at an exaggerated rate. This T-cell proliferation is maintained by the spontaneous release of interleukin 2 (IL-2), the T-cell growth factor, by activated T-helper cells in the local milieu. In this regard, sarcoidosis is a remarkable example of compartmentalization of the immune system and a dramatic illustration of why disease activity of sarcoidosis cannot be assessed by evaluating the immune system only in the blood. Whereas the T-helper cells in the involved organs are releasing IL-2 and proliferating at an enhanced rate, the T cells in other sites, such as blood, are quiescent. Furthermore, while there is a marked enhancement of the number of T-helper cells at the sites of disease, the numbers of T-helper cells in the blood are normal or slightly reduced. In this regard, in the involved organs, the ratio of T-helper to T-suppressor cells may be as high as 10:1 compared to the ratio of 2:1 found in normal tissues or in the blood of affected individuals.

In addition to driving other T-helper cells in the affected organs to proliferate, the T-helper cells at the sites of disease are activated and release mediators that both recruit and activate mononuclear phagocytes. The T-helper cells accomplish this by releasing a variety of mediators (lymphokines) including monocyte chemotactic factor, a protein capable of recruiting blood monocytes to the local milieu of the activated T cells, and gamma interferon, a protein that, among its many actions, activates mononuclear phagocytes. Together, these mediators recruit blood monocytes to the affected organs and activate them, providing the building blocks for the formation of the granuloma.

In addition to these aberrant cellular immune processes, active sarcoid is also characterized by hyperglobulinemia. Included among the immunoglobulins are antibodies against a variety of infectious agents as well as IgM anti-T-cell antibodies; there is no evidence that they play a role in the pathogenesis of the disease, and they are thought to result from the nonspecific polyclonal stimulation of B cells by the activated T cells at the site of disease.

If the damage in the affected organs is sufficiently extensive so that the remaining parenchymal cells cannot reestablish the normal tissue architecture, the usual result is fibrosis, the proliferation of mesenchymal cells and deposition of their connective tissue products. The current concepts relating to this process are described in Chap. 209.

CLINICAL MANIFESTATIONS Sarcoidosis is a systemic disease, and thus the clinical manifestations may be generalized or focused on one or more organs. However, because the lung is almost always involved, most patients have symptoms referable to the respiratory system. Independent of the site, the clinical manifestations of the disease relate directly to the exaggerated T-helper cell–mononuclear phagocyte granulomatous inflammatory process itself, or to the sequela resulting from the permanent damage caused by this process.

Sarcoidosis is occasionally discovered in a completely asymptomatic individual, but more commonly it presents abruptly over 1 to 2 weeks or the affected individual develops symptoms insidiously over several months. Independent of the mode of presentation, about 75 percent of all cases present when the individual is less than 40 years of age.

The asymptomatic form is usually detected by a routine examination, such as a chest film. In the United States, this represents about 10 to 20 percent of all cases, but in countries where chest films are mandatory in preemployment screening programs, the proportion of asymptomatic patients is higher.

So-called acute or subacute sarcoidosis develops abruptly over a period of a few weeks and represents 20 to 40 percent of all cases. These individuals usually have constitutional symptoms such as fever, fatigue, malaise, anorexia, or weight loss. These symptoms are usually mild, but in approximately 25 percent of these acute cases, the constitutional complaints are extensive. Many have respiratory symptoms, including cough, dyspnea, or a vague retrosternal chest discomfort. Two syndromes have been identified in the acute group. Löfgren's syndrome, frequent in Scandinavian, Irish, and Puerto Rican females, includes the complex of erythema nodosum and x-ray findings of bilateral hilar adenopathy, often accompanied by joint symptoms. The Heerfordt-Waldenstrom syndrome describes individuals with fever, parotid enlargement, anterior uveitis, and facial nerve palsy.

The insidious form of sarcoidosis develops over months and is associated usually with respiratory complaints without constitutional symptoms. About 10 percent of these individuals have symptoms referable to organs other than the lung. It is the individuals who present with the insidious form of sarcoidosis that most commonly go on to develop chronic sarcoidosis, with permanent damage to the lung and other organs.

Despite the fact that sarcoidosis is a systemic disease and some evidence of inflammation can be detected in most organs in the majority of patients, sarcoidosis is important clinically because of the pulmonary abnormalities and, to a lesser extent, lymph node, skin, and eye involvement. Far less commonly, other organs are involved significantly.

Lung Of individuals with sarcoidosis, 90 percent have an abnormal chest x-ray at some time during their course. Overall, approximately 50 percent develop permanent pulmonary abnormalities and 10 to 20 percent have progressive fibrosis of the lung parenchyma. Sarcoidosis of the lung is primarily an interstitial lung disease (see Chap. 209) in which the inflammatory process involves the alveoli, small bronchi, and small blood vessels. These individuals typically have symptoms of dyspnea, particularly with exercise, and a dry cough. Physical examination reveals dry rales. Hemoptysis is rare, as is production of sputum. Occasionally, the large airways are involved to a degree sufficient to cause dysfunction. Distal atelectasis can result from endobronchial sarcoidosis or from external compression from enlarged intrathoracic nodes. Rarely, wheezing is heard, incorrectly suggesting asthma. Large-vessel pulmonary granulomatous arteritis is common, but it rarely causes major problems. If it dominates the pulmonary lesions, it is sometimes called "necrotizing sarcoidal granulomatosis." The pleura is involved in 1 to 5 percent of cases, almost always manifesting as a unilatereal pleural effusion with characteristics of an exudate containing lymphocytes. The effusions usually clear within a few weeks, but chronic pleural thickening can result. Pneumothorax is very rare.

Lymph nodes Lymphadenopathy is very common in sarcoidosis. Intrathoracic nodes are enlarged in 75 to 90 percent of all patients; usually this involves the hilar nodes, but the paratracheal nodes are commonly involved. Less frequently, there is enlargement of subcarinal, anterior mediastinal, or posterior mediastinal nodes. Peripheral lymphadenopathy is very common, particularly involving the cervical, axillary, epitrochlear, and inguinal nodes. The nodes in the retroperitoneal area and in the mesenteric chain can also enlarge. All of these nodes are nonadherent, with a firm, rubbery texture. Palpation causes no pain. Unlike nodes in tuberculosis, the nodes do not ulcerate. The lymphadenopathy rarely causes a problem for the affected individual; however, if it is massive, it can be disfiguring and can impinge on other organs and lead to functional impairment.

Skin Sarcoidosis involves the skin in about 25 percent of cases. The most common lesions are erythema nodosum, plaques, maculopapular eruptions, subcutaneous nodules, and lupus pernio. Erythema nodosum, comprising bilateral, tender red nodules on the anterior surface of the legs, is not specific for sarcoidosis but is common, particularly in acute sarcoidosis, in combination with systemic symptoms and polyarthralgias. The plaques are purple, indolent lesions, often raised, and usually occur on the face, buttocks, and extremities. The maculopapular eruptions occur on the face around the eyes and nose, on the back, and on the extremities. These are elevated lesions less than 1 cm in diameter with a flat, waxy top. Subcutaneous nodules are most common on the trunk and extremities. Lupus pernio is characterized by indurated blue-purple, swollen, shiny lesions on the nose, cheeks, lips, ears, fingers, and knees. The lesions on the tip of the nose cause a bulbous appearance, sometimes associated with varicosities. The nasal mucosa is usually involved, and underlying bone can be destroyed. Sarcoidosis can also involve old surgical scars and tattoos. Although it may be disfiguring, cutaneous sarcoidosis rarely causes major problems.

Eye Eye involvement occurs in approximately 25 percent of patients with sarcoidosis and it can cause blindness. The usual lesions involve the uveal tract, iris, ciliary body, and choroid. Of those cases with eye involvement, approximately 75 percent have anterior uveitis and 25 to 35 percent have posterior uveitis. There is blurred vision, tearing, and photophobia. The uveitis can develop rapidly and may clear spontaneously over a 6- to 12-month period. It can also develop insidiously and be chronic. Conjunctival involvement is also common, usually with small, yellow nodules. When the lacrimal gland is involved, a keratoconjunctivitis sicca syndrome, with dry, sore eyes, can result.

Upper respiratory tract The nasal mucosa is involved in up to 20 percent of patients, usually presenting with nasal stuffiness. Any of the structures of the mouth can be involved, particularly the tonsils. Sarcoidosis involves the larynx in about 5 percent of cases. The epiglottis and areas around the true vocal cords are usually involved, but the cords themselves are not. These individuals are usually hoarse and they have dyspnea, wheezing, and stridor; complete obstruction can occur.

Bone marrow and spleen Sarcoidosis of the marrow is reported in 15 to 40 percent of cases, but it rarely causes hematologic abnormalities other than a mild anemia and occasionally thrombocytopenia. Although splenomegaly occurs in only 5 to 10 percent of patients, celiac angiography or splenic biopsy reveals involvement in 50 to 60 percent of cases. The presentation and complications of splenomegaly in sarcoidosis are similar to those of splenomegaly in general.

Liver Although liver biopsy reveals liver involvement in 60 to 90 percent of cases, usually it is not important clinically. Sarcoidosis involves generally the periportal areas. Approximately 20 to 30 percent have hepatomegaly and/or biochemical evidence of liver involvement. Usually these changes reflect a cholestatic pattern and include an elevated alkaline phosphatase level; the bilirubin and aminotransferases are only mildly elevated, and jaundice is rare. Rarely, portal hypertension can occur, as can intrahepatic cholestasis with cirrhosis.

Kidney Clinically apparent primary renal involvement in sarcoidosis is rare, although tubular, glomerular, and renal artery disease have been reported. More commonly, but still in only 1 to 2 percent of all cases, there is a disorder of calcium metabolism with hypercalcinuria, with or without hypercalcemia. If chronic, nephrocalcinosis and nephrolithiasis can result. It is believed that the calcium abnormalities are associated with enhanced calcium absorption in the gut, which is related to an abnormally high level of circulating 1,25-dihydroxyvitamin D.

Nervous system All components of the nervous system can be involved in sarcoidosis. Neurologic findings are observed in about 5 percent of patients. Seventh nerve involvement with unilateral facial paralysis is most common. It occurs suddenly and is usually transient. Other common manifestations of neurosarcoid include optic nerve dysfunction, papilledema, palate dysfunction, hearing abnormalities, hypothalamic and pituitary abnormalities, chronic meningitis, and occasionally, space-occupying lesions. Psychiatric disturbances have been described, and seizures can occur. Rarely, multiple lesions which mimic multiple sclerosis, spinal cord abnormalities, and peripheral neuropathy can occur.

Musculoskeletal system The bones, joints, and/or muscles can be involved in sarcoidosis. Bone lesions are observed in 5 percent of patients and include variable-sized cysts in areas of expanded bone, well-defined round punched-out lesions, or lattice-like changes. Hand and foot bones are the common sites, but most bones can be involved.

Occasionally, the bone lesions are tender and painful. Joint involvement is more common, with an incidence of 25 to 50 percent in known cases of sarcoidosis. Arthralgias and frank arthritis occur mostly in large joints; they can be migratory and are usually transient, but then can be chronic and result in deformities. Although muscle biopsy frequently demonstrates granulomatous inflammation, muscle dysfunction is rare. However, nodules, polymyositis, and chronic myopathy have been described.

Heart Approximately 5 percent of patients have significant heart involvement, with clinical evidence of cardiac dysfunction. Left ventricular wall involvement is common. Arrhythmias are frequent, and serious conduction disturbances, including complete heart block, can occur. Papillary muscle dysfunction, pericarditis, and congestive heart failure are also observed. Cor pulmonale secondary to chronic pulmonary fibrosis may occur but is uncommon.

Endocrine and reproductive system The hypothalamic-pituitary axis is the part of the endocrine system most commonly involved; this usually presents as diabetes insipidus. Anterior pituitary dysfunction is also seen, manifesting as a deficiency in one or more pituitary hormones. Complete hypopituitarism is rare. Much less frequently, sarcoidosis can cause primary dysfunction of other endocrine glands. Adrenal cortical involvement resulting in Addison's syndrome has been described. Involvement of the reproductive organs occurs, but infertility is rare. Pregnancy is rarely affected by sarcoidosis, and patients with sarcoidosis who become pregnant usually improve during pregnancy. However, the disease may flare post partum; presumably this variation results from fluctuations in endogenous corticosteroid production.

Exocrine glands Parotid enlargement is a classic feature of sarcoidosis, but clinically apparent parotid involvement occurs in less than 10 percent of patients. Bilateral involvement is the rule. The gland is usually nontender, firm, and smooth. Xerostomia can occur; other exocrine glands are affected only rarely.

Gastrointestinal tract Although sarcoidosis involvement of the gastrointestinal tract is found occasionally at autopsy, it rarely has clinical importance. Occasionally, patients have esophageal or gastric symptoms.

COMPLICATIONS The respiratory tract abnormalities cause most of the morbidity and mortality associated with sarcoidosis. The major problems are those characteristic of interstitial lung disease (see Chap. 209), particularly dyspnea and insufficient oxygen delivery to vital organs. Respiratory failure with carbon dioxide retention is rare. In some patients, lung destruction results in formation of bullae that may harbor mycetomas, which are usually aspergillomas; erosion into the parenchyma can result in massive bleeding. The most common complications apart from the lung are associated with the eye; however, with therapy blindness is rare. Complications of other organs include a gamut of abnormalities. The most serious are central nervous system lesions or cardiac involvement leading to congestive heart failure or sudden death.

LABORATORY ABNORMALITIES Abnormalities in the blood include lymphocytopenia, an occasional mild eosinophilia, an increased erythrocyte sedimentation rate, hyperglobulinemia, and an elevated level of angiotensin-converting enzyme. Hypercalcemia is rare. Other serum abnormalities relate to involvement of specific organs such as liver, kidney, or endocrine glands.

Because the lung is involved so commonly, the routine chest film is almost always abnormal (Fig. 270-2A). The three classic x-ray patterns of pulmonary sarcoidosis are type I—bilateral hilar adenopathy with no parenchymal abnormalities; type II—bilateral hilar adenopathy with diffuse parenchymal changes; and type III—diffuse parenchymal changes without hilar adenopathy. The type III pattern is sometimes split into two categories with films that show fibrosis and upper lobe retraction classified separately. Although patients with type I x-rays tend to have the acute, reversible form of the disease while those with types II and III often have the chronic, progressive disease, these patterns do not represent the "stages" of sarcoidosis. Except for epidemiologic purposes, this x-ray categorization is mostly of historic interest. The hilar adenopathy is almost always bilateral, but unilateral node enlargement can be seen. Nodes are also common in the paratracheal region. The diffuse parenchymal changes are typically reticulonodular infiltrates, but an acinar pattern is observed occasionally. Large nodules, similar to those of metastatic disease, are unusual but can occur. When there is massive fibrosis, the hila are pulled upward and there are conglomerate masses in the mid-lung zones. Some of the unusual chest x-ray findings in sarcoidosis include "egg shell" calcification of hilar nodes, pleural effusions, cavitation, atelectasis, pulmonary hypertension, pneumothorax, and cardiomegaly.

The lung function abnormalities of sarcoidosis are typical for interstitial lung disease (see Chap. 209) and include decreased lung volumes and diffusing capacity with a normal ratio of the forced expiratory volume in 1 s to the forced vital capacity. Occasionally there is evidence of airflow limitation. There is usually mild hypoxemia and a mild, compensated hypocarbia.

The gallium 67 lung scan is usually abnormal, showing a pattern of diffuse uptake. If present, enlarged nodes are detected in these scans, as is inflammation in a variety of extrathoracic sites that usually have no clinical importance (Fig. 270-2B). Bronchoalveolar lavage demonstrates typically an increased proportion of lymphocytes, most

of which are activated helper T lymphocytes. The remainder of the cells are mostly alveolar macrophages. In patients with significant fibrosis, a small number of neutrophils are also found. Eosinophils are rare.

The other laboratory features of sarcoidosis depend on the specific organ involved.

DIAGNOSIS For a typical case, the diagnosis of sarcoidosis is made by a combination of clinical, radiographic, and histologic findings. In a young adult with constitutional complaints, respiratory symptoms, erythema nodosum, blurred vision, and bilateral hilar adenopathy, the diagnosis is almost always sarcoidosis. Commonly, however, the findings are more subtle. Furthermore, because sarcoidosis can occur in almost any place in the body, like tuberculosis or syphilis, it can be confused with many other disorders. In this context, the differential diagnosis of sarcoidosis must cover a wide range. However, it is confused most commonly with disorders characterized also by a mononuclear cell granulomatous inflammatory process, such as the mycobacterial and fungal disorders.

The chest x-ray cannot be used as the sole criterion for the diagnosis of sarcoidosis. While the finding of bilateral hilar adenopathy is the hallmark of this disease, a similar pattern can be found in lymphoma, tuberculosis, coccidioidomycosis, brucellosis, and bronchogenic carcinoma.

Whether or not the presentation is "classic," biopsy evidence of a mononuclear-cell granulomatous inflammatory process is mandatory

FIGURE 270-2 *Common laboratory findings of sarcoidosis. A. Schematic view of the abnormal findings on the chest x-ray. Shown are changes observed with the average frequency of occurrence. B. Typical gallium 67 scan of an individual with active sarcoidosis. The isotope has accumulated in the lung parenchyma (LP), liver (L), spleen (S), parotid (P), hilar nodes (HN), and pelvic nodes (PN).*

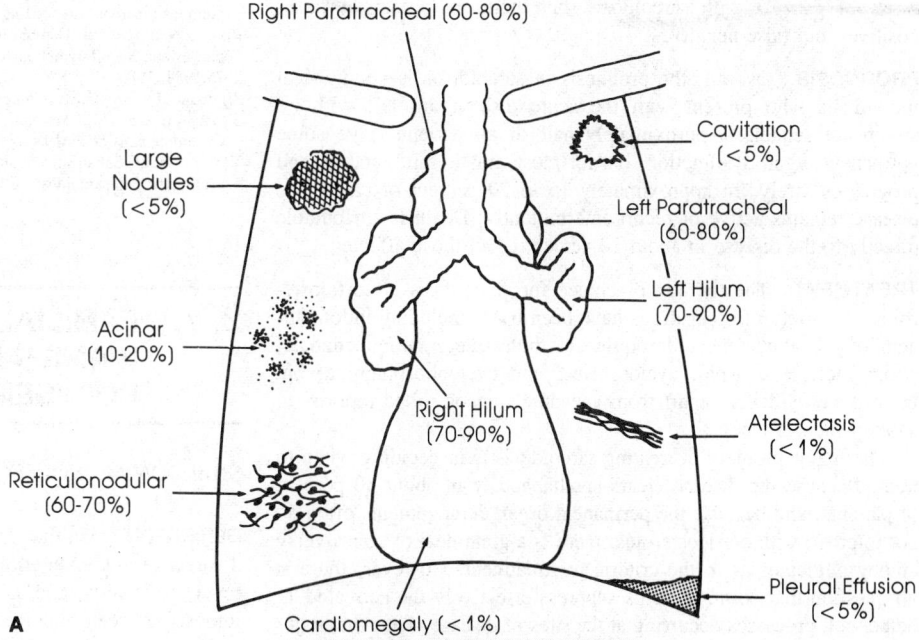

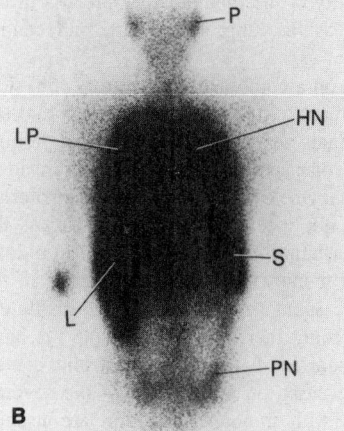

in order to make a definitive diagnosis of sarcoidosis. Because the lung is involved so frequently, it is the most common site to be biopsied, usually through a fiberoptic bronchoscope. Less common, but acceptable, sites for biopsy are the hilar nodes (by mediastinoscopy), the skin, conjunctiva, or lip. Rarely, the spleen, intraabdominal nodes, muscle, parotid or other salivary glands, upper respiratory tract, or the heart are biopsied for diagnostic purposes. At any of these sites, the findings must include the typical noncaseating granulomas. However, although histologic evidence is mandatory for a definitive diagnosis of sarcoidosis, the histologic findings are not sufficiently specific to make the diagnosis by themselves, as noncaseating granulomas are found in a number of other diseases, including infections and malignancy. Furthermore, although the liver or scalene nodes often reveal ''positive'' biopsies in cases of sarcoidosis, noncaseating granulomas from other causes are so frequent in these sites that they are not considered acceptable sites for establishing the diagnosis.

The presence of skin anergy is typical but not diagnostic of sarcoidosis. The Kveim-Siltzbach skin test, the intradermal injection of a heat-treated suspension of a sarcoidosis spleen extract which is biopsied 4 to 6 weeks later, yields sarcoidosis-like lesions in 70 to 80 percent of individuals with sarcoidosis with less than 5 percent false-positives. However, the material is not available for general use, and with the widespread use of the transbronchial biopsy to obtain lung parenchyma for diagnostic purposes, the Kveim-Siltzbach test is now only of historic interest.

No blood findings are diagnostic of the disease. Angiotensin-converting enzyme is elevated in the serum in approximately two-thirds of patients with sarcoidosis, but there are numerous false-positives and false-negatives.

PROGNOSIS   Overall, the prognosis in sarcoidosis is good. Most individuals who present with the acute disease are left with no significant sequela. Approximately half of all patients have some permanent organ dysfunction, but for most, this is mild, stable, and progresses rarely. In approximately 15 to 20 percent of cases, the disease remains active or recurs intermittently. Death is attributable directly to the disease in about 10 percent of all those affected.

TREATMENT   The therapy of choice for sarcoidosis is corticosteroids. A variety of other drugs have been tried, including indomethacin, oxyphenbutazone, chloroquine, methotrexate, p-aminobenzoate, allopurinol, levamisole, cyclosporine, and cyclophosphamide, but there is no evidence, apart from anecdotal, uncontrolled reports, to support their efficacy.

The major problem in treating sarcoidosis is in deciding when to treat. Because the disease clears spontaneously in about 50 percent of patients, and because the permanent organ derangements often do not improve with corticosteroids, there is a great deal of controversy among clinicians as to the criteria for treatment. However, there is no question that corticosteroids suppress effectively the activated T-helper cell processes occurring at the sites of disease. Thus the major problem in making decisions concerning therapy in sarcoidosis is to determine the extent and activity of the inflammatory process in the organs at greatest risk, such as the lung, eye, heart, and central nervous system.

For the lung, this is based on a combination of history, physical findings, chest x-ray, and pulmonary function tests. Centers that see large numbers of these individuals also use criteria based on gallium 67 lung scans and bronchoalveolar lavage findings. The serum level of the angiotensin-converting enzyme has been suggested as a criterion for disease activity, but it is not specific for the lung. Unless the respiratory impairment is devastating, active pulmonary sarcoidosis is observed usually without therapy for 2 to 3 months; if the inflammation does not subside spontaneously, therapy is instituted. For the eye, decisions concerning therapy are based on slit lamp examination and tests for visual acuity. For the heart and central nervous system, decisions are based on an estimate of the severity of the involvement; patients with minor dysfunction are usually observed, while patients with significant cardiac or neurologic abnormalities are treated. Usually, it is not necessary to treat the systemic symptoms, but occasionally the extent of the fevers, fatigue, and/or weight loss will necessitate therapy.

The usual therapy for sarcoidosis is prednisone, 1 mg/kg, for 4 to 6 weeks followed by a slow taper over 2 to 3 months. This is repeated if the disease again becomes active. Alternate-day therapy is used by some clinicians, but there is no evidence that it is any better or avoids complications in these patients. High-dose bolus intravenous corticosteroids are used occasionally, but are probably not as effective as oral therapy. Inhaled corticosteroids are not efficacious. Mild ocular disease responds usually to local therapy but suppression of the uveitis often requires systemic corticosteroids.

REFERENCES

CHRETIEN J et al (eds): *Ninth International Conference on Sarcoidosis and Other Granulomatous Disorders*. Paris, Pergamon, 1981

CRYSTAL RG et al: Interstitial lung disease of unknown etiology: Disorders characterized by chronic inflammation of the lower respiratory tract. N Engl J Med 310:154, 235, 1984

———— et al: Pulmonary sarcoidosis: A disease characterized and perpetuated by activated lung T-lymphocytes. Ann Intern Med 94:73, 1981

FANBURG BL (ed): *Sarcoidosis and Other Granulomatous Diseases of the Lung*. New York, Marcel Dekker, 1983

FRASER RG, PARE JAP: *Diagnosis of Diseases of the Chest*. Philadelphia, Saunders, 1979, vol 3, p 1658

HUNNINGHAKE GW et al: Maintenance of granuloma formation in pulmonary sarcoidosis by T-lymphocytes within the lung. N Engl J Med 302:594, 1980

MITCHELL DN et al: Sarcoidosis: Histopathologic definition and clinical diagnosis. J Clin Pathol 30:395, 1977

PINKSTON P et al: Spontaneous release of interleukin-2 by lung T-lymphocytes in active pulmonary sarcoidosis. N Engl J Med 308:793, 1983

ROBINSON BWS et al: Gamma interferon is spontaneously released by alveolar macrophages and lung T-lymphocytes in patients with pulmonary sarcoidosis. J Clin Invest 75:1488, 1985

SHARMA OP: *Sarcoidosis: Clinical Management*. London, Butterworths, 1984

SILTZBACH LE (ed): *Seventh International Conference on Sarcoidosis and Other Granulomatous Disorders*. New York, NY Acad Sci, 1976

VENET A et al: Enhanced alveolar macrophage-mediated antigen-induced T-lymphocyte proliferation in sarcoidosis. J Clin Invest 75:293, 1985

271   FAMILIAL MEDITERRANEAN FEVER (FAMILIAL PAROXYSMAL POLYSEROSITIS)

SHELDON M. WOLFF

DEFINITION   Familial Mediterranean fever (FMF) is an inherited disorder of unknown etiology, characterized by recurrent episodes of fever, peritonitis, and/or pleuritis. Arthritis, skin lesions, and amyloidosis are seen in some patients.

TERMINOLOGY   The variety of names given to FMF has led to confusion concerning its clinical features. None of the names, including FMF, is completely satisfactory. Such terms as *periodic disease, periodic peritonitis, la maladie périodique* are inaccurate because the disease often is not cyclical. *Benign paroxysmal peritonitis* is inappropriate because many of the patients have involvement of serosal surfaces other than the peritoneum, and some die of amyloidosis. *Familial paroxysmal polyserositis* is an acceptable alternative for the term *familial Mediterranean fever*.

ETHNOLOGY AND GENETICS   FMF occurs predominantly in patients of non-Ashkenazi (Sephardic) Jewish, Armenian, and Arabic ancestry. However, the disease is not restricted to these groups, and has been seen in patients of Italian, Ashkenazi Jewish, and Anglo-Saxon descent as well as others.

The best studies of the genetics of FMF have been done in Israel, where the disease appears to be inherited as an autosomal recessive.

Nevertheless, approximately 50 percent of patients give no family history of the disease. Consanguinity among the parents of FMF patients is as high as 20 percent, a figure which may be an underestimate because most patients came from very inbred ethnic groups. Approximately 60 percent of patients are male.

ETIOLOGY Although numerous pathogenetic mechanisms have been suggested, the etiology of FMF is unknown. Fever and inflammation are such prominent signs that frequent attempts have been made to implicate infectious agents and/or their products. However, extensive studies utilizing modern microbiologic and serologic techniques have failed to implicate these or any other specific infectious agents.

It has been reported that FMF is due to an allergy or to hypersensitivity, but such hypersensitive states have not been substantiated. There is no firm evidence favoring an autoimmune etiology.

It has been suggested that FMF may be a pathologic exaggeration of normal periodic temperature rhythmicity. However, extensive studies of temperature and other circadian rhythms in FMF patients have failed to demonstrate alterations from normal.

Because many FMF patients note that certain emotional or environmental changes may have profound effects on the frequency with which episodes of their disease occur, a psychosomatic basis has been suggested for the illness. There is no question that most patients eventually have transient or even permanent psychological alterations, which probably reflect their reaction to a chronic recurring illness that is forever threatening their social, economic, and personal well-being, but there is no evidence for a functional etiology for FMF.

The demonstration that FMF is inherited as an autosomal recessive disorder has led to the thesis that it is another inborn error of metabolism. Despite extensive studies, no such error has been found. Reported instances of excessive urinary excretion of porphyrins in FMF are probably examples of true porphyria and not FMF.

It has been reported that blood levels of unconjugated etiocholanolone were elevated during fever in six patients with FMF. Subsequent studies, however, showed no correlation between levels of etiocholanolone and fever.

PATHOLOGY Despite the striking clinical manifestations during an acute attack of FMF, no specific pathologic alterations have been found. At laparotomy, only acute peritoneal inflammation in which the exudate contains a predominance of polymorphonuclear leukocytes is found to be present. A disproportionately large number of male patients develop gallbladder disease with and without cholelithiasis, but extensive histopathologic examination has failed to reveal any specific pathologic changes. Pleural and joint inflammation are also nonspecific.

In the amyloidosis which accompanies FMF, amyloid is deposited in the intima and media of the arterioles, the subendothelial region of venules, the glomeruli, and the spleen. Aside from their vessels, the heart and liver are uninvolved.

MANIFESTATIONS In the majority of patients, the symptoms of FMF begin between the ages of 5 and 15, although attacks sometimes commence during infancy, and onset has occurred as late as age 52. The duration and frequency of attacks vary greatly in the same patient, and there is no set rhythm or periodicity to their occurrence. The usual acute episode lasts 24 to 48 h, but some may be prolonged for 7 to 10 days. The attacks range in frequency from twice weekly to once a year, but 2 to 4 weeks is the commonest interval. Spontaneous remissions lasting years have been seen. In the majority of cases, pregnancy is associated with an absence of acute episodes, and many patients note less frequent attacks in the summer than in the winter. There may be a decrease in the severity and frequency of the attacks with age or with development of amyloidosis.

Fever Fever is a cardinal manifestation of FMF and is present during most but not all attacks. Rarely, fever may be present without serositis. The temperature may be preceded by a chill and will peak in 12 to 24 h. Defervescence is often accompanied by diaphoresis. The fever ranges from 38.5 to 40°C but is quite variable.

Abdominal pain Abdominal pain occurs in more than 95 percent of patients, and may vary in severity in the same patient. Minor premonitory discomfort may precede an acute episode by 24 to 48 h. The pain usually starts in one quadrant and then spreads to involve the whole abdomen. The initial site is usually very tender. Tenderness may remain localized with referred pain in other areas, and there may be radiation to the back. There may be splinting of the chest and pain in one or both shoulders, typical of diaphragmatic irritation. Nausea and vomiting sometimes occur. The abdomen is usually distended, and may become rigid with decreased or absent bowel sounds. On x-ray, the wall of the small intestine may appear edematous, transit of barium is slowed, and fluid levels may be seen. Because the manifestations of an acute abdominal attack can simulate those of a perforated viscus so closely, patients should be advised to have an elective appendectomy between attacks so that acute appendicitis will not obfuscate the picture at a later date. An abdominal operation may precipitate an acute attack of FMF which may be confused with other postoperative complications.

Chest pain Most patients with abdominal attacks have referred chest pain at one time or another, and 75 percent also develop acute pleuritic pain with or without abdominal symptoms. In 30 percent, the attacks of pleuritis precede the onset of abdominal attacks by varying periods of time, and a small number of patients never develop abdominal attacks. Chest pain is usually unilateral and is associated with diminished breath sounds, a friction rub, or a transient pleural effusion.

Joint pain In Israel, 75 percent of patients report at least one episode of acute arthritis. Arthritis can be distinct from abdominal or pleural attacks, can be acute or, rarely, chronic, and may involve one or several joints. Effusions are common and the large joints are involved most frequently. Radiologic findings are nonspecific. Despite careful search, frank arthritis rarely has been seen in the United States. Some patients have a history of rheumatic fever–like illness in childhood, but in a large series of patients, including 30 from the Middle East, acute arthritis was not observed. Mild arthralgia is common during acute attacks but is nonspecific.

Skin manifestations Skin involvement is reported by 25 to 35 percent of patients. These lesions consist of painful, erythematous areas of swelling from 5 to 20 cm in diameter, usually located on the lower legs, the medial malleolus, or the dorsum of the foot. They may occur without abdominal or pleural pain and subside within 24 to 48 h.

Other signs and symptoms Involvement of other serosal membranes has been reported, but pericarditis is rare, and it is probable that descriptions of recurrent meningitis have been diseases other than FMF. Hematuria, splenomegaly, and small white dots called *colloid bodies* in the ocular fundus are among the findings of questionable significance. Rarely migraine-like headaches accompany acute abdominal attacks, and some patients have become somewhat irrational or show extreme emotional lability during attacks. Whether these are primary manifestations of FMF or secondary effects of pain and fever is not known.

Complications A serious complication of FMF is drug addiction or habituation, and obviously efforts should be made to avoid use of narcotics. Depression and lack of motivation are common, and patients with FMF require considerable encouragement and support. A striking number of patients in one American series have developed gallbladder disease.

Amyloidosis has been reported in Israel, North Africa, and elsewhere in the Middle East, but there have been only rare reported instances of amyloidosis complicating FMF in the United States. These findings are even more striking because there are probably as many known FMF patients in the United States as in Israel. These differences are unexplained and suggest that environmental or nutritional, as well as genetic, factors may play a role in the development of amyloidosis in FMF.

LABORATORY FINDINGS There is no specific diagnostic test. Polymorphonuclear leukocytosis ranging from 15,000 to 30,000 cells per cubic millimeter is almost invariable during acute attacks. The erythrocyte sedimentation rate is elevated during attacks but returns to normal between attacks. Plasma fibrinogen, serum haptoglobin, ceruloplasmin, and C-reactive protein increase during the episodes. Plasma lipids are normal, and there are no consistent abnormalities of hepatic or renal function. When amyloidosis is present, laboratory findings are typical of a nephrotic syndrome followed by renal insufficiency. Electrocardiographic and electroencephalographic changes are inconstant and nonspecific.

DIAGNOSIS When the typical acute attacks of FMF occur in an individual of appropriate ethnic background who has a family history of FMF, the diagnosis is easy. When a patient is seen for the first time, a variety of other febrile illnesses must be excluded by appropriate study or observation. These include acute appendicitis, acute pancreatitis, porphyria, cholecystitis, intestinal obstruction, and other major abdominal catastrophes.

Some of the inherited forms of the hyperlipidemias may mimic the clinical picture of FMF, but lipid analysis will eliminate them from consideration. The patient with FMF is not immune to other diseases, and when an attack differs from the usual pattern or is more prolonged, consideration should be given to other diagnostic possibilities. The pleural form of the disease is sometimes difficult to differentiate from acute pulmonary infection or infarction, but the rapid disappearance of signs and symptoms resolves the problem. The joint manifestations may be more prolonged than other forms of FMF, and differentiation from septic arthritis, gout, and acute rheumatoid disease may be necessary. The erythema is sometimes difficult to differentiate from superficial thrombophlebitis or cellulitis.

Whether or not the patient is of the appropriate ethnic group, the most difficult diagnostic problem in FMF is the patient who presents with fever alone. In this situation, an extensive diagnostic workup for fever of unknown origin may be required. Fortunately, such patients are rare, and all eventually develop serosal involvement. Until specific diagnostic tests for FMF are available, patients with recurrent fever but without signs of inflammation of one of the serosal membranes should not be categorized as having FMF.

PROGNOSIS Despite the severity of the symptoms during some acute attacks, most patients are remarkably free of any debilitation during the intervals between attacks. With encouragement and an understanding of their disease, most FMF patients lead fairly normal lives. The greatest hazard to patients is prolonged periods of hospitalization due to erroneous diagnoses or failure to understand the disease. In the United States, the prognosis of patients with FMF does not seem to be different from that of patients with other chronic nonfatal illnesses. Death usually results from causes unrelated to the underlying disease.

The complication of amyloidosis in Israel, parts of North Africa, Turkey, and other parts of the Middle East makes the prognosis quite different from that in America. In the past, approximately 25 percent of FMF patients in Israel were known to have amyloidosis, and this complication usually led to death. However, there is now evidence to suggest that the widespread use of colchicine has resulted in dramatically decreasing the incidence of amyloidosis.

TREATMENT Among the therapies tried have been antibiotics, hormones (including estrogens and adrenal corticosteroids), antipyretic drugs, immunotherapy, psychotherapy, elimination and low-fat diets, chloroquine, and phenylbutazone. When carefully studied and followed up, none of these therapies proved effective.

During the past 14 years, the outlook of patients with FMF has been altered dramatically. Goldfinger reported in 1972 that the prophylactic use of colchicine in five patients dramatically reduced the number of attacks. Subsequently, controlled trials in the United States and Israel have shown that chronic administration of colchicine will greatly reduce the number of acute attacks of FMF. It is recommended that 0.6 mg colchicine be taken by mouth three times a day. Patients often develop gastrointestinal side effects with this dose, however, in which case the dose should be reduced to 0.6 mg taken twice a day. Although an occasional patient will respond to 0.6 mg taken only once a day, this amount is less likely to be beneficial. Most but not all FMF patients will respond favorably to colchicine prophylaxis.

Since colchicine is known to occasionally result in nondisjunction of chromosomes and in azospermia, patients who are attempting to have children should be advised to withhold the drug during the time of conception. In some patients, intermittent therapy may be beneficial. The patient should take 0.6 mg colchicine by mouth every hour for 4 h, then every 2 h for 4 h, and every 12 h thereafter for 48 h. The colchicine should be given at the first premonitory sign of an attack. If both acute and prophylactic colchicine therapy fail, supportive therapy is all that can be offered. Except for unusual circumstances, narcotics should not be given to FMF patients.

The mechanism of colchicine's action against acute attacks of FMF is unknown. It is postulated that it may work by preventing the normal cellular response to inflammation. There are strong suggestions that as colchicine therapy becomes more widespread, the incidence of amyloidosis is decreasing.

REFERENCES

DINARELLO CA et al: Colchicine therapy for familial Mediterranean fever. A double-blind trial. N Engl J Med 291:934, 1974

MEYERHOFF J: Familial Mediterranean fever: Report of a large family, review of the literature, and discussion of the frequency of amyloidosis. Medicine 59:66, 1980

SCHWABE AD, PETERS RS: Familial Mediterranean fever in Armenians. Analysis of 100 cases. Medicine 53:453, 1974

WRIGHT DG et al: Efficiency of intermittent colchicine therapy in familial Mediterranean fever. Ann Intern Med 86:162, 1977

ZEMER D et al: Colchicine in the prevention and treatment of the amyloidosis of familial Mediterranean fever. N Engl J Med 314:1001, 1986

272   MIDLINE GRANULOMA

SHELDON M. WOLFF

DEFINITION Midline granuloma is an uncommon disease characterized by localized inflammation, destruction, and often mutilation of the tissues of the upper respiratory tract and face. This condition has also been referred to as *lethal midline granuloma, malignant granuloma,* and *granuloma gangrenescens,* none of which is an appropriate term.

ETIOLOGY The etiology of midline granuloma is unknown. In view of the intense granulomatous inflammation, the disease is thought to represent a localized hypersensitivity reaction which leads to tissue destruction and mutilation. However, the responsible antigen(s) is unknown, and there is no immunologic evidence supporting this hypothesis. A variety of microorganisms have been considered as possible causative agents, but detailed microbiologic investigations have failed to detect the consistent presence of pathogenic organisms. In view of the clinical and pathologic features of the illness as well as the fact that some upper-airway tumors can elicit a similar intense inflammatory response, some authors have suggested a neoplastic basis for midline granuloma. However, when malignant tissue (usually of a lymphomatous nature) is found in the lesions, the diagnosis of midline granuloma is no longer tenable.

PATHOLOGY The most characteristic pathologic finding is acute or chronic inflammation with necrosis. Superimposed pyogenic infection of the involved tissues, including the sinuses, may contribute to nonspecific histologic findings. The pathologic hallmark, noncaseating granulomas, with or without giant cells, may be obscured by the inflammatory reaction, but when present this is strong evidence in favor of the diagnosis. Primary vasculitis is seen rarely; when it occurs, a search for other causes, most notably Wegener's granulomatosis, should be made. The presence of malignant cells makes the diagnosis of midline granuloma unacceptable. Until an etiology is established, the diagnosis of midline granuloma will rest on the characteristic clinical features outlined below.

CLINICAL FEATURES The disease may occur at any age, but the majority of patients are in the fifth and sixth decades. It is more common in women than men and has been reported in all races. Many patients report recurrent "sinus" problems, and some have histories of allergic rhinitis, although the significance of these features is unknown.

The major symptoms are usually related to the nose. Patients frequently complain of nasal stuffiness and occasionally of discharge. The first symptom in a smaller percentage of patients relates to ulceration of the mucosa of the nose, the buccal mucosa, or the gums. This has led to loosening of the teeth, and dentists are often first consulted by these patients. Rarely, patients will present first with eye findings related to conjunctival inflammation or even ulceration. Although the progression of symptoms in some patients may be slow, all too often the disease steadily, and sometimes rapidly, progresses. The characteristic symptoms of nasal discharge, difficulty in breathing through the nose, and pain over the sinuses, nose, or eye become more prominent with time. Once ulceration begins, the disease often progresses rapidly. The ulcers frequently involve the nasal septum and will lead to the characteristic septal perforation and a saddlenose deformity. The majority of patients develop ulceration and eventually perforations of the soft and hard palates. Untreated, the disease can lead to massive destruction and mutilation of the tissues involved, including the skin of the face and the eyes. Frequently, the necrotic tissue becomes infected, and systemic symptoms such as fever and anorexia appear. The destructive lesions can become very malodorous. The disease extends to involve local tissues and does not progress below the neck; if this happens, other diseases should be considered. As the necrotic process progresses and involves vital organs, patients may lose sight in the affected eye, experience dysphagia, and have difficulty in speech. Although spontaneous temporary remissions have been reported, untreated midline granuloma is fatal. The progression of the disease can be rapidly accelerated by surgical procedures in the affected areas. The patient usually dies from secondary infection, although erosion by the process into a major blood vessel or penetration into the central nervous system with superimposed meningitis can also cause death.

Aside from the granulomatous inflammation, necrosis, and destruction, no other specific clinical or pathologic findings are associated with midline granuloma. Occasionally, with superimposed infection, local lymphadenopathy may be noted, but it is not characteristic of the disease per se.

LABORATORY FINDINGS With progression of the disease, a variety of nonspecific abnormalities may be noted. These changes are characteristic of inflammatory processes in general or of secondary infections. For example, mild anemia, leukocytosis, elevated sedimentation rate, and hyperglobulinemia are common in these patients. Radiographic examination reveals pansinusitis, and as the disease advances, destruction of bone in the involved areas is characteristic.

DIFFERENTIAL DIAGNOSIS The diagnosis of midline granuloma is made by finding the characteristic histologic lesions in biopsies of the affected tissues. When the specimens show only inflammatory tissue, a presumptive diagnosis of midline granuloma can be made only when the characteristic clinical picture is present and other diseases with similar presentation have been excluded. The diagnosis of Wegener's granulomatosis is ruled out by the absence of vasculitis in the biopsy specimens and the localized nature of midline granuloma (i.e., no pulmonary or renal involvement). In addition, Wegener's granulomatosis rarely, if ever, causes erosion through facial tissues. It is often difficult to differentiate true midline granuloma from neoplasms of the upper airways such as malignant reticulosis and certain lymphomas. These may be clinically similar to midline granuloma and are often associated with granulomatous inflammation. Careful examination of generous biopsy material as well as concomitant workup for disseminated neoplasm often provides the clinicopathologic distinction. Other diseases to be excluded by appropriate laboratory techniques are histoplasmosis, blastomycosis, coccidioidomycosis, leprosy, tuberculosis, syphilis, mucocutaneous leishmaniasis, rhinoscleroma, and pseudotumor of the orbit.

TREATMENT The complications of midline granuloma such as superimposed infections can be treated specifically. Although adrenal corticosteroids are often used in the therapy of midline granuloma, they are of no value and probably are contraindicated if infection is present. Sporadic reports of therapy with cytotoxic agents are difficult to interpret, since some of the patients reported clearly had lymphoma or Wegener's granulomatosis, diseases where such agents are of definite value. Surgical removal of the involved tissue has been attempted but is useless and may, in fact, cause rapid progression of the disease.

The treatment of choice is radiotherapy to the local lesion. Although low dosages [10,000 mGy (1000 rads) and below] have been reported to be effective, many patients relapse after such therapy. Radiotherapy should be given in a dose of 50,000 mGy (5000 rads) to the involved areas. Where such a regimen is employed, long-lasting remissions (more than 15 years) and possible cures have been achieved. Following irradiation and after an appropriate period to allow for tissue healing (usually 1 year), reconstructive and plastic surgery, which may be of enormous cosmetic and functional value, can be undertaken.

REFERENCES

FAUCI AS et al: Radiation therapy of midline granuloma. Ann Intern Med 84:140, 1976

FECHNER RE, LAMPPIN DW: Midline malignant reticulosis. Arch Otolaryngol 95:467, 1972

273 APPROACH TO DISORDERS OF THE JOINTS AND MUSCULOSKELETAL DISORDERS

JOHN J. CUSH / PETER E. LIPSKY

Musculoskeletal complaints account for nearly 10 percent of all outpatient evaluations in general medical practice. In the United States, musculoskeletal disorders are among the leading causes of disability and absenteeism from work. Many of the musculoskeletal complaints that cause patients to seek medical attention are related to self-limited conditions requiring minimal evaluation and only symptomatic therapy and reassurance. However, others with similar symptoms may require additional laboratory testing to confirm a suspected diagnosis or document the extent and nature of the pathologic process. The initial goal of the clinician is to diagnose accurately and provide timely therapy while avoiding excessive diagnostic testing and unnecessary treatment.

Individuals with musculoskeletal complaints should be evaluated in a uniform, logical manner with a thorough history, a comprehensive physical examination, and appropriate laboratory testing. With such an approach and an understanding of the pathophysiologic processes underlying musculoskeletal complaints, an adequate diagnosis can be made in 90 percent of individuals. Approximately 10 percent of patients will not fit immediately into an established diagnostic category. Moreover, many musculoskeletal disorders resemble each other at the outset and may take months or even years to evolve fully into a specific recognizable syndrome. Such knowledge should temper the desire to establish a definitive diagnosis at the first encounter.

A paramount objective during the initial encounter is to determine whether the condition requires additional evaluation or immediate therapy. To make this decision, a knowledge of the particular anatomic

TABLE 273-1 Musculoskeletal disorders

I Tissue involvement
  A Articular
    1 Synovium
    2 Articular cartilage
    3 Juxtaarticular bone
    4 Other—menisci, capsule
  B Periarticular
    1 Ligaments
    2 Tendons
    3 Bursae
  C Extraarticular
    1 Muscle
    2 Fascia
    3 Bone
    4 Nerve
    5 Skin and subcutaneous tissue
II Pathologic processes
  A Inflammatory
    1 Infectious
    2 Crystal-induced
    3 Immunologic
    4 Reactive
    5 Idiopathic
  B Noninflammatory
    1 Traumatic
    2 Mechanical or degenerative
    3 Neoplastic
    4 Functional
    5 Other

sites of involvement (articular, periarticular, or extraarticular) and the nature of the pathologic processes (inflammatory or noninflammatory) is important (Table 273-1). Information derived from the patient's symptoms and signs allows the clinician to narrow the diagnostic considerations and assess the need for therapeutic intervention, immediate diagnostic testing, or continued observation over a period of time.

MUSCULOSKELETAL DISORDERS: HISTORIC FEATURES Historic features of the disorder are important in establishing the nature and extent of the pathologic process and may also provide important clues to the diagnosis. Aspects of the patient profile including age, sex, race, and family history can provide important information. Certain diagnoses are more frequent in different age groups. Systemic lupus erythematosus and Reiter's syndrome occur more frequently in the young, while fibrositis is most frequent in middle age and osteoarthritis and polymyalgia rheumatica are more prevalent among the elderly. Diagnostic clustering is also evident when *sex* and *race* are considered. Gout and the spondyloarthropathies are more common in men, whereas rheumatoid arthritis and fibrositis are more frequent in women. Racial predilections are noted with disorders such as polymyalgia rheumatica (whites) and sarcoidosis (blacks). *Familial aggregation* may be seen in disorders such as ankylosing spondylitis, gout, rheumatoid arthritis, and Heberden's nodes of osteoarthritis.

Features of the clinical presentation also provide important diagnostic clues. The *mode of onset* is characteristically acute in infection or gout, while osteoarthritis and fibrositis may have more indolent presentations. The length of time the patient has had signs and symptoms alters the diagnostic considerations. Thus, the signs and symptoms of the arthritis associated with hepatitis B virus infection may be identical with those of rheumatoid arthritis, but rarely persist beyond 2 weeks.

Precipitating events such as trauma, drug administration, or antecedent illnesses should be sought. The *number and pattern* of involved structures often provide useful information. Disorders such as trauma and gout are typically focal, whereas others, such as polymyositis and fibrositis, involve more than a single site. Rheumatoid arthritis tends to be symmetric, whereas the spondyloarthropathies are asymmetric. The upper extremities are frequently involved in rheumatoid arthritis, while lower extremity arthritis is characteristic of gout at its onset. Involvement of the axial skeleton is common in ankylosing spondylitis but is infrequent in rheumatoid arthritis with the notable exception of the cervical spine. The *chronology and evolution* of the patient's complaints may also be useful in suggesting diagnostic categories. Chronic (osteoarthritis), intermittent (gout), migratory (rheumatic fever), and additive (Reiter's syndrome) patterns are suggestive of certain disease processes.

Associated features outside the musculoskeletal systems may also provide useful diagnostic information. A variety of musculoskeletal disorders may be associated with systemic features such as fever (systemic lupus erythematosus, infection), rash (systemic lupus erythematosus, Reiter's syndrome, rheumatic fever), or morning stiffness (inflammatory arthritis). In addition, some are associated with involvement of other organs including ocular (Reiter's syndrome), gastrointestinal (scleroderma, inflammatory bowel disease), genitourinary (Reiter's syndrome, gonococcemia), or neurologic involvement (rheumatoid arthritis, vasculitis).

PHYSICAL EXAMINATION The goal of the physical examination is to document the structures involved, the nature of the disorder, the extent and functional consequences of the process, and the presence of systemic manifestations. A knowledge of topographic anatomy is necessary to identify the primary site(s) of involvement and differentiate between articular, periarticular, and extraarticular disease. The musculoskeletal evaluation is largely dependent on careful inspection, palpation, and a variety of physical maneuvers to elicit diagnostic signs.

Examination of involved and uninvolved joints will determine the absence or presence of *warmth, erythema,* or *swelling.* The examination should distinguish true articular swelling caused by synovial effusion or synovial proliferation from periarticular involvement which usually extends beyond the normal joint margins. Synovial effusion can be distinguished from synovial hypertrophy or bony hypertrophy by palpation. Bursal effusions (i.e., olecranon, prepatellar) overlie bony prominences and are fluctuant with sharply defined borders. Joint *stability* can be assessed by palpation and by the application of manual stress. Subluxation or dislocation, which may be secondary to traumatic, mechanical, or inflammatory causes, can be assessed by inspection and palpation. Joint *volume* can be assessed by palpation. Distention of the articular capsule by various processes causes pain. The patient will attempt to minimize the pain by maintaining the joint in the position of greatest volume and least intraarticular pressure, usually flexion. Clinically, this may be reflected as obvious swelling, voluntary or eventually fixed flexion deformities, or diminished range of motion, especially on extension when joint volumes are decreased. Active and passive *range of motion* should be assessed in all planes and is best quantified by a goniometer with contralateral comparison. Joint *crepitus* may be felt during these maneuvers and may be prominent in degenerative disorders. Limitation of motion is frequently caused by effusion, pain, deformity, or contracture. Contractures may be an indication of antecedent synovial inflammation. Joint *deformity* usually indicates a long-standing pathologic process. Deformities may result from ligament destruction, soft tissue contracture, bony enlargement, ankylosis, erosive disease, or subluxation. Examination of the musculature will document strength and the presence of atrophy, and also will elicit pain or spasm.

ADDITIONAL INVESTIGATIONS The vast majority of musculoskeletal disorders can be easily diagnosed by a complete history and physical examination. However, in a number of circumstances, additional investigations may be required to establish the diagnosis or confirm a suspected etiology. A number of features indicate the need for additional evaluation. Patients with *acute monarticular* conditions require additional evaluation, as do those who present with *traumatic* or *inflammatory* conditions or those with *neurologic changes* or *systemic manifestations* of serious disease. Finally individuals with *chronic (>6 weeks)* symptoms, even of minor severity, are candidates for additional evaluation. The extent and nature of the additional investigation should be dictated by the pattern of the involvement and suspected pathologic process. Broad batteries of diagnostic tests and radiographic procedures are rarely a useful or cost-effective means to establish a diagnosis.

Besides a complete blood count including a white blood cell and differential count, the routine evaluation should include a determination of the erythrocyte sedimentation rate, which can be useful in discriminating inflammatory from noninflammatory musculoskeletal disorders. A radiographic evaluation is indicated when there is a history of prior trauma, suspected chronic infection, progressive disability, monarticular involvement, or when therapeutic alterations are considered. Early in most inflammatory disorders radiographs are rarely helpful in establishing a diagnosis and often reveal only soft tissue swelling and juxtaarticular demineralization. As the disease progresses, calcification (soft tissue, cartilage, or bone), joint space narrowing, erosions, bony ankylosis, new bone formation (sclerosis, osteophytes, or periostitis), or subchondral cysts can be demonstrated.

Synovial fluid aspiration and analysis is always indicated in acute monarthritis or when a septic or crystal-induced arthropathy is suspected. Synovial fluid can be classified according to its appearance, cell count, glucose level, and viscosity. Noninflammatory synovial fluid is clear, amber-colored, with a white blood cell count of <3000

cells per cubic millimeter and a mononuclear cell predominance. The glucose and viscosity are normal. Such effusions are typical of osteoarthritis and trauma. Inflammatory fluid is turbid and yellow with an increased white cell count (3000 to 50,000 cells per cubic millimeter) and a polymorphonuclear leukocyte predominance. The protein is elevated, the glucose is normal or low, and the viscosity is poor. Such effusions are found in rheumatoid arthritis, gout, other inflammatory arthritides, and occasionally septic arthritis. Infectious fluid is turbid and opaque, with a white cell count >50,000 cells per cubic millimeter, and a polymorphonuclear leukocyte predominance. The protein is elevated, the glucose is low, and viscosity is poor. Such effusions are typical of septic arthritis but may rarely occur with sterile arthritides such as rheumatoid arthritis. Additionally, hemorrhagic synovial fluid may be seen with hemarthrosis or trauma. Synovial fluid should be analyzed immediately for crystals using a polarizing microscope. Monosodium urate, seen in gouty effusions, appears as long, needle-shaped, negatively birefringent, usually intracellular crystals, whereas calcium pyrophosphate dihydrate found in chondrocalcinosis and pseudogout is usually seen as short, rhomboid-shaped, positively birefringent crystals. When infection is suspected, synovial fluid should be Gram-stained and cultured appropriately. Whenever gonococcal arthritis is suspected, immediate plating out of the fluid on appropriate culture media is indicated. It should be noted that on occasion both crystal-induced arthritis and infection may occur in the same joint.

Serologic tests for rheumatoid factor (antibodies to IgG), antinuclear antibodies, complement levels or antistreptolysin O titers should only be carried out when there is clinical evidence to suggest a specific diagnosis.

EVALUATION OF THE ELDERLY FOR RHEUMATIC DISEASES
Musculoskeletal disorders in geriatric patients are often not diagnosed since complaints in the elderly may be insidious in onset and chronic in nature. In addition, older individuals frequently possess multiple interactive variables, including other medical conditions and therapies that may obscure the nature of the problem. This is compounded by the diminished reliability of laboratory testing in the elderly, owing to the wider range of nonpathologic serologic variability, including elevated erythrocyte sedimentation rates and low titers of rheumatoid factor or antinuclear antibodies. Although nearly all rheumatic disorders can afflict the elderly, certain diseases and drug-induced disorders are more common in this age group (Table 273-2). The elderly should be approached in the same uniform manner used for all patients with musculoskeletal complaints, with additional inquiry to exclude common geriatric musculoskeletal disorders. An emphasis on identifying intercurrent medical conditions and therapies is extemely important. Drug-induced lupus erythematosus, gout, and chronic salicylate toxicity all are more common in the elderly. The physical examination should emphasize coexistent disease that may influence subsequent diagnosis and treatment.

TABLE 273-2 Common musculoskeletal disorders in the elderly

I Inflammatory
    Polymyalgia rheumatica
    Temporal (giant cell) arteritis
    Gout
    Calcium pyrophosphate dihydrate deposition disease
II Mechanical
    Degenerative joint disease
    Spinal stenosis
III Metabolic
    Osteoporosis
    Myxedema
    Paget's disease
IV Associated with neoplastic disease
    Carcinomatous arthropathy or neuromyopathy
    Dermatomyositis
    Hypertrophic osteoarthropathy
V Drug-induced
    Diuretics (gout)
    Drug-induced lupus
    Corticosteroids (osteopenia, myopathy)

REFERENCES

BLUESTONE R: The patient who hurts all over: Practical approach to diagnosis and management. Postgrad Med 72:71, 1982

FRIES JF, MITCHELL DM: Joint pain or arthritis. JAMA 235:199, 1976

GATTER RA: *Practical Handbook of Joint Fluid Analysis.* Philadelphia, Lea & Febiger, 1984

HALL H: Examination of the patient with low back pain. Bull Rheum Dis 33:1, 1983

HUGHES GRV: Auto antibodies in lupus and its variants: Experience in 1000 patients. Lancet 289:339, 1984

POLLEY HF, HUNDER GG: *Rheumatologic Interviewing and Physical Examination of the Joints.* Philadelphia, Saunders, 1978

STEVENS MB: Rheumatic disease: An overview of geriatric problems. Geriatrics 38:67, 1983

TAN EM: Antinuclear antibodies in diagnosis and management. Hosp Pract 18:79, 1983

WILSON FC: Principles of diagnosis and treatment of musculoskeletal trauma, in *The Musculoskeletal System: Basic Processes and Disorders,* FC Wilson (ed). Philadelphia, Lippincott, 1983, pp 270–274

274   DEGENERATIVE JOINT DISEASE

BRUCE C. GILLILAND

Degenerative joint disease (osteoarthritis), is the most common form of arthritis and affects almost all joints, especially weight-bearing and frequently used joints. The disorder is characterized by progressive deterioration and loss of articular cartilage accompanied by proliferation of new bone and soft tissue in and around the involved joint. Osteoarthritis is divided into a primary or idiopathic form in which no underlying predisposing factor(s) are apparent and into a secondary form in which a predisposing cause such as previous trauma, congenital abnormality, or metabolic disorder is present.

EPIDEMIOLOGY   Osteoarthritis affects both men and women, being slightly more frequent in men before the age of 45 and in women after age 55. The prevalence of osteoarthritis increases with age and is almost universal in individuals over the age of 75. Osteoarthritis is found in all races. The placement of stress on joints is thought to be a factor in the development of osteoarthritis. For example, osteoarthritis of shoulders and knees is more frequent in coal miners, presumably because of stress placed on these joints during work. On the other hand, studies have shown no increase in osteoarthritis in runners or in persons performing heavy physical work. Hereditary factors also appear to play a role in some forms of osteoarthritis. Heberden's nodes are twice as frequent in mothers and three times more frequent in sisters of the affected individual. The inheritance of Heberden's nodes appears to involve a single autosomal dominant gene.

PATHOGENESIS   Articular cartilage together with subchondral bone, joint capsule, and muscle absorb the energy of weight bearing. Normal articular cartilage is compressible and elastic and able to lubricate its surfaces under high-pressure loads, providing smooth and almost frictionless movement. The materials which give cartilage these properties are primarily collagen, proteoglycans, and hyaluronic acid. The form and tensile strength of cartilage is due to collagen. The type of collagen in articular cartilage is type II, which is unique to joints. The other major component of cartilage is proteoglycan. The proteolglycan molecule is composed of glucosaminoglycans, chondroitin sulfate, and keratin sulfate, which extend from a protein core in a configuration that has been likened to a bottle brush. Most of the proteoglycan molecules exist in aggregates in which individual molecules are noncovalently linked to a long chain of hyaluronic acid. The large aggregates of proteoglycans are extremely hydrophilic and bind most of the water present in cartilage. Water represents approximately 70 percent of the total weight of articular cartilage. The large hydrophilic proteoglycan aggregates are interwoven and constrained within the network of collagen fibers, giving cartilage the property of resiliency.

Normal articular cartilage undergoes continuous internal remodeling. Chondrocytes secrete collagen and proteoglycans as well as enzymes that degrade matrix. Enzymes include cathepsin D, neutral proteases, and collagenase. A substance named catabolin, which is released from mononuclear cells in synovium, stimulates chondrocytes to produce enzymes that degrade cartilage matrix. The degradative process is kept under control by small proteins that inhibit these enzymes secreted by cells in synovium. Chondrocytes in normal cartilage are metabolically active but do not synthesize DNA or divide unless their microenvironment is altered.

The initiating event in primary osteoarthritis that leads to stimulation of chondrocytes and the changes in cartilage is not known. The first event may be microfractures of subchondral bone which occur from repeated impact loading. The healing of these fractures results in stiff and thickened subchondral bone which poorly absorbs the energy of weight bearing. Chondrocytes in articular cartilage therefore are subjected to increased pressure, which stimulates cell division and synthesis of DNA, collagen, and proteoglycans as well as degradative enzymes. Others have suggested that the initial changes occur in cartilage, leading to loss of cartilage resiliency. Microfractures of subchondral bone occur as a consequence of decreased cartilage compressibility. Initially, in the development of osteoarthritis, the reparative process is able to keep pace with degradation. Eventually, the degradative process predominates, resulting in loss of cartilage.

Inflammation plays a role in the pathogenesis of osteoarthritis. Breakdown products of cartilage stimulate the release of collagenase and other hydrolytic enzymes from cells in the synovium. The finding of immunoglobulin and complement in the superficial layer of cartilage suggests that immune complexes may induce an inflammatory response. Hydroxyapatite, calcium pyrophosphate crystals, or both are often found in the synovial fluid. These crystals have been proposed as a possible factor in the production or exacerbation of osteoarthritis.

PATHOLOGY   In the early stages of osteoarthritis, cartilage shows fissuring and pitting which progress to focal erosions. Cartilage is disrupted along the planes of collagen fibrils, resulting in flaking, fibrillation, and eventually denuded areas. The proteoglycan and water content of cartilage is decreased in proportion to the severity of the disease. Clusters of chrondrocytes are observed followed later by a decreased number of cells. Subchondral bone shows osteoblastic and osteoclastic activity resulting eventually in a thickened, dense bony plate. The development of this ivory-like bone is termed *eburnation*. Subchondral cysts represent focal areas of necrosis and may also develop from the penetration of synovial fluid through microfractures in the bone. New bone proliferation at the joint margins forms osteophytes (spurs) which are covered by a layer of articular cartilage. The synovium is thickened by an increase of lining cells and a mild to moderate infiltration of lymphocytes, plasma cells, and occasional multinucleated giant cells. Fibrotic thickening of the joint capsule and ligaments is present.

CLINICAL FEATURES   The clinical manifestations are usually limited to one or a few joints. Osteoarthritis can also be more generalized, suggesting a systemic form of arthritis. Symptoms usually begin insidiously in the form of a deep, aching, poorly localized pain occurring with use of the involved joint and relieved by rest. Stiffness of the affected joint(s) occurs in the morning and after periods of inactivity during the day, usually lasting 15 min or less. Joint pain, which may be due to the absence of protective splinting of the joint and/or to increased intraosseous venous pressure frequently awakens the patient at night. Patients may experience joint pain with changes in the weather. Crepitus may occur with joint movement due to loss of cartilage and joint surface irregularities. The involved joint may give way on weight bearing. Subsequently, joint motion becomes limited, and subluxation and deformity of joints appear. Flares of acute arthritis may occur in involved joints from trauma or crystal-induced synovitis due to either calcium pyrophosphate or hydroxyapatite crystals.

The most common finding in primary osteoarthritis is *Heberden's nodes,* which usually appear after age 45 (see Fig. 274-1). They usually develop slowly over months or years in association with osteoarthritis of the distal interphalangeal joints. Heberden's nodes are firm enlargements appearing on the dorsomedial and dorsolateral aspect of the distal interphalangeal joint, and are composed of bone covered by cartilage. Similar enlargements at the proximal interphalangeal joint are called *Bouchard's nodes.* Gelatinous cysts may precede the development of Heberden's nodes. These cysts initially communicate with the distal interphalangeal joint, but may lose their connection later. Heberden's and Bouchard's nodes usually develop with little or no pain, but in some patients may be associated with pain, paresthesias, erythema, and swelling.

Osteoarthritis of interphalangeal joints of the hands causes symptoms of pain, swelling, and stiffness. Nodes develop at the joint margins along with flexor and lateral deviation of fingers. When ankylosis develops, joints become asymptomatic. A syndrome termed erosive osteoarthritis is characterized by recurrent episodes of acute inflammation and progressive destruction of the interphalangeal joints. Middle-aged women are most often affected.

Primary generalized osteoarthritis is characterized by involvement of three or more joints or group of joints. The proximal interphalangeal joints are considered as one group and the distal interphalangeal joints as another. This form of osteoarthritis also appears most often in middle-aged women and involves distal and proximal interphalangeal joints of hands, first carpometacarpal joint, knees, hips, and first metatarsophalangeal joint. The spine may also be involved. The joints may be episodically warm and swollen and the erythrocyte sedimentation rate mildly elevated.

Osteoarthritis of the hip is more common in men than women and is often initially unilateral. The opposite side will eventually be affected in approximately 20 percent of patients. It has been estimated that 80 percent of cases are secondary to an underlying congenital or developmental abnormality. These abnormalities include hip dysplasia, slipped capital femoral epiphysis, and Legg-Calvé-Perthes disease. Avascular necrosis related to deep-water diving, glucocorticoid therapy, alcohol, or sickle cell disease leads to collapse of the femoral head and severe osteoarthritis. The pain of hip disease is felt in the groin or inguinal area. Hip pain may also be experienced over the greater trochanter, in the buttock, or down the anterior and inner thigh. In some patients, involvement may manifest as pain in the distal thigh or knee since the obturator nerve and its branches supply both hip and knee. Patients may limp as the disease progresses and complain of difficulty in rising from a sitting position. On examination, internal rotation is limited initially, followed by decreased extension, adduction, and flexion. Adduction and/or flexion contractures may lead to a functional shortening of the leg on the involved side, causing the patient to walk with a shuffling gait.

Osteoarthritis of the knee involves the medial, lateral, and/or patellofemoral compartments. Pain may be diffuse or localized to a compartment and is aggravated by motion. Stiffness occurs after periods of inactivity. The knee may lock due to a loose body or give way suddenly because of a pain reflex. Small joint effusions are often present. With progression, ligamentous laxity, limitation of motion, and flexion contractures subsequently develop. Chondromalacia patellae is a clinical syndrome occurring in adolescents and young adults, being more common in women. The cartilage on the undersurface becomes softened, fibrillated, and eroded. The changes are indistinguishable from early osteoarthritis but usually do not progress. The lesion is thought to result from trauma or abnormal forces on the patella from lateral displacement of the patella as it moves through the shallow groove between the femoral condyles.

Osteoarthritis of the first carpometacarpal joint causes pain and tenderness at the base of the thumb. Enlargement and radial subluxation give the hand a squared appearance. Osteoarthritis also involves the scaphotrapezoid joint. The first metatarsophalangeal joint is another common site for osteoarthritis.

Osteoarthritis of the spine affects the intervertebral disks, apophyseal joints, and paraspinal ligaments. In the neck, the joints of Luschka (uncovertebral joints) may also be affected. The term *spondylosis* is preferred by some for disease of the intervertebral disks while disease in the apophyseal joints is considered true osteoarthritis. Cervical spine involvement produces localized pain or pain referred to the interscapular region, occiput, shoulder, and arm, depending upon the level of involvement. Compression of the spinal cord by posteriorly protruding disk or osteophytes as well as occlusion of the anterior spinal artery by a herniated disk will cause long tract signs. A congenitally narrowed cervical spinal cord may contribute to cord compression. Osteophytes extending from the joint of Luschka may impinge on the vertebral arteries producing symptoms of basilar artery insufficiency. Symptoms include vertigo, nystagmus, diplopia, scotomas, tinnitus, and ataxia. Symptoms are usually intermittent and related to position of the head. Osteoarthritis of the thoracic spine is less common. Costovertebral joints may be affected. Neoplasm, infection, or osteoporosis should be considered in the differential diagnosis of thoracic spine pain. Symptoms of lumbar spine involvement include localized pain and stiffness and radicular pain radiating into the buttocks and legs depending on the level of disease (see Chaps. 7, 353).

Lumbar stenosis causes cord compression, affecting older-age patients. Posterior vertebral osteophytes impinge on the cord particularly in those persons who have congenitally narrowed spinal canals. Symptoms develop gradually and include bilateral paresthesias and weakness of lower extremities. Symptoms may be induced by hyperextension of the lumbar spine and relieved by flexion. Lumbar

FIGURE 274-1 *Osteoarthritis. A. Heberden's nodes of the distal interphalangeal joints and Bouchard's nodes of the proximal interphalangeal joints are present. The carpometacarpal joint is radially subluxed giving the hand a squared appearance. There is also angulation of the distal and proximal interphalangeal joints. B. Radiograph of the second, third, and fourth proximal and distal interphalangeal joints. Loss of joint space, osteophytes, and subchondral sclerosis and cysts are evident.*

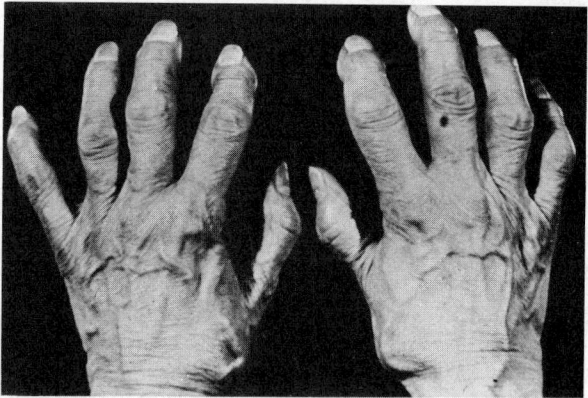

A

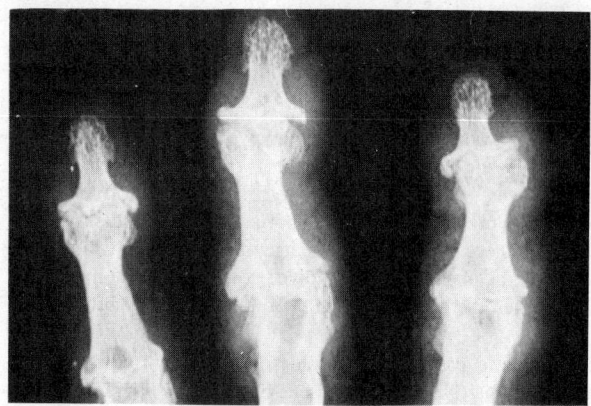

B

stenosis is differentiated from vascular insufficiency by these positional symptoms and by the presence of weakness and paresthesia. Laminectomy may be required if symptoms and signs persist or progress.

Secondary osteoarthritis may be due to traumatic, systemic, or congenital disorders. The arthritis may be unilateral, appear at an earlier age, and involve joints that are not commonly observed in primary osteoarthritis. Previous trauma to a joint, resulting, for example, in a torn knee meniscus or ligamentous instability leads to joint surface incongruity and subsequent osteoarthritis. Joint damage caused by septic arthritis or noninfectious inflammatory arthritis, for example, rheumatoid arthritis, also predisposes the involved joint(s) to osteoarthritis. Neuropathic joint disease (Charcot's joint) is a severe form of osteoarthritis associated with loss of pain sensation, proprioception, or both (see Chap. 278). Joint hypermobility syndromes, either inherited or idiopathic, may be associated with early onset of osteoarthritis. Metabolic disorders associated with osteoarthritis include hemochromatosis, Wilson's disease, calcium pyrophosphate deposition disease, Paget's disease, and ochronosis (alkaptonuria). Acromegaly and hyperparathyroidism are also associated with osteoarthritis.

LABORATORY AND RADIOGRAPHIC FINDINGS   Routine laboratory work is normal in patients with primary osteoarthritis. The erythrocyte sedimentation rate is usually normal, but may be mildly elevated in patients with primary generalized or erosive osteoarthritis. The synovial fluid is straw colored and has good viscosity. The leukocyte count is usually less than 2000 per cubic millimeter with the majority of cells being mononuclear. Elevated leukocyte counts are found during acute episodes of calcium pyrophosphate deposition disease associated with osteoarthritis. Calcium pyrophosphate and/or hydroxyapatite crystals may be found in some synovial fluids (see Chap. 275). Radiographs of the involved joints are initially normal, but as the disease progresses, joint space narrowing, subchondral bone sclerosis (eburnation), and osteophytes are observed. Erosions are found on the joint surfaces in association with sclerosis of subchondral bone, and bony ankylosis may be present. Radiographic findings may not correlate with clinical symptoms.

DIAGNOSIS   Osteoarthritis can usually be distinguished from other arthropathies by the pattern of joint involvement (especially in the hands), normal laboratory tests, low leukocyte counts in synovial fluid, and characteristic radiographic findings. The erythrocyte sedimentation rate is usually normal for the age of the patient, and rheumatoid factor and antinuclear antibody tests are negative. Primary generalized and erosive osteoarthritis may have inflammatory features suggesting a systemic arthritis such as rheumatoid arthritis. The involvement of distal and proximal interphalangeal joints and the absence of wrist disease in osteoarthritis differs from rheumatoid arthritis, in which metacarpophalangeal, proximal interphalangeal, and wrist joints are characteristically affected. Painful swelling and erythema of a distal or proximal interphalangeal joint associated with Heberden's or Bouchard's nodes may mimic gout. Both entities, however, may coexist.

TREATMENT   The goals of treatment are to decrease pain and maintain and improve function. Management of osteoarthritis requires coordinating the patient's care which at various times in the course of the disease may involve physical therapy, occupational therapy, social services, and orthopedics. Patient education is extremely important. Patients should be advised to protect the involved joints from overuse. Weight reduction is important in those patients with back, hip, and knee involvement. The use of a cane also reduces the amount of weight placed on an involved joint. Isometric exercises help to strengthen the muscles around a joint and thereby protect the joint.

In symptomatic patients, salicylates or other nonsteroidal anti-inflammatory drugs (NSAIDs) are used. Salicylates should be given in an adequate dose in the range of 2 to 4 g per day. NSAIDs are ibuprofen (400 to 600 mg qid), fenoprofen (600 mg qid), naproxen (250 to 500 mg bid), diflunisal (500 mg bid), indomethacin (25 to 50 mg tid), tolmetin (200 to 400 mg qid), sulindac (200 mg bid), meclofenamate (50 mg qid), and piroxicam (10 to 20 mg once a day). The NSAIDs share several similar side effects, including gastrointestinal bleeding and sodium retention (see Chap. 263). Drugs that are primarily analgesic, such as acetaminophen or propoxyphene, may also be beneficial at times. Phenylbutazone, because of the increased risk of agranulocytosis, should only be used after all other NSAIDs have been found to be ineffective. If given, the physician and patient should be well aware of its toxicity and the need for only short-term usage.

Intraarticular steroid injections may be very effective in reducing pain and swelling. They should be used judicially in weight-bearing joints and limited to no more than three injections per year. Injection of glucocorticoids into the juxtaarticular soft tissue may benefit some patients. Orthopedic surgery may provide patients with improved pain relief and function. Osteotomy of the knee will correct a valgus or varus deformity and improve weight distribution within the knee. Replacement of the hip with a prosthetic joint has been one of the most dramatic forms of surgery for patients with osteoarthritis. Total knee replacements also have been helpful in some patients, although not nearly as successful as the total hip. Debridement, removal of loose bodies, and placement of partial prostheses are other procedures that may benefit individual patients. Splinting of a joint for short periods of time, for example, the carpometacarpal joint of the thumb, often alleviates pain. Hot packs, ultrasound, and other physical therapy modalities also provide pain reduction and improvement of joint motion.

REFERENCES

BLAND JH, COOPER SM: Osteoarthritis: A review of the cell biology involved and evidence for reversibility: Management rationally related to known genesis and pathophysiology. Semin Arthritis Rheum 14:106, 1984

BRANDT KD: Pathogenesis of osteoarthritis in *Textbook of Rheumatology*, WN Kelley et al (eds). Philadelphia, Saunders, 1985, chap 88, pp 1417–1431

———: Osteoarthritis: Clinical patterns and pathology in *Textbook of Rheumatology*, WN Kelley et al (eds). Philadelphia, Saunders, 1985, chap 89, pp 1432–1448

GIBILISCO PA et al: Synovial fluid crystals in osteoarthritis. Arthritis Rheum 28:511, 1985

HOWELL DS: Etiopathogenesis of osteoarthritis, in *Osteoarthritis: Diagnosis and Management*, RW Moskowitz et al (eds). Philadelphia, Saunders, 1984, chap 7, pp 129–146

PAINE KWT et al: Clinical features of lumbar spinal stenosis. Clin Orthop 115:77, 1976

WARD J, SAMUELSON CO: Nonsteroidal anti-inflammatory drugs, in *Update II: Harrison's Principles of Internal Medicine*, KJ Isselbacher et al (eds). New York, McGraw-Hill, 1982, pp 91–110

275   CALCIUM PYROPHOSPHATE (PSEUDOGOUT) AND CALCIUM HYDROXYAPATITE DEPOSITION DISEASES

BRUCE C. GILLILAND

The deposition of calcium pyrophosphate dihydrate crystals in the joint is referred to as *calcium pyrophosphate deposition disease* (CPDD) and is characterized by acute and chronic inflammatory joint disease, usually affecting older individuals. The acute or subacute form of this arthritis is called *pseudogout*, but this term is also used as a synonym for CPDD. The calcium deposits in articular cartilage (chondrocalcinosis) are detected radiographically in most patients with CPDD. Knee and other large joints are the most frequent sites of involvement.

In *hydroxyapatite arthropathy*, arthritis is induced by deposition of calcium hydroxyapatite crystals. Differential diagnosis is based on crystal identification.

EPIDEMIOLOGY, PATHOGENESIS, AND PATHOLOGY   CPDD occurs in persons of either sex, usually over age 50; its prevalence increases sharply with age. Approximately one symptomatic CPDD patient is observed for every two to three patients with gouty arthritis. An indication of the prevalence of chondrocalcinosis comes from autopsy studies, which have shown that approximately 3 to 5 percent of the adult population have calcium pyrophosphate dihydrate deposits in the knee joints.

CPDD is classified into three groups: a hereditary type, CPDD associated with metabolic disease, and idiopathic CPDD. Reports of hereditary CPDD have come from outside the United States; this disease occurs in individuals in the fourth to sixth decade. Sometimes it is severe, crippling, and involves many joints. Another form of familial disease is oligoarticular and affects older patients.

CPDD appears to have a definite association with primary hyperparathyroidism and hemochromatosis. CPDD has been reported in up to approximately 40 percent of patients with both of these disorders. Other associated metabolic disorders include hypophosphatasia, hypomagnesemia, hypothyroidism, gout, ochronosis, and Wilson's disease. In hypothyroidism, acute arthritis attacks usually occur only after treatment with thyroid hormone. The relationship of these disorders to the pathogenesis of chondrocalcinosis is unknown; furthermore, the association of some of them with chondrocalcinosis may not be greater than with osteoarthritis alone. In general, CPDD has a close association with degenerative joint disease.

Levels of inorganic pyrophosphate are elevated in the synovial fluid of many patients with CPDD but are also elevated in patients with osteoarthritis without evident chondrocalcinosis. Elevated levels of inorganic pyrophosphate most likely reflect increased metabolic activity of cartilage. The concentrations of calcium and pyrophosphate ions in joint fluid do not exceed their solubility product, and therefore it is unlikely that crystals form within synovial fluid. The initial site of crystal formation is believed to be in articular cartilage; however, the mechanism has not been elucidated. It is not yet clear whether idiopathic CPDD is a primary event or a secondary effect of osteoarthritis. Some investigators have suggested that mineral formation is a consequence of disturbed cartilage metabolism occurring in osteoarthritis.

The crystals in synovial fluid are believed to be shed from crystals in the cartilage. Several mechanisms have been postulated for the release of crystals from cartilage into the joint fluid. Lowering of either calcium or pyrophosphate ions in synovial fluid may result in the shedding of crystals from cartilage into synovial fluid. This hypothesis is supported by two observations: (1) lowering of the concentration of ionized calcium in joint fluid brings on an acute attack of crystal-induced arthritis, and (2) acute attacks of arthritis are associated with illness in which blood calcium concentrations decrease. Crystals may also enter the joint fluid as a consequence of mechanical disruption of cartilage secondary to microfractures of subchondral bone. The occurrence of acute attacks following trauma supports this concept. Another proposed mechanism is the release of crystals resulting from degradation of the cartilage matrix by enzymes. This mechanism may explain the occurrence of pseudogout superimposed on infectious arthritis, gout, or osteoarthritis. The finding of calcium pyrophosphate crystals may sometimes be the result and not the primary cause of joint inflammation.

The presence of calcium pyrophosphate crystals in the synovial fluid leads to an inflammatory response. Acute arthritis can be induced experimentally by the injection of calcium pyrophosphate crystals into a normal joint. Phagocytosis of the crystals by polymorphonuclear leukocytes leads to release of lysosomal enzymes and a chemotactant for leukocytes.

The *pathologic changes* in the joint involve deposits of calcium pyrophosphate dihydrate crystals in the joint capsule, synovium, tendons, and ligaments, in the midzonal area of articular hyaline cartilage, and diffusely in fibrocartilage. The menisci of the knee are a common site of crystal deposition. Crystals can be seen at the margin of degenerating cartilage and surrounding the lacunae of chondrocytes; this site is considered the earliest detectable lesion. The deposition of crystals varies from microcrystalline aggregates to large masses intermixed with fibrous tissue. Crystals may also be observed in normal-appearing cartilage.

The synovium in acute arthritis is edematous, with numerous polymorphonuclear leukocytes. In chronic arthritis, mononuclear cell infiltration and fibroblastic proliferation are present; crystals are rarely observed.

CLINICAL MANIFESTATIONS   Several patterns of joint involvement are recognized in calcium pyrophosphate deposition disease. Acute attacks occur in approximately 25 percent of patients, and this clinical picture is commonly called *pseudogout*. The onset of the acute attack of pseudogout is rapid, and it reaches a peak usually in 12 to 36 h. The involved joint is erythematous, swollen, warm, and painful. The acute attack is usually confined to a single joint, but in some patients involvement of other joints may follow in rapid progression. The knee is by far the most frequent site of acute arthritis, but attacks occur in the ankles, wrists, elbows, hips, and cervical and lumbar spine. As in gout, the metatarsophalangeal joint of the great toe may be a site of involvement. Furthermore, attacks may be provoked by trauma, surgery, or medical illness. The acute arthritis is usually intermittent, and the same joint is often involved in subsequent attacks. The acute episode usually subsides in 1 to 2 weeks. Between attacks the involved joint appears relatively normal. Most patients have radiographic evidence of chondrocalcinosis.

Approximately 5 percent of patients with calcium pyrophosphate deposition disease have what is termed *pseudorheumatoid disease*, which is characterized by multiple joint involvement with subacute attacks lasting several weeks to several months. The attacks affect one or several joints, then move on to involve other joints. Patients may complain of morning stiffness and fatigue. Synovial proliferation, limitation of joint motion, and flexion deformities can develop. Rheumatoid arthritis and CPDD may coexist.

Another group, predominantly middle-aged and elderly women and representing half the patients with calcium pyrophosphate deposition disease, has a chronic form of the disease. Progressive degenerative joint changes occur in multiple joints. The knees are the most frequently involved, followed by the wrists, metacarpophalangeal joints, hips, shoulders, elbows, and ankles. The joint involvement is usually symmetric, and flexion contractures may develop. Approximately one-half of the patients with this form of the disease experience intermittent acute attacks. Another group of patients has typical articular chondrocalcinosis without any symptoms. Finally, CPDD may resemble neuropathic arthropathy; in these patients a severe oligo- or polyarticular destructive arthropathy is seen without neurologic deficits. Calcium pyrophosphate deposits, however, are also seen in neuropathic arthropathies.

DIAGNOSIS   The microscopic examination of *synovial fluid* in an acute attack shows large numbers of polymorphonuclear leukocytes. Calcium pyrophosphate dihydrate crystals are frequently found extracellularly and in polymorphonuclear leukocytes. In chronic arthritis, the crystals are observed less frequently and are most often extracellular. With polarized light, the crystals appear as short blunt rods, rhomboids, and cuboids. They have weakly positive birefringence under compensated polarized light, in contrast to the strongly negative birefringence of sodium urate crystals. The diagnosis is made by finding typical crystals under compensated polarized light and is supported by radiographic evidence of chondrocalcinosis.

Radiographically, calcifications in articular hyaline cartilage appear as fine linear densities parallel to and separated from the underlying subchondral bone surface. Sites commonly involved are the knee, wrist, elbow, hip, and glenohumeral joints. Calcifications in fibrocartilage usually appear as thick and irregular densities within the central portion of the joint cavity. Common sites of fibrocartilage involvement include the menisci of the knee, triangular cartilage of the wrist, symphysis pubis, and the annulus fibrosis of the intervertebral disk. Calcifications in tendons are thin and linear, affecting most often the Achilles, supraspinatus, and triceps tendons. Calcification in the synovium has a cloudy appearance. Evidence for chondrocalcinosis can usually be obtained with radiographs of the knees, wrists, and symphysis pubis. Radiographs of the joints in chronic CPDD are similar to those in osteoarthritis, showing sclerosis of the subchondral bone, joint space narrowing, and subchondral cysts. The latter are often larger and more numerous than in osteoarthritis.

Gout and septic arthritis are the main considerations in the *differential diagnosis* of the acute arthritis. Gout and pseudogout are frequently indistinguishable clinically, and the diagnosis depends on the identification of their characteristic crystals under compensated polarized light. Both crystals occasionally have been found together in the synovial fluid of patients with typical radiographic articular calcifications of chondrocalcinosis. Bacterial smears and cultures should be performed on synovial fluid in all patients with an acute monarticular arthritis even if crystals are present, since crystals may be shed into synovial fluid during septic arthritis. The symptoms of osteoarthritis and chronic CPDD are very similar, and radiographic evidence for both is often present. The role played by each is difficult to determine. Features that may distinguish CPDD from osteoarthritis are the involvement in CPDD of non-weight-bearing joints such as the elbows, wrists, and shoulders and the rapid progression of joint destruction. Pseudogout should be considered when intermittent attacks of acute arthritis occur in a patient presumed to have osteoarthritis. The finding of a chronic effusion in patients with symptoms of osteoarthritis also suggests the possibility of pseudogout. The diagnosis should not be made only on the radiographic findings of intraarticular calcific deposits; it depends also on the identification of the characteristic crystals, since other forms of inflammatory arthritis may affect the same joints. Attacks of pseudogout may occur in patients without radiographic evidence of chondrocalcinosis, requiring a careful search for calcium pyrophosphate dihydrate crystals in any case of acute arthritis, especially in older patients. On the other hand, radiographic evidence of calcific deposits is found not infrequently in the knees of elderly patients who have no joint symptoms. Intraarticular calcifications and joint inflammation may be caused by deposition of calcium hydroxyapatite crystals. Hydroxyapatite arthropathy tends to affect one or only a few joints, while chronic CPDD may be more generalized. Intraarticular calcifications in hydroxyapatite arthropathy tend to have a more diffuse and amorphous pattern than that in CPDD. Differential diagnosis requires identification of the respective crystals. The arthritis of hemochromatosis and CPDD may be difficult to distinguish, since both affect the metacarpophalangeal joints, especially the second and third, and have similar changes on x-ray.

TREATMENT Indomethacin, 75 to 150 mg per day, or other nonsteroidal anti-inflammatory drugs (NSAIDs) are usually effective and should be given for approximately 10 to 14 days. Aspiration of the synovial fluid, followed by intraarticular injection of glucocorticosteroids, also may be effective. Results of treatment with colchicine are variable, but this drug may be useful in those patients who require parenteral therapy. In chronic arthritis, salicylates or the newer NSAIDs may give symptomatic relief. The deposition of calcium pyrophosphate crystals in articular tissues cannot be prevented or reversed.

HYDROXYAPATITE ARTHROPATHY Crystal-induced arthritis is also observed with calcium hydroxyapatite crystals. This arthritis has been mainly described in the knee and shoulder. A group of elderly women who were studied in Milwaukee, Wisconsin, were found to have glenohumeral osteoarthritis, rotator cuff defects, joint effusions with few cells, and the presence of calcium hydroxyapatite crystals in the fluid. This constellation of findings was termed "Milwaukee shoulder." The joint fluid of these and other patients studied subsequently also contained collagenase, neutral proteases, and particulate collagen, types I, II, and III. Similar findings have been noted in synovial fluid of involved knees. Hydroxyapatite and calcium pyrophospate crystals have been found together in synovial fluid in some patients, suggesting that both crystals may be involved in the inflammatory process. Diagnosis is based on crystal identification. Hydroxyapatite crystals cannot be recognized by light microscopy because of their small size (0.1 to 1 μm in length). Electron-microscopic or x-ray diffraction studies are required for the accurate diagnosis of this crystal. Alizarin red S staining can be used as a screening test to detect calcium components in synovial fluid. Radiographic changes are as described above for CPDD. Treatment consists of administration of a nonsteroidal anti-inflammatory drug, repeated joint aspiration, and rest of the affected joint.

REFERENCES

HALVERSON PB et al: Milwaukee shoulder syndrome: Eleven additional cases with involvement of the knee in seven (basic calcium phosphate crystal deposition disease). Semin Arthritis Rheum 14(1):36, 1984

HOWELL DS: Diseases due to the deposition of calcium pyrophosphate and hydroxyapatite, in *Textbook of Rheumatology*, WN Kelley et al (eds). Philadelphia, Saunders, 1985, chap 87, pp 1398–1416

MCCARTHY DJ: Pseudogout and pyrophosphate metabolism, in *Advances in Internal Medicine*, GH Stollerman (ed). Chicago, Year Book, 1980, pp 363–390

PAUL H et al: Alizarin red S staining as a screening test to detect calcium compounds in synovial fluid. Arthritis Rheum 26:191, 1983

RESNICK D, NIWAYAMA G: Calcium pyrophosphate dihydrate (CPDD) crystal deposition disease, in *Diagnosis of Bone and Joint Disorders*, D Resnick, G Niwayama (eds). Philadelphia, Saunders, 1981, chap 44, pp 1520–1574

276 PSORIATIC ARTHRITIS AND ARTHRITIS ASSOCIATED WITH GASTROINTESTINAL DISEASES

BRUCE C. GILLILAND

PSORIATIC ARTHRITIS The prevalence of arthritis in patients with psoriasis is higher than that found in the general population, even when degenerative joint disease and rheumatoid arthritis are excluded. Arthritis related to psoriasis occurs in approximately 5 percent of patients with skin disease.

The *etiology* and *pathogenesis* of psoriatic arthritis are not known; however, studies showing aggregation of psoriatic arthritis in first-degree relatives of psoriatic patients suggest that hereditary factors may play a role. Approximately 50 percent of psoriatic patients with spondylitis have the HLA-B27 antigen. The presence of HLA-B27 apparently does not predispose to peripheral arthritis in psoriatic patients.

The age of onset of psoriatic arthritis is usually in the third or fourth decade, and the sex ratio is approximately equal. Psoriasis usually precedes the onset of arthritis by months or years. In approximately 15 percent of patients, the arthritis precedes the skin lesions. Simultaneous onset of arthritis and skin lesions is uncommon, but arthritis and nail abnormalities often begin together. In general, the prognosis of psoriatic arthritis is more favorable than that of rheumatoid arthritis, except in patients with the severe destructive form of psoriatic arthritis (arthritis mutilans). The course of psoriatic arthritis in most patients is mild, intermittent, and affects only a few joints. Spontaneous remission may occur.

Several patterns of joint involvement are observed in psoriatic arthritis. Approximately 70 percent of patients will have an asymmetric oligoarticular arthritis involving two or three joints at a time. The proximal joints of the hands and feet are frequently affected. "Sausage" digits are also present as seen in Reiter's syndrome. Another pattern observed in about 15 percent of patients consists of a symmetric polyarthritis similar to rheumatoid arthritis. The rheumatoid factor test in these patients is negative. Patients with psoriasis and symmetric polyarthritis who have rheumatoid factor are considered to have coexistent rheumatoid arthritis and psoriasis. Another pattern of arthritis found in approximately 10 percent of patients has prominantly distal interphalangeal joint involvement. The adjacent nail usually has changes of psoriasis. A very few patients have a pattern of disease referred to as "arthritis mutilans," which is characterized by a severe destructive and deforming polyarthritis. These patients have ankylosis of joints, dissolution of bone, and "telescoping" of fingers. In addition, they may have ankylosis of the spine.

Approximately 20 percent of patients with psoriatic arthritis have spine involvement in the form of sacroiliitis and/or spondylitis, which in some patients may be asymptomatic and evident only on x-ray. The spondylitis tends to be more asymmetric than in ankylosing spondylitis and may occur even in the absence of peripheral arthritis.

The peripheral joints in psoriatic arthritis are warm, swollen, and tender. Flexion contractures and ankylosis of joints may occur, with long periods of persistent joint inflammation. No definite correlation exists between the degree of skin involvement and joint disease, but in some patients the activity of both tends to be parallel. A closer temporal relationship has been found between psoriatic nail lesions and arthritis than between the skin lesions and arthritis. Psoriatic nail changes include onycholysis, pits, and ridges.

Laboratory abnormalities include hypoproliferative anemia and an elevated erythrocyte sedimentation rate. Tests for rheumatoid factor are negative. Hyperuricemia is observed in 10 to 20 percent of patients, similar to uncomplicated psoriasis, and reflects the severity of skin involvement. Synovial fluid and biopsy findings are those of nonspecific inflammation.

Several *radiographic* features are characteristic of psoriatic arthritis. These include severe destruction of isolated joints, osteolysis, bony ankylosis, whittling of the tufts of the terminal phalanges, and the "pencil-in-cup" deformity, which is most commonly observed in the joints of the fingers and toes. Whittling of the distal end of the middle phalanx produces the "pencil" which projects into a widened, cuplike erosion in the joint surface of the terminal phalanx. Bony absorption of phalanges produces the opera-glass deformity of the hands (telescoped fingers). The radiographic findings in spondylitis associated with psoriatic arthritis are similar to those found in spondylitis with Reiter's syndrome (Chap. 268).

The *diagnosis* of psoriatic arthritis is suggested by the presence of an inflammatory arthritis in a patient with typical skin or nail lesions of psoriasis. Skin lesions may be quite small and hidden in the scalp, intergluteal fold, or umbilicus. The asymmetry of joint involvement, negative test for rheumatoid factor, and the absence of rheumatoid nodules help to distinguish psoriatic arthritis from rheumatoid arthritis. Psoriatic arthritis presenting as monarticular arthritis or asymmetric oligoarthritis may be differentiated from Reiter's syndrome by the chronic nature of the skin lesions, the absence of urethritis and conjunctivitis, and the rarity of mucous membrane lesions. At times, however, differentiation of these two diseases may not be possible. Psoriatic arthritis presenting as an acute arthritis in a toe or finger may be mistaken for gouty arthritis especially in the presence of hyperuricemia due to psoriatic skin disease. The appearance of the joint also may suggest septic arthritis. These diagnostic considerations are easily excluded by examining synovial fluid for sodium urate crystals and for microorganisms with appropriate cultures. Development of acute Heberden's nodes may be confused with psoriatic arthritis, but other features such as Bouchard's nodes at the proximal interphalangeal joints, involvement of the first carpometacarpal joint, and a normal erythrocyte sedimentation rate (ESR) point to the diagnosis of primary osteoarthritis. Fungal disease of the toenails may be mistaken for psoriatic nails; the distinction may require examination of nail scrapings for mycelia.

In the *treatment* of psoriatic arthritis, patient education and physical and occupational therapy are all important. Aspirin or other nonsteroidal anti-inflammatory drugs are recommended initially. Intraarticular injection of glucocorticoids may be of value in patients with few joints involved, but should be limited to three injections per year for

any one joint. In patients with more progressive and severe peripheral arthritis, gold salts may be indicated and have resulted in clinical improvement in greater than 50 percent of patients in some studies. Methotrexate has been shown to be beneficial for both the skin and joint disease of psoriasis but because of its potential serious liver toxicity, should be used only in patients with severe psoriatic disease. The most widely used regimen of methotrexate is three oral doses 12 h apart once a week beginning with three 2.5-mg doses (7.5 mg) and with the maximum being three 5-mg doses (15 mg) per week. Patients should have a complete blood count, blood urea nitrogen, creatinine, and liver function tests done monthly. This drug should be used cautiously, if at all, in patients with creatinine greater than 2.0 mg/dL since the risk of toxicity greatly increases. Cirrhosis of the liver is a major concern. It is seldom seen before a total dose of 1.5 g. Alcohol abusers and patients with underlying liver disease should not be given methotrexate. Some have recommended that a liver biopsy be obtained before treatment and then annually. However, its value in identifying patients at risk for cirrhosis is not proven. Other immunosuppressive agents, azathioprine or 6-mercaptopurine, have been reported to be beneficial. Gold, methotrexate, and other immunosuppressive agents should only be given under the supervision of experienced clinician. Adequate control of skin disease may lead to improvement of the joint disease in an occasional patient.

ARTHRITIS ASSOCIATED WITH GASTROINTESTINAL DISEASES

Inflammatory bowel disease The articular manifestations of ulcerative colitis and regional enteritis (Crohn's disease, granulomatous colitis) are similar and will be discussed together. Two patterns of joint involvement may be distinguished: arthritis of peripheral joints and spondylitis. The frequency of peripheral arthritis in regional enteritis is approximately 20 percent and in ulcerative colitis, 10 percent. The frequency of spondylitis in both bowel disorders is 4 percent.

The peripheral arthritis of inflammatory bowel disease (IBD) most commonly begins between the ages of 25 and 45 years and affects both sexes equally. Arthritis usually follows the onset of colitis by 6 months to several years, but uncommonly the onset of both may coincide or the arthritis may precede colitis. Arthritis is more frequent in ulcerative colitis patients who have pseudopolyps or perianal disease and also is more common with extensive colitis than disease limited to the rectum. In regional enteritis, arthritis is more frequent in patients with colon disease and less common with disease limited to the small bowel. Patients with aphthous stomatitis, erythema nodosum, or uveitis are likely also to have arthritis. These extraintestinal manifestations often flare up with exacerbation of colitis.

The typical attack of arthritis presents acutely, reaching a peak within 24 h, and often affects a single joint in the lower extremity. Involvement of other joints, without definite symmetry, may follow over the next few days. Usually fewer than four joints are involved during an episode. The involved joint is usually red, swollen, and painful. The knee and ankle are most frequently affected, followed by the proximal interphalangeal, elbow, shoulder, and wrist joints. The arthritis usually subsides within several weeks, but occasionally lasts for months. Complete resolution without residual damage is the general rule. Some patients may experience only migratory arthralgias as evidence of an attack.

Spondylitis with IBD is indistinguishable from ankylosing spondylitis. However, the usual male preponderance observed in ankylosing spondylitis is not seen in patients with IBD and spondylitis. The onset of spondylitis antedates IBD in approximately one-third of patients. The HLA-B27 antigen is found in approximately 70 percent of these patients. In some patients, spondylitis and bowel disease may have a nearly simultaneous onset, while in others spondylitis follows the onset of colitis. Spondylitis usually progresses regardless of remission of the bowel disease or colectomy. The disease may progress to complete ankylosis of the spine.

Radiographic evidence of sacroiliitis without symptoms is found in patients with IBD, the prevalence ranging from 4 to 15 percent.

The majority of these patients will probably not become symptomatic or progress to ankylosing spondylitis. In this group of patients the prevalence of HLA-B27 is not increased.

Radiographs of involved peripheral joints usually are normal except for soft tissue swelling. An occasional patient with recurrent or persistent disease will show small bony erosions and joint space narrowing. Films of the spine show changes indistinguishable from those of ankylosing spondylitis.

The peripheral white blood cell count, anemia, and erythrocyte sedimentation rate usually reflect the intestinal disease. Tests for rheumatoid factor are negative. Synovial fluid shows a moderate leukocytosis, in the range of 10,000 cells per cubic millimeter, consisting predominantly of polymorphonuclear leukocytes.

Treatment should be directed primarily at the underlying IBD. Joint symptoms can usually be managed with salicylates or other nonsteroidal anti-inflammatory drugs. Glucocorticoids used for control of colitis and extraintestinal manifestations, such as erythema nodosum, may lead to suppression of arthritis. Colectomy or systemic glucocorticoids are not indicated for treatment of the arthritis alone. Physical therapy is directed toward maintenance of posture in spondylitis and prevention of contractures in the peripheral form of arthritis.

Intestinal bypass arthritis   Approximately one-third of patients with jejunocolic and a somewhat smaller percentage of patients with jejunoileal bypass develop arthritic manifestations which occur from several weeks to years following the surgery. These consist of recurrent episodes of migratory polyarthralgia, polyarthritis, and, sometimes, tenosynovitis. Episodes last from a few days to a few weeks. Some patients may experience persistent arthritis for months. The knees, ankles, wrists, and shoulders are most commonly affected. Neck and back symptoms may also occur. Joint damage usually does not occur. However, in some patients with persistent arthritis, erosions of the joint margins have been described. The arthritis may be accompanied by vasculitic skin lesions which can be urticarial, pustular, or nodular. Raynaud's phenomenon also occurs in some of these patients.

Examination of synovial fluid has shown a mild leukocytosis with polymorphonuclear white cells predominating. Circulating immune complexes and cryoglobulins are found in the serum of many bypass patients with arthritis. Immunoglobulins, complement, and antibodies to *Escherichia coli* and other bacteria have been identified in cryoglobulins from these patients.

The pathogenesis of bypass arthritis and vasculitis is postulated to be mediated by immune complexes. Bacterial growth in the blind loop of the intestine leads to absorption of bacterial antigens, and subsequent development of antibodies to these antigens results in formation of immune complexes.

The definitive treatment of bypass arthritis is reconnecting the bowel. When this is not possible, treatment with tetracycline or other appropriate antibiotics to reduce the bacterial growth in the blind loop has produced clinical improvement. Aspirin or other nonsteroidal anti-inflammatory drugs may help to control symptoms. Arthritis and vasculitis are also suppressed with systemic glucocorticoids in most patients.

Whipple's disease   Whipple's disease (intestinal lipodystrophy) is a rare disorder affecting predominantly middle-aged males and is characterized by arthritis, serositis, diarrhea, malabsorption, weight loss, skin hyperpigmentation, and lymphadenopathy. The diagnosis is confirmed by the identification of periodic acid Schiff (PAS) staining of bacilliform structures intercellularly or as inclusions in foamy macrophages. Electron microscopy has demonstrated rod-shaped organisms in the lamina propria of the small intestine. The PAS-staining material is thought to consist of partially degraded bacteria. PAS-staining granules can also be seen in abdominal and peripheral lymph nodes and in other tissues.

Arthritis occurs in approximately two-thirds of the patients and usually precedes the appearance of intestinal symptoms by months or years. With the onset of intestinal symptoms, the arthritis may subside. The joint disease involves predominantly peripheral joints, affecting knees and ankles most commonly, followed by fingers, hips, shoulders, elbows, and wrists. It is typically acute, migratory, and transient, lasts only a few days, and causes no permanent joint damage. Long, irregular periods of remission are common. Joints may be quite tender and erythematous. Arthritis may be chronic in other patients. Some patients with peripheral joint involvement have radiographic changes in the sacroiliac joints similar to those of ankylosing spondylitis. Synovial fluid analysis has shown leukocyte counts ranging from 450 to 36,000 per cubic millimeter with 30 to 95 percent neutrophils. Synovial fluid, however, may only show a mild monocytosis without characteristic foamy macrophages. PAS-positive macrophages have been seen in synovial biopsy tissue. This disease, including the joint manifestations, responds well to therapy with penicillin, 1.2 million units, and streptomycin, 1 g daily for 2 weeks, followed by tetracycline, 1 g daily for 1 year. Relapse while on tetracycline requires administration again of penicillin and streptomycin. Glucocorticoids may be necessary in addition to antimicrobials in severely ill patients but are not indicated for the treatment of arthritis alone. Salicylates or other nonsteroidol anti-inflammatory drugs may be helpful in controlling joint symptoms.

REFERENCES

Arnett FC: HLA and the spondylarthropathies, in *Spondylarthropathies*. New York, Grune & Stratton, 1984, chap 15, pp 297–321

Calin A: Diagnosis and treatment—HLA-B27: To type or not to type? Ann Intern Med 92:208, 1980

———: Reiter's syndrome, in *Textbook of Rheumatology*, WN Kelley et al (eds). Philadelphia, Saunders, 1985, chap 65, pp 1007–1020

Good AE, Utsinger PD: Enteropathic arthritis, in *Textbook of Rheumatology*, 2d ed, WN Kelley et al (eds). Philadelphia, Saunders, 1985, chap 67, pp 1031–1041

Kammer GM et al: Psoriatic arthritis: A clinical, immunologic and HLA study of 100 patients. Semin Arthritis Rheum 9:75, 1979

Wright V: Psoriatic arthritis, in *Textbook of Rheumatology*, 2d ed, WN Kelley et al (eds). Philadelphia, Saunders, 1985, chap 166, pp 1021–1031

277   INFECTIOUS ARTHRITIS

BRUCE C. GILLILAND / ROBERT G. PETERSDORF

ACUTE BACTERIAL ARTHRITIS   Septic arthritis is a serious medical problem requiring prompt recognition and appropriate treatment to avoid permanent joint damage. All ages are affected.

Etiology and Pathogenesis   Bacteria most often infect the joint during an episode of bacteremia. A source of bacteremia can be identified in the majority of patients. Because the synovium is very vascular and does not have a limiting basement membrane, bacteria can enter the joint freely. Host factors, however, must be important since joint infection is not a common sequel of bacteremic episodes. Certain bacteria, such as *Neisseria gonorrhoeae* and *Staphylococcus aureus*, have a propensity to infect a joint during bacteremia. Joint sepsis may also result from a penetrating wound, direct extension of adjacent osteomyelitis, arthroscopy, intraarticular steroid injection, or prosthetic joint surgery.

An increased susceptibility to joint infection occurs in patients with diabetes, cancer, hypogammaglobulinemia, or chronic liver disease, and in those receiving corticosteroids or immunosuppressive drugs. Patients with chronic alcoholism are more prone to develop infections in general, and bacterial arthritis in particular. In addition, joints previously damaged by trauma or by chronic arthritis, especially rheumatoid arthritis, are more susceptible to infections.

Pathology The synovium in the early stages of infection is edematous and infiltrated by neutrophils. An effusion with many neutrophils forms rapidly. Enzymes released from neutrophils or synovial cells destroy articular cartilage, subchondral bone, and joint capsule. Increased intraarticular pressure also contributes to joint damage. Small abscesses appear in the synovium and subchondral bone, and necrotic debris collects in the joint space. During healing, proliferation of fibroblasts may lead to ankylosis.

Acute *bacterial arthritis* is caused by many different types of bacteria; the ones most commonly encountered are *N. gonorrhoeae, S. aureus, Streptococcus pneumoniae, Streptococcus pyogenes, Haemophilus influenzae,* and gram-negative bacilli (*Escherichia coli, Salmonella, Pseudomonas* spp.). Septic arthritis due to *H. influenzae* occurs mostly in neonates. *S. aureus* is the most common nongonococcal infecting agent in adults. Joint sepsis with gram-negative bacilli tends to occur in patients with underlying infection of the urinary, biliary, or intestinal tract, in patients with impaired resistance to infection, and in intravenous drug abusers. Osteomyelitis is also a feature of infections with gram-negative bacilli, and joint infection is a common sequel. Patients with *Salmonella* arthritis often have evidence of underlying osteomyelitis. Infectious arthritis of the spine is most often caused by staphylococci. Brucellosis, tuberculosis, and *Salmonella* also preferentially involve the spine.

Manifestations The onset of bacterial arthritis usually occurs over several days and is accompanied by fever. Shaking chills are uncommon. One or a few joints may be involved. The affected joint is warm, erythematous, swollen, and painful; however, these signs may be less marked in elderly patients or in patients receiving corticosteroids or immunosuppressive drugs. Marked guarding of the joint and muscle spasms are common. The knee is involved in approximately one-half of the cases. Other commonly involved joints include hips, shoulders, wrists, ankles, and elbows. Sternoclavicular and sacroiliac joints are affected less often; however, predilection of these two joints for septic arthritis has been observed in intravenous drug abusers. The articulations of the spine or any peripheral joint may be a site of infection. In the spine, infection involves the vertebral body and adjacent intervertebral disk space, and may extend to the adjacent apophyseal joint. Localized tenderness and spasm of the paraspinal or psoas muscles are often present. The diagnosis of septic arthritis of the hip is often delayed, because swelling of this joint is not readily detected. Pain from the hip may be felt in the groin, buttock, or lateral upper thigh, or referred to the anterior knee. The thigh is usually held in adduction, flexion, and internal rotation. In some instances, the thigh becomes edematous and swelling appears in the anterior groin.

Laboratory and x-ray findings Aspiration and examination of joint fluid should be performed immediately in any patient suspected of having a septic joint. The needle should not be inserted into the joint through an overlying area of cellulitis or an infected bursa. The appearance of synovial fluid in infectious arthritis is usually cloudy or grossly purulent. The white blood cell count ranges from 10,000 to greater than 100,000 per cubic millimeter, and more than 90 percent of the cells are neutrophils. The peripheral blood often shows a leukocytosis; however, the leukocyte count may be normal. The concentration of glucose in the joint cavity is often less than 50 percent of a simultaneous blood sugar reading when obtained at least 6 h after a meal, or after cessation of intravenous glucose infusions to allow equilibrium of glucose between blood and synovial fluid. In some patients with gonococcal arthritis, the reduction of synovial fluid glucose may be less marked. Gram's stain frequently reveals microorganisms in patients with nongonococcal infections. Blood and synovial fluid should be cultured for aerobes and anaerobes. Cultures of the synovial fluid and blood should be performed even if Gram's stain is negative. Radiographs of the joint early in infection show soft tissue swelling and distention of the joint capsule, and later show juxtaarticular osteoporosis, periosteal elevation, joint space narrowing due to cartilage destruction, and bony erosions on the articular surface.

Radiographic evidence of coexisting osteomyelitis may be present. In the spine, radiographic changes may not be seen for several months. The first changes consist of narrowing of the involved disk space or vertebra and proliferation of bone at the vertebral margins. Subsequently, lytic lesions appear in the vertebra and may extend to the disk space. During healing adjacent vertebrae may become fused. Radioisotope scanning techniques utilizing technetium polyphosphonate or gallium may be useful in distinguishing whether the site of the infection is cellulitis, osteomyelitis, or septic arthritis. Both types of scan are positive in septic arthritis and osteomyelitis, but only the gallium scan is positive in cellulitis. Radioisotope scans may point to infection in such joints as hip, shoulder, spine, and sacroiliac. A positive scan, however, is not specific for infection, since other causes of inflammatory joint disease as well as degenerative joint disease will give a positive scan.

Diagnosis The diagnosis of acute bacterial arthritis can be made by finding microorganisms on Gram's stain of synovial fluid or in synovial tissue, and is confirmed by a positive culture. With involvement of the spine or sacroiliac joint, needle biopsy or open surgical biopsy may be required to obtain tissue for examination and culture. The possibility of infectious arthritis should be entertained in a patient with fever and unilateral sacroiliac or back pain. Other forms of acute arthritis may be mistaken for infectious arthritis. These include gout, pseudogout, Reiter's syndrome, psoriatic arthritis, peripheral arthritis of inflammatory bowel disease, and rheumatic fever. These disorders usually are not associated with chills, high fever, and marked leukocytosis. Crystal deposits of sodium urate or calcium pyrophosphate may be found in fluid of a septic joint, and may have played a role in predisposing this joint to infection. On the other hand, the enzymes of the inflammatory process of infectious arthritis may have released into the joint fluid preexisting crystal deposits from synovial tissue or cartilage, a process referred to as "enzymatic strip mining." In patients with rheumatoid arthritis who develop chills and fever and have one or two joints disproportionately more inflamed than others, superimposed infectious arthritis in those joints should be carefully excluded by examination and culture of synovial fluid.

Infection of a bursa or juxtaarticular soft tissue and skin should be distinguished from infectious arthritis. Bursae and tendon sheaths become infected with the same types of microorganisms that invade joints. Care must be taken not to infect a bursa or joint by passing a needle through an overlying area of cellulitis.

Treatment Septic arthritis requires prompt treatment with appropriate antibiotics. The preferred antibiotic regimens for the more common organisms are given in the chapters dealing with these organisms as well as in Chap. 88, which summarizes the properties of each antibiotic. When no organisms are seen on Gram's stain, the patient should be given a penicillinase-resistant penicillin and gentamicin until culture and sensitivities dictate the appropriate antibiotic. Bactericidal levels of antibiotics are achieved with systemic administration; therefore, direct administration of an antibiotic into the joint is not necessary and may in itself produce a chemical synovitis. During treatment, bactericidal assays of synovial fluid may be performed to ensure that therapeutic levels of antibiotic have been achieved. Drainage, recommended when the joint is tightly distended or when the fluid contains a high neutrophil count, reduces pressure and removes pus that generates proteolytic enzymes. Needle aspiration, during which the joint cavity can be irrigated with sterile saline to enhance removal of inflammatory substances, usually provides adequate drainage. The frequency of aspiration depends on the amount of fluid and the cell count of that which reaccumulates. Aspiration ordinarily is necessary only during the first few days of treatment. Open surgical drainage is usually not indicated except in septic arthritis of the hip or in a joint with chronic suppuration and loculated pus. Splinting of the affected joint may make the patient more comfortable and reduce the degree of flexion deformity. Passive range of motion should be performed once pain has decreased, followed later by active exercises to restore mobility and strength. A severely damaged weight-bearing joint may require bony fusion.

GONOCOCCAL ARTHRITIS (See Chap. 104) Gonococcal arthritis is the most common cause of arthritis in young adults, especially women. Pregnancy and menstruation are predisposing factors for bacteremia and arthritis. Patients with homozygous deficiency of a terminal complement component (C5 to C8) or those with low levels due to excessive complement consumption are also more susceptible to disseminated *Neisseria* infections, since these organisms are killed by complement-mediated cell lysis requiring the terminal complement components.

Patients with gonococcal arthritis may present with fever, chills, skin lesions, and polyarthritis. The polyarthritis usually evolves in a few days to a monarticular septic arthritis. The clinical picture, however, is quite variable, and some patients present with monarticular septic arthritis and few if any systemic manifestations. The leukocyte count in synovial fluid may not be as high as in nongonococcal infections, but usually is above 50,000 cells per cubic millimeter. Diagnosis is confirmed by positive cultures of blood, synovial fluid, or skin lesion. Cultures of synovial fluid, however, are positive in less than half the cases and blood cultures in less than 20 percent. Skin lesions are usually sterile. The diagnosis is often assumed when culture of cervix, urethra, or throat is positive for gonococcus. Arthritis usually responds to antibiotic therapy. The gonococcal organisms associated with disseminated infection are usually very sensitive to penicillin.

TUBERCULOUS ARTHRITIS (See also Chap. 119) Tuberculous arthritis is a chronic destructive form of septic arthritis caused by *Mycobacterium tuberculosis*. Approximately 1 percent of patients with tuberculosis have skeletal involvement. Many patients with skeletal tuberculosis do not have evidence for active or even inactive pulmonary disease. Tuberculous arthritis occurs more frequently in nonwhites and men, and tends to involve an older population of patients, in their fifth and sixth decades. Tuberculous arthritis, however, can occur at any age.

The most frequently involved joints are the spine, hips, knees, sacroiliac, wrists, and ankles. In the spine (Pott's disease) the infection begins in the margins of the vertebral bodies and extends into the adjacent disk space. Destruction of bone leads to vertebral collapse and angulation of the spine resulting in kyphosis or gibbus. Extension of the infection into the paraspinal muscles produces a cold abscess which can spread up or down the spine or along the rib and eventually point in the groin, neck, chest wall, or sternum. Cord compression may cause paraplegia, and extension into the meninges results in tuberculous meningitis. A rare complication is the formation of a mycotic aneurysm by the erosion of a cold abscess into the aorta. Common clinical manifestations of spinal involvement are back pain, muscle spasm, local tenderness, kyphosis, and referred pain from spinal nerve root compression.

Peripheral or axial joints are infected by direct hematogenous spread or by extension from a tuberculous process in the adjacent bone. A combination of arthritis and osteomyelitis often occurs in skeletal tuberculosis. The tuberculous process produces synovitis with the formation of a pannus of granulation tissue over the articular cartilage. Destruction of articular cartilage initially occurs at the joint margins and gradually progresses. The rate of destruction is slower than in other acute infectious bacterial arthritis. The subchondral bone is involved and areas of necrosis develop. The joint infection can extend to the juxtaarticular soft tissues to produce a cold abscess and eventually a sinus tract.

Tuberculous arthritis has an insidious onset and is usually monarticular, and hips and knees are the most commonly affected peripheral joints. A low-grade fever and night sweats may be present, but most patients do not have prominent constitutional symptoms. The affected peripheral joint is swollen, warm, and tender and has a decreased range of motion. Erythema is minimal, and pain is initially mild. The hypertrophied synovium gives the joint a boggy, doughy feeling. Muscle atrophy, spasm, and contracture of the affected extremity occur. Tenosynovitis of the flexor tendon sheaths of the wrist may compress the median nerve and produce a carpal tunnel syndrome.

The synovial fluid white cell count is usually greater than 10,000 per cubic millimeter, with polymorphonuclear cells predominating. The tubercle bacilli are seen on smears of synovial fluid in approximately 20 percent of patients but are more likely to be found on biopsy of synovial tissue.

Radiographs of peripheral joints in early disease show joint capsule distention and juxtaarticular osteoporosis. Bony erosions at the joint margin, subchondral bone destruction, and joint space narrowing are observed later in the disease. Films of the spine show destruction of the vertebral body, vertebral collapse, and loss of intervertebral disk space.

The diagnosis of tuberculous arthritis is made by demonstrating tubercle bacilli in synovial fluid or tissue by smear, histology, or culture. The tuberculin skin test is almost always positive. Anergy may occur in advanced disease, old age, or severe malnutrition.

Nontuberculous (atypical) mycobacteria (see Chap. 121) (e.g., *M. kansasii, M. marinum, M. intracellulare*) can also cause septic arthritis and infect bursae and tendons. Microorganisms usually reach the joint by hematogenous spread but also can be introduced into the bone or joint by direct inoculation. Involvement of the tendon sheaths in the hand and wrist often occurs and may result in a carpal tunnel syndrome. Peripheral joint involvement is similar to that in tuberculosis. The correct diagnosis depends on a positive culture from synovial or bursal fluid or tissue. Treatment of tuberculosis and nontuberculous mycobacterial infections is described in Chaps. 119 and 121.

MYCOTIC, SYPHILITIC, AND VIRAL ARTHRITIS **Mycotic arthritis** The systemic mycoses (coccidioidomycosis, histoplasmosis, blastomycosis, cryptococcosis, candidiasis, and sporotrichosis) may involve bone and joints. In the primary phase of coccidioidomycosis, a transient polyarthritis, lasting up to 1 month, may occur in association with erythema nodosum (desert arthritis), but no residual joint damage ensues. However, with chronic disseminated disease, arthritis may occur alone or secondary to adjacent bone infection. The arthritis is usually monarticular, affects the knee predominantly, and leads in time to joint destruction. Sporotrichosis arthritis occurs in two distinct clinical forms: in the unifocal form, one or a few joints are chronically affected; while in the multifocal form, multiple joints, skin, and other tissues are involved. Progressive joint damage ensues in the absence of treatment. Young infants receiving parenteral nutrition or patients receiving glucocorticosteroids or immunosuppressive or antibiotic drugs are at risk for *Candida* infections which can involve joints. In other mycotic diseases, joint involvement is infrequent.

Actinomycosis infection due to an anaerobic bacteria-like obligate parasite may involve the spine. The diagnosis of fungal arthritis is established by the identification of the organisms in synovial fluid or in a biopsy specimen. Treatment with amphotericin B is usually successful; however, surgical debridement may be necessary. Penicillin is the drug of choice for actinomycosis.

Syphilitic arthritis This form of arthritis (see Chap. 122) occurs in congenital, secondary, or tertiary syphilis. During the first year of life, congenital syphilis may produce an osteochondritis in the juxtaepiphyseal region which results in the breakdown of bone and articular cartilage (Parrot's pseudoparalysis). At puberty, congenital disease may cause a synovitis which most commonly involves the knees and elbows (Clutton's joints). The joint is often red, swollen, and tender, but pain may be minimal. Synovial fluid shows a leukocytosis, predominantly lymphocytes.

In secondary syphilis, transient polyarthritis and polyarthralgia occur. Gummatous involvement of the synovium may occur in tertiary syphilis and most often involves the larger joints.

In addition to direct involvement of the joint, syphilis also produces a neuropathic joint (Charcot's joint).

The proper diagnosis of the joint disease can be established only after the correct diagnosis of syphilis. A positive serologic test for syphilis is not diagnostic, since biologic false-positive tests may occur in rheumatic diseases such as systemic lupus erythematosus.

Viral arthritis A self-limited polyarthritis may be a manifestation of several viral diseases. Three viral infections especially are accompanied by significant arthritis: rubella, type B hepatitis, and arboviruses not found in the western hemisphere (chikungunya and o'nyongnyong in Africa, and Ross River arthritis in Australia). Other viral infections with arthritis include mumps, infectious mononucleosis, varicella, and adenoviral infections.

Rubella infection (see Chap. 133) may present with a polyarthritis, usually involving the fingers, wrists, and knees symmetrically. The arthritis is seen most often in young adults, especially women. Arthritis is also observed in children and young adults after vaccination with live, attenuated rubella vaccine, and is similar to that observed with natural disease. The onset of arthritis coincides with or shortly follows the appearance of the rash. The arthritis lasts up to 2 weeks or occasionally a month. In a few patients, the arthritis may be recurrent for months to years. Permanent joint damage does not usually occur even with chronic disease. Joint effusions are usually small, and synovial fluid shows mild leukocytosis with either lymphoctyes or neutrophils predominating. Rheumatoid factor tests may be positive.

Arthritis is a relatively common manifestation of type B hepatitis (serum hepatitis). It is often accompanied by a rash, may precede the onset of clinical jaundice by a few days to 2 weeks, or coincide with the appearance of jaundice. Jaundice may not appear in some patients with arthritis; however, liver function tests are abnormal in such patients. The rash is most often urticarial, but can be macular, papular, or petechial. The onset of arthritis is usually abrupt, with symmetric involvement of both small and large joints. The most commonly involved joints are the fingers, followed by the knee, shoulder, ankle, elbow, and wrist. The arthritis can also be asymmetric or migratory. Permanent joint damage does not occur. Synovial fluid shows a varying degree of leukocytosis with polymorphonuclear cells. Rheumatoid factor tests usually are negative.

Serum and joint fluid complement levels are usually low during arthritis. Serum complement level returns to normal with the appearance of overt liver disease. Hepatitis B antigen (Australia antigen, hepatitis-associated antigen) can usually be detected in both serum and joint fluid during the prodromal period of hepatitis. The synovitis is thought to be induced by immune complexes consisting of viral antigens and their antibodies.

LYME DISEASE Lyme disease is a multisystem disorder caused by a spirochete transmitted by the bite of *Ixodes dammini* or related ticks. The spirochete has been recovered from skin lesions, blood, and cerebrospinal fluid. The disease is characterized by skin lesions and neurologic and cardiac abnormalities and arthritis. It is described in detail in Chap. 127.

REFERENCES

GOLDENBERG DL, REED JI: Bacterial arthritis. N Engl J Med 312:764, 1985

HOFFMAN GS: Mycobacterial and fungal infections of bones and joints, in *Textbook of Rheumatology*, WN Kelley et al (eds). Philadelphia, Saunders, 1985, pp 1527–1540

JOHNSTON YE et al: Lyme arthritis: Spirochetes found in synovial microangiopathic lesions. Am J Pathol 118:26, 1985

SCHNITZER TJ: Viral arthritis, in *Textbook of Rheumatology*, WN Kelley et al (eds), Philadelphia, Saunders, 1985, pp 1540–1556

STEERE AC, MALAWISTA SE: Lyme disease, in *Textbook of Rheumatology*, WN Kelley et al (eds). Philadelphia, Saunders, 1985, pp 1557–1563

278 MISCELLANEOUS ARTHRITIDES AND EXTRAARTICULAR RHEUMATISM

BRUCE C. GILLILAND

NEUROPATHIC JOINT DISEASE Neuropathic joint disease (Charcot's joint) is a severe form of osteoarthritis associated with loss of pain sensation, proprioception, or both. In addition, normal muscular reflexes which modulate joint movement are decreased. Without these protective mechanisms, joints are subjected to repeated trauma, resulting in progressive cartilage damage. The distribution of joint involvement depends on the underlying neurologic disorder. In tabes dorsalis, knees, hips, and ankles are most commonly affected; in syringomyelia, the glenohumeral joint, elbow, and wrist; and in diabetes mellitus, the tarsal and tarsometatarsal joints. Resorption of metatarsals and phalanges is also seen in diabetic patients. In children, neuropathic joint disease is caused by congenital indifference to pain or meningomyelocele. Neuropathic joint disease is also observed in patients with amyloidosis and leprosy or following repeated intraarticular glucocorticoid injections. The mechanism of injury in this situation is thought to be an analgesic effect of steroids leading to overuse of a previously damaged joint which results in accelerated cartilage deterioration.

Neuropathic joint disease usually begins in a single joint and then progresses to involve other joints, depending on the underlying neurologic disorder. The involved joint progressively becomes enlarged from bony overgrowth and synovial effusion. Loose bodies may be palpated in the joint cavity. Joint instability, subluxation, and crepitus occur as the disease progresses. Charcot's joints may develop rapidly, and a totally disorganized joint with multiple bony fragments may evolve in a patient within weeks or days. The amount of pain experienced by the patient is less than would be anticipated based on the degree of joint involvement. Patients may experience sudden joint pain from intraarticular fractures of osteophytes or condyles. Initially, radiographs show early features of osteoarthritis followed subsequently by marked destructive and hypertrophic changes. Large, bizarre-shaped osteophytes and intraarticular bone fragments are observed. The radiographic findings of the diabetic Charcot's foot may be difficult to distinguish from those of osteomyelitis. Osteomyelitis is often suspected when the diabetic patient has an infected cutaneous ulcer on the foot. The Charcot's joint radiographically shows osteopenia, sharp cortical margins, and severe disruption and disorganization of the midtarsal and tarsometatarsal joints. In osteomyelitis, the bone margins are indistinct. The synovial fluid is usually noninflammatory, may be bloody or xanthochromic, and may contain fragments of synovium, cartilage, and/or bone.

The primary focus of treatment is to provide stabilization of the joint. Treatment of the underlying disorder, even if successful, usually does not alter the joint disease. Braces and splints are helpful. Their use requires close surveillance since patients may be unable to appreciate pressure from a poorly adjusted brace. Fusion of a very unstable joint may improve function, but nonunion is frequent especially when immobilization of the joint is inadequate.

RELAPSING POLYCHONDRITIS Relapsing polychrondritis is an inflammatory disorder of unknown etiology affecting cartilaginous structures as well as the cardiovascular system, eyes, and ears. The onset is usually between 40 and 60 years of age and the disorder occurs predominantly in whites. No familial tendency is apparent, and both sexes are equally affected.

Histologically, the cartilage matrix has decreased basophilic staining indicating a loss of glucosaminoglycans. Lymphocytes and plasma cells are found at the edge of cartilage destruction. Granulation tissue invades degenerating cartilage followed by fibrosis. Both humoral and cell-mediated immunity are considered to be operative in tissue damage.

The cartilage of the ears and nose is involved in 80 to 90 percent of patients. The patient may experience the sudden onset of pain, tenderness, and swelling of the cartilaginous portion of the ear. Prolonged or recurrent episodes lead to floppy ears and saddle deformity of the nose. Swelling may narrow the external auditory meatus, interfering with hearing. The eustachian tube may also be closed off, leading to otitis media. Arteritis of the internal auditory artery and its cochlear branch produces hearing loss, vertigo, ataxia, nausea, and vomiting.

Eye manifestations include conjunctivitis, episcleritis, scleritis, and iritis. Oral and/or genital ulcerations may occur. Patients also may experience an episodic nondeforming polyarthritis which lasts a few days to several weeks and involves both large and small peripheral joints. Synovial fluid is noninflammatory. Destruction of the cartilage in the larynx and trachea leads to hoarseness and stridor and may necessitate tracheostomy. Respiratory insufficiency and recurrent pulmonary infections develop because of collapse of the supporting bronchial cartilage rings. Aortic regurgitation occurs in 25 percent of patients, predominantly men, and is due to progressive dilatation of the aortic ring or to destruction of the valve cusps. Other heart valves can be affected. Vasculitis of either medium or large vessels may lead to aneurysm formation and thrombosis. Focal proliferative glomerulonephritis may occur, and in some patients may dominate the clinical picture. The clinical course is highly variable. The prognosis usually depends on the extent of pulmonary and cardiac involvement.

A mild leukocytosis and a normocytic, normochromic anemia may be present. The erythrocyte sedimentation rate is usually elevated. Rheumatoid factor and antinuclear antibody tests may be positive, and circulating immune complexes have been identified in some patients. Radiographs may show calcifications in the cartilage of the nose, larynx, and trachea. Bronchography and computed tomography can be used to demonstrate tracheal stenosis and bronchial narrowing.

The diagnosis is based on the recognition of the typical clinical features. Biopsy of involved cartilage from the ear, nose, or respiratory tract will confirm the diagnosis but is only necessary when clinical features are not typical. Polychondritis may be associated with a variety of connective tissue disorders including systemic vasculitis (Wegener's granulomatosis, Takayasu's arteritis), rheumatoid arthritis, or systemic lupus erythematosus. The connective tissue disorder usually precedes polychrondritis by months to years. It is not clear whether this association represents two separate disorders which coexist or whether the polychrondritis is a manifestation of one of these connective tissue disorders.

Prednisone in a dose of 40 to 60 mg per day is often effective in suppressing disease activity and is tapered gradually once the disease is controlled. If not controlled by steroids, cyclophosphamide or azathioprine may be beneficial.

HYPERTROPHIC OSTEOARTHROPATHY Hypertrophic osteoarthropathy is characterized by the presence of periosteal new bone formation, clubbing of the digits, and arthritis. In adults, this syndrome is seen almost always in its secondary form associated with a pulmonary neoplasm; rarely, it is seen with chronic lung or liver disease. In children, it occurs in association with a variety of congenital heart, lung, and liver conditions. Idiopathic and familial forms also occur in which no underlying associated disorder can be found.

In hypertrophic osteoarthropathy, the periosteum is elevated. Mononuclear cell infiltration is present in the adjacent soft tissue. New bone is deposited beneath the periosteum while at the same time endosteal bone is resorbed. These changes occur primarily at the distal ends of metacarpals, metatarsals, and the long bones. Occasionally, scapulas, clavicles, ribs, and pelvic bones are also affected. Proliferation of connective tissue occurs in the nail bed and soft tissue of the volar pad of the digits, giving the distal phalanges a clubbed appearance. The small blood vessels are dilated and

thickened. The number of arteriovenous anastomoses in the soft tissue of the digits is increased. The synovium of involved joints is edematous and may contain a mild infiltration of lymphocytes and plasma cells.

The etiology of hypertrophic osteoarthropathy is unknown. Stimulation of the vagal neural arc is suggested by the reversal of this syndrome by vagotomy. Furthermore, disorders associated frequently with clubbing have in common sites of involvement innervated in part by the vagus. A circulating vasodilator, hormones, or immune complexes have also been proposed as etiologic factors.

While hypertrophic osteoarthropathy is usually associated with clubbing, it can occur alone either in primary or secondary forms. Primary clubbing occurs in familial and idiopathic forms. Secondary clubbing is most often associated with chronic bronchitis, diffuse infiltrative diseases of the lung, and bacterial endocarditis, and usually has a more rapid onset than primary clubbing.

The syndrome of hypertrophic osteoarthropathy is less common, occurring most often in association with bronchogenic carcinoma and is also observed with the disorders mentioned above. It occurs rarely with metastases to the lung or with pleural tumors. The frequent occurrence of hypertrophic osteoarthropathy with pulmonary disorders has led to this syndrome being referred to as hypertrophic pulmonary osteoarthropathy. The number of cases associated with chronic pulmonary infections has declined markedly with early diagnosis and effective antibiotic therapy.

Hyperthyroidism may occasionally be associated with clubbing and periostitis of the bones of the hands and feet. The condition is referred to as *thyroid acropachy*. Periostitis is asymptomatic and occurs in the midshaft and diaphyseal portion of the metacarpal and phalangeal bones. The long bones of the extremities are seldom affected.

Familial hypertrophic osteoarthropathy, also referred to as *pachydermoperiostosis,* usually begins insidiously during puberty and is characterized by thickening of the skin of the face, scalp, and extremities along with features of hypertrophic osteoarthropathy. The skin of the face and scalp is greasy, and excessive sweating of the palms and soles occurs. The distal extremities are enlarged due to proliferation of new bone and connective tissue. The disorder is inherited as an autosomal dominant with variable expression.

The onset of hypertrophic osteoarthropathy is often insidious and may precede clinical features of the associated disorder by months. The onset is more rapid than in the idiopathic syndrome or clubbing alone. Patients may experience burning pain or deep aching in the distal extremities which is aggravated by dependency and relieved by elevation of the affected limbs. Joint manifestations vary from arthralgias to severe pain and swelling, most often affecting metacarpophalangeal and metatarsophalangeal joints, wrists, ankles, and knees. The skin over the distal extremities may be warm, erythematous, and edematous. Pressure applied over the distal ends of the forearms and legs may be quite painful. Clubbing of digits is manifested by widening of the fingertips, enlargement of the distal volar pads, convexity of the nail, and loss of the normal 15° angle between the nail and cuticle. The nails and surrounding skin become shiny. Nails become brittle and grow more rapidly.

The laboratory abnormalities reflect the underlying disorder. The synovial fluid of involved joints has less than 500 predominantly mononuclear white cells per cubic millimeter. Radiographs show periosteal thickening with new bone formation along the shaft of long bones at their distal ends. The ends of the distal phalanges show hypertrophic changes and in more advanced cases, osteolysis. Radionuclide studies show pericortical linear uptake along the shafts of long bones which may be present in advance of any x-ray changes.

The treatment of hypertrophic osteoarthropathy is to identify the associated disorder and treat it appropriately. Symptoms and signs of hypertrophic osteoarthropathy may disappear completely with removal or effective chemotherapy of a tumor or with antibiotic therapy and drainage of a chronic pulmonary infection. Vagotomy or percutaneous block of the vagus nerve may be beneficial in some patients. Aspirin, other nonsteroidal antiinflammatory drugs, or analgesics may help control symptoms of hypertrophic osteoarthropathy.

FIBROSITIS Fibrositis is a commonly encountered disorder characterized by pain, aching, and stiffness of the trunk and extremities and the presence of a number of specific tender sites. The disorder is more common in women between the ages of 25 and 45 years. The etiology is unknown, but may be produced or exacerbated by a sleep disturbance. Symptoms of fibrositis were produced in normal subjects by disturbing normal slow wave sleep with a buzzer without awakening them.

Symptoms are generalized aching and stiffness, often referred to muscle and bony prominences. Patients may feel that their joints are swollen; however, joint examination is normal. Patients complain of exhaustion and wake up tired. They also awake frequently at night and have difficulty falling asleep. Patients often attribute their lack of a refreshing night's sleep to pain. Some complain of urinary frequency and a sensation of bladder fullness. Irritable bowel syndrome has been associated with fibrositis.

The characteristic physical feature is the demonstration of specific tender sites or trigger points, which are exquisitely more tender than adjacent areas. The patient may suddenly jump or withdraw when the site is palpated. The sites of tenderness are remarkably constant in location. Common sites of tenderness are over the midpoint of the upper fold of the trapezius, lateral epicondyles, supraspinatus, lower cervical spine, lumbar spine, posterior iliac spine, costochondral junctions, especially the second, gluteus maximus, and medial fat pad of the knee. Skinfold tenderness may be present, particularly over the upper scapular region. Tender subcutaneous nodules may be felt in these regions. Nodules in similar location are present in normal persons but are not tender.

The diagnosis of fibrositis is made by recognizing the clinical manifestations. The joint and muscle examination is normal, and there are no laboratory abnormalties. The disease must be distinguished from polymyositis, in which weakness occurs and muscle enzyme levels are elevated, and from polymyalgia rheumatica, in which pain and an elevated sedimentation rate are present.

Patients should be informed that they have a treatable condition which is not a crippling, deforming, or degenerative process. Salicylates or other nonsteroidal anti-inflammatory drugs along with a benzodiazepine at bedtime may help. The sleep disturbance may improve with the use of tricyclic agents such as amitriptyline or imipramine. These drugs are more effective if taken early in the evening instead of at bedtime. Local measures such as heat, massage, injection of trigger points with corticosteroids or lidocaine, or acupuncture may help to relieve pain. Fibrositis can occur in patients with rheumatoid arthritis or other connective tissue diseases and should be treated appropriately.

PSYCHOGENIC RHEUMATISM Patients may experience severe joint pain involving a few to several joints without physical findings of arthritis. These patients are often convinced that they have rheumatoid arthritis or systemic lupus erythematosus. This disorder is recognized by the inconsistencies, exaggerations, and emotional lability of the patient during the history and physical examination. Laboratory studies are normal. Organic disease needs to be excluded, which requires seeing the patient at intervals. This condition also needs to be distinguished from fibrositis. Anti-inflammatory or other drugs are not helpful.

CARPAL TUNNEL SYNDROME Carpal tunnel syndrome is an entrapment neuropathy of the median nerve at the wrist producing paresthesias and weakness in the hands. The syndrome is caused by pressure on the median nerve where it passes in company with the flexor tendons of the fingers through the tunnel formed by carpal bones and the transverse carpal ligament.

Compression of the median nerve is produced by any process that encroaches on the carpal tunnel. Localized tenosynovitis of the flexor tendons of the fingers is a frequent cause of carpal tunnel syndrome, particularly in middle-aged women. Premenstrual edema or edema occurring in pregnancy may also cause these symptoms. Symptoms can be precipitated by activities which require repeated flexion,

pronation, and supination of the wrist, for example, sewing, driving, and operating computers. Other causes of carpal tunnel syndrome include trauma, tuberculosis, rheumatoid arthritis, gout, acromegaly, hypothyroidism, and amyloidosis.

Patients experience numbness or paresthesias of the palmar surface of the thumb, index, middle, and radial half of the ring finger. Numbness or paresthesias of the whole hand may occur. Pain may be referred to the forearm and less commonly to the shoulder and neck regions. Pain or tingling of the fingers often occurs at night and is relieved by shaking the hand. Weakness and atrophy of the thenar muscles usually appear later and can occur without significant sensory symptoms.

Thenar muscle weakness is manifested by decreased strength of abduction, opposition, and flexion of the thumb. On examination, symptoms of paresthesia or pain in the fingers may be reproduced by percussion over the volar surface of the wrist (Tinel's sign) or by full flexion of the wrist for over 1 min (Phalen's maneuver). Decreased touch or hyperpathia to pinprick may be demonstrated over the fingers supplied by the median nerve. Nerve conduction studies of the median nerve show delayed latency across the wrist, confirming the diagnosis.

Treatment of patients with only sensory symptoms and minor nerve conduction abnormalities consists of wrist splints to be worn mainly at night, anti-inflammatory drugs, and local injection of steroids. If symptoms persist or motor abnormalities are present, surgical decompression of the carpal tunnel with release of the transverse carpal ligament and debridement is indicated.

REFLEX SYMPATHETIC DYSTROPHY SYNDROME The reflex sympathetic dystrophy syndrome (RSDS) is characterized by pain and tenderness usually of a distal extremity accompanied by signs and symptoms of vasomotor instability, trophic skin changes, and the rapid development of bony demineralization. A precipitating event can be identified in two-thirds of the cases. These include local trauma, myocardial infarction, strokes, and peripheral nerve injuries. RSDS is observed most often in individuals over the age of 50, reflecting the frequency of the underlying disorder. The sex distribution is equal. An entire hand or foot is usually affected. Occasionally, RSDS will involve an isolated site such as the patella, hip, or one or two rays of a foot or hand. The contralateral side may be affected in up to 50 percent of patients, and subclinical disease may be present in virtually all patients.

The first clinical manifestation of RSDS is pain and swelling of a distal extremity which develops weeks to months following the precipitating event. The pain is of a burning quality (causalgia). The involved extremity is warm, edematous, and tender especially around joints. Increased sweating and hair growth are observed. Later in the course, the skin becomes thin, shiny, and cool. Flexion contractures of the fingers develop, and thickening of the palmar fascia results in a Dupuytren's contracture. The shoulder on the involved side frequently becomes painful and restricted in motion (shoulder-hand syndrome).

The course of RSDS is divided into three overlapping phases. The first phase, which lasts 3 to 6 months, is characterized by pain, swelling, warmth, and sweating of the involved extremity, followed later by a cool shiny skin in the second phase. In the third phase, the skin and subcutaneous tissue become atrophic, and irreversible flexion contractures of the hand or foot develop. Fluctuation occurs between the first two phases during which time the disorder is potentially reversible if treated.

The laboratory abnormalities are those of the associated disorder. Radiographs of the involved distal extremity demonstrate mottled osteopenia referred to as Sudeck's atrophy. Later in the course, diffuse osteopenia develops. Similar changes, however, are observed in an immobilized limb following a fracture or paralysis. Bone scans with radionuclides show increased uptake in periarticular bone on the involved side. Uptake may also be increased on the contralateral side indicating subclinical involvement.

Early recognition and treatment are important to prevent permanent disability. Appropriate mobilization of the patient following a myocardial infarction, stroke, or injury may help to prevent this syndrome. Pain should be properly controlled. Application of heat or cold along with exercises are useful. Sympathetic nerve block may be effective and if it is, can be followed by surgical sympathectomy. The response, however, may not be sustained. A short course of high-dose prednisone in conjunction with physical therapy has been beneficial in some patients. Prednisone is started at 60 mg for 4 days and gradually tapered over a 3-week period.

TSIETZE'S SYNDROME Tsietze's syndrome is manifested by painful swelling of one or more costochondral articulations. Age of onset is usually before 40, and both sexes are equally affected. Most patients have only one joint involved, usually the second or third costochondral joint. The onset of anterior chest pain may be sudden or gradual. The pain may radiate to the arms or shoulder and is aggravated by sneezing, coughing, deep inspirations, or twisting motions of the chest. The term *costochondritis* is often used interchangeably with Tsietze's syndrome, but some restrict the former term to pain of the costochondral articulations without swelling. This disorder is observed in patients over age 40, tends to affect the third, fourth, and fifth costochondral joints, and occurs more often in women. Both syndromes may mimic cardiac or upper abdominal causes of pain. Rheumatoid arthritis, ankylosing spondylitis, or Reiter's syndrome may involve costochondral joints but are distinguished easily by their clinical features. Other skeletal causes of anterior chest wall pain are xyphodynia and the slipping rib syndrome, which usually involves the tenth rib. Analgesics, anti-inflammatory drugs, or local steroid injections usually relieve symptoms.

MUSCULOSKELETAL DISORDERS ASSOCIATED WITH HYPERLIPIDEMIA Patients with familial hypercholesterolemia (type II hyperlipidemia) may experience a recurrent transient migratory arthritis involving the proximal interphalangeal joints, knees, ankles, wrists, shoulders, or elbows. Achilles tendinitis may also be present. The onset of arthritis is sudden and lasts approximately 48 h in each affected joint. The episodes of arthritis are of approximately 1-week duration, and several attacks occur a year without residual joint deformity. Patients may also have tendinous xanthomas in the Achilles, patellar, and extensor tendons of the hands and feet, and tuberous xanthomas over the elbows, knees, or buttocks. A mild inflammatory arthritis affecting a few peripheral joints in an asymmetric pattern has been observed in a few patients with familial hypertriglyceridemia (type IV hyperlipidemia). Large juxtaarticular bone cysts have been noted in a few patients. The cause of arthritis in both groups of patients is not known. Analgesics or anti-inflammatory drugs provide relief of symptoms.

PERIARTICULAR DISORDERS Bursitis Bursitis is inflammation of a bursa, which is a thin-walled sac lined with synovial tissue. The function of the bursa is to facilitate movement of tendons and muscles over bony prominences. Excessive frictional forces, trauma, systemic disease (e.g., rheumatoid arthritis, gout), or infection may cause bursitis. Subacromial bursitis (subdeltoid bursitis) is the most common form of bursitis. Another is trochanteric bursitis, which involves the bursa around the insertion of the gluteus medius to the greater trochanter of the femur. Patients experience pain over the lateral aspect of the hip and upper thigh and are tender over the posterior aspect of the greater trochanter. External rotation and resisted abduction of the hip elicit pain. Olecranon bursitis occurs over the posterior elbow, and when the area is acutely inflamed, infection should be excluded. Achilles bursitis involves the bursa located above the insertion of the tendon to the calcaneus and results from wearing tight shoes. Ischial bursitis (weaver's bottom) affects the bursa separating the gluteus medius from the ischial tuberosity and develops from prolonged sitting on hard surfaces. Anserine bursitis is an inflammation of the sartorius bursa over the medial side of the tibia just below the knee and is manifested by pain on climbing stairs. Tenderness is present over the insertion of the conjoint tendon of the

sartorius, gracilis, and semitendinosus. Prepatellar bursitis (housemaid's knee) occurs over the patellar tendon and is caused by kneeling on hard surfaces. Treatment of bursitis consists of prevention of the aggravating condition, rest of the involved part, a nonsteroidal anti-inflammatory drug, and local steroid injection.

Rotator cuff tendinitis Tendinitis of the rotator cuff is the major cause of a painful shoulder. Of the tendons forming the rotator cuff, the supraspinatus tendon is most often affected, probably because of its repeated impingement between the acromion and humeral head as well as its reduced blood supply occurring with abduction of the arm. The process evolves through inflammation, fibrosis, and tears of the tendon. Symptoms usually occur after injury or overuse, particularly in individuals over age 40. Patients complain of a dull aching in the shoulder that may interfere with sleep. Severe pain is experienced when the arm is actively abducted into an overhead position. Tenderness is present over the lateral aspect of the humeral head just below the acromion. Nonsteroidal anti-inflammatory drugs, local steroid injection, and physical therapy may relieve symptoms.

Patients may tear the supraspinatus tendon acutely by falling on an outstretched arm or lifting a heavy object. Symptoms are pain, along with weakness of abduction and external rotation of the shoulder. Atrophy of the supraspinatus muscles develops. The diagnosis is established by arthrogram. Surgical repair may be necessary in patients who fail to respond to conservative measures.

Calcific tendinitis This is characterized by deposition of calcium salts, primarily hydroxyapatite, within a tendon. The exact mechanism for calcification is not known but may be due to ischemia or degeneration of the tendon. The supraspinatus tendon is most often affected because of its frequent impingement and reduced blood supply when the arm is abducted. It usually develops after age 40. Calcification within the tendon may evoke acute inflammation, producing sudden and severe pain in the shoulder. Tendon calcification, however, may be asymptomatic or not related to the patient's symptoms.

Bicipital tendinitis and rupture Bicipital tendinitis, or tenosynovitis, is produced by friction on the tendon of the long head of the biceps as it passes through the bicipital groove. When the inflammation is acute, patients experience anterior shoulder pain which radiates down the biceps into the forearm. Abduction and internal rotation of the arm are painful and limited. The bicipital groove is very tender to palpation. Pain may be elicited along the course of the tendon by resisting supination of the forearm with the elbow at 90° (Yergason's supination sign). Acute rupture of the tendon may occur with vigorous exercise of the arm and is often painful. In a young patient, it should be repaired surgically. Rupture of the tendon in an older person may be associated with little or no pain and is recognized by the presence of persistent swelling of the biceps ("Popeye" muscle). Surgery is usually not necessary in this setting.

Adhesive capsulitis Often referred to as "frozen shoulder," adhesive capsulitis is characterized by pain and restricted movement of the shoulder usually in the absence of intrinsic shoulder disease. Adhesive capsulitis, however, may follow bursitis or tendinitis of the shoulder or be associated with systemic disorders such as chronic pulmonary disease, myocardial infarction, and diabetes mellitus. Prolonged immobility of the arm contributes to the development of adhesive capsulitis, and reflex sympathetic distrophy is thought to be a pathogenic factor. The capsule of the shoulder is thickened, and a mild chronic inflammatory infiltrate and fibrosis may be present.

Adhesive capsulitis occurs more commonly in women after age 50. Pain and stiffness usually develop gradually over several months to a year, but may progress rapidly in some patients. Pain may interfere with sleep. The shoulder is tender to palpation, and both active and passive movement are restricted. Radiograph of the shoulder shows osteopenia. The diagnosis is confirmed by arthrogram, in that only a limited amount of contrast material, usually less than 15 mL, can be injected under pressure into the shoulder joint.

The majority of patients improve spontaneously 12 to 18 months after the onset of disease, but some may have permanent restriction of movement. Early mobilization of the arm following an injury to the shoulder may prevent the development of this disease. Slow but forceful injection of contrast material into the joint may lyse adhesions and stretch the capsule, resulting in improvement of shoulder motion. Manipulation under anesthesia may be helpful in some patients. Once established, therapy may have little effect on the natural course of the disease. Local injections of corticosteroids, nonsteroidal anti-inflammatory drugs, and physical therapy may provide relief of symptoms.

TUMORS OF JOINTS Primary tumors and tumorlike disorders of synovium are uncommon but should be considered in the differential diagnosis of monarticular joint disease. In addition, metastases to bone and primary bone tumors adjacent to a joint may produce joint symptoms.

Pigmented villonodular synovitis is characterized by exuberant proliferation of synovial cells usually involving a single joint. It occurs most often in young adults and affects both sexes equally. The etiology of this disorder is unknown.

The synovium is a brownish color and has numerous large, fingerlike villi which fuse to form pedunculated nodules. There is marked hyperplasia of synovial cells within the stroma of the villi. Hemosiderin granules and lipids are found in the cytoplasm of macrophages and in the interstitial tissue. Multinucleated giant cells may be present. The proliferative synovium grows into the subsynovial tissue and invades adjacent cartilage and bone.

The clinical picture of pigmented villonodular synovitis is characterized by the insidious onset of swelling and pain in one joint, most commonly the knee. Other joints affected include the hips, ankles, calcaneocuboid joints, elbows, and small joints of the fingers or toes. The disease may also involve the common flexor sheath of the hand. Symptoms may be mild, intermittent, and present for years before the patient seeks medical attention. Radiographs may show joint space narrowing, erosions, and subchondral cysts. The joint fluid contains blood and is dark-red or almost black in color. Lipid containing macrophages may be present in the fluid. The joint fluid may be clear if hemorrhages have not occurred.

The treatment of pigmented villonodular synovitis is complete synovectomy. With incomplete synovectomy, the villondular synovitis recurs, and the rate of tissue growth may be faster than occurred originally. Irradiation of the involved joint has been successful in some patients.

Synovial chondromatosis is a disorder characterized by multiple focal metaplastic growths of normal-appearing cartilage in the synovium or tendon sheath. Segments of cartilage break loose and continue to grow as loose bodies. When calcification and ossification of loose bodies occur, the disorder is referred to as synovial osteochondromatosis. The disorder is usually monarticular and affects young to middle-aged individuals. The knee is most often involved followed by hip, elbow, and shoulder. Symptoms are pain, swelling, and decreased motion of the joint. Radiographs may show several rounded calcifications within the joint cavity. Treatment is synovectomy; however, the tumor may recur.

Hemangiomas occur in synovium and in tendon sheaths. The knee is affected most commonly. Recurrent episodes of joint swelling and pain usually begin in childhood. The joint fluid is bloody. Treatment is excision of the lesion. *Lipomas* occur most often in the knee, originating in the subsynovial fat on either side of the patellar tendon. Lipomas also appear in tendon sheaths of the hands, wrists, feet, and ankles.

Synovial sarcoma (malignant synovioma) is a neoplasm of connective origin arising from tissue adjacent to large joints and seldom from the joint itself. It occurs most often in young adults and is more common in men. The tumor presents as a slowly growing mass near a joint, without much pain. The tumor spreads along tissue planes. The most common site of visceral metastasis is lung. The diagnosis is made by biopsy. Treatment is wide resection of the tumor including adjacent muscle and regional lymph nodes. Amputation of the involved distal extremity may be required. Chemotherapy may be beneficial in some patients with metastatic disease.

Synovial chondrosarcoma may arise in the synovium, tendon sheath, or bursa and is very rare. Treatment is radical excision or amputation.

REFERENCES

ALTMAN RD, TENENBAUM J: Hypertrophic osteoarthropathy, in *Textbook of Rheumatology*, WN Kelley et al (eds). Philadelphia, Saunders, 1985, chap 103, pp 1594–1603

HERMAN JH: Polychondritis, in *Textbook of Rheumatology*, WN Kelley et al (eds). Philadelphia, Saunders, 1985, chap 91, pp 1458–1467

KOZIN F et al: The reflex sympathetic dystrophy syndrome (RSDS). III. Scintigraphic studies, further evidence for the therapeutic efficacy of systemic corticosteroids, and proposed diagnostic criteria. Am J Med 70:23, 1982

MYERS BW et al: Pigmented villonodular synovitis and tenosynovitis: A clinical epidemiologic study of 166 cases and literature review. Medicine 59:223, 1980

NEER CS II: Impingement lesions. Clin Orthop 173:70, 1983

RODNAN GP: Neuropathic joint disease (Charcot joints), in *Arthritis and Allied Conditions*, 9th ed, DJ McCarty (ed). Philadelphia, Lea & Febiger, 1979, chap 58, pp 892–904

ROONEY PJ et al: Transient polyarthritis associated with familial hyperbetalipoproteinemia. Q J Med 47:249, 1978

SCHILLER AL: Tumors and tumor-like lesions involving joints, in *Textbook of Rheumatology*, WN Kelley et al (eds). Philadelphia, Saunders, 1985, chap 108, pp 1711–1732

SCHUMACHER HR JR: Articular manifestations of hypertrophic pulmonary osteoarthropathy in bronchogenic carcinoma: A clinical and pathological study. Arthritis Rheum 19:629, 1976

THORNHILL TS: The painful shoulder, in *Textbook of Rheumatology*, WN Kelley et al (eds). Philadelphia, Saunders, 1985, chap 29, pp 435–448

YUNUS M et al: Primary fibromyalgia (fibrositis): Clinical study of 50 patients with matched normal controls. Semin Arthritis Rheum 11:151, 1981

section 1 Clotting disorders

279 DISORDERS OF THE PLATELET AND VESSEL WALL

ROBERT I. HANDIN

Patients with platelet or vessel wall disorders usually bleed into superficial sites such as the skin, mucous membranes, genitourinary tract, and gastrointestinal tract. Bleeding begins immediately after trauma and either responds to simple measures like pressure and packing or requires therapy with corticosteroids, plasma fractions, or platelet concentrates. The most common platelet/vessel wall disorders are (1) various forms of thrombocytopenia, (2) von Willebrand's disease, and (3) drug-induced platelet dysfunction. This chapter reviews the diagnosis and treatment of quantitative and qualitative platelet disorders as well as vessel wall defects which cause bleeding. The physiology of normal hemostasis and the cardinal manifestations of bleeding from the primary hemostatic disorders have been reviewed in Chap. 54.

PLATELET PRODUCTION AND KINETICS Platelets arise from the fragmentation of megakaryocytes, which are very large, polyploid bone marrow cells produced by several cycles of chromosomal duplication without cytoplasmic division. After leaving the marrow space, approximately one-third of the platelets are sequestered in the spleen, while the other two-thirds circulates for 7 to 10 days. Normally, only a small fraction of the platelet mass is consumed in the process of hemostasis, so that most platelets circulate until they become senescent and are removed by phagocytic cells. The normal blood platelet count is maintained between 150,000 and 450,000 per cubic millimeter. Although the regulatory signals are not well-defined, a decrease in platelet mass stimulates an increase in the number, size, and ploidy of megakaryocytes releasing additional platelets into the circulation.

The platelet count varies during the menstrual cycle, rising following ovulation and falling at the onset of menses. It is also influenced by the patient's nutritional state and can be decreased in severe iron, folic acid, or vitamin B_{12} deficiency. Platelets are *acute phase reactants* and patients with systemic inflammation, tumors, bleeding, and mild iron deficiency may have an increased platelet count, a benign condition called *secondary or reactive thrombocytosis*. In contrast, the increase in platelet count that is characteristic of the myeloproliferative disorders such as polycythemia vera, chronic myelogenous leukemia, myeloid metaplasia, and essential thrombocytosis can cause either severe bleeding or thrombosis.

MECHANISM OF THROMBOCYTOPENIA Thrombocytopenia is caused by one of three mechanisms—decreased bone marrow production, increased splenic sequestration, or accelerated destruction of platelets. In order to determine the etiology of thrombocytopenia, each patient should have a careful examination of the peripheral blood film, an assessment of marrow morphology by examination of an aspirate or biopsy, and an estimate of splenic size by bedside palpation. A scheme for classifying patients with thrombocytopenia based on these clinical observations and laboratory tests is outlined in Fig. 279-1.

Impaired production Disorders that injure stem cells or prevent their proliferation in marrow frequently cause thrombocytopenia. They usually affect multiple hematopoietic cell lines so that throm-

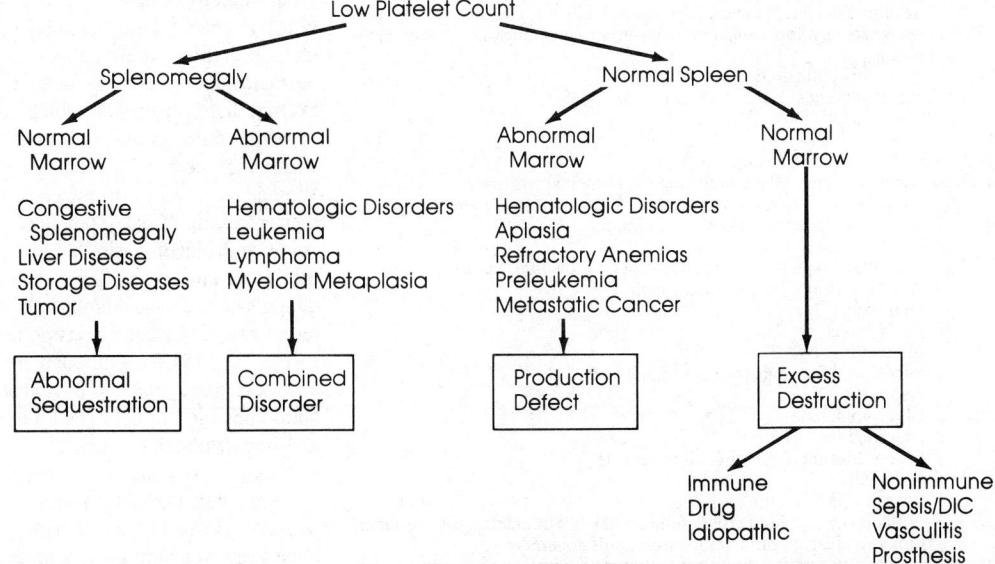

FIGURE 279-1 *The clinical evaluation of patients with thrombocytopenia [Modified from RI Handin, in W Beck (ed). Hematology, 4th ed, MIT Press, Cambridge, Mass., 1985.]*

bocytopenia is accompanied by varying degrees of anemia and leukopenia. Diagnosis of a platelet production defect is readily established by examination of a bone marrow aspirate or biopsy, which should show a reduced number of megakaryocytes. The most common causes of decreased platelet production are marrow aplasia, fibrosis, or infiltration with malignant cells; these produce highly characteristic marrow abnormalities. Occasionally, thrombocytopenia is the presenting laboratory abnormality in these disorders. Cytotoxic drugs, which are frequently used in cancer chemotherapy, impair megakaryocyte proliferation and maturation and frequently cause thrombocytopenia. There are also rare marrow disorders like congenital amegakaryocytic hypoplasia and thrombocytopenia with absent radii (TAR syndrome), which selectively decrease megakaryocyte production.

Splenic sequestration Since one-third of the platelet mass is normally sequestered in the spleen, splenectomy will increase the platelet count by 30 percent. In contrast, when the spleen enlarges, the fraction of sequestered platelets increases, lowering the platelet count. The most common causes of splenomegaly are portal hypertension secondary to liver disease, splenic infiltration with tumor cells in myeloproliferative or lymphoproliferative disorders, or with macrophages in storage disorders like Gaucher's disease. Isolated splenomegaly is rare and, in most patients, splenomegaly is accompanied by other clinical manifestations of the underlying disease. Many patients with leukemia, lymphoma, or a myeloproliferative syndrome have both marrow infiltration and splenomegaly and develop thrombocytopenia from a combination of impaired marrow production and splenic sequestration of platelets.

Accelerated destruction Abnormal vessels, fibrin thrombi, or intravascular prostheses can all shorten platelet survival and cause *nonimmunologic thrombocytopenia*. For example, thrombocytopenia is common in patients with vasculitis, the hemolytic uremic syndrome, thrombotic thrombocytopenic purpura (TTP), as a manifestation of disseminated intravascular coagulation (DIC), and in patients with prosthetic cardiac valves. In addition, platelets coated with antibody, immune complexes, or complement are rapidly cleared by mononuclear phagocytes in the spleen or other tissues inducing *immunologic thrombocytopenia*. The most common causes of immune thrombocytopenia are viral infections, drugs, and a chronic autoimmune disorder referred to as idiopathic thrombocytopenic purpura (ITP). These patients do not usually have splenomegaly and have an active bone marrow with an increased number of megakaryocytes.

TABLE 279-1 Drugs implicated in thrombocytopenia

I Suppression of platelet production
  A Myelosuppressive drugs
    1 Severe: cytosine arabinoside, daunorubicin
    2 Moderate: cyclophosphamide, busulfan, methotrexate, 6-mercaptopurine
    3 Mild: vinca alkaloids
  B Thiazide diuretics
  C Ethanol
  D Estrogens
II Immunologic platelet destruction
  A Clinical suspicion plus convincing experimental evidence
    1 Antibiotics: sulfathiazole, novobiocin, *p*-aminosalicylate
    2 Cinchona alkaloids: quinidine, quinine
    3 Foods: beans
    4 Sedatives, hypnotics, anticonvulsants: apronalide, carbamazepine
    5 Arsenical drugs used to treat syphilis
    6 Digitoxin
    7 Methyldopa
    8 Stibophen
  B Clinical suspicion (major drugs implicated)
    1 Aspirin
    2 Chlorpropamide
    3 Chloroquine
    4 Chlorothiazide and hydrochlorothiazide
    5 Gold salts
    6 Insecticides
    7 Sulfadiazine, sulfisoxazole, sulfamerazine, sulfamethazine, sulfamethoxypyridazine, sulfamethoxazole, sulfatolamide

DRUG-INDUCED THROMBOCYTOPENIA Many common drugs can cause thrombocytopenia (see Table 279-1). As previously mentioned, some chemotherapeutic agents are cytotoxic and depress megakaryocyte production. Ingestion of large quantities of alcohol has a similar marrow-depressing effect leading to transient thrombocytopenia, which is particularly common in binge drinkers. Thiazide diuretics, which are commonly used to treat hypertension or congestive heart failure, impair megakaryocyte production and can produce mild thrombocytopenia (50,000 to 100,000 per cubic millimeter), which may persist for several months after the drug is discontinued.

Most drugs induce thrombocytopenia by eliciting an immune response in which the platelet is an innocent bystander. The platelet is damaged by complement activation following the formation of drug-antibody complexes. Current laboratory tests can identify the causative agent in 10 percent of patients with clinical evidence of drug-induced thrombocytopenia. The best proof of a drug-induced etiology is a prompt rise in the platelet count when the suspected drug is discontinued. Patients with immune-mediated platelet destruction may also have a secondary increase in megakaryocyte number without other marrow abnormalities.

Although most patients recover within 7 to 10 days and do not require therapy, occasional patients with platelet counts below 10,000 to 20,000 per cubic millimeter have severe hemorrhage and may require temporary support with corticosteroids, plasmapheresis, or platelet transfusions while waiting for the platelet count to rise. A patient who has recovered from drug-induced immune thrombocytopenia should be instructed to avoid the offending drug in the future since only minute amounts of drug are needed to set up subsequent immune reactions. Certain drugs like diphenylhydantoin and gold salts may induce prolonged thrombocytopenia, since the drugs are cleared from body storage depots quite slowly.

IDIOPATHIC THROMBOCYTOPENIC PURPURA (ITP) The immune thrombocytopenias can be classified on the basis of the pathologic mechanism, the inciting agent, or the duration of the illness. The explosive onset of severe thrombocytopenia following recovery from a viral exanthem or upper respiratory illness is common in children and accounts for 90 percent of the pediatric cases of immune thrombocytopenia. This syndrome is usually called *acute idiopathic thrombocytopenic purpura* (Acute ITP). Of these patients, 60 percent recover in 4 to 6 weeks and over 90 percent recover within 3 to 6 months. Transient immune thrombocytopenia also complicates some cases of infectious mononucleosis, acute toxoplasmosis, or cytomegalovirus infection and can be part of the prodromal phase of viral hepatitis. Acute ITP is rare in adults and accounts for less than 10 percent of postpubertal patients with immune thrombocytopenia. Acute ITP is caused by immune complexes containing viral antigens which bind to platelet Fc receptors or by antibodies produced against viral antigens which cross react with the platelet. In addition to the viral disorders described above, the differential diagnosis should include atypical presentations of aplastic anemia, acute leukemias, or metastatic tumor. A bone marrow examination is essential to exclude these disorders, which can occasionally mimic acute ITP.

Most adults present with a more indolent form of thrombocytopenia which may persist for many years and is referred to as *chronic ITP*. Women aged 20 to 40 are most commonly afflicted and outnumber men by a ratio of 3:1. They may present with an abrupt fall in platelet count and bleeding similar to patients with acute ITP. More often they have a prior history of easy bruising or menometrorrhagia. These patients have an autoimmune disorder with antibodies directed against target antigens on the glycoprotein IIb-IIIa complex or glycoprotein Ib (see Fig. 54-2). Although most antibodies function as opsonins and accelerate platelet clearance by phagocytic cells, occasional antibodies bind to epitopes on critical regions of these glycoproteins and impair platelet function.

Since a low platelet count may be the initial manifestation of systemic lupus erythematosus (SLE) or the first sign of a primary hematologic disorder, all patients with chronic ITP should have a bone marrow examination and an antinuclear antibody determination.

In addition, patients with hepatic or splenic enlargement, lymphadenopathy, or atypical lymphocytes should have serologic studies for hepatitis, cytomegalovirus, Epstein-Barr virus, toxoplasma, and HTLV III.

Treatment of patients with ITP must be planned taking into account the age of the patient, the severity of the illness, and the suspected natural history. Although adults have a higher incidence of intracranial bleeding than children, specific therapy may not be necessary unless the platelet count is under 20,000 per cubic millimeter or there is extensive bleeding. Hemorrhage in patients with either acute or chronic ITP can usually be controlled with corticosteroids but, in rare cases, may require plasmapheresis to reduce the antibody or immune complex level, or temporary phagocytic blockade with intravenous gamma globulin. Emergency splenectomy is usually reserved for patients with chronic ITP who are desperately ill and have not responded to any medical measures to improve hemostasis.

Symptomatic patients with chronic ITP are usually placed on corticosteroids. In one standard regimen, 60 mg of prednisone is administered for 2 to 4 weeks and rapidly decreased over another week. Approximately 50 percent of patients with chronic ITP will normalize their platelet count on these high doses of prednisone. However, the majority will have a fall in platelet count following steroid withdrawal. Patients with chronic ITP who fail to maintain a normal platelet count after 2 to 3 weeks of steroids are eligible for elective splenectomy. These steroid-responsive but steroid-dependent patients are very likely to respond to splenectomy, and 70 percent will have a normal platelet count within 1 week after surgery. Some patients who do not respond to corticosteroids may still respond to splenectomy.

Patients who are still thrombocytopenic after steroid therapy or splenectomy or who relapse months to years after initial therapy have received a variety of immunosuppressive drugs including azathioprine, cyclophosphamide, vincristine, and vinblastine. More recently danazol, an impeded androgen, has been used with some success. Although each of these drugs may be beneficial, it is important to use some restraint as they have serious side effects. If a patient is not bleeding and maintains a platelet count over 20,000 per cubic millimeter consideration should be given to withholding therapy since there are many patients with severe chronic thrombocytopenia who have lived with their disease for two or three decades.

VON WILLEBRAND'S DISEASE Von Willebrand's disease (vWD) is the most common inherited bleeding disorder and may occur in as many as 1 in 800 to 1000 individuals. The von Willebrand's factor (vWF) is a heterogeneous multimeric plasma glycoprotein with two major functions. It facilitates platelet adhesion under conditions of high shear stress by forming a bridge between platelet membrane receptors and the vascular subendothelium; it also serves as the plasma carrier for factor VIII, the antihemophilic factor, a critical blood coagulation protein. The normal plasma vWF level is 10 μg/mL. The vWF activity is distributed among a series of plasma multimers with estimated molecular weights ranging from 400,000 to over 20 million. A single large vWF precursor subunit is synthesized in endothelial cells and megakaryocytes, where it is cleaved and assembled into the disulfide-linked multimers present in plasma and the vascular subendothelium. A modest reduction in plasma vWF concentration, or a selective loss in the high-molecular-weight multimers, decreases platelet adhesion and causes clinical bleeding.

Although vWD is heterogeneous, there are certain clinical features which are common to all the syndromes. With one exception (type III disease), all forms are inherited as autosomal dominant traits. In mild cases, bleeding occurs only after surgery or trauma. More severely affected patients have spontaneous epistaxis or oral mucosal, gastrointestinal, or genitourinary bleeding. The laboratory findings are variable. The most diagnostic pattern is the combination of (1) a prolonged bleeding time, (2) a reduction in plasma vWF concentration, (3) a parallel reduction in ristocetin cofactor activity, and (4) reduced factor VIII activity. The variability in laboratory tests is related both to the heterogeneous nature of the defects in vWD and the fact that

vWF synthesis or release is increased by central nervous disorders, systemic inflammation, or pregnancy. Since vWD is an autosomal dominant disorder, some vWF is produced by the remaining normal allele. Thus, patients with mild defects may have laboratory values that fluctuate over time and may occasionally be within the normal range.

Although vWF cDNA has been cloned and the gene localized to chromosome 12, there is no information regarding the molecular genetics of the von Willebrand syndromes. There are three major types of vWD. Patients with *type I disease,* the most common abnormality, have a mild to moderate decrease in plasma vWF. In the milder cases, although hemostasis is clearly impaired, the vWF level is just below the lower limit of normal (50 percent activity, or 5 μg/mL). In type I disease there is a parallel decrease in vWF antigen, factor VIII activity, and ristocetin cofactor activity, with a normal spectrum of multimers detected by sodium dodecyl sulfate–agarose (SDS-agarose) gel electrophoresis.

The variant forms of vWD (*type II disease*), which are much less common, are characterized by normal or near-normal levels of dysfunctional protein. Patients with the *type IIa variant* of vWD have a deficiency in the high-molecular-weight forms of vWF multimer detected by SDS-agarose electrophoresis. This is due either to an inability to assemble the high-molecular-weight multimers or to a premature catabolism after they leave the endothelial cell and enter the circulation. The quantity of vWF antigen and the amount of associated factor VIII are usually normal. In the *type IIb variant,* there is also a loss in high-molecular-weight multimers. However, in type IIb cases, it is due to the inappropriate binding of vWF to platelets. This forms intravascular platelet aggregates which are rapidly cleared from the circulation causing mild, cyclic thrombocytopenia. Levels of vWF antigen and factor VIII usually remain normal.

Approximately 1 in 1 million individuals have a very severe form of vWD that is phenotypically recessive (*type III disease*). Type III patients are usually the offspring of two parents with mild type I disease. They may actually inherit a different abnormality from each parent (a doubly heterozygous state) or be homozygous for a single defect. Type III patients have severe mucosal bleeding, no detectable vWF antigen or activity, and may have sufficiently low factor VIII levels to have occasional hemarthroses like mild hemophiliacs.

Appropriate therapy of vWD depends on the symptoms and the underlying type of disease. There are two therapeutic options. One involves the use of cryoprecipitate, which is a plasma fraction enriched in vWF and is appropriate treatment for all the inherited forms of vWD. During surgery or after major trauma, patients should receive ten bags of cryoprecipitate. This regimen should be continued twice daily for 48 to 72 h to ensure optimal hemostasis. Minor bleeding episodes such as prolonged epistaxis or severe menorrhagia may respond to a single transfusion of cryoprecipitate. Recurrent menorrhagia, a major problem for women with severe vWD, can be effectively treated with oral contraceptive agents that suppress menses.

A second therapeutic option is the use of 1-desamino-8-D-arginine vasopressin (DDAVP), a vasopressin analogue which has minimal blood pressure–elevating and fluid-retaining properties and raises the plasma vWF level in normal individuals and patients with mild vWD. Patients with type I disease are the best candidates for DDAVP therapy. However, they must be tested for an adequate response prior to anticipated surgery, and vWF levels must be closely monitored during therapy since the patient may develop tachyphylaxis when therapy is continued for more than 48 h. DDAVP should not be given to patients with vWD variants, since it does not improve multimer pattern or hemostasis in type IIa patients, and it may actually worsen the defect or cause thrombotic complications in type IIb patients, since it increases the number of platelet-vWF aggregates and the degree of thrombocytopenia.

Although most cases of vWD are inherited, there are acquired forms of vWD caused by antibodies which block vWF function or by lymphoid or other tumors which selectively adsorb vWF multimers onto their surfaces. Anti-vWF antibodies have developed in patients with severe vWD following multiple transfusions, as well as in patients with autoimmune and lymphoproliferative disorders. Adsorption of vWF to tumor surfaces has been documented in patients with Waldenstrom's macroglobulinemia and Wilm's tumor and inferred in other patients with lymphoma. Treatment of acquired vWD should focus on controlling the underlying disease, since cryoprecipitate and DDAVP are usually not effective and the disorder can be fatal.

PLATELET MEMBRANE DEFECTS   Receptors which modulate platelet adhesion and aggregation are located on the two major platelet surface glycoproteins. As previously discussed (see Chap. 54), vWF facilitates platelet adhesion by binding to glycoprotein Ib, while fibrinogen links platelets into aggregates via sites on the glycoprotein IIb-IIIa complex. There are two rare but well-defined platelet defects characterized by the loss of these glycoprotein receptors. Patients with the *Bernard-Soulier syndrome* have markedly reduced platelet adhesion and cannot bind vWF to their platelets owing to a deficiency in glycoprotein Ib. They also have reduced levels of several other membrane proteins, mild thrombocytopenia, and extremely large, lymphocytoid platelets. Platelets from patients with *Glanzmann's disease* or *thrombasthenia* are missing or markedly deficient in the glycoprotein IIb-IIIa complex. Their platelets do not bind fibrinogen and cannot form aggregates. The platelets undergo shape change and secretion and are of normal size.

Both of these disorders are inherited as autosomal recessive traits and are characterized by markedly impaired hemostasis and lifelong episodes of severe mucosal hemorrhage. In keeping with the selective nature of the defects, Bernard-Soulier platelets react normally to all stimuli except ristocetin. In contrast, thrombasthenic platelets adhere normally and will agglutinate with ristocetin but will not aggregate with any of the agonists which require fibrinogen binding, such as adenosine diphosphate (ADP), thrombin, or epinephrine.

The only effective therapy for hemorrhagic episodes in these two disorders is transfusion with normal platelets. This is usually effective, although alloimmunization will eventually limit the lifespan of infused platelets. In addition, a few patients have developed inhibitor antibodies with specificity for the missing protein. These antibodies bind to the protein which is expressed on the transfused normal platelets and impair their function.

PLATELET RELEASE DEFECTS   The most common mild bleeding disorders arise from the ingestion of nonsteroidal anti-inflammatory drugs (NSAIDS) which inhibit platelet production of thromboxane A_2, an important mediator of platelet secretion and aggregation (see Figs. 54-3, 54-4). These drugs inhibit platelet cyclooxygenase, which converts arachidonic acid to a labile endoperoxide intermediate that is critical for thromboxane formation. Aspirin is the most potent agent, since it irreversibly acetylates the platelet enzyme; a single dose impairs hemostasis for 5 to 7 days. The other agents are competitive and reversible inhibitors with more transient effects. Blocking thromboxane A_2 synthesis partially inhibits platelet release and aggregation with weak agonists such as ADP and epinephrine and produces a mild hemostatic defect.

Patients generally have minimal symptoms such as easy bruising, and bleeding is usually confined to the skin. Occasional patients will have prolonged oozing after surgery, particularly with procedures involving mucous membranes such as periodontal, oral, or reconstructive plastic surgery. Not surprisingly, the antiplatelet effect of drugs like aspirin is more dramatic when they are administered to patients with underlying defects like vWD or hemophilia. Patients with drug-induced cyclooxygenase deficiency have a prolonged bleeding time, and their platelets fail to aggregate when incubated with arachidonic acid, epinephrine, or low doses of ADP. Platelet responses to collagen and thrombin are impaired at low doses but normal at higher doses. Symptomatic patients should be encouraged to use drugs like acetaminophen which do not impair platelet function. Although most cases of cyclooxygenase deficiency are drug-induced,

occasional patients have inherited disorders in platelet cyclooxygenase activity which impair thromboxane production or receptor level defects which prevent platelets from responding to thromboxane A_2.

STORAGE POOL DEFECTS   Platelet granules have considerable amounts of adenine nucleotides, calcium, and adhesive glycoproteins like thrombospondin, fibronectin, and vWF, all of which promote platelet adhesion and aggregation. Thus, it is not surprising that patients with defective platelet granules have a mild bleeding disorder. Platelet storage pool defects may be inherited as an isolated disorder or be part of systemic granule packaging defects such as oculocutaneous albinism or the Chediak-Higashi syndrome. Clinically, these patients cannot be distinguished from those with other functional platelet disorders since they all have easy bruising, mucosal bleeding, and a prolonged bleeding time. They can be differentiated from patients with the cyclooxygenase defects since their platelets will usually aggregate in response to arachidonic acid. In addition, their platelets have decreased levels of specific granule constituents like ADP and serotonin and abnormalities in granule morphology that are best visualized by electron microscopy.

Occasionally, patients with acute and chronic leukemia or one of the myeloproliferative disorders develop an acquired storage pool disorder due to dysplastic megakaryocyte development. In addition, patients with liver disease and some patients with systemic lupus or other immune complex–mediated disorders may have circulating platelets which have degranulated prematurely. Platelet degranulation and a transient storage pool disorder have also been described following prolonged cardiopulmonary bypass.

VESSEL WALL DISORDERS   Bleeding from vascular disorders (nonthrombocytopenic purpura) is usually mild and confined to the skin and mucous membranes. The pathogenesis of bleeding is poorly defined in many of the syndromes, and classical tests of hemostasis, including the bleeding time and tests of platelet function, are usually normal. Vascular purpura arises from damage to capillary endothelium, abnormalities in the vascular subendothelial matrix or extravascular connective tissues which support blood vessels, or from the formation of abnormal blood vessels. There are also several idiopathic disorders which involve the vessel wall and which can cause more severe bleeding and organ dysfunction.

Thrombotic thrombocytopenic purpura   Thrombotic thrombocytopenic purpura (TTP) is a fulminant, often lethal disorder that may be initiated by endothelial injury and subsequent release of vWF and other procoagulant materials from the endothelial cell. In addition, some patients with TTP have a unique circulating protein which induces platelet aggregation. Characteristic findings include the microvascular deposition of hyaline thrombi which stain for fibrin, thrombocytopenia, microangiopathic hemolytic anemia, fever, renal failure, fluctuating levels of consciousness, and evanescent focal neurologic deficits. The presence of hyaline thrombi in arterioles, capillaries, and venules without any inflammatory changes in the vessel wall is diagnostic. Gingival biopsies are positive in 30 to 40 percent of patients, and marrow biopsies are occasionally helpful. The presence of a severe Coombs negative hemolytic anemia, coupled with thrombocytopenia, and minimal activation of the coagulation system help to confirm the clinical suspicion of TTP. This disorder should be distinguished from vasculitis and systemic lupus erythematosus, which can predispose patients to TTP and ITP. Levels of platelet-associated IgG and complement are usually normal in TTP.

The treatment of acute TTP has changed radically in the past few years. The use of steroids and heparin or emergency splenectomy have been abandoned, and the enthusiasm for antiplatelet therapy has diminished. Increasingly, treatment has involved the use of exchange transfusion or intensive plasmapheresis coupled with infusion of fresh frozen plasma. With this therapeutic approach, the overall mortality has been markedly reduced, and over half the patients with TTP are recovering from this formerly fatal disorder. Most patients surviving the acute illness recover completely with no residual renal or neurologic disease. Occasional patients with a chronic relapsing form of TTP require maintenance plasmapheresis and plasma infusion, and a few patients are only controlled with corticosteroids.

Hemolytic-uremic syndrome Hemolytic-uremic syndrome (HUS) is a disease of infancy and early childhood which closely resembles TTP. Patients present with fever, thrombocytopenia, microangiopathic hemolytic anemia, hypertension, and varying degrees of acute renal failure. In many cases, onset is preceded by a minor febrile or viral illness, and an infectious or immune complex–mediated etiology has been proposed. As in TTP, there is no evidence of disseminated intravascular coagulation. In contrast to TTP, the disorder remains localized to the kidney where hyaline thrombi are seen in the afferent aterioles and glomerular capillaries. Such thrombi are not present in other vessels, and neurologic symptoms, other than those associated with uremia, are uncommon. There is no effective therapy; however, with dialysis for acute renal failure, the initial mortality is only 5 percent. Between 10 and 50 percent of patients are left with some chronic renal impairment.

Henoch-Schönlein purpura Henoch-Schönlein or anaphylactoid purpura is a distinct, self-limited type of vasculitis which occurs in children and young adults. Patients have an acute inflammatory reaction in capillaries, mesangial tissues, and small arterioles which leads to increased vascular permeability, exudation, and hemorrhage. Vessel lesions contain IgA and complement components. The syndrome may be preceded by an upper respiratory infection or streptococcal pharyngitis or be associated with food or drug allergies. Patients develop a purpuric or urticarial rash on the extensor surface of the arms and legs and on the buttocks; they also have polyarthralgias or arthritis, colicky abdominal pain, and hematuria from focal glomerulonephritis. Despite the hemorrhagic features, all coagulation tests are normal. A small number of patients may develop fatal acute renal failure, and 5 to 10 percent develop chronic nephritis. Corticosteroids provide symptomatic relief of the joint and abdominal pains but do not alter the course of the illness.

Metabolic and inflammatory disorders A number of acute febrile illnesses cause capillary fragility and skin bleeding. Immune complexes containing viral antigens, or the viruses themselves, may damage endothelial cells. In addition, certain pathogens such as the rickettsiae which cause Rocky Mountain spotted fever replicate in endothelial cells and damage them. Thrombocytopenia is also a frequent finding in acute infectious disorders and may contribute to skin bleeding. In addition, whenever the platelet count falls below 10,000 per cubic millimeter gaps which develop between endothelial cells allow the diapedesis of red cells into the dermis leading to the formation of petechiae. Drugs such as the sulfonamides, penicillin, and allopurinol may cause vascular inflammation resulting in maculopapular or urticarial rashes. Some of these mechanisms are additive, and drug reactions in thrombocytopenic individuals cause an intensely hemorrhagic rash.

Occasionally, patients with diffuse polyclonal hyperglobulinemia will develop purpuric lesions on the lower limbs—a benign condition referred to as *hyperglobulinemic purpura*. Vascular purpura may occur in patients with various monoclonal plasma protein abnormalities including Waldenstrom's macroglobulinemia, multiple myeloma, and cryoglobulinemia. These proteins markedly increase serum viscosity and may impair blood flow through capillaries. Thus, retinal hemorrhage, central nervous system dysfunction, and skin necrosis have all been described in these syndromes due to the marked elevation in viscosity. In addition, the globulins may impair platelet aggregation and adhesion and interfere with fibrin polymerization. Patients with mixed cryoglobulinemia develop a more extensive maculopapular lesion due to immune complex–mediated damage to the vessel wall. The mixed cryoglobulinemia (usually IgG and anti-IgG) may be associated with arthralgias, diffuse weakness, and unexplained nephritis. Plasmapheresis will temporarily lower the level of globulins, remove immune complexes, and improve symptoms in these patients.

However, long-term management must include control of the underlying disease which produces the abnormal globulins or immune complexes.

Patients with *scurvy* (vitamin C deficiency) develop painful episodes of perifollicular skin bleeding as well as bleeding into muscles and, occasionally, into the gastrointestinal and genitourinary tracts. The diagnosis is confirmed by the presence of hyperkeratosis of skin, gum swelling, and low levels of the vitamin in leukocytes. Vitamin C–deficient patients have markedly defective collagen synthesis, since ascorbic acid is needed to synthesize hydroxyproline, an essential constituent of collagen. Patients with *Cushing's syndrome*, which is characterized by excess production of glucocorticoids, or patients on large doses of corticosteroids develop generalized protein wasting and may show skin bleeding or easy bruising due to atrophy of the supporting connective tissue around blood vessels. Aging causes a similar atrophy of perivascular connective tissue on the extensor surface of the hands and arms, leading to "senile purpura." These patients develop dark purple, irregularly shaped hemorrhagic areas due to abnormal skin mobility which tears small blood vessels.

Patients with inherited disorders of the connective tissue matrix such as *Marfan's syndrome, Ehlers-Danlos syndrome,* and *pseudoxanthoma elasticum* also have easy bruising. In addition to having fragile skin vessels and easy bruising, patients with Ehlers-Danlos syndrome may develop aneurysms in intraabdominal vessels and apoplectic rupture and hemorrhage due to defects in the vascular collagen network. Primary vascular abnormalities can also lead to bleeding. Patients with *Osler-Rendu-Weber disease* (hereditary hemorrhagic telangiectasia), an inherited autosomal dominant disorder, have frequent episodes of nasal and gastrointestinal bleeding from abnormal telangiectatic capillaries; patients with *angiodysplasia* of the colon have increased incidence of gastrointestinal bleeding. In the *Kasabach-Merritt syndrome* patients may have very extensive and progressively enlarging vascular malformations which may involve large portions of their extremities. Bleeding is secondary to disseminated intravascular coagulation triggered by stagnant blood flow through the tortuous abnormal vessels.

REFERENCES

GEORGE JN et al: Molecular defects in interactions of platelets with the vessel wall. N Engl J Med 311:1084, 1984

HOLMBERG L et al: Platelet aggregation induced by 1-desamino-8-D-arginine vasopressin (DDAVP) in type IIb von Willebrand's disease. N Eng J Med 309:816, 1983

KING DJ, KELTON JG: Heparin-associated thrombocytopenia. Ann Intern Med 100:535, 1984

KITCHENS CS: The purpuric disorders. Semin Thromb Hemost 10:173, 1984

LIND SE: Prolonged bleeding time. Am J Med 77:305, 1984

MCMILLAN R: Chronic idiopathic thrombocytopenic purpura. N Eng J Med 304:1135, 1982

MOAKE JL et al: Unusually large plasma factor VIII: von Willebrand's factor multimers in chronic relapsing thrombotic thrombocytopenia purpura. N Eng J Med 307:1432, 1982

VON SCHACKY C, WEBER PC: Metabolism and effects on platelet function of the purified eicosapentaenoic and docosahexaenoic acids in humans. J Clin Invest 76:2446, 1985

ZIMMERMAN TS, RUGGIERI ZM: von Willebrand's disease. Prog Hemost Thromb 6:203, 1983

---

280 COAGULATION DISORDERS

ROBERT I. HANDIN

Patients with congenital plasma coagulation defects characteristically bleed into muscles, joints, and body cavities, hours or days after an injury. The *inherited* plasma coagulation disorders result from rare defects in single coagulation proteins, with the two X-linked disorders, factors VIII and IX deficiency, accounting for almost all of the known congenital coagulation defects. These patients merit special attention since they may have severe bleeding and chronic disability and require specialized medical therapy. With the exception of factor XIII deficiency, each of the known disorders prolongs either the prothrombin time (PT) or partial thromboplastin time (PTT), the two important screening laboratory tests. If they are abnormal, quantitative assays of specific coagulation proteins are then carried out using PT or PTT tests with plasma from congenitally deficient individuals as substrate. The corrective effect of varying concentrations of patient plasma is measured and expressed as a percentage of a normal pooled plasma standard. The interval range for most coagulation factors is from 50 to 150 percent of this average value, and the minimal level of most individual factors needed for adequate hemostasis is 25 percent.

Acquired coagulation disorders are both more frequent and more complex, arising from deficiencies of multiple coagulation proteins and simultaneously affecting both primary and secondary hemostasis. The most common acquired hemorrhagic disorders are (1) disseminated intravascular coagulation, (2) the hemorrhagic diathesis of liver disease, and (3) vitamin K deficiency and complications of anticoagulant therapy. This chapter reviews the diagnosis, natural history, and therapy of congenital and acquired disorders of secondary hemostasis or plasma coagulation. The physiology of normal hemostasis and the cardinal manifestations of hemorrhagic and thrombotic disorders are described in Chap. 54.

FACTOR VIII DEFICIENCY—HEMOPHILIA A Pathogenesis and clinical manifestations

The antihemophilic factor (AHF) or factor VIII coagulant protein is a large (265,000-dalton), single-chain protein which regulates the activation of factor X by proteases generated in the intrinsic coagulation pathway (see Figs. 54-5, 54-6). It is synthesized in liver parenchymal and endothelial cells and circulates complexed to the von Willebrand protein (vWF). Previous efforts to purify and characterize the factor VIII molecule were limited by its low concentration (10 ng/mL) and susceptibility to proteolysis. However, the cloning and sequencing of complementary DNA (cDNA) encoding the factor VIII molecule and the mapping of the factor VIII gene on the X chromosome have provided the first detailed picture of its structure and have resulted in improved methods for carrier detection and prenatal diagnosis.

One in 10,000 males is born with a deficiency or dysfunction of the factor VIII molecule. The resulting disorder, hemophilia A, is characterized by bleeding into soft tissues, muscles, and weight-bearing joints. Although normal hemostasis requires 25 percent factor VIII activity, symptomatic patients usually have factor VIII levels below 5 percent, with a close correlation between the clinical severity of hemophilia and plasma AHF level. Patients with <1 percent factor VIII activity have *severe* disease; they bleed frequently even without discernible trauma. Patients with levels between 1 and 5 percent have *moderate* disease with less frequent bleeding episodes. Those with levels over 5 percent have *mild* disease with infrequent bleeding that is usually secondary to trauma. Occasional patients with factor VIII levels as high as 25 percent are discovered when they bleed after major trauma or surgery, although the vast majority of patients with hemophilia A have factor VIII levels below 5 percent.

Hemophilic bleeding occurs hours or days after injury, can involve any organ, and, if untreated, may continue for days or weeks. This can result in large collections of partially clotted blood putting pressure on adjacent normal tissues and can cause necrosis of muscle (compartment syndromes), venous congestion (pseudophlebitis), or ischemic damage to nerves. For example, hemophiliacs often develop femoral neuropathy due to pressure from an unsuspected retroperitoneal hematoma. They can also develop large calcified masses of blood and inflammatory tissue that are mistaken for soft tissue sarcomas (pseudotumor syndrome).

Patients with severe hemophilia are usually diagnosed shortly after birth because of an extensive cephalhematoma or profuse bleeding at circumcision. However, patients with moderate disease may not bleed until they begin to walk or crawl, and mild hemophiliacs may not be diagnosed until they are adolescents or young adults. Typically, a hemophiliac patient presents with pain followed by swelling in a weight-bearing joint, like the hip, knee, or ankle. The presence of blood in the joint (hemarthrosis) causes synovial inflammation, and repetitive bleeding erodes articular cartilage and causes osteoarthritis, articular fibrosis, joint ankylosis, and eventually muscle atrophy. Although bleeding may occur into any joint, after a joint has been damaged it may become a site for subsequent bleeding episodes.

Hematuria, in the absence of any genitourinary pathology, is also common. It is usually self-limited and may not require specific therapy. The most feared complications of hemophilia are oropharyngeal and central nervous system bleeding. Patients with oropharyngeal bleeding may require emergency intubation to maintain an adequate airway. Central nervous system bleeding can occur without antecedent trauma or without evidence of a specific lesion.

Therapy There are several tenets regarding the treatment of bleeding in hemophiliac patients: (1) Symptoms often precede objective evidence of bleeding. (2) Signs of bleeding may not appear until several days after well-documented trauma. Physicians caring for these patients have learned to rely on their patients to inform them of early symptoms, usually pain, and to begin treatment at that time. Early treatment is more effective, less costly, and can be lifesaving. (3) It is critical to avoid the use of aspirin or aspirin-containing drugs which impair platelet function and may cause severe hemorrhage.

Plasma products enriched in factor VIII have revolutionized the care of hemophilia patients, reduced the degree of orthopedic deformity, and permitted virtually any form of elective and emergency surgery. The widespread use of factor VIII concentrates has also produced serious complications including viral hepatitis, chronic liver disease, and the acquired immunodeficiency syndrome (AIDS). The standard therapeutic products are cryoprecipitate and factor VIII concentrate. *Cryoprecipitate,* which contains about half the factor VIII activity of fresh frozen plasma in one-tenth the original volume, is simple to prepare and is produced in hospital or regional blood banks. It must be stored frozen and is thawed and pooled prior to administration. However, most patients utilize partially purified *factor VIII concentrate* prepared from multiple donors and supplied as a lyophilized powder. It can be refrigerated and reconstituted just prior to use. Each unit of factor VIII, which is the amount present in 1 mL of normal plasma, will raise the plasma level of the recipient by 2 percent per kilogram of body weight. Factor VIII has a half-life of 8 to 12 h, making it necessary to infuse it continuously or at least twice daily to sustain a chosen factor VIII level. In patients with mild hemophilia an alternative to the use of plasma products is DDAVP (1-desamino-8-D-arginine vasopressin) which transiently increases the factor VIII level.

An uncomplicated episode of soft tissue bleeding, or an early hemarthrosis, can be treated with one infusion of cryoprecipitate or factor VIII concentrate, raising the factor VIII level to 15 or 20 percent. A more extensive hemarthrosis or retroperitoneal bleeding requires twice-daily or continuous infusions in order to keep the factor VIII level between 25 and 50 percent for at least 72 h. Life-threatening bleeding into the central nervous system or major surgery may require therapy for 2 weeks with levels kept at a minimum of 50 percent of normal. In addition to the prompt infusion of factor VIII–enriched plasma products, patients need skilled orthopedic care with immobilization of inflamed joints to promote healing and to prevent contractures, and physical therapy to strengthen muscles and maintain joint mobility. Prior to surgery every patient should be screened for the presence of an inhibitor to factor VIII.

Patients with hemophilia who do not have an inhibitor should receive factor VIII infusions just prior to surgery and will require daily monitoring so that the factor VIII level is maintained above 50 percent for 10 to 14 days after surgery. When patients undergo joint replacement or other major orthopedic surgery, therapy should be continued for 3 weeks. This permits adequate wound healing and the institution of necessary joint mobilization and physical therapy.

Hemophiliacs also require treatment prior to dental procedures. Filling of a carious tooth can be managed by a single infusion of cryoprecipitate or factor VIII concentrate coupled with the administration of 4 to 6 g of ε-aminocaproic acid (EACA) four times daily for 72 to 96 h after the dental procedure. EACA is a potent antifibrinolytic agent which will inhibit plasminogen activators present in oral secretions and stabilize clot formation in oral tissue. For major oral and periodontal surgery and extractions of permanent teeth, patients should be hospitalized and treated with factor VIII. Therapy should begin just prior to surgery and be continued for a minimum of 48 to 72 h.

Many centers have organized home care programs so that patients can administer their own factor VIII infusions with the onset of symptoms. Occasional patients with very frequent bleeding receive regularly scheduled infusions. However, the expense and inconvenience usually limit the use of "prophylactic" infusions. Concern regarding transmission of AIDS has complicated therapy of hemophilia. Some patients are reluctant to treat themselves, and many centers have returned to the use of cryoprecipitate to limit donor exposure. Recently, a commercial heating process has been introduced which appears to inactivate the AIDS-associated retrovirus, HTLV III, without destroying factor VIII activity, and all hemophilia centers now use heat-treated material.

Complications Most hemophiliacs have had multiple episodes of hepatitis, and a majority have elevated hepatocellular enzyme levels and abnormalities on liver biopsy. Ten to twenty percent of hemophiliacs also have hepatosplenomegaly, and a small number develop chronic active or persistent hepatitis or cirrhosis. Recently, a few patients with hemophilia and end-stage liver disease have received liver transplants with cure of both diseases. Along with homosexuals and intravenous drug abusers, hemophiliacs are at high risk for AIDS since they frequently receive blood products. Hemophiliacs also present with the full range of AIDS-related syndromes including diffuse lymphadenopathy and immune thrombocytopenia.

Despite frequent bleeding, severe iron-deficiency anemia is uncommon since most of the bleeding is internal and iron is effectively recycled. Mild iron deficiency from chronic epistaxis or gastrointestinal bleeding has been noted in some hemophiliacs. In addition, after receiving large doses of factor VIII concentrate, some patients develop a mild Coombs'-positive hemolytic anemia due to anti-A and anti-B antibody present in commercial concentrates which bind to red cells and cause hemolysis.

Following multiple transfusions, between 10 and 20 percent of patients with severe hemophilia develop inhibitors to factor VIII. Inhibitors are, generally, IgG antibodies which rapidly neutralize factor VIII activity and prevent effective transfusion therapy. There are two types of inhibitors which have different biologic characteristics and lead to different clinical presentations. Patients with type I inhibitors have a typical anamnestic response in that they raise their antibody titer after exposure to factor VIII. Patients with a type II inhibitor have a low antibody titer which cannot be stimulated by factor VIII infusion. Patients with the type I inhibitor should not receive factor VIII. In an emergency, control of bleeding may require intensive plasmapheresis, or infusion of prothrombin complex concentrates which contain trace quantities of activated coagulation factors and can bypass the block in coagulation produced by the inhibitor. Patients with low-titer type II antibodies may respond to higher than normal doses of factor VIII.

Genetic counseling and carrier detection Until recently, carrier detection required biologic and immunologic assays which compared the ratio of factor VIII to vWF (von Willebrand factor) protein and were predictive in only 70 to 80 percent of cases. It is now possible to trace the defective allele in some families by examining the inheritance of restriction fragment length polymorphisms (RFLPs) linked to the factor VIII gene. In addition, certain families have been identified with specific mutations and deletions in the factor VIII gene that can be detected by restriction enzyme digestion of their DNA. Previously, prenatal diagnosis required sampling fetal blood for coagulant activity. Now, in families with an identifiable RFLP linked to the gene or a gene deletion or rearrangement, precise diagnosis is possible early in pregnancy from either chorionic villus biopsy or amniocentesis.

Most women carriers of hemophilia produce sufficient factor VIII for normal hemostasis from the factor VIII allele on their normal X chromosome. However, occasional hemophilia carriers will have factor VIII levels far below 50 percent due to random inactivation of normal X chromosomes in tissue producing factor VIII. These symptomatic carriers may bleed with major surgery or occasionally with menses. Rarely, true female hemophiliacs arise from consanguinity within families with hemophilia, or from concomitant Turner's syndrome or XO mosaicism in a carrier female.

FACTOR IX DEFICIENCY—HEMOPHILIA B Factor IX is a single-chain 55,000-dalton proenzyme which is converted to an active protease (IXa) by factor XIa. Factor IXa then activates factor X in conjunction with activated factor VIII. Factor IX is one of a group of six proteins, synthesized in the liver, which require vitamin K for biologic activity. As previously discussed (see Chap. 54), vitamin K serves as cofactor for a unique posttranslational modification which inserts a second carboxyl group onto certain glutamic acid residues on factor IX. This modification permits calcium binding and adsorption onto phospholipid surfaces. Factor IX cDNA has been cloned, the gene mapped on the X chromosome, linked RFLPs identified, and several patients with deletions and mutations in the IX gene have been discovered.

Factor IX deficiency or dysfunction (hemophilia B, Christmas disease) occurs in 1 in 100,000 male births. Accurate laboratory diagnosis is critical, since it is clinically indistinguishable from factor VIII deficiency (hemophilia A) but requires treatment with a different plasma fraction. Either fresh frozen plasma or a plasma fraction enriched in the prothrombin complex proteins is used. In addition to the expected complications of hepatitis, chronic liver disease, and AIDS, the therapy of factor IX deficiency has a special hazard. Trace quantities of activated coagulation factors in prothrombin complex concentrates may activate the coagulation system and cause thrombosis and embolism. This is particularly common in immobilized surgical patients and patients with liver disease. As a result, some centers have returned to fresh frozen plasma for factor IX–deficient surgical patients; others have recommended the addition of small doses of heparin to the concentrate to activate antithrombin III during the infusion and reduce hypercoagulability.

FACTOR XI DEFICIENCY Factor XI is a 160,000-dalton, dimeric protein which is activated via the intrinsic coagulation pathway. It is converted to an active protease (XIa) by factor XIIa, in conjunction with high-molecular-weight kininogen and kallikrein (see Figs. 54-4 and 54-5). Factor XI deficiency is inherited as an autosomal recessive trait and is especially common in Ashkenazi Jews. In contrast to factors VIII and IX deficiency, the correlation between factor level and propensity to bleed is not as precise, and there is minimal spontaneous bleeding and hemarthroses are rare. Many patients with factor XI deficiency present with posttraumatic bleeding or with bleeding in the perioperative period, and occasional factor XI–deficient women have menorrhagia. Daily infusions of fresh frozen plasma are sufficient since the half-life of factor XI is approximately 24 h.

OTHER FACTOR DEFICIENCIES Deficiencies in factors V, VII, X, and prothrombin (factor II) are all exceedingly rare autosomal recessive disorders. Although spontaneous or posttraumatic musculoskeletal bleeding or menorrhagia can occur with these deficiencies, hemarthroses are uncommon. Fresh frozen plasma is the appropriate therapy, although prothrombin concentrates may be employed for patients with severe prothrombin or factors VII or X deficiency so long as the risks of hepatitis and thrombosis are recognized.

Defects in the contact activation pathway involving Hageman factor (factor XII), high-molecular-weight kininogen, and prekallikrein cause laboratory abnormalities but no clinical bleeding. Despite dramatic prolongation of the PTT, which is often greater than 100 s, deficient individuals have normal hemostasis and can undergo major surgery without plasma replacement therapy. It is important to

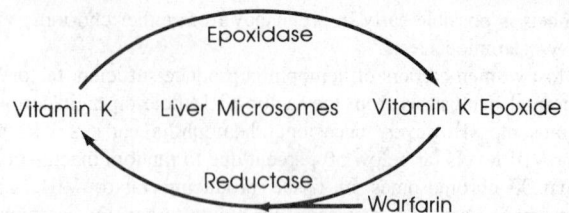

FIGURE 280-1   *The mechanism of action of vitamin K, which is a cofactor in the formation of di,γ-carboxyglutamic acid residues on coagulation proteins, is depicted. Vitamin K is converted to an epoxide in liver microsomes. The epoxide is the active form and is reduced back to vitamin K by a liver membrane reductase. Warfarin blocks the action of the reductase and competitively inhibits the effects of vitamin K.*

recognize and diagnose these disorders since the patients should neither be inappropriately treated with plasma nor denied indicated surgery on the basis of these laboratory abnormalities.

AFIBRINOGENEMIA AND DYSFIBRINOGENEMIA   Fibrinogen is a 340,000-dalton dimeric molecule made up of two sets of three covalently linked polypeptide chains. Thrombin sequentially cleaves fibrinopeptides A and B from the α and β chains of fibrinogen to produce fibrin monomer, which then polymerizes to form a fibrin clot. Although fibrinogen is needed for platelet aggregation and fibrin formation, severe fibrinogen deficiency, paradoxically, does not usually cause serious bleeding except after surgery. Patients with afibrinogenemia, who have no detectable fibrinogen in plasma or platelets, may have infrequent, mild spontaneous bleeding episodes. Preliminary genetic analyses do not show any deletion or structural changes in the genes encoding the α, β, and γ chains of fibrinogen despite the total absence of plasma fibrinogen.

Fibrinogen is an abundant plasma protein (250 mg/dL) that has been purified and completely sequenced. Mutations have been identified which alter the release of fibrinopeptides from the α and β chains of fibrinogen, the rate of polymerization of fibrin monomers, and the sites for fibrin cross-linking. These dysfibrinogenemias are almost always inherited as autosomal dominant traits, so that patients have approximately equal concentrations of normal and mutant fibrinogen in their plasma. Patients with dysfibrinogenemia have a slightly prolonged PT and PTT, a prolonged thrombin time, and a disparity between the quantity of fibrinogen measured with functional and immunologic assays. Despite these abnormalities most patients have no symptoms while other patients have moderate bleeding. A

few dysfibrinogenemias induce a hypercoagulable state and increase the risk of thrombosis, and others have been associated with an increased incidence of abortion (see Chap. 281).

FACTOR XIII DEFICIENCY AND DEFECTIVE FIBRIN CROSS-LINKING   Factor XIII is a transglutaminase which stabilizes fibrin clots by forming ε-amino-γ-glutamyl cross-links between adjacent α and γ chains of fibrin. Factor XIII deficiency is an extremely rare inherited syndrome with only a few hundred documented cases. Patients usually bleed in the neonatal period from their umbilical stump or circumcision. In addition to hemorrhage, these patients may have poor wound healing, a high incidence of infertility among males and abortion among affected females, and a high incidence of intracerebral hemorrhage. These observations suggest that the enzyme may be important in other physiologic and pathologic processes beyond hemostasis, including placental implantation, spermatogenesis, and wound healing. Several drugs, including isoniazid, may bind to cross-linking sites on fibrinogen and mimic factor XIII deficiency by blocking enzyme activity. Normal hemostasis requires only 1 percent of normal enzyme activity, which can be achieved with small amounts of fresh frozen plasma.

VITAMIN K DEFICIENCY   Vitamin K is a fat-soluble vitamin which plays a critical role in hemostasis. Dietary vitamin K is absorbed in the small intestine and stored in the liver. The vitamin is also synthesized by endogenous bacterial flora resident in the small intestine and colon; however, there is controversy regarding the quantity of endogenous vitamin K that is absorbed from the large intestine. Following absorption and transport, vitamin K is converted to an active epoxide in liver microsomes and serves as a cofactor in the enzymatic carboxylation of glutamic acid residues on prothrombin complex proteins (Fig. 280-1).

There are three major causes of vitamin K deficiency—inadequate dietary intake, intestinal malabsorption, and loss of storage sites due to hepatocellular disease. Neonatal vitamin K deficiency, which causes hemorrhagic disease of the newborn, has disappeared from western countries with the routine administration of vitamin K to all newborn infants. Although there is, theoretically, a 30-day store of vitamin K in the normal liver, acutely ill patients can become deficient within 7 to 10 days. Acute vitamin K deficiency is particularly common in patients recovering from biliary tract surgery who have no dietary intake of vitamin K, have T-tube drainage of bile, and are on broad-spectrum antibiotics, especially the newer cephalosporins. Vitamin K deficiency is also seen in chronic liver disease, particularly primary biliary cirrhosis, and in some malabsorption states (see Chaps. 237 and 249).

With the onset of vitamin K deficiency, plasma levels of the prothrombin complex proteins (factors II, VII, IX, X; protein C and protein S) decrease. Factor VII, which has the shortest half-life, decreases first. Thus, patients with mild vitamin K deficiency may have a prolonged PT and a normal PTT. Later, as the levels of the other factors fall, the PTT also becomes prolonged. Parenteral administration of 10 mg of vitamin K rapidly restores vitamin K levels in the liver and permits normal production of prothrombin complex proteins with 8 to 10 h. Severe hemorrhage can be treated with fresh frozen plasma, which immediately corrects the hemostatic defect. If the cause of vitamin K deficiency cannot be eliminated, patients may need monthly injections. Purified prothrombin complex concentrates should be avoided as they can cause thrombosis in patients with liver disease and will expose patients to an increased risk of hepatitis.

DISSEMINATED INTRAVASCULAR COAGULATION   Disseminated intravascular coagulation (DIC) may be an explosive and life-threatening bleeding disorder. Although there is a long list of diseases complicated by DIC, it is most frequently associated with obstetrical catastrophes, disseminated malignancy, massive trauma, and bacterial sepsis (Table 280-1). In each case, a tentative triggering mechanism has been identified. For example, tumors and traumatized or necrotic

TABLE 280-1   Etiologic factors and disorders causing disseminated intravascular coagulation

Liberation of tissue factors	Obstetrical syndromes—abruptio placentae, amniotic fluid embolism, retain dead fetus, second trimester abortion
	Hemolysis
	Neoplasms, particularly mucinous adeno-carcinomas, acute promyelocytic leukemia
	Intravascular hemolysis
	Fat embolism
	Tissue damage—burns, frostbite, head injury, gunshot wounds
Endothelial damage	Aortic aneurysm
	Hemolytic uremic syndrome
	Acute glomerulonephritis
	Rocky Mountain spotted fever
Vascular malformation and decreased blood flow	Kasabach-Merritt syndrome
Infections	Bacterial: staphylococci, streptococci pneumococci, meningococci, gram-negative bacilli
	Viral: arboviruses, varicella, variola, rubella
	Parasitic: malaria, kala-azar
	Rickettsial: Rocky Mountain spotted fever
	Mycotic: acute histoplasmosis

SOURCE: *Modified from RI Handin, RD Rosenberg, in Hematology, 4th ed, WS Beck (ed), Cambridge, MA, MIT Press, 1985.*

tissue release materials resembling tissue factor into the circulation, while endotoxin from gram-negative bacteria activates several steps in the coagulation cascade. These potent thrombogenic stimuli cause the deposition of small thrombi and emboli throughout the microvasculature. This early thrombotic phase of DIC is then followed by a phase of secondary fibrinolysis. Continued fibrin formation and fibrinolysis leads to hemorrhage from the depletion of coagulation proteins and platelets and the antihemostatic effects of fibrin degradation products (see Fig. 280-2).

The clinical presentation varies with the stage and severity of the syndrome. Most patients have extensive skin and mucous membrane bleeding and hemorrhage from multiple sites—usually surgical incisions, venipuncture, or catheter sites. Less often, patients present with peripheral acrocyanosis, thrombosis, and pregangrenous changes in digits, genitalia, and nose—areas where blood flow is markedly reduced by vasospasm or microthrombi. Occasional patients, particularly those with chronic DIC secondary to malignancy, have laboratory abnormalities without any evidence of thrombosis or hemorrhage.

The laboratory manifestations include thrombocytopenia and the presence of schistocytes or fragmented red blood cells which arise from cell trapping and damage within fibrin thrombi; prolonged PT, PTT, and thrombin time and a reduced fibrinogen level from depletion of coagulation proteins; and elevated fibrin degradation products (FDPs) from intense secondary fibrinolysis. The cardinal manifestation of DIC, which correlates most closely with bleeding, is the plasma fibrinogen level.

Treatment DIC can cause life-threatening hemorrhage and requires prompt treatment. This should include (1) an attempt to correct any reversible cause of DIC; (2) measures to control the major symptom, either bleeding or thrombosis, and (3) a prophylactic regimen to prevent recurrence in cases of chronic DIC. Treatment will vary with the clinical presentation. In patients with an obstetric complication like abruptio placentae or acute bacterial sepsis, the underlying disorder is easy to correct, and prompt delivery of the fetus and placenta or treatment with appropriate antibiotics will reverse the DIC syndrome. In patients with a metastatic tumor causing DIC, control of the primary disease may not be possible and long-term prophylaxis may be necessary.

Patients with bleeding as a major symptom should receive fresh frozen plasma and cryoprecipitate to replace depleted clotting factors and platelet concentrates to correct thrombocytopenia. Those with acrocyanosis and incipient gangrene or thrombosis need immediate anticoagulation with intravenous heparin. The use of heparin in the treatment of bleeding is still controversial, although it is a logical way to reduce thrombin generation and prevent further consumption of clotting proteins. It should be reserved for patients with thrombosis or those rare patients who continue to bleed despite vigorous treatment with plasma and platelets.

Patients with mild DIC, who may not be symptomatic, may begin to bleed following stresses such as surgery or chemotherapy. For example, mild DIC, without clinical bleeding, can be documented during saline- or prostaglandin-induced midtrimester abortions. Prophylactic treatment of patients with heparin may prevent progression of the DIC syndrome and has been used in the treatment of patients with acute promyelocytic leukemia and in some patients with a retained dead fetus who require surgical extraction. Chronic DIC does not respond to oral warfarin anticoagulants, but it can be controlled with long-term heparin infusion. Occasional patients with indolent tumors and severe DIC have been maintained on heparin administered by intermittent subcutaneous injection or continuous infusion with portable pumps.

Despite our detailed understanding of the pathophysiology of DIC and a vigorous approach to therapy, there is little evidence that its treatment will change the natural history of the underlying disorder. Therapy will only stabilize the patient, prevent exsanguination or massive thrombosis, and permit institution of definitive therapy.

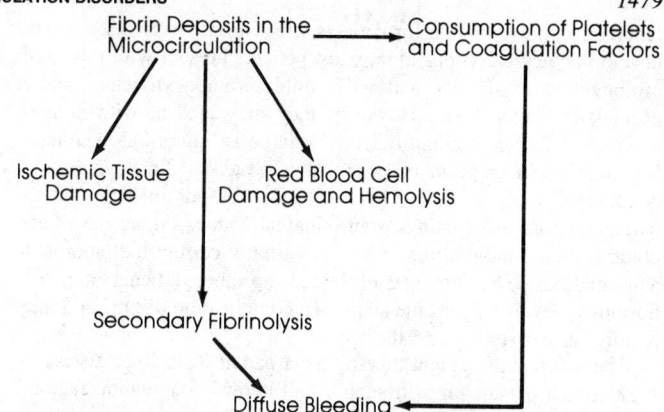

FIGURE 280-2 *The pathophysiology of disseminated intravascular coagulation (DIC). Shown are the interactions between coagulation and fibrinolytic pathways which result in bleeding in patients with DIC.*

COAGULATION DISORDERS IN LIVER DISEASE Since the liver plays a central role in the synthesis and metabolism of coagulation proteins, liver dysfunction is frequently accompanied by a hemostatic defect. The major causes of hemorrhage in patients with liver disease are outlined in Table 280-2. It is important to recognize that bleeding is usually due to an anatomic lesion, which is then exacerbated by the hemostatic defect. Most patients bleed from complications of portal hypertension such as esophageal varices, or from gastritis and peptic ulceration of the gastrointestinal tract. Portal hypertension also causes splenomegaly, with splenic sequestration of platelets and thrombocytopenia, which contributes to the hemostatic defect (see Chap. 249).

Patients with hepatocellular liver disease cannot store vitamin K optimally and may have some degree of vitamin K deficiency. Cholestasis, which is a frequent feature of liver disease, impairs vitamin K absorption and further decreases liver vitamin K stores. Patients also may have decreased production of other coagulation proteins including fibrinogen and factor V. The liver also produces inhibitors of coagulation such as antithrombin III, proteins C and S and is the clearance site for activated coagulation factors and fibrinolytic enzymes. Thus, patients with liver disease are both "hypercoagulable" and predisposed to developing DIC and may develop systemic fibrinolysis. For these reasons coagulation defects in advanced liver failure are often difficult to distinguish from those of DIC.

Each patient with hemorrhage and liver disease should have a PT, PTT, platelet count, and fibrinogen determination, although it is not always possible to determine the major hemostatic abnormality from a single set of laboratory values. It is helpful to have previous

TABLE 280-2 Causes of bleeding in liver disease

I Anatomic factors
  A Portal hypertension
    1 Varices
    2 Splenomegaly and secondary thrombocytopenia
  B Peptic ulceration
  C Gastritis
II Hepatic function abnormalities
  A Decreased synthesis of procoagulant systems: fibrinogen, prothrombin, factors V, VII, IX, X, XI
  B Decreased synthesis of coagulation inhibitors: protein C, protein S, antithrombin III
  C Impaired absorption and metabolism of vitamin K
  D Failure to clear activated coagulation proteins leading to
    1 Disseminated intravascular coagulation
    2 Systemic fibrinolysis
III Complications of therapy
  A Dilution of platelets and coagulation proteins from massive transfusions
  B Infusion of activated coagulation proteins in prothrombin complex concentrates
  C Bleeding from heparin; thrombosis from ϵ-aminocaproic acid (EACA)

laboratory data available for patients with chronic liver disease who develop an acute complication. Most patients present with moderate prolongation of the PT and PTT, mild thrombocytopenia, and a normal fibrinogen level. However, they may present with a more complex defect combining defective synthesis, abnormal clearance, and active consumption of coagulation proteins. Since vitamin K deficiency is so common, it is advisable to administer a single parenteral dose of vitamin K after initial laboratory studies have been obtained, even though this may only partially correct the laboratory abnormalities. The presence of severe thrombocytopenia or a low fibrinogen level suggests the additional complication of DIC and may require further studies and therapy.

The safest replacement therapy for a patient with liver disease is fresh frozen plasma since it supplies all known coagulation factors. However, even this form of therapy has drawbacks since large quantities of plasma may precipitate hepatic encephalopathy and cause fluid and sodium overload. Prothrombin complex concentrates should be avoided since they only replace the vitamin K–dependent factors, may be contaminated with hepatitis and AIDS virus, and contain trace quantities of activated coagulation proteins. Similarly, fibrinogen concentrates or cryoprecipitate, which are rich in factor VIII and fibrinogen should not be used without additional fresh frozen plasma. Anticoagulation with heparin has been advocated to control DIC, but this is particularly hazardous and not recommended in cirrhosis since heparin is metabolized erratically and may thus lead to severe bleeding.

FIBRINOLYTIC DEFECTS Bleeding can also occur from defects in the fibrinolytic system. Patients with alpha$_2$ plasmin inhibitor deficiency have excess fibrinolysis when it is triggered by fibrin deposition after trauma or surgery and so may experience recurrent hemorrhage. Patients with cirrhosis have an impaired clearance of tissue plasminogen activator and systemic fibrinolysis which may contribute to their hemorrhagic defect. Rarely, patients with tumors such as metastatic prostatic carcinoma may develop diffuse bleeding from primary fibrinolysis rather than DIC. Clues to the diagnosis include a disproportionately low fibrinogen with a relatively normal PT and PTT and the presence of a normal or nearly normal platelet count. However, at times it is difficult or impossible to differentiate primary fibrinolysis from the secondary fibrinolysis accompanying DIC. Patients with clearly established primary fibrinolysis should not receive heparin; they do require plasma therapy and, occasionally, fibrinolytic inhibitors like EACA. However, EACA should not be given to patients suspected of having DIC unless they are also receiving heparin, since EACA can cause massive, often fatal, thrombosis in a patient with DIC.

CIRCULATING ANTICOAGULANTS Circulating anticoagulants, or inhibitors, are usually IgG antibodies which interfere with coagulation reactions. Specific inhibitors inactivate individual coagulation proteins and may cause severe hemorrhage. As discussed above, they arise in 15 to 20 percent of patients with factor VIII or IX deficiency who have received plasma infusions. Specific inhibitors also occur in previously normal individuals. Although the most common target protein is factor VIII, inhibitors have been described with a specificity for each of the coagulation proteins. Anti-factor VIII antibodies in nonhemophiliacs are seen in postpartum females, in patients on various drugs, as part of the spectrum of autoantibodies in systemic lupus erythematosus patients, and in normal elderly individuals. *Nonspecific* (lupuslike) inhibitors prolong coagulation tests by binding to phospholipids; they do not perturb hemostasis in vivo, unless associated with thrombocytopenia or prothrombin deficiency. While they are most often encountered in patients with systemic lupus erythematosus, nonspecific inhibitors have also been noted in patients with many other disorders and also in otherwise normal individuals.

The critical laboratory feature, which identifies the presence of either type of inhibitor, is the failure of normal plasma to correct a prolonged PT, PTT, or both. Plasma from patients with a specific inhibitor will progressively inactivate a coagulation protein and thus prolong whichever of these screening tests require the participation of that clotting factor. This effect persists after dilution. Nonspecific inhibitors immediately prolong the PT and PTT and, at low dilution, block multiple coagulation reactions. However, these effects can be overcome by altering the quantity or type of phospholipid or by diluting the plasma.

Hemorrhage in patients with specific inhibitors may require treatment with massive plasma or concentrate infusion, the use of activated prothrombin complex concentrates to bypass the antibodies against factors VIII or IX, and plasmapheresis or exchange transfusion to lower antibody titer. Chronic immunosuppressive regimens have been sometimes employed, and have been particularly useful in otherwise normal elderly individuals with an acquired factor VIII antibody. Many patients lose their antibody and recover within 6 to 12 months, although the acute mortality rate from uncontrollable bleeding may approach 10 percent. Patients with nonspecific anticoagulants have normal hemostasis and do not require any therapy, unless they are concomitantly thrombocytopenic or prothrombin deficient. There is some evidence that nonspecific anticoagulants may also predispose patients to thrombosis and are associated with habitual abortions in some women.

REFERENCES

GIDDINGS JC, PEAKE IR: Laboratory support in the diagnosis of coagulation disorders. Clin Haematol 14:571, 1985

KASPER CK, DIETRICH SL: Comprehensive management of haemophilia. Clin Haematol 14:489, 1985

LAWN R: The molecular genetics of hemophilia. Sci Am 254:48, 1986

MAMMEN E: Congenital coagulation disorders. Semin Thromb Hemost 9:1, 1983

SHAPIRO SS, TIAGARAJAN P: Lupus anticoagulants. Prog Hemost Thromb 6:263, 1982

WHITE GC II et al: Factor VIII inhibitors: A clinical overview. Am J Hematol 13:335, 1982

281 INHERITED THROMBOTIC DISORDERS AND ANTITHROMBOTIC THERAPY

ROBERT I. HANDIN

Venous and arterial thrombosis and embolism are common medical disorders which have been recognized for over 100 years. Although risk factors such as atherosclerotic vascular disease, congestive heart failure, malignancy, and immobility predispose patients to thrombosis, specific coagulation defects have not yet been identified in most patients with thromboembolism. Several inherited deficiencies of coagulation inhibitors or abnormalities of coagulation proteins have now been described which induce a hypercoagulable or prethrombotic state and predispose patients to thrombosis. These disorders merit special attention since they affect young people, cause recurrent episodes of thromboembolism, and may involve multiple members of a single family. An understanding of the biochemical basis of thromboembolism is also important, since anticoagulant and antithrombotic regimes are based on the premise that modifying critical coagulation reactions will reduce the incidence of thrombosis. This chapter reviews both the inherited prethrombotic disorders and the use and complications of anticoagulant and antithrombotic therapy.

INHERITED PRETHROMBOTIC DISORDERS As previously discussed (see Chap. 54), coagulation is carefully regulated by a series of inhibitors which limit thrombin generation and fibrin formation and by the fibrinolytic system which effectively removes fibrin thrombi (see Figs. 54-5 and 54-7). Inherited defects of the natural coagulation inhibitors (i.e., antithrombin, protein C, and protein S), abnormalities in the fibrinolytic system, and certain dysfibrinogenemias predispose patients to thrombosis (see Table 281-1). Although they are an important and rapidly expanding group of disorders, they account for less than 10 percent of patients with recurrent thromboembolism. The known disorders are all inherited as autosomal dominant traits, so that heterozygous individuals, who have a 50 percent reduction in protein concentration or a mixture of mutant and normal molecules, will have an increased risk of thrombosis. These patients all have similar clinical presentations with a strong family history of thrombosis, episodes of recurrent venous thromboembolism, and symptoms by their early twenties. Any patient with this distinctive history should be tested for the molecular abnormalities described below.

ANTITHROMBIN DEFICIENCY Antithrombin III complexes with activated coagulation proteins and blocks their biologic activity (see Fig. 54-5). The rate of this reaction is enhanced by heparin-like molecules within the vessel wall or on endothelial cells. Plasma antithrombin III content varies from 5 to 15 µg/mL (50 to 150 percent), with values only slightly below normal increasing the risk of thrombosis. For optimal screening, it is important to assess both the antithrombin III concentration by immunoassay and the plasma antithrombin and heparin cofactor activity with functional assays. The most common defect is mild (heterozygous) antithrombin deficiency, which occurs in 1 out of 2000 individuals. In addition, dysfunctional antithrombin molecules, with mutations affecting either the serine protease–binding site or the heparin-binding site, or activation of inhibitor by heparin have been described. Some investigators have suggested that another molecule called heparin cofactor II may also be a clinically important thrombin inhibitor. In fact, some patients have been described who are heparin cofactor II–deficient.

Patients with antithrombin deficiency who develop acute thrombosis or embolism can be treated with intravenous heparin, since there is usually sufficient normal antithrombin to act as a heparin cofactor. Following their first episode of thromboembolism, patients should be placed on oral anticoagulants for life to prevent recurrent thrombosis. Family studies should be conducted when an antithrombin-deficient individual is discovered, since up to one-half the members of a kindred group may be affected. Asymptomatic individuals with antithrombin deficiency should receive prophylactic anticoagulation with heparin or plasma infusions to raise their antithrombin level prior to medical or surgical procedures which may increase their risk of thrombosis. Chronic oral anticoagulation is not recommended until patients have a clinical thrombotic episode.

DEFICIENCIES OF PROTEINS C AND S Protein C is a vitamin K–dependent hepatic protein which binds to the endothelial cell surface protein thrombomodulin and is converted to an active protease by thrombin (Fig. 54-5). Activated protein C, in conjunction with protein S, proteolyzes factors Va and VIIIa, which shuts off fibrin formation. Activated protein C may also stimulate fibrinolysis and accelerate clot lysis. Deficiencies of proteins C and S are autosomal dominant disorders which may be more common than antithrombin deficiency and may cause identical problems—recurrent venous thrombosis and pulmonary embolism. No dysfunctional molecules have as yet been definitely identified in patients with thrombosis. However, protein S activity may be reduced when there is an excess of C4b binding protein.

Heterozygous patients with acute thrombosis and moderate protein C or S deficiency should be heparinized and then placed on oral anticoagulants. There are, however, two potential problems with the use of coumarin anticoagulants in these patients. First, these vitamin K antagonists (see Fig. 280-1 and Fig. 54-5), which lower the level of the procoagulant factors II, VII, IX, and X, may also reduce the concentration of proteins C and S and nullify the described antithrombotic effect. In addition, there are patients with coumarin-induced skin necrosis who have protein C deficiency, suggesting that this defect may predispose patients to a rare but serious complication of oral anticoagulants.

Homozygous protein C deficiency, which is very rare, can cause

TABLE 281-1 Inherited prethrombotic disorders

Antithrombin III deficiency and dysfunction
Protein C deficiency
Protein S deficiency
Dysplasminogenemia
Dysfibrinogenemia
Defective release of plasminogen activator
Diminished venous content of plasminogen activator
Heparin cofactor II deficiency

fulminant intravascular coagulation in the neonatal period. Patients with homozygous protein C deficiency may require periodic plasma infusions rather than oral anticoagulants to prevent recurrent intravascular coagulation and thrombosis.

DYSFIBRINOGENEMIAS AND FIBRINOLYTIC DEFECTS Several families have been described with recurrent venous thrombosis and embolism due to defects in fibrinogen or plasminogen or with decreased synthesis or release of tissue plasminogen activator. While the majority of dysfibrinogenemias cause bleeding, one variant, fibrinogen New York, is characterized by excessively rapid release of fibrinopeptides and recurrent thromboembolism. Patients with this disorder as well as those with an abnormal plasminogen which resists activation by streptokinase and urokinase have been successfully treated with heparin and oral anticoagulants. Defects in tissue plasminogen activator content or release have not been completely characterized. One group of patients with recurrent venous thrombosis and embolism failed to increase venous blood fibrinolytic activity when challenged with local ischemia or physical exercise. The other group had impaired fibrinolytic activity in extracts prepared from biopsied veins. The recent cloning of cDNA for tissue plasminogen activator (TPA) and the availability of immunoassays for TPA should facilitate more detailed studies of this class of defects.

ANTICOAGULANT AND FIBRINOLYTIC THERAPY Anticoagulation with heparin, followed by treatment with oral vitamin K antagonists, has become the standard treatment for acute venous thrombosis and pulmonary embolism. In addition, chronic oral anticoagulation is used to prevent cerebral arterial embolism from cardiac sources such as mural thrombi, atrial thrombi, a stenotic mitral valve, or from an atherosclerotic, partially stenosed carotid or vertebral artery. Anticoagulants are also used, but less successfully, to treat peripheral or mesenteric arterial thrombosis. These agents retard fibrin deposition on established thrombi and prevent the formation of new thrombi. The induction of a fibrinolytic state by the infusion of recombinant TPA or pharmacologic agents such as streptokinase (SK) and urokinase (UK) has become an accepted mode of therapy for some thromboembolic disorders. This approach has been advocated for some patients with massive pulmonary embolism and circulatory instability and to restore the patency of acutely occluded peripheral and coronary arteries.

ACUTE ANTICOAGULATION WITH HEPARIN Heparin is a naturally occurring mucopolysaccharide polymer which has tetrasaccharide sequences that bind to and activate antithrombin III. It is an extremely potent anticoagulant which can dramatically reduce thrombin generation and fibrin formation in patients with acute venous and arterial thrombosis or embolism. Heparin is usually administered by continuous intravenous infusion at a rate sufficient to raise the partial thromboplastin time (PTT) to 1.5 to 2 times the control value. This usually requires 1000 U.S.P. units per hour and is continued for 7 to 10 days while patients are begun on oral anticoagulants. Alternatives include the administration of 5000 U.S.P. units four times a day either subcutaneously or intravenously. Long-term heparin administration via portable external or implantable pumps is occasionally needed for patients with recurrent thromboembolism that is refractory to oral anticoagulants, for pregnant women with thromboembolism, and for patients with chronic disseminated intravascular coagulation (DIC). Lower doses of heparin (5000 units every 12 h) have also been used to prevent deep venous thrombosis in high-risk surgical and medical patients.

The major complication of heparin therapy is bleeding—especially from surgical sites and into the retroperitoneum. It is important to avoid aspirin or aspirin-containing drugs, which impair platelet function, and to avoid intramuscular injections in these patients. Heparin's anticoagulant effect can be rapidly reversed by the administration of protamine sulfate. However, in most cases this is not necessary and reduction or omission of heparin will improve hemostasis and stop bleeding. Thrombocytopenia occurs in about 10 percent of heparin recipients; it can occasionally be very severe and be accompanied by intravascular platelet agglutination and arterial thrombosis. Recognition of this rare complication—thrombocytopenia and paradoxical thrombosis—is critical, since discontinuing heparin can reverse the syndrome and may be lifesaving. Heparin administration for longer than 2 months carries a risk of osteoporosis and osteomalacia.

CHRONIC ORAL ANTICOAGULATION The coumarin group of anticoagulants, which includes drugs like warfarin and dicumarol, prevents the reduction of vitamin K epoxides in the liver microsomes and induces a state analogous to vitamin K deficiency (see Fig. 280-1). They slow thrombin generation and clot formation by impairing the biologic activity of the prothrombin complex proteins and are frequently used to prevent the recurrence of venous thrombosis and pulmonary embolism. Although regimens employing loading doses of drug have been advocated, the simplest way to induce anticoagulation is to administer a single dose of a coumarin compound and monitor the prothrombin time (PT) until the desired prolongation is achieved. For example, treatment can be initiated with 5 to 10 mg per day of warfarin or equivalent, with the goal of prolonging the PT to 1.5 to 2 times the control value. Although the PT may reach this value after a few days of therapy, effective anticoagulation, with stable reduction of all the prothrombin complex proteins, requires at least 1 week of coumarin administration. Most patients require a daily maintainence dose of 2.5 to 7.5 mg of warfarin to remain anticoagulated.

Although warfarin anticoagulants reduce the recurrence of deep venous thrombosis and pulmonary or cerebral embolism, they also cause bleeding. Any patient who takes oral anticoagulants requires frequent monitoring of the PT. Despite the most careful management, frequent fluctuations in PT can occur. Various drugs which alter liver microsomal metabolism of coumarins or compete for albumin binding sites can increase or decrease the biologic potency of a given warfarin dose (Table 281-2).

TABLE 281-2 Effect of drugs and metabolic changes on oral anticoagulant potency

I Factors leading to enhanced potency and increased prothrombin time
  A Reduced coumarin clearance
    1 Disulfiram (Antabuse)
    2 Metronidazole (Flagyl)
    3 Trimethoprim-sulfamethoxazole (Bactrim, Septra)
  B Reduced albumin binding
    1 Phenylbutazone
  C Additive hemostatic effect of certain drugs or disorders
    1 Aspirin
    2 Heparin
    3 Liver disease
    4 Thrombocytopenia
    5 Vitamin K deficiency
  D Increased turnover of vitamin K
    1 Clofibrate
    2 Hypermetabolism (e.g., hyperthyroidism)
II Factors leading to diminished potency and decreased prothrombin time
  A Accelerated coumarin clearance—induction of hepatic metabolizing enzymes
    1 Barbiturates
    2 Rifampin
  B Reduced absorption
    1 Cholestyramine
  C Impaired metabolism
    1 Genetic coumarin resistance

There is a direct relationship between the duration of anticoagulation and the risk of recurrent thrombosis. Although recommendations vary somewhat, most patients with a single uncomplicated thromboembolic event will have derived maximal benefit after 3 to 6 months of anticoagulation. It is estimated that 10 percent of patients on an oral anticoagulant for 1 year will have a serious complication requiring medical supervision, and 0.5 to 1 percent may have a fatal hemorrhagic event despite the most careful medical management. The anticoagulant effect of coumarins can be reversed by infusion of fresh frozen plasma or by the administration of vitamin K. In many cases, reduction or omission of several doses will improve hemostasis and stop hemorrhage. Despite the risk of bleeding, many patients with prosthetic heart valves, tight mitral stenosis, cardiomyopathy, chronic congestive heart failure, recurrent atrial fibrillation or with an inherited prethrombotic disorder will require lifelong anticoagulation.

One devastating complication of oral anticoagulation is hemorrhagic skin necrosis which in the past was thought to represent an allergic reaction. As previously discussed, several studies have found that patients with this complication are deficient in protein C, which may be the predisposing factor. There are some patients who have an inherited trait associated with coumarin resistance; they may require extemely high doses to get an anticoagulant effect. Psychologically disturbed patients may surreptitiously ingest coumarin and present with unexplained bleeding and a prolonged PT. Plasma coumarin levels can be measured by a quantitative spectrofluorometric assay to confirm such ingestion.

FIBRINOLYTIC THERAPY Fibrinolysis, an important part of the hemostatic process, is initiated by the release of TPA from endothelial cells. TPA preferentially activates plasminogen when it is adsorbed to fibrin clots; this helps to localize the lytic process to sites containing fibrin thrombi. Although fibrinolysis begins immediately after vascular injury, clot lysis and vessel recanalization may not be complete for 7 to 10 days. As previously discussed, this pathway is important for normal hemostasis since defects in the fibrinolytic pathway can predispose patients either to hemorrhage or to recurrent thrombosis. In addition, pharmacologic activators like SK and UK are used to accelerate clot lysis in patients with massive pulmonary embolism, acute arterial and coronary thrombosis, and peripheral venous thrombosis.

SK is a bacterial enzyme, and UK is a product of renal tubular epithelial cells. In contrast to TPA, these agents cannot discriminate between free and fibrin-bound plasminogen; when they are used for localized clot lysis, they produce hypofibrinogemenia and a systemic lytic state. SK is an indirect activator which forms an equimolar complex with plasminogen. Following the binding of SK, plasminogen develops proteolytic activity which activates additional plasminogen molecules and intiates fibrinolysis. In contrast, UK (like TPA) has intrinsic proteolytic activity and can directly convert plasminogen to plasmin. The major complication of fibrinolytic therapy is hemorrhage due to severe hypofibrinogenemia and intense systemic fibrinolysis. Such lytic therapy is not recommended for patients with recent surgery, indwelling cannulas or a history of neurologic lesions or gastrointestinal bleeding.

Fibrinolytic therapy is recommended for patients with massive pulmonary emboli complicated by hypotension, severe hypoxemia, and strain of the right side of the heart. In addition, fibrinolytic agents have been successfully administered to patients with acute peripheral arterial embolism and to patients with extensive iliofemoral thrombophlebitis. In the case of SK, one usually administers a total loading dose of 250,000 units; with UK one gives a loading dose of 4400 units per kilogram of body weight over 10 to 30 min. This will induce an intense lytic state as evidenced by a drop in fibrinogen, a prolongation of the thrombin time, and a prolongation of the euglobulin lysis time—a measure of fibrinolytic activity, predominantly the presence of plasminogen activator activity. After the initial loading dose, hourly doses of 100,000 units of SK or 4400 units of UK per kilogram of body weight are continued for 24 to 72 h. At the desired time, the lytic state is reversed by discontinuing UK or SK, and heparinizing the patient for 7 to 10 days. Heparin can be started 6 h after the fibrinolytic agent has been stopped. To maximize the likelihood of success, fibrinolytic therapy should be initiated as soon as possible after the onset of thrombosis or embolism.

Fibrinolytic therapy is also gaining favor among cardiologists since there is evidence that prompt institution of intracoronary lytic therapy with broad-spectrum agents such as SK or UK or systemic administration of a fibrin-specific agent like TPA may restore coronary arterial patency and reduce myocardial damage following acute coronary occlusion. It has been suggested that TPA, which is now produced by recombinant DNA techniques, may be a more useful pharmacologic agent than SK or UK since, in theory, it should lyse fibrin clots without causing systemic fibrinolysis and bleeding. As more experience is gained with TPA, it is apparent that some systemic lysis occurs with doses needed to lyse localized thrombi. In addition, TPA cannot discriminate between pathologic (and therefore undesirable) thrombi and vitally important hemostatic plugs, since both contain fibrin and may coexist in the same patient. Until more definitive results are obtained, TPA should be considered an important but experimental form of fibrinolytic therapy.

REFERENCES

CLOUSE LJ, COMP PC: The regulation of hemostasis: The protein C system. N Engl J Med 314:1298, 1986

HIRSH J: Effectiveness of anticoagulants. Semin Thromb Hemost 12:21, 1986

LAFFEL GL, BRAUNWALD E: Thrombolytic therapy: A new strategy for the treatment of acute myocardial infarction. N Engl J Med 311:710, 770, 1984

LEVINE MN, HIRSH J: Hemorrhagic complications of anticoagulant therapy. Semin Thromb Hemost 12L:39, 1986

ROSENBERG RD, ROSENBERG JS: Natural anticoagulant mechanisms. J Clin Invest 74:1, 1984

SCHAFER AI: The hypercoagulable states. Ann Int Med 102:814, 1985

AMERICAN COLLEGE OF PHYSICIANS, Health and Public Policy Committee: Thrombolysis for evolving myocardial infarction. Ann Int Med 103:463, 1985

WINTER JH et al: Familial antithrombin III deficiency. Q J Med 51:373, 1982

282 BLOOD GROUPS AND BLOOD TRANSFUSION

ELOISE R. GIBLETT

BLOOD GROUP ANTIGENS AND ANTIBODIES

INTRODUCTION Human red blood cell membranes contain over 300 different antigenic determinants, the molecular structure of which is dictated by genes at an unknown number of chromosomal loci. The term *blood group* is applied to any well-defined system of red blood cell antigens controlled by a locus having a variable number of allelic genes, such as *A*, *B*, and *O* in the ABO system. Twenty-one blood group systems are currently recognized. The term *blood type* refers to the antigen phenotype, which is the serologic expression of the inherited blood group genes.

Alloantibodies specific for the blood group antigens may occur "naturally" (i.e., in the absence of known stimulus by foreign red blood cells) or in response to transfusion or pregnancy. Naturally occurring antibodies tend to be IgM molecules, and many of them (notably excepting anti-A and anti-B) react poorly at body temperature but readily agglutinate red blood cells at 5 to 20°C. Antibodies formed in response to exposure to another person's red blood cells or soluble blood group substances initially belong to the IgM class but usually change to the IgG class within a few weeks or months. In general, these "immune" antibodies react best at body temperature, and special laboratory procedures are required for their detection.

BLOOD GROUP SYSTEMS ABO system: Genes and antigens

There are four major allelic genes in this system: A^1, A^2, B, and O. The locus for these alleles is on the long arm of chromosome 9. The actual products of the first three genes are glycosyltransferases which select specific sugars, N-acetyl-D-galactosamine (GalNAc) by the A^1 and A^2 transferases and D-galactose (Gal) by the B transferase, attaching them by alpha-linkage to short (oligo) saccharide chains. These chains comprise the carbohydrate moiety of glycolipid and glycoprotein molecules on the red blood cells or in other tissues and fluids. Although the A^1 and A^2 transferases perform the same function, they have different rate constants, so people who inherit an A^1 gene have more A-reactive sites than those with an A^2 gene. The O gene product is a protein which cross-reacts immunologically with the A and B transferase molecules but has no detectable enzyme activity; thus it is functionally "silent."

Nearly all individuals produce "naturally occurring" antibodies against the A or B antigens not present on their own red blood cells, as shown in Table 282-1. This fact is used as the basis for confirming the red blood cell type. Most of the major phenotypes represent more than one genotype. In the absence of family studies, it is possible to infer the genotype from only three phenotypes: A_1B, A_2B, and O. In routine practice, the ABO type is determined by testing the red blood cells with anti-A and anti-B and by testing the serum against A, B, and O red blood cells. Under special circumstances, a further distinction between A and AB types is made by using anti-A_1, an antiserum prepared by absorbing anti-A typing serum with A_2 red blood cells. The remaining unabsorbed antibodies have A_1 specificity, reacting with A_1 and A_1B, but not with A_2 and A_2B cells. (Alternatively, anti-A_1 is prepared as a lectin from extracts of certain seeds.) The frequencies of the various phenotypes in two American blood donor populations are also given in Table 282-1.

Red blood cells of types O and A_2 have large amounts of another antigen, called H, which is the immediate precursor to A and B. H specificity depends on the presence of a fucose (Fuc) residue attached to the oligosaccharides by a transferase that is the product of a very common gene called H. (The H and ABO loci are not genetically linked.) In very rare individuals who fail to inherit an H gene from either parent (i.e., they are homozygous for its allele, h), the H transferase is not made, and the H-determining fucose is not attached. This prevents the addition of specific sugars by the A and B transferases. As a result, even if an A or B gene has been inherited, the red blood cells are not agglutinated by anti-A, anti-B, or anti-H, while the serum contains all three antibodies. When a patient requiring transfusion has this so-called O_h (or Bombay) phenotype, special arrangements are necessary to obtain blood of the same rare type from a source such as the Red Cross.

About 80 percent of people are either homozygous or heterozygous for the "secretor," or Se, gene, which has no effect on the formation of antigens intrinsic to red blood cells but which activates the H gene to produce its fucosyltransferase in secretory tissues. Homozygotes for the apparently inactive allele se are called *nonsecretors* because their secretory cells do not produce a very weakly reactive H transferase, so their body fluids virtually lack H, A, and B antigen activities.

Antibodies in ABO system Red blood cells of newborn infants have a decreased number of H, A, and B reactive sites, and their plasma normally contains very little anti-A or anti-B. This finding is due to the fact that fetal immunoglobulin production is minimal, while most of the anti-A and anti-B produced in the mother are IgM molecules which cannot cross the placenta. However, in some type O adults, the anti-A, anti-B, and anti-AB (a cross-reacting antibody sometimes called anti-C) are of the IgG class. For this reason, ABO hemolytic disease of the newborn usually occurs in A (or B) infants of O mothers.

It is not acceptable medical practice to transfuse A, B, or AB blood into patients whose red blood cells lack the corresponding antigens, since their plasma contains incompatible antibodies. However, it is acceptable to give A or B blood (preferably as packed red

TABLE 282-1 Blood types of the ABO system (including Hh)

Genotype*	Phenotype	Antigens on red blood cells†	Antibodies in serum‡	Phenotype frequencies in Americans, %	
				Western European descent	African descent
A^1A^1 A^1A^2 A^1O }	A_1	A_1, (H)	Anti-B (anti-H)	35	23
A^2A^2 A^2O }	A_2	A_2, H	Anti-B (anti-A_1)	10	6
BB BO }	B	B, (H)	Anti-A, -A_1	8	17
A^1B	A_1B	A, A_1, B	(Anti-H)	3	3
A^2B	A_2B	A, B, H	(Anti-A_1)	1	1
OO	O	H	Anti-A, -A_1 Anti-B	43	50
hh	O_h	None	Anti-A, -A_1 Anti-B Anti-H	Very rare	Very rare

* In all types except the last, the H allele is present as HH or Hh.
† (H) indicates occasional presence of weakly reacting H antigen.
‡ Antibodies in parentheses are, if present, weak cold agglutinins.
SOURCE: Race and Sanger.

blood cells) to AB recipients, or to give O packed red blood cells (*not* whole blood, except in severe emergencies) to patients of type A, B, or AB when the transfusion requirement exceeds the supply of type-specific blood. Although antibodies with A_1 specificity frequently occur in the plasma of A_2 and A_2B subjects, they are almost always weak cold agglutinins. Therefore, if anti-A_1 has been identified in a transfusion patient, it can be ignored unless it reacts in vitro with A_1 red blood cells at 37°C.

Lewis system Antigens in the Lewis system are not produced by red blood cells but are taken up as glycosphingolipid molecules from the surrounding plasma. About 80 percent of western Europeans are either homozygous or heterozygous for the *Le* gene. The other 20 percent are homozygous for its presumably inactive allele, *le*. There are two well-defined Lewis antigenic determinants, Le^a and Le^b, both of which are structurally related to the H, A, and B antigens. The *Le* gene product, like the *H* gene product, is a fucosyltransferase, but it attaches fucose to a different sugar (N-acetyl-D-glucosamine instead of D-galactose) in the oligosaccharide chains. The Le^a determinant is a monofucosyl structure which lacks the fucose attached by the *H* transferase. The Le^b determinant has two fucose residues placed there by the *H* and *Le* transferases, in that order.

Anti-Le^a and anti-Le^b are fairly common naturally occurring antibodies, produced mainly by subjects of phenotype O, Le(a − b −). Nearly all examples of these antibodies are of the IgM class, so they rarely, if ever, can cross the placenta during pregnancy. Were they to do so, destruction of the infant's red blood cells would be highly unlikely, since the Lewis glycosphingolipids are very poorly developed during fetal life.

Lewis antibodies (particularly anti-Le^a) are complement-binders; anti-Le^a is rarely the cause of a transfusion reaction with intravascular hemolysis. However, the plasma of Le(a +) donors usually contains enough soluble Le^a antigen to neutralize the patient's anti-Le^a before it can attack the vulnerable red blood cells. Nevertheless, patients whose plasma contains an anti-Le^a that strongly hemolyzes Le(a +) red blood cells or agglutinates them at temperatures above 30°C should be given blood from either Le(a − b +) or Le(a − b −) donors. Anti-Le^b is virtually never a transfusion hazard.

P system Several structurally related antigens are considered together under the heading of a single system called P. As in the ABO and Lewis systems, the gene products are glycosyltransferases, attaching either D-galactose, N-acetyl-D-galactosamine, or N-acetyl-D-glucosamine to glycosphingolipids on the red blood cell membrane. P_1 and P, the major antigenic determinants, were previously thought to represent the expression of two allelic genes at the same locus, analogous to A^1 and A^2 in the ABO system. However, these two antigens represent quite different sugar sequences, and the genetic interpretation is complex.

Anti-P_1, which occurs frequently, almost never causes red blood cell destruction—the exceptions being those rare examples which react strongly with P_1 red blood cells in vitro at 37°C. In patients with paroxysmal cold hemoglobinuria, the so-called Donath-Landsteiner autoantibodies frequently react with globoside, a very common red blood cell glycosphingolipid with P specificity.

I system The I and i antigenic determinants are structurally heterogeneous, biochemically related to the H, A, B, Le, and P antigens. Most people inherit a gene associated with I antigen production, but the red blood cells of newborn infants react very weakly with anti-I and strongly with anti-i. A gradual reversal occurs during the first year or two, representing the development of I antigen in association with branching of carbohydrate chains on the cell membrane. In patients with certain kinds of "marrow stress," particularly thalassemia and hypoplastic anemia, red blood cell I activity increases.

Anti-I is a common antibody, frequently found as a weak cold agglutinin of no clinical concern. In patients with the cold type of autoimmune hemolytic anemia, autoantibodies usually have anti-I or anti-I plus i specificity, and most of them belong to the IgM class (see Chap. 287). Anti-i production is associated mainly with lymphoid cell diseases, especially infectious mononucleosis and lymphosarcoma. A patient already having a "marrow-stressing" disorder such as thalassemia may develop an intense autoimmune hemolytic anemia due to anti-i. When transfusions are required, finding compatible blood poses no problem, since the red blood cells of most adults are i-negative. Even patients with strong cold-reacting anti-I antibodies are usually not difficult to transfuse safely if they are kept warm during the infusion. However, since anti-I often fixes complement, washed red cells may be preferable for transfusion to prevent exposure to additional complement components.

MNS system Closely linked genes on chromosome 4 determine the MN and Ss antigens, respectively. There are four inherited haplotypes: MS, Ms, NS, and Ns. Glycophorin A carries M and N specificity, while S and s are on glycophorin B. Absence of these sialoglycoproteins is associated with rare phenotypes such as En(a-), S^u, and M^k, but there are no accompanying hematologic abnormalities.

Anti-M and anti-N are usually naturally occurring IgM agglutinins with little capability of destroying red blood cells. Patients on long-term renal dialysis tend to form anti-N as either an auto- or alloantibody. These N-specific autoantibodies have no hemolytic potential, but they are alleged to cause rejection of kidneys kept refrigerated before transplantation.

Formation of anti-S or anti-s usually requires the stimulus of transfusion or pregnancy, and accordingly these antibodies often belong to the IgG class. A third antibody, anti-U, behaves serologically somewhat like anti-S plus anti-s, being formed in sensitized black subjects whose red blood cells have the S^u phenotype lacking S and

TABLE 282-2 Rh alleles, their antigenic determinants, and frequencies

Allele	Associated antigenic determinants*		Approximate allele frequencies in Americans†		
	R-S	W	Western European descent	African descent	Oriental descent
R^1	D, C, e	Rh_0, rh', hr''	0.45	0.10	0.55
r	c, e	hr', hr''	0.37	0.15	0.10
R^2	D, c, E	Rh_0, hr', rh''	0.14	0.10	0.35
R^0	D, c, e	Rh_0, hr', hr''	0.02	0.60	Low
r''	c, E	hr', rh''	0.01	Low	Low
r'	C, e	rh', hr''	0.01	Low	
R^z	D, C, E	Rh_0, rh', rh''	Low	Low	Low
r^y	C, E	rh', rh''	Low	Low	Low

* R-S = Race and Sanger; W = Wiener (see references).
† Low frequency means less than 0.01. Individuals of African descent have other alleles not listed here, thus accounting for failure of their frequencies to total 1.0.

s antigens. All three of these antibodies can hemolyze incompatible red blood cells in vivo, but they are readily detectable by adequate compatibility testing.

Rh system The Rh locus is on chromosome 1. Rh antigenic determinants may be dependent on interaction between red blood cell membrane protein and phospholipid molecules. Many Rh phenotypes have been described serologically, but the underlying biochemical genetics is unknown. It is convenient to envision a stretch of nucleotides at the Rh locus which dictates the structure of a set of three antithetical determinants: C or c, E or e, and D or d (the latter having no corresponding antibody and therefore being simply the absence of D). These sets are inherited from each parent as a haplotype, such as CDe, cde, cDE, and so forth. This nomenclature, used by Race and Sanger, is compared with the alternative nomenclature of Wiener in Table 282-2, which also gives the approximate frequencies of the corresponding alleles in Americans of western European, African, and Oriental origins.

The $D(Rh_0)$ antigen is by far the most immunogenic of this or any other blood group system (except for those previously described systems in which the formation of antibodies does not depend on exposure to foreign red blood cells). About 15 percent of Caucasians lack the $D(Rh_0)$ antigen and are Rh-negative. When transfused only once with Rh-positive blood, these Rh-negative persons have about a 50 percent chance of forming anti-$D(Rh_0)$ antibodies, which could cause destruction of any subsequently transfused Rh-positive red blood cells. For this reason, Rh-negative patients are always given Rh-negative blood except when the transfusion requirements of a male or postmenopausal female exceed the available supply. Giving Rh-positive blood to Rh-negative premenopausal females is a very serious matter, because, unless adequate amounts of Rh immuno-

globulin are given to prevent immunization, any subsequent pregnancy with an Rh-positive infant will almost always stimulate a secondary immune response, resulting in hemolytic disease of the newborn.

The Rh antigens C, c, E, and e are considerably less immunogenic than D, and it is impractical to match these antigens in donors and recipients. Of course, when previously sensitized patients form the corresponding antibodies, it is necessary to find donor blood lacking the specific antigens. The difficulty of this search varies. For example, about 20 percent of the population lack the c antigen and thus are compatible donors for a patient whose plasma contains anti-c. However, only 2 percent lack the e antigen, so patients with anti-e pose serious problems, especially when large amounts of blood are required. Blood banks often maintain donor calling lists or frozen red blood cells for use in such cases.

A large proportion of patients with acquired hemolytic anemia of the warm type have IgG autoantibodies which react with one or more Rh-associated antigens. In some instances, the specificity is clear-cut (for example, anti-e), but more often the antibodies react with all red blood cells except those of the rare type known as Rh_{null}. These cells lack all known Rh antigens, and the cell membrane is defective, reinforcing the belief that in normal red blood cells, molecules bearing the Rh determinants are an intrinsic part of the membrane protein structure.

Kidd, Kell, Duffy, and Lutheran systems The major antigens of these four clinically important systems and their average phenotype frequencies in Americans of western European and African origins are presented in Table 282-3 along with the frequencies of S and s in the MNS system. Anti-K and anti-Fyᵃ are frequently encountered antibodies capable of marked alloimmune red blood cell destruction. Even more dangerous are the antibodies in the Kidd system, anti-Jkᵃ

TABLE 282-3 The major antigens and phenotypes in five clinically important blood group systems (excepting ABO and Rh)*

System	Major antigens	Phenotypes	Approximate phenotype frequencies in Americans, %†	
			Western European descent	African descent
Kidd	Jkᵃ Jkᵇ	Jk(a+b−)	26	55
		Jk(a−b+)	24	7
		Jk(a+b+)	50	38
Kell	K, k, Jsᵃ	K−k+Js(a−)	91	83
		K−k+Js(a+)	Low	15
		K+k−Js(a−)	Low	Low
		K+k+Js(a−)	9	2
		K+k+Js(a+)	Low	Low
Duffy	Fyᵃ, Fyᵇ	Fy(a+b−)	18	10
		Fy(a−b+)	33	20
		Fy(a+b+)	49	2
		Fy(a−b−)	Low	68
Lutheran	Luᵃ, Luᵇ	Lu(a+b−)	Low	Low
		Lu(a−b+)	92	97
		Lu(a+b+)	8	3
(MN) Ss	S, s	S−s+	47	65
		S+s−	10	9
		S+s+	43	24
		S−s−	Low	2

* See Tables 282-1 and 282-2 for information about ABO and Rh types.
† Low means less than 1 percent.
SOURCE: ER Giblett, Genetic Markers in Human Blood, Philadelphia, Davis, 1969.

and anti-Jk^b, which are notoriously difficult to detect. Whenever a patient has a hemolytic transfusion reaction after transfusion of blood found to be compatible by the usual laboratory tests, the most likely cause is anti-Jk^a. Antibodies in the Lutheran system have only rarely been reported to cause red blood cell destruction.

Other blood group antigens Many other red blood cell antigens have been described. The Xg^a antigen is of considerable importance, since its locus is on the X chromosome. Other antigens are of clinical interest because they occur on the red blood cells of 95 percent or more of most populations, making it difficult to find compatible blood when their antibodies are present in patients requiring transfusion. Many of these antibodies have little ability to destroy red blood cells, even though they consist of IgG molecules and react in vitro at 37°C. Included in this category are most examples of anti-Sd^a (Sid), anti-Yt^a (Cartwright), anti-Yk^a (York), and many others. Nevertheless, both caution and experience are necessary when considering the transfusion of serologically incompatible blood, particularly when the antibodies react in vitro at body temperature. Antibodies with Chido (Ch^a) and Rodgers (Rg^a) specificity are incapable of causing hemolysis. Their respective antigenic determinants are located on the C4d fragment of the fourth component of complement and are thereby taken up from the plasma by red cells.

BIOLOGIC SIGNIFICANCE OF BLOOD GROUPS

Immune reactions The relationship of blood group antigens and antibodies to alloimmune red blood cell destruction has been briefly discussed in the previous sections. Because antigens in the ABO system are present in other tissues, they play a role in determining *histocompatibility,* so that transplantation of ABO-incompatible kidneys and other organs carries a risk of rejection (see Chap. 221). However, successful grafting of ABO-incompatible bone marrow is possible when the patient is immunosuppressed and either given exchange transfusions of plasma compatible with the donor's red blood cells or the patient's own plasma is passed over a column containing oligosaccharides with A and/or B specificity.

Infertility and early fetal loss Both of these effects have been ascribed to ABO incompatibility, although in some instances the data are of marginal significance. Nevertheless, many population geneticists believe that this factor plays a significant role in the processes of natural selection.

Disease-related phenotype changes A and, to a lesser extent, B determinants are subject to certain biochemical changes, such as those caused by bacterial glycosidases and other enzymes. As a result, the red blood cells may develop new specificities, becoming either "polyagglutinable" or having "pseudo-B" characteristics. Another acquired alteration in ABO type occurs in some patients with acute myelocytic leukemia whose original type is A$_1$ or B. This change in phenotype, with partial or complete loss of agglutinability by anti-A or anti-B, can be a diagnostic aid in the early hypoplastic phase of leukemia. The changes in Ii specificity associated with "marrow stress" are described above (see "I System").

Other disease relationships The incidence of certain diseases is related to blood type. For example, type O "nonsecretors" have about twice the incidence of duodenal ulcer than do secretors of types A or B. On the other hand, type A carries a higher incidence of tumors of salivary glands, stomach, and pancreas than does type O. Persons with the rare Rh$_{null}$ type, whose red cells lack all the Rh antigens, have some degree of increased hemolysis, as do people with the McLeod phenotype. McLeod red blood cells react only weakly with antibodies against antigens of the autosomally controlled Kell system, and they lack Kx, a very common X-linked antigen. Some boys with the X-linked form of chronic granulomatous disease have the McLeod phenotype and others do not. In both instances, the Kx antigen, also a normal granulocyte component, is not detectable on these cells. Individuals (mainly of African origin) who lack both Fy^a and Fy^b—the major antigens in the Duffy system—are protected against infestation by the malarial parasite, *Plasmodium vivax,*

presumably because Fy^a and Fy^b act as specific recognition or acceptor sites for the merozoites.

Chromosome mapping Blood genetic markers, including the red and white blood cell allotypes as well as the plasma and blood cell enzyme phenotypes, are very useful for mapping the human chromosomes. Some of these markers are genetically linked to loci for genes causing metabolic diseases, and, as more markers are identified, it will be increasingly possible to predict the development of inherited malfunctions from specimens obtained in utero or from newborn infants. For example, the secretor gene locus is closely linked to the locus of the gene causing myotonic dystrophy, and a determination of the secretor status of a baby at risk can be used to predict the likelihood of its developing this disease, since both characters are inherited as autosomal dominants.

Medicolegal applications When the red blood cell antigens are combined with the other genetic markers in blood, the probability of distinguishing one person from another is about 2 million to 1. This high degree of individuality promotes the usefulness of genetic markers for ruling out paternity, maternity, and monozygosity in nearly all cases where those relationships do not exist.

BLOOD TRANSFUSION

INTRODUCTION Considerable morbidity and, to a lesser extent, mortality are associated with blood transfusion therapy. Responsible medical practice dictates that physicians have sufficient background information to make soundly reasoned judgments concerning the risks as well as the benefits of this procedure. They must decide not only what blood components (if any) are indicated but also what quantities are needed.

WHOLE BLOOD A unit of whole blood consists of approximately 450 mL blood collected into a plastic bag containing 63 mL of either citrate-phosphate-dextrose (CPD) or citrate-phosphate-dextrose–adenine (CPD-A) solution as anticoagulant and preservative. Blood collected in CPD has a refrigerated storage life of only 3 weeks, while CPD-A blood may be kept 5 weeks. At the end of these periods, about 70 to 80 percent of red blood cells are still viable, white blood cells and platelets are nonviable, and clotting factors V and VIII have low levels of activity. The storage time for packed red blood cells harvested from blood collected in CPD can be increased to 49 days by the addition of preservative solutions that contain mannitol.

Virtually the only reason to transfuse whole blood is to restore blood volume lost through recent hemorrhage, as with gastrointestinal bleeding, major surgery, or trauma. For assessing blood loss, routine laboratory tests are misleading for several hours after hemorrhage. Both hemoglobin and hematocrit measurements reflect the ratio of red blood cell mass to blood volume, rather than indicating the total circulating red blood cells. Since the compensatory vasoconstriction evoked by hemorrhage initially prevents extravascular fluids from replacing intravascular fluid loss, both laboratory measurements may be falsely high. Clinically, postural hypotension provides a warning that blood transfusion may be required. Pallor, syncope, tachycardia, thirst, and air hunger are useful indicators of massive blood loss (i.e., 1500 mL or more in adults), sometimes requiring immediate transfusion of type O red blood cells that have not been cross-matched. In less severe cases, maintaining the blood volume with saline or plasma expanders provides time for accurate blood typing and compatibility testing.

During surgery, blood loss can be measured quite accurately, and there is a tendency to "keep up" or even to "stay ahead" of lost volume by transfusion. Such practices lead to unwarranted use of blood with its attendant hazards. In most adult subjects, blood loss of 500 mL is easily tolerated, being equivalent to the amount given by a blood donor. Judicious use of crystalloid infusions is frequently all that is required to circumvent blood transfusion, even with blood losses up to a liter. In modern medicine, ordering "fresh" blood at any time is not acceptable practice, since proper component therapy is both safer and more scientifically based.

PACKED RED BLOOD CELLS The preparation of packed red blood cells from whole blood involves sedimentation or centrifugation followed by removal of plasma into a satellite bag, all in a closed system. Such packed cells have the same storage periods as whole blood. Removal of the plasma provides protection against circulatory overload as well as against excessive loads of sodium, potassium, citrate, ammonia, and antibodies (particularly anti-A) which might be harmful to the patient. Furthermore, the removed plasma can be used for preparing such products as cryoprecipitate, albumin, and immunoglobulins.

In the absence of recent blood loss, most transfusions are given to patients who need replacement of oxygen-carrying capacity. Packed red blood cells are much preferred to whole blood for this purpose, since the plasma serves no useful purpose and may be detrimental, especially in hypervolemic subjects. Diagnoses most frequently associated with the need for packed red blood cells fall into two major categories of anemia, hypoplastic and hemolytic.

Red blood cell hypoplasia Chronic bone marrow depression may, under favorable circumstances, be treated by bone marrow transplantation (see Chap. 291). However, many patients either have no access to a marrow donor or are unsuitable candidates. The red blood cell mass of these patients can be maintained at functional levels for long periods, provided they do not develop multiple antibodies against red blood cell antigens. These patients are in general more liable to become immunologically refractory to platelets and white blood cells than to red blood cells. Patients whose red blood cell hypoplasia is secondary to marrow invasion by malignancy and/or to various chemo- or radiotherapeutic agents also require red blood cell transfusions. Again, sensitization to transfused platelets and white blood cells creates a greater problem than red blood cell immunization.

Hemolytic anemia In severe cases of inherited nonimmune hemolysis due to intrinsic red blood cell defects (e.g., sickle cell anemia, thalassemia, or severe deficiencies of glucose 6-phosphate dehydrogenase), the only hope of maintaining oxygen-carrying capacity through a crisis is the careful use of red blood cell transfusion. Patients with other forms of nonimmune hemolysis or ineffective erythropoiesis (e.g., vitamin B_{12}, folate, or iron deficiencies) are candidates for transfusion only if they are severely anemic and if the cause cannot be corrected by specific replacement therapy. Whenever any infusion is given to a patient with severe anemia, the possibility of precipitating heart failure must be circumvented by careful monitoring.

Patients with autoimmune hemolytic anemia are not good candidates for red blood cell transfusion. Not only are they liable to develop new alloantibodies, but they may have already formed such antibodies as the result of earlier transfusion or pregnancy. In the presence of circulating *auto*antibodies, alloantibodies are often difficult to detect, and transfused red blood cells may be rapidly destroyed. Consultation with a blood transfusion expert is desirable in cases where severe anemia with hypoxemia or cardiac failure poses an immediate threat to life.

PLATELETS Platelet concentrates are prepared by centrifugation of platelet-rich plasma to yield about 5×10^{10} platelets from each donor unit. More porous plastic bags and gentle agitation facilitate gas transport across the container walls during storage at room temperature. A continuous supply of oxygen maintains aerobic platelet metabolism and prevents harmful drops in pH due to lactic acid production and CO_2 retention. These factors permit platelet storage for up to 7 days with posttransfusion survivals of 6 to 7 days. In adult thrombocytopenic patients without consumptive coagulopathy or platelet-specific antibodies, 1 unit of platelet concentrate raises the platelet count by about 10,000 per microliter.

Patients with idiopathic thrombocytopenic purpura produce auto-antibodies which react with all human platelets (see Chap. 279), and therefore derive little or no benefit from platelet transfusion. Similarly, in patients with thrombocytopenia due to a consumptive coagulopathy (as in infection or metastatic malignancy) the usefulness of platelet therapy is limited, unless its purpose is to keep the patient from bleeding while the primary cause is being treated.

The most rational use of platelets is to control bleeding in patients either with a temporary loss of platelets not due to immunity (e.g., massive blood replacement, prolonged surgery) or with suppressed platelet production (leukemia, lymphoma, treatment with radio- or chemotherapy). Since platelets are very immunogenic, and typing and cross-matching techniques are not yet practical, this blood component should not be given in the absence of clear indication. Most nonbleeding patients with platelet counts above 10,000 per microliter can maintain adequate hemostasis. Patients in the immediate postoperative period may need to have their platelet counts elevated to as high as 100,000 per microliter. In other bleeding situations, a platelet count of 50,000 per microliter or more suggests other causes for hemorrhage, especially if there is no recent history of ingestion of aspirin or other drugs that interfere with platelet function, which would be reflected by a prolonged bleeding time. The effectiveness of platelet transfusion is assessed by comparing the platelet count before the infusion with counts obtained about 1 and 24 h later.

Choice of blood type Ideally, donors of platelets should have the same ABO and Rh types as the patient, since it is impossible to remove all red blood cells and plasma from the platelet concentrate. When it is necessary to use O donors for A, B, or AB recipients, the plasma may contain sufficient anti-A (or anti-B) to destroy some of the patient's red blood cells. Although this possibility is small, it deserves consideration in children or in adults receiving large numbers of platelet concentrates. When platelets of A, B, or AB donors are given to patients of unlike ABO type, the posttransfusion platelet increment may be somewhat diminished, although this is rarely a major problem. However, it is important that the number of red blood cells in such ABO-incompatible preparations be kept as small as possible.

Since some red blood cells are inevitably present in platelet concentrates, Rh-negative patients should receive platelets from Rh-negative donors whenever feasible, particularly if there is a possibility of subsequent pregnancy. However, lack of platelets from Rh-negative donors should not preclude transfusing Rh-positive donor platelets in a life-threatening situation. Patients who have the potential of becoming mothers can be protected against Rh alloimmunization by an injection of Rh immunoglobulin, about 20 μg for each milliliter of Rh-positive red blood cells present in the infusion. In other Rh-negative patients given platelets from Rh-positive donors, Rh-antibody formation can be expected to occur with a high frequency, but these antibodies do not interfere with the survival of subsequently transfused Rh-positive donor platelets, since they do not themselves contain Rh antigens.

Refractory state Patients who receive random donor platelets on more than one or two occasions frequently develop alloantibodies with either HLA or platelet antigen specificities. Such refractory patients can often be maintained with concentrates prepared by plateletpheresis from family members or HLA-compatible community pheresis donors. Failure to achieve a good response to histocompatible platelets suggests the presence of platelet-specific alloantibodies, nonimmune causes of platelet refractoriness, or hypersplenism.

WHITE BLOOD CELL TRANSFUSIONS Since it is now possible with platelet transfusions to control bleeding in many patients with hematologic malignancies, hemorrhage has been supplanted by infection as the most frequent cause of death. In general, neutrophil transfusion therapy should be considered in patients with severe neutropenia who have documented bacterial infections not responsive to appropriate antibiotic therapy. A course of neutrophil support usually consists of daily transfusion of 10 to 30×10^9 neutrophils, obtained from normal donors by leukapheresis. Problems of maintaining patients for long periods in this way are even more difficult than those associated with platelets. Neutrophils have a very short life span in the bloodstream, and many questions remain unanswered about the best dosage schedules, the feasibility of neutrophil storage, the efficacy of neutrophils for fungal infections, and the recognition and management of alloimmunization. Hazards include alloimmunization to HLA and other antigens, pulmonary damage and other transfusion reactions, as well as transmission of infection, particularly cytomegalovirus, to immunosuppressed recipients.

PLASMA COMPONENT THERAPY Fresh frozen plasma and cryoprecipitate are major blood component preparations because they are necessary for the care of patients with coagulation disorders. Plasma can be used for expanding intravascular volume, but it carries the risk of viral transmission. Commercially prepared albumin solutions are preferable as volume expanders, as they have been heated to inactivate viruses. They are useful in special cases, such as nephrosis, certain gastroenteropathies, and severe malnutrition. Immunoglobulin preparations are also commercially made, including specific hyperimmune globulin for preventing the development of certain infectious diseases and for blocking the immune response to Rh antigen.

PLASMAPHERESIS The introduction of cell separators has made plasmapheresis a simple procedure wherein as much as one to two plasma volumes may be exchanged in 1 to 3 h. The procedure has generally been used to reduce the plasma concentration of proteins, lipids, protein-bound hormones or toxins, antibodies, antigens, or immune complexes. While the number of different diseases that have been managed by this procedure is considerable, there are only a few in which the role of plasmapheresis is generally accepted. Even then, there is controversy regarding the frequency and volume of exchange as well as the nature of replacement fluids.

The most established indication is symptomatic hyperviscosity syndrome; plasmapheresis in this setting reproducibly results in clinical improvement. Plasmapheresis can also be used successfully in selected patients with myasthenia gravis, Goodpasture's syndrome, thrombotic thrombocytopenic purpura, and immune-complex-mediated vasculitis.

COMPLICATIONS OF BLOOD TRANSFUSION Transfusion reactions are classified as immune or nonimmune. The immunologically mediated reactions may be directed against red or white blood cells, platelets, or at least one of the immunoglobulins, IgA. Other less well defined hypersensitivity reactions also occur. The major nonimmune reactions are due to circulatory overload, massive transfusion, or transmission of an infectious agent.

Immunologically mediated reactions Hemolysis due to red blood cell alloantibodies may occur within the circulation or extravascularly. The very rapid cell destruction associated with *intravascular hemolysis* is usually due to incompatibility within the ABO system, since both anti-A and anti-B fix complement, regardless of whether they are IgM or IgG molecules. Other possibilities to consider are anti-Jk^a, anti-Fy^a, and anti-Le^a. Rh antibodies are only rarely associated with hemoglobinemia. Symptoms include restlessness, anxiety, flushing, chest or lumbar pain, tachypnea, tachycardia, and nausea, followed by the typical findings of shock and renal failure. In comatose or anesthetized patients, the first sign of danger is often oozing of blood from the mucous membranes or operative site, due to intravascular coagulation.

Extravascular hemolysis is most commonly caused by antibodies of the Rh system, but several other antibodies, especially of the Kell, Duffy, and Kidd systems, are among the offenders. The clinical manifestations are usually milder, consisting of malaise and fever. Shock and renal complications rarely occur. Some patients have delayed reactions in which the transfused red blood cells have normal survival initially, but about a week later they are rapidly destroyed in the reticuloendothelial system. Such delayed reactions are commonly due to an anamnestic rise in antibodies previously stimulated by transfusion or pregnancy. Rarely, patients are found to have

destroyed all the transfused cells in the absence of demonstrable antibodies.

LABORATORY INVESTIGATION Of first importance in the investigation of a hemolytic transfusion reaction is a careful check on the identity of both the donor and the recipient, since clerical errors, especially mistakes in identity, are most frequently involved. Then the necessary steps include demonstrating that red blood cell destruction has occurred, investigating its cause, and determining the status of the patient's renal and coagulation mechanisms.

With recent *intravascular* lysis, the hemoglobin level is elevated in both plasma and urine (blood must be drawn cautiously to avoid red blood cell rupture). Also, depending on the number of red blood cells destroyed, there may be methemalbuminemia accompanied by marked reduction of serum haptoglobin and hemopexin. (Measuring the latter two substances is rarely necessary, and to be meaningful, both tests require knowledge of the pretransfusion levels for comparison.) The best indicator of *extravascular* lysis is a rise in unconjugated bilirubin, accompanied by failure of the hematocrit to reach the expected posttransfusion level.

Having a *pretransfusion* specimen of the patient's blood is very helpful, so that determination of both donor and recipient blood types can be repeated, along with the compatibility test. If antibodies are detected, this pretransfusion specimen is also valuable for determining specificity, aided by knowledge of the full antigen composition, since alloantibodies are formed only against antigens not present on the patient's own cells. The *posttransfusion* specimen may not contain the offending antibodies, since they could have been completely absorbed by the donor's incompatible red blood cells. However, it is desirable to examine the red blood cells in the posttransfusion sample, both microscopically for agglutinates and by the direct antiglobulin (Coombs) test. A positive result usually means that some of the donor's red blood cells, coated by the patient's antibodies, were still present when the blood was drawn. But it is also possible that the *donor's* plasma contained antibodies, missed during the donor screening procedure, which reacted with the red blood cells of the patient. Thus, if the direct antiglobulin test on the posttransfusion specimen is positive, the plasma of both donor and recipient should be examined for the responsible antibodies. In the absence of ABO incompatibility, significant destruction of a patient's red blood cells by a donor's alloantibodies is distinctly rare. More typically, the antibody-coated red blood cells survive well in vivo, but their presence can lead to a misdiagnosis of acquired hemolytic anemia.

TREATMENT The care of patients with extravascular hemolysis should be conservative, avoiding additional transfusion unless the patient's life is otherwise threatened. Intravascular hemolysis is a far greater hazard, since shock and renal failure can occur. Immediate treatment with an osmotic diuretic is indicated unless acute tubular necrosis has already occurred. Renal blood flow can be increased with appropriate agents, shock controlled symptomatically, and disseminated intravascular coagulation treated appropriately. Management of the coagulopathy is discussed in Chap. 281, and treatment of renal shutdown in Chap. 219.

In the absence of red blood cell destruction, most febrile reactions can be ascribed to immunity against white blood cell, platelet, or plasma antigens. Further laboratory workup is required only when the reaction is unusually severe. For example, patients with antibodies against IgA molecules sometimes undergo severe shock upon exposure to the blood of other human subjects. Such individuals must be transfused only with blood that lacks IgA or with repeatedly washed red blood cells. Patients with antibodies against white blood cells or platelets can usually be given packed red blood cells from which the buffy layer has been removed after centrifugation or by filtration. Some centers use frozen and thawed red blood cells for transfusing patients sensitized to white blood cells, or to retard the occurrence of such sensitization in candidates for bone marrow transplantation. However, in patients who are candidates for renal transplantation, prior transfusions with white cell–containing products are often associated with improved prognosis—especially if the blood donor is subsequently used as the kidney donor.

Nonimmune transfusion reactions Included in this category are circulatory overload, adverse effects of massive transfusion, infections, metabolic shock, air and fat embolisms, thrombophlebitis, and siderosis. The first three are by far the most common.

CIRCULATORY OVERLOAD Patients with renal or cardiac insufficiency are liable to develop circulatory failure and pulmonary edema with even modest amounts of intravenous infusion. Infants are also vulnerable, since their vasculature does not accommodate rapidly to infusions. The onset may be immediate or delayed for up to 24 h after transfusion, with dyspnea and chest pain progressing to the full-blown picture of pulmonary edema. Susceptible patients should be transfused in a sitting position, with the rate of red blood cell flow not exceeding 2 mL/min, depending on body size and degree of impairment. A rise in central venous pressure heralds the danger of administering more red blood cells unless they are exchanged with whole blood removed from the patient.

MASSIVE TRANSFUSION When the amount of stored blood transfused to bleeding patients exceeds the amount of their normal blood volume, complications can include hyperkalemia, ammonia and citrate toxicity, and dilutional coagulopathy, which is most commonly associated with thrombocytopenia. Platelet concentrates are frequently indicated for this condition, while fresh frozen plasma is only rarely useful. If the factor 8 level or fibrinogen content is low, concentrates such as cryoprecipitate should be considered.

INFECTION Many diseases, such as hepatitis, cytomegalovirus infection, syphilis, malaria, toxoplasmosis, brucellosis, and the acquired immunodeficiency syndrome (AIDS) can be transmitted by transfusion. In addition, blood that becomes infected during handling and storage can cause very severe shock, owing to toxic bacterial metabolites. Testing donated blood for evidence of transmissible infection is increasingly important to reduce transfusion risks. Tests for hepatitis B virus and syphilis, as well as for the antibody to HTLV III (the AIDS-associated virus), are now routinely performed on all donor units. No tests for non-A, non-B hepatitis are available. Immunocompromised patients, including low birthweight neonates, are candidates to receive blood found negative for the cytomegalovirus antibody. To reduce the risk of AIDS transmission, patients at high risk for the disease are asked to defer serving as donors. In addition, all blood is tested for the antibody using an ELISA technique. Confirmatory tests, such as the western blot technique, are performed before the donor is informed of a positive result, but blood found positive by the ELISA test is discarded.

REFERENCES

ANSTEE DJ: The blood group MNSs-active sialoglycoproteins. Semin Hematol 18:13, 1981

CASH JD: Blood replacement therapy, in *Haemostasis and Thrombosis*, AL Bloom, DP Thomas (eds). Edinburgh, Churchill Livingston, 1981, pp 473–490

GIBLETT ER: Blood group alloantibodies: An assessment of some laboratory practices. Transfusion 17:299, 1977

HAKOMORI S: Blood group ABH and Ii antigens of human erythrocytes: Chemistry, polymorphism and their developmental change. Semin Hematol 18:39, 1981

MARSH WL: Molecular defects associated with the McLeod blood group phenotype, in *Blood Groups and Other Red Cell Surface Markers in Health and Disease*, C Salmon (ed). New York, Masson, 1982

McKUSICK VA: Human gene map, in *Genetic Maps, 1984*, SJ O'Brien (ed). New York, Cold Spring Harbor Laboratory, 1984, pp 417–446

MOHN JF et al (eds): *Human Blood Groups*. New York, Karger, 1977

MOLLISON PL: *Blood Transfusion in Clinical Medicine*, 7th ed. Philadelphia, Lippincott, 1983

MOURANT AE et al: *The Distribution of the Human Blood Groups and Other Biochemical Polymorphisms*, 2d ed. New York, Oxford University Press, 1975

PETZ LD, SWISHER SN (eds): *Clinical Practice of Blood Transfusion*. New York, Churchill Livingston, 1981

Provisional public health service interagency recommendations for screening donated blood and plasma for antibody to the virus causing acquired immunodeficiency syndrome. Morb Mort Week Rep 34:1, 1985

RACE RR, SANGER R: *Blood Groups in Man*, 6th ed. Oxford, Blackwell, 1975

SLICHTER SJ: Controversies in platelet transfusion therapy. Ann Rev Med 31:509, 1980

WATKINS WM: Biochemistry and genetics of the ABO, Lewis, and P blood group systems, in *Advances in Human Genetics*, H Harris, K Hirschhorn (eds). New York, Plenum, 1980, vol 10, pp 1–136, 379–385

section 2 Disorders of the hematopoietic system

283 PATHOPHYSIOLOGY OF THE ANEMIAS

H. FRANKLIN BUNN

There is a large and coherent body of information on the birth, life, and death of red cells. A thorough familiarity with erythropoiesis and erythrocyte structure and function is necessary to understand the pathogenesis of the various anemias as well as to develop an orderly approach to diagnosis and management. Conversely, investigation of specific red cell disorders has provided unique insights into normal erythroid physiology.

RED CELL PRODUCTION Red cells are derived from an undifferentiated progenitor cell in the bone marrow called the *pluripotent stem cell* (Fig. 283-1). A stem cell is one which is capable of both self-renewal and differentiation. *Pluripotent* implies that granulocytes, monocytes, and platelets also evolve from this ancestor cell. The pluripotent stem cell has the morphologic characteristics of a mature lymphocyte. The control of proliferation into differentiated cell lines is poorly understood. Experiments have been hampered by difficulty in isolating early red cell precursors from the bone marrow. However, considerable advances have been made in culturing erythroid progenitor cells in vitro. As Fig. 283-1 shows, the most primitive erythroid progenitor which has been cultured from both bone marrow and peripheral blood is called the *erythroid burst-forming unit* (BFU_e). After 10 to 15 days in tissue culture it produces a large colony of recognizable red cell precursors. The BFU_e is responsive to high doses of the erythroid-promoting hormone erythropoietin, which acts synergistically with other growth factors which are derived from lymphocytes and monocytes. A more mature cell, the *erythroid colony-forming unit* (CFU_e), produces a smaller clone of erythroid cells after 4 to 7 days in culture and is very sensitive to erythropoietin. Various other factors such as catecholamines, steroids, thyroid hormone, growth hormone, and cyclic nucleotides may also influence erythropoiesis. Well-designed experiments involving incubation of uniform cell populations with purified growth factors should provide considerably more information about the mechanisms underlying the

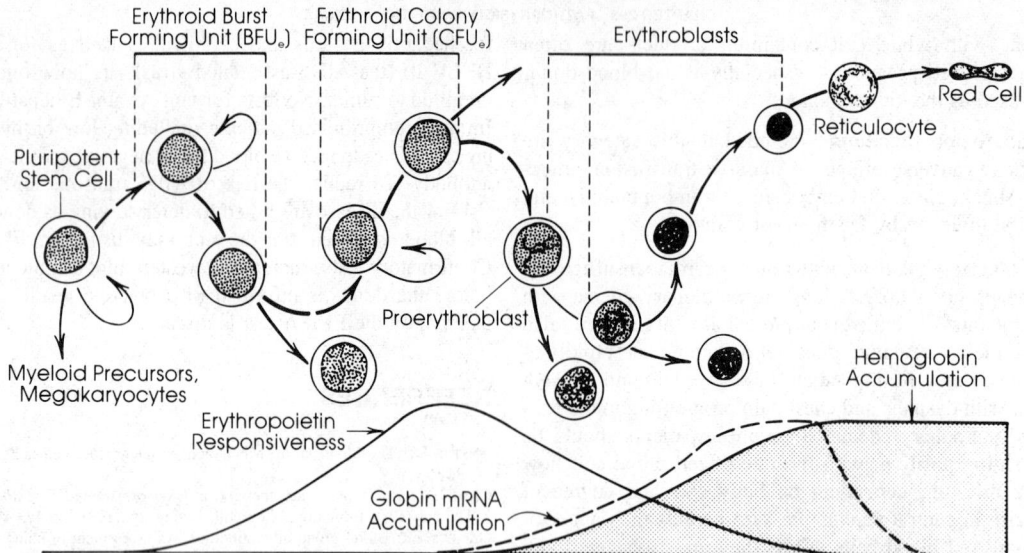

FIGURE 283-1 *Differentiation and morphologic maturation of erythroid cells. Erythroid cells are derived from pluripotent stem cells shown on left. Under the influence of erythropoietin, erythroid stem cells ($BFU_e \rightarrow CFU_e$)* *differentiate into proerythroblasts, the earliest recognizable red blood cell precursors in the bone marrow. During further maturation, globin mRNA accumulates, directing the cell to synthesize hemoglobin.*

differentiation and maturation of erythroid cells, as well as insights into certain disorders of erythropoiesis.

Erythropoietin, a glycoprotein having a molecular weight of about 36,000, has been purified to homogeneity. The cloning of the erythropoietin gene has made possible the synthesis of large amounts of biologically active hormone. Erythropoietin is produced primarily by the kidneys in response to hypoxic stimuli. The purification of erythropoietin has permitted the development of a radioimmunoassay which is more accurate and sensitive than conventional bioassays. Reliable measurements of erythropoietin will have a number of diagnostic applications and will also provide new information about the pathogenesis of several types of anemias.

Erythropoietin probably interacts with specific receptors on the surfaces of committed erythroid stem cells, inducing them to differentiate into pronormoblasts, the earliest red cell precursor that can be recognized on examination of the bone marrow. In addition, erythropoietin acts on later red cell precursors, stimulating hemoglobin synthesis. Normally the transition from the proerythroblast to the most mature normoblast involves three or four cell divisions over a

4-day period (Fig. 283-1). During this time, the nucleus becomes smaller, and an increasing amount of hemoglobin is produced in the cytoplasm. Following the last division, the pyknotic nucleus is removed from the normoblast, forming the reticulocyte which stays in the bone marrow for 2.5 to 3 days. The reticulocyte is then released into the general circulation, where it remains for another 24 h before it loses its mitochondria and ribosomes and assumes the morphologic appearance of a mature red cell.

Erythroid precursor cells ranging from the pronormoblast to the reticulocyte possess a specific surface receptor for the iron-transferrin complex, enabling them to incorporate sufficient iron for hemoglobin production (Fig. 238-2). The use of a radioactive iron label such as ^{59}Fe permits a quantitative assessment of erythropoiesis. From the rate at which injected ^{59}Fe-labeled transferrin disappears from the plasma, plasma iron turnover can be calculated. This parameter is generally proportional to the total developing erythroid cell mass. Normally, about 80 percent of ^{59}Fe bound to plasma transferrin goes to erythroid cells in the marrow (Fig. 284-3B). After 4 to 6 days the labeled iron reappears in circulating erythrocytes. The extent to which

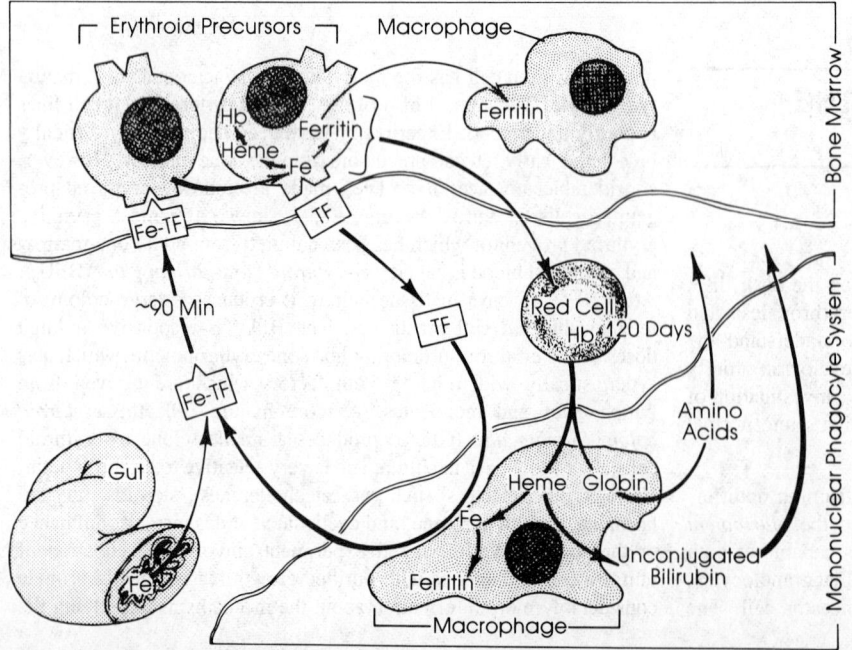

FIGURE 283-2 *Erythrocyte production, circulation, and destruction. Circulating iron-bound transferrin (TF) is bound to specific receptors on the surface of red blood cell precursors in the marrow. Most of this iron is incorporated into hemoglobin; the remainder is stored as ferritin. Following maturation of the erythroid precursor, the nucleus is shed and the red blood cell emerges from the marrow into the plasma where it circulates for approximately 120 days. The senescent red blood cell is taken up by the mononuclear phagocyte system and is destroyed. The heme iron is initially incorporated into ferritin. This storage iron is available for transport to the marrow via transferrin.*

circulating red cells acquire the label provides an index of the efficiency or effectiveness of erythropoiesis.

The normal marrow is capable of increasing its red cell production to about three to five times the normal rate within a week or two following maximal stimulation. In chronic hemolytic anemias, erythropoiesis may increase five- to sevenfold. As the erythroid marrow expands, fat is replaced by erythroid cells, and formerly inactive or "yellow" marrow becomes active or "red."

HEMOGLOBIN BIOSYNTHESIS Erythroid cell development involves the production of hemoglobin-containing cells. About 98 percent of the protein in the cytoplasm of circulating red cells is hemoglobin. This protein is a tetramer composed of two pairs of polypeptide chains designated α, β, γ, and δ, each of which is covalently linked to a heme group. The synthesis of a particular globin subunit is directed by a corresponding gene inherited from each parent. As shown in Fig. 283-1, there is a marked amplification in the transcription of globin chain mRNA during the development of proerythroblasts.

In the red cells of normal adults, hemoglobin A ($\alpha_2\beta_2$) composes about 97 percent of the total hemoglobin. The remaining 3 percent is primarily hemoglobin A_2 ($\alpha_2\delta_2$). As discussed in Chap. 288, this minor component is increased in patients with β thalassemia. Fetal hemoglobin (HbF or $\alpha_2\gamma_2$) usually accounts for less than 1 percent of total hemoglobin in normal adult red cells. HbF is localized to 1 to 7 percent of red cells. In contrast, it is the main hemoglobin component of fetal red cells. During the last 3 months of gestation, γ-chain synthesis switches to β-chain synthesis. However, in certain types of congenital hemolytic anemias such as the β thalassemias and sickle cell anemia, the production of γ chains (and therefore of HbF) persists. In addition, increased levels of HbF may also be encountered in certain acquired anemias in which there is disordered red cell proliferation.

Normally α- and β-chain synthesis in erythroid precursors is evenly balanced. In contrast, the thalassemias (Chap. 288) are characterized by imbalance in globin chain synthesis.

The synthesis of *heme* in red cell precursors is closely matched to globin chain production. As shown in Fig. 283-3 the initial and rate-limiting step is the condensation of succinyl coenzyme A (CoA) and glycine to form δ-aminolevulinic acid. This reaction, which takes place in mitochondria, requires that glycine be activated by pyridoxal phosphate. Accordingly, patients with sideroblastic anemia in whom heme synthesis is usually defective may sometimes respond to pyridoxine therapy (Chap. 284). The next steps of heme synthesis take place in the cytosol. Two molecules of δ-aminolevulinic acid condense to form a ring structure, prophobilinogen. This colorless pyrrole is elevated in acute intermittent porphyria and can be detected in urine by the Watson-Schwartz test. The subsequent steps in prophyrin synthesis are also shown in Fig. 283-3. The last three reactions take place in mitochondria. Iron is inserted into protoporphyrin IX to form heme. In iron deficiency, as well as in lead poisoning, increased levels of protoporphyrin can be detected in red cells. Disorders of porphyrin synthesis and metabolism are discussed in Chap. 312.

HEMOGLOBIN STRUCTURE AND FUNCTION The primary role of red cells is to transport oxygen from lungs to tissues and to transport carbon dioxide in the reverse direction. Both of these functions are assumed by hemoglobin. The three-dimensional structure of human hemoglobin has been determined from x-ray crystallographic analysis. The important functional properties of hemoglobin such as heme-heme interaction, the pH dependency of oxygen affinity (the Bohr

FIGURE 283-3 *The biosynthesis of heme. The following abbreviations are used: CoA, coenzyme A; GTP, guanosine triphosphate; GDP, guanosine diphosphate; Pi, inorganic phosphorus; GSH, glutathione; Δ-ALA-DH, Δ-aminolevulinate dehydrase; UIS, uroporphyrinogen I synthetase; UIII CoS, uroporphyrinogen III cosynthetase; UD, uroporphyrinogen decarboxylase; CO, coproporphyrinogen oxidase; HS, heme synthetase; A, acetate; P, proportionate; M, methyl; V, vinyl. Enzymatic steps that occur in mitochondria are shown.*

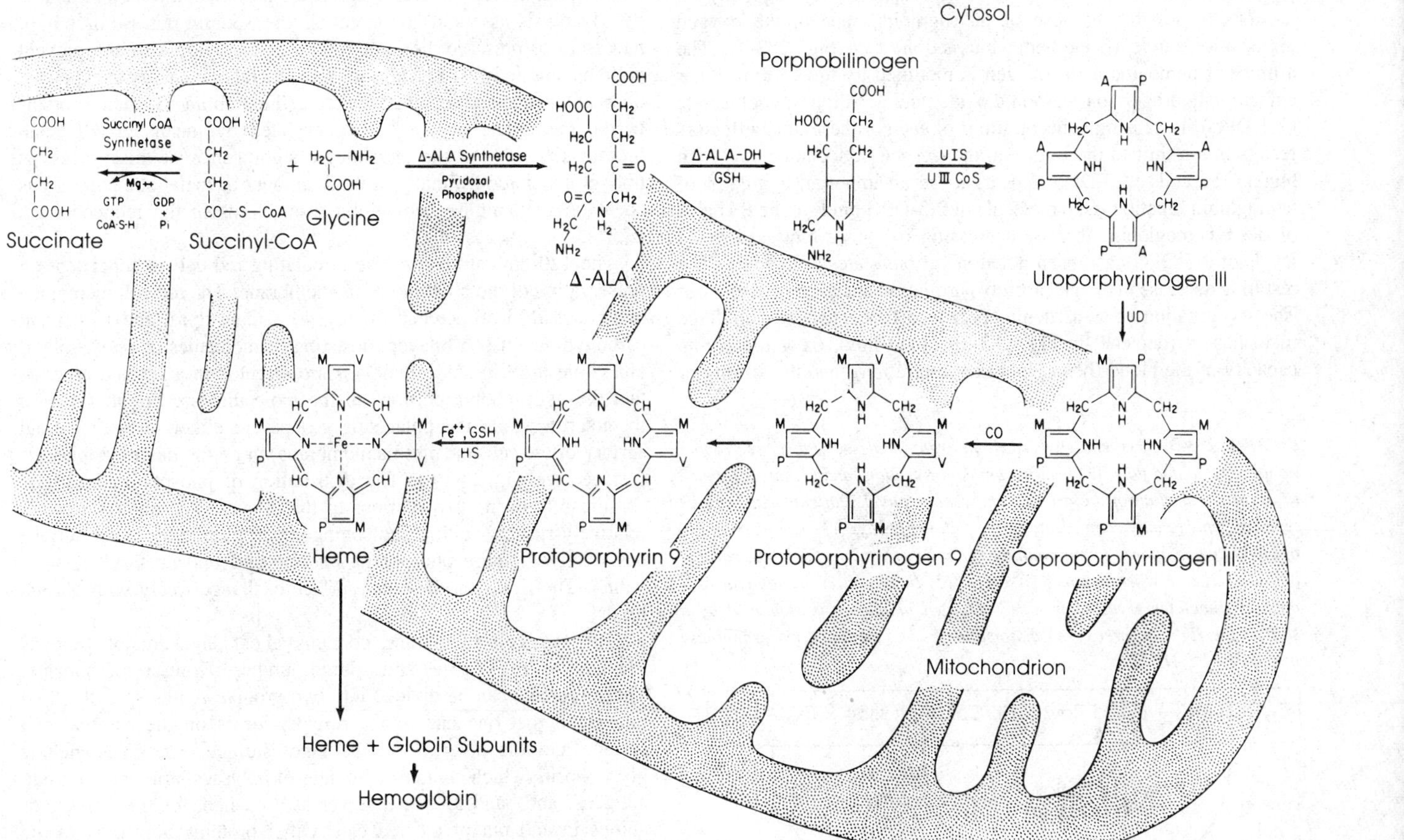

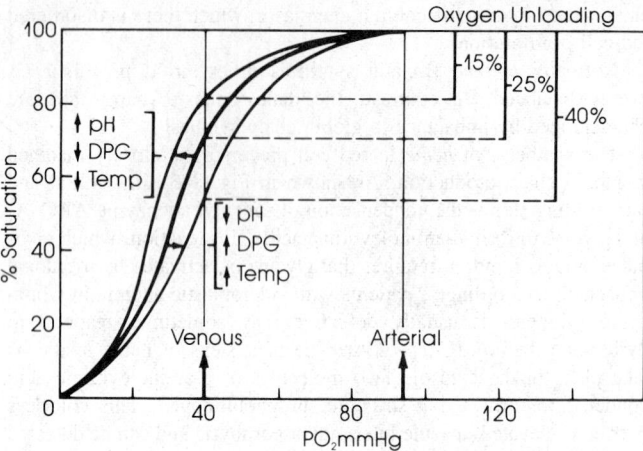

FIGURE 283-4 *The oxyhemoglobin dissociation curve of normal blood. The major factors influencing the position of the curve are pH, temperature, and the intracellular concentration of 2,3-DPG. An increase in plasma pH or a decrease in temperature and 2,3-DPG causes an increase in oxygen affinity (shift to the left) and a relative decrease in oxygen unloading when going from an arterial P_{O_2} of 95 mmHg to a venous P_{O_2} of 40 mmHg. Conversely, a decrease in pH or an increase in temperature and 2,3-DPG causes a decrease in oxygen affinity (shift to the right) and a relative increase in oxygen unloading.*

effect), and the interaction with 2,3-diphosphoglycerate can now be understood on a stereochemical basis. This structural information has also been useful in explaining the abnormal functional properties of a number of human hemoglobin variants which are associated with clinical and hematalogic manifestations (see Chap. 288).

During the circulation through the lungs, hemoglobin becomes almost fully saturated with oxygen (1.34 mL O_2 per gram of hemoglobin). As red cells perfuse the capillary beds, oxygen is extracted. Efficient unloading of oxygen at relatively high oxygen tensions is possible because of the sigmoid shape of the oxygen dissociation curve (heme-heme interaction) (see Fig. 283-4). The affinity of hemoglobin for oxygen is modified by three intracellular cofactors: hydrogen ion, carbon dioxide, and 2,3-diphosphoglycerate (2,3-DPG). Increasing concentrations of each of these three effectors results in a "shift to the right" in the oxygen dissociation curve. In human red cells, 2,3-DPG appears to be an important regulator of hemoglobin function. One molecule of 2,3-DPG binds to the β chains of deoxyhemoglobin, thereby decreasing oxygen affinity. Elevated levels of 2,3-DPG have been noted in various states of hypoxia. The resulting decrease in oxygen affinity permits enhanced oxygen release. The oxygenation of a particular organ or tissue depends on three main factors (depicted in Fig. 283-5): blood flow, oxygen-carrying capacity of the blood (hemoglobin concentration), and the affinity of

FIGURE 283-5 *Oxygen delivered to an organ or tissue is directly proportional to (1) blood flow, (2) hemoglobin concentration, and (3) the difference in oxygen saturation of the arterial and venous blood. Patients with various types of hypoxia may compensate in the following ways: (1) The distribution of blood flow is altered to maintain oxygenation of vital organs; total cardiac output increases when hypoxia is severe. (2) Increased erythropoietin production stimulates erythropoiesis. (3) Oxygen unloading is enhanced by a shift to the right in the oxygen dissociation curve, mediated by an increase in red cell 2,3-DPG.*

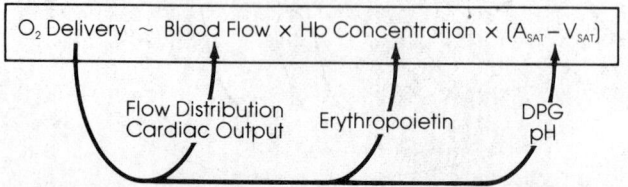

the hemoglobin for oxygen. Patients with a primary abnormality of one of these three factors depend on adjustments in one or both of the other two in order to maintain optimal tissue oxygenation. For example, patients with anemia have two available modes of compensation: enhanced blood flow and decreased oxygen affinity, mediated by increased levels of 2,3-DPG. Conversely, individuals with a hemoglobin variant having increased oxygen affinity have a primary defect in oxygen unloading. As discussed in Chap. 288, such patients compensate by developing secondary erythrocytosis.

RED BLOOD CELL METABOLISM As the red cell emerges from the bone marrow, it loses its nucleus, ribosomes, and mitochondria and therefore all capability for cell division, protein synthesis, and oxidative phosphorylation. Compared with other cells, the erythrocyte has a rather simple scheme of intermediary metabolism. Glucose is virtually the only fuel utilized by the red cell. It readily enters the red cell by facilitated diffusion and is then converted to glucose 6-phosphate. There are two major pathways available for glucose 6-phosphate (Fig. 287-2). About 80 to 90 percent of this intermediate is converted to lactate by means of the glycolytic (or Embden-Meyerhof) pathway. Two moles of adenosine triphosphate (ATP) are generated for every mole of glucose that is metabolized. The intracellular mediator of hemoglobin function, 2,3-diphosphoglycerate, is synthesized in a side reaction shown in Fig. 287-2. About 10 percent of intracellular glucose 6-phosphate undergoes oxidation by means of the hexose-monophosphate shunt. This pathway maintains glutathione in the reduced form, thereby protecting sulfhydryl groups in hemoglobin and the red cell membrane from oxidation by peroxides and superoxide as well as by certain drugs and toxins. Such oxidant stress can compromise red cell function and viability in patients with a deficiency in glucose 6-phosphate dehydrogenase, the first enzymatic step in the hexose-monophosphate shunt (see Chap. 287). Less commonly, individuals may have a deficiency in one of the enzymes of the glycolytic pathway or in one of the other enzymes of the hexose-monophosphate shunt.

The red cell has rather modest metabolic obligations in keeping with its simplified structure. A significant portion of the ATP generated by glycolysis is spent in operating the sodium-potassium pump, necessary to preserve the ionic milieu in the cytoplasm and prevent colloid osmotic lysis. In addition, some metabolic energy is expended on maintenance and repair of the red cell membrane. Certain proteins in the membrane become phosphorylated by means of ATP and protein kinases, but the physiologic significance of this process is not yet understood. Finally, a small amount of metabolic currency is spent on maintaining hemoglobin iron atoms in the reduced form (Fe^{2+}).

The 120-day survival of the circulating red cell is dependent on preservation of the pliability of its membrane. The red cell membrane is composed of 50 percent protein, 40 percent lipid, and 10 percent carbohydrate. It is a bilayer consisting of molecules of phospholipid and cholesterol in a 1.2:1 molar ratio oriented in a stacked array so that the hydrophobic portions of the molecules are oriented toward the interior while the polar side groups are either on the external surface of the cell (the plasma membrane) or on the inner cytoplasmic surface (see Fig. 283-6). The distribution of phospholipids differs significantly in the two portions of the bilayer. The outer surface is relatively rich in lecithin and sphingomyelin while the inner surface has relatively more phosphatidyl serine and phosphatidyl ethanolamine. The lipids on the outer surface exchange freely with plasma lipids.

The red cell membrane contains about eight major proteins (depicted in Fig. 283-6) and a large number of minor components. These proteins can be divided into two groups. A few span the lipid bilayer so that one end of the polypeptide is on the external cell surface and the other is on the inner surface. Examples include glycophorin, which contains a number of polysaccharide blood group antigens, and band 3, which serves as a channel for the passage of anions in and out of the red cell. Other proteins bind only to the inner surface of the red cell membrane. These include several enzymes

FIGURE 283-6 *Diagram of a cross section of the red blood cell membrane. Spectrin, actin, and protein 4.1 form a meshwork which laminates the inner surface of the membrane. In contrast, other proteins such as the glycophorins (GP) and the anion transport protein traverse the lipid bilayer. Long polysaccharide chains are covalently attached to these proteins on the outer surface of the cell and also to glycolipid. The protein ankyrin forms a bridge between spectrin and a fraction of the anion transport proteins. Protein 4.1 binds to GP. Phospholipids in the lipid bilayer include phosphatidylcholine (PC) and sphingomyelin (SM), which are located primarily on the outer surface of the membrane, and phosphatidyl serine (PS) and phosphatidyl ethanolamine (PE), which are located primarily on the inner surface of the membrane.*

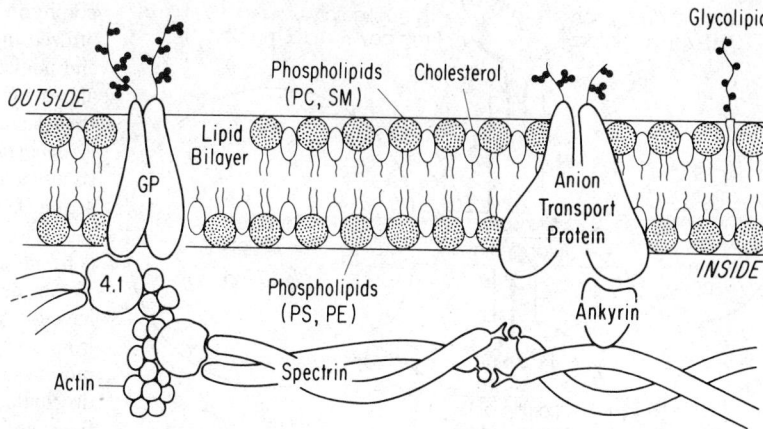

as well as structural proteins such as spectrin and actin, which interact to form a meshwork that laminates the cytoplasmic surface of the membrane.

It is likely that the physiologic demise of 120-day-old red cells is due to a loss of membrane flexibility preventing them from negotiating the narrow-bore channels of the microcirculation, including the sinusoids of the spleen. The factors responsible for red cell senescence are poorly understood. Experimental evidence indicates that deterioration of the red cell's metabolic machinery, sufficient to deplete it of ATP, can cause the cell to become spiculated (ecchinocytic) and lose its normal pliability. Depletion of ATP disrupts the spectrin and actin meshwork lining the inner membrane surface, resulting in aggregation of these proteins. Other factors such as enhanced rigidity and, perhaps, coating with immunoglobulin may also contribute to the recognition of the senescent red cell by the mononuclear phagocyte system. In contrast to normal red cells, there is a large and well-documented body of information on the mechanisms responsible for red cell destruction in various hemolytic anemias. These are discussed in Chap. 287.

Once the senescent red cell is sequestered (Fig. 283-2), hemoglobin is readily catabolized. Amino acids are released by proteolytic digestion and subsequently metabolized. The heme group is catabolized by a microsomal oxidizing system. The porphyrin ring is converted to bile pigments which are excreted almost quantitatively by the liver. One mole of carbon monoxide is formed per mole of heme that is broken down. Endogenous carbon monoxide production correlates directly with erythroid cell destruction. As Fig. 283-2 shows, the iron that is released during heme catabolism is initially incorporated into the storage protein ferritin, but it is eventually transported to marrow erythroid precursors by transferrin, the plasma iron–binding protein.

If red cell production is disordered, there may be significant destruction of erythroid cells within the bone marrow. A number of anemias are chararcterized by *ineffective erythropoiesis,* particularly those in which erythroid maturation is morphologically abnormal and the circulating red cells are abnormal in size. Examples discussed in detail elsewhere include megaloblastic anemias, sideroblastic anemias, and β thalassemia major. Such disorders are characterized by erythroid hyperplasia in the bone marrow and rapid uptake of labeled iron into the marrow but a low recovery of the labeled iron in circulating red cells. Endogenous carbon monoxide production and plasma levels of unconjugated bilirubin are generally elevated in ineffective erythropoiesis.

REFERENCES

BABIOR BM, STOSSEL TP: *Hematology: A Pathophysiological Approach.* New York, Churchill Livingston, 1984

BECK WS (ed): *Hematology,* 4th ed. Boston, MIT Press, 1985

BENNETT V: The membrane skeleton of human erythrocytes and its implications for more complex cells. Ann Rev Biochem 54:273, 1985

BUNN HF, FORGET BG: *Hemoglobin: Molecular, Genetic and Clinical Aspects.* Philadelphia, Saunders, 1986

COHEN CM: The molecular organization of the red cell membrane skeleton. Semin Hematol 20:141, 1983

CROSBY WH: Red cell mass: Its precursors and perturbations. Hosp Pract 15:2, 71, 1980

EAVES AC, EAVES CJ: Erythropoiesis in culture. Clin Haematol 13:371, 1984

ERSLEV AJ, GABUZDA TG: *Pathophysiology of Blood,* 3 ed. Philadelphia, Saunders, 1985

FINCH CA: Erythropoiesis, erythropoietin and iron. Blood 60:1241, 1982

FRIED W, MORLEY C: Update on erythropoietin. Int J Art Org 8:79, 1985

WILLIAMS WJ et al (ed): *Hematology,* 2 ed. New York, McGraw-Hill, 1983

284 ANEMIAS OF IRON DEFICIENCY AND IRON OVERLOAD

ANDREW I. SCHAFER / H. FRANKLIN BUNN

Among the transition metals that are essential to life, iron is the most abundant and important, being used in a broad repertoire of biochemical reactions. When complexed with porphyrin and inserted into an appropriate protein, iron not only binds oxygen reversibly but also participates in a number of vital oxidation-reduction reactions. Since inorganic iron is highly toxic, specific processes have evolved for its assimilation, transport, and storage. Under normal circumstances iron homeostasis is precisely maintained but can go awry in a variety of clinical settings, leading either to iron deficiency or iron overload.

IRON METABOLISM

The amount of iron obtained from the diet must replace the obligatory losses from the skin and gastrointestinal and genitourinary tracts; these losses generally do not exceed 1 mg daily in the adult male or nonmenstruating female. Additional iron requirements due to menstrual blood loss vary greatly but average about 0.5 mg daily. The amount of iron present in the diet, about 10 to 20 mg daily in the United States, greatly exceeds that required to meet physiologic demands. Thus, the widespread prevalence of iron deficiency is due in part to the inefficient absorption of dietary iron. Heme iron is better absorbed than is nonheme iron. Unfortunately, the diet of most of the population of the world is virtually devoid of meats and hence of heme iron. Even in the more developed countries, only 5 to 10 percent of the iron in the diet is absorbed.

ABSORPTION Because there is no major physiologic route for the excretion of iron, body iron content normally is largely determined by its absorption. Iron is absorbed mainly in the duodenum and proximal jejunum. The absorption of nonheme iron is modified by several factors in the diet and in gastrointestinal secretions. Iron-binding anions in food, such as ethylenediaminetetraacetic acid (EDTA), which is used as a preservative in a number of foodstuffs, tannates (contained in tea), carbonates, oxalates, and phosphates all

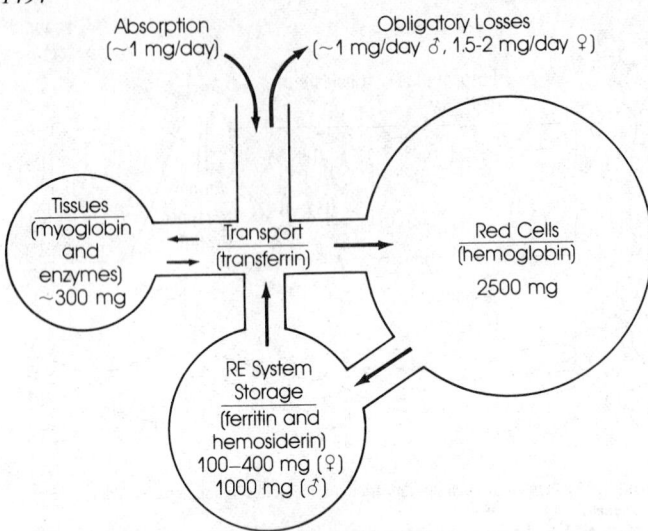

FIGURE 284-1 *The distribution of iron in normal adults and internal iron kinetics. Bold arrows indicate major pathways of iron movement.*

inhibit iron absorption. Medicinal antacids, such as magnesium trisilicate, and clay may also impair iron absorption. In contrast, other substances in the diet, including ascorbic acid, citric acid, amino acids, and sugars, enhance iron absorption. Gastric secretions and hydrochloric acid facilitate nonheme iron absorption by poorly understood mechanisms which probably involve the stabilization of ionic iron, thereby preventing its precipitation as insoluble ferric hydroxide. Most of these dietary and secretory factors do not affect the absorption of heme iron, which is taken up by the mucosal cells as the intact metalloporphyrin.

Intestinal iron absorption depends on both the amount and bioavailability of dietary iron and is controlled by the gut mucosal "setting" which is responsive to the state of body iron stores. The amount of iron entering the mucosal cell and passing into the portal circulation is regulated to maintain a normal body iron content. The signals which determine this "mucosal intelligence" are largely unknown. However, when the demand for iron is increased by depletion of body reserves due to growth spurts, pregnancy, or menstrual and pathologic hemorrhage, the efficiency of iron absorption can increase to about 10 to 20 percent. Conversely, when excessive body stores of iron are present, intestinal iron absorption is markedly reduced.

DISTRIBUTION   The distribution of iron in normal adults is shown in Fig. 284-1. Most of the body iron is found in red cells as the iron

FIGURE 284-2 *Serum iron and iron-binding capacity in various disorders.*

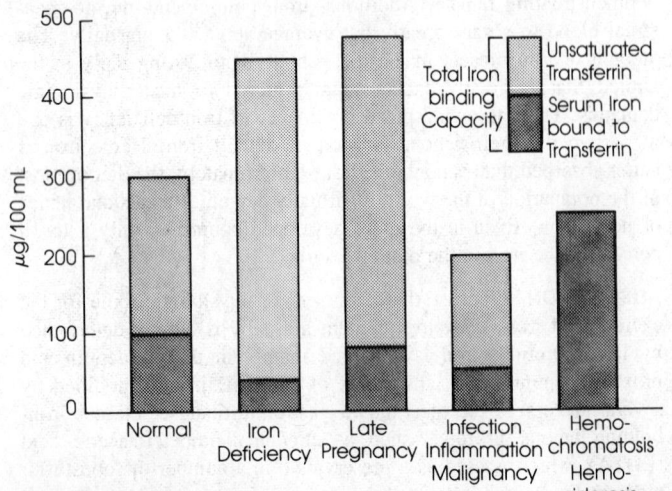

porphyrin complex of hemoglobin. Smaller quantities of iron are utilized in various tissues in the form of myoglobin as well as heme and nonheme enzymes. Excess iron is stored in the body as ferritin and hemosiderin. The iron in ferritin is enclosed within a protein shell, apoferritin, which can take up Fe^{2+} and oxidize it so that Fe^{3+} is deposited within the iron core. The synthesis of apoferritin is stimulated by iron. Small quantities of ferritin can be measured in serum. Under normal conditions there is a close correlation between serum ferritin concentration and body iron stores, with serum ferritin concentration of 1 μg/L equivalent to 10 mg of storage iron. Hemosiderin is a degraded form of ferritin in which the molecules have lost part of their protein shell and have aggregated. Most storage iron is normally present as ferritin, but an increasing proportion is present as hemosiderin as iron overload progresses. Storage iron is distributed primarily in mononuclear phagocyte cells of the spleen, liver, and bone marrow and in hepatic parenchymal cells. Exchange of iron between these communicating tissue compartments is effected by the carrier plasma protein transferrin, a beta globulin synthesized in the liver.

TRANSPORT   The major destination of plasma transferrin–bound iron is the erythron, where immature red cell precursors assimilate the iron for hemoglobin synthesis. A much smaller amount of transferrin iron is delivered to other sites, particularly the parenchymal cells of the liver. Transferrin has two iron-binding sites. Diferric transferrin is more effective in donating iron to the developing erythron than is monoferric iron. When transferrin iron saturation is increased, tissue iron uptake is increased. Virtually no iron is deposited in mononuclear phagocyte cells from the plasma transferrin pool. These cells derive most of their iron from the phagocytosis of senescent red cells. Following phagocytosis, the iron is liberated from the porphyrin ring by heme oxygenase and is either released to the plasma to be bound by transferrin or is stored in the form of ferritin and hemosiderin. Therefore, the passage of iron through the mononuclear phagocyte system is unidirectional (see Fig. 284-1). Iron metabolism is characterized by conservation of body iron, so that the iron of hemoglobin degradation is continually reutilized for erythropoiesis. Storage iron is readily mobilized in response to increased demand by the erythron, but chronic infection, inflammation, or malignancy can interfere with the release of iron from mononuclear phagocyte stores.

LABORATORY EVALUATION   In the laboratory assessment of body iron status, the most direct and sensitive tests involve *examination of tissues for iron content*. Depletion of bone marrow iron stores is the earliest stage in the development of iron deficiency and can be detected by the absence of Prussian blue–stainable iron in an aspirate of bone marrow. Histochemical assessment of increased bone marrow iron does not correlate as well with body iron stores in disorders of transfusional iron overload, and it is an unreliable index of iron overload in idiopathic hemochromatosis. The most sensitive test of iron loading in hemochromatosis (Chap. 310) is quantitative measurement of liver iron content in a liver biopsy specimen. Computerized tomography can show increased density of the liver.

Measurement of *serum iron and total iron-binding capacity* (or transferrin) is useful in the diagnosis of both iron deficiency and overload states (Fig. 284-2). The degree to which transferrin is saturated with iron represents a reliable indicator of iron supply to the developing red cell. Transferrin is normally about 20 to 45 percent saturated. The serum iron is characteristically decreased both in iron deficiency and in association with chronic disorders; however, in the latter the iron-binding capacity is generally also decreased to maintain a transferrin saturation of over 15 percent, while in the former it is usually increased so that transferrin saturation falls below 10 percent. In hypoproliferative and iron-overload states, serum iron is elevated and transferrin saturation may approach 100 percent. A disadvantage of this test is that serum iron (and hence transferrin saturation) is subject to pronounced diurnal and day-to-day variations.

Assay of *serum ferritin* correlates closely with total-body iron stores. The "normal range" of serum ferritin is not clearly established since it depends on age and sex; however, serum ferritin concentrations of 15 to 300 μg/L can be generally considered to be normal in adults. The finding of a low ferritin level is diagnostic of iron deficiency and obviates the need to perform bone marrow aspiration for the purpose of assessing stainable iron. Measurement of serum ferritin is also useful in detecting and determining the degree of iron overload, although it may underestimate iron stores in some patients with early hemochromatosis. The serum ferritin level depends not only on tissue iron stores but also on the rate of release of ferritin from the tissues. Therefore, in cases of extensive tissue damage, as may occur in patients with inflammation, liver disease, and certain malignancies, the ferritin level is usually elevated in the absence of iron overload and may be normal in the presence of coexisting iron deficiency.

Ferrokinetics *Ferrokinetic studies,* using tracer amounts of a radioactive isotope of iron, provide a more dynamic laboratory assessment of iron supply to the marrow and erythropoiesis in general than do the static methods described above. Radioactive iron (^{59}Fe) is injected intravenously and binds readily to plasma transferrin. From serial samples of the peripheral blood following injection the plasma iron turnover can be determined as well as the subsequent incorporation of iron into the hemoglobin of circulating red cells. In normal subjects, injected radioiron disappears rapidly and exponentially from plasma, with a half-time of 60 to 90 min. Figure 284-3A shows the linear clearance of plasma radioiron when it is plotted semilogarithmically. Plasma iron turnover (PIT) is the measure of the absolute amount of iron released from plasma transferrin per unit of time and is calculated from the rate of disappearance of iron label from the plasma, the plasma iron content, and the plasma volume. In normal individuals 30 to 40 mg of iron leaves the plasma daily. The PIT reflects the rate of *total* erythropoiesis. The *effectiveness* of erythropoiesis is indicated by the extent that the iron label is incorporated into hemoglobin in circulating red cells (Fig. 284-3B). In about a week, red cells normally accumulate 80 to 90 percent of the injected dose of radioiron.

In conditions of severe bone marrow failure (hypoplastic anemias) plasma iron clearance is slow, PIT is decreased, and there is very little incorporation of ^{59}Fe into hemoglobin. In iron deficiency, ^{59}Fe is removed from plasma more rapidly than normal and is almost entirely utilized by the hemoglobin of newly formed red cells. A similar pattern of ferrokinetics is seen in polycythemia vera, which is characterized by increased effective erythropoiesis. In hemolytic states, radioiron is rapidly cleared from the plasma and rapidly appears in circulating red cells, but because of the premature removal of red cells from the circulation, the apparent maximal recovery is less than normal. In disorders of hemoglobin synthesis, such as thalassemia and the sideroblastic anemias, plasma iron clearance is likewise rapid

and PIT is increased; however, because of ineffective erythropoiesis, red cell radioiron utilization is low. A similar ferrokinetic profile is seen in megaloblastic anemias and myeloid metaplasia, which are likewise characterized by ineffective erythropoiesis.

IRON-DEFICIENCY ANEMIA

When the supply of iron to the bone marrow falls short of that required for the production of red blood cells, anemia will ensue. Iron deficiency is the most common cause of anemia throughout the world. This condition is particularly prevalent in tropical areas where the dietary intake of meat is low and where infestation with hookworm is endemic. In the United States, about 20 percent of women in the childbearing age group are iron-deficient, while the overall prevalence in adult males is about 2 percent.

ETIOLOGY The development of iron deficiency depends upon one or more of the following factors: (1) increased requirements, (2) inadequate dietary intake, (3) decreased intestinal absorption, and (4) blood loss. Accordingly, certain groups of individuals can be readily identified to be at increased risk for developing iron deficiency.

Increased requirements for iron occur during the growth spurts of infancy and adolescence and during pregnancy. Up to 10 percent of pre-school-age children in the United States are iron-deficient, with a peak incidence at 1 to 2 years of age. The increased demand for iron during infancy is not adequately met by a diet rich in milk and cereals and poor in meat and vegetables. The iron content of such a diet is low, and assimilation may be further impaired by the presence of iron-binding anions, particularly phosphates. Accordingly, an infant's diet should be supplemented with iron. During adolescence, iron intake also may be compromised owing to irregular dietary habits and the current predilection for "junk food." During pregnancy the growing fetus usurps about 500 mg of iron from the mother, even if she is already iron-deficient. The daily iron requirement increases about threefold during pregnancy. Currently, the vast majority of pregnant women who seek medical attention are routinely given prophylactic treatment with iron salts. Among pregnant women who do not receive adequate antenatal care, the incidence of iron deficiency exceeds 50 percent.

Inadequate intake of iron is prevalent in certain parts of the world where diets are low in animal proteins. The low iron content of the diets of infants and adolescents is mentioned above. Among indigent and elderly individuals, iron intake is often suboptimal, owing to a combination of economic constraints, poor dentition, and apathy.

FIGURE 284-3 *Ferrokinetics in normal subjects and patients with disorders of erythropoiesis. A. Plasma radioiron clearance. B. Red cell radioiron utilization.*

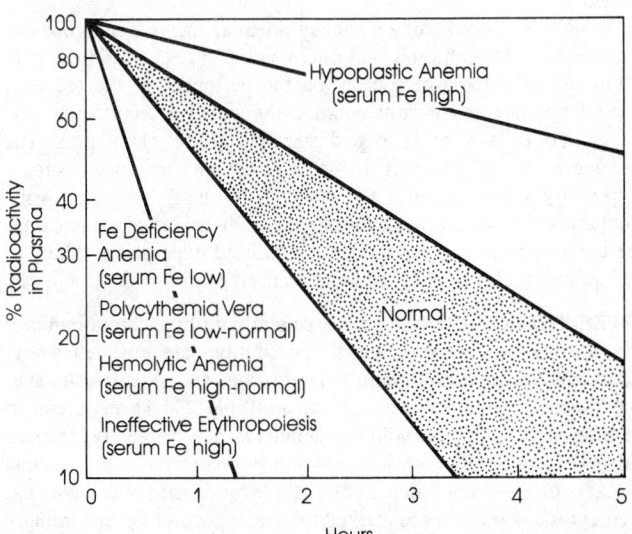

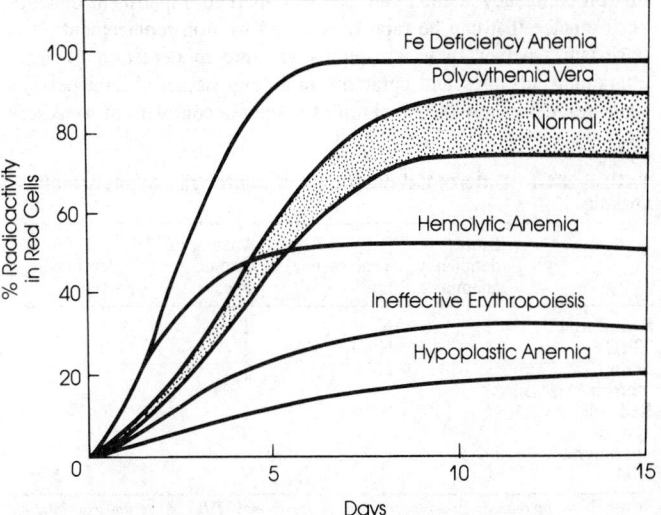

Decreased absorption of iron can occur in many clinical settings. After partial or total gastrectomy, the assimilation of dietary iron is impaired, owing primarily to increased motility and bypass of the proximal intestine, which is the primary site of iron absorption. Achlorhydria also contributes to decreased iron absorption. Patients with chronic diarrhea or intestinal malabsorption may also develop iron deficiency, particularly if the duodenum and proximal jejunum are involved. Sometimes iron-deficiency anemia is a harbinger of nontropical (celiac) sprue.

Blood loss is by far the most important cause of iron deficiency in adults. Among women in the childbearing age group, menstrual blood loss is responsible for most cases of iron deficiency. Women who take estrogen-progesterone birth control pills tend to have reduced menstrual blood loss, whereas those with intrauterine devices have increased menstrual blood flow.

Gastrointestinal blood loss is the primary cause of iron deficiency among adult males but must be carefully considered in any iron-deficient patient. The testing of stool for occult blood is an indispensable part of the evaluation of all patients with iron deficiency or unexplained anemia. Since gastrointestinal bleeding can be intermittent, it may be necessary to test multiple specimens over an extended time span. The most common causes of gastrointestinal blood loss are peptic ulcer, hiatus hernia, diverticulosis, and cancer. Hemorrhoids and salicylate ingestion are often responsible for the presence of occult blood in the stool but rarely cause significant blood loss. In about 15 percent of patients with documented gastrointestinal bleeding, no source can be determined, even after extensive radiologic and endoscopic investigation. In tropical areas parasitic infestations, particularly hookworm, are a major cause of blood loss. Occasionally, as in patients with hereditary telangiectasia or in those with a bleeding diathesis, gastrointestinal bleeding arises from multiple sites. Thrombocytopenia, qualitative platelet disorders, and von Willebrand's disease are more apt to cause gastrointestinal bleeding than are deficiencies of the soluble coagulation factors.

Regular blood donors undergo a progressive depletion of iron reserves, and menstruating female donors in particular may develop frank iron-deficient erythropoiesis. The prevalence of iron depletion increases progressively with the rate of donations.

In rare patients, iron deficiency may be caused by impaired incorporation of transferrin-bound iron by erythroid precursors. This may be a congenital condition or it may be acquired with the development of autoantibodies to transferrin receptors.

CLINICAL FINDINGS   Because iron deficiency usually develops insidiously, anemic patients are often relatively free of symptoms. In general, the signs and symptoms of iron-deficiency anemia are shared by other anemias of comparable severity (Chap. 53). Weakness, fatigue, lassitude, palpitations, and lightheadedness are common complaints. Subtle behavioral changes may occur. Even mild degrees of iron deficiency anemia can lead to a marked impairment of work performance that can be rapidly reversed by iron replacement. It is uncertain whether these symptoms are due to depletion of iron-containing enzymes and cofactors in certain tissues. Many persons with iron deficiency but no significant anemia complain of weakness

and fatigue, but such nonspecific symptoms are difficult to evaluate. Iron deficiency is sometimes associated with pica, a desire to gnaw on solid substances. Patients develop a craving for clay (geophagia), cornstarch (amylophagia), or ice (pagophagia). This peculiar symptom subsides when iron deficiency is corrected. Iron deficiency may also be associated with a variety of gastrointestinal symptoms. Following severe and prolonged deficiency, patients sometimes develop dysphagia owing to thin membranous webs at the postcricoid area (Plummer-Vinson syndrome). More commonly, iron-deficient patients develop a variety of less specific gastrointestinal symptoms, such as anorexia, nausea, eructation, and constipation, but it is uncertain whether these complaints are caused by iron deficiency per se. Those with prolonged iron deficiency often have achlorhydria and gastric atrophy. Menorrhagia is a common symptom in iron-deficient women. Gastric atrophy and menorrhagia may contribute toward the development of iron deficiency rather than being sequelae.

Physical findings may include pallor, tachycardia, and a "hemic" flow murmur, signs shared by patients with other types of anemia. Those with prolonged iron deficiency often have dry, brittle, and ridged nails which occasionally assume a concave surface (koilonychia). The epithelium at the edges of the lips may be cracked (angular stomatitis), and the tongue may become atrophic and even tender (glossitis). The spleen is seldom enlarged. The nonhematologic manifestations of iron deficiency, such as koilonychia, angular stomatitis, glossitis, and esophageal webs, are rarely encountered nowadays, probably because iron deficiency is more readily diagnosed and more promptly treated than in earlier times.

LABORATORY FINDINGS   A variety of laboratory tests can be used to assess varying degrees of iron deficiency. The development of iron deficiency progresses in an orderly sequence of events, each of which correlates with clinical laboratory abnormalities. *Storage iron depletion* occurs first, during which iron reserves are lost without compromise of the iron supply for erythropoiesis. At this stage, a bone marrow aspirate stained with Prussian blue will show markedly reduced or absent deposits of iron in macrophages. This finding is accompanied by a decrease in the level of serum ferritin. The next stage is *iron-deficient erythropoiesis*, during which the erythroid iron supply is reduced without the development of anemia. The iron-binding capacity of the serum (TIBC) first rises, followed by a drop in serum iron. As a result, the fractional saturation of transferrin falls markedly. The circulating red cells become microcytic and hypochromic. This is accompanied by an increase in free erythrocyte protoporphyrin (FEP). Protoporphyrin IX accumulates in the red cell because there is insufficient iron to convert it to heme (see Fig. 283-3). The fluorometric assay of FEP is a reliable and cost-effective way of screening large groups of individuals such as schoolchildren for iron deficiency. The final stage is the development of *iron-deficiency anemia*.

In well-developed iron-deficiency anemia, the red cells become more severely hypochromic and microcytic (Fig. A5-4). Often, only a thin rim of cytoplasm appears on the periphery of the red cell. Small fragments and bizarre poikilocytes are also seen. Such misshapen red cells have shortened survival in the circulation. The percentage of reticulocytes is usually normal but may increase temporarily following an acute episode of blood loss. The white count is usually normal, while the platelet count is normal or increased. The bone marrow displays moderate erythroid hyperplasia. Many of the late normoblasts appear to have scanty cytoplasm.

DIFFERENTIAL DIAGNOSIS   In a patient with hypochromic microcytic anemia, the major diagnostic possibilities are iron deficiency, thalassemia, anemia of chronic inflammation, and sideroblastic anemia. Several laboratory tests (shown in Table 284-1) are useful in the differential diagnosis. Mild iron deficiency may be readily confused with β-thalassemia trait or with the two-deletion forms of α thalassemia ($\alpha-/\alpha-$ or $--/\alpha\alpha$) (Chap. 288). In these mild forms of thalassemia, microcytosis is much more marked than is hypochromia; accordingly the mean corpuscular hemoglobin concentration (MCHC) is usually

TABLE 284-1   Differential diagnosis of microcytic hypochromic anemia

	Iron-deficiency anemia	β-Thalassemia trait	Anemia of chronic disease	Sideroblastic anemia
Serum iron	↓	N	↓	↑
TIBC	↑	N	↓	N
Serum ferritin	↓	N	↑	↑
Red cell protoporphyrin	↑	N	↑	↑ or N
HbA₂	↓	↑	N	↓

NOTE: ↑ = *increased;* ↓ = *decreased;* N = *normal;* TIBC = *serum iron binding capacity.*

normal. The red cell size distribution is more uniform than that in iron deficiency. Target cells and basophilic stippling are more prominent in thalassemia than in iron deficiency. Hemoglobin A_2 is elevated in β-thalassemia trait and decreased in iron deficiency and α thalassemia. β-Thalassemia trait may be masked by the finding of a normal level of hemoglobin A_2 if the patient has coexisting iron deficiency. The serum iron is normal or elevated in the thalassemias and decreased in both iron deficiency and in the anemia of chronic disease. However, as Fig. 284-2 shows, the transferrin level is also decreased in the latter. The laboratory tests shown in Table 284-1 are not very helpful in determining whether a patient with a chronic inflammatory disease, such as rheumatoid arthritis, has become iron-deficient. The finding of a low serum ferritin level or absent iron stores in a bone marrow aspirate would be diagnostic of iron deficiency. A trial of iron therapy may be necessary to settle the issue. The diagnosis of sideroblastic anemia rests on the demonstration of ringed sideroblasts in the bone marrow. These patients often have a population of hypochromic microcytic red cells, even though the red cell indexes are usually normal.

TREATMENT   Iron-deficiency anemia responds very effectively to iron therapy. However, an equally important part of management is to elicit and, if possible, correct the cause of the iron deficiency. Unless the patient has a clear-cut history of menorrhagia or bleeding from an obvious local site such as prolonged epistaxis or hemorrhoids, the gastrointestinal tract must be evaluated with appropriate radiologic and endoscopic studies.

Among the many iron preparations available, ferrous sulfate taken by mouth is the simplest and preferred treatment for most patients. The addition of extraneous minerals (copper, molybdenum) or vitamins or the addition of slow-release forms adds to the cost of the preparation but adds little to its efficacy. In some prenatal multivitamin preparations, calcium carbonate and magnesium oxide may actually interfere with the absorption of the iron. Most patients respond well to ferrous sulfate, 300 mg (60 mg elemental iron) three times daily. Absorption is somewhat enhanced if the iron is administered between meals. Conversely, patients experience less gastric distress if the iron is taken with meals. Some patients tolerate therapy better if it is begun with only one tablet per day and gradually increased over several days. About 15 percent of orally administered iron is absorbed during the first 3 weeks of therapy. Thereafter, absorption decreases, averaging about 5 percent. Treatment for at least 6 months is needed in most cases if body stores are to be replenished.

The response to treatment is generally very satisfactory. A peak reticulocytosis is generally seen at about day 10 with a gradual increase in hemoglobin and correction of red cell indexes.

Failure to respond to therapy usually means that (1) the diagnosis was incorrect; (2) the patient has failed to take the prescribed iron; (3) blood loss has exceeded the buildup of hemoglobin; (4) erythropoiesis has been suppressed by infection, inflammation, or tumor; or (5) the iron has not been properly absorbed.

Parenteral therapy is rarely required. When iron is absorbed poorly, as in some patients who have undergone gastrectomy or those with proximal intestinal disease, particularly celiac sprue, iron-dextran complex may be given intramuscularly. The first dose should be limited to 50 mg because severe reactions sometimes occur. By repeated injections, a total of 1.5 to 2.0 g may be given in this way. Although more likely to produce an adverse reaction, intravenous administration is also possible in patients who cannot tolerate intramuscular injections. The iron-dextran solution can be given by direct infusion, or it can be diluted in about 20 mL sterile saline solution and administered by intravenous drip. One or two drops should be given intravenously, and then, if no untoward symptoms develop in the next 5 min, 500 mg is infused slowly. With intravenous iron-dextran complex, the total replacement dose of iron can be infused at one time. The total amount of parenteral iron that should be given is based on the calculated deficit in red blood cell mass, plus an additional 1000 mg to replenish iron stores. Transfusion of blood is seldom indicated, unless the patient has evidence of cardiovascular compromise, such as congestive heart failure or coronary or cerebral ischemia.

IRON-LOADING ANEMIAS

Dependence on multiple blood transfusions by some patients with acquired or congenital anemias can lead to a state of generalized iron overload. One unit of blood contains about 200 to 250 mg iron. Therefore, in a patient with failure of bone marrow erythroid activity who requires about 4 units of blood every month, at least 20 g of elemental iron can be expected to accumulate within 2 years; this is enough iron to produce clinical symptoms in some patients with idiopathic hemochromatosis. Hyperabsorption of dietary iron in idiopathic hemochromatosis (Chap. 310), in which excess iron is distributed predominantly in parenchymal cells, leads to earlier signs of clinical organ damage than does transfusional iron loading, in which excess iron initially is deposited in the mononuclear phagocyte system. However, most patients who have received more than 100 units of blood exhibit evidence of organ damage in a pattern which resembles that observed in idiopathic hemochromatosis. The most common clinical manifestations of iron overload include hyperpigmentation of the skin, abnormal liver function and cirrhosis, diabetes mellitus, anterior pituitary insufficiency manifesting as hypogonadism, adrenal insufficiency or hypothyroidism, and cardiomyopathy manifesting as congestive heart failure, arrhythmias, or conduction disturbances.

In anemias associated with ineffective erythropoiesis, transfusional iron overload is compounded by excessive intestinal iron absorption. The importance of this factor is exemplified by patients with sideroblastic anemia or thalassemia intermedia who can develop advanced hemochromatosis even in the absence of transfusions. The mechanisms responsible for the inappropriate hyperabsorption of dietary iron in patients with ineffective erythropoiesis are unknown, but iron absorption can be reduced if the anemia is corrected and erythropoiesis is suppressed by transfusion. Thalassemia is discussed in Chap. 288.

SIDEROBLASTIC ANEMIA   Sideroblastic anemia consists of a group of disorders of diverse etiologies (Table 284-2) characterized by ringed sideroblasts in the nucleated red cell population of the bone marrow. Ringed sideroblasts are normoblasts which contain iron deposits within mitochondria. The partial or complete rings of Prussian blue–staining granules are produced by the perinuclear distribution of these iron-laden mitochondria. A number of metabolic abnormalities has been noted in the sideroblastic anemias, including defects in one or more of the enzymatic steps in heme synthesis. Since the initial and terminal steps in heme porphyrin synthesis are localized in the mitochondria, it is difficult to determine whether such abnormalities are the cause or the result of mitochondrial iron loading. In addition to the presence of ringed sideroblasts in the bone marrow, these disorders share certain other characteristics: a population of microcytic and hypochromic red cells in the peripheral smear due to defective heme synthesis; bone marrow erythroid hyperplasia as a result of ineffective erythropoiesis; increased levels of red cell porphyrins; and marked increase in the serum iron and transferrin saturation often accompanied by evidence of generalized iron overload.

Hereditary sideroblastic anemia may be either X-linked or autosomal recessive and is often pyridoxine-responsive. Severe anemia is usually first noted in young adulthood, although the age of detection

TABLE 284-2   The sideroblastic anemias

1 Hereditary or congenital sideroblastic anemias
2 Acquired sideroblastic anemias
  a Associated with drugs and toxins (e.g., alcohol, lead, isoniazid, chloramphenicol)
  b Associated with neoplastic and inflammatory disease (e.g., carcinoma, leukemia, myeloproliferative disorders, Hodgkin's disease, other lymphomas, myeloma, rheumatoid arthritis)
  c Idiopathic refractory sideroblastic anemia

may vary greatly even within a single kindred. Large doses of vitamin B_6 result in at least a partial correction of the anemia in patients with hereditary pyridoxine-responsive sideroblastic anemia. The genetic lesion may affect the first and rate-limiting enzyme of porphyrin synthesis, δ-aminolevulinic acid synthetase (ALA-S), either directly or through metabolism of its essential cofactor, pyridoxal 5′-phosphate.

A variety of drugs and toxins can cause a reversible sideroblastic anemia which usually resolves following removal of the offending agent. These include isoniazid (INH) and alcohol, which cause abnormalities in pyridoxine metabolism, and lead, which interferes with several reactions in the pathway of heme synthesis. Sideroblastic anemia occurs in about 30 percent of hospitalized alcoholics; ringed sideroblasts in the bone marrow disappear within several days after cessation of alcohol ingestion. Sideroblastic changes in the bone marrows of alcoholics usually occur in the setting of coexisting malnutrition and folate deficiency. Secondary sideroblastic anemia has also been observed occasionally in association with a variety of inflammatory, neoplastic, and preleukemic states; in these disorders the clinical picture is dominated by the underlying illness.

Sideroblastic anemia is a common form of refractory anemia in older patients in whom other associated diseases, drugs, or toxins cannot be identified. Many of these patients have an indolent course and die of nonhematologic causes. However, some patients become transfusion-dependent and develop complications of iron overload. Unlike the other types of sideroblastic anemia, this can be a preleukemic disorder which is frequently associated with chromosomal abnormalities and transforms into acute nonlymphocytic leukemia in approximately 10 percent of cases.

TREATMENT   In cases of secondary sideroblastic anemia, withdrawal of the offending drug or toxin or treatment of the underlying disease is usually beneficial. Patients with acquired idiopathic sideroblastic anemia rarely respond to pyridoxine, although a 2- to 3-month trial of this vitamin in a dose of 200 mg daily should be attempted. A trial of androgens, in a regimen similar to that used in aplastic anemia, may ameliorate the anemia in some cases. In idiopathic refractory sideroblastic anemia, therapy is usually supportive. Many patients require frequent blood transfusions, and measures to reduce transfusional iron loading are required.

While phlebotomy is the most effective treatment for hemochromatosis, in anemic patients with transfusional iron overload, in whom phlebotomy is precluded, elimination of excess iron can be achieved only with iron-chelating agents. Deferoxamine is presently the only clinically effective iron chelator available. Deferoxamine-chelated iron is excreted primarily in the urine and to a lesser extent in the stool. Because the drug is not well absorbed when given orally and has a short half-life, it should be administered by continuous parenteral infusion. Deferoxamine can be administered to ambulatory patients by means of a subcutaneous infusion delivered by a portable pump. Doses are generally 1.5 to 2.5 g daily, infused over 16 to 24 h; however, there is considerable individual variation, and the optimal regimen should be established for individual patients. Adverse effects from deferoxamine are unusual. Patients may develop cataracts after long-term use, and periodic slit-lamp eye examinations are indicated in patients on chronic therapy. Local erythema and discomfort at the subcutaneous injection site can usually be prevented by the addition of hydrocortisone to the deferoxamine solution. Hypersensitivity reactions occur rarely.

Oral ascorbic acid supplementation may markedly enhance the iron-chelating efficiency of deferoxamine, presumably by liberating more free intracellular iron which becomes available for chelation. However, increased amounts of free iron may also damage cells by generating free oxygen radicals. This may be manifested clinically by cardiac irritability or congestive heart failure. Therefore, the administration of ascorbic acid to patients with iron overload may be hazardous.

Manipulation of blood transfusions to selectively infuse young red cells (neocytes), and thereby prolong the interval between transfusions, is a promising measure for the avoidance of iron overload in transfusion-dependent patients, but its application to adult patients has not been established.

REFERENCES

Bothwell TH et al: *Iron Metabolism in Man*. Oxford, Blackwell Scientific, 1979

Bottomley SS: Sideroblastic anaemia. Clin Haematol 11:389, 1982

Cook JD: Clinical evaluation of iron deficiency. Semin Hematol 19:6, 1982

Crosby WH: Current concepts in nutrition: Who needs iron? N Engl J Med 297:543, 1977

Dallman PR: Manifestations of iron deficiency. Semin Hematol 19:19, 1982

Finch CA, Huebers H: Perspectives in iron metabolism. N Engl J Med 360:1520, 1982

Huebers HA, Finch CA: Transferrin: Physiologic behavior and clinical implications. Blood 64:763, 1984

Lanzkowsky P: Problems in diagnosis of iron deficiency anemia. Pediatr Ann 14:618, 622, 627, 1985

Schafer AI: Iron overload, in *Current Hematology*. New York, Wiley, 1981 vol 1, chap 5

Schwartz S et al: Chromosome abnormalities in acquired idiopathic sideroblastic anemia with subsequent leukemic transformation. Cancer Genet Cytogenet 19:291, 1986

Worwood M: Iron and hemochromatosis. J Inherited Metab Dis 6(Suppl 1):63, 1983

---

285   MEGALOBLASTIC ANEMIAS

BERNARD M. BABIOR / H. FRANKLIN BUNN

The megaloblastic anemias are disorders caused by impaired deoxyribonucleic acid (DNA) synthesis. Cells primarily affected are those having a relatively rapid turnover, especially hematopoietic precursors and gastrointestinal epithelial cells. Cell division is sluggish, but cytoplasmic development progresses normally, so megaloblastic cells tend to be large, with an increased ratio of ribonucleic acid (RNA) to DNA. Megaloblastic erythroid cells tend to be destroyed in the marrow in excessive numbers, an abnormality termed *ineffective erythropoiesis* (Chaps. 53 and 283).

Most megaloblastic anemias are due to a deficiency of vitamin B_{12} and/or folic acid. The various clinical entities associated with megaloblastic anemia are listed in Table 285-1. This classification is easier to comprehend if the physiologic and biochemical principles discussed below are kept in mind.

PHYSIOLOGIC CONSIDERATIONS

FOLIC ACID   Folic acid is the common name for pteroylmonoglutamic acid. It is synthesized by many different plants and bacteria. Fruits and vegetables constitute the primary dietary source of the vitamin. Some forms of dietary folic acid are labile and may be destroyed by cooking. The minimum daily requirement is normally about 50 μg but may be increased severalfold during periods of enhanced metabolic demand such as pregnancy.

The assimilation of adequate amounts of folic acid is dependent on the nature of the diet and its means of preparation. Folates in various foodstuffs are largely conjugated to polyglutamic acid. This highly polar side chain impairs the intestinal absorption of the vitamin. However, conjugases (γ-glutamyl carboxypeptidases) in the lumen of the gut convert polyglutamates to mono- and diglutamates, which are readily absorbed in the proximal jejunum.

There are binding proteins in plasma for folates, but their physiologic significance is unclear. Plasma folate is primarily in the form of N^5-methyltetrahydrofolate, a monoglutamate. N^5-Methyltetrahydrofolate is transported into cells by a carrier which is specific for the tetrahydro forms of the vitamin. Once in the cell, the folate is reconverted to the polyglutamate form, after removal of the N^5-methyl group in a vitamin B_{12}–requiring reaction (see below). The polyglutamate form may be useful for retention of folate by the cell.

Normal individuals have about 5 to 20 mg folic acid in various body stores, half in the liver. In light of the minimum daily

TABLE 285-1 Classification of the megaloblastic anemias

I Vitamin B_{12} deficiency
  A Inadequate intake: vegetarians (rare)
  B Malabsorption
    1 Inadequate production of intrinsic factor (IF)
      a Pernicious anemia
      b Gastrectomy
      c Congenital absence or functional abnormality of IF (rare)
    2 Disorders of terminal ileum
      a Tropical sprue
      b Nontropical sprue
      c Regional enteritis
      d Intestinal resection
      e Neoplasms and granulomatous disorders (rare)
      f Selective vitamin B_{12} malabsorption (Imerslund's syndrome) (rare)
    3 Competition for vitamin B_{12}
      a Fish tapeworm
      b Bacteria: blind loop syndrome
    4 Drugs: *p*-Aminosalicylic acid, colchicine, neomycin
  C Other
    1 Nitrous oxide
    2 Transcobalamin II deficiency (rare)
II Folic acid deficiency
  A Inadequate intake: Unbalanced diet (common in alcoholics, teenagers, some infants)
  B Increased requirements
    1 Pregnancy
    2 Infancy
    3 Malignancy
    4 Increased hematopoiesis (chronic hemolytic anemias)
    5 Chronic exfoliative skin disorders
    6 Hemodialysis
  C Malabsorption
    1 Tropical sprue
    2 Nontropical sprue
    3 Drugs: Phenytoin, barbiturates, (?) ethanol
  D Impaired metabolism
    1 Inhibitors of dihydrofolate reductase: Methotrexate, pyrimethamine, triamterene, pentamidine, etc.
    2 Alcohol
    3 Rare enzyme deficiencies: Formiminotransferase, dihydrofolate reductase, others
III Other causes
  A Drugs which impair DNA metabolism
    1 Purine antagonists: 6-mercaptopurine, azathioprine, etc.
    2 Pyrimidine antagonists: 5-fluorouracil, cytosine arabinoside, etc.
    3 Others: Procarbazine, hydroxyurea
  B Metabolic disorders (rare)
    1 Hereditary orotic aciduria
    2 Others
  C Megalobastic anemia of unknown etiology
    1 Refractory megaloblastic anemia
    2 Di Guglielmo's syndrome*
    3 Congenital dyserythropoietic anemia

* A form of acute nonlymphocytic leukemia with atypical, dysplastic changes in erythroid series.

requirement, it is not surprising that a deficiency will occur within months if dietary intake or intestinal absorption is curtailed.

VITAMIN B_{12} This vitamin is a complex organometallic compound in which a cobalt atom is situated within a corrin ring, a structure similar to the porphyrin from which heme is formed (Fig. 283-3). As with heme, both δ-aminolevulinic acid and porphobilinogen are precursors in the biosynthesis of vitamin B_{12}. However, unlike heme, vitamin B_{12} cannot be synthesized in the human body and must be supplied in the diet. The only dietary source of vitamin B_{12} is animal products: meat and dairy foods. The minimum daily requirement for vitamin B_{12} is about 2.5 μg.

During gastric digestion, vitamin B_{12} in food is released and forms a stable complex with gastric R binder, one of a group of closely related glycoproteins of unknown function which are found in secretions (e.g., saliva, milk, gastric juice, bile), phagocytes, and plasma. On entering the duodenum, the vitamin B_{12}–R binder complex is digested, releasing the vitamin B_{12}, which then binds to intrinsic factor (IF). This glycoprotein of molecular weight 50,000 is produced by the parietal cells of the stomach. The secretion of intrinsic factor generally parallels that of hydrochloric acid. The vitamin B_{12}–IF complex is resistant to proteolytic digestion and travels to the distal ileum, where specific receptors on the mucosal brush border bind the

vitamin B_{12}–IF complex, thereby enabling the vitamin to be absorbed. Thus, intrinsic factor serves as a cell-directed carrier protein. Vitamin B_{12} is transferred from the ileal receptor across the mucosa to the capillary circulation where it binds initially to another transport protein, transcobalamin II (TC II). The vitamin B_{12}–TC II complex is rapidly taken up by the liver, the bone marrow, and other cells. Normally, about 2 mg vitamin B_{12} is stored in the liver, and another 2 mg is stored elsewhere in the body. In view of the minimum daily requirement, about 3 to 6 years would be required for a normal individual to become deficient in vitamin B_{12} if absorption were to cease abruptly.

Although TC II is the acceptor for newly absorbed vitamin B_{12}, most circulating vitamin B_{12} is bound to transcobalamin I (TC I), a glycoprotein closely related to gastric R binder. TC I appears to be derived in part from leukocytes. The paradox that most circulating vitamin B_{12} is bound to TC I rather than TC II, even though TC II receives all the vitamin B_{12} which is absorbed by the intestine, is explained by the fact that vitamin B_{12} bound to TC II is rapidly cleared from the blood ($t_{1/2}$ about 1 h), while clearance of vitamin B_{12} bound to TC I requires many days. The function of TC I is unknown.

BIOCHEMICAL CONSIDERATIONS

FOLATE The *prime function* of this vitamin is to transfer one-carbon moieties such as methyl and formyl groups to various organic compounds (see Fig. 285-1). The source of these one-carbon moieties is usually serine, which reacts with tetrahydrofolate to produce glycine and $N^{5,10}$-methylenetetrahydrofolate. An alternative source is formiminoglutamic acid, an intermediate in histidine catabolism, which gives up its formimino group to tetrahydrofolate to yield N^5-formiminotetrahydrofolate and glutamic acid. These derivatives provide entry into an interconvertible donor pool consisting of tetrahydrofolate derivatives carrying various one-carbon moieties (see Fig. 285-1). The constituents of this pool can donate their one-carbon moieties to appropriate acceptor compounds to form metabolic intermediates which are ultimately converted to building blocks used in the synthesis of biologic macromolecules. The most important building blocks are (1) purines, in which the C-2 and C-8 atoms are introduced in folate-dependent reactions; (2) deoxythymidylate monophosphate (dTMP), synthesized from $N^{5,10}$-methylenetetrahydrofolate and deoxyuridylate monophosphate (dUMP); and (3) methionine, formed by the transfer of a methyl group from N^5-methyltetrahydrofolate to homocysteine. Vitamin B_{12} is also required for the formation of methionine from homocysteine (see below).

In all but one of the one-carbon transfer reactions, tetrahydrofolate is produced. It can immediately accept a one-carbon moiety and reenter the donor pool. The single exception is the thymidylate

FIGURE 285-1 *Scheme of folate metabolism.*

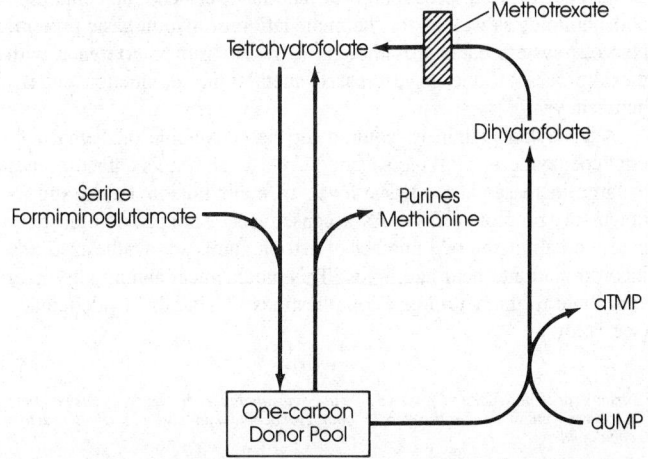

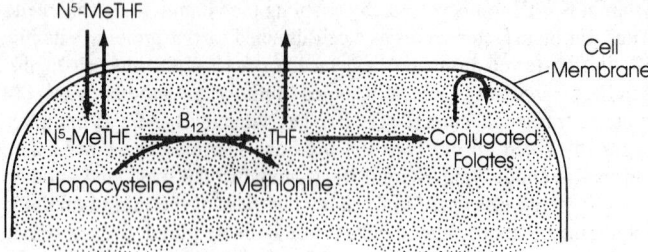

FIGURE 285-2 *Diagram showing the interrelationship between vitamin B$_{12}$ (methylcobalamin) and folate metabolism within the cell.*

synthetase reaction (dUMP → dTMP), in which dihydrofolate is the product (Fig. 285-1). This must be reduced to tetrahydrofolate by the enzyme dihydrofolate reductase before it can reenter the donor pool. A number of drugs are able to inhibit dihydrofolate reductase, thereby diverting folate from the donor pool and producing what amounts to a state of folate deficiency in the face of normal tissue folate concentrations.

VITAMIN B$_{12}$ In humans there are two metabolically active forms of vitamin B$_{12}$, identified by the alkyl group attached to the sixth coordination position of the cobalt atom: methylcobalamin and adenosylcobalamin. The vitamin preparation which is used therapeutically is cyanocobalamin. Cyanocobalamin has no known physiologic role and must be converted to a biologically active form before it can be used by tissues.[1]

Methylcobalamin is an essential cofactor in the conversion of homocysteine to methionine (Fig. 285-2). When this reaction is impaired, folate metabolism is deranged, and it is this derangement which is thought to underlie the defect in DNA synthesis and the megaloblastic maturation pattern in patients who are deficient in vitamin B$_{12}$ (see Fig. 285-2). What appears to happen in vitamin B$_{12}$ deficiency is that the unconjugated N^5-methyltetrahydrofolate newly taken from the bloodstream cannot be converted to other forms of tetrahydrofolate by methyl transfer. This is the so-called folate trap hypothesis. Since N^5-methyltetrahydrofolate is a poor substrate for the conjugating enzyme (this has been shown in rats but has not yet been demonstrated in humans), it largely remains in the unconjugated form and slowly leaks from the cell. Tissue folate deficiency therefore develops, and this results in megaloblastic hematopoiesis. This hypothesis explains the fact that tissue folate stores in vitamin B$_{12}$ deficiency are substantially reduced, with a disproportionate reduction in conjugated as compared with unconjugated folates, despite normal or supranormal serum folate levels. It also explains why large doses of folate can produce a partial hematologic remission in patients with vitamin B$_{12}$ deficiency.

Impairment in the conversion of homocysteine to methionine may also be partly responsible for the neurologic complications of vitamin B$_{12}$ deficiency (see below). The methionine formed in this reaction is needed for the production of choline and choline-containing phospholipids as well as for the methylation of myelin basic protein. Nervous system damage is thought to result from interference with these processes due to decreased methionine production in B$_{12}$ deficiency.

Adenosylcobalamin is required for the conversion of methylmalonyl coenzyme A (CoA) to succinyl CoA. Lack of this cofactor leads to large increases in the tissue levels of methylmalonyl CoA and its precursor, propionyl CoA. As a consequence, nonphysiologic fatty acids containing an odd number of carbon atoms are synthesized and incorporated into neuronal lipids. This biochemical abnormality may contribute to the neurologic complications of vitamin B$_{12}$ deficiency (see below).

CLINICAL DISORDERS

CLASSIFICATION OF MEGALOBLASTIC ANEMIAS   The etiology of megaloblastic anemia varies in different parts of the world. In temperate zones, folate deficiency in alcoholics and pernicious anemia are the common types of megaloblastic anemias. In certain areas close to the equator, tropical sprue is endemic and an important cause. In Scandinavia, megaloblastic anemia is sometimes secondary to infestation by the fish tapeworm *Diphyllobothrium latum.*

The dietary intake of vitamin B$_{12}$ is more than adequate for the body's requirements, except in true vegetarians (individuals who live on a purely vegetable diet) and their breast-fed infants. Thus, deficiency of vitamin B$_{12}$ is almost always due to malabsorption. As explained in the section above, the absorption of vitamin B$_{12}$ depends upon a specific binding protein produced in the stomach and uptake by a specific receptor in the mucosa of the distal ileum. Accordingly, several steps in this process can go awry and lead to malabsorption. These are listed in Table 285-1. In contrast, the dietary intake of folic acid is marginal in many parts of the world. Furthermore, since the body's stores of folate are relatively low, folic acid deficiency can arise rather suddenly during periods of decreased dietary intake or increased metabolic demand. Finally, folic acid deficiency may be due to malabsorption. Often two or more of these factors coexist in a given patient.

Combined deficiencies of vitamin B$_{12}$ and folic acid are not uncommon. Patients with tropical sprue are often deficient in both vitamins. The biochemical lesion that results in megaloblastic maturation of bone marrow cells also causes structural and functional abnormalities of the rapidly proliferating epithelial cells of the intestinal mucosa. Thus, severe deficiency of one vitamin can lead to malabsorption of the other. Furthermore, as discussed above, a deficiency of vitamin B$_{12}$ causes a secondary reduction in cellular folic acid.

Finally, megaloblastic anemias may occasionally be induced by factors unrelated to a vitamin deficiency. Most such cases are caused by one or more of the many drugs which interfere with DNA synthesis. Less commonly, megaloblastic maturation is encountered in certain acquired defects of hematopoietic stem cells. Rarest of all are specific congenital enzyme deficiencies in which megaloblastic anemia is characteristically encountered.

VITAMIN B$_{12}$ DEFICIENCY   There are many conditions in which vitamin B$_{12}$ deficiency may develop. Although each has its own characteristic manifestations, certain clinical features are common to all. These clinical features involve the blood, the gastrointestinal tract, and the nervous system.

The hematologic manifestations are almost entirely the result of anemia although very rarely purpura may appear, due to thrombocytopenia. Symptoms of anemia may include weakness, lightheadedness, vertigo, and tinnitus, as well as palpitations, angina, and the symptoms of congestive failure. On physical examination, the patient with florid vitamin B$_{12}$ deficiency is pale, with slightly icteric skin and eyes. The pulse is rapid, and the heart may be enlarged; auscultation will reveal a systolic flow murmur. The spleen and liver may be somewhat enlarged. There may be a slight fever.

The gastrointestinal manifestations reflect the effect of vitamin B$_{12}$ deficiency on the rapidly turning over gastrointestinal epithelium. The patient sometimes complains of a sore tongue, which on inspection will be smooth and beefy red. Anorexia with moderate weight loss may also be evident, possibly accompanied by diarrhea and other gastrointestinal symptoms. These latter manifestations may be in part caused by megaloblastosis of the small intestinal epithelium, which results in malabsorption.

The neurologic manifestations are the most worrisome of all, because they often fail to remit completely on treatment. They begin pathologically with demyelination, followed by axonal degeneration and eventual neuronal death; the final stage, of course, is irreversible. Sites of involvement include peripheral nerves, the spinal cord, where

---

[1] *Strictly speaking, vitamin B$_{12}$ refers only to cyanocobalamin. However, in this chapter, the term vitamin B$_{12}$ will refer to both cyanocobalamin and biologically active cobalamins.*

the posterior and lateral columns undergo demyelination, and the cerebrum itself. Signs and symptoms include numbness and paresthesias in the extremities (the earliest neurologic manifestations), weakness, ataxia, and poor finger coordination. There may be sphincter disturbances. Reflexes may be diminished or increased. The Romberg and Babinski signs may be positive, and position sense and vibration sense are usually diminished. Disturbances of mentation will vary from mild irritability and forgetfulness to severe dementia or frank psychosis. It should be emphasized that occasionally *neurologic disease may occur in a patient with a normal hematocrit.*

In the usual patient, in whom hematologic problems predominate, the blood and bone marrow show characteristic megaloblastic changes which are described under "Diagnosis" below. The anemia may be very severe—hematocrits of 15 to 20 are not infrequent—but is surprisingly well tolerated by the patient because it develops so slowly.

Pernicious anemia The most common cause of vitamin B_{12} deficiency in temperate climates is pernicious anemia, in which intrinsic factor secretion ceases owing to atrophy of the gastric mucosa. It is most frequently seen in individuals of northern European descent and is much less common in southern Europeans, blacks, and Orientals. Men and women are equally affected. It is a disease of the elderly, the average patient presenting near age 60; it is rare under 30, although typical pernicious anemia can be seen in children under 10 (juvenile pernicious anemia). Inherited conditions in which a histologically normal stomach secretes either an abnormal intrinsic factor or none at all will cause vitamin B_{12} deficiency which appears in infancy or early childhood.

On the basis of incomplete evidence, pernicious anemia is currently thought to be caused by an autoimmune reaction against gastric parietal cells. There is considerable evidence for immunologic abnormalities in pernicious anemia. The incidence of pernicious anemia is substantially increased in patients with other diseases thought to be of immunologic origin, including Graves' disease, myxedema, thyroiditis, idiopathic adrenocortical insufficiency, vitiligo, and hypoparathyroidism. Patients with pernicious anemia also have abnormal circulating antibodies related to their disease: 90 percent have antiparietal cell antibody while 60 percent have anti-intrinsic factor antibody. Antiparietal cell antibody is also found in 50 percent of patients with gastric atrophy without pernicious anemia as well as in 10 to 15 percent of an unselected patient population, but anti-intrinsic factor antibody is usually absent from these patients. Relatives of patients with pernicious anemia show an increased incidence of the disease, and even clinically unaffected relatives may have anti-intrinsic factor antibody in their serum. A final point supporting an immunologic basis for pernicious anemia is the fact that corticosteroids have been reported to reverse the disease both pathologically and clinically.

The destruction of parietal cells in pernicious anemia is thought to be mediated by the cellular immune system. Humoral factors such as anti-intrinsic factor antibody probably have little role in the pathogenesis of the disease, a view supported by the observation that pernicious anemia is unusually common in patients with agammaglobulinemia.

Pathologically, the most characteristic finding in pernicious anemia is gastric atrophy which involves only the acid- and pepsin-secreting portion of the stomach; the antrum is spared. Other pathologic changes, which are secondary to the deficiency of vitamin B_{12}, include megaloblastoid alterations in the gastric and intestinal epithelium and the neurologic changes described above. The abnormalities in the gastric epithelium are evident as cellular atypia in gastric cytology specimens, a finding which must be carefully distinguished from the cytologic abnormalities seen in gastric malignancy.

The *clinical manifestations* are primarily those of vitamin B_{12} deficiency, as described above. The disease is of insidious onset and progresses slowly. An additional physical finding is the tendency of patients with pernicious anemia to be fair-haired or prematurely gray.

Laboratory examination will reveal hypergastrinemia and pentagastrin-fast achlorhydria as well as the hematologic and other laboratory abnormalities discussed below in "Diagnosis."

Through appropriate replacement therapy, patients with pernicious anemia should experience complete and lifelong correction of all abnormalities which are due to vitamin B_{12} deficiency, except to the extent that irreversible changes in the nervous system may have occurred prior to treatment. These patients, however, are unusually subject to gastric polyps and have about twice the normal incidence of cancer of the stomach. In view of the latter complication, patients should be followed with frequent stool guaiac examinations together with further diagnostic studies when indicated.

Postgastrectomy Following total gastrectomy or extensive damage to gastric mucosa as, for example, by ingestion of corrosive agents, megaloblastic anemia may develop because the source of intrinsic factor has been removed. In such patients the absorption of orally administered vitamin B_{12} is impaired. Megaloblastic anemia may also follow partial gastrectomy, but the incidence is lower than after total gastrectomy, in which vitamin B_{12} malabsorption occurs in 100 percent of patients. The cause of vitamin B_{12} deficiency after partial gastrectomy may be intestinal overgrowth of bacteria, but it does not always respond to antibiotics.

Intestinal organisms The macrocytic anemia seen in association with intestinal strictures, diverticula, anastomoses, and "blind loops" may be attributed to colonization of the small intestine by large masses of bacteria which divert vitamin B_{12} from the host. Steatorrhea may also be seen under these circumstances, because bile salt metabolism is disturbed when the intestine is heavily colonized with bacteria. Hematologic responses have been observed after administration of oral antibiotics such as tetracycline and ampicillin.

Megaloblastic anemia is seen, in Scandinavia especially, in persons harboring the tapeworm *D. latum.* The anemia has been attributed to competition by the worm for vitamin B_{12}. Destruction of the worm eliminates the problem.

Ileal abnormalities Vitamin B_{12} deficiency is commonly found in tropical sprue, while it is an unusual complication of nontropical sprue (gluten-sensitive enteropathy; see Chap. 237). Virtually any disorder which compromises the absorptive capacity of the distal ileum can result in vitamin B_{12} deficiency. Specific entities include regional enteritis, Whipple's disease, and tuberculosis. Segmental involvement of the distal ileum by disease can cause megaloblastic anemia without any other manifestations of intestinal malabsorption such as steatorrhea. Vitamin B_{12} malabsorption is also seen after ileal resection. The Zollinger-Ellison syndrome (intense gastric hyperacidity due to a gastrin-secreting tumor) may cause vitamin B_{12} malabsorption by acidifying the small intestine. This will retard the transfer of the vitamin from R binder to intrinsic factor and will impair the binding of the vitamin B_{12}–IF complex to the ileal receptors. Chronic pancreatitis may also cause vitamin B_{12} malabsorption by impairing the transfer of the vitamin from R binder to intrinsic factor. This abnormality can be detected by tests of vitamin B_{12} absorption (see below, Schilling test), but it is invariably mild and never causes clinical vitamin B_{12} deficiency. Finally, there is a rare congenital disorder, described by Imerslund, in which a selective defect in vitamin B_{12} absorption is accompanied by proteinuria.

FOLIC ACID DEFICIENCY Patients with folic acid deficiency are more apt to be malnourished than those with vitamin B_{12} deficiency. Accordingly, they are likely to appear wasted. The gastrointestinal manifestations are similar to, but may be more widespread and more severe than those of, pernicious anemia. Diarrhea is often present, and cheilosis and glossitis are also encountered. However, in contrast to vitamin B_{12} deficiency, neurologic abnormalities do not occur.

The hematologic manifestations of folic acid deficiency are the same as those of vitamin B_{12} deficiency. Folic acid deficiency can generally be attributed to one or more of the following factors: increased demand for folate, inadequate intake, and malabsorption.

Inadequate intake Folic acid malnutrition is commonly encountered among a number of groups. Alcoholics frequently become folate-deficient because their main source of caloric intake is in the form of alcoholic beverages. Distilled spirits are virtually devoid of folic acid, while beer and wine do not contain enough of the vitamin to satisfy the daily requirement. In addition, alcohol may interfere with folate metabolism. Narcotic addicts are also prone to become folate-deficient because of malnutrition. Many indigent and elderly individuals who subsist primarily on canned foods or "tea and toast" and occasional teenagers whose diet consists of soft drinks and potato chips develop folate deficiency.

Increased demand Tissues with a relatively high rate of cell division such as the bone marrow or gut mucosa have a large requirement for folate. Therefore, patients with chronic hemolytic anemias or other causes of very active erythropoiesis may become deficient if their high folate requirement is not met by dietary intake. Likewise, a pregnant woman may become deficient in folic acid because of the high demand of the developing fetus. Folate deficiency may also occur during the growth spurts of infancy and adolescence.

Malabsorption Folic acid deficiency is a common accompaniment of tropical sprue. Both the gastrointestinal symptoms and malabsorption are improved by the administration of either folic acid or antibiotics by mouth. Patients with nontropical sprue (gluten-sensitive enteropathy) may also develop significant folic acid deficiency which parallels other parameters of malabsorption. Similarly, alcohol-related folate deficiency may be due in part to malabsorption. In addition, other primary small-bowel disorders are sometimes associated with vitamin deficiency. These entities are all discussed in Chap. 237.

DRUGS Next to deficiency of folate or vitamin B_{12}, the most common cause of megaloblastic anemia is drug ingestion. Drugs which cause megaloblastic anemia do so by interfering with DNA synthesis, either directly or by antagonizing the action of folate. They can be classified as follows:

1 Direct inhibitors of DNA synthesis. The drugs in this category are used in the treatment of malignancy. Their efficacy depends on their ability to disrupt DNA synthesis. They include purine analogues (6-thioguanine, azathioprine, 6-mercaptopurine), pyrimidine analogues (5-fluorouracil, cytosine arabinoside), and certain other drugs which interfere with DNA synthesis by a variety of mechanisms (hydroxyurea, procarbazine).

2 Folate antagonists. The most toxic of these is methotrexate, an exceedingly powerful inhibitor of dihydrofolate reductase which is used in the treatment of certain malignancies. Much less toxic, but still capable of inducing a megaloblastic anemia, are several weak dihydrofolate reductase inhibitors which are used to treat a variety of nonmalignant conditions. These include pentamidine, trimethoprine, triamterene, and pyrimethamine.

The megaloblastic changes in methotrexate poisoning appear to result from the following sequence of events. In methotrexate-poisoned cells, the methylation of dUMP to dTMP is grossly impaired. As a consequence, the phosphorylation of dUMP to dUTP, normally a very minor reaction, becomes a major route of dUMP metabolism. The capacity of a highly specific dUTP pyrophosphatase to degrade dUTP back to dUMP is exceeded under these conditions, and dUTP accumulates in the cell. This dUTP is incorporated into newly synthesized DNA, because DNA polymerase cannot distinguish between dUTP and the closely related normal substrate, dTTP. As a result, defective strands of DNA are produced in which T is partly replaced by U. The U-containing regions of these defective strands are recognized by a specific repair system, which excises them and attempts to replace them with normal DNA. In methotrexate-poisoned cells, however, there is so much dUTP and so little dTTP that the new DNA is also likely to be defective. It is this futile cycle of faulty replication, error excision, faulty repair, etc., which explains the megaloblastic pattern of DNA synthesis in methotrexate-poisoned cells. The

megaloblastic changes in folate and vitamin B_{12} deficiency might have a similar biochemical origin.

3 Nitrous oxide. Nitrous oxide inhalation causes the destruction of endogenous vitamin B_{12}. As ordinarily used, this anesthetic does not destroy enough of the vitamin to cause clinical manifestations. Repeated or protracted exposure, however, may lead to a megaloblastic anemia. Fatal megaloblastic anemia has been reported in patients with tetanus who were given nitrous oxide continuously for weeks.

4 Others. A number of drugs antagonize folate by mechanisms which are poorly understood but are thought to involve an effect on absorption of the vitamin by the intestine. In this category are certain anticonvulsants [phenytoin (Dilantin), primidone (Mysoline)] and phenobarbital (Luminal). Megaloblastic anemia induced by these agents is mild.

OTHER Hereditary Megaloblastic anemia may be seen in several hereditary disorders. It is a regular feature of orotic aciduria, a defect in pyrimidine metabolism which is also characterized by retarded growth and development as well as the excretion of large amounts of orotic acid, and which is due to a deficiency of orotidylic decarboxylase and phosphorylase. Megaloblastic anemia has been reported in a single case of the Lesch-Nyhan syndrome, a condition resulting from a deficiency of hypoxanthine-guanine phosphoribosyltransferase whose clinical manifestations include gout, mental retardation, and self-mutilation. It has also been described in methylmalonic aciduria due to a defect in the biosynthesis of the two metabolically active alkyl cobalamins, though it is not seen in methylmalonic aciduria due to methylmalonyl CoA mutase deficiency. Congenital folate malabsorption causes megaloblastic anemia, accompanied by ataxia and mental retardation. Megaloblastic anemia has been reported to accompany the congenital deficiency of other folate-metabolizing enzymes including formiminotransferase, dihydrofolate reductase, and N^5-methyltetrahydrofolate reductase. These deficiencies are less well documented than is congenital folate malabsorption. Megaloblastic changes as well as multinuclearity of red blood cell precursors are seen in the marrow of certain patients with congenital dyserythropoietic anemia, a group of inherited disorders characterized by mild to moderate anemia presenting at any age and pursuing a benign course.

Transcobalamin II deficiency, as well as the congenital abnormalities in vitamin B_{12} absorption described previously, causes pronounced deficiencies in vitamin B_{12} in infancy or early childhood, with all the accompanying manifestations. Megaloblastic anemia is not seen in hereditary transcobalamin I deficiency.

Acquired idiopathic anemia Some patients with acquired sideroblastic anemia and other forms of refractory anemia show megaloblastic erythropoiesis. Megaloblastic changes are restricted to the red blood cell series; large granulocyte precursors and giant metamyelocytes are not seen (see below). Both are associated with an increased incidence of acute leukemia.

Megaloblastic changes are seen in erythremic myelosis and acute erythroleukemia (di Guglielmo) where red blood cell precursors are prominently involved. Here, the marrow is characterized by bizarre erythroid maturation, with multinuclearity and multipolar mitotic figures in the red blood cell precursors. Erythremic myelosis is discussed further in Chap. 292.

DIAGNOSIS The finding of significant macrocytosis [mean corpuscular volume (MCV) > 96 fl] suggests the presence of a megaloblastic anemia. Other causes of macrocytosis include hemolysis, liver disease, alcoholism, hypothyroidism, and aplastic anemia. If the macrocytosis is marked (MCV > 110 fl), the patient is much more likely to have a megaloblastic anemia. The reticulocyte count is low, and the leukocyte and platelet count may also be decreased, particularly in severely anemic patients. The blood smear (Fig. A5-2) demonstrates marked anisocytosis and poikilocytosis, together with macroovalocytes which are large, oval, fully hemoglobinized erythrocytes typical of megaloblastic anemias. There is some basophilic stippling, and an occasional nucleated red blood cell may be seen. In the white blood cell series, the neutrophils show hypersegmentation of the nucleus. This is such a typical finding that a single cell with a nucleus of six lobes or more should raise the immediate suspicion of a megaloblastic anemia. A rare myelocyte may also be seen. Bizarre, misshapen platelets are also observed. The bone marrow examination is very helpful in the diagnosis of megaloblastic anemia. The marrow is hypercellular with a decreased myeloid/erythroid ratio and abundant stainable iron. Red blood cell precursors are abnormally large and have nuclei that appear much less mature than would be expected from the development of the cytoplasm (nuclear-cytoplasmic asynchrony). The nuclear chromatin is more dispersed than it should be and consequently stains less intensely than normal. To the extent that it is aggregated, it condenses in a peculiar fenestrated pattern which is very characteristic of megaloblastic erythropoiesis. Abnormal mitoses may be seen. Granulocyte precursors are also affected, many being larger than normal, including giant bands and metamyelocytes. Megakaryocytes are decreased and show abnormal morphology.

Megaloblastic anemias are characterized by ineffective erythropoiesis (Chaps. 283 and 284). In a severely megaloblastic patient as many as 90 percent of the red blood cell precursors may be destroyed before they are released into the bloodstream, compared with 10 to 15 percent in the normal subject. Enhanced intramedullary destruction of erythroblasts results in an increase in unconjugated bilirubin and lactic acid dehydrogenase (isoenzyme 1) in plasma. Abnormalities in iron kinetics also attest to the presence of ineffective erythropoiesis, with increased iron turnover but low incorporation of labeled iron into circulating red blood cells.

In evaluating a patient with megaloblastic anemia, it is important to determine whether there is a specific vitamin deficiency by measuring serum B_{12} and folate levels. At one time the assay for B_{12} was unreliable, giving false-normal values in B_{12} deficiency because of its inability to distinguish authentic B_{12} from biologically inactive B_{12} analogues present in serum. Within the past few years, however, this problem with the B_{12} assay has been corrected.

The normal range of vitamin B_{12} in serum is 200 to 900 pg/mL; values less than 100 pg/mL indicate clinically significant deficiency. The normal serum concentration of folic acid ranges from 6 to 20 ng/mL; values of 4 ng/mL or less are generally considered to be diagnostic of folate deficiency. Unlike serum vitamin B_{12}, serum folate levels may reflect recent alterations in dietary intake. Measurement of red blood cell folate occasionally provides useful information since it is not subject to short-term fluctuations in folate intake and is, therefore, a better index of tissue folate stores than serum folate.

A test which is occasionally used in the diagnosis of megaloblastic anemia is the deoxyuridine (dU) suppression test. This test is based on the observation that the uptake of tritiated thymidine by bone marrow cells, suppressed sharply (10 times or more) by deoxyuridine under normal circumstances, is affected to a much smaller extent in megaloblastic anemia. The abnormality in deoxyuridine suppression is probably related in some way to alterations in nucleotide pool sizes in megaloblastic cells.

Once vitamin B_{12} deficiency has been established, its pathogenesis can be delineated by means of a Schilling test. A patient is given radioactive vitamin B_{12} by mouth followed shortly thereafter by an intramuscular injection of unlabeled vitamin B_{12}. The proportion of the administered radioactivity excreted in the urine during the next 24 h provides an accurate measure of absorption of vitamin B_{12}, assuming that a complete urine sample has been collected. Since vitamin B_{12} deficiency is almost always due to malabsorption (Table 285-1), this first stage of the Schilling test should be abnormal. The patient is then given labeled vitamin B_{12} bound to intrinsic factor. Absorption of the vitamin will now approach normal if the patient has pernicious anemia or some other type of intrinsic factor deficiency. If vitamin B_{12} absorption is still decreased, the patient may have bacterial overgrowth (blind loop syndrome) or ileal disease (including

an ileal absorptive defect secondary to the B_{12} deficiency itself). Vitamin B_{12} malabsorption due to bacterial overgrowth can frequently be corrected by the administration of antibiotics. The Schilling test can provide equally reliable information after the patient has had adequate therapy with parenteral vitamin B_{12}.

TREATMENT

VITAMIN B_{12} DEFICIENCY Apart from specific therapy related to the underlying disorder (e.g., antibiotics for intestinal overgrowth with bacteria), the mainstay of treatment for B_{12} deficiency is replacement therapy. Since the defect is one of absorption, replacement should be administered parenterally, specifically in the form of intramuscular cyanocobalamin. (If intramuscular administration is contraindicated or refused, vitamin B_{12} deficiency can be managed by oral replacement therapy, but at doses of 300 to 1000 µg daily, it is an exceedingly expensive mode of treatment which requires very close medical supervision to avoid relapse.) Treatment should be started with 100 µg vitamin B_{12} per day for a week. The frequency of administration of the vitamin may then be decreased, the goal being to give a total of 2000 µg during the first 6 weeks. The patient may then be placed on 100 µg cyanocobalamin intramuscularly every month, a regimen that must be maintained for the rest of the patient's life. If necessary, larger doses may be given at less frequent intervals (e.g., 1 mg every 2 to 4 months), but the risk of relapse is substantially greater than if the vitamin is given monthly.

The response to treatment is gratifying. Shortly after treatment is begun, and several days before a hematologic response is evident in the peripheral blood, the patient will experience an increase in strength and an improved sense of well-being. Marrow morphology begins to revert toward normal within a few hours after treatment is initiated. Reticulocytosis begins 4 to 5 days after therapy is started and peaks at about day 7 (Fig. 285-3), with subsequent remission of the anemia over the next several weeks. If a reticulocytosis does not occur, or if it is less brisk than expected from the level of the hematocrit, a search should be made for other factors contributing to the anemia (e.g., infection, coexisting folate deficiency, or hypothyroidism). The sudden development of hypokalemia and salt retention may occur early in the course of therapy; usually these are of no consequence, but occasionally they may represent clinical problems.

In most cases, replacement therapy is all that is needed for the treatment of vitamin B_{12} deficiency. Occasionally, however, a patient with a severe anemia will have such a precarious cardiovascular status that emergency transfusion is necessary. This must be done with great care, since it is very easy to precipitate florid congestive failure in such patients by fluid overload. Blood must be administered slowly in the form of packed cells, with very close observation, giving as an initial dose no more than 100 mL. This small volume will frequently be enough to ameliorate the cardiovascular problems sufficiently that further therapy can be restricted to vitamin B_{12} replacement. If necessary, blood may be administered by exchanging patient blood (mostly plasma) for packed cells.

With lifelong treatment, patients should experience no further manifestations of B_{12} deficiency. As previously stated, neurologic symptoms may not be fully corrected even by optimal therapy. The potential for late development of gastric carcinoma in pernicious anemia necessitates careful follow-up of the patient.

FOLATE DEFICIENCY Like vitamin B_{12} deficiency, folate deficiency is treated by replacement therapy. The usual dose of folate is 1 mg per day, by mouth, but higher doses (up to 5 mg per day) may be required for folate deficiency due to malabsorption. Parenteral folate is rarely necessary. The hematologic response is similar to that seen after replacement therapy for vitamin B_{12} deficiency—that is, a brisk reticulocytosis after about 4 days, followed by correction of the anemia over the next 1 to 2 months. The duration of therapy depends on the basis of the deficiency state. Patients with a continuously

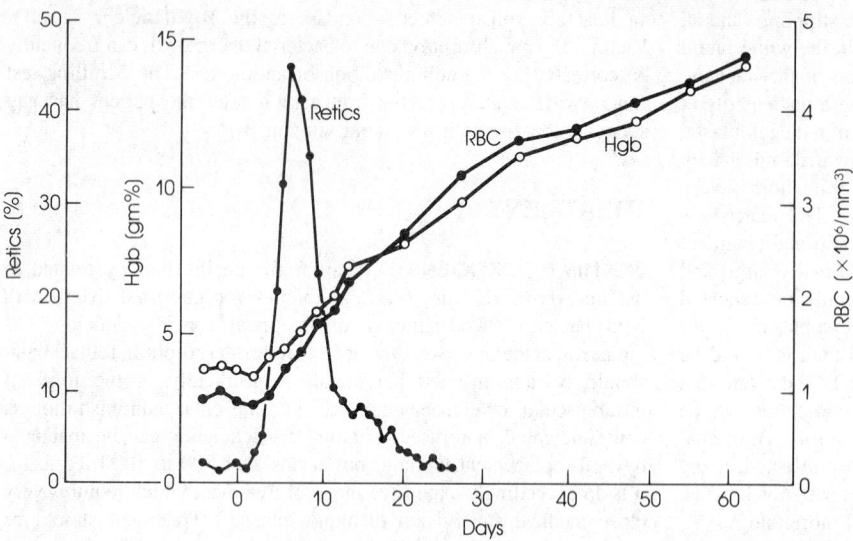

FIGURE 285-3 *Hematologic response of a patient with pernicious anemia to an intramuscular injection of 100 μg vitamin B_{12} on day 0. (From A Erslev, TG Gabuzda, Pathophysiology of Blood, Philadelphia, Saunders, 1975.)*

increased requirement (such as patients with hemolytic anemia) or those with malabsorption or chronic malnutrition should continue to receive oral folic acid indefinitely. In addition, the patient should be encouraged to maintain an optimal diet containing adequate amounts of folate.

Folate, particularly in large doses, can correct the megaloblastic anemia of vitamin B_{12} deficiency without altering the neurologic abnormalities. The neurologic manifestations may even be aggravated by folate therapy. Vitamin B_{12} deficiency can thus be masked in patients who for one reason or another are taking large doses of folate. For this reason, a hematologic response to folate must never be used to rule out vitamin B_{12} deficiency in a given patient; vitamin B_{12} deficiency can be excluded only by appropriate laboratory evaluation.

OTHER CAUSES OF MEGALOBLASTIC ANEMIA Megaloblastic anemia due to drugs can be treated, if necessary, by reducing the dose of the drug or eliminating it altogether. The effects of folate antagonists which inhibit dihydrofolate reductase can be counteracted by folinic acid (citrovorum factor) in a dose of 100 to 200 mg per day. Since folinic acid is a derivative of tetrahydrofolate, it circumvents the block in folate metabolism imposed by dihydrofolate reductase inhibitors, replenishing the tissues with a form of folate which can directly enter the one-carbon donor pool.

Certain of the congenital megaloblastic anemia–producing enzyme deficiencies can be treated by appropriate specific therapeutic regimens. The anemia of orotic aciduria is corrected by uridine, and the anemia in one case of Lesch-Nyhan syndrome responded to adenine. Both congenital folate malabsorption and homocystinuria have been treated successfully with oral folate, the former with very large doses (40 mg per day). Transcobalamin II deficiency can be treated with cyanocobalamin, but the vitamin has to be administered parenterally in very large doses so that it can enter cells by mass action without the aid of TC II.

For the megaloblastic forms of sideroblastic anemia, pyridoxine in pharmacologic doses (as high as 300 mg per day) should be tried. A few patients will respond to this therapy. Simple supportive measures are all that appear to be in order for treatment of refractory megaloblastic anemia. Acute erythroleukemia (di Guglielmo's disease) is usually treated like other types of acute nonlymphocytic leukemia (see Chap. 292).

REFERENCES

ALLEN RH: The plasma transport of vitamin B_{12}. Br J Haematol 36:153, 1976
BECK WS: The megaloblastic anemias, in *Hematology*, WJ Williams et al (eds). New York, McGraw-Hill, 1983
BORCH K: Epidemiologic, clinicopathologic, and economic aspects of gastroscopic screening of patients with pernicious anemia. Scand J Gastroenterol 21:21, 1986
CHANARIN I et al: Cobalamin folate interactions: A critical review. Blood 66:474, 1985
ERIKSSON S et al: Pernicious anemia as a risk factor in gastric cancer: The extent of the problem. Acta Med Scand 210:481. 1981
LAWSON DH et al: Early mortality in the megaloblastic anemias. Q J Med 41:1, 1972
LINDENBAUM J: Status of laboratory testing in the diagnosis of megaloblastic anemia. Blood 61:624, 1983
———: Aspects of vitamin B_{12} and folate metabolism in malabsorption syndromes. Am J Med 67:1037, 1979
———: Folate and vitamin B_{12} deficiencies in alcoholism. Semin Hematol 17:119, 1980
ROSENBERG LE: Disorders of propionate and methylmalonate metabolism, in *Metabolic Basis of Inherited Disease*, JB Stanbury et al (eds). New York, McGraw-Hill, 1983
SCOTT JM, WEIR DG: Drug induced megaloblastic change. Clin Haematol 9:587, 1980

286   ANEMIA ASSOCIATED WITH CHRONIC DISORDERS

H. FRANKLIN BUNN

Among the most commonly encountered anemias are those that accompany a variety of chronic underlying diseases. They can be corrected only if the primary condition is reversible. As shown in Table 286-1, these anemias can be subdivided into several groups. Those associated with chronic inflammation are characterized by an abnormality in iron metabolism.

ANEMIA OF CHRONIC INFLAMMATION

CLINICAL FEATURES Patients who have a chronic systemic inflammatory disorder persisting more than a month usually develop a mild or moderate anemia. The extent of the anemia is roughly proportional to the duration and severity of the inflammatory process. These disorders include chronic infections such as subacute infective endocarditis, osteomyelitis, lung abscess, tuberculosis, and pyelonephritis. Among noninfectious causes of anemia of chronic inflammation, the most common is rheumatoid arthritis. Other noninfectious inflammatory disorders often associated with chronic anemia include systemic lupus erythematosus, vasculitides (such as temporal arteritis), sarcoidosis, regional enteritis, and tissue injury such as fractures.

This kind of anemia is also commonly encountered in neoplastic disorders, including Hodgkin's disease and a variety of solid tumors such as carcinoma of the lung and breast. Other factors may contribute to the development of more severe anemia in cancer patients. In those with gastrointestinal cancer, blood loss can be the predominant factor. Chronic gastrointestinal bleeding will lead to iron deficiency. Furthermore, cancer patients may develop progressive anemia if the bone marrow is invaded with tumor cells. Myelophthisic anemia is discussed in Chap. 290. Cancer patients are often malnourished and may develop folate deficiency. Rarely, patients with disseminated malignancy develop severe traumatic hemolytic anemia (Chap. 287). Finally, suppression of hematopoiesis by chemotherapeutic agents or radiation therapy may aggravate anemia.

HEMATOLOGIC FEATURES Hemoglobin values generally range between 9 and 11 g/dL. A hemoglobin level less than 8 g/dL indicates the presence of one or more of the aggravating factors mentioned above. Although this group of anemias is generally classified as normocytic-normochromic, red blood cells are often slightly microcytic. The mean corpuscular hemoglobin concentration is about 32 g/dL (normal $\cong$ 34 g/dL). Examination of the bone marrow reveals normal erythroid maturation. However, the red blood cell precursors have less stainable iron than normal (i.e., fewer sideroblasts), while the macrophages in the marrow usually contain increased amounts of iron. Myeloid hyperplasia and an increase in plasma cells are often seen in chronic infections.

The reticulocyte count is usually normal (<3 percent). Careful measurement of red blood cell survival generally reveals moderately shortened erythrocyte life span. Cross-transfusion studies point to an extracorpuscular mechanism, probably hyperplasia of the mononuclear-phagocyte system. There is seldom any other evidence of significant hemolysis. However, in certain chronic infections such as subacute infective endocarditis and miliary tuberculosis, splenomegaly can contribute to further shortening of the red blood cell life span, thereby increasing the severity of the anemia. In this setting spherocytes are often seen on the blood smear.

Serum iron is characteristically subnormal in this group of anemias, but in contrast to iron deficiency, the total transferrin level is also reduced (see Fig. 284-2). The fractional saturation of transferrin is lower than normal. The serum iron falls within hours or days following the onset of the inflammation, whereas several weeks elapse before the transferrin level falls. Serum ferritin is increased in patients with inflammatory disorders. Certain other plasma proteins are characteristically elevated in chronic inflammation, probably under the stimulus of interleukin 1, a protein hormone released by activated macrophages. These "phase reactants" include gamma globulin, the third component of complement, haptoglobin, alpha$_1$ antitrypsin, orosomucoid, and fibrinogen. The latter is usually not measured since protein electrophoresis is routinely done on serum rather than plasma. Elevation of these proteins is responsible for the increased rate of red blood cell sedimentation which is so commonly observed.

It is often difficult to detect iron deficiency in a patient with chronic inflammation. The serum iron is low, and red blood cell protoporphyrin is increased in both conditions. When iron deficiency is superimposed on a chronic inflammatory state, the serum ferritin falls and transferrin level rises, usually to within normal limits. Under such circumstances, the amount of storage iron in the bone marrow is unpredictable. This problem is commonly encountered in patients with rheumatoid arthritis who may have developed iron deficiency owing to gastrointestinal blood loss. Because of this diagnostic uncertainty, it is often prudent to give such a patient a trial of iron and ascertain whether the hemoglobin level increases. However, it is important to avoid prolonged administration of iron unless a true deficiency state persists.

PATHOGENESIS The anemia of chronic inflammation is primarily due to defective red blood cell production and failure to compensate for the slightly decreased red blood cell life span. The subnormal amounts of iron in erythroblasts, in spite of an abundance of storage iron, suggests a defect in the transfer of iron to the developing erythroid cells. The cells that are formed are somewhat "iron deficient," and therefore tend to be small and pale. As in true iron deficiency, increased red blood cell protoporphyrin reflects the reduced availability of iron for heme synthesis. This defect can be quantitated by iron kinetic studies. If radioactive iron bound to transferrin is administered, there is normal uptake into erythroblasts and incorpo-

ration into circulating red cells. In contrast, if hemoglobin labeled with radioactive iron is injected, the incorporation of label into circulating red cells is only half normal. The hyperplastic mononuclear phagocyte system which is responsible for decreased survival of circulating red cells probably traps the hemoglobin iron and prevents its transfer to the bone marrow. The macrophages' increased avidity for iron may be due to one of the actions of interleukin 1, i.e., release of lactoferrin from neutrophils. The iron-binding protein lactoferrin captures free iron and rapidly transfers it to macrophages.

The modest suppression of red blood cell production is caused in part by decreased availability of iron. In addition, erythropoietin levels tend to be lower than expected for the degree of anemia. However, erythropoietin levels are not as low as in the anemia of renal failure (see below) and probably do not play a significant role in the pathogenesis of the anemia.

MANAGEMENT The anemia of chronic inflammation is not responsive to hematinic agents such as iron, folic acid, or vitamin B$_{12}$. Since the anemia is seldom severe, blood transfusion is rarely indicated. Efforts should be directed toward correcting the underlying disorder. In addition, if the anemia is more severe than expected, it is essential to search for other factors such as blood loss or drug-induced myelosuppression that could contribute to the reduction of red blood cell mass.

ANEMIA OF UREMIA

Anemia almost always accompanies the uremic syndrome (Chap. 220). Although the hemoglobin level is highly variable among uremic patients, the severity of the anemia is roughly proportional to the degree of azotemia. The etiology of the renal failure usually has little bearing on the extent of anemia. However, for any level of serum creatinine patients with polycystic disease tend to be less anemic than those with other types of renal disease. In contrast to anemias associated with other chronic disorders discussed in this chapter, the anemia of uremia can be very severe, with hemoglobin levels as low as 4 g/dL. However, patients often tolerate such marked anemia fairly well. This is largely due to compensatory adjustments such as redistribution of blood flow and a decrease in the oxygen affinity of the blood (see Chap. 53).

The anemia of uremia is normochromic and normocytic. Examination of the bone marrow seldom reveals any abnormalities. Red blood cell morphology is usually normal. In about one-third of patients, so-called burr cells are seen in the peripheral blood smear. These red blood cells have a characteristic evenly scalloped border (see Fig. A5-9). Neither the degree of anemia nor the red blood cell life span is influenced by the presence of burr cells. In most patients the reticulocyte count is normal and the red blood cell survival is only modestly decreased. Thus the low red blood cell mass is due to decreased red blood cell production. The primary basis for this defect is that the diseased kidneys are unable to secrete adequate amounts of erythropoietin. Plasma erythropoietin levels are lower than those of nonuremic patients with a comparable degree of anemia. Erythropoiesis is further impaired but not abolished in patients who have undergone bilateral nephrectomy. In addition, red blood cell production may be suppressed by the accumulation of substances that are normally cleared by the kidneys. Iron kinetic measurements reveal impaired incorporation of iron into circulating red blood cells. Thus, it is likely that the anemia is due in part to ineffective erythropoiesis

TABLE 286-1 Anemias secondary to chronic systemic diseases

1 Anemia of chronic inflammation
   a Infection
   b Connective tissue disorders, etc.
   c Malignancy
2 Anemia of uremia
3 Anemia due to endocrine failure
4 Anemia of liver disease

(see Chap. 283). Improvement in the rate of utilization of iron by the bone marrow has been noted following hemodialysis.

A small minority of uremic patients, particularly those with advanced disease, have brisk hemolysis. Red blood cell survival studies indicate that the hemolysis is due to extracorpuscular factors. Both metabolic and mechanical factors contribute to the hemolysis. Some patients may acquire a defect in the hexose monophosphate shunt which renders the red blood cell vulnerable to the formation of Heinz bodies (see Chap. 287). The hemolysis can be aggravated by oxidant drugs or oxidant compounds such as chloramine in the dialysis bath. If the renal failure is due to thrombotic thrombocytopenic purpura or hemolytic-uremic syndrome, patients will have a severe form of microangiopathic hemolytic anemia, with characteristic abnormalities of red blood cell morphology (see Chap. 287).

Treatment of the anemia of uremia should focus on an attempt to reverse the renal failure. The anemia may be modestly improved following hemodialysis. A prompt and dramatic correction of the anemia follows successful renal transplantation. Occasionally, polycythemia may be encountered following the renal engraftment, and may be a harbinger of impending rejection. In those patients who are not candidates for renal transplantation the administration of androgens has proved effective in stimulating erythropoiesis, particularly in patients who have not undergone bilateral nephrectomy. The recent development of synthetic erythropoietin offers the hope of definitive therapy in the near future.

It is important to be aware of other factors that may aggravate the anemia of renal disease. Uremic patients have a propensity to hemorrhage, owing to a qualitative defect in platelet function. Thus, gastrointestinal blood loss is commonly encountered. Furthermore a small but significant amount of blood loss occurs during hemodialysis. For these reasons some uremic patients become iron deficient. Folic acid deficiency may also occur, owing to the poor nutrition of many patients or to the loss of this vitamin during dialysis.

ANEMIA SECONDARY TO ENDOCRINE FAILURE

A number of hormones, including thyroxine, glucocorticoids, testosterone, and growth hormone are known to affect proliferation of human erythroid cells in vitro. Therefore it is not surprising that a mild to moderate normochromic-normocytic anemia generally accompanies a number of endocrine deficiency states, including hypothyroidism, Addison's disease, hypogonadism, and panhypopituitarism. It is possible that the anemias associated with hypothyroidism and hypopituitarism are related to the decreased need for oxygen transport, since oxygen consumption is reduced when thyroid hormone or growth hormone is lacking.

The anemia of *myxedema* is usually normocytic. Red blood cell life span is normal and erythropoiesis is effective. A minority of patients have macrocytic red blood cells which can usually be attributed to either folic acid or B_{12} deficiency. Patients with myxedema have an increased incidence of pernicious anemia. Hypothyroid patients, particularly females with menorrhagia, often develop iron deficiency and a microcytic anemia. Because the plasma volume may be reduced along with the red blood cell mass, the anemia of hypothyroidism may be masked. Since the signs and symptoms of myxedema are sometimes elusive, this diagnosis should be considered in the evaluation of any patient with unexplained anemia.

The anemia of *Addison's disease* is also masked by a decrease in plasma volume. Untreated patients have an average hemoglobin level of about 13 g/dL. Upon hormone replacement, the plasma volume is rapidly reconstituted and the hemoglobin level falls to 80 percent of its pretreatment value. With continued therapy, the red blood cell mass returns to normal.

Testosterone has a physiologic influence on red blood cell mass. During passage through adolescence the mean hemoglobin level of males increases from 13 to 15 g/dL. Eunuchoid males generally have a mild decrease in hemoglobin, averaging 13 g/dL. Pituitary dys-

function or ablation is associated with a mild normochromic normocytic anemia as well as occasional leukopenia.

The anemias secondary to endocrine failure are all readily corrected when adequate hormone replacement is given.

ANEMIA OF LIVER DISEASE

Patients with chronic liver disease, regardless of etiology, usually have a mild to moderate anemia which is normocytic or slightly macrocytic. An increased plasma volume may artificially lower the hematocrit and make the anemia seem worse than it is. Red blood cell morphology is normal, except for the presence of target cells (see Fig. A5-3) and occasional stomatocytes, which have increased membrane surface area owing to increased deposits of cholesterol and phospholipid. The bone marrow is usually normal. Erythropoiesis fails to compensate for a moderate shortening of red blood cell life span. The anemia persists as long as hepatic function is defective, but it may be corrected if normal hepatic function can be restored.

The situation is much more complex in patients with *alcoholic liver disease*. Many factors can contribute to the development of anemia. Alcohol is a direct suppressor of erythropoiesis. In alcoholics who have continued to drink up to the time of clinical evaluation, the bone marrow often reveals vacuoles in the cytoplasm of red and white blood cell precursors. In addition, ringed sideroblasts may be observed, particularly in patients who are malnourished. In alcoholics there is often suboptimal intake of dietary folic acid and impairment of folate utilization. Furthermore, alcoholics commonly develop significant hemorrhage from gastritis, esophageal varices, or duodenal ulcer, which contributes to the anemia. The risk of gastrointestinal blood loss is further increased by the presence of thrombocytopenia or deficiencies in soluble clotting factors. Although alcoholics usually have increased iron stores, they may become iron-deficient after prolonged gastrointestinal bleeding. Rarely patients with alcoholic cirrhosis develop a severe hemolytic anemia accompanied by the appearance of rigid red blood cells with irregular borders called acanthocytes or "spur" cells (see Fig. A5-8). This entity is discussed in detail in Chap. 287. In addition, alcoholics may acquire a defect in the erythrocyte hexose monophosphate shunt, similar to that encountered in patients with uremia.

REFERENCES

BUDMAN DR, STEINBERG AD: Hematologic aspects of systemic lupus erythematosus. Ann Intern Med 86:220, 1977

COLMAN D, HERBERT V: Hematologic complications of alcoholism: Overview. Semin Hematol 17:164, 1980

ESCHBACH JW, ADAMSON J: Anemia of end-stage renal disease. Kideny Int 28:1, 1985

LEE GR: The anemia of chronic disease. Semin Hematol 20:61, 1983

MOWAT AG: Hematologic abnormalities in rheumatoid arthritis. Semin Arthritis Rheum 1:195, 1972

NEFF MS et al: A comparison of androgens for anemia in patients on hemodialysis. N Engl J Med 304:871, 1981

———: Anemia in chronic renal failure. Acta Endocrinol 271(Suppl):80, 1985

ORREGO H et al: Interrelation of the hypermetabolic state, necrosis, anemia and cell enlargement as determinants of severity of alcoholic liver disease. Acta Med Scand 703(Suppl):81, 1985

287 HEMOLYTIC ANEMIAS

RICHARD A. COOPER / H. FRANKLIN BUNN

Red blood cells undergo premature destruction by two general mechanisms. First, red blood cells may lyse in the circulation and release their contents directly into the plasma. Intravascular hemolysis may be caused by trauma to the red blood cell, by fixation of complement to the red blood cell, or by exogenous toxins. Second, and more commonly, red blood cells are taken up by macrophages in the spleen and liver (mononuclear-phagocyte system), where they are destroyed and digested (extravascular lysis). The mononuclear-phagocyte system clears the cells from the circulation under two general conditions: first, the presence of surface abnormalities such as bound immunoglobulin for which macrophages have specific receptors; second, the presence of physical characteristics that limit the deformability of red blood cells, thereby impeding their ability to traverse the fine filtering system of the spleen.

The discoid shape of red blood cells favors deformability, providing a surface area that is 60 to 70 percent in excess of the minimum that is necessary to encompass the content of the cell. Deformability is determined by three independent variables: (1) the viscoelastic properties of the red blood cell membrane, (2) the ratio of surface area to volume, and (3) the intracellular concentration of hemoglobin or the aggregation of hemoglobin into polymers or precipitates.

One or more of these factors play a role in the pathogenesis of the various hemolytic anemias that are described in this chapter. A classification of these anemias is shown in Table 287-1. A number of clinical and laboratory features are shared by various types of hemolytic anemia. Patients with congenital hemolysis often have lifelong anemia and may have a positive family history. Splenomegaly is seen in most chronic hemolytic anemias, both congenital and acquired. Patients with significant red blood cell turnover may be icteric, owing to an increase in unconjugated bilirubin.

LABORATORY EVALUATION OF HEMOLYSIS

The reticulocyte count is the single most useful test in the initial evaluation (Table 287-2). Patients with hemolytic anemia generally have a brisk reticulocytosis. The bone marrow predictably reveals erythroid hyperplasia. Since it seldom provides useful additional information, a bone marrow examination is generally not indicated in the evaluation of a patient with hemolytic anemia, unless an associated disorder such as lymphoma is suspected.

A number of serum tests are useful in establishing the presence of hemolysis (see Table 287-2), most importantly, the measurement of bilirubin, a tetrapyrrole formed from the oxidative catabolism of heme. *Unconjugated* or "*indirect*" *bilirubin* circulates in the plasma in transit from the mononuclear-phagocyte system to the liver where it is conjugated. When measured accurately, unconjugated bilirubin is a reliable guide to the presence of increased heme catabolism and is usually elevated in patients with hemolysis. The serum level of conjugated or "direct" bilirubin is normal unless the patient has associated hepatic or biliary dysfunction. Unconjugated bilirubin is also increased in patients with ineffective erythropoiesis, a condition in which there is enhanced destruction of red cell precursors within the bone marrow. Since circulating unconjugated bilirubin is tightly bound to albumin, it does not pass through renal glomeruli. Thus, patients with hemolytic anemia have acholuric jaundice, whereas the hyperbilirubinemia of liver disease is associated with bilirubin in the urine.

Other serum tests are also useful in the assessment of hemolysis. *Haptoglobin* is an alpha globulin which is present in high concentration (~100 mg/dL) in the plasma (and serum). It binds specifically and tightly to the protein (globin) in hemoglobin. The hemoglobin-haptoglobin complex is cleared within minutes by the mononuclear-phagocyte system, while free haptoglobin has a long circulation time ($t_{1/2}$ = 4 days). Thus, patients with significant hemolysis, either intravascular or extravascular, have low or absent levels of serum haptoglobin. Haptoglobin synthesis is decreased in patients with hepatocellular disease. Conversely, synthesis is enhanced in inflammatory states. Haptoglobin, like alpha$_1$ antitrypsin, orosomucoid, and the third component of complement are acute phase reactants. These facts must be considered in the interpretation of serum haptoglobin. *Hemopexin* is a plasma beta globulin which binds specifically to heme. It becomes depleted in patients with moderate and severe hemolysis. In addition to that bound by hemopexin, some of the heme from circulating free hemoglobin is transferred to albumin,

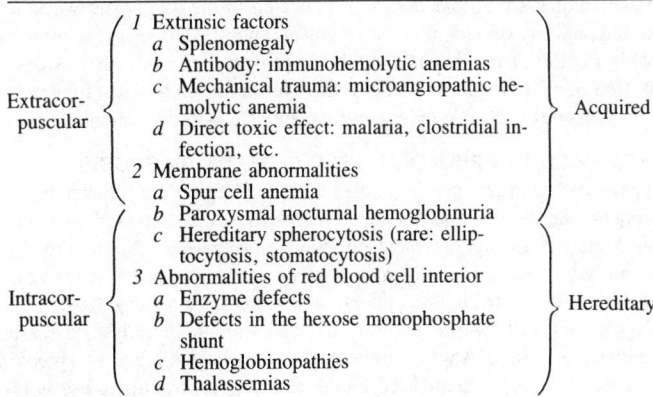

TABLE 287-1 Hemolytic anemias

Extracorpuscular	*1* Extrinsic factors
	  a Splenomegaly
	  b Antibody: immunohemolytic anemias
	  c Mechanical trauma: microangiopathic hemolytic anemia
	  d Direct toxic effect: malaria, clostridial infection, etc.

Intracorpuscular	*2* Membrane abnormalities
	  a Spur cell anemia
	  b Paroxysmal nocturnal hemoglobinuria
	  c Hereditary spherocytosis (rare: elliptocytosis, stomatocytosis)
	3 Abnormalities of red blood cell interior
	  a Enzyme defects
	  b Defects in the hexose monophosphate shunt
	  c Hemoglobinopathies
	  d Thalassemias

(Acquired; Hereditary — bracketed grouping at right)

resulting in the formation of *methemalbumin*. This complex is encountered only in severe intravascular hemolysis. Plasma hemoglobin is increased in proportion to the degree of hemolysis, but may be falsely elevated owing to lysis of red cells in vitro.

Once the haptoglobin binding capacity of the plasma is exceeded, free hemoglobin permeates renal glomeruli, primarily as $\alpha\beta$ dimers with a molecular weight of 32,000. This filtered hemoglobin is reabsorbed by the proximal tubule, where it is catabolized in situ, and the heme iron is incorporated into storage proteins (ferritin and hemosiderin). The presence of hemosiderin in the urine, detected by staining the sediment with Prussian blue, indicates that a significant amount of circulating free hemoglobin has been filtered by the kidneys. When the absorptive capacity of the tubular cells is exceeded, hemoglobinuria ensues. The presence of hemoglobinuria indicates severe intravascular hemolysis. Sometimes the clinician is faced with the dilemma of whether benzidine-positive heme pigment in the urine is hemoglobin or myoglobin. The easiest way to distinguish between these alternatives is to examine an anticoagulated blood specimen after centrifiguration. Because of its higher molecular weight, hemoglobin has lower glomerular permeability than myoglobin and is less rapidly cleared by the kidneys. The plasma of patients with hemoglobinuria has a reddish-brown color. Conversely, patients with myoglobinuria have normal-appearing plasma.

Tagging red cells with an appropriate isotopic label provides the most direct and precise measure of cell survival. The most commonly used label is sodium [^{51}Cr]chromate. Since it does not bind irreversibly to red cells, the measured survival of normal red cells ($t_{1/2}$ = 26 to

TABLE 287-2 Laboratory evaluation of hemolysis

	Moderate hemolysis (RBC life span 20–40 days)	Severe hemolysis (RBC life span 5–20 days)
HEMATOLOGIC		
Routine blood film	Polychromatophilia	Polychromatophilia
Reticulocyte count	↑	↑ ↑
Bone marrow examination	Erythroid hyperplasia	Erythroid hyperplasia
PLASMA OR SERUM		
Bilirubin	↑ Unconjugated	↑ Unconjugated
Haptoglobin	↓, absent	Absent
Hemopexin	Normal, ↓	↓, absent
Plasma hemoglobin	↑	↑ ↑
Lactate dehydrogenase	↑ (variable)	↑ ↑ (variable)
Methemalbumin	0	+ *
URINE		
Bilirubin	0	0
Urobilinogen	Variable	Variable
Hemosiderin	0	+
Hemoglobin	0	+ *

* Intravascular hemolysis.

32 days) is shorter than the true red cell survival ($t_{1/2} \simeq 60$ days). Such studies are not necessary or indicated in the diagnostic workup of the majority of patients with hemolytic anemia. However, scanning with a collumnated detector can be employed to monitor the sequestration of ^{51}Cr-tagged red cells in the liver and spleen. This approach is sometimes useful in evaluating patients for possible splenectomy.

RED CELL MORPHOLOGY AS A CLUE TO DIAGNOSIS Most hemolytic disorders are associated with a change in the morphologic appearance of red blood cells. Some of these are depicted in Atlas 5. Spherocytes are the most common morphologic abnormality in hemolytic diseases, and small numbers occur in many disorders. They are most striking in patients with hereditary spherocytosis and in patients with warm antibody-induced immunohemolytic disease (Figs. A5-10 and A5-11). Spherocytes are the hallmark of splenic conditioning. Fragmented red blood cells suggest traumatic injury of the red cell including valve hemolysis or one of the microangiopathic hemolytic anemias such as thrombotic thrombocytopenic purpura (Fig. A5-7), hemolytic uremic syndrome, or disseminated intravascular coagulation. Target-shaped red blood cells which are well filled with hemoglobin occur in patients with hemoglobin C. They are prevalent in sickle cell anemia, where they were first described, and they are found in patients with the underhydrated form of hereditary stomatocytosis. The most common cause of target cells is liver disease (Fig. A5-3). Target cells which are deficient in hemoglobin (hypochromic) are the hallmark of the thalassemia syndromes (Fig. A5-5).

Spiculated red blood cells often cause confusion because of the frequency with which they are induced as an artifact during the preparation of a blood smear. Under these conditions, they are particularly frequent at the edges of the smear. When surrounded by otherwise normal-appearing red blood cells, spiculated red blood cells can be a clue to diagnosis. They occur, usually in small numbers, in conjunction with uremia or following splenectomy even in the absence of an underlying red blood cell disorder. Bizarrely spiculated red blood cells (acanthocytes) occur in the rare condition abetalipoproteinemia (Chap. 315) and in anorexia nervosa; however, in each of these instances minimal hemolysis is present. As discussed below, acanthocytes are a striking feature of spur-cell anemia (Fig. A5-8).

Permanently sickled, crescent-shaped red blood cells (Fig. A5-6) are the hallmark of sickle cell anemia (see Chap. 288). Boat-shaped red cells are a clue to the double heterozygous state of hemoglobin SC disease (see Chap. 288). The presence of both crescent-shaped cells and hypochromic target cells on the same smear is suggestive of the doubly heterozygous state, sickle cell–β thalassemia (see Chap. 288).

While in no case can the peripheral blood smear be totally diagnostic, in many it is a low-cost, important clue to the diagnosis. In addition to red blood cell morphology, a large battery of specific diagnostic tests are available for determining the etiology of the various hemolytic anemias. These are discussed in broad outline in Chap. 53 (Table 53-1) and in detail in this chapter.

EXTRINSIC CAUSES OF HEMOLYSIS

SPLENOMEGALY The spleen is particularly efficient in trapping and destroying red blood cells which have minimal defects, often so mild as to be undetectable by in vitro techniques. This unique ability of the spleen to filter mildly damaged red blood cells results from its unusual vascular anatomy. Almost all the blood circulating through the spleen flows rapidly from arterioles in the white pulp to sinuses in the spleen's red pulp, and then on into the venous system. In contrast, a small portion of splenic blood flow (normally 1 to 2 percent) leaves the arterioles of the white pulp to enter a nonendothelialized portion of the spleen. In this sense, it is extravascular, although the entire spleen may be considered as a specialized part of the vascular system. This blood passes into the "marginal zone" of the lymphatic white pulp. Although the cells which occupy this zone are not phagocytic, they serve as a mechanical filter hindering the

progress of severely damaged red blood cells. As red blood cells leave this zone and enter the red pulp, they flow into narrow cords which end blindly but which communicate with sinuses through small openings between the lining cells of the sinuses. These openings, averaging 3 µm in diameter, test the ability of red blood cells to undergo a deformation of shape. Red blood cells which do not pass the stringent test imposed upon them by the spleen filter are engulfed by phagocytic cells and destroyed.

The normal spleen poses no threat to normal red blood cells. However, splenomegaly exaggerates the adverse conditions to which red blood cells are exposed. Splenic enlargement may be considered in three broad categories. In the first are infiltrative disease (such as myeloproliferative disorders, Chap. 289), lymphomas (Chap. 294), and storage diseases (such as Gaucher's disease, Chap. 316). In the second are systemic inflammatory diseases leading to splenic hypertrophy. In the third are diseases which cause congestive splenomegaly. Hemolysis may occur whenever the spleen is enlarged. Its occurrence is least predictable in infiltrative diseases of the spleen where substantial splenomegaly may exist with no apparent hemolysis. Inflammatory and congestive splenomegaly are commonly associated with mild to moderate shortening of red blood cell survival.

RED CELL ANTIBODIES Immune hemolysis in the adult may be induced by three general types of antibodies:

1 Alloantibodies acquired by blood transfusions or pregnancies and directed against transfused red blood cells (Chap. 282).

2 Antibodies reactive at body temperature and directed against the patient's own red blood cells (Table 287-3).

3 Antibodies reactive in the cold and directed against the patient's own red blood cells (Table 287-3).

Coombs' antiglobulin test is the major tool for diagnosing these disorders. This test relies on the ability of antibodies prepared in animals and directed against specific human serum proteins to agglutinate red blood cells if these human serum proteins are present on the red blood cell surface. The serum proteins of particular interest are IgG and C3. The ability of anti-IgG or anti-C3 antiserums to agglutinate the patient's red blood cells is referred to as the *direct Coombs test*. At times it is advantageous to know whether there is antibody in the serum of patients which is reactive against other human red blood cells. This is important in cross matching prior to blood transfusion (Chap. 282), and it is of prognostic significance in patients with warm-antibody hemolytic anemia. To determine this, an *indirect Coombs test* is performed by incubating normal ABO- and Rh-compatible red blood cells with the patient's serum and subsequently performing a direct Coombs test on these incubated red cells.

"Warm" antibodies Antibodies which react at body temperature are usually of the IgG class, although occasionally they are IgA. They induce a pattern of hemolysis which affects both the patient's own cells and normal transfused cells. This acquired syndrome is frequently designated *autoimmune hemolytic anemia*. In recent years, as a number of drugs which induce this clinical syndrome have become recognized, attention has focused on the exogenous factors which may underlie the formation of these red blood cell antibodies, and the expression *immunohemolytic anemia* is preferred.

CLINICAL MANIFESTATIONS Warm-antibody immunohemolytic anemia occurs at all ages but is most common in adults, particularly women and older individuals. In approximately one-fourth of patients this disorder occurs as a complication of an underlying disease affecting the immune system, especially chronic lymphocytic leukemia, non-Hodgkin's lymphoma, and systemic lupus erythematosus (SLE). Occasionally, immunohemolytic anemia is seen in patients with advanced, active Hodgkin's disease. Case reports link it to a variety of nonlymphoid neoplasms.

The presentation and course of immunohemolytic anemia are quite variable. In its mildest form, the only manifestation is a positive direct Coombs test. In this instance, insufficient antibody is present on the red blood cell surface to permit the reticuloendothelial system to recognize the cell as abnormal. This is particularly common in SLE. A large fraction of patients with immunohemolytic anemia have a chronic mild anemia and splenomegaly. The direct Coombs test is positive for IgG but seldom for C3, and the indirect Coombs test is negative. In other cases this disorder may be more severe, with hemoglobin levels less than 7.0 g/dL and reticulocyte counts of 30 percent and higher. Spherocytosis is usually marked (Fig. A5-11). Coombs' test is positive for IgG and frequently for C3 as well. Large quantities of antibody are present not only on the patient's red blood cells but also in the patient's serum as demonstrated by the indirect Coombs test. Thrombocytopenia may also be present. The coexistence of immune destruction of red blood cells and platelets is referred to as *Evans' syndrome,* a disorder in which separate antibodies are directed against platelets and red blood cells. In its most severe form, immunohemolytic anemia presents with fulminant, overwhelming hemolysis associated with hemoglobinemia, hemoglobinuria, and shock, a syndrome which may be fatal.

Associated findings include hyperbilirubinemia, decreased or absent haptoglobin levels, and occasionally hepatomegaly. Fever and abdominal pain occur in some patients. Venous thrombosis occurs commonly, the most frequent site being the deep veins of the legs, but thrombosis of mesenteric and portal veins has also been reported. Arterial thromboses occur as well.

PATHOGENESIS Little is known about the origin of red blood cell antibodies in the immunohemolytic anemias. Much more information exists concerning the mechanism of destruction of red blood cells coated with IgG antibodies. Although spherocytosis is often a prominent feature of hemolysis in vivo, the simple exposure of normal red blood cells to IgG antibodies does not lead to spherocytosis in vitro. However, human red blood cells coated with IgG antibodies are bound to the surface of monocytes or splenic macrophages and undergo a spherical transformation. The ability to cause this red blood cell–leukocyte interaction is greatest with IgG of subclasses 1 and 3 (the most common subclasses). It is not shared by IgM or IgA. However, C3 on the red blood cell surface also promotes this cell-cell interaction, but binding may be more transient because of the ability of the plasma C3 inactivator to release bound cells. Indeed, IgG and C3 behave in a synergistic fashion in this regard, accounting for the more severe hemolytic disease in patients in whom both IgG and C3 are present on the red blood cell surface. The slow flow compartment of the spleen is particularly efficient in trapping red blood cells which are coated with IgG antibodies, and the spleen is the major site of red blood cell destruction in this disorder.

THERAPY AND PROGNOSIS In the initial evaluation of the patient, it is important to rule out drugs which are known to cause immuno-hemolytic anemia. This topic is discussed below.

Patients having a mild degree of hemolysis usually do not require therapy. In those with clinically significant hemolysis, initial therapy consists of corticosteroids (e.g., prednisone, 1.0 mg/kg per day). A rise in hemoglobin is frequently noted within 3 or 4 days and occurs in most patients within 1 week. Prednisone is continued until the hemoglobin level has risen to normal values, and thereafter it is tapered slowly over the course of several months. More than 75 percent of patients will achieve a significant and sustained reduction in hemolysis; however, in half of these patients the disease will relapse either during the period of steroid tapering or following the cessation of steroid therapy. Steroids appear to have two modes of action: an immediate effect due to inhibition of the clearance of IgG-coated red blood cells by the mononuclear phagocyte system, and a later effect due to steroid-induced inhibition of antibody synthesis.

Patients with severe anemia may require blood transfusions. Because the antibody in this disease is a "panagglutinin," reacting with all normal donor cells, the usual cross matching is impossible. The goal in selecting blood for transfusion is to avoid administering red cells with antigens to which patients have previously been sensitized and which are known to be associated with complement

lysis and intravascular hemolysis. In addition to A and B, Kell, Kidd (Jk^a), and Duffy (Fy) account for almost all examples of this type of hemolysis. A common procedure is to adsorb the panagglutinin present in patient's serum using the patient's own red cells from which antibody has previously been eluted. Serum freed of autoantibody in this way can then be tested for the presence of alloantibody to specific donor blood groups. ABO-compatible red cells matched in this fashion are administered slowly with attention paid to the possibility of an immediate-type transfusion reaction.

Splenectomy is the second line of therapy in this disorder. It is recommended for patients who cannot tolerate steroid therapy, in whom steroid therapy has been insufficient to control the disease process, or in whom a normal hematologic status can be maintained only with excessive doses of steroids. When red blood cells are labeled with chromium, their site of destruction can be determined. In 75 percent of patients, the spleen is the dominant site, whereas the liver predominates in the remaining patients. However, this test is not generally useful for selecting those patients who would respond to splenectomy. Rather, a favorable response to splenectomy is obtained in approximately two-thirds of patients in whom a splenic pattern of localization is found and in approximately one-third of patients in whom it is not found. Therefore, splenectomy must be undertaken on clinical grounds alone. To provide prophylaxis against pneumococcal infection, a risk in splenectomized individuals, patients should be immunized with polyvalent pneumococcal antiserum.

In recent years, patients who have been refractory to steroid therapy and to splenectomy have been treated with immunosuppressive drugs. The greatest experience is with azathioprine (Imuran) and cyclophosphamide (Cytoxan). A variable success rate has been reported with each.

In the majority of patients, this disease is controlled by steroid therapy alone, by splenectomy, or by a combination. In most of the remaining patients, a partial degree of control is achieved. Fatalities occur among three categories: first, rare patients with overwhelming hemolysis in whom death is directly attributable to anemia; second, those with major thrombotic events coincident with active hemolysis; third, those whose host defenses are impaired by corticosteroids, splenectomy, and/or immunosuppressives. In patients in whom immunohemolysis develops as a complication of an underlying disorder, the prognosis is dominated by that of the primary disease.

Immunohemolytic anemia secondary to drugs Drugs which have been directly related to immunohemolytic anemia are of three kinds, as distinguished by their three mechanisms of actions: (1) Drugs, such as α-methyldopa (Chap. 196), which induce a disorder identical almost in every respect to the warm-antibody immunohemolytic anemia described above. (2) Drugs of the penicillin type which can become associated with the red blood cell surface and induce the formation of an antibody directed against the red blood cell–drug complex. (3) Drugs, such as quinidine, that form a complex with plasma proteins to which an antibody forms; this drug–plasma protein–antibody complex settles out on red blood cells or platelets to involve them in a destructive process on an "innocent bystander" basis.

TABLE 287-3 Hemolysis due to antibodies

I Warm-antibody immunohemolytic anemia
  A Idiopathic
  B Lymphomas: Chronic lymphocytic leukemia, non-Hodgkin's lympho-
    mas, Hodgkin's disease (infrequent)
  C Systemic lupus erythematosus
  D Tumors (rare)
  E Drugs
    1 α-Methyldopa type
    2 Penicillin type (hapten)
    3 Quinidine type (innocent bystander)
II Cold-antibody immunohemolytic anemia
  A Cold agglutinin disease
    1 Acute: Mycoplasma infection, infectious mononucleosis
    2 Chronic: Idiopathic, lymphoma
  B Paroxysmal cold hemoglobinuria

α-METHYLDOPA-TYPE ANTIBODIES   A positive direct Coombs test is observed in up to 10 percent of patients receiving α-methyldopa therapy in a dose of 2.0 g daily. A small minority of these patients develop spherocytosis and hemolysis, often of severe degree. This "autoimmune" disorder may be triggered by a deficiency of suppressor T lymphocytes. Two distinctive features are that the indirect Coombs test is positive in almost all patients with hemolysis and that the red cells are coated with IgG but not C3. The IgG antibody is directed against the Rh complex as it is in most patients with idiopathic immunohemolytic anemia due to IgG. Hemolysis decreases over the course of several weeks after cessation of drug therapy, although the direct Coombs test may remain positive for more than 1 year.

PENICILLIN (HAPTEN)-INDUCED IMMUNOHEMOLYSIS   An antibody directed against "penicillinized" red blood cells induces hemolysis in patients receiving large, intravenous doses of penicillin and penicillin-type antibiotics (e.g., 15 to 20 million units of penicillin per day, or 12 to 15 g oxacillin per day). Hemolysis usually begins 7 to 14 days after the start of penicillin therapy and is associated with spherocytosis and hyperbilirubinemia. The patient's red blood cells are Coombs-positive for IgG during the period of penicillin therapy. An indirect Coombs test can be demonstrated with the patient's serum using normal red blood cells "penicillinized" in vitro. Hemolysis ceases abruptly when penicillin therapy is stopped, although the serum antibody can be demonstrated for many weeks.

INNOCENT BYSTANDER IMMUNOHEMOLYSIS   Innocent bystander antibodies may be of either the IgG or IgM class, and the antigen-antibody complexes which adhere to the red blood cell surface are capable of fixing complement. The drug-antibody complex dissociates from the red blood cell, leaving only C3 to be detected by Coombs' test. The pattern of hemolysis may be primarily extravascular red blood cell destruction, or it may be intravascular hemolysis due to complement lysis with hemoglobinemia, hemoglobinuria, and acute renal failure. This is an uncommon form of hemolysis despite the fact that the drugs associated with it are in very common usage. They include quinine and quinidine, isoniazid, sulfonamides, phenacetin, stibophen, p-aminosalicylic acid, dipyrone, and various insecticides.

Immune hemolysis due to cold-reactive antibodies   Antibodies which are reactive in the cold induce hemolysis under two general conditions. First, in cold agglutinin disease IgM antibodies, usually reactive with the I antigen, occur spontaneously, in the course of a lymphoproliferative disease or as a complication of infectious mononucleosis or mycoplasma pneumonia. Second, in paroxysmal cold hemoglobinuria, antibodies of the IgG class (Donath-Landsteiner) occur spontaneously or as a complication of certain viral diseases or of syphilis.

COLD AGGLUTININ DISEASE   *Clinical manifestations.* Agglutination of red blood cells by IgM cold agglutinins is most profound at very low temperatures, and disagglutination occurs quickly upon warming. In most patients agglutination ceases at 32°C. The fixation of complement is a warm-reactive process. Therefore, patients may have very high titers of cold agglutinins as measured at low temperatures, but these antibodies may be inefficient in fixing complement to the cell surface and totally unable to induce agglutination at temperatures achieved in the bloodstream. Most cold agglutinins cause little or no shortening of red blood cell survival.

In mycoplasma pneumonia, cold agglutinins are very common, whereas only the occasional patient will have significant hemolysis about 5 to 10 days after recovery from the infection. Spherocytes may be seen occasionally, but the red blood cell morphology is usually normal. The antibody is directed against the I antigen, and the entire process is self-limited.

The cold agglutinin in infectious mononucleosis is most frequently directed against the i antigen, an antigen accessible on the surface of fetal red blood cells but not adult red blood cells. Therefore, this cold agglutinin is of serologic interest, but rarely induces hemolysis in humans. Antibody directed against the I antigen and complex

antibodies involving both antigens have also been reported, with hemolysis.

A chronic form of cold-induced hemolysis occurs in patients de novo or in association with lymphoid neoplasms. It most commonly affects individuals in their seventh or eighth decades. The clinical manifestations relate to hemolysis and less commonly to agglutination of red blood cells in capillaries in those portions of the body exposed to low temperature, causing acrocyanosis. Gangrene is uncommon. Hemoglobin levels are usually above 10 g/dL and rarely below 7 g. Reticulocytes are fewer in number than might be anticipated, presumably because of the selective destruction of young cells (including reticulocytes) in this disorder.

In most patients with cold agglutinin disease, the antibody titer is very high (e.g., 1:10,000) at 4°C and very low (e.g., 1:16) at 37°C. In some patients the antibody shows a flatter thermal spectrum with a moderately high titer at 4°C (e.g., 1:320) and a readily demonstrable titer at 37°C (e.g., 1:64). Hemolysis tends to be more severe in this latter group. The Coombs test demonstrates the presence of C3 on the red blood cell surface, but IgM (which is responsible for the C3 coating of red cells) is not found.

Pathogenesis. The etiology of the antibody is unknown. It appears to exert its hemolytic effect not through agglutination per se but rather by the fixation of C3 to the red blood cell surface. The liver is particularly efficient at detecting red blood cells coated with C3 in the form of C3b and clearing them from the circulation. A plasma enzyme, C3 inactivator, is capable of cleaving C3b into a small fragment (C3c) which leaves the cell surface and reenters the plasma, and C3d, which adheres to the red blood cell surface where it is recognized as C3 in Coombs' test but not as C3 by the mononuclear phagocyte system. The presence of C3d on the red blood cell surface decreases the ability of IgM anti-I to begin anew the complement sequence and thereby reestablish C3b on the red cell surface. Because of this, red blood cells that have survived in the circulation for a period of time have become "protected," while the younger red blood cells are in greater jeopardy.

Therapy. The cutaneous manifestations of this disorder are best treated by maintaining the patient in a warm environment. Because transfusion of normal blood presents to the patient a large number of red blood cells which have not previously been exposed to the cold agglutinin and are therefore not "protected," transfusion may be associated with an acceleration of the hemolytic process. Splenectomy is usually not of value in this disorder. Corticosteroids are of limited value, although patients with the panthermal variety of cold agglutinin disease may respond favorably to this therapy. Chlorambucil and cyclophosphamide are the most commonly employed agents in those patients in whom therapy is indicated. Although some patients have experienced a dramatic improvement, the effectiveness of this therapy is usually marginal.

Cold agglutinin disease tends to be chronic and unremitting. The overall prognosis is dominated by the underlying lymphoproliferative disease, if present. In those patients in whom cold agglutinin disease appears to arise spontaneously, lymphoproliferative disease may become apparent after several years.

PAROXYSMAL COLD HEMOGLOBINURIA (PCH)   Now a rare disorder, PCH was more frequent at a time when tertiary syphilis was more prevalent. It results from the formation of the Donath-Landsteiner antibody, an IgG antibody which is directed against the P antigen complex and which can induce complement-mediated lysis. Attacks are precipitated by exposure to cold and are associated with hemoglobinemia and hemoglobinuria, chills and fever, back, leg, and abdominal pain, headache, and malaise. Recovery from the acute episode is prompt, and between episodes patients are asymptomatic. When this syndrome accompanies acute viral infections (e.g., measles and mumps), it is self-limited. When secondary to syphilis, it responds favorably to specific therapy for this disorder. No specific therapy exists for idiopathic cases. Despite the severity of individual episodes, the natural history of this disease extends over many years.

TRAUMA IN THE CIRCULATION Mechanical trauma can cause hemolysis in three ways: (1) when red blood cells flow through small vessels over the surface of bony prominences and are subject to external impact during various physical activities; (2) when they flow across a pressure gradient created by an abnormal heart valve or valve prosthesis and are disrupted by a shear stress; and (3) when the deposition of fibrin in the microvasculature exposes them to a physical impediment that fragments them (Table 287-4).

External impact Hemoglobinemia and hemoglobinuria have been observed in individuals who have undergone a prolonged march or a prolonged jog, most typically on a hard surface and while wearing thin-soled shoes. The role of direct external trauma in this process has been demonstrated by the fact that hemolysis can be prevented by the insertion of a soft inner sole in the runner's shoes. Similar types of hemolysis have been described following karate and the playing of bongo drums. No abnormality of red blood cell morphology has been demonstrated, even during the acute episode, and no underlying red blood cell abnormality has been uncovered. A large percentage of individuals will develop hemoglobinemia and hemoglobinuria when exposed to the conditions described above. As a result of muscle damage that occurs during some of these activities, myoglobinuria commonly occurs, but renal function is preserved. No specific therapy is required.

Cardiac hemolysis Hemolysis associated with fragmented red blood cells (Fig. A5-7) occurs in approximately 10 percent of patients with artificial aortic valve prostheses. This incidence is somewhat greater with valves having stellite rather than silastic occluders, greater with small valves as compared with larger valves, and greater when valves are cloth-covered or when there is a paravalvular leak with increased flow across the prosthesis. Traumatic hemolysis is much less common in recipients of porcine valves. Severe hemolysis may occur after repair of ostium primum or endocardial cushion defects with a prosthetic patch. Mitral valve prostheses have also been associated with hemolysis, but since the pressure gradient across these is lower than across aortic prostheses, the incidence is lower. A moderately shortened red blood cell survival with little or no anemia occurs in some patients with severe calcific aortic stenosis. Indeed, almost any intracardiac lesion which alters hemodynamics may lead to some shortening of red blood cell survival. In addition, traumatic hemolysis has been observed in patients who have undergone aortofemoral bypass.

CLINICAL MANIFESTATIONS In severe cases hemoglobin levels fall to 5.0 to 7.0 g/dL with reticulocytosis, fragmented red blood cells in the peripheral blood, depressed haptoglobin, elevated serum lactic dehydrogenase, and hemoglobinemia and hemoglobinuria. Iron loss (as hemoglobin or hemosiderin) in the urine may lead to iron deficiency. Direct Coombs test may rarely become positive.

PATHOGENESIS A number of factors combine to cause the fragmentation and destruction of red blood cells in this disorder. Direct mechanical trauma of red blood cells at the time of seating of the occluder of the prosthetic valve, the deposition of fibrin across disrupted attachment points, but probably most important, the shear stress resulting from turbulent blood flow may all result in the fragmentation of red blood cells. The last explains the higher incidence of hemolysis in patients who have a paravalvular leak and therefore greater velocity of blood flow across the aortic orifice during systole.

THERAPY AND PROGNOSIS Iron deficiency should be corrected by the administration of oral iron. The elevated hemoglobin which results may permit a decrease in the cardiac output and a slowing of the hemolytic rate. Limitation in physical activity also lessens the hemolytic rate. When these measures fail, any paravalvular leak must be repaired or the prosthetic valve replaced.

Deposition of fibrin in the microvasculature Fibrin becomes deposited in the microvasculature where it traps platelets and fragments red blood cells, under three general conditions: (1) abnormalities of the vessel wall in recognized disorders, such as malignant hypertension, eclampsia, rejection of a renal allograft, disseminated cancer, and hemangiomas; (2) two potentially fatal syndromes of unknown etiology, thrombotic thrombocytopenic purpura and the hemolytic uremic syndrome; and (3) disseminated intravascular coagulation.

ABNORMALITIES OF THE VESSEL WALL The degree of hemolysis induced by this family of disorders is usually quite mild, although the number of fragments in the peripheral blood may be striking. In occasional patients, thrombocytopenia may be severe. In each case, therapy is best directed at the primary disease. Thus, reversal of renal graft rejection, treatment of malignant hypertension and eclampsia, control of cancer, etc., lead to a cessation of the hemolytic process. The relative importance of the primary vascular abnormality and of the deposition of fibrin in causing hemolysis is unclear.

Thrombotic thrombocytopenic purpura (TTP) This disease of unknown etiology affects individuals of all ages but primarily young adults, more often women.

CLINICAL MANIFESTATIONS Hemolysis is a striking feature of this disease. Anemia occurs in association with fragmented red blood cells, nucleated red cells in the peripheral blood, an elevated reticulocyte count, and thrombocytopenia of varying degree. Platelet counts range from 5000 to 100,000 per cubic millimeter. Jaundice is common, and petechiae may be present, although usually to a less striking degree than in idiopathic thrombocytopenic purpura (ITP). Tests of coagulation, such as the prothrombin time, partial thromboplastin time, fibrinogen concentration, and the level of fibrinogen split products, are usually normal or only mildly abnormal. If the coagulation tests indicate disseminated intravascular coagulation, the diagnosis of TTP is doubtful. Erythroid hyperplasia and an increased number of megakaryocytes are present in the bone marrow. The life span of platelets is decreased to hours, and no site of organ localization of destroyed platelets is observed. A positive antinuclear antibody (ANA) is obtained in approximately 20 percent of patients. Some patients experience significant bleeding of uterine, gastrointestinal, or other origin, but severe bleeding is not common. Fever is present in almost all patients, and many experience nonspecific constitutional symptoms such as nausea, abdominal pain, and arthralgias. The spleen and liver may be palpable.

The course of TTP spans days to weeks in most patients, but occasionally continues for months. As the disease progresses, the brain and kidneys become progressively involved, and their dysfunction is the ultimate cause of death in the majority of patients. Proteinuria and a moderate elevation of blood urea nitrogen may be found on initial presentation, and there is a continued rise in blood urea nitrogen and a fall in urine output as the disease progresses. Neurologic symptoms evolve in more than 90 percent of patients

TABLE 287-4 Disturbances of the formed elements of blood secondary to intravascular trauma

Etiology	Fragments	Hemolysis	Thrombo-cytopenia
Impact: march hemoglobinuria, etc.	0	+	0
Cardiac (turbulence):			
Aortic valve prosthesis	+ + + +	+ + + +	0
Ostium primum repair	+ + + +	+ + + +	0
Mitral valve prosthesis	+ +	+ +	0
Calcific aortic stenosis	+	±	0
Vessel disease:			
Malignant hypertension			
Eclampsia			
Renal graft rejection	+ + +	+	+
Hemangiomas			
Immune disease (scleroderma)			
Thrombotic thrombocytopenic purpura	+ + + +	+ + + +	+ + + +
Hemolytic uremic syndrome	+ + + +	+ + + +	+ + + +
Disseminated intravascular coagulation	+ +	±	+ + + +

whose disease terminates in death. Initially, there may be changes in mental status such as confusion, delirium, or altered states of consciousness. Focal findings include seizures, hemiparesis, aphasia, and visual field defects. These neurologic symptoms may fluctuate and terminate in coma. Involvement of myocardial blood vessels may be a cause of sudden death in some patients.

PATHOGENESIS The etiology of TTP is unknown. Arterioles are filled with hyalin material, presumably fibrin and platelets, and similar material may be seen beneath the endothelium of otherwise uninvolved vessels. Immunofluorescence studies have shown the presence of immunoglobulin and complement in arterioles. Microaneurysms of arterioles are often present. Controversy exists concerning the specificity of these changes, some authorities noting them in the hemolytic uremic syndrome and in disseminated intravascular coagulation. An association with systemic lupus erythematosus (SLE), scleroderma, and Sjögren's syndrome suggests an immunologic etiology.

DIAGNOSIS The combination of hemolytic anemia with fragmented and nucleated red blood cells, thrombocytopenia, fever, neurologic disorders, and renal dysfunction is virtually pathognomonic of TTP. The diagnosis is further supported by the finding of normal coagulation tests, although occasional patients have an isolated abnormality of coagulation. Although they are not usually required for diagnosis, biopsies of skin and muscle, gingiva, lymph node, or bone marrow will frequently reveal the pathologic abnormalities described above. TTP should be considered in every patient in whom the diagnosis of ITP or Evans' syndrome (ITP plus immunohemolytic anemia) is made. The finding of fragmented red blood cells in the peripheral blood is particularly helpful in this regard. Because the clinical course can fluctuate widely, therapy is difficult to evaluate.

THERAPY AND PROGNOSIS Until recently, this disease was almost universally fatal. A large number of therapeutic modalities have been attempted with variable success. These include corticosteroids, plasma exchange, splenectomy, and antiplatelet drugs. Patients are initially treated with high doses of corticosteroids (100 to 1000 mg prednisone per day). However, additional therapy is indicated once the diagnosis has been established. The most consistent improvement (60 to 75 percent) has been noted with exchange transfusion or plasmapheresis. In most patients plasmapheresis is as effective as exchange transfusion. In others the response may depend upon the infusion of plasma. Splenectomy is also effective, but with a lower frequency of response and with additional risk in these critically ill patients. The benefit of antiplatelet drugs (dipyridamole, sulfinpyrazone, dextran, aspirin) is unclear, but they are commonly used together with the therapeutic measures described above. Aspirin may increase the risk of bleeding and should be employed with caution. Vincristine may be effective in otherwise refractory patients. In addition, rare responses to heparin infusion have been reported. Because of the ever-present risk of sudden death, therapy should be instituted promptly. Even deep coma is not a contraindication to therapy since full neurologic recovery is the rule in patients responding to therapy. If treatment is instituted early in the disease, remission occurs in approximately two-thirds of patients. Relapses have been noted in approximately 10 percent of patients but are usually responsive to therapeutic intervention.

Hemolytic uremic syndrome The hemolytic uremic syndrome is a disorder usually encountered in young children with laboratory features similar to those of TTP. Often the patient has a prodrome of a viral-like illness. Less commonly, the disorder appears to be familial. Patients present with acute hemolytic anemia, thrombocytopenic purpura, and acute oliguric renal failure. Most patients have either hemoglobinuria or anuria. Unlike TTP, neurologic manifestations are uncommon. The peripheral blood findings, coagulation tests, and pathologic changes on biopsy specimens are usually indistinguishable from those of TTP. Patients are treated with dialysis and transfusions. The efficacy of corticosteroids, dextran, and heparin is uncertain. The mortality in children ranges from 5 to 20 percent, but is

considerably higher in adults. A disorder resembling the hemolytic-uremic syndrome has recently been described in adults treated with the antineoplastic drug mitomycin C, usually in combination with other drugs.

Disseminated intravascular coagulation (DIC) Red blood cell fragmentation in the microvasculature (microangiopathic hemolytic anemia) is seen in about one-third of patients with DIC (Chap. 281). The degree of hemolysis is much less in DIC than in either TTP or the hemolytic uremic syndrome, and anemia with reticulocytosis and nucleated red blood cells is distinctly rare.

DIRECT TOXIC EFFECTS A variety of infections may be associated with severe hemolysis. The microorganisms in bartonellosis (Chap. 116) and malaria (Chap. 154) directly parasitize red blood cells. Babesiosis (Chap. 159) also may cause a mild to moderate hemolytic anemia by direct parasitization of red blood cells.

Other infectious organisms exert their damaging effects on red blood cells indirectly. The most striking is that resulting from septicemia with *Clostridium welchii* (Chap. 101). The phospholipase produced by this organism is capable of cleaving the phosphoryl bond of lecithin thereby lysing human red blood cells. A mild, transient hemolysis frequently accompanies bacteremia with diverse organisms such as pneumococci, staphylococci, and *Escherichia coli*.

Hemolysis may result from the direct action of snake and spider venoms on the red blood cell. Although cobra venom is directly lytic in vitro, the clinical disease induced by the bite of the cobra is one of moderate hemolysis associated with spherocytosis. Spider bites are known to induce acute intravascular hemolysis associated with spherocytosis. It is thought that the brown recluse spider which inhabits the central and southern portions of the United States and portions of South America is responsible. The hemolytic disease continues for several days up to 1 week.

Copper has a direct hemolytic effect on red blood cells. Hemolysis has been observed following exposure of individuals to copper salts (such as during hemodialysis). In addition, the transient episodes of hemolysis observed in patients with Wilson's disease are probably due to copper toxicity.

The red blood cell membrane is unstable at temperatures above 49°C due to denaturation of the cytoskeletal protein, spectrin. When studied in vitro, the red blood cell undergoes a process of budding, cleavage, and resealing above this temperature. The same process is observed in individuals who have suffered extensive burns. These patients have prominent spherocytosis as well as hemoglobinemia and sometimes hemoglobinuria.

MEMBRANE ABNORMALITIES

ACQUIRED DISORDERS OF THE MEMBRANE There are two well-defined acquired disorders of the red blood cell membrane: spur cell anemia and paroxysmal nocturnal hemoglobinuria (PNH).

Spur cell anemia Hemolytic anemia with bizarre-shaped red blood cells occurs in some patients with severe hepatocellular disease. Most patients with spur cell anemia have advanced Laennec's cirrhosis. This hemolytic disorder is observed in approximately 5 percent of patients with manifestations of severe cirrhosis, such as ascites, jaundice, and hepatic encephalopathy. Spur cell anemia has also been reported in neonatal hepatitis.

CLINICAL MANIFESTATIONS Anemia is moderate to severe, with hematocrit levels ranging from 16 to 30 percent. Thus, the anemia is more severe than is observed in otherwise uncomplicated cirrhosis, in which hematocrit levels are rarely below 28 percent, unless there is accompanying folic acid deficiency, blood loss, iron deficiency, etc. (Chap. 286). Splenomegaly is a constant feature, and the spleen is generally more prominent than in patients who have cirrhosis but who do not have spur cell anemia. Jaundice is also a constant feature, and hepatic encephalopathy is common. Other tests of liver function are similar to values obtained in most patients with severe cirrhosis, although there is a tendency to longer prothrombin times. Chromium half-survival times of red blood cells are decreased to as short as 6 days (normal being 26 to 32 days), and red cell destruction is localized to the spleen. Normal transfused red blood cells have a survival similar to that of the patient's own red blood cells. Red blood cells are irregularly shaped with multiple spicules, and a small number of bizarre-shaped fragments are commonly seen on peripheral blood smears (see Fig. A5-8). Reticulocytes range from 5 to 15 percent.

PATHOGENESIS The surface membrane of spur cells contains 50 to 70 percent excess cholesterol, but its total phospholipid content is normal. In this way, spur cells are distinct from the more usual target red blood cells in liver disease, which possess an excess of both cholesterol and phospholipid. Cholesterol out of proportion of phospholipid decreases the fluidity of the spur cell membrane, and cell deformability is also decreased. Normal red blood cells acquire the spur abnormality when incubated in serum from affected patients. This results from the presence in serum of an abnormal low-density lipoprotein with an increased mole ratio of free (unesterified) cholesterol to phospholipid. Thus, red blood cells in spur cell anemia may be considered to be "innocent bystanders." These rigid, cholesterol-laden red blood cells are detected by the filtering system of the spleen, aided by congestive splenomegaly in cirrhosis. In contrast to circulating spur cells, normal red blood cells which have acquired cholesterol in vitro have an increased surface area and a decreased osmotic fragility, and they have a regular pattern of spicule deformity. This is also true in vivo for normal red blood cells during their initial 24 h in the circulation. However, during continued circulation in vivo in the presence of the spleen, cholesterol-rich spur cells lose surface area and transform to the irregular pattern of spiculation associated with acanthocytes (see "Red Blood Cell Morphology" above). This process of membrane "conditioning" by the spleen continues, and the cell is destroyed in the spleen.

DIAGNOSIS Increasing anemia in a patient with chronic cirrhosis most commonly results from blood loss, folic acid deficiency, or iron deficiency. The hemolytic rate may increase transiently during periods of acute fatty liver. The combination of an elevated reticulocyte count and elevated bilirubin in the presence of the characteristic morphologic abnormality on peripheral blood smear is diagnostic. Red blood cells of similar morphologic appearance are seen in patients with abetalipoproteinemia. However, these individuals have a minimal amount of hemolysis.

Spur cells and acanthocytes must be distinguished from regularly scalloped, crenated red blood cells (echinocytes). These are a frequent artifact on blood smears, and they are present in some patients with uremia ("burr cells") (Fig. A5-9). Small, dense crenated spheres (spheroechinocytes) are sometimes seen in congenital nonspherocytic hemolytic anemia due to enzyme deficiencies in the Embden-Meyerhof pathway.

TREATMENT Since normal red blood cells acquire the spur abnormality when transfused into patients with this form of anemia, transfusion therapy is of limited benefit. Attempts to influence red blood cell cholesterol by the use of various lipid-lowering agents have thus far been unsuccessful. Splenectomy has been reported to prevent both the conditioning of red blood cells in the spleen and their premature destruction. However, splenectomy carries a high risk in patients with severe liver disease complicated by portal hypertension and coagulation defects, and it must be reserved for selected patients in whom hemolysis is a major clinical problem and who appear to be relatively good surgical risks.

PROGNOSIS In most patients spur cell anemia occurs during the late stages of cirrhosis, and more than 90 percent of patients succumb to their underlying liver disease within 1 year of the diagnosis of spur cell anemia.

Paroxysmal nocturnal hemoglobinuria (PNH) This condition is distinctive among hemolytic disorders in humans because it is an intracorpuscular defect acquired at the stem cell level. It occurs primarily in young adults.

CLINICAL MANIFESTATIONS Anemia is of exceedingly variable degree with hematocrit values of 20 percent and lower in occasional patients and normal values in others. Mild granulocytopenia and thrombocytopenia are commonly present. Although regarded as a classic feature of this disease, gross hemoglobinuria is present only intermittently in most patients, and never occurs in some. Hemosiderinuria is usually present. Other features of diagnostic significance are a low leukocyte alkaline phosphatase and a low red blood cell acetylcholinesterase. Red blood cells are normochromic and normocytic unless iron deficiency has occurred from the chronic loss of iron in the urine. The diagnosis is established by a positive acid hemolysis test or sucrose lysis test, both of which demonstrate the enhanced sensitivity of PNH red blood cells to complement (see below). Venous thromboses are a common complication of this disorder, and they have been reported in peripheral veins as well as in mesenteric, hepatic, portal, and cerebral veins. Thromboses are a common cause of death in patients severely affected with PNH. A second manifestation, possibly related to thromboses in small veins, is the occurrence of back and abdominal pain similar in character to that which occurs in sickle cell anemia. Headache has also been reported. Since the widespread use of the sucrose lysis test, many patients have been discovered with mild, chronic disease.

PATHOGENESIS The underlying abnormality which affects red blood cells, granulocytes, and platelets in PNH is an inordinate sensitivity to complement. This may be demonstrated in vitro using a complement-fixing antibody. PNH red blood cells fix more C1 than normal red cells per unit of antibody present, and this C1 promotes more C3 fixation per molecule of C1 than is seen with normal red cells. However, antibody is not necessary for the lysis of red blood cells in PNH. Rather, C3 is readily fixed to the red blood cell surface by means of the alternate (properdin) pathway. Careful analytic procedures have demonstrated two and in some cases three separate populations of red blood cells with varying sensitivities to complement in patients with PNH. The clinical manifestations relate directly to the proportion of the red blood cells produced that are most sensitive to complement. Although platelets share with red blood cells this sensitivity to complement, platelet survival is normal in PNH. However, a functional modification of platelets induced by complement may underlie the thrombotic complications of this disease. The increased sensitivity of red blood cells to complement has been demonstrated to result from the lack of a red cell membrane regulatory protein, decay-accelerating factor (DAF), which is partially responsible for the rapid conversion of C3b to the inactive C3d.

Since it affects granulocytes, platelets, and red blood cells but not lymphocytes, this defect is thought to occur because of an acquired change in the pluripotent stem cell which generates these cells. In this respect it is similar to both acute myelogenous leukemia and the myeloproliferative syndromes, disorders which appear to affect the stem cells responsible for platelet, granulocyte, and red blood cell production. Both acute myelogenous leukemia and PNH may be secondary manifestations of a primary bone marrow injury that is manifested initially as aplastic anemia. Moreover, a number of patients with PNH have subsequently developed acute myelogenous leukemia. The red blood cell abnormality characteristic of PNH (complement sensitivity) occurs to a mild degree in some patients with aplastic anemia and in some with myelofibrosis, further linking this series of bone marrow disorders. The precise mechanism has not been identified. It appears likely that PNH results from a somatic mutation in the marrow stem cell pool. The phenotypic representation of this presumed mutation is not known.

DIAGNOSIS As indicated above, PNH is commonly undiagnosed for a period of months to years. The classic manifestation of gross hemoglobinuria may be present only intermittently, and an awareness of its presence may be obtained only by repeated questioning of the patient. In some patients, a chronic hemolytic process occurs without gross hemoglobinuria. Therefore, diagnoses such as refractory anemia, hemolytic anemia of unknown etiology, and pancytopenia are common in patients subsequently proven to have PNH. A decreased leukocyte alkaline phosphatase is a clue to the diagnosis, and the presence of hemosiderin in the urine sediment is strongly suggestive. Hemosiderinuria may occur with intravascular hemolysis of any etiology. However, only a few disorders in humans result in intravascular hemolysis. These are PNH, paroxysmal cold hemoglobinuria, hemolytic transfusion reaction, traumatic hemolysis, and hemolysis due to lysins (snake venom, *C. welchii* bacteremia) or to extensive acute burns. The acid hemolysis test is also positive in the rare congenital disorder hereditary erythrocytic multinuclearity with positive acidified-serum test (HEMPAS). In this latter disorder, complement sensitivity results from an inordinate fixation of C4 molecules per molecule of C1. Since this sensitivity exists in the classic (antibody-mediated) pathway but not in the alternate (properdin) pathway, spontaneous fixation of complement with lysis in vivo is not a feature of the HEMPAS disorder.

It should be noted that chromium survival studies often produce information which is confusing in PNH. This results from the bi- or trimodal population of red blood cells. The cells most sensitive to complement have a very short survival, and they account for a minority of circulating red blood cells, whereas the cells less sensitive to complement have a more normal survival and account for the majority of circulating cells. Thus, the chromium survival is longer than might be anticipated from other measures of hemoglobin turnover.

TREATMENT   Transfusion therapy is useful in PNH not only for raising the hemoglobin level but also for suppressing the marrow production of red blood cells during episodes of sustained hemoglobinuria or of sustained painful crisis. The transfusion of blood prior to surgery may reduce the incidence of postoperative thrombotic complications. For reasons that are still unclear, whole blood transfusions frequently cause an exacerbation of the hemolytic process. This can be prevented by using washed red blood cells rather than whole blood.

Therapy with androgens frequently results in a rise of hemoglobin level. Adrenocortical steroids may also be effective in reducing the rate of hemolysis.

Because of iron loss in the urine, iron deficiency is common. An exacerbation of hemolysis often follows the administration of iron because of the formation of a large number of young red blood cells, many of which are sensitive to complement. This may be minimized by suppressing the bone marrow with transfusions.

Splenectomy has been undertaken in some patients with the hope of decreasing the hemolytic rate and the transfusion requirement. However, because of the limited therapeutic benefit and the high risk attendant upon surgery in patients with PNH, splenectomy cannot be recommended.

Anticoagulation with coumarin-type drugs may have some benefit in preventing thromboses, particularly in the postsurgical patient. On the other hand, therapy with heparin has been noted to cause an increased amount of hemolysis in some patients with PNH, and caution must be exercised when using this drug.

PROGNOSIS   Most patients with classic PNH have a life expectancy of less than 10 years, although some survive for much longer. A series of 17 patients surviving more than 20 years has been compiled by questioning hematologists nationally. In more than one-third of these patients, there had been an amelioration of disease symptoms, and in two patients PNH was totally quiescent. The major morbidity relates to venous thromboses. Despite the overwhelming degree of iron deposition in the kidney, death from renal failure is rare. The prognosis is uncertain in patients in whom the manifestations of PNH are more subtle and in whom the diagnosis was made because of the widespread use of the sucrose lysis test. Some patients may lead a normal life.

CONGENITAL ABNORMALITIES OF THE RED CELL MEMBRANE

There are four types of inherited abnormalities of the red cell membrane: hereditary spherocytosis, hereditary elliptocytosis, hereditary pyropoikilocytosis, and hereditary stomatocytosis. Each syndrome may represent a group of disorders with a differing structural basis. The molecular pathogenesis of these disorders has not been completely defined.

Hereditary spherocytosis

This is a disease of autosomal dominant inheritance in which intrinsically abnormal red blood cells are destroyed in the presence of an otherwise normal spleen. Its incidence is approximately 1:4500. In 20 percent of patients the absence of hematologic abnormalities in family members suggests that a spontaneous mutation has occurred. The disorder is sometimes clinically apparent in early infancy, but often escapes detection until adult life.

CLINICAL MANIFESTATIONS   The major clinical features of hereditary spherocytosis are anemia, splenomegaly, and jaundice. The prominence of the latter finding accounts for its prior designation "congenital hemolytic jaundice" and is due to an increased concentration of unconjugated (indirect-reacting) bilirubin in plasma. Jaundice may be intermittent and tends to be less pronounced in early childhood. Because of the increased bile pigment production, gallstones of pigment type are common, even in childhood. Compensatory normoblastic hyperplasia of the bone marrow occurs with the extension of red marrow into the midshafts of long bones and occasionally with extramedullary erythropoiesis, at times leading to the formation of paravertebral masses visible on chest x-ray. Because the bone marrow's capacity to increase erythropoiesis by six- to tenfold exceeds the usual rate of hemolysis in this disease, anemia is usually mild or moderate and may even be absent in an otherwise healthy individual. Compensation may be temporarily interrupted by episodes of erythroid hypoplasia precipitated by infections, often of a minor nature. Splenomegaly is a constant feature of hereditary spherocytosis. The hemolytic rate may increase transiently during systemic infections which induce further splenic enlargement. Chronic leg ulcers, similar to those observed in sickle cell anemia, occasionally occur.

The characteristic erythrocyte abnormality is the spherocyte (Fig. A5-10). The mean corpuscular volume (MCV) is usually normal or

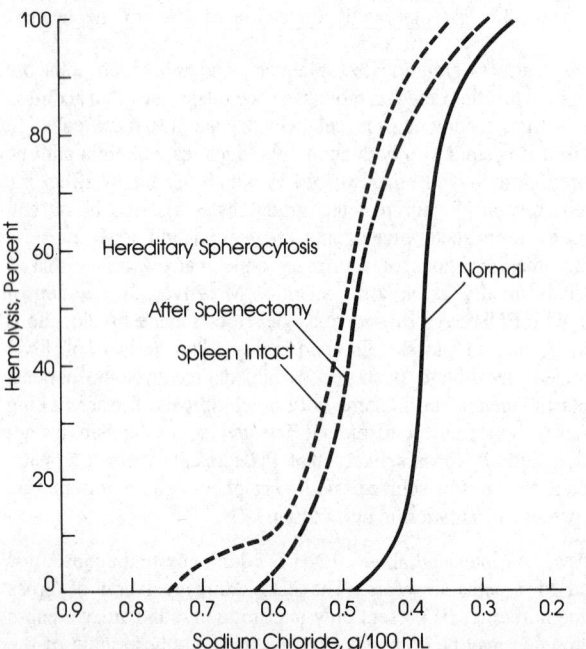

FIGURE 287-1 *Osmotic fragility of red blood cells in hereditary spherocytosis. When the spleen is present, a small subpopulation of cells which are "conditioned" in the spleen form the fragile "tail" of the osmotic fragility curve. After splenectomy a single population exists which is more osmotically fragile than normal.*

slightly decreased, and the mean corpuscular hemoglobin concentration (MCHC) is increased to 35 to 38 g/dL. Spheroidicity may be quantitatively assessed in terms of osmotic fragility (Fig. 287-1). Because spherocytes have a decreased surface area per unit volume, they lyse more readily when exposed to solutions of low salt concentration. On microscopic examination spherocytes are usually detected even when present in very small numbers. However, they will ordinarily not influence the osmotic fragility test unless they constitute more than 1 or 2 percent of the total cell population. A prominent increase in the osmotic fragility of red blood cells following sterile incubation of whole blood for 24 h at 37°C is also characteristic of hereditary spherocytosis. The autohemolysis test is an extension of this latter procedure and measures the amount of spontaneous hemolysis occurring after 48 h of sterile incubation. In hereditary spherocytosis about 10 to 50 percent of the red blood cells are lysed (versus less than 4 percent of normal red blood cells). Autohemolysis of these red blood cells is largely prevented by the addition of glucose prior to incubation.

PATHOGENESIS   Although not well understood, the molecular abnormality in hereditary spherocytosis involves the proteins of the cytoskeleton. Nearly all patients have a significant deficiency of spectrin (see Fig. 283-6) which correlates with the severity of the anemia. The spheroidal contour and rigid structure of the red blood cells impede their passage through the spleen. There, the red blood cells are exposed to an environment in which their increased metabolic rate cannot be sustained. The first injury imposed upon them by the spleen is a further loss of surface membrane "conditioning," which produces a subpopulation of hyperspheroidal red blood cells in the peripheral blood. These are subsequently destroyed in the spleen. The intracorpuscular nature of the red blood cell defect in hereditary spherocytosis is demonstrated by a diminished life span of the patient's red cells in normal subjects when the spleen is present and a normal survival of normal cells transfused into patients with hereditary spherocytosis.

DIAGNOSIS   Hereditary spherocytosis must be distinguished from the spherocytic hemolytic anemias associated with red blood cell antibodies. The family history is helpful, when present. The diagnosis of immune spherocytosis is usually readily established by a positive direct Coombs test. Spherocytes, often in considerable numbers, are seen in association with hemolysis induced by splenomegaly in patients with cirrhosis or chronic infections, and a few spherocytes are seen in the course of a wide variety of hemolytic disorders, particularly glucose 6-phosphate dehydrogenase deficiency.

TREATMENT AND PROGNOSIS   Splenectomy reliably corrects the anemia, although the red blood cell defect persists. The operative risk is low. Red blood cell survival after splenectomy is normal or nearly so. Rare relapses have been reported and are probably attributable to postoperative growth of splenic autotransplants or to hyperplasia of secondary spleens which were overlooked at operation. Because of the potential for gallstones and for episodes of bone marrow hypoplasia or hemolytic crises, splenectomy should be performed in most individuals with hereditary spherocytosis, even those with mild anemia. Splenectomy in children should be postponed until the age of 4 years, if possible, although it may be performed at any age. Beyond age 3, severe infections following splenectomy in hereditary spherocytosis are rare. Nonetheless, polyvalent pneumococcal vaccine should be administered to all patients who are to undergo splenectomy. Because of the increased requirement for folic acid in patients with hemolysis, they sometimes become deficient in this vitamin. Therapy with folic acid may result in an increased hemoglobin level.

Hereditary elliptocytosis and hereditary pyropoikilocytosis   Red blood cells of oval or elliptic shape are normally found in birds, reptiles, camels, and llamas; however, they occur in appreciable numbers in humans only in *hereditary elliptocytosis,* a disorder which is transmitted as an autosomal dominant and affects 1 per 4000 to 5000 of the population, a frequency similar to that of hereditary

spherocytosis. It is also referred to as *hereditary ovalocytosis.* Less commonly, homozygotes have been encountered with an absence of a red cell membrane protein (band 4.1) that is important in stabilizing the interaction of spectrin and actin in the cytoskeleton (see Fig. 283-6).

The great majority of patients manifest only mild hemolysis, with hemoglobin levels above 12 g/dL, reticulocytes less than 4 percent, depressed haptoglobin levels, and red blood cell survivals within or just under the normal range. In 10 to 15 percent of patients the rate of hemolysis is substantially increased with chromium half-survival times of red blood cells as short as 5 days and reticulocytes ranging to 20 percent. Hemoglobin levels rarely fall below 9 to 10 g/dL. Red blood cell destruction occurs predominantly in the spleen, which is enlarged in patients with overt hemolysis, and hemolysis is corrected by splenectomy.

In both the anemic and nonanemic varieties of this disorder the red blood cells are normochromic and normocytic. At least 25 percent and, more commonly, greater than 75 percent of red blood cells are elliptic, with an axial ratio (width/length) of less than 0.78. Patients with hemolysis frequently have microovalocytes, bizarre-shaped red blood cells, and red cell fragments, and these increase in number following splenectomy. The degree of hemolysis does not correlate with the percentage of elliptocytes. Osmotic fragility is usually normal but may be increased in patients with overt hemolysis. The pathogenesis of the red blood cell defect probably involves abnormalities of assembly of spectrin subunits.

Hereditary pyropoikilocytosis (HPP) is thought to be related to hereditary elliptocytosis, since both have been reported in the same family. HPP is a rare disorder characterized by bizarre-shaped, microcytic red cells which undergo disruption at temperatures of 44 to 45°C (in contrast to the normal thermal instability at 49°C). This results from an abnormality of spectrin structure. Hemolysis, which is usually severe, is recognized in childhood and is partially responsive to splenectomy.

Hereditary stomatocytosis   Stomatocytes are red blood cells having a slit-like central zone of pallor on dried smears. The syndrome of hereditary hemolytic anemia and stomatocytic red blood cells is inherited in an autosomal dominant pattern. It may represent a number of discrete entities. Two major red blood cell defects have been delineated in this syndrome. First, the red blood cells have an increased permeability to sodium and potassium, which is compensated for by an increased active transport of these cations. Second, red cells have an increased surface area associated with an increase in membrane lipid content, particularly phosphatidylcholine. In some patients, the red blood cell is swollen with an excess of ions and water and a decreased mean corpuscular hemoglobin concentration (overhydrated stomatocytes, "hydrocytosis"); in other patients the red cell is shrunken with a decreased ion and water content and an increased mean corpuscular hemoglobin concentration (dehydrated stomatocytes, "desiccytosis"). Those patients in whom the red blood cells are overhydrated have true stomatocytes on dried smears. Dehydrated stomatocytes assume the morphology of target cells on dried smears. In both instances, red blood cells are cup- or bowl-shaped when examined in wet preparation. Osmotic fragility is increased in overhydrated stomatocytes and decreased in underhydrated stomatocytes. Autohemolysis is increased and is corrected by glucose.

Most patients have splenomegaly and mild anemia. Splenectomy decreases but does not totally correct the hemolytic process. Its indications are similar to those for hereditary spherocytosis.

DISORDERS OF THE INTERIOR OF THE RED CELL

RED CELL ENZYME DEFECTS   During its maturation, the red blood cell loses its nucleus, ribosomes, and mitochondria and thus its capability for protein synthesis and oxidative phosphorylation. The mature circulating red blood cell has a relatively simple pattern of intermediary metabolism (Fig. 287-2) in keeping with its modest metabolic obligations. As discussed in Chap. 283, some ATP must be generated from the Embden-Meyerhof pathway to drive the cation pump which maintains the ionic milieu within the red blood cell. Smaller amounts of energy are needed for the preservation of hemoglobin iron in the ferrous (Fe^{2+}) state, and perhaps for the renewal of the lipids in the red blood cell membrane. About 10 percent of the glucose consumed by the red blood cell is metabolized via the hexose-monophosphate shunt (Fig. 287-2). This pathway protects both hemoglobin and the membrane from exogenous oxidants including certain drugs.

Studies of red blood cell enzyme defects have provided valuable information on the metabolic control of normal erythrocytes. Figure 287-2 shows a large number of recognized specific enzyme deficiency states affecting the glycolytic pathway or the hexose-monophosphate shunt. Many of these enzyme abnormalities appear to be restricted to red blood cells. The long life span of the red blood cell and its inability to synthesize proteins pose a challenge to the stability of its enzymes. Therefore, a mutation resulting in decreased stability will be expressed more readily in the red blood cell compared with other tissues.

Defects in the Embden-Meyerhof pathway   Deficiencies of most of the enzymes of the Embden-Meyerhof (or glycolytic) pathway have been reported. In general, all these enzymopathies have similar pathophysiologic and clinical features. Patients present with a congenital nonspherocytic hemolytic anemia of variable severity. The red blood cells are often relatively deficient in ATP, considering their young age. As a result, there is an increased leak of potassium ion from inside these cells. Abnormalities in red blood cell morphology (see below) indicate that the red cell membrane is secondarily affected by the enzyme defect. These red blood cells are apt to be rigid and thus more readily sequestered by the mononuclear-phagocyte system.

Some of these glycolytic enzyme deficiencies such as pyruvate kinase (PK) deficiency and hexokinase deficiency are localized to the red blood cell. There is no apparent metabolic abnormality in leukocytes or other cells that have been studied. In other disorders, the enzyme deficiency is more widespread. Glucose phosphate isomerase deficiency and phosphoglycerate kinase deficiency also involve leukocytes, although affected individuals have no apparent abnormalities of white blood cell function. Individuals with deficiency of triose phosphate isomerase have decreased levels of enzyme in leukocytes, muscle cells, and central nervous system fluid. Furthermore, they have a progressive neurologic disorder. Some patients with phosphofructokinase deficiency have a myopathy.

Among the reported defects of glycolytic enzymes, about 95 percent are due to PK deficiency and about 4 percent are due to glucose phosphate isomerase deficiency. The remainder shown in Fig. 287-2 are extremely rare. Most have been encountered in isolated families. There is considerable variability in the clinical manifestations

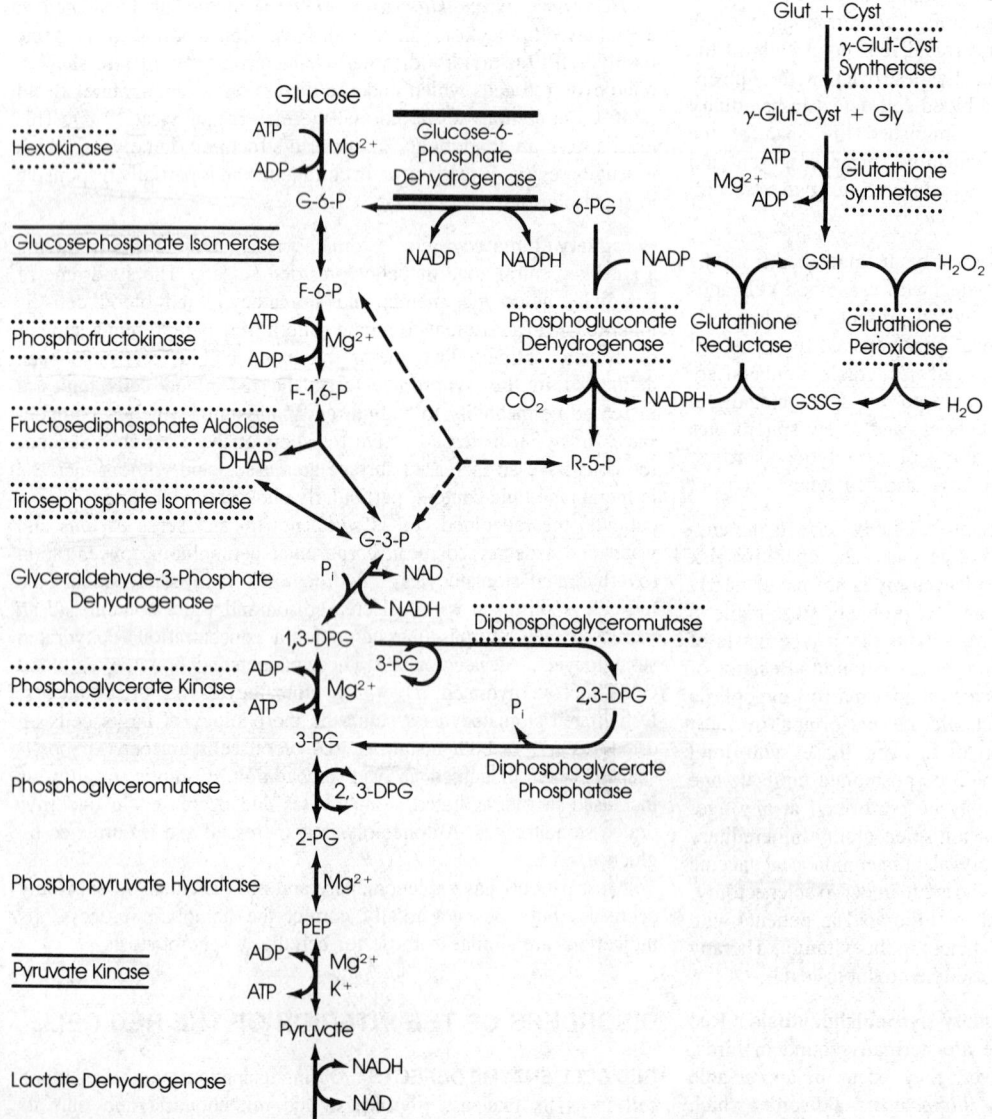

FIGURE 287-2 *Metabolic pathways in the red blood cell. The glycolytic pathway is outlined vertically from glucose to lactate. The pentose phosphate pathway is shown on the right. Known enzyme deficiency states are shown. Bold solid lines denote common states, light solid lines less common ones, and dotted lines rare ones. (From WN Valentine, Semin Hematol 8:309, 1971.)*

and laboratory findings among reported cases of PK deficiency. This is probably due to the fact that a number of different PK variants have been reported. This heterogeneity probably also applies to the other less common glycolytic enzyme defects. Accordingly, the clinical manifestations of these disorders are quite variable.

GENETICS Most of the glycolytic enzyme defects are inherited in an autosomal recessive pattern. Thus, the parents of affected patients are heterozygotes. Heterozygotes generally possess half-normal levels of enzyme activity which are more than adequate for normal metabolic function. Thus, these individuals are entirely asymptomatic. Since the gene frequency for this group of enzymopathies is low, it is not surprising that true homozygotes are often the offspring of a consanguineous mating. Alternatively, affected individuals may be double heterozygotes, inheriting an abnormal allele from each parent. Phosphoglycerate kinase deficiency is inherited as a sex-linked disorder. Affected males have a severe hemolytic anemia while female carriers may have a mild hemolytic process.

CLINICAL MANIFESTATIONS Patients with severe hemolysis usually present during early childhood with anemia, icterus, and splenomegaly. Other stigmata of chronic hemolysis are occasionally seen. Occasionally, siblings are similarly affected.

LABORATORY FINDINGS Patients have a normocytic (or slightly macrocytic) normochromic anemia with reticulocytosis. In those with PK deficiency, bizarre erythrocytes are noted on the peripheral smear with large numbers of spiculated red blood cells. Spherocytes are usually infrequent or absent. Hence, the term *congenital nonspherocytic hemolytic anemia* has been applied to these disorders. Unlike hereditary spherocytosis, the osmotic fragility of freshly drawn blood is usually normal. Incubation brings out an osmotically fragile population of red blood cells.

The diagnosis of this group of anemias depends upon specific enzymatic assays. An abnormality in enzyme kinetics may be demonstrated. In addition, differences in electrophoretic mobility, pH optimum, or heat stability may be noted. This information is useful in documenting heterogeneity among enzyme variants.

TREATMENT Most patients do not require therapy. Those with severe hemolysis should be given a daily supplement of folic acid (1 mg per day). Blood transfusions may be necessary during a hypoplastic crisis. Patients with PK deficiency may be benefited by splenectomy. Because of their enzymatic defect, the younger cells (reticulocytes) depend on mitochondrial respiration rather than glycolysis for maintenance of ATP. However, in the hypoxic environment of the spleen, aerobic metabolism is curtailed and the ATP-depleted cells are destroyed in situ. It is of interest that following splenectomy patients with PK deficiency often have a marked increase in circulating reticulocytes. Patients with deficiency of glucose phosphate isomerase may also be improved by splenectomy. There is not sufficient information to indicate whether this operation would help individuals with other glycolytic enzymopathies.

Defects in the hexose-monophosphate shunt The normal red blood cell is well endowed to protect itself against oxidant stress. Upon exposure to an offending drug or toxin, the amount of glucose that is metabolized via the hexose-monophosphate shunt is increased severalfold. In this way reduced glutathione is regenerated, protecting the sulfhydryl groups of hemoglobin and the red blood cell membrane from oxidation. Individuals with an inherited defect in the hexose-monophosphate shunt are unable to maintain an adequate level of reduced glutathione in their red blood cells. As a result, hemoglobin sulfhydryl groups become oxidized, and the hemoglobin tends to precipitate within the red blood cell forming Heinz bodies.

Among the congenital shunt defects, by far the most common is *G6PD deficiency*. It affects millions of people throughout the world. Like the glycolytic enzymopathies, there is considerable genetic heterogeneity among affected individuals. Indeed, over 250 variants of G6PD have been described. In contrast to the hemoglobin variants

(Chap. 288) abnormalities in primary structure have been established in only a few of the G6PD variants. The remainder are presumed to have abnormal structure because of differences in electrophoretic mobility, enzyme kinetics, pH optimum, and heat stability. Like many of the hemoglobin variants, some G6PD mutants were discovered by chance and are not associated with any significant functional abnormalities. The normal or "wild" form of G6PD is designated by type B. About 20 percent of blacks have a G6PD (designated A+) which differs electrophoretically but is functionally normal. Among the clinically significant G6PD variants, the most common is the so-called A− type encountered primarily in blacks who originated from central Africa. The A− G6PD has the same electrophoretic mobility as the A+ type, but it is unstable and has abnormal kinetic properties. Like the HbS gene, the A− type of G6PD may confer protection against malaria. This variant is found in about 15 percent of black males in the United States. A second relatively common G6PD variant is encountered among peoples of the eastern Mediterranean area, particularly Sephardic Jews. A third relatively common variant occurs in the Chinese.

The G6PD gene is located on the X chromosome. Thus the deficiency state is a sex-linked trait. Affected males (hemizygotes) inherit the abnormal gene from their mothers who are usually carriers (heterozygotes). Because of inactivation of one of the two X chromosomes (Lyon hypothesis, see Chap. 57), the heterozygote has two populations of red blood cells: normal and deficient in G6PD. Most female carriers are asymptomatic. Those who happen to have a high proportion of deficient cells resemble the male hemizygotes.

G6PD activity normally declines about 50 percent during the 120-day life span of the red blood cell. This decay is moderately accelerated in A− red blood cells and markedly so in red blood cells containing the Mediterranean variant. Individuals with the A− variant may have a slightly shortened red blood cell survival, but they are not anemic. Clinical problems arise only when the affected individual is subjected to some type of environmental stress. Most often, hemolytic episodes are triggered by viral and bacterial infections. The mechanism for this is unknown. Drugs or toxins which pose an oxidant threat to the red blood cell by serving as oxidation-reduction catalysts also cause hemolysis in individuals deficient in G6PD (see Table 287-5). Of these, sulfa drugs, antimalarials, and nitrofurantoin are most commonly incriminated. Although aspirin is frequently mentioned as a likely offender, it has no deleterious effect in A− individuals. Occasionally, accidental ingestion of toxic compounds such as naphthalene (found in moth balls) can cause severe hemolysis. Finally, metabolic acidosis can precipitate an episode of hemolysis in subjects deficient in G6PD.

CLINICAL AND LABORATORY FEATURES The patient may experience an acute hemolytic crisis within hours of exposure to the oxidant stress. In severe cases, hemoglobinuria and peripheral vascular collapse can develop. Since only the older population of red blood cells is rapidly destroyed, the hemolytic crisis is usually self-limited, even if the exposure to the oxidant continues. Among black males with the A− variant, the red cell mass decreases by a maximum of 25 to 30 percent. During the period of acute hemolysis, a rapid drop in hematocrit is accompanied by a rise in plasma hemoglobin and unconjugated bilirubin and a decrease in plasma haptoglobin. The oxidation of hemoglobin leads to the formation of Heinz bodies visualized by means of a supravital stain such as crystal violet. However, Heinz bodies are usually not seen after the first day or so,

TABLE 287-5 Drugs causing hemolysis in subjects deficient in G6PD

Antimalarials: Primaquine, pamaquine, chloroquine, dapsone
Sulfonamides: Sulfanilamide, sulfasoxazole, etc.
Nitrofurantoin
Analgesics: Phenacetin, acetanilid
Miscellaneous: Vitamin K (water-soluble form), probenecid, methylene blue,
  p-aminosalicylic acid, nalidixic acid, quinine,* quinidine,* chloramphenicol*

* Not known to cause hemolysis in blacks with A− type G6PD.

since these inclusions are readily removed by the spleen. Their removal leads to the formation of "bite cells," red cells which have lost a peripheral portion of the cell. Multiple bites cause the formation of fragments. Small numbers of spherocytes may also be present.

Individuals with the *Mediterranean type G6PD* have a more unstable enzyme and, therefore, a much lower overall enzyme activity than blacks with the A− variant. As a result, they have more severe clinical manifestations. Some have a chronic hemolytic anemia, even in the absence of any exposure to oxidants. A minority of patients are exquisitely sensitive to fava beans and will develop a fulminant hemolytic crisis following exposure. Sensitivity to *Vicia fava* is a poorly understood phenomenon that appears to be determined by a separate gene. Favism is not encountered in blacks with the A− variant. Individuals with the Mediterranean variant sometimes have a temporary episode of hemolysis during the newborn period.

The *diagnosis* of G6PD deficiency should be considered in any individual, particularly a black male, who experiences an acute hemolytic episode. The patient should be thoroughly questioned about possible exposure to oxidant agents. A number of screening tests are available to establish the diagnosis. However, since the deficiency occurs primarily in older red blood cells, a false-negative test may be seen during a hemolytic episode when there is a high proportion of young red blood cells. It may be necessary to repeat these diagnostic tests after the patient has recovered. Unusual features in the case should prompt further investigation including a more complete and specific characterization of the enzyme.

TREATMENT   Since hemolysis in patients deficient in A− G6PD is usually self-limited, no specific treatment is necessary. Splenectomy does not appear to be of benefit to Mediterranean patients with chronic hemolysis. Blood transfusions are rarely indicated. If a patient develops a severe hemolytic episode with hemoglobinuria, maintaining adequate urine output is important.

Attention should be directed toward the *prevention* of hemolytic episodes. Infections ought to be treated promptly. Subjects deficient in G6PD should be warned about risks posed by oxidant drugs and fava beans. Any black patient about to be given an oxidant drug should be screened for G6PD deficiency.

OTHER DEFECTS OF THE HEXOSE-MONOPHOSPHATE SHUNT   A few kindreds have been found to have congenital deficiency in red blood cell glutathione due to a defect in either of the two enzymes responsible for the synthesis of this tripeptide. Affected individuals have a hemolytic anemia with Heinz bodies that is aggravated by oxidant drugs. Deficiency of glutathione reductase has been reported, but its relationship to clinically significant hemolysis is not well established. Sometimes the deficiency state can be corrected by the administration of riboflavin (5 mg per day). There are also isolated reports of deficiencies of glutathione peroxidase and 6-phosphogluconate dehydrogenase, but, again, their association with hemolysis is uncertain.

Other enzyme defects   Hemolytic anemia may sometimes be caused by abnormalities in enzymes of nucleotide metabolism. A growing number of individuals with pyrimidine 5′-nucleotidase deficiency have been encountered. Their red cells have marked basophilic stippling. Hemolytic anemia has also been noted in individuals whose red blood cells have supranormal levels of adenosine deaminase and relatively low levels of ATP.

HEMOGLOBINOPATHIES   The sickling disorders constitute an important form of congenital hemolytic anemia. Less commonly, hemolysis may be due to the inheritance of an unstable hemoglobin variant. These disorders of hemoglobin are discussed in Chap. 288.

REFERENCES

ANTMAN KH et al: Microangiopathic hemolytic anemia and cancer: A review. Medicine 58:377, 1979
BEUTLER E: Red cell enzyme defects as nondiseases and as diseases. Blood 54:1, 1979
BUKOWSKI RM et al: Therapy of thrombotic thrombocytopenic purpura: An overview. Semin Throm Hemo 7:1, 1981
COOPER RA: Abnormalities of cell-membrane fluidity in the pathogenesis of disease. N Engl J Med 297:371, 1977
——: Hemolytic syndromes and red cell membrane abnormalities in liver disease. Semin Hematol 17:103, 1980
MIWA S, FUJII H: Molecular aspects of erythroenzymopathies associated with hereditary hemolytic anemias. Am J Hemat 19:293, 1985
PALEK J, LUX SE: Red cell membrane skeletal defects in hereditary and acquired hemolytic anemias. Semin Hematol 20:189, 1983
PANGBURN et al: Paroxysmal nocturnal hemoglobinuria: Deficiency in factor H–like functions of the abnormal erythrocytes. J Exp Med 157:1971, 1983
PETZ LD, GARRATTY G: *Acquired Immune Hemolytic Anemias.* New York, Churchill Livingstone, 1980
PISCIOTTA AV: Thrombotic thrombocytopenic purpura. Ann Intern Med 92:249, 1980
ROSSE WF: Autoimmune hemolytic anemia. Hosp Prac 20:105, 1985
——, PARKER CG: Paroxysmal nocturnal hemoglobinuria. Clin Haematol 14:105, 1985
SCHRIER SL (ed): The red blood cell membrane. Clin Haematol 14:1, 1985
VALENTINE WN et al: Hemolytic anemias and erythrocyte enzymopathies. Ann Intern Med 103:245, 1985

288   DISORDERS OF HEMOGLOBIN

H. FRANKLIN BUNN

In 1910, Herrick described a medical student from Jamaica who had a hemolytic anemia in conjunction with elongated "sickled" red blood cells. Subsequently, it was shown that all the red blood cells of such patients assume a classic holly leaf or sickle shape following deoxygenation of the blood. In 1949, Itano and Pauling discovered the association of sickle cell anemia with an electrophoretically abnormal hemoglobin. Eight years later, Ingram demonstrated that this hemoglobin (designated Hb S) differed from normal Hb A by the substitution of valine for glutamic acid at the sixth position of the β chain. Since then, over 400 structurally different human hemoglobin variants have been discovered in widely scattered parts of the world. Generally, a new hemoglobin is named after the place where it is first encountered. No more than a third of these mutant hemoglobins are associated with significant clinical manifestations. The remainder have been discovered by serendipity or as a result of large population surveys. All told, the hemoglobinopathies have taught us many valuable lessons in such diverse areas as the mechanisms of hemolysis, the pathophysiology of oxygen transport, the stereochemistry of hemoglobin function, and the genetic bases of protein synthesis.

This chapter focuses on the clinically significant variants. In addition, disorders of the biosynthesis of globin (the thalassemias) and methemoglobinemia are discussed.

GENETIC CONSIDERATIONS   The synthesis of each of the subunits of hemoglobin (α, β, γ, δ, ϵ, ζ) is governed by separate genes. The ϵ and ζ subunits are found only in embryonic hemoglobin. Normal individuals inherit two β-chain genes (one from each parent), four α-chain genes, and four γ-chain genes. The ϵ-, γ-, δ-, and β-chain genes occupy adjacent loci on chromosome 11 (see Fig. 288-1). The ζ and α genes are located on chromosome 16. The structure and function of normal hemoglobin ($\alpha_2\beta_2$) are discussed in Chap. 283. The inheritance of abnormal hemoglobins follows classic mendelian genetics. If two parents are heterozygous for a hemoglobin variant such as Hb S, statistically one-quarter of the offspring will be SS homozygotes, another quarter will be normal (AA genotype), and half will have sickle trait (AS). The commonly encountered hemoglobinopathies such as S, C, and E are β-chain variants. Occasionally, an individual inherits two different β-chain variants, one from each parent. Hemoglobin SC disease is an example of such a double heterozygous state. Genes for β thalassemia are located on the β-chain structural gene. Accordingly, an individual can inherit from one parent (and pass on to a child) either β thalassemia or a β-chain variant, but not both. Among the hemoglobinopathies associated with sickling (described below), only the homozygous state (Hb SS) or double heterozygous state (Sβ thalassemia or SC) has important

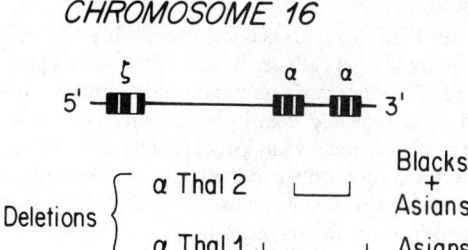

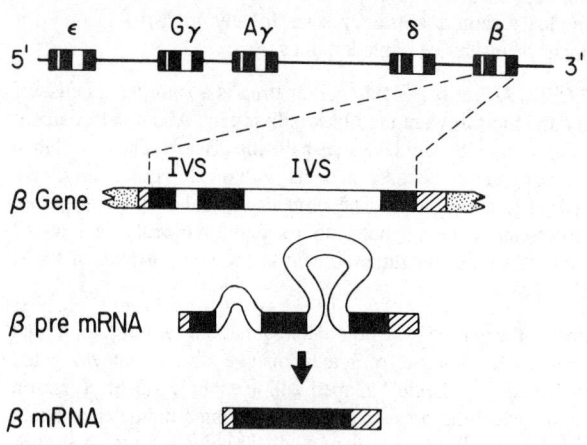

β^+ Thal: Impairment of IVS splicing

β^0 Thal: Nonsense mutation in coding region

FIGURE 288-1 *Diagram of human globin genes. Left: The α-globin gene complex includes the embryonic ζ gene as well as two α genes. In the vast majority of individuals with α thalassemia 2 (α−) one α gene is deleted owing to a nonhomologous crossover between adjacent α genes. In α thalassemia 1 (− −) both α genes are deleted. Right: The β-globin gene complex includes the embryonic ε gene, two fetal genes (ᴳγ and ᴬγ), the δ gene, and the β gene. Below is a diagram of the β gene showing the coding regions (■), the intervening segments (IVS, □) and the flanking regions (▨) that are transcribed into mRNA, shown below. Most cases of β⁺ thalassemia in Mediterranean individuals involve a base substitution causing partial impairment of splicing of an IVS. Most cases of β⁰ thalassemia in Mediterraneans involve a base substitution that creates either a stop codon or a frame shift.*

clinical manifestations. In contrast, the unstable variants and those having abnormal oxygen-binding properties are encountered only in heterozygotes. In many cases, the homozygous state would be incompatible with life.

About 90 percent of these abnormal hemoglobins are single amino acid replacements, due to a single base substitution in the corresponding triplet codon. The structural information accumulated on human mutant hemoglobins has provided ample verification of the fidelity of the genetic code. Other genetic mechanisms must be invoked to explain the structure of a few interesting hemoglobin variants. The Lepore hemoglobins have arisen because of nonhomologous crossover between the adjacent δ- and β-chain genes, giving rise to a fusion subunit in which the *N*-terminal end has the amino acid sequence of the δ chain and the *C*-terminal end has the sequence of the β chain (see Fig. 288-1). Some of the unstable hemoglobins have deletions of one or more residues in sequence within a subunit. Finally there are a few variants which have elongated subunits (e.g., Hb Constant Spring). These have arisen either because of a base substitution in the termination codon or because of a frame shift which puts the termination codon out of phase.

CLINICAL CLASSIFICATION The clinically significant hemoglobin variants are classified in Table 288-1. By far the most important and prevalent type of hemoglobinopathy is due to the presence of sickle hemoglobin, either in the homozygous state or in conjunction with another type of hemoglobin abnormality. The inheritance of an unstable hemoglobin variant may give rise to congenital hemolytic anemia associated with the presence of inclusions of precipitated hemoglobin within the red blood cells (Heinz bodies). Finally, hemoglobin variants may have abnormal functional or spectral properties, resulting in familial erythrocytosis or familial cyanosis.

SICKLE SYNDROMES

SICKLE CELL TRAIT About 8 percent of black Americans are heterozygous for Hb S. The gene frequency is highest in central Africa, particularly in regions where malaria is endemic. In some

parts of Nigeria, over 30 percent of the population has sickle trait. The gene has persisted because heterozygotes gain slight protection against falciparum malaria. This is an example of balanced polymorphism.

The diagnosis of sickle trait or any of the other sickle syndromes depends upon the demonstration of sickling under reduced oxygen tension. In the widely used sickle preparation, sickled cells can be visualized microscopically after the addition of an oxygen-consuming reagent such as metabisulfite. Many clinical laboratories prefer a solubility test which depends on the fact that deoxyhemoglobin S has a low solubility at high ionic strength. These tests are reasonably specific for Hb S although some of the unstable variants may give a false-positive solubility test. Therefore, if one of these screening tests is positive, hemoglobin electrophoresis should be performed. Individuals with sickle trait usually have about 35 to 40 percent Hb S and 55 to 60 percent Hb A.

Hemoglobin S heterozygotes have minimal clinical problems. Their overall life expectancy and frequency of hospitalization are no different from those of a comparable group of individuals with hemoglobin A. AS red blood cells require a much lower oxygen tension for sickling than SS red cells. Accordingly, individuals with sickle trait may develop sickle cell crises only if they become severely hypoxic. They may occasionally sustain a splenic infarct. As discussed below, the renal medulla is particularly susceptible to sickling. Many AS individuals have impaired ability to form concentrated urine, and a few have recurrent episodes of painless hematuria as a result of medullary infarction. Infarction due to sickling has been encountered

TABLE 288-1 Clinically important hemoglobin variants

I Sickle syndromes
  A Sickle cell trait (AS)
  B Sickle cell anemia (SS)
  C Double heterozygous states: Sickle β thalassemia, sickle C disease (SC), sickle D disease (SD)
II Unstable hemoglobin variants: congenital Heinz body hemolytic anemia
III Variants with high oxygen affinity: familial erythrocytosis
IV M hemoglobins: familial cyanosis (see Table 288-3)

in other organs in sickle trait but is extremely rare. For these reasons, AS individuals should not be placed in any high-risk group for employment or insurance considerations.

SICKLE CELL ANEMIA Sickle cell anemia is a significant cause of morbidity and mortality among black individuals. About 0.15 percent of black children in the United States have the disease. The prevalence is lower among adults because patients with sickle cell anemia have a decreased life expectancy. The protean clinical manifestations of this disorder can all be attributed to a specific molecular lesion: the substitution of valine for glutamic acid at the sixth residue of the β chain (Fig. 288-2).

Molecular pathogenesis Upon deoxygenation, a red blood cell containing Hb S changes from a biconcave disk to an elongated crescent-shaped or "sickle"-shaped cell (see Fig. A5-6). Electron micrographs reveal the presence of fibers having a diameter of about 20 nm. Each sickle fiber consists of a helical polymer with 14 strands The polymer is stabilized by hydrophobic bonding between β6 valine and a complementary site on another portion of the β chain on an adjacent strand (Fig. 288-2). In addition, there are many other interactions between neighboring molecules. Sickling, both within the intact red blood cell and in free solution, is greatly affected by the presence of non-S hemoglobin. Hb A participates more readily than Hb F in copolymerization with Hb S.

Cellular pathogenesis As discussed in Chap. 283, the ability of red blood cells to traverse the microcirculation depends in large part on their pliability. As a red blood cell sickles, it becomes rigid, and, as a result, may obstruct capillary blood flow. The deoxygenation of blood from patients with sickle cell disease is associated with a marked increase in viscosity. It is likely that obstruction to flow leads to local tissue hypoxia. As a result, further deoxygenation takes place, leading to further sickling. This vicious cycle may result in the amplification of microscopic obstruction into a larger area of infarction. The oxygen-dependent sickle cycle is ordinarily reversible. However, the membrane of SS red blood cells may become sufficiently damaged so that the cells lose potassium and water, leading to the formation of irreversibly sickled forms. In these cells, the characteristic sickle shape persists even after they are exposed to ambient oxygen tension at room temperature and can readily be seen on examination of Wright-stained blood films (see Fig. A5-6). The proportion of irreversibly sickled cells varies considerably among homozygous sicklers and is not correlated with clinical severity. Hemoglobin F is distributed unevenly among red blood cells of SS patients, and composes between 2 and 20 percent of the total hemoglobin (the remainder is almost entirely Hb S). Since Hb F inhibits the polymerization of Hb S, those cells that are relatively rich in Hb F are protected from sickling, whereas those cells that have relatively small

amounts of Hb F are likely to become irreversibly sickled. It is not surprising that these rigid cells are readily culled from the circulation and destroyed. The continuous formation and destruction of irreversibly sickled cells probably contributes significantly to the severe hemolytic anemia shared by all patients with sickle cell anemia. Furthermore, these rigid cells may initiate small-vessel occlusions.

Factors such as acidosis or increased erythrocyte 2,3-diphosphoglycerate, which lower the oxygen affinity of red blood cells, will enhance the formation of deoxyhemoglobin and, therefore, promote intracellular polymerization and eventual sickling. In addition, sickling is highly dependent on hemoglobin concentration. Any pathophysiologic process which tends to pull water out of sickle red blood cells will greatly increase their tendency to sickle. Thus, the hypertonic environment of the renal medulla can cause local sickling and the formation of papillary infarcts, even in individuals with sickle trait.

Clinical manifestations Patients with homozygous sickle cell anemia have a variety of clinical problems broadly outlined in Table 288-2. Signs and symptoms usually do not appear until after the sixth month of life, at which time most of the Hb F has been replaced by Hb S. Among the *constitutional* manifestations of sickle cell anemia are delay of growth and development and a general failure to thrive. In addition, these patients have an increased tendency to develop serious infections, particularly due to pneumococcus. SS patients have marked impairment of splenic function, preventing effective clearance of circulating bacteria. With the passage of time, the organ sustains recurrent infarcts and eventually becomes a nubbin of fibrous tissue.

ANEMIA SS homozygotes have a severe hemolytic anemia with hematocrit values between 18 and 30 percent. The destruction of red blood cells is independent of cell age. The mean red blood cell survival is about 10 to 15 days. Those cells having relatively low levels of Hb F have a shorter life span, in part due to a greater chance of becoming irreversibly sickled. As a result of accelerated red blood cell breakdown, patients with sickle cell disease have characteristic clinical and laboratory findings discussed in Chap. 283. Even though hemolysis is primarily extravascular, plasma haptoglobin is generally low or absent, and plasma hemoglobin levels are moderately elevated.

The anemia becomes increasingly severe if erythropoiesis is suppressed. There are two main causes of "aplastic crises"—infection and folic acid deficiency. As discussed in Chap. 286, infection brings about a transient reduction in red blood cell production. In particular, parvovirus causes an abrupt suppression of erythropoiesis. In SS patients with severe ongoing hemolysis, this usually results in a rapid drop in hematocrit (Table 288-2).

VASOOCCLUSIVE PHENOMENA The morbidity and mortality of sickle cell disease are due primarily to recurrent vasoocclusive phenomena.

FIGURE 288-2 *Polymerization of sickle hemoglobin. When the red cell (A) is deoxygenated, deoxyhemoglobin S aggregates to form domains of elongated rodlike polymers (B). In most cells these fibers align and distort the cell into the classic sickle shape (C). The individual Hb S molecules form a closely* *packed polymer consisting of 14 strands having a helical configuration (D). A close-up of the contacts between a pair of aligned strands (E) shows the abnormal β6 valine forming a hydrophobic contact with an acceptor site on the β chain of a molecule on the adjacent strand.*

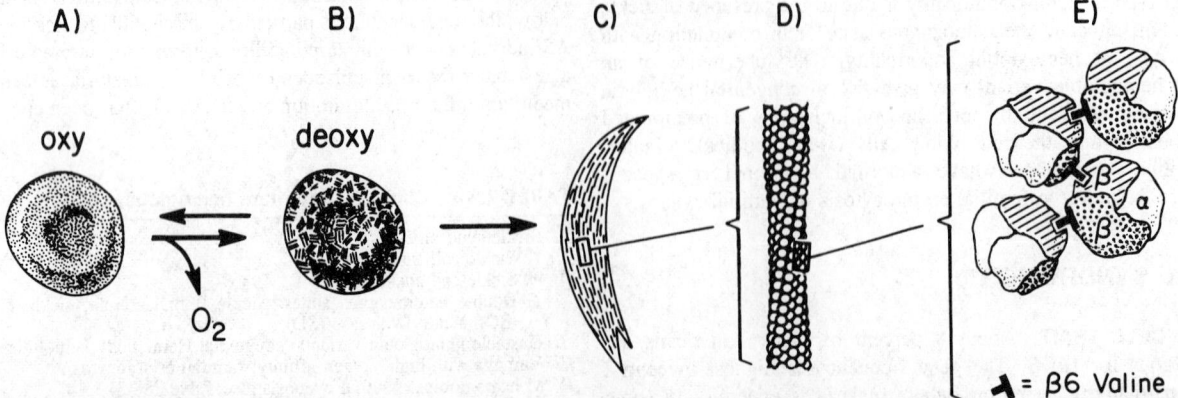

A)   B)   C)   D)   E)

oxy   deoxy

O₂

= β6 Valine

As shown in Table 288-2, these can be divided into two groups. Throughout their lives, SS patients are plagued by recurrent *painful crises.* These episodes may appear with explosive suddenness and attack various parts of the body, particularly the abdomen, chest, and joints. About a third of painful crises are preceded by a viral or bacterial infection (Table 288-2). The frequency of painful crises is highly variable. A given patient may have months or even years without a crisis and then have a cluster of frequent severe attacks. In some individuals, crises occur more frequently in cold weather, perhaps precipitated by reflex vasospasm. In others, crises come more often in warm weather, during times when patients are likely to become dehydrated. It is often difficult to distinguish between painful sickle crisis and some other type of acute process such as biliary colic, appendicitis, or a perforated viscus. Many patients have undergone exploration because they were considered to have an acute surgical problem. Patients having abdominal sickle crises usually have normal bowel sounds and no rebound tenderness. If the abdominal pain is due to sickling, the surgeon usually finds no gross evidence of infarction or ischemia.

SS homozygotes frequently develop attacks of acute pleuritic chest pain with fever. Although the initial chest x-ray is often unremarkable, an infiltrate may evolve. The important differential is between pneumonitis and pulmonary infarction. Culture and Gram's stain of the sputum will be helpful in establishing the presence of pneumonia. In these patients, pulmonary infarctions are much more likely due to thrombosis in situ than to emboli. Occasionally, pulmonary infarcts become secondarily infected.

When a sickle crisis is localized in the extremities, it may mimic osteomyelitis or an acute arthritis such as gout or rheumatoid arthritis. Patients commonly develop acute synovitis with joint effusion. Examination of the joint fluid is helpful in this differential diagnosis. If the effusion is due to sickling, the fluid will be clear and yellow, with a low white blood cell count (100 to 1000 mononuclear cells per cubic millimeter) and an absence of crystals or bacteria. Synovial biopsy may show sickled red blood cells in the lumen of small vessels.

Sickle crises may occasionally involve the central nervous system. Patients can present with a seizure, stroke, or coma. Although such crises are frequently reversible, they may be fatal.

CHRONIC ORGAN DAMAGE By the time that patients reach adulthood, there is often objective evidence of anatomic or functional damage to various tissues, due to the cumulative effect of recurrent vasoocclusive episodes. Almost any organ may be involved, but most commonly the lungs, kidneys, liver, skeleton, and skin.

Cardiopulmonary. Impairment of pulmonary function is a common complication of sickle cell disease. Resting arterial P_{O_2} is usually reduced in part because of intrapulmonary arterial-venous shunting. Since SS red blood cells have decreased oxygen affinity, arterial blood will be significantly undersaturated, leading to an increased tendency for red cells to sickle when they reach the peripheral circulation. SS homozygotes frequently develop congestive heart failure. The chronic severe anemia and hypoxemia impose a sustained burden on the heart. Most patients have a systolic ejection murmur as a result of their hyperdynamic circulation. Even though more oxygen is extracted by the myocardium than any other tissue, SS patients rarely develop myocardial infarction.

Hepatobiliary. Like other patients with congenital hemolytic anemia, those with sickle cell anemia have icterus and an increased tendency to form gallstones. It is often difficult to distinguish between the abdominal pain of acute cholecystitis and that due to a sickle crisis. Jaundice deepens markedly if a patient develops choledocholithiasis, and bilirubin levels as high as 50 mg/dL have been reported. As a rule, cholecystectomy is not recommended unless gallstones cause symptoms. In addition, patients with sickle cell anemia may develop hepatic infarcts which occasionally become infected, resulting in abscess formation. If a significant portion of hepatic parenchyma becomes infarcted, fibrosis and deterioration of liver function may result, with deepening of jaundice.

Genitourinary (see also Chaps. 224 and 227). The hypertonic and acidic environment of the renal medulla promotes sickling, resulting in microinfarcts. Virtually all patients have isosthenuria. The inability to form concentrated urine increases the risk of significant dehydration. In addition, like those with sickle trait or SC disease, SS homozygotes may develop significant and prolonged painless hematuria as a result of papillary infarcts. Hematuria may be so extensive that iron deficiency develops. ε-Aminocaproic acid has proved to be effective in severe cases but must be used with caution since it may prevent the lysis of clots in the renal pelvis.

A small number of patients develop frank renal failure, sometimes following the nephrotic syndrome. The pathogenesis of the glomerular lesions is not well understood. Mild nitrogen retention is commonly encountered, accompanied by moderate hyperuricemia. However, patients rarely have uric acid nephropathy or gout. Male patients with sickle cell anemia occasionally develop priapism (spontaneous and painful engorgement of the penis). This distressing complication occurs with about equal frequency in prepubertal and postpubertal patients, although the latter are more difficult to treat and may develop impotence following the acute episode. Patients should be treated conservatively with sedation, analgesia, and intravenous fluids. The administration of packed red blood cells may also be effective. Surgical intervention is rarely indicated.

Skeletal. Like other patients with congenital hemolytic anemia, patients with sickle cell anemia demonstrate radiologic abnormalities due to the expansion of red marrow. However, the development of bony infarcts results in more characteristic x-ray abnormalities. The biconcave or "fishmouth" vertebrae are pathognomonic of sickle cell disease. Skeletal infarction generally leads to increased bony trabeculation and sclerosis. Aseptic necrosis of the head of the femur is particularly common in patients with sickle cell disease and can lead to considerable disability. Like infarcts in other organs, bony infarctions are more likely to become infected. In patients who develop osteomyelitis, salmonella is a frequent pathogen.

Ocular. A variety of ocular abnormalities are encountered in patients with SS and SC disease. These include retinal infarcts, peripheral vessel disease, arteriovenous anomalies, vitreous hemorrhage, retinitis proliferans, and retinal detachment. In addition, when viewed with a strong magnifying lens, angulated and "corkscrew" vessels can be seen in the bulbar conjunctiva. The major ocular complications are more commonly encountered in SC and Sβ thalassemia patients than in SS patients. The early diagnosis of retinal lesions in sickle disease is important since retinal detachment may be prevented by appropriate therapy.

Skin. Chronic skin ulcers often occur in the distal lower extremities. The lesions appear to be commoner in patients with more severe anemia. Ankle ulcers have also been encountered in rare patients with other types of congenital hemolytic anemia. This complication is more commonly seen in tropical areas. Ankle ulcers generally respond to conservative management, such as elevation of the leg, maintenance of strict cleanliness, and application of a mild chemical debriding agent such as Dakin's solution. The weekly application of Unna boots has been effective. In patients with refractory ulcers, a hypertransfusion regimen is probably indicated. Skin grafting should be undertaken only after all other measures have failed.

Neurologic. A variety of central nervous system manifestations

TABLE 288-2 Clinical manifestations of sickle cell anemia

I Constitutional
   A Impaired growth and development
   B Increased susceptibility to infection

II Vasoocclusive
   A Microinfarcts → Painful crises
   B Macroinfarcts

              → Organ damage

III Anemia
   A Severe hemolysis
   B Aplastic crises

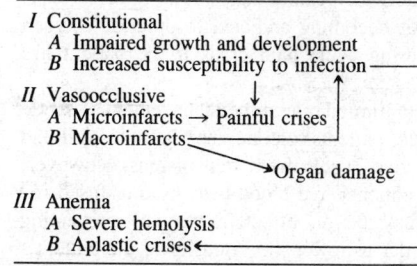

may be encountered in sickle cell anemia. Although cerebral thrombosis is the principal neurologic complication, SS patients also have an increased incidence of subarachnoid hemorrhage. A patient has about a 25 percent chance of developing some type of neurologic complication during a lifetime. Hemiplegia is encountered more frequently than coma, convulsions, or visual disturbances. Patients generally make a full recovery, particularly from their first cerebral vascular accident. Preliminary studies in children indicate that a hypertransfusion program is beneficial to those who have sustained a major neurologic complication.

Diagnosis The diagnosis of sickle cell anemia should be considered in any black patient with a hemolytic anemia. The history of painful crises, arthropathy, ankle ulcers, etc., can be very helpful. If a patient has a relatively mild form of the disease, the diagnosis may not have been made during childhood. A number of laboratory tests are useful in distinguishing sickle cell anemia from other hemoglobinopathies. Examination of the peripheral blood smear reveals normochromic normocytic red blood cells, many of which appear as targets. The presence of irreversibly sickled forms is very helpful (see Fig. A5-6). In addition, the presence of Howell-Jolly bodies, siderocytes, and occasional normoblasts suggests the absence of effective splenic function. A positive test for sickling, such as the metabisulfite preparation or the solubility test, indicates the presence of Hb S but does not distinguish between SS, AS, and double heterozygotes (SThal, SC). Hemoglobin electrophoresis is necessary to establish the diagnosis. Patients with homozygous sickle cell anemia have about 2 to 20 percent Hb F and 2 to 4 percent Hb A_2. The remainder is Hb S. No Hb A is detected unless the patient has been transfused within the past 4 months. Patients with sickle β thalassemia will have hypochromic microcytic red blood cells, fewer irreversibly sickled forms, and a variable proportion of Hb A (0 to 30 percent). SC diseases can be readily diagnosed by hemoglobin electrophoresis. In hemoglobin SD disease, the two hemoglobin variants comigrate during conventional electrophoresis at pH 8.6 but can be separated by agar gel electrophoresis at pH 6.0.

Treatment Understanding the molecular pathogenesis of sickling has not yet led to an effective form of therapy. A large array of antisickling regimens has been proposed, but thus far none has stood the test of time. Recent investigation has focused on drugs that alter cell division and thereby increase the proportion of F cells. Currently accepted management of sickle cell anemia is primarily supportive and conservative. Since patients with sickle cell anemia are at increased risk of developing infections, many of which trigger painful and aplastic crises, it is very important to detect infection early and give appropriate antibiotics promptly. Malaria prophylaxis should be administered in endemic areas. The development of pneumococcal sepsis in children may be prevented by the administration of the polyvalent vaccine.

The anemia of sickle cell disease increases markedly if the patient becomes deficient in folic acid. Since these patients have a continuous increased requirement for folic acid, it is reasonable to maintain them on a daily oral supplement. Testosterone increases the red blood cell mass in patients with sickle cell anemia. However, the potential risk of hepatotoxicity, and of priapism in males, limits its utility.

Painful crises should be treated promptly with adequate analgesia and hydration. Some patients feel that their crises can be aborted if treated early. Therefore, it is expedient to give patients a supply of an analgesic such as codeine which can be taken at home. However, these patients are at risk of becoming addicted to opiates. Oxygen should be administered during acute pain crisis if the patient has arterial hypoxemia.

Blood transfusions play a limited role in the management of sickle cell anemia. Between crises, patients tolerate anemia quite well and do not derive much subjective benefit from transfusions. However, partial replacement of the patients' red blood cells by transfused red cells (hypertransfusion) may be an effective way of preventing vasoocclusive crises. In order to lower the viscosity of the patient's blood significantly, it is necessary that over 50 percent of the patient's red blood cells be of donor origin. Hypertransfusion is a reasonable approach to getting a patient through a limited period of risk such as surgery. However, the problems of isoimmunization, iron overload, and hepatitis dictate against its widespread use.

Prevention Genetic counseling can play an important role in the prevention of sickle cell anemia. Parents who are both AS heterozygotes should be informed that there is a 25 percent chance that their offspring will be homozygous. The antenatal diagnosis of sickle cell anemia can be made in the second trimester of pregnancy by obtaining fetal cells from the amniotic fluid and analyzing the DNA following digestion with a restriction endonuclease that recognizes the β6 valine mutation. If it is established that the fetus is an SS homozygote, the parents may decide to interrupt the pregnancy.

Prognosis The clinical course of patients with sickle cell anemia is highly variable. Many assessments of prognosis that have appeared in the literature have been unduly pessimistic. During the past 30 years there has been considerable improvement in the care of patients with sickle cell anemia. An increasing number of patients are surviving into adulthood and even bearing offspring. There has also been a decline in the mortality of SS mothers during pregnancy and childbirth. However, in underdeveloped nations, the mortality in sickle cell anemia remains very high.

No single clinical or laboratory finding is a consistent predictor of prognosis in sickle cell disease. Although those patients who have relatively high amounts of Hb F tend to have milder clinical manifestations, this relationship is of no prognostic value in any given patient. Considerable variation in the severity of sickle cell disease has been reported among different ethnic and geographical groups. A group of Shi Arabs from Saudi Arabia has been found to have a benign form of sickle cell anemia with very high levels of Hb F (15 to 30 percent). A mild type of sickle cell anemia has also been seen among the Veddoids of India. SS patients with coexisting α thalassemia have less severe hemolysis but do not appear to have a significant reduction in vasoocclusive phenomena.

SICKLE β THALASSEMIA This disease is highly variable in its clinical severity and complications. It is commonly encountered in people from the Mediterranean countries as well as those from central Africa. Sickle β thalassemia tends to be milder in blacks, just as homozygous β thalassemia is much less severe in blacks than in the Mediterranean populations. Patients have a congenital hemolytic anemia of variable severity, accompanied by splenomegaly in about 70 percent of cases. They may have all the various types of vasoocclusive phenomena described above for homozygous sickle cell anemia. However, painful crises are generally less frequent and less severe.

Examination of the blood film reveals hypochromic microcytic red blood cells, with polychromatophilia, target cells, stippling, and rare fixed sickle forms. The electrophoretic pattern shows from 60 to 90 percent Hb S and 10 to 30 percent Hb F. Hemoglobin A will be about 10 to 30 percent if the β-thalassemia gene is capable of producing some β^A chains (β$^+$ thalassemia, see below). In patients who have sickle β^0 thalassemia, no Hb A will be present, and therefore the disorder may be difficult to distinguish from homozygous sickle cell anemia. Hemoglobin A_2 is moderately elevated in sickle β thalassemia, but it is difficult to measure this minor component accurately in the presence of Hb S. Sickle β^0 thalassemia is significantly more severe than sickle β$^+$ thalassemia. Occasional patients may derive benefit from splenectomy if the spleen is sequestering a significant amount of red blood cells.

SICKLE C DISEASE Although the gene frequency for Hb C (β6 Glu→Lys) is only one-fourth that for Hb S, the prevalence of SC disease among adults is almost as high as SS disease since the former group of patients has a nearly normal life expectancy. These individuals have a mild to moderate hemolytic anemia, usually accompanied by splenomegaly. On peripheral blood smears, target cells and occasional plump sickled forms are seen. Hemoglobin electrophoresis reveals 50 percent Hb S, 50 percent Hb C. Hemoglobin S copolymerizes with Hb C to the same extent as with Hb A. The increased tendency of SC red cells to sickle, compared with sickle trait cells, can be explained by two phenomena: increased intracellular hemoglobin concentration and significantly higher percent Hb S. Patients with SC disease may occasionally have painful crises or organ infarcts. They are at particular risk of developing ocular complications described above, including proliferative retinopathy and retinal detachment. In addition, patients with SC disease are at relatively high risk of developing hematuria from renal medullary infarcts and avascular necrosis of the femoral head. Pregnant women with SC disease have a high rate of complications during pregnancy. Individuals with an electrophoretic pattern suggestive of Hb SC disease but with more severe clinical manifestations are likely to be double heterozygotes for Hb S and Hb O Arab (β121 Glu$\rightarrow$Lys).

SICKLE D DISEASE   A number of hemoglobins comigrate with Hb S on routine electrophoresis. The most commonly encountered variant is Hb D Los Angeles (β121 Glu$\rightarrow$Gln). Hemoglobins S and D can be separated by special electrophoretic methods. The diagnosis of Hb SD disease is suggested by the demonstration of a positive sickle cell preparation in only one of the patient's two parents. SD double heterozygotes have moderately severe anemia.

HOMOZYGOUS Hb C DISEASE   Patients have a mild congenital hemolytic anemia accompanied by splenomegaly. Hemoglobin C has a tendency to form intracellular crystals, particularly if red blood cells are suspended in a hypertonic medium. The intracellular hemoglobin concentration is markedly increased owing to loss of potassium and water from the cytoplasm. As a result, the blood film reveals striking target cells. Red blood cell osmotic fragility is decreased. Patients rarely develop significant complications. No specific therapy is indicated.

UNSTABLE HEMOGLOBIN VARIANTS

In the early 1950s several patients in England were found to have congenital nonspherocytic hemolytic anemia associated with inclusions of precipitated hemoglobin (Heinz bodies) within red blood cells. The presence of an abnormal hemoglobin was suspected by the fact that a precipitate was formed when the patients' hemolysates were gently heated. Currently, over 90 different unstable hemoglobin variants have been identified. The great majority are single amino acid substitutions in the β chain. A few are due to deletion of one or more amino acids within the β chain. Patients present with a hemolytic anemia of variable degree. Severe cases are usually detected in late infancy or early childhood and have jaundice, splenomegaly, and dark-colored urine. An autosomal dominant mode of inheritance can usually be established, although about a fifth of the cases appear to be spontaneous mutants.

Pathogenesis   These hemoglobin variants have structural alterations at sites in the molecule that drastically affect its stability and solubility. Many involve an amino acid substitution in the portion of the subunit where heme is inserted. In such instances, the heme may be displaced from the heme pocket. As a result, the abnormal hemoglobin has decreased solubility and forms an intracellular precipitate (Heinz body). Red blood cells which contain this type of inclusion are recognized by the mononuclear phagocyte system and are either cleansed of their intracellular debris (pitting) or destroyed. The displaced heme moiety is aberrantly catabolized, forming dipyrroles, such as mesobilifuscin, instead of bilirubin. Pigmenturia is probably due to the excretion of these dipyrroles. The degree of instability of these hemoglobin variants and, therefore, the extent of hemolysis vary considerably. In some, such as Hb Zürich, an additional oxidant stress, such as the ingestion of certain drugs, is required for significant

hemolysis. In contrast, patients with Hb Hammersmith have continuous and marked red blood cell breakdown. The degree of anemia is influenced not only by the severity of the hemolysis but also by the ability of the blood to unload oxygen. Thus, patients having unstable variants with increased oxygen affinity, such as Hb Köln, may have a near-normal hemoglobin level, i.e., compensated hemolysis.

Diagnosis   The red blood cell morphology is somewhat variable. Often, patients with a functioning spleen have normal-appearing red blood cells. Slight hypochromia and basophilic stippling are not uncommon. The blood may have to be incubated in order to bring out Heinz bodies. In some cases, red blood cells appear as if a bite had been taken from a margin. It is tempting to speculate that at this site a Heinz body had been pitted. Following splenectomy, red blood cells appear much more abnormal, and Heinz bodies are larger and more numerous.

The diagnosis of a congenital Heinz body hemolytic anemia is established by the following laboratory tests and results:

1 *Hemoglobin electrophoresis* will often reveal an abnormal component, usually composing less than 30 percent of the total.
2 *Heinz bodies* can be demonstrated by incubating a freshly drawn sample of blood with a supravital stain.
3 A significant *precipitate* is formed when the hemolysate is incubated at 50°C, or in the presence of 17% isopropanol.
4 The unstable hemoglobins often have an abnormal *oxygen dissociation curve*.

If these tests are negative in a patient with congenital nonspherocytic hemolytic anemia, a defect of the membrane or one of the red blood cell enzymes is likely.

Treatment   The treatment of congenital Heinz body hemolytic anemia is primarily supportive. Anemia is rarely severe enough to warrant blood transfusion. Oxidant drugs should be avoided. Like others with chronic hemolysis, these patients have an increased requirement for folic acid. Those with severe hemolysis often benefit from prophylactic folate therapy. The red blood cell mass may fall during a period of bone marrow suppression, such as that resulting from folate deficiency or acute infection. Although patients with severe hemolysis may benefit from splenectomy, this operation is not curative. Because of the risk of bacterial sepsis in infants and young children who have been splenectomized, this treatment should be postponed until the child is over 4 years old. The diagnostic tests cited above become more abnormal following splenectomy. For this reason, in some cases the diagnosis may not be definitely established until after the operation.

STABLE VARIANTS HAVING ABNORMAL OXYGEN AFFINITY

In 1966 certain members of a large family were discovered to have erythrocytosis in association with an electrophoretically abnormal hemoglobin, Hb Chesapeake, which had a very high affinity for oxygen. Since then, more than 40 other stable high-affinity hemoglobin variants have been encountered in families with erythrocytosis. Their structural alterations tend to be at sites which influence hemoglobin's functional behavior. As a result of the hemoglobin's increased oxygen affinity, oxygen unloading to tissues is decreased, and there is an erythropoietin-mediated stimulus to erythropoiesis. This disorder is manifested in the heterozygous state and follows an autosomal codominant pattern of inheritance. Hematocrit levels are rarely high enough to cause a significant increase in blood viscosity. Thus, affected individuals are generally asymptomatic and lack any pertinent physical findings other than a ruddy complexion. The diagnosis should be suspected in all patients with unexplained erythrocytosis, particularly when other family members are similarly affected, and can be established by the demonstration of increased oxygen affinity of the whole blood. About two-thirds of the high-affinity variants can be readily separated from Hb A by electrophoresis. No treatment is indicated. The patient should be reassured that the disorder is benign.

Hemoglobin variants having a marked decrease in oxygen affinity cause one form of familial cyanosis (Table 288-3). Because of the abnormality of hemoglobin function, arterial blood is partially unsaturated despite normal oxygen tension. Thus, the cyanosis is due to increased levels of deoxyhemoglobin in the blood. Except for this cosmetic problem, affected individuals have no other clinical manifestations. Blood values are otherwise normal.

METHEMOGLOBINEMIA

Oxygen transport depends on the maintenance of intracellular hemoglobin in the reduced (Fe^{2+}) state. When hemoglobin is oxidized to methemoglobin, the heme iron becomes Fe^{3+} and is incapable of binding oxygen. Normal red cells contain less than 1 percent methemoglobin. A small amount of hemoglobin autooxidizes as red cells circulate. This process probably occurs by the dissociation of the superoxide anion from oxyhemoglobin:

$$Hb^{2+}O_2 \rightarrow Hb^{3+} + O_2^-$$

Normally, the methemoglobin that is formed is reduced by the following reaction:

$$Hb^{3+} + RedCyt\ b_5 \rightarrow Hb^{2+} + OxCyt\ b_5$$

Reduced cytochrome b_5 (RedCyt b_5) is regenerated by the enzyme cytochrome b_5 reductase (methemoglobin reductase):

$$OxCyt\ b_5 + NADH \xrightarrow[\text{reductase}]{\text{Cytochrome } b_5} RedCyt\ b_5 + NAD$$

Hereditary methemoglobinemia is due either to the presence of one of the M hemoglobins or to the deficiency of the enzyme cytochrome b_5 reductase (Table 288-3). These inherited disorders are clinically mild, while the induction of methemoglobinemia by drugs or toxins can be life-threatening.

If methemoglobin exceeds 1.5 g/dL (10 percent of the total hemoglobin), affected individuals will have clinically obvious cyanosis. The color of the skin is indistinguishable from the much commoner cyanosis due to impairment of oxygen saturation that may occur in pulmonary and cardiac disorders (Table 288-3). With higher amounts of methemoglobin, patients become symptomatic. At a methemoglobin level of about 35 percent, the affected individual experiences headache, weakness, and breathlessness. Levels in excess of 80 percent are usually incompatible with life.

The toxicity of methemoglobinemia can be readily explained in terms of hemoglobin function. The fact that a certain proportion of the heme moieties is no longer able to bind oxygen is not a serious physiologic handicap per se. A proportion of 30 percent methemoglobin is much more deleterious than a 30 percent decrement in red cell mass, because the oxidized hemes have a profound effect on the remaining functional hemes in the hemoglobin tetramer. The confor-

mation of methemoglobin (like that of carboxyhemoglobin) is very similar to that of oxyhemoglobin. Thus, a partially oxidized hemoglobin tetramer has the same tertiary and quaternary structure as a molecule which is comparably oxygenated. In each case, the affinity of the remaining hemes for oxygen is increased. For this reason, methemoglobinemia (as well as carbon monoxide) causes a "shift to the left" of the oxyhemoglobin dissociation curve and, consequently, impaired unloading of oxygen to tissues.

M Hemoglobins Five hemoglobin variants have abnormal absorbance spectra, owing to the oxidation of the heme iron in the affected subunit. They involve amino acid substitutions of residues responsible for the binding of the heme iron to the globin. These so-called M hemoglobins (Table 288-3) result in a rare form of congenital and familial cyanosis. Individuals with the α-chain variants Hb M Boston and Hb M Iwate are cyanotic at birth, while cyanosis does not appear in those with the β-chain variants (Hb M Saskatoon, Hb M Hyde Park, and Hb M Milwaukee) until about 4 to 6 months of age, when fetal hemoglobin has been replaced by adult hemoglobin. As with the unstable and high-affinity variants, an autosomal codominant inheritance pattern is found. Except for cyanosis, patients are asymptomatic.

CYTOCHROME b_5 REDUCTASE (METHEMOGLOBIN REDUCTASE) DEFICIENCY This condition is inherited in an autosomal recessive pattern. The enzyme is a flavoprotein having properties similar to those of liver microsomal cytochrome b_5 reductase. The soluble erythrocyte enzyme is formed by cleavage of a hydrophobic tail from the microsomal enzyme.

Individuals with cytochrome b_5 reductase deficiency have lifelong cyanosis of variable degree, depending on the level of methemoglobin, but usually have no associated symptoms or other physical findings. Some may have mild polycythemia owing to increased oxygen affinity. Others have been noted to be mentally retarded. Untreated individuals usually have 15 to 30 percent methemoglobin. Methemoglobin levels are higher in the older population of red cells because the activity of the abnormal enzyme declines markedly with red cell age. There appears to be considerable heterogeneity in the variant enzymes from different families, as shown by differences in their electrophoretic mobility and kinetic parameters. In these ways, cytochrome b_5 reductase deficiency resembles glucose 6-phosphate dehydrogenase deficiency (Chap. 287).

ACQUIRED METHEMOGLOBINEMIA This disorder is generally due to exposure to certain drugs or toxins. Compounds which can cause clinically significant methemoglobinemia are listed in Table 288-3. Some agents such as nitrite and chlorate oxidize the heme iron directly. Others such as sulfa drugs and aniline must undergo biochemical transformation before they cause methemoglobinemia. Few drugs currently in use cause significant methemoglobinemia, unless the individual is unusually susceptible. Exposure to local anesthetics such as procaine and to nitroprusside occasionally causes severe methemoglobinemia. As might be expected, individuals heterozygous for methemoglobin reductase deficiency are much more likely than normal individuals to develop clinically apparent methemoglobinemia after exposure to an oxidant stress. Thus, the extent of methemoglobinemia depends not only on the dose of the toxic agent but also on the susceptibility of the exposed individual.

DIAGNOSIS Methemoglobinemia should be considered in any cyanotic patient with no evidence of heart or lung disease. If the cyanosis is due to decreased oxygen saturation, a blood specimen will change from a purple to a red color upon mixing with air. In contrast, a blood specimen from a methemoglobinemic individual remains a chocolate brown color irrespective of exposure to air. Methemoglobinemia can be documented by spectroscopic examination of the hemolysate. Individuals with hereditary methemoglobinemia will have lower levels than patients symptomatic from acquired methemoglobinemia. Patients who have ingested an oxidant drug may have an additional hemoglobin derivative called sulfhemoglobin

---

TABLE 288-3 Differential diagnosis of cyanosis

I Decreased oxygenation of hemoglobin (↑ deoxyhemoglobin)
  A Reduced arterial oxygen tension (common)
    1 Pulmonary disease
    2 Cardiac right-to-left shunt
  B Hemoglobin variant having decreased oxygen affinity (rare)
II Methemoglobinemia (rare)
  A Hereditary
    1 M hemoglobins
    2 Cytochrome b_5 reductase deficiency
  B Acquired
    1 Nitrites and nitrates: sodium nitrite, amyl nitrite, nitroglycerin, nitroprusside, silver nitrate
    2 Aniline dyes
    3 Acetanilid and phenacetin
    4 Sulfonamides
    5 Other: lidocaine, chlorate, phenazopyridine

in which the protoporphyrin has been chemically modified. Sulfhemoglobinemia tends to cause cyanosis even more readily than methemoglobinemia. Unlike methemoglobin, the absorbance of sulfhemoglobin at 620 to 630 nm is not decreased by the addition of cyanide. The M hemoglobins have characteristic spectral abnormalities which differ from those obtained when normal Hb A is partially oxidized. Furthermore, these hemoglobin variants can be detected by hemoglobin electrophoresis.

Treatment In individuals with methemoglobin reductase deficiency, the oral administration of methylene blue (100 to 300 mg per day) or ascorbic acid (300 to 500 mg per day) will result in a marked reduction in the level of methemoglobin. The purpose of treatment is primarily cosmetic. Severe toxic methemoglobinemia is treated by the intravenous administration of methylene blue (2 mg/kg, repeat if needed). Within an hour, the methemoglobin level is usually reduced by at least 50 percent. Treatment is neither necessary nor possible in individuals having Hb M.

THALASSEMIAS

The thalassemias are a diverse group of congenital disorders in which there is a defect in the synthesis of one (or more) of the subunits of hemoglobin. As a result of decreased production of hemoglobin, the red blood cells are microcytic and hypochromic (Table 53-2). The thalassemias involve a spectrum ranging from subtle morphologic abnormalities to life-threatening disease. In contrast to the qualitative hemoglobin abnormalities listed in Table 288-1, the thalassemias are quantitative abnormalities of subunit synthesis. Thus, the β chains of patients with β thalassemia have normal structure but are produced in reduced and sometimes undetectable amounts. Conversely, patients with α thalassemia have impaired production of α chains. The reduction in globin chain synthesis can be demonstrated in vitro by incubating reticulocytes with labeled amino acids and determining the incorporation of radioactivity into globin subunits (Table 288-4). Most forms of thalassemia can be identified from the information summarized in Table 288-4. Occasionally, establishing a definitive diagnosis requires measurement of globin chain synthesis or analysis of globin gene structure.

α THALASSEMIA As mentioned at the beginning of this chapter, normal individuals inherit two α-chain genes from each parent. The great majority of cases of α thalassemia can be explained by deletions of α-chain genes, owing to nonhomologous crossover (Fig. 288-1). Specific gene deletions can be identified by analysis of patients' DNA following digestion by restriction endonucleases. The clinical manifestations of α thalassemia depend upon the number of genes deleted (Table 288-4). In the silent carrier state, heterozygous α thalassemia 2 (α−/αα), one of the four genes is deleted. Affected individuals have no hematologic abnormalities. Individuals with deletion of two of the four α-chain genes (α-thalassemia trait) have either homozygous

α thalassemia 2 (α−/α−) or heterozygous α thalassemia 1 (−−/αα). They have microcytic and slightly hypochromic red blood cells but no significant hemolysis or anemia. Hemoglobin electrophoresis is normal except for a decreased amount of Hb A₂. Deletion of three α-chain genes (−−/α−) produces a well-compensated hemolytic state with microcytic hypochromic red blood cells including many target cells. Intracellular inclusions or Heinz bodies are formed by the precipitation of Hb H, a tetramer composed of β chains which accumulates because of the marked impairment of α-chain synthesis. The most severe form of α thalassemia, hydrops fetalis, is usually due to deletion of all four α-chain genes. The affected fetus has red blood cells containing only Hb Barts, a tetramer composed of γ chains. This condition is incompatible with life, since oxygen transport depends upon the presence of heterotetramers such as $\alpha_2\beta_2$ and $\alpha_2\gamma_2$. In orientals both the α− and the −− haplotypes are relatively common; thus both Hb H disease and hydrops fetalis are frequently encountered. In contrast, blacks commonly have the α− haplotype (gene frequency ≅ 0.15) but rarely have the −− haplotype. Therefore Hb H disease is very rare in blacks and hydrops fetalis has not been reported. Homozygous α thalassemia 2 is encountered in about 2 percent of blacks and is therefore a relatively common cause of microcytosis in an individual who is otherwise healthy and not iron-deficient.

The elongated α-chain variant Hb Constant Spring, commonly encountered among southeast Asians, also has an α-thalassemia phenotype, and when inherited with the −− haplotype can cause Hb H disease.

β THALASSEMIA Since individuals inherit only one β-chain gene from each parent, affected individuals are either heterozygotes, homozygotes, or double heterozygotes. The gene frequency for β thalassemia approaches 0.1 in southern Italy and certain Mediterranean islands. β Thalassemia is also encountered quite commonly in central Africa, Asia, the south Pacific, and certain parts of India. Statistically, one-quarter of the offspring of two heterozygotes (β-thalassemia trait) will have the homozygous state: β thalassemia major or Cooley's anemia. An individual may inherit a β-thalassemia gene from one parent and a β-chain structural variant from the other (Fig. 288-1). Sickle β thalassemia (discussed above) is a commonly encountered example of such a double heterozygous state.

The molecular pathogenesis of the β thalassemias is more complex and heterogeneous than that of α thalassemia. In contrast to α thalassemia, gene deletion is an uncommon cause of β thalassemia. Among the recognized types of β-gene deletion, an entity known as "pancellular hereditary persistence of fetal hemoglobin" has minimal clinical manifestations owing to efficient synthesis of γ chains on the chromosome in which the β and δ genes are deleted. Hemoglobin Lepore is a fusion protein formed from a nonhomologous crossover between the δ and β genes resulting in the absence of normal β-chain synthesis and therefore a β-thalassemia phenotype (Fig. 288-1). In the great majority of cases of β thalassemia, restriction endonuclease maps reveal no gross abnormalities of the β-globin

TABLE 288-4 Classification of the thalassemias

Diagnosis	Globin chain synthesis in reticulocytes	RBC morphology	Hb electrophoresis	Clinical severity
α Thalassemia:	α/β*			
Silent carrier (α−/αα)	0.9	Normal	Normal, ↓ A₂	0
α-thalassemia trait [(α−/α−) or (−−/αα)]	0.7	↓ MCV†	Normal, ↓ A₂	0
Hb H disease (−−/α−)	0.3	↓ MCV Heinz bodies, targets	↑ Hb H (β₄) (10–15%)	2+
Hydrops fetalis (−−/−−)	0	↑↑ Nucleated RBC	↑↑ Hb Barts (γ₄)	4+
β thalassemia:	β/α*			
Heterozygous	0.5	↓ MCV, stippling	↑ A₂ (± ↑ HbF)	0 to +
Homozygous (or double heterozygous)	0–0.3	↓ MCV, hypochromic Nucleated RBC, targets bizarre shapes	↑↑ HbF	4+ (major) 2–3+ (intermedia)

* *Normal = 1.*
† *MCV = mean corpuscular volume.*

gene complex. Nevertheless, there are several steps in β-globin synthesis that could go awry and lead to a thalassemic phenotype. A number of cases involve mutations in or near one of the intervening sequences of the β-globin gene, leading to errors in the processing of mRNA. Often β^A chains are made but in reduced amounts (β^+ thalassemia) (see Fig. 288-1). Others have nonsense mutations in the coding region, causing premature termination of β-globin chains. This is the most common cause of β^0 thalassemia (Fig. 288-1).

Cellular pathogenesis   As a result of imbalance in globin chain synthesis, the β thalassemias have varying degrees of ineffective erythropoiesis (Chap. 283) and hemolysis. In β thalassemia major there is a marked relative excess of α-chain production. Free α chains have decreased solubility and will form insoluble aggregates or inclusions within red blood cell precursors in the bone marrow. Like congenital Heinz body hemolytic anemia due to unstable hemoglobin variants, the inclusion bodies in thalassemia bring about abnormalities in membrane permeability as well as entrapment and destruction of red blood cells by the macrophages in the mononuclear phagoycte system. As a result, β thalassemia is characterized by both intramedullary erythroid destruction and also a shortening of the life span of circulating red blood cells that emerge from the bone marrow. Thus, these patients have the characteristic parameters of both ineffective erythropoiesis (increased plasma iron turnover, decreased incorporation of iron into red blood cells) and peripheral hemolysis. Because these red blood cells are under double jeopardy, there is an enormous compensatory stimulus to erythropoiesis, resulting both in expansion of the red marrow and in extramedullary hematopoiesis in the liver and spleen. Chain imbalance in β thalassemia is attenuated to a variable degree by the "compensatory" synthesis of γ chains which are able to combine with excess free α chains and form a stable tetramer (Hb F). Patients with Cooley's anemia who have a relatively high rate of γ-chain production have a less severe clinical course. Individuals with β thalassemia minor have absent or very mild ineffective erythropoiesis and hemolysis, detectable in some patients by a slight elevation in fecal urobilinogen and a modest shortening of the red blood cell life span.

In the α thalassemias a relative excess production of non-α chains can be detected, leading to the formation of Hb Barts (γ_4) in the newborn and young infant. Children and adults with deletion of 3 α-globin genes usually have Hb H (β_4). In contrast to the α-chain inclusions found in β thalassemia, the Heinz bodies due to Hb H are more stable and develop in mature circulating red blood cells. As a result, Hb H disease is primarily a hemolytic disorder without a significant amount of ineffective erythropoiesis.

β thalassemia minor   This common entity, also referred to as β-*thalassemia trait*, is rarely associated with significant clinical manifestations. The diagnosis is generally made in patients being evaluated for mild anemia or in follow-up of abnormalities found on routine blood studies. Most individuals with β-thalassemia trait escape diagnosis. About one-fifth of affected individuals have splenomegaly. Icterus is occasionally noted, particularly in those individuals who also have Gilbert's disease, another common and benign congenital disorder (Chap. 246).

In otherwise healthy individuals with β-thalassemia trait, the mean hemoglobin level is about 15 percent lower than in normal persons of the same age and sex; the red blood cell count is usually elevated, and the cells are microcytic. Indeed, at any level of hematocrit, patients with β thalassemia minor have more marked microcytosis than those with iron deficiency. In contrast, the mean corpuscular hemoglobin concentration is normal. In addition to microcytosis, examination of the blood film reveals occasional target cells, cigar-shaped cells, and a moderate amount of basophilic stippling; the reticulocyte count is normal. Special isotope techniques are required to demonstrate a slightly reduced red blood cell life span. The red blood cells have decreased osmotic fragility. Serum iron is normal unless the patient also happens to be iron-deficient. Hemoglobin electrophoresis is very useful in establishing the diagnosis of β

thalassemia minor. Most affected individuals will have a twofold increase in Hb A_2 (5 percent versus normal of 2.5 percent). In contrast, Hb A_2 is subnormal in α thalassemia, iron deficiency, and sideroblastic anemias. Patients with β-thalassemia trait who become iron-deficient usually have a "normal" level of Hb A_2 which increases to above normal after correction of the deficiency. Almost half of individuals with β thalassemia minor also have moderate elevation of Hb F (2 to 5 percent). In the less common state, δβ thalassemia, in which there is a deletion of the adjacent δ and β chain genes, Hb A_2 levels will be normal or decreased, but Hb F is increased (5 to 15 percent).

No treatment is indicated for individuals with β-thalassemia trait. They should be reassured that they do not have a serious hematologic problem. The genetic implications of thalassemia should be explained, particularly to those of childbearing age. Many individuals have been given long-term iron treatment on the mistaken impression that they had iron-deficiency anemia. These patients may gradually develop clinically significant siderosis. Establishing the diagnosis of β thalassemia minor should prevent such inappropriate therapy.

β thalassemia major   Also termed Cooley's anemia, this is probably the most severe form of congenital hemolytic anemia. Clinical manifestations generally appear after the first 4 to 6 months of life when the switch from γ-chain to β-chain production usually occurs. Patients develop a severe anemia with a hematocrit of less than 20 unless they are supported by transfusions. Accordingly, patients have all the signs and symptoms associated with severe anemia. In addition, they have findings related to severe intramedullary and peripheral hemolysis and to iron overload. Patients with β thalassemia major often have marked wasting and appear malnourished. Children have slow rates of growth and development. In adolescents, the onset and development of secondary sex characteristics are delayed. Patients have a peculiar skin color due to a combination of icterus, pallor, and increased melanin deposition. They usually have skeletal abnormalities, secondary to expansion of the erythroid marrow. Enlargement of the malar bones may give the characteristic "chipmunk" facies or cause malocclusion of the jaw. Patients invariably have cardiomegaly which may be accompanied by signs of congestive heart failure. Marked hepatomegaly and splenomegaly are always found in these patients.

The *diagnosis* of β thalassemia major should be considered in any patient with a severe hemolytic anemia and hypochromic microcytic red blood cells. Examination of the peripheral blood smear reveals marked variations in the size and shape of red blood cells, including many target cells as well as teardrop and cigar-shaped cells (Plate 9-5). Normoblasts are usually seen, particularly if the patient has undergone splenectomy. Hemoglobin electrophoresis shows the presence of large amounts of Hb F and variable amounts of Hb A. In patients who are homozygous for β^0 thalassemia, no Hb A can be detected. Hemoglobin A_2 is usually increased about twofold, although it can be normal in β thalassemia major.

Patients with β thalassemia major have a short life expectancy. It is unusual for a patient with the most severe form of the disease to survive into adulthood. Most patients have such severe anemia that they are dependent upon transfusions. The chronic administration of large amounts of blood along with an inappropriate increase in iron absorption from the gastrointestinal tract inevitably leads to clinically significant hemosiderosis. As a result of iron overload, these patients develop abnormalities in cardiac, endocrine, and hepatic function. The combination of chronic hypoxia and myocardial siderosis leads to cardiac arrhythmias, congestive failure, and ultimately death.

Homozygotes who survive into adulthood are likely to have a less severe form of the disease, designated as β *thalassemia intermedia*. There are several genetic subtypes which are associated with less severe clinical manifestations: (1) β thalassemia with unusually high levels of Hb F synthesis, (2) δβ thalassemia in which there is absence of δ-chain as well as β-chain synthesis, and (3) the presence of α thalassemia in combination with homozygous β thalassemia, leading to more balanced subunit synthesis. A milder clinical course is also seen in individuals who are doubly heterozygous for β thalassemia and hereditary persistence of Hb F. Patients with the above genotypes usually have moderately severe anemia, but do not require transfusions.

Treatment of β thalassemia major is primarily supportive. The obvious benefits of transfusion therapy are partially offset by the risk of iron overload, hepatitis, and alloimmunization. Despite these problems, children with Cooley's anemia fare better if their hemoglobin is maintained at greater than 9 g/dL. In view of the increased demands of the hyperplastic marrow, it is reasonable to maintain these patients on a daily supplement of folic acid. Since splenic sequestration contributes to shortened red blood cell survival, many patients derive some benefit from splenectomy. The prevention and treatment of iron overload is a continuing concern in these patients. Transfusion of young low-density red blood cells, "neocytes," reduces the rate of iron accumulation. Continuous subcutaneous injection of desferrioxamine permits the mobilization and excretion of significant amounts of iron and, when administered over a prolonged period, can prevent or retard the development of chronic iron toxicity.

Considerations of genetic counseling and antenatal diagnosis are as relevant in the *prevention* of β thalassemia major as they are for sickle cell anemia (see above). Because of linkages between β thalassemias and restriction enzyme polymorphisms, prenatal diagnosis can often be made by DNA analysis of amniotic fluid cells. However, in some cases it is necessary to take the risk of obtaining fetal red blood cells for globin chain synthesis measurements.

REFERENCES

ALTER BP: Advances in the prenatal diagnosis of hematologic diseases. Blood 64:329, 1984

BENZ ES, FORGET BG: The thalassemia syndromes: Models for the molecular analysis of human disease. Ann Rev Med 33:363, 1982

BUNN HF, FORGET BG: *Hemoglobin: Molecular, Genetic and Clinical Aspects.* Philadelphia, Saunders, 1986

CASTLE WB: From man to molecule and back to mankind. Semin Hematol 13:159, 1976

CHARACHE S: Advances in the understanding of sickle cell anemia. Hosp Pract 21:173, 182, 1986

JAFFE EF: Methemoglobinemia. Clin Hematol 10:99, 1981

KAN YW: Thalassemia: Molecular mechanism and detection. Am J Hum Genet 38:4, 1986

LEY TJ, NIENHUIS AW: Induction of Hb F synthesis in patients with β thalassemia. Ann Rev Med 36:485, 1985

NIENHUIS AW et al: Advances in thalassemia research. Blood 63:738, 1984

NOGUCHI CT, SCHECHTER AN: The intracellular polymerization of sickle hemoglobin and its relevance to sickle cell disease. Blood 58:1057, 1981

POWARS DR: Natural history of sickle cell disease: The first ten years. Semin Hematol 12:267, 1975

SCHECHTER AN, BUNN HF: What determines severity in sickle cell disease. N Engl J Med 306:295, 1982

SERJEANT GR: *The Clinical Features of Sickle Cell Disease.* New York, American Elsevier, 1986

WEATHERALL DJ, CLEGG JB: *The Thalassemia Syndromes.* Oxford, Blackwell, 1982

289 THE MYELOPROLIFERATIVE DISEASES

JOHN W. ADAMSON

DEFINITION The myeloproliferative diseases are neoplasms of the multipotent hematopoietic stem cell. They include chronic myelogenous leukemia (CML), polycythemia vera (PV), agnogenic myeloid metaplasia with myelofibrosis (AMM/MF), and essential thrombocytosis (ET). In addition to their common stem cell origin, other features are shared which occasionally lead to a blurring between the various disorders. However, apparent transitions from one disorder to another are uncommon. With the exception of CML, the diseases tend to run a chronic course over many years.

The stem cell origin and clonal nature of these diseases have been shown through cytogenetic analyses and through studies in female patients who are heterozygous for glucose 6-phosphate dehydrogenase (G6PD). Consistent with the stem cell origin and neoplastic nature of these diseases a single G6PD enzyme is found in peripheral blood granulocytes, platelets, red cells, and monocytes in patients who have been shown to be G6PD heterozygotes by analysis of skin fibroblasts. In at least some patients, the level of stem cell involvement includes a progenitor capable of giving rise to lymphocytes, as well. In patients with characteristic cytogenetic abnormalities, abnormal metaphases may be found in precursors of platelets, red cells, and granulocytes. These findings indicate that the diseases arise as clonal expansions of single transformed stem cells. At the time of diagnosis, virtually all of the myeloid cells of the blood are derived from the neoplastic clone.

CHRONIC MYELOGENOUS LEUKEMIA

DEFINITION AND ETIOLOGY CML is characterized by marked splenomegaly and the production of increased numbers of granulocytes, particularly neutrophils. The disorder is associated with a characteristic chromosomal abnormality (see below) and runs a generally mild course until it transforms to a frankly leukemic (blastic) phase. No specific etiologic agent can usually be identified; however, an increased incidence of CML in atomic bomb survivors has been noted. CML occurs at any age, but the peak incidence occurs in the third and fourth decades. The sexes are affected equally.

PATHOPHYSIOLOGY AND SYMPTOMATOLOGY The natural course of CML can be divided into a chronic and a blastic or acute phase. The chronic phase of CML is characterized by an excessive proliferation and accumulation of granulocytes and their precursors in the marrow and blood. Typically, the white blood cell count is markedly elevated, often exceeding 200,000 per cubic millimeter. At this stage, myeloblasts are less than 5 percent of the cells in the marrow and blood. The diagnosis often is made because of incidental laboratory tests which reveal an elevated white blood count, or because a patient complains of left upper quadrant discomfort due to an enlarged spleen. About 20 percent of cases are diagnosed on the basis of an elevated blood count in the absence of symptoms. In the majority, however, the signs and symptoms of the disease are related to the expanded myeloid mass in the marrow and spleen. Presenting symptoms are related to splenomegaly, anemia, or hypermetabolism manifested by weight loss and fever. Arthralgias may be severe. Lymphadenopathy is rare in this phase. Thrombohemorrhagic complications such as excessive bleeding, either spontaneously or with surgical or dental procedures, are found occasionally. Ninety percent of patients have palpable splenomegaly.

During the course of the chronic phase of CML the disease transforms to the more malignant blastic phase. After the first 6 to 12 months following diagnosis, the rate of transformation to the blastic phase is about 25 percent of the remaining patients per year and over 85 percent of patients with CML will eventually die in this phase. Occasionally, patients may present in the blastic phase of the disease. The chronic phase may be restored if such patients respond successfully to chemotherapy. There is no single test which predicts precisely when a patient's disease will transform to the blastic phase, but certain features associated with early transformation include the degree of leukocytosis, the presence of an excessively large liver and spleen, the percentage of immature cells in the marrow, and the presence of large numbers of eosinophils or basophils. Overall survival for patients from the time of diagnosis averages 3½ years.

The blastic phase of CML represents an evolution in the disease from hyperplasia of mature marrow elements of the marrow to increased numbers of blasts and promyelocytes. Half of the patients progress to blast crisis through an "accelerated" phase characterized by progressively increasing leukocytosis, thrombocytosis or thrombocytopenia, and splenomegaly, which are refractory to previously effective drugs. In some patients, the transition to a state resembling acute myelogenous leukemia may take only a few weeks. A minority of patients will present with or develop extramedullary tumors, usually in lymph nodes or skin, or osteolytic bone lesions. Meningeal leukemia is rare.

The blastic phase may be lymphoid or myeloid in origin. One-third of cases have characteristics of lymphoblasts including the enzyme terminal deoxynucleotidyl transferase (TdT), a DNA-synthesizing enzyme associated with acute lymphoblastic leukemia and normal thymic lymphocytes, as well as the common acute lymphoblastic leukemia antigen (CALLA). This is consistent with the known level of stem cell involvement in the original disease. Lymphoid blast crisis in some patients is associated with arrested rearrangements of the immunoglobulin genes typical of pre-B cells. Myeloid blast crisis resembles acute myelogenous leukemia, but a few patients will have a basophilic or erythroleukemic conversion from the chronic phase of the disease. The latter, and the fact that the blasts may react positively with monoclonal antibodies to erythroid- or megakaryocyte-associated antigens, emphasize the diversity of this phase and the stem cell nature of the disease. Auer rods are virtually never seen in the myeloblasts of CML in blastic phase.

LABORATORY FINDINGS Table 289-1 summarizes the distinguishing laboratory features of the various myeloproliferative diseases. The most prominent laboratory finding in CML is the leukocytosis. Unlike the finding in leukemoid reactions, there is generally a bimodal distribution of neutrophils in the blood with a peak of mature polymorphonuclear neutrophils (PMNs) and a second peak of myelocytes or metamyelocytes. Platelet morphology is more normal than in the other myeloproliferative disorders, and in vitro platelet function, as marked by aggregation in the presence of agents such as epinephrine, is also generally normal. Basophilia, typical of all of the myeloproliferative disorders, may be prominent. A number of unique biochemical abnormalities are also found. Accompanying the leukocytosis of CML is a marked elevation of serum vitamin B_{12} levels, as well as an increased serum vitamin B_{12}–binding capacity. This is due to excessive serum levels of transcobalamin I, a glycoprotein of alpha globulin electrophoretic mobility. A vitamin B_{12}–binding protein with similar properties has been shown to be produced by mature normal and leukemic granulocytes in vitro. Elevated levels in the serum of patients with CML are probably derived from the turnover of the increased granulocytic mass. The high levels of vitamin B_{12}, as well as the increased serum binding capacity, return toward normal with treatment of the disease. Leukocyte alkaline phosphatase, an enzyme in granulocytes, is markedly reduced in the granulocytes of nearly all patients with CML. However, with infection or steroid administration, the level of the enzyme in granulocytes may rise to the normal range. The levels of the enzyme may also return toward normal with successful therapy of the disease and reduction of the white cell count. The only other hematologic disorder with low or absent leukocyte alkaline phosphatase is paroxysmal nocturnal hemoglobinuria. The marrow as well as the spleen of patients with CML may contain glycolipid-laden phagocytes which resemble Gaucher cells. Hyperuricemia related to the increased cell turnover may occur in all the myeloproliferative diseases prior to therapy and can be exacerbated by treatment. The mature granulocyte in CML is a cell that is functionally normal with respect to phagocytosis and bactericidal activity. Granulocyte kinetics in CML have been studied with isotope-labeling techniques, and there is clear evidence for increased production of mature granulocytes. The numbers of primitive myeloid progenitors (colony-forming cells) in the marrow and blood of patients with CML are also increased. This includes both committed erythroid

as well as granulocytic progenitors, and their numbers in the blood may be 10,000 times the normal number.

CYTOGENETICS More than 95 percent of patients with CML have a unique and characteristic chromosome marker in metaphases of marrow—the Philadelphia chromosome (Ph^1). This chromosomal abnormality represents a reciprocal translocation of genetic material between the long arms of chromosome 22 and chromosome 9. This particularly interesting chromosomal rearrangement involves break points near two cellular proto-oncogenes, c-abl on chromosome 9 and c-sis on chromosome 22. The proto-oncogene c-sis is the cellular homologue of the simian sarcoma virus oncogene and encodes sequences for platelet-derived growth factor (PDGF). The proto-oncogene c-abl is translocated to a specific region of chromosome 22, the breakpoint cluster region (bcr). As a result, a fusion gene product of bcr/abl is formed which has tyrosine kinase activity and may have a role in the development or persistence of the disease. This chromosome abnormality persists throughout the course of the disease, in remission and relapse, and is unaffected by the usual therapies. It is present in virtually all metaphases of granulocytic, megakaryocytic, and erythroid precursors but not in traditionally prepared lymphocyte preparations or skin fibroblasts. In addition to the Ph^1 chromosome, the blastic phase of CML is often associated with the acquisition of other chromosomal abnormalities, such as aneuploidy, which reflect the more malignant character of this phase of the disease. Double Ph^1 chromosomes also may be seen. Less than 5 percent of patients with clinically typical CML lack the Ph^1 chromosome. These patients are generally younger and have a more rapidly progressive clinical course. Although considered with CML, this disease is probably a distinct myeloproliferative disorder.

While the Ph^1 chromosome is a consistent feature of CML, there is evidence, using other cell markers such as G6PD, that the appearance of the chromosomal abnormality is not the primary event in the acquisition of the disease. Thus, some lymphocyte populations which appear by G6PD analysis to be clonally derived lack the Ph^1 chromosome. These and other results suggest a multistep pathogenesis in CML with the acquisition of the Ph^1 chromosome as a secondary event.

DIAGNOSIS CML which presents with splenomegaly, a markedly elevated white cell count, a low leukocyte alkaline phosphatase, and the Ph^1 chromosome is an easy diagnosis. Atypical presentations must be differentiated from leukemoid reactions associated with infections or neoplasms. In the latter, the leukocyte alkaline phosphatase is usually elevated and the Ph^1 chromosome is absent. A closely related myeloproliferative disorder is agnogenic myeloid metaplasia (AMM/MF) (see below). This disease usually presents with marked myelofibrosis and splenomegaly. The white blood cell count and platelet count may be elevated, but leukocyte alkaline phosphatase is normal or increased and the Ph^1 chromosome is absent. Among the myeloproliferative diseases, the serum vitamin B_{12} level cannot be used as a differential diagnostic test in patients with elevated white cell counts.

THERAPY Chronic phase CML can be controlled by a number of alkylating agents such as busulfan, cyclophosphamide, or melphalan. Splenic irradiation is not as effective as chemotherapy for control of the disease. The most commonly used drug is busulfan. It may be administered on an intermittent schedule or on a continuous daily basis with approximately the same results. The most serious compli-

TABLE 289-1 The myeloproliferative diseases

Disease	Hematocrit	White blood cell count	Platelet count	Splenomegaly	Leukocyte alkaline phosphatase	Marrow fibrosis	Ph¹ chromosome
CML	Normal or ↓	↑↑↑	↑ to ↓	+ + +	↓ to 0	±	+
PV	↑↑	↑↑	↑ to ↓	+	↑↑	±	0
AMM/MF	↓↓	↑ to ↓	↑ to ↓	+ + +	↑ or normal	+ + +	0
ET	Normal	Normal	↑↑↑	+	↑ or normal	±	0

cation of busulfan therapy is prolonged myelosuppression. Occasionally, remission of the disease for periods in excess of 1 year may follow a single course of treatment. The principal side effects include increased skin pigmentation resembling adrenal insufficiency and, rarely, pulmonary or retroperitoneal fibrosis. An initial daily oral dose of 4 to 8 mg will reduce the white cell count to less than 20,000 per cubic millimeter in 2 to 3 weeks. The dose of busulfan should be reduced progressively, roughly in proportion to the reduction in white blood cell count. Patients achieve an excellent hematologic remission, with return of blood counts to normal and reduction in organomegaly. The Ph¹ chromosome remains, however. A true remission of the disease does not occur; rather, the proliferating granulocyte mass is reduced to the point where immature cells disappear from the peripheral blood. Furthermore, neither conventional therapy nor high-dose combination chemotherapy designed to eradicate the Ph¹-positive clone significantly prolongs survival. Encouraging results with interferon have been reported, but more extensive trials with this or similar agents will be necessary.

Splenectomy has little place in the primary management of CML but may be reserved for those patients with evidence of hypersplenism or repeated painful splenic infarctions or for the rare instance in which prolonged thrombocytopenia follows busulfan therapy. Splenectomy in the chronic phase of CML does not prolong survival or delay the onset of blastic transformation.

Acceleration of the disease is reflected by progressive refractoriness to chemotherapy, increased leukocytosis with a larger proportion of immature forms, thrombocytosis, and increasing splenomegaly. Prior to blastic transformation, the drug hydroxyurea can effectively control the proliferative aspects of the disease. The dose ranges from 1 to 3 g per day by mouth. The blastic phase of CML is refractory to most drug regimens, but short-lived remissions in about 20 percent of cases have been obtained with the use of vincristine and prednisone or other intensive combination chemotherapy programs useful in the treatment of acute leukemia (see Chap. 292). There is a correlation between the appearance of TdT in the blast cells and the response to vincristine and prednisone, drugs commonly used for acute lymphoblastic leukemia in childhood. However, the correlation is not perfect, and therapy for the blastic phase should begin with vincristine and prednisone, regardless of the presence or absence of TdT or the morphology of the blasts. Hydroxyurea may be used here, as well, to suppress the proliferation of blasts; however, meaningful remissions are rarely, if ever, obtained and patients die of infection or bleeding. Symptomatic extramedullary myeloblastic tumors can be controlled with local radiation therapy.

It has been demonstrated that eradication of Ph¹-positive cells can be achieved in the majority of chronic phase patients treated with intensive chemotherapy and radiation and transplanted with bone marrow from an identical twin or sibling compatible for human histocompatibility leukocyte antigens (HLA). Analysis of patients receiving bone marrow transplantation suggests that the best results are obtained in patients transplanted in chronic phase within the first year of diagnosis. Long-term disease-free survival in good-risk transplant patients is approximately 70 percent, although late relapses have been reported with reappearance of the Ph¹ chromosome. Progressively poorer results with higher relapse rates are obtained in patients when they are transplanted in the accelerated or blastic phase of the disease.

POLYCYTHEMIA VERA

DEFINITION AND ETIOLOGY Polycythemia vera (PV) is characterized by splenomegaly and an increased production of all myeloid elements; however, the disease is generally dominated by an elevated hemoglobin concentration. PV is gradual in onset and runs a chronic but usually slowly progressive course.

The disease generally begins in late middle life and is slightly more common in males. Only rarely is PV found in children or

multiple members of a single family. The disease is relatively uncommon in Blacks and occurs with increased frequency in Jews of European extraction.

PATHOPHYSIOLOGY AND SYMPTOMATOLOGY None of the recognized physiologic mechanisms of increased red blood cell production is present in PV. The disease must be distinguished from secondary forms of polycythemia, in which an elevated hemoglobin concentration results from increased erythropoietin production. Secondary polycythemia may arise through hypoxia or occasionally may be found with certain neoplasms. PV is also distinct from spurious (relative) polycythemia, which results from a decrease in the plasma volume rather than a true increase in red blood cell mass. Also, secondary causes of polycythemia are not associated with splenic enlargement or increased leukocytes and platelets, which are typical of PV.

In PV there is a unique relationship of erythropoietin to red blood cell production. As opposed to the findings in secondary forms of polycythemia, urine and serum levels of erythropoietin in patients with PV are substantially reduced or absent. Presumably, erythropoietin production is suppressed by the elevated hemoglobin concentration, since phlebotomy results in a rise in both erythropoietin excretion and red blood cell production (provided that there is no deficiency in iron). This demonstrates the marrow's ability to respond to humoral regulation.

In cell culture, marrow from patients with PV forms colonies of hemoglobin-synthesizing cells in the absence of added erythropoietin. This is rarely the case with marrow cells from normal persons or from patients with secondary polycythemia. A reduced production of erythropoietin, the appearance of ''endogenous'' erythroid colonies in marrow cultures, and the clonal origin from the pluripotent hematopoietic stem cell indicate that hematopoiesis in PV is not regulated by the usual mechanisms.

PV produces symptoms associated with increased blood volume and blood viscosity. The hemoglobin concentration, hematocrit, and total blood volume may become markedly elevated, a consequence of the sharply increased red blood cell mass. The plasma volume is usually normal but may be increased. Associated with the expanded blood volume is a consistently elevated increase in cardiac output and a less uniform, but significant, increase in cardiac index. Reduction of the hematocrit and blood volume by phlebotomy leads to a reduction in the stroke volume and cardiac output in these patients and generally to an improvement in exercise tolerance. The increased cardiac output occurs in association with an increase in blood viscosity and, presumably, in vascular resistance associated with the elevated hematocrit.

Complaints related to the increased viscosity and/or decreased cerebral perfusion include headache, dizziness, vertigo, a sense of fullness of the head, rushing in the ears, visual alterations (scotomas, double vision, or blurred vision), tinnitus, syncope, and even chorea. Peripheral vascular symptoms of both arterial and venous insufficiency are common; in one large series, more than 35 percent of patients gave a history of some thrombotic or hemorrhagic event during the course of their disease. The risk of thrombosis may be increased by the accelerated atherosclerosis in this disease. Bleeding is common and comes most often from the nose or from peptic ulcer disease. Intramuscular hemorrhages and bruising also are seen. The tendency to increased bleeding may be due to the distended vasculature resulting from the increased blood volume. However, intrinsic platelet dysfunction also may contribute to bleeding, particularly from the gastrointestinal tract. The incidence of peptic ulcer disease is estimated to be four to five times higher in patients with PV than it is in the general population, although the reasons are unclear.

Late in the disease, the spleen may become greatly enlarged, producing symptoms of early satiety, a sense of abdominal fullness, and pleuritic chest or left upper quadrant pain secondary to capsular stretching or infarction. Pruritus, particularly after bathing, is reported frequently and may be disabling. Occasionally, urticaria is seen.

The increased cellular proliferation seen with PV results in hyperuricemia in 25 to 30 percent of patients and may be associated with formation of urate stones and uric acid nephropathy.

LABORATORY FINDINGS   The most prominent laboratory feature is the elevated hemoglobin concentration. Unless altered by iron deficiency, the red blood cells are normochromic and normocytic. Polychromasia is frequently seen, and nucleated red blood cells may be found in the later stages of the disease. These findings represent cells released from extramedullary sites of hematopoiesis or reflect damage to marrow stroma due to fibrosis. The erythrocyte sedimentation rate is frequently very low (0 to 3 mm/h).

The white cell count is elevated in two-thirds of patients and is usually in the range of 15,000 to 25,000 per cubic millimeter but may be as high as 60,000 per cubic millimeter. An increase in the absolute basophil count (to more than 100 per cubic millimeter) is found in about 70 percent of patients. The leukocyte alkaline phosphatase is increased in more than 80 percent of cases. Serum vitamin B_{12} levels vary and are increased in about one-third of the patients; however, the binding capacity is increased in as many as 75 percent. In addition to increased transcobalamin I, transcobalamin III is also increased.

Thrombocytosis is seen in over half of all patients with PV. In vitro studies of platelet function demonstrate defective platelet adhesiveness and impaired secondary release of adenosine diphosphate (ADP) in response to epinephrine. These are poorly correlated with the bleeding time, and the contribution of these functional abnormalities to the thrombotic and hemorrhagic events in patients with PV is uncertain. Abnormal liver function studies, including an elevated alkaline phosphatase, may occur if there is massive hepatomegaly.

Splenomegaly occurs in 75 percent of patients but is usually not as marked as in CML or AMM/MF. Splenomegaly persists even when the elevated hemoglobin concentration has been reduced by repeated phlebotomies. Microscopic examination of the spleen reveals multiple foci of extramedullary hematopoiesis and fibrosis. The follicular pattern of the organ is retained, unlike the loss of normal architectural structure observed in CML. Foci of extramedullary hematopoiesis also may be found in the liver.

Bone marrow examination shows either erythroid hyperplasia or panhyperplasia without distinctive morphologic features. There is increased megakaryocyte nuclear ploidy in the face of thrombocytosis. This pattern of platelet regulation is different from that observed in the reactive thrombocytosis associated with inflammation or neoplasia, where megakaryocyte nuclear ploidy is inversely related to the peripheral platelet count. As PV progresses, fibrosis may appear in central areas of the marrow, and scanning techniques will demonstrate expansion of hematopoietic tissue to more peripheral skeletal sites.

Cytogenetic abnormalities, including trisomy 1, 8, or 9 and 20q −, have been reported in about 10 percent of untreated patients. Prior treatment with myelosuppressive agents or radioactive phosphorus (^{32}P) appears to increase the incidence of such abnormalities.

DIAGNOSIS   The plethoric patient with pancytosis and splenomegaly, and without evidence of chronic cardiac or pulmonary disease, presents few diagnostic problems. However, it is more common to see patients with PV who have less than the full clinical disease or in whom an elevated hemoglobin or hematocrit has been discovered at the time of routine laboratory evaluation. Under these circumstances, it is important that the diagnosis of PV be made with certainty in order to direct therapeutic efforts appropriately.

First, there is little statistical likelihood that hematocrits consistently near or greater than 60 percent represent a simple decrease in plasma volume. When hematocrit levels are in the range of 50 to 55 percent, however, the likelihood of true erythrocytosis is reduced to about 50 percent and the red blood cell mass should be determined directly by isotope dilution using ^{51}Cr-labeled autologous red blood cells. While the plasma volume may be calculated indirectly from the red blood cell mass, it is preferable to measure this compartment

independently using a second label. The results for red blood cell mass are best expressed as a function of the lean body mass, which may be estimated from the patient's height and weight. If the results of such a study are equivocal, the clinical findings must establish whether the patient has a true increase in red blood cell production or else the patient should be restudied at a later time.

The patient who presents with a hematocrit or hemoglobin in the high normal range, microcytosis, leukocytosis, and iron deficiency should be considered as possibly having PV. Evaluation of red and white blood cell morphology, basophil count, and platelet morphology should be carried out to make certain that this is not a patient with PV who has bled.

While measurements of red blood cell mass distinguish spurious from true erythrocytosis, the results do not distinguish between the various forms of polycythemia. If the diagnosis is uncertain, additional indexes which may be helpful include the absolute basophil count, the leukocyte alkaline phosphatase score, and results of radioisotope scanning to quantitate spleen size. This last is particularly useful in obese individuals or patients in whom the spleen is enlarged but not palpable.

If the diagnosis of PV remains obscure, an intravenous pyelogram or abdominal CT scan should be obtained to exclude hypernephroma or other renal pathology which might result in increased erythropoietin production. Arterial blood gas measurements should be obtained, including carboxyhemoglobin levels if the patient is a smoker. Perhaps 20 percent of patients with PV may have a hemoglobin oxygen saturation below 92 percent, but almost all will have a saturation equal to or greater than 88 percent. This modest impairment of oxygen loading may be due to decreased diffusing capacity of the lung, possibly triggered by repeated episodes of thromboembolism or thrombosis in situ.

When the diagnosis is not clear following routine investigation, measurement of serum levels or of urinary excretion of erythropoietin may be helpful. Patients with PV excrete little or no measurable erythropoietin, whereas patients with secondary forms of polycythemia excrete at least normal and frequently elevated amounts. Measurements of serum erythropoietin may be performed using a bioassay or a radioimmunoassay. Other types of immunologic assays are not helpful. In vitro growth characteristics of bone marrow cells from patients with PV suggest that such determinations may be useful in diagnosis, but experience with these tests is limited.

COURSE AND PROGNOSIS   The course of PV has been a subject of disagreement, some observers believing that later complications are hastened by myelosuppressive therapy. About 15 to 20 percent of patients will progress to marrow fibrosis, marked splenomegaly, and anemia; one view holds that if patients live long enough, all will enter this so-called spent phase of the disease. However, the majority of patients die of vascular complications of their disease or of unrelated causes. Although the incidence is low, there is a statistically significant association of second hematologic neoplasms in patients with PV; these include lymphocytic and histiocytic lymphomas and multiple myeloma. Of patients with PV, 1 to 2 percent experience transformation into acute leukemia even without prior radiation or chemotherapy.

THERAPY   Optimal therapy of PV remains unsettled. The median survival has been extended to 10 to 12 years with phlebotomy alone, while patients receiving no therapy at all survive only 2 years. However, neither myelosuppressive therapy nor phlebotomy holds a clear advantage for survival. For many years after its introduction in 1940, ^{32}P was the therapy of choice. However, a retrospective analysis of a large number of cases suggested that ^{32}P increased the incidence of acute leukemia to nearly 15 percent while not clearly enhancing survival over other forms of therapy. In order to resolve the major questions regarding the most effective therapy, the incidence of complicating factors, and the prognostic implication of certain features such as thrombocytosis or cytogenetic abnormalities, the International

Polycythemia Vera Study Group was established. This group prospectively assigned patients who met strict diagnostic criteria into three treatment programs at random: ^{32}P therapy augmented by phlebotomy, myelosuppressive therapy plus phlebotomy, and phlebotomy alone. Analysis of the survival curves demonstrated similar survivals for the various treatment groups until the seventh year after randomization. At that point, patients treated with alkylating agents had poorer survival. The findings indicated that those patients in the phlebotomy-only group suffered from increased risk of death due to hemorrhage or thrombosis within the first four years, while leukemia and other neoplasms were more prevalent later in the course of the patients treated with chemotherapy or ^{32}P. However, a simultaneous European cooperative therapy trial did not demonstrate increased leukemia in patients treated with chemotherapy, and the survival in those patients was superior to that of patients treated with phlebotomy alone.

Despite the controversy, certain therapeutic tenets meet with agreement. Phlebotomy is safe, can be done repeatedly, and is preferred in individuals with mild disease, young patients, or those with polycythemia of uncertain etiology. Myelosuppression is best in patients with extreme symptomatic thrombocytosis, rapidly enlarging spleen, or symptoms of hypermetabolism. It may also spare elderly patients the symptoms associated with phlebotomy. Regardless of eventual decisions involving therapy, phlebotomy should be used initially to reduce the red blood cell mass and blood volume. The end point of phlebotomy therapy should be a hematocrit or hemoglobin value in the low-normal range. This form of treatment may lead to prolonged clinical remission. Iron should not be given if phlebotomy is the primary mode of therapy. Phlebotomy is especially important if a patient with PV must undergo emergency surgery, since intra- and postoperative morbidity and mortality are four to five times greater in uncontrolled as opposed to controlled (phlebotomized) patients. Under these circumstances, the red blood cell mass should be reduced acutely by exchange phlebotomies and the blood replaced with a suitable plasma expander. This will prevent the vascular instability associated with too rapid a reduction in total blood volume.

Marrow suppression may be achieved by radiation or chemotherapy. The administration of ^{32}P is easy, provides long, trouble-free remissions in most cases, and successfully reduces the morbidity associated with the disease. The regimen recommended by the International Polycythemia Vera Study Group consists of the intravenous administration initially of 85.2 MBq of ^{32}P per square meter of body surface area. The patient is then followed for a period of 3 months and retreated at that time, as needed, with a dose 25 percent greater than that given originally. This program may be repeated 3 months later but is rarely required. Remissions may last 6 to 24 months, during which time the patient is often symptom-free. This ^{32}P therapy may be repeated if relapse occurs. Exposure to ^{32}P increases the incidence of leukemia in patients with PV, and the risk of leukemic transformation may be related to the cumulative dose of isotope.

Suppression of marrow function with chemotherapy has been common during the last 15 years. Effective drugs include melphalan, busulfan, and chlorambucil. Busulfan, in doses of 4 to 6 mg per day orally, reduces the white blood cell and platelet counts, but suppression may be unpredictable and prolonged and the drug is relatively less effective in suppressing erythropoiesis. Moreover, continued use of this drug may lead to pulmonary fibrosis and a syndrome resembling adrenal insufficiency. Chlorambucil, originally employed in the prospective treatment trial by the International Polycythemia Vera Study Group, resulted in a high incidence (over 10 percent) of acute leukemia, and the study group has recommended against the routine use of this or other alkylating agents in this disease. Currently, no form of treatment is clearly better than any other in terms of patient survival, but management with ^{32}P may be simpler. Hydroxyurea, a drug active in the DNA synthetic phase of the cell cycle and not known to be leukemogenic, is currently being evaluated. Hydroxyurea

given orally in doses of 1 to 3 g per day may control symptoms of hypermetabolism and the elevated leukocyte and platelet counts, but phlebotomy is generally required for adequate control of the red cell mass.

Other symptoms associated with PV may be managed conservatively. In the case of pruritus, cyproheptadine, 12 to 16 mg per day, may be effective. Allopurinol in doses of 300 mg per day will reduce serum uric acid. Symptomatic splenomegaly is usually improved with treatment, although splenectomy may be indicated in rare instances.

AGNOGENIC MYELOID METAPLASIA/MYELOFIBROSIS

DEFINITION AND ETIOLOGY AMM/MF is characterized by the tendency of the neoplastic stem cells to lodge and grow in multiple sites outside the marrow. Typically, there is progressive splenomegaly, the gradual replacement of marrow elements by fibrosis, progressive anemia, and variable changes in the number of granulocytes and platelets. The disease begins in late middle life and is gradual in onset, chronic, and progressive. Males and females are equally involved, and there is only rare familial occurrence.

While erythrocytes, granulocytes, and platelets are members of a single neoplastic clone, the fibrosis is reactive and not part of the abnormal clone. AMM is an integral part of the disease and is seen early in its course. There is no evidence that AMM arises in compensation for replacement of the marrow by fibrous tissue.

PATHOPHYSIOLOGY AND SYMPTOMATOLOGY AMM/MF presents most commonly with vague constitutional symptoms associated with anemia, such as fatigue, weakness, and anorexia, or with splenomegaly. An enlarged spleen is seen in virtually all patients; however, the disease progresses slowly and splenomegaly may be present for years prior to diagnosis. The enlargement may become so extensive as to produce symptoms of pain, abdominal fullness, and dyspnea. Hepatomegaly occurs in more than 50 percent of patients and also may become massive, but enlargement of the liver due to AMM does not occur in the absence of splenomegaly. Petechiae are found in 20 percent of patients as a result of thrombocytopenia, and a history of bleeding is obtained in 10 percent. Less common findings include lymphadenopathy, jaundice, ascites, and bone pain. Weight loss, fever, sweating, and extremity pain may occur occasionally and are associated with a hypermetabolic state. The increased cellular turnover results in hyperuricemia in 25 to 30 percent of patients.

LABORATORY FINDINGS The blood counts of patients with AMM/MF are variable. Mild anemia is observed in over one-half of the patients at the time of diagnosis and progresses during the course of the disease. Eventually, almost all patients become anemic. The recognized mechanisms leading to anemia include ineffective erythropoiesis, increased splenic pooling of red cells, and a decrease in red blood cell survival. Low serum folate and megaloblastic maturation may contribute. The peripheral blood smear usually shows dramatic changes in red cell and platelet morphology. Basophilic stippling is prominent and bizarre red cell shapes, including teardrop poikilocytes, fragmented cells, and nucleated red cells, are common, as are giant platelet forms.

An elevation in the white blood cell count is found in about 50 percent of patients, and values as high as 50,000 per cubic millimeter may be seen. However, 20 percent of patients are leukopenic, with white blood cell counts less than 4000 per cubic millimeter. Generally, there is a shift toward immature forms in granulocyte maturation, and circulating blast forms may be found. The appearance of these cells does not imply a bad prognosis. An increase in the absolute basophil count may be observed in 25 percent of patients. The leukocyte alkaline phosphatase activity is elevated in about half the patients, the remainder being equally distributed between having normal or low values. Serum vitamin B_{12} levels are normal or slightly elevated, as are vitamin B_{12}-binding proteins. These values usually do not approach those seen with CML.

A normal or elevated platelet count is frequently found early in the course of the disease, but thrombocytopenia eventually develops in most patients, owing to ineffective production and splenic pooling. The circulating platelets vary considerably in size and shape, and megakaryocyte nuclei may be found on the peripheral blood smear. In vitro studies of platelet function reflect defective platelet adhesiveness and impaired secondary release of ADP in response to epinephrine. Abnormal liver function tests, including elevated bilirubin and alkaline phosphatase, may be associated with massive hepatomegaly.

The spleen may become massive. There are multiple foci of extramedullary hematopoiesis on pathologic examination, but the normal follicular architecture of the spleen is maintained. Other organs which may be involved include the kidneys, lymph nodes, adrenal glands, and lungs. Bone marrow examination early in the course of the disease reveals a hypercellular marrow in about 20 percent of patients and may be difficult to distinguish from PV. Special stains of the marrow reveal increased reticulin deposition. However, a minority of patients develops obvious patchy collagen fibrosis separating areas of hyperplastic marrow, or diffuse fibrosis with osteosclerosis. Megakaryocytes may be preserved remarkably well in the areas of fibrosis. One hypothesis to account for the marrow fibrosis is that neoplastic megakaryoblasts and megakaryocytes release growth factors, such as PDGF, which stimulate fibroblasts or other connective tissue cells to synthesize collagen or reticulin. This is also consistent with the fact that successful bone marrow transplantation leads to the reversal of established fibrosis.

The fibrosis and osteosclerosis of the marrow generally correlate with one another and also with the degree of splenomegaly. However, there is no clear relationship between the histopathology of the marrow and the peripheral blood counts. In 40 to 50 percent of patients, the appearance of marrow sclerosis is reflected on x-ray examination by increased bone density involving particularly the axial skeleton and proximal long bones. These x-ray changes result from thickened cortical bone and the loss of medullary spaces due to increased and thickened bony trabeculae.

No unique cytogenetic abnormalities have been described in AMM/MF; however, certain nonrandom abnormalities, including monosomy 7 and trisomy 9, have been found. Reports of the Ph^1 chromosome in this disorder probably reflect examples of atypical CML.

DIAGNOSIS   A bone marrow biopsy is essential to the evaluation of this disease, and without it the diagnosis cannot be made with certainty. This disorder may be difficult to distinguish from other myeloproliferative diseases.

In CML the white blood cell count is usually greater than 20,000 per cubic millimeter, while in AMM/MF it is generally 10,000 to 20,000 per cubic millimeter. Leukocyte alkaline phosphatase is usually lower in CML, and this determination may be useful in distinguishing between the two disorders. Fibrosis of the marrow is found in only 10 to 15 percent of patients with CML and is usually present only as a preterminal event; osteosclerosis is almost never seen. In the absence of the Ph^1 chromosome, however, the distinction between these diseases is occasionally difficult.

The separation of PV and essential thrombocytosis (ET) from AMM/MF occasionally is troublesome because all may present with thrombocytosis, splenomegaly, leukocytosis, and anemia. However, ET generally is not associated with advanced fibrosis. The most difficult distinction is between AMM/MF and the late stages of PV, and attempts to separate them are probably unwarranted. Approximately 15 to 25 percent of patients with PV progress to advanced marrow fibrosis and marked splenomegaly. It is impossible to be certain that a patient with typical AMM/MF did not initially have PV. Postpolycythemia myeloid metaplasia with myelofibrosis has a poorer prognosis.

Secondary causes of myelofibrosis include metastatic carcinoma, leukemia and lymphomas, tuberculosis, Gaucher's disease, Paget's disease, and exposure to toxins such as benzene or to x-rays. These associations are usually not difficult to distinguish from AMM/MF.

THERAPY   There is no definitive therapy for this disorder, and no treatment has been shown to affect life span favorably. Anemia is treated with transfusions as required. Androgens may be administered to improve the anemia, although they are helpful in less than half of the cases. Oxymetholone (2 to 4 mg/kg per day) or fluoxymesterone may be given, particularly if there is marked ineffective erythropoiesis. Corticosteroids may enhance the response to androgens but alone are not helpful. Myelosuppressive therapy is only occasionally indicated, but it may be used to control painful splenomegaly or marked thrombocytosis. Chlorambucil or melphalan may be employed, but other blood elements may be depressed and the period of remission is relatively short (4 to 5 months). External radiation to the spleen will reduce its size, but the effects are transient and therapy may lead to severe pancytopenia. Allopurinol may be given to reduce a high uric acid level.

The role of splenectomy in the treatment of AMM/MF is controversial. Late in the course of the disease the hazards of removing a massively enlarged organ are considerable, and intraoperative mortality and postoperative complications, particularly thrombosis and infection, are frequent. Some clinicians have advocated early removal of the spleen, as soon as the diagnosis is made, believing that this will reduce later complications and make management easier. This is unlikely. The only clear indications for splenectomy are hemolysis, severe thrombocytopenia, and intractable symptoms related to spleen size.

COURSE AND PROGNOSIS   AMM/MF generally follows a prolonged course, with a median survival of 4 to 5 years from the time of diagnosis; 25 percent of patients may live 15 years. Anemia occurs eventually in most patients, and many will require transfusions. Complicating features of the disease include gout or other problems related to hyperuricemia and symptoms related to the enlarging spleen. Portal hypertension may be seen due to hepatic fibrosis, hepatic vein thrombosis, or the markedly increased blood flow through the spleen. Clinically evident bleeding occurs in about 25 percent, and it is important for thrombocytopenic patients to avoid drugs such as aspirin or nonsteroidal anti-inflammatory agents which further impair platelet function. While the degree of splenomegaly appears to be of no prognostic importance, a platelet count of less than 100,000 per cubic millimeter, hemoglobin of less than 10 g/dL, and hepatomegaly are associated with poorer survival.

The major causes of death include infection, congestive heart failure, renal failure, portal hypertension, and hemorrhage. Transformation to acute leukemia occurs in 5 to 10 percent of patients and may be related to radiation or chemotherapy. A particularly fulminant variant of AMM/MF, known as acute myelofibrosis, is characterized by rapid progression of fibrosis and pancytopenia without splenic enlargement. Death due to marrow failure usually occurs within 1 year of diagnosis. This disorder is now more correctly recognized as acute megakaryoblastic leukemia.

ESSENTIAL THROMBOCYTOSIS

DEFINITION AND ETIOLOGY   Essential thrombocytosis (ET) is dominated clinically by a markedly elevated platelet count which is invariably above 400,000 per cubic millimeter and which may reach levels of 3 to 4 million per cubic millimeter. The disease closely resembles PV and AMM/MF. Although an elevated platelet count is the dominant laboratory feature, all cell lines are involved in the expansion of the neoplastic clone.

As opposed to secondary forms of thrombocytosis, which arise in response to inflammation, acute bleeding, iron deficiency, or neoplasms, ET represents the overproduction of platelets in the absence of a recognizable stimulus. However, no specific etiologic agent has been implicated. In cultures of bone marrow cells from patients with

ET, colonies of megakaryocytes from megakaryocytic progenitors often form in the absence of added stimulus. This does not happen with marrow cell cultures from normal individuals or patients with secondary thrombocytosis.

PATHOPHYSIOLOGY AND SYMPTOMATOLOGY Symptoms associated with ET are linked to the platelet dysfunction and perhaps to platelet aggregation in the microvasculature of the central nervous system. Patients with ET may present with erythromelalgia, venous or arterial thromboses, or spontaneous bleeding. This may be seen as easy bruisability, unusual bleeding following minor dental procedures or other surgery, or large-vessel bleeding into soft tissues or muscles in the absence of a history of trauma. The first clue may be such a hemorrhagic or thrombotic episode. Transient ischemic attacks or even frank strokes may occur in patients with markedly elevated platelet counts. In general, there is a correlation between symptomatology and platelet counts in patients with this disease. However, the correlation is imperfect and individual patients will manifest symptoms at different platelet levels.

LABORATORY FINDINGS The most prominent laboratory feature is the elevated platelet count. Examination of the peripheral blood smear reveals platelets of markedly different morphology with many large forms and forms which appear hypogranular. In vitro platelet function tests typically reveal an abnormality in platelet aggregation in response to epinephrine, collagen, or ADP. The epinephrine defect is the most characteristic. These in vitro aggregation abnormalities do not correlate with the history of bleeding or thrombosis or with a prolonged bleeding time. Splenomegaly is seen in a large number of patients with this disease but is generally modest, and the spleen does not achieve the size observed in CML or AMM/MF. Bone marrow examination reveals large numbers of hyperploid megakaryocytes and, with disease progression, there may be evidence of fibrosis. This is rarely as marked as in AMM/MF.

DIAGNOSIS A markedly elevated platelet count with typical platelet morphology in the absence of a cause for secondary thrombocytosis is generally sufficient to make the diagnosis. Confirmation may be obtained by in vitro platelet function tests, measurement of bleeding time, or the association of splenomegaly. Cytogenetic abnormalities are uncommon with this disease. A useful feature is the matching of megakaryocyte size to platelet number on examination of a marrow aspirate and biopsy. Secondary thrombocytosis is associated with increased numbers of megakaryocytes which are of generally small diameter and lower ploidy. In ET, the elevated platelet number is associated with increased numbers of large, hyperploid megakaryocytes.

COURSE AND PROGNOSIS The median survival of patients with ET is not well-defined. A prospective study evaluating therapy in this disease is being conducted by the Polycythemia Vera Study Group. It is anticipated that survival will be at least as good as for those patients with PV and possibly better. Complications of the disease, such as hemorrhage or fatal thrombosis, represent the terminal event in the majority of cases. In less than 10 percent of cases does the disease transform to a more aggressive or frankly leukemic phase. If this does occur, aggressive chemotherapy is rarely effective.

THERAPY The indications for therapy in ET are unsettled and the effect of therapy in prolonging survival has not been quantitated. However, there is agreement that patients with symptomatic thrombocytosis who have had bleeding or thrombotic episodes should be treated. Previous therapy has employed alkylating agents such as busulfan or chlorambucil. However, because of the concern that these drugs may result in or enhance the likelihood of leukemic transformation, therapy with hydroxyurea is being evaluated. The available data suggest good control of the disease, but the overall effect on survival cannot be judged as yet. If patients are symptomatic at a particular platelet count, their counts should be maintained well below that level through the use of myelosuppression. Alkylating agents or

^{32}P may be used if hydroxyurea becomes ineffective. Treatment of acute events such as thrombosis or hemorrhage in an uncontrolled or previously undiagnosed patient with ET should be by emergent plateletpheresis. Although it appears anomalous, the use of aspirin and dipyridamole may prove useful in preventing symptoms in some patients with ET.

REFERENCES

ADAMSON JW, FIALKOW PJ: Pathogenesis of the myeloproliferative syndromes. Brit J Haematol 38:299, 1978

BERK PD et al: Increased incidence of acute leukemia in polycythemia vera associated with chlorambucil therapy. N Engl J Med 304:441, 1981

CHAMPLIN RE, GOLDE DW: Chronic myelogenous leukemia (CML): Recent advances. Blood 65:1039, 1985

GOLDE DW et al: Polycythemia: Mechanisms and management. Ann Intern Med 95:71, 1981

JACOBSON RJ et al: Agnogenic myeloid metaplasia: A clonal proliferation of hematopoietic stem cells with secondary myelofibrosis. Blood 51:189, 1978

Polycythemia vera: An update I and II. In *Seminars in Hematology*, vol. 23, PA Miescher, ER Jaffe (eds). Orlando, Grune & Stratton, Nos. 2 (April) and 3 (July), 1986

SILVERSTEIN MK: Primary thrombocythemia, in *Hematology*, WJ Williams et al (eds). New York, McGraw-Hill, 1983, pp 218–222

STAM K et al: Evidence of a new chimeric *bcr/abl* mRNA in patients with chronic myelocytic leukemia and the Philadelphia chromosome. N Engl J Med 313:1429, 1985

TALPAZ M et al: Hematologic remission and cytogenetic improvement induced by recombinant human interferon alpha-a in chronic myelogenous leukemia. N Engl J Med 314:1065, 1986

THOMAS ED et al: Marrow transplantation for the treatment of chronic myelogenous leukemia. Ann Intern Med 104:155, 1986

290 BONE MARROW FAILURE: APLASTIC ANEMIA AND OTHER PRIMARY BONE MARROW DISORDERS

JOEL M. RAPPEPORT / H. FRANKLIN BUNN

An important group of anemias is caused by primary disorders of the bone marrow which impair the formation of erythropoietic precursors. The term *aplastic anemia* should be restricted to conditions in which an acellular or markedly hypocellular bone marrow results in pancytopenia (anemia, neutropenia, and thrombocytopenia). Rare patients develop selective aplasia of only erythroid cells (*pure red blood cell aplasia*). Alternatively, in *myelophthisic anemia*, erythropoiesis is suppressed because the marrow is infiltrated with tumor, granulomas, or fibrosis. The pathophysiology, differential diagnosis, and treatment of these entities are discussed in this chapter.

APLASTIC ANEMIA

ETIOLOGY Aplastic anemia is thought to be due to injury or destruction of a common pluripotential stem cell affecting all subsequent cell populations. The diverse factors associated with the development of aplastic anemia are listed in Table 290-1. In approximately half of the cases of aplastic anemia in the United States, no etiologic agent is identifiable, although this figure may vary with the vigor with which an agent is sought. In other areas of the world where a larger percentage of the population may be exposed to toxins such as insecticides and benzenes in uncontrolled dose, the percentage of idiopathic cases is probably smaller.

Congenital causes Fanconi's anemia, the most common type of constitutional aplastic anemia, is an autosomal recessively inherited disease usually appearing in childhood. This disorder is often associated with multiple congenital somatic anomalies, including hypoplasia or other malformations of the kidney, hyperpigmentation of the skin, and bony abnormalities, particularly hypoplastic or absent thumbs or radii. Many patients have chromosomal abnormalities owing to a defect in DNA repair. Patients who survive the complications of progressive marrow failure are at high risk of developing leukemia. Other syndromes associated with bone marrow failure include dyskeratosis congenita as well as constitutional predisposition to aplasia without the stigmata of Fanconi's anemia.

Immune causes A number of clinical observations have led to the concept that a significant proportion of cases of aplastic anemia may be mediated by immunologic mechanisms. These include autologous recovery following immunosuppressive preparation for marrow grafting, failure of hematopoietic reconstitution in some patients following marrow transplantation from identical twin donors in the absence of immunosuppression, and the identification of antibodies which inhibit the growth of hematopoietic cells in culture. A variety of in vitro culture techniques have also supported the concept of a cellular autoimmune process in some patients with aplasia. However, in any given case the identification of an immune process may be difficult.

Drugs and toxins Multiple and seemingly unrelated drugs and chemical agents have been incriminated as etiologic agents in aplastic anemia. The association varies from a predictable dose-related aplasia to idiosyncratic reactions unrelated to dose.

The agents which in an adequate dose will predictably produce bone marrow depression are the antineoplastic and immunosuppressive drugs along with ionizing radiation. The degree of aplasia is dose related but may vary from individual to individual. These drugs include folic acid antagonists, alkylating agents, the anthracyclines, the nitrosoureas as well as purine and pyrimidine analogues. The effects of combination chemotherapy may be additive. Withdrawal of the drug usually permits recovery of the marrow elements, although irreversible aplasia is occasionally noted. Marrow aplasia may also be induced by therapeutic x-rays or, less commonly, by acute exposure from a laboratory or industrial accident. The severity of aplasia is dependent upon the dose and rate of the exposure as well as the extent of marrow irradiated.

Benzene derivatives have been associated with multiple hematologic abnormalities including aplastic anemia. Safety regulations in the United States control industrial exposure but not the domestic use of benzene-containing products. Benzene-induced marrow aplasia may be reversible, although mild abnormalities such as macrocytosis may persist.

Chloramphenicol, a commonly used broad-spectrum antibiotic, is associated with two forms of bone marrow toxicity. The more common effect upon the bone marrow is a reversible dose-related suppression of erythroid and, on occasion, granulocytic and megakaryocytic precursors. This condition is characterized by a transient anemia, associated with a drop in reticulocytes and elevation of serum iron. The bone marrow is normocellular with vacuolization of the cytoplasm of early erythroid and occasionally granulocytic precursors. This bone marrow suppression is related to the dose and duration of administration of chloramphenicol. Similar features are seen much more commonly in some patients who have ingested large amounts of alcohol.

The more serious form of bone marrow failure associated with chloramphenicol is an "idiosyncratic" reaction. This nitrobenzene compound has been the single most commonly incriminated drug in cases of aplastic anemia. These patients develop severe pancytopenia and often irreversible, fatal marrow aplasia. This complication occurs in approximately 1 in 50,000 patients who take the drug. The development of aplastic anemia seems to be unrelated to dose or duration of administration. Marrow aplasia cannot be anticipated or prevented by hematologic monitoring, since it may appear long after cessation of the drug. Unfortunately, many cases of fatal aplastic anemia have occurred in patients who received chloramphenicol for trivial or dubious reasons. Therefore, this antibiotic should not be used when there are reasonable alternatives.

Other unrelated chemicals and drugs may be responsible for the development of aplastic anemia. These agents can be placed into two classes: those in which a number of associations have been reported and, therefore, a definite toxic potential has been established, and those in which only a few reported cases exist and, therefore, only a possibility of toxic potential exists at present. The establishment of these relationships is often further confused by the fact that many of the patients have taken multiple drugs. Those agents in which a definite potential toxicity exists are shown in Table 290-1.

Infectious hepatitis A number of cases of aplastic anemia have been reported following infectious hepatitis. The antecedent hepatitis is not distinguished by its severity, and the aplastic anemia commonly appears as the hepatitis resolves. Aplasia has usually followed non-A, non-B hepatitis but on occasion has been associated with types A and B. The aplasia tends to be severe and frequently has a fatal outcome. Other viruses, including Epstein-Barr virus, have been implicated in aplastic anemia. Many cases of so-called "idiopathic aplastic anemia" are preceded by a benign-appearing viral respiratory illness. Parvovirus selectively infects erythroblasts and therefore acutely aggravates anemia in patients with hemolysis (Chap. 287).

Aplastic anemia has also been reported in association with a number of other illnesses (Table 290-1). The clinical and laboratory findings associated with paroxysmal nocturnal hemoglobinuria may accompany or precede the development of aplasia. Aplastic anemia that develops during pregnancy may remit following delivery of the fetus.

CLINICAL MANIFESTATIONS The onset of aplastic anemia is usually insidious. Initial presenting symptoms include mild progressive weakness and fatigue attributable to the anemia and/or hemorrhage from the skin, nose, gums, vagina, or gastrointestinal tract due to the thrombocytopenia. The bleeding is usually mild, but occasionally retinal or central nervous system hemorrhage may be the initial mode of presentation. Although the patient may be severely neutropenic, it is less common for the initial presentation to be a bacterial infection.

Physical examination generally reveals pallor. Petechiae or ecchymoses may be noted in the skin, mucous membranes, the conjunctivae, and fundi. Lymphadenopathy and hepatosplenomegaly are notably absent. Fever may be present, but despite the presence of an infection, the usual signs of inflammation may be absent because of neutropenia.

The *course* of the disease is generally determined by the severity of the aplasia, rather than by the etiology. Mild disease can progress to a more severe disorder. Conversely, complete recovery or partial recovery of one or more cell lines may develop. It is important to obtain an accurate assessment of the degree of aplasia. Severe aplasia is defined as marked pancytopenia with at least two of the following criteria: granulocytes fewer than 500 per cubic millimeter, platelets

---

TABLE 290-1 Causes of pancytopenia

I Aplastic anemia
  A Idiopathic anemias
  B Constitutional anemias (Fanconi's anemia)
  C Chemical and physical agents
    1 Dose-related: benzene, ionizing irradiation, alkylating agents, antimetabolites (folic acid antagonists, purine and pyrimidine analogues), mitotic inhibitors, anthracyclines, inorganic arsenicals
    2 Idiosyncratic: chloramphenicol, phenylbutazone, sulfa drugs, methylphenylethylhydantoin, gold compounds, organic arsenicals, insecticides
  D Immunologically mediated aplasia
  E Other associations: hepatitis, other viral infections, systemic lupus erythematosus, diffuse eosinophilic faciitis
II Pancytopenia with normal or increased bone marrow cellularity
  A Myelodysplastic syndromes (Chap. 292)
  B Hypersplenism (Chap. 55)
  C Vitamin B_{12} and folate deficiencies (Chap. 285)
III Paroxysmal nocturnal hemoglobinuria (Chap. 287)
IV Bone marrow replacement
  A Hematologic malignancies (Chaps. 292 to 294)
  B Nonhematologic metastatic tumor
  C Storage cell disorders (Chap. 316)
  D Osteopetrosis (Chap. 339)
  E Myelofibrosis (Chap. 289)

fewer than 20,000 per cubic millimeter, or anemia with corrected reticulocyte count less than 1 percent. The bone marrow is markedly hypoplastic and depleted of hematopoietic cells. Patients with severe disease have a high risk of dying from bleeding and/or infections in a matter of months, while patients with a milder form of the disease may live for years. The clinical course of the disease is affected primarily by infections and by the nature and location of bleeding. Although infections may not dominate the clinical picture initially, they assume greater importance with the passage of time. Because of the need for multiple red blood cell and platelet transfusions, over a period of time one may encounter the sequelae of hemosiderosis and/or hepatitis. Other clinical manifestations may be due to side effects from the administration of corticosteriods and androgens. Even those patients who recover may have mild thrombocytopenia and persistent macrocytosis for many years.

LABORATORY DIAGNOSIS The diagnosis of aplastic anemia and the assessment of its relative severity depend upon a thorough laboratory evaluation. The peripheral blood usually shows pancytopenia. The absolute granulocyte count is low, or becomes progressively depressed during the illness. The red blood cells are normochromic and normocytic or mildly macrocytic reflecting stress erythropoiesis, and the reticulocyte count is very low or zero. Since the incidence of serious bleeding and/or infection correlates with the degree of thrombocytopenia or neutropenia, these values must be determined initially and followed serially. A bone marrow aspirate may yield a "dry tap," but a bone marrow biopsy will reveal a severely hypocellular or aplastic marrow with replacement by fat. There is usually a severe depression of megakaryocytes and myeloid cells and a marked but relatively less severe depression of the erythroid precursors.

The serum iron concentration is elevated, and the iron-binding capacity is normal. There is no evidence of increased red blood cell destruction. As predicted from the nature of this disease, plasma iron clearance is prolonged, and incorporation of iron into red blood cells is markedly decreased.

DIFFERENTIAL DIAGNOSIS The diagnosis of aplastic anemia implies the exclusion of the other causes of pancytopenia that are listed in Table 290-1. Splenomegaly and/or lymphadenopathy argue strongly against aplastic anemia. Malignant and nonmalignant invasion of the bone marrow must be excluded by microscopic examination of the marrow. Paroxysmal nocturnal hemoglobinuria and systemic lupus erythematosus should be ruled out by appropriate tests including the sugar water and acid hemolysis tests. Vitamin B_{12} and folate deficiencies can be excluded by serum assays and morphologic changes. Pancytopenia rarely may be secondary to various infections. Before aplastic anemia can be classified as idiopathic, a careful history must exclude exposure to all known and suspected agents. In our complex society, all patients are exposed to potentially toxic agents in their environment. Nevertheless this difficulty should not discourage a careful and extensive search for a cause.

TREATMENT The management of aplastic anemia has become one of the most challenging aspects of modern medicine, requiring a diligent multidisciplinary team of care givers in a well-equipped tertiary care center. For patients with mild aplasia, every effort should be made to do as little as possible except to remove possible etiologic agents in expectation of spontaneous recovery. As noted below, androgens may be of value in mild aplasia. Patients with severe aplasia should be considered for a bone marrow transplantation, if a suitable donor is available. The efficacy of this treatment with complete correction of the hematopoietic defect has been most clearly demonstrated in younger patients (Chap. 291).

Supportive care Regardless of the therapy chosen, the mainstay of treatment is good supportive care. The first and most immediate step is the removal of any suspected etiologic agent. If the disease is mild at presentation, no further supportive care need be instituted, unless there is a subsequent further deterioration. If a severe neutropenia

exists (polymorphonuclear leukocytes fewer than 500 per cubic millimeter), the patient should be shielded from potential infections. Prophylactic systemic antibiotics should not be utilized. Intramuscular injections should be minimized and, if necessary, should be administered with care. Established infections should be treated vigorously with specific antibiotics, and fever of undetermined etiology may, after appropriate evaluation, call for broad-spectrum antibiotic coverage until a specific diagnosis is established. Menstruating females should be placed on suppressive doses of birth control pills.

TRANSFUSIONS These should be used *judiciously* and restricted to appropriate component therapy, since future therapy and ultimate survival may be affected by transfusions. Red blood cells should be administered to maintain the well-being of the patient rather than to establish a certain hemoglobin level. Transfusions pose significant risks such as risk of hepatitis, hemosiderosis, and sensitization to both red blood cell antigens and transplantation antigens. Platelet transfusions should be administered in the face of serious hemorrhage. Some groups employ prophylactic transfusions when the platelet count is lower than 20,000 per cubic millimeter. Others fearful of the development of resistance to future transfusions administer platelets only when faced with hemorrhage. Responses to platelet transfusions may be blunted by the presence of infection. Over a period of time many patients will develop immune resistance to subsequent transfusion at which time HLA-compatible platelet transfusions may be useful (Chap. 282). Should a bone marrow transplant be considered, family members should be avoided as a source of blood products, since the patient may develop antibodies to minor transplantation antigens. Leukocyte transfusions are not administered prophylactically. However, white blood cell infusions may be of value in patients with documented gram-negative infections and severe neutropenia who have failed to respond to antimicrobial therapy.

Marrow-stimulating agents Although patients with mild aplasia sometimes respond to androgens, and a few appear to be androgen-dependent, those with severe aplasia are unresponsive. Patients with mild aplasia should be treated with androgens as the initial mode of therapy. The most widely used drugs at present are oxymetholone, fluoxymesterone, and nandrolone decanoate. Responses may occur 3 to 6 months after the initiation of therapy.

Immunosuppressive agents Increasing clinical and laboratory evidence suggests that 40 to 50 percent of patients will have a complete or partial response to immunosuppressive therapy. The specificity and mechanism of this therapy is as yet undefined. The most commonly administered therapy is animal antiserums directed against human lymphocytes and thymocytes. The effectiveness as well as the dose and duration of administration of these heterogeneous serums is variable from batch to batch as are the not inconsequential side effects. Although very high doses of adrenal corticosteroids may yield similar responses, these agents increase the predisposition to opportunistic infections.

In general, splenectomy has no role in the management of aplastic anemia.

Bone marrow transplantation (see Chap. 291)

OTHER PRIMARY BONE MARROW DISORDERS

PURE RED CELL APLASIA Pure red cell aplasia involves a selective failure in the production of erythroid elements in the bone marrow. Granulopoiesis and megakaryocytopoiesis remain normal. Patients have a normochromic normocytic anemia with normal granulocyte count and platelet count. Severe reticulocytopenia exists, and the bone marrow is characterized by a virtual absence of any erythroid precursors in the face of otherwise normal cellular elements. An increase in lymphocytes may be seen in the marrow.

Constitutional red cell aplasia　Blackfan-Diamond syndrome, a rare chronic constitutional red blood cell aplasia, may appear in infants from the time of birth to the age of 2 years. Twenty-five percent of patients have minor congenital anomalies. The disorder is of unknown etiology.

Acquired red cell aplasia　The rare acquired form of pure red blood cell aplasia is seen predominantly in middle-aged adults. About one-third of patients have thymomas. Five percent of all patients with thymomas have pure red blood cell aplasia. The association between thymoma and myasthenia gravis is somewhat stronger. In many patients both with and without thymomas, erythropoiesis is inhibited by a complement-fixing IgG immunoglobulin which has selective cytotoxicity for marrow erythroblasts. A much smaller group of patients has been noted to have an inhibitor against erythropoietin. Occasionally, pure red cell aplasia is encountered in a patient with non-Hodgkins lymphoma.

TREATMENT　Since these patients have virtually no endogenous red blood cell production, they are totally dependent on red blood cell transfusion. If thymic enlargement is noted, a thymectomy may induce a remission in approximately 50 percent of patients. If the thymus is normal, thymectomy is of no benefit. Patients without thymoma or those with an unsuccessful thymectomy should receive a combination of corticosteroids and an immunosuppressive agent such as cyclophosphamide. Treatment often results in both prolonged clinical remission and disappearance of the inhibitor.

MYELOPHTHISIC ANEMIA　Infiltration of the bone marrow with tumor, fibrosis, or granulomas can result in the development of a severe anemia. Tumor may be derived from cell lines indigenous to the bone marrow, as in leukemia, lymphoma, or myeloma, or the marrow may be invaded by metastatic deposits of solid tumor, usually carcinoma. Among the solid tumors most frequently associated with myelophthisic anemia are carcinoma of the breast, stomach, prostate, lung, and thyroid. Hepatomegaly and splenomegaly may develop in this setting, along with marrow fibrosis.

A myelophthisic anemia may accompany the development of fibrosis in the bone marrow, usually in association with myeloid metaplasia. This entity is discussed in Chap. 289. Granulomatous involvement of the bone marrow is usually due to advanced tuberculosis. Primary lipid storage disorders, such as Gaucher's disease and Niemann-Pick disease, occasionally produce a myelophthisic anemia, and the rare disorder osteopetrosis, or marble bone disease, may also give a similar hematologic picture.

The invasion of the bone marrow by tumor or granulomas impairs both erythropoiesis and thrombopoiesis. In contrast, neutrophil production is generally normal or increased. It is unlikely that the anemia and thrombocytopenia are due merely to "crowding" of the bone marrow space by extrinsic cells. Myelophthisis also causes a distortion of the microcirculation of the marrow, with premature release of immature cells.

Myelophthisis usually results in a severe normochromic normocytic anemia. A variety of misshapen erythrocytes are noted, particularly teardrop cells and fragmented cells with some basophilic stippling. In addition, normoblasts are usually seen in the peripheral blood. The reticulocyte percentage is often slightly increased (4 to 7 percent). However, when corrected for the anemia and the premature release from the bone marrow, the absolute reticulocyte count is actually reduced and reflects a decrease in red blood cell production. While thrombocytopenia is usually present, the white blood cell count is often elevated, with a marked shift to the left in the differential count. The combination of immature myeloid cells and normoblasts in the peripheral blood constitutes the "leukoerythroblastic" morphology so characteristic of myelophthisic anemia. Striking abnormalities are usually seen on examination of the bone marrow. Often an aspirate yields a "dry tap" owing to the infiltration of the marrow with abnormal tissue. Marrow biopsy is more likely to be diagnostic, revealing leukemia, lymphoma, or foci of metastatic tumors or granulomas. However, marrow involvement is often segmental, so that the primary pathologic process may be missed on a single biopsy.

Treatment　Treatment consists of attempts to reverse the primary pathologic process. Disseminated tumors of the breast or prostate may respond remarkably well to appropriate hormonal therapy. It is particularly important to search for the presence of tuberculosis, since this disease is readily treatable. More often, however, the disease is not amenable to therapy, and supportive measures, such as blood transfusions, must be employed.

REFERENCES

ANASETTI C et al: Marrow transplantation for severe aplastic anemia. Long-term outcome in fifty "untransfused" patients. Ann Intern Med 104:461, 1986

CAMITTA BM et al: Aplastic anemia: Pathogenesis, diagnosis, treatment and prognosis. N Engl J Med 306:645, 1982

CLARK DA et al: Studies on pure red cell aplasia. XI. Results of immunosuppressive treatment of 37 patients. Blood 63:277, 1984

ELLMAN L: Bone marrow biopsy in the evaluation of lymphoma, carcinoma and granulomatous disease. Am J Med 60:1, 1976

HUMPHRIES RK, YOUNG N: Aplastic anemia and stem cell biology, in Aplastic Anemia. New York, AR Liss, 1984

KRANTZ SB, DESSYPRIS EN: Pure red cell aplasia, in Hematopoietic Stem Cells, DW Golde and F Takaka (eds). New York, Dekker, 1985

RAPPEPORT JM, NATHAN DG: Acquired aplastic anemia: Pathophysiology and treatment. Adv Intern Med 27:547, 1982

SPECK B et al: Treatment of severe aplastic anemia. Exp Hematol 14:126, 1986

WILLIAMS DM et al: Drug induced aplastic anemia. Semin Hematol 10:195, 1973

291　BONE MARROW TRANSPLANTATION

E. DONNALL THOMAS

SELECTION OF THE PATIENT　Marrow transplantation is a rational therapeutic option only if the patient's disease involves the marrow or if hazard to the normal marrow is the limiting factor in aggressive treatment of a disease. A marrow transplant involves a transplant not only of the donor myeloid, erythroid, and megakaryocytic systems but also of the donor lymphoid and macrophage systems. The rationale is illustrated by the three types of disease for which marrow transplantation has been widely utilized:

1　*Genetic disease.* For immunologic deficiency diseases, the objective is to replace the recipient's genetically defective lymphoid system with the normal lymphoid system of the donor. For genetic diseases such as thalassemia major, the abnormal marrow must be destroyed and replaced by normal marrow.
2　*Aplastic anemia.* Regardless of etiology, the disease process results in loss of the marrow, and the objective is to replace the defective organ with a normal functioning organ.
3　*Acute leukemia.* For leukemia (and other hematologic malignancies) the objective is the complete destruction of the leukemic cell population and, unavoidably, normal marrow cells by intensive chemoradiotherapy with restoration of normal marrow function by the transplanted marrow.

TYPES OF TRANSPLANTS　A *syngeneic* graft describes a graft in which donor and recipient are genetically identical, i.e., identical twins. An *allogeneic* graft is one in which donor and recipient are of different genetic origins. A *chimera* is an individual whose body contains living, proliferating cells of different genetic origin. An *autologous* marrow graft refers to the removal of a patient's marrow, administration of chemo- and/or radiotherapy, and then return of the patient's own marrow.

SELECTION OF THE DONOR　The donor must be in good health, and the donor, or an appropriate advocate, must be capable of giving informed consent. The principal risk is the anesthesia. Beyond these considerations, selection of the donor is largely determined by histocompatibility testing. Red blood cell incompatibility is not a barrier to marrow transplantation.

Histocompatibility typing (see Chap. 63) The HLA region is composed of a series of closely linked genetic loci on chromosome 6. The array of antigens encoded by this region on a chromosome is known as a haplotype. Each individual has two haplotypes, one inherited from each parent. The antigens encoded at HLA-A, HLA-B, and HLA-C are detected on lymphocytes by serologic techniques in a microcytotoxicity assay and those at HLA-D by the mixed leukocyte culture. Loci within the D region can now be recognized serologically by typing of B lymphocytes. These closely linked genetic loci, each with a large number of known alleles, make the HLA region the most complex genetic polymorphism yet described. Despite this complexity, within a family there can be only four haplotypes. Therefore, for a given patient, each sibling has one chance in four of being HLA-identical with the patient. The most widely used transplants are those between HLA-identical siblings.

PREPARATION OF THE PATIENT Infants with severe combined immunologic deficiency are conditioned to accept a transplant by the nature of their disease. All other patients are immunologically competent, to a greater or lesser degree, and are able to reject the marrow graft unless prepared with some form of immunosuppressive therapy. An immunosuppressive regimen commonly used for patients with aplastic anemia uses large doses of cyclophosphamide. Preparation of the patient with leukemia involves high-dose chemoradiotherapy for immunosuppression and to kill leukemic cells. A commonly used regimen involves cyclophosphamide followed by total-body irradiation (TBI). Approximately 10 gray (Gy) must be used for immunosuppression sufficient to permit consistent engraftment of marrow even though only 4 to 5 Gy will cause lethal marrow injury. Patients with genetic disease of the marrow may be prepared with busulfan or dimethyl busulfan to destroy the abnormal marrow along with cyclophosphamide for immunosuppression.

Marrow aspiration and infusion The pelvic bones are the most readily accessible sites for procurement, although marrow may be obtained from the sternum, ribs, or, in the case of children, the tibia. In the operating room and under general or spinal anesthesia multiple marrow aspirations are performed on the iliac crests. For adult donors, the volume of the mixture of blood and marrow cells is from 500 to 800 mL. As each aspiration is performed, the marrow is mixed with heparin and tissue culture medium. When the collection is completed, the marrow is passed through stainless steel screens to break up particles. It is then given to the recipient by intravenous infusion. The marrow stem cells pass through the lungs and subsequent growth and reconstitution of the marrow is confined almost exclusively to the medullary cavities.

Support for the patient without marrow function Usually 2 to 4 weeks are required before the transplanted marrow starts to produce the critical formed elements of the peripheral blood. Supportive care is crucial for survival. The patient should be cared for using the most effective available isolation facilities. Platelet transfusions are usually unnecessary at levels above 20,000 per cubic millimeter (see Chap. 279). Below that level, they should be used until values above 20,000 are sustained, especially if there is any evidence of bleeding. If the patient becomes refractory to random donor platelets, the use of platelets from HLA-matched unrelated donors may be necessary. Aspirin, and other drugs that depress platelet function, should be avoided. Routine use of prophylactic granulocyte transfusions is controversial and impractical. Granulocyte transfusions (see Chaps. 56 and 84) may be indicated for therapy of any significant infection in a granulocytopenic patient. Packed red blood cells should be given as needed to control symptoms of anemia, usually to keep the hematocrit above 25 percent. All blood products should be irradiated with 1.5 Gy to inactivate lymphocytes that might cause a graft-versus-host reaction.

Since infection is an ever-present danger, bacteriologic cultures should be obtained frequently. Onset of significant fever (38.5°C) should arouse a strong suspicion of infection in the granulocytopenic patient. Fever with clinical signs of bacteremia or fever sustained more than 24 h is an indication for starting systemic antibacterial therapy even if cultures are negative. Initial therapy usually includes an aminoglycoside active against *Pseudomonas* (gentamicin, tobramycin, amikacin) and carbenicillin or ticarcillin with additional antibiotics added as indicated by culture results (see Chaps. 84 and 88). Subsequently, if cultures are negative but fever persists, therapy with a combination of trimethoprim and sulfamethoxazole or with amphotericin may be considered. Once broad-spectrum antibiotic therapy has been initiated, it should be continued until the granulocyte count rises above 200 per cubic millimeter even if clinical signs of infection disappear.

Many patients coming to marrow transplantation have had inadequate nutrition because of their disease or the efforts to treat it. The preparation for marrow grafting results in nausea, vomiting, and mucositis which results in poor oral intake for at least several weeks. A Hickman modification of the Broviac catheter is installed routinely. The catheter makes it possible to administer hyperalimentation, medications, and blood products and is also used for drawing blood samples. Although some catheters are removed because of infection or suspected infection, about 90 percent of the patients have the catheter in place for approximately 3 months, the period of time when it is needed.

ENGRAFTMENT AND PROOF OF ENGRAFTMENT Engraftment is signaled by a rise in granulocytes and platelets and the reappearance of reticulocytes. The median time required to reach a granulocyte count of 1000 per cubic millimeter is 26 days. The rise in platelet count usually occurs a week or two later.

Proof of engraftment depends upon use of cytogenetics, blood genetic markers, and/or restriction enzyme fragment length polymorphisms to distinguish donor from host cells. The regenerating marrow is usually entirely of host type. Occasional patients show persistence of some host cells for a few weeks. Rare patients have an increasing number of host cells, and eventually the marrow is repopulated by host cells.

COMPLICATIONS FOLLOWING ENGRAFTMENT The complications that may follow successful marrow engraftment are (1) graft rejection, a problem primarily occurring in patients with aplastic anemia; (2) infection, including early bacterial infections or later opportunistic infections such as cytomegalovirus interstitial pneumonia; (3) acute graft-versus-host disease (GVHD), the result of the immunologic reaction of the engrafted lymphoid elements against tissues of the recipient; (4) chronic GVHD; (5) recurrence of leukemia; and (6) miscellaneous complications such as hemorrhagic cystitis, cardiomyopathy, cataract formation, venocclusive liver disease, leukoencephalopathy, and sterility.

CLINICAL RESULTS OF MARROW TRANSPLANTATION Immunodeficiency diseases Despite the rarity of these disorders, these patients are unique in that immunosuppressive therapy is not necessary to condition the patient to accept a graft, and because some myeloid function is usually present, rapid marrow engraftment is not essential. One such patient was the first to be transplanted from an HLA-identical sibling and some 100 similar patients have been successfully reconstituted in the intervening 15 years.

Genetically determined hematologic diseases Marrow grafts have now been reported for Kostmann's syndrome, chronic granulomatous disease, Chédiak-Higashi syndrome, Blackfan-Diamond syndrome, congenital aplastic anemia, and sickle cell disease (one patient, transplanted because of leukemia). Of particular interest is marrow transplantation for thalassemia major. Thalassemia major is a significant cause of death in children in many parts of the world. In developed countries, therapy with transfusions and chelating agents can prolong life for one to three decades but at great expense. In 1981, a patient with thalassemia major was prepared with dimethyl busulfan and cyclophosphamide and given a marrow graft from an HLA-identical older sister who did not have the thalassemia trait. There was prompt resolution of laboratory and clinical evidence of thalassemia, and the patient's growth and development have been normal. Since then, some 80 marrow transplants for thalassemia major have been reviewed. Approximately 10 percent of the children died of complications of marrow grafting and 15 percent regenerated their own marrow and again developed thalassemia major. Seventy-five percent of the patients appear to be cured of the disease although some 10 to 15 percent of the cured patients are under treatment for chronic GVHD. These results indicate that marrow grafting can cure genetically determined hematopoietic disorders which, at present, cannot be cured in any other way. Gene transfer for therapy of these diseases is an exciting possibility currently under investigation in many laboratories.

Transplantation for severe aplastic anemia (see Chap. 290)   Because of the poor prognosis on conventional therapy, patients with severe aplastic anemia are logical candidates for marrow transplantation.

HLA-IDENTICAL SIBLING DONORS   Patients with severe aplastic anemia must be prepared for engraftment with immunosuppressive therapy. The most widely used regimen is cyclophosphamide 50 mg/kg on each of 4 days followed 36 h later by donor marrow. The first two successful transplants were reported in 1972, and these recipients are alive and well 14 years later.

For ethical reasons the initial marrow transplants were carried out in patients who had failed to benefit from conventional therapy. As a consequence these end-stage patients had already received multiple transfusions, and many were severely infected at the time of transplantation. One-third of the patients rejected the graft, and the long-term survival of these end-stage patients was 40 to 50 percent.

Studies of marrow transplantation in dogs showed that blood transfusions could sensitize an intended marrow transplant recipient, resulting in rejection of the marrow graft. Accordingly, patients with severe aplastic anemia were identified early in the course of the disease so that marrow transplantation could be carried out before blood transfusions were given. The long-term survival of these patients has been approximately 80 percent. Therefore, patients with severe aplastic anemia and their families should have tissue typing performed immediately upon diagnosis. If a suitable donor can be identified, marrow transplantation should be carried out promptly before transfusions become necessary.

However, many patients with severe aplastic anemia present to the physician with bleeding and/or infection, and transfusions must be given as an urgent medical necessity. Therefore, marrow transplant teams are investigating other preparative regimens designed to prevent graft rejection and to improve survival. These include procarbazine and antithymocyte globulin administered before the standard cyclophosphamide regimen, cyclophosphamide followed by 3-Gy TBI, a cyclophosphamide regimen followed by 8-Gy TBI with shielding of the lung to 4 Gy, and the use of cyclophosphamide followed by 7.5 Gy of total-nodal irradiation. Another regimen is based on the fact that patients given a smaller number of marrow cells have had an increased probability of graft rejection. Since it was not practical to get more marrow cells from the donor, peripheral blood mononuclear cells have been used as an added source of donor cells. The standard cyclophosphamide regimen was administered followed by the marrow transplant. Then, on each of 3 to 5 days following marrow transplantation, buffy coat white blood cells were collected from 4 units of donor blood by a leukapheresis technique and administered intravenously to the recipient without in vitro irradiation. For patients who have been transfused, these modified regimens have largely solved the problem of graft rejection. Reported long-term survival ranges from 50 to 75 percent.

IDENTICAL TWIN DONORS   Aplastic anemia is not a common disease, and to find a patient with it who has an identical twin is even more uncommon. Nevertheless, a number of transplants have been carried out for severe aplastic anemia using an identical twin as the marrow donor. In some patients the simple intravenous infusion of marrow without any immunosuppressive treatment resulted in recovery. These results reinforce the concept that aplastic anemia is due to an acquired abnormality of the stem cell which can be corrected by transplantation of normal syngeneic stem cells. However, some patients did not recover after simple intravenous marrow infusion. These patients were then treated with the cyclophosphamide regimen and given a second infusion of marrow from the twin which resulted in complete hematopoietic reconstitution. The results suggest that some cases may be due to an immune mechanism or abnormal regulators of cell growth. Whatever the mechanism, the rare patient with aplastic anemia who has a genetically identical twin has a 90 percent chance of being cured with marrow transplantation.

Transplantation for acute leukemia   Acute leukemia (see Chap. 292) has served as a prototype malignant disease of the marrow for treatment by intensive chemoradiotherapy and marrow transplantation. Almost all regimens used for preparing leukemic patients for marrow transplantation have employed supralethal TBI. This has been done for several reasons: (1) much of the laboratory experience with marrow transplantation in animals has used supralethal TBI; (2) irradiation is an effective means of eradicating leukemic cells; (3) irradiation penetrates to the so-called privileged sites where leukemic cells may be inaccessible to chemotherapeutic agents; and (4) irradiation is a powerful immunosuppressive agent.

ACUTE LEUKEMIA IN RELAPSE USING HLA-IDENTICAL SIBLING DONORS   For ethical reasons, marrow transplantation was initially attempted only in patients with acute leukemia in relapse after combination chemotherapy. These end-stage patients were poor candidates for any therapeutic procedure because they usually presented with a heavy body burden of leukemic cells, were usually granulocytopenic and thrombocytopenic, and often already infected with antibiotic-resistant bacteria and fungi. In early studies 10-Gy total-body irradiation was given in preparation for grafting. Then an attempt was made to kill more leukemic cells by giving cyclophosphamide a few days before administration of TBI and the marrow transplant. For these end-stage patients there were many deaths related to advanced illness at the time of transplantation, graft-versus-host disease, opportunistic infections, or recurrence of leukemia. An analysis of survival shows that 10 percent of these patients are long-term survivors with the leading patients now 14 years postgrafting. It appears that these patients, on no maintenance chemotherapy, are cured of their disease. Marrow transplant teams have utilized several different chemoradiotherapy preparative regimens for end-stage patients, but the long-term survival rate remains at 5 to 15 percent.

ACUTE LYMPHOBLASTIC LEUKEMIA (ALL) IN REMISSION USING HLA-IDENTICAL SIBLING DONORS   The fact that some patients in the end stages of acute leukemia could apparently be cured led to transplantation earlier in the course of disease. Many patients with ALL, particularly children in the "good-risk" category, can be cured by combination chemotherapy, but once marrow relapse has occurred, long-term survival is rare. Therefore, the decision was made to transplant patients in the second or subsequent remission. It was recognized that some of these patients would be lost early to transplant complications, but this risk seemed acceptable if some patients could, in fact, be cured. Most marrow transplant teams are reporting long-term survival and apparent cure of 25 to 40 percent of these patients. Recurrent leukemia is a major problem. These recurrences, in host-type cells, show that the preparative regimen was often ineffective in eradicating the residual leukemic cell population.

ACUTE NONLYMPHOBLASTIC LEUKEMIA (ANL) IN REMISSION USING HLA-IDENTICAL SIBLING DONORS   In contrast to patients with ALL, patients with ANL in first remission are known to have a poor prognosis. With combination chemotherapy the median duration of the first remission in most reported series is approximately 12 to 15 months, and only 20 percent of the patients are alive at 5 years after initial chemotherapy. Therefore, a study of marrow transplantation in these patients in first remission was considered to be ethically acceptable. In an initial series of 19 consecutive patients transplanted in first remission, 11 (58 percent) are in continued disease-free remission 6 to 9 years after grafting. Several hundred such transplants have now been carried out with various transplant teams reporting 45 to 70 percent long-term survival.

PATIENTS WITH CHRONIC GRANULOCYTIC LEUKEMIA (CGL) The term *chronic* is inappropriate in describing the clinical course of patients with CGL. The conversion to blast crisis and death occurs at a fairly constant rate, and the median survival in most series of patients is approximately 30 to 40 months (see Chap. 289). Although a small fraction of patients may live for a long time in the chronic phase, in general, the outlook for most patients with CGL is quite grim. When blast crisis appears, therapy is usually ineffective. A subset of patients whose blasts appear to be more like lymphoblasts (terminal transferase-positive) and with a hypodiploid number of chromosomes may respond for a period of a few months to treatment with vincristine and prednisone.

Marrow transplantation from HLA-identical donors has been carried out in patients with CGL in blast crisis. As expected from the experience with acute leukemia in relapse, there were many deaths. However, 10 to 20 percent of these patients are long-term survivors without the Philadelphia chromosome and appear to be cured.

A study of marrow transplantation during the chronic phase of the disease for patients with an identical twin to serve as marrow donor was initiated. The twin donors were clinically and hematologically normal. After preparation with cyclophosphamide and irradiation, a complete hematologic and cytogenetic remission was induced in 11 of 12 patients. One patient relapsed 30 months after transplantation and died of leukemia at 51 months. Two others have relapsed into the chronic phase. The other eight patients are clinically and cytogenetically normal 5 to 9 years after transplantation. These results of syngeneic marrow transplantation, indicating that the Philadelphia chromosome–positive leukemic clone can be eliminated, suggested that it may be reasonable to carry out marrow transplantation in the chronic phase of CGL utilizing allogeneic donors. Seven marrow transplant teams have now reported HLA-identical grafts in approximately 200 patients in the chronic phase of CGL. Long-term survival ranges from 50 to 70 percent and absence of the Philadelphia chromosome indicates cure in the majority of these patients.

PATIENTS WITH ACUTE LEUKEMIA USING DONORS OTHER THAN HLA-IDENTICAL SIBLINGS The general experience in the United States has been that only one-third of the patients with acute leukemia will have an HLA-identical sibling, but the majority of patients will not. Therefore, a cautious exploration of the use of other donors has been initiated by several marrow transplant teams. One such study involved marrow transplantation in family member donor-recipient pairs in which one of the HLA haplotypes was genetically identical and the other haplotype phenotypically identical for one or more of the HLA loci. The results of these transplants when donor and recipient are mismatched at only one locus are quite similar to the results using an HLA-identical sibling donor. The outcome is largely a function of the stage of the disease in which the transplant was carried out. The incidence of acute GVHD was greater, but the causes of death were not significantly different. There are too few patients to permit an analysis according to the family relationship of the donor or according to the HLA locus involved in the mismatch.

Serologic HLA typing makes it technically possible to find a suitably matched unrelated donor, at least for patients with the more common HLA haplotypes, given a large panel of potential donors whose HLA types have been determined. A few transplants using unrelated donors have been reported. Some have been successful, but others have failed because of GVHD. These results indicate the feasibility of utilizing unrelated donors for marrow transplantation.

Autologous marrow transplantation The technique for procuring and cryopreserving marrow has been established for 20 years. The patient's own marrow can be cryopreserved during intensive chemoradiotherapy and then returned to the patient in order to avoid subsequent lethal marrow aplasia. The concept is attractive because use of the patient's own marrow avoids the risk of GVHD. The following points are pertinent in considering autologous marrow transplantation: (1) The patient's marrow should not be contaminated with malignant cells. (2) Autologous marrow is of value only in protecting the patient against lethal hematopoietic toxicity. If the regimen of chemoradiotherapy involves lethal toxicity to other organ systems, autologous marrow will not be of benefit. (3) The tumor being treated must show a dose-response curve such that supralethal chemoradiotherapy can be expected to result in a significantly enhanced antitumor response. Unfortunately, with currently available agents, only a few tumors appear to fall into this category. (4) The protocol must be designed so that the role of autologous marrow can be demonstrated. In animals it is feasible to administer "supralethal" therapy and to demonstrate that animals given syngeneic marrow will survive while those not given marrow will die. For obvious reasons, this kind of controlled experiment cannot be done in humans. Failure to recognize these four principles accounts for much of the current uncertainty about the value of autologous marrow transplantation in the treatment of patients with malignant disease.

Nevertheless, the potential use of autologous marrow is the subject of a new wave of interest and some results are encouraging. The tumors that might be expected to show a significant improvement in response to high-dose chemoradiotherapy include the leukemias, Hodgkin's disease, non-Hodgkin's lymphoma, small cell cancer of the lung, breast cancer, testicular tumors, and ovarian tumors. Techniques being explored for removal of tumor cells from the marrow include physical separation, destruction by chemotherapeutic agents, and destruction by monoclonal antibodies. Several transplant centers are conducting studies of the utility of cryopreserved autologous marrow, and all have reported successful hematopoietic reconstitution in most patients. It is too early to evaluate the clinical impact of these studies on the course of the several diseases.

IMMUNOLOGIC ASPECTS OF MARROW TRANSPLANTATION Marrow graft rejection "Marrow graft rejection" describes a phenomenon in which the transplanted marrow graft begins to function, but after a few days or weeks, the peripheral blood counts suddenly drop and marrow biopsy shows the marrow to be devoid of myeloid elements. Immunologically mediated marrow graft rejection is usually a consequence of sensitization by transfusions. In addition, inadequate immunosuppressive therapy before grafting may facilitate marrow graft rejection. Marrow graft rejection is a common problem in patients with aplastic anemia, but is very uncommon in patients with leukemia, which may be due to several factors: (1) Transfusions are usually given to leukemic patients while they are receiving antileukemic chemotherapy which is also immunosuppressive. This chemotherapy may prevent sensitization to transplantation antigens contained in blood products. (2) Leukemia may damage the lymphoid system so that the disease process itself interferes with sensitization. And (3) leukemic patients receive a more intensive immunosuppressive regimen before grafting.

Marrow graft failure may be due to causes other than immunologic mechanisms. With a solid organ, such as the kidney, histologic proof of graft rejection is easily obtained, but such proof usually cannot be obtained with a marrow graft since the myeloid marrow simply disappears. Other possible mechanisms of graft failure include (1) defective or inadequate numbers of "stem cells" in the donor marrow; (2) defective microenvironment in the marrow recipient; (3) allogeneic resistance not associated with HLA; and (4) susceptibility of the donor marrow to the same etiologic mechanism(s) responsible for the original disease process.

Acute graft-versus-host disease (GVHD) A "wasting disease" or "runt disease" was described many years ago in newborn mice or in rodents exposed to lethal TBI and given infusions of allogeneic hematopoietic cells. These observations were later confirmed for other species, including humans, and were recognized to be due to an immunologic reaction of engrafted lymphoid cells, presumably T cells, against the tissues of the host. This graft-versus-host reaction and its consequences, referred to as GVHD, is one of the major complications of marrow transplantation in humans. In patients given a marrow graft from an HLA-identical sibling and postgrafting immunosuppression, approximately one-half develop moderate to severe GVHD.

Acute GVHD in humans usually involves the skin, gastrointestinal tract, and/or the liver. A skin rash is usually the first sign of GVHD. Intestinal involvement results in diarrhea and may progress to abdominal pain and ileus. Liver disease is characterized by rises of bilirubin, serum glutamic oxaloacetic transaminase, and alkaline phosphatase. Severe immunologic deficiency accompanies GVHD, and death from infection is frequent.

Since GVHD is immunologically mediated, efforts to prevent its development have involved the use of immunosuppressive therapy. Of the many agents studied, methotrexate and cyclophosphamide were found to be useful. A standard regimen consists of methotrexate, 15 mg/m² on day 1 postgrafting and 10 mg/m² on days 3, 6, 11, and 18, and weekly thereafter through day 102. An alternative consists of cyclophosphamide, 7.5 mg/kg for five doses on alternate days, beginning on the first day after marrow grafting followed by additional doses at irregular intervals. Despite these regimens, acute GVHD remains a serious problem.

Cyclosporine has been shown to be a potent new immunosuppressive agent. It is particularly valuable in organ grafts such as kidney, heart, and liver. Randomized trials have been carried out to compare cyclosporine with methotrexate post grafting for their effectiveness in preventing acute GVHD. These trials have not shown a difference in patient survival between the two regimens. However, cyclosporine is useful because it does not cause mucositis as methotrexate does, and it does not suppress the marrow graft so that effective marrow function is evident approximately 1 week earlier. Cyclosporine is nephrotoxic, and marrow graft recipients often receive other nephrotoxic agents such as amphotericin for suspected fungal infection. Creatinine level and serum cyclosporine level must be monitored carefully with prompt reduction of dosage if renal function is threatened.

A number of studies have been carried out in an effort to treat acute GVHD once it becomes established. Recipients of HLA-identical marrow have been treated with rabbit or goat antithymocyte globulin with improvement in some patients. In a clinical trial, without untreated controls because of ethical considerations, prednisone, horse antithymocyte globulin, and cyclosporine gave equivalent results in the treatment of established human GVHD. Despite these efforts, about one-third of the patients who develop moderate to severe GVHD will die with this complication. It is clear that the treatment of acute GVHD is unsatisfactory and that new approaches in preventing or treating GVHD must be found.

Experiments are underway designed to eliminate from the marrow inoculum the T cells believed to be responsible for GVHD while retaining hematopoietic stem cells. One approach involves treatment of the donor marrow with lectins for agglutination and separation of the T cells. Monoclonal antibodies that react with human T cells or subsets of T cells are being used in conjunction with complement, or are bound to toxins, such as the A chain of ricin, to create an immunotoxin. The preliminary results of these studies indicate a reduction in the incidence and severity of GVHD. However, the incidence of graft failure is significantly increased. The nature of the graft failure is under investigation.

Chronic GVHD Chronic GVHD occurs in approximately one-fourth of those recipients of marrow from an HLA-identical sibling who survive beyond 100 days. The manifestations include skin disease, keratoconjunctivitis, buccal mucositis, esophageal strictures, small- and large-intestinal involvement, pulmonary insufficiency, chronic liver disease, and generalized wasting. Histologically, the disease resembles the systemic collagen vascular diseases, especially morphea and lupus erythematosus profundus. Chronic GVHD may be associated with recurrent and occasionally fatal bacterial infections.

Initial efforts to treat chronic GVHD with short courses of antithymocyte globulin or prolonged treatment with prednisone were ineffective. Recently, treatment with prednisone and either procarbazine, cyclophosphamide, or azathioprine has resulted in recovery of about 80 percent of the patients, although treatment may be required for 1 or even 2 years. Twenty percent continue to have problems which may be disabling, and cyclosporine and steroids are being tried for the refractory patients.

Recovery of immunologic function Almost all patients given a marrow transplant from an HLA-identical sibling develop a functional graft with adequate levels of circulating granulocytes and platelets. Nevertheless, particularly in the first 3 months after grafting, these patients are susceptible to a wide variety of opportunistic infections. Approximately one-third of patients develop an interstitial pneumonia, and cytomegalovirus can be demonstrated in approximately one-half of these pneumonias. The mortality rate is approximately 80 percent. The high incidence of infection is the result of a very slow return of immunologic function, which may be made worse by GVHD and by efforts to prevent or treat GVHD. Fortunately, by the end of the first year after grafting, most patients have recovered immunologically and are able to lead normal lives without an increased incidence of infection.

Tolerance The long-term healthy human recipients of allogeneic marrow transplants are true chimeras. Their myeloid, lymphoid, and monocyte-macrophage systems are entirely made up of cells of donor origin. Clearly, these donor cells in the recipient are "tolerant" of the hosts' tissues. Studies of tolerance constitute a fascinating story in immunobiology, but a clear understanding of the state of tolerance has not emerged. At least three mechanisms may be operative, including classical central tolerance, tolerance maintained by "blocking factors," and tolerance related to the presence of "suppressor" cells.

The effect of age The success of allogeneic marrow grafting is inversely proportional to the age of the recipient. For example, for patients transplanted in first remission of ANL, long-term survival for those under age 20 is approximately 75 percent and for patients aged 30 to 50, 40 percent. The most apparent explanation for this difference is the increased incidence and severity of GVHD in older patients. Most marrow transplant centers do not transplant patients over the age of 50. These age restrictions do not apply to syngeneic transplants since these patients do not have GVHD, although patients over the age of 50 do not tolerate intensive treatment as well as younger patients.

RECURRENT LEUKEMIA AFTER GRAFTING **Frequency of recurrence of leukemia** For patients with leukemia transplanted in relapse or in second remission, an actuarial analysis shows a rather constant rate of recurrence of leukemia in the first year, a decreasing rate in the second year, and few recurrences thereafter. If there were no other causes of death, approximately 35 percent of the patients would be cured, while 65 percent would be destined to relapse. However, only about 25 percent of patients with ANL transplanted in first remission subsequently relapse. It is evident that recurrent leukemia after grafting is a major problem for patients transplanted in relapse or in second or subsequent remission. The low incidence of recurrent leukemia for those patients transplanted in the first remission may be explained by the presence of only a very small number of residual leukemic cells at the time of transplant and/or by the possibility that the leukemic cells of patients in first remission may not as yet have acquired resistance to therapeutic agents.

Nature of recurrent leukemia Blood genetic makers, cytogenetic techniques, and restriction enzyme fragment length polymorphisms can be used to identify the donor or host origin of the leukemic cells in patients who relapse after marrow transplantation. In the vast majority of patients the recurrent leukemia is in host-type cells. However, 10 cases have now been reported in which the recurrent leukemic cells were shown to be of donor origin. The mechanism of donor-cell transformation is unknown. However, in three cases a lymphoblastic lymphoma occurred in donor cells. The presence of Epstein-Barr virus genomes indicated transformation by this virus.

Graft-versus-leukemia   In recipients of allogeneic marrow grafts, evidence supporting the existence of a graft-versus-leukemia effect has been difficult to obtain because of the large number of deaths from other causes among patients with severe GVHD. Sophisticated statistical methods have shown that the relative relapse rate for patients transplanted in relapse or for ALL in second remission was 2.5 times greater in recipients without GVHD than in those with GVHD. Recipients of allogeneic marrow who did not develop GVHD had approximately the same relapse rate as recipients of syngeneic marrow, indicating that subclinical GVHD did not reduce the relapse rate.

SOME GENERALIZATIONS ABOUT MARROW TRANSPLANTATION   Because of the complexity of the marrow grafting regimens, transplantation should be undertaken only by teams with all of the resources needed to ensure an optimal result. The number of such teams has increased rapidly over the past few years.

Marrow transplantation is obviously an expensive undertaking, primarily because of hospital costs, but cost has been reduced appreciably by transplantation earlier in the course of the disease when the patient is in relatively good condition. Three centers (UCLA, Children's Orthopedic Medical Center of Seattle, and the Royal Marsden Hospital) have carried out cost analysis studies comparing marrow transplantation with combination therapy and have found marrow transplantation to be less expensive than current chemotherapy regimens.

The ethical problems of exposing a patient and donor to the marrow transplant regimen and the risk of death in the first 1 to 3 months after grafting have limited the use of marrow transplantation. However, the demonstration of better long-term survival rates with marrow transplantation compared to conventional therapy for several diseases and the cure of some diseases not cured by conventional therapy should alleviate the ethical concern. Extension of this form of therapy to other malignant diseases and to a variety of genetic disorders is being reported, and the current rapid rate of progress may soon make a much broader application of marrow grafting a reality.

REFERENCES

APPELBAUM FR et al: Treatment of aplastic anemia by bone marrow transplantation in identical twins. Blood 55:1033, 1980

BEATTY PG et al: Marrow transplantation from donors other than HLA genotypically identical siblings: The immunogenetics of acute graft versus host disease, in *Histocompatibility Testing 1984*, ED Albert et al (eds). New York, Springer-Verlag, 1984, p 670

BLUME KG et al: Bone-marrow ablation and allogeneic marrow transplantation in acute leukemia: Clinical candidacy and outcome. N Engl J Med 302:1041, 1980

BORTIN MM, RIMM AA for the Advisory Committee of the International Bone Marrow Transplant Registry: Severe combined immunodeficiency disease: Characterization of the disease and results of transplantation. JAMA 238:591, 1977

FEFER A et al: Treatment of chronic granulocytic leukemia with chemoradiotherapy and transplantation of marrow from identical twins. N Engl J Med 306:63, 1982

MARTIN P et al: Effects of in vitro depletion of T cells in HLA-identical allogeneic marrow grafts. Blood (in press)

MEYERS JD, THOMAS ED: Infection complicating bone marrow transplantation, in *Clinical Approach to Infection in the Immunocompromised Host*, RH Rubin, LS Young (eds). New York, Plenum, 1981, p 507

O'REILLY RJ: Allogeneic bone marrow transplantation: Current status and future directions. Blood 62:941, 1983

POWLES RL et al: The curability of acute leukaemia, in *Topical Reviews of Haematology*, S Roath (ed). London, Wright & Sons, 1980, p 186

RAPPEPORT JM et al: Application of bone marrow transplantation in genetic diseases. Clin Haematol 12:755, 1983

SCHUBACH WH et al: A monoclonal immunoblastic sarcoma in donor cells bearing Epstein-Barr virus genomes following allogeneic marrow grafting for acute lympho-blastic leukemia. Blood 60:180, 1982

SHIELDS AF et al: Adenovirus infections in patients undergoing bone-marrow transplantation. N Engl J Med 312:529, 1985

STORB R et al: Marrow transplantation for aplastic anemia. Semin Hematol 21:27, 1984

SULLIVAN KM et al: Chronic graft-versus-host disease in 52 patients: Adverse natural course and successful treatment with combination immunosuppression. Blood 57:267, 1981

THOMAS ED et al: Bone-marrow transplantation. N Engl J Med 292:832, 895, 1975

——————: Marrow transplantation for malignant diseases (Karnofsky Memorial Lecture). J Clin Oncol 1:517, 1983

—————— et al: Marrow transplantation for thalassemia. Lancet 2:227, 1982

WEIDEN PL et al: Antileukemic effect of graft-versus-host disease in human recipients of allogeneic-marrow grafts. N Engl J Med 300:1068, 1979

---

292   THE LEUKEMIAS

RICHARD CHAMPLIN / DAVID W. GOLDE

The leukemias are a heterogeneous group of neoplasms arising from the malignant transformation of hematopoietic (blood-forming) cells. Leukemic cells proliferate primarily in the bone marrow and lymphoid tissues where they interfere with normal hematopoiesis and immunity. Ultimately they emigrate into the peripheral blood and infiltrate other tissues.

Leukemias are classified according to the cell types primarily involved (*myeloid* or *lymphoid*) and as *acute* or *chronic* based upon the natural history of the disease. Acute leukemias have a rapid clinical course, resulting in death within a matter of months without effective treatment, whereas chronic leukemias have a more prolonged natural history. This chapter will cover acute lymphocytic leukemia (ALL), acute myelogenous leukemia (AML), chronic lymphocytic leukemia (CLL), and hairy-cell leukemia. Chronic myelogenous leukemia (CML) is discussed in Chap. 289.

ETIOLOGY   The cause of leukemia is not known in most patients, although both genetic and environmental factors may be important. There is a high concordance rate among identical twins if acute leukemia develops in the first year of life, and families with an excessive incidence of leukemia have been identified. Acute leukemia occurs with an increased frequency in a variety of congenital disorders, including Down's, Bloom's, Klinefelter's, Fanconi's, and the Wiskott-Aldrich syndromes.

Environmental factors are also known to play a role in the etiology of leukemia. Ionizing radiation causes leukemia in experimental animals, and there is a clear relationship between such exposure and the development of leukemia in humans. For example, individuals with occupational exposure, patients receiving radiation therapy, or Japanese survivors of the atomic bomb explosions have a predictable and dose-related increased incidence of leukemia. Radiation exposure increases the risk of developing CML, AML, and possibly ALL, but there is no known relationship to CLL or to hairy-cell leukemia. Chemicals such as benzene and other aromatic hydrocarbons have also been associated with the development of AML.

While leukemias induced by retroviruses (RNA viruses) have been studied in laboratory animals for many years, it was not until very recently that a viral etiology was established for a form of human leukemia. A unique human retrovirus, referred to as human T-cell leukemia virus (HTLV) (see Chap. 293) has been isolated from the cells of patients with adult T-cell leukemia (ATL), an aggressive malignancy composed of mature T-lymphoid cells. There is overwhelming evidence that HTLV I causes ATL in many parts of the world. The disease is endemic in southwestern Japan and parts of the Caribbean and central Africa. Except for the HTLV family, no other virus has been causally associated with the more common human acute and chronic leukemias.

INCIDENCE AND PREVALENCE   The incidence of all leukemias is approximately 13 per 100,000 people per year, and the age-related incidence of the various forms of leukemia is shown in Fig. 292-1. The incidence of both acute and chronic leukemias is somewhat higher in men than in women. Acute lymphoblastic leukemia is primarily a disease of children and young adults, whereas AML

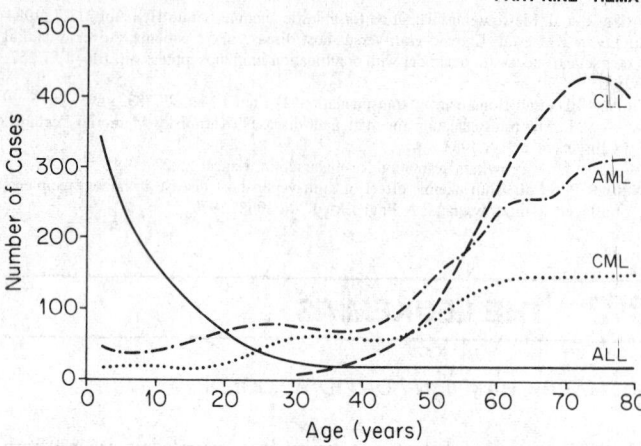

FIGURE 292-1 *Age-related incidence of various forms of leukemia: ALL = acute lymphoblastic leukemia, AML = acute myelogenous leukemia, CLL = chronic lymphocytic leukemia, CML = chronic myelogenous leukemia. (From Surveillance and Mortality Data 1973–1977, U.S. Department of Health and Human Resources.)*

occurs primarily in adults. Chronic lymphocytic leukemia and hairy-cell leukemia tend to occur in the elderly.

There have been several epidemiologic reports of case clustering of leukemias within communities and even in successive occupants of the same house. The bulk of evidence, however, indicates that the common forms of acute and chronic leukemias are not contagious and the incidence of leukemia is not increased among close contacts, such as marital partners or in the offspring of women who develop leukemia during pregnancy. The clear exception, ATL, is caused by HTLV I; in this type of leukemia there is evidence of passage of virus from infected to uninfected individuals.

PATHOPHYSIOLOGY Acute leukemia is characterized by proliferation of immature myeloid or lymphoid cells. The leukemia arises

TABLE 292-1 Chromosomal abnormalities associated with acute leukemias

Abnormalities	Leukemia subtype	Relative prognosis
AML		
t(8;21)	M2 (myelocytic)	Good
+8	M1, M2, M4, M5	—
t(15;17)	M3 (promyelocytic)	Good if remission is achieved
t(9;11)	M5 (monocytic)	Poor
inv 16	AML usually M4 with eosinophilia	Good
t(6;9)	AML with basophilia	—
5q−, −5, −7	AML following preleukemic syndrome or treatment-related leukemia	Poor
Ph¹, t(9;22)	Occasionally present in M1, M2, M4, M5, M6; must distinguish from CML blast crisis	Poor
ALL		
Hyperdiploidy	L1, L2	Good
6 q−	L1, L2	Good
14q+	L1, L2	—
t(8;14)	L3 (B cell)	Poor
Ph¹, t(9;22)	L1, L2	Poor
t(4;11)	L2 (or M4 form AML)	Poor
CLL		
+12	B-cell type	Good
+12, 14 q+	B-cell type	Poor
+12, + other abnormalities	B-cell type	Poor
t(11;14)	B-cell type	Poor

following malignant transformation of a single hematopoietic or lymphoid progenitor, followed by cellular replication and expansion of the transformed clone. A fundamental characteristic of the malignant cells in acute leukemia is their failure to mature beyond the myeloblast or promyelocyte level in AML and the lymphoblast level in ALL. Leukemic cells accumulate in the bone marrow due both to excessive proliferation and to a defect in terminal differentiation. The failure to mature to nonreplicating end cells is the primary reason for the accumulation of leukemic cells in AML. The leukemic cells proliferate primarily in the bone marrow, circulate in the blood, and may infiltrate into other tissues such as lymph nodes, liver, spleen, skin, viscera, and the central nervous system.

The mechanism of neoplastic transformation producing leukemia is poorly understood but involves a fundamental alteration of DNA conferring hereditable malignant characteristics to the transformed cell and its progeny. The neoplastic phenotype can be induced in nonmalignant cells in vitro by transfer (transfection) of DNA from the leukemic cells. In animals, leukemias can be induced by retroviruses which either carry a transforming gene (viral oncogene) or integrate into specific sites in DNA causing activation of cellular proto-oncogenes (insertional mutagenesis). The role of oncogenes in the pathogenesis of neoplasia is discussed in Chap. 59. With sensitive techniques, clonal cytogenetic abnormalities can be detected in most patients with acute and chronic leukemias. A wide range of cytogenetic abnormalities is associated with the various forms of leukemias, and distinctive nonrandom chromosomal abnormalities are associated with AML, ALL, and CLL, as shown in Table 292-1. Chromosomal rearrangements in leukemic cells may alter the structure or regulation of cellular oncogenes, producing quantitative or qualitative changes in their gene products, which may play a role in initiating or maintaining the leukemic state. Most data suggest the development of leukemia is a multistep process. In many cases, acute leukemia develops in patients with a preexisting myelodysplastic or myeloproliferative disorder.

The pathophysiology of bone marrow failure in leukemia is complex. Pancytopenia is typically present and results at least in part from physical replacement of the normal precursor cells by leukemic cells. Some patients with acute leukemia and pancytopenia have a hypocellular bone marrow indicating that marrow failure is not simply due to overcrowding by leukemic cells. Leukemic cells may directly inhibit normal hematopoiesis via cell-mediated or humoral mechanisms. Alternatively, leukemic cells may occupy critical niches in the bone marrow (stromal) microenvironment and interfere with normal cellular interactions. Normal hematopoietic stem cells do remain in the bone marrow and are capable of proliferating and restoring hematopoiesis following effective antileukemic treatment.

ACUTE LEUKEMIAS—ACUTE LYMPHOCYTIC LEUKEMIA (ALL) AND ACUTE MYELOGENOUS LEUKEMIA (AML)

PATHOLOGY AND CLASSIFICATION The diagnosis of acute leukemia requires the demonstration of leukemic cells in the bone marrow, peripheral blood, or extramedullary tissues. The bone marrow is typically hypercellular with a monomorphic infiltration of leukemic blasts and a marked reduction in normal bone marrow elements. It is critical to distinguish ALL from AML since these two diseases differ in natural history, prognosis, and response to various therapeutic agents.

Acute lymphocytic leukemia can be identified and classified on the basis of morphology and immunologic phenotype related to the stage of lymphoid differentiation. The leukemic lymphoblasts in ALL are typically smaller than myeloblasts (10 to 15 μm in diameter) and often have only a thin rim of agranular cytoplasm. The nucleus may be round or convoluted (see Fig. A5-24). Three morphologic subtypes have been described in the French-American-British classification: L1 cells are small and homogeneous with a regular nuclear membrane and a small nucleolus. L2 cells are larger and have a lower nuclear-cytoplasmic ratio with more pleomorphic size and shape. L2 cells typically have one or more prominent nucleoli. The L3 form of ALL is uncommon, occurring in less than 5 percent of cases; the leukemic cells in this variant contain large vesicular nuclei with basophilic, often vacuolated cytoplasm. L3 cells have a high mitotic index and represent the leukemic form of Burkitt's lymphoma.

Leukemic lymphoblasts in more than 90 percent of patients with ALL contain a nuclear enzyme *terminal deoxynucleotidal transferase* (TdT) which is only rarely present in AML cells. The functional role of this enzyme is not known. TdT is normally found in 1 percent of normal bone marrow cells and is present in immature T and B lymphocytes; it is absent in mature lymphocytes, hairy-cell leukemia, and CLL. The leukemic cells from approximately half of patients with ALL react with the periodic acid Schiff stain showing blocklike inclusions of glycogen. Lymphoblasts do not contain granulocytic or monocytic lysosomal enzymes and therefore do not react with cytochemical stains for peroxidase, Sudan black, and nonspecific esterase.

Several forms of ALL can be defined based upon immunologic phenotype. Approximately 60 percent of cases are termed *common ALL;* the cells are TdT-positive and have the common ALL antigen (CALLA) but do not express surface membrane immunoglobulin or T-cell antigens. These cells are usually derived from precursors of the B-cell lineage, as they may express immature B-cell antigens and have immunoglobulin gene rearrangements. CALLA is not a leukemia-specific antigen since it is present on immature lymphoid cells including approximately 1 percent of cells in the normal bone marrow. About 20 percent of cases of ALL are of the *T-cell type,* where the T lymphoblasts express the E-rosette receptor or other T-lymphocyte-related antigens; these cells are TdT-positive, usually CALLA-negative, and stain positively for acid phosphatase. T-cell ALL typically occurs in adolescent males and is frequently associated with a high leukocyte count and an anterior mediastinal mass. Less than 5 percent of cases of ALL are *B-cell type.* The cells in this variant produce a monoclonal immunoglobulin which is bound to the surface membrane and have L3 morphology. In B-cell ALL, the cells are usually negative for TdT and contain the t(8;14) chromosomal abnormality characteristic of Burkitt's lymphoma. Approximately 15 percent of cases of ALL are termed *null cell type* because the cells do not elaborate CALLA or T- or B-cell antigens.

The leukemic cells in AML are 12 to 20 μm in diameter, larger than lymphoblasts, and have a lower nuclear-cytoplasmic ratio. The leukemic myeloblasts typically have discrete nuclear chromatin and multiple nucleoli. The presence of Auer rods, abnormal primary granules, in the cytoplasm of leukemic cells is diagnostic of AML; these inclusions are present in 10 to 20 percent of patients with AML (see Fig. A5-22). Dysplastic morphologic abnormalities may be prominent in residual granulocytic, erythroid, and megakaryocytic cells. Cytochemical stains are often helpful in distinguishing AML from ALL and in classifying the pathologic subtypes of AML. Myeloperoxidase, α-naphthyl-AS-D-chloracetate esterase, and Sudan black are primarily present in cells undergoing granulocytic differentiation. Nonspecific esterase (α-naphthyl butyrate esterase) stains cells of the monocyte-macrophage lineage. A number of cell surface antigens present in AML cells have also been described. These stains and markers, however, may be negative in leukemias of undifferentiated cells.

A collaborative French-American-British group has divided AML into seven pathologic subtypes based upon the degree of differentiation and maturation of the predominant cells toward granulocytes, monocytes, erythrocytes, or megakaryocytes. The characteristics of each subtype are summarized in Table 292-2. There are only subtle differences in the clinical features of each subtype. Patients with the acute promyelocytic subtype (M3) typically present with disseminated intravascular coagulation (DIC) induced by thromboplastic material released by the leukemic cells; DIC is usually present at the time of diagnosis and may be markedly exacerbated during chemotherapy. Acute myelomonocytic leukemia (M4) and acute monocytic leukemia (M5) are more likely than other subtypes to have extramedullary involvement of the skin, gingiva, central nervous system, and other tissues.

It is often difficult to distinguish the undifferentiated form of AML (M1) from the L2 form of ALL by morphology alone. In these cases additional studies including cytochemical stains and analysis of myeloid and lymphoid antigens are required. Electron microscopy may be helpful in some cases to demonstrate small numbers of promyelocytic granules in cells that appear undifferentiated by light microscopy.

The cellular blood elements are derived from pluripotent and committed hematopoietic stem cells which reside in the bone marrow.

TABLE 292-2 Morphologic subtypes of AML

Subtype	% of AML	Morphology	Peroxidase Sudan black	Nonspecific esterase	PAS*
			Reactivity with special strains		
M1 Acute undifferentiated leukemia	20	Few if any azurophilic granules	+/−	+/−	−
M2 AML with differentiation	30	Blasts with promyelocytic granules, Auer rods may be present	+++	+/−	+
M3 Promyelocytic leukemia	5	Hypergranular promyelocytes often with multiple Auer rods per cell	+++	+	+
M4 Acute myelomonocytic leukemia	30	Monocytoid-appearing cells in peripheral blood associated with serum lysozyme	++	+++	+ +/+
M5 Acute monocytic leukemia	10	Two subtypes identified: (a) undifferenitated; (b) differentiated associated with serum lysozyme	+/−	+++	+ +/+
M6 Acute erythroleukemia	5	Predominance of erythroblasts and markedly dysplastic erythroid precursors	−	−	++
M7 Acute megakaryocytic leukemia	5	Undifferentiated blasts react with antiplatelet antibodies and contain platelet peroxidase	−	+/−	+

* *Periodic acid Schiff.*

Leukemic transformation may occur in cells at several levels of differentiation. In some patients with AML who are heterozygous for glucose 6-phosphate dehydrogenase (G6PD) isoenzymes, the granulocytes, macrophages, erythrocytes, and megakaryocytes all contain the single G6PD isoenzyme present in the leukemic cells, suggesting that these cells are derived from the malignant clone and that leukemic transformation involved a pluripotent stem cell. In other AML patients, only granulocytes and/or macrophages appear monoclonal, and in these patients, transformation may have occurred at the level of the committed granulocytic-macrophage progenitor. Some patients appear to have a *biphenotypic acute leukemia*. In these patients, subpopulations of malignant cells contain both myeloid and lymphoid markers. These cells may represent leukemias of primitive pluripotent stem cells, or more likely they result from aberrant gene expression in a transformed myeloid or lymphoid progenitor.

Some patients develop AML after a preleukemic syndrome. The preleukemic and myelodysplastic syndromes are a heterogeneous group of disorders, and the nomenclature describing them is confusing and poorly standardized. These syndromes generally occur in middle-aged or elderly patients. Sometimes included under the heading of myelodysplastic syndromes are refractory anemia with excessive blasts, chronic myelomonocytic leukemia, and acquired idiopathic sideroblastic anemia. The term *preleukemia* should be reserved to refer to a recognizable syndrome of hematopoietic dysfunction that typically precedes the classic findings of AML. This syndrome is usually characterized by a picture of ineffective hematopoiesis with anemia, thrombocytopenia, and sometimes granulocytopenia associated with a hypercellular, dysplastic bone marrow. In preleukemia, the leukemic clone is already established, and usually there is progressive impairment of hematopoiesis and accumulation of blasts. Megaloblastic hematopoiesis is common, and folate or vitamin B_{12} deficiency must be ruled out. Cytogenetic abnormalities are frequent; the most common chromosomal abnormalities are $5q-$, -5, -7, and trisomy 8. When $5q-$ exists as the sole abnormality, the patient usually presents with refractory anemia associated with mild thrombocytosis. Many patients with preleukemic or myelodysplastic syndromes never develop overt AML but die from complications of bone marrow failure. Smoldering AML refers to a syndrome in which the diagnostic features of acute leukemia are present, but the disease follows an indolent or subacute course. This disorder also tends to occur in elderly patients.

CLINICAL AND LABORATORY FEATURES   Acute lymphocytic leukemia (ALL) and AML share many clinical features. In the majority of patients, the initial symptoms of acute leukemia are present for less than 3 months. A preleukemic syndrome can be identified in approximately 25 percent of patients with AML; in these patients, anemia and other cytopenias are usually present for months to years preceding the development of overt leukemia.

Patients with ALL and AML may present with pancytopenia without circulating blasts, with a normal leukocyte count, or with marked leukocytosis. Leukostasis due to occlusion of the microcirculation by leukemic blast cells can lead to hypoperfusion of vital tissues, most commonly lung and brain. Leukostasis becomes increasingly common when the number of circulating blasts exceeds 100×10^9 per liter. Patients may complain of manifestations of anemia such as pallor, easy fatigability, and dyspnea on mild exertion. The metabolic activity of large numbers of blasts can lead to artifactual results in laboratory tests, especially glucose and potassium concentrations and arterial blood gas analysis.

Bleeding is a major problem in patients with acute leukemia and is primarily related to thrombocytopenia. Coagulation defects may also be present. In some patients, megakaryocytes are derived from the leukemic clone and produce platelets with abnormal function. Petechiae and easy bruisability are common. Hemorrhage becomes increasingly common when the platelet count is less than 20×10^9 per liter, typically occurring from oral (particularly gingiva) and gastrointestinal mucous membranes. Spontaneous bleeding involving the central nervous system, lungs, or other viscera may also occur.

Infection is a frequent complication of acute leukemia. The incidence of infection is inversely related to the number of circulating granulocytes and becomes a major risk in patients with granulocyte counts less than 0.5×10^9 per liter. Granulocytes derived from leukemic progenitors may also function abnormally, further compromising host defenses. The leukemia and its treatment cause a breakdown of mucosal barriers, and systemic infections usually develop from organisms colonizing the skin, throat, and gastrointestinal tract. Common sites of infections in patients with acute leukemia include the skin, gingiva, perirectal tissues, lung, and urinary tract. Septicemia often occurs without an apparent source. Gram-negative bacteria, gram-positive cocci, and *Candida* species are frequent pathogens.

Hepatomegaly and splenomegaly due to leukemic infiltration are present in approximately one-half to three-fourths of patients with ALL and a minority of patients with AML. This visceral involvement can produce symptoms of nausea, abdominal fullness, or early satiety. Lymphadenopathy is more common in ALL than in AML. An anterior mediastinal mass is usually present in patients with the T-cell variant of ALL, and rarely occurs in other forms of ALL or in AML. Acute leukemia may infiltrate into extramedullary tissues such as the skin, lung, eye, nasopharynx, or kidneys. Testicular involvement is particularly common in males with ALL. Soft tissue masses of leukemic cells, "chloromas," can develop in any location. Occasionally, extramedullary leukemia can precede detectable involvement in the bone marrow.

Symptoms related to the expanding malignant cell mass, such as bone pain and sternal tenderness, occur in approximately half of patients with acute leukemia; osteolytic lesions are rare. Renal abnormalities can develop as a result of leukemic infiltration, ureteral obstruction by uric acid stones or enlarged lymph nodes, urate nephropathy, or from infectious or hemorrhagic complications. Gastrointestinal symptoms of early satiety, distention, and constipation may result from organomegaly or from leukemic infiltration or bleeding into the bowel and other viscera.

In acute leukemia, the neoplastic cells may infiltrate into the subarachnoid space, causing leukemic meningitis or direct involvement of the brain or spinal cord parenchyma. Neurologic involvement can only rarely be demonstrated at the time of diagnosis, but the central nervous system is a frequent site of relapse, particularly in patients with ALL. The first symptoms of leukemic meningitis are usually headache and nausea. Papilledema, cranial nerve palsies, seizures, and altered mentation develop with disease progression. Cytocentrifuge preparations of cerebrospinal fluid (CSF) characteristically reveal leukemic blast cells, the CSF protein concentration is increased, and the glucose reduced.

Patients with acute leukemia often develop metabolic abnormalities. Hyponatremia and hypokalemia are common due to renal tubular abnormalities induced by lysozyme or other products of the leukemic cells. The serum lactic acid dehydrogenase (LDH) level may be increased. Hyperuricemia may be present due to accelerated turnover of cells with increased purine release, and lactic acidosis rarely occurs in patients with a large burden of leukemic cells.

TREATMENT OF ACUTE LEUKEMIA: GENERAL CONSIDERATIONS   The growth of leukemic cells follows a Gompertzian growth curve with near exponential growth at a lower cell mass and progressive slowing of the growth rate at higher leukemic cell burdens. The leukemic mass is usually between 10^{11} to 10^{12} cells at the time of diagnosis. Chemotherapeutic agents produce a fractional cell kill, that is, a percentage of tumor cells (not an absolute number) is killed with each course of treatment. Most chemotherapeutic regimens employed for acute leukemias are probably capable of a 3 to 5 log kill, resulting in the elimination of 99.9 to 99.999 percent of the leukemia cells. Another potential effect of some chemotherapeutic drugs is to induce differentiation and maturation of the leukemic cells to mature nonproliferating cells. When the leukemia cell mass is reduced below approximately 10^9 cells, leukemia can no longer be detected in the blood or bone marrow, and the patient appears to be in complete remission. The clinical criteria for complete remission include (1) less than 5 percent blasts in the bone marrow and absence of leukemic cells in the peripheral blood, (2) the restoration of normal peripheral blood counts, and (3) the absence of physical findings attributable to extramedullary involvement of the leukemia. If no further treatment is given, however, the residual clonogenic leukemic cells will proliferate, leading to relapse.

The treatment of acute leukemia is divided into distinct phases. *Remission induction chemotherapy* is the most critical phase. Intensive systemic chemotherapy is administered with the goal of reducing the leukemic cell mass below the level of detection. After remission is achieved, additional systemic chemotherapy must be given to further reduce the leukemic cell mass and, ideally, eradicate the leukemia. Intensive chemotherapy administered immediately following remission induction is referred to as *consolidation* or *early intensification* treatment. Lower dose chemotherapy that is generally continued over several years is referred to as *maintenance treatment*. Intensive chemotherapy administered more than 6 months after remission induction is termed *late intensification*. Another aspect of treatment involves local chemotherapy or radiation to frequent sites of relapse which are considered to be sanctuary sites, such as the central nervous system where systemic treatment may fail to eradicate the disease. The value of these forms of treatment for ALL and AML will be discussed separately.

Supportive care The supportive care of patients with pancytopenia is a critical aspect of the treatment of acute leukemia. This primarily involves the appropriate administration of blood products and management of infections.

Adequate levels of hemoglobin can usually be maintained with transfusions of packed red blood cells. An adequate number of circulating platelets can initially be attained by transfusions of platelets from unselected donors, but some transfused patients eventually develop antiplatelet antibodies which shorten platelet survival and render the patient unresponsive to further platelet transfusions. Patients who fail to respond to transfusions of platelets from unselected donors may respond to platelets from an HLA-identical donor. The risk of spontaneous hemorrhage is directly related to the degree of thrombocytopenia. It is generally advisable to transfuse platelets to maintain the platelet count above 20×10^9 per liter. Also, uterine bleeding should be minimized in menstruating women with thrombocytopenia by administering an anovulatory agent.

The potential therapeutic benefit of granulocyte transfusions has been extensively studied in patients receiving treatment for acute leukemia. Most data indicate that survival is not improved by granulocyte transfusions either to prevent infections or to treat documented infections, and that their routine use cannot be recommended. The major limitations in the use of granulocyte transfusions are the current technical difficulty in collecting sufficient numbers of granulocytes from normal donors and the adverse effects associated with their transfusion such as fever, leukoagglutination, pulmonary infiltrates, and transmission of cytomegalovirus (CMV) and other infections.

The prevention and treatment of infections is of critical importance in the management of patients with acute leukemia. Since most infections are caused by organisms colonizing the skin and gastrointestinal tract, a variety of approaches have been evaluated to suppress the endogenous flora in these sites. Most centers recommend the use of face masks, careful hand washing, oral nonabsorbable antibiotics, and reverse isolation for granulocytopenic patients. The development of bacterial and fungal infections may be delayed or avoided by these measures.

Granulocytopenic patients who develop fever or other signs of infection require prompt evaluation and treatment. Fever is usually due to a bacterial, fungal, or viral infection. Gram-negative sepsis is common in this setting and may be rapidly fatal. Granulocytopenic patients with unexplained fever or overt infections should be evaluated and receive empiric treatment for a presumed bacterial infection until a definitive diagnosis can be established. A combination of broad-spectrum antibiotics, such as an aminoglycoside or a third-generation cephalosporin in combination with a semisynthetic penicillin, should be employed and modified when the results of bacterial and fungal cultures are available. Systemic fungal infections are also common in granulocytopenic patients with leukemia and should be suspected in patients who fail to respond to antibiotic or who respond and develop recurrent fever. Definitive diagnosis of fungal infections may be difficult, and a therapeutic trial of amphotericin B is often indicated. The problem of infections in the immunocompromised host is discussed in Chap. 84.

TREATMENT OF ACUTE LYMPHOBLASTIC LEUKEMIA The treatment of ALL is one of the major successes in modern oncology. Forty years ago the disease was uniformly fatal and had a median survival of only 3 months. With current therapy, more than 50 percent of children with ALL achieve long-term remissions and probable cure. Adults and high-risk subgroups of children with ALL do not have a good prognosis, and long-term remissions are only achieved in a minority of patients. Therapy for ALL consists of three phases: (1) remission induction chemotherapy (2) central nervous system prophylaxis, and (3) continuation (maintenance) chemotherapy.

The goal of remission induction chemotherapy is to eliminate all clinical signs and morphologic evidence of leukemia, as well as to restore normal bone marrow function. The intensity of treatment is important, because the duration of remission is prolonged by reducing the leukemic cell burden to the smallest possible fraction.

The combination of vincristine and prednisone plus either L-asparaginase or daunorubicin induces complete remissions in over 90 percent of children with ALL within 4 weeks. Some patients with persistent leukemia may achieve remission with 2 to 4 additional weeks of treatment with the same or alternate drugs. Failure to achieve remission can be attributed primarily to the development of drug resistance, severe infections, or central nervous system (CNS) leukemia.

In patients who achieve remission, local prophylactic treatment to the CNS is required to prevent leukemic meningitis. The rationale for this treatment is based on the hypothesis that circulating leukemic cells infiltrate into the CNS and cerebrospinal fluid early in the course of the disease. Since the drugs used in remission induction in ALL penetrate poorly into the cerebrospinal fluid, these leukemic cells are sheltered from the effects of systemic chemotherapy. Over the ensuing months these cells may proliferate, producing overt leukemic meningitis. Leukemic meningitis is the initial site of relapse in up to two-thirds of patients with ALL who do not receive prophylactic therapy. Prophylactic treatment to the CNS, instituted immediately after remission induction, has been successful in dramatically reducing the incidence of CNS relapse. Most centers employ 24-Gy (2400-rad) whole-brain radiation in combination with intrathecal methotrexate. Cranial irradiation does produce subtle abnormalities in neurologic function, particularly in young children, and there is considerable interest in evaluating lower-dose radiotherapy regimens or alternative methods of CNS treatment. Preliminary data suggest that the combination of intrathecal and high-dose systemic methotrexate may provide adequate prophylactic treatment to the CNS.

Since patients in remission still harbor leukemia cells, further systemic treatment is required to prevent or delay leukemic relapse. The optimal approach to continuation therapy involves the administration of combination chemotherapy given in doses approaching maximal tolerance. As a rule, the drugs that are effective in inducing remission in ALL have not been useful in maintenance chemotherapy. The combination of 6-mercaptopurine and methotrexate is the most frequently employed maintenance regimen, but more intensive consolidation and maintenance regimens are required for adult patients and children with poor prognostic features.

The optimal duration of maintenance chemotherapy is unknown. Many patients can discontinue chemotherapy after 2 to 3 years and remain in long-term remission. Up to one-quarter of patients will relapse, however, after maintenance therapy is discontinued. It is not known whether maintenace therapy given for more than 3 years will further reduce the likelihood of relapse. Since there is currently no method to reliably detect small numbers of residual leukemic cells, there is no objective means to determine when therapy can be safely discontinued.

Complications of therapy for ALL   Chemotherapy-induced myelo-suppression and immunosuppression are inevitable side effects of the treatment for ALL. The chemotherapy directed toward the leukemic lymphoblasts also affects normal T and B lymphocytes, resulting in lymphocytopenia and immunodeficiency. Peripheral blood B cells generally recover to normal levels within several months after treatment is discontinued, but T-cell numbers and function may remain depressed for up to 1 year. *Pneumocystis carinii* pneumonia can occur while patients are in remission; trimethoprim-sulfamethox-azole prophylaxis is effective in preventing this complication. Growth in children is somewhat retarded during the administration of chemo-therapy. Catch-up growth generally occurs once therapy is discontin-ued, and most children ultimately attain normal height and weight. Sterility may result from treatment with most chemotherapeutic agents and irradiation. Gonadal function may recover after a prolonged interval. The gonads in prepubertal patients are relatively resistant to the effects of chemotherapy, and most patients undergo normal puberty after therapy is discontinued.

Prognosis in ALL   The two factors most affecting prognosis are age and the leukocyte count at the time of diagnosis. Children between the ages of 3 and 9 years with white blood counts less than 10×10^9 per liter have the best prognosis; 50 to 70 percent achieve long-term survival and probable cure with current treatment. Older patients and those with higher leukocyte counts have a poorer prognosis. Fewer than 20 percent of adults with ALL are long-term survivors in most series, and it is uncertain whether the maintenance therapy which is effective in children is of benefit for adults. Males have a worse prognosis than females, due in part to the problem of testicular relapse. In children, patients with the L1 morphologic subtype have a better prognosis than the L2 form, but this is probably not true in adults. Patients with T-cell ALL tend to have a poorer prognosis than the common ALL (CALLA) subgroup. These patients are generally older and present with a high white blood count, and it is uncertain if T-cell type, per se, is an independent poor prognostic factor. The B-cell (L3) variant of ALL has the worst prognosis.

Chromosomal abnormalities provide independent prognostic in-formation. Approximately one-half of the patients with ALL have detectable cytogenetic abnormalities, including hypodiploidy, pseu-dodiploidy, or hyperdiploidy. A number of nonrandom chromosomal abnormalities are associated with ALL. Approximately 10 percent of patients with ALL have the Philadelphia (Ph¹) chromosome, an abnormality typical of chronic myelogenous leukemia. Associated with ALL, and possibly with hybrid (biphenotypic) leukemias, is t(4;11). Patients with pseudodiploidy, particularly t(4;11) and t(9;22), have a poor prognosis, while patients with hyperdiploidy have a better prognosis.

Remission and survival rates in adult patients with ALL (those over 15 years of age) are significantly lower than for children with the same disease. Remission induction rates in adults and high-risk children are generally between 50 to 70 percent following treatment with vincristine, prednisone, and daunorubicin; the median duration of remission is 10 to 12 months, and the 5-year survival rate is 10 to 30 percent with standard maintenance chemotherapy. Several centers have reported improved results with more intensive, multiple-drug consolidation and maintenance programs, but the optimal therapy for high-risk forms of ALL is uncertain.

Treatment of recurrent ALL   Leukemia may recur either in the bone marrow or in extramedullary sites. Patients who relapse while receiving maintenance therapy have a very poor prognosis with little possibility of a long-term second remission. Combination chemo-therapy with a three- or four-drug regimen including vincristine, prednisone, L-asparaginase, and/or daunorubicin results in a second remission in 50 to 70 percent of these patients. Remission duration,

however, is usually brief, and subsequent relapse is inevitable. Patients who relapse after discontinuation of maintenance therapy have a better prognosis. Second remissions can be induced in about 90 percent of these patients. Although most will relapse again, some have achieved long-term survival. These patients should probably have CNS prophylaxis repeated to prevent recurrent disease in this extramedullary site.

Meningeal leukemia is the most common site of extramedullary relapse in patients with ALL. Cranial irradiation plus intrathecal methotrexate alone or in combination with cytarabine is the standard therapy for CNS leukemia. Testicular relapse is common in male patients with ALL and may occur during or after cessation of maintenance therapy. The treatment of choice is irradiation of the affected testicle. Patients with extramedullary relapse involving the CNS, testes, or other tissues are at very high risk for subsequent relapse in the bone marrow. Systemic reinduction therapy is indicated and may prevent generalized relapse of ALL.

TREATMENT OF ACUTE MYELOGENOUS LEUKEMIA   The initial goal in the treatment of AML is to induce a complete hematologic remission. The drugs active in AML have little selectivity for leukemic cells over their normal bone marrow counterparts. Induction of severe myelosuppression is necessary in order to achieve a complete remis-sion. The two most active drugs are cytarabine and daunorubicin. The combination of these agents with or without 6-thioguanine results in a complete remission rate of 60 to 80 percent. If residual leukemia is present 2 to 4 weeks after chemotherapy, the treatment is repeated. Patients who fail to enter remission with this approach have a poor prognosis.

Patients with AML who achieve complete remission still have a substantial number of residual leukemic cells. Further therapy is required to reduce and hopefully to eradicate these occult leukemia cells. The benefits of available forms of consolidation and maintenance treatment are controversial. The best results have been achieved in patients receiving one to three intensive cycles of consolidation chemotherapy using agents such as daunorubicin, cytarabine, 6-thioguanine, 5-azacitidine, and amsacrine. Median remission du-ration varies from 9 months to 2 years in most series. Ten to thirty percent of patients survive over 5 years free of disease, and most of these patients are probably cured. Better results have been reported in preliminary studies using very intensive consolidation regimens, including high-dose cytarabine alone or in combination with other drugs. The results of these studies suggest a benefit for patients receiving consolidation treatment when compared to historical con-trols, but these observations remain to be confirmed in prospectively controlled clinical trials.

Although some uncontrolled studies suggested that maintenace therapy with lower doses of these same agents or late intensification treatment improved remission duration, recent prospective controlled studies reported no benefit for patients receiving this form of treatment. Current data suggest that the major benefit in therapy is achieved with intensive induction and consolidation treatment.

Most patients who achieve complete remission will ultimately relapse. At that point, the disease is usually much less responsive to therapy; only a minority of patients achieve a brief second remission, and median survival is 3 to 6 months.

Central nervous system leukemia in AML occurs in 10 to 20 percent of patients at some point in their disease, and most commonly develops in patients with monocytic (M5) or myelomonocytic (M4) subtypes. Unlike ALL, the CNS is rarely an isolated site of relapse in AML; CNS involvement usually occurs in the setting of systemic relapse. This may not be a biologically important leukemic sanctuary in patients with AML, and prophylactic treatment to the CNS has not improved remission duration or survival. Patients who develop meningeal leukemia are treated with cranial irradiation and intrathecal chemotherapy with cytarabine and/or methotrexate.

Prognostic factors in AML   Chromosomal abnormalities in AML are of prognostic value; patients with abnormalities such as t(8;21), t(15;17), or inv 16 tend to have a relatively good prognosis, while −5, −7, t(9;22), and complex chromosomal abnormalities are associated with a poor prognosis.

Age is a major prognostic factor in many series; elderly patients (over 70 years of age) are less likely to achieve complete remission. This group also tolerates intensive therapy poorly and is more difficult to support through the complications of pancytopenia. In addition, elderly patients are more likely to have leukemic cells with poor-risk chromosomal abnormalities such as −7, −5 and are more likely to have a defined preleukemic syndrome. However, elderly patients who do achieve remission have a similar remission duration and survival as younger patients. Since the major factor influencing survival is the achievement of complete remission, intensive chemotherapy should be administered to most elderly patients.

The leukemic subtype is of limited prognostic significance. Acute promyelocytic leukemia (M3) is typically associated with disseminated intravascular coagulation, and fatal CNS hemorrhage is a common complication during remission induction chemotherapy for this type of leukemia. Prophylactic heparin therapy is generally indicated during induction treatment to suppress DIC and prevent hemorrhagic complications. Patients with promyelocytic leukemia who do achieve remission appear to have a greater chance of long-term survival than other subgroups. Patients with monocytic or myelomonocytic leukemia may have a poorer prognosis than the M1 to M3 subgroups.

Patients with preleukemia evolving into AML or smoldering leukemia respond poorly to chemotherapy; less than half of these patients achieve complete remission. Such patients also tend to have prolonged bone marrow aplasia following treatment and often succumb to complications of pancytopenia. Patients who do achieve remission have a similar remission duration as patients with de novo AML, and intensive induction therapy is usually indicated. No treatment has been consistently effective during the preleukemic phase, and chemotherapy should be withheld until progressive overt leukemia develops. Low-dose cytarabine has been reported to be successful in selected patients with preleukemia or smoldering AML; this therapy will transiently worsen cytopenias, and responses tend to be brief. An innovative approach to therapy for preleukemia involves agents such as retinoic acid which induce cellular diferentiation. A small number of patients with preleukemia have had improvement in peripheral blood counts with retinoic acid therapy, but it is uncertain whether progression to overt leukemia is delayed or if survival is improved. Patients who develop acute leukemia after a preexisting myeloproliferative disorder or paroxysmal nocturnal hemoglobinuria also have a poor prognosis.

Patients who receive cytotoxic chemotherapy with or without concomitant extensive radiation therapy have an increased risk of developing AML. Secondary or treatment-related leukemia is most commonly associated with prolonged therapy with alkylating agents, nitrosoureas, or procarbazine, and has been seen primarily in patients with Hodgkin's disease, multiple myeloma, and ovarian carcinoma. Almost all of the patients with treatment-related AML have chromosomal abnormalities, usually hypodiploidy with −5 and/or −7. These patients typically develop a preleukemic syndrome with pancytopenia several months before overt AML is recognized. They respond poorly to chemotherapy, and despite treatment, median survival is only 3 months after development of AML.

Other factors such as white blood and platelet counts, LDH level, and the presence of fever and hemorrhage have been reported to have prognostic importance. The impact of each of these variables is uncertain.

IMMUNOTHERAPY FOR ACUTE LEUKEMIAS Immunotherapy has been reported to be capable of suppressing small numbers of tumor cells in experimental animals. As such, immunotherapy has been evaluated to prevent leukemic relapse from the residual leukemic cells remaining after induction treatment in patients with ALL and AML. Unfortunately, clinical trials with nonspecific immune potentiating agents such as bacillus Calmette-Guérin (BCG), *Corynebacterium parvum*, or levamisole have not shown any benefit in prolonging the duration of remission. There are no convincing data to support the use of currently available immunotherapy in patients with either ALL or AML.

BONE MARROW TRANSPLANTATION FOR ACUTE LEUKEMIAS Bone marrow transplantation from an identical twin or an HLA-identical sibling donor is effective treatment for both ALL and AML. The objective of this approach is to administer very high doses of chemotherapy alone or with total-body irradiation, and then to rescue the patient from severe myelosuppression by the transplantation of bone marrow from a normal donor. In addition, the transplantation of allogenic bone marrow may confer an immune-mediated graft-versus-leukemia effect. The current results with bone marrow transplantation are summarized in Table 292-3. Bone marrow transplantation is discussed in detail in Chap. 291.

Allogeneic bone marrow transplantation is associated with substantial risks. Approximately one-third of patients transplanted for leukemia will die from transplant-related complications including graft-versus-host disease, interstitial pneumonitis, and opportunistic infections. Most centers limit the use of bone marrow transplantation to patients under 45 years of age, since older patients generally have a poor outcome. Reports from several centers indicate that 10 to 15 percent of otherwise end-stage patients with refractory leukemia have achieved long-term disease-free survival and probable cure following bone marrow transplantation. Although only a small proportion of patients in this category benefit, the results compare favorably to those obtained with other forms of treatment.

These survival figures are substantially improved when bone marrow transplantation is performed during remission, the burden of leukemic cells is low, and the patients are in relatively good general condition. Because many patients with ALL can achieve a prolonged initial remission with chemotherapy, bone marrow transplantation has generally been reserved for patients in second remission; in this group 30 to 60 percent have achieved prolonged survival with marrow transplantation. It is uncertain whether patients with high-risk forms of ALL should receive marrow transplants in first complete remission.

Approximately 30 percent of patients with AML transplanted in early relapse or second remission have achieved long-term survival. There is controversy whether patients with AML should receive allogenic bone marrow transplantation or postremission chemotherapy while in first complete remission. Over 500 marrow transplants have been reported in this setting. It is clear that the risk of recurrent leukemia is lower following bone marrow transplantation than with postremission chemotherapy; however, bone marrow transplantation is more likely to be associated with fatal treatment complications. Overall 3- to 5-year survival is 40 to 60 percent with bone marrow transplantation compared with 10 to 50 percent survival achieved with optimal chemotherapy. Patient age appears to be a major prognostic factor with bone marrow transplantation; the best results have been reported in children and young adults. Although young patients probably have better results with bone marrow transplantation

TABLE 292-3 Representative results of bone marrow transplantation (BMT) compared with conventional chemotherapy for AML and ALL

	Survival >3 Years, %	
	BMT	Chemotherapy
ALL		
First remission	30–60	20–70*
Second remission	30–50	<10
Third remission or relapse	10–20	0
AML		
First remission	40–60	10–50
Second remission or early relapse	30	<10
Third remission or relapse	10–20	0

* Best results in children with low white blood count.

than with chemotherapy, it is uncertain whether this is true for patients over 30 years of age. One major limitation of bone marrow transplantation as a general therapeutic approach is that only a minority of patients are currently eligible; most patients are either too old to be considered or lack an HLA-identical donor.

Autologous bone marrow transplantation has been evaluated in patients with acute leukemia who lack a histocompatible donor for allogeneic transplantation. With this therapy, remission bone marrow is collected and cryopreserved. The patient may then receive intensive chemoradiotherapy followed by reinfusion of the cryopreserved bone marrow. Since remission bone marrow is likely to contain small numbers of residual leukemic cells, the bone marrow has usually been treated with antileukemic monoclonal antibodies or chemotherapy prior to cryopreservation. Selected patients with ALL and AML transplanted in first or second remission have achieved prolonged survival, but further studies are required to critically assess the efficacy of autologous marrow transplantation for acute leukemia.

SUMMARY AND FUTURE DIRECTIONS IN ACUTE LEUKEMIA   Effective induction chemotherapy capable of inducing remission in most patients with ALL and AML is now available, but long-term survival has been achieved in only a minority of patients. In the next decade, the focus of clinical research should be toward measures to prolong the duration of remission. Innovative methods of consolidation treatment with intensive chemotherapy or high-dose chemoradiotherapy and bone marrow transplantation must be evaluated for their effect on remission duration and survival. It will also be important to develop effective but less toxic approaches for favorable prognostic groups such as children with low-risk forms of ALL to improve the quality of life in long-term survivors. Innovative new therapies are required for poor-risk groups, particularly the elderly and patients with preleukemic syndromes.

Sensitive techniques to detect residual leukemia during morphologic complete remission must also be developed to help guide the intensity and duration of treatment. Most importantly, new and effective drugs are required with selectivity toward leukemic cells which would spare the host from morbidity and mortality attendant to the currently available agents.

CHRONIC LYMPHOCYTIC LEUKEMIA

Chronic lymphocytic leukemia (CLL) is a hematologic neoplasm characterized by the accumulation of mature-appearing lymphocytes in the peripheral blood associated with infiltration of the bone marrow, spleen, and lymph nodes. The disease is uncommon before the fourth decade of life and is usually seen in patients over 50 years of age. It is the most common form of chronic leukemia in the United States but is rare in Orientals. CLL is more frequent in males than females.

CLL represents a clonal expansion of neoplastic B lymphocytes in more than 95 percent of cases. These cells commonly have trisomy 12 alone or with additional chromosomal abnormalities. Clonality has also been demonstrated by expression of a single light chain (kappa or lambda) or immunoglobulin idiotype specificity. In less than 5 percent of cases, CLL may be due to an expansion of T lymphocytes. An unusual type of T-cell CLL is seen in patients with ataxia-telangiectasia and is often associated with a translocation of genetic material between the number 14 chromosomes (t14;14).

The diagnosis of CLL can usually be made on the basis of physical examination and a review of the peripheral blood smear. Leukocytosis is present, and the malignant cells characteristically appear as morphologically normal small lymphocytes (see Fig. A5-23). They have markers of B lymphocytes. In most cases a monoclonal immunoglobulin can be demonstrated on the cell surface, although immunofluorescent staining is usually weak. Monoclonal surface IgM with or without IgD is characteristically present, and a small amount of this IgM paraprotein can often be detected in the serum with sensitive techniques. The CLL cells also have receptors for the Fc portion of IgG, and complement receptors may or may not be present.

Most patients develop some degree of hypogammaglobulinemia. Approximately 5 percent of patients have the T-cell form of CLL. The neoplastic cells form rosettes with sheep erythrocytes and contain other T-cell surface markers. T-cell CLL cannot usually be distinguished from B-cell CLL morphologically.

It is important to distinguish early CLL from reactive lymphocytosis in asymptomatic patients. In reactive lymphocytosis, the cells are polyclonal and predominantly T lymphocytes, whereas in CLL they are usually B cells. The demonstration of monoclonal surface membrane immunoglobulin unambiguously defines a B-cell lymphocytosis as neoplastic. T-cell CLL must be distinguished from Sézary syndrome where the cells have a characteristic lobulated nucleus and there is extensive skin involvement. T-cell CLL also must be distinguished from adult T-cell leukemia (ATL). Prolymphocytic leukemia is a CLL variant seen in older people and is characterized by massive splenomegaly, usually in the absence of lymphadenopathy. The neoplastic cell in prolymphocytic leukemia usually is of B-cell origin. It is larger than that seen in CLL and has a prominent nucleolus. Prolymphocytic leukemia is typically associated with very high white counts (in excess of 200×10^9 per liter) and a poor response to therapy. Lymphosarcoma cell leukemia represents a leukemic phase of lymphocytic lymphoma and is typically an aggressive disease (Chap. 294). The cellular morphology is suggestive of an acute rather than a chronic leukemia. Monoclonal immunoglobulin is usually easily detected on these cells, and the fluorescent staining is bright, often with spontaneous capping. Hairy-cell leukemia is distinguished on the basis of the typical cellular morphology and the presence of tartrate-resistant acid phosphatase in the hairy cells. Waldenström's macroglobulinemia is differentiated from CLL on the basis of bone marrow morphology and lower white blood cell counts, and the secretion of a large amount of a monoclonal IgM paraprotein.

CLINICAL FEATURES   The clinical features of CLL are very different from acute leukemia. In more than 25 percent of patients with CLL, the disorder is discovered as an incidental finding. The common practice of ordering routine complete blood counts in adults has led to an earlier diagnosis of CLL in asymptomatic patients. The signs and symptoms of CLL usually relate to tissue infiltration, peripheral blood cytopenias, or immunosuppression. Patients may present with symptoms of anemia, lymph node enlargement, or intercurrent infection. Splenomegaly seldom leads to symptoms, and the liver is minimally enlarged in only about half of patients.

The white cell count ranges between 15×10^9 and 200×10^9 per liter, with a preponderance of mature-appearing lymphocytes. There is little correlation between the leukocyte count and symptomatology. Patients with advanced disease may present with anemia, granulocytopenia, and thrombocytopenia resulting from bone marrow infiltration by the leukemic cells. About 20 percent of patients develop a Coombs-positive autoimmune hemolytic anemia during the course of their disease. Occasionally, autoimmune thrombocytopenia may occur. Rarely, CLL evolves into an aggressive lymphocytic lymphoma referred to as *Richter's syndrome*, which is believed to be due to a clonal evolution of the original leukemia.

TREATMENT   The therapeutic objectives in CLL differ sharply from those for the acute leukemias. The available drugs and radiation therapies are incapable of eradicating the leukemia and producing true complete remissions. Current therapy is effective to reduce the lymphocyte count and lymphadenopathy and to palliate symptoms produced by the leukemia. There is little evidence, however, that survival is substantially affected.

Although a number of prognostic classifications of CLL have been suggested, the new international classification appears most useful (Table 292–4). Prognosis correlates well with stage of disease; however, the rate of progression of patients from one stage to another is highly variable. Patients with stage A disease, in which the disease is limited to lymphocytosis alone or lymphocytosis plus limited lymphadenopathy, have a good prognosis. Median survival exceeds 7 years; these patients usually require no treatment. Patients with

TABLE 292-4 International workshop on CLL staging classification

Stage	Description	Median survival, years
A	Lymphocytosis with clinical involvement of fewer than 3 lymph node groups*; no anemia or thrombocytopenia	>10
B	More than 3 lymph node groups* involved	5
C	Anemia or thrombocytopenia regardless of number of lymph node groups involved	2

* Lymph node groups—cervical, axillary, inguinal, liver, spleen.

more substantial lymphadenopathy and hepatosplenomegaly (stage B) have an intermediate prognosis with a median survival of approximately 5 years. Patients with anemia or thrombocytopenia (stage C) have a worse prognosis with a median survival of less than 2 years.

The indications for therapy in CLL include hemolytic anemia, important cytopenias, disfiguring lymphadenopathy, symptomatic organomegaly, or marked systemic symptoms. When treatment is required, the cornerstone of therapy is usually an alkylating agent. Chlorambucil is the most frequently prescribed drug for CLL at a recommended daily dose of 0.1 to 0.2 mg/kg per day. The chlorambucil dose is generally reduced and the drug is eventually stopped when the lymphocyte count falls below 20×10^9 per liter. The drug may also be given in pulses every 3 to 6 weeks, or continuously in low daily doses. Cyclophosphamide appears to be as effective as chlorambucil in the treatment of CLL. Maintenance therapy has no definite value, and continuing alkylating agent therapy may increase the risk of future development of AML.

Glucocorticosteroids are useful for CLL in special circumstances. These drugs do not have a prominent lympholytic effect in CLL and are therefore not effective as primary therapy. Glucocorticosteroids are useful, however, in the treatment of associated Coombs-positive hemolytic anemia or immune thrombocytopenia, and may be transiently effective in treating patients with pancytopenia and the "packed marrow" syndrome. Glucocorticosteroids have important side effects, including a predisposition to opportunistic infection. In more advanced CLL, combination chemotherapy may be useful. Regimens that include an alkylating agent, vincristine, and prednisone are often employed. Splenectomy may be indicated in patients with hypersplenism, refractory hemolytic anemia, or thrombocytopenia. Radiation therapy may occasionally be useful for control of localized disease, and total-body radiation has rarely been useful in palliating end-stage disease. In preliminary trials, interferon does not appear to be effective in this disease, although agents such as deoxycoformycin, an adenosine deaminase inhibitor, are promising.

Hypogammaglobulinemia is common in patients with CLL, and life-threatening infectious complications may occur. Intramuscular injections of gamma globulin have not been effective, but it is uncertain whether the recently developed intravenous immunoglobulin preparations will be useful in preventing infections in these patients.

HAIRY-CELL LEUKEMIA

Hairy-cell leukemia is a lymphoid neoplasm characterized by peripheral blood cytopenias, splenomegaly, and morphologically typical malignant cells in the blood and bone marrow. The disease superficially resembles CLL but has distinct clinical features and requires different therapy. Hairy-cell leukemia is usually seen in patients over 40 years of age, and there is a very definite male preponderance. Originally, this disorder was thought to account for about 2 percent of all leukemias; however, the disease is now recognized with increased frequency, and many large series have been reported. Hairy-cell leukemia has been reported to occur worldwide.

The disease was originally referred to as leukemic reticuloendotheliosis; however, the term hairy-cell leukemia is now widely accepted because it is descriptive of the characteristic cytoplasmic projections seen on the leukemic cell. The disorder is due to expansion of neoplastic B lymphocytes which often produce monoclonal immunoglobulin; however, rare T-cell variants have been reported. The etiology of hairy-cell leukemia is unknown; a single case of T-cell hairy-cell leukemia has been reported, from which a unique species of human T-cell leukemia virus (HTLV II) was recovered.

CLINICAL FEATURES AND PATHOLOGY Patients with hairy-cell leukemia usually present with symptoms due to splenomegaly, infection caused by impaired host defense, or vasculitis. Many asymptomatic patients are detected on routine complete blood counts. More than three-quarters of patients will have palpable splenomegaly and, in some cases, splenic involvement is massive. Lymphadenopathy is rare, and substantial hepatomegaly is uncommon at the time of diagnosis, although infiltration of the portal triads by hairy cells is often seen microscopically. Occasionally bone lesions may cause symptoms of hip pain. Approximately 30 percent of patients with hairy-cell leukemia have an associated vasculitis-like disorder. Common manifestations include erythema nodosum and cutaneous nodules due to perivasculitis. Visceral involvement similar to polyarteritis nodosa may occur.

Moderate pancytopenia is usually present at diagnosis. The leukocyte count is normal or low, and characteristic hairy cells are seen in the peripheral blood. These cells are about 15 to 20 μm in diameter and have an eccentrically placed nucleus with characteristic foamy cytoplasm. Cytoplasmic projections may be seen on smear, but they are best appreciated by phase microscopy. These cells stain positively for tartrate-resistant acid phosphatase (TRAP), which is a cytochemical stain for the isoenzyme 5 of acid phosphatase. Bone marrow aspiration is seldom successful because of reticulin fibrosis. The biopsy typically shows replacement of the normal architecture by mononuclear cells that are not packed together but maintain spaces between the intercellular contacts. Splenic histology is typical, consisting of mononuclear cell infiltration of the red pulp and engorgement of the sinuses.

Hairy-cell leukemia must be distinguished from chronic lymphocytic leukemia, Waldenström's macroglobulinemia, and acute leukemia. Some patients with hairy-cell leukemia present with a hypocellular bone marrow which may be misdiagnosed as aplastic anemia. The diagnosis depends on identifying the characteristic cells in the bone marrow and peripheral blood.

TREATMENT OF HAIRY-CELL LEUKEMIA The course of hairy-cell leukemia can be quite indolent; however, there is a wide spectrum of severity and rate of progression of the disease among patients. Approximately one-quarter of patients present without significant cytopenias and without other complications of the disease; these patients require no immediate treatment. They should be followed at intervals and closely observed for infections. Infection is the primary cause of death in patients with hairy-cell leukemia. Common infections include *Legionella* pneumonitis, toxoplasmosis, tuberculosis, and atypical mycobacterial disease, nocardiosis, and pyogenic infections. Patients probably benefit from pneumococcal vaccination. Any significant fever should be thoroughly evaluated and aggressively treated with antibiotics. Since *Legionella* pneumonitis is relatively common in these patients, high-dose erythromycin should usually be administered to patients with pulmonary infiltrates.

Therapy directed at the leukemia is indicated in patients presenting with marked pancytopenia, a history of infections, massive splenomegaly, or a rapid rate of disease progression. The cornerstone of therapy is splenectomy, which appears to ameliorate the disease in a majority of patients. The role of splenectomy in patients with no splenic enlargement is uncertain. Patients with progressive disease following splenectomy or those in whom splenectomy is contraindicated should be treated with α-interferon. Interferon is an experimental drug which has recently been shown to be effective in hairy-cell leukemia. Virtually all treated patients have responded to α-interferon.

Patients requiring interferon therapy should be referred to research centers specializing in such treatment. Glucocorticosteroids are not effective in hairy-cell leukemia, and they are potentially dangerous because they further predispose these patients to infections. Short courses of glucocorticosteroids may be useful, however, in controlling the vasculitis or autoimmune manifestations that are often associated with the disease. Chemotherapy with alkylating agents or other myelotoxic drugs is hazardous in patients with hairy-cell leukemia because of poor bone marrow reserve. The adenosine deaminase inhibitor deoxycoformycin has been shown to be useful for selected patients. Aggressive chemotherapy may be tried when other therapeutic interventions have failed, and there is anecdotal information that some patients respond to treatment with lithium and androgens. Bone marrow transplantation has also been successful in a small number of patients with advanced hairy-cell leukemia.

The prognosis in hairy-cell leukemia is variable, and published series are outdated because of the recent improvements in diagnosis and treatment. At least 50 percent of patients will survive more than 8 years from diagnosis, and this prognosis should improve further with the application of new treatments and better supportive care.

SELECTED REFERENCES

General

GALE RP (ed): *Leukemia Treatment*. Boston, Blackwell, 1986
———, GOLDE DW (eds): *Leukemia: Recent Advances in Biology and Treatment*. New York, Alan R Liss Inc., 1985
GOLDE DW, TAKAKU E (eds): *Hematopoietic Stem Cells*. New York, Marcel Dekker Inc, 1985
GUNZ FW, HENDERSON ES (eds): *Leukemia*, 4th ed. New York, Grune & Stratton, 1983
ROWLEY JD: Biological implications of consistent chromosome rearrangements in leukemia and lymphoma. Cancer Res 44:3159, 1984
WONG-STAAL F, GALLO RC: The family of human T-lymphotropic leukemia viruses: HTLV-I as the cause of adult T cell leukemia and HTLV-III as the cause of acquired immunodeficiency syndrome. Blood 65:253, 1985
YUNIS JJ: The chromosomal basis of human neoplasia. Science 221:227, 1983

Acute leukemias

BENNETT JM et al: Proposals for the classification of the acute leukaemias. Br J Haematol 33:451, 1976
BENNETT JM et al: Criteria for the diagnosis of acute leukemia of megakaryocytic lineage. Ann Intern Med 103:460, 1085
CHAMPLIN RE, GALE RP: Role of bone marrow transplantation in the treatment of hematologic malignancies and solid tumors: Critical review of syngeneic, autologous, and allogeneic transplants. Cancer Treat Rep 68:145, 1984

ALL

JACOBS AD, GALE RP: Recent advances in the biology and treatment of acute lymphoblastic leukemia in adults. N Engl J Med 311:1219, 1984

JOHNSON FL et al: A comparison of marrow transplantation with chemotherapy for children with acute lymphoblastic leukemia in second or subsequent remission. N Engl J Med 305:846, 1981
MAUER AM: Therapy of acute lymphoblastic leukemia in childhood. Blood 56:1, 1980
RITZ J et al: Autologous bone marrow transplantation in CALLA-positive acute lymphoblastic leukemia after in vitro treatment with J5 monoclonal antibody and complement. Lancet 2:60, 1982
SHAUER P et al: Treatment of acute lymphoblastic leukemia in adults; results of the L-10 and L-10M protocols. J Clin Oncol 1:462, 1983

AML

APPELBAUM FR et al: Bone marrow transplantation or chemotherapy after remission induction for adults with acute nonlymphoblastic leukemia. Ann Intern Med 101:581, 1984
CHAMPLIN RE et al: Treatment of acute myelogenous leukemia: A prospective controlled trial of bone marrow transplantation versus consolidation chemotherapy. Ann Intern Med 102:285–291, 1985
——— et al: Prolonged survival in acute myelogenous leukaemia without maintenance chemotherapy. Lancet 1:894, 1984
FIALKOW PJ et al: Acute nonlymphocytic leukemia: Heterogeneity of stem cell origin. Blood 57:1068, 1981
FOON KA et al: The role of immunotherapy in acute myelogenous leukemia. Arch Intern Med 143:1726, 1983
GALE RP: Progress in acute myelogenous leukemia. Ann Intern Med 101:702, 1984
———, CHAMPLIN RE: How does bone marrow transplantation cure leukaemia? Lancet 2:28, 1984
GREENBERG PL: The smoldering myeloid leukemic states: Clinical and biologic features. Blood 61:1035, 1983
HERZIG RH et al: High-dose cytosine arabinoside therapy for refractory leukemia. Blood 62:361, 1983
KOEFFLER HP: Induction of differentiation of human acute myelogenous leukemia cells: Therapeutic implications. Blood 62:709, 1983
WEINSTEIN HJ et al: Chemotherapy for acute myelogenous leukemia in children and adults: VAPA update. Blood 62:315, 1983
WISCH JS et al: Response of preleukemic syndromes to continuous infusion of low-dose cytandine. N Engl J Med 309:599, 1983

Chronic lymphocytic leukemia

BINET J-L et al: Chronic lymphocytic leukaemia: Proposals for a revised prognostic staging system. Br J Haematol 48:365, 1981
CALIGARIS-CAPPIO F, JANOSSY G: Surface markers in chronic lymphoid leukemias of B cell type. Semin Hematol 22:1, 1985
FOON K GALE RP: Chronic lymphocytic leukemia: Recent advances in biology and treatment. Ann Intern Med 101:120, 1985
HAN T et al: Prognostic importance of cytogenetic abnormalities in patients with chronic lymphocytic leukemia. N Engl J Med 310:288, 1984

Hairy-cell leukemia

GOLOMB HM (ed): Hairy cell leukemia. Semin Oncol 11, 1984
——— et al: Hairy cell leukemia: A five year update on seventy-one patients. Ann Intern Med 99:485, 1983
JACOBS AD et al: Recombinant alpha-2 interferon for hairy-cell leukemia. Blood 65:1017, 1985
QUESADA JR et al: Alpha interferon for induction of remission in hairy-cell leukemia. N Engl J Med 310:15, 1984

section 3   Neoplastic diseases

293   THE HUMAN T-LYMPHOTROPIC VIRUSES

ROBERT C. GALLO / ANTHONY S. FAUCI

BIOLOGY OF THE RETROVIRUSES   Retroviruses were first isolated from chickens at the beginning of this century. In the 1950s the first mammalian retroviruses were isolated from mice with leukemia, and these are now known to be associated with malignancies in many species and with some nonmalignant disorders. Retroviruses may be subdivided according to the types of disease they cause: malignant, nonmalignant, both malignant and nonmalignant, and nonpathogenic. Nonpathogenic retroviruses are often transmitted in the germ line as normal genetic mendelian elements, a unique feature of this class of viruses, i.e., endogenous retroviruses. An example of a retrovirus causing malignant and nonmalignant disease is feline leukemia virus (FeLV), which can cause T-cell leukemia but more frequently causes a disorder mimicking the acquired immunodeficiency syndrome (AIDS) of human beings (see Chap. 257). Retroviruses of a class that causes nonmalignant disease, e.g., encephalitis, other neurologic abnormalities, arthritis, and lung disease, are the slow-acting lenti-retroviruses. Lentiretroviruses occur in ungulates, in human beings (human T-lymphotropic virus type III [HTLV III]), and in nonhuman primates (simian T-lymphotropic virus type III [STLV III]).

Retroviruses are enveloped, bud from cell membranes, and contain an electron-dense, central core structure surrounding a viral RNA genome. The *sine qua non* of a retrovirus is the DNA polymerase, known as reverse transcriptase (RT), which is complexed to the RNA in the viral core and catalyzes the transcription of the RNA genome into a DNA form (the provirus). The DNA form usually migrates from the cytoplasm to the nucleus and then, after becoming a double-stranded circular form, integrates into the host cell DNA, where the viral genes may remain for the lifetime of the cell (Fig. 293-1). Because the provirus is duplicated with the cell DNA during the S phase of the cell cycle, the viral genes are passed to daughter cells. Therefore, infection of an organism is generally lifelong. When the provirus is expressed, viral RNA and proteins are found in the cell cytoplasm and assembled at the cell membrane, where budding and release of the viruses completes the virus's life cycle. Sometimes deletions of the provirus occur, and this may be followed by the acquisition of host cellular sequences by normal or abnormal processing of RNA. As a consequence, the virus subsequently formed with these newly acquired nucleotide sequences acquires some properties that differ from the original virus.

Structural features of the retroviral genome determine the molecular mechanism by which these viruses alter a cell. The most common are the chronic leukemia viruses which contain only the three essential genes for virus replication: *gag, pol,* and *env* (Fig. 293-2) (see Chap. 59). *Gag* codes for the viral internal structural proteins, *pol* codes for RT, and *env* codes for the glycoprotein envelope of the virus. The properties of the envelope have a major influence on the kind of cell the virus can infect, and production of antibodies against the envelope is one of the essential features sought for in a vaccine. The viral genes are flanked at each end by nucleotide sequences called *long terminal repeats* (LTR), which contain regulatory elements that influence the expression of the viral genes and sometimes of nearby cellular genes. The LTRs contain the signals determining proviral integration into the host cell DNA and form the terminals of the integrated proviral sequence. Some examples of chronic leukemia viruses are FeLV, mouse leukemia virus, and avian leukosis virus (ALV). These viruses replicate extensively in the host prior to the induction of leukemia. There is evidence that they cause leukemia by integration into a specific region of a chromosome so that the associated LTRs act to promote continual expression of a cellular gene involved in growth. The best example of this *cis* mechanism is in chickens, where the LTR of ALV promotes expression of a cellular

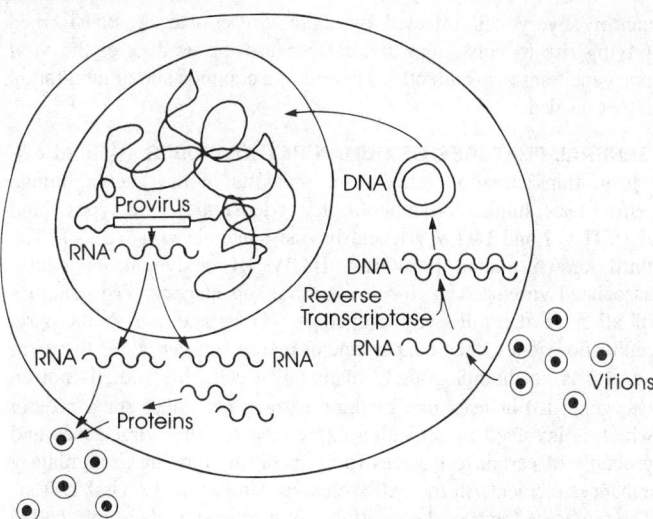

FIGURE 293-1 *Life cycle of a retrovirus. Intact virions are endocytosed via a specific cellular receptor. The uncoated viral single-stranded RNA is then transcribed into double-stranded DNA, enters the cell nucleus, and integrates into the host genome. The DNA provirus in some conditions is unexpressed. In other cases it is transcribed, giving rise to viral RNA encoding viral proteins and to genome-length viral RNA molecules which then reassemble with viral proteins to make complete virions. These progeny are released by budding from the cell membrane.*

oncogene believed to be the first step in the induction of leukemia by this virus. Since integration by retroviruses is random, a high rate of replication favors the chance of integration into regions sufficiently near the cellular oncogene to enable the LTR to activate this gene. This may explain the apparent need for extensive virus replication prior to the development of malignancy.

When retroviruses acquire through genetic recombination a host cell gene which rapidly transforms cells and induces acute malignancies, the virus is often called an acute leukemia or sarcoma virus, and the gene is called a viral *onc* gene (Fig. 293-2) (see Chaps. 58 and 59). Viruses with *onc* genes are rare, have never been identified in humans, and are of interest in animals chiefly for investigating neoplastic transformation rather than as causes of naturally occurring

FIGURE 293-2 *Genetic structure and proposed classification of retroviruses.* gag, *core proteins;* pol, *reverse transcriptase;* env, *envelope;* LTR, *long terminal repeat;* gag, env, *incomplete genes;* src, *one of the* onc *genes;* BLV, *bovine leukemia virus;* tat, *transacting transcriptional activator gene;* sor, *short open reading frame;* 3' orf, *3' open reading frame. The latter two are genes in HTLV III of unknown function.*

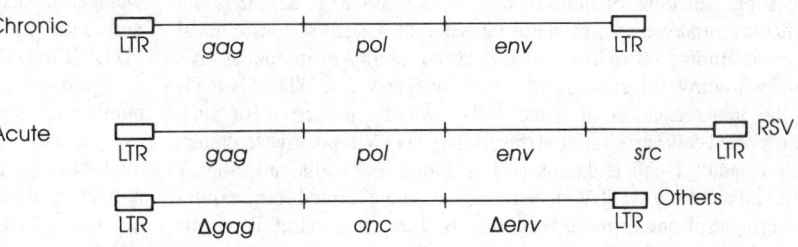

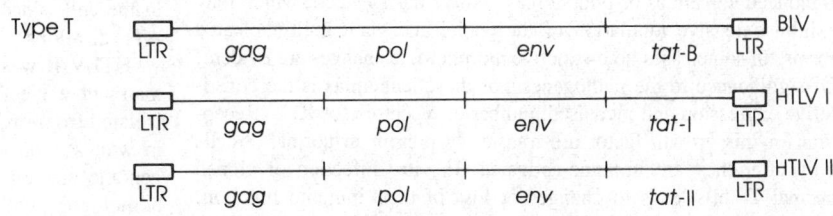

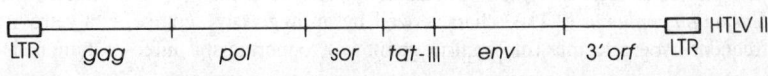

cancer. Every cell infected by these viruses can be transformed (giving rise to polyclonal tumors) because the product of the viral *onc* gene transforms directly. Therefore, a common site of integration is not needed.

GENERAL FEATURES OF HUMAN RETROVIRUSES   A third category, transactivation retroviruses, consists of the known human retroviruses, human T-lymphotropic (or leukemia) virus types I and II (HTLV I and HTLV II), and bovine leukemia virus (BLV). The third known human retrovirus, HTLV III or lymphadenopathy-associated virus (LAV), forms a special subcategory. The genomes of all have the following properties: (1) in addition to the viral replication genes, they contain one or more extra genes; (2) the extra gene(s) is not homologous to mammalian cell gene, i.e., is not an *onc* gene; (3) at least one of these extra genes codes for a protein which is involved in activating expression of other viral genes and probably of certain cell genes (presumably by binding to regulatory enhancer elements in the cell which are similar to the viral LTRs). The biologic effects of these viruses are mediated by this gene, called *transacting transcriptional activator* or *tat*. Since *tat* codes for a nuclear protein which can activate other genes, these viruses do not need to integrate in a special region to induce disease. This may explain why extensive virus replication is not essential for them to cause neoplastic or nonneoplastic disease. A similar phenomenon is seen in bovine lymphoma induced by BLV. HTLV III not only contains the three genes for virus replication and a *tat* gene but also contains at least two other genes of undefined function.

HTLV I and HTLV II are similar in structure, HTLV III differs in its mature form, containing a highly condensed cylindrical core. HTLV I, the first human retrovirus to be identified, was isolated in 1978 from a man with an aggressive T-cell malignancy. Techniques for virus detection were based on the use of reverse transcriptase as a "footprint" of a retrovirus, since this assay can be much more sensitive than electron microscopy. In addition, the necessary prerequisite for the growth of the target T lymphocytes, which allow virus replication, was fulfilled with the discovery of T-cell growth factor, now called interleukin 2 (IL-2). This same basic technique was used for the isolation of the virus that causes AIDS.

A striking feature of all known human retroviruses is their tropism for the T4$^+$ helper lymphocyte. Although other cells can be infected, this helper T cell is preferentially infected in vitro by all three types of human retroviruses and the diseases caused by them almost always involve this cell. Since the T4$^+$ cell regulates many immune functions and some functions of nonlymphoid cells (see Chap. 62), it is not difficult to understand why these viruses induce such serious clinical disease. Human retroviruses also have the ability to mimic in vivo effects in vitro. Infection of T4$^+$ cells by HTLV I or HTLV II leads to the transformation of some cells, and the properties of such transformed cells are similar to the primary HTLV I–positive leukemic cells in adult T-cell leukemia (ATL). Other T4$^+$ cells and other T cells infected by HTLV I may not be transformed but exhibit impairment of one or more functions. In vitro infection of T4$^+$ cells by HTLV III can lead to their premature death when the viral genes are expressed, resembling what is assumed to be the case in AIDS.

DISEASES ASSOCIATED WITH HTLV I   The majority of HTLV I–induced leukemias or lymphomas involve the T4$^+$ cell, which may exhibit extensive lobulation of the nuclei and giant multinucleated forms. In some cases no distinctive morphologic changes are evident. Of significance to the pathogenesis of these leukemias is the constitutive expression and increased number of receptors for IL-2. Receptors for this growth factor are transiently present in normal T cells only after they are immune-activated. In vitro infection of cloned normal T cells leads to changes or loss of their immune function. These findings parallel the opportunistic infections that occur in these viral leukemias. Leukemias/lymphomas caused by HTLV I usually fit a particular form of lymphoid malignancy known as *adult T-cell leukemia/lymphoma* (ATL), characterized by an aggressive course, frequent hypercalcemia (mechanism unknown), opportunistic infec-

tion, and, in over half the cases, leukemic skin infiltrates (see Chap. 294).

HTLV I may also be involved in T4-cell leukemias/lymphomas that exhibit a more chronic course (15 to 20 percent of cases) and have other features differing from ATL. These may be indistinguishable pathologically or clinically from T-cell chronic lymphocytic leukemia (CLL), diffuse histiocytic lymphoma, large and mixed cell lymphomas, and mycosis fungoides or Sézary leukemias. In the United States only a small percentage of these diseases are HTLV I–positive, whereas close to 100 percent of ATL cases are virus-positive. In areas of the world where HTLV I is endemic, some B-cell lymphoid malignancies and certain other cancers are associated with HTLV I infection more frequently than expected from the prevalence of the virus in the general population. In contrast to virus-positive T-cell leukemias where the viral genes are integrated into the DNA of the leukemic cell, HTLV I was not found in the DNA of these B-cell tumors. Instead, the virus was found in the normal T cells of these patients. The malignant B cells in this disorder make a single type of antibody directed against a protein of HTLV I. Therefore, the B-cell tumors may arise in part by an indirect effect of HTLV I, i.e., by chronic antigenic stimulation combined with diminished T-cell immune surveillance, thereby increasing the chance for a neoplastic transformation in the expanding B-cell compartment.

ORIGIN AND EPIDEMIOLOGY OF HTLV I   Although HTLV I was originally discovered in two sporadic cases of T-cell malignancies in blacks in the United States and although the first clusters of this disease were found in Japanese and later in Caribbean-born blacks, the virus likely originated in Africa for the following reasons: (1) it is widely distributed throughout Africa, (2) in the Americas and Europe, ATL occurs chiefly in people with African ancestry, and (3) a closely related virus (STLV I) has been found in African old world monkeys. HTLV I is also prevalent in the two small southwestern islands of Japan, Kyushu and Shikoku, where it may have been brought by Africans in the sixteenth century. The geographic distribution of HTLV I is relatively restricted, e.g., less than 1 percent of whites in the United States and Europe are infected, and the virus is unusual in most of Asia. Thus, it was not complicated to establish an epidemiologic link of this virus to the diseases caused. Transmission is by intimate contact, by blood or blood products, and by infection of the developing fetus in utero. It has been speculated that the virus may also be transmitted by insect vectors, but there are no data bearing on this important question. Because of increase in travel, changes in sexual habits, drug abuse (blood-contaminated needles), and wide use of blood and blood products, the prevalence of HTLV I infection may be increasing.

Upon infection of T cells with HTLV I or HTLV II a small number of these cells become immortalized, losing their need for exogenous IL-2 to maintain growth. This phenomenon appears to be mediated by the *tat* gene product, which is believed to bind to regulatory elements of T cells which activate the expression of gene(s) involved in T-cell proliferation. One such gene is the IL-2 receptor, which, as noted earlier, is constitutively expressed in these transformed cells. Since cells other than T4 can be infected, the reason for the frequency of transformation of the T4$^+$ cell is unclear. The maintenance of malignancy is believed to require additional genetic changes in the cell, since the HTLV I genes are usually not expressed after ATL develops.

HTLV II was originally isolated from a cell line derived from a man with a T-cell variant of hairy-cell leukemia. The virus was again isolated from two more cases of chronic forms of T-cell malignancies in whites. Considerable details exist on the nature of the HTLV-II genome and on its in vitro effects (it is overall about 50 percent homologous with HTLV I), and a few major biologic differences have been found between the two viruses.

THE ETIOLOGIC AGENT OF AIDS   The etiologic agent of AIDS is a retrovirus called HTLV III. Other designations for the virus are lymphadenopathy-associated virus (LAV) and AIDS-associated retrovirus (ARV). The pathogenesis of the syndrome relates to the infection of the T4$^+$ inducer/helper subset of lymphocytes with the virus, leading to the premature death of these critical cells. The resulting immune defect predisposes the patient to overwhelming opportunistic infections and certain malignancies. For a detailed description of AIDS, see Chap. 257.

OTHER HTLV III–ASSOCIATED DISEASES In addition to full-blown AIDS, with its opportunistic infections and increased incidence of Kaposi's sarcoma, and to the AIDS-related complex of disease (Chap. 257), infection with HTLV III/LAV can also be associated with other diseases. The virus can infect the brain and lead to severe neuropsychiatric abnormalities. A lymphoid interstitial pneumonitis has been associated with HTLV III/LAV infection. AIDS patients have an increased incidence of certain B-cell lymphomas. Furthermore, the incidence of Hodgkin's disease and certain carcinomas (cloacogenic squamous-cell carcinoma and head and neck tumors) may be increased in patients with HTLV III/LAV infection. The reason for the increase in these malignancies is not understood. HTLV III/LAV is not the direct cause because viral sequences are not found in the DNA from the majority of tumor cells. For the B-cell lymphomas, the mechanism may be similar to the indirect role described above for HTLV I. HTLV III/LAV infection may also cause autoimmune thrombocytopenia and congenital abnormalities.

THE CYTOPATHIC EFFECT OF HTLV III/LAV ON T4$^+$ CELLS Infection of T4$^+$ cells by HTLV III/LAV leads to the premature death of these cells, and there is evidence that one or more genes of HTLV III/LAV leads to T4-cell death upon transfection of the DNA provirus into these cells. It is impossible to induce a productive viral infection of T4$^+$ cells in vitro unless the T cells are immune-activated. The activated, infected T cells appear to go through the same process of cell gene expression as do uninfected cells, except that the viral genes are eventually expressed. When this occurs, a higher percentage of the cells than normal terminally differentiate, and the rate of terminal differentiation is faster than that in the uninfected T cells. This process may involve the *tat*-III gene (Fig. 293-2). Expression of this gene may in turn activate an extremely high level of transcription of another viral gene or of cellular genes that augment terminal differentiation.

HETEROGENEITY OF HTLV III/LAV Molecular analysis of various HTLV III/LAV isolates reveals variation of nucleotide sequences of certain parts of the genome, especially in the envelope gene. Detailed analysis of different isolates indicates that there is a continuum from very closely related isolates (1 to 2 percent variation) to those that vary more than 5 percent. Variation develops after successive infections and does not occur during prolonged tissue culture, suggesting that these changes occur during transcription of the viral RNA genome to the DNA form and/or during the recombinational process when the DNA provirus integrates into the host cell DNA. RTs are DNA polymerases that tend to be error prone. The RT of HTLV III/LAV may be particularly error prone. It may be that variation in other parts of the viral genome leads to noninfectious particles.

PREVENTION AND TREATMENT OF HTLV III/LAV INFECTION There are three special problems in the prevention and treatment of HTLV III/LAV infection: (1) T cells are the principal cells involved in protection against a virus, and these are the cells destroyed by the virus. If infection occurs by cell-cell contact, there may be little one can do to augment defense against the virus. (2) The envelope heterogeneity among different HTLV III/LAV isolates presents a problem, but the nucleotide sequences of the envelope of several isolates have been recently compared and analysis reveals that there are conserved areas of the envelope gene, some of which should be immunogenic. It is conceptually feasible, therefore, to develop a vaccine to induce protective antibodies. (3) Since infection may mean integration of the viral genes into the DNA of the infected cell and these are transmitted to progeny cells, infection with HTLV III/LAV

is likely lifelong. More than one million people in the United States are known to be infected by HTLV III/LAV. Avoidance of other infections which could activate already infected T cells, promoting both their death and spread of virus, is important. Antiviral compounds are being developed, including those which utilize RT inhibitors and agents that interact with the viral envelope. Other approaches result from structural-functional studies of the viral genome, e.g., inhibitors of *tat*-III gene expression or function. Treatment will probably have to be lifelong, and to avoid toxicity and reduce the chances for viral resistance, it may be necessary to use a combination of compounds with different mechanisms of action. Another approach would be to kill infected cells. Hypothetically, if this could be achieved for all infected cells, a cure could be effected. However, this may not be possible with human retroviruses because most infected cells do not express viral proteins and hence would not be distinguishable from uninfected cells.

HTLV III/LAV is a new infection of humans with severe and often fatal consequences. Like HTLV I (and probably HTLV II), it is likely that HTLV III/LAV entered African humans from African green monkeys or related primates directly or through intermediary vectors and subsequently spread to other regions. Also similar to HTLV I is its mode of transmission, T4 tropism, in vitro mimicry of the disease, and presence of the *tat* gene. Unlike HTLV I or HTLV II, the AIDS virus contains at least two additional genes, has strong cytopathic effects, has greater structural similarities to the lentiretroviruses, and is generally more infectious.

REFERENCES

BALTIMORE D: RNA-dependent DNA polymerase in virions of RNA tumor viruses. Nature 226:1209, 1970

BRODER S, GALLO RC: A pathogenic retrovirus (HTLV-III) linked to AIDS. N Engl J Med 311:1292, 1984

Cold Spring Harbor Symposia on Quantitative Biology, vol 39: *Biology of Tumor Viruses*. Cold Spring Harbor, New York, Cold Spring Harbor, 1975

GALLO RC: Introduction: Human T-lymphotropic retroviruses, in *Human T-Cell Leukemia/ Lymphoma Virus*, RC Gallo et al (eds). Cold Spring Harbor, New York, Cold Spring Harbor, 1984, pp 1–8

GROSS L: *Oncogenic Viruses*, 3d ed. Oxford, Pergamon Press, 1983

HAHN BH et al: Genomic diversity of the acquired immune deficiency syndrome virus HTLV-II: Different viruses exhibit greatest divergence in their envelope genes. Proc Natl Acad Sci USA 83:4813, 1985

ROBERT-GUROFF M et al: T-cell growth factor, in *Growth and Maturation Factors*, G Guroff (ed). New York, Wiley, 1984, vol 2, pp 267–308

SAXINGER WC, GALLO RC: Human T-cell growth factor (TCGF): Its discovery, properties and some basic and applied uses in the long term propagation of human mature T-cells, in *Human Cancer Immunology*, B Serou, CL Rosenfeld (eds). Amsterdam, North-Holland, 1981, pp 463–568

SHAW GM et al: Human T-cell leukemia virus: Its discovery and role in leukemogenesis and immunosuppression, in *Advances in Internal Medicine*, GH Stollerman et al (eds). Chicago, Year Book, 1984, vol 30, pp 1–27

TEMIN HM, MIZUTANI S: RNA-directed DNA polymerase in virions of Rous sarcoma virus. Nature 226:1211, 1970

WONG-STAAL F, GALLO RC: The family of human T-lymphotropic leukemia and HTLV-III as the cause of acquired immunodeficiency syndrome. Blood 65:253, 1985

———: Human T lymphotropic retrovirus. Nature 317:395, 1985

294 HODGKIN'S DISEASE AND THE LYMPHOCYTIC LYMPHOMAS

VINCENT T. DeVITA, JR. / JOHN E. ULTMANN

DEFINITION The lymphomas should be considered tumors of the immune system. They include tumors of lymphocytes and Hodgkin's disease. They rarely include tumors thought to be derived from histiocytes. While they have been referred to as Hodgkin's disease and the non-Hodgkin's lymphomas, more sophisticated diagnostic tools can precisely delineate the subcategories of disease. The old terminology should be abandoned.

EPIDEMIOLOGY About 34,000 new cases of lymphoma were diagnosed in 1985; 40 percent of these were Hodgkin's disease. The most common lymphocytic lymphomas are those of follicular morphology followed by diffuse large-cell lymphomas, each constituting about 40 percent of the remaining cases. Because of the young average age of the population (32 years for Hodgkin's disease and 42 for the other adult lymphomas), the toll in person-years of life lost because of deaths from lymphomas ranks them fourth among cancers in terms of economic impact. Although the incidence of lymphomas is increasing each year, mortality is falling because of improvements in treatment. In Hodgkin's disease, survival has improved markedly since 1970, and national mortality has fallen 58 percent since 1973. In diffuse large cell lymphomas, national 5-year survival rates have improved from less than 5 percent to over 40 percent in the past decade.

Worldwide, there are differences in the prevalence of lymphomas. In the United States, Hodgkin's disease has a bimodal age-specific incidence rate, one mode occurring at ages 15 to 35 years and the second above 50. A disproportionate number of patients in the first modal peak have the nodular sclerosing variety of Hodgkin's disease. The first peak is absent in Japan. Hodgkin's disease in children under 10 years is seen much more frequently in underdeveloped countries and, when it is observed, the histologic varieties and stages are characteristic of more advanced disease in the United States. These observations and the occasional report of clusters of Hodgkin's disease suggest environmental and/or genetic influences operating on the development of these diseases. Following reports of several clusters of Hodgkin's disease in the United States, population-based studies using the cancer registries of Connecticut and California indicated that these reported clusters probably occurred by chance alone. Medical personnel who specialize in the care of patients with lymphoma do not seem to have a higher incidence of these diseases than do others. An excellent epidemiologic study, however, has made a strong case for the hypothesis that Hodgkin's disease may be a rare manifestation of a common infection. Factors that increase the risk of early exposure to infections, such as large family size or multiple families per dwelling, decrease the risk of Hodgkin's disease. The data also suggest that different risk factors are involved for Hodgkin's disease among the young and in the old. These data may explain several curious epidemiologic associations, such as the absence of the early peak in Japan. Some of the lymphocytic lymphomas have unique epidemiologic characteristics. Burkitt's lymphoma occurs characteristically in children of central Africa, although a small number of cases have been reported in this country, but with a different clinical presentation. Abdominal lymphomas with associated production of heavy chains of immunoglobulin occur in the Mediterranean region but are rarely seen in other parts of the world.

SITE OF ORIGIN OF THE LYMPHOMAS The lymphomas arise in the lymph nodes or in the lymphoid tissues of parenchymal organs such as the gut, lung, or skin. Ninety percent of cases of Hodgkin's disease originate in lymph nodes; 10 percent are of extranodal origin. In the lymphocytic lymphomas, the tissues of the parenchymal organs are more often involved; 60 percent of these lymphomas originate in the nodes and 40 percent are of extranodal origin.

Phenotype With the availability of more specific antiserums, the lymphomas can be classified by their cells of origin (Table 294-1). Sixty-five percent of lymphomas of lymphocyte origin derive from a monoclonal population of B cells and as many as 30 to 40 percent from T cells. With DNA probes to the immunoglobulin gene and the β-chain T-cell receptors, the lineage of most lymphoid tumors can now be precisely delineated. In some series as many as 10 percent of tumors have been found to be biclonal. Only a few appear to be true derivatives of tissue histiocytes despite the morphologic similarity of some malignant lymphomas to these cells. It is also possible to relate B-cell tumors to functional subsets of B-cell populations. Follicular lymphomas are derived from the proliferative site of the B-cell system, the lymphoid follicle, while the diffuse small lymphocytic lymphomas relate to the secretory compartment of the medullary cords. B-cell lymphomas are recognized by the demonstration of monoclonal surface immunoglobulin or, if absent, by immunoglobulin gene rearrangement using specific DNA probes. Lymphomas of T-cell origin are less common in the United States than in other parts of the world. Approximately 15 to 35 percent of diffuse large cell lymphomas are of T-cell origin and are referred to as peripheral T-cell lymphomas, in contrast to the immature T-cell lymphomas of thymic origin, such as lymphoblastic lymphoma of adolescence and childhood. They are identified by their characteristic rosetting with sheep red blood cells and T cell–specific monoclonal antibodies. In some cases the phenotypic expression of the T cell is matched by functional capabilities. In mycosis fungoides/Sézary syndrome, which is a peripheral T-cell lymphoma, a helper cell phenotype and comparable function has been identified. While many monoclonal antibodies have been developed that allow characterization of T cells, a smaller number are available that recognize antigens specific for B cells. The monoclonal antibody with the broadest activity is anti-B1, a pan-B cell antibody. Another commonly used monoclonal antibody, J5, was at first thought to react exclusively with common acute lymphoblastic leukemia antigen (CALLA). Further studies have shown that this antigen is expressed in many B-cell malignancies, including most follicular lymphomas and Burkitt's lymphoma. The origin of the Hodgkin's disease (HD) cell may be the antigen-presenting interdigitating reticulum cell found in the paracortex regions of lymph nodes. Sternberg-Reed cells in culture and their mononuclear variants have Fc and C3 receptors and Ia antigens. They do not synthesize immunoglobulins, are not phagocytic, and lack diffuse activity for nonspecific esterase and acid phosphatase, all characteristics that support an origin from antigen-presenting cells. Sternberg-Reed cells, even in paraffin sections, stain with the monoclonal antibody anti-Leu M1, which also stains interdigitating reticulum cells after neuraminidase digestion, and rosette with T cells. Anti-Leu M1 does not react with morphologically similar T cells. A monoclonal antibody Ki1 prepared against HD cell lines also reacts with HD cells in frozen sections of involved nodes but has also been found to react with antigens on the surface of some large cell lymphomas of B-cell origin. Several monoclonal antibodies are available that detect the common leukocyte antigen, expressed

TABLE 294-1 Cellular origins of malignant lymphomas

Neoplasms of B-cell origin	Neoplasms of T-cell origin	Neoplasms of histiocytic/reticulum cell origin
Chronic lymphocytic leukemia (98%)	Chronic lymphocytic leukemia (2%)	Malignant histiocytosis (histiocytic medullary reticulosis)
Small lymphocytic (well-differentiated lymphoma)	Mycosis fungoides/Sézary syndrome	Monocytic leukemia
Lymphocytic lymphoma, intermediate and/or small cleaved cell type	Diffuse aggressive lymphomas of adults (25%) Mixed cell type Large cell, immunoblastic	Large cell lymphomas (<5%)
Follicular lymphomas	Adult T-cell leukemia/lymphoma	Hodgkin's disease
Diffuse aggressive lymphomas of adults (65%) Mixed cell type Large cell type Large cell immunoblastic Small noncleaved cell	Antiocentric lymphomas (lymphomatoid granulomatosis) (polymorphic reticulosis)	
Burkitt's (small noncleaved cell) lymphoma		
Acute lymphocytic leukemia (70%)	Acute lymphocytic leukemia (25%)	
Lymphoblastic lymphomas (10%)	Lymphoblastic lymphomas (85%)	

on all normal lymphoreticular cells. These antibodies can be useful in distinguishing carcinomas and sarcomas from malignant lymphomas.

ETIOLOGY There is clear evidence that viruses are the cause of lymphomas in rodents, birds, cats, and cows. Such a relationship has now been demonstrated in humans for the first time by American and Japanese investigators who isolated a unique retrovirus from patients with mycosis fungoides in the United States and acute T-cell lymphomas in Japan. The latter disease is a relatively new syndrome rarely found in the United States but common in Japan and in blacks from the Caribbean. This class of virus has been termed human T-cell leukemia/lymphoma virus (HTLV). There is reason to believe that other lymphomas of humans may be due to viruses of the HTLV class. Cases of diffuse immunoblastic lymphoma have been reported in patients with acquired immunodeficiency syndrome (AIDS). While HTLV viruses thus far identified are T cell–trophic in humans, a distantly related virus, the bovine lymphoma/leukemia virus, causes a B-cell lymphoma in cows and HTLV-like viruses have been isolated from cells of human B-cell lymphomas. With new technology to grow lymphoma cells in long-term culture, the viral association with human lymphomas is undergoing reexamination. A virus may be related to the causation of Hodgkin's disease, in which the immune defect that accompanies the disease is in T cells and could result from an infection from a T cell–trophic virus. There is also a strong association between the Epstein-Barr DNA virus (EBV) and the rare lymphoma described by Burkitt in east Africa (anti-EBV antibodies appear in serum of patients, and complementary DNA appears in the human genome of Burkitt's cells), but the association is less strong in Burkitt's lymphomas diagnosed in the United States. In addition, in large series of patients with infectious mononucleosis, a disease caused by the Epstein-Barr virus, after long follow-up a small but consistent increase in the incidence of lymphomas has been noted compared to controls who have not had infectious mononucleosis. A lymphomatous disease of chickens, Marek's disease, is known to be caused by another herpes-like DNA virus and can now be prevented by vaccination.

A hereditary influence on the incidence of lymphomas is suggested by their higher incidence in patients with inherited immunologic deficiency diseases and by a slightly increased incidence in families of patients with immunologic disorders. In one study, a significantly increased incidence of Hodgkin's disease was noted in siblings of the index case, particularly in siblings of the same sex. A slight increase in incidence of lymphomas has been noted in large series of patients with collagen-vascular diseases compared with the general population adjusted for age. This increased incidence approached 10 percent in patients with long-standing Sjögren's syndrome, who tend to develop diffuse lymphomas or immunoblastic sarcomas.

Lymphoma-like syndromes have been found in patients who take phenytoin. Although in most cases the disease regresses when the patient stops taking the drug, a significant fraction proceed to develop frank lymphoma of several different varieties, including Hodgkin's disease. Such observations suggest that the drug is acting on patients with an inherited tendency to develop the disease. Patients who are chronically immunosuppressed, particularly those who have received renal or heart transplants or have AIDS, have a higher incidence of diffuse large cell lymphomas and immunoblastic lymphomas (often of the brain).

Cytogenetics of lymphomas The cells of Hodgkin's disease have been shown to be aneuploid although no specific chromosomal abnormality has been identified. In contrast, almost all of the lymphocytic lymphomas have nonrandom chromosomal abnormalities, usually translocations involving chromosome 14 (8;14, 11;14, and 14;18). The first translocation was described in Burkitt's lymphoma, where a portion of the 8 chromosome is translocated to chromosome 14. This translocation brings the c-*myc* oncogene, on chromosome 8, in close proximity to the promoter sequence of the heavy chain gene and results in the constitutive expression of c-*myc*.

Other, less common translocations (8;2, 8;22), bring the same gene under the control of the κ and λ light chain promoter, respectively. The 14;11 and 14;18 translocations are common in the follicular lymphomas, and two previously undescribed genes, which may be lymphoma-specific oncogenes, have been identified on chromosomes 11 and 18 (called BCL 1 and BCL 2) in close proximity to the breakpoint. The breakpoints of these translocations have now been cloned, and specific DNA probes have been made that should serve as diagnostic tools to identify lymphocytes that have the specific chromosomal abnormality.

HODGKIN'S DISEASE

NATURAL HISTORY AND CLINICAL MANIFESTATIONS There are two theories about the origin and spread of Hodgkin's disease. Careful mapping of sites involved by tumor suggest that the disease is unifocal in origin and spreads initially by involving contiguous lymph node areas. This hypothesis has two flaws—the high degree of involvement of retroperitoneal lymph and left cervical nodes without intervening mediastinal involvement and the common involvement of the spleen, which has no afferent lymphatics. Kaplan has proposed that retroperitoneal lymph nodes are involved by retrograde spread through the thoracic duct due to obstructing cervical nodes. This explanation is difficult to accept because almost total occlusion of the duct's flow would be required. Smithers has proposed an alternative hypothesis, referred to as "the susceptibility hypothesis." He suggests that the malignant Hodgkin's cell freely circulates but grows only in preferential sites, giving the appearance of contiguous spread; this theory is supported by the finding of early involvement of the spleen with tumor. The fact that this multifocal disease can be cured by irradiation, a local form of treatment, seems improbable if one accepts Smithers' proposal, but a possible explanation may be that preferential sites of involvement are destroyed by irradiation, thereby limiting future growth of the tumor.

Hodgkin's disease usually presents either with asymptomatic, discrete, painless, rubbery enlargement of lymph nodes or with symptoms of fever, night sweats, weight loss, and sometimes pruritus associated with adenopathy. Asymptomatic adenopathy may be noted by the patient or by the doctor on routine physical examination. Often mediastinal adenopathy is noted on a routine chest x-ray or a film taken because the patient has a dry, nonproductive cough. These presentations are more common in young people, and such patients often have the nodular sclerosing variety of the disease. Other, usually older, patients present with fever and night sweats or both, followed by increasing malaise and weight loss. Whereas superficial adenopathy is present in most such patients at some time in the course of the disease, in some cases, the enlarging lymph nodes are located exclusively in the abdomen, and these patients often present to the physician with a differential diagnosis of fever of undetermined origin. When diagnosed, they are usually found to have the lymphocyte-depleted variety of Hodgkin's disease.

The fever in Hodgkin's disease is usually remittent. While commonly discussed, a cyclical pattern of fever, called Pel-Ebstein fever, which is characterized by several days or weeks of fever, alternating with afebrile periods, is rarely observed. Fever, night sweats, and weight loss (referred to as B symptoms) have been found to correlate with a poorer prognosis in Hodgkin's disease than the absence of symptoms. The prognostic significance of pruritus is uncertain. It rarely occurs in the absence of fever and/or night sweats and has been dropped as a staging criterion indicating the presence of more advanced disease. Alcohol-induced pain in Hodgkin's disease is uncommon but has been reported to coincide with heavy eosinophilic infiltration at the sites involved by tumor. If alcohol-associated pain occurs, it may serve to direct the physician's attention to a site of involvement which can be biopsied. Occasionally a patient with Hodgkin's disease will present with obstruction of the superior vena cava as the first symptom. Sudden spinal cord compression can be a presenting complaint in patients with Hodgkin's disease but is usually a complication of progressing disease in a patient with known disease.

Asymptomatic patients may have their adenopathy for extended periods of time with waxing and waning of lymph node size. Old x-ray films, in retrospect, may reveal that evidence of mediastinal widening had been present for several years. Slow progression of the disease, usually by extension to contiguous lymph node areas, occurs, especially in the nodular sclerosing variety of the disease. With the invasion of the hilar lymph nodes, the gateway to the lungs, the tumor mass may invade the pulmonary parenchyma. At some point in the progression of the disease, blood vessel invasion may occur. Vascular invasion can be easily demonstrated in biopsy specimens of lymphoid tissue stained with Weigert's stain, especially in patients with more advanced histologic subtypes. Unsuspected involvement of the spleen, an organ which has no afferent lymphatics, suggests that vascular invasion and circulation of the malignant cell may be a common occurrence, even in patients with apparently localized disease. Later, with further progression of disease and clear evidence of vascular invasion, the bone marrow, liver, and other viscera become involved. Symptoms, if they were not present initially, appear as the volume of tumor increases, and if the patient is not successfully treated, cachexia and widespread involvement of visceral organs by tumor occurs, infections complicate the course, and the patient dies. Patients symptomatic at the outset seem to have disease which progresses more rapidly, have smaller-sized but more widespread lymphadenopathy, and more often have the lymphocyte-depleted or mixed cellularity varieties of Hodgkin's disease. Bone and visceral involvement occurs earlier in such patients. Bone lesions are often osteoblastic, and the "ivory" vertebra is characteristic of Hodgkin's disease. Bone pain is common, but pathologic fractures are rare.

DIFFERENTIAL DIAGNOSIS Adenopathy in young people occurs more often as a result of infectious diseases with symptoms of fever, headache, or pharyngitis, and is often due to infectious mononucleosis, viral syndromes, or infection by *Toxoplasma gondii*. In older patients, cervical adenopathy may occur as a result of local spread of head and neck cancers. A good rule is that any lymph node of 1 cm or greater in diameter which does not show signs of regression after 6 weeks of observation should be biopsied.

Mediastinal and hilar adenopathy should be distinguished from sarcoidosis, which is almost always panhilar, erythema nodosum, and primary tuberculosis, which, although unilateral like Hodgkin's disease, is almost always accompanied by a resolving pulmonary

TABLE 294-2 Evolution of histopathologic classification of Hodgkin's disease*

Jackson-Parker (1947)	Lukes-Butler (1966)	Rye classification (1966)
Paragranuloma	Lymphocytic and/or histiocytic *1* Nodular *2* Diffuse	Lymphocytic predominance
	Nodular sclerosis	Nodular sclerosis
Granuloma	Mixed	Mixed cellularity
	Diffuse fibrosis	
		Lymphocytic depletion
Sarcoma	Reticular	

* *The current classification by Lukes et al. provides greater prognostic information than the old Jackson-Parker classification by virtue of identifying those patients whose tissue shows intense fibrosis in nodules.*

infection and usually does not cause mediastinal lymph node enlargement. In older patients, the differential diagnosis includes primary tumors of the lung and mediastinum, specifically oat cell and epidermoid carcinomas. Reactive mediastinitis and hilar adenopathy from histoplasmosis can be confused with lymphoma, particularly in regions where histoplasmosis is endemic, since it occurs in otherwise asymptomatic young people. Histoplasma mediastinitis usually involves the esophagus and should be suspected by obtaining a history of difficulty in swallowing; the diagnosis is confirmed by an abnormal esophagogram or node calcification. Biopsy may be complicated by hemorrhage. Hodgkin's disease presenting as "fever of undetermined origin" may remain undiagnosed despite extensive investigations until an exploratory celiotomy is done.

DIAGNOSIS AND PATHOLOGY The diagnosis and classification of a lymphoma can be made only by biopsy and histopathologic examination under a light microscope. Needle aspiration of lymph nodes, while it may suggest the diagnosis, does not yield sufficient tissue to classify lymphoma accurately, and the error rate is high. Needle aspiration, however, may be useful to distinguish recurrent disease from reactive hyperplasia and to supply tissue samples for analysis of gene rearrangements characteristic of lymphomas of B- and T-cell origin. Even experienced pathologists, using fixed sections of lymph nodes, disagree on classification of 25 percent of cases and on whether the resected tissue shows evidence of malignancy in as many as 6 percent of cases. Frozen section material should not be used alone when lymphoma is suspected because slightly crushed normal lymphoid tissue in frozen sections mimics malignancy. Frozen sections, however, can now be used with a panel of monoclonal antibodies to phenotype lymphocytic lymphomas.

Hodgkin's disease is unique among cancers because the tumor observed by the physician contains largely normal tissue, reactive lymphocytes, plasma cells, and the fibrous stroma of the lymph node and only a scattering of the characteristic malignant cell of Hodgkin's disease, the Sternberg-Reed cell. In the absence of Sternberg-Reed cells, the diagnosis of Hodgkin's disease should rarely be made, although the presence of such a cell by itself is not pathognomonic of the disease, since cells simulating Sternberg-Reed cells have been found in patients with infectious mononucleosis and breast cancer. The presence of the mononuclear variety of the Sternberg-Reed cell, which has a large eosinophilic nucleolus, is sufficient to demonstrate Hodgkin's disease involving the liver or bone marrow in a patient known to have Hodgkin's disease elsewhere; however, the finding of mononuclear Sternberg-Reed cells is not sufficient for the diagnosis of the primary tumor itself.

On the basis of histologic classification and knowledge of the rates of spread of tumor, the likelihood that an apparently localized lesion will be disseminated can often be predicted. The histologic classification by Lukes and Butler used for Hodgkin's disease is shown in Table 294-2, along with the older Jackson-Parker classification. The original, more complete version of the Lukes and Butler classification was modified at the Rye Staging Conference to include the four major histologic subgroups shown in the right column of Table 294-2.

IMMUNOLOGIC ABNORMALITIES In the 1950s, patients with Hodgkin's disease were shown to have a higher incidence of cutaneous anergy to a battery of intradermal skin tests than did normal controls. In most studies, the immunologic defect has been shown to have no influence on the prognosis within a given clinical stage, when modern therapy is used. This is an important observation because it indicates that immunosuppressive chemotherapy has no adverse effect, even when the patients are already immunosuppressed by their disease, as long as it effectively eradicates the malignant cell, an observation that pertains to other cancers as well.

The functional T-lymphocyte defect can now be detected even in patients with very early stage I Hodgkin's disease, if dose-response curves are done with topical dinitrochlorobenzene (DNCB) and with lymphocyte response to phytohemagglutinin (PHA) in vitro. These data show that a T-cell defect is always a concomitant of Hodgkin's disease. Following successful treatment with chemotherapy or radiation therapy, a permanent immunologic defect, both in number and function of T lymphocytes, remains even in patients who have been free of tumor for many years; this does not occur in other lymphoma patients cured with the same treatments. Antibody production is normal in most patients with Hodgkin's disease, but antibody production can be influenced by therapy. Combined multidrug chemotherapy and radiotherapy, especially in patients who have undergone splenectomy, have been shown to diminish the primary response to capsular antigens of *Haemophilus influenzae* type B. This may lead to a higher incidence of sepsis with *H. influenzae* and other encapsulated pathogens and accounts for the failure of pneumococcal vaccines to prevent infection in treated patients after splenectomy. While no firm data exist, vaccination with pneumococcal vaccine prior to staging and treatment should be considered if patients will undergo splenectomy.

HEMATOLOGIC ABNORMALITIES A moderate, normochromic, normocytic anemia associated with low serum iron and low iron-binding capacity, but normal or increased iron stores in the bone marrow, may be present in patients with Hodgkin's disease. This profile is similar to that found in other patients with malignancy. A Coombs-positive hemolytic anemia occurs in less than 1 percent of patients with advanced disease. The erythrocyte sedimentation rate (ESR) is usually rapid and serves as a useful test to follow disease activity; however, it has limited sensitivity and returns to normal when residual disease is still present. It can be useful in monitoring patients who are in remission to determine the early evidence of recurrence. Extensive radiation therapy may cause the ESR to be elevated for as long as 1 year after treatment without evidence of recurrent tumor. Numerous more complicated and usually more expensive laboratory tests of disease activity have not been shown to be superior to the ESR. A moderate to marked leukemoid reaction is common in Hodgkin's disease, particularly in symptomatic patients. White blood cell counts as high as 67,000 per deciliter, a level which can easily be confused with the level found in chronic granulocytic leukemia, may be seen. The leukemoid reaction disappears with successful treatment. Mild peripheral eosinophilia is not uncommon especially in patients with pruritus. Absolute lymphocytopenia (<1000 cells per cubic millimeter) usually occurs in patients with more advanced disease.

Marrow aspiration has not yielded results comparable to those obtained by biopsy, probably because of the fibrosis and granuloma formation in the marrow of patients with Hodgkin's disease. On smear or section, the myeloid/erythroid ratio may be increased, and marrow eosinophilia is common; neither is sufficient to diagnose marrow involvement by tumor. Involvement of the marrow by tumor is demonstrated by finding either classic Sternberg-Reed cells or their mononuclear variant, distributed focally or diffusely throughout the bone marrow. Marrow involvement is often associated with reticular fibrosis, which sometimes obscures the architecture of the marrow. In a patient with known Hodgkin's disease, intense marrow fibrosis, even in the absence of the characteristic malignant cells, is strong evidence of tumor in the bone marrow. Surprisingly, effective treatment by chemotherapy often leads to total resolution of marrow fibrosis in patients who achieve remission.

SELECTED CLINICAL PROBLEMS Infections are common in patients with Hodgkin's disease. Those who have progressive tumor usually die of the complications of bone marrow failure, bacteremia, or disseminated fungal infections. Diffuse pulmonary infiltrates may appear in patients who are in remission between cycles of chemotherapy due to infection with the protozoan *Pneumocystis carinii*, a disease now so commonly reported in patients with AIDS. The first cases of pneumonia caused by the protozoan *P. carinii* were reported in adults under these circumstances and subsequently in children with leukemia. In rodents, the appearance of this infection between cycles of treatment seems to be related to a rebound inflammatory response

to the growing organism. Patients with Hodgkin's disease are prone to develop cryptococcosis, either in the form of meningitis or as a primary pulmonary infiltrate with or without meningitis. Herpes zoster (shingles) occurs in 10 percent of treated Hodgkin's patients and in 20 percent of treated patients who have had a splenectomy. Most patients who develop herpes zoster have a few scattered papules outside the involved dermatome; this minimal evidence of spread usually does not require systemic treatment.

Cord compression is the most serious acute complication caused by growing tumor masses and is usually seen in patients with progressive tumor who have failed primary treatment. It can be caused by vertebral body involvement with collapse, which is easily seen on x-ray or bone scan, or by invasion of the epidural space from retroperitoneal lymph nodes with compression of the cord or compression of the vascular supply to the cord. Computerized tomograph (CT) scanning can be useful in detecting encroachment on the spinal cord from the retroperitoneal area. Selective electromyography is a useful way to detect regional denervation, but a myelogram is usually needed to confirm the diagnosis. Tumor masses can also obstruct the superior vena cava. This may occur as a presenting syndrome or late in the course of the disease when the diagnosis is obvious.

STAGING The staging classification developed for Hodgkin's disease and used for all lymphomas is shown in Table 294-3. Accurate staging of Hodgkin's patients is vital for planning long-term management. The primary physician must take a detailed history, do a thorough physical examination, and seek evidence of systemic symptoms such as fever, night sweats, and weight loss. Weight loss of 10 percent or greater, with no attempt at dieting, usually indicates serious disease in this young population. Soaking night sweats can occur in anxious patients, and a history of sweats preceding knowledge of the diagnosis should be sought carefully. Every lymph node area of the body should be examined carefully, and the presence or absence of enlargement noted for future reference; the size, shape, and consistency should be recorded. Reactive hyperplasia is a cause for lymph node enlargement around the lymph nodes involved with tumor, especially in the neck region; the largest lymph nodes in a group should be marked for biopsy. These may be less accessible to the surgeon, who should be urged nonetheless to seek them out. Nodes in areas other than the primary site, that might change the patient's stage from local to generalized disease, should be biopsied at the same time. Unfortunately, internists are prone to omit examination of the oro- and nasopharynx by indirect laryngoscopy. Such

TABLE 294-3 Staging classification for lymphomas

Stage	Definition
I	Involvement of a single lymph node region (I) or of a single extralymphatic organ or site (I_E).
II	Involvement of two or more lymph node regions on the same side of the diaphragm (II) or localized involvement of an extralymphatic organ or site and of one or more lymph node regions on the same side of the diaphragm (II_E).
III	Involvement of lymph node regions on both sides of the diaphragm (III), which may also be accompanied by involvement of the spleen (III_S) or by localized involvement of an extralymphatic organ or site (III_E) or both (III_{SE}).
III_1	Involvement limited to the lymphatic structures in the upper abdomen, that is, spleen, or splenic, celiac, or hepatic portal nodes, or any combination of these.
III_2	Involvement of lower abdominal nodes, that is, paraaortic, iliac, or mesenteric nodes, with or without involvement of the splenic, celiac, or hepatic portal nodes.
IV	Diffuse or disseminated involvement of one or more extralymphatic organs or tissues, with or without associated lymph node involvement.

NOTE: *E = extralymphatic site; S = splenic involvement. The presence of fever, night sweats, and/or unexplained loss of 10 percent of body weight in the 6 months preceding admission is denoted by the suffix letter B. The letter A indicates the absence of these symptoms. Biopsy-documented involvement of stage IV sites is also denoted by letter suffixes; marrow = M+; lung = L+; liver = H+; pleura = P+; bone = 0+; skin and subcutaneous tissue = D+.*

examination is essential to uncovering Waldeyer's ring involvement by lymphoma, although this finding is more common in the lymphocytic lymphomas than in Hodgkin's disease. Epitrochlear nodes are also more likely to indicate a lymphocytic lymphoma. The size of the liver and spleen should be noted. In Hodgkin's disease, palpable splenomegaly is significant because, in most cases, it indicates more generalized disease. The procedures required for staging patients with Hodgkin's disease under various circumstances are shown in Tables 294-3 to 294-6.

Radiologic examination should include a routine chest film. When any evidence of disease is noted on this x-ray, whole-chest CT scanning is performed to identify the extent of mediastinal or hilar adenopathy or evidence of contiguous invasion of the lung from the hilar nodes. Lower extremity lymphogram should always be done unless medically contraindicated. On occasion, the lymphogram will not fill high retroperitoneal lymph nodes. CT scans and ultrasound have been shown to be effective in delineating the status of the retroperitoneal lymph nodes in these upper node regions and should supplement lymphography. Bone involvement can be assessed using the lymphogram films in most cases. Symptomatic patients should have a separate skeletal survey and/or bone scan. The latter is the more sensitive test for identifying bone lesions.

Routine blood counts, ESR, urinalysis, liver function studies, and renal function studies are all necessary parts of the medical workup, but by themselves do not provide information about the extent of Hodgkin's disease or specific organ involvement. Liver function abnormalities, in particular, are poor indicators of Hodgkin's involvement of the liver but are helpful in ruling out the presence of other complicating illnesses. Bone marrow biopsy, not aspiration, should be done in all symptomatic patients with Hodgkin's disease and in those asymptomatic patients with evidence of generalized adenopathy and in patients who are undergoing staging laparotomy. Asymptomatic patients who have disease clinically localized above the diaphragm, that is, whose lymphography, CT scan, and sonogram are found to be negative, rarely have bone marrow involvement, and the biopsy can be omitted in such cases.

In 1968, a group of investigators at Stanford University introduced routine staging laparotomy as a research tool to evaluate the extent of Hodgkin's disease, to define its mode of spread, and to determine the implications of such information for therapy. In one-third of patients with normal-sized spleens, Hodgkin's disease was found in the spleen removed at surgery; conversely, in those patients with clinically enlarged spleens, up to 25 percent had no evidence of tumor in the spleen but appeared instead to have reactive hyperplasia. Splenic enlargement due to involvement by HD has been linked to liver involvement. The liver is rarely involved when splenic involvement is not associated with splenomegaly (<0.5 percent). Liver involvement is present in as many as 28 percent of patients with positive lymphograms and enlarged spleens. The Stanford data also showed that the lymphogram is an accurate test to detect lymph node

TABLE 294-4   Staging the lymphomas: Required evaluative procedures

1 Adequate surgical biopsy, reviewed by an experienced hematologist
2 A detailed history recording the absence or presence of and duration of fever, unexplained sweating and its severity, unexplained pruritus, and unexplained weight loss
3 A careful and detailed physical examination; special attention to all node-bearing areas, including Waldeyer's ring (indirect laryngoscopy), and determination of size of liver and spleen
4 Necessary laboratory procedures:
  a Complete blood count, including an erythrocyte sedimentation rate
  b Serum alkaline phosphatase
  c Evaluation of renal function
  d Evaluation of liver function
5 Radiologic studies
  a Chest roentgenogram (posteroanterior and lateral)
  b Bilateral lymphogram of lower extremities
  c CT scan of abdomen, with or without ultrasonography
  d Views of skeletal system to include thoracic and lumbar vertebrae, the pelvis, proximal extremities, and any area of bone tenderness

TABLE 294-5   Staging the lymphomas: Procedures required under certain conditions

1 Whole-chest CT scan if any abnormality is noted or suspected on routine chest roentgenogram
2 Bone marrow *biopsy* (needle or surgical) in the presence of
  a An elevated alkaline phosphatase
  b Unexplained anemia or other blood count depression
  c Other evidence of bone disease (scan or x-ray)
  d Disease of stage III or greater
3 Exploratory laparotomy and splenectomy, if management decisions will depend on the identification of abdominal disease

involvement by tumor. Only 15 percent of patients with positive lymphograms are found to have normal lymph node biopsies at surgery. Even in these patients, an explanation may be found in the reactive lymphoid hyperplasia normally found adjacent to tumor.

Staging laparotomy should not be considered a routine concomitant of staging. Knowledge of the type of treatment to be used by the radiotherapist or medical oncologist, for the variety of stages of Hodgkin's disease, should be known *in advance* of a decision to operate, since general treatment strategy may markedly influence the decision to perform a staging laparotomy. When it is performed, the laparotomy should always be complete and include at least two needle biopsies of each lobe of the liver, a wedge biopsy of edge of the right lobe of the liver and biopsies of other suspicious areas in the liver, splenectomy, and biopsy of selected lymph nodes in the retroperitoneal area, marked on the lymphogram prior to the operation. A postoperative film should confirm that the proper lymph nodes were removed. Nodes in the porta hepatis should also be biopsied and in female patients in the reproductive period the ovaries should be moved laterally or centrally to avoid the major part of the radiation ports. The spleen should be sectioned in 0.3-cm slices and, if tumor is found, the number of nodules enumerated. Determining whether or not the liver is involved with tumor can have a major influence on the selection of therapy and obviate the need for splenectomy or examination of the retroperitoneum. Laparoscopy has been shown to be a useful alternative approach to laparotomy in staging abdominal disease. Results from laparotomy may change the stage in as many as 35 percent of patients. It should be emphasized that the change of stage following laparotomy infrequently results in a change in the plan of therapy, especially if chemotherapy is to be used alone or in combination with radiotherapy. Nationwide, the mortality from staging laparotomy in Hodgkin's disease is 1.5 percent, with a complication rate of approximatley 12 percent. However, mortality rates up to 6.6 percent and morbidity rates of greater than 25 percent have been reported from institutions where laparotomies are done infrequently. In some stages and types of Hodgkin's disease, the operative mortality may exceed the expected death rate at 5 years from the disease itself. Splenectomy itself has not been shown to have a beneficial side effect either in the delivery or outcome or radiotherapy or combination chemotherapy.

The Ann Arbor Conference on Staging of Hodgkin's Disease recommended that results of staging should be reported using both the clinical stage (CS, i.e., all tests leading up to invasive studies) and the final pathologic stage (PS), which includes the results of invasive tests such as liver biopsy, peritoneoscopy, and laparotomy. This was recommended to ensure that investigators, using different staging approaches, could make comparisons of the results of therapy based on the clinical stage of the patient.

TABLE 294-6   Staging the lymphomas: Useful ancillary procedures

1 Skeletal scintigrams*
2 Hepatic and splenic scintigrams*
3 Gallium whole-body scans*
4 Serum chemistries to include serum calcium and uric acid for overall management of patient

* *Cannot be used as evidence of Hodgkin's disease without biopsy confirmation.*

TREATMENT More than 70 percent of all patients with Hodgkin's disease are now curable using either radiotherapy or combination chemotherapy, or both. Because of the stringent requirements for shielding and field piecing, the radiotherapy used for Hodgkin's disease is the most difficult treatment a radiation therapist performs. The treatment of Hodgkin's disease by radiotherapy requires extensive experience with more than a few patients a year and adequate equipment. A linear accelerator, preferably a 4- to 8-MeV model is the preferred instrument. Kilovoltage equipment is inadequate and should no longer be used. Cobalt 60 equipment can be used, but is associated with an increase in side effects from greater scatter of the radiotherapy beam.

Current drug treatment programs require precise metering of doses using a sliding scale for increases and decreases of dosage, based on nadir blood counts and blood counts determined the day a new cycle is to begin. Consistently safe delivery of chemotherapy requires experience in treating the disease and using the drugs, and therefore, should not be attempted by anyone not expert in the field. Inexperienced physicians will often use reduced doses, omit drugs, and use improper sequencing and disrupted schedules, all of which have been shown to diminish the chance of cure.

Although highly successful, treatment of Hodgkin's disease is still in transition. Clinical trials are in progress to develop and study ways to make both drugs and radiation treatment safer, to further facilitate their general use, and to evaluate the role of each alone and together in various stages and histologic subtypes. Some general principles have, however, emerged. At the present time, the best approach to treatment is to use either radiotherapy or combination chemotherapy alone in the appropriate stage. Studies comparing both types of treatment used together to each used alone have shown that patients who relapse after radiotherapy can be retreated successfully with combination chemotherapy with survival results equivalent to those obtained in previously untreated patients of the same stage and histologic subtype. This means that patients cured by radiotherapy alone can be spared exposure to drugs and those patients treated with radiotherapy who relapse have a second chance for cure. Interpretation of results of radiotherapy of localized disease is complicated by the fact that with the success of combination chemotherapy, patients who are inadequately treated with radiotherapy can be salvaged by chemotherapy. Until the results are in, less-than-standard radiotherapy should not be given intentionally just because of the potential for salvage by chemotherapy of those patients who fail this treatment. Studies are now underway to determine the effectiveness of chemotherapy alone in patients with early stages of disease.

The role of radiotherapy as a supplement to drug treatment of stages III and IV disease is also experimental. Such an approach has not yet been proved to be superior to chemotherapy alone and runs the risk of increasing the rate of late complications. Adding full-dose radiotherapy to combination chemotherapy has not proved useful in any study so far. Interesting results have been reported from low-dose radiotherapy given to organs involved with tumors between cycles of chemotherapy.

The dose of radiotherapy is important, because the risk of relapse in a treated field is inversely proportional to dose, falling to about 1 percent at 44 Gy (4400 rad). Because of the sharpness of the field edge with minimal scatter achieved by a linear accelerator, the large fields required to treat Hodgkin's disease can be given with less toxicity to the bone marrow and less scatter to uninvolved but susceptible essential organs. In spite of shielding and sharp field edges, scatter to the entire lung fields is often in the range of 2 Gy (200 rad), and similar scatter doses are routinely received by the testes if the lower abdomen is irradiated, even when extensive shielding is used.

Three types of radiation fields are used for all lymphomas. Involved-field (IF) radiotherapy treats only the tumor mass with a minimal margin of normal tissue. Mantle-field irradiation gives radiation treatment to the cervical, axillary, mediastinal, and upper paraaortic nodes, as well as preauricular nodes, usually as one field.

When used in this way, it is referred to as extended-field (EF) radiotherapy. The "inverted-Y" field is used to irradiate the retroperitoneal lymph nodes as a single field, and when used with the mantle field, is referred to as total-nodal irradiation (TNI). Actually, TNI is a misnomer since many lymph nodes are outside the usual TNI fields; total-axial lymph node irradiation (TANI) is a more accurate designation. Critical to applying these treatments is the shielding of the spinal cord at the field match sites, the cervical region, and the heart. Field overlap can result in delivery of sufficient radiation to the spine to cause radiation myelitis.

There is little role for single-agent chemotherapy as the primary treatment in patients with advanced disease unless they are medically infirm for reasons other than Hodgkin's disease. The four-drug program with the acronym MOPP [nitrogen *m*ustard, vincristine (*O*ncovin), *p*rednisone, and *p*rocarbazine] has emerged as the standard treatment program for stages III and IV Hodgkin's disease. Through the use of the MOPP combination program, 80 percent of patients with advanced stages can achieve complete remissions; 63 percent of patients at risk for 20 years have remained free of their disease after remission was induced with only six cycles of treatment. Most patients who relapse do so in the first 4 years of follow-up. Numerous variations on the MOPP program using similar drugs to diminish toxicity without sacrificing results have not proved superior, but can be used under special circumstances. A detailed review of these programs is to be found in DeVita et al. Non-cross-resistant drug combinations are now available and are being tested along with MOPP treatment to determine whether alternating cycles of non-cross-resistant drug combinations are superior to combining drug combinations with radiation therapy in patients with advanced disease. The combination ABVD (*A*driamycin, *b*leomycin, *v*inblastine, and *d*acarbazine) may be as effective as MOPP. Its use in alternating cycles with MOPP is under study. A new approach using hybrid half-cycles of MOPP and Adriamycin, bleomycin, and vinblastine (MOPP-ABV) shows early promise. Other combinations of old and new single drugs are also used to salvage those patients who relapse after MOPP-induced remission, or who fail to achieve remission.

Many variables influence the outcome of patients within a given stage. These include the presence or absence of symptoms and the various histologic subtypes in the treatment groups. Symptoms adversely affect prognosis since they generally indicate a greater volume of tumor as well as rapidity of spread. Volume is a clinical variable that is difficult to assess in current staging classifications. However, a large mediastinal mass, occurrence of more than four splenic nodules, and PS III$_2$ are poor prognostic factors. Histology is also important. The nodular sclerosing variety of Hodgkin's disease favorably influences the prognosis of patients treated by radiotherapy alone. The selection of treatment for patients presenting with a large mediastinal mass, contiguous involvement of the lung (E), more than four splenic nodules, CS III, or PS III$_2$ is not settled, and these patients are often considered for combined-modality therapy.

Use of specific radiation treatment approaches INVOLVED-FIELD RADIOTHERAPY Patients with single-node involvement in the high right neck, especially those who have lymphocyte-predominant Hodgkin's disease, do not require a laparotomy, since they rarely have splenic or retroperitoneal lymph node involvement by tumor and can be rendered free of disease for extended periods 95 percent of the time when treated with 35 to 40 Gy (3500 to 4000 rad) to the involved field.

EXTENDED-FIELD RADIOTHERAPY Patients with CS IA and IIA, with nodular sclerosing or mixed cellular Hodgkin's disease, limited to lymph node areas above the diaphragm, can be rendered free of disease more than 90 percent of the time for periods extending beyond a decade, by EF radiotherapy alone, without the need for laparotomy. However, the normal-sized spleen needs to be included in the EF port. Those patients who present with single sites of involvement in the groin should be treated with EF radiotherapy (in this case the inverted-Y field) rather than IF radiotherapy. Some assessment of the status of the liver should also be made in such patients, either by laparoscopy or laparotomy.

TOTAL-AXIAL LYMPH NODE RADIOTHERAPY (TANI)   TANI has provided results superior to EF or mantle-field radiotherapy when relapse-free survival is the major criterion of effectiveness. TANI includes a splenic port and should not be used in patients with enlarged spleens. All symptomatic patients with localized disease (CS and PS IB and IIB), if they are to receive radiotherapy alone, should receive TANI, even if a laparotomy demonstrated no evidence of disease below the diaphragm, since there is evidence that withholding radiation therapy to retroperitoneal nodes is not safe in patients with negative random lymph node biopsies. Laparotomy is therefore unnecessary in most of these cases. The type of radiotherapy to be given for supradiaphragmatic CS and PS IIA mixed-cellularity and lymphocyte-predominant Hodgkin's disease is debatable. Equivalent results are achievable with TANI in clinically staged patients and EF in patients staged by laparotomy.

Patients with large mediastinal masses   If the mediastinum is involved with Hodgkin's disease and the mass exceeds one-third of the diameter of the chest on a posteroanterior (PA) film, the control rate by radiotherapy alone in patients with stage II disease is poor. Some evidence exists to suggest that survival of relapsing patients is not compromised because they can be salvaged with chemotherapy, but the weight of evidence now favors the use of combination chemotherapy and radiotherapy in these patients as the primary treatment. One of two sequences can be used: radiotherapy first with a shrinking field to minimize lung damage, or chemotherapy first to shrink the mass. Combination chemotherapy alone may prove sufficient, but this point is presently under study. It is suggested by the fact that in some series patients with stages III *and* IV disease and massive mediastinal disease do as well with chemotherapy alone as those patients with advanced disease but without massive mediastinal involvement.

Combination chemotherapy   Stage IIIA responds well to MOPP or variants of MOPP chemotherapy; recent studies report a superior remission rate and fewer relapses over a decade of follow-up compared to the use of TANI alone, and the results equal those from the use of TANI and combination chemotherapy together. Several studies clearly show that patients with CS and PS IIIB Hodgkin's disease have a better chance of relapse-free survival with MOPP chemotherapy than with TANI and that the addition of full doses of radiotherapy to chemotherapy does not appear to provide much benefit. An exception may be found in patients with nodular sclerosing stage IIIB Hodgkin's disease, with bulky tumor, especially in the mediastinum. These patients may profit from the combined use of MOPP and TANI radiotherapy.

All patients with stage IV disease are best treated with MOPP chemotherapy or other drug combinations that have been equally effective in producing relapse-free survivals beyond 5 years with no treatment beyond the initial induction cycles. Remission rate and duration are not influenced by specific organs involved with tumor. A patient with bone marrow involvement by Hodgkin's disease should receive full doses of chemotherapy and can expect the same frequency and duration of remission as those patients who have liver or lung involvement. Other drug combinations such as ABVD may be useful in patients who fail the MOPP chemotherapy program. It has been shown to produce a significant fraction of durable complete remissions in MOPP treatment failures. When a patient has failed treatment with both MOPP and ABVD, the greater side effects produced by combinations of drugs must be weighed more carefully against the use of single-agent treatment as palliation. Because of the lack of durability of remissions achieved after resistance has developed to the first two trials of combination drug treatment, cure by standard chemotherapy alone is no longer a reasonable expectation. Under these circumstances, it is sometimes helpful to return to the use of single-agent chemotherapy, including drugs used in previous combinations, but given in a different dose or by a new schedule. For

example, patients with advancing MOPP-resistant Hodgkin's disease may still respond to daily oral procarbazine or intermittent large doses of alkylating agents.

Some institutions are investigating the use of high-dose chemotherapy and total-body irradiation in conjunction with autologous bone marrow transplantation in patients who have failed primary chemotherapy. Some long-term remissions have been realized. Clinical trails with biologicals are also under study. Monoclonal antibody therapy with anti-Ki1 antibody armed with alpha-emitting isotopes hold great promise.

Side effects   Acute side effects of radiotherapy are nausea and vomiting, marrow suppression, and gastrointestinal ulceration. All of these are troublesome but usually subside shortly after radiation therapy is terminated. After completion of radiotherapy, the more serious side effects, radiation myelitis, pneumonitis, and rarely pericarditis may occur 6 weeks to several months following completion of therapy. Late complications include fibrosis of soft tissue and lungs within the radiation field, coronary artery disease, persistent bone marrow fibrosis, and pancytopenia, as well as an increased incidence of tumors within the treated field.

With chemotherapy, marrow suppression is the most life-threatening acute side effect. It should be monitored carefully, and drug doses adjusted using sliding scales provided in publications reporting the results of treatment. Nausea, vomiting, and alopecia are the most troublesome complications of drug therapy to patients. Delta-9-tetrahydrocannabinol and metaclopramide have been shown to be useful in ameliorating nausea and vomiting associated with cancer chemotherapy. Most patients respond to emotional support and reassurance from their physicians that the symptoms are temporary, hair grows back, and they will return to normal post treatment. Sterility, more commonly seen in males, is a consequence of chemotherapy. The effective use of drugs requires experience; it is unacceptable to give smaller or widely spaced doses of chemotherapy, both of which adversely affect the probability of cure, because of convenience or to avoid nausea and vomiting, especially if the patient is not fully aware of the consequences of altering the treatment.

In combined treatment with radiation and chemotherapy, particularly in patients with early disease, one of the late complications is an increased incidence of acute myelocytic leukemia. The actuarial incidence is 5 to 7 percent at 10 years following completion of therapy. An increased incidence of lymphocytic lymphoma following combined-modality treatment has also been reported. While such a risk may be acceptable in patients who would otherwise have died without treatment, it may not be acceptable in patients who might have been effectively treated with either chemotherapy or radiotherapy alone.

THE LYMPHOCYTIC LYMPHOMAS

This group of diseases, like Hodgkin's disease, have their origin in lymphoreticular tissue. There are differences among them in the cell of origin, age distribution, presentation, stage at onset, complications, and response to therapy. They encompass a wide spectrum of disorders, ranging from Burkitt's lymphoma in children in Africa to follicular and diffuse lymphomas in adults. Lymphocytic lymphoma is the correct designation, not non-Hodgkin's lymphomas. The majority of cases of lymphocytic lymphomas are monoclonal B-cell neoplasms (see Table 294-1).

CLINICAL FEATURES   The lymphocytic lymphomas usually present as painless, localized, or generalized enlargements of lymph nodes with or without hepatosplenomegaly and not infrequently as an abdominal mass. Involvement of Waldeyer's ring is more common in lymphocytic lymphomas than in Hodgkin's disease and is often associated with gastrointestinal involvement. A discrete lesion or multiple lesions of the lung, bone, gastrointestinal system, skin, or other parenchymal sites may be the presenting feature. The systemic symptoms described for Hodgkin's disease are less common in patients with lymphocytic lymphomas, but their presence is also thought to influence the prognosis negatively. In the follicular lymphomas, the lymphadenopathy may have been present for a long period of time; often a previous lymph node biopsy may have been interpreted as "atypical" or "hyperplastic." Review of such material by a hematopathologist at a later time and comparison with a second biopsy often reveals that a lymphoma was present from the start.

DIFFERENTIAL DIAGNOSIS The differential diagnosis of lymphocytic lymphomas as a cause of adenopathy is similar to that of Hodgkin's disease. Since the average age of the population is a decade and a half older than for Hodgkin's disease, other malignancies are more likely prospects in the differential diagnosis.

DIAGNOSIS AND PATHOLOGY The diagnosis of a lymphocytic lymphoma is made by histopathologic examination of biopsy material usually obtained from lymph nodes; diagnosis and classification of material obtained from other sites may be more difficult. This is a most important step because, in contrast to Hodgkin's disease, selection of therapy depends on the histologic type more than the stage of disease. The histologic classification proposed by Rappaport has been generally employed because it was reproducible and useful in predicting prognosis (Table 294-7). Familiarity with this system is important since it has been employed in the majority of clinical trials. In addition to the Rappaport classification, six other classifications have been proposed, leading to considerable confusion. The National Cancer Institute sponsored a study to develop a "Working Formulation for Clinical Usage" that amalgamates the best of each classification system. This classification is now used widely and will be used throughout this chapter with the Rappaport classification given in brackets when necessary. The basic approach in the Working Formulation is similar to that of Rappaport in dividing lymphocytic lymphomas on the basis of follicular or diffuse patterns and cytologic composition. Immunologic terminology is not used, but correlations with immunologic phenotypes, when established, are easily drawn. In addition, the Formulation divides the lymphocytic lymphomas into three grades: low, intermediate, and high, depending on the aggressiveness of their growth behavior; low-grade lymphomas are more indolent and high-grade the most aggressive. Utilizing this system makes cross-correlations between studies easier. Most older data, however, have been reported in the Rappaport system and when specific studies are cited, the terminology in those studies will be used.

The presence of a follicular or a diffuse pattern in the nodal architecture is a most influential prognostic factor. Follicular lymphomas tend to follow a more indolent course than those with a diffuse pattern of equivalent cytologic appearance. The pace of evolution and response to treatment within the follicular variety is also influenced by the cytologic features of the cells within the follicles—slower for small cleaved cells and more rapid for large cells. The diffuse lymphomas are clinically more aggressive than the follicular lymphomas, except for the small lymphocytic lymphoma, which resembles chronic lymphocytic leukemia and follows a chronic course. At the time of initial clinical staging, 40 percent of patients with diffuse large cell lymphomas appear to have regional disease, although if treated only locally, the relapse rate is high (see below). In contrast, patients with follicular, predominantly small cleaved cell lymphomas show a propensity for widespread dissemination, easily demonstrated with routine tests, and for a pattern of continuous, late recurrence extending over a period of 5 to 10 years.

IMMUNOLOGIC ABNORMALITIES Immune function is less affected in lymphocytic lymphomas than in Hodgkin's patients, although a defect in delayed hypersensitivity reactions can be found in patients with intermediate- and high-grade lymphomas such as diffuse large cell lymphoma. Skin reactivity and phytohemagglutinin response in follicular, predominantly small cleaved cell lymphoma are sometimes depressed but usually only in association with advanced tumor. A

defect in humoral immune function can be demonstrated more frequently in patients with diffuse small lymphocytic lymphomas than with Hodgkin's disease and is manifest as a monoclonal gammopathy or hypogammaglobulinemia.

STAGING The stage of disease must be determined prior to treatment after the confirmation of the histologic diagnosis. The extent of clinical evaluation is guided by histologic subtype and the type of therapy proposed for a particular patient. The staging classification developed for Hodgkin's disease (Ann Arbor Staging Classification, Table 294-3) is used in lymphocytic lymphomas as well; however, the sequence of staging procedures differs because extralymphatic presentations occur more frequently in lymphocytic lymphomas than in Hodgkin's disease. Further, since many approach stages II, III, and IV disease therapeutically in a similar manner, utilizing systemic therapy with or without radiotherapy, this distinction may be far less relevant. For those occasional patients who, after clinical staging, still appear to have localized disease (less than 10 percent of all lymphocytic lymphoma patients) and are considered eligible for radiotherapy alone, extensive staging, even employing laparotomy, may be justified. For the remainder, documentation of advanced disease is usually quite simple, with few or no invasive tests indicated. In those whose age or general medical problems limit therapy to local palliation with radiotherapy or systemic treatment with a single drug, even fewer invasive staging procedures are indicated. Thus, surgical staging should never be considered a routine procedure in patients with lymphocytic lymphomas. The major task of staging is to determine whether the patient has limited nodal or extranodal (E) disease, which is radiocurable (stage I or contiguous stage II), or disseminated disease, which requires systemic therapy (discontiguous stage II or stages III and IV).

Because the histologic patterns correlate well with specific disease patterns, response to therapy, and prognosis, the histologic diagnosis

TABLE 294-7

Working formulation	Rappaport terminology
LOW-GRADE	
A Malignant lymphoma, small lymphocytic, consistent with chronic lymphocytic leukemia; plasmacytoid	Diffuse well-differentiated lymphocytic (DWDL)
B Malignant lymphoma, follicular, predominantly small cleaved cell; diffuse areas, sclerosis	Nodular poorly differentiated lymphocytic (NPDL)
C Malignant lymphoma, follicular, mixed, small cleaved and large cell; diffuse areas, sclerosis	Nodular mixed lymphocytic histiocytic (NML)
INTERMEDIATE-GRADE	
D Malignant lymphoma, follicular, predominantly large cell; diffuse areas, sclerosis	Nodular histiocytic (NHL)
E Malignant lymphoma, diffuse small cleaved cell	Diffuse poorly differentiated lymphocytic (DPDL)
F Malignant lymphoma, diffuse mixed, small and large cell; sclerosis, epithelioid cell component	Diffuse mixed lymphocytic-histiocytic (DML)
G Malignant lymphoma, diffuse large cell; cleaved cell, non-cleaved cell, sclerosis	Diffuse histiocytic (DHL)
HIGH-GRADE	
H Malignant lymphoma, large cell, immunoblastic; plasmacytoid, clear cell, polymorphous, epithelioid cell component	Diffuse histiocytic (DHL)
I Malignant lymphoma, lymphoblastic; convoluted cell, nonconvoluted cell	Diffuse lymphoblastic
J Malignant lymphoma small non-cleaved cell; Burkitt's follicular areas	Diffuse undifferentiated (DUL)

can be used to determine the appropriate staging procedures needed to choose the appropriate treatment strategy for a particular patient. For example, 80 percent of patients with a follicular pattern have a histopathologic diagnosis of follicular, predominantly small cleaved cell [nodular, poorly differentiated lymphoma (NPDL)] or follicular mixed, small cleaved and large cell lymphoma [nodular mixed lymphoma (NML)], and 80 to 90 percent of these patients will be in stages III and IV after clinical staging and simple needle biopsy techniques. Early in the patient's staging evaluation, only diagnostic studies that have a low morbidity and a high probability of disclosing advanced disease should be employed. Lymphograms, bone marrow biopsies, and liver biopsy meet these requirements and can usually obviate the need for staging laparotomy. Approximately 90 percent of patients with follicular and 60 to 70 percent with diffuse lymphocytic lymphomas have positive lymphograms. For patients with positive lymphograms, the incidence of spleen, liver, and/or bone marrow involvement is high (90 percent); in contrast, in patients with negative lymphograms, such involvement is 10 percent or less. Bone marrow aspirates are inadequate for diagnosis, and bilateral posterior iliac crest biopsies are recommended. In low-grade lymphomas, follicular or diffuse, the incidence of bone marrow involvement is at least 50 to 60 percent, even though there is usually no evidence of peripheral blood count abnormalities.

Search for liver involvement should be pursued if the bone marrow biopsies prove to be negative and if the therapeutic plan is to treat the patient with less than a systemic approach. Nondirected percutaneous biopsies detect 20 percent of cases with liver involvement, peritoneoscopy-directed multiple biopsies detect an additional 20 to 30 percent of cases, and finally, if no evidence of stage IV disease has been shown after these procedures, and if it is important to detect microscopic liver involvement, liver biopsies at laparotomy detect the remaining 50 percent of cases. Liver involvement occurs in 65 percent of cases with low-grade lymphomas, whether the architecture is nodular or diffuse. In contrast are the findings in patients diagnosed as having intermediate- or high-grade lymphomas of the diffuse large cell variety. Some 20 percent of patients with diffuse large cell disease appear to be in clinical stage I after clinical staging and may be candidates for megavoltage radiotherapy alone; in such patients, laparotomy is advisable to ensure that patients are truly stage I since radiotherapy alone for stage II disease is inferior to radiotherapy with chemotherapy or chemotherapy alone. Extranodal presentations in Waldeyer's ring and extralymphatic local presentations in bone, brain, testes, or other sites are more frequent in high-grade large cell lymphomas than in low-grade lymphoma.

TYPES OF LYMPHOCYTIC LYMPHOMAS **Follicular, predominantly small cleaved cell [nodular poorly differentiated lymphocytic type (NPDL)]** This is the most common follicular lymphoma and presents a more uniform clinical picture than the other follicular types. The disease afflicts adults, usually over the age of 40, and is very rare in children, though instances below the age of 15 are known. Follicular, small cleaved cell lymphomas are usually asymptomatic at the onset and are characterized by painless adenopathy in the cervical, axillary, inguinal, and femoral regions. In some patients, large abdominal masses of retroperitoneal or mesenteric lymph nodes cause acute gastrointestinal problems, including obstruction, hemorrhage, and intussusception. Some patients present with ureteral obstruction and consequent renal failure. Even though the patient may notice only one or several enlarged lymph nodes, examination and study with lymphography or other tests usually reveals widespread, often symmetric, lymphadenopathy. In some patients, the lymph node enlargement may have been present for several years but is so gradual or fluctuating that patients were not sufficiently concerned to seek medical attention. The spleen is often enlarged but rarely produces symptoms at the onset of the disease. Later in the course of the disease, it may become considerably larger and result in local symptoms and significant hypersplenism. Involvement of the lymphoid tissue in Waldeyer's ring is much more common than in Hodgkin's disease. Epitrochlear and popliteal adenopathy usually indicates the disease is a low-grade lymphocytic lymphoma. Lymphoid masses may result in chylous pleural effusions and/or ascites presumably because of lymphatic obstruction. It is extremely rare for the central nervous system to become involved, though peripheral nerve compression and epidural tumor masses may develop. The peripheral blood picture is usually normal at the onset of the disease, but careful examination of the blood smear may reveal typical notched or cleft, so-called buttock cells, thought to be characteristic, but not diagnostic of follicular lymphomas. Ordinary bone marrow aspirations are usually normal. However, study of the bone marrow by the needle or open biopsy technique will reveal bone marrow involvement with the cells located in the paratrabecular area of the marrow (in contrast to the centrally placed normal lymphoid follicles) in up to 85 percent of patients with low-grade, follicular lymphoma, even at the onset of the disease.

The clinical course of follicular lymphoma is variable, and affected by the cytologic appearance of cells within the follicles. In some it is indolent, and lymphadenopathy may have been present for years prior to the diagnosis, and may be well tolerated for 5 years or more after the diagnosis is established. In other patients the tempo of the disease is accelerated from the start, and such patients may experience early difficulties that require prompt therapy. It is also now clear that follicular low-grade lymphomas evolve in time to high-grade diffuse large cell lymphomas. In all cases the disease is malignant, however, and though there may be spontaneous regression of lymphadenopathy, in rare cases, in the majority of patients clinical problems appear within the first year after diagnosis, especially in those who show evidence of a mixture of large and small cells in the follicles. When the disease accelerates, lymph node masses grow rapidly, often in localized or asymmetric locations. They cause serious local problems and are less responsive to treatment which was previously effective. Fever, night sweats, and weight loss may appear. Involvement of the nonlymphoid organs and tissues occurs. If biopsy is repeated when the tempo of clinical progression increases, the histologic picture commonly shows a change in cytology to larger, less differentiated cells with a persistent follicular pattern or effacement of the nodal architecture with diffuse large cells. Clinical evolution of this type occurs in 60 percent of all cases of low-grade follicular, small cleaved lymphomas. Autopsy studies of such patients reveal that fewer than 10 percent of patients whose initial diagnosis was NPDL have evidence of a follicular pattern at the time of death.

Low-grade follicular, mixed small cleaved and large cell [nodular mixed lymphoma (NML)] There are many similarities between follicular, small cleaved lymphoma and the less frequently occurring follicular, mixed small cleaved and large cell lymphoma. The latter differs in overall prognosis, frequency of initial bone marrow involvement, and type and location of lymph node enlargement. The difference may relate to the lessened propensity of large, blastic-type lymphocytes to migrate. Bone marrow involvement at the onset is less common, and unusual large abdominal masses may be seen more often. In contrast to the predominantly small cleaved lymphomas, combination chemotherapy has been found to yield a significant percentage of complete remissions with long-term disease-free intervals, suggesting cure.

Intermediate-grade follicular, predominantly large cell lymphomas [nodular "histiocytic" (NH) lymphomas] This group of intermediate-grade lymphomas generally is considered together with the diffuse large cell lymphomas since the course and prognosis are unlike those of the low-grade follicular lymphomas. The cells in this lymphoma are large and poorly differentiated, indicating a more aggressive growth pattern although follicle structure is preserved.

Diffuse lymphomas The diffuse lymphocytic lymphomas consist of a number of diseases with variable presentation and clinical evolution. Low-grade small lymphocytic lymphoma is generally considered the most indolent lymphocytic lymphoma and in its outcome is usually indistinguishable from chronic lymphocytic leukemia. The low-grade diffuse small cleaved cell lymphoma (DPDL) presents and behaves like the follicular variant. When the patient is first seen, the disease usually is disseminated to all lymph node areas, the liver, spleen, and bone marrow. The incidence of bone marrow and liver involvement is over 50 percent. Low-grade diffuse small cleaved lymphoma is not generally curable by chemotherapy. In contrast, intermediate- and high-grade diffuse and mixed cell lymphomas (diffuse histiocytic lymphomas of Rappaport) often present with localized lymph node enlargement, or local extralymphatic manifestations. The lymph nodes are most prominently located in the neck or in abdominal masses. Presentations in the gastrointestinal tract, bone, thyroid, testes, brain, and the lymph node tissue of Waldeyer's ring also occur frequently. The bone marrow is involved initially in less than 10 percent of the patients and is not commonly involved, even late in the course of the disease. In 20 percent of the patients, even after extensive diagnostic efforts, the disease is found to be relatively localized. Diffuse large cell lymphoma is, however, highly invasive locally, and involvement of peripheral nerves, epidural tumors, compression of the vena cava or airways, and destruction of the osseous tissue occur during the course of the disease. The skin, liver, kidneys, lung, and even the brain may be involved. Occasionally bone marrow invasion results in the appearance of large undifferentiated cells in the peripheral blood.

Truly localized diffuse large cell lymphoma may be curable by megavoltage radiotherapy. In some studies, over 70 percent 5-year actuarial disease-free survival has been achieved in patients with true stage I disease, of whom 75 percent will have 5-year actuarial disease-free survival.

The diffuse lymphoblastic lymphomas of T-cell origin and Burkitt's and diffuse undifferentiated non-Burkitt's lymphomas that occur in children, adolescents, and young adults must be separated from those that occur in the older age groups because of differences in clinical patterns and in response to therapy. Several unique clinical pathologic entities have been recognized.

High-grade diffuse lymphocytic lymphomas (lymphoblastic lymphoma) These tumors constitute about 30 percent of all childhood lymphocytic lymphomas and 5 to 10 percent of lymphocytic lymphomas in adolescents and adults. Males predominate in this group. The characteristic presentation is supradiaphragmatic with cervical, supraclavicular, or axillary lymph nodes; in half the cases, a massive anterior mediastinal mass is found. Pleural effusions may occur. Some patients may present with inguinal nodes or with disease in extranodal sites (breast, gonads, long bones, skin, etc.). Initially, the blood and bone marrow may not be involved but a leukemia-like picture is inevitable if the disease is not successfully treated. The tumors are composed of convoluted or nonconvoluted lymphocytes, but all are associated with T-cell characteristics. Following a 2- to 3-month period, 30 to 50 percent of cases develop acute leukemia cytologically identical with common acute lymphocytic leukemia of childhood. Central nervous system involvement occurs frequently. These T-cell tumors of children and young adults are also cytologically

distinct from the B-cell Burkitt's and undifferentiated non-Burkitt's lymphomas. Patients identified by clinical and histopathologic criteria as having lymphoblastic lymphoma require only minimal staging procedures since all stages require chemotherapy. Newer combination chemotherapy, together with central nervous system prophylaxis have recently improved results to the extent that half of all patients may have long disease-free survival (see Table 294-8).

Burkitt's lymphoma Burkitt first described this diffuse lymphoma of follicular center B cells in children in Africa. It has unique clinical and epidemiologic features. Although found worldwide, Burkitt's lymphoma is endemic in certain areas of east Africa and New Guinea. In endemic regions, serologic evidence of infection with Epstein-Barr virus has been documented repeatedly. It is associated with specific cytogenetic abnormalities (see "Cytogenetics").

The disease appears to predominate in males (the male/female ratio in Africa is 8:5; in America it is 2:1). The median age at onset in African children is 7 years, whereas in American children it is 11 years. In its typical African form, the disease presents primarily as an extralymphatic tumor arising in the bones of the jaw. In addition, there appears to be a predilection for spread to the abdominal viscera, particularly the ovaries, as well as the breasts and meninges. Bone marrow involvement occurs but is not common; leukemia is seen infrequently. In American children, bony tumors of the jaw are less frequent, and abdominal or pelvic sites, particularly in the gastrointestinal tract, are involved with tumor at the time of presentation. Bone marrow and/or cerebrospinal fluid involvement occurs eventually in one-third of patients.

The diagnosis is made by recognition of the clinical picture and the characteristic histologic and cytochemical findings. The tumor is very responsive to chemotherapy. Response to therapy depends on stage and tumor volume. Regardless of stage, all patients are now treated with combination chemotherapy, and long-term complete remissions occur without maintenance therapy in half of all cases and in 90 percent of patients with minimal tumor masses in one site.

TREATMENT Treatment approaches to the lymphocytic lymphomas have undergone considerable change in the past decade. Various treatments, including regional radiotherapy, total-lymphoid irradiation, single-drug chemotherapy, combination chemotherapy, and combinations of both modalities have been tested. Treatment strategies based on clinical stage and pathologic classification have been developed. These strategies address three issues: (1) Most localized lymphomas with the exception of pathologic stage I large cell lymphoma are *not* cured by radiotherapy alone; thus an attempt to cure by radiotherapy must be planned with ports which will not harm bone marrow function often required later to administer effective chemotherapy. (2) The treatment of low-grade (follicular) lymphomas is controversial. Although current research focuses on curability with initial aggressive treatment versus no initial treatment, present data dictate a conservative approach with treatment only as required by

TABLE 294-8 Primary chemotherapy of advanced stages of diffuse aggressive lymphomas

Regimen	Number of patients	Percent complete remissions	Percent disease-free at 2 years	Comments
ProMACE-MOPP*	79	74	65	—
M-BACOD†	101	72	59	—
COP-BLAM‡	33	73	—	Average follow-up < 2 years
CHOP-HOAP-Bleo-IM VP-16§	56	100 (stages I–III) 66 (stage IV)	93 (stages I–III) 55 (stage IV)	—
APO¶	21	95	58	For lymphoblastic lymphomas
Modified LSA₂-L₂	15	73	64	For lymphoblastic lymphomas

* *ProMACE-MOPP = prednisone, methotrexate, Adriamycin, cyclophosphamide, epipodophyllotoxin (VP-16); nitrogen mustard, Oncovin (vincristine), procarbazine, and prednisone in altering cycles.*
† *M-BACOD = methotrexate, bleomycin, Adriamycin, cyclophosphamide, Oncovin, and dexamethasone.*
‡ *COP-BLAM = cyclophosphamide, Oncovin, prednisone, bleomycin, Adriamycin, and Matulane (procarbazine).*
§ *CHOP-HOAP-Bleo-IM VP-16 = CHOP = cyclophosphamide, hydroxydaunorubicin (Adriamycin), Oncovin, prednisone; HOAP = hydroxydaunorubicin, Oncovin, arabinosyl cytosine, prednisone, bleomycin; IM VP-16 = iphosphamide, methotrexate, VP-116.*
¶ *APO and LSA₂-L₂ are acronyms for cyclical ten-drug combinations reviewed in detail in Blaney et al.*

symptoms. (3) There is no controversy regarding an aggressive approach to attempt to *cure* the intermediate- and high-grade lymphomas using third-generation drug combinations.

Involved-field (IF) radiotherapy The principles of delivery of effective radiotherapy described for Hodgkin's disease pertain for lymphocytic lymphomas when irradiation is selected as the primary treatment with curative intent. The effectiveness of regional radiotherapy alone depends largely on the histologic type of lymphoma. For follicular lymphomas following treatment with 44 Gy (4400 rad), the local recurrence rate in the treated field is close to zero but the occurrence of distant relapse is continuous at 10 to 15 percent per year of treated cases. The local recurrence rate (21 to 37 percent) for patients with large cell lymphoma does not appear to be dose-related for doses between 25 and 65 Gy (2500 and 6500 rad). Local control with radiotherapy translates into long-term disease-free survival in 60 to 80 percent of patients with laparotomy staged PS I but in only 30 percent with pathologic stage II disease.

Chemotherapy For the follicular variety of the lymphomas, three treatment options are available; no treatment initially, treatment with a single drug, or treatment with combinations of drugs. Even when patients with indolent disease are carefully selected, most will require treatment within 12 to 24 months.

When chemotherapy first became available for the treatment of cancer, the most responsive tumors were the lymphomas, and continuous oral single-agent chemotherapy evolved initially as the treatment of choice. Two well-established facts now dictate the aggressive use of combination chemotherapy when treatment does become necessary, as the initial treatment for patients with advanced follicular lymphocytic lymphoma. First, modern combination chemotherapy induces a greater fraction of complete remissions in the first year of treatment than does single-agent chemotherapy. Second, patients who attain a complete remission survive longer than those patients who achieve partial responses; therefore the therapy that induces the greatest fraction of complete remissions is always the superior choice, provided toxicity is not too severe. Continuous chlorambucil, the single-agent most often used in the past, is frequently associated with development of bone marrow aplasia, a side effect which is not noted when intermittent cyclical combination chemotherapy is used. Once older forms of chemotherapy of patients with low-grade follicular lymphomas is discontinued, the rate of relapse tends to be persistent at 10 to 15 percent per year, as in patients with localized disease. While maintenance drug treatment of patients with low-grade follicular lymphomas prolongs the duration of initial remissions, it is not generally recommended, since it has not been shown to prolong survival when compared with intermittent reinduction of remission. With the uncertainty over whether more aggressive newer approaches to drug treatment or the use of biologicals such as anti-idiotypic monoclonal antibodies will control low-grade lymphomas, and the certainty that continuous oral alkylating agents or older drug combinations of cyclophosphamide, vincristine, and prednisone (CVP) alone or combined with Adriamycin (CHOP) will not, the decision to start chemotherapy should not be taken lightly. Recent studies, employing κ-λ analyses to detect circulating monoclonal B cells, have shown a high incidence (90 to 100 percent) of monoclonal B cells in the blood of lymphoma patients prior to therapy, regardless of histologic subtype. In patients with low-grade follicular (nodular) lymphomas in complete remission for longer than 18 months, 16 to 25 showed circulating monoclonal B cells. This contrasts sharply with the fact that no circulating B cells were found in 14 patients with intermediate- or high-grade lymphomas in complete remission. These laboratory findings offer an explanation for the persistent relapse rate in the low-grade lymphomas in contrast to the curability of intermediate- and high-grade lymphomas and serve as a rationale for clinical trials of initial intensive chemotherapy. Presently most patients with low-grade follicular lymphoma should be entered into clinical trials comparing more intensive initial chemotherapy, which shows some promising early results, to expectant management using

intensive chemotherapy only where necessary. In either case, when chemotherapy is offered, combinations of the type shown in Table 294-8 are preferred to older programs. Recently, high-dose 5-day pulses of chlorambucil have produced a complete remission rate and relapse-free survival equivalent to combination chemotherapy and are under evaluation.

The situation is clearly different for patients with the low- and intermediate-grade follicular mixed cell lymphomas (NML) and follicular large cell (nodular histiocytic lymphoma). Here studies have shown that combination chemotherapy is clearly more effective than single agents. At the National Cancer Institute, patients achieved complete remission in 75 percent of cases. In contrast to patients with follicular, predominantly small cleaved lymphomas (NPDL), these patients remain in complete remission for periods up to 10 years after therapy is discontinued, and the relapse rate diminishes after 2 years.

Selection and results of treatment in patients who have diffuse lymphomas again depends, in a major way, on the cytologic characteristics of the individual tumor cell. Patients with low-grade small lymphocytic lymphomas have a long, indolent course that waxes and wanes in a manner similar to the course of patients with chronic lymphocytic leukemia. Conservative single-agent treatment, usually with chlorambucil or cyclophosphamide, employed only when disease progression dictates its use, is the treatment of choice. For patients with advanced stages of intermediate-grade diffuse small cleaved cell lymphomas, the approach should be similar to that for follicular predominantly small cleaved cell types and treatment is the same.

Intermediate- and high-grade diffuse lymphomas such as diffuse large cell, diffuse mixed cell, immunoblastic, and diffuse small noncleaved cell have been known to be highly curable diseases since 1974, and the treatment of choice is one of several third-generation drug combinations shown in Table 294-8. In these lymphomas, the poor differentiation of the cellular component that leads to the more aggressive clinical behavior apparently makes the tumor cells more vulnerable to the cytocidal effects of chemotherapy. Complete remissions in patients with these poorly differentiated diffuse lymphomas are possible in up to 80 percent of treated patients. Failure to achieve a complete remission in these patients is associated with an extremely short survival time, usually 6 months to 2 years. Relapses rarely occur in patients who have been in remission for more than 2 years after therapy is discontinued. In some studies, relapse-free survival has been reported to extend for more than 15 years beyond the end of drug treatment. Patients with the diffuse lymphomas who achieve a complete remission do not benefit from maintenance therapy.

Combined modality treatment of lymphocytic lymphomas Involved-field radiotherapy with combination chemotherapy (RT + CT) has been shown to be superior to radiotherapy (RT) alone in stage II intermediate- and high-grade lymphomas in several United States and European centers. For stage I intermediate- and high-grade lymphoma, radiotherapy can be used alone. There appears to be no significant improvement, however, in relapse-free survival for patients with low-grade lymphomas of the follicular variety treated with chemotherapy in addition to radiotherapy.

Whole-body radiotherapy (WBR) This modality has been employed for the management of patients with low-grade lymphocytic lymphomas in stages III and IV. The 56 percent complete remission rate achieved is similar to that obtained in parallel studies using various older drug regimens. This approach is prone to long-term complications. Moreover, the difficulty in retreatment of relapse with drugs dictates the use of WBR only when other treatments have failed.

Biological therapy of lymphocytic lymphomas For the past decade, numerous studies have been carried out to determine the role of nonspecific immunotherapy in the management of lymphocytic lymphoma. A controlled study shows that combination chemotherapy combined with bacillus Calmette-Guérin (BCG) vaccination produced a slightly better overall survival than the use of that particular combination chemotherapy alone. While this observation is of some interest, other drug programs alone now produce superior results and BCG use is not recommended for any patients with lymphoma. In recent years, interest has been heightened with the use of pure biologicals to treat lymphomas. Early positive results using crude interferon preparations in low-grade, follicular, small cleaved cell lymphomas have been confirmed using purified recombinant alpha interferon. A significant fraction of patients will achieve complete remission that can be maintained for periods of 1 year or more. More aggressive varieties of the disease do not respond well. Interferon can be used as an alternative to chemotherapy as an early treatment in indolent lymphoma, but its use is complicated by the requirement for continuous parenteral administration, and side effects such as extreme fatigue, fever, and leukopenia—in addition to the uncertainty over long-term benefit. Thus its exact role in patient management is not clear.

Interesting results have been obtained using monoclonal antibodies to the idiotypic protein unique to each monoclonal B-cell line in patients with B-cell lymphomas. Although many patients have been treated, only one completely durable remission has been reported. Resistance to this therapy develops because of biclonal lymphoma cell populations now recognized by immunoglobulin gene rearrangement, and the ability of point mutations to alter the idiotypic target. Further studies are underway to exploit labeling of monoclonal antibodies with radioisotopes. Monoclonal antibodies to T cell–specific antigens have been used in T-cell lymphomas with transient responses.

Bone marrow transplantation Studies are in progress utilizing autologous bone marrow transplantation coupled with very intensive chemotherapy and/or total-body irradiation in patients with lymphocytic lymphomas. This approach is reserved for patients who have failed chemotherapy. Autologous marrow is generally harvested after a second chemotherapy remission has been achieved, and purge of lymphoma cells from the marrow is accomplished using monoclonal antibodies to the specific cell type (anti-B1 antibodies for B-cell lymphomas, or T cell–specific antibodies for T-cell lymphomas) or chemicals such as 4-hydroperoxycyclophosphamide and/or phototherapy with hematoporphyrins. After further very high dose chemotherapy and/or total-body irradiation, the marrow is reinfused. Interesting results have been achieved in small series sufficient to warrant using this approach in clinical trials in follicular lymphoma patients with an accelerated course or who have failed chemotherapy and in patients with diffuse large cell lymphomas in their first relapse.

NEWLY RECOGNIZED LEUKEMIA/LYMPHOMA SYNDROMES
Acute T-cell leukemia/lymphomas Acute T-cell leukemia/lymphomas (ATL) is a relatively newly recognized syndrome caused by a unique T cell–trophic human retrovirus, HTLV I. The syndrome was originally described in southwest Japan, where it is endemic, and has since been identified in the Caribbean and the southeast United States. It is characterized by highly pleomorphic and polylobulated cells in the peripheral blood (65 percent of cases). Generalized adenopathy, hepatosplenomegaly, cutaneous involvement, hypercalcemia, and lytic bone lesions also occur associated with secretion of osteoclast activating factor. ATL is a neoplasm of the postthymic T cell which expresses a helper cell phenotype T4+ T8−, but functionally, in vitro, the cells behave as suppressor cells. The course is rapidly progressive, and although combination chemotherapy of the types used in diffuse large cell lymphomas produces remissions, they are usually temporary, and experience is limited to a few patients. ATL deserves to be recognized as a separate entity in the high-grade lymphoma category in the Working Formulation. It is likely that in the past a few such cases were classified as high-grade, diffuse large cell immunoblastic lymphomas.

Histiocytic medullary reticulosis (HMR) HMR, also called malignant histiocytosis, is a rare, usually rapidly progressive systemic disease characterized by abrupt onset, fever, progressive pancytopenia, splenomegaly, and mild lymphadenopathy. It is a malignancy of true histiocytes of the reticuloendothelial system. The malignant cells exhibit phagocytic activity of erythrocytes and leukocytes associated with progressive pancytopenia. Occasional long-term remissions have been observed with high doses of the alkylating agent cyclophosphamide.

Angioimmunoblastic lymphadenopathy with dysproteinemia (AILD) Angioimmunoblastic lymphadenopathy is a lymphoma-like, systemic disorder characterized by acute onset, generalized lymphadenopathy, hepatomegaly, splenomegaly, and severe constitutional symptoms including fever, sweats, and weight loss. Pruritus and skin rashes may be present. These clinical features closely mimic many of the presenting symptoms and signs of advanced Hodgkin's disease and of the other lymphomas. The disorder occurs in adults (age 28 to 92, median 62). In half the patients, a generalized pruritic maculopapular rash precedes the onset of the other signs and symptoms by weeks or a few months. In some patients, ingestion of drugs, including penicillin or other antibiotics, phenytoin, sulfonamide, halothane, methyldopa, and aspirin, antedates the onset of the disease. AILD is not considered a histologically malignant disease but rather an extreme form of hypersensitivity (hyperimmune) reaction. Some have considered this a clinical example of a graft-versus-host reaction. A proliferation of B cells and a profound deficiency of T cells have been demonstrated. The laboratory data show anemia, which in one-quarter of the cases is due to Coombs-positive hemolytic anemia. A majority of the patients have a polyclonal hypergammaglobulinemia. Leukocytosis and eosinophilia may be present.

Characteristic lesions are found in biopsy specimens of lymph nodes and consist of alterations of nodal architecture or complete effacement with a pleomorphic cellular proliferation in which immunoblasts, lymphocytes, and plasma cells predominate. In addition, vascular proliferation and prominent eosinophilic interstitial material are seen. The changes in the liver, spleen, and bone marrow do not have the diagnostic specificity of the lesions seen in the lymph nodes.

The course of AILD is usually fulminant. Some patients (approximately 25 percent) appear to have a long survival (20 to 45 months) with or without small doses of corticosteroids and do not require intensive chemotherapy. Others (25 percent), although requiring intensive cytotoxic chemotherapy, nevertheless have a long survival (28 to 67 months). A third group of patients (50 percent of cases) have a rapid course (1 to 20 months) terminating in death, regardless of the therapeutic approach employed. Many patients die of overwhelming infections often with pneumonia due to *Pseudomonas* and other gram-negative organisms, *Pneumocystis carinii*, cytomegalovirus, or mycoses. Acute hepatic failure or acute renal failure have also been reported to occur as terminal events.

The correct treatment of AILD has not been devised. Treatment should be initiated with corticosteroids. If there is no response, a combination chemotherapy regimen effective in lymphomas has been advocated. Radiotherapy may be employed for control of local problems. In view of the high failure rate of cytotoxic drugs, brief use of corticosteroids has been recommended to diminish the hyperimmune response along with levamisole to stimulate T-cell function.

COMPLICATIONS OF HODGKIN'S DISEASE AND LYMPHOCYTIC LYMPHOMAS

The complications of lymphoma may be due to progressive enlargement of lymph nodes, involvement of parenchymal organs, and hematologic, metabolic, or immunologic abnormalities. Complications may also result from therapy.

Progressive lymph node enlargement causes compression or obstruction of surrounding structures such as vascular structures (superior vena cava syndrome), airway, esophagus, urinary tract, or gastrointestinal tract. Serious complications may ensue depending on the site affected. Direct infiltration of the lymphoma from involved mediastinal lymph nodes into the parenchyma of the lung, pleura, pericardium, and heart may occur. Infiltration from retroperitoneal lymph nodes through lymphatic channels leads to involvement of the gastrointestinal tract and may result in ulceration, perforation, hemorrhage, intussusception, or malabsorption. Jaundice may be caused by obstruction of the biliary duct by portal lymph nodes or by infiltration of the liver secondary to hematogenous spread.

Central nervous system involvement may occur by direct extension of tumor from the mediastinum or retroperitoneum to the spinal canal. Symptoms of cord compression which are produced in this way occur more frequently in Hodgkin's disease than in the lymphocytic lymphomas and, in the latter, most often in the diffuse large cell lymphomas. Cranial nerves and brain may be affected by Hodgkin's disease and the lymphocytic lymphomas. Occasionally, lymphomatous meningitis may occur, and lymphoma cells, high protein, and low glucose appear in the spinal fluid. In diffuse large cell lymphomas with demonstrated bone marrow involvement, meningeal carcinomatosis occurs with sufficiently high frequency to recommend prophylactic therapy, although this complication has diminished with the more modern chemotherapy programs. More rarely, bizarre neurologic manifestations may occur without demonstrable direct involvement by lymphoma. Progressive multifocal leukoencephalopathy, subacute cerebellar degeneration, myelopathy, and neuropathy have been described. Occasionally, polymyositis may occur. The differential diagnosis of these central and peripheral nervous system complications includes bacterial and viral meningitis, herpes zoster, and drug toxicity, particularly with the vinca alkaloids.

The lung may be involved by direct extension from the mediastinal-hilar lymph nodes or by hematogenous spread. In the lymphocyte-predominant type of Hodgkin's disease and in follicular lymphomas the lungs are rarely involved; in contrast, nodular sclerosis–type Hodgkin's disease with hilar node involvement frequently involves the lung. Pneumonia is a frequent complication of treatment and constitutes the major differential diagnostic problem. Bleomycin, methotrexate, and other drugs may cause pulmonary manifestations and must be considered in the differential diagnosis of lung disease.

Skin involvement occurs as part of hematogenous dissemination of the lymphoma, especially in the newly described acute T-cell lymphoma syndrome. A number of nonspecific skin lesions also occur in lymphoma, including excoriations secondary to pruritus, urticaria, erythema multiforme, erythema nodosum, exfoliative dermatitis, and dermatomyositis.

Bone marrow involvement occurs most frequently in low-grade lymphomas (50 to 60 percent) but less frequently in intermediate- or high-grade lymphomas (10 percent). In Hodgkin's disease, initial bone marrow involvement is rare; it is seen most often in patients with symptoms (B category) and in patients with the lymphocyte-depleted subtype. Anemia, neutropenia, and thrombocytopenia are the consequences of bone marrow replacement but usually only occur late in the course of the disease; however, these conditions may also be caused by hypersplenism, immunologic mechanisms, blood loss, or complications of therapy.

Hematologic complications occur frequently. Anemia may be caused by blood loss secondary to gastrointestinal infiltration and ulceration or nonspecific lesions, malabsorption of iron or folate, bone marrow infiltration by lymphoma, or hemolysis. Coombs-positive hemolytic anemia is seen most often with diffuse low-grade lymphomas; it occurs less frequently with diffuse large cell lymphomas or in the follicular lymphomas and Hodgkin's disease. Chronic illness and radiotherapy or chemotherapy result in diminished or ineffective erythropoiesis. Changes in white blood cell counts are frequent. The leukemic phase of lymphoma is seen most frequently in the low-grade lymphomas; rarely, in the intermediate- or high-grade lymphomas. Leukopenia in an untreated patient suggests hypersplenism. In the patient undergoing therapy, leukopenia is usually due to the therapy. Thrombocytosis occurs occasionally in Hodgkin's disease and lymphocytic lymphoma. Frequently following staging splenectomy, the platelet count rises briefly. More often, thrombocytopenia

occurs because of bone marrow replacement by lymphoma, hypersplenism, or therapy.

Metabolic abnormalities may occur as a consequence of the lymphoma or of therapy. Hyperuricemia is seen in patients with large volume of lymphoma. Effective therapy with rapid reduction of the tissue mass may exacerbate the hyperuricemia and lead to a decrease in renal function or acute renal failure and infrequently to gouty arthritis. Hydration and administration of allopurinol can prevent these complications.

Hypercalcemia occurs in less than 10 percent of cases and is usually related to bone destruction. It is seen most frequently in diffuse large cell lymphoma and Hodgkin's disease of the lymphocytic-depletion and mixed cellularity varieties. Occasionally, the hypercalcemia may be due to release of a parathyroid-like substance. It is a common concomitant of the rare syndrome of acute T-cell lymphoma caused by the human retrovirus HTLV I. In this disease, it appears to be due to tumor release of lymphokines and osteoclast activating factor rather than direct bone invasion. Hypercalcemia requires prompt and appropriate treatment to lower the serum calcium level and specific therapy appropriate for the management of the lymphoma.

Serum protein abnormalities occur frequently. Particularly in Hodgkin's disease, but also in lymphocytic lymphomas, the $alpha_1$, $alpha_2$, and beta fractions of globulins may be increased. The $alpha_2$ increase in Hodgkin's disease has been shown to be due to increases in haptoglobin and ceruloplasmin. Polyclonal gamma globulin elevation is seen in 40 percent of patients with Hodgkin's disease; it is less frequent in lymphocytic lymphoma. Paraproteinemia may occur in lymphocytic lymphoma, especially in low-grade diffuse types and occasionally in Hodgkin's disease. Hypogammaglobulinemia may precede the onset of some low-grade diffuse lymphomas, occurs eventually in 60 percent of patients, but is seen less frequently in advanced Hodgkin's disease. Antibody production is usually decreased in response to both primary and recall challenge.

Complications of treatment include radiation damage associated with therapy of specific sites, toxicity due to chemotherapeutic agents, sterility, and second malignancies. Chemotherapy with multidrug regimens leads to some decrease in ovarian or testicular function in most patients. Amenorrhea, inability to conceive, or hypo- or aspermia may result; however, in those patients who have achieved a complete remission and are off all chemotherapy, these functions may return.

Second malignancies, particularly nonlymphocytic acute leukemias, have been reported to occur in patients with Hodgkin's disease and lymphocytic lymphomas treated with radiation alone, combination chemotherapy alone, or with both modalities. The incidence is estimated to be 1 to 8 percent of cases, with time of onset 1.2 to 19 years and a mean interval of 7 years following initial therapy. Hypoplastic or aplastic bone marrow may antedate the occurrence of frank leukemia. In the preleukemic phase, chromosome analysis employing chromosome banding techniques has demonstrated a high incidence of abnormalities in chromosomes 5, 8, and 7.

REFERENCES

BLAYNEY DW et al: The human T-cell leukemia/lymphoma virus (HTLV) defines a distinct clinical entity. Blood 62(2):401, 1982

BLOOMFIELD CD et al (eds): Proceedings of the Symposium on Contemporary Issues in Hodgkin's Disease: Biology, Staging and Treatment. San Francisco, California, September 9–12, 1981. Cancer Treat Rep 66(4):601, 1982

——— et al: Nonrandom chromosome abnormalities in lymphoma. Cancer Res 43:2975, 1983

DEVITA VT: The consequences of the chemotherapy of Hodgkin's disease (10th David A. Karnofsky Memorial Lecture). Cancer 47(1):1, 1981

——— et al: Hodgkin's disease and the non-Hodgkin's lymphomas, in Cancer: Principles and Practice of Oncology, 2d ed, VT DeVita et al (eds). Philadelphia, Lippincott, 1985, pp 1623–1697

FISHER RI et al: Advances in the treatment of diffuse aggressive lymphoma, in UT M.D. Anderson Clinical Conference on Cancer, vol. 27, RJ Ford et al (eds). New York, Raven, 1984, pp 377–390

GOLOMB HM (ed): Non-Hodgkin's lymphoma. Semin Oncol 7(3):221, 1980

HORNING SJ, ROSENBERG SA: The natural history of initially untreated low-grade non-Hodgkin's lymphomas. N Engl J Med 311(23):1471, 1984

KAPLAN HS: Hodgkin's Disease, 2d ed. Cambridge, Harvard University, 1980

LONGO DL et al: What is so good about the "good prognosis" lymphomas? in *Recent Advances in Clinical Oncology No 1*, CS Williams et al (eds). New York, Churchill Livingstone, 1982, pp 223–231

ROSENBERG SA, KAPLAN HS (eds): *Malignant Lymphomas: Etiology, Immunology, Pathology, Treatment*, vol 3: *Bristol-Myers Cancer Symposia*. New York, Academic, 1982, pp 1–682

——— et al: National Cancer Institute sponsored study of classifications of non-Hodgkin's lymphomas. Cancer 49:2112, 1982

SMITH BR et al: Circulating monoclonal B lymphocytes in non-Hodgkin's lymphoma. N Engl J Med 311:1476, 1984

VOKES EE et al: Long-term survival of patients with localized diffuse histiocytic lymphoma. J Clin Oncol 3:1309, 1985

295 BREAST CANCER

JANE E. HENNEY / VINCENT T. DeVITA, JR.

Breast cancer is a major public health problem in the western hemisphere. In 1985, in the United States, 119,000 women and approximately 1000 men were diagnosed as having this disease. Until it was surpassed by lung cancer, it had been the most common cause of cancer death in women and accounted for 38,400 deaths each year in the United States.

RISK FACTORS: ETIOLOGY AND EPIDEMIOLOGY In the United States, no woman is at such a low risk from breast cancer that she can be excluded from education and screening programs appropriate for her age. Even if no risk factors are present, one woman of every 11 develops this disease.

At risk for the development of breast cancer (in decreasing order) is the woman whose mother had bilateral breast cancer diagnosed prior to menopause, the woman with a first-degree relative who developed bilateral or unilateral breast cancer but was postmenopausal, the woman older than 50 who is nulliparous or whose first parity occurred after age 30, the woman with a history of chronic breast disease, particularly epithelial hyperplasia, the woman exposed to ionizing radiation of more than 0.5 Gy (50 rad) during adolescence, and finally the woman who is obese.

Except for a plateau at age 50, the risk of breast cancer increases with age. Early menstruation, late menopause (after 55) and/or irregularity in the menstrual cycle also increase a woman's chances of developing breast cancer. Artificial menopause before age 35 confers some degree of protection; such women have only one-third the risk of developing breast cancer of those who undergo natural menopause. Women who bear their first child before age 18 have one-third the risk of those who bear their first child after age 30. The older primiparas, however, are at slightly higher risk of developing breast cancer than women who are nulliparous.

With respect to the familial association of breast cancer, the cause is not understood, although a gene that is transmitted in an autosomal dominant manner through either maternal or paternal line has been described in rare families. This particular gene is felt to have wide distribution but low penetrance. The allele that increases the susceptibility for this penetrance may be linked to the glutamic pyruvate transaminase locus.

The breast is one of the most susceptible organs to the effects of ionizing radiation. Exposure of the breast to ionizing radiation is a major risk enhancer for the development of malignancy. Data which support these observations are derived from studies of survivors of the bombings at Hiroshima and Nagasaki and women who have undergone radiation therapy, as well as those who have had multiple fluoroscopies during pneumothorax treatment for tuberculosis. The dose-effect relationship appears to be linear with an increased risk present in women who have received as small a dose as 0.5 Gy.

There also appears to be an additional risk for those women who are exposed to radiation during adolescence. Fractionated or intermittent dosing does not appear to diminish this risk, nor does time since exposure, even after 45 years. The interval between exposure and the appearance of breast cancer is likely mediated by many factors including the age of the woman and related hormonal factors.

The occurrence of breast cancer varies greatly among different geographic areas and is influenced markedly by migration patterns. For example, Asian women living in eastern countries are at low risk for developing breast cancer. Yet Asian women whose ancestors migrated to Hawaii or the continental United States develop breast cancer at rates observed in populations native to these areas. Although no etiologic hypothesis has been established unequivocally, dietary factors (high fat intake and obesity) may be a main cause of the differing incidences by affecting the metabolism of estrogens which act as promoters of tumor growth.

The incidence of breast cancer varies among racial groups within the United States; it is highest in whites, intermediate in blacks, and lowest in American Indians in New Mexico and Filipinos in Hawaii. The extent to which different dietary habits may influence these variations in incidence rates has not been well studied.

High doses of diethylstilbestrol have been implicated in the development of breast cancer and benign uterine tumors. However, estrogens in conventional doses do not cause an increased incidence of breast cancer, and estrogen with added progesterone therapy may afford some protection for the postmenopausal woman with no prior history of breast cancer. Similarly, oral contraceptives of the combination type have no associated risk for the development of breast cancer and may confer some degree of protection.

Hair dyes and other chemicals frequently used by women have been shown to be mutagenic but their role in the etiology of breast cancer has not been established.

Because of the relatively low incidence of breast cancer in males, its epidemiology and etiology have been largely unexplored. It is known, however, that males with altered estrogen metabolism, gynecomastia, and/or Klinefelter's syndrome, or who have testicular damage or atrophy from mumps orchitis, injury, or aging, are at greatest risk.

NATURAL HISTORY AND PROGNOSTIC FACTORS One important characteristic of breast cancer is multicentricity, that is, in approximately 13 percent of patients with breast cancer, microscopic foci of invasive and noninvasive tumor can be detected in quadrants of the breast other than that in which the dominant primary lesion is discovered. The clinical significance of such nondominant lesions is unclear; it is unusual for multiple cancers in a single breast to become clinically overt or for bilateral cancers to occur synchronously. In women over 70 who have died from other causes, the incidence of clinically inapparent intraductal carcinoma is 19 times the reported incidence of breast cancer. Whether these cancers are controlled by the body's own defense mechanisms because they represent a low tumor burden or undergo regression for other reasons, such as removal of a dominant primary, has not been elucidated. Data linking invasion of lymph nodes to the presence of receptors for the basement membrane protein laminen suggest that multiple steps may be involved in the development of a fully invasive and metastasizing cancer; such events may not have occurred in nondominant microscopic foci. This observation of multicentricity has been central to the debate about the extent of treatment necessary for breast cancer with local modalities. Long-term follow-up of the women who were treated with segmental mastectomy only in a trial comparing this approach to segmental mastectomy and radiation therapy conducted by the National Surgical Adjuvant Breast Project (NSABP) should provide an answer to the clinical relevance of multicentricity in breast cancer (see "Surgical Options" below).

The size of the primary tumor, a clinical predictor of outcome, can be determined easily by palpation combined with mammography. Tumors less than 2 cm in size are generally associated with the most favorable outcome. Tumor size is also correlated with the likelihood of axillary lymph node involvement, another prognostic indicator. Lesions <1.5 cm are less likely to have nodal metastases (38 percent) than are large lesions (≥ 5.5 cm), which have metastasized to axillary lymph nodes 70 percent of the time. A correlation also exists between increased tumor size and the presence of four or more positive axillary lymph nodes.

Establishing whether there is nodal involvement and the number of axillary nodes involved is critical (Table 295-1). In those patients with no histologic involvement of axillary nodes, an 83 percent rate of 5-year disease-free survival has been found; those with one to three positive nodes have a 50 percent disease-free, 5-year survival rate. Those patients with four or more positive nodes have a 21 percent disease-free survival at 5 years. Further analysis indicates that the group with four or more positive nodes should be split because there is a 25 percent greater disease-free survival or 18 percent overall survival) in those with four to six positive nodes than in those with 13 or more positive nodes. In contrast to measuring the size of the primary, the physical examination of the axillary nodes is an inaccurate predictor of histologic involvement. In approximately 25 percent of cases examined, when axillary nodes are palpable, histologic evidence of disease is not found. Likewise, in 30 percent of cases in which axillary nodes are not palpable, histologic involvement with tumor is discovered. Axillary involvement can be assessed accurately only by surgically removing the nodes.

In addition to the size of the tumor and the number of positive axillary nodes, an important prognostic factor is the presence or absence of the estrogen receptor (ER) and the progesterone receptor (PR). Unlike the size of tumor, receptor content is not predictive of the degree of axillary nodal involvement. The ER is capable of binding and transferring the steroid molecule into nuclei to exert specific hormonal functions. The PR production in breast cancer cells is likely an end product in the pathway regulated by estrogens and involving the ER. The degree of ER binding capacity is expressed in femtomoles per milligram of cytosol protein. Values above 10 are positive, 3 to 10 intermediate, and less than 3 negative. The degree of positivity is proportional to the degree of cellular differentiation and subtype and is also a measure of potential responsiveness of the tumor to hormonal manipulation. The ER expression tends to increase with the age of the patient while PR shows no such relationship to age. Women who have ER levels in the positive range have a more favorable prognosis than those whose ER is either in the intermediate or negative range. Observations from women who have more advanced disease indicate that approximately 60 percent of patients who are ER-positive respond to hormonal manipulation while fewer than 10 percent of patients who are ER-negative respond to hormonal therapy.

Other factors which are predictive of outcome of breast cancer are the patient's age and menopausal status. The group found to be most likely to have a favorable outcome are those postmenopausal women whose primary cancer is less than 2 cm and positive for ER, and who have no evidence of spread to the axillary lymph nodes.

SCREENING In order to detect earlier clinical stages of breast cancer (Table 295-2), which confer a more favorable outcome, major emphasis is being placed on screening large asymptomatic populations for breast cancer. Ninety percent of breast masses are found by the patient either accidentally or during deliberate self-examination. The

TABLE 295-1 Disease-free survival related to lymph node status

Axillary node status	Percent surviving disease-free	
	5 years	10 years
Negative	82	76
Positive:	35	24
1–3 nodes	50	35
≥ 4 nodes	21	11

SOURCE: *National Surgical Adjuvant Breast Project.*

TABLE 295-2 Breast cancer clinical stage and prognosis

Stage	American Joint Committee staging	Approximate frequency of stage at presentation, %	Approximate 5-year survival, %
I	Primary tumor <2 cm; nodes, if palpable, not felt to contain metastases; no distant metastases	55–70	80
II	Primary tumor >2 cm and <5 cm; nodes, if palpable, not fixed; no distant metastases evident	20–25	65
III	Tumor >5 cm or fixed to chest wall or skin invasion present; supraclavicular nodes palpable; no distant metastases evident	10	40
IV	Distant metastases	10	10

remaining 10 percent are discovered during examination by health professionals or by mass screening techniques such as mammography.

The Health Insurance Plan of New York evaluated mammography as a screening tool in 62,000 patients; their screening included physical examination as well. A 10-year follow-up period showed a 30 percent reduction in mortality for women 50 or older who had been screened compared to a control group. The risk/benefit ratio involved in exposing large populations of asymptomatic women to ionizing radiation has been widely debated. High-quality mammograms can be performed which expose the patient to radiation doses which do not exceed 0.01 Gy. In general, annual mammograms are recommended for asymptomatic women over 50, with annual mammograms of women from 40 to 49 who are considered to be at high risk. This high-risk group is defined as those who have had prior breast cancer or have a mother or sibling with the disease. Regardless of the age, a patient with a palpable breast mass or other symptom suggestive of breast cancer should have a biopsy. Mammography prior to biopsy is not required, but it can provide supplemental preoperative information to the surgeon. Other screening techniques such as thermography pose a lesser risk to the patient but are not considered sufficiently accurate to be used as the sole screening tool. In addition, ultrasound and computerized tomography (CT) are currently being evaluated as screening techniques.

PATHOLOGY The anatomic units of the female breast are the small, medium, and large ducts. Tumors can arise from any of these structures, but carcinoma of the breast most frequently arises in a large duct. In 70 to 75 percent of cases, no distinctive histologic structure can be distinguished and these infiltrating duct carcinomas are designated NOS (not otherwise specified). In spite of the small size of the primary, these cancers frequently metastasize to axillary lymph nodes and their prognosis is the worst of all breast cancer types. To palpation these lesions are firm, and a fibrotic response within the tumor is characteristic. Lobular invasive, medullary, and colloid or mucinous tumors of the breast are generally seen in their pure form but can appear in combinations and make up 20 percent of all breast cancers.

Lobular carcinoma makes up approximately 5 percent of breast cancers and arises in the small end ducts. This carcinoma may be either invasive, with tumor extending beyond the duct in which it arises, or noninvasive. In the noninvasive form, carcinoma in situ, the anaplastic cells are contained within the lobules. In the invasive form the tumor extends beyond the lobule or end duct from which it arises. This type of lobular carcinoma has a poor prognosis.

Medullary carcinoma comprises 5 to 7 percent of all breast cancers. Unlike intraductal carcinomas, these tumors are well-circumscribed and often attain large size but are not as likely to infiltrate, and patients generally have a good prognosis. Another slow-growing invasive carcinoma that reaches large, bulky proportion is the colloid carcinoma, a mucinous-producing tumor which comprises 3 to 5 percent of breast cancers. The tumor occurs in older women (over the age of 70) and has a tendency to occur in areas readily accessible to palpation.

Rare histologic types of breast cancer with a favorable outcome are tubular, adenocystic, and secretory carcinoma. The latter occurs primarily in children and adolescents. Tumors with unfavorable rare histologies are squamous metaplasia and carcinomas with sarcomatoid, osseous, or chondrometaplastic elements; these tend to be quite large when discovered. Other significant histologic forms of breast cancer are inflammatory breast cancer and Paget's disease.

Inflammatory breast carcinoma presents with a unique clinical picture in which much of the skin overlying the breast becomes erythematous and thickened. The diagnosis must be confirmed pathologically. Biopsies of the erythematous areas of the breast as well as normal-appearing skin will reveal undifferentiated cancer cells in the subdermal lymphatics. In Paget's disease, the nipple epithelium contains nests of tumor cells, but the tumor may be either intraductal or of the invasive duct type. The prognosis is related to the histologic type of the tumor.

Staging following the histologic confirmation of breast cancer using both the clinical and surgical staging systems illustrated in Table 295-2 is essential. In addition, receptor status should be determined for establishing the patient's prognosis and prescribing an appropriate form of treatment. Frequently, metastases to distant sites occur early and metastatic spread follows no predictable pattern. The axillary lymph nodes, liver, bones, skin, and lungs are the most common sites of metastases while the adrenal glands, kidneys, ovaries, spleen, and thyroid are less frequently involved.

DIAGNOSIS In 70 to 80 percent of cases, the patient presents with a hard, circumscribed mass in the breast. If this mass is fixed to skin or deep muscle, or if there is edema of the skin or retraction of the nipple, cancer is almost a certainty. However, 75 percent of all breast lumps are benign. Breast cancer presents most frequently (in 45 percent of cases) in the upper outer quadrant of the breast; it is present in the central or subareolar portion of the breast in 25 percent of cases, in the upper inner quadrant in 15 percent of cases, and in the lower inner quadrant in only 5 percent of cases. A mobile mass with well-defined margins in a woman under 30 is much more likely to be a fibroadenoma, a benign condition. On rare occasions, infectious mastitis may be mistaken for adenoma.

Once a well-defined breast mass has been detected, a complete history and physical examination should be followed by a biopsy or needle aspiration. A breast mass is an indication for biopsy regardless of the results of mammography. There is no necessity for the biopsy and definitive surgical treatment to be undertaken as a single operative procedure. Prior custom was to perform the initial biopsy while the patient was under general anesthesia, examine a frozen section of the tissue, and proceed with a radical mastectomy if the biopsy was positive. Biopsy can be done using local anesthesia and the interval between diagnostic biopsy and definitive surgery or radiation therapy provides a period during which metastatic disease can be ruled out and the physician can discuss all of the options for further management with the patient. In the workup for metastatic disease, the patient should be questioned and examined thoroughly for signs and symptoms of bone pain, neurologic deficit, or behavioral changes which would indicate the need to search for distant metastases. However, routine scanning of the bones in patients who are asymptomatic has not proved to be cost-effective. Likewise, radioisotopic or CT scans of the liver and brain should be undertaken only in patients with abnormal physical findings or liver function studies.

Two infrequent but nonetheless important clinical presentations of breast cancer are *inflammatory breast carcinoma* and *Paget's disease*, which have been briefly described above. With inflammatory breast disease there is increased local temperature, redness, and a visible erysipeloid margin; the entire breast is often indurated and firm to hard. This particular type of breast cancer implies systemic disease; axillary and supraclavicular node involvement and distant metastases are invariably present and require an initial systemic rather than surgical approach. Patients with inflammatory breast cancer have had an extremely poor prognosis. Results of combination chemotherapy as the initial treatment appear promising. In Paget's disease eczematoid changes in the nipple, including itching, burning, oozing, and bleeding, occur over a relatively long period and a mass can be palpated in two-thirds of patients. The prognosis is related to the treatment of the disease.

Extremely rare, but clinically distinctive, is *cystosarcoma phyllodes,* a form of sarcoma which can arise from a fibroadenoma. This tumor presents as a warm, tender, cystic mass. In the presence of a breast mass, a bloody discharge from the nipple is usually a classic sign of cancer. However, *intraductal papilloma*, a benign lesion, is associated with a bloody discharge from the nipple, without a palpable mass. These tumors are generally exceedingly small but can be located by noting the area which, when palpated, results in bleeding from the nipple. Infrequently, sarcomas, or nonepithelial malignancies, including fibrosarcomas, lymphomas, liposarcomas, and hemangiosarcomas, may be associated with breast masses.

Inflammatory lesions Mammary duct ectasia is a benign condition, usually seen in elderly women with atrophic breasts, in which the mammary ducts in or just beneath the nipple become dilated and filled with cellular debris and lipid-containing material. Intermittent pain and local inflammatory changes may be present, and because a discharge, at times bloody, and retraction of the nipple may occur, this condition must be differentiated from carcinoma. Excision of the nipple is usually indicated.

Fat necrosis is a common occurrence following trauma that may be so slight as to have not been noticed. It presents as a painful lump usually associated with some ecchymosis and may be followed by local atrophy and dimpling of the skin, at which stage biopsy must be performed to distinguish it from carcinoma.

Thrombosis of the thoracoepigastric veins and sclerosing subcutaneous phlebitis (Mondor's disease) occur after trauma or for no apparent reason and are manifested by the appearance of long cord-like structures, initially tender, in the outer half of the breast, frequently extending up into the axilla or down toward the epigastrium. They may persist for up to a year, but no treatment is indicated.

Sarcoid may very rarely involve the skin of the chest, and secondary amyloidosis may involve the breast tissue itself. Eosinophilic granuloma may occur in the submammary folds.

Fibrocystic disease With each menstrual cycle there is a recurring biphasic stimulation, first of proliferation of breast tissue by estrogens, then of alveolar secretory activity by progesterone, followed by a period of involution. In most women these changes are of such slight degree as to cause few if any clinical symptoms. Not infrequently, however, inflammatory changes may precede each menses, with tenderness, engorgement, and increasing nodularity of the breasts. This is more often seen in nulliparous women and may subside after childbearing and lactation. Suspected cysts in the breast may be aspirated safely in the office with local anesthesia if biopsy is done promptly in any of the following circumstances: (1) no fluid is obtained; (2) the cyst fluid is grossly bloody; (3) the mass does not completely disappear with aspiration; and (4) the fluid reaccumulates during succeeding days. Cytologic examinations of cyst aspirates are of little value if negative.

In the later years of reproductive life the continued recurrent stimulation and involution of the breasts in the course of each menstrual cycle may result in diffuse and nodular fibrosis and the formation of cysts of varying sizes, called chronic cystic mastitis. This condition may simulate carcinoma but is usually distinguishable by the fact that it is intermittently painful and may subside to some extent following menstruation. Nevertheless, carcinoma may coexist and be masked by the diffuse nodularity of the cystic disease.

Moreover, the incidence of mammary carcinoma is greater in patients with fibrocystic disease of the breasts, and it is unwise to delay biopsy of suspicious areas in the hope that they may subside by the end of the next menstrual cycle.

LOCAL MANAGEMENT OF BREAST CANCER (STAGE I AND STAGE II) Background

Until a decade ago, the radical mastectomy, which involves removal of the breast, both the major and minor pectoralis muscles, ipsilateral axillary lymph nodes, and, in the medial lesions, the ipsilateral supraclavicular and mediastinal lymph chains, was considered the sole therapeutic option for breast cancer. This treatment was based on the rationale that breast cancer begins as a single focus of disease which, after a considerable period of time, will spread in an orderly fashion from the breast to the axillary nodes and from there into the systemic channels of the blood and lymphatic systems. With this underlying assumption, treatment was targeted at arresting the spread of tumor by removing the primary breast tumor and the surrounding tissue en bloc.

Data from many studies have changed the conceptual underpinnings for such radical therapy. Breast cancer is now appreciated to be a disease which is localized for only a brief period and then disseminates into the circulatory and lymphatic channels early in its course. The current emphasis in the management of breast cancer is removal of the primary site of tumor with the minimum disfigurement necessary to gain local control by surgical or radiation therapy and control of the distant microscopic foci of disease with adjuvant systemic therapy. No single procedure can be recommended as ideal for all patients. It is estimated that annually approximately 50,000 women in the United States have breast cancer masses of 4 cm or less in diameter and are eligible for breast-preserving therapy.

Surgical options   The radical mastectomy described previously not only confers no increased benefit in terms of survival, but often, because of the removal of the pectoralis minor, results in edema of the arm and a shallow, shrunken chest which make fitting a prosthesis difficult. Various other surgical options attain survival outcomes similar to those in patients treated with the radical mastectomy while obtaining a more acceptable cosmetic result. The radical mastectomy is occasionally useful in patients with locally invasive tumors.

If the surgical option selected includes removal of a breast, many forms of external prosthesis are available, but they are often clumsy and uncomfortable. Alternatively, reconstructive surgical techniques are available. The nature and timing of the procedure should be tailored to the requirements of the patient.

The modified radical mastectomy is the most common primary surgical treatment for breast cancer in this country. This operation differs from the radical mastectomy in that the pectoralis muscles are spared but an axillary dissection is done en bloc. Women with little breast tissue often favor complete removal of the breast with subequent reconstruction since the amount of tissue removed even in the more conservative procedures such as the quadrantectomy or segmental resection can result in a distorted-appearing breast.

The total or simple mastectomy is an operation in which the breast is removed but the pectoralis muscles are not excised, and the axillary lymph nodes are removed through a separate incision. In comparative clinical trials conducted by NSABP, this operation produced survival benefits similar to that of the radical mastectomy. Total or simple mastectomy without axillary dissection is generally not recommended because an informed judgment regarding the necessity for further adjuvant therapy cannot be made without this information.

The segmental mastectomy (lumpectomy) and the tylectomy involve removal of the primary tumor and a minimal amount of surrounding tissue. Both operative procedures are aimed at preserving most of the breast. These procedures are appropriate for women who have small lesions, <2 cm, located in the periphery of the breast,

and who have ample breast tissue remaining so that the desired aesthetic effect can be achieved. The segmental mastectomy has been evaluated in a randomized prospective clinical study. Patients eligible for a segmental mastectomy were randomized into three groups; one group received the segmental mastectomy, the second the segmental mastectomy plus radiation to the breast, and the third a total mastectomy. In all patients entered in this trial, an axillary dissection was performed and chemotherapy given to those with nodes positive for tumor.

After five years, the results indicate that segmental mastectomy followed by breast irradiation in all patients plus adjuvant chemotherapy given to those with positive nodes is acceptable therapy for tumors of 4 cm or less when margins of resected specimens are tumor-free. In fact, in this group the overall survival was better than overall survival after total mastectomy.

A quadrantectomy is the removal of the breast quadrant in which the primary occurs along with the overlying skin and the fascia of the pectoralis major. In this study no difference was observed in the 9-year survival rate of two groups of women with breast cancer, one that had been treated by a radical mastectomy and the other by quadrantectomy plus axillary dissection coupled with radiotherapy. Local control of disease in those treated with the less-extensive surgical procedures was not markedly different from patients treated with radical mastectomy, and when local recurrences did occur, they could be treated effectively with further surgery or irradiation.

Radiation therapy   Other nonsurgical means of achieving local-regional control of tumor, such as radiation therapy, have been under investigation for over 50 years. A study by United States investigators has evaluated a selected group of women with stages I and II breast cancer. This group of 357 women received local treatment consisting of external beam radiation therapy utilizing tangential and nodal fields to deliver 44 to 50 Gy (2 Gy daily, four to five times per week) plus a booster dose of 10 to 20 Gy from either an external beam or radium implants. At 6 years, the rate of local control of tumor is similar to that of the historical controls who underwent extensive surgical treatment.

However, a subgroup of patients at increased risk of local recurrence when treated by radiation therapy has been defined. The histologic features include poor nuclear grade, extensive mitoses, and intraductal carcinoma in the primary tumor and adjacent tissue. While the breast remains intact in those women who received primary radiation therapy, this procedure can cause fibrosis and hardening of the affected breast and the shrinkage caused by this technique may result in an asymmetric appearance in the patient with small breasts. This treatment modality also raises the possibility of tumor induction in the irradiated area; data in patients who had received postoperative radiation suggest that this risk is slight. Whether the primary breast cancer is treated with surgery or radiation, sampling of the ipsilateral axillary lymph nodes should be undertaken to ascertain whether any nodes are positive for carcinoma, indicating the need for further therapy.

ADJUVANT THERAPY OF BREAST CANCER Background

Because only 80 percent of patients with stage I disease and 65 percent of those with stage II disease (Table 295-2) attained a 5-year survival following surgery, clinicians began to investigate other modalities such as postoperative radiation and hormonal manipulation in an effort to improve these results. Radiation therapy was aimed at achieving survival by increasing local-regional control of tumor, while hormonal manipulation by means of prophylactic castration was designed to reach deposits of tumor that had already undergone systemic dissemination. Neither of these modalities has improved the overall survival of treated patients. Radiation proved ineffective because it could only affect local disease. Hormonal manipulation failed as well, probably because it was not applied selectively to only those patients who were ER-positive, a technology that was not available at the time. Animal experiments with chemotherapeutic agents suggested these drugs administered systemically might be effective in patients with micrometastatic breast cancer.

Selected adjuvant chemotherapy trials Two prospective randomized studies of the efficacy of postoperative chemotherapy were initiated first by the NSABP in 1972 and then by the Cancer Institute of Milan, Italy in 1973. The first group of investigators studied the agent melphalan (L-phenylalanine mustard or L-PAM) versus placebo, the second studied a combination of cyclophosphamide, methotrexate, and 5-fluorouracil (CMF). After nearly a decade of follow-up, both studies demonstrate a statistically significant improved relapse-free survival, particularly for patients with one to three positive nodes. Not only was adjuvant therapy successful in preventing distant recurrence of disease but local-regional control was similar to that achieved in women who received postoperative radiation therapy.

Subsequent sequential studies completed by the NSABP group included a combination of melphalan and 5-FU compared to melphalan alone. The two-drug combination proved superior to the single agent not only in those patients under 50 but also in those patients over 50 with four or more positive lymph nodes in whom a 40 percent reduction in mortality was observed at 5 years. The third study was a comparison of the two-drug combination to a three-drug combination of melphalan, 5-FU, and methotrexate. This three-drug combination showed no distinct advantage over two drugs. However, in a fourth study, tamoxifen—an antiestrogen—was substituted for methotrexate and compared to the two-drug combination. A significant improvement in relapse-free survival and overall survival was noted. This improvement was largely attributable to improved results in patients older than 50 with four or more positive nodes. Five additional studies are still in progress.

Numerous other clinical trials were initiated by other investigators. During the fall of 1985, a review of all randomized trials (approximately 100) comparing adjuvant therapy with either antiestrogen therapy or cytotoxic chemotherapy to untreated controls was sponsored by the United Kingdom Breast Cancer Trials Coordinating Subcommittee. This analysis indicated a significant reduction in mortality among those women receiving either form of therapy, but the reduction was greatest in premenopausal women who received cytotoxic chemotherapy, for the most part CMF or slight variations of CMF. Systemic adjuvant chemotherapy produced not only significant reductions in early mortality in women with breast cancer under the age of 50 but was also effective in the postmenopausal group. In postmenopausal women, antiestrogens alone also produced a significant reduction in early mortality. A consensus development conference held at the National Institutes of Health concluded that all women with positive nodes should receive some sort of adjuvant treatment, preferably in a clinical trial designed to define better regimens. Another piece of confirmatory evidence of the effectiveness of adjuvant chemotherapy is the change in age-specific breast cancer mortality rates among white females in the United States. From 1976 to 1981, a 20 percent decline in mortality in women below age 50 occurred. Mortality has always been closely linked to nulliparity rates of women between the ages of 20 and 25. Because nulliparity was high in the early 1960s due to increased use of birth control agents, an increase in mortality in this cohort of women would have been predicted. This first-time divergence in mortality and nulliparity trends suggest that the major influences on decreasing mortality in premenopausal women between 1976 and 1981 was the widespread use of adjuvant chemotherapy. It has been estimated that wide application of adjuvant therapy could save approximately 5000 lives a year in the United States.

Investigators at the Cancer Institute of Milan have suggested that a dose-response effect may be responsible for the less promising results in postmenopausal patients. When they reviewed those patients who had received 85 percent of the planned dose, 77 percent had a relapse-free survival at 5 years. However, the patients who received only 65 percent of the planned dose had only a 48 percent rate of relapse-free survival, a result no different from the controls. An analysis of dose intensity of the drug regimens used as adjuvant treatment showed that there is a direct correlation between dose intensity and relapse-free survival at 3 years. These data suggest that adjuvant chemotherapy should be administered early and used as aggressively as possible to ensure the most favorable results. Short courses of chemotherapy may be as effective and are certainly tolerated better than longer ones. The Milan group has demonstrated that 6 months of therapy provides similar results to treatment of women for 12 months.

Selecting adjuvant chemotherapy CMF for 6 to 12 months' duration has been studied extensively and is probably the most commonly used combination. Although other combinations of drugs have yielded similar results, the combination of drugs that appears most promising in postmenopausal patients is a modification of CMFVP (cyclophosphamide, methotrexate, 5-fluorouracil, vincristine, and prednisone). Although each patient's clinical situation must be considered individually, those recommended for adjuvant chemotherapy are stage II (node-positive) premenopausal patients and stage II postmenopausal patients who are ER- and PR-negative. Adjuvant therapy is not commonly recommended for stage I (node-negative) patients. These patients, however, should be considered candidates for clinical trials. One of the most profound predictors of outcome is that of nuclear grade. This characteristic exceeds other major prognostic factors such as tumor stage, menopausal status, or estrogen receptor status in predicting aggressiveness of tumor as measured by disease-free interval or survival. Prospective studies of the future will likely test the utility of this index for selection of patients for treatment.

Side effects of chemotherapy Acute side effects of adjuvant therapy such as malaise, nausea, and vomiting are common. Nausea and vomiting can often be relieved by the administration of phenothiazines prior to and during treatment. Alopecia must be anticipated and can be minimized by cooling the scalp with a cap specifically designed for this purpose, 30 min prior to, during, and 30 min after the administration of chemotherapy. The long-term side effects of adjuvant therapy have not yet been fully delineated, but the adverse long-term effects appear to be low. Analyses of 8483 women entered into NSABP trials indicate only 36 patients (0.4 percent) developed leukemia and 7 (0.1 percent) a myeloproliferative syndrome. The cumulative risk of leukemia before or after the development of metastatic disease or a second primary tumor was 0.27 percent at 10 years. Cardiotoxicity from anthracycline-containing combinations should be watched for. Clearly, long-term follow-up will continue to be required to elucidate the risk/benefit ratio of each adjuvant regimen.

Adjuvant radiotherapy Postoperative radiotherapy, a common practice in the past, is effective only in decreasing the rate of local-regional recurrence. If a patient has four or more positive nodes, the local-regional recurrence rates range from 15 to 25 percent. If one to three nodes are positive, 5 to 10 percent of patients develop local-regional recurrence. If the nodes are negative, only 2 to 8 percent develop recurrence. Radiation delivered postoperatively can reduce the overall local-regional recurrence rate to less than 5 percent but does not increase overall survival. Patients who have received adjuvant chemotherapy have an incidence of local-regional recurrence similar to that observed in women treated with local-regional radiation therapy and have the additional benefit of longer survival. Should a patient who has received adjuvant chemotherapy develop a local-regional recurrence, radiation therapy is effective in controlling the lesion in 60 to 70 percent.

Postoperative radiotherapy should only be considered if clinically apparent tumor remains following surgery, if the tumor is >5 cm, or if the histologic type is undifferentiated or inflammatory.

Adjuvant hormone therapy   Prior attempts to evaluate hormonal manipulation as an adjuvant therapy were done without the benefit of the assay for the ER protein and were, for the most part, inconclusive. One trial, however, has yielded positive findings. After 10 years of follow-up, an improvement in overall survival was observed in those stage II premenopausal patients whose ovaries were ablated by radiation (20 Gy in five daily fractions) plus prednisone (7.5 mg per day) after surgery and postoperative regional radiation. The survival rate for women in this treatment group was 77 percent, in contrast to a survival rate of 61 percent in women who received only primary surgery and a postoperative regimen of radiation. Evaluation of the antiestrogens, such as tamoxifen, as adjuvant therapy is limited. A worldwide analysis conducted in Bethesda, Maryland, in September 1985 did indicate a highly significant benefit in reduction of mortality in postmenopausal women who received tamoxifen as adjuvant therapy. The reduction in mortality was slightly superior in postmenopausal women who received adjuvant combination chemotherapy. Women most likely to benefit from the addition of an antiestrogen to a chemotherapy combination are ER-positive and postmenopausal, and women with the greatest tumor burden (i.e., a primary >3 cm and/or four or more nodes involved). Which combination of drugs should be used in addition to antiestrogen therapy and what the duration of antiestrogen treatment (continuous versus 1 to 2 years) should be are under study, although administration of antiestrogens for at least 2 years appears to be the treatment of choice at present.

MANAGEMENT OF DISSEMINATED BREAST CANCER   While fewer than 10 percent of patients present with stage IV breast cancer, approximately one-third to one-half of all breast cancer patients treated with surgery or radiation alone will eventually have recurrence of the disease. Therefore, it is important to document the extent and location, ER status, and rate of progress of the cancer since it is useful in determining a patient's prognosis and in selecting the proper approach to management if metastases appear. Once systemic disease has occurred, nearly half of the patients with metastatic disease will respond to chemotherapy, one-third with complete remissions. While survival has improved, the duration of response is generally limited to 6 months to 1 year.

Hormone receptors and hormonal management   Conventional forms of hormonal manipulation are aimed at abolishing estrogen or estrogen precursors. In the majority of patients the initial ER determination remains unchanged and the ER values of the primary and metastatic sites are similar. A woman who has changed menopausal status since the original ER determination is the most likely candidate to have changed ER status from negative to positive or vice versa. Although on a statistical basis women who are ER-positive are more likely to respond to estrogen deprivation, in any given patient, the absence or presence of ER should not totally influence the choice of therapy. Certainly patients with absent estrogen receptors may respond to estrogen deprivation therapy, and those with receptors present may not. If, at the time of relapse, tissue for ER evaluation is not obtainable, the therapeutic plan should consider the results from earlier evaluation of breast tissue. Even if the ER status of a patient is unknown, a 30 percent response rate of approximately 12 to 18 months' duration has been observed after either additive or ablative hormonal manipulation. In the absence of ER data, clinical findings which predict a favorable response to hormonal manipulation are postmenopausal status, a disease-free interval longer than 2 years, metastases which are confined to the soft tissue or bones, and a prior positive response to hormone therapy. In general, the response to hormone therapy is not rapid, but 90 percent of those patients who are going to respond do so within an 8-week period. Hypercalcemia may develop during hormone therapy (see ''Hypercalcemia'' below) and may indicate a favorable response. The x-ray picture created by

bone lesions which are responding favorably to hormone treatment, i.e., a healing osteoblastic lesion, can easily be confused with tumor progression.

ANTIESTROGENS   These estrogen analogues are the hormonal treatment of choice; they bind to the ER, are translocated like estrogens with the receptor into the cell's nucleus, and block the action of estrogens. Tamoxifen, 10 mg twice daily, is considered the antiestrogen of choice. Although sixty percent of patients who are ER-positive respond to antiestrogens, patients with visceral metastases, especially hepatic lesions, are the least likely to respond. Common side effects of tamoxifen are mild nausea, vomiting, and, occasionally, hot flashes. Corneal opacities and retinal degeneration have been observed only rarely at normal dose levels.

MEDICAL ADRENALECTOMY/AMINOGLUTETHIMIDE   Women who are postmenopausal should be considered for such therapy to reduce estrogen production. Approximately half the patients who had previously been hormone-sensitive respond to this treatment. Medical adrenalectomy using aminoglutethimide (AG) is an alternative to surgical adrenalectomy for ablating adrenal function, reducing estrogen production by inhibiting adrenal androgen synthesis, and thereby depleting the substrate for aromatization to estrogen. While achieving the same response rate as surgical ablation (a procedure that is now rarely indicated), the drug can be withdrawn should the treatment fail without the patient's being rendered permanently hypoadrenal. The recommended dosage of AG is 250 mg every 6 h. Hydrocortisone 20 to 40 mg per day is administered to mimic glucocorticoid administration and to prevent the reflex ACTH rise (see Chap. 325). Hydrocortisone is preferred to dexamethasone because this drug's metabolism is accelerated by AG, thereby reducing availability of the steroid. Side effects of AG include lethargy, rash, transient ataxia, and dizziness; most of these are acute and transient.

Hormones   ESTROGEN   If a patient is no longer responding to tamoxifen or AG, one hormonal approach to be considered is the use of estrogen. Estrogens such as diethylstilbestrol, 15 mg daily, or ethinyl estradiol, 3 mg daily, are most effective in postmenopausal women with soft-tissue and slowly progressive visceral metastases. Acute side effects include nausea, vomiting, and uterine bleeding, which can be controlled with cyclic administration of progesterone.

ANDROGENS   Androgens can be considered for some premenopausal patients, but their greatest utility is in the postmenopausal patient with bony metastases.

Surgical approaches   The advent of antiestrogens and aminoglutethimide has diminished the use of surgical procedures such as castration, adrenalectomy, or hypophysectomy.

CASTRATION   Premenopausal females who relapse after having achieved a response to tamoxifen and other hormonal manipulations and who have no evidence of hepatic metastases or lymphatic spread to the lungs may be candidates for castration. The response rate to this procedure in ER-positive women is 50 percent, while 20 percent of men respond. The average duration of such a response is 15 to 18 months.

SURGICAL ADRENALECTOMY/HYPOPHYSECTOMY   If, after having responded to antiestrogen therapy and/or castration, a premenopausal patient develops recurrent tumor, hypophysectomy should be considered. Surgical adrenalectomy is appropriate only for the rare patient who cannot comply with the medical adrenalectomy regimen.

Chemotherapy   Patients who have failed or exhausted prior hormonal manipulation, or who are ER-negative, and those with visceral disease that is progressing rapidly should be considered for chemotherapy. Single-agent chemotherapy with drugs such as 5-fluorouracil, methotrexate, doxorubicin, or cyclophosphamide produces partial responses in 20 to 40 percent of patients. While the overall response rates to doxorubicin hydrochloride and cyclophosphamide may approach that of some combination programs, the responses are usually only partial. Overall response rates of the common drug combinations are illustrated in Table 295-3 and range from 50 to 75 percent, with 15 to 20 percent of patients achieving a complete response with a fraction remaining disease-free. Combination chemotherapy is therefore the treatment of choice in patients with metastatic disease. The "Cooper regimen," CMFVP, was originally reported to attain a response rate of 90 percent with nearly all responses being complete. However, numerous clinical trials using these same drugs in a variety of schedules have attained an overall response rate of 40 percent and only 10 to 20 percent of patients achieved a complete response. An analysis of the relative dose intensity of these drug combinations compared to the Cooper regimen shows a decreased dose intensity that correlates with the lower response rate. Other combinations of drugs show similar results. The median duration of response of patients who achieve a complete remission is 1 year, while for those who have partial regression of tumor it is 6 to 9 months. Should the patient initially respond to chemotherapy and then fail, subsequent chemotherapy regimens produce responses of brief duration in 25 to 40 percent of cases. The high relapse rate and diminished sensitivity to second-line chemotherapy are strong indicators of cells which have become or were inherently resistant. Experimental approaches, including monoclonal antibodies, in a protocol setting should be considered for these patients. At some cancer centers, high-dose chemotherapy and autologous bone marrow transplantation have yielded a significant number of complete responses in previously treated patients.

Clinical predictors of a favorable response to chemotherapy include a disease-free interval of more than 2 years and pre- or perimenopausal status. All sites of metastatic disease are not equally responsive to chemotherapy; metastases to soft tissue, such as skin and lymph modes, are most responsive; visceral sites of metastases show intermediate responsiveness, and bone lesions are least likely to respond to chemotherapy, although pain relief often results.

Selecting an appropriate combination depends primarily on two factors: the patient's prior exposure to drugs in the adjuvant setting, and a medical history which would contraindicate the use of specific drugs in combination. Patients exposed to melphalan in the adjuvant setting can respond to a non-cross-resistant drug or drug combination such as doxorubicin or CMF if metastases occur. Patients exposed previously to CMF remain responsive to doxorubicin-containing combinations, but are unlikely to respond to standard doses of single-agent alkylating therapy once combination therapy has failed. Such regimens should be considered for the patient with a prior history of congestive heart failure only if the patient has failed to respond to non-anthracycline-containing combinations. A maximum total dose of 550 mg per square meter of body surface should be used in all patients who receive doxorubicin.

MANAGEMENT OF COMPLICATIONS DUE TO BREAST CANCER

Skeletal system Painful and destructive lesions of the skeleton often occur in breast cancer patients with advanced disease. Bone scans are the most sensitive test for detecting early signs of metastatic disease but have not proved to be cost effective in asymptomatic patients. When following a patient, x-rays of sites which become symptomatic are appropriate. Bone-scanning is required only if x-rays are negative.

Limited field irradiation is effective for palliation of pain. The extent of disease, the patient's requirements for narcotics, and the overall health status should be carefully evaluated before radiation for pain relief is recommended. Preventing fractures of weight-bearing bones can also be accomplished by limited field irradiation. Total dosage in this instance is generally 20 to 40 Gy over 3 to 4 weeks. If the site of involvement is a weight-bearing bone and if the lesion is approximately 2.5 cm or larger, stabilization by internal fixation or, in some cases, replacement of the femoral head should be considered.

If the patient complains of back pain, a careful neurologic examination should be carried out and, if the findings are equivocal, a CT scan and occasionally a myelogram should be performed to rule out compression of the spinal cord due to pathologic fracture of a vertebra or epidural involvement by tumor. Prevention of paralysis is preferable to treatment after the fact.

Hypercalcemia Elevated levels of calcium occur in breast cancer patients for many reasons. Skeletal metastases which result in destruction of bone can result in hypercalcemia, but the severity of the hypercalcemia does not necessarily correlate with the extent of bone destruction. A response to hormonal therapy, dehydration, and immobilization because of increased bone reabsorption of calcium, as well as use of long-term prednisone can also cause hypercalcemia in breast cancer patients.

The severity of symptoms dictates the urgency and measures that should be employed to treat the hypercalcemia. The more common symptoms—nausea, vomiting, anorexia, lethargy, confusion, stupor, and eventually coma—may be confused with side effects due to

TABLE 295-3 Commonly used combination chemotherapies for the treatment of breast cancer

Combination	Dose and schedule*	Overall response rate, %	Complete response rate, %
CMFVP:		50–90	10–20
Cyclophosphamide	80 mg/m² PO daily		
Methotrexate	20 mg/m² IV weekly × 8 weeks		
5-Fluorouracil	500 mg/m² IV weekly		
Vincristine	1.0 mg/m² IV weekly × 4–5 weeks		
Prednisone	30 mg/m² PO daily × 15 (then taper)		
CMFP (repeat every 4 weeks):		65	26
Cyclophosphamide	100 mg/m² PO days 1–14		
Methotrexate	60 mg/m² IV days 1 & 8		
5-Fluorouracil	700 mg/m² IV days 1 & 8		
Prednisone	40 mg/m² PO days 1 & 14		
CMF (repeat every 4 weeks):		50	15
Cyclophosphamide	100 mg/m² PO days 1–14		
Methotrexate	30–40 mg/m² IV days 1 & 8		
5-Fluorouracil	600 mg/m² IV days 1 & 8		
CAF (repeat every 4 weeks):		80	18
Cyclophosphamide	100 mg/m² PO days 1–14		
Doxorubicin	40 mg/m² IV day 1		
5-Fluorouracil	400 mg/m² IV days 1 & 8		
AC (repeat cycle every 3–4 weeks):		80	12
Doxorubicin	40 mg/m² IV day 1		
Cyclophosphamide	200 mg/m² PO days 3–6		

These are doses appropriate to a patient whose marrow is not compromised and must be adjusted according to a sliding scale if marrow, hepatic, or renal functions are abnormal.

therapy or with a terminal state of cancer. In patients who are relatively asymptomatic or have only mild elevation of calcium, administration of fluids and/or diuretics such as furosemide, as well as increasing the patient's level of activity, may be sufficient. If hypercalcemia is due to additive hormonal agents, glucocorticoids (40 to 100 mg of prednisone or its equivalent in divided doses) are recommended. In patients with hypercalcemia, substitutes should be found for medications such as thiazide, antacids which contain calcium, and lithium, which also tends to increase the serum calcium level. Dose adjustments should be made in drugs like digoxin which are dependent on calcium for their action. In breast cancer as in other malignancies, treatment of the tumor is the most effective means to control complications such as hypercalcemia. Because effects of such treatment take days to weeks, it may be necessary to administer plicamycin (mithramycin) 25 μg per kilogram of body weight as a rapid intravenous infusion to achieve a lowering of calcium levels in the more severe cases. This drug usually acts to lower serum calcium within 48 h of administration, and the effect may last for a week or more. If, however, it has not had the desired effect within that period, a similar dose (not to exceed two doses per week) should be given. These dosages of plicamycin rarely cause toxic side effects.

Central nervous system   Changes in behavior or evidence of cranial or peripheral neurologic deficit should raise the possibility of brain or spinal involvement. A thorough neurologic examination, CT scan, and lumbar puncture should be undertaken and, if lesions can be localized, whole-brain radiotherapy is generally the treatment of choice. If metastases appear to be soiitary, the possibility of surgical removal followed by cranial radiotherapy should be considered. Cytologic examination should be carried out on the spinal fluid as well as culture for opportunistic infections. If leptomeningeal metastases are observed, intrathecal administration of methotrexate is recommended.

Eye   Breast cancer is the most common cause of retro- or intraorbital metastases. Visual impairment with or without proptosis in the breast cancer patient is an indication for further evaluation. Intraorbital metastases can be revealed by careful fundoscopic examination, but retroorbital metastases require evaluation by CT scan.

REFERENCES

BONADONNA G et al: Adjuvant CFM chemotherapy inoperable breast cancer: Ten years later. Lancet 1:976, 1985

Consensus Conference. Adjuvant chemotherapy for breast cancer. JAMA 254(24):3461, 1985

FISHER B et al: A summary of findings from NSABP trials of adjuvant therapy, in *Adjuvant Therapy of Cancer IV*, S. Jones et al (eds). New York, Grune & Stratton, 1984, p 185

————: Five-year results of a randomized clinical trial comparing total mastectomy and segmental mastectomy with or without radiation in the treatment of breast cancer. N Engl J Med 312:665, 1985

————: Ten-year results of a randomized clinical trial comparing radical mastectomy and total mastectomy with or without radiation. N Engl J Med 312:674, 1985

HARRIS J et al: The role of radiation therapy in the primary treatment of carcinoma of the breast. Semin Oncol 5:403, 1978

———— et al: Cancer of the breast, in *Cancer: Principles and Practices in Oncology*, VT DeVita et al (eds). New York, Lippincott, 1985, p 1119

MILLER A et al: The epidemiology and etiology of breast cancer. N Engl J Med 303:1246, 1980

Review of mortality results in randomized trials in early breast cancer, editorial. Lancet 2:1205, 1984

SANTEN R et al: A randomized trial comparing surgical adrenalectomy with aminoglutethimide plus hydrocortisone in women with advanced breast cancer. N Engl J Med 305:545, 1981

SORACE R et al: The management of nonmetastatic locally advanced breast cancer using primary induction chemotherapy with hormonal synchronization followed by radiation therapy with or without debulking surgery. World J Surg (in press)

296 CARCINOMA OF THE OVARY

FRED J. HENDLER

The occurrence rate of ovarian cancer is relatively low, only 1.5 percent, and it is only the seventh most common cause of cancer in women. However, cancer of the ovary is the leading cause of death from gynecologic malignancies and the fourth most common cause of cancer-related death among women. Survival is excellent with early stage disease and poor when extensive disease is present. The apparent discrepancy between incidence and survival reflects the fact that most women at diagnosis have extensive disease. The high death rate associated with advanced disease has led to the development of aggressive multimodal therapy encompassing surgery, radiation, and/ or chemotherapy. As a result, survival in patients with advanced disease has improved, and some advanced ovarian carcinomas may be cured.

INCIDENCE AND EPIDEMIOLOGY

Each year 18,500 new cases are diagnosed, and about 11,500 women die in the United States from ovarian cancer (Table 296-1). The disease is responsible for a fifth of all pathologically documented ovarian masses and is the most frequent ovarian mass detected in postmenopausal women. The peak incidence is in the sixth and seventh decades, with the disease eventually affecting 1 in 70 women. The incidence and death rate have remained fairly constant during the past 20 years, namely 14 and 9, respectively, per 100,000 women per year.

The epidemiology varies with histologic cell type. In the United States ovarian germ cell tumors are more frequent in young nonwhite women, and epithelial tumors are more common among postmenopausal white women. The epidemiology of epithelial tumors is similar to that of breast cancer. The highest incidence of ovarian cancer is in the western industrialized countries, and the lowest incidence is in Japan and the Mediterranean countries. The rate of ovarian cancer is increased in Japanese immigrants to the United States and in their descendants, suggesting that environmental factors are important epidemiologic variables. Hormones may also influence the incidence. Risk is higher in nulliparous women, women who have difficulty conceiving, and women with fewer pregnancies. However, no conclusive data link birth control pills or exogenous estrogen administration with an increased incidence. Familial ovarian cancer is not as common as familial breast cancer. Genetic disorders that affect the intestinal epithelium, such as Peutz-Jeghers syndrome, are associated with a five- to tenfold increased risk. Some chromosomal abnormalities (pure gonadal dysgenesis of the 46,XY type and mixed gonadal dysgenesis of the 46,XY/45,X type) are associated with an increased incidence of gonadoblastomas, while others (gonadal dysgenesis of the 46,XX and 45,X types) are not associated with ovarian malignancies (see Chap. 333). Chromosomal changes have been described in ovarian cancer tissue, but these appear to be acquired defects.

TABLE 296-1   Incidence and death rate of invasive gynecologic cancer

Tissue	Incidence, per year	Deaths, per year
Ovarian	18,500	11,600
Cervix, invasive	15,000	6,800
Uterine corpus and endometrium	37,000	2,900
Other	4,400	1,100

SOURCE: *Modified from the National Cancer Institute's Surveillance, Epidemiology, and End Results Program (1977–1981).*

HISTOLOGIC CLASSIFICATION

Tumors can arise from all of the component cells of the ovary—epithelial, germinal, and stromal (Table 296-2). They may be benign, have a borderline malignancy (i.e., have some but not all the features of malignancy), or be truly neoplastic. Even in the neoplastic category, many gradations exist. The histologic grade of the tumor is based on the most aggressive cytologic and histologic pattern that is identified. Approximately 85 percent of ovarian carcinomas are of epithelial origin, derived from the coelomic epithelium or mesothelium from the embryonal gonadal ridge. The remaining 15 percent encompass a wide variety of cell types. In most, the tissue of origin can be identified, and, when more than one cell type is present, tumors are classified by the predominant cell type.

EPITHELIAL TUMORS

CLINICAL FEATURES AND DIAGNOSIS Tumors derived from epithelial cells represent 85 percent of ovarian carcinoma. These malignancies most frequently occur in peri- or postmenopausal women. Frequently, the symptoms at presentation are nonspecific and usually include abdominal pain, increasing abdominal girth, and/or dysfunctional uterine bleeding. The symptoms have often been present for long periods and have been ignored. Thus, 75 percent of these tumors are widely disseminated at diagnosis. When the tumors are detected in premenopausal women they may be more limited because menstrual abnormalities are associated with an earlier diagnosis.

Epithelial ovarian malignancies are rarely confined to one ovary and may be multifocal. Dissemination may occur early with small primary tumors. In limited disease, the tumors are confined to the ovaries and pelvic tissue. With extensive disease, the mode of spread is by diffuse peritoneal implantation of serosal surfaces and metastasis to regional lymphatics. The inferior surface of the right diaphragm is a frequent site for extrapelvic metastases. Hematogenous metastases are infrequent at the time of diagnosis. Careful examination of the entire abdominal cavity and retroperitoneal lymph nodes is required for accurate staging. Development of ascites with advanced disease is due to increased exudation and to blockage of diaphragmatic lymphatics.

PROGNOSTIC FACTORS Tumor stage A staging classification for all ovarian cancer was developed by the International Federation of Gynecology and Obstetrics (FIGO) in 1969. Tumor stage for epithelial carcinomas correlates the extent of disease with prognosis (Table 296-3). With a thorough and systematic diagnostic staging evaluation, many patients previously designated as stage I are now shown to have stage III disease. Similarly, malignant peritoneal washings in the presence of limited disease (stages Ic and IIc) probably indicate extensive disease outside the true pelvis, and such tumors should now be viewed as stage III. In short, many patients with apparent Ib, Ic, and IIc disease, when carefully staged, are at least stage III, and the prevalence of IIa and IIb disease has thereby been reduced. Apparently, only 20 to 30 percent of patients have limited ovarian cancer at presentation. By separating patients with previously unrecognized advanced disease, the prognosis in stages I and II has apparently improved to projected cure rates of approximately 80 percent and 60 percent, respectively. In addition, the prognosis of patients with stage II disease has improved because patients with less bulky disease have been added to this stage. These stage shifts have no effect on true prognosis. Nevertheless, the staging system has documented the importance of the tumor burden to the prognosis. Furthermore, modern chemotherapy has altered the natural history of ovarian cancer, prolonging the time to relapse. As a result, 5-year survical may no longer be synonymous with cure.

Tumor burden Confined disease, although bulky, has a better prognosis than does disease of similar total burden that is diffusely distributed. Survival is better for stage Ia than for Ic, and survival for stage IIa is better than for IIb or IIc. When extensive disease is present (stages III or IV), survival correlates with the tumor burden at presentation and with the minimal residual tumor burden following surgical debulking (Table 296-4).

Histologic grade and cell type The histologic grade of the tumor is an important prognostic factor. Histologic grading systems are applied to tumors with proliferative activity (not borderline malignancies) and are based on the ability of tumors to form papillary structures and glands and on the degree of cellular atypia (Broder's classification). The histologic grade correlates with survival (Fig.

TABLE 296-2 Primary ovarian neoplasms

Cell type	Incidence, percent
I Epithelial cell	85
A Serous	
B Mucinous	
C Endometrioid	
D Mesonephroid (clear cell)	
E Brenner	
F Undifferentiated	
G Carcinosarcoma	
II Stromal cell	<10
A Granulosa	
B Thecoma	
C Arrhenoblastoma	
D Sertoli	
E Gynandroblastoma	
F Lipoid	
III Germ cell	<5
A Teratoma	
1 Not otherwise specified	
2 Dermoid cyst	
3 Struma ovarii	
B Teratocarcinoma	
C Dysgerminoma	
D Embryonal carcinoma	
E Endodermal sinus	
F Choriocarcinoma	
G Gonadoblastoma	
H Mixed tumors	
IV Mesenchymal cell	2

TABLE 296-3 Pathologic staging of ovarian cancer

Stage	Extent of disease	Incidence, percent	Projected 5-year survival, percent
I	Involvement of ovaries only	15	80
a	Limited to one ovary, no ascites		
b	Both ovaries involved, no ascites		
c	Ia or Ib with ascites and/or malignant cells in peritoneal washings		
II	Ovarian involvement and extension into true pelvis	10	60
a	Extension or metastasis to uterus and/or tubes		
b	Extension to other pelvic tissues		
c	IIa or IIb with ascites and/or malignant cells in peritoneal washings		
III	Ovarian involvement with extension and/or metastasis into abdominal cavity including metastic implantation on the peritoneal surfaces of the liver and diaphragm and the serosal surface of the bowel	70	40
IV	Ovarian involvement with distant metastasis; pleural effusions must contain malignant cells; liver involvement must be parenchymal	5	0

TABLE 296-4   Five-year survival with respect to residual tumor size in stage III ovarian cancer

Tumor size, cm	Number of patients	Survival, percent	
		Two years	Five years
0	31	80	63
0–1	84	70	41
1–2	46	49	15
3–6	144	28	8
7	309	16	3

SOURCE: *Smith and Day, 1979*

296-1). Well-differentiated tumors (lower histologic grades) have a better prognosis than do poorly differentiated tumors (higher histologic grades). The tumors with higher histologic grade are usually stages III and IV at presentation and respond poorly to radiation and/or chemotherapy.

The histologic cell type similarly appears to be an important prognostic factor (Fig. 296-1). Mucinous and endometrial tumors with good prognosis can be distinguished from those with moderately poor prognosis, such as serous tumors, and from those more-undifferentiated carcinomas with poor prognosis.

Biologic markers   Alpha fetoprotein and human chorionic gonadotropin (hCG) are useful tumor markers in germ cell tumors but not in epithelial carcinoma of the ovary. Carcinoembryonic antigen is often detectable in patients with epithelial cell tumors who have ascites and/or liver involvement, but it does not fluctuate consistently with tumor burden. Using a monoclonal antibody (OC125), a mucin-like glycoprotein (CA125) can be detected in normal coelomic epithelium, in normal müllerian duct cells, and in serum in about 80

percent of patients with epithelial ovarian malignancies. CA125 is also present in serum from some patients with other adenocarcinomas, in some subjects with melanomas, and in some women who do not have carcinoma. The antigen level correlates with the extent of disease and fluctuates with therapy; it may be useful in quantitating tumor burden and documenting responses to therapy.

STAGING EVALUATION   A standard schema for evaluating suspected ovarian cancer is outlined in Table 296-5. Noninvasive diagnostic studies are of limited usefulness in detecting minimal abdominal involvement but are helpful in designing the surgical procedure.

The usual approach to staging an ovarian mass is to proceed directly to surgery once the diagnosis is suspected (Table 296-5). Paracentesis preoperatively is contraindicated in patients with ascites and a pelvic mass unless there is concern that the patient is infected. Once an epithelial cancer is diagnosed, the surgery should include (1) bilateral salpingo-oophorectomy, (2) hysterectomy, (3) omentectomy, (4) inspection and biopsy of the liver, diaphragmatic surfaces, and peritoneal gutters, and (5) cytologic examination of abdominal fluid and washings. Attempts should be made to remove all residual disease. When patients with bulk disease present following a diagnostic procedure, an aggressive surgical procedure should be undertaken. When patients present following an incomplete staging procedure with no clinical evidence of residual or bulk disease, peritoneoscopy should be performed; if disease is present a second, more complete surgical procedure is indicated for complete staging and debulking.

THERAPEUTIC CONSIDERATIONS   Stage I   Stage I disease is adequately treated by a bilateral salpingo-oophorectomy and total abdominal hysterectomy done in the context of a staging procedure (Table 296-5). When the tumor is a borderline grade malignancy (approximately 25 percent of the stage I disease) and the patient is premenopausal and desires to have children, removal of the involved ovary and biopsy of the contralateral ovary may be adequate therapy. However, if the lesion is frankly malignant, if tumor involves both ovaries (Ib), or if ascites is present (Ic) a complete staging procedure should be performed. The prognosis for stage I disease treated with surgery alone may be as high as 90 percent for 5-year survival. Postoperative therapy has not been shown to be beneficial.

Stage II   With a careful staging procedure less than 10 percent of epithelial tumors are stage II. Survival at 5 years may approach 60 percent. The standard approach is to treat stage II patients with postoperative radiation and/or chemotherapy. Clinical trials evaluating the benefits of postoperative therapy in stage II disease are ongoing.

Stages III and IV   At least 70 percent of patients with ovarian carcinoma present with advanced disease. Multiagent chemotherapy may result in improved survival if the total measurable tumor mass is reduced to less than 2 cm in diameter prior to chemotherapy. Reduction of the tumor mass to a diameter between 0.5 and 1.5 cm may be associated with additional survival benefits. When the tumor

FIGURE 296-1   *Prognosis factors in carcinomas of the ovary. (From K. Sigurdsson et al. Reprinted with permission.)*

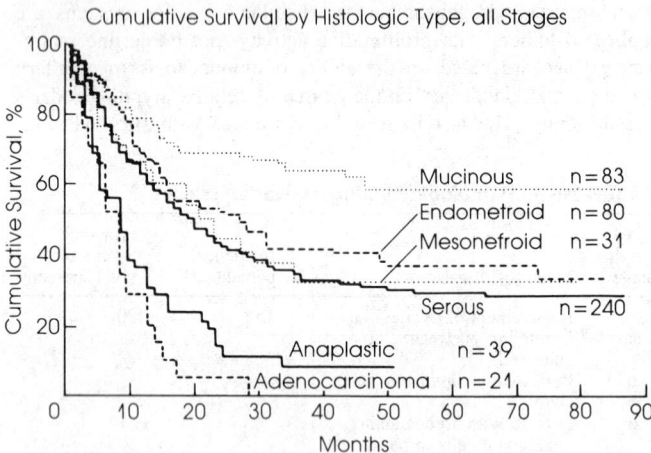

Cumulative Survival by Histologic Type, all Stages

Mucinous   n = 83
Endometroid   n = 80
Mesonefroid   n = 31
Serous   n = 240
Anaplastic   n = 39
Adenocarcinoma   n = 21

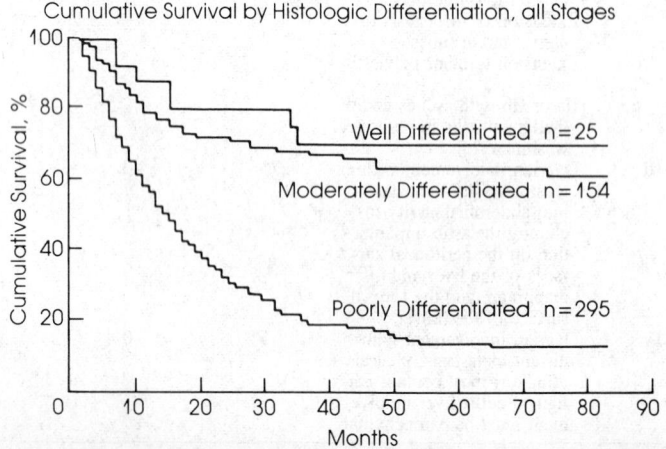

Cumulative Survival by Histologic Differentiation, all Stages

Well Differentiated   n = 25
Moderately Differentiated   n = 154
Poorly Differentiated   n = 295

TABLE 296-5   Evaluation of epithelial ovarian carcinoma

A Staging evaluation:
   1 History and physical examination
   2 Ultrasound and/or computerized tomography of entire abdomen, including liver
   3 Chest x-ray
   4 Surgery
      a Bilateral salpingo-oophorectomy
      b Infracolic omentectomy, inspection of small bowel
      c Periaortic node sampling
      d Biopsy of liver, diaphragm, peritoneal gutters
      e Peritoneal surface washing for cytologic examination
B Pathologic evaluation:
   1 Review of all tissue and peritoneal fluid blocks by at least two independent observers
   2 Determination of histologic type
   3 Determination of histologic grade
   4 Review by ovarian cancer referral center

bulk is reduced to microscopic disease, some patients may be cured. If a complete remission is not achieved, cytoreductive surgery may prolong survival but not alter the cure rate.

Chemotherapy in advanced ovarian cancer has improved the 5-year survival to between 20 and 30 percent and altered the natural history of the disease. It can palliate and probably cure some patients with advanced disease. The chemotherapeutic regimens induce approximately a 60 percent complete clinical response rate, and 30 percent of patients attain a pathologic complete remission. About 20 percent of tumors of stages III and IV, typically histologic grade IV, do not respond. The most effective drugs are cisplatin, doxorubicin, alkylating agents (cyclophosphamide, melphalan, and chlorambucil), and hexamethylmelamine. Cisplatin-containing multiagent regimens appear to be most effective, but an ideal drug regimen has not yet been developed (Table 296-6). Thus, patients with stages III and IV disease should be entered into cooperative group clinical trails.

To achieve complete remissions in patients with residual disease following cytoreductive surgery and chemotherapy, many modes of therapy have been evaluated. Radiation therapy can reduce mass disease in stages III and IV patients and has a role in the treatment of advanced disease. Furthermore, radiation therapy following cytoreductive surgery and multiagent chemotherapy may increase the remission rate in patients with bulk residual disease but has not improved survival or cure rates. Intraperitoneal administration of chemotherapeutic or radioactive agents requires further evaluation. Selection of appropriate chemotherapeutic agents in an assay utilizing cloned tumor cells can aid in the management of a fraction (10 percent) of patients who fail conventional treatment.

STROMAL TUMORS

Stromal tumors constitute only a tenth of ovarian malignancies but account for most of the hormone-secreting tumors. The majority have either masculinizing or feminizing effects, and the severity of the clinical syndrome is dependent in part on the patient's age (see Chaps. 46 and 331). Tumors that secrete hormones have a better prognosis because the tumors are relatively well-differentiated and because of the earlier clinical awareness that is associated with the hormonal effects. Feminizing tumors of the granulosa-theca-cell variety are readily detected in prepubescent children because of the resultant precocious puberty, with breast development and uterine bleeding, and in postmenopausal women as a result of dysfunctional uterine bleeding. However, in the reproductive years these tumors are usually insidious since menstrual irregularities are often disregarded. Androgen-secreting tumors, which include arrhenoblastoma, lipoid and hilar cell tumors, adrenal-rest tumors, and gynandroblastomas, are more readily diagnosed because of the hirsutism and virilization (see Chap. 46). The endocrine syndromes may be caused by secretions of a steroid hormone that acts directly as an estrogen or an androgen (e.g., estradiol synthesis by granulosa cell tumors, testosterone synthesis by arrhenoblastomas), by secretion of a hormone that must be converted peripherally to active androgens or estrogens (e.g., androstenedione by thecomas), or by secretion of a peptide hormone that induces the synthesis of steroid hormones by uninvolved ovarian tissue (e.g., hCG by germ cell tumors).

As a result of the endocrine abnormalities, stromal tumors are detected at earlier stages than are epithelial tumors. Prospective clinical studies on the response to therapy are not available, but the prognosis for a given tumor stage appears to be no different than that of epithelial tumors (Table 296-3). When stromal tumors are confined to one ovary in reproductive or prepubescent women, a conservative approach is warranted. Removal of the involved ovary with a biopsy of the contralateral ovary may be adequate and will maintain ovarian and reproductive function without jeopardizing survival. Since chemotherapy and radiation therapy have no significant benefit in these tumors, extensive disease and late recurrences are often managed by surgical debulking.

GERM CELL TUMORS

Germ cell tumors comprise less than 5 percent of ovarian malignancies, occur in young women, and have a higher incidence in blacks than in whites. They are usually unilateral with metastases to regional lymph nodes, hematogenous spread to the lungs, and direct extension to other pelvic organs. Peritoneal implantation and ascites are rare. Tumors that contain yolk sac epithelium produce alpha fetoprotein, and those with syncytiotrophoblasts produce hCG. These tumor markers make it possible to monitor the disease status and response to therapy. High levels of hCG are associated with feminizing syndromes and with hyperthyroidism because of structural similarities of the hCG alpha chain with alpha chains of follicle-stimulating hormone and thyroid-stimulating hormone (see Chap. 303). Hyperthyroidism also occurs in struma ovarii which are derived from specialized thyroid tissue within teratomas. Struma carcinoid tumors can arise from argentaffin tissue in teratomas, although carcinoid syndrome is more frequently associated with metatasis to the ovary from a primary intestinal tumor than from strumal carcinoid. Pure choriocarcinoma of the ovary is rare and is due to a primary ovarian gestation, to metastasis from a choriocarcinoma of the uterus, or to direct germ cell derivation. Most commonly, elements of choriocarcinoma are observed as a component of a mixed germ cell tumor.

When germ cell tumors are clinically stage I, surgical removal of the involved ovary, biopsy of the contralateral ovary, and a limited node dissection should be performed. However, these tumors tend to be disseminated at presentation. They are responsive to multiagent chemotherapy and poorly controlled by surgery and radiation therapy. Mot patients with disseminated germ cell tumors have been treated primarily with vincristine, actinomycin D, and cyclophosphamide. However, cisplatin-containing chemotherapeutic regimens that are effective in testicular cancer appear to be similarly effective in ovarian germ cell tumors (see Chap. 297).

REFERENCES

Bast RC et al: A radioimmunoassay using a monoclonal antibody to monitor the course of epithelial ovarian cancer. N Engl J Med 309:883, 1983

Berek JS et al: Survival of patients following secondary cytoreductive surgery in ovarian cancer. Obstet Gynecol 61:189, 1983

Decker DG: Mayo Clinic experience with epithelial ovarian cancer. Clin Obstet Gynecol 10:337, 1981

Dembo AJ: Radiation therapy in the management of ovarian cancer. Clin Obstet Gynecol 10:261, 1983

TABLE 296-6 Responses to combination chemotherapy in advanced ovarian carcinoma

Regimen*	Investigators	No. of patients	Overall responses, percent	Complete responses, percent	Pathologic complete responses, percent
Hexa-CAF	Young, 1978	40	75	—	33
H-CAP	Greco, 1981	46	96	76	30
CHAD	Vogl, 1983	26	92	42	22
PAC	Ehrlich, 1983	56	79	41	18
CHEX-UP	Young, 1984	51	75	41	20

* Hexa-CAF: altretamine, cyclophosphamide, methotrexate, 5-fluorouracil; H-CAP: altretamine, cyclophosphamide, doxorubicin, cisplatin; CHAD: cyclophosphamide, altretamine, doxorubicin, cisplatin; PAC: cisplatin, doxorubicin, cyclophosphamide; CHEX-UP: cyclophosphamide, altretamine, 5-fluorouracil, cisplatin.

FUKS A et al: The multimodal approach to the treatment of stage IV ovarian cancer. Int J Radiat Oncol Biol Phys 8:903, 1982

GRIFFITHS CT et al: Role of cytoreductive surgical treatment in the management of advanced ovarian cancer. Cancer Treat Rep 63:235, 1979

HACKER NF et al: Primary cytoreductive surgery for epithelial ovarian cancer. Obstet Gynecol 61:413, 1983

LONGO DL, YOUNG RC: The natural history and treatment of ovarian cancer. Ann Rev Med 32:475, 1981

KATZ ME et al: Epithelial carcinoma of the ovary: Current strategies. Ann Intern Med 95:98, 1981

OZOLS RF et al: Advanced ovarian cancer—correlation of histologic grade with response to therapy. Cancer 45:572, 1980

—— et al: Phase I and pharmacologic studies of adriamycin administered intraperitoneally to patients with ovarian cancer. Cancer Res 42:4265, 1983

SIGURDSSON K et al: Prognostic factors in malignant epithelial tumors. Gynecol Oncol 15:370, 1983

SMITH JP, DAY TG: Review of ovarian cancer at The University of Texas System Cancer Center, M.D. Anderson Hospital and Tumor Institute. Am J Obstet Gynecol 135:984, 1979

SORBE B et al: Importance of histologic grading in the prognosis of epithelial ovarian carcinoma. Obstet Gynecol 59:576, 1982

WHARTON JT, HENSON J: Surgery for common epithelial tumors of the ovary. Cancer 48:582, 1981

YOUNG RC: Ovarian carcinoma. Semin Oncol 9:209, 1984

—— et al: Staging laparotomy in early ovarian cancer. JAMA 250:3072, 1983

—— et al: Cancer of the ovary, in Cancer Principles and Practice of Oncology, VT DeVita, Jr. et al (eds). Philadelphia, Lippincott, 1985, pp 1083–1117

297   TESTICULAR CANCER

MARC B. GARNICK

Carcinoma of the testis is a disease that serves as a model of a curable, solid neoplasm. Patients with localized forms of germinal cell cancer have a high cure rate when treated either with surgery or radiation therapy, and the advanced, metastatic forms, which in the past were almost universally fatal, are now also potentially curable. In 1977 testicular cancer was the third leading cause of cancer death in men between the ages of 15 and 34, but by 1981 the disease was no longer among the top five causes of cancer death in the same age group. The multidisciplinary principles and strategies that evolved for the management of patients with advanced testicular cancer are now being applied to other cancers.

Approximately 5000 new cases are diagnosed annually. The incidence in blacks is substantially lower than in whites. There is a peak frequency in early childhood and a larger peak incidence between 20 and 35 years. The disease is uncommon after age 40. A lesion suggestive of testicular neoplasm in a patient over the age of 50 should suggest a lymphoma rather than primary germinal cell carcinoma. This is especially true if there is bilateral involvement of the testes.

Several factors are known to predispose to development of testicular tumor. Men with a history of cryptorchid (undescended) testes have a several-fold increased risk, intraabdominal testes being more at risk than high inguinal testes. Both the cryptorchid testis itself and the contralateral normally descended testis are at risk, suggesting that some underlying testicular defect may predispose both to maldescent and to tumor development. Although the effectiveness of orchiopexy in reducing risk is not established, it is generally agreed that a high inguinal testis should be brought into the scrotum so that it can be followed carefully. Abdominal testes that cannot be treated in this manner should probably be removed. Other predisposing factors include a prior history of mumps orchitis, inguinal hernia in childhood, and a history of prior testicular cancer in the contralateral testis. In the majority of cases no predisposing factor can be identified.

CLINICAL FEATURES AND DIAGNOSIS   The manifestations of testicular cancer range from an asymptomatic nodule or swelling detected while performing testicular self-examination to dyspnea secondary to massive pulmonary metastases. Most testicular cancers are diagnosed because of symptoms related to the testes, but significant delay in making a diagnosis is common and is the result of oversight by physicians and by patients. Most testicular cancers occur in men under age 40, and the public should be educated to the need to seek prompt medical advice for any change in previously normal testes, including the presence of a mass, a feeling of heaviness, pain, swelling, or any other unusual findings. Other causes of testicular masses include hydrocele, epididymitis, spermatocele, and orchitis, but to reduce delay in reaching a diagnosis, physicians should consider any testicular mass to be malignant until proven otherwise. Testicular pain occurs in many men with testicular neoplasms (for example, due to associated torsion or epididymitis) and hence does not rule out cancer.

Back or abdominal pain secondary to retroperitoneal adenopathy, weight loss, dyspnea secondary to pulmonary metastases, gynecomastia, supraclavicular lymphadenopathy, and urinary obstruction may also be present at diagnosis.

A testicular ultrasound can aid in establishing the presence of a testicular parenchymal abnormality. Once the diagnosis of a testicular neoplasm in suspected, a blood sample should be set aside, prior to orchiectomy, for subsequent determination of the tumor marker glycoproteins, alpha fetoprotein (AFP) and human chorionic gonadotropin (hCG). The correct operative approach is a high radical inguinal orchiectomy. A transscrotal biopsy of the testis or a transscrotal orchiectomy should never be performed if the diagnosis of testicular cancer is likely. Because the lymphatic drainage of the testis (to the retroperitoneal lymphatics between L1 and L3) differs from that of the scrotum (to superficial and deep inguinal groin nodes), a scrotal incision in the presence of a testicular cancer may predispose to the development of local recurrences and metastases to the inguinal lymphatics. This rarely, if ever, happens if a radical, high inguinal orchiectomy is performed.

CLASSIFICATION AND PATHOLOGY   The most widely used classification of testicular tumors is that of Mostofi and is based on the cell type from which the tumor is derived, namely germinal or stromal (Leydig and Sertoli) cells (Table 297-1). Germinal cell tumors, the most common of these tumors and the focus of this chapter, can be subdivided into seminomas and nonseminomas. Seminomas are characterized by large cells with clear cytoplasm in a delicate fibrovascular stroma infiltrated with lymphocytes. Indeed, the granulomatous reaction around the tumor can be so intense as to suggest a graft-versus-host reaction. These tumors account for about half of all testicular neoplasms and can be divided into spermatocytic and anaplastic varieties. Germinal cell tumors of the nonseminoma type can be divided into embryonal cell tumors (yolk sac tumors), teratomas, and choriocarcinomas. Embryonal carcinomas are common in children and resemble embryonal carcinomas of the ovary. Choriocarcinomas contain syncytiotrophoblastic cells. Teratomas contain at least two types of germinal cell layers and in childhood are second in frequency to embryonal tumor. Mixed tumors that contain combinations of germinal cell types account for 40 percent of germinal

TABLE 297-1   Classification of testicular tumors

I Germinal cell tumors (95%)
A Single cell tumors
1 Seminomas
2 Nonseminomas
a Embryonal cell tumors (yolk sac tumors)
b Teratomas
c Choriocarcinomas
B Combination tumors
II Tumors of gonadal stroma (1–2%)
A Leydig cell
B Sertoli cell
C Primitive gonadal structures
III Gonadoblastoma: germinal cell + stomal cell

SOURCE: *After FK Mostofi, Cancer 45:1735, 1980.*

cell tumors; the biology of such tumors is usually determined by the least differentiated (most malignant) elements. All four types of germinal cell tumors can also originate in extragonadal sites, most commonly the mediastinum or brain. Such extragonadal tumors are presumed to arise either from aberrant migration of germinal cells during embryogenesis or, alternatively, from some common precursor stem cell line that gives rise to the germinal cells, the thymus, and the pineal.

From the clinical standpoint, the critical distinction is between *seminomas* and *nonseminomas*, based upon the histopathology of the orchiectomy specimen. The former must be in pure form; the latter may either be a mixed cancer with both seminomatous and nonseminomatous components or a pure form of a nonseminoma, such as embryonal cell carcinoma, teratoma, or choriocarcinoma. The term *teratocarcinoma* generally refers to a mixed nonseminomatous cancer consisting of teratoma and embryonal cell cancer.

The distinction between seminoma and nonseminoma is important because the staging evaluation and subsequent management in the two differ as a consequence of the relative radioresponsiveness of seminomas compared to the radioresistance of nonseminomas. Radiation therapy to the lymphatics of the abdomen and/or chest is the mainstay of therapy in patients with pure seminoma but is rarely utilized in patients with nonseminoma. In addition, seminomas usually spread via the regional lymphatics to the retroperitoneal nodes of the abdomen and/or to the mediastinal and supraclavicular lymph nodes before gaining access to other visceral structures. Pulmonary and other hematogenous metastases are more common in patients with nonseminomas than in patients with seminomas. In advanced disease patients with nonseminoma may have pulmonary, hepatic, central nervous system, and, rarely, osseous metastases during the course in addition to lymphatic metastases in the retroperitoneum.

BIOLOGIC TUMOR MARKERS   Germinal cell cancers of the testis often secrete biologic tumor markers that can be detected in the peripheral blood (see Chap. 303). Following orchiectomy, the presence of such markers in blood reflects the presence of metastatic disease. Such assays can also be valuable in monitoring therapy (marker levels fall with disease regression and increase with disease progression), and elevated levels in blood may predate the detection of new clinical or radiologic metastatic disease by weeks to months. The two most common markers are AFP and hCG. AFP is commonly secreted by embryonal cell cancer: its biologic half-life is approximately 6 days. AFP is not produced by pure seminoma, and its detection implies the presence of nonseminomatous elements, either in the primary lesion itself or in the metastatic site, even when the primary orchiectomy specimen is thought to be a pure seminoma. hCG is secreted by syncytiotrophoblastic giant cells present most commonly in choriocarcinomas; such giant cells may be present in embryonal cell components and occasionally in so-called pure seminomas. The biologic half-life of hCG is approximately 24 h. hCG may be biologically active, and hCG-enhanced secretion of estrogen by the testis is the cause of gynecomastia in such patients (see Chap. 332).

Clinicopathologic correlations can be drawn from immunohistochemical staining of primary testis cancers for AFP and hCG. Pure seminomas usually stain negatively for both AFP and hCG. Approximately 5 percent of pure seminomas may stain positively for hCG, helping to explain the clinical situation of a patient with a pure seminoma and an elevated hCG value. These patients often have syncytiotrophoblastic giant cells within the primary lesion. Nonseminomatous components, such as embryonal cell carcinoma, stain for AFP, and choriocarcinomas stain positively for hCG. Teratomas usually stain for neither AFP nor hCG.

STAGING EVALUATION   The function of staging is to determine whether or not the cancer is localized to the testis or to regional lymphatics or is widely disseminated. Such information is necessary to determine if disease is amenable to local or regional therapy. If the disease is disseminated at presentation, the initial staging evalu-

ation serves as a baseline in assessing subsequent response. Since the approach to staging and management is dictated by the pathologic diagnosis of the orchiectomy specimen, the appropriate evaluation will be outlined for each.

Pure seminoma   The routine workup involves careful physical examination, an abdominal-pelvic computerized tomographic (CT) scan to determine the presence of retroperitoneal adenopathy or visceral involvement, a chest x-ray with or without lung tomography, measurement of routine chemistries, and assessment of the biologic markers (AFP and hCG). In most cases, the biologic markers are undetectable. If AFP is elevated, the patient should be treated as having a nonseminoma, even though the pathologic interpretation is pure seminoma.

The portals for radiation therapy for pure seminomas were traditionally determined on the basis of bipedal lymphangiography. However, the necessity of lymphangiography for such purposes is less imperative today because computerized tomographic scanning may provide similar information.

If plasma hCG is elevated in a patient with a diagnosis of pure seminoma, a search should be made for syncytiotrophoblastic giant cells. Otherwise, there may be some uncertainty of whether occult foci of nonseminomatous components are responsible for the hCG production. Also, if the physical or radiographic examinations fail to reveal any evidence of metastatic disease and the hCG is elevated before orchiectomy, it is necessary to follow the level of hCG sequentially. If the marker does not decline as predicted by its biologic half-life, the presence of occult metastatic cancer should be considered.

Nonseminoma   The staging evaluation outlined for the seminoma is employed for the patient with a nonseminomatous germinal cell tumor of the testis. On the basis of these noninvasive staging studies, patients can be categorized as having stage I, early stage II, advanced stage II, or stage III disease. Patients with stage I disease have no clinical, radiographic, or marker evidence of tumor presence beyond the confines of the testis. Patients with early stage II have nonpalpable, small, retroperitoneal adenopathy on computerized tomographic scans, usually measuring <4 to 5 cm. Advanced stage II is defined as retroperitoneal lymphadenopathy measuring >5 cm on CT scan or palpable retroperitoneal adenopathy with disease limited to lymphatics below the diaphragm. Stage III disease includes visceral involvement below the diaphragm (e.g., liver or bowel) or above the diaphragm (e.g., lung or supraclavicular lymphadenopathy). Furthermore, patients with stage III disease can be further subdivided according to anatomic location of disease and disease bulk. Stage III disease of "minimal" to "moderate" risk involves supraclavicular lymphadenopathy (stage IIIA), gynecomastia ± elevated biologic markers (IIIB1), or more than five pulmonary lesions, none of which is >2 cm in greatest diameter (IIIB2). More advanced forms of stage III disease include pulmonary involvement with mediastinal or hilar lesions, positive pleural effusion or pulmonary metastases greater than 2 cm, palpable abdominal mass, ureteral displacement or hydronephrosis (IIIB4), and hepatic, gastrointestinal, central nervous system, bone, or vena caval involvement (IIIB5).

Conceptually, patients with testicular cancer can be categorized pathologically as having either *seminoma* or *nonseminoma* and staged as having either "early" or "advanced" disease. Patients with *early* disease would be considered to have stage I and early stage II disease, while patients with *advanced* disease have advanced stage II or any form of stage III disease. This formulation allows rational decision making for nearly all categories of disease.

TREATMENT MODALITIES ACCORDING TO HISTOLOGY AND STAGE (Table 297-2)   **Early seminoma**   These patients have either a normal abdominal CT scan or retroperitoneal lymphadenopathy measuring less than 5 cm in greatest diameter. Most such patients are treated with abdominal radiotherapy, delivering 30 Gy (3000 rad) to the subdiaphragmatic lymph nodes and ipsilateral groin and a 6-Gy (600-rad) boost in areas of known disease. Although prophylactic medias-

TABLE 297-2   Testicular cancer: General approach to management*

	Seminoma	Nonseminoma
Stage I	XRT	RPLND or orchiectomy alone/observation
Early stage II	XRT	RPLND ± Chemo^a or Chemo^a
Advanced stage II Stage III	Chemo^a	Chemo^a ± TRS ± Chemo^b

* *XRT = radiation therapy, delivered to subdiaphragmatic lymphatics [30 Gy (3000 rad)]; RPLND = retroperitoneal lymph node dissection; chemo^a = combination chemotherapy (see Table 297-3); TRS = tumor-reductive surgery; chemo^b = additional chemotherapy given if surgical specimen reveals viable cancer.*

tinal and supraclavicular radiation therapy was used in the past, this practice is generally not employed today. When treated with radiation following orchiectomy, patients with clinical stage I have a 95 to 97 percent cure rate, and patients with early stage II disease have an 85 to 90 percent survival rate.

Advanced seminoma   In the past, patients with large retroperitoneal masses or mediastinal involvement were often treated with radiation therapy to fields including the subdiaphragmatic lymph nodes, whole abdomen, mediastinum, and supraclavicular nodes; however, survival rates were only 40 to 70 percent. If these patients subsequently suffered a relapse in an area outside the radiation therapy field, the ability to administer myelosuppressive combination chemotherapy was diminished and was associated with drug-related morbidity. Today, most patients with advanced forms of seminoma are treated initially with combination chemotherapy that includes cisplatin. Substantial tumor shrinkage occurs in the majority of patients. However, the proper management for partially regressed retroperitoneal masses following chemotherapy is controversial. Some patients are treated with postchemotherapy radiation to areas of bulk disease, and, in rare instances, debulking of residual tumor masses is undertaken. However, residual masses following chemotherapy may continue to shrink after therapy is discontinued. Nonetheless, one treatment strategy allows for cisplatin-combination chemotherapy to be given over a span of 12 to 14 weeks. Patients are then restaged; decisions regarding further chemotherapy, radiation therapy, or surgery are then made.

Stage I nonseminoma   Patients with stage I nonseminoma are routinely treated with a retroperitoneal lymph node dissection (RPLND), using either a transabdominal or a thoracoabdominal approach. The rationale for this operation is based upon the inexact data generated from the noninvasive staging evaluation of the retroperitoneal lymphatics. The false-negative rate of abdominal CT scans in patients with clinical stage I is 35 to 50 percent. Thus, surgical removal of the retroperitoneal lymph nodes not only serves as therapy but also

TABLE 297-3   Commonly used chemotherapy programs for advanced testicular cancer

PVB

Vinblastine	0.15 mg/kg body weight per day	IV days 1, 2
Bleomycin	30 mg	IV days 1, 8, 15
Cisplatin	20 mg/m² surface area per day	IV days 1–5

Repeat cycles q 21 days × 4 cycles.

VAB-6

Cyclophosphamide	600 mg/m² surface area	IV day 1
Bleomycin	30 mg bolus	IV day 1, then
	20 mg/m² surface area/ day	IV* days 1–3†
Actinomycin D	1 mg/m² surface area	IV day 1
Vinblastine	4 mg/m² surface area	IV day 1
Cisplatin	120 mg/m² surface area	IV day 4

Repeat cycles 21–28 days × 3–5 cycles.

* *Continuous intravenous infusion.*
† *Bleomycin omitted after cycle 2.*

determines the need for possible additional therapy. If microscopic disease is detected and surgically removed, an 85 to 90 percent cure rate can be expected following RPLND.

Stage II nonseminoma   The optimal management of patients with retroperitoneal lymphadenopathy measuring between 2 and 5 cm on the CT scan is controversial. While RPLND may be curative, a relapse rate of 30 to 45 percent can be expected. If relapse occurs after RPLND, combination chemotherapy can be administered, or chemotherapy may sometimes be given as an adjuvant to RPLND. Alternatively, combination chemotherapy can be given prior to RPLND. If complete resolution of disease is achieved following chemotherapy, RPLND would not be performed, obviating the need for the operation in this subset of patients.

Advanced stage (bulky stage II or stage III) nonseminoma   Testicular cancer has been responsive to varying antineoplastic agents of differing mechanisms of action. The early encouraging results using chlorambucil, methotrexate, and actinomycin D were followed by the more successful programs of vinblastine and bleomycin. The introduction of cisplatin was associated with further improvement in both the response rate and duration of response of advanced testicular cancer. Cisplatin-containing programs are in nearly universal use today, either with vinblastine and bleomycin (PVB) or the combination of cisplatin with vinblastine, actinomycin D, bleomycin, and cyclophosphamide (VAB program) (Table 297-3). The use of these agents is associated with complete remission in as many as 80 to 85 percent of patients with advanced nonseminomatous germ cell cancer.

Following such therapy, patients are then restaged (with physical, radiographic, and biochemical examinations) to assess the response of areas which previously contained disease and to determine the need for additional therapy. Large abdominal masses may undergo astonishing regression. Pulmonary nodules often resolve completely, and biologic markers frequently return to normal after 12 weeks of such chemotherapy. If after chemotherapy, a residual abdominal or pulmonary mass persists in the setting of normal levels of plasma markers, surgical removal of the mass(es) should be undertaken. Table 297-4 outlines current recommendations. Preoperatively, it is difficult to determine the nature of such residual masses. Approximately 20 percent contain residual, viable cancer; 40 percent contain fibrosis, necrosis, or hemorrhage, and an additional 40 percent demonstrate the phenomenon of "teratomatous transformation." The latter is thought to result either from chemotherapy-induced differentiation of the primary mass into a teratoma or from the selective elimination of the more malignant elements of the mass but persistence of residual teratomatous components. If either fibrosis, hemorrhage, or teratoma is found following chemotherapy, additional postsurgical chemotherapy is usually not indicated. If, however, residual cancer is demonstrated, additional cisplatin combination chemotherapy is required.

If biologic markers are persistently positive following remission induction chemotherapy, additional chemotherapy is also indicated. "Tumor-reductive" surgery should not be attempted until biologic markers return to normal. Some patients experience complete resolution of physical, radiographic, and biochemical marker abnormalities

TABLE 297-4   Advanced testicular cancer, nonseminoma: Approach to management after initial chemotherapy

Biologic "markers"*	Radiographic abnormalities	Therapeutic choice
Positive	Present or absent	Additional chemotherapy†
Normal	Present	TRS‡ ± chemotherapy§
Normal	Absent	Observation

* *Alpha fetoprotein and human chorionic gonadotropin.*
† *Chemotherapy with a "second-line" program, with attempts to "normalize" biologic markers.*
‡ *Tumor-reductive surgery.*
§ *Additional chemotherapy determined by presence of "viable" cancer in surgical specimen. Chemotherapy withheld if surgical specimen contains only fibrosis or teratoma.*

after cisplatin-containing chemotherapy and may require no additional chemotherapy or surgery following their program of chemotherapy.

All patients with testicular cancer, regardless of pathology or stage, require meticulous follow-up with monthly physical exams, chest x-rays, and assessment of markers for 18 to 24 months. The frequency of these tests can be decreased in the third or fourth year following diagnosis. The goal is to detect relapse when the tumor burden is minimal. Most relapses from testicular cancer occur within the first 2 years following diagnosis, but late relapses do occur.

Approximately 85 percent of patients with advanced nonseminomatous testicular cancer have a complete remission and are potentially cured (Fig. 297-1), and the relapse rate from a complete remission status is low. However, certain subsets of patients with "high-risk" forms of advanced disease have a lower complete remission, a low cure rate, and a high relapse rate. Such patients require different treatment strategies. These include patients with extragonadal presentations (e.g., with extensive nonseminomatous germinal cell cancer in the anterior mediastinum or brain, but with normal testes), or patients with high levels of biologic markers in serum, such as high hCG titers (usually >5000 mIU/mL). Alterations in the duration of therapy and doses of chemotherapy are being tested in hopes of improving treatment results in this "high-risk" population.

Testicular cancer which is refractory to PVB or VAB-6 programs may sometimes respond to the addition of the epipodophyllotoxin derivative, etoposide. The combination of cisplatin with etoposide will cause a second remission, which may be durable, in approximately 25 to 30 percent of patients.

SIDE EFFECTS OF THERAPY Radiation therapy and surgery
Infertility can result both from radiation therapy and RPLND. Because these modalities are generally reserved for the management of early stage patients, a full discussion with patients about the potential loss of fertility is appropriate. Although of questionable benefit, the possiblity of sperm banking should be considered prior to the initiation of either definitive radiation therapy for early stage seminomas or RPLND for early stage nonseminomas. Modifications in the surgical technique of RPLND (limited dissection) may decrease the incidence of fertility loss and ejaculatory disturbances.

Combination chemotherapy When standard cisplatin-vinblastine-bleomycin programs are employed, the major side effects are myelosuppression, potential for nephrotoxicity, nausea and vomiting, weight loss, anemia, ileus, pulmonary toxicity, ototoxicity, peripheral neuropathy, Raynaud's phenomenon, alopecia, hypomagnesemia, and stomatitis. Infertility is usual during therapy, although fertility may return years after completion of therapy. The use of the chemotherapy programs requires skill on the part of the treating physician and should not be attempted by the occasional user. With proper expertise these side effects can often be minimized.

Bleomycin is known to cause pulmonary toxicity (see Chap. 203), and special precautions must be taken in patients who have received bleomycin and are scheduled for a surgical procedure. The acute respiratory distress syndrome has occurred in some and is thought to be related to excessive fluid overload and high inspired oxygen concentration (FIO_2) during the operative procedure. Current recommendations now call for the FIO_2 to be maintained at ≤24 percent and for patients to be kept in a hypovolemic or euvolemic state in the perioperative period. Such measures seem to minimize the postoperative pulmonary complications.

ORCHIECTOMY ALONE FOR CLINICAL STAGE I DISEASE Because combination chemotherapy with or without tumor-reductive surgery can cure 80 to 85 percent of patients with advanced disease, the possibility of orchiectomy alone for stage I patients has gained support. Treatment with chemotherapy (or radiation therapy) is instituted if relapse occurs. Such an approach prevents RPLND or radiation therapy from being performed in the 60 to 70 percent of patients who have negative nodes and are already cured by the orchiectomy. Patients who do relapse can nearly always be treated

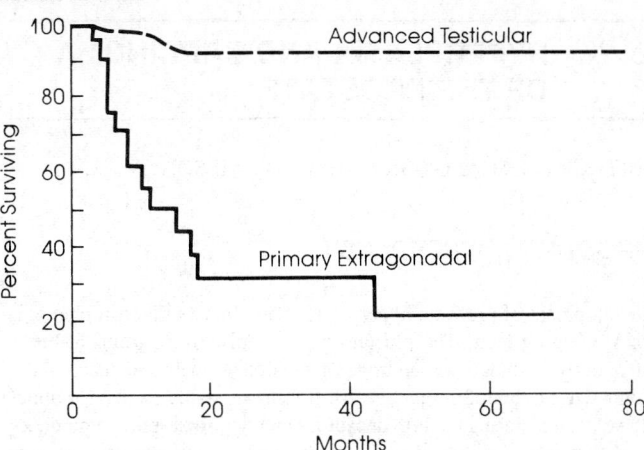

FIGURE 297-1 *Survival curves of patients with advanced primary testicular nonseminoma and extragonadal germinal cell cancer treated at the Dana Farber Institute and Brigham and Women's Hospital, Boston. Relapses are unusual in the primary testicular patients after 2 years following diagnosis. In contrast, extragonadal patients have a lower survival rate, and many continue to relapse years after the original diagnosis. (Adapted from MB Garnick et al, JAMA 250:1733, 1983.)*

successfully with chemotherapy at the time of first relapse, assuming patient compliance. However, patients selected for an orchiectomy-only policy must satisfy strict criteria relating to the clinical stage of disease, pathologic interpretation of the primary lesion, and willingness to undergo meticulous follow-up.

THE EXTRAGONADAL GERMINAL CELL SYNDROME Patients with extragonadal germinal cell tumors may present with a large anterior mediastinal mass, central nervous system abnormalities, or retroperitoneal disease. The response to therapy is generally lower when compared to primary testicular cancer, justifying the need for more intensive therapy. However, a proportion of these patients may be cured when treated with chemotherapy and tumor-reductive surgery. In addition, patients with "undifferentiated" cancer of the mediastinum or retroperitoneum may have an unrecognized form of extragonadal germinal cell cancer. Biologic markers and immunohistochemical staining of the biopsy material for AFP or hCG may provide useful clues. If positive, these patients should be treated as if they have potentially curable advanced testicular cancer.

REFERENCES

BOSL GJ: Treatment of germ cell tumors at Memorial Sloan-Kettering Cancer Center: 1960 to present, in *Genitourinary Cancer: Contemporary Issues in Clinical Oncology,* vol 5, MB Garnick (ed). New York, Churchill Livingstone, 1985

EINHORN EH (ed): *Testicular Tumors: Management and Treatment.* New York, Masson, 1980

———, DONOHUE JP: Cis-diamminedichloroplatinum, vinblastine, and bleomycin combination chemotherapy in disseminated testicular cancer. Ann Intern Med 87:293, 1977

GARNICK MB: Advanced testicular cancer: Treatment choices in the "land of plenty" (editorial). J Clin Oncol 3:294, 1985

——— et al: The treatment and surgical staging of testicular and primary extragonadal germ cell cancer. JAMA 250:1733, 1983

HAINSWORTH JD et al: Advanced extragonadal germ-cell tumors. Ann Intern Med 97:7, 1982

———, GRECO FA: Testicular germ cell neoplasms. Am J Med 75:817, 1983

LOEHRER PJ, EINHORN LH: Management of testicular cancer, in *Harrison's Principles of Internal Medicine Update VI*, RG Petersdorf et al (eds). New York, McGraw-Hill, 1985

PECKHAM MJ et al: Orchiectomy alone for stage I testicular nonseminoma. Br J Urol 55:754, 1983

POTTERN LM et al: Testicular cancer risk among young men: Role of cryptorchidism and inguinal hernia. J Natl Cancer Inst 74:377, 1985

298 HYPERPLASIA AND CARCINOMA OF THE PROSTATE

ARTHUR I. SAGALOWSKY / JEAN D. WILSON

PROSTATIC HYPERPLASIA

Development of prostatic hyperplasia is an almost universal phenomenon in aging men. The prostate weighs only a few grams at birth; at puberty it undergoes androgen-mediated growth and reaches the adult size of about 20 g by age 20. It remains stable in size for about 25 years, and during the fifth decade a second growth spurt commences in the majority of men. Consequently, the disease affects men over the age of 45 and increases in frequency with age so that by the eighth decade more than 90 percent of men have prostatic hyperplasia at autopsy. Because of refinements in prostatic surgery, the disorder is not a major cause of death, but it is a leading cause of morbidity in elderly men. The prostate surrounds the urethra, and any enlargement is a potential cause of urinary tract obstruction; indeed, prostatic hyperplasia is the most common cause of obstruction to urinary outflow in men. Overall, about 10 percent of men at some time require prostatic surgery to relieve urinary tract obstructions. The disorder occurs in all populations but is less common in the orient. The mean age for development of symptomatic disease is about 65 years for whites and about 60 years for blacks. It is probable that prostatic hyperplasia does not predispose to the development of prostatic cancer.

PATHOGENESIS   Unlike the pubertal growth spurt which involves the gland diffusely, prostatic hyperplasia begins in the periurethral region as a localized proliferation and progresses to compress the remaining normal gland. Histologically, the hyperplastic tissue is nodular and composed of varying amounts of glandular epithelium, stroma, and smooth-muscle elements. The hyperplastic process can compress and obstruct the urethra; rarely, the hyperplastic gland grows posteriorly to obstruct the rectum and cause constipation.

The pathogenesis is not well-understood, but two necessary features for the process are aging and the presence of testes; whether the testes play a direct or permissive role is not known, but the active androgen that mediates prostatic growth at all ages is dihydrotestosterone, which is formed within the prostate from plasma testosterone (see Chap. 330). In the castrated dog, hormonal therapy that increases dihydrotestosterone levels in the prostate causes prostatic enlargement comparable to that seen in spontaneous canine prostatic hyperplasia. Estradiol levels in men increase with age (absolutely or relative to testosterone levels), and in dogs estrogen acts synergistically with dihydrotestosterone to induce prostatic growth by enhancing the amount of androgen receptor protein in the tissue. Consequently, the role of aging in the development of prostatic hyperplasia in men would be explained if dihydrotestosterone is the mediator of the hyperplasia and if estradiol augments dihydrotestosterone action.

DIAGNOSIS   Urethral obstruction results from the elongation, tortuosity, and compression of the posterior urethra, but there is no straightforward relationship between obstruction and prostatic size; indeed, severe obstruction can occur when the hyperplasia does not exceed the size of the normal gland. Early symptoms can be minimal because compensatory hypertrophy of the detrusor musculature of the bladder is capable of compensating for the increased resistance to urine flow. With increasing obstruction, diminution in the caliber and force of the urinary stream, hesitancy in initiating voiding, postvoiding dribbling, the sensation of incomplete emptying, and on occasion, urinary retention supervene. These *obstructive* symptoms must be distinguished from *irritative* symptoms such as dysuria, frequency, and urgency that can result from inflammatory, infectious, or neoplastic causes. As the amount of residual urine increases,

nocturia, overflow urinary incontinence, and a mass in the lower abdomen may develop. Eventually, the manifestations of chronic urinary retention and obstruction supervene, or acute urinary retention can be precipitated by infection, the ingestion of tranquilizing drugs, or alcohol. On occasion, significant obstruction can be compensated to the extent that symptoms are minimal or absent, and patients present with obstructive uropathy.

The prostate is palpated during digital rectal examination with attention to size, consistency, and shape. Hyperplasia commonly produces a smooth, firm, elastic enlargement, recognizing that obstruction can occur in the absence of abnormalities on rectal examination. Ultrasonography with a rectal probe allows a quantitative estimate of prostate size but ordinarily provides no information beyond that provided by rectal examination. An intravenous pyelogram with postvoiding film will document the degree of upper urinary tract obstruction and the extent of bladder emptying. To evaluate vesicle neck obstruction, cystourethroscopy is indicated. Measurement of urine flow rate and/or residual urine volume is recommended to document the degree of obstruction to outflow. More detailed urodynamic evaluation is occasionally required to rule out other causes of voiding dysfunction such as neurogenic bladder.

TREATMENT   The treatment is surgical, and when surgery is indicated, transurethral prostatectomy is the usual procedure of choice. In the case of massive glands, open prostatectomy may be employed using either retropubic, suprapubic, or perineal approaches. Because the majority of men above age 60 have some degree of prostatic hyperplasia, the presence of the disorder is not an indication for treatment. Indications for surgery include decrease in urine flow of sufficient magnitude to cause men to seek relief, persistent residual urine, acute urinary retention due to obstruction with no reversible precipitating cause, and hydronephrosis. In men who lack definite indications for prostatectomy, it is advisable that they be examined periodically to determine the natural history of the process; many patients who receive no therapy experience no progression in symptoms over many years.

PROSTATIC CARCINOMA

Cancer of the prostate is the second most common malignancy in men and is the third most common cause of cancer death in men older than age 55 (after carcinomas of the lung and colon). In 1980 there were some 66,000 newly diagnosed cases and 21,500 deaths from the disorder in the United States. Only about a third of cases identified at autopsy are manifest clinically. The disease is rare before age 50, and the incidence increases with advancing age.

The frequency varies in different parts of the world. In terms of age-adjusted mortality rates, the United States has 14 deaths per 100,000 men per year compared to 22 for Sweden and 2 for Japan. However, Japanese immigrants to the United States develop prostatic cancer at a frequency similar to the rest of the men in this country, suggesting that an environmental factor is the principal cause for population differences. The disease is more common among black men than white men in the United States; the reason for this difference is not known.

CLASSIFICATION   Some carcinomas of the prostate are slow-growing and may persist for long periods without causing significant symptoms, whereas others behave aggressively. It is not known whether tumors can become more malignant with time. Insight into the natural history of a given tumor is provided by careful histopathologic grading of the lesion combined with surgical evaluation of the pelvic lymph nodes.

Histologic grading   Over 95 percent of prostatic cancers are adenocarcinomas that arise in the prostatic acini. Adenocarcinoma may begin anywhere in the prostate but has a predilection for the periphery. The tumors are frequently multifocal. Variability in cellular size, nuclear and nucleolar shape, glandular differentiation, and the content of acid phosphatase and mucin may occur within a single specimen, but the most poorly differentiated area of tumor (i.e., the area with the highest histologic grade) appears to determine its biologic behavior. In the Gleason grading scheme the dominant and any other glandular histologic patterns are independently assigned numbers from 1 to 5 (best- to least-differentiated), and these numbers are summed to give a total score of 2 to 10 for each tumor. Such grading is reproducible and correlates with the course of the disease and with patient survival.

The remainder of prostatic cancers are comprised of squamous-cell and transitional-cell carcinomas that arise in the prostatic ducts, carcinoma of the prostatic utricle (a müllerian duct remnant), carcinosarcomas that arise in the mesenchymal elements of the gland, and occasional metastatic tumors (usually carcinoma of the lung, melanoma, or lymphoma). These tumors will not be considered further.

Surgical staging Adenocarcinoma of the prostate may spread by three routes: direct extension, the lymphatics, and the bloodstream. The prostatic capsule is a natural boundary against growth of tumor into adjacent structures, but direct extension occurs upward into the seminal vesicles and bladder floor. Lymphatic spread can best be assessed by surgical exploration; the frequency with which it occurs correlates with the size and the histologic grade of the tumor. Only about one-tenth of tumors with a grade of less than 5 have lymph node involvement, while more than 70 percent of tumors with a Gleason grade of 9 or 10 have coexisting lymphatic invasion at the time of diagnosis. The route of lymphatic spread (in decreasing order) is to obturator, internal iliac, common iliac, presacral, and paraaortic nodes. Hematogenous metastases occur to bone (pelvis > lumbar vertebrae > thoracic vertebrae > ribs) more frequently than to viscera (lung > liver > adrenal gland). Diffuse pulmonary involvement is infrequent.

The standard staging scheme is that of Whitmore. Stage A represents cancer not detectable by rectal examination but found in a surgical specimen obtained during operation for prostatic hyperplasia or at autopsy. Stage A is subdivided into two groups: stage A_1, in which well-differentiated tumor is present in only a few transurethral chips from one lobe; and stage A_2, in which involvement is more diffuse. Stage B disease is palpable but confined to the prostate. Stage B_1 disease is a single nodule involving only one lobe and surrounded by tissue that is normal to palpation; stage B_2 involves the gland more diffusely. In stage C, palpable tumor extends beyond the prostate, but there are no distant metastases. In stage D, metastatic disease is present. Stage D_1 refers to involvement of pelvic nodes only with no other metastases, whereas in the D_2 category metastatic disease is more widespread. Any of the lower stages (A, B, or C) may progress directly to stage D. Failure to include pelvic lymphadenectomy in the staging process results in marked underestimation of the frequency of lymph node metastases; for example, about one-fifth of tumors tentatively classified as A_2 solely on the basis of prostate pathology actually constitute stage D disease when appropriate surgical staging is performed. The frequency with which early hematogenous metastases are missed with the current staging procedures is uncertain.

DIAGNOSIS Symptoms and signs Both early and advanced carcinoma of the prostate may be asymptomatic at the time of diagnosis, and more than 80 percent of patients have stage C or D disease at the time of diagnosis. In symptomatic subjects common presenting complaints (in descending order) include dysuria, difficulty in voiding, increased urinary frequency, complete urinary retention, back or hip pain, and hematuria. A high index of suspicion should be entertained in all men over age 40 with dysuria, frequency, or difficulty in voiding in the absence of mechanical urethral obstruction.

Palpation of the prostate is the best predictor for the diagnosis of all stages of disease other than stage A. Indeed, the importance of the rectal examination in the routine physical examination of men cannot be stressed too strongly. The posterior surfaces of the lateral lobes, where carcinoma begins most often, are easily palpable on digital rectal examination. Carcinoma characteristically is hard, nodular, and irregular, but induration may be due to fibrous areas in benign prostatic hyperplasia, to focal infarcts, or to calculi as well as to tumor. The midline furrow between the lateral lobes may be obscured by either benign or malignant enlargement. Local extraprostatic extension of tumor into the seminal vesicles can also be detected by rectal exam. Scrotal and/or lower extremity lymphedema secondary to infiltration of pelvic lymph nodes are manifestations of extensive disease.

When a transrectal probe is used for pelvic sonography, carcinoma is manifested by asymmetric densities within the prostate. The procedure is not a sensitive means of establishing a diagnosis but is useful for documenting the degree of extension of the tumor into bladder and seminal vesicles. Computerized tomography (CT) of the prostate may also be helpful in defining the extent of tumor and locating nodes for aspiration needle biopsy.

Biopsy Biopsy of the prostate is essential for establishing the diagnosis and is indicated when a palpable abnormality is detected or when lower urinary tract symptoms occur in men who have no know cause of obstruction. Core-needle biopsy may be performed transperineally or transrectally with less risk of bacterial contamination with the former and more precise sampling with the latter. Fine-needle aspiration cytology offers immediate diagnosis with minimal patient discomfort and morbidity. Open perineal biopsy is performed infrequently because it carries risk of at least temporary impotence and is a more extensive surgical procedure. Transurethral biopsy is also used infrequently because most early lesions are in the peripheral regions of the gland.

Biochemical markers Several biochemical markers provide ancillary information in diagnosing prostatic cancer. Elevated serum acid phosphatase is present in some localized disease, more commonly with bony metastases. However, no technique of assay for the enzyme (including counterimmune electrophoresis and radioimmunoassay) is sufficiently specific or sensitive for use in screening, and the major application of the assay is in following the progress of the disease. Likewise, none of the other biochemical markers studied—bone marrow acid phosphatase, hydroxyproline, cholesterol, isoleucine, glycine, aspartic acid, glutamic acid, methionine, or spermidine— has sufficiently high specificity or sensitivity for routine screening.

Assessment of metastic disease Bony metastases from prostatic carcinoma usually contain both osteoblastic and osteolytic components. The bony pelvis and lumbar vertebrae are involved most often, and metastases also occur in thoracic vertebrae, ribs, skull, and long bones. Skeletal survey has a low sensitivity of detection because a significant portion of bone must be involved to permit detection on a routine x-ray. Bone scans using radionuclides such as technetium 99 are more sensitive, but the specificity is not high because positive scans may occur in any metabolically hyperactive bone; this includes sites of inflammation, healing fractures, osteoarthritis, and Paget's disease. Therefore, when a positive radionuclide scan is obtained during an initial survey for bone metastases, the presence of other lesions must be excluded by conventional radiography of the affected site. Radionuclide bone scans are also useful for monitoring progression and response to therapy.

Surgical staging is the common modality for assessing lymph node involvement and determining therapy. The procedure usually includes removal of the external iliac, internal iliac, and obturator lymph node chains and is either performed by itself or in conjunction with prostatic surgery or implantation of radioactive beads. In some centers the initial procedure is either lymphangiography or pelvic computerized tomography (CT) scan, followed when positive by confirmatory thin-needle biopsy of the affected lymph nodes. When the CT scan or the lymphangiogram is negative, however, operative staging is mandatory.

TREATMENT Surgery Total prostatoseminovesiculectomy is the oldest treatment for carcinoma of the prostate. Radical perineal prostatectomy allows an easier vesicourethral anastomosis and less bleeding, while radical retropubic prostatectomy affords access to the pelvic lymph nodes. In experienced hands both procedures have a low risk of urinary incontinence ($\sim$ 1 percent for radical perineal and 1 to 4 percent for radical retropubic prostatectomy). Formerly both operations caused impotence in most patients. Improvements in surgical technique for the retropubic procedure allow preservation of the neurovascular supply to the corpora cavernosa and preservation of potency in the majority of patients without compromising the thoroughness of the operation.

Radical prostatectomy is not indicated for stage A_1 cancer, since this disease is cured definitively by the simple prostatectomy at which the diagnosis is made. The role of radical prostatectomy in stage A_2 is unsettled. However, true stage A_2 disease in which pelvic nodes show no evidence of metastases may behave aggressively and be benefited by radical surgery, particularly when the neoplasm is anaplastic. Indeed, 5- and 10-year survivals equivalent to those of age-matched controls have been reported following such treatment for stage A_2 disease.

Radical prostatectomy has its clearest indication in stage B disease. Nearly all of the apparent surgical cures in this stage are in men who have 1- to 2-cm nodules involving only one lobe of the prostate (e.g., stage B_1), a group comprising only 5 percent of prostatic carcinoma patients. In addition, subjects with true stage B_2 disease may also be appropriate candidates for radical prostatectomy.

The effectiveness of radical prostatectomy for stage C disease is less certain. Morbidity rates from local pelvic symptoms, bladder outlet obstruction, hematuria, and ureteral obstruction may be decreased by radical prostatectomy in stage C disease, but controlled studies comparing morbidity rates after surgery with those following other therapies are lacking. Radical prostatectomy has no place in the treatment of stage D disease, and lymph node removal has no therapeutic benefit. Therefore, other means of therapy should be tried.

Radiation   Radiation therapy was developed as a primary treatment in prostatic carcinoma because of a desire to avoid the impotence and occasional incontinence that followed radical prostatectomy. In most series, approximately 60 to 70 Gy (6000 to 7000 rad) are administered to the prostate over 6 weeks by a variety of delivery patterns. Radiation to the pelvic nodes may or may not be performed. Acute proctitis and urethritis are common side effects but are usually controllable by local measures and adjustments in radiation therapy. Chronic complications after full courses of external beam radiation include impotence in 30 to 60 percent; chronic proctitis in 10 to 15 percent; and occasional rectal stricture, rectal fistula, or rectal bleeding. It is not clear whether external beam radiation actually eradicates prostatic carcinoma, because many patients in whom progression of the tumor is slowed or halted have persistent tumor on rebiopsy, and the biologic potential of these persistent tumors is not clear.

The largest series on external beam radiation for prostatic cancer is that of Bagshaw; a variety of delivery techniques and doses were utilized in nearly 1300 patients, many of whom had received prior hormone manipulation. There was about 50 percent 10-year survival in stages A and B and a mean 10-year survival of 30 percent in stage C. The 5-year survival in stage D patients who received radiation to the pelvis as well was 58 percent. Several smaller studies have reported responses that in the aggregate are similar. The best results are obtained when the tumors are less than 2 cm in size at the time of therapy. There appears to be no consistent correlation between tumor grade and radiosensitivity.

Focal external beam radiation may be palliative for bone pain due to metastases. The duration of relief is variable. Radiation is less effective for alleviating ureteral obstruction secondary to metastatic tumor because the time lag for a successful response may be 6 to 8 weeks.

Interstitial radiation involves retropubic implantation of seeds of ^{125}I. This treatment avoids major extirpative surgery and provides a concentrated delivery of radiation to the target tissue. Successful ^{125}I implantation requires a well-defined primary tumor with a diameter less than 5 cm, a tumor volume less than 30 to 40 mL, and uniform distribution of ^{125}I seeds throughout the prostate. In the initial reports, 5-year survival following staging pelvic lymphadenectomy and retropubic implantation of ^{125}I seeds was comparable to survival rates after other forms of treatment, but the incidence of tumor progression is higher. Potency is preserved in more than 90 percent, and early complications are fewer and less severe than those after external beam radiation.

In summary, except for impotence following external beam radiation, serious morbidity is infrequent following either form of radiation therapy. Practical considerations make ^{125}I seed implantation most suited to stage B_1 disease. The long-term efficacy of either form of radiation as compared to radical prostatectomy for treatment of localized carcinoma (stages A_2, B_1, and B_2) is not clear, but current data suggest that radiotherapy may be less curative than radical prostatectomy.

Androgen deprivation   Since growth of the normal prostate is dependent upon testicular androgens (see Chap. 330), it was logical to try androgen deprivation for treatment of prostatic cancer. Androgen deprivation can be achieved in four ways: (1) surgical extirpation of the glands that synthesize androgens (castration and adrenalectomy), (2) inhibition of pituitary gonadotropin (and/or adrenocorticotropic hormone, ACTH) production [estrogen therapy, hypophysectomy, or treatment with luteinizing hormone–releasing hormone (LHRH) analogues such as leuprolide or buserelin], (3) inhibition of androgen synthesis by the testes and adrenals (aminoglutethimide), and (4) inhibition of androgen binding to its receptor protein (cyproterone or flutamide).

The common means of achieving androgen deprivation at the clinical level are castration and estrogen therapy. Since testicular secretion accounts for more than 95 percent of testosterone production, bilateral orchiectomy results in a decline of plasma levels from approximately 5 ng/mL to 0.3 to 0.5 ng/mL. Estrogens such as diethylstilbestrol are potent inhibitors of the release from the pituitary gland of luteinizing hormone, the gonadotropin that regulates testosterone production, and consequently its administration also causes a fall in plasma testosterone to castration levels. Maximum depression of plasma testosterone is achieved with 3 mg of diethylstilbestrol per day. Other estrogens (conjugated estrogens, ethinyl estradiol, diethylstilbestrol diphosphate) are no more effective in lowering plasma testosterone than is diethylstilbestrol. Luteinizing hormone–releasing hormone analogues also inhibit leuteinizing hormone secretion and lower plasma testosterone levels.

Androgen depletion beyond that achieved by surgical castration, estrogen administration, or ACTH analogues can be accomplished by adrenalectomy. Since adrenal androgen production is under the control of POMC, the adrenal sources of androgen can also be eliminated by hypophysectomy. The alternative to surgical ablation is the induction of a medical adrenalectomy and/or castration with drugs that inhibit the synthesis and/or binding of androgen to its cytoplasmic receptor protein. While these ancillary surgical and medical means have theoretical benefits for enhancing androgen deprivation, their usefulness in treating prostatic cancer is not established.

Androgen deprivation therapy utilizing bilateral orchiectomy, diethylstilbestrol therapy, or combined orchiectomy plus diethylstilbestrol was a standard form of treatment for carcinoma of the prostate for many years, based largely upon clinical reports comparing treatment groups with historical controls. Subsequently, the role of such therapy was assessed in three controlled prospective studies conducted by the Veterans Administration Cooperative Urological Research Group. These studies failed to establish the effectiveness of high-dose diethylstilbestrol or orchiectomy, alone or in combination, in enhancing survival in any stage of prostatic cancer. (Low-dose diethylstilbestrol, 1 mg per day, may decrease deaths from cancer; since this dosage does not uniformly suppress testosterone levels, the drug may work by means other than or in addition to inhibiting testosterone formation.)

A prospective, randomized multicenter trial comparing an LHRH analogue to 3 mg diethylstilbestrol per day for metastatic prostate cancer suggests equivalent response rates and patient survival in the two groups at 1 year. Cardiovascular complications were fewer in the LHRH analogue group. Whether the duration of response with LHRH analogue therapy will be equal to that with orchiectomy or estrogen is not known.

Even when there is no beneficial effect upon survival, androgen deprivation causes decreased bone pain in two-thirds of symptomatic stage D patients. Whether androgen deprivation therapy should be administered early (asymptomatic phase) or late (symptomatic phase) in stage D disease is unsettled.

Chemotherapy The age group at greatest risk for prostatic cancer has poor tolerance for chemotherapy. This feature, coupled with the variable course of the disease, makes it difficult to determine the effectiveness of such therapy. However, several comprehensive trials utilizing chemotherapy have been undertaken in stage D disease following relapse after hormonal treatment, a situation in which mean survival time is only 7 to 8 months. The agents studied most extensively are estramustine phosphate, prednimustine, and cisplatin; more limited trials have been conducted with 5-fluorouracil, melphalan, and hydroxyurea. Complete response is rare, and only one-tenth of stage D patients have an objective partial response. In other trials combinations of chemotherapeutic agents have been tested in stage D disease, most commonly estramustine phosphate plus prednimustine or cyclophosphamide plus another agent. Complete response is again rare, and only one-fourth of patients or fewer show any objective improvement. For progressive, symptomatic stage D prostatic cancer, endocrine ablation therapy should be undertaken first, but chemotherapeutic agents may provide some benefit when such patients relapse.

REFERENCES

Benign prostatic hyperplasia

Horton R, Coffey DS: *Benign Prostatic Hyperplasia,* Washington, DC, US Department of Health Education, and Welfare, in press, 1986
Walsh PC: Benign prostatic hyperplasia, in *Campbell's Urology,* PC Walsh et al (eds). Philadelphia, Saunders, 1986, p 1248–1267
Wilson JD: The pathogenesis of prostatic hyperplasia. Am J Med 68:745, 1980

Carcinoma of the prostate

Bagshaw MA: External radiation therapy of carcinoma of the prostate. Cancer 45:1912, 1980
Byar DP, Corle DK: VACURG randomized trial of radical prostatectomy for Stages I and II prostate cancer. Urology 17(4) (Suppl):7, 1981
Catalona WJ, Scott WW: Carcinoma of the prostate, in *Campbell's Urololgy,* PC Walsh et al (eds). Philadelphia, Saunders, 1985
Guinan P et al: The accuracy of the rectal examination in the diagnosis of prostatic carcinoma. N Engl J Med 303:499, 1980
Herr HW: Iodine 125 implantation in the management of localized prostatic carcinoma. Urol Clin North Am 7:605, 1980
Jewett HJ: Radical perineal prostatectomy for palpable clinically localized, non-obstructive cancer. Experience at the Johns Hopkins Hospital, 1909–1963. J Urol 124:492, 1980
Klein LA: Prostatic carcinoma. N Engl J Med 300:824, 1979
Murphy GP et al: Current status of classification and staging of prostate cancer. Cancer 45:1889, 1980
Sagalowsky AI, Wilson JD: Carcinoma of the prostate: The therapeutic dilemma, in *Update IV: Harrison's Principles of Internal Medicine,* KJ Isselbacher et al (eds.) New York, McGraw-Hill, 1982
Schmidt JD: Chemotherapy of hormone-resistant stage D prostatic cancer. J Urol 123:797, 1980
Stamey TA: Cancer of the prostate. An analysis of some important contributions and dilemmas. 1982 Monographs in Urology 3:67, 1983
Walsh PC: Physiologic basis for hormonal therapy in carcinoma of the prostate. Urol Clin N Am 2:125, 1975
——— et al: Radical surgery for prostatic cancer. Cancer 45:1906, 1980

299 CARCINOID SYNDROME

JOHN A. OATES / L. JACKSON ROBERTS II

The association of carcinoid tumors with cutaneous flushes, telangiectasia, diarrhea, cardiac valvular lesions, and bronchial constriction suggested that the peripheral manifestations are mediated by release of one or more biologically active agents by the tumor. Serotonin was the first such agent to be discovered, and overproduction of this amine is the most consistent biochemical indicator of the carcinoid syndrome. Serotonin, however, is not the sole mediator of the symptoms. These tumors may elaborate additional indoles and chemically unrelated agents including vasoactive peptides and histamine. Furthermore, unidentified substances may participate in the flushing. Within the broad classification of carcinoid tumors there is great diversity in the substances produced and in the mechanisms for their storage and release. Accordingly, there is a varied spectrum of clinical manifestations.

THE TUMOR Carcinoid tumors are slowly growing neoplasms of enterochromaffin cells. The metastatic tumors associated with carcinoid syndrome usually arise from small primary tumors in the ileum. The syndrome is also produced by neoplasms arising from the remainder of the small intestine, from organs derived from the embryonic foregut (e.g., bronchus, stomach, pancreas, and thyroid), and from ovarian or testicular teratomas.

Carcinoid tumors have an unusual proclivity for metastasis to the liver and may involve this organ extensively, with minimal metastatic disease elsewhere. Extrahepatic metastases occur in bone, where they are often osteoblastic, and in lung, pancreas, spleen, ovaries, adrenals, and other organs.

Primary carcinoid tumors of the appendix are common, but they rarely metastasize. Those from the large intestine may metastasize but almost never exhibit endocrine effects.

The usual carcinoid tumor arising from the ileum has the histologic pattern of dense nests of cells with uniform size and nuclear appearance. Histochemically, they typically exhibit an argentaffin reaction in which the cells convert a silver salt to metallic silver. A positive argentaffin reaction is not required for the diagnosis, however, and carcinoid tumors arising from organs of the embryonic foregut usually contain few if any argentaffin cells. Tumors from these organs also have a broad histologic spectrum, which in the lung ranges from typical bronchial carcinoid to a form indistinguishable from oat cell carcinoma. Ultrastructural examination of carcinoid tumors reveals electron-dense secretion granules.

CLINICAL FEATURES Unlike most metastatic neoplasms, carcinoid tumors have an unusually slow rate of growth; many patients survive for 5 to 10 years after the disease is recognized. For much of the duration of the illness, morbidity may result largely from the endocrine function of the tumor. Death results from cardiac or hepatic failure and from complications associated with tumor growth.

Vasomotor paroxysms The most common clinical feature is cutaneous *flushing.* The typical flush is erythematous and involves the head and neck (blush area). The color may change from red to violaceous to pallor during its course. Prolonged flushing attacks may be associated with lacrimation and periorbital edema. The systemic effects of the flush are variable. It may be accompanied by tachycardia, and the blood pressure may fall or not change. A rise in blood pressure during flushing is rare, and carcinoid syndrome is not a cause of sustained hypertension.

Flushing may be provoked by excitement, exertion, eating, and ethanol ingestion. In addition, the administration of pentagastrin and beta-adrenoceptor agonists such as epinephrine can trigger episodes of vasodilatation; as the hemodynamic changes associated with such pharmacologically induced attacks may be severe, these drugs should be administered with great caution.

Telangiectasia   In addition to paroxysms of cutaneous vasodilatation, some patients also develop purple telangiectasia, primarily on the face and neck and most marked in the malar area.

Gastrointestinal symptoms   Intestinal hypermotility with borborygmi, cramping, and explosive diarrhea may accompany the episodic flushes. Chronic diarrhea is more common and may have a secretory component. When this is severe, malabsorption may occur.

Cardiac manifestations   There is a unique deposition of fibrous tissue on the endocardium of the valvular cusps and cardiac chambers. It occurs primarily in the right side of the heart but may involve the left side to a minimal degree. The plaque-like thickening of the endocardium is composed of smooth-muscle cells embedded in a stroma rich in mucopolysaccharides, collagen, and microfibrils and does not penetrate the internal elastic membrane. Distortion of the valve cusps, chordae tendineae, and papillary muscles interferes with valvular function in the right side of the heart and may lead to regurgitation, stenosis, or combined functional lesions. The fibrosing process tends to produce incompetence at the tricuspid valve and stenosis of the smaller pulmonary orifice, a deleterious hemodynamic combination. A high cardiac output, with its attendant imposition on cardiac function, may be due either to a continuing release of a vasodilator or to excessive flow in the metastatic tumors.

Pulmonary symptoms   Bronchoconstriction is a less common feature of the syndrome, but it may be severe. It is usually most pronounced during flushing attacks.

General   In addition to the endocrine effects, the tumors themselves may cause intestinal obstruction or bleeding. Necrosis of intestinal

FIGURE 299-1   *Metabolic pathway of serotonin.*

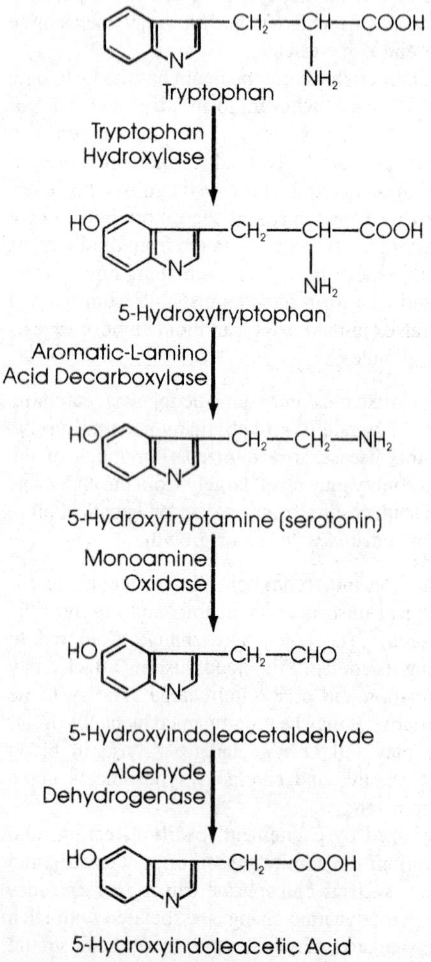

or hepatic tumor masses may produce abdominal pain, tenderness, fever, and leukocytosis. Hepatomegaly from the metastatic disease is usually present with the syndrome. Extensive metastatic involvement of the liver by these slowly growing tumors may occur before the liver function test results become abnormal. Rarely, a tumor-associated myasthenia accompanies the carcinoid syndrome.

ENDOCRINE FUNCTION OF THE TUMORS   The most constant biochemical characteristic of carcinoid tumors is the presence of tryptophan hydroxylase, which catalyzes the formation of 5-hydroxytryptophan (5-HTP) from tryptophan (Fig. 299-1). Most tumors also contain the enzyme aromatic L-amino acid decarboxylase, which catalyzes the formation of 5-hydroxytryptamine (serotonin). Carcinoids from the stomach and from other organs derived from the embryonic foregut, however, are frequently deficient in this decarboxylase and release 5-HTP from the tumor. Following its release from the tumor, serotonin is inactivated primarily by the enzyme monoamine oxidase; uptake into platelets also contributes to removal of free serotonin from blood. Monoamine oxidase oxidizes serotonin to 5-hydroxyindoleacetaldehyde, which is rapidly converted to 5-hydroxyindoleacetic acid (5-HIAA) by aldehyde dehydrogenase. This acid is rapidly excreted in the urine, and almost all circulating serotonin can be accounted for as urinary 5-HIAA. Carcinoid tumors vary widely in their capacity to store serotonin, with concentrations of the amine in tumors ranging from a few micrograms per gram to 3 mg/g. The concentration in the tumor appears unrelated to the rate of synthesis of serotonin as reflected by urinary 5-HIAA. Generally, tumors from the ileum have a higher storage capacity for serotonin than do tumors from organs of the embryonic foregut.

Peptides in the class of tachykinins have been found in the tumors and blood of patients with carcinoid syndrome. There are numerous vasodilator peptides in the tachykinin group, including the undecapeptide substance P, and the specific structure(s) associated with the tachykinins in carcinoid syndrome has not been classified.

Bradykinin, also a vasodilator peptide, is released during flushes in some, but not all, cases of carcinoid syndrome. Accordingly, it is not likely to be the principal agent causing flushing.

Some carcinoid tumors, particularly those of gastric origin, produce and release excessive amounts of histamine. This can be detected by an increased excretion of this amine in the urine. In such patients, the release of histamine from the tumors is responsible for the episodic vasodilatation with flushing, tachycardia, and hypotension.

Carcinoid syndrome has been associated with hyperadrenocorticism in a number of instances. This results from ectopic production of adrenocorticotropic hormone or of a corticotropin-releasing factor by the tumors, which usually originate from sites other than the ileum (bronchus, pancreas, ovary, and stomach) (see Chap. 303 and Chap. 321).

In a few cases, "multiple endocrine adenomas" have been seen in conjunction with carcinoids arising from organs of the embryonic foregut. The associated tumors have included parathyroid adenomas and pancreatic tumors, producing Zollinger-Ellison syndrome (see Chap. 334).

Neoplasms of foregut origin with histologic features resembling carcinoids may produce excessive amounts of gastrin, insulin, calcitonin, glucagon, corticotropin, growth hormone, a growth hormone–releasing factor, and vasoactive intestinal polypeptide without exhibiting the usual features of carcinoid syndrome. These carcinoid tumors probably share a common embryologic origin with those producing carcinoid syndrome.

PATHOPHYSIOLOGY   Serotonin contributes to those aspects of the syndrome related to intestinal hypermotility, and the fibrous deposits on the endocardium may result from increased levels of circulating serotonin.

A secondary effect of serotonin overproduction occurs when a large fraction of dietary tryptophan is shunted into the hydroxylation pathway, leaving less tryptophan available for the formation of nicotinic acid and protein. When urinary excretion of 5-HIAA exceeds

200 to 300 mg daily, low levels of plasma tryptophan and evidence of nicotinamide deficiency are seen (see Chap. 76).

Mechanism of the flush Although the flushes of patients with gastric carcinoids that secrete histamine can be attributed to this amine, the mechanism of the flush in the more typical carcinoid syndrome has not yet been elucidated. Current evidence suggests that serotonin is not the mediator of the flush.

Release of the flush-provoking substance(s) can be triggered by catecholamines, and this probably accounts for the association of flushing with excitement and emotional stimuli. For experimental induction of flushing, injection of isoproterenol in amounts of as little as 0.5 μg may be effective. Pentagastrin in doses as small as 0.25 μg also can trigger flushing, an action that may explain the provocation of flushes by eating in some patients. Flushing episodes can be blocked by somatostatin, probably by inhibition of the release of the vasodilator substance(s).

DIAGNOSIS With its full constellation of clinical features, carcinoid syndrome is easily recognized. The diagnosis also must be considered when any one of its features is present. The diagnostic hallmark is *overproduction of 5-hydroxyindoles* with *increased urinary excretion of 5-hydroxyindoleacetic acid.* Normally, excretion of 5-HIAA does not exceed 9 mg daily. Ingestion of foods containing serotonin may complicate the biochemical diagnosis of carcinoid syndrome; walnuts and bananas contain enough serotonin to produce elevated urinary excretion of 5-HIAA after their ingestion. Some drugs also interfere with the analysis of urinary 5-HIAA; cough syrups containing guaiacolate cause falsely elevated values, and phenothiazines interfere with the colorimetric test. When dietary 5-hydroxyindoles are excluded, a urinary excretion of more than 25 mg 5-HIAA daily is diagnostic of carcinoid. Elevations in the range of 9 to 25 mg may be seen with carcinoid syndrome, nontropical sprue, or acute intestinal obstruction.

Measurement of *serotonin in blood or platelets* is of less diagnostic value than assay of the major metabolite of serotonin in the urine.

Measurement of an increased concentration of *serotonin in tumor tissue* is a useful and sometimes necessary supplement to histologic examination. A portion of suspected tumor should always be frozen for serotonin analysis (see Table 299-1).

Differential diagnosis Attacks of flushing in a patient with normal urinary excretion of 5-HIAA raises other diagnostic possibilities. Disorders associated with systemic mastocyte activation, including mastocytosis, produce flushing, hypotension, and even syncope and are a consideration when 5-HIAA excretion is not elevated. Flushing also occurs in the postmenopausal state and in conjunction with other tumors, particularly medullary carcinoma of the thyroid.

VARIANTS OF THE SYNDROME The origin of the tumor influences the biologically active substances produced and their storage and release. Carcinoid tumors arising from organs derived from the embryonic foregut (bronchus, stomach, and pancreas) tend to differ from those arising distal to the midduodenum (midgut). The typical carcinoid syndrome usually results from tumors of midgut origin, which almost invariably secrete serotonin with little or no 5-HTP. Tumor serotonin content is likely to be high, and the tumor usually contains dense nests of argentaffin-positive cells.

In contrast, tumors arising from the embryonic foregut contain fewer argentaffin cells, have lower serotonin content, and may secrete 5-HTP. Hyperadrenocorticism and multiple endocrine adenomas are more likely to be associated with this group.

In addition to the general characteristics of the foregut group, certain clinical and biochemical features have been associated with gastric and bronchial carcinoids. Patients with gastric carcinoids frequently exhibit unique flushing which begins as a bright-red patchy erythema with sharply delineated serpentine borders; these patches tend to coalesce as the blush heightens. Food ingestion is especially likely to produce flushes. The tumors usually are deficient in decarboxylase enzyme and secrete 5-HTP; histamine secretion is also

common, as is a high incidence of peptic ulcers. Diarrhea and heart lesions are not prominent features in the patients who secrete largely 5-HTP from the tumor without much preformed serotonin.

When the carcinoid tumor arises from the bronchus, attacks of flushing tend to be prolonged and severe and may be associated with periorbital edema, excessive lacrimation and salivation, hypotension, tachycardia, anxiety, and tremulousness. Nausea, vomiting, explosive diarrhea, and bronchoconstriction may progress to a severe degree. This group is distinctive in that the severe flushes often can be prevented by glucocorticoids, and chlorpromazine may relieve the symptoms.

TREATMENT Treatment of the carcinoid syndrome is directed toward (1) reducing tumor mass by surgical and/or chemotherapeutic approaches and (2) relief of humorally mediated symptoms.

Recognition of the carcinoid syndrome has led to complete surgical cure of a few patients with tumors arising in ovarian or testicular teratomas or in the bronchus. By releasing their secretions directly into the systemic circulation, tumors from these locations can produce the syndrome before metastatic disease occurs. As the humoral substances released by tumors draining into the portal circulation are largely metabolized by the liver, tumors arising in this location produce the syndrome only after metastasis, usually to the liver. Because of the relatively slow growth of carcinoid tumors, palliative resection of hepatic metastases may be beneficial in selected cases. Resection of large isolated hepatic metastases has led to relief of the symptoms of carcinoid syndrome and reduction in urinary 5-HIAA excretion for periods of several years. In some cases with multiple metastases, removal of as much as a hepatic lobe may be considered when the metastases are located primarily in the portion of the liver to be resected, as indicated by arteriography, radionuclide scanning of the liver, ultrasonography, computerized tomography or inspection of the hepatic surface at surgical exploration.

In patients with diffuse metastatic disease involving both lobes of the liver, reduction of tumor mass and control of symptoms has been accomplished by surgical ligation or percutaneous embolization of the hepatic artery. Experience with these approaches, however, is limited, and further studies are required to define efficacy and associated complications.

There is no universally effective chemotherapeutic regimen, and none will eradicate carcinoid tumors. Palliation has been achieved in some patients with 5-fluorouracil, cyclophosphamide, streptozotocin, doxorubicin, and methotrexate, used singly or in combination. Objective response rates to chemotherapy are low, the average duration of remission is usually less than 1 year, and associated toxicity of drug therapy is high. An occasional patient may respond to 5-fluorouracil alone with minimal toxicity. Initial doses of chemotherapeutic agents should be low in patients with 5-HIAA levels over 150 mg per day or florid manifestations of the carcinoid syndrome, because rapid lysis of tumor may result in massive mediator release ("carcinoid crisis"). Radiation therapy can be effective in the treatment of symptomatic metastases, e.g., bone. The antiestrogen tamoxifen and leukocyte interferon have been tried in a few patients.

Pharmacologic therapy directed at the humoral mediators of the

---

TABLE 299-1 Outline of diagnostic approach to a patient with suspected carcinoid syndrome

1 Quantitative determination of 24-h urinary excretion of 5-HIAA (5-hydroxyindoleacetic acid).

2 When elevated 5-HIAA confirms carcinoid syndrome, curable ovarian, testicular, or bronchial primary tumors should be sought.

3 Consideration of possible treatment of the syndrome by surgical resection of hepatic metastases requires
  a Assessment of the location and character of hepatic metastases with computerized tomography, scintillation scanning of the liver, arteriography, and ultrasonography.
  b Evaluation of hepatic and cardiac function.
  c A search for extrahepatic metastases in bone and other sites.

4 In patients with substantial diarrhea, possible malabsorption of nutrients should be investigated.

syndrome may be useful. When the flush is associated with release of histamine, as may be the case with gastric carcinoids, combined treatment with an H-1 antagonist (e.g., diphenhydramine) and an H-2 antagonist (cimetidine or ranitidine) will block the vasodilator action of histamine. Diarrhea should be treated symptomatically if possible, e.g., with loperamide. Treatment with serotonin antagonists such as cyproheptadine and methysergide can also be helpful in controlling diarrhea. Prolonged therapy with methysergide, however, can produce retroperitoneal fibrosis. Blockade of serotonin synthesis with the tryptophan hydroxylase inhibitor *p*-chlorophenylalanine (an experimental drug) also ameliorates the diarrhea. Somatostatin (also an experimental agent) decreases flushing, diarrhea, and broncho-constriction and may contribute to the management of episodes with massive mediator release or "carcinoid crisis." The prevention of severe flushing by glucocorticoids and amelioration of the syndrome by phenothiazines are limited largely to patients with tumors arising from the bronchus and other organs derived from the embryonic foregut.

There are no known means to reverse or halt the progression of endocardial fibrosis. Surgical replacement of damaged cardiac valves is associated with technical problems because of the marked fibrosis of the endocardium.

In patients with urinary 5-HIAA levels about 100 mg per day supplemental niacin therapy prevents the development of pellagra.

Hypotensive episodes should not be treated with catecholamines; by stimulating the release of vasoactive substances from the tumor, norepinephrine, epinephrine, and other agents with adrenergic activity can exaggerate and prolong the circulatory disturbance. If hypotension requires therapy, volume expansion or methoxamine infusion is the preferred approach.

REFERENCES

MARTIN JK et al: Surgical treatment of functioning metastatic carcinoid tumors. Arch Surg 118:537, 1983

MELIA WM et al: Use of arterial devascularization and cytotoxic drugs in 30 patients with the carcinoid syndrome. Br J Cancer 46:331, 1982

MOERTEL CG, HANLEY JA: Combination chemotherapy trials in metastatic carcinoid tumor and malignant carcinoid syndrome. Cancer Clin Trials 2:327, 1979

OATES JA, BUTLER TC: Pharmacologic and endocrine aspects of carcinoid syndrome. Adv Pharmacol 5:109, 1967

SJOERDSMA A et al: A clinical, physiologic and biochemical study of patients with malignant carcinoid. Am J Med 20:520, 1956

SKRABANEK P et al: Substance P in ovarian carcinoid. J Clin Pathol 33:160, 1980

300 CUTANEOUS MANIFESTATIONS OF INTERNAL MALIGNANCY

HARLEY A. HAYNES

One of the most satisfying aspects of dermatologic diagnosis is the detection of previously unknown malignant disease in a treatable stage by recognition of an apparently irrelevant alteration of the skin as a clue to the presence of the neoplasm. Although less satisfying, the recognition of the probability of a neoplastic disease may be of great assistance in clarifying a difficult diagnostic problem, even if the neoplasm should be untreatable when discovered. Sometimes these skin changes are induced directly by infiltration of the neoplasm into the skin, but more often they are induced indirectly by a variety of mechanisms.

This chapter is an attempt to classify the wide range of skin signs of internal malignancy in a logical fashion (Table 300-1). Since the types of skin alterations and the number of neoplasms are extremely large, grouping of the alterations by pathogenetic mechanisms was selected. There remains a substantial idiopathic category; the entities therein will be grouped by pathogenesis when this becomes understood. The skin alterations induced by neoplasms of the endocrine organs are not included here as they generally are the alterations one would expect from excess or deficiency of the hormone in question and are mentioned in the appropriate chapters.

SKIN INFILTRATION BY AN INTERNAL MALIGNANCY

METASTASES FROM CARCINOMA Cutaneous metastases of malignant lesions occur in 3 to 5 percent of patients with metastatic disease. These lesions may provide the first indication of recurrence

---

TABLE 300-1 Classification of skin signs of internal malignancy

I Skin infiltration by an internal malignancy
  A Metastatic: lymphatic, hematogenous, or by surgical implantation
    1 Carcinoma
    2 Leukemia
  B Metastatic: intraepidermal
    1 Paget's disease of the breast
    2 Extramammary Paget's disease
  C Autochthonous or metastatic (?)
    1 Lymphoma
    2 Malignant histiocytosis
II Skin changes due to exposure to a carcinogen that also induces internal malignancy
  A Arsenical keratoses
  B Bowen's disease
III Skin malignancies associated with increased risk of separate primary internal malignancy
  A Bowen's disease
  B Kaposi's sarcoma
  C Any skin malignancy (??)
IV Skin changes due to metabolic products of malignancies
  A Malignant carcinoid syndrome
  B Addisonian hyperpigmentation with Cushing's syndrome, from carcinomas producing MSH- and ACTH-like peptides
  C Generalized dermal melanosis (slate gray), from malignant melanoma
  D Nodular fat necrosis, due to lipases from pancreatic carcinoma
  E Raynaud's syndrome with cryoproteinemia, from multiple myeloma
  F Amyloidosis, from multiple myeloma
  G Necrolytic migrating erythema, from functioning glucagonoma
  H Porphyria cutanea tarda secondary to primary hepatoma
V Skin changes due to functional disturbances in other systems induced by nonendocrine malignancies
  A Jaundice, obstructive
  B Addisonian hyperpigmentation from adrenal infiltration by a tumor
  C Purpura, thrombocytopenic
  D Pallor, from anemia
  E Herpes zoster
  F Herpes simplex, severe, protracted, recurrent
  G Pyoderma, recurrent
  H Delayed hypersensitivity, exaggerated to mosquito bites
VI Skin changes, idiopathic
  A Changes frequently related to internal malignancy
    1 Dermatomyositis, adult-onset
    2 Acanthosis nigricans
    3 Thrombophlebitis, migratory
    4 Ichthyosis, adult-onset
    5 Alopecia mucinosa, adult
    6 Pachydermoperiostosis, acquired
    7 Hypertrichosis lanugosa, acquired ("malignant down")
    8 Erythema gyratum repens
  B Changes occasionally related to internal malignancy
    1 Pruritus, without causative skin lesions
    2 Clubbing, with and without hypertrophic osteoarthropathy
    3 Erythroderma
    4 Normolipemic xanthomatosis
    5 Erythema multiforme
    6 Urticaria and erythema perstans
    7 Pyoderma gangrenosum, atypical and acute febrile neutrophilic dermatosis
    8 Bullous disease (bullous pemphigoid and dermatitis herpetiformis)
    9 Seborrheic keratoses, multiple, sudden onset (sign of Leser-Trelat)
    10 Dermatoses, bizarre
VII Heritable diseases with skin manifestations and the propensity to develop internal malignancy (see Table 300-2)

---

in a patient with a known primary tumor or may be the presenting lesions of a hitherto unsuspected tumor. Typical skin metastases are dermal nodules, varying from skin color to purple, which are more easily felt than seen and are very firm to the touch; they ulcerate rarely. Metastases from renal and thyroid carcinomas may be pulsatile and have a bruit. Breast carcinomas may produce an erysipelas-like appearance on the chest. The location of skin metastases may give a clue to the origin of the primary tumor. The abdominal wall is the most common site in both sexes for lesions initially presenting as metastases. In this situation, the primary sites are usually the lung, stomach, or kidney in men, and the ovary in women. In women with metastases on the chest wall, the most likely primary site is the breast. Other skin areas that tend to be involved by metastases are the scalp, from lung, kidney, or breast; the chest, in men, from lung; the back, from lung or breast; the extremities, from malignant melanomas; and the face, from oropharyngeal carcinomas. Histologic examination of a skin metastasis may reveal the identity of the primary tumor.

METASTASES FROM LEUKEMIA Leukemic deposits in skin are more common in myelomonocytic leukemia than in lymphocytic or granulocytic leukemias (Chap. 292). Firm papules or nodules ranging in color from pink to purple are the usual lesions, although ulcerations may develop. If thrombocytopenia is present, purpura often occurs in the nodules. Leukemic infiltrates may develop in recent scars, in traumatized areas, and in lesions of herpes zoster and herpes simplex. Cytologic examination of "touch" preparations from the cut surface of a nodule more readily identifies the cell type than does examination of histologic sections. The only clinically pathognomonic lesion of any of the leukemias is chloroma, named for its green color, which is due to myeloperoxidase in the cells of acute granulocytic leukemia. In addition to specific leukemic cell infiltrates, a variety of lesions occur that are nonspecific on biopsy.

INTRAEPIDERMAL METASTASES: PAGET'S DISEASE *Paget's disease of the nipple* and areola is an uncommon but well-known skin sign of underlying intraductal carcinoma of the breast. The primary ductal carcinoma extends upward within the epithelium of the mammary ducts and into the epidermis, where it causes the skin lesion. The clinical appearance is that of an eczematous, weeping, crusted, or scaly lesion resembling atopic eczema or contact dermatitis. Paget's disease is unaffected by topical corticosteroids, in contrast to the responsiveness of eczema. Therefore, any such "eczematous" lesions that fail to respond to treatment must be biopsied. The histopathologic appearance of Paget's disease is diagnostic; the presence in the epidermis of clear cells containing mucopolysaccharides is apparent.

Extramammary Paget's disease is a similar eczematous-appearing lesion occurring on the pubis, perineum, thighs, or genitalia. It is related usually to underlying apocrine or eccrine sweat gland carcinoma but occasionally to rectal or urethral adenocarcinoma. Occasionally, a primary malignant origin cannot be found. The histopathologic appearance of extramammary Paget's disease of apocrine gland origin is identical to that of Paget's disease of the breast, which is an apocrine gland. Special staining of the mucopolysaccharides will permit differentiation between Paget's disease of cloacogenic and apocrine gland origin.

LYMPHOMA Lymphomatous deposits in the skin secondary to an internal lymphoma are seen most often in histiocytic lymphoma and lymphoblastic lymphoma. Such cutaneous deposits are rare in Hodgkin's disease. Mycosis fungoides, the most frequent lymphomatous skin disorder, is discussed in Chap. 301. Lymphoma lesions in the skin are dermal or subcutaneous nodules that typically have a purple or red-brown color. The lesions usually are covered by relatively normal intact epidermis. Skin infiltrates may be the initial manifestations or may appear at any time in the course of the disease. Biopsy of these lesions is necessary to establish the correct diagnosis. The nonspecific skin changes in lymphoma are discussed below.

MALIGNANT HISTIOCYTOSIS In the Letterer-Siwe, Schüller-Christian disease complex, a variety of skin lesions may occur: (1) scaly papules or vesicles with or without purpura on trunk or scalp; (2) pruritic seborrheic or eczematous lesions in intertriginous areas that do not respond to local treatment for the benign conditions; (3) petechiae due to perivascular infiltrates, thrombocytopenia, or both; (4) scaly or exudative eruptions of the scalp; and (5) xanthomas, usually late in the course. When there is lack of response to local therapy, directed at presumptive diaper dermatitis, seborrheic dermatitis, moniliasis, or intertrigo, early biopsy of these various lesions should be done and is usually diagnostic if histiocytosis is present. Skin lesions may be the presenting sign and may lead to the correct diagnosis, or they may appear late in the course of the disease if it is not controlled.

SKIN CHANGES DUE TO EXPOSURE TO A CARCINOGEN THAT ALSO INDUCES INTERNAL MALIGNANCY

ARSENICAL KERATOSES Inorganic arsenicals are the only well-recognized carcinogens which cause both skin and visceral malignancies. These salts were widely used in medicine a few decades ago for the treatment of a large variety of disorders, such as arthritis, asthma, and psoriasis, and were also used as herbicides in agriculture. Arsenic contamination of drinking water occurs in many parts of the world. Exposure may therefore be intentional and known or accidental and wholly unsuspected. Multiple, discrete, hard hyperkeratotic wartlike lesions, termed *arsenical keratoses,* on the palms and soles occur characteristically in patients a decade or more after exposure to arsenic. These lesions are similar to actinic or solar keratoses in that they are premalignant lesions, but they have a very low incidence of malignancy. The histopathologic changes produced by these two types of keratosis also are similar.

BOWEN'S DISEASE Squamous-cell carcinoma of the skin in situ is known as Bowen's disease. The lesions are single or multiple sharply defined plaques that are slightly thickened and brownish red and have a varying amount of scale. At times the lesions of Bowen's disease resemble eczema or psoriasis but fail to respond to local therapy. Such lesions must be biopsied. Arsenical exposure is definitely the cause of many cases of Bowen's disease and may be the cause of nearly all. The lesions are easily treated by surgical excision or by various methods of local destruction. Although about 5 percent become invasive, less than 2 percent metastasize. More important is the recognition of the fact that the patient is at significant risk of developing carcinomas of the respiratory, genitourinary, and gastrointestinal systems. This risk is especially high in patients in whom Bowen's disease develops on skin that is not usually exposed to sunlight. Thorough examinations to detect visceral neoplasia must be performed at intervals, as the average latent period between the onset of Bowen's disease and the development of visceral neoplasia is more than 8 years. Even without a history or stigmata of arsenical exposure, there is an increased risk of visceral neoplasms in patients with this condition.

SKIN MALIGNANCIES ASSOCIATED WITH INCREASED RISK OF SEPARATE PRIMARY INTERNAL MALIGNANCY

BOWEN'S DISEASE See preceding section.

KAPOSI'S SARCOMA Initially Kaposi's sarcoma may be a multiple, autochthonous, reactive, lymphoreticular and endothelial cell proliferation rather than a neoplasm. It usually behaves in an indolent fashion, although frank, aggressive, sarcomatous change develops in a small percentage of patients. The lesions begin on the feet or ankles, then may progress proximally and also be found on the hands and arms. Extracutaneous lesions are most frequently seen in the gastrointestinal tract, where bleeding is the major complication. The respiratory tract is the second most frequently involved extracutaneous site. Generally these extracutaneous lesions are not clinically significant, unless frankly sarcomatous. There is a marked genetic predisposition to the disease among Jews, Italians, and the Bantus in the Congo. A pronounced male predominance of 9:1 has been noted. The skin lesions of Kaposi's sarcoma are rather distinctive dark blue or purple-brown nodules or plaques, primarily located on the distal extremities. The color is due to the vascular nature of the lesions and the chronic extravasation of erythrocytes, resulting in hemosiderin deposition. Almost invariably, chronic lymphedema is associated with, and at times precedes, the lesions. Lymphoma and leukemia are associated in about 10 percent of cases in the western hemisphere, but not in the eastern. The histopathologic picture is sufficiently characteristic for confirmation of the clinical diagnosis. For the average case, very conservative therapy, such as elastic support hose to reduce edema and low-dose x-ray treatment of symptomatic skin lesions, is all that is required. Chemotherapy should be considered only in the presence of clinically significant visceral lesions or aggressive sarcomatous behavior.

In recent years Kaposi's sarcoma has been described with increasing frequency in homosexual males. This type of Kaposi's sarcoma is quite aggressive and occurs in association with suppressor T-cell-induced immunologic suppression and HTLV infection in approximately one-third of patients with AIDS. Immunosuppression and HTLV III infection have also been identified in the Zaire African type of Kaposi's sarcoma. Therapeutic immunosuppression with prednisone and azathioprine for renal transplants also has been reported to result in the development of Kaposi's sarcoma in genetically predisposed individuals. Thus, the mechanism in AIDS and in therapeutic immunosuppression is similar.

ANY SKIN MALIGNANCY Neoplasia of the skin of any type may be an indication of increased risk of visceral neoplasia, but the exact relationship is difficult to ascertain because of the high incidence of skin malignancies.

SKIN CHANGES DUE TO METABOLIC PRODUCTS ASSOCIATED WITH MALIGNANCIES

MALIGNANT CARCINOID SYNDROME The hallmark of the syndrome (Chap. 299) is the sudden onset of bright red flushing of the skin, especially of the face, neck, and upper part of the chest.

ADDISONIAN HYPERPIGMENTATION WITH CUSHING'S SYNDROME (See Chap. 325) Some nonendocrine tumors, particularly oat cell carcinoma of the lung, secrete polypeptide hormones. The most commonly observed syndrome is Addisonian hyperpigmentation with Cushing's syndrome. Intense hyperpigmentation combined with proximal muscle weakness, hypertension, diabetes mellitus, edema, and confusion are typical features. Hypokalemic alkalosis and elevated serum cortisol levels are more frequent findings than are the usual physical signs of Cushing's disease. The syndrome is caused by the production of adrenocorticotropic hormone and β-melanocyte-stimulating hormone by the tumor.

GENERALIZED DERMAL MELANOSIS (SLATE GRAY) In some patients with widespread metastases from malignant melanoma, metabolic precursors of melanin enter the circulation and are deposited in all tissues, where they become oxidized to melanin. Excretion of these intermediates results in urine that turns black upon exposure to air. Inasmuch as most of the visible melanin in this type of melanosis is in the dermis, the Tyndall effect causes the skin to look gray or blue-black rather than brown.

NODULAR FAT NECROSIS The syndrome of tender subcutaneous nodules, fever, eosinophilia, and polyarthritis of the small joints is produced by pancreatic adenocarcinoma as well as by pancreatitis.

In this syndrome, the subcutaneous nodules are various shades of red and may undergo central necrosis with discharge of oily material. The increased circulating levels of lipase and other pancreatic enzymes are probably responsible for the syndrome. The histopathologic picture of the nodules usually permits the diagnosis of pancreatic fat necrosis but does not permit differentiation of benign from malignant etiology.

RAYNAUD'S PHENOMENON (See Chap. 198) The production of cryoglobulins in patients with myeloma may cause Raynaud's phenomena. Such an etiology should be especially suspected when the syndrome is atypical, appears in men, or begins in individuals over 50 years of age.

SYSTEMIC AMYLOIDOSIS From 10 to 20 percent of patients with multiple myeloma develop amyloidosis (Chap. 259). The characteristic presentation resembles "primary" amyloidosis and includes macroglossia, extraordinarily easy bruising, and, occasionally, yellowish papules or plaques visible in the skin. All organs may be affected. The purpura appears to result from vascular fragility as a consequence of deposition of amyloid. Purpura may often be induced by gentle stroking or pinching of apparently normal skin, particularly the eyelids and body folds. When the skin lesions of amyloidosis are isolated rather than scattered diffusely, the etiology is unlikely to be systemic. Such local skin amyloidosis is not rare and must be differentiated from systemic amyloidosis.

NECROLYTIC MIGRATING ERYTHEMA The glucagonoma syndrome includes a characteristic dermatitis, somewhat resembling chronic mucocutaneous candidiasis and acrodermatitis enteropathica. The skin lesions are often most severe on the lower abdomen, groin, and perineum and about the mouth. Their morphology consists of vesicles or bullae with a migrating erythematous, scaly margin. There is a tendency to heal centrally. A red, smooth, painful tongue is common (see Chap. 329).

PORPHYRIA CUTANEA TARDA The cutaneous manifestations of porphyria cutanea tarda include hyperpigmentation (especially on the dorsum of the hands in sun-exposed areas), blisters, erosions, superficial scars with milia as a result of minimal trauma, periorbital erythema, hypertrichosis, and occasionally sclerodermoid changes in exposed skin. Patients do not generally note photosensitivity. Most patients with porphyria cutanea tarda have hepatic dysfunction; a few cases have been reported secondary to primary hepatoma.

SKIN CHANGES DUE TO FUNCTIONAL DISTURBANCES IN OTHER SYSTEMS INDUCED BY NONENDOCRINE MALIGNANCIES

See Table 300-1.

IDIOPATHIC SKIN SIGNS OF INTERNAL MALIGNANCY

SIGNS FREQUENTLY RELATED TO INTERNAL MALIGNANCY
Dermatomyositis (see Chap. 370) Adults with dermatomyositis have an associated malignancy in at least 15 percent of cases, the association being slightly higher in men than in women. The skin changes may be either subtle and transient initially or widespread, persistent, and rapid in onset. Transient, blotchy, red or violaceous areas, with or without fine scaling, may be incorrectly diagnosed as contact dermatitis, eczema, or seborrheic dermatitis. When the initial lesions are sudden in onset and marked on the face, neck, and other sun-exposed areas, a photosensitivity dermatitis or contact dermatitis may be simulated. Indeed, photosensitivity is frequently noted in dermatomyositis. Later, telangiectasia develops in the lesions, and often edema and telangiectasia of the malar area or the eyelids may result in the violaceous (heliotrope) color. Linear telangiectasia adjacent to the cuticles on the nail folds within areas of periungual

erythema are usually seen, as in systemic lupus erythematosus. Accentuation of cutaneous lesions over the joints on the dorsum of the hands, as well as over large joints, is often noted.

Acanthosis nigricans   This skin sign is a highly significant marker of probable malignant disease when it develops in adults. The clinical problem is to differentiate between the different types of acanthosis nigricans, all of which look the same clinically and histopathologically. The lesions typically involve the axilla, groin, umbilicus, and nipples, but more extensive lesions may occur. The epidermis shows brown to black hyperpigmentation in areas of multiple confluent papillomas, resulting in a velvety elevation of the surface of the epidermis. Pruritus is sometimes present. The histopathologic appearance of the lesions confirms the diagnosis of acanthosis nigricans but does not permit differentiation between the various types. It is the history, the family history, and the physical examination which provide the most helpful data in classifying the type of acanthosis nigricans. Lesions present at birth or developing in childhood or at puberty are genetically determined and not related to malignancy. Obese individuals may develop intertriginous acanthosis nigricans without underlying disease. Various endocrinopathies, particularly Cushing's syndrome, acromegaly, and Stein-Leventhal syndrome, may be associated with acanthosis nigricans. When these conditions are absent and acanthosis nigricans develops in an adult, an underlying malignancy will be associated in most of the cases. Adenocarcinomas are the usual type of malignancy, and 60 percent of these are gastric (Chap. 236). Occasionally an undifferentiated or squamous-cell carcinoma or a lymphoma is the associated neoplasm. Though the course of the acanthosis nigricans in two-thirds of cases tends to parallel the course of the neoplasm, including remission with cure, intervals as long as 6 years between the skin lesion and the onset of the malignancy have been observed. If no benign explanation can be found for acanthosis nigricans in an adult, periodic efforts to locate a neoplasm are mandatory.

Migratory thrombophlebitis   Superficial and multiple deep venous thromboses, not readily explained by the usual causes, are likely to be associated with a malignancy, usually pancreatic carcinoma (Chap. 255). Involvement of atypical sites, such as upper extremities, should also alert the physician to this possible association. An involved area may resolve in a few days. Pulmonary embolism is not a frequent complication. The migratory thrombophlebitis may precede detection of the neoplasm by several months. Unfortunately, the neoplasms associated with recurrent phlebitis tend to be inoperable.

Ichthyosis   The development of ichthyosis in adults having no personal or family history of the disorder is very likely to be associated with lymphoma (usually Hodgkin's disease), although occasionally other types of malignancy have been reported. Hypothyroidism can result in similar skin changes. The skin appears dry, and the stratum corneum cracks to produce rhomboidal scales with flaky edges. Hyperkeratosis of the palms and soles may occur as well. The histopathologic changes are epidermal atrophy and hyperkeratosis, but they do not distinguish ichthyosis as a manifestation of malignancy from certain hereditary types. Although the association of this ichthyosiform alteration with lymphoma is strong, only a small number of cases have been reported.

Alopecia mucinosa   Dermal papules, often with follicular accentuation and usually with hair loss in affected areas, are the typical findings. Usually this disorder is benign and self-limited, especially in patients under 40 and with a small number of lesions. In patients over 40 and when there are multiple infiltrated plaques with alopecia, the lesions are likely to represent a lymphoma with associated follicular mucinosis. However, alopecia mucinosa may develop before the lymphoma can be diagnosed in a certain number of patients.

Pachydermoperiostosis   This term describes hypertrophic osteoarthropathy combined with acromegaloid features (Chap. 322). Thickening of the skin of the hands, forearms, and legs, as well as marked accentuation of facial folds, is typical. When the scalp is involved, the skin is reduplicated and furrowed (cutis verticis gyrata). A familial form of the disorder occurs and is unrelated to malignant disease. The acquired form usually occurs in men over 40 years of age who have bronchogenic carcinoma. Some acquired cases are associated with pulmonary infections, congenital heart disease, and hepatic disease.

Hypertrichosis lanugosa   This sign is quite rare but so striking in its appearance and in its association with internal malignancy that it deserves discussion. A congenital form, often familiarly known as "dog face" or "monkey face," is inherited as an autosomal dominant trait and has no association with malignancy. Acquired hypertrichosis of lanugo hair type in adults has been associated with malignant disease. The associated neoplasms have been carcinomas of the breast, urinary bladder, lung, gallbladder, colon, and rectum. The hypertrichosis in this condition is composed of extremely fine, silky, and lightly pigmented hairs of the lanugo type. This hair growth is most apparent on the face and ears but may occur on the trunk and extremities. Care must be taken to differentiate this lanugo hair growth from adult-type hair growth in women with disorders of androgen excess and in either sex with porphyria cutanea tarda, erythropoietic porphyria (Chap. 52), and phenytoin administration.

Erythema gyratum repens   See "Urticaria" below.

SIGNS OCCASIONALLY RELATED TO INTERNAL MALIGNANCY

Pruritus   Since pruritus is one of the major symptoms expressed in the skin (Chap. 50), obviously most causes of pruritus are not related to malignant disease. Yet pruritus may be a significant symptom in up to 30 percent of patients with Hodgkin's disease. Other lymphomas are less frequently associated with pruritus, excepting mycosis fungoides, in which pruritus is almost universal. Occasionally carcinomas of the lung, stomach, colon, breast, or prostate are associated with pruritus. In such patients the pruritus usually is not limited to a small discrete area. An association with malignancy should be considered in any patient in whom pruritus cannot be explained by the finding of a metabolic cause (Chap. 50) or a local skin disease, aside from excoriations, which could explain it. Hodgkin's disease is the most likely malignancy in patients in their teens through the thirties. In the elderly, xerosis (dry skin) is common and presents a tempting explanation of pruritus. However, if decreased frequency of bathing and the use of emollients do not eliminate the pruritus, then a malignant disease must be considered. The pruritus of malignant disease will cease upon successful therapy of the malignancy.

Clubbing   This alteration of the fingers and toes may sometimes be a manifestation of tumors arising either intrathoracically or metastatic to the thorax (Chap. 213).

Erythroderma   This dramatic reaction of the skin is a response to a variety of stimuli (Chap. 48). Approximately 8 percent of persons with generalized erythroderma are patients with lymphoma, particularly mycosis fungoides, or leukemia. Only occasionally is erythroderma a manifestation of a carcinoma. In patients with erythroderma due to mycosis fungoides, atypical cells are present in the skin and a skin biopsy will often be diagnostic. In erythroderma related to other types of lymphoma, leukemia, or carcinoma, there is not usually a definable infiltration of the skin by the atypical cells, and the diagnosis must be made from the blood smear, the bone marrow, involved lymph nodes, or other such tissue. In such cases, this erythroderma syndrome may represent an expression of a hypersensitivity reaction to tumor products. The course of the erythroderma parallels the response of the malignant disease to therapy, but it may precede the detection of the malignancy by a year or more, making repeated diagnostic investigations necessary.

Normolipemic xanthomatosis   Malignant diseases of the reticuloendothelial system have been reported in approximately one-half the reported cases of normolipemic plane xanthomatosis. Multiple myeloma is the most frequent type of associated malignant process, but several cases of lymphoma and malignant histiocytosis have been reported. Lesions are yellow to yellow-brown, flat or slightly elevated plaques. There is marked variation in size, and the lesions may be sharply demarcated or may have indistinct borders. The eyelids, sides of the neck, and upper trunk are favored sites, but lesions may appear on any portion of the body. The histopathologic appearance of these xanthomas does not differ from that of clinically similar lesions not associated with malignant disease.

Erythema multiforme (see Chap. 48)   This skin reaction occasionally occurs days to weeks after deep radiation therapy of internal malignant disease, perhaps representing a hypersensitivity reaction to components of tumor tissue. Erythema multiforme is also occasionally reported as an apparent manifestation of a lymphoma, leukemia, or carcinoma, in the absence of radiation therapy. The number of cases which are related to malignant disease is a very small fraction of the total number. The skin reaction tends to resolve spontaneously even in the presence of persistent malignant disease.

Urticaria (see Chap. 48)   This frequent skin reaction is an uncommon manifestation of malignant disease. A cause-effect relationship is difficult to establish unless a clear effect on the urticaria results from therapy of the associated condition. In a few patients with chronic urticaria in whom investigation disclosed a malignant disease, removal of the malignant process was associated with remission of the urticaria. Variants of urticaria present with wheal-like lesions that persist for days to months in the same site, possibly slowly changing position to form annular, arcuate, polycyclic, concentric, or other patterns. This reaction pattern is often classified under the heading of *erythema perstans*. One clinically spectacular but rare syndrome is known as *erythema gyratum repens,* in which concentric, arcuate lesions look like the grain of a soft wood. Only a few cases have been reported, but all were associated with a malignant disease, and in several the skin reaction cleared after successful treatment of the malignancy. These urticarial cutaneous vascular reactions are presumed to represent a hypersensitivity reaction to some component of the malignant disease.

Pyoderma gangrenosum, atypical (neutrophilic dermatosis)   Various myeloproliferative disorders have been found in association with pyoderma gangrenosum. Myelogenous and myeloblastic leukemia, myeloma, myeloid metaplasia, monoclonal gammopathy, and polycythemia have been so described. The lesions begin as papules,

TABLE 300-2   Heritable diseases with skin manifestations and propensity to develop internal malignancy

Disorder	Skin signs	Alterations of other systems	Predominant malignancy
DOMINANT INHERITANCE			
Multiple hamartoma syndrome (Cowden's disease)	Acral verrucous papules, trichilemmomas of face, fibromas of oral mucosa	Multiple hamartomas: Lipomas, hemangiomas, fibrocystic disease of breast, thyroid adenomas, neuromas	Thyroid carcinoma, breast carcinoma
Gardner's syndrome	Epidermal cysts, sebaceous cysts, dermoid tumors, lipomas, fibromas	Polyposis of colon, osteomas	Colonic adenocarcinomas (very high incidence, unless colectomy done)
Multiple mucosal neuromas	Neuromas on eyelids, lips, tongue, nasal or laryngeal mucosae	Parathyroid adenomas, hypertension	Pheochromocytoma, medullary carcinoma of thyroid (high incidence)
Neurofibromatosis (Recklinghausen's)	Neurofibromas, café au lait spots, axillary "freckles," giant nevi	Acoustic and spinal neuromas, meningiomas, osseous fibrous dysplasia	Malignant neurilemmoma (5% incidence), pheochromocytoma (uncommon), astrocytoma, glioma (uncommon)
Nevoid basal-cell carcinoma syndrome	Multiple basal-cell carcinomas, epidermoid cysts, "pits" on palms and soles	Jaw cysts, rib and vertebral abnormalities, short metacarpals, ovarian fibromas, hypertelorism	Medulloblastoma, fibrosarcoma of jaw (low incidence)
Palmar-plantar hyperkeratosis (tylosis)	Hyperkeratosis of palms and soles (usually onset after age 10)	None	Esophageal carcinoma (95% incidence)
Peutz-Jeghers syndrome	Pigmented macules on lips, oral mucosa, digits	Intestinal polyposis (predominantly small intestine)	Gastric, duodenal, and colonic adenocarcinomas (low incidence)
Tuberous sclerosis	Hypopigmented macules, shagreen patches, adenoma sebaceum, subungual fibromas	Epilepsy, mental retardation, hamartomas in brain, kidneys, heart	Astrocytomas, glioblastomas (low incidence)
AUTOSOMAL RECESSIVE INHERITANCE			
Ataxia-telangiectasia	Telangiectasia: neck, malar, antecubital fossae, popliteal fossae, ears	Cerebellar ataxia, sinopulmonary infections, IgA deficiency, ± IgE deficiency	Lymphoma, leukemia (10% incidence)
Bloom's syndrome	Telangiectasia of sun-exposed skin, photosensitivity	Short stature, fine features, dolichocephaly	Leukemia (high incidence)
Chédiak-Higashi syndrome	Dilution of skin and hair color, recurrent pyoderma, giant melanosomes	Recurrent infections, azurophilic leukocytic inclusions, nystagmus, iris translucence, photophobia, pancytopenia	Lymphoma (high incidence)
Fanconi's anemia	Patchy hyperpigmentation	Bone anomalies, chromosomal aberrations	Leukemia (high incidence)
Werner's syndrome (adult progeria)	Premature aging, scleroderma-like changes, graying hair and baldness, leg ulcers	Arteriosclerosis, cataracts	Sarcoma, meningiomas (10% incidence)
SEX-LINKED RECESSIVE INHERITANCE			
Bruton's sex-linked agammaglobulinemia	Recurrent infections	Recurrent infections, agammaglobulinemia	Leukemia, lymphoma (5% incidence)
Dyskeratosis congenita	Reticulate hyperpigmentation, leukoplakia of mucosae, loss of nails, hyperkeratosis of palms and soles, atrophy of skin of extensor surfaces	Pancytopenia	Carcinomas (high incidence), leukemia (occasional)
Wiscott-Aldrich syndrome	Eczematous dermatitis, petechiae–purpura, recurrent pyoderma	Decreased IgM, thrombocytopenia	Leukemia, lymphoma (10% incidence)

nodules, or bullae and progress rapidly to central necrosis and ulceration with an epithelial rim of violaceous hue, undermined edge, and occasionally peripheral bulla formation. The lesions are quite often tender. Bacterial cultures and skin biopsy should be done to evaluate possible sepsis, vasculitis, or leukemia cutis. In pyoderma gangrenosum the biopsy is not diagnostic, but there is a neutrophilic dermal infiltrate with varying degrees of tissue necrosis. Another neutrophilic dermatosis with pustules and/or areas resembling cellulitis (Sweet's syndrome) has also been associated with myeloproliferative disease. The atypical pyoderma gangrenosum and Sweet's syndrome have occurred simultaneously, suggesting they are related neutrophilic dermatoses.

Bullous disease Blistering disorders of various types may occur as a manifestation of malignant disease. The most common type is the subepidermal bullous disease known as *bullous pemphigoid* (Chap. 48). This disorder usually occurs in the elderly and may affect any of or all the skin and mucosal surfaces. Although there appears not to be an increased incidence of malignant disease in such patients, this point is not proved. Removal of a neoplasm has been associated with remission of the dermatosis in a few cases. Another bullous reaction which should cause the physician to think of the possibility of a malignant disease is *dermatitis herpetiformis*. The disease is characterized by intensely pruritic, grouped vesicles which tend to be symmetrically distributed on the extensor surfaces of the limbs and over the scalp, buttocks, and back. Any patient over 40 or 50 years of age who has a dermatitis herpetiformis–like disorder which is atypical and which does not respond well to sulfone or sulfapyridine therapy should be suspected of having an occult malignant process. This situation is distinctly uncommon.

Seborrheic keratoses, multiple, sudden-onset This cutaneous lesion (sign of Leser-Trelat) is a rare occurrence, while seborrheic keratoses are very common. The suspicion of any paraneoplastic significance should be reserved for the very sudden appearance of unusually large numbers of seborrheic keratoses and/or a rapid increase in their size. This syndrome can occur along with acanthosis nigricans and may be related. No consistent tumor type has been associated with the sign of Leser-Trelat.

Dermatoses, bizarre From time to time patients present very strange skin reactions, difficult to identify, and are discovered to have a malignant process. Some of these patients appear to have a cutaneous vasculitis, but this eventually is recognized to be a lymphoma. The variety of such skin reactions is great and cannot be clearly defined. The major importance of including this category is to alert the physician to the possibility of occult malignancy in a patient who presents an unusual, or atypical, or bizarre skin reaction.

HERITABLE DISORDERS WITH SKIN MANIFESTATIONS AND THE PROPENSITY TO DEVELOP INTERNAL MALIGNANCY

The role of heredity in neoplasia is interesting and complex. At times congenital immunologic deficiency states predispose to malignancy, as does acquired immune deficiency. In other cases the relationship between the hereditary condition and neoplasia is unclear. Both types are listed here to increase the awareness of the association. The list is not complete but has been selected to include the most significant syndromes. The manifestations in the skin and other organ systems, as well as the predominant type of malignancy, are presented in Table 300-2. The reader should refer to specific discussion of these entities for more complete information.

REFERENCES

BARNES BE: Dermatomyositis and malignancy: A review of the literature. Ann Intern Med 84:68, 1976
CALLEN JP: Skin signs of internal malignancy, in *Cutaneous Aspects of Internal Disease*, JP Callen (ed). Chicago, Year Book, 1981, pp 207–222
———, HEADINGTON J: Bowen's and non-Bowen's squamous intraepidermal neoplasia of the skin. Relationship to internal malignancy. Arch Dermatol 116:422, 1980
CAUGHMAN W et al: Neutrophilic dermatoses of myeloproliferative disorders. J Am Acad Dermatol 9:751, 1983
CROCKER AC: The histiocytosis syndromes, in *Dermatology in General Medicine*, 3d ed, TB Fitzpatrick et al (eds). New York, McGraw-Hill, 1987
DIGIOVANNA JJ, SAFAI B: Kaposi's sarcoma: Retrospective study of 90 cases with particular emphasis on the familial occurrence, ethnic background, and prevalence of other diseases. Am J Med 71:779, 1981
FRIEDMAN-KIEN AE, GREEN JB: The acquired immune-deficiency syndrome, in *Update V, Harrison's Principles of Internal Medicine*, RG Petersdorf et al (eds). New York, McGraw-Hill, 1984
KAHAN RS et al: Necrolytic migratory erythema. Distinctive dermatosis of the glucagonoma syndrome. Arch Dermatol 113:792, 1977
LEWIS SJ et al: Atypical pyoderma gangreenosum with leukemia. JAMA 239:935, 1978
MCLEAN DJ, HAYNES HA: Cutaneous manifestations associated with malignant internal disease, in *Dermatology in General Medicine*, 3d ed, TB Fitzpatrick et al (eds). New York, McGraw-Hill, 1987
MINNA JD, BUNN PA Jr: Paraneoplastic syndromes, in *Cancer, Principles and Practice of Oncology*, VT DeVita Jr, et al (ed). Philadelphia, Lippincott, 1985, pp 1823–1842
RIGEL DS, JACOBS MI: Malignant acanthosis nigricans: A review. J Dermatol Surg Oncol 6:923, 1980
STONE SP, SCHROETER AL: Bullous pemphigoid and associated malignant neoplasms. Arch Dermatol 111:991, 1975

301 PRIMARY CANCER OF THE SKIN

HARLEY A. HAYNES

Carcinoma of the skin is the most common carcinoma occurring in white individuals. Inasmuch as the lesions can be seen with the naked eye when they are in an early stage, the potential for cure is well over 90 percent. Although not responsible for all carcinomas of the skin, chronic exposure to ultraviolet radiation of the sunburn wavelengths (290 to 320 nm) in individuals not protected by intense melanin pigmentation is the most important single etiologic factor (Chap. 52). Hence, most of these cancers occur on areas of the skin that remain uncovered when the individual is fully clothed. As discussed in Chap. 52, genetic factors markedly mediate this tendency for carcinogenesis. Heritable diseases such as albinism, xeroderma pigmentosum, and the nevoid–basal-cell carcinoma syndrome are less common conditions associated with a greater risk of skin cancer. The routine local use of effective sun-screen preparations by individuals at risk can undoubtedly reduce tumor incidence. Chemical carcinogens, especially inorganic arsenicals and certain organic hydrocarbons, are separate and additional causes of skin cancers, particularly of the squamous-cell variety. Chemical and ultraviolet (UV) carcinogenesis may share some mechanisms as UV radiation is both an initiator and a promotor of carcinoma of the skin. Ionizing radiation, including x-rays, grenz rays, and gamma rays, is also carcinogenic. As with other organ systems, the skin is predisposed to the development of malignant lesions in immunologic deficiency states, such as those associated with lymphoma or immunosuppressive therapy. In fact, there is increasing evidence that UV radiation of the skin is in itself immunosuppressive by several mechanisms: (1) destruction of lymphocyte-activating Ia antigens on the surface of lymphoid cells, (2) impairment of antigen-processing function, (3) induction of suppressor lymphocytes that prevent the rejection of UV-induced tumors in mice, and (4) depletion from the epidermis of functional Langerhans cells, the bone marrow–derived dendritic cells which serve as the sentinel cells for contact dermatitis and other types of delayed hypersensitivity. Although any of the cell types in the skin may give rise to malignant neoplasms, the most common are basal cell and squamous cell carcinomas.

BASAL CELL CARCINOMA Basal cell carcinoma accounts for over 75 percent of all skin cancers. These carcinomas arise from the epidermis, cytologically resemble the normal basal cells, and show little tendency to undergo the usual differentiation into squamous cells which produce keratin. Although these tumors very rarely metastasize, they are locally invasive and, if neglected, may invade widely and deeply into underlying structures, including nerves, bone, and brain. Like most cancers these tumors are remarkably painless in their course. This lack of symptoms often leads to prolonged neglect of a lesion. The typical basal cell carcinoma is a noninflamed, smooth, waxy nodule that appears translucent, usually has numerous telangiectatic vessels visible near the surface, and may have variable amounts of melanin pigment in the form of small dots. Such nodules often ulcerate and form a crust. This ulceration may reepithelialize, causing the patient to assume that the nodule is resolving. Basal cell carcinomas may take many other forms, including subtle infiltrating lesions that do not produce elevated nodules, as well as fibrosing lesions resembling cicatrices. Biopsy for confirmation of the diagnosis should be routine. The patient with one basal cell carcinoma is likely to have others, either at the same time or in following years. Some patients come to the physician with a dozen or more concurrent primary basal cell carcinomas. Although there is no visible premalignant lesion that precedes a basal cell carcinoma, the lesion is usually seen in patients who manifest the stigmata of skin damage from sunlight (or x-rays). Treatment is selected according to the size, depth, type, and location of the lesion; the age, gender, and complexion of the patient; and the particular abilities of the physician. If a simple excision will suffice, there is no other procedure that can equal the cosmetic result. Curettage and electrodesiccation for small lesions give a cure rate of more than 95 percent in experienced hands, as does x-ray treatment. Cryosurgery with liquid nitrogen seems to give cure rates similar to those of curettage and electrodesiccation and often yields a better cosmetic result. The specialized technique of microscopically controlled serial shave excision (Mohs' technique) gives the highest cure rate known (about 99 percent) and is recommended for difficult or recurrent lesions not manageable by the usual forms of therapy. Local chemotherapy with 5-fluorouracil is not recommended as routine treatment of basal cell carcinomas, but may have a role in the treatment of multiple superficial lesions. Immunotherapy is investigational.

Education of the patient as to the role of UV radiation and strategies to reduce future such exposure by proper clothing, avoidance of noonday sun, and regular use of potent sunscreens with a sun protection factor (SPF) of 15 is important. Physician follow-up at 6- to 12-month intervals for 5 years following each new carcinoma of the skin is desirable. Recurrences of treated basal cell carcinomas occur within 5 years in 97 percent of recurrent lesions and will be seen in 3 to 5 percent of all treated lesions. More importantly, the patient with a previous carcinoma of the skin is at high risk for the development of additional such lesions.

SQUAMOUS CELL CARCINOMA   Squamous cell carcinoma also arises from the epidermis but shows significant squamous differentiation and usually keratin production. These tumors have a variable tendency to metastasize, depending upon their size, extent of invasion, location, and whether they arise from a premalignant lesion, a burn scar, a chronic inflammatory condition, or from apparently normal skin. The typical squamous cell carcinoma is a painless, firm, red nodule or plaque with visible scales on the surface. Ulceration and crusting may occur. Relatively undifferentiated lesions that do not produce much keratin may fail to show noticeable scaling on the surface. In contrast to the basal cell variety, squamous cell carcinomas most commonly arise from preexisting *actinic* or *solar keratoses.* These premalignant keratoses are scaly, rough, red plaques that occur in chronically sun-damaged skin. Although very few of these keratoses progress to carcinoma, most squamous cell carcinomas on exposed skin do arise from such keratoses. This type of squamous cell carcinoma has the lowest frequency of metastasis (under 2 percent). However, because of the potential of malignant change in solar keratoses, which though small is real, it seems prudent to remove them, especially in younger patients. At present, the local application of 5-fluorouracil (1 to 5%) in cream or lotion seems to be the most effective method and one that generally produces no scarring. Cryosurgery with liquid nitrogen is also effective, but carries a higher

risk of scarring. Squamous cell carcinomas arising from mucous membranes, mucocutaneous junctions, burn scars, chronic ulcers, or sinus tracts or from apparently normal skin have a much higher tendency to metastasize. An in situ stage of cutaneous squamous cell carcinoma is known as Bowen's disease (Chap. 300). Although some of these in situ lesions are the result of chronic sun damage, a significant proportion occurs in patients who had received inorganic arsenic preparations either accidentally or for medicinal purposes a decade or more before. In these patients there is also an increased risk of carcinomas of the respiratory, genitourinary, and gastrointestinal systems.

Patients with squamous cell carcinoma must be examined carefully for the presence of metastases so that therapy may be appropriate. In the absence of metastases, therapy of the local lesion may generally be as indicated for basal cell carcinoma, with preference for surgical excision or x-irradiation in view of the potential for metastasis. Extensive local or metastatic lesions may benefit from systemic chemotherapy, sometimes via local perfusion.

Patients with squamous cell carcinoma should be instructed in methods of reducing their UV radiation exposure, and should be followed for a minimum of 5 years to check for local recurrence, additional new primary lesions, and the infrequent development of metastatic disease.

MYCOSIS FUNGOIDES LYMPHOMA   *Lymphoma of the skin* may be a primary or secondary manifestation of various types of lymphoma. Histiocytic lymphoma and lymphoblastic lymphoma may occasionally begin with only skin lesions, but Hodgkin's disease rarely does so. The most common lymphoma of the skin is *mycosis fungoides,* which always begins with cutaneous lesions, usually with no evidence of visceral infiltration for several years. The initial lesions may be clinically confused with eczema, contact dermatitis, or psoriasis, and the biopsy may not be diagnostic. Later, more typical patches of infiltrated skin develop, often with a tendency for central clearing or an arciform or polycyclic arrangement. At this point, the biopsy may be diagnostic. In some patients, diffuse exfoliative erythroderma develops, and there may be circulating mycosis fungoides cells in the blood, at times causing diagnostic confusion with chronic lymphocytic leukemia. The skin biopsy may resolve the confusion if it is sufficiently characteristic, as may electron microscopy of the atypical cells, which are quite distinct in mycosis fungoides. The atypical cells found in the skin appear to be the same cells found in the blood or in visceral infiltrates. These cells have been identified as thymus-dependent lymphocytes and are usually of the helper/inducer type as determined by the monoclonal antibody technique. In blood smears these cells resemble large lymphocytes with scant cytoplasm and folded nuclei. In routine tissue sections these cells sometimes look like lymphocytes and sometimes like reticulum cells with the characteristic infolded nucleus. Electron-microscopic examination shows the nucleus of this cell to be highly irregular, convoluted, lobulated, and drawn into narrow threads and ribbons. At some point in time, most patients develop larger tumors as well. Although any of the viscera may be affected, disability from internal involvement usually does not occur until quite late in the course of the disease. For a patient with the early stage of the disease, the prognosis is for survival for several decades. Once the histologic diagnosis of mycosis fungoides is confirmed, the median survival for all patients is 5 years. Patients with skin tumors, ulceration, or lymphatic involvement have a median survival of 30 months.

Treatment is best planned so as to not restrict unnecessarily the future options of therapy. Topical applications of dilute, nonvesicant concentrations of mechlorethamine are often very effective for months or even years. Photochemotherapy with psoralens and long-wave UV radiation (PUVA) is often helpful (see Chap. 300). Selected lesions can be treated with grenz rays. Whole-skin electron beam treatment may be given without hematologic suppression, since the voltage is regulated to control the depth of penetration of electrons. The use of orthovoltage x-irradiation of multiple sites should be carefully restricted, so as not to compromise the marrow or complicate further therapy with electron beam. Electron beam followed by topical mechlorethamine is probably the most effective therapy for disease limited to cutaneous plaques. Systemic chemotherapy with agents such as methotrexate, cyclophosphamide, vinca alkaloids, procarbazine, chlorambucil, steroids, and combinations of these agents often can cause dramatic objective regression of disease but has not yet been proved to prolong life expectancy. Even though most patients at necropsy are found to have infiltrates in various viscera, early systemic chemotherapy has not been found advantageous, as a rule, perhaps because of the adverse effect of such therapy on the clinically very apparent resistance of the host to this lymphoma. In fact, this lymphoma was the first human malignancy to regularly show regression of lesions that were challenged locally with delayed hypersensitivity reactions.

REFERENCES

Burn PA Jr et al: Prospective staging evaluation of patients with cutaneous T-cell lymphomas: Demonstration of a high frequency of extracutaneous dissemination. Ann Intern Med 93:223, 1980

Edelson RL: Cutaneous T-cell lymphoma (mycosis fungoides, Sézary syndrome, and related presentations), in *Update: Dermatology in General Medicine*, TB Fitzpatrick et al (eds). New York, McGraw-Hill, 1983, pp 143–158

Fitzpatrick TB et al (eds): Neoplasms of the dermis, in *Dermatology in General Medicine*, 3d ed. New York, McGraw-Hill, 1987

Granstein RD, Sober AJ: Current concepts in ultraviolet carcinogenesis. Proc Soc Exp Biol Med 170:115, 1982

Haynes HA et al: Cancers of the skin, in *Cancer, Principles and Practice of Oncology*, 2d ed, VT DeVita Jr et al (eds). Philadelphia, Lippincott, 1985

Honigsmann H et al: Photochemotherapy for cutaneous T-cell lymphoma. A follow-up study. J Am Acad Dermatol 10:238, 1984

McDonald CJ, Bertino JR: Treatment of mycosis fungoides lymphoma—effectiveness of infusions of methotrexate followed by oral citrovorum factor. Cancer Treat Rep 62:1009, 1978

Price NM et al: Ointment-based mechlorethamine treatment for mycosis fungoides. Cancer 52:2214, 1983

302 MALIGNANT MELANOMA OF THE SKIN

THOMAS B. FITZPATRICK / ARTHUR J. SOBER / MARTIN C. MIHM, JR.

Primary malignant melanoma of the skin is the leading cause of death from all diseases arising in the skin, and the detection of early lesions must be the task of every physician, regardless of specialty. At every occasion when the entire cutaneous surface can be viewed, a careful search for suspicious pigmented lesions should be made.

Pigmented moles are among the most common growths on the skin, and yet cancer involving pigment cells (i.e., malignant melanoma) is relatively uncommon, constituting about 2 percent of all cancers. There has been a disturbing increase in the incidence of primary melanoma of the skin. The rate has doubled in the past 10 years, possibly due to increased "weekend" exposure to sunlight, especially among persons in professional and managerial positions. During 1985, 22,000 cutaneous melanomas are estimated for the population of the United States. Primary cutaneous malignant melanoma, moreover, does not respond or responds only poorly to chemotherapy or radiation therapy, and, so far, hope for survival has been based on surgical excision during the very early primary stages before deep invasion occurs. The problem for the physician, therefore, is to recognize early primary malignant melanoma and also those precancerous lesions that will develop into malignant melanoma among the large number of pigmented lesions that occur on the skin.

Primary malignant melanoma of the skin, even in the early stages, is now considered relatively easy to detect by clinical examination alone. In the past, the clinical description of primary cutaneous malignant melanoma was presented incompletely. Physicians and patients were told to have concern only for those pigmented lesions that showed changes in growth pattern or color or were bleeding or ulcerated—criteria indicating deep invasion in the skin and, usually, a poor prognosis.

Follow-up study of more than 1100 patients with primary melanoma has provided evidence indicating that a primary cutaneous melanoma may exist in a "silent," intraepidermal, preinvasive form for several years. These early "silent" primary malignant melanomas, even when 3 to 4 mm in size, can be recognized by certain simple criteria, which are delineated below.

Two criteria, *variegation of color* and *irregular border* often with a "notch," are so characteristic of primary cutaneous malignant melanoma that histologic examination is advised when they are present. The important colors that are signs of primary malignant melanoma *include shades of red, white, or blue* and the shades resulting from their mixture with brown or black. Furthermore, a lesion may be uniformly colored, e.g., *bluish black or bluish red.*

The diagnostic significance of various shades of brown or black, or both, in pigmented primary cutaneous malignant melanoma has been stressed in the past. It is, however, the diagnostic significance of the various shades of red, white, or blue, or all three mixed with brown or black, that requires emphasis. Of the colors present in pigmented primary cutaneous malignant melanomas, shades of blue (bluish red, bluish gray, and bluish black) are the most significant in the diagnosis. Variegation in the pigment pattern with unevenness and disarray is another important sign. *Examination with a magnifying lens and bright lighting* may assist greatly in recognizing the diagnostic feature of melanoma (Table 302-1).

Before 1967, malignant melanoma was considered a single morphologic entity with a uniformly grave prognosis. Later histopathologic investigations, especially by Clark, McGovern, Mihm, and colleagues, have permitted a new approach to the classification of primary human cutaneous malignant melanomas, based on the correlation of the clinical and histologic features with prognosis. Four types of primary malignant melanoma have been delineated (Table 302-2) and have been placed in two groups, depending on the presence or absence of an adjacent intraepidermal component around the tumor nodule:

Malignant melanoma with adjacent intraepidermal component:

1 Superficial spreading melanoma
2 Lentigo maligna melanoma
3 Acral lentiginous melanoma

Malignant melanoma without an adjacent intraepidermal component:

4 Nodular melanoma

It should be emphasized that lentigo maligna melanoma and superficial spreading melanoma may exist for several years in the preinvasive stage. Hence, early diagnosis of malignant melanoma of the skin makes excision of the identified lesions possible before deep invasion has occurred. The survival rate of malignant melanoma is related to the level of invasion of the tumor or the thickness of the primary tumor expressed in millimeters (see Table 302-3). These levels of invasion have been classified on the basis of anatomic structure as follows:

TABLE 302-1 Indications for excision or diagnostic biopsy of pigmented lesions

I History
  A Change in size or color, bleeding
  B Symptoms
    1 Itching (25%)
    2 Tenderness
  C Congenital, raised pigmented lesions
II Lesion characteristics
  A Color
    1 Uniform blue or gray
    2 Variegated: blue, gray, white, red, mixed with brown or black
    3 Variegation in pigment pattern
  B Border: irregular, often with a notch
  C Surface: irregular

TABLE 302-2 Clinical features of malignant melanoma

Type	Site	Average age at diagnosis, years	Duration of known existence, years	
Superficial spreading melanoma	Any site (more common on upper back and in women on lower legs)	40–50	1–7	Shades of brown and black mixed with bluish red (violaceous), bluish black, reddish brown, and often whitish pink, and the border of lesion is at least in part visibly and/or palpably elevated
Lentigo maligna melanoma	Exposed surfaces usually, and particularly malar region of cheek and temple	70	5–20* or longer	In flat portions, shades of brown and black predominant, but whitish gray occasionally present; in nodules, shades of reddish brown, bluish gray, bluish black
Acral lentiginous melanoma	Palm, sole, nailbed, mucous membrane	64	1–10	In flat portions, dark brown predominantly; in raised lesions (plaques), brown-black or blue-black color predominantly
Nodular melanoma	Any site	40–50	Months to less than 5 years	Reddish blue (purple) or bluish black, either uniform in color or mixed with brown or black

* During much of this time the precursor stage, lentigo maligna, is actively confined to the epidermis.

Level 1: Intraepidermal melanocytic atypism, a level recognized for purposes of research. Patients with this finding are at present labeled with the diagnosis melanoma in situ by some pathologists and severely atypical intraepidermal melanocytic hyperplasia by others.

Level 2: Tumor invading the papillary layer but not extending to the reticular layer.

Level 3: Tumor filling and expanding the papillary layer but not invading the reticular layer.

Level 4: Tumor penetrating into the reticular layer of the dermis.

Level 5: Tumor invading the subcutaneous fat.

When thickness of the primary tumor is determined by measuring the vertical thickness with a light microscope fitted with an ocular micrometer, tumors measuring less than 0.85 mm in thickness have a uniformly favorable outcome, while patients with tumors greater than 3.65 mm are at high risk for recurrent disease and death. At the present time, the determination of prognosis by thickness is the most practical (see Table 302-3 for survival by thickness).

Suspicious lesions require biopsy, which will confirm the benign or malignant nature of the lesion. Simple excisional biopsy with narrow margins is the procedure of choice, but trephine (punch) or incisional biopsies are also acceptable depending on the situation and

TABLE 302-3 Summary data on malignant melanoma of skin

I Incidence: 2% of all cancers (excluding nonmelanoma skin cancer)
  A Annual incidence rates (United States) for 1985: 22,000
  B Increasing with time (Connecticut Registry)
    1 1935–1939: 1.2/10⁵/year
    2 1965–1969: 4.8/10⁵/year
    3 1976–1977: 7.2/10⁵/year
    4 1979–1980: 9/10⁵/year
  C Latitude-dependent crude incidence rates:
    1 Northern United States (Connecticut):9/10⁵/year
    2 Southern United States (Arizona):26/10⁵/year
II Frequency for type of melanoma
  A Superficial spreading: 70%
  B Nodular: 16%
  C Lentigo maligna melanoma: 5%
  D Unclassified (includes acral lentiginous type): 10%
III Five-year survival
  A Stage III (distant metastases): <10%
  B Stage II (regional lymph nodes clinically enlarged): 30%
  C Stage I (clinically localized disease): 85%
    1 Based on level of invasion
      a Level 2: 99%
      b Level 3: 95%
      c Level 4: 75%
      d Level 5: 39%
    2 Based on thickness of primary tumor
      a <0.85 mm: 99%
      b 0.85–1.69 mm: 94%
      c 1.70–3.60 mm: 78%
      d ≥3.65 mm: 42%

the experience of the physician performing the procedure. Table 302-1 lists the indications for biopsy of cutaneous lesions.

Treatment of malignant melanoma at the present is primarily by surgical excision of the primary lesion; there is no agreement as to whether prophylactic lymph node dissection affects the course of the disease. Data of Breslow and Macht suggest that limited excision may be effective for thin (≤0.75 mm) lesions. We have been recommending surgical margins of 1.5 cm for tumors smaller than 0.85 mm and margins of up to 3 cm for tumors greater than 0.85 mm. Elective lymph node dissection is considered when the tumor drains to only one lymph node group in patients with primary tumors thicker than 1.7 to 2.0 mm. Age, patient preference, and convictions of the surgeon are also factors which are weighed in the decision to perform elective nodal dissection. No benefit from dissection has mostly been shown in randomized trials. However, retrospective or nonrandomized prospective trials show a small benefit in survival favoring patients who have received node dissection. Surgery for lentigo maligna melanoma is less aggressive; the recommendation is for surgical margins of 1 cm and lymph node dissection only if therapeutically indicated.

In the past few years, considerable interest has been directed toward the factors that influence both the development of primary malignant melanomas of the skin and also the rate and degree of dissemination of the tumor. The possibility that there is a population with a high risk for the development of these melanomas is being studied. It is suspected that persons, both male and female, who have poor tolerance to sunlight and who develop sunburn on short exposures and who tan poorly have a higher incidence of malignant melanoma (Table 302-3). Risk for melanoma is increased by having had blistering sunburns in childhood or adolescence. It has recently been demonstrated that within countries an inverse relationship exists between melanoma incidence and latitude. For example, incidence rates of 9 per 100,000 per year in Connecticut can be contrasted to rates greater than 20 per 100,000 per year in the white population of the southwestern United States.

Families have been studied in the members of which malignant melanomas have aggregated. Many of these family members appear to have a type of nevus which resembles clinically miniature early superficial spreading melanomas. These lesions, termed *dysplastic nevi*, may be a genetically determined precursor lesion for malignant melanomas. The dysplastic nevus also occurs sporadically in patients with malignant melanoma and is currently thought to be the associated precursor lesion in up to 40 percent of cases. (For clinical illustrations of dysplastic nevi, see Greene et al.) Patients with large congenital melanocytic nevi are also at recognized higher risk for melanoma development in these lesions.

Several well recognized patterns of spread are observed for cutaneous melanoma. The most frequent pathway of spread is up the lymphatic channels within the skin to produce satellite, intransit, and regional nodal metastases. This pattern of recurrence tends to occur earlier than the second pattern of spread—hematogenous, blood-borne metastases to distant sites (cutaneous and/or visceral). Preferential visceral sites include liver, lung, bone, and brain, and perhaps half of the deaths from melanoma can now be attributed to central nervous system metastases.

Currently about 80 to 90 percent of patients present with clinical stage I disease (localized disease). Work-up for dissemination should include a detailed history and physical examination and a chest x-ray. Other studies should be obtained (scans, other biopsies, liver function tests) if there is a suggestion of disease at a location other than the primary site. Follow-up involves careful evaluation of the operative sites for local recurrence, palpation of the skin for intransit or disseminated intracutaneous metastases, palpation of lymph node areas, palpation of viscera, and a complete cutaneous examination to look for second primary tumors.

Only a few factors are presently known to influence the dissemination of melanoma. Incidence of melanoma by sex is equal, but the death rate is higher among men. When multifactorial analyses are performed, the primary tumor site appears to be important in outcome. Torso lesions have a worse prognosis than lower extremity lesions. The most common site for melanoma in males is the torso. The immune status of the patient is another factor under investigation. The possibility that immunologic factors are involved in the course of malignant melanoma is suggested by the high rate of spontaneous regressions of melanoma, by the long periods of freedom from the time of excision of the primary lesion to the development of metastases, and by the improved prognosis of those lesions in which on histologic examination a marked lymphocytic response is found. Both cellular and hormonal immunities to melanoma cells have been demonstrated by in vitro techniques.

The management of metastatic disease presents real problems since chemo- and immunotherapeutic techniques are ineffective in the majority of patients. The most effective single agent, dacarbazine (dimethyltriazenoimidazole carboxamide or DTIC), induces a partial remission in only 20 percent and complete responses in less than 5 percent of cases. Remissions are usually of only a few months duration. Many experimental chemotherapeutic combinations are now undergoing clinical trial. At the present time the best strategy in the management of melanoma is early recognition, which will prevent the development of metastases.

The physician examining a patient with many pigmented lesions should recognize the features that are highly suggestive of primary melanoma of the skin and indicate that the lesion be removed, or, if it is very large, at least biopsied (see Table 302-1). If these early lesions can be detected and excised, the 5-year survival rate of patients with malignant melanoma should approach 90 to 95 percent.

REFERENCES

BALCH CM et al: Tumor thickness as a guide to surgical management of clinical stage I melanoma patients. Cancer 43:883, 1979

———, MILTON GW: *Cutaneous Melanoma*. Philadelphia, Lippincott, 1985

BRESLOW A, MACHT SD: Optimum size of resection margin for thin cutaneous melanoma. Surg Gynecol Obstet 145:691, 1977

DAY CL JR et al: The natural breakpoints for primary tumor thickness in clinical stage I melanoma. N Engl J Med 305:1155, 1981

———: Prognostic factors for melanoma patients with lesions 0.76 through 1.69 mm in thickness: An appraisal of thin level IV lesions. Ann Surg 195:30, 1982

GREENE MH et al: Acquired precursors of cutaneous malignant melanoma: The familial dysplastic nevus syndrome. N Engl J Med 312:91, 1985

MIHM MC JR et al: Early detection of primary cutaneous malignant melanoma: Color atlas. N Engl J Med 289:989, 1973

REIMER RR et al: Precursor lesions in familial melanoma. JAMA 239:744, 1978

SOBER AJ et al: Early recognition of cutaneous melanoma. JAMA 242:2795, 1979

———: Primary melanoma of the skin: Recognition and management. J Am Acad Dermatol 2:179, 1980

———: Primary melanoma of the skin: Recognition of precursor lesions and estimation of prognosis in stage I, in *Update: Dermatology in General Medicine*, TB Fitzpatrick et al (eds). New York, McGraw-Hill, 1983

VERONESI U et al: Inefficacy of immediate node dissection in stage I melanoma of the limbs. N Engl J Med 297:627, 1977

303 ENDOCRINE MANIFESTATIONS OF NEOPLASIA

LAWRENCE A. FROHMAN

Hormone secretion by tumors derived from nonendocrine tissue has been recognized for more than 50 years. Initially, the majority of reported cases were associated with hypoglycemia and hypercalcemia, but the term *ectopic hormone secretion* was first used in relation to Cushing's syndrome caused by adrenocorticotropic hormone (ACTH) secretion from a variety of tumors. The spectrum of ectopic hormone secretion is now expanded as a result of increased clinical awareness and the availability of more sophisticated and sensitive assay techniques. However, the use of the term *ectopic* in this regard has been questioned with the recognition that hormones once believed to be tissue-specific may have widespread sites of production, i.e., gonadotropins are produced by the normal gonad and intestine, thyrotropin-releasing hormone (TRH) and ACTH by the pancreas, and somatostatin by the kidney and thyroid C cells. Nevertheless, the original term serves to distinguish tumor-associated hormone production from syndromes due to excess secretion of the major and characteristic hormone of a particular endocrine tissue.

THEORIES OF ECTOPIC HORMONE SECRETION Several possible pathogenetic mechanisms have been proposed to explain ectopic hormone secretion. The "sponge" theory assumed a selective update of the circulating hormone by tumor tissue with subsequent release upon tumor cell death. This concept was abandoned, however, after the demonstration of arteriovenous differences of hormones across tumor vascular beds and of hormone biosynthesis by tumor preparation in vitro. The theory that random mutations resulted in abnormal DNA sequences and gene products was also discounted when it became apparent that the production of ectopic hormones by tumors is not random, i.e., that certain tumors produce specific endocrinopathies. A third theory, that of gene derepression, proposed that regions of the genome not normally expressed become active and are transcribed in tumors presumably as a result of loss of a normal suppressive mechanism during neoplastic transformation; in fact, however, there is no overall increase in gene transcription (derepression) in neoplastic cells. Two other explanations have also been proposed: *cellular dedifferentiation*, a theory that neoplastic cells revert to a more primitive level and again produce peptide hormones that were produced normally at an earlier developmental stage, and *arrested differentiation*, whereby hormone secretion is due to persistence of a function present during development because of a failure (arrest) of the developmental process. Arguments against these theories include an absence of evidence that cells can retrace their pathways of differentiation or that incompletely differentiated cells routinely secrete the hormone in question. The pathogenesis of ectopic hormone secretion is thus unclear.

CRITERIA FOR DIAGNOSIS Criteria for the diagnosis of ectopic hormone secretion have changed as more sophisticated laboratory methodology has made it possible to recognize clinically inapparent cases (Table 303-1). Although many of these criteria cannot be

TABLE 303-1 Criteria for establishing the diagnosis of ectopic hormone secretion

1 Association of a nonendocrine neoplasm with a syndrome attributable to excessive hormone secretion or with inappropriately elevated plasma and/or urine hormone levels

2 Failure of plasma and/or urine hormone levels to respond to normal homeostatic suppression

3 Exclusion of other possible causal mechanisms for hormone hypersecretion

4 Reduction in hormone levels after tumor-specific therapy

5 Arteriovenous step-up gradients across tumor

6 Demonstration of hormone in tumor tissue

7 Biosynthesis and/or secretion of hormone by tumor tissue in vitro

8 Demonstration in the tumor of hormone-specific messenger RNA by cell-free translation or by hybridization with cDNA

satisfied in individual cases, the majority have been fulfilled in the commonly recognized syndromes.

TUMOR TYPES ASSOCIATED WITH ECTOPIC HORMONE SECRETION Ectopic secretion of hormones is associated with a large variety of tumors. Although original reports of these syndromes described primarily lung carcinomas, carcinoids, thymomas, and fibrosarcomas, virtually all tumor types have the potential of hormone secretion. Nevertheless, the frequency of occurrence of ectopic hormone secretion among various tumor types is not random. The tumors most frequently associated with clinically recognized ectopic hormone production are small cell lung carcinomas, carcinoids, and pancreatic islet tumors. Carcinoid tumors are generally found in the lung or in the gastrointestinal tract. Gastrointestinal carcinoids may be present in either the foregut or the hindgut, though it is primarily those in the former location that are hormonally active and tend to be malignant. In the lung these tumors are usually endobronchial and may remain undetected for long periods of time. There are many morphologic similarities between bronchial carcinoid tumors and small cell carcinoma of the lung. Indeed, the two types may have a common cell of origin, namely the Kulchitsky cell, a bronchial mucosal cell that has been called a neuroendocrine cell of the lung because of its peptide-containing granules observed on electron microscopy. Bombesin (gastrin-releasing peptide) or a bombesin-like peptide is present in Kulchitsky cells during fetal life and is the most frequent peptide produced by small cell carcinoma of the lung. Ectopic hormone secretion is also associated with other types of lung tumors, most commonly the squamous type of bronchogenic carcinomas.

In the 1960s Pearse proposed the theory that certain hormone-secreting cells are components of a "diffuse neuroendocrine system". Such cells were originally considered to be of neural crest or neuroectodermal origin, and were designated APUD (amine precursor uptake and decarboxylation) cells on the basis of their ability to decarboxylate precursors of biogenic amines. Later it was discovered that many of these cells also produce the enzyme neuron-specific enolase. A corollary of the APUD theory was that tumors derived from APUD cells had the capability of hormone secretion. At present, there is doubt concerning the validity of the APUD theory on several grounds. First, all APUD cells are not of neuroectodermal origin. Second, the APUD function of these cells is not inherently linked with peptide hormone production, and third, some ectopic hormone-secreting tumors do not possess APUD characteristics. Nevertheless, the association of particular tumor types with the secretion of certain hormones is useful in evaluating these syndromes.

CHARACTERIZATION OF ECTOPIC HORMONES   **Type of hormone secreted**   Of the four classes of hormones—steroids, monoamines, substituted amino acids, and peptides/proteins—only the latter are secreted ectopically. Although the explanation is not known with certainty, the ectopic production of peptide/protein hormones may require less complicated derangements in cell metabolism. For example, an oncogene containing an initiator or inducer of gene transcription may be responsible for the expression of a gene coding for a peptide hormone. In contrast, the synthesis of steroids, thyroid hormones, or monoamines requires multiple enzymatic steps and specifically targeted translocation of the precursor molecules through various cell compartments. The likelihood that this degree of cell specialization would occur as a consequence of neoplastic change is much less than the possibility that a process (protein synthesis) common to all cells might be initiated aberrantly.

Ectopic secretion of nearly all peptide hormones has been reported. These hormones may be grouped according to their usual site of origin (Table 303-2). The first group of hormones, common to the central nervous system and gastrointestinal tract, are most frequently secreted by carcinoids, small cell lung carcinomas, and pancreatic islet tumors. The second group, normally produced by the fetoplacental unit and/or the anterior pituitary, tends to be produced by gastrointestinal, hepatic, adrenal, and gonadal tumors. The third group, which includes insulin-like growth factors and parathyroid hormone–like factors, tends to be produced by mesenchymal, hepatic, genitourinary, and squamous cell lung tumors. In addition to the hormones listed, other humoral factors are believed responsible for tumor-associated syndromes such as hypertrophic osteoarthropathy, polyneuropathy, hypophosphatemic osteomalacia, and anorexia.

Relation to naturally secreted hormones   The primary amino acid sequences of all ectopically secreted hormones analyzed to date are identical to those of the native hormones. However, other differences in structure between ectopically secreted and native hormones can occur as a result of incomplete or abnormal processing of the precursor hormone. Several abnormal forms of ectopic hormones have been defined: (1) large-molecular-weight species due to incomplete enzymatic cleavage of the precursor; (2) small-molecular-weight fragments due to unregulated intracellular processing; and (3) altered glycosylation species (microheterogeneity) due either to failed cleavage of carbohydrate residues during postribosomal hormone processing (glycosylated ACTH) or failure of normal glycosylation (the glycosylated alpha subunit common to the gonadotropins and TSH). The usual consequence is a hormone variant with diminished or aberrant biologic activity. If modification of hormone structure is sufficient to cause loss of all biologic activity, ectopic secretion is not accompanied by clinical manifestations. Even if a neoplastic cell can synthesize and store a biologically active hormone, a syndrome of hormone excess may not result if an intact secretory mechanism is absent. The frequency with which either an inactive hormone is synthesized or an active hormone is synthesized but not secreted is probably greater than that of classical ectopic hormone secretion since only a small percentage of tumors that contain ectopic hormones cause clinically recognizable syndromes.

Other considerations   Hormones may be secreted by both benign and malignant tumors. Although hormone secretion normally requires a high level of cellular differentiation, an incompletely differentiated tumor may still be able to secrete some hormone. For example, the process of granule formation and hormone storage is not generally expressed by hormone-secreting tumors; consequently the concentration of hormone in the tumor is usually low compared to that in endocrine glands. Overall hormone secretion per unit weight is also less and, as a result, considerable tumor mass is usually present before ectopic hormone secretion is clinically apparent. One notable exception is the relatively benign, highly differentiated neoplasm, usually a carcinoid or pancreatic islet tumor, that contains and secretes hormone at a level comparable to that of normal endocrine tissue and that is sufficiently small to escape detection for long periods.

Many tumors produce multiple hormones. In some this is due to the existence of a common precursor for multiple hormones, e.g., ACTH, lipotropins, melanocyte-stimulating hormones (MSHs), and endorphins are all derived from a single precursor, proopiomelanocortin (POMC), and both vasoactive intestinal peptide (VIP) and peptide histidyl-methionine (PHM) are encoded in a single precursor. In other instances multiple hormones are produced in the absence of common precursors, e.g., production of ACTH, calcitonin, and somatostatin by medullary thyroid carcinoma and by small cell carcinoma of the lung. In some tumors separate cells secrete individual hormones, whereas in others multiple hormones are produced by the same cell. Furthermore, variation may occur in cell lines cloned from such tumors, suggesting that gene expression may change with succeeding generations of tumor cells.

FREQUENCY   The frequency of ectopic hormone secretion varies with the criteria used for its definition. The most frequently encountered syndromes are those of ACTH hypersecretion, hypercalcemia, and organic hypoglycemia. Ectopic ACTH secretion occurs in approximately 15 to 20 percent of patients with Cushing's syndrome. Thus, consideration of this diagnosis is of great importance. Similarly, nearly half of patients with hypercalcemia unrelated to volume depletion, excess ingestion of vitamin D, or sarcoidosis have a malignancy rather than hyperparathyroidism, and of these about 70

TABLE 303-2 Spectrum of ectopic hormone production

Group/hormone	Tumor type — Common	Tumor type — Infrequent	Group/hormone	Tumor type — Common	Tumor type — Infrequent
1 Neuroendocrine-gastrointestinal			*2* Fetoplacental and/or anterior pituitary		
a ACTH, β-lipotropin, endorphins, MSHs, enkephalins	Lung carcinoma (small cell) Thymoma Pancreatic islet tumors Carcinoid Thyroid medullary carcinoma Pheochromocytoma Parotid tumor Prostatic carcinoma Renal carcinoma	Squamous cell, adenocarcinoma, and large cell carcinoma of the lung Breast carcinoma Colonic carcinoma Gallbladder tumors Testicular carcinoma Uterine carcinoma Laryngeal carcinoma Plasmacytoma	*a* Chorionic gonadotropin (and subunits)	Lung carcinoma Gastric carcinoma Ovarian carcinoma Adeno- and islet cell carcinoma of the pancreas Hepatoma	Testicular carcinoma Ovarian carcinoma Adrenocortical carcinoma Breast carcinoma Bladder carcinoma Melanoma Carcinoid
b Vasopressin, oxytocin, neurophysin	Lung carcinoma (small cell, anaplastic, adenocarcinoma) Carcinoid	Pancreatic carcinoma Duodenal carcinoma	*b* Placental lactogen	Lung carcinoma (small cell)	Lymphoma Pheochromocytoma Hepatoma
c Corticotropin-releasing factor	Lung carcinoma (small cell) Carcinoid	Pituitary gangliocytoma	*c* Growth hormone		Lung carcinoma (large cell) Carcinoid Pancreatic islet tumor
d Growth hormone–releasing factor	Carcinoid Pancreatic islet adenoma Lung carcinoma (small cell)	Adrenocortical adenoma Neurofibroma Endometrial carcinoma Pheochromocytoma Pituitary gangliocytoma	*d* Prolactin		Lung carcinoma Renal carcinoma
			3 Others		
e Somatostatin	Lung carcinoma (small cell) Carcinoid Pheochromocytoma		*a* Tissue growth factors (somatomedins)	Mesenchymal tumors (i.e., fibrosarcoma) Hepatoma Adrenocortical carcinoma Pancreatic/bile duct carcinoma	Lung carcinoma Ovarian carcinoma Neuroblastoma Wilms's tumor
f Calcitonin	Lung carcinoma (small cell) Carcinoid	Breast carcinoma	*b* Erythropoietin	Cerebellar hemangioblastoma Uterine fibroma Renal carcinoma	Adrenocortical carcinoma Hepatoma Pheochromocytoma
g Gastrin	Lung carcinoma (small cell)	Ovarian carcinoma	*c* Parathyroid hormone, osteoclast-activating factor, and humoral hypercalcemic factor of malignancy	Renal carcinoma Lung carcinoma (squamous) Hepatoma	GI tract tumors Parotid tumors Genitourinary tract tumors Melanoma Lymphoma
h Vasoactive intestinal peptide	Lung carcinoma (small cell) Pancreatic islet tumors				
i Insulin		Gastric carcinoma Lung carcinoma Carcinoid			
j Glucagon		Lung carcinoma Carcinoid			
k Gastrin-releasing peptide (Bombesin)	Lung carcinoma Carcinoid				

percent have a humoral hypercalcemic factor that is not parathyroid hormone but has parathyroid hormone–like biologic activity. In contrast, hypoglycemia due to ectopic production of an insulin-like growth factor is infrequent in patients suspected of having an insulinoma, and ectopic growth hormone–releasing factor (GRH) secretion is a rare (<1 percent) cause of acromegaly.

CONSEQUENCES OF ECTOPIC HORMONE SECRETION The consequences of ectopic hormone secretion may be of greater significance than the tumor itself. This is particularly true for patients with benign ACTH- or gastrin-producing tumors in whom fulminant Cushing's syndrome or bleeding peptic ulceration may be life-threatening. In others, the hormone may cause medical problems that shorten the life span beyond that attributable to the tumor itself, i.e., severe hypercalcemia, hyponatremia, or hypoglycemia.

The symptoms of ectopic hormone secretion may be the presenting manifestations of the neoplasm or occur late in the course of the disease. The rapidity of onset of the clinical features of hormone hypersecretion affects the frequency with which the syndrome is recognized. For example, excessive secretion of ACTH or vasopressin is clinically evident within weeks or months; thus, a fully developed syndrome can be associated with rapidly growing malignant tumors as well as with benign tumors. In contrast, acromegaly due to ectopic GRH secretion typically requires years to become apparent and

therefore is observed only when caused by slowly growing malignant neoplasms. Ectopic hormone secretion, once established, does not necessarily persist for as long as the tumor is present. Hormone secretion may cease or decline to clinically insignificant levels either spontaneously or in response to radiation or chemotherapy. With tumor relapse, hormone secretion usually, but not invariably, recurs.

In addition to effects on the host, ectopic hormone secretion has numerous important biologic implications. Since tumor-secreted factors that exhibit biologic effects are unlikely to be unique substances, their identification and characterization can assist in the search for the naturally occurring (eutopic) peptide. For example, tumor-secreted GRH was the source for the purification, isolation, and structural characterization of hypothalamic GRH. Relatively little attention has been given to possible effects of ectopically secreted hormones on the growth or survival of the tumor.

DIAGNOSIS Occasionally, the clinical manifestations of ectopic hormone secretion are so distinctive that they suggest the diagnosis before any hormone measurements have been performed. The development of gynecomastia in the absence of associated diseases such as cirrhosis or testicular failure may suggest the presence of ectopic gonadotropin secretion, while Cushing's syndrome and increased pigmentation or severe muscle weakness (due to hypokalemia) point to ectopic ACTH secretion.

More commonly, however, clinical manifestations of hormone excess are subtle or absent. In such instances basal levels of hormones, e.g., ACTH, may be elevated out of proportion to the biologic effects observed. This may be the result of ACTH precursor molecules that have little or no biologic activity. Identification of these hormonal forms can be accomplished by molecular sieve chromatography or by multiple, site-specific radioimmunoassays. Similarly, disproportionate elevations of hCG may reflect the presence of the glycoprotein alpha subunit, which is biologically inactive but exhibits cross-reactivity in some radioimmunoassays. A specific alpha-subunit assay is used to confirm the diagnosis.

In other instances the diagnosis of ectopic hormone secretion may be suggested by finding suppressed levels of hormones that are subject to feedback inhibition. Low or undetectable levels of insulin or parathyroid hormone in the presence of hypoglycemia or hypercalcemia are suggestive of tumors that secrete an insulin-like growth factor or a humoral hypercalcemic factor of malignancy, respectively.

Alterations in normal feedback regulation may also provide clues that elevated circulating hormone levels are derived from ectopic sources. Patients with ectopic ACTH production do not respond to suppression by glucocorticoids (presumably because of the absence of glucocorticoid receptors in the tumor tissue), an observation that helps distinguish them from patients with pituitary-dependent Cushing's disease. Apparent suppression of ACTH, which has been noted in several case reports, could be explained by intermittent secretion of ACTH by the tumor (an uncommon and poorly understood phenomenon of ectopic hormone secretion) or by the coproduction of corticotropin-releasing factor.

If the diagnosis is still in doubt, or if the source of ectopic secretion is unknown, differential venous catheterization, often with fluoroscopic control, may be an effective means of locating the tumor. As long as the tumor is actually secreting hormone at the time of study, a step-up gradient in the concentration of the hormone is of value in tumor localization and/or a search for metastases.

THERAPY Primary treatment of ectopic hormone–secreting tumors should be directed, if possible, toward removal of the tumor. Measurement of circulating hormone levels can serve as a marker for completeness of tumor excision or of the effect of radiation and chemotherapy for tumors considered inoperable, i.e., small cell carcinoma of the lung. In addition recurrence of tumor may be heralded by reappearance of elevated hormone levels prior to clinical evidence of the tumor mass. However, occasional tumors may not secrete hormones at the time of recurrence, so that one cannot rely entirely on hormone measurements as a marker of tumor activity.

Frequently, the tumor cannot be removed or is already metastatic at the time of diagnosis. In such cases, two other approaches are available for eliminating the effects of ectopic hormone secretion. Pharmacologic agents may be used to inhibit hormone release. Somatostatin and a long-acting somatostatin analogue have been used effectively in inhibiting gastrin secretion, VIP secretion, and the clinical symptoms of the carcinoid syndrome. This drug is being investigated in the United States at the time of this writing.

The other approach involves blocking the action of the hormone when its secretion cannot be altered. Pharmacologic agents may interfere with hormone effects on target tissues. Examples include (1) demeclocycline to inhibit vasopressin action on the renal tubule in the syndrome of inappropriate antidiuretic hormone (SIADH) associated with malignancy, and (2) aminoglutethimide amd metyrapone and/or mitotane to inhibit adrenal steroidogenesis in the ectopic ACTH syndrome. Alternatively, surgical removal of the target tissue may avoid life-threatening complications and permit relatively symptom-free long-term survival if the tumor itself is benign or is slowly growing. Examples include adrenalectomy for the ectopic ACTH syndrome and gastrectomy for recurrent gastrointestinal bleeding caused by gastrin-producing tumors. This form of therapy will be used with decreasing frequency as newer and more specific pharmacologic agents become available.

ECTOPIC HORMONES AS MARKERS FOR NEOPLASIA With the initial recognition of ectopic hormone secretion it was hoped that by measuring these hormones a generally applicable means of screening for clinically silent tumors would become available. As knowledge of the spectrum of ectopic hormone secretion has increased, however, this hope has faded. The list of hormones that are secreted ectopically has lengthened to the point that cost considerations preclude the use of this form of screening. Even if the number of hormones were not as extensive, the limited correlation of tumor site and type with secretion of specific hormones means that an extensive workup to localize the tumor would still be necessary. Screening programs, when performed, have yielded relatively few positive results. Moreover evidence is lacking that earlier diagnosis, as a result of such procedures, reduces subsequent morbidity or mortality. Consequently, screening for ectopic hormone production is not part of routine cancer detection programs.

REFERENCES

BAYLIN SB, MENDELSOHN G: Ectopic (inappropriate) hormone production by tumors: Mechanisms involved and the biological and clinical implications. Endocr Rev 1:45, 1980

FROHMAN LA: Ectopic hormone production by tumors: Growth hormone-releasing factor, in Neuroendocrine Perspectives, EE Muller et al (eds). Amsterdam, Elsevier, 1984 vol 3

HANSEN M et al: Diagnostic and therapeutic implications of ectopic hormone production in small cell carcinoma of the lung. Thorax 35:101, 1980

HEITZ PU et al: Ectopic hormone production by endocrine tumors: Localization of hormones at the cellular level by immunocytochemistry. Cancer 48:2029, 1981

IMURA H: Ectopic hormone production viewed as an abnormality in regulation of gene expression. Adv Cancer Res 33:39, 1980

LOKICH JJ: The frequency and clinical biology of the ectopic hormone syndromes of small carcinoma. Cancer 50:2111, 1982

MUNDY GR et al: The hypercalcemia of cancer. Clinical implications and pathogenetic mechanisms. N Engl J Med 310:1718, 1984

ODELL WD, WOLFSEN AR: Humoral syndromes associated with cancer: Ectopic hormone production. Prog Clin Cancer 8:57, 1982

ORTH D: Ectopic hormone production, in Endocrinology and Metabolism, P Felig et al (eds). New York, McGraw-Hill, 1981

SORENSEN GS: Hormone production by cultures of small cell carcinoma of lung. Cancer 47:1289, 1981

STEVENS RE, MOORE GE: Inadequacy of APUD concept in explaining production of peptide hormones by tumours. Lancet 1:118, 1983

304   NEUROLOGIC MANIFESTATIONS OF SYSTEMIC NEOPLASIA

KARI STEFANSSON / BARRY G.W. ARNASON

INTRODUCTION Neurologic disorders commonly complicate systemic neoplasia. Tumors metastasize to brain with distressing frequency. Radiation treatment in doses exceeding 4500 rad may cause delayed necrosis of central nervous tissue secondary to occlusion of small- or intermediate-sized blood vessels. Chemotherapy of cancer may also be followed by nervous system damage; intrathecal methotrexate enhances radiosensitivity and can cause central nervous system necrosis directly, and cytosine arabinoside and 5-fluorouracil treatment may cause cerebellar damage. Many anticancer drugs cause peripheral neuropathy, and vincristine invariably does so. Opportunistic infections of the nervous system may also complicate cancer in persons immunosuppressed by the tumor or its treatment. When tumors damage vital organs, metabolic derangements may follow, and these too may compromise nervous system function (see Chap. 345).

In addition to the above, systemic tumors may occasionally be complicated by neurologic disorders not ascribable to invasion or compression of nervous tissue by tumor, to drugs used in cancer treatment, to infection, or to metabolic disturbance. Such neurologic disorders are termed paraneoplastic syndromes. Those that are currently recognized are summarized in Table 304-1.

TABLE 304-1 Remote effects of cancer on the nervous system

Site	Evolution	Clinical features	Cancer	Pathology
BRAIN				
Limbic encephalitis	Weeks to months	Confusional state followed by loss of retentive memory and dementia; anxiety, depression, and agitation common early in course	Oat cell tumor of lung	Neuronal loss in medial temporal lobe and other parts of limbic system; perivascular and meningeal infiltration
Photoreceptor degeneration	Months	Visual loss progressing to blindness	Oat cell tumor, rarely cervical cancer	Loss of rods and cones with retinal infiltration of mononuclear cells
CEREBELLUM AND BRAINSTEM				
Subacute cortical cerebellar degeneration	Weeks to months	Cerebellar ataxia Dysarthria	Oat cell tumor, ovarian and breast cancer, Hodgkin's disease	Loss of Purkinje cells with perivascular and leptomeningeal lymphocytic infiltration
Opsoclonus-myoclonus	Weeks	Dancing eyes, myoclonic jerks, cerebellar ataxia, (in children)	Neuroblastoma	Loss of Purkinje cells
Bulbar encephalitis	Days to weeks	Nystagmus, diplopia, vertigo, ataxia, (in adults)	Lung tumor	Neuronal loss in pons and medulla, mononuclear infiltration
SPINAL CORD				
Necrotizing myelopathy	Hours, days, or weeks	Paraplegia or quadriplegia with sensory loss and bladder dysfunction	Oat cell tumor lymphomas	Severe necrosis of white and gray matter
Subacute motor neuronopathy	Weeks or months	Flaccid weakness and muscle atrophy; legs affected more than arms	Non-Hodgkin's lymphoma	Degeneration and loss of anterior horn cells
ROOT AND PERIPHERAL NERVE				
Subacute sensory neuronopathy	Weeks or months	Severe sensory loss with areflexia; often precedes the discovery of the malignant tumor	Oat cell tumor, other lung tumors	Degeneration and loss of neurons in dorsal root ganglia; infiltration with mononuclear cells
Acute polyneuritis (Guillain-Barré syndrome)	Days to weeks	Ascending weakness with minimal sensory findings	Hodgkin's disease	Segmental demyelination; inflammatory infiltration of peripheral nerves
Sensory motor neuropathy	Weeks to months	Distal motor and sensory loss; distal reflex loss	Oat cell tumor	Segmental demyelination, Wallerian degeneration
Peripheral neuropathy associated with monoclonal gammopathy	Weeks to months	Heterogeneous group; some predominantly sensory, others motor	Proliferative disorders of plasma cells and B lymphocytes	Segmental demyelination or axonal degeneration
Neuropathy with insulinoma	Weeks to months	Weakness, without sensory loss	Insulinoma	Axonal degeneration
NEUROMUSCULAR JUNCTION				
Myasthenia gravis	Weeks to months	Weakness, fatigability, normal sensory findings, normal reflexes	Thymoma, breast cancer, gastric cancer	Destruction of motor end plate and postsynaptic junctional folds
Eaton-Lambert syndrome	Weeks to months	Weakness, fatigability proximal leg muscles	Oat cell tumor	Abnormalities of presynaptic membrane of myoneural junction
MUSCLE				
Polymyositis	Months to years	Proximal muscle weakness, tender muscles, arrhythmias, heart failure	Breast, ovarian, lung cancer, lymphomas	Degeneration of muscle fibers with mononuclear cellular infiltration

Three of these paraneoplastic syndromes are considered elsewhere and need only be mentioned briefly here: *myasthenia gravis,* which in 10 percent of cases occurs against a background of thymoma (see Chap. 358); *acute idiopathic polyradiculoneuropathy* (Guillain-Barré syndrome), the incidence of which is increased in Hodgkin's disease (see Chap. 355); and *polymyositis,* which in older people is associated with an increased probability of neoplasm in the breast, ovary, lung, or lymphoid tissue (see Chap. 356). All three occur far more often in the absence of cancer than in its presence, indicating that neoplasia, while favoring these complications, cannot be their sole cause. Even though the link to cancer is tighter in several other paraneoplastic syndromes, cases in which no cancer can be found, even at autopsy, have been reported, and all probably occur in the absence of cancer. More than one paraneoplastic complication may occur simultaneously in the same individual, and the histopathology of the various syndromes overlap. All may precede the detection of a tumor by months to years, and all can develop at any time during its course.

The paraneoplastic syndromes pose difficult diagnostic problems, and other complications that plague cancer patients (e.g., metastasis, infections, drug toxicity) must be excluded before the definitive diagnosis can be made. This is particularly important since the paraneoplastic syndromes are less likely to respond to therapeutic intervention than are the other problems.

NEUROMUSCULAR DISORDERS Eaton-Lambert syndrome (see also Chap. 358) The syndrome is characterized by weakness and fatigability, primarily of the muscles of the pelvic girdle and thighs. It occurs often in conjunction with dry mouth, impotence, aching thighs, peripheral paresthesias, and diminished or absent tendon reflexes. The tensilon test may be weakly positive. Electromyograms show a pathognomonic increase in amplitude on repetitive stimulation at high rates. Electron-microscopic studies show characteristic abnormalities of the presynaptic membrane of the myoneural junction.

The basic physiologic defect in Eaton-Lambert syndrome is a failure of quantal release of acetylcholine from the terminal axons of motor neurons although quantum, when released, is normal. There is reason to believe that Eaton-Lambert syndrome, like myasthenia gravis, may be caused by autoantibodies. Mice injected with serum IgG from patients develop the electrophysiologic and electron-microscopic characteristics of the Eaton-Lambert syndrome. The syndrome is associated with cancer in 70 percent of cases; half of these are small cell cancers of the lung. The prognosis for the tumor itself is remarkably favorable; patient survival for a small cell cancer of the lung in the presence of Eaton-Lambert syndrome averages 4 years versus less than 2 years in its absence. The tumor mass is often remarkably small, and may be found only at autopsy.

Eaton-Lambert syndrome patients without cancer have a significant increase over expected values in the frequency of the HLA-B8 and HLA-DR3 histocompatibility alleles. It appears that humoral immunity plays a major role in the pathogenesis of Eaton-Lambert syndrome and that immunogenetic factors influence propensity to develop the syndrome in noncancer cases.

Tumor removal often brings about some relief from Eaton-Lambert syndrome; spontaneous remissions also occur both in tumor and nontumor cases. Guanidine hydrochloride, a drug that facilitates acetylcholine release, may give symptomatic relief. Plasmapheresis and immunosuppressive medications may be beneficial, in keeping with the proposed autoimmune nature of the disease.

Sensorimotor polyneuropathy The most common paraneoplastic syndrome is a combined sensorimotor symmetric distal polyneuropathy characterized by weakness, sensory loss, and absence of distal tendon reflexes. Pathologic studies show segmental demyelination in most examined cases, but Wallerian degeneration can also occur. The clinical features are indistinguishable from those seen in other forms of sensorimotor neuropathy. Since the etiology of the disorder is unknown in one-third to one-half of patients who present with polyneuropathy without cancer, it is uncertain what role the tumor has when present in the evolution of the clinical syndrome. The distal polyneuropathy associated with cancer is refractory to treatment with vitamins, and does not usually improve, even after removal of the tumor. Most commonly associated with the distal polyneuropathy are tumors arising in the lung (oat cell), breast, stomach, and thymus, and rarely Hodgkin's disease and multiple myeloma.

Subacute sensory neuronopathy (Chap. 355) The clinical characteristics include profound sensory loss, most often developing over a period of weeks although sometimes more slowly. Muscle strength is relatively preserved. Numbness, paresthesias, dysesthesias, and pain begin distally in the extremities and spread proximally. The legs are affected more severely than the arms. Loss of position sense of the feet invariably leads to profound gait ataxia. Deep tendon reflexes are diminished or absent. Patients with subacute sensory neuronopathy often have signs and symptoms that indicate dysfunction of the central nervous system, particularly of the brainstem and cerebral cortex. Most patients have lymphocytosis and an increased concentration of protein in the cerebrospinal fluid (CSF).

The main histopathologic findings occur in the dorsal root ganglia with loss of neurons, reactive proliferation of supporting satellite cells, and infiltration by lymphocytes and macrophages. It is not uncommon to find inflammatory cell infiltrates elsewhere in the neuraxis. Small cell cancer of the lung has been the underlying neoplasm in half the reported cases; most of the remainder have been accompanied by other types of lung tumors. The onset of the neuronopathy has preceded detection of the tumor by an interval of 1 year or more in better than half the cases.

Attempts to culture viruses from dorsal root ganglia of patients with subacute sensory neuronopathy have been unsuccessful. Patients with the disorder often have IgG in their serum that reacts with neurons in dorsal root ganglia, spinal cord, and brain. It has been postulated, but not proven, that these antibodies play a role in the pathogenesis of the neuronopathy. Disease progression sometimes ceases with tumor resection.

Subacute motor neuropathy of lymphomas This syndrome is characterized by subacute progressive lower motor neuron weakness, more pronounced in legs than arms with sparing of the bulbar musculature. A small proportion of patients complain of sensory symptoms, but sensory signs are absent. The neuropathy is rarely severe enough to disable the patient. It does at times precede the detection of the lymphoma and can appear at any time during its course. In most cases it resolves or stabilizes after a few months to a year. The course of the neuropathy is independent of the course of the underlying lymphoma. The CSF is usually normal. Patients with subacute motor neuropathy are remarkably sensitive to the neurotoxic effects of vinca alkaloids, and therefore their neuropathic problems may fluctuate with treatment of the underlying lymphoma.

Autopsies of a few cases have revealed degeneration and loss of anterior horn cells and to a lesser extent loss of cells in Clarke's column and the intermediolateral column of the spinal cord. Areas of demyelination and reactive gliosis are seen in the white matter. There is demyelination of anterior spinal roots accompanied by reactive proliferation of Schwann cells. A rare Schwann cell has a peculiar hyperchromatic giant nucleus. Striated muscles in involved areas show neurogenic atrophy. The etiology and pathogenesis of subacute motor neuropathy are unknown; it has been postulated that it may be caused by a viral infection, but no direct evidence supports this hypothesis. There is no effective treatment for subacute motor neuropathy.

Peripheral neuropathies accompanying plasma cell dyscrasias Peripheral neuropathy is common among patients suffering from plasma cell dyscrasias. In prospective studies, for example, 13 percent of patients with multiple myeloma suffer from clinical peripheral neuropathies and between 40 and 60 percent have slowed nerve conduction velocities and/or histopathologic changes in peripheral nerves. Fifty percent of patients with sclerosing myeloma and 25 percent of patients with Waldenström's macroglobulinemia have peripheral neuropathies. Viewed from another perspective, 10 percent of patients with chronic peripheral neuropathies not readily ascribed to other causes have plasma cell dyscrasias. Because the neuropathies that accompany plasma cell dyscrasias are highly pleomorphic in their clinical features, a search for plasma cell dyscrasias is warranted in any patient with chronic peripheral neuropathy of unknown origin. The clinical course is usually independent of that of the underlying plasma cell dyscrasia. There is no reliable treatment, but plasmapheresis is said to be beneficial in some cases.

Two distinct neuropathic syndromes have emerged from the heterogeneous group of neuropathies that accompany plasma cell dyscrasias.

DISTAL SENSORIMOTOR NEUROPATHY IN PATIENTS WITH WALDENSTRÖM'S MACROGLOBULINEMIA. The peripheral neuropathy is usually a slowly evolving distal sensorimotor neuropathy without significant pain or autonomic involvement. Nerve conduction velocities are considerably slowed. Cerebrospinal fluid is acellular and the protein concentration is normal. The histopathology of the sural nerves is characterized by evidence of demyelination and remyelination with relative sparing of axons and by deposition of monoclonal IgM on the myelin. Electron microscopy shows a characteristic increase in the distance between the major dense lines of the outermost lamellae of some myelin sheaths, a change not described in other human diseases.

The monoclonal IgM in the serum of patients with this syndrome binds to an epitope(s) shared by myelin-associated glycoprotein, a minor component of both central and peripheral myelin, and to a glycolipid and several low-molecular-weight proteins confined to peripheral nerves. Preliminary work indicates that this monoclonal IgM can induce demyelination in peripheral nerves of animals. It is likely, therefore, that the monoclonal IgM plays a direct role in the pathogenesis of the neuropathy.

PERIPHERAL NEUROPATHY IN PATIENTS WITH OSTEOSCLEROTIC MYELOMA. The neuropathy is a symmetric, predominantly motor neuropathy that can lead to profound weakness of the extremities within months or years. There may be some involvement of all sensory modalities, but pain and autonomic dysfunction are rare. Thirty percent of patients develop papilledema. A small proportion of patients with osteosclerotic myeloma also have one or more of the following; hypogonadism, gynecomastia, hyperpigmentation, hypertrichosis, hyperhidrosis, effusions into body cavities, hepatosplenomegaly, generalized lymphadenopathy, and clubbing. Most of these patients have been Japanese but several cases have also been reported in the United States and in Europe. Nerve conduction velocities are moderately to severely slowed, and CSF contains an increased concentration of protein.

Nerve biopsies show a mixture of axonal degeneration and segmental demyelination. No monoclonal immunoglobulin is found within nerves. Only 60 percent of patients with osteosclerotic myeloma have circulating monoclonal immunoglobulins, and antineural antibodies have not been found in their sera. When a monoclonal gammopathy is detected, it is of IgG or IgA class. It is probable that the pathogenesis of this neuropathy differs from that accompanying Waldenström's macroglobulinema. The peripheral neuropathies of sclerotic myeloma respond poorly to chemotherapy; radiation of the sclerotic bone lesion, which may be small and solitary, is sometimes followed by significant relief.

Peripheral neuropathy associated with insulinomas. This rare syndrome is characterized by acute or subacute loss of strength of all extremities. The arms are usually weaker than the legs. Weakness is followed by atrophy but fasciculations are rare. Although sensory complaints are prominent, minimal sensory signs are found. There is mild to moderate slowing of nerve conduction and electromyograms show denervation. The cerebrospinal fluid is normal. Removal of the insulinoma may be followed by a considerable recovery of strength; apart from this no treatment is known for this neuropathy.

CENTRAL NERVOUS SYSTEM DISORDERS

SPINAL CORD DISORDERS   Necrotizing myelopathy   Necrosis of the spinal cord occurs rarely on a background of cancer. The clinical syndrome is one of severe, acute, or subacute transverse myelopathy. Necrosis begins most often in the thoracic region and progresses both rostrally and caudally until the greater part of the vertical extent of the spinal cord is destroyed. Occasionally, it begins as a Brown-Séquard syndrome (see Chap. 353) which evolves into paraplegia or quadriplegia. Protein concentration and the cell count in the cerebrospinal fluid may be increased. Myelography sometimes shows swelling of the cord, as in other acute myelopathies. An identical syndrome occurs in the absence of cancer.

The basic histologic lesion is necrosis of both gray and white matter with relative sparing of the periphery of the cord. In some cases necrotic lesions have been found in cerebral cortex and brainstem in addition to spinal cord.

One-third of tumor-associated cases occur in patients with lymphoma, another one-third in patients with lung tumors, and the remaining one-third in patients with other neoplasms. Necrotizing myelopathy may present months to years before the neoplasm becomes detectable and may also appear after the patient's tumor has been cured. There is no effective treatment.

CEREBELLUM AND BRAINSTEM   Subacute cortical cerebellar degeneration   This condition presents as a subacute progressive cerebellar ataxia which can stabilize after a few weeks or months. The patient may be rendered quite helpless. Half have upper motor neuron signs, mental disturbances are frequent, and 10 percent become deaf. Most patients have an increased number of lymphocytes and an elevation of protein in the cerebrospinal fluid. Cerebellar atrophy is often evident on computerized tomography or magnetic resonance imaging a few weeks after onset of the disease. This condition may account for up to 50 percent of patients with nonfamilial idiopathic cerebellar degeneration of late onset (over 45 years of age).

The histopathology is characterized by loss of Purkinje and granule cells and by thinning of the molecular layer. Frequently there are perivascular and leptomeningeal lymphocytic infiltrates in the cerebellum and elsewhere in the neuraxis. Occasionally there is also loss of anterior horn cells and of neurons in the dorsal root ganglia.

Subacute cortical cerebellar degeneration occurs in association with various neoplasms, but half the reported cases have been associated with small cell carcinoma of the lung. Other cases have been described with ovarian and breast cancer, and with Hodgkin's disease and other tumors. There are reports of patients who have developed subacute cerebellar degeneration up to a year before their tumor was diagnosed. Attempts to culture viruses from the cerebellum of affected individuals have been unsuccessful. Several reports have appeared describing antineural antibodies in the serum of patients with subacute cerebellar degeneration, and it has been proposed that these antibodies may play a role in the pathogenesis of the syndrome; this hypothesis has not been proven. There is no effective treatment for the condition; tumor resection may arrest progression in some patients.

Opsoclonus-myoclonus   Patients with opsoclonus-myoclonus suffer from rapid and irregular involuntary movements of the eyes and limbs. The condition has consequently been called the "dancing eyes–dancing feet syndrome." Most patients with opsoclonus-myoclonus have normal cerebrospinal fluid although lymphocytosis and an increased concentration of immunoglobulins may occur. Elevation of serum immunoglobulins has also been reported in a few cases.

Most cases occur in children, and half of the childhood cases accompany a well-differentiated neuroblastoma. Although neuroblastomas are secretory tumors, the secretion (of catecholamines) is less conspicuous in cases of neuroblastoma accompanied by opsoclonus-myoclonus than in those that are not associated with the condition. Opsoclonus-myoclonus can occur in adults with neoplasms other than neuroblastoma, and a similar syndrome has been described in both children and adults following upper respiratory and gastrointestinal illnesses. As with other paraneoplastic entities, opsoclonus-myoclonus may occur months to years before the tumor is recognized.

The histopathology of active childhood opsoclonus-myoclonus has yet to be described, but two reports of the histopathology of opsoclonus-myoclonus in adults indicate that the lesions resemble those that cause subacute cerebellar degeneration. Why children with neuroblastomas are prone to develop the clinical syndrome of opsoclonus-myoclonus while adults with other neoplasms (small cell cancer, ovarian cancer, breast cancer, etc.) and the same histologic lesions are more likely to develop subacute cerebellar ataxia is not understood. Successful treatment of the underlying neoplasm by resection and/or radiation has resulted in relief from opsoclonus-myoclonus in some patients. Glucocorticosteroid treatment is frequently effective. Children who recover from opsoclonus-myoclonus often have residual mild mental retardation.

Bulbar encephalitis.   Brainstem symptoms and signs including diplopia, vertigo, nystagmus, dysarthria, and dysphagia may rarely develop insidiously or subacutely in patients with cancer, usually of the lung. Neuronal loss in the pons and medulla and perivascular infiltration are present. The cause is unknown, and no effective treatment has been found.

Limbic encephalitis. Limbic encephalitis usually presents as an agitated confusional state followed by a loss of retentive memory. The clinical picture is similar to herpes simplex encephalitis, but there is no concomitant rise in titer of antiherpes antibody, and the disease evolves more slowly. The cerebrospinal fluid often contains mononuclear cells, and the protein concentration is elevated. The histopathology is marked by a loss of neurons in the medial aspect of the temporal lobes and by perivascular and leptomeningeal infiltration with lymphocytes and phagocytes. There is also reactive astrocytosis in the involved brain areas. Similar histopathology is seen in the cerebellum in half of the cases. Most reported instances have occurred in association with small cell cancer of the lung. There is no effective treatment.

PHOTORECEPTOR DEGENERATION   Patients with neoplasms arising outside of the nervous system can lose vision due to direct compression by metastases to the leptomeninges or choroid, or indirectly due to increased cerebrospinal fluid pressure from intracranial metastases. Radiation damage to the eyes or visual pathways can also cause loss of vision. Paraneoplastic photoreceptor degeneration presents yet another mechanism whereby the cancer patient may lose vision. It is a rare condition that presents with a gradual and painless loss of vision progressing to blindness. Electroretinograms are abnormal, and the cerebrospinal fluid may show pleocytosis. There is loss of rods and cones, and the retina is infiltrated by lymphocytes and macrophages. Reported cases have occurred in association with lung tumors or cervical cancer. Antiretinal antibodies have been found in the serum of patients with photoreceptor degeneration, but their role in the pathogenesis of the syndrome is unknown. There is no effective treatment for paraneoplastic photoreceptor degeneration.

Several other neurologic disorders have been reported in the past as occurring with increased frequency in patients with various neoplasms. These include optic neuritis, thalamic degeneration, and amyotrophic lateral sclerosis. Most of these reports have been anecdotal, and it is likely that the association of cancer with these neurologic problems is coincidental.

REFERENCES

ARNASON BGW: Paraneoplastic syndromes of muscle, nerve and brain: Immunological considerations, in *Clinical Neuroimmunology*, FC Rose (ed). Oxford, Blackwell, 1979

GRAUS F et al: Sensory neuronopathy and small cell lung cancer. Am J Med 80:45, 1986

GREENLEE JE, BRASHEAR HR: Antibodies to cerebellar Purkinje cells in patients with paraneoplastic cerebellar degeneration and ovarian carcinoma. Ann Neurol 14:609, 1983

GRUNWALD GB et al: Autoimmune basis for visual paraneoplastic syndrome in patients with small-cell lung carcinoma. Lancet 1:65, 1985

HENSON RA, URICH H: *Cancer and the Nervous System.* Oxford, Blackwell, 1982

JAECKLE KA et al: Autoimmune response of patients with paraneoplastic cerebellar degeneration to a Purkinje cell cytoplasmic protein antigen. Ann Neurol 18:592, 1985

JASPAN JB et al: Hypoglycemic peripheral neuropathy in association with insulinoma: Implication of glycopenia rather than hyperinsulinism. Medicine 61:33, 1982

KELLY JJ et al: The spectrum of peripheral neuropathy in myeloma. Neurology 31:24, 1981

KINSBOURNE M: Myoclonic encephalopathy of infants. J Neurol Neurosourg Psych 25:271, 1962

MANCALL EL, ROSALES RK: Necrotizing myelopathy associated with visceral carcinoma. Brain 87:639, 1964

PRIOR C et al: Action of Lambert-Eaton myasthenic syndrome IgG at mouse motor nerve terminals. Ann Neurol 17:587, 1985

SHY M et al: Specificity of human IgM M-proteins that bind to myelin associated glycoprotein: Peptide mapping, deglycosylation and competitive binding studies. J Immunol 133(5):2509, 1984

ZEROMSKI J: Immunological findings of sensory carcinomatous neuropathy: Application of peroxidase labeled antibody. Clin Exp Immunol 6:663, 1970

PART TEN ENDOCRINOLOGY AND METABOLISM

section 1 Disorders of metabolism

305 OVERVIEW OF INHERITED METABOLIC DISEASES

LEON E. ROSENBERG

GENE-ENVIRONMENT INTERACTION Metabolism comprises all the processes by which living matter is built up (anabolism) or broken down (catabolism). These processes begin with the earliest chemical reactions leading to the formation of the sperm and egg; continue throughout fertilization, growth, maturation, and senescence; and end inexorably with the death of cell, tissue, organ, and finally the individual. Metabolic processes are controlled by two integrated inputs: the *genes,* which delimit the capacity of any given cell (and pari passu of any organism), and the *environment,* which determines how those genes will be expressed. It follows that all metabolic disorders result from some disturbance in the interaction between genetic and environmental factors, and, in the strictest sense, that no metabolic disorder can be classified as either purely *inherited* or *acquired.* When we have little or no information about the genetic determinants of a disease, as in susceptibility to tuberculosis or to traumatic fractures of bones, we think of the condition as acquired. Conversely, when a metabolic disorder is due to a primary abnormality of a specific protein (and hence to a mutation of a specific gene) and when this abnormality is inherited as a simple mendelian trait (as in acute intermittent porphyria or phenylketonuria), we consider the metabolic derangement inherited. In fact, neither acute intermittent porphyria nor phenylketonuria would be significant clinically were it not for precipitating and modifying factors in the environment (drugs and hormones in porphyria; dietary phenylalanine in phenylketonuria). Appreciation of this gene-environment continuum is of more than nosologic interest. Identification of genes controlling susceptibility to tuberculosis would enable us to identify individuals and groups at risk, and additional information about age-related dietary phenylalanine requirements would permit more effective nutritional treatment of phenylketonuria.

CHARACTER OF INBORN ERRORS Literally hundreds of inherited metabolic diseases or, as they were originally designated by Garrod, "inborn errors of metabolism," are now recognized, and new ones continue to be described at a rapid rate. As a group, these conditions affect all phases of metabolism and have contributed enormously to the understanding of normal metabolic pathways. They share only the two common features mentioned earlier: each is inherited as a simple mendelian trait, and each has been traced (or is attributed) to a functional abnormality of a specific protein. In other ways the conditions are diverse. Most are inherited as autosomal recessive traits, implying that a double dose of the mutant gene is required for the disorder to be phenotypically manifest (see Chap. 57); others are inherited as X-linked or autosomal dominant traits. Some have an incidence as high as 1:500 (familial hypercholesterolemia); others have an incidence as low as 1:1,000,000 (alcaptonuria). Some demonstrate prominent racial or ethnic clustering (sickle cell anemia, thalassemia, Tay-Sachs disease), and others appear to be uniformly distributed in races and groups. Some produce clinical manifestations at birth (or even before), others only in adult life (or not at all). Some are uniformly lethal regardless of treatment; others are compatible with a normal life span and health.

LEVELS OF UNDERSTANDING Since the clinical and chemical abnormalities observed with a given inherited metabolic disease reflect the mutation of a specific gene, it is theoretically possible to understand each inborn error at four levels: the gene, the protein coded for by the gene, the metabolic step at which the protein works, and the clinical or chemical phenotype produced by abnormalities at that step. A number of defects in globin-chain synthesis (the thalassemias and hemoglobinopathies) have been explored at each of these levels (see Chap. 288). In hemoglobin S disease (sickle cell anemia), for example, the specific nucleotide base change in the structural gene for β globin and the precise amino acid substitution in the β-globin polypeptide have been identified. Furthermore, physicochemical studies with hemoglobin S have shown why this mutant protein has a tendency to gel in the deoxygenated state and form the tactoids that distort the erythrocyte and lead to the hyperviscosity, sludging, tissue infarction, and hemolysis characteristic of this disorder. Until recently, information at the level of the gene was available only for disorders of globin-chain synthesis. The development of recombinant DNA technology has led to an explosive increase in the number of human genes that have been cloned and isolated (see Chap. 58) and in the number of inherited disorders understood at the level of the gene. This list now includes loci coding for such proteins as α_1-antitrypsin, argininosuccinate synthetase, collagen, growth hormone, hypoxanthine-guanine phosphoribosyltransferase, insulin, ornithine transcarbamylase, and phenylalanine hydroxylase. For many loci, however, understanding stops at the level of the gene product and, even there, is incomplete. For example, in the "classic" form of galactosemia, galactose 1-phosphate uridyltransferase activity is markedly deficient; this deficiency leads to accumulation of galactose and galactose 1-phosphate, which results in serious hepatic and central nervous system dysfunction. However, we know little about the molecular nature of the transferase deficiency or the means by which metabolite accumulation leads to cirrhosis and mental retardation. In other instances, such as Wilson's disease or cystinosis, the particular protein whose function is deranged is unknown, although it is recognized that copper and cystine, respectively, accumulate in tissues of affected patients. In the case of Huntington's disease we still have no biochemical "handle" with which to confront its therapeutic, diagnostic, and prognostic dilemmas, but a genetic marker of the disease has been identified (see Chap. 58).

PROTEINS AS GENE PRODUCTS

SPECTRUM OF MUTANT PROTEINS Genes and messenger RNAs are polymers of nucleic acids often referred to as "informational macromolecules." Along similar lines proteins and polypeptides can be called "functional macromolecules." These polymers of amino acids convert the informational potential of genes and messengers into chemical and physiologic work. Proteins are ubiquitous. They are a vital constituent of the membranes that separate tissues, cells, and organelles from one another. In the blood, lymph, and cerebrospinal fluid they maintain osmotic pressure and selectively bind and transport a large number of small molecules. As enzymes and hormones, whether extracellular or intracellular, they catalyze or regulate reactions that allow anabolic and catabolic pathways to proceed. Proteins display almost limitless variation in size, shape, and function. Molecular weights vary from a few hundred for the pituitary hormone-releasing factors to more than a million for gamma macroglobulin. Some are monomeric; others are oligomers of two, three, four, or more like or unlike polypeptide chains. Some are globular while others are helical; still others have both globular and helical regions. Some have metal ions as prosthetic groups or cofactors, while others require organic constituents for activity. Each, however, owes its unique structural features and functional specificity to a single feature—the primary amino acid sequence. Since this primary sequence is dependent on the nucleotide sequence of the gene and messenger RNA that codes for the polypeptide, inherited variations in protein structure or function are the visible expression of gene mutation. Mutations occur in all genes, and hence variation must occur in all proteins. Some variants are detected easily because they lead to obvious chemical or clinical disturbance. Others are detected with great difficulty, either because they produce early lethality or because they are clinically or chemically silent.

In general, mutations responsible for inherited metabolic disorders affect the structural genes that code for the *primary structure* of the protein (see Chap. 57). Single codon changes usually lead to single amino acid substitutions and are referred to as *missense* mutations. Other point mutations (those leading to inappropriately placed terminator codons) as well as deletions and insertions (of codons, segments, or entire genes) result in absence of the gene product or one so incomplete or distorted as to be essentially functionless. Alternatively, mutations can modify the *rate* at which a protein is made. Such rate control may be exerted either by modifying control genes or by changing codons in structural genes in a way that leads to accelerated or retarded transcription or translation. Finally, mutations can influence the posttranslational modification of proteins. Since most proteins destined for secretion, for membrane insertion, or for transport to organelles such as lysosomes or mitochondria are synthesized as precursors which must be processed, trimmed, or glycosylated as part of their delivery system, mutations can alter such "traffic." Hyperproinsulinemia and I-cell disease are examples of defective processing of secretory and lysosomal proteins, respectively.

Inborn errors have been described for all types of proteins. Enzymatic defects that produce a block in an anabolic or catabolic pathway were the first to be recognized. Hundreds of examples of this type of defect are known (see subsequent chapters), and new enzymatic deficiencies are described at a rate of about 10 per year. Inborn errors of transport affecting gut and kidney may selectively impair transmembrane movement of sugars, amino acids, phosphate, vitamins, or water (see Chap. 308). Disorders like cystinuria or glycosuria reflect deficiency of specific membrane carrier proteins required for transepithelial movement of dibasic amino acids or glucose, respectively. Other transport defects lead to abnormal binding of hormones to membrane receptors as in vasopressin-resistant diabetes insipidus or of protein-ligand complexes as in the cell surface receptor defect for low-density lipoprotein in familial hypercholesterolemia (see Chap. 315). Still other mutations alter circulating proteins rather than membrane or intracellular constituents. Analbuminemia, trans-

cobalamin II deficiency, and abetalipoproteinemia are examples of such deficiencies.

FUNCTIONAL DERANGEMENTS Increased activity Simply put, metabolic disorders can be thought of as resulting from too much or too little of a specific protein (or of that protein's activity). Variant forms of glucose 6-phosphate dehydrogenase (G6PD), pseudocholinesterase, and phosphoribosylpyrophosphate synthetase have been described in which enzyme activity is *increased*. In these instances, mutations result in an increase in intracellular enzyme content because either the mutant protein is synthesized more rapidly than normal or it is degraded more slowly. In acute intermittent porphyria and familial hypercholesterolemia, rate-controlling enzymes are increased as well (see Chaps. 312 and 315). In the latter disorders, however, enzyme overactivity is a secondary event, reflecting impaired feedback regulation produced by other primary genetic disturbances.

Decreased activity Most inborn errors are associated with decreased activity (or content) of a protein. The deficiency may be *virtually complete* (as in the classic forms of phenylketonuria and galactosemia) or *partial* (as in the benign variants of those disorders). It should be emphasized that complete loss of enzyme activity cannot be equated with complete absence of a protein. For example, in classic galactosemia, no galactose 1-phosphate uridyltransferase activity can be detected in tissues of affected patients, but such tissues contain a protein that cross-reacts with antibody to the native transferase molecule. Numerous examples of cross-reacting material positive (CRM$^+$) abnormalities are recognized. They indicate that the mutation has resulted in the synthesis of a protein that has lost catalytic activity but retains antigenic specificity. Other metabolic disorders characterized by complete enzyme deficiency such as muscle phosphorylase deficiency or von Willebrand's disease are CRM$^-$, implying either that no protein is made or that the gene product is so altered that both catalytic and antigenic functions have been lost.

Most inborn errors are characterized by partial, rather than complete, loss of activity. Such partial deficiency may result from several different mechanisms. First, it may reflect a reduced rate of synthesis of normal or abnormal enzyme molecules. Second, it may result from accelerated destruction of a structurally altered enzyme. Third, reduced activity may reflect reduced affinity of the active enzyme for substrate or cofactor. Fourth, for oligomeric enzymes, reduced activity can result from impaired interaction of identical or nonidentical subunits. Fifth, for those enzymes in which more than a single isoenzyme exists in a tissue, reduced activity can reflect isolated loss of one form of the enzyme. Examples of each of these mechanisms exist among inherited metabolic disorders. Moreover, the same phenotypic manifestations can result from different mechanisms. For example, some G6PD variants exhibit increased lability, others abnormal affinity for substrate, and still others impaired oligomer formation. These abnormalities result from different structural alterations in a single polypeptide chain.

CONSEQUENCES OF TRANSPORT OR ENZYMATIC DEFECTS

The effect of a given genetic alteration on cellular metabolism and clinical status depends on the role that the mutant protein plays and the severity of the defect. As mentioned earlier, most inborn errors are the result of intracellular enzymatic defects or of membrane transport abnormalities. Since these kinds of mutations are discussed repeatedly in the following chapters, it is appropriate to summarize the possible consequences of inherited transport or enzyme defects. The model reaction sequence shown in Fig. 305-1 is used for illustrative purposes. A, B, C, D, F, and G are substrates or products of a series of enzymatic reactions; T_A, E_{AB}, E_{BC}, and E_{CD} refer to specific transport systems or enzymes catalyzing specific reactions in this sequence. The major pathway involves the conversion of A to

D via intermediates B and C. F and G are products of an alternate metabolic pathway. The arrow from D to E_{AB} represents negative feedback control of the first enzyme in the pathway by the final product of the sequence. Where possible, examples of specific inborn errors that illustrate specific consequences of transport or enzyme defects will be cited.

PRECURSOR DEFICIENCY If T_A, the receptor or carrier system that transports A into the cell, is defective, the intracellular concentration of A may be so low that E_{AB} will not be saturated with its substrate. This could slow the entire reaction sequence and result in inadequate formation of B, C, and D. In Hartnup's disease (see Chap. 308), intestinal transport of tryptophan is defective. This transport defect has important chemical and clinical consequences, since tryptophan is converted to nicotinamide intracellularly. Patients with this disorder may exhibit cerebellar ataxia and temporary or permanent dementia due to nicotinamide deficiency if they do not receive supplements of niacin in the diet. Similarly, patients with inherited defects in intestinal absorption of vitamin B_{12} develop megaloblastic anemia unless the vitamin is supplied parenterally. Precursor or substrate deficiency may also occur if the defect involves a circulating protein that transports substance A in the blood and carries it to the cell surface.

PRECURSOR ACCUMULATION Let us next consider the effect of reduced activity of one of the intracellular enzymes (E_{AB}, E_{BC}, or E_{CD}). Such a defect might lead to intracellular and extracellular accumulation of the immediate or remote precursors of the reaction. If E_{AB} is defective, only A will accumulate. Such a result is illustrated by the marked increase in lysosomal glucocerebroside content in Gaucher's disease (see Chap. 316) and of blood galactose concentration in galactokinase deficiency (see Chap. 314). Defects of E_{BC} may result in accumulation of A as well as B, and a defect of E_{CD} could lead to the pileup of A, B, and C. In homocystinuria due to cystathionine synthase deficiency, methionine, a remote precursor, accumulates, as does homocystine, the immediate precursor of the blocked reaction (see Chap. 306).

ALTERNATE PATHWAY UTILIZATION If the conversion of A to B is impaired by deficiency of E_{AB}, not only will A accumulate, but the usually minor, alternate pathway to F and G may become prominent. Phenylketonuria represents an excellent example of this phenomenon. The absence of phenylalanine hydroxylase activity leads to gross overproduction and excretion of phenylpyruvic, phenylacetic, and phenyllactic acids, compounds not usually detectable in blood or urine (see Chap. 306). Such alternate pathway augmentation may have important physiologic significance if the products of the alternate pathway interfere with cell processes when present in more than minute concentrations.

PRODUCT DEFICIT If D is the physiologically active product of the hypothetical reaction sequence, a block at any of the steps from A to D results in inadequate synthesis of D. The formation of thyroxine in the thyroid gland proceeds through just such a series of reactions, involving first the transport of iodide into the gland and then its subsequent oxidation and organification. Several enzymatic defects lead to goitrous cretinism due to impaired synthesis of thyroxine. Similarly, in some patients with congenital adrenal hyperplasia due to a defect in hydroxylation on carbon 21 of the steroid nucleus, aldosterone production is impaired, leading to renal salt wasting and hyponatremic crises. Deficient synthesis of product may cause overproduction of precursors, as in acute intermittent porphyria, because of loss of feedback control (D → E_{AB}).

PRODUCT EXCESS As shown in Fig. 305-1, the end product of the reaction sequence D is presumed to regulate the activity of E_{AB}, the first enzyme in this biosynthetic pathway. Several inborn errors demonstrate abnormalities in feedback regulation, but the biochemical events involved are not well understood. In some patients with primary gout, urate is overproduced, presumably because the first enzyme in the purine pathway is defective and does not respond to its normal feedback inhibitors, hypoxanthine and adenine. Abnormal feedback control occurs in the congenital adrenal hyperplasias and congenital goitrous cretinism as well, presumably by different chemical mechanisms. In these disorders the formation or release of adrenocorticotropic hormone (ACTH) and thyroid-stimulating hormone (TSH), respectively, is not impeded by their usual "servo" regulators, cortisol and thyroxine, resulting in hyperplasia and functional disturbances in the two target glands.

Faulty feedback control is not the only mechanism capable of producing product excess. In those disorders characterized by enzyme excess, such as hyperuricemia resulting from increased phosphoribosylpyrophosphate (PRPP) synthetase activity (see Chap. 309), product excess is a consequence of a primary acceleration in conversion of precursor to product.

GENETIC HETEROGENEITY

A given abnormal phenotype may be produced by more than one genotype. This genetic heterogeneity is ubiquitous and important. Clinically, an appreciation of genetic heterogeneity has important implications for diagnosis, treatment, and counseling. Elucidation of the mechanisms of heterogeneity is also imperative for understanding the ways in which the human genome can be modified. As noted in Table 305-1, heterogeneity has been discerned using three approaches: clinical, biochemical, and genetic.

FIGURE 305-1 *Schematic representation of metabolic pathway including transport system, enzymes, alternate route, and feedback regulation. (From Rosenberg.)*

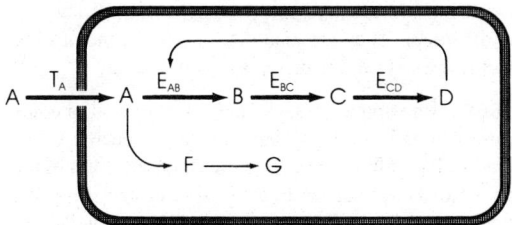

A, B, C, D - Substrate and Products of Major Pathway

F, G - Products of Minor Pathway

T_A - Transport System for A

E_{AB}, E_{BC}, E_{CD} - Enzymes Catalyzing Conversion of A to B, B to C, and C to D

▮ - Cell Membrane

TABLE 305-1   Methods of demonstrating genetic heterogeneity

1 Clinical analysis
  a Age of onset
  b Severity
  c Specific features
2 Biochemical analysis
  a Constituents of blood, urine, and cerebrospinal fluid
  b Enzymatic activity
  c Protein characterization
  d DNA-RNA or DNA-DNA hybridization
3 Genetic analysis
  a Chance matings
  b Mode of inheritance
  c Manifestations in heterozygotes
  d Linkage relationships
  e Complementation in mixed cells or heterokaryons

CLINICAL EVIDENCE   In the absence of independent biochemical or genetic information, it is often impossible to determine whether subtle variations in clinical expression of a given metabolic disorder in affected individuals reflect the presence of different mutations or result from modification of an identical mutation by other genetic and environmental influences. However, information gleaned from biochemical techniques may support the clinical evidence of heterogeneity. For example, patients with juvenile Gaucher's disease probably have an earlier age of onset and a more rapid downhill course than do those with adult Gaucher's disease because the mutant glucocerebrosidase in the former group is distinct from and retains less catalytic activity than that in cells from the latter (see Chap. 316). It follows that tissue glucocerebroside content will increase more rapidly if glucocerebrosidase activity is 3 percent of normal than if it is 15 percent of normal. Similarly, the reason that patients with Hunter's disease do not have corneal clouding, whereas patients with the phenotypically similar Hurler's disease do, almost certainly depends on the different enzymatic dysfunctions in the two disorders: iduronate sulfatase deficiency in Hunter's, α-L-iduronidase deficiency in Hurler's.

BIOCHEMICAL TECHNIQUES   More often, heterogeneity is first defined through chemical or biochemical assays. Such assays vary in design and complexity—from identification of compounds in blood, urine, or cerebrospinal fluid to molecular hybridization analyses. Illustrative examples of disorders shown to be heterogeneous by each of the four kinds of biochemical assays are noted in Table 305-1. For example, the "ketotic hyperglycinemia" syndrome, characterized by episodic ketoacidosis, protein intolerance, and hyperglycinemia, was shown by chemical analyses of blood and urine to be a feature of several different disturbances of organic acid metabolism— α-methylacetoacetic acidemia, propionic acidemia, and methylmalonic acidemia. Patients from different families with "congenital, nonspherocytic hemolytic anemia" were found to have deficiencies in different glycolytic enzymes in the erythrocyte. The nature of the heterogeneity in patients with G_{M2} gangliosidosis did not become apparent until the lysosomal hexoseaminidases were subdivided into A and B isoenzymes whose activities could be measured individually in patients with Tay-Sachs or Sandhoff's disease. Another approach is directed at the gene rather than the gene product. Molecular hybridization experiments employing DNA and RNA provided the evidence for two general categories of β-thalassemia: β^0, characterized by the apparent absence of β-globin mRNA, and β^+, characterized by reduced but detectable amounts of β-globin mRNA. As gene probes for more and more human loci become available, we can anticipate a sharp increase in the use of DNA-DNA hybridization analysis as a means of identifying heterogeneity. Such techniques have already been useful in defining heterogeneity in α- and β-thalassemia, Lesch-Nyhan syndrome, phenlyketonuria, and ornithine transcarbamylase deficiency.

GENETIC METHODS   Genetic methods have also been important in demonstrating heterogeneity (Table 305-1). One of the earliest and most convincing evidences of such heterogeneity came from the chance mating of two individuals each affected with autosomal recessively inherited nerve deafness. None of their progeny was deaf, demonstrating conclusively that the mutations that produced deafness in the parents were different and likely nonallelic. In several instances heterogeneity was suggested by different modes of inheritance of phenotypically similar (or identical) disorders. For example, Hunter's and Hurler's diseases were differentiated early because the former is inherited as an X-linked trait, the latter as an autosomal recessive. Similarly, at least three forms of spastic diplegia are now recognized: one inherited as an autosomal dominant, a second as an autosomal recessive, and a third as an X-linked trait. In a few instances heterogeneity was first appreciated by studying obligate heterozygotes for a recessive phenotype. For example, cystinuria was shown to be heterogeneous by the observation that all obligate heterozygotes in some families excreted increased amounts of cystine and lysine,

whereas in other pedigrees urinary findings in obligate heterozygotes were normal. A fourth genetic tool that has revealed heterogeneity is linkage analysis. Through this type of investigation hereditary elliptocytosis was divided into two forms—one closely linked to the Rh blood group locus, the other not. Finally, heterogeneity has been demonstrated by complementation analyses. The general strategy of such studies is simple. Cultured fibroblasts from two affected individuals are cocultivated in the same dish or are fused into heterokaryons. If the abnormal phenotype expressed in both cell strains remains in the mixed culture, the defect in the two patients is assumed to be identical; if correction occurs in the mixed culture, the defects in the original strains must be different. This approach has been used to define heterogeneity in a wide variety of disorders, including the mucopolysaccharidoses, the G_{M2} gangliosidoses, the methylmalonic acidemias, the propionic acidemias, xeroderma pigmentosum, and branched-chain ketoaciduria. Theoretically, positive complementation tests could reflect either of two general mechanisms: intergenic complementation, in which two different loci are involved, or interallelic complementation, in which two different mutations at the same locus are mutually corrective. The majority of positive complementation tests probably reflects the intergenic mechanism.

COMPOUND HETEROZYGOTES   Some individuals with a given metabolic disorder are "compound heterozygotes" rather than true homozygotes. Compound heterozygotes are individuals who have received a different mutant allele at a given locus from each parent rather than identical mutant alleles. Patients with hemoglobin SC disease were the first compound heterozygotes identified, having inherited the gene for hemoglobin S from one parent and that for hemoglobin C from the other. These individuals have a double dose of a mutation for β-globin-chain synthesis and thus make no normal β chains. They are clinically and chemically distinct from true SS or CC homozygotes. Compound heterozygotes have also been identified in patients with cystinuria, iminoglycinuria, galactose 1-phosphate uridyltransferase deficiency, L-iduronidase deficiency, methylmalonyl-CoA mutase deficiency, and cystathionine synthetase deficiency. Some, but not all, compound heterozygotes are as severely affected as true homozygotes, depending on the nature of the mutant alleles inherited.

DIAGNOSTIC TECHNIQUES AND TARGETS

PHYSIOLOGIC FLUIDS   Most of the early information concerning the inborn errors and their mode of detection came from chemical studies of blood or urine. Such chemical determinations identified specific biochemical abnormalities and provided the clues in many instances for enzymatic studies that clarified the specific defect involved. They also allowed large populations to be screened for specific disorders, thereby facilitating the detection of affected subjects prior to the onset of overt clinical problems. The use of screening tests in blood and urine has allowed the detection of heterozygous carriers for many disorders. They are also often useful in monitoring the effects of specific dietary, drug, or replacement therapy.

TISSUE ANALYSES   Enzymatic assays and biochemical studies using human tissue obtained by biopsy have revealed specific enzymatic defects in more than a hundred metabolic diseases. Membrane transport defects have also been demonstrated in vitro in such disorders as hereditary spherocytosis, cystinuria, and the glucose-galactose malabsorption syndrome. These assays have often identified the biochemical and genetic heterogeneity characteristic of the inborn errors, in addition to documenting specific gene product abnormalities. Tissue studies do not lend themselves to population surveys and have the greatest impact when combined with investigations of abnormalities in blood and urine.

CELL CULTURE   Human fibroblasts grown in tissue culture have also yielded important insights into the biochemistry and genetics of inborn metabolic disorders. In some instances (acatalasia, galactosemia, glucose 6-phosphate dehydrogenase deficiency, glycogen storage disease type II, branched-chain ketoaciduria, and orotic aciduria), enzymatic defects initially described in other tissues were confirmed in cultured fibroblasts. In citrullinemia and Refsum's disease, specific enzymatic defects were first demonstrated in fibroblasts, while in the Lesch-Nyhan syndrome defective hypoxanthine-guanine phosphoribosyl transferase activity was demonstrated coincidently in erythrocytes, leukocytes, and cultured fibroblasts. Abnormalities found in cells from heterozygous carriers have also been of significance. For example, the study in obligate heterozygotes of several X-linked traits provided evidence confirming the validity of the Lyon hypothesis.

DNA ANALYSIS   Use of DNA-DNA blot hybridization techniques for diagnosis of inherited metabolic disorders constitutes one of the most powerful applications of recombinant DNA technology to medicine (see Chap. 58). This approach, often referred to as "Southern blotting," employs DNA isolated from such accessible tissues as peripheral blood leukocytes, cultured fibroblasts, or amniotic fluid cells. The DNA, after being "cut" with restriction endonucleases and sized by gel electrophoresis, is reacted with labeled gene probes specific for particular loci (and, therefore, for particular disorders). When the precise molecular defect responsible for a disorder is known, as in sickle cell disease or the Z variant of α_1-antitrypsin, disease-precise oligonucleotide probes can be employed. In other instances, diagnosis can be accomplished by taking advantage of *restriction fragment length polymorphisms* (RFLP) that segregate in families and constitute useful linkage markers for disease detection (see Chap. 58). Such RFLPs have been employed in detection of Huntington's disease, phenylketonuria, citrullinemia, Lesch-Nyhan syndrome, and ornithine transcarbamylase deficiency.

HETEROZYGOTE DETECTION   The detection of heterozygous carriers contributes to the study of inborn errors in two important ways. First, such detection provides the most convincing evidence for a recessive mode of inheritance of a disorder, whether the mutation is autosomal or X-linked. Second, the identification of heterozygous carriers in a single pedigree provides valuable information for counseling family members. In those diseases in which clinical manifestations may be observed in the carriers (i.e., in dominantly inherited conditions such as acute intermittent porphyria or familial hypercholesterolemia) heterozygote detection has direct clinical relevance.

Identification of heterozygotes can be made by many of the methods employed for the recognition of defects in affected subjects. In a few instances, blood or urine screening techniques may be sufficient to detect carriers. Enzymatic assays using blood cells or serum have been helpful in other conditions. In some disorders blood or urine analyses fail to discriminate between normal subjects and heterozygous carriers, but carriers can be detected after administration of oral or parenteral loads of the metabolic precursor involved in the chemical defect. Thus, heterozygotes for galactosemia and phenylketonuria respond to oral loads of galactose and phenylalanine, respectively, with higher plasma concentrations of these substances than observed in normal subjects. Carriers for a number of diseases have been detected by enzymatic assays or phenotypic appearance of cells in biopsy material. Finally, DNA-DNA hybridization techniques are being used frequently for carrier detection and, importantly, for carrier exclusion. These techniques for carrier detection have usually been worked out and utilized in one laboratory or, in some instances, a few centers. Because of their complexity, they have not been employed for carrier detection in large populations.

PRENATAL DETECTION   There is now considerable interest in the detection of genetic diseases in utero (see Chap. 58). More than 50 inherited metabolic disorders have been identified by chemical examination of amniotic fluid or enzymatic assays on amniotic fluid cells. The largest group of disorders so detected are those mucopolysaccharide or lipid storage diseases due to deficiency of particular lysosomal hydrolases, but disorders of amino acid, organic acid, carbohydrate, and purine metabolism have been identified as well. A few inborn errors have been diagnosed by examination of fetal blood obtained by placental puncture or under fetoscopic control. Sickle cell anemia, β-thalassemia, and hemophilia have been detected in this way. Whereas the above techniques examine gene products or metabolites, diagnosis of other disorders are being accomplished using DNA-DNA blot hybridization techniques. These techniques hold great promise because they can be used on cells such as cultured amniotic fluid cells that contain, but do not express, the genes for many highly differentiated functions including globin and polypeptide hormone synthesis. DNA-DNA blot hybridization has been used prenatally to detect phenylketonuria, α_1-antitrypsin deficiency, hemophilia, sickle cell anemia, thalassemia, and ornithine transcarbamylase deficiency.

GENETIC SCREENING

Genetic screening is the search in a population for persons possessing genotypes that are known to be associated with or to predispose to disease in the individuals or their descendants. As a research tool, screening can define the incidence of a particular genotype in the population and can be used to search for polymorphisms. In the context of discussion of inherited metabolic diseases, however, screening has two important applications: early identification of at-risk patients with treatable disease prior to onset of clinical symptoms and identification of at-risk couples who may benefit from appropriate genetic counseling. A prototypic example of the former application is neonatal screening for phenylketonuria. The features of this screening application include a relatively common disease (about 1:10,000 in whites) with serious clinical consequences (severe mental retardation); evidence that institution of dietary phenylalanine restriction by age 30 days can return blood phenylalanine concentrations to values commensurate with normal or near normal development; and a simple, sensitive, and specific assay that can be performed in the neonatal period. More than 90 percent of neonates in North America and western Europe are screened for phenylketonuria using the bacterial inhibition assay. The human and monetary savings of this screening program have been enormous and have prompted extension to neonatal detection of other treatable diseases such as galactosemia, hypothyroidism, and homocystinuria. Such "secondary" prevention emphasizes the interaction between environment and heredity and raises no serious ethical problems.

That statement, however, cannot be made with regard to the other screening application—identification of couples at risk for having offspring with untreatable (or nearly untreatable) disorders. The prototype is Tay-Sachs disease in Ashkenazi Jews. When two Ashkenazim marry, there is a 1:900 chance that both individuals are carriers for the Tay-Sachs gene. Theoretically, if all Ashkenazim were screened before marriage, if all pregnancies in at-risk couples were monitored by prenatal diagnosis, and if all affected fetuses were aborted, the incidence of Tay-Sachs disease could be decreased to zero. However, mandatory screening is not possible, and compliance for voluntary testing is poor. Education, motivation, and effective follow-up are crucial to the success of such a venture. Similar programs have been mounted in the black community, where 1:100 couples are at risk for having children with sickle cell anemia. Early programs were not only ineffective but indeed counterproductive, owing to inadequate pretesting educational programs, misunderstanding about the difference between sickle trait and sickle cell disease, and penalties for diagnosis levied by employers and insurance companies. This debacle points out the importance of ethical and social issues in such screening programs.

TREATMENT

Effective therapy is available for many inherited metabolic disorders, particularly those in which the biochemical abnormalities have been defined. As more is learned about the mutations responsible for specific disorders and about the chemical consequences of the mutations, other inborn errors will surely be controlled or modified by specific therapeutic programs. Two potential levels of treatment exist: the first is directed to means by which the basic genotype of the affected subject can be altered; the second aims to manipulate the environment so as to mitigate the harmful effect of the mutant phenotype. Successful therapy of the inborn errors has, thus far, been achieved only at the latter level. Although there is great interest in the possibility of genotypic alteration in humans, clinical application remains only a hope.

Several prerequisites are necessary for successful therapy at the phenotypic level. The correct diagnosis must be established. Some inborn errors such as phenylketonuria have harmless phenocopies that produce transient but similar biochemical abnormalities in the newborn. Whereas a low-phenylalanine diet mitigates the central nervous system complications of true phenylketonuria, such a diet may have catastrophic effects on the growth and development of a newborn with transient hyperphenylalaninemia due to delayed maturation of phenylalanine hydroxylase. Next, the physician must be convinced that the disorder is harmful and requires therapy. As stated earlier, some inborn errors such as pentosuria or iminoglycinuria do not appear to cause any significant clinical pathology and require no treatment. Finally, any therapeutic program must be continually scrutinized for evidence of harmful effects as well as for documentation of beneficial effects of therapy. These may be difficult parameters to dissociate. Penicillamine is an effective drug in Wilson's disease because of its ability to chelate copper; it is also efficacious in solubilizing and preventing the formation of cystine stones in cystinuria. Unfortunately, penicillamine also causes untoward effects that limit its usefulness and demand careful medical follow-up.

MODALITIES EMPLOYED Phenotypic modification has been approached in many ways, depending on the nature of the defect and the timing of its deleterious effects. Both medical and surgical modalities have been employed, the range and experience with the former far exceeding those with the latter. Five medical modalities have been used and will be described briefly.

Avoidance For several disorders, clinical consequences can be mitigated or forestalled entirely by avoiding exposure to particular environmental influences. For example, the hemolytic episodes in patients with G6PD deficiency can be modified significantly by avoiding exposure to such drugs as primaquine or sulfonamides and to such foods as fava beans. Similarly, the prolonged apnea that occurs after succinylcholine administration in individuals deficient in pseudocholinesterase activity will not occur if this anesthetic is not used. Avoiding barbiturates and many other drugs in acute intermittent porphyria and avoidance of tobacco smoke and other noxious fumes in alpha$_1$-antitrypsin deficiency are examples of this approach.

Restriction There are numerous disorders in which the phenotypic abnormalities result from the accumulation of a specific substrate or its metabolic by-products. Such disorders may respond to restriction of intake of the injurious substrate or its precursors, providing that the substrate is essential in the dietary sense and thus cannot be manufactured by the organism. Phenylketonuria, branched-chain ketoaciduria, homocystinuria, galactosemia, essential fructosuria, and Refsum's disease are examples of inborn errors that have been effectively treated in this way. Similarly, patients with the glucose-galactose malabsorption syndrome who develop profound diarrhea when fed lactose-containing foods do well if their source of dietary carbohydrate is changed. In contrast, dietary restriction is of no value in hyperprolinemia, hydroxyprolinemia, or citrullinemia, because these amino acids are synthesized extensively de novo. Even in those conditions in which dietary restriction is of value, there may be uncertainty about the needed duration of such restriction. The injurious effects of excess phenylalanine, galactose, or branched-chain amino acids or keto acids may be limited to the early years of life when brain development and organization are proceeding at a maximal

rate. If this is so, it should be possible to modify or even discontinue dietary restrictions after a given age. More experience is needed before meaningful recommendations can be made.

Replacement Many disorders caused by the failure to make a specific protein or small-molecular-weight product have responded dramatically to replacement therapy. Hemophilia and agammaglobulinemia are examples of inborn errors that respond to parenteral protein replacement. These disorders are amenable to such replacement because the proteins involved normally circulate in abundance. In most instances, however, the missing protein or enzyme is confined to some intracellular organelle and is present in very small amounts. Replacement therapy in these instances may be difficult or impossible for three reasons: first, because large amounts of the protein are difficult to purify or synthesize; second, because mere parenteral administration of the protein will not ensure its delivery to that portion of the cell in which it is required; and third, because the protein may initiate unfavorable immunologic reactions. Despite these drawbacks, attempts along these lines continue to be made. For example, pure human glucocerebrosidase has been administered intravenously to a few patients with Gaucher's disease. Tissue glucocerebroside content fell modestly in these patients, suggesting that some enzyme was being taken up by cells and was active intracellularly, for a brief interval. As we learn more about the mechanisms by which proteins are targeted to different cellular organelles, such replacement strategies may become more effective.

The clinical stigmata of a disorder may be related not to the protein whose synthesis is defective but rather to the product of the blocked pathway. Cortisol synthesis is blocked in several variants of congenital adrenal hyperplasia, and replacement therapy with this steroid produces dramatic improvement. Similarly, administration of thyroid hormone and uridine reverses the serious clinical disturbances in familial goitrous cretinism and orotic aciduria, respectively.

Supplementation Some metabolic disorders respond clinically and/or chemically to supplementary amounts of specific vitamins. Infants with seizures controlled only by supraphysiologic amounts of pyridoxine provided the first evidence for this phenomenon. Now more than 20 different disorders are known to respond to supplements of a single vitamin. Most of these disorders are caused by primary enzymatic disturbances that result in impaired affinity for cofactor. Others are caused by primary abnormalities in the pathway of coenzyme or metabolite synthesis from vitamin precursors. Several disorders responsive to cobalamin (vitamin B$_{12}$), folate, or vitamin D fall in this category. Long-term experience with such vitamin supplements is limited.

Drug administration Clinical disturbances in several inherited metabolic disorders result from deposition of a specific substance in one or more tissues. Successful treatment of these conditions may be achieved by enhancing the excretion of the stored chemical or by preventing its formation. Copper deposition in Wilson's disease can be controlled by drugs such as penicillamine, which chelates copper and enhances its urinary excretion. The excretion of iron in hemochromatosis is augmented by phlebotomy and by the administration of deferoxamine. Penicillamine is also effective in solubilizing cystine calculi in cystinuria by reacting with cystine to form the more soluble cysteine-penicillamine disulfide. In this instance, the amount of cystine excreted is not changed, but its chemical form is altered in a therapeutically advantageous fashion. Uric acid deposition in gout responds both to drugs that enhance its excretion, such as sulfinpyrazone and probenecid, and to metabolic inhibitors like allopurinol that inhibit uric acid biosynthesis.

Surgical intervention The use of surgery is restricted to a few conditions, such as gout, cystinuria, and oxalosis, in which nephrolithotomy or ureterolithotomy may provide important symptomatic relief while other programs of therapy are initiated. Several reports indicate that tissue transplants may be beneficial in some diseases. Thus, kidney transplants have been undertaken in cystinosis, hyperoxaluria, and Fabry's disease. Here the aim is restoration of renal function in conditions which produce progressive, and ultimately lethal, renal injury. Results have been variable. In hyperoxaluria, the transplanted kidney has been destroyed by oxalate deposition. In cystinosis, this has not occurred. A second, and different, goal of transplantation involves restitution of normal function. Thus, in combined immune deficiency, administration of fetal liver cells or thymocytes has produced clinical improvement. Similar beneficial results of bone marrow transplantation have been reported in other immune deficiency diseases and in β-thalassemia. In the future, spleen transplantation may provide lasting benefit to patients with hemophilia or agammaglobulinemia by providing a constant source of antihemophilic globulin or gamma globulin, respectively. Likewise, hepatic transplantation has been used successfully to cure Wilson's disease, tyrosinemia, and the homozygous form of familial hypercholesterolemia. This modality will surely be tried in other inborn errors as its morbidity and mortality fall to the range where risk-benefit assessment favors its application in conditions such as glycogen storage disease, branched-chain ketoaciduria, and disorders of urea cycle enzymes.

REFERENCES

HARRIS H: *The Principles of Human Biochemical Genetics*, 3d ed. Amsterdam, North-Holland, 1980

ROSENBERG LE: Inborn errors of metabolism, in *Metabolic Control and Disease*, 8th ed, PK Bondy, LE Rosenberg (eds). Philadelphia, Saunders, 1980, pp 73–102

STANBURY JB et al: Inborn errors of metabolism in the 1980s, in *The Metabolic Basis of Inherited Disease*, 5th ed, JB Stanbury et al (eds). New York, McGraw-Hill, 1983, pp 3–59

306 INHERITED DISORDERS OF AMINO ACID METABOLISM

LEON E. ROSENBERG

All polypeptides and proteins are polymers of 20 different amino acids. Eight of these, referred to as *essential,* cannot be synthesized by humans and must be obtained from dietary sources. The others are formed endogenously. Although most of the body's amino acids are "tied up" in proteins, small intracellular pools of *free* amino acids are in equilibrium with extracellular reservoirs in plasma, cerebrospinal fluid, and the lumina of the gut and kidney. Physiologically, amino acids are more than mere "building blocks." Some (glycine, γ-aminobutyric acid) are neurotransmitters. Others (phenylalanine, tyrosine, tryptophan, glycine) are precursors of hormones, coenzymes, pigments, purines, or pyrimidines. Each has a unique degradative pathway by which its nitrogen and carbon components are used for the synthesis of other amino acids, carbohydrates, and lipids.

Current concepts of inherited metabolic diseases are based to a considerable degree on investigations of amino acid disorders. More than 70 inherited aminoacidopathies are now known, the catabolic defects (approximately 60) discussed in this and the following chapter far outnumbering the transport abnormalities (approximately 10) considered in Chap. 308. Each of these disorders is rare—the incidences range from 1 in 10,000 for phenylketonuria to 1 in 200,000 for alkaptonuria. Collectively, however, they occur in perhaps 1 in 500 to 1 in 1000 live births.

The salient features of inherited disorders of amino acid catabolism are summarized in Table 306-1. In general, these disorders are named for the compound which accumulates to highest concentration in blood (*-emias*) or urine (*-urias*). For many conditions the parent amino acid is found in excess; for others, products in the catabolic pathway accumulate. Which process takes place depends, of course,

on the site of the enzymatic block, the reversibility of the reactions proximal to the lesion, and the existence of alternate pathways of metabolic "run-off." For some amino acids, such as the sulfur-containing or branched-chain molecules, defects at nearly each step in the catabolic pathway have been described. For others numerous gaps in our knowledge remain. Biochemical and genetic heterogeneity are common among the aminoacidopathies. Four distinct forms of hyperphenylalaninemia, three variants of homocystinuria, and five types of methylmalonic acidemia are recognized—variants of both chemical and clinical interest.

The manifestations of these conditions differ widely (Table 306-1). Some, such as sarcosinemia or hyperprolinemia, appear to produce no clinical consequences. At the other extreme, complete deficiency of ornithine transcarbamylase or of branched-chain keto acid dehydrogenase causes neonatal death in the untreated patient. Central nervous system dysfunction, in the form of developmental retardation, seizures, alterations in sensorium, or behavioral disturbances, occurs in more than half of the disorders. Protein-induced vomiting, neurologic dysfunction, and hyperammonemia occur in many disorders of urea cycle intermediates. Metabolic ketoacidosis often accompanied by hyperammonemia is a frequent presenting finding in the disorders of branched-chain amino acid metabolism. Occasional disorders produce focal tissue or organ involvement such as liver disease, renal failure, cutaneous abnormalities, or ocular lesions.

The clinical manifestations in many of these conditions can be prevented or mitigated if diagnosis is achieved early and appropriate treatment (i.e., dietary protein or amino acid restriction or vitamin supplementation) is instituted promptly. For this reason, aminoacidopathies are screened for in mass newborn surveys which analyze blood or urine with an array of chemical and microbiologic techniques. Once a presumptive diagnosis is made, confirmation can be provided by direct enzyme assay on extracts of leukocytes, erythrocytes, cultured fibroblasts, or liver or by DNA-DNA hybridization studies. The latter approach has been used to diagnose and characterize phenylketonuria, ornithine transcarbamylase deficiency, citrullinemia, and propionic acidemia. As additional genes are cloned, DNA-based analysis will become more common. Several disorders (cystinosis, branched-chain ketoaciduria, propionic acidemia, methylmalonic acidemia, phenylketonuria, ornithine transcarbamylase deficiency, citrullinemia, and argininosuccinic aciduria) have been diagnosed in utero by chemical analysis or by DNA-DNA blot hybridization on cultured amniotic fluid cells. The remainder of this and the subsequent chapter are focused on selected disorders that illustrate the problems posed by aminoacidopathies.

THE HYPERPHENYLALANINEMIAS

DEFINITION The hyperphenylalaninemias (Table 306-1), result from impaired conversion of phenylalanine to tyrosine. The most important is phenylketonuria, which is characterized by an increased concentration of phenylalanine in blood, increased concentrations of phenylalanine and its by-products (notably phenylpyruvate, phenylacetate, phenyllactate, and phenylacetylglutamine) in urine, and severe mental retardation.

ETIOLOGY AND PATHOGENESIS Each of the hyperphenylalaninemias results from reduced activity of the enzyme complex called *phenylalanine hydroxylase.* This system is found in appreciable amounts only in liver and kidney. Phenylalanine and molecular oxygen are substrates for the enzyme which requires a reduced pteridine, tetrahydrobiopterin, as a cofactor. Tyrosine and dihydrobiopterin are the products of this catalytic system, the latter being reconverted to tetrahydrobiopterin by a second enzyme, dihydropteridine reductase. In classic phenylketonuria, activity of the hydroxylase apoenzyme is almost totally deficient but the hydroxylase gene is present and not grossly rearranged or deleted. Benign hyperphenylalaninemia results from a less complete deficiency, whereas transient hyperphenylalaninemia (sometimes called transient phenylketonuria)

TABLE 306-1   Inherited disorders of amino acid catabolism

Amino acid(s) affected	Disorder or condition	Enzyme defect	Clinical manifestations*			
			Mental retardation	Neuropsychiatric dysfunction	Protein intolerance	Metabolic ketoacidosis
AROMATIC—HETEROCYCLIC						
Phenylalanine	Classic phenylketonuria	Phenylalanine hydroxylase	+	+	−	−
	Benign hyperphenylala-ninemia	Phenylalanine hydroxylase	−	−	−	−
	Transient hyperphenylala-ninemia	Phenylalanine hydroxylase	−	−	−	−
	Variant phenylketonuria	Dihydropteridine reductase	+	+	−	−
	Variant phenylketonuria	Dihydrobiopterin synthetase (?)	+	+	−	−
Tyrosine	Hypertyrosinemia	Tyrosine aminotransferase (cytosol)	+	−	−	−
	Tyrosinosis	Tyrosine aminotransferase (?)	−	−	−	−
	Hereditary tyrosinemia	Unknown	−	−	−	−
	Alkaptonuria	Homogentisic acid oxidase	−	−	−	−
	Albinism (oculocuta-neous)	Tyrosinase	−	−	−	−
	Albinism (ocular)	Unknown	−	−	−	−
Tryptophan	Tryptophanuria	Unknown	+	+	−	−
	Xanthurenic aciduria	Kynureninase	?	−	−	−
Histidine	Histidinemia	Histidine-ammonia lyase	±	±	−	−
	Urocanic aciduria	Urocanase	+	+	−	−
	Formiminoglutamic aciduria	Formiminotransferase	?	+	−	−
GLYCINE-IMINO ACIDS						
Glycine	Hyperglycinemia	Glycine cleavage	+	+	−	−
	Sarcosinemia	Sarcosine dehydrogenase	−	−	−	−
	Hyperoxaluria (type I)	α-Ketoglutarate: glyoxylate carboligase	−	−	−	−
	Hyperoxaluria (type II)	D-Glyceric acid dehydrogen-ase	−	−	−	−
Imino acids	Hyperprolinemia (type I)	Proline oxidase	−	−	−	−
	Hyperprolinemia (type II)	Δ′-Pyrroline dehydrogenase	−	−	−	−
	Hyperhydroxyprolinemia	Hydroxyproline reductase	−	−	−	−
	Iminopeptiduria	Prolidase	+	−	−	−
SULFUR-CONTAINING						
Methionine	Hypermethioninemia	Methionine adenosyltransfer-ase	−	−	−	−
Homocystine	Homocystinuria	Cystathionine β-synthase	±	±	−	−
	Homocystinuria	5,10-Methylenetetrahydro-folate reductase	±	±	−	−
	Homocystinuria and methylmalonic acidemia (cbl C, D, E)‡	Cobalamin (vitamin B$_{12}$) re-ductase (cytosol) (?)	±	±	−	−
Cystathionine	Cystathioninuria	Cystathionase	±	−	−	−
Cystine	Cystinosis	Unknown	−	−	−	−
S-Sulfo-L-cys-teine	S-Sulfo-L-cysteine, sul-fite, and thiosulfaturia	Sulfite oxidase	+	+	−	−
CATIONIC						
Lysine	Hyperlysinemia (type I)	Lysine dehydrogenase	−	+	+	−
	Hyperlysinemia (type II)	Lysine: α-ketoglutarate re-ductase	±	±	−	−
	Saccharopinuria	Saccharopine dehydrogenase	−	−	−	−
	Hydroxylysinemia	Unknown	+	−	−	−
	Pipecolic acidemia	Unknown	+	+	−	−
	α-Ketoadipic aciduria	α-Ketoadipic acid decarbox-ylase	±	±	−	−
	Glutaric aciduria (type I)	Glutaryl CoA dehydrogenase	−	+	−	−
	Glutaric aciduria (type II)	Medium-chain acyl CoA de-hydrogenase (?)	−	+	−	−
Ornithine	Hyperornithinemia (type I)	Ornithine decarboxylase	+	+	+	−
	Hyperornithinemia (type II)	Ornithine aminotransferase	−	−	−	−
UREA CYCLE						
Carbamyl-phosphate	Hyperammonemia (type I)	Carbamylphosphate synthe-tase I	+	+	+	−
N-acetylgluta-mate	Hyperammonemia (type IA)	N-acetylglutamate synthetase	?	+	+	−

* +, regularly present; ±, sometimes present; −, absent; ?, uncertain; all designations refer to manifestations in untreated disorder.
† AR, autosomal recessive; XL, X-linked; (AR), probably autosomal recessive.
‡ Designations in parentheses refer to complementation groups assigned by genetic analysis with cultured cells.

Ammonia intoxication	Other	Inheritance pattern†
−	Hypopigmented skin and hair, eczema	AR
−		AR
−		(AR)
−		(AR)
−		(AR)
−	Palmar keratosis, corneal dystrophy	(AR)
−	Myasthenia gravis	?
−	Cirrhosis, hepatic failure, renal tubular dysfunction	AR
−	Ochronosis, arthritis	AR
−	Hypopigmentation of hair, skin, and optic fundus	AR
−	Hypopigmentation of optic fundus	XL
−	Photosensitive skin rash	AR
−		?
−	Hearing and speech deficit	AR
−		?
−		(AR)
−		AR
−		AR
−	Renal failure	AR
−	Calcium oxalate nephrolithiasis, renal failure	AR
−		AR
−		AR
−		AR
−	Crusting erythematous, ecchymotic dermatitis	AR
−		?
−	Dislocated lenses, osteoporosis, thrombotic vascular disease	AR
−		(AR)
−	Megaloblastic anemia	(AR)
−		AR
−	Fanconi syndrome, renal failure, photophobia	AR
−	Dislocated lenses	AR
+		?
−		AR
−		?
−		(AR)
−	Hepatomegaly, dysplastic optic disks	?
−		?
−		AR
−	Hypoglycemia	?
+		(AR)
−	Gyrate atrophy of choroid and retina	AR
+		AR
+		XL

(Table continues next page)

is caused by a delayed maturation of the hydroxylase apoenzyme. In two variants of phenylketonuria, however, persistently impaired hydroxylating activity results not from abnormality in the apohydroxylase but from a lack of tetrahydrobiopterin. The tetrahydrobiopterin deficiency has two distinct metabolic bases: a block in the pathway by which biopterin is synthesized from its precursors or deficiency of dihydropteridine reductase, the enzyme that regenerates tetrahydrobiopterin from dihydrobiopterin.

As a group the hyperphenylalaninemias occur in about 1 in 10,000 births. Classic phenylketonuria, which accounts for nearly half of these, is an autosomal recessive trait and is widely distributed among whites and Orientals. It is rare in blacks. Phenylalanine hydroxylase activity in obligate heterozygotes is less than normal but higher than it is in homozygotes. Heterozygous carriers are clinically well but usually have slightly increased phenylalanine concentrations in plasma. The other hyperphenylalaninemias also appear to be inherited as autosomal recessive traits.

Phenylalanine accumulation in blood and urine and reduced tyrosine formation are direct consequences of the impaired hydroxylation. In untreated phenylketonuria and in its tetrahydrobiopterin-deficient variants, plasma concentrations of phenylalanine become sufficiently high (greater than 20 mg/dL) to activate alternate pathways of metabolism and lead to formation of phenylpyruvate, phenylacetate, phenyllactate, and other derivatives that are rapidly cleared by the kidney and excreted in urine. Plasma concentrations of several other amino acids are moderately reduced, probably secondary to inhibition of gastrointestinal absorption or impairment of renal tubular reabsorption by the excess phenylalanine in body fluids. The severe brain damage appears to be related to several consequences of phenylalanine accumulation: deprivation of other amino acids required for protein synthesis, impaired polyribosome formation or stabilization, reduced myelin synthesis, and inadequate formation of norepinephrine and serotonin. Phenylalanine is a competitive inhibitor of tyrosinase, a key enzyme in the pathway of melanin synthesis. This block plus reduced availability of the melanin precursor, tyrosine, accounts for the hypopigmentation of hair and skin.

CLINICAL MANIFESTATIONS No abnormalities are apparent at birth. Untreated children with classic phenylketonuria fail to attain early developmental milestones and demonstrate progressive impairment of cerebral function. Most require chronic institutionalization within a few years of birth because of the hyperactivity and seizures that accompany the severe mental retardation. Electroencephalogram abnormalities, "mousy" odor of skin, hair, and urine (due to phenylacetate accumulation), and a tendency to hypopigmentation and eczema complete the devastating clinical picture. In contrast, children who are detected at birth and treated promptly show none of these abnormalities. Children with transient hyperphenylalaninemia or with the benign variant are not at risk for any of the clinical consequences seen in untreated classic phenylketonuria. Those children with tetrahydrobiopterin deficiency, however, are the most unfortunate. Seizures appear early, followed by progressive cerebral and basal ganglia dysfunction (rigidity, chorea, spasms, hypotonia). Each has succumbed to secondary infection within a few years despite early diagnosis and standard treatment.

Occasionally, women with untreated classic phenylketonuria have reached adulthood and had children. More than 90 percent of the offspring are markedly retarded, and many exhibit other congenital anomalies such as microcephaly, growth retardation, and congenital heart defects. Since these children are heterozygous, not homozygous for the phenylketonuria mutation, the clinical manifestations must be attributed to damage produced by the elevated maternal concentrations of phenylalanine to which they have been exposed in utero.

DIAGNOSIS Plasma phenylalanine concentrations may be normal at birth in all the hyperphenylalaninemias but rise rapidly after institution of protein feedings and are usually abnormal by day 4. Since diagnosis and initiation of dietary treatment of classic phenylketonuria must be completed before the child is 30 days of age if

TABLE 306-1 Inherited disorders of amino acid catabolism (continued)

Amino acid(s) affected	Disorder or condition	Enzyme defect	Clinical manifestations*			
			Mental retardation	Neuropsychiatric dysfunction	Protein intolerance	Metabolic ketoacidosis
UREA CYCLE (continued)						
Ornithine	Hyperammonemia (type II)	Ornithine transcarbamylase	±	+	+	−
Citrulline	Citrullinemia	Argininosuccinate synthetase	+	+	+	−
Argininosuccinic acid	Argininosuccinic aciduria	Argininosuccinase	+	+	+	−
Arginine	Argininemia	Arginase	+	+	+	−
BRANCHED-CHAIN						
Valine	Hypervalinemia	Valine aminotransferase	+	+	+	−
Leucine, isoleucine	Hyperleucine-isoleucinemia	Leucine-isoleucine aminotransferase	+	+	+	−
Valine, leucine, isoleucine	Classic branched-chain ketoaciduria	Branched-chain ketoacid dehydrogenase	+	+	+	
	Intermittent branched-chain ketoaciduria	Branched-chain ketoacid dehydrogenase	±	−	+	+
Leucine	Isovaleric acidemia	Isovaleryl CoA dehydrogenase	±	±	+	+
	β-Methylcrotonyl glycinuria	β-Methylcrotonyl CoA carboxylase	+	+	−	+
	β-Hydroxy-β-methylglutaric aciduria	β-Hydroxy-β-methylglutaryl CoA lyase	−	+	+	+
Isoleucine, valine	α-Methylacetoacetic aciduria	β-Ketothiolase	±	±	+	+
	Propionic acidemia (pcc A, B, C)‡	Propionyl CoA carboxylase	±	±	+	+
	Propionic acidemia (bio)‡	Holocarboxylase synthetase; biotinidase	+	±	+	+
	Methylmalonic acidemia (mut)‡	Methylmalonyl CoA mutase	±	±	+	+
	Methylmalonic acidemia (cbl A)‡	Cobalamin (vitamin B_{12}) reductase (mitochondrial) (?)	±	±	+	+
	Methylmalonic acidemia (cbl B)‡	Cobalamin (vitamin B_{12}): ATP adenosyltransferase	±	±	+	+
DICARBOXYLIC						
Glutamic acid	Glutathionemia	γ-Glutamyl-transpeptidase	+	−	−	−
5-Oxoprolinuria	Glutathione synthetase	±	±	±		

* +, regularly present; ±, sometimes present; −, absent; ?, uncertain; all designations refer to manifestations in untreated disorder.
† AR, autosomal recessive; XL, X-linked; (AR), probably autosomal recessive.
‡ Designations in parentheses refer to complementation groups.

developmental retardation is to be prevented, most newborns in North America and Europe are screened by determinations of blood phenylalanine concentration using the Guthrie bacterial inhibition assay. Infants with abnormal values are followed up with more quantitative fluorometric or chromatographic assays. In classic phenylketonuria and in tetrahydrobiopterin deficiency, values greater than 20 mg/dL are regularly observed. In transient or benign hyperphenylalaninemia concentrations are usually lower but above control values of less than 1 mg/dL. Distinction of classic phenylketonuria from its benign variants depends on following serial plasma phenylalanine concentrations as a function of age and dietary restriction. In transient hyperphenylalaninemia plasma values return to normal within 3 to 4 months. In benign hyperphenylalaninemia dietary restriction produces a more profound fall in plasma phenylalanine than that observed in classic phenylketonuria. Deficiency of tetrahydrobiopterin must be considered in any child with hyperphenylalaninemia who develops progressive neurologic impairment despite prompt diagnosis and dietary treatment. Diagnostic confirmation of these variants, which account for 1 to 5 percent of phenylketonuric children, can be achieved by enzyme assay on cultured fibroblasts. Of potentially greater therapeutic value, however, is the observation that administration of oral tetrahydrobiopterin loads can distinguish children with classic phenylketonuria (who show no chemical response) from those with tetrahydrobiopterin deficiency (who exhibit a sharp fall in plasma phenylalanine). Prenatal diagnosis of classic phenylketonuria is now feasible using restriction length polymorphisms identified by DNA-DNA blot hybridization.

TREATMENT Classic phenylketonuria is the first inherited metabolic disease in which it was demonstrated that mitigating the accumulation of the offending metabolite prevented the clinical abnormalities. This is accomplished by a special diet in which the bulk of protein is replaced by an artificial amino acid mixture low in phenylalanine. By supplementing this formula with a small amount of natural foods, an amount of dietary phenylalanine is provided that is sufficient for normal growth but is insufficient to produce markedly increased quantities of phenylalanine in blood. Ordinarily, plasma phenylalanine concentrations are maintained between 3 and 12 mg/dL.

Until it is determined whether dietary treatment can be terminated safely at any age, dietary restriction in classic phenylketonuria should be continued indefinitely. The transient and benign forms of hyperphenylalaninemia do not require long-term dietary restriction. As mentioned earlier, children with tetrahydrobiopterin deficiency deteriorate despite dietary phenylalanine restriction; efficacy of pteridine cofactor replacement is under study.

THE HOMOCYSTINURIAS

The homocystinurias are three biochemically and clinically distinct disorders (Table 306-1), each characterized by increased concentration of the sulfur-containing amino acid, homocystine, in blood and urine. The most common form results from reduced activity of cystathionine β-synthase, an enzyme in the transsulfuration pathway by which methionine is converted to cysteine. The two other forms are the

Ammonia intoxication	Other	Inheritance pattern†
+		AR
+		AR
+		AR
+		
−		?
−		?
−	"Maple syrup" odor	AR
−		AR
±	"Sweaty feet" odor	AR
−	"Cat's urine" odor	AR
−		?
+		AR
+		AR
−		?
+		AR
+		AR
+		AR
−		?
−		AR

of patients synthase activity in liver, brain, leukocytes, and cultured fibroblasts is undetectable. In the remaining patients, tissues retain 1 to 5 percent of normal activity, and this residual activity can often be stimulated by pyridoxine supplementation. Heterozygous carriers of this autosomal recessive trait show no reproducible chemical abnormalities in body fluids but have reduced tissue synthase activity.

Homocysteine interferes with the normal cross-linking of collagen, an effect that likely plays an important role in the ocular, skeletal, and vascular complications. Altered collagen in the suspensory ligament of the optic lens and in bone matrix may account for the dislocated lenses and osteoporosis. Similarly, interference with normal ground substance metabolism in vascular walls may predispose to the arterial and venous thrombotic diathesis. Recurrent cerebrovascular accidents secondary to thrombotic disease may account for the mental retardation, but direct chemical effects on cerebral cell metabolism have not been excluded.

Clinical manifestations   More than 80 percent of homozygotes for complete synthase deficiency have dislocated optic lenses. This abnormality usually appears by 3 to 4 years of age and often results in acute glaucoma as well as impaired visual acuity. Mental retardation occurs in about half of such patients, often accompanied by ill-defined behavioral disturbances. Osteoporosis is a common radiologic finding (seen in 64 percent of patients by age 15) but rarely causes clinical disease. Life-threatening vascular complications, probably initiated by damage to vascular endothelium, are the major cause of morbidity and mortality. Occlusion of coronary, renal, and cerebral arteries with attendant tissue infarction can occur during the first decade of life. Nearly one-quarter of patients die of vascular disease before age 30. These vascular complications seem to be exacerbated by angiographic procedures. Importantly, pyridoxine-responsive patients have milder clinical manifestations in all regards. Heterozygous carriers for synthase deficiency (about 1 in 70 in the population) may be at increased risk for premature peripheral and cerebral occlusive vascular disease.

Diagnosis   The cyanide-nitroprusside test is a simple way of demonstrating increased excretion of sulfhydryl-containing compounds in urine. Since cystine and S-sulfocysteine also give a positive test, other disorders of sulfur metabolism must be excluded, but this is usually possible on clinical grounds. Distinction of cystathionine β-synthase deficiency from other causes of homocystinuria can usually be accomplished by measurements of plasma methionine, which tend to be increased in synthase-deficient patients and normal or low in those with impaired methionine formation (see below). Diagnostic confirmation depends on measurements of synthase activity in tissue extracts. Heterozygotes can be identified by measurement of peak serum homocystine after an oral methionine load and by measurement of tissue synthase activity.

Treatment   As with classic phenylketonuria, effective treatment depends on early diagnosis. A few infants diagnosed in the newborn period have been treated successfully with methionine-restricted, cystine-supplemented diets. Their clinical course has, thus far, been benign compared with that of untreated affected siblings. In approximately half of patients, oral supplements of pyridoxine (25 to 500 mg per day) produce a fall in plasma and urinary methionine and homocystine and an increase in cystine concentration in body fluids. This effect probably reflects a modest increase in synthase activity in cells of patients in whom the enzymatic defect is characterized by either reduced affinity for cofactor or accelerated degradation of mutant enzyme. Since such vitamin supplementation is simple and apparently harmless, it should be tried in all patients. There are no reports of the effect of pyridoxine supplementation therapy that has been initiated soon after birth. Similarly, there are no data regarding pyridoxine supplements in heterozygous carriers.

5,10-METHYLENETETRAHYDROFOLATE REDUCTASE DEFICIENCY Definition   In this form of homocystinuria, methionine concentrations in body fluids are normal or decreased because

result of impaired conversion of homocysteine to methionine, a reaction catalyzed by homocysteine:methyltetrahydrofolate methyltransferase and two essential cofactors methyltetrahydrofolate and methylcobalamin (methyl–vitamin B_{12}). Depending on the underlying disorder, some patients with each of the homocystinurias show chemical and, in some instances, clinical improvement following administration of specific vitamin supplements (pyridoxine, folate, or cobalamin).

CYSTATHIONINE β-SYNTHASE DEFICIENCY Definition   Deficiency of this enzyme leads to increased concentrations of methionine and homocystine in body fluids and to decreased concentrations of cysteine and cystine. The clinical hallmark is dislocated optic lenses. Mental retardation, osteoporosis, and thrombotic vascular disease are frequent.

Etiology and pathogenesis   The sulfur atom of the essential amino acid methionine is transferred ultimately to cysteine by a series of reactions designated as the transsulfuration pathway. In one of these steps, homocysteine condenses with serine to form cystathionine. This reaction is catalyzed by the pyridoxal phosphate–dependent enzyme, cystathionine β-synthase. More than 600 patients have been described with deficiency of this enzyme. The condition is common in Ireland (1 in 40,000 births) but rare elsewhere (less than 1 in 200,000 births).

Homocysteine and methionine accumulate in cells and body fluids; cysteine synthesis is impaired, resulting in reduced concentrations of this amino acid and its disulfide form, cystine. In approximately half

deficiency of 5,10-methylenetetrahydrofolate reductase leads to impaired synthesis of 5-methyltetrahydrofolate, a cofactor in the enzymatic formation of methionine from homocysteine. Central nervous system dysfunction occurs in most patients.

Etiology and pathogenesis   5-Methyltetrahydrofolate:homocysteine methyltransferase catalyzes the conversion of homocysteine to methionine. The methyl group transferred in this reaction comes from 5-methyltetrahydrofolate, which is converted to tetrahydrofolate in the process. 5-Methyltetrahydrofolate, in turn, is synthesized enzymatically from 5,10-methylenetetrahydrofolate by another enzyme, 5,10-methylenetetrahydrofolate reductase. Thus, reductase activity controls both methionine synthesis and tetrahydrofolate generation. This series of reactions is critical to normal DNA and RNA synthesis. A primary defect in the reductase activity results, secondarily, in deficient methyltransferase activity and impaired conversion of homocysteine to methionine. Methionine deficiency and impaired nucleic acid synthesis may contribute to the central nervous system dysfunction. The disorder appears to be inherited as an autosomal recessive trait.

Clinical manifestations   Fewer than 10 children with homocystinuria due to reductase deficiency have been reported. The most severely affected have presented with profound developmental retardation and cerebral atrophy early in life. Others manifested behavioral disturbances (catatonia) during the second decade or mild retardation. Presumably the severity of the clinical manifestations reflects the severity of the reductase deficiency.

Diagnosis and treatment   The combination of increased concentrations of homocystine in body fluids with normal or decreased concentrations of methionine should suggest this entity. Serum folate concentrations are low in some patients. Confirmation requires direct reductase assays in tissue extracts (brain, liver, cultured fibroblasts). Although therapeutic experience is limited, one teenage girl with a catatonic psychosis responded dramatically, both chemically and clinically, to folate supplements (5 to 10 mg per day). When the folate was withdrawn, behavior worsened. This observation suggests that early diagnosis followed by folate supplementation may forestall neurologic or psychiatric disturbances.

DEFICIENCY OF COBALAMIN (VITAMIN B₁₂) COENZYME SYNTHESIS   Definition   This form of homocystinuria also reflects impaired conversion of homocysteine to methionine. The primary defect is in the synthesis of methylcobalamin, a cobalamin (vitamin B_{12}) coenzyme required by methyltetrahydrofolate:homocysteine methyltransferase. Methylmalonic acid accumulates in body fluids as well because synthesis of a second coenzyme, adenosylcobalamin, required for isomerization of methylmalonyl coenzyme A (CoA) to succinyl CoA is also impaired.

Etiology and pathogenesis   As with 5,10-methylenetetrahydrofolate reductase deficiency, this disorder impairs remethylation of homocysteine. The primary defect concerns deficient synthesis of cobalamin coenzymes. Since methylcobalamin is required for methyl-group transfer from methyltetrahydrofolate to homocysteine, impaired cobalamin metabolism leads to deficient methyltransferase activity. The defect responsible for impaired synthesis of methylcobalamin involves some early step in lysosomal or cytosolic activation of the vitamin precursor. Somatic cell genetic studies indicate that three distinct lesions can cause deficient coenzyme formation, each of which appears to be inherited as an autosomal recessive trait.

Clinical manifestations   The first reported patient died of infection at age 6 weeks following severely arrested development. Clinical manifestations in the other affected children vary: two had megaloblastic anemia and pancytopenia; three had significant spinocerebellar neurologic impairment; one exhibited little clinical abnormality.

Diagnosis and treatment   Homocystinuria, hypomethioninemia, and methylmalonic aciduria are the chemical hallmarks. These findings may also be present in juvenile- or adult-onset pernicious anemia in which intestinal cobalamin absorption is impaired. Measurement of serum cobalamin concentrations, low in pernicious anemia and normal in patients with defective conversion of cobalamin vitamin to coenzymes, helps in the differential diagnosis. Definitive diagnosis depends on demonstrating impaired coenzyme synthesis in cultured cells. Treatment of affected children with cobalamin supplements (1 to 2 mg per day) shows promise: homocystine and methylmalonate excretion fall to near normal values; the hematologic and neurologic deficits have also lessened to a variable degree.

REFERENCES

Boers GHJ et al: Heterozygosity for homocystinuria in premature peripheral and cerebral occlusive arterial disease. N Engl J Med 313:709, 1985

McKusick VA: Homocystinuria, in *Heritable Disorders of Connective Tissue*, 4th ed. St. Louis, Mosby, 1972, pp 224–281

Mudd SH, Levy HL: Disorders of transsulfuration, in *The Metabolic Basis of Inherited Disease*, 5th ed, JB Stanbury et al (eds). New York, McGraw-Hill, 1983, pp 552–559

——— et al: Natural history of homocystinuria due to cystathionine β-synthase deficiency. Am J Hum Genet 37:709, 1985

Rosenberg LE, Scriver CR: Disorders of amino acid metabolism, in *Metabolic Control and Disease*, 8th ed, PK Bondy, LE Rosenberg (eds). Philadelphia, Saunders 1980, pp 583–776

Scriver CR, Clow CL: Phenylketonuria: Epitome of human biochemical genetics. N Engl J Med 303:1336, 1394, 1980

Woo SLC et al: Cloned human phenylalanine hydroxylase gene allows prenatal diagnosis and carrier detection of classical phenylketonuria. Nature 306:151, 1983

307   STORAGE DISEASES OF AMINO ACID METABOLISM

LEON E. ROSENBERG

A number of inherited metabolic disorders are characterized by deposition or storage of particular metabolites in tissues. In most, storage reflects impaired degradation of the substance in question; in others, the mechanism is unknown. Many storage diseases involve large molecules such as glycogen, sphingolipids, mucolipids, cholesterol esters, and mucopolysaccharides (see Chaps. 313, 315, and 316); in others, metals such as iron and copper are deposited (see Chaps. 310 and 311). Finally, there is a group of storage diseases in which relatively small organic molecules are deposited. These include gout (see Chap. 309) and a group of disorders of amino acid metabolism.

ALKAPTONURIA

DEFINITION   Alkaptonuria is a rare disorder of tyrosine catabolism. Deficiency of the enzyme homogentisic acid oxidase leads to excretion of large amounts of homogentisic acid in urine and to accumulation of oxidized homogentisic acid pigment in connective tissues (ochronosis). After many years ochronosis produces a distinctive form of degenerative arthritis.

ETIOLOGY AND PATHOGENESIS   Homogentisic acid is an intermediate in the catabolism of tyrosine to fumarate and acetoacetate. Activity of homogentisic acid oxidase, the enzyme that catalyzes the opening of the phenolic ring yielding maleylacetoacetic acid, is deficient in liver and kidney of patients with alkaptonuria, and homogentisic acid accumulates in cells and body fluids. Patients have minimally increased concentrations of homogentisic acid in blood because it is rapidly cleared by the kidney. As much as 3 to 7 g homogentisic acid may be excreted in the urine per day, but this is of little pathophysiologic significance. However, homogentisic acid and its oxidized polymers bind to collagen, leading to the progressive deposition of a gray to bluish-black pigment. The mechanism(s) by which degenerative changes develop in cartilage, intervertebral disk, and other connective tissues is unknown but may involve direct chemical irritation or an impairment of normal connective tissue metabolism.

Alkaptonuria was the first human disease shown to be inherited as an autosomal recessive trait. Affected homozygotes occur with a frequency around 1 in 200,000. Heterozygous carriers are clinically well and excrete no homogentisic acid in urine, even after loading doses of tyrosine.

CLINICAL MANIFESTATIONS   Alkaptonuria may go unrecognized until middle life when degenerative joint disease develops in the majority. Prior to this time the tendency of the patient's urine to darken on standing may go unnoticed, as may slight discoloration of the sclerae and ears. The latter manifestations are generally the earliest external evidence of the disorder and develop after age 20 to 30. Foci of gray-brown scleral pigment and generalized darkening of the concha, antihelix, and, finally, helix of the ear are typical. Ear cartilages may be irregular and thickened. *Ochronotic arthritis* is heralded by pain, stiffness, and some limitation of motion of the hips, knees, and shoulders. Intermittent periods of acute arthritis, which may resemble rheumatoid arthritis, occur, but small joints are usually spared. Limitation of motion and ankylosis of the lumbosacral spine are common late manifestations. Pigmentation of heart valves, larynx, tympanic membranes, and skin occurs, and occasional patients develop pigmented renal or prostatic calculi. An increased incidence of degenerative cardiovascular disease may occur in older patients.

DIAGNOSIS   A patient whose urine darkens to blackness on standing must be suspected of having alkaptonuria, but because of modern plumbing conditions this finding is not often observed. The diagnosis is usually made from the triad of degenerative arthritis, ochronotic pigmentation, and urine which turns black upon alkalinization. Homogentisic acid in urine may be identified presumptively by other tests: upon addition of ferric chloride, a purple-black color is observed; treatment with Benedict's reagent yields a brown color; addition of a saturated silver nitrate solution produces an immediate black color. These screening tests can be confirmed by chromatographic, enzymatic, or spectrophotometric determinations of homogentisic acid. X-rays of the lumbar spine are virtually pathognomonic. They show degeneration and dense calcification of the intervertebral disks and narrowing of the intervertebral spaces.

TREATMENT   There is no specific treatment for ochronotic arthritis. Joint manifestations might be mitigated if homogentisic acid accumulation and deposition could be curbed by dietary restriction of phenylalanine and tyrosine, but the long course of the disease has discouraged such therapeutic attempts. Since ascorbic acid impedes oxidation and polymerization of homogentisic acid in vitro, its use has been suggested as a possible means of decreasing pigment formation and deposition. The efficacy of this form of treatment has not been established. Symptomatic treatment is similar to that for osteoarthritis (Chap. 274).

CYSTINOSIS

DEFINITION   Cystinosis is a rare disorder characterized by the intralysosomal accumulation of free cystine in body tissues. This results in the appearance of cystine crystals in the cornea, conjunctiva, bone marrow, lymph nodes, leukocytes, and internal organs. Three variants have been identified: an infantile (nephropathic) form leading to the Fanconi syndrome and renal insufficiency in the first decade; a juvenile (intermediate) form in which renal disease becomes manifest during the second decade; and an adult (benign) form characterized by deposition of cystine in the cornea but not in the kidney.

ETIOLOGY AND PATHOGENESIS   The basic defect in cystinosis involves impaired efflux of cystine from lysosomes rather than an

abnormality in cystine catabolism. Lysosomal cystine efflux is an active, ATP-dependent process. The cystine content of tissues may be more than 100 times normal in the infantile form, more than 30 times normal in the adult form. Intracellular cystine appears to be located in lysosomes and does not exchange with other intracellular or extracellular pools of this amino acid. Neither plasma nor urinary concentrations of cystine are particularly elevated.

The extent of cystine crystal deposition varies from patient to patient, depending on the form of the disease and on the methods used to prepare pathologic specimens. Cystine accumulation in the kidney causes renal insufficiency in the infantile and juvenile forms. The kidneys are pale and shrunken, the capsule is adherent, and the corticomedullary junction is obscured. Microscopically, nephron organization is interrupted, glomeruli are hyalinized, connective tissue is increased, and the normal epithelium of the tubules is replaced by cuboidal cells. Narrowing and shortening of the proximal tubule produces the swan neck deformity that is characteristic of but not specific for cystinosis. Patchy depigmentation and degeneration of the peripheral retina occurs in the infantile and juvenile forms. Cystine crystals may also be deposited in the ocular conjunctiva or uvea.

Each form of cystinosis appears to be inherited as an autosomal recessive trait. Obligate heterozygotes have intracellular cystine contents intermediate between those of normal persons and affected patients but are free of clinical abnormalities.

CLINICAL MANIFESTATIONS   In the infantile form abnormalities are usually apparent by 4 to 6 months of age. Growth retardation, vomiting, fever, vitamin D–resistant rickets, polyuria, dehydration, and metabolic acidosis are prominent. Generalized proximal tubular dysfunction (the Fanconi syndrome) leads to hyperphosphaturia and hypophosphatemia, renal glycosuria, generalized aminoaciduria, hypouricemia, and often hypokalemia. Pyelonephritis may contribute, along with interstitial fibrosis, to progressive glomerular insufficiency. Death due to uremia or intercurrent infection usually occurs before age 10. Ocular manifestations are prominent. Photophobia is usually demonstrable within the first few years of life due to cystine deposits in the cornea, and retinal degeneration may appear even earlier.

In contrast, patients with the adult form manifest only ocular abnormalities. Photophobia, headache, and burning or itching of the eyes are major complaints. Glomerular and tubular function and the integrity of the retina are preserved. The findings in the juvenile variant fall between these extremes. These patients have both ocular and renal manifestations, but the latter do not become significant until the second decade. The renal lesion, albeit milder than that seen in the infantile form, eventually leads to renal insufficiency.

DIAGNOSIS   Cystinosis must be considered in any child with vitamin D–resistant rickets, the Fanconi syndrome, or glomerular insufficiency. Hexagonal or rectangular cystine crystals can be detected in the cornea (by slit-lamp examination), in leukocytes from peripheral blood or bone marrow, or in biopsies of rectal mucosa. Diagnosis can be confirmed by quantification of cystine in peripheral blood leukocytes or cultured fibroblasts. The infantile form has been diagnosed prenatally by the demonstration of increased cystine content in cultured amniotic fluid cells.

TREATMENT   The adult form is benign and requires no treatment. Symptomatic treatment of renal disease in the infantile or juvenile form of cystinosis does not differ from that of other forms of chronic renal insufficiency: maintenance of adequate fluid intake to prevent dehydration; correction of the metabolic acidosis; and ingestion of supplementary calcium, phosphate, and vitamin D to heal the rickets. Such measures are effective in maintaining growth, development, and well-being in affected children for a time. Two types of more specific therapy have been attempted without much success. Cystine-restricted diets have not prevented progression of renal disease. Likewise, the use of sulfhydryl reagents (penicillamine, dimercaprol) and reducing agents (vitamin C) have yielded no long-term benefit.

The most promising form of therapy for nephropathic cystinosis is renal transplantation. More than 20 affected children with end-stage renal disease have been so treated. Those patients who tolerated the procedure and did not develop immunologic problems have shown return of kidney function toward normal. The transplanted kidneys have not developed the functional abnormalities typical of cystinosis (i.e., the Fanconi syndrome or glomerular insufficiency). They may, however, reaccumulate some cystine, apparently owing to migration of interstitial or mesangial cells from the host. This experience justifies offering renal transplantation to patients with terminal renal failure.

PRIMARY HYPEROXALURIA

DEFINITION Primary hyperoxaluria is the designation for two rare disorders characterized by chronic excessive urinary excretion of oxalic acid and by calcium oxalate nephrolithiasis and nephrocalcinosis. Typically, patients with both forms develop renal insufficiency early in life and die of uremia. At postmortem examination, calcium oxalate deposits are widespread in renal and extrarenal tissues, a condition referred to as *oxalosis*.

ETIOLOGY AND PATHOGENESIS The metabolic basis for the primary hyperoxalurias involves pathways of glyoxylate metabolism. In type I hyperoxaluria, urinary excretion of oxalate and of the oxidized and reduced forms of glyoxylate is increased. The excessive synthesis of these substances results from a block in an alternate route of glyoxylate metabolism. Activity of α-ketoglutarate:glyoxylate carboligase, which catalyzes the formation of α-hydroxy-β-ketoadipic acid, is reduced in liver, kidney, and spleen. The resulting expansion of the glyoxylate pool leads to enhanced oxidation of glyoxylate to oxalate and to enhanced reduction of glyoxylate to glycolate. Each of these 2-carbon acids is then excreted in excess in the urine. In type II hyperoxaluria, L-glyceric acid is excreted in excess along with oxalate. In this condition, activity of D-glyceric acid dehydrogenase, which catalyzes the reduction of hydroxypyruvate to D-glyceric acid in the catabolic pathway of serine metabolism, is absent in leukocytes (and presumably other tissues). The accumulated hydroxypyruvate is instead reduced by lactic dehydrogenase to the L-isomer of glycerate, which is excreted in the urine. The reduction of hydroxypyruvate is coupled in some way to the oxidation of glyoxylate to oxalate, thus causing the formation of increased oxalate. Both disorders appear to be inherited as autosomal recessive traits. Heterozygotes are asymptomatic.

The pathogenesis of stone formation, nephrocalcinosis, and oxalosis relates directly to the insolubility of calcium oxalate. Extrarenal deposits of oxalate are prominent in the heart, walls of arteries and veins, male urogenital tract, and bone.

CLINICAL MANIFESTATIONS Nephrolithiasis and oxalosis may be manifest during the first year of life. Most patients experience renal colic or hematuria between ages 2 and 10 and succumb to uremia before age 20. With the onset of uremia, patients may develop severe peripheral arterial spasm and necrosis with resulting vascular insufficiency. Oxalate excretion falls as renal failure worsens. In patients with delayed onset of symptoms, survival to age 50 or 60 has been reported, despite recurrent nephrolithiasis.

DIAGNOSIS Oxalate excretion in normal children or adults is less than 60 mg per 1.73 square meters of surface area per day. Patients with type I or type II hyperoxaluria generally excrete two to four times this amount. Distinction between the two types of primary hyperoxaluria depends on measurements of the other organic acids that identify them: glycolic acid in type I and L-glyceric acid in type II. Since patients with pyridoxine deficiency or chronic ileal disease may excrete excessive amounts of oxalate, these conditions must be excluded.

TREATMENT There is no satisfactory treatment. Urinary oxalate concentration can be transiently reduced by increasing the urinary flow rate. Large doses of pyridoxine (100 mg per day) may reduce urinary oxalate, but long-term effects are not dramatic. A diet high

in phosphate content seems to reduce the frequency of attacks of renal colic, but oxalate excretion is unaffected. Finally, after renal transplantation renal function is lost because of calcium oxalate deposition in the transplanted kidney.

REFERENCES

GAHL WA: Cystine transport is defective in isolated leukocyte lysosomes from patients with cystinosis. Science 217:1263, 1982

JONAS AJ: ATP-dependent lysosomal efflux is defective in cystinosis. J Biol Chem 257:12185, 1982

LADU NB: Alcaptonuria, in *The Metabolic Basis of Inherited Disease*, 4th ed, JB Stanbury et al (eds). New York, McGraw-Hill, 1978, pp 268–282

SCHNEIDER JA, SCHULMAN, JD: Cystinosis, in *The Metabolic Basis of Inherited Disease*, 5th ed, JB Stanbury et al (eds). New York, McGraw-Hill, 1983, pp 1844–1866

WILLIAMS HE, SMITH LH JR: Primary hyperoxaluria, in *The Metabolic Basis of Inherited Disease*, 5th ed, JB Stanbury et al (eds). New York, McGraw-Hill, 1983, pp 204–228

308   INHERITED DEFECTS OF MEMBRANE TRANSPORT

LEON E. ROSENBERG / ELIZABETH M. SHORT

The passage of certain molecules across plasma cell membranes depends on specific transport systems that owe their specificity to membrane receptor and "carrier" proteins. These membrane constituents recognize individual molecules or structurally related substances and catalyze their transmembrane movement by mechanisms poorly understood. The disorders considered in this chapter have three features in common: each is characterized by a specific defect in the transport of one or more compounds; each is inherited as a dominant or recessive trait, implying that a single genetic locus is involved; and each is presumed to reflect a primary alteration in a specific membrane protein. Many of these defects have been well characterized physiologically, but in none has the putative mutant transport protein been isolated.

More than 20 inherited disorders of membrane transport have been described in humans (Table 308-1). Most affect the gut and/or kidney only. Numerous classes of substrates are represented, including amino acids, sugars, cations, anions, vitamins, and water. Some are discussed elsewhere in this text. Those impairing the transport of amino acids, hexoses, urate, and chloride are discussed here as examples of the abnormalities encountered.

DISORDERS OF AMINO ACID TRANSPORT

As noted in Table 308-1, 10 disorders of amino acid transport have been described. Five of these (cystinuria, dibasicaminoaciduria, Hartnup disease, iminoglycinuria, and dicarboxylicaminoaciduria) show transport abnormalities for structurally related amino acids, thereby implying the existence of group-specific membrane receptors or carriers. With the exception of iminoglycinuria and dicarboxylicaminoaciduria, these defects have important clinical consequences. The remaining five disorders affect the transport of only one amino acid, implying the existence of substrate-specific transport systems. Each of these conditions affects transport in the kidney, gut, or both; none has been shown to alter transport in other tissues.

CYSTINURIA   **Definition**   Cystinuria is the most common inborn error of amino acid transport. It is characterized by excessive urinary excretion of the dibasic amino acids: lysine, arginine, ornithine, and cystine. This aminoaciduria results from impaired tubular reabsorption of these amino acids. A similar transport defect exists in the intestinal mucosa. Because cystine is the least soluble of the naturally occurring amino acids, its overexcretion predisposes to the formation of renal, ureteral, and bladder calculi. Such calculi are responsible for the signs and symptoms of the disorder.

Etiology and pathogenesis Massive excretion of cystine and the other dibasic amino acids occurs only in classic cystinuria. The disorder, inherited as an autosomal recessive trait, is believed to result from alterations in a membrane carrier protein essential for transport of this group of amino acids in the apical brush border of proximal renal tubule and small intestinal cells. The putative protein has a greater affinity for ornithine and arginine than for lysine and cystine. Although the renal clearance of all four amino acids is increased in homozygotes, the presence of some residual transport capacity for these compounds plus the existence of three other disorders marked by selective excretion of members of this group (dibasicaminoaciduria, hypercystinuria, lysinuria) argues for the existence of at least three discrete renal transport systems for these amino acids: one for each amino acid alone; one shared by lysine, arginine, and ornithine; and one for all four amino acids.

Whereas urinary excretion patterns and renal clearance abnormalities in all homozygotes are similar, evidence for three allelic variants has come from studies of intestinal transport in homozygotes and of urinary excretion in obligate heterozygotes. Type I homozygotes lack mediated intestinal transport of cystine, lysine, arginine, and ornithine; heterozygotes have normal urinary amino acid excretion patterns. Type II homozygotes lack mediated lysine transport in the gut but retain some capacity for cystine transport; heterozygotes have moderately increased urinary excretion of each of the four amino acids. Type III homozygotes retain some capacity for mediated intestinal transport of the four involved substrates; heterozygotes have modestly increased urinary lysine and cystine.

Clinical manifestations Cystinuria is among the most common inborn errors, homozygotes occurring with a frequency of 1 in 10,000 to 1 in 15,000 in many ethnic groups. Two-thirds of adults with cystinuria are type I homozygotes. Cystine stones account for 1 to 2 percent of all urinary tract calculi. The maximum solubility of cystine in the physiologic urinary pH range of 4.5 to 7.0 is about 300 mg per liter. Since affected homozygotes regularly excrete 600 to 1800 mg per day, crystalluria and calculus formation are a constant threat. Cystine stone formation usually becomes manifest in the second or third decade but may occur in the first year of life. Symptoms and signs are those typical of urolithiasis: hematuria, flank pain, renal colic, obstructive uropathy, and infection. Recurrent urolithiasis may lead to progressive renal insufficiency.

Diagnosis The presence of cystine in a urinary tract stone is pathognomonic of cystinuria. However, since 50 percent of the stones excreted by cystinuric subjects are of mixed composition and since as many as 10 percent may contain *no* detectable cystine, a urinary nitroprusside test should be done on all patients with urolithiasis to exclude this diagnosis. The nitroprusside test is also positive (appearance of a cherry red color) in some heterozygotes for cystinuria, in patients with hypercystinuria, homocystinuria, and cysteine β-mercaptolactate disulfiduria, and in the presence of acetone in the urine. When cystine content exceeds 250 mg per liter, cystine crystals may be seen in the sediment of acidified, concentrated, chilled urine. These hexagonal crystals are pathognomonic of cystine overexcretion in patients not taking sulfonamides.

Diagnostic confirmation of cystinuria depends upon the demonstration of the characteristic amino acid excretion pattern in the urine. Selective excretion of cystine, lysine, arginine, and ornithine can be demonstrated by paper chromatography or electrophoresis, and quantitative determinations can be made by column chromatography. Quantitation is important for differentiating some heterozygotes from homozygotes and documenting the reduction of free cystine excretion during therapy.

Treatment Medical management is aimed at reducing the concentration of cystine in urine. The most important treatment is maintenance of a large urine volume. Fluid ingestion in excess of 4 liters per day

is essential, and 5 to 7 liters per day is optimal. Urinary cystine excretion should measure less than 250 to 300 mg per liter. The daily fluid ingestion necessary to maintain this dilution of excreted cystine should be spaced over the waking hours, with one-quarter to one-third of the total volume ingested at bedtime. Stones can be prevented and even dissolved by such hydration. It must be made clear to the cystinuric subject that water is a drug. Solubility of cystine rises sharply in urine above pH 7.5, and urinary alkalinization can be therapeutic in some situations. Vigorous administration of sodium bicarbonate, acetazolamide, and polycitrates is required to maintain a persistently alkaline pH, but this measure introduces the danger of inducing formation of other "alkaline" stones (calcium oxalate, calcium phosphate, magnesium ammonium phosphate) and even of producing nephrocalcinosis.

Another treatment involves administration of penicillamine which undergoes sulfhydryl-disulfide exchange with cystine to form the mixed disulfide of penicillamine and cysteine. Since this disulfide is more than 50 times as soluble as cystine, penicillamine (in doses of 1 to 3 g per day) has the capacity to reduce free cystine excretion markedly, thereby preventing new stone formation and promoting dissolution of existing calculi. Unfortunately, allergic manifestations include acute serum sickness, agranulocytosis, pancytopenia, immune glomerulitis, and the Goodpasture syndrome. Thus, its use should be reserved for patients who fail to respond to hydration alone or who are in a high-risk category (one remaining kidney, renal insufficiency). Those patients unable to tolerate penicillamine may benefit from α-mercaptopropionylglycine, an experimental drug whose mechanism of action is similar to that of penicillamine but whose structure, and hence toxicity, is different. When medical management fails, urologic surgery is required. An occasional patient may require renal transplantation because of renal failure.

DIBASICAMINOACIDURIA Families have been described in which affected members have a defect in renal tubular reabsorption of lysine, arginine, and ornithine but *not* of cystine. The disorder almost surely reflects mutations in the genes coding for a renal transport protein used by the three dibasic amino acids only. Two variants have been observed, each apparently inherited as an autosomal recessive trait. Manifestations are related to the losses of ornithine, arginine, and perhaps lysine.

In the common form of dibasicaminoaciduria (type II), also known as lysinuric protein intolerance, homozygotes show defective intestinal transport of dibasic amino acids as well as exaggerated renal losses. The transport defect may affect renal basolateral rather than luminal membrane transport. A defect in hepatic cell uptake of these substances has also been proposed. Affected patients present in childhood with hepatosplenomegaly, protein intolerance, and episodic ammonia intoxication. Plasma concentrations of lysine, arginine, and ornithine are reduced. The clinical findings have been attributed to hyperammonemia resulting from insufficient amounts of arginine and ornithine to maintain proper function of the urea cycle. Treatment includes dietary protein restriction and supplementation with citrulline, a neutral amino acid that has unimpaired intestinal and hepatic transport, that when metabolized to arginine and ornithine fuels the urea cycle. With 2.0 to 3.0 g of oral citrulline daily, dietary protein intake can be increased and growth improved in pediatric patients. Obligate heterozygotes are healthy and show no excess urinary loss of dibasic amino acids.

Type I dibasicaminoaciduria has been described in only one homozygote. She was moderately mentally retarded but had no clear history of protein intolerance or hyperammonemia. Her urinary losses of dibasic amino acids were not as great as those seen in type II homozygotes. The condition was distinguished from type II by the presence of modest excesses of dibasic amino acids in urine of both asymptomatic parents. Other pedigrees containing asymptomatic heterozygotes have been identified by urinary screening programs. Type I disease may involve a renal luminal membrane transport defect.

TABLE 308-1 Genetic disorders of membrane transport

Class of substance and disorder	Individual substrates	Tissues manifesting transport defect	Proposed molecular basis of defect	Major clinical manifestations	Mode of inheritance	Location of discussion
AMINO ACIDS						
Classic cystinuria	Cystine, lysine, arginine, ornithine	Proximal renal tubule, jejunal mucosa	Mutation of shared dibasic-cystine transport protein	Cystine nephrolithiasis	Autosomal recessive	Chap. 308
Dibasicamino-aciduria	Lysine, arginine, ornithine	Proximal renal tubule, jejunal mucosa	Mutation of dibasic transport protein	Type I: Moderate retardation. Type II: Protein intolerance, hyperammonemia, retardation	Autosomal recessive	Chap. 308
Hypercystinuria	Cystine	Proximal renal tubule	Mutation of cystine transport protein	Some risk of cystine nephrolithiasis	Autosomal recessive	Chap. 308
Lysinuria	Lysine	Proximal renal tubule, jejunal mucosa	Mutation of lysine transport protein	Seizures, physical and mental retardation	Possible autosomal recessive	Chap. 308
Hartnup disease	Neutral amino acids	Proximal renal tubule, jejunal mucosa	Mutation of shared neutral amino acid transport protein	Constant neutral aminoaciduria, intermittent symptoms of pellagra	Autosomal recessive	Chap. 308
Tryptophan malabsorption	Tryptophan	Jejunal mucosa	Mutation of tryptophan transport protein	Indoluria, ?hypercalcemia, ?nephrocalcinosis	Probable autosomal recessive	Chap. 308
Methionine malabsorption	Methionine	Jejunal mucosa	Mutation of methionine transport protein	α-Hydroxybutyricaciduria, white hair, mental retardation, convulsions, hyperpneic attacks, edema	Probable autosomal recessive	Chap. 308
Histidinuria	Histidine	Proximal renal tubule, jejunal mucosa	Mutation of histidine transport protein	Mental retardation	Autosomal recessive	Chap. 308
Iminoglycinuria	Glycine, proline, hydroxyproline	Proximal renal tubule, jejunal mucosa	Mutation of shared glycine–imino acid transport protein	None	Autosomal recessive	Chap. 308
Dicarboxylic-aminoaciduria	Glutamic acid, aspartic acid	Proximal renal tubule, jejunal mucosa	Mutation of shared dicarboxylic amino acid transport protein	None	Probable autosomal recessive	Chap. 308
HEXOSES						
Renal glycosuria	D-Glucose	Proximal renal tubule	Mutation of D-glucose transport protein	Glycosuria with normal blood glucose	Autosomal recessive	Chap. 308
Glucose-galactose malabsorption	D-Glucose, D-Galactose	Jejunal mucosa, proximal renal tubule	Mutation of shared glucose-galactose transport protein	Watery diarrhea on feeding glucose, lactose, sucrose, or galactose	Autosomal recessive	Chaps. 237, 308
LIPIDS						
Familial hypercholesterolemia	Cholesterol	Fibroblasts, lymphoid lines, leukocytes	Mutation of membrane LDL–cholesterol receptor protein	Hypercholesterolemia, tendon xanthomas, arcus corneae, coronary artery atherosclerosis	Autosomal dominant	Chap. 315
URATE						
Hypouricemia	Uric acid	Proximal renal tubule	Mutation of urate transport protein	Hypouricemia, hyperuricosuria, ?hypercalcinuria	Autosomal recessive	Chap. 308
ANIONS						
Familial hypophosphatemic rickets	Inorganic phosphate	Proximal renal tubule, jejunal mucosa	Mutation of inorganic phosphate transport protein	Hypophosphatemia, phosphaturia, phosphatopenic rickets/osteomalacia	X-linked dominant	Chap. 337
Congenital chloridorrhea	Chloride	Ileal and colonic mucosa	Mutation of Cl^-/HCO_3^- exchange pump carrier protein	Hydramnios, watery diarrhea, elevated fecal chloride, achloriduria, metabolic alkalosis with volume depletion, hyperaldosteronism	Autosomal recessive	Chaps. 237, 308

TABLE 308-1 Genetic disorders of membrane transport (*continued*)

Class of substance and disorder	Individual substrates	Tissues manifesting transport defect	Proposed molecular basis of defect	Major clinical manifestations	Mode of inheritance	Location of discussion
ANIONS (*continued*)						
Familial goiter	Inorganic iodide	Thyroid gland, salivary gland, gastric mucosa	Mutation of iodide transport protein	Congenital hypothyroidism (cretinism), goiter	Probable autosomal recessive	Chap. 324
CATIONS						
Distal renal tubular acidosis (type I—gradient)	Hydrogen ion	Distal renal tubule	Mutation of distal tubule H^+ pump carrier protein	Hyperchloremic acidosis, hypokalemia, acquired nephrocalcinosis, and hypercalcinuria	Autosomal dominant	Chap. 228
Proximal renal tubular acidosis (type II—HCO_3^- wasting)	Hydrogen ion	Proximal renal tubule	Mutation of proximal tubule H^+ pump carrier protein	Hyperchloremic acidosis, bicarbonate wasting	Probable autosomal recessive	Chap. 228
Menkes' disease	Copper	Duodenal and jejunal intestinal cells	Possible serosal transport protein or intracellular transport defect	Severe mental retardation, pili torti (kinky hair), typical facies, arterial tortuosity, excess Wormian bones, thermal instability	X-linked recessive	Chaps. 77, 319
Hereditary Spherocytosis Elliptocytosis Ovalocytosis Stomatocytosis	Sodium	Red blood cell (RBC) membranes	Mutation of membrane structure (? lipid or protein) resulting in increased sodium permeability	Increased RBC fragility resulting in variable degrees of hemolytic anemia, splenomegaly, and jaundice; RBC shape respectively spherocytic, elliptocytic, ovalocytic, or stomatocytic (target-shaped)	Each of these diseases of RBC morphology is a separately inherited autosomal dominant	Chap. 287
WATER						
Nephrogenic diabetes insipidus (AVP-resistant)	Water	Distal renal tubule	Lack of activation of AVP-responsive luminal membrane adenylate cyclase, possible defect in receptor or enzyme protein	Polyuria, polydipsia, hyposthenuria	X-linked recessive	Chap. 228
VITAMINS						
Juvenile pernicious anemia	Cobalamin (vitamin B_{12})	Ileal mucosa	Mutation of receptor for intrinsic factor–cobalamin complex	Megaloblastic anemia	Autosomal recessive	Chap. 285
Folate malabsorption	Folic acid	Small bowel	Mutation of folate transport protein	Megaloblastic anemia	Autosomal recessive	Chap. 285
Multiple carboxylase deficiency (type II)	Biotin	Small bowel	Mutation of biotin transport protein	Ketoacidosis, alopecia, eczematoid eruption	Undefined	

HARTNUP DISEASE Pellagra-like skin lesions, variable neurologic manifestations, and aminoaciduria for the monoaminomonocarboxylic amino acids with neutral or aromatic side chains characterize Hartnup disease. Alanine, serine, threonine, valine, leucine, isoleucine, phenylalanine, tyrosine, tryptophan, glutamine, asparagine, and histidine are excreted in urine in quantities 5 to 10 times normal, and intestinal transport for these same amino acids is defective. The clinical manifestations result from nutritional deficiency of the essential amino acid tryptophan, caused by the combination of intestinal malabsorption and renal loss. Disease manifestations are episodic, related, at least in part, to metabolic demands for tryptophan.

The major pathway of tryptophan metabolism leads to the synthesis of niacin and nicotinamide-adenine dinucleotide (NAD). This pathway supplies about 50 percent of daily niacin needs. In patients with Hartnup disease, the renal and intestinal transport defect for tryptophan leads to niacin deficiency. The transport defect likely reflects abnormalities of a group-specific system for neutral amino acids. Some residual reabsorptive capacity persists for each involved amino acid. This suggests that they are transported by other carrier systems as well, a conclusion supported by the identification of patients with substrate-specific transport errors for tryptophan, methionine, and histidine.

Hartnup disease is inherited as an autosomal recessive trait. Homozygotes occur with a frequency of about 1 in 16,000 births. Heterozygotes exhibit no clinical or chemical abnormalities.

Pellagra is the clinical syndrome produced by dietary niacin deficiency, and its clinical features are those that characterize Hartnup disease (see Chap. 76). The diagnosis should be suspected in any patient with pellagra without a history of dietary niacin deficiency. The neurologic and psychiatric manifestations range from attacks of cerebellar ataxia to mild emotional lability to frank delirium and usually accompany exacerbations of the erythematous, eczematoid skin rash. Fever, sunlight, stress, and sulfonamide therapy provoke clinical relapses. Diagnosis is made by detection of the neutral aminoaciduria that does not occur in dietary niacin deficiency. Treatment is directed at niacin repletion and includes a high-protein diet and daily nicotinamide supplementation (50 to 250 mg).

IMINOGLYCINURIA This trait is characterized by excessive urinary excretion of glycine and the imino acids proline and hydroxyproline. Homozygotes for this autosomal recessive disorder occur with a frequency of about 1 in 16,000. The exaggerated renal clearance of glycine, proline, and hydroxyproline reflects a defect in the tubular transport system shared by these three compounds. An intestinal transport defect may also be present. This suggests that more than one mutation may lead to persistent iminoglycinuria, a thesis corroborated by the demonstration that obligate heterozygotes from some but not all families manifest glycinuria. No consistent clinical abnormalities have been reported in homozygotes, who are usually detected by urinary amino acid screening programs. Individuals with iminoglycinuria should be reassured as to the benign nature of the disturbance.

DICARBOXYLICAMINOACIDURIA Selective urinary loss and exaggerated endogenous renal clearance of glutamic and aspartic acids have been described in two unrelated children. Intestinal absorption of these dicarboxylic amino acids was impaired in one. This patient suffered from recurrent hypoglycemia; the other was asymptomatic.

SUBSTRATE-SPECIFIC DEFECTS IN AMINO ACID TRANSPORT
Rare pedigrees exist in which individuals have defective renal tubular reabsorption and/or impaired intestinal absorption of a single free amino acid. These disorders, each apparently inherited as an autosomal recessive trait, suggest that transport of amino acids is catalyzed by substrate-specific as well as group-specific transport mechanisms.

Hypercystinuria Two siblings exhibited modest cystinuria without excessive urinary excretion of lysine, arginine, or ornithine. Fractional tubular reabsorption of cystine was reduced to about 80 percent of the filtered load, and up to 250 mg per day was excreted in the urine. Neither showed any abnormality in intestinal absorption of cystine. Both were clinically well, although the cystine excretion places them at risk for cystine urolithiasis. Urinary cystine excretion by the parents was normal.

Lysinuria A child with selective impairment of renal tubular reabsorption of lysine has been described. Endogenous lysine clearance was increased; intestinal transport was impaired; plasma lysine was reduced. Mental and growth retardation and seizures were present. A lysine-supplemented diet stimulated growth. Urinary lysine excretion was normal in the parents.

Histidinuria Two siblings, each with mental retardation, exhibited a renal transport defect for histidine only. Urinary loss of histidine approached 40 to 50 percent of the filtered load, and an intestinal transport defect for histidine was also present. The clinically normal parents had normal urinary excretion but a modest defect in intestinal absorption of histidine. In two additional cases of isolated histidinuria myoclonic seizures occurred.

Methionine malabsorption Single children from two pedigrees have shown an intestinal transport defect for methionine. One may have had a renal transport defect as well. This disorder was detected because of urinary excretion of α-hydroxybutyric acid, a by-product of the intestinal bacterial breakdown of the unabsorbed methionine. This compound, which gives an odor resembling malt or dried celery to the urine, appears to be responsible for the white hair, attacks of hyperpnea, convulsions, edema, and mental retardation. Treatment of one of these children with a methionine-restricted diet caused improvement in all clinical manifestations.

Tryptophan malabsorption An isolated defect in intestinal absorption of tryptophan has been described in two siblings. The renal tubular reabsorption of tryptophan was normal. A variety of indoles were excreted in stool and urine. These compounds result from chemical degradation of unabsorbed tryptophan by intestinal bacteria and may be present in patients with Hartnup disease as well. Because of concomitant renal disease, hydrolytic enzymes were released into the urine, acted upon the indoles found there, and led to the formation of a blue pigment, indigotin. This sequence of events earned this condition the sobriquet "blue-diaper syndrome." No pellagra-like symptoms were described. The mother also excreted indole compounds, suggesting that she is a carrier of this trait.

DISORDERS OF HEXOSE TRANSPORT

Nondiabetic melituria occurs in a number of conditions. Pentoses, hexoses, heptoses, and disaccharides have been identified in the urine; all except sucrose yield a positive test for reducing substances. Some meliturias result from diffuse renal injury, others from ingestion of nonmetabolizable sugars. In still others the sugars accumulate in blood owing to deficient activity of catabolizing enzyme systems and "spill" into the urine. Only among the hexoses have specific inherited disorders of sugar transport been identified. The existence of renal glycosuria and intestinal glucose-galactose malabsorption as heritable, autosomal recessive disorders points to the existence of at least two specific carrier proteins for hexoses in human jejunal and renal brush border membranes: one for glucose and one shared by glucose and galactose.

RENAL GLYCOSURIA To avoid confusion with diabetes mellitus, Marble's criteria for the diagnosis of renal glycosuria should be followed: (1) glycosuria in the absence of hyperglycemia, (2) constant glycosuria with little fluctuation related to diet, (3) normal (or slightly flat) oral glucose tolerance test, (4) identification of urinary reducing substance as glucose, and (5) normal storage and utilization of carbohydrates. The Fanconi syndrome, in which renal glycosuria occurs as part of generalized proximal tubular dysfunction, should also be excluded. The incidence is less than 1 in 500. The condition is benign, but occasionally glycosuria may be great enough to cause polyuria and polydipsia. Even more rarely, dehydration or ketosis may develop under conditions of stress such as pregnancy or starvation.

In normal persons glucose is present in the glomerular filtrate at a concentration equal to that in plasma water and is reabsorbed throughout the proximal renal tubule by a sodium-dependent, phlorizin-inhibitable transport process. Reabsorptive capacity exceeds normal plasma glucose concentration. Thus, glucose does not appear in the urine until the threshold for reabsorption is reached. The plasma concentration at which filtered glucose begins to escape proximal tubular reabsorption is 200 to 240 mg/dL. Maximal renal reabsorptive capacity is exceeded at a filtered load of 325 ± 36 mg/min per 1.73 square meters of body surface area, and this value is defined as the tubular maximum for glucose (TmG).

Two patterns of glycosuria are recognized: type A characterized by a reduced tubular maximum reabsorptive capacity and type B showing a reduced threshold for glycosuria, an increased "splay" in the titration curve, and a normal TmG. Marked renal glycosuria occurs in individuals homozygous for either of these recessively inherited mutations and in genetic compounds for these presumably allelic mutations. Modest reduction in renal threshold or TmG is present in obligate heterozygotes in some pedigrees; modest glycosuria occurs in such family members when plasma glucose is elevated. The gene responsible for renal glycosuria segregates with the human histocompatibility leukocyte antigen (HLA) haplotype suggesting its location on chromosome 6. No linkage disequilibrium was observed, and no specific HLA antigens have been associated with renal glycosuria.

GLUCOSE-GALACTOSE MALABSORPTION In this condition, infants develop a profuse, watery diarrhea when fed milk or foods containing lactose, sucrose, glucose, or galactose. Fructose or carbohydrate-free formulas are well tolerated. A specific defect in intestinal absorption of glucose and galactose can be demonstrated by oral tolerance tests that produce little or no increase in plasma glucose or galactose. Treatment with a glucose- and galactose-free diet leads to resolution of symptoms in childhood. Although the basic transport defect is present throughout life, most patients show an improved tolerance for glucose and galactose with age.

Active D-glucose and D-galactose transport is absent in affected children, and intermediate transport capacity is present in their parents. These findings confirm the specificity and the autosomal recessive inheritance of the disorder.

A number of these patients have renal glycosuria at normal plasma glucose concentrations. Renal titration studies generally demonstrate a reduced threshold for glucose reabsorption (type B renal glycosuria) with a normal TmG. Urinary glucose loss is not as severe as in isolated renal glycosuria. This finding suggests the presence of multiple glucose transport proteins in the kidney. One, responsible for the bulk of glucose reabsorption and specific for glucose only, is affected in renal glycosuria; another, shared by glucose and galactose and responsible for transporting less of the filtered load of glucose, is affected in glucose-galactose malabsorption. Either the former is not present in intestinal mucosa, or the shared system is more important in that tissue. In both disorders transport of sugars in all other tested tissues is normal, reflecting the multiplicity and tissue specificity of membrane transport proteins.

DEFECTIVE URATE TRANSPORT: HYPOURICEMIA

Individuals with a selective defect in renal tubular reabsorption of sodium urate have marked hypouricemia. Since little serum urate is bound to plasma proteins, failure to reabsorb filtered urate results in a serum urate ranging from 0.2 to 1.8 mg/dL. Moderate uricosuria is present, and half of patients have renal calculi.

Renal urate clearance normally averages 15 percent of glomerular filtration rate, and the excreted urate is composed both of filtered urate that has escaped reabsorption and secreted urate. Subjects with isolated hypouricemia have urate clearances averaging from 33 to 85 percent of the filtration rate; in some, urate clearance exceeds the glomerular filtration rate. Studies with probenecid, which blocks tubular reabsorption of urate, and pyrazinamide, which blocks tubular secretion, reveal that six of the eight families described have a presecretory urate reabsorptive defect, and two have defective transport affecting the entire tubule. In four families hypercalciuria due to enhanced intestinal calcium absorption is also present, but in others only uricosuria has been demonstrated. The defect is inherited as an autosomal recessive trait. Urate transport has not been studied in nonrenal tissue or in obligate heterozygotes. The defect is presumed to reflect mutation of one or both of the proximal renal tubular membrane proteins that transport sodium urate. The findings in these families support the hypothesis that renal urate reabsorption is controlled by more than one transport protein.

DEFECTIVE ANION TRANSPORT: CHLORIDORRHEA

This rare, autosomal recessive disease results from impairment of active transport of chloride in the ileum and colon. Absence of the chloride-bicarbonate ion exchange ''pump'' causes profound symptoms even before birth (polyhydramnios and absence of meconium). Massive watery diarrhea is apparent from the first days of life. This fluid loss, with its attendant impairment of electrolyte homeostasis, is life-threatening. A hypokalemic, hypochloremic, hyponatremic metabolic alkalosis develops with dehydration and secondary hyperaldosteronism. Fecal fluid contains an excess of chloride ion over the sum of the accompanying cations, sodium and potassium. Fecal chloride concentration always exceeds 90 mmol per liter when volume and serum electrolyte disturbances are corrected, and this chloridorrhea is diagnostic. Renal chloride transport is normal. Decreased urine chloride results from the kidney's attempts to conserve salt and water.

Treatment requires adequate, life-long repletion of electrolyte and fluid losses, since no way has yet been found to mitigate the transport disorder. Exact replacement of water, sodium chloride, and potassium chloride can prevent the growth and psychomotor retardation and the development of progressive renal damage. The renal lesion, with hyalinized glomeruli, juxtaglomerular hyperplasia, calcifications, and arteriolar changes, is probably a result of chronic volume depletion. Treatment of hyperreninemia and hypokalemia with prostaglandin inhibitors may reduce renal damage but does not alter intestinal symptoms or the need for chronic sodium chloride repletion.

REFERENCES

DeMarchi S et al: Close genetic linkage between HLA and renal glycosuria. Am J Nephrol 4:280, 1984

Elsas LJ, Rosenberg LE: Renal glycosuria, in *Strauss and Welt's Diseases of the Kidney*, 3d ed, LE Earley, CW Gottschalk (eds). Boston, Little, Brown, 1979, pp 1021–1028

Holmberg C, Perheentupa J: Congenital chloride diarrhoea (CCD), in *Population Structure and Genetic Disorders*, AW Erikson et al (eds). New York, Academic, 1980, pp 596–599

Kamoun PP et al: Renal histidinuria. J Inherited Metab Dis 4:217, 1981

Rajantie J et al: Lysinuric protein intolerance: A 2-year trial of dietary supplementation therapy with citrulline and lysine. J Pediatr 97:927, 1980

Rajantie J et al: Lysinuric protein intolerance: Basolateral transport defect in renal tubuli. J Clin Invest 67:1078, 1981

Rosenberg LE: Intestinal hexose transport in familial glucose-galactose malabsorption, in *Membranes and Disease*, L Bolis et al (eds). New York, Raven Press, 1976, pp 253–262

———, Scriver CR: Disorders of amino acid metabolism, in *Metabolic Control and Disease*, 8th ed, PK Bondy, LE Rosenberg (eds). Philadelphia, Saunders, 1980, pp 616–645

Segal S, Thier SO: Cystinuria, in *The Metabolic Basis of Inherited Disease*, 5th ed, JB Stanbury et al (eds). New York, McGraw-Hill, 1983, pp 1774–1791

Short EM, Rosenberg LE: Renal aminoaciduria, in *Strauss and Welt's Diseases of the Kidney*, 3d ed, LE Earley, CW Gottschalk (eds). Boston, Little, Brown, 1979, pp 975–1020

Weitz R, Sperling O: Hereditary renal hypouricemia: Isolated tubular defect of urate reabsorption. J Pediatr 96:850, 1980

309 GOUT AND OTHER DISORDERS OF PURINE METABOLISM

WILLIAM N. KELLEY / THOMAS D. PALELLA

Gout is a term representing a heterogeneous group of diseases, which in their full development are manifested by (1) an increase in the serum urate concentration; (2) recurrent attacks of a characteristic acute arthritis, in which crystals of monosodium urate monohydrate are demonstrable in leukocytes of synovial fluid; (3) aggregated deposits of monosodium urate monohydrate (tophi) chiefly in and around the joints of the extremities and sometimes leading to severe crippling and deformity; (4) renal disease involving interstitial tissues and blood vessels; and (5) uric acid nephrolithiasis. These may occur singly or in combination.

PREVALENCE AND EPIDEMIOLOGY The serum urate value is elevated in an absolute sense when it exceeds the limit of solubility of monosodium urate in serum. At 37°C the saturation value of urate in plasma is about 7.0 mg/dL; a value above this represents supersaturation in a physicochemical sense. The serum urate concentration is relatively elevated when it exceeds the upper limit of an arbitrary normal range, usually defined as the mean serum urate value plus 2 standard deviations in a healthy population matched for age and sex. In most studies the upper limit is about 7.0 mg/dL in men and 6.0 mg/dL in women. In epidemiologic terms a serum urate value in excess of 7.0 mg/dL carries an increased risk of gouty arthritis or renal stones.

Sex and age influence urate levels. In both boys and girls the serum urate concentration before puberty averages approximately 3.6 mg/dL. After puberty, levels increase in boys more than in girls. Values in men reach a plateau in the early twenties and are essentially stable thereafter. Values in women are constant from age 20 through 40, but with menopause the values rise and approach or equal those in men. These age and sex differences are thought to be related to differences in the renal clearance of urate, perhaps influenced by the levels of estrogens and androgens. Certain physiologic variables such as height, body weight, creatinine, blood urea nitrogen, serum creatinine, and blood pressure correlate with serum urate concentration. Other factors, including warm ambient temperature, alcohol intake, high social status, and achievement or intelligence also appear to correlate with a higher serum urate concentration.

Hyperuricemia by one or more of the above definitions is present in 2 to 18 percent of the population. In one hospitalized group, 13 percent of adult men exhibited a serum urate concentration in excess of 7.0 mg/dL.

The incidence and prevalence of gout are less than those of hyperuricemia. In most of the western world the incidence of gout ranges from 0.20 to 0.35 per 1000, resulting in an overall prevalence of 0.13 to 0.37 percent of the population. The prevalence relates both to the degree of elevation of the serum urate and to the duration over which this elevation is sustained. Gout is therefore primarily a disease of adult men, and only about 5 percent of cases occur in women; it occurs rarely in the prepubertal child of either sex. The usual form is uncommon before the third decade, and the peak incidence is in the fifth decade.

INHERITANCE   In the United States a family history of gout is obtained in 6 to 18 percent of gouty subjects, and figures as high as 75 percent are noted after persistent questioning. A precise definition of the inheritance of gout is complicated by the environmental factors that alter the serum urate concentration. In addition, the identification of several specific causes of gout indicates that the disorder is the common clinical manifestation of a heterogeneous group of diseases. Accordingly, analysis of the inheritance of hyperuricemia and gout in the population or even within families is difficult. Two specific enzymatic causes of gout, hypoxanthine-guanine phosphoribosyltransferase deficiency and 5-phosphoribosyl-1-pyrophosphate (PRPP) synthetase overactivity, are X-linked. In other families the inheritance is consistent with an autosomal dominant mode. More commonly, genetic studies suggest multifactorial inheritance.

CLINICAL FEATURES   The full natural history of gout comprises four stages: asymptomatic hyperuricemia, acute gouty arthritis, intercritical gout, and chronic tophaceous gout. Nephrolithiasis may occur in any stage but the first.

Asymptomatic hyperuricemia   Asymptomatic hyperuricemia is that stage in which the serum urate level is raised but arthritic symptoms, tophi, or uric acid stones have not yet appeared. In men vulnerable to classic gout, hyperuricemia begins at puberty, whereas in women at risk hyperuricemia is usually delayed until menopause. In contrast, patients with certain of the enzyme defects to be described later may be hyperuricemic from birth. While asymptomatic hyperuricemia may last throughout the lifetime with no recognizable consequences, the tendency toward acute gouty arthritis increases as a function of the level and the duration of hyperuricemia. The risk of nephrolithiasis also increases as serum urate values increase and correlates with the magnitude of uric acid excretion. While virtually all gouty subjects are hyperuricemic, only about 5 percent of hyperuricemics ever develop gout.

The phase of asymptomatic hyperuricemia ends with the first attack of gouty arthritis or nephrolithiasis. In most, gout comes before stone, usually after at least 20 to 30 years of sustained hyperuricemia. However, between 10 and 40 percent of gouty subjects have renal colic prior to the first episode of arthritis.

Acute gouty arthritis   The primary manifestation of acute gout is exquisitely painful arthritis, at first usually monoarticular and associated with few constitutional symptoms but later often polyarticular and accompanied by fever. Estimates vary as to the percentage of patients in whom the initial gouty episode is polyarticular. Some authors' estimates are as high as 40 percent, and the majority of reports range from 3 to 14 percent. Attacks last a variable but limited period of time and are separated by asymptomatic intervals. In at least half the initial attack occurs in the first metatarsal phalangeal joint. Ultimately, 90 percent of patients experience an acute attack in the great toe (podagra).

Acute gouty arthritis is predominantly a disease of the lower extremities. The more distal the site of involvement the more typical are the attacks. Following the toe in order of frequency as sites of initial involvement are the insteps, ankles, heels, knees, wrists, fingers, and elbows. Acute attacks in the shoulder, hips, spine, sacroiliac, sternoclavicular, and mandibular joints are rare except in patients with established, severe disease. Gouty bursitis also occurs, the prepatellar and olecranon bursae being the most commonly involved sites. The patient may report trivial episodes of pain, often described as "twinges," preceding the first dramatic gouty attack. More commonly, the initial attack is unheralded and explosive. Often, the major attack begins at night, is exquisitely painful with inflamed joints, and may be triggered by a specific event such as trauma, alcohol ingestion, certain drugs, dietary excess, or surgery. The pain reaches peak intensity within several hours, and the associated signs of inflammation progress. The inflammatory response is typically so intense as to suggest pyogenic arthritis. Systemic signs may include fever, leukocytosis, and an elevated sedimentation rate. It is difficult to improve upon Syndenham's classic description:

The victim goes to bed and sleeps in good health. About two o'clock in the morning he is awakened by a severe pain in the great toe; more rarely in the heel, ankle or instep. This pain is like that of a dislocation, and yet the parts feel as if cold water were poured over them. Then follow chills and shivers, and a little fever. The pain, which was at first moderate, becomes more intense. With its intensity the chills and shivers increase. After a time this comes to its height, accommodating itself to the bones and ligaments of the tarsus and metatarsus. Now it is a violent stretching and tearing of the ligaments—now it is a gnawing pain and now a pressure and tightening. So exquisite and lively meanwhile is the feeling of the part affected, that it cannot bear the weight of bedclothes nor the jar of a person walking in the room. The night is passed in torture, sleeplessness, turning of the part affected, and perpetual change of posture; the tossing about of the body being as incessant as the pain of the tortured joint, and being worse as the fit comes on. Hence the vain effort by change of posture, both in the body and the limb affected, to obtain an abatement of the pain.

The initial gouty episode indicates the serum urate concentration has been sufficiently elevated for a long enough period of time to result in tissue deposition of substantial amounts of urate.

Intercritical period   The attack of gout may last only a day or two or up to several weeks but characteristically subsides spontaneously. No sequelae ensue, and resolution is complete. An asymptomatic phase termed the *intercritical period* then commences. The patient is totally free of symptoms during this stage, a feature that is diagnostically important. While approximately 7 percent never have a second attack, approximately 60 percent experience a recurrence within 1 year. However, the intercritical period may last up to 10 years and is terminated by successive attacks each of which may last longer and resolve less completely than its predecessors. Later attacks tend to be polyarticular, more severe, more prolonged, and associated with fever. In this stage gout may be difficult to differentiate from

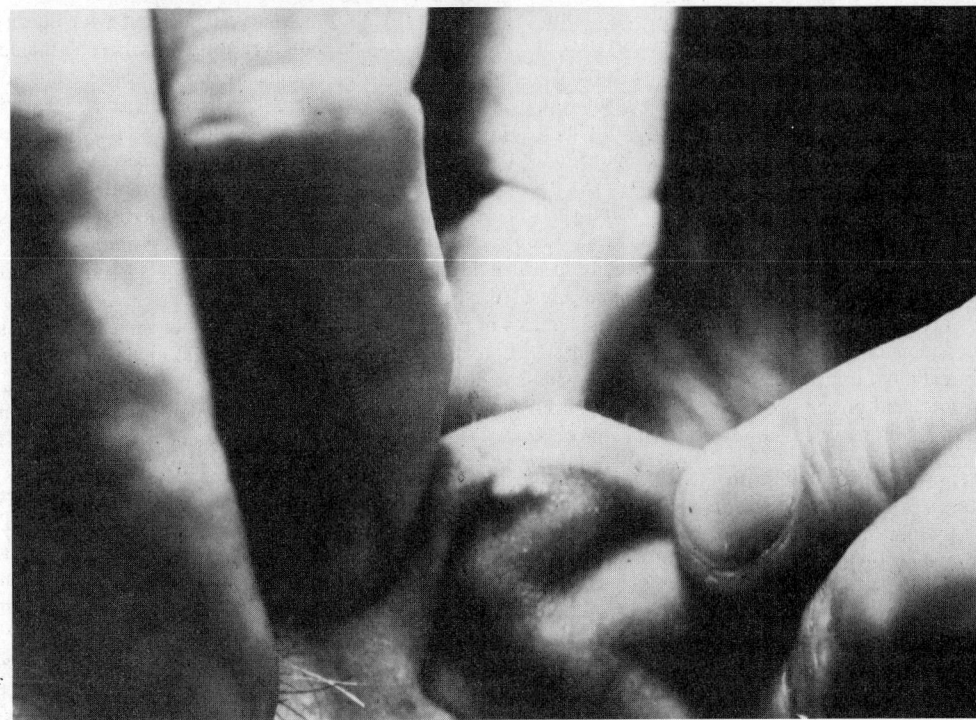

FIGURE 309-1 *Tophus of the helix of the ear adjacent to the auricular tubercle.*

other types of polyarticular arthritis such as rheumatoid arthritis. Rare patients progress directly from the initial acute attack to chronic polyarticular disease with no remissions.

Tophi and chronic gouty arthritis   In the untreated patient the rate of urate production exceeds the rate of urate disposition. As a result, the urate pool expands, and crystal deposits of monosodium urate eventually appear in cartilage, synovial membranes, tendons, and soft tissues. The rate of formation of these tophaceous deposits is a function of the degree and duration of hyperuricemia and of the severity of renal disease. The classic, but by no means the most common, location of a tophus is the helix or antihelix of the ear (Fig. 309-1). Tophi also commonly occur along the ulnar surface of the forearm, as saccular distensions of the olecranon bursae (Fig. 309-2), as enlargements of the Achilles tendon, or at other pressure points. Patients with the most severe tophi, interestingly, often have sparing of the helix and antihelix of the ear.

Tophi are difficult to differentiate from rheumatoid nodules and other types of subcutaneous nodules. They may ulcerate and exude chalky or pasty material rich in monosodium urate crystals. In contrast to other subcutaneous nodules, tophi are rarely transient although they may resolve slowly in response to treatment of hyperuricemia. Documentation of monosodium urate crystals by polarizing microscopy of an aspirate establishes the nodule in question as a tophus. It is rare for a tophus to become infected. Patients with severe tophaceous disease appear to have milder and less frequent attacks of acute gouty arthritis than do nontophaceous subjects. Chronic tophaceous gout rarely occurs prior to the onset of gouty arthritis.

Effective therapy alters the natural history of the disease. Since the advent of effective antihyperuricemic therapy, only a minority of patients develop visible tophi, permanent joint changes, or chronic symptoms.

Nephropathy   Some renal dysfunction occurs in up to 90 percent of subjects with gouty arthritis. Prior to the advent of chronic hemodialysis, renal failure accounted for 17 to 25 percent of deaths in the gouty population. The initial manifestation of renal involvement may be albuminuria or isosthenuria. If the patient presents in an advanced stage of renal failure it may be difficult to determine whether renal failure is a consequence of hyperuricemia or hyperuricemia is the result of renal disease.

Several types of parenchymal renal damage have been described. The first, urate nephropathy, has been attributed to the deposition of monosodium urate crystals in the renal interstitial tissue. The second, obstructive uropathy, is due to the formation of uric acid crystals in the collecting tubules, renal pelvis, or ureter, with resulting blockage of urine flow.

There is considerable controversy over the pathogenesis of urate nephropathy. While crystals of monosodium urate have been demonstrated in the interstitium of kidneys from some gouty subjects, such crystals are not present in the kidneys of most people with gout. Conversely, renal interstitial urate deposition occurs in the absence of gout, although the clinical significance of such deposition is unclear. Unidentified factors may participate in the formation of urate deposits in the kidney. Further, there is a close correlation between the development of renal disease and the presence of hypertension in patients with gout. It is frequently not clear whether the hypertension causes the renal disease or the gouty renal disease is the cause of the hypertension.

FIGURE 309-2 *Effusions of olecranon bursae of patient with gout. Note also the cutaneous deposits of urate and the minimal inflammatory response.*

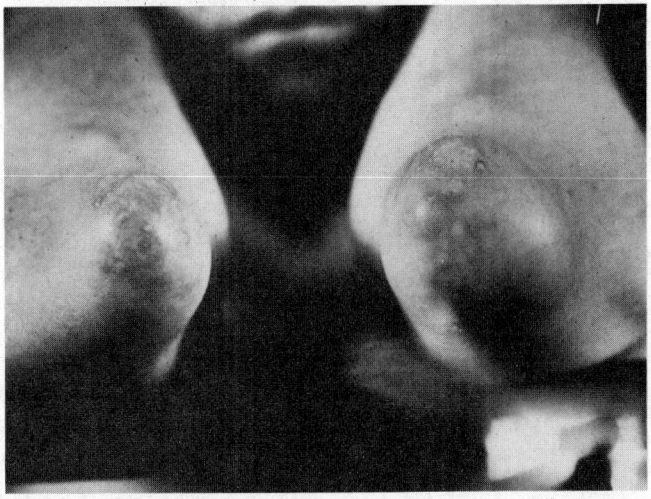

Acute obstructive uropathy is a severe form of acute renal failure due to the precipitation of uric acid crystals in collecting ducts and ureters. Renal failure in this setting correlates more strongly with hyperuricaciduria than with hyperuricemia. This condition occurs most commonly in (1) patients with profound overproduction of uric acid, particularly subjects with leukemia or lymphoma who are subjected to aggressive chemotherapy, (2) patients with gout and marked hyperuricaciduria, and (3) (possibly) patients following severe exercise, rhabdomyolysis, or convulsions. Aciduria favors the formation of the relatively insoluble nonionized uric acid and, hence, may contribute to crystal precipitation in any of these conditions. Postmortem studies reveal intraluminal precipitates of uric acid with dilatation of proximal tubules. Therapy designed to decrease the formation of uric acid, accelerate urine flow, and increase the fraction of uric acid present as the more soluble ionized form, monosodium urate, is effective in the reversal of this process.

Nephrolithiasis While the prevalence of subjects with uric acid stones in the United States is about 0.01 percent, the prevalence in gouty subjects ranges from 10 to 25 percent. The major factor favoring formation of uric acid stones is the increased urinary excretion of uric acid. Hyperuricaciduria may be due to primary gout, inborn errors of metabolism resulting in the overproduction of uric acid, myeloproliferative disease, and other neoplastic disorders. When the urinary uric acid exceeds 1100 mg per day, the incidence reaches 50 percent. There is also correlation with increasing serum urate concentrations, the prevalence reaching approximately 50 percent at a serum urate value of 13 mg/dL or above. Other factors contributing to the formation of uric acid stones include (1) undue acidity of the urine, (2) increased urine concentration, and (3) (perhaps) abnormalities of urinary constituents that affect the solubility of uric acid itself.

Gouty subjects also have an increased frequency of calcium-containing stones; the occurrence in gout is 1 to 3 percent, while that in the general population is about 0.1 percent. While the mechanisms for this association are unclear, there is a high frequency of hyperuricemia and hyperuricaciduria in patients seen because of calcium stones. Uric acid crystals may serve as a nidus for calcium stone formation.

Associated conditions Obesity, hypertriglyceridemia, and hypertension are common. The hypertriglyceridemia of primary gout is strongly associated with obesity or alcohol ingestion and not with hyperuricemia itself. The incidence of hypertension in the nongouty population is correlated with age, sex, and obesity; when these factors are appropriately scored, there appears to be little or no direct relationship between hyperuricemia and hypertension. The increased frequency of diabetes is also probably related to factors such as age and obesity and not to hyperuricemia itself. Finally, the increased incidence of atherosclerosis has been attributed to the concomitant obesity, hypertension, diabetes, and hypertriglyceridemia.

Independent analysis of these variables suggests that obesity is most important. Hyperuricemia in the obese subject appears to be related to both increased production and reduced excretion of uric acid. Chronic alcohol ingestion also results in both overproduction and underexcretion of uric acid.

Rheumatoid arthritis, systemic lupus erythematosus, and amyloidosis rarely coexist with gout. The reasons for these negative associations are not known.

Acute gout should be suspected in any patient presenting with the sudden onset of monoarthritis, particularly in a distal joint of the lower extremity. Synovial aspiration should be performed in all such patients. The diagnosis of gout is established with certainty upon demonstration of monosodium urate crystals in leukocytes of synovial fluid from the involved joint by compensated polarized light microscopy (Fig. 309-3). The crystals are typically needle-shaped and negatively birefringent. Such crystals can be identified in synovial fluid of over 95 percent of patients with acute gouty arthritis. Failure to demonstrate urate crystals in synovial fluid after careful search under appropriate conditions makes the diagnosis unlikely. The presence of intracellular urate crystals establishes the diagnosis but does not exclude the possibility that another type of arthropathy is present concurrently.

Infection or pseudogout (calcium pyrophosphate dihydrate deposition) may coexist with gout. A Gram stain of the synovial fluid should be examined, and cultures should be obtained to exclude coexistent infection. Calcium pyrophosphate dihydrate is weakly positively birefringent and is more rectangular than monosodium urate. With polarized light microscopy, the crystals are easily differentiated. Synovial aspiration need not be repeated with subsequent episodes unless an alternative diagnosis is being considered.

During asymptomatic intercritical periods, synovial aspiration may still be helpful. Extracellular urate crystals can be found in more than two-thirds of aspirates from the first metatarsophalangeal joints of asymptomatic gouty patients Less than 5 percent of hyperuricemic patients without gout have such crystals.

Synovial fluid analysis may also be helpful in other ways. The total leukocyte count may range from 1000 to more than 70,000 per milliliter. The predominant cell type is the polymorphonuclear leukocyte. As with other inflammatory fluids, the mucin clot is fair to poor. The concentrations of glucose and uric acid are the same as in serum.

In the patient in whom synovial fluid cannot be obtained or in whom intracellular crystals cannot be demonstrated, a presumptive diagnosis of gout can be seriously entertained if the patient has (1) hyperuricemia, (2) the classic clinical features described above, and (3) a dramatic response to colchicine. In the absence of crystals or this highly suggestive triad, the diagnosis of gout should be considered tentative. A dramatic therapeutic response to colchicine is strongly suggestive of the diagnosis of gouty arthritis but is not pathognomonic by itself.

Acute gouty arthritis must be differentiated from other causes of monoarticular and polyarticular arthritis. A common initial presentation in the gouty patient is podagra, but many conditions mimic the painful, swollen big toe characteristic of the disease. These include soft tissue infection, pyogenic arthritis, inflamed bunions, local trauma, rheumatoid arthritis, degenerative arthritis with acute inflammation, acute sarcoidosis, psoriatic arthritis, pseudogout, acute calcific tendonitis, palindromic rheumatism, Reiter's disease, and sporotrichosis. Rarely, confusion may be caused by cellulitis, gon-

FIGURE 309-3 *Crystals of monosodium urate monohydrate in joint aspirate.*

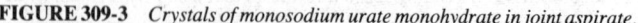

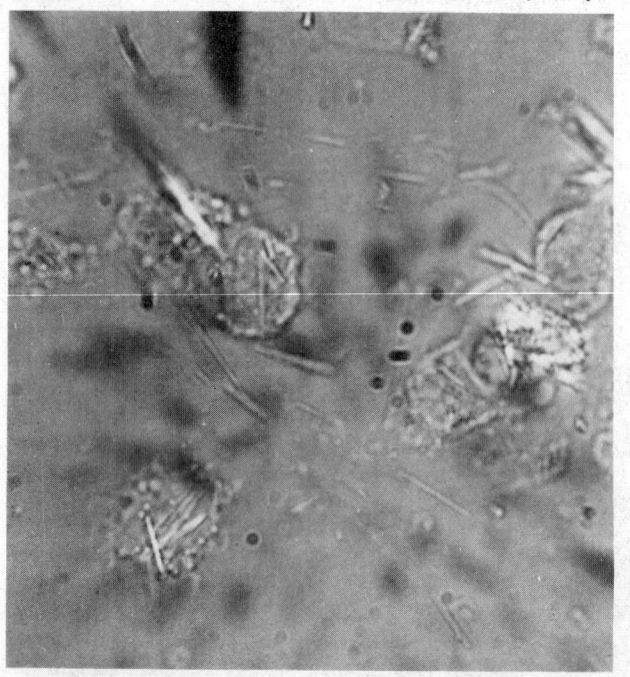

orrhea, fibrosis of the sole and heel, hematoma, and subacute bacterial endocarditis with embolization or suppurative arthritis. Gouty involvement of other joints such as the knee must also be differentiated from acute rheumatic fever, serum sickness, hemarthrosis, and the peripheral joint involvement of ankylosing spondylitis or inflammatory bowel disease.

Chronic gouty arthritis must be differentiated from rheumatoid arthritis, inflammatory osteoarthritis, psoriatic arthritis, enteropathic arthritis, and the peripheral arthritis associated with the spondyloarthropathies. A history of antecedent, self-limited monoarticular arthritis, the presence of tophi, typical radiographic changes, and the demonstration of hyperuricemia add support to the diagnosis of chronic gout. Chronic gout can be similar to other inflammatory arthropathies. The existence of effective therapy for gout justifies a vigorous workup to establish or exclude this diagnosis.

PATHOPHYSIOLOGY OF HYPERURICEMIA Classification The biochemical hallmark and prerequisite of gout is hyperuricemia. The concentration of uric acid in body fluids is determined by the balance between rates of production and elimination. Uric acid is formed by oxidation of purine bases, which may be exogenous or endogenous in origin. About two-thirds of uric acid is excreted into the urine (300 to 600 mg per day), and approximately one-third is excreted into the gastrointestinal tract, where it is ultimately destroyed by bacteria. Hyperuricemia may be due to an excessive rate of uric acid production, a decrease in the renal excretion of uric acid, or a combination of both events.

Hyperuricemia and gout may be classified as metabolic or renal (Table 309-1). In those patients with hyperuricemia of metabolic origin, there is an increased production of uric acid, whereas in those with hyperuricemia of renal origin, decreased renal excretion of uric acid causes the hyperuricemia. The distinction between metabolic and renal origins of hyperuricemia is not always clear-cut. A large number of gouty subjects have evidence of both mechanisms when thoroughly investigated. In such cases, the dominant component—renal or metabolic—directs classification. In the classification used here *primary* refers to those cases in which gout or hyperuricemia is the central manifestation of the disease, namely, gout that is neither secondary to another acquired disorder nor a subordinate manifestation of an inborn error that leads initially to a major disease unlike gout. While some cases of primary gout have a defined genetic basis, others do not. *Secondary* hyperuricemia or gout refers to those cases which develop in the course of another disease or as a consequence of drugs.

Overproduction of uric acid Overproducers of uric acid by definition excrete in excess of 600 mg per day after a 5-day period of dietary purine restriction; such patients probably represent less than 10 percent of the gouty population. In these patients there is an acceleration in the rate of purine biosynthesis de novo or an increased turnover of purines. Understanding the basic mechanisms responsible for these abnormalities requires an understanding of purine metabolism (Fig. 309-4).

The purine nucleotides, adenylic acid (AMP), inosinic acid (IMP), and guanylic acid (GMP), are the end products of purine biosynthesis. They can be synthesized in one of two ways: either directly from the purine bases, e.g., guanine to GMP, hypoxanthine to IMP, and adenine to AMP; or they may be synthesized de novo, beginning with nonpurine precursors and progressing through a series of steps to the formation of IMP, which is the common intermediate purine nucleotide. IMP can be converted either to AMP or to GMP. Once the purine nucleotides are formed, they are utilized for the synthesis of nucleic acids, adenosine triphosphate (ATP), cyclic AMP, cyclic GMP, and certain cofactors.

The various purine components are degraded to the purine nucleotide monophosphates. GMP is degraded via guanosine, guanine, and xanthine to uric acid. IMP is degraded through inosine, hypoxanthine, and xanthine to uric acid. AMP can be deaminated to IMP and further catabolized through inosine to uric acid, or it may be degraded to inosine by an alternate pathway with the intermediate formation of adenosine.

While the purine pathway is regulated in a complex manner, the intracellular concentration of 5-phosphoribosyl-1-pyrophosphate (PRPP) appears to be a major determinant of the rate of synthesis of uric acid in humans. Generally, when the concentration of PRPP in the cell is elevated, uric acid synthesis is elevated; when the concentration of PRPP is reduced, the synthesis of uric acid is also reduced. Although exceptions are recognized, this concept is applicable to most situations.

Overproduction of uric acid in a small minority of adult gouty subjects occurs as either a primary or a secondary manifestation of an inborn error in metabolism. Hyperuricemia and gout occur as a primary manifestation of partial hypoxanthine-guanine phosphoribosyltransferase deficiency (reaction 2, Fig. 309-4) and of PRPP synthetase superactivity (reaction 3, Fig. 309-4). In the Lesch-Nyhan syndrome, the virtually complete deficiency of hypoxanthine-guanine phosphoribosyltransferase results in secondary hyperuricemia. These important inborn errors are discussed more fully below.

These two inborn errors of purine metabolism, hypoxanthine-guanine phosphoribosyltransferase deficiency and PRPP synthetase overactivity, account for less than 15 percent of all patients with primary hyperuricemia associated with an overproduction of uric acid. The cause of the overproduction in the majority of patients has not been defined.

There are numerous causes of secondary hyperuricemia associated with an increased production of uric acid. In some, the increased excretion of uric acid is related, as it is in primary gout, to an accelerated rate of purine biosynthesis de novo. Patients with glucose 6-phosphatase deficiency (type I glycogen storage disease) uniformly

TABLE 309-1 Classification of hyperuricemia and gout

Type	Metabolic disturbance	Inheritance
Metabolic (10%):		
Primary		
Molecular defects undefined	Not established	Polygenic
Associated with specific enzyme defects		
PRPP synthetase variants, increased activity	Overproduction of PRPP and of uric acid	X-linked
Hypoxanthine-guanine phosphoribosyltransferase deficiency, partial	Overproduction of uric acid, increased purine biosynthesis de novo driven by surplus PRPP	X-linked
Secondary		
Associated with increased purine biosynthesis de novo		
Glucose 6-phosphatase deficiency or absence	Overproduction plus underexcretion of uric acid; glycogen storage disease, type I (von Gierke)	Autosomal recessive
Hypoxanthine-guanine phosphoribosyltransferase deficiency, "virtually complete"	Overproduction of uric acid; Lesch-Nyhan syndrome	X-linked
Associated with increased nucleic acid turnover	Overproduction of uric acid	
Renal (90%):		
Primary		
Secondary		

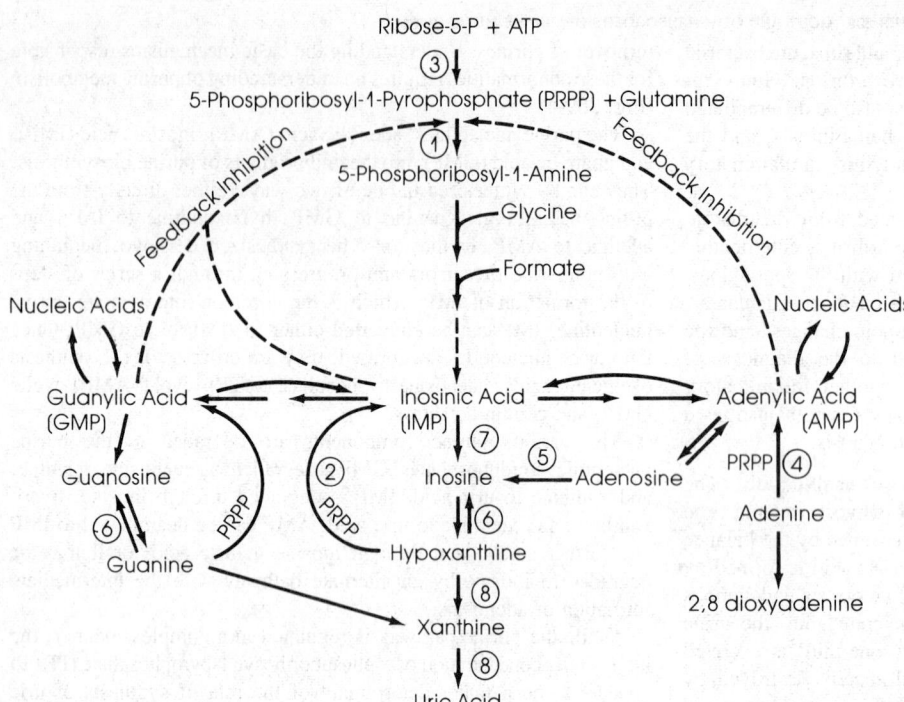

FIGURE 309-4 *Outline of purine metabolism: (1) amidophosphoribosyltransferase; (2) hypoxanthine-guanine phosphoribosyltransferase; (3) PRPP synthetase; (4) adenine phosphoribosyltransferase; (5) adenosine deaminase; (6) purine nucleoside phosphorylase; (7) 5'-nucleotidase; (8) xanthine oxidase.*

exhibit an increased production of uric acid as well as an accelerated rate of purine biosynthesis de novo (see Chap. 313). Overproduction of uric acid in patients with this enzyme defect is multifactorial. An accelerated rate of de novo purine synthesis may be due in part to accelerated synthesis of PRPP. Additionally, accelerated degradation of purine nucleotides contributes to an increased rate of uric acid excretion. Both of these mechanisms are due to the deficiency of

FIGURE 309-5 *Rate of uric acid excretion at various plasma urate levels in nongouty (solid symbols) and gouty (open symbols) subjects. Large symbols represent mean values; small symbols represent individual data of a few mean values selected to illustrate the degree of scatter within groups. Studies were conducted under basal conditions, after RNA feeding, and after infusions of lithium urate. (From Wyngaarden. Reproduced by permission of Academic Press.)*

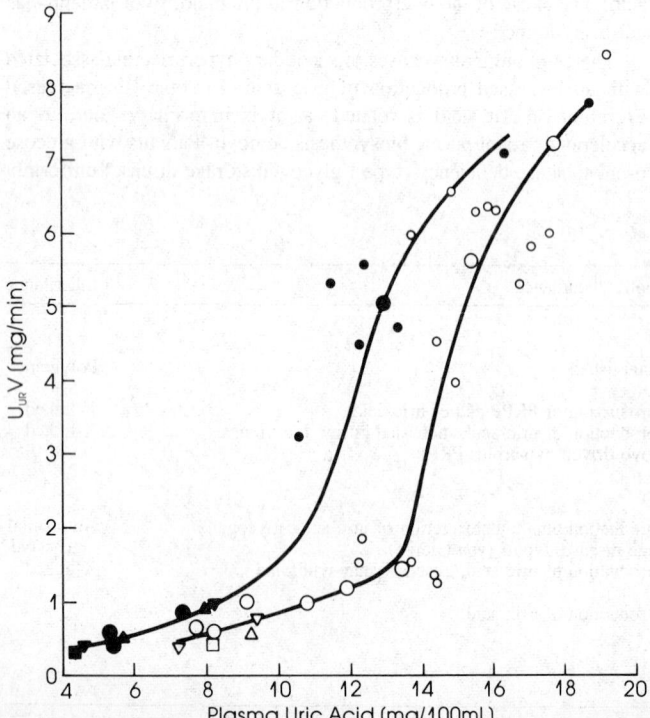

glucose as an energy source, and the production of uric acid can be decreased by the sustained correction of hypoglycemia in this disorder.

In the majority of patients with secondary hyperuricemia due to an overproduction of uric acid, the predominant abnormality appears to be an increased turnover of nucleic acids. A number of diseases, including the myeloproliferative and lymphoproliferative disorders, multiple myeloma, secondary polycythemia, pernicious anemia, certain hemoglobinopathies, thalassemia, other hemolytic anemias, infectious mononucleosis, and some carcinomas, may be associated with increased marrow activity or increased cell turnover at other sites and an associated increased turnover of nucleic acids. The increased turnover in nucleic acids leads in turn to hyperuricemia, hyperuricaciduria, and a compensatory increase in the rate of purine biosynthesis de novo.

Reduced excretion A large proportion of gouty subjects require a plasma urate value 1 to 2 mg/dL higher than normal subjects to achieve a given rate of uric acid excretion (Fig. 309-5). This abnormality is most prominent in the gouty subject with a normal production of uric acid and is not present in most subjects with overproduction of uric acid.

The excretion of urate is dependent on glomerular filtration, tubular reabsorption, and tubular secretion. Uric acid appears to be completely filtered at the glomerulus and reabsorbed in the proximal tubule (i.e., presecretory reabsorption). Uric acid secretion then occurs in a subsequent segment of the proximal tubule, and partial reabsorption takes place at a second reabsorptive site in the distal portion of the proximal tubule (i.e., postsecretory reabsorption). While some uric acid reabsorption may also occur in the ascending limb of the loop of Henle and in the collecting duct, these latter two sites are thought to be quantitatively less important. Attempts to define further the location and nature of these latter sites and to quantify their contribution to uric acid transport in normal humans or in various disease states have been largely unrewarding.

Theoretically, the altered renal excretion of uric acid exhibited by most patients with gout could be due to (1) reduced filtration of uric acid, (2) enhanced reabsorption, or (3) decreased secretion. No unequivocal data establish any one of these mechanisms as the basic defect, and it is likely that all three are operative within the gouty population.

Numerous secondary causes of hyperuricemia and gout can also be attributed to a decrease in the renal excretion of uric acid. A reduction in the glomerular filtration rate leads to a decrease in the filtered load of uric acid and thus to hyperuricemia; patients with renal disease are hyperuricemic on this basis. Other factors, such as decreased secretion of uric acid, have been postulated in patients with some types of renal disease (e.g., polycystic kidney disease and lead nephropathy). Gout is a rare complication of the secondary hyperuricemia due to renal disease.

Diuretic therapy is one of the most important causes of secondary hyperuricemia. Diuretic-induced volume depletion leads to enhanced tubular reabsorption of uric acid as well as decreased uric acid filtration. Decreased secretion of uric acid may also be a mechanism in diuretic-induced hyperuricemia. A number of other drugs lead to hyperuricemia by undefined renal mechanisms; these agents include low-dose aspirin, pyrazinamide, nicotinic acid, ethambutol, and ethanol.

Impaired renal excretion of uric acid is thought to be an important mechanism for the hyperuricemia associated with several disease states. Volume depletion may be important in patients with hyperuricemia associated with adrenal insufficiency and nephrogenic diabetes insipidus. In some situations hyperuricemia has been attributed to competitive inhibition of uric acid secretion by excess organic acids thought to be secreted by the same renal tubular mechanism responsible for uric acid secretion. Examples include starvation (ketosis and free fatty acids), alcoholic ketosis, diabetic ketoacidosis, maple syrup urine disease, and lactic acidosis of any cause. Hyperuricemia in conditions such as hyperparathyroidism, hypoparathyroidism, pseudohypoparathyroidism, and hypothyroidism may also have a renal basis, but the mechanism is unclear.

PATHOGENESIS OF ACUTE GOUTY ARTHRITIS The events leading to the initial crystallization of monosodium urate in a joint after an average of 30 years of asymptomatic hyperuricemia are not completely understood. Sustained hyperuricemia leads eventually to the development of microtophi in the synovial lining cells and perhaps to an accumulation in cartilage of monosodium urate on proteoglycans that have a high affinity for urate. By one of several mechanisms, probably including trauma with disruption of the microtophi and increased turnover of the cartilage proteoglycans, there is an episodic release of urate crystals into the synovial fluid. Other factors, such as a lower temperature in the joint space or an unequal reabsorption of water and urate from the synovial fluid, may accelerate urate precipitation.

A sufficient amount of crystals in the joint space triggers the acute attack by a process that appears to include (1) phagocytosis of the crystals by leukocytes with the rapid release of a chemotactic protein from the leukocytes, (2) activation of the kallikrein system, (3) activation of complement with the consequent formation of the chemotactic complement components, and (4) the ultimate urate-mediated disruption of lysosomes within the leukocytes, leading to destruction of white blood cells and release of lysosomal products into the synovial fluid. While progress in the understanding of acute gouty arthritis has occurred, questions about factors responsible for spontaneous resolution of the acute attack and the effect of colchicine remain to be answered.

TREATMENT The therapeutic aims in gout are (1) to terminate the acute attack as promptly and gently as possible; (2) to prevent recurrences of acute gouty arthritis; (3) to prevent or reverse complications of the disease resulting from deposition of monosodium urate crystals in joints, kidneys, and other sites; (4) to prevent or reverse associated features such as obesity, hypertriglyceridemia, or hypertension; and (5) to prevent formation of uric acid kidney stones.

Treatment of the acute gouty attack Acute gouty arthritis is treated with an anti-inflammatory agent. Colchicine is the drug most frequently employed. Standard therapy involves administration of 0.5 mg each hour or 1.0 mg every 2 h by mouth until one of three things occurs: (1) the patient improves, (2) gastrointestinal side effects develop, or (3) a maximum of 6 mg is taken without relief. Colchicine is most effective if therapy is begun shortly after the onset of symptoms. Over 75 percent of patients with gout show major improvement in symptoms within the first 12 h of treatment. However, as many as 80 percent of patients are unable to tolerate an optimal dose because of gastrointestinal side effects, which may precede or coincide with clinical improvement. Orally administered colchicine results in peak plasma levels in approximately 2 h. Consequently, it has been suggested that 1.0 mg every 2 h is less likely to lead to the accumulation of toxic levels before the onset of therapeutic effect. However, since therapeutic benefit relates to colchicine levels within leukocytes rather than plasma levels, the efficacy of this regimen requires further evaluation.

Intravenous administration of colchicine eliminates gastrointestinal side effects and provides a more rapid response. Colchicine levels become high in leukocytes, remain constant for 24 h, and are detectable for over 10 days after a single intravenous infusion. As an initial dose 2 mg should be given intravenously, followed by two additional doses of 1 mg at 6-h intervals if needed. Special care must be taken in the intravenous administration of colchicine. The drug is irritative and can lead to severe pain and necrosis if allowed to extravasate to surrounding tissues. It is important to make certain that the intravenous route is secure and that the drug is diluted with 5 to 10 volumes of normal saline solution and infused over a period of no less than 5 min. Colchicine by either oral or parenteral route may cause bone marrow depression, alopecia, hepatocellular failure, mental depression, seizures, ascending paralysis, respiratory depression, and death. Toxic effects are more likely in patients with hepatic, bone marrow, or renal disease and in those subjects on maintenance colchicine. The dosage should be reduced for these individuals, and the drug should not be used in neutropenic patients.

Other anti-inflammatory agents, including indomethacin, phenylbutazone, naproxen, and fenoprofen, are also effective in the treatment of acute gouty arthritis. Indomethacin may be given at a dose of 75 mg orally, followed by 50 mg every 6 h and continued at that dose for 24 h after relief is obtained. The drug is then tapered to 50 mg every 8 h for three doses and then to 25 mg every 8 h for three doses. Side effects of indomethacin include gastrointestinal toxicity, sodium retention, and complaints referable to the central nervous system. While the incidence of side effects may be as high as 60 percent in patients taking the doses described above, the drug is generally better tolerated than colchicine and probably is the treatment of choice in the patient with a well-established diagnosis of acute gouty arthritis. To improve the therapeutic response and thus diminish morbidity of the disease, the patient may be instructed to begin therapy with an anti-inflammatory agent at the first twinge of an acute attack. Uricosuric drugs and allopurinol have no role in the treatment of the acute gouty attack.

Systemic or locally administered (i.e., intraarticular) glucocorticoids are useful in treating acute gout particularly when colchicine and nonsteroidal anti-inflammatory drugs are contraindicated or ineffective. When given systemically, moderate doses should be administered either by the oral or intravenous route for several days at most before the drug is rapidly tapered and discontinued. An isolated monoarthritis or bursitis can be terminated within 24 or 36 h by the intraarticular instillation of a long-acting steroid preparation (e.g., triamcinolone hexacetonide, 15 to 30 mg). This is particularly useful when standard drug regimens are not practical.

Prophylaxis Once the acute episode has resolved, a number of measures can reduce the likelihood of recurrence: (1) the institution of prophylactic daily colchicine or indomethacin, (2) controlled weight reduction for the obese patient, (3) avoidance of known precipitating factors such as heavy alcohol consumption or a diet rich in purines, and (4) the institution of antihyperuricemic therapy.

The administration of small daily doses of colchicine is effective prophylaxis against further acute attacks. A program of 1 to 2 mg colchicine a day is successful in about three-fourths of patients with gout and fails completely in only about 5 percent. In addition, this program is safe and essentially free of side effects. However, unless serum urate is maintained at normal levels, the patient is spared only acute arthritis and may develop other manifestations of gout. Maintenance colchicine therapy is particularly helpful during the first year or two after institution of antihyperuricemic drugs.

Prevention or reversal of the deposition of monosodium urate in tissues Antihyperuricemic agents are effective in reducing serum urate concentration and should be used in patients with (1) one or more attacks of acute gouty arthritis, (2) one or more tophi, and (3) uric acid nephrolithiasis. The aim of antihyperuricemic therapy is to maintain the serum urate below 7.0 mg/dL, the minimal concentration at which urate saturates the extracellular fluid. Reduction to these levels may be achieved by use of drugs that increase the renal excretion of uric acid or decrease uric acid production. Antihyperuricemic drugs generally do not have anti-inflammatory properties. Uricosuric agents reduce serum urate by enhancing the renal excretion. While a large number of drugs exhibit this property, the most effective agents available in the United States are probenecid and sulfinpyrazone. Probenecid is usually started in doses of 250 mg twice a day; it is increased over a period of several weeks to the dose necessary to achieve effective reversal of the hyperuricemia. A total dose of 1 g per day is appropriate for half of patients; the maximum dose should not exceed 3.0 g per day. Because the half-life is 6 to 12 h, it should be given in two to four evenly spaced doses per day. Hypersensitivity, skin rash, and gastrointestinal complaints are the major side effects. Although serious toxicity is rare, side effects may cause up to a third of the patients to discontinue probenecid.

Sulfinpyrazone is a metabolite of phenylbutazone with no anti-inflammatory activity. The drug is usually started at a dose of 50 mg twice a day and gradually increased to a maintenance level of 300 to 400 mg per day given in three or four divided doses. The maximum effective daily dose is 800 mg. Side effects are similar to those with probenecid, although the incidence of bone marrow toxicity may be higher. Approximately a fourth of patients stop the drug for one reason or another.

Probenecid and sulfinpyrazone are effective in most patients with hyperuricemia and gout. In addition to intolerance, failures can result from poor patient compliance, concomitant salicylate ingestion, or impaired renal function. Aspirin at any dose blocks the uricosuric effect of probenecid and sulfinpyrazone. These agents begin to lose effectiveness as the creatinine clearance falls below 80 mL/min and are ineffective when clearance reaches 30 mL/min.

During the negative urate balance induced by uricosuric therapy, the serum urate value drops and urinary uric acid excretion is elevated above pretreatment levels. With continuation of therapy excess urate is mobilized and eliminated, the serum urate falls, and uric acid excretion returns essentially to pretreatment levels. The transient increase in uric acid excretion, which usually lasts for only a few days, may lead to the development of renal calculi in a tenth of patients so treated. To avoid this complication uricosuric agents should be started at low doses and gradually increased as described. Maintaining an ample urine flow with adequate hydration and alkalinizing the urine with oral sodium bicarbonate alone or in combination with acetazolamide reduce the likelihood of stone formation. The ideal candidate for uricosuric agents is under 60 and has normal renal function, uric acid excretion of less than 700 mg per day on a general diet, and no history of renal stones.

Hyperuricemia may also be controlled by allopurinol, a drug that decreases uric acid synthesis. Allopurinol inhibits xanthine oxidase (reaction 8, Fig. 309-4), the enzyme that catalyzes the oxidation of hypoxanthine to xanthine and xanthine to uric acid. While allopurinol has a half-life in vivo of only 2 to 3 h, it is metabolized largely to oxipurinol, which also is an effective inhibitor of xanthine oxidase and has a half-life ranging from 18 to 30 h. In most patients 300 mg per day is an effective antihyperuricemic dose. Because of the long half-life of the major metabolite the drug may be administered once a day. Since oxipurinol is largely excreted in the urine, its half-life is prolonged in patients with renal insufficiency. The dose of allopurinol should, therefore, be reduced by half in patients with significant renal dysfunction.

Significant side effects of allopurinol include gastrointestinal distress, skin rashes, fever, toxic epidermal necrolysis, alopecia, bone marrow suppression, hepatitis, jaundice, and vasculitis. The overall incidence of side effects is about 20 percent; they are more common in the presence of renal insufficiency. In only 5 percent of patients the side effects are sufficient to force discontinuation of the drug. Important drug-drug interactions involving allopurinol include prolongation of the half-lives of mercaptopurine and azathioprine and enhancement of the toxicity of cyclophosphamide.

Specific indications for choosing allopurinol over a uricosuric drug include (1) an increased urinary uric acid excretion (greater than 700 mg per day on a general diet), (2) impairment of renal function with a creatinine clearance less than 80 mL/min, (3) tophaceous gout regardless of renal function, (4) uric acid nephrolithiasis, and (5) gout not controlled by uricosuric agents because of ineffectiveness or intolerance. Allopurinol and a uricosuric drug may be used simultaneously in the rare patient who cannot be controlled by a single medication. Such combination therapy requires no modification in the dosage of either agent and usually results in further lowering of the serum urate concentration.

Acute gouty arthritis may occur whenever there is a rapid and substantial change in the serum urate concentration. Thus, the initiation of antihyperuricemic therapy with any agent may precipitate acute gouty arthritis. In addition, recurrent attacks may occur for a year or longer when large tophaceous deposits are present, even if hyperuricemia is controlled. For these reasons, it is prudent to begin prophylactic therapy with colchicine prior to initiation of antihyperuricemic drugs and to continue it until the serum urate is controlled for at least a year or until all tophi have resolved. Patients should be warned of the possibility of flare-up during the early phase of therapy. While it is not necessary in most gouty patients, strict dietary purine restriction should be instituted in patients with severe tophaceous gout and/or renal failure.

Prevention and treatment of acute uric acid nephropathy Immediate and vigorous therapy is essential for acute uric acid nephropathy. The first step is to increase urine flow by vigorous hydration coupled with administration of a potent diuretic such as furosemide. The urine should be alkalinized to achieve conversion of uric acid to the more soluble monosodium urate. Alkalinization can be accomplished by the administration of sodium bicarbonate alone or in combination with acetazolamide. Allopurinol should also be administered to reduce uric acid formation. The initial dose in this setting should be 8 mg per kilogram of body weight per day given as a single daily dose. The dose should be decreased after 3 or 4 days to 100 to 200 mg per day if renal insufficiency persists. Treatment for uric acid kidney stones is similar to that for acute uric acid nephropathy. In most cases allopurinol combined only with high fluid intake is effective.

WORKUP OF THE HYPERURICEMIC PATIENT Evaluation of the patient with hyperuricemia is directed toward (1) defining the cause of the hyperuricemia (which may disclose an important disease other than gout), (2) assessing the presence and extent of damage to tissues and organs, and (3) identifying associated abnormalities. From a practical standpoint these inquiries are pursued simultaneously, since decisions about the significance of hyperuricemia and about therapy depend on the answers to all of these.

The most important single test in the hyperuricemic patient is analysis of the urine for uric acid. If a history of stone disease is present, a flat plate of the abdomen and intravenous pyelogram may be indicated. If a renal stone is recovered, analysis for uric acid and other constituents is useful. If joint disease is present, synovial fluid analysis and x-rays of the involved joints are helpful. If there is a history of exposure to lead, measurement of urinary lead excretion after an infusion of calcium edetate may be useful in documenting the presence of gout due to lead exposure. In cases where the patient appears to be an overproducer, measurement of erythrocyte hypoxanthine-guanine phosphoribosyltransferase and PRPP synthetase levels may be indicated.

Management of asymptomatic hyperuricemia   There is considerable controversy about the indications for therapy of the patient with asymptomatic hyperuricemia. Generally, treatment should be withheld unless the patient (1) becomes symptomatic; (2) has a strong family history for gout, nephrolithiasis, or renal failure; or (3) excretes large quantities of uric acid (greater than 1100 mg per day).

OTHER DISORDERS OF PURINE METABOLISM ASSOCIATED WITH HYPERURICEMIA AND GOUT   Hypoxanthine-guanine phosphoribosyltransferase deficiency states

Hypoxanthine-guanine phosphoribosyltransferase catalyzes the conversion of hypoxanthine to inosinic acid and guanine to guanosinic acid (reaction 2, Fig. 309-4). PRPP serves as the phosphoribosyl donor. The deficiency of hypoxanthine-guanine phosphoribosyltransferase leads to decreased consumption of PRPP which accumulates to higher than normal levels. The excess PRPP accelerates de novo purine biosynthesis and consequently increases uric acid production.

The Lesch-Nyhan syndrome is an X-linked disorder. The characteristic biochemical abnormality is a profound deficiency of the enzyme hypoxanthine-guanine phosphoribosyltransferase (reaction 2, Fig. 309-4). Affected patients have hyperuricemia and a profound overproduction of uric acid. In addition, they have a bizarre neurologic disorder characterized by self-mutilation, choreoathetosis, spasticity, and retardation of growth and mental function. The incidence is estimated at 1:100,000 births.

From 0.5 to 1.0 percent of adult gouty subjects with overproduction of uric acid have a partial deficiency of hypoxanthine-guanine phosphoribosyltransferase. These patients typically have the onset of gouty arthritis at a young age (15 to 30 years), a high incidence of uric acid stones (75 percent), and the occasional occurrence of mild neurologic dysfunction characterized by dysarthria, hyperreflexia, incoordination, and/or mental retardation. This disease is inherited as an X-linked trait so that men are affected through carrier females.

The enzyme whose deficiency results in these disorders, hypoxanthine-guanine phosphoribosyltransferase, is of considerable interest in genetics. With the possible exception of the globin gene family, the hypoxanthine-guanine phosphoribosyltransferase locus is the single most studied human gene.

Human hypoxanthine-guanine phosphoribosyltransferase has been purified to homogeneity, and its amino acid sequence has been determined. The normal enzyme has a native subunit molecular weight of 24,470 and consists of 217 amino acid residues. The normal enzyme is a tetramer with four identical subunits. Four variant forms of hypoxanthine-guanine phosphoribosyltransferase from deficient patients have been sequenced as well (Table 309-2). In each a single amino acid substitution leads to either a catalytically incompetent protein or decreased steady-state concentrations of hypoxanthine-guanine phosphoribosyltransferase as a result of diminished synthesis or accelerated degradation of the mutant protein.

The DNA sequence complementary to messenger RNA (mRNA) encoding hypoxanthine-guanine phosphoribosyltransferase has been cloned and sequenced as well. As a molecular probe, this cDNA sequence has been used to identify carrier status in a female at risk for whom conventional carrier detection techniques were not successful. The human gene has been transferred to mice via retroviral vector–infected bone marrow transplantation. Expression of the human hypoxanthine-guanine phosphoribosyltransferase in mice so treated has been conclusively demonstrated. A transgenic strain of mice has also recently been established in which the human enzyme is expressed with a tissue distribution characteristic of humans.

The associated biochemical abnormalities leading to the devastating neurologic consequences of the Lesch-Nyhan syndrome are incompletely understood. Evidence obtained from postmortem examination of brains from subjects with the Lesch-Nyhan syndrome indicates a specific defect in the central dopaminergic pathways, particularly those found in the basal ganglia and nucleus accumbens. Corroborating in vivo evidence is emerging from positron emission tomography (PET) studies of subjects deficient in hypoxanthine-guanine phosphoribosyltransferase. A defect in the metabolism of 2'-fluorodeoxyglucose in the caudate nuclei is present in the majority of subjects studied with this technique. The relationships between dopaminergic nervous system abnormalities and the aberrant metabolism of purines remain unknown.

The hyperuricemia resulting from partial or complete deficiency of hypoxanthine-guanine phosphoribosyltransferase can be successfully controlled with allopurinol, an inhibitor of xanthine oxidase. A few patients have developed xanthine stones with such therapy, but in the majority the renal stones and gout are effectively treated. No specific therapy exists for the neurologic abnormalities in the Lesch-Nyhan syndrome.

PRPP synthetase variants   Several families are described in which there is increased activity of the enzyme PRPP synthetase (reaction 3, Fig. 309-4). The mutant enzymes, of which three different types are recognized, all exhibit increased activity, resulting in increased intracellular concentrations of PRPP, accelerated purine biosynthesis, and elevated excretion of uric acid. The inheritance pattern in this disease is also X-linked. These patients, like those with partial hypoxanthine-guanine phosphoribosyltransferase deficiency, generally develop gout in the second or third decade and have a high incidence of uric acid stones. Several kindred have been described in which nerve deafness is associated with PRPP synthetase overactivity groups.

OTHER DISORDERS OF PURINE METABOLISM   Adenine phosphoribosyltransferase deficiency

Adenine phosphoribosyltransferase catalyzes the conversion of adenine to AMP (reaction 4, Fig. 309-4). The first subjects described with a deficiency of this enzyme were heterozygous for deficiency of the enzyme and had no associated disease. It subsequently became apparent that heterozygosity for this deficiency is common, perhaps as frequent as 1:100. A homozygous deficiency of this enzyme has now been described in 11 patients with a history of renal stones composed of 2,8-dioxyadenine. Because of chemical similarity, 2,8-dioxyadenine may be confused with uric acid, and in each of these patients an incorrect diagnosis of uric acid nephrolithiasis was made initially.

Adenosine deaminase deficiency and purine nucleoside phosphorylase deficiency   See Chap. 256.

TABLE 309-2   Structural and functional abnormalities in mutant forms of human hypoxanthine-guanine phosphoribosyltransferase

| Mutant enzyme | Clinical presentation | Mutation | | Functional abnormalities | | Michaelis constants | |
		Amino acid substitution	Position	Intracellular concentration	Maximal velocity	Hypoxanthine	PRPP
HPRT$_{Toronto}$	Gout	Arg→Gly	50	Decreased	Normal	Normal	Normal
HPRT$_{London}$	Gout	Ser→Leu	109	Decreased	Normal	↑ 5-fold	Normal
HPRT$_{Ann Arbor}$	Nephrolithiasis	ND	ND	Decreased	Normal	Normal	Normal
HPRT$_{Munich}$	Gout	Ser→Arg	103	Normal	↓ 20-fold	↑ 100-fold	Normal
HPRT$_{Kinston}$	Lesch-Nyhan Syndrome	Asp→Asn	193	Normal	Normal	↑ 200-fold	↑ 200-fold

NOTES: *PRPP denotes 5-phosphoribosyl-1-pyrophosphate; Arg, arginine; Gly, glycine; Ser, serine; Leu, leucine; Asn, asparagine; Asp, aspartic acid; ND, not determined; →, is replaced by.*
SOURCE: *Wilson et al.*

Xanthine oxidase deficiency   Xanthine oxidase catalyzes the oxidation of hypoxanthine to xanthine, xanthine to uric acid, and adenine to 2,8-dioxyadenine (reaction 8, Fig. 309-4). Xanthinuria, the first inborn error of purine metabolism to be defined at the enzyme level, is due to a deficiency of xanthine oxidase. As a result, affected patients with xanthinuria have hypouricemia and hypouricaciduria as well as an increased urinary excretion of the oxypurines, hypoxanthine, and xanthine. Half are asymptomatic and a third have urinary xanthine stones. Several patients have been noted to have a myopathy. Three patients have been reported with polyarthritis, which may represent a crystal-induced synovitis. Precipitation of xanthine is thought to be the important factor in the development of each of these clinical manifestations.

Four patients have been described with combined congenital deficiencies of xanthine oxidase and sulfate oxidase. The clinical presentation is dominated by the serious neurologic abnormalities in the neonatal period seen in isolated sulfate oxidase deficiency. Although deficiency of a molybdate cofactor required by both enzymes has been postulated as the primary abnormality, therapy with ammonium molybdate has little effect on the neurologic manifestation. An acquired disorder mimicking combined xanthine oxidase and sulfate oxidase deficiency has been described in a patient on chronic total parenteral nutrition. Therapy with oral ammonium molybdate successfully restored enzymatic function and resulted in clinical resolution.

Myoadenylate deaminase deficiency   Myoadenylate deaminase is an isozyme of adenylate deaminase found only in skeletal muscle. This enzyme catalyzes the conversion of adenylate (AMP) to inosinic acid (IMP). This reaction is a component of the purine nucleotide cycle and is probably important in the maintenance of energy production and utilization in skeletal muscle.

Deficiency of this enzyme is limited to skeletal muscle. The majority of deficient patients demonstrate exercise-induced myalgias, muscle cramps, and fatigue. Approximately one-third report weakness even in the absence of exercise. A few patients are apparently asymptomatic.

The disorder typically presents in childhood or adolescence. The clinical manifestations are those of a metabolic myopathy. Creatine kinase is elevated in less than half of subjects. Electromyograms and routine histology of muscle biopsies show nonspecific abnormalities. Presumptive evidence of adenylate deaminase deficiency can be obtained from performance of an ischemic forearm exercise test. Ammonia production is reduced in deficient patients since AMP deamination is blocked. The diagnosis must be confirmed by actual assay of AMP deaminase activity in a skeletal muscle biopsy since reduced ammonia production with exercise occurs in other myopathies. The disorder is slowly progressive, leading to mild disability in most cases. No specific therapy has been shown to be effective.

Adenylosuccinase deficiency   Subjects deficient in adenylosuccinase are mentally retarded and often autistic. Additional neurologic abnormalities include seizures, psychomotor retardation, and other movement disorders. Urinary excretion of succinylamino-imidazole carboxamide riboside (SAICAR) and succinyladenosine is elevated. Diagnosis depends upon demonstration of partial or complete absence of enzyme activity in liver, kidney, or skeletal muscle. Lymphocytes and fibroblasts show a partial deficiency. The prognosis is not known, and no specific therapy exists.

REFERENCES

KELLEY WN: Crystal-induced arthropathies, in *The Clinics in Rheumatic Diseases.* Philadelphia, Saunders, 1977, vol 3, pp 1–171
————, FOX IH: Gout and related disorders of purine metabolism, in *Textbook of Rheumatology,* WN Kelley et al (eds). Philadelphia, Saunders, 1985, pp 1359–1397
————, HOLMES EW: Antihyperuricemic drugs, in *Textbook of Rheumatology,* WN Kelley et al (eds). Philadelphia, Saunders, 1985, pp 857–870
———— et al: Hypoxanthine-guanine phosphoribosyltransferase deficiency in gout. Ann Intern Med, 70:155, 1969
PALELLA TD, KELLEY WN: Purine and deoxypurine metabolism, in *Textbook of Rheumatology,* WN Kelley et al (eds). Philadelphia, Saunders, 1985, p 337

SEEGMILLER JE: Diseases of purine and pyrimidine metabolism, in *Duncan's Diseases of Metabolism,* 8th ed, PK Bondy, LE Rosenberg (eds). Philadelphia, Saunders, 1980, p 777
TALBOTT JH, YU TF: *Gout and Uric Acid Metabolism.* New York, Grune & Stratton, 1976
WILSON JM et al: Hypoxanthine-guanine phosphoribosyltransferase deficiency: The molecular basis of the clinical syndromes. N Engl J Med 309:900, 1983
WYNGAARDEN JB: Gout, in *Advances in Metabolic Disorders,* R Levine and R Luft (eds). New York, Academic, 1965, vol 2, pp 2–78
————, KELLEY WN: *Gout and Hyperuricemia.* New York, Grune & Stratton, 1976
————, ————: Gout, in *The Metabolic Basis of Inherited Diseases,* 5th ed, JB Stanbury et al (eds). New York, McGraw-Hill, 1983

---

310   HEMOCHROMATOSIS

LAWRIE W. POWELL / KURT J. ISSELBACHER

DEFINITION   Hemochromatosis is an iron-storage disorder in which an inappropriate increase in intestinal iron absorption results in deposition of iron with eventual tissue damage and functional insufficiency of the organs involved, especially the liver, pancreas, heart, and pituitary. In 1889, von Recklinghausen named the disease *hemochromatosis* and the iron-storage pigment *hemosiderin* because he believed that the pigment was derived from the blood. The terms *hemosiderosis* or *siderosis* are often used to describe the presence of stainable iron in tissues, but quantitative measurement of tissue iron is necessary for accurate assessment of body iron status (see below and Chap. 284). *Hemochromatosis* implies progressive and massive iron overload leading to fibrosis and organ failure. Although there is debate about definitions, it seems logical to use the following terminology: (1) *genetic hemochromatosis*—the inherited disease now known to be associated with an abnormal iron-loading gene tightly linked to the A locus of the HLA complex on chromosome 6, (2) *acquired hemochromatosis*—iron overload with tissue injury arising secondarily to other disease, usually thalassemia or sideroblastic anemia. It should be emphasized, however, that in these acquired iron-loading disorders massive iron deposits in parenchymal tissues can lead to the same clinical and pathologic features that are seen in genetic hemochromatosis.

The metabolic defect leading to increased iron absorption in hemochromatosis is unknown. The genetic disease can now be recognized during its early stages when the iron overload is of lesser degree and organ damage is minimal. At this stage the disease is best referred to as *latent* or *precirrhotic hemochromatosis* (see Fig. 310-1).

PREVALENCE   Genetic hemochromatosis is not as rare as previously believed. In white Anglo-Saxon populations the gene frequency is approximately 5 percent, the disease (homozygote) frequency is 0.3 percent, and the carrier (heterozygote) frequency is 10 percent. However, expression of the disease is modified by several factors, especially blood loss associated with menstruation and pregnancies in women. The disease is observed 5 to 10 times more frequently in males than in females. Nearly 70 percent of patients develop their first symptoms between ages 40 and 60. The disease is rarely clinically evident below age 20, although with family screening (see below) asymptomatic subjects with iron overload can be identified, including young menstruating women.

PATHOGENESIS   Normally the body iron content of 3 to 4 g is maintained such that intestinal mucosal absorption of iron is equal to loss. This amount is approximately 1 mg per day in men and 1.5 mg per day in menstruating women. In hemochromatosis mucosal absorption is inappropriate to body needs, amounting to 4 mg per day or more. The resulting progressive accumulation of iron is reflected in an early elevation in the plasma iron and an increased saturation of transferrin. In advanced disease, the body may contain over 20 g iron. This excess iron is deposited mainly in parenchymal cells of

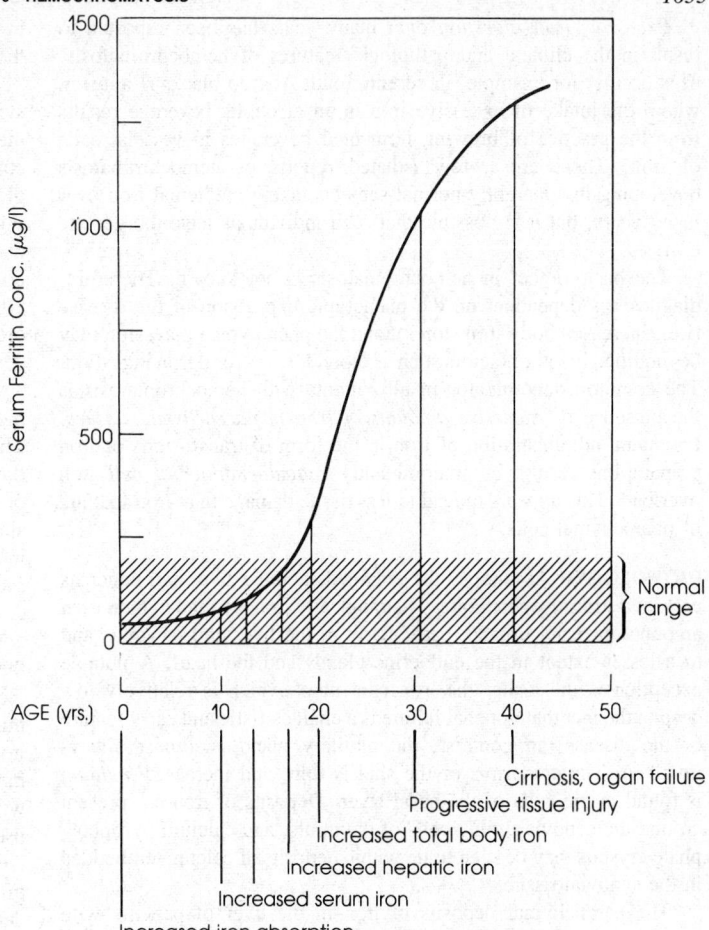

FIGURE 310-1 *Sequence of events in genetic hemochromatosis and their correlation with the serum ferritin concentration. Increased iron absorption is present throughout life. Overt, symptomatic disease usually develops between ages 40 and 60, but latent precirrhotic disease can be detected long before this.*

the liver, pancreas, and heart. Iron in the liver and pancreas increases 50 to 100 times; in the heart, 5 to 25 times; in the spleen, kidney, and skin, about 5 times. Tissue injury may result from disruption of iron-laden lysosomes and lipid peroxidation of subcellular organelles by excess iron. The demonstration of an association between hemochromatosis and the histocompatibility antigens HLA-A3, HLA-B14, and HLA-B7 has confirmed the genetic basis for the disease. The mode of inheritance is autosomal recessive, with homozygotes usually developing severe iron overload and symptomatic disease and heterozygotes developing only minor derangements in iron metabolism without progressive iron overload or clinical evidence of the disease.

Gross parenchymal iron overload leading to *acquired* hemochromatosis occurs in association with chronic disorders of erythropoiesis, particularly in those with a defect in hemoglobin synthesis and ineffective erythropoiesis such as sideroblastic anemia and thalassemia. In this group of disorders the absorption of iron is increased, and these patients are also frequently treated with iron and blood transfusions. Porphyria cutanea tarda, a disorder characterized by a defect in porphyrin biosynthesis (Chap. 312), is also sometimes

associated with excessive parenchymal iron deposits; however, the magnitude of the iron load is usually insufficient to produce tissue damage.

Alcoholic subjects with chronic liver disease may show evidence of increased tissue iron stores. They can be divided into two groups. The first group comprises patients who have a mild to moderate increase in stainable hepatic iron but relatively normal body iron stores. These patients have alcoholic liver disease (usually cirrhosis) but not hemochromatosis. The reason for the increased iron may be related in part to cell necrosis and uptake of iron released from adjacent Kupffer and parenchymal cells. The second (less common) group of alcoholic subjects with increased hepatic iron have gross iron deposition and increased body iron stores and are usually found to have genetic hemochromatosis with or without superimposed alcoholic liver disease. Hemochromatosis occurring in a heavy drinker may be distinguished from alcoholic liver disease by two means: (1) by measurement of hepatic iron concentration (see below and Table 310-1) and (2) by studying relatives for evidence of the disease, including HLA typing of family members.

TABLE 310-1 Representative iron values in normal subjects, patients with hemochromatosis, and patients with alcoholic liver disease

Determination	Normal	Symptomatic hemo-chromatosis	Homozygotes with early, asymptomatic hemochromatosis	Alcoholic liver disease
Plasma iron, μg/dL	50–150	180–300	Usually elevated	Often elevated
Total iron-binding capacity, μg/dL	250–370	200–300	200–300	250–370
Percent transferrin saturation, μg/dL	22–46	50–100	50–100	22–60
Serum ferritin, ng/mL	10–200	900–6000	200–500	10–500
Urinary iron,* mg/24 h	0–2	9–23	2–5	Usually < 5
Liver iron, μg/100 mg dry wt	30–140	600–1800	200–400	30–200

* *After intramuscular administration of 0.5 g deferoxamine.*

Excessive iron ingestion over many years has been reported to result in the clinical and pathologic features of hemochromatosis. This occurs, for example, in certain South African blacks (Bantu) in whom the intake of excessive iron in an alcoholic beverage results from the practice of brewing fermented beverages in vessels made of iron. There are a few isolated reports of hemochromatosis developing in apparently normal subjects taking medicinal iron over many years, but it is possible that such individuals have the genetic trait.

The basic defect in hemochromatosis is not known. Therefore, diagnosis is dependent on the phenotypic expression of the disease (i.e., increased body iron stores), and the phenotypic expression may be modified by other factors such as blood loss and oral iron ingestion. The common denominator in all patients with hemochromatosis is the presence of *excessive amounts of iron in parenchymal tissues*. Parenteral administration of iron in the form of transfusions or iron preparations results in predominantly *reticuloendothelial cell* iron overload. This appears to lead to less tissue damage than iron loading of parenchymal cells.

PATHOLOGY   At autopsy the enlarged, nodular liver and pancreas present a striking ochre color. Histologically iron is found in increased amounts in many organs, particularly in the liver and pancreas and to a lesser extent in the endocrine glands and the heart. A notable exception is the testis, the iron content of which is relatively low despite the fact that gonadal failure is a characteristic and early feature of the disease. In contrast, the pituitary gland is almost always involved. The epidermis of the skin is thin, and increased *melanin* is found in the cells of the basal layer. Deposits of iron are present around the synovial lining cells of the joints, and calcium pyrophosphate crystals may be seen to lie within deposits of calcium embedded in the synovial tissue.

The parenchymal deposits of iron in the liver of patients with genetic hemochromatosis are in the form of ferritin and hemosiderin. In the early stages, these deposits are found in the periportal parenchymal cells, especially within lysosomes in the pericanalicular cytoplasm of the hepatocytes. This stage progresses to perilobular fibrosis and deposition of iron in bile duct epithelium, Kupffer cells, and fibrous septa. Inflammatory cells are few in contrast to prominent proliferation of bile ductules. Wedge biopsy specimens show a characteristic pattern of fibrosis with dense fibrous septa surrounding groups of lobules somewhat analogous to the pattern in chronic biliary disease. In the advanced stage, a macronodular or mixed macro- and micronodular cirrhosis develops.

CLINICAL MANIFESTATIONS   The symptoms and signs of hemochromatosis include skin pigmentation, diabetes, liver and cardiac impairment, arthropathy, and hypogonadism. The initial symptoms most frequently encountered are weakness, lassitude, weight loss, change in skin color, abdominal pain, loss of libido, and symptoms related to the onset of diabetes. Hepatomegaly, pigmentation, spider angiomas, splenomegaly, arthropathy, ascites, cardiac arrhythmias, congestive heart failure, loss of body hair, testicular atrophy, and jaundice are the most prominent physical signs in the fully established disease.

The *liver* is usually the first organ to be affected, and hepatomegaly is present in more than 95 percent of symptomatic cases. Hepatic enlargement may exist in the absence of symptoms or in the presence of normal liver function tests. Indeed, over half the patients with symptomatic hemochromatosis have little or no laboratory evidence of functional impairment of the liver, in spite of hepatomegaly and fibrosis. Loss of body hair, palmar erythema, testicular atrophy, and gynecomastia are common. Manifestations of portal hypertension and esophageal varices occur less commonly than in Laennec's cirrhosis. Splenomegaly is present in approximately half the symptomatic cases. Hepatocellular carcinoma develops in about 30 percent. The incidence of this complication increases with age and is now the most common cause of death in treated patients. However, it appears to occur only

in cirrhotic patients; hence the importance of early diagnosis and therapy.

Excessive *skin pigmentation* is present in about 90 percent of symptomatic patients at the time the diagnosis is established. The melanin deposition in the skin usually gives rise to bronzing. The characteristic metallic gray hue is believed to result from the presence of increased melanin or both melanin and iron in the dermis. Pigmentation usually is diffuse and generalized, but frequently it is deeper on the face, neck, extensor aspects of the lower forearms, dorsa of the hands, lower legs, genital regions, and in scars. In only 10 to 15 percent of cases is there demonstrable pigmentation of the oral mucosa. Pigmentation of the hard palate and retina has been described.

Diabetes mellitus occurs in about 65 percent of patients and is more likely to develop in patients with a family history of diabetes. The presence of a family history of diabetes and direct damage to the pancreas by iron deposition both may contribute to the development of diabetes in hemochromatosis. The management of the diabetes is similar to that of idiopathic diabetes mellitus except for a higher incidence of insulin resistance and of fat atrophy. Late degenerative sequelae are the same as in diabetes mellitus.

Arthropathy develops in 25 to 50 percent of patients. It most commonly occurs after the age of 50 but may occur at any time in the course of the disease, even as a first manifestation or long after therapy. The small joints of the hands, especially the second and third metacarpophalangeal joints, are usually the first joints to be involved. A progressive polyarthritis involving wrists, hips, and knees may ensue. Acute brief attacks of synovitis may occur, associated with deposition of calcium pyrophosphate (chondrocalcinosis or pseudogout), chiefly in the knees. Roentgenologic manifestations consist of cystic changes of sclerosis of the subchondral bones, loss of articular cartilage with narrowing of the joint space, diffuse demineralization, hypertrophic bone proliferation, and calcification of the synovium. The mechanism of these abnormalities and their relationship to iron metabolism are not known.

Cardiac involvement is the presenting manifestation in about 15 percent of patients. The most common cardiac manifestation, congestive heart failure, is observed in about 10 percent of young adults with the disease. Symptoms of congestive failure may develop suddenly, with rapid progression to death if untreated. The heart is diffusely enlarged, and such cases may be misdiagnosed as idiopathic cardiomyopathy if other overt manifestations are absent. A variety of cardiac arrhythmias may be present, particularly supraventricular beats and paroxysmal tachyarrhythmias. Atrial flutter, atrial fibrillation, and varying degrees of atrioventricular block have also been described.

Loss of libido and *testicular atrophy* are common. The former may antedate the other clinical manifestations of the disease. Testicular atrophy is usually due to the decreased production of gonadotropins associated with impaired hypothalamic-pituitary function due to iron deposition. Adrenal insufficiency, hypothyroidism, and hypoparathyroidism have been described but are rare.

DIAGNOSIS   The association of (1) hepatomegaly, (2) skin pigmentation, (3) diabetes mellitus, (4) heart disease, (5) arthritis, and (6) evidence of hypogonadism should suggest the diagnosis of hemochromatosis. However, a parenchymal iron overload of comparatively short duration or modest degree may exist without any of these clinical manifestations, or with only some of them [e.g., in young subjects (see Fig. 310-1)]. Therefore, the diagnosis should be considered in any patient with unexplained hepatomegaly, idiopathic cardiomyopathy, abnormal skin pigmentation, loss of libido, diabetes, or arthritis.

The history should be particularly detailed in regard to disease in other members of the family, alcohol ingestion, iron intake, and the ingestion of large doses of ascorbic acid which promotes iron absorption. The blood should be examined for evidence of anemia and abnormal erythropoiesis to rule out iron loading secondary to a hematologic disorder. Confirmation of the presence of liver, pancreatic, cardiac, and joint disease should be obtained by physical examination, roentgenologic examination, and routine function tests of these organs. It then remains to be demonstrated that there is an increase in total body iron stores and, in particular, an increased parenchymal iron concentration associated with tissue damage.

The methods available for the demonstration of excessive parenchymal iron stores include (1) measurement of serum iron, (2) determination of percent saturation of transferrin, (3) estimation of chelatable iron stores using the agent deferoxamine, (4) measurement of serum ferritin concentration, (5) liver biopsy (Table 310-1), and (6) computerized tomography. Each has its inherent advantages and limitations. The serum iron level and percent saturation of transferrin are elevated early in the course of the disease, but their specificity is reduced by relatively high false-positive and false-negative rates. In particular, an increased serum iron concentration may be present in patients with alcoholic liver disease without iron overload; in this situation, however, the iron-binding capacity is usually not decreased as in hemochromatosis (Table 310-1).

The serum ferritin concentration is usually a good index of body iron stores, whether they are decreased or increased. In untreated patients with hemochromatosis, the serum ferritin level is greatly increased (Fig. 310-1 and Table 310-1). This test is also useful as a noninvasive screening test for the diagnosis of early disease, since it is usually abnormal before there is any morphologic evidence of liver damage and the ferritin concentration correlates with the magnitude of body iron stores. It has, therefore, generally replaced the more cumbersome screening tests involving measurement of urinary iron excretion. However, in patients with inflammation and hepatocellular necrosis serum ferritin levels may be elevated out of proportion to body iron stores due to increased rate of release from tissues. Also, some families have been reported in whom serum ferritin levels in symptomatic relatives are normal despite increased iron stores; the reason for this finding is unclear, but it would appear to be unusual. In clinical practice, the *combined measurements* of the (1) serum iron concentration, (2) percent transferrin saturation, and (3) serum ferritin level provide the simplest and most reliable screening test for hemochromatosis, including the precirrhotic phase of the disease. If any of these tests are abnormal, liver biopsy should be performed since it is the *definitive* test for the diagnosis of hemochromatosis. It permits histochemical estimation of tissue iron, measurement of hepatic iron concentration, and assessment of the extent of tissue damage. Computerizd tomography shows increased density of the liver due to iron deposition. However, dual-energy scanning and experienced personnel are required, and the lower limits for accurate detection of increased tissue iron are unclear.

It is of particular importance to examine family members at risk when the diagnosis of hemochromatosis is established. Asymptomatic as well as symptomatic family members with the disease will usually have an increase in plasma iron, a decrease in total iron-binding capacity, an increased saturation of transferrin, and an increased or increasing serum ferritin concentration. These changes occur even before the iron stores are greatly increased (see Fig. 310-1). A liver biopsy should then be performed, since it is imperative to establish the diagnosis and begin therapy before tissue damage occurs. HLA typing may be helpful in evaluating families with the disease. Affected siblings usually have both HLA haplotypes identical with those of the proband, and where children of a proband are affected, a homozygous-heterozygous mating probably occurred.

The distinction between hemochromatosis and alcoholic cirrhosis associated with increased tissue iron is discussed above. It is usually not difficult if measurement of liver iron concentration is made, and the deferoxamine excretion test can provide additional diagnostic information (Table 310-1).

TREATMENT The therapy of genetic hemochromatosis involves the removal of the excess body iron and supportive treatment of damaged organs.

Iron is best removed from the body by weekly or twice weekly phlebotomy of 500 mL. Although there is an initial modest decline in the volume of packed red blood cells to about 35 mL/dL, the level stabilizes after several weeks. The plasma iron concentration remains increased until the available iron stores are depleted. The plasma ferritin concentration falls progressively, reflecting the gradual decrease in body iron stores. Since one 500-mL unit of blood contains from 200 to 250 mg iron and about 25 g iron must be removed, 2 or 3 years of weekly phlebotomy are usually required. When the plasma iron and ferritin levels become normal, phlebotomies are performed at such time intervals as are required to maintain a plasma iron concentration of less than 150 µg/dL. Usually one phlebotomy every 3 months will suffice. The adequacy of the therapy may be evaluated at any time by measuring the plasma iron, the percentage of saturation of transferrin with iron, or the serum ferritin concentration. These measurements become abnormal promptly with iron reaccumulation.

Chelating agents such as deferoxamine, when given parenterally, remove 10 to 20 mg iron per day, less than half that mobilized by one weekly phlebotomy. Phlebotomy is also generally a less expensive, more convenient, and safer treatment for patients with genetic hemochromatosis, but chelating agents are indicated when anemia or hypoproteinemia is severe enough to preclude phlebotomy. Subcutaneous infusions of deferoxamine using a portable slow pump are most effective.

The management of the hepatic failure, cardiac failure, and diabetes differs little from conventional management of these conditions. Loss of libido and change in secondary sex characteristics are partially relieved by testosterone therapy or gonadotropin therapy.

PROGNOSIS The principal causes of death in *untreated* patients are cardiac failure (30 percent), hepatocellular failure or portal hypertension (25 percent), and hepatocellular carcinoma (30 percent).

Life expectancy of symptomatic patients is extended to an average of more than 8 years by removal of the excessive stores of iron and maintenance of these stores at near-normal levels. The 5-year survival rate with therapy is increased from 33 to 89 percent. With removal of iron by repeated phlebotomy, the liver and spleen decrease in size, liver function studies return to normal, pigmentation of skin decreases, and cardiac failure is reversed. Carbohydrate tolerance improves in about 40 percent. Removal of excess iron has little or no effect on hypogonadism or arthropathy. The fibrosis in the liver may decrease, but cirrhosis is irreversible. Hepatocellular carcinoma occurs as a late sequela in about one-third of the patients despite adequate iron removal. The apparent increase in its incidence in treated patients is probably related to their increased life span. This complication does not appear to develop if the disease is treated in the precirrhotic stage. Hence, the importance of family screening and early therapy cannot be emphasized too strongly. Asymptomatic subjects who are detected by family studies should have phlebotomy therapy if iron stores are moderately to severely increased. Screening for increasing iron stores at appropriate intervals is also important. With this approach most manifestations of the disease can be prevented. Indeed, the life expectancy of such treated precirrhotic patients appears to be similar to that of the normal population.

REFERENCES

BASSETT ML et al: HLA typing in idiopathic hemochromatosis: Distinction between homozygotes and heterozygotes with biochemical expression. Hepatology 1:120, 1981
——— et al: Diagnosis of hemochromatosis in young subjects: Predictive accuracy of biochemical screening tests. Gastroenterology 87:628, 1984
BOTHWELL TH et al: *Iron Metabolism in Man.* Oxford, Blackwell, 1979
EDWARDS CQ et al: Hereditary hemochromatosis. N Engl J Med 297:7, 1977
MILDER MS et al: Idiopathic hemochromatosis, an interim report. Medicine 59:1, 34, 1980
POWELL LW, KERR JFR: The pathology of liver in hemochromatosis, in *Pathobiology Annual*, H Joacim (ed). New York, Appleton-Century-Crofts, 1975
SIMON M et al: Idiopathic hemochromatosis: Demonstration of recessive transmission and early detection by family HLA typing. N Engl J Med 297:1017, 1977

311 WILSON'S DISEASE

I. HERBERT SCHEINBERG

Wilson's disease is an autosomal recessive abnormality in the hepatic excretion of copper that results in toxic accumulations of the metal in liver, brain, and other organs. The disease occurs in populations of every ethnic and geographic origin and has a worldwide prevalence of about 1 in 30,000. Deficiency of the plasma copper protein ceruloplasmin is a characteristic feature.

NATURAL HISTORY Normal babies have low levels of plasma ceruloplasmin and high concentrations of hepatic copper. During the first year of life ceruloplasmin values rise, and hepatic copper concentrations fall to normal adult levels. In contrast, serum ceruloplasmin changes very little in homozygotes for the Wilson's disease gene, and the concentration of hepatic copper remains elevated. However, clinical manifestations of copper excess are rare before age 6, and one-half of untreated patients remain asymptomatic through adolescence.

Wilson's disease presents with hepatic involvement in about one-half of patients. The toxic effects of copper in the liver may be manifest as acute hepatitis, cirrhosis of the liver, or asymptomatic hepatosplenomegaly. The acute hepatitis is similar to viral hepatitis, can be mistaken for infectious mononucleosis, and may evolve in three different ways. The first is a fulminant, sometimes lethal disease characterized by jaundice, malaise, and at times ascites, hypoalbuminemia, and elevated levels of liver enzymes in plasma. In the acute phase sufficient copper may be released into plasma to cause a hemolytic anemia. The disease may not be diagnosed until autopsy or until the diagnosis in a younger sibling leads to copper analysis of preserved tissues. Second, parenchymal liver disease may develop insidiously and result in a clinical and histologic picture indistinguishable from chronic active hepatitis. Third, patients may apparently recover from the hepatitis, although cirrhosis always develops. Years or decades may elapse with no sign or symptom of disease. In these patients the past history of an episode of hepatitis can be overlooked unless they are questioned carefully or unless the cirrhosis becomes clinically manifest.

More frequently, the copper-induced hepatic disease evolves to cirrhosis without any recognized hepatitis. In these patients the initial manifestations are extrahepatic. Neurologic or psychiatric disturbances are the first clinical signs in most of this group and are always accompanied by Kayser-Fleischer rings (Fig. A4-16). These green or golden deposits of copper in Descemet's membrane of the cornea do not interfere with vision but indicate that hepatic copper has been released and has caused the brain damage. Rarely Kayser-Fleischer rings may be accompanied by sunflower cataracts. If a patient with frank neurologic or psychiatric disease does not have Kayser-Fleischer rings when examined by a trained observer using a slit lamp, the diagnosis of Wilson's disease can be excluded.

The primary neurologic manifestations are those of a movement disorder, particularly resting and intention tremors. Spasticity, rigidity, chorea, drooling, dysphagia, and dysarthria are common. Babinski

responses and absent abdominal reflexes are occasionally noted; sensory changes never occur. Psychiatric disturbances, in part due to the toxic effects of copper on the brain and in part to the reactions to a life-threatening disease, are present in most patients with symptomatic disease. Syndromes indistinguishable from schizophrenia, manic-depressive psychoses, and classic neuroses may occur, and some bizarre behavioral disturbances defy classification. Improvement in the psychiatric state can occur with pharmacologic reduction of the copper excess, but psychotherapy is often also required.

In occasional patients the clinical onset reflects neither a hepatic nor a central nervous system disturbance. For example, primary or secondary amenorrhea may be the first evidence of disease in some young women; in others, repeated spontaneous abortions may result from excess free copper in intrauterine secretions. Routine ophthalmologic examination in patients without symptomatic liver or neurologic disease occasionally reveals Kayser-Fleischer rings, leading to the diagnosis.

PATHOGENESIS The metabolic defect in Wilson's disease is an inability to maintain a near-zero balance of copper. Excess copper accumulates possibly because hepatic lysosomes lack the normal mechanism to excrete into bile the copper that has been catabolically cleaved from ceruloplasmin. This may cause deficiency of ceruloplasmin since a stoichiometric excess of copper inhibits the formation of ceruloplasmin from apoceruloplasmin and copper. The capacity of hepatocytes to store copper is eventually exceeded, and release into blood and uptake in extrahepatic sites occurs (Table 311-1).

Under normal circumstances essentially all tissue copper is present as the prosthetic element of copper proteins such as cytochrome oxidase, tyrosinase, superoxide dismutase, and ceruloplasmin. There is normally little or no free (non-protein-bound) copper. In Wilson's disease more copper is present than can be bound by specific copper proteins; such copper is as toxic as excess iron, zinc, mercury, or lead. Toxicity of these cations is probably effected in large degree by pathologic combinations with proteins that ordinarily do not contain metal.

The pathologic consequences of the accumulated copper occur first in the liver. Abnormal fat and glycogen deposits are the earliest findings by light microscopy (Fig. 311-1). With electron microscopy mitochondrial abnormalities are observed early and appear to be specific for Wilson's disease (Fig. 311-2). Later, necrosis, inflammation, fibrosis, bile duct proliferation, and cirrhosis occur. Abnormalities in liver chemistries develop later than the histologic changes.

Death can occur from the effects of copper toxicosis in the central nervous system with little or no evidence of liver dysfunction, but significant liver disease usually becomes apparent sometime during the course. Patients with prolonged survival always show hepatic cirrhosis.

In the brain the excess copper is distributed ubiquitously. Necrosis of neurons with cavitation may be preceded by the appearance of Opalski and Alzheimer type II cells; however, neither is specific for Wilson's disease.

Increased copper in the kidney produces little if any structural change and commonly does not alter renal function. Hematuria,

TABLE 311-1 Summary of analytic data in patients with Wilson's disease, heterozygous carriers, and control subjects

Group	Serum ceruloplasmin			Hepatic copper concentration		
	No. of patients	Range, mg/dL	Mean ± SD, mg/dL	No. of patients	Range, μg/g dry weight	Mean ± SD, μg/g dry weight
Wilson's disease:						
Asymptomatic	31	0–19.5	3.6 ± 5.3	36	152–1828	983.5 ± 368
Symptomatic	84	0–43.0	5.9 ± 7.1	33	94–1360	588.3 ± 304
Heterozygous carriers	95*	1–50.1	28.4 ± 8.5	14	39–213	117.0 ± 51
Normal subjects	180	18.5–65.9	30.7 ± 3.5	16	20–45	31.5 ± 6.8

* *71 parents of patients with Wilson's disease and 24 children, each of whom had one parent with Wilson's disease.*
SOURCE: *Sternlieb and Scheinberg, 1968.*

proteinuria, the Fanconi syndrome, and renal tubular acidosis occur rarely. Pathologic effects in other organs and tissues are minor.

DIAGNOSIS The diagnosis is easy—*provided it is suspected*. Wilson's disease should be considered in any patient under the age of 40 with an unexplained disorder of the central nervous system, signs or symptoms of chronic active hepatitis, unexplained persistent elevations of serum transaminase, hemolytic anemia in the presence of hepatitis, or unexplained cirrhosis, or in any patient who has a relative with Wilson's disease.

The diagnosis is confirmed in suspected cases by the demonstration either of (1) a serum concentration of ceruloplasmin less than 20 mg/dL and Kayser-Fleischer rings, or (2) a serum ceruloplasmin less than 20 mg/dL and a concentration of copper in a liver biopsy sample greater than 250 μg per gram of dry weight. Most patients also excrete more than 100 μg copper per day in urine and exhibit histologic abnormalities on liver biopsy.

About 5 percent of patients have a serum concentration of ceruloplasmin greater than 20 mg/dL, and some patients with other hepatic disorders have elevated hepatic copper levels and Kayser-Fleischer rings. In either circumstance measurement of the ability to incorporate radioactive copper into ceruloplasmin is useful as a discriminating test. Even in the presence of a normal concentration of ceruloplasmin, patients with Wilson's disease incorporate little or no isotope into the protein, while patients with other liver disorders and elevated hepatic copper incorporate the isotope normally.

TREATMENT Treatment consists of removing the deposits of copper as rapidly as possible and should be instituted once the diagnosis is secure whether the patient is ill or asymptomatic. The drug of choice is D-penicillamine. It is administered orally in an initial dose of 1 g daily, usually in divided doses before meals and at bedtime. Since penicillamine has an antipyridoxine effect in animals, 25 mg per day of vitamin B₆ is also given. Effectiveness of therapy should be assayed chemically and clinically. Initially, the 24-h urinary excretion of copper should increase fivefold or more over the pretreatment level, and 1 to 3 mg copper per day may be excreted during the first months of therapy.

White blood cell and platelet counts, urinalysis, and body temperature should be monitored several times weekly for the first month of therapy and at intervals thereafter. Sensitivity to penicillamine usually appears within the first 14 days of treatment and may cause rash, fever, leukopenia, thrombocytopenia, lymphadenopathy, or proteinuria. Discontinuation of treatment is required if sensitivity develops. Therapy can often be resumed if the drug is reinstituted in small and gradually increasing dosage, although reactions are less likely to recur if 20 mg of prednisone is given daily for the first 2 weeks of penicillamine treatment and subsequently gradually discontinued. Reactions requiring a desensitizing regimen may recur several times before penicillamine can be administered without a steroid.

Lifelong treatment is required. Inadequate treatment or interruption of therapy causes relapse that may be irreversible. Reinstitution of penicillamine after temporary interruption of therapy may be accompanied by the appearance or reappearance of sensitivity reactions. At any time—even after years of uneventful administration—granulocytopenia (or agranulocytosis), thrombocytopenia, the nephrotic syndrome, Goodpasture's syndrome, systemic lupus erythematosus, severe arthralgias, or myasthenia gravis may supervene. Toxicity is sometimes dose-related, and reduction of the dose to a level that is therapeutically effective but nontoxic may be possible. Continued low dosage of steroids may control penicillamine-associated lupus or arthralgias. After temporary interruption of the drug in patients with the nephrotic syndrome, it is sometimes possible to reinstitute therapy without recurrence of proteinuria. However, although irreversible intolerance to D-penicillamine is rare, the toxicity may be such that

FIGURE 311-2 *Electron micrograph of a liver biopsy sample from a 6-year-old asymptomatic boy. There are prominent vacuoles, containing granular material, in mitochondria (M). P, peroxisome; PM, plasma membrane.*

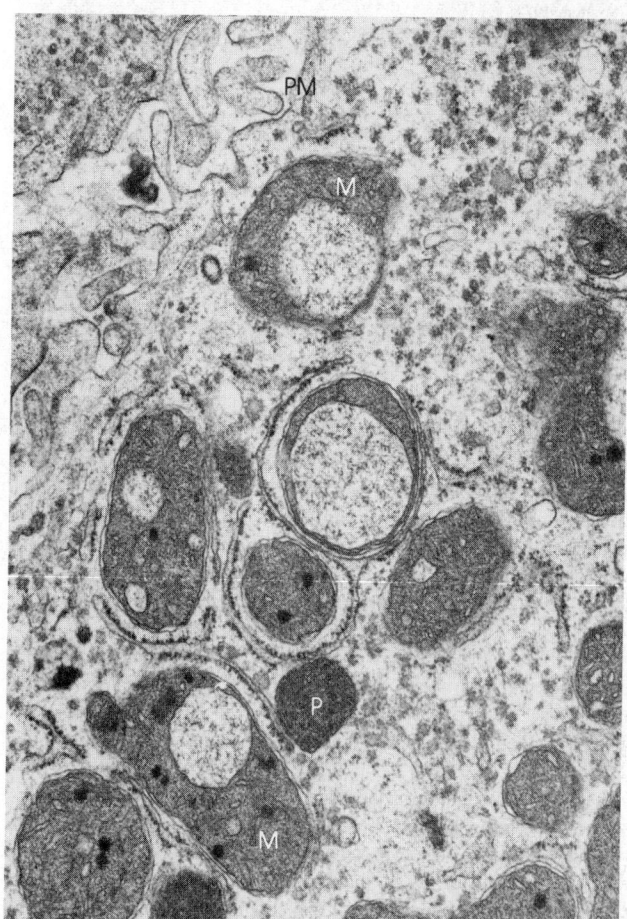

FIGURE 311-1 *Fatty changes, glycogen deposits, and cellular infiltrates in a hematoxylin and eosin–stained section of liver from an asymptomatic boy with Wilson's disease.*

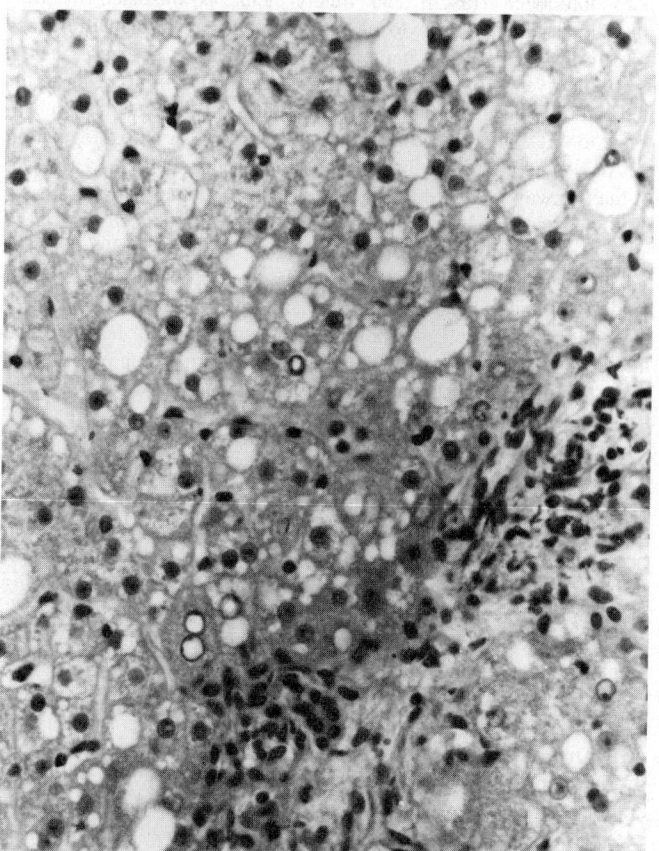

the drug must be withdrawn permanently. The lifelong administration of dimercaprol by injection is impractical, and the only other alternative mode of therapy is trientine.

After therapy with penicillamine has been successfully instituted, the patient should be seen indefinitely at 1- to 3-month intervals to detect drug toxicity and to manage the disease. Physical examination, including relevant neurologic assessment and inspection of the corneas with a slit lamp, and the patient's own evaluation provide the best indicators of the efficacy of treatment. Serial determinations of serum transaminase levels, albumin, and bilirubin are useful in following the course of liver function. Lack of clinical improvement or worsening of the disease may be due to irreversible damage present before therapy was begun, poor compliance, or inadequate dosage of penicillamine. Quantitative determinations of urinary copper excretion and of free copper in serum (total serum copper minus ceruloplasmin-bound copper) can help determine which is the case. After treatment for long periods, the level of urinary copper should be lower than at the onset of therapy, and rarely exceeds 1.5 mg per day. Even more helpful, the concentration of free serum copper is generally less than 10 μg/dL in the adequately treated patient. After a patient has remained asymptomatic with no laboratory evidence of liver dysfunction for a year and in patients with minimal residual disease that has not changed, the dose of penicillamine may be reduced to 0.75 g per day.

Treatment of more than 100 asymptomatic patients with a confirmed diagnosis has established that continued administration of D-penicillamine can prevent virtually every manifestation of this disease.

REFERENCES

SCHEINBERG IH, STERNLIEB I: Wilson's disease, in *Major Problems in Internal Medicine.* Philadelphia, Saunders, 1984, vol XXIII

STERNLIEB I: Evolution of the hepatic lesion in Wilson's disease (hepatolenticular degeneration), in *Progress in Liver Diseases,* H Popper et al (eds). New York, Grune & Stratton, 1972, vol IV, pp 511–526

————, SCHEINBERG IH: Prevention of Wilson's disease in asymptomatic patients. N Engl J Med 278:352, 1968

————, ————: Chronic hepatitis as a first manifestation of Wilson's disease. Ann Intern Med 76:59, 1972

WALSHE JM: Wilson's disease (hepatolenticular degeneration), in *Handbook of Clinical Neurology,* PJ Vinken et al (eds). New York, American Elsevier, 1976, vol 27

312 PORPHYRIAS

URS A. MEYER

The porphyrias are disorders associated with inherited or acquired disturbances in heme biosynthesis. Porphyrins are tetrapyrrole pigments that serve as intermediates in this pathway and are formed from the precursors δ-aminolevulinic acid (ALA) and porphobilinogen. Heme, the ferrous iron complex of protoporphyrin IX, functions as a prosthetic group for hemoproteins such as hemoglobin, cytochromes, catalase, and tryptophan oxygenase. Heme biosynthesis is essential to life and is operative in all aerobic cells.

Each of the porphyrias is characterized by a unique pattern of overproduction, accumulation, and excretion of intermediates of heme biosynthesis. These patterns are the metabolic expression of deficiencies of specific enzymes of the heme biosynthetic pathway (Table 312-1, Fig. 312-1).

The main clinical manifestations are intermittent attacks of nervous system dysfunction and/or sensitivity of the skin to sunlight. The *neurologic syndrome* is characteristically precipitated by drugs such as barbiturates and results in abdominal pain, peripheral neuropathy, and mental disturbance. The neuropsychiatric symptoms occur only in those porphyrias in which there is great overproduction of the porphyrin precursors ALA and porphobilinogen. The pathogenesis of the neurologic lesion is unclear. The *skin photosensitivity* is related directly to increased porphyrin accumulation, although the lesions differ among the different disorders. The photosensitivity is due to the photodynamic action of porphyrins and is probably mediated through the formation of singlet-oxygen with consequent destructive processes such as the peroxidation of lipids in the membranes of lysosomes. The dominantly inherited human porphyrias exhibit variable expressivity. Only the biochemical or enzymatic abnormalities may be apparent. Such latent disease may occur as a phase or persist throughout life, or manifestations can be precipitated by factors such as drugs, hormones, or liver disease.

CLASSIFICATION   The porphyrias are usually divided into two main groups, erythropoietic and hepatic, according to the two major sites of heme synthesis where the error of metabolism is expressed (Table 312-1). The only pure erythropoietic form of porphyria is the rare *congenital erythropoietic porphyria* (CEP). In *protoporphyria* (PP) porphyrins accumulate in both erythropoietic and hepatic tissue. In *intermittent acute porphyria* (IAP), *hereditary coproporphyria* (HCP), and *variegate porphyria* (VP), dominantly inherited enzyme deficiencies impair heme biosynthesis predominantly in the liver, apparently without affecting hemoglobin formation. *Porphyria cutanea tarda* (PCT) was previously considered to be an acquired hepatic porphyria. However most if not all patients with this disease have been found to have hereditary deficiency of uroporphyrinogen decarboxylase. Acquired porphyria resembling PCT occurs in individuals exposed to polychlorinated hydrocarbons and in association with hepatic tumors. Poisoning with lead also produces abnormalities in porphyrin and heme synthesis (see Chap. 172). Small increases in urinary excretion of porphyrins or precursors and accumulation of porphyrins in erythrocytes may accompany numerous clinical conditions; these secondary phenomena do not produce symptoms or signs of porphyria.

BIOCHEMICAL CONSIDERATIONS   The sequence of reactions that leads from the substrates glycine and succinyl coenzyme A to ALA, porphobilinogen (PBG), and finally heme is mediated by four mitochondrial and four cytosolic enzymes (Fig. 312-2). Differences exist in the regulation of heme biosynthesis among tissues.

In the liver ALA synthase catalyzes the rate-limiting reaction for heme formation under physiologic conditions. The enzymes subsequent to ALA synthase are present in excess. The principal regulation of ALA synthase is feedback repression by heme, the end product of the pathway. Increased demands for heme are met by the synthesis of ALA synthase. Hepatic ALA synthase can be induced by a large number of lipid-soluble drugs, steroids, and chemicals that are substrates and inducers of cytochrome P_{450} hemoproteins, the terminal oxidases in microsomal drug metabolism. This induction is modulated by multiple genetic, metabolic, and environmental factors. The interdependence of heme synthesis and microsomal drug oxidation is important in some hepatic porphyrias where symptoms are precipitated by these drugs.

In the bone marrow ALA synthase is also rate-limiting in cells with fully expressed heme synthesis, but little is known of the role of the enzyme in heme synthesis during division, differentiation, and maturation of erythroid cells. With maturation of erythroid cells the nuclei and mitochondria are extruded, and the mitochondrial enzymes of heme synthesis disappear, while the cytosolic enzymes catalyzing the reactions between ALA and coproporphyrinogen persist. Therefore, erythrocytes can be used for the diagnosis of porphyrias due to a defect in a cytosolic enzyme.

Control of heme synthesis differs in bone marrow and liver. The level of ALA synthase is the major determinant of heme formation in the liver, while heme synthesis in the bone marrow is triggered by the complex process of erythroid differentiation. These considerations probably explain the different manifestations of enzyme defects of heme synthesis in erythroid cells and liver.

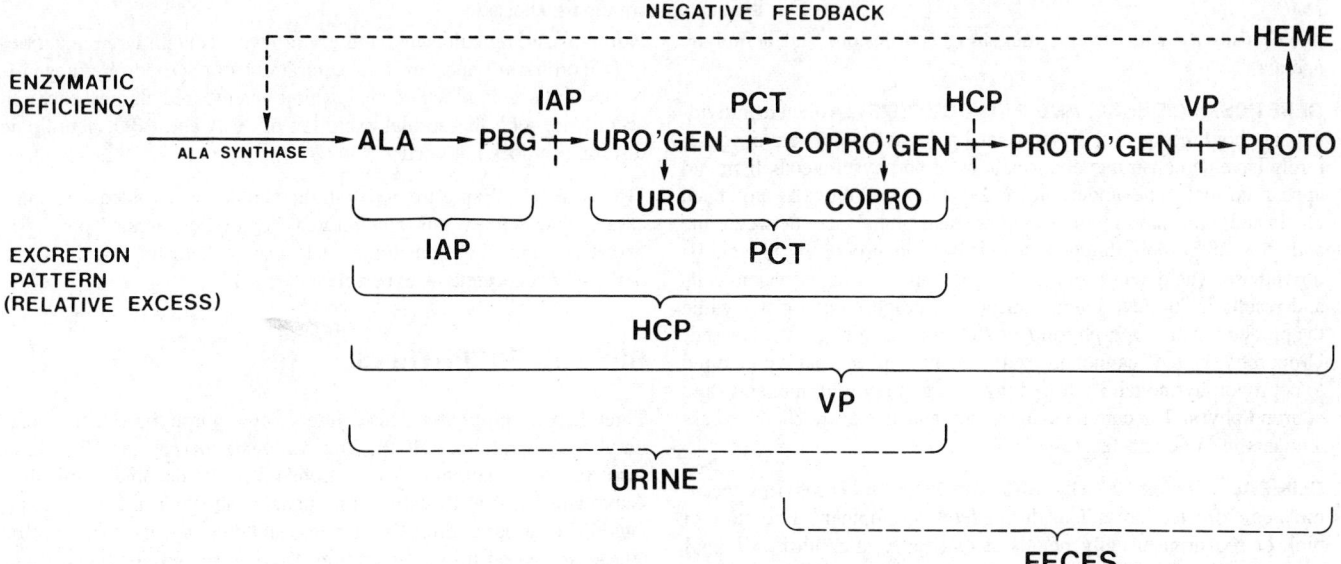

FIGURE 312-1 *Patterns of urinary porphyrin and porphyrin precursor excretion in the hepatic porphyrias in relation to the enzymatic deficiency in the pathway of heme biosynthesis. Intermediates of the pathway excreted excessively during the acute phase of each of the hepatic porphyrias are within the respective brackets. (ALA, δ-aminolevulinic acid; PBG, porpho- bilinogen; URO'GEN, uroporphyrinogen; COPRO'GEN, coproporphyrino- gen; PROTO'GEN, protoporphyrinogen; PROTO, protoporphyrin; IAP, in- termittent acute porphyria; PCT, porphyria cutanea tarda; HCP, hereditary coproporphyria; VP, variegate porphyria.)*

The porphyrinogens serve as intermediates between porphobilin- ogen and protoporphyrin. Porphyrinogens are colorless and nonflu- orescent. With the exception of protoporphyrin porphyrins are by- products that have escaped from the biosynthetic path by irreversible oxidation of the corresponding porphyrinogen. Porphyrins do not possess physiologic function but are responsible, through their pigment and fluorescent properties, for the spectacular appearance of urine and erythrocytes in some patients.

The arrangement of two substituent side chains on the pyrrole ring of porphyrins determines the structural isomer types, numbered I to IV. In nature only types I and III have been identified, and only

type III serves as substrate for the terminal steps of the pathway leading to protoporphyrin IX and heme. The catabolism of heme does not lead to porphyrins but to noncyclic tetrapyrroles referred to as *bile pigments*.

CONGENITAL ERYTHROPOIETIC PORPHYRIA

DEFINITION Congenital erythropoietic porphyria (CEP; Günther's disease, congenital photosensitive porphyria, erythropoietic uropor- phyria) is a rare, recessively inherited defect that causes chronic

TABLE 312-1 Characteristics of the porphyrias

	Erythropoietic porphyria	Hepatic porphyrias				Erythrohepatic porphyria
	Congenital erythropoietic porphyria (CEP)	Intermittent acute porphyria (IAP)	Hereditary coproporphyria (HCP)	Variegate porphyria (VP)	Porphyria cutanea tarda (PCT)	Protoporphyria (PP)
Enzyme deficiency	Porphobilinogen deaminase and/or uroporphyrinogen III cosynthase (?)	Porphobilinogen deaminase	Coproporphyri- nogen oxidase	Protoporphyri- nogen oxidase	Uroporphyrino- gen decarboxyl- ase	Ferrochelatase
Inheritance	Autosomal reces- sive	Autosomal domi- nant	Autosomal domi- nant	Autosomal domi- nant	Autosomal domi- nant	Autosomal domi- nant
Metabolic expression	Erythroid cells	Liver	Liver	Liver	Liver	Erythroid cells and liver
Signs and symptoms:						
Photosensitive cuta- neous lesions	Yes	No	Infrequent	Yes	Yes	Yes
Attacks of abdomi- nal pain, neuropsy- chiatric syndrome	No	Yes	Yes	Yes	No	No
Laboratory abnormalities:						
Red blood cells:						
Uroporphyrin	+++	N	N	N	N	N
Coproporphyrin	++	N	N	N	N	+
Protoporphyrin	(+)	N	N	N	N	+++
Urine:						
δ-Aminolevulinic acid	N	(+++)	(+++)	(+++)	N	N
Porphobilinogen	N	(+++)	(+++)	(+++)	N	N
Uroporphyrin	+++	++	+	+	+++	N
Coproporphyrin	++	N	++	++	+	(+)
Feces:						
Coproporphyrin	+	N	+++	+	(+)	(+)
Protoporphyrin	+	N	+	+++	N	++

NOTE: *N, normal; +, increased levels or excretion; ++, moderately increased; +++, markedly increased; (+), increased in some patients only; (+++), frequently increased only during acute attacks.*

photosensitivity with severe, mutilating skin lesions and hemolytic anemia.

GENETICS, INCIDENCE, AND PATHOGENESIS Affected individuals are homozygous for an autosomal recessive gene; heterozygotes rarely have demonstrable abnormalities in porphyrin metabolism and appear normal. The underlying enzyme abnormality has not been elucidated but may involve a functional imbalance between the activities of porphobilinogen deaminase and uroporphyrinogen III cosynthase. The defect is expressed solely in maturing erythroid cells and results in massive overproduction of uroporphyrinogen I while the production of uroporphyrinogen III is normal or slightly increased. Uroporphyrinogen I cannot be used for heme synthesis but is converted to coproporphyrinogen I. Uroporphyrin I, coproporphyrinogen I, and coproporphyrin I accumulate in tissues and are excreted in excess amounts in urine and feces.

CLINICAL PRESENTATION AND DIAGNOSIS Porphyrins accumulate in affected individuals during fetal development. Excretion of pink or red urine usually begins at or shortly after birth, whereas cutaneous photosensitivity, intermittent hemolysis, and splenomegaly may be manifested later. Hypertrichosis and red discoloration of the teeth and bones are common. Death may occur in childhood. With longer survival, severe scarring and mutilation occur, mostly affecting fingers, nose, and ears. The urine contains high concentrations of uroporphyrin I, coproporphyrin, and porphyrins with seven, six, five, and three carboxyl groups, whereas the excretion of ALA and PBG is normal. Large amounts of coproporphyrin I are found in the feces.

Normoblasts, reticulocytes, and erythrocytes contain large quantities of uroporphyrin I and lower concentrations of coproporphyrinogen I. Normoblasts and reticulocytes exhibit intense red fluorescence. In accordance with the normal excretion of ALA and PBG, neurologic disturbance does not occur.

TREATMENT Exposure to sunlight should be avoided. In some cases, splenectomy has ameliorated hemolytic anemia, porphyrin excretion, and photosensitivity. The use of hematin infusions and oral β-carotene remains experimental.

HEPATIC PORPHYRIAS

Three hepatic porphyrias, intermittent acute porphyria (IAP), hereditary coproporphyria (HCP), and variegate porphyria (VP), have many features in common. All are transmitted as autosomal dominants. Acute attacks of a life-threatening neurologic syndrome are precipitated by a variety of drugs, hormones, and other agents. During acute attacks increased urinary excretion of ALA and PBG occurs in all, but the patterns of porphyrins in urine and feces differ (Fig. 312-1).

INTERMITTENT ACUTE PORPHYRIA Definition Intermittent acute porphyria [IAP, acute intermittent porphyria (AIP), pyrroloporphyria] is characterized by recurrent attacks of neurologic and psychiatric dysfunction. Photosensitivity does not occur. The primary defect is in porphobilinogen deaminase.

Genetics, incidence, and pathogenesis IAP is an autosomal dominant trait with variable expressivity. The frequency of the abnormal

FIGURE 312-2 *Outline of heme biosynthesis. (ALA, δ-aminolevulinic acid; PBG, porphobilinogen; URO'GEN, uroporphyrinogen.)*

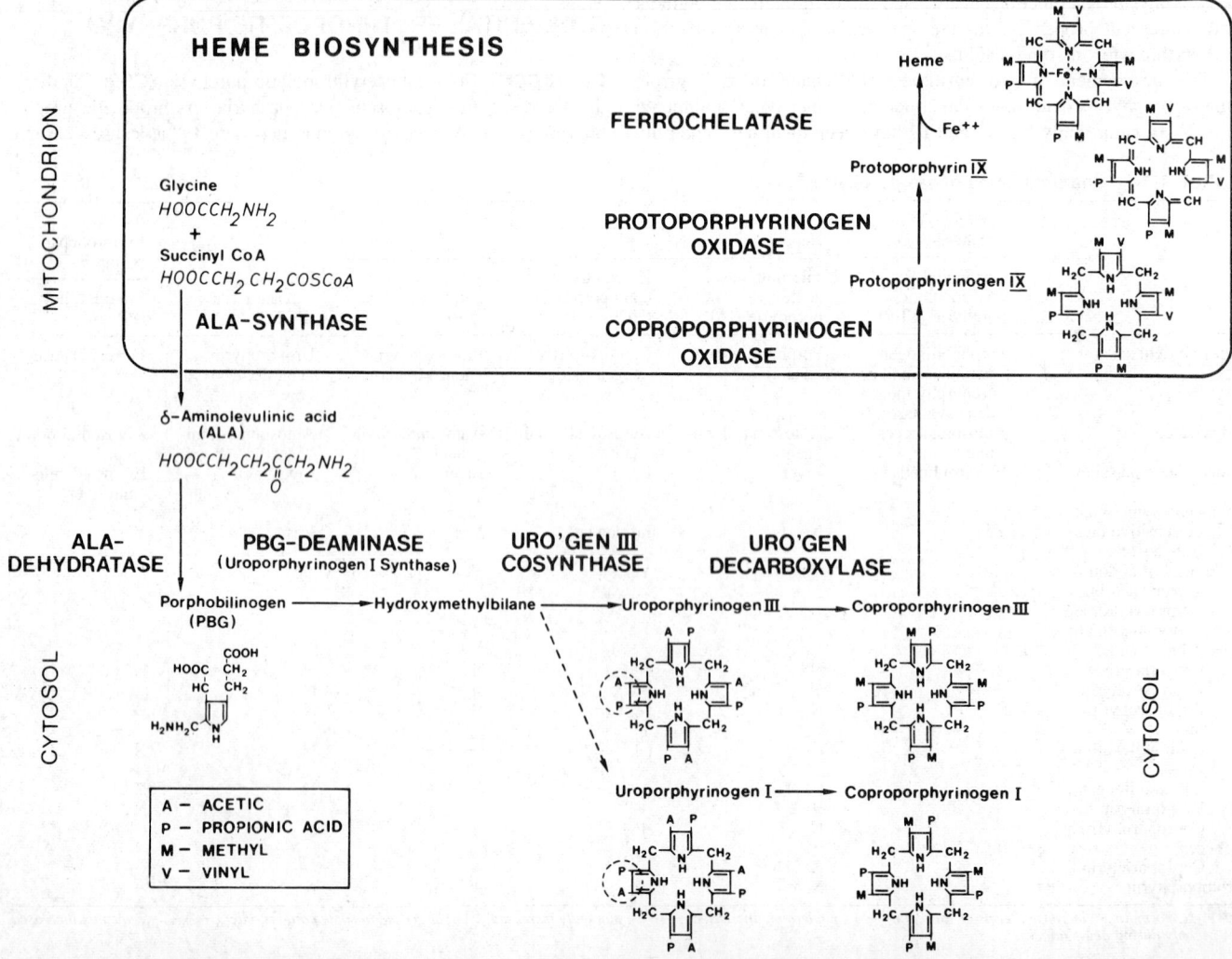

gene is estimated to be between 1 in 10,000 and 1 in 50,000, but in certain regions the incidence may be higher. Homozygous cases have not been observed. The defect consists of a partial (50 percent) deficiency of porphobilinogen deaminase, the enzyme that converts PBG to uroporphyrinogen I. More than one mechanism at the gene level can cause this deficiency, the most common mutation resulting in a decreased amount of immunoreactive enzyme protein. In the liver a partial deficiency of the enzyme leads to increased activity and/or inducibility of ALA synthase by drugs and other factors and, consequently, to increased formation and urinary excretion of ALA and PBG. Preformed porphyrins do not accumulate, and, therefore, cutaneous photosensitivity does not occur. Decreased porphobilinogen deaminase activity is present in liver, erythrocytes, cultured skin fibroblasts, lymphocytes, and amniotic cells of patients with IAP. Thus, the enzymatic defect is present, albeit metabolically unexpressed, in tissues other than liver. Deficiency of the enzyme does not necessarily result in clinical manifestations of acute porphyria without additional acquired factors, and only a third or less of individuals with the genetic defect ever experience an attack of porphyria. The relation between the genetic defect and the neurologic lesions is unknown.

Clinical presentation and diagnosis Symptoms rarely occur before puberty. Abdominal pain is frequently the initial and most prominent symptom of the porphyric attack. It may be moderate or severe, colicky, localized or generalized; radiation to the back or loins may occur. The pain probably results from autonomic neuropathy causing disturbed gastrointestinal motility with alternate areas of spasm and dilatation. The abdomen is usually soft, and tenderness is not marked. Because it is often accompanied by fever and leukocytosis, the acute porphyric attack can mimic any inflammatory abdominal disease. Severe vomiting and persistent constipation are common. Neurologic manifestations and mental disturbance are variable. Peripheral nerves, the autonomic nervous system, brainstem, cranial nerves, or cerebral function may be involved. Sinus tachycardia and labile hypertension with postural hypotension, urinary retention, and excessive sweating are frequent. Hypertension and tachycardia correlate with increased excretion of catecholamines. Peripheral neuropathy is predominantly motor, but sensory components may be present. Deep tendon reflexes are diminished or absent. Neuritic pain in the extremities, areas of hypesthesia and paresthesia, and foot and wrist drop are typical. Paraplegia or complete flaccid quadriplegia may ensue. In the past, respiratory paralysis was a leading cause of death. Cranial nerve involvement may lead to optic nerve atrophy, ophthalmoplegia, and dysphagia. With more severe CNS involvement, delirium, coma, and seizures occur. Although the neuropathy is reversible to a surprising degree, residual paresis may last for years following an acute attack. Many patients have a long history of vague nervousness, emotional instability, and functional disturbances. Signs of mental disturbance occur in one-third, and an organic brain syndrome with restlessness, disorientation, and visual hallucinations may supervene. Hyponatremia can be severe. Multiple mechanisms (including gastrointestinal loss of sodium, imprudent fluid therapy, and a sodium-losing nephropathy related to a toxic effect of ALA) have been implicated, but the major mechanism appears to be inappropriate release of antidiuretic hormone. Hypomagnesemia may be severe enough to cause tetany.

Acute attacks may last from days to months and vary in frequency and severity. In periods of remission symptoms may be slight or completely absent. Clinical (and biochemical) manifestations may be precipitated by usual therapeutic doses of barbiturates, anticonvulsants, estrogens, contraceptives, or alcohol. All these drugs are oxidized by hemoproteins of the cytochrome P_{450} system. Impaired hepatic metabolism of some of these drugs can occur during acute attacks. In some women, exacerbations correlate with the menstrual cycle, and latent porphyria may become manifest late in pregnancy or shortly after delivery. Prolonged periods of decreased caloric intake (fasting) and infections may also provoke attacks.

Laboratory findings Excessive excretion of ALA and PBG in the urine is characteristic during acute attacks and does not differentiate IAP from HCP and VP. The levels do not correlate with the severity of the symptoms. The qualitative determination of porphobilinogen in the urine by the Watson-Schwartz or the Hoesch test is a simple and valuable screening aid for the diagnosis of an acute attack in IAP, HCP, and VP. These tests are almost always positive during episodes of neuropsychiatric dysfunction but are positive only when the concentration of PBG in the urine is three to five times the upper limit of normal; as a consequence, both assays may be negative in latent cases and in patients in whom urinary excretion of PBG becomes normal following recovery from an acute attack. In these instances urinary ALA and PBG excretion should be measured quantitatively by chromatographic methods. In latent IAP with normal excretion of ALA and PBG, diagnosis is possible by measuring the activity of porphobilinogen deaminase in erythrocytes, lymphocytes, or cultured skin fibroblasts. However, there is an overlap between the activities of the enzyme in erythrocytes from normals and patients with IAP, and definite diagnosis is not always possible.

In IAP the porphyrin precursors ALA and PBG are excreted in increased amounts, consistent with the enzymatic defect. Freshly passed urine is, therefore, usually colorless and contains little preformed uro- or coproporphyrin. The urine may darken on standing because PBG polymerizes spontaneously to uroporphyrin and porphobilin, a dark-brown pigment of unknown structure. However, some patients have enough nonenzymatically formed pigments to impart a dark-red appearance to freshly voided urine. The fecal porphyrin concentration is usually normal.

Conventional liver function tests are normal except for increased Bromsulphalein (BSP) retention. A moderate reduction in red blood cell mass and blood volume or a transient normochromic, normocytic anemia are the only hematologic disturbances. Metabolic abnormalities during acute attacks include hypercholesterolemia with increased low-density lipoprotein levels, increased serum thyroxine (without hyperthyroidism), impaired glucose tolerance, and defective 5α-reduction of testosterone in liver. The relationship of these abnormalities to the genetic defect is unknown.

Treatment The treatment of the acute attack is identical in IAP, HCP, and VP. Some acute attacks seemingly can be aborted by administration of large quantities (500 g per day) of carbohydrates (glucose effect), although no objective study of the efficacy of this therapy has been performed. Intravenous administration of glucose at a rate of 20 g/h is recommended. If the patient does not improve within 48 h of continued glucose infusion or if neuropsychiatric symptoms progress, intravenous infusion of hematin (4 mg per kilogram of body weight infused over 10 to 15 min every 12 h for 3 to 6 days) should be tried. Hematin is commercially available (Panhematin) as lyophilized powder; solutions are prepared immediately before infusion. Complications of hematin treatment with the recommended doses seem to be exceedingly rare. Thrombophlebitis at the site of infusion, a coagulopathy (manifested by thrombocytopenia, prolonged prothrombin time, abnormal partial thromboplastin time, and hypofibrinogenemia), and hemolysis have been reported rarely. Both hematin and glucose prevent the induction of hepatic ALA-synthase in experimental animals, and both may reverse the biochemical abnormalities and cause improvement within 48 h. Supportive treatment with careful monitoring of fluid and electrolytes is important to prevent and/or correct hyponatremia, hypomagnesemia, and azotemia. Tachycardia and hypertension should be treated with beta-adrenergic blocking drugs. A list of agents considered to be "safe" or "probably safe" in patients with latent and acute IAP, HCP, and VP is given in Table 312-2. Acute attacks carry a substantial risk of fatality if the diagnosis is delayed and neurologic lesions progress. Complete recovery occurs in the majority, but neurologic deficits may require months or years to resolve. The most important measure in the management is prevention of acute attacks by instructing the patient to avoid provocative factors, such as drugs, steroids, alcohol excess, and deliberate fasting.

TABLE 312-2 Drugs considered to be safe (or probably safe) in patients with intermittent acute porphyria, hereditary coproporphyria, and variegate porphyria

Analgesics:
  Salicylates, ibuprofen
  Morphine and related opiates (meperidine)
Antibiotics:
  Penicillins, cephalosporins,
  Methenamide mandelate, aminoglycosides
Psychoactive drugs:
  Phenothiazines (chlorpromazine)
Antihistamines:
  Diphenhydramine
Antihypertensives:
  Guanethidine
  Propranolol
  Reserpine, thiazides
Miscellaneous:
  Atropine
  Neostigmine
  Propanidid
  Procaine
  Succinylcholine
  Ether
  Nitrous oxide
  Corticosteroids
  Oxazepam
  Chlordiazepoxide
  Insulin
  Heparin

HEREDITARY COPROPORPHYRIA Definition and genetics Hereditary coproporphyria (HCP) is a hepatic porphyria characterized by attacks of neuropsychiatric dysfunction identical with those of IAP and VP. In addition, photosensitivity occurs in some. The primary genetic defect is a partial deficiency of coproporphyrinogen oxidase. The disease is inherited as an autosomal dominant trait. The incidence of HCP is uncertain since the majority of affected individuals remain asymptomatic.

Pathogenesis and clinical picture HCP is characterized by the excretion of large amounts of coproporphyrin III, mainly in feces but also in urine. Excretion of ALA and PBG is increased during acute attacks (positive Watson-Schwartz or Hoesch test) but usually returns to normal during remission. Acute attacks are indistinguishable from those of IAP and VP and are precipitated by the same factors. Skin photosensitivity occurs in approximately one-third of patients with overt disease. Its onset is frequently associated with intercurrent hepatic disease. A partial deficiency of coproporphyrinogen oxidase can be demonstrated in leukocytes and cultured skin fibroblasts.

Treatment Treatment is identical with that described for IAP.

VARIEGATE PORPHYRIA Definition Variegate porphyria (VP; South African genetic porphyria) is characterized both by acute attacks of neuropsychiatric dysfunction and by chronic skin sensitivity to sunlight and to mechanical trauma. The primary enzymatic lesion in heme biosynthesis is a partial deficiency of protoporphyrinogen oxidase.

Genetics, incidence, and pathogenesis VP is inherited as an autosomal dominant trait. The disease is particularly common among the white population of South Africa, where its incidence is estimated at 1 in 400, and many cases have been identified as descendants of a woman who emigrated to Cape Town from the Netherlands in 1688. Elsewhere the disease is less frequent, but VP has been recognized in many countries. The defect leads to the excretion of large amounts of protoporphyrin in bile and feces (with lesser increases in the fecal excretion of coproporphyrin) and to increased urinary excretion of ALA, PBG, and coproporphyrin during acute attacks.

Clinical presentation and diagnosis Overt cases with VP usually present in the second or third decade. The features include acute attacks of abdominal pain and neuropsychiatric symptoms, coupled with photocutaneous lesions. Neurologic and cutaneous manifestations may occur simultaneously or at different times. Most South African patients have cutaneous involvement, consisting of dermal abrasions, superficial erosions, and blister formation after trivial mechanical trauma. The mechanical fragility usually is limited to light-exposed parts of the skin. The lesions often leave depigmented or pigmented scars. Secondary infection may delay healing. Hyperpigmentation of the face and hands is common, and women often have hirsutism. The skin lesions are indistinguishable from those of porphyria cutanea tarda (PCT). Severe exacerbations of the cutaneous lesions may be associated with intercurrent hepatic disease, presumably related to decreased fecal excretion and a concomitant increase in the urinary excretion of porphyrins. Acute attacks of neuropsychiatric dysfunction are indistinguishable from those of IAP and HCP and are precipitated by the same factors. The characteristic chemical finding in VP is the continuous excretion of large amounts of proto- and coproporphyrin, even when clinical manifestations are minimal or absent. The levels of protoporphyrin exceed those of coproporphyrin, the reverse of the situation in HCP. Urinary excretion of ALA, PBG, and porphyrins is either normal or moderately increased in asymptomatic patients or those who have only skin symptoms. During acute attacks the urinary excretion of ALA and PBG is increased (positive Watson-Schwartz or Hoesch test), and there also is increased urinary excretion of coproporphyrin and uroporphyrin. Erythrocyte porphyrins are normal, allowing distinction from protoporphyria.

Treatment Prophylactic measures and treatment of the acute attack with glucose and possibly hematin infusions are the same as for IAP and HCP, although the experience with hematin in VP is limited. Avoidance of exposure to direct sunlight and use of protective clothing (gloves, hats) are advocated. The prognosis is similar to or better than that of patients with IAP.

PORPHYRIA CUTANEA TARDA Definition Porphyria cutanea tarda (PCT; symptomatic cutaneous hepatic porphyria, symptomatic porphyria) is the most common form of porphyria. The disease is characterized by chronic skin lesions, the frequent presence of hepatic disease (and hepatic siderosis), and a distinct pattern of urinary excretion of porphyrins. The disorder is probably caused by an inherited or acquired deficiency of hepatic uroporphyrinogen decarboxylase. Neurologic manifestations are absent.

Genetics, incidence, and pathogenesis PCT was considered to be an acquired disorder because of its sporadic (and usually nonfamilial) occurrence late in life and its common association with alcoholic liver disease and hepatic siderosis.

The incidence of the disease is not established, but PCT is frequent where both alcoholism and iron overload are common, as among the Bantus in South Africa. PCT can be a familial disease, inherited in an autosomal dominant fashion with variable expressivity (familial PCT). The inherited defect consists of a partial decrease of demonstrable uroporphyrinogen decarboxylase activity in liver, erythrocytes, and cultured fibroblasts; clinically and chemically latent carriers of the defect have been identified. In sporadic PCT a partial deficiency of uroporphyrinogen decarboxylase is found only in liver. It is unknown if this is a consequence of a genetic or acquired (toxic) mechanism. Deficiency (of whatever etiology) in uroporphyrinogen decarboxylase, which catalyzes the conversion of uroporphyrinogen to coproporphyrinogen, leads to a disturbance of hepatic heme synthesis and consequent skin photosensitivity only in the presence of additional factors such as iron overload, usually in association with liver disease and the prolonged administration of estrogens. The mechanism by which iron overload and hormones cause clinical expression of latent PCT is unknown. In contrast to IAP, HCP, and VP, the enzymatic defect in PCT does not result in altered regulation of the hepatic heme synthetic pathway, and ALA synthase activity remains normal or only minimally increased even in overt cases. This probably accounts for the absence of acute neuropsychiatric attacks, the usually normal urinary ALA and PBG, and the lack of sensitivity to drugs such as barbiturates.

Clinical presentation and diagnosis Photosensitivity is the only major manifestation. The skin lesions are indistinguishable from those in VP. Skin symptoms usually begin insidiously, most often in men aged 40 to 60, and consist of enhanced facial pigmentation, increased fragility to trauma, erythema, and vesicular and ulcerative lesions. Sclerodermatous changes and increased hair on the forehead, malar region, or forearms are common.

Liver disease, frequently related to alcohol, is common, and hepatic siderosis is an almost constant finding, although the degree of iron deposition is variable and rarely severe. Spontaneous remission may occur. Occasionally, estrogens (including contraceptive pills) or known hepatotoxic drugs precipitate the clinical disease. The incidence of diabetes mellitus is increased in PCT, and association with systemic lupus erythematosus and other autoimmune syndromes has been noted.

The excretion in urine of uroporphyrin and, to a lesser extent, coproporphyrin is increased. The urine may be pink or brown. The excretion of ALA and PBG in urine is usually normal (negative Watson-Schwartz or Hoesch test). Although uroporphyrin is the major porphyrin in the urine, intermediary porphyrins (particularly hepta-carboxylic porphyrin) are also found. Increases in fecal porphyrins are less marked and usually restricted to the coproporphyrin fraction. The diagnosis is established by the combined presence of skin photosensitivity, liver disease, increased urinary uroporphyrin excretion, the lack of an increase in porphyrin precursors (ALA, PBG), and absence of a history of neuropsychiatric attacks.

Toxic acquired porphyria resembling PCT can occur in individuals accidentally exposed to hexachlorobenzene, polychlorinated biphenyls, tetrachlorodibenzo-*p*-dioxin (TCDD), and other polychlorinated hydrocarbons. Moreover, several instances of PCT in association with benign or malignant primary tumors of the liver have been observed.

Treatment Abstinence in alcoholic patients usually leads to improvement of PCT. Removal of hepatic iron by repeated phlebotomy may lead to long-lasting remissions: 400 mL of blood (or the equivalent amount of erythrocytes) is removed weekly or less frequently with careful monitoring of the hemoglobin and plasma protein levels. For patients unable to tolerate phlebotomy, the administration of small doses of chloroquine (125 mg twice weekly) apparently removes uroporphyrins from the liver and has produced remissions. However, chloroquine carries the risk of hepatotoxicity. Chelation therapy with desferoxamine is another alternative to remove iron. Topical sunscreens and oral carotenoids are not effective in protecting against the skin lesions of PCT.

PROTOPORPHYRIA

DEFINITION Protoporphyria (PP; erythropoietic protoporphyria, erythrohepatic protoporphyria), a disorder in which mild skin photosensitivity is associated with high concentrations of protoporphyrin in erythrocytes, is due to a deficiency of ferrochelatase. Protoporphyrin may also accumulate in the liver.

GENETICS, INCIDENCE, AND PATHOGENESIS PP is inherited as an autosomal dominant trait with variable expressivity. Activity of ferrochelatase, the mitochondrial enzyme that catalyzes the incorporation of ferrous iron into protoporphyrin, is deficient in bone marrow, peripheral blood, liver, and cultured skin fibroblasts. This deficiency results in the excessive accumulation of protoporphyrin in late normoblasts, reticulocytes, and young erythrocytes; protoporphyrin leaks into the plasma from erythrocytes as they age. Photosensitivity is mediated by protoporphyrin in plasma and skin and is evoked by visible light (380 to 560 nm). Skin photosensitivity shows seasonal variability. The liver participates in excess porphyrin production in some patients or, alternatively, may take up protoporphyrin from plasma. Many carriers of the defect remain clinically (and chemically) asymptomatic, and diagnosis may be possible only through enzymatic studies.

CLINICAL PRESENTATION AND DIAGNOSIS Mild photosensitivity usually begins in childhood. Exposure to sunlight is followed by pruritus, erythema, and occasional edema (solar urticaria). The lesions subside over hours or days without scarring. Cutaneous manifestations may occur only after prolonged exposure to sunlight; alternatively, the initial skin lesions may progress to a chronic eczematous phase (solar eczema). There is no abnormal mechanical fragility or blister formation in skin as is characteristic for VP and PCT. Erythrodontia, hypertrichosis, and hyperpigmentation are absent. Attacks of neuropsychiatric dysfunction do not occur.

PP is generally benign, but may be associated with abnormalities of liver, biliary tract, or blood. The incidence of cholelithiasis is increased, and the gallstones contain protoporphyrin. Liver disease due to massive deposition of protoporphyrin may rarely progress to fatal cirrhosis. All patients therefore should have routine evaluation of liver function. Mild anemia is common.

PP is diagnosed by the detection of high concentrations of protoporphyrin in erythrocytes. Large numbers of red-fluorescing erythrocytes are seen by fluorescent microscopy. Protoporphyrin may also be elevated in plasma and feces, while urinary porphyrins, ALA, and PBG are usually normal.

TREATMENT Topical sunscreens usually are ineffective. Orally administered β-carotene (usually as a mixture of β-carotene and canthaxanthine) substantially improves the tolerance to sunlight. Serum carotene levels should be maintained between 600 and 800 μg/dL.

REFERENCES

BONKOWSKY KL, SCHADY W: Neurologic manifestations of acute porphyria. Semin Liver Dis 2:108, 1982
DEAN G: *The Porphyrias*, 2d ed. London, Pitman Medical Publishing Company, 1972
DeLeo VA et al: Erythropoietic protoporphyria: 10 years' experience. Am J Med 60:8, 1976
ELDER GH: The porphyrias: Clinical chemistry, diagnosis and methodology. Clin Haematol 9:371, 1980
KAPPAS A et al: The porphyrias, in *The Metabolic Basis of Inherited Disease*, 5th ed, JB Stanbury et al (eds). New York, McGraw-Hill, 1983
PIERACH CA: Hematin therapy for the porphyric attack. Semin Liver Dis 2:125, 1982

313 THE GLYCOGEN STORAGE DISEASES

ARTHUR L. BEAUDET

The glycogen storage diseases are a group of genetic disorders involving the pathways for storage of carbohydrate as glycogen and for its utilization to maintain blood sugar and to provide energy. Some forms are not associated with actual increases in glycogen content in tissues.

Glycogen is a highly branched polymer of glucose with the majority of residues in 1,4 linkage and with 7 to 10 percent of residues in 1,6 linkage. The treelike structure undergoes addition and removal of residues at its periphera. Glycogen molecules have molecular weights of many millions, and molecules may aggregate to form structures recognizable by electron microscopy. Liver generally contains less than 70 mg glycogen per gram of tissue, and muscle usually contains less than 15 mg/g, but these levels fluctuate as a consequence of feeding and hormonal stimuli. Abnormalities of glycogen structure can result either from decreased or increased branching.

The metabolic pathways involved in glycogen synthesis and breakdown are outlined in Fig. 313-1. These pathways differ among tissues; for example, certain reactions are active in liver but trivial or absent in muscle, and some enzyme functions are encoded by

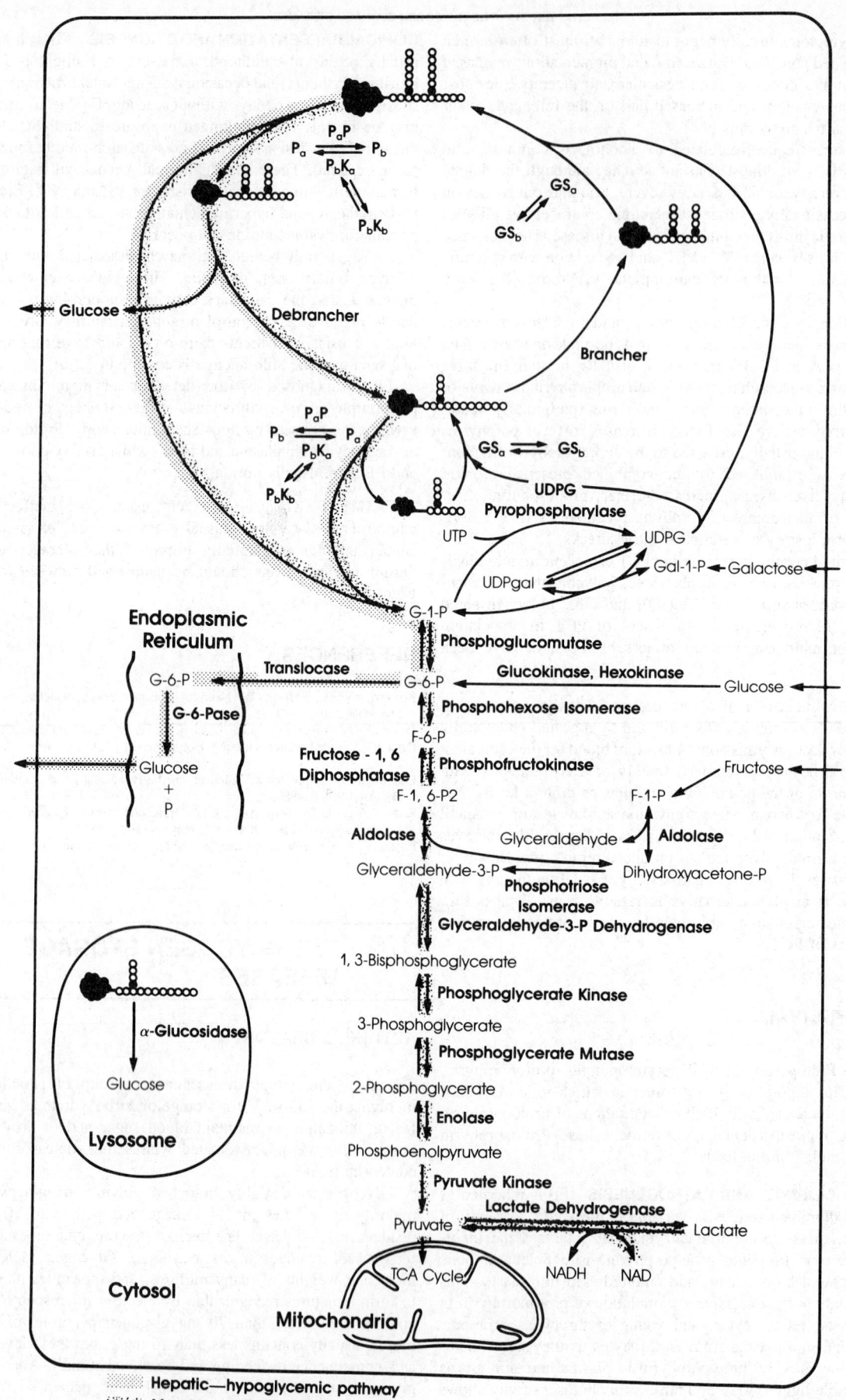

FIGURE 313-1 *Metabolic pathways related to glycogen storage disease. A hypothetical composite cell is shown depicting both hepatic and muscle pathways. The shaded areas depict pathways that are blocked in the hepatic-hypoglycemic diseases or in the muscle-energy diseases. Nonstandard abbre-* *viations are as follows: GS_a, active glycogen synthase; GS_b, inactive glycogen synthase; P_a, active phosphorylase; P_b, inactive phosphorylase; P_aP, phosphorylase a phosphatase; P_bK_a, active phosphorylase b kinase; P_bK_b, inactive phosphorylase b kinase.*

different genes in muscle and liver. Plasma glucose enters the cell and is phosphorylated by glucokinase or hexokinase. The former enzyme is found in liver where it accomplishes the majority of phosphorylation of glucose, while multiple hexokinases are distributed more widely in tissues. Glucose 6-phosphate (G6P) is converted to glucose 1-phosphate (G1P) in a reversible reaction catalyzed by phosphoglucomutase. Uridine diphosphate glucose (UDPG) is synthesized from G1P and UTP by UDPG pyrophosphorylase. Genetic deficiency has not been documented for any of the hepatic enzymes. Glycogen is then elongated by the addition from UDPG of individual glucose residues to an existing polymer. This reaction is catalyzed by glycogen synthase, which exists in an active dephosphorylated form and in an inactive phosphorylated form. Synthesis of a normally branched glycogen structure also requires the action of a branching enzyme (1,4-α-glucan:1,4-α-glucan 6-glucosyltransferase) which transfers a 1,4-linked oligosaccharide to a 1,6-linkage position.

Glucose is mobilized from glycogen by a complex group of enzyme reactions. Glycogen is acted upon directly by the active form of phosphorylase, phosphorylase *a,* to remove individual glucose units and yield G1P. Phosphorylase is encoded by different gene products in muscle and in liver. In both tissues, the enzyme can exist in an active phosphorylated form and in an inactive dephosphorylated form. Phosphorylase is a dimer of identical subunits, and both forms of the enzyme are subject to complex allosteric regulation. The inactive phosphorylase *b* is converted to the active form by phosphorylase *b* kinase. Phosphorylase *b* kinase also exists in an active phosphorylated form and in an inactive dephosphorylated form. Phosphorylase *b* kinase is composed of four nonidentical subunits $(\alpha,\beta,\gamma,\delta)_4$, and the δ chain is identical with the calcium-binding protein calmodulin. The rate of glucose mobilization by this system is regulated by a cascade of kinase reactions, including cyclic AMP–dependent protein kinase. Epinephrine and glucagon act to increase blood sugar via this cascade system by activation of phosphorylase and simultaneous inactivation of glycogen synthase. Glycogen also is acted upon directly by a debranching enzyme which carries out the debranching process by first transferring an oligosaccharide from a branch point to leave a single 1,6-linked glucose residue and then hydrolyzing the 1,6 linkage. Thus, the debrancher enzyme has both glucan transferase activity (oligo-1,4 → 1,4-transferase) and a glucosidase (amylo-1,6-glucosidase) activity and yields a single residue of glucose for each branch point removed. The G1P generated by phosphorylase, as mentioned above, must be further metabolized to G6P by phosphoglucomutase. In the liver G6P is transported by a specific translocase to the inner surface of the endoplasmic reticulum for hydrolysis by glucose 6-phosphatase. Glucose is then free to exit the hepatic cell to maintain blood levels. Many genetic deficiencies occur in the enzymes required for the conversion of glycogen to free glucose in the liver, and these cause the hepatic-hypoglycemic forms of glycogen storage disease.

If glycogen is used as a direct energy source, as in muscle, G6P and G1P must enter the pathways for glycolysis. Again, numerous enzymes are required in muscle for proper breakdown of glycogen and entry into the glycolytic pathway and tricarboxylic acid cycle. The enzymatic steps known to be associated with genetic deficiency states in muscle include muscle phosphorylase, debranching enzyme, muscle phosphofructokinase (PFK), and probably muscle phosphoglycerate mutase (PGAM) and lactate dehydrogenase (LDH) M subunit.

The lysomal enzyme α-glucosidase, which is structurally and metabolically separate from the above-described pathways, is capable of degrading both 1,4 and 1,6 linkages in glycogen to give free glucose. This enzyme has widespread distribution in tissues, but its deficiency affects primarily skeletal and cardiac muscle.

CLASSIFICATION The clinical manifestations, diagnostic criteria, and therapy for glycogen storage diseases can be formulated in terms of the metabolic pathway outlined above (Table 313-1). According to this schema, two broad categories of disease can be delineated—those with a *hepatic-hypoglycemic* pathophysiology and those with a

muscle-energy pathophysiology. Diseases with individualized pathophysiology also occur. It is suggested that disorders be designated by the specific protein deficiency, i.e., glucose 6-phosphatase deficiency. Although the roman numeral designations for types I through VII are in widespread use, numbering for higher types is confused and is to be avoided. Eponyms are of historical interest.

The hepatic-hypoglycemic disorders include glucose 6-phosphatase deficiency (type Ia), G6P microsomal translocase deficiency (type Ib), debrancher enzyme deficiency (type III), hepatic phosphorylase deficiency (type VI), and phosphorylase *b* kinase deficiency. Within this group, a distinction can be made between those disorders in which G6P and its metabolites are likely to be elevated (types Ia and Ib) and those disorders where G6P and related metabolites are likely to be decreased. This explains why increased glycolysis and lactic acidosis occur in types Ia and Ib disease but not in other forms of hepatic-hypoglycemic disease. Likewise, types Ia and Ib disease are distinct because gluconeogenesis, galactose, and fructose cannot contribute effectively to maintenance of blood sugar, in contrast to the other forms of hepatic-hypoglycemic disease. The glycemic response to epinephrine or glucagon tends to be blunted in the hepatic-hypoglycemic disorders. Dietary therapy with frequent feeding is a rational approach to the hepatic-hypoglycemic disorders and is tailored to reduce protein and to eliminate sources of galactose and fructose in types Ia and Ib disease.

The muscle-energy disorders include muscle phosphorylase deficiency (type V), phosphofructokinase deficiency (type VII) phosphoglycerate mutase deficiency, and LDH M-subunit deficiency. The clinical picture is one of muscle pain, myoglobinuria, and elevation of muscle enzymes in serum following vigorous exercise. The interruption of the pathway from glycogen to lactate with the accompanying failure to oxidize NADH is the unifying theme in these disorders. The failure of blood lactate to increase in response to exercise is a useful diagnostic test for the muscle-energy deficiency disorders. Debrancher enzyme deficiency constitutes an overlap syndrome; it presents primarily as a hepatic-hypoglycemic disorder, and the glucose released by phosphorylase appears to be sufficient to prevent myoglobinuria but not to prevent skeletal myopathy and weakness.

Two other disorders are best considered individually. Deficiency of lysosomal α-glucosidase is a lysosomal storage disease without major impact on either carbohydrate metabolism or maintenance of blood sugar (see Chap. 316). The major pathologic process in branching enzyme deficiency is a severe hepatic cirrhosis, possibly due to the harmful effects of the abnormal glycogen that accumulates. Glycogen content is generally normal, and the ability to maintain a normal blood sugar is not impaired.

HEPATIC-HYPOGLYCEMIC DISEASES Glucose 6-phosphatase deficiency, type Ia CLINICAL FEATURES Glucose 6-phosphatase deficiency, or von Gierke disease, is an autosomal recessive genetic disorder with an incidence of 1 in 100,000 to 400,000. The disorder is usually manifested during the first 12 months of life by symptomatic hypoglycemia or by the recognition of hepatomegaly. Occasional patients experience hypoglycemia in the immediate neonatal period, and rare patients never have hypoglycemia. Characteristic findings include a full-cheeked, rounded facial appearance; a protuberant abdomen due to marked hepatomegaly; and thin extremities. Hyperlipidemia may cause eruptive xanthomas and lipemia retinalis. Splenomegaly is usually mild or absent, although massive enlargement of the left lobe of the liver may be mistaken for enlargement of the spleen. Growth is usually normal for the first few months of life; growth retardation then supervenes, and adolescence is delayed. Mental development is usually normal except for injury from hypoglycemia.

The characteristic profound symptomatic hypoglycemia may be associated with blood glucose levels below 15 mg/dL. Liver enzymes are mildly elevated if at all. The presence of lactic acidosis is helpful in diagnosing this disorder, although blood lactate may be normal in the fed state in young infants. However, these patients are relatively

TABLE 313-1 Glycogen storage diseases

Type	Basic defect*	Clinical findings	Laboratory	Diagnosis	Treatment	Comments
DISORDERS WITH HEPATIC-HYPOGLYCEMIC PATHOPHYSIOLOGY						
Ia von Gierke	Glucose 6-phosphatase deficiency	Hypoglycemia, hepatomegaly, bleeding diathesis, short stature, delayed adolescence, hepatic adenomas, enlarged kidneys	Increased lactate, cholesterol, triglyceride, and uric acid	Enzyme assay on liver or intestine, increased glycogen with normal structure in liver	Frequent feeding, nighttime tube feeding, 60–70% carbohydrate, restrict sucrose and lactose, bicarbonate and allopurinol as needed	Common, severe, autosomal recessive
Ib	G6P microsomal translocase deficiency	As for Ia with addition of neutropenia and recurrent infection	As for Ia	Enzyme assay on liver with and without detergent	As for Ia	Rare, severe, autosomal recessive
III Cori	Debrancher enzyme deficiency	Hypoglycemia, hepatomegaly, some short stature and delayed adolescence, mild myopathy worsening in some adults	Normal lactate and uric acid; increased cholesterol, triglyceride, and SGOT	Enzyme assay on liver, muscle, or fibroblasts; leukocytes variable; increased glycogen with abnormal structure in liver and muscle	Frequent feeding, nighttime tube feeding, 50% carbohydrate and 15–20% protein	Common, intermediate severity, some hepatic fibrosis
VI Hers	Hepatic phosphorylase deficiency	Hepatomegaly, variable hypoglycemia	Minimal changes, ? hyperlipidemia	Enzyme assay on liver, increased hepatic glycogen with normal structure	Dietary therapy as for type III, often little treatment required	Rare and poorly characterized; ? autosomal recessive
Formerly VIb, VIII, or IX	Hepatic phosphorylase b kinase deficiency	Hepatomegaly, variable hypoglycemia, occasional findings in heterozygous females	Minimal changes	Enzyme assay on leukocytes, fibroblasts, or liver; increased hepatic glycogen with normal structure	Dietary therapy as for type III, often little treatment required	Very mild but may be fairly common, X-linked
DISORDERS WITH MUSCLE-ENERGY PATHOPHYSIOLOGY						
V McArdle	Muscle phosphorylase deficiency	Pain, cramps, and myoglobinuria on strenuous exercise	Increased CPK with episodes, deficient lactate production with ischemic exercise test	Muscle enzyme assay, increased muscle glycogen with normal structure	Avoid exercise, glucose or fructose before exercise	Some clearly autosomal recessive, male preponderance
VII	Muscle phosphofructokinase deficiency	As for type V, mild hemolytic anemia	As for type V	Muscle enzyme assay, increased muscle glycogen with normal structure	As for type V	Rare, autosomal recessive
	Muscle phosphoglycerate mutase deficiency	As for type V	As for Type V	Muscle enzyme assay, normal glycogen content	? As for type V	Based on one affected male
	LDH-M subunit deficiency	As for type V	Increased CPK with episodes; pyruvate but not lactate rises with ischemic exercise test	LDH isozymes on serum, erythrocytes or leukocytes; enzyme assay on muscle; ? glycogen content normal	? As for type V	Based on sibship of 3 males and 1 female affected
DISORDERS WITH INDIVIDUAL PATHOPHYSIOLOGY						
II Pompe	Lysosomal α-glucosidase deficiency	*Infantile:* hypotonia, muscle weakness, cardiac enlargement and failure, enlarged tongue, fatal early; *juvenile:* progressive skeletal muscle weakness; *adult:* progressive skeletal muscle weakness, pulmonary insufficiency presentation	Increased CPK, no hypoglycemia	Enzymes assay on muscle or fibroblasts, enzyme assay on leukocytes possible but pitfalls are serious	No effective treatment	Common, autosomal recessive, prenatal diagnosis available and widely utilized in infantile
IV Andersen	Brancher enzyme deficiency	Infantile failure to thrive, cirrhosis and liver failure, extreme hypotonia and weakness in some, fatal early	No hypoglycemia, changes of liver disease	Enzyme assay on liver, muscle, leukocytes or fibroblasts; glycogen content not remarkable but structure abnormal	No effective treatment	Very rare, autosomal recessive

These defects provide the preferred nomenclature for the diseases.

resistant to development of ketosis. Hyperlipidemia is frequent and involves elevation of both cholesterol and triglycerides. Hypertriglyceridemia can be extreme with levels as high as 5000 to 6000 mg/dL. Hyperuricemia due both to decreased renal excretion and increased production is frequent and often becomes more severe after adolescence. The rise in plasma glucose following administration of epinephrine or glucagon is impaired, as is the rise in blood glucose following administration of galactose by mouth. Renal enlargement can be demonstrated by radiologic or sonographic techniques. Mild renal tubular dysfunction or the Fanconi syndrome may occur. Moderate anemia is usually due to recurrent nosebleeds and chronic acidosis but may become severe after prolonged acidosis. A bleeding diathesis is due to a platelet dysfunction.

Once type Ia disease is suspected clinically, the diagnosis is established by liver biopsy. The diagnosis is suggested by lactic acidosis, an abnormal galactose tolerance test, or renal enlargement. Proper handling of biopsy material should be arranged to distinguish types Ia and Ib. Sufficient material for enzyme assay may be obtained by needle biopsy provided the bleeding time is normal, or alternatively, open liver biopsy provides more tissue for analysis. Microscopic examination of liver reveals increased glycogen in cytoplasm and nuclei; lipid vacuoles in hepatocytes are prominent, and fibrosis is usually absent.

The hypoglycemia and lactic acid acidosis may be life-threatening. Other troublesome features include short stature, delayed adolescence, and hyperuricemia. During adult years uric acid nephropathy and hepatic adenomata may develop. The latter lesions are often large and either palpable or demonstrable by radioisotopic scan. There is a significant risk of malignant degeneration, often during the third decade, and subjects who live long enough are probably at increased risk for atherosclerosis.

TREATMENT   The mainstay of management is frequent feeding. The most widely used approach in children has been the combination of frequent daytime feeding by mouth and continuous nighttime feeding by nasogastric tube (see Chap. 74). The regimen should include approximately 60 percent carbohydrate, and no significant portion of carbohydrate should come from sources containing galactose or fructose, which cannot be utilized effectively to maintain blood sugar. The ability of a family to carry out such a program is a significant variable, but in some instances the metabolic abnormalities and the rate of growth have improved substantially. Raw cornstarch feeding provides a convenient, economical, and palatable source of slowly digested glucose polymer, and cornstarch therapy may become the primary dietary treatment for this disease. Optimal management requires a team attentive to the dietary and psychosocial needs of patient and family. Control of elevated plasma urate may require the addition of allopurinol. This regimen provides a reasonably optimistic short-term prognosis, but it is not known whether the long-term risks of hepatic malignancy and atherosclerosis are ameliorated. Portacaval anastomosis was previously used in the management of some forms of glycogen storage disease, but the enthusiasm for the procedure has declined. Prenatal diagnosis is not possible at present.

G6P microsomal translocase deficiency, type Ib   G6P microsomal translocase deficiency, historically referred to as *pseudo type I*, has an incidence of perhaps one-tenth or less that of type Ia. The term *microsomal translocase* describes the capacity to transport G6P into the endoplasmic reticulum. The clinical features are similar to those in type Ia, but unique features include neutropenia, impaired neutrophil migration, and recurrent pyogenic infections; in general, type Ib is more severe than Ia. Laboratory findings, responses to tolerance tests, and management are similar in the two disorders.

Type Ib disease was initially distinguished from type Ia by the presence of normal glucose 6-phosphatase activity on assay of biopsy tissue in the presence of detergent. However, glucose 6-phosphatase activity is low in type Ib disease when fresh tissue is homogenized and assayed in the absence of detergent. These results have been interpreted to imply a genetic deficiency of a microsomal glucose 6-

phosphate transport system as a primary defect in type Ib glycogen storage disease. The cause for the neutropenia and abnormal neutrophil migration is unknown, although the disease suggests a role for G6P transport in these cells.

Debrancher deficiency, type III   CLINICAL FEATURES   Debrancher enzyme deficiency, also known historically as Cori disease, is an autosomal recessive disorder and is one of the more frequent forms of glycogen storage diseases, occurring with a particularly high frequency in North African Jews. Symptomatic disease in the newborn period is unusual, and patients usually present with hypoglycemia or hepatomegaly during the first year of life. The physical findings are similar to those in type Ia, except that splenomegaly is more prominent, but the clinical course tends to be less severe. The skeletal myopathy is usually mild or insignificant in childhood but may be disabling and progressive in adults. Some patients with myopathy are first diagnosed as adults because the features in childhood were mild and overlooked.

Fasting hypoglycemia occurs in about 80 percent of patients. The glucose response after glucagon or epinephrine is abnormal in the fasting state but may be normal shortly after eating since the terminal glucose residues in glycogen can be mobilized. The galactose tolerance test is usually normal. Ketosis is prominent, and blood lactate is normal. Serum transaminase is elevated, and further increases may occur with minor illnesses. Blood cholesterol and triglyceride are elevated in about two-thirds. Hyperuricemia is rare.

Two diagnostic modalities are used to establish the diagnosis— analysis of glycogen and measurement of debranching enzyme in tissue samples. The glycogen content of red blood cells and liver is increased in almost all, whereas glycogen content of muscle is increased only in some. Documentation of abnormal structure of glycogen with the use of spectrophotometric techniques is a more consistent finding than the increase in glycogen content. The establishment of the diagnosis by enzymatic assay is complicated both by methodologic problems and what is believed to be genetic heterogeneity. Both debrancher functions—the glucan transferase activity and glucosidase activity—are believed to reside in a single polypeptide, but as many as six subtypes of the disease may occur. While the diagnosis can be made in some patients using red cells, leukocytes, or fibroblasts, it is generally preferable to document the abnormal glycogen structure and the enzyme deficiency directly in biopsy material from liver or muscle. The pathologic findings in liver are similar to those in type Ia except for less lipid deposition and more prominent fibrous septae.

In regard to growth retardation and abdominal protuberance, the course is one of progressive improvement following adolescence, so that the adult appearance may be normal and hypoglycemia is less frequent. Liver tumors are not reported, and there is no information regarding the long-term risks of hyperlipidemia. The fraction of adult patients who develop a debilitating myopathy is probably low. Affected patients have had children.

TREATMENT   Frequent feeding is also the mainstay of therapy for type III in childhood. Gluconeogenesis is normal, and as described above patients can ingest galactose, fructose, or protein to help maintain blood glucose. Thus, dietary therapy can include a larger percentage of calories as protein, but carbohydrate intake should be 40 to 50 percent of the total. An evening feeding is often sufficient to avoid hypoglycemia, but nighttime nasogastric tube feeding or cornstarch therapy may be required in severely affected children. Attempts to lower blood lipids using dietary means are desirable. Prenatal diagnosis is possible.

Hepatic phosphorylase deficiency, type VI   The diagnosis of hepatic phosphorylase deficiency, or Hers disease, was previously applied to a diverse group of patients with reduced hepatic phosphorylase levels due to a variety of causes but is now limited to patients in whom deficiency of hepatic phosphorylase is the primary defect. This nosologic difficulty is a consequence of the fact that phosphorylase exists in both active and inactive forms, and many factors may inhibit the activation of the enzyme secondarily. Consequently, diagnosis requires documentation that phosphorylase is absent and that the phosphorylase *b* kinase responsible for its activation is normal. The disorder is probably due to an autosomal recessive mutation.

Most patients have features similar to those in type III but in a milder form. The diagnosis is suspected because of hepatomegaly or hypoglycemia, and patients generally respond to dietary management similar to that employed in type III disease.

Phosphorylase *b* kinase deficiency Phosphorylase *b* kinase deficiency, now known to be a separate entity, was previously included in the type VI category. Various authors have designated this disorder as type VIa, type VIII, or type IX, but it is best termed *phosphorylase b kinase deficiency*. The best characterized form of the disorder is the X-linked variety, but there is potential for genetic heterogeneity, since the enzyme is composed of four nonidentical subunits. This disorder is relatively benign and is manifested in affected males by hepatomegaly, occasional fasting hypoglycemia, and some growth retardation, all of which tend to resolve spontaneously at the time of adolescence. Mild hepatomegaly may occur in female heterozygotes. The diagnosis can be established by specific enzyme assay of leukocytes, cultured skin fibroblasts, or liver. Muscle phosphorylase *b* kinase is believed to be normal in this condition. Dietary management similar to that employed in type III can be employed for hypoglycemia or growth retardation. It is possible that this condition is relatively common and passes undiagnosed. Healthy adults with a history of abdominal protuberance in childhood are often identified during family studies of patients with this condition.

MUSCLE-ENERGY DISEASES (See also Chap. 357) In recognizing the various glycogen storage diseases that affect muscle, the *ischemic exercise test* is of particular use in the initial evaluation. A blood pressure cuff is inflated above arterial pressure, and the ischemic hand is exercised to maximum effort. The pressure cuff is released, and blood is drawn from the other arm at 2, 5, 10, 20, and 30 min for assay of lactate and pyruvate, muscle enzymes, and myoglobin.

Myophosphorylase deficiency, type V Myophosphorylase deficiency, or McArdle disease, is uncommon. Symptoms of pain and cramps after exercise usually develop during the second or third decade. A history of myoglobinuria is present in most, and on occasion myoglobinuria can cause renal failure. Affected individuals are otherwise healthy, without evidence of hepatic, cardiac, or metabolic disturbance. Performance of an ischemic exercise test usually causes painful cramping, which is helpful diagnostically. In addition, blood lactate does not rise whereas serum creatine phosphokinase is elevated after strenuous exercise.

The diagnosis is established by documentation of elevated glycogen content and reduced phosphorylase activity in biopsied muscle tissue. The glycogen is usually deposited in subsarcolemmal regions of the muscle. The gene for human myophosphorylase has been cloned and is located on chromosome 11, in keeping with the autosomal recessive nature of the disease. There is an excess of male patients, which may be due to better ascertainment in males, genetic heterogeneity, or other factors. A fatal infantile form of hypotonia in association with myophosphorylase deficiency also has been described.

Management of myophosphorylase deficiency requires the avoidance of strenuous exercise. Glucose or fructose ingestion prior to exercise can reduce symptoms.

Muscle phosphofructokinase deficiency, type VII There are two genetically distinct forms of phosphofructokinase. Activity in muscle is due to a distinct muscle isoenzyme, whereas activity in red cells is due both to a red cell isoenzyme and to the muscle form of the enzyme. A small number of families have been identified with deficiency of the muscle isoenzyme. Symptoms similar to those in myophosphorylase deficiency were present with pain and cramps, myoglobinuria, and elevated muscle enzymes in serum after strenuous exercise. Lactate production was impaired, and a mild nonspherocytic hemolytic anemia was present. Other patients have the anemia but

no muscle symptoms; the latter phenomenon might be due to a qualitatively abnormal, unstable enzyme that rapidly disappears from the anucleate red cell but is replaced effectively in muscle cells and consequently prevents muscle symptoms.

Other muscle-energy diseases A group of even rarer familial metabolic disorders must be considered in the differential diagnosis of patients with myoglobinuria and elevated muscle enzymes in serum after exercise. These include phosphoglycerate mutase deficiency, LDH M-subunit deficiency, and carnitine palmityl transferase deficiency. (Older reports of phosphoglucomutase deficiency and phosphohexoseisomerase deficiency seem inconclusive by current standards.) When myophosphorylase, phosphofructokinase, or phosphoglycerate mutase are deficient, neither lactate nor pyruvate rises following exercise, whereas in deficiency of LDH M subunit there is a rise in pyruvate in the face of a failure of lactate production. Carnitine palmityl transferase deficiency is a disorder of lipid metabolism and is discussed in Chap. 329. Definitive diagnosis of these disorders must be established by enzyme assay of muscle tissue. Some patients with this clinical presentation have none of the above-mentioned enzyme deficiencies, and identification of other defects in muscle metabolism is likely in the future.

DISORDERS WITH INDIVIDUAL PATHOPHYSIOLOGY α-Glucosidase deficiency, type II Alpha-glucosidase deficiency, or Pompe disease, is a lysosomal storage disease, and the pathophysiology is discussed in Chap. 316. The incidence is not known but may exceed 1 in 100,000. The disorder is not associated with hypoglycemia, ketosis, or other abnormalities of intermediary metabolism.

The infantile form presents within the first 6 months of life and may be manifested at birth. Clinical features include skeletal muscle hypotonia and weakness, massive cardiac enlargement, enlargement of the tongue, and varying degrees of hepatomegaly. Muscle enzymes such as creatine phosphokinase and aldolase are usually elevated, and the ECG may show large QRS complexes and a shortened PR interval. Motor weakness and developmental delay may be present. Death occurs in the first 2 to 3 years in most cases due to the cardiac involvement.

The juvenile form has features suggestive of a progressive form of muscular dystrophy. These patients have gait abnormalities but no cardiac symptoms. Plasma creatine phosphokinase and aldolase are elevated, and the length of survival is variable. An even milder adult form presents as skeletal muscle weakness in the third to the fifth decade. Again, cardiac symptoms are absent, and serum muscle enzymes are elevated. Some patients have respiratory failure due to involvement of the muscles of respiration and are often misdiagnosed as having some form of muscular dystrophy.

Vacuolization of muscle and increased glycogen content are demonstrable on muscle biopsy. Electron-microscopic studies demonstrate membrane-bound vacuoles containing glycogen, a finding strongly suggestive of the disorder. Excessive glycogen is also found in other tissues including liver and central nervous system, particularly in the anterior horn cells of the spinal cord. Specific diagnosis is made by enzyme assay in biopsy material from muscle or liver or in cultured skin fibroblasts. In general, some residual enzyme activity is present in patients with the adult form of disease, but the exact level is not of prognostic significance. Prenatal diagnosis is reliable and has been used extensively for the infantile form. Various forms of enzyme infusion therapy have been tried but are ineffective.

Brancher deficiency, type IV Brancher enzyme deficiency, or Andersen disease, is a rare, autosomal recessive disorder. Features in infants include hepatomegaly, failure to thrive, and hypotonia in the first few months of life with subsequent development of progressive cirrhosis. In other patients the predominant feature is cardiac involvement and/or extreme hypotonia similar to that observed in spinal muscular atrophy and anterior horn cell degeneration. Death occurs within the first 2 or 3 years.

The symptoms are thought to be related primarily to the abnormal glycogen structure that results from a generalized deficiency of brancher enzyme. The presence of long outer chains on the glycogen molecules has led to the designation of the disease as amylopectinosis. The laboratory findings are generally those associated with severe liver disease except that hypoglycemia usually does not occur. The absence of hypoglycemia and the presence of normal glycogen content in the liver make the diagnosis difficult to establish. The diagnosis is suggested by finding abnormally structured glycogen in biopsy material and is established by direct assay of the enzyme in liver, leukocytes, or cultured skin fibroblasts. No effective treatment is known, but prenatal diagnosis is possible using cultured amniotic cells.

Other possible disorders of glycogen metabolism Deficiency of glycogen synthase has been reported in a small number of families. Affected patients usually have fasting hypoglycemia, seizures, and some degree of mental impairment. The presence of some hepatic glycogen, the increase in plasma glucose in response to glucagon or galactose, and the known lability of the activation system for glycogen synthase have all led to skepticism as to whether such a disorder actually exists. This syndrome may be confused with ketotic hypoglycemia of childhood (see Chap. 329).

There are also reports of more than one enzyme defect in the same patient and of different enzyme defects among siblings. Many of these reports may be related to difficulties inherent in measuring enzymes of glycogen metabolism in human pathologic tissue. At present no specific syndrome of multiple primary enzyme deficiency is documented.

REFERENCES

CHEN Y-T et al: Cornstarch therapy in type I glycogen-storage disease. N Engl J Med 310:171, 1984

FERNANDES J: Hepatic glycogen storage diseases, in *The Treatment of Inherited Metabolic Disease*, DN Raine (ed). New York, American Elsevier, 1974

GREENE HL et al: Type I glycogen storage disease: A metabolic basis for advances in treatment. Adv Pediatr 26:63, 1979

HOWELL RR, WILLIAMS JC: The glycogen storage diseases, in *The Metabolic Basis of Inherited Disease*, 5th ed, JB Stanbury et al (eds). New York, McGraw-Hill, 1983, pp 141–166

314 GALACTOSEMIA, GALACTOKINASE DEFICIENCY, AND OTHER RARE DISORDERS OF CARBOHYDRATE METABOLISM

KURT J. ISSELBACHER

DEFINITION Galactosemia refers to either of two inborn errors of galactose metabolism. "*Classic*" *galactosemia* is due to the deficiency of galactose 1-phosphate uridyl transferase (GALT) and is typically associated with cataract formation, mental retardation, and cirrhosis. The second disorder, *galactokinase deficiency*, leads primarily to cataract formation.

PATHOGENESIS Lactose, the main carbohydrate in milk, is a disaccharide containing galactose and glucose; when ingested it is hydrolyzed by intestinal lactase. Normally the absorbed galactose is converted to glucose in the liver. The first reaction in this pathway is the phosphorylation of galactose to galactose 1-phosphate by galactokinase (specified by a gene on chromosome 17):

$$\text{Galactose} + \text{ATP} \xrightarrow{\text{galactokinase}} \text{galactose 1-phosphate}$$

The next step involves the conversion of galactose 1-phosphate to glucose 1-phosphate by GALT, the gene for which is on chromosome 9:

$$\text{Galactose 1-phosphate} + \text{UDP-glucose} \xrightarrow{\text{GALT}}$$
$$\text{UDP-galactose} + \text{glucose 1-phosphate}$$

The UDP sugars can be reversibly interconverted by an epimerase reaction:

$$\text{UDP-galactose} \xrightarrow{\longleftarrow} \text{UDP-glucose}$$

Galactose can also be metabolized by alternate pathways. It can be converted (reduced) in the presence of NADPH (or NADH) to galactitol (dulcitol) by aldose reductase. It can also be oxidized to a limited extent by galactose dehydrogenase, leading to the formation of galactonic acid, xyulose, and CO_2. These pathways account for limited galactose metabolism in patients with galactosemia.

In galactokinase deficiency, galactose accumulates in the blood and tissues. In the lens galactose is converted by aldose reductase to galactitol, a sugar to which the lens is impermeable. As a consequence, excessive hydration occurs which, together with a decrease in glutathione in the lens, leads to cataract formation.

In classic galactosemia, GALT deficiency results in tissue accumulation of galactose 1-phosphate and galactose. As in galactokinase deficiency, cataracts develop secondary to galactitol accumulation in the lens. It is assumed that the cirrhosis and mental retardation of classic galactosemia are related to increased amounts of galactose 1-phosphate in these tissues. Elevated blood galactose levels may lead to a decreased hepatic output of glucose and hence to hypoglycemia. In the kidney and intestine accumulation of galactose and galactose 1-phosphate appears to lead to an inhibition of amino acid transport. In some women ovarian malfunction develops in association with hypergonadotrophic hypogonadism; the pathogenesis is unclear.

Both galactokinase and GALT deficiencies are transmitted as autosomal recessive traits. Heterozygotes for these disorders have half-normal enzyme levels but are asymptomatic. Maternal deficiency of galactokinase, together with lactose intake during pregnancy, may contribute to cataract formation during fetal development. However, not all persons with half-normal GALT enzymes in their cells are carriers of classic galactosemia. Some individuals homozygous for another gene, called the *Duarte variant,* normally have half-normal GALT levels and are asymptomatic. This group can be differentiated from classic galactosemia heterozygotes on the basis of the electrophoretic properties of the mutant enzyme. In both galactokinase deficiency and classic galactosemia there is a functional deficiency or absence of the involved enzyme. Classic galactosemia is due to a structural gene mutation, and the altered enzyme (GALT) protein does not function normally. Other clinical variants with altered enzyme electrophoretic mobility have been described.

The incidence of classic galactosemia is about 1 per 80,000 births in the white population. Approximately 0.8 to 1.3 percent of the population are heterozygotes for the galactosemia (GALT) gene, and about 10 percent carry the Duarte variant. During screening of newborns for galactosemia the most frequent cause of an abnormal result is compound heterozygosity for the Duarte variant and for classic galactosemia in which GALT levels are about 17 percent of normal. Such individuals are clinically asymptomatic.

CLINICAL FEATURES Symptoms of classic galactosemia usually begin within days to weeks after birth. The infant usually is reluctant to ingest breast milk or milk formulas, develops vomiting, shows poor nutrition, and fails to thrive. Jaundice, hepatomegaly, and evidence of liver disease may develop. Cataracts are usually not present at birth but develop gradually over weeks to months. Mental retardation becomes evident after 6 to 12 months. Infants with classic galactosemia are subject to bacterial sepsis (especially with *Escherichia coli*), and this may be the leading cause of death in the neonatal period. The only consistent feature of galactokinase deficiency is cataract formation.

DIAGNOSIS Galactokinase deficiency should be suspected in infants or children with cataract formation who have non-glucose-reducing substances in the urine. The diagnosis is made by demonstrating the deficiency of galactokinase in red blood cells.

TABLE 314-1 Some other disorders of carbohydrate metabolism

Disorder	Metabolic defect	Manifestations
Hereditary fructose intolerance	Deficiency of fructose-l-phosphate aldolase leads to accumulation of fructose-1-PO$_4$ in tissues.	Liver disease, renal tubular damage, and hypoglycemia.
Fructose 1,6-diphosphatase deficiency	Deficiency of the enzyme prevents gluconeogenesis from its normal precursors, lactate, glycerol, and alanine. Thus, maintenance of blood sugar is dependent upon exogenous glucose.	Lactic acidosis leads to hyperventilation, somnolence, and coma, usually with hypoglycemia and ketosis.

Classic galactosemia must be considered when one or more of the clinical features described above are found. If the patient is ingesting milk, reducing sugar is present in the urine but gives a negative glucose oxidase reaction (i.e., is not glucose) and is identified as galactose by other techniques, such as chromatography. If the child is vomiting, has a poor food intake, or is on intravenous glucose feedings, galactose may not be present in the urine. The definitive diagnosis is made by demonstrating a lack or deficiency of red cell GALT by one of several techniques. The disease can also be diagnosed prenatally by enzyme studies on culture amniocentesis cells or by demonstrating increased galactitol in amniotic fluid.

In the neonatal period galactosemia needs to be differentiated from primary liver disease. With liver damage, galactose removal from the blood is impaired, and elevated blood galactose levels and galactosuria may be present. However, GALT levels are normal in patients with liver damage.

TREATMENT The treatment of galactosemia consists of the removal of galactose-containing foods from the diet, especially milk. Milk substitutes such as Nutramigen are often used. Although soybean preparations contain polysaccharide-bound galactose, they appear to be well tolerated because the bound galactose is not readily liberated. In general, the red cell levels of galactose 1-phosphate are not increased in affected infants fed soybean formulas.

The institution of a galactose-free diet usually leads to a dramatic improvement in all clinical features except for mental retardation. Patients should be kept on galactose-free diets indefinitely or at least until they have attained adequate physical and neurologic development.

OTHER DISORDERS OF CARBOHYDRATE METABOLISM Features of hereditary fructose intolerance and fructose 1,6-diphosphatase deficiency, two autosomal recessive disorders of fructose metabolism that lead to hypoglycemia, are summarized in Table 314-1 (also see Chaps. 313 and 329).

REFERENCES

ALLEN TJ et al: Evidence of galactosemia in utero. Lancet 1:603, 1980

BURMAN D et al (eds): *Inborn Errors of Carbohydrate Metabolism.* Lancaster, MTP Press, 1979

GITZELMANN R et al: Galactose metabolism in a patient with hereditary galactokinase deficiency. Eur J Clin Invest 4:79, 1974

——— et al: Essential fructosuria, heredity fructose intolerance, and fructose 1,6-diphosphatase deficiency, in *The Metabolic Basis of Inherited Disease,* 5th ed, JB Stanbury et al (eds). New York, McGraw-Hill, 1983, p 118

SCHWARTZ HP et al: Galactose intolerance in individuals with double heterozygosity for Duarte variant and galactosemia. J Pediatr 100:704, 1982

SEGAL S: Disorders of galactose metabolism, in *The Metabolic Basis of Inherited Disease,* 5th ed, JB Stanbury et al (eds). New York, McGraw-Hill, 1982, p 167

315 THE HYPERLIPOPROTEINEMIAS AND OTHER DISORDERS OF LIPID METABOLISM

MICHAEL S. BROWN / JOSEPH L. GOLDSTEIN

The *hyperlipoproteinemias* are disturbances of lipid transport that result from accelerated synthesis or retarded degradation of lipoproteins that transport cholesterol and triglycerides through plasma. Elevated plasma lipoprotein levels are important clinically because they can cause two life-threatening diseases: atherosclerosis and pancreatitis. A reduction in plasma lipoprotein-cholesterol levels, achieved by diet and drugs, reduces the risk of myocardial infarction in subjects with hyperlipoproteinemia. Some hyperlipoproteinemias are the direct result of *primary* defects in the synthesis or degradation of lipoprotein particles. Other hyperlipoproteinemias are *secondary*, that is, the elevated plasma lipoprotein level occurs as part of a constellation of abnormalities caused by an underlying disorder in a related metabolic system, such as thyroid hormone deficiency or insulin deficiency. The primary hyperlipoproteinemias can be divided into two broad categories: (1) *single-gene disorders* that are transmitted by simple dominant or recessive mechanisms and (2) *multifactorial disorders* with complex inheritance patterns in which multiple variant genes, each having a subtle effect, interact with environmental factors to produce varying degrees of hyperlipoproteinemia in members of a family.

ROLE OF LIPOPROTEINS IN LIPID TRANSPORT The lipoproteins are globular particles of high molecular weight that transport nonpolar lipids (primarily *triglycerides* and *cholesteryl esters*) through the plasma. A general model for the structure of a lipoprotein particle is shown in Fig. 315-1. Each lipoprotein particle contains a nonpolar *core,* in which many molecules of hydrophobic lipid are packed to form an oil droplet. This hydrophobic core, which accounts for most of the mass of the particle, consists of triglycerides and cholesteryl esters in varying proportions. Surrounding the core is a polar *surface coat* of phospholipids that stabilize the lipoprotein particle so that it can remain in solution in the plasma. In addition to phospholipids, the polar coat contains small amounts of unesterified cholesterol. Each lipoprotein particle also contains specific proteins (termed *apoproteins*) that are exposed at the surface. The apoproteins bind to specific enzymes or transport proteins on cell membranes, thus directing the lipoprotein to its sites of metabolism.

Table 315-1 describes the characteristics of the five major classes of lipoproteins that normally circulate in human plasma. These lipoprotein classes differ in the composition of the nonpolar lipids in the core; in the composition of the apoproteins; and in density, size, and electrophoretic mobility.

Lipid transport: The exogenous pathway Figure 315-2 shows the pathways by which lipoproteins transport lipids in plasma. The largest amounts of lipoproteins are involved in the transport of dietary fat, which amounts to more than 100 g triglyceride and about 1 g cholesterol per day. Within intestinal epithelial cells, dietary triglycerides and cholesterol are incorporated into large lipoprotein particles called *chylomicrons.* The chylomicrons are secreted into the intestinal lymph and pass into the general circulation for transport to the capillaries of adipose tissue and skeletal muscle, where they adhere to binding sites on the capillary walls. While bound to these endothelial surfaces, the chylomicrons are exposed to the enzyme *lipoprotein lipase.* The chylomicrons contain an apoprotein, apoprotein CII, that activates the lipase, liberating free fatty acids and monoglycerides (Fig. 315-3). The fatty acids pass through the endothelial cells and enter the underlying adipocytes or muscle cells, where they are either reesterified to triglycerides or oxidized.

After the core triglycerides have been removed, the remainder of the chylomicron dissociates from the capillary endothelium and

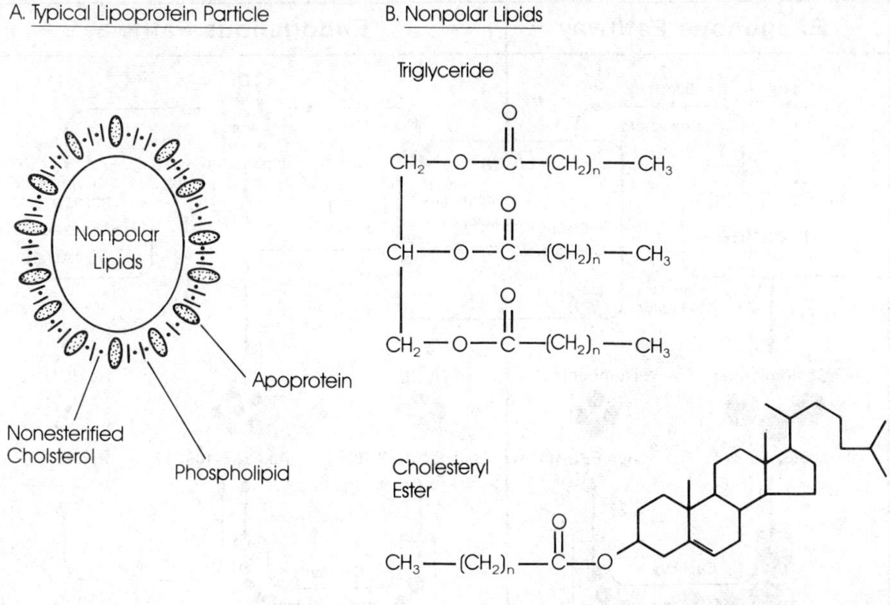

FIGURE 315-1 *A. Diagrammatic representation of the structure of a typical plasma lipoprotein particle. The core of the spherical lipoprotein particle is composed of two nonpolar lipids, triglyceride and cholesteryl ester, which are present in different lipoproteins in varying amounts. The nonpolar core is surrounded by a surface coat composed primarily of phospholipids. Apoproteins are exposed at the surface and extend into the core. Variable amounts of unesterified cholesterol are interdigitated with the phospholipids of the surface coat. The qualitative composition of each of the five major classes of lipoprotein particles in human plasma is summarized in Table 315-1. B. Structures of the two nonpolar lipids, triglyceride and cholesteryl ester. In order for these nonpolar lipids to be assimilated into tissues, the ester bonds between the fatty acids and either glycerol (triglycerides) or cholesterol (cholesteryl esters) must be broken by lipoprotein lipase and the lysosomal cholesterol esterase, respectively.*

reenters the circulation. It has now been transformed into a particle that is relatively poor in triglyceride and enriched in cholesteryl esters. It has also undergone an exchange of apoproteins with other plasma lipoproteins. The net result is the conversion of the chylomicron to a *chylomicron remnant particle,* enriched in cholesteryl esters and apoproteins B48 and E. This remnant travels to the liver, where it is taken up with great efficiency. This uptake is mediated by the binding of apoprotein E to specific receptors, called *chylomicron remnant receptors,* on the surface of the hepatocytes. The surface-bound remnants are taken into the cell and degraded within lysosomes by a process called receptor-mediated endocytosis (Fig. 315-3). The overall result of the chylomicron transport process is to deliver dietary triglyceride to adipose tissue and cholesterol to the liver.

Some of the cholesterol that reaches the liver is converted to bile acids, which are excreted into the intestine to act as detergents and facilitate the absorption of dietary fat. In addition, some cholesterol is excreted into the bile without metabolism to bile acids. The liver also distributes cholesterol to other tissues by the endogenous pathway, which is discussed below.

Lipid transport: The endogenous pathway   Triglyceride synthesis in the liver is enhanced when the diet contains excess carbohydrates. The liver converts the carbohydrate to fatty acids, esterifies the fatty acids with glycerol to form triglycerides, and secretes the triglyceride into the bloodstream in the core of *very low density lipoprotein* (VLDL). The VLDL particles are relatively large, carry 5 to 10 times more triglycerides than cholesteryl esters, and contain a form of apoprotein B, designated B100, that differs from the apoprotein B48 of chylomicrons (Table 315-1).

The VLDL particles are transported to tissue capillaries, where they interact with the same lipoprotein lipase enzyme that catabolizes chylomicrons. The core triglycerides of the VLDL are hydrolyzed, and the fatty acids are used for triglyceride synthesis within adipose tissue. The remnants generated from the action of lipoprotein-lipase on VLDL are designated *intermediate-density lipoprotein (IDL)*. A portion of the IDL particles are catabolized by the liver through binding to receptors called *low-density lipoprotein (LDL) receptors,* which are distinct from the chylomicron remnant receptors. The remaining IDL remain in plasma, where they undergo a further transformation in which nearly all the residual triglycerides are removed. During this conversion, all the apoproteins are removed from the particle with the exception of apoprotein B100. The result is the transformation of the IDL particle into cholesterol-rich LDL. The core of LDL is composed almost entirely of cholesteryl esters, and the surface coat contains only one apoprotein, apoprotein B100. In humans a relatively high fraction of IDL escapes hepatic uptake, and consequently humans have relatively high circulating levels of LDL. Indeed, about three-fourths of the total cholesterol in normal human plasma is contained within LDL particles.

One function of LDL is to supply cholesterol to a variety of extrahepatic parenchymal cells, such as adrenal cortical cells, lymphocytes, muscle cells, and renal cells. These cells have *LDL receptors* localized on the cell surface. LDL that binds to this receptor is taken up by receptor-mediated endocytosis and digested by lysosomes within the cells (Fig. 315-3). The cholesteryl esters of LDL are hydrolyzed by a lysosomal cholesteryl esterase (acid lipase), and the liberated cholesterol is used both for membrane synthesis and as a precursor for steroid hormone synthesis. Like extrahepatic tissues, the liver also has abundant LDL receptors; it uses the LDL-cholesterol for synthesis of bile acids and for generation of free cholesterol, which is secreted into the bile. In humans 70 to 80 percent of LDL is removed from the plasma each day by the LDL receptor pathway. The remainder is degraded by a scavenger cell system in phagocytic cells in the reticuloendothelial system. In contrast to the receptor-mediated pathway for LDL degradation, the scavenger cell pathway is thought to function solely to degrade LDL when the lipoprotein

TABLE 315-1   Characteristics of the major classes of lipoproteins in human plasma

Lipoprotein class	Major lipids	Apoproteins	Density, g/mL	Diameter, Å	Electrophoretic mobility
Chylomicrons and remnants	Dietary triglycerides	AI, AII, B48, CI, CII, CIII, E	<1.006	800–5000	Remains at origin
VLDL	Endogenous triglycerides	B48, CI, CII, CIII, E	<1.006	300–800	Pre-β
IDL	Cholesteryl esters, triglycerides	B100, CIII, E	<1.019	250–350	Slow pre-β
LDL	Cholesteryl esters	B100	1.019–1.063	180–280	β
HDL	Cholesteryl esters	AI, AII	1.063–1.210	50–120	α

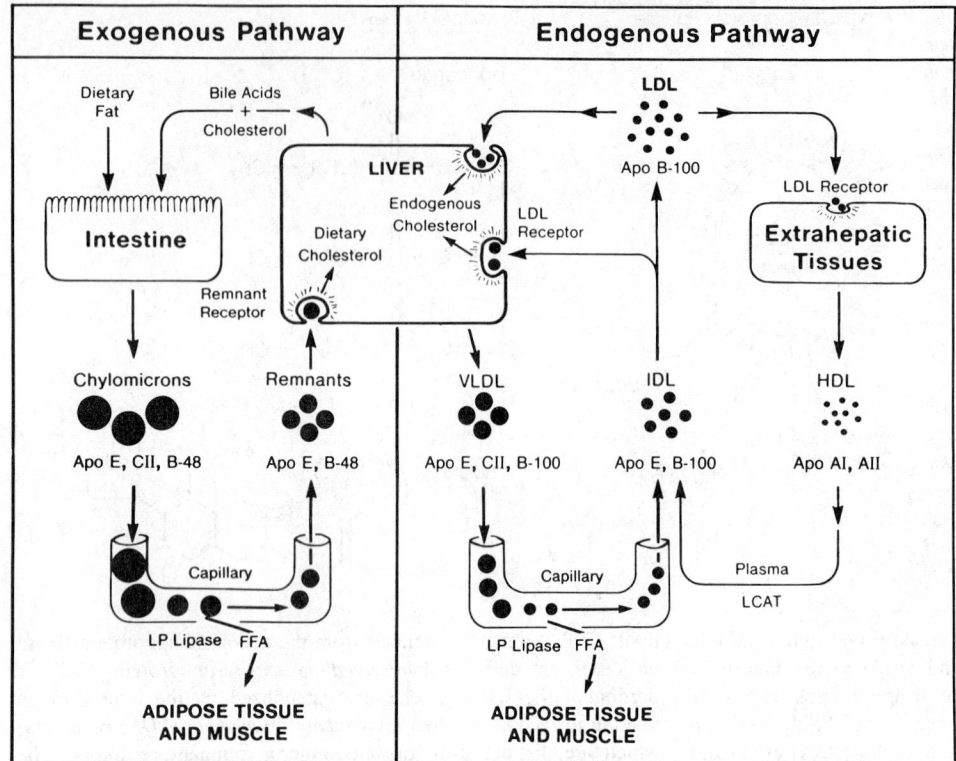

FIGURE 315-2 *Model for plasma triglyceride and cholesterol transport in humans. The details of this model are described in the text. VLDL, very low density lipoprotein; IDL, intermediate-density lipoprotein; LDL, low-density lipoprotein; HDL, high-density lipoprotein; LCAT, lecithin:cholesterol acyltransferase; LP lipase, lipoprotein lipase; FFA, free fatty acids. The major apoprotein for each class of lipoproteins is shown. Other apoproteins are also present, and these are listed in Table 315-1.*

reaches high concentrations in plasma rather than to supply cholesterol to cells.

As the membranes of parenchymal and scavenger cells undergo turnover and as cells die and are renewed, unesterified cholesterol is released into plasma, where it binds initially to *high-density lipoprotein* (*HDL*). This unesterified cholesterol is then coupled to a fatty acid in an esterification reaction catalyzed by the plasma enzyme *lecithin:cholesterol acyltransferase* (*LCAT*). The cholesteryl esters that are formed on the surface of HDL are transferred to VLDL and eventually appear in LDL. This establishes a cycle by which LDL delivers cholesterol to extrahepatic cells and by which cholesterol is returned to LDL from extrahepatic cells via HDL. Most of the cholesterol released from extrahepatic tissues is transported to the liver for excretion in the bile.

DIAGNOSIS OF HYPERLIPOPROTEINEMIA   A variety of diseases cause elevations in the concentrations of one or more lipoprotein

classes in plasma. In general, these abnormalities are detected by the finding of an elevated concentration of triglycerides or cholesterol in fasting plasma, a condition called *hyperlipidemia*. The value for plasma cholesterol represents the total cholesterol, which includes both cholesteryl esters and unesterified cholesterol. The plasma cholesterol and triglyceride levels provide information regarding the nature of the lipoprotein particle that is increased. An isolated elevation in plasma triglycerides indicates that the concentrations of chylomicrons or VLDL are increased. On the other hand, an isolated elevation of plasma cholesterol nearly always indicates that the concentration of LDL is increased. Frequently, both triglycerides and cholesterol are elevated. Such a combined abnormality may be produced by a marked elevation in chylomicrons or VLDL, in which case the ratio of triglyceride to cholesterol in plasma will be greater than 5:1. Alternatively, there may be an elevation of both VLDL and LDL, in which case the triglyceride/cholesterol ratio in plasma is usually less than 5:1.

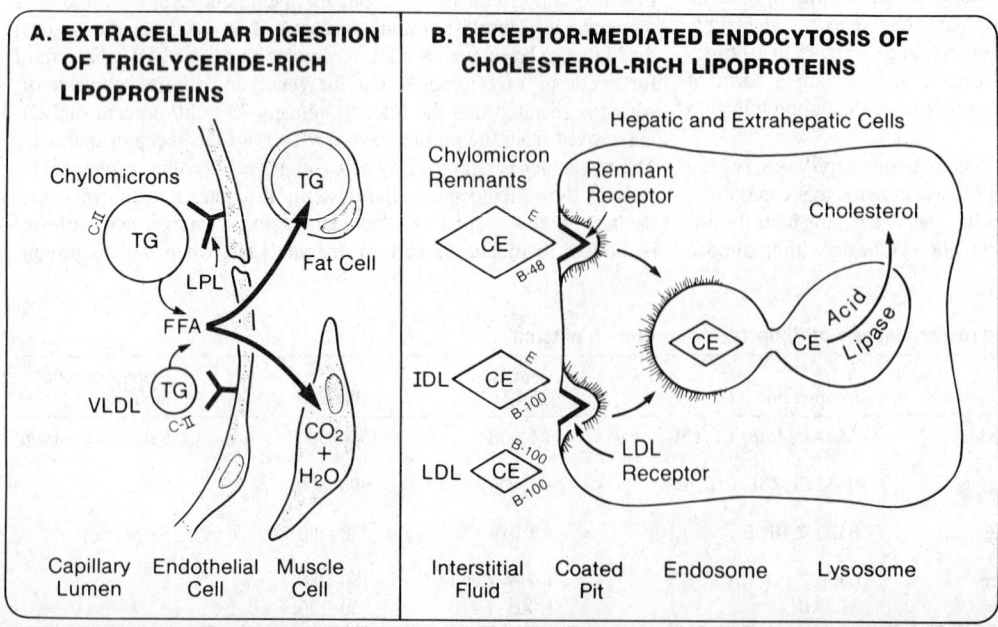

FIGURE 315-3 *Comparison of the mechanisms by which triglyceride-rich lipoproteins and cholesterol-rich lipoproteins deliver their core lipids to target tissues. Triglycerides are hydrolyzed by an extracellular enzyme (LPL) that is attached to endothelial cells and operates at the endothelial surface. Cholesteryl esters are hydrolyzed by an intracellular enzyme, acid lipase, that is located in lysosomes and cleaves the esters that enter cells via receptor-mediated endocytosis. TG, triglycerides; LPL, lipoprotein lipase; VLDL, very low density lipoproteins; CE, cholesteryl esters; IDL, intermediate-density lipoproteins; LDL, low-density lipoproteins; FFA, free fatty acid. The apoproteins responsible for the interactions (CII, B, and E) are indicated.*

TABLE 315-2 Patterns of lipoprotein elevation in plasma (lipoprotein types)

Lipoprotein pattern	Major elevation in plasma	
	Lipoprotein	Lipid
Type 1	Chylomicrons	Triglycerides
Type 2a	LDL	Cholesterol
Type 2b	LDL and VLDL	Cholesterol and tri-glycerides
Type 3	Remnants	Triglycerides and cholesterol
Type 4	VLDL	Triglycerides
Type 5	VLDL and chy-lomicrons	Triglycerides and cholesterol

The definition of hyperlipoproteinemia is arbitrary because plasma lipid and lipoprotein levels exhibit a bell-shaped distribution in the population, without clear separation between normal and abnormal values. Since lipoprotein concentrations are influenced by diet and other environmental factors, standards must be established for the population under consideration. Usually, arbitrary statistical limits of normal concentrations are selected, based on the examination of a large number of healthy-appearing subjects of different ages. The usual cut-off limit is the upper 5 to 10 percent of values (i.e., the 90th to 95th percentile values). However, analysis of blood lipid levels in individuals from industrialized and more agrarian cultures indicates that lipid and lipoprotein concentrations that are "normal" in a statistical sense are not necessarily healthy. As a working rule, significant hyperlipoproteinemia is considered to be present in any individual below the age of 20 whose total plasma cholesterol level exceeds 190 mg/dL or whose triglyceride level exceeds 140 mg/dL. In individuals above the age of 20, significant hyperlipoproteinemia exists whenever the plasma cholesterol level exceeds 220 mg/dL or the triglyceride level exceeds 200 mg/dL.

The various combinations of elevated lipoproteins that occur in disease states have been divided into six lipoprotein types or patterns (Table 315-2). Most of the lipoprotein types can be caused by several different genetic diseases (Table 315-3); conversely, some genetic diseases can produce more than one lipoprotein type. In addition, each of the abnormal lipoprotein types can occur as a secondary consequence of another metabolic disease (Table 315-4). Hence, the lipoprotein type must be considered a shorthand notation to describe an abnormal lipoprotein pattern in plasma and not a designation of a specific disease.

Ordinarily, the simple measurement of plasma lipid levels, coupled with a clinical assessment, is sufficient to classify the type of lipoprotein abnormality present (Table 315-2). Occasionally, paper electrophoresis of the plasma is useful either when an elevation in remnant particles is suspected (type 3 lipoprotein pattern giving a "broad beta" band on electrophoresis) or when chylomicronemia is a possibility (type 1 pattern). On occasion, HDL levels are measured, since high levels of this lipoprotein class are statistically associated with a decreased risk of myocardial infarction (see Chap. 195). The level of HDL can be estimated in clinical laboratories using standardized lipoprotein separation techniques, but the value of such measurement for predicting the occurrence of myocardial infarction in the individual patient has not been established.

PRIMARY HYPERLIPOPROTEINEMIAS RESULTING FROM SINGLE-GENE MUTATIONS

FAMILIAL LIPOPROTEIN LIPASE DEFICIENCY This rare autosomal recessive disorder is attributable to the absence or marked reduction in the activity of the enzyme lipoprotein lipase. This deficiency leads to a metabolic block in the metabolism of chylomicrons, causing these lipoproteins to accumulate to massive levels in plasma.

Clinical features The disease usually presents in infancy or childhood with recurrent attacks of abdominal pain. The pain is caused by pancreatitis occurring as a consequence of the massive elevation of chylomicrons in plasma. Affected individuals intermittently develop eruptive xanthomas, small yellowish papules, frequently surrounded by an erythematous base, that appear predominantly on the buttocks and other pressure-sensitive surfaces. The xanthomas are caused by the deposition of large amounts of chylomicron triglycerides in cutaneous histiocytes. Triglycerides are also deposited in phagocytes of the reticuloendothelial system, producing hepatomegaly, splenomegaly, and foam cell infiltration of the bone marrow. When the level of chylomicrons in the blood is massively elevated (i.e., plasma triglyceride level greater than 2000 mg/dL), the blood appears pale and creamy and is said to be *lipemic*. When viewed with the ophthalmoscope, the retina is pale, and the retinal vessels are white, producing the appearance of lipemia retinalis. Despite the massive elevation of plasma triglycerides, accelerated atherosclerosis does not occur.

Pathogenesis Affected individuals are homozygous for a mutation that prevents normal expression of lipoprotein lipase activity. The primary genetic defect appears to involve the structure of the enzyme itself; the activator of lipoprotein lipase, apoprotein CII, is present in normal amounts. The parents are obligate heterozygotes for the lipoprotein lipase defect, but they are clinically normal. As a result of the deficiency of lipoprotein lipase in homozygotes, chylomicrons cannot be metabolized normally, and the level of chylomicrons in

TABLE 315-3 Characteristics of the primary hyperlipoproteinemias resulting from single-gene mutations

Genetic disorder	Primary biochemical defect	Plasma lipoprotein elevation	Lipoprotein pattern	Typical clinical findings			Lipoprotein pattern in affected relatives
				Xanthomas	Pancreatitis	Premature atherosclerosis	
Familial lipoprotein lipase deficiency	Deficiency of lipoprotein lipase	Chylomicrons	1	Eruptive	+		1
Familial apoprotein CII deficiency	Deficiency of apoprotein CII	Chylomicrons and VLDL	1 or 5		+		1 or 5
Familial type 3 hyperlipoproteinemia	Abnormal apoprotein E of VLDL	Chylomicrons and IDL	3	Xanthelasma; tuberous; palmar creases		+	3, 2a, 2b, or 4
Familial hypercholesterolemia	Deficiency of LDL receptor	LDL	2a (rarely 2b)	Xanthelasma; tendon		+	2a (rarely 2b)
Familial hypertriglyceridemia	Unknown	VLDL (rarely chylomicrons)	4 (rarely 5)	(Eruptive)	(+)	+	4 (rarely 5)
Multiple lipoprotein-type hyperlipidemia (familial combined hyperlipidemia)	Unknown	LDL and VLDL	2a, 2b, or 4 (rarely 5)			+	2a, 2b, or 4 (rarely 5)

Underlying disorder	Plasma lipoprotein elevation				Lipoprotein type	Proposed mechanism for hyperlipoproteinemia	Associated abnormality of carbohydrate metabolism
	Chylomicrons	IDL	VLDL	LDL			
ENDOCRINE AND METABOLIC							
Diabetes mellitus	+		+ + +		4 (rarely 5)	Increased secretion of VLDL Decreased catabolism of VLDL and chylomicrons due to reduced lipoprotein lipase activity	Insulin deficiency or resistance
von Gierke's disease (glycogen storage disease, type I)	+		+ + +		4 (rarely 5)	Increased secretion of VLDL Decreased catabolism of VLDL and chylomicrons due to reduced lipoprotein lipase activity	Hypoglycemia with decreased insulin secretion
Lipodystrophies (congenital and acquired forms)			+ +		4	Increased secretion of VLDL	Insulin resistance
Cushing's syndrome			+	+ +	2a or 2b	Increased secretion of VLDL with conversion to LDL	Insulin resistance
Sexual ateliotic dwarfism (isolated growth hormone deficiency)			+ +	+ +	2b	Increased secretion of VLDL with conversion to LDL	Insulin deficiency or resistance
Acromegaly			+		4	Increased secretion of VLDL	Insulin resistance
Hypothyroidism		+		+ + +	2a (rarely 3)	Decreased catabolism of VLDL and IDL	
Anorexia nervosa				+ +	2a	Reduced biliary excretion of cholesterol and bile acids	
Werner's syndrome				+ +	2a	Unknown	Insulin resistance
Acute intermittent porphyria				+ +	2a	Unknown	
DRUG-INDUCED							
Alcohol	+		+ + +		4 (rarely 5)	Increased secretion of VLDL in individuals genetically predisposed to hypertriglyceridemia	
Oral contraceptives	+		+ + +		4 (rarely 5)	Increased secretion of VLDL in individuals genetically predisposed to hypertriglyceridemia	Insulin resistance
Glucocorticoids			+	+ +	2a or 2b	Increased secretion of VLDL with conversion to LDL	Insulin resistance

the blood rises to high levels after a fat meal. In normal individuals chylomicrons disappear from the blood after a 12-h fast. However, in affected patients high levels of chylomicrons are found in the plasma even after several days of fasting or ingestion of a fat-free diet.

The circulating chylomicrons inflame the pancreas when they pass through its capillaries. Within the capillary lumen in the pancreas, chylomicrons are exposed to small amounts of pancreatic lipase that leaks from the tissue. Partial hydrolysis of the triglycerides and phospholipids of the chylomicron produces toxic products, including fatty acids and lysolecithin, that break down tissue membranes, produce further leakage of lipase from the pancreatic acinar cells, and eventually cause fulminant pancreatitis.

Diagnosis The diagnosis of familial lipoprotein lipase deficiency is suggested by the finding of lipemic plasma in a young individual who has been fasting for at least 12 h. This lipemic plasma, when collected in the presence of EDTA, has a characteristic appearance after it has incubated overnight in a refrigerator at 4°C. A white layer of cream (which consists of chylomicrons) appears at the top of the tube. The layer beneath the cream is clear. The diagnosis of familial

lipoprotein lipase deficiency is supported by the finding of a type 1 pattern on lipoprotein electrophoresis. It is confirmed by the demonstration that lipoprotein lipase levels in plasma fail to increase following the infusion of heparin. In normal individuals, intravenous heparin releases lipoprotein lipase from its binding sites within the capillary endothelium, and increased amounts of enzyme can then be assayed in the plasma. Gel electrophoresis of VLDL apoproteins in patients with lipoprotein lipase deficiency shows a normal amount of activator apoprotein CII, thus distinguishing these patients from those with the related disorder, familial apoprotein CII deficiency (see below).

Treatment The symptoms and signs of the disease recede when the patient is placed on a fat-free diet. Every attempt should be made to maintain the fasting plasma triglyceride level below 1000 mg/dL to prevent pancreatitis. It has been found empirically that the chronic fat intake in affected adults must be less than 20 g per day to prevent symptomatic hyperlipemia. Since medium-chain triglycerides are not incorporated into chylomicrons, they have been employed to help achieve normal caloric intake. The diet should be supplemented with fat-soluble vitamins.

TABLE 315-4   Clinical disorders associated with secondary hyperlipoproteinemia *(continued)*

Underlying disorder	Plasma lipoprotein elevation				Lipoprotein type	Proposed mechanism for hyperlipoproteinemia	Associated abnormality of carbohydrate metabolism
	Chylomicrons	IDL	VLDL	LDL			
RENAL							
Uremia			+ + +		4	Decreased catabolism of VLDL due to reduced lipoprotein lipase activity	Insulin resistance
Nephrotic syndrome			+ +	+ + +	2a or 2b	Increased secretion of VLDL Direct secretion of LDL from liver Decreased catabolism of VLDL and LDL	
HEPATIC							
Primary biliary cirrhosis and extrahepatic biliary obstruction					↑ Cholesterol ↑ Phospholipids ↑ Lipoprotein X	Diversion of biliary cholesterol and phospholipids into bloodstream	
Acute hepatitis (nonfulminant)			+ + +		4	Decreased hepatic secretion of lecithin:cholesterol acyltransferase (LCAT)	
Hepatoma				+ +	2a	Lack of feedback inhibition of hepatic cholesterol synthesis by dietary cholesterol	
IMMUNOLOGIC							
Systemic lupus erythematosis	+ +				1	Presence of IgG or IgM that binds heparin, thereby decreasing activity of lipoprotein lipase	
Monoclonal gammopathies (myeloma, macroglobulinemia, lymphoma)	+ +	+ +	+ +		3 or 4	Presence of IgG or IgM that forms immune complex with chylomicron remnants and/or VLDL, thereby decreasing their catabolism	
STRESS-INDUCED							
Emotional stress, acute myocardial infarction, extensive burns, acute gram-negative sepsis			+ +		4	Increased secretion and decreased catabolism of VLDL	

FAMILIAL APOPROTEIN CII DEFICIENCY This rare autosomal recessive disorder is due to the absence of apoprotein CII, an essential cofactor for lipoprotein lipase. Deficiency of this peptide creates a functional lipoprotein lipase deficiency, thus producing a syndrome that is similar but not identical to familial lipoprotein lipase deficiency (see above). Because of the apoprotein CII deficiency, lipoprotein lipase is not activated, and its two substrate lipoproteins, chylomicrons and VLDL, accumulate in the blood, thus causing hypertriglyceridemia (type 1 or type 5 lipoprotein pattern). The disorder is diagnosed in children or adults on the basis of recurrent attacks of pancreatitis or by milky plasma detected by chance. The diagnosis is made by showing an absence of apoprotein CII on gel electrophoresis of VLDL apoproteins. Transfusion of normal plasma (which contains abundant apoprotein CII) into the patient is followed by a dramatic fall in plasma triglyceride levels. Heterozygotes, who have 50 percent reduction in apoprotein CII levels, may exhibit slightly elevated triglyceride concentrations but do not have pancreatitis. Treatment involves use of a fat-restricted diet throughout life. In case of severe pancreatitis, transfusion of one or two units of normal plasma is helpful. As compared with patients with familial lipoprotein lipase

deficiency, subjects with homozygous apoprotein CII deficiency are generally detected at a later age, accumulate more VLDL in their plasma, and rarely show cutaneous eruptive xanthomas. The reason for these clinical differences is not known.

FAMILIAL TYPE 3 HYPERLIPOPROTEINEMIA This is an inherited disorder in which the plasma concentrations of both cholesterol and triglycerides are elevated owing to the accumulation in plasma of remnant-like particles derived from the partial catabolism of VLDL. Also called familial dysbetalipoproteinemia, the disorder is transmitted by a single-gene mechanism, but its expression appears to require the presence of contributory environmental and/or genetic factors (discussed below).

Clinical features Affected individuals characteristically do not manifest hyperlipidemia or any clinical feature of the disease until after age 20. A unique clinical feature is the occurrence of two types of cutaneous xanthomas: xanthoma striata palmaris, which appear as orange or yellow discolorations of the palmar and digital creases, and tuberous or tuberoeruptive xanthomas, which are bulbous cutaneous xanthomas that may vary from pea to lemon size. The tuberous xanthomas are characteristically located over the elbows and knees. Xanthelasmas of the eyelids also occur but are not unique to this disorder (see "Familial Hypercholesterolemia" below).

Severe and fulminant atherosclerosis involves the coronary arteries, the internal carotids, and the abdominal aorta and its branches. The sequelae include premature myocardial infarctions, strokes, intermittent claudication, and gangrene of the lower extremities. Patients who develop clinical manifestations of this disorder often have hypothyroidism, obesity, or diabetes mellitus as aggravating factors.

Pathogenesis The hyperlipidemia is caused by the accumulation of large lipoprotein particles that contain both triglycerides and cholesteryl esters. These particles consist of chylomicron remnants produced from the catabolism of chylomicrons and IDL produced from the catabolism of VLDL through the action of lipoprotein lipase. In normal subjects, chylomicron remnant particles are rapidly taken up by the liver, and hence they are barely detectable in plasma. A portion of the IDL is also taken up by the liver while the rest is converted to LDL. In patients with type 3 hyperlipoproteinemia the uptake of IDL and chylomicron remnants by the liver is blocked, and these lipoproteins accumulate to high levels in plasma and tissues, producing xanthomas and atherosclerosis.

The mutation responsible for this disease involves the gene that encodes the structure of apoprotein E, a protein normally found in IDL and chylomicron remnants. This protein binds with very high affinity to both the chylomicron remnant receptor and the LDL receptor. Apoprotein E thus mediates the rapid uptake for both chylomicron remnants and IDL by the liver. The gene for apoprotein E is polymorphic in the population. There are three common alleles, designated E^2, E^3, and E^4, with approximate frequencies of 0.12, 0.75, and 0.13 in the population. Each allele specifies a distinctive form of apoprotein E that can be detected by isoelectric focusing. The three alleles create six genotypes: E^2/E^2, E^3/E^3, E^4/E^4, E^2/E^3, E^2/E^4, and E^3/E^4. Type 3 hyperlipoproteinemia occurs only in individuals who are homozygous for the E^2 allele (genotype, E^2/E^2). The protein produced by the E^2 allele is defective in its ability to bind to the liver receptors that mediate uptake of chylomicron remnants and IDL, as a result of which these particles accumulate in plasma.

The frequency of the E^2/E^2 genotype in the population is about 1 in 100. Yet the frequency of type 3 hyperlipoproteinemia is only about 1 in 10,000. Thus, only 1 percent of the individuals having genotype E^2/E^2 have symptomatic disease. It seems that most homozygotes for the E^2 allele are somehow able to compensate for the abnormal apoprotein E, because other apoproteins such as apoproteins B48 and B100 can also mediate binding to liver receptors, albeit less efficiently than apoprotein E. Familial type 3 hyperlipoproteinemia occurs only in those individuals who are homozygous for the E^2 allele and who are also unable to compensate for the abnormal function of the E protein. The inability to compensate may be caused by the independent inheritance of another defect in lipoprotein metabolism, such as familial hypercholesterolemia or multiple lipoprotein–type hyperlipoproteinemia (see below). When an individual is a heterozygote for one of these dominant diseases and is also homozygous for the E^2 allele, he or she expresses the syndrome of type 3 hyperlipoproteinemia. The expression of hyperlipoproteinemia is also brought out when an individual of genotype E^2/E^2 develops hypothyroidism, diabetes mellitus, or obesity. It should be emphasized that heterozygotes for the E^2 allele never show the clinical syndrome of familial type 3 hyperlipoproteinemia.

Diagnosis The diagnosis is suggested by the finding of palmar or tuberous xanthomas in a patient with elevated plasma levels of both cholesterol and triglyceride. Approximately 80 percent of symptomatic patients exhibit these xanthomas. The diagnosis is also suggested when a moderate elevation in the plasma concentration of both cholesterol and triglyceride occurs in such a way that the absolute concentrations of cholesterol and triglyceride are nearly equal (e.g., the plasma cholesterol and triglyceride level are both about 300 mg/dL). However, this finding does not always hold true and becomes especially unreliable when the disease is in severe exacerbation, in which case the plasma triglyceride tends to rise higher than the cholesterol.

The diagnosis is supported by the finding of a so-called broad beta band on lipoprotein electrophoresis (type 3 pattern). This appearance results from the presence of chylomicron remnants and IDL. The diagnosis can be established in specialized laboratories by two procedures. First, the plasma can be subjected to ultracentrifugation, and the chemical composition of the VLDL fraction can be measured. In affected patients, the VLDL fraction contains IDL and chylomicron remnants that have a relatively high ratio of cholesterol to triglyceride. Second, the diagnosis can be confirmed by the finding of homozygosity for the E^2 allele on isoelectric focusing of the proteins extracted from the remnant particles.

Treatment A vigorous search for occult hypothyroidism should be made, including measurement of plasma thyroid stimulating hormone (TSH) levels. If hypothyroidism exists, levothyroxine should be instituted. Patients who have hypothyroidism show a dramatic lowering of lipid levels with treatment. In addition, attempts should be made to control obesity and diabetes mellitus through diet and insulin treatment. If these measures are not successful, patients with type 3 hyperlipoproteinemia should be treated with clofibrate. Affected patients usually show a dramatic and sustained reduction in plasma lipid levels when treated with this drug.

FAMILIAL HYPERCHOLESTEROLEMIA This common autosomal dominant disorder affects approximately 1 in every 500 persons. It is caused by a mutation in the gene for the LDL receptor. Heterozygotes manifest a two- to threefold elevation in the concentration of total plasma cholesterol which is attributable to an elevation in the level of LDL. Patients with two mutant LDL receptor genes (called familial hypercholesterolemia homozygotes) have six- to eightfold elevations in plasma LDL-cholesterol levels.

Clinical features Heterozygotes with familial hypercholesterolemia can be diagnosed at birth because their umbilical cord blood contains a two- to threefold increase in the concentration of LDL and hence a similar increase in total cholesterol. The elevated levels of plasma LDL persist throughout life, but symptoms typically do not develop until the third or fourth decade. The most important feature is the occurrence of premature and accelerated coronary atherosclerosis. Myocardial infarctions begin to occur in affected men in the third decade and peak in the fourth and fifth decades. By age 60, approximately 85 percent have experienced a myocardial infarction. In women the incidence of myocardial infarction is also increased, but the mean age of onset is delayed 10 years as compared with men. Heterozygotes for this disorder constitute about 5 percent of all patients who have a myocardial infarction.

Xanthomas of the tendons constitute the second major clinical manifestation of the heterozygous state. These xanthomas are nodular swellings that typically involve the Achilles and other tendons about the knee, elbow, and dorsum of the hand. They are formed by the deposition of LDL-derived cholesteryl esters in tissue macrophages. The macrophages are swollen with lipid droplets and form foam cells. Cholesterol is also deposited in the soft tissue of the eyelid, producing xanthelasma, and within the cornea, producing arcus corneae. Whereas tendon xanthomas are essentially diagnostic of familial hypercholesterolemia, xanthelasma and arcus corneae also occur in many adults with normal plasma lipid levels. The incidence of tendon xanthomas in familial hypercholesterolemia increases with age, and up to 75 percent of heterozygotes display this sign. The absence of tendon xanthomas does not rule out familial hypercholesterolemia.

Approximately 1 in 1 million persons in the general population inherits two copies of the familial hypercholesterolemia gene and is a homozygote for the disorder. These individuals have marked elevations in the plasma level of LDL from birth. A unique type of planar cutaneous xanthoma is often present at birth and always develops within the first 6 years of life. These xanthomas are raised, yellow, plaque-like lesions at points of cutaneous trauma, such as the knees, elbows, and buttocks. Xanthomas are almost always present in the interdigital webs of the hands, particularly between the thumb and index finger. Tendon xanthomas, arcus corneae, and xanthelasma are also characteristic. Coronary artery atherosclerosis frequently has its clinical onset before age 10, and myocardial infarction has been reported as early as 18 months of age. In addition, cholesterol deposition in the aortic valve may produce symptomatic aortic stenosis. Homozygotes usually succumb to the complications of myocardial infarction before age 20.

Obesity and diabetes mellitus do not occur with increased frequency in familial hypercholesterolemia. A slender body habitus is the rule.

Pathogenesis The primary defect resides in the gene for the LDL receptor. Studies of cultured cells suggest that at least 12 mutant alleles occur at this locus. These mutant alleles can be grouped into three classes. The most common, designated receptor-negative, specifies a gene product that is nonfunctional. The second most frequent mutant, designated receptor-defective, produces a receptor that has 1 to 10 percent of normal LDL binding activity. The third type, designated internalization-defective, produces a receptor that binds LDL normally but is unable to transport the receptor-bound lipoprotein into the cell. This rare allele produces the so-called internalization defect.

Phenotypic homozygotes possess two mutant alleles at the LDL receptor locus, and hence their cells show a total or near-total inability to bind or take up LDL. Heterozygotes have one normal allele and one mutant allele at the LDL receptor locus, and hence their cells are able to bind and take up LDL at approximately half the normal rate.

Because of the reduction in LDL receptor activity, LDL catabolism is blocked, and the level of LDL in plasma rises in a manner that is inversely proportional to the reduction in LDL receptors. In addition to the impaired catabolism of LDL, LDL production is increased in homozygotes. Enhanced production of LDL has been attributed to the lack of an LDL receptor on liver cells. The liver fails to remove IDL from the plasma normally, with the result than an increased amount of IDL is converted to LDL. This overproduction of LDL, together with its inefficient catabolism, accounts for the high concentrations in affected patients. The elevated LDL levels cause an increase in the uptake of LDL by scavenger cells, which accumulate at various sites in the body, producing xanthomas.

The accelerated coronary atherosclerosis in familial hypercholesterolemia also results from the high LDL levels, which lead to an enhanced infiltration of LDL into the artery wall following episodes of endothelial damage. The large amounts of LDL that penetrate the artery wall cannot be cleared from the interstitial space by the scavenger cells, and atherosclerosis ultimately results. High LDL levels may also act to accelerate platelet aggregation at sites of endothelial injury, thereby enhancing the growth of the atherosclerotic plaque (see Chap. 195).

Diagnosis The diagnosis of heterozygous familial hypercholesterolemia is suggested by the finding of an isolated elevation of plasma cholesterol, with a normal concentration of plasma triglycerides. Such an isolated elevation in plasma cholesterol is usually due to an elevation in the plasma concentration of LDL alone (type 2a pattern). However, most individuals in the general population with type 2a hyperlipoproteinemia do not have familial hypercholesterolemia. Rather, they have a form of polygenic hypercholesterolemia that puts them on the upper end of the bell-shaped curve for the general population (see ''Polygenic Hypercholesterolemia'' below). Type 2a hyperlipoproteinemia is also caused by multiple lipoprotein-type hyperlipidemia (discussed below). In addition, a variety of metabolic disorders, including hypothyroidism and nephrotic syndrome, can cause type 2a hyperlipoproteinemia (Table 315-4).

Among individuals who have a type 2a lipoprotein pattern, those with heterozygous familial hypercholesterolemia can be distinguished from those with polygenic hypercholesterolemia and multiple lipo-protein-type hyperlipidemia on several grounds. (1) In familial hypercholesterolemia the plasma cholesterol level tends to be higher. A plasma cholesterol level in the range of 350 to 400 mg/dL is more suggestive of heterozygous familial hypercholesterolemia than of the other disorders. However, many patients with heterozygous familial hypercholesterolemia have cholesterol levels of 285 to 350 mg/dL, a range in which the other disorders cannot be excluded. (2) The occurrence of tendon xanthomas virtually establishes the diagnosis of familial hypercholesterolemia, since such xanthomas usually do not occur in patients with other forms of hyperlipidemia. (3) In cases in which the diagnosis is in doubt, other family members should be surveyed. In familial hypercholesterolemia half of the first-degree relatives show an elevated plasma cholesterol level. Hypercholester-olemia in relatives is particularly informative when it occurs in children, since elevated levels of cholesterol in childhood are characteristic of familial hypercholesterolemia but not of the other disorders.

Approximately 10 percent of heterozygotes with familial hyper-cholesterolemia have a concomitant elevation in plasma triglyceride levels (type 2b pattern). In these cases, the disease is difficult to differentiate from multiple lipoprotein-type hyperlipidemia. The finding of a tendon xanthoma or a hypercholesterolemic child in the family establishes the diagnosis of familial hypercholesterolemia.

The diagnosis of homozygous familial hypercholesterolemia ordinarily affords no problem, providing the physician is familiar with the clinical picture. Most patients are first seen by dermatologists in childhood because of the cutaneous xanthomas. Occasionally, the presentation is delayed until the onset of angina pectoris or until the child suffers a syncopal episode owing to the xanthomatous aortic stenosis. The finding of a cholesterol level greater than 600 mg/dL with normal triglyceride values in a nonjaundiced child is highly suggestive of the diagnosis. Both parents should have elevated cholesterol levels and other features of heterozygous familial hyper-cholesterolemia.

In specialized laboratories the diagnosis of both heterozygous and homozygous familial hypercholesterolemia can be made by direct measurement of the number of LDL receptors on cultured skin fibroblasts or freshly isolated blood lymphocytes. Homozygous familial hypercholesterolemia has been diagnosed in utero by the absence of LDL receptors on cultured amniotic fluid cells. The mutant genes for the LDL receptor can also be visualized directly in genomic DNA from affected individuals by using restriction enzyme digests and so-called southern blots (see Chap. 58).

Treatment Inasmuch as the atherosclerosis in this disorder is a consequence of the long-standing elevation in plasma LDL levels, every effort should be made to lower the plasma LDL level into the normal range. Patients should be placed on a diet that is low in cholesterol, low in saturated fats, and high in polyunsaturated fats. This generally means the avoidance of milk, butter, cheese, chocolate, shellfish, and fatty meats and the addition of polyunsaturated cooking oils such as corn oil and safflower oil. With such a diet heterozygotes usually show a 10 to 15 percent drop in plasma cholesterol level.

Bile acid–binding resins, such as cholestyramine, should be added to the regimen when dietary therapy fails to lower the cholesterol levels to the normal range. These resins trap the bile acids excreted by the liver into the intestine and prevent their reabsorption. The liver responds to bile acid depletion by converting additional cholesterol into bile acids. This leads to an enhanced production of LDL receptors by the liver, which in turn lowers the plasma level of LDL. Unfortunately, affected subjects also respond to bile acid depletion by enhancing cholesterol synthesis in the liver, and this compensatory response ultimately limits the long-term success of bile acid sequestrant therapy. With the combination of diet and bile acid–binding resins, the extent of reduction in plasma cholesterol level usually is in the range of 15 to 20 percent in heterozygotes. The addition of nicotinic acid may help to block the compensatory increase in hepatic cholesterol synthesis, thus allowing a further lowering of the cholesterol. Major side effects of bile acid–binding resins include gastrointestinal bloating, cramps, and constipation. The major side effect of nicotinic acid is hepatotoxicity; it also produces flushing and headaches in most patients. Probucol has also been used for the treatment of familial hypercholesterolemia. Its mechanism of action is unknown.

A new class of experimental drugs shows great promise for treatment of hypercholesterolemia. These drugs inhibit 3-hydroxy-3-methylglutaryl coenzyme A reductase, an enzyme in the cholesterol biosynthetic pathway. When cholesterol synthesis is inhibited, the production of LDL is diminished and the clearance of LDL by the liver is enhanced as a result of an increased production of LDL receptors. These two effects combine to lower plasma LDL levels by 30 to 50 percent. The HMG CoA reductase inhibitors are even more effective when given together with a bile acid binding resin such as cholestyramine. One of the inhibitors, mevinolin, is undergoing clinical trial.

Heterozygotes often show a moderate to marked lowering of plasma cholesterol level in response to the creation of an intestinal anastomosis that bypasses the ileum. This operation has the same functional effect as bile acid–binding resins, i.e., it accelerates the loss of bile acids in the stool. In certain patients in whom drug therapy is not tolerated, the creation of an ileal bypass may be indicated.

Homozygotes tend to be more resistant to treatment, probably because they are unable to increase production of LDL receptors. In general, combination therapy consisting of diet, a bile acid–binding resin, and nicotinic acid has little effect. Ileal bypass is uniformly ineffective. Several children have responded to surgical creation of a portacaval anastomosis. However, this procedure is still experimental. The use of a continuous-flow blood cell centrifuge to perform plasma exchanges at monthly intervals lowers the cholesterol in all homozygotes. After each plasma exchange, the plasma cholesterol level drops to about 300 mg/dL and then gradually rises over the ensuing 4 weeks to the pretreatment level. If facilities are available, plasma exchange is the treatment of choice for homozygotes. One child has been treated with liver transplantation, which provided LDL receptors and lowered LDL levels by 80 percent.

FAMILIAL HYPERTRIGLYCERIDEMIA

This is a common autosomal dominant disorder in which the concentration of VLDL is elevated in the plasma, causing hypertriglyceridemia.

Clinical features Affected individuals do not usually express hypertriglyceridemia until puberty or early adulthood. Thereafter, the fasting plasma triglyceride level tends to be moderately elevated in the range of 200 to 500 mg/dL (type 4 lipoprotein pattern). The typical patient exhibits the clinical triad of obesity, hyperglycemia, and hyperinsulinemia. Hypertension and hyperuricemia are also frequent.

The incidence of atherosclerosis is increased. In one study affected patients constituted 6 percent of all individuals with myocardial infarction. However, it has not been established that the hypertriglyceridemia per se causes the increased atherosclerosis. As discussed above, many patients with this disease have diabetes, obesity, and hypertension. Each of these disorders by itself may predispose to atherosclerosis. Xanthomas are not a characteristic feature of familial hypertriglyceridemia.

Affected patients ordinarily have mild to moderate hypertriglyceridemia but may develop a severe exacerbation when exposed to a variety of precipitating factors. These include poorly controlled diabetes mellitus, excessive consumption of alcohol, ingestion of birth control pills containing estrogen, and the development of hypothyroidism. In response to any of these stimuli, the plasma triglyceride level can rise to more than 1000 mg/dL. During exacerbations such patients develop *mixed hyperlipidemia;* that is, they show an elevation in the concentration of both VLDL and chylomicrons (type 5 lipoprotein pattern). Whenever the concentration of chylomicrons rises to high levels, patients are predisposed to the formation of eruptive xanthomas and the development of pancreatitis. With treatment of the exacerbating condition, the chylomicron-like particles

disappear from plasma, and the concentration of triglycerides returns to the moderately elevated basal condition.

In certain families some patients exhibit a severe mixed hyperlipidemia, even in the absence of known exacerbating factors. This is the so-called familial type 5 hyperlipidemia. Other individuals in the same family may have only the mild form of the disease with moderate hypertriglyceridemia and no hyperchylomicronemia (type 4 pattern).

Pathogenesis Familial hypertriglyceridemia is transmitted as an autosomal dominant trait, implying a mutation in a single gene. However, the nature of the mutant gene and the mechanism by which it produces hypertriglyceridemia have not been identified. It is likely that the disorder is genetically heterogeneous; that is, the hypertriglyceridemia phenotype in different families may result from different mutations.

Some patients with familial hypertriglyceridemia seem to have an underlying defect in the ability to catabolize the triglycerides of VLDL. When VLDL production rates become elevated due to obesity or diabetes, they are unable to increase the catabolism of VLDL proportionately, and hypertriglyceridemia results. The reason for this defect in catabolism is not apparent. Lipoprotein lipase activity increases normally in plasma after the administration of heparin, and no abnormalities of lipoprotein structure have been identified.

The increased prevalence of diabetes and obesity in this syndrome is believed to be fortuitous, owing to the fact that both conditions tend to increase VLDL production and hence to exacerbate hypertriglyceridemia. In family studies, one can find relatives who have diabetes without hypertriglyceridemia and relatives who have hypertriglyceridemia without diabetes, indicating that the two are inherited by independent mechanisms. When an individual inherits the gene(s) for diabetes as well as the gene for hypertriglyceridemia, the hypertriglyceridemia is more severe, and such a person is more apt to come to medical attention. Similarly, an individual with familial hypertriglyceridemia who has a normal weight usually has mild hypertriglyceridemia and is less likely to come to medical attention. However, if obesity develops, the hypertriglyceridemia worsens, and a diagnosis is more likely to be made.

Diagnosis A moderate elevation in the plasma triglyceride level, together with a normal cholesterol level, raises the possibility of familial hypertriglyceridemia. In most patients, the plasma is clear to somewhat cloudy on inspection. Chylomicrons typically are not found at the top of the plasma after overnight refrigeration. Electrophoresis of the plasma reveals an increase in the pre-β fraction (type 4 lipoprotein pattern). As mentioned above, an occasional patient exhibits severe hypertriglyceridemia with an elevation in both chylomicrons and VLDL. In this case, a cream layer develops on top (chylomicrons) and a cloudy infranatant (VLDL) is present after overnight storage of plasma in the refrigerator (type 5 lipoprotein pattern).

Given an individual who has an elevation in VLDL levels with or without an elevation in chylomicrons, there is no simple test to determine whether this subject has familial hypertriglyceridemia or hypertriglyceridemia due to some other genetic or acquired cause, such as multiple lipoprotein-type hyperlipidemia or sporadic hypertriglyceridemia. In a typical case of familial hypertriglyceridemia, half of the first-degree relatives have hypertriglyceridemia and no relatives have isolated hypercholesterolemia. Measurement of plasma lipid levels in children is not helpful inasmuch as the disease is typically not manifest until the time of puberty.

Treatment Attempts should be made to control all the exacerbating conditions. Caloric restriction is required in the obese subject. The dietary content of saturated fat should also be limited. Alcohol and oral contraceptives should be avoided. Diabetes mellitus, if present, should be treated vigorously. Thyroid function should be checked, and hypothyroidism treated if found. If the above measures fail, some patients respond to the administration of nicotinic acid or gemfibrozil. The mechanism of action of neither drug is well defined. Patients with severe hypertriglyceridemia frequently show a dramatic response to a fish oil diet.

MULTIPLE LIPOPROTEIN-TYPE HYPERLIPIDEMIA This common disorder, which is also called familial combined hyperlipidemia, is inherited as an autosomal dominant trait. Affected individuals in a single family characteristically show one of three different lipoprotein patterns: hypercholesterolemia (type 2a), hypertriglyceridemia (type 4), or both hypercholesterolemia and hypertriglyceridemia (type 2b).

Clinical features Hyperlipidemia is not present in childhood. Elevations in the plasma cholesterol and/or triglyceride level appear at puberty and continue throughout life. The lipid elevations tend to be mild and vary from time to time so that affected individuals may have a mildly elevated cholesterol level at one examination and/or a mildly elevated triglyceride level at another time. Xanthomas are not a feature. However, premature atherosclerosis occurs, and the incidence of myocardial infarction in middle age is elevated in affected women as well as men.

Patients usually have a strong family history of premature coronary artery disease. This disorder is found in about 10 percent of all patients who have a myocardial infarction. The frequency of obesity, hyperuricemia, and glucose intolerance is increased in affected individuals, especially those with hypertriglyceridemia. However, this association is not as striking as in familial hypertriglyceridemia.

Pathogenesis The disease is transmitted within families as an autosomal dominant trait, implying a mutation in a single gene. Family studies show that about half of the first-degree relatives of an affected individual have hyperlipidemia. However, blood lipid levels are variable among affected individuals in the same family as well as in the same individual at different times. About one-third of hyperlipidemic relatives have hypercholesterolemia (type 2a lipoprotein pattern), one-third hypertriglyceridemia (type 4), and one-third both hypercholesterolemia and hypertriglyceridemia (type 2b). In most affected relatives the plasma lipid levels tend to be just above the 95th percentile for the population and to dip into the normal range intermittently.

While the extent (if any) of the genetic heterogeneity and the nature of the underlying biochemical mechanisms are not known, affected individuals may have an elevated rate of secretion of VLDL by the liver. Depending on the interplay of factors governing the efficiency of conversion of VLDL to LDL and the efficiency of catabolism of LDL, this overproduction of VLDL may manifest itself alternatively as an elevation in plasma VLDL levels (hypertriglyceridemia), an elevation in LDL levels (hypercholesterolemia), or both. The hyperlipidemia is worsened by diabetes, alcoholism, and hypothyroidism.

Diagnosis No clinical or laboratory methods exist by which to determine whether an individual with hyperlipidemia has the multiple lipoprotein-type disorder. The 2a, 2b, and 4 lipoprotein patterns can each occur in patients with several other diseases (see Tables 315-3 and 315-4). However, this disorder should be suspected in any individual whose hyperlipoproteinemia is mild and whose lipoprotein type changes with time. The diagnosis is supported by the finding of multiple abnormal lipoprotein types in relatives. The diagnosis can be ruled out by the finding of tendon xanthomas in the patient or the patient's relatives or by the finding of hypercholesterolemia in a relative under the age of 10 years.

Treatment Therapy should be directed at the predominant lipid elevated at the time of examination. General measures such as weight reduction, restriction of dietary saturated fat and cholesterol, and avoidance of alcohol and oral contraceptives are useful. Triglyceride elevations may respond to nicotinic acid or gemfibrozil. When only the cholesterol level is elevated, a bile acid–binding resin should be given. However, in some individuals the lowering of cholesterol levels with such a drug is accompanied by an increase in triglyceride levels.

PRIMARY HYPERLIPOPROTEINEMIAS OF UNKNOWN ETIOLOGY

POLYGENIC HYPERCHOLESTEROLEMIA By definition, 5 percent of individuals in the general population have LDL-cholesterol levels that exceed the 95th percentile and therefore have hypercholesterolemia (type 2a or type 2b lipoprotein patterns). On the average, among every 20 such hypercholesterolemic persons, 1 person has the heterozygous form of familial hypercholesterolemia, and 2 have multiple lipoprotein-type hyperlipidemia. The remaining 17 have a form of hypercholesterolemia, designated polygenic hypercholesterolemia, that owes its origin not to a single mutant gene but rather to a complex interaction of multiple genetic and environmental factors.

Most of the factors that place an individual in the upper part of the bell-shaped curve for cholesterol levels are not known. It is likely that subtle genetic differences exist among people with regard to many processes governing cholesterol metabolism. For example, among normal people there may be genetic polymorphisms in the proteins that govern the rates of intestinal cholesterol absorption, bile acid synthesis, cholesterol synthesis, and LDL synthesis or catabolism. Certain unfavorable combinations of these mildly altered proteins, coupled with an environmental challenge, such as a diet high in cholesterol or saturated fat, may raise the plasma cholesterol level.

Clinically, polygenic hypercholesterolemia can be distinguished from familial hypercholesterolemia and multiple lipoprotein-type hyperlipidemia in two ways: (1) family studies (hyperlipidemia is present in no more than 10 percent of first-degree relatives in polygenic hypercholesterolemia in contrast to 50 percent in the other two disorders) and (2) examination for tendon xanthomas (absent in both polygenic hypercholesterolemia and multiple lipoprotein-type hyperlipidemia but present in about 75 percent of adult heterozygotes with familial hypercholesterolemia).

Certain patients with polygenic hypercholesterolemia respond to dietary restriction of saturated fat and cholesterol. Other patients require drug therapy. Probucol is sometimes effective in this latter group. Cholestyramine with or without nicotinic acid may also be used.

SPORADIC HYPERTRIGLYCERIDEMIA In addition to the forms of primary hypertriglyceridemia that show familial aggregation, endogenous hypertriglyceridemia with or without hyperchylomicronemia is sometimes seen in individuals whose relatives do not manifest hyperlipidemia. For purposes of classification, this disorder is called sporadic hypertriglyceridemia. Affected patients comprise a heterogeneous group. Some would undoubtedly be classified under one of the genetic disorders described above if a larger number of relatives were available for lipid measurements. Other than an absence of hyperlipidemic relatives, patients with sporadic hypertriglyceridemia cannot be distinguished clinically from patients with the single-gene forms of primary hypertriglyceridemia. Inasmuch as patients with sporadic hypertriglyceridemia may develop hyperchylomicronemia and pancreatitis, they should be treated with diet and drugs as in the familial disease.

FAMILIAL HYPERALPHALIPOPROTEINEMIA This entity is characterized by elevated plasma levels of HDL, also called alpha lipoprotein. The plasma levels of LDL, VLDL, and triglycerides are normal. The elevated HDL causes a slight elevation in the total plasma cholesterol level. Although a selective elevation in plasma HDL cholesterol can be observed in individuals after exposure to chlorinated hydrocarbon pesticides, in alcoholism and after administration of estrogen, most cases of hyperalphalipoproteinemia have a genetic basis. In some families, hyperalphalipoproteinemia is inherited as an autosomal dominant trait, while in others a multifactorial or polygenic basis is suspected. Individual subjects with familial hyperalphalipoproteinemia show no distinctive clinical features.

Hyperalphalipoproteinemia is associated with a slightly increased longevity and an apparent protection against myocardial infarction.

The mechanism for the increase in plasma HDL levels in this disorder has not been determined.

SECONDARY HYPERLIPOPROTEINEMIAS

A variety of clinical disorders produce secondary hyperlipoproteinemias. These are summarized in Table 315-4. The most frequently encountered forms of secondary hyperlipoproteinemia occur in association with diabetes mellitus, consumption of alcohol, and ingestion of oral contraceptives.

DIABETES MELLITUS Three distinct patterns of hypertriglyceridemia occur in patients with diabetes mellitus. Classic "diabetic hyperlipemia" consists of a massive elevation in the plasma triglyceride level that occurs in patients who have suffered from insulin deficiency or insulin resistance for many weeks or months. Such insulin-deprived patients develop a progressive increase in concentration of plasma VLDL and eventually of chylomicrons as well. Triglyceride levels as high as 25,000 mg/dL are seen. Eruptive xanthomas, lipemia retinalis, and hepatomegaly can occur. Ketosis is frequently present, but severe acidosis is not characteristic. This form of massive hyperlipemia is seen only in partial insulin deficiency. Patients with this form of diabetic hyperlipidemia usually respond to a fat-free diet and to the administration of insulin, although triglyceride levels may not return entirely to normal.

The second type of hypertriglyceridemia in diabetics is associated with acute ketoacidosis. Such patients usually exhibit a mild hyperlipidemia with elevations of VLDL but not chylomicrons. On occasion, however, marked elevations of triglyceride are seen with lipemia retinalis. In this case both VLDL and chylomicrons are present.

The third type of hypertriglyceridemia is a mild to moderate elevation in plasma VLDL that persists even when patients appear to be adequately treated for their diabetes. This chronic triglyceride elevation generally occurs in patients who are obese. Inasmuch as most patients with well-controlled diabetes have normal plasma triglyceride levels, the occasional patient with persistent hypertriglyceridemia is likely to have an underlying familial hyperlipoproteinemic disorder. Indeed, family studies indicate that many of these patients have inherited the trait for familial hypertriglyceridemia in a pattern independent of the inheritance of diabetes mellitus.

The insulin deficiency or insulin resistance of diabetes produces a high VLDL level by two mechanisms. With acute insulin deprivation there is an increase in VLDL secretion from the liver as a secondary response to the increased mobilization of free fatty acids from adipose tissue. As the state of insulin deprivation becomes prolonged, the rate of removal of VLDL and chylomicrons from the circulation declines because lipoprotein lipase activity becomes diminished.

ALCOHOL CONSUMPTION In any individual the daily consumption of large amounts of ethanol can produce a mild, asymptomatic elevation in the plasma triglyceride level due to an elevation of VLDL. However, in a subgroup ethanol ingestion regularly produces massive and clinically significant hyperlipidemia with elevations in both VLDL and chylomicrons (type 5 lipoprotein pattern). In most of this group, the VLDL level remains mildly elevated (type 4 lipoprotein pattern), even in the basal state after recovery from the severe alcoholic hyperlipidemia. This suggests that these individuals have a form of familial hypertriglyceridemia or multiple lipoprotein-type hyperlipidemia that is exacerbated and converted to a type 5 pattern by the ethanol ingestion.

Ethanol elevates the plasma triglyceride level primarily because it inhibits fatty acid oxidation and enhances fatty acid synthesis in the liver. The excess fatty acids are esterified to triglyceride. Some of this excess triglyceride accumulates in the liver, producing the characteristic enlarged fatty liver of alcoholics. The remainder of the

TABLE 315-5 Rare autosomal recessive disorders of lipid metabolism

Disorder	Typical age of onset	Plasma lipid abnormality	Major clinical manifestations	Pathogenesis	Treatment
Abetalipoproteinemia	Early childhood	Cholesterol, ~50 mg/dL; triglycerides, <10 mg/dL	Malabsorption of fat, ataxia, neuropathy, retinitis pigmentosa, acanthocytosis	Defective synthesis of apoprotein B leads to absence of chylomicrons, VLDL, and LDL in plasma	Vitamin E
Tangier disease	Childhood	Cholesterol, 40 to 125 mg/dL; triglycerides, normal to slightly elevated	Large orange tonsils, corneal opacities, relapsing polyneuropathy No premature atherosclerosis	Absence of HDL from plasma leads to generation of abnormal chylomicron remnants, which are taken up and stored as cholesteryl esters in phagocytic cells	None
Lecithin:cholesterol acyltransferase (LCAT) deficiency	Young adult	Total plasma cholesterol level variable with marked decrease in esterified cholesterol and increase in unesterified cholesterol; elevated VLDL level; structure of all lipoproteins is abnormal	Corneal opacities, hemolytic anemia, renal insufficiency, premature atherosclerosis	Decreased LCAT activity in plasma leads to accumulation of excess unesterified cholesterol in plasma and body tissues	Fat-restricted diet, kidney transplantation
Cerebrotendinous xanthomatosis	Young adult	None	Progressive cerebellar ataxia, dementia and spinal cord paresis, subnormal intelligence, tendon xanthomas, cataracts	Defective synthesis of primary bile acids in liver leads to increased hepatic synthesis of cholesterol and cholestanol, which accumulate in brain, tendons, and other tissues	None
Sitosterolemia	Childhood	Elevated levels of plant sterols in plasma, elevated or normal levels of cholesterol, normal triglyceride levels	Tendon xanthomas	Increased intestinal absorption of dietary sitosterol and other plant sterols with accumulation in plasma and tendons	Diet low in plant sterols

newly formed triglyceride is secreted into plasma, resulting in an increased secretion of VLDL. In those who develop massive alcoholic hyperlipidemia, there appears to be a partial defect in the catabolism of these VLDL particles. As the concentration of VLDL increases, the lipoprotein begins to compete with chylomicrons for hydrolysis by lipoprotein lipase, and the plasma concentration of chylomicrons also rises.

In severe alcoholic hyperlipidemia, eruptive xanthomas and lipemia retinalis are frequent. The most serious complication, pancreatitis, may be difficult to diagnose, since elevated triglyceride levels can interfere with the estimation of serum amylase. There is no evidence to indicate that pancreatitis can cause hyperlipidemia; rather the hyperlipidemia is the cause of the pancreatitis.

Plasma from patients with alcoholic hyperlipidemia is creamy in appearance. If a blood sample is drawn in calcium edetate and the plasma placed in the refrigerator at 4°C overnight, the chylomicrons float to the top, and the infranatant layer is turbid, owing to the combined elevation of VLDL and chylomicrons (type 5 pattern).

ORAL CONTRACEPTIVES The ingestion of estrogen-containing birth control pills causes an increase in the VLDL secretion rate from the liver. In most women the catabolism of VLDL also increases, so that the overall increase in plasma triglyceride level is modest. However, in women who have an underlying genetic disorder (such as familial hypertriglyceridemia or multiple lipoprotein-type hyperlipidemia) the plasma VLDL-triglyceride level can increase markedly, and hyperchylomicronemia can develop when estrogen-containing medications are taken. These women generally have mild hypertriglyceridemia prior to the institution of oral contraceptive therapy, and they presumably are unable to increase VLDL catabolism in response to the stimulation of VLDL production. The elevated VLDL prevents the normal catabolism of chylomicrons by lipoprotein lipase, and secondary hyperchylomicronemia ensues. When the latter develops, severe pancreatitis can occur.

Ingestion of oral contraceptives may be a risk factor in promoting thromboembolic disease in young women, especially those with preexisting hypercholesterolemia. Thus, it is important to measure the plasma cholesterol and triglyceride levels prior to the institution of birth control therapy. The finding of hyperlipidemia is a contraindication to the use of these drugs.

RARE DISORDERS OF LIPID METABOLISM

Table 315-5 summarizes the clinical and pathophysiologic features of five rare autosomal recessive disorders of lipid metabolism. In two—abetalipoproteinemia and Tangier disease—the major effect of the abnormality is to cause a decrease in lipid levels in plasma. In two—cerebrotendinous xanthomatosis and sitosterolemia—the major effect of the inborn error is to cause an accumulation of unusual sterols in tissues. In LCAT deficiency, the underlying mutation produces both an abnormal pattern of lipoproteins in plasma and an accumulation of unesterified cholesterol in tissues.

REFERENCES

BILHEIMER DW: Treatment of hyperlipidemia, in *Harrison's Principles of Internal Medicine, Update VI*, RG Petersdorf et al (eds). New York, McGraw-Hill, 1985, p 215

BROWN MS, GOLDSTEIN JL: How LDL receptors influence cholesterol and atherosclerosis. Sci Am 212:58, 1984

———, ———: Drugs used in the treatment of hyperlipoproteinemias, in *The Pharmacological Basis of Therapeutics*, 7th ed, AG Gilman et al (eds). New York, Macmillan, 1986, pp 827–845

CONNOR WE et al: Reduction of plasma lipids, lipoproteins and apoproteins by dietary fish oils in patients with hypertriglyceridemia. N Engl J Med 312:1210, 1985

GOLDSTEIN JL, BROWN MS: Familial hypercholesterolemia, in *The Metabolic Basis of Inherited Disease*, 5th ed, JB Stanbury et al (eds). New York, McGraw-Hill, 1983, pp 672–712

MAHLEY RW, ANGELIN B: Type III hyperlipoproteinemia: Recent insights into the genetic defect of familial dysbetalipoproteinemia. Adv Intern Med 29:385, 1984

NIKKILA E: Familial lipoprotein lipase deficiency and related disorders of chylomicron metabolism, in *The Metabolic Basis of Inherited Disease*, 5th ed, JB Stanbury et al (eds). New York, McGraw-Hill, 1983, pp 622–642

STANBURY JB et al (eds): *The Metabolic Basis of Inherited Disease*, 5th ed. New York, McGraw-Hill, 1983

316 LYSOSOMAL STORAGE DISEASES

ARTHUR L. BEAUDET

GENERAL FEATURES

DEFINITION Lysosomes are cytoplasmic organelles that enclose an acidic environment containing numerous enzymes capable of hydrolyzing most biologic macromolecules (Fig. 316-1). Primary lysosomes, the original bodies derived from the Golgi apparatus, may fuse with other membrane-bound vesicles to form secondary lysosomes. Secondary lysosomes contain material derived from outside the cell through endocytosis or material from within the cell through autophagy. A major function of the lysosome is degradation of used macromolecules related to normal turnover and tissue remodeling. Studies of the metabolism of vitamin B_{12}, lipoproteins, peptide hormones, and growth factors indicate that the lysosome is also important in the uptake of molecules through the process of adsorptive endocytosis. The initial cellular vacuole resulting from adsorptive endocytosis is the receptosome, or endosome, and this vacuole fuses with lysosomes. The lysosomal enzymes are glycoproteins which are synthesized within the endoplasmic reticulum. The initial products of protein synthesis undergo extensive modification including proteolytic cleavage, addition of complex oligosaccharides, synthesis of recognition markers (mannose 6-phosphate in some instances), and compartmentalization into primary lysosomes. These processes occur in the endoplasmic reticulum, in the Golgi apparatus, and probably in the primary, if not secondary, lysosomes as well.

The concept of lysosomal storage diseases arose from the studies of type II (Pompe) glycogen storage disease. The demonstration of lysosomal accumulation of glycogen as the result of α-glucosidase deficiency and data from other disorders led Hers to define an inborn lysosomal disease as one in which (1) a single lysosomal enzyme is deficient and (2) abnormal deposits (of substrate) are present within vacuoles related to lysosomes. This definition can be modified to include single-gene defects affecting one or more lysosomal enzymes and thus encompass disorders such as the mucolipidoses and multiple sulfatase deficiency. The concept also can be expanded to include the deficiency of other proteins necessary for lysosomal function such as sphingolipid activator proteins. Biochemical and genetic evidence indicates that these activator proteins are essential for hydrolysis of some substrates.

The lysosomal storage diseases include most of the lipid storage disorders, the mucopolysaccharidoses, the mucolipidoses, glycoprotein storage diseases, and others, as indicated in Table 316-1. The enzyme deficiencies have an autosomal recessive basis with the exception of Hunter's mucopolysaccharidosis II (MPS II), which is X-linked recessive, and Fabry's disease, which is X-linked with frequent manifestations in females. The target organs are determined by the usual sites of degradation for a macromolecule. For example, cerebral white matter is affected in patients with defects in degradation of myelin, hepatosplenomegaly develops in those with defects in degradation of glycolipids from red cell stroma, and generalized tissue involvement may occur in patients with defects in the degradation of ubiquitous mucopolysaccharides. The accumulated material often causes visceromegaly or macrocephaly, but secondary atrophy also can occur, particularly in brain or muscle. In simple terms, the symptoms appear to be due to damage from stored material, but exactly how this causes cell death or dysfunction often is unclear.

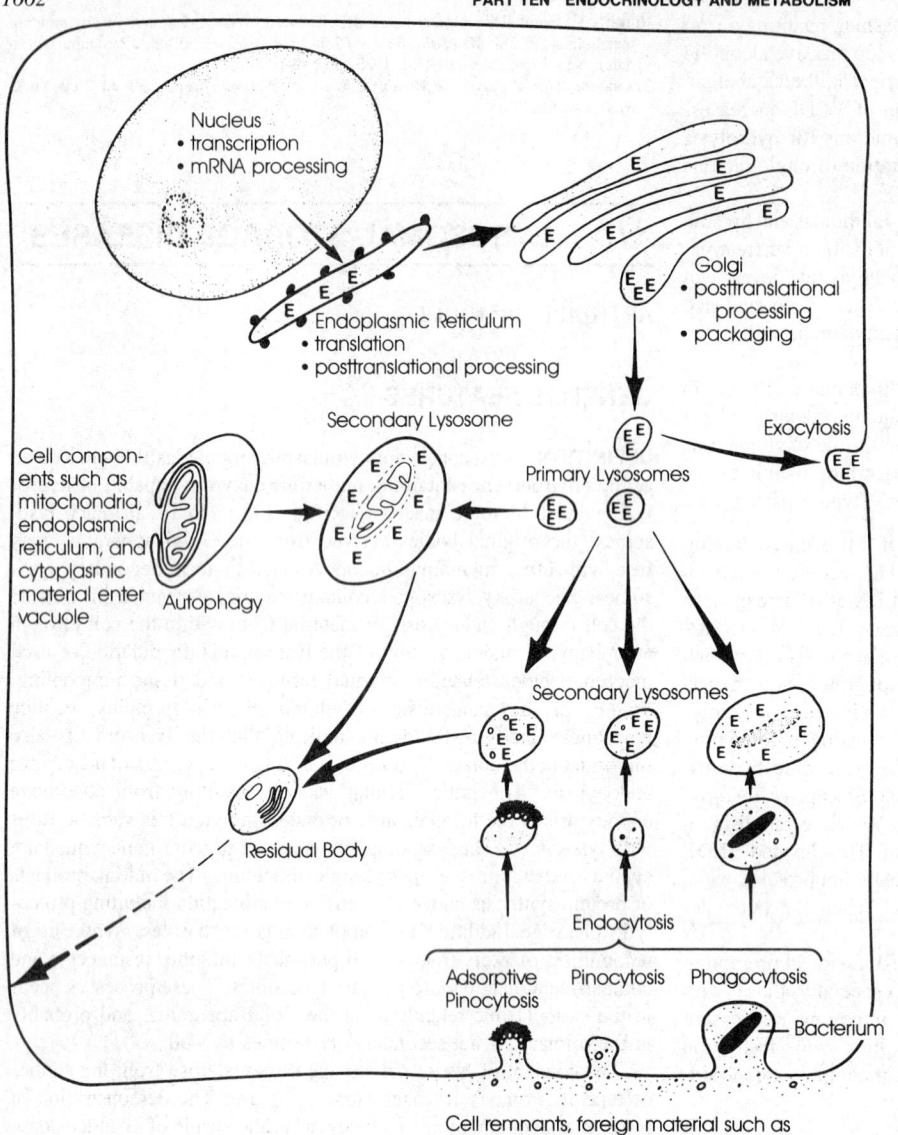

FIGURE 316-1 *Biology of lysosomes. E represents lysosomal enzymes, including precursor forms. Lysosomal enzymes are synthesized in the endoplasmic reticulum and then undergo posttranslational processing that allows packaging into the primary lysosomes. The primary lysosomes can then undergo any of the several fates outlined.*

All the disorders are progressive, and many are fatal in childhood or adolescence. Definitive diagnosis is accomplished best by specific enzyme assays on serum, leukocytes, or cultured skin fibroblasts, selecting the appropriate tests on clinical grounds. There is extensive phenotypic variation within disorders with infantile, juvenile, and adult forms of many entities. In addition, varying combinations of visceral, skeletal, and neurologic involvement can occur within a single enzyme disorder.

DIAGNOSIS A lysosomal storage disease is usually suspected on the basis of progressive neurologic dysfunction, visceromegaly, skeletal dysostosis, or some more specific finding, as outlined in Table 316-1. Progressive or degenerative disease is the hallmark of these disorders. The superimposition of degeneration upon normal childhood development results in a slowing of progress prior to loss of previously acquired abilities. The history should focus on the course of childhood development, neurologic symptoms, including seizures and visual or auditory impairment, the course of physical growth, and more specific findings such as coarsening facies, corneal clouding, exaggerated startle response, abdominal distention, joint pain, joint stiffness, hernias, and recurrent infection. The family history may reveal similarly affected siblings or consanguinity in autosomal recessive disease or other affected male family members in X-linked disorders. Ethnic background may be helpful because

several lipid storage diseases are more frequent in Ashkenazi Jews and mannosidosis and aspartylglucosaminuria may occur with increased frequency in Scandinavian populations. The juvenile form of sialidosis is frequent in the Japanese.

On physical examination the head circumference may be enlarged. Gigantism occurs early in the course of some mucopolysaccharidoses and glycoprotein storage diseases, while short stature is a later finding in many disorders. Ophthalmologic examination should include slit-lamp and careful funduscopic examination. Enlargement of the tongue, coarsening of the facies, and hepatosplenomegaly may occur. Skeletal findings may include gibbus deformity, broadening of the long bones, and joint stiffness. Cutaneous findings are rare except in fucosidosis, sialidosis, Fabry's disease, and Hunter's disease. Careful neurologic examination should attempt to distinguish the extent of involvement of gray matter, white matter, and peripheral nerves. Preliminary diagnostic studies should include examination of the peripheral blood smear for vacuolated or granulated leukocytes, urinary spot test for mucopolysaccharide, and radiologic bone survey. The preferred method of diagnosis is to use the above information to select specific enzyme assays in serum, leukocytes, or cultured skin fibroblasts. If a mucopolysaccharide screening test is positive or if clinical findings are suggestive, quantitative mucopolysaccharide analysis can be carried out. If a specific diagnosis is not readily established, biopsy of skin, bone marrow, rectal mucosa, liver, peripheral nerve, conjunctiva, or other tissue for light and electron microscopy can be helpful. Electron-microscopic findings can direct one toward or away from the general category of lysosomal storage diseases based on the presence or absence of engorged lysosomes. Again, enzyme assay is the proper method for diagnosis of the standard disorders. When significant evidence favors a lysosomal storage disease but no enzyme deficiency is demonstrable, chemical analysis of biopsy tissue from liver or brain may be an appropriate research starting point.

HETEROGENEITY There is extensive clinical and biochemical heterogeneity within the lysosomal storage diseases. The biochemical genetic principles underlying this heterogeneity are reviewed in Chaps. 57 and 305. In general, a structural gene for lysosomal enzyme produces products which undergo posttranslational modification to become glycoproteins, often resulting in a series of electrophoretic variants, or isozymes. These isozymes may hydrolyze one or a variety of substrates, and the substrate specificity of particular isozymes may vary. Differences in substrate specificity also arise from the occurrence of similar but genetically distinct enzymes, for example, the β-galactosidases. Mutations within a gene may totally eliminate or reduce enzyme activity, alter the ability of the enzyme to undergo posttranslational modification, or alter the activity of the enzyme for specific substrates.

In most instances different mutations within the structural genes for lysosomal enzymes account for varying degrees of severity from individual to individual as well as for the diverse combinations of visceral, skeletal, neurologic, ocular, and other manifestations. The heterogeneity is increased further by the recessive nature of most of the conditions in that each affected individual must have two mutant genes at the same locus. The exact mutation may vary in the two copies of the gene, making the patient a genetic compound heterozygote. In this instance either one or both genes may encode some form of residual enzyme activity for one or more substrates. Patients with intermediate clinical phenotypes with mucopolysaccharidosis type I (MPS I) have been cited as likely examples of compound heterozygotes. At a molecular level the majority of lysosomal storage disease patients might prove to be compound heterozygotes. Although it is useful to characterize clinical phenotypes as infantile, juvenile, adult, neuropathic, or nonneuropathic, the existence of different mutant alleles and of genetic compounds provides an explanation for those occasional patients who appear aberrant or intermediate as compared with the usual phenotype. Another type of heterogeneity is illustrated by MPS III A, B, C, and D, which are very similar disorders caused by different gene defects. Thus, biochemical heterogeneity can underlie apparent clinical homogeneity.

Further complexity results from the fact that certain enzyme activities are derived from complexes of nonidentical subunits. As a consequence, different mutations can cause deficiency of the same enzyme, as for example, hexosaminidase A deficiency in Tay-Sachs and Sandhoff's diseases, and can explain multiple enzyme deficiencies due to a single-gene defect as in Sandhoff's disease. Genetic disorders involving the posttranslational modification of lysosomal enzymes and general defects in the integrity and function of the lysosome may also cause lysosomal storage diseases. The mucolipidoses II and III represent situations in which a single-gene defect alters the ability of a number of lysosomal enzymes to enter the lysosome. Thus, mutations outside the structural genes for the enzymes themselves can account for further heterogeneity. Better biochemical understanding of the identity, subunit structure, posttranslational processing, and substrate specificities of lysosomal enzymes should provide further insight into phenotypic and genotypic heterogeneity.

Clinical diagnosis is facilitated but also somewhat complicated by the widespread use of synthetic substrates for measuring lysosomal enzyme activities. These substrates often measure a group of related activities attributable to different enzymes. Thus, the activity of β-galactosidase using an artificial substrate may represent the sum of various β-galactosidases encoded by different structural genes and having different substrate specificities. Clinical reliability generally is achieved by manipulating in vitro conditions to reflect that enzyme activity whose deficiency is characteristic of a clinical disorder. Genetic heterogeneity has, however, resulted in individuals with a mutant enzyme that either hydrolyzes the natural substrate and not the artificial substrate, or vice versa. This is exemplified by the normal individuals who have hexosaminidase A deficiency using artificial substrate and by patients with Tay-Sachs disease who have substantial levels of hexosaminidase A activity with artificial substrates. The presence or absence of disease correlates with ability to hydrolyze the natural G_{M2} ganglioside substrate. These phenomena have considerable significance for identification of affected patients, for heterozygote screening, and for prenatal diagnosis. They indicate the need to go beyond artificial substrate enzyme assays if normal results occur in the face of overwhelming clinical, electron-microscopic, or chemical evidence of a storage disease.

MANAGEMENT AND PREVENTION Specific therapy is not effective in lysosomal storage diseases at present, and care is largely symptomatic. The relentless, progressive course in many instances represents a tragic burden. Transplantation is effective in reversing the renal failure that commonly occurs in Fabry's disease, and splenectomy frequently is helpful in adult Gaucher's disease. Considerable attention has been focused on enzyme replacement for lysosomal storage diseases using organ or fibroblast transplantation or the infusion of either plasma, leukocytes, purified enzyme itself, or enzyme trapped in erythrocytes or liposomes. Although these approaches offer promise for treatment of manifestations outside the central nervous system, they are not of proven efficacy. The most distressing aspects of lysosomal storage diseases involve the central nervous system, where the blood-brain barrier presents an additional obstacle to the development of effective enzyme replacement therapy.

Genetic counseling is important in the management of these disorders. All the lysosomal storage diseases in which the specific enzyme deficiency is known either have been or presumably could be diagnosed in utero, since lysosomal enzyme activities appear to be expressed in cultured amniotic fluid cells as well as in cultured skin fibroblasts. Prenatal diagnosis can also be made using chorionic villus biopsy. Although the incidence of miscarriage after this procedure may be slightly higher, the possibility of earlier diagnosis is very attractive to families with high genetic risks. Heterozygote detection in close relatives is sometimes possible, although it can be difficult to achieve adequate statistical confidence for such determinations. Heterozygote detection is further complicated by random inactivation of X chromosomes in 46,XX carriers of X-linked diseases, but counseling of females at risk in such families should be pursued vigorously. More effective approaches to prevention require identification of heterozygous couples prior to the birth of an affected offspring. The feasibility of this approach has been demonstrated by heterozygote testing programs for Tay-Sachs disease. Such programs could result in a decreased frequency of these disorders through extensive testing and appropriate reproductive decisions on the part of the rare couples at risk for having affected offspring; the high frequency of the heterozygous state in Ashkenazi Jews and favorable biochemical aspects of carrier detection for Tay-Sachs disease have facilitated this program. Efficient, accurate heterozygote detection methods would be needed to apply this approach to other diseases and to populations with lower heterozygote frequencies. Even under optimal conditions genetic variants might cause false-positive or false-negative results in any screening process.

CLONING OF LYSOSOMAL ENZYME GENES The cloning of DNAs that encode several lysosomal enzymes has been reported, and the majority of these genes will be cloned eventually. These developments should increase the understanding of the biochemistry and genetics for the lysosomal disorders, although clinical diagnosis and prenatal diagnosis are not likely to be altered significantly. The major hope would be that availability of the cloned genes might allow for some form of gene replacement therapy.

TABLE 316-1 Summary of lysosomal storage diseases

Disorder	Heterogeneity (onset)	Enzyme deficiency	Stored material	Neurologic
G_{M1} gangliosidosis	Infantile (birth) Juvenile (6–20 mo) Adult	β-Galactosidase	G_{M1} ganglioside Glycoproteins Keratan sulfate	Mental retardation, seizures, blindness; later in juvenile form, variable in adults
Tay-Sachs and variants, G_{M2} gangliosidosis	Infantile (3–6 mo) Juvenile Adult forms	Hexosaminidase A	G_{M2} ganglioside	Mental retardation, seizures, blindness; later in juvenile form
Sandhoff, G_{M2} gangliosidosis	Infantile (3–6 mo)	Hexosaminidase A and B	G_{M2} ganglioside Globoside	Mental retardation, seizures, blindness
G_{M2} gangliosidosis, AB variant	Findings similar to Tay-Sachs except primary defect is a ganglioside activator protein.			
Krabbe, galactosylceramide lipidosis	Infantile (2–6 mo) Late onset	Galactosylceramide β-Galactosidase	↑ Galactoscerebroside/sulfatide ratio	Mental retardation, leukodystrophy; variable in late onset
Metachromatic leukodystrophy, sulfatide lipidosis	Late infantile (1–4 yr) Juvenile (4–20 yr) Adult	Arylsulfatase A (cerebroside sulfatase)	Galactosyl sulfatides	Mental retardation, leukodystrophy, psychosis and dementia in adults
Sphingolipid activator protein 1 deficiency	Findings similar to metachromatic leukodystrophy except primary defect is activator protein.			
Niemann-Pick, sphingomyelin lipidosis	Infantile neuropathic (1–4 mo) Late onset neuropathic Visceral	Sphingomyelinase ? Specific isozymes in some	Sphingomyelin	Mental retardation, ataxia, and seizures in neuropathic forms
Gaucher, glucosylceramide lipidosis	Infantile (1–12 mo) Juvenile (2–6 yr) Adult	β-Glucocerebrosidase	Glucosylceramide	Mental retardation; spastic, later flaccid, ataxia in juvenile; no neurologic symptoms in adult form
Fabry, trihexosyl ceramidosis	Hemizygous males Heterozygous females	α-Galactosidase A	Trihexosylceramide	Painful neuropathy
Acid lipase deficiency	Infantile Wolman's disease (0–3 mo) Late onset cholesteryl ester storage disease (CESD)	Acid lipase	Cholesteryl ester Triglyceride	Mental retardation but mild related to growth failure in Wolman; none in CESD
Farber, ceramide deficiency	Infantile (0–4 mo) Rare juvenile	Ceramidase	Ceramide	Occasional mental retardation, but may be secondary to somatic features
Pompe, glycogen storage type II	Infantile (0–6 mo) Juvenile Adult	Acid maltase (α-1,4- and 1,6-glucosidase)	Glycogen	Probably normal mentally
Acid phosphatase deficiency	Infantile (0–3 mo)	Acid phosphatase	Not characterized	Mental retardation
Fucosidosis	Infantile (3–12 mo) Juvenile	α-Fucosidase	Glycopeptides Glycolipids Oligosaccharides	Mental retardation

* AR = autosomal recessive.

Liver and/or spleen enlargement	Skeletal dysplasia	Ophthalmic	Hematologic	Genetics	Unique manifestations	References
++++ Less in juvenile, variable in adult	++++ Variable in juvenile and adult forms	Cherry-red spot in 50% of infantile; corneal clouding variable but more in adults	Foam cells Vacuolated lymphocytes	AR*	Coarse facies, edema, macroglossia, mucopolysacchariduria; early blindness in infantile, milder in juvenile; in adults often spondyloepiphyseal dysplasia +/− mucopolysacchariduria	Hers and Van Hoof, chap 12 Stanbury et al, chap 46 Ho et al
0	0	Cherry-red spot in infantile form, rare in juvenile	0	AR	Macrocephaly, hyperacusis in infantile; increased in Ashkenazi Jews	Hers and Van Hoof, chap 13 Stanbury et al, chap 46 Ho et al
0	0	Cherry-red spot	0	AR	Macrocephaly, hyperacusis, visceral histiocytosis	Hers and Van Hoof, chap 14 Stanbury et al, chap 46 Ho et al
0	0	Optic atrophy	0	AR	Extreme irritability, ↑ CSF protein, fever, globoid cell neuropathology	Hers and Van Hoof, chap 17 Stanbury et al, chap 43 Ho et al
0	0	Optic atrophy, less in juvenile and adult forms	0	AR	↑ CSF protein and early gait abnormalities in late infantile; peripheral neuropathy	Hers and Van Hoof, chap 18 Stanbury et al, chap 44
++++ Less prominent in late onset forms	0	Macular degeneration and cherry-red spot in neuropathic forms	Distinctive foam cell Vacuolated lymphocytes	AR	Pulmonary infiltrates, brownish skin, infantile neuronopathic form increased in Ashkenazi Jews, sea-blue histiocytes	Hers and Van Hoof, chap 19 Stanbury et al, chap 41
++++ Hypersplenism common	++	Usually normal	Distinctive foam cell	AR	Adult form includes ↑ acid phosphatase, pathologic fractures; Ashkenazi Jewish predilection	Hers and Van Hoof, chap 16 Stanbury et al, chap 42 Ho et al
0	0	Corneal dystrophy, vascular lesions, cataracts	0	X-linked dominant	Cutaneous angiokeratoma, vascular thromboses, hypohidrosis	Hers and Van Hoof, chap 15 Stanbury et al, chap 45 Ho et al
+++	0	0	Foam cells Vacuolated lymphocytes	AR	Adrenal calcification, anemia, vomiting and poor growth in Wolman; hepatic fibrosis and ↑ blood cholesterol in CESD	Hers and Van Hoof, chap 20 Stanbury et al, chap 39
+/−	?	Mild macular degeneration	0	AR	Arthropathy—subcutaneous, periarticular and visceral nodules (lipogranulomatosis); ↑ CSF protein	Hers and Van Hoof, chap 24 Stanbury et al, chap 40 Ho et al
Mild hepatomegaly	0	0	0	AR	Lethal skeletal and cardiac myopathy in infantile; primarily skeletal myopathy in adults	See chap 313 Hers and Van Hoof, chap 7 Stanbury et al, chap 6
++	0	0	0	AR?	Lethal disorders described in two families	Hers and Van Hoof, chap 21 Hirschhorn and Weissmann
++	++	0	Vacuolated lymphocytes Foam cells	AR	Coarse facies, increased sweat electrolytes, angiokeratoma in juvenile	Hers and Van Hoof, chap 11 Ho et al Stanbury et al, chap 38

(Table continues next page)

TABLE 316-1 Summary of lysosomal storage diseases (continued)

Disorder	Heterogeneity (onset)	Enzyme deficiency	Stored material	Neurologic
Mannosidosis	Infantile (6–18 mo) Milder form	α-Mannosidase	Oligosaccharides	Mental retardation
Aspartylglucosaminuria	Young adult onset	Aspartylglucosamine amidase	Aspartylglucosamine Glycopeptides	Mental retardation
Mucopolysaccharidosis IH and IS	Infantile Hurler (6–12 mo) Intermediate Adult Scheie	α-Iduronidase	Dermatan sulfate Heparan sulfate	Mental retardation, absent in Scheie
Hunter, mucopolysaccharidosis II	Severe infantile (6–12 mo) Mild juvenile	Iduronosulfate sulfatase	Dermatan sulfate Heparan sulfate	Mental retardation, less in mild form
Sanfilippo A, mucopolysaccharidosis III A	Late infantile (1–4 yr)	Heparan N-sulfatase (sulfamidase)	Heparan sulfate	Severe mental retardation
Sanfilippo B, mucopolysaccharidosis III B		N-Acetyl-α-glucosaminidase		
Sanfilippo C, mucopolysaccharidosis III C		Acetyl-CoA:α-glucosaminide N-acetyltransferase		
Sanfilippo D, mucopolysaccharidosis III D		N-Acetylglucosamine 6-sulfate sulfatase		
Morquio, mucopolysaccharidosis IV	Some variation	N-Acetylgalactosamine 6-sulfate sulfatase	Keratan sulfate	0
Maroteaux-Lamy, mucopolysaccharidosis VI	Variation in severity and cardiovascular involvement	N-Acetylhexosamine 4-sulfate sulfatase (arylsulfatase B)	Dermatan sulfate	0
β-Glucuronidase deficiency, mucopolysaccharidosis VII	Few patients; infantile to adult forms	β-Glucuronidase	Dermatan sulfate ? Heparan sulfate	Mental retardation ? absent in some adults
Multiple sulfatase deficiency	Late infantile (1–4 yr)	Arylsulfatases A, B, and C Other sulfatases	Sulfatides Mucopolysaccharides	Mental retardation
Sialidosis	Congenital, infantile, juvenile, cherry-red spot myoclonus	Glycoprotein neuraminidase (sialidase)	Sialyloligosaccharides	Mental retardation, myoclonus
Mucolipidosis II, I cell disease	Infantile (0–3 mo)	UDP-N-acetylglucosamine (GlcNAc):glycoprotein GlcNAc1-phosphotransferase	Glycoproteins Glycolipids	Mental retardation
Mucolipidosis III, pseudo-Hurler polydystrophy	Late infantile (>2 yr)		Glycoproteins Glycolipids	Mild mental retardation
Mucolipidosis VI	Infantile	? Ganglioside neuraminidase	? Multiple	Mental retardation
Neuronal ceroid lipofuscinoses	Late infantile Juvenile Adult	Unknown	"Ceroid" "Lipofuscin"	Mental retardation, dementia variable in adults, seizures

SPECIFIC DISORDERS

SPHINGOLIPIDOSES G_{M1} gangliosidosis G_{M1} gangliosidosis is due to deficiency of β-galactosidase. Prominent features of the infantile form are the presence of abnormalities at or near birth, developmental delay, seizures, coarse facies, edema, hepatosplenomegaly, macroglossia, ocular cherry-red spot, and a distinctive mucopolysaccharidosis-like dysostosis multiplex. Death usually occurs in the first or second year of life. The juvenile form is characterized by a later onset, survival to the latter half of the first decade, neurologic impairment and seizures, and milder skeletal and ocular findings. In the adult form, spondyloepiphyseal dysplasia similar to that in MPS IV, corneal clouding and normal intelligence are common. Joint pain and limitation of motion, particularly at the hips, can be disabling in these patients. Prominent spasticity and ataxia with mild bony abnormalities may be present. A high index of suspicion is necessary

Liver and/or spleen enlargement	Skeletal dysplasia	Ophthalmic	Hematologic	Genetics	Unique manifestations	References
+++	++	Cataracts, corneal clouding	Vacuolated lymphocytes Granulated neutrophils	AR	Coarse facies, enlarged tongue	Hers and Van Hoof, chap 11 Stanbury et al, chap 38
0	++	Lens opacities	Vacuolated lymphocytes	AR	Coarse facies, detectable by urine amino acid analysis	Hers and Van Hoof, chap 24 Stanbury et al, chap 38
+++	++++	Corneal clouding	Granulated lymphocytes	AR	Coarse facies, cardiovascular involvement, joint stiffness	Hers and Van Hoof, chaps 8 and 9 Stanbury et al, chap 36 McKusick
+++	++++	Retinal degeneration, no significant corneal clouding	Granulated lymphocytes	X-linked	Coarse facies, cardiovascular involvement, joint stiffness	
+	+	0	Granulated lymphocytes	AR	Mild coarsening of facies	
+	Severe, distinctive	Corneal clouding	Granulated neutrophils	AR	Severe deformity, odontoid hypoplasia, aortic regurgitation	
++	++++	Corneal clouding	Granulated neutrophils and lymphocytes	AR	Mild coarsening of facies, joint stiffness, valvular heart disease	
+++	+++	Corneal clouding	Granulated neutrophils	AR	Coarse facies, ↑ vascular involvement	
+	MPS features	Retinal degeneration	Vacuolated and granulated cells	AR	Icthyosis, combined MPS and metachromatic leukodystrophy phenotype	Hers and Van Hoof, chaps 8 and 18 Stanbury et al, chap 44
++ Less in late form	++ Less or absent in late form	Cherry-red spot	Vacuolated lymphocytes	AR	MPS phenotype in all but cherry-red spot myoclonus	Hers and Van Hoof, chap 8 Stanbury et al, chap 38
0/+	++++	Corneal clouding	Vacuolated and granulated neutrophils	AR	Coarse facies, inclusions in cultured fibroblasts, normal mucopolysacchariduria	Hers and Van Hoof, chap 8 Stanbury et al, chap 37
0	+++	Corneal clouding	Vacuolated plasma cells	AR	Coarse facies, inclusions in cultured fibroblasts, joint contractures, valvular heart disease, normal mucopolysacchariduria	
0	0	Corneal clouding, retinal degeneration	0	AR	Diagnosis based on electron microscopy; ? Ashkenazi Jewish predilection	Stanbury et al, chap 37
0	0	Optic atrophy, macular degeneration, retinitis pigmentosa	Vacuolated lymphocytes Granulated neutrophils	AR AR	Electron microscopy helpful, degree of genetic heterogeneity unknown	Hers and Van Hoof, chap 23

to recognize the diverse phenotypes caused by β-galactosidase deficiency in juvenile and adult patients, since almost any combination of skeletal, ocular, neurologic, and visceral findings can occur. Isozymes of β-galactosidase occur, and the diversity of phenotypes is due to different mutations in the same structural gene. All forms of G_{M1} gangliosidosis have an autosomal recessive inheritance. There is no ethnic predilection. The frequency of the disease is low, with fewer than 50 patients reported for any given phenotype. Some

patients originally reported to have β-galactosidase deficiency were subsequently shown to have combined deficiency of neuraminidase and β-galactosidase.

G_{M2} gangliosidosis Tay-Sachs disease is a relatively common inborn error of metabolism with thousands of documented cases. Although it is clinically very similar to Sandhoff's disease, the two are genetically distinct with deficiency of hexosaminidase A in the former and hexosaminidase A and B in the latter. An additional disorder, called the AB variant of G_{M2} gangliosidosis, occurs with normal hexosaminidase A and B activity. This variant is due to a deficiency of a protein factor (activator) necessary for activity of the enzyme against natural substrate. The presenting features are similar in all of the infantile disorders and include a developmental delay beginning in the third to sixth month with subsequent, rapidly progressive neurologic deterioration. Macrocephaly, seizures, retinal cherry-red spot, and an augmented startle response to sound suggest the diagnosis. The diagnosis is confirmed by enzyme assay. Most juvenile-onset patients with hexosaminidase deficiency present with dementia, seizures, and ocular findings, and some have an atypical spinocerebellar degeneration. Some juvenile and adult patients have presented with clinical features of spinal muscular atrophy.

Sandhoff's disease is nonallelic with Tay-Sachs disease, whereas the juvenile forms of hexosaminidase deficiency are usually allelic with Tay-Sachs disease. Tay-Sachs disease is the most frequent form of hexosaminidase deficiency, the risk being about 100 times higher in Ashkenazi Jews than in other ethnic groups. All forms of G_{M2} gangliosidosis are autosomal recessive. Hexosaminidase B is composed of β subunits whose structural locus is on chromosome 5, while hexosaminidase A is composed of α and β subunits with the structural locus for the α subunit on chromosome 15. Thus there is a defect in the α subunit in Tay-Sachs disease and in the β subunit in Sandhoff's disease.

Although no specific therapy is available, extensive programs for heterozygote detection to prevent Tay-Sachs disease have been carried out throughout the world. As of 1982, more than 400,000 people had been tested, and more than 15,000 heterozygotes and 333 couples at risk for Tay-Sachs in their offspring had been identified. Six hundred sixty-seven pregnancies had been monitored by prenatal diagnosis because of a previous affected child, and 391 pregnancies had been monitored based on results of carrier screening by 1982.

LEUKODYSTROPHIES　Krabbe's galactosylceramide lipidosis or globoid cell leukodystrophy is an infantile disease due to deficiency of galactosylceramide β-galactosidase. The disorder is characterized by onset at 2 to 6 months of age, with irritability, hyperesthesia, hypersensitivity to external stimuli, unexplained fever, optic atrophy, and sometimes seizures. Spinal fluid protein is usually increased. Initially there is hypertonicity and increased deep tendon reflexes with progression to a hypotonic state. Rapid neurologic deterioration and death occur within 1 to 2 years of onset. Premortem diagnosis is accomplished by enzyme assay. The presence of globoid cells on neuropathologic examination is characteristic and possibly specific for this enzyme deficiency. Galactosylceramide β-galactosidase functions in the degradation of sulfatides derived from myelin. Myelin synthesis is so impaired by tissue damage that the absolute amount of the galactocerebroside substrate is usually not increased in postmortem tissue. Galactosylceramide β-galactosidase is genetically distinct from the β-galactosidase that is deficient in G_{M1} gangliosidosis.

Krabbe's disease is relatively rare, with about 150 reported cases. It has an autosomal recessive genetic basis and is present in all ethnic groups with a possible increased frequency in the Scandinavian countries. Although no specific therapy is available, prenatal diagnosis has been accomplished.

Deficiency of arylsulfatase A (cerebroside sulfatase) is the basis of metachromatic leukodystrophy, a lipid storage disease with a frequency of 1 in 40,000. The age of onset is later than that in Tay-Sachs disease or Krabbe's disease. Patients develop the ability to walk and frequently present with gait abnormalities in the second to fourth year of life. Initially the patients may be hypotonic with decreased deep tendon reflexes, the latter reflecting peripheral nerve involvement. The disease progresses over the first decade to include ataxia, increased muscle tone, decorticate or decerebrate posturing, and eventual loss of all contact with surroundings. Duration of survival depends on nursing care and support such as nasogastric or gastrostomy feeding.

Although some diagnostic studies have been performed on urine, leukocytes or fibroblasts are preferable for diagnostic enzyme assay. Changes demonstrable on metachromatic staining of nerve tissue are nonspecific and not an adequate substitute for enzyme assay. Rare patients with a juvenile form of metachromatic leukodystrophy have the onset between 4 and 20 years of age and a slower progression. The adult form deserves special mention as an example of the difficulties presented by subtle, slowly progressive forms of lysosomal storage diseases. The onset is in the second to fifth decade with a slowly progressive dementia. Emotional difficulties, motor dysfunction, and indistinct speech are often present. Even though conduction velocity in peripheral nerves is usually diminished, the deep tendon reflexes are often increased. Typical premortem diagnoses include organic dementia, schizophrenia, and multiple sclerosis; a correct premortem diagnosis is made rarely.

Arylsulfatase A is routinely measured using artificial substrate, and complexities involving low levels of activity in normal individuals and moderate levels of residual activity in symptomatic patients have been described. Heterogeneity involving mutations in multiple components of the cerebroside sulfatase activity may exist, but the majority of patients probably have simple allelic disorders on an autosomal recessive basis. A few patients with a phenotype similar to metachromatic leukodystrophy have been shown to have deficiency of a sphingolipid activator protein. Arylsulfatase A deficiency also occurs in multiple sulfatase deficiency discussed below.

NIEMANN-PICK DISEASE　Niemann-Pick disease is a sphingomyelin lipidosis. In type A and B disease, there is a clear deficiency of sphingomyelinase, an enzyme that hydrolyzes sphingomyelin to yield ceramide and phosphorylcholine. The most common disorder, Niemann-Pick A, begins shortly after birth with hepatosplenomegaly, failure to thrive, and neurologic impairment. Retinal cherry-red spots occur, but seizures and hypersplenism are rare. The diagnosis can be made by recognition of the distinctive Niemann-Pick cell in the bone marrow but should be confirmed by enzyme assay. Niemann-Pick B disease is a relatively benign disorder with hepatosplenomegaly, sphingomyelinase deficiency, and sometimes pulmonary infiltrates; but there is no neurologic involvement. Niemann-Pick C disease is characterized by sphingomyelin lipidosis, progressive neurologic deterioration in childhood, and substantial or normal sphingomyelinase activity. Niemann-Pick D disease resembles type C but is separated primarily on the basis of occurrence in a Nova Scotian population. Niemann-Pick E disease causes visceral sphingomyelin lipidosis without neurologic involvement and without sphingomyelinase deficiency. The biochemical basis for Niemann-Pick types C, D, and E is not understood. Many patients described with the sea-blue histiocyte syndrome may have had sphingomyelinase deficiency; other patients with the sea-blue histiocyte syndrome may have defects not yet characterized.

GAUCHER'S DISEASE　Gaucher's disease is a glucosylceramide lipidosis caused by deficiency of glucosylceramidase. An infantile form is characterized by early onset, marked hepatosplenomegaly, and severe neurologic progression to early death. A juvenile form with milder neurologic involvement exists. The adult form of the disease may be the most common lysosomal storage disease. Patients with juvenile and adult Gaucher's disease have been observed within the same family but not within the same sibships, suggesting that these are allelic disorders.

All forms of Gaucher's disease have an autosomal recessive genetic basis. The adult disorder is about 30 times more frequent in Ashkenazi Jews, with an incidence in this group of about 1 in 2500 births. Although commonly termed "adult Gaucher's disease," this variant frequently has its onset in childhood. Absence of neurologic involvement is the criterion for inclusion in this category. Adult Gaucher's disease is one of the lysosomal storage diseases most likely to present in the practice of internal medicine, although patients may be diagnosed at almost any age. The clinical presentation is usually either the incidental discovery of splenomegaly or the occurrence of thrombocytopenia secondary to hypersplenism. In addition, bone pain or pathologic fractures may occur including aseptic necrosis of the femoral heads and vertebral collapse. Bone pain with fever has been described as pseudoosteomyelitis. Pulmonary infiltrates, pulmonary hypertension, and moderate hepatic dysfunction may be present. Serum acid phosphatase is characteristically elevated. A distinctive storage cell occurs in the bone marrow in all forms of Gaucher's disease, but enzyme assay should be performed because the Gaucher cell may also be found in patients with granulocytic leukemia and myeloma.

The clinical course is variable; pulmonary involvement may lead to early death, but in many patients life span is not shortened. Bleeding secondary to thrombocytopenia frequently responds to splenectomy. Bone marrow transplantation may be considered in the face of life-threatening complications from the disease. Because of the frequency of the disease and the lack of neurologic involvement, the adult form of Gaucher's disease is particularly worthy of efforts to develop enzyme replacement therapy.

FABRY'S DISEASE Fabry's disease involves the accumulation of a trihexoside, galactosylgalactosylglucosylceramide, due to deficiency of α-galactosidase A. The disorder is X-linked, and the most severe symptoms are in affected males. Fabry's disease usually presents during adulthood. If symptoms occur during childhood, they are likely to take the form of a painful neuropathy. During adolescence and early adulthood, patients often experience hypohidrosis, and a history of heat stroke during military training is frequent. A characteristic corneal dystrophy allows for diagnosis by the astute ophthalmologist, but the patients rarely have visual complaints. Frequently the disease is diagnosed only after development of progressive renal impairment in the third to fifth decade. Vascular thromboses may occur even in childhood. Death most often results from renal failure, typically in the fourth or fifth decade. Heterozygous females are affected more mildly. Corneal dystrophy is the most frequent finding, but all other manifestations may be seen also. Life expectancy is greater in women, although fatal complications can occur rarely.

Therapeutic intervention of several types may be helpful. Counseling regarding the risks of hypohidrosis is important. Painful neuropathy frequently responds to administration of phenytoin. Renal failure can be treated by chronic dialysis, and the patients are acceptable candidates for transplantation since the donor kidney will not be impaired by the disease. The disease in the future might be amenable to enzyme replacement therapy, since the central nervous system is spared.

ACID LIPASE DEFICIENCY Acid lipase deficiency is the basis for two disorders with different phenotypic features. Wolman's disease is a severe disorder of early onset, with prominent hepatosplenomegaly, anemia, vomiting, failure to thrive, and characteristic adrenal calcification. Neurologic involvement is minimal compared with the severe somatic handicap. Cholesteryl ester storage disease is a rare disorder with mild phenotypic features by comparison. The most constant features are hepatosplenomegaly and increased plasma cholesterol. Hepatic fibrosis, esophageal varices, and poor growth have occurred. One reported sibship may represent an intermediate phenotype, since two females died at 7 and 9 years of age with unexplained acute hepatic failure, and a third sibling developed adrenal calcification and pulmonary hypertension early in life. Tissues from patients with acid lipase deficiency demonstrate inability to hydrolyze triglycerides as well as cholesteryl esters. Possibly a single enzyme hydrolyzes multiple substrates, but the subunit structure and hydrolytic capacities of various lysosomal lipases are not well studied. Deficiency of acid lipase results in impairment of low-density lipoprotein degradation as described in Chap. 315 and may be associated with premature atherosclerosis. Both Wolman's and cholesteryl ester storage diseases have an autosomal recessive basis.

GLYCOPROTEIN STORAGE DISORDERS Fucosidosis, mannosidosis, and aspartylglucosaminuria are rare, autosomal recessive disorders involving hydrolases that degrade polysaccharide linkages. Glycolipids as well as glycoproteins are accumulated in fucosidosis. All are characterized by neurologic impairment and varying somatic involvements, as outlined in Table 316-1. Fucosidosis and mannosidosis are most often lethal disorders in childhood, while aspartylglucosaminuria presents as a late-onset lysosomal storage disease with prominent mental retardation and a prolonged course. Abnormal sweat electrolytes and cutaneous angiokeratomas are distinctive in fucosidosis, and an unusual cartwheel-type cataract occurs in mannosidosis. Aspartylglucosaminuria is remarkable in that urinary amino acid analysis is diagnostic with an increase of aspartylglucosamine; it is more frequent in the Finnish population. Sialidosis encompasses a group of phenotypes associated with glycoprotein neuraminidase (sialidase) deficiency. The phenotypes include an adult cherry-red spot myoclonus syndrome, infantile and juvenile presentations with mucopolysaccharidosis-like phenotypes, and a congenital presentation with hydrops fetalis. Many patients previously classified as having mucolipidosis I have been proven to have mannosidosis or sialidosis. Some patients with sialidosis have β-galactosidase deficiency as well as neuraminidase deficiency. The molecular basis for the combined β-galactosidase and neuraminidase deficiency is uncertain, but a defect in a "protective protein" has been proposed. Each of the glycoprotein storage diseases can be diagnosed by appropriate enzyme assay.

MUCOPOLYSACCHARIDOSIS (MPS) The mucopolysaccharidoses represent a broad spectrum of disorders due to deficiencies of one of a group of enzymes which degrade three classes of mucopolysaccharides: heparan sulfate, dermatan sulfate, and keratan sulfate. The general MPS phenotype includes coarse facies, corneal clouding, hepatosplenomegaly, joint stiffness, hernias, dysostosis multiplex, mucopolysaccharide excretion in the urine, and metachromatic staining in peripheral leukocytes and bone marrow. Various components of the MPS phenotype are also found in the mucolipidoses, glycoprotein storage disorders, and other lysosomal storage diseases. Detailed clinical and radiologic evaluation and identification of the type of MPS excreted in the urine help to narrow the diagnostic possibilities. Definitive diagnosis requires assay of specific enzymes in various tissues such as cultured skin fibroblasts.

Hurler's or MPS IH disorder is the prototype MPS. Virtually all the components of the phenotype mentioned above are present and expressed in a severe degree. Nasal congestion and grossly visible corneal clouding are early features. Excessive growth during the first year of life is followed by poor growth late in the course. Radiologic features include enlargement of the sella turcica with a distinctive "shoe-shaped" fossa, broadening and shortening of the long bones, and hypoplasia and beaking of the vertebrae in the lumbar area. The vertebral beaking gives rise to an accentuated kyphosis or gibbus deformity. Death occurs within the first decade; postmortem findings include hydrocephalus and cardiovascular disease with occlusion of the coronary arteries. The biochemical defect is α-iduronidase deficiency with accumulation of heparan sulfate and dermatan sulfate.

MPS IS, or Scheie's syndrome, a clinically distinct disorder with childhood onset but adult survival, is characterized by joint stiffness, corneal clouding, aortic regurgitation, and usually normal intelligence. Surprisingly, this much milder disorder is also the result of α-iduronidase deficiency; it is allelic with Hurler's syndrome, as shown by lack of cross-correction of enzyme activity in cocultures of skin fibroblasts. Phenotypes occur that are clearly intermediate between Hurler's and Scheie's syndromes. It is believed that patients with an intermediate phenotype represent genetic compounds with one Hurler's allele and one Scheie's allele. Although genetic compounds must occur, in any one case their existence is difficult to distinguish from still other mutations of intermediate severity.

Hunter's, or MPS II, syndrome is distinguishable from Hurler's phenotype by the absence of gross corneal clouding and the X-linked recessive inheritance. The infantile form resembles the Hurler's disease phenotype, and a milder form allows survival into adulthood.

The severe and mild forms may be allelic, since both are X-linked and share the same enzyme deficiency (iduronosulfate sulfatase).

Sanfilippo's mucopolysaccharidoses (MPS IIIA, IIIB, IIIC, and IIID) are distinguished by the accumulation of heparan sulfate without dermatan or keratan sulfate and by the marked central nervous system involvement with milder somatic involvement. Sanfilippo's mucopolysaccharidosis usually is diagnosed in the evaluation of mental retardation in childhood. Because the somatic features of this MPS are mild, the condition can be overlooked in the evaluation of an apparently isolated central nervous system problem. Death usually occurs during the second or third decade. The MPS III disorders are approximate genocopies. That is, four different enzyme deficiencies give rise to relatively indistinguishable clinical phenotypes with the same storage product. The four MPS III disorders can be diagnosed and distinguished by enzyme assay (Table 316-1).

Morquio's or MPS IV syndrome is distinguished by the absence of mental retardation and the presence of a distinctive bony dystrophy which can be classified as a spondyloepiphyseal dysplasia. Marked hypoplasia of the odontoid process can cause cervical dislocation and usually leads to some degree of spinal cord compression. Aortic regurgitation is frequent. The deficiency of N-acetylgalactosamine 6-sulfate sulfatase is the basis for this condition. Bone changes somewhat suggestive of Morquio's syndrome may also occur in β-galactosidase deficiency and in other forms of spondyloepiphyseal dysplasia. Maroteaux-Lamy's or MPS VI disorder is characterized by prominent osseous involvement, corneal clouding, and normal intellect. Allelic forms with variable severity but the same deficiency of arylsulfatase B (N-acetylhexosamine 4-sulfate sulfatase) have been described. MPS VII, or β-glucuronidase deficiency, has been described in only a few patients with a rather complete MPS phenotype. Extreme variability from a lethal infantile form to a mild adult disease occurs.

MULTIPLE SULFATASE DEFICIENCY Multiple sulfatase deficiency is a unique disorder, which, although autosomal recessive, is characterized by deficiency of five or more cellular sulfatases. Arylsulfatase A, arylsulfatase B, other mucopolysaccharide sulfatases, and a nonlysosomal steroid sulfatase are deficient in this condition. The clinical picture combines features of metachromatic leukodystrophy, an MPS phenotype, and ichthyosis. The last feature presumably relates to the steroid sulfatase deficiency which also occurs as an isolated X-linked enzyme deficiency characterized by abnormal parturition and ichthyosis. Biochemical studies of this condition should provide further insight into biochemical and clinical genetic heterogeneity.

MUCOLIPIDOSES Mucolipidosis is a general term for lysosomal storage diseases involving some combination of MPS, glycoprotein, oligosaccharide, and glycolipids. The category of mucolipidosis I probably can be abandoned since most or all of these patients actually have a specific glycoprotein storage disease.

Mucolipidosis II, or I-cell disease, is an early onset disorder with mental retardation and an MPS phenotype. The distinctive features are striking inclusions in cultured skin fibroblasts and markedly elevated serum levels of lysosomal enzymes. The disorder has an autosomal recessive basis and is now known to represent a defect in the posttranslational processing of lysosomal enzymes. Mucolipidosis III, or pseudo-Hurler's polydystrophy, is a milder disorder with many aspects of the MPS phenotype, particularly dysostosis multiplex. The disorder presents in the first decade with joint stiffness, the diagnosis of rheumatoid arthritis often being considered. The major handicaps are progressive physical disabilities, particularly claw hand deformity and hip dysplasia. Mild mental retardation is common. Aortic and/or mitral valvular disease is routinely present, although often not functionally significant. Survival into adult life with possible stabilization of the condition is characteristic, with greater disability in males than in females. Inclusions in cultured skin fibroblasts and elevation of serum lysosomal enzymes are essentially identical with the findings in mucolipidosis II, suggesting that these are allelic disorders. The primary defect in mucolipidosis II and III is deficiency of UDP-N-acetylglucosamine (GLcNAc):glycoprotein GLcNAc 1-phosphotransferase, an enzyme involved in posttranslational synthesis of the oligosaccharide portion of the lysosomal enzymes.

Mucolipidosis IV is a disorder with mental retardation, corneal clouding, and retinal degeneration without other somatic features. Diagnosis has been made primarily on electron-microscopic findings. A small number of patients, all of Ashkenazi Jewish origin, have been described. The disorder may be due to deficiency of a neuraminidase which is active against ganglioside substrates.

NEURONAL CEROID LIPOFUSCINOSES The neuronal ceroid lipofuscinosis disorders include a wide clinical spectrum with onset in childhood, juvenile, or adult periods. It is uncertain if these disorders are true lysosomal storage diseases, indeed whether single or multiple biochemical genetic disorders are present. The clinical features include central nervous system deterioration with cerebral atrophy, usually commensurate with degree of impairment. Seizures, particularly myoclonic jerks, are prominent. Ocular involvement with optic atrophy, retinitis pigmentosa, and macular degeneration is present in the infantile and juvenile disorders but often absent in adult forms. Autosomal recessive inheritance is likely in most instances. The neuropathologic findings form the basis for the descriptive term for the disease. Electron microscopy demonstrates abnormal inclusions within lysosomes throughout a wide variety of tissues, despite the rather isolated neurologic clinical involvement. The presence of curvilinear bodies, electron-dense material, and fingerprint profiles on electron microscopy of white blood cells, liver biopsy, or muscle biopsy can be helpful diagnostically.

OTHER LYSOSOMAL STORAGE DISEASES Glycogen storage disease type II (Pompe's disease) is the prototype lysosomal storage disease. The predominant clinical features of skeletal and cardiac myopathy are described in Chap. 313. Acid phosphatase deficiency and Farber's lipogranulomatosis are included in Table 316-1. Lactosyl ceramidosis appears to represent a variant of Niemann-Pick disease; in vitro hydrolysis of lactosyl ceramide is accomplished by those enzymes that are deficient in G_{M1} gangliosidosis or in Krabbe's disease, depending upon the in vitro conditions used. Reports of N-acetylglucosamine 6-sulfate sulfatase deficiency causing a type VIII mucopolysaccharidosis may be incorrect. Adrenoleukodystrophy is a distinct X-linked disorder with accumulation of long-chain fatty acid cholesteryl esters in tissues, but it may not represent a lysosomal storage disease. The recognition of females with the Hunter's MPS II phenotype and identical enzyme deficiency has raised the possibility of an autosomal recessive form of Hunter's syndrome. Such could occur if the enzyme in question had nonidentical subunits coded for by one autosomal and one X-linked gene or if regulatory genetic elements were invoked. On the other hand phenotypic manifestations in females could be caused by a variety of X-chromosome aberrations. One family has been described with G_{M3} gangliosidosis. This is not a lysosomal storage disease but does possibly represent a defect in ganglioside synthesis. The clinical features are similar to those seen in lysosomal storage diseases, but inconsistencies between siblings leave the question of whether this is a unique genetic disorder. Other neurodegenerative diseases may eventually become classifiable as lysosomal storage diseases. Disorders such as juvenile dystonic lipidosis, neuroaxonal dystrophy, Hallervorden-Spatz disease, Pelizaeus-Merzbacher disease, and other candidates exist. In addition, it is not unusual to identify patients with distinctive clinical features suggestive of lipidosis, mucolipidosis, or mucopolysaccharidosis, in which none of the present biochemically identifiable disorders can be identified. For these reasons, the number of distinct lysosomal storage diseases is likely to continue to increase.

REFERENCES

HERS HG, VAN HOOF F (eds): *Lysosomes and Storage Diseases*. New York, Academic, 1973

HIRSCHHORN R, WEISSMANN G: Genetic disorders of lysosomes, in *Progress in Medical Genetics*, AG Steinberg et al (eds). Philadelphia, Saunders, 1976, vol 1

Ho MW et al: Glycosphingolipid hydrolases: Properties and molecular genetics. Mol Cell Biochem 17:125, 1977

McKusick VA: *Heritable Disorders of Connective Tissue*, 4th ed. St Louis, Mosby, 1972

Stanbury JB et al (eds): *The Metabolic Basis of Inherited Disease*, 5th ed. New York, McGraw-Hill, 1983

Warner TG, O'Brien JS: Genetic defects in glycoprotein metabolism. Ann Rev Genet 17:395, 1983

317 OBESITY

JERROLD M. OLEFSKY

The ability to store food energy as fat provides survival value when the food supply is scarce or sporadic. Unlike glycogen or protein, triglyceride does not require water or electrolytes for storage purposes and can be retained essentially as pure fat; 1 g adipose tissue yields close to the full theoretical equivalent of 9 kcal. Because of the efficient storage of energy in adipose tissue, an individual of normal weight can survive up to 2 months of total starvation. However, western society is generally not characterized by periodic or insufficient food supply but rather by constant and abundant food. As a consequence, the ability to store fat all too frequently is of negative survival value because of overconsumption and the resulting obesity.

DEFINITION AND INCIDENCE Obesity can most easily be assessed in terms of height and weight. One way is to relate weight to an average range for height and age. This measure of *relative weight* can lead to an underestimation of the incidence of obesity, since in the United States the "average" individual is somewhat obese. Tables of *ideal* and *desirable* weight are based on actuarial estimates of what is consistent with normal life expectancy. Such tables are more useful if adjusted for differences in body build. An alternative method of estimating obesity is the *body mass index* or *BMI* [(body weight in kg) divided by (height in meters)^2]. For adults ages 20 to 29, the 85th percentile for BMI is 27.8 for males and 27.3 for females. Although relative weight and BMI correlate with the degree of adiposity, excess poundage can be either lean or fat tissue. For example, heavily muscled individuals would be considered obese with these measurements. Nevertheless, such assessments correlate fairly well with the risk of adverse effects on health and longevity. More precise assessment of obesity can be made with measurements of body density or with isotopic dilution methods, but these are unsuitable for routine use. Alternatively anthropometry can be utilized for assessing the degree of adiposity. Assessment of skin-fold thickness over various areas of the body together with height, weight, and age can be used to assess the degree of adiposity. Triceps and subscapular skin folds are most commonly employed (see Chap. 71). From a health standpoint, certain patterns of obesity may be less desirable than others. Fat deposition about the waist and flank, as evidenced by a high ratio of waist to hip circumference, is associated with a greater health risk than fat deposition at the hips.

The term *obesity* implies an excess of adipose tissue, but the meaning of excess is hard to define. Aesthetic considerations aside, obesity can best be viewed as any degree of excess adiposity that imparts a health risk. This cutoff between normal and obese can only be approximated. The Framingham Study demonstrated that a 20 percent excess over desirable weight imparted a health risk. A National Institutes of Health consensus panel on obesity agreed with this definition and concluded that a 20 percent increase in relative weight or a BMI above the 85th percentile for young adults constitutes a health risk; by use of these criteria 20 to 30 percent of adult men and 30 to 40 percent of adult women are obese. Significant health risks at lower levels of obesity can occur in the presence of diabetes, hypertension, heart disease, or other associated risk factors.

ETIOLOGY When caloric intake exceeds expenditure, the excess calories are stored in adipose tissue, and if this net positive caloric balance is prolonged, obesity results, i.e., there are two components to weight balance, and an abnormality on either side (intake or expenditure) can lead to obesity.

The regulation of eating behavior is incompletely understood. To some extent, appetite is controlled by discrete areas in the hypothalamus: a feeding center in the ventrolateral nucleus of the hypothalamus (VLH) and a satiety center in the ventromedial hypothalamus (VMH). The cerebral cortex receives positive signals from the feeding center that stimulate eating (Fig. 317-1), and the satiety center modulates this process by sending inhibitory impulses to the feeding center. In animals destruction of the feeding center results in decreased food intake, and destruction of the satiety center leads to overeating and obesity. Several regulatory processes may influence these hypothalamic centers. The satiety center may be activated by the increases in plasma glucose and/or insulin that follow a meal. It is of interest in this regard that the VMH contains insulin receptors and is insulin-sensitive. Meal-induced gastric distention is another possible inhibitory factor. The total adipose tissue mass may also influence the activity of the hypothalamic centers; i.e., there is a relatively fixed "set point" for body adiposity. An elevated set point may account for the frequent recidivism in obese patients who have lost weight. How the "set point" is established and how the hypothalamus senses total fat stores are unknown. Glycerol release from fat cells and ascending neural impulses may be signals of adipose tissue size. Additionally, the hypothalamic centers are sensitive to catecholamines, and beta-adrenergic stimulation inhibits eating behavior. This provides at least one rationale for the anorexiant effects of amphetamines.

Ultimately, the cerebral cortex controls eating behavior, and impulses from the feeding center to the cerebral cortex are only one input. Psychological, social, and genetic factors also influence food intake. In many obese subjects these influences are overriding; indeed, obese subjects usually respond to external signals such as time of day, social setting, and smell or taste of food to a greater extent than do persons of normal weight.

Although overeating is the usual cause of obesity, other factors may participate. Daily caloric needs range between 31 and 35 kcal per kilogram of body weight; this figure is higher in active and lower in sedentary individuals. Physical activity clearly modulates overall caloric balance, and obese individuals tend to be less active. This

FIGURE 317-1 *The regulation of eating. The ventromedial satiety center is considered to be inhibitory, and the ventrolateral feeding center stimulatory. See text for discussion.*

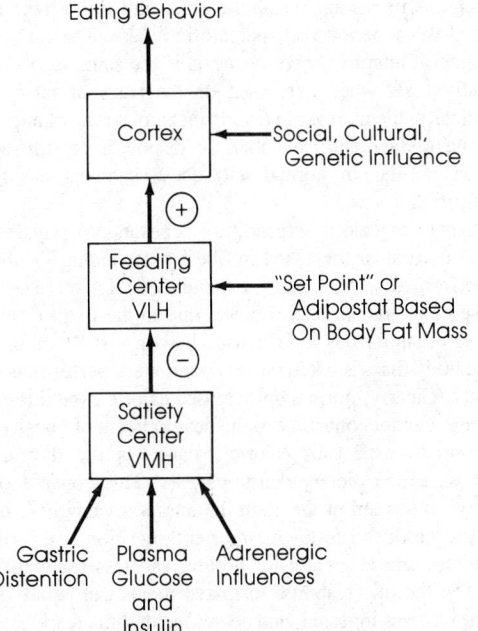

can be a contributory factor in the maintenance of excess weight, but decreased physical activity is unlikely to be an important cause of major weight gain in the most obese subjects. Rather, obesity leads to inactivity. The modest increase in weight that often accompanies the middle years may be related more directly to diminished physical activity. Injury or illness may lead to chronic restricted activity and predispose to weight gain unless caloric intake is appropriately curtailed. Perhaps the greatest factor tending to diminish the output side of the equation is simply a sedentary life-style.

Decreased caloric expenditure and a metabolic abnormality associated with overefficient caloric utilization have also been postulated to be involved in the pathogenesis of obesity. With rare exceptions major metabolic abnormalities have not been detected in obese individuals, although subtle defects may be undetected. There are three major components to overall energy expenditure: resting metabolic rate, exercise-induced thermogenesis, and the thermic response to food.

The resting metabolic rate accounts for 60 to 75 percent of daily caloric expenditure and is measured in a thermoneutral environment while the subject is at rest following an overnight fast and several hours after any significant physical activity. The resting metabolic rate should be expressed as a function of fat-free body weight (by subtracting the subject's total adipose mass from body weight), since triglyceride mass is metabolically inert. When expressed in this way, the resting metabolic rate is normal in most obese subjects. However, a distinction must be made between static obesity and the actual process of gaining weight. When normal subjects consume hypercaloric diets, less weight is gained than would be predicted on the basis of the excess calories ingested. This effect is most marked when carbohydrate is consumed and disappears when the excess calories consist of fat. Thus, humans can apparently partially adapt to chronic excessive carbohydrate and protein intake, and this protective effect attenuates the weight gain. Part of this adaptive response is related to an increase in thermogenesis manifested as an increase in the resting metabolic rate. The mechanism of adaptive thermogenesis is unknown, but overeating of carbohydrate or mixed nutrients leads to increased plasma levels of triiodothyronine (T_3) and decreased levels of reverse T_3 (rT_3). A converse effect is seen in starvation with decreased T_3 and increased rT_3 levels. The conversion of thyroxine to T_3 occurs largely in the liver; excess food may induce adaptive thermogenesis by increasing the concentration of T_3 relative to that of T_4 and rT_3. Increased central or peripheral sympathetic outflow leading to increased catecholamine-induced caloric utilization and increased heat production may also play a role in the thermogenic response to overnutrition. Adaptive thermogenesis can lead to a 10 to 15 percent increase in resting metabolic rate, and this effect is seen after a 2- to 3-week period of hypercaloric intake. The rate of onset and the degree of adaptive thermogenesis is the same in obese and nonobese individuals when expressed on the basis of fat-free body mass. Specifically, the increase in resting metabolic rate, changes in thyroid hormone metabolism, and thermic responses to infused catecholamines are similar in normal and obese subjects during periods of overnutrition.

Work performance, or caloric expenditure per standard physical work load, can be normal or increased in obesity depending on the kind of work performed. The energy expenditure of exercise is increased in obese compared to lean subjects due to the extra effort involved in moving or supporting an increased body mass. When this effect of increased body mass is taken into account, work performance is normal in obesity. Clearly, normal or increased caloric expenditure during physical work cannot contribute to the development of obesity.

The third important aspect of caloric balance is the thermic response to food, so-called dietary thermogenesis. This consists of the heat, or energy, expended in the assimilation and metabolism of foodstuffs. The heat produced following nutrient ingestion is a form of caloric expenditure and is greater for protein and less for carbohydrate and fat. The thermic response to mixed meals can equal 10 to 15 percent of the calories ingested, and decreased thermic responses

have been described in human obesity. This difference may be due to altered flux rates through different pathways of intermediary metabolism, with more energy-efficient pathways such as those leading to caloric storage being favored in obesity. As an example, the rate of glucose utilization is related to the extent of the thermic response to carbohydrate-containing meals, and small decreases in the thermic response to food may be due to insulin resistance and decreased glucose disposal in obese subjects. It is clear that small differences in caloric utilization maintained over years can lead to a significant net positive caloric balance. However, while it is tempting to postulate that this decreased thermic response may contribute to obesity, the published comparisons have been made between normal persons and subjects who are already obese. Thus, the obesity-associated changes in thermic response to food may be secondary to the obese state rather than a primary abnormality. More importantly, differences in the thermic response to meals between the obese and nonobese are at most in the range of 30 to 50 kcal per day. Such minor differences can easily be counterbalanced by minor decreases in food intake and/or increases in exercise-induced thermogenesis. Since such compensation does not occur, it seems more probable that obesity is the result of impaired coupling between caloric intake and expenditure.

Another potential regulatory process in the control of adipose tissue mass involves adipose tissue lipoprotein lipase (ATLPL). This enzyme is synthesized within adipocytes, secreted into the extracellular space, and attached to the luminal surface of nearby endothelial cells. At this location ATLPL hydrolyzes fatty acids from the triglycerides of circulating triglyceride-rich lipoproteins. The released fatty acids are taken up by adipocytes, converted to triglycerides, and stored. Thus, ATLPL participates in the storage of excess fat calories in adipose tissue. The *lipoprotein lipase hypothesis* holds that in some obese states excessive levels of this enzyme induce obesity by causing preferential deposition of fat calories in adipose tissue. In support of this hypothesis, ATLPL levels are increased in obese rodents and humans. More importantly, levels of this enzyme do not return to normal following weight reduction. This latter finding is of particular interest since it is one of the few characteristics of the obese state that is not corrected by weight reduction and could explain the propensity of obese patients to regain lost weight.

Certain types of obesity in animals have clear-cut genetic causes, but the role of genetic influences in most human obesity is difficult to evaluate because of confounding social and cultural factors.

SECONDARY OBESITY **Hypothyroidism** Obesity can result from hypothyroidism because of decreased caloric needs. However, only a minority of hypothyroid patients are truly obese, and an even smaller proportion of obese patients are hypothyroid. Indiscriminate use of thyroid hormone in the treatment of obesity is to be deplored and should never be instituted in the absence of documentation of decreased thyroid function.

Cushing's disease Cushing's disease is a rare cause of obesity. Hyperadrenocorticism elicits a typical pattern of obesity with predominantly centripetal fat stores, characteristic rounded or moon facies, and cervical or supraclavicular fat deposits.

Insulinoma Hyperinsulinemia, secondary to an insulinoma, can occasionally cause obesity, presumably because of increased caloric intake secondary to recurrent hypoglycemia. Most patients with islet-cell tumors and hypoglycemia are not obese.

Hypothalamic disorders Froehlich's syndrome in boys is characterized by obesity and hypogonadotrophic hypogonadism with other variable features such as diabetes insipidus, visual impairment, and mental retardation. The anterior pituitary is usually normal, and the syndrome is thought to be the result of hypothalamic dysfunction. This syndrome likely includes a number of overlapping disorders having in common hypothalamic lesion that leads to overeating and to hypogonadotrophism. Occasionally pituitary tumors are present (as in Froehlich's original case) which may physically impair the hypothalamus.

Other rare causes of obesity include the Laurence-Moon-Biedl syndrome characterized by retinitis pigmentosa, mental retardation, skull deformities, polydactyly and syndactyly, and the Prader-Willi syndrome which is associated with hypotonia, mental retardation, and a predilection for diabetes mellitus. Both of these disorders also feature obesity and hypogonadism that are thought to be hypothalamic in origin.

PATHOLOGIC SEQUELAE Increased adipose tissue stores are deposited subcutaneously, around all internal organs, throughout the omentum, and in the intramuscular spaces. Obese individuals also have an expansion of lean body mass as evidenced by increased size of the kidneys, heart, liver, and skeletal muscle mass. Fatty livers are common in extreme obesity.

Adipocyte size and number Attempts have been made to classify obese individuals on the basis of the relative degree of adipocyte hypertrophy versus hyperplasia. This classification scheme was generated as the result of experimental data indicating that in several rodent species and in humans the capacity to increase adipocyte number exists for only a limited period in early life and perhaps at the time of puberty. Thus, prior to reaching adulthood the ability to increase the number of adipocytes declines, and after this time expansion of adipose tissue mass is accompanied primarily by an increase in fat-cell size. Individuals with severe obesity have both increased adipocyte size and number, and those with the greatest degree of adipocyte hyperplasia have a strong tendency toward onset of obesity early in life. Patients having mild to moderate obesity show predominantly adipocyte hypertrophy, and the onset is usually during adult life. Weight reduction leads to a decrease in adipocyte size with no change in cell number. The above observations led to the concept of the existence of a "critical period" in early life when final adipocyte number is determined and after which cell number cannot be changed. This formulation implies that alterations in adipocyte number can only be induced during this critical period. However, the concept of a strictly defined critical period for hyperplasia of the adipocytes is only partially correct. When severe obesity is induced in adult rats, both adipocyte number and cell size increase. Adipocyte hypercellularity also occurs in some patients with adult-onset obesity.

Thus while substantial overnutrition at any stage of life can lead to hypertrophy of individual existing adipocytes, there are periods during childhood and adolescence when overnutrition has an enhanced ability to induce the development of new adipocytes. Furthermore, even in adult life, if the degree of overnutrition is sufficient to induce existing adipocytes to enlarge to some limiting size, then new adipocytes will form. Whether this latter population of cells represents new cell formation or simply the filling with lipid of previously undetectable preadipocytes formed earlier in life is not known. Regardless of the cause or time of development of increased adiposity (adipocyte hypertrophy with or without hyperplasia), subsequent weight reduction only leads to a decrease in the size of existing adipocytes and not a decrease in adipocyte number. Thus, once a given complement of adipocytes is attained, this number is fixed and cannot be reduced.

METABOLIC SEQUELAE Obesity has a profound impact on diabetes mellitus and on various hyperlipoproteinemic states primarily through its influences on insulin secretion and insulin sensitivity.

Hyperinsulinemia: Insulin resistance Increased insulin secretion is a common feature of obesity. It occurs in the basal state and in response to a wide variety of insulinogenic agents. A correlation exists between the degree of obesity and the magnitude of the hyperinsulinemia—particularly the basal insulin levels. Some obese patients exhibit hyperglycemia or frank diabetes in the face of hyperinsulinemia. The combination of hyper- or euglycemia and hyperinsulinemia indicates an insulin-resistant state, and decreased hypoglycemic responses to insulin are common in obese humans and animals. Insulin resistance could be due to an abnormal beta-cell product, circulating insulin antagonists, or tissue insulin insensitivity. Since abnormal islet secretory products or circulating antagonists have not been identified, it is thought that the insulin resistance of obesity is primarily due to tissue insensitivity. The initial step in the cellular action of insulin involves binding to cell surface receptors in target tissues. Cells from obese animals and humans contain decreased numbers of insulin receptors, and this decrease doubtless plays a role in the insulin resistance. However, other factors participate. The enlarged adipocytes of obese rats have both a decrease in insulin receptors and an even greater defect in the capacity to metabolize glucose, suggesting a major biochemical abnormality distal to the receptor mechanism. A similar postreceptor defect presumably exists in other insulin target tissues such as muscle and liver. In the obese human insulin resistance is due to a combination of receptor and postreceptor defects in insulin action. In those obese patients with the mildest degree of hyperinsulinemia and insulin resistance, the decrease in insulin action is predominantly due to a decreased number of insulin receptors. As the insulin-resistance state worsens, a postreceptor defect emerges, and in obese subjects with the most severe degree of insulin resistance, the postreceptor defect is the predominant abnormality.

Diabetes mellitus (see also Chap. 327) Although only a minority of obese patients are diabetic, the converse is not the case. Non-insulin-dependent, or type II, diabetes comprises about 90 percent of the diabetic population in the United States, and 80 to 90 percent of type II diabetics are obese. Obesity is an important contributory factor to the diabetes in these patients, predominantly through its influences on insulin resistance. Obesity exacerbates the diabetic state, and in many cases diabetes can be ameliorated by weight reduction.

Hyperlipoproteinemia (see also Chap. 315) Most plasma cholesterol circulates in the low-density lipoprotein (LDL) fraction, and, in the fasting state, very low density lipoproteins (VLDL) contain most of the circulating triglyceride. The association between obesity and elevated LDL levels is modest at best, especially when the relationship is corrected for factors such as age. Total body cholesterol is increased in obesity, but this is mainly accounted for by adipose tissue cholesterol stores. Cholesterol turnover may be increased, leading to increased biliary excretion of cholesterol. This may contribute to the increased incidence of gallstone formation. Obesity has a more pronounced effect on VLDL metabolism. Hypertriglyceridemia is frequent, and the degree of obesity correlates with the level of hypertriglyceridemia. The increased triglyceride levels are due to increased hepatic VLDL production with no defect in the removal of VLDL from plasma. As discussed above, plasma insulin levels are elevated, particularly in the portal venous blood. Hyperinsulinemia can promote increased hepatic VLDL synthesis and secretion. In addition, increased plasma free fatty acid (FFA) turnover exists in obesity, and FFA extraction by the liver provides an important precursor for hepatic triglyceride synthesis. Thus, the hypertriglyceridemia in obesity may be secondary to increased hepatic VLDL secretion due to hyperinsulinemia and augmented FFA availability.

MANIFESTATIONS AND COMPLICATIONS Gross obesity produces mechanical and physical stresses that aggravate or cause a number of disorders including osteoarthritis (especially the hips) and sciatica. Varicose veins, thromboembolism, ventral and hiatal hernias, and cholelithiasis are also more common.

Hypertension In significantly obese persons, use of the standard size blood pressure cuff leads to erroneously high readings; an oversize cuff should always be used. A strong association between hypertension and obesity is observed even when accurate measurements are obtained. The mechanism by which obesity causes hypertension is uncertain, but peripheral vascular resistance is usually normal while blood volume is increased. Weight loss leads to reductions in systemic blood pressure independent of changes in sodium balance.

Hypoventilation syndrome (Pickwickian syndrome)   The obesity-hypoventilation syndrome is a heterogeneous group of disorders with differing clinical manifestations. The hypersomnolence that can occur in obesity is a manifestation of nighttime sleep apnea. In these individuals, once sleep begins, upper airway obstruction leads to hypoxemia and hypercapnia, causing arousal with return of normal respiration. Many such episodes occur each night, leading to chronic sleep deprivation and daytime somnolence. The combination of the obese habitus plus sleep-induced relaxation of the pharyngeal musculature is believed to be the cause of the intermittent upper airway obstruction. Occasionally such episodes are life-threatening (causing serious cardiac arrhythmias) and require long-term tracheostomy therapy. Chronic daytime hypoventilation is usually not as severe as that occurring during sleep and may be due to abnormalities of the respiratory control centers. Patients with hypoventilation display blunted ventilatory responses to hypercapnia and hypoxia and often develop hypercapnia and hypoxemia due to decreased basal ventilation; in addition, ventilation-perfusion mismatch may result from mechanical factors. In severe cases polycythemia, pulmonary hypertension, and cor pulmonale can result. Weight reduction will reverse these abnormalities if instituted before permanent cardiac damage develops. Some obese patients with sleep apnea and hypersomnolence do not have daytime hypoventilation and have normal ventilatory responses to hypoxia and hypercapnia. Progestational agents have been used therapeutically in the obesity-hypoventilation syndrome since they stimulate the ventilatory response to hypercapnia and hypoxia in normal subjects. Medroxyprogesterone increases ventilation and improves heart failure and erythrocytosis in these patients, although obstructive sleep apnea continues.

Adrenal function   Although Cushing's disease can usually be distinguished from simple obesity on clinical grounds, laboratory testing is occasionally necessary. This can lead to confusion since 24-h urinary 17-hydroxycorticoid excretion is often elevated in obesity. Less commonly, plasma cortisol levels are also increased. Corticosteroid levels are usually suppressible with dexamethasone in obesity, but occasionally suppression is incomplete, rendering the diagnosis difficult (also see Chap. 325).

Growth hormone   Secretory responses of growth hormone to a variety of stimuli such as hypoglycemia, exercise, and arginine infusion are reduced, and the starvation-induced rise in plasma growth hormone levels is attenuated.

Atherosclerosis   Obesity is a risk factor for the development of coronary artery disease and stroke. Most of the risk is mediated through the associated hypertension, hyperlipoproteinemia, and diabetes. Nevertheless, even when these abnormalities are factored out, an additional, smaller risk can be ascribed to obesity per se.

TREATMENT   Amelioration of hyperinsulinemia, insulin resistance, diabetes, hypertension, and hyperlipidemia can occur following weight loss. These changes are significant and enduring provided the weight loss is maintained. During weight loss all adipose tissue depots diminish proportionately. Sometimes generalized loss does not produce the attractive cosmetic effects desired. Many techniques have been proposed to effect selective adipose tissue reduction over particular regions of the body, but none is effective.

Methods of weight reduction   In instances where obesity is secondary, the appropriate therapy is to treat the underlying disease. Most of the time the difficult problem of primary weight reduction must be undertaken.

Diet   Caloric restriction is the cornerstone of weight reduction. From the standpoint of patient and physician this is a frustrating and demanding undertaking. The basic principles are simple. If caloric intake is less than caloric expenditure, stored calories, predominantly in the form of fat, will be consumed. In general, a deficit of 7700 kcal leads to loss of about 1 kg fat. By estimating the patient's daily caloric needs (approximately 30 to 35 kcal per kilogram of body weight) one can calculate the daily deficit necessary to achieve a given rate of weight loss.

Dietary restriction can range from total starvation to mild caloric deprivation, and these approaches will be discussed separately. Dietary recommendations are most effective when they are specific and geared to the patient's life-style. A dietitian or a similarly trained health professional should interview each patient and estimate average daily caloric intake, identify food preferences, and characterize the eating patterns. The amount of calories to be consumed on the restricted diet should be carefully explained in terms of quantities of specific foodstuffs. Frequently, the therapist must balance the degree of restriction against potential noncompliance. The more restrictive the diet, the more rapid the weight loss, but this often leads to a greater rate of nonadherence. It is preferable to design a diet with which the patient is comfortable and that produces a modest but steady weight loss.

Schemes for weight reduction have become a multimillion-dollar business in the United States, and there are almost as many diets as there are therapists. Each proponent claims that the presence or absence of certain foodstuffs is desirable for more effective weight loss. However, little evidence exists to support the claim that calorie for calorie one hypocaloric diet will lead to a greater weight loss than another. The relationship between the patient and the therapist, plus patient education and encouragement, are more important to success than are the specific dietary constituents. The major virtue of "fad" diets is that patients are usually motivated to try them, at least initially, and patient cooperation is often better. Provided a particular diet is not harmful, probably the best course for the therapist is to maintain flexibility in the treatment program. Nevertheless, diets markedly deficient in any major class of foodstuff are to be avoided. For example, whole-food diets that are exceedingly low in carbohydrate are by nature high in fat and, depending on the type and quantity of fat ingested, may lead to hypercholesterolemia. The major virtue of a low-carbohydrate diet is the attendant ketosis (ketone bodies have a central anorexant effect). This provides part of the rationale for the widely touted liquid or powdered protein diets. These diets have been dubbed "protein-sparing modified fasts," and claims have been made that they allow drastic long-term caloric restriction without inducing negative nitrogen balance. These claims have not been substantiated, nor has it been shown that the diets lead to a greater degree of tissue weight loss than mixed diets of equal caloric value. Basically a calorie is a calorie whether it comes from protein, carbohydrate, or fat. Furthermore, deaths have been reported in otherwise healthy individuals participating in such long-term dietary programs, even under medical supervision. This has been attributed to the fact that some of these diets contain mostly protein of low biologic value. Other very low calorie diets involve formula preparations containing 350 to 800 kcal per day, with 40 to 80 g of high-quality protein. The remaining calories consist of carbohydrate and fat. Vitamin and micronutrient supplements are incorporated in the formula or provided as an added supplement. Such very low calorie diets lead to relatively rapid weight loss but should not be taken continuously as the sole caloric source for more than 6 weeks. In the absence of coexisting diseases such as gout, renal insufficiency, cardiac arrhythmias, etc., such diets are safe when taken under medical supervision.

Prior to therapy it is wise to warn patients that when caloric restriction is started there is usually a marked initial weight loss, in large part due to fluid loss, but that such rapid rates of loss will not persist. Likewise, positive shifts in fluid balance can sometimes mask loss of adipose mass, a fact that can sometimes be demonstrated to the patient's satisfaction by recording skin-fold thickness at periodic intervals.

Total-starvation diets have been advocated for the treatment of obesity; provided gout, renal insufficiency, and ketosis-prone diabetes are not present, short-term (2- to 3-day) fasts are usually well tolerated. Ketonemia and hyperuricemia regularly develop during starvation but rarely lead to acidosis or gout. Because of these potential complications, total fasting should be carried out only under medical supervision. Probably the major usefulness of total fasting is as a motivational aid at the beginning of a dietary program or when weight loss has stopped. Even though much of the weight loss during short-term fasting represents fluid, this weight loss can be encouraging to frustrated patients and motivate them to improve compliance with the long-term weight reduction program.

The major problem in the treatment of obesity is not weight reduction but maintenance of the reduced weight. Provided the therapist works hard and long enough, most motivated patients can eventually lose weight. Unfortunately, only the rare patient maintains the weight loss permanently. Obesity is an eating disorder, and the underlying mechanisms are not reversed by limiting food intake.

Behavior modification In recognition of the problems involved, the techniques of behavior modification have been devised to treat abnormal patterns of eating behavior. Many studies demonstrate that obese individuals respond less well than normal individuals to internal cues that regulate eating behavior such as gastric contractions, fear, and previous food ingestion. Conversely, obese subjects overrespond to external cues such as taste, smell, food attractiveness, food abundance, and the ease of obtaining food. Given the fact that the obese individual is unusually susceptible to external stimuli, food intake may be altered by changing the pattern and nature of these external cues, and this is the major premise underlying the behavior modification approach to weight reduction.

Behavior modification begins with a detailed individual history of the patient's eating patterns with respect to time of day, length of eating period, place of ingestion (restaurant, dining table, standing in front of open refrigerator), simultaneous activities (watching television, reading, idleness), emotional state, companions (relatives, friends, or alone), and finally the kinds and quantities of foods ingested. Once this detailed record is obtained, the therapist and patient can design specific behavioral changes aimed at disrupting or aborting recurring behavior patterns which initiate or prolong abnormal eating activity. As examples: if a patient eats in response to certain emotional states, then other activities can be substituted when the patient perceives such a state; if the patient snacks frequently from readily available food storage areas (refrigerators, cookie jars, etc.), then he or she is encouraged to eat only while sitting down at a table

with a fixed place setting; if eating frequently occurs while watching television alone, then efforts to avoid this activity can be initiated. Many other examples of specific and general interventions could be given. Results with behavior modification techniques indicate that many patients can maintain long-term weight reduction providing the new behavior patterns are truly "learned."

Exercise Exercise has a place in any weight reduction program. However, the importance of exercise in terms of caloric balance must be clearly understood. Even moderate daily exercise would not lead to a large enough increase in caloric expenditure to alter significantly the initial rate of weight reduction (Table 317-1). This does not mean exercise is unimportant in weight reduction, since even modest increases in caloric expenditure can lead to large long-term differences in caloric balance, provided exercise is performed on a regular basis. For example, a daily increase in caloric expenditure of 300 kcal over a period of 4 months could lead to a 4.5-kg weight loss. More importantly, incorporation of regular exercise into the overall weight reduction program improves the chances that the patient will maintain the weight loss.

Drugs Two classes of drugs are frequently used in the treatment of obesity: anorexants and thyroid hormone supplements. The addition of L-thyroxine or triiodothyronine to a weight reduction program is of no benefit. These drugs are ineffective in promoting adipose tissue loss and, if anything, accentuate lean tissue loss and cause negative nitrogen balance. In susceptible individuals, cardiotoxicity may occur. Thus, unless clear-cut hypothyroidism is present, thyroid supplementation has no role in the treatment of obesity.

The major anorexants are amphetamine-like agents that presumably exert their effect at the level of the hypothalamus. They probably have a modest effect in promoting short-term weight loss in some individuals. However, they are effective only for short periods, and problems of habituation, addiction, and generalized drug abuse limit their usefulness. Two anorexants, diethylpropion and fenfluramine, may be less addictive and, therefore, somewhat more useful. However, none of these agents treats the underlying eating disorder, and they are of little use in maintenance of weight reduction.

Injections of human chorionic gonadotropin (hCG) have been tried as an adjunct to weight reduction, but no evidence exists to indicate

TABLE 317-1 Energy equivalents of food calories expressed in minutes of activity

Food	Calories, kcal	Walking*	Riding bicycle†	Swimming‡	Running§	Reclining¶
Apple, large	101	19	12	9	5	78
Bacon, 2 strips	96	18	12	9	5	74
Beer, 1 glass	114	22	14	10	6	88
Bread and butter	78	15	10	7	4	60
Carbonated beverage, 1 glass	106	20	13	9	5	82
Carrot, raw	42	8	5	4	2	32
Cheese, cottage, 1 tbsp	27	5	3	2	1	21
Chicken, fried, ½ breast	232	45	28	21	12	178
Cookie, chocolate chip	51	10	6	5	3	39
Egg, fried	110	21	13	10	6	85
Ham, 2 slices	167	32	20	15	9	128
Ice cream, ⅙ qt	193	37	24	17	10	148
Mayonnaise, 1 tbsp	92	18	11	8	5	71
Milk, skim, 1 glass	81	16	10	7	4	62
Milk shake	421	81	51	38	22	324
Orange, medium	68	13	8	6	4	52
Pancake with syrup	124	24	15	11	6	
Peas, green, ½ cup	56	11	7	5	3	43
Pizza, cheese, ¼	180	35	22	16	9	138
Potato chips, 1 serving	108	21	13	10	6	83
Sandwiches:						
Hamburger	350	67	43	31	18	269
Tuna fish salad	278	53	34	25	14	214
Sherbet, ⅙ qt	177	34	22	16	9	136

* *Energy cost of walking for 70-kg individual = 5.2 kcal/min at 3.5 mph.*
† *Energy cost of riding bicycle = 8.2 kcal/min.*
‡ *Energy cost of swimming = 11.2 kcal/min.*
§ *Energy cost of running = 19.4 kcal/min.*
¶ *Energy cost of reclining = 1.3 kcal/min.*

a beneficial effect. The primary effectiveness of the hCG-diet program is due to the calorically restricted diet, frequent physician contact, and placebo effects. Comparable weight loss is achieved if saline injections are substituted for hCG, suggesting a placebo or physiologic effect of the act of parenteral injection.

Jejunoileal shunt   Small-bowel bypass is an effective means of achieving weight reduction in morbidly obese patients. However, it is an experimental procedure and should be attempted only in institutions where a trained team is committed to regular, systematic, and long-term follow-up.

The most common operative procedures involve end-to-end or end-to-side anastomosis of about 38 cm of proximal jejunum to 10 cm of terminal ileum. Weight loss is initially rapid, reaching a plateau at 18 to 24 months. While all patients lose weight, few return to ideal weight. The mean weight loss is about 30 to 50 percent of initial excess weight, leaving patients still about 50 percent overweight once a steady state is reached. Although some degree of malabsorption occurs, the major portion of the weight loss is due to decreased food intake.

Most teams performing this surgery select patients who are at least 50 kg overweight and in whom adequate attempts at medical management have failed repeatedly. Because of postoperative morbidity, older patients (>50 years) and psychologically unstable individuals are usually excluded.

The overall surgical mortality ranges from 0.5 to 7.8 percent with an average of around 4 percent. Mortality is inversely related to the experience of the surgical team. The major postoperative morbidity is related to wound infection and thromboembolism. The common serious medical complications are cirrhosis and hepatic failure, nephrolithiasis, electrolyte imbalances, cholelithiasis, and arthritis (Table 317-2). Severe liver disease probably occurs in 5 percent of patients, and milder degrees of hepatic dysfunction are more common. The long-range implications of mild hepatic abnormalities are unknown. Possible causes of liver damage following small-bowel bypass include (1) protein and particularly essential amino acid deficiency, (2) accumulation of hepatotoxic, secondary bile salts, and (3) release of unknown toxic substances from the excluded bowel. Hypokalemia

is most likely secondary to diarrhea. Persistent deficiency of calcium and magnesium can result from malabsorption and must be treated with appropriate replacement. Transient depression of plasma 25-hydroxyvitamin D levels may also contribute to abnormal mineral metabolism. Nephrolithiasis occurs in up to 30 percent of patients and is due to hyperoxaluria secondary to calcium malabsorption. It can be treated by calcium supplements and a low oxalate intake. Migratory polyarthritis occurs in up to 6 percent of patients and may be due to circulating immune complexes. This operation is now rarely performed, in part due to the decision of many insurance companies not to render compensation for this procedure.

Gastric surgery   Gastroplasty establishes a small upper gastric remnant connected to a larger lower gastric pouch by a narrow 1- to 1.5-cm channel. Gastric bypass excludes the lower 90 percent of the stomach pouch and maintains intestinal continuity of the upper 10 percent via a retrocolic gastrojejunostomy. Both of these procedures cause patients to limit food intake by delaying gastric emptying and providing a small gastric reservoir so that fullness is experienced after a small meal. Weight loss with these procedures is comparable with that achieved with small-bowel bypass operations but without the complications related to malabsorption, diarrhea, and hepatic dysfunction. The procedure can be reversed if a decision to restore normal anatomy is made at a later time. For these reasons, gastroplasty is frequently performed for the surgical treatment of morbid obesity, especially since the number of intestinal bypass procedures has decreased.

SUMMARY   For most patients obesity is an eating disorder, and a major hope for effective long-term treatment of this disease lies in understanding the causes of overeating. No single etiology explains all cases, and different causes exist for different individuals. At present a variety of techniques are available to effect initial weight loss. Unfortunately, initial weight loss is not the real therapeutic goal. Rather, the problem is that most obese patients eventually regain their weight. An effective means to sustain weight loss is the major challenge in the treatment of obesity today. The technique of behavioral modification, when professionally and rigorously applied, is the best tool for this task. As information develops concerning the hypothalamic "set point," or *adipostat*, and the factors that regulate it, other therapies may emerge that will effect long-term correction of abnormal eating patterns.

TABLE 317-2   Complications of bypass surgery

Complication	Percentage
EARLY	
Perioperative mortality	2–6
Thromboembolic disease	1–5
Wound infection	2–5
Renal failure	3
Severe nausea, vomiting	3
Wound dehiscence	1–3
LATE	
Urinary calculi	3–10
Severe electrolyte imbalance	5–8
Acute cholecystitis	0–5
Progressive liver disease	2–4
Intestinal obstruction	2
Peptic ulcer	1–2
Osteoporosis	?
Tuberculosis	1
MINOR	
Diarrhea	100
Weakness	80
Hypokalemia	80
Hypoproteinemia	50
Vomiting	50
Thirst	50
Hypocalcemia	30
Arthralgias	15
Incisional hernias	3
Hyperuricemia	<10
Anemias	<10

REFERENCES

ASSIMACOPOULOS-JEANNET F, JEANRENAUD B: The hormonal and metabolic basis of experimental obesity. Clin Endocrinol Metab 5:337, 1976

BRAY GA: Current status of intestinal bypass surgery in the treatment of obesity. Diabetes 26:1072, 1977

FOSTER DW: Eating disorders: Obesity and anorexia nervosa, in *Williams Textbook of Endocrinology,* 7th ed, JD Wilson, DW Foster (eds). Philadelphia, Saunders, 1985, p 1081

HASHIM SA, PORIKOS K: Food intake behavior in man: Implications for treatment of obesity. Clin Endocrinol Metab 5:503, 1976

HENRY RR et al: Metabolic consequences of very low calorie diet therapy in obese non-insulin dependent diabetic and non-diabetic subjects. Diabetes 35:155, 1986

HORTON ES, DANFORTH E JR: Energy metabolism and obesity, in *Diabetes Mellitus and Obesity,* SJ Bleicher, BN Brodoff (eds). Baltimore, Williams & Wilkins, 1981, p 261

KOLTERMAN OG et al: Mechanisms of insulin resistance in human obesity. Evidence for receptor and postreceptor defects. J Clin Invest 65:1272, 1980

MANN GV: The influence of obesity on health. N Engl J Med 291:226, 1974

NATIONAL INSTITUTES OF HEALTH CONSENSUS DEVELOPMENT PANEL ON THE HEALTH IMPLICATIONS OF OBESITY: Health implications of obesity. Ann Intern Med 103:147, 1985

OLEFSKY JM et al: Insulin action and insulin resistance in obesity and non-insulin dependent, type II diabetes mellitus. Am J Physiol 243:E15, 1982

SALANS L: The obesities, in *Endocrinology and Metabolism,* P Felig et al (eds). New York, McGraw-Hill, 1981, p 891

WOO R et al: Regulation of energy balance, in *Annual Review of Nutrition,* vol 5. Palo Alto, Annual Reviews Inc, 1985, pp 411–433

318 THE LIPODYSTROPHIES AND OTHER RARE DISORDERS OF ADIPOSE TISSUE

DANIEL W. FOSTER

This chapter is concerned with abnormalities in adipose tissue. The disorders are rare, the pathophysiology is frequently not clear, and only clinical descriptions can be given.

THE LIPODYSTROPHIES

The lipodystrophies are characterized by generalized or partial loss of body fat and metabolic abnormalities, including insulin resistance, hyperglycemia, and hypertriglyceridemia. A classification is shown in Table 318-1. In *generalized lipodystrophy* essentially all body fat is lost, while in *partial lipodystrophy* fat atrophy is limited. The common acquired form of partial lipodystrophy ordinarily involves half the body, usually the upper segment. Dominantly transmitted partial lipodystrophy tends to spare the face. One variant is associated with eye and tooth malformations, the Rieger anomaly. *Localized lipodystrophy* may be either inflammatory or noninflammatory. The best-studied syndrome is *centrifugal lipodystrophy* in which fat atrophy begins in the groins or axillae of children under the age of 3 and spreads centrally to involve the entire abdomen. The edge of the lesion is red and scaly with an inflammatory infiltrate demonstrable on histologic examination. Fat atrophy usually disappears spontaneously when the patient is around 13 years of age.

GENERALIZED LIPODYSTROPHY   Generalized lipodystrophy (also called lipoatrophic diabetes) may be either congenital or acquired. The congenital form is transmitted as an autosomal recessive trait. Males and females are equally affected. Rates of parental consanguinity are high. Loss of fat is usually obvious at birth, but the rest of the clinical picture may not appear until later (up to 30 years). The acquired disease often develops after some other illness. Measles, chicken pox, whooping cough, or infectious mononucleosis are common precipitating events, but hypothyroidism, hyperthyroidism, and pregnancy have been implicated. Some cases begin with the appearance of painful nodular swellings of adipose tissue resembling acute panniculitis (see below). The congenital and acquired forms are similar in clinical manifestations (Table 318-2).

Fat atrophy   Loss of body fat is the characteristic feature. In congenital cases the skin of the face is tightly drawn over the bony structures, and the entire body is devoid of adipose tissue. Rarely, a small amount of breast fat remains. In the acquired form the face may be spared, but all other fat disappears. Adipose tissue cells can be identified microscopically, but they contain no triglyceride stores. Paradoxically the liver is engorged with fat, and the reticuloendothelial system contains lipid-laden macrophages (foam cells). The cause of the fat atrophy is not known. Fat-mobilizing polypeptides have been reported in the urine of patients with generalized lipodystrophy, but their role in the disease is uncertain.

A candidate molecule for the induction of lipodystrophy is a compound similar to cachectin (tumor necrosis factor), which has powerful inhibitory effects on lipoprotein lipase and results in fat depletion and hypertriglyceridemia when injected into animals. Lipoprotein lipase activity is low in generalized lipodystrophy, as would be predicted if a cachectin-like inducer were the cause. Hepatic lipase is not impaired. Since triglyceride content of the adipocyte is the result of a balance between fat synthesis and fat breakdown, an alternative mechanism might involve activation of the hormone-sensitive lipase that catalyzes hydrolysis of triglycerides in the fat cell. For example, a defect in a natural inhibitor of the lipase, such as adenosine, could result in enhanced response to physiologic (nonelevated) concentrations of lipolytic hormones. Release of free fatty acids into plasma following norepinephrine infusion is impaired, but this may simply reflect the depleted triglyceride stores.

Although an inducing molecule could act as a circulating hormone in generalized lipodystrophy, such an etiology is unlikely in partial lipodystrophy where autotransplantation of adipocytes from an affected area to a nonaffected site resulted in reaccumulation of fat, and reverse transplantation from normal to affected site resulted in fat atrophy. An autocrine or paracrine function may be involved. In the former a cellular product would act on the cell of origin while in the latter a cellular product would act on adjacent cells, but in neither case would the putative inducer of lipodystrophy enter the circulation to act as a typical hormone.

Growth and maturation   Linear growth is accelerated in the first few years of life in the congenital disorder and in acquired disease that begins early in childhood. Epiphyses close early, however, so that the final height is usually normal. True muscular hypertrophy is present, and patients may have an acromegalic appearance with coarse facial features and large hands and feet. The ears tend to be prominent in the congenital form. Many viscera are enlarged, and generalized lymphadenopathy may be present. The cause of the growth disorder is not known. Levels of growth hormone and insulin-like growth factor I (IGF-I/SM-C) are normal or low. Insulin-like growth factor II has not been systematically assessed. One possibility is that abnormal growth and pseudoacromegaly are due to high concentrations of insulin in plasma secondary to insulin resistance (see below). The elevated insulin might cross-react with the IGF-I/SM-C receptor in muscle and cartilage and promote growth via this mechanism.

Liver   Enlargement of the liver causes protuberance of the abdomen. Fatty liver may progress to cirrhosis, especially in the acquired disorder. Several patients have died from bleeding esophageal varices. Splenomegaly does not occur in the absence of portal hypertension.

Kidneys   The kidneys are usually enlarged. Subjects with the acquired disorder may have proteinuria and the nephrotic syndrome, although not as frequently as in partial lipodystrophy. Moderate hypertension is common.

Genitalia   The external genitalia (penis and testes in males, clitoris and labia majora in females) are usually hypertrophied in congenital disease. In women polycystic ovaries are common, resulting in the clinical picture of Stein-Leventhal syndrome. The cause of the genital abnormalities is not known. Systematic investigation of gonadotropin, estrogen, and androgen metabolism has not been carried out.

Skin   Acanthosis nigricans is present in most. Hypertrichosis of face, neck, trunk, and limbs is frequent. Scalp hair is usually thick and curly, particularly early in life.

Central nervous system   Mental retardation is present in about half the congenital cases. Dilatation of the third ventricle and basal cisterns has been demonstrated by pneumoencephalography. Central nervous system involvement appears to be less marked in the acquired disease, although two patients had astrocytomas arising in the floor of the third ventricle. Few patients have been examined with computerized tomography or magnetic resonance imaging.

TABLE 318-1   The lipodystrophies

1 Generalized lipodystrophy
   a Congenital (familial or sporadic)
   b Acquired (sporadic)
2 Partial lipodystrophy
   a Common (sporadic)
   b Dominant (familial)
      (*1*) Limb and trunk
      (*2*) With Rieger anomaly
3 Localized lipodystrophy
   a Inflammatory
   b Noninflammatory

TABLE 318-2 Characteristics of the lipodystrophies

Finding	Congenital general	Acquired general	Acquired partial	Dominant partial
Inheritance	Autosomal recessive	Sporadic	Usually sporadic	Autosomal dominant
Age of onset	Infancy	Childhood to adult	Childhood to adult	Puberty
Sex incidence	Males and females equal	Female preponderance	Female preponderance	Female preponderance
Lipoatrophy	Face, trunk, limbs	Face, trunk, limbs	Face, upper trunk, upper limbs	Trunk and limbs
Liver involvement	+	+ +	Rare	0
Renal disease	+	+	+ +	0
Insulin resistance	+	+	+	+
Hyperglycemia	+	+	+	+
Hypertriglyceridemia	+	+	+	+
Acanthosis nigricans	+	+	Rare	+
Genital hypertrophy	+	+	Rare	+
Bone age	Accelerated	Normal to accelerated	Normal	Normal

Other abnormalities Bones tend to be sclerotic in generalized lipodystrophy, and cystic angiomatosis may be present. Cardiomegaly is common, but heart failure appears to be rare. Goiter is frequent. The associated abnormalities in generalized lipodystrophy are summarized in Table 318-3.

Metabolic and endocrine abnormalities Three major metabolic disturbances are characteristic.

1 *Severe insulin resistance with hyperglycemia.* Insulin resistance may be mild or severe. Insulin and C-peptide concentrations are relatively or absolutely elevated, and response to exogenous insulin is impaired. Resistance is due to several causes, and affected siblings may exhibit different mechanisms. Increased insulin clearance, decreased number of insulin receptors, diminished affinity of the receptor for insulin, and postreceptor defects have all been reported. Insulin in the plasma of affected subjects is biologically active. Although glucagon levels are high (indicating insulin resistance in the alpha cell of the islets of Langerhans) and free fatty acid concentrations are elevated, ketoacidosis is unusual. One patient had recurrent epidoses of metabolic acidosis considered to be ketoacidosis, but concentrations of acetoacetate and β-hydroxybutyrate were characteristic of fasting ketosis, not ketoacidosis; presumably lactate or other organic acids were involved.

Ketoacidosis may be infrequent because insulin resistance spares liver and skeletal muscle (or is less severe); glycogen levels in the liver are high (insulin stimulates glycogen synthesis), and branched-chain amino acids fall normally in response to injected insulin. Elevated insulin levels in portal vein plasma would counteract the actions of glucagon in the insulin-responsive hepatocyte. This would prevent activation of the ketone body synthesis in liver and assure utilization of incoming fatty acids for triglyceride synthesis and production of very low density lipoproteins. The elevated long-chain fatty acids in the plasma are of dietary origin and fall toward normal with restriction of dietary fat. The diabetes mellitus accompanying lipodystrophy appears to be typical apart from insulin resistance, including the propensity to develop late degenerative complications.

2 *Hypertriglyceridemia with accumulation of both chylomicrons and very low density lipoproteins in the blood.* Eruptive xanthomas, lipemia retinalis, and recurrent pancreatitis may be seen. Although lipoprotein lipase is low, as noted, and there is a defect in disposal of triglycerides in the atrophied fat tissue, the major cause for the hypertriglyceridemia is overproduction of very low density lipoproteins (VLDL) in the liver. This overproduction is probably driven by the elevated free fatty acids in blood since dietary fat restriction results in a fall of VLDL production rates toward normal. Hyperinsulinemia may contribute by enhancing hepatic fat synthesis.

3 *A hypermetabolic state with normal thyroid function.* Basal metabolic rates are usually elevated although thyroid hormone values (thyroxine, triiodothyronine, reverse triiodothyronine) are normal. Patients do not gain weight with excessive caloric intake, indicating a facile capacity to waste calories as heat. Food intakes as high as 5000 kcal per day are not unusual. One 16-month-old child ate 2400 kcal/day. Following thyroidectomy in one patient, the basal metabolic rate decreased but did not return to normal; symptoms and signs of hypothyroidism supervened requiring treatment with thyroid hormone despite continued high metabolic rates. It thus seems clear that hypermetabolism is not due to hyperthyroidism. There is also no evidence of mitochondrial disease. Abnormal dietary thermogenesis is the likely cause of the increased metabolic rate. Metabolic rates are increased by fat, carbohydrate, and protein in the diet, but protein is the most important. There is no evidence for adrenal medullary dysfunction.

Course and treatment Patients with generalized lipodystrophy may die at an early age. Hepatic failure, hemorrhage from esophageal varices, and renal failure are common causes of death. Despite the almost constant hypertriglyceridemia, symptomatic coronary artery disease is rare. There is no specific treatment for lipodystrophy, although moderate caloric and fat restriction (sufficient to maintain weight) is generally recommended. Medium-chain triglyceride supplementation has been reported to be of benefit. Pimozide therapy, hypophysectomy, and plasmapheresis are ineffective.

ACQUIRED PARTIAL LIPODYSTROPHY This is the most common of the lipodystrophies and usually affects women. Fat atrophy occurs in the upper half of the body, including the face, but spares the lower extremities. Rarely the lower half of the body is affected, leaving the upper torso intact. Occasionally the lesion affects only one side. The other anatomic features of generalized lipodystrophy are usually absent, and liver disease is unusual. Proteinuria, with or without the nephrotic syndrome, occurs more frequently than in other forms. The complement system is abnormal, and C3 levels tend to be low. C3 nephritic factor, a polyclonal IgG immunoglobulin that interacts with alternative pathway convertase to augment C3 activation, is present in serum. C3 levels may be low in unaffected first-degree relatives, but C3 nephritic factor is absent. Complement abnormalities disappeared after renal transplantation in one subject. Dermatomyositis and Sjögren's syndrome may occur. Rarely partial lipodystrophy progresses to the generalized form of the disease.

LIPODYSTROPHY WITH DOMINANT TRANSMISSION This variant is characterized by fat atrophy of the limbs and trunk with sparing of the face, which may actually be rounded. The neck may also be exempt. The disease usually begins at puberty but may not appear until middle age. Males are rarely affected. In families with the Rieger anomaly onset tends to be in infancy. Insulin resistance and hyperglycemia are usual, and severe hypertriglyceridemia with eruptive xanthoma may occur. The labia majora are hypertrophied, and polycystic ovaries may be seen. Acanthosis nigricans is usually present. Liver and renal disease do not occur.

TABLE 318-3 Accompanying abnormalities of lipodystrophy

Bone	Sclerosis, cystic angiomatosis
Brain	Mental retardation, third ventricle dilatation
Genitalia	Clitoromegaly, polycystic ovaries, penile hypertrophy
Heart	Cardiomegaly
Kidneys	Hypertrophy without renal failure
Liver	Hepatomegaly, fatty liver, cirrhosis, hepatic failure
Lymph nodes	Generalized lymphadenopathy
Skin	Acanthosis nigricans, hypertrichosis
Thyroid	Goiter, euthyroid state

MULTIPLE SYMMETRIC LIPOMATOSIS

Multiple symmetric lipomatosis, a disease found predominantly in men, is characterized by formation of multiple nonencapsulated lipomas in various areas. Two patterns of distribution are noted. In the *type I* variant, lipomas are primarily in the nape of the neck and in the supraclavicular and deltoid regions, resulting in an extraordinary bull-necked appearance (*Madelung collar*). Extension into the mediastinum may produce obstruction of the trachea or vena cava. Fat over the remainder of the body appears normal. In the *type II* pattern, lipomas are not localized to the neck but extend down over the body giving the appearance of simple obesity. Correct diagnosis requires recognition that the fat masses are symmetric and that the distal arms and legs are spared. Deep lipomatosis is absent in type II disease, and vena caval and tracheal compression do not occur.

Multiple symmetric lipomatosis may occur sporadically or in families. Autosomal dominant transmission has been postulated in the latter. Alcoholism is common. Coexisting folate deficiency, macrocytic anemia, and abnormal liver function may be due to alcohol and not lipomatosis. Neuropathy, which may be sensory, motor, or autonomic, is prominent, and neuropathic foot ulcers may be present.

Metabolic abnormalities include hyperuricemia, hypertriglyceridemia (VLDL, chylomicrons) and, paradoxically, an elevation of high-density lipoproteins (HDL) as well. Diabetes has not been reported, although hyperinsulinism may be present. A few patients have had renal tubular acidosis.

The cause of multiple symmetric lipomatosis is not known. The fat cells are slightly smaller than normal, suggesting hyperplasia. Isolated adipocytes appear to have a marked increase in lipoprotein lipase activity and a defect in adrenergic lipolysis. Lipolytic response to cyclic AMP is intact, suggesting an abnormality at the hormone receptor/adenylate cyclase unit. The biochemical abnormalities are not present in all cases.

There is no treatment except for surgical removal of lipomas that cause compression. They may also be removed for cosmetic reasons.

MEDIASTINO-ABDOMINAL LIPOMATOSIS

This syndrome may be a variant of multiple symmetric lipomatosis. The features include (1) exertional dyspnea due to compression of airways by lipomas of the mediastinum, (2) massive enlargement of the abdomen (pseudoascites) due to intraperitoneal and retroperitoneal fat, and (3) abnormal glucose tolerance or diabetes mellitus. The metabolic abnormalities and enzymic changes in adipocytes are identical with those in multiple symmetric lipomatosis except that HDL levels are not elevated.

ACUTE PANNICULITIS (NODULAR FAT NECROSIS)

The appearance of single or multiple crops of tender nodules in subcutaneous fat with a histologic picture of fat-cell necrosis, infiltration of inflammatory cells, and development of fat-filled macrophages (foam cells) is the hallmark of acute panniculitis. The nodules range in size from 0.5 to 10 cm and may be firm or fluctuant. They are usually, but not always, tender. On occasion they drain an oily solution, and suppuration may occur. Individual lesions last from 1 to 8 weeks before disappearing, and a pigmented depressed area may be left at the involved site. While some patients have only nodular panniculitis, which may or may not be relapsing, others develop fever, abnormal liver function, involvement of the bone marrow with leukemoid response, bleeding tendencies, nodular pulmonary lesions, and evidence of pancreatic disease with elevated plasma amylase and lipase levels. In the past this constellation of findings was called *Weber-Christian disease*. However, since painful or nonpainful panniculitis may result from a variety of conditions, Weber-Christian disease is not a specific entity, and the term should probably be abandoned.

It is not possible to develop a firm classification of acute panniculitis

since the lesions may appear in sporadic fashion with many conditions. One classification system is given in Table 318-4.

Panniculitis without systemic disease is usually due to trauma (sometimes factitiously induced) or cold. For example, in equestrian cold panniculitis the lesions appear in the outer thighs of persons riding horseback for several hours in icy weather. One variant, subcutaneous fat necrosis of the newborn, may be due to a combination of obstetric trauma and hypothermia.

Panniculitis with systemic disease can be divided into several large categories. Collagen vascular disease is a frequent cause, although few patients with connective tissue disorders develop this complication. Lupus is probably most common, and scleroderma is second. About 2 to 3 percent of patients with lupus have nodular fat necrosis; it is more common in discoid lupus than in the systemic variant. Lymphomas and histiocytosis represent a second category. Cytophagic histiocytic panniculitis, an illness characterized by severe hemorrhagic diathesis and high mortality rates, may occur in association with lymphoma or as a separate disease. Deficiencies of α_1-antitrypsin have been found in a number of patients with acute panniculitis. It is postulated that the α_1-antitrypsin deficiency predisposes to panniculitis secondary to trauma and induces a hyperactive immune response. Severe pancreatic disease may also cause acute panniculitis. One distinct syndrome has been called *disseminated fat necrosis* and is described below. Finally, panniculitis may be associated with generalized lipodystrophy, especially the acquired type.

Acute panniculitis can be diagnosed only histologically. Once the lesion is identified a search for the cause must be made. If systemic symptoms are present and the course is rapidly downhill, the primary differential diagnosis is between collagen vascular disease, lymphoproliferative disorder, and pancreatitis or pancreatic cancer. Milder cases raise the possibility of α_1-antitrypsin deficiency.

Treatment is unsatisfactory, but steroids and immunosuppression may be tried.

DISSEMINATED FAT NECROSIS

Disseminated fat necrosis (also called metastatic fat necrosis) is a syndrome in which patients with pancreatitis (two-thirds) or carcinoma of the pancreas (one-third) develop lesions that appear to be similar to or identical with nodular panniculitis. The fat necrosis has a predilection for periarticular sites. Fever is almost invariably present. Arthritis occurs in about 60 percent of cases and may be severe, resulting in destruction of the joint. Often there are sinus tracts running from the site of subcutaneous fat necrosis into the joint space, leading to deposition of necrotic material. Lytic bone lesions may underlie the site of fat necrosis. Polyserositis and vasculitis may be present. Since complement levels are low and immunofluorescent staining shows deposition of complement and IgG, the syndrome resembles, in some respects, lupus-associated panniculitis. Serologic studies for lupus have not been systematically carried out. Antinuclear antibody (ANA) and rheumatoid factor were negative in one patient.

Disseminated fat necrosis may be due to release of pancreatic enzymes into blood or lymph, and these enzymes may initiate fat necrosis at distal sites. Presumably free fatty acids released by pancreatic lipase and phospholipase A, both of which may be elevated in serum, induce tissue necrosis, with trypsin playing an ancillary role. Necrosis in pericardial, subpleural, and subcutaneous fat can be produced by ligation of pancreatic ducts, and amylase and lipase

TABLE 318-4 Causes of panniculitis

1 Panniculitis without systemic disease
  a Trauma
  b Cold
  c Subcutaneous fat necrosis of the newborn
2 Panniculitis with systemic disease
  a Connective tissue disorders (lupus erythematosus, scleroderma)
  b Lymphoproliferative disease (lymphoma, histocytosis)
  c α_1-Antitrypsin deficiency
  d Pancreatic disease (cancer, pancreatitis)
  e Generalized lipodystrophy

levels may be elevated in pleural, pericardial, and ascitic fluid. These enzymes have also been found in fluid aspirated from subcutaneous nodules. A fistula developed between a pancreatic pseudocyst and the portal vein in one patient; shortly thereafter nodular fat necrosis appeared over most of the body. On the other hand an immune mechanism may be causal, given that polyserositis is common and that low complement levels and vasculitis may be present. The meaning of the eosinophilia that frequently accompanies disseminated fat necrosis is not known.

Mortality rates are high (even in the absence of pancreatic carcinoma), and death may occur in weeks to months. No treatment is known. Infusion of the protease inhibitor aprotinin appeared to have beneficial effects in one patient.

ADIPOSIS DOLOROSA

Adiposis dolorosa (Dercum's disease) is characterized by painful circumscribed adipose tissue deposits in subcutaneous tissues of the extremities and of other parts of the body. Juxtaarticular areas, particularly the knees, are the most common sites. Lesions vary from 0.5 to 5.0 cm. Pain and paresthesias may occur spontaneously or result from pressure. Affected subjects are frequently women (30:1). They are usually obese. The syndrome is associated with weakness, fatigue, emotional instability, and occasional dementia and rarely begins until after menopause. Most cases are sporadic, but familial occurrence has been noted with a presumed dominant inheritance. Multiple associations have been reported, but they are probably chance phenomena. Autopsy reports from early in the century suggested abnormalities of the pituitary and other endocrine glands, but modern endocrinologic evaluations have not been undertaken.

Biopsy of affected sites may show no abnormalities, but granulomas with giant cell formations are usually seen. Fat necrosis is rare, thus separating the condition from acute panniculitis.

Treatment is unsatisfactory, although intravenous lidocaine has apparently provided relief in two cases.

REFERENCES

Lipodystrophy

AARSKOG D et al: Autosomal dominant partial lipodystrophy associated with Rieger anomaly, short stature, and insulinopenic diabetes. Am J Med Genet 15:29, 1983

BEUTLER B et al: Purification of cachectin, a lipoprotein lipase-suppressing hormone secreted by endotoxin-induced raw 264.7 cells. J Exp Med 161:984, 1985

DUNNIGAN MG et al: Familial lipoatrophic diabetes with dominant transmission: A new syndrome. Q J Med 43:33, 1974

FRANKLIN B et al: Very low-density lipoprotein metabolism in an unusual case of lipoatrophic diabetes. Metabolism 33:814, 1984

LILLYSTONE D, WEST RJ: Lipodystrophy of limbs associated with insulin resistance Arch Dis Child 50:737, 1975

SEIP M: Generalized lipodystrophy, in Ergebnisse der Inneren Medizin und Kind kunde, P Frick et al (eds). Berlin, Springer Verlag, 1971, pp 59–95

SOLER NG et al: Lipoatrophic diabetes: Endocrine dysfunction and the response to control of hypertriglyceridemia. Metabolism 31:19, 1982

WACHSLICHT-RODBARD H et al: Heterogeneity of the insulin-receptor interaction in lipoatrophic diabetes. J Clin Endocrinol Metab 52:416, 1981

WILSON DE et al: Eucaloric substitution of medium chain triglycerides for dietary long chain fatty acids in acquired total lipodystrophy: Effects on hyperlipoproteinemia and endogenous insulin resistance. J Clin Endocrinol Metab 57:517, 1983

Multiple symmetric lipomatosis

ENZI G: Multiple symmetric lipomatosis: An updated clinical report. Medicine 63:56, 1984

Mediastino-abdominal lipomatosis

ENZI G et al: Mediastino-abdominal lipomatosis: Deep accumulation of fat mimicking a respiratory disease and ascites. Clinical aspects and metabolic studies in vitro. Q J Med 53:453, 1984

Acute panniculitis

ARONSON IK et al: Panniculitis associated with cutaneous T-cell lymphoma and cytophagocytic histiocytosis. Br J Dermatol 112:87, 1985

BLEUMINK E, KLOKKE HA: Protease-inhibitor deficiencies in a patient with Weber-Christian panniculitis. Arch Dermatol 120:936, 1984

WINKELMANN RK: Panniculitis in connective tissue disease. Arch Dermatol 119:336, 1983

Disseminated fat necrosis

PHILLIPS MR JR et al: Inflammatory arthritis and subcutaneous fat necrosis associated with acute and chronic pancreatitis. Arthritis Rheum 23:355, 1980

WILSON HA et al: Pancreatitis with arthropathy and subcutaneous fat necrosis. Evidence for the pathogenicity of lipolytic enzymes. Arthritis Rheum 26:121, 1983

Adiposis dolorosa

ATKINSON RL: Intravenous lidocaine for the treatment of intractable pain of adiposis dolorosa. Int J Obes 6:351, 1982

---

319   HERITABLE DISORDERS OF CONNECTIVE TISSUE

DARWIN J. PROCKOP

Heritable disorders of connective tissues are among the most common genetic diseases. The most general in their manifestations are osteogenesis imperfecta (OI), Ehlers-Danlos syndrome (EDS), and Marfan's syndrome.

The usual classification of OI, EDS, and Marfan's syndrome is based on the work of McKusick, who analyzed signs, symptoms, and pathologic changes in a large number of patients. Such an attempt to classify the diseases is complicated by their heterogeneity. For example, some families lack one or more of the cardinal features of a disease. Other families have features characteristic of two or three different diseases. Heterogeneity may also exist among members of the same family. For example, some individuals from one family can have joint dislocations characteristic of EDS, other members can have increased brittleness of bone characteristic of OI, and still others with the same gene defect can be asymptomatic. Because of these problems, classifications based upon clinical features will eventually be replaced by analyses based upon molecular defects in specific genes.

ORGANIZATION AND CHEMICAL COMPOSITION OF CONNECTIVE TISSUES   Connective tissues are loosely defined as the extracellular components that provide the structural support of the body and bind together its cells, organs, and tissues. The major connective tissues are bone, skin, tendons, ligaments, and cartilage. The term is also applied to blood vessels and to synovial spaces and fluids. Indeed, all organs and tissues contain connective tissue in the form of membranes and septa.

Connective tissues contain large amounts of fluid in the form of a filtrate of blood that includes about half the body albumin. Most connective tissues are filled with, or surrounded by, fibrils or fibers of collagen (Table 319-1). Most connective tissues also contain proteoglycans.

To a degree, the differences among connective tissues are due to subtle differences in the size and orientation of collagen fibrils. In tendons collagen fibrils are packed into thick, parallel bundles of fibers. In skin the collagen fibrils are oriented more randomly. In bone, the fibrils are organized into an orderly architecture around the haversian canals that is made rigid by the presence of hydroxyapatite. The principal collagen of tendons, skin, and bone, type I collagen, comprises two polypeptide chains that are the products of different structural genes. The differences among these tissues are in large part due to differences in how the structural genes for type I collagen are expressed, namely, how much collagen is synthesized, the thickness and length of the fibrils formed, and how the fibrils are oriented.

Some of the differences among connective tissues reflect the presence of tissue- or organ-specific gene products. Bone contains proteins that have a critical role in the mineralization of the collagen. Aorta contains elastin and an associated microfibrillar protein, several different types of collagen, and other components. The basal lamina found beneath all epithelial and endothelial cells contains type IV collagen and other tisse-specific macromolecules. Skin and several other connective tissues contain small amounts of additional kinds of collagen.

BIOSYNTHESIS OF CONNECTIVE TISSUE The synthesis of connective tissues involves the self-assembly of molecular subunits of the correct size, shape, and surface properties. In the case of collagen, the molecule is a long, thin rod comprising three α-polypeptide chains wrapped into a rigid, ropelike structure (Fig. 319-1). Each α chain has a simple, repetitive amino acid sequence in which glycine (Gly) appears as every third amino acid. Since each α chain has about 1000 amino acids, the amino acid sequence of each α chain can be designed as (-Gly-X-Y-)$_{333}$, where X and Y represent amino acids other than glycine. It is essential that every third amino acid be glycine, the smallest amino acid, since this residue must fit in a sterically restricted space where the three chains of the triple helix come together. Two of the α chains in type I collagen are identical and are called α1(I). One has a slightly different amino acid sequence and is called α2(I). Some collagens contain three identical α chains whereas others contain three different α chains. Sequences in the α chains in which the X position is occupied by proline or the Y position is occupied by hydroxyproline give rigidity to the molecule and hold it in the triple-helical conformation. The hydrophobic and charged amino acids in the X and Y positions appear as clusters on the surface of the molecule and define the manner in which one molecule spontaneously binds to other molecules to form the cylindrical arrays characteristic of every collagen fibril (Fig. 319-1).

The simplicity of the structure and function of the collagen molecule is in contrast to the complexity of its synthesis (Fig. 319-1). The protein is first assembled as a precursor called procollagen, which has a mass about 1.5 times that of the collagen molecule. The additional mass is due to amino acid sequences at both the N terminus and C terminus of the procollagen molecule. To generate collagen fibrils, the N-terminal propeptides must be cleaved by a specific N-proteinase, and the C-terminal propeptides must be cleaved by a specific C-proteinase. As the proα chains of procollagen are assembled on ribosomes, they pass into the cisternae of the rough endoplasmic reticulum. Hydrophobic "signal peptides" at the N terminus are cleaved, and a series of additional posttranslational reactions begin. Proline residues in the Y position are converted to hydroxyproline by a specific hydroxylase requiring ascorbic acid. Lysine residues in

the Y position are similarly hydroxylated to hydroxylysine by another hydroxylase requiring ascorbic acid. The requirement for ascorbic acid by the two hydroxylases probably explains why wounds fail to heal in scurvy (see Chap. 76). Many of the hydroxylysine residues are further modified by glycosylation with galactose or with galactose and glucose. A large mannose-rich oligosaccharide is added to the C-terminal propeptide of each chain. The C-terminal propeptides associate and become disulfide-linked. When each proα chain acquires a critical level of about 100 hydroxyproline residues, the protein spontaneously folds into a triple-helical conformation. Once the protein is folded, it is processed to collagen by N-proteinase and C-proteinase.

The fibrils formed by the self-assembly of the collagen molecule have considerable tensile strength, and the strength is increased by cross-linking reactions that form covalent bonds between α chains in one molecule and the α chains in adjacent molecules. The first step in cross-linking is oxidation by the enzyme lysyl oxidase of amino groups on lysine or hydroxylysine residues to form aldehydes; the aldehydes then interact to form stable covalent bonds.

The collagen fibrils and fibers in tissues other than bone are stable throughout most of adult life and turn over only with marked starvation or tissue wastage. However, fibroblasts, synovial cells, and other cells can produce collagenases that cleave the collagen molecule at a point about three-quarters of the distance from its N terminus and thereby trigger further degradation of collagen fibrils and fibers by additional proteinases. In bone, there is continual degradation and resynthesis of collagen fibrils as part of bone remodeling. In summary, the assembly and maintenance of collagen fibrils in tissues require the coordinated expression of a series of genes whose products are required in the posttranslational assembly of collagen fibrils or are involved in the metabolic turnover of collagen.

The assembly of type I collagen fibrils is similar to that for type II collagen fibrils in cartilage and the type III collagen fibrils in aorta and skin. Assembly of nonfibrillar collagens such as the type IV of basement membranes does not involve cleavage of globular domains at the ends of the molecules. Instead, these domains participate in the self-assembly of the monomers into interlocking networks. Elastin

TABLE 319-1 Constituents of connective tissue in various tissues

Connective tissue	Known constituents	Approximate amounts (% dry wt)	Characteristics
Skin (dermis), ligaments, tendons	Type I collagen	80	Bundles of fibers of high tensile strength
	Type III collagen	5 to 15	Thin fibrils
	Type IV collagen, laminin, entactin, nidogen	<5	In basal laminae under epithelium and in blood vessels
	Types V to VII	<5	Distributions and functions unclear
	Fibronectin	<5	Associated with collagen fibers and cell surfaces
	Proteoglycans*	0.5	Provides resiliency
	Hyaluronate	0.5	Provides resiliency
Bone (demineralized)	Type I collagen	90	Complex organization of fibrils
	Type V collagen	1 to 2	Function unclear
	Proteoglycans	1	Function unclear
	Sialoproteins	1	Function unclear
	Osteonectin	2 to 3	Role in ossification
	Osteocalcin	1	Probable role in ossification
	α$_2$-Glycoprotein	1	Possible role in ossification
Aorta	Type I collagen	20 to 40	
	Type III collagen	20 to 40	Thin fibrils
	Elastin, microfibrillar protein	20 to 40	Amorphous, elastic fibrils
	Type IV collagen, laminin, entactin, nidogen	<5	In basal lamina
	Types V and VI collagens	<2	Functions unclear
	Proteoglycans	<3	Mucopolysaccharides, mainly chondroitin sulfate and dermatan sulfate; heparan sulfate in basal lamina
Cartilage	Type II collagen	40 to 50	Thin fibrils
	Types IX and X collagen	5 to 25	Possible role in maturation
	Proteoglycans	15 to 50	Provides resiliency
	Hyaluronate	0.5 to 2	Provides resiliency

* *Proteoglycan structures are incompletely defined. About five different protein cores have been identified, and each has one or more kind of mucopolysaccharides attached. Major mucopolysaccharides of skin and tendon are dermatan sulfate and chondroitin 4-sulfate; of aorta, chondroitin 4-sulfate and dermatan sulfate; of cartilage, chondroitin 4-sulfate, chondroitin 6-sulfate, and keratan sulfate. Basal lamina contains heparan sulfate.*

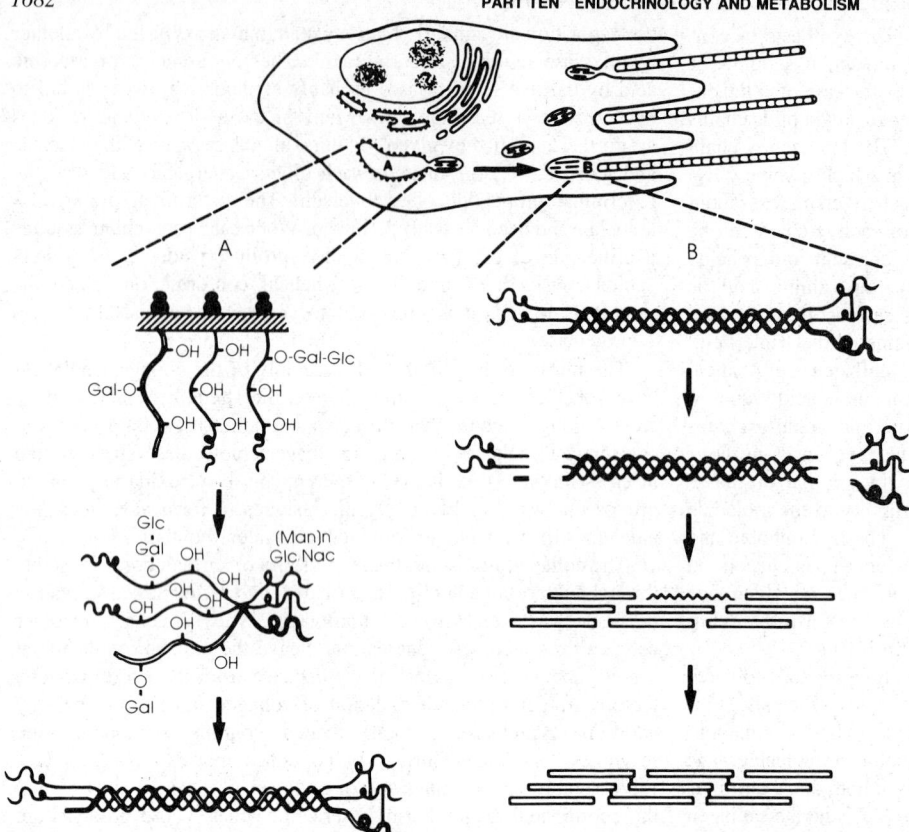

FIGURE 319-1 *Schematic representation of synthesis of a type I collagen fibril by a fibroblast. A. Intracellular steps in the assembly of the procollagen molecule. Hydroxylations and glycosylations of the proα chains begin soon after the N termini pass into the cisterni of the rough endoplasmic reticulum and continue after the three chains associate through their C-propeptides and become disulfide-linked. B. Cleavage of procollagen to collagen, self-assembly of the collagen molecule into quarter-staggered fibrils, and crosslinking of the molecules in the fibrils. Cleavage of the propeptides may occur within crypts of the fibroblast, as shown here, or some distance from the cell. (Reproduced with permission from Prockop and Kivirikko.)*

fibers are also assembled by a similar pathway. The elastin monomer, however, is a single polypeptide chain without a defined three-dimensional structure, and it self-assembles into amorphous elastic fibers.

Proteoglycan synthesis is similar to collagen synthesis in that it

FIGURE 319-2 *Approximate locations of mutations in the structure of type I procollagen. EDS denotes the Ehlers-Danlos syndrome, OI, osteogenesis imperfecta; and MS, Marfan's syndrome. Other symbols: proα1^S, mutation giving rise to a shortened proα1 chain; proα2^S, mutation giving rise to a shortened proα2 chain; proα1^{cys}, mutation introducing a cysteine residue; proα$^{c\text{-}man}$, mutation introducing excess mannose into one or both proα chains; proα2^x, unknown structural mutation that prevents cleavage of the chain by N-proteinase; proα2^L, mutation giving rise to a lengthened proα2 chain; proα2^{CX}, mutation altering the structure of the C-terminal propeptide of the proα2 chain. Roman numerals indicate specific type of EDS or OI as discussed in text. Exons where specific deletions occur are indicated with the exons being numbered from the 3' end to the 5' end of the gene. Other deletions are defined in terms of the approximate number of amino acids deleted from the chain. The symbol aa 988 indicates that the glycine residue in amino acid position 988 of the α1 chain is replaced by cysteine. As discussed in the text, the proα2^L mutation involves insertion of 38 base pairs into an intervening sequence and was found in a patient with atypical Marfan's syndrome. Proα2$^{S-100\ aas}$ refers to an apparent deletion of about 100 amino acids in a variant of type II osteogenesis imperfecta. (Modified and reproduced with permission from Prockop and Kivirikko.)*

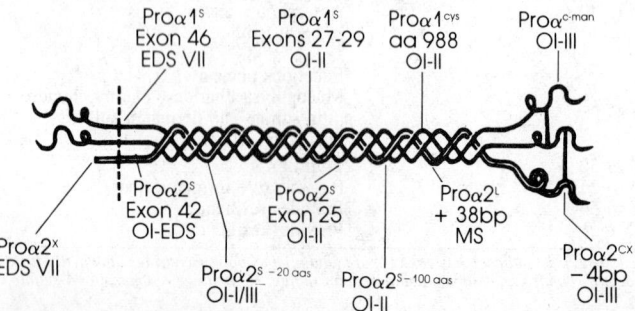

begins with assembly of a polypeptide chain, called the protein core, in the cisternae of the rough endoplasmic reticulum, and the protein core undergoes modification by addition of sugar residues and sulfate that generate large mucopolysaccharide side chains on the protein core. After secretion into the extracellular space, the core protein with its mucopolysaccharide side chains binds to a link protein and then to a long chain of hyaluronic acid to form the mature proteoglycan with a molecular weight of several millions.

The assembly of bone follows the same principles as that for other connective tissues (see also Chap. 335). The first step is deposition of osteoid tissue that consists largely of type I collagen (Fig. 319-1). Mineralization of the osteoid occurs by steps that are still incompletely defined; specific proteins such as osteonectin bind to specific sites on the collagen fibril and then chelate calcium to initiate mineralization.

CONSEQUENCES FOR HERITABLE DISEASES Our understanding of the chemistry and biochemistry of connective tissues is incomplete but nevertheless provides insight into the clinical features of heritable diseases of connective tissue. For example, it explains why many of the diseases are systemic in their manifestations. Since all type I collagen is synthesized from the same two structural genes, any mutation in these genes must be expressed in all the tissues containing type I collagen. Tissue or organ specificity of the diseases can be explained by either of two major mechanisms. One is that the diseases are produced by mutations in genes expressed in only one or two connective tissues. For example, patients with the type IV form of Ehlers-Danlos syndrome have mutations in genes for the type III procollagen, and the symptoms are confined to skin, aorta, and intestine—tissues rich in type III collagen. A second reason for tissue specificity of the diseases is more subtle. Different regions of collagen molecules have different biologic functions. In the case of type I collagen, removal of the N-terminal propeptides is necessary for assembly of large collagen fibrils and fibers in ligaments and tendons. If the N-propeptides are incompletely cleaved, the protein self-assembles into thin fibrils. Hence, patients with mutations in type I procollagen genes that prevent efficient cleavage of the N-propeptides suffer primarily from dislocations of hips and other large joints. They rarely have fractures, because assembly of thick fibrils of type I

TABLE 319-2 Classification of osteogenesis imperfecta (OI) based on clinical manifestations and mode of inheritance as proposed by Sillence

Type	Bone fragility	Blue sclerae	Abnormal dentition	Hearing loss	Inheritance*
I	Mild	Present	Absent in IA, present in IB	Present in some	AD
II	Extreme	Present	Present in some	Unknown	AR or S
III	Severe	Bluish at birth	Present in some	Low incidence	AR
IV	Variable	Absent	Absent in IVA, present in IVB	Low incidence	AD

AD, autosomal dominant; AR, autosomal recessive; S, sporadic.

collagen appears to be less important for the normal function of bone than for normal joint ligaments. In contrast, patients with mutations altering the structure of other regions of the type I procollagen molecule may have primary manifestations in bone.

The current information about the chemistry of matrix also provides insight into the heterogeneity of signs and symptoms in patients with identical gene defects. The expression of a collagen or proteoglycan gene depends on coordinated expression of genes for posttranslational enzymes and on the expression of genes for other components of the same matrix. Therefore, the ultimate effect of a given mutation on the functional properties of a complex structure such as bone or a large blood vessel is influenced by differences in the "genetic background" among individuals, namely, differences in the expression of a large family of other genes whose products influence the same structure. The manifestations must also be subject to other factors that influence connective tissues such as exercise, trauma, nutrition, and hormonal changes. Hence, there is broad scope for variable manifestations in patients with the same defect.

DEFINITION OF THE MOLECULAR DEFECTS Defining the defect in patients with heritable disorders of connective tissue requires an intensive research effort (Fig. 319-2). One reason is that no two unrelated patients have the same molecular defects even when the clinical manifestations appear identical. Another is that the proteins and proteoglycans in connective tissues are large molecules that are difficult to solubilize and obtain in pure form. Also, in many patients the defect causes synthesis of an abnormal protein that is rapidly degraded. Therefore, it is difficult to establish which gene product is at fault by analysis of tissues. Still another reason is that the genes for matrix components are large. In the case of type I procollagen, the gene for the $\text{pro}\alpha1(\text{I})$ chain contains 18,000 base pairs, and the gene for the $\text{pro}\alpha2(\text{I})$ chain contains 38,000 base pairs. Each of these genes has about 50 exons, most of which have a very similar structure. With the recombinant DNA technologies currently available, locating a mutation of one or more bases in a collagen gene is a formidable

challenge. However, newer technologies will probably overcome most of these problems.

OSTEOGENESIS IMPERFECTA

General features The term osteogenesis imperfecta (OI) is used for heritable defects that make bones brittle (Fig. 319-3). The diagnosis is made by excluding other heritable defects or environmental factors that produce osteopenia or osteoporosis and by establishing that the mutation is expressed in more than one connective tissue. The increased fragility of bone is usually associated with blue sclerae, hearing loss, abnormalities of dentition, or a combination of these features (Table 319-2). The presence of blue sclerae and fractures early in life is usually sufficient to establish the diagnosis. Also, fractures together with the characteristic dental abnormalities (dentinogenesis imperfecta) are sufficient for a diagnosis. Some consider brittleness of bone associated with early hearing loss in the patient or members of the same family as diagnostic, and others make the diagnosis on the basis of fragile bones that cannot be attributed to environmental facts such as physical inactivity or malnutrition or to any other heritable syndromes, such as the skeletal dysplasias (Table 319-3). Since some individuals from families with OI do not develop fractures until after menopause, mild forms of OI may not be distinguishable from postmenopausal osteoporosis. Some individuals with osteoporosis may be heterozygous carriers for gene defects that produce OI in homozygotes. Therefore, it may prove useful to include postmenopausal osteoporosis in the same spectrum of diseases as OI.

The most common classification scheme for OI is the one developed by Sillence (Table 319-2). Type I disease has a frequency of about 1:30,000. It is a mild to moderately severe disorder that is inherited as an autosomal dominant trait and is associated with blue sclerae. Type II is the most severe form of the disease. Types III and IV OI are intermediate in severity between types I and II.

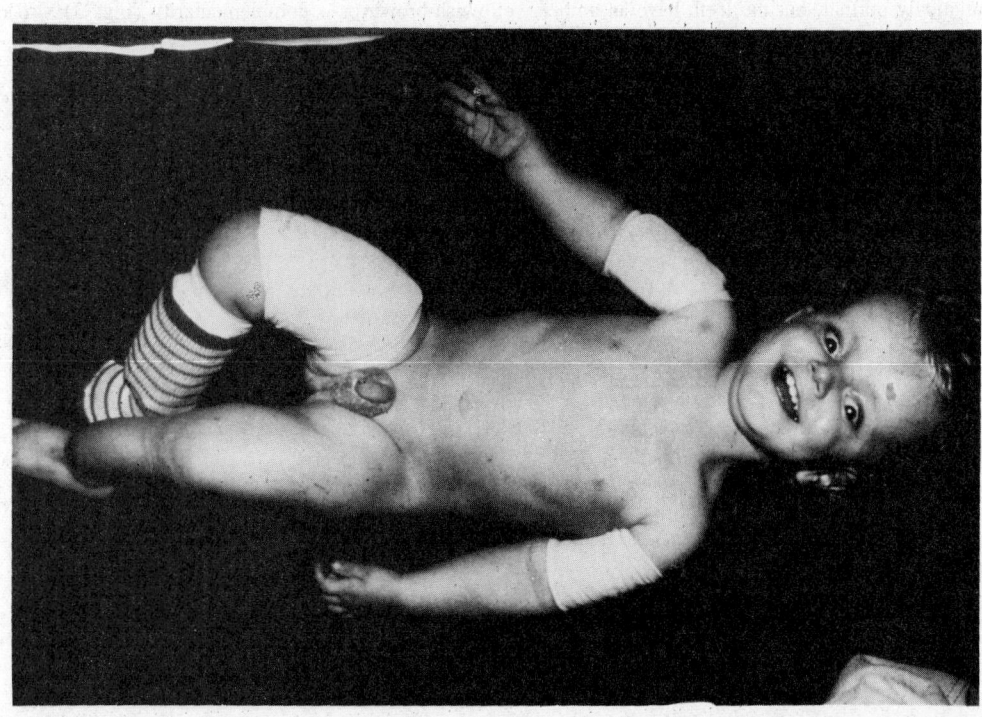

FIGURE 319-3 *A 21-month-old boy with type III OI. Child has had multiple fractures of arms and legs. He is homozygous for a four-base-pair deletion in the genes for $\text{pro}\alpha2(\text{I})$ chains that changes the sequence of the last 33 amino acids in these proteins. Therefore, the $\text{pro}\alpha2(\text{I})$ chains do not associate with $\text{pro}\alpha1(\text{I})$ chains, and the only type I procollagens formed are trimers of $\text{pro}\alpha1(\text{I})$ chains that have a partially unfolded C-terminal region. (Reproduced with permission from Nicholls et al.)*

TABLE 319-3   Partial differential diagnosis of OI

Age	Diagnosis	Distinguishing features
At birth	Hypophosphatasia	Unmineralized skull
	Achondrogenesis	Unmineralized vertebrae
	Thanatophoric dwarfism	H-shaped vertebrae
	Asphyxiating thoracic dystro-phy	Cylindrical thorax
	Achondroplasia	Large head, short, tubular bones
Infancy	Battered child syndrome	Skull and rib fractures more common
	Immobilization osteogenesis	
	Scurvy	
	Congenital syphilis	
Childhood	Idiopathic juvenile osteogene-sis	Prepubertal and self-limiting
	Homocystinuria	Marfanoid appearance and mental deficiency
	Celiac disease	Steatorrhea, anemia
	Adrenal cortical tumor	
	Corticosteroid therapy	

SOURCE: *Modified from Smith et al., p. 126*

Skeletal changes   In type I OI the fragility of bones may be so marked as to limit physical activity or so mild that individuals may be unaware of any debility. In type II OI, bones and other connective tissues are so fragile that death occurs in utero, during delivery, or within a few weeks after birth. In types III and IV disease, multiple fractures resulting from minor physical stress can lead to a stunting of growth and to skeletal abnormalities. Many patients have an increase in fractures during childhood, a decrease after puberty, and then an increase with pregnancy and after menopause. Severe kyphoscoliosis may cause respiratory impairment and predispose to pulmonary infections. Bone density is decreased in unfractured bone, but there is no consensus about specific morphologic changes. The general impression is that the repair of fractures is normal. The skull of some patients with relatively mild symptoms has a mottled appearance, apparently because of small islands of ossification.

Ocular changes   The sclerae can vary in color from normal to a slightly bluish or slate color to a bright blue. The blueness is caused by a thinness or transparency of the collagen fibers of the sclera that allows the choroid layer to be seen. Some patients also have other ocular changes. Blue sclerae can be an inherited trait in some families without any evidence of increased bone fragility.

Dentinogenesis imperfecta   The enamel of the lamina dura is relatively normal, but the teeth have an amber, yellowish-brown or translucent bluish-gray color because of improper deposition of dentine. The deciduous teeth are usually smaller than normal whereas the permanent teeth are bell-shaped and constricted at the base. Indistinguishable tooth defects can be inherited independently of OI.

Presenile hearing loss   The deafness usually begins in the second decade of life or later. It arises from impaired transmission through the middle ear as far as the footplate of the stapes. The histologic features include deficient ossification, persistence of cartilage areas normally ossified, and calcified strial deposits.

Associated features   Many patients and families show involvement of other connective tissues. Some patients show skin and joint changes indistinguishable from those of EDS (see below). A few patients have cardiovascular manifestations such as aortic regurgitation, floppy mitral valves, mitral incompetence, and fragility of large blood vessels. Hypermetabolic states can occur with elevated serum thyroxine levels, hyperthermia, and excessive sweating. In mild forms of OI, the associated features can be the presenting symptom.

Mode of inheritance   The type I form of OI has an autosomal dominant mode of inheritance with variable expressivity so that apparent skipping of a generation may occur. In the lethal type II variant, the inheritance may be autosomal recessive, but in the few cases of type II OI in which the genetic defect has been defined new mutations are involved. The mode of inheritance is a primary criterion for distinguishing type III from type IV (Table 319-2), but it may be difficult to distinguish recessive inheritance from a new autosomal dominant mutation.

Molecular defects   Because most of the affected tissues are rich in type I collagen, most forms of the disease are believed to be caused by mutations in the structural genes for the protein, in genes for its posttranslational processing, or in genes regulating its expression. Mutations in the genes for type I procollagen have now been identified in four variants of type II OI. One variant had a deletion mutation in one allele for the proα1(I) gene (Fig. 319-4A). The deletion removed three exons but did not interfere with the transcription of the gene. As a result, the proα1(I) chain was 84 amino acids shorter than normal. The mutation was lethal because the shortened proα1(I) chain associated with normal proα1(I) and proα2(I) chains (Fig. 319-4B). The shortening in the proα1(I) chain prevented molecules from folding in the triple-helical conformation. As a result, most of the procollagen remained nonhelical and was rapidly degraded in a process that has been referred to as "protein suicide" or negative complementarity (Fig. 319-4B). In a second lethal type II variant,

FIGURE 319-4   *Schematic representation of the molecular defect in a patient with type II OI. A. Schematic representation of the gene deletion. As indicated, the human proα1(I) gene is about 18,000 base pairs long and contains about 50 exons (vertical dark bars). The deletion removed three exons containing 252 base pairs of coding sequences. B. Scheme of "protein" suicide or negative complementarity. Shortened proα1(I) chains were synthesized, and* they associated with and became disulfide-bonded to normal proα chains. Procollagen molecules containing one or two shortened proα1(I) chains did not fold into a triple helix at 37°C and were degraded. Hence, a sporadic homozygous defect reduced the amount of functional procollagen by about 75 percent. (Modified from and reproduced with permission from Prockop and Kivirikko.)

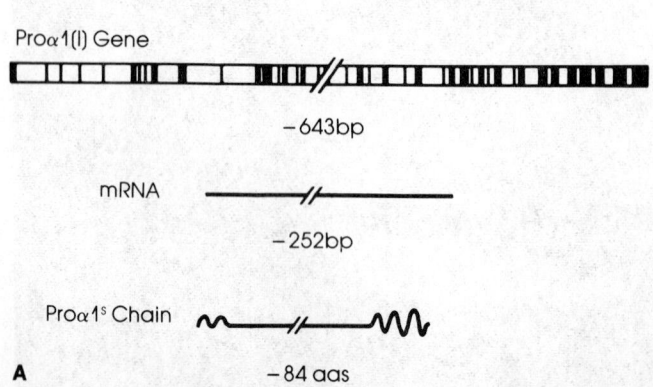

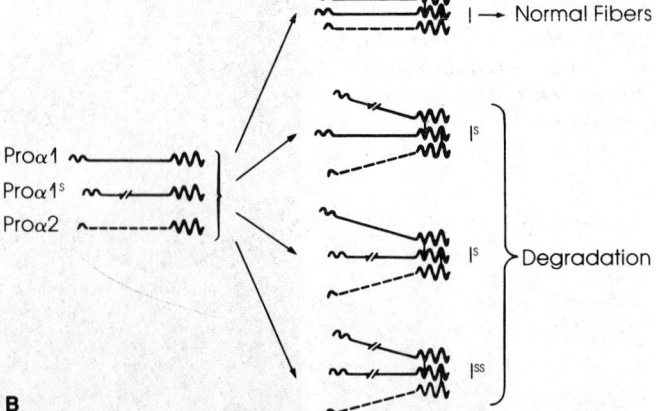

the mutation led to the synthesis of a proα2(I) chain that was about 20 amino acids shorter than normal. The other allele was nonfunctioning, and therefore all the proα2 chains were shortened. In a third type II variant, a deletion mutation in an allele for proα2(I) chains caused the synthesis of proα2 chains that were shortened by about 100 amino acids. In a fourth type II variant, a single-base substitution introduced a cysteine residue instead of a glycine residue in the α1(I) chain and thereby disrupted the triple-helical conformation of the protein.

Mutations in genes for type I procollagen have also been detected in two variants of type III. In one, the mutation was a four-base-pair deletion that produced a change in the reading frame for the last 33 amino acids of the proα2(I) chain. The patient was homozygous for the defect, and none of the proα2(I) chains were incorporated in procollagen molecules. Instead, the type I procollagen consisted of a trimer of proα1(I) chains. The trimer of proα1(I) chains was triple-helical but unstable. The parents, who were third cousins, were heterozygous for the same mutation and had osteoporosis while in their thirties. In another type III variant, a structural alteration in the C-terminal propeptide caused increased mannose in the C-propeptides. In a patient who had some manifestations of the type I disorder and some of type II, proα2(I) chains were shortened by about 100 amino acids.

These data suggest several generalizations about mutations in collagen genes. One is that a mutation that causes synthesis of an abnormal protein can be more deleterious than a nonfunctioning allele. Another is that mutations that give rise to shortened polypeptide chains may be more frequent than in other gene systems. Nevertheless, the molecular defects in most patients with OI have not been identified. Many may be RNA-splicing mutations or single-base mutations that are difficult to detect in genes as large as those for type I procollagen. Other variants of OI may be due to mutations in other genes whose expression is required for the assembly and maintenance of bone and other connective tissues.

Diagnosis Diagnosis is difficult in patients who lack the cardinal features of the disease and is probably often missed. Other conditions that produce brittle bones in infancy and childhood must be considered (Table 319-3). In a third of patients, abnormal proα can be identified by polyacrylamide gel electrophoresis of type I procollagen synthesized by cultured skin fibroblasts. In most instances, the altered migration reflects posttranslational modification and does not define the exact nature of the mutation or the type of OI.

Treatment No convincing data have been presented that OI can be effectively treated. Patients with mild forms may need little treatment after fractures decrease at the age of 15 to 20 years, but they may need special attention during pregnancy or after menopause when fractures again increase. More severely affected children require a comprehensive program of physical therapy, surgical management of fractures and skeletal deformities, vocational education, and emotional support for the patients and their parents. Many patients appear to be unusually intelligent and have successful careers in spite of severe deformities. A program for orthotic management developed by Bleck is a useful guide. Many of the fractures are minimally displaced and have little soft tissue swelling. Therefore, they can be treated with minimal support or traction for a week or two followed by a light cast. If fractures are relatively painless, physical therapy can be initiated early. There is controversy over correcting limb deformities with steel rods inserted into long bones. The rationale for the procedure is that correcting deformities during childhood may make it possible to align the limbs adequately for walking during adulthood.

Genetic counseling may be difficult in families with types II, III, and IV because of uncertainty about the mode of inheritance. OI has been identified in fetuses as early as 20 weeks of pregnancy with x-rays and sonography. In the few families in which the precise gene defect has been defined, DNA can be analyzed for prenatal diagnosis in the research laboratories that have studied the defects. Restriction fragment length polymorphisms have been identified for the type I

procollagen genes and may be useful for prenatal diagnosis. Cultured amniotic fluid cells synthesize collagen, but it appears impractical to use such cultures to detect mutations.

EHLERS-DANLOS SYNDROME

General features The Ehlers-Danlos syndrome (EDS) describes a group of heritable disorders characterized by hypermobile joints and abnormalities of skin (Fig. 319-5). Beighton initially identified five types of EDS (Table 319-4). Type I is the classical, severe form of the disease with both joint hypermobility and characteristically velvety and hyperextensible skin. Type II is similar to type I but milder. In type III joint hypermobility is more prominent than the skin changes. Type IV is characterized by a striking thinness of skin and a

FIGURE 319-5 *Schematic of the skin and joint changes in EDS. Girl in upper right has type VIIB EDS with dislocations of both hips that were not corrected by surgery. (Reproduced with permission from Prockop and Guzman, Hosp Prac, 12(12):61, 1977.)*

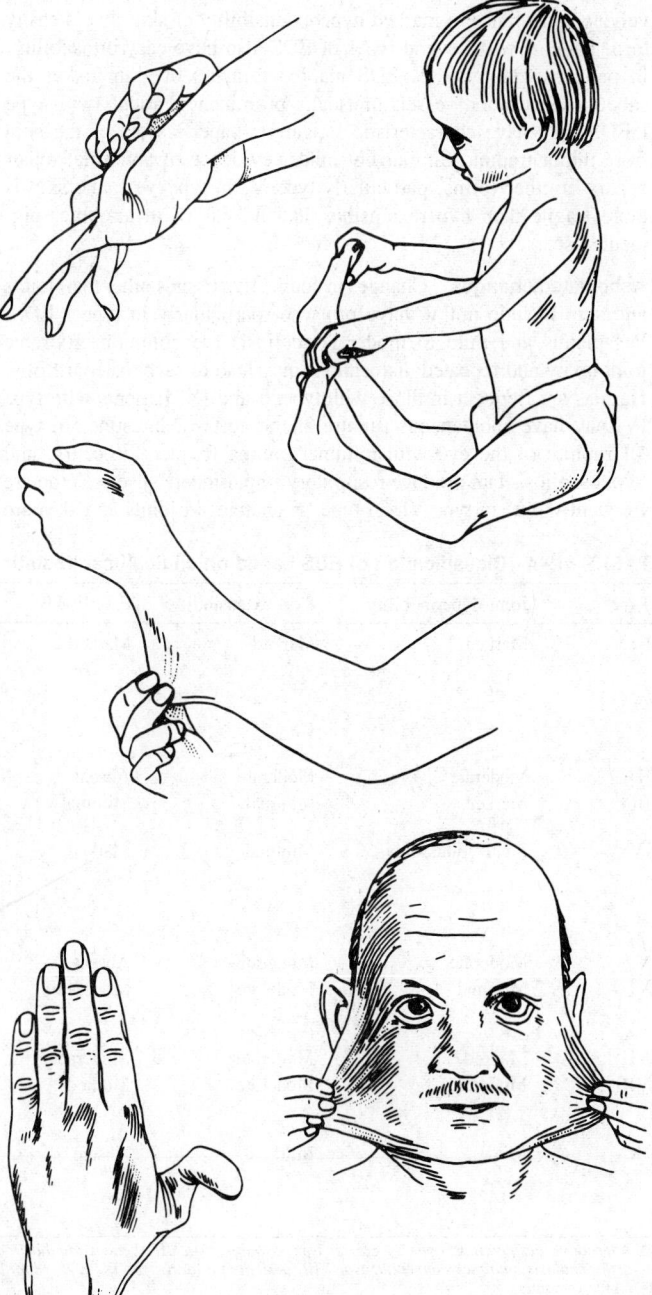

predisposition to sudden death from rupture of large blood vessels or the large bowel. Type V is similar to type II but characterized by X-linked inheritance.

The additional types VI, VII, and IX were defined because of the presence of biochemical defects and phenotypes that did not fit into the types defined by Beighton. However, not all patients with these phenotypes have the molecular defect initially used to establish the classification. Type VIII was identified by the presence of generalized periodontitis together with moderate joint and skin changes. Many patients and families cannot be assigned to any of the nine defined types of EDS.

Ligaments and joint changes Laxity and hypermobility of joints can vary from mild changes to those that are severe enough to produce unreducible dislocations of hips and other joints. In milder forms, patients learn to reduce dislocations themselves or to avoid them by limiting physical activity. In more severe forms, surgical repair is required. Some patients have progressive difficulty with increasing age, but severe joint laxity can be compatible with a normal life span.

Skin The skin changes vary from a slight thinness and soft or velvety appearance to marked hyperextensibility or skin that is easily torn. Patients with several types of EDS also have easy bruisability. In patients with type IV EDS marked thinness of skin makes the subcutaneous blood vessels unusually prominent. Patients with type I EDS may have characteristic "cigarette-paper" scars of the skin from minor trauma. Similar but milder evidence of abnormal repair occurs in other forms, particularly type V. In type VIII, the skin is more fragile than hyperextensible, and it heals with atrophic, pigmented scars.

Associated changes Changes in connective tissues other than joints and skin include mitral valve prolapse, particularly in type I EDS. Pes planus and mild to moderate scoliosis are common. Extreme joint laxity and repeated dislocations may lead to early osteoarthritis. Hernias are frequent in those with types I and IX. Patients with type IV may have spontaneous rupture of the aorta or intestine. In type VI rupture of the eye with minimal trauma frequently occurs, and kyphoscoliosis can produce respiratory impairment. Also, sclerae are frequently blue in type VI. In type IX changes in joints and skin are

minimal. This type is primarily defined by the presence of abnormalities in copper metabolism and includes diseases previously classified as X-linked cutis laxa, X-linked EDS, and Menkes's syndrome. Patients frequently have bladder diverticuli that can rupture, hernias, skeletal abnormalities that include characteristic occipital horns, and laxity of skin. In the variants formerly defined as cutis laxa, skin laxity is the most prominent finding and results in an appearance of premature senescence. These patients frequently develop pulmonary emphysema and pulmonary stenosis.

Molecular defects The molecular defects in the type I, type II, and type III variants of EDS are unknown. Electron microscopy of the skin from some patients has shown an unusual morphology of collagen fibers, but similar types of collagen fibrils are occasionally seen in normal skin.

Patients with the type IV variant appear to have a defect either in the synthesis or the structure of type III collagen. This is consistent with the fact that they are prone to spontaneous rupture of the aorta and intestines, tissues that are rich in type III collagen. In one variant of type IV EDS, the defect involves synthesis of structurally abnormal proα(III) chains. The abnormal proα(III) chains were incorporated into molecules of type III procollagen in an equal stoichiometry with normal proα(III) chains so that most of the type III procollagen molecules contained one or more abnormal proα(III) chains. These molecules underwent "protein suicide" or negative complementarity, so that the skin contained no detectable type III collagen. In other variants of type IV EDS, the synthesis or secretion of type III procollagen is defective.

Type VI EDS was first characterized in two sisters by the fact that their collagen contained a decreased amount of hydroxylysine secondary to a deficiency of lysyl hydroxylase; a similar enzyme deficiency has been detected in other patients. Some patients with the clinical features of type VI EDS, however, do not have deficiency of lysyl hydroxylase.

Type VII EDS was first identified as a defect in the conversion of procollagen to collagen in patients with joint hypermobility and joint dislocations. At the molecular level, two kinds of genetic changes produce this disease. One, defined as type VIIA, is a deficiency of procollagen N-proteinase, the enzyme that removes the N-terminal peptide from type I procollagen. This form is inherited

TABLE 319-4 Classification of EDS based on clinical manifestations and mode of inheritance

Type*	Joint hypermobility	Skin extensibility	Fragility	Bruisability	Other manifestations	Inheritance†
I	Marked	Marked	Marked	Marked	Skin characteristically soft, velvety; cigarette-paper scars; hernias; varicose veins; premature birth because rupture of fetal membranes	AD
II	Moderate	Moderate	Absent	Moderate	Milder than type I	AD
III	Marked	Minimal	Minimal	Minimal	Joint dislocations with minimal changes in skin	
IV	Small joints only	Minimal	Marked	Marked	Rupture of large arteries and bowel; thin skin with prominent venous network; characteristic facies in some	AD or AR
V	Moderate	Moderate	Absent	Moderate	Similar to type II	XL
VI	Minimal	Moderate	Moderate	Moderate	Similar to type II; intramuscular hemorrhage or keratoconus in some	XL
VII	Marked	Moderate	Moderate	Moderate	Multiple dislocations	AR or AD
VIII	Moderate	Moderate	Marked	Moderate	Advanced periodontitis; atrophic pigmented scars of skin	AD
IX	Mild	Mild	Absent	Absent	Bladder diverticuli with spontaneous rupture; hernias; skeletal abnormalities; skin laxity	XL

* *Alternative designations; type I, gravis; type II, mitis; type III, benign familial hypermobility; type IV, ecchymotic or aortic; type V, X-linked; type VI, ocular; type VII, arthrochalosis multiplex congenita; type VIII, periodontal form; type IX, EDS with abnormal copper metabolism, Menkes's steely-hair syndrome (some variants) and cutis laxa (some variants).*
† *AD, autosomal dominant; AR, autosomal recessive; XL, X-linked.*

as an autosomal recessive trait. The second form, defined as type VIIB, involves a series of different mutations that make the type I procollagen resistant to cleavage by N-proteinase. The enzyme requires a protein substrate in a native conformation, and it will not cleave type I procollagen that has an abnormal conformation. The change in amino acid sequences of the proα chains of type I procollagen can be located as much as 90 amino acids away from the site at which the enzyme cleaves the protein. In both type VIIA and type VIIB variants, the persistence of the N-propeptide on the molecule causes the formation of fibrils that are unusually thin. As discussed above, such thin fibrils can provide a scaffolding for bone but do not provide the necessary tensile strength for ligaments and joint capsules.

A defect in copper metabolism is present in most patients studied with type IX EDS (see Chap. 77). Low levels of serum copper and serum ceruloplasmin are accompanied by marked elevation of copper within cells. The molecular defects in some patients appear to be linked to synthesis of a diffusable factor involved either in regulation of the metallothionein gene or in some other aspect of copper metabolism.

Diagnosis Diagnosis is still based primarily on clinical evaluation of patients. Biochemical assays for known defects in EDS are still difficult and time-consuming. In type IV variants, incubation of cultured skin fibroblasts with radioactive proline or glycine followed by gel electrophoresis of the newly synthesized proteins will usually demonstrate a defect in the synthesis or secretion of type III procollagen. The approach is not currently applicable to prenatal diagnosis. A protocol for observing both the secretion and the rate of processing of type I procollagen in cultures of skin fibroblasts provides a simple method of identifying deficiencies of procollagen N-proteinase and structural mutations that prevent cleavage of the N-propeptide. It should therefore be useful in the diagnosis of both type VIIA and type VIIB EDS. However, some patients with OI are also positive by this assay. In patients suspected of having type IX EDS, the assignment to this general category can be confirmed by assays of copper and ceruloplasmin in serum and in fibroblast cultures. Specific DNA tests should soon be available for families in which the exact mutations in type I genes have been defined. Also, it is likely that restriction fragment length polymorphisms will be applicable for prenatal diagnosis in families with severe forms of EDS (see also Chap. 58).

Treatment There are no specific treatments for the disease. Surgical repair and tightening of the joint ligament require careful evaluation of individual patients since the ligaments frequently will not hold sutures. The cardiovascular status should be evaluated in all patients, particularly those suspected of having type IV. Patients with bruisability should be evaluated for specific bleeding disorders, but such tests are usually negative.

MARFAN'S SYNDROME

Diagnosis Marfan's syndrome is defined on the basis of characteristic changes in three connective tissue systems: the skeleton, the eyes, and the cardiovascular system (Fig. 319-6). The disease is inherited as an autosomal dominant trait, and 15 to 30 percent of cases may be due to new mutations. "Skipped generations" due to variable expressivity is relatively common. Also, the typical marfanoid habitus, lens dislocations, and cardiovascular abnormalities can each be inherited independently in some families. Therefore, the diagnosis is usually not made unless at least one member of a family has characteristic changes in at least two of the three connective tissue systems.

Skeletal changes Patients are unusually tall compared to other members of the same family and have unusually long limbs. The ratio of the upper segment (top of head to top of pubic ramus) to the lower segment (top of pubic ramus to floor) is usually 2 standard deviations below mean for age, race, and sex. The patients usually have long and slender fingers and toes (called arachnodactyly or dolichostenomelia), but these are difficult to evaluate objectively.

Because of longitudinal overgrowth of the ribs, many patients have chest deformities, including depression (pectus excavatum), protrusion (pectus carinatum), or marked asymmetry. Scoliosis is usually present, often accompanied by kyphosis.

Patients fall into three categories in terms of joint mobility. Most have moderate hypermobility of most joints. Some have marked hypermobility similar to that in EDS, but a few have exceptionally tight joints with contractures of hands and fingers. The group with the latter disorder, which is known as contractual arachnodactyly, appears to be less prone to cardiovascular problems.

Cardiovascular changes Mitral valve prolapse and aortic dilatation are common. Dilatation of the aorta begins in the root and is usually progressive so that dissection and rupture are common. Echocardiography is particularly helpful in evaluation.

Ocular changes The characteristic finding is subluxation of the lens (ectopia lentis), usually in an upward direction. The lens dislocation, however, may be detectable only by slit lamp examination. Displacement of the lens into the anterior chamber may cause glaucoma, but glaucoma is more frequent after surgical removal of the lens. The axial length of the globe is greater than normal, predisposing to myopia and retinal detachment.

Associated changes Striae may occur over the shoulders and buttocks. Otherwise the skin is normal. A number of patients develop

FIGURE 319-6 *A 16-year-old boy with Marfan's syndrome. Manifestations include dislocated lens; long, thin face; long fingers (arachnodactyly) and extremities (dolichostenomelia); and inward displacement of the sternum (pectus excavatum). (Courtesy of JG Hall.)*

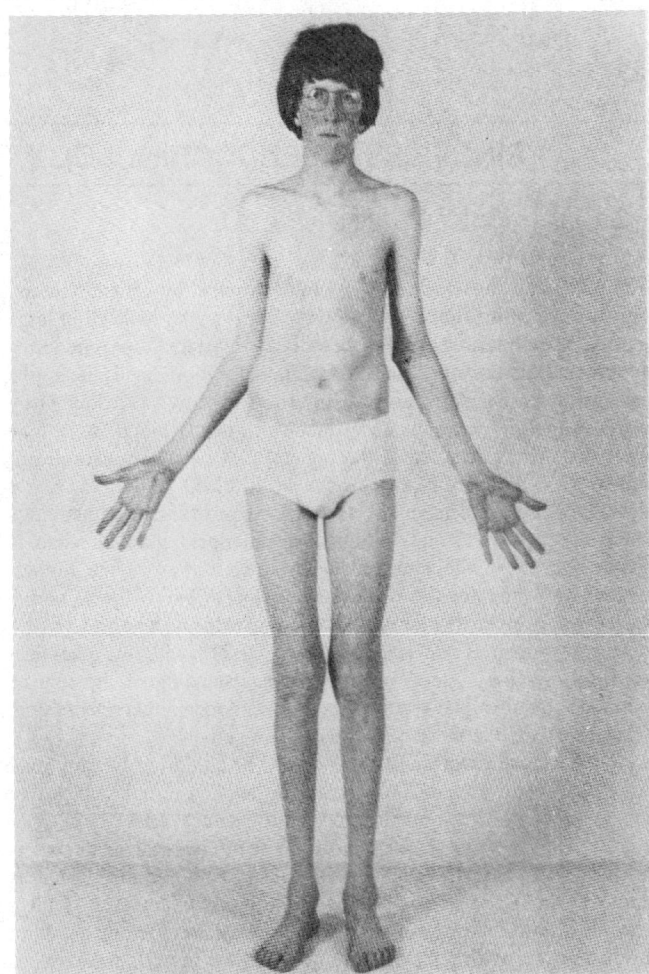

spontaneous pneumothorax. High-arched palate and high pedal arches are frequent.

Diagnosis   The diagnosis is easiest to establish if the patient or members of the family have objective evidence of subluxed lenses, aortic dilatation, and severe kyphoscoliosis or chest deformities. The diagnosis is frequently made if ectopia lentis and an aneurysm of the ascending aorta are present without evidence of a Marfan habitus or a positive family history. All patients in whom the diagnosis is suspected should have a slip lamp examination and an echocardiogram. Also, homocystinuria (Table 319-3) should be ruled out by a negative cyanide-nitroprusside test for disulfides in the urine. Patients with types I, II, and III EDS may have ectopia lentis but lack the Marfan habitus and have characteristic skin changes not present in Marfan's syndrome.

Treatment   As with other heritable disorders of connective tissue, there is no established treatment. Several investigators have recommended use of propranolol to delay or prevent the severe aortic complications, but the therapy is unproven. Surgical replacement of the aorta, aortic valve, and mitral valve has been undertaken in a number of patients.

The scoliosis tends to be progressive and should be treated by mechanical bracing and physical therapy if greater than 20° or by surgery if it continues to progress and becomes greater than 45°. Estrogen to induce menarche has been tried in girls with progressive scoliosis, but the results are inconclusive.

The subluxated lens rarely requires surgical removal, but patients should be followed closely for signs of retinal detachment.

Counseling is based on a 50 percent probability of passing on the defective gene. Because of the heterogeneity of the disease, offspring may be more or less severely affected than their parents. Women should be advised that the cardiovascular risk of pregnancy is high.

REFERENCES

Bleck EE: Non-operative treatment of osteogenesis imperfecta: Orthotic and mobility management. Clin Orthop 159:115, 1981

Byers PH et al: Ehlers-Danlos syndrome, in *Principles and Practice of Medical Genetics,* vol 2, AEH Emery, DL Rimoin (eds). New York, Churchill Livingston, 1983, p 36

McKusick VA: *Heritable Disorders of Connective Tissue,* 4th ed. St. Louis, Mosby, 1972

Prockop JD, Kivirikko KI: Heritable diseases of collagen. N Engl J Med 311:376, 1984

Pyeritz RE: Marfan syndrome, in *Principles and Practice of Medical Genetics,* vol 2, AEH Emery DL Rimoin (eds). New York, Churchill Livingston, 1983, p 57

Sillence DO: Osteogenesis imperfecta: An expanding panorama of variance. Clin Orthop 191:11, 1981

———: Disorders of bone density, volume and mineralization, in *Principles and Practice of Medical Genetics,* vol 2, AEH Emery, DL Rimoin (eds). New York, Churchill Livingston, 1983, p 736

Smith R et al: *The Brittle Bone Syndrome: Osteogenesis Imperfecta.* London, Butterworths, 1983

Uitto J, Bauer EA: Diseases associated with collagen abnormalities, in *Collagen in Health and Disease,* JB Weiss, MID Jayson (eds). New York, Churchill Livingston, 1982, p 289

section 2   Endocrinology

320   PRINCIPLES OF ENDOCRINOLOGY

JEAN D. WILSON

The functional capacities of cells are determined by genetic factors, but the rates of the metabolic pathways in cells are regulated in large part by two interlocking and coordinated systems, the endocrine system and the nervous system. As originally formulated, these two systems were considered distinct, information being carried either by neural impulses or by chemical mediators in the blood. It is now clear that this conception is incomplete. Not only may neurotransmitters such as norepinephrine circulate in blood as hormones, but neural impulses have major effects on the release of chemical mediators such as testosterone and insulin. This interlocking relationship is most apparent in the hypothalamus, which serves as the highest integrative center for the two systems. Hence, one neuroendocrine system has evolved to integrate and coordinate the metabolic activities of the organism. Endocrinology deals largely with the chemical mediators in this system, but proper understanding of the role of hormones requires knowledge of both the autonomic nervous system (Chap. 66) and the metabolic capacities of cells.

The formulation of endocrinology has been blurred in additional ways. The term *hormone* was originally applied to substances that are secreted into the circulation and act as chemical effectors in other tissues. However, the capacity to form such chemical mediators is not limited to so-called endocrine organs. Some hormones such as angiotensins II and III are formed in the bloodstream itself. Others such as testosterone in women and dihydrotestosterone and estradiol in men are in part secreted and in part formed in peripheral tissues

from circulating precursors, so-called prohormones. Still other chemical mediators circulate only in restricted compartments such as the hypothalamic-pituitary portal system and do not reach the systemic circulation in appreciable quantities. Finally, certain hormones such as insulin, dihydrotestosterone, and thyrotropin-releasing hormone (TRH) have paracrine actions in the same tissues in which they are formed and exert different actions at distal sites. Therefore, the action as well as the origins should be considered when deciding whether or not a given effector should be classified as a hormone.

BIOCHEMISTRY   Synthesis   The mammalian hormones, now recognized to be more than 60 in number, fall into three major categories—peptides or peptide derivatives, steroids, and amines—and are synthesized in one of two ways. In the case of peptide hormones, genes code for messenger RNA, which is then translated into protein precursors. These proteins undergo posttranslational cleavage (preproparathyroid hormone → proparathyroid hormone → parathyroid hormone and proinsulin → insulin) and/or processing (thyroglobulin → thyroxine → triiodothyronine) to form the active hormone recognized by the target tissue. The distinct feature of peptide hormones is that one (or a few) genes code for the amino acid sequence of the peptide while other genes are responsible for the alteration of the peptide to its final form. In the case of peptide hormones with subunits, the different subunits may either be derived from a single precursor (insulin) or from separate precursors [luteinizing hormone (LH)]. Furthermore, the same peptide hormone (somatostatin) can be formed from different prohormones encoded by distinct genes, and individual prohormones such as pro-opiomelanocortin can be metabolized to different hormones in different cells, depending on the complement of processing enzymes in the cell in question (see Chap. 69). Peptide hormones can also be formed ectopically in malignancies of nonendocrine origin such as carcinoma of the lung (see Chap. 303).

In the case of steroid hormones the fundamental precursor—cholesterol (for most steroid hormones) or 7-dehydrocholesterol (for vitamin D metabolites)—undergoes a series of enzymatic transformations to form the final products. At least six enzymes (or enzyme complexes) and consequently six or more genes are required to transform cholesterol to estradiol. Because of the number of enzymes required the synthesis of steroids from cholesterol is unusual in malignancies of nonendocrine tissues. However, many tissues that cannot form steroid hormones de novo from cholesterol do contain enzymes that convert circulating steroids to other hormones, for example, the conversions of androgens to estrogens by trophoblastic tumors and the conversion of progesterone to deoxycorticosterone by the kidney.

The amine hormones are synthesized by a similar series of reactions to those involved in steroid hormone synthesis except that the precursors are amino acids. For example, tyrosine is the precursor for epinephrine and norepinephrine (see Chap. 66).

Storage Most tissues that synthesize hormones have a limited capacity to store the completed product. For example, the normal adult testes contain only about one-sixth of the quantity of testosterone needed for daily turnover, and consequently the testicular pool turns over several times to provide the normal daily output of hormone. Even when tissues have special storage organelles for hormone, the amount of hormone stored is usually limited: the insulin granules in the pancreatic beta cell ordinarily contain amounts of insulin sufficient only for short-term, reserve needs, whereas nerve endings may contain a several-day supply of norepinephrine. The limited capacity to store hormones is a chemical consequence of their unsuitability for incorporation into any of the three main storage compartments of the body (lipids, glycogen, or protein). For example, most steroid hormones are too polar to be stored in large quantities in lipid compartments, and peptide and amine hormones are unsuitable for incorporation into proteins. As a consequence of these factors the body pools of most hormones tend to be small. The major exceptions to this rule are those instances in which the precursor forms of hormone can be stored either as protein or in neutral lipid compartments; the normal thyroid gland contains the equivalent of a 2-week supply of thyroid hormones in the form of the protein thyroglobulin, and the precursor and intermediate forms of vitamin D can be stored in considerable quantity in hepatic lipid.

Release The biochemical mechanisms involved in the release process are poorly understood. In some instances they are thought to involve conversion of insoluble to soluble derivatives (proteolysis of thyroglobulin to thyroid hormones). In others, release is due to exocytosis of storage granules (insulin, glucagon, prolactin, growth hormone). Finally, release may involve passive diffusion of newly synthesized molecules such as steroid hormones down activity gradients into plasma; under this circumstance the rate of hormone release may be determined in part by the rate of blood flow to the tissue.

Because of the limited capacity for storage, most hormones are released into plasma as a reflection of the rates of formation. The pituitary trophic hormones [LH, adrenocorticotropin (ACTH) thyrotropin (TSH)] act in their target tissues to influence rates of both hormone synthesis and release. Even when peptide hormones are stored in granules, initial release of the stored material is followed by an enhanced rate of synthesis (as, for instance, the two-phase release of insulin induced by glucose infusion). For some hormones, major diurnal, sleep-related, developmental, and neural factors influence hormone release; again it is assumed that in most of these instances synthesis and release are tightly linked.

In many instances, the regulation of hormone release on a short-term basis is poorly understood. Some hormones are released in a pulsatile fashion with bursts of secretion occurring in a repetitive pattern; whether this intermittent release is a function of alterations in synthetic rates, alterations in blood flow, or other mechanisms is uncertain. While the physiologic significance of pulsatile release is not fully understood, changes in frequency or in amplitude of the release pattern may have profound effects on hormone function; i.e., the pulsatile administration of luteinizing hormone–releasing hormone (LHRH) stimulates the release of LH by the pituitary whereas the constant infusion of the same amount of hormone per unit time has the opposite effect. Furthermore, changes in frequency or amplitude of hormone release may characterize specific disease states; loss of the diurnal rhythm of cortisol release is characteristic of the early phase of Cushing's disease.

Transport Hormones are transported via lymph, blood, and extracellular fluids from sites of synthesis to sites of cellular action and ultimately of metabolic inactivation and degradation. The plasma is probably a passive diluent for most peptide and amine hormones but provides specific proteins for binding and transport of certain steroid and thyroid hormones. The generalization can be made that the more insoluble a hormone in water, the more important the role of transport proteins. No transport protein yet characterized is exclusive; for example, testosterone can be transported both by a specific binding protein [testosterone-binding globulin (TeBG)] and by albumin; thyroxine can be transported both by prealbumin and by thyroxine-binding globulin (TBG). Protein-bound hormone (HP) cannot enter most cellular compartments and serves as a reservoir from which free hormone (H) is liberated in sufficient quantities for diffusion into intracellular compartments:

$$H + P \rightleftharpoons HP$$

Distribution of bound and free hormone in plasma is determined by the amount of hormone, the amount of binding protein, and the binding affinity of hormone for the protein. However, in the intact organism the effective level of free hormone is influenced by additional factors. When the rate of dissociation of a hormone from a binding protein is rapid (more rapid than the capillary transit time for a specific organ), then the functional free fraction in vivo is also influenced by capillary transit time and membrane permeability.

Understanding the relation between free and bound hormone is essential for assessment of endocrine function. First, the free (dialyzable) fraction in vitro is generally less than the actual free fraction available for transport in vivo; this is because the portion of hormone bound to weak binding proteins such as albumin (in contrast to that portion bound to specific, high-affinity binding proteins) rapidly dissociates from the albumin as the free fraction diffuses from the capillary; consequently the albumin-bound hormone may function in vivo as a free fraction. Under many conditions, measurement of the dialyzable fraction does provide a useful index of the in vivo apparent free fraction. However, in hypoalbuminemic states, the in vitro free (dialyzable) fraction may increase when the in vivo free hormone level is diminished. In addition, in those tissue compartments such as liver in which proteins including hormone-transport protein complexes are cleared (in contrast to the situation in peripheral tissues in which only the free hormone enters the cell) free hormone levels have lesser effects on hormone uptake by the tissue.

Second, the net distribution of hormones between plasma and tissue is a function of the balance between tissue binding proteins and plasma binding proteins. Therefore, levels of true or apparent free hormone do not reflect the amounts of hormone within cells.

Third, only the free hormone interacts with peripheral cells and participates in the regulatory feedback mechanisms that control the rates of hormone synthesis. As a consequence, changes in the amount of transport protein alone cannot cause endocrine pathology in the steady state, provided the remainder of the endocrine feedback loop is intact. For example, profound elevations or decreases in TBG (either because of genetic or other factors) are both compatible with a euthyroid state. To illustrate, a sudden increase in TBG lowers the level of free (dialyzable) hormone and of the amount bound to albumin; as a consequence TSH secretion increases, and the output of thyroxine by the thyroid is increased *until* TBG is again saturated so that the level of free hormone returns to the normal range, at which time TSH levels and thyroid hormone secretion also return to normal. Likewise, a decrease in TBG temporarily increases the level of free hormone, and TSH secretion and thyroxine output fall until the free level returns to normal. To summarize, a change in the amount of a specific, high-affinity binding protein can cause profound alterations in hormone levels but by itself cannot cause either a steady-state hormone excess or deficiency, provided the regulatory feedback mechanisms that control hormone synthesis are intact. However, alteration of the amount of a binding protein may cause endocrine pathology in those instances in which hormone formation is not regulated by ordinary feedback control mechanisms. For example, testosterone production in women is not regulated directly by testosterone levels, and alterations in TeBG levels in women may alter the steady state levels of free testosterone.

Degradation and turnover   The plasma level (PL) of any hormone is dependent on two factors—the secretion rate (SR) of the hormone and the rates of metabolism and excretion, the so-called metabolic clearance rate (MCR):

$$PL = \frac{SR}{MCR} \quad \text{or} \quad SR = MCR \times PL$$

Metabolic clearance of hormones is accomplished by several mechanisms. Only small fractions of hormones are excreted intact in urine or bile. Degradation and inactivation of the hormone can take place in target tissues, in nontarget tissues such as liver and kidneys, or in both target and nontarget tissues. In many instances hormone metabolism facilitates excretion by rendering the hormone soluble in urine or bile. Peptide hormones are in general inactivated by proteases, largely in target tissues. Thyroid hormones are deiodinated, deaminated, and deconjugated primarily by the liver. Steroid hormones are reduced, hydroxylated, and converted into glucuronide and sulfate conjugates. On occasion biliary conjugates may be hydrolyzed in the gastrointestinal tract and reabsorbed into the circulation. The degradative mechanisms for different hormones have one common feature, namely, that alternative pathways exist for the catabolism of all hormones described to date.

Because of the nature of the feedback control of hormone secretion, changes in rates of hormone degradation alone do not cause endocrine pathology, provided the feedback loops that regulate synthesis are intact. For example, in severe liver disease and in myxedema, the degradation of glucocorticoids by the liver is impaired; as a consequence the turnover of cortisol slows, but the plasma level does not rise because secretion of ACTH is inhibited. Thus, a normal level of free hormone is maintained by decreasing the rate of cortisol secretion. The opposite is the case when glucocorticoid degradation is enhanced

(as in thyrotoxicosis); in this situation cortisol secretion rises to keep the level of the hormone normal.

Although changes in rates of hormone degradation alone do not result in hormone deficit or excess, such changes may cause profound alterations in endocrine pharmacology. Thus, ordinary doses of glucocorticoids may cause the Cushing syndrome in patients with myxedema or liver disease, and consequently glucocorticoid dosage must be reduced in both conditions. Likewise, doses of glucocorticoids may have to be increased in the presence of hyperthyroidism. In addition, the development of hyperthyroidism in a patient with inadequate adrenal reserve might precipitate an adrenal crisis by accelerating the rate of glucocorticoid catabolism. Thus, in circumstances in which the normal servomechanisms that regulate hormone synthesis are either circumvented or inoperative, changes in rates of hormone degradation may aggravate or cause pathology.

REGULATION OF HORMONE PRODUCTION   As stated above, fluctuations of hormone levels in the normal person are determined primarily by changes in rates of production. A unifying feature of all endocrine systems is the fact that the production of most hormones is regulated directly or indirectly by the metabolic activity of the hormone itself. This regulation is accomplished through a series of negative feedback loops (Fig. 320-1). In some cases a fairly constant blood level of hormone is required, and some sensing device must exist to monitor either the hormone level itself or some related function such as plasma osmolality, blood glucose, plasma calcium, or body sodium content. For example, hormones produced in response to pituitary trophic hormones (cortisol, thyroxine, gonadal steroids) feed back on the hypothalamic-pituitary system to regulate their own rates of secretion. Similarly, parathyroid hormone and insulin are secreted in response to feedback signals from serum calcium and glucose levels, respectively. Feedback systems are generally more complex than this description indicates, sometimes operating indirectly by several steps; in those instances in which the hormone itself acts as the direct regulator of feedback (testosterone on the pituitary), the effect is mediated by the same cellular machinery by which the action of the hormone is accomplished in other target tissues.

Both negative and positive feedback can occur; an example of positive feedback is the stimulation of LH release by estradiol prior to ovulation. Nonhormonal and environmental factors may alter either positive or negative feedback control mechanisms or the response to such control.

A usual feature of the feedback systems is rapidity of action; indeed, most respond within minutes or hours to varying metabolic demands to maintain homeostatic control within a narrow range. The main exceptions relate to gametogenesis in the ovary and testis (see Chaps. 330 and 331). In both instances, a complex differentiative process is involved. The steady-state operation of these systems is such that sperm production tends to be relatively constant from day to day whereas ovulation is cyclic. However, spermatogenesis requires approximately a month to complete so that changes in FSH levels may not result in altered rates of sperm production for long periods.

The fact that the secretion of hormones is under regulatory control has several important clinical implications. First, the clinical significance of plasma levels of hormones may be interpretable only if the appropriate regulatory factors are taken into account (Fig. 320-2). The meaning of a borderline low testosterone value may become clear only when LH is measured simultaneously; likewise, plasma insulin and parathyroid hormone levels may be interpretable only in conjunction with simultaneous measurements of plasma glucose and calcium, respectively. Second, the finding of simultaneous elevations of hormone pairs (or hormone-regulatory factor pairs) in the absence of signs of hormone excess suggests the presence of a hormone-resistance state. For example, simultaneous elevation of plasma glucose and insulin is characteristic of insulin resistance; simultaneous elevation of LH and testosterone suggests androgen resistance, etc. Third, insight into the regulatory control of hormone secretion is the basis for the various dynamic tests of hormone reserve and hormone secretion.

FIGURE 320-1 *Feedback control of an endocrine organ such as the adrenal, thyroid, or gonads by the pituitary.*

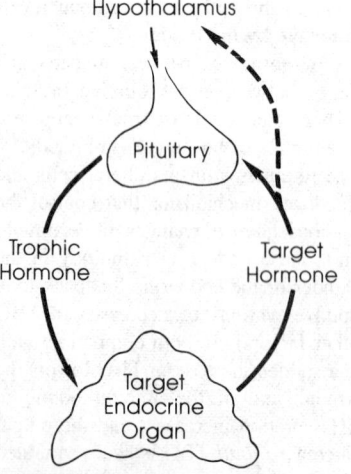

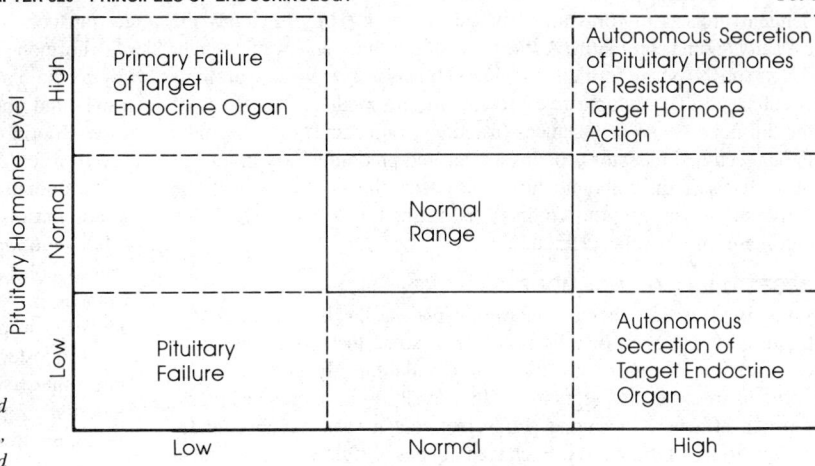

FIGURE 320-2 *Relation between target hormone level and trophic hormone level in normal and disease states (e.g., TSH and thyroid hormones, ACTH and cortisol, LH and testosterone).*

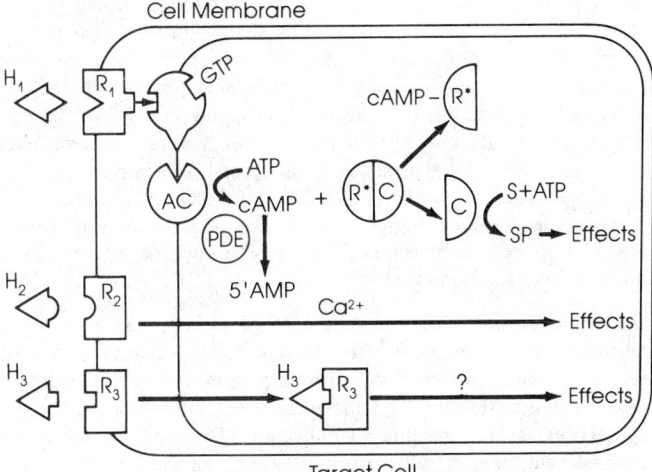

FIGURE 320-3 *Schema of action of hormones with cell surface receptors. H = hormone; R = receptor; C = catalytic subunit of protein kinase; R* = cAMP-binding subunit of protein kinase; cAMP = cyclic AMP; AC = adenylate cyclase; S = substrate; SP = phosphorylated substrate; PDE = phosphodiesterase.*

MECHANISMS OF HORMONE ACTION The first step in hormone action is the interaction of the hormone with specific macromolecules in the cell, so-called hormone receptors either on the plasma membrane of the cell surface or in the cell cytoplasm.

Hormones with cell surface receptors The hormones of the first type bind to surface receptors localized on the plasma membrane (Fig. 320-3). At least three categories of plasma membrane–hormone interaction can be distinguished. In the first category (H_1 in Fig. 320-3) the hormone-receptor complex on the cell surfaces causes the production of a so-called second messenger, cyclic adenosine 3′,5′-monophosphate (cAMP), and the subsequent actions of the hormone are mediated by cAMP (for details see Chap. 67). This mechanism applies to several protein hormones and to the biogenic amines. In the second category (H_2 in Fig. 320-3) the cell surface receptor causes the production or release of other second messengers, for example, calcium. This mechanism applies to certain neurotransmitters and TRH. The precise mechanism of calcium release and action in such systems is not known; the latter may involve binding of calcium to the enzyme-regulating protein calmodulin. In the third category (H_3 in Fig. 320-3) the cell surface receptor–hormone complex is internalized within the cell, but the subsequent events have not been defined. A hormone of the last category is insulin (see Chap. 327).

The best understood of these systems is that in which cAMP serves as the second messenger (Fig. 320-3). Cellular concentration of cAMP is controlled by two enzymes with opposite activities. Adenylate cyclase (AC), localized in the plasma membrane, converts

adenosine triphosphate (ATP) into cAMP. Phosphodiesterase (PDE), found largely in the cell cytosol, inactivates cAMP by converting it to 5′-adenosine monophosphate (5′-AMP). Hormones (H_1) that act at the cell surface form a reversible complex with specialized membrane protein receptors (R_1). These proteins bind the hormone with high affinity but limited capacity. The formation of the hormone-receptor complex causes stimulation of the adenylate cyclase. The H_1R_1 complex binds the N subunit of the adenylate cyclase (a protein that also binds GTP) and activates the catalytic subunit of the enzyme AC, thus stimulating cAMP synthesis. Phosphorylating enzymes—known as protein kinases—appear to play an important role in the overall process; these kinases (RC) are composed of catalytic (C) and regulatory (R) subunits. Binding of cAMP to R frees C and allows phosphorylation of various proteins (S) with consequent activation or inactivation.

Hormones with intracellular receptors Steroid and thyroid hormones are transported in plasma bound to carrier proteins (Fig. 320-4). The protein-bound hormones (HP) are in dynamic equilibrium with small amounts of free hormones (H) that diffuse by a passive mechanism into cells where they act by fundamentally different mechanisms than do the peptide hormones. In most instances the principal form of the hormone secreted into plasma (cortisol, progesterone, aldosterone, estradiol) undergoes no further metabolism within the cell and is responsible for hormone action within the target cell. Other hormones (thyroxine, testosterone) undergo chemical conversion to more active forms (triiodothyronine and dihydrotestosterone).

H binds to specific receptor proteins (R) in the cytoplasm to form a hormone-receptor complex (HR). The hormone-receptor complex undergoes transformation by a poorly understood, temperature-de-

FIGURE 320-4 *Mechanism of action of hormones with intracellular receptors. H = hormone; P = plasma transport protein; R = receptor; R* = activated receptor; mRNA = messenger RNA.*

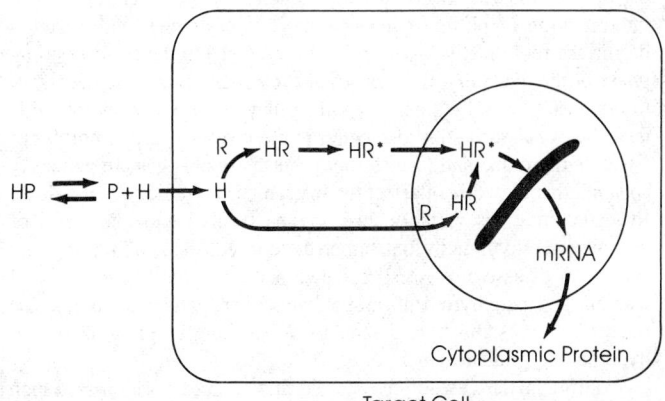

pendent process to form an activated complex (HR*) that has the capacity to bind chromatin. As the result of this binding new messenger RNAs (mRNAs) are formed, and the synthesis of cytoplasmic proteins is enhanced. The cytoplasmic proteins in turn mediate the effects of the hormone. In some instances (triiodothyronine and some steroids) the unoccupied receptor proteins are located predominantly in nuclei; in such cases the unbound hormone enters the nucleus where the active hormone-receptor complex is formed and attaches to the chromatin in a similar fashion.

ASSESSMENT OF HORMONE FUNCTION In practice endocrine status is assessed either by measuring plasma levels of a hormone, the urinary excretion of a hormone or of some metabolite, the rates of secretion of hormones into the circulation, dynamic tests of hormone reserve and regulation, the levels of hormone receptors, selected effects of hormone action in target tissues, or appropriate combinations of these tests. Each technique is useful in certain clinical situations.

Plasma levels The plasma levels of steroid and thyroid hormones range between 1 nM and 1 μM, while those of peptide hormones are generally in the range of 1 pM to 0.1 nM. The application of modern chemical, chromatographic, radioreceptor, and radioimmunoassay techniques for the assessment of plasma constituents in low concentrations constitutes one of the significant advances of modern medicine and has transformed endocrinology to a more quantitative discipline. In the case of hormones whose plasma levels are relatively constant from moment to moment and day to day (thyroxine and triiodothyronine), the measurement of isolated plasma levels alone provides a reliable assessment of the hormone status in most clinical situations.

For several reasons, however, care must be exercised in assessing isolated plasma levels. First, for hormones with relatively simple structures (steroid and thyroid hormones) chemical and radioimmunoassay techniques are reliable so that measured values usually reflect the plasma levels as of a given moment. In the case of the more complex peptide hormones, however, considerable variability may exist in the structure of physiologically active hormone molecules in the circulation, some of which may be measured poorly in specific radioimmunoassay procedures; for example, standard radioimmunoassays for LH and for parathyroid hormone may on occasion either underestimate or overestimate the amount of biologically active hormone in plasma. In such situations, radioreceptor assays or in vitro bioassays may be employed to assess endocrine status.

Second, in the case of hormones that undergo pulsatile secretion (LH, testosterone) a single value may or may not be representative of mean plasma levels. In these instances it is necessary either to measure levels in several samples drawn at random or to pool aliquots of three or more samples of plasma drawn at 20- to 30-min intervals for a single determination.

Third, when plasma levels exhibit a characteristic, predictable fluctuation such as the diurnal variation of plasma cortisol, the timing of plasma sampling can be designed to provide a useful index of the hormone status. Even here, however, it is important to recognize that plasma levels may exhibit diurnal variation only during certain phases of life (plasma LH levels in early puberty). In women appropriate interpretation of plasma gonadotropins, progesterone, and estradiol during the reproductive years requires reference to the corresponding phase of the ovulatory and menstrual cycles, and it may be necessary to obtain sequential studies over many days to provide interpretable data. Seasonal variations also occur in the levels of certain hormones (such as thyroxine and testosterone), but these changes are generally so small that they do not affect the interpretation of individual values. In some situations variation in hormone levels is not the result of any obvious rhythmicity but rather the consequences of waxing and waning of disease processes; repeated measurements of cortisol or of calcium and parathyroid hormone levels over many months may be necessary to establish a diagnosis of Cushing's syndrome or of hyperparathyroidism.

Fourth, in the case of the steroid and thyroid hormones, which are transported in plasma largely bound to proteins, measurement of total hormone concentration provides an index of endocrine status *only* to the extent that it allows a deduction of the level of the free or unbound hormone. Indeed, direct measurements of the free levels of these hormones (usually 1 percent or less of the total) can be done only in a few labs. Since the amount of free hormone is a function of the amount and the affinity of binding of transport proteins and the amount of hormone, the total hormone level reflects the amount of free hormone only as long as the amount of binding protein(s) remains constant or fluctuates only within narrow limits. In those instances in which the level of binding protein is increased (TBG and TeBG in pregnancy) or decreased [hereditary decreases in TBG and corticosteroid-binding globulin (CBG)] it is essential to utilize some other assessment of the amount of binding protein to allow deduction of the free hormone level (T$_3$ resin uptake for TBG or direct measurement of TBG, TeBG, or CBG).

Fifth, the range of plasma levels of most hormones within the normal population is broad. As a consequence, the level of a hormone in an individual may be halved or doubled (and thus be grossly abnormal for that person) but still be within the so-called normal range. For this reason it is frequently useful to assess appropriate hormone pairs simultaneously (LH and testosterone, thyroxine and TSH); a borderline low testosterone level in the presence of elevated plasma LH is indicative of testicular failure, whereas the same level of testosterone in the presence of a normal LH implies that the endocrine status is normal (Fig. 320-2). Likewise, in women with increased testosterone production and secondary decrease in TeBG, plasma testosterone concentration may be normal despite increased production of the hormone.

Urinary excretion The measurement of urinary excretion of a hormone or a hormone metabolite that reflects plasma levels or secretory rates offers certain advantages over the measurement of isolated plasma levels, e.g., the urinary excretion reflects average plasma levels over the time of collection. Thus, a 24-h urine free cortisol value may provide a better estimate of the function of the adrenal cortex than isolated measurements of plasma cortisol. Again, however, certain limitations of the use of urinary measurements must be kept in mind. (1) Creatinine determinations should be done routinely to document the adequacy of the urine collection. Women excrete on average about 1 g, and men about 1.8 g per day. Day-to-day variation should not exceed 20 percent. (2) The excretion of individual metabolites may not reflect changes in hormone secretion under all conditions. For example, the formation of the 18-oxo derivative of aldosterone may be influenced by drugs that do not alter secretion or plasma levels of the hormone. (3) Urine values are obviously meaningless for those hormones (thyroxine, triiodothyronine) excreted into bile. Of more importance is the fact that peptide hormones such as gonadotropins may be metabolized differently in different individuals prior to excretion into the urine so that establishment of the range of normal is difficult. (4) Hormones from more than one source may be excreted as common metabolites; urinary 17-ketosteroids are derived from both adrenal and gonadal androgens, and consequently their measurement is of little value in assessing testicular androgen production in men. (5) Changes in renal function may influence rates of hormone excretion into urine. Such changes can in part be corrected by measurement of urine creatinine, but in the case of metabolites or conjugates formed in the kidney itself excretion patterns may be distorted out of proportion to the decrease in creatinine clearance.

Secretion and production rates The measurement of the actual secretion rate of a hormone circumvents most problems inherent in measurement of plasma levels and urinary excretion. Such measurements involve the administration of radioactive hormone and measuring the dilution that such a hormone undergoes as a consequence of mixture with endogenously secreted, nonradioactive hormones over a given period of time. In practice the plasma hormone itself or a unique metabolite of the hormone from urine is isolated, purified to radiochemical homogeneity, and used to calculate the amount of the hormone secreted during the time of study. In the case of hormones formed principally in peripheral tissues (estradiol and dihydrotestosterone in men, triiodothyronine in both sexes) radioactive precursors can be administered, and the rates of conversion to the metabolites in question can be measured for assessment of overall production rates. Alternatively, as described above, clearance rates of hormones can be measured and, together with mean plasma levels, used to estimate secretion rates. Unfortunately, these various techniques are complex and expensive to perform, require use of radioactive isotopes, and can be done in only a few centers.

Dynamic tests of hormone reserve and regulation When hypo- or hyperfunction is severe, measurement of the level of hormone in blood or urine may be satisfactory for making a diagnosis, particularly when the tests demonstrate appropriate feedback relationships; e.g., low plasma testosterone coupled with high plasma LH indicates primary testicular failure. In less clear-cut instances, however, stimulation tests are useful in establishing the significance of borderline low values. Likewise, suppression tests are used to document the presence of hyperfunction of endocrine systems. All such dynamic tests are designed to take advantage of the known feedback control mechanisms for various hormones (Fig. 320-1).

Two types of stimulation tests are in common usage. In one, endogenous hormone production or action is blocked (cortisol production by metyrapone, estradiol action by clomiphene), and the capacity of the pituitary to respond by increasing endogenous production of the trophic hormone and/or the capacity of the target tissue to respond are then assessed; ideally such tests measure the integrity of an entire hypothalamic–pituitary–target tissue loop. In the other type of stimulation test, the trophic hormone itself is administered under some standardized regimen, and the capacity of the target tissue to respond is determined (cortisol levels before and after ACTH administration). Stimulation tests are particularly useful in four situations: (1) assessing hormone status when precise quantification of plasma levels is difficult or imperfect (ACTH), (2) assessing endocrine status when static tests are borderline low, (3) distinguishing primary from secondary (pituitary) causes of endocrine failure, and (4) assessing gonadal reserve in prepubertal patients in whom plasma gonadotropins and gonadal steroids are difficult to interpret.

Suppression tests are useful for the diagnosis of hyperfunction because the hyperfunctioning gland by definition does not operate under normal control mechanisms. Suppression can either be quantitatively or qualitatively abnormal. For example, the feedback control of the pituitary may be reset to respond to high levels of the suppressing hormone (pituitary ACTH secretion in Cushing's disease), or secretion can be autonomous (ACTH secretion by carcinoma of the lung). In principle, the feedback regulator is administered, and the capacity of the secretion of the hormone to be inhibited is assessed for the endocrine system in question (change in ^{131}I uptake after administration of thyroid hormones, change in cortisol secretion after the administration of potent exogenous glucocorticoids, suppressibility of plasma growth hormone by glucose).

The clinical usefulness of dynamic tests of endocrine function is limited by the fact that they are altered by a multitude of secondary factors. Age, coexisting disease states, and concurrent drug regimens all interact to influence responsiveness and hence to limit the specificity of such tests.

Hormone receptors and antibodies The measurement of hormone receptors in biopsy material from target tissues or in fibroblasts propagated from biopsy material is useful—for example, in the diagnosis of partial hormone-resistance states such as rickets due to vitamin D resistance, hyperglycemia and hyperinsulinemia associated with insulin resistance, and male pseudohermaphroditism due to androgen resistance. Likewise, under selected conditions measurement of antibodies to hormones (such as antibodies to thyroid hormones that can cause hypothyroidism) or antibodies to target tissues (adrenal gland, gonads, thyroid) may be essential for the assessment of

endocrine status. With certain exceptions (antibodies to thyroid tissue) these tests are not widely available.

Tissue effects The ideal hormone test perhaps is the measurement of the peripheral end result of hormone action in the target tissues for the hormone. For example, demonstration of the capacity to concentrate urine maximally following water restriction indicates that the hypothalamic control mechanisms are intact, that the posterior pituitary has a normal capacity to secrete vasopressin, that the vasopressin receptor is intact, and that the postreceptor effector mechanisms for the hormone are operative. Optimally such a test assesses the function of the entire pathway of hormone secretion and action. In practice, many such tests are imperfect. For example, even though vasopressin secretion is normal, intrinsic renal disease can result in a fixed low urine osmolality and thus distort the interpretation of the functional test of vasopressin action. In other instances the tests are difficult to perform and subject both to artifact and to influences from diverse parameters (for example, the metabolic rate is increased by fever even when thyroid function is normal). For these reasons, the identification of additional specific tissue markers for hormone action would be very useful.

CLINICAL SYNDROMES Endocrinopathy can result from hormone deficiency, hormone excess, or resistance to hormone action, and abnormalities in more than one endocrine system commonly coexist in the same individual.

Deficiency states With few exceptions (calcitonin) hormone deficiency results in pathologic manifestations. The study of clinical disorders that result from hormone deficiency or absence played an important role in the evolution of endocrinology as a discipline. Such studies were followed by attempts to extract the responsible hormone from normal endocrine tissues, characterize its chemical nature (and ultimately synthesize it), and administer the hormone to replace the deficit. The routine treatment of hypothyroidism by the administration of thyroid hormone is probably as successful as any therapeutic measure in medicine. Because clinical deficiency states can be induced in experimental animals by appropriate destruction or removal of the endocrine organ, an enormous amount is known about the pathophysiology of the deficiency states (diabetes mellitus, pituitary and adrenal insufficiency, hypothyroidism, and hypogonadism).

The nature of the destructive processes involved in the failure of the endocrine organs is also understood in many instances; these include infections (adrenal insufficiency due to tuberculosis), infarction (postpartum pituitary failure) and tissue death of other causes (diabetes secondary to pancreatitis), tumors (chromophobe adenomas of the pituitary), autoimmune processes (Hashimoto's thyroiditis), dietary inadequacy (hypothyroidism due to iodine deficiency), and hereditary defects (pituitary dwarfism). In certain forms of diabetes mellitus, the cause may be a hereditary predisposition that renders the pancreas subject to destruction by several mechanisms (see Chap. 327). In other endocrine-deficiency diseases the etiology of the defect is unidentified (ordinary myxedema and congenital anorchia).

Hormone excess With few exceptions (testosterone in men, progesterone in men and women) hormone excess causes pathologic effects. Four general types of hormone excess are recognized. In one, the hormone is overproduced by the gland that is the usual site of its production (hyperthyroidism, acromegaly, Cushing's disease); such excess production results from failure or circumvention of the feedback control mechanisms that regulate production of the hormone in the normal state, but the underlying mechanism is often obscure because animal models for the diseases are rare. The second type of hormone excess results when a hormone is produced by a tissue (usually malignant) that ordinarily is not a major endocrine organ (for example, ACTH production in oat cell carcinoma of the lung, thyroid hormone secretion by struma ovarii). Such hormone-excess states have been described for many hormones (see Chap. 303). A third type of hormone-excess state involves the overproduction of hormones in peripheral tissues from circulating precursors; for example, overproduction of estrogen in liver disease because of diversion of the precursor androstenedione from its usual sites of catabolism in the liver to sites of extraglandular estrogen formation. Finally, hormone excess all too commonly results from iatrogenic causes; for example, the complications resulting from glucocorticoid therapy constitute a major clinical problem (see Chap. 325).

Excess of a given hormone may result from more than one cause. Thyrotoxicosis can result from overproduction of hormone by the thyroid as a result of overproduction of TSH (rare), from stimulation by extrapituitary thyroid-stimulating factors, from autonomous thyroid hyperfunction; from leakage of preformed hormone from the thyroid due to an inflammatory injury; or from excess hormone from sources other than the thyroid itself, as in thyroid hormone overdosage or struma ovarii (see Chap. 324). The unraveling of the cause of specific hormone-excess states can be one of the most challenging problems of clinical endocrinology.

Production of abnormal hormones In some instances abnormal hormones can cause endocrine disease. One form of diabetes mellitus is the result of a single-gene mutation that results in the production of an abnormal insulin molecule that is ineffective because of defective binding to the insulin receptor. In other cases, hormone precursors or incompletely processed peptide hormones may be released into the circulation, as is common in so-called ectopic hormone production of neoplasia (see Chap. 303). Alternatively, immunoglobulins may bind to hormone receptors and thus exert hormonal actions, for example, the thyroid-stimulating immunoglobulins in hyperthyroidism (Chap. 324) or the antibodies to the insulin receptor that have some insulin-like actions (Chap. 327).

Hormone resistance The concept that an endocrinopathy could result because the tissues cannot respond to normal (or increased) levels of a hormone evolved from the deduction that pseudohypoparathyroidism is due to peripheral resistance to the action of parathyroid hormone (see Chaps. 67 and 336). This concept has had far-reaching implications. First, the concept of hormone resistance has served as a major stimulus for the study of how hormones act within cells. Second, more and more forms of hormone resistance have been identified so that diseases are now recognized to result from resistance to most hormones. Such hormone resistance is frequently due to hereditary causes. Third, hormone resistance can be due to a variety of causes, including defects in receptors and in postreceptor effector mechanisms for hormones, development of antibodies to hormones or hormone receptors, and the absence of target cells. Fourth, abnormalities of receptors are now implicated in the pathogenesis of diseases outside the endocrine domain, such as myasthenia gravis and familial hypercholesterolemia.

A common feature of hormone-resistance states is the coexistence of a normal or *elevated* level of the hormone in the circulation with evidence of deficient hormone action (Fig. 320-1). This feature is a consequence of the fact that most hormones are under regulatory feedback control, and failure of hormone action usually leads to increased hormone production.

However, hormone resistance does not necessarily involve equally all target tissues for the hormone. For example, selective resistance to thyroid hormone can be restricted to the pituitary itself, and in one form of androgen resistance androgen action is more severely impaired in the testis than in other target tissues. Elucidation of the pathogenesis of these selective defects will doubtlessly provide insight into the factors that determine the nature of "target tissues" for hormones.

Diseases affecting multiple endocrine systems The fact that disorders can affect more than one endocrine system has been known since the description of panhypopituitarism in the nineteenth century. Such disorders encompass diverse etiologies including autoimmunity (autoimmune polyglandular dysfunction, or Schmidt's syndrome), receptor abnormalities (gonadotropin and thyrotropin resistance in pseudohypoparathyroidism), tumors (multiple endocrine neoplasia,

or MEN), and hereditary disorders of unknown etiology (lipodystrophies) (see Chap. 334). They may include both hypo- and hyperfunctioning states, and some clinical syndromes may occur in the context of more than one polyendocrine state (pheochromocytoma in MEN II and MEN III, diabetes mellitus in Schmidt's syndrome and in lipodystrophy).

Because each endocrinopathy in such a constellation can also occur alone, all endocrine patients must be approached with a high index of suspicion for abnormalities of multiple systems. This is of particular importance because treatment of one condition may cause worsening of another (surgical procedures such as thyroidectomy can cause worsening of unrecognized pheochromocytoma) and because in certain of the familial syndromes it is mandatory to make systematic searches for the disease in potentially affected family members.

REFERENCES

CLARK JH et al: Mechanisms of steroid hormone action, in *Williams' Textbook of Endocrinology*, 7th ed, JD Wilson, DW Foster (eds). Philadelphia, Saunders, 1985, pp 33–75

GILMAN AG: Guanine nucleotide-binding regulatory proteins and dual control of adenylate cyclase. J Clin Invest 73:1, 1984

GORDEN P, WEINTRAUB BD: Radioreceptor and other functional hormone assays, in *Williams' Textbook of Endocrinology*, 7th ed, JD Wilson, DW Foster (eds). Philadelphia, Saunders, 1985, pp 133–146

HABENER JF: Genetic control of hormone formation, in *Willimas' Textbook of Endocrinology*, 7th ed, JD Wilson, DW Foster (eds). Philadelphia, Saunders, 1985, pp 9–32

KRIEGER DT, ASCHOFF J: Endocrine and other biological rhythms, in *Endocrinology*, vol 3, LJ DeGroot et al (eds). New York, Grune & Stratton, 1979, pp 2079–2109

PARDRIDGE WM: Transport of protein-bound hormones into tissues in vivo. Endocr Rev 2:103, 1981

ROTH J, GRUNFELD C: Mechanism of action of peptide hormones and catecholamines, in *Williams' Textbook of Endocrinology*, 7th ed, JD Wilson, DW Foster (eds). Philadelphia, Saunders, pp 76–122

VERHOEVEN GFM, WILSON JD: The syndromes of primary hormone resistance. Metabolism 28:253, 1979

YALOW RS: Radioimmunoassay of hormones, in *Williams' Textbook of Endocrinology*, 7th ed, JD Wilson, DW Foster (eds). Philadelphia, Saunders, 1985, pp 123–132

321 NEUROENDOCRINE REGULATION AND DISEASES OF THE ANTERIOR PITUITARY AND HYPOTHALAMUS

GILBERT H. DANIELS / JOSEPH B. MARTIN

The pituitary, appropriately titled the master gland, produces six major hormones and stores an additional two hormones. Growth hormone (GH) regulates growth and has important influences on intermediary metabolism (see Chap. 322). Prolactin (PRL) is necessary for lactation. Luteinizing hormone (LH) and follicle-stimulating hormone (FSH) control the gonads in men and women. Thyroid-stimulating hormone (TSH, thyrotropin) controls the function of the thyroid gland. Adrenocorticotropic hormone (ACTH) is responsible for controlling glucocorticoid function of the adrenal cortex. These hormones are all synthesized in the anterior pituitary. Antidiuretic hormone (AVP, arginine vasopressin) and oxytocin are produced in neurons of the hypothalamus and stored in the posterior lobe of the pituitary (see Chap. 323). AVP controls water conservation by the kidneys; oxytocin is necessary for milk let-down during lactation (Fig. 321-1).

An important feedback relationship exists between the anterior pituitary and its three target glands—the gonads, the adrenal cortex, and the thyroid. When the gonads fail or are removed the concentrations of LH and FSH rise, a condition known as primary hypogonadism. When the adrenal cortex is removed or destroyed, primary adrenal insufficiency (or Addison's disease) results, and the serum ACTH concentration increases. Thyroid failure results in the characteristic TSH rise of primary hypothyroidism.

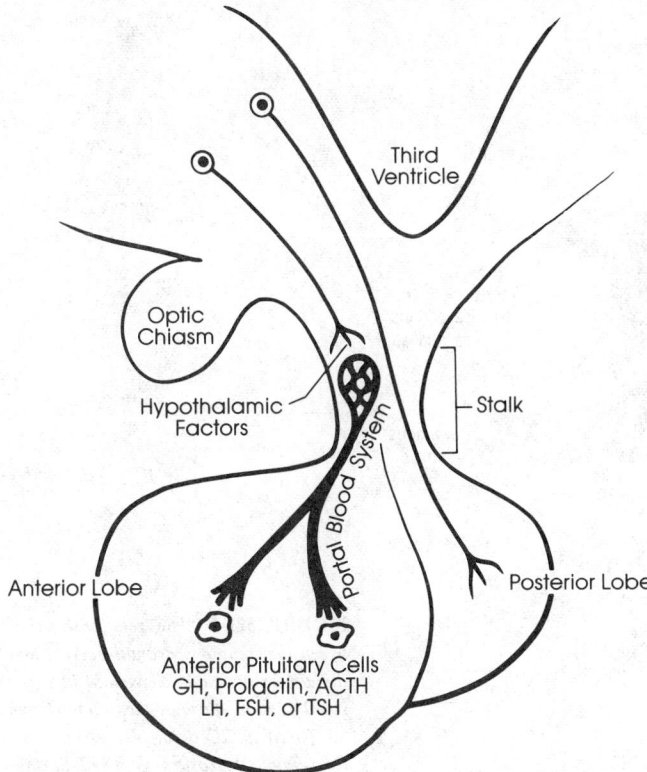

FIGURE 321-1 *The relationship between the hypothalamus and pituitary. See text for details.*

When the pituitary gland is removed or destroyed, loss of the trophic hormones results in secondary hypogonadism, adrenal insufficiency, or hypothyroidism. Growth hormone and prolactin function are also lost. AVP and oxytocin function are not affected by destruction of the pituitary provided their site of origin in the hypothalamus is not disturbed.

The pituitary is in turn under the control of the hypothalamus, which produces a number of chemical mediators. These hormones are synthesized in the hypothalamus and enter the portal vascular system which carries them through the pituitary stalk to the anterior lobe (Fig. 321-1). Interruption of the pituitary stalk is followed by reduction in the release of GH, LH, FSH, TSH, and ACTH from the anterior pituitary. This implies that stimulatory influences from the hypothalamus are necessary for release of these hormones. In contrast, the level of prolactin rises after interruption of the stalk, implying a normal tonic inhibitory hypothalamic influence on prolactin secretion. The rise in prolactin secretion also provides evidence that stalk section does not lead to pituitary destruction. If the stalk section is not performed at too high a level, AVP and oxytocin release continue principally from axons that terminate in the median eminence of the hypothalamus. With hypothalamic ablation, the levels of GH, LH, FSH, TSH, ACTH, AVP, and oxytocin fall, whereas prolactin levels increase (Fig. 321-1).

Most hypothalamic factors that control secretion of the pituitary hormones are peptides (Table 321-1). Growth hormone–releasing hormone (GRH) is the dominant influence on GH release; in addition, somatostatin acts as an inhibitory hormone for GH release. Although LH and FSH levels vary independently in physiologic states, a single releasing hormone [luteinizing hormone–releasing hormone (LHRH), also called gonadotropin-releasing hormone (GnRH)] plays a major role in controlling their release. Thyrotropin-releasing hormone (TRH) controls TSH release and may also influence prolactin release, and corticotropin releasing hormone (CRH) controls ACTH release. In addition, dopamine acts as the prolactin inhibitory factor (PIF).

Pituitary tumors may lead to hormonal over- or underproduction or may cause mechanical problems by impinging on neighboring structures. The most common hormones produced by pituitary tumors are prolactin and GH, the two hormones that lack simple end-organ feedback inhibitory loops. Prolactin excess leads to galactorrhea and/or hypogonadism; GH excess leads to gigantism and acromegaly. ACTH-secreting tumors produce Cushing's disease. TSH-secreting tumors are rare causes of hyperthyroidism. Gonadotropin-secreting tumors are paradoxically most often associated with hypogonadism. Large pituitary tumors may cause partial or complete hypopituitarism by compression of the adjacent normal gland or pituitary stalk and are associated with visual field disturbances due to compression of the optic chiasm with other neurologic disturbances caused by invasion of cavernous sinuses or cranial fossae.

Hypothalamic disease may cause hypopituitarism with the exception that secretion of prolactin may be increased. AVP deficiency leading to diabetes insipidus is virtually diagnostic of hypothalamic disease or of high interruption of the pituitary stalk. Disturbances of thirst, temperature regulation, appetite, and blood pressure may occur with hypothalamic disorders as well. Large hypothalamic masses may lead to visual field disturbances, obstruction of the third ventricle, and invasion of surrounding brain tissue.

ANATOMY AND EMBRYOLOGY

The pituitary gland (hypophysis) sits within the sella turcica (''Turkish saddle'') of the sphenoid bone at the base of the skull and is composed principally of the anterior (adenohypophysis) and posterior lobes (neurohypophysis). The intermediate lobe is rudimentary in humans. The normal pituitary gland weighs between 0.5 and 0.9 g.

The pituitary is separated from the brain by the diaphragma sella, an extension of the dura mater, and from the sphenoid sinus anteriorly and inferiorly by a thin layer of bone. The lateral walls of the sella abut on the cavernous sinuses, which contain the internal carotid arteries and cranial nerves III, IV, V, and VI. The optic chiasm is slightly anterior to the pituitary stalk, just above the diaphragma sella. Thus, tumors of the pituitary may lead to visual field defects, to cranial nerve palsies, or to invasion of the sphenoid sinus (Figs. 321-2 and 321-3).

The hypothalamus extends anteriorly to the margin of the optic chiasm and posteriorly to include the mammillary bodies. Superiorly, the hypothalamic sulcus of the third ventricle separates the thalamus from the hypothalamus. The rounded inferior base of the hypothalamus

TABLE 321-1 Anterior pituitary and hypophysiotrophic hormones

Pituitary hormone	Hypophysiotrophic hormones	
	Name	Structure
Thyrotropin (TSH)	Thyrotropin-releasing hormone (TRH)	Tripeptide
Adrenocorticotropin (ACTH)	Corticotropin-releasing hormone (CRH)	41 Amino acids
Luteinizing hormone (LH)	Luteinizing hormone–releasing hormone (LHRH)	Decapeptide
Follicle-stimulating hormone (FSH)	LHRH	Decapeptide
Growth hormone (GH)	Growth hormone–releasing hormone (GRH)	44 Amino acids
	Growth hormone release–inhibiting hormone* (somatostatin, GIH)	14 Amino acids
Prolactin	Prolactin release–inhibiting factor (PIF)	Dopamine
	Prolactin-releasing factor (PRF)†	Peptide ? Vasoactive intestinal polypeptide (VIP)

* *Somatostatin also inhibits TRH-stimulated TSH release*
† *TRH stimulates prolactin release*

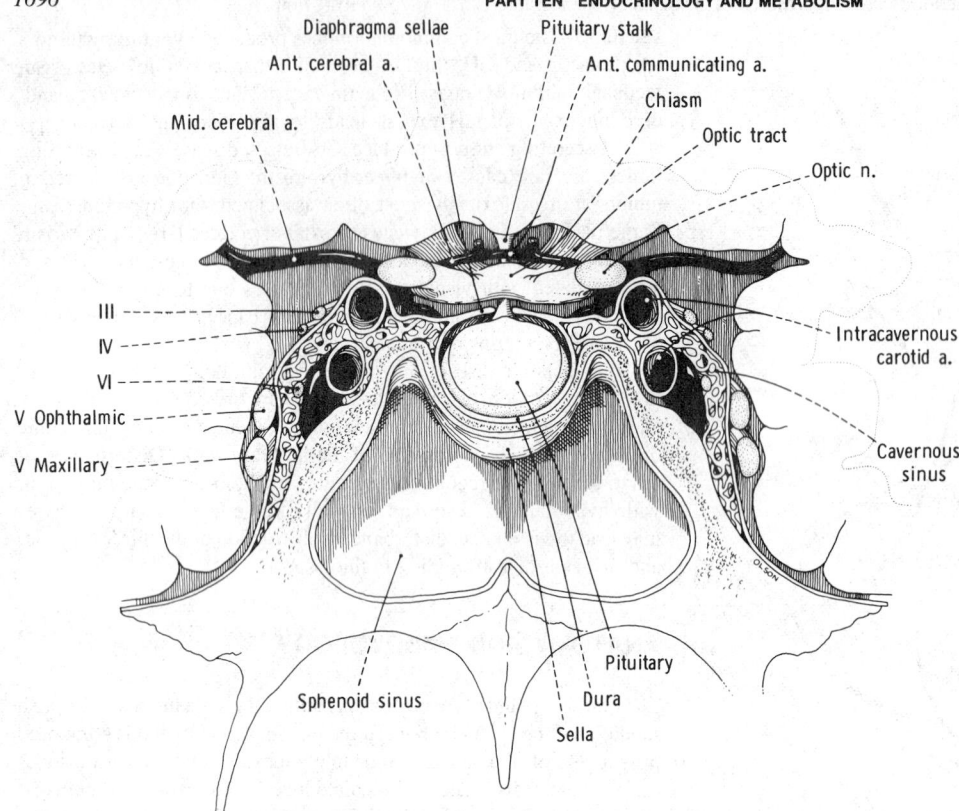

FIGURE 321-2 *The relationship between the pituitary, cranial nerves, and the cavernous sinus as viewed in a coronal section through the sella. (From JA Taren in RC Schneider et al (eds). Correlative Neurosurgery, 3d ed, Springfield, Ill., Charles C Thomas, 1982.)*

forms the tuber cinereum. The central portion of the base (termed the infundibulum or median eminence) is formed by the floor of the third ventricle (Fig. 321-3) and continues inferiorly to form the pituitary stalk. The releasing factors are synthesized in neurons that are located along the margins of the third ventricle and that project fibers which terminate in the median eminence adjacent to the portal capillaries.

The cell bodies of the supraoptic and paraventricular nuclei of the hypothalamus produce vasopressin and oxytocin, which travel down nerve axons in the supraopticohypophysial and paraventriculohypophysial nerve tracts to reach the posterior lobe.

The communication between the hypothalamus and the anterior pituitary is chemical rather than physical. Releasing factors produced by hypothalamic neurons reach the anterior pituitary via the portal system to stimulate or inhibit hormone production. Some of the vasopressin-containing neurons also terminate in the median eminence, and vasopressin can stimulate release of ACTH and GH.

The anterior pituitary has the highest blood flow of any tissue in the body [0.8 (mL/g)/min]. The blood supply reaches the anterior pituitary by a circuitous route through the hypothalamus. Two derivatives of the internal carotid arteries, the superior hypophysial arteries (SHA), branch in the subarachnoid space around the pituitary

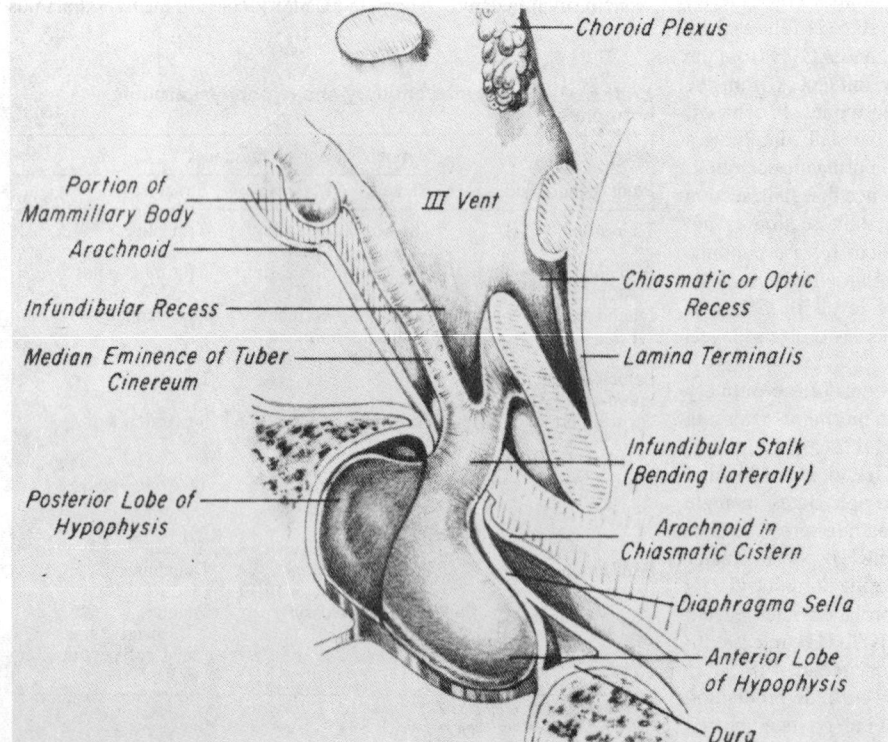

FIGURE 321-3 *Sagittal view of the human hypothalamic-pituitary unit, demonstrating the anatomic relationships between optic chiasm and pituitary stalk. (From Reichlin in Post et al.)*

stalk and terminate in the capillary network of the median eminence. These capillaries have a fenestrated endothelium which allows easy access to the hypothalamic releasing hormones. Transport of substances from the capillaries to the median eminence is also facilitated because the median eminence lies outside the blood-brain barrier. The capillaries then coalesce to form 6 to 10 straight veins known as the hypothalamic-pituitary portal circulation. These veins constitute the main direct blood supply to the anterior lobe and supply it with nutrients as well as information from the hypothalamus. A minor arterial blood supply to the anterior lobe comes from the trabecular branches of the SHA. The posterior pituitary is supplied entirely by blood from the inferior hypophysial arteries.

The anterior lobe of the pituitary is formed predominantly from the lateral proliferation of Rathke's pouch, an embryologic outpouching from the floor of the primitive oral cavity. Rathke's pouch is met by a diverticulum extending downward from the floor of the third ventricle, which forms the posterior lobe.

Rathke's pouch is closed off by proliferation of the anterior and posterior lobe and forms a thin residual cleft in the gland (Rathke's cleft). This small cleft may persist as a cyst lined with cuboidal or columnar epithelium. Since the pituitary gland rotates as it grows, these cysts usually lie in a position superior to the pituitary gland. The further growth and proliferation of these cysts can give rise to craniopharyngiomas, tumors that generally occupy a suprasellar position. Development of the sphenoid bone separates the pituitary from the oral cavity. Remnants of the pituitary, known as pharyngeal pituitaries, occasionally persist within or below the sphenoid bone. These remnants may produce pituitary hormones and occasionally develop into pituitary tumors.

Five distinct cell types in the anterior pituitary secrete six different hormones: lactotrophs (prolactin), somatotrophs (GH), gonadotrophs (LH and FSH), thyrotrophs (TSH), and corticotrophs (ACTH).

PROLACTIN

PHYSIOLOGY The lactotrophs constitute 10 to 25 percent of the normal pituitary and increase to 70 percent of the gland during pregnancy. The prolactin gene on chromosome 6 codes for a precursor molecule that is larger than the circulating hormone. The predominant form of the processed hormone contains 198 amino acids (23,000 mol wt) in a single polypeptide chain containing three intrachain disulfide bonds. Higher-molecular-weight forms of prolactin, up to 100,000 mol wt, ("big" and "big-big" prolactin) may be present in small amounts in the circulation of normal persons and in larger amounts in patients with pituitary adenomas; these molecules react in prolactin immunoassays but do not have normal biologic potency.

Prolactin is essential for lactation. Receptors for the hormone are present in human breast and gonads, whereas in other animals they are found in a variety of tissues. Prolactin is an important promoter of breast cancer in rodents; a similar connection has not been established in human breast cancer (see Chap 295).

During pregnancy increasing placental estrogen production stimulates the growth and replication of the pituitary lactotrophs and causes increased prolactin secretion. The pituitary doubles in size during a normal pregnancy and returns to normal after delivery. Prolactin secretion during pregnancy prepares the breast for postpartum lactation. Estrogen inhibits prolactin action at the breast, so that lactation does not occur until estrogen levels decline post partum.

Prolactin levels rise in the fetus beginning at about 25 weeks, probably owing to maternal estrogen transfer and stimulation of the fetal pituitary. The level falls rapidly after delivery, reaching a nadir by 2 to 4 weeks post partum. High concentrations of prolactin are present in amniotic fluid, although the origin and functional significance are unknown.

Under normal circumstances, prolactin secretion by the anterior pituitary is restrained by the hypothalamus. With hypothalamic destruction or pituitary stalk section, prolactin secretion increases and

serum concentrations rise. The hypothalamic inhibitory factor for prolactin appears to be dopamine, although peptide inhibitory factors have been described. The arcuate nucleus of the hypothalamus is the primary hypothalamic site of dopamine synthesis; dopamine travels down axons to nerve terminals in the median eminence where it is released (tuberoinfundibular dopamine system). Dopamine enters the portal circulation and reaches the anterior pituitary to inhibit prolactin release. The intravenous administration of dopamine (2 μg/min per kilogram of body weight) or the oral administration of dopamine precursors (e.g., levodopa) or dopamine agonists (e.g., bromocriptine) inhibits prolactin release. Increased blood prolactin appears to increase hypothalamic dopamine production, which in turn partially inhibits prolactin release via a "short" feedback loop.

The prolactin rise during suckling appears to require a prolactin-releasing factor, which has not yet been conclusively identified. Vasoactive intestinal peptide (VIP) may be responsible, as it is a potent stimulator of prolactin release. Suckling-induced prolactin rise is blocked by serotonin antagonists, such as methysergide, which suggests an influence of serotonin on prolactin release. TRH is also a potent stimulator of prolactin release; indeed the lowest dose of TRH capable of stimulating TSH stimulates prolactin release as well. However, TSH and prolactin release are under independent control in most physiologic states; lactation does not lead to TSH elevation, and primary hypothyroidism is rarely associated with prolactin excess.

Prolactin concentrations rise during sleep, a phenomenon which requires the input of higher centers into the hypothalamus. Stress-related prolactin release can be blocked by opiate antagonists such as naloxone and is probably mediated by endogenous opioids. Morphine can stimulate prolactin release, which may contribute to the amenorrhea that occurs with narcotic addiction, but basal prolactin secretion is not influenced by opiate antagonists.

HYPERPROLACTINEMIA Clinical features Prolactin excess (hyperprolactinemia) is associated with hypogonadism and/or galactorrhea and may be an important clue to the presence of a pituitary adenoma or hypothalamic disease. Of women with amenorrhea, 10 to 40 percent have hyperprolactinemia, and as many as one-third of women with amenorrhea and galactorrhea have prolactin-secreting pituitary tumors.

The hypogonadism associated with hyperprolactinemia appears to be due to inhibition of hypothalamic release of LHRH, resulting in a decrease in LH and FSH secretion. This functional hypogonadism can be regarded, in part, as a physiologic mechanism since breast feeding causes decreased fertility and delayed resumption of menses. In general, the higher the plasma prolactin, the greater the likelihood of amenorrhea. Milder degrees of hyperprolactinemia in women cause irregular menses or infertility due to a shortened luteal phase. The estrogen deficiency associated with hyperprolactinemia may lead to osteoporosis.

Prolactin excess in men can cause impotence and infertility. In some series 8 percent of men with impotence and 5 percent of men with infertility have hyperprolactinemia. With prolactin elevation, FSH and LH levels in men also decline, and serum testosterone is often low.

Galactorrhea, defined as milk production in a patient who is not postpartum, is present in 30 to 90 percent of hyperprolactinemic women (see Chap. 332). The variation in incidence reflects, in part, variation in the intensity with which clinicians search for this finding. Galactorrhea may occur without hyperprolactinemia, particularly in parous women. However, galactorrhea is often an important clue to prolactin excess; when galactorrhea is coupled with amenorrhea, hyperprolactinemia is present in 75 percent of patients. Hyperprolactinemia in men rarely causes gynecomastia or galactorrhea (see Chap. 332).

Differential diagnosis Prolactin excess has several causes: (1) autonomous production (pituitary adenomas), (2) decreased dopamine or dopamine inhibitory action (e.g., due to hypothalamic disease or drugs that block dopamine synthesis or release or inhibit dopamine action), (3) stimuli that overcome the normal dopaminergic inhibition (e.g., estrogens, possibly hypothyroidism), and (4) decreased clearance of prolactin (renal failure). No single suppression test can separate physiologic from pharmacologic or pathologic causes of hyperprolactinemia (Table 321-2).

Prolactin concentrations are slightly higher (<20 ng/mL) in women than in men (<15 ng/mL). During pregnancy, prolactin concentrations begin to increase during the second trimester and peak at term; maximal values are 100 to 300 ng/mL, usually less than 200 ng/mL. A pregnancy test is mandatory in all patients with hyperprolactinemic amenorrhea, as it is with amenorrhea alone. The mean prolactin concentration declines post partum but rises with each suckling episode. Gradually, over several months, basal and suckling-stimulated prolactin concentrations diminish; by 4 to 6 months post partum, basal prolactin levels are normal, and the suckling-induced rise is absent despite continued nursing.

A careful drug history should be obtained in hyperprolactinemic patients. Dopamine-blocking drugs (e.g., phenothiazines, butyrophenones, metoclopramide) and dopamine-depleting drugs (e.g., methyldopa and reserpine) are important causes of hyperprolactinemia. Prolactin concentrations are rarely greater than 100 ng/mL with these agents, provided renal failure is not present. Although high-dose estrogens cause hyperprolactinemia, oral contraceptives containing low doses of estrogen do not.

End-stage renal failure is associated with elevated serum prolactin in 70 to 90 percent of women and 25 to 60 percent of men. This contributes to hypogonadism in some patients with renal failure. Both decreased prolactin clearance and increased prolactin secretion may contribute to this elevation. The increased prolactin in cirrhosis has not been adequately explained.

Severe primary hypothyroidism may cause a mildly elevated serum prolactin concentration, either due to elevated TRH levels or due to decreased dopaminergic tone. Since primary hypothyroidism may also cause enlargment of the sella turcica, mimicking a pituitary adenoma, thyroid function tests are essential in all patients with elevated serum prolactin. Rarely, primary adrenal insufficiency causes reversible serum prolactin elevation.

TABLE 321-2   Causes of hyperprolactinemia

I Physiologic states
  A Pregnancy
  B Nursing (early)
  C "Stress"
  D Sleep
  E Nipple stimulation
II Drugs
  A Dopamine receptor antagonists
    1 Phenothiazines
    2 Butyrophenones
    3 Thioxanthenes
    4 Metoclopramide
  B Dopamine-depleting agents
    1 Methyldopa
    2 Reserpine
  C Estrogens
  D Opiates
III Disease states
  A Pituitary tumors
    1 Prolactinomas
    2 Adenomas secreting GH and prolactin
    3 Adenomas secreting ACTH and prolactin (Nelson's syndrome and Cushing's disease)
    4 Nonfunctioning chromophobe adenomas with pituitary stalk compression
  B Hypothalamic and pituitary stalk disease
    1 Granulomatous diseases especially sarcoidosis
    2 Craniopharyngiomas and other tumors
    3 Cranial irradiation
    4 Stalk section
    5 Empty sella
    6 Vascular abnormalities including aneurysm
  C Primary hypothyroidism
  D Chronic renal failure
  E Cirrhosis
  F Chest wall trauma (including surgery, *herpes zoster*)

If a hyperprolactinemic patient is not pregnant, postpartum, cirrhotic, on medications, hypothyroid, or in renal failure, that patient is likely to have disease of the pituitary or hypothalamus. Ectopic production of prolactin by nonpituitary tumors occurs rarely if at all. Diseases of the hypothalamus or pituitary stalk cause moderate prolactin elevation (usually less than 150 ng/mL). Hyperprolactinemia occurs in 20 to 50 percent of patients with hypothalamic tumors.

Prolactin-secreting pituitary adenomas (prolactinomas) may either be small tumors within the parenchyma of the gland (so called microadenomas) or cause enlargement of the pituitary gland (macroadenomas). Large, nonfunctioning pituitary adenomas may also cause modest prolactin elevation as a result of stalk compression and a consequent impedence of delivery of dopamine to the gland. Acromegalics (25 to 45 percent) and patients with Nelson's syndrome (postadrenalectomy pituitary tumors in Cushing's disease) commonly also have elevated serum prolactin. Hyperprolactinemia is less common in untreated Cushing's disease.

Laboratory evaluation   Serum prolactin levels should be measured in all patients with hypogonadism or galactorrhea. If basal prolactin concentration is elevated, further evaluation is warranted after establishing that minimal prolactin elevations (e.g., less than 30 ng/mL) are not stress-related. Although there is no simple test to distinguish the various causes of hyperprolactinemia, a serum prolactin level of over 300 ng/mL is diagnostic of a pituitary adenoma; a serum prolactin of over 100 ng/mL in a nonpregnant patient is usually caused by a pituitary adenoma. Administration of dopamine agonists, such as bromocriptine, lowers prolactin regardless of the etiology and, therefore, is not useful as a differential test (Fig. 321-4). Prolactin stimulation tests do not distinguish among the various etiologies of hyperprolactinemia. For example, the majority of patients with prolactinomas have only a minimal or no rise in prolactin in response to TRH, as compared to the normal rise of 200 percent or more and the intermediate response (usually a doubling at serum prolactin) in patients with hypothalamic disease and those on dopamine-blocking agents. Unfortunately, the response to TRH is too variable to be useful in individual patients.

All patients with unexplained hyperprolactinemia require contrast-enhanced computerized tomography (CT) scanning of the hypothalamus and pituitary or magnetic resonance imaging (MRI) of this area. Pituitary macroadenomas are easily visualized on CT scans, but microadenomas (<10 mm) may be more difficult to delineate. When no radiologic abnormalities are found the disorder is designated "idiopathic hyperprolactinemia," although it is recognized that a small microadenoma may still be present. Sella tomography is not a useful screening test for small pituitary adenomas because of the high prevalence of false-positive and false-negative results.

Microprolactinomas do not cause hypopituitarism (except for hypogonadism). If a small pituitary lesion is seen in a patient with hypopituitarism and hyperprolactinemia, sarcoidosis or other lesions involving the pituitary stalk should be suspected, rather than a microprolactinoma. In patients with macroprolactinomas or hypothalamic lesions, evaluation of pituitary function and formal visual field examinations are essential.

Prolactinomas   PATHOLOGY   Prolactinomas are the most common type of functional pituitary adenomas. Small unsuspected microadenomas are found in 15 to 25 percent of unselected autopsies; 40 percent of these small tumors contain prolactin by immunologic staining techniques, but the percentage that actually secrete prolactin is unknown. About 70 percent of macroadenomas previously thought to be nonfunctioning are, in fact, prolactinomas. Prolactin-secreting pituitary carcinomas are rare.

Prolactinoma size correlates with hormonal output; in general, the larger the tumor, the higher the prolactin levels. Large pituitary tumors with modest prolactin elevation (50 to 100 ng/mL) are not true prolactinomas and differ in their biologic behavior. Microprolactinomas cause only hyperprolactinemia and hypogonadotropism, whereas macroprolactinomas may influence other pituitary hormones and cause headaches, visual field disturbances, and other structural problems.

CLINICAL PRESENTATION Microprolactinomas are more common than macroprolactinomas, and 90 percent of patients with microprolactinomas are women. In contrast, 60 percent of patients with macroprolactinomas are men. Irregular menses, amenorrhea, and galactorrhea are likely to result in early diagnosis, and this probably explains the preponderance of microadenomas in women. Sexual dysfunction occurs in most men with prolactinomas, but this is the presenting complaint in 15 percent or less. Although delay in seeking medical help probably explains the larger tumors in men, more aggressive tumor behavior in men has not been excluded.

Estrogens promote the growth of lactotrophs, but an etiologic role has not been established for oral contraceptives in the pathogenesis of prolactinomas. Many women with prolactinomas first develop galactorrhea while on oral contraceptives or develop amenorrhea when the drug is discontinued. Some of these women may have been started on oral contraceptives for irregular menses that were the consequence of a prolactinoma. Although amenorrhea after discontinuing oral contraceptives is rare (about 2 percent), about one-third of patients with postpill amenorrhea have prolactinomas. Development of galactorrhea in a woman on oral contraceptives mandates a prolactin determination. About 5 to 7 percent of prolactinoma patients have never menstruated (primary amenorrhea), making this an important treatable cause of primary amenorrhea. Prolactinomas may grow during pregnancy, and 15 percent of prolactinoma patients are first diagnosed in the postpartum period.

Women with prolactinomas who desire pregnancy need special consideration. Medical treatment of patients with microprolactinomas results in uneventful pregnancies 95 to 98 percent of the time; the remainder may develop headaches or visual field disturbances due to tumor enlargement that rarely requires therapy. Asymptomatic enlargement of microprolactinomas, as ascertained by radiologic studies, occurs in about 5 percent. With macroprolactinomas, the complications of tumor growth during pregnancy are more common. Symptomatic tumor enlargement occurs in about 15 percent of these patients, although individual series report complications in up to 35 percent. The majority of patients who develop symptoms do so during the first trimester.

In prolactinoma patients, the effect of pregnancy on prolactin secretion is variable. A further rise in prolactin during pregnancy may not occur even in some patients in whom tumor growth occurs.

Prolactin concentrations should be measured periodically throughout pregnancy in women with prolactinomas. If marked prolactin rise occurs (greater than 300 to 400 ng/dL), then postpartum prolactin is usually greater than the prepartum level, and tumor growth is likely. Patients with stable or declining prolactin concentrations during pregnancy may have lower prolactin concentrations after pregnancy than before. In such patients infarction or involution of the adenomas may have occurred during pregnancy.

The therapy of prolactinomas is influenced by the natural history of the disorder. Although large pituitary adenomas must begin as small tumors, most microadenomas do not progress to macroadenomas. Knowledge of the natural history of untreated microprolactinomas is incomplete; 90 to 95 percent may remain stable or demonstrate decreased serum prolactin concentrations after 7 years of follow-up. Most patients with "idiopathic hyperprolactinemia" are presumed to harbor small microadenomas. Serum prolactin returns to normal in one-third of patients with idiopathic hyperprolactinemia followed for 5 years without therapy; in two-thirds of patients in whom the basal prolactin is less than 40 ng/mL serum prolactin levels return to normal over this time span.

THERAPY Not all patients with microprolactinomas need therapy. Women with microprolactinomas require therapy when they desire pregnancy, have decreased libido or troublesome galactorrhea, desire regular menses, or are at risk for osteoporosis. Men with microadenomas should be treated for decreased potency or libido or when infertility is a problem. Most patients with macroprolactinomas require therapy.

Dopamine agonist drugs lower prolactin concentrations in virtually all hyperprolactinemic patients (Fig. 321-4). Ovulatory menses and fertility are restored in 90 percent of premenopausal women, underscoring the direct relationship between hyperprolactinemia and amenorrhea. Bromocriptine, an ergot derivative with dopamine agonist actions, is the only effective prolactin-lowering agent licensed in the United States at this time. Bromocriptine should be given twice daily with food or a snack to prevent gastrointestinal irritation. Therapy should begin with 1.25 mg at bedtime to minimize the side effects of nausea, vomiting, fatigue, nasal stuffiness, and postural hypotension. The dosage is gradually increased to an average of 2.5 mg twice daily. However, doses up to 15 mg per day may be required to return the prolactin concentration to normal in some patients with macroprolactinomas. Although the drug is expensive, it is effective in all forms of hyperprolactinemia and often abolishes nonhyperpro-

FIGURE 321-4 *Changes in serum prolactin concentration in a woman with "idiopathic" hyperprolactinemia after an initial 5 mg dose of bromocriptine and when maintained on 7.5 mg daily. (From GH Besser and MO Thorner. Postgrad Med J, 52:66, 1976.)*

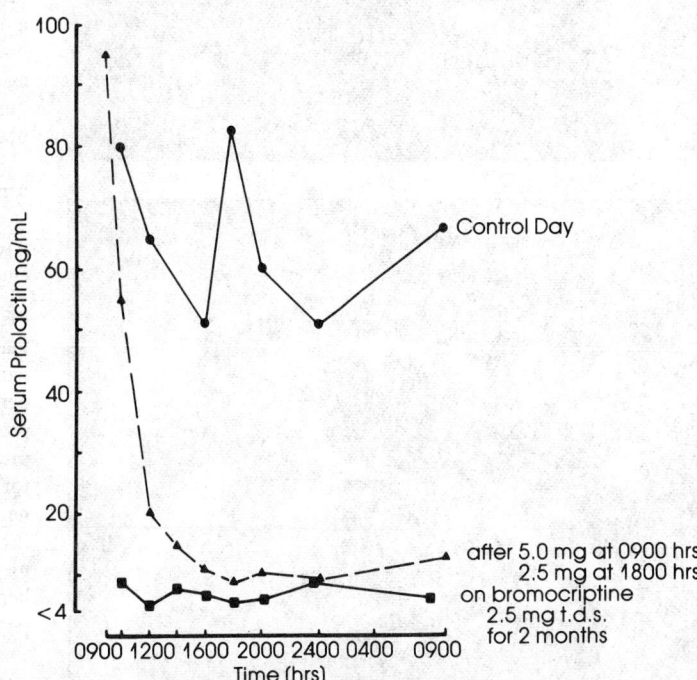

lactinemic galactorrhea as well. Pergolide, a longer-lasting dopamine agonist, can be administered once daily but is not available in the United States. Although pergolide and bromocriptine have similar side effects, individuals may tolerate one but not the other.

Bromocriptine is the therapy of choice for patients with microprolactinomas who have one of the indications for treatment discussed above. Prolactin concentrations return to normal in almost all who tolerate the medication, usually within days of achieving full therapeutic dosages (Fig. 321-4). Menses usually resume within 2 months but may be delayed up to a year. Since pregnancy may occur without resumption of menses, a barrier contraceptive is recommended until menses become regular. In this way, bromocriptine can be stopped with the first missed period when pregnancy has occurred. Bromocriptine use during pregnancy is not, however, associated with an increased risk of congenital anomalies or fetal wastage. The effects of bromocriptine are usually not permanent, but one-sixth of microprolactinoma patients maintain normal prolactin concentrations after stopping the drug.

In patients with macroprolactinomas, bromocriptine usually lowers the serum prolactin and may cause the tumor mass to shrink. In men testosterone concentrations usually begin to increase after 3 months of therapy and may reach normal levels by 6 to 8 months. Normal sperm counts are achieved in some.

One series of patients with large prolactinomas and suprasellar

FIGURE 321-5 *Frontal CT scan of a man with a large prolactin-secreting macroadenoma. Top, pretreatment scan. Bottom, scan after 1 year of treatment with bromocriptine. The upper border of the tumor is shown by arrows. (From Molitch et al.)*

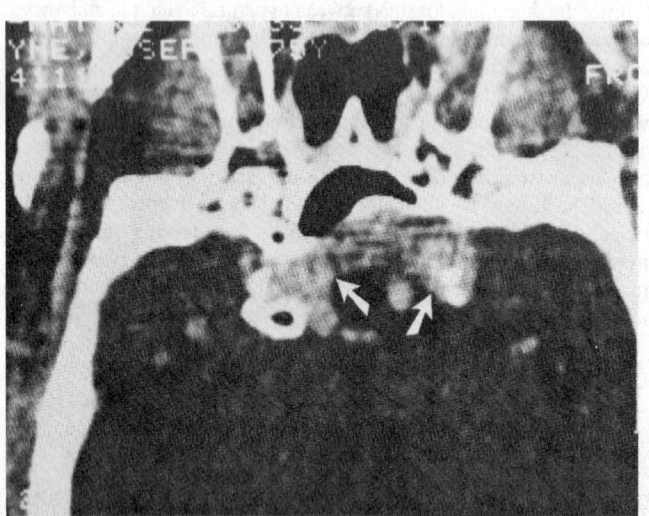

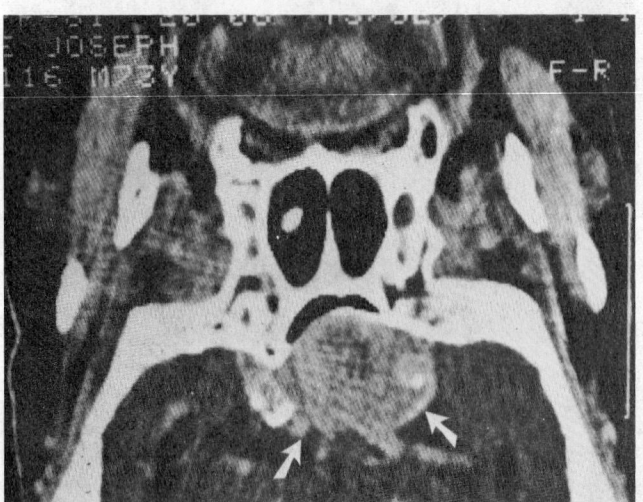

extension (mean prolactin of 1441 ng/mL in women, 3451 ng/mL in men) is of particular interest. Although prolactin levels fell to 10 percent of baseline in 96 percent of patients, most did not return to the normal range despite bromocriptine dosages of 7.5 to 20 mg per day. Visual field defects improved in 90 percent of those with field cuts. Tumor mass decreased by half or more in 60 percent of patients (see Fig. 321-5). This is a reasonable choice of therapy for patients with small macroprolactinomas. However, for patients with larger tumors who have persistent visual field defects or persistent symptomatic hyperprolactinemia, or in those women with large tumors who desire pregnancy, we do not recommend bromocriptine as the sole form of therapy. In such patients, tumor regrowth is likely when bromocriptine is stopped either inadvertently or for pregnancy or because other medical illnesses preclude its administration. Large nonfunctioning pituitary adenomas associated with hyperprolactinemia due to stalk compression usually do not shrink with bromocriptine therapy, although prolactin concentrations return to normal. Patients with large prolactinomas, refractory to bromocriptine and other modalities of therapy, may partially respond to tamoxifen, an estrogen antagonist.

Following transsphenoidal resection of microprolactinomas, serum prolactin concentration returns to normal in up to 80 to 90 percent of patients, usually within 24 h. This procedure has low morbidity and mortality. Unfortunately, recurrence rates average 17 percent after ''successful'' surgery and may be as high as 40 percent after 6 years of follow-up. Surgery is a reasonable alternative for women with microprolactinomas who desire pregnancy and who cannot tolerate or do not wish to take dopamine agonist drugs.

Surgery, combined with bromocriptine and/or radiation therapy, is indicated in all macroprolactinoma patients with suprasellar extension and persistent visual field defects and particularly in those women desiring pregnancy. However, surgical resection, whether by transsphenoidal or transcranial approach, is rarely curative in patients with macroprolactinomas. Prolactin concentrations return to normal in about 30 percent, but even when they do, recurrence rates of up to 80 percent have been reported. In all patients in whom prolactin levels do not return to normal following surgery, long-term bromocriptine therapy and/or radiation should be given.

Conventional radiation therapy [4500 cGy (4500 rad) over 25 days] for prolactinomas causes a slow decline in serum prolactin concentration. Prolactin concentration returns to normal in about 30 percent of microprolactinoma patients 2 to 10 years post therapy. We do not favor this approach in patients with microprolactinomas because of the risk of their developing hypopituitarism. Radiation therapy is a useful adjunct to surgical or medical therapy in patients with macroprolactinomas; further growth is usually prevented, and shrinkage occurs in about half the patients. This therapy usually prevents tumor growth during subsequent pregnancies, but exceptions have been noted.

Heavy particle therapy with protons or alpha particles may be useful in treatment of macroprolactinomas without suprasellar extension or after surgical debulking of larger tumors. Occasional patients with microprolactinomas opt for this form of therapy. Long-term studies in prolactinoma patients are not available.

PROLACTIN DEFICIENCY Prolactin deficiency is manifested as an inability to lactate. Failure of lactation is often the earliest clue to panhypopituitarism resulting from pituitary destruction during the peripartum period. The lateral wings of the pituitary gland have a precarious blood supply; most lactotrophs reside in this area. During pregnancy, the hypertrophied and hyperplastic lactotrophs are at risk for necrosis. If systemic hypotension develops, as with postpartum hemorrhage, the hypertrophic and hyperplastic lactotrophs may infarct (Sheehan's syndrome). Patients with diabetes mellitus are susceptible to peripartum pituitary infarction even in the absence of significant hemorrhage. Autoimmune pituitary destruction (lymphocytic hypophysitis) may also occur during late pregnancy.

Commercial prolactin radioimmunoassays cannot easily distinguish normal from low concentrations; hence, prolactin stimulation tests are needed to diagnose prolactin insufficiency. After administration of TRH or chlorpromazine, a rise in serum prolactin of less than 200 percent suggests prolactin deficiency. If prolactin deficiency is present, evaluation of other pituitary hormones is necessary as well to define other manifestations of hypopituitarism.

GROWTH HORMONE

PHYSIOLOGY Growth hormone (GH, somatotropin) is secreted by somatotrophs which make up about 50 percent of the anterior pituitary cells. The normal pituitary contains 3 to 5 mg of GH and secretes 500 to 875 μg of GH per day. The gene coding for GH is on chromosome 17; additional GH-related genes are of uncertain significance. Human growth hormone is a single polypeptide chain at 191 amino acids (22,000 mol wt) and contains two intrachain disulfide bonds. A larger (28,000 mol wt) precursor molecule is cleaved to yield GH. GH is stored in cytoplasmic granules in a high-molecular-weight polymeric form.

The structure of GH is similar to that of human placental lactogen (hPL, chorionic somatomammotropin), there being a 92 percent structural homology between the two. GH and hPL genes are found on the same chromosome and appear to have originated by gene duplication.

In the circulation, monomeric GH (22,000 mol wt) predominates. Larger molecular weight forms may represent dimers (i.e., "big" GH, 44,000 mol wt) that appear to be secreted by the pituitary gland into the circulation. Although "big" GH is measured by the GH radioimmunoassay, its biologic activity is reduced. Pulsatile release is characteristic, and circulating levels are low for much of the day. The half-life of the hormone in plasma is 20 to 30 min.

GH is necessary for normal linear growth. Growth hormone deficiency causes short stature; growth hormone excess (prior to epiphyseal closure) leads to gigantism. GH does not appear to be the principal direct stimulator of growth but acts indirectly through serum factors. These factors, known as somatomedins (SM, somatotropin-mediating hormones) or insulin-like growth factors (IGF) are growth hormone–dependent and appear to be responsible for growth stimulation (also see Chap. 322). Somatomedin C (insulin-like growth factor 1, IGF-1/SM-C), the most important somatomedin for growth, is produced in the liver and by other tissues as well. IGF-1/SM-C is a small basic protein (7600 mol wt) which circulates bound to a large carrier molecule (140,000 mol wt). The complex has a half-life of 3 to 18 h, as compared to the half-life of 20 to 30 min for unbound hormone. As a consequence, the concentration of IGF-1/SM-C remains relatively constant throughout the 24 h period, in contrast to the fluctuating levels of GH itself. How the liver integrates GH pulses into somatomedin production is not known. Furthermore, local tissue generation of IGF-1/SM-C may play an important role in mediating growth through paracrine effects.

Somatomedin C and a second somatomedin (somatomedin A) have structural homology with proinsulin, and the somatomedins share some insulin-like actions. Furthermore, GH is a trophic factor for insulin release, facilitating its release in response to various secretagogues, and GH-deficient individuals have impaired insulin release to glucose challenge. Technically, one might consider insulin a somatomedin.

During the prenatal and neonatal period growth is independent of GH, as shown by the normal birth length of GH-deficient children born to GH-deficient mothers. Nevertheless IGF-1/SM-C levels rise during pregnancy, and its concentration correlates with that of hPL, which may regulate somatomedin production. Whether the somatomedins play a physiologic role in utero is uncertain. IGF-1/SM-C levels at birth are about half those of adults and rise gradually during childhood to reach the adult range by age 8 to 10 years. IGF-1/SM-C levels are dependent upon nutritional status, declining in states of malnourishment. Elevated serum IGF-1/SM-C concentrations are present during the pubertal growth spurt, presumably accounting for the growth acceleration during this period. With estrogen deficiency, the pubertal rise of IGF-1/SM-C does not occur.

Although IGF-1/SM-C concentrations correlate with linear growth, the correlation is inexact, and therefore GH may have some direct influence on growth or cause somatomedin generation in target cells.

Other metabolic actions of GH are important. GH is an anabolic hormone that stimulates the incorporation of amino acids into protein. Although most of this action is somatomedin-mediated, GH can directly stimulate amino acid uptake in certain systems. It is not surprising, therefore, that some amino acids, such as arginine, are potent stimuli for GH release.

GH may have a direct effect as an insulin antagonist. Patients with GH deficiency are sensitive to insulin-induced hypoglycemia; patients with GH excess develop insulin resistance. GH is one of the counterregulatory hormones that help restore a low blood sugar to normal (see Chap. 329) and is probably involved in the "dawn" phenomenon in which plasma glucose increases in the early morning in patients with diabetes mellitus. Hypoglycemia is a potent GH stimulus, and an acute rise in blood sugar inhibits GH release. GH causes increased free fatty acid release from adipocytes. The absence of this effect may be responsible for the pudgy appearance of children with GH deficiency. Increased serum free fatty acid concentrations tend to blunt GH release. GH opposes the action of insulin on sugar uptake and fatty acid release and complements the anabolic action of insulin on amino acid uptake.

Serum GH is undetectable much of the day, peaks after meals, and undergoes a sustained rise during sleep. Integrated 24-h GH levels are higher in growing children than in adults.

GH has a dual hypothalamic regulation (Table 321-3). Secretion is stimulated by growth hormone–releasing factor (GRH, somatocrinin) and inhibited by growth hormone release–inhibitory hormone (somatostatin, somatotropin release–inhibitory factor, SRIF). GRH appears to play the more important role, as stalk section leads to failure of GH release. In animals treated with anti-GRH antibodies the GH peaks disappear, and growth ceases; following treatment with antisomatostatin antibodies, the peaks remain, but the baseline values rise. After treatment with both anti-GRH and antisomatostatin antibodies, the peaks disappear but the baseline rises. Although GRH- and somatostatin-containing neurons are separate, their nerve endings interconnect.

TABLE 321-3 Growth hormone regulation

Class of agent	Stimulation	Inhibition
Hypothalamic factors	GRH	Somatostatin
Amines	Alpha-adrenergic stimuli (norepinephrine, clonidine)	Beta-adrenergic stimuli
	Beta-adrenergic blockers (propranolol)	Alpha-adrenergic blockers (phentolamine, dibenzyline)
	Dopaminergic stimuli (levodopa, bromocriptine, apomorphine)	Dopamine blockers (chlorpromazine)
	Serotonergic stimuli (L-tryptophan)	Serotonin blockers (methysergide, cyproheptadine)
Hormones	Decreased IGF-1/SM-C	Increased IGF-1/SM-C (obesity)
	Estrogen	Progestogens
	Vasopressin	Glucocorticoids
	Glucagon	
Fuels	Hypoglycemia*	Increased blood sugar
	Decreased free fatty acids	Increased free fatty acids
	Amino acids (arginine)*	
Others	Exercise*	
	Stress*	
	Sleep	

* Probably mediated through alpha-adrenergic stimulation.

Growth hormone–releasing factor   GRH was initially isolated from an acromegalic patient with a GRH-secreting adenoma of the pancreatic islet cells. The clue to the diagnosis came from analysis of the pituitary pathology: Somatotroph hyperplasia was present rather than an adenoma that is characteristic for acromegaly. GRH has since been identified in the human hypothalamus.

GRH has 44 amino acids, 29 of which are necessary for full potency. GRH belongs to a family of molecules that includes secretin, glucagon, vasoactive intestinal peptide (VIP), and gastric inhibitory peptide (GIP). The arcuate nucleus of the hypothalamus is the major site of GRH production, although a few neurons are found in the ventromedial nucleus as well. Axons containing the peptide project to the median eminence and terminate on the portal vessels. GRH is also present in normal pancreas.

GRH stimulates GH release in vitro and in vivo, an effect that is calcium-dependent and appears to be mediated by cyclic adenosine monophosphate (cyclic AMP). Intravenous injection of GRH (0.1 to 3.3 μg per kilogram of body weight) produces a peak GH response at 30–60 min with a return to baseline by 2 to 3 h postinjection (Fig. 321-6). The GH response to GRH decreases with age, particularly after age 40.

Somatostatin   Somatostatin is a cyclic tetradecapeptide and is the most widely distributed of the hypothalamic releasing hormones. The primary hypothalamic sources are the periventricular and medial preoptic areas of the anterior hypothalamus. Somatostatin is found in neurosecretory granules of axons that terminate in the median eminence. In addition to its function as a hormone, somatostatin is synthesized and distributed throughout the brain and serves as a neurotransmitter in many areas including the spinal cord, brain stem, and cerebral cortex. Somatostatin is also present in the gastrointestinal tract. Specific somatostatin-secreting cells (D cells) of the pancreatic islets participate in the regulation of insulin and glucagon secretion, an example of paracrine regulation by this hormone (see Chap. 327).

Somatostatin is produced by processing of a larger precursor molecule and exists in both 28– and 14–amino acid forms. The 28–amino acid somatostatin has a longer half-life and is a more potent inhibitor of GH and insulin secretion. Somatostatin 14 has a greater affinity for hypothalamic and cortical receptors and is more potent in inhibition of glucagon release. Somatostatin and analogues of somatostatin are being evaluated for efficacy in the therapy of acromegaly, secretory pancreatic tumors, pancreatitis, acute gastric ulcers and stress gastritis.

Somatostatin inhibits GH secretion and decreases the GH response to secretagogues. Somatostatin also lowers serum TSH in normal and hypothyroid individuals and blunts TSH release in response to TRH. Somatostatin probably mediates the secondary hypothyroidism that may develop in GH-deficient children treated with GH. Somatostatin has no significant effect on the release of prolactin, gonadotropins, or ACTH in normal subjects but may lower ACTH concentrations in patients with Nelson's syndrome. Somatostatinomas are rare pancreatic islet-cell or duodenal tumors that secrete somatostatin (see Chap. 329).

Growth hormone release is under complex physiologic control. (Table 321-3) The various mediators appear to act through GRH and somatostatin. IGF-1/SM-C has an important feedback effect on GH secretion. An increased IGF-1/SM-C concentration inhibits GH release both through increased somatostatin production and by a direct action on the pituitary. A decrease in IGF-1/SM-C, as induced by starvation, leads to a compensatory increase in GH release.

A number of neurotransmitters influence GH release:

1 Hypothalamic dopamine, the important prolactin inhibitory factor, stimulates GH through an effect on GRH. Dopamine has a direct but weak inhibitory effect on GH release; this effect is overwhelmed by its hypothalamic stimulation of GRH secretion. Oral administration of dopamine precursors or agonists that cross the blood-brain barrier, such as levodopa, apomorphine, or bromocriptine, causes an increase in serum GH concentration. The effects of these stimuli can be utilized to test the adequacy of GH secretion (GH reserve).
2 Alpha-adrenergic agonists, such as clonidine, stimulate GRH and GH release whereas phentolamine, an alpha blocker, prevents the GH rise. A number of GH stimulators, including insulin hypoglycemia, arginine, and exercise, act through alpha-adrenergic mechanisms. Beta-adrenergic blockers potentiate the GH-stimulatory effect of clonidine (and of many other agents including levodopa), possibly by inhibiting somatostatin secretion.
3 Serotonin agonists stimulate GH release, and the nocturnal surge in GH secretion may be mediated by serotonin, as cyproheptadine (a serotonin antagonist) blocks the sleep-induced GH rise.

Obesity blunts GH release in response to many stimuli, including GRH itself. Weight reduction restores normal GH dynamics. In contrast, malnourished individuals, including women with anorexia nervosa, often have an increased GH concentration, probably as a result of decreased serum IGF-1/SM-C levels. Oral glucose administration decreases serum GH and the GH response to GRH.

A number of hormones influence GH release. Most factors that stimulate GH release are more potent in women than in men, an effect mediated by estrogen. In testing GH reserve in children, estrogen priming may be necessary before adequate GH release can be demonstrated. Although estrogen increases GH concentration, it decreases its biologic effect by blocking somatomedin production. This is similar to the estrogen effect on prolactin in which secretion

FIGURE 321-6 *Response to GRH-44 (1 μg/kg) in eight men and eight women. The shaded area shows the full range of responses at each time point and the error bars indicate the mean ± 1 SD. (From MC Gelato et al, J Clin Endocrinol Metab 59:200, 1984.)*

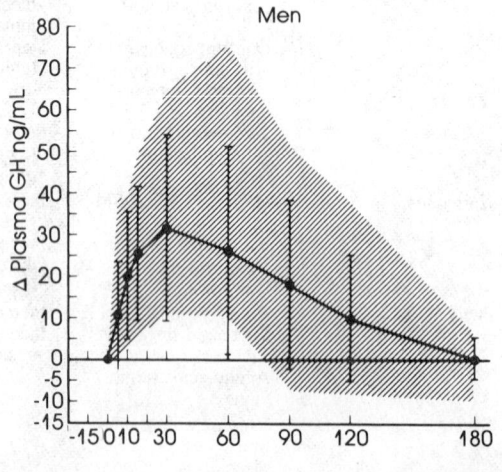

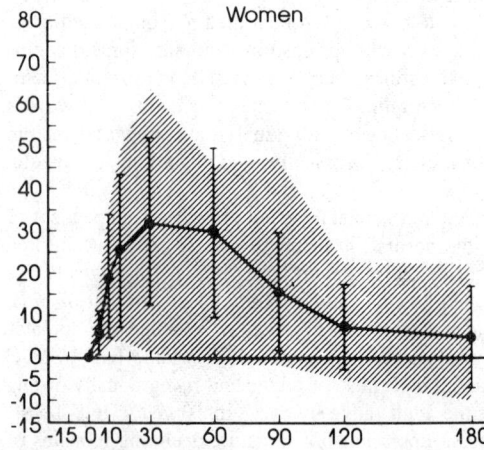

Elapsed Time, minutes

is stimulated, but its action in promoting lactation is inhibited. Glucocorticoids inhibit GH release and may blunt somatomedin action as well, explaining the potent growth-inhibiting effects of these agents in children.

GROWTH HORMONE EXCESS: ACROMEGALY AND GIGANTISM

Clinical features GH excess results in acromegaly, an insidious, chronic debilitating disease associated with bony and soft tissue overgrowth (Table 321-4). Acromegaly occurs most frequently in middle age. It is uncommon with a prevalence of 40 cases per million and an incidence of 3 cases per million per year. When GH excess develops prior to epiphyseal closure in children, increased linear growth and gigantism develop.

Most patients have soft tissue and bone enlargement which results in increased hand, foot, and hat size, prognathism, enlargement of the tongue, wide-spacing of the teeth, and coarsening of facial features. Acromegalics are said to look more like each other than their own family members (Fig. 321-7). Laryngeal hypertrophy and sinus enlargement lead to a hollow-sounding voice. A moist, doughy handshake, increased skin tags, acanthosis nigricans, and oily skin are common.

Acromegaly is more than a cosmetically disfiguring disease. Patients feel weak and tired. The basal metabolic rate increases, which in turn causes increased sweating. Obstructive sleep apnea may be an important cause of hypersomnolence. The majority have neurologic and musculoskeletal symptoms including headaches, paresthesias (often due to carpal tunnel syndrome), muscle weakness, and arthralgias (particularly involving the shoulders, back, and knees). The cartilage hypertrophy and osseous overgrowth often lead to degenerative arthritis. Hypertension occurs in about one-third and is characterized by suppressed renin and aldosterone secretion associated with expansion of plasma volume and total body sodium. Almost all

hypertensive acromegalics and about half of nonhypertensive acromegalics have increased left ventricular mass or left ventricular wall thickness. Although it is not established whether a specific cardiomyopathy occurs, acromegalics may develop congestive heart failure in the absence of other known underlying heart disease. Many organs, including the liver and kidneys, increase in size with no evidence of functional impairment. Goiter develops in about one-fourth of patients, and 3 percent are hyperthyroid. Some series report abdominal pain and inguinal hernias each in about one-third of patients. Intracranial aneurysms coexist in 10 percent or less.

Patients with acromegaly have a shortened life expectancy. In older studies, 25 to 50 percent of acromegalics died by age 50 and 65 to 90 percent died by age 60. Increased mortality in men is due mainly to cardiovascular and respiratory disease, whereas mortality in women is principally due to cerebrovascular and respiratory disease. Patients with coexisting diabetes mellitus have increased mortality, as expected, and diabetes may contribute to the atherosclerosis. An increased number of malignancies might be expected in these patients, as acromegaly is associated with increased concentrations of circulating growth factors. However, although increased prevalence of carcinoma has been reported in some series, the differences are not statistically significant. Skin tags correlate with increased prevalence of colonic polyps and possibly with carcinoma of the colon.

Laboratory investigation Insulin resistance occurs in 80 percent, although abnormal glucose tolerance (20 to 40 percent) and clinical diabetes mellitus (13 to 20 percent) are less common. Hypercalciuria is frequent, apparently due to increased levels of circulating 1,25-dihydroxyvitamin D; renal stones occur in about one-fifth of patients. Hypercalcemia, when it occurs, is not due to acromegaly per se but

FIGURE 321-7 *Serial photographs of a patient with acromegaly taken at ages 28, 49, 55, and 65 years, 6 months after removal of a GH-secreting adenoma. Note the gradual increase in the size of the nose, lips, and skin folds, particularly the nasolabial skin fold and forehead. (From Reichlin 1982.)*

TABLE 321-4 Acromegaly—Manifestations

Location	Symptoms	Signs
General	Fatigue Increased sweating Heat intolerance Weight gain	
Skin and subcutaneous tissue	Enlarging hands, feet Coarsening facial features Oily skin Hypertrichosis	Moist, warm, fleshy, doughy handshake Skin tags Acanthosis nigricans Increased heel pad
Head	Headaches	Parotid enlargement, frontal bossing
Eyes	Decreased vision	Visual field defects
Ears		Otoscope speculum cannot be inserted
Nose-throat–paranasal sinuses	Sinus congestion	Enlarged furrowed tongue
	Increased tongue size	Tooth marks on tongue
	Malocclusion Voice change	Widely spaced teeth Prognathism
Neck		Goiter Obstructive sleep apnea Enlarged sinuses
Cardiorespiratory system	Congestive heart failure	Hypertension Cardiomegaly Left ventricular hypertrophy
Genitourinary system	Decreased libido Impotence Oligomenorrhea Infertility Kidney stones	
Neurologic system	Paresthesias Hypersomnolence	Carpal tunnel syndrome
Muscles	Weakness	Proximal myopathy
Skeletal system	Joint pains (shoulders, back, knees)	Osteoarthritis

suggests primary hyperparathyroidism as part of the multiple endocrine neoplasia I (MEN I) syndrome (see Chap. 334). GH causes increased renal tubular reabsorption of phosphate by an undefined mechanism. Elevation of serum phosphate occurs in about one-half. Hyperprolactinemia occurs in up to one-half of patients and is responsible for much of the associated galactorrhea, amenorrhea, and decreased libido.

Pathophysiology Well-defined pituitary adenomas are found in almost all patients with acromegaly and gigantism. The tumors tend to occur in the lateral wings of the sella where normal somatotrophs are found in abundance. Occasionally, tumors are found in ectopic locations along the lines of migration of Rathke's pouch, such as the sphenoid sinus or parapharyngeal regions.

GH levels correlate on average with tumor size. Tumors tend to be larger in younger patients, suggesting more rapid growth in this population. At the time of diagnosis 75 percent of somatotroph adenomas are macroadenomas, whereas two-thirds or more of prolactinomas are microadenomas at the time of diagnosis. Aggressive screening for acromegaly on the basis of subtle clinical clues might lead to early diagnosis while tumors are still small.

Immunohistochemical staining and electron microscopy of somatotroph tumors help to predict their behavior. Patients with densely granulated tumors have typical acromegaly, with slow, nonaggressive tumor growth. The sparsely granulated tumors also cause acromegaly but grow more quickly and often invade the sella locally or produce extrasellar extension. Mixed GH- and prolactin-secreting adenomas contain mixtures of somatotrophs and lactotrophs. These mixed cell tumors cause acromegaly, are associated with moderate prolactin elevation, and do not usually demonstrate aggressive growth behavior. In contrast, acidophil stem-cell adenomas, individual cells of which stain for both GH and prolactin, represent poorly differentiated precursors of the somatotrophs and lactotrophs. These tumors grow rapidly, are often invasive, and are associated with marked hyperprolactinemia. Although the cells stain for GH, clinical acromegaly is usually not present. The well-differentiated acidophil adenoma also contains cells that stain for both prolactin and GH and seems to be a slowly growing, more mature variant of the stem-cell adenoma; acromegaly is present with variably elevated prolactin concentrations. Growth hormone–secreting carcinomas are rare and should be diagnosed only in the presence of distant metastases. Tumors that cause local invasion are called invasive adenomas.

Although hypothalamic GRH excess or somatostatin deficiency has been postulated to be the underlying abnormality leading to acromegaly, most acromegalics in fact have primary disease of the pituitary. The evidence for a pituitary etiology includes (1) low serum GRH in patients with acromegaly, (2) absence of somatotroph hyperplasia in the cells outside the adenomas, and (3) return of GH dynamics to normal upon successful removal of the somatotroph adenomas.

GRH-induced acromegaly is rare (less than 1 percent in a recent series). This diagnosis should be considered when pituitary somatotroph hyperplasia, rather than an adenoma, is diagnosed histologically. Bronchial carcinoids and pancreatic islet-cell tumors are the most likely to secrete GRH. Hypothalamic gangliocytomas also produce GRH (as well as somatostatin) and may cause somatotroph hyperplasia and acromegaly. A number of other tumors (including small cell carcinoma of the lung, medullary carcinoma of the thyroid, and thymic carcinoid) contain GRH as shown by immunologic staining, but the amount of secretion from these tumors is unknown. These tumors are also commonly associated with ectopic ACTH production.

Ectopic production of GH is rare but has been described in a patient with a pancreatic islet-cell tumor; the tumor size in this instance (420 g) suggested inefficient GH production since GH-secreting pituitary tumors that cause acromegaly are usually small.

Diagnosis Patients with acromegaly have symptoms for an average of 7 to 8 years and often see several doctors before the diagnosis is made. Newly consulted physicians are more likely to suspect the diagnosis than is a physician or family member who has watched the insidious progress of the disease. When suggestive facial features are noted, a comparison with old pictures may be helpful (Fig. 321-7).

Basal or random GH determinations may be elevated in normal persons, particularly in active women, and should not be used to screen for acromegaly. A physiologic test of the capacity to inhibit GH release must be utilized. The standard screening test is the measurement of serum GH concentrations 60 to 120 min after the oral administration of 100 g glucose. A serum GH concentration of less than 5 ng/mL is usually taken as a normal response, although a postsuppression value of less than 2 ng/mL is a more rigorous criterion. Acromegalics usually have a GH concentration after glucose administration of greater than 10 ng/mL; however, some suppress to values below 5 but rarely below 2 ng/mL.

GH concentrations in acromegaly may vary during the day, although they are never undetectable as in normal persons. After glucose administration to acromegalics the GH concentrations usually are unchanged or increase, but some GH lowering may occur. GH levels increase in response to insulin-induced hypoglycemia and arginine infusion, and the response to GRH is enhanced in most acromegalics. Somatostatin infusion lowers GH concentration but usually not to normal values. In addition, GH-secreting pituitary tumors respond to stimuli that do not affect normal somatotrophs: TRH increases GH in the majority (80 percent), and LHRH increases GH in about 10–15 percent. Dopamine agonists stimulate GH release in normal persons but inhibit GH release in 75 percent of acromegalics. Somatotroph tumors that cosecrete prolactin are most likely to show GH stimulation with TRH and GH inhibition with dopamine agonists.

Measurement of serum IGF-1/SM-C is useful, although clinical experience with this assay is limited; concentrations seem to correlate with disease activity even in patients with basal GH concentrations below 10 ng/mL. Acromegalics usually have IGF-1/SM-C values greater than 2.6 units per milliliter, whereas normal persons have values less than 1.4 units per milliliter. The level does not correlate well with basal GH concentrations but does correlate with heel pad thickness and fasting blood sugar. IGF-1/SM-C is less useful in following acromegalics after therapy.

All patients with large pituitary adenomas should be screened with GH measurements, preferably after glucose ingestion. In rare cases patients with elevated serum GH and IGF-1/SM-C concentrations may have large pituitary tumors, without clinical evidence of acromegaly. This syndrome is unexplained.

Radiologic investigation is necessary once the laboratory tests confirm the clinical suspicion of acromegaly. Conventional skull x-rays or coned-down views of the sella turcica are abnormal in 90 percent of patients with acromegaly. CT scanning or MRI provides better definition of tumor size and is necessary for appropriate therapeutic planning. Additional clues to the diagnosis of acromegaly can be found on conventional skull x-rays and include thickening of the skull with increased bone density, enlargement of the paranasal sinuses and proliferation of the mastoid air cells, and prognathism if the jaw is included. On bone x-rays one may see enlarged vertebral bodies with anterior lipping, tufting of the distal phalanges of the hands and feet, increased thickness and lengthening of the ribs and clavicles, and bowing of the femur, tibia, and fibula. Soft tissue x-rays demonstrate increased thickness of the heel pad (greater than 18 mm in women and 21 mm in men).

Testing of anterior pituitary function for hypopituitarism and for increased prolactin should be performed at some point in the evaluation of all acromegalics. Large somatotrope adenomas commonly cause neurologic abnormalities. In addition, acromegaly may be associated with hyperparathyroidism and pancreatic islet-cell tumors in the MEN I syndrome and rarely with pheochromocytomas or aldosteronomas. The alpha subunit of the glycoprotein hormones may be oversecreted in acromegaly and may serve as an additional marker of tumor regrowth.

Therapy The objectives of therapy are (1) return of GH levels to normal, (2) stabilization or decrease in tumor size, and (3) preservation of normal pituitary function. The available modalities are variably successful in achieving these goals, and none is perfect. Although GH values of less than 5 ng/mL are frequently interpreted as representing cures, a value of less than 2 ng/mL is a better criterion; patients with GH values between 2 and 5 ng/mL may have persistent symptoms and increased IGF-1/SM-C concentrations.

Transsphenoidal surgery has the advantage of producing a rapid therapeutic response and is the procedure of choice. GH concentrations fall to normal with hours, and soft tissue (but not bony) enlargement may melt away, even before the patient has been discharged from the hospital. The success of this procedure depends upon the preoperative GH concentration. In expert hands, apparent cure rates (GH below 5 ng/mL) average 75 percent in patients with preoperative GH levels of less than 40 ng/mL but only 35 percent in those with a GH level greater than 40 ng/mL. The occurrence of tumor regrowth and recurrent acromegaly after successful surgery may be higher than previously appreciated. Persistent GH response to TRH stimulation appears to have predictive value in assessing risk of relapse, even in those patients with normal postoperative GH concentrations. Hypopituitarism may occur in 10 to 20 percent of patients with larger tumors, but up to 10 percent of patients with pituitary insufficiency prior to surgery regain normal function.

Heavy particle pituitary radiation is successful in lowering GH concentrations in acromegaly but is slow in accomplishing this goal. Patients with suprasellar extension of the pituitary adenoma are generally excluded from this therapy. The Harvard cyclotron utilizes the Bragg peak with proton irradiation, achieving up to 12,000 cGy (12,000 rad) to the center of the pituitary adenoma. In patients with mean pretherapy GH concentration of 60 ng/mL, GH concentrations are below 5 ng/mL in 29 percent of patients at 2 years, 40 percent at 4 years, 75 percent at 10 years and 92 percent by 20 years. Hypopituitarism occurs in about 20 percent. The Lawrence Radiation Laboratory at Berkeley uses alpha particles and delivers 9000 cGy (9000 rad) to the adenoma. GH values are less than 5 ng/mL in 30 percent of patient at 1 year and 70 percent by 6 years (mean pretherapy GH of 24 ng/mL).

Conventional pituitary radiation [4500 cGy (4500 rad)] also has its proponents. GH concentrations of less than 5 ng/mL occur in 50 percent of acromegalics at 5 years and in 70 percent at 10 years (mean pretherapy GH 60 ng/mL). Hypopituitarism is a sequela, and up to 50 percent of patients require replacement therapy. The hypopituitarism is most likely due to hypothalamic damage, which is less likely to occur with focused heavy particle radiation. We use heavy particle or conventional radiation in patients who have failed surgery or when surgery is contraindicated or refused by the patient.

Bromocriptine is a useful adjunct to other modalities of therapy but rarely is used alone. Clinical improvement is reported in up to 90 percent of patients when dosages of 20 to 60 mg per day are utilized. Objective decrease in hand and ring size as well as improvement in diabetes mellitus may occur in the absence of decreasing GH values. However, GH concentrations fall to less than 10 ng/mL in only 35 percent, and values of less than 5 ng/mL are achieved in only 15 percent. Those patients who demonstrate GH increase after TRH administration are more likely to respond to bromocriptine. A decrease in tumor size is noted in about 25 percent.

Estrogen administration is an older form of therapy which is empirically successful but is rarely used now. Its clinical efficacy is probably explained by the blockade of somatomedin production by estrogen. Although intravenous somatostatin lowers GH concentration, GH concentrations do not return to normal. Subcutaneous injections of newer long-acting analogues of somatostatin have been effective in lowering GH over the short term. It is not known whether analogues can be developed that suppress GH but not insulin or glucagon.

GH DEFICIENCY AND PITUITARY DWARFISM GH is often the first hormone to be lost in pituitary and hypothalamic disorders. In adults, GH deficiency is often cryptic and can only be diagnosed on the basis of stimulation tests for GH release. GH deficiency is probably responsible for the fine wrinkling of facial skin in patients with hypopituitarism. Diabetics with GH deficiency show a reduction in insulin requirements and may develop hypoglycemia. In children, GH deficiency leads to impaired growth and short stature (see Chap. 322).

GONADOTROPINS

PHYSIOLOGY The gonadotropins, LH and FSH, are secreted by the gonadotrophs (also see Chaps. 330 and 331). These cells, which make up about 10 percent of anterior pituitary cells, are dispersed throughout the anterior lobe, often situated close to the lactotrophs. Most gonadotrophs produce both LH and FSH, although a few cells produce only one hormone.

LH and FSH are glycoprotein hormones of similar size (about 30,000 mol wt), which share a common alpha subunit [also present in TSH and human chorionic gonadotropin (hCG)] but have unique beta subunits. The alpha and beta chains are encoded in separate genes on separate chromosomes, and alpha chains are often produced in excess. The carbohydrate content of the molecules influences the biologic behavior and duration of action and may vary throughout the menstrual cycle. Although both FSH and LH are secreted in pulsatile fashion, the longer FSH half-life (3 to 4 h versus 50 min) means that FSH concentrations fluctuate less throughout the day. FSH and LH regulate ovarian and testicular function.

FSH stimulates the growth of the granulosa cells of the ovarian follicle and controls estrogen formation within these cells. LH stimulates the ovarian theca cells to produce androgens, which diffuse to the granulosa cells where they are converted to estrogens. Estradiol, the principal estrogen, peaks about 1 day prior to the LH surge, which in turn triggers ovulation. Postovulation, LH contributes to corpus luteum formation. Once conception has occurred, pituitary gonadotropin function is no longer necessary to sustain pregnancy.

In the testis LH is primarily responsible for controlling testosterone production in the Leydig cells. FSH, in conjunction with intratesticular testosterone, stimulates the seminiferous tubules to produce sperm. Thus LH and FSH are necessary for normal spermatogenesis, whereas testosterone production requires only LH.

Luteinizing hormone–releasing hormone (LHRH, gonadotropin-releasing hormone), a decapeptide produced by the arcuate nuclei of the hypothalamus, is responsible for the release of both LH and FSH. Extrahypothalamic LHRH is present in other areas of the brain and in the gonads as well. Norepinephrine appears to facilitate, whereas dopamine and the endorphins inhibit, LHRH release.

LHRH interacts with high-affinity pituitary receptors to stimulate LH and FSH production and release, a process mediated through an increase in cytosolic calcium and possibly an effect on cyclic AMP. The pituitary response to LHRH varies greatly throughout life. LHRH and the gonadotropins first appear in the fetus at about 10 weeks of gestation. During the first 3 months after birth, LHRH elicits a brisk gonadotropin rise. The sensitivity to LHRH then declines until the onset of puberty. Before puberty, the FSH response to LHRH is greater than that of LH. With the onset of puberty sensitivity to LHRH increases, and pulsatile LH secretion, first noted during sleep ensues. Later in puberty and during the reproductive years, pulsations are present throughout the day, with LH responsiveness being greater than that of FSH. After the menopause FSH and LH concentrations rise, and postmenopausal FSH levels are higher than those of LH. LHRH may also have direct effects on the gonads, leading to a decreased number of LH, FSH, and prolactin receptors.

Pulsatile LHRH release results in pulsatile LH and FSH release. However, sustained infusion of LHRH and its analogues results in inhibition of LH and FSH release. This phenomenon has been utilized in the successful treatment of gonadotropin-mediated precocious puberty by the sustained administration of LHRH or its analogues. Conversely, in monkeys with experimental hypothalamic defects and in humans with LHRH deficiency, the pulsatile administration of

LHRH can restore a normal menstrual cycle or normal sperm and testosterone production.

The feedback relationship between the gonadal steroids and the hypothalamus and pituitary is detailed in Chaps. 330 and 331. Low doses of estrogens decrease the frequency of LHRH pulses and, more importantly, decrease the pituitary response to LHRH; this phenomenon is seen most clearly in castrated individuals or in postmenopausal women with elevated gonadotropins. However, sustained elevation of estrogens results in a positive feedback signal that stimulates LHRH and LH release; this phenomenon is responsible for the LH surge prior to ovulation. The sensitivity of LHRH to this positive feedback by estrogen increases during mid to late puberty. Progesterone in high concentrations decreases the frequency of LHRH release and to a lesser extent diminishes the pituitary response to LHRH. In castrated men testosterone administration usually suppresses LH to undetectable levels and less often lowers FSH to normal (but not undetectable) concentrations. Inhibin, a peptide produced by the testes and ovaries, is probably the dominant physiologic inhibitor of FSH release. Testosterone decreases the frequency of LH pulsations, probably by a direct effect on LHRH release, and is converted to estradiol which inhibits the pituitary response to LHRH.

Gonadotropin measurements In postmenopausal women and men with primary hypogonadism, gonadal failure results in a marked increase in FSH and LH concentrations, providing an endogenous stimulation test. Such elevated gonadotropin concentrations assure the adequacy of pituitary gonadotroph function. On the other hand, gonadotropin measurements are rarely indicated in a woman with ovulatory menses and in men with normal sperm counts. In evaluating gonadal failure associated with low testosterone concentrations in men or low estradiol levels in women, gonadotropin measurements help separate primary from central (secondary, hypogonadotropic) hypogonadism: high gonadotropin concentrations are indicative of primary gonadal failure; low or normal gonadotropin concentrations suggest hypothalamic or pituitary disease (see Chap. 320).

HYPOGONADOTROPIC (CENTRAL, SECONDARY) HYPOGONADISM Gonadotropin deficiency may be present at birth as a congenital or hereditary disorder. Kallmann's syndrome is inherited as a single gene trait, afflicts men more severely than women, and is characterized by gonadotropin deficiency frequently associated with anosmia and midline anatomic defects. Kallmann's syndrome appears to be due to LHRH deficiency, as most patients secrete gonadotropins in response to LHRH administration after suitable priming. Acquired defects of LHRH production are common: hyperprolactinemic amenorrhea is due to inhibition of LHRH release, possibly mediated by increased hypothalamic dopamine. Anorexia nervosa and starvation inhibit LHRH release as well. Gonadotropin deficiency may be a relatively early defect in patients with large pituitary adenomas. Gonadotropin deficiency also occurs in patients with polyglandular endocrine deficiencies, presumably on an autoimmune basis (see Chap. 334) and in patients with hemochromatosis.

Patients with LHRH deficiency who desire fertility may respond to pulsatile therapy with LHRH or its analogues. When gonadotropin deficiency is due to pituitary disease, injections of FSH (menotropin) and choronic gonadotropin (a hormone with LH-like activity) are necessary to achieve fertility.

ECTOPIC GONADOTROPIN SECRETION AND GONADOTROPIN-SECRETING TUMORS Ectopic gonadotropin production (usually hCG) can be secreted by germinomas of the nonseminoma type (see Chap. 297), lung carcinomas, hepatomas, and other tumors. Children may develop precocious puberty, and men may develop gynecomastia. No distinct clinical syndrome occurs in women. Pituitary gonadotropin-secreting tumors, previously thought to be rare, are now known to be relatively common. Approximately 4 percent of all pituitary adenomas demonstrate gonadotropins or their subunits on immunologic staining; how often these tumors secrete gonadotropins is not clear.

FSH-secreting pituitary adenomas are large tumors, most commonly diagnosed in men with decreased libido, decreased serum testosterone, and normal prolactin levels. The finding of an increased FSH concentration may be misinterpreted as indicating primary hypogonadism if a pituitary adenoma is not suspected. The majority of these tumors overproduce the beta subunit of FSH, and 40 percent demonstrate increased FSH secretion after TRH administration. Normal subjects and patients with primary hypogonadism do not have increased FSH secretion after TRH. Despite the normal or elevated LH concentrations in these patients, testosterone concentrations are low and respond normally to hCG administration. This suggests that the LH measured by radioimmunoassay is biologically inactive or that it represents immunologic cross-reactivity due to subunit overproduction.

LH-secreting pituitary adenomas are usually large tumors and are characterized by increased serum testosterone, elevated LH levels, and normal or low FSH concentrations, often with partial hypopituitarism. It is often difficult to diagnose gonadotropin-secreting pituitary adenomas in postmenopausal women because of the elevated gonadotropins associated with menopause.

THYROTROPIN

PHYSIOLOGY TSH is a glycoprotein hormone (28,000 mol wt) composed of an alpha subunit which it shares with LH, FSH, and hCG and a unique beta subunit that confers specificity (also see Chap. 324). The genes coding for the alpha and beta subunits are on different chromosomes. TSH is produced by thyrotrophs which constitute about 10 percent of the cells of the anterior pituitary. TSH regulates the biosynthesis, storage, and release of thyroid hormones and determines thyroid gland size. TSH first appears in the fetal pituitary at about 10 weeks of gestation. TSH levels in normal subjects average 0.5 to 3.5 μU per milliliter, with a slight increase in the nocturnal hours.

Thyrotropin-releasing hormone (TRH), the major hypothalamic mediator of TSH release, is a tripeptide found in highest concentrations in the medial division of the hypothalamic paraventricular nuclei and in the median eminence. Extrahypothalamic TRH is found in the posterior pituitary, in other parts of the brain and spinal cord, and in the gastrointestinal tract. TRH stimulates TSH secretion by increasing cytoplasmic free calcium; phosphatidylinositol and membrane phospholipids probably participate in TRH-stimulated TSH secretion. TRH stimulates the release of prolactin as well as that of TSH. The prolactin response is enhanced in hypothyroidism and diminished in hyperthyroidism. TRH-induced GH stimulation may occur in acromegaly, renal failure, or depression.

The thyroid hormones thyroxine (T_4) and triiodothyronine (T_3) inhibit TSH production directly at the pituitary level. Both T_3 and T_4 bind to receptors on pituitary nuclei, but T_3 has a 40-fold greater affinity for these receptors than does T_4. Nevertheless, exogenous T_4 is more potent than T_3 in inhibiting TSH release because circulating T_4 is a more effective means of delivering T_3 to the pituitary than is T_3 itself. Half of intrapituitary T_3 is derived from T_4 conversion within the pituitary. The effects of T_4 and T_3 on hypothalamic TRH release are unknown. In hyperthyroidism TSH is suppressed, and the TSH response to TRH is absent; in primary hypothyroidism the basal TSH concentration is elevated, and the response to TRH is exaggerated.

Somatostatin decreases basal TSH release, the TSH response to TRH, and the nocturnal TSH peak. Dopamine and glucocorticoids decrease basal TSH concentration and the TSH response to TRH. Patients with untreated primary adrenal insufficiency may have slightly elevated TSH levels.

TSH concentrations can be interpreted only when serum thyroid hormone concentrations are known (see Chap. 320). In hyperthyroidism, thyroid hormone levels are elevated and TSH release is inhibited. Unfortunately, most TSH assays cannot differentiate between low and normal concentrations. However, since TRH administration causes no rise of serum TSH in hyperthyroidism, a normal TSH response to TRH excludes conventional hyperthyroidism. Low thyroid hormone and elevated serum TSH concentrations are characteristic of primary hypothyroidism. Since the basal TSH concentration is elevated, a TRH stimulation test is superfluous. Low thyroid hormone concentrations with a "normal" or "low" TSH concentration are found in central (secondary) hypothyroidism. The TRH stimulation test is not useful in the diagnosis of secondary hypothyroidism or in differentiating pituitary from hypothalamic disease.

PRIMARY HYPOTHYROIDISM Thyroid gland failure (primary hypothyroidism) leads to compensatory hypertrophy of the thyrotrophs. With thyroid failure of long duration, the pituitary gland and the sella turcica may enlarge. Although TSH-secreting tumors may develop in animals after thyroid gland removal, the increased TSH and pituitary size in human hypothyroidism is not autonomous and decreases with thyroid hormone replacement. Since hyperprolactinemia may also occur in patients with primary hypothyroidism, pituitary enlargement (hyperplasia) may be incorrectly diagnosed as a prolactinoma. Severe primary hypothyroidism may occasionally cause impaired release of GH and ACTH after appropriate stimuli (so-called pituitary myxedema), and hypothyroid children may develop precocious puberty. These abnormalities are all corrected with thyroid hormone therapy.

SECONDARY HYPOTHYROIDISM Hypothyroidism due to pituitary or hypothalamic disease may be difficult to diagnose. With primary hypothyroidism serum TSH commonly rises before thyroid hormone concentrations decline below the normal range. No similar early laboratory clue exists in secondary hypothyroidism. Patients with central hypothyroidism usually do not have goiter, and many have deficiencies of other pituitary trophic hormones.

Some patients with hypothalamic hypothyroidism have mild TSH elevations, rather than normal or low concentrations as expected. Although the TSH elevations rarely exceed 10 μU/mL, they are above the expected range for hypothyroidism due to TSH deficiency. Biologically inactive but immunologically active thyrotropin is present in such cases. After TRH injection, TSH concentration rises, and the biologic potency of the TSH is increased. This suggests an additional role for TRH in controlling the biologic activity of the TSH molecule.

PITUITARY (TSH-INDUCED) HYPERTHYROIDISM Hyperthyroidism is not usually a disease of TSH overproduction. However, two types of TSH-mediated hyperthyroidism are recognized:

1 Pituitary tumors. These are usually macroadenomas with autonomous TSH secretion, unresponsive to thyroid hormone suppression or TRH stimulation. A hallmark of such tumors is overproduction of the glycoprotein hormone alpha subunit (TSH alpha), with a serum molar ratio of alpha to intact TSH of greater than 1:1. The free alpha subunit may be an important tumor marker and differs from the native alpha subunit in that one of its amino acids is carbohydrate-blocked and hence cannot combine with beta subunits. These tumors may produce other pituitary hormones in addition to TSH, most commonly GH.
2 Pituitary resistance to thyroid hormone. In this situation thyroid hormone fails to inhibit TSH secretion appropriately in the absence of a pituitary adenoma. Since TSH secretion is not inhibited, TSH rises and stimulates thyroid hormone overproduction. The peripheral tissues are not resistant to thyroid hormone, and clinical hyperthyroidism results. The pituitary resistance to thyroid hormone is incomplete since TSH can be suppressed with supraphysiologic levels of thyroid hormone and stimulated further with TRH; bromocriptine may lower TSH as well. Pituitary resistance is usually diagnosed after thyroid gland ablation, when TSH cannot be lowered to normal values with the usual therapeutic doses of thyroid hormone. However, once the hyperthyroidism has been treated, pituitary resistance is of no clinical consequence.

ADRENOCORTICOTROPHIC HORMONE

PHYSIOLOGY ACTH is produced by corticotrophs which comprise about 15 percent of anterior pituitary cells, located principally in the central portion. ACTH is synthesized as part of a large precursor molecule termed proopiomelanocortin (POMC, 265 amino acids) (see Chaps. 69 and 325). ACTH contains 39 amino acids, with near complete biologic activity residing in the N-terminal 26 amino acids. In the anterior pituitary POMC is cleaved to yield ACTH, β-lipotropin, and an N-terminal precursor (see Chap. 325).

ACTH controls the release of cortisol from the adrenal cortex. Although aldosterone is primarily controlled by the renin-angiotensin system, ACTH also stimulates aldosterone release acutely. Other derivatives of the POMC molecule, such as γ-melanocyte-stimulating hormone (γ-MSH), also influence aldosterone production and are found in increased concentrations in the plasma of patients with idiopathic hyperaldosteronism. Patients with ACTH deficiency have near-normal aldosterone production and do not require mineralocorticoid replacement therapy.

Corticotropin releasing hormone (CRH) is the major regulator of ACTH release. CRH contains 41 amino acids on a single polypeptide chain. CRH is produced primarily by neurons of the paraventricular nuclei of the hypothalamus but is also present in other areas of the brain, including the limbic system and cortex, as well as in the pancreas, gut, and adrenal medulla. CRH stimulates cyclic AMP production and increases the concentration of POMC messenger RNA. Vasopressin potentiates the ACTH-releasing properties of CRH through a noncyclic AMP–dependent mechanism and may play a physiologic role in ACTH release. Beta-adrenergic stimuli and oxytocin cause ACTH release as well. Somatostatin blocks CRH-induced ACTH release.

ACTH is released in pulses with an overriding circadian rhythm. With a normal sleeping pattern, ACTH concentration is highest in the early morning (around 4 A.M.) and lowest in late evening. The characteristic diurnal rhythm of plasma cortisol occurs in response to these ACTH changes. In primary adrenal insufficiency (Addison's disease), cortisol concentrations fall and ACTH concentrations rise. This results in hyperpigmentation owing to the melanocyte-stimulating properties of ACTH. Cortisol administration inhibits ACTH release, a phenomenon dependent upon both the rate of rise of cortisol and its absolute concentration. Increased plasma cortisol inhibits CRH-induced ACTH release and may also inhibit CRH release. When supraphysiologic doses of glucocorticoids (e.g., cortisone, prednisone, dexamethasone) are given for prolonged periods, the hypothalamic-pituitary–adrenal cortex axis may remain suppressed for months after the drugs have been stopped, probably as the result of prolonged hypothalamic CRH suppression (see Chap. 325).

Stress, including hypoglycemia, surgery, and psychic distress, stimulates ACTH release, via increased CRH release. With severe illness, the requirements for cortisol may increase tenfold; failure to achieve these levels of cortisol during such periods may result in clinical adrenal insufficiency in subjects with diminished ACTH reserve.

In normal persons ACTH circulates in low concentrations (10 to 80 pg/mL). It is difficult to measure ACTH in plasma and usually not possible to separate low from normal values using commercial assays. Random ACTH measurements have little clinical significance. Tests for adrenal insufficiency and excess rely primarily on measurements of cortisol and its metabolites rather than on measurement of ACTH.

ACTH EXCESS (CUSHING'S DISEASE AND NELSON'S SYNDROME) Clinical features Cortisol excess is characterized by a central distribution of adipose tissue, muscle weakness, purplish striae, hypertension, amenorrhea, osteoporosis, fatigue, and psychiatric abnormalities. This syndrome may be caused by pituitary or ectopic ACTH overproduction, adrenal tumors, or exogenous glucocorticoid administration.

The presence of cortisol excess is established by the finding of increased excretion of urine free cortisol and/or 17-hydroxycorticosteroids that fails to decrease appropriately after low-dose dexamethasone administration (0.5 mg every 6 h for 8 doses). Additional suppression (and occasionally stimulation) tests are required to determine whether the Cushing's syndrome is due to a pituitary lesion. In patients with pituitary ACTH hypersecretion, high-dose dexamethasone administration (2 mg every 6 h for 8 doses) results in suppression of urine 17-hydroxycorticosteroids and free cortisol, usually by greater than 50 percent. Urine 17-hydroxycorticosteroids increase after metyrapone administration in Cushing's disease. Plasma ACTH levels are normal or high-normal and show an exaggerated increase after CRH administration. Pituitary ACTH hypersecretion (Cushing's disease) is caused by a corticotroph microadenoma in 90 percent of patients and by a macroadenoma in most of the rest. Corticotroph hyperplasia has been documented in a few cases. The microadenomas are often small (3 mm or less) and may be missed on CT scanning. Thus pituitary surgery must often be recommended on the basis of dynamic testing along. However, bilateral inferior petrosal sinus catheterizations to localize the site of ACTH production may prove to be useful in patients in whom an adenoma is not radiographically detectable.

Treatment Transsphenoidal microsurgery is successful in treating microadenomas in about 75 percent of patients. When surgery is successful, plasma cortisol concentrations fall almost to zero and often remain low for many months owing to delayed recovery of CRH and ACTH secretion by the hypothalamus and normal remaining pituitary. However, adrenal function eventually returns to normal in most patients. Previously, bilateral adrenalectomy was the therapy of choice for patients with pituitary Cushing's disease. Unfortunately, after this procedure enlarging pituitary adenomas with increased skin pigmentation (Nelson's syndrome) develop in 10 to 30 percent of patients.

Ectopic ACTH production is a relatively common disorder and can cause great difficulty in diagnosis (see Chaps. 303 and 325). When ACTH production by such tumors is of short duration (e.g., when caused by rapidly growing tumors such as oat cell carcinoma of the lung), symptoms of Cushing's syndrome are blunted. Rather, patients often demonstrate hypokalemia, muscle weakness, weight loss, and hyperpigmentation. ACTH concentrations often exceed 300 pg/mL and do not change with dexamethasone administration. When slow-growing tumors such as thymic carcinoids, bronchial carcinoids, medullary carcinoma of the thyroid, and pancreatic islet-cell tumors produce ACTH the typical features of Cushing's syndrome are common. In the latter group ACTH measurements and cortisol response to dexamethasone administration may mimic those found in patients with pituitary adenomas. However, with ectopic ACTH production ACTH concentrations generally do not change after CRH administration. When differentiation between pituitary and ectopic ACTH production is uncertain, bilateral inferior petrosal sinus catheterization is necessary. Production of Cushing's syndrome by ectopic production of CRH itself and by factors that enhance CRH action has also been reported.

ACTH DEFICIENCY (SECONDARY ADRENAL INSUFFICIENCY)
ACTH deficiency may be isolated or occur in association with other anterior pituitary hormone deficiencies. Reversible isolated ACTH deficiency is common after long-term glucocorticoid administration. If glucocorticoids are withdrawn suddenly in this situation or continued in physiologic doses when severe illness is present, adrenal insufficiency may occur. Symptoms include nausea, vomiting, fatigue, and dizziness and there may be fever, hypotension, hyponatremia, and hypoglycemia. Although cortisol is necessary for free water excretion, it is not needed for potassium excretion. Hence patients with ACTH deficiency are not hyperkalemic as are patients with primary adrenal insufficiency. Hyperpigmentation also does not occur. These factors make diagnosis of secondary adrenal insufficiency more difficult than that of primary adrenal insufficiency. Isolated ACTH deficiency may occur without prior glucocorticoid therapy.

All patients undergoing pituitary surgery need to be treated with "stress" doses of glucocorticoids until normal adrenal function can be demonstrated postoperatively. All patients with pituitary macroadenomas or hypothalamic disease require testing of the pituitary-adrenal axis but when pituitary surgery is planned, testing can be limited in focus until after surgery is completed.

ENDORPHINS (ENDOGENOUS OPIOIDS)

Endogenous peptides that interact with opioid receptors are termed endorphins, enkephalins, or endogenous opioids (see Chap. 69). In the anterior pituitary the precursor molecule POMC is cleaved to ACTH and β-lipotropin, both of which are secreted into plasma. A small fraction (about 15 percent) of β-lipotropin is cleaved to β-endorphin. In other parts of the brain and in the intermediate pituitary lobe of animals, most POMC is cleaved to β-endorphin. Dynorphin, a potent endogenous opioid, is produced by the same magnocellular neurons of the hypothalamus that synthesize vasopressin and is stored along with vasopressin in the posterior pituitary. Pituitary ablation is successful in relieving pain in about one-third of patients with metastatic carcinoma, independent of any effect on tumor growth. Although the mechanism for this effect is uncertain, most patients who respond to this therapy develop concomitant diabetes insipidus.

Although some endorphins originate in the pituitary and hypothalamus, the role of these compounds in regulating pituitary and hypothalamic function is uncertain. Endorphins appear to inhibit LH and FSH release; naloxone, an opiate antagonist, increase LH and FSH concentrations in men and women. Naloxone can restore LH pulsations to normal in hyperprolactinemic patients with absent LH pulsations. Whereas in trained athletes exogenous opiates (e.g., morphine) stimulate prolactin and GH release, naloxone does not influence basal or stimulated prolactin or GH. Exogenous opioids inhibit ACTH release but endogenous opioids have little influence on ACTH or TSH release.

DISEASES OF THE HYPOTHALAMUS AND PITUITARY

Diseases that affect the hypothalamus and pituitary can have both endocrine and nonendocrine manifestations.

HYPOTHALAMUS The human hypothalamus weighs about 4 g; hypothalamic dysfunction occurs only when disease is bilateral. Tumors in this region are often slow-growing and may achieve large size before symptoms appear. Signs of hydrocephalus or focal cerebral dysfunction may coexist with hypopituitarism and hypothalamic dysfunction and may produce a confusing clinical picture.

The hypothalamus exerts both endocrine and nonendocrine functions. Hypothalamic control of the pituitary gland has already been discussed. Nonendocrine functions that are influenced by the hypothalamus are as follows:

1 Caloric intake and feeding behavior. The basal hypothalamus is necessary for maintenance of a stable weight. The ventromedial nucleus is involved with satiety; the lateral hypothalamus with hunger. Hypothalamic obesity is usually associated with lesions of the ventromedial nucleus; this obesity appears to involve a resetting of the weight set point. Marked hyperphagia, possibly related to rapid gastric emptying, occurs until the new weight set point is reached. Patients often demonstrate decreased activity and finicky eating once the new set point is reached. Lateral hypothalamic lesions may cause aphagia. Other factors that influence eating behavior include hypothyroidism and adrenal insufficiency, both of which can diminish appetite.

2 Temperature regulation. The anterior hypothalamus contains warm- and cold-sensitive neurons that respond to local and environmental thermal gradients. The posterior hypothalamus generates the signals necessary for heat dissipation. The temperature increase associated with infections is generated by the hypothalamus. Phagocytic cells throughout the body produce interleukin 1 (endogenous pyrogen) which stimulates the anterior hypothalamus to produce prostaglandin E_2. Prostaglandin E_2 raises the thermostat set point, leading to heat conservation (e.g., vasoconstriction) and increased heat production (e.g., muscle shivering) until blood and core temperatures match the new hypothalamic set point.

Abnormalities of temperature regulation may occur with hypothalamic disease. Hypothermia is a rare consequence of diffuse hypothalamic disease. Paroxysmal hypothermia with sweating, flushing, and a fall in body temperatures may occur, and sustained hyperthermia without tachycardia is reported with acute pathologic processes such as hemorrhage into the third ventricle. Poikilothermia (a change in body temperature of greater than 1°C with change in environmental temperature) is usually a consequence of posterior hypothalamic disease. Paroxysmal hyperthermia with episodic shaking chills, spiking fevers, and autonomic phenomena is a rare manifestation. It is important to remember that adrenal insufficiency can cause fever or hypothermia and that hypothyroidism may cause hypothermia.

3 Sleep-wake cycle. The anterior hypothalamus contains a sleep center; lesions in this region result in insomnia. The posterior hypothalamus is important for arousal and maintenance of the waking state; posterior hypothalamic destruction due to ischemia, encephalitis, or trauma can result in a hypersomnolent state from which arousal is possible. Larger lesions extending to the reticular formation of the rostral midbrain cause coma (see Chap. 21).

4 Memory and behavior. Lesions of the ventromedial hypothalamus and premammillary region result in loss of short-term memory, often with Korsakoff's syndrome. Longer-term memory is often intact. Hypothalamic lesions may also cause a more typical picture of dementia. Rage reactions may result with ventromedial lesions, and lateral hypothalamic destruction may cause an apathetic state.

5 Thirst. The hypothalamus is the center for AVP production and for the control of thirst by serum osmolality. Impaired thirst may occur with hypothalamic lesions; rarely primary polydipsia without diabetes insipidus is a consequence of hypothalamic lesions.

6 Autonomic nervous system function. Parasympathetic pathways are stimulated by the anterior hypothalamus; sympathetic pathways are stimulated by the posterior hypothalamus. Diencephalic epilepsy is a rare syndrome associated with paroxysms of autonomic hyperactivity.

A diencephalic syndrome in children, characterized by emaciation, hyperkinesis and inappropriate affect, often with a cheerful disposition, is usually associated with invasive tumors of the anterior and basal hypothalamus. Most of these children die by the age of 2 years, but in those who survive the clinical picture changes to one of increased appetite with obesity, irritability, and rage reactions.

In general, slow-growing tumors are more likely to produce dementia, disturbances of food intake (obesity or emaciation), and endocrine dysfunction. Acute destructive processes are more likely to produce coma or disturbances of the autonomic nervous system.

Diseases of the anterior hypothalamus include craniopharyngiomas, gliomas of the optic nerve, sphenoid ridge meningiomas, granulomatous disease (including sarcoidosis), germinomas, and aneurysms of the internal carotid artery. Suprasellar pituitary adenomas and tuberculum sella meningiomas may grow into the hypothalamus as well. Lesions of the posterior hypothalamus include gliomas, hamartomas, ependymomas, germinomas, and teratomas.

Precocious puberty, particularly in males, has often been associated with "pinealomas," leading to the speculation that the pineal is important for gonadotropin regulation. However, these pinealomas actually are germinomas, and the precocious puberty appears to result from the ectopic production of hCG by these tumors rather than from an effect on pituitary gonadotropins.

Craniopharyngiomas Craniopharyngiomas arise from remnants of Rathke's pouch. Most of these tumors are suprasellar, but about 15 percent are intrasellar. The tumors are usually cystic or partially cystic, often contain calcium, and are lined with stratified squamous epithelium. Although craniopharyngiomas are typically thought to be a disease of childhood, 45 percent of patients are over the age of 20, and 20 percent are over the age of 40 at the time of diagnosis.

Children usually present with signs of increased intracranial pressure due to hydrocephalus (80 percent) with headache, vomiting, and papilledema. Visual abnormalities such as loss of vision and field cuts are found in 60 percent. Short stature is sometimes found (7 to 40 percent), but retarded bone age is more common. Delayed sexual development occurs in about 20 percent, and diabetes insipidus may be present.

About 80 percent of adults present with visual complaints and an additional 10 percent have visual abnormalities on careful testing. Papilledema is present in about 15 percent of adults. Headaches (40 percent), mental deterioration or personality change (26 percent), and hypogonadism (35 percent) are relatively common in adults. Hyperprolactinemia is present in one-third to one-half of patients, but prolactin levels rarely exceed 100 to 150 ng/mL. Diabetes insipidus (15 percent), weight gain (15 percent), and panhypopituitarism (7 percent) may occur as well. Rarely, the cyst contents spill into the cerebrospinal fluid, causing a picture of aseptic meningitis.

Suprasellar calcification (see Fig. 321-14) in a flocculent, granular, or curvilinear pattern is present on skull x-rays in most children and in some adults with craniopharyngioma. Calcification is evident on CT scan in most of these adults, however. Hypothalamic germinomas may calcify as well. Skull x-ray abnormalities include calcification, sellar enlargement, and signs of increased intracranial pressure in 90 percent of children and 60 percent of adults.

Therapy of craniopharyngiomas remains controversial. Many advocate total removal whereas others suggest biopsy and partial resection followed by conventional radiation. Tumors less than 3 cm in diameter have a better prognosis.

Germ-cell tumors Germinomas originate in the posterior third ventricle, anterior third ventricle (supra- or intrasellar), or in both locations (also see Chap. 297). Germinomas (also known as atypical teratomas) were previously confused with parenchymal tumors of the pineal (pinealomas); when located in the anterior third ventricle they were known as "ectopic pinealomas." Germinomas often infiltrate the hypothalamus and occasionally metastasize to the CSF or distant sites.

The majority of patients have diabetes insipidus in association with variable anterior pituitary insufficiency. Precocious puberty may occur in males, probably due to hCG production by these tumors. Diplopia, headache, vomiting, lethargy, weight loss, and hydrocephalus are common. The tumors usually begin in childhood but may be diagnosed in young adults. Because germinomas are radiosensitive, early recognition is important. When the tumor is located in the anterior third ventricle, biopsy by the transsphenoidal route is often possible. Tumors in the pineal region are more difficult to biopsy, leading some authors to recommend empirical radiation therapy or chemotherapy, whereas others prefer surgical biopsy or debulking followed by radiation and chemotherapy. Germinomas of the nonseminoma type may produce hCG and/or α-fetoprotein, whereas pure seminomas rarely produce tumor markers (see Chap. 297).

PITUITARY ADENOMAS Pituitary adenomas account for about 10 to 15 percent of all intracranial neoplasms. They can cause anterior pituitary hormonal imbalance, structural problems related to invasion of surrounding structures, or syndromes of hormone excess. Occasionally, the diagnosis is the result of incidental findings during skull x-ray examinations.

Pathology For many years pituitary tumors were classified as basophilic, acidophilic, or chromophobic on the basis of hematoxylin and eosin straining. Corticotroph adenomas are generally basophilic; the more densely granulated prolactin-secreting tumors are acidophilic; the majority of prolactinomas, sparsely granulated GH-secreting tumors. TSH-secreting and gonadotropin-secreting tumors and nonsecreting tumors are all chromophobic. Because this classification provides little specific information about hormone production, it has been abandoned. Many nonfunctioning pituitary tumors are, however, still referred to as "chromophobes." Classification based upon immunohistochemical staining makes it possible to identify and localize specific hormones. Pituitary tumors can also be classified according to hormonal secretion, based upon hormone measurements in serum.

Furthermore, pituitary tumors can be classified according to size and invasive characteristics. Stage I tumors are microadenomas (less than 10 mm in diameter) that may cause hormonal oversecretion but do not cause hypopituitarism and are not associated with structural problems. Stage II tumors are macroadenomas (greater than 10 mm) with or without suprasellar extension. Stage III tumors are macroadenomas that locally invade the floor of the sella and may cause sellar enlargement and suprasellar extension. Stage IV tumors are invasive macroadenomas with diffuse destruction of the sella, with or without suprasellar extension. The difficulty with this system of classification is that not all pituitary tumors fall neatly into one of these categories. For example, it is often difficult to separate thinning of the sellar floor (stage II) from erosion through the floor (stage III).

Endocrine manifestations Anterior pituitary hormone overproduction is suspected on clinical grounds and confirmed by appropriate laboratory evaluation (see Table 321-5). The most common secretory pituitary tumors are prolactinomas. They cause galactorrhea and hypogonadism, including amenorrhea, infertility, and impotence. GH-secreting tumors are the next most common secretory pituitary tumors and cause acromegaly or gigantism. Next in frequency are corticotroph (ACTH-secreting) adenomas which cause cortisol excess (Cushing's disease). Glycoprotein hormone–secreting pituitary adenomas (secreting TSH, LH, or FSH) are the least common. TSH-secreting adenomas are a rare cause of hyperthyroidism. Paradoxically, most patients with gonadotropin-secreting adenomas have hypogonadism.

About 15 percent of patients with tumors that come to surgery have adenomas that secrete more than one pituitary hormone. The most common combination is GH and prolactin, and other common patterns are GH-TSH, GH-prolactin-TSH, and ACTH-prolactin. Most of these tumors have one cell secreting two hormones (unimorphous), but some tumors have two or more cell types, each of which produces a single hormone (polymorphous).

Prolactinomas in women and corticotroph adenomas in both sexes are usually diagnosed while still microadenomas. In contrast, the majority of patients with acromegaly and most men with prolactinomas have macroadenomas at the time of diagnosis. Glycoprotein hormone–secreting tumors are also usually quite large at the time of diagnosis.

About 25 percent of pituitary adenomas that come to surgery are apparently nonsecretory, although some stain immunologically for pituitary hormones. In some cases, particularly in the case of gonadotropin-secreting tumors, hormonal secretion is overlooked. Some of the "nonfunctioning" pituitary tumors, as well as some functional ones, secrete part of the glycoprotein hormone molecule, most commonly the alpha subunit. Alpha subunit excess is a frequent finding in patients with TSH-secreting adenomas, and FSH beta may be hypersecreted in patients with gonadotropin-secreting tumors.

Null cell tumors (no specific hormones identified by immunostaining) are generally large when diagnosed, since no hormonal

TABLE 321-5   Pituitary hormone evaluation

Hormone	Excess	Deficiency
Growth hormone	1 Measurement of plasma growth hormone 1 h following glucose PO	1 Measurement of plasma growth hormone 30, 60, and 120 min after one of the following: a Regular insulin 0.1 to 0.15 unit per kilogram IV b Levodopa 10 mg/kg PO c L-Arginine 0.5 mg/kg intravenously over 30 min
	2 Measurement of IGF-1/SM-C	2 ?Measurement of IGF-1/SM-C
Prolactin	1 Measurement of basal serum prolactin	1 Measurement of serum prolactin 10 to 20 min after one of the following: a TRH 200 to 500 μg IV b Chlorpromazine 25 mg IM
TSH	1 Measurement of T_4, free T_4 index, T_3, TSH	1 Measurement of T_4, free T_4, free T_4 index, TSH
Gonadotropins	1 Measurement of FSH, LH, Testosterone, FSH beta, FSH response to TRH	1 Measurement of basal LH, FSH in postmenopausal women; no measurements in menstruating, ovulating women 2 Testosterone, FSH, and LH in men
ACTH	1 Measurement of urine free cortisol*	1 Measurement of serum cortisol at 30 and 60 min following regular insulin 0.1 to 0.15 units per kilogram IV
	2 Dexamethasone suppression by one of the following: a Measurement of 8 A.M. plasma cortisol after administration of 1 mg dexamethasone at midnight b Measurement of 8 A.M. plasma cortisol or 24-h urine 17-hydroxysteroids after 0.5 mg dexamethasone PO q 6 h for 8 doses	2 Metyrapone response by one of the following: a Measurement of plasma 11-deoxycortisol at 8 A.M. after 30 mg metyrapone at midnight (maximal dose 2 g) b Measurement of 24-h urinary 17-hydroxycorticoids day of and day after 750 mg metyrapone q 4 h for 6 doses c Measurement of 24-h urinary 17-hydroxycorticoids day of and day after 500 mg metyrapone q 2 h for 12 doses
	3 High-dose dexamethasone suppression by one of the following: a Measurement of plasma cortisol after 8 mg dexamethasone PO at midnight b Measurement of 8 A.M. plasma cortisol or 24 h urine 17-hydroxysteroids after 2 mg dexamethasone q 6 h for 8 doses	3 ACTH stimulation test: Measurement of plasma cortisol at 0 and 60 min after IM or IV administration of 0.25 mg cosyntropin
	4 Metyrapone response (same protocol as for deficiency testing) 5 Response of plasma ACTH to corticotropin releasing hormone (no standard protocol)	
Arginine vasopressin (AVP)	1 Measurement of serum sodium and osmolality, urine osmolality in presence of normal renal, adrenal, thyroid function 2 Simultaneous measurement of serum osmolality and ADH levels	1 Comparison of urine osmolality and serum osmolality under conditions of increased AVP secretion† 2 Simultaneous measurement of serum osmolality and AVP levels

* Tests 1 and 2 establish the diagnosis of Cushing's syndrome. Tests 3, 4, and 5 localize the Cushing's disease to the pituitary gland. Occasionally bilateral inferior petrosal sinus catheterization will be necessary.

† May be achieved by water deprivation or saline administration.

overproduction is present to provide early clues to diagnosis. Onco-cytomas are nonsecretory pituitary adenomas with abundant mito-chondria, commonly found in older men.

Pituitary adenomas are occasionally part of the multiple endocrine neoplasia (MEN I) syndrome (see Chap. 334). This dominantly inherited disease causes adenomas of the pituitary gland, secretory tumors of the endocrine pancreas, and hyperparathyroidism due to generalized parathyroid hyperplasia. Pituitary adenomas secreting GH or prolactin are common, but nonfunctioning tumors also occur. Insulinomas and gastrinomas are the most common tumors in MEN I. Pancreatic GRH-secreting tumors that cause acromegaly and pituitary hyperplasia may superficially resemble the MEN I syndrome.

Mass effects of pituitary tumors

VISUAL FIELD DEFECTS The optic chiasm lies anterior and superior to the pituitary gland and in 80 percent of normal persons overlies the pituitary fossa; in about 10 percent the chiasm is anterior to the tuberculum sella (prefixed), and in another 10 percent it overlaps the dorsum sella posteriorly (postfixed). The chiasm is found at a variable distance above the diaphragma sella, with up to 1 cm of separation in some patients.

The most common visual field defect in patients with pituitary adenomas is a bitemporal hemianopsia, and about 8 percent of patients develop complete loss of vision in one eye with a temporal defect in the opposite eye. Alternatively, patients may demonstrate bitemporal scotomas rather than hemianopsia, particularly with a rapidly growing lesion in association with a prefixed chiasm (see Chap. 13). For this reason careful visual field examinations must assess more than the lateral fields of vision. Of those patients with field defects about 9 percent have a single eye defect, most commonly with a superior temporal defect. Occasionally, there is a monocular field loss such as a central scotoma that mimics nonpituitary lesions. When pituitary adenomas cause visual field defects sellar enlargement is the rule.

OCULOMOTOR PALSIES Pituitary adenomas may extend laterally, invade the cavernous sinuses, and cause oculomotor palsies. When this occurs, visual field defects are usually not present. Involvement of the third cranial nerve is most common and may mimic diabetic third nerve neuropathy in that pupillary reactivity is usually preserved. Additional findings associated with lateral extension of the adenoma may include involvement of the fourth and sixth cranial nerves, pain or numbness in the distribution of the fifth cranial nerve, and compression or obstruction of the carotid artery.

Headaches are common in patients with larger tumors and are also present in the majority of patients with acromegaly. Headaches tend to be dull and annoying and may be exacerbated by coughing. Headaches are thought to be due to stretching of the diaphragma sella and may be referred to several locations, including the vertex of skull and to retroorbital, frontooccipital, frontotemporal, or occipital-cervical areas.

Very large pituitary tumors may invade the hypothalamus and cause hyperphagia, abnormal temperature regulation, loss of con-sciousness, and loss of hormonal input from the hypothalamus. Obstructive hydrocephalus involving the third ventricle is less common with pituitary adenomas than with craniopharyngiomas. Tumor in-vasion of the temporal lobe may cause complex partial seizures; invasion of the posterior fossa may be associated with brainstem dysfunction, and invasion into the frontal lobes causes alterations in mental state and frontal release signs.

PITUITARY APOPLEXY Acute hemorrhagic infarction of a pituitary adenoma may cause a dramatic syndrome including severe headache, nausea, vomiting, and depression of consciousness. Ophthalmoplegia, visual and pupillary disturbances, and meningismus may be present. Most of these symptoms are caused by direct pressure from the tumor, whereas meningismus results from blood in the CSF. The syndrome may either evolve slowly over a period of 24 to 48 h or may lead to sudden death.

Pituitary apoplexy is most commonly found in patients with somatotroph or corticotroph adenomas, but it may be the first clinical manifestation of a pituitary tumor. Both anticoagulation and radio-therapy predispose to hemorrhagic infarction. Rarely, pituitary apo-plexy produces "autohypophysectomy" with "cure" of clinical acromegaly, Cushing's disease, or hyperprolactinemia. Hypopitui-tarism is a common sequela; although acute hormonal measurements may be normal during the acute phase, cortisol and gonadal steroid concentrations decline over the ensuing days, and thyroxine concen-trations decline over weeks. Diabetes insipidus is rare.

It is important to differentiate between pituitary apoplexy and a leaking aneurysm; angiography is often required in this situation. Acute pituitary apoplexy is generally considered a neurosurgical emergency and may require acute decompression of the pituitary, generally via the transsphenoidal route.

Therapy of pituitary adenomas

Ideal therapy for pituitary adenomas would permanently correct hormonal hypersecretion without causing hypopituitarism and would shrink or remove the tumor mass without additional morbidity or mortality. Therapy for microadenomas may achieve both of these goals, whereas therapy for macroadenomas is usually less successful. In considering therapy it is critical to weigh the disability due to the tumor against any disability that may arise from the treatment. Regardless of tumor size the therapy should not be worse than the disease. Potentially lethal diseases such as Cushing's disease or acromegaly may require more aggressive treatment than do prolactinomas.

MEDICAL THERAPY Bromocriptine, a dopamine agonist, is currently the therapy of choice for patients with microprolactinomas who require therapy. Bromocriptine corrects hyperprolactinemia in almost all patients with microprolactinomas; however, when the drug is stopped, prolactin levels usually return to pretreatment levels. It is uncertain if bromocriptine use affects the success of future surgery.

Bromocriptine side effects of nausea, gastric irritation, and postural hypotension can be minimized by initially giving a low dose (1.25 mg) at bedtime with a snack. Other side effects include headache, fatigue, abdominal cramps, nasal congestion, and constipation. The dosage is gradually increased to a twice-daily schedule (most com-monly 2.5 mg bid).

Bromocriptine is also effective in larger prolactin-secreting ma-croadenomas. Bromocriptine lowers prolactin levels by about 90 percent in most patients with large tumors but usually not to normal. Tumor shrinkage of 50 percent or greater occurs in about half the patients, and visual field defects may return to normal. Tumor shrinkage is occasionally accompanied by reversal of hypopituitarism. With giant adenomas, bromocriptine-induced tumor shrinkage may rarely cause a devastating intracranial hemorrhage. Unfortunately macroadenomas usually regrow when bromocriptine is stopped. When pregnancy is desired or when mass effects of the tumor are not reversed with bromocriptine, additional therapy (surgery or radiation) is often necessary.

Bromocriptine is a useful therapeutic adjunct in some patients with acromegaly, particularly in those with coexistent hyperprolac-tinemia. GH concentrations rarely return to normal, but symptomatic improvement is common and tumor shrinkage may occur. Bromo-criptine should be considered in acromegalic subjects whose GH levels remain elevated following surgery or who are waiting for radiation therapy to take effect. Nonfunctioning chromophobe ad-enomas usually do not shrink in response to bromocriptine, even when high doses are used.

Tamoxifen is occasionally useful as an adjunct in the therapy of large prolactinomas refractory to therapy with dopamine antagonists. Cyproheptadine, a serotonin antagonist, has been reported to induce remissions in occasional patients with corticotroph adenomas.

SURGERY Transsphenoidal surgery of pituitary microadenomas is safe and frequently corrects hormonal oversecretion. Hormonal over-production is corrected within 24 h in 75 percent of patients with Cushing's disease due to corticotroph microadenomas, acromegaly with GH concentration less than 40 ng/mL, and microprolactinomas associated with serum prolactin concentrations less than 200 ng/mL. The initial success rate varies among institutions, with reported figures ranging from 50 to 95 percent. Unfortunately, after initially successful surgery hyperprolactinemia recurs in about 17 percent of patients followed for 3 to 5 years and possibly in 50 percent after 5 to 10 years. The recurrence rate after initially successful surgery in acromegaly and Cushing's disease is less well-established.

The mortality rate for transsphenoidal surgery of microadenomas is 0.27 percent with a morbidity rate of about 1.7 percent based on 2600 surgical procedures. Major complications include cerebrospinal fluid rhinorrhea, oculomotor palsy, and visual loss.

Pituitary surgery is less successful with larger secretory tumors. In patients with serum prolactin greater than 200 ng/mL or GH greater than 40 ng/mL, hormone concentrations return to normal in only 30 percent following surgery. Surgery is successful in about 60 percent of patients with Cushing's disease due to corticotroph macroadenomas. Recurrence rates with these secretory macroadenomas after a surgery-induced remission are uncertain; in the case at prolactin-secreting tumors, hyperprolactinemia recurs in 10 to 80 percent of patients.

Mass effects of large tumors are also rarely cured with surgery alone; in cases where surgery is the exclusive therapy, the 10-year recurrence of symptoms is 85 percent in patients not treated with radiation and/or bromocriptine. When radiation therapy is used in combination with surgery, the 10-year recurrence is 15 percent.

Surgery for macroadenomas has a mortality rate of around 0.86 percent and a morbidity rate of about 6.3 percent. Hypopituitarism occurs in an additional 10 percent of patients. Transient diabetes insipidus occurs in about 5 percent, and permanent diabetes insipidus occurs in 1 percent. Major complications of surgery for macroadenoma include cerebrospinal rhinorrhea (3.3 percent), permanent visual loss (1.5 percent), permanent oculomotor palsy (0.6 percent), and meningitis (0.5 percent).

RADIATION THERAPY Conventional radiation therapy is effective in preventing tumor growth (70 to 100 percent) but is unsatisfactory in the acute management of pituitary hyperfunction. Therapy consists of delivery of 4500 cGy (4500 rad) over 4.5 to 5 weeks, using rotational techniques. GH values of less than 5 ng/mL can be achieved in half of acromegalics after 5 years and in 70 percent after 10 years. Conventional radiation alone is rarely successful in treating corticotroph adenomas in adults. Long-term efficacy of radiation in patients with prolactinoma is currently being studied. Complications of conventional radiation therapy include hypopituitarism in up to 50 percent of patients.

Heavy particle therapy with proton beam or alpha particles is effective in treating secretory adenomas but response is slow. Tumors with suprasellar extension or tissue invasion are generally excluded from such series. With proton beam therapy at the Harvard cyclotron, radiation doses of up to 14,000 cGy (14,000 rad) can be given safely without damage to surrounding structures. At 2 years, 28 percent of acromegalics achieve GH values of less than 5 ng/mL; the percentages increase to 56 percent at 5 years and 75 percent by 10 years. With Cushing's disease proton beam corrects the hypercortisolism in 55 percent at 2 years and in 80 percent by 5 years. Proton beam therapy effectively lowers ACTH and stops growth of most corticotroph adenomas in patients with Nelson's syndrome with the exception of adenomas that are invasive at the time of therapy. Long-term results for treatment of prolactinomas with proton beam therapy are not available.

Complications of heavy particle therapy include hypopituitarism in at least 10 percent of patients, although the exact long-term prevalence of this complication is uncertain. Visual field defects and oculomotor dysfunction, usually temporary, have been reported in about 1.5 percent of patients. The major draw-back of this form of therapy is the length of time that must elapse before hormonal hypersecretion is corrected.

We generally treat microprolactinomas with bromocriptine. However, we recommend surgery for those patients with microprolactinoma who require therapy and are intolerant of dopamine agonists. Surgery generally does not result in hypopituitarism in this relatively benign disease. Surgery is usually our treatment of choice in patients with acromegaly or Cushing's disease because in most instances rapid reversal of hormonal hypersecretion is essential. Since Cushing's disease and acromegaly are potentially lethal diseases, more extensive surgery that results in hypopituitarism may be required.

Many patients with macroprolactinomas are treated with bromocriptine alone, and a trial of this agent should be given. We recommend transsphenoidal surgery and/or radiation therapy for patients with large prolactinomas who desire pregnancy, show persistent structural abnormalities or symptomatic hyperprolactinemia despite dopamine agonists, and who are intolerant of dopaminergic agents. Patients with nonfunctioning pituitary adenomas with structural abnormalities require transsphenoidal surgery, generally followed by conventional radiation therapy. Heavy particle therapy is an effective alternative to surgery in patients with acromegaly or Cushing's disease who have contraindications to or refuse surgery. Heavy particle or conventional radiation therapy is effective in treating patients with persistent GH elevation after transsphenoidal surgery. Heavy particle therapy is effective in persistent Cushing's disease as well. Proton beam therapy is effective in most patient's with Nelson's syndrome and may be a desirable alternative to conventional radiation therapy in patients with macroprolactinomas and nonsecretory macroadenomas. Transfrontal surgery is occasionally required, particularly in patients with giant adenomas.

HYPOPITUITARISM *Hypopituitarism* refers to deficiency of one or more pituitary hormones and has many etiologies (see Table 321-6). Pituitary hormone deficiency may be congenital or acquired. Isolated GH or gonadotropin deficiency is common. Temporary ACTH deficiency as a consequence of long-term glucocorticoid therapy is also common, but permanent isolated deficiency of ACTH or TSH is rare. Deficiency of any of the anterior pituitary hormones may occur at the level of the pituitary gland or the hypothalamus. When diabetes insipidus is present the primary defect is almost invariably in the hypothalamus or high pituitary stalk, often in conjunction with mild hyperprolactinemia and anterior pituitary hypofunction.

Manifestations of hypopituitarism depend upon the specific pituitary hormones that are lacking. Growth failure due to GH deficiency is a common presenting complaint in children. GH deficiency in adults causes more subtle manifestations such as fine wrinkling around the eyes and mouth and in subjects with diabetes mellitus increased sensitivity to insulin. Complaints related to gonadotropin deficiency include amenorrhea and infertility in women and testosterone deficiency and decreased libido, decreased beard and body hair, and preservation of a youthful scalp hairline in men. TSH deficiency

---

TABLE 321-6 Causes of hypopituitarism

A Isolated hormone deficiencies
  1 Congenital or acquired deficiencies
B Tumors
  1 Large pituitary adenomas
  2 Pituitary apoplexy
  3 Hypothalamic tumors, e.g., craniopharyngiomas, germinomas, chordomas, meningiomas, gliomas, and others
C Inflammatory diseases
  1 Granulomatous disease, e.g., sarcoidosis, tuberculosis, syphilis, granulomatous hypophysitis
  2 Histiocytosis X
  3 Lymphocytic hypophysitis (autoimmune)
D Vascular diseases
  1 Sheehans post-partum necrosis
  2 ? Diabetic peripartum necrosis
  3 Carotid aneurysm
E Destructive-traumatic events
  1 Surgery
  2 Stalk section
  3 Radiation (conventional—hypothalamus; heavy-particle—pituitary)
F Developmental anomalies
  1 Pituitary aplasia
  2 Basal encephalocoele
G Infiltration
  1 Hemochromatosis
  2 Amyloidosis
H "Idiopathic" causes
  1 ?Autoimmune disease

causes hypothyroidism with fatigue, cold intolerance, and puffy skin in the absence of goiter. ACTH deficiency results in cortisol deficiency, manifested by fatigue; decreased appetite; weight loss; decreased skin and nipple pigmentation; abnormal response to stress characterized by fever, hypotension, and hyponatremia; and a high mortality rate. Unlike primary adrenal insufficiency (Addison's disease) ACTH deficiency does not cause hyperpigmentation, hyperkalemia, or salt loss. With combined ACTH and gonadotropin deficiency, axillary and pubic hair may be lost. Children with combined GH and cortisol deficiency often develop hypoglycemia. AVP deficiency causes diabetes insipidus with polyuria and increased thirst. When pituitary adenomas impair anterior pituitary function GH is often the first hormone to be compromised, followed by deficiencies of gonadotropins, TSH, and ACTH.

Etiology Damage to the anterior pituitary is commonly due to a pituitary adenoma (with or without infarction), pituitary surgery, heavy particle pituitary irradiation, or infarction during the postpartum period (Sheehan's syndrome). Postpartum pituitary infarction occurs because the enlarged pituitary gland of pregnancy becomes vulnerable to ischemia; postpartum hemorrhage with systemic hypotension can destroy the pituitary gland. Inability to lactate is the first and most common clinical clue, and other symptoms of hypopituitarism may unfold over months or years. The condition is sometimes diagnosed years after the primary event. Although clinical diabetes insipidus is rare in this setting, a decreased AVP response to appropriate stimuli is common. Patients with diabetes mellitus are also prone to develop hypopituitarism late in pregnancy.

Another cause of hypopituitarism is lymphocytic hypophysitis, a syndrome that usually occurs during pregnancy or in the postpartum period. In this syndrome, a mass lesion is often seen on CT scanning which, when biopsied, consists of lymphocytic infiltration. Lymphocytic hypophysitis is thought to represent autoimmune pituitary destruction and often occurs with other autoimmune diseases such as Hashimoto's (autoimmune) thyroiditis and gastric atrophy (see Chap. 334). Circulating antibodies to prolactin cells have been identified in some of these patients. Although fewer than 20 cases of lymphocytic hypophysitis have been diagnosed, about 7 percent of patients with other autoimmune diseases have prolactin antibodies in serum. It is not yet clear whether autoimmune hypophysitis is a common cause of "idiopathic" hypopituitarism in adults.

Hypothalamic or pituitary stalk damage has many causes (see Table 321-6). Certain lesions in this region, such as sarcoidosis, metastatic carcinoma, germinomas, histiocytosis, and craniopharyngiomas, commonly cause diabetes insipidus along with hypofunction of the anterior pituitary. Pituitary insufficiency, resulting from conventional radiation to the brain or the pituitary, is thought to be largely hypothalamic in origin.

Diagnosis (see Table 321-5) To diagnose GH deficiency, the most reliable GH stimulus is insulin-induced hypoglycemia in which the blood sugar declines to less than 40 mg/dL (Fig. 321-8). A GH concentration of greater than 10 ng/mL after hypoglycemia, levodopa, or arginine effectively excludes GH deficiency. Measuring the basal GH or serum IGF-1/SM-C concentration is less reliable, because GH levels are undetectable in normal persons for much of the day and because IGF-1/SM-C concentrations in patients with GH deficiency may overlap the normal range.

Cortisol deficiency is potentially life-threatening. Basal cortisol function may be preserved in the face of extensive pituitary destruction; consequently, the ability of pituitary ACTH secretion to increase in response to "stress" must be assessed. Either the insulin tolerance test or the metyrapone test can be used to determine the adequacy of ACTH reserve.

The insulin tolerance test is safely performed on an outpatient basis in younger patients without heart disease or diseases predisposing to seizures (Fig. 321-8 and Table 321-5). Both cortisol and GH responses are measured. If hypopituitarism is strongly suspected a lower dose of regular insulin (0.05 to 0.1 units per kilogram of body

weight) should be employed. After adequate hypoglycemia, the peak plasma cortisol should be greater than 19 μg/dL, although other criteria have been suggested. Since the metyrapone test can precipitate acute adrenal insufficiency in patients with low basal cortisol secretory rates, it should always be performed in the hospital setting when the 8 A.M. basal plasma cortisol is less than 9 μg/dL. Furthermore, metyrapone administration in most patients should be preceded by a rapid ACTH stimulation test to ensure that the adrenals can respond to ACTH. In patients with an 8 A.M. basal plasma cortisol less than 4 to 5 μg/dL, metyrapone tests should not be performed. A normal response to metyrapone administration (see Table 321-5) is an increase of plasma 11-deoxycortisol to greater than 10 μg/dL and of the urinary 17-hydroxysteroids to at least twofold over baseline, usually to a value greater than 22 mg per 24 h. The plasma cortisol must concomitantly fall to less than 4 μg/dL to ensure that there has been an adequate stimulus for ACTH release. Although ACTH responses to insulin-hypoglycemia and metyrapone have not been well-standardized, a peak ACTH concentration of greater than 200 pg/mL is considered normal.

The rapid ACTH stimulation test (see Table 321-5) may be a safer and more convenient screening test for determining the adequacy of the pituitary-adrenal axis than is insulin tolerance or metyrapone testing. Since the response of the adrenal gland to exogenous ACTH is dependent upon prior endogenous ACTH exposure, patients with profound ACTH deficiency in fact do have a deficient adrenal response to exogenous ACTH stimulation. However, the rapid ACTH stimulation test may be normal in some patients with abnormal insulin tolerance tests and therefore may not detect all who are at risk for stress-induced adrenal insufficiency. Thus, whereas an abnormal

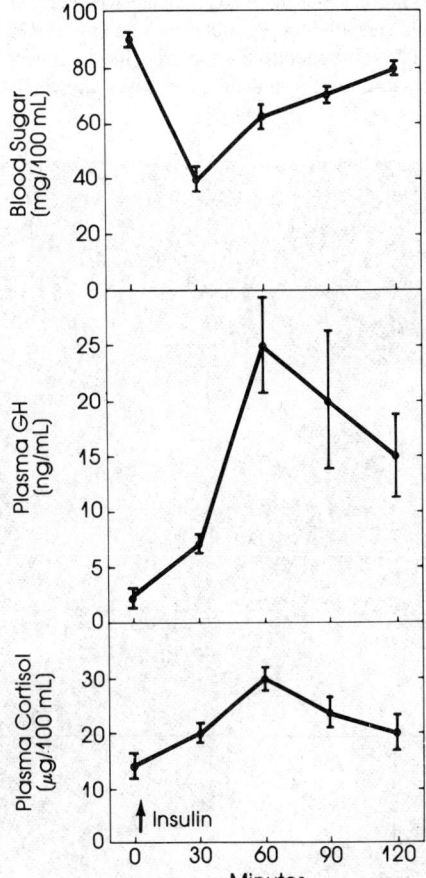

FIGURE 321-8 *The insulin tolerance test. After an intravenous injection of regular insulin (0.1 unit per kilogram of body weight) a fall in blood sugar and rise in plasma GH and cortisol is expected. This test permits evaluation of both GH and ACTH in patients with pituitary disease (After KJ Catt, Lancet 1:933, 1970.)*

ACTH stimulation test is indicative of an abnormal pituitary-adrenal axis, a normal response in the rapid ACTH stimulation test (cortisol greater than 19 μg/dL) does not always confirm that there is a normal pituitary-adrenal axis.

Gonadotropin function is easier to evaluate. In women with regular menses gonadotropin secretion is normal and gonadotropin measurements are superfluous. Likewise, a man with a normal serum testosterone and normal spermatogenesis need not have gonadotropins measured. In postmenopausal women gonadotropin levels are elevated (an endogenous stimulation test); ''normal'' levels suggest gonadotropin deficiency. Estrogen deficiency in women and testosterone deficiency in men in the absence of elevated gonadotropins imply gonadotropin deficiency.

To diagnose central hypothyroidism (thyrotropin deficiency), the serum T_4 and free T_4 (or T_3 resin uptake and free T_4 index) should first be measured. If these are in the midnormal range, TSH function is normal. If T_4 and free T_4 are low and the serum TSH is not elevated, central hypothyroidism is present. Mild central hypothyroidism, a consideration in patients with known pituitary disease who have low normal T_4 and free T_4 concentrations, remains a clinical diagnosis. Before considering the diagnosis of isolated TSH deficiency in patients with the biochemical features of central hypothyroidism without evidence of other pituitary hormone deficiency, it is important to exclude the thyroxine-binding globulin (TBG) deficiency syndrome (low T_4, increased T_3 resin uptake, low to low-normal free T_4 index, normal TSH) and the ''sick euthyroid'' syndrome (low T_4, low free T_4 or free T_4 index, normal TSH) (see Chap. 324).

Several diagnostic tests utilize hypothalamic-releasing hormones to assess pituitary reserve. While these tests are not helpful in assessing the adequacy of anterior pituitary function, they can be useful in certain situations. In GH deficient children documentation of a GH response to GRH may be helpful in deciding which children can be treated with GRH rather than GH. Likewise, in patients with isolated gonadotropin deficiency, the gonadotropin response to LHRH may be useful in predicting which patients will respond to therapy with LHRH analogues. CRH testing may be useful in the differential diagnosis of Cushing's syndrome but does not indicate whether the pituitary-adrenal axis will respond appropriately to stress. TRH stimulation testing is useful in some patients in supporting the diagnosis of hyperthyroidism or of acromegaly and in those cases in which documentation of prolactin deficiency is necessary to support a diagnosis of more generalized anterior pituitary hormone deficiency (e.g., mild central hypothyroidism). TRH testing is not necessary in the evaluation for central hypothyroidism and is not reliable in separating pituitary from hypothalamic hypothyroidism.

Therapy   A number of hormones must be replaced in patients with panhypopituitarism, but cortisol replacement is most important. We prefer prednisone for matters of convenience and cost, but many physicians use cortisone acetate. Prednisone (5 to 7.5 mg) or cortisone acetate (20 to 37.5 mg) can be given to some patients as a single morning dosage, whereas others require divided doses (two-thirds at 8 A.M., one-third at 3 A.M.). Hypopituitary patients may require lower daily glucocorticoid dosages than do patients with Addison's disease and do not require mineralocorticoid replacement. In stress situations or when preparing these patients for pituitary or other surgery, higher doses of glucocorticoids should be administered (e.g., for major surgery, hydrocortisone hemisuccinate 75 mg IM/IV every 6 h or methyl prednisolone sodium succinate 15 mg IM/IV every 6 h). Levothyroxine is the therapy of choice in patients with central hypothyroidism (0.1 to 0.2 mg per day). Since thyroxine accelerates the degradation of cortisol and can precipitate adrenal crisis in patients with limited pituitary reserve, glucocorticoid replacement should always precede levothyroxine therapy in subjects with panhypopituitarism. Hypogonadism in women is treated with estrogen/progestogen combinations and in men with testosterone esters by injection. To achieve fertility gonadotropins must be administered by injection in patients with pituitary disease, whereas LHRH or its analogues may be successful in those with hypothalamic disease. GH deficiency is not treated in adults; in children GH administration usually is required, but GRH injections may be effective in those with hypothalamic disease. Diabetes insipidus is treated with nasal desmopressin (usually 0.05 to 0.1 mL twice a day) (see Chap. 323).

RADIOLOGY OF THE PITUITARY   Conventional posteroanterior and lateral skull x-rays define the contours of the sella turcica (Fig. 321-9). Abnormalities that may be identified on these films include enlargement, erosions, and calcifications in the region of the sella. CT scanning or magnetic resonance imaging (MRI) is necessary to define further intrapituitary and suprasellar lesions. Angiography is routinely used when an aneurysm or vascular malformation is

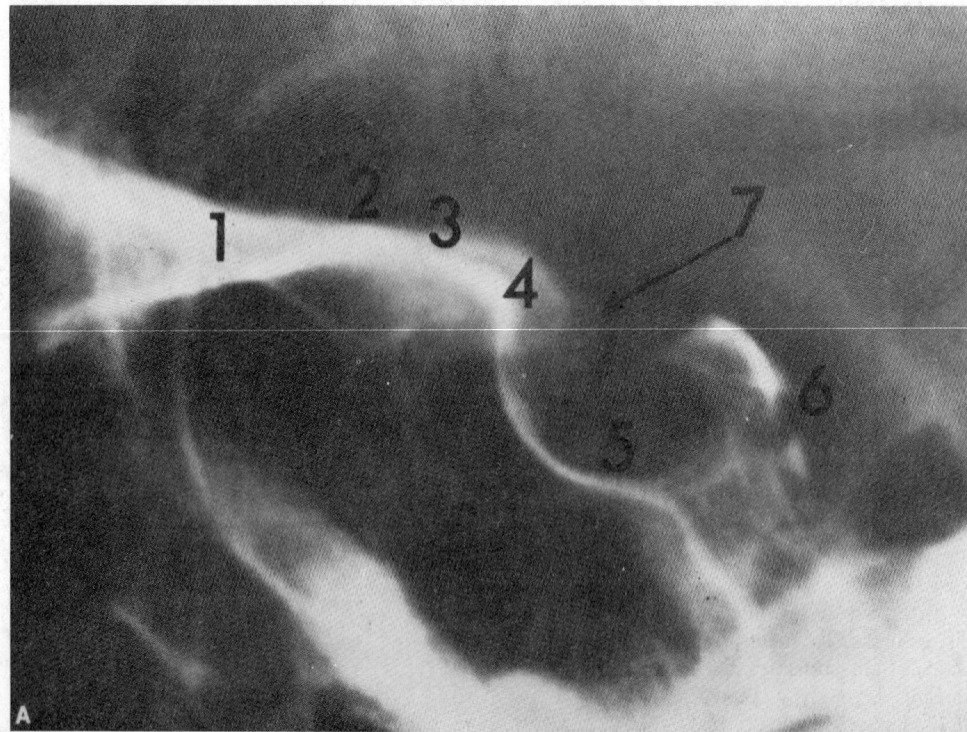

FIGURE 321-9   *X-ray of the sella, lateral view. Note (1) planum sphenoidal, (2) limbus sphenoidal, (3) sulcus chiasmaticus, (4) tuberculum sellae, (5) sella floor with distinct lamina dura, (6) dorsum sella, (7) anterior clinoid, and (8) sphenoid sinus. (From SM Wolpert in Post et al.)*

suspected as the cause of an enlarged sella and is occasionally necessary in patients with large pituitary or hypothalamic tumors. Metrizamide cisternography, in which CT scanning is performed following intrathecal injection of the water-soluble dye metrizamide has largely replaced pneumoencephalography in the delineation of the suprasellar region. Sella tomography is not recommended, as it has a high frequency of false-positive and false-negative findings and exposes the lens of the eye to excessive radiation. MRI may eventually supercede current methods of pituitary evaluation (Fig. 321-10).

The volume of the normal sella turcica (233 to 1092 mm³, mean 594 mm³) does not change in patients with pituitary microadenomas. With conventional radiography, pituitary microadenomas may be suspected on the basis of focal erosions or blistering of the floor of the sella, but these findings may also be present in normal individuals. Larger microadenomas may cause the floor of the sella to "tilt" when viewed in the frontal projection and may create the appearance of a double floor on lateral view (Fig. 321-11).

However, since most microadenomas neither affect the volume of the sella nor produce specific radiographic findings, high resolution CT scanning is necessary for localization (Fig. 321-12). On CT scanning the normal pituitary gland has a height of 3 to 7 mm. The upper aspect is flat or concave. The stalk is midline with a maximum

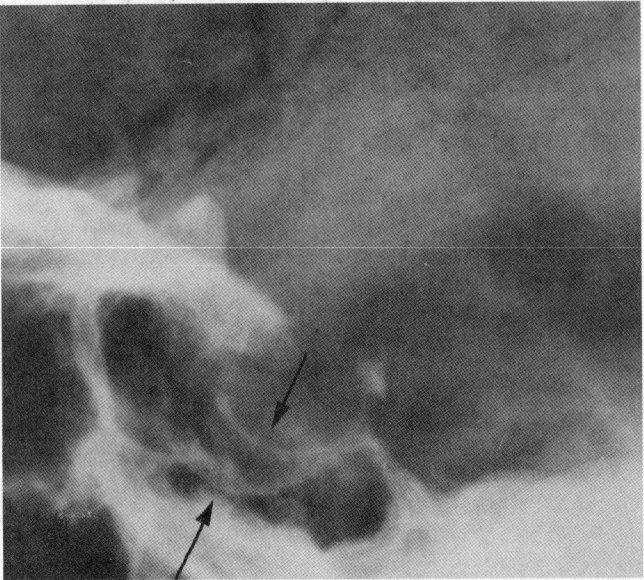

FIGURE 321-11 *Lateral view of the sella turcica demonstrating a "double floor" due to downward displacement by a pituitary adenoma. Top arrow points to normal floor; bottom arrow points to floor displaced by tumor.*

FIGURE 321-10 *Magnetic resonance imaging (MRI) in patient with a large pituitary adenoma. The arrow points to the adenoma which is seen on axial (A), sagittal (B), and coronal (C) views. (From G Gerard et al, Hosp Pract 19:151, 1984.)*

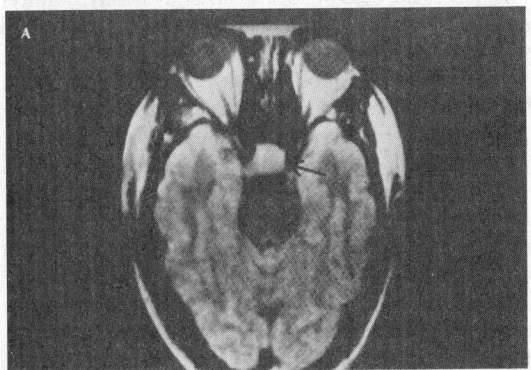

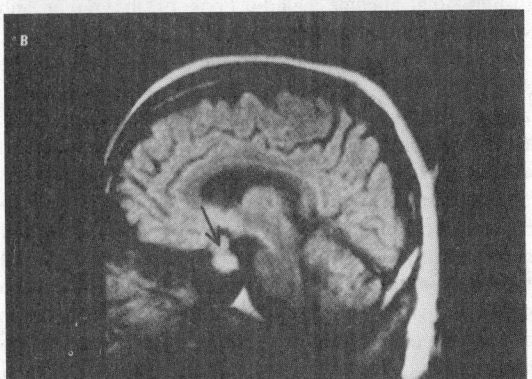

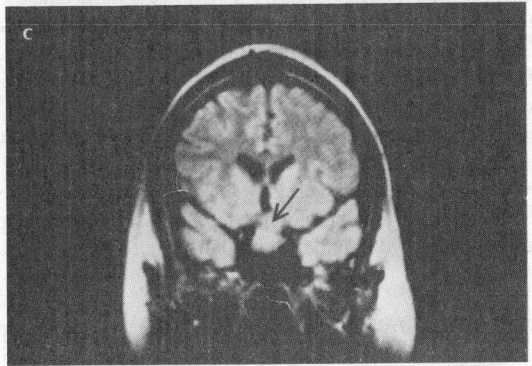

stalk diameter of 4 mm on axial selections. After intravenous contrast administration, the normal pituitary shows homogeneous enhancement in 60 percent of patients and heterogeneous enhancement in 40 percent. Up to 20 percent of normal persons show discrete low-density areas on contrast-enhanced CT scanning. In a random selection of autopsies up to 24 percent of individuals demonstrate small pituitary abnormalities (e.g., microadenomas, cysts, metastatic tumors, pituitary infarcts), but it is unclear whether such abnormalities correspond to the focal abnormal areas on CT scanning.

Microadenomas are best demonstrated on direct coronal views taken in 1 mm sections after rapid infusion of contrast material. The normal pituitary is hyperdense but less so than the cavernous sinus. Microadenomas, particularly microprolactinomas, usually appear to be hypodense using this technique (see Fig. 321-12). Small corticotroph adenomas are particularly difficult to visualize. Larger microadenomas may cause upward convexity of the diaphragma sella and contralateral deviation of the pituitary stalk (Fig. 321-13). If marked intrasellar enhancement is noted angiography is required to exclude an aneurysm or transsellar intercarotid anastamosis.

Pituitary macroadenomas generally cause sella enlargement, with or without bony erosion, seen on conventional radiography. However, the presence of an enlarged sella in itself is not sufficient to diagnose a pituitary adenoma (see below). Additional findings in plain skull x-rays in patients with acromegaly may include prognathism, enlarged paranasal sinuses, hyperostosis of the external occipital protuberance,

FIGURE 321-12 *Sagittal CT scan of sella in patient with small microprolactinoma. The tumor has decreased density, and minimal erosion of the sella floor is demonstrated. Arrow points to tumor.*

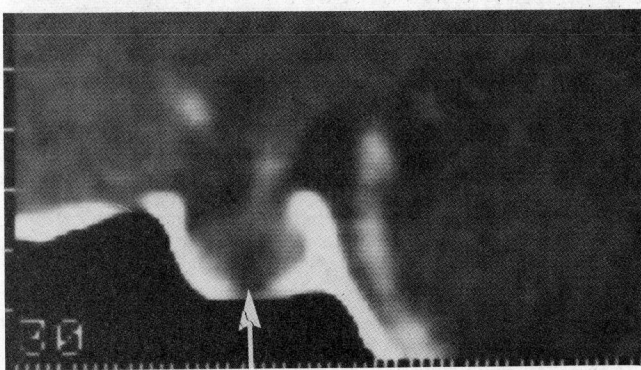

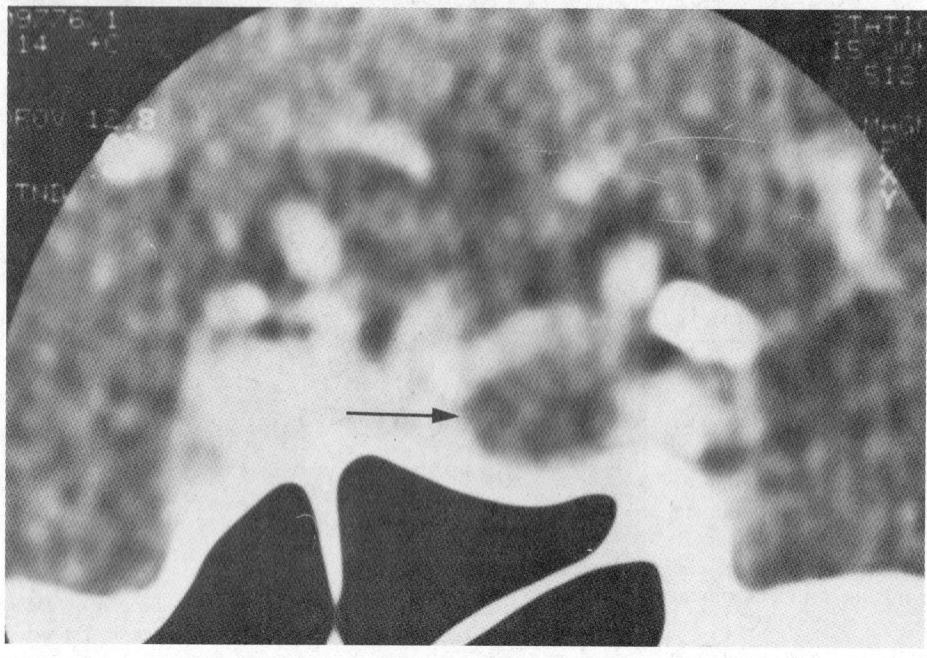

FIGURE 321-13 *Coronal CT scan demonstrating 1.3 cm macroprolactinoma in a 30-year-old woman. Note decreased density of the tumor (arrow). The pituitary stalk is displaced to the left, and the floor of the sella slopes to the left as well.*

increased density of the central bone on the sella, and an enlarged square sella with tapered tuberculum. GH-secreting adenomas may calcify and regress to leave a pituitary calculus or stone. Larger corticotroph adenomas may cause depression of the central floor of the sella.

CT scanning of macroadenomas reveals a mass in the sella that generally enhances after contrast administration (Fig. 321-5). An area of decreased density within an enhancing mass is present in about 20 percent of patients and suggests cystic degeneration of an adenoma. An additional 20 percent of patients with macroadenomas have a partially empty sella with CSF density within the sella (see below). Larger invasive tumors may extend into the cavernous sinus, sphenoid sinus, or any of the cranial fossae. Pituitary hyperplasia (e.g., thyrotroph hyperplasia in primary hypothyroidism) appears on CT as an enlarged, filled sella that does not enhance after contrast administration.

Pituitary apoplexy is caused by a sudden increase in the size of a pituitary macroadenoma due to hemorrhage or infarction. Enlargement

FIGURE 321-14 *Lateral skull x-ray in a patient with a craniopharyngioma. Note dense calcification in suprasellar region (arrow).*

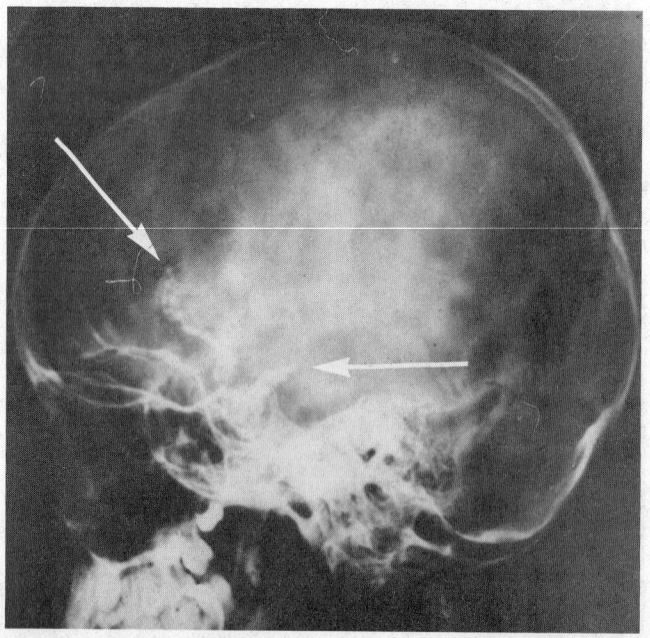

of the sella on plain films is almost always evident. In the case of hemorrhage CT scanning reveals a high-density area within the adenoma during the acute phase and a decreased density, with or without marginal enhancement, as the hematoma is resorbed. With infarction low-density areas are seen with or without enhancement.

Craniopharyngiomas can often be suspected on plain skull x-rays on the basis of nodular or curvilinear calcification in the suprasellar region (Fig. 321-14). This calcification is visible in 80 to 90 percent of children but in less than 50 percent of adults. Although the sella may be enlarged and ballooned, the cortical bone is usually preserved. With intrasellar craniopharyngiomas, the dorsum sella is often displaced backwards. On CT scanning cystic components are prominent with ring or nodular calcification demonstrable in almost all children and in 80 percent of adults. The noncystic areas show variable enhancement which is usually more prominent in children.

Most meningiomas of the sellar region cause abnormalities on routine skull films that include calcifications of the tumor and hyperostosis of the planum sphenoidale or of the chiasmatic sulcus. Meningiomas may also cause sella enlargement and thereby mimic pituitary adenomas. On CT scanning, meningiomas may give the appearance of an aneurysm because of their dense homogeneous enhancement. Angiography may be required to exclude an aneurysm and to delineate the feeding vessels.

Aneurysms in the region of the sella contain concentric calcifications demonstrable on plain skull films in about 30 percent of patients. Aneurysms may cause sella enlargement, usually with lateral depression and erosion of the sella floor; a "double floor" is therefore seen on lateral films. On CT scanning the aneurysm is hyperdense with homogeneous contrast enhancement. Most patients with hyperdense lesions that enlarge the sella need to be studied with digital subtraction or conventional angiography. When aneurysms clot the CT appearance may change: new clots show no enhancement whereas old clots enhance like adenomas. Complete thrombosis of an aneurysm is sometimes radiologically indistinguishable by radiographic criteria from a pituitary adenoma.

On CT scanning enhancing masses of the suprasellar region include optic chiasm or hypothalamic gliomas, metastases to the hypothalamus or pituitary stalk, germinomas, sarcoid granulomas, histiocytosis, aneurysms, and craniopharyngiomas. Nonenhancing suprasellar masses include dermoid tumors, epidermoid tumors, and arachnoid cysts.

THE ENLARGED SELLA—EMPTY SELLA SYNDROME Enlargement of the sella can be caused by pituitary adenomas, hypothalamic

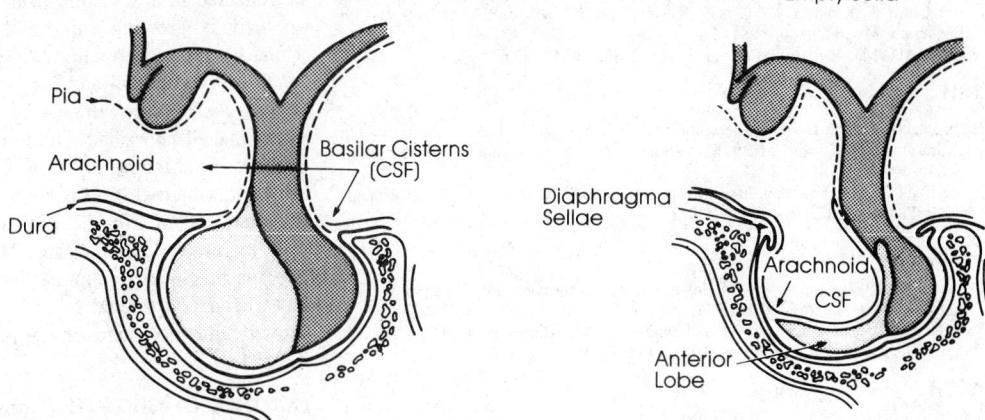

FIGURE 321-15 *The findings in patients with the empty sella syndrome. The left panel shows the normal anatomic relationships. With the empty sella syndrome, right panel, ballooning of the sella results when an arachnoid diverticulum herniates through an incompetent diaphragma sellae. (After Jordan et al.)*

masses and cysts, aneurysms, primary hypothyroidism or hypogonadism, and increased intracranial pressure. It can also occur in patients with the primary empty sella syndrome (Fig. 321-15). In this situation the sella tends to be symmetrically ballooned without evidence of bony erosion. The suprasellar subarachnoid space herniates through an incomplete diaphragma sella (Fig. 321-15) so that the sella becomes filled with CSF within an arachnoid-lined sac. An incomplete diaphragma sella is thought to be a prerequisite for this to occur. It is not clear whether transient or persistent increased CSF pressure is necessary to produce sella enlargement in these patients, but CSF pressure is generally normal when measured. The pituitary gland is flattened and pushed to one side but tends to function normally. The fact that the CSF fills the sella can be demonstrated on metrizamide cisternography, high-resolution CT scanning, or MRI.

It is important to separate the primary empty sella from the enlarged partially empty sella due to a degenerated pituitary adenoma. In the former the pituitary volume is usually normal, in the latter the pituitary volume is generally increased.

The vast majority of patients with the primary empty sella syndrome are obese, multiparous women with headaches; about 30 percent of these women have hypertension. It is of interest that multiparity, obesity, and hypertension are associated with increases in CSF pressure. Selection bias cannot be excluded in case reports since skull x-rays may be obtained in patients with headaches, which in turn uncovers the enlarged sella. Endocrine symptoms are uncommon. Hyperprolactinemia occurs on occasion, possibly due to stalk stretching or coincidental microprolactinomas. GH secretory reserve is often abnormal in these patients, probably the result of obesity. Spontaneous CSF rhinorrhea and pseudotumor cerebri have each been reported in about 10 percent of the cases. CSF rhinorrhea often requires surgical correction. Visual field defects have occasionally been reported and are thought to be caused by herniation of the optic chiasm into the sella turcica. Once the diagnosis of the empty sella syndrome has been established by CT scan, metrizamide cisternography, or MRI further diagnostic studies are superfluous, and the only therapy needed is reassurance.

REFERENCES

General

BESSER GM: The hypothalamus and pituitary. Clin Endocrinol Metab 6:1, 1977

BLACK PMcL et al: *Secretary Tumors of the Pituitary Gland.* New York, Raven Press, 1984

BURROW GN et al: Microadenomas of the pituitary and abnormal sellar tomograms in an unselected autopsy series. N Engl J Med 304:156, 1981

DANIEL PM, PRICHARD MML: The human hypothalamus and pituitary stalk after hypophysectomy or pituitary stalk section. Brain 59:813, 1972

IMURA H (ed): *The Pituitary Gland.* New York, Raven Press, 1985

KRIEGER DT, MARTIN JB: Brain peptides. N Engl J Med 304:876, 1981

MARTIN JB, REICHLIN S: *Clinical Neuroendocrinology,* 2d ed. Philadelphia, FA Davis, 1987

POST KD et al (eds): *The Pituitary Adenoma.* New York, Plenum Medical Book Company, 1980

SCANLON ME: Neuroendocrinology. Clin Endocrinol Metab 12:467, 1983

VANCE ML et al: Bromocriptine. Ann Intern Med 100:78, 1984

Prolactin

CARTER JN et al: Prolactin secreting tumors and hypogonadism in 22 men. N Engl J Med 299:847, 1978

FERRARI C et al: Functional characterization of hypothalamic hyperprolactinemia. J Clin Endocrinol Metab 55:897, 1982

GROSSMAN A et al: Treatment of prolactinomas with megavoltage radiotherapy. Br Med J 288:1105, 1984

KLEINBERG DS et al: Galactorrhea: 235 cases including 48 with pituitary tumor. N Engl J Med 296:589, 1977

KLEINBERG DL et al: Pergolide for the treatment of pituitary tumors secreting prolactin or growth hormone. N Engl J Med 309:704, 1983

KLIBANSKI A et al: Decreased bone density in hyperprolactinemic women. N Engl J Med 303:1511, 1980

MOLITCH ME: Hyperprolactinemia. Med Grand Rounds 1:307, 1982

——— : Pregnancy and the hyperprolactinemic woman. N Engl J Med 321:1364, 1985

——— et al: Bromocriptine as primary therapy for prolactin-secreting macroadenomas: Results of a prospective multicenter study. J Clin Endocrinol Metab 60:698, 1985

MORIONDO P et al: Bromocriptine treatment of microprolactinomas: Evidence of stable prolactin decrease after drug withdrawal. J Clin Endocrinol Metab 60:764, 1985

SCHLECTE J et al: Prolactin-secreting pituitary tumors in ammenorrheic women: A comprehensive study. Endocr Rev 1:294, 1980

Growth hormone

ASA SL et al: A case for hypothalamic acromegaly: A clinicopathological study of six patients with hypothalamic gangliocytomas producing growth hormone–releasing factor. J Clin Endocrinol Metab 58:796, 1984

CLEMMONS DR et al: Evaluation of acromegaly by radioimmunoassay of somatomedin-C. N Engl J Med 301:1138, 1979

EASTMAN RC et al: Conventional supervoltage irradiation is an effective treatment for acromegaly. J Clin Endocrinol Metab 48:931, 1979

EDDY RL et al: Human growth hormone release: Comparison of provocative test procedures. Am J Med 56:179, 1974

GELATO MC et al: Effects of a growth hormone releasing factor in man. J Clin Endocrinol Metab 57:674, 1983

——— et al: Effects of growth hormone-releasing factor on growth hormone secretion in acromegaly. J Clin Endocrinol Metab 60:251, 1985

GROSSMAN A et al: Growth hormone releasing factor: Comparison of two analogues and demonstration of hypothalamic defect in growth hormone release after radiotherapy. Br Med J 288:1785, 1984

JADRESIC A: Recent developments in acromegaly. A review. J R Soc Med 76:947, 1983

LAWRENCE JH et al: Successful treatment of acromegaly. Metabolic and clinical studies in 145 patients. J Clin Endocrinol Metab 31:180, 1970

MARTIN, JB: Neural regulation of growth hormone secretion. N Engl J Med 288:1384, 1973

MELMED S et al: Pathophysiology of acromegaly. Endocr Rev 4:271, 1983

——— et al: Acromegaly due to secretion of growth hormone by an ectopic pancreatic islet-cell tumor. N Engl J. Med 312:9, 1985

MOSES AC et al: Bromocriptine therapy in acromegaly. Use in patients resistant to conventional therapy and effect on serum levels of somatomedin C. J Clin Endocrinol Metab 53:752, 1981

PHILLIPS LS, VASILOPOULOU-SELLIN R: Somatomedins. N Engl J Med 302:371, 1980

REICHLIN S: Acromegaly. Med Grand Rounds 1:9, 1982

——— : Somatostatin. N Engl J Med 309:1495, 1983

RUDMAN D et al: Children with normal-variant-short stature: Treatment with human growth hormone for six months. N Engl J Med 305:123, 1981

THORNER MO et al: Somatotroph hyperplasia: Successful treatment of acromegaly by removal of a pancreatic islet tumor secreting a growth hormone releasing factor. J Clin Invest 70:965, 1982

——— et al: Extrahypothalamic growth-hormone-releasing factor (GRF) secretion is a rare cause of acromegaly: Plasma GRF levels in 177 acromegalic patients. J Clin Endocrinol Metab 59:846, 1984

WRIGHT AD et al: Mortality in acromegaly. Q J Med 39:1, 1970

TSH

BECK-PECCOZ P et al: Decreased receptor binding of biologically inactive thyrotropin in central hypothyroidism. Effect of treatment with thyrotropin-releasing hormone. N Engl J Med 312:1085, 1985

BIGOS ST et al: Spectrum of pituitary alterations with mild and severe thyroid impairment. J Clin Endocrinol Metab 46:317, 1978

Gonadotropins

CUTLER GB JR: Therapeutic applications of luteinizing-hormone-releasing hormone and its analogs. Ann Intern Med 102:643, 1985

SNYDER PJ et al: Secretion of uncombined subunits of luteinizing hormone by gonadotroph cell adenomas. J Clin Endocrinol Metab 59:1169, 1984

ACTH

BORST GC et al: Discordant cortisol response to exogenous ACTH and insulin-induced hypoglycemia in patients with pituitary disease. N Engl J Med 306:1462, 1982

CHROUSOS GP et al: The corticotropin-releasing factor stimulation test: An aid in the evaluation of patients with Cushing's syndrome. N Engl J Med 310:622, 1984

STREETEN DHP et al: Normal and abnormal function of the hypothalamic-pituitary-adrenal system in man. Endocr Rev 5:371, 1984

Endorphins

MORLEY JE: The endocrinology of the opiates and opioid peptides. Metabolism 30:195, 1981

Alpha Subunits

KLIBANSKI A et al: Pure alpha subunit-secreting pituitary tumors. J Neurosurg 59:585, 1983

Hypothalamus

BRAY GA, GALLAGHER TFJ: Manifestations of hypothalamic obesity in man: A comprehensive investigation of eight patients and a review of the literature. Medicine 54:301, 1974

DINARELLO CA: Interleukin-1 and the pathogenesis of the acute phase response. N Engl J Med 54:301, 1984

———, WOLFF SM: Molecular basis of fever in humans. Am J Med 72:799, 1982

PLUM F, VAN UITERT R: Nonendocrine diseases and disorders of the hypothalamus, in The Hypothalamus, S Reichlin et al (eds). New York, Raven Press, 1978, pp 415–473

Craniopharyngiomas

BANNA M: Craniopharyngiomas in adults. Surg Neurol 1:202, 1973

———: Craniopharyngioma: Based on 160 cases. Br J Radiol 49:206, 1976

Hypopituitarism

ASA SL et al: Lymphocytic hypophysitis of pregnancy resulting in hypopituitarism: A distinct clinicopathologic entity. Ann Intern Med 95:166, 1981

BOTTAZZO GF et al: Autoantibodies to prolactin secreting cells of human pituitary. Lancet 2:97, 1975

VELDHUIS JD, HAMMOND JM: Endocrine function after spontaneous infarction of the human pituitary: Report, review, and reappraisal. Endocr Rev 1:100, 1980

Radiology

BRUNETON JN et al: Normal variants of the sella turcica. Radiology 131:99, 1979

HEMINGHY S et al: Computed tomographic study of hormone-secreting microadenomas. Radiology 146:65, 1983

JORDAN RM et al: The primary empty sella syndrome. Analysis of the clinical characteristics, radiographic features, pituitary function, and cerebrospinal fluid adenohypophysial hormone concentrations. Am J Med 62:569, 1977

KENDALL B: Current approaches to hypothalamic-pituitary radiology. Clin Endocrinol Metab 12:535, 1983

WOLPERT SM: The radiology of pituitary adenomas. Semin Roentgenol 19:53, 1984

322 DISORDERS OF GROWTH

RAYMOND L. HINTZ

NORMAL GROWTH Children undergo rapid changes in size over relatively short periods of time, and the physician must be aware of normal standards for growth and development as a function of age. A record of these dynamic changes can be utilized as a sensitive indicator of general health: minimal aberrations in health may initially be reflected in a deviation from the normal growth rate; conversely, an actively growing child seldom has a serious systemic disease. Thus, height and growth rate provide important information.

Both longitudinal and cross-sectional studies indicate that differences exist in growth among different ethnic groups. However, normal well-nourished children have remarkably similar growth patterns. One interesting approximation is that the average length of children, which at birth is about 50 cm, increases by about 25 cm in the first year of life, 12.5 cm in the second year, and 6.2 cm per year thereafter until puberty. This formula can be used to estimate average height up to about 10 years of age. A variety of nomograms have been constructed to give a more accurate picture of average growth and the range of normal deviations from the mean (Figs. 322-1 and 322-2).

CONTROL OF GROWTH Growth involves both an increase in the total number of cells in an organism and the synthesis of macromolecules by individual cells. The relative importance of these processes varies from organ to organ and with age. The control and integration of growth also vary among tissues and with the stage of development. Understanding the control of growth is important to understanding the variations in normal growth patterns as well as the mechanisms of aging and oncogenesis.

Prenatal growth Prenatal development exemplifies the complexities of the integration and control of growth. During this time, a single cell becomes a complex organism with billions of cells working in harmonious concert. The growth rate is astounding; the most rapid growth rate occurs during the second trimester. Prenatal growth may have different control mechanisms from those in the postnatal period. Growth hormone and thyroid hormone have relatively minor effects on growth during prenatal life. Prenatal growth rates are dependent on uterine blood flow and other maternal influences and are less dependent on the factors that determine ultimate stature. At birth the correlation ($r = 0.3$) between body length and adult height is weak; by 2 years of age the correlation with adult height is stronger ($r = 0.7$), indicating that the factors influencing adult stature begin operating early in postnatal life.

Genetic factors Stature is a polygenic trait (see Chap. 57), so that there is no simple method of predicting on the basis of genetic factors the adult height of any given child. However, on average there is a correlation between the mean height of parents and the mean height attained by their children.

Nutrition The next most important factor affecting growth is nutrition. Severe nutritional deprivation, such as in those with marasmus or kwashiorkor (see Chap. 72), severely impairs growth. Selective deficiencies of vitamins and minerals, such as vitamin D, may also cause major abnormalities of growth. In some instances, a subclinical deficiency of a nutrient may retard growth. The trend toward increased adult stature in several countries over the last century may be due to improvement in diet, especially to an increase in protein intake during the growth period.

Hormones GROWTH HORMONE Growth hormone (GH, or somatotropin) plays the central role in the modulation of growth of children from birth until the completion of puberty. In the total absence of GH, linear growth occurs at about half to a third the normal rate. GH may also play a role in the control of body anabolism throughout life.

GH is a member of a family of hormones that includes pituitary prolactin and human placental lactogen (hPL) (see Chap. 321). The most common form of GH in the pituitary and in the circulation is the 22,000-dalton ("22K") form. This is the 191-amino-acid form that was purified and sequenced from human pituitary glands. The second most common form is a 20,000-dalton ("20K") form. This variant is coded by the same gene sequence as the 22K growth hormone, but a segment of an exon (expressed part of the gene) in the growth hormone gene is not transcribed, thus resulting in a shorter

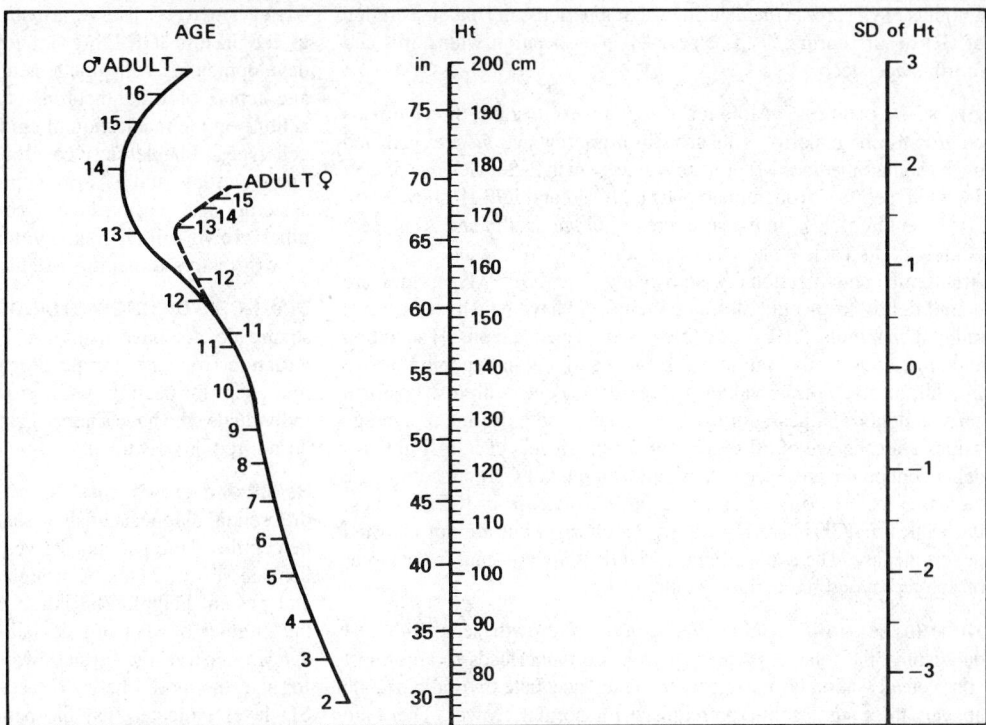

FIGURE 322-1 *Nomogram for height of boys and girls.*

form of growth hormone. Whether this variant fulfills some important metabolic function is not yet clear; the 20K form seems to have equivalent growth promoting activity but may have a lesser effect on carbohydrate function than the 22K form.

GH secretion is under both positive and negative hypothalamic control (see Chap. 321). The somatotropin release–inhibiting factor (somatostatin, SRIF) is a 14-amino-acid peptide that is widely distributed in tissues outside the hypothalamus and is a potent inhibitor of the secretion of other hormones including insulin, glucagon, and gastrin.

The biologic action of GH-releasing hormone (GRH, somatocrinin) is contained in the first 29 amino acids of the 44-amino acid peptide, and the aminoterminal amino acid is crucial for its biologic action.

Patients with idiopathic GH deficiency may have a deficiency of GRH rather than an inability to make GH in the pituitary. Indeed, half or more of subjects with GH deficiency respond to prolonged pulsatile administration of GRH with an increase in plasma GH and with an accelerated growth rate.

The secretion of somatostatin and GRH, and hence the release of GH, is under the influence of several factors (Fig. 322-3). Higher centers in the central nervous system have synapses which terminate on hypothalamic cells that secrete somatostatin and GRH and exert both positive and negative influences. In addition, both GH and the GH-controlled somatomedin peptides influence the secretion or action of GRH and somatostatin. The secretion of GH is episodic with a relatively short (10- to 15-min) half-life in plasma. Although small

FIGURE 322-2 *Nomogram for growth rate in boys and girls.*

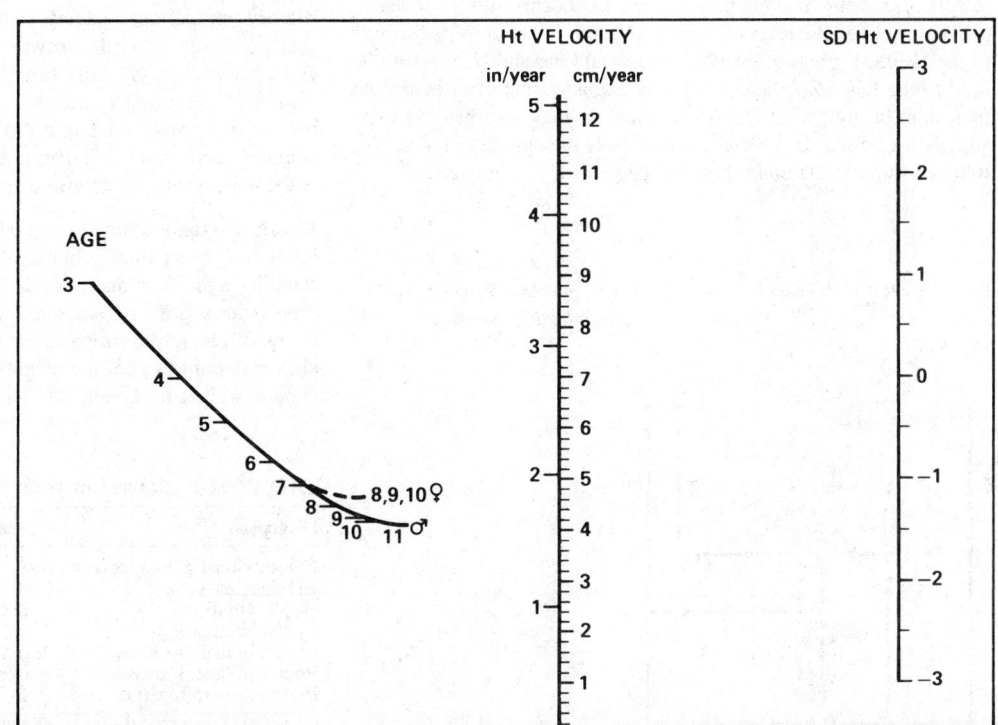

amounts of GH are secreted during waking periods, the major secretion of GH occurs during sleep, especially in association with third- and fourth-stage sleep.

THE SOMATOMEDINS   Although GH may exert some direct effects on growth, the majority of its growth-promoting actions are mediated by the somatomedin (SM) or insulin-like growth factor (IGF) peptides. Two IGF peptides from human plasma, IGF-I and IGF-II, show about 50 percent homology to the structure of human insulin and 70 percent homology to each other. Somatomedin C (SM-C) and IGF-I are structurally and functionally equivalent. The IGF/SM peptides are bound tightly to specific plasma proteins and have half-lives of hours rather than minutes. IGF-I/SM-C levels are dependent on GH secretion and are consequently high in acromegaly and low in hypopituitarism. In addition, the normal values are age-dependent, with low levels in early childhood, a peak during adolescence, and a decline in average values after the age of 50 years. The plasma levels of IGF-II are also dependent on the presence of a minimal amount of GH, but pathologic increases in GH do not result in a further increase in IGF-II. Thus, the values of IGF-II are low in hypopituitarism but are not elevated in acromegaly. The average levels of IGF-II are constant from 1 year of age to beyond the eighth decade of life.

THYROID HORMONE   Unlike the pattern of growth seen with GH deficiency, the total absence of thyroid hormone leads to an almost complete cessation of linear growth. Thus, adequate thyroid hormone appears to be an absolute prerequisite for normal growth. There are several potential mechanisms for this phenomenon. Thyroid hormones exert direct effects on cell metabolism, and thyroid hormone deficiency results in diminished GH secretion in response to stimulation. Finally, the action of IGF-I/SM-C on cartilage cells may be dependent on thyroid hormone.

GONADAL STEROIDS   Androgens and estrogens exert their major role in the stimulation of growth at the time of puberty. Much of the pubertal growth spurt is due to these hormones. Androgens have a direct stimulatory effect on the growth and maturation of bone, cartilage, and muscle. Estrogens appear to have a biphasic action, stimulating growth at low levels and inhibiting growth at high levels.

INSULIN   Insulin has strong anabolic actions separate from its effects on carbohydrate metabolism. These actions include stimulation of protein synthesis and cell division. The excessive growth of some infants of diabetic mothers may be the consequence of high levels of plasma insulin in the fetus. The close structural relationship of insulin to the IGF/SM group of growth factors, and the ability of insulin to bind to the IGF-I/SM-C receptor may explain some of these actions of insulin at high levels. However, insulin may also have growth-stimulating actions of its own at low levels in some cells types. The role of insulin in the control of normal growth is still unclear.

OTHER FACTORS   Nerve growth factor which is structurally related to the insulin-IGF-I/SM-C family of peptides has actions on the development of sympathetic neurons and possibly on the maintenance and repair of other neurons. Epidermal growth factor has potent actions on the maturation of epidermal features but also acts on other cell types. Platelet-derived growth factor is released from platelets upon clotting and is also a potent mitogen in many cell culture systems. The plasma levels, control mechanisms, interactions with other growth-stimulating hormones, and physiologic roles of these growth factors remain to be elucidated.

DIAGNOSIS OF GROWTH DISORDERS   Most individuals with short stature do not have a disease in the usual sense but exhibit some variation from the normal growth pattern (Table 322-1). Thus, the first step in dealing with growth disorders is to identify those individuals who have a normal variation in stature and who presumably do not require treatment.

Height and growth rate   One of the most important factors in the differential diagnosis of short stature is the determination of the height percentile of the patient, derived by a comparison to others of his or her age (Fig. 322-1). A straightedge is placed on the patient's age and present height. The intercept on the right-hand scale estimates the number of standard deviations (SD) from the mean height for age. In general, the further away the patient is from the mean height for age, the more likely a disease is present. A height above the -2-SD level indicates that the patient is likely normal. The patient's growth rate also should be determined, if possible, either from existing growth data or by observation (Fig. 322-2).

Because of the large number of normal children with short stature, clinical judgment plays a large role in the approach to this problem. Individuals with severe short stature (> -3 SD for age) should undergo immediate evaluation, while those with less severe short stature may be serially observed so that the growth rate can be assessed. A consistently low growth rate should lead to further investigation. The diagnosis of constitutional delay is one of exclusion. In general, if the physician has excluded hypothyroidism, GH deficiency, and the more common systemic diseases, it is reasonable to observe the patient. However, the boundaries between "normal" and "disease" may be blurred, and the indications for treatment may change. Furthermore, continued failure to maintain a normal growth rate is an indication for reinvestigation.

History   Important features in the history include the weight and gestational age at birth, growth and development in early infancy, and presence of systemic disease. It is also crucial to assess the stature of the parents and first- and second-degree relatives and to review the growth and pubertal development patterns of parents, siblings, and other relatives. A family history or late pubertal development may be helpful diagnostically.

Physical examination   The body proportions must be evaluated. Relatively short limbs compared to the trunk suggest either long-standing hypothyroidism or one of the chondrodystrophies. Achondroplastic dwarfism is an extreme example of this, but more subtle forms of chondrodystrophy may elude the casual examination. It is also important to note the height-to-weight ratio. A short child who is underweight for height may have malnutrition or systemic disease.

FIGURE 322-3   *Feedback control of growth hormone secretion. GH = growth hormone; GRH = growth hormone–releasing hormone; SM = somatomedin.*

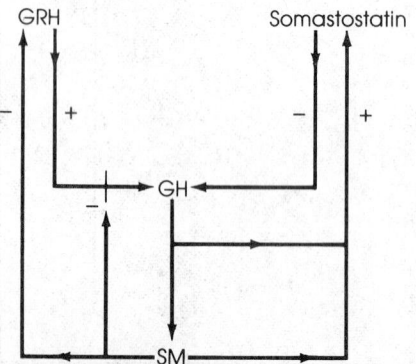

TABLE 322-1   Causes of short stature

Diagnosis	Usual practice, %	Referral center, %
Constitutional growth delay	98	80
GH deficiency	0.1	10
Hypothyroidism	0.2	4
Systemic disease	0.3	3
Chromosomal disorders	0.1	1
Bone-cartilage dysplasia	0.3	1
Psychosocial disorders	1	1

SOURCE: *Modified from Horner et al., 1978.*

On the other hand, a child who is short but overweight is more likely to have endocrine disease. Patients with Cushing's syndrome, GH deficiency, or hypothyroidism are frequently relatively overweight for their height. Specific physical findings may suggest hypothyroidism, GH deficiency, or other specific syndromes (Table 322-2).

Laboratory evaluation Laboratory tests may either confirm the clinical impression or reveal unsuspected pathology. Assessment of bone age is useful to indicate possible pathology and to estimate final adult height. Because the manifestations of hypothyroidism may be minimal, a serum thyroxine should be obtained routinely. IGF-I/SM-C measurements are also useful screening procedures, since most patients with GH deficiency have low values. There are also syndromes of GH resistance, such as Laron dwarfism, that are characterized by low IGF-I/SM-C levels and high GH levels. Specific chemistries may be ordered to screen for other disease states. Any girl with unexplained short stature should have a chromosomal karyotype. Useful laboratory studies for the evaluation of short stature are summarized in Table 322-3. Abnormalities of these tests should lead to more specific investigations.

TESTING OF GH SECRETION Because GH secretion is episodic and therefore variable, random measurements of plasma GH are not adequate tests of GH deficiency. Some GH stimulation tests for outpatient screening for GH deficiency are summarized in Table 322-4 (also see Chap. 321). Because of the long half-life of IGF-I/SM-C, a random measurement of this hormone during the day is an accurate reflection of the mean plasma concentration. If care is taken to use age-related standards, measurement of IGF-I/SM-C provides a reasonable screen for GH deficiency. Low levels of IGF-I/SM-C should lead to more extensive evaluation. The other tests listed are indirect and largely nonphysiologic ways of provoking the release of GH. In our clinic, a GH level of 7 ng/mL after an exercise or clonidine test is interpreted as a normal response. If that level is not achieved, more definitive testing of GH reserve should be carried out as described in Chap. 321.

TREATMENT WITH GH **GH deficiency** The only established use of human GH is in the treatment of children who are GH-deficient. Only between 1 in 4000 and 1 in 20,000 children have a GH deficiency. About half of these cases are due to idiopathic GH deficiency, and the other half are secondary to tumor and/or radiation therapy. In approximately one-third of the latter cases, only GH is deficient, and in the other two-thirds, there are multiple pituitary hormone deficiencies. If short stature is due to a systemic disease such as renal failure, treatment is directed toward the underlying disease state. Similarly, short stature due to hypothyroidism or cortisol excess is managed by treatment of the primary endocrine disorder. In general, the earlier the disorder is diagnosed and treated, the more successful the growth response will be; if treatment of the underlying disease is delayed until after puberty, little or no improvement in stature can be expected.

Unlike the broad species specificity characteristic of peptide hormones such as insulin, GH exhibits limited species specificity.

TABLE 322-2 Physical findings in syndromes of short stature

Syndrome	Specific physical findings
GH deficiency	Frontal bossing, central obesity, high-pitched voice
Hypothyroidism	Dry skin, coarse hair, immature facies
Cushing's syndrome	Central obesity, striae, hypertension
Gonadal dysgenesis	Webbed neck, multiple pigmented nevi, shield chest, delayed sexual development
Pseudohypoparathyroidism	Moon facies and obesity, short metacarpals, mental retardation
Bone-cartilage dysplasia	Abnormal proportions, macrocephaly
Russell-Silver dwarfism	Small at birth, "pointed" facies, asymmetry

TABLE 322-3 Screening laboratory investigations in short stature

Test or x-ray	Disorder
Serum thyroxine	Hypothyroidism
IGF-I/SM-C	GH deficiency
Bone age	Constitutional delay, hypothyroidism, GH deficiency
Lateral skull film	Craniopharyngioma or other central nervous system lesion
Serum Ca	Pseudohypoparathyroidism
Serum phosphate	Vitamin D–resistant rickets
Serum bicarbonate	Renal tubular acidosis
Blood urea nitrogen	Renal failure
Complete blood count	Anemia, nutritional disorder
Sedimentation rate	Inflammatory disease of bowel
Chromosomal karyotype	Gonadal dysgenesis or other abnormality

Human GH stimulates linear growth in children with GH deficiency, whereas the bovine hormone is ineffective in humans. The need for human GH led to the formation of the National Pituitary Agency to facilitate the collection of pituitary glands from autopsy material and the preparation of human GH and other pituitary hormones. This effort did not supply adequate amounts of hormone for the treatment of all children who had GH deficiency, let alone provide sufficient material for the study of GH as a therapeutic agent for other conditions. Furthermore, the distribution of human pituitary GH in the United States and several other countries was discontinued in 1984 because of the development of Creutzfeldt-Jakob disease in four subjects who had been treated with human GH. Since this degenerative central nervous system disease is rare in this age group, the concern is that previous and/or present methods of GH extraction allowed contamination of GH preparations with the causative agent of this disease. The availability since 1985 of synthetic GH produced by recombinant DNA in bacteria has relieved the supply problem. Hormone is again available for patients with GH deficiency, and its relatively unlimited supply will allow the exploration of other therapeutic uses of GH.

Despite the difficulties generated by inadequate supplies, there is an extensive experience with the use of pituitary GH for treating GH deficiency. Most children with GH deficiency respond to GH treatment with an acceleration of growth rate to normal or even above normal

TABLE 322-4 Screening tests for assessing GH secretion

1 IGF-I/SM-C radioimmunoassay
Age-related normals (may vary with method):

Age, years	Range (units/mL)
<1	0.17–0.62
1–5	0.14–1.44
6–11	0.50–2.06
12–17	0.78–3.73
18–25	0.92–2.06
26–40	0.70–2.04

2 Exercise test:
Vigorous exercise (running or stairsteps) for 20 min
20-min rest
Samples for measurement of GH by radioimmunoassay at 0, 20, and 40 min from beginning
Normal response: GH greater than or equal to 7 ng/mL on any sample

3 Clonidine test:
NPO after midnight
Administration of clonidine by mouth

Body weight, kg	Dose, mg
5 to 15	0.05
15 to 25	0.1
25 to 35	0.15
35 to 50	0.2
>50	0.25

Samples for measurement of GH by radioimmunoassay at 0, 60, and 90 min
Side effects: Postural hypotension and somnolence
Keep patient supine until after postural hypotension is gone
Normal response: Greater than or equal to 7 ng/mL on any sample

rates. As with other peptide hormones, there is a dose-response curve to GH. The doses that have been tested range from 0.02 to 0.2 units (0.01 to 0.1 mg) per kilogram of body weight administered as an intramuscular injection three times a week. There is a wide variation in response, but the higher dosages in general result in higher average growth rates. It is possible that in selected clinical circumstances dosages of GH higher than those currently recommended should be administered. Now that synthetic GH is available, treatment should be started at the 0.1 unit per kilogram of body weight dosage, since the majority of GH-deficient patients have a good growth response to this amount of GH. If the patient fails to show an adequate growth rate, the GH dose can be increased until an adequate growth response is obtained or until the upper limit of 0.25 units per kilogram of body weight three times per week is achieved. As doses of GH are increased above this level, the risk of glucose intolerance increases, particularly in children who are prediabetic. An unsettled therapeutic issue is whether daily use of GH results in a greater growth response than with the schedule of three doses a week. Preliminary data suggest that daily subcutaneous injections may lead to better responses. Furthermore, subcutaneous GH may be as effective and safe as when administered intramuscularly.

An alternative method for the treatment of GH deficiency now under study is the use of long-term, subcutaneous infusion of GH-releasing hormone (GRH). Since at least half of children with GH deficiency are able to secrete GH in response to GRH, this approach may ultimately be useful for those patients.

Short stature of other causes IDIOPATHIC SEVERE SHORT STATURE   GH hormone treatment has been used for the treatment of some patients with growth failure not due to GH deficiency. Many children with severe short stature (more than 2.5 SD below the mean for age) do not have GH deficiency. Some workers propose that a subgroup of children without GH deficiency but with low IGF-I/SM-C levels are responsive to GH treatment. These patients are believed to have a relatively inactive GH or to have a partial defect in the control of GH secretion. For example, although they do not fulfill the usual criteria for GH deficiency, they may not have normal bursts of GH secretion during certain physiologic circumstances such as sleep. Whatever the etiology, some of these children have a short-term increase in growth rate in response to GH therapy; whether the final height of these children after GH treatment is greater than their predicted height is not established. Furthermore, it is not known whether there are serious side effects associated with the rise of GH levels to the supraphysiologic range. At present such therapy should be undertaken only as part of a research protocol.

GONADAL DYSGENESIS   GH may also have a therapeutic role in the treatment of gonadal dysgenesis (see Chap. 60). The majority of women with gonadal dysgenesis have an average adult height between 135 and 142 cm. Androgens can cause a short-term increase in the rate of growth of girls with the disorder but do not result in an increase in final adult stature. The use of GH at modest doses is also associated with a small increase in the rate of growth. Preliminary results of a multicenter group study utilizing a somewhat higher dose of synthetic GH are even more encouraging in terms of initial growth response. However, it is not known whether GH therapy results in an increase in adult stature.

SKELETAL DISORDERS   GH hormone has also been used to treat small numbers of subjects with a wide variety of other growth disorders including bone-cartilage dysplasias and other genetic syndromes associated with short stature. It is not clear whether GH is of use in any of these disorders.

REFERENCES

BROWN P: Potential epidemic of Creutzfeldt-Jacob disease from human growth hormone therapy. N Engl J Med 313:728, 1985

FRASIER SD: A review of growth hormone stimulation tests in children. Pediatrics 53:929, 1974

———— et al: A dose response curve for human growth hormone. J Clin Endocrinol Metab 53:1213, 1981

FURLANETTO R et al: Estimation of somatomedin-C levels in normals and patients with pituitary disease by radioimmunoassay. J Clin Invest 60:648, 1977

GERTNER J et al: Prospective clinical trial of human growth hormone in short children without growth hormone deficiency. J Pediatr 104:172, 1984

HINTZ RL: The somatomedins. Adv Pediatr 28:293, 1980

———— et al: Biosynthetic methionyl-human growth hormone is biologically active in adult man. Lancet 1:1276, 1982

HORNER JM et al: Growth deceleration patterns in children with constitutional short stature: An aid to diagnosis. Pediatrics 62:529, 1978

KASTRUP KW et al: Increased growth rate following transfer to daily sc administration from three weekly im injections of hGH. Acta Endocrinol (Copenh) 104:148, 1983

LEWIS UJ et al: Human growth hormone: A complex of proteins. Recent Prog Horm Res 36: 477, 1980

RINDERKNECHT R, HUMBEL RE: Primary structure of human IGF-II. FEBS Lett 89:283, 1978

ROSENFELD RF et al: A prospective, randomized trial of methionyl human growth hormone and/or oxandrolone in Turner's syndrome. Pediatr Res 19:A102, 1985

RUDMAN D et al: Children with normal variant short stature: Treatment with human growth hormone for 6 months. N Eng J Med 305:123, 1981

TANNER JM, ISREALSOHN WJ: Parent-child correlations for body measurements of children between the ages of one month and 7 years. Ann Hum Genet 26:245, 1963

———— et al: Effect of human growth hormone treatment for 1 to 7 years on growth of 100 children with growth hormone deficiency, inherited smallness, Turner's syndrome, and other complaints. Arch Dis Child 46:745, 1971

————, DAVIS PSW: Clinical longitudinal standards for height and height velocity for North American children. J Pediatr 107:317, 1985

THORNER MO et al: Acceleration of growth in two children treated with human growth hormone releasing factor. N Engl J Med 312:4, 1985

VIMPANI OV et al: Prevalence of severe growth hormone deficiency. Br Med J 2:427, 1977

WILSON DM et al: Subcutaneous versus intramuscular growth hormone therapy: Growth and acute somatomedin response. J. Pediatr 76:361, 1985

323   DISORDERS OF THE NEUROHYPOPHYSIS

DAVID H. P. STREETEN / ARNOLD M. MOSES / MYRON MILLER

There are two largely independent hypothalamic-neurohypophyseal systems composed of neurons in the supraoptic and paraventricular nuclei, from which axons extend through the pituitary stalk to the posterior pituitary. Hormones (vasopressin and oxytocin), formed within separate ganglion cells, migrate down the axons as part of precursor proteins that include the neurophysins. They are stored in secretory granules within the nerve terminals in the neurohypophysis. The hormones with their neurophysins are released by exocytosis from the granules into the bloodstream. Vasopressin or antidiuretic hormone (AVP or ADH) is predominantly concerned with the control of water conservation, and its release is coordinated with the activity of the thirst center that regulates fluid intake. Oxytocin stimulates uterine contractions and milk ejection.

VASOPRESSIN RELEASE AND ACTION

CHEMISTRY   Arginine vasopressin (AVP) is a nonapeptide composed of six amino acids in a ring attached to a side chain of three amino acids.

ACTIONS   Via actions on its V_2 receptors in the distal renal tubules, AVP conserves water and concentrates the urine by enhancing the hydroosmotic flow of water from the luminal fluid through the cells of the collecting tubule of the kidney to the medullary interstitium. This action assists in maintaining constancy of the osmolality and volume of body fluids. High concentrations of AVP acting on V_1 receptors can cause vasoconstriction, as may occur in response to severe hypotension or to infusion of vasopressin for treatment of bleeding esophageal varices.

AVP, perhaps from axons that terminate in the cerebrum, may play a role in learning and memory, and AVP from fibers in the median eminence may influence corticotropin secretion.

NORMAL HORMONE LEVELS

AVP concentrations in plasma and urine can be measured by radioimmunoassay. The results may be expressed either as units based on pressor activity in the rat or in terms of weight of purified vasopressin. Arginine vasopressin has a biologic activity of approximately 400 units per milligram (1 μU = 2.5 pg). The human neurohypophysis under conditions of random fluid intake contains approximately 8 units of AVP. Under the same conditions peripheral plasma AVP concentration in humans ranges from 1 to 3 μU/mL. The AVP concentration of blood fluctuates, with a maximum late at night and in the early morning and a minimum in the early afternoon. Under conditions of normal hydration, healthy subjects release approximately 400 to 550 mU from the pituitary and excrete 10 to 35 mU AVP in urine in 24 h. During 24 to 28 h of dehydration the amount released increases three to five times with consequent increases in plasma and urinary levels.

METABOLISM

Inactivation of AVP occurs largely in liver and kidneys, a major mechanism being the cleavage of the terminal glycinamide to produce a biologically inactive substance. Approximately 7 to 10 percent of secreted AVP is excreted in the urine as active hormone.

CONTROL OF AVP RELEASE

The release of AVP is influenced by a number of stimuli (Fig. 323-1).

Osmoregulation   Under normal conditions AVP release is primarily regulated by osmoreceptors in the hypothalamus. Changes in the concentrations of plasma solutes to which the cellular membrane is impermeable cause alterations in the volume of the osmoreceptor cells, which in turn alter the electric activity of the neurons and control AVP release. Osmotic changes that stimulate release also enhance production of AVP. The servomechanism between effective plasma osmolality and AVP release normally maintains plasma osmolality within a very narrow range. The mean plasma osmolality of normal subjects following a water load of 20 mL per kilogram of body weight is 281.7 mosmol/kg, and the osmolality that initiates AVP release following infusion of hypertonic saline solution into water-loaded subjects is 287.3 mosmol/kg. Thus, the increase in plasma osmolality from full diuresis to the initiation of antidiuresis by hypertonic saline solution is only 5.6 mosmol/kg, or 2 percent.

The infusion of hypertonic saline solution at a constant rate into water-loaded subjects causes a linear rise in plasma osmolality with time. After an interval that depends on the infusion rate and the concentration of the saline solution, there is an abrupt, progressive fall in free water clearance without a significant change in solute or creatinine excretion. We have defined the osmotic threshold for AVP release as the plasma osmolality at the onset of antidiuresis under these conditions. In 73 normal subjects, this occurred at a mean plasma osmolality of 287 mosmol/kg.

Volume regulation   Decreases in plasma volume, through effects on stretch receptors in the left atrium and perhaps in the pulmonary veins, stimulate the release of AVP by reducing the tonic inhibitory impulses from the left atrium to the hypothalamus. The neural impulses travel via the vagi to the reticular formation of the midbrain and diencephalon and thence to the supraoptic and paraventricular nuclei, where they are integrated with the other stimuli that affect AVP release. Positive pressure breathing, quiet standing, and vasodilatation due to a warm environment may activate this mechanism, which serves to restore plasma volume, even at times overriding osmotic inhibition of AVP release. Following volume contraction, circulating AVP concentrations may reach 10 times the levels induced by hypertonicity. Increased plasma volume inhibits AVP release by the reverse mechanisms, leading to a diuresis and correction of the hypervolemia. Negative pressure breathing, recumbency, lack of gravitational force (as occurs in space travel), submersion in water, and exposure to cold may activate this mechanism.

Baroreceptor regulation   Activation of carotid and aortic baroreceptors in response to hypotension causes release. Hypotension due to blood loss is the most potent stimulus and may raise plasma levels of AVP to 1000 μU/mL at times. These concentrations of AVP may cause marked vasoconstriction, which probably plays a role in the restoration of blood pressure.

Neural regulation   Neurotransmitters and peptide neuromodulators such as angiotensin II, dopamine, and endorphins may mediate some of the stimulatory and inhibitory input into the hypothalamus and thus alter AVP release. Acetylcholine appears to be the final link connecting neural pathways to the supraoptic neurons involved in AVP release. Both cholinergic and beta-adrenergic stimuli release AVP, while atropine and alpha-adrenergic stimulation inhibit AVP release, apparently by actions on the hypothalamus. Emotional stress, emesis, and pain may overcome a diuresis. A diuresis may follow hypnotic suggestion, psychological conditioning, and inhalation of carbon dioxide.

Aging   The aging process is associated with enhanced AVP release in response to a rising plasma osmolality and a progressive increase in plasma AVP concentration. These physiologic changes appear to place the older individual under greater risk of developing water retention and hyponatremia, despite a concomitant decline in maximal renal concentrating capacity in response to AVP, which is usually evident and progressive beyond 60 years of age.

Pharmacologic influences   Pharmacologic agents that can stimulate AVP release include nicotine, morphine, vincristine, vinblastine, cyclophosphamide, clofibrate, chlorpropamide, and some of the

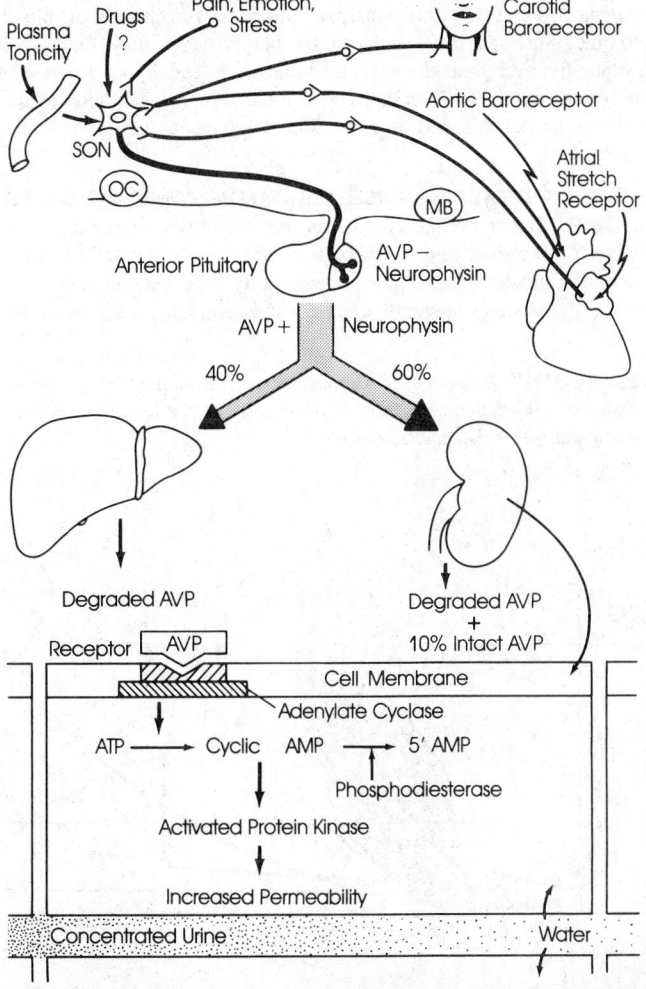

FIGURE 323-1 *Schematic representation of control of AVP release and cellular action of AVP. OC, optic chiasma; MB, mamillary body.*

tricyclic anticonvulsants and antidepressants. Ethanol has diuretic properties and inhibits neurohypophyseal function under a variety of conditions. Some narcotic antagonists also inhibit AVP release. Experimentally chlorpromazine, reserpine, and phenytoin all diminish the loss of AVP from the pituitary and the rise in urinary excretion of AVP that result from water deprivation. In humans, phenytoin and chlorpromazine may inhibit AVP release and produce diuresis.

AVP RESPONSE TO WATER DEPRIVATION AND TO WATER LOAD

Water deprivation provides both an osmotic and a volume stimulus to vasopressin release by increasing plasma osmolality and decreasing plasma volume. The maximum urinary osmolality after water deprivation varies, depending on renal medullary osmolality and other intrarenal factors. In response to fluid deprivation for 18 to 24 h, in normal individuals, plasma osmolality rarely rises above 292 mosmol/kg. The resultant stimulation of AVP release increases plasma AVP concentration to 6 to 10 µU/mL.

The administration of water lowers plasma osmolality and expands blood volume, inhibiting the release of AVP via both the osmoreceptor and the atrial volume receptor mechanisms. An oral water load of 20 mL/kg in normal adults results in a fall in plasma osmolality to a mean of 281.7 mosmol/kg and causes a maximum diuresis in 1 to 1½ h with free water clearance rising to approximately 12 mL/min and urine osmolality falling to 40 to 60 mosmol/kg. The delay in reaching maximal diuresis is accounted for by the time involved in absorption of water from the gut, in metabolizing previously secreted vasopressin, and in renal recovery from the action of vasopressin.

INTERACTION OF OSMOTIC AND VOLUME INFLUENCES

Under conditions of water deprivation and of water loading, volume and osmotic influences act in parallel to influence AVP release. In other circumstances volume and osmotic influences may be competitive, and minor changes in plasma volume can modify hypertonic stimuli to AVP release. Osmotic factors ordinarily predominate to maintain plasma osmolality within a narrow range. Larger changes in blood volume, such as those induced by hemorrhage, may blunt and eventually overcome the osmotic influences, and hypotension can activate arterial baroreceptors and exert a powerful stimulus to the elaboration of AVP and thus override simultaneous inhibiting influences.

RELATION BETWEEN AVP RELEASE AND THIRST-INDUCED WATER INTAKE

Under normal conditions there is close coordination between AVP release and thirst, both of which are regulated by small increases and decreases in plasma osmolality. The perception of thirst generally becomes apparent when plasma osmolality rises to values greater than 292 mosmol/kg. Angiotensin II increases thirst and AVP release, at least under experimental conditions. When AVP release is impaired, water losses lead to hypernatremia, which increases thirst and fluid intake to an extent sufficient to restore and maintain normal plasma osmolality. On the other hand, loss of thirst (adipsia) leads to uncorrected fluid losses and hypernatremia despite increased AVP release and excretion of a maximally concentrated urine.

EFFECTS OF GLUCOCORTICOIDS

Hormones of the adrenal cortex and the posterior pituitary have antagonist effects on water excretion. Cortisol elevates the osmotic threshold for AVP release elicited by hypertonic saline infusion in water-loaded normal subjects, and glucocorticoids protect against water intoxication and overcome the impaired response to water loading in adrenal insufficiency.

Although the subnormal ability to dilute the urine in patients with adrenal insufficiency may in part be due to excessive circulating AVP, glucocorticoids can also act directly on the renal tubules to decrease water permeability and increase solute-free water in the absence of AVP.

CELLULAR MECHANISM OF AVP ACTIVITY

The biochemical basis for the action of AVP on the renal tubule is shown in Fig. 323-1: (1) AVP binds to specific contraluminal V_2 receptor sites; (2) the receptor-hormone complex is coupled to and activates adenylate cyclase in the same contraluminal membrane via a guanine nucleotide regulatory protein (see Chap. 67); (3) the production of cyclic AMP is increased; (4) the cyclic AMP is translocated to the luminal cell membrane where it causes the activation of membrane-bound protein kinase; (5) the activated protein kinase causes the phosphorylation of membrane proteins; and (6) permeability of the luminal membrane to water is increased. The AVP-generated cyclic AMP may be inactivated by a phosphodiesterase that converts cyclic AMP to 5'-AMP. AVP also stimulates prostaglandin E_2 production which, in turn, acts as a feedback inhibitor of adenylate cyclase activation.

The transtubular movement of water depends on the integrity of the microtubular system of the epithelial cells. The above biochemical events lead to the passive flow of water along an osmotic gradient across the collecting tubule. The physiologic action of AVP is accompanied by anatomic changes, including cell swelling, vacuolization, expansion of the medullary interstitium, and widening of the lateral intercellular spaces of the collecting ducts. The latter changes indicate that fluid resorption during AVP-induced antidiuresis occurs in part by way of intercellular channels.

Various cations and drugs can influence the action of AVP. Calcium and lithium inhibit the adenylate cyclase response to vasopressin. Lithium also interferes with a subsequent biochemical action, as does potassium deficiency. Demeclocycline inhibits adenylate cyclase stimulation by AVP and also inhibits the cyclic AMP–dependent protein kinase. In contrast, chlorpropamide increases AVP-induced activation of adenylate cyclase.

DEFICIENCY OF VASOPRESSIN: DIABETES INSIPIDUS

In central diabetes insipidus renal conservation of water is impaired because of deficient AVP release in response to normal physiologic stimuli.

PATHOPHYSIOLOGY

Deficiency of vasopressin release in response to the appropriate stimuli may result from lesions at several functional sites in the physiologic chain of events which regulates discharge of the hormone into the bloodstream. For conceptual purposes four types of central diabetes insipidus can be defined. Patients of the first type show very little rise in urine osmolality with increasing plasma osmolality (1, Fig. 323-2) and no evidence of AVP release during hypertonic saline infusion. They are essentially devoid of releasable AVP. In the second type there is an abrupt increase in urine osmolality during dehydration (2, Fig. 323-2), but there is no evidence of an osmotic threshold during saline infusion. These patients have a

FIGURE 323-2 *Relation of plasma and urinary osmolality during varying conditions of hydration in normal adult subjects (shaded area) and in four types of patients with diabetes insipidus.*

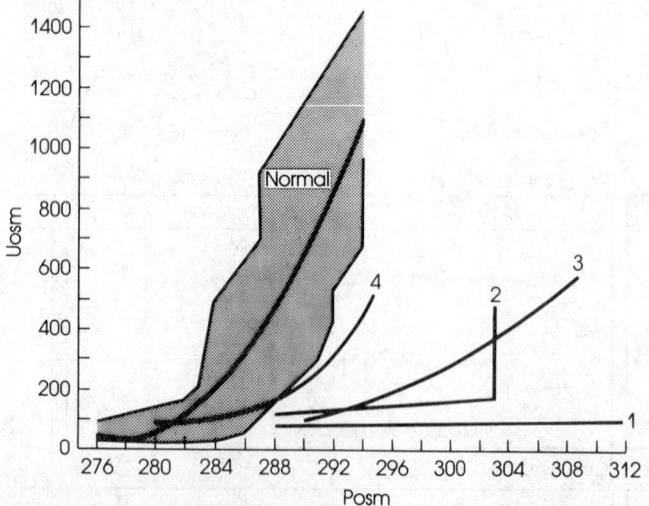

defective osmoreceptor mechanism but are capable of releasing AVP in response to the hypovolemia of severe dehydration. The third type of patient has some rise in urine osmolality with increasing plasma osmolality (3, Fig. 323-2) and has an elevated osmotic threshold for AVP release. These patients have a sluggish release mechanism and may be said to have a high-set osmoreceptor. In the fourth type of patient, urine and plasma osmolality coordinates are shifted to the right of normal (4, Fig. 323-2). AVP release in these patients is initiated at a normal plasma osmolality but is subnormal in amount.

The second to fourth types of patients may develop a good antidiuresis in response to nausea, nicotine, methacholine, chlorpropamide, or clofibrate, indicating that the synthesis and storage of AVP are sufficient to allow for adequate urinary concentrating ability in the presence of an appropriate stimulus to release. In rare instances patients of the second to fourth types may present with asymptomatic hypernatremia associated with mild or absent evidence of diabetes insipidus.

ETIOLOGY   The causes of diabetes insipidus in 100 consecutive patients who satisfied the criteria described under ''Diagnostic Tests'' (below) and who had had diabetes insipidus for at least 6 months are shown in Table 323-1. Diabetes insipidus frequently starts in childhood or early adult life (median age of onset 21 years) and is more common in males than females. The major causes are as follows: (1) *Neoplastic or infiltrative lesions* of the hypothalamus or pituitary, including chromophobe adenomas, craniopharyngiomas, germinomas, pinealomas, metastatic tumors, leukemia, histiocytosis X, and sarcoidosis, caused diabetes insipidus in 32 patients (in groups 1, 3, 7, and 9 in Table 323-1). In approximately 60 percent of these patients evidence of partial or complete loss of anterior pituitary function was present. (2) *Pituitary or hypothalamic surgery or isotopic ablative therapy* caused diabetes insipidus in 20 patients and almost invariably was associated with anterior hypopituitarism. Surgically induced diabetes insipidus usually develops between 1 and 6 days after surgery and often disappears after a few days and may remain absent or may recur and become chronic after an ''interphase'' of 1 to 5 days. Removal of the posterior lobe of the pituitary induces permanent diabetes insipidus only if the pituitary stalk is sectioned high enough to induce retrograde degeneration of most of the neurons of the supraoptic nucleus. (3) *Severe head injuries,* usually associated with fractures of the skull, caused diabetes insipidus in 17 patients and were associated with anterior hypopituitarism in only about one-sixth of patients. Spontaneous remissions of traumatic diabetes insipidus occurred in a fourth of patients, presumably because of regeneration of disrupted axons within the pituitary stalk. (4) *Vascular lesions* were a rare cause of diabetes insipidus (4 patients). Three patients had diabetes insipidus associated with cerebral malacia from cardiac asystole followed by resuscitation. (5) *Idiopathic diabetes insipidus* (in 27 patients) usually starts in childhood and is seldom (<20 percent) associated with anterior pituitary dysfunction. This diagnosis can be made only after a careful search has failed to reveal evidence of a tumor, infiltrative lesion, vascular lesion, or other presumptive cause of the AVP deficiency. The presence of anterior hypopituitarism or hyperprolactinemia or radiologic evidence of lesions within or above the sella should stimulate a continuing search for a causative lesion at 3- to 12-month intervals. The diagnosis of idiopathic diabetes insipidus is made with increasing confidence as the duration of negative findings on follow-up increases. A decrease in the number of neurons in the supraoptic and paraventricular nuclei has been reported in idiopathic diabetes insipidus. In rare instances, dominant inheritance has been documented.

CLINICAL MANIFESTATIONS   *Polyuria, excessive thirst,* and *polydipsia* are almost invariably present in diabetes insipidus. Characteristically, these symptoms are sudden in onset, both when the disorder first presents itself and whenever the effects of administered vasopressin disappear during long-term therapy. In severe cases the urine is pale in color, and its volume may be immense (up to 16 to 24 liters per day), requiring micturition every 30 to 60 min throughout the day and night. More frequently, however, the urine volume is only moderately increased (2.5 to 6 liters per day), and occasionally it may be less than 2 liters per day, causing no complaints on the part of the patient. Urinary concentration (less than 290 mosmol/kg, specific gravity less than 1.010) is below that of the serum in severe cases but may be higher than that of serum (290 to 600 mosmol/kg) in patients with mild diabetes insipidus.

The slight rise in serum osmolality resulting from hypotonic polyuria stimulates thirst. Large volumes of fluid are imbibed, and cold drinks are preferred, patients often going to great trouble to secure cold fluids. Although thirst is probably secondary to loss of water, the administration of vasopressin often relieves or reduces thirst, even in the absence of fluid intake.

Normal function of the thirst center ensures that polydipsia closely matches polyuria, so that dehydration is seldom detectable except in the mild elevation of serum sodium concentration. However, when adequate replenishment of excreted water is interfered with, dehydration may become severe, causing weakness, fever, psychic disturbances, prostration, and death. These features are associated with a rising serum osmolality and serum sodium concentration, the latter sometimes exceeding 175 meq per liter. Adipsia is not found in idiopathic diabetes insipidus, but it may result from impaired function of the hypothalamic thirst center because of extension of the same abnormality that caused the diabetes insipidus. More frequently, dehydration occurs during unconsciousness produced by surgical anesthesia, head trauma, or other causes. It is particularly hazardous to administer large volumes of isotonic saline solution intravenously or of hyperosmolar protein by nasogastric tube unless adequate amounts of water are administered simultaneously in unconscious patients with untreated diabetes insipidus.

Hydronephrosis is a rare complication of the polyuria, especially in patients who fail to empty their bladders adequately because of bladder atony, uretheral strictures, or other causes.

DIAGNOSTIC TESTS   The principle that underlies diagnostic tests for diabetes insipidus is that elevation of the plasma osmolality by fluid deprivation or hypertonic saline infusion elicits subnormal AVP release. This may be documented by plasma or urinary AVP measurements (Fig. 323-3) or by demonstrating that urinary osmolality fails to rise to the extent that occurs when exogenous vasopressin is administered in supramaximal amounts. Measurements of plasma and urinary osmolalities are so simple and reliable that AVP measurements are only occasionally needed, when osmolality measurements are inconclusive.

Assessment of the relation of plasma to urine osmolality   The normal relationship between plasma osmolality (assuming no increase

TABLE 323-1   Characteristics of 100 consecutive patients with permanent diabetes insipidus

		Age of onset, years		Total number	Males	Females
		Median*	Range			
1	Histiocytosis X	1.5	1–20	4	2	2
2	Idiopathic causes	12	Infancy–66	27	16	11
3	Primary tumor of brain or pituitary	17.5	3–58	18	15	3
4	Trauma	22	5–48	17	11	6
5	Pituitary surgery	24	6–68	20	7	13
6	Ruptured intracranial aneurysm	39		1		
7	Sarcoidosis	42		1		1
8	Cerebral hypoperfusion	49	37–73	3	1	2
9	Metastatic tumors including leukemia	57	44–71	9	5	3
	Totals			100	59	41

* *Median age of onset for all 100 patients =21.*
NOTE: *Evaluated by authors at SUNY, Upstate Medical Center, Syracuse, New York (arranged in order of increasing median age of onset).*

in blood urea or glucose) and urine osmolality is indicated in Fig. 323-2. If several simultaneously determined plasma and urine osmolalities in a patient with polyuria fall substantially to the right of the shaded area, the patient has central or nephrogenic diabetes insipidus. The latter diagnosis can be made if plasma or urinary AVP concentration is increased or if the response to injected vasopressin is subnormal (see "Dehydration Test" below). The practice of relating plasma to urine osmolality is useful, particularly in postoperative neurosurgical cases or after head trauma, where its use can lead quickly to the differentiation of diabetes insipidus from parenteral fluid excess. In such patients, intravenous hydration can be slowed temporarily, and repeated plasma and urine osmolalities can be obtained and plotted as in Fig. 323-2, to determine whether the relationship is normal.

Dehydration test   Comparison of the urinary osmolality after dehydration with that after vasopressin administration is a simple and reliable way of diagnosing diabetes insipidus and of differentiating vasopressin deficiency from other causes of polyuria.

The maximal urinary concentrating capacity varies widely between individuals, and no absolute lower limits of "normal" can be defined in patients with nonspecific illnesses in whom AVP is produced in adequate amounts. It is impossible to distinguish between deficiency and sufficiency of AVP release solely by the level of the urinary osmolality attained after specified periods of water deprivation. On the other hand, if after prolonged dehydration vasopressin administration induces a further rise in urinary osmolality, there is a strong implication that vasopressin deficiency exists.

PROCEDURE

1 Fluids are withheld long enough to result in stable hourly urinary osmolalities (an hourly increase of <30 mosmol/kg for at least three successive hours). This is usually associated with a loss in body weight of at least 1 kg. In patients whose daily urinary volumes exceed 10 liters, the fluid deprivation should begin between 4 A.M. and 6 A.M. so that the patient can be carefully watched and the test terminated if weight loss exceeds 2 kg or the clinical condition deteriorates. In polyuric patients whose urinary volumes are less than 10 liters per day, it is preferable to start fluid deprivation between 6 P.M. and midnight and to continue to withhold fluids until noon the following day.

2 Urine specimens are collected hourly for osmolality measurements from 6 A.M. at least until noon and preferably until the osmolality has been stable for three consecutive hours.

3 At 11 A.M. (if dehydration started at 6 P.M.) or after the third hour of stable urinary osmolalities, the patient is given vasopressin as 5 units aqueous vasopressin or 1 μg desmopressin by subcutaneous injection or 10 μg desmopressin by nasal spray.

4 Plasma osmolality is determined immediately before the injection of vasopressin, and urinary osmolality is measured on the specimen collected during the hour after the injection.

Vital signs should be monitored during the dehydration procedure, but when the test has been performed as described, adverse effects are rare.

INTERPRETATION   In subjects with normal pituitary function, urinary osmolality does not rise by more than 9 percent after the injection of vasopressin, whatever the maximal urinary osmolality might be after dehydration alone (Fig. 323-3). In central diabetes insipidus, the rise in urinary osmolality after vasopressin exceeds 9 percent. To ensure adequacy of dehydration, plasma osmolality before the vasopressin injection should be above 288 mosmol/kg. Patients who have polyuria from renal diseases, potassium depletion, or nephrogenic diabetes insipidus (see below) usually show little rise in urinary osmolality with dehydration and no further rise after vasopressin injection. Patients with compulsive water drinking (primary polydipsia) often require prolonged water deprivation before plasma osmolality reaches 288 mosmol/kg and before a plateau in urinary osmolality is reached; urinary osmolality fails to rise by >9 percent after the administration of exogenous vasopressin.

Hypertonic saline infusions   Assessment of the renal response to hypertonic saline infusion is required to determine whether AVP deficiency is due to a defect in osmoreceptor function. Urinary and plasma osmolality should be measured before and immediately after the infusion of 5% saline solution to calculate changes in free water clearance and thus obtain conclusive results from the procedure (Fig. 323-4). The test is dangerous in patients who are unable to tolerate a saline load.

PROCEDURE

1 Administer a water load (20 mL/kg by mouth), and subsequently replace the urine voided every 15 min by an equal volume of water by mouth.

2 Infuse 5% sodium chloride solution intravenously into one arm, preferably by infusion pump, at approximately 0.5 mL/min—to replace solute lost in the urine—until urine flow rate is stabilized, usually at 8 to 20 mL/min, for at least four 15-min periods.

3 Increase the rate of infusion of 5% saline solution to 0.05 (mL/kg)/min and continue the infusion until urine flow rate undergoes an abrupt, sustained decrease lasting for at least two 15-min periods, or until ten 15-min periods of the more rapid infusion have elapsed, or until headache, nausea, or other unpleasant symptoms have supervened, whichever comes first.

4 Draw blood through an indwelling cannula or needle in a vein in the other arm every 15 min, starting at least 15 min before the onset of the more rapid rate of infusion.

FIGURE 323-3 *Relationship between plasma osmolality (Posm) and urinary AVP excretion (U$_{AVP}$) in normal subjects (shaded area on left), patients with central diabetes insipidus (shaded area on right), and patients with nephrogenic diabetes insipidus (individual data points). Correlates in patients with SIADH fall to the left of the normal range. [From AM Moses, in P Czernichow and AG Robinson (eds), Frontiers of Hormone Research, vol 13: Diabetes Insipidus in Man, Basel, Karger, 1985.]*

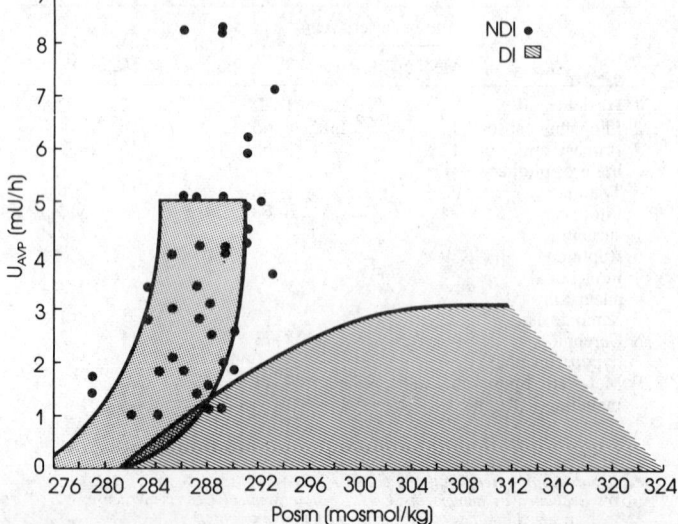

5 Measure urinary and plasma (or serum) osmolality in all specimens. Calculate free water clearances and plot the data.

6 Measurement of plasma AVP concentration in each of the blood samples drawn for plasma osmolality determinations is useful, provided a reliable radioimmunoassay is available.

INTERPRETATION Inspection of the data will show whether a sudden, clear-cut onset of a progressive fall in free water clearance can be identified. The osmotic threshold for AVP release is deduced by interpolation on the best straight line representing plasma osmolality measurements plotted against time, at the onset of the fall in free water clearance (Fig. 323-4). When defined in this way in water-loaded subjects, the osmotic threshold is normally 287.3 ± 3.3 mosmol/kg (mean ± standard deviation). The osmotic threshold may also be computed by plotting plasma AVP against simultaneous plasma osmolality measurements and determining the level of plasma osmolality at which the linear rise in plasma AVP concentration commences. Urinary AVP measurements may be used in the same way. In most patients with diabetes insipidus there is no detectable osmotic threshold, i.e., no fall in free water clearance even after plasma osmolality rises above 300 mosmol/kg (Fig. 323-4). However, some patients may have a high or normal osmotic threshold and yet have diabetes insipidus (3 and 4, Fig. 323-2).

DIFFERENTIAL DIAGNOSIS Diabetes insipidus must be distinguished from other types of polyuria (Table 323-2), in all of which there is loss of the renal tubular response to endogenous vasopressin. The other types of polyuria can, therefore, be recognized by failure of response to administered AVP. Several are recognizable by the history (e.g., recent lithium or mannitol administration, recent surgery under methoxyflurane anesthesia, or recent renal transplantation). In others the physical examination or simple laboratory procedures will indicate the diagnosis (evidence of glycosuria, renal disease, sickle cell anemia, hypercalcemia, or potassium depletion, including primary aldosteronism).

Congenital nephrogenic diabetes insipidus is a rare, usually familial, form of polyuria resulting from unresponsiveness to AVP.

TABLE 323-2 Major polyuric syndromes

I Primary disorders of water intake or output
  A Excessive water intake
    1 Psychogenic polydipsia
    2 Hypothalamic disease: histiocytosis X, sarcoidosis
    3 Drug-induced polydipsia
      a Thioridazine
      b Chlorpromazine
      c Anticholinergic drugs (dry mouth)
  B Inadequate tubular reabsorption of filtered water
    1 Vasopressin deficiency
      a Central diabetes insipidus
      b Drug-induced inhibition of AVP release
        (1) Narcotic antagonists
    2 Renal tubular unresponsiveness to AVP
      a Nephrogenic diabetes insipidus (congenital and familial)
      b Nephrogenic diabetes insipidus (acquired)
        (1) Several chronic renal diseases, after obstructive uropathy, unilateral renal arterial stenosis, after renal transplantation, after acute tubular necrosis
        (2) Potassium deficiencies, including primary aldosteronism
        (3) Chronic hypercalcemias, including hyperparathyroidism
        (4) Drug-induced: lithium, methoxyflurane anesthesia, demeclocycline
        (5) Various systemic disorders: multiple myeloma, amyloidosis, sickle cell anemia, Sjögren's syndrome
II Primary disorders of renal absorption of solutes (osmotic diuresis)
  A Glucose: diabetes mellitus
  B Salts, especially sodium chloride
    1 Various chronic renal diseases, especially chronic pyelonephritis
    2 After various diuretics, including mannitol

It is usually diagnosed from the lack of a reduction in polyuria or rise in urinary osmolality after an injection of vasopressin, as described in the "Dehydration Test" above. These patients can also be distinguished from patients with vasopressin-deficient diabetes insipidus by the familial nature of the disorder (rare in diabetes insipidus) and by lack of the dramatic reduction in daily urine volume when vasopressin or desmopressin is administered to patients with vasopressin-deficient diabetes insipidus. Occasionally patients with nephrogenic diabetes insipidus respond to vasopressin that is injected at the plateau in urinary osmolality with a 40 to 50 percent increase in

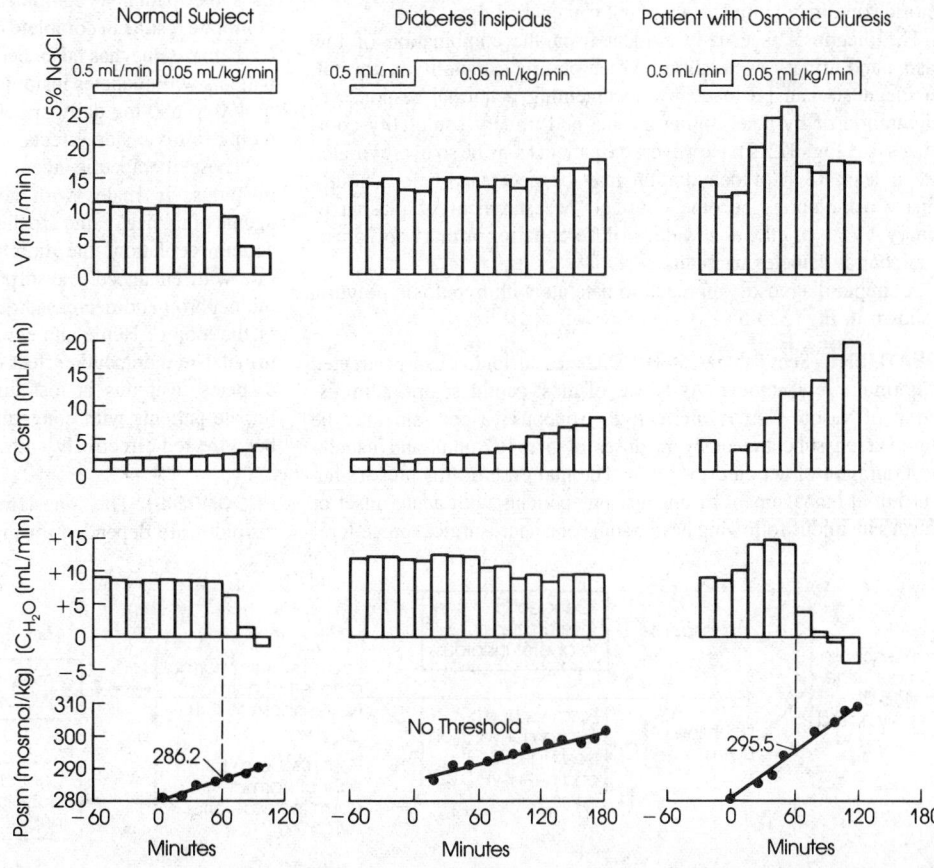

FIGURE 323-4 Diagnostic use of responses to 5% saline infusion in subjects preloaded with water (20 mL/kg). In the normal subject (left) 5% NaCl, infused at 0.05 (mL/kg)/min, caused a gradual rise in osmolal clearance (Cosm) and an abrupt fall in urine flow rate (V) and free water clearance (C_{H_2O}) when the plasma osmolality (Posm) had been raised to the osmotic threshold for AVP release (286.2 mosmol/kg). In the patient with diabetes insipidus (middle), 5% NaCl infusion failed to cause a fall in V or C_{H_2O} despite elevation of Posm above 300 mosmol/kg. In the third subject (right) 5% NaCl infusion induced a rapid rise in Cosm resulting from osmotic diuresis which prevented a fall in V. This finding might have suggested diabetes insipidus but the fall in C_{H_2O} indicated AVP release at an osmotic threshold (295.5 mosmol/kg) which was elevated because of steroid therapy. (From AM Moses, DHPS Streeten, Am J Med 42:368, 1967.)

urinary osmolality. This response is intermediate between the responses of patients with mild and severe diabetes insipidus. When nephrogenic and central diabetes insipidus cannot be differentiated with certainty by these procedures, documentation of an appropriately elevated plasma or urinary AVP concentration in relation to plasma osmolality (Fig. 323-3) or of a high AVP concentration in relation to urinary osmolality will establish the diagnosis of nephrogenic diabetes insipidus.

Primary polydipsia Primary or psychogenic polydipsia is occasionally difficult to differentiate from diabetes insipidus and may occur in two forms. Chronic overingestion of water results in hypotonic polyuria and is often confused with diabetes insipidus. Intermittent ingestion of very large volumes of water may also lead to dilutional hyponatremia even though a very dilute urine is excreted.

Polydipsia and polyuria in this disorder are usually somewhat erratic, in contrast to the sustained polydipsia and polyuria of diabetes insipidus. These patients usually have no nocturnal polyuria because polyuria of long duration may result in the development of large bladder capacities and consequently infrequent urination. The patients are often emotionally disturbed. The syndrome may be seen in occasional patients with anorexia nervosa, who may drink huge quantities of water while eating very little. Fluid intake may decrease markedly when food intake increases. Rarely, a patient with chronic fluid overingestion may have a central nervous system lesion, although adipsia or hypodipsia is more common in central nervous system disease.

The intermittent ingestion of large quantities of fluid may lead to water intoxication and dilutional hyponatremia even though there is normal urinary diluting capacity. This phenomenon is rare because normal adults can excrete between 10 and 14 mL/min of solute-free water, and it is an unusual circumstance which results in the ingestion of sufficiently more water than this to cause dilutional hyponatremia. The syndrome of water intoxication with normal diluting capacity has been reported in persons who take large enemas, drink excessive amounts of beer, or are given thioridazine. The phenothiazine drugs have parasympathetic effects and may cause dryness of the mouth, which aggravates tendencies toward compulsive water drinking. Thioridazine may stimulate the thirst center directly.

The diagnosis is usually evident from the combination of low plasma and urinary osmolalities. When plasma osmolality is normal, the diagnosis can be made by documenting a normal response to dehydration or by determining plasma and urinary osmolality coordinates (see Fig. 323-2). However, the patients may be so overhydrated that at least 18 h of dehydration may be necessary before hourly urinary osmolalities become constant. Measurement of plasma or urinary AVP is of little or no value in differentiating primary polydipsia from central diabetes insipidus.

A simple diagnostic approach to patients with hypotonic polyuria is shown in Fig. 323-5.

TREATMENT (See Table 323-3) Diabetes insipidus can be treated by hormone replacement. As is true of most peptides, oral administration of vasopressin is ineffective. Aqueous vasopressin may be administered subcutaneously in doses of 5 to 10 units and usually has a duration of action of 3 to 6 h. The main use of this preparation is in initial management of unconscious patients with acute onset of diabetes insipidus following head trauma or a neurosurgical procedure.

Its short duration of action allows recognition of the recovery of neurohypophyseal function and prevents the development of water intoxication in patients receiving intravenous fluids.

Desmopressin has prolonged antidiuretic activity and is almost completely devoid of pressor effects. When used intranasally in amounts between 10 and 20 μg (0.1 to 0.2 mL) or by subcutaneous injection (1 to 4 μg), it has an antidiuretic action for 12 to 24 h in most patients. This analogue is the drug of choice in the treatment of most patients with diabetes insipidus. Lypressin is a nasal spray; a single application may result in an antidiuresis lasting approximately 4 to 6 h. Nasal absorption of both analogues may be decreased in the presence of an upper respiratory infection or allergic rhinitis with edema of the nasal mucosa. In such circumstances and in the unconscious patient with diabetes insipidus, desmopressin should be given by subcutaneous injection.

In the past, patients with an established diagnosis of diabetes insipidus were usually treated with intramuscular injections of vasopressin tannate in oil (2.5 or 5 units), which has an antidiuretic effect for 24 to 72 h. Since this material is a suspension of vasopressin tannate in peanut oil, it is essential that the ampul be warmed and then thoroughly shaken or inverted repeatedly until the brownish deposit of pituitary powder in the ampul is evenly distributed as a slightly cloudy suspension in the oil. A dry syringe should be used.

Patients with diabetes insipidus who have some residual releasable AVP (types 2 to 4) may respond to oral treatment with several nonhormonal agents. Chlorpropamide stimulates AVP release from the neurohypophysis and potentiates the action of submaximal amounts of AVP on the renal tubule, properties that make it of use in many patients with diabetes insipidus. Doses of 200 to 500 mg, usually taken once daily, are sufficient for an antidiuretic response. Its action starts within several hours of administration and usually lasts for 24 h. Chlorpropamide may also restore thirst perception and thus be useful in patients with thirst center defects. Hypoglycemia may occur but can usually be avoided by adherence to a regular schedule of meals. Clofibrate is capable of stimulating AVP release and has also been used in the treatment of diabetes insipidus. Doses of 500 mg four times a day often result in a prompt and sustained antidiuresis. In some patients, combined treatment with chlorpropamide and clofibrate results in complete restoration of water regulation to normal. Carbamazepine has also been observed to produce antidiuresis in patients with diabetes insipidus by stimulation of AVP release. Doses of 400 to 600 mg daily are effective, but the drug is not widely used owing to toxic side effects.

These therapeutic agents are effective only in central diabetes insipidus. In males with nephrogenic diabetes insipidus the only agents of clinical value are thiazides and other diuretics. By producing sodium depletion, the diuretics cause a fall in glomerular filtration rate with enhanced reabsorption of fluid in the proximal portion of the nephron and decreased delivery of sodium to the ascending limb of the loop of Henle and consequently reduced capacity to dilute the urine. The therapeutic effect of diuretics in patients with nephrogenic diabetes insipidus is lost unless sodium intake is restricted. Two female patients with congenital nephrogenic diabetes insipidus have been treated effectively with large doses of desmopressin.

PROGNOSIS The long-term prospects of a patient with diabetes insipidus are dependent primarily upon the underlying cause. In the

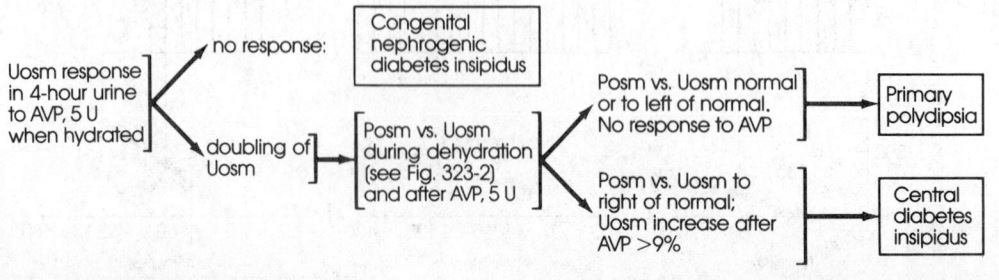

FIGURE 323-5 *Approach to hypotonic polyurias*

TABLE 323-3 Agents used in treatment of diabetes insipidus

	Dose form	Usual dose	Duration of action, h
CENTRAL DIABETES INSIPIDUS			
Hormone replacement:			
Aqueous vasopressin	10 or 20 units/ampul	5–10 units subcutaneously	3–6
Desmopressin	2.5-mL bottle, 0.1 mg/mL	10–20 μg intranasally or 1–4 μg subcutaneously	12–24
Lypressin	5-mL bottle, 50 units/mL	2–4 units intranasally	4–6
Vasopressin tannate in oil	5 units/ampul	5 units intramuscularly	24–72
Nonhormonal agents:			
Chlorpropamide	100- and 250-mg tablets	200–500 mg daily	
Clofibrate	500-mg capsules	500 mg four times daily	
Carbamazepine	200-mg tablets	400–600 mg daily	
NEPHROGENIC DIABETES INSIPIDUS			
Hydrochlorothiazide	50-mg tablets	50–100 mg daily	
Chlorthalidone	50-mg tablets	50 mg daily	

absence of brain tumor or systemic disease, ready access to water and proper treatment of the polyuria usually lead to a normal life and life expectancy. Early recognition and treatment are important to prevent bladder distention, hydroureter, and hydronephrosis which may develop in patients with long-standing polyuria, particularly in patients with nephrogenic diabetes insipidus. The rare patient with adipsia or hypodipsia in association with diabetes insipidus is in danger of developing severe dehydration, which may lead to vascular collapse or central nervous system damage. Similarly severe complications may occur in patients with diabetes insipidus who develop impairment of consciousness. For this reason, all patients with diabetes insipidus should carry identification indicating the presence of the disorder and the necessity for treatment and fluid administration.

SYNDROME OF INAPPROPRIATE AVP SECRETION (SIADH)

The syndrome of inappropriate AVP secretion (known as SIADH) is characterized by hyponatremia that results from water retention attributable to persistent AVP release. In SIADH the vasopressin is released either autonomously or in response to potent stimuli that override the inhibitory influence of hypoosmolality. Since these patients are unable to excrete a dilute urine, ingested fluids are retained, with consequent expansion of the extracellular fluid volume without edema. The continued release of AVP and the consequent elevation of urinary osmolality are considered to be inappropriate only in relationship to the lowered plasma osmolality or sodium concentration.

Water retention can be mediated by AVP through excessive AVP secretion or enhanced renal action of AVP. It can also result from mechanisms unrelated to AVP. A fall in renal blood flow or glomerular filtration rate can increase the percentage reabsorption of sodium and water in the proximal portion of the nephron, with consequent decrease in delivery of sodium and water to the diluting segment. This impairs urinary dilution and leads to water retention.

ETIOLOGY AND PATHOPHYSIOLOGY The various causes of SIADH operate through three pathophysiologic mechanisms (Table 323-4).

In the first of these, AVP is synthesized, stored, and autonomously released from tumor tissue, in amounts that are determined largely by the tumor mass and not by osmolal, volume, pressure, or known chemical stimuli. Small-cell or oat cell carcinoma of the lung accounts for 80 percent of such patients. In prospective studies of patients with oat cell carcinoma, more than half have impaired water excretion and elevated plasma AVP levels, even though many do not have evident hyponatremia. The AVP produced by the neoplasms is identical with arginine vasopressin produced by the normal neurohypophyseal system and may be associated with neurophysin. Other malignancies that can cause SIADH include pancreatic and duodenal carcinomas, lymphosarcoma, reticulum cell sarcoma, Hodgkin's disease, and thymoma.

In the second type of SIADH, nontumorous lung tissue either acquires the capacity to synthesize and release AVP autonomously or reduces left atrial filling which stimulates central AVP release. This type of hyponatremia is a common feature of pulmonary tuberculosis, pneumonias, and other pulmonary or pleural diseases. AVP has been demonstrated in tuberculous lung tissue but not in uninvolved lung or in suspensions of tubercle bacilli.

The third type of SIADH involves release of AVP from the patient's neurohypophysis due to neighboring inflammatory, neoplastic, or vascular lesions (group III, Table 323-4) or of drugs (group IV, Table 323-4), and independently of the normal stimuli.

Chlorpropamide stimulates AVP release, enhances the antidiuretic action of submaximal concentrations of AVP, and can cause water intoxication in patients with diabetes mellitus, particularly in elderly individuals who may be more sensitive to this effect of the drug. The antineoplastic drugs vincristine, vinblastine, and cyclophosphamide produce SIADH by causing release of AVP from the neurohypophysis. The severity of water retention in these patients is aggravated by the

TABLE 323-4 Causes of SIADH

I Malignant neoplasms with autonomous AVP release
  A Oat cell carcinoma of lung
  B Carcinoma of pancreas
  C Lymphosarcoma, reticulum cell sarcoma, Hodgkin's disease
  D Carcinoma of duodenum
  E Thymoma
II Nonmalignant pulmonary diseases
  A Tuberculosis
  B Lung abscess
  C Pneumonia
  D Viral pneumonitis
  E Empyema
  F Chronic obstructive airways disease
III Central nervous system disorders
  A Skull fracture
  B Subdural hematoma
  C Subarachnoid hemorrhage
  D Cerebral vascular thrombosis
  E Cerebral atrophy
  F Acute encephalitis
  G Tuberculous meningitis
  H Purulent meningitis
  I Guillain-Barré syndrome
  J Lupus erythematosus
  K Acute intermittent porphyria
IV Drugs
  A Chlorpropamide
  B Vincristine
  C Vinblastine
  D Cyclophosphamide
  E Carbamazepine
  F Oxytocin
  G General anesthesia
  H Narcotics
  I Tricyclic antidepressants
V Miscellaneous causes
  A Hypothyroidism
  B Positive pressure respiration

common practice of recommending a large fluid intake to prevent formation of uric acid calculi. Carbamazepine can cause water intoxication by stimulating AVP release. Tricyclic compounds can also produce SIADH. Clofibrate is capable of stimulating AVP release but only rarely causes SIADH. Oxytocin possesses inherent antidiuretic activity and, when administered in large amounts to obstetric patients, may cause water intoxication. Patients who have been exposed to general anesthetics or narcotics in association with surgical procedures may release excessive amounts of AVP. Hypothyroidism may produce hyponatremia with all of the features of SIADH by mechanisms involving either increased AVP release or impaired capacity of the kidneys to generate a dilute urine. Elevated plasma AVP concentrations may also occur when AVP release is an appropriate response to hypovolemia, as in sodium depletion (such as after diuretic therapy), adrenal insufficiency, and perhaps congestive heart failure. To consider these conditions as types of SIADH might be technically correct but may lead to the misguided use of fluid restriction.

The excessive AVP release in this syndrome, in the presence of water intake in amounts greater than can be excreted at the existing level of urinary osmolality, results in water retention and extra- and intracellular hypotonicity. Sodium excretion is enhanced because of increased glomerular filtration rate and, probably, suppression of aldosterone secretion. In addition, atrial natriuretic factors may be released by volume expansion and may further contribute to the sodium loss. These urinary losses, which may be profound, aggravate the hypotonicity of body fluids. This combination of factors leads to what many authors describe as a state of euvolemic hyponatremia (in contrast with states of hypovolemic and hypervolemic hyponatremia).

CLINICAL AND LABORATORY FEATURES Patients with SIADH may present with weight gain, weakness, lethargy, and mental confusion, ultimately progressing to convulsions and coma. Edema and hypertension are rare. Laboratory features include low serum levels of BUN, creatinine, uric acid, and albumin. The serum sodium concentration is generally less than 130 meq per liter, and the plasma osmolality is below 270 mosmol/kg. The urine is almost always hypertonic to plasma. Urinary sodium concentration is usually more than 20 meq per liter but may initially be less when chronic sodium depletion is due to poor intake or excessive losses.

DIAGNOSIS SIADH should be suspected in any patient with hyponatremia who excretes urine that is hypertonic relative to plasma. The finding that urinary sodium concentration is greater than 20 meq per liter provides further support for the diagnosis. To make the diagnosis of SIADH it is essential to exclude (1) depletional hyponatremias, especially due to adrenal insufficiency, salt-losing nephritis, diarrhea, and previous diuretic therapy; (2) hyponatremic edema states (congestive heart failure, cirrhosis, nephrosis); (3) pseudohyponatremia (associated with hyperlipemia); (4) severe hyperglycemia; (5) hypothyroidism; (6) primary polydipsia, in which the urine is invariably dilute; and (7) the sick-cell syndrome (essential hyponatremia). In the last disorder the chronic debilitating diseases which it accompanies (congestive heart failure, hepatic cirrhosis, pulmonary tuberculosis, and some malignancies) are thought to reduce osmolality of the intracellular fluid (including that of the hypothalamic osmoreceptors), thereby "setting" the osmoreceptors at a subnormal level. Thus, AVP is released at levels of plasma osmolality below the normal osmotic threshold. These patients show normal renal responses to water loading and deprivation, though the changes occur at subnormal levels of plasma osmolality.

In contrast with patients who have SIADH, patients with depletional hyponatremia are often clearly dehydrated and usually have elevated BUN levels, hemoconcentration, and urinary sodium concentrations below 20 meq per liter (see Chap. 41). Since SIADH is associated with hypervolemia, while primary sodium depletion usually lowers plasma volume, orthostatic hypotension is not a feature of SIADH and is common in depletional hyponatremia. For the same reason, plasma renin activity and plasma aldosterone concentrations

are low in SIADH and elevated in sodium depletion except in adrenal insufficiency where plasma renin activity may be high but plasma aldosterone level is usually low. Severe hypertension with hyponatremia may be due to high plasma angiotensin II levels resulting from renovascular stenosis or other forms of angiotensinogenic hypertension, which may increase AVP release. Hypokalemia is uncommon in SIADH.

In patients with the features of SIADH in whom central nervous system disease, pulmonary infections, and the use of drugs capable of causing water retention can be excluded, the possibility of malignancy must be seriously considered, especially oat cell carcinoma of the lung. Water retention and hyponatremia may occur before malignancy can be detected on chest x-ray.

The response to water loading is a useful means of establishing the diagnosis of SIADH. Before water loading is carried out, the serum sodium must be brought to a safe level, generally above 125 meq per liter, by appropriate fluid restriction and sodium administration (if necessary), and the patient must be free of symptoms of hyponatremia. An oral water load of 20 mL per kilogram of body weight is given over a period of 15 to 20 min, and urine is collected hourly for the next 5 h while the patient is recumbent. In normal individuals given such a water load, more than 80 percent of the water is excreted by the end of the fifth hour, and the osmolality of at least one urine specimen, usually in the second hour, falls to less than 100 mosmol/kg (specific gravity 1.005). Patients with hyponatremia who excrete the water load normally may be considered to have essential hyponatremia. In contrast, patients with SIADH have impaired excretion of the water load (often excreting less than 40 percent in 5 h) and fail to dilute the urine to hypotonic levels. When a water load is given to a patient with SIADH, no further water intake should be permitted over the next 24 h or until the serum sodium concentration returns to the pretest value. In this way, production of water intoxication can be avoided. Adrenal insufficiency cannot be distinguished from SIADH by the water load test. A small group of patients with hyponatremia and hypertonic urine demonstrate normal renal excretory and diluting capacity in response to a water load. These individuals should be considered not to have a variant of SIADH but rather to have a downward resetting of their osmoreceptor mechanism so that they dilute and concentrate urine in a normal fashion but around a lowered osmoreceptor set point. In these patients AVP suppresses normally in response to further reduction of plasma osmolality.

Measurements of AVP in patients with SIADH have revealed persistence of inappropriately elevated levels of AVP in plasma and urine when hypoosmolality should normally have inhibited AVP release. In response to further reduction of plasma osmolality after a water load, AVP has remained detectable in plasma and urine, confirming that indeed the secretion is inappropriate relative to plasma osmolality. In SIADH the correlates of plasma osmolality (P_{osm}) versus urinary AVP levels (U_{AVP}) (Fig. 323-3) fall to the left of the values in normal individuals. The initial diagnostic procedures and the more definitive tests for SIADH are summarized in Fig. 323-6.

SIADH cannot be diagnosed with confidence in the presence of severe "stress," pain, hypovolemia, hypotension, and other stimuli that evoke physiologic release of AVP, even in the presence of hypotonicity.

TREATMENT Patients with mild or moderate water intoxication should be treated by restricting fluid intake to about 800 to 1000 mL daily. If water restriction is adequate, a steady increase in serum sodium concentration or osmolality occurs as body weight decreases. Occasional patients with severe water intoxication associated with mental confusion, convulsions, or coma must be treated more vigorously. Intravenous administration of 200 to 300 mL of 5% saline solution is usually sufficient to raise the serum sodium to a level at which the symptoms will improve. This should be accomplished over a period of several hours to avoid the complication of pontine myelinosis, which may result from more rapid increases in serum sodium concentration. When there is the possibility of congestive heart failure due to the fluid overload, the simultaneous administration of large doses of furosemide usually causes a diuresis sufficient to reduce cardiac overload. When furosemide is given, careful attention must be paid to correction of potassium and other electrolyte losses induced by the drug. If, for any reason, intravenous fluid administration is considered necessary when the serum sodium has been raised to an appropriate level, isotonic saline solution and not 5% dextrose solution should be infused slowly to maintain normality of the serum sodium concentration.

Once the initial hyponatremia is improved, careful adherence to a regimen of fluid restriction is necessary to prevent recurrence of water intoxication. Treatment should be directed at the underlying problem. The withdrawal of drugs which might have caused water retention usually results in prompt clearing of SIADH. The SIADH occurring with central nervous system disorders is usually transient and clears with improvement of the underlying disease. In patients with hypothyroidism, correction of the thyroid deficiency by appropriate replacement therapy leads to resolution of hyponatremia. Treatment of pulmonary tuberculosis with appropriate antituberculous therapy results in gradual disappearance of SIADH. Similarly, antibiotic treatment of lung abscess or pneumonia results in resolution of SIADH.

In patients with SIADH due to malignancy, surgical resection, irradiation, or chemotherapy may be successful in alleviating water retention. Sometimes, these measures should be carried out even when there is little likelihood of curing the malignancy, since tumor debulking may correct life-threatening water intoxication and prevent the necessity for rigid fluid restriction. In patients in whom treatment is judged to have been curative, the disappearance of SIADH may confirm the success of treatment. Periodic water load tests may be valuable in following such patients for evidence of recurrence of malignancy.

No drugs are clinically useful in suppressing AVP release from the neurohypophyseal system or from a tumor. Phenytoin inhibits AVP release but is rarely clinically effective. Several opioid agonists, including butorphanol are capable of inhibiting AVP release from the neurohypophysis. Their role in the treatment of SIADH remains to be determined. Drugs capable of blocking AVP effect on the renal tubule may be of value in the chronic management of patients with hyponatremia. Lithium can interfere with the antidiuretic action of AVP on the kidney but is too toxic for use in SIADH. Demeclocycline is effective in interfering with the renal action of AVP. Administration of the drug in doses of 900 to 1200 mg per day to patients with SIADH due to lung malignancy has resulted in diuresis with excretion of an isotonic or hypotonic urine and improvement in hyponatremia. The only untoward effect has been azotemia without other evidence of renal toxicity, which has disappeared promptly on discontinuation of the drug. Thus, demeclocycline may be useful in the management of SIADH when fluid restriction is difficult to accomplish.

PROGNOSIS The prognosis of SIADH depends on the underlying cause of the syndrome. Transient or reversible SIADH as in central nervous system disorders or following use of water-retaining drugs is usually benign as long as proper treatment of acute water intoxication is effectively carried out. SIADH in association with malignancy is ominous, since the malignancies most commonly associated are oat cell carcinoma of the lung and adenocarcinomas of the pancreas, both usually associated with rapid spread and early death.

PARAVENTRICULAR-NEUROHYPOPHYSEAL SYSTEM AND OXYTOCIN

CHEMISTRY AND PHYSIOLOGY Oxytocin, a nonapeptide that differs by two amino acids from vasopressin, is produced predominantly in the cell bodies of the paraventricular nuclei and to a lesser extent in those of the supraoptic nuclei. It is synthesized and transported in neurosecretory granules by way of neuronal axons to the neurohypophysis, where it is stored or released, in conjunction with an oxytocin-specific neurophysin. Oxytocin release is stimulated by nerve impulses originating in the hypothalamus, which cause depolarization of the neurosecretory terminals of the posterior pituitary and subsequent release of oxytocin through a calcium-dependent process, similar to the mechanism for vasopressin. Estrogen stimulates release of oxytocin and its neurophysin. The secretion of oxytocin, as well as of vasopressin, is inhibited by ethanol. Some stimuli such as pain apparently release oxytocin and vasopressin simultaneously, but most stimuli release the two hormones independently. Oxytocin is primarily liberated during suckling, whereas vasopressin is released in much greater quantities than is oxytocin after an osmotic stimulus or hemorrhage. Manipulation or distention of the female genital tract, artificially or during parturition, is a more effective stimulus to oxytocin release than suckling.

Oxytocin acts on the membranes of myometrial and myoepithelial cells and results in an increased force of contraction. Sensitivity of the myometrium to oxytocin increases with the duration of pregnancy, but oxytocin per se probably is not responsible for the initiation and maintenance of labor. Oxytocin may have survival value to the offspring since it may hasten the final stages of birth and lessen the chances of anoxia. Oxytocin also exerts a contractile action on the myometrium post partum and contracts the myoepithelial cells of the mammary alveoli, causing them to expel milk from the secretory tissue to the nipple. Oxytocin is 100 times more potent than vasopressin in its milk-ejecting activity in the human. In contrast, the antidiuretic potency of oxytocin relative to vasopressin is about 1:200. It is unlikely that oxytocin exerts any significant physiologic effect other than on the uterus and breast.

One milligram of purified preparation of oxytocin contains 450 IU of hormone, and the amount of oxytocin in the posterior pituitary ranges from 10 to 15 units. In spite of the fact that there is no known role of oxytocin in the male, the male neural lobe stores oxytocin in amounts similar to those in the female. Plasma oxytocin concentration in both men and women exhibits episodic increases, with values

FIGURE 323-6 *Approach to diagnosis of SIADH in patients with hyponatremia.*

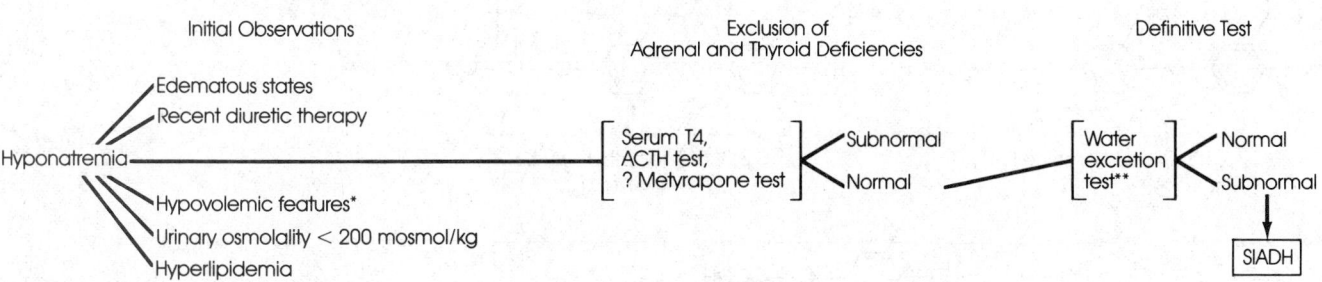

*Orthostatic hypotension and tachycardia, prerenal azotemia, etc.

**Water excretion test should only be performed when serum Na concentration has risen above 125 mEq/L, after water deprivation for as long as may be necessary.

ranging from a low of approximately 0.5 to a high of 2.0 μU/mL but with no diurnal variation. In normal women there is a midcycle increase in plasma oxytocin concentration from a preovulatory value of approximately 1.0 μU/mL to a peak value of 2 to 4 μU/mL at the time of ovulation. During labor, plasma oxytocin concentrations may reach several hundred microunits per milliliter, with a rapid fall to prepartum levels after delivery. During suckling, plasma oxytocin levels of the mother vary but are usually about 5 to 10 μU/mL. The half-life of oxytocin in plasma is about 3 to 5 min. Removal of oxytocin from the circulation is mainly by the kidneys and liver, although the uterus and mammary gland may remove some.

CLINICAL USE OF OXYTOCIN The clinical use of oxytocin is limited to the induction of labor, control of hemorrhage following incomplete abortion and curettage, and treatment of impaired milk ejection. For discussion of the obstetric uses of oxytocin, the reader is referred to textbooks on obstetrics. Care must be taken because oxytocin may cause uterine rupture and fetal death. The antidiuretic action of oxytocin can be elicited with single intravenous doses of as little as 100 mU. Maximal antidiuresis is reached with 40 to 50 mU/min. Since 10 to 40 units of oxytocin per liter of dextrose is often used in obstetric practice, water intoxication may result. The vasodilatory action of oxytocin may cause sudden death of obstetric patients with heart disease because of hypotension, tachycardia, and arrhythmias. Anesthetics may modify the cardiovascular responses to oxytocin. For instance, in patients under cyclopropane anesthesia, oxytocin produces more hypotension but less tachycardia than in unanesthetized subjects. The vasodilatory effect of oxytocin can be blocked by vasopressin.

REFERENCES

BARTTER FC, SCHWARTZ WB: The syndrome of inappropriate secretion of antidiuretic hormone. Am J Med 42:790, 1967

CROSS BA, LENG G: *Progress in Brain Research*, vol 60: *The Neurohypophysis: Structure, Function and Control*. Amsterdam, Elsevier, 1983

KNOBIL E, SAWYER WH (eds): *Handbook of Physiology*, sec 7: *Endocrinology*, vol IV: *The Pituitary Gland—Its Neuroendocrine Control*, part I. Washington, DC, American Physiological Society, 1974

MILLER M et al: Recognition of partial defects in antidiuretic hormone secretion. Ann Intern Med 73:721, 1970

MOSES AM et al: Pathophysiologic and pharmacologic alterations in the release and action of ADH. Metabolism 25:697, 1976

OZERNICHOW P, ROBINSON AE: *Frontiers of Hormone Research*, vol 13: *Diabetes Insipidus in Man*. Basel, Karger, 1985

REICHLIN S: *The Neurohypophysis. Physiological and Clinical Aspects*. New York, Plenum, 1984

ROBERTSON GL: The regulation of vasopressin function in health and disease. Rec Progr Hormone Res 33:333, 1977

SCHRIER RW: *Vasopressin*. New York, Raven, 1985

324 DISEASES OF THE THYROID

SIDNEY H. INGBAR

Normal function of the thyroid gland is directed to the secretion of L-thyroxine (T_4) and 3,5,3'-triiodo-L-thyronine (T_3), iodinated amino acids that are the active thyroid hormones and that influence a diversity of metabolic processes (Fig. 324-1). Diseases of the thyroid gland are manifested by qualitative or quantitative alterations in hormone secretion, enlargement of the thyroid (goiter), or both. Insufficient hormone secretion results in the syndrome of *hypothyroidism* or *myxedema*, in which decreased caloric expenditure (hypometabolism) is a principal feature. Conversely, excessive secretion of active hormone results in hypermetabolism and other features of a syndrome termed *hyperthyroidism* or *thyrotoxicosis*. Enlargement of the thyroid gland (normally 15 to 25 g in adults) may be generalized or focal. Generalized enlargements may not be absolutely symmetric, however, the right lobe tending to enlarge more than the left. They are associated with increased, normal, or decreased hormone secretion, depending upon the underlying disturbance. Truly focal enlargement usually reflects neoplastic disease, either benign or malignant, the former sometimes being responsible for hypersecretion of hormone and hyperthyroidism, the latter very rarely so. Any type of goiter may result in compression of adjacent structures in the neck or mediastinum.

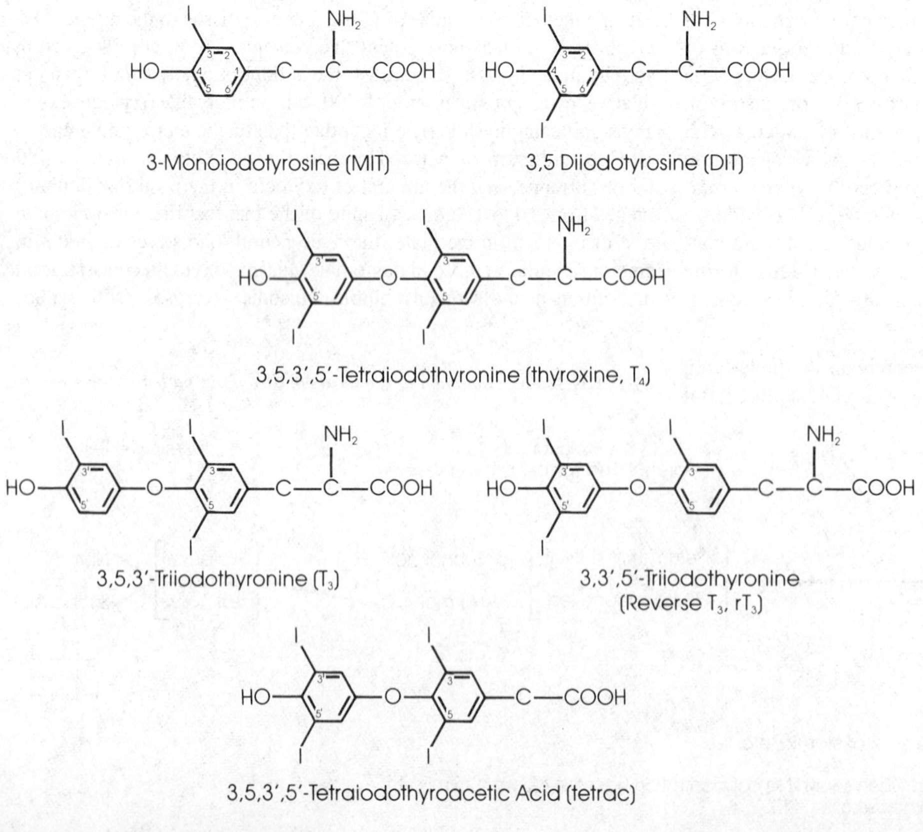

FIGURE 324-1 *Structural formulas of thyroxine, its precursors, and certain of its metabolites.*

3-Monoiodotyrosine (MIT)

3,5 Diiodotyrosine (DIT)

3,5,3',5'-Tetraiodothyronine (thyroxine, T_4)

3,5,3'-Triiodothyronine (T_3)

3,3',5'-Triiodothyronine (Reverse T_3, rT_3)

3,5,3',5'-Tetraiodothyroacetic Acid (tetrac)

EMBRYOLOGY, ANATOMY, AND HISTOLOGY

The human thyroid originates embryologically from an evagination of the pharyngeal epithelium with some cellular contributions from the lateral pharyngeal pouches. Progressive descent of the midline thyroid anlage gives rise to the thyroglossal duct, which extends from the foramen cecum near the base of the tongue to the isthmus of the thyroid. Remnants of tissue may persist along the course of this tract as "lingual thyroid," as thyroglossal cysts or nodules, or as a structure contiguous with the thyroid isthmus called the *pyramidal lobe*. The latter is usually not discernible, except when the remainder of the gland is enlarged. In some individuals, lingual thyroid may be the sole functioning thyroid tissue. In such cases, its secretion may or may not be sufficient to maintain a normal metabolic (euthyroid) state. Thyroid aplasia and functional failure of ectopic thyroid tissue are causes of sporadic neonatal hypothyroidism, an important disorder because of its frequency (1 in every 4000 or 5000 newborns) and its response to early treatment.

The fetal thyroid acquires the capacity to collect and organify iodine at about 10 weeks gestation. Both T_4 and thyroid-stimulating hormone (thyrotropin, TSH) are detectable in the blood soon thereafter and increase in concentration during the second trimester. The increase in serum T_4 is due both to increasing thyroid secretion and to the appearance in plasma of thyroxine-binding globulin (TBG), and the increase in TSH is a reflection of the maturation of the fetal hypothalamus with resulting secretion of thyrotropin-releasing hormone (TRH). Maternal TRH readily crosses the placenta and could play a role in the development of the fetal pituitary-thyroid axis. Maternal TSH, by contrast, does not cross the placenta. T_3 is detectable in the blood later during the second trimester, but its concentration in blood and amniotic fluid remains low until shortly after parturition. By contrast, the concentration of its analogue, 3,3',5'-triiodo-L-thyronine (reverse T_3, rT_3), is increased in fetal blood and amniotic fluid relative to that in maternal blood (Fig. 324-1). These differences are due to qualitative alterations in T_4 metabolism in the fetus that are discussed below. The low T_3 concentration in fetal blood and amniotic fluid in the face of a high maternal concentration indicates that maternal-fetal transfer of T_3 is minimal, and the same is true of T_4. Hence, T_4 derived from the fetal thyroid is the major thyroid hormone available to the fetus. Except for the possible effect of maternal TRH, therefore, the fetal pituitary-thyroid axis is a functional unit distinct from that of the mother.

The normal adult thyroid contains two lobes joined by an isthmus and lies just anterior and caudad to the cartilages of the larynx. Fibrous septa divide the gland into pseudolobules which, in turn, are composed of vesicles, called *follicles* or *acini*, surrounded by a capillary network. Normally, the follicle walls are composed of cuboidal epithelium. Their lumen is filled with a proteinaceous material termed *colloid*, which contains a protein peculiar to the thyroid, *thyroglobulin*, within the peptide sequence of which T_4 and T_3 are synthesized and stored. The thyroid contains a second population of cells, the C cells. They are the source of calcitonin and give rise to medullary thyroid carcinoma when they undergo malignant transformation.

THYROID HORMONE ECONOMY: NORMAL PHYSIOLOGY

The term *thyroid hormone economy* denotes the complex processes involved in the synthesis of hormones within the thyroid gland; their transport in the circulation; their action and metabolism within the peripheral tissues; and the regulatory mechanisms that maintain a normal supply of thyroid hormones to tissues. This section describes the normal physiology and biochemistry of the thyroid hormone economy. Abnormalities in transport, action, and metabolism are described in the sections dealing with laboratory tests or specific disorders.

HORMONE SYNTHESIS AND SECRETION Thyroid hormone synthesis depends on entry into the thyroid of adequate quantities of iodine, a constituent of the active hormones T_4 and T_3; normality of pathways for iodine metabolism within the gland; and concurrent synthesis of a normal receptor protein for iodine, thyroglobulin. The structure of thyroglobulin favors iodinations and particularly formation of T_4 and T_3. Secretion of normal quantities of hormone, in turn, requires both a normal rate of hormone synthesis and the integrity of processes within the gland by which thyroglobulin is hydrolyzed and the active hormones thereby liberated. Iodine enters the thyroid from the bloodstream in the form of inorganic or ionic iodide whose source is twofold: iodide derived either from the deiodination of thyroid hormones or from iodinated agents that the patient may have received and iodide ingested in food, water, or medication. Formerly, a dietary iodine intake of approximately 200 µg was considered normal within the continental United States, and this was sufficient to sustain a plasma iodide concentration of approximately 0.5 µg/dL. However, owing to iodine contamination of some foods, and to the widespread use of iodine in drugs, vitamin preparations, and antiseptic agents, the average iodine intake has increased to values as high as 1000 µg daily, with corresponding increases in plasma iodide concentration. Iodide is removed from the plasma by the thyroid, kidneys, and salivary and gastrointestinal glands, but since iodide that enters gastrointestinal secretions is reabsorbed, net clearance is effected only by the thyroid and kidneys. In effect, the thyroid and kidneys compete for plasma iodide. Renal clearance is largely a function of glomerular filtration rate and is not influenced by humoral factors or plasma iodide concentration; therefore, the kidney is normally a passive participant in this competition. Hence, adjustments in the rate of entry of iodide into the thyroid relative to the rate of urinary excretion are mediated by changes in thyroid, rather than renal, avidity.

The reactions involved in the synthesis and secretion of the active thyroid hormones can be divided into four sequential steps (Fig. 324-2). The first involves active inward transport of iodide from the

FIGURE 324-2 *Schema depicting pathways in the synthesis and secretion of thyroid hormones and mechanisms for the suprathyroidal and intrathyroidal regulation of thyroid function. Small, solid arrows indicate pathways of iodine metabolism; open arrows indicate stimulation; cross-hatched arrows indicate inhibitory influences. TRH, thyrotropin-releasing hormone; TSH, thyroid-stimulating hormone; IPO, iodide peroxidase; prot., thyroid protease; peptid., thyroid peptidase; MIT, monoiodotyrosine; DIT, diiodotyrosine; T_4, thyroxine; T_3, 3,5,3'-triiodothyronine.*

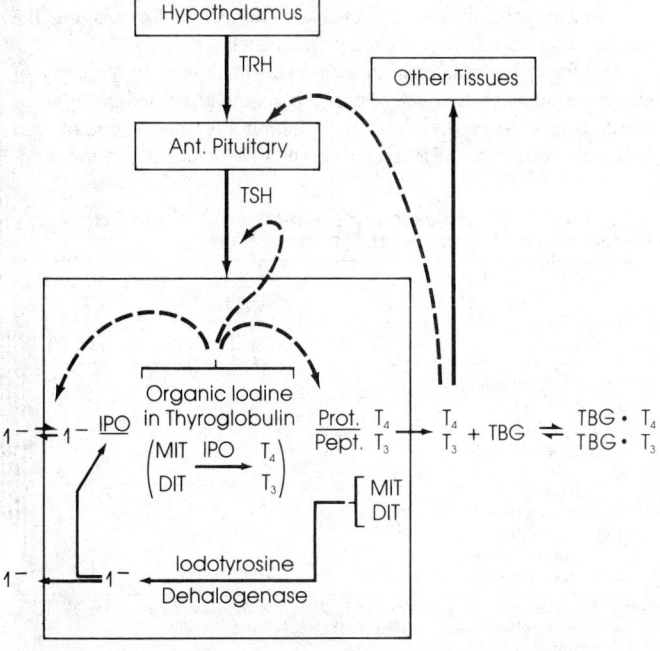

plasma into the thyroid cell and follicular lumen. This occurs at a rate that exceeds passive diffusion of iodide out of the gland, with the result that the thyroid is capable of maintaining concentration gradients for iodide (thyroid/plasma concentration ratios) of substantial magnitude (up to 500, or more, under certain conditions). Energy for iodide transport is phosphate bond–derived and therefore depends upon oxidative metabolism within the gland. The second step in hormone biosynthesis involves oxidation of iodide to a higher valence form that is capable of iodinating tyrosyl residues in thyroglobulin, a glycoprotein of approximately 650,000 mol wt that is synthesized within the follicular cell. Oxidation of iodide is effected by an iodide peroxidase, which utilizes hydrogen peroxide generated during the course of oxidative metabolism within the gland. Organic iodinations occur at the cell-colloid interface, where they take place to a large extent in newly synthesized thyroglobulin undergoing exocytosis into the follicular lumen. They result in the formation of the peptide-bound, hormonally inactive precursors, monoiodotyrosine (MIT) and diiodotyrosine (DIT). Subsequently, these iodotyrosines undergo oxidative condensation, again through the mediation of peroxidase. This coupling reaction occurs within the thyroglobulin molecule and yields a variety of iodothyronines, including T_4 and T_3. Although minute quantities of thyroglobulin are detectable in the blood, most thyroglobulin is retained for a time within the gland, serving as a storage form of thyroid hormone, or "prohormone." Liberation of the active hormones into the blood involves pinocytosis of follicular colloid at the apical margin of the cells to form colloid droplets. Functioning microtubules are necessary for this process. The colloid droplets fuse with thyroid lysosomes to form "phagolysosomes," in which thyroglobulin is hydrolyzed by proteases and peptidases. The final step is release of the free iodothyronines, T_4 and T_3, into the blood. The thyroid gland is the only source of endogenous T_4; in contrast, thyroid secretion normally accounts for only about 20 percent of the T_3 produced, the remainder being generated in extraglandular tissues by the enzymatic removal of the 5'-iodine from the outer ring of T_4. Inactive iodotyrosines liberated by the hydrolysis of thyroglobulin are stripped of their iodine by an intrathyroid enzyme, iodotyrosine dehalogenase. Normally, iodide so liberated is largely reutilized in the synthesis of hormone, but a small proportion is lost into the blood (iodide leak); this proportion may become large in abnormal circumstances.

The thyroid is also capable of concentrating other monovalent anions such as pertechnetate, which is available as the radioactive isotope, sodium [^{99m}Tc]pertechnetate. Unlike iodide, little pertechnetate is organically bound; hence, its duration of stay within the thyroid is short. This property, together with its short physical half-life, makes pertechnetate a valuable radionuclide for imaging the thyroid with scintillation scanning techniques.

The foregoing reactions are subject to inhibition by a variety of chemical compounds. Such agents are generally termed *goitrogens*, since, by virtue of their ability to inhibit hormone synthesis and indirectly stimulate TSH secretion, they induce goiter formation.

Certain inorganic anions, notably perchlorate and thiocyanate, inhibit the iodide transport mechanism and thereby reduce substrate availability for hormone formation. The goiter and hypothyroidism that follow, however, can be prevented or relieved by doses of iodide sufficiently large to enable adequate quantities to enter the gland by simple diffusion. The commonly employed antithyroid agents, such as the derivatives of thiourea and mercaptoimidazole, exert more complex actions upon hormone biosynthesis. These agents, as well as certain aniline derivatives, inhibit the initial oxidation (organic binding) of iodide, decrease the proportion of DIT relative to MIT, and block coupling of iodotyrosines to form the hormonally active iodothyronines. The latter reaction is the most sensitive. Thus, it is possible for the synthesis of hormonally active iodothyronines to be decreased greatly, although the total incorporation of iodine by the thyroid is inhibited but little. In contrast to the effect of the monovalent anions, the goitrogenic action of inhibitors of organic binding is not overcome by large quantities of iodine. Indeed, certain weak goitrogens, such as sulfonamides and antipyrine, are more potent when given with iodide, an effect not understood. Iodine itself, when given acutely in large doses, is capable of blocking the organic-binding and coupling reactions. This action (Wolff-Chaikoff effect) is normally transient, but in some normal individuals, prolonged administration of iodide is associated with continued inhibition of hormone synthesis and development of goiter, with (iodide myxedema) or without hypothyroidism. Most patients with Graves' disease, especially after treatment with radioiodine or surgery, as well as patients with Hashimoto's disease, are inordinately sensitive to the blocking effect of iodide and develop hypothyroidism when given iodides chronically. The fetal thyroid is similarly sensitive, and consequently pregnant women should not be given iodide in large doses because of the danger of inducing goitrous hypothyroidism in the fetus. Iodide in large doses is capable of inhibiting proteolysis of thyroglobulin and hormone release, an effect that is most readily demonstrable in hyperfunctioning thyroids and that is responsible for the rapid ameliorative action of iodides in most patients with hyperthyroidism. Lithium, which is administered as the carbonate salt in some patients with depressive states, has several effects on intrathyroidal iodine metabolism, one of which is to inhibit hormone release. Dexamethasone in large doses also inhibits hormone release and, in conjunction with iodide, can effect a rapid reduction in the degree of thyrotoxicosis.

HORMONE TRANSPORT AND METABOLISM

HORMONE TRANSPORT In the blood, T_4 and T_3 are almost entirely bound to plasma proteins. T_4 is bound, in decreasing order of intensity, to an inter-alpha globulin, termed thyroxine- or thyronine-binding globulin (TBG), to a T_4-binding prealbumin (TBPA), and to albumin. By virtue of its intense affinity for T_4, TBG is normally the major determinant of overall binding intensity. The interaction between T_4 and its binding proteins conforms to a reversible binding equilibrium in which the majority of the hormone is bound and a small proportion (normally about 0.03 percent) is free. T_3 is not significantly bound by TBPA and is bound less firmly than T_4 by TBG. As a consequence, the normal proportion of free T_3 (approximately 0.3 percent) is 8 to 10 times greater than that of T_4. Only the free or unbound hormone is available to tissues; therefore, the metabolic state correlates more closely with the concentration of free than with the total concentration of hormone in plasma, and homeostatic regulation of thyroid function is directed toward maintenance of a normal concentration of free rather than total hormone. Moreover, the relatively weak binding of T_3 accounts for its failure to contribute materially to the total hormonal iodine concentration in the blood and possibly for its more rapid onset and offset of action. Disturbances of the thyroid hormone–plasma protein interaction are of two general types (see Table 324-1). In the first, the thyroid-pituitary axis is intrinsically normal, and the homeostatic control of thyroid hormone secretion is intact. Under these circumstances, disordered binding

TABLE 324-1 Classification of the varieties of disordered thyroid hormone–plasma protein interactions

Type of abnormality	Serum T_4 and T_3	Percent FT_4 and FT_3 or RT_3U	FT_4 and FT_3 or FT_4I and FT_3I
I Primary abnormality in TBG			
A Increased concentration	↑	↓	N
B Decreased concentration	↓	↑	N
II Primary disorder of thyroid function			
A Hypothyroidism	↓		↑
B Hyperthyroidism	↑	↑	↑

NOTE: FT_4 = free T_4; FT_3 = free T_3; FT_4I = free T_4 index; FT_3I = free T_3 index; RT_3U = resin-T_3 uptake; TBG = thyroid-binding globulin.

interactions result from alterations in thyroid hormone binding. For example, an increase in TBG initially lowers the concentration of free hormone and thus diminishes the quantity of hormone available to tissues. Total hormone concentration in serum then increases until the concentration of free hormone is restored to normal. At this time, the proportions of free T_4 and T_3 are decreased. The increase in total hormone concentration counterbalances the decrease in the free proportion; as a result, the absolute concentration of free hormone is normal, and the metabolic state of the patient is normal. Converse changes occur when the concentration of TBG declines. Table 324-2 summarizes those states associated with primary alterations in the concentration of TBG. Primary disturbances in thyroid hormone binding also occur when other binding proteins in blood are increased, or when abnormal binding proteins appear. These are discussed below.

The second type of disturbance of thyroid hormone–binding interactions results from a primary alteration in the concentration of thyroid hormones in the blood, as in hypothyroidism or thyrotoxicosis. Here, normal homeostatic control of thyroid hormone secretion is lost, either because of disease within the control mechanism itself or because an intact control mechanism is incapable of overcoming the effects of disease elsewhere. Under these circumstances, the concentration of TBG is changed little, if at all, and the concentration of free hormone varies directly with the total concentration of hormone. Since homeostatic mechanisms cannot restore the concentration of free hormone to normal, primary changes in thyroid function are associated with persistent changes in the concentration of total and free hormone, and, consequently, with alterations in the metabolic state. In these disorders, the proportion of free hormone changes in a direction similar to that of the change in hormone supply.

HORMONE METABOLISM Following their penetration into the cell, T_4 and T_3 undergo a variety of reactions that lead ultimately to their excretion or inactivation. Thyroid hormones undergo metabolism mainly through the sequential removal of single iodine atoms (monodeiodinations) that ultimately yields the thyronine nucleus stripped of its iodine content. Deiodinative pathways account for approximately 70 percent of T_4 and T_3 disposal. In the case of T_4, the most important of these is the 5'-monodeiodination that leads to the generation of T_3 (T_3-neogenesis). Since approximately 30 percent of T_4 is converted to T_3 and since T_3 has approximately three times the metabolic potency of T_4, virtually all of the metabolic action of T_4 can be ascribed to the action of the T_3 that it gives rise to. Normally, T_3-neogenesis accounts for about 80 percent of the T_3 in the blood and of overall T_3 production, the remainder coming from direct thyroid secretion. As a consequence, abnormal states and pharmacologic agents that impair T_3-neogenesis lower the serum T_3 concentration (Table 324-3). When patients with thyroid hypofunction are treated with doses of synthetic T_4 (levothyroxine) sufficient to sustain serum T_4 concentrations within or somewhat above the normal range, normal or nearly normal serum T_3 concentrations are maintained. The generalization that the thyroid secretes relatively little T_3 does not apply to states in which the thyroid is hyperfunctioning or under increased stimulation by TSH or when thyroid iodine content is reduced. Under these conditions, the T_3:T_4 ratio of the secretory product and the serum concentration of T_3 relative to that of T_4 are increased. In addition, when T_4 production is decreased, as in early thyroid failure or iodine deficiency, the T_3:T_4 concentration ratio in blood is increased still further by an autoregulatory mechanism that leads to an increase in the efficiency of T_3-neogenesis.

Approximately 40 percent of T_4 disposal is accounted for by monodeiodination at the 5 position of its inner ring to yield 3,3',5'-triiodo-L-thyronine (reverse T_3,rT_3); this process accounts for nearly all rT_3 produced. rT_3 has little if any metabolic potency; therefore, the relative poise between outer- and inner-ring monodeiodination of T_4 determines the quantity of metabolically active hormone available. Factors that impair T_3-neogenesis almost invariably increase serum rT_3 concentrations. This increase is not due to an increase in the production of rT_3 from T_4, but rather to a decrease in the 5'-monodeiodination of rT_3 to yield 3,3'-diiodothyronine (3,3'T_2), i.e., both the decreased conversion of T_4 to T_3 and the decreased degradation of rT_3 are due to a selective impairment of 5'-monodeiodination.

A second major pathway of metabolism of T_4 and T_3 and of their metabolites is conjugation in the liver, principally with glucuronate and sulfate. Conjugates either undergo deiodination locally or are secreted into the bile, but the magnitude of the enterohepatic circulation in humans is unknown. Reabsorption is incomplete at best, since the fecal excretion of T_4, T_3, and their iodine-containing metabolites accounts for approximately 20 percent of overall T_4 disposal. A small proportion of T_4 and T_3 (approximately 20 percent) undergoes oxidative deamination and decarboxylation of the alanine side chain to yield the acetic acid analogues tetraiodo- and triiodothyroacetic acid (tetrac and triac, respectively).

Under certain circumstances, changes in hormone accumulation and metabolism are the major determinant of changes in the rates of metabolic clearance of T_4 and T_3. Both phenobarbital and phenytoin increase the metabolic clearance of thyroid hormones without increasing the proportion of free hormone in the blood. Indeed, in the case of phenytoin, both total and free T_4 concentrations are diminished. Nevertheless, a normal metabolic state is maintained possibly because of an increase in T_3-neogenesis.

HORMONE ACTION The thyroid hormones influence the growth and maturation of tissues, total energy expenditure, and the turnover of essentially all substrates, vitamins, and hormones, including the thyroid hormones themselves. The primary mechanisms whereby these effects are initiated remain uncertain, but the hormones appear to act in a coordinated manner at the level of the nucleus to alter genomic expression, at the level of the mitochondrion to influence oxidative metabolism, and at the level of the plasma membrane to influence the transcellular flux of substrates and cations.

REGULATION OF THYROID FUNCTION Regulation of thyroid function is effected by two general mechanisms, one suprathyroid and one intrathyroid in locus (Fig. 324-2). The proximate mediator of suprathyroid regulation is thyrotropin (thyroid-stimulating hormone, TSH), a glycoprotein secreted by basophilic (thyrotropic) cells in the anterior pituitary. TSH stimulates thyroid hypertrophy and hyperplasia; accelerates most aspects of intermediary metabolism in the thyroid; enhances synthesis of nucleic acid and protein, including

TABLE 324-2 Circumstances associated with altered concentration of TBG

Increased TBG	Decreased TBG
Pregnancy	Androgenic and anabolic steroids
Newborn state	Large doses of glucocorticoid
Oral contraceptives and other sources of estrogen	Chronic liver disease
Tamoxifen	Severe systemic illness
Infectious and chronic active hepatitis	Active acromegaly
Biliary cirrhosis	Nephrosis
Acute intermittent porphyria	Genetically determined
Perphenazine	Asparaginase
Genetically determined	

TABLE 324-3 States associated with decreased peripheral conversion of T_4 to T_3

I Physiologic
  A Fetal and early neonatal life
  B ? Old age
II Pathologic
  A Fasting
  B Malnutrition
  C Systemic illness
  D Physical trauma
  E Postoperative state
  F Drugs (propylthiouracil, dexamethasone, propranolol, amiodarone)
  G Radiographic contrast agents (Oragrafin, Telepaque)

thyroglobulin; and stimulates all steps in the synthesis and secretion of thyroid hormones. These actions of TSH result from binding of the hormone to specific receptors in the surface of the follicular cell and subsequent activation of the plasma membrane enzyme adenylate cyclase. The resulting increase in the cellular cyclic $3',5'$-adenosine monophosphate (cyclic AMP) concentration initiates most or all of the responses that characterize the action of TSH.

Regulation of TSH secretion, in turn, is effected by two opposing influences at the level of the thyrotropic cell. Thyrotropin-releasing hormone (TRH), a tripeptide of hypothalamic origin, stimulates the secretion and synthesis of TSH, whereas thyroid hormones both inhibit the TSH secretory mechanism directly and antagonize the action of TRH. Thus, homeostatic control of TSH secretion is exerted in a negative-feedback manner by thyroid hormones, and the threshold for feedback inhibition is apparently set by TRH. TRH is synthesized in the ventromedial hypothalamus, reaches the pituitary via the hypophyseal portal blood system, and binds to specific receptors on the plasma membrane of the thyrotropic cell. Either activation of the adenylate cyclase system or a concomitant translocation of extracellular calcium into the cell initiates release of TSH. To what extent, if any, suprahypothalamic centers influence the secretion of TRH is uncertain. The negative-feedback effect of the thyroid hormones appears to take place entirely at the level of the thyrotropic cell. Thyroid hormones do not directly affect the hypothalamic secretion of TRH but reduce the number of TRH receptors on the thyrotrophic cell, thus impairing its responsiveness to TRH. The negative-feedback action of the thyroid hormones is apparently mediated by an inhibitory protein whose synthesis is induced by binding of the hormones to specific receptors in the nucleus of the thyrotrophic cell. The principal arbiter of thyroid hormone action within the pituitary is T_3, both that generated locally from intrapituitary T_4 and that derived from the pool of free T_3 in the plasma. To what extent T_4 itself is effective within the pituitary is uncertain, but other factors modify the secretion of TSH and its response to TRH. Both somatostatin and dopamine appear to be physiologic inhibitors of TRH secretion. Estrogens enhance responsiveness to TRH, whereas glucocorticoids inhibit this function.

Intrathyroid regulation of thyroid function is also important. In some manner, changes in glandular organic iodine content cause reciprocal changes in thyroid iodide transport activity and regulate growth, amino acid uptake, glucose metabolism, and nucleic acid synthesis. These influences are evident in the absence of TSH stimulation and hence may be termed *autoregulatory*, but their most important role is to modify (iodine-enrichment inhibiting and iodine-depletion enhancing) the response to TSH, probably by modifying the generation of cyclic AMP consequent to TSH stimulation.

LABORATORY TESTS

Laboratory tests of thyroid hormone economy can be divided into five major categories: direct tests of thyroid function, tests related to the concentration and binding of thyroid hormones in blood, metabolic indexes, tests of the homeostatic control of thyroid function, and various tests that do not fit into other categories.

DIRECT TESTS OF THYROID FUNCTION   Among all tests designed to assess thyroid status, only those that involve in vivo administration of radioactive iodine test glandular function per se, and measurement of the *thyroid radioactive iodine uptake* (RAIU) is the most common. ^{131}I has been used for this purpose for decades, but ^{123}I is preferable because of the lower radiation dose that it delivers. The administered radioiodine mixes uniformly with the endogenous iodide in the extracellular fluid and, in the steady state, can be used to assess what percentage of the iodide entering and leaving the extracellular space per unit time is accumulated by the thyroid. The RAIU is usually measured 24 h after administration of the isotope since it has usually reached a plateau value at this time, but in states of severe thyroid hyperfunction it may peak early. The RAIU varies inversely with the

plasma iodide concentration and directly with the functional state of the thyroid. At usual levels of iodine intake in the United States (up to 1000 µg per day), the normal range for the 24-h RAIU is approximately 5 to 30 percent of the administered dose. Consequently, this test discriminates poorly between normal and hypothyroid states. Values above the normal range, however, indicate thyroid hyperfunction and are useful in the diagnosis of hyperthyroidism. The RAIU is also used as part of the thyroid suppression test.

The principal value of the test, however, is in the diagnosis of disorders in which thyrotoxicosis is associated with a low value of the RAIU. These include iodine-induced hyperthyroidism, thyrotoxicosis factitia, and the spontaneously resolving thyrotoxicosis that is associated with painless chronic thyroiditis or subacute thyroiditis.

TESTS RELATED TO HORMONE CONCENTRATION AND BINDING IN BLOOD   Measurement of the concentration of one or both thyroid hormones in serum, T_4 and T_3, in conjunction with some assessment of hormone binding, is generally the most reliable means of confirming a diagnosis of hyperthyroidism or hypothyroidism. Highly specific and sensitive radioimmunoassays are used to measure *serum T_4 and T_3* concentrations and when indicated for measuring *serum rT_3* concentration. The approximate normal ranges are 4 to 12 µg/dL for T_4, 80 to 100 ng/dL for T_3, and 10 to 40 ng/dL for rT_3.

Measurements of serum *protein-bound iodine* (PBI) were once used as an indirect means of assessing serum T_4 concentration. At present, the serum PBI is occasionally measured as a means of detecting release from the thyroid of abnormal iodoproteins, such as occurs in various forms of thyroiditis or as the result of an intrathyroid biosynthetic defect.

As mentioned in a previous section, alterations in the intensity of hormone binding by plasma proteins, as well as alterations in the rate of hormone secretion, influence the concentration of hormone in the blood. However, only alterations in hormone secretion lead to steady-state alterations in the concentration of free hormone. Because they most consistently reflect the rate of hormone production, free hormone concentrations usually correlate better with the metabolic state than do total hormone concentrations. The free T_4 concentration (FT_4) can be measured by equilibrium dialysis of serum enriched with a tracer quantity of labeled T_4. The percent of T_4 that is dialyzable or free is thereby determined, and the product of this value and the total T_4 is the FT_4. However, the dialysis technique is cumbersome; for clinical purposes, the *in vitro uptake test* is simple to perform and usually provides the same information. Here, the serum is enriched with labeled T_4 or labeled T_3 and is then incubated with an insoluble, particulate matter, such as resin or charcoal, that binds free hormone. The percent of labeled hormone taken up by the particulate material varies inversely with both the concentration of unoccupied sites among the serum proteins and their affinity for the particular hormone being used. Labeled T_3 is usually used in preference to labeled T_4, since it is less strongly bound in the serum and hence yields higher, and therefore more nearly accurate, uptake values (resin T_3 uptake, RT_3U). In most clinical conditions, values of the RT_3U are proportionate to those of the percent of FT_4 and percent of FT_3. This proportionality reflects the fact that in normal serum T_4 and T_3 are mainly bound by a common binding site on TBG. Therefore, alterations in binding produced by an excess or deficiency of TBG, or by an excessive or insufficient supply of T_4, do not seriously disturb the relationship between the intensity of T_4 binding and that of T_3. Under these conditions, therefore, one may calculate a *free T_4 index* (FT_4I) and a *free T_3 index* (FT_3I) as the product of the RT_3U and the total T_4 and T_3 concentrations, respectively, and these are proportional to the actual FT_4 and FT_3. (In practice, values of the FT_3 and FT_3I are rarely determined.)

Primary alterations in plasma TBG concentration (Table 324-2) produce changes in the RT_3U that are inverse and approximately proportionate to those in the serum T_4 and serum T_3; as a result, the FT_4I and FT_3I remain normal. By contrast, alterations in T_4 secretion cause changes in the percent FT_4 and RT_3U that are in the same direction as those in serum T_4. As a result, the FT_4 and FT_4I deviate from normal values more markedly than do the percent FT_4 and RT_3U alone. Radioimmunoassay methods for the direct measurement of FT_4 have been developed; some provide reliable results in a wide range of disorders and can replace measurement of the FT_4I in the diagnosis of thyrotoxicosis and hypothyroidism.

As noted earlier, several disorders are characterized by increased plasma binding of T_4 in which, because the protein involved is not TBG, the intensity of T_4 binding relative to that of T_3 is abnormal. Most commonly, binding of T_4 is greatly enhanced, while that of T_3 is increased little, if at all. Included among these disorders is *familial dysalbuminemic hyperthyroxinemia (FDH)*, transmitted by autosomal dominant inheritance, in which the plasma concentration of an albumin variant with an unusually high affinity for T_4 is increased. As a result, the serum T_4 is markedly elevated, but in keeping with the euthyroid state FT_4 is normal. Because the RT_3U does not reflect the increase in the intensity of T_4 binding, calculated values of the FT_4I are greatly increased, often leading to a mistaken diagnosis of thyrotoxicosis. Similar findings occur when there is *increased T_4 binding by TBPA* or when the patient, usually one with autoimmune thyroid disease, develops *circulating antibodies* against T_4 itself.

In the foregoing disorders, in which the serum T_4 is increased owing to an increase in T_4 binding, the FT_4 and the metabolic state are normal. They are therefore classified among the disorders that lead to a state of *euthyroid hyperthyroxinemia*, a term that implies the presence of hyperthyroxinemia not caused by intrinsic thyroid disease (Table 324-4). The mechanism responsible for these findings is variable and in some cases uncertain. Also uncertain is the impact of these increases in FT_4 on the metabolic state, but the clinician should be aware of these causes of euthyroid hyperthyroxinemia lest hyperthyroidism be mistakenly diagnosed.

Some states are associated with an increased thyroid secretion of T_3, at least relative to the secretion of T_4. As a result, the serum T_3 concentration is disproportionately high relative to the prevailing serum T_4 concentration. This is apparently a consequence of hyperfunction of the follicular cell, since it is seen in all varieties of hyperthyroidism and in early thyroid failure, in which the gland is exposed to enhanced stimulation by TSH. Accordingly, the serum T_3 concentration and the derived FT_3I are generally superior to the corresponding values for T_4 in the diagnosis of hyperthyroidism. In *early* hypothyroidism, by contrast, the serum T_3 concentration and FT_3I may be normal despite subnormal values for the serum T_4 concentration and FT_4I.

Measurement of the serum rT_3 concentration is valuable in differentiating the low T_3 syndrome from intrinsic hypothyroidism; in the former state, the serum rT_3 concentration is increased, whereas in the latter it is usually subnormal.

METABOLIC INDEXES Tests in this category assess the metabolic impact of thyroid hormone in the peripheral tissues. Though tests of this type have value in the investigative setting, none of sufficient sensitivity, specificity, and ease of performance is available for routine use. Measurements of oxygen consumption in the basal state (basal metabolic rate, BMR) were once a mainstay in the diagnosis of thyroid disease but are now of historic interest. Serum concentrations of the MM isoenzyme of creatine phosphokinase and, less frequently, lactic dehydrogenase and aspartate aminotransferase are increased in hypothyroidism and may be slightly decreased in hyperthyroidism. The changes are nonspecific, and appreciation of them is important only in avoiding the inference that other diseases that produce similar changes are present. The concentrations in serum of testosterone-binding globulin (TeBG) and of angiotensin-converting enzyme are thyroid hormone–dependent and are, therefore, increased in thyrotoxicosis, but their utility in the diagnosis of thyroid disease has not been demonstrated. Increases in the *serum cholesterol concentration* are common in hypothyroidism of thyroid origin; however, decreases in serum cholesterol are of little value in the diagnosis of thyrotoxicosis. *Systolic time indexes*, such as the preejection period and pulse-wave arrival time, are prolonged in hypothyroidism and shortened in hyperthyroidism. They are of value in monitoring thyroid replacement therapy in elderly patients or in patients with coexisting heart disease.

TESTS OF HOMEOSTATIC CONTROL Measurement of the basal *serum TSH concentration* by radioimmunoassay is useful in the diagnosis of both advanced and subclinical hypothyroidism. The latter state represents a stage in the evolution of hypothyroidism, in which a structural or functional abnormality that impairs hormone synthesis is compensated for by hypersecretion of TSH and activation of the thyroid. The normal TSH level is less than 5 μU/mL. In thyrotoxic states, serum TSH concentration is almost always low or undetectable. This is of little diagnostic value, since most assays cannot distinguish between normal and subnormal values. Serum TSH concentrations are absolutely or inappropriately elevated, relative to serum FT_4 and FT_3 values, in patients with TSH-induced hyperthyroidism. This rare syndrome results either from a TSH-secreting pituitary adenoma or resistance of the TSH secretory mechanism to feedback inhibition by T_4 and T_3. Measurement of serum TSH is the best means of distinguishing between untreated hypothyroidism of thyroid origin, in which the values are invariably increased, and pituitary or hypothalamic hypothyroidism, in which the values are usually undetectable or within the normal range. Occasional patients with hypothyroidism of hypothalamic or pituitary origin secrete a form of TSH that is immunoactive but not bioactive. Here, serum TSH concentrations may be elevated rather than depressed.

TABLE 324-4 States associated with euthyroid hyperthyroxinemia

Disorder	FT_4	FT_4I	T_3	TSH	Comments
I Increased T_4 binding					
A Increased TBG	N	N	↑	N	See Tables 324-1 and 324-2
B FDH	N	↑	N,Sl ↑	N	Autosomal dominant inheritance
C Increased TBPA binding	N	↑	N	N	Increased concentration (islet-cell tumor) or affinity
D Anti-T_4 antibody	N	↑	N	N	Anti-T_3 antibody may be present
II Pituitary and peripheral thyroid hormone resistance	↑	↑	↑	↑	If only pituitary resistant, patient thyrotoxic
III Various disorders					
A Sick euthyroid syndrome	↑	↑	↓	N,↓	Uncommon; poorly understood
B Acute psychiatric illness	↑	↑	N, ↑	N,↑	Remits without treatment in several weeks
C Hyperemesis gravidarum	↑	↑	N		Remits in several weeks
IV Drugs					
A Inhibitors of T_3-neogenesis					
1 X-ray contrast agents	↑	↑	↓	↑	Particularly ipodate and iopanoate
2 Propranolol	↑	↑	↓	N, ↑	Especially with large doses
3 Amiodarone	↑	↑	↓	↑	Increased TSH during first several months
B Heparin	↑		N	—	Requires only small intravenous doses
C Levothyroxine therapy	↑	↑	N	↓	Hyperthyroxinemia in about 50% of cases

NOTE: *FT_4 = free T_4 concentration; FT_4I = free T_4 index calculated from an in vitro T_3 uptake test; TSH = basal serum TSH concentration and response to TRH; N = normal; Sl = slightly.*

The *thyrotropin-releasing hormone (TRH) stimulation test* assesses the functional state of the TSH-secretory mechanism, and has diagnostic value in diverse circumstances. Following the intravenous injection of TRH in normal subjects, the serum TSH begins to increase at 10 min, reaches a maximum between 20 and 45 min, and then rapidly declines. The nature of the pituitary feedback mechanism is such that, when hypothalamic-pituitary function is normal, one would expect an increased response to TRH when the thyrotropic cell senses a deficiency of thyroid hormone, particularly T_3, and a decreased or absent response when there is thyroid hormone excess. Thus, except in the rare instances of pituitary resistance to thyroid hormone, in which responses are usually normal, thyrotoxicosis is invariably accompanied by a blunted or absent TSH response to TRH. Owing to extreme sensitivity of the TSH-secretory mechanism to feedback inhibition, diminished responses to TRH commonly occur in clinically euthyroid patients with autonomously functioning toxic adenomas or toxic multinodular goiters and possibly in some patients with euthyroid Graves' disease. In addition, responses to TRH are often decreased in elderly individuals, especially men. Despite these exceptions, a subnormal or absent response to TRH is an excellent confirmatory test for thyrotoxicosis. TRH tests are of lesser value in the diagnosis of hypothyroidism. Responses are increased in patients with primary hypothyroidism, but the magnitude of increase is generally proportional to the extent of increase in basal serum TSH. Some patients with pituitary hypothyroidism have subnormal responses, and some with TRH deficiency owing to hypothalamic disease have a near normal response, but these expected responses are not seen consistently. Further, in as many as one-fourth of patients with hypothyroidism due to hypothalamic-pituitary disease, basal serum TSH concentrations are normal or slightly elevated, and the response to TRH is exaggerated.

The *thyroid suppression test* is used to assess whether thyroid function is controlled by normal homeostatic mechanisms. Normally, exogenous thyroid hormone suppresses pituitary TSH secretion, resulting in a decrease in the RAIU. Since liothyronine is usually employed (100 µg daily for 10 days), the resulting decline in serum T_4, as well as in the RAIU, can serve as an index of suppression. A normal suppressive response is a decrease of the RAIU to less than half of the control value and a decline of the serum T_4 to low normal or subnormal values. An abnormal suppression test is always present in hyperthyroidism, irrespective of the underlying cause; this indicates either autonomy of thyroid function, the presence of an abnormal stimulator, or unremitting hypersecretion of TSH. A normal suppression test, on the other hand, is incompatible with and excludes a diagnosis of hyperthyroidism. An abnormal suppression test is not pathognomonic of hyperthyroidism, however, since it is seen after treatment of hyperthyroidism in Graves' disease, in about half of the euthyroid patients with the ophthalmopathy of Graves' disease, and in seemingly euthyroid patients in whom autonomous hyperfunctioning adenomas suppress the remainder of the gland.

Because of the risk of adverse effects of exogenous thyroid hormone in elderly patients and in those with cardiovascular disease, and since the TRH test is almost entirely devoid of undesirable side effects, the latter test has almost entirely supplanted the thyroid suppression test as an aid in the diagnosis of hyperthyroidism.

MISCELLANEOUS TESTS   Various tests that do not assess thyroid function are of value in defining the nature of the thyroid disorder or in planning therapy. For example, high titers of *antimicrosomal antibodies* or *antithyroglobulin antibodies* are found in the serum of most adults with Hashimoto's disease and in many patients with primary thyroprivic hypothyroidism or Graves' disease. In the latter, the serum also contains antibodies aginst the TSH receptor in the thyroid plasma membrane. In general, these are capable of inhibiting the receptor binding of TSH (TSH-binding inhibitory immunoglobulins, TBII) and of stimulating the production of cyclic AMP therein (thyroid-stimulating immunoglobulins, TSI). The clinical utility of tests for TBII and TSI stems from the fact that the disappearance of

the factors from the serum during a course of antithyroid therapy implies the likelihood of a long-term remission of hyperthyroidism when therapy is withdrawn. In some patients, analogous antibodies have no intrinsic stimulatory effect but block the response to endogenous TSH and produce nongoitrous hypothyroidism. Both stimulatory and blocking anti-TSH receptor antibodies have the ability to cross the placenta and, as a consequence, to produce transient hyperthyroidism (neonatal Graves' disease) or hypothyroidism, respectively, in the newborn.

Some patients, most commonly those with autoimmune thyroid disease, develop *circulating antibodies against T_3 or T_4*, or both. In radioimmunoassays for these hormones, because the endogenous antibody competes with the exogenous antibody for binding of the added labeled ligand, spurious values for the concentration of the hormone are obtained. These may be grossly elevated or greatly depressed, depending on the technique of radioimmunoassay used. The true concentration of the hormone, as determined in extracts of the serum, is increased owing to the additional binding sites provided by the antibody, but antibody-bound hormone is unavailable for metabolic action. In the case of anti-T_3 antibodies, which are the more common, values of the RT_3U are low because endogenous antibody competes with the resin for binding of the added labeled T_3. Such antibodies can be detected by adding labeled hormone to serum, separating the immunoglobulins from other serum proteins by any of several techniques, and demonstrating that they bind the labeled hormone.

Along with several other thyroid disorders, differentiated carcinomas of the thyroid release thyroglobulin into the bloodstream. As a consequence, measurements of the *serum thyroglobulin concentration* by radioimmunoassay have value not in the initial diagnosis of thyroid carcinoma but in assessing the adequacy of initial therapy and in monitoring for recurrence or dissemination of the disease. In patients with thyrotoxicosis, subnormal serum thyroglobulin concentrations together with decreased values of the RAIU suggest the presence of thyrotoxicosis factitia.

Imaging by *scintiscanning* permits localization of sites of accumulation of radioiodine or sodium [^{99m}Tc]pertechnetate. This technique is useful for defining areas of increased or decreased function within the thyroid and for detecting retrosternal goiter, ectopic thyroid tissue, hemiagenesis of the thyroid, and functioning metastases of thyroid carcinoma. Ultrasonic examination of the thyroid is also a valuable technique for differentiating cystic nodules from those that are solid. Since ultrasonic scans provide an accurate indication of size, are noninvasive, and apparently have no injurious effects, sequential scans can be employed to assess changes in the size of the thyroid as a whole or of discrete nodules over time or in response to treatment.

SICK EUTHYROID SYNDROME

Severe illness, physical trauma, or physiologic stress can induce changes in one or more aspects of thyroid hormone economy, leading to findings referred to as the sick euthyroid syndrome (SES). Abnormalities in SES include alterations in the peripheral transport and metabolism of the thyroid hormones; the regulation of TSH secretion; and in some cases changes in thyroid function itself. Acting alone or together, these lead to changes in the concentrations of the circulating thyroid hormones, both total and free, that serve to define the several variants of the SES. Because of the frequency of illness in the general population and the nonspecificity of the disorders that cause it, SES is probably a more common cause of abnormalities in the concentration of thyroid hormones in the blood than intrinsic thyroid disease.

NORMAL T_4 VARIANT OF SES   Decreased production of T_3 owing to inhibition of the peripheral 5'-monodeiodination of T_4 is a consistent feature of the SES. This is reflected in a decrease in the serum total

T_3 concentration that varies in severity with that of the illness. In moderately ill patients, serum total T_4 concentration is within the normal range. A decrease in the intensity of protein binding, greater for T_4 than T_3, is an additional accompaniment. As a result, values of the RT_3U are moderately increased, and the percent FT_4 is increased to a proportionately greater extent. As a consequence, values of the free T_4 index (FT_4I) and those of the free T_4 concentrations (FT_4) are often increased. Serum rT_3 concentrations are increased, owing to a decrease in the plasma clearance of rT_3 secondary to inhibition of its 5'-monodeiodination. The plasma clearance rate of T_4 is increased, probably as a result of decreased T_4 binding, and this, in the face of normal T_4 concentrations, indicates that the overall rate of T_4 degradation and production is increased. Production rates for T_3 are decreased, and those for rT_3 are normal. Serum TSH concentration and the response of serum TSH to TRH are generally normal, though they may increase to supranormal values and then return to normal as recovery from the illness takes place. Despite the reduction in the serum T_3 concentration, this variant of the SES can be separated from intrinsic thyroid disease because the serum T_4 and TSH are normal and because the serum T_3 is not useful for diagnosing hypothyroidism in any event.

LOW T_4 VARIANT OF SES In more seriously ill patients, T_3 production rates and serum total and free T_3 concentrations decrease still further, and abnormalities in hormone binding increase in severity. As a consequence, serum T_4 concentrations decrease into the hypothyroid range, sometimes markedly so. This is partly but not entirely due to decreased T_4 binding since values of the FT_4 are frequently subnormal. These are probably the result of decreased T_4 production that occurs in the most severely ill patients. Decreased production of T_4 appears to be secondary to decreased secretion of TSH. Serum TSH concentrations appear normal by conventional assay but are low with sensitive TSH assays, and TRH responses may be blunted. Hence, in this variant of the SES, there is an inappropriate hyposecretion of TSH, considering the low serum total and free T_4 and T_3 concentrations; its cause is unknown, but a diagnosis of organic pituitary hypothyroidism may be suggested. Production rates for rT_3 are diminished, owing to the decreased availability of its precursor T_4; nonetheless, serum rT_3 concentrations are increased, owing to retardation of its degradation, and this provides an important means of differentiating the SES from pituitary hypothyroidism, in which serum rT_3 concentrations are low. In patients with primary hypothyroidism who have associated illness, serum TSH concentrations remain elevated, though their concentrations are generally lower than they otherwise would be.

HIGH T_4 VARIANT OF SES An unusual variant of the SES (approximately 1 percent of sick patients) is associated with increased serum total and free T_4 concentrations during acute illness and return to normal thereafter. This variant is most often seen in elderly women, many of whom have received medications that contain iodine. The principal source of diagnostic confusion is with the syndrome of "T_4 toxicosis," i.e., illness superimposed on true thyrotoxicosis, so that serum T_4 concentrations are increased and serum T_3 concentrations are normal. In the latter, however, serum rT_3 concentrations are higher, values of the serum total T_3 and FT_3I are higher, and TRH responses are blunted.

ABNORMALITIES IN HORMONE BINDING IN SES Multiple factors are responsible for the decreased binding of T_4 and, to a lesser extent, T_3 that occurs in the SES. Illness is associated with decreased synthesis of TBPA and a decrease in its serum concentration, but the extent to which this contributes to decreased T_4 binding is uncertain. In chronically ill patients, serum TBG concentration is subnormal. When present, this undoubtedly is a contributory factor. Most often, however, the extent of decreased T_4 binding cannot be explained by decreases in serum TBPA and TBG, and an inhibitor of hormone binding may be responsible. Its nature is uncertain, but it may be

one or more fatty acids, which may also be responsible for diminished conversion of T_4 to T_3.

The importance of the SES is that the changes in circulating thyroid hormone concentrations that result should not be confused with those due to intrinsic thyroid or pituitary disease. Unresolved questions are whether the metabolic impact of thyroid hormone in peripheral tissues is decreased in the SES, whether the syndrome is a beneficial or adverse response to illness, and whether some patients would benefit from treatment with thyroid hormones.

SIMPLE (NONTOXIC) GOITER

Endemic goiter implies an etiologic factor or factors common to a particular geographic region. The term has been defined as the presence of generalized or localized thyroid enlargement in more than 10 percent of the population. The connotation of *sporadic* goiter is that goiter arises in nonendemic areas as a result of a stimulus that does not affect the population generally. Since these terms fail to define or distinguish the causes of such goiters and since thyroid enlargement of diverse etiology may exist in both endemic and nonendemic regions, it is prudent to employ a general term such as *simple* or *nontoxic goiter*. This all-inclusive category can be further subdivided into specific etiologic groups as defined by objective procedures. Simple or nontoxic goiter can be defined as any enlargement of the thyroid gland that does not result from an inflammatory or neoplastic process and that is not initially associated with thyrotoxicosis or myxedema.

ETIOLOGY AND PATHOGENESIS Simple goiter is sometimes due to a definable cause of impaired thyroid hormone synthesis, such as iodine deficiency, ingestion of a goitrogen, or a demonstrable defect in a hormone biosynthetic pathway, but in most instances its cause cannot be determined. Whatever the cause, however, the clinical manifestations are thought to reflect the operation of a common pathophysiologic mechanism. Simple goiter occurs when one or more factors impair the capacity of the thyroid gland to secrete quantities of active hormones sufficient to meet the needs of the peripheral tissues. Although this has been presumed to lead to increased secretion of TSH, concentrations of TSH in the serum of patients with established simple goiter are usually normal. Hence, some other mechanism of goitrogenesis may be operative. A likely possibility is that depletion of glandular organic iodine accompanying impaired hormone synthesis increases the responsiveness of thyroid structure and function to levels of TSH that remain within the normal range. The resulting increases in both functioning thyroid mass and cellular activity overcome mild impairment of hormone synthesis; thus, the patient is metabolically normal, though goitrous. When the underlying disorder is severe, compensatory responses, now including hypersecretion of TSH, are inadequate to overcome the impairment, and the patient is both goitrous and hypothyroid. Thus, simple goiter cannot be clearly separated in the pathogenetic sense from goitrous hypothyroidism. Specific causes of simple goiter may exist with or without hypothyroidism (Table 324-5). Defective iodination of thyroglobulin may be an important pathogenetic factor in many patients. The concept that goiter can be due to antibodies that stimulate thyroid growth but not function remains to be fully evaluated.

PATHOLOGY The histopathology of the thyroid in simple goiter varies with the severity of the etiologic factor and the stage at which the examination is made. In its initial stages, the gland exhibits a uniform hypertrophy, hyperplasia, and hypervascularity. As the disorder persists or undergoes repeated exacerbations and remissions, uniformity of thyroidal architecture is lost. Occasionally, the greater part of the gland may display a reasonably uniform degree of involution or hyperinvolution with colloid accumulation. More often such areas are interspersed with patchy areas of focal hyperplasia. Fibrosis may demarcate hyperplastic or involuted nodules. These may resemble true neoplasms (adenomas). Areas of hemorrhage and irregular calcification may be present. The evolution of the multinodular stage is almost always accompanied by the development of functional autonomy. Indeed, heterogeneity of structure and function and a greater or lesser degree of functional autonomy are the hallmarks of the mature stage of this disorder. As a result, hyperthyroidism may ensue spontaneously (toxic multinodular goiter) or be induced by large quantities of iodine (jodbasedow phenomenon).

CLINICAL MANIFESTATIONS In simple goiter the clinical manifestations arise solely from enlargement of the thyroid since the metabolic state is normal. In goitrous hypothyroidism, symptoms caused by thyromegaly are accompanied by signs and symptoms of hormonal insufficiency. Mechanical sequelae include compression and displacement of the trachea or esophagus, occasionally with obstructive symptoms if the goiter becomes sufficiently large. Superior mediastinal obstruction may occur with large retrosternal goiters. Signs of compression can be induced in the case of large retrosternal goiters when the patient's arms are raised above the head (Pemberton's sign); suffusion of the face, giddiness, or syncope may result from this maneuver. Compression of the recurrent laryngeal nerve leading to hoarseness is rare in simple goiter and suggests neoplasm. Sudden hemorrhage into a nodule may lead to an acute, painful swelling in the neck and may produce or enhance compressive symptoms. Hyperthyroidism may supervene in long-standing multinodular goiter (toxic multinodular goiter). In both endemic and sporadic multinodular goiter, the ingestion of excess iodide may result in the development of thyrotoxicosis (jodbasedow phenomenon).

In geographic regions where iodine deficiency is severe, goitrous enlargement may also be associated with varying degrees of hypothyroidism. Cretinism, both goitrous and nongoitrous, occurs with increased frequency in the children of goitrous parents in many countries where goiter is common. Although iodine deficiency is doubtless a necessary factor in the etiology of endemic goiter, the frequency of goiter may differ greatly among areas of equally severe iodine deficiency. In such instances, dietary or waterborne goitrogens appear to be important conditioning factors. In some areas, these goitrogens may be sufficient to cause goiter in the absence of iodine deficiency.

DIAGNOSIS The diagnosis of simple goiter requires, first, demonstration of a euthyroid state and, second, demonstration of normal serum T_4 and T_3 concentrations. The former may be difficult because manifestations of thyrotoxicosis may be subtle or atypical, especially among the elderly (see section on "Toxic Multinodular Goiter"). The latter may be problematic, since serum T_4 and especially T_3 concentrations may be near the upper limit of the normal range. In addition, the fact that serum T_3 concentrations decrease in the euthyroid elderly complicates interpretation of this test. The RAIU is usually normal but may be increased in the presence of iodine deficiency or

a biosynthetic defect. Exclusion of thyrotoxicosis is further complicated by the significant functional autonomy and consequent decrease in response to TRH that often accompany long-standing multinodular goiter. Differentiation of nontoxic goiter from Hashimoto's disease is facilitated by the greater frequency of multinodularity in the former and by the presence of high titers of circulating antimicrosomal or antithyroglobulin antibodies in the latter. In some instances, emergence of a strongly dominant nodule may suggest the presence of a carcinoma. This is especially true if bleeding has caused it to increase in size rapidly and to lose the ability to accumulate iodine or pertechnetate.

TREATMENT The object of treatment is to reduce the size of the goiter, either by relieving external encumbrances to hormone formation or by providing sufficient quantities of exogenous hormone to inhibit TSH secretion and thereby put the thyroid gland almost completely at rest. In disorders characterized by decreased thyroid iodide stores, such as iodine deficiency or impairment of the thyroid iodide-concentrating mechanism, small doses of iodide may prove effective. Occasionally, a known extrinsic goitrogen can be withdrawn. Most commonly, however, no specific etiologic factor can be detected, and suppressive thyroid therapy is required. For this purpose, sodium L-thyroxine (levothyroxine) is the agent of choice. In the younger patient with the early diffuse stage of simple goiter, treatment can be instituted with 100 μg of levothyroxine daily, and the dose is increased over the next month or so to a maximum of 150 or 200 μg daily. Adequacy of suppression can be assessed by measuring the RAIU, which should decrease to less than 5 percent of the administered dose at 24 h. Lesser decreases indicate only partial suppression, reflecting the presence of autonomous foci demonstrable by scanning techniques. In the elderly patient or the patient with long-standing multinodular goiter, a TRH stimulation test should be undertaken before initiating treatment with levothyroxine to determine whether or not significant functional autonomy is present. If such is indicated by diminished or absent TSH responsiveness to TRH, suppressive therapy with levothyroxine is contraindicated since such patients are or will eventually become thyrotoxic. Rather, consideration should be given to radioiodine ablation of the autonomous foci (see later section on "Toxic Multinodular Goiter"). On the other hand, if the TSH response to TRH is normal, excluding significant functional autonomy, treatment with levothyroxine can be initiated. In the elderly patient, the initial dose should not exceed 50 μg daily, and the dosage should be gradually increased, partial rather than complete suppression of the value for the RAIU being the end point. It is the practice to obtain a thyroid scan as part of the initial evaluation of all patients with multinodular goiter and to repeat the RAIU and scan (suppression scan), when practical, in all patients receiving suppressive thyroid hormone therapy.

Reported results of therapy vary widely. There is general agreement that the early diffuse, hyperplastic goiter responds well, with regression or disappearance in 3 to 6 months. In the author's experience, the later, nodular stage responds less favorably, and significant reduction in gland size is achieved only in about one-third of the cases; however, in the remainder, suppressive treatment may forestall further glandular growth. Internodular tissue regresses more often than do nodules themselves. The latter may therefore become more prominent during treatment. After maximum regression of the goiter, suppressive medication may be maintained for prolonged periods, reduced to minimal levels, or at times withdrawn. In an unpredictable manner, goiter in some cases remains relieved while in others it recurs. In the latter instances, suppressive therapy should be reinstituted and continued indefinitely.

In areas of endemic iodine deficiency, the size and prevalence of goiter and the frequency of cretinism can be reduced by the provision of iodized salt or water or the periodic injection of iodized oil.

Surgical therapy of simple goiter is physiologically unsound, but it may occasionally be necessary to relieve obstructive symptoms,

---

TABLE 324-5 Classification of the causes of hypothyroidism

I Thyroid
  A Thyroprivic
    1 Congenital development defect
    2 Primary idiopathic
    3 Postablative (radioiodine, surgery)
    4 Postradiation (lymphoma)
  B Goitrous
    1 Heritable biosynthetic defects
    2 Maternally transmitted (iodides, antithyroid agents)
    3 Iodine deficiency
    4 Drug-elicited (p-aminosalicylic acid, iodides, phenylbutazone, iodoantipyrine, lithium)
    5 Chronic thyroiditis (Hashimoto's disease)
II Suprathyroid (trophoprivic)
  A Pituitary
  B Hypothalamic
III Self-limited
  A Following withdrawal of suppressive thyroid therapy
  B Subacute thyroiditis and chronic thyroiditis with transient hypothyroidism (usually after a phase of thyrotoxicosis)

especially those that persist after a conscientious trial of medical therapy. Surgical exploration of nodular goiter may be indicated in some individuals when evidence suggests carcinoma. However, the concept that subtotal resection of multinodular nontoxic goiter affords effective prophylaxis against the development of thyroid carcinoma is unsound. If for some reason subtotal thyroidectomy has been performed, levothyroxine in a usual dose of about 150 μg daily is recommended to inhibit regenerative hyperplasia and further goitrogenesis.

HYPOTHYROIDISM

Hypothyroidism can result from any of a variety of structural or functional abnormalities that lead to insufficient synthesis of thyroid hormone. Hypothyroidism dating from birth and resulting in developmental abnormalities is termed *cretinism*. The term *myxedema* connotes severe hypothyroidism in which there is accumulation of hydrophilic mucopolysaccharides in the ground substance of the dermis and other tissues, leading to thickening of the facial features and doughy induration of the skin.

ETIOLOGY AND PATHOGENESIS   A classification of the causes of hypothyroidism is presented in Table 324-5. Overall, the thyroid varieties account for approximately 95 percent of cases, only 5 percent or less being suprathyroid in origin. In thyroprivic hypothyroidism, loss of thyroid tissue leads to inadequate synthesis of thyroid hormone, despite maximum stimulation of any thyroid remnant by TSH. The most common cause of thyroprivic hypothyroidism is surgical or radioiodine ablation of the thyroid gland in the treatment of Graves' disease. Thyroprivic hypothyroidism may also occur as a primary idiopathic phenomenon. Primary hypothyroidism is frequently associated with circulating antithyroid antibodies and in some cases may result from the action of antibodies that block the TSH receptor. It may coexist with other diseases in which circulating autoantibodies are found. These diseases include pernicious anemia, systemic lupus erythematosus, rheumatoid arthritis, Sjögren's syndrome, and chronic hepatitis. In addition, hypothyroidism can be one manifestation of a polyglandular endocrine deficiency state in which autoantibodies cause variable insufficiency of thyroid, adrenal, parathyroid, and gonadal function (see Chap. 334). All these diseases, including isolated primary hypothyroidism, are associated with an increased frequency of specific HLA haplotypes and may be diverse reflections of disordered immune regulation. Finally, a developmental defect may result in failure of the gland to function adequately, leading to sporadic nongoitrous cretinism or juvenile hypothyroidism. A self-limited period of hypothyroidism is common in the course of subacute thyroiditis and in the syndrome of ''painless thyroiditis,'' usually after a temporary period of thyrotoxicosis. Owing to a persisting lack of TSH stimulation, intrinsically euthyroid patients from whom chronic suppressive therapy is abruptly withdrawn experience a several-week period of thyroid hypofunction.

Impairment in the ability to synthesize adequate quantities of thyroid hormone leads to hypersecretion of TSH and hence goiter. If this compensatory response is inadequate, goitrous hypothyroidism ensues. The commonest cause of goitrous hypothyroidism in North America is Hashimoto's disease, in which defective organic binding of iodide and abnormal secretion of iodoproteins are frequent abnormalities. Iodide-induced goiter with or without hypothyroidism appears to arise from an intrinsic defect in the organic binding mechanism, which permits a persistent Wolff-Chaikoff effect. Patients with Graves' disease, especially after radioiodine treatment, those with Hashimoto's disease, and the normal fetus are particularly susceptible to iodide-induced goiter. In view of the susceptibility of the fetal thyroid to iodide, with resulting goiter and hypothyroidism, iodine in large doses should not be given during pregnancy. Less common causes of goitrous hypothyroidism are hereditary defects in hormone biosynthesis and ingestion of drugs that induce defects in

hormone biosynthesis, such as *p*-aminosalicylic acid and lithium carbonate. Finally, in areas of environmental iodine deficiency, goitrous cretinism and hypothyroidism can occur on an endemic basis. Diminished thyroid reserve occurs as a stage in the evolution of both thyroprivic and goitrous hypothyroidism.

In hypothyroidism of suprathyroid origin, the thyroid is intrinsically normal but is deprived of stimulation by TSH. Deprivation of TSH, most commonly the result of postpartum pituitary necrosis or a tumor of the pituitary or adjacent regions, results in pituitary hypothyroidism. Hypothalamic hypothyroidism is less common and results from inadequate secretion of TRH.

CLINICAL PICTURE   The appearance of children with hypothyroidism depends on the age at which the deficiency began and the promptness with which replacement therapy was instituted. Cretinism may be manifested at birth but usually becomes evident within the first several months, depending upon the extent of thyroid failure. Hypothyroidism is present in approximately 1 of every 5000 neonates and manifests itself in abnormally long persistence of physiologic jaundice, hoarse cry, constipation, somnolence, and feeding problems; all neonates should be screened for hypothyroidism with measurements of the serum T_4 or TSH, since clinical diagnosis is difficult and early treatment is crucial for normal intellectual development. In later months, delay in reaching the normal milestones of development becomes evident, and the physical characteristics of the cretin appear. These include short stature, coarse features with protruding tongue, broad flat nose, widely set eyes, sparse hair, dry skin, protuberant abdomen with an umbilical hernia, and impaired mental development. X-ray examination reveals retarded bone age, epiphyseal dysgenesis, and delayed dentition.

In the older child, the clinical manifestations of hypothyroidism are intermediate between those of infantile and adult hypothyroidism. Retardation of linear growth is manifested by shortness of stature, and retardation of sexual maturation results in delay in the onset of puberty. Poor performance at school may call attention to the diagnosis. The manifestations of adult hypothyroidism are present to a variable degree. X-ray examination reveals delayed union of the epiphyses.

In the adult, early symptoms of hypothyroidism are nonspecific and of insidious onset. They may include lethargy, constipation, cold intolerance, stiffness and cramping of the muscles, the carpal tunnel syndrome, and menorrhagia. Over the succeeding months, intellectual and motor activity slows, appetite declines, and weight increases. The hair becomes dry and tends to fall out, and the skin becomes dry. The voice becomes deeper and hoarse, and auditory acuity may deteriorate. Obstructive sleep apnea may occur. Ultimately, the clinical picture of florid myxedema appears, with dull expressionless face, sparse hair, periorbital puffiness, large tongue, and pale, cool skin that feels rough and doughy. Thyroid tissue is not readily palpable, except in the goitrous variety of hypothyroidism. The heart is enlarged owing to both dilation and pericardial effusion; if the heart is small, pituitary hypothyroidism should be considered. Adynamic ileus may occur, producing megacolon or intestinal obstruction. Rarely, psychiatric symptoms or cerebellar ataxia may dominate the clinical picture. The relaxation phase of the deep tendon reflexes is characteristically prolonged, the so-called hung-up reflex. If left untreated, the patient with severe long-standing hypothyroidism may pass into a hypothermic, stuporous state (*myxedema coma*) that is frequently fatal. Respiratory depression is an important component of this state, and hence arterial P_{CO_2} may be increased. Factors that predispose to myxedema coma include cold exposure, trauma, infection, and administration of central nervous system depressants. Dilutional hyponatremia is common and results from impaired water excretion and from disordered regulation of vasopressin secretion.

LABORATORY TESTS   A decrease in serum T_4 and in the FT_4I is common to all varieties of hypothyroidism. In the thyroid varieties, the serum T_3 may be decreased to a lesser extent than is the serum T_4, the presumption being that the compensatory hypersecretion of

TSH leads to a relative preponderance of T_3 secretion. In thyroprivic hypothyroidism the decreased RAIU is of limited diagnostic utility because of the low value for the lower limit of the normal range. In goitrous hypothyroidism, the RAIU may be increased or display an abnormal pattern of accumulation or retention. The serum TSH is invariably increased in the thyroprivic and goitrous varieties and is usually normal or undetectable in pituitary or hypothalamic hypothyroidism. In the latter instances, hyposecretion of TSH is usually accompanied by hyposecretion of other pituitary hormones (see Chap. 321). A subnormal response of the serum TSH to the administration of TRH confirms the presence of pituitary hypothyroidism.

Frequent manifestations of the hypothyroid state include an increased serum cholesterol in hypothyroidism of thyroid (but not pituitary) origin and increased concentrations in serum of creatine phosphokinase (MM variant), aspartate transaminase, and lactic dehydrogenase. Systolic time intervals are altered in that the pre-ejection period is distinctly prolonged and the ratio of the preejection period to left ventricular ejection time is increased. Electrocardiographic changes include bradycardia, low amplitude QRS complexes, and flattened or inverted T waves. In primary thyroprivic hypothyroidism, overt pernicious anemia occurs in about 12 percent of patients; histamine-fast achlorhydria and circulating antigastric parietal cell antibodies are even more common.

In addition to patients who are clinically hypothyroid, some patients who appear clinically euthyroid display laboratory evidence of early thyroid failure (subclinical hypothyroidism). In mild cases serum TSH and its response to TRH administration are increased while serum T_4 and T_3 concentrations are normal. When there is a greater degree of thyroid failure, serum T_4 concentration is decreased, but the serum T_3 concentration is normal or nearly so owing to TSH-induced hypersecretion of T_3 relative to T_4, and perhaps to more efficient conversion of T_4 to T_3. Subclinical hypothyroidism is most often seen in patients with Hashimoto's disease or those with Graves' disease who have been treated with ^{131}I or surgery and are usually stages in the evolution of frank hypothyroidism.

DIFFERENTIAL DIAGNOSIS   Little difficulty will be experienced in diagnosing the classic picture of cretinism or juvenile and adult hypothyroidism. Occasionally, an infant with Down's syndrome may be confused with a cretin. However, the characteristic mongoloid eyes, Brushfield's spots in the iris, hyperextensibility of the joints, and normal skin and hair texture distinguish Down's syndrome from hypothyroid cretinism. Chronic nephritis and the nephrotic syndrome may simulate myxedema, particularly because of the facial puffiness and pallor. The nephrotic patient may also have anemia, hypercholesterolemia, and anasarca. In addition, the serum T_4 concentration may be decreased if there is significant loss of TBG into the urine, but the FT_4I is normal or increased. The serum T_3 concentration is often subnormal, as it might be in any severe systemic illness, owing to impaired peripheral generation from T_4, but the serum TSH concentration is not increased.

TREATMENT   Two types of hormone are available for the treatment of hypothyroidism, synthetic hormone and thyroprotein derived from animal thyroids (Table 324-6). Synthetic hormones include L-thyroxine (levothyroxine), L-triiodothyronine (liothyronine), and a combination of the two (liotrix). The preparation of natural origin most commonly used is thyroid extract, USP. Because of their uniform

TABLE 324-6 Approximate therapeutic equivalence of various thyroid hormone preparations

Preparation	Average daily oral maintenance dose	Serum T_4
Thyroid extract, USP	120–180 mg	Normal
Levothyroxine	150 μg	Normal or slightly increased
Liothyronine	50 μg	Decreased
Liotrix (T_4: T_3 = 4:1)	2 units	Normal

potency, the author prefers the synthetic preparations and specifically levothyroxine. Unlike liothyronine, liotrix, and even thyroid extract, ingestion of levothyroxine does not lead to abrupt increases in serum T_3 concentration, which could be dangerous in the older patient or in the patient with coexisting heart disease. Rather, a stable T_3 concentration is attained through continuous generation from administered T_4.

In most instances, a normal metabolic state should be restored gradually, especially in the elderly or the patient with heart disease, since sudden increases in metabolic rate may tax cardiac or coronary reserve. In adults, an initial daily dose of 25 μg levothyroxine can be increased by 25- to 50-μg increments at 2- to 3-week intervals, until a normal metabolic state is attained. The dose necessary to sustain a normal metabolic state is usually about 150 μg per day, and this usually results in a serum T_4 at or somewhat above the upper limit of the normal range. The serum T_3 is superior to the serum T_4 as an indicator of the metabolic state in the patient receiving levothyroxine. Because of its long half-life, levothyroxine is generally administered as a single daily dose. The optimum dose for the individual patient should be based on clinical criteria and on measurements of serum TSH or T_3 concentration. Elevations of the former indicate that treatment is insufficient and of the latter that it is excessive.

In neonatal, infantile, and juvenile hypothyroidism it is essential that full replacement therapy be begun as soon as possible; otherwise the chances of normal intellectual development and growth are poor. Infants and children require doses of levothyroxine that are disproportionately large in relation to body size. *In known or strongly suspected pituitary and hypothalamic hypothyroidism, thyroid replacement should not be instituted until treatment with hydrocortisone has been initiated*, since acute adrenocortical insufficiency may be precipitated by an increase in metabolic rate.

In some patients, hypothyroidism should be treated rapidly. This includes patients with myxedema coma and, because of the extreme sensitivity to central nervous system depressants, hypothyroid patients being prepared for emergency surgery. Here, intravenous administration of levothyroxine, in conjunction with the use of hydrocortisone, is indicated.

THYROTOXICOSIS

The term *thyrotoxicosis* denotes the clinical, physiologic, and biochemical findings that result when the tissues are exposed to, and respond to, an excess supply of active thyroid hormone. Rather than a specific disease, thyrotoxicosis is a syndrome that can originate in a variety of ways. In general, three main categories of disorder can produce the thyrotoxic state (Table 324-7). The first, and most important, encompasses those diseases that lead to sustained overproduction of hormone by the thyroid gland itself. Here, hyperfunction

TABLE 324-7 Varieties of thyrotoxicosis

I Disorders associated with thyroid hyperfunction*
  A Excess production of TSH (rare)
  B Abnormal thyroid stimulator
    1 Graves' disease
    2 Trophoblastic tumor
  C Intrinsic thyroid autonomy
    1 Hyperfunctioning adenoma
    2 Toxic multinodular goiter
II Disorders not associated with thyroid hyperfunction†
  A Disorders of hormone storage
    1 Subacute thyroiditis
    2 Chronic thyroiditis with transient thyrotoxicosis
  B Extrathyroid source of hormone
    1 Thyrotoxicosis factitia
    2 Ectopic thyroid tissue
      a Struma ovarii
      b Functioning follicular cacinoma

---

* *Associated with increased RAIU unless body iodine burden is excessive.*
† *Associated with decreased RAIU.*

of the gland variously results from excessive secretion of TSH, a rare cause associated with pituitary tumor or with resistance to thyroid hormone or the pituitary but not in peripheral tissues; the action of an abnormal, homeostatically unregulated thyroid stimulator of extrapituitary origin, as in patients with Graves' disease, patients who develop hyperthyroidism in association with Hashimoto's disease, or patients with trophoblastic tumors; or the development of one or more areas of autonomous hyperfunction within the gland itself. The second category encompasses the thyrotoxic states associated with subacute thyroiditis and the syndrome termed *chronic thyroiditis with spontaneously resolving thyrotoxicosis;* an excess of preformed hormone leaks from the gland owing to the presence of inflammatory disease. New hormone formation is decreased, however, owing to the suppression of TSH secretion by the hormone excess, and in some cases to the inflammatory injury itself. Since the inflammatory disorders are transitory and since stores of preformed hormone are ultimately depleted, the thyrotoxicosis in these disorders is self-limited and is often followed by a transient period of thyroid hormone insufficiency. The third category of thyrotoxic state is one in which the source of excess hormone is outside of the thyroid gland itself, as in thyrotoxicosis factitia, the rare functioning metastatic thyroid carcinoma, or struma ovarii.

Although all of the foregoing disorders are associated with thyrotoxicosis, not all are associated with hyperthyroidism, a term which should be used to denote only those conditions in which sustained hyperfunction of the thyroid leads to thyrotoxicosis. Thus, thyrotoxic states can be classified according to whether or not they are associated with hyperthyroidism. This distinction has practical implications for diagnosis and for treatment. In hyperthyroidism, hyperfunction of the thyroid is reflected in an increased RAIU, whereas in the nonhyperthyroid thyrotoxic states, thyroid function (as reflected in the RAIU) is subnormal. Further, treatment of thyrotoxicosis by means intended to decrease hormone synthesis (antithyroid agents, surgery, or radioiodine) is appropriate in hyperthyroidism but is inappropriate and ineffective in other forms of thyrotoxicosis.

Though the specific diseases that cause thyrotoxicosis each make their own imprint on the clinical picture, the manifestations of the thyrotoxic state are largely the same. In the discussion that ensues, the major diseases that lead to a thyrotoxic state are individually described. Since the first considered and most important is Graves' disease, the common manifestations of thyrotoxicosis are described in relation to Graves' disease.

GRAVES' DISEASE

Graves' disease, also known as Parry's or Basedow's disease, is a disorder of unknown etiology with a triad of major manifestations: hyperthyroidism with diffuse goiter, ophthalmopathy, and dermopathy. Although part of the same disease complex, the three major manifestations need not appear together. Indeed, one or two need never appear, and moreover, the three tend to run courses that are largely independent of one another.

PREVALENCE Graves' disease is a relatively common disorder that occurs at any age but is especially common in the third and fourth decades. The disease is more frequent in women than in men. In nongoitrous areas the ratio of predominance in women may be as high as 7:1. In areas of endemic goiter the ratio is lower. Genetic factors play an important role; there is an increased frequency of haplotypes HLA-B8 and DRw3 in Caucasian, HLA-Bw36 in Japanese, and HLA-Bw46 in Chinese patients with the disease. Not surprisingly, there is a distinct familial predisposition to Graves' disease. In addition, among family members of patients with Graves' disease, a clinical and immunologic overlap exists with respect to Hashimoto's disease, primary thyroprivic hypothyroidism, and pernicious anemia and probably with respect to other diseases in which autoimmune

features are prominent. In occasional patients, the disease picture may change from Graves' disease to Hashimoto's disease, or vice versa, and rarely patients with primary myxedema later become hyperthyroid. Thus, it is proper to consider Graves' disease, Hashimoto's disease, and primary myxedema as closely related autoimmune thyroid diseases.

ETIOLOGY AND PATHOGENESIS The cause is unknown. In view of the varied manifestations of Graves' disease and their differing courses, it is possible that no single factor is responsible for the entire syndrome. With respect to hyperthyroidism, the central disorder is a disruption of homeostatic mechanisms that normally adjust hormone secretion to meet the needs of peripheral tissues; if such were able to operate, hyperthyroidism could not be sustained. This homeostatic disruption results from the presence in plasma of an abnormal thyroid stimulator. The existence of such was first recognized when it was shown that the serums of patients with Graves' disease release radioiodine from the prelabeled guinea pig or mouse thyroid. In view of its prolonged duration of action relative to that of TSH in this bioassay system, this material was designated the long-acting thyroid stimulator (LATS). LATS activity is present in one or more immunoglobulins of the class IgG elaborated by lymphocytes of patients with Graves' disease. It soon became apparent, however, that LATS could be detected only in about half of patients with this disorder, and consequently its pathogenetic role was questioned. This failure to detect LATS in all patients with Graves' disease is due to the fact that the stimulator has variable actions in other species and is not uniformly detectable, therefore, in the conventional bioassay. When human thyroid tissue is used as the assay system, however, one or more in vitro responses can be demonstrated in the plasma of most patients. These responses and the corresponding names given to the responsible factors are as follows: prevention of the adsorption of LATS activity by human thyroid particulate fractions (LATS-protector, LATS-p), stimulation of colloid droplet or cyclic AMP generation in thyroid cells, slices, or membranes (thyroid-stimulating immunoglobulins, TSI), and inhibition of the binding of TSH to its receptors in human thyroid tissue (TSH-binding inhibitory immunoglobulins, TBII). The underlying nature of these factors, their number, and their relationship to one another are uncertain, but they are probably antibodies against the thyroid TSH receptor. Activities of this type are also found in serums of some patients with euthyroid ophthalmic Graves' disease, an occasional patient with Hashimoto's disease, and some euthyroid relatives of patients with Graves' disease, though the reason for the absence of thyrotoxicosis in such instances is uncertain. Disappearance of these stimulatory factors from the serum during antithyroid treatment augurs well for long-term remission after treatment is withdrawn. Thus, while the basic cause of Graves' disease is not understood, an immunoglobulin or family of immunoglobulins directed against the TSH receptor mediates the thyroid stimulation of Graves' disease. A heritable abnormality in immune surveillance may permit particular lymphocytes to survive, proliferate, and secrete the stimulatory immunoglobulins in response to some precipitating factors.

The pathogenesis of the ophthalmic component of Graves' disease is even more enigmatic. One proposed mechanism is the development of antibodies against the extraocular muscles. A second postulate invokes lymphatic transport of thyroglobulin from the thyroid to orbital tissues, at which site an immune response is evoked. Nothing is known of the pathogenesis of the dermopathy of Graves' disease.

PATHOLOGY In Graves' disease, the *thyroid gland* is diffusely enlarged, soft, and vascular. The essential pathology is that of parenchymatous hypertrophy and hyperplasia, characterized by increased height of the epithelium and redundancy of the follicular wall, giving the picture of papillary infoldings and cytologic evidence of increased activity. Such hyperplasia is usually accompanied by lymphocytic infiltration that reflects the immune aspect of the disease and that correlates in severity with levels of antithyroid antibodies in the blood. Following iodine medication, there is colloid storage, which sometimes causes enlargement and increased firmness of the gland. Graves' disease is associated with generalized lymphoid hyperplasia and infiltration and occasionally with enlargement of the spleen or thymus. Thyrotoxicosis may lead to degeneration of skeletal muscle fibers, enlargement of the heart, fatty infiltration or diffuse fibrosis of the liver, decalcification of the skeleton, and loss of body tissue (including fat deposits, osteoid, and muscle).

The *ophthalmopathy* of Graves' disease is characterized by an inflammatory infiltrate of the orbital contents, exclusive of the globe, with lymphocytes, mast cells, and plasma cells being the predominant cellular components. The orbital musculature is mainly involved and often is enlarged, largely accounting for the increased volume of the orbital contents that causes the globe to protrude. Muscle fibers show degeneration and loss of striations, with ultimate fibrosis.

The *dermopathy* of Graves' disease is characterized by thickening of the dermis, which is infiltrated with lymphocytes and with hydrophilic, metachromatically staining mucopolysaccharides.

CLINICAL MANIFESTATIONS The manifestations comprise those that reflect the associated thyrotoxicosis and those specifically related to Graves' disease. The former vary in intensity with the severity of the thyrotoxicosis, the age of the patient, and the presence of disease in other organs, such as the heart.

Manifestations of thyrotoxicosis Common manifestations include nervousness, emotional lability, inability to sleep, tremors, frequent bowel movements, excessive sweating, and heat intolerance. Weight loss is usual despite a well-maintained or increased appetite. Loss of strength is often manifested by difficulty in climbing stairs. In premenopausal women, oligomenorrhea and amenorrhea tend to occur. Dyspnea, palpitations, and, in patients over the age of 40, enhancement of angina pectoris or cardiac failure may occur. In general, nervous symptoms dominate the clinical picture in younger individuals, whereas cardiovascular and myopathic symptoms predominate in older subjects.

Usually, the patient appears anxious, restless, and fidgety. The skin is warm and moist with a velvety texture, and palmar erythema is present. Separation of the fingernail from the nailbed (Plummer's nail) is common, especially on the ring finger. The hair is fine and silky. A fine tremor of the fingers and tongue, together with hyperreflexia, is characteristic. *Ocular signs* include a characteristic stare with widened palpebral fissures, infrequent blinking, lid lag, and failure to wrinkle the brow on upward gaze. These signs result from sympathetic overstimulation and usually subside when the thyrotoxicosis is corrected. They are to be distinguished from the *infiltrative ophthalmopathy* characteristic of Graves' disease, discussed below.

Cardiovascular findings include a wide pulse pressure, sinus tachycardia, atrial arrhythmias (especially atrial fibrillation), systolic murmurs, increased intensity of the apical first sound, cardiac enlargement, and, at times, overt heart failure. A to-and-fro, high-pitched sound may be audible in the pulmonic area and may simulate a pericardial friction rub (Means-Lerman scratch).

Manifestations of Graves' disease The three distinctive manifestations of Graves' disease, diffuse hyperfunctioning goiter, ophthalmopathy, and dermopathy, appear in varying combinations and with varying frequency, goiter being the most common. Premature graying of the hair and patchy vitiligo are not specific to Graves' disease per se since they are also common in other autoimmune disorders, whether of the thyroid or other organ systems.

The *diffuse toxic goiter* may be asymmetric and lobular. The presence of a bruit over the gland usually signifies that the patient is thyrotoxic, but it may also rarely be present in other disorders in which the thyroid is markedly hyperplastic. Venous hums and carotid souffles should be distinguished from true thyroid bruits. An enlarged pyramidal lobe of the thyroid may be palpable.

The clinical signs associated with the *ophthalmopathy* of Graves'

disease may be divided into two components: the spastic and the mechanical. The former includes the stare, lid lag, and lid retraction that accompany thyrotoxicosis and account for the "frightened" facies and classic eye signs previously described. These findings need not be associated with proptosis and usually return to normal after correction of thyrotoxicosis. The mechanical component includes proptosis of varying degrees with ophthalmoplegia and congestive oculopathy characterized by chemosis, conjunctivitis, periorbital swelling, and the resultant complications of corneal ulceration, optic neuritis, and optic atrophy. When exophthalmos progresses rapidly and becomes the major concern in Graves' disease, it is usually referred to as *progressive,* and if severe, *malignant exophthalmos.* The term *exophthalmic ophthalmoplegia* refers to the ocular muscle weakness that commonly accompanies this disorder and results in strabismus with varying degrees of diplopia. Exophthalmos may be unilateral early in the course of the disorder but usually progresses to bilateral involvement.

The *dermopathy* of Graves' disease usually occurs over the dorsum of the legs or feet and is termed *localized* or *pretibial myxedema.* It occurs in patients with past or present Graves' disease and is not a manifestation of hypothyroidism. About half of cases occur during the active stage of thyrotoxicosis; in the remainder the lesions develop after treatment. The affected area is usually well demarcated from normal skin by the fact that it is raised, thickened, has a *peau d'orange* appearance, and may be pruritic and hyperpigmented. The lesions are usually discrete, assuming a plaquelike or nodular configuration but in some instances becoming confluent. Clubbing of the fingers and toes with characteristic bony changes that differ from those of hypertrophic pulmonary osteoarthropathy may accompany the dermal changes (*thyroid acropachy*). This disorder is usually self-limited.

DIAGNOSIS When severe, Graves' disease presents little difficulty in diagnosis. Florid thyrotoxicosis is manifested by weakness, weight loss despite good appetite, nervous instability, tremor, intolerance to heat, sweating, palpitations, and hyperdefecation. When associated with diffuse thyroid enlargement, often accompanied by a bruit, and particularly when associated with ophthalmopathy, the clinical picture of Graves' disease is virtually unique. In such instances, laboratory tests documenting increased RAIU, serum T_4 and T_3, RT_3U, and FT_4I serve as baselines for evaluation of therapy, rather than necessary diagnostic aids. Occasionally, laboratory tests reveal a normal RAIU, normal serum T_4 and RT_3U, and elevated serum T_3 and FT_3I (T_3 toxicosis).

In less severe cases, particularly when ophthalmopathy is lacking, the diagnosis may be more difficult, since the symptoms of mild thyrotoxicosis are similar to those of other disorders (see "Differential Diagnosis" below). Presence of a goiter makes the diagnosis of hyperthyroidism likely, but careful palpation is necessary to determine whether toxic multinodular goiter, toxic adenoma, or subacute thyroiditis is present, since treatment of these disorders may differ from that of diffuse toxic goiter. Absence of thyroid enlargement makes the diagnosis of Graves' disease unlikely but does not exclude it. In mild cases, confirmatory laboratory tests assume great importance. Unfortunately, mild thyrotoxicosis is often associated with marginal abnormalities in laboratory tests or values within the upper limit of the normal range. In such instances, the TRH stimulation test assumes crucial importance.

In a few patients, the clinical picture may be one of apathy rather than hyperactivity, and evidence of hypermetabolism may be slight. In such patients, myopathic features may be pronounced. More often, cardiovascular manifestations predominate since mild hyperthyroidism may produce severe disability in patients with underlying heart disease. Hence, *all patients with unexplained cardiac failure or irregularities in rhythm, especially if atrial in origin, should be examined for thyrotoxicosis.* Clues to the diagnosis include a relatively rapid circulation time and resistance to the usual doses of digitalis, but laboratory confirmation is required.

DIFFERENTIAL DIAGNOSIS Signs and symptoms in a number of nonthyroid disorders may simulate certain aspects of the thyrotoxic syndrome. Anxiety is a prominent feature of thyrotoxicosis, and there is thus some overlap in the symptomatology of thyrotoxicosis with that of anxiety states of emotional origin. Such symptoms as tachycardia, tremulousness, irritability, weakness, and fatigue are common to both disorders. In anxiety of emotional origin, however, the peripheral manifestations of excessive thyroid hormones are absent; the skin is usually cold and clammy rather than warm and moist. Weight loss, when present in emotional anxiety, is characteristically accompanied by anorexia, whereas in thyrotoxicosis the appetite is generally, but not invariably, increased. Thyrotoxicosis can occasionally be confused with such disorders as metastatic carcinoma, cirrhosis of the liver, hyperparathyroidism, sprue, myasthenia gravis, and muscular dystrophy. Hypokalemic periodic paralysis is more common in thyrotoxic patients, especially in the case of Oriental and Latin American men. Signs and symptoms of thyrotoxicosis may overlap with those of pheochromocytoma, which may cause heat intolerance, excessive perspiration, tachycardia with palpitations, and a severe hypermetabolic state. In all the above disorders, and in other conditions considered in the differential diagnosis, the judicious application of laboratory tests usually makes it possible to differentiate them from thyrotoxicosis.

When bilateral ophthalmopathy is accompanied by goiter and thyrotoxicosis, the origin of the ophthalmopathy in Graves' disease is virtually certain. The presence of unilateral ophthalmopathy, even when associated with thyrotoxicosis, raises the possibility of some other intraorbital or intracranial disease. In the euthyroid patient with either unilateral or bilateral ophthalmopathy other causes must be excluded. These include cavernous sinus thrombosis, sphenoidal ridge meningioma, retrobulbar tumors, including leukemic deposits, and the rare granulomatous disorder, pseudotumor oculi. Exophthalmos may also be seen in certain systemic disorders, such as uremia, accelerated hypertension, chronic alcoholism, chronic obstructive pulmonary disease, superior mediastinal obstruction, and Cushing's syndrome. Ophthalmoplegia in the absence of overt infiltrative manifestations can be confused with that which occurs in diabetes mellitus, myasthenia gravis, and myopathies. When doubt exists about the cause of ophthalmopathy, the demonstration of an abnormal TRH stimulation test or thyroid suppression test suggests that the cause is Graves' disease, though not all patients with "euthyroid Graves' disease" demonstrate abnormal responses. In such cases, ultrasonography or computerized tomography of the orbits is valuable in demonstrating characteristic thickening of the extraocular muscles.

When a thyrotoxic state occurs in a patient lacking the characteristic ophthalmopathy of Graves' disease, other causes of thyrotoxicosis must be considered. Careful palpation of the thyroid and studies with radioactive iodine are important in this regard. A symmetric, diffuse goiter of moderate or large size suggests the diagnosis of Graves' disease, especially if a bruit is present. However, the uncommon patient whose hyperthyroidism is secondary to an excess of TSH (associated with a *pituitary tumor* or resistance to feedback suppression of TSH secretion) or an abnormal stimulator of trophoblastic origin (*hydatidiform mole* or *choriocarcinoma of uterus* or *testis;* see Chap. 303) may present in this way. A single, prominent thyroid nodule or multiple nodules suggest *toxic adenoma* or *toxic multinodular goiter,* respectively. Tenderness of the thyroid associated with firm nodularity strongly suggests *subacute thyroiditis,* while a small, firm, nontender goiter is consistent with the syndrome of chronic thyroiditis with spontaneously resolving thyrotoxicosis. The foregoing disorders are discussed more fully in later sections. Absence of a palpable thyroid gland suggests an extrathyroid source of hormone, such as ectopic thyroid tissue (*struma ovarii*) or, more commonly, self-administration of hormone (*thyrotoxicosis factitia*). Studies with radioactive iodine are also helpful. Except when hormone overproduction is secondary to increased iodine intake, values of the RAIU are increased in all disorders producing hyperthyroidism, and scintillation scanning may aid in differentiating among them. Conversely, thyrotoxicosis that is not the result of hyperthyroidism is characterized by subnormal values of the RAIU. Subacute thyroiditis and chronic thyroiditis with spontaneously resolving thyrotoxicosis are the more common. Ectopic thyroid tissue producing thyrotoxicosis is rare. Here, the RAIU, as measured over the thyroid, is low since TSH secretion is suppressed, but despite this, urinary excretion of the dose of ^{131}I is slowed, owing to accumulation of ^{131}I by the ectopic tissue. Functioning ectopic tissue can be located by direct counting or scintillation scanning. Thyrotoxicosis factitia most frequently occurs in medical or paramedical personnel or in those who have easy access to thyroid hormone preparations. Physiologically, it resembles thyrotoxicosis caused by ectopic thyroid tissue in that the patient's thyroid gland is suppressed. By contrast, however, most of an administered dose of ^{131}I is excreted promptly in the urine. When the disorder is caused by ingestion of preparations containing T_4, such as levothyroxine or thyroid extract, the serum T_4 is increased. On the other hand, when caused by liothyronine, the serum T_4 is subnormal. Irrespective of the preparation, the serum T_3 is increased but more so when liothyronine is the offending agent. Owing to thyroid suppression, serum thyroglobulin concentration is subnormal.

The demonstration of elevated titers of antithyroid antibodies or of TSI or TBII activity in the blood also provides strong evidence that Graves' disease is the cause of thyrotoxicosis.

TREATMENT Hyperthyroidism The hyperthyroidism in Graves' disease is often characterized by cyclic phases of exacerbation and remission, each of unpredictable onset and duration. Moreover, longstanding disease may be associated with progressive thyroid failure, probably consequent to chronic thyroiditis, with the result that hypothyroidism or decreased thyroid reserve supervenes. These characteristics of Graves' disease have important implications in the choice of and response to therapy.

The two major approaches to the treatment are directed to limiting the quantity of thyroid hormones the gland can produce. The use of antithyroid agents interposes a chemical blockade to hormone synthesis, the effect of which is operative only as long as the drug is administered or until a spontaneous remission occurs. Thus, the agents can control a given phase of active thyrotoxicity but probably do not prevent exacerbation at some subsequent period. The second major approach is ablation of thyroid tissue, thereby limiting hormone production. This may be achieved either by surgery or by means of radioactive iodine. Since these procedures induce permanent anatomic alterations of the thyroid, they can control the individual active phase and are more likely to prevent a later exacerbation or recurrence. On the other hand, the permanency of the effects of surgery or radiation makes these modes of therapy more likely to lead to hypothyroidism, either shortly after treatment or with the passage of years.

Each therapy has advantages and disadvantages, indications and contraindications. The latter are more often relative than absolute. In general, a trial of long-term antithyroid therapy is desirable in children, adolescents, young adults, and pregnant women but may also be employed in older patients. Indications for ablative procedures include relapse or recurrence following drug therapy, a large goiter, drug toxicity, failure to follow a medical regimen, or failure to return for periodic examinations. Subtotal thyroidectomy may be elected for patients under the age of 40 in whom ablative therapy is required; however, opinions differ, and some authorities employ radioactive iodine in the treatment of patients in the second or third decades. Radioactive iodine is the ablative procedure of choice in older patients, in patients who have had previous thyroid surgery, and in those in whom systemic disease contraindicates elective surgery.

In patients selected for *long-term antithyroid therapy,* satisfactory control can almost always be achieved if sufficient drug is administered. Most patients can be managed with propylthiouracil, 100 to 150 mg every 6 or 8 h. In occasional patients with severe disease, larger doses are required for initial control. Methimazole is at least as effective as propylthiouracil when administered in one-tenth the dosage. However, propylthiouracil has the advantage of inhibiting the peripheral conversion of T_4 to T_3, thereby bringing about more rapid symptomatic improvement. Once euthyroidism is achieved, the daily dosage may be reduced to the smallest doses that control the thyrotoxicosis. In some clinics the initial dose is continued and is supplemented with levothyroxine. By this latter regimen, hypothyroidism from overdosage of antithyroid drugs can be prevented. The undesirable consequences of hypothyroidism, such as enhancement of ophthalmopathy and enlargement of the goiter, may thereby be forestalled. The duration of therapy is difficult to predict in the individual patient and may be a function of the spontaneous course of the disease. If this is the case, the longer the course of therapy, the more likely it is that the patient will remain well when the drug is discontinued. In general a 12- to 24-month course is employed, following which one-third or one-half of patients remain well for a prolonged period or indefinitely. The likelihood of a prolonged remission is increased by a decrease in goiter size, reversion of the thyroid suppression test to normal, or disappearance of Graves' disease–related immunoglobulins (TSI and TBII) from the serum during treatment.

Leukopenia is the principal undesirable side effect of antithyroid drugs. Mild transient leukopenia may occur in approximately 10 percent of patients and is not necessarily an indication for discontinuing therapy. When the absolute number of polymorphonuclear leukocytes reaches 1500 or less, antithyroid medication should be discontinued. Allergic rashes and drug sensitivity occur in a small percentage of patients. These may disappear with antihistamine therapy at the same or reduced dosage of antithyroid agent, but it is probably preferable when sensitivity reactions occur to change to another drug. On rare occasions (in less than 0.2 percent), agranulocytosis occurs. This may be sudden in onset. Hepatitis, drug fever, and arthralgias occur on occasion. In the author's view, severe sensitivity reactions, including agranulocytosis, dictate the abandonment of antithyroid therapy, rather than recourse to an alternate drug.

Iodide inhibits the release of hormones from the hyperfunctioning thyroid gland, and its ameliorative effects occur more rapidly than those of agents that inhibit hormone synthesis. Hence, its main use is in patients with actual or impending thyrotoxic crisis and in patients with severe thyrocardiac disease. The response to iodide is often incomplete and transient. Furthermore, by expanding the thyroid store of hormone, iodide may prolong the latency of response to antithyroid therapy. Therefore, iodide should be used in conjunction with the antithyroid agents. If the clinical course is sufficiently severe to require iodide administration, antithyroid drugs are usually the primary therapeutic agents and should be given in large doses prior to iodide. Since iodide appears to synergize with radiation, it is also useful in controlling thyrotoxicosis following ^{131}I administration, during the period in which the therapeutic effect of radioiodine has not yet taken place. By a poorly understood mechanism, large doses of *glucocorticoids* (2 mg of dexamethasone every 6 h) reduce the serum T_4 concentration and should be added to the regimen when relief of thyrotoxicosis is urgent. The iodinated x-ray contrast agent sodium ipodate has a similar effect. Iodine liberated from this agent inhibits thyroid secretion of T_4 and T_3, and serum T_3 is further reduced by the inhibition by ipodate of peripheral T_3-neogenesis. Daily doses of 1 g orally are effective, but the same precautions concerning the use of iodine therapy are applicable to ipodate as well.

Owing to the pronounced adrenergic component in thyrotoxicosis, various *adrenergic antagonists* have been employed in its management. Of these, propranolol is the agent of choice because of its relative freedom from side effects. In doses of 40 to 120 mg daily, propranolol alleviates such adrenergic manifestations as sweating, tremor, and tachycardia and may reduce to some extent the conversion of T_4 to T_3. However, propranolol should be used only as adjunctive therapy rather than sole therapy, as some have suggested, since the underlying metabolic abnormalities are not affected. Moreover, although the diminution in heart rate and cardiac work may be beneficial, the blocking of adrenergic support of myocardial contractility contraindicates its use in the patient with coexisting heart failure, unless rate- or rhythm-related. As adjunctive therapy, the major usefulness of propranolol is during the period when the response to conventional antithyroid agents or to radioiodine therapy is being awaited and in the management of thyrotoxic crisis. It has been employed as the sole agent in preparation for thyroidectomy, but its use in this setting is not recommended since it does not render the patient euthyroid, with a likely greater risk of surgically induced crisis.

Radioactive iodine (^{131}I) affords a relatively simple, effective, and economical means of treating thyrotoxicosis. It can produce the ablative effects of surgery without the immediate operative and postoperative complications. The principal disadvantage of ^{131}I therapy, in the dosage usually employed, is its tendency to produce hypothyroidism with a frequency that increases with time. As many as 40 to 70 percent of patients may develop this complication within 10 years after treatment. Although hypothyroidism is treatable, once diagnosed, the insidious onset may obscure the diagnosis until serious complications have developed. Hence, some recommend that all patients be treated with large doses of ^{131}I to ensure relief of thyrotoxicosis and then placed on permanent physiologic replacement doses of thyroid hormone.

There is no evidence of carcinogenic or leukemogenic effects of radioiodine when it is given to adults in the doses commonly used in treating hyperthyroidism. However, the susceptibility to carcinogenesis may be increased in the thyroids of children. Mutagenic effects have not been reported and would be difficult to document. For these reasons, many physicians prefer to reserve radioiodine therapy for patients over 30 years of age or those unlikely to have children subsequently. Moreover, the longer the life expectancy after ^{131}I therapy, the greater the likelihood that hypothyroidism will develop. Among younger patients, therefore, those with recurrent thyrotoxicosis following surgery, those who refuse surgery, and those with complicating illness that contraindicates surgery are candidates for radioiodine therapy. In elderly patients, treatment with large doses of radioiodine is the general method of choice, so that the undesirable effects of incomplete treatment or recurrence can be avoided. There is general agreement that patients with coexisting cardiac disease should receive ^{131}I in large doses in view of the hazard of recurrent thyrotoxicosis.

The usual therapeutic dose of ^{131}I [approximately 5.92 MBq (160 µCi) per gram of estimated gland weight] has led to the disturbingly high frequency of hypothyroidism. As a result, though continuing to use this dose, some authorities regularly administer prophylactic replacement doses of thyroid hormone. On the other hand, others have administered smaller doses [approximately 2.96 MBq/g (80 µCi/g)]. However, this does not diminish the frequency of late hypothyroidism but merely delays its onset. Moreover, the smaller dose is less likely to relieve thyrotoxicosis within a relatively short period. Antithyroid agents can be employed, however, to speed the attainment of a eumetabolic state, and propranolol can be given to relieve symptoms, while the effect of the ^{131}I is taking hold.

Radiation thyroiditis is an occasional immediate complication of ^{131}I therapy. When present, it commonly appears within 7 to 10 days and is associated with excessive release of hormone into the blood. For this reason, patients with severe hyperthyroidism or underlying heart disease should be rendered eumetabolic with antithyroid agents before ^{131}I is administered. Interruption of antithyroid therapy for several days before and after ^{131}I treatment suffices to permit adequate accumulation and retention of administered ^{131}I. Propranolol may be used as an adjunct both before and after ^{131}I administration but should not be relied upon to provide adequate prophylaxis if given alone. The swelling that accompanies radiation thyroiditis may contraindicate the use of large doses of ^{131}I in patients with large retrosternal goiters.

Before radioactive iodine was introduced, *subtotal thyroidectomy* was the standard form of ablative therapy, and it is still employed in younger patients in whom antithyroid therapy is unsuccessful. Although precise preoperative programs differ, several general principles should be emphasized. Patients should first be rendered fully euthyroid by means of antithyroid agents. Only then should iodide (five drops of Lugol's solution a day for approximately 10 days) be administered concomitantly to effect an involutional response in the gland. Antithyroid drugs should not be discontinued merely because treatment with iodide is instituted. The response of the patient, and not the calendar, should dictate when surgery is performed.

Hazards of subtotal thyroidectomy include immediate complications, such as anesthetic accidents, hemorrhage sometimes leading to respiratory obstruction, and damage to the recurrent laryngeal nerve leading to vocal cord paralysis. Later complications include wound infection, hemorrhage, hypoparathyroidism, or hypothyroidism. Subtotal thyroidectomy should be performed by a surgeon experienced in this procedure; under this condition surgery is effective and relatively safe. Postoperative recurrences are uncommon. However, carefully conducted follow-up studies reveal that hypothyroidism follows surgery more frequently than previously suspected, although not as commonly as following treatment with [131]I.

The *treatment of hyperthyroidism during pregnancy* is a subject of some disagreement. Most physicians believe that antithyroid therapy is preferable to surgery, which should not be performed in any event during the first and third trimesters. Antithyroid agents carry less risk to the patient and the pregnancy. Further, since they traverse the placental barrier, they have the theoretical advantage of preventing fetal and neonatal hyperthyroidism when maternal titers of thyroid-stimulating IgG are high. As a clue to the risk of fetal hyperthyroidism, assays of such stimulators should be conducted in pregnant women with a history of Graves' disease, whether treated or not. On the other hand, the major disadvantage of antithyroid therapy is the possibility of inducing hypothyroidism in the fetus. T_4 and T_3 traverse the human placenta from mother to fetus only slowly, if at all, and simultaneous administration of thyroid hormone and antithyroid drugs to the mother will not protect the fetus from developing hypothyroidism. Hence, the cardinal rule in using the antithyroid agents in pregnancy is that the dosage should be the smallest necessary to control hyperthyroidism in the mother. From the laboratory standpoint, the physician should aim to keep the serum FT_4 concentration or the FT_4I within the normal limits, remembering that pregnancy is normally associated with some elevation of the serum total T_4, owing to an increase in serum TBG concentration. Since pregnancy appears to attenuate the severity of hyperthyroidism, control can often be achieved with maintenance doses of 200 mg of propylthiouracil daily or less. At this dose level, fetal goiter or hypothyroidism has not been a problem. Patients who require doses of 300 mg daily or more during the first trimester should probably be treated by subtotal thyroidectomy during the middle trimester. Although some would disagree, the author believes that patients carried through pregnancy on antithyroid agents should not be given propranolol as adjunctive treatment, in view of reports that the agent may cause fetal growth retardation and neonatal respiratory depression. Radioiodine should never be administered to a pregnant woman, and all women of childbearing age who are about to receive ^{131}I should have a pregnancy test performed first.

Ophthalmopathy, dermopathy When severe and progressive, ophthalmopathy is the most difficult component of Graves' disease to treat satisfactorily. Fortunately, in most patients the disorder runs a benign course that is largely independent of the course of the hyperthyroidism. In most instances, the activity of even moderately severe disease declines and disappears with time, although some exophthalmos and ophthalmoplegia may persist. In mild disease, considerable benefit may be obtained from simple measures, such as elevating the head at night, administering diuretics to reduce edema, and providing tinted glasses for protection from sun, wind, and foreign bodies. A 1% solution of methylcellulose or plastic shields may prevent corneal drying in patients unable to oppose the lids

during sleep. In more severe cases, as evidenced by progressive exophthalmos, chemosis, ophthalmoplegia, or loss of vision, large doses of prednisone (120 to 140 mg daily) should be administered, since this is usually effective in reducing the edematous and infiltrative components. With improvement, the dosage is reduced to the lowest effective level, since prolonged administration of large doses leads to adverse accompaniments of glucocorticoid excess. Orbital radiation may be helpful in some patients with acute, severe infiltrative manifestations. In cases that progress despite these measures, orbital decompression, i.e., removal of part of the bony orbit to relieve intraorbital pressure, usually halts progression of the disease. The management must always be conducted in concert with an ophthalmologist.

In general, treatment of associated hyperthyroidism should be carried out much as would be the case were ophthalmopathy not present, since the mode of treatment of the hyperthyroidism does not influence the course of the ocular disease. The suggestion that total thyroid ablation by surgery and large doses of ^{131}I is beneficial to the ophthalmic disease has not been borne out. It is agreed, however, that hyperthyroidism should be treated and that hypothyroidism be avoided.

Severe dermopathy can be alleviated by the topical application of glucocorticoids.

TOXIC MULTINODULAR GOITER

Toxic multinodular goiter is an occasional consequence of long-standing simple goiter, although the exact proportion of cases in which this complication arises is uncertain. In areas of nonendemicity, the etiology of nontoxic multinodular goiter is usually indeterminate. Hence, it is unclear whether a specific etiologic factor underlies those cases of nontoxic multinodular goiter that progress to thyrotoxic phase. Common to many nontoxic multinodular goiters, even in areas of iodine sufficiency, is a decrease in the iodine content of thyroglobulin, suggesting either a conditioned deficiency of iodine or an impairment of its normal incorporation into iodinated amino acids. There is no pathologic feature to distinguish the nontoxic from the toxic multinodular goiter. However, the transition from nontoxic to toxic nodular goiter involves the development of a sufficient degree of functional autonomy, i.e., independence from TSH stimulation in one or more areas of the gland. Scattered foci of functional autonomy are present, even early in the disease process. These increase in size and frequency as time passes so that even among seemingly euthyroid patients with nontoxic nodular goiter, approximately a fourth display, as evidence of functional autonomy, subnormal or absent responses to TRH administration. As judged from scintillation scanning studies, functional patterns may be of two types. In the first and more common, iodine accumulation occurs diffusely but in patchy foci throughout the gland. The second, less common, pattern is that of iodine accumulation in one or more discrete nodules within the gland, the remainder appearing to be essentially nonfunctional. Histologic and autoradiographic studies reveal marked heterogeneity of structure and function, the two being poorly correlated. In both endemic and sporadic nontoxic multinodular goiter, administration of iodides may lead to the development of thyrotoxicosis, a complication that is consonant with the functional autonomy that characterizes this disorder.

Because it arises in long-standing simple goiter, toxic multinodular goiter is a disease of the aging or elderly. For this reason and because of the nature of the underlying disease, the clinical presentation differs from that in Graves' disease. Ophthalmopathy is rare and would signal the emergence of Graves' disease superimposed on simple goiter. Some patients have typical thyrotoxicosis. Often, however, the degree of thyrotoxicosis is less severe than that in Graves' disease, although its physiologic impact upon specific organ systems may be great. Notable among these is the cardiovascular system, in which arrhythmias or congestive failure may be precipitated or accentuated by thyrotoxicosis that may be manifested only by subtle findings in other areas (apathetic hyperthyroidism). Weakness and wasting may predominate, frequently with loss of appetite rather than hyperphagia, suggesting the presence of a carcinoma.

In some patients, a definitive diagnosis of toxic nodular goiter is difficult to establish. On the one hand, enlargement or nodularity of the gland may escape detection because the patient has a short neck or is kyphotic or because the thyroid is located substernally. When this is the case and when the clinical findings suggest thyrotoxicosis, RAIU and scintiscan may prove illuminating. On the other hand, even when a nodular goiter is palpable, the presence of mild but clinically significant thyrotoxicosis may be difficult to confirm, since values of the serum total T_4, FT_4, and FT_4I, as well as the serum T_3 concentration, are often only near or slightly above the upper limit of the normal range. For example, a value for the serum T_3 that would be considered normal for a young adult may represent an increase in the elderly patient, since serum T_3 usually declines with age. Despite their value in situations such as this, thyroid suppression tests should not be undertaken in the elderly patient because of the hazard of adverse cardiovascular responses. Unfortunately, although a normal response to TRH would exclude a diagnosis of thyrotoxicosis in a patient with a nodular goiter, subnormal responses do not establish the diagnosis. Responses to TRH decline in the elderly, especially in men, and a high proportion of patients with nodular goiter who otherwise seem euthyroid respond subnormally to TRH as a reflection of at least partial functional autonomy of the thyroid gland. When laboratory findings do not permit a clear diagnosis of thyrotoxicosis but suggestive clinical findings are present, a therapeutic trial of antithyroid drugs is indicated.

Radioactive iodine is the treatment of choice for toxic multinodular goiter. Large doses [740 to 1110 MBq (20 to 30 mCi)] are usually required, owing to the generally lower RAIU and to the variable degree of function throughout the gland. Moreover, the physiologic instability of the elderly patient makes definitive treatment desirable. For the same reason, it is usually wise to initiate therapy with antithyroid agents, withholding radioiodine until a euthyroid state has been achieved and thereby forestalling an exacerbation of thyrotoxicosis, should radiation thyroiditis occur. Unless contraindicated, propranolol is often useful in controlling manifestations of thyrotoxicosis both before and after radioiodine therapy, while its therapeutic effect is awaited. Hypothyroidism is an uncommon consequence of radioiodine treatment of toxic multinodular goiter, owing to the variable activity of differing portions of the gland, which permits previously quiescent areas to replace functionally those that have been destroyed by ^{131}I.

UNUSUAL VARIETIES OF THYROTOXICOSIS

In addition to Graves' disease and toxic multinodular goiter, thyrotoxicosis is seen in other disorders, including follicular adenoma of the thyroid and various forms of thyroiditis, which are discussed in later sections. This section will consider still other infrequent causes of thyrotoxicosis and unusual ways in which thyrotoxicosis may present from the laboratory standpoint.

UNUSUAL CAUSES OF THYROTOXICOSIS Rarely, hyperthyroidism and thyrotoxicosis are the result of sustained hypersecretion of TSH from either a *TSH-secreting pituitary adenoma* or a selective *resistance of the TSH-secretory mechanism* to feedback inhibition by thyroid hormones. The resistance syndrome may be a variant of one in which both the pituitary and peripheral tissues are relatively resistant to thyroid hormones. TSH-secreting pituitary adenomas can be distinguished, in many cases, by radiologic evidence of pituitary tumor, by the fact that the concentration of free alpha subunits of TSH in serum is elevated, and by the fact that the response of the serum TSH to TRH is negligible. In the variant caused by pituitary resistance, subunit concentrations are not grossly elevated, and the TSH response to TRH is usually normal.

Patients with *trophoblastic tumor,* either choriocarcinoma or hydatidiform mole, frequently display elevations, sometimes marked, of serum total and free T_4 and T_3 concentrations. Clinical evidence of thyrotoxicosis may be lacking. Thyroid hyperfunction is caused by a circulating thyroid stimulator of trophoblastic origin, which is probably a variant of human chorionic gonadotropin (hCG), and abnormalities remit promptly after removal of the tumor.

Thyrotoxicosis factitia is a form of thyrotoxicosis without hyperthyroidism and results from purposeful or inadvertent ingestion of supraphysiologic quantities of thyroid hormone. The syndrome is usually a form of malingering and occurs most commonly in women with an underlying psychiatric disorder, usually paramedical personnel, or in patients who have taken thyroid hormones in the past or who have relatives that take thyroid hormones. In such patients, endogenous thyroid function is suppressed, as evidenced by subnormal values of the RAIU and serum thyroglobulin concentration. Both serum T_4 and T_3 concentrations are increased if the patient is taking a preparation that contains T_4, whereas the serum T_3 concentration is elevated and the serum T_4 depressed in patients taking T_3 alone.

Very rarely, thyrotoxicosis with a low RAIU is the result of excess hormone secretion by *ectopic thyroid tissue,* either widespread functioning metastases of thyroid carcinoma or struma ovarii.

Jodbasedow phenomenon refers to the induction of thyrotoxicosis in a previously euthyroid patient as a result of exposure to increased quantities of iodine. It typically occurs in areas of endemic iodine deficiency when measures to increase iodine intake or body iodine stores are implemented. The presumption is that the supplemental iodine permits functionally autonomous thyroid tissue to produce and secrete excessive hormone. A similar phenomenon can occur in patients with nontoxic multinodular goiter who have received large doses of iodide. Since such patients tend to be elderly with the danger of serious cardiovascular manifestations should thyrotoxicosis ensue, large doses of iodine should not be given to those with multinodular goiter. Similarly, in such patients, pharmaceuticals containing iodine, most often x-ray contrast media, should be used only when indicated and with consideration of the possible hazard of inducing the jodbasedow phenomenon. When a contrast study is indicated under these conditions, it may be judicious to administer large doses of propylthiouracil (450 to 600 mg per day) prior to and for a week after the procedure. Some patients may develop hyperthyroidism following exposure to large quantities of iodine despite the fact that after iodine is withdrawn, they recover, their thyroid function appears to be entirely normal, and evidence of functional autonomy is lacking.

UNUSUAL PRESENTATIONS OF THYROTOXICOSIS T_3 **toxicosis** Thyrotoxicosis in which serum T_4 is normal or low in the absence of a deficiency of TBG, while the serum T_3 is increased, is termed T_3 toxicosis. Although the production rate of T_3 is disproportionately increased relative to that of T_4 in all patients with hyperthyroidism, in some this discrepancy is exaggerated. This may occur in association with Graves' disease, multinodular goiter, or hyperfunctioning adenoma. The diagnosis should be suspected in a patient with clinical manifestations of thyrotoxicosis in whom the serum T_4 and FT_4 are normal or low and the RAIU is normal or increased. This, together with the frequently palpable goiter, serves to differentiate this disorder from liothyronine-induced thyrotoxicosis factitia. In contrast to patients with nonthyroidal disorders that mimic thyrotoxicosis, patients with this disorder, as would be expected, demonstrate both nonsuppressibility of thyroid function in response to exogenous T_3 and blunted or absent responses to TRH. In many patients, thyrotoxicosis with increased serum T_3 and normal serum T_4 antecedes emergence of typical increases in both, either during an initial episode of hyperthyroidism or more commonly during recurrence after previous treatment. In some patients in whom symptoms of thyrotoxicosis fail to regress completely during antithyroid therapy despite return of the serum T_4 concentration to normal, the serum T_3 concentration is persistently elevated. Such patients are prone to experience a recurrence of thyrotoxicosis when antithyroid therapy is withdrawn.

T_4 toxicosis In most patients with hyperthyroidism, the serum T_3 is increased to a relatively greater extent than is the serum T_4. This reflects the fact that in hyperthyroidism T_3 generated from T_4 peripherally is supplemented by release of substantial quantities of T_3 from the thyroid. However, thyrotoxicosis may sometimes be associated with a clear elevation of serum T_4 and a seemingly normal serum T_3 concentration. This syndrome of T_4 toxicosis occurs most commonly in patients who are elderly, ill, or both, and is, therefore, usually seen in a hospital setting. Presumably, the combination of high serum T_4 and normal serum T_3 concentration reflects inhibition of peripheral T_3 generation from T_4, with persistence of T_3 secretion along with T_4 from the thyroid.

MAJOR COMPLICATIONS OF THYROTOXICOSIS

THYROCARDIAC DISEASE Thyrotoxicosis imposes a variety of burdens upon the heart. Hypermetabolism of the peripheral tissues increases both the metabolic and nonmetabolic (heat-loss) circulatory load, while direct effects of thyroid hormone on the myocardium increase the force, velocity, and rate of ventricular contraction. As a result, cardiac work and cardiac output are increased. Moreover, atrial irritability is enhanced, leading to tachydysrhythmias, most importantly atrial fibrillation. In the patient with a normal heart, these burdens are usually tolerated. In the patient with underlying heart disease, however, cardiac insufficiency may be precipitated or aggravated. As would be expected, this complication is more common in the elderly patient and is common in the patient with toxic multinodular goiter, sometimes as the most prominent manifestation of the thyrotoxic state. In patients with cardiac insufficiency, clues to the presence of thyrotoxicosis include atrial fibrillation, relatively rapid circulation time, increased cardiac output (high-output failure), and resistance to the usual therapeutic doses of digitalis.

Treatment is directed at rapid alleviation of thyrotoxicosis and restoration of cardiac compensation. The former objective is best met by initiation of treatment with large doses of an antithyroid agent, followed by iodine if the clinical situation is urgent. In less severe cases, radioiodine treatment is preceded by antithyroid drug treatment alone. Management of the cardiac decompensation is carried out in the usual manner, employing larger than usual doses of digitalis but with care to avoid digitalis intoxication as thyrotoxicosis is alleviated. Adrenergic antagonists should not be employed in the presence of cardiac failure, unless it is felt that failure is the consequence primarily of disturbance of cardiac rate or rhythm.

THYROTOXIC CRISIS Thyrotoxic crisis or storm causes a fulminating increase in the signs and symptoms of thyrotoxicosis. In the past, this disturbance was most often observed postoperatively in patients poorly prepared for surgery. However, with the preoperative use of antithyroid drugs and iodide and with appropriate measures directed to control of metabolic factors, weight, and nutritional status, postoperative thyrotoxic crisis should not occur. At present, so-called medical storm is more common and occurs in untreated or inadequately treated patients. It is precipitated by surgical emergency or complicating illness, usually sepsis. The syndrome is characterized by extreme irritability, delirium or coma, fever to 41°C or more, tachycardia, restlessness, hypotension, vomiting, and diarrhea. Rarely, the picture may be more subtle, with apathy, prostration, and coma, but with only slight elevation of temperature. Such postoperative complications as sepsis, septicemia, hemorrhage, and transfusion or drug reactions may mimic thyrotoxic crisis. The physiologic factor(s) that initiates thyrotoxic crisis is unknown. It does not appear to be an acute increase in the severity of thyroid hyperfunction.

Treatment consists in providing general supportive therapy while undertaking measures for alleviating thyrotoxicosis as rapidly as possible. Supportive therapy includes treatment of dehydration and the intravenous administration of glucose and saline, vitamin B complex, and glucocorticoids. The latter are indicated because of the increased glucocorticoid requirements in thyrotoxicosis and because adrenocortical reserve is reduced in this disorder. Patients should be placed in a cooled, humidified oxygen tent, and, if hyperpyrexia is present, a cooling blanket should be used. Digitalization is required to control ventricular rate in those with atrial fibrillation. If shock exists, intravenous pressor agents should be employed. Therapy of the hyperthyroidism consists of induction of blockade of hormone synthesis by the immediate and continued administration of large doses of an antithyroid agent (e.g., 100 mg propylthiouracil every 2 h). If the patient is unable to swallow the medication, the tablets should be triturated and given by nasogastric tube, as parenteral preparations are unavailable. Following initiation of antithyroid therapy, inhibition of hormone release is sought through the administration of large doses of iodine intravenously or by mouth. The iodinated x-ray contrast agent sodium ipodate can be administered instead of iodine and has the added action of also inhibiting the peripheral conversion of T_4 to T_3. Doses of 1 g daily are effective. Adrenergic antagonists are an important, and perhaps critical, part of the therapeutic regimen, in the absence of cardiac failure. The beta-adrenergic blocking agent propranolol can be administered in doses of 40 to 80 mg every 6 h. If medications cannot be taken orally, 2 mg of propranolol may be given intravenously, with careful electrocardiographic monitoring. Large doses of dexamethasone (e.g., 2 mg every 6 h) should also be administered, since they inhibit hormone release, impair the peripheral generation of T_3 from T_4, and provide adrenal support. Indeed, with the combined use of propylthiouracil, iodine, and dexamethasone, the serum T_3 concentration generally returns to normal within 24 to 48 h. Antithyroid therapy, iodine, and dexamethasone must be continued until a normal metabolic state is approached, at which time iodine is progressively withdrawn and plans are made for definitive treatment.

THYROIDITIS

Thyroiditis embraces disorders of differing etiology. Two are exceedingly uncommon, *pyogenic thyroiditis* and *chronic fibrosing (Riedel's) thyroiditis*. Pyogenic thyroiditis is usually anteceded by a pyogenic infection elsewhere and is characterized by tenderness and swelling of the thyroid, redness and warmth of the overlying skin, and constitutional signs of infection. Treatment consists of antibiotic therapy and incisional drainage if a fluctuant area within the thyroid should occur. Riedel's thyroiditis is a rare disorder in which intense fibrosis of the thyroid and surrounding structures, leading to induration of the tissues of the neck, may be associated with mediastinal and retroperitoneal fibrosis. The principal importance of this disorder is that it requires differentiation from thyroid neoplasia.

The other forms of thyroiditis, comprising subacute thyroiditis, chronic thyroiditis with transient thyrotoxicosis (CT/TT), and Hashimoto's thyroiditis, are more common. They are notable for their different clinical courses and for the fact that each can be associated, at one time or another, with a euthyroid, thyrotoxic, or hypothyroid state.

SUBACUTE THYROIDITIS This disorder, also termed *granulomatous, giant cell,* or *de Quervain's thyroiditis,* appears to be viral in origin. Symptoms of thyroiditis usually follow those of an upper respiratory infection and include pronounced asthenia, malaise, and symptoms referable to stretching of the thyroid capsule, principally pain over the thyroid or pain referred to the lower jaw, ear, or occiput. Referred pain may predominate. These symptoms may smolder for weeks before the diagnosis is suspected. Less commonly, the onset is acute, with severe pain over the thyroid, accompanied by fever and occasionally symptoms of thyrotoxicosis. Physical findings include exquisite tenderness and nodularity over the thyroid, which may be unilateral but which usually involves other areas of the gland. Although local or referred pain is the commonest symptom, occasional patients have other features typical of the disease but have no pain.

Two laboratory findings are characteristic: a high erythrocyte sedimentation rate (ESR) and a depressed RAIU. Values for the remaining tests depend upon the stage of the disease in which they are obtained. Early, many patients are mildly thyrotoxic owing to leakage of hormone from the gland. The serum T_4 and T_3 are high. Later, as glandular hormone is depleted, the patient may pass through a hypothyroid phase, in which serum T_4 and T_3 are low and TSH increased. Diagnosis of the thyrotoxic phase is especially troublesome in patients with the uncommon, painless variant since the patient may be thought to have Graves' disease or toxic nodular goiter and therapy inappropriate for subacute thyroiditis may be instituted. Demonstration of a low RAIU usually serves to differentiate subacute thyroiditis from these other causes of hyperthyroidism. Differentiation of painless subacute thyroiditis from the syndrome of chronic thyroiditis with transient thyrotoxicosis is discussed below.

The disorder may smolder for months but eventually subsides with a return of normal thyroid function. In mild cases, aspirin suffices to control the symptoms. In more severe cases, glucocorticoid (prednisone, 20 to 40 mg daily) is generally effective. Propranolol can be used to control associated thyrotoxicosis. When the RAIU returns to normal, therapy can be withdrawn without recurrence of symptoms.

CHRONIC THYROIDITIS WITH TRANSIENT THYROTOXICOSIS

This term denotes a disorder in which a self-limited episode of thyrotoxicosis is associated with a histologic picture of chronic lymphocytic thyroiditis that differs from that of Hashimoto's disease. This syndrome has been variously designated as painless thyroiditis, silent thyroiditis, hyperthyroiditis, chronic thyroiditis with spontaneously resolving hyperthyroidism, or, as the author prefers, chronic thyroiditis with transient thyrotoxicosis (CT/TT). Designations that imply the existence of hyperthyroidism are inappropriate, since ongoing production of thyroid hormone is negligible and the RAIU is decreased.

The syndrome occurs in patients of any age, and although it occurs mainly in women, the female/male ratio is not as high as in Graves' disease. Manifestations of thyrotoxicosis are usually mild but may be severe. The thyroid is nontender, firm, symmetrical, and enlarged only slightly or moderately. Laboratory features include elevations of the serum T_4 and T_3 concentrations consonant with the thyrotoxicosis and a markedly depressed RAIU. The ESR is normal or only slightly elevated, rarely exceeding 50 mm/h, and antithyroid antibodies, when present, are present in low titer.

The etiology, pathogenesis, and pathophysiology of this disorder are unclear. Viral antibody titers show no characteristic patterns. It is presumed that thyrotoxicosis results from leakage of hormone from the gland, as in subacute thyroiditis. Low values for the RAIU, in turn, reflect suppression of TSH secretion, since urinary iodine excretion is not greatly elevated. Some degree of thyroid malfunction is indicated by failure of the RAIU to respond briskly to exogenous TSH stimulation.

Thyrotoxicosis in CT/TT usually abates within 2 to 5 months. Many patients have recurrent episodes of thyrotoxicosis of similar nature, sometimes following pregnancy. The thyrotoxic phase may be followed in several months by a phase of self-limited hypothyroidism. The latter, which has been noted particularly in the postpartum period, may be the only component of the disease that is diagnosed. In Japan, as many as 5 percent of pregnant women may experience the syndrome post partum.

This disorder, in the thyrotoxic phase, needs differentiation, first from Graves' disease; this can be accomplished by demonstration of a depressed RAIU and absence of increased urinary iodine excretion. The latter serves also to exclude the jodbasedow syndrome. When these data are available, the disorder must be differentiated from other causes of thyrotoxicosis with a low RAIU, principally subacute thyroiditis. Lack of tenderness or nodularity of the thyroid and absence of marked elevation of the ESR tend to exclude the latter diagnosis.

Patients with functioning ectopic thyroid tissue and thyrotoxicosis factitia characteristically respond to exogenous TSH stimulation with a brisk increase in RAIU. Definitive diagnosis of CT/TT can be made by thyroid biopsy.

Since the thyroid is not hyperfunctioning in this disorder, measures used in the treatment of hyperthyroidism are useless. Symptomatic treatment with propranolol or mild sedatives is administered until the thyrotoxicosis abates. In patients with frequently recurrent disease, thyroid ablation with ^{131}I during a period of remission followed by long-term replacement therapy has been advocated by some.

HASHIMOTO'S THYROIDITIS

This disorder, also termed *lymphadenoid goiter,* is a common chronic inflammatory disease of the thyroid in which autoimmune factors play a prominent role, occurring most frequently in women of middle age. It is also the most common cause of sporadic goiter in children. Evidence of the participation of autoimmune factors includes the lymphocytic infiltration of the gland and the presence in the serum of increased concentrations of immunoglobulins and of antibodies against several components of thyroid tissue. Of these, the most important from the clinical standpoint are the antithyroglobulin antibody detected by the tanned red cell agglutination technique and the antimicrosomal antibody detected by immunofluorescence or complement fixation techniques. This disorder also coexists with some frequency with other diseases of a presumed autoimmune nature, including pernicious anemia, Sjögren's syndrome, chronic active hepatitis, systemic lupus erythematosus, rheumatoid arthritis, nontuberculous Addison's disease, diabetes mellitus, and Graves' disease itself (see Chap. 334). These disorders, as well as Hashimoto's disease itself, also occur frequently in family members of patients with Hashimoto's disease.

Goiter is the outstanding feature. The enlargement involves the entire gland but not necessarily symmetrically. Typically, the consistency is rubbery, the margins are scalloped, and the general outline of the gland is preserved. The pyramidal lobe may be prominent. Early in the disease the patient is metabolically normal; however, even then decreased thyroid reserve is often manifest in an increase in serum TSH. The RAIU may be elevated early in the disease, reflecting the secretion of calorigenically inactive iodoproteins, but the serum T_4 and T_3 are normal and the patient is euthyroid. As the disease progresses, thyroid failure, at first subclinical, gradually supervenes owing to progressive replacement of thyroid parenchyma by lymphocytes or fibrous tissue. The thyroid failure is evident first in a rise in serum TSH concentration. With time, the serum T_4 concentration declines though the serum T_3 remains normal. Eventually, the serum T_3 concentration falls below normal, and the patient is frankly hypothyroid. High titers of antimicrosomal antibody are almost always present. High titers may also occur in other thyroid disorders, particularly primary thyroprivic hypothyroidism and Graves' disease but with lesser frequency. Although the foregoing findings usually suffice to permit a diagnosis, histologic confirmation by needle biopsy may be required. In view of the frequency with which hypothyroidism is either present or eventually develops, treatment with replacement doses of levothyroxine is indicated. In some patients, such therapy is associated with regression of goiter.

Occasional patients present with hyperthyroidism in association with a thyroid gland that is unusually firm and with high titers of circulating antithyroid antibodies, a combination which suggests, probably correctly, the concurrence of Graves' disease and Hashimoto's thyroiditis ("Hashitoxicosis"). In others, hyperthyroidism may supervene in a patient known to have Hashimoto's thyroiditis, presumably due to the emergence of clones of lymphocytes that produce anti-TSH receptor antibodies. Hyperthyroidism in association with Hashimoto's thyroiditis is treated in a conventional manner, but ablative therapy is less commonly employed, since the associated chronic thyroiditis tends to limit the duration of thyroid hyperfunction and also predisposes the patient to the development of hypothyroidism after surgical or radioiodine treatment.

NEOPLASMS

THYROID ADENOMAS True adenomas, as contrasted with localized adenomatous areas, are encapsulated and usually compress contiguous tissue. Adenomas vary in size and histologic characteristics and are often classified into three major types: papillary, follicular, and Hürthle cell. The follicular adenomas can be subdivided according to the size of the follicles into colloid or macrofollicular, fetal or microfollicular, and embryonal varieties. There is variation in physiologic differentiation, as judged by the ability to concentrate radioiodine. The more highly differentiated adenomas (follicular) are the most common and are the most likely to mimic the function of normal thyroid tissue. Though their function may be responsive to TSH stimulation, it differs from that of normal thyroid tissue in being autonomous, i.e., the basal activity is independent of TSH stimulation. Adenomas of this type are usually unifocal, presenting as a single nodule. Often the patient reports that the nodule has grown slowly over many years. Initially, its function is insufficient to disturb hormonal equilibrium though its capacity to accumulate radioiodine is evident in scintiscans as an area of increased density within the still-functioning extranodular tissue (*"warm" nodule*). At this stage, demonstration of the inherent autonomy of the nodule's function requires scintiscanning while the patient is receiving suppressive doses of exogenous thyroid hormone (suppression scan). With time the nodule grows larger, its function increasing until it is sufficient to suppress TSH secretion. Consequently, the remainder of the gland undergoes atrophy and loss of function, and the scintiscan then reveals radioiodine accumulation only in the region of the nodule (*"hot" nodule*). At this time, the patient may or may not be overtly thyrotoxic, but frank thyrotoxicosis usually supervenes eventually (*toxic adenoma*). Relative to its overall rate of occurrence, hyperfunctioning adenoma is a frequent cause of T_3 toxicosis. Hyperfunctioning adenomas are amenable to ablation by surgery or ^{131}I. Large doses of the latter are usually required to bring about prompt cure. Before such treatment it is desirable to administer TSH and demonstrate by scintiscan the latent functional capacity of the extranodular tissue. Although it has been thought that radiation damage would be confined solely to the hyperfunctioning nodule being treated with ^{131}I, the remaining tissue being spared, this may not always be the case, since some patients with hyperfunctioning adenoma become euthyroid after treatment with ^{131}I only to become hypothyroid years later.

Hyperfunctioning nodules are rarely the seat of carcinoma. However, hyperfunctioning adenomas not infrequently undergo hemorrhagic necrosis. The resulting pain and nodularity may suggest subacute thyroiditis. Subsequently, there is loss of function and the appearance of a *"cold" nodule* on scintiscanning, since the remainder of the thyroid will have resumed function. When this happens, the nodule is likely to be mistaken for a carcinoma. Indeed, hypofunctioning, hemorrhagic adenomas and thyroid cysts account for the majority of cold nodules initially suspected of being carcinomas.

THYROID CARCINOMAS Thyroid carcinoma may be classified into two varieties, depending upon whether the lesion arises in thyroid follicular epithelium or whether it arises from the parafollicular or C cells. The latter disorder, medullary thyroid carcinoma, has distinctive physiologic and clinical characteristics and is discussed separately (see Chap. 334). The thyroid may also be the site of one or another of the lymphoproliferative diseases or of carcinoma metastatic from a diagnosed or undiagnosed primary tumor elsewhere.

Carcinomas of follicular epithelium The three general histologic types differ in their clinical course. The least common is *anaplastic carcinoma*, which is histologically undifferentiated, usually afflicts the elderly, and is highly malignant. The lesion is rapidly fatal, owing to extensive local invasion which is refractory to radiation. The second type of tumor, *follicular carcinoma*, is also uncommon

and histologically mimics normal thyroid tissue. This lesion usually undergoes early hematogenous spread, and the patient may present with a distant metastasis, usually in lung or bone. Follicular carcinoma or follicular elements in papillary carcinoma are responsible for those instances in which thyroid carcinoma, in situ or in metastases, accumulates significant quantities of ^{131}I. The third and most common type of tumor, *papillary carcinoma*, has a bimodal frequency, peaks occurring in the second or third decades and again in later life. This lesion is slowly growing and typically spreads to the regional lymph nodes, where it may remain indolent for many years. Acceleration of the disease may take place at any time. Follicular elements are usually present in both the primary lesion and its metastases.

DIAGNOSIS AND MANAGEMENT The diagnosis and management of thyroid carcinoma are interwoven with the management of the nodular goiter. In the past, this subject has evoked a wide disparity of views among authorities, stemming from seemingly contradictory data. On the one hand, surgically excised specimens of thyroid nodules, particularly solitary nodules, revealed a high frequency of carcinoma (as much as 20 percent in some series). On the other hand, despite the frequency of nodular goiter in the general population (approximately 4 percent), the frequency of thyroid carcinoma, either newly diagnosed or as a cause of death, is very low. These respective data led either to vigorous or to conservative approaches to the management of nodular goiter. It now appears that this discordance can be explained, by the ability of the physician to select for surgery those patients who are at high risk of harboring thyroid carcinoma, with consequent weighting of statistics from surgical series. This capability has increased, the as yet unrealized aim being to operate on only those patients whose thyroids harbor carcinoma and to avoid surgery in patients whose thyroids do not.

Several features suggest the presence of thyroid carcinoma. Recent growth of a thyroid nodule or mass, especially if rapid and unaccompanied by tenderness and hoarseness, is a source of suspicion. Of particular importance is a history of x-ray to the head or neck or upper mediastinum in infancy or childhood, since this is associated with a high incidence of thyroid disease, including carcinoma, later in life. Nodular disease develops in approximately 20 percent of patients so exposed and may not be apparent until 30 years or more after the radiation exposure. Among patients in this group who have palpable nodules, approximately a third have thyroid carcinoma at surgery, often multicentric and sometimes metastatic.

Skillful palpation of the thyroid provides important information. A nodule in an otherwise normal gland (solitary nodule) creates more suspicion of thyroid tumor than does one nodule among many, since the latter is more likely to be part of a diffuse process, such as simple goiter. In addition, carcinomas are usually firm or hard in consistency and nontender. Fixation to surrounding structures and lymphadenopathy are late features. Since purely cystic lesions, especially those that are less than a few centimeters in diameter, are less likely to reflect malignancy than solid lesions, transillumination is sometimes helpful, and ultrasonograms (see below) are particularly so. Age and sex of the patient also influence the clinical decision. Benign nodular lesions are more common in women than in men, malignant nodular lesions less so. Hence, nodular lesions in men create more suspicion of carcinoma than in women.

Laboratory tests are of little assistance in differentiating between malignant and nonmalignant thyroid nodules. Overall thyroid function is usually normal. Except in patients with medullary thyroid carcinoma, in whom serum calcitonin concentrations may be elevated, tumor markers are of little value. Elevations of serum thyroglobulin are present in many patients with differentiated thyroid carcinoma but are not useful in the initial diagnosis, since they may be elevated in patients with benign adenoma, simple goiter, or Graves' disease. Soft-tissue x-rays of the neck may be of assistance, since finely stippled calcification within the thyroid suggests the presence of psammoma bodies within a papillary carcinoma.

Scintillation scanning is a keystone in the approach to the management of the patient with nodular goiter. Although only approximately 20 percent of nonfunctioning thyroid nodules prove to be malignant, demonstration that a nodule is cold adds substantial weight to the other factors suggesting carcinoma. Nodules that are hyperfunctioning are rarely malignant. Ultrasonograms of the thyroid have value in demonstrating whether nodules are cystic, solid, or a mixture of the two. Cystic nodules can be aspirated, a procedure that is often curative, and their contents should be subjected to cytopathologic examination. Solid or mixed lesions are consistent with tumor but may be either benign or malignant.

At this point in the evaluation, the physician must decide whether to continue to observe the patient; whether to administer suppressive doses of thyroid hormone in the hope that the suspect nodule will shrink or disappear, a hope that in the author's experience is usually unrealized; whether to obtain a closed biopsy; or whether to proceed to excisional biopsy and thyroidectomy. There are some patients in whom the author would choose the latter course. In general, these include patients with a history of radiation to the thyroid and one or more clearly palpable nodules, as well as young men and women with solitary cold nodules, particularly if hard, nontender, and changing rapidly in size. In the remainder, the author recommends either aspiration or cutting-needle biopsy. The former is simpler to learn, free of complications, and applicable to smaller nodules. Optimum application of that technique rests upon the availability of experienced histopathologic interpretation of the specimen obtained. When such is available, aspiration biopsy provides a reliable means of differentiating between benign and malignant nodules in all except highly cellular lesions or follicular lesions, where evidence of vascular invasion may be required to differentiate benign from malignant forms. Despite the occasional occurrence of false-positives and -negatives, the procedure can reduce the number of operations performed for nodules that prove to be benign. Further, a diagnosis of carcinoma permits planning of the surgery to be undertaken preoperatively and is often useful in providing an impetus to surgery when the patient or physician is uncertain if surgery should be performed.

Regardless of the operative procedure planned, surgery for thyroid carcinoma should be performed by a surgeon experienced in the procedure. A several-week period of suppressive therapy with levothyroxine is often recommended preoperatively to facilitate the operative procedure and perhaps to decrease the likelihood of tumor dissemination. In patients in whom a definitive preoperative diagnosis, such as by biopsy, has not been made, the suspected lesion is removed en bloc with a wide margin of surrounding tissue and is examined by frozen section. Opinions vary as to the type of procedure that is preferable when carcinoma is found. For lesions that are not multicentric and that have not metastasized, some recommend ipsilateral lobectomy, isthmectomy, and possibly contralateral partial lobectomy. Despite its higher rate of morbidity, the author prefers that a near-total thyroidectomy be performed, in view of the frequency of seeding of tumor throughout the gland by transglandular lymphatic spread and of evidence that both recurrence rates and subsequent mortality are lower after the more extensive operation. Regional lymph nodes should be explored and removed if there is evidence of involvement, but radical neck dissection is not justified. If permanent sections reveal carcinoma when frozen sections had failed to do so, secondary surgery should be undertaken to remove residual thyroid tissue.

Approximately 3 weeks after surgery, liothyronine (75 to 100 μg daily) is substituted for levothyroxine, since it permits a more rapid return of TSH secretion when withdrawn some 3 weeks later. After an additional 2 or 3 weeks, when the serum TSH concentration has risen to the range of 50 μU/mL, a large scanning dose of ^{131}I [185 to 370 MBq (5 to 10 mCi)] is administered and whole-body scans are obtained at 24, 48, and 72 h. If residual thyroid tissue is found, as is usually the case, a thyroid ablating dose of 1850 MBq (50 mCi) of ^{131}I is administered, and if functioning metastases are present, the

dose is doubled. Suppressive therapy with levothyroxine is reinstituted 24 to 48 h later. Approximately 1 week after administration of the second dose of ^{131}I, whole-body scans are repeated, as the larger dose of radioiodine may permit demonstration of functioning metastases not seen after the smaller initial dose. If this proves to be the case, suppressive therapy is withdrawn, an additional 3700 MBq (100 mCi) of ^{131}I is administered, and suppressive therapy with levothyroxine reinstituted.

Patients are reexamined approximately 6 months after the initial operation and at least every 6 months for several years thereafter. At these examinations, the neck is palpated for evidence of recurrence of metastases, which often can be treated with selective surgical removal. Blood is drawn for a serum thyroglobulin measurement, since elevated values in patients receiving suppressive therapy signal the presence of metastatic disease. At the initial 6-month examination, patients in whom metastases had previously been found are prepared for a whole-body scan as described above. Those in whom no metastases had been demonstrated by earlier scans are not rescanned unless the serum thyroglobulin is elevated but are rescanned approximately 1 year after the initial surgery. Patients in whom whole-body scans are positive are reentered into the therapeutic algorithm, as described above. Those in whom scans are negative continue to be reexamined and have measurements of serum thyroglobulin concentrations at regular intervals. If both serum thyroglobulin concentrations and scans are unrevealing, patients are scanned for the last time after approximately 3 years, unless serum thyroglobulin concentrations rise. In some patients, serum thyroglobulin may be elevated despite the absence of demonstrable functioning metastases. Such patients obviously cannot be treated with ^{131}I but should be studied with x-rays and bone scans to ascertain the site of the thyroglobulin-secreting metastases.

A program of this nature, involving near-total thyroidectomy, long-term suppressive therapy, and treatment of functioning metastases with radioiodine reduces the recurrence rate and prolongs survival in patients with papillary carcinoma of the thyroid. Follicular carcinoma should be treated with at least equal vigor, though the results are generally less favorable. Treatment of anaplastic carcinoma is largely palliative; most patients with this disease die within 6 months from the time of diagnosis.

REFERENCES

BEIERWALTES WH: The treatment of thyroid carcinoma with radioactive iodine. Semin Nucl Med 8:79, 1978

BILEZEKIAN JP, LOEB JN: The influence of hyperthyroidism and hypothyroidism on the α- and β-adrenergic receptor system and adrenergic responsiveness. Endocr Rev 4:378, 1983

DUNN JT: Choice of therapy in young adults with hyperthyroidism of Graves' disease. Ann Intern Med 100:891, 1984

FISHER DA, KLEIN AH: Thyroid development and disorders of thyroid function in the newborn. N Engl J Med 304:702, 1981

INGBAR SH, BORGES M: Peripheral metabolism of the thyroid hormones, in Free Thyroid Hormones, R Ekins et al (eds). Amsterdam, Excerpta Medica, 1979, p 17

KIDD A et al: Immunologic aspects of Graves' and Hashimoto's diseases. Metabolism 29:80, 1980

MAZZAFERRI EL et al: Papillary thyroid carcinoma: The impact of therapy in 576 patients. Medicine 56:171, 1977

MILLER JM et al: Diagnosis of thyroid nodules. Use of fine-needle aspiration and needle biopsy. JAMA 241:481, 1979

RAJATANAVIN R, BRAVERMAN LE: Euthyroid hyperthyroxinemia. J Endocrinol Invest 6:493, 1983

SCHNEIDER AB et al: Sequential serum thyroglobulin determinations, ^{131}I scans, and ^{131}I uptakes after triiodothyronine withdrawal in patients with thyroid cancer. J Clin Endocrinol Metab 53:1199, 1981

STERLING K: Thyroid hormone action at the cell level. N Engl J Med 300:117, 173, 1979

STUDER H, RAMELLI F: Simple goiter and its variants: Euthyroid and hyperthyroid multinodular goiters. Endocr Rev 3:440, 1980

WARTOFSKY L, BURMAN KD: Alterations in thyroid function in patients with systemic illness: The "euthyroid sick syndrome." Endocr Rev 3:164, 1982

WITT JR et al: The approach to the irradiated thyroid. Surg Clin N Am 59:45, 1979

WOOLF PD: Transient painless thyroiditis with hyperthyroidism: A variant of lymphocytic thyroiditis. Endocr Rev 1:411, 1980

325 **DISEASES OF THE ADRENAL CORTEX**

GORDON H. WILLIAMS / ROBERT G. DLUHY

BIOCHEMISTRY AND PHYSIOLOGY

STEROID NOMENCLATURE Steroids contain as their basic structure a cyclopentenoperhydrophenanthrane nucleus consisting of three 6-carbon hexane rings and a single 5-carbon pentane ring (D in Fig. 325-1). The carbon atoms are numbered in a sequence beginning with ring A (Fig. 325-1). Adrenal steroids contain either 19 or 21 carbon atoms. The C_{19} steroids have methyl groups at positions C-18 and C-19. C_{19} steroids that have a ketone group at C-17 are termed *17-ketosteroids.* The C_{19} steroids have predominant androgenic activity. The C_{21} steroids have a 2-carbon side chain (C-20 and C-21) attached at position 17 and methyl groups at C-18 and C-19. C_{21} steroids that also possess a hydroxyl group at position 17 are termed *17-hydroxycorticosteroids* or *17-hydroxycorticoids.* The C_{21} steroids have either glucocorticoid or mineralocorticoid properties. *Glucocorticoid* signifies a C_{21} steroid with predominant action on intermediary metabolism; *mineralocorticoid* indicates a C_{21} steroid with predominant action on the metabolism of sodium and potassium.

BIOSYNTHESIS OF ADRENAL STEROIDS Cholesterol, derived from the diet and from endogenous synthesis via acetate, is the starting compound in steroidogenesis. The three major adrenal biosynthetic pathways lead to the production of glucocorticoids (cortisol), mineralocorticoids (aldosterone), and adrenal androgens (dehydroepiandrosterone). Separate zones of the adrenal cortex synthesize specific hormones; this reflects the enzymatic capacity of each zone to carry out certain transformations and hydroxylations (Fig. 325-2). The outer (glomerulosa) zone is mainly involved in aldosterone biosynthesis, and the inner (fasciculata-reticularis) zone is the site of cortisol and androgen biosynthesis.

STEROID TRANSPORT Some steroid hormones, e.g., testosterone and cortisol, circulate to a considerable extent bound to plasma proteins. Cortisol occurs in the plasma in three forms: free cortisol, protein-bound cortisol, and cortisol metabolites. *Free cortisol* refers to that quantity which is physiologically active but not protein-bound and, therefore, represents a form of cortisol acting directly on tissue sites. Normally, less than 5 percent of circulating cortisol is free. The diffusible fraction ranges between 0.7 and 1.0 µg/dL. Only the unbound cortisol and its metabolites are filtrable at the glomerulus. Increased quantities of free steroid are excreted in the urine in states characterized by hypersecretion of cortisol, as the unbound fraction of plasma cortisol rises. *Protein-bound cortisol* is that reversibly bound to circulating plasma proteins. There are two cortisol-binding systems of plasma. One is a high-affinity, low-capacity alpha$_2$ globulin termed *transcortin* or *cortisol-binding globulin* (CBG), and the other is a low-affinity, high-capacity protein, albumin. Cortisol-binding globulin in normal humans can bind approximately 20 to 25 µg of cortisol per deciliter of plasma. When the concentration of cortisol exceeds this level, the excess becomes bound in part to albumin, and a greater proportion circulates unbound. The CBG level is increased in high-estrogen states (e.g., pregnancy, oral contraceptive administration). The rise in CBG is accompanied by a parallel rise in protein-bound cortisol, with the result that the plasma cortisol concentration is elevated. However, the free cortisol levels probably remain normal, and signs and symptoms of glucocorticoid excess are absent. Most synthetic glucocorticoid analogues bind less efficiently to CBG (approximately 70 percent binding). This may explain the propensity of some synthetic analogues to produce cushingoid side effects at low dosage. *Cortisol metabolites* are biologically inactive and bind only weakly to circulating plasma proteins.

Aldosterone is bound to proteins to a smaller extent than either testosterone or cortisol, and an ultrafiltrate of plasma contains as much as 50 percent of the circulating aldosterone. The limited binding of aldosterone by plasma protein is significant in the metabolism of this hormone.

STEROID METABOLISM AND EXCRETION Glucocorticoids The daily secretion of cortisol ranges between 15 and 30 mg, with a pronounced diurnal cycle. Cortisol is distributed in a volume of body fluids approximating the total extracellular fluid space. The total plasma concentration of cortisol in the morning hours is approximately 15 µg/dL, with more than 90 percent in the protein-bound fraction. The plasma concentration of cortisol is determined by the rate of secretion, the rate of inactivation, and the rate of excretion of free cortisol. The liver is the major organ responsible for steroid inactivation, by reduction of ring A and conjugation of the reduced products with glucuronic acid at position C-3 to form water-soluble compounds. The 11-dehydrogenase system converts cortisol to the inactive cortisone and is influenced by the level of circulating thyroid hormone, the oxidative reaction being increased in hyperthyroidism.

Mineralocorticoids In normal subjects on a normal salt intake, the average daily secretion of aldosterone ranges between 50 and 250 µg, and the plasma concentration ranges between 5 and 15 ng/dL. Since aldosterone is only weakly bound to proteins, its volume of distribution is larger than that of cortisol and approximates 35 liters. During a single passage through the liver, more than 75 percent of circulating aldosterone is normally inactivated by ring A reduction and conjugation with glucuronic acid. However, under certain conditions, such as congestive failure, this inactivation is reduced.

From 7 to 15 percent of aldosterone is excreted in the urine as a glucuronide conjugate, from which free aldosterone is released on standing at pH 1. This *acid-labile conjugate* is formed in the liver and in the kidney. For average salt intake, the 24-h urine excretion of the acid-labile conjugate ranges from 2 to 20 µg, that of the reduced derivative from 25 to 35 µg, and that of the nonconjugated, nonreduced free aldosterone from 0.2 to 0.6 µg.

FIGURE 325-1 *Basic steroid structure and nomenclature.*

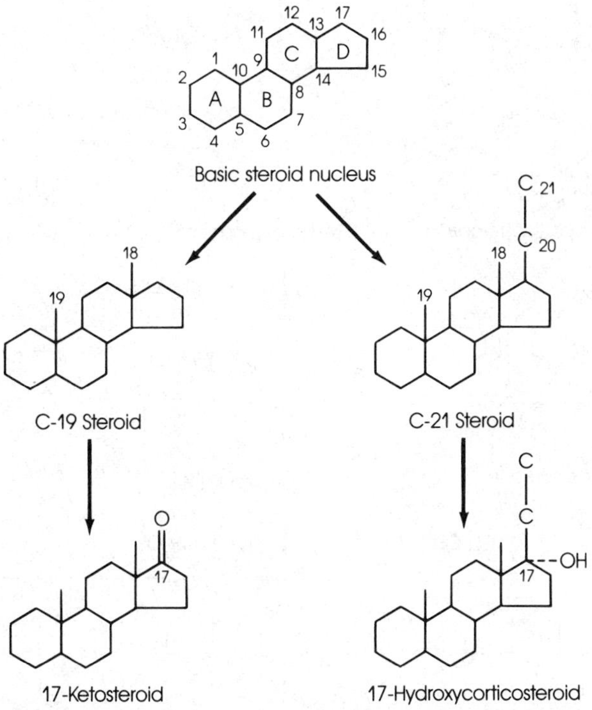

Basic steroid nucleus

C-19 Steroid

C-21 Steroid

17-Ketosteroid

17-Hydroxycorticosteroid

Adrenal androgens   The major androgen secreted by the adrenal is dehydroepiandrosterone (DHEA) and its C-3 sulfuric acid ester. From 15 to 30 mg of these compounds is secreted daily. Smaller amounts of Δ^4-androstenedione, 11β-hydroxyandrostenedione, and testosterone are secreted. DHEA is the major precursor of the urinary 17-ketosteroids. Two-thirds of the urine 17-ketosteroids in the male is derived from adrenal metabolites, and the remaining one-third comes from testicular androgens. In the female, almost all urine 17-ketosteroids are derived from the adrenal.

ACTH PHYSIOLOGY   Corticotropin (ACTH) (see Chap. 321) is an unbranched polypeptide containing 39 amino acids. ACTH and a number of other peptides (lipotropins, endorphins, and melanocyte-stimulating hormones) are processed from a larger precursor molecule of 31,000 mol wt—pro-opiomelanocortin (POMC) (see Chaps. 69 and 321 and Fig. 325-3). ACTH is synthesized and stored in basophilic cells of the anterior pituitary gland. The basophilic staining of the corticotrophs is the result of the glycosylation of ACTH and related peptides. Much of the potential for the corticotropic actions of ACTH is present in smaller polypeptide fragments; the *N*-terminal 18-amino-acid structure retains full biologic potency, and shorter *N*-terminal fragments exhibit partial biologic activity. Release of ACTH and related peptides from the anterior pituitary gland is governed by a "corticotropin-releasing center" in the median eminence of the

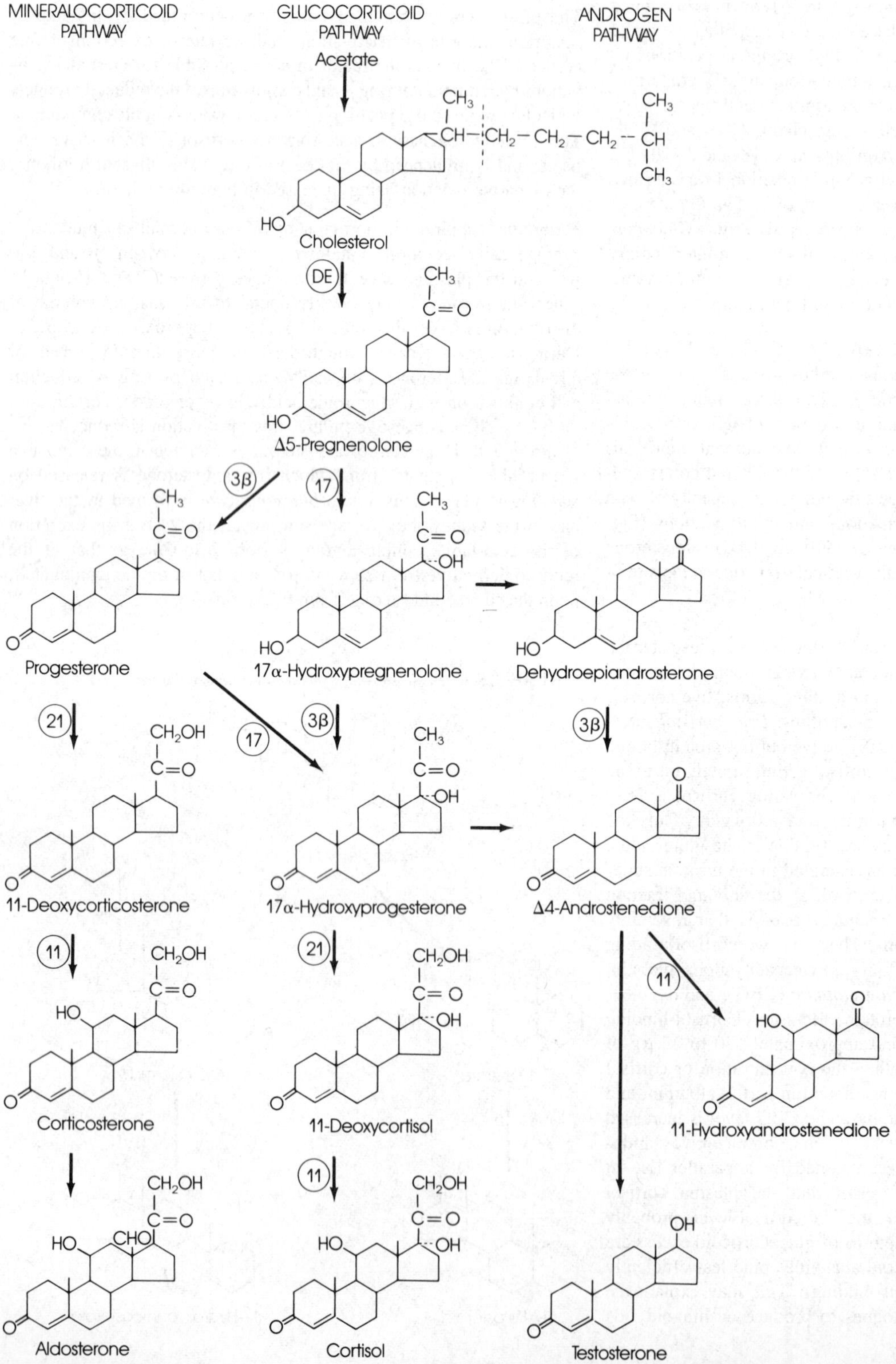

FIGURE 325-2 *Biosynthetic pathways for adrenal steroid production; major pathways to mineralocorticoids, glucocorticoids, and androgens. Circled letters and numbers denote specific enzymes: DE = cholesterol side chain cleavage enzyme; 3β = 3β-ol-dehydrogenase with Δ^{4,5}-isomerase; 11 = C-11 hydroxylase; 17 = C-17 hydroxylase; 21 = C-21 hydroxylase.*

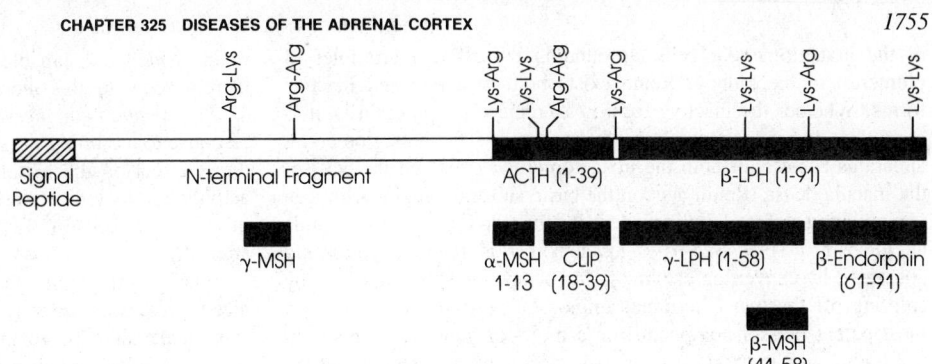

FIGURE 325-3 *Schematic representation of the probable structure of the 31,000–mol wt pro-opiomelanocortin molecule. (From DT Krieger, JB Martin, N Engl J Med 304:880, 1981. By permission of the New England Journal of Medicine.)*

hypothalamus, which upon stimulation releases a peptide with a chain of 41 amino acids (corticotropin-releasing hormone, CRH) that travels via the pituitary-stalk portal bloodstream to the anterior pituitary, where it effects the release of ACTH (Fig. 325-3). Some related peptides such as β-lipotropin (β-LPH) are released in equimolar concentrations with ACTH, suggesting enzymatic cleavage from the parent POMC prior to or concomitant with the secretory process. However, beta endorphin levels may vary disparately with circulating levels of ACTH depending on the nature of the stimulus. The functions and regulation of secretion of the related peptides derived from POMC are not understood.

The major factors controlling ACTH release include CRH, free cortisol concentration in plasma, stress, and the sleep-wake cycle (Fig. 325-4). The plasma level of ACTH varies during the day as a result of its pulsatile secretion but roughly follows a diurnal pattern, with a peak occurring just prior to awaking and a nadir shortly before retiring. After several days on a new sleep-wake cycle, the pattern is altered to conform to the new cycle. ACTH and cortisol levels also increase in response to eating. Stress (e.g., pyrogens, surgery, hypoglycemia, exercise, and severe emotional trauma) can also enhance ACTH release. Stress-related secretion of ACTH abolishes circadian periodicity but is in turn suppressed by prior high-dose glucocorticoid administration. The secretion of ACTH following stress and the normal pulsatile, diurnal ACTH release are regulated by CRH; this is the so-called open feedback loop. CRH secretion, in turn, is influenced by hypothalamic neurotransmitters. For example, serotoninergic and cholinergic systems stimulate the secretion of CRH and ACTH; there is contradictory evidence regarding the inhibitory effects of α-adrenergic agonists and gamma-aminobutyric acid (GABA) on CRH release. In addition, there may be direct pituitary effects of these neurotransmitters. There is also evidence for peptidergic regulation of ACTH release. For example, beta endorphin and enkephalin inhibit and vasopressin and angiotensin II augment the secretion of ACTH. Finally, ACTH release is regulated by the free cortisol level in plasma. Cortisol decreases the responsiveness of adrenal corticotropic cells to CRH; i.e., in the presence of cortisol more CRH is required to produce a given increment of ACTH. Glucocorticoids also inhibit CRH release. This servomechanism establishes the primacy of blood cortisol concentration in the control of ACTH secretion. The inhibition of ACTH occurs in two phases: (1) an early fast feedback, possibly a membrane effect, lasting less than 10 min and dependent on the rate of increase of glucocorticoid levels; and (2) a time-dependent delayed feedback response, probably due to inhibition of synthesis of the precursor protein. The suppression of ACTH secretion that results in adrenal atrophy following *prolonged* glucocorticoid therapy may be primarily related to suppression of hypothalamic CRH release, since exogenous CRH administration in this circumstance still produces a rise in plasma ACTH. Cortisol also exerts feedback on higher brain centers (hippocampus, reticular system, and septum) and perhaps on the adrenal cortex as well (Fig. 325-4).

The biologic half-life of ACTH in the circulation is less than 10 min. The action of ACTH is also rapid; within minutes of its release, the concentration of steroids in the adrenal venous blood increases.

ACTH stimulates steroidogenesis via activation of the membrane-bound adenyl cyclase. Adenosine 3′,5′-monophosphate (cyclic AMP) in turn activates protein kinase enzymes, thereby resulting in the phosphorylation of proteins that activate steroid biosynthesis (see Chap. 67).

RENIN-ANGIOTENSIN PHYSIOLOGY (See also Chap. 196)   Renin is a proteolytic enzyme that is produced and stored in the granules

FIGURE 325-4 *The hypothalamic-pituitary-adrenal axis. The dominant feedback control of plasma cortisol is on the pituitary gland (1) and on the hypothalamic corticotropin-releasing center (2). Feedback of plasma cortisol may also act on higher nerve centers (3) and/or on the adrenal gland itself (4). There also may be a short feedback inhibition of CRH by ACTH (5). Hypothalamic neurotransmitters influence CRH release; serotoninergic and cholinergic systems stimulate the secretion of CRH and ACTH; alpha-adrenergic agonists and gamma-aminobutyric acid (GABA) probably inhibit CRH release. The opioid peptides, beta endorphin and enkephalin, inhibit and vasopressin and angiotensin II augment the secretion of CRH and ACTH. CRH = corticotropin-releasing hormone; β-LPH = beta lipotropin; POMC = pro-opiomelanocortin.*

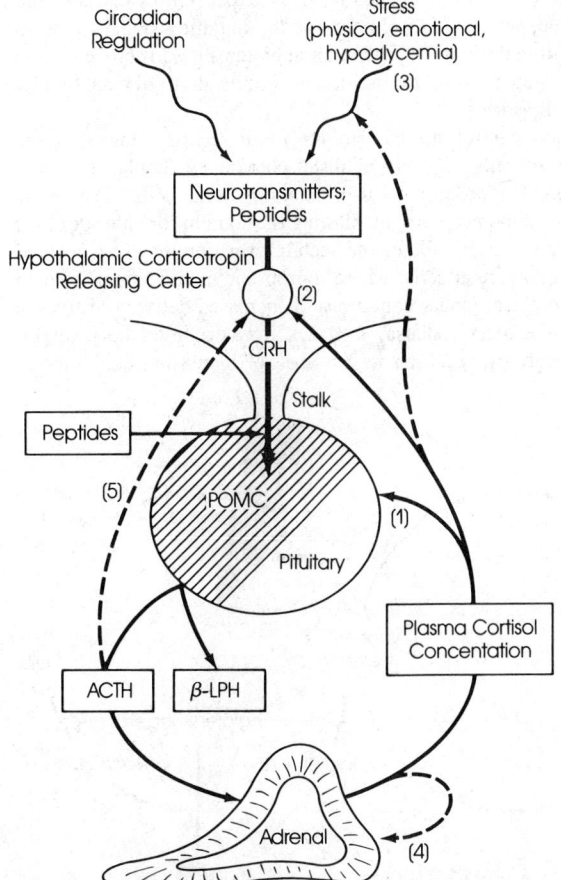

of the juxtaglomerular cells surrounding the afferent arterioles of glomeruli in the kidney. Renin exists both in active and inactive forms. Whether the inactive form is a precursor (''prorenin'') or is a product formed after release is uncertain. The juxtaglomerular apparatus consists of both the juxtaglomerular cells and the cells of the macula densa. Renin acts on the basic substrate angiotensinogen (a circulating alpha$_2$ globulin made in the liver) to form the decapeptide angiotensin I (Fig. 325-5). Angiotensin I is then enzymatically converted by converting enzyme to the octapeptide angiotensin II by splitting off the two C-terminal amino acids. Angiotensin II is the most potent pressor compound (on a mole-for-mole basis) made in the body, and it exerts this pressor action by a direct effect on arteriolar smooth muscle. In addition, angiotensin II is a potent stimulus to the production of aldosterone by the zona glomerulosa of the adrenal cortex; the nonapeptide, angiotensin III, may also stimulate aldosterone production. Angiotensinases rapidly destroy angiotensin II (half-life approximately 1 min), while the half-life of renin is more prolonged (10 to 20 min). Other tissues, such as uterus, vascular tissue, brain, and salivary glands, also produce renin-like substances, the significance of these so-called isorenins is not known.

Renin release is controlled by four interdependent factors, and the amount of renin released is a composite of the effects of all four. The *juxtaglomerular cells,* which are specialized myoepithelial cells cuffing the afferent arterioles, act as miniature pressure transducers, sensing renal perfusion pressure and corresponding changes in afferent arteriolar perfusion pressures. For example, under conditions of a reduction in circulating blood volume, there is a corresponding reduction in renal perfusion pressure and, therefore, in afferent arteriolar pressure (Fig. 325-5). This is perceived by the juxtaglomerular cells as a decreased stretch exerted on the afferent arteriolar walls. The juxtaglomerular cells then release increasing quantities of renin within the kidney circulation. This results in the formation of angiotensin I, which is converted in the kidney and peripherally to angiotensin II by a peptidyldipeptide hydrolase (so-called converting enzyme). Angiotensin II stimulates the adrenal cortex to release aldosterone. Increasing plasma levels of aldosterone lead to increasing renal sodium retention and thus result in expansion of extracellular fluid volume, which, in turn, dampens the initiating signal for renin release. Within this context, the renin-angiotensin-aldosterone system subserves volume control by appropriate modifications of renal tubular sodium transport.

A second control mechanism for renin release centers in the *macula densa* cells, a group of distal convoluted tubular epithelial cells in direct apposition to the juxtaglomerular cells. They may function as chemoreceptors, monitoring the sodium (or chloride) load presented to the distal tubule, and such information may be conveyed to the juxtaglomerular cells, where appropriate modifications in renin release take place. Under conditions of increased delivery of filtered sodium to the macula densa, feedback may occur to the juxtaglomerular apparatus, resulting in a release of increasing quantities of

renin, which are capable of decreasing glomerular filtration rate, thereby reducing the filtered load of sodium.

The *sympathetic nervous system* regulates release of renin in response to assuming the upright posture. The mechanism is either a direct effect on the juxtaglomerular cell to increase adenyl cyclase activity or an indirect effect on either the juxtaglomerular or the macula densa cells by way of a vasoconstrictive action on the afferent arteriole.

Finally, circulating factors may alter renin release. Increasing dietary *potassium* directly decreases renin release; decreasing potassium intake increases renin release. The significance of this potassium effect is unclear. *Angiotensin II* itself can exert a negative feedback control on renin release independent of alterations in renal blood flow, pressure, or aldosterone secretion. Atrial natriuretic peptides also may inhibit renin release. Thus, the control of renin release is complex, consisting of both *intrarenal* (pressor receptor and macula densa) and *extrarenal* (sympathetic nervous system, potassium, angiotensin, etc.) mechanisms. A given level of renin secretion probably reflects all these factors, with the intrarenal mechanism predominating.

GLUCOCORTICOID PHYSIOLOGY   The division of adrenal steroids into glucocorticoids and mineralocorticoids is arbitrary in that most glucocorticoids have some mineralocorticoid-like properties, and vice versa. The descriptive term *glucocorticoid* is applied to those adrenal steroids having a predominant action on intermediary metabolism. The principal glucocorticoid is cortisol (hydrocortisone). Cortisol enters the target cell by diffusion, combines with a specific high-affinity cytoplasmic receptor protein, and is transferred to a specific acceptor site on the chromatin tissue of the nucleus, which then produces an increase in RNA synthesis and later in protein synthesis. Thus, an alternative way of defining a glucocorticoid effect is one mediated by a class of high-affinity cytoplasmic receptors (glucorticoid receptors) (see Chap. 320). The physiologic actions of the glucocorticoids on intermediary metabolism include the regulation of protein, carbohydrate, lipid, and nucleic acid metabolism. The actions appear to be mainly catabolic in effect, with an increased protein breakdown and nitrogen excretion. Glucocorticoids increase hepatic glycogen content and promote the hepatic synthesis of glucose (gluconeogenesis). These actions are in large part explained by the mobilization of glycogenic amino acid precursors from peripheral supporting structures, such as bone, skin, muscle, and connective tissue, due to protein breakdown and inhibition of protein synthesis and amino acid uptake. Glucocorticoid-induced hyperaminoacidemia also facilitates gluconeogenesis by stimulating glucagon secretion. Glucocorticoids act directly on the liver to stimulate the synthesis of certain enzymes, such as tyrosine amino transferase and tryptophan pyrrolase. Corticoids inhibit the synthesis of nucleic acids in most body tissues, but in the liver ribonucleic acid (RNA) synthesis is stimulated. Glucocorticoids regulate fatty acid mobilization by enhancing activation of

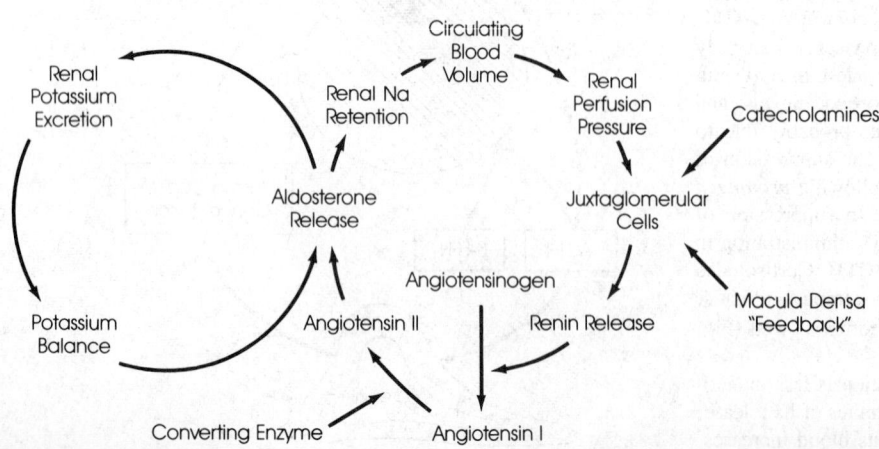

FIGURE 325-5 *The interrelationship of the volume and potassium feedback loops on aldosterone secretion. Integration of signals from each loop determines the level of aldosterone secretion.*

cellular lipase by lipid-mobilizing hormones (e.g., catecholamines and pituitary peptides).

The actions of cortisol on structural protein and on adipose tissue vary in different parts of the body. For example, pharmacologic doses of cortisol may deplete the protein matrix of the vertebral column (trabecular bone), but long bones (primarily compact bone) are affected only minimally; peripheral adipose tissue may diminish, whereas abdominal and interscapular fat may accumulate.

Cortisol levels are responsive within minutes to a variety of physical stresses (trauma, surgery, exercise) and psychological stresses (anxiety, depression). Hypoglycemia and fever are also potent stimuli of ACTH and cortisol secretion. The reasons why elevated glucocorticoid levels protect the organism under stress are not understood, but in their absence such stresses may cause hypotension, shock, and death. For these reasons, glucocorticoid administration should always be increased in individuals with hypofunction of the pituitary-adrenal axis during stress.

Glucocorticoids have anti-inflammatory properties, which are probably related to their actions on the microvasculature as well as to cellular effects. Cortisol maintains normal vascular responsiveness to circulating vasoconstrictor factors and opposes the increase in capillary permeability characteristic of acute inflammation. Glucocorticoids cause a polymorphonuclear leukocytosis; the circulating leukocyte mass is increased due to a release from the bone marrow of mature cells as well as to an inhibition of egress through the capillary wall. Cortisol also inhibits the production of interleukin 2 by macrophages. Reduced adherence of macrophages to vascular endothelium following glucocorticoid administration is probably secondary to antagonism to the action of migration-inhibiting factor (MIF). Glucocorticoids produce a depletion of circulating eosinophils and of lymphoid tissue, specifically T cells or the small lymphocytes derived from the thymus. The mechanism is by redistribution from the circulation into other compartments. Thus, cortisol impairs cellular-mediated immunity. It is probably only at pharmacologic dosages that antibody production is suppressed and stabilization of lysosomal membranes occurs, thereby suppressing the release of proteolytic acid hydrolases stored in these cytoplasmic organelles. Cortisol has a major action on the distribution and excretion of body water. It subserves the extracellular fluid volume by retarding the migration of water into cells. It affects renal water excretion by suppressing the secretion of antidiuretic hormone, increasing the rate of glomerular filtration, and acting directly on the renal tubule, the consequence being to increase solute-free water clearance. Glucocorticoids also have weak mineralocorticoid-like properties, and increasing doses produce renal tubular sodium reabsorption and increased urine potassium excretion. Glucocorticoids can also influence behavior; emotional disorders may occur with either excesses or deficits of cortisol. Lastly, cortisol suppresses the secretion of pituitary ACTH and hypothalamic CRH.

MINERALOCORTICOID PHYSIOLOGY The major mineralocorticoid, aldosterone, has two important activities: (1) It is a major regulator of extracellular fluid volume, and (2) it is a major determinant of potassium metabolism. These effects are mediated by binding of aldosterone to specific, high-affinity mineralocorticoid receptor proteins in target tissues. Volume is regulated through a direct effect on the renal tubular transport of sodium. Aldosterone acts predominantly at the distal convoluted tubule, where it causes a decrease in the excretion of sodium and an increase in excretion of potassium. The reabsorption of sodium ions causes a fall in the transmembrane potential, thus enhancing the flow of positive ions out of the cell into the lumen. The major intracellular singly charged positive ion is potassium. Since its concentration in the cell is forty- to eightyfold greater than in the lumen, potassium passively follows this relative electric gradient to restore the normal positive charge to the lumen. The reabsorbed sodium ions are then transported out of the tubular epithelial cells into the interstitial fluid of the kidney and from there into the renal capillary circulation. Water passively follows the transported sodium.

Hydrogen ion is also abundant in the tubular epithelial cell. Since its concentration is greater in the lumen than in the cell, it is actively secreted, but the reduced intraluminal positivity allows more hydrogen to be secreted with the same amount of energy. Aldosterone and other mineralocorticoids also act on the epithelium of the salivary ducts, sweat glands, and gastrointestinal tract to cause reabsorption of sodium in "exchange" for potassium ions.

When normal individuals are given aldosterone (or deoxycorticosterone acetate), an initial period of sodium retention is followed by a natriuresis, and sodium balance is reestablished after 3 to 5 days. As a result, edema does not develop. This phenomenon is referred to as the "escape phenomenon," signifying an "escape" by the renal tubules from the sodium-retaining action of chronically administered aldosterone.

Three mechanisms control aldosterone release—the renin-angiotensin system, potassium, and ACTH (Table 325-1). The renin-angiotensin system is the major system for control of extracellular fluid volume, via regulation of aldosterone secretion (Fig. 325-5). In effect, the renin-angiotensin system maintains the circulating blood volume constant by causing aldosterone-induced sodium retention during periods registered as volume deficiencies and by decreasing aldosterone-dependent sodium retention under conditions in which volume is registered as being ample.

Potassium ions directly regulate aldosterone secretion independently of the renin-angiotensin system (Fig. 325-5). In normal humans, oral potassium loading increases aldosterone secretion, excretion, and plasma levels. In addition, an increase in serum potassium of as little as 0.1 meq per liter increases plasma aldosterone levels under certain circumstances.

Physiologic amounts of ACTH acutely stimulate aldosterone secretion, but this action is not sustained if ACTH is infused for periods greater than 10 to 12 h. Most studies relegate ACTH to a minor role in the control of aldosterone. For example, subjects on high-dose steroid therapy for several years and with presumably complete suppression of ACTH have normal aldosterone-secretory responses to sodium restriction. Therefore, chronic ACTH deficiency per se does not alter glomerulosa cell responsiveness.

The prior dietary intake of both potassium and sodium can alter the magnitude of the aldosterone response to acute stimulation. Increasing potassium intake or decreasing sodium intake sensitizes the response of the glomerulosa cells to acute stimulation by ACTH, angiotensin II, and/or potassium.

Neurotransmitters (dopamine and serotonin) and some peptides, such as atrial natriuretic factor, γ-melanocyte-stimulating hormone (γ-MSH), beta endorphin, and an unidentified pituitary aldosterone-stimulating factor, also participate in the regulation of aldosterone secretion (Table 325-1). Thus, the control of aldosterone secretion involves both stimulatory and inhibitory factors.

TABLE 325-1 Factors regulating aldosterone biosynthesis

Factors	Effects
I Renin-angiotensin system	Stimulate
II Sodium ion	Inhibit (?physiologic)
III Potassium ion	Stimulate
IV Neurotransmitters	
A Dopamine	Inhibit
B Serotonin	Stimulate
V Pituitary hormones	
A ACTH	Stimulate
B Non-ACTH pituitary hormones (e.g., growth hormone)	Permissive (for optimal response to sodium restriction)
C Unidentified pituitary factors	Stimulate
D Beta endorphin	Stimulate
E γ-MSH	Permissive
VI Natriuretic factors	
A Atrial factors	Inhibit
B Ouabain-like factors	Inhibit

ANDROGEN PHYSIOLOGY   Androgens are substances that stimulate male secondary sexual characteristics. They produce these actions by binding to high-affinity cytoplasmic receptors. The secondary sexual characteristics are affected through inhibition of the female characteristics (defeminization) and accentuation of the male characteristics (masculinization). These are seen clinically as hirsutism and virilization in the female with amenorrhea, atrophy of the breasts and uterus, enlargement of the clitoris, deepening of the voice, acne, increased muscle mass, and receding hairline (Chap. 46).

Steroids with predominant androgenic activity have 19 carbon atoms (Fig. 325-1). The principal adrenal androgens are dehydroepiandrosterone (DHEA), androstenedione, and 11-hydroxyandrostenedione. DHEA and its sulfate are *quantitatively* the major androgens secreted by the adrenal; DHEA and androstenedione are weak androgens, and they exert their effects via conversion in extraglandular tissues to the potent androgen, testosterone. The release of adrenal androgens is stimulated by ACTH, not by gonadotropins. With ACTH stimulation, 17-ketosteroids increase but to a lesser extent than do urine 17-hydroxycorticosteroids. It follows that adrenal androgens are suppressed by exogenous glucocorticoid administration.

LABORATORY EVALUATION OF ADRENOCORTICAL FUNCTION

The basic assumption in the measurement of plasma or urinary steroids is that they accurately reflect adrenal *secretory* rates of that steroid. A disadvantage of urine *excretion* values is that they may not truly reflect the secretion rate because of improper collection or altered metabolism. Measurement of the actual adrenal secretory rate of a given steroid would be preferable but is more difficult, involving isotope dilution techniques following administration of a radioactive steroid. Plasma levels reflect the level of secretion only at the time of measurement. The plasma level (PL) is dependent on two factors: the secretion rate (SR) of the hormone and the rate at which it is metabolized, i.e., its metabolic clearance rate (MCR). These three factors can be related mathematically as follows:

$$PL = \frac{SR}{MCR} \quad \text{or} \quad SR = MCR \times PL$$

BLOOD LEVELS (See Table 352-2)   **Peptides**   ACTH and angiotensin II can be measured by radioimmunoassay, but the measurements are technically difficult because of their low concentrations and their instability in human plasma. In addition, ACTH levels fluctuate from moment to moment, and a circadian rhythm is superimposed on basal ACTH secretion, with lower levels in the early evening than in the morning. Angiotensin II levels also vary diurnally but more importantly are influenced by dietary sodium intake and posture. Both upright posture and sodium restriction elevate angiotensin II levels.

Most clinical determinations of the renin-angiotensin system, however, involve measurements of peripheral "plasma renin activity" (PRA) in which the renin activity is gauged by the generation of angiotensin I during a standardized incubation period. This method depends on the presence of sufficient angiotensinogen in the patient's plasma as substrate. The generated angiotensin I is then measured by radioimmunoassay. Plasma renin activity depends on dietary sodium intake and whether the patient is ambulatory. In normal humans a diurnal rhythm for plasma renin activity is characterized by peak values in the morning with decreases in activity in the afternoon.

Steroids   Cortisol and aldosterone are both secreted episodically, and levels generally decline during the day with peak values in the morning and low levels in the evening. In addition, the plasma level of aldosterone, but not of cortisol, is increased by dietary potassium loading, sodium restriction, or assuming the upright posture. Measurement of the sulfate conjugate of DHEA is a useful index of adrenal androgen secretion since little is formed in the gonads and the half-life is prolonged (7 to 9 h).

URINE LEVELS   The urine *17-hydroxycorticoids* are determined as Porter-Silber chromogens; this reaction is specific for steroids with a "dihydroxyacetone" C-17 side chain, i.e., with hydroxyl groups on C-17 and C-21 and a ketone group on C-20. Therefore, this determination includes cortisol, cortisone, tetrahydrocortisol, tetrahydrocortisone, and 11-deoxycortisol (Fig. 325-2). Normally, daytime (7 A.M. to 7 P.M.) excretion exceeds night values (7 P.M. to 7 A.M.).

The urine *17-ketosteroids* are those containing a ketone group at C-17 (Fig. 325-1). They originate either in the adrenal gland or the gonad. In normal women, 90 percent or more of total urinary 17-ketosteroids is derived from the adrenal gland, while in men only 60 to 70 percent is of adrenal origin. Urine 17-ketosteroid values are highest in young adults and decline with age.

The determination of urinary free cortisol is perhaps more useful than 17-hydroxysteroid measurements since elevated excretion values correlate with states of hypercortisolism, reflecting changes in the unbound, physiologically active, circulating levels of cortisol.

A carefully timed urine collection is a prerequisite for all excretory determinations. Urinary creatinine should be measured simultaneously to demonstrate the accuracy and adequacy of the collection procedure. Adjustments for body size can be made; e.g., normal subjects excrete 3 to 7 mg of 17-hydroxycorticosteroids per gram of creatinine.

STIMULATION TESTS   Stimulation tests are useful in documenting the existence of a hormonal deficiency state. A standardized and specific stimulus for the production and release of a given hormone is applied, and the quantity of the released hormone can then be measured.

Tests of glucocorticoid reserve   Within minutes after initiation of an infusion of ACTH, cortisol levels increase in adrenal venous blood. This responsiveness of the adrenal gland to ACTH is utilized as an index of the "functional reserve" of the gland for production of cortisol. Under maximal ACTH stimulation the cortisol secretion increases tenfold to 300 mg per day. Such maximal stimulation can be obtained only with prolonged ACTH infusions. For clinical purposes, the functional adrenal reserve for cortisol production is

TABLE 325-2   Range of normal values for tests of adrenal function

Test	Normal value, range
Plasma cortisol, μg/dL:	
8 A.M.	9–24
4 P.M.	3–12
Cortisol secretory rate, mg/24 h	5–25
Urinary free cortisol, μg/24 h	20–100
17-Hydroxycorticoids, mg/24 h	2–10
Plasma testosterone, μg/dL:	
Men	0.3–1.0
Women	0.01–0.1
17-Ketosteroids, mg/24 h:	
Men	7–25
Women	4–15
Plasma dehydroepiandrosterone (DHEA) μg/dL	0.2–0.9
Plasma DHEA sulfate, μg/dL	50–250
Plasma 11-deoxycortisol (S), μg/dL	<1.0
Plasma 17αOH progesterone, ng/dL:	
Women	
Follicular phase	6–110
Luteal phase	50–350
Men	6–300
Plasma aldosterone, ng/dL (100 meq Na, 60–100 meq K, 8 A.M.)	1–5
Aldosterone secretion, μg/24 h (100 meq Na, 600–100 meq K)	50–250
Aldosterone excretion, μg/24 h (100 meq Na, 60–100 meq K)	2–10
Plasma renin activity, (ng/mL)/h (100 meq Na, 60–100 meq K, supine, 8 A.M.)	1–2.5
Plasma angiotensin II, pg/mL (100 meq Na, 60–100 meq K, supine, 8 A.M.)	10–30
Plasma ACTH, pg/mL (8 A.M.)	<80

standardized with a 24-h ACTH infusion. Synthetic α^{1-24}-ACTH (cosyntropin) is usually given in 500 to 1000 mL normal saline solution at a rate of 2 units per hour for 24 h. Normal subjects increase 17-hydroxysteroid excretion rates to at least 25 mg per 24 h, and plasma cortisol levels exceed 40 μg/dL. In patients with secondary adrenal insufficiency, the maximal 17-hydroxysteroid excretion rate is 3 to 20 mg per 24 h, and the plasma cortisol value at 24 h ranges between 10 and 40 μg/dL. Patients with primary adrenal insufficiency have smaller responses.

A rapid screening test is to administer 25 units (0.25 mg) cosyntropin intravenously or intramuscularly and measure plasma cortisol levels before and 30 and 60 min later. An increment of at least 7 μg/dL above base line is observed in normal subjects.

Tests of mineralocorticoid reserve and stimulation of the renin-angiotensin system
Stimulation tests utilize protocols of programmed volume depletion, such as sodium restriction, diuretic administration, or upright posture. A simple potent test consists of severe sodium restriction and upright posture. After 3 to 5 days of a 10-meq sodium intake, aldosterone secretion or excretion rates should increase two- to threefold over control. Supine morning plasma aldosterone levels usually increase three- to sixfold. In addition, plasma levels increase two- to fourfold in response to 2 to 3 h of upright posture.

Stimulation tests on normal dietary sodium intake may be carried out by the administration of a potent diuretic, such as 40 to 80 mg furosemide, followed by 2 to 3 h of upright posture. The normal response is a two- to fourfold rise in plasma aldosterone levels.

SUPPRESSION TESTS
Suppression tests to document hypersecretion of adrenocortical hormones are based on the demonstration of a decrease in the target hormone following standardized suppression of its tropic hormone.

Tests of pituitary-adrenal suppressibility
The ACTH release mechanism is sensitive to the circulating blood level of glucocorticoids. When such blood levels are increased in the normal individual, less ACTH is released from the anterior pituitary, and secondarily, less steroid is produced by the adrenal gland. The integrity of this feedback mechanism can be tested clinically by giving a potent glucocorticoid and judging suppression of ACTH secretion by analysis of urine steroid excretory values and/or plasma cortisol and ACTH levels. A potent glucocorticoid such as dexamethasone is utilized in order that the administered compound can be given in such small amounts that it does not contribute significantly to the steroids to be analyzed.

The best *screening* procedure is the overnight dexamethasone suppression test. This involves the measurement of plasma cortisol levels at 8 A.M. following the oral administration of 1 mg dexamethasone the previous midnight. The 8 A.M. value for plasma cortisol in normal subjects should be less than 5 μg/dL.

The definitive test of adrenal suppressibility is to administer 0.5 mg dexamethasone every 6 h for two successive days while collecting urine over a 24-h period for determination of creatinine, 17-hydroxysteroids and/or free cortisol and/or measuring plasma cortisol levels. In a patient with a normal hypothalamic pituitary ACTH release mechanism, a fall in the urine 17-hydroxycorticoids to less than 3 mg a day on the second day of dexamethasone administration, urinary free cortisol to less than 30 μg per day, or plasma cortisol to less than 5 μg/dL is seen.

Normal responses to either of the suppression tests implies that the ACTH control of the adrenal glands is physiologically normal. However, an isolated abnormal result, particularly when the overnight suppression test is being used, does not in itself imply pituitary and/or adrenal disease.

Tests of mineralocorticoid suppressibility
Mineralocorticoid suppression procedures have been devised using saline infusions, oral salt loading, or deoxycorticosterone acetate (DOCA) administration for expansion of the extracellular fluid volume. With expansion of extracellular fluid volume, there is a decrease in renal renin release, a decrease in circulating plasma renin activity, and a decrease in aldosterone secretion and/or excretion. Various tests differ in the rate at which extracellular fluid volume is expanded. One convenient suppression test is the intravenous infusion of 500 mL normal saline solution per hour for 4 h, which normally suppresses plasma aldosterone levels to < 8 ng/dL on a sodium-restricted diet or to < 5 ng/dL on a normal sodium intake. This test should not be performed in potassium-depleted subjects.

TESTS OF PITUITARY-ADRENAL RESPONSIVENESS
Stimuli such as insulin hypoglycemia, arginine vasopressin, and pyrogen, cause release of ACTH from the pituitary by an action on higher nerve centers, the hypothalamus, or the pituitary itself. By measuring plasma ACTH or plasma glucocorticoids the status of pituitary ACTH can be evaluated. Insulin-induced hypoglycemia is particularly useful, since the release of growth hormone and of ACTH is stimulated. In this test 0.05 to 0.1 unit of regular insulin per kilogram of body weight is administered intravenously as a bolus to reduce fasting glucose levels at least 50 percent below basal. The normal cortisol response is a rise to more than 18 μg/dL.

Metyrapone is a drug that inhibits 11β-hydroxylase in the adrenal gland. As a result, the conversion of 11-deoxycortisol (compound S) to cortisol is interfered with, and increased amounts of 11-deoxycortisol accumulate while blood levels of cortisol decrease (Fig. 325-2). The hypothalamic-pituitary axis responds to the declining cortisol blood levels by releasing more ACTH. The metabolites of 11-deoxycortisol are excreted in increasing amounts in the urine, where they are measured as 17-hydroxycorticoids. Alternatively, changes in plasma 11-deoxycortisol levels can be measured. *Note that the adrenal glands must be capable of being stimulated by ACTH, since assessment of the response depends both on an intact hypothalamic-pituitary axis and on adrenal steroid production.*

The metyrapone test involves administering orally 750 mg of the drug every 4 h over a 24-h period and comparing the control and the post-metyrapone 17-hydroxysteroid excretion rates and/or plasma 11-deoxycortisol levels. Normal individuals respond with at least a doubling of their basal 17-hydroxysteroid excretion; 11-deoxycortisol levels in the blood should exceed 10 μg/dL following metyrapone administration. The metyrapone test does not accurately reflect ACTH reserve if subjects are ingesting exogenous glucocorticoids or drugs that accelerate the metabolism of metyrapone (e.g., phenytoin).

A direct and selective test of the pituitary corticotrophs can be achieved with the investigational agent corticotropin-releasing hormone (CRH). The bolus injection of 1 μg per kilogam of body weight of ovine CRH stimulates ACTH and beta endorphin secretion in normal human subjects within 60 to 180 min. However, the magnitude of the ACTH response is less than that produced by the insulin tolerance test, which implies that additional factors (such as vasopressin) augment stress-induced increases in ACTH secretion.

A test that distinguishes between primary and secondary adrenal insufficiency takes advantage of the preservation of relatively normal aldosterone secretion in secondary adrenal insufficiency. Twenty-five units of cosyntropin is given intravenously or intramuscularly, and plasma cortisol and aldosterone levels are obtained before and 30 and 60 min later. The cortisol increment is less than 7 μg/dL in both groups, but only patients with primary insufficiency fail to increase aldosterone levels above control by at least 5 ng/dL.

HYPERFUNCTION OF THE ADRENAL CORTEX

Distinct clinical syndromes are produced when excess amounts of the principal adrenocortical hormones are secreted. Thus, excess production of cortisol is associated with Cushing's syndrome, excess production of aldosterone with clinical and chemical signs of aldosteronism, and excess production of adrenal androgens with adrenal virilism. These syndromes do not always occur in the ''pure'' form but may have overlapping features.

CUSHING'S SYNDROME   Etiology   Cushing described a syndrome characterized by truncal obesity, hypertension, fatigability and weakness, amenorrhea, hirsutism, purplish abdominal striae, edema, glucosuria, osteoporosis, and a basophilic tumor of the pituitary. As awareness of this syndrome increased, the diagnosis of Cushing's syndrome has been broadened into the classification shown in Table 325-3. Regardless of etiology, all cases of Cushing's syndrome are due to increased production of cortisol by the adrenal gland. The majority are due to *bilateral adrenal hyperplasia,* secondary to adrenocortical stimulation by hypersecretion of pituitary ACTH or the production of ACTH by nonendocrine tumors. The incidence of pituitary-dependent adrenal hyperplasia in women is three times that in men, with the most frequent age of onset being the third or fourth decade. The cause of the hypersecretion pituitary ACTH is still unclear, but the primary defect probably resides in the hypothalamus or in higher nerve centers, leading to release of CRH inappropriate to the level of circulating cortisol. Consequently, a higher level of cortisol is required to reduce ACTH secretion to normal. This primary defect leads to hyperstimulation of the pituitary resulting, in some cases, in tumor formation. As the pituitary tumor grows, it may become independent of the regulating influence of central nervous system factors and/or circulating cortisol levels. Thus, individuals with hypersecretion of pituitary ACTH may have a microadenoma (<10 mm) or a macroadenoma (>10 mm) of the pituitary, or diffuse hyperplasia of the corticotropic cells (hypothalamic-pituitary dysfunction). Since microadenomas of the pituitary are often difficult to detect by usual radiologic procedures, the frequency of pituitary adenomas as a cause of Cushing's syndrome is uncertain. Traditionally, only an individual who has an ACTH-producing pituitary tumor has been defined as having *Cushing's disease.* However, in some centers, anyone who has hypersecretion of pituitary ACTH regardless of whether a tumor is present is classified as having Cushing' disease. In this chapter, we will use the traditional definition.

Nonendocrine tumors may secrete polypeptides that are biologically, chemically, and immunologically indistinguishable from either ACTH or CRH and that cause bilateral adrenal hyperplasia (see also Chap. 303). The ectopic production of CRH results in clinical, biochemical, and radiologic features indistinguishable from those caused by hypersecretion of pituitary ACTH. Often, but not invariably, the typical signs and symptoms of Cushing's syndrome are absent with ectopic ACTH production, and hypokalemic alkalosis and glucose intolerance are the prominent manifestations. The majority of these cases are associated with the primitive small-cell (oat cell) type of bronchogenic carcinoma or with tumors of the thymus, pancreas, or ovary, medullary carcinoma of the thyroid, or bronchial adenomas. The onset of Cushing's syndrome may be sudden, particularly in patients with oat cell carcinoma of the lung, and this feature accounts in part for the failure of these patients to exhibit the classic physical findings. On the other hand, patients with carcinoid tumors or pheochromocytomas have longer clinical courses and usually exhibit the typical cushingoid features. The secretion of ACTH by nonendocrine tumors is also accompanied by the accumulation of ACTH fragments in plasma and by elevated plasma levels of ACTH precursor molecules. Since such tumors may produce large amounts of ACTH,

baseline urinary steroid values are usually markedly elevated, and increased skin pigmentation is usually present. Indeed, hyperpigmentation in patients with Cushing's syndrome almost always points to an extraadrenal tumor, either in an extracranial location or within the cranium.

Approximately 20 to 25 percent of patients with Cushing's syndrome have primary overproduction of cortisol and other adrenal steroids due to an adrenal neoplasm. These tumors are usually unilateral, and about half are malignant. Occasionally, patients have biochemical features both of hypersecretion of pituitary ACTH and of an adrenal adenoma. These individuals usually have micro- or macro-nodularity of both adrenal glands resulting in *nodular hyperplasia.*

The most common cause of Cushing's syndrome is *iatrogenic* administration of steroids for other reasons. While the clinical features bear some resemblance to those of an individual with an adrenal adenoma, these patients are usually readily distinguishable on the basis of history and initial laboratory studies.

Clinical signs, symptoms, and laboratory findings   Many of the signs and symptoms of Cushing's syndrome logically follow from the known action of glucocorticoids (Table 325-4). As a result of mobilization of peripheral supportive tissue, muscle weakness and fatigability, osteoporosis, cutaneous striae, and easy bruisability result. The latter two signs are secondary to weakening and rupture of collagen fibers in the dermis. The osteoporosis may be so severe that collapse of vertebral bodies and pathologic fractures of other bones occur. Increased hepatic gluconeogenesis and insulin resistance can cause impaired glucose tolerance. Frank diabetes occurs in less than 20 percent of patients, probably in individuals with a familial predisposition to this disorder. Hypercortisolism promotes the deposition of adipose tissue in characteristic sites, notably in the upper part of the face, the classic "moon" facies; in the interscapular area, the "buffalo" hump; and in the mesenteric bed, where it produces the classic "truncal" obesity (Fig. 325-6). Rarely, there may be episternal fatty tumors and mediastinal widening secondary to fat accumulation. The reason for this peculiar distribution of adipose tissue is not known. The face appears plethoric, even in the absence of any increase in red blood cell concentration. Hypertension is common, and frequently there are profound emotional changes, ranging from irritability or emotional lability to severe depression, confusion, or even frank psychosis. In women, increased adrenal androgen secretion can cause acne, hirsutism, and oligomenorrhea or amenorrhea. The most common signs and symptoms in patients with hypercortisolism, i.e., obesity, hypertension, osteoporosis, and diabetes, are nonspecific and therefore less helpful in diagnosing this condition. On the other hand, easy bruising, typical striae, myopathy, and androgen effects (although less frequent) are, if present, more suggestive of Cushing's syndrome.

Except in iatrogenic Cushing's syndrome, plasma and urine cortisol and urinary 17-hydroxycorticoid levels are variably elevated. Occasionally, hypokalemia, hypochloremia and metabolic alkalosis are present, particularly in individuals who have ectopic production of ACTH.

Diagnosis   The diagnosis of Cushing's syndrome depends on the demonstration of increased cortisol production and the failure to suppress endogenous cortisol secretion normally when dexamethasone is administered. Once the diagnosis is established, further testing is

TABLE 325-3   Causes of Cushing's syndrome

I Adrenal hyperplasia
  A Secondary to pituitary ACTH overproduction
    1 Pituitary-hypothalamic dysfunction
    2 Pituitary ACTH-producing micro- or macroadenomas
  B Secondary to ACTH or CRH-producing nonendocrine tumors (bronchogenic carcinoma, carcinoid of the thymus, pancreatic carcinoma, bronchial adenoma)
II Adrenal nodular hyperplasia
III Adrenal neoplasia
  A Adenoma
  B Carcinoma
IV Exogenous, iatrogenic causes
  A Prolonged use of glucocorticoids
  B Prolonged use of ACTH

TABLE 325-4   Incidence of signs and symptoms in Cushing's syndrome, percent

Typical habitus	97	Amenorrhea	77
Increased body weight	94	Cutaneous striae	67
Fatigability and		Personality changes	66
weakness	87	Ecchymoses	65
Hypertension		Edema	62
(>150/90)	82	Polyuria, polydipsia	23
Hirsutism	80	Hypertrophy of clitoris	19

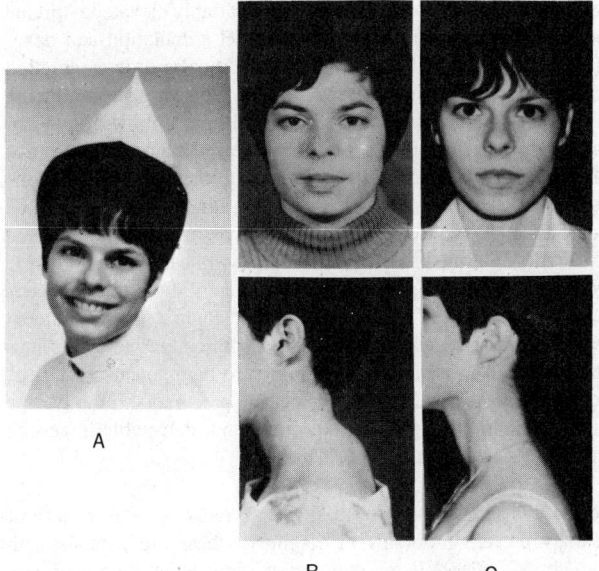

FIGURE 325-6 *A 20-year-old woman with Cushing's syndrome due to a right adrenal cortical adenoma. A. Two years prior to surgery, age 18. B. One month prior to surgery, age 20. C. One year after surgery, age 21.*

TABLE 325-5 Diagnostic tests to determine the type of Cushing's syndrome

Test	Pituitary macroadenoma	Pituitary-hypothalamic dysfunction or microadenoma	Ectopic ACTH or CRH production	Adrenal tumor
Measurement of plasma ACTH	↑ to ↑↑	N to ↑	↑ to ↑↑↑	↓
Response to high-dose dexamethasone, %	<10	>80	<10	<10
Response to metyrapone, %	>80	>90	<10	<10
Response to CRH, %	>90	>90	<10	<10

NOTE: *N, normal;* ↑, *elevated;* ↓, *decreased.*

designed to determine the etiology of the hypercortisolism (see Fig. 325-7 and Table 325-5).

For initial screening, the overnight dexamethasone suppression test is recommended (see above). In difficult cases (e.g., in obesity) measurement of a 24-h free cortisol excretion rate can also be used as a screening test. A level greater than 100 μg per day is suggestive

of Cushing's syndrome. The definitive diagnosis is then established by failure to suppress urinary cortisol to less than 30 μg per day, plasma cortisol to less than 5μg/dL, or 17-hydroxysteroid excretion to less than 3 mg per 24 h after a standard low-dose dexamethasone suppression test (0.5 mg every 6 h for 48 h). Owing to diurnal variability, plasma cortisol and, to a certain extent, ACTH determinations are not meaningful when performed in isolation, but demonstration that the normal fall in bedtime blood levels does not occur may be useful.

Determining the etiology of Cushing's syndrome is complicated by the lack of specificity of all tests available and the spontaneous changes in hormonal secretion, often dramatic, that may occur in the tumors producing this syndrome (periodic hormonogenesis). No test has a specificity greater than 95 percent, and it may be necessary to

FIGURE 325-7 *Diagnostic flowchart for evaluating patients suspected of having Cushing's syndrome.*

*The 17-hydroxycorticosteroid response to metyrapone (750 mg given orally every 4 h for six doses) may be used as an alternative test to the high-dose dexamethasone test (2 mg given orally every 6 h). Increased urinary 17-hydroxycorticosteroid excretion following metyrapone occurs in the majority of patients with adrenal hyperplasia secondary to pituitary ACTH secretion; no response suggests an adrenal neoplasm or adrenal hyperplasia secondary to a non-endocrine ACTH-producing tumor.

**This group of patients probably contains subjects with both pituitary-hypothalamic dysfunction and pituitary microadenomas. In some instances, a pituitary microadenoma may be visualized by CT scanning of the sella turcica.

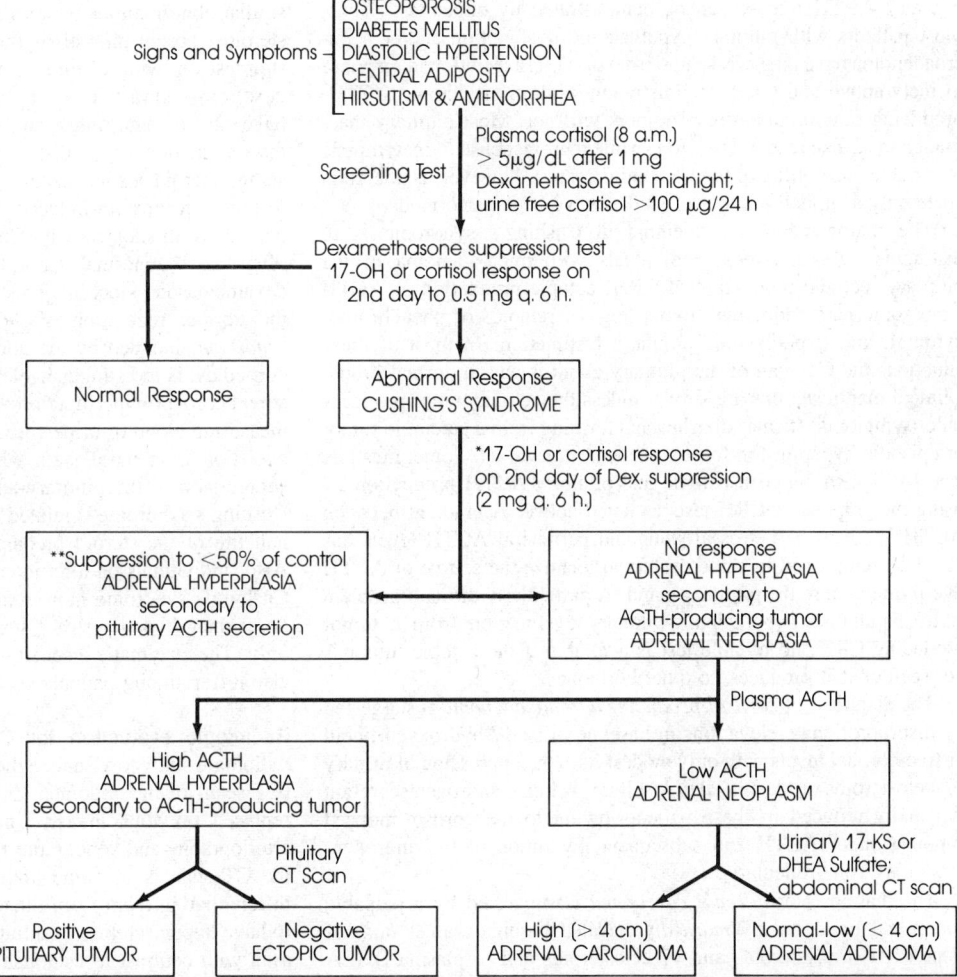

use a combination of tests to arrive at the correct diagnosis. A particularly useful first step is to determine the response of cortisol output to high-dose dexamethasone administration (2 mg every 6 hours for 2 days). In most series, more than half of the patients so tested have a suppression of urine cortisol and or 17-hydroxysteroid levels to less than 50 percent of basal values. These individuals usually have either an ACTH-secreting pituitary microadenoma or hypothalamic-pituitary dysfunction. Occasionally, in individuals with bilateral nodular hyperplasia and/or ectopic CRH production steroid output is also suppressed. Failure to suppress cortisol production after low- and high-dose dexamethasone administration (see Table 325-5) is usual in patients with adrenal hyperplasia secondary to an ACTH-secreting pituitary macroadenoma or ACTH-producing tumors of nonendocrine origin, and in adrenal neoplasms.

Theoretically, plasma ACTH levels should be useful in distinguishing the various causes of Cushing's syndrome, particularly in separating the ACTH-dependent from the ACTH-independent etiologies of the syndrome. In general, this is true for the ACTH-independent etiologies of the syndrome since most adrenal tumors have low or undetectable ACTH levels. Furthermore, ACTH-secreting pituitary macroadenomas and ACTH-producing nonendocrine tumors usually have elevated ACTH levels. However, at least two problems hinder the utilization of ACTH levels in the differential diagnosis of Cushing's syndrome. First, reliable ACTH assays are still not widely available, and second, ACTH levels may be similar in individuals with hypothalamic-pituitary dysfunction, pituitary microadenomas, ectopic CRH production, and ACTH production from some nonendocrine tumors (especially carcinoid tumors) (Table 325-5).

Because of these difficulties, several additional tests have been advocated, e.g., the metyrapone and the CRH infusion tests. The rationales underlying these tests are similar: Steroid hypersecretion secondary to an adrenal tumor or the ectopic production of ACTH will suppress the hypothalamic-pituitary axis so that inhibition of pituitary ACTH release can be demonstrated by either test. Thus, most patients with pituitary-hypothalamic dysfunction and/or a microadenoma have an increase in steroid or ACTH secretion in response to metyrapone and CRH administration while most ectopic ACTH-producing tumors and adrenal tumors will not. Most pituitary macroadenomas also respond to CRH, while their response to metyrapone is variable. The utility of the CRH infusion test, however, is uncertain since only a limited number of studies have been performed.

The major diagnostic dilemma in Cushing's syndrome is to distinguish between those individuals with microadenoma of the pituitary, ectopic production of CRH, ectopic production of ACTH from some para-endocrine tumors (e.g., carcinoids or pheochromocytoma), and hypothalamic pituitary dysfunction. In most of these situations the CT scan of the pituitary gland is within normal limits. Clinical manifestations are similar unless the ectopic tumor produces other symptoms, such as diarrhea and flushing from a carcinoid tumor or episodic hypertension from a pheochromocytoma. Sometimes one can distinguish between ectopic and pituitary ACTH production by using metyrapone or CRH tests as noted above. A gradient between ACTH level in the petrossal sinus and peripheral ACTH levels has also been employed in some centers to localize the source of ACTH overproduction to the pituitary gland. A particularly difficult problem is to distinguish hypothalamic-pituitary dysfunction from a tumor producing CRH; no reliable test is available if the ectopic tumor is not seen or if it produces no other hormones.

The diagnosis of *cortisol-producing adrenal adenoma* is suggested by disproprotionate elevations in baseline urine 17-hydroxycorticoid or free-cortisol levels with only modest rises or suppression of urinary 17-ketosteroids or plasma DHEA sulfate. Adrenal androgen secretion is usually reduced in these patients owing to the cortisol-induced suppression of ACTH and subsequent involution of the androgen-producing zona reticularis.

The diagnosis of *adrenal carcinoma* is suggested by a palpable abdominal mass and by *markedly* elevated baseline values *both* of urine 17-hydroxysteroids and 17-ketosteroids and of plasma DHEA

sulfate. Plasma and urine cortisol levels are variably elevated. Adrenal carcinoma is usually resistant to both ACTH stimulation and dexamethasone suppression. Markedly elevated adrenal androgen secretion often leads to virilization in the female. Feminizing estrogen-producing adrenocortical carcinoma in the male usually presents with gynecomastia. These adrenal tumors secrete increased amounts of androstenedione which is peripherally converted to the estrogens, estrone and estradiol (see Chap. 332). Functioning adrenal carcinomas that produce Cushing's syndrome are most often associated with elevated values for the intermediates of steroid biosynthesis (especially 11-deoxycortisol), suggesting inefficient conversion of the intermediates to the final product. It is also important to recognize that 20 percent of adrenal carcinomas are not associated with endocrine syndromes and are presumed to be nonfunctioning or to be associated with the production of biologically inactive steroid precursors. Finally, the excessive production of gonadal steroids is not detectable in certain situations (e.g., androgens in adult men).

Differential diagnosis PSEUDOCUSHING'S SYNDROME A variety of groups may present problems in diagnosis; these are patients with obesity, chronic alcoholism, depression, and acute illness of any type. Extreme *obesity* is uncommon in Cushing's syndrome; furthermore, with exogenous obesity, the adiposity is generalized, not truncal. On adrenocortical testing, abnormalities in patients with exogenous obesity are usually modest. Basal urine steroid excretion levels in obese patients are either normal or slightly elevated, a finding similar to their cortisol secretory values. Some patients have elevated conversion of secreted cortisol into excreted metabolites. *Urinary* and *blood cortisol* levels are normal, and the diurnal pattern in blood and urine levels is normal. Exogenous obesity may *cause* alterations in the secretion and metabolism of steroids; this points up the secondary nature of altered steroid testing patterns sometimes encountered. Patients with *chronic alcoholism* and *depression* share similar abnormalities in steroid output: elevated urinary 17-hydroxysteroids, absent diurnal rhythm of cortisol levels, and resistance to suppression with dexamethasone (particularly overnight and low dose). In contrast to alcoholic subjects, depressed patients do not have clinical signs and symptoms of Cushing's syndrome. Following discontinuation of alcohol and/or improvement of the emotional status, steroid testing usually returns to normal. A normal cortisol response to insulin-induced hypoglycemia may distinguish these patients from subjects with Cushing's syndrome. *Acutely ill* subjects often have abnormal laboratory tests and fail to suppress with dexamethasone since major stress (such as pain or fever) interrupts the normal regulation of ACTH secretion. *Iatrogenic Cushing's syndrome*, induced by the administration of potent synthetic glucocorticoids, is indistinguishable by physical findings from endogenous adrenocortical hyperfunction. This situation can be distinguished by measuring blood or urine cortisol levels or urinary 17-hydroxysteroid excretion in a basal state where the levels are low secondary to suppression of the pituitary-adrenal axis. The severity of iatrogenic Cushing's syndrome is related to the total steroid dose, to the biologic half-life of the steroid preparation, and to the duration of therapy. Also, individuals on afternoon and evening doses of steroid develop Cushing's syndrome more readily and on smaller total daily steroid doses than do patients on a steroid program limited to morning doses only. The enzymatic disposition and binding of administered steroids also differ among patients.

Radiologic evaluation for Cushing's syndrome The preferred radiologic study to visualize the adrenals is computerized tomography (CT scan) of the abdomen (Fig. 325-8). This procedure has largely replaced previous invasive procedures (such as selective adrenal arteriography and venography) and 19-[131I]iodocholesterol scanning; the CT scan is of value both in localizing adrenal tumors and in differentiating them from bilateral hyperplasia. All patients believed to have hypersecretion of pituitary ACTH should have a pituitary CT scan with contrast to establish whether a pituitary tumor is present.

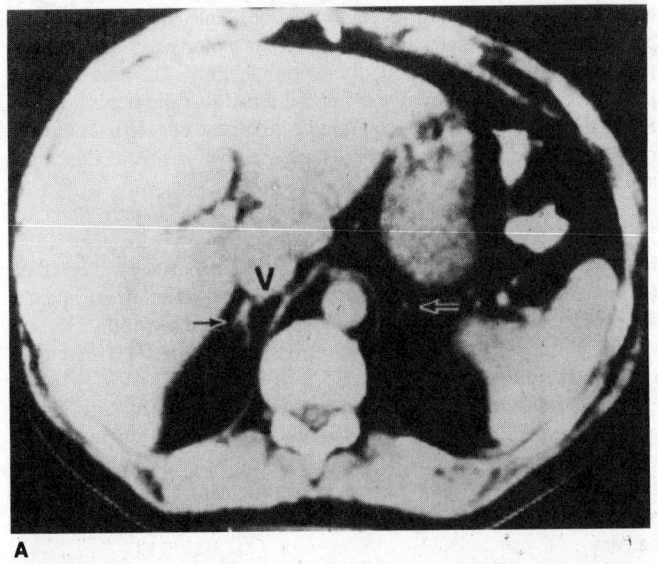

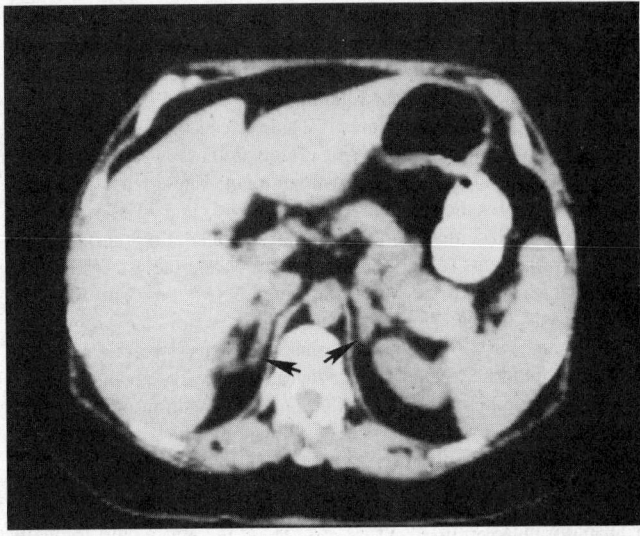

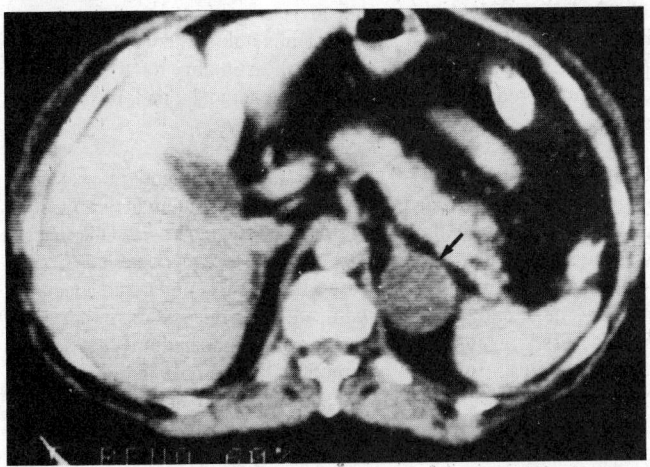

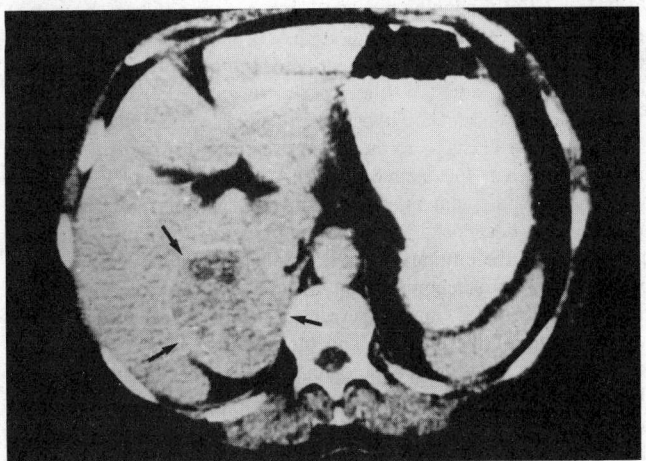

FIGURE 325-8 *Computerized tomography is the preferred method for visualizing the adrenal glands. The adrenal glands are indicated by arrows. A. The normal right adrenal gland is adjacent to the inferior vena cava (V) as it emerges from the liver. Approximately 90 percent of the right adrenal glands appear as linear structures extending posteriorly from the inferior vena cava into the space between the right lobe of the liver and the crus of the diaphragm. The normal left adrenal gland is lateral to the left crus of the diaphragm and below the stomach. The majority of left adrenal glands are shaped like an inverted "V" or "Y." B. Adrenal CT scan of a patient with ectopic ACTH production. Both adrenal glands (arrows) are enlarged (compare with A). In contrast, only 50 percent of patients with bilateral adrenal hyperplasia secondary to pituitary ACTH hypersecretion show enlargement of the adrenals when imaged by CT scan. C. CT scan of a patient with Cushing's syndrome with biochemical evidence only of cortisol overproduction. The left adrenal has been replaced by a racquet-shaped 2-cm tumor (arrow). Attenuation of the tumor is low because of its high lipid content. D. CT scan in a patient with Cushing's syndrome and biochemical evidence of an adrenal carcinoma. In contrast to C, the left-sided mass has a heterogeneous appearance and is larger in size—usual characteristics of an adrenal carcinoma.*

Even with the best CT scanners presently available small microadenomas may be undectable.

Evaluation of asymptomatic adrenal masses With abdominal CT scanning, many incidental adrenal masses are discovered. This is not surprising, since 10 to 20 percent of subjects at autopsy have adrenal cortical adenomas. The first step in evaluating such patients is to determine if the tumor is functioning by appropriate screening tests. However, in 90 percent of the cases tumors detected incidentally at the time of abdominal CT scanning are nonfunctioning. Fortunately, they also are seldom malignant. Yet, nonfunctioning tumors raise difficult therapeutic questions. Since 20 percent of adrenal carcinomas are nonfunctioning, one could argue that all such lesions should be removed. However, the frequency of adrenal carcinomas is low compared with the frequency of benign cortical adenomas (less than 1 percent), and surgery is not indicated in most cases. The size of the tumor sometimes is of value: Adrenal carcinomas are rarely smaller than 3 cm in diameter, and adrenal adenomas are usually smaller than 6 cm (Fig. 325-8). If surgery is not performed, a repeat CT scan in 3 to 6 months is usually required for followup.

Therapy ADRENAL NEOPLASMS When an adenoma or carcinoma is diagnosed, adrenal exploration is performed with excision of the tumor. Because of the possible atrophy of the contralateral adrenal, the patient is treated pre- and postoperatively for total adrenalectomy even when a unilateral lesion is suspected, the routine being similar to that for an Addisonian patient undergoing elective surgery (Table 325-11).

Despite operative intervention, most patients with adrenal carcinoma die within 3 years of diagnosis. Metastases occur most often to liver and lung. The principal antitumor drug used to treat metastatic adrenocortical carcinoma is mitotane (*o,p'*-DDD), an isomer of the insecticide DDT. This drug suppresses cortisol production and decreases plasma and urine steroid levels. Although its cytotoxic action is relatively selective for the glucocorticoid-secreting zone of the adrenal cortex, the zona glomerulosa may also be inhibited.

Because mitotane also alters the extraadrenal metabolism of cortisol, plasma and urinary cortisol levels must be assessed to titrate the effect. The drug is usually given in divided doses three to four times a day, with the dose increased gradually to 8 to 10 g daily. Almost all patients experience gastrointestinal side effects (anorexia, diarrhea, or vomiting) or neuromuscular side effects (lethargy, somnolence, or dizziness). All patients treated with mitotane should be placed on long-term maintenance glucocorticoid therapy, and in some mineralocorticoid replacement should also be instituted. In approximately one-third of patients regression of both tumor and metastases occurs, but long-term survival is limited, as noted above. In many patients, mitotane only inhibits steroidogenesis and does not cause regression of tumor metastases. Osseous metastases are usually refractory to the drug and should be treated with radiation therapy. Mitotane can also be given as adjunctive therapy after surgical resection of an adrenal carcinoma even in the absence of known metastases because the prognosis of this neoplasm is so poor.

BILATERAL HYPERPLASIA   Patients with hyperplasia have a relative or absolute increase in ACTH levels. Since therapy would logically be directed at reducing ACTH levels, the ideal primary treatment for ACTH- or CRH-producing tumors, whether in the pituitary or ectopic, is surgical removal. Occasionally, this is not possible because the disease, particularly with ectopic ACTH production, is often far advanced. In this situation "medical" or surgical adrenalectomy may be indicated to correct the hypercortisolism.

Controversy exists as to the proper treatment for bilateral adrenal hyperplasia when the source of the ACTH overproduction is not apparent. In some centers, these patients (especially patients with a positive high-dose dexamethasone suppression test) have surgical exploration of the pituitary via a transsphenoidal approach in anticipation of a microadenoma being found. These explorations prove fruitful in between 20 and 70 percent of the cases, depending on the level of skill of the surgeon and the ability of the radiologist to localize the microadenoma preoperatively. However, in the event that a microadenoma is not found, total hypophysectomy may be needed. Complications of transsphenoidal surgery include rhinorrhea, diabetes insipidus, panhypopituitarism, and optic or cranial nerve injuries. Furthermore, these pituitary neoplasms may recur if the primary abnormality actually resides in the hypothalamus.

In other centers, total adrenalectomy is the treatment of choice. Cure with this procedure is close to 100 percent. The adverse effects include the certain need for lifelong mineralocorticoid as well as glucocorticoid replacement therapy and a 10 to 20 percent probability of a pituitary tumor developing over the next 10 years, many requiring surgical therapy (Nelson's syndrome). It is uncertain whether in these individuals (see Chap. 321) the tumor develops de novo or is present prior to bilateral adrenalectomy but is so small that it is not detected by radiologic procedures. Periodic radiologic evaluation of the pituitary gland by CT scanning and serial ACTH levels should be obtained in any individual who has undergone bilateral adrenalectomy for Cushing's syndrome. Often, such pituitary tumors that become apparent following adrenalectomy become locally invasive and impinge on the optic chiasm or extend into the cavernous or sphenoid sinuses. Thus, an aggressive surgical approach is often followed by postoperative irradiation.

In a few centers, pituitary irradiation is the primary treatment for pituitary ACTH overproduction, with the use of either conventional external or alpha (proton beam) radiation. The latter, while more effective, has a greater incidence of ocular motor palsy and hypopituitarism than does conventional radiation therapy. The long lag time between treatment and remission and the fact that the remission rate is less than 50 percent often contraindicate the use of external pituitary radiation in the presence of rapidly progressive or severe Cushing's syndrome.

Finally, in occasional patients in whom a surgical approach is not feasible, medical therapy directed at reducing hypothalamic CRH release either by administering the serotonin antagonist cyproheptadine or by administering an inhibitor of GABA transaminase, sodium valproate, has been successful in reducing cortisol secretion. Bromocriptine, a dopaminergic agonist, also suppresses ACTH output in occasional patients.

If ACTH levels cannot be successfully lowered by any of the above treatment modalities, then medical or surgical adrenalectomy may be indicated (Table 325-6). Chemical adrenalectomy may be accomplished by the administration of mitotane (2 or 3 g per day) and/or aminoglutethimide (1 g per day) and metyrapone (2 or 3 g per day).

ALDOSTERONISM   Aldosteronism is a syndrome associated with hypersecretion of the major adrenal mineralocorticoid, aldosterone. *Primary* aldosteronism signifies that the stimulus for the excessive aldosterone production resides within the adrenal gland; in *secondary* aldosteronism the stimulus is extraadrenal.

Primary aldosteronism   The signs and symptoms of excessive inappropriate aldosterone production were first summarized by Conn in 1956. In the original case and many subsequent cases, the disease was the result of an *aldosterone-producing adrenal adenoma* (Conn's syndrome). The majority of cases involved a unilateral adenoma, usually small and occurring with equal frequency on either side. Rarely, primary aldosteronism occurs in association with adrenal carcinoma. It is twice as common in women as in men, occurs between the ages of 30 and 50, and is present in approximately 1 percent of unselected hypertensive patients. Many cases have clinical and biochemical features characteristic of primary aldosteronism, but a solitary adenoma is not found at surgery. Instead, these patients have *bilateral cortical nodular hyperplasia*. In the literature this disease has been alternatively termed "pseudo" primary aldosteronism, idiopathic hyperaldosteronism, or nodular hyperplasia. The cause is unknown.

SIGNS AND SYMPTOMS   The continual hypersecretion of aldosterone increases the renal distal tubular exchange of intratubular sodium for secreted potassium and hydrogen ions, with progressive depletion of body potassium and development of hypokalemia. Most patients have diastolic hypertension, usually not of marked severity, and complain of headaches. The hypertension is probably due to the increased sodium reabsorption and extracellular volume expansion. Potassium depletion is responsible for the muscle weakness and fatigue and is related to the effect of intra- and extracellular potassium ion depletion on muscle membrane. The polyuria results from impairment of concentrating ability and is often associated with polydipsia. Electrocardiographic and roentgenographic signs of left ventricular enlargement are secondary to the hypertension. Electrocardiographic signs of potassium depletion, such as prominent U waves, cardiac arrhythmias, and premature contractions, are common. In the absence of associated congestive heart failure, renal disease, or preexisting abnormalities (such as thrombophlebitis), edema is characteristically absent. In cases of long duration, nephropathy with azotemia may be associated with congestive heart failure and edema.

LABORATORY FINDINGS   Laboratory findings are dependent on both the duration and the severity of the potassium depletion. An overnight concentration test often reveals impaired ability to concentrate the urine. Urine pH is neutral to alkaline, because of excessive secretion of ammonium and bicarbonate ions to compensate for a metabolic

TABLE 325-6 Treatment modalities for patients with adrenal hyperplasia secondary to pituitary ACTH hypersecretion

I Reduce pituitary ACTH production
  A Transsphenoidal resection of microadenoma
  B Radiation
  C Treatment with hypothalamic serotonin antagonist (cyproheptadine) or GABA-transaminase inhibitor (sodium valproate)*
II Reduce or eliminate adrenocortical cortisol secretion
  A Bilateral adrenalectomy
  B Medical adrenalectomy (metyrapone, mitotane, aminoglutethimide)*

* *Not curative but effective as long as chronically administered in selected patients.*

alkalosis. Tests of glucocorticoid and androgen secretion are within the normal range.

Hypokalemia may be severe (less than 3 meq potassium per liter) and reflects significant body potassium depletion, usually in excess of 300 meq. *Hypernatremia* is due to both sodium retention and a concomitant water loss from polyuria. Metabolic alkalosis and elevation of serum bicarbonate are a result of hydrogen ion loss into the urine and migration into potassium-depleted cells. The alkalosis is perpetuated by potassium deficiency, which increases the capacity of the proximal convoluted tubule to reabsorb filtered bicarbonate. If hypokalemia is severe, serum magnesium levels are also reduced. In the absence of azotemia, serum uric acid is normal.

Total body sodium content and total exchangeable sodium are increased, while total exchangeable body potassium is usually reduced. The expanded extracellular fluid volume may be responsible for the reversed diurnal excretory pattern for salt and water, with predominant salt and water excretion occurring during the night.

DIAGNOSIS The diagnosis is suggested by persistent hypokalemia in a nonedematous patient on a normal sodium intake who is not receiving potassium-wasting diuretics (furosemide, ethacrynic acid,

thiazides) or potassium-sparing diuretics (triamterene, spironolactone). If hypokalemia occurs in a hypertensive patient on a potassium-wasting diuretic, the diuretic should be discontinued and the patient should be given potassium supplements. After 1 to 2 weeks the potassium level should be remeasured, and if hypokalemia persists, the patient should be evaluated for a mineralocorticoid excess syndrome (Fig. 325-9).

The criteria for the diagnosis of primary aldosteronism are (1) diastolic hypertension without edema, (2) hyposecretion of renin (as judged by low plasma renin activity levels) that fails to increase appropriately during volume depletion (upright posture, sodium depletion), and (3) hypersecretion of aldosterone that fails to suppress appropriately during volume expansion (salt loading).

Patients with primary aldosteronism characteristically *do not have edema*, since they exhibit an "escape" phenomenon from the sodium-retaining aspects of mineralocorticoids. Rarely, pretibial edema may be present in patients with associated nephropathy and azotemia.

The estimation of plasma renin activity is of limited value in separating patients with primary aldosteronism from those with other causes of hypertension. While the failure of plasma renin activity to rise normally during volume-depletion maneuvers is a criterion for

FIGURE 325-9 *Diagnostic flowchart for evaluating patients with suspected primary aldosteronism.*

*Serum K+ may be normal in some patients with hyperaldosteronism who are taking potassium-sparing diuretics (spironolactone, triamterene) or ingesting low sodium–high potassium intakes.

†This step should not be taken if hypertension is severe (diastolic pressure >115 mmHg) or if cardiac failure is present. Also, serum potassium levels should be corrected before the infusion of saline solution. Alternative methods producing comparable suppression of aldosterone secretion include oral sodium loading (200 meq per day for 3 days) or 10 mg deoxycorticosterone acetate (DOCA) intramuscularly every 12 h for 3 days.

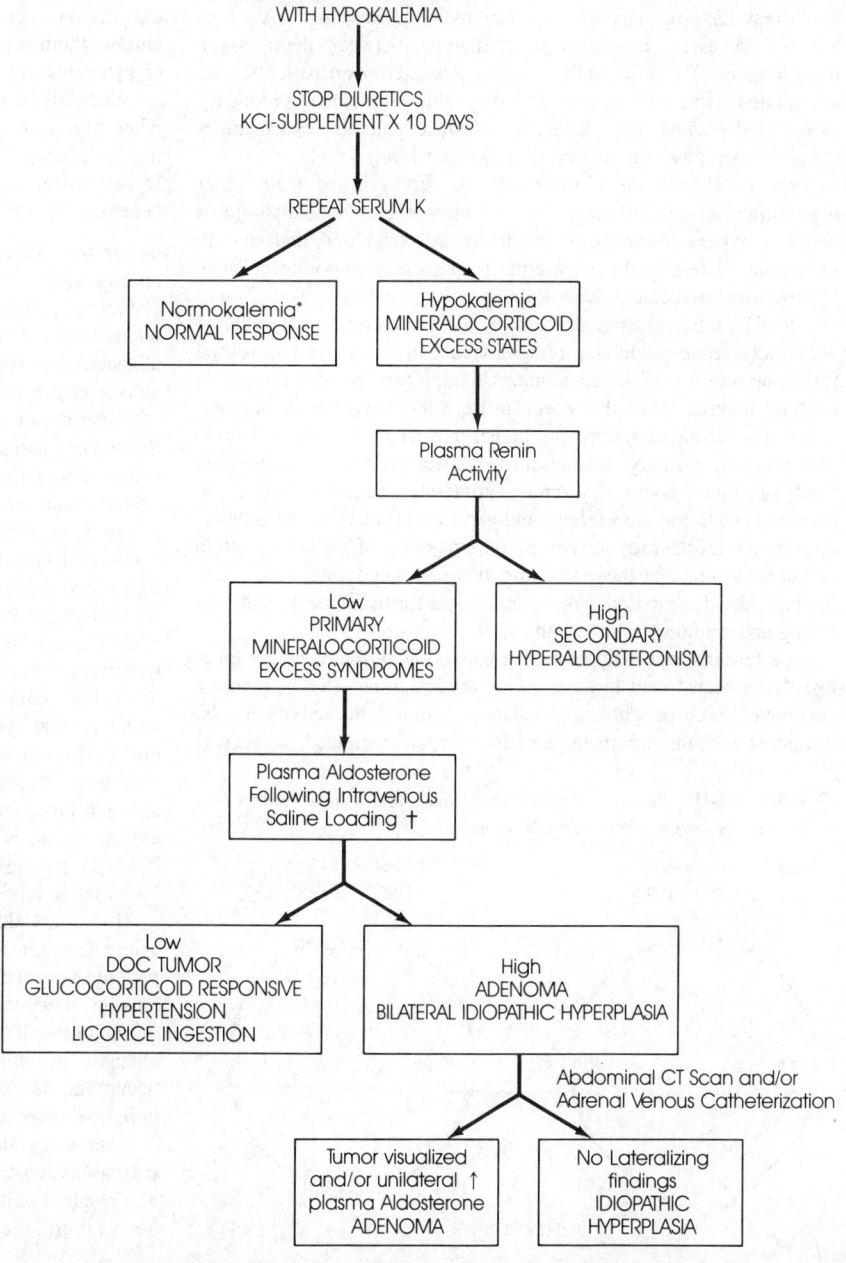

primary aldosteronism, suppressed renin activity also occurs in about 25 percent of patients with essential hypertension.

Since the determination of plasma renin responsiveness is not sufficient, the demonstration of lack of suppression of aldosterone secretion is necessary to diagnose primary aldosteronism (Fig. 325-9). The autonomy exhibited by aldosterone tumors in these patients refers only to the resistance to suppression of secretion during volume expansion; such tumors can and do respond in normal or supernormal fashion to the stimuli of potassium loading or ACTH infusion.

Once hyposecretion of renin and failure to suppress aldosterone secretion are demonstrated, localization of aldosterone-producing adenomas should be determined preoperatively by abdominal CT scan or by percutaneous transfemoral bilateral adrenal vein catheterization with simultaneous adrenal venography. The latter technique permits radiologic localization, and, in addition, the adrenal vein sampling may demonstrate a two- to threefold increase in plasma aldosterone concentration on the involved side compared with the uninvolved side. In cases of hyperaldosteronism secondary to cortical nodular hyperplasia, no localization is found. It is important for samples to be obtained simultaneously if possible and for cortisol levels to be measured to ensure that false localization does not reflect an ACTH- or stress-induced rise in aldosterone levels.

DIFFERENTIAL DIAGNOSIS   Patients with hypertension and hypokalemia may have primary or secondary hyperaldosteronism (see Fig. 325-10). A useful maneuver to distinguish between them is the measurement of plasma renin activity. Aldosteronism patients with accelerated hypertension and secondary aldosteronism is secondary to elevated plasma renin levels; in contrast, patients with primary aldosteronism have suppressed plasma renin levels.

Primary aldosteronism must also be distinguished from other *hypermineralocorticoid states*. The common problem is to distinguish between hyperaldosteronism due to an adenoma and that due to idiopathic bilateral nodular hyperplasia. This is of importance, since hypertension associated with idiopathic hyperplasia is usually not benefited by bilateral adrenalectomy, whereas hypertension associated with aldosterone-producing tumors is usually improved or cured following removal of the adenoma. Although patients with idiopathic bilateral nodular hyperplasia tend to have less severe hypokalemia, lower aldosterone secretion, and higher plasma renin activity than do patients with primary aldosteronism, differentiation is impossible solely on clinical and/or biochemical grounds. An anomalous postural decrease in plasma aldosterone and elevated plasma 18-hydroxycorticosterone levels are present in the majority of patients with a unilateral lesion, but these tests are also of limited diagnostic value in the individual patient. A definitive diagnosis is best made by radiographic studies as noted above.

In a few instances, hypertensive patients with hypokalemic alkalosis have been found to have deoxycorticosterone (DOC)-secreting adenomas. Such patients have reduced plasma renin activity levels, but aldosterone measurements are either normal or reduced, suggesting

the diagnosis of mineralocorticoid excess due to a hormone other than aldosterone. Rarely, hypermineralocorticoidism is due to a defect in cortisol biosynthesis, specifically 11- or 17-hydroxylation. ACTH levels are increased, with a resultant increase in the production of the mineralocorticoid 11-deoxycorticosterone. *Hypertension and hypokalemia can be corrected by glucocorticoid administration.* The definitive diagnosis is made by demonstrating an elevation of precursors of cortisol biosynthesis in the blood or urine. Occasionally, glucocorticoid administration produces normotension and normokalemia although a hydroxylase deficiency cannot be identified (Fig. 325-9).

The ingestion of candies or chewing tobacco containing certain forms of licorice produces a syndrome mimicking primary aldosteronism. The sodium-retaining principle in such agents is glycyrrhizinic acid, which causes sodium retention, expansion of the extracellular fluid volume, hypertension, depressed plasma renin levels, and suppressed aldosterone levels. The diagnosis is established or excluded by a careful history.

TREATMENT   Primary aldosteronism due to an adenoma is usually treated by surgical excision. However, dietary sodium restriction and the administration of an aldosterone antagonist, spironolactone, are effective in many cases. Hypertension and hypokalemia are usually controlled by doses of 25 to 100 mg spironolactone every 8 h. Some patients have been successfully managed medically for years, but chronic therapy in men is usually limited by the common occurrence of gynecomastia, decreased libido, and impotence.

When bilateral hyperplasia is suspected, surgery is indicated only when significant, symptomatic hypokalemia cannot be controlled with medical therapy, e.g., by spironolactone, triamterene, or amiloride. Hypertension associated with idiopathic hyperplasia is usually not benefited by bilateral adrenalectomy.

Secondary aldosteronism   Secondary aldosteronism refers to an appropriately increased production of aldosterone in response to activation of the renin-angiotensin system (Fig. 325-10). The production rates of aldosterone are often higher in patients with secondary aldosteronism than in those with primary aldosteronism. Secondary aldosteronism usually occurs in association with the accelerated phase of hypertension or on the basis of an underlying edema disorder. Secondary aldosteronism in pregnancy is a normal physiologic response to estrogen-induced increases in circulating levels of renin substrate and plasma renin activity, and to the antialdosterone actions of the progestogens.

Secondary aldosteronism in hypertensive states either is secondary to a primary overproduction of renin (primary reninism) or is caused by an overproduction of renin which is secondary to a decrease in renal blood flow and/or perfusion pressure (Fig. 325-5). Secondary hypersecretion of renin can be due to a narrowing of one or both of the major renal arteries either by an atherosclerotic plaque or by fibromuscular hyperplasia. Overproduction of renin from both kidneys also occurs in association with severe arteriolar nephrosclerosis (malignant hypertension) or secondary to profound renal vasoconstriction (accelerated phase of hypertensive disease). The secondary aldosteronism is characterized by hypokalemic alkalosis, moderate to severe increases in plasma renin activity, and moderate to marked increases in aldosterone levels (see Chap. 196).

Secondary aldosteronism with hypertension can also be caused by a rare renin-producing tumor, in so-called primary reninism. These patients have the biochemical characteristics of renal vascular hypertension; however, the primary defect is renin secretion by a juxtaglomerular-cell tumor. The diagnosis can be made by the absence of changes in renal vasculature and/or demonstration of a space-occupying lesion in the kidney by radiographic techniques and unilateral increases in renal vein renin activity.

Secondary aldosteronism is present in many forms of *edema*. Increased aldosterone secretion rates are usual in patients with edema as a result of either cirrhosis or the nephrotic syndrome. In congestive heart failure, elevated aldosterone secretion varies depending on the

FIGURE 325-10 *Responses of the renin-aldosterone volume control loop in primary versus secondary aldosteronism.*

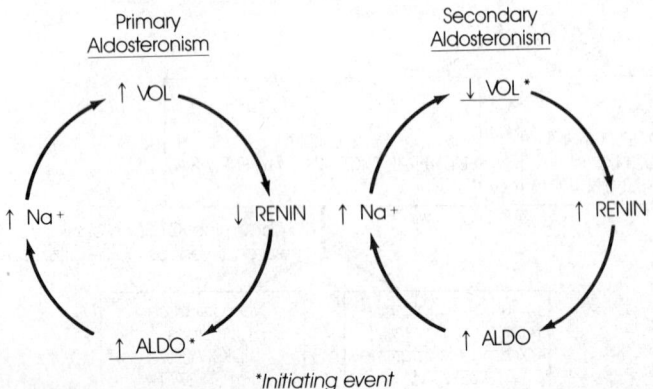

Primary Aldosteronism

↑ VOL

↑ Na⁺   ↓ RENIN

↑ ALDO*

Secondary Aldosteronism

↓ VOL*

↑ Na⁺   ↑ RENIN

↑ ALDO

*Initiating event

severity of cardiac decompensation. The stimulus for aldosterone release in these conditions appears to be *arterial hypovolemia* and/or hypotension. Diuretic therapy often exaggerates the secondary aldosteronism via volume depletion; when this happens hypokalemia and on occasion alkalosis can become prominent features.

Secondary hyperaldosteronism rarely occurs without edema or hypertension (Bartter's syndrome). This syndrome is characterized by the signs of severe hyperaldosteronism (hypokalemic alkalosis) with moderate to marked increases in renin activity but normal blood pressure and absence of edema. Renal biopsy shows juxtaglomerular hyperplasia. The pathogenesis may be a defect in the renal conservation of sodium or chloride. The renal loss of sodium is thought to stimulate renin secretion and subsequent aldosterone production. Hyperaldosteronism produces potassium depletion, with the hypokalemia further elevating plasma renin activity. In some cases, the hypokalemia may be potentiated by a defect in renal conservation of potassium. One associated abnormality is an increased production of prostaglandins. (See Chap. 228.)

SYNDROMES OF ADRENAL ANDROGEN EXCESS   The syndromes of adrenal androgen excess result from excess production of dehydroepiandrosterone and androstenedione, which are converted to testosterone in extraglandular tissues; the elevated testosterone levels account for most of the androgenic effects. Adrenal androgen excess may be associated with the secretion of greater or smaller amounts of other adrenal hormones and may, therefore, present as "pure" syndromes of virilization or as "mixed" syndromes associated with excessive production of glucocorticoids and some characteristics of Cushing's syndrome.

Clinical signs and symptoms   The signs and symptoms of androgen excess can be divided into four areas: hirsutism, oligomenorrhea, acne, and virilization. Clinically, it is important to distinguish between simple hirsutism and hirsutism associated with virilization. In most cases of simple hirsutism, there is no known cause for the increased hair growth. On the other hand, if the patient is virilized as well as hirsute, increased levels of androgens are usually present. Hirsutism, commonly defined as an excess of body hair in a female in a male pattern of distribution (see Chap. 46), may result from androgen excess syndromes either of ovarian or adrenal etiologies or from drug ingestion, or it may be familial or idiopathic. Excess androgen secretion as a cause of hirsutism is probably uncommon in the absence of other signs of increased androgen production.

The four components of virilization are temporal balding, change in body habitus from a female to a male pattern (i.e., loss of pelvic fat and increase in upper torso muscular development), clitoral enlargement, and deepening of the voice. In general, the degree of virilization reflects both the duration and the degree of excess androgen secretion, although significant virilization can result from minimal changes in testosterone production, and a significant increase in testosterone production may be associated with minimal signs of virilization. The occurrence of oligomenorrhea in a hirsute patient increases the probability that an excess secretion of androgens will be found. Thus, the evaluation of the hirsute patient should include a careful history of the onset of menarche, past and present menstrual history, and reproductive capacity and a careful physical examination for signs and symptoms of androgen excess.

Etiology   As in other states of adrenocortical hyperfunction, the syndromes associated with androgen excess may result from hyperplasia, adenoma, or carcinoma (the latter two having been discussed above). Adrenal androgen overproduction may also arise from *congenital adrenal hyperplasia*, owing to enzymatic defects. In these patients, increased adrenal androgen production is associated either with excess or decreased secretion of mineralocorticoids or decreased production of glucocorticoids. Since, in humans, cortisol is the principal adrenal steroid regulating ACTH elaboration, and since ACTH stimulates both cortisol and adrenal androgen production, an enzymatic interference with cortisol synthesis may result in the enhanced secretion of adrenal androgens. In severe congenital virilizing hyperplasia, the adrenal output of cortisol may be so compromised as to cause glucocorticoid deficiency despite anatomic adrenal hyperplasia.

Congenital adrenal hyperplasia is the most common adrenal disorder of infancy and childhood. These children usually have severe enzyme deficiencies (see Chap. 333). The deficiency of enzymes is the result of autosomal recessive mutations. Partial adrenal enzyme deficiencies can be expressed after adolescence, predominantly in women with hirsutism and oligomenorrhea but minimal virilization. Late onset adrenal hyperplasia may account for as many as 25 percent of adult women with hirsutism and oligomenorrhea.

Congenital adrenal hyperplasia is secondary to one of several defects in steroid synthesis. To date, defects have been described in the C-21, C-18, C-17, and C-11 hydroxylase enzymes, as well as in the 3β-ol-dehydrogenase enzyme (see Fig. 325-2). These enzyme deficits usually occur singly. C-21 hydroxylase deficiency has a characteristic histocompatibility leukocyte antigen (HLA) association (HLA-B locus of chromosome 6) so that HLA typing can be used to detect the heterozygous carriers in affected families (see Chap. 63). The clinical expression in the different disorders is variable, ranging from virilization of the female (C-21 deficiency) to feminization of the male (3β-ol-dehydrogenase deficiency). (See also Chap. 333.)

Adrenal virilization in the female at birth is associated with ambiguous external genitalia (*female pseudohermaphroditism*). The onset of virilization is most probably after the fifth month of embryonic development. At birth there may be macrogenitosomia in the male infant, and in the female enlargement of the clitoris, partial or complete fusion of the labia, and sometimes a urogenital sinus. If the labial fusion is nearly complete, the female infant has external genitalia resembling a penis with hypospadias. In the *postnatal* period, congenital adrenal hyperplasia is associated with virilization in the female and isosexual precocity in the male. The excessive androgens result in accelerated growth, with bone age exceeding chronologic age. Since epiphyseal closure is hastened by excessive androgens, growth stops, but truncal development continues, giving the characteristic appearance of a child of short stature with well-developed trunk.

The most common form of congenital adrenal hyperplasia (95 percent of cases) is a result of impairment of *C-21 hydroxylation*. In addition to cortisol deficiency, there is an associated reduction in aldosterone secretion in approximately one-third of the patients. Thus, with C-21 hydroxylase deficiency, adrenal virilization occurs with or without an associated salt-losing tendency due to aldosterone deficiency (see Fig. 325-2).

C-11 hydroxylase deficiency causes a "hypertensive" variant of congenital adrenal hyperplasia. Hypertension and hypokalemia occur because of the impaired conversion of 11-deoxycorticosterone to corticosterone, resulting in the accumulation of 11-deoxycorticosterone, a potent mineralocorticoid. Increased shunting again occurs into the androgen pathway.

The *C-17 hydroxylase* deficiency is characterized by hypogonadism, hypokalemia, and hypertension. This rare deficiency causes decreased production of cortisol and shunting of precursors into the mineralocorticoid pathway with hypokalemic alkalosis, hypertension, and suppressed plasma renin activity. Usually, 11-deoxycorticosterone production is elevated. Because C-17 hydroxylation is required for biosynthesis of adrenal androgens as well as for biosynthesis of gonadal testosterone and estrogen, this defect is associated with sexual immaturity, high urinary gonadotropin levels, and low urinary 17-ketosteroid excretion. Female patients have primary amenorrhea and lack of development of secondary sexual characteristics. Because of deficient androgen production, male patients either have ambiguous external genitalia or a female phenotype (male pseudohermaphroditism). Exogenous glucocorticoids can correct the hypertensive syndrome, and treatment with appropriate gonadal steroids results in sexual maturation.

With 3β-ol-dehydrogenase deficiency, conversion of pregnenolone to progesterone is impaired, with the result that pathways to both cortisol and aldosterone are "blocked," with shunting then occurring into the adrenal androgen pathway via 17α-hydroxypregnenolone to dehydroepiandrosterone. Since dehydroepiandrosterone is a weak androgen and because this enzyme deficiency is also present in the gonad, the genitalia of the male fetus may be incompletely virilized or feminized. Conversely, in the female, overproduction of dehydroepiandrosterone may produce partial virilization.

Diagnosis The diagnosis of *congenital adrenal hyperplasia* should be considered in all infants exhibiting "failure to thrive," particularly those having episodes of acute adrenal insufficiency or salt wasting or showing sustained hypertension. The diagnosis is further suggested by the finding of hypertrophy of the clitoris, fused labia, or urogenital sinus in the female and isosexual precocity in the male. In infants and children with a *C-21 hydroxylation block,* increased urine 17-ketosteroid excretion and plasma DHEA sulfate are typically associated with an increase in the blood levels of 17α-hydroxyprogesterone and the urinary excretion of the metabolite of this steroid, pregnanetriol.

The diagnosis of a *salt-losing form of congenital adrenal hyperplasia* due to defects in C-21 hydroxylase enzyme is suggested by episodes of acute adrenal insufficiency with hyponatremia, hyperkalemia, dehydration, and vomiting. These infants and children often crave salt and exhibit laboratory signs of concomitant deficits in both cortisol and aldosterone secretion.

With the *hypertensive form of congenital adrenal hyperplasia* due to impaired C-11 hydroxylation, 11-deoxycorticosterone and 11-deoxycortisol accumulate. Both urine 17-ketosteroid and 17-hydroxycorticoid excretion may be elevated, since 11-deoxycortisol is included in the analysis of Porter-Silber chromogens. The diagnosis is secured by demonstrating increased levels of 11-deoxycortisol in the blood or increased amounts of tetrahydro-11-deoxycortisol in the urine.

The finding of very high levels of urine dehydroepiandrosterone with low levels of pregnanetriol and of cortisol metabolites in urine is characteristic of patients with 3β-ol-dehydrogenase deficiency. Marked salt wasting may also occur.

Patients with *late onset adrenal hyperplasia* (partial deficiency of C-21 hydroxylase) are characterized by normal or moderately elevated urinary 17-ketosteroids and plasma DHEA sulfate. A high basal level of a precursor of cortisol biosynthesis (such as 17-hydroxyprogesterone) or elevation of the precursor after ACTH stimulation confirms the diagnosis of a partial hydroxylase deficiency. It is uncertain how long the ACTH needs to be infused to unmask the enzyme deficiency. Adrenal androgen output is easily suppressed by the standard low-dose (2 mg) dexamethasone test.

Differential diagnosis The causes of hirsutism can be divided into four broad categories: familial, idiopathic, due to androgen excess, and due to drugs. In general, the first two conditions are not associated with other signs of androgen excess, i.e., oligomenorrhea, significant acne, or virilization. Likewise, drug-induced hirsutism is usually not associated with other signs and symptoms of androgen excess, unless the drug is an androgen. The drugs that produce an increase in body hair include phenothiazines, minoxidil, and phenytoin. Each of these drugs, particularly minoxidil, produces a generalized increase in hair growth, not just an increase in hair growth in androgen target areas.

TABLE 325-7 Causes of hirsutism in women

I Familial
II Idiopathic
III Ovarian
   A Polycystic ovaries; hilus-cell hyperplasia
   B Tumor: arrhenoblastoma, hilus cell, adrenal rest
IV Adrenal
   A Congenital adrenal hyperplasia
   B Noncongenital adrenal hyperplasia (Cushing's)
   C Tumor: virilizing carcinoma or adenoma

The mechanism may be related to the ability of these drugs to convert vellus into terminal hair follicles.

If drugs are excluded, the only known causes of hirsutism amenable to treatment are those secondary to excess production of androgens by either the adrenal or the ovary.

In the female, the differential diagnosis of hirsutism and virilization is between adrenal and ovarian etiologies (Table 325-7). *Sudden onset of progressive hirsutism and virilization* suggests an adrenal or ovarian neoplasm. *Adrenal adenomas and carcinomas* may cause a pure or mixed virilizing syndrome. Since adrenal androgens are weak compared with gonadal androgens, adrenal virilization is characterized by *large increments in urine 17-ketosteroid excretion.* Virilizing adrenal adenomas are rare. *Virilizing adrenal carcinomas,* the most common adrenal tumors causing virilization, are associated with high plasma DHEA sulfate levels and high urinary 17-ketosteroid excretion rates; cortisol levels and 17-hydroxycorticosteroid excretion are normal or moderately elevated. Clinical differentiation between virilizing adrenal adenoma and carcinoma can usually be made preoperatively by CT scanning since carcinomas as a rule exceed 6 cm in size. Failure to reduce 17-ketosteroid levels and plasma DHEA sulfate levels to normal following dexamethasone suppression (0.5 mg given orally every 6 h for 2 days) further supports a diagnosis of virilizing adrenal tumor and excludes congenital adrenal hyperplasia. The most common virilizing *ovarian tumor* is the arrhenoblastoma, but other ovarian tumors, such as adrenal rest tumor, granulosa-cell tumor, hilar-cell tumor, and Brenner tumor, have been associated with virilization. Virilization due to ovarian tumors is usually characterized by normal levels of urinary 17-ketosteroids and DHEA sulfate, since the neoplasm usually secretes the potent androgen testosterone. Occasionally increases in 17-ketosteroid excretion occur in some patients with ovarian neoplasms, but baseline 17-ketosteroid excretion in excess of 30 mg per day is rare with the exception of adrenal rest tumors. Like adrenal neoplasms, ovarian tumors are not suppressed by dexamethasone. With the exception of adrenal rest tumors, these tumors are largely independent of ACTH stimulation. Elevations of plasma testosterone or urinary testosterone excretion do not localize the neoplasm to the ovary, since testosterone can be elevated subsequent to peripheral conversion of adrenal precursors, such as DHEA (see Chap. 331).

The most common ovarian cause of excess androgen production is ovarian hyperplasia or polycystic ovaries (see Chap. 331). As opposed to ovarian or adrenal tumors, virilization is less common with polycystic ovaries, whereas hirsutism is quite frequent. In most cases, the 17-ketosteroid excretion rate is greater than normal. Although the 17-ketosteroid excretion is partially reduced by dexamethasone, the residual level is often greater than in normal subjects. Plasma levels and production rates of androstenedione and to a lesser extent testosterone are usually increased. Follicle-stimulating hormone (FSH) levels tend to be lower than normal, and luteinizing hormone (LH) levels are tonically elevated, leading to the characteristic increased LH/FSH ratio. The laboratory findings in patients with hirsutism-virilizing syndromes are summarized in Table 325-8.

Treatment Treatment of adrenal virilism is dictated by the type of lesion. Patients with *congenital adrenal hyperplasia* have a fundamental defect of cortisol deficiency with resultant excessive ACTH stimulation, producing hyperplasia of the adrenal glands and causing additional "shunting" into the adrenal androgen pathway. Therapy in these patients consists of daily administration of glucocorticoids to suppress pituitary ACTH secretion. Because of its cost and intermediate half-life, prednisone is the drug of choice except in infants, when hydrocortisone is usually used. In adult patients with late-onset adrenal hyperplasia, a single bedtime dose of an intermediate-acting glucocorticoid, such as 2.5 or 5 mg of prednisone, suppresses pituitary ACTH secretion. The amount of steroid required by children with congenital adrenal hyperplasia is approximately 1 to 1.5 times the normal cortisol production rate of 12 to 13 mg cortisol per square meter of body surface area per day and is given

TABLE 325-8 Laboratory evaluation of hirsutism-virilizing syndromes

	Ovarian		Adrenal			
	PCO	Ovarian tumor	CAH	Adrenal neoplasm	Cushing's syndrome	Idiopathic
Urinary 17-ketosteroids, plasma DHEA sulfate	N↑	N	N↑	↑↑↑	N↑	N
Plasma testosterone	N↑	↑↑	N↑	N↑	N↑	N
LH/FSH ratio	N↑	N	N	N	N	N
Precursors of cortisol biosynthesis:						
Basal	N	N	N↑	N↑	N	N
Following ACTH infusion	N	N	↑↑	N↑	N	N
Cortisol following overnight dexamethasone suppresion test	N	N	N	↑	↑	N

NOTE: *CAH, congenital adrenal hyperplasia; PCO, polycystic ovary syndrome; N, normal; ↑, elevated.*

in divided doses two or three times per day. The dosage schedule is governed by repetitive analysis of the urinary 17-ketosteroids, plasma DHEA sulfate, and/or precursors of cortisol biosynthesis. Skeletal growth and maturation must also be closely monitored since over-treatment with glucocorticoid replacement therapy retards linear growth.

HYPOFUNCTION OF ADRENAL CORTEX

Adrenocortical hypofunction includes all conditions in which the secretion of adrenal steroid hormones falls below the requirements of the body. Adrenal insufficiency may be divided into two general categories: (1) those associated with primary inability of the adrenal to elaborate sufficient quantities of hormone and (2) those associated with a secondary failure due to a primary failure in the elaboration of ACTH (Table 325-9).

PRIMARY ADRENOCORTICAL DEFICIENCY (ADDISON'S DISEASE) Addison's description of "general languor and debility, remarkable feebleness of the heart's action, irritability of the stomach, and a peculiar change of the color of the skin," summarizes the dominant clinical features of the disease. Advanced cases are usually easy to diagnose, but recognition of the disease in its earlier phases may present a real challenge.

Incidence Primary adrenocortical insufficiency is relatively rare. It may occur at any age and affects both sexes with equal frequency. Because of increasing therapeutic use of exogenous steroids, secondary adrenal insufficiency is relatively common.

Etiology and pathogenesis Addison's disease results from progressive adrenocortical destruction, which must involve more than 90 percent of the glands before signs of adrenal insufficiency appear. The adrenal is a frequent site for chronic granulomatous diseases, predominantly tuberculosis but also histoplasmosis, coccidioidomycosis, and cryptococcosis. In previous years, tuberculosis was found at postmortem examination in 70 to 90 percent of cases; however, the most frequent finding at present is *idiopathic* atrophy, and an

autoimmune mechanism is probably responsible. Rarely, other lesions are encountered, such as bilateral tumor metastases, amyloidosis, or sarcoidosis.

The possibility that primary adrenal insufficiency can have an autoimmune basis is strengthened by the finding that half of patients have circulating adrenal antibodies. Some patients also have circulating antibodies to thyroid, parathyroid, and/or gonadal tissue (see also Chap. 334). Cellular immunity may also be altered in patients with idiopathic adrenal insufficiency; for example, the expression of the Ia (immune-associated) antigen on T lymphocytes has been described in patients with recent-onset Addison's disease, probably reflecting activation of the immune system. There is also an increased incidence of chronic lymphocytic thyroiditis (Hashimoto's disease) and an increased incidence of premature ovarian failure, type I diabetes mellitus, Graves' disease, and primary hypoparathyroidism in patients with idiopathic adrenal insufficiency. The occurrence of two or more of these autoimmune endocrine disorders in the same individual defines the polyglandular autoimmune syndrome type II. Additional disorders in these patients include pernicious anemia, vitiligo, alopecia, nontropical sprue, and myasthenia gravis. Within families, multiple generations are affected by one or more of the above diseases. The inheritance of diseases in the type II polyglandular syndrome is associated with the HLA alleles B8 and Dw3.

The combination of parathyroid and adrenal insufficiency and chronic mucocutaneous moniliasis constitutes a distinct familial syndrome (type I polyglandular autoimmune syndrome). Other autoimmune diseases also occur in higher frequency in these patients (e.g., pernicious anemia, chronic active hepatitis, thyroid disease, alopecia, and premature gonadal failure). There is no HLA association; this syndrome is inherited in an autosomal recessive pattern, often with multiple affected siblings within a family. The type I syndrome usually presents during childhood, whereas the peak incidence of expression of the type II syndrome is 20 to 60 years. The mechanisms by which genetic predisposition and/or autoimmunity interact in the pathogenesis of these disease states are unknown.

Clinical signs and symptoms Adrenocortical insufficiency is characterized by an insidious onset of slowly progressive fatigability, weakness, anorexia, nausea and vomiting, weight loss, cutaneous and mucosal pigmentation, hypotension, and occasionally hypoglycemia (Table 325-10). However, the spectrum may vary, depending on the duration and degree of adrenal hypofunction, from a complaint of mild chronic fatigue to the fulminating shock associated with acute

TABLE 325-9 Classification of adrenal insufficiency

I Primary adrenal insufficiency
  A Anatomic destruction of gland (chronic and acute)
    1 "Idiopathic" atrophy (autoimmune)
    2 Surgical removal
    3 Infection (tuberculous, fungous)
    4 Hemorrhage
    5 Invasion: metastatic
  B Metabolic failure in hormone production
    1 Congenital adrenal hyperplasia
    2 Enzyme inhibitors (metyrapone)
    3 Cytotoxic agents (mitotane)
II Secondary adrenal insufficiency
  A Hypopituitarism due to hypothalamic-pituitary disease
  B Suppression of hypothalamic-pituitary axis
    1 Exogenous steroid
    2 Endogenous steroid from tumor

TABLE 325-10 Incidence of symptoms and signs in Addison's disease, percent

Weakness	99	Hypotension	
Pigmentation of skin	98	(<110/70)	87
Pigmentation of		Abdominal pain	34
mucous membranes	82	Salt craving	22
Weight loss	97	Diarrhea	20
Anorexia, nausea, and		Constipation	19
vomiting	90	Syncope	16
		Vitiligo	9

massive destruction of the glands in the syndrome described by Waterhouse and Friderichsen.

Asthenia is the cardinal symptom. Early it may be sporadic, usually most evident at times of stress; as adrenal function becomes more impaired, weakness progresses until the patient is continuously fatigued, necessitating bed rest.

Hyperpigmentation may be a striking sign, but its absence does not exclude this diagnosis. It commonly appears as a diffuse brown, tan, or bronze darkening of both exposed and unexposed parts such as elbows or creases of the hand and of areas normally pigmented such as the areolas about the nipples. Bluish-black patches may appear on the mucous membranes. Some patients develop dark freckles, and occasionally irregular areas of vitiligo may appear paradoxically. As an early sign, patients may notice an unusually persistent tanning following exposure to the sun.

Arterial hypotension is frequent, and in severe cases blood pressures may be in the range of 80/50 or less. Postural accentuation of hypotension is common.

Abnormalities of gastrointestinal function often are the presenting complaint. Symptoms may vary from mild anorexia with weight loss to fulminating nausea, vomiting, diarrhea, and ill-defined abdominal pain, which at times may be so severe as to be confused with an acute abdomen. In addition, patients with adrenal insufficiency frequently have marked personality changes, usually in the form of excessive irritability and restlessness. Enhancement of the sensory modalities of taste, olfaction, and hearing is often present and is reversible with therapy. A decrease in axillary and pubic hair is common in women due to loss of adrenal androgen production.

Laboratory findings In the milder forms, there may be no demonstrable abnormalities in the routine laboratory parameters, and even plasma and urinary steroid determinations may indicate values relatively low yet within normal range. However, studies of adrenal stimulation with ACTH show abnormalities even in this stage of the disease. In the more advanced stages, serum sodium, chloride, and bicarbonate are reduced while serum potassium is elevated. The hyponatremia is due to both loss of sodium into the urine (due to aldosterone deficiency) and movement into the intracellular compartment. This extravascular sodium loss depletes extracellular fluid volume and accentuates hypotension. Elevated plasma vasopressin and angiotensin II levels may be contributing factors to hyponatremia through impairment of free water clearance. The hyperkalemia is due to a combination of factors, including aldosterone deficiency, impaired glomerular filtration, and acidosis. Mild to moderate hypercalcemia is seen in 10 to 20 percent of patients; the reason for this is not understood. The electrocardiogram may show nonspecific changes, and the electroencephalogram exhibits a generalized reduction and slowing. There may be a normocytic anemia, a relative lymphocytosis, and usually a moderate eosinophilia.

Diagnosis The diagnosis of adrenal insufficiency should be made only with ACTH stimulation testing to assay the adrenal reserve

capacity for steroid production (see above for ACTH test protocols). In *severe adrenal insufficiency* the cortisol secretory rate is markedly decreased, and this may be ascertained indirectly by the finding of low to absent 24-h urine cortisol, 17-hydroxycorticoids, and 17-ketosteroids. With *mild or moderate adrenal insufficiency*, urine steroid excretion values overlap into the normal range; a diagnosis of adrenal insufficiency should never be excluded solely on the basis of normal basal urine steroid determinations. Plasma cortisol values vary from zero to the lower range of normal. Aldosterone secretion is usually low, resulting in salt wasting and secondary rises in plasma renin levels. In primary adrenal insufficiency, plasma ACTH and associated peptides are elevated because of loss of the usual cortisol-hypothalamic-pituitary feedback relationship, whereas in secondary adrenal insufficiency, plasma ACTH values are low, or ''inappropriately'' normal (Fig. 352-11).

Differential diagnosis Since weakness and fatigue are common complaints, clinical diagnosis of early adrenocortical insufficiency is frequently difficult. However, mild gastrointestinal distress with weight loss, anorexia, and a suggestion of increased pigmentation make mandatory ACTH stimulation testing to rule out adrenal insufficiency, particularly before steroid treatment is begun. Weight loss is useful in evaluating the significance of weakness and malaise. Weight gain associated with lassitude is more characteristic of depressive syndromes. Racial pigmentation in many individuals may be a problem, but a *recent* and progressive *increase* is usually reported by the Addisonian patient. Hyperpigmentation in other diseases may also present a problem, but the appearance and distribution of pigment in Addison's disease are usually characteristic. When doubt exists, measurement of ACTH levels and testing of adrenal reserve with the infusion of ACTH provide clear-cut differentiation.

Treatment All patients with Addison's disease should receive specific hormone replacement. Like diabetics, these patients require careful and persistent education in regard to their disease. Since the adrenal gland elaborates three general classes of hormone, of which two, glucocorticoids and mineralocorticoids, are of primary clinical importance, replacement therapy should correct both deficiencies. Cortisone (or cortisol) is the mainstay of treatment. Cortisone dosage varies from 12.5 to 50 mg daily, with the majority of patients taking 25 to 37.5 mg in divided doses. Cortisol (30 mg daily) or prednisone (7.5 mg daily) in divided doses may also be given for substitution therapy. Because of its effect on gastric mucosa, patients are advised to take their cortisone with meals or, if this is impractical, with milk or an antacid preparation. In addition, the larger proportion of the dose (e.g., 25 mg of cortisone) is taken in the morning and the remainder (12.5 mg of cortisone) in the late afternoon, to simulate the normal diurnal adrenal rhythm. Some patients exhibit insomnia, irritability, and mental excitement after initiation of therapy; in these, the dosage should be reduced. Other indications for smaller amounts of glucocorticoids are hypertension, diabetes, or active tuberculosis.

Since this amount of cortisone or cortisol fails to replace the

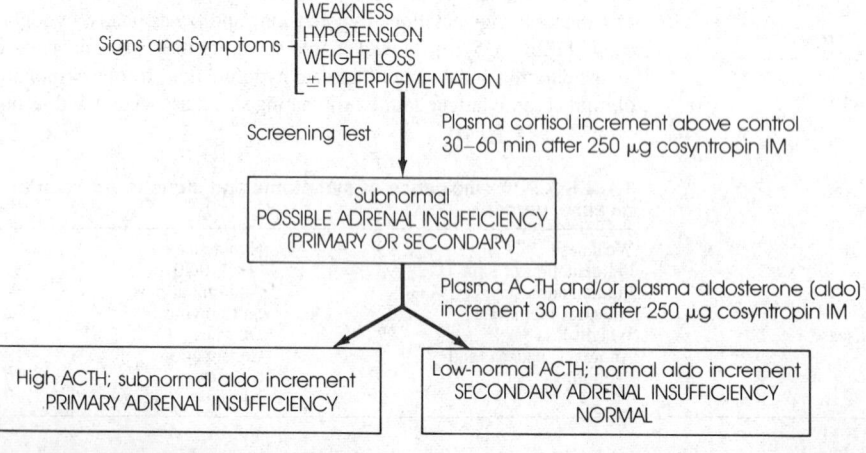

FIGURE 325-11 *Diagnostic flowchart for evaluating patients with suspected adrenal insufficiency. Plasma ACTH levels are low in secondary adrenal insufficiency. In adrenal insufficiency secondary to pituitary tumors or idiopathic panhypopituitarism, other pituitary hormone deficiencies are present. On the other hand, ACTH deficiency may be isolated, as seen following prolonged use of exogenous glucocorticoids.*

Since the isolated blood levels obtained in these screening tests may not be definitive, the diagnosis should always be confirmed by a continuous 24-h ACTH infusion. Normal subjects and patients with secondary adrenal insufficiency may be distinguished by insulin tolerance or metyrapone testing.

mineralocorticoid component of the adrenal gland, supplementary hormone is usually needed. This is accomplished by the daily oral administration of 0.05 to 0.1 mg fludrocortisone. If parenteral administration is indicated, a dosage of 2 to 5 mg deoxycorticosterone acetate in oil may be given every day intramuscularly.

Complications of glucocorticoid therapy, with the exception of gastritis, are *rare* in the dosage used in the treatment of Addison's disease. Complications of mineralocorticoid therapy occur more frequently and include hypokalemia, edema, hypertension, cardiac enlargement, or even congestive failure due to sodium retention. In the management of patients with Addison's disease, periodic measurements of body weight, serum potassium, and blood pressure are useful.

All patients with adrenal insufficiency, including bilaterally adrenalectomized patients, should carry medical identification, should be instructed in the parenteral self-administration of steroids, and should be registered with a national medical alerting system.

Special therapeutic problems During periods of intercurrent illness, the dose of cortisone or cortisol should be increased to 75 to 150 mg per day. When oral administration is not possible, parenteral routes should be employed. Likewise, before surgery or dental extractions, supplemental glucocorticoids should be administered. Patients should also be advised to increase the dose of fludrocortisone and to add excess salt to their otherwise normal diet during periods of excessive exercise with sweating, during extremely hot weather, and with gastrointestinal upsets. For a representative program of steroid therapy for the patient with adrenal insufficiency who is undergoing a major operation, see Table 325-11. This schedule is designed to mimic on the day of surgery the output of cortisol in normal individuals undergoing prolonged major stress (10 mg/h, 250 to 300 mg per 24 h). Thereafter, if the patient is progressing well and is afebrile, the dose of cortisol is tapered by 20 to 30 percent daily. Parenteral mineralocorticoid administration is unnecessary at cortisol doses greater than 100 mg per day because of the mineralocorticoid effects of cortisol at such dosages.

SECONDARY ADRENOCORTICAL INSUFFICIENCY Pituitary ACTH deficiency causes *secondary* adrenocortical insufficiency. ACTH deficiency may be selective, as is seen following prolonged administration of excess glucocorticoids, or may occur in association with multiple pituitary tropic hormone deficiencies (panhypopituitarism) (see Chap. 321). Patients with secondary adrenocortical hypofunction may have many symptoms and signs in common with Addisonian patients but are *characteristically not hyperpigmented* since ACTH and related peptide levels are low. In fact, plasma ACTH levels distinguish between primary and secondary adrenal insufficiency, since they are elevated in the former and decreased to absent in the latter. Patients with total pituitary insufficiency also have signs and symptoms suggestive of multiple hormone deficiencies. An additional feature distinguishing primary from secondary adrenocortical insufficiency is the *near-normal level of aldosterone secretion* seen in the presence of pituitary and/or isolated ACTH deficiencies (Fig. 325-11). Patients with pituitary insufficiency may present with hyponatremia, which may be dilutional or secondary to subnormal increments in aldosterone secretion in response to severe sodium restriction. However, the findings of severe dehydration, *hyponatremia,* and *hyperkalemia* are characteristic of severe mineralocorticoid insufficiency and favor a diagnosis of primary adrenocortical insufficiency.

Patients receiving long-term steroid therapy, despite physical findings of Cushing's syndrome, develop adrenal insufficiency because of prolonged pituitary-hypothalamic suppression and adrenal atrophy secondary to the loss of endogenous ACTH. Thus, these patients have two deficits, a loss of adrenal responsiveness to ACTH and a failure of pituitary ACTH release. These patients are characterized by low blood cortisol and ACTH levels, low baseline steroid excretion, and abnormal ACTH and metyrapone test results. Most patients with steroid-induced adrenal insufficiency eventually recover normal hypothalamic-pituitary-adrenal responsiveness, but individual response time varies from days to months. The rapid ACTH test can be used as a convenient assessment of recovery of hypothalamic-pituitary-adrenal function. Since the plasma cortisol concentrations after injection of cosyntropin and during insulin-induced hypoglycemia correlate closely, the rapid ACTH test assesses the integrated hypothalamic-pituitary-adrenal function. Additional testing to assess endogenous pituitary ACTH reserve includes the standard metyrapone and the insulin tolerance tests.

Substitution glucocorticoid therapy in patients with secondary adrenocortical insufficiency does not differ from that for Addisonian patients. Mineralocorticoid replacement therapy is usually not necessary, since aldosterone secretion is preserved. Otherwise, the same basic principles should be applied to patients with secondary adrenocortical insufficiency.

ACUTE ADRENOCORTICAL INSUFFICIENCY Acute adrenocortical insufficiency may result from several processes. One of these, termed *adrenal crisis,* is a rapid and overwhelming intensification of chronic adrenal insufficiency, usually precipitated by sepsis or surgical stress. Another involves an acute hemorrhagic destruction of both adrenal glands, usually associated with an overwhelming septicemia (Waterhouse-Friderichsen syndrome). Adrenal hemorrhage associated with anticoagulant therapy in patients with increased adrenocortical activity has also been reported, as in the period immediately following a myocardial infarction. Occasionally, adrenal hemorrhage in the newborn results from birth trauma. Hemorrhage also has been observed during pregnancy, following idiopathic adrenal vein thrombosis, and as a complication of venography (e.g., infarction of an adenoma). A third, and probably the most frequent, cause of acute insufficiency results from the rapid withdrawal of steroids from patients with adrenal atrophy secondary to chronic steroid administration. In the presence of severe stress, acute adrenocortical insufficiency may also occur in patients with congenital adrenal hyperplasia and those receiving pharmacologic agents that are capable of inhibiting steroid synthesis (such as mitotane).

TABLE 325-11 Steroid therapy schedule for Addisonian patient undergoing a major operation*

	Cortisone acetate (intramuscularly)		Cortisol infusion, continuous, mg/h	Cortisone acetate (orally)		Fludro-cortisone (orally), 8 A.M.
	7 A.M.	7 P.M.		8 A.M.	4 P.M.	
Routine daily medication				25	12.5	0.1
Day before operation		50		25	12.5	0.1
Day of operation	50	50	10			
Postoperative:						
Day 1	50	50	5–7.5			
Day 2	50	50	2.5–5			
Day 3	50	50				
Day 4	50				25	0.1
Day 5				37.5	25	0.1
Day 6				25	25	0.1
Day 7				25	12.5	0.1

* *All steroid doses are given in milligrams.*

Adrenal crisis The long-term survival of patients with Addison's disease largely depends upon prevention and treatment of adrenal crisis. Consequently, the occurrence of infection, trauma (including surgery), gastrointestinal upsets, or other forms of stress requires an immediate increase in hormone. In untreated patients, preexisting symptoms are intensified. Nausea, vomiting, and abdominal pain may become intractable. Fever may be severe or absent. Lethargy deepens into somnolence, and the blood pressure and pulse fail as hypovolemic vascular shock ensues. In contrast, patients previously maintained on chronic glucocorticoid therapy may not exhibit severe dehydration or hypotension until preterminally, since mineralocorticoid secretion is usually preserved. In all patients in crisis, a precipitating cause should be sought. Intercurrent infection associated with omission or failure to increase maintenance therapy is common.

Treatment is primarily directed toward the rapid elevation of circulating glucocorticoid and the replacement of the sodium and water deficits. Hence, an intravenous infusion of 5% glucose in normal saline solution should be immediately started with a bolus intravenous infusion of 100 mg cortisol followed by a continuous infusion of cortisol at a rate of 10 mg/h; 50 mg cortisone acetate should be given intramuscularly in case the infusion becomes infiltrated or inadvertently stopped. Effective treatment of hypotension consists of aggressive repletion of sodium and water deficits. If the crisis was preceded by prolonged nausea, vomiting, and dehydration, several liters of saline solution may be required within the first few hours. Vasoconstrictive agents (such as dopamine) may be indicated in extreme conditions as adjuncts to volume replacement. With large doses of steroid, as for example 100 to 200 mg cortisol, the patient receives a maximal mineralocorticoid effect, and supplementary mineralocorticoid is superfluous. Following improvement, the patient can be offered oral fluids and the steroid dosage is tapered over the next few days to maintenance levels, with reinstitution of supplementary mineralocorticoid if needed (Table 325-11).

HYPOALDOSTERONISM

Isolated aldosterone deficiency accompanied by normal cortisol production occurs in association with hyporeninism, as an inherited biosynthetic defect, postoperatively following removal of aldosterone-secreting adenomas, during protracted heparin or heparinoid administration, in pretectal disease of the nervous system, and in severe postural hypotension.

The feature common to all patients with hypoaldosteronism is the inability to increase aldosterone secretion appropriately during salt restriction. Most patients present with unexplained hyperkalemia often exacerbated by restriction of dietary sodium intake. In severe cases urine sodium wastage occurs on a normal salt intake, whereas in milder forms excessive losses of urine sodium occur only during salt restriction.

Most cases of isolated hypoaldosteronism occur in patients with a deficiency in renin production (so-called hyporeninemic hypoaldosteronism). This syndrome is most commonly seen in adults with mild renal failure and diabetes mellitus in association with hyperkalemia and metabolic acidosis out of proportion to the state of renal impairment. Plasma renin levels fail to rise normally following sodium restriction and postural changes. The pathogenesis is uncertain. Possibilities include renal disease (most likely), autonomic neuropathy, extracellular fluid volume expansion, and a defect in conversion of presumed renin precursors into active renin. Aldosterone levels also fail to rise normally following salt restriction and volume contraction; this is probably related to the hyporeninism since biosynthetic defects in aldosterone secretion cannot usually be demonstrated. In these patients, aldosterone secretion increases promptly following ACTH stimulation, but it is uncertain whether the magnitude of the response is normal. On the other hand, the level of aldosterone appears to be subnormal in relationship to the hyperkalemia.

Hypoaldosteronism can also be associated with high renin levels.

In many of these subjects, a biosynthetic defect has been noted where there is an inability to transform the C-18 methyl group of corticosterone to the C-18 aldehyde of aldosterone due to a deficiency of the enzyme 18-hydroxysteroid dehydrogenase. These patients manifest not only low to absent aldosterone secretion and elevated plasma renin levels but also elevated values for the intermediates of aldosterone biosynthesis (corticosterone and 18-hydroxycorticosterone).

Before considering the diagnosis of isolated hypoaldosteronism in a patient with hyperkalemia, "pseudohyperkalemia" (e.g., hemolysis, thrombocytosis) should be excluded by measuring plasma potassium. The next step is to demonstrate a normal cortisol response to ACTH stimulation. Then stimulated (upright posture, sodium restriction) renin and aldosterone levels are obtained. Low renin–low aldosterone levels establish a diagnosis of hyporeninemic hypoaldosteronism. High renin–low aldosterone levels are consistent with an aldosterone biosynthetic defect or a selective unresponsiveness of the glomerulosa to angiotensin II. Finally, elevated renin and aldosterone levels suggest primary renal unresponsiveness to aldosterone, so-called pseudohypoaldosteronism.

Treatment of patients with isolated hypoaldosteronism would logically be to replace the mineralocorticoid deficiency. For practical purposes, the oral administration of fludrocortisone in a dose of 0.1 to 0.2 mg daily should restore electrolyte balance. However, patients with hyporeninemic hypoaldosteronism usually require greater doses of mineralocorticoid to normalize the hyperkalemia. This poses a risk in these patients who usually have hypertension and mild renal insufficiency. Therefore, an alternative approach is to administer furosemide, which can ameliorate the acidosis and the hyperkalemia. Occasionally a combination of these two approaches may be efficacious.

NONSPECIFIC CLINICAL USE OF ADRENAL STEROIDS AND ACTH

The widespread utilization of glucocorticoids and ACTH emphasizes the need for a thorough understanding of the metabolic effects of these agents when used nonspecifically, if optimum effectiveness is to be obtained and if undesirable side reactions are to be minimized. Before instituting adrenal hormone therapy, the gains that can reasonably be expected should be weighed against the potentially undesirable metabolic actions of pharmacologic doses of hormone.

HOW SERIOUS IS THE DISORDER? In a patient whose life is threatened by unexplained shock or in whom other measures have failed, the physician need not hesitate to employ large-dosage steroid therapy. On the other hand, one should exercise restraint in administering steroids to a patient with early rheumatoid arthritis who as yet has not been exposed to the possible benefits of physiotherapy, analgesics, and a well-organized program of general medical care.

HOW LONG WILL GLUCOCORTICOID THERAPY BE REQUIRED? The use of intravenously administered steroids for a period of 24 to 48 h in the treatment of such life-threatening situations as status asthmaticus or pseudotumor cerebri has little or no contraindication, in contrast to the initiation of a program of chronic steroid therapy for asthma, arthritis, or psoriasis. In the latter instances, the almost certain complication of a Cushing's syndrome of some degree must be weighed against the potential benefit. These side effects should be minimized by a careful choice of steroid preparations, alternate-day or interrupted therapy programs, and the judicious use of supplementary adjuvants.

WHICH ADRENAL PREPARATION IS PREFERABLE? At least five considerations need to be taken into account in deciding which steroid preparation to use:

1 The biologic half-life of the compound. The rationale behind every-other-day therapy is to decrease the metabolic effects of the steroids for a significant amount of time over the 2-day period, yet at the same time to produce pharmacologic suppression of sufficient duration to maintain the disease in remission. Too long a half-life would defeat the first purpose, and too short a half-life would defeat the second. In general, the more potent the steroid, the longer its biologic half-life.

2 The importance of the mineralocorticoid effects of the steroid. Synthetic steroids have less mineralocorticoid effect relative to their glucocorticoid effect than do cortisol or cortisone (Table 325-12). This may be an important consideration in certain disease states.

3 The biologically active form of the steroid. Cortisone and prednisone, in contrast to the other glucocorticoids, have to be converted to biologically active equivalents before anti-inflammatory effects can occur. Because of this, in a condition in which steroids are known to be effective and when an adequate dose has been given without response, one should consider substituting cortisol or prednisolone for cortisone or prednisone.

4 The cost of the medication. This is a serious consideration if chronic administration is to be undertaken. Prednisone is the least expensive of available steroid preparations.

5 The variation in the manner in which preparations of glucosteroids are formulated. This factor may modify absorption. Thus, it is advisable for a patient whose steroid dosage has been standardized to continue to utilize the same pharmaceutical preparation to avoid relapse or overdosage.

ACTH VERSUS STEROIDS In general, adrenal steroid therapy is effective by mouth and can be regulated more accurately than ACTH therapy. The amount of steroid produced in response to ACTH varies from day to day, depending on the rate and extent of absorption of ACTH and on the state of the adrenal cortex. ACTH therapy stimulates the secretion of adrenal androgens as well as of hydroxysteroids. Sodium retention with ACTH is often more marked than with cortisone or prednisone therapy.

While some studies imply that ACTH may be superior to oral steroid therapy in the treatment of certain disorders such as dermatomyositis and multiple sclerosis, it is generally believed that the two agents are equally effective (or ineffective). Both ACTH and steroid therapy induce hypothalamopituitary suppression; however, in ACTH therapy adrenal gland size and activity are maintained, in contrast to the adrenal atrophy usually associated with steroid therapy.

EVALUATION OF PATIENT PRIOR TO INITIATING STEROID THERAPY (See Table 325-13) **Chronic infection** Three problems de-

TABLE 325-12 Glucocorticoid preparations

Commonly used name*	Estimated potency†	
	Glucocorticoid	Mineralocorticoid
SHORT-ACTING		
Cortisol	1	1
Cortisone	0.8	0.8
INTERMEDIATE-ACTING		
Prednisone	4	0.25
Prednisolone	4	0.25
Methylprednisolone	5	±‡
Triamcinolone	5	±
LONG-ACTING		
Paramethasone	10	±
Betamethasone	25	±
Dexamethasone	30–40	±

* *The steroids are divided into three groups according to the duration of biologic activity. Short-acting preparations have a biologic half-life of less than 12 h; long-acting, greater than 48 h; and intermediate, between 12 and 36 h. Triamcinolone has the longest half-life of the intermediate-acting preparations.*

† *Relative milligram comparisons with cortisol, setting the glucocorticoid and mineralocorticoid properties of cortisol as 1. Sodium retention is insignificant in usual doses employed of methylprednisolone, triamcinolone, paramethasone, betamethasone, and dexamethasone.*

‡ *±, Too low to measure with accuracy.*

TABLE 325-13 A "checklist" for use prior to the administration of glucocorticoids in pharmacologic dosages

1 Presence of tuberculosis or other chronic infection (chest x-ray, tuberculin test)
2 Evidence of glucose intolerance or history of gestational diabetes mellitus
3 Evidence of preexisting osteoporosis (spine x-ray or bone density assessment, if available, in postmenopausal patients)
4 History of peptic ulcer, gastritis, or esophagitis (stool guaiac test)
5 Evidence of hypertension or cardiovascular disease
6 History of psychological disorders

mand attention: (1) Any active infection, particularly tuberculosis, should be identified. If tuberculosis is present, steroid therapy can be employed, if indicated, in conjunction with antituberculous chemotherapy. (2) The chest film and tuberculin test provide baseline information for future comparison. Since high-dosage steroids minimize the tuberculin reaction, serial chest roentgenograms may be indicated. (3) Infection due to "opportunistic" low-virulence pathogens should be constantly considered in patients on high steroid dosage, especially when steroid therapy is combined with other immunosuppressive agents.

Diabetes mellitus Prolonged glucocorticoid therapy may unmask latent diabetes mellitus or aggravate preexisting disease. The presence of diabetes mellitus or the demonstration of impaired glucose tolerance may affect the decision to institute adrenal hormone therapy.

Osteoporosis All patients receiving long-continued steroid therapy are likely to develop some degree of osteoporosis. Indeed osteoporosis, with vertebral fractures or compression, is one of the most serious potential hazards of long-term steroid therapy. For patients at high risk (postmenopausal women, elderly men, and patients with restricted physical activity) initial films of the thoracolumbar segment of the spine are mandatory. Alternate-day or interrupted steroid therapy minimizes this complication (Table 325-14), and adjunctive therapies may be effective in the therapy of steroid osteoporosis (see Chap. 339).

Peptic ulcer, gastric hypersecretion, or esophagitis In conventional therapeutic doses (equivalent to 15 mg prednisone per day or less) glucocorticoids probably do not cause peptic ulceration; whether higher doses are associated with increased incidence of peptic ulcer disease is not established and probably depends on duration of treatment (as well as dose) and the presence of predisposing factors such as hypoalbuminemia or cirrhosis. However, even in conventional doses patients with a history of ulcer may experience aggravation of symptoms while receiving glucocorticoids. Consequently, all individuals with a positive history or with known risk factors should be given a vigorous "ulcer combating" program (antacids, cimetidine) along with glucocorticoids. *The development of anemia in a patient receiving glucocorticoids should suggest gastrointestinal bleeding as a cause, and patients should be cautioned to note black stools.*

Hypertension or cardiovascular disease In general, the sodium-retaining propensity of many adrenal steroid preparations requires

TABLE 325-14 Supplementary measures to minimize undesirable metabolic effects of glucocorticoids

I Monitor caloric intake to prevent weight gain.
II Restrict sodium intake to prevent edema and minimize hypertension and potassium loss.
III Supplement potassium if necessary.
IV Give antacid therapy and/or histamine receptor antagonist therapy.
V Institute alternate-day steroid schedule if possible. Patients on steroid therapy over a prolonged period should be protected by an appropriate increase in hormone level during periods of acute stress. A rule of thumb is to *double* the maintenance dose.
VI Minimize osteopenia by (not proved effective):
  A Estrogen therapy for postmenopausal women; 0.625–1.25 mg conjugated estrogens, may be given "cyclically." Regular Papanicolaou smear and breast examination mandatory (see Chap. 331).
  B Consider supplementary vitamin D and calcium.

that caution be used when they are given to patients with preexisting hypertension or cardiovascular or renal disease. Use of preparations in which sodium-retaining activity is minimal, restriction of dietary sodium intake, and the use of diuretic agents and supplementary potassium salts will minimize the mineralocorticoid actions of steroid therapy. However, hypertension may still be exacerbated by steroid-induced increases in renin substrate and consequently in angiotensin II levels.

Psychological difficulties Steroid therapy may be complicated by minor or severe psychological disturbances. In general, serious psychological disturbances are more closely related to the patient's personality structure than to the actual dose of hormone, although, as might be anticipated, larger doses of hormone are associated with more frequent serious reactions. At present there is no reliable method of determining beforehand a patient's psychological reaction to steroid therapy; moreover, previous tolerance of steroids does not necessarily ensure immunity to subsequent courses of therapy. Likewise, untoward psychological reactions on one occasion do not invariably mean that the patient will respond unfavorably to a second course of treatment; however, prophylactic treatment with lithium may be indicated.

Sleeplessness is a common complication and can be minimized by using the shorter-acting steroids and by prescribing the total dose as a single early-morning medication.

ALTERNATE-DAY STEROID THERAPY The single most effective measure in minimizing the cushingoid effects of glucocorticoid therapy is to administer the total 48-h dose as a *single* dose of *intermediate-acting steroid* in the morning, *every other day*. If symptoms of the underlying disorder can be controlled by this technique, the therapeutic program offers a distinct advantage. Three special considerations deserve mention: (1) The alternate-day schedule may be approached through a series of transition dose schedules that permit the patient an opportunity to adjust to the ultimate program. (2) The physician should provide the patient with supplementary nonsteroid medications, if required, on the "off day" to minimize symptoms of the underlying disorder. (3) The physician and the patient should recognize that many symptoms noted during the off day (e.g., fatigue, joint pain, muscle stiffness or tenderness, and fever) are those of relative adrenal insufficiency, rather than an exacerbation of the underlying disease. Knowing this is of vital importance, since the physician can reassure the patient and avoid giving up the program on the basis of a misconception.

The alternate-day concept capitalizes on the fact that cortisol secretion and plasma levels normally are highest in the early morning and lowest in the evening. The normal pattern is mimicked by administering an intermediate-acting steroid in the morning (7 to 8 A.M.) (Table 325-12).

Initially the steroid program usually requires daily or more frequent doses of steroid to accomplish the desired anti-inflammatory or immunity-suppressing action. *Only after this desired effect has been achieved is an attempt made to switch over to an alternate-day program.* A number of programs may be employed for transferring a patient from a daily to an alternate-day program. The key points to be considered are flexibility in arranging a program and the use of supportive measures on the off day. One may attempt a transition by a series of gradations rather than by an abrupt complete changeover. One approach is to keep the steroid dose constant on one day and gradually reduce the level on the alternate day. Alternatively, the steroid dose can be increased on one day while being reduced on the alternate day. In any case it is important to anticipate that the patient will experience some increase in pain or discomfort between the 36 to 48 h following the last dose of steroid.

The general principles advocated in the long-term use of steroids and in implementing an alternate-day schedule are as follows:

1 Utilize intermediate-acting steroids such as prednisone or predni-solone.
2 Give the total daily steroid as a single morning dose.

3 Begin a transition program as soon as the manifestations of the diseases are under reasonable control.
4 If possible, eliminate steroid medication on the alternate day.

WITHDRAWAL OF CORTICOSTEROIDS FOLLOWING THEIR LONG-TERM USE AS PHARMACOLOGIC AGENTS Complete withdrawal of steroids should be initiated by implementing an alternate-day schedule. Patients on an alternate-day program for a month or more experience less difficulty during a subsequent termination regimen as far as pituitary-adrenal function is concerned. The dosage is gradually reduced and finally discontinued after a normal replacement dosage has been reached (e.g., 5 to 7.5 mg prednisone). Complications rarely ensue unless undue stress is experienced, and patients should understand that for 1 year or longer after the complete withdrawal from long-term high-dosage steroid therapy, they should receive supplementary hormone in the presence of serious infection, operation, or injury.

In patients on high-dose daily steroid therapy, it is frequently advised to reduce total steroid dosage to approximately 20 mg prednisone daily before beginning the transition to every-other-day therapy. If a patient cannot tolerate an alternate-day program, it is debatable as to whether complete discontinuance should be considered. Under these circumstances a daily dose of steroid could be continued, and at some future date another trial of gradual transition to the alternate-day schedule should be attempted. In patients with life-threatening disorders, it may be desirable to consider life-long daily maintenance therapy at an Addisonian replacement dosage. These patients will not require mineralocorticoid therapy, as aldosterone secretion is usually adequate.

REFERENCES

BLOOM E et al: Nuclear binding of glucocorticoid receptors: Relations between cytosol binding, activation in the biologic response. J Steroid Biochem 12:175, 1980

BRAVO E et al: The changing clinical spectrum of primary aldosteronism. Am J Med 74:641, 1983

CHROUSOS GP et al: Late onset of 21-hydroxylase deficiency mimicking idiopathic hirsutism or polycystic ovary disease. Ann Intern Med 96:143, 1982

EDELMAN IS, MARVER D: Mediating events in the action of aldosterone. J Steroid Biochem 12:219, 1980

EISENBARTH GS et al: The polyglandular failure syndrome: Disease inheritance, HLA-type and immune function. Ann Intern Med 91:528, 1979

KNOX FG et al: Escape from the sodium retaining effects of mineralocorticoids. Kidney Int 17:263, 1980

KRIEGER DT: Physiopathology of Cushing's disease. Endocr Rev 4:22, 1983

LITRA SN et al: Corticotrophin releasing factor: Responses in normal subjects and patients with disorders of the hypothalamus and pituitary. Clin Endocrinol 20:71, 1984

NEW MI, LEVINE LS: Recent advances in 21-hydroxylase deficiency. Ann Rev Med 35:649, 1984

NOLAN PM et al: Therapeutic problems with transsphenoidal pituitary surgery for Cushing's disease. Clev Clin Q 49:199, 1982

PARRILLO JE, FAUCI AS: Mechanisms of glucocorticoid action on immune processes. Ann Rev Pharmacol Toxicol 19:179, 1979

PEDERSEN RC et al: Pro-adrenocorticotropin/endorphin-derived peptides: Coordinated action on adrenal steroidogenesis. Science 208:1044, 1980

RABINOWE SL et al: Ia-positive T lymphocytes in recently diagnosed idiopathic Addison's disease. Am J Med 77:597, 1984

ROSS EJ, LYNCH DC: Cushing's syndrome—killing disease: Discriminatory value of signs and symptoms aiding early diagnosis. Lancet 2:646, 1982

SCHAMBELAN M et al: Prevalence, pathogenesis and functional significance of aldosterone deficiency in hyperkalemic patients with chronic renal insufficiency. Kidney Int 17:89, 1980

SINDLER BH et al: The superiority of the metyrapone test vs the high dose dexamethasone test in the differential diagnosis of Cushing's syndrome. Am J Med 74:657, 1983

THOMAS JP, RICHARDS SH: Long term results of radical hypophysectomy for Cushing's disease. Clin Endocrinol 19:629, 1983

WEINBERGER MH: Primary aldosteronism: Diagnosis and differentiation of subtypes. Ann Intern Med 100:300, 1984

WILLIAMS GH, DLUHY RG: Control of aldosterone secretion, in *Hypertension*, 2d ed, J Genest et al (eds), New York, McGraw-Hill, 1983, p 320

WILLIAMS GH, DLUHY RG: Diagnostic imaging of the adrenal gland, in *Endocrinology*, 2d ed, LG DeGroot et al (eds), Orlando Fla., Grune and Stratton (in press)

326 PHEOCHROMOCYTOMA

LEWIS LANDSBERG / JAMES B. YOUNG

Pheochromocytomas, also known as chromaffin tumors, produce, store, and secrete catecholamines and are derived most often from the adrenal medulla. Pheochromocytomas that develop outside the adrenal arise from chromaffin cells in or about sympathetic ganglia and are known as extraadrenal pheochromocytomas or paragangliomas. Related tumors that secrete catecholamines and produce similar clinical syndromes include chemodectomas derived from the carotid body and ganglioneuromas derived from the postganglionic sympathetic neurons.

The clinical features and morbidity of these tumors are due predominantly to the release of catecholamines. Hypertension is the most common manifestation, and hypertensive paroxysms or crises, often spectacular and alarming, occur in over half the cases.

Pheochromocytoma occurs only in approximately 0.1 percent of the hypertensive population, but it is, nevertheless, an important correctable cause of high blood pressure. Indeed, it is usually curable if properly diagnosed and treated, but may be fatal if undiagnosed or mistreated. Postmortem series indicate that the majority of pheochromocytomas are unsuspected clinically and that in many of these cases the tumor is related to the fatal outcome.

PATHOLOGY   Location and morphology   In adults approximately 80 percent occur as a unilateral solitary lesion, 10 percent are bilateral, and 10 percent are extraadrenal. In children a fourth of tumors are bilateral, and an additional fourth are extraadrenal. Solitary lesions inexplicably favor the right side. Although pheochromocytomas may grow to large size (over 3 kg) most weigh less than 100 g and are less than 10 cm in diameter. The tumors are highly vascular with an arterial supply derived from any of the three arteries that normally supply the adrenal.

The tumors are made up of large, polyhedral, pleomorphic chromaffin cells. Less than 10 percent are malignant. As with other endocrine tumors malignancy cannot be determined by the histologic appearance; local invasion of surrounding tissues or distant metastases indicate malignancy.

FAMILIAL PHEOCHROMOCYTOMA   In approximately 5 percent of cases pheochromocytoma is inherited as an autosomal dominant trait either alone or in combination with other abnormalities such as multiple endocrine neoplasia (MEN) type II (Sipple's syndrome) or type III (mucosal neuroma syndrome) (see Chap. 334), von Recklinghausen's neurofibromatosis, or von Hippel–Lindau's retinal cerebellar hemangioblastomatosis. Bilateral adrenal pheochromocytomas are common in the familial syndromes; within MEN kindreds over half with pheochromocytomas have bilateral lesions. A familial syndrome should be suspected in any patient presenting with bilateral pheochromocytomas.

EXTRAADRENAL PHEOCHROMOCYTOMAS   Extraadrenal pheochromocytomas have an average weight of 20 to 40 g and are usually less than 5 cm in diameter. Most are located within the abdomen in association with the celiac, superior mesenteric, and inferior mesenteric ganglia. Approximately 1 percent are located within the thorax in relation to the paravertebral sympathetic ganglia, 1 percent are located within the urinary bladder, and less than 1 percent are within the neck, usually in association with the sympathetic ganglia or the extracranial branches of the ninth or tenth cranial nerves.

Catecholamine synthesis, storage, and release   Pheochromocytomas synthesize and store catecholamines by processes resembling those of the normal adrenal medulla (Chap. 66). Little is known about the mechanisms of catecholamine release from pheochromocytomas, but changes in blood flow and necrosis within the tumor may be the cause in some instances. These tumors are not innervated, and catecholamine release does not result from neural stimulation.

EPINEPHRINE, NOREPINEPHRINE, AND DOPAMINE   Most pheochromocytomas contain and secrete both norepinephrine and epinephrine, and the percentage of norepinephrine is usually greater than in the normal adrenal. Most extraadrenal pheochromocytomas secrete norepinephrine exclusively. Rarely, pheochromocytomas produce epinephrine alone, particularly in association with MEN. Although epinephrine-producing tumors may be associated with a preponderance of metabolic and beta-receptor effects, in general the predominant catecholamine secreted cannot be predicted from the clinical presentation. Increased production of dopamine and homovanillic acid (HVA) is uncommon with benign lesions; the excretion of these precursors is, however, increased in some patients with malignant pheochromocytoma.

CLINICAL FEATURES   Pheochromocytoma occurs at all ages but is most common in young to midadult life. Some series show a slight female preponderance. Although the presentation is characteristically unpredictable, most patients come to medical attention as a result of hypertensive crisis, paroxysmal symptoms suggestive of seizure disorder or anxiety attacks, or hypertension that responds poorly to conventional treatment. Less commonly, unexplained hypotension or shock in association with surgery or trauma will suggest the diagnosis.

Hypertension   Hypertension is the most common manifestation. In approximately 60 percent of cases the hypertension is sustained, although significant blood pressure lability is usually present and half of patients with sustained hypertension have distinct crises or paroxysms. The other 40 percent have blood pressure elevations only during an attack. The hypertension is often severe, occasionally malignant, and usually resistant to treatment with standard drugs used for therapy of essential hypertension.

Paroxysms or crises   The paroxysm or crisis is a typical manifestation, occurring in over half of patients. In an individual patient the symptoms are often similar with each attack. The paroxysms are commonly frequent but may be sporadic at intervals as long as weeks or months. With time the paroxysms usually increase in frequency, duration, and severity.

The attack usually has a sudden onset. It may last from a few minutes to several hours or longer. Headache, profuse sweating, palpitations, and apprehension, often with a sense of impending doom, are common. Pain in the chest or abdomen may be associated with nausea and vomiting. Either pallor or flushing may occur during the attack. The blood pressure is elevated, often to alarming levels, and is usually accompanied by tachycardia.

The paroxysm may be precipitated by any activity that displaces the abdominal contents. In some cases a particular stimulus may reproduce an attack in a characteristic fashion, but no clearly defined precipitating event may be found. Although anxiety may accompany the attacks, mental stress or psychological tension does not usually provoke a crisis.

Other distinctive clinical features   Symptoms and signs of an increased metabolic rate, such as profuse sweating and mild to moderate weight loss, are common. Orthostatic hypotension is a consequence of diminished plasma volume and blunted sympathetic reflexes. Both of these factors predispose the patient with unsuspected pheochromocytoma to hypotension or shock during surgery or major trauma.

CARDIAC MANIFESTATIONS   Sinus tachycardia, sinus bradycardia, supraventricular arrhythmias, and ventricular premature contractions have all been noted. Angina and acute myocardial infarction may occur even in the absence of coronary artery disease. Catecholamine-induced increase in myocardial oxygen consumption and, perhaps, coronary spasm may be involved in the pathogenesis of these ischemic events. Electrocardiographic changes, including nonspecific ST-T wave changes, prominent U waves, left ventricular strain patterns, and right and left bundle branch blocks may be present in the absence of demonstrable ischemia or infarction. Cardiomyopathy, either congestive with myocarditis and myocardial fibrosis or hypertrophic with concentric or asymmetric hypertrophy, may be associated with heart failure and cardiac arrhythmias.

CARBOHYDRATE INTOLERANCE   Over half of patients have impaired carbohydrate tolerance due to suppression of insulin and stimulation of hepatic glucose output. The impaired glucose tolerance almost never requires specific treatment and disappears after removal of the tumor.

HEMATOCRIT   Patients may have an elevated hematocrit secondary to diminished plasma volume. Rarely production of erythropoietin by the pheochromocytoma may cause a true erythrocytosis.

PHEOCHROMOCYTOMA OF THE URINARY BLADDER   Pheochromocytoma within the wall of the urinary bladder may result in typical paroxysms in relation to micturition. The unique location of these tumors within the bladder wall is responsible for the production of symptoms while the tumors are quite small, and consequently, urinary catecholamine excretion may be normal or only minimally elevated. Hematuria is present in over half, and the tumor can often be visualized at cystoscopy.

Adverse drug interactions   Severe and occasionally fatal paroxysms have been induced by opiates, histamine, ACTH, saralasin, and glucagon. These agents appear to release catecholamines directly from the tumor. Indirect-acting sympathomimetic amines, including methyldopa (when administered intravenously), may cause an increase in blood pressure by releasing catecholamines from the augmented stores within nerve endings. Drugs that block neuronal uptake of catecholamines, such as tricyclic antidepressants or guanethidine, may enhance the physiologic effects of circulating catecholamines. These drugs should be avoided in patients with known or suspected pheochromocytoma; indeed all medications should be carefully considered and cautiously administered in such patients.

Associated diseases   Pheochromocytoma is associated with medullary carcinoma of the thyroid in the familial MEN syndromes types II and III and with hyperparathyroidism in MEN II (see Chap. 334). Hypercalcemia, resolving after tumor resection, has also been described in patients with pheochromocytoma in the absence of parathyroid disease. Every member of MEN II and III kindreds should be screened periodically for pheochromocytoma by assay of a 24-h urine sample for catecholamines, including measurement of epinephrine. Pheochromocytoma should be excluded or removed before thyroid or parathyroid surgery.

The association of pheochromocytoma and neurofibromatosis is uncommon. Nevertheless, since incomplete forms of neurofibromatosis may be associated with pheochromocytoma, minor manifestations such as five to six café au lait spots, vertebral abnormalities, or kyphoscoliosis should increase the suspicion of pheochromocytoma in a patient with hypertension. The incidence of pheochromocytoma in some kindreds with von Hippel–Lindau disease may be as high as 10 to 25 percent. Many of these are unsuspected clinically and diagnosed postmortem.

The incidence of cholelithiasis is about 15 to 20 percent in patients with pheochromocytoma. Cushing's syndrome is rarely associated with pheochromocytoma, usually a consequence of ectopic secretion of ACTH either by the pheochromocytoma or, less commonly, by a coexistent medullary carcinoma of the thyroid.

DIAGNOSIS   The diagnosis is established by the demonstration of increased amounts of catecholamines or catecholamine metabolites in a 24-h urine collection. The diagnosis can usually be made by the analysis of a single 24-h urine sample, provided the patient is hypertensive or symptomatic at the time of collection.

Biochemical tests   The determinations employed in the diagnosis include vanillylmandelic acid (VMA), the metanephrines, and unconjugated or "free" catecholamines (Chap. 66). Although much has been written about the relative specificity and sensitivity of the different measurements, they are probably equivalent provided the assays are properly performed. Accuracy of diagnosis is improved when two of the three determinations are employed, although this is not essential as a screening procedure. The following considerations apply to all the urinary tests: (1) Despite claims for the adequacy of determinations made on random urine samples and expressed per milligram of creatinine, analysis of a full 24-h urine sample is preferable. Creatinine should be determined as well to assess the adequacy of collection. (2) Where possible the collection should be obtained when the patient is at rest, on no medication, and without recent exposure to radiographic contrast media. Where it is not practical to discontinue all medications, those drugs known specifically to interfere in the assays (as noted above) should be avoided. (3) The urine collection should be properly acidified and kept cold during and after collection. (4) With specific high-quality assays dietary restrictions are minimal and should be specified by the laboratory performing the analyses. (5) Although the majority of patients with pheochromocytoma excrete increased quantities of catecholamines and catecholamine metabolites each day, in patients with paroxysmal hypertension the yield is increased if a 24-h urine collection is initiated during a crisis.

FREE CATECHOLAMINES   The upper limit of normal for total catecholamines is between 100 and 150 μg per 24 h. In most patients with pheochromocytoma values in excess of 250 μg per day are obtained. Specific measurement of epinephrine is often of value since increased epinephrine excretion (over 50 μg per 24 h) is usually due to an adrenal lesion and may be the only abnormality in cases associated with MEN. False-positive increases in catecholamine excretion result from exogenous catecholamines such as methyldopa, levodopa, and sympathomimetic amines, which may elevate catecholamine excretion for up to 2 weeks. Endogenous catecholamines from stimulation of the sympathoadrenal system may also increase urinary catecholamine excretion and result in a false-positive test. The relevant clinical situations include hypoglycemia, strenuous exertion, central nervous system disease with increased intracranial pressure, and clonidine withdrawal.

METANEPHRINES AND VMA   In most laboratories the upper limit of normal is 1.3 mg of total metanephrine and 7.0 mg of VMA excretion per 24 h. In most patients with pheochromocytoma the increase in excretion of these metabolites is considerable, often more than three times the normal range. Metanephrine excretion is increased by exogenous and endogenous catecholamines and by treatment with monoamine oxidase inhibitors; propranolol may cause a spurious increase in metanephrine excretion, since a propranolol metabolite interferes in the commonly utilized spectrophotometric assay. VMA is less affected by endogenous and exogenous catecholamines but is spuriously increased by a variety of drugs, including carbidopa. VMA excretion is decreased by monoamine oxidase inhibitors.

PLASMA CATECHOLAMINES   Measurement of plasma catecholamines has a limited application in the diagnosis. The care required in obtaining basal catecholamine levels (Chap. 66), the lack of readily available, reliable plasma catecholamine assays, and the satisfactory results obtained with urinary determinations make measurement of plasma catecholamines unnecessary in most cases. Plasma catecholamine levels are affected by the same drugs and physiologic perturbations that increase urinary catecholamine excretion. In addition, alpha- and beta-adrenergic receptor blocking agents may elevate plasma catecholamines by impairing catecholamine clearance.

In occasional patients, when the clinical features suggest pheochromocytoma and the urinary assays are borderline, measurement of plasma catecholamines may be worthwhile. Basal levels of total catecholamines over 2000 pg/mL support the diagnosis, although approximately one-third of patients with pheochromocytoma have basal values below this level. The usefulness of plasma catecholamine determinations may be increased by agents that suppress sympathetic nervous system activity. Clonidine and ganglionic blocking agents (Chap. 66) both markedly reduce plasma catecholamine levels in normal subjects and in patients with essential hypertension. These drugs have little effect on catecholamine levels in patients with pheochromocytoma. In patients with elevated basal plasma catecholamines failure to suppress plasma levels with clonidine supports the diagnosis of pheochromocytoma.

Pharmacologic tests Reliable methods for the measurement of catecholamines and catecholamine metabolites in urine have rendered obsolete both the provocative and adrenolytic tests, which are nonspecific and entail considerable risk. A modified version of the adrenolytic test may be of some use, however, as a therapeutic trial in a patient in hypertensive crisis with features suggestive of pheochromocytoma. A positive response to phentolamine (5-mg bolus following a 0.5-mg test dose) is a reduction in blood pressure of at least 35/25 mmHg that becomes maximal after 2 min and persists for 10 to 15 min. The response to a pharmacologic agent is never diagnostic, and biochemical confirmation must always be obtained. Provocative tests in normotensive patients are potentially dangerous and rarely indicated. However, a glucagon provocative test may be of use in patients with paroxysmal hypertension and basal catecholamine levels below those usually found in patients with pheochromocytoma (less than 1000 to 1500 pg/mL). Glucagon has a negligible effect on blood pressure or on plasma catecholamine levels in normal or hypertensive subjects. In patients with pheochromocytoma, on the other hand, glucagon may substantially increase both blood pressure and circulating catecholamine levels. The elevation in plasma catecholamine concentration, moreover, may occur in patients without a blood pressure response. It must be emphasized, however, that life-threatening pressor crises have occurred after administration of glucagon to patients with pheochromocytoma so that the test should never be performed casually. Careful continuous monitoring of the blood pressure is required, intravenous access must be adequate, and phentolamine must be at hand to terminate the test if a significant pressor reaction enuses.

Differential diagnosis Since the manifestations may be protean, the diagnosis must be considered and excluded in many patients with suggestive clinical features. In patients with essential hypertension and "hyperadrenergic" features such as tachycardia, sweating, and increased cardiac output, and in patients with anxiety attacks associated with blood pressure elevations, analysis of a 24-h urine collection is usually decisive in excluding the diagnosis. Repeated determinations on urine collected during attacks may be necessary, however, before the diagnosis can be excluded with certainty. The clonidine suppression and glucagon stimulation tests may occasionally be helpful in excluding the diagnosis in difficult cases. Pressor crises associated with clonidine withdrawal or the use of monoamine oxidase inhibitors (Chap. 66) may mimic the paroxysms of pheochromocytoma. Factitious crises may be produced by self-administration of sympathomimetic amines in psychiatrically disturbed patients, particularly among those employed in the health care professions.

Intracranial lesions, particularly posterior fossa tumors or subarachnoid hemorrhage, may be associated with hypertension and increased excretion of catecholamines or catecholamine metabolites. While this is most common in patients who have suffered an obvious neurologic catastrophe, the possibility of subarachnoid or intracranial hemorrhage secondary to pheochromocytoma should be considered. Diencephalic or autonomic epilepsy may be associated with paroxysmal spells, hypertension, and increased plasma catecholamine levels. This rare entity may be difficult to distinguish from pheochromocytoma, but an aura, an abnormal electroencephalogram, and

a beneficial response to anticonvulsant medications will often suggest the proper diagnosis.

MANAGEMENT **Preoperative management** The induction of stable alpha-adrenergic blockade is the basis of preoperative management and provides the foundation for successful surgical treatment. Once the diagnosis is established, the patient should be placed on phenoxybenzamine to induce a long-lived, noncompetitive alpha-receptor blockade. The usual initial dose is 10 mg every 12 h with increments of 10 to 20 mg added every few days until the blood pressure is controlled and the paroxysms disappear. Because of the long duration of action the therapeutic effects are cumulative, and the optimal dose must be achieved gradually with careful monitoring of supine and upright blood pressures. Most patients require between 40 and 80 mg of phenoxybenzamine per day although in some cases 200 mg or more may be necessary. Phenoxybenzamine should be administered for at least 10 to 14 days prior to surgery. Over this time the combination of alpha-receptor blockade and a liberal salt intake will restore the contracted plasma volume to normal. Before adequate alpha-adrenergic blockade with phenoxybenzamine is achieved, paroxysms may be treated with intravenous phentolamine. Prazosin, the selective alpha$_1$ antagonist, has been employed in the preoperative management of a small number of patients. Doses in the range of 1.5 to 2.5 mg every 6 h have effectively controlled blood pressure and paroxysms. The role of this agent in the management of pheochromocytoma has not been established; the relatively short duration of action may be a disadvantage compared with phenoxybenzamine. Prazosin may be useful as an antihypertensive agent in patients with suspected pheochromocytoma while workup is in progress, since it is usually better tolerated than phenoxybenzamine and prevents serious pressor crises if pheochromocytoma is present. Nitroprusside is the only other antihypertensive agent that reliably reduces blood pressure in patients with pheochromocytoma and may be useful on occasion.

Beta-adrenergic receptor-blocking agents should be given only after alpha blockade has been established, since administration of such agents by themselves may cause a paradoxic increase in blood pressure by antagonizing beta-mediated vasodilatation in skeletal muscle. Beta blockade is usually initiated when tachycardia develops during the induction of alpha-adrenergic blockade. Low doses often suffice, and a reasonable starting dose is 10 mg propranolol 3 to 4 times per day, increased as needed to control the pulse rate. Beta blockade is effective treatment for catecholamine-induced arrhythmias, particularly those potentiated by anesthetic agents.

Preoperative localization of the tumor Surgical removal of pheochromocytoma is facilitated if the location of the tumor, or tumors, can be established preoperatively. Once pheochromocytoma is diagnosed, localization should be undertaken while the patient is being prepared for surgery by the administration of alpha receptor-blocking agents. Computerized tomography of the adrenals is usually successful in identifying the intraadrenal lesions. Conventional chest roentgenograms and computerized tomography of the chest usually suffice to identify intrathoracic lesions. If these studies are negative, abdominal aortography (once alpha-adrenergic blockade is complete) may be useful in identifying extraadrenal pheochromocytomas within the abdomen, since these lesions are often supplied by a large aberrant artery. If aortography and computerized tomography fail to localize the lesion, venous sampling at different levels of the inferior and superior vena cava may reveal a step-up in catecholamine concentration in the region drained by the tumor; this area may then be restudied by selective angiography or directed scanning by computerized tomography. An additional localization technique involves a radionuclide scintiscan after administration of an investigational radiopharmaceutical ^{131}I-metaiodobenzylguanidine (MIBG). This agent is concentrated by the amine uptake process and produces an external scintigraphic image at the site of the tumor. This type of scanning has no advantages over computerized tomography in the diagnosis of adrenal lesions but may have a role in localizing extraadrenal pheochromocytomas.

Surgery　Surgery is best performed in centers with experience in the preoperative, anesthetic, and intraoperative management of pheochromocytoma patients. In experienced hands surgical mortality is below 2 or 3 percent.

Adequate monitoring during the surgical procedure should include continuous recording of arterial pressure, central venous pressure, and electrocardiogram; in the presence of cardiac disease or if congestive failure has been present, pulmonary capillary wedge pressure should be monitored as well. Adequate fluid replacement is crucial. Intraoperative hypotension responds better to volume replacement than to the administration of vasoconstrictors. Hypertension and cardiac arrhythmias are most likely to occur during induction of anesthesia, intubation, and manipulation of the tumor. Intravenous phentolamine is usually sufficient to control the blood pressure, but nitroprusside may be required. Propranolol may be given in the treatment of tachycardia or ventricular ectopy.

PHEOCHROMOCYTOMA IN PREGNANCY　Spontaneous labor and vaginal delivery in unprepared patients are usually disastrous for mother and fetus. In early pregnancy it seems reasonable to prepare the patient with phenoxybenzamine and remove the tumor as soon as the diagnosis is confirmed. The pregnancy need not be terminated, but the operative procedure itself may result in spontaneous abortion. In the third trimester, treatment with adrenergic blocking agents should be undertaken; when the fetus is of sufficient size cesarean section followed by extirpation of the tumor may be undertaken. Although the safety of adrenergic blocking drugs in pregnancy has not been established, these agents have been administered in several cases without obvious adverse effect.

UNRESECTABLE TUMOR　In cases of metastatic or locally invasive tumor or in patients with intercurrent illness that precludes surgery, long-term medical management is required. When the manifestations of pheochromocytoma cannot be adequately controlled by the chronic administration of adrenergic blocking agents, the concomitant administration of metyrosine may be required. This agent inhibits tyrosine hydroxylase, diminishes catecholamine production by the tumor, and often simplifies chronic management. At present there are no practical ways of destroying the tumor by radiotherapy or chemotherapy.

PROGNOSIS　The 5-year survival after surgery is usually over 95 percent, and the recurrence rate is less than 10 percent. After successful surgery catecholamine excretion returns to normal in about 1 week and should be measured to ensure complete tumor removal. In malignant pheochromocytoma the 5-year survival is less than 50 percent.

Complete removal of the pheochromocytoma cures the hypertension in approximately three-fourths. In the remainder hypertension recurs but is usually well controlled by standard antihypertensive agents. In this group either underlying essential hypertension or irreversible vascular damage induced by catecholamines may cause the persistence of the hypertension.

REFERENCES

BRAVO EL, GIFFORD RW: Pheochromocytoma: Diagnosis, localization, and management. N Engl J Med 311:1298, 1984

BROWN MJ et al: Increased sensitivity and accuracy of phaeochromocytoma diagnosis achieved by use of plasma-adrenaline estimations and a pentolinium-suppression test. Lancet 1:174, 1981

ENGELMAN K: Phaeochromocytoma. Clin Endocrinol Metab 6:769, 1977

FUDGE TL et al: Current surgical management of pheochromocytoma during pregnancy. Arch Surg 115:1224, 1980

GLUSHIEN AS et al: Pheochromocytoma: Its relationship to the neurocutaneous syndromes. Am J Med 14:318, 1953

HAMILTON BP et al: Measurement of urinary epinephrine in screening for pheochromocytoma in multiple endocrine neoplasia type II. Am J Med 65:1027, 1978

HORTON WA et al: Von Hippel-Lindau disease: Clinical and pathological manifestations in nine families with 50 affected members. Arch Intern Med 136:769, 1976

JONES DH et al: The biochemical diagnosis, localization and followup of phaeochromocytoma: The role of plasma and urinary catecholamine measurements. Q J Med 49:431, 1980

KHAIRI MRA et al: Mucosal neuroma, pheochromocytoma and medullary thyroid carcinoma: Multiple endocrine neoplasia type 3. Medicine 54:89, 1975

LAURSEN K, DAMGAARD-PEDERSON K: CT for pheochromocytoma diagnosis. AJR 134:277, 1980

MANGER WM, GIFFORD RW JR: Pheochromocytoma. New York, Springer-Verlag, 1977

PALUBINSKAS AJ et al: Localization of functioning pheochromocytomas by venous sampling and radioenzymatic analysis. Radiology 136:495, 1980

REMINE WH et al: Current management of pheochromocytoma. Ann Surg 179:740, 1974

ROSS EJ et al: Preoperative and operative management of patients with pheochromocytoma. Br Med J 1:191, 1971

ST JOHN WM, GIFFORD RW JR: Prevalence of clinically unsuspected pheochromocytoma. Mayo Clin Proc 56:354, 1981

SISSON JC et al: Scintigraphic localization of pheochromocytoma. N Engl J Med 305:12, 1981

SJOERDSMA A et al: Pheochromocytoma: Current concepts of diagnosis and treatment. Ann Intern Med 65:1302, 1966

STEINER AL et al: Study of a kindred with pheochromocytoma, medullary thyroid carcinoma, hyperparathyroidism and Cushing's disease: Multiple endocrine neoplasia, type 2. Medicine 47:371, 1968

327　DIABETES MELLITUS

DANIEL W. FOSTER

Diabetes mellitus is the most common of the serious metabolic diseases. The true frequency is difficult to ascertain because of differing standards of diagnosis but probably is around 1 percent. The disease is characterized by metabolic abnormalities; by long-term complications involving the eyes, kidneys, nerves, and blood vessels; and by a lesion of the basement membranes demonstrable by electron microscopy. Patients fulfilling these criteria are not a homogeneous group, and several distinct diabetic syndromes have been delineated.

DIAGNOSIS　The diagnosis of symptomatic diabetes is not difficult. When a patient presents with signs and symptoms attributable to an osmotic diuresis and is found to have hyperglycemia, essentially all physicians agree that diabetes is present. There is likewise little disagreement about an asymptomatic patient with persistently elevated fasting plasma glucose concentrations. The problem arises with the asymptomatic patient who for one reason or another is considered to be a potential diabetic but has a normal fasting glucose concentration in plasma. Such patients are often given an oral glucose tolerance test, and, if abnormal values are found, diagnosed as having "chemical" diabetes. There seems to be little question that normal glucose tolerance is strong evidence against the presence of diabetes, the predictive value of a positive test is less certain. Much evidence suggests that the standard oral glucose tolerance test overdiagnoses diabetes to a remarkable degree, probably because a variety of stresses can produce an abnormal response. The operative mechanism is thought to be epinephrine discharge. Epinephrine blocks insulin secretion, stimulates glucagon release, activates glycogen breakdown, and impairs insulin action in target tissues such that hepatic glucose production is increased and the capacity to dispose of an exogenous glucose load is impaired. Even anxiety over venipunctures may generate sufficient epinephrine to produce an abnormal test. Concomitant illness, inadequate diet, and lack of physical exercise also contribute to false-positive examinations.

In an attempt to deal with these problems, the National Diabetes Data Group of the National Institutes of Health in 1979 provided revised criteria for the diagnosis of diabetes following a challenge with oral glucose:

1　*Fasting* (*overnight*): Venous plasma glucose concentration ≥ 140 mg/dL on at least two separate occasions.[1]

[1] *Venous whole blood concentrations are 15 percent lower than plasma values. Capillary whole blood, utilized in patient self-monitoring, is equivalent to venous plasma.*

2 Following ingestion of 75 g of glucose: Venous plasma glucose concentration ≥200 mg/dL at 2 h and on at least one other occasion during the 2-h test (i.e., *two* values ≥200 mg/dL must be obtained for diagnosis).

If the 2-h value is between 140 and 200 mg/dL and one other value during the 2-h test period is equal to or greater than 200 mg/dL, a diagnosis of "impaired glucose tolerance" is suggested. The interpretation would be that persons in this category are at increased risk for the development of fasting hyperglycemia or symptomatic diabetes but that such progression is not predictable in an individual patient. Most patients (~75 percent) with impaired glucose tolerance never develop diabetes, and subjects diagnosed as having diabetes by the second criterion may never manifest fasting hyperglycemia or symptomatic deterioration. Consequently, the oral glucose tolerance test is rarely indicated in clinical practice although it is useful as a research tool.

CLASSIFICATION A classification of diabetes is given in Table 327-1. The basic categories are those recommended by the National Diabetes Data Group except for division into primary and secondary types. Primary implies that no associated disease is present while in the secondary type some other identifiable condition causes or allows a diabetic syndrome to develop. Insulin dependence in this classification is not equivalent to insulin therapy. Rather, the term means that the patient is at risk for ketoacidosis in the absence of insulin. Many patients classified as non-insulin-dependent require insulin for control of hyperglycemia although they do not become ketoacidotic if insulin is withdrawn.

The term *type 1* has often been used as a synonym for insulin-dependent diabetes (IDDM), and *type 2* diabetes has been considered equivalent to non-insulin-dependent disease (NIDDM). This probably is not ideal since some patients with apparent non-insulin-dependent diabetes may in fact be destined to become fully insulin-dependent and prone to ketoacidosis. The subset of patients in this category are nonobese subjects who carry the HLA-DR3/DR4 phenotype and exhibit islet cell antibodies in the blood (see "Pathogenesis" below). For this reason it has been suggested that the classification shown in Table 327-1 be modified such that the terms *insulin-dependent* and *non-insulin-dependent* describe physiologic states (ketoacidosis-prone and ketoacidosis-resistant, respectively) while the terms *type 1* and *type 2* refer to pathogenetic mechanisms (immune-mediated and non-immune-mediated, respectively). Using such a classification three major forms of primary diabetes would be recognized: (1) type 1 insulin-dependent diabetes, (2) type 1 non-insulin-dependent diabetes and (3) type 2 non-insulin-dependent diabetes. Category 2 can be considered as type 1 insulin-dependent diabetes in evolution; i.e., autoimmune beta-cell destruction occurs slowly rather than rapidly with the result that there is a delay in reaching the ketoacidotic threshold of insulin deficiency.

Secondary forms of diabetes encompass a host of conditions. *Pancreatic disease,* particularly chronic pancreatitis in alcoholics, is a common cause. Destruction of the beta-cell mass is the etiologic mechanism. *Hormonal abnormalities* include pheochromocytoma, acromegaly, and Cushing's syndrome or arise consequent to therapeutic administration of steroid hormones. "Stress hyperglycemia,"

associated with severe burns, acute myocardial infarctions, and other life-threatening illnesses, is due to endogenous release of glucagon and catecholamines. Mechanisms of hormonal hyperglycemia include varying combinations of impairment of insulin release and induction of insulin resistance. A large number of *drugs* can lead to hyperglycemia, but most simply produce impaired glucose tolerance. Hyperglycemia and even ketoacidosis may occur as a result of abnormalities at the level of the *insulin receptor.* The dysfunction may be due to quantitative or qualitative defects in the receptor itself or to antibodies directed against it. The mechanism is essentially pure insulin resistance. A number of *genetic syndromes* are associated with impaired glucose tolerance or hyperglycemia. The three most common are the lipodystrophies, myotonic dystrophy, and ataxia-telangiectasia. The final category, *other,* is poorly defined and is meant to include any condition which does not fit elsewhere in the etiologic scheme. The appearance of abnormal carbohydrate metabolism in association with any of the secondary causes does not necessarily indicate the presence of underlying diabetes although in some cases a mild, asymptomatic primary diabetes may be made overt by the secondary illness.

PREVALENCE Prevalence of diabetes is difficult to determine because numerous standards, many now no longer acceptable, have been used in diagnosis. As noted above the overall prevalence in western societies is thought to be about 1 percent. Estimates for insulin-dependent diabetes are more reliable than for the non-insulin-dependent form since most patients are diagnosed after the abrupt appearance of symptoms. In England prevalence of the type 1 illness has been estimated to be 0.22 percent by age 16, and a study in the United States suggested a prevalence of 0.26 percent by age 20. If the prevalence of diabetes is actually 1 percent, it follows that about one-fourth of cases have insulin-dependent disease while three-fourths are non-insulin-dependent. The relative frequency of insulin-dependent to non-insulin-dependent diabetes varies with age, being higher if a young population is studied and lower in the older age range.

PATHOGENESIS OF TYPE 1 DIABETES MELLITUS By the time insulin-dependent diabetes mellitus appears, most of the beta cells in the pancreas have been destroyed. The destructive process is almost certainly autoimmune in nature. An overview of the pathogenetic sequence is given in Table 327-2. *First,* genetic susceptibility to the disease must be present. *Second,* an environmental event initiates the process in genetically susceptible individuals. Viral infection is believed to be a common triggering mechanism. The best evidence that an environmental insult is required comes from studies in monozygotic twins, in whom the concordance rate for diabetes is no more than 50 percent. If diabetes were a purely genetic illness, concordance rates would be approximately 100 percent. The *third* step in the sequence is an inflammatory response in the pancreas called "insulitis." The cells that infiltrate the islets are activated T lymphocytes. The *fourth* step is an alteration or transformation of the surface of the beta cell such that it is no longer recognized as "self" but is seen by the immune system as a foreign cell or "nonself." The *fifth* step is the development of an immune response. Because

TABLE 327-1 Classification of diabetes

A Primary
  1 Insulin-dependent diabetes mellitus (IDDM, type 1)
  2 Non-insulin-dependent diabetes mellitus (NIDDM, type 2)
    a Nonobese NIDDM (type 1 IDDM in evolution?)
    b Obese NIDDM
    c Maturity-onset diabetes of the young (MODY)
B Secondary
  1 Pancreatic disease
  2 Hormonal abnormalities
  3 Drug or chemical induced
  4 Insulin receptor abnormalities
  5 Genetic syndromes
  6 Other

TABLE 327-2 The pathogenesis of type 1 diabetes mellitus

Step	Event	Agent or response
1	Genetic susceptibility	HLA-DR3, DR4 (T-cell receptor?)
2	Environmental event	Virus (?)
3	Insulitis	Infiltration of activated T lymphocytes
4	Activation of autoimmunity	Self → nonself transition
5	Immune attack on beta cells	Islet cell antibodies, cell-mediated immunity
6	Diabetes mellitus	> 90 percent beta cells destroyed (alpha cells unopposed)

the islets are now considered "nonself," cytotoxic antibodies develop and act in concert with cell-mediated immune mechanisms. The end result is the destruction of the beta cell and the appearance of diabetes.

In the summary, the pathogenetic sequence is genetic predisposition → environmental insulitis → conversion of beta cell from "self" to "nonself" → activation of the immune system → destruction of the beta cell → diabetes mellitus.

Genetics Although insulin-dependent diabetes aggregates in families, the mechanism of inheritance is unclear in mendelian terms. Transmission has been postulated to be autosomal dominant, recessive, and mixed, but none has been proven. The genetic predisposition is probably permissive and not causal.

Analysis of pedigrees shows a low prevalence of direct vertical transmission. In one series of 35 families in which there was a child with classic insulin-dependent diabetes only four of the index cases had a parent with diabetes and two had a diabetic grandparent. Of the 99 siblings of these diabetic children only 6 had overt disease. Overall the chance of a child developing type 1 diabetes when another first-degree relative has the disease is only 5 to 10 percent. The presence of non-insulin-dependent disease in a parent increases the risk for insulin-dependent diabetes in the offspring. It is not known whether the intermixing of IDDM and NIDDM in the same family represents a single genetic trait (i.e., the apparent NIDDM is really type 1 NIDDM) or whether two common genetic predispositions coexist in the same family by chance, each perhaps influencing the expression of the other. Low rates of transmission of IDDM make it difficult to discern mechanisms of inheritance through study of families but are reassuring to diabetic parents who may wish to have children.

One of the susceptibility genes in IDDM likely resides on the sixth chromosome in view of strong associations between diabetes and certain human leukocyte antigens (HLA) coded by the major histocompatibility region on this chromosome (see Chap. 63). Four loci designated by the letters A, B, C, and D are recognized with alleles at each site identified by numbers. Major alleles conferring enhanced risk for IDDM are HLA-DR3, HLA-Dw3, HLA-DR4, HLA-Dw4, HLA-B8, and HLA-B15. The D locus is considered of primary importance with the B and A loci being involved through nonrandom associations with D (*linkage disequilibrium*). When compared with the general population the risk for IDDM imposed by the presence of DR3 or DR4 is 4 to 10 times. If the comparison is made not against a control population but against a subset of persons not bearing the predisposing antigen, relative risks are as high as thirtyfold. However, many persons carrying "high-risk" alleles never develop diabetes. It is likely that further probing of the genes in the D region will sharpen the ability to identify risk; i.e., a particular variant of an HLA-DR or -DQ antigen, not identified by routine screening, may be more tightly associated with diabetes than would be indicated by the mere presence of the antigen. Not all HLA-DR4, for example, may confer risk for diabetes but only a certain subset. It must also be emphasized that diabetes can develop in the absence of HLA determinants shown to be high risk in population studies.

Antigens B7 and DR2 (Dw2) have been called "protective" since they are found with less frequency in diabetic subjects than in the general population. It is likely, however, that they are acutally "low-risk" alleles (rather than protective) because they are present in inverse relationship with DR3/DR4; i.e., if DR2, Dw2 is present, high-risk alleles will be absent.

Current terminology divides the D region into DP, DQ, and DR (Fig. 327-1). (DP was formerly designated SB and DQ was called DC.) The HLA-associated susceptibility gene may be more closely linked to the DQ region than to DR. If so, the relationship to DR3 and DR4 is due to linkage disequilibrium. Many investigators believe that a second susceptibility gene is required for development of diabetes. The second gene might code for an abnormality in the T-cell receptor.

A word is necessary about the function of the cell surface molecules derived from genes in the HLA region. Antigens derived from regions A, B, and C are called class I molecules. They are present on nucleated cells and function primarily in the defense against infections, expecially viruses. D region antigens are called class II molecules. They function in the regulatory (helper/suppressor) T-cell system and in the response to alloantigens (e.g., the rejection of transplanted organs). Class II molecules are normally present only on B lymphocytes and circulating or tissue macrophages.

Class I and II molecules are best considered as recognition/programming signals for initiation and amplification of immune responses in the body. Thus, activation of cytotoxic T lymphocytes to fight a viral infection requires the presence of the same class I molecule on infected cell and cytotoxic T cell; i.e., a "self" class I molecule plus viral antigen yields a recognizable neoantigen to which the T lymphocyte can respond. If exposed to a cell bearing viral antigen but a "nonself" class I HLA antigen, the T cell would not respond. Similarly the helper T cell becomes activated only when exposed to antigen-presenting cells (macrophages) bearing a recognizable class II molecule and an antigen for which it has a correct recognition site.

The appearance of class II molecules on endocrine cells, where they are normally not present, has been thought to play an important role in the autoimmune destructive process that leads to diabetes mellitus and other endocrine conditions such as Hashimoto's thyroiditis. The presence of a "self" class II molecule coupled with a foreign or autoantigen is recognized by a helper T lymphocyte which then initiates activation of the immune system including antibody formation against the cell bearing the class II/foreign (or autologous) antigen combination (see below).

Environmental event As noted earlier, the fact that a significant proportion of monozygotic twins remain discordant for diabetes (one twin with, the other without) has suggested that nongenetic factors are required for expression of diabetes in humans. Similar arguments derive from the fact that HLA haploidentity does not ensure concordance.

The environmental factor in most cases is believed to be a virus capable of infecting the beta cell. A viral etiology was originally suggested by seasonal variations in the onset of the disease and what appeared to be more than a chance relationship between appearance of diabetes and preceding episodes of mumps, hepatitis, infectious mononucleosis, congenital rubella, and coxsackievirus infections. The viral hypothesis gained support from studies showing that certain strains of encephalomyocarditis virus cause diabetes in genetically susceptible mice. The isolation of a coxsackievirus B4 from the pancreas of a previously healthy boy who died following an episode of ketoacidosis and the induction of diabetes in experimental animals inoculated with the isolated virus also suggest that viruses can cause diabetes in humans. A rise in titer of neutralizing antibody to coxsackievirus over the weeks prior to death of the patient indicated that the virus was recently acquired. Further support for the viral theory comes from the observation that congenital rubella is associated with subsequent development of IDDM in about 20 percent of affected individuals in the United States. Presumably viral infections of the

FIGURE 327-1 *A schematic representation of the major histocompatibility complex on chromosome 6. Courtesy of Dr. J. Harold Helderman.*

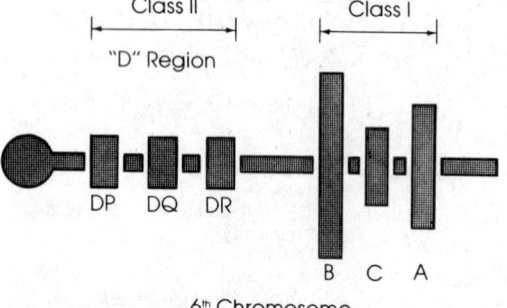

pancrease could induce diabetes by two mechanisms: direct inflammatory disruption of islets or induction of an immune response.

Despite its attractiveness, considerable caution should be reserved for the viral theory. Serologic studies seeking evidence of recent viral infection in patients with new-onset insulin-dependent diabetes are inconclusive at best. If viruses are commonly involved, those producing acute disease may not be the major inducers but a slow virus not yet identified.

Insulitis   In animals activated T lymphocytes infiltrate the pancreatic islets prior to or simultaneous with development of diabetes. Lymphocytes are also found in the islets of young persons dying from new-onset diabetes, and radioactively labeled lymphocytes localize in the pancrease in humans with IDDM. These findings are in accord with the observation that immune endocrinopathies in general are associated with lymphocytic infiltration of the affected tissue. However, the insulitis might be an epiphenomenon not causally related to the pathogenetic sequence. This follows from the fact that in the low-dose streptozocin model of diabetes in rodents, which is immunologically mediated, loss of beta-cell mass occurs prior to development of insulitis. Moreover, experiments in mice with immune deficiency indicate that T lymphocytes are not necessary for the beta-cell destruction induced by low-dose streptozocin.

Conversion of the beta-cell from "self" to "nonself" and activation of the immune system   HLA-DR3 and -B15, known to be associated with immune endocrinopathy, are found with increased frequency in insulin-dependent diabetic subjects. Moreover, there is a frequent coexistence of IDDM and other forms of autoimmune endocrinopathy such as Addison's disease, Hashimoto's thyroiditis, hyperthyroidism, pernicious anemia, vitiligo, myasthenia gravis, and collagen-vascular disease (see Chap. 334). All of these conditions tend to run in families. In addition, islet cell antibodies are found in a high percentage of patients with insulin-dependent diabetes who are examined during the first year after diagnosis. These antibodies are also present in the blood of nonconcordant monozygotic twins or triplets destined to become concordant in the future. The same is true for siblings of patients with insulin-dependent diabetes mellitus. Killer T cells are present in 50 to 60 percent of recently diagnosed diabetic children, a value higher than in control populations. It is noteworthy that diabetes similar to human type 1 disease develops spontaneously in the BB rat. Affected animals exhibit insulitis, thyroiditis, and autoantibodies to pancreatic islets, smooth muscle, thyroid colloid, and gastric parietal cells. Diabetes in these animals can be prevented or reversed by immune modulation.

What causes the autoimmune process? First, there is an increase in the ratio of helper to suppressor T cells in the circulation. This may be a general phenomenon in immune endocrine disease. The increase in this ratio is likely due to a deficiency of suppressor T cells. An unbalanced helper-T-cell population would predispose to exuberant antibody formation on exposure to antigen.

Second, class II HLA molecules appear on the surface of the beta cell. It will be recalled that activation of helper T cells requires the presence of a class II molecule and a foreign or autoantigen. The idea is that the normal islet cell does not express class II molecules but that in response to a virus (probably through the production of γ interferon) the cell develops such molecules, rendering it potentially recognizable as "nonself." Depending on the allele expressed the immune system may be activated. Thus, if HLA-DR2 is present, it would be unlikely that diabetes would develop, as suggested by population studies. Conversely, if HLA-DR3 or -DR4 (or the putative DQ antigen) were present, then the system could be activated. Presumably susceptibility is linked to the fit between newly appearing class II molecules, the requisite membrane antigen (foreign or autologous), and a particular form of the T-cell receptor on the helper T cell. This may account for the appearance of IDDM in the absence of high-risk HLA genes; i.e., in certain cases the class II molecule–T-cell receptor fit occurs even with an ordinarily low-risk allele.

As is true in other immune-mediated endocrinopathies, evidence of an activated immune system may disappear with time. Thus, the islet cell antibodies present in newly diagnosed patients with type 1 IDDM disappear within a year or so. The presence of islet cell antibodies correlates with residual beta-cell mass as assessed in vivo by the capacity to release endogenous insulin in response to a fuel stimulus. As the capacity for endogenous insulin secretion disappears, so do islet cell antibodies. The implication is that as beta cells die, the stimulus to the immune response disappears.

Destruction of beta cells and development of IDDM   Because persons developing insulin-dependent diabetes often have a rather abrupt onset of symptomatic hyperglycemia with polyuria and/or ketoacidosis, it was long assumed that beta-cell damage occurred rapidly. In many cases (most?) there may be a slow loss of insulin reserve over many years. This insight came from studies of discordant monozygotic diabetic twins and triplets where one twin or triplet developed diabetes many years after the index case. In the slow course the earliest sign of abnormality is the development of islet cell antibodies at a time when there is no elevation of the blood sugar and glucose tolerance is normal. Insulin responses to a glucose load are intact. A phase then ensues in which the only metabolic abnormality is decreased glucose tolerance. Fasting blood sugar remains normal. In the third stage fasting hyperglycemia develops, but ketosis does not occur even when the diabetes is poorly controlled. The clinical appearance is that of non-insulin-dependent diabetes mellitus. With time, however, insulin dependence and ketoacidosis may develop, especially with stress. Many nonobese patients with non-insulin-dependent diabetes mellitus may have a slow autoimmune form of the disease as mentioned earlier.

The immune-directed destruction of beta cells probably involves both humoral and cell-mediated mechanisms. Initially, antibodies are probably dominant. Two types of antibodies have been identified: cytoplasmic and surface. Usually both are present simultaneously in a given patient, but either can occur alone. Islet cell surface antibodies have the capacity to fix complement and lyse beta cells. Surface antibodies appear to impair insulin release even before the beta cell is physically damaged. They interact with a membrane antigen that has not been precisely characterized. At some point in the course cytotoxic T lymphocytes and antibody-dependent killer T cells participate in and complete the destructive process. By the time overt diabetes appears, most insulin-producing cells have disappeared. In one study pancreatic mass at autopsy averaged 40 g in type 1 diabetes versus 82 g in controls. Endocrine cell mass in subjects with IDDM decreased from 1395 to 413 mg, and beta cells, which averaged 850 mg in normals, were unmeasurable. Since alpha cells remained essentially intact, the ratio of glucagon- to insulin-producing cells approached infinity.

PATHOGENESIS OF TYPE 2 NON-INSULIN-DEPENDENT DIABETES   Little progress has been made in understanding the pathogenesis of non-insulin-dependent diabetes mellitus. Although the disease runs in families, modes of inheritance are not known except for the variant known as *maturity-onset diabetes of the young* (MODY). This disease is manifested by mild hyperglycemia in young persons who are resistant to ketosis. Four lines of evidence suggest transmission as an autosomal dominant trait. First, three-generation direct transmission has been demonstrated in over 20 families. Second, a 1:1 ratio of diabetic to nondiabetic children is found when one parent has the disease. Third, about 90 percent of obligate carriers have diabetes. Fourth, direct male-to-male transmission excludes X-linked inheritance.

No HLA relationship has been identified in type 2 NIDDM, and autoimmune mechanisms are not believed to be operative. The 5' flanking region of the structural gene for insulin, located on the short arm of the eleventh chromosome, is polymorphic in regard to varying number and arrangement of tandemly repeated nucleotides beginning some 363 base pairs before the transcription site (see Chap. 58). It was initially thought that homozygosity for a long insert (>1500 base pairs) correlated with the presence of type 2 NIDDM, but subsequent studies failed to confirm a unique relationship. Alcohol-induced flushing after priming with chlorpropamide has also been suggested as a genetic marker for certain forms of the type 2 illness. Whatever its nature, the genetic influence is powerful, since the concordance rate for diabetes in monozygotic twins with type 2 disease approaches 100 percent. It is likewise thought that risk to offspring and siblings of patients with NIDDM is higher than the risk in type 1 diabetes.

Patients with type 2 NIDDM have two physiologic defects: abnormal insulin secretion and resistance to insulin action in target tissues. The primacy of the secretory defect versus the insulin resistance is not established. Most patients with type 2 diabetes are obese, often massively so, and it has been speculated that obesity-induced insulin resistance leads to exhaustion of the beta cell; i.e., the secretory defect is secondary. On the other hand, many massively obese patients do not have diabetes or glucose intolerance, suggesting that obesity does not lead to diabetes in the presence of normal beta-cell responsiveness. The picture is further complicated by the observations that hyperglycemia per se may induce a beta-cell secretory defect and that relative insulin deficiency can cause insulin resistance. A period of aggressive dietary or insulin therapy leading to return of the blood sugar to normal may partially restore insulin secretory capacity as well as sensitivity to insulin action. Unfortunately this does not help in deciding primacy between a secretory defect and insulin resistance. The author favors the view that an islet cell abnormality is primary and necessary for development of diabetes but that acquired insulin resistance, usually obesity-related, is required for overt hyperglycemia to develop. This view is consistent with the observation that beta-cell mass is intact in type 2 NIDDM, in contrast to the situation with type 1 IDDM.

Although insulin resistance in type 2 NIDDM is associated with decreased numbers of insulin receptors, the bulk of the resistance is postreceptor in type. If experiments in animals apply to humans, the postreceptor defect is likely due to a deficiency of microsome-bound glucose transport units. These units, which facilitate diffusion of glucose across the plasma membrane, are normally rapidly mobilized when insulin binds to its receptor on the plasma membrane. Intracellular stores of the transporter are depleted in rats with either obesity or experimental diabetes and can be restored by weight loss and insulin therapy, respectively.

A rare form of type 2 NIDDM, clinically mild, is due to production of an abnormal insulin that does not bind well to insulin receptors. Such persons respond normally to exogenous insulin.

CLINICAL FEATURES The manifestations of symptomatic diabetes mellitus vary from patient to patient. Most often medical help is sought because of symptoms related to hyperglycemia (polyuria, polydipsia, polyphagia), but the first event may be an acute metabolic decompensation resulting in diabetic coma. Occasionally, the initial expression is a degenerative complication such as neuropathy in the absence of symptomatic hyperglycemia. The metabolic derangements of diabetes are due to a relative or absolute deficiency of insulin and a relative or absolute excess of glucagon. Normally it is a rise in the molar ratio of glucagon to insulin that leads to metabolic decompensation. Changes in this ratio can be caused by a fall in insulin or a rise in glucagon concentration, separately or together. Conceptually

alteration in biologic response to either hormone would have the same effect. Thus insulin resistance could cause metabolic effects expected of an elevated glucagon:insulin ratio even though the ratio assessed by immunoassay of the two hormones in plasma was not markedly abnormal or even decreased (the glucagon being biologically active, the insulin relatively inactive). The relationship between metabolic abnormalities and degenerative complications will be discussed subsequently. Typically, the clinical features of IDDM and NIDDM are distinctive.

Insulin-dependent diabetes Insulin-dependent diabetes usually begins before the age of 40; in the United States peak incidence is around age 14. Onset of symptoms may be abrupt, with thirst, excessive urination, increased appetite, and weight loss developing over a several-day period. In some cases the disease is heralded by the appearance of ketoacidosis during an intercurrent illness or following surgery. As outlined in Table 327-3, type 1 patients vary from normal weight to wasted, depending on the length of time between onset of symptoms and start of treatment. Characteristically the plasma insulin is low or immeasurable. Glucagon levels are elevated but suppressible with insulin. Once symptoms have developed, insulin therapy is required. Occasionally an initial episode of ketoacidosis is followed by a symptom-free interval (the "honeymoon" period) during which no treatment is required. The likely explanation for this phenomenon is shown in Fig. 327-2.

Non-insulin-dependent diabetes This disorder usually begins in middle life or beyond. The typical patient is overweight. Symptoms begin more gradually than in IDDM, and the diagnosis is frequently made when an asymptomatic person is found to have an elevated plasma glucose on routine laboratory examination. In contrast to insulin-dependent disease, plasma insulin levels are normal to high in absolute terms, although they are lower than predicted for the level of the plasma glucose; i.e., relative insulin deficiency is present. Stated in another way, if plasma glucose concentrations in nondiabetic subjects were raised to levels equivalent to those found in diabetic patients, insulin values would be higher in the normal group. This reflects the previously mentioned insulin secretory defect in NIDDM. Glucagon metabolism in non-insulin-dependent diabetes is complex. While the elevated fasting plasma concentrations can be lowered by large amounts of insulin, the exaggerated glucagon response to

FIGURE 327-2 *Schematic representation of the "honeymoon" period. In this graph insulin secretory capacity is shown gradually decreasing in a patient destined to develop diabetes. At approximately 13½ years insulin would become insufficient to maintain plasma glucose in the normal range. An initial episode of ketoacidosis, for example, in association with acute appendicitis, is shown occurring in the twelfth year. Presumably stress-induced epinephrine release blocks insulin secretion and causes the syndrome. In normal subjects insulin reserve is such that hormone release is adequate, even in the face of stress. Following recovery from the stressful episode insulin secretory capacity returns to the previous level and remains sufficient for an additional year as indicated by the shaded area—the "honeymoon" period.*

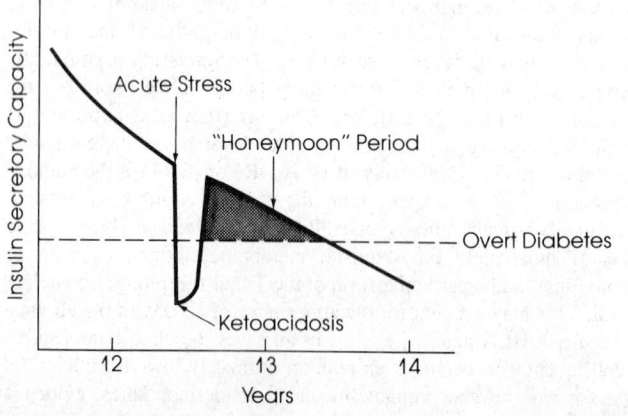

TABLE 327-3 General characteristics of IDDM and NIDDM diabetes

	IDDM	NIDDM
Genetic locus	Chromosome 6	Chromosome 11 (?)
Age of onset	< 40	> 40
Body habitus	Normal to wasted	Obese
Plasma insulin	Low to absent	Normal to high
Plasma glucagon	High, suppressible	High, resistant
Acute complication	Ketoacidosis	Hyperosmolar coma
Insulin therapy	Responsive	Responsive to resistant
Sulfonylurea therapy	Unresponsive	Responsive

ingested nutrients cannot be suppressed; i.e., alpha-cell function remains abnormal. For unknown reasons non-insulin-dependent diabetics do not develop ketoacidosis. In the decompensated state they are susceptible to the syndrome of hyperosmolar, nonketotic coma. One hypothesis to explain the absence of ketoacidosis during stress is that the liver is resistant to glucagon so that malonyl-CoA levels remain high, inhibiting the fatty acid oxidation–ketogenic pathway (see below). If weight loss can be induced, patients may be managed by diet alone. The majority of patients failing dietary therapy respond to sulfonylureas, but improvement of hyperglycemia in many is not sufficient for control of diabetes. For this reason a high percentage of patients with NIDDM are treated with insulin.

TREATMENT Diet An estimate is made of the total number of calories needed per day based on ideal body weight (determined from life insurance tables). A decision is then made regarding carbohydrate, fat, and protein content, and an appropriate diet is constructed from the exchange system provided by the American Diabetes Association. Caloric recommendations from the Food and Nutrition Board for adults carrying out "average" activity decrease with age and range from 42 kcal per kilogram of body weight in 18-year-old men to 33 kcal per kilogram for 75-year-old women. Intakes slightly less than official recommendations are usually preferable; 36 kcal per kilogram for men and 34 kcal per kilogram for women are reasonable initial values in most patients, but upward or downward adjustments may be necessary to achieve desired weight.

The minimal protein requirement for good nutrition is about 0.9 g per kilogram of body weight per day. Recommended carbohydrate content is 40 to 60 percent of total calories, although fractional intakes as high as 85 percent have been prescribed. Protein and carbohydrate calories are supplemented with sufficient fat to bring caloric intake to the desired level. Although sucrose is ordinarily not allowed in diabetic diets, a number of reports indicate that in moderation ordinary sugar does not exaggerate postprandial hyperglycemia. Currently most diabetic diets emphasize polyunsaturated fats as an antiatherogenic measure. Increased amounts of fiber are also often prescribed.

Once the desirable caloric intake and the fractional distribution between fat, protein, and carbohydrate are decided, a diet is constructed using the exchange lists shown in Table 327-4.[2] For example, a 2200-kcal diet with 50 percent of the calories as carbohydrate and 1 to 1.5 g protein per kilogram of body weight can be met by providing 2 milk exchanges, 7 fruit exchanges, 12 bread exchanges, 8 meat exchanges, 4 fat exchanges, and unlimited type A vegetables (Table 327-5). In practice, precalculated diets of given caloric content prepared by the American Diabetes Association are usually used. Care must be taken to emphasize foods the patient likes and can obtain. Initially it is helpful to weigh and measure foods until visual estimates can be made accurately. As in any dietary regimen it is important to emphasize that it is the long-term, overall dietary pattern which counts. Deviation for one meal or two meals does not matter much. Thus a teenage diabetic may be allowed to eat a dessert,

[2] *Copies of* Exchange Lists for Meal Planning *may be ordered from the American Diabetes Association, National Service Center, 1660 Duke Street, P.O. Box 25757, Alexandria, VA 22313, or from any local affiliate of the association.*

ordinarily forbidden, as a special treat with the understanding that resumption of the diet will be necessary the next day. Even in adults the "treat" technique often ensures better dietary cooperation than more rigid demands. Ideally patients should be trained by dieticians in a formal teaching program. Such classes are available in most large hospitals. If a patient is from a smaller community, it will probably be helpful to refer to a larger center for initial training.

In insulin-requiring diabetics the distribution of calories is also important if hypoglycemia is to be avoided. A typical pattern might include 20 percent of the total calories for breakfast, 35 percent for lunch, 30 percent for dinner, and 15 percent as a late-evening feeding. Occasionally a midafternoon snack is necessary. Different distributions may be required for different lifestyles; i.e., a person employed on a late-evening or night shift would not eat the major meal at noon.

The traditional approach to dietary therapy has come under question as a result of experiments designed to measure actual blood sugar responses to ingested foods. It is now clear that the exchanges are not necessarily equivalent; i.e., foods of the same weight and similar fat, carbohydrate, or protein content may result in different postprandial increases in the plasma glucose. The term *glycemic index* has been coined to express these differences. In calculating a glycemic index the mean plasma glucose is measured over a 2- to 3-h period after ingestion of a test food and compared to the response with a reference standard of defined composition such as bread. Although in principle the approach is attractive because it measures actual glycemic response to foods, its applicability to the general diabetic population is not established. Many foods and combinations must be tested before diets based on glycemic indexes can be compared to standard exchange-based diets under ordinary conditions.

The importance of diet in the management of diabetes varies with type of disease. In insulin-dependent patients, particularly those on intensive insulin regimens, the composition of the diet is not of critical importance since adjustment of insulin can cover wide variations in food ingestion. In non-insulin-dependent patients not treated with exogenous insulin more rigorous adherence to a fixed diet is required since endogenous insulin reserve is limited. Such patients cannot respond to increased demand produced by excess calories or increased intake of rapidly absorbed carbohydrate. Thus diet is of primary importance in non-insulin-dependent subjects.

Insulin Insulin is required for treatment of all type 1 patients and many patients with non-insulin-dependent disease. If the physician does not use oral agents (see below), all diet-unresponsive NIDDM subjects must be given the hormone. It is fairly easy to control the symptoms of diabetes with insulin, but it is difficult to maintain a normal blood sugar throughout 24 h even if one utilizes multiple injections of regular insulin or infusion pumps. It is even more difficult to maintain normal blood sugars utilizing traditional insulin therapy given as one or two injections a day. Nondiabetic subjects maintain the plasma glucose concentration within a narrow range at all times despite episodic food intake. When a meal is eaten, a prompt rise in insulin release occurs such that absorbed carbohydrate is rapidly transported into the liver and other tissues. Even after meals, therefore, the plasma glucose in normal subjects does not rise into the hyperglycemic or glycosuric range. As the plasma glucose

TABLE 327-4 Composition of food exchanges*

Exchange	Calories	Carbohydrate, g	Fat, g	Protein, g
Milk	170	12	10	8
Vegetable[†]	35	7	—	2
Fruit	40	10	—	—
Bread	70[‡]	15	—	2
Meat	75[‡]	—	5	7
Fat	45	—	5	—

* *Composition listed for one exchange.*
† *Type A vegetables contain little carbohydrate, fat, or protein and can be eaten in any amount. Exchange values are for type B vegetables.*
‡ *Calculated value for bread exchange is 68 cal and for meat exchange is 73 cal using 4 kcal/g for carbohydrate and protein and 9 kcal/g for fat. The values 70 and 75 cal were adapted to facilitate computations.*

TABLE 327-5 A 2200-cal diabetic diet (50 percent carbohydrate)

Exchange	No.	Calories	Carbohydrate, g	Fat, g	Protein, g
Milk	2	340	24	20	16
Vegetable*		Unlimited amounts of type A vegetables			
Fruit	7	280	70	—	—
Bread	12	840	180	—	24
Meat	8	600	—	40	56
Fat	4	180	—	20	—
Total		2240	274	80	96
			(50%)	(33%)	(17%)

* *Type B vegetables include beets, carrots, onions, green peas, pumpkin, rutabagas, winter squash, and turnips. If these are desired, ½ to 1 cup can be substituted for one fruit exchange. All other common vegetables can be eaten as desired.*

falls under the influence of insulin, release of the hormone is damped, and counterregulatory hormones enter the circulation to prevent hypoglycemia, ensuring smooth control of plasma glucose throughout the absorptive process. The diabetic treated with insulin by injection cannot reproduce these physiologic responses. If enough insulin is given to keep the postprandial glucose normal, inevitably too much insulin will be present during the postabsorptive phase and hypoglycemia will result. The same problem exists when insulin infusion pumps or multiple injections of insulin are utilized in an attempt to control diabetes tightly.

Because evidence suggests that some of the complications of diabetes may be prevented or partially reversed by maintenance of normal or near normal plasma glucose concentrations throughout the day, aggressive insulin therapy is frequently prescribed despite these difficulties. Three treatment regimens will be described: conventional, multiple subcutaneous injections (MSI), and continuous subcutaneous insulin infusion (CSII). *Conventional insulin therapy* involves the administration of one or two injections a day of intermediate acting insulin such as zinc insulin (lente insulin) or isophane insulin (NPH insulin) with or without the addition of small amounts of regular insulin. If the newly diagnosed diabetic is not in acute distress, therapy can be started as an outpatient, provided instruction in diet and insulin use and monitoring are adequate, and the physician can be reached by telephone for consultation. Adults of normal weight may be started on 15 to 20 units a day (the estimated daily insulin production rate in nondiabetic subjects of normal size is about 25 units a day). Obese patients, because of insulin resistance, may be started on 25 to 30 units a day. It is preferable to use the same quantity of insulin for several days before changing, the one exception being the hypoglycemic patient, for whom the dose should be immediately decreased unless a nonrecurrent cause of hypoglycemia (such as excessive exercise) is present. Generally changes should be no more than 5 or 10 units per step. It is probable that a single injection of insulin provides adequate control only in patients who have some residual capacity for insulin secretion. Poorly controlled patients should be placed on split therapy with about two-thirds of the total insulin given before breakfast and the remainder before supper. Two injections are almost always used when the total dose reaches 50 or 60 units a day but may be helpful at smaller doses as well since the peak action of intermediate insulins appears to be dose-related, i.e., a low dose may exhibit maximal activity earlier and disappear sooner than a large dose. Many physicians routinely add regular insulin to the intermediate dose even at initiation of therapy. Thus in a single-dose schedule one might begin with 20 units of intermediate and 5 units of regular insulin rather than 25 units of intermediate alone. This practice is based upon the concept that the regular insulin lowers the plasma glucose rapidly after which the more slowly absorbed insulin maintains the lowered level. Most patients on twice-daily insulin injections are also treated with a mixture of intermediate and regular insulin; e.g., 25 units NPH plus 10 units of regular before breakfast and 10 units of NPH plus 5 units of regular before supper. All patients should be taught to decrease

insulin when significant extra activity or exercise is anticipated. The proper decrement must be determined by trial and error, although a reduction of 5 to 10 units is a reasonable first step. The blood glucose–lowering effect of excercise is primarily due to increased energy demands in previously non-contracting muscle; enhanced absorption of insulin from depot sites secondary to increased blood flow plays a minor role. Conversely a small amount of extra regular insulin can be taken before a meal that contains extra calories or food ordinarily not allowed (e.g., when the diabetic must eat out at a banquet or the teenager goes out on a date). For patients willing to self-monitor plasma glucose an algorithm for adjusting insulin can be provided. Atypical protocol is shown in Table 327-6. Patients with complicated control problems may require hospitalization, where frequent plasma glucose determinations can guide therapy.

The *multiple subcutaneous insulin injection technique* most commonly involves administration of intermediate or long-acting insulin in the evening as a single dose together with regular insulin prior to each meal. Home glucose monitoring by the patient is necessary if the goal is the return of the plasma glucose to normal. One approach to initiation of therapy involves administration of 25 percent of the previous daily insulin dose in the patient's conventional regimen at bedtime as intermediate insulin (NPH or lente) with the other 75 percent given as regular insulin divided such that 40, 30, and 30 percent is given 30 min before breakfast, lunch, and supper, respectively. Alternatively, a three-injection schedule can be designated by omitting the night intermediate insulin and giving a long-acting insulin, such as insulin zinc extended (ultralente insulin) or protamine zinc insulin (PZI insulin), before the evening meal. Adjustments of dosage depend on response of the plasma glucose. A number of different protocols have been utilized, all of which represent sliding scales of insulin based on the plasma glucose. A typical schedule based on home monitoring of plasma glucose is shown in Table 327-7. Individual patients may require different dosages. For specific details the reader should consult one of the published papers utilizing the technique (e.g., Schriffrin and Belmont or the monograph by Schade et al.). MSI can be effective in controlling the plasma glucose and in some studies appears to match goals achieved with CSII.

Continuous subcutaneous insulin infusion involves use of a small battery-driven pump that delivers insulin subcutaneously into the abdominal wall, usually through a 27-gauge butterfly needle. With CSII insulin is delivered at a basal rate continuously throughout the day with increased rates programmed prior to meals. Adjustments in dosage are made in response to measured capillary glucose values in a fashion similar to that used in MSI. Ordinarily about 40 percent of

TABLE 327-6   Adjusting insulin dosage in conventional insulin therapy*

Blood sugar, mg/dL	Regular insulin, units	
	Breakfast	Supper
	(to be mixed with intermediate dosage)	
51–100	8	4
101–150	10	5
151–200	12	6
201–250	14	7
251–300	16	8
>300	20	10

* Once the patient has most blood sugars in the reasonable range (60–200 mg/dL), a prescription can be written for varying the regular insulin dosage as illustrated. The prescription in this case was for a patient in reasonable control on 25 units of NPH plus 10 units of regular before breakfast and 10 units of NPH plus 5 units of regular before supper. Change in metabolic status may require adjustments in both intermediate insulin and the sliding scale of regular insulin.

TABLE 327-7   Adjusting insulin dosage in a multiple-injection schedule*

I Initiation of therapy
  A 0.6 to 0.7 units insulin per kilogram body weight
  B 25% NPH at 9 P.M.; 75% regular in divided doses
    (40% before breakfast, 30% before lunch, 30% before supper)
  C Adjust NPH every 48 h based on fasting blood glucose
    <60 mg/dL − 2 units
    >90 mg/dL + 2 units
  D Adjust regular insulin every 48 h based on 1-h postprandial glucose
    < 60 mg/dL − 2 units
    >140 mg/dL + 2 units
II Daily therapy

Preprandial glucose, mg/dL	Regular insulin, units
<60	− 2
61– 90	No change
91–120	+ 1
121–150	+ 2
151–200	+ 3
201–250	+ 4
>250	+ 6

* With initiation of therapy insulin dosage is changed until target range is reached (see Table 327-8). After initial stabilization a variable insulin schedule is prescribed to maintain tight control. For example, if the patient after initiation is found to generally require 12 units of regular insulin before breakfast but has a prebreakfast blood sugar of 160 mg/dL, 15 units of regular insulin instead of the usual 12 would be taken.
SOURCE: Adapted from Schiffrin and Belmonte.

the total daily dose is given at the basal rate, the remainder being administered as preprandial boluses. There is little question that CSII can improve diabetic control relative to conventional therapy. Most patients report positive feelings of well-being as control improves. Nevertheless, although insulin infusion pumps have caught the attention of the public and many physicians, they should not be used indiscriminately. The danger of hypoglycemia is real, especially during the night in patients who maintain the plasma glucose consistently below 100 mg/dL. A fall in plasma glucose of 50 mg/dL may not be important if the starting value is 150 mg/dL but may be fatal if it occurs against a steady-state level of 60 mg/dL. Several deaths from hypoglycemia have occurred in pump users. In the author's opinion pumps should be prescribed only in highly disciplined and motivated patients who are followed by physicians with extensive experience in their use. Apart from problems of hypoglycemia, local insulin reactions and abscess formation may occur.

In one or two centers catheters for the insulin infusion pumps have been placed intravenously rather than subcutaneously. While few difficulties have been reported, this procedure appears unwise for routine use. Intraabdominal insulin pumps with reservoirs refillable from outside the body have been tried on experimental protocols. At present no advantage is apparent except that a pump does not have to be worn externally.

Who should be recommended for meticulous control utilizing either MSI or CSII? There are only two absolute indications: pregnancy and renal transplantation. Maintenance of a normal plasma glucose during pregnancy prevents fetal macrosomy and respiratory distress and lowers perinatal mortality. Unfortunately, congenital malformations due to diabetes cannot be prevented by control of the blood sugar after conception occurs. This means that maximal safety for the fetus can only be provided by meticulous treatment of diabetes *prior* to impregnation. Routine treatment of diabetes in pregnancy is not an option, and aggressive treatment should be started at the time pregnancy is planned. Inclusion of patients with renal transplants in the nonoptional category follows from the fact that diabetic nephropathy develops early in normal transplanted kidneys. The hope is that with improved metabolic control the acquired lesions can be slowed or prevented.

Meticulous control is an option for most other patients with insulin-dependent diabetes. Since the treatment schedules require much effort on the part of the patient, reliability and willingness to accept responsibility for self-care must be assessed ahead of time. Glucose monitoring is not inexpensive, and the financial status of the patient also has to be considered. Even if meticulous control does not achieve the goal of preventing late complications, in properly chosen patients it seems worthwhile in and of itself both because patients generally feel better when metabolically normal and because attention to clinical detail provides a sense of self-sufficiency and independence that is otherwise easily lost in diabetes. Meticulous control is rarely appropriate for patients whose life expectancy is shortened because of age, cardiovascular, cerebrovascular, or diabetic complications.

For surgical procedures in diabetic patients, intermediate insulin is omitted, and treatment is carried out with regular insulin alone. An effective method is to add 10 to 20 units of insulin to a liter of 5% glucose in water with infusion at a rate of 100 to 150 mL/h. Measurements of plasma glucose in capillary blood allows change of rate to avoid significant hypo- or hyperglycemia. It is also possible to administer 10 units of regular insulin subcutaneously and infuse 5 or 10% glucose at rates sufficient to avoid major changes in glucose concentration.

Types of insulin A variety of insulins are available for use in the treatment of diabetes. Rapidly acting preparations are used in diabetic emergencies and in CSII and MSI programs. Intermediate preparations are used in conventional and MSI regimens. As noted, long-acting formulations are used in three-injection MSI schedules. Peak effects and duration vary from patient to patient and depend not only on route of administration but on dose. Hypoglycemic effects in insulin-

treated diabetics appear to be delayed relative to normal subjects, probably because of the presence of anti-insulin antibodies in plasma. In one study in diabetics, regular insulin given subcutaneously had its onset of action at about 1 h, reached a peak at 6 h, and had measurable effects on average for 16 h, whereas in normal persons onset is within minutes, maximal action is around 2 h, and duration is only 6 to 8 h. With NPH insulin, diabetics exhibited an onset of action at 2.5 h, a peak at 11 h, and a total period of action of 25 h, more closely approximating values in normal subjects.

Commercial insulins are prepared in concentrations of 100 units per milliliter (U100) although higher concentrations can be obtained (e.g., U500). All commercial insulins are now "purified," meaning that they have a contamination with proinsulin <10 parts per million. Some preparations contain as little as 1 part per million. Animal insulins (beef, pork) are still in wide use, but insulin identical to the human molecule is now available. The advantages of purified animal insulins (beef, pork) are still in wide use, but insulin identical to the human molecule is now available. The advantages of purified animal It is possible that anti-insulin antibody (IgG) formation is slightly less with the "human" hormone. Given equivalent price structure it is appropriate to prescribe "human" insulin routinely. As stated above, the various insulins are available as rapid, intermediate, and long-acting preparations, although not all manufacturers offer all varieties. Lente and NPH insulin are used in most conventional therapy and are roughly equivalent in biologic effects, although lente appears to be slightly more immunogenic and to mix less well with regular insulin than does NPH.

Self-glucose monitoring For many years effectiveness of treatment for diabetes was followed by reviewing symptoms (such as frequency of nocturia) and measurement of glucose in the urine by semiquantitative techniques. Since the renal threshold for glucose in normal persons is in the range of 180 to 200 mg/dL plasma glucose and may increase with the appearance of renal disease, assessment of glycosuria is of little value if the goal of therapy is to maintain the plasma glucose near normal. In consequence most insulin-requiring patients now monitor control and alter therapy based on self-measurement of the capillary blood sugar. In addition to the fact that such measurements are necessary in all treatment schedules utilizing variable insulin dosage the ability to assess the blood glucose as needed has other positive benefits. It bestows a sense of confidence and independence in the patient, has a reinforcing effect on therapeutic goals (for example, the effect of dietary indiscretion can be immediately seen), serves to give early warning of incipient hypoglycemia, and allows documentation of hypoglycemia when suggestive symptoms are present.

Although blood glucose can be estimated visually utilizing reagent strips, it is generally preferable to use an instrument for readings. This is because it is difficult for many patients to extrapolate accurately between the color changes and because subjective wishes may influence the extrapolation. It is harder to ignore a number appearing in a machine. A variety of glucose analyzers are available. The system chosen should be "dry" (i.e., not require washing of the reagent strip). In general, the cost of a machine, spring-driven lancet holder, and lancets is less than $200, and many insurance carriers reimburse for the purchase. The patient needs to have supervised training in the technique, and simultaneous checks of the blood sugar in a laboratory should be done periodically to test accuracy of the self-analysis. Repeated studies show that patients can measure blood glucose accurately using these techniques.

Although urine testing for glucose is now rarely used to follow diabetes, the measurement of ketones in the urine remains important.

Goals of therapy Target levels for glucose control vary amongst diabetologists. The schedule shown in Table 327-8 lists the ranges considered acceptable and ideal by the author. The "acceptable" category would apply in conventional therapy utilizing a two-dose schedule of intermediate and regular insulin. The upper limit of 200 mg/dL postprandially is arbitrary but is based on the finding in the

Pima Indian population that complications of diabetes are rare if the 2-h value in the oral glucose tolerance test is less than 200 mg/dL. The "ideal" column represents values targeted in meticulous control regimens. Although some authors are more stringent and prefer the 1-h postprandial value to be no more than 140 mg/dL, the risk of hypoglycemia is greater under these circumstances. In general avoidance of serious hypoglycemia is more important than avoidance of hyperglycemia because the former has immediate consequences that may threaten the life of the patient or others (e.g., through an automobile accident) while the detrimental effects of hyperglycemia are long-term and less certain.

Hypoglycemia, the Somogyi effect, and the dawn phenomenon

(see also Chap. 329) The problem of hypoglycemia is common in insulin-dependent diabetics, particularly when aggressive efforts are made to keep both the fasting plasma glucose and postprandial hyperglycemia within the normal range. Hypoglycemia may be caused by missing a meal or doing unexpected exercise but can occur in the absence of known precipitating events. Daytime episodes of hypoglycemia are usually recognized by adrenergic symptoms, such as sweating, nervousness, tremor, and hunger. Hypoglycemia during sleep may produce no symptoms or cause night sweats, unpleasant dreams, and early-morning headache. In one study of insulin-dependent diabetic children monitored throughout 24 h, 18 percent had asymptomatic nocturnal hypoglycemia. If hypoglycemia is not aborted by the countercurrent regulatory mechanisms or by ingestion of carbohydrate, central nervous system symptoms ensue: confusion, abnormal behavior, loss of consciousness, or convulsions. As diabetes progresses, particularly with the development of neuropathy, epinephrine-induced symptoms may become blunted and lose their effectiveness as warning signals, with the consequence that central nervous system signs predominate. Up to 7 percent of deaths in insulin-dependent diabetic subjects have been attributed to hypoglycemia.

Protection against hypoglycemia is normally provided by two mechanisms as plasma glucose concentrations fall: cessation of insulin release and mobilization of counterregulatory hormones. The latter act to increase hepatic glucose production and decrease glucose utilization in nonhepatic tissues. Glucagon is the primary counterregulatory hormone, and epinephrine (and norepinephrine released from the sympathetic nervous system) serves as the major backup. Epinephrine is not required for maintenance of the plasma glucose provided glucagon is available but becomes critical in its absence. Cortisol and growth hormone do not function acutely but come into play with prolonged fasting or sustained hypoglycemia. Diabetic patients are vulnerable to hypoglycemia because of both insulin excess and counterregulatory failure. Since insulin is given by injection or infusion, the capacity to decrease plasma concentrations of the hormone as glucose levels fall is not available. Very early on the diabetic subject with type 1 insulin-dependent disease loses the capacity to increase glucagon release in response to hypoglycemia. Protection is thus dependent on epinephrine. Unfortunately, many patients also lose the capacity to secrete epinephrine in response to hypoglycemia. In most circumstances the epinephrine deficiency is probably due to diabetic autonomic neuropathy, but the defect may occur in the absence of clinically demonstrable nerve dysfunction. Failure of catecholamine release is usually a late event in diabetes but can occur early. It is thought that beta-adrenergic blocking agents have the same effects as deficiencies of epinephrine, although a prospective

clinical trial on the dangers of such agents in producing hypoglycemia under real life circumstances has not been carried out.

Counterregulatory hormone failure is of particular significance when intensive insulin therapy is prescribed. The incidence of hypoglycemia is inversely related to the mean level of plasma glucose. Unfortunately there is no easy way to predict the occurrence of clinically significant counterregulatory failure. Experimentally an insulin infusion test can be used for this purpose but is probably not practical for routine use. In this test neuroglycopenic symptoms or delay in return of plasma glucose from nadir after infusion of a standard amount of insulin are utilized to identify defects in the response system. Perhaps the best clue to counterregulatory failure is the presence of frequent hypoglycemia not explicable by change in diet or exercise. Of additional concern are reports that intensive insulin therapy (meticulous control) may itself produce abnormal glucose counterregulation.

An important question is whether hypoglycemia symptoms can occur in the absence of low plasma glucose levels, for example, in response to a rapid fall in glucose concentrations. While this question cannot be answered with certainty, the evidence suggests that neither rate nor magnitude of the fall signals counterregulatory release, only a low plasma glucose. Although the triggering level of plasma glucose may vary from patient to patient, counterregulatory hormone release is not induced at normal or elevated levels of glucose. Adrenergic symptoms occurring in the presence of hyperglycemia are likely due to anxiety or cardiovascular mechanisms.

Hypoglycemia can occur in diabetic patients consequent to other mechanisms. Diabetic renal disease is not infrequently accompanied by diminished insulin requirements and may lead to frank hypoglycemia if adjustments in dosage are not made. The mechanism is not known. Although half-times for insulin in plasma are increased in diabetic nephropathy, other factors doubtless play a role.

Hypoglycemia may be due to the development of autoimmune adrenal insufficiency as part of the Schmidt syndrome (see Chap. 334), which is more frequent in diabetics than in the population as a whole. Some patients develop hypoglycemia in association with high levels of circulating insulin antibodies. The exact mechanism has not been established. Occasionally an insulinoma may develop in a diabetic patient. Very rarely, permanent remission of apparently typical diabetes occurs. The reason is not known, but the initial sign may be frequent hypoglycemia in a previously well controlled patient.

It must be emphasized that hypoglycemic attacks are dangerous and if frequent portend a serious or even fatal outcome.

The *Somogyi phenomenon* refers to rebound hyperglycemia following an episode of hypoglycemia due to counterregulatory hormone release. It should be suspected whenever wide swings in the plasma glucose occur over short time intervals even if symptoms are not reported. Such rapid changes contrast with the alterations seen following insulin withdrawal in previously well-controlled diabetic patients in whom hyperglycemia and ketosis develop gradually and smoothly over a 12- to 24-h period. Excessive hunger and weight gain occurring in the context of worsening hyperglycemia are clues that the insulin dosage may be too high, since poor control due to underinsulinization usually results in weight loss (because of osmotic diuresis and glucose wastage). If the Somogyi phenomenon is suspected, the insulin dose should be decreased as a trial, even when specific symptoms of overinsulinization are absent. The Somogyi phenomenon probably occurs less frequently in patients utilizing insulin infusion pumps than in those treated by conventional or multiple injections of insulin as a bolus.

The *dawn phenomenon* refers to an early morning rise in plasma glucose requiring increased amounts of insulin to maintain euglycemia. Although similar early morning hyperglycemia may result from hypoglycemia, as just described, the dawn phenomenon itself is thought to be independent of the Somogyi mechanism. The nocturnal surge of growth hormone release is thought to be a major factor. Increased clearance of insulin also occurs in the early morning hours, but the changes are probably not of major importance. Differentiation

TABLE 327-8   Goals for blood glucose in the control of diabetes*

Goal	Acceptable, mg/dL	Ideal, mg/dL
Fasting	60–130	70–100
Preprandial	60–130	70–100
Postprandial (1 h)	<200	<160
3 A.M.	> 65	> 65

* Values for healthy patients below the age of 65. Goals my be shifted upward in older patients.

between the dawn phenomenon and posthypoglycemic hyperglycemia can usually be accomplished by measuring the blood glucose at 3 A.M. This is important since the Somogyi phenomenon is avoided by decreasing insulin dosages for the critical time period while the dawn phenomenon usually requires increased insulin to maintain glucose in the normal range.

Oral agents Non-insulin-dependent diabetes that cannot be controlled by dietary management often responds to sulfonylureas. The drugs are easy to use and appear to be safe. Fear that sulfonylureas might increase deaths from heart attacks, prompted by reports of the University Group Diabetes Program (UGDP), has largely dissipated because of questions about the design of that study. On the other hand use of the oral drugs has decreased concomitant with the emphasis on better control as a possible means of slowing the development of late complications. While some patients with relatively mild disease have return of plasma glucose to normal on oral drugs, those with significant hyperglycemia tend to improve but do not approach the normal range. Thus a high percentage of non-insulin-dependent diabetics are now treated with insulin.

Sulfonylureas act primarily by stimulating release of insulin from the beta cell. They have the capacity to increase the number of insulin receptors in target tissues, but also enhance insulin-mediated glucose disposal independent of an increase in insulin binding. Since mean levels of plasma insulin do not increase following treatment with sulfonylureas despite significantly improved mean plasma glucose concentrations, extrapancreatic effects of the drugs may be significant. However, the paradox of improved glucose metabolism in the absence of higher steady-state levels of insulin has been resolved by studies which show that elevation of plasma glucose to pretreatment values results in a rise of plasma insulin to levels higher than those seen pretreatment. Thus, the initial action of the drugs is to increase insulin release with lowering of the plasma glucose. As glucose concentrations fall, insulin levels also decrease since plasma glucose is the major stimulus to insulin release, thereby masking the initial stimulation of insulin secretion. The insulinogenic effect can then be unmasked by raising the plasma glucose to the previous elevated levels. The fact that sulfonylureas are ineffective in IDDM, where beta-cell mass is diminished, supports the pancreatic effect as primary, although extrapancreatic mechanisms doubtless play a role.

The characteristics of the sulfonylureas are summarized in Table 327-9. The newer drugs such as glipizide and glyburide are effective in smaller doses but otherwise differ little from agents in long use such as chlorpropamide and tolbutamide. In patients who have significant renal disease it is preferable to treat with tolbutamide or tolazamide since these agents are exclusively metabolized and inactivated by the liver. Chlorpropamide has the capacity to sensitize the renal tubule to antidiuretic hormone. It thus is helpful in some patients with partial diabetes insipidus but may cause water retention in patients with diabetes mellitus. Hypoglycemia is less common with oral agents than with insulin, but when it occurs it tends to be severe and prolonged. Some patients have required massive glucose infusions for days following the last dose of sulfonylurea. For this reason hospitalization is mandatory in patients with sulfonylurea-induced hypoglycemia.

The only other oral agents effective in the treatment of maturity-onset diabetes are the biguanides. They presumably lower plasma glucose by inhibiting gluconeogenesis in the liver although phenformin may increase the number of insulin receptors in some tissues. The drugs are ordinarily used only in combination with sulfonylureas under circumstances in which control is inadequate with sulfonylurea alone. Because of many reports linking phenformin to the appearance of lactic acidosis, the Food and Drug Administration removed the agent from clinical use in the United States except for certain special patients who continue to take it as an investigational drug. Phenformin and other biguanides are still used elsewhere in the world. Biguanides should not be given to patients with renal disease and should be stopped if nausea, vomiting, diarrhea, or any intercurrent illness appears.

Monitoring control of diabetes For those patients who measure blood glucose frequently for adjustment of insulin dosage an estimate of mean ambient glucose concentrations is readily available. For other patients, and as a check on accuracy of the self measurements, most diabetologists now measure hemoglobin A_{1c} to assess long-term control. Hemoglobin A_{1c}, a fast-moving minor hemoglobin component, is present in normal persons but increases in the presence of hyperglycemia. Its enhanced electrophoretic mobility is due to nonenzymatic glycosylation of the amino acids valine and lysine. The reaction is as follows:

$$
\begin{array}{ccccc}
HC{=}O & & HC{=}N{-}\beta A & & CH_2{-}N^+H_2{-}\beta A \\
| & & | & & | \\
HCOH & & HCOH & & C{=}O \\
| & & | & & | \\
HOCH & & HOCH & & HOCH \\
\beta\text{-}NH_2 + \quad | & \rightleftharpoons & | & \longrightarrow & | \\
HCOH & & HCOH & & HCOH \\
| & & | & & | \\
HCOH & & HCOH & & HCOH \\
| & & | & & | \\
CH_2OH & & CH_2OH & & CH_2OH \\
\text{Glucose} & & \text{Aldimine} & & \text{Ketoamine} \\
& & \text{(Schiff base)} & & \\
Hb\ A & \overset{Rapid}{\rightleftharpoons} & pre\ A_{1c} & \overset{Slow}{\longrightarrow} & Hb\ A_{1c}
\end{array}
$$

In this scheme $\beta\text{-}NH_2$ stands for the terminal valine of the β chain of hemoglobin. Aldimine formation is reversible so that pre-A_{1c} is labile while ketoamine formation is irreversible and thus stable. Pre-A_{1c} levels depend on the ambient glucose concentrations and do not reflect long-term control although they are measured in chromatographic methods for determining hemoglobin A_{1c}. Pre-A_{1c} must thus be removed to assess true Hb A_{1c} values accurately. Many laboratories employ high-performance liquid chromatography (HPLC) to make the measurement. A colorimetric method utilizing thiobarbituric acid also does not measure the labile pre-A_{1c} fraction. When properly assayed, the percent of glycosylated hemoglobin gives an estimate of diabetic control for the preceding 3-month period. Normal values must be obtained for each lab; on average nondiabetic subjects have Hb A_{1c} values of around 6 percent, and levels in poorly controlled diabetics may reach 10 to 12 percent. Measurement of glycosylated

TABLE 327-9 The sulfonylureas

Agent	Daily dose, mg	Doses per day	Duration of hyperglycemic action, h	Metabolism/excretion
Acetohexamide	250–1500	1–2	12–18	Liver/kidney
Chlorpropamide	100–500	1	60	Kidney
Tolazamide	100–1000	1–2	12–14	Liver
Tolbutamide	500–3000	2–3	6–12	Liver
Glyburide	1.25–20	1–2	Up to 24	Liver/kidney
Glipizide	2.5–40	1–2	Up to 24	Liver/kidney
Glibornuride	12.5–100	1–2	Up to 24	Liver/kidney

SOURCE: *RH Unger, DW Foster, Diabetes mellitus, in Williams' Textbook of Endocrinology, 7th ed, JD Wilson, DW Foster (eds), Philadelphia, Saunders, 1985, pp 1018–1080. Adapted from HE Lebovitz and MN Feinglos.*

hemoglobin gives an objective assessment of metabolic control. Discrepancies between reported plasma glucose values and hemoglobin A_{1c} concentrations suggest either that measurement or reporting of the former is not accurate. Measurement of glycosylated albumin, because of its short half-life, can be used to monitor diabetic control over a 1- to 2-week period but clinically is rarely used.

ACUTE METABOLIC COMPLICATIONS   In addition to hypoglycemia, diabetics are susceptible to two major acute metabolic complications: diabetic ketoacidosis and hyperosmolar, nonketotic coma. The former is a complication of insulin-dependent diabetes, while the latter usually occurs in the setting of non-insulin-dependent disease. Ketoacidosis rarely, if ever, develops in true type 2 diabetes.

Diabetic ketoacidosis   Diabetic ketoacidosis appears to require insulin deficiency coupled with a relative or absolute increase in glucagon concentration. It is often caused by cessation of insulin intake but may result from physical (e.g., infection, surgery) or emotional stress despite continued insulin therapy. In the former case the concentration of glucagon rises secondary to insulin withdrawal, while in stress the operative stimulus is probably epinephrine and/or norepinephrine. In addition to stimulating glucagon secretion epinephrine presumably blocks release of the small amount of residual insulin found in some subjects with IDDM and inhibits insulin-induced glucose transport in peripheral tissues. These hormonal changes have multiple effects, but two are critical: (1) They induce maximal gluconeogenesis and impair peripheral utilization of glucose, causing severe hyperglycemia. Glucagon facilitates gluconeogenesis by inducing a fall in fructose 2,6-bisphosphate, an intermediate that stimulates glycolysis through activation of phosphofructokinase and blocks gluconeogenesis by inhibiting fructose bisphosphatase. When fructose 2,6-bisphosphate concentrations fall, glycolysis is inhibited, and gluconeogenesis is enhanced. The resultant hyperglycemia induces an osmotic diuresis that leads to the volume depletion and dehydration that characterize the ketoacidotic state. (2) They activate the ketogenic process and thus initiate development of metabolic acidosis. For ketosis to occur, changes must be produced in both adipose tissue and the liver. Free fatty acids from adipose stores represent the primary substrate for ketone body formation, and plasma levels of free fatty acids must rise if high rates of ketogenesis are to develop. However, fatty acids delivered to the liver are simply reesterified and stored as hepatic triglyceride or converted into very low density lipoproteins and transported back into the circulation unless the hepatic oxidative machinery for fatty acids is activated. While free fatty acid release is enhanced directly by insulin deficiency, accelerated fatty acid oxidation in the liver is primarily induced by glucagon, via action on the carnitine acyltransferase system of enzymes responsible for the transport of fatty acids into the mitochondria following their esterification to coenzyme A. As shown in Fig. 327-3 carnitine acyltransferase I (carnitine palmitoyltransferase I) transesterifies fatty acyl-CoA to fatty acylcarnitine, which then freely traverses the inner mitochondrial membrane. Reversal of the reaction occurs internally under the influence of carnitine acyltransferase II (carnitine palmitoyltransferase II). In the fed state carnitine acyltransferase I is inactive, and, as a consequence, long-chain fatty acids cannot reach the β-oxidative enzymes for ketone body production. During starvation or uncontrolled diabetes the system is activated; under these circumstances the rate of ketogenesis is a first-order function of the concentration of fatty acids reaching transferase I.

Glucagon (or a change in the glucagon/insulin ratio) activates the transport system in two ways. First, glucagon causes a rapid fall in hepatic malonyl-CoA content. It does so by interrupting the sequence glucose 6-phosphate → pyruvate → citrate → acetyl CoA → malonyl CoA via the previously mentioned decrease in fructose 2,6-bisphosphate. Malonyl-CoA, the first committed intermediate in the synthesis of fatty acids from glucose, is a competitive inhibitor of carnitine acyltransferase I, and a fall in its concentration activates the enzyme. Second, glucagon causes a rise in hepatic carnitine concentration, which then drives the reaction toward fatty acylcarnitine formation by mass action. These events are summarized schematically in Fig. 327-4. At high plasma fatty acid concentrations hepatic uptake of fatty acids is sufficient to saturate both oxidative and esterifying pathways, resulting in fatty liver, hypertriglyceridemia, and ketoacidosis. Overproduction of ketones by the liver is the primary event in ketotic states, but limitation of peripheral utilization also plays a role at high concentrations of acetoacetate and β-hydroxybutyrate.

Clinically ketoacidosis begins with anorexia, nausea, and vomiting, coupled with increased rate of urine formation. Abdominal pain may be present. If untreated, altered consciousness or frank coma may occur. Initial examination usually shows Kussmaul's respiration, together with signs of volume depletion. Rarely the latter is sufficient to cause vascular collapse and renal shutdown. Body temperature is normal or below normal in uncomplicated ketoacidosis, and fever suggests the presence of infection. Leukocytosis, frequently very marked, is a feature of diabetic acidosis per se and may not indicate infection.

The characteristic metabolic abnormalities of diabetic coma are shown in Table 327-10. Several features deserve comment. The metabolic acidosis and anion gap are almost totally accounted for by the elevated plasma levels of acetoacetate and β-hydroxybutyrate, although other acids (e.g., lactate, free fatty acids, phosphates) contribute. Despite initial potassium concentrations that are normal to high, there is a total body potassium deficit of several hundred millimoles. Similarly, initial serum phosphorus may be high despite depletion of body stores. Magnesium deficiency may also be present. The serum sodium concentration tends to be low in the face of modest osmolar concentration because of the hyperglycemia that draws intracellular water into the plasma space. A low serum sodium (e.g., 110 meq per liter) suggests an artifact due to severe hypertriglyceridemia. The latter is common in ketoacidosis and is the consequence of both impaired activity of lipoprotein lipase (a disposal defect) and the hepatic overproduction of very low density lipoproteins. If a fat meal has been ingested prior to the onset of ketoacidosis, chylomicrons may make up a major portion of the circulating fat. Lipemia is usually visible if triglyceride concentration is above 400 mg/dL. True hyponatremia may occur if the patient has vomited repeatedly and continued to drink water. Prerenal azotemia, reflecting volume

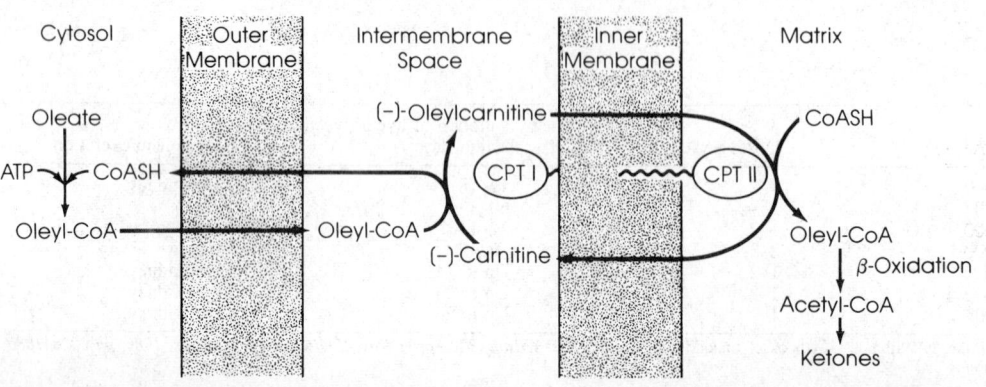

FIGURE 327-3   *The carnitine palmitoyltransferase system for the transfer of long-chain fatty acids into the mitochondria. CPT I-carnitine palmitoyltransferase I; CPT II-carnitine palmitoyltransferase II. (From JD McGarry et al, J Clin Invest 55:1202, 1975. Used by permission.)*

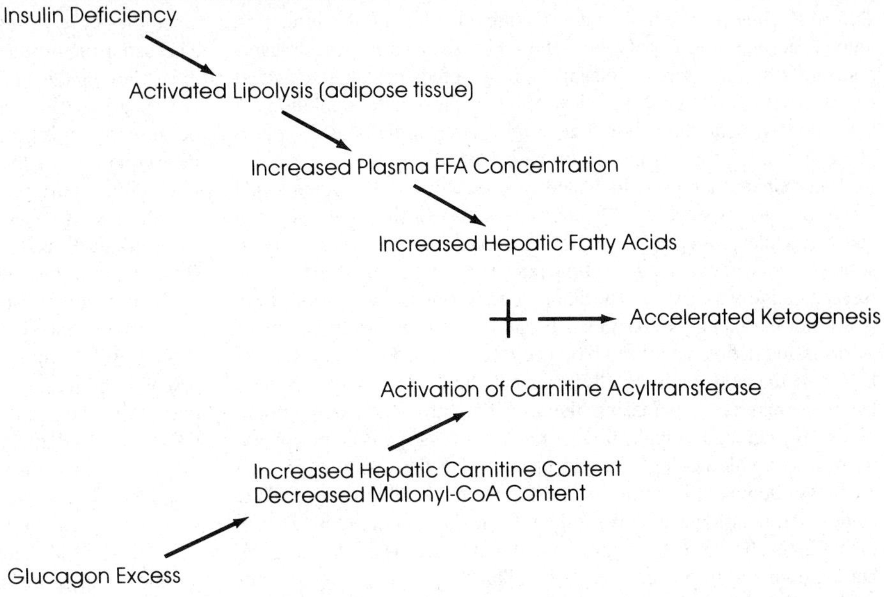

Insulin Deficiency

Activated Lipolysis (adipose tissue)

Increased Plasma FFA Concentration

Increased Hepatic Fatty Acids

+ ——→ Accelerated Ketogenesis

Activation of Carnitine Acyltransferase

Increased Hepatic Carnitine Content
Decreased Malonyl-CoA Content

Glucagon Excess

FIGURE 327-4 *The regulation of ketogenesis. Significant production of acetoacetate and β-hydroxybutyrate by the liver requires provision of adequate free fatty acid substrate and activation of fatty acid oxidation. Lipolysis is primarily increased by insulin deficiency while the fatty acid oxidative sequence is activated primarily by glucagon. The immediate signal for oxidation is a fall in malonyl CoA content. (After JD McGarry, DW Foster, Am J Med 61:9, 1976.)*

depletion, is usually modest in degree and reversible with treatment. The serum amylase may be elevated, and frank pancreatitis can occur.

The diagnosis of ketoacidosis in a known diabetic is not difficult. Its appearance in a patient not previously known to have diabetes requires differentiation from the other common causes of metabolic acidosis with an anion gap: lactic acidosis, uremia, alcoholic ketoacidosis, and certain poisonings. The first step is to test the urine for glucose and ketones. If urine ketones are negative, another cause for the acidosis is likely. If positive, plasma examination is required to be certain that something more than starvation ketosis is present. Since quantitative determinations of acetoacetate and β-hydroxybutyrate are not routinely available, semiquantitative tests must be done using ketone reagent strips. Serial dilutions of plasma can be made and tested. A strong test may occur in undiluted plasma owing to starvation alone; a strong reaction beyond 1:1 dilution is presumptive evidence for ketoacidosis. Apart from diabetes the only other common ketoacidotic state is alcoholic ketoacidosis. This syndrome, which by definition occurs in chronic alcoholics, usually follows a debauch, but the patient may not have had alcohol for 24 h or longer. It never occurs in the absence of starvation and frequently is associated with severe vomiting and abdominal pain. Pancreatitis is present in up to 75 percent of patients. A plasma glucose of less than 150 mg/dL was found in three-fourths of cases and in 15 percent was less than 50 mg/dL on arrival at the hospital. Hyperglycemia may occur but is usually mild and rarely, if ever, above 300 mg/dL. Plasma free fatty acid concentrations are higher (mean 2.9 mM) than in normal starvation (range 0.7 to 1.0 mM), reaching levels seen in diabetic ketoacidosis. Presumably the liver is activated for ketogenesis by starvation in these patients and driven to maximal rates of ketone formation by the high fatty acid levels. Why some alcoholics mobilize fatty acids excessively is not known. In contrast to diabetic acidosis, the syndrome is rapidly reversible by the intravenous administration of glucose. As in all alcoholics given glucose, thiamine should be supplied to avoid precipitation of acute beriberi. (Other water-soluble vitamins, though not as critical, should also be infused.) Insulin is required only if hyperglycemia persists during therapy.

Diabetic ketoacidosis cannot be reversed without insulin. For decades 50 or more units of insulin were given per hour until ketosis was reversed, but now most patients are treated by "low-dose" insulin schedules in which 8 to 10 units of insulin are infused intravenously each hour. Most diabetic acidosis can be reversed adequately with low-dose treatment, but some patients do not respond. Presumably the insulin resistance that is characteristic of diabetic ketoacidosis is more pronounced in these patients than in responsive subjects. The problem is that resistant subjects cannot be identified prospectively. For this reason it is probably preferable to treat

ketoacidosis with 25 to 50 units of regular insulin intravenously hourly until the acidosis is reversed. There are no known toxic effects of larger insulin doses, since maximal physiologic response is obtained once insulin receptors are saturated regardless of how much insulin is given. The advantage of the higher dosage schedule is that it ensures saturation of the receptors in the face of competing antibodies or other resistance factors. If physicians choose to use the low-dose insulin schedule, they should be alert to the possibility of resistance. Should acidosis persist unabated after several hours of treatment, larger amounts of insulin are clearly indicated. Ketoacidosis can also be adequately treated with intramuscular (but not subcutaneous) insulin.

Therapy of ketoacidosis also requires intravenous fluids. The usual fluid deficit is 3 to 5 liters, and both salt solutions and free water are needed. One to two liters of isotonic saline or Ringer's lactate should be given rapidly intravenously on arrival, with additional amounts determined by urine output and clinical assessment of the fluid state. When the plasma glucose falls to about 300 mg/dL, 5% glucose solutions should be given, both as a source of free water and as a prophylactic measure to prevent the late cerebral edema syndrome. The latter is a rare complication of ketoacidosis occurring most often in children. It is suspected when the patient remains comatose or lapses into coma following reversal of acidosis.

Potassium replacement is always necessary, but the time of administration will vary. The initial potassium is often high despite a total body deficit because of the severe acidosis. In this case the cation will ordinarily not be needed until 3 to 4 h after initiation of therapy, when reversal of acidosis and the action of insulin cause a

TABLE 327-10 Initial laboratory findings in diabetic ketoacidosis

Series	Dallas*	Los Angeles†	Washington‡
Age	38	36	43
Glucose, mg/dL	475	675	733
Sodium, mM	132	131	132
Potassium, mM	4.8	5.3	6.0
Bicarbonate, mM	<10	6	10
BUN, mg/dL	25	32	42
Acetoacetate, mM	4.8	—	—
β-Hydroxybutyrate, mM	13.7	—	—
Free fatty acids, mM	2.1	—	2.3
Lactate, mM	4.6	—	—
Osmolarity, mosmol/liter	310	323	331

* *Eighty-eight consecutive episodes of ketoacidosis at Parkland Memorial Hospital (DW Foster, unpublished observations).*
† *Mean data from 308 episodes of nonfatal ketoacidosis (PM Beigelman, Diabetes 20:490, 1971).*
‡ *Mean data from 10 episodes of ketoacidosis (JE Gerich et al, Diabetes 20:228, 1971).*

shift of K^+ into intracellular water. On the other hand if the admission value is normal or low, potassium should be given early, since plasma concentrations fall rapidly during therapy, predisposing the patient to cardiac arrhythmias. In view of the phosphate depletion of ketoacidosis, potassium should be administered initially as the phosphate salt rather than as potassium chloride.

Bicarbonate therapy is indicated in severely acidotic patients (pH 7.0 or below), especially if hypotension is present (acidosis itself can cause vascular collapse). It is not used routinely in less acutely ill subjects since rapid alkalinization may have detrimental effects on oxygen delivery to tissues. The hemoglobin-oxygen dissociation curve is normal in diabetic ketoacidosis because of the opposing effects of acidosis and deficiency of red blood cell 2,3-diphosphoglycerate (2,3-DPG). If the acidosis is rapidly reversed, the deficiency of 2,3-DPG becomes manifest, increasing the avidity with which hemoglobin binds oxygen and impairing the release of oxygen in peripheral tissues. In a volume-depleted patient with poor tissue perfusion such a change theoretically could predispose to the development of lactic acidosis. If bicarbonate is given, the infusion should be stopped when the pH reaches 7.2 to minimize effects on oxygen binding by hemoglobin and to prevent metabolic alkalosis as circulating ketones are metabolized to bicarbonate with reversal of ketoacidosis.

In following the response to treatment, two points should be emphasized. (1) Plasma glucose invariably falls more rapidly than plasma ketones. Insulin should not be stopped because glucose concentrations approach normal; rather, as mentioned, glucose should be infused and insulin continued until the ketosis has cleared. (2) Plasma ketone values are not very helpful. The testing materials measure acetoacetate and acetone but not β-hydroxybutyrate. Since β-hydroxybutyrate must be oxidized to acetoacetate prior to utilization, it is characteristic for the plasma ketones measured by reagent strip to remain stable or even rise early in therapy at a time when total ketone concentration (acetoacetate plus β-hydroxybutyrate) is steadily falling. Because β-hydroxybutyrate and acetoacetate represent a redox couple in equilibrium with mitochondrial NADH/NAD concentrations, vascular collapse or severe hypoxia may mask the presence of ketoacidosis as acetoacetate is reduced to β-hydroxybutyrate. Under these circumstances the β-hydroxybutyrate/acetoacetate ratio, normally about 3:1, may reach 7:1 or 8:1. Paradoxically, in such a situation, ketosis may seem to worsen as the patient gets better because of conversion of β-hydroxybutyrate to acetoacetate when the circulation is reestablished and tissue oxygenation is restored. The key parameters to follow are the pH and the calculated anion gap since these give a more accurate assessment of therapeutic progress. The usual picture is for the pH to rise and the anion gap to narrow even though the plasma bicarbonate remains low. The persistently low bicarbonate is the consequence of hyperchloremia that develops because of rapid infusion of sodium chloride, the loss of potential bicarbonate from the body in urine as ketones, and exchanges with intracellular buffers.

All patients should be followed with a flow sheet outlining amounts and timing of insulin and fluids together with a record of vital signs, urine volume, and blood chemistries. Without such a record therapy tends to become chaotic.

Most patients with diabetic ketoacidosis recover when properly treated. While mortality in large series is reported to be around 10 percent, the majority of deaths result from late complications rather than from ketoacidosis itself. The major causes are myocardial infarction and infection, particularly pneumonia. Poor prognostic signs on admission include hypotension, azotemia, deep coma, and associated illness. In children, cerebral edema is a common cause of death (less frequent in adults). The cause of the brain swelling is not known. Theories include osmotic disequilibrium between brain and plasma as glucose is rapidly lowered, decreased plasma oncotic pressure due to infusion of large amounts of saline, and insulin-induced ion flux across the blood-brain barrier. Whatever the mechanism, mortality rates are high. Diagnosis is usually made by CT scan. Treatment involves the bolus infusion of 1 g mannitol per kilogram of body weight in the form of a 20% solution. Although of questionable benefit, dexamethasone is also usually given: 12 mg initially then 4 mg every 6 h. If there is no response, hyperventilation to an arterial P_{CO_2} of about 28 mmHg should be carried out by an anesthesiologist or pulmonary specialist.

Other acute complications of ketoacidosis include vascular thrombosis and the adult respiratory distress syndrome. The former is induced by volume depletion, hyperosmolarity, increased viscosity of blood, and changes in clotting factors favoring thrombosis. The cause of the pulmonary lesion is not known; it is probably not related to the metabolic acidosis since respiratory distress syndrome occurs in hyperosmolar coma as well. Acute gastric dilatation is another rare complication. A rare infection associated with ketoacidosis is mucormycosis (see below). Table 327-11 summarizes the complications of diabetic ketoacidosis and its treatment.

Hyperosmolar coma Hyperosmolar nonketotic diabetic coma is usually a complication of non-insulin-dependent diabetes. It is a syndrome of profound dehydration resulting from a sustained hyperglycemic diuresis under circumstances in which the patient is unable to drink sufficient water to keep up with urinary fluid losses. Commonly an elderly diabetic—often living alone or in a nursing home—develops a stroke or infection, which worsens hyperglycemia and prevents adequate water intake. The full-blown syndrome probably does not occur until volume depletion has become severe enough to decrease urine output. Hyperosmolar coma has also been precipitated by therapeutic procedures such as peritoneal dialysis or hemodialysis, tube feeding of high-protein formulas, high-carbohydrate infusion loads, and the use of osmotic agents such as mannitol and urea. Phenytoin, steroids, immunosuppressive agents, and diuretics have also been reported to initiate the disorder.

The absence of ketoacidosis is important in the pathophysiology. When ketoacidosis occurs in an insulin-dependent diabetic, nausea, vomiting, and air hunger bring the patient to the physician before extreme dehydration can occur. Such a protective mechanism is not operative in the ketoacidosis-resistant, maturity-onset diabetic. Interestingly, hyperosmolar coma can occur in insulin-dependent diabetic patients given sufficient insulin to prevent ketosis but insufficient to control hyperglycemia. Although unusual, the same patient may present on one occasion with ketoacidosis and on the next with hyperosmolar coma.

The reason for the absence of ketoacidosis in maturity-onset diabetics is not known. The hepatic ketogenic machinery is not

TABLE 327-11   Clues to complications in diabetic ketoacidosis

Complication	Clues
Acute gastric dilatation or erosive gastritis	Vomiting of blood or coffee-ground material
Cerebral edema	Obtundation or coma with or without neurologic signs, especially if occurring after initial improvement
Hyperkalemia	Cardiac arrest
Hypoglycemia	Adrenergic or neurologic signs; rebound ketosis
Hypokalemia	Cardiac arrhythmias
Infection	Fever
Insulin resistance	Unremitting acidosis after 4–6 h of adequate therapy
Myocardial infarction	Chest pain, appearance of heart failure; appearance of hypotension despite adequate fluids
Mucormycosis	Facial pain, bloody nasal discharge, blackened nasal turbinates, blurred vision, proptosis
Respiratory distress syndrome	Hypoxemia in the absence of pneumonia, chronic pulmonary disease, or heart failure
Vascular thrombosis	Strokelike picture or signs of ischemia in nonnervous tissue

SOURCE: *Adapted from DW Foster, Diabetic ketoacidosis, in* Current Therapy in Endocrinology and Metabolism 1985–1986, *DT Krieger, CW Bardin (eds), Toronto/Philadelphia, Decker, 1985, pp 268–270.*

impaired since the patients frequently have ketone concentrations in the starvation range (2 to 4 mM). Free fatty acid levels are lower in hyperosmolar coma than in ketoacidosis, and substrate deficiency may limit ketone formation. That this is the sole mechanism seems unlikely since some patients with hyperosmolar coma have high levels of free fatty acids in plasma. A more likely explanation is that insulin concentrations in the portal vein of type 2 diabetics are higher than those of insulin-dependent subjects and prevent full activation of the hepatic carnitine acyltransferase system. Another possibility is that glucagon resistance plays a role.

Clinically patients present with extreme hyperglycemia, hyperosmolality, and volume depletion, coupled with central nervous system signs ranging from clouded sensorium to coma. Seizure activity—sometimes Jacksonian in type—is not unusual, and transient hemiplegia may be seen. Infections, particularly pneumonia and gram-negative sepsis, are common and indicate a grave prognosis. Pneumonia is often due to gram-negative organisms. A high index of suspicion for infection should be maintained, and routine culture of the blood and spinal fluid is indicated. Because of the extreme dehydration plasma viscosity is high, and widespread in situ thrombosis has been found at post mortem. Bleeding, probably the consequence of disseminated intravascular coagulation and acute pancreatitis may accompany the illness.

The laboratory findings in two large series are shown in Table 327-12. Plasma glucose is generally around 1000 mg/dL, about twice the value seen in ketoacidosis. The serum osmolality is extremely high, but because of the hyperglycemia the absolute serum sodium concentration is often not elevated.[3] Prerenal azotemia with marked elevation of BUN and creatinine is characteristic. A mild metabolic acidosis is present, plasma bicarbonate on the average being about 20 meq per liter. The acidosis is due to a combination of starvation ketosis, retention of inorganic acids secondary to the azotemia, and modest elevation of plasma lactate, the latter the consequence of volume depletion. If the bicarbonate is less than 10 meq per liter and plasma ketones are not elevated, it can be assumed that lactic acidosis is present.

The mortality rate in hyperosmolar coma is high (>50 percent). As a consequence immediate treatment is urgent. The most important measure is rapid administration of large amounts of intravenous fluids to reestablish the circulation and urine flow. The average fluid deficit is 10 liters. While free water will ultimately be needed, initial therapy should be with isotonic salt solutions, and 2 to 3 liters should be

[3] *Serum osmolality can be estimated from the formula*

Serum osmolality (mosmol/liter)

$$= 2([Na^+] + [K^+]) + \frac{glucose\ (mg/dL)}{18} + \frac{BUN\ (mg/dL)}{2.8}$$

In practice the contribution of the BUN is often ignored since it contributes to total osmolality but does not reflect the free water deficit. There are situations in clinical medicine in which an increased osmolality is not equivalent to dehydration. Severe alcohol intoxication is the classic example, the ethanol itself providing the measured milliosmoles.

given over the first 1 to 2 h. Subsequently half-strength saline can be used. As the plasma glucose approaches normal levels, 5% dextrose can be given as a vehicle for free water. While hyperosmolar coma may be reversed by fluids alone, insulin should be given to control the hyperglycemia more rapidly. Many authors recommend small doses of insulin, but larger amounts may be necessary, particularly in the obese patient. Potassium salts are usually required earlier in the treatment of hyperosmolar coma than in ketoacidosis because the intracellular shift of plasma K$^+$ during therapy is accelerated in the absence of acidosis. If lactic acidosis is present, sodium bicarbonate should be given until tissue perfusion can be reestablished (see Chap. 328). Antibiotics are required if infection complicates the picture.

LATE COMPLICATIONS OF DIABETES The diabetic patient is susceptible to a series of complications that cause morbidity and premature mortality. While some patients may never develop these problems and others note their onset early, on the average symptoms develop 15 to 20 years following the appearance of overt hyperglycemia. A given patient may experience several complications simultaneously, or a single problem may dominate the picture.

Circulatory abnormalities Arteriosclerosis of the type seen in nondiabetics occurs more extensively and earlier than in the general population. The cause for this accelerated atherosclerosis is not known, although, as discussed below, nonenzymatic glycosylation of lipoproteins may be important. Atherosclerotic lesions produce symptoms in a variety of sites. Peripheral deposits may cause intermittent claudication, gangrene, and, in men, organic impotence on a vascular basis. Surgical repair of large vessel lesions may be unsuccessful because of the simultaneous presence of widespread disease of the small vessels. Coronary artery disease and stroke are common. Silent myocardial infarction is thought to occur with increased frequency in diabetics and should be suspected whenever symptoms of left ventricular failure appear suddenly. Diabetes may also be associated with the clinical picture of cardiomyopathy, in which heart failure occurs in the face of angiographically normal coronary arteries and the absence of other identifiable causes of heart disease. As in nondiabetic subjects, smoking is a major risk factor for both coronary and peripheral vascular disease and should be avoided.

Retinopathy Diabetic retinopathy is a leading cause of blindness in the United States. On the other hand, most diabetics never become blind. Retinopathic lesions are divided into two large categories, *simple* (background) and *proliferative* (Table 327-13). The earliest sign of retinal change is an increased capillary permeability that is evidenced by leakage of dye into the vitreous humor after fluorescein injection. Occlusion of retinal capillaries follows, with subsequent formation of saccular and fusiform aneurysms. Arteriovenous shunts also occur. The vascular lesions are accompanied by proliferation of lining endothelial cells and a loss of the pericytes that surround and

TABLE 327-12   Initial laboratory findings in hyperosmolar coma

Series	Brooklyn*	Washington†
Age	60	57
Glucose, mg/dL	1166	976
Sodium, mM	144	142
Potassium, mM	5	5
Chloride, mM	99	98
Bicarbonate, mM	17	22
BUN, mg/dL	87	65
Creatinine, mg/dL	5.5	—
Free fatty acids, mM	0.73	0.96
Osmolarity, mosmol/liter	384	374

* *Mean data from 33 episodes of hyperosmolar coma (AA Arieff, HJ Carroll, Medicine 51:73, 1972).*
† *Mean data from 20 episodes of hyperosmolar coma (JE Gerich et al, Diabetes 20:228, 1971).*

TABLE 327-13   Lesions of diabetic retinopathy

BACKGROUND

Increased capillary permeability
Capillary closure and dilatation
Microaneurysms
Arteriovenous shunts
Dilated veins
Hemorrhages (dot and blot)
Cotton-wool spots
Hard exudates

PROLIFERATIVE

New vessels
Scar (retinitis proliferans)
Vitreal hemorrhage
Retinal detachment

support the vessels. Hemorrhages into the inner retinal areas are dot-shaped, while bleeding into the more superficial nerve fiber layer causes flame-shaped, blot, or linear lesions. Preretinal hemorrhages characteristically have a boat-shaped appearance. Exudates are of two types. Cotton-wool spots can be shown by angiography to be microinfarcts—nonperfused areas surrounded by a ring of dilated capillaries. A sudden increase in the number of cotton-wool spots represents an ominous prognostic sign and may herald the appearance of rapidly advancing retinopathy. Hard exudates are more common than cotton-wool spots and probably represent leakage of protein and lipids from damaged capillaries.

The fundamental characteristics of proliferative retinopathy are new vessel formation and scarring. The stimulus for neovascularization may be hypoxia secondary to capillary or arteriolar occlusion. Two serious complications of proliferative retinopathy are vitreal hemorrhage and retinal detachment. Either may cause a sudden loss of vision in one eye.

The frequency of diabetic retinopathy appears to vary with the age of onset as well as the duration of the disease. Approximately 85 percent of patients eventually develop the complication, but some never develop lesions even after 30 years of disease. Retinopathy appears to develop earlier in older patients, but proliferative retinopathy is less common. Some 10 to 18 percent of patients with simple retinopathy progress to proliferative disease in a 10-year period. About half of patients with proliferative disease progress to blindness within 5 years.

Treatment for diabetic retinopathy is photocoagulation. Such treatment decreases the incidence of hemorrhage and scarring and is always indicated when new vessel formation occurs. Photocoagulation is also useful in treatment of microaneurysms, hemorrhages, and edema even if the proliferative stage has not begun. Panretinal photocoagulation is sometimes used to diminish retinal demands for oxygen in the hope that the stimulus for neovascularization will be decreased. In this technique several thousand lesions are produced over a 2-week period. Complications of photocoagulation are within the acceptable range. Some loss of peripheral vision is inevitable with extensive burns. Another surgical technique, pars plana vitrectomy, is utilized for treatment of nonresolving vitreal hemorrhage and retinal detachment. Postoperative complications are more frequent than with photocoagulation and include retinal tears, retinal detachment, cataracts, recurrent vitreal hemorrhage, glaucoma, infection, and loss of the eye. Hypophysectomy, once widely performed for diabetic retinopathy, is no longer recommended. All patients with diabetic retinopathy should be followed by retinal specialists.

Diabetic nephropathy   Renal disease is a leading cause of death and disability in diabetes. One-fourth or more of end-stage renal disease in the United States is now due to diabetic nephropathy. Approximately 40 to 50 percent of patients with insulin-dependent diabetes develop this complication. Prevalence may be somewhat less with the non-insulin-dependent form of the disease, possibly because duration of illness tends to be shorter. However, two-thirds of diabetic Pima Indians (who have non-insulin-dependent diabetes) have diabetic glomerulosclerosis at autopsy.

Diabetic nephropathy involves two distinct pathologic patterns that may or may not coexist: diffuse and nodular. The former, which is more common, consists of widening of the glomerular basement membrane together with generalized mesangial thickening. In the nodular form large accumulations of PAS-positive material are deposited at the periphery of the glomerular tufts, the Kimmelstiel-Wilson lesion. In addition, there may be hyalinization of afferent and efferent arterioles, "drops" in Bowman's capsule, fibrin caps, and occlusion of glomeruli. Deposition of albumin and other proteins occurs in both glomeruli and tubules. The most specific lesions of diabetic glomerulosclerosis are hyalinization of afferent glomerular arterioles and the Kimmelstiel-Wilson nodules. Clinical renal dysfunction in diabetes does not correlate well with the histologic abnormalities.

Diabetic nephropathy may be functionally silent for long periods (~10 to 15 years). At onset of diabetes the kidneys are usually enlarged with "superfunction," i.e., glomerular filtration rates may be 40 percent above normal. The next stage is the appearance of *microproteinuria* (microalbuminuria), the excretion of albumin in the range of 30 to 300 mg per 24 h. Normal persons excrete less than 30 mg per 24 h. Microalbuminuria is not detected by reagent sticks for urinary protein, which generally become positive only when proteinuria is greater than 550 mg per 24 h, a degree of leakage termed *macroproteinuria*. Since microalbuminuria is initially transient and can be induced by mechanisms other than diabetes, diagnosis requires an excretion rate of albumin greater than 20 μg/h (~30 mg per 24 h) in two of three samples collected in a 6-month period. Persistent leakage of protein >50 mg per 24 h is statistically predictive of subsequent macroproteinuria. Once the macroproteinuric phase begins, there is a steady decline in renal function with glomerular filtration rate falling, on average, about 1 mL/min per month. A plot of the reciprocal of the serum creatinine against time usually results in a straight line and allows assessment of the rate of deterioration. Ordinarily azotemia begins about 12 years after diagnosis of diabetes. The nephrotic syndrome may occur prior to azotemia. Progression of renal disease is accelerated by hypertension.

There is no specific treatment for diabetic nephropathy. Meticulous control of diabetes can reverse microalbuminuria in some patients, but there is no evidence that diabetic nephropathy can be prevented by intensive insulin therapy. Hypertension must be treated aggressively whenever present. Low-protein diets may be useful, based on experimental studies in animals, but no prospective study has appeared testing protein restriction in diabetic humans. Once the azotemic phase is reached, treatment does not differ from other forms of renal failure. Chronic dialysis and renal transplantation are routine in patients with renal failure due to diabetes. Hyporeninemic hypoaldosteronism, which is associated with renal tubular acidosis, may require alkalinizing solutions (Shohl's solution) and avoidance of external potassium loads. Rarely, fludrocortisone may be required to control hyperkalemia.

Diabetic neuropathy   Diabetic neuropathy may affect every part of the nervous system with the possible exception of the brain. While it is rarely a direct cause of death, it is a major cause of morbidity. Distinct syndromes can be recognized, and several different types of neuropathy may be present in the same patient. The most common picture is that of *peripheral polyneuropathy*. Usually bilateral, the symptoms include numbness, paresthesias, severe hyperesthesias, and pain. The pain, which may be deep-seated and severe, is often worse at night. It is occasionally lancinating or lightning in type, resembling tabes dorsalis (pseudotabes). Fortunately extreme pain syndromes are usually self-limited, lasting from a few months to a few years. Involvement of proprioceptive fibers leads to abnormalities of gait and development of typical Charcot joints, particularly in the feet. Loss of arch with multiple fractures of tarsal bones is a common finding by x-ray. On physical examination absent stretch reflexes and loss of vibratory sense are early signs. Diabetic neuropathy may also cause delay in return of the ankle reflex identical to that seen in hypothyroidism. *Mononeuropathy,* though less common than polyneuropathy, may also occur. Characteristically there is a sudden wrist drop, foot drop, or paralysis of the third, fourth, or sixth cranial nerves. Other single nerves, including the recurrent laryngeal, have been reported to be involved. Mononeuropathy is characterized by a high degree of spontaneous reversibility, usually over a several-week period. *Radiculopathy* is a sensory syndrome in which pain occurs over the distribution of one or more spinal nerves, usually in the chest wall or abdomen. The severe pain may mimic herpes zoster or an acute surgical abdomen. Like mononeuropathy, the lesion is usually self-limited. *Autonomic neuropathy* may present in a variety of ways. The gastrointestinal tract is a prime target, and there may be esophageal dysfunction with difficulty in swallowing, delayed gastric emptying, constipation, or diarrhea. The last is often nocturnal.

Incompetence of the internal anal sphincter may mimic diabetic diarrhea. Patients may suffer from orthostatic hypotension and frank syncope. Cardiorespiratory arrest and sudden death, thought to be due solely to autonomic neuropathy, have been reported. Bladder dysfunction or paralysis is particularly distressing and often leads to the necessity of chronic catheter drainage. Impotence and retrograde ejaculation are additional manifestations in the male. Clues to autonomic neuropathy can be obtained by clinical tests such as measuring response of the heart rate to the Valsalva maneuver or standing. In both tests the subject has an electrocardiograph running for assessment of heart rate. In the former the subject blows against an anaeroid or mercury manometer to 40 mmHg pressure for 15 s. The test is performed three times with a rest period of 1 min in between. Normally the heart rate speeds during Valsalva such that the ratio of the longest interval between beats after release to the shortest interval during the test is >1.2. In autonomic neuropathy involving the parasympathetic system the ratio is <1:1. Similarly the ratio at the thirtieth beat after standing relative to that at the fifteenth beat should be >1.0. It is <1 in autonomic neuropathy. Diabetic *amyotrophy* is likely a form of neuropathy, although atrophy and weakness of the large muscles in the upper leg and pelvic girdle resemble primary muscle disease. Anorexia and depression may accompany amyotrophy.

Treatment of diabetic neuropathy is unsatisfactory in most respects. When pain is severe, it is easy for the patient to become habituated or addicted to narcotics or powerful nonnarcotic analgesics such as pentazocine. If the pain requires something more powerful than aspirin, acetaminophen, or other nonsteroidal anti-inflammatory agents, codeine is the drug of choice. Phenytoin is used by some physicians, but others have not found it helpful. Combination therapy with amitriptyline and fluphenazine causes significant relief of pain in some patients and should always be tried. The recommended dosage is 75 mg amitriptyline at bedtime and 1 mg fluphenazine three times a day. Mononeuropathies and radiculopathies usually require no specific therapy since they are self-limited. Diabetic diarrhea often responds to treatment with diphenoxylate and atropine or loperamide. Orthostatic hypotension is best treated by having the patient sleep with the head of the bed elevated, avoidance of sudden assumption of the upright position, and the use of full-length elastic stockings. Occasionally volume expansion with fludrocortisone is required as in other forms of orthostatic hypotension.

Symptoms of neuropathy may improve following administration of oral myoinositol, an inhibitor of aldose reductase, the enzyme responsible for formation of sorbitol in tissues. These approaches remain experimental at the time of this writing.

Diabetic foot ulcers A special problem in the diabetic patient is the development of ulcers of the feet and lower extremities. The ulcers appear to be primarily due to abnormal pressure distribution secondary to diabetic neuropathy. The problem is accentuated when there is bony distortion in the feet. Callus formation is usually the initial abnormality. Alternatively the ulcer may be initiated by ill-fitting shoes which cause blister formation in patients whose sensory deficits preclude recognition of pain. Cuts and punctures from foreign bodies such as needles, tacks, and glass are common, and a foreign body of which the patient is unaware may be found in the soft tissue. For this reason all patients with ulcers should have x-rays made of the feet. Vascular disease with diminished blood supply contributes to development of the lesion, and infection is common, often with multiple organisms. While no specific therapy is available for diabetic ulcers, aggressive supportive treatment can often lead to salvation of the leg without amputation. One approach is to simply put the patient to bed using frequent foot soaks and debridement to remove nonviable tissue. Others recommend casting the leg with plaster to remove weight bearing and protect the lesion.

All diabetics should be instructed about proper foot care in an attempt to prevent ulcers. Feet should be kept clean and dry at all times. Patients with neuropathy should not be allowed to walk barefoot, even in the home. Properly fitted shoes are essential. This is a particular problem with women, since an adequate shoe for the diabetic is not often stylish. The feet should be carefully inspected daily for callus, infection, abrasions, or blisters and the physician consulted for any potentially troublesome lesion.

What causes diabetes complications? The cause of diabetic complications is not known and may be multifactorial. Major emphasis has been placed on the polyol pathway wherein glucose is reduced to sorbitol by the enzyme aldol reductase. Sorbitol, which appears to function as a tissue toxin, has been implicated in the pathogenesis of retinopathy, neuropathy, cataracts, nephropathy, and aortic disease. The mechanism is perhaps best worked out in experimental diabetic neuropathy where sorbitol accumulation is associated with a decrease in myoinositol content, abnormal phosphoinositide metabolism, and a decrease in $[Na^+ + K^+]$-ATPase activity. In experimental models primacy of the polyol pathway in initiating neuropathy was proven by showing that inhibition of aldol reductase prevented the fall in tissue myoinositol content and the decrease in ATPase activity. Aldol reductase inhibition has also been shown to prevent experimental cataracts and retinopathy. It thus seems possible that neuropathy and retinopathy are primarily due to activation of the polyol pathway. The latter may also play a role in diabetic nephropathy.

A second mechanism of potential pathogenetic importance is nonenzymatic glycosylation of proteins. The effect of such glycosylation on hemoglobin has been mentioned, but multiple proteins in the body are altered in the same way, often with disturbed functions. Examples include plasma albumin, lens protein, fibrin, collagen, lipoproteins, and the glycoprotein recognition system of hepatic endothelial cells. Particularly intriguing is the effect of glycosylation on lipoproteins. Glycosylated low-density lipoprotein (LDL) is not recognized by the normal LDL receptor, and its plasma half-life is increased. Conversely, glycosylated high-density lipoprotein (HDL) turns over more rapidly than native HDL. It has also been reported that glycosylated collagen traps LDL at rates two to three times greater than normal collagen. Conceivably the accelerated atherosclerosis of diabetes might be related to the combined effect of a glycosylated LDL that did not bind normally to LDL receptors but would be trapped to a greater than normal extent in macrophages and glycosylated collagen of blood vessels and other tissues. Dysfunctional HDL could contribute by diminishing cholesterol transport out of affected sites.

Glycosylated collagen is less soluble and more resistant to degradation by collagenase than native collagen. However, it is not clear that this is related either to the basement membrane thickening or the tight, waxy skin syndrome with limited joint mobility (scleroderma-like) seen in some patients with insulin-dependent diabetes (see ''Miscellaneous Abnormalities,'' below). Although it is attractive to presume that nonenzymatic glycosylation of proteins plays a role in some degenerative complications, the evidence is less direct than with the polyol pathway.

Increased blood flow has been postulated to play an initiating role in diabetic complications, possibly by increasing filtration of macromolecules that function as tissue toxins. There is supportive evidence for a role of hyperperfusion in diabetic nephropathy, but the hemodynamic hypothesis does not appear as attractive as the first two.

Can diabetic complications be prevented by meticulous control of diabetes? The critical question in diabetic therapy is whether hyperglycemia or some associated metabolic disorder causes or accelerates the development of the long-term complications just discussed. The alternative possibility is that complications are primarily determined by genetic factors independent of hyperglycemia. Perhaps the strongest evidence that the metabolic environment per se causes complications comes from the observation that kidneys from donors who have neither diabetes nor a family history of diabetes develop characteristic lesions of diabetic nephropathy within 3 to 5 years after transplantation into a diabetic recipient. Diabetic nephropathy did not develop when a kidney was transplanted into a diabetic subject whose disease had been reversed by pancreatic transplantation prior to renal transplantation. It has also been reported that kidneys with the lesions of diabetic nephropathy demonstrated reversal of the lesion when transplanted into normal recipients. All of these findings suggest that hyperglycemia or some other aspect of the abnormal metabolism of diabetes causes or influences the development of complications. On the other hand additional factors, probably genetic, must play a role. This follows from the fact that diabetic subjects with decades of poor control may escape the ravages of the late complications and from the fact that typical diabetic complications may be found in patients at the time of diagnosis of diabetes or even in the absence of hyperglycemia.

Meticulous control with insulin infusion pumps has been reported to decrease microalbuminuria, alter motor nerve conduction velocity, lower plasma lipoproteins, and decrease capillary leakage of fluorescein in the retina. Width of the capillary basement membrane in skeletal muscle has also been decreased. The changes are small in general, however, and of questionable biologic significance. Firm evidence does not exist to show that late complications can be either prevented or reversed by long-term near-normalization of the plasma glucose. Hopefully, definitive answers to this question may be forthcoming from a large multicenter trial now underway under the sponsorship of the National Institutes of Health.

Until the issue is clarified it is prudent to maintain the plasma glucose as near normal as possible in all diabetic patients. About this there appears to be no disagreement. The only question is whether insulin therapy should be routinely aggressive to the point where recurrent hypoglycemia occurs. A mild insulin reaction consisting of nervousness, tremor, hunger, and sweating that is rapidly interrupted by carbohydrate intake is probably not harmful except for the possibility of worsening diabetic control via the Somogyi reaction. Unfortunately, as stated earlier, many diabetics, particularly those with long-standing disease and autonomic neuropathy, do not have or do not recognize the usual warning signals and progress to altered central nervous system function with abnormal behavior, loss of consciousness, or even convulsions. The latter reactions are dangerous for both patient and society. Every effort should be made to control hyperglycemia, but the limit of therapy should be the appearance of hypoglycemic reactions. It does not seem wise to induce a condition that can cause immediate and irreversible damage to a patient in the unproven hope that late complications might be prevented.

Miscellaneous abnormalities of diabetes   Diabetes affects almost every system in the body. Space limitations preclude discussion of all associated features, but several deserve comment. *Infections* in diabetics may not occur more frequently than in normal subjects, but they tend to be more severe. This may be due to impaired leukocyte function, a frequent accompaniment of poor control. In addition to common infections of the skin, urinary tract, lungs, and bloodstream, three unusual conditions appear to have specific relationship with diabetes. *Malignant external otitis,* usually due to *Pseudomonas aeruginosa,* tends to occur in older patients and is characterized by severe pain in the ear, drainage, fever, and leukocytosis. Soft tissues around the ear are swollen and tender. A mound of granulation tissue is characteristically present internally at the junction of the osseous and cartilaginous portions of the ear. The facial nerve becomes paralyzed in half the cases, and other cranial nerves may also be involved. Facial nerve paralysis is a poor prognostic sign, and mortality approximates 50 percent in this subset of patients. A 6-week course of ticarcillin or carbenicillin together with tobramycin is the treatment of choice. Surgical debridement is often necessary. *Rhinocerebral mucormycosis* is a rare fungal infection which usually develops in patients during or following an episode of diabetic ketoacidosis. Organisms are from the genera *Mucor, Rhizopus,* and *Absidia.* Onset is sudden with periorbital and perinasal swelling, pain, bloody nasal discharge, and increased lacrimation. The nasal mucosa and underlying tissues become black and necrotic. Cranial

nerve palsies are not uncommon. There may be thrombosis of the internal jugular vein or sinuses of the brain. Proptosis, chemosis, and retinal vein engorgement indicate cavernous sinus thrombosis. Untreated, death usually occurs in a week to 10 days. Amphotericin B and aggressive debridement are the indicated therapies. *Emphysematous cholecystitis* tends to affect diabetic men (in contrast to ordinary cholecystitis, a disease predominantly present in women). Gangrene of the gallbladder is 30 times more frequent than in the usual forms, accounting for high rates of perforation and a mortality rate 3 to 10 times higher than in ordinary cholecystitis. Diagnosis is made when gas is seen in the gallbladder wall on plain films of the abdomen. Clostridial species are frequently cultured from bile, but other organisms may be present. Treatment is cholecystectomy coupled with broad-spectrum antibiotics. Clindamycin and an aminoglycoside are adequate coverage until cultures are returned.

Hypertriglyceridemia is common in diabetes and is usually due to insulin deficiency. Both overproduction of very low density lipoproteins in the liver and a disposal defect in the periphery appear to be operative. The latter is a consequence of lipoprotein lipase deficiency, an insulin-dependent enzyme. Some diabetics exhibit hyperlipemia even when diabetic control is adequate, and these patients may have a primary familial hyperlipoproteinemia that is independent of diabetes. Clofibrate is the drug of choice for treatment in subjects unresponsive to diet and insulin therapy.

Some diabetics have *recurrent hyperkalemia* in association with hyperglycemia. Hyperkalemia can occur in the absence of potassium loads, and serum potassium concentrations may rise acutely in response to oral glucose in contrast to normals in whom glucose ingestion produces a fall in potassium levels. The presumption is that potassium shifts from intracellular to extracellular water under these circumstances. Traditionally these patients have been considered to have hyporeninemic hypoaldosteronism although basal renin and aldosterone concentrations may be normal. Since the capacity to increase aldosterone production in response to stimulatory signals is impaired even when basal levels are normal, probably functional hypoaldosteronism plays a central role in the syndrome. With a deficiency of aldosterone, renal secretion of potassium is impaired and disposal of a potassium load is dependent on insulin-mediated transport of the cation into the intracellular space. Administration of potassium salts or triamterene to such patients may be dangerous. Whether potassium transport is directly regulated by insulin or is secondary to glucose movement is not clear.

A variety of skin lesions occur in diabetes. *Necrobiosis lipoidica diabeticorum* is a plaque-like lesion with a central yellowish area surrounded by a brownish border. It is usually found over the anterior surfaces of the legs. Ulceration may occur (see Fig. A1-28). *Diabetic dermopathy* is also usually located over the anterior tibial surface. The lesions are small rounded plaques with a raised border which may crust at the edges and ulcerate centrally. Several plaques may be arranged in linear fashion. Pigmentation is not prominent early, but as the lesion heals a depressed scar occurs with diffuse brown discoloration. A rarer abnormality is *bullosis diabeticorum.* The bullae may be superficial with clear serum or may be mildly hemorrhagic. The cause is unknown. *Infestations of the skin* with Candida and dermatophytes are common, and bacterial infections of a variety of types occur. In women *vaginal moniliasis* may be troublesome during hyperglycemic-glycosuric periods. While the symptoms respond to nystatin or gentian violet, recurrence is inevitable unless glycosuria is reversed. *Atrophy of adipose tissue* may occur at the site of insulin injections. The lipoatrophy is said to respond to injection of purified insulin into the atrophic area.

Hyperviscosity occurs in diabetes, and *platelets aggregate abnormally.* The latter may be caused by increased prostaglandin synthesis. *Wound healing* is impaired in experimental diabetes but probably is not a major factor clinically. An interesting accompaniment of insulin-dependent diabetes is the presence of *joint contractures* coupled with *tight, waxy skin* over the dorsum of the hands. The hands resemble those in patients with scleroderma. The cause of the tendon contractures is unknown although alterations of cross-linking in collagen has been proposed. Patients with the joint contracture–waxy skin syndrome appear to have accelerated development of other diabetic complications. *Scleredema* is a common finding in diabetes. The lesion is a thickening of the skin over the shoulders and upper back that resembles scleroderma. The lesion is benign.

Future directions Research aimed at therapy of established diabetes continues. From the pharmacologic standpoint the search for an orally active antiglucagon is ongoing. Likewise development of a somatostatin analogue that would be relatively specific in blocking glucagon release with lesser activity against growth hormone is of high priority. Such an analogue would have to be orally absorbed and have a longer biologic half-life than native somatostatin. Insulin has been successfully given by nasal insufflation, but the clinical usefulness of this approach in the broad spectrum of diabetic patients is uncertain.

Hopes remain that transplantation of islet cells will be possible in humans. Considerable success has been achieved in experimental animals, but human trials have thus far been unpromising. Segmental transplantation of the vascularized whole human pancreas has also been carried out, but overall complication rates have been high. Techniques for islet cell transplantation that remove antigen-presenting cells (such that immunosuppression is not required) may eventually be applicable in humans, but the problem of islet cell supply will be a formidable obstacle. There is also concern that in type 1 patients the transplanted islets will succumb to the same immunologic mechanism that caused diabetes, as mentioned earlier. An alternative approach would be to activate insulin production in cells in which the gene is normally turned off utilizing techniques of molecular biology. This has already been achieved in vitro, but for maintenance of a normal plasma glucose the activated gene would have to be placed in a cell that is fuel-responsive, i.e., releases hormones only in response to substrate signal. Uncontrolled insulin release would mimic an insulinoma.

The possibility of preventing type 1 diabetes by suppression of the immune system prior to destruction of the beta-cell mass has also received attention. In one study treatment with cyclosporine restored insulin secretory capacity and reversed diabetes in about two-thirds of patients treated within the first 6 weeks of diagnosis. Unfortunately, hyperglycemia returned when cyclosporine was stopped, suggesting that immunosuppression must be constant. Continual use of cyclosporine, even at low doses, would appear to be an unacceptable risk, but it might be possible to modulate the immune system with safer drugs and accomplish the same aims. In an ideal program persons at increased risk for developing type 1 diabetes, primarily first-degree relatives of a patient with this disease, would be typed for genetic susceptibility. Persons with haploidentity to the index case would be followed prospectively for appearance of islet cell antibodies and diminution of insulin reserve. At the earliest sign of immune attack against the beta cell, immunosuppression would be started. Careful double-blind trials would be required to prove effectiveness.

INSULIN RESISTANCE Insulin resistance is arbitrarily said to exist when more than 200 units per day are required to control hyperglycemia and prevent ketosis. Relative insulin resistance occurs with lower insulin requirements, but therapy for the resistant state is usually not considered necessary below the 200-unit level. Insulin antibodies of IgG type are present in essentially all diabetics within 60 days of the initiation of insulin therapy. The titer of these antibodies fluctuates for reasons that are not clear. Although the correlation between antibody titer and functional resistance is not close, insulin binding by high levels of antibody is presumed to be the primary mechanism in most cases. Probably less than 0.1 percent of insulin-treated diabetics ever have significant resistance. The problem may appear within a few weeks of the start of therapy or many years later. The onset may be abrupt, resulting in ketoacidosis, but usually is gradual, with uncontrollable hyperglycemia being the major problem. About 20 to 30 percent of patients have concomitant insulin allergy. Therapy of the syndrome requires prednisone in large

amounts—80 to 100 mg per day initially. Response often occurs in 48 to 72 h but may take longer. If no improvement has resulted after 3 to 4 weeks it can be assumed that steroids will not be effective. Once insulin requirements begin to fall, prednisone dosage can be rapidly decreased by 10 to 20 mg every 3 to 7 days until a maintenance level of 5 to 10 mg per day is reached. These levels may be required for many months. Whether remission has occurred, allowing cessation of therapy, can only be determined by trial. On rare occasions insulin resistance in diabetics appears to be due to enhanced destruction of the hormone at the subcutaneous injection site. Such patients tend to respond normally to insulin given intravenously or intraperitoneally. In some patients addition of a protease inhibitor (aprotinin) to the insulin mixture has been helpful. When resistance is extreme, U500 regular insulin should be used in order to control the volume of the injection.

Insulin resistance may occur in diseases other than diabetes. The physiologic consequences can be minor or severe. A variety of insulin-resistant syndromes are associated with *acanthosis nigricans,* a brown to black, velvety hyperpigmentation of the skin in the axilla, groin, neck, umbilicus, and other areas. Although acanthosis nigricans may be a sign of occult malignancy, it is not associated with neoplasia in the insulin-resistant states. A classification of insulin resistance based on the absence or presence of acanthosis nigricans is given in Table 327-14. *Obesity* and *antibodies* to insulin are by far the most common causes of insulin resistance, and neither is accompanied by acanthosis. Obesity is associated with diminished insulin receptor number and affinity but also has postreceptor hormone resistance. *Werner's syndrome* is an autosomal recessive illness with a high incidence of hyperglycemia despite elevated concentrations of plasma insulin (see Chap. 334). There is little response to exogenous hormone. Other features include growth retardation, alopecia or premature graying of the hair, cataracts, hypogonadism, leg ulcers, atrophy of muscle, fat, and bone, soft-tissue calcification, and a high frequency of sarcomas and meningiomas.

Of the rare conditions associated with acanthosis nigricans, women with *insulin receptor abnormalities* have attracted the greatest interest. Type A patients are tall young women with a tendency to hirsutism and abnormalities of the reproductive tract who most probably have polycystic ovaries. However, other causes of androgen excess can induce the syndrome. The absolute number of insulin receptors is diminished. Type B subjects are older women with evidence of immunologic disease. The clinical picture includes arthralgias, alopecia, enlarged salivary glands, proteinuria, leukopenia, and antinuclear and anti-DNA antibodies. Insulin resistance in these patients is due to blocking antibodies to the insulin receptor (not to insulin itself). Interestingly, antireceptor antibodies may also cause hypoglycemia. The determinant of agonist (hypoglycemia) or antagonist (insulin resistance) activity presumably depends on the site of binding to the insulin receptor. Both A and B patients have high plasma insulin concentrations.

Generalized and *partial lipodystrophies* are fat depletion syndromes differing primarily in the extent of fat atrophy (see Chap.

TABLE 327-14 Insulin-resistant states

I Insulin resistance without acanthosis nigricans
  A Obesity
  B Diabetes mellitus with insulin antibodies
  C Werner's syndrome
II Insulin resistance with acanthosis nigricans
  A Insulin resistance with receptor abnormality
    1 Receptor deficiency (type A abnormality)
    2 Antibody to insulin receptor (type B abnormality)
  B Lipodystrophic states
    1 Generalized lipodystrophy (congenital or acquired)
    2 Partial lipodystrophy (congenital or acquired)
  C Syndrome of familial insulin resistance, somatic abnormalities, and pineal hyperplasia
  D The Alström syndrome
  E Ataxia-telangiectasia
  F Rabson-Mendenhall syndrome

318). In the generalized form essentially all body fat is missing, while the more common partial type exhibits atrophy of fat in the face and trunk with normal or increased adiposity in the lower half of the body. The disease can be either congenital or acquired. Typically the patients develop hyperglycemia at puberty, but ketoacidosis never occurs. Marked hypertriglyceridemia with eruptive xanthoma is a frequent feature. Characteristic features are hepatomegaly, splenomegaly, cardiomegaly, hirsutism, lymphadenopathy, hypertrophy of the external genitalia, varicose veins, and (in the congenital forms) muscle hypertrophy. Mental retardation is common, and renal disease may develop. The term *lipoatrophic diabetes* is synonymous with total lipodystrophy. All patients have elevated plasma insulin levels. Resistance may be due to decreased number of receptors, diminished affinity of the receptor for insulin, or a postreceptor defect.

The *pineal hypertrophy syndrome* is characterized by insulin resistance, early dentition with malformed teeth, dry skin, thick nails, hirsutism, and a peculiar sexual precocity with enlargement of the external genitalia. The latter may reach near adult size by age 3 or 4. The insulin resistance is severe, and ketoacidosis may occur despite high endogenous insulin levels. The *Alström syndrome* is a rare autosomal recessive disease characterized by childhood blindness due to retinal degeneration, nerve deafness, vasopressin-resistant diabetes insipidus, and, in males, hypogonadism with high plasma gonadotropin levels. The patients thus appear to have end organ resistance to multiple hormones. Other features include baldness, hyperuricemia, hypertriglyceridemia, and aminoaciduria. Superficially the patients may resemble subjects with the Lawrence-Moon-Biedl syndrome but can be differentiated on initial exam by the absence of polydactyly and mental deficiency. Insulin resistance in the Alström syndrome is mild. *Ataxia-telangiectasia* is characterized by cerebellar ataxia, telangiectasia, and a variety of abnormalities in the immune system in addition to insulin resistance. The *Rabson-Mendenhall syndrome* consists of dental dysplasia, dystrophic nails, premature puberty, and acanthosis nigricans. The insulin resistance is probably due to an insulin receptor abnormality. Not listed in Table 327-14 is insulin resistance due to hormone excess (acromegaly, Cushing's syndrome), myotonic dystrophy, and leprechaunism. The insulin resistance in these conditions is usually not clinically significant.

INSULIN ALLERGY Insulin allergy is due to IgE antibodies to insulin. Manifestations include immediate reactions with local stinging or itching, delayed local reactions with brawny swelling lasting up to 30 h, and generalized urticaria or frank anaphylaxis. Systemic reactions are usually seen in patients who have stopped insulin therapy for one reason or another and have then resumed treatment. The allergic reaction may occur as early as the second injection on resumption of therapy. Mild reactions can be treated with antihistamines. If the problem is severe, desensitization procedures are required. A 1-day insulin desensitization procedure is shown in Table 327-15. Once the patient is desensitized, insulin therapy should not be interrupted.

TABLE 327-15   Insulin desensitization*

Time, h	Dose, units	Route
0	0.001	Intradermal
0.5	0.002	Intradermal
1	0.004	Subcutaneous
1.5	0.01	Subcutaneous
2	0.02	Subcutaneous
2.5	0.04	Subcutaneous
3	0.1	Subcutaneous
3.5	0.2	Subcutaneous
4	0.5	Subcutaneous
4.5	1	Subcutaneous
5	2	Subcutaneous
5.5	4	Subcutaneous
6	8	Subcutaneous

* *Following desensitization, use 2 to 10 units of regular insulin every 4 to 6 h for 24 to 36 h after the 6-h injection before switching to intermediate-acting insulin.*
SOURCE: *Schedule of JA Galloway. For detailed information see JA Galloway, R Bressler, Med Clin North Amer 62:663, 1978.*

THE EMOTIONAL RESPONSE TO DIABETES Acceptance of the fact that a person has a chronic disease that requires a change in lifestyle is always difficult. This is particularly true in the case of diabetes since patients generally are aware that they are vulnerable to late complications and that life expectancy is shortened. It is not surprising that the emotional response to diabetes often hampers treatment. On the one hand, the primary reaction may be denial with an accompanying refusal to cooperate. At the other extreme is excessive preoccupation with the illness. The physician should make every effort to define a middle ground wherein the patient acknowledges his or her disease and responds prudently without becoming obsessed. The goal is to live with diabetes not for it. Diabetics are no different from other patients in that they may attempt to use their disease manipulatively with both family and physician. The problems are particularly acute with children and adolescents. While the psychiatric aspects of diabetes are not discussed here, most problems can be anticipated and handled if common sense is coupled with sympathy and firmness. It is also appropriate to offer cautious hope that the disease will be handled better in the future than is possible now.

REFERENCES

General review

UNGER RH, FOSTER DW: Diabetes mellitus, in *Williams' Textbook of Endocrinology*, 7th ed, JD Wilson, DW Foster (eds). Philadelphia, Saunders, 1985, pp 1018–1080

Pathophysiology

BOTTAZZO GF: β-Cell damage in diabetic insulitis: Are we approaching a solution? Diabetologia 26:241, 1984
——— et al: In situ characterization of autoimmune phenomena and expression of HLA molecules in the pancreas in diabetic insulitis. N Engl J Med 313:353, 1985
CAHILL GF JR, MCDEVITT HO: Insulin-dependent diabetes mellitus: The initial lesion. N Engl J Med 304:1454, 1981
DEFRONZO RA, FERRANNINI E: The pathogenesis of non-insulin-dependent diabetes: An update. Medicine 61:125, 1982
LERNMARK A: Molecular biology of type 1 (insulin-dependent) diabetes mellitus. Diabetologia 28:195, 1985
WARD WK et al: Diminished β-cell secretory capacity in patients with non-insulin-dependent diabetes. J Clin Invest 74:1318, 1984

Treatment

BANTLE JP et al: Postprandial glucose and insulin responses to meals containing different carbohydrates in normal and diabetic subjects. N Engl J Med 309:7, 1983
CRYER PE, GERICH JE: Glucose counterregulation, hypoglycemia, and intensive insulin therapy in diabetes mellitus. N Engl J Med 313:232, 1985
LEBOVITZ HE, FEINGLOS MN: The oral hypoglycemic agents, in *Diabetes Mellitus: Theory and Practice*, 3d ed, M Ellenberg, H Rifkin (eds). New Hyde Park, Medical Examination Publishing, 1983, pp 591–610
RASKIN P: Treatment of insulin-dependent diabetes mellitus with portable insulin infusion devices. Med Clin North Am 66:1269, 1982
SCHADE DS et al: *Intensive Insulin Therapy*. Princeton, Excerpta Medica, 1983
SCHIFFRIN A, BELMONTE MM: Comparison between subcutaneous insulin infusion and multiple injections of insulin: A one year prospective study. Diabetes 31:255, 1982
SIMONSON DC et al: Intensive insulin therapy reduces counterregulatory hormone responses to hypoglycemia in patients with type 1 diabetes. Ann Intern Med 103:184, 1985
SKYLER JS et al: Algorithms for adjustment of insulin dosage by patients who monitor blood glucose. Diabetes Care 4:311, 1981
WOLEVER TMS et al: Prediction of the relative blood glucose response of mixed meals using the white bread glycemic index. Diabetes Care 8:418, 1985

Acute complications

CARROLL P, MATZ R: Uncontrolled diabetes mellitus in adults: Experience in treating diabetic ketoacidosis and hyperosmolar nonketotic coma with low-dose insulin and a uniform treatment regimen. Diabetes Care 6:579, 1983
FOSTER DW: From glycogen to ketones—and back. Diabetes 33:1188, 1984
———, MCGARRY JD: The metabolic derangements and treatment of diabetic ketoacidosis. N Engl J Med 309:159, 1983
FRANKLIN B et al: Cerebral edema and ophthalmoplegia reversed by mannitol in a new case of insulin-dependent diabetes mellitus. Pediatrics 69:87, 1982

Late complications

BROWNLEE M et al: Nonenzymatic glycosylation and the pathogenesis of diabetic complications. Ann Intern Med 101:527, 1984
DORMAN JS et al: The Pittsburgh insulin-dependent diabetes mellitus (IDDM) morbidity and mortality study: Case-control analyses of risk factors for mortality. Diabetes Care 8 (Suppl 1):54, 1985

GREENE DA et al: Glucose-induced alterations in nerve metabolism: Current perspective on the pathogenesis of diabetic neuropathy and future directions for research and therapy. Diabetes Care 8:290, 1985

LESTRADET H et al: Long-term study of mortality and vascular complications in juvenile-onset (type 1) diabetes. Diabetes 30:175, 1981

LOGERFO FW, COFFMAN JD: Vascular and microvascular disease of the foot in diabetes. N Engl J Med 311:1615, 1984

MOGENSEN CE, CHRISTENSEN CK: Predicting diabetic nephropathy in insulin-dependent patients. N Engl J Med 311:89, 1984

PARVING HH et al: Hemodynamic factors in the genesis of diabetic microangiopathy. Metabolism 32:943, 1983

STEFFES MW et al: Studies of kidney and muscle biopsy specimens from identical twins discordant for type 1 diabetes mellitus. N Engl J Med 312:1282, 1985

VIBERTI G, KEEN H: The patterns of proteinuria in diabetes mellitus. Relevance to pathogenesis and prevention of diabetic nephropathy. Diabetes 33:686, 1984

Future directions

ALEJANDRO R et al: Successful long-term survival of pancreatic islet allografts in spontaneous or pancreatectomy-induced diabetes in dogs. Cyclosporine-induced immune unresponsiveness. Diabetes 34:825, 1985

EISENBARTH GS: Immunotherapy of type 1 diabetes. Diabetes Care 6:521, 1983

FAUSTMAN D et al: Prolongation of murine islet allograft survival by pretreatment of islets with antibody directed to Ia determinants. Proc Natl Acad Sci USA 78:5156, 1981

LAFFERTY KJ, PROWSE SJ: Theory and practice of immunoregulation by tissue treatment prior to transplantation. World J Surg 8:187, 1984

STILLER CR et al: Effects of cyclosporine immunosuppression in insulin-dependent diabetes mellitus of recent onset. Science 223:1362, 1984

Insulin resistance

FLIER JS et al: Acanthosis nigricans in obese women with hyperandrogenism. Characterization of an insulin-resistance state distinct from the types A and B syndromes. Diabetes 34:101, 1985

KAHN CR: Role of insulin receptors in insulin-resistant states. Metabolism 29:455, 1980

KURTZ AB, NABARRO JDN: Circulating insulin-binding antibodies. Diabetologia 19:329, 1980

MISBIN RI et al: Resistance to subcutaneous and intramuscular insulin associated with deficiency of insulin-like growth factor (IGF) 2. Metabolism 32:537, 1983

PAULSEN EP et al: Insulin resistance caused by massive degradation of subcutaneous insulin. Diabetes 28:640, 1979

TAYLOR SI et al: Insulin resistance associated with androgen excess in women with autoantibodies to the insulin receptor. Ann Intern Med 97:851, 1982

328 LACTIC ACIDOSIS

DANIEL W. FOSTER

Lactic acidosis is common. This follows from the fact that lactic acid is produced at accelerated rates in skeletal muscle and other tissues whenever oxygenation is inadequate to supply energy needs. Thus

FIGURE 328-1 *Schematic view of aerobic metabolism. Subcellular compartments are not indicated. Glycolysis occurs in the cytosol while enzymes of fatty acid oxidation and the Krebs cycle are located intramitochondrially. The dotted line indicates that glycogenolysis and glycolysis are inactive in the presence of oxygen. (See text.)*

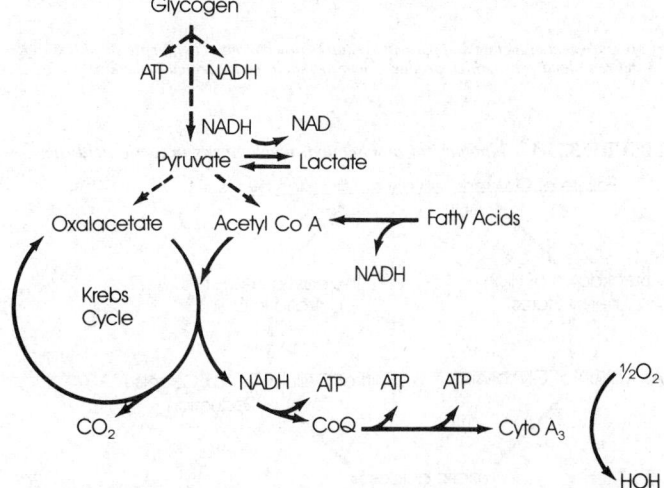

lactic acidosis represents a final common pathway for any disease resulting in circulatory collapse or hypoxia. Lactic acidosis can also occur when tissue hypoxia is not apparent. In most cases an etiology can be established, but in some the lactic acidosis is "idiopathic."

BIOCHEMICAL BACKGROUND In the narrowest sense biologic life can be defined as the capacity to generate high-energy phosphate bonds within the cell. Adenosine triphosphate (ATP) is the most important high-energy compound, but other nucleotides, such as guanosine triphosphate, also play important roles. Structure and function of every tissue in the body are directly or indirectly dependent on ATP or equivalent high-energy nucleotides. During tissue hypoxia ATP cannot be generated in adequate amounts, and lactic acidosis results. The acidosis is the metabolic consequence of activation of a back-up system for the generation of ATP when the primary energy-forming pathway is impaired. The normal mechanism of ATP generation under aerobic conditions is shown in Fig. 328-1. When substrates such as free fatty acids or glucose are oxidized to acetyl CoA, the constituent hydrogen atoms are transferred to nicotinamide adenine dinucleotide (NAD), producing the reduced form of the pyridine nucleotide (NADH). Oxidation of acetyl CoA to CO_2 in the Krebs cycle generates additional NADH. The bulk of NADH is formed intramitochondrially, where fatty acid oxidizing and tricarboxylic acid cycle enzymes are located; cytosolic NADH must be transported into the mitochondria by "shuttle" systems because NADH cannot directly penetrate the inner mitochondrial membrane. In the presence of oxygen, NADH is oxidized by the electron transport chain, the end product being water ("metabolic water"). For each mole of NADH passing through the cytochrome sequence 2 to 3 moles of ATP are formed. When oxygen content of tissues is normal and ATP stores are high, rates of glycogen breakdown and glucose oxidation are low (the *Pasteur effect*). Conversely, when oxygen content is low, ATP stores fall, and glycogen breakdown and glycolysis are activated.

Control of glycolysis is primarily vested in the enzyme phosphofructokinase (PFK). As shown in Fig. 328-2, this enzyme catalyzes the conversion of fructose 6-phosphate to fructose 1,6-bisphosphate. Several allosteric modulators regulate the activity of PFK. In muscle and other tissues ATP is the primary physiologic inhibitor, and AMP is a prominent activator. In liver fructose 2,6-bisphosphate is the major regulator of PFK (see Chap. 327). When fructose 2,6-bisphosphate concentrations are normal, rates of glycolysis (glucose 6-phosphate → pyruvate) are high, and gluconeogenesis (pyruvate → glucose 6-phosphate) is inhibited. Concentrations of fructose 2,6-bisphosphate are low in muscle, and it is not thought to play a primary regulatory role in that tissue. Fructose 2,6-bisphosphate concentrations in the liver fall with hypoxia and thus shift metabolism of the hepatocyte toward gluconeogenesis. This adaptation favors lactate uptake and utilization under circumstances in which lactate production is accelerated in nonhepatic tissues. Muscle contraction causes activation of glycogen breakdown and lactic acid production, but, paradoxically, it also causes a fall in fructose 2,6-bisphosphate concentration. This supports the view that phosphofructokinase ac-

FIGURE 328-2 *Phosphofructokinase and glycolysis. The minus sign indicates inhibition; the plus sign indicates activation. (See text.)*

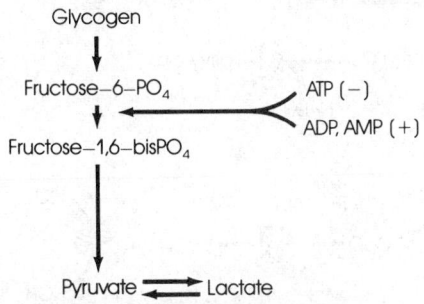

tivity and glycolysis are controlled primarily by the ATP/AMP ratio in muscle and not by fructose 2,6-bisphosphate.

The sequence of events occurring during tissue hypoxia is schematically shown in Fig. 328-3. If blood flow to peripheral tissues is diminished such that oxygen delivery is insufficient to meet metabolic demands, electron flow through the transport chain is impaired or blocked (all cytochromes become reduced). Because of the block, NADH, which for a finite period continues to be generated, cannot be oxidized, resulting in high NADH/NAD ratios in both mitochondrial and cytosolic compartments. As a result all near-equilibrium reactions utilizing NADH as cofactor shift to the reduced side (e.g., oxaloacetate → malate, pyruvate → lactate), slowing substrate flux at a number of critical sites. In addition, ATP cannot be synthesized, and tissue ATP concentrations fall. There is a reciprocal rise in ADP and AMP. As a result, phosphofructokinase is activated, with rapid glycogen breakdown and glucose oxidation. Accelerated glycolysis leads to overproduction of pyruvic acid, which, because of the elevated NADH content of the cell, is reduced to lactic acid. Put simply, the acidosis of tissue hypoxia is due to the conversion of neutral substrate, glycogen/glucose, to a strong acid, pyruvate. It is a lactic acidosis because the high NADH/NAD ratio drives the lactic dehydrogenase reaction to the right. These points are shown schematically in Fig. 328-4.

Even in the fully oxygenated subject lactate is produced by a variety of tissues. This lactate passes to the liver, where it enters the gluconeogenic pathway for conversion to glucose (*Cori cycle*). Diminished hepatic uptake of lactate undoubtedly plays a role in the pathogenesis of lactic acidosis (especially in patients with vascular collapse, severe hepatocellular disease, or enzymic defects in the gluconeogenic pathway), but significant acidosis probably never occurs in the absence of peripheral overproduction. Whether lactate overproduction in lactic acidosis is generalized or limited to specific tissues such as muscle and intestine is not resolved.

Conceptually the accelerated glycolysis induced by hypoxia can be considered an alternative system for the generation of ATP when the normal mitochondrial mechanism is impaired. The glycolytic system is not efficient, however. A mole of glucose derived from glycogen and oxidized completely through the Krebs cycle generates about 37 mol ATP, while the yield from glycogen to pyruvate is only 3 mol. Nevertheless, over the short run, this ATP may be lifesaving.

CLINICAL PICTURE   Lactic acidosis is usually heralded by the onset of nausea, vomiting, restlessness, and driven respiration of the Kussmaul type. Stupor or coma is sometimes seen. Huckabee, who in 1961 brought the problem of lactic acidosis to the attention of clinicians, recognized that there were two major groups of patients with elevated lactate concentrations in the blood. The first had proportionate increases of lactate and pyruvate and were not considered to be hypoxic. The second group had lactate levels disproportionately elevated when compared with the simultaneously measured pyruvate concentration. Huckabee coined the term "excess lactate" for any increase in lactate that could not be accounted for by a rise in pyruvate concentration and interpreted its presence to mean tissue hypoxia (a high NADH/NAD ratio). The relationship of the lactate/pyruvate concentration to the cytoplasmic NADH/NAD ratio is obvious when the lactate dehydrogenase reaction is rearranged:

$$\text{Pyruvate} + \text{NADH} + \text{H}^+ \rightleftharpoons \text{lactate} + \text{NAD}^+ \quad (1)$$

$$K \times \frac{[\text{NADH}] [\text{H}^+]}{[\text{NAD}^+]} = \frac{[\text{lactate}]}{[\text{pyruvate}]} \quad (2)$$

A sample calculation of "excess lactate" is given in Fig. 328-5.

The mean level of lactate in venous blood normally is about 1 mM (range 0.6 to 1.5 mM), and the pyruvate concentration is about 0.1 mM (range 0.05 to 0.15 mM)[1]. Accurately determined lactate/pyruvate ratios above 10 to 15 usually mean some degree of hypoxia. In practice pyruvate is usually not measured because instability and low concentrations make assay difficult. As a consequence, excess lactate is rarely quantitated. The concept was seminal, however, in providing the insight that led to understanding of the pathophysiology of lactic acidosis.

Cohen and Woods have suggested a classification of lactic acidosis based on clinical findings rather than on the lactate/pyruvate ratio (Table 328-1). Type A lactic acidosis is associated with poor tissue perfusion or oxygenation. Most patients with lactic acidosis fall into this category. Vascular collapse is the most common cause, and any condition leading to shock (e.g., myocardial infarction, pulmonary embolism, hemorrhage, septicemia, poisoning) can produce the disorder. Hypoxia does not have to be present. Importantly, diminished tissue perfusion may occur in the absence of a measurable fall in the blood pressure. Lactic acidosis occurs physiologically whenever muscular exercise is sufficient to contract an oxygen debt. The pathologic counterpart is lactic acidosis produced by convulsions or hypothermia with prolonged shivering. All type A patients have "excess lactate" in the Huckabee terminology.

Type B patients have elevated blood lactate concentrations without evidence of diminished tissue perfusion. Acidosis may be absent, mild, or severe. Pyruvate and lactate may both be elevated, but high lactate/pyruvate ratios are present when acidosis is severe. Systemic clinical disorders associated with elevations of blood lactate include uncontrolled diabetes mellitus, severe liver disease, leukemia, thiamine deficiency, and metabolic or respiratory alkalosis. Lactic acidosis

---

[1] *Measurement of lactate and pyruvate requires precautions. The sample should be iced, and red blood cells (which produce lactate) should be separated immediately.*

FIGURE 328-3 *Schematic view of anaerobic metabolism. Diagonally striped boxes indicate metabolic blocks secondary to failure of delivery of oxygen to tissues and high NADH/NAD ratios. Heavy arrows indicate accelerated glycogenolysis, glycolysis, and lactate production. Glycolysis is permitted to continue in the face of high NADH/NAD ratios in the cytosol because one molecule of NAD (required in the glyceraldehyde 3-phosphate dehydrogenase reaction) is produced for each molecule of lactate formed.*

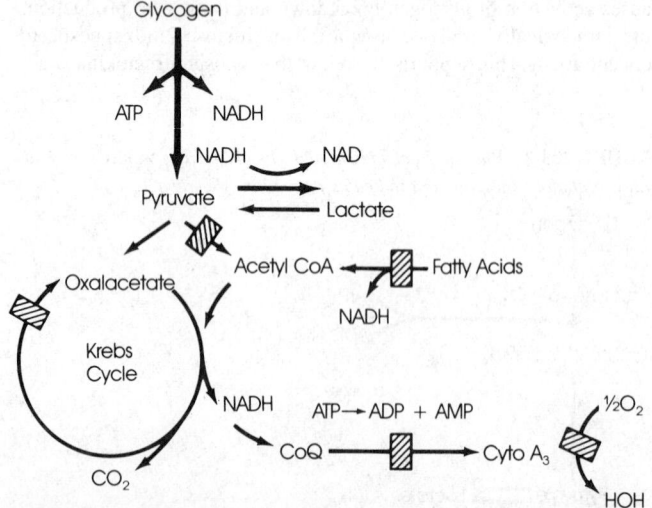

FIGURE 328-4 *Summary of biochemical mechanisms in lactic acidosis.*

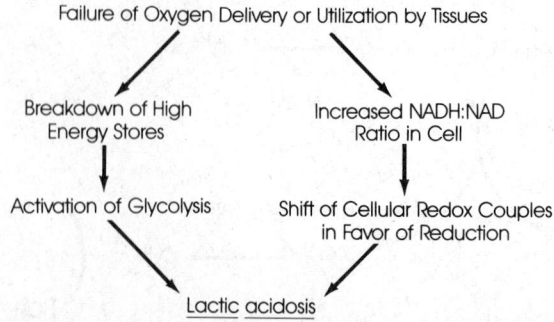

was commonly reported with biguanide therapy of diabetes, and because of this, phenformin was removed from clinical use in the United States by the Food and Drug Administration. The syndrome also occurs with nitroprusside therapy of hypertension, with epinephrine overdosage, and in isolated instances with other drug intoxications. Most of the latter are doubtless associated with hypoxia or shock and rightfully belong in the type A category. Ethanol is often listed as a cause of lactic acidosis but in fact rarely induces the syndrome. The oxidation of ethanol by the liver results in the generation of high NADH/NAD ratios in the cell and presumably blocks the recycling of lactate (and alanine) to glucose. Infants with enzyme defects in the glycolytic-gluconeogenic-tricarboxylic acid pathway appear to be particularly vulnerable to lactic acidosis, and early death is common. Recurrent lactic acidosis occurs in certain primary myopathies characterized by mitochondrial abnormalities. The mitochondrial myopathies typically show "ragged-red fibers" with the modified Gomori trichromic stain and exhibit bizarre-looking mitochondria (see Chap. 355). A variety of defects in the electron transport chain presumably cause lactic acidosis because of inability to generate ATP in the face of increased demand, as in exercise. Subtle mitochondrial disease is likely present in most cases of so-called idiopathic lactic acidosis.

The pathophysiology of lactate accumulation in other forms of type B disease is varied and often incompletely understood. The enzyme defects and alcohol may involve diminished hepatic uptake of lactate as a primary mechanism; i.e., modest increases in lactate production induced by hormones or exercise cause acidosis because of limited capacity for extraction in the liver. Drugs that do not cause perfusion problems probably alter mitochondrial function in some fashion. Hormones such as glucagon and epinephrine raise lactate by stimulating glycolysis. Leukemia probably acts both by direct overproduction of lactate in the white cell mass and through increased blood viscosity that diminishes capillary perfusion.

Most chronic type B conditions cause only mild to moderate hyperlactatemia in themselves, and an additional insult is required for acidosis to develop. The latter might include infection, dehydration, volume depletion, starvation, or unusual exertion. The effect of such an insult would be to add a mild inadequacy of tissue perfusion (insufficient to qualify as type A disease) to the primary abnormality and in combination to cause frank acidosis.

DIAGNOSIS   The diagnosis of lactic acidosis requires that a significant metabolic acidosis be present and that the measured lactate concentration be sufficient to account for the bulk of the decrease in plasma bicarbonate content. In general the arterial pH is less than 7.2, and the plasma lactate concentration is greater than 12 mM. Unfortunately, in many case reports of "lactic acidosis" plasma lactate concentrations are only modestly elevated (3 to 6 mM), and pH values are near normal. There are many causes of elevated plasma lactate levels, but the term *lactic acidosis* should be reserved for situations in which acidosis is present. Confusion also occurs when severe acidosis is present but lactate concentrations do not account for the decrement of bicarbonate (i.e., a mixed acidosis is present). In diabetic ketoacidosis, for example, lactate concentrations of 3 to 6 mM are common, but acetoacetate and β-hydroxybutyrate are primarily responsible for the low pH.

FIGURE 328-5   *The concept of excess lactate (XL). The symbols L_t and P_t indicate plasma concentrations of lactate and pyruvate, respectively, in the patient. L_n and P_n refer to mean values in normal subjects.*

$$XL = (L_t - L_n) - (P_t - P_n) \cdot \frac{L_n}{P_n}$$

	Pyruvate	Lactate
Normal	0.1 mM	1.0 mM
Patient	0.3 mM	11.0 mM

$$XL = (11 - 1) - (0.3 - 0.1)\frac{1.0}{0.1} = 8 \text{mM}$$

Lactic acidosis should be suspected whenever a metabolic acidosis is associated with an "anion gap" in the absence of an explanation for the unmeasured anions. The anion gap can be calculated in several ways, the simplest of which is $[Na^+] - ([Cl^-] + [HCO_3^-])$. The normal range is 8 to 16 mmol per liter, with the mean about 12. The four most common causes of metabolic acidosis with anion gap are diabetic or alcoholic ketoacidosis, uremic acidosis, lactic acidosis, and acidosis associated with toxin ingestion (salicylates, methanol, ethylene glycol, paraldehyde). Thus if ketoacidosis and uremia are not present and there is nothing to suggest a poisoning, the chances are good that a metabolic acidosis with significant anion gap is due to lactic acid.

TREATMENT   If lactic acidosis is caused by shock or hypoxia, reversal of the primary condition cures the secondary acidosis. Traditionally treatment has also involved the infusion of large amounts of sodium bicarbonate intravenously. Questions about this practice have been based on experiments showing a detrimental effect of bicarbonate therapy in dogs with lactic acidosis induced by hypoxia. The applicability of these results to humans is not clear, although bicarbonate therapy is not very effective. Until this issue is clarified, it may be prudent to initiate treatment with 1 to 2 liters of 0.9% saline solution to expand volume and then switch to bicarbonate infusion if improvement is not forthcoming. The recommendation to use bicarbonate follows from the observation that severe and prolonged acidosis in and of itself can cause vascular collapse. If administered, straight bicarbonate solutions should be used. A near isotonic solution can be prepared by adding three 50-mL vials of sodium bicarbonate (1 mmol/mL) to 850 mL of sterile distilled water. Hypertonic (5%) solutions are commercially available and may be required in certain cases.

Because large volumes of bicarbonate are required, the problem of fluid overload often arises, especially in elderly patients and in subjects with impaired renal function. Diuretics should be routinely given with vigorous alkali therapy after it is clear that any volume deficits have been repaired. Occasionally peritoneal dialysis or hemodialysis with hypertonic solutions may be required to prevent pulmonary edema. Dialysis is not indicated as a treatment of lactic acidosis per se.

An experimental drug, dichloroacetate, has been successfully used to reverse lactic acidosis in humans. The drug is thought to stimulate pyruvate/lactate oxidation through activation of pyruvate dehydrogenase. Although the drug causes polyneuropathy, testicular damage,

TABLE 328-1   Some causes of hyperlactatemia

A Hyperlactatemia with hypoxia
  1 Strenuous muscle exercise (convulsions, hypothermia)
  2 Inadequate tissue perfusion or oxygenation of any cause*
B Hyperlactatemia without apparent hypoxia
  1 Systemic clinical disorders
    a Alkalosis (respiratory or metabolic)
    b Uncontrolled diabetes mellitus
    c Leukemia, lymphoma, other cancers
    d Severe liver disease
    e Thiamine deficiency
  2 Drugs, hormones, toxins
    a Phenformin and other biguanides
    b Salicylates
    c Sodium nitroprusside
    d Ethanol
    e Epinephrine, glucagon
    f Fructose, sorbitol
  3 Enzyme defects
    a Glucose 6-phosphatase
    b Fructose 1,6-bisphosphatase
    c Pyruvate carboxylase
    d Pyruvate dehydrogenase
    e Unclassified tricarboxylic acid defect
  4 Certain primary myopathies
  5 Idiopathic

* *The most common causes of perfusion-oxygenation defects are myocardial infarction, sepsis, hemorrhage, volume depletion, pulmonary embolism, and heart failure. Hypoxia due to severe pulmonary disease, chronic anemia, carbon monoxide inhalation, and cyanide poisoning are much less frequent.*
SOURCE: *After Cohen and Woods, 1976.*

cataracts, and disturbed oxalate metabolism when used chronically, Stacpoole and colleagues observed no serious toxicity with bolus doses at the 50 mg per kilogram of body weight level. The effects of a single dose lasted for a number of hours. Unfortunately, despite improvement in the acidosis, most of the patients went on to die. Such a course would be in accord with the view that lactic acidosis is usually a marker of impending demise from some underlying disease as opposed to being the primary cause of death. Further experience with dichloroacetate will be required before its efficacy can be determined.

REFERENCES

CLAUS TH et al: The role of fructose 2,6-bisphosphate in the regulation of carbohydrate metabolism. Curr Top Cell Regul 23:57, 1984

COHEN RD, WOODS HF: *Clinical and Biochemical Aspects of Lactic Acidosis.* Oxford, Blackwell, 1976

———: Lactic acidosis revisited. Diabetes 32:181, 1983

GABOW PA et al: Diagnostic importance of an increased anion gap. N Engl J Med 303:854, 1980

GRAF H et al: Evidence for a detrimental effect of bicarbonate therapy in hypoxic lactic acidosis. Science 227:754, 1985

HUCKABEE WE: Abnormal resting blood lactate. Am J Med 30:833, 1961

KENNAWAY NG et al: Lactic acidosis and mitochondrial myopathy associated with deficiency of several components of complex III of the respiratory chain. Pediatr Res 18:991, 1984

KREISBERG RA: Lactate homeostasis and lactic acidosis. Ann Intern Med 92:227, 1980

STACPOOLE PW et al: Treatment of lactic acidosis with dichloroacetate. N Engl J Med 309:390, 1983

329   HYPOGLYCEMIA, INSULINOMA, AND OTHER HORMONE-SECRETING TUMORS OF THE PANCREAS

DANIEL W. FOSTER / ARTHUR H. RUBENSTEIN

Maintenance of the plasma glucose concentration within narrow bounds is essential for health. Hypoglycemia is dangerous (in the short run more serious than hyperglycemia) because glucose is the primary energy substrate of the brain. Its absence, like that of oxygen, produces deranged function, tissue damage, or even death if the deficit is prolonged. The vulnerability of the brain to hypoglycemia is due to the fact that it cannot utilize circulating free fatty acids as an energy source in contrast to other tissues of the body. Short-chain metabolites of the free fatty acids, acetoacetic and β-hydroxybutyric acids (the "ketone bodies"), are efficiently oxidized by brain and can protect the central nervous system from damage by hypoglycemia when present at moderate concentrations in plasma. However, development of ketosis requires a number of hours in humans. Ketogenesis is not, therefore, an effective protective mechanism against acute hypoglycemia. Preservation of central nervous system function in the early phases of fasting or during hypoglycemia thus requires a prompt increase in the production of glucose by the liver. At the same time glucose utilization in other tissues is diminished by provision of free fatty acids as alternative substrate. These adaptive mechanisms are hormonally controlled and, under ordinary circumstances, are extremely effective. Occasionally, however, the system breaks down or is overwhelmed, resulting in the clinical syndrome of hypoglycemia.

DEFENSE AGAINST HYPOGLYCEMIA   The mechanisms underlying the hypoglycemic states can best be understood by briefly reviewing normal fuel metabolism. Under ordinary circumstances energy needs are met by exogenous substrate derived from food. Oxidation of the constituent molecules of absorbed foodstuffs to carbon dioxide and water is accompanied by the generation of adenosine triphosphate (ATP), the principal high-energy compound of the body. In one sense, life can be defined as the continued ability to generate ATP

(and related high-energy nucleotides) for the preservation of cellular integrity in all its manifestations. When caloric intake is greater than immediate oxidative needs, as after the usual meal, excess substrate is stored as fat, structural protein, and glycogen. Substrate flux in this phase of metabolism, called *anabolic,* proceeds from intestine to liver to utilization and storage sites. Insulin is the primary hormone mediating the anabolic phase, during which counterregulatory hormone levels are suppressed.

The *catabolic* phase of metabolism begins about 5 to 6 h after a meal. Normally the only significant period of catabolism is during the overnight fast, but under other circumstances, particularly serious illness, it may be prolonged. During fasting/catabolism a series of metabolic adjustments begin that are designed to maintain the plasma glucose in a safe range for central nervous system metabolism while at the same time providing energy for other tissues in the body. This is accomplished by two mechanisms. First, the liver is activated for glucose production, and second, a lipid economy is established for most other tissues of the body. Initially glucose release from the liver is derived almost exclusively from hepatic glycogen. Because there is only about 70 g of glycogen available in the average human liver, glycogenolysis can only sustain the plasma glucose for a short time, ordinarily 8 to 10 h. Exercise may shorten the protective period significantly, as may the stress of severe illness. To compensate for glycogen depletion gluconeogenesis begins early with flux of substrate from muscle and adipose tissue stores to liver and then to utilization sites. The precursors for glucose synthesis are lactate/pyruvate and amino acids (primarily alanine) derived from muscle and glycerol released from adipose tissue consequent to lipolysis.

The switch to fat metabolism is accomplished by activation of the hormone-sensitive lipase in adipose tissue, which hydrolyzes stored triglycerides to long-chain fatty acids and glycerol. The long-chain fatty acids have two fates. The bulk (normally about 120 g per day) is utilized directly while the remainder (about 40 g per day) is oxidized in the liver to acetoacetic and β-hydroxybutyric acids. The ketones can be utilized efficiently as an energy source by most tissues (liver only minimally), but their primary importance is as backup substrate for the brain, as noted above. The shift of most tissues to lipid metabolism is important since the preferential utilization of free fatty acids and ketones in place of glucose spares the latter for utilization by the central nervous system.

Catabolic metabolism is initiated by a fall in insulin concentration in plasma coupled with secretion of the four counterregulatory hormones glucagon, epinephrine, cortisol, and growth hormone. In addition norepinephrine is released directly in tissues from sympathetic neurons. Glucagon is considered the primary hormone of glucose maintenance with epinephrine playing a backup or secondary role. The latter is particularly important in the defense against hypoglycemia in diabetes mellitus where the glucagon response is lost early (see Chap. 328).

The anabolic and catabolic phases of metabolism are summarized in Table 329-1. Breakdown in any of the adaptive mechanisms can lead to hypoglycemia.

SYMPTOMATOLOGY OF HYPOGLYCEMIA   Symptoms of hypoglycemia fall into two main categories: those induced by an *excessive secretion of epinephrine* and those due to *dysfunction of the central nervous system.* Rapid epinephrine release causes sweating, tremor, tachycardia, anxiety, and hunger. Central nervous system symptoms include dizziness, headache, clouding of vision, blunted mental acuity, confusion, abnormal behavior, convulsions, and loss of consciousness. When the onset of hypoglycemia is gradual central nervous system symptoms predominate, and the epinephrine phase may not be recognizable. With more rapid drops in plasma glucose (as in insulin reactions), adrenergic symptoms are prominent. In the diabetic subject adrenergic symptoms may not be manifest if severe neuropathy is present.

CLASSIFICATION   It has been traditional to classify hypoglycemia as either *postprandial* (reactive) or *fasting.* Pathologically low plasma

TABLE 329-1 The feeding-fasting cycle

Phase	Primary hormone	Plasma substrates	Substrate flux	Active process
Anabolic*	Insulin	↑ Glucose ↑ Triglycerides ↑ Branched-chain amino acids ↓ Free fatty acids ↓ Ketones	Splanchnic bed → storage and utilization sites	Glycogen storage Protein synthesis Triglyceride formation
Catabolic†	Glucagon	↓ Glucose ↓ Triglycerides ↑ Alanine and glutamine‡ ↑ Free fatty acids ↑ Ketones	Storage sites → liver and utilization sites	Glycogenolysis Gluconeogenesis Proteolysis Lipolysis Ketogenesis

* *Expected findings during the first several hours after ingestion of a mixed meal of fat, carbohydrate, and protein.*
† *The major catabolic phase occurs during the overnight fast, although partial catabolic cycles occur between meals.*
‡ *Arrows indicate plasma concentrations except for alanine and glutamine. While arterial concentrations of these amino acids are relatively constant, uptake by the liver and intestine is increased in the catabolic phase.*

glucose concentrations occur in the former only in response to meals, while in the latter fasting for a few to many hours is necessary to demonstrate the abnormality. Patients with fasting hypoglycemia (particularly those with insulinomas) may exhibit a reactive component, but reactive patients do not have symptoms when food is withdrawn. Fasting hypoglycemia usually means that an identifiable disease process is associated with the lowered plasma glucose, but symptoms suggestive of postprandial hypoglycemia are often found in the absence of recognizable disease.

CAUSES OF HYPOGLYCEMIA **Postprandial hypoglycemia** Some causes of postprandial hypoglycemia are shown in Table 329-2. The most common category is alimentary hyperinsulinism. Patients who have undergone gastrectomy, gastrojejunostomy, pyloroplasty, or vagotomy are subject to hypoglycemia following meals, presumably because of rapid gastric emptying with brisk absorption of glucose and excessive insulin release. Glucose concentrations fall more rapidly than insulin under these circumstances, and the resulting insulin-glucose imbalance leads to hypoglycemia. Ingestion of fructose or galactose induces hypoglycemia in children with fructose intolerance and galactosemia (Chap. 314), respectively. Leucine intake can rarely cause the syndrome in susceptible infants in the absence of insulinoma. Diabetes mellitus in its early phase is usually listed as a cause of reactive hypoglycemia. In our experience symptomatic hypoglycemia as a premonitory symptom of diabetes is uncommon if it occurs at all. Prediabetics, who by definition have normal glucose tolerance, may have a late fall in plasma glucose after oral glucose tolerance testing, but this does not mean hypoglycemia. In fact, this pattern is similar to that frequently present in asymptomatic, healthy individuals (see below).

The fifth cause, idiopathic alimentary hypoglycemia, has in the past been broken down into two categories, *true hypoglycemia* and *nonhypoglycemia*. The former represents a condition in which adrenergic symptoms appear postprandially and are accompanied by a measurably low plasma glucose at the time the symptoms appear spontaneously during everyday life. The symptoms are relieved by ingestion of carbohydrate which raises the plasma glucose. Such patients are extraordinarily rare. The mechanism is unknown, although subtle (nonanatomic) dysfunction of the gastrointestinal tract might be operative. Some patients with true postprandial hypoglycemia turn out to have insulinomas (see below). *Nonhypoglycemia* describes a large number of patients who reproducibly develop adrenergic symptoms suggestive of hypoglycemia 2 to 5 h after a meal but who do not have low plasma glucose concentrations when symptoms appear spontaneously in everyday life. The condition is often self-diagnosed by those who have read the extensive lay-oriented literature that describes hypoglycemia as a common cause of ill health. Further, in almost every community there are physicians who specialize in "hypoglycemia" and make the diagnosis frequently. This is usually based on a 5-h glucose tolerance test that reveals a lower than "normal" plasma glucose between 2 and 5 h.

Two questions have to be asked about nonhypoglycemia. First, what are the symptoms (which may be incapacitating) due to? Second,

can a diagnosis of hypoglycemia be made by glucose tolerance test? The symptoms of nervousness, weakness, tremor, tachycardia, dizziness, and sweating reported by these patients are probably due to epinephrine release. Many otherwise normal persons experience similar symptoms at some time in their lives and may even have gained relief by eating. Patients with nonhypoglycemia, on the other hand, develop the symptoms regularly and repetitively. In one study 80 consecutive subjects with reproducible postprandial symptoms by history were studied by 5-h glucose tolerance testing. Hypoglycemia was considered to be present if (1) the plasma glucose fell below 60 mg/dL during the test, (2) symptoms or signs compatible with hypoglycemia were present, and (3) at least a doubling of plasma cortisol occurred 39 to 90 min after the nadir of plasma glucose (suggesting hypoglycemia sufficient to activate the hypothalamic-pituitary-adrenal axis). Only 18 of the 80 (23 percent) who by history were candidates for postprandial hypoglycemia fulfilled these criteria. Twenty-five percent of asymptomatic matched normal controls also met all three criteria. When the patients and controls were tested after a mixed meal, no subject in either group had a plasma glucose below 60 mg/dL, yet 14 of the 18 patients (78 percent) had symptoms typical of those occurring spontaneously and after glucose tolerance testing. The absence of hypoglycemia after mixed meals despite the presence of typical symptoms has been confirmed in other studies. Thus, the syndrome termed *nonhypoglycemia* has been correctly named since the symptoms occur in the absence of chemical hypoglycemia after mixed meals. Most of these patients doubtless have stress and/or anxiety as the primary disorder, with epinephrine released in consequence thereof. However, it is conceivable that some persons discharge epinephrine abnormally in response to meals to account for the syndrome. Sucrose or glucose overfeeding can cause stimulation of the sympathetic nervous system, but in normal subjects it is primarily norepinephrine and not epinephrine that is released. One possibility is that affected subjects have increased sensitivity to the normal postmeal epinephrine secretion. It is suggested that the terms *idiopathic postabsorptive hypoglycemia* and *nonhypoglycemia* be abandoned and the designation *idiopathic postprandial syndrome* be substituted to avoid confusion with true hypoglycemic disorders.

Fasting hypoglycemia The causes of fasting hypoglycemia are many, but in all there is an imbalance between the production of glucose by the liver and its utilization in peripheral tissues. In some, hypoglycemia is due primarily to a defect in glucose production, while in others the problem is due to excess glucose utilization. The two forms can be distinguished by the amount of glucose required to prevent hypoglycemia during a 24-h period. If this is more than 200 g, it can be assumed that overutilization is present. This follows

TABLE 329-2 Causes of postprandial (reactive) hypoglycemia

I Alimentary hyperinsulinism
II Hereditary fructose intolerance
III Galactosemia
IV Leucine sensitivity
V Idiopathic

TABLE 329-3 Major causes of fasting hypoglycemia

I Conditions primarily due to underproduction of glucose
  A Hormone deficiencies
    1 Hypopituitarism
    2 Adrenal insufficiency
    3 Catecholamine deficiency
    4 Glucagon deficiency
  B Enzyme defects
    1 Glucose 6-phosphatase
    2 Liver phosphorylase
    3 Pyruvate carboxylase
    4 Phosphoenolpyruvate carboxykinase
    5 Fructose 1,6-diphosphatase
    6 Glycogen synthetase
  C Substrate deficiency
    1 Ketotic hypoglycemia of infancy
    2 Severe malnutrition, muscle wasting
    3 Late pregnancy
  D Acquired liver disease
    1 Hepatic congestion
    2 Severe hepatitis
    3 Cirrhosis
    4 Uremia (probably multiple mechanisms)
  E Drugs
    1 Alcohol
    2 Propranolol
    3 Salicylates
II Conditions primarily due to overutilization of glucose
  A Hyperinsulinism
    1 Insulinoma
    2 Exogenous insulin
    3 Sulfonylureas
    4 Immune disease with insulin antibodies
    5 Quinine in falciparum malaria
    6 Endotoxic shock
  B Appropriate insulin levels
    1 Extrapancreatic tumors
    2 Systemic carnitine deficiency
    3 Deficiency in enzymes of fat oxidation
    4 Cachexia with fat depletion

from the fact that hepatic glucose output after an overnight fast is normally about 2 (mg/kg)/min or 196 g per 24 h in a 70-kg person.[1] Since this is sufficient to prevent hypoglycemia, the presence of a low plasma glucose in the face of a 200-g glucose intake strongly suggests enhanced glucose utilization. The diseases that can cause accelerated glucose utilization usually also have an element of underproduction (relative or absolute), and in some cases the latter may predominate. The hepatic response to increased glucose demand may be impaired in conditions of glucose overutilization by several mechanisms, but persistent release of insulin sufficient to blunt the effect of glucagon in the liver is likely of key importance. Other factors include inadequate release of amino acids from muscle (necessary for gluconeogenesis) and/or impairment of fatty acid delivery or oxidation (necessary for maximal rates of gluconeogenesis).

To summarize, if glucose demand is more than 200 g per day, increased glucose flux into peripheral tissues is present. If less than 200 g per day prevents hypoglycemia, no diagnostic implications can be drawn since a condition capable of causing overutilization may, in a given case, function primarily by impairing glucose production. A classification of fasting hypoglycemia based on underproduction or overutilization of glucose is given in Table 329-3. Hypoglycemia occurs in other conditions in isolated fashion.

UNDERPRODUCTION OF GLUCOSE As discussed earlier, the production of glucose by the liver initially involves the breakdown of stored glycogen and subsequently depends on gluconeogenesis, the synthesis of glucose from precursors delivered to the liver from peripheral tissues. The causes of inadequate production of glucose during fasting can be grouped into five general categories: (1) hormone deficiencies, (2) specific defects in glycogenolytic or gluconeogenic enzymes, (3)

inadequate substrate delivery, (4) acquired liver disease, and (5) drugs. Hypopituitarism and adrenal insufficiency are the most common of the hormone deficiency states causing hypoglycemia. Defects in catecholamine or glucagon release are rare. Enzymic abnormalities causing hypoglycemia are generally seen in children and not adults. Glucose 6-phosphatase deficiency is the classic example of a defect in glycogen breakdown, but hypoglycemia may occur in young children with deficiencies of hepatic glycogen phosphorylase and in other forms of glycogen storage disease (Chap. 313). The inability to make glycogen because of inadequate glycogen synthetase activity also renders the infant susceptible to fasting hypoglycemia. In addition to glucose 6-phosphatase, three other enzymes are necessary for gluconeogenesis: pyruvate carboxylase, phosphoenolpyruvate carboxykinase, and fructose 1,6-bisphosphatase (fructose 1,6-diphosphatase) (Fig. 329-1). Hypoglycemia can occur with decreased activities of each of these enzymes, often in association with lactic acidosis. Substrate deficiency appears to be one of the mechanisms operative in ketotic hypoglycemia of infancy, since alanine turnover in such patients is low. Inadequate substrate supply may also contribute to hypoglycemia in malnutrition, muscle-wasting states, chronic renal failure, and late pregnancy. Acquired liver disease can cause serious hypoglycemia. Hepatic congestion due to right-sided heart failure is particularly troublesome, but severe viral hepatitis or cirrhosis may also cause symptomatic hypoglycemia. The hypoglycemia of renal failure has been attributed to suppression of hepatic compensatory functions by uremia, but other mechanisms may also play a role.

A number of drugs cause hypoglycemia. By far the most common, apart from insulin and sulfonylureas, is alcohol. Alcohol only induces hypoglycemia after a period of fasting sufficient to deplete liver glycogen stores. In this circumstance hepatic glucose production is dependent on gluconeogenesis. The oxidation of ethanol in the liver is accompanied by generation of high concentrations of NADH, the reduced form of nicotinamide adenine dinucleotide (NAD), in the cytosol of the cell. The increased NADH/NAD ratio diverts oxaloacetate into malate formation, diminishing its availability to the gluconeogenic sequence via the action of phosphoenolpyruvate carboxykinase (Fig. 329-1). The normal pathway of gluconeogenesis from pyruvate is thus blocked, leading to a drop in hepatic glucose output and hypoglycemia. Large amounts of ethanol are not required to produce this syndrome, and plasma alcohol concentrations may be as low as 25 mg/dL at the time symptoms occur. Ethanol-induced hypoglycemia usually occurs in adults but can be seen in children who drink alcohol unknowingly. Salicylates (in children) and pro-

---

FIGURE 329-1 *Scheme of hepatic carbohydrate metabolism. Only the sequence for gluconeogenesis, glycogen synthesis, and glycogenolysis is shown.*

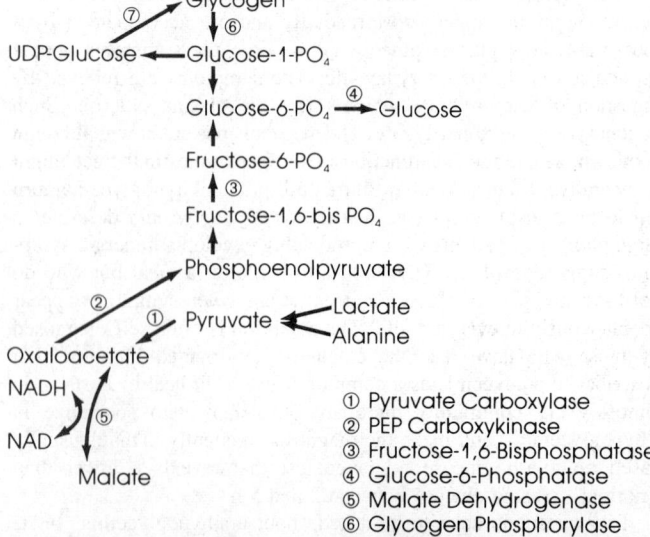

① Pyruvate Carboxylase
② PEP Carboxykinase
③ Fructose-1,6-Bisphosphatase
④ Glucose-6-Phosphatase
⑤ Malate Dehydrogenase
⑥ Glycogen Phosphorylase
⑦ Glycogen Synthetase

---

[1] *Much more than 200 g of glucose can be disposed of by normal humans without development of hyperglycemia. Therefore, the rule is valid only if large quantities of glucose are required to avoid hypoglycemia, i.e., if plasma glucose falls below fasting levels and continues at a low concentration despite the infusion of 200 g of glucose per day.*

pranolol are the next most frequently involved drugs. Propranolol presumably causes difficulty in fasting patients or insulin-requiring diabetics by impairing the glycogenolytic response. In diabetes the drug may also prevent recognition of impending hypoglycemia by blunting the symptomatic response to epinephrine release. Other drugs have been reported to cause hypoglycemia in isolated cases, but the relationship is often unproved.

OVERUTILIZATION OF GLUCOSE Overutilization of glucose occurs in two settings. In the first, hyperinsulinism is present, and in the second, plasma insulin concentrations are low. There are basically four causes of hyperinsulinemic hypoglycemia: insulinoma, exogenous insulin administration, sulfonylureas, and a peculiar form of insulin autoimmunity. In areas of endemic malaria some patients develop hyperinsulinemic hypoglycemia when treated with quinine, but this is not a problem elsewhere. Hypoglycemia in a diabetic taking prescribed insulin or oral agents is not a diagnostic problem. The difficulty comes when a nondiabetic subject induces hypoglycemia deliberately and surreptitiously because of psychiatric disturbance, raising the possibility of an insulin-producing tumor. The differential diagnosis between insulinoma and factitious hypoglycemia is considered below. Rarely hypoglycemia with hyperinsulinism occurs in autoimmune disease with antibodies to endogenous insulin. Mechanisms are not well understood, although dissociation of free insulin from hormone-antibody complexes at inappropriate times may play a role. By binding insulin, antibodies may also induce excessive insulin release from the pancreas.

Hypoglycemia in the context of glucose overutilization and appropriately low plasma insulin concentrations occurs in two situations. The first is in association with solid extrapancreatic tumors, usually of large size. The most common are of mesothelial origin and include a variety of fibromas and sarcomas. The syndrome can also be seen with hepatomas, carcinomas of the gastrointestinal tract, and adrenal cancers. The mechanism of the hypoglycemia is not clear, although high levels of insulin-like growth factors (''nonsuppressible insulin-like activity'') may play a role in some.

Symptomatic hypoglycemia due to overutilization may also occur in situations where free fatty acids are not available for oxidation in muscle and other tissues. Patients with *systemic carnitine deficiency* may have severe hypoglycemia. In this condition carnitine, which is necessary to transport fatty acids into mitochondria for oxidation, is low in plasma, muscle, liver, and other tissues. As a consequence, peripheral tissues cannot utilize fatty acids for energy production, and the liver cannot make ketone bodies as alternative substrate. The result is that all tissues become glucose-dependent, exceeding the capacity of the liver to meet the demand. Other features of systemic carnitine deficiency include nausea, vomiting, hyperammonemia, and hepatic encephalopathy. The illness thus constitutes one form of Reye's syndrome. (In *myopathic carnitine deficiency* only muscle is involved, and a polymyositis-like syndrome without hypoglycemia is produced.) Hypoglycemia is less common with deficiency of *carnitine palmitoyltransferase*, the enzyme that transesterifies fatty acyl coenzyme A (CoA) to carnitine for oxidation. Presumably the defect is not complete in most patients, allowing some fatty acid oxidation to occur so that the tendency to hypoglycemia is minimized. The clinical picture is that of an exercise-induced myopathy with myoglobinuria. Nonketotic (or hypoketotic) hypoglycemia may also

occur with diminished activity of other enzymes of fatty acid oxidation such as deficiency of medium- or long-chain acyl CoA dehydrogenase. Interestingly, these enzyme deficiencies appear to cause secondary decrease of carnitine levels in tissue and blood. Hypoglycemia also occurs in patients with cachexia due to advanced cancer. At autopsy no recognizable triglyceride stores are present in adipose tissue, suggesting free fatty acid deficiency as the primary mechanism.

DIAGNOSIS Fasting hypoglycemia If a nondiabetic presents with symptoms suggestive of hypoglycemia—particularly if confusion, loss of consciousness, or convulsions are present—the most important rule is to draw blood for simultaneous determinations of plasma glucose and insulin before intravenous glucose is administered, since the critical diagnostic issue will be the presence or absence of hyperinsulinism. Plasma cortisol should be determined at the same time since an elevation demonstrates intact pituitary/adrenal function. In addition to these tests, plasma should be separated and frozen. The stored samples can then be used for drug screening and measurement of insulin, C peptide, proinsulin, counterregulatory hormones, and substrates (e.g., free fatty acids, lactate, carnitine, amino acids) should the diagnosis not be clear after initial workup. Although storage of plasma at the time of spontaneous hypoglycemia is rarely done, it should be routine. *The best time to obtain diagnostic laboratory tests with spontaneous hypoglycemia is at presentation.* Once the patient has become alert (assuming altered mental status is present on arrival) it is important to take a detailed history and carry out a thorough physical examination. Special emphasis should be placed on food intake in the preceding 24 h and the possibility of drug ingestion. Signs of heart failure and hepatic congestion should be sought, and the presence and thickness of the adipose tissue mass should be noted. Pigmentation of the skin may suggest Addison's disease. Workup includes liver function studies and computed tomography (CT) scanning or abdominal sonography (to look for solid tumors in the retroperitoneal space or abdominal cavity). Patients with enzyme defects and rare hormonal deficiencies (epinephrine, glucagon) usually require evaluation in referral centers, since definitive assays for these hormones and enzymes are not routinely available. For reasons cited above it is important to quantitate the amount of glucose required to prevent recurrent hypoglycemia during acute phase therapy.

If the patient has a history compatible with hypoglycemia but does not have symptoms at the time of examination, hospitalization for fasting is generally required. The fast should be carried out for at least 72 h unless symptoms develop. Plasma glucose, insulin, and cortisol should be measured every 6 h. Occasionally quantitation of plasma free fatty acids, glucagon, and total ketones is helpful. (For glucagon, a protease inhibitor such as aprotinin must be added.) Two points are at issue. First, does the patient have fasting hypoglycemia? And second, is the hypoglycemia associated with hyperinsulinism? Neither question is easy to answer. There is no definitive lower limit of plasma glucose that unequivocally defines pathologic hypoglycemia. The mean minimal level of glucose attained during a 72-h fast in one study is shown in Table 329-4. Women usually develop lower levels than men. Another series reported mean minimal levels of 62 mg/dL in men and 52 mg/dL in women during a 72-h fast. However, values as low as 22 mg/dL may occur in normal women without symptoms. On balance, a presumptive diagnosis of hypoglycemia is

TABLE 329-4 Plasma glucose and insulin during fasting

Test	Subjects	Hours of fast				
		0*	24	36	48	72
Glucose, mg/dL	Men	85 ± 1.5	83 ± 3.6	78 ± 3.4	78 ± 3.3	71 ± 2.4
	Women	83 ± 1.3	63 ± 1.6	50 ± 1.7	46 ± 1.7	48 ± 1.4
Insulin, μU/mL	Men	14 ± 0.9	9 ± 0.8	8 ± 1.1	8 ± 0.9	6 ± 0.7
	Women	12 ± 0.8	6 ± 0.4	4 ± 0.5	3 ± 0.4	4 ± 0.5

* *Zero values obtained after overnight fast. Results represent means ± SEM for 20 normal men and 60 normal women.*
SOURCE: *TJ Merimee, JE Tyson, Diabetes 26:161, 1977.*

probably justified if the plasma glucose falls below 50 mg/dL in men and 45 mg/dL in women at any time during the fast, provided typical symptoms are induced. The diagnosis of hypoglycemia is strengthened if symptoms are rapidly relieved by administration of carbohydrate. If symptoms are not produced, the diagnosis of hypoglycemia should be made with caution.

In interpreting plasma insulin concentrations absolute values are not very helpful. In normal subjects when glucose concentrations rise insulin levels also increase, and when plasma glucose concentrations fall insulin release is inhibited. This means that plasma insulin concentrations must be interpreted in the light of the simultaneously determined glucose value. Thus, a "normal" absolute insulin level may be abnormal in the face of hypoglycemia, while high absolute levels may be appropriate if the glucose concentration is elevated. In an attempt to relate the two parameters the concept of the insulin/glucose ratio

$$\frac{\text{Plasma insulin } (\mu U/mL)}{\text{Plasma glucose } (mg/dL)}$$

was developed. In normal persons the ratio is always less than 0.4, while most (but not all) patients with insulinoma have ratios greater than 0.4—often above 1.0. Patients with insulinoma may secrete insulin episodically; the ratio may, therefore, be normal on one occasion and abnormal on another. Multiple sampling is required. The insulin/glucose ratio tends to fall during fasting in normal individuals but increases in patients with insulinoma.

Pancreatic insulin release ceases when the glucose concentration is decreased much below 90 mg/dL, and plasma insulin concentration generally reaches background levels for the assay when the plasma glucose falls below about 80 mg/dL. While some studies have shown lower cutoff points, it is probable that any measurable insulin concentration (>5 to 6 $\mu U/mL$) should be considered suspicious if the plasma glucose is below 50 mg/dL in men or 45 mg/dL in women, regardless of the value of the insulin/glucose ratio. If hyperinsulinism is not demonstrated, one of the other causes of fasting hypoglycemia must be sought.

Should hypoglycemia not develop during fasting, an insulinoma or other hypoglycemia-producing organic disease is unlikely, although insulinomas may rarely present solely as postprandial hypoglycemia with no depression of the plasma glucose even during a prolonged fast. Diagnosis usually is suspected in such cases because inappropriate insulin levels are shown during the postmeal episodes. Some authors recommend provocative tests with tolubutamide, glucagon, or leucine in suspected islet-cell tumors, but overlap between normal subjects and patients with insulinoma is so great as to render the tests of little value in a given individual.

Most patients who come to an emergency room with true postabsorptive hypoglycemia have a ready explanation for the problem. In one prospective study in a metropolitan hospital 125 cases of unequivocal hypoglycemia were seen in a 12-month period; 108 had hypoglycemia associated with diabetes or alcohol ingestion or a combination of the two. This experience is in accord with the view that insulinomas and other causes of hypoglycemia are uncommon and that only a minority of patients with hypoglycemia require extensive workup to determine the cause.

Postprandial hypoglycemia In patients presumed to have postprandial hypoglycemia the most widely used test has been a 5-h oral glucose tolerance examination. Since normal persons may have chemical hypoglycemia without symptoms in the glucose tolerance test while subjects with idiopathic postprandial syndrome have symptoms in the absence of hypoglycemia following meal testing, the 5-h glucose tolerance test should be abandoned as a tool for diagnosis. The only unequivocal diagnostic test for true idiopathic postprandial hypoglycemia is the demonstration of a low plasma glucose concentration (less than 50 mg/dL) during spontaneously developed symptoms. Patients with idiopathic postprandial syndrome (anxiety) usually have slightly elevated glucose concentrations during spontaneous attacks because of the hyperglycemic action of epinephrine, the stress hormone that induces the symptoms.

Insulinoma versus factitious hypoglycemia The self-induction of hypoglycemia by the injection of insulin or the ingestion of sulfonylureas is so common as to equal or exceed the incidence of insulinoma. The demonstration of hyperinsulinism during hypoglycemia cannot, therefore, be taken as definitive evidence of the presence of an islet-cell tumor. Factitious disease should always be suspected when hypoglycemic symptoms appear in medical personnel or families of diabetic patients. Several tests are helpful in distinguishing insulinoma from factitious disease once hyperinsulinism has been established. Patients with insulinoma tend to have high concentrations of proinsulin in plasma (>20 percent of total insulin). Plasma proinsulin is not elevated by the administration of commercial insulin preparations or sulfonylureas. Measurement of the insulin connecting peptide (C peptide) will indicate whether the insulin circulating in plasma is of endogenous or exogenous origin. When insulin is cleaved from its precursor proinsulin molecule, C peptide is released into the portal vein in a 1:1 ratio with insulin. Thus, patients with insulinoma should have high C-peptide concentrations which parallel the plasma insulin values. The characteristic pattern in factitious hypoglycemia due to insulin injection would be a high circulating level of insulin with relatively suppressed C-peptide values because exogenous insulin suppresses endogenous insulin release in normal persons, both directly and by inducing hypoglycemia. Suppression does not usually occur in insulinoma. For this reason some investigators recommend a C-peptide suppression test in equivocal situations. In this test 0.1 unit of insulin per kilogram of body weight is infused intravenously over 60 min. C-Peptide concentration should be less than 1.2 ng/mL at the end of the test, provided the plasma glucose has dropped to 40 mg/dL or less. As part of the test counterregulatory hormone response should also be measured 30 min after the nadir of the plasma glucose. Animal and human insulins can be distinguished by some radioimmunoassays and by high performance liquid chromatography. The presence of animal insulin is strong evidence of factitious disease. Antibodies to insulin are helpful if present since they usually indicate chronic insulin injection. Unfortunately sulfonylureas also elevate both the C-peptide and insulin concentrations in plasma. Therefore, factitious hypoglycemia due to oral agents can only be diagnosed by a high index of suspicion coupled with assay of the drug in plasma or urine. The differential characteristics of insulinoma and the two types of factitious hypoglycemia are shown in Table 329-5.

TREATMENT The initial treatment of serious hypoglycemia (producing confusion or coma) is the intravenous administration of a bolus of 25 or 50 g glucose as a 50% solution followed by constant infusion of glucose until the patient is able to eat a meal. The importance of the meal resides in the fact that hepatic glycogen repletion is not effective with small quantities of intravenous glucose. Patients in the overutilization category may require large quantities of intravenous glucose to maintain consciousness. It is not enough to infuse 5% dextrose at a rate of 1 to 2 mL/min and assume the patient is protected (20 to 30% dextrose solutions may be required

TABLE 329-5 Differential diagnosis of insulinoma and factitious hyperinsulinism

Test	Insulinoma	Exogenous insulin	Sulfonylurea
Plasma insulin	High	Very high*	High
Insulin/glucose ratio	High	Very high	High
Proinsulin	Increased	Normal or low	Normal
C peptide	Increased	Normal or low†	Increased
Insulin antibodies	Absent	± Present‡	Absent
Plasma or urine sulfonylurea	Absent	Absent	Present

* Total plasma insulin in patients with insulinoma is rarely above 200 $\mu U/mL$ in the basal state and often much lower. Values greater than 1000 $\mu U/mL$ are highly suggestive of exogenous insulin injection.

† C peptide may be normal in absolute terms, but low in relation to the increased insulin value. See text for C-peptide suppression test.

‡ Insulin antibodies may not be present if only a few injections have been given, especially with purified insulins.

in some cases). Frequent measurement of capillary glucose concentrations should be carried out using glucose-sensitive reagent strips to assess effectiveness of glucose infusion rates. Intravenous glucose can usually be stopped once the patient has eaten, but this can only be determined by trial. Adrenergic reactions without central nervous system abnormalities can be treated with oral carbohydrate and do not require parenteral therapy.

Hypoglycemia from sulfonylureas may last for prolonged periods (days), particularly with chlorpropamide (Fig. 329-2). It is common for patients to lapse back into coma if glucose infusions are stopped too soon. The reason for the prolonged effect is not always clear, though drug interactions, hepatic disease, and renal failure may play a role in some cases.

Surgery is the treatment of choice for insulinoma. Localization should be attempted with CT scan or sonography prior to exploration. Arteriography (celiac or superior mesenteric) is less effective. In some centers preoperative or operative sampling of insulin concentrations by selective pancreatic vein catheterization has been performed but appears to be of minimal benefit even if a rapid insulin assay is available. If the tumor cannot be palpated in the pancreas or located in an extrapancreatic site at the time of surgery, stepwise pancreatectomy (from tail to head) should be carried out with frozen sections made of sequential slices. Capillary glucose should be measured frequently (at each stage of the resection if the tumor is not obvious). A rise in plasma glucose may indicate removal of a small, nonpalpable lesion. In general, resection is stopped with an 85 percent pancreatectomy, even if the tumor is not found, to avoid malabsorptive complications. Evaluation of 1012 cases of insulinoma cited in the literature indicated the following outcomes from surgery: operative mortality, 11 percent; cure, 63 percent; postoperative diabetes, 10 percent; and persistent hypoglycemia, 16 percent. Postoperative complications included acute pancreatitis, peritonitis, fistulas, and pseudocyst formation.

Medical treatment is indicated in insulinoma only in preparation for surgery or after failure to find the tumor at operation. The drug of choice is diazoxide, which can be given intravenously or orally in doses of 300 to 1200 mg per day. Because of this drug's salt-retaining properties a diuretic must always be added when diazoxide is administered. Treatment of metastatic insulin-producing carcinomas is unsatisfactory. Streptozocin, plicamycin, and doxorubicin have been tried, but the results are dismal. One multicenter trial reported improved results when streptozocin was combined with fluorouracil.

Despite the generally poor prognosis, occasional patients with insulin-producing islet-cell carcinomas survive for long periods.

Therapy of other forms of recurrent hypoglycemia, apart from hormone replacement in pituitary or adrenal insufficiency, is dietary. In most cases avoidance of fasting is all that is required. A high-protein, low-carbohydrate diet is frequently prescribed for patients with the idiopathic postprandial syndrome and often relieves symptoms. With true alimentary hypoglycemia it is probably important to keep the size of the individual meals small. The practice of giving massive amounts of vitamin E, crude adrenocortical extract, and trace metals to patients with the idiopathic postprandial syndrome is useless even if harmless (which has not been proved).

OTHER HORMONE-SECRETING TUMORS OF THE PANCREAS

Tumors of the pancreatic islets can synthesize a variety of hormones other than insulin. Almost all benign tumors are thought to be hormone-secreting, but a fifth or more of islet carcinomas produce no clinically detectable product. Histologically the tumors may be of a single-cell type or of mixed derivation. Despite the capacity of mixed tumors to produce several hormones, one hormone usually predominates so that distinct syndromes result. Tumors are generally named after the primary hormone released. If multiple hormones are produced and none dominates the clinical picture, the tumor is simply classified as "multiple hormone producing." Pancreatic tumors may be part of the multiple endocrine neoplasia syndrome (Chap. 334). This is particularly true of the ulcerogenic islet-cell tumor which is now considered to be a typical manifestation of the multiple endocrine neoplasia type I (MEN I). In addition to insulin, islet-cell tumors have been associated with the production of gastrin, secretin, vasoactive intestinal polypeptide, human pancreatic polypeptide, gastric inhibitory polypeptide, glucagon, ACTH, melanocyte stimulatory hormone, serotonin, neurotensin, enkephalin, and calcitonin. Chorionic gonadotropin and its β subunit may also be elevated in the plasma. A summary of the major tumors is given in Table 329-6.

Ulcerogenic islet-cell tumor (Zollinger-Ellison syndrome, gastrinoma) This is likely the most common of the non-insulin-secreting tumors. The clinical picture is that of intractable ulcer symptoms, hypersecretion of gastric acid, and diarrhea, which may be watery or due to steatorrhea. Complications such as perforation and hemorrhage occur commonly. X-ray frequently shows the stomach to be filled with fluid, and giant gastric rugae are seen. The ulcer may be atypically located in the second or third portion of the duodenum.

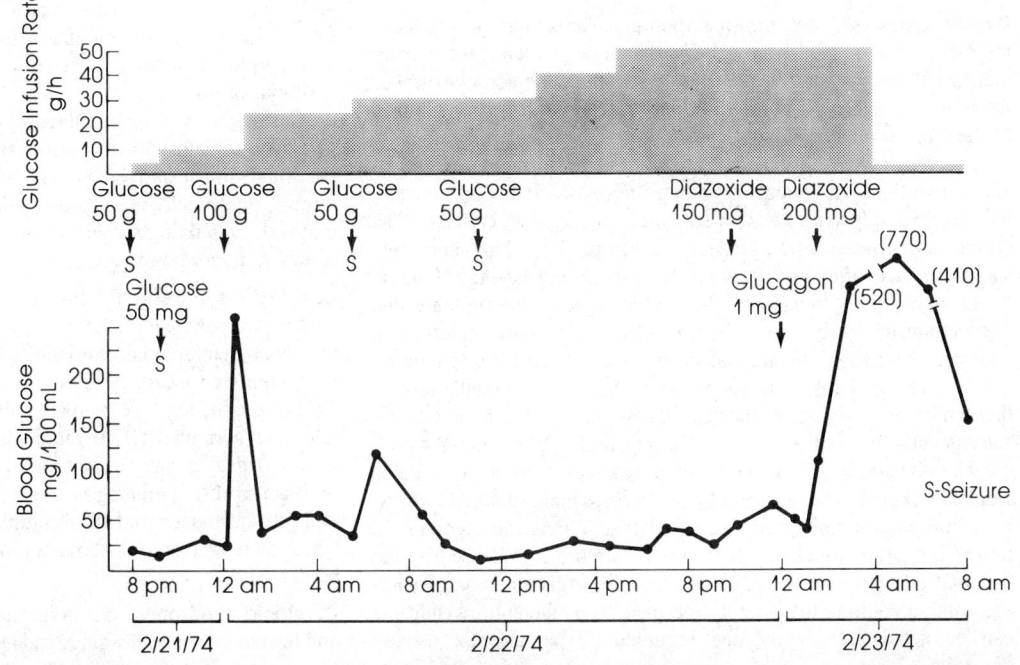

FIGURE 329-2 *Prolonged and refractory hypoglycemia in factitious hypoglycemia due to chlorpropamide in an alcoholic. Note continued hypoglycemia despite the infusion of glucose at rates up to 50 g/h. (From RM Jordan et al, Arch Intern Med 137:390, 1977. Copyright 1977, American Medical Association. Used by permission.)*

TABLE 329-6   Non-insulin-producing tumors of the pancreas

Tumor	Clinical syndrome
Gastrinoma	Severe peptic ulcer disease, secretory diarrhea, steatorrhea, hypersecretion of gastric acid, associated endocrine findings (MEN I)
Vipoma	Secretory diarrhea, hypokalemia, low or absent gastric acid, metabolic acidosis, hypercalcemia, hyperglycemia, dilated gallbladder, flushing
Glucagonoma	Migrating skin rash (necrolytic migratory erythema), sore tongue, cheilosis, weight loss, anemia, mild hyperglycemia, decreased plasma amino acids
Somatostatinoma	Dyspepsia, diarrhea, hyperglycemia, anemia, hypochlorhydria, gallstones, steatorrhea
Corticotropinoma	Cushing's syndrome
Carcinoid tumor	Diarrhea, flushing, tachycardia No asthma
Calcitoninoma	Diarrhea (?)
Parathyrinoma	Hypercalcemia
Neurotensinoma	Esophageal reflux (?)
PP-oma (pancreatic polypeptide)	Asymptomatic

Multiple ulcers may be present. Development of ulcer disease in the very young or very old should always raise suspicion of the Zollinger-Ellison syndrome. Associated endocrine abnormalities of the MEN I syndrome are present in half the patients and in a high percentage of first-degree relatives. Hypercalcemia due to parathyroid adenoma is the most common accompanying abnormality. A careful family history designed to elicit evidence of hypoglycemia, renal stones, and pituitary adenomas is imperative. All first-degree relatives of patients with gastrinomas should be examined by the physician. Multiple lipomas can be a clue to the presence of multiple endocrine neoplasia. Minimal screening should probably include CT scan of the pituitary and measurement of stimulated serum gastrin, cortisol, prolactin, calcium, and phosphorus. If hypercalcemia is present, workup for hyperparathyroidism can be completed. Evaluation for insulinoma is not indicated in the absence of symptoms suggesting hypoglycemia. Details of diagnosis and treatment for the Zollinger-Ellison syndrome are discussed in Chap. 235. Basically patients undergo total gastrectomy followed by treatment with a histamine H-2 receptor–blocking agent (cimetidine or ranitidine). Some authorities believe that gastrectomy is not indicated and that vagotomy plus H-2 blockers gives equally good results.

Diarrheogenic islet-cell tumor (vipoma)   The syndrome produced by these tumors has been called pancreatic cholera, the watery diarrhea syndrome, and the WDHA syndrome. The acronym stands for *w*atery *d*iarrhea, *h*ypokalemia, and *a*chlorhydria, major features of the clinical picture. Acid secretion in the basal state may actually be low rather than absent, and stimulation by histamine is intact. About two-thirds of patients have hypercalcemia, and approximately half are hyperglycemic. A dilated gallbladder is characteristic. The secretory diarrhea is often profuse and can produce shock and renal shutdown. It is often nocturnal and persists during fasting. Hypokalemia may be life-threatening. Metabolic acidosis, presumably due to bicarbonate loss but possibly also related to volume depletion, is common. Attacks of flushing occur in about 20 percent of patients.

Considerable confusion has existed about the hormonal cause of the syndrome. Originally secretin was thought to be involved, but subsequently vasoactive intestinal polypeptide (VIP), human pancreatic polypeptide, gastric inhibitory polypeptide, and prostaglandins were all reported to be associated with diarrheogenic islet-cell tumors. It is now almost universally accepted that VIP is the mediator in most cases. The attractiveness of this possibility is enhanced by the fact that the hormone is known to cause hyperglycemia and hypercalcemia in addition to secretory diarrhea. Thus the entire syndrome can be accounted for by one hormone. Hypercalcemia usually

disappears after removal of the pancreatic neoplasm and in most cases is not due to concomitant hyperparathyroidism.

Diagnosis requires demonstration of a secretory diarrhea, the presence of a pancreatic tumor, and elevation of plasma VIP levels on more than one occasion. Secretory diarrhea can essentially be ruled out if stool volume is less than 750 mL per 24 h. The diarrheogenic tumors tend to be larger than other islet adenomas and may be more easily localized by CT scan or ultrasonography.

Treatment is surgical removal of the tumor after fluid and electrolyte balance has been restored. Steroids ameliorate the diarrhea in some cases but should be used only if the patient is at risk for life despite conservative management preparatory to surgery. Diarrhea disappears, and gastric acid secretion and potassium concentration return to normal if the tumor is completely removed. Somatostatin analogues may be helpful when the tumor is not resectable.

Glucagonoma   Glucagonomas, a high percentage of which appear to be malignant and metastasizing, cause a distinctive skin lesion (necrolytic migratory erythema) on the face, lower abdomen, perineum, buttocks, or distal extremities. The characteristic picture is of multiple crusts, scaly macules and papules, occasional pustules, flaccid bullae, and generalized erythema. Glossitis, stomatitis, and angular cheilosis are common. Spontaneous exacerbations and remissions occur, and hyperpigmentation follows healing. Weight loss and normochromic, normocytic anemia are common. Elevated fasting blood glucose concentrations or abnormal glucose tolerance tests are present in most patients. Plasma amino acid levels are depressed, and hypocholesterolemia may be present. Plasma ketones may be elevated despite normal plasma free fatty acid concentrations. Glucagon levels in plasma are high (5 to 10 times normal) and show abnormal responses to a number of provocative tests. It is of interest that four asymptomatic first-degree relatives of one patient with a proved glucagonoma had persistently elevated glucagon concentrations and abnormal responses to glucose suppression and arginine stimulation. Transmission appeared to follow an autosomal dominant pattern. Whether the asymptomatic subjects had small (undetectable) adenomas or whether the alpha cells were functionally abnormal but not neoplastic is not known. Glucagonomas have also been reported in a family with multiple endocrine neoplasia type I.

Treatment of glucagonoma is surgical removal. Chemotherapy of metastatic disease is unsatisfactory. Experimentally a long-acting somatostatin analogue has been tried and may be of benefit.

Somatostatinoma   The secretion of somatostatin by islet-cell tumors causes a picture that includes dyspepsia, diarrhea, weight loss, cholelithiasis with a dilated gallbladder, mild hyperglycemia, anemia, and hypochlorhydria. Steatorrhea and abdominal pain may be present. In addition to a pancreatic mass, liver metastases are usually present at the time of diagnosis. Because somatostatinomas often produce additional hormones, some patients may have hypoglycemia, flushing, or Cushing's syndrome. Diagnosis requires demonstration of high levels of somatostatin in plasma together with a pancreatic tumor. Intestinal somatostatinomas, which histologically are psammomatous tumors, do not release somatostatin into plasma. Treatment is surgical removal. Debulking surgery may be carried out even when complete resection is not possible.

Cushing's syndrome   Adrenocorticotropic hormone (ACTH) production by pancreatic islet tumors causes less severe clinical manifestations than are characteristic of other forms of ectopic Cushing's syndrome (see Chap. 325). Pigmentation may be a clue to ectopic ACTH production. Occasionally the tumor produces corticotropin-releasing hormone (CRH) rather than ACTH. Mixed hormone production (insulin, gastrin, serotonin) is common in these tumors. The problem of differentiating between a single islet tumor that produces multiple hormones and the multiple endocrine neoplasia syndrome where two or more adenomas each produce a single hormone may be difficult.

Carcinoid syndrome   Serotonin may be synthesized in islet tumors and lead to diarrhea, flushing, and tachycardia. Asthma is not present.

Some of these patients may actually have a diarrheogenic tumor with symptoms primarily due to vasoactive intestinal polypeptide, and serotonin production may represent a second hormone synthesized by a mixed adenoma (see Chap. 299).

General principles of treatment Brief comments about treatment have been made for the major syndromes. It is not always clear what the best therapy might be, especially if metastases to liver are present. A reasonable approach might be the following in all tumors except gastrinoma (which, as noted, requires gastrectomy or vagotomy): (1) resect all primary tumors; (2) resect all primary tumors and follow with partial hepatectomy if the hepatic lesion is localized; (3) utilize antisecretory drugs in inoperable cases or in preparation for surgery if the patient is in poor shape. These would include H-2 receptor antagonists in gastrinoma and somatostatin analogues in vipoma and glucagonoma (somatostatin probably should be tried in all diarrheal forms); (4) reserve chemotherapy for "last resort" conditions.

REFERENCES

Hypoglycemia and insulinoma

AVRAM MM et al: Uremic hypoglycemia. A preventable life-threatening complication. NY State J Med 84:593, 1984

BAUMAN WA, YALOW RS: Hyperinsulinemic hypoglycemia. Differential diagnosis by determination of the species of circulating insulin. JAMA 252:2730, 1984

BOLLI G et al: Role of hepatic autoregulation in defense against hypoglycemia in humans. J Clin Invest 75:1623, 1985

CHARLES MA et al: Comparison of oral glucose tolerance tests and mixed meals in patients with apparent idiopathic postabsorptive hypoglycemia. Absence of hypoglycemia after meals. Diabetes 30:465, 1981

CRYER PE: Glucose counterregulation in man. Diabetes 30:261, 1981

————: Glucose homeostasis and hypoglycemia, in *Williams' Textbook of Endocrinology*, 7th ed., JD Wilson, DW Foster (eds). Philadelphia, Saunders, 1985, pp 989–1017

GOLDMAN J et al: Characterization of circulating insulin and pro-insulin-binding antibodies in autoimmune hypoglycemia. J Clin Invest 63:1050, 1979

GORDEN P et al: Hypoglycemia associated with non-islet-cell tumor and insulin-like growth factors. A study of the tumor types. N Engl J Med 305:1452, 1981

HALE DE et al: Long-chain acyl coenzyme A dehydrogenase deficiency: An inherited cause of nonketotic hypoglycemia. Pediatr Res 19:666, 1985

HANSEN IL et al: Differential diagnosis of hypoglycemia in children by responses to fasting and 2-deoxyglucose. Metabolism 32:960, 1983

HOELZER DR et al: Glucoregulation during exercise: Hypoglycemia is prevented by redundant glucoregulatory systems, sympathochromaffin activation, and changes in islet hormone secretion. J Clin Invest 77:212, 1986

HOGAN MJ et al: Oral glucose tolerance test compared with a mixed meal in the diagnosis of reactive hypoglycemia. A caveat on stimulation. Mayo Clin Proc 58:491, 1983

JORDAN RM et al: Sulfonylurea-induced factitious hypoglycemia. A growing problem. Arch Intern Med 137:390, 1977

KLEIN RF et al: High performance liquid chromatography used to distinguish the autoimmune hypoglycemia syndrome from factitious hypoglycemia. J Clin Endocrinol Metab 61:571, 1985

LEV-RAN A, ANDERSON RW: The diagnosis of postprandial hypoglycemia. Diabetes 30:996, 1981

MALOUF R, BRUST JCM: Hypoglycemia: Causes, neurological manifestations, and outcome. Ann Neurol 17:421, 1985

McGARRY JD, FOSTER DW: Systemic carnitine deficiency. N Engl J Med 303:1413, 1980

MERIMEE TJ, TYSON JE: Hypoglycemia in man. Pathologic and physiologic variants. Diabetes 26:161, 1977

MOERTEL CG et al: Streptozocin alone compared with streptozocin plus fluorouracil in the treatment of advanced islet-cell carcinoma. N Engl J Med 303:1189, 1980

NAYLOR JM, KRONFELD DS: In vivo studies of hypoglycemia and lactic acidosis in endotoxic shock. Am J Physiol 248:E309, 1985

RIZZA RA et al: Pathogenesis of hypoglycemia in insulinoma patients. Suppression of hepatic glucose production by insulin. Diabetes 30:377, 1981

SCARLETT JA et al: Factitious hypoglycemia. Diagnosis by measurement of serum C-peptide immunoreactivity and insulin-binding antibodies. N Engl J Med 297:1029, 1977

SERVICE FJ et al: Insulinoma. Clinical and diagnostic features of 60 consecutive cases. Mayo Clin Proc 51:417, 1976

————: *Hypoglycemia Disorders*, Boston, G. K. Hall, 1983

STEFANINI P: Beta-islet cell tumors of the pancreas: Results of a study on 1067 cases. Surgery 75:597, 1974

Other hormone-secreting islet-cell tumors

CREUTZFELDT W: Endocrine tumors of the pancreas: Clinical, chemical and morphological findings, in *The Pancreas*, PJ Fitzgerald, AB Morrison (eds). Baltimore, Williams & Wilkins, 1980, pp 185–207

FRIESEN SR: Tumors of the endocrine pancreas. N Engl J Med 306:580, 1982

JASPAN JB et al: Clinical features and diagnosis of islet cell tumors, in *Tumors of the Pancreas*, AR Moosa (ed). Baltimore, Williams & Wilkins, 1980, pp 469–504

KREJS GJ: Non-insulin-secreting tumors of the pancreatic islets, in *William's Textbook of Endocrinology*, 7th ed., JD Wilson, DW Foster (eds). Philadelphia, Saunders, 1985, pp 1301–1308

SANTANGELO WC et al: Pancreatic cholera syndrome: Effect of a synthetic somatostatin analog on intestinal water and ion transport. Ann Intern Med 103:363, 1985

STACPOOLE PW et al: A familial glucagonoma syndrome: Genetic, clinical and biochemical features. Am J Med 70:1017, 1981

---

330 DISORDERS OF THE TESTIS

JAMES E. GRIFFIN III / JEAN D. WILSON

The testis produces sperm and the steroid hormones that regulate male sexual life. Both functions are under complex feedback control by the hypothalamic-pituitary system so that the testis has biosynthetic and regulatory features similar to those of the ovary and the adrenal. Testicular hormones are also responsible for the formation of the basic male phenotype during embryogenesis. The function of the embryonic testis and the disorders that result from abnormalities of testicular function or androgen action during embryogenesis are described in Chap. 333.

PHYSIOLOGY AND REGULATION OF TESTICULAR FUNCTION

The testis consists of two components—a system of spermatogenic tubules for the production and transport of sperm and clusters of interstitial or Leydig cells that produce androgenic steroids.

THE LEYDIG CELL Testosterone synthesis The biochemical pathway by which the 27-carbon sterol cholesterol is converted to androgens and estrogens is depicted in Fig. 330-1. Cholesterol can either be synthesized de novo in the Leydig cell or derived from plasma lipoproteins. Five enzymes or enzyme complexes are required for the conversion of cholesterol to testosterone. In this process the side chain of cholesterol is cleaved in two steps to reduce the size from 27 to 19 carbons, and the A ring of the steroid is converted to the Δ^4-3-keto configuration. The five enzymes are the 20,22-desmolase, the 3β-hydroxysteroid dehydrogenase-$\Delta^{4,5}$-isomerase complex, 17α-hydroxylase, 17,20-desmolase, and 17β-hydroxysteroid dehydrogenase. The first four enzymes are also present in the adrenal.

The rate-limiting reaction in testosterone synthesis is the conversion of cholesterol to pregnenolone by the 20,22-desmolase; luteinizing hormone (LH) from the pituitary regulates the activity of this enzyme and of other enzymes in the pathway. Other steroids including estradiol are synthesized in small amounts in the Leydig cell.

Testosterone secretion and transport Only about 0.02 mg of testosterone is stored in the normal testes so that the total hormone content turns over about 200 times each day to provide the average of 5 to 6 mg that is secreted into plasma in normal young men (Fig. 330-2). Testosterone is transported in plasma bound to protein, largely to albumin and to a specific transport protein, testosterone-binding globulin (TeBG). The bound and unbound fractions in plasma are in dynamic equilibrium, only about 1 to 3 percent being present in the free fraction. The fraction of circulating testosterone available for entry into tissues approximates the sum of the free and albumin-bound fractions or about 40 to 50 percent of the total plasma testosterone in normal men.

Peripheral metabolism of androgens Testosterone serves as a circulating precursor (or prohormone) for the formation of two other types of active metabolites which mediate many of the physiologic processes involved in androgen action (Fig. 330-1). On the one hand, testosterone can be 5α-reduced to dihydrotestosterone, which performs many of the differentiative, growth-promoting, and functional

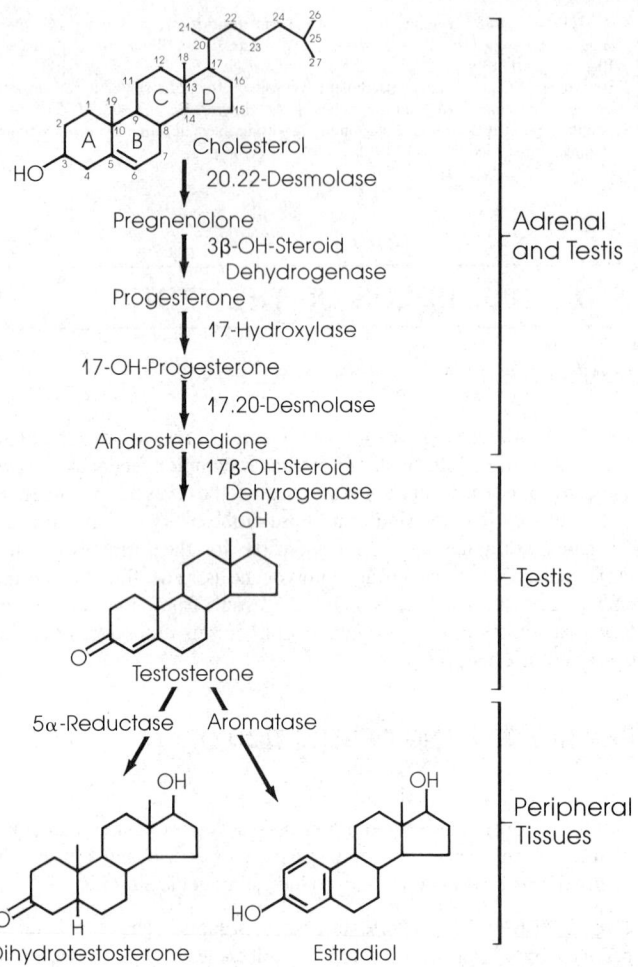

FIGURE 330-1 *Pathways of androgen formation in the testis and the conversion of androgens to other active hormones in peripheral tissues.*

actions involved in male sexual differentiation and virilization. Circulating androgens in both sexes can also be converted to estrogens in extraglandular tissues. In men estrogens act in some instances in concert with androgens but can also have effects independent of or opposite to those of androgens. Thus, the physiologic effects of testosterone are the result of the combined effects of testosterone itself plus those of the active androgen and estrogen metabolites of the parent molecule. (In normal men small amounts of estradiol and dihydrotestosterone are also derived by direct secretion from the testis and indirectly from the weak adrenal androgen androstenedione.)

The quantitative relation between circulating androgens and the formation of estrogen in normal young men is illustrated diagrammatically in Fig. 330-2. The production rates of testosterone and androstenedione average about 6 and 3 mg, respectively, per day. All of estrone production (averaging about 66 μg per day) can be accounted for by formation from circulating precursors. The mean estradiol production rate is about 45 μg per day; about 35 percent of this amount is derived from circulating testosterone, 50 percent is derived from the weak estrogen estrone, and 15 percent is secreted directly into the circulation by the testes. When gonadotropin levels are elevated, the amount of estradiol secretion by the testis is increased.

The 5α-reduced and estrogenic metabolites can exert local (paracrine) actions in the tissues in which they are formed or enter the circulation and act as hormones at other sites. Circulating dihydrotestosterone is formed principally in the androgen target tissues, and estrogen formation takes place in many tissues, the most significant being adipose tissue. The overall rate of extraglandular estrogen formation increases with increasing amounts of adipose tissue and with age.

Plasma testosterone and its active metabolites are converted to inactive metabolites in the liver and excreted predominantly in the urine; approximately half of the daily turnover is excreted in the form of urinary 17-ketosteroids (primarily androsterone and etiocholanolone), and the remainder is excreted as a series of polar compounds (diols, triols, and conjugates).

Gonadotropin regulation and testosterone secretion Testosterone secretion is regulated by pituitary LH (Fig. 330-3). (For the details of pituitary function, see Chap. 321.) Follicle-stimulating hormone (FSH) may also augment testosterone secretion, possibly by inducing maturation of the Leydig cell. Testosterone also regulates the sensitivity of the pituitary to the hypothalamic-releasing factor luteinizing hormone–releasing hormone (LHRH). Although the pituitary can convert testosterone to dihydrotestosterone and to estrogens, testosterone itself is the primary regulator of gonadotropin secretion.

FIGURE 330-2 *Androgen and estrogen production in normal young men. Average production of androstenedione and testosterone are shown in the top boxes, and mean daily production of estrone and estradiol is shown in the lower boxes. Estrogen is formed by extraglandular aromatization (braces) or by direct secretion from the testes. Vertical arrows indicate the rates of extraglandular aromatization of androgens, and the horizontal arrows indicate the interconversion of androgen and estrogens by 17β-hydroxysteroid dehydrogenase. Thus estradiol arises from plasma testosterone, from estrone, and from direct secretion by the testes. (Adapted from PC MacDonald et al.)*

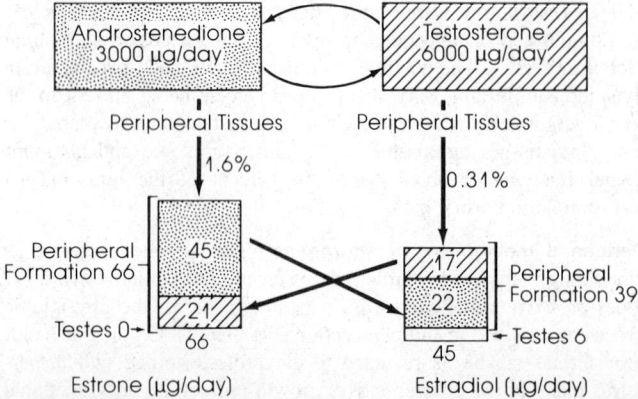

FIGURE 330-3 *Regulation of testosterone and sperm production by LH and FSH. (C, cholesterol; T, testosterone.)*

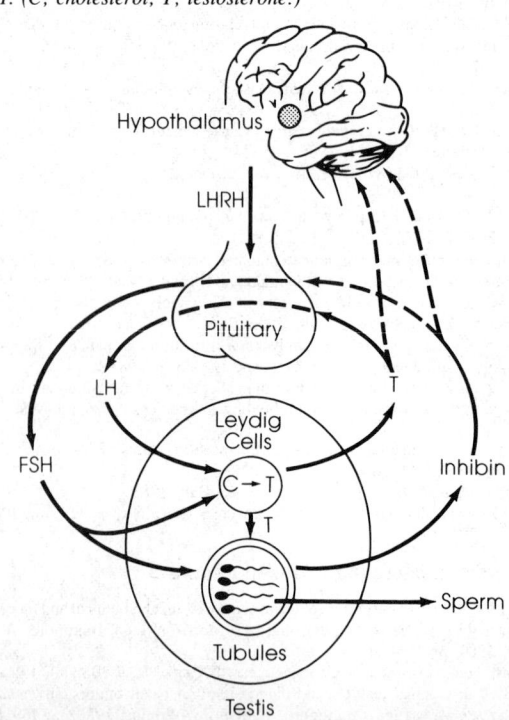

Testosterone also acts in the central nervous system to slow the rate of LHRH formation or secretion and consequently to decrease the frequency of pulsatile LH release. Under ordinary circumstances, LH secretion is exquisitely sensitive to the feedback effects of testosterone, with complete suppression following the administration of amounts of exogenous androgen that approximate the normal daily secretory rate of testosterone (about 6 mg). However, prolonged elevation of plasma LH (as in testicular deficiency) renders the pituitary less sensitive to negative feedback control by exogenous androgen.

Neither the plasma concentration of testosterone nor that of LH is constant, each showing fluctuations of a pulsatile nature that reflect changes in secretory rates (Fig. 330-4). Major sleep-related surges in the pulsatile secretion of both LH and testosterone signal the initiation of male puberty. In the adult the diurnal variation in the magnitude of this episodic secretion of LH and testosterone is minor with peak morning levels only about 10 to 15 percent higher than during the rest of the day.

Androgen action The major functions of androgen are the regulation of gonadotropin secretion, the formation of the male phenotype during sexual differentiation, and the induction of sexual maturation and function following puberty. The cellular mechanisms by which androgens perform these functions are summarized schematically in Fig. 330-5. Testosterone (T) enters the cell by passive diffusion. Inside the cell T can be converted to dihydrotestosterone (D) by the 5α-reductase enzyme. T or D is then bound to the androgen-receptor protein in the cytosol (R). The hormone-receptor complex (TR or DR) is transformed to the DNA-binding state (TR* or DR*) and translocated to the nucleus, where it attaches to specific chromosomal sites; as a result, new messenger RNA is transcribed, and new protein appears within the cytoplasm of the cell.

Although testosterone and dihydrotestosterone bind to the same receptor, their physiologic roles differ. The testosterone-receptor complex regulates gonadotropin secretion and is responsible for the Wolffian stimulation phase of sexual differentiation (see Chap. 333), whereas the dihydrotestosterone-receptor complex is responsible for external virilization during embryogenesis and the major portion of androgen action during sexual maturation and adult sexual life, including the initiation and maintenance of spermatogenesis. The mechanism by which testosterone and dihydrotestosterone mediate these different functions is not known. The mechanisms by which estrogens act to augment or block androgen effects are also not known. It is presumed that estradiol acts by a mechanism similar to that of androgens but involving its own receptor protein (see Chap. 331).

THE SEMINIFEROUS TUBULE AND SPERMATOGENESIS Normal function of the seminiferous tubule is dependent both on the pituitary and on normal function of the adjacent Leydig cells, both FSH and androgen being essential for initiating and maintaining normal spermatogenesis (Fig. 330-3). The major site of FSH action is the Sertoli cell in the seminiferous tubules. The seminiferous tubule also contains

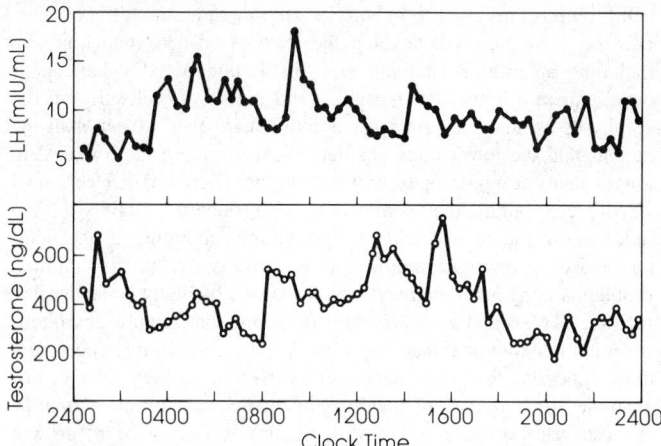

FIGURE 330-4 *Twenty-four-hour pattern of plasma LH and testosterone in a normal man sampled every 20 min. (Reprinted from Griffin and Wilson, 1980.)*

specific androgen receptors. Androgen appears to be essential for the initial phase of spermatogenesis, whereas FSH is required for the terminal phases of spermatid development. In the normal adult male this machinery produces more than 200 million sperm per day.

The Sertoli cell cannot synthesize steroid hormones de novo and is dependent on testosterone that diffuses in from adjacent Leydig cells. Sertoli cells can convert testosterone to estradiol and to dihydrotestosterone. The seminiferous tubules also produce the peptide hormone inhibin that regulates the secretion of FSH by the hypothalamic-pituitary axis (Fig. 330-3). Whether inhibin is the primary physiologic regulator of FSH is unclear; testosterone and estradiol also can inhibit FSH secretion, and altered frequency of LHRH pulses can result in selective increases of FSH.

The interlocking system in which two pituitary hormones regulate testicular function provides a precise dual-control mechanism by which plasma testosterone and sperm production feed back upon the hypothalamic-pituitary system to regulate their own rates of production (Fig. 330-3).

ASSESSMENT OF TESTICULAR FUNCTION

LEYDIG CELL FUNCTION **History of physical examination** The assessment of Leydig cell function and androgen status should include inquiry about the presence at birth of developmental abnormalities of the urogenital tract, the timing and extent of sexual maturation at puberty, the rate of beard growth, and the current libido, sexual function, strength, and energy. Inadequate Leydig cell function or androgen action during embryogenesis may manifest itself by the presence of hypospadias, cryptorchidism, or microphallus. If Leydig

FIGURE 330-5 *Current concepts of androgen action. (T, testosterone; D, dihydrotestosterone; E, estradiol; R, receptor protein; R*, transformed receptor protein; LH, luteinizing hormone; 5α-Red, 5α-reductase.)*

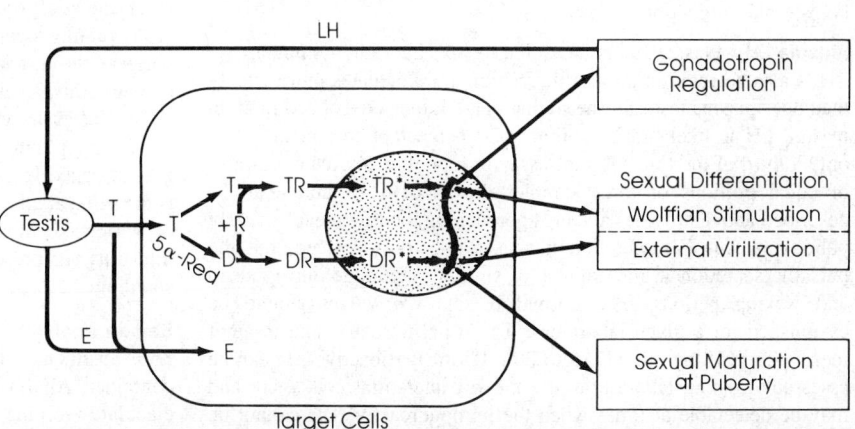

cell failure occurs prior to puberty, sexual maturation will not occur, and the individual will develop the features termed eunuchoidism, including an infantile amount and distribution of body hair, poor development of skeletal muscles, and failure of closure of the epiphyses so that the arm span is more than 2 in greater than the height, and the lower body segment (heel to pubic) more than 2 in longer than the upper body segment (pubic to crown). Detection of Leydig cell failure that commences after puberty requires a high index of suspicion and usually appropriate laboratory assessment. One reason is that decreased sexual function is a relatively common problem among adult men and may be caused by many nonendocrine factors. The second is that certain functions that require androgens for initiation continue unabated when Leydig cell failure occurs, and those functions that eventually regress may do so very slowly. For example, the frequency of shaving may not decrease for many months or even years because of the slow decline in rate of beard growth once established.

Plasma testosterone and dihydrotestosterone levels Plasma testosterone is measured by a specific radioimmunoassay. Testosterone is secreted into plasma in a pulsatile fashion every 60 to 90 min (Fig. 330-4); a single random sample provides a result within ±20 percent of the true mean value only two-thirds of the time while three equally spaced samples 15 to 20 min apart provide a more accurate assessment. The samples do not need to be assayed separately, and aliquots of the three samples can be pooled for a single determination. The range of plasma testosterone in normal adult men is 300 to 1000 ng/dL. In adult men the plasma values vary slightly throughout the day and at different times of the year, but these variations are not as great as those for plasma cortisol and are not significant in routine clinical assessment. Plasma levels of testosterone correlate in general with testosterone secretory rates as measured by isotope infusion. Estimation of TeBG concentration is sometimes useful in the interpretation of total plasma testosterone levels. Such assays can be done either by measuring the binding capacity of radioactive androgen or with a specific radioimmunoassay.

The plasma testosterone value in prepubertal children is statistically higher in boys than girls, the range in both being 5 to 20 ng/dL. The rise in plasma testosterone at the beginning of puberty occurs as a result of sleep-related nocturnal gonadotropin surges so that during the initial phases plasma testosterone and LH are higher at night than during the day. The random daytime levels of plasma testosterone increase gradually as puberty progresses and reach adult levels at about age 17.

Dihydrotestosterone is also measured by radioimmunoassay. In normal young men the plasma dihydrotestosterone level is about one-tenth that of the testosterone value and averages around 50 ng/dL. In older men with benign prostatic hyperplasia, plasma dihydrotestosterone levels are higher and average about 90 ng/dL.

Urinary 17-ketosteroids The measurement of urinary 17-ketosteroids is not a valid way to assess testicular function. Urinary 17-ketosteroids are mainly weak adrenal androgens or their metabolites, and testosterone contributes only about 40 percent of daily 17-ketosteroid production in men.

Plasma LH Plasma LH is measured by specific radioimmunoassay. LH is also secreted in a pulsatile fashion and fluctuates more widely than does plasma testosterone so that in adult men an isolated random plasma LH is likely to be within ±20 percent of true mean value only a third of the time. Again, assay of a pool of plasma comprised of equal portions of three samples drawn 6 to 18 min apart as described above provides a value approaching the true mean. In early puberty plasma LH secretion increases only during sleep, but the pulsatile secretion in the adult is of similar magnitude during sleep and waking periods. The normal plasma LH values should be established for a given laboratory. The usual normal range in adult men is 26 ±18 ng/mL SD (5 to 20 mIU/mL). Bioactive LH can be assessed in some laboratories by the rat interstitial cell assay and may be detectable at times when the immunoreactive LH cannot be

measured. A low plasma testosterone concentration can be interpreted correctly only if plasma LH is also measured simultaneously, and likewise the "appropriateness" of a given plasma LH must be interpreted in relation to the plasma testosterone. For example, a low plasma testosterone coupled with a low LH implies hypothalamic or pituitary disease, whereas the finding of a low plasma testosterone and a high LH suggests primary testicular insufficiency (see Chap. 320).

Response to gonadotropin stimulation Leydig cell function is difficult to assess prior to puberty when both LH and testosterone levels are low, and it is common to measure response of plasma testosterone to gonadotropin stimulation as an index of Leydig cell capacity. Normal prepubertal boys respond to 3 to 5 days of injection of 1000 to 2000 IU human chorionic gonadotropin (HCG) with an increase in plasma testosterone to about 200 ng/dL; the magnitude of the response increases with the initiation of puberty and peaks in early puberty.

Response to luteinizing hormone–releasing hormone The response of plasma LH (and/or FSH) to the administration of luteinizing hormone–releasing hormone (LHRH) is utilized in some centers to assess the functional integrity of the pituitary-testicular axis. The responsiveness of the pituitary gland to LHRH changes at the time of puberty. Prior to puberty quantitative responses to LH and FSH are similar. With pubertal development the LH response to acute administration of LHRH increases while the FSH response remains the same. The amount of LH released following acute administration of LHRH probably reflects the amount of stored hormone in the pituitary. When 100 μg of LHRH is given subcutaneously or intravenously to normal men, there is, on average, a four- to fivefold increase in LH with the peak level at 30 min. However, the range of response is broad with some normal men having less than a doubling of LH levels. In general, the peak LH following a single LHRH injection correlates with the basal levels. In patients with primary testicular failure measurement of basal LH is usually sufficient, and measurement of LHRH response adds little to aid the diagnosis. Men who have either pituitary disease or hypothalamic disease may have either a normal or an abnormal LH response to an acute dose of LHRH. Therefore, a normal response is of no diagnostic value, either in determining the presence or absence of disease or in distinguishing hypothalamic from pituitary disease. A subnormal response is of value in determining that an abnormality exists, even though the site is not determined. The LHRH test is most useful in the evaluation of men with secondary hypogonadism and subnormal LH response to an acute dose of LHRH. If daily infusions of LHRH for a week lead to the development of a normal LH response to an acute dose, a hypothalamic etiology is likely.

SEMINIFEROUS TUBULE FUNCTION Examination of the testes Evaluation of the testes is an essential portion of the physical examination. The seminiferous tubules account for about 95 percent of testicular volume. The prepubertal testis measures about 2 cm in length and 2 mL in volume and increases in size during puberty to reach the adult proportions by age 16. When damage to the seminiferous tubules occurs prior to puberty the testes are small and firm, whereas the testes are usually small and soft following postpubertal damage (the capsule, once enlarged, does not contract to its previous size). Testes in adults average 4.6 cm in length (range, 3.5 to 5.5 cm), corresponding to a volume of 12 to 25 mL. Advanced age does not influence testicular size, so that the significance of small testes is the same at all ages in the adult. Because of the frequent occurrence of varicocele among infertile men and its possible causal role in infertility, its presence should be sought by palpation with the patient standing.

Semen analysis Seminal fluid analysis is performed after 24- to 36-h abstinence on samples obtained by masturbation into a glass container. Analysis should be performed within an hour. The normal ejaculate volume is 2 to 6 mL. Immediately after ejaculation, coagulation of the seminal fluid occurs, followed within 15 to 30 min by liquefaction. Estimation of motility should be made on undiluted seminal fluid; more than 60 percent of the sperm should be motile and of normal morphology. The normal range for sperm density is generally considered to be greater than 20 million per milliliter with a total count per ejaculate of more than 60 million, but a major difficulty in the interpretation of a semen analysis is the definition of the minimally adequate ejaculate. Some men with low sperm counts are nevertheless fertile. This uncertainty as to the lower level of sperm density, percent motility, and percent normal forms in fertile semen stems from two issues. First, many factors produce temporary aberrations in sperm count, and in men who present with semen of equivocal quality it is necessary to examine three or more ejaculates to determine whether abnormal findings are permanent or temporary. Second, routine evaluation of the seminal fluid is dependent on tests that do not assess the functional capacity of the sperm. Although methods to measure sperm penetration of bovine cervical mucus and zona-free hamster ova have been developed, they are not sufficiently standardized to permit general use.

Plasma FSH   Plasma FSH as measured by specific radioimmunoassay usually correlates inversely with spermatogenesis. In normal adult men, the range of plasma FSH is 102 ± 55 ng/mL SD (5 to 20 mIU/mL). Men with intact hypothalamic-pituitary axes have elevations of FSH when damage to the germinal epithelium is severe.

Testicular biopsy   Testicular biospy is useful in some patients with oligospermia and azoospermia both as an aid in diagnosis and as an indication of feasibility of treatment. For example, a normal testicular biopsy and a normal FSH in an azoospermic man suggest the presence of obstruction of the vas deferens, which may be surgically correctible. Tissue culture of the biopsy material with subsequent karyotypic analysis is necessary to identify those instances of Klinefelter syndrome secondary to chromosomal mosaicism in which the abnormality is limited to the testes. Testicular biopsy is often followed by a transient decrease in sperm counts, but there are no permanent adverse effects.

ESTROGENIC FUNCTION   Examination of the breasts   Breast enlargement is the most consistent feature of feminizing states in men (see Chap. 332). Gynecomastia, enlargement of the male breast, is due to the proliferation of glandular tissue. The presence of gynecomastia should be sought by examining the patient while he is in the sitting position using the fingers to grasp glandular tissue. Palpation with the flat of the hand while the patient is supine may result in failure to detect early or minimal breast enlargement. In obese men it is important to try to define the edge of the rim of glandular tissue that separates it from adipose tissue of the chest wall.

Plasma estrogen   As discussed above, most of the estradiol and all of the estrone produced in normal men is formed by extraglandular aromatization of circulating androgens. Plasma estradiol is usually less than 50 pg/mL in normal men; plasma estrone is somewhat higher but usually less than 80 pg/mL. Elevated estrogen production and elevated plasma levels can be due to elevations in plasma precursors (liver or adrenal disease), to increases in peripheral aromatization (obesity), or to increased production by the testes (testicular tumors or androgen resistance).

PHASES OF NORMAL TESTICULAR FUNCTION

The phases of male sexual life can be defined in terms of the plasma testosterone value (Fig. 330-6). In the male embryo the production of testosterone by the testis commences at about 7 weeks of gestation. Shortly thereafter plasma testosterone attains a high value that is maintained until it falls late in gestation so that at the time of birth plasma testosterone is only slightly higher in males than in females. Shortly after birth, plasma testosterone in the male infant again begins to rise and remains elevated for approximately 3 months, falling to low levels by age 1 year. The concentration then remains low (but slightly higher in boys than girls) until the onset of puberty, when it begins to rise in boys, reaching adult levels by age 17 or thereabouts. The mean plasma level remains more or less constant in the adult until late middle age and then declines slowly during the later decades of life. It is only during the third or adult phase of male sexual life that sperm production becomes sufficient to allow reproduction to take place. The physiologic events that take place during these various phases differ, as do the pathologic consequences of derangements in testicular function at different stages of life. Male sexual differentiation during embryogenesis is considered in Chap. 333. The role of the neonatal surge of testosterone formation during the first year of life is unknown. The focus of this chapter is on testicular pathophysiology during puberty, mature sexual life, and old age.

ABNORMALITIES OF TESTICULAR FUNCTION

PUBERTY   The factors that ultimately determine the onset of puberty are poorly understood and may reside in the hypothalamic-pituitary system, the testis, or the adrenal. Prior to the onset of puberty, gonadotropin secretion by the pituitary is low but appears to be under regulatory control by the testis, as prepubertal castration results in a rise in plasma gonadotropin levels. This suggests that prior to puberty the negative feedback control of gonadotropin secretion is exquisitely

FIGURE 330-6   *Phases of male sexual life. (Reprinted from Griffin and Wilson, 1980.)*

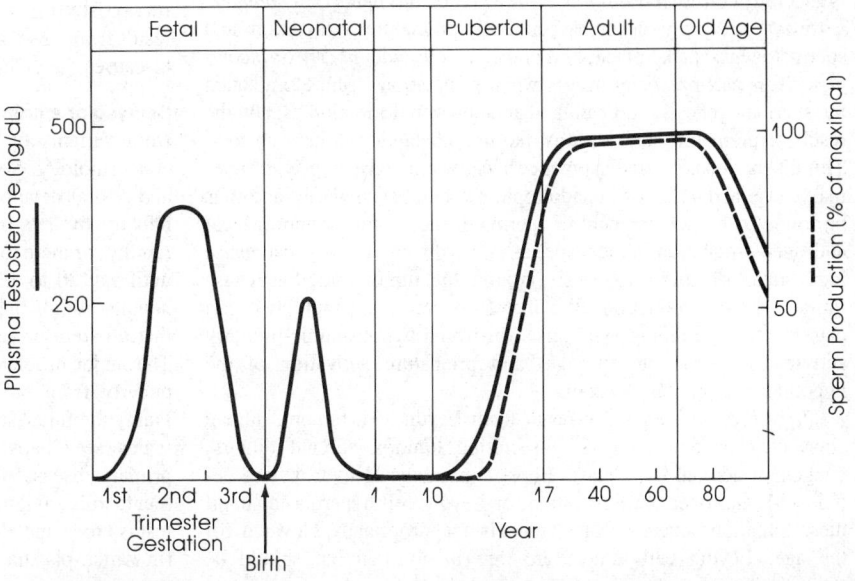

sensitive to the small amount of circulating testosterone. The onset of puberty is heralded by sleep-associated surges in gonadotropin secretion. Later in puberty the rises in LH and FSH persist throughout the day. Thus, with maturation the hypothalamic-pituitary system becomes less sensitive to negative feedback control, and the consequences are a higher mean plasma testosterone, maturation of the testes, and the onset of spermatogenesis. The rise in gonadotropin secretion is believed to be the consequence both of an increase in LHRH secretion and an increased sensitivity of the pituitary to LHRH. Plasma levels of bioactive LH increase even more than those of the immunoreactive hormone. The remaining anatomic and functional changes at the time of puberty are secondary to the rise in plasma testosterone. Maturation of the accessory organs of male reproduction (the penis, the prostate, the seminal vesicles, and the epididymides) accounts for about one-fourth of androgen-mediated nitrogen retention during puberty. The characteristic hair growth of male puberty involves development of mustache and beard, regression of the scalp line, appearance of body, extremity, and perianal hair, and extension of the pubic hair upward into a diamond-shaped pattern. Growth of axillary and pubic hair is initiated under the control of adrenal androgens and promoted by testicular androgens. The larynx enlarges, and the vocal cords become thickened, resulting in a lowering of the pitch of the voice. Linear growth is accelerated and is accompanied by growth of muscle and connective tissue which accounts for the major portion of nitrogen retention at puberty. The principal androgen-sensitive muscles are those of the pectoral region and the shoulder. There is, in addition, an increase in the hematocrit. These various androgen-mediated growth and maturation processes reach some limiting value so that once puberty is completed the administration of pharmacologic doses of androgen has no further effect. The entire process is usually heralded by testicular enlargement at age 11 to 12 and is usually completed within 5 years, although some aspects of virilization, such as growth of the chest hair, may continue over a decade or more.

The events of normal male puberty are variable in onset, duration, and sequence. The central issue in dealing with disorders of puberty is separating instances of true absence or precocity from subjects at the extremes of normal variation. The use of staging criteria that correlate developmental and anatomic landmarks with chronologic age is useful in making this distinction. (See Marshall and Tanner.)

Sexual precocity   Those disorders in which the developing sexual characteristics are appropriate for the phenotype, i.e., virilization in boys, are termed *isosexual precocity*. Heterosexual precocity refers to feminizing syndromes occurring in boys with early sexual development.

ISOSEXUAL PRECOCITY   Sexual development prior to age 9 in boys is generally considered abnormal. *True precocious puberty* or *complete isosexual precocity* occurs when both premature virilization and spermatogenesis take place, and *precocious pseudopuberty* or *incomplete isosexual precocity* occurs when virilization is unaccompanied by spermatogenesis, indicating that androgen formation is not the result of premature activation of the hypothalamic-pituitary system. This distinction is blurred in practice because pure virilizing syndromes may cause activation of gonadotropin secretion secondarily and thus be followed by development of spermatogenesis. Furthermore, local androgen production in the testis, as in Leydig cell tumors, can cause local areas of spermatogenesis around the tumor and thus cause limited sperm production. We therefore prefer a simple two-part classification: virilizing syndromes (in which hypothalamic-pituitary activity is appropriate for age) and premature activation of the hypothalamic pituitary system.

Virilizing syndromes can result from Leydig cell tumors, human chorionic gonadotropin (hCG)–secreting tumors, adrenal tumors, congenital adrenal hyperplasia (most commonly 21-hydroxylase deficiency), androgen administration, or Leydig cell hyperplasia. In all these situations plasma testosterone is inappropriately elevated for the age. Leydig cell tumors are rare in children but should be suspected when the testes are asymmetric in size (see Chap. 297). Virilizing adrenal tumors are usually associated with the production of large amounts of adrenal androgen (mainly androstenedione and dehydroepiandrosterone, some of which is converted to testosterone) and consequently with elevated 17-ketosteroid secretion. Glucocorticoid administration does not suppress 17-ketosteroid excretion to normal in either testicular or adrenal tumors, in contrast to the prompt decrease that occurs following such treatment in congenital adrenal hyperplasia. Congenital adrenal hyperplasia leads to elevated 17-hydroxyprogesterone levels and as a consequence elevated androgen levels (see Chaps. 325 and 333). In this disorder enhanced gonadotropin secretion can be initiated secondarily so that true precocious puberty can then result.

Gonadotropin-independent sexual precocity in boys may occur as a result of autonomous Leydig cell hyperplasia in the absence of Leydig cell tumor formation. The disorder is inherited as a male-limited autosomal disorder either from father to son or from mothers who are unaffected carriers. Virilization begins usually by age 2. Testosterone levels are elevated, often to the adult male range; however, immunoreactive and bioactive LH levels and the response to LHRH are prepubertal. Many of these boys were mistakenly thought to have true precocious puberty in the past because of the presence of spermatogenesis.

Since sexual precocity is defined as the occurrence of any sign of sexual maturation at an age less than 2 SD below the mean (age 9 in North America), by definition a fraction of normal boys have activation of the hypothalamic-pituitary system before this age. *Premature activation of the hypothalamic-pituitary system* may be "idiopathic" or due to central nervous system tumors, infections, or injuries. Such early hypothalamic-pituitary activation typically is associated with characteristics of normal puberty, i.e., sleep-related gonadotropin secretion, elevated plasma bioactive LH, and enhanced gonadotropin response to LHRH. Since the diagnosis of idiopathic true precocious puberty is one of exclusion, some patients later prove to have been misclassified and to have an identifiable central nervous system abnormality. With improved means of diagnosis, such as CT scans, delays in diagnosis will probably be less frequent.

Management of sexual precocity due to steroid- or gonadotropin-producing tumors, congenital adrenal hyperplasia, or an identified CNS abnormality is directed toward the primary disease. In boys with Leydig cell hyperplasia attempts have been made to lower plasma testosterone with medroxyprogesterone acetate or ketoconazole, but the long-term efficacy and safety of these agents is unknown. Idiopathic true precocious puberty and true precocious puberty due to inoperable CNS lesions are treated with LHRH analogue therapy, resulting in reversal of the pubertal maturation including decreased rate of skeletal development.

HETEROSEXUAL PRECOCITY   Feminization in prepubertal boys can result from absolute or relative increases in estrogen due to a variety of causes (see Chap. 332).

Delayed or incomplete puberty   The separation of failure of puberty from variants of normal is one of the most difficult problems in endocrinology. Some patients fail to show the normal spurt of growth and sexual development at the usual time but eventually commence puberty by age 16 or older. Adolescence may then either progress rapidly, or there may be a slow development and growth that continues until age 20 to 22. Many men with delayed onset of puberty attain heights within the normal adult range. At times the history reveals that a parent or sibling has shown a similar pattern of development. The major problem is to separate this group of patients with delayed puberty from patients with organic disorders that impair puberty. Panhypopituitarism and hypothyroidism can cause pubertal failure in males (see Chaps. 321 and 324). Absent puberty can also result from primary disease of the testis including defects in testicular development; this diagnosis is suspected on the basis of low plasma testosterone and elevated FSH and LH. Hereditary androgen resistance (in which plasma testosterone and LH are both high) usually results in hereditary male pseudohermaphroditism, but in milder cases may be manifested by absent puberty (see Chap. 333).

The most frequent finding in boys with absent puberty is both low plasma testosterone and low gonadotropin levels; in these patients it is necessary to distinguish those with delayed puberty from those with *hypogonadotropic hypogonadism (the Kallman syndrome)*. The manifestation of hypogonadotropic hypogonadism varies from boys with eunuchoidal features and testes of prepubertal size to those with partial manifestations of LH and FSH deficiency. Anosmia or hyposmia and cryptorchidism are common. Histologic examination of the testis reveals undifferentiated Leydig cells and immature germinal epithelium similar to a normal prepubertal testis. The disorder is inherited as an X-linked recessive trait or an autosomal dominant trait with variable expressivity. Serum FSH and LH levels are usually below the normal male range, and plasma testosterone levels are low for the age. The secretion of other pituitary hormones is usually normal. The defect appears to be in the synthesis or release of LHRH, and the administration of synthetic LHRH for a sufficient period corrects the endocrine abnormalities and initiates spermatogenesis. If untreated, these patients usually remain in the prepubertal state indefinitely. A prepubertal manifestation of this disorder is microphallus, in which the size of the penis is below the fifth percentile for the age. Indeed, in a fourth or more of prepubertal patients with isolated microphallus the underlying etiology is hypogonadotropic hypogonadism. Distinction between this disorder and delayed puberty is particularly difficult in patients of early or midpubertal age; the presence of microphallus, anosmia, or a family history of hypogonadotropic hypogonadism may make it possible to establish the diagnosis. In the absence of such evidence, differentiation of the two states may become clear only after several years of observation. In some cases the response of plasma LH to LHRH stimulation may be helpful in suggesting that puberty is imminent.

One less severe form of hypogonadotropic hypogonadism is the so-called *fertile eunuch syndrome* in which spermatogenesis is present despite deficient androgen production. Plasma FSH levels are within the normal adult male range, whereas plasma testosterone and plasma LH levels are low. However, LHRH administration to such patients causes an increase in plasma LH as well as FSH. This implies that the defect in this disorder, as in the Kallman syndrome, is defective LH release. *Isolated FSH deficiency* is a rare disorder in which virilization, plasma LH, and plasma testosterone are normal but plasma FSH is persistently low; testicular biopsy in one individual revealed a maturation arrest at the spermatid stage. In some, FSH levels increased following administration of LHRH.

ADULT ABNORMALITIES OF TESTICULAR FUNCTION At the time of the completion of puberty, plasma testosterone levels reach the adult level of 300 to 1000 ng/dL throughout the day, plasma gonadotropins are 5 to 20 mIU/mL each for LH and FSH, and sperm production is sufficient to allow reproduction. The adult set of the complex regulatory system (Fig. 330-3) is sustained in the normal man for more than 40 years. However, the system is subject to a variety of influences, both at the level of the testis and of the hypothalamic-pituitary system. Spermatogenesis is exquisitely sensitive to alterations in temperature, and brief increases either in systemic or local temperature (as in a hot bath) can be followed by temporary decreases in sperm production. The system is likewise subject to influence by diet, drugs, alcohol, environmental agents, and psychological stress, all of which may cause temporary decreases in sperm count.

Persistent abnormalities of testicular function after the time of normal puberty can be due to hypothalamic-pituitary abnormalities (see Chap. 321), testicular defects, or to abnormalities of sperm transport. Certain of these conditions tend to affect Leydig cell function or spermatogenesis selectively, but most influence both aspects of testicular function and cause both underandrogenization and infertility (Table 330-1). The interlocking of defective Leydig cell function with infertility is a consequence of the dependence of

spermatogenesis on androgen formation. Even partial decreases in testosterone production can cause infertility. Certain disorders (hyperprolactinemia, radiation, cyclophosphamide therapy, autoimmunity, paraplegia, androgen resistance) can cause either isolated infertility or a combined defect in testicular function in different subjects.

Hypothalamic-pituitary disorders Disorders of the hypothalamus and pituitary can impair secretion of gonadotropins (and cause as a consequence decreased androgen production and defective spermatogenesis) either as an isolated defect (hypogonadotropic hypogonadism) or as a portion of more complex endocrine and systemic manifestations (see Chap. 321). Alternatively, gonadotropin secretion can be altered by factors other than hypothalamic pituitary pathology. For example, elevation of plasma cortisol in the *Cushing syndrome* can depress LH secretion independent of a space-occupying lesion of the pituitary. Some patients with *congenital adrenal hyperplasia* have early activation of gonadotropin secretion and true precocious puberty, while other patients have suppressed gonadotropin secretion and consequent infertility. *Hyperprolactinemia* (either as the consequence of pituitary adenomas or of drugs such as phenothiazines) has been associated with combined Leydig cell and seminiferous tubule dysfunction, presumably the consequence of inhibition of LH

TABLE 330-1 Classification of abnormalities of testicular function in the adult

Site of defect	Presentation	
	Infertility with underandrogenization	Infertility with normal virilization
Hypothalamic-pituitary	Panhypopituitarism Hypogonadotropic hypogonadism Cushing's syndrome	Isolated FSH deficiency Congenital adrenal hyperplasia
	Hyperprolactinemia Hemochromatosis	Hyperprolactinemia
Testicular	Developmental and structural defects: Klinefelter's syndrome* XX male	Germinal cell aplasia Cryptorchidism Varicocele Immotile cilia syndrome Other structural defects of sperm
	Acquired defects: Viral orchitis* Trauma Radiation Drugs (spironolactone, alcohol, ketoconazole, cyclophosphamide)	*Mycoplasma* infection Radiation Drugs (cyclophosphamide)
	Autoimmunity (polyglandular endocrine failure) Granulomatous disease	Autoimmunity
	Associated with systemic diseases: Liver disease Renal failure Sickle cell disease Neurologic diseases (myotonic dystrophy and paraplegia) Androgen resistance	Febrile illness Celiac disease Neurologic disease (paraplegia) Androgen resistance
Sperm transport		Obstruction of the epididymis or vas deferens (cystic fibrosis, diethylstilbesterol exposure, congenital absence)

* *The common testicular causes of underandrogenization and infertility in adults—Klinefelter's syndrome and viral orchitis—are associated with small testes.*

and FSH secretion by prolactin. Occasionally, impaired fertility in hyperprolactinemia is associated with normal gonadotropin and androgen levels and is presumed to result from direct inhibition of spermatogenesis by prolactin. *Hemochromatosis* impairs testicular function most commonly as the result of effects on the pituitary, less often it affects the testis directly (see Chap. 310).

Testicular defects   Abnormalities of testicular function in the adult can be grouped into several categories: developmental and structural defects of the testes, acquired testicular defects, and those abnormalities secondary to systemic and/or neurologic disease.

DEVELOPMENTAL ABNORMALITIES   The *Klinefelter syndrome* (both the classic and mosaic forms) and the *XX male syndrome* are usually not recognized until after the time of expected puberty (see Chap. 333). Some developmental defects cause infertility in the presence of normal androgen production. These include varicocele, germinal cell aplasia, and cryptorchidism. *Varicocele* is probably the most common treatable cause of male infertility and may be of etiologic importance in as much as one-third of all male infertility. It is caused by retrograde flow of blood into the internal spermatic vein that eventuates in progressive, often palpable dilatation of the peritesticular pampiniform plexus of veins. The incidence of varicocele is about 10 to 15 percent in the general population and 20 to 40 percent in men with infertility. It is thought to result from incompetence of the valve between the internal spermatic vein and the renal vein and is more common on the left (85 percent). Unilateral varicocele increases the blood flow and the temperature of both testes as a result of the extensive anastomoses of the venous systems. The findings on semen analysis are usually nonspecific with all parameters showing some abnormality. The increased scrotal (and testicular) temperature is believed to be the cause of the poor-quality semen and infertility (the testes do not have the usual 2°C lower temperature than that of the abdominal cavity). In some studies, surgical resection results in improved fertility, with the best results (70 percent pregnancy rate) obtained in men whose preoperative sperm counts are over 10 million per milliliter.

Some patients with *germinal cell aplasia* (the Sertoli cell–only syndrome) have a positive family history and may constitute a specific entity in which the germinal epithelium is missing with resulting azoospermia; plasma testosterone and LH values are normal, and plasma FSH levels are elevated. Other patients with identical histologic and clinical findings have androgen resistance or a history of viral orchitis or cryptorchidism. Consequently a variety of conditions are commonly lumped under this term. The syndrome accounts for less than 10 percent of patients with azoospermia.

Unilateral *cryptorchidism,* even when corrected prior to puberty, is associated with abnormal semen in many individuals. This suggests that even in unilateral cryptorchidism the testicular abnormality is usually bilateral.

The *immotile cilia syndrome* is an autosomal recessive defect characterized by immotility or poor motility of the cilia of the airways and of the sperm. Kartagener's syndrome is a subgroup of the immotile cilia syndrome associated with situs inversus. The immotile cilia in the airways result in chronic sinusitis and bronchiectasis, and the immotile sperm cannot fertilize. The structural abnormality leading to impaired motility of cilia can usually be defined by the electron-microscopic appearance. The specific defects that are known to cause the syndrome include defects in the dynein arms, spokes, or microtubule doublets. Cilia from epithelia and sperm tails from the same individual exhibit the same defects, but the pulmonary manifestations may be minor. *Other structural defects of sperm* that are less well understood can apparently lead to immotile sperm without involvement of cilia in the lung.

ACQUIRED TESTICULAR DEFECTS   Most acquired testicular failure in the adult results from *viral orchitis.* Mumps is the virus most frequently responsible, although other viruses act in a similar fashion, including echovirus, lymphocytic choriomeningitis virus, and group B arbo-

viruses. The orchitis is due to actual infection of the tissue by virus rather than indirect effects of the infection. Orchitis is the most common complication of mumps in adult men, occurring in as many as one-fourth of men who have the disease. In about two-thirds of the cases it is unilateral, and in the remainder it is bilateral. It usually develops within a few days after the onset of parotitis but may precede it. The testis may return to normal size and function or undergo atrophy. Atrophy is believed to be due both to direct effects of the virus on the seminiferous tubules and to ischemia secondary to pressure and edema within the taut tunica albuginea. Semen analysis returns to normal in three-fourths of men with unilateral involvement and in only one-third of men with bilateral orchitis. Atrophy is usually perceptible within 1 to 6 months after the orchitis subsides, and the degree of atrophy is not necessarily proportional to the severity of the acute orchitis or the development of infertility. Unilateral atrophy occurs in approximately one-third of cases of mumps orchitis, and bilateral atrophy occurs in about one-tenth.

Trauma is the second most common cause of secondary atrophy of the testes. The exposed position of the testis in the scrotum renders it susceptible to both thermal and physical trauma—particularly in individuals with hazardous occupations.

Both the seminiferous tubules and the Leydig cells are sensitive to *radiation damage;* the diminished secretion of testosterone appears to be a consequence of diminished testicular blood flow. Doses higher than 200 mGy (20 rad) cause increases in plasma FSH and LH levels and damage to the spermatogonia. With doses of about 800 mGy (80 rad) oligospermia or azoospermia develops. Higher doses may result in virtual obliteration of the germinal epithelium except for occasional stem and Sertoli cells. Still higher doses [6000 mGy (600 rad)] can cause an increase in the number of Leydig cells. Complete recovery of sperm density to preirradiation levels may require as long as 5 years. Permanent infertility can apparently occur after amounts of radiation used for therapy of malignant lymphoma in spite of shielding the testes. Permanent androgen deficiency in adult men is uncommon from doses of radiation in the therapeutic range; however, most boys receiving direct testicular radiation for acute lymphoblastic leukemia have permanently low plasma testosterone levels.

In general, *drugs* interfere with testicular function in one of four ways—inhibition of testosterone synthesis, blockade of the peripheral action of androgen, enhancement of estrogen levels, or direct inhibition of spermatogenesis. Certain drugs have multiple effects, and agents such as guanethidine that block the sympathetic nervous system can impair sexual function in men whose pituitary-testicular axis is normal.

Spironolactone and ketoconazole block the synthesis of androgen by interfering with the late reactions in androgen biosynthesis. Spironolactone and cimetidine also compete with androgen for the cytoplasmic receptor protein and thus interfere with androgen action in the target cell. Testosterone levels may be low and estradiol levels may be elevated in patients taking large amounts of marijuana, heroin, or methadone, although the exact reasons are unclear. Alcohol, when consumed in excess for prolonged periods, causes decreased plasma testosterone, independent of liver disease or malnutrition. Elevated plasma estradiol levels and decreased plasma testosterone levels have been reported in men taking digitalis.

Antineoplastic and chemotherapeutic agents, especially cyclophosphamide, commonly interfere with spermatogenesis. Cyclophosphamide causes azoospermia or extreme oligospermia within a few weeks after the initiation of therapy. Cessation of drug therapy is followed by a return of spermatogenesis within 3 years in about half of patients. Combination chemotherapy for acute leukemia, Hodgkin's disease, and other malignancies may also impair Leydig cell function. In pubertal boys this is manifested by decreased serum testosterone and elevated LH levels while in adult men testosterone levels do not decline and the impaired Leydig cell function may only be detected by an exaggeration of LH response to LHRH. The alkylating agents in the chemotherapeutic regimens seem to be responsible for the toxic effects on the Leydig cell.

Testicular failure also occurs as a part of a generalized disorder of *autoimmunity* in which multiple primary endocrine deficiencies coexist (Schmidt's syndrome) and in which circulating antibodies to the basement membrane of the testes are present (see Chap. 334). Sperm antibodies are a rare cause of isolated male infertility (less than 1 percent of cases). In some instances such antibodies may be secondary phenomena resulting from duct obstruction or vasectomy. *Granulomatous diseases* can also destroy the testes, the most common such disorder being leprosy. Testicular atrophy occurs in 10 to 20 percent of men with lepromatous leprosy, the result of direct invasion of the tissue by the mycobacteria. The tubules are involved initially, followed by endarteritis and destruction of Leydig cells.

TESTICULAR ABNORMALITIES ASSOCIATED WITH SYSTEMIC DISEASE
The common systemic diseases that cause combined underandrogenization and infertility are liver disease and renal failure. In *cirrhosis of the liver* a combined testicular and pituitary lesion leads to decreased testosterone production independent of the direct toxic effects of ethanol. Although plasma LH is elevated, the level may be below the expected range given the degree of androgen deficiency. This is most likely the result of inhibition of LH secretion by the higher estrogen concentrations found in patients with chronic liver disease. Increased estrogen production results from impaired hepatic extraction of adrenal androstenedione and subsequent increased peripheral conversion to estrone and estradiol. In effect there is shunting of estrogen precursors to aromatization sites in peripheral tissues. Testicular atrophy and gynecomastia are present in about half of men with cirrhosis, and many such men are impotent.

In chronic *renal failure* decreased androgen synthesis and diminution of sperm production develop in the setting of elevated plasma gonadotropins. The elevated LH is due to increased production as well as reduced clearance but is incapable of effecting normal testosterone production. In addition, about half of men with chronic renal failure have hyperprolactinemia. Low testosterone levels coupled with normal or increased plasma estrogen levels probably account for the presence of gynecomastia in about half of men on chronic hemodialysis. The role of the hyperprolactinemia in decreasing testosterone production is unclear. About half of men with renal failure on dialysis experience decreased libido and impotence. The etiology of the testicular abnormalities in renal failure is not well understood. Only slight improvement in testosterone production occurs with hemodialysis, but successful transplantation may lead to return of testicular function to normal.

Men with *sickle cell anemia* usually have impaired secondary sexual development, and testicular atrophy is present in one-third. The defect may be either at the testicular or hypothalamic-pituitary level. Abnormalities in Leydig cell function, frequently accompanied by decreased sperm density, have been noted in a variety of chronic systemic diseases including protein-calorie *malnutrtion*, advanced *Hodgkin's disease* and *cancer* prior to chemotherapy, and *amyloidosis*. Most of these disorders cause a lowered plasma testosterone coupled with a normal to increased plasma LH, suggesting combined hypothalamic-pituitary and testicular defects. The low plasma testosterone is not the result of inhibitors that interfere with the binding to TeBG and hence is not analogous to the euthyroid sick syndrome. Similar hormone changes occur following *surgery, myocardial infarction,* and severe *burns,* and thus may be a nonspecific effect of illness.

The temporary decrease in sperm density that occurs following *acute febrile illness* usually occurs in the absence of any changes in testosterone production. Men with *celiac disease* may have infertility associated with a hormonal pattern typical of androgen resistance with elevated testosterone and LH levels on average. The major *neurologic diseases* associated with altered testicular function are myotonic dystrophy and paraplegia. In myotonic dystrophy small testes may be associated with abnormalities of both spermatogenesis and Leydig cell function. Spinal cord lesions resulting in paraplegia lead to a temporary decrease in testosterone levels that tend to return to normal but persistent defects in spermatogenesis; some patients retain the capacity to obtain erection and to ejaculate.

ANDROGEN RESISTANCE Defects of the androgen receptor cause resistance to the action of androgen usually associated with defective male phenotypic development as well as infertility and underandrogenization (see Chap. 333). However, some men with familial Reifenstein's syndrome have a less complete androgen resistance with no abnormalities of phenotypic development except for azoospermia but with endocrine and tissue culture evidence of a defective androgen receptor. An even less severe form of androgen resistance is associated with infertility due to oligo- or azoospermia in otherwise phenotypically normal men; this form of androgen resistance may be the etiology in a significant fraction of men with infertility previously classified as having idiopathic azoospermia.

Impairment of sperm transport Disorders of sperm transport may lead to infertility in as many as 6 percent of infertile men with normal virilization. The obstruction may be unilateral or bilateral, congenital or acquired. In men with unilateral obstruction of sperm transport the infertility may result from antisperm antibodies. Obstructive azoospermia at the level of the epididymis also occurs in association with chronic sinopulmonary infections. Tuberculosis, leprosy, and gonorrhea are rare causes of acquired obstruction of Wolffian duct–derived structures. Congenital defects of the vas deferens can occur as an isolated abnormality associated with absence of the seminal vesicles (and consequently absence of fructose in the ejaculate), in patients with *cystic fibrosis,* or in men whose mothers received *diethylstilbestrol* during pregnancy.

At least 40 percent of infertile men have infertility of unknown etiology; none of the above conditions is found on careful search. The therapy in these patients, as in all infertile men except those with surgically correctable varicocele, vas deferens obstruction, or treatable endocrinopathy, is unsatisfactory. Empirical therapy with androgens or gonadotropins probably has no significant effect on fertility. Although the semen quality may improve with such treatment, the pregnancy rate is usually no greater than in infertile men given no therapy (25 percent fertility in patients followed for a year). This latter fact should be kept in mind, namely that spontaneous resolution may occur in one-fourth of patients with idiopathic infertility followed with no treatment. The extent to which the sperm from men with idiopathic infertility can be used successfully for in vitro fertilization and embryo transfer is unclear (see Chap. 331).

Fertility control in the male Although a variety of approaches to fertility control in men have been tried, the most practical means is ligation of the vas deferens, a procedure that has been utilized successfully in large numbers of men and that can be performed on an outpatient basis. The time required for azoospermia to occur following the operation depends upon the number of sperm in the terminal vas deferens and ejaculatory ducts at the time of surgery but is usually less than 40 days. Azoospermia should be documented in each case to prove effectiveness. No deleterious effects on either testosterone production or the hypothalamic-pituitary axis have been documented. Despite reports of immune-complex-associated accelerated atherosclerosis in vasectomized nonhuman primates, there does not appear to be any association of vasectomy and atherosclerosis in men. Vasectomy should only be recommended for men requesting permanent sterilization. Vasovasostomy for reanastomosis of the vas has a success rate of about 80 to 90 percent as judged by return of sperm to the ejaculate, but only about 30 to 40 percent subsequently achieve fertility. This discrepancy is possibly due to the development of antisperm antibodies as a consequence of the vasectomy.

OLD AGE Beginning at about age 70 mean plasma testosterone concentrations decline. This decrease occurs despite an elevation in TeBG so that the level of free testosterone decreases even more than the total. Though statistically lower than average, both total and free concentrations of testosterone usually remain within the normal range. There is, however, an associated rise in plasma LH and an increase in the rate of conversion of androgen to estrogen in peripheral tissues so that the effective ratio of androgen to estrogen decreases. These endocrine changes in the aging man are believed to be critical for the development of prostatic hyperplasia and probably for development of gynecomastia in aging men (see Chap. 332), but there is no convincing evidence that such changes have any direct bearing on sexual function in the elderly.

Prostatic hyperplasia   See Chap. 298.

Cancer of the prostate   See Chap. 298.

DISORDERS OF ALL AGES   Testicular tumors (see Chap. 297) Chorionic gonadotropin is present in normal testes, and it is therefore not surprising that plasma gonadotropins are elevated in testicular tumors. Indeed, an elevated plasma level of the beta subunit of human chorionic gonadotropins (hCG-β) serves as a sensitive and specific marker of tumor activity in some men with germ cell tumors. Plasma levels of the beta subunit are elevated in all patients with choriocarcinoma, in one-third of embryonal carcinomas and teratocarcinomas, and rarely in seminomas. There is a good correlation between change in hCG-β levels and response to therapy.

Elevated estradiol and testosterone production in patients with testicular tumors can arise by at least two mechanisms. In trophoblastic tumors and in tumors of Leydig and Sertoli cells production of both hormones occurs autonomously in the tumor tissue itself; in these instances plasma gonadotropin levels and hormone production by the uninvolved portions of the testes are depressed, and azoospermia is common. However, when gonadotropins are secreted by the tumor, the gonadotropin acts to increase estradiol and testosterone production in the unaffected areas of the testes, and azoospermia is uncommon. When potent estrogens and androgens are formed (directly or indirectly) by the tumors, feminization, virilization, or no obvious change may result, depending on the pattern of hormones produced and the age of the patients involved. Other cellular markers of testicular tumor activity have been described in individual cases, including alpha fetoprotein.

Gynecomastia   See Chap. 332.

HORMONAL THERAPY

ANDROGENS   Pharmacologic preparations   Effective androgen therapy requires the use of chemically modified analogues of testosterone. When testosterone itself is administered by mouth, it is absorbed into the portal blood and degraded promptly by the liver so that insignificant amounts reach the systemic circulation; when injected parenterally testosterone is rapidly absorbed from the injection vehicle so that it is difficult to sustain effective levels in the plasma. Therefore, it is necessary to modify the molecule so as to retard the rate of absorption or catabolism, so as to sustain effective blood levels or to enhance the androgenic potency of each molecule, so that full androgenic effects can be achieved at a lower blood level of the drug. Three types of modification of the molecule have received widespread clinical application (Fig. 330-7), namely esterification of the 17β-hydroxyl group, alkylation at the 17α position, and modification of the ring structure, particularly substitutions at the 2, 9, and 11 positions. Esterification serves to decrease the polarity of the molecule. Consequently, the steroid is more soluble in the fat vehicles used for injection, and release of the steroid into the circulation is slowed. Esters cannot be administered by mouth and must be injected parenterally. The more carbon molecules in the acid esterified, the more prolonged the action. Currently available esters such as testosterone cypionate and testosterone enanthate can be injected every 1 to 3 weeks. Because the esters are hydrolyzed before the hormones act, the effectiveness of therapy can be monitored by assaying the plasma level of testosterone with time following administration.

The effectiveness of 17α-alkylated androgens (such as methyltestosterone and methandrostenolone) when given by mouth is due to slower hepatic catabolism than occurs with testosterone itself so that the alkylated derivatives escape degradation by the liver and reach the systemic circulation. For this reason 17α-methyl or -ethyl substitution is a common feature of most orally active androgens.

Unfortunately, all 17α-alkylated steroids may cause abnormalities of liver function, and for this reason they have a limited role in medicine.

Other alterations of the ring structure of the androgen molecule have been adopted empirically; in some instances the modification slows the rate of inactivation, in others it enhances the potency of a given molecule, and in still others it alters the conversion to other active metabolites. For example, the potency of fluoxymesterone may be due to the fact that, unlike most androgens, it is a poor precursor for conversion to estrogens in peripheral tissues.

Side effects of androgens   All androgens carry the risk of inducing virilization in women. Among the early manifestations are acne, coarsening of the voice, and development of hirsutism. Menstrual irregularities are common. If treatment is discontinued as soon as these effects develop, the manifestations may slowly subside. With prolonged treatment, male-pattern baldness, worsening of the hirsutism and voice changes, and hypertrophy of the clitoris develop and are largely irreversible. There is considerable variation in the frequency and the degree to which these signs develop in women. The variation in response probably results from several factors including individual differences in susceptibility, variability in steady-state blood levels among individuals, and variable duration of therapy. In general, the younger the patient, the more striking the virilizing signs; nevertheless, florid virilization can also occur in adult women.

Retention of a limited amount of sodium is an inevitable consequence of androgen therapy, but in patients with underlying heart disease or renal failure or when androgens are administered in enormous amounts, as in some patients with carcinoma of the breast, the degree of sodium retention may be sufficient to produce edema. Although androgens do not cause malignancy, they may promote growth of and intensify pain from carcinoma of the prostate and from breast carcinoma in men.

Feminizing side effects of androgen therapy in men are poorly

FIGURE 330-7   *Some of the androgen preparations available for pharmacologic use.*

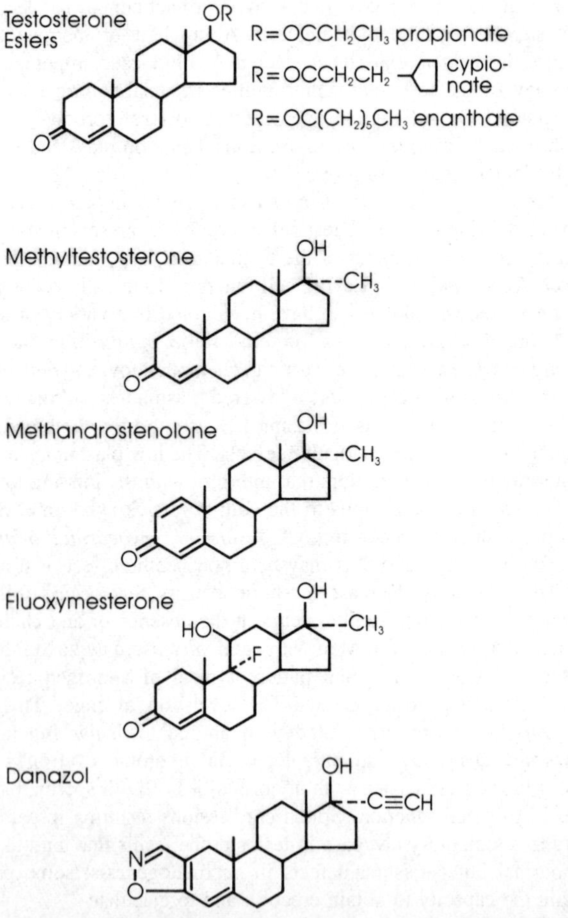

understood. Testosterone itself can be converted (aromatized) in peripheral tissues to estradiol. In contrast, 5α-reduction of the molecule precludes estrogen formation. The commonest manifestation of feminization is development of gynecomastia. Such breast enlargement is common in children given androgens and correlates with an increase in urinary estrogens, possibly because of a greater capacity to convert androgens to estrogens in childhood. The administration of testosterone esters to men results in an increase in plasma estrogen levels. In men with normal liver function, gynecomastia usually develops only after high doses of androgens.

All 17α-alkylated androgens produce sodium sulfobromophthalein retention and frequently cause elevation of plasma alkaline phosphatase and conjugated bilirubin. The incidence of clinically manifest liver disease probably depends upon the previous integrity of the liver, but jaundice may occur even in the absence of preexisting liver disease. 17α-Alkylated drugs also cause an increase in a variety of plasma proteins that are synthesized in the liver. The most serious complications of oral androgen therapy are the development of peliosis hepatis (blood-filled cysts in the liver) and hepatoma. These disorders were initially described in patients with aplastic anemia, many of whom have Fanconi anemia, itself a predisposing factor for the development of malignancy. However, both lesions have also been reported in patients who received oral androgens for a variety of other causes, including use by athletes. There may be a similar increased incidence of hepatocellular neoplasms in women taking oral contraceptives. Although in some individuals these tumors regress and follow a benign course after discontinuation of the drugs, in others the course is rapidly fatal.

One indication for the use of 17α-alkylated androgens is in hereditary angioneurotic edema; in this disorder the desired therapeutic benefit (increase in the level of the inhibitor of the first component of complement) may actually be a side effect of the 17-alkylated steroid rather than an effect of the parent androgen itself. As a consequence, weak androgens such as danazol are effective in this disorder (Fig. 330-6). Another indication for danazol is in the management of endometriosis (see Chap. 43).

Replacement therapy The aim of androgen therapy in hypogonadal men is to restore or bring to normal male secondary sexual characteristics (beard, body hair, external genitalia) and male sexual behavior and to mimic the hormonal effects on somatic development (hemoglobin, muscle mass, nitrogen balance, and epiphyseal closure). Since an assay for plasma testosterone is available for monitoring therapy, the treatment of androgen deficiency is almost universally successful. The parenteral administration of a long-acting testosterone ester such as 100 to 200 mg testosterone enanthate at 1- to 3-week intervals results in a sustained increase in plasma testosterone to the normal male range. Such esters act only through the release of testosterone itself into the circulation. If the hypogonadism is primary and of long duration (as in the Klinefelter syndrome) suppression of plasma LH to the normal range may not occur for many weeks, if at all. Considerable variability exists in the relation between plasma testosterone and male sexual behavior, but in postpubertal testicular failure (even of many years duration) resumption of normal sexual activity is usual following adequate replacement. Androgen does not restore spermatogenesis in hypogonadal states, but the volume of the ejaculate (derived largely from the prostate and seminal vesicles) and male secondary sex characteristics return to normal. The effects of endogenous androgen on hemoglobin, nitrogen retention, and skeletal development are also reproduced.

In patients of all ages in whom hypogonadism developed prior to expected puberty (such as patients with hypogonadotropic hypogonadism), it is appropriate to bring plasma testosterone slowly into the adult range. When therapy is commenced at the time of expected puberty in such patients, the normal events of male puberty proceed in the usual fashion. If therapy is delayed until long after the time of usual puberty, the degree to which normal virilization will occur is variable, but many patients undergo a relatively complete anatomic and functional maturation. Intermittent low-dose androgen therapy is indicated in prepubertal hypogonadal boys with microphallus to bring the external genitalia into the normal range. If such patients are monitored closely and given androgens only for short periods, such therapy usually has no adverse effects on somatic growth.

In boys of pubertal age with either isolated hypogonadotropic hypogonadism or primary testicular deficiency, the usual practice is to institute androgen therapy between the ages of 12 and 14 years, depending on the subjective need for sexual development. The initial administration of small doses of testosterone esters followed by a gradual increase to 100 to 150 mg/m² of body surface area every 1 to 3 weeks should result in a normal pubertal growth spurt. The time from the start of treatment to the appearance of secondary sex characteristics is variable. Penile development, deepening of the voice, and other secondary sexual characteristics usually commence during the first year of treatment. In normal boys puberty extends over several years, and treatment designed to replicate normal development does not shorten the process greatly.

Testosterone exerts its full action only in the presence of a balanced hormonal environment and, particularly, in the presence of adequate levels of growth hormone. Consequently, prepubertal patients who have coexisting growth hormone deficiency exhibit a diminished response to androgens both in regard to growth and to the development of secondary sex characteristics unless sufficient growth hormone is given simultaneously.

Pharmacologic uses Androgens have been used for a variety of disorders unassociated with hypogonadism, in the hope that potential benefits from the nonvirilizing actions of the agents (such as increase in nitrogen retention and muscle mass, increased hemoglobin, etc.) would outweigh any deleterious actions of the drugs. The most common nonreplacement uses of androgen have been attempts to improve nitrogen balance in catabolic states, self-administration by athletes in the belief that muscle mass and/or athletic performance will be improved, attempts to enhance erythropoiesis in refactory anemias including the anemia of renal failure, adjuvant therapy in carcinoma of the breast, treatment of hereditary angioneurotic edema and endometriosis, and management of growth retardation of various etiologies. Most expectations of beneficial effects in these disorders have been illusory for two reasons. First, pharmacologic doses of androgens do little if anything in men beyond the normal testicular androgen, and in women the virilizing side effects of all agents are formidable. Second, no androgen has been devised that exhibits only the nonvirilizing effects of the hormone. This is not surprising in view of the fact that all known action of androgens are mediated by a single high-affinity receptor protein in the cytoplasm (Fig. 330-5).

The most pervasive form of androgen abuse is by male athletes in the expectation that muscle development and athletic performance will be improved. In fact, however, in most adequately controlled studies such therapy does not improve performance, and in those rare instances in which it does, such improvement may be the consequence of sodium retention and expansion of the blood volume rather than of an effect on muscle development or strength. Under no circumstances do putative benefits outweigh the risks associated with the use of oral androgens, a practice that cannot be condemned too harshly. At present, the only established indications for androgen therapy outside of male hypogonadism are in selected patients with anemia due to bone marrow failure and in patients with hereditary angioneurotic edema or endometriosis.

Parenteral administration of testosterone esters to normal men results in little effects of any kind, except for the suppression of gonadotropin secretion by the hypothalamic-pituitary system and a consequent decrease in the production of sperm. There is no established contraindication to their administration to men with those disorders (such as short stature) where their use has been advocated, but the efficacy is not yet established. However, the virilizing side effects in women of androgens in usual dosages preclude their use in all except life-threatening situations. Even in potentially fatal diseases in women such as bone marrow failure and carcinoma of the breast great care must be exercised in androgen use.

GONADOTROPINS Treatment with gonadotropins is utilized to establish or restore fertility in patients with gonadotropin deficiency of all causes. Two gonadotropin preparations are available: human menopausal gonadotropins (hMG) (purified from the urine of postmenopausal women) and human chorionic gonadotropin (hCG) (purified from the urine of pregnant women). hMG contains 75 IU FSH and 75 IU LH per vial. hCG has little FSH activity and resembles LH in its ability to stimulate testosterone production by Leydig cells. Because of the expense of hMG, treatment is usually begun with hCG alone, and hMG is added later to stimulate the FSH-dependent stages of spermatid development. A high ratio of LH to FSH activity and a long duration of treatment (3 to 6 months) are necessary to bring about the maturation of the prepubertal testis. Once spermatogenesis has been restored in hypophysectomized patients or initiated in hypogonadotropic hypogonadal men by combined therapy, spermatogenesis can usually be maintained with hCG alone.

Men with oligospermia of unknown etiology have been treated with human gonadotropins; the incidence of fertility in patients so treated is probably no greater than would occur in similar groups of untreated controls.

The dosage of hCG required to maintain a normal testosterone level is variable, ranging from 1000 to 5000 IU weekly. A variety of treatment regimens have been utilized to induce maturation of spermatogenesis. Most involve starting with 2000 IU hCG three or more times a week until most of the clinical parameters, including plasma testosterone, indicate normal adult male development. hMG (usually one ampul) is then added three times a week to complete the development of spermatogenesis. After regression of spermatogenesis has occurred the length of therapy required to bring about restoration of spermatogenesis is variable and may be as long as 12 months.

LUTEINIZING HORMONE–RELEASING HORMONE LHRH (gonadorelin) is now available for endocrine testing. LHRH therapy is now used by some physicians for chronic therapy of the infertility of hypogonadotropic hypogonadism. It is necessary to administer LHRH in frequent boluses (25 to 200 ng/kg of body weight every 2 h), requiring the use of portable infusion pumps or periodic nasal application. The relative efficacies of LHRH and gonadotropin therapy have yet to be defined.

REFERENCES

AIMAN J, GRIFFIN JE: The frequency of androgen receptor deficiency in infertile men. J Clin Endocrinol Metab 54:725, 1982

BAKER HWG et al: Testicular control of follicle-stimulating hormone secretion, in *Recent Progress in Hormone Research*, RO Greep (ed). New York, Academic, 1976, vol 32, pp 429–476

CARR BR, GRIFFIN JE: Fertility control and its complications, in *Williams' Textbook of Endocrinology*, 7th ed, JD Wilson, DW Foster (eds). Philadelphia, Saunders, 1985, pp 452–475

CUTLER GB et al: Therapeutic applications of luteinizing-hormone-releasing hormone and its analogs. Ann Intern Med 102:643, 1985

DAVIS JE: Male sterilization. Clin Obstet Gynaecol 6:97, 1979

DE KRETSER DM: The effects of systemic disease on the function of the testis. Clin Endocrinol Metab 8:487, 1979

GOLDZIEHER JW et al:Improving the diagnostic reliability of rapidly fluctuating plasma hormone levels by optimized multiple-sampling techniques. J Clin Endocrinol Metab 43:824, 1976

GRIFFIN JE, WILSON JD: Disorders of the testes and male reproductive tract, in *Williams' Textbook of Endocrinology*, 7th ed, JD Wilson, DW Foster (eds). Philadelphia, Saunders, 1985, pp 259–312

MACDONALD PC et al: Origin of estrogen in normal men and in women with testicular feminization. J Clin Endocrinol Metab 49:905, 1979

MARSHALL WA, TANNER JM: Variation in the pattern of pubertal changes in boys. Arch Dis Child 45:13, 1970

MASSEY FJ et al: Vasectomy and health: Results from a large cohort study. JAMA 252:1023, 1984

ROSENBERG E: Gonadotropin therapy of male infertility, in *Human Semen and Fertility Regulation in Men*, ESE Hafez (ed). St Louis, Mosby, 1976, pp 464–475

RYAN AJ: Anabolic steroids are fool's gold. Fed Proc 40:2682, 1981

SHERINS RH et al: Male infertility, in *Campbell's Urology*, 5th ed, PC Walsh et al (eds). Philadelphia, Saunders, 1985, pp 640–699

SNYDER PF, LAWRENCE DA: Treatment of male hypogonadism with testosterone enanthate. J Clin Endocrinol Metab 51:1335, 1980

SPRATT DI, CROWLEY WF: Hypogonadotropic hypogonadism: GnRH therapy, in *Current Therapy in Endocrinology and Metabolism 1985–1986*, DT Krieger, CW Bardin (eds). Toronto, Decker, 1985, pp 155–159

STYNE DM, GRUMBACH MM: Puberty in the male and female: Its physiology and disorders, in *Reproductive Endocrinology: Physiology, Pathophysiology and Clinical Management*, SSC Yen, RB Jaffe (eds). Philadelphia, Saunders, 1978, pp 189–240

WIERMAN ME et al: Puberty without gonadotropins: A unique mechanism of sexual development. N Engl J Med 312:65, 1985

WILSON JD, GRIFFIN JE: The use and misuse of androgens. Metabolism 29:1278, 1980

331 DISORDERS OF THE OVARY AND FEMALE REPRODUCTIVE TRACT

BRUCE R. CARR / JEAN D. WILSON

The ovary is the source of ova for reproduction and of the hormones that regulate female sexual life. The anatomic structure, response to hormonal stimuli, and secretory capacity of the ovary are different at different periods of life. This chapter will review normal ovarian physiology as a background for understanding the abnormalities of the ovary and other tissues of the female reproductive tract.

DEVELOPMENT, STRUCTURE, AND FUNCTION OF THE OVARY

EMBRYOLOGY During the third week of gestation the primordial germ cells arise from the endoderm lining the yolk sac at the caudal end of the embryo. The germ cells migrate to the genital ridge adjacent to the mesonephric kidney by the fifth week of gestation and undergo mitotic divisions. The gonads exist in an undifferentiated state until the seventh week of fetal life, at which time the primitive ovary can be differentiated from the testis (see Chap. 333). Estrogen formation in the ovary commences between weeks 8 and 10, and by 10 to 11 weeks of gestation some oogonia in the developing ovarian cortex begin developing into primary oocytes. The ovary contains a finite number of germ cells, the maximal number of about 7 million oogonia being reached by the fifth to sixth month of gestation. Afterward, the germ cells begin to decrease in number through a process of atresia such that only 1 million remain at birth, 400,000 are present at the time of menarche, and only a few remain at menopause. Two X chromosomes are required for normal development of the ovary; in individuals with a 45,X karyotype ovarian development occurs, but the rate of atresia is accelerated so that only a fibrous streak remains at the time of birth (see Chap. 333).

After the oogonia cease to proliferate, meiosis commences, proceeds until the diplotene stage of the first meiotic division is completed, and then remains stationary until the time of onset of ovulation at puberty. During the fifth month of fetal life, the primordial follicle is formed, consisting of the primary oocyte arrested in meiosis, a single layer of granulosa cells, and a basement membrane that separates the primordial follicle from surrounding stromal (interstitial) tissues.

PUBERTAL MATURATION Final maturation of ovarian follicles commences during puberty. The two major hormones that regulate follicular development are the pituitary gonadotropins—follicle-stimulating hormone (FSH) and luteinizing hormone (LH) (Fig. 331-1). During the second trimester of fetal development the plasma gonadotropins rise to levels equivalent to those at menopause. This peak in gonadotropin levels may be causally related to the simultaneous peak in replication of oocytes. The hypothalamic-pituitary axis (the so-called gonadostat) undergoes maturation and becomes sensitive after the second trimester to negative feedback by circulating steroid hormones, particularly estrogen and progesterone produced in the placenta. The circulating gonadotropins decrease thereafter and are almost undetectable at the time of birth. In the neonate, concomitant with the decrease in estrogen and progesterone levels due to separation from the placenta at birth, there is a rebound increase in gonadotropin secretion that persists for the first few months of life. With continued maturation of the hypothalamic-pituitary system the gonadostat becomes sensitive to negative feedback control by the low levels of circulating steroid hormones, and plasma gonadotropins again decrease.

As the time of puberty nears, a decrease in the sensitivity of the gonadostat allows for increased secretion of FSH and LH, possibly secondary to increased production of luteinizing hormone–releasing hormone (LHRH) by the hypothalamus (see Chap. 321). A sleep-induced, pulsatile pattern of LH secretion then ensues, the first step in the development of a cyclic pattern of gonadotropin secretion (Fig. 331-1). The increase in estrogen secretion subsequently exerts a positive feedback which leads to an exaggeration of the pulsatile release of LH and eventually to ovulation and the menarche, after which mean plasma gonadotropin concentrations reach adult values in which day and night levels are similar. After the menopause plasma gonadotropin levels rise, plateau 5 to 10 years later, and remain fairly constant until the eighth to ninth decade of life when the plasma levels may fall. Although ovarian function is regulated primarily by LH and FSH, the ovary contains receptors for prolactin and LHRH, and both hormones inhibit steroidogenesis in in vitro preparations of human ovary, raising the possibility that they play a role in ovarian pathophysiology.

With the development at puberty of decreased sensitivity of the hypothalamic-pituitary centers to circulating steroid hormones, LHRH release by the hypothalamus increases, gonadotropin secretion by the pituitary is enhanced, ovarian estrogen secretion increases, and the anatomic changes of puberty ensue. At age 10 to 11 the first secondary sexual characteristics begin to appear in girls, namely development of the breast buds (thelarche), followed by the development of pubic hair (pubarche), and later by the development of axillary hair (adrenarche). The appearance of pubic and axillary hair is believed to be the result of an increase in adrenal androgens, commencing at approximately 6 to 8 years of age. A growth spurt ensues, and peak growth rate is attained at a mean age of 12 years.

The culmination of puberty is the onset of predictable, cyclic menses. The average time between the beginning of breast development and the onset of menses (menarche) is 2 years. The age of menarche is variable and is determined in part by socioeconomic as well as by genetic factors and general health. In the United States the mean age of menarche is believed to have decreased at a rate of 3 to 4 months per decade over the last 100 years and is now around

13 years, a decrease believed to be due to an improvement in nutrition in the population at large. A critical body weight of around 48 kg or a critical combination of weight, body water, and body fat is associated with development of hypothalamic insensitivity to circulating steroids that leads to increased secretion of gonadotropins and finally to menarche. Obese girls with a body weight 20 to 30 percent above ideal have earlier menarche than do girls with normal weights. In contrast, participation in certain sports or ballet, malnutrition, and chronic debilitating disease commonly cause delayed menarche.

MATURE OVARY Morphology The anatomic components and function of the adult ovary are illustrated schematically in Fig. 331-2. Under the influence of gonadotropins, a group of primary follicles is recruited, and by day 6 to 8 of the menstrual cycle one follicle becomes mature or "dominant," a process characterized by accelerated growth of granulosa cells and enlargement of the fluid-filled antrum. The recruited follicles not destined to ovulate begin to undergo degeneration, similar to the atresia observed in other follicles during embryogenesis. Just prior to ovulation, meiosis resumes in the ova of the dominant follicle, and the first meiotic division is completed with formation of the first polar body. Rapid enlargement of the antrum (up to 10 to 15 mm in size) occurs with an associated increase in follicular fluid, followed by a thinning of the follicular surface and formation of a conical stigma. Ovulation from the dominant follicle occurs some 16 to 23 h after the LH peak or 24 to 38 h after the onset of the LH surge as the result of rupture of the follicular wall at the area of the stigma, followed by expulsion of the ovum together with a mass of surrounding granulosa cells called cumulus cells. The rupture is believed to result from the action of hydrolyzing enzymes on the surface of the follicle, possibly under the control of prostaglandins. The second meiotic division begins after the egg is fertilized by a sperm, and a second polar body is then extruded. Following ovulation, the formation of the corpus luteum begins in the retained remnant of the ovulated follicle; the remaining granulosa and theca cells increase in size and accumulate lipids and a yellow pigment, lutein, to become "luteinized." The basement membrane that separated the granulosa cells from the stroma and blood vessels breaks, and capillaries, fibroblasts, and lymphatics from the theca invade the granulosa cells and reach the central cavity, thereby filling it with blood. After a period of 14 ± 2 days (the functional life of the corpus luteum) regression of vessels and atrophy of the corpus luteum commence and eventuate in replacement of the corpus luteum by a fibrous scar, the corpus albicans. The factors that

FIGURE 331-1 *Pattern of gonadotropin secretion during different stages of life in women. FSH (follicle-stimulating hormone), LH (luteinizing hormone). The secretory patterns of LH during the waking hours (clear area) and night (stippled area) for each stage are indicated in the upper insets. (After C Faiman et al.)*

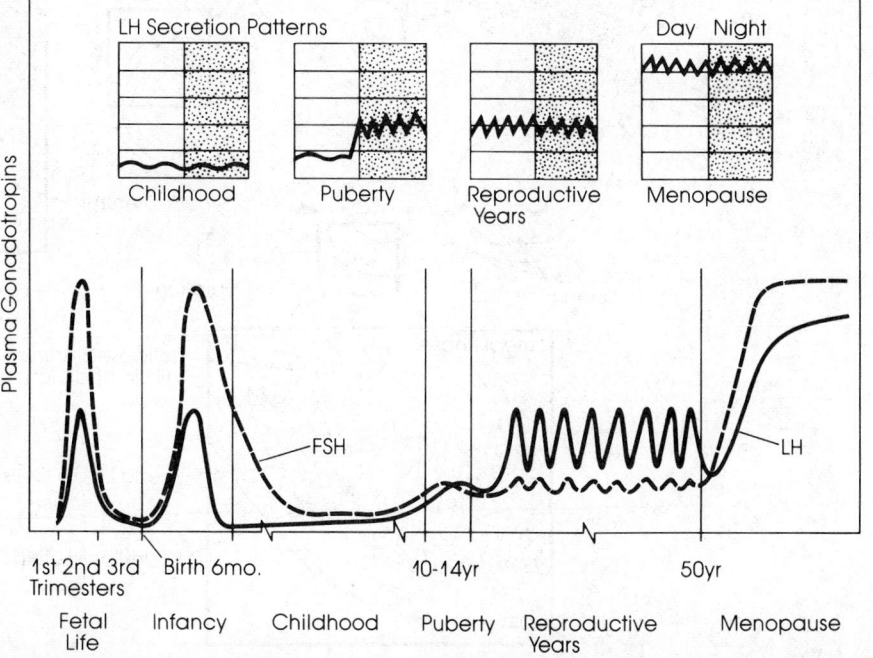

limit the life span of the corpus luteum are not known. However, if pregnancy occurs, the corpus luteum persists under the influence of placental or chorionic gonadotropins, and progesterone is produced by the corpus luteum for the support of early pregnancy.

Hormone formation STEROID HORMONES   Like other steroid hormones, ovarian steroids are derived from cholesterol (Fig. 331-3). The ovary can synthesize cholesterol de novo from 2-carbon precursors and can also utilize cholesterol from circulating low-density lipoproteins (LDL) as substrate for steroid hormone formation (Fig. 331-4). Virtually all ovarian cells are believed to possess the complete enzymatic complement required for the conversion of cholesterol to estradiol (Fig. 331-3); however, different cell types within the ovary contain different amounts of these enzymes so that the predominant steroids produced differ in the various compartments. For example, the corpus luteum forms progesterone and 17-hydroxyprogesterone predominantly, whereas theca and stromal cells convert cholesterol to the androgens androstenedione and testosterone. Granulosa cells are particularly rich in the aromatase activity responsible for conversion of androgens to estrogen and utilize as substrates for this process androgens synthesized within the granulosa cells and in the adjacent theca cells.

The principal sites of action of LH and FSH are also illustrated in Figs. 331-3 and 331-4. LH acts primarily to regulate the first step in steroid hormone biosynthesis, namely the conversion of cholesterol to pregnenolone, and also induces subsequent enzymes in the pathway. FSH acts to regulate the final process by which androgens are aromatized to estrogens. As a consequence, in the absence of FSH LH enhances substrate flow and the formation of androgens and/or progesterone, whereas FSH action is impeded in the absence of LH because of diminished substrate for aromatization.

Estrogens. Naturally occurring estrogens are 18-carbon steroids characterized by an aromatic A ring, a phenolic hydroxyl group at C-3, and either a hydroxyl group (estradiol) or a ketone (estrone) at C-17 (Fig. 331-3). (For the numbering of the steroid ring see Fig. 330-1.) The principal estrogen secreted by the ovary and the most potent naturally occurring estrogen is estradiol. Estrone is also secreted by the ovary, but the principal source of estrone is from extraglandular conversion of androstenedione in peripheral tissues. Estriol (16-

hydroxyestradiol), the most abundant estrogen in urine, arises from the 16-hydroxylation of estrone and estradiol. Catechol estrogens are formed by hydroxylation of estrogens at the C-2 or C-4 position and may act as the intracellular mediators of some estrogen action. Estrogens promote development of the secondary sexual characteristics in women and cause uterine growth, thickening of the vaginal mucosa, thinning of the cervical mucus, and development of the ductular system of the breasts. The mechanism of estrogen action in target tissues is similar to that for other steroid hormones and involves the binding to a specific cytosolic receptor protein, subsequent conformational change and translocation of the hormone-receptor complex to the nucleus, attachment of the complex to DNA, and initiation of the transcription of messenger RNA, which in turn causes increased protein synthesis in the cell cytoplasm (see Chap. 320).

Progesterone. Progesterone, a 21-carbon steroid (Fig. 331-3), is the principal hormone secreted by the corpus luteum and is responsible for progestational effects, namely induction of secretory activity in the endometrium of the estrogen-primed uterus in preparation for implantation of the fertilized egg. Progesterone also induces a decidual reaction in endometrium. Other effects include inhibition of uterine contractions, increased viscosity of cervical mucus, glandular development of the breasts, and increase in basal body temperature (thermogenic effect).

Androgens. The ovary synthesizes a variety of 19-carbon steroids including dehydroepiandrosterone, androstenedione, testosterone, and dihydrotestosterone, principally in stromal and thecal cells. The major ovarian 19-carbon steroid is androstenedione (Fig. 331-3), part of which is secreted into plasma and the remainder of which is converted to estrogen in granulosa cells or to testosterone in the interstitium. In peripheral tissues androstenedione can also be converted to testosterone and to estrogens. Only testosterone and dihydrotestosterone are true androgens with the capacity of interacting with the androgen receptor and thus inducing virilizing signs in women (see Chaps. 46 and 330).

OTHER HORMONES   Other ovarian hormones play an uncertain role in human physiology. *Relaxin,* a polypeptide hormone produced by

FIGURE 331-2 *Developmental changes in the adult ovary during a complete 28-day cycle.*

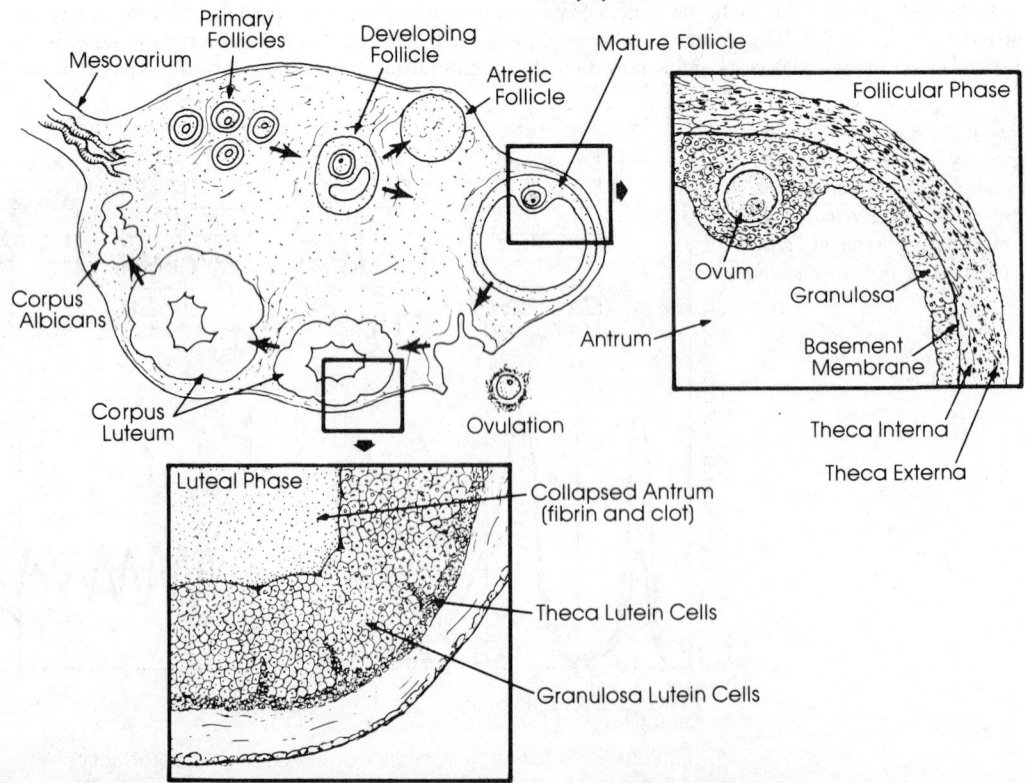

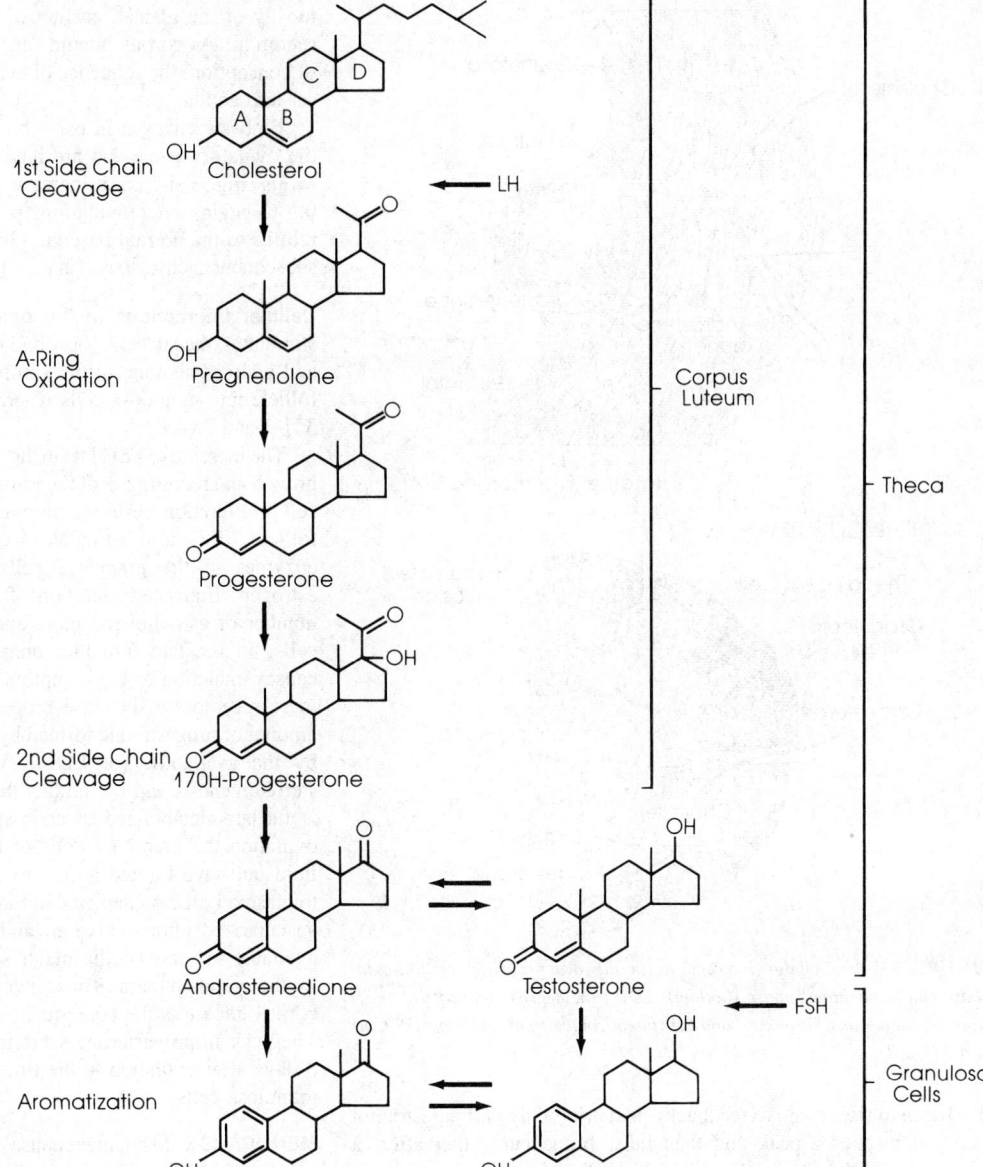

FIGURE 331-3 *The principal pathway of steroid hormone biosynthesis in the ovary. Although every ovarian cell probably contains the complete enzyme complement required for the formation of estradiol from cholesterol, the amounts of the various enzymes and consequently the predominant hormones formed differ among the various cell types. The major enzyme complements for the corpus luteum, stroma, and granulosa cells are shown by the brackets; as a consequence these cells produce predominantly progesterone and 17-OH progesterone, androgen, and estrogen, respectively. The major sites of action of LH and FSH in mediating this pathway are shown in the horizontal arrows.*

the human corpus luteum as well as by the decidua, causes softening of the cervix and loosening of the symphysis pubis in preparation for parturition in animals. *Follicular inhibin* or *folliculostatin* (the equivalent of testicular inhibin) is secreted by the follicle and is believed to regulate the release of FSH by the hypothalamic-pituitary unit. *Follicle regulatory protein* (FRP) of human follicular fluid inhibits granulosa secretion and growth. *Gonadocrinins*, peptides purified from rat follicular fluid, stimulate the release of both FSH and LH from the pituitary in vitro and in vivo. In addition, in the gonads of both sexes a *meiosis-inducing substance* (MIS) triggers the onset of meiosis, an event that occurs earlier in ovarian than in testicular development. In contrast, male fetal testes secrete predominantly a *meiosis-preventing substance* (MPS) that prevents meiosis until the onset of puberty at which time MIS is formed predominantly.

The normal menstrual cycle   The menstrual cycle is usually divided into a follicular or proliferative phase and a luteal or secretory phase (Fig. 331-5). The secretion of FSH and LH is fundamentally under negative feedback control by ovarian steroids (particularly estradiol) and probably by inhibin, but the response of gonadotropins to different levels of estradiol varies. FSH secretion is inhibited progressively as

estrogen levels increase—typical negative feedback. In contrast, LH secretion is suppressed maximally by estrogen in low amounts and is enhanced in response to a rising and sustained elevation of estradiol—so-called positive feedback control. Negative feedback of estrogen involves both the hypothalamus and pituitary, whereas positive feedback operates primarily at the level of the pituitary.

The length of the normal menstrual cycle is defined as the time from the onset of one menstrual bleeding episode to the onset of the next. In women of reproductive age the menstrual cycle averages 28 ± 3 days, and the mean duration of flow is 4 ± 2 days. Longer menstrual cycles occur at menarche and prior to menopause. At the end of one menstrual cycle and in the face of a waning corpus luteum, plasma levels of estrogen and progesterone fall, and circulating levels of FSH increase concomitantly. Under the influence of increasing levels of FSH, follicular recruitment is initiated to effect development of the follicle that will be dominant during the next cycle.

After the onset of menses, follicular development continues, but FSH levels decrease. Approximately 8 to 10 days prior to the midcycle LH surge, plasma estradiol levels begin to rise as the result of secretion of estradiol by the granulosa cells of the enlarging dominant follicle. During the second half of the follicular phase, LH levels

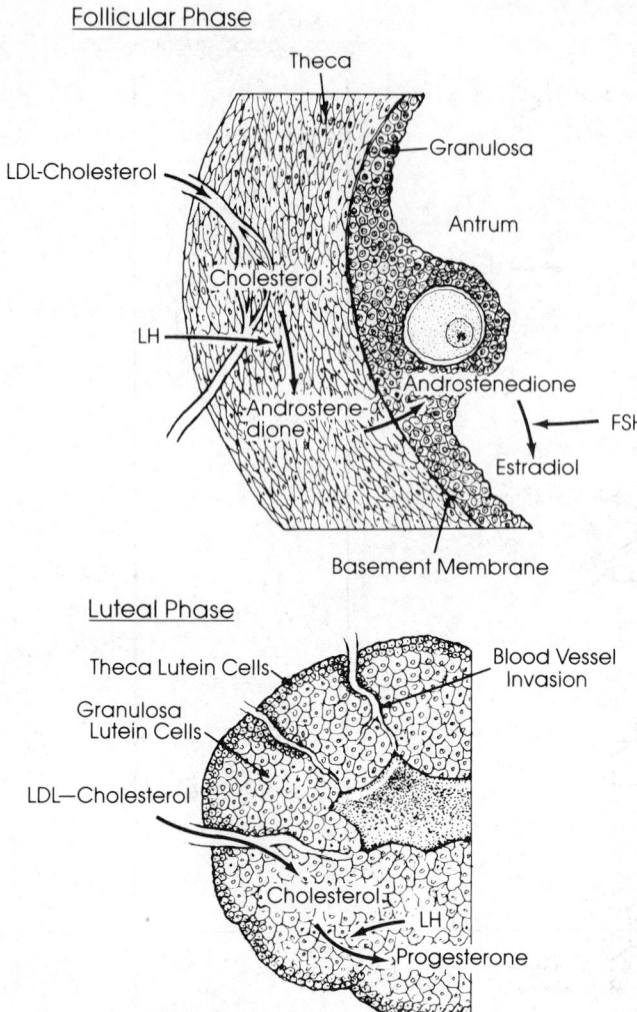

Follicular Phase

Theca

Granulosa

LDL-Cholesterol

Antrum

Cholesterol

LH

Androstene-
dione

Androstenedione

FSH

Estradiol

Basement Membrane

Luteal Phase

Theca Lutein Cells

Blood Vessel
Invasion

Granulosa
Lutein Cells

LDL—Cholesterol

Cholesterol

LH

Progesterone

FIGURE 331-4 *Cellular interactions in the ovary during the follicular phase (top) and luteal phase (bottom); LDL (low-density lipoprotein), FSH (follicle-stimulating hormone), and LH (luteinizing hormone). (From BR Carr et al, 1982.)*

also begin to rise (positive feedback). Just prior to ovulation, estradiol secretion reaches a peak and then falls. Immediately thereafter, a further rise in the plasma level of LH mediates the final maturation of the follicle, followed by follicular rupture and ovulation 16 to 23 h after the LH peak. Concomitant with the rise in LH is a smaller increase in the level of plasma FSH, the physiologic significance of which is unclear. Plasma progesterone also begins to rise just prior to midcycle and facilitates the positive feedback action of estradiol on LH secretion.

At the onset of the luteal phase plasma gonadotropins decrease, and plasma progesterone increases. A secondary rise in estrogens causes further gonadotropin suppression. Near the end of the luteal phase progesterone and estrogen levels fall, and FSH levels begin to rise to initiate the development of the next follicle (usually in the contralateral ovary) and the next menstrual cycle.

The endometrium lining the uterine cavity undergoes marked alterations in response to the changing plasma levels of ovarian hormones (Fig. 331-5). Concomitant with the decrease in plasma estrogen and progesterone and the decline of corpus luteum function in the late luteal phase, intense vasospasm occurs in the spiral arterioles supplying blood to the endometrium, followed by an ischemic necrosis, endometrial desquamation, and bleeding. This vasospasm is caused by locally synthesized prostaglandins. The onset of bleeding marks the first day of the menstrual cycle. By the fourth to fifth day of the cycle the endometrium is thin. During the proliferative phase glandular growth of the endometrium is mediated

by estrogen. After ovulation increased progesterone leads to further thickening of the endometrium, but the rapid growth slows. The endometrium then enters the secretory phase characterized by tortuosity of the glands, curling of the spiral arterioles, and glandular secretion. As corpus luteum function begins to wane in the absence of conception, the sequence of events leading to menstruation is again set into action.

Biphasic changes in basal body temperature are characteristic of the ovulatory cycle and are mediated by alterations in progesterone levels (Fig. 331-5). An increase in basal body temperature of 0.3 to 0.5°C begins after ovulation, persists during the luteal phase, and returns to the normal baseline (36.2 to 36.4°C) after the onset of the subsequent menses (see Chap. 9).

Cellular interactions in the ovary during the normal cycle LH stimulates thecal cells surrounding the follicle to form androgens, and androstenedione diffuses across the basement membrane of the follicle into granulosa cells where it is aromatized to estrogen (Figs. 331-3 and 331-4).

The increase of FSH late in the preceding menstrual cycle stimulates growth and recruitment of the primary follicles by enhancing granulosa cell proliferation, resulting ultimately in the formation of the dominant follicle. FSH also stimulates activity and amount of aromatizing enzymes in the granulosa cells that convert androstenedione to estrogen. Enhanced secretion of estradiol causes an increase in the number of estradiol receptors and further proliferation of granulosa cells. In the late follicular phase FSH, in concert with estradiol, causes induction of LH receptors on the granulosa cells. LH acts via these receptors to increase progesterone secretion at midcycle. The amount of progesterone formed by the follicle is believed to be limited by the availability of LDL-cholesterol to serve as substrate for steroidogenesis and by the fact that most of the progesterone formed is further metabolized to androstenedione by thecal cells. Prior to ovulation the granulosa cells of the follicle are bathed in follicular fluid but have limited access to circulating blood and consequently to plasma LDL. As depicted in Fig. 331-4, the granulosa cells become vascularized after ovulation, and plasma LDL-cholesterol becomes available to serve as the major substrate for progesterone synthesis by the corpus luteum. Thus, increased progesterone synthesis by the corpus luteum is the consequence of increased substrate availability. The peak in progesterone secretion by the corpus luteum is attained 8 days after ovulation at the time of maximal vascularization of the granulosa cells.

MENOPAUSE The menopause is defined as the final episode of menstrual bleeding in women. However, the term is used commonly to refer to the period of the female climacteric that encompasses the transitional period between the reproductive years up to and beyond the last episode of menstrual bleeding. During this period there is a gradual but progressive loss of ovarian function and a variety of endocrine, somatic, and psychological changes.

The median age of women at the time of cessation of menstrual bleeding is 50 to 51 years. Since the life expectancy in women is now close to 80 years, approximately one-third of life occurs after cessation of reproductive function. Preceding the menopause, the pattern of menstrual cycles is variable, but the interval between menses usually becomes shorter due to a decrease in the length of the follicular phase of the cycle. In addition, there is an increase in the mean levels of plasma FSH and LH, despite the continuation of ovulatory cycles. Thus, the ovary appears to become less responsive to gonadotropins prior to the menopause.

The menopause is the consequence of the exhaustion of ovarian follicles. The decrease in the number of ova begins in intrauterine life; by the time of the menopause few ova remain, and these appear to be nonfunctional. Only a small number of ova are lost as the result of ovulation during reproductive life, the majority of follicles and associated ova being lost by atresia. The cessation of follicular development results in a drop in the production of estradiol and other hormones, which in turn causes a loss of negative feedback on the

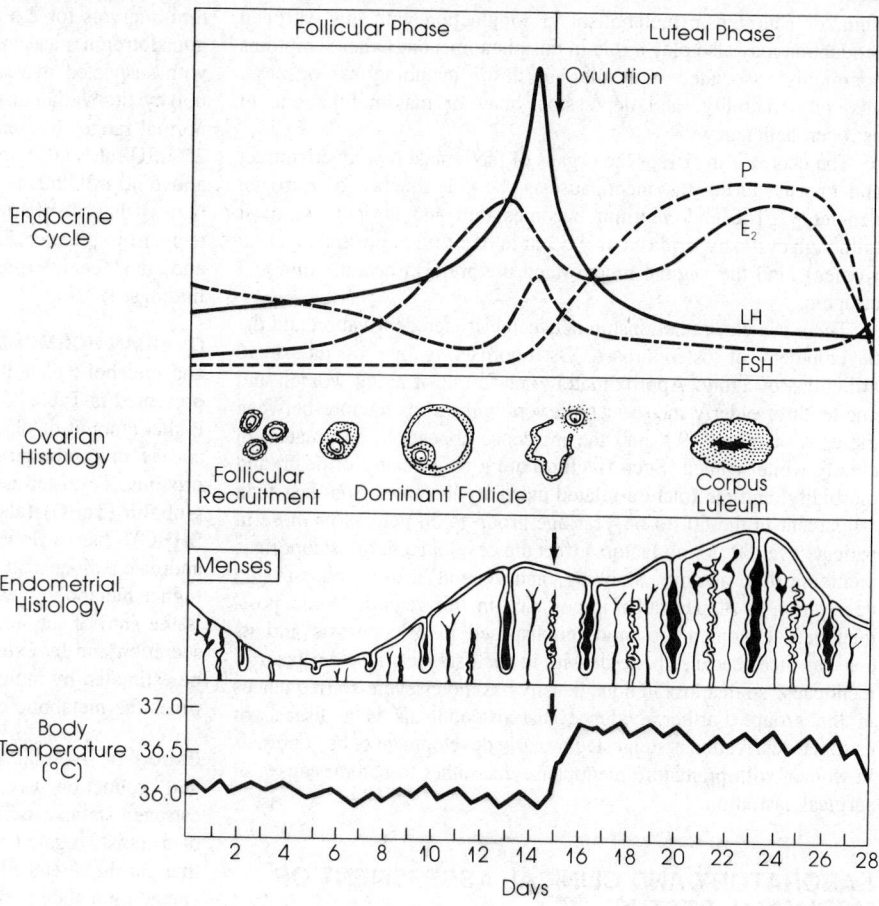

FIGURE 331-5 *The hormonal, ovarian, endometrial, and basal body temperature changes and relationship throughout the normal menstrual cycle.*

hypothalamic-pituitary centers. In turn, the levels of plasma gonadotropins increase with FSH levels rising earlier and to a greater extent than those of LH (Figs. 331-1 and 331-6). The higher concentration of FSH than LH in postmenopausal women may result from the decrease in inhibin secretion by the ovary, from the fact that FSH is cleared from plasma less rapidly than LH due to its higher sialic acid content, and possibly from the loss of positive feedback on LH production by estradiol. Intravenous administration of LHRH to menopausal women results in a pronounced increase in the secretion of both FSH and LH, consistent with the enhanced hypothalamic-pituitary secretory activity in other forms of primary ovarian failure.

The ovaries of postmenopausal women are small, and the residual cells are predominantly stromal in type. Estrogen and androgen levels in plasma are reduced but not absent from the circulation (Fig. 331-6). Prior to the menopause, plasma androstenedione is derived almost equally from the adrenals and the ovaries; after menopause the ovarian contribution ceases so that the plasma levels of androstenedione fall by 50 percent (Fig. 331-6). However, the menopausal ovary continues to secrete testosterone, presumably formed in stromal cells.

Circulating estrogens in the ovulating woman are derived from two sources. Sixty percent of mean estrogen formation during the menstrual cycle is in the form of estradiol formed primarily by ovaries, and the remainder is estrone formed mainly in extraglandular tissues from androstenedione. After menopause, extraglandular estrogen formation becomes the major pathway for estrogen synthesis. Estrogen production by the menopausal ovary is minimal, and subsequent oophorectomy is not followed by any further decrease in estrogen levels. Plasma levels of estradiol, the principal estrogen secreted by the follicle, are lower in postmenopausal women than are the levels of estrone. The rate of peripheral formation of estrone increases somewhat in menopausal women so that estrone production is usually only slightly less than prior to the menopause, despite the fall in plasma androstenedione. Because a major site of extraglandular

estrogen production is adipose tissue, peripheral estrogen formation may actually be enhanced in obese postmenopausal women, so that total estrogen production rates may be as great or greater than in premenopausal women. The predominant estrogen formed is estrone rather than estradiol.

The most common menopausal symptoms are those of vasomotor instability (hot flash), atrophy of the urogenital epithelium and skin, decreased size of the breasts, and osteoporosis. Approximately 40 percent of women in the postmenopausal period develop symptoms serious enough to seek medical assistance.

The pathogenesis of the hot flash is uncertain. There is a close temporal relationship between the onset of the hot flash and pulses of LH secretion. Alterations in catecholamine, prostaglandin, endor-

FIGURE 331-6 *Differences in hormone concentration in women during the reproductive years and in women during the menopause. FSH (follicle-stimulating hormone), LH (luteinizing hormone), E₂ (estradiol-17β), E₁ (estrone), Δ⁴-A (androstenedione), T (testosterone). (From SSC Yen and RB Jaffe, 1986, and from DR Mishell Jr and V Davajan.)*

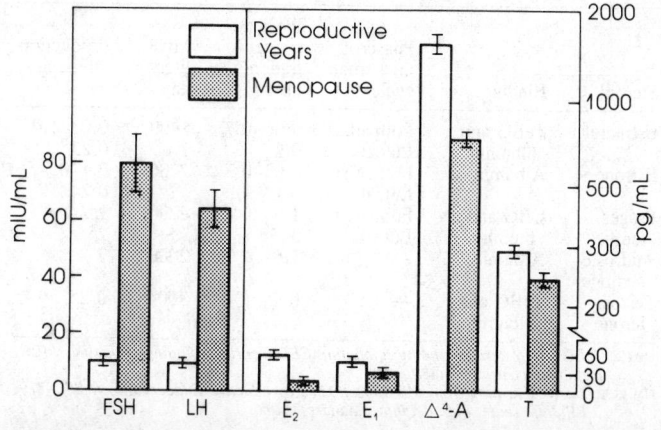

phin, or neurotensin metabolism in conjunction with low estrogen production may also play a role in this phenomenon. Other symptoms commonly associated with the hot flash, including nervousness, anxiety, irritability, and depression, may or may not be due to estrogen deficiency.

The decrease in size of the organs of the female reproductive tract and breasts during the menopause is the consequence of estrogen deficiency. The endometrium becomes thin and atrophic in most (although cystic hyperplasia may occur in one-fifth of postmenopausal women), and the vaginal mucosa and urethra also become thin and atrophic.

There is a close relationship between estrogen deprivation and the development of osteoporosis. Osteoporosis is one of the dread afflictions of aging. Approximately one-fourth of aging women and one-tenth of elderly men sustain a vertebral or hip fracture between the ages of 60 and 90, and the incidence appears to be greatest in elderly white women. Such fractures are a major cause of death and morbidity, and the fracture-related mortality increases from less than 10 percent in the 60- to 64-year age group to 30 percent or more in patients over 80. Many factors affect the development of osteoporosis including diet, activity, smoking, and general health, and estrogen deprivation is of particular importance in this regard. White postmenopausal women are more predisposed to osteoporosis and its consequences because bone density in such subjects is lower prior to menopause so that loss in bone density has more severe consequences in the group. Further evidence that osteoporosis is a disease of estrogen deprivation is suggested by early development of osteoporosis in women with premature menopause due either to natural causes or surgical castration.

LABORATORY AND CLINICAL ASSESSMENT OF HORMONAL STATUS

Assessment of the hormonal status of women can usually be made by obtaining a thorough history and physical examination. In general, presence of secondary sexual characteristics such as normal female breast development indicates adequate estrogen secretion in the past, and the presence of regular, predictable, cyclic menses implies that ovulation and the production of gonadotropins, estrogen, progesterone, and androgens are adequate and that the outflow tract is intact. Such a history may be more valuable than laboratory tests in evaluating ovarian hormone status. However, laboratory tests provide valuable ancillary information in the workup of women with endocrine dysfunction or infertility.

PITUITARY GONADOTROPINS Plasma gonadotropins are assessed by radioimmunoassay. Because both FSH and LH are secreted in pulsatile manner, the results obtained from a single serum sample may be difficult to interpret. Consequently, multiple samples at 20-min intervals for 2 h may be pooled to obtain a mean value. Serum gonadotropin measurements are of most use in evaluating women with suspected ovarian failure and in establishing the diagnosis of polycystic ovarian disease and hypogonadotropic hypogonadism. The normal ranges for serum LH and FSH in ovulating women are 5 to 25 mIU/mL and 5 to 30 mIU/mL, respectively. A persistent FSH above 40 mIU/mL is diagnostic of ovarian failure, and an LH value of less than 5 mIU/mL is suggestive of hypogonadotropic hypogonadism. In practice, however, gonadotropin values may be equivocal and must be interpreted in light of the remainder of the clinical findings.

OVARIAN HORMONES The mean plasma levels, production rates, and metabolic clearance rates of the principal ovarian hormones are presented in Table 331-1. The metabolic clearance rate of a hormone is that amount of plasma that is cleared of hormone per unit of time and is inversely proportional to the degree of binding to plasma proteins. Testosterone, which is tightly bound to testosterone-binding globulin (TeBG) (also known as sex hormone–binding globulin or SHBG), has a low metabolic clearance rate. Steroids such as androstenedione that are not tightly bound to carrier proteins have higher metabolic clearance rates. The production rate of a hormone is the sum of the amount of hormone produced by direct glandular secretion and by extraglandular conversion of prohormones and can be estimated by multiplying the concentration of hormone in plasma times the metabolic clearance rate of that hormone.

Estrogen Normal secondary sexual characteristics imply that estrogen production was adequate in the past. Indication of the current estrogen status can be obtained by pelvic examination. The presence of a moist, rugated vagina with copious, clear, thin cervical mucus that can be stretched and that exhibits arborization or ferning when spread on a slide is strong evidence of adequate estrogen production. Cytologic demonstration of mature vaginal epithelial cells and abundant cornified squamous epithelial cells with pyknotic nuclei confirms the presence of adequate estrogen levels.

The progesterone-withdrawal test provides a functional assessment of estrogen status. If menses appear within a week to 10 days after the end of a trial of medroxyprogesterone acetate (10 mg by mouth once or twice a day for 5 days) or after a single intramuscular injection of progesterone (100 mg), then prior estrogen priming was adequate to allow withdrawal bleeding.

Due to its variable level in plasma during the normal cycle and the difficulty of estimating the day of the cycle in women with abnormal cycles, the determination of estrogen levels in plasma or urine by radioimmunoassay is of little use in the routine assessment of estrogen status. Plasma estradiol is measured during attempts to induce ovulation with human menopausal gonadotropins to prevent the development of the ovarian hyperstimulation syndrome and is utilized along with ultrasound assessment to monitor follicular growth in women who are to undergo in vitro fertilization.

Progesterone Cyclic, predictable menses also imply that adequate progesterone is secreted during the luteal phase of the menstrual cycle. The indications for specific assay of progesterone are to document ovulation or evaluate the adequacy of the luteal phase in the evaluation of infertile women and to separate subjects with müllerian agenesis from those with the testicular feminization syndrome. Several functional assays of progesterone secretion can be utilized. The least expensive and most useful is the daily measurement of basal body temperature throughout a cycle. Due to the thermogenic properties of progesterone, documentation of the monthly biphasic curve with an elevated temperature for approximately 2 weeks after ovulation is a valid indication of progesterone secretion during the luteal phase (Fig. 331-5). Presence of viscous cervical mucus that does not stretch or fern and the presence of predominant intermediate cells on vaginal cytology or demonstration of a secretory epithelium in an endometrial biopsy during the luteal phase on day 20 to 22 of the cycle provide additional evidence of progesterone secretion. In

TABLE 331-1 Concentrations, metabolic clearance rates, and production rates of the major ovarian steroid hormones in blood of ovulatory women

Steroid	Binding	Phase of menstrual cycle	Plasma concentration, ng/mL	MCR, liters/day	Production rate, mg/day
Estradiol	TeBG and albumin	Follicular Luteal	0.06–0.7 0.2	1400	0.08–1.0 0.25
Estrone	Albumin	Follicular Luteal	0.05–0.3 0.1	2200	0.1–0.7 0.24
Progesterone	CBG and albumin	Follicular Luteal	1.0 3–25	2200	2 25
Androstenedione	Albumin	—	1.6	2000	3
Testosterone	TeBG and albumin	—	0.4	700	0.25

NOTE: *TeBG, testosterone-binding globulin; CBG, cortisol-binding globulin; MCR, metabolic clearance rate.*
SOURCE: *Derived in part from MB Lipsett, in Reproductive Endocrinology, SSC Yen, RB Jaffe (eds). Philadelphia, Saunders, 1986.*

addition measurement of serum progesterone by radioimmunoassay can be used to estimate progesterone secretion by the corpus luteum.

Androgen   Under normal conditions the ovary secretes androstenedione, testosterone, and dehydroepiandrosterone. In conditions of androgen excess, hirsutism and/or virilization are common. The laboratory evaluation of androgen excess is discussed in Chap. 46.

DIAGNOSIS OF PREGNANCY   Pregnancy is usually suspected and diagnosed on the basis of the history and findings on physical examination. Namely, a woman with previous cyclic, predictable menses develops amenorrhea accompanied by breast tenderness, malaise, lassitude, and nausea, and on physical examination a softening and enlargement of the uterus is found.

Laboratory assays of placental products excreted in urine facilitate the diagnosis of pregnancy. Human chorionic gonadotropin (hCG) is secreted by the trophoblastic cells of the placenta into the maternal plasma and excreted in the urine. Assays of urinary hCG make it feasible to detect the presence of functioning trophoblasts earlier than can be recognized by clinical assessments. Assays for measurement of hCG content of serum or urine utilize either antibody against hCG or receptor for hCG. With some radioimmunoassays it is possible to detect pregnancies 8 to 10 days after ovulation and before the first missed menstrual period. Radioimmunoassay of the β subunit of hCG in serum or urine makes it possible to differentiate between excess LH and hCG, an important distinction in evaluating women with trophoblastic disease such as hydatidiform mole or choriocarcinoma.

DISORDERS OF OVARIAN FUNCTION

PREPUBERTAL YEARS   Puberty is said to be precocious if the onset of breast budding occurs before age 8 or if menarche commences before age 9. Those disorders in which the developing sexual characteristics are appropriate for the genetic and gonadal sex, i.e., feminization in girls or virilization in boys, are termed *isosexual precocity*, whereas *heterosexual precocity* occurs when sexual characters are not in accord with the genetic sex, namely virilization in girls or feminization in boys. Pubertal disorders of boys are described in Chap. 330.

Isosexual precocious puberty   Isosexual precocious puberty in girls can be divided into three major categories (Table 331-2).

TRUE PRECOCIOUS PUBERTY   True precocious puberty is characterized by an early but otherwise normal sequence of pubertal development, including increased secretion of gonadotropins and ovulatory menstrual cycles. Constitutional or idiopathic precocious puberty comprises 90 percent of cases. In these individuals no cause for the premature maturation of the central nervous system–hypothalamic-pituitary axis can be identified, and the diagnosis is one of exclusion. As many as half of these individuals have abnormal electroencephalograms. Premature appearance of secondary sexual characteristics and of ovulatory cycles with the accompanying risk of fertility may result in significant emotional disturbances. Therefore, prompt initiation of therapy is imperative. The usual treatment is medroxyprogesterone acetate in doses of 100 to 200 mg given intramuscularly every 2 to 4 weeks to suppress gonadotropin secretion. Such a regimen is usually effective in inhibiting ovarian estrogen production and ovulation but does not consistently control bone growth or prevent premature epiphyseal closure and the resultant short stature. LHRH analogues have been utilized to inhibit estrogen synthesis and thus inhibit precocious puberty, and early evidence suggests that they also prevent premature closure of the epiphyses.

About 10 percent of cases are due to organic brain diseases, including brain tumors (hypothalamic gliomas, astrocytomas, ependymomas, germinomas, and hamartomas), encephalitis, meningitis, hydrocephalus, head injury, tuberous sclerosis, and neurofibromatosis. It is essential to separate this group of patients from those with the idiopathic disorder, and patients designated as idiopathic occasionally

prove to have such tumors. Fortunately, most patients with organic lesions serious enough to cause precocious puberty have obvious neurologic signs and symptoms. Evaluation of all patients with precocious puberty should include, at a minimum, skull films and computerized tomography scans of the brain. The success of treatment depends upon the nature of the lesion, but surgical and radiation treatment of well-localized tumors is occasionally successful.

A rare cause of isosexual precocity is virilizing congenital adrenal hyperplasia due to 21-hydroxylase deficiency in girls in whom treatment is delayed until 4 to 8 years of age. After initiation of glucocorticoid replacement, such individuals may undergo true isosexual precocious puberty (see Chap. 325).

PRECOCIOUS PSEUDOPUBERTY   Precocious pseudopuberty occurs when girls feminize as a consequence of enhanced estrogen formation but do not ovulate or develop cyclic menses. Ovarian cysts or tumors that secrete estrogen (granulosa-theca cell tumors) are the most frequent cause of precocious pseudopuberty. Granulosa-theca-cell tumors associated with intestinal polyps and pigmentation of the mucous membranes occur in the Peutz-Jeghers syndrome. Other ovarian tumors that secrete estrogens (or androgens that can be converted to estrogens at extraglandular sites) include dysgerminomas, teratomas, cystadenomas, and ovarian carcinomas (also see Chap. 296). Ovarian tumors can usually be detected by rectoabdominal examination, and sonography, computerized tomography, and/or laparoscopy may also be of help. Ovarian teratomas and choriocarcinomas and other carcinomas that secrete hCG do not cause precocious puberty in girls unless there is concomitant secretion of estrogen by the tumor (hCG or LH in the absence of FSH does not induce ovarian estrogen production). Rarely, feminizing tumors of the adrenal cause isosexual precocious puberty, either by formation of estrogens directly or by secretion of weak androgens to serve as estrogenic precursors in extraglandular tissues.

Other causes of precocious pseudopuberty include the following: (1) The McCune-Albright syndrome (polyostotic fibrous dysplasia), characterized by café au lait spots, cystic fibrous dysplasia of bones, and sexual precocity. Some of these individuals have increased gonadotropin secretion, but the majority have low gonadotropins and a form of gonadotropin-independent sexual precocity. Occasionally, this disorder leads to true precocious puberty (see Chap. 334). (2) Primary hypothyroidism in which secretion of thyrotropin-releasing hormone (TRH) as well as the secretion of other hypothalamic hormones is enhanced, leading to increased FSH levels and ovarian estrogen secretion, frequently with galactorrhea. (3) The Silver syndrome, or congenital asymmetry associated with short stature and precocious feminization. (4) Estrogen-containing medications including use of estrogen-containing creams for diaper rash or the ingestion of any estrogen by mouth.

INCOMPLETE ISOSEXUAL PRECOCITY   This term is used to describe the premature development of a single pubertal event and encompasses

TABLE 331-2   Differential diagnosis of sexual precocity

I Isosexual precocity
   A True precocious puberty
      1 Constitutional
      2 Organic brain disease
      3 Congenital adrenal hyperplasia
   B Precocious pseudopuberty
      1 Ovarian tumors
      2 Adrenal tumors
      3 McCune-Albright syndrome
      4 Hypothyroidism
      5 Silver syndrome
      6 Estrogen-containing medications
   C Incomplete sexual precocity
      1 Premature thelarche
      2 Premature adrenarche
      3 Premature pubarche
II Heterosexual precocity
   A Ovarian tumors
   B Adrenal tumors
   C Congenital adrenal hyperplasia

several entities. The appearance of breast budding prior to the age of 8 (premature thelarche) without other evidence of estrogen secretion and without premature bone maturation is believed to be due to a transient increase in estrogen secretion or a temporary increase in sensitivity to the small amounts of circulating estrogens formed prior to puberty. Usually the disorder is self-limited and resolves spontaneously. Occasionally axillary hair and/or pubic hair (so-called *premature adrenarche* and *pubarche*) appear without any other secondary sexual development. The phenomenon is associated with adrenal androgen secretion in the range of normal puberty and can be distinguished from syndromes of virilization by the absence of clitoromegaly. It requires no treatment, and patients enter puberty at about the average time.

Heterosexual precocity Virilization in a prepubertal female is usually due to congenital adrenal hyperplasia or to androgen secretion by an ovarian or adrenal tumor. The manifestations of virilization are described in Chap. 46. Virilization in girls with congenital adrenal hyperplasia usually takes place in a background of variable sexual ambiguity (see Chap. 333).

Evaluation of sexual precocity The evaluation of sexual precocity involves a careful history and physical examination including rectoabdominal examination, abdominal sonography, determination of bone age, and measurement of gonadotropins (and androgen or estrogen levels when appropriate). Skull films and further diagnostic tests are indicated if a neurologic disorder is suspected and no evidence of ovarian or adrenal tumor is found.

REPRODUCTIVE YEARS Disorders of the menstrual cycle
ABNORMAL UTERINE BLEEDING Between menarche and the menopause, almost every woman experiences one or more episodes of abnormal uterine bleeding, here defined as any bleeding pattern that differs in frequency, duration, or amount from the pattern observed during a normal menstrual cycle. A variety of descriptive terms (such as *menorrhagia*, *metrorrhagia*, and *menometrorrhagia*) have been used to characterize patterns of abnormal uterine bleeding. A more logical approach is to divide abnormal uterine bleeding into those patterns associated with ovulatory cycles and those associated with anovulatory cycles.

Ovulatory cycles. Normal menstrual bleeding with ovulatory cycles is spontaneous, regular, cyclic, and predictable and frequently associated with discomfort (dysmenorrhea). Deviations from this pattern associated with cycles that are still regular and predictable are most often due to organic disease of the outflow tract. For example, regular but prolonged and excessive bleeding episodes unassociated with bleeding dyscrasias (hypermenorrhea or menorrhagia) can result from abnormalities of the uterus such as submucous leiomyomas, adenomyosis, or endometrial polyps. Regular, cyclical, predictable menstruation characterized by spotting or light bleeding is termed *hypomenorrhea* and is due to obstruction of the outflow tract as from intrauterine synechiae or scarring of the cervix. Intermenstrual bleeding between episodes of regular, ovulatory menstruation is also often due to cervical or endometrial lesions. An exception to the association between organic disease of the uterus and abnormal uterine bleeding is the occurrence of episodes of regular bleeding more frequently than 21 days apart (polymenorrhea). These cycles may be a normal variant.

Anovulatory cycles. Uterine bleeding that is unpredictable with respect to amount, onset, and duration and is usually painless is described as *dysfunctional uterine bleeding*. This disorder is not due to abnormalities of the uterus but rather to chronic anovulation and occurs when there is interruption of the normal progressive sequence of follicular and luteal phases under the influence of a dominant follicle and its resulting corpus luteum. As discussed above normal uterine bleeding in ovulatory cycles is due to progesterone withdrawal and requires that the endometrium first be primed with estrogen (when castrates or postmenopausal women are given progesterone withdrawal bleeding usually does not occur).

Dysfunctional uterine bleeding can occur in women who have a transient disruption of the synchronous hypothalamic-pituitary-ovarian patterns necessary for regular ovulatory cycles, most often at the extremes of the reproductive life, namely in the early menarche and in the perimenopausal period, but also as the secondary consequence of temporary stresses intercurrent illnesses.

On the other hand, primary *dysfunctional uterine bleeding* can result from at least three pathophysiologic mechanisms.

1 *Estrogen withdrawal bleeding* occurs when estrogen is given to a castrate or postmenopausal woman and then withdrawn. As in other types of dysfunctional uterine bleeding, this form of menstrual bleeding is usually painless.

2 *Estrogen breakthrough bleeding* occurs when there is prolonged continuous estrogen stimulation of the endometrium not interrupted by cyclic progesterone secretion and withdrawal. This is the most common type of dysfunctional uterine bleeding and is usually due to anovulation associated with chronic acyclic estrogen production as in women with polycystic ovarian disease. Such women may have histories of irregular, unpredictable menses, oligomenorrhea, or amenorrhea (see below). Alternatively, estrogen breakthrough bleeding can occur in hypogonadal women given estrogens chronically rather than intermittently or in women with estrogen-secreting tumors of the ovary. Estrogen breakthrough bleeding may be profuse and is unpredictable with respect to duration, amount of flow, and time of occurrence. The endometrium is typically thin because its repair between episodes of bleeding is incomplete.

3 *Progesterone breakthrough bleeding* occurs in the presence of abnormally high ratios of progesterone to estrogen, for example, in women on continuous low-dose oral contraceptives.

The approach to a patient with dysfunctional uterine bleeding in the reproductive years begins with a careful history of menstrual patterns and prior hormonal therapy. Since not all bleeding from the urogenital tract is from the uterus, rectal, bladder, and vaginal or cervical sources must be excluded by physical examination. If the bleeding is from the uterus a pregnancy-related disorder such as abortion or ectopic pregnancy must also be excluded. Once the diagnosis of dysfunctional uterine bleeding is established a rational approach to management is as follows. During a first episode of dysfunctional bleeding the patient can simply be observed, provided the bleeding is not copious and no evidence of bleeding dyscrasia is present. If bleeding is moderately severe, control can be achieved with relatively high dose estrogen oral contraceptives for 3 weeks. Alternatively, a regimen of three or four low-dose oral contraceptive pills per day for 1 week followed by tapering to the usual dosage for up to 3 weeks is also effective. If uterine bleeding is more severe, hospitalization, bed rest, and intramuscular injections of estradiol valerate (10 mg) and 17α-hydroxyprogesterone caproate (500 mg) or intravenous or intramuscular conjugated estrogens (25 mg) usually control the bleeding. After initial treatment iron replacement should be instituted, and recurrence can be prevented by cyclic oral contraceptives for 2 to 3 months (or more if pregnancy is not desired). Alternatively, menses should be induced every 2 to 3 months with medroxyprogesterone acetate 10 mg by mouth once or twice a day for 5 days. If hormone therapy fails to control uterine bleeding, an endometrial biopsy or dilatation and curettage may be required for diagnosis and therapy. Indeed, uterine sampling may be indicated prior to hormone therapy in women at risk for endometrial cancer (i.e., in women approaching the age of menopause or in the massively obese); endometrial cancer is rare in ovulatory women of reproductive age.

AMENORRHEA An acceptable definition of amenorrhea is failure of menarche by age 16, irrespective of the presence or absence of secondary sexual characteristics, or the absence of menstruation for 6 months in a woman with previous periodic menses. However, women who do not fulfill these criteria should be evaluated if (1) the subject and/or her family are greatly concerned, (2) no breast development has occurred by age 14, or (3) any sexual ambiguity or virilization is present (Chap. 333). Amenorrhea is usually categorized as either primary (in a woman who has never menstruated) or secondary (in a woman in whom menstruation is present for a variable time and then ceases); some disorders can cause either primary or secondary amenorrhea. For example, most women with gonadal dysgenesis have primary amenorrhea, but occasional such patients have some follicles and ovulate for short periods so that pregnancies may rarely occur. Furthermore, patients with chronic anovulation (polycystic ovarian disease) most often have secondary amenorrhea but occasionally present with primary amenorrhea. For these reasons, categorization of amenorrhea into primary and secondary types is less helpful in the differential diagnosis than a classification based upon the major underlying physiologic derangements: (1) anatomic defects, (2) ovarian failure, and (3) chronic anovulation with or without estrogen present.

Anatomic defects. A variety of anatomic or structural defects of the female genital tract can preclude menstrual bleeding. Starting from the caudal end of the female genital tract, labial agglutination or fusion is often associated with disorders of sexual development, particularly female pseudohermaphroditism (congenital adrenal hyperplasia or exposure to maternal androgens in utero). (See Chap. 333.) Congenital defects of the vagina, imperforate hymen, and transverse vaginal septae can also cause amenorrhea. These women frequently have accumulation of menstrual blood behind the obstruction and may have cyclic, predictable episodes of abdominal pain.

More severe müllerian anomalies include müllerian agenesis (the Mayer-Rokitansky-Küster-Hauser syndrome) (see Chap. 333), second in frequency only to gonadal dysgenesis as a cause of primary amenorrhea. Women with this syndrome have a 46,XX karyotype, female secondary sex characteristics, and normal ovarian function, including cyclical ovulation, but have absence or severe hypoplasia of the vagina. The uterus usually consists of only rudimentary bicornuate cords, but if the uterus contains endometrium, cyclic abdominal pain and accumulation of blood may occur as in other forms of outlet obstruction. One-third of patients have abnormalities of the urogenital tract, and one-tenth have skeletal anomalies, usually involving the spine. The major diagnostic problem is separating müllerian agenesis from complete testicular feminization in which 46,XY genetic males with testes differentiate as phenotypic women with a blind vaginal pouch and an absent uterus. Women with testicular feminization have feminized breasts but a paucity of pubic and axillary hair. The disorder is due to a defect in the intracellular cytoplasmic androgen-receptor protein that results in profound resistance to the action of testosterone (see Chap. 333). Testicular feminization can be diagnosed by demonstrating a male level of serum testosterone or a 46,XY karyotype, whereas the diagnosis of müllerian agenesis is established by demonstrating a 46,XX karyotype, biphasic basal body temperatures characteristic of ovulating women, and elevated levels of progesterone during the luteal phase.

A rare cause of absence of uterus in 46,XY phenotypic women who are sexually infantile is the so-called testicular regression syndrome or testicular agenesis (see Chap. 333).

Other abnormalities of the uterus that cause amenorrhea include obstruction due to scarring or stenosis of the cervix, often resulting from surgery, electrocautery, or cryosurgery. Destruction of the endometrium (Asherman's syndrome) may follow vigorous curettage, usually in association with postpartum hemorrhage or therapeutic abortion complicated by infection. This diagnosis is confirmed by hysterosalpingography or by direct vision of the endometrial scarring or synechiae using a hysteroscope.

Treatment of disorders of the outflow tract is surgical. Repair of vaginal agenesis results in normal menstruation and potential fertility only if an intact uterus is present.

Ovarian failure. Primary ovarian failure is associated with elevated plasma gonadotropins and can result from several causes. The most frequent cause is *gonadal dysgenesis,* in which the germ cells are lacking and the ovary is replaced by a fibrous streak. (Also see Chaps. 60 and 333.) Women with gonadal dysgenesis can be divided

into two broad groups on the basis of karyotype. The most common is due to deletion of genetic material in the X chromosomes and accounts for about two-thirds of gonadal dysgenesis. A 45,X karyotype is found in about half, and most have somatic defects including short stature, webbed neck, shield chest, and cardiovascular defects, collectively termed the Turner phenotype. The remainder of patients with identifiable abnormalities of the X chromosome have chromosomal mosaicism with or without associated structural abnormalities of the X chromosome. The most common form of mosaicism is 45,X/46,XX. Gonadal tumors are rare in 45,X patients, but gonadal malignancies have been reported in women with chromosomal mosaicism involving the Y chromosome. Therefore, a chromosomal analysis should be obtained in all cases of amenorrhea associated with ovarian failure, and the streak gonad should be removed if a Y chromosome is present. Approximately 90 percent of individuals with gonadal dysgenesis associated with deletion of genetic material in the X chromosome never have menstrual bleeding, and the remaining 10 percent have sufficient residual follicles to experience menses and, rarely, fertility; the menstrual and reproductive lives of such individuals are invariably brief.

A tenth of subjects with bilateral streak gonads have a normal 46,XX or 46,XY karyotype and are said to have *pure gonadal dysgenesis.* These individuals have either normal or above-average stature due to failure of estrogen-mediated epiphyseal closure in the presence of a normal chromosomal constitution. Pure gonadal dysgenesis does not constitute a phenotypic or chromosomally homogenous disorder. Some are the result of X-linked or autosomal gene defects. Other possible causes include chromosomal mosaicism limited to gonadal tissue and destruction of germinal tissue in utero by environmental or infectious processes. Approximately one-tenth of such individuals with a 46,XY karyotype develop signs of virilization including clitoromegaly and have an increased incidence of tumors in the gonadal streaks; as a consequence gonadal streaks should be removed prophylactically as previously discussed when a Y chromosome is present. Approximately two-thirds of individuals with 46,XX karyotype experience no menses while the remainder have one or more menstrual episodes and are occasionally fertile.

Other causes of ovarian failure and amenorrhea include 17α-hydroxylase or 17,20-desmolase deficiency, premature ovarian failure, the resistant-ovary syndrome, and ovarian failure secondary to chemotherapy or radiation therapy for malignancy. *17α-Hydroxylase deficiency* is characterized by primary amenorrhea, sexual infantilism, and hypertension that is due to increased production of desoxycorticosterone (DOC), whereas women with 17,20-desmolase deficiency have primary amenorrhea and sexual infantilism with normal blood pressure (see Chaps. 325 and 333). The diagnosis of *premature ovarian failure* or *premature menopause* is applied to women who cease menstruating prior to the age of 40. The ovaries are similar to the ovaries of postmenopausal women, namely paucity or absence of follicles as the result of accelerated follicular atresia. Premature ovarian failure due to ovarian antibodies may be one component of polyglandular failure together with adrenal insufficiency, hypothyroidism, and other autoimmune disorders (see Chap. 334). A rare form of ovarian failure is the *resistant-ovary syndrome* in which the ovaries contain many follicles arrested in development prior to the antral stage, possibly because of resistance to the action of FSH in the ovary. To differentiate this disorder from the 46,XX variety of pure gonadal dysgenesis, both of which are associated with sexual immaturity, it is necessary to perform ovarian biopsy. However, such a distinction is not clinically useful since the treatment of infertility in both conditions is usually unsuccessful.

Chronic anovulation. At least 80 percent or more of gynecologic endocrine problems result from chronic anovulation. Women with chronic anovulation fail to ovulate spontaneously but may ovulate with appropriate therapy. The ovaries of such women do not secrete estrogen in a normal cyclic pattern; it is clinically useful to differentiate those women who produce sufficient estrogen to have withdrawal bleeding after progesterone therapy from those who fail to produce enough estrogen to have progesterone withdrawal bleeding and who often have hypothalamic-pituitary dysfunction.

Chronic anovulation with estrogen present. Women with chronic anovulation who experience withdrawal bleeding after progesterone administration are said to be in a state of "estrus" due to the acyclic production of estrogen, largely estrone, by extraglandular aromatization of circulating androstenedione. The most common term for this disorder is *polycystic ovarian disease* (PCOD), a syndrome characterized by infertility, hirsutism, obesity, and amenorrhea or oligomenorrhea. When spontaneous uterine bleeding occurs in subjects with PCOD, it is unpredictable with respect to time of onset, duration, and amount, and on occasion the bleeding can be severe. The dysfunctional uterine bleeding is usually due to estrogen breakthrough (see above).

The disorder, which may be transmitted as an autosomal dominant or X-linked trait, was originally described by Stein and Leventhal as characterized by enlarged, polycystic ovaries, but the syndrome and its accompanying endocrine abnormalities are now known to be associated with a variety of pathologic findings in the ovaries, only some of which result in enlargement of the ovaries and none of which are pathognomonic. The most common finding is a white, smooth, sclerotic ovary with a thickened capsule, multiple follicular cysts in various stages of atresia, a hyperplastic theca and stroma, and rare or absent corpora albicans. Other ovaries have hyperthecosis in which the ovarian stroma is hyperplastic and may contain lipid-laden luteal cells. Thus, the diagnosis of PCOD is a clinical one, based upon the coexistence of chronic anovulation and varying degrees of androgen excess.

In most women with PCOD menarche occurs at the expected time, but uterine bleeding is unpredictable in onset, duration, and amount. Amenorrhea ensues after a variable time, although primary amenorrhea occurs in some women. Signs of androgen excess (hirsutism) usually become evident around the time of menarche. One formulation suggests that this disorder originates as an exaggerated adrenarche in obese girls (Fig. 331-7). The combination of elevated adrenal androgens and obesity would result in increased formation of extraglandular estrogen and lead to an acyclic positive feedback on LH secretion and negative feedback on FSH secretion so that the characteristic LH/FSH ratios in plasma would be greater than 2. The increased LH levels could then lead to hyperplasia of the ovarian stroma and theca cells and increased androgen production,

which in turn would provide more substrate for peripheral aromatization and perpetuate the chronic anovulation. In the advanced state the ovary is the major site of androgen production, but the adrenal may continue to secrete excess androgen as well. The greater the obesity, the more this sequence would be perpetuated because adipose tissue stromal cells aromatize androgens to estrogens, which in turn exaggerates inappropriate LH release by positive feedback.

Thus, the fundamental defect in PCOD is viewed as one of inappropriate signals to the hypothalamus and pituitary. In fact, the hypothalamic-pituitary axis responds appropriately to high levels of estrogen, and ovulation can be induced with antiestrogens such as clomiphene citrate. Increased levels of plasma endorphins and inhibin may contribute to the perpetuation of the defect. The concept that the fundamental defect is one of inappropriate signals is supported by the findings in the ovary itself. Ovarian follicles from women with PCOD have low aromatase activity, but normal aromatase can be induced when the follicles are treated with FSH. In short, the anovulation is not due to an intrinsic abnormality in the ovary itself but rather the result of FSH deficiency and LH excess. An association exists between PCOD or hyperthecosis, acanthosis nigricans, and diabetes mellitus due to insulin resistance. The meaning of this association is not clear.

Treatment of PCOD is directed toward interrupting this self-perpetuating cycle and can be accomplished in several ways, including decreasing ovarian androgen secretion (wedge resection or oral contraceptive agents), decreasing peripheral estrogen formation (weight reduction), enhancing FSH secretion [administration of clomiphene, human menopausal gonadotropin (hMG), or LHRH (gonadorelin) by portable infusion pump]. The choice of therapy depends on the clinical findings and the needs of the patient. Attempt at weight reduction is appropriate in all who are obese. If the woman is not hirsute and does not desire pregnancy, periodic withdrawal menses can be induced with medroxyprogesterone acetate every 2 to 3 months; such treatment prevents development of endometrial hyperplasia. If the woman is hirsute but does not desire pregnancy, the ovarian (and possibly the adrenal) component of androgen production can be suppressed with combined estrogen-progestogen oral contraceptive agents. Combined oral contraceptives are also indicated if prolonged or excessive menstrual bleeding is present. Once androgen excess is controlled, treatment of previously existing hair growth by shaving, depilatories, or electrolysis may be indicated (see Chap. 46). If the

FIGURE 331-7 *Proposed mechanism for the initiation and perpetuation of chronic anovulation in polycystic ovarian disease (PCOD). This cycle may be entered or initiated via adrenal androgen excess or obesity, both of which result in enhanced extraglandular formation of estrogens. The therapy of PCOD involves interruption of the cycle at various sites. (From SSC Yen and RB Jaffe, 1986, and from U Goebelsmann in DR Mishell Jr and V Davajan.)*

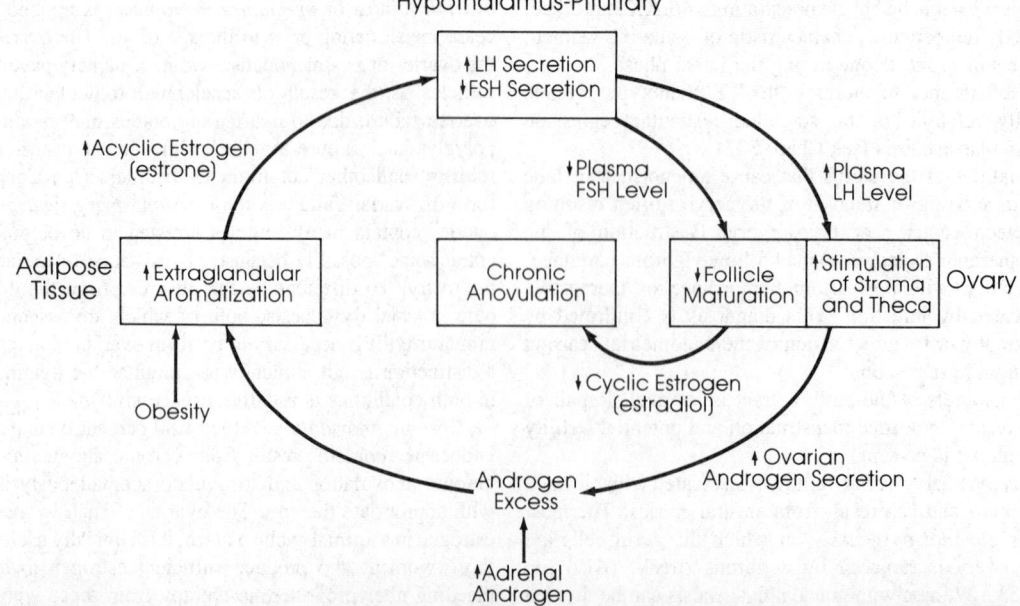

woman wants to become pregnant, induction of ovulation is necessary. The drug of choice for this purpose is clomiphene, which promotes ovulation in three-fourths of cases, and treatment with hMG, gonadorelin, or wedge resection of the ovaries may be successful in the remainder.

Chronic anovulation with estrogen present may also occur with tumors of the ovary. These include granulosa-theca cell tumors, Brenner tumors, cystic teratomas, mucous cystadenomas, and Krukenberg tumors (also see Chap. 296). These tumors can either secrete excess estrogen themselves or produce androgens that can then be aromatized in extraglandular sites. As a result, chronic anovulation and the clinical features of PCOD are produced. Occasionally areas of the ovary not involved with tumors show the characteristic histologic changes of PCOD. Other causes of chronic anovulation with estrogen present include adrenal production of excess androgen and various thyroid disorders.

Chronic anovulation with estrogen absent. Women with chronic anovulation who have low or absent estrogen production and do not experience withdrawal bleeding after progestogen treatment usually have hypogonadotropic hypogonadism due either to pituitary disease or to any of several organic or functional disorders of the central nervous system.

Isolated hypogonadotropic hypogonadism associated with defects of smell (olfactory bulb defects) is known as the Kallman syndrome (see Chaps. 321 and 330). Affected women are sexually infantile with a eunuchoid habitus and appear to have a defect in either the synthesis or release of LHRH. A variety of rare hypothalamic lesions can also impair LHRH production and cause hypogonadotropic hypogonadism; these include craniopharyngioma, germinoma (pinealoma), glioma, Hand-Schüller-Christian disease, teratomas, endodermal-sinus tumors, tuberculosis, sarcoidosis, and metastatic tumors that cause suppression or destruction of the hypothalamus. Central nervous system trauma and radiation can also cause hypothalamic amenorrhea and deficiencies in secretion of growth hormone, ACTH, and thyroid hormone.

More commonly, gonadotropin deficiency leading to chronic anovulation is believed to arise from functional disorders of the hypothalamus or higher centers. A history of a stressful event in a young woman is frequent. For example, chronic anovulation can begin suddenly in a woman who leaves home for the first time or experiences the death of a loved one. Gonadotropin and estrogen levels are in the low to low-normal range as compared to normal women in the early follicular phase of the cycle. In addition, rigorous exercise such as jogging or ballet and diets that result in excessive weight loss may lead to the development of chronic anovulation particularly in girls with a history of prior menstrual irregularity. The amenorrhea in these women does not appear to be due to weight loss alone but to a combination of a decrease in the percentage of body fat and chronic stress. An extreme form of weight loss with chronic anovulation is seen in anorexia nervosa. Anorexia nervosa is characterized by the development in a young woman of amenorrhea with associated severe weight loss, distorted attitudes toward eating and weight gain, self-induced vomiting, extreme emaciation, and distorted body image. Amenorrhea in anorexia nervosa can precede, follow, or appear coincidently with the loss in body weight (see Chap. 73). During successful therapy gonadotropin changes recapitulate those observed during normal puberty (Fig. 331-1).

In addition, chronic debilitating diseases such as end-stage kidney disease, malignancy, or the malabsorption syndrome are believed to lead to development of hypogonadotropic hypogonadism via a hypothalamic mechanism.

Treatment of chronic anovulation due to hypothalamic disorders includes reversal of the stressful situation, reducing exercise, or correction of weight loss if appropriate. These women appear to be susceptible to the development of osteoporosis, and estrogen replacement therapy to induce and maintain normal secondary sexual characteristics and prevent bone loss is recommended in those who do not desire pregnancy, and gonadotropin or gonadorelin therapy is

indicated when pregnancy is desired (see therapy section). When appropriate, therapy is directed at the primary disease of the hypothalamus.

Disorders of the pituitary can lead to the estrogen-deficient form of chronic anovulation by at least two mechanisms—direct interference with gonadotropin secretion by lesions that either obliterate or interfere with the gonadotropic cells (chromophobe adenomas, Sheehan's syndrome) or inhibition of gonadotropin secretion in association with excess prolactin (prolactinoma). *Pituitary tumors* make up approximately 10 percent of all intracranial tumors and may secrete no hormone, one hormone, or more than one hormone (see Chap. 321). In the past most pituitary tumors were assumed to be nonfunctional chromophobe adenomas, but prolactin levels are elevated in 50 to 70 percent of cases, either because of prolactin secretion by the tumor (prolactinomas) or interference by tumor mass with the normal inhibitory influence of the hypothalamus on prolactin secretion.

Prolactinomas can be divided into microadenomas (less than 10 mm in diameter) and macroadenomas (greater than 10 mm). Prolactin excess associated with low levels of LH and FSH constitutes a specific subgroup of hypogonadotropic hypogonadism. One-tenth or more of amenorrheic women have increased levels of serum prolactin, and more than half of women with both galactorrhea and amenorrhea have elevated prolactin levels. The amenorrhea in this disorder is most often associated with decreased or absent estrogen production, but prolactin-secreting tumors may on occasion be associated with normal ovulatory menses or chronic anovulation with estrogen present. Most prolactin-secreting adenomas grow slowly, and some cease growth after attainment of a certain size. The increased frequency of diagnosis of prolactin-secreting adenomas is probably due to several factors, including increased awareness, improved radiographic detection methods, and availability of radioimmunoassays for prolactin. However, since in older autopsy series a 9 to 23 percent prevalence of pituitary adenomas was observed in asymptomatic women, the clinical and prognostic significance of small microadenomas remains to be established. When tumors of any size are associated with symptoms of amenorrhea or galactorrhea, however, therapy should be considered, and when visual field defects or severe headaches are present bromocriptine therapy or neurosurgical evaluation is mandatory. The evaluation, differential diagnosis, and management of hyperprolactinemia is described in Chap. 321. In the latter half of pregnancy, prolactin-secreting pituitary tumors may expand, leading to headaches, compression of the optic chiasm, and blindness. Therefore, prior to induction of ovulation for the purposes of achieving pregnancy, it is mandatory to exclude the presence of a pituitary tumor.

Large pituitary tumors such as chromophobe adenomas—whether or not hyperprolactinemia is present—are likely to be associated with deficiency of hormones in addition to gonadotropins (Chap. 321).

Craniopharyngiomas, thought to arise from remnants of Rathke's pouch, account for 3 percent of intracranial neoplasms, occur most frequently in the second decade of life, and may extend into the suprasellar region. A large percentage of these tumors calcify and can be diagnosed by conventional skull films. Patients often present with sexual infantilism, delayed puberty, and amenorrhea due to gonadotropin deficiency. Craniopharyngioma may also result in impaired secretion of TSH, ACTH, growth hormone, and vasopressin.

Panhypopituitarism may occur spontaneously, result from surgical or radiation treatment of pituitary adenomas, or develop after postpartum hemorrhage (Sheehan's syndrome). The latter patients exhibit characteristic clinical manifestations including failure to lactate or ovulate, loss of genital and axillary hair, hypothyroidism, and adrenal insufficiency (see Chap. 321).

Evaluation of amenorrhea. A general schema for the evaluation of women with amenorrhea is given in Fig. 331-8. In the initial physical examination, special attention should be given to three features: (1) degree of maturation of the breasts, the pubic and axillary hair, and the external genitalia; (2) the current estrogen status; and (3) the presence or absence of a uterus. All women with amenorrhea should be assumed to be pregnant until proven otherwise. Even when history and physical examination are not suggestive, it is prudent to exclude pregnancy by a suitable screening test. Once this is done, the cause of amenorrhea can frequently be diagnosed by history and physical examination. For example, Ashermans syndrome is suggested by a history of curettage in a woman who previously menstruated; in women with primary amenorrhea and sexual infantilism the essential differential diagnosis is between gonadal dysgenesis and hypopituitarism, and, in addition, the diagnosis of gonadal dysgenesis (Turner's syndrome) or of anatomic defects of the outflow tract (müllerian agenesis, testicular feminization, and cervical stenosis) is frequently suggested on the basis of physical findings. When a specific cause is suspected, it is appropriate to proceed directly to confirm the diagnosis (such as obtaining a chromosomal karyotype or measurement of plasma gonadotropins). It is also useful to measure serum prolactin level during the initial evaluation.

Estrogen status is evaluated by determining if the vaginal mucosa is moist and rugated and if the cervical mucus can be stretched and shown to fern upon drying. If these criteria are indeterminate a progestational challenge is indicated, most often administration of 10 mg of medroxyprogesterone acetate by mouth once or twice daily for 5 days or 100 mg of progesterone in oil intramuscularly. (It should be emphasized that progestogen should never be administered until pregnancy is excluded.) If estrogen levels are adequate (and the outflow tract is intact) menstrual bleeding should occur within 1 week of ending the progestogen treatment. If withdrawal bleeding occurs, the diagnosis is chronic anovulation with estrogen present, usually polycystic ovarian disease.

If no withdrawal bleeding occurs, the nature of the subsequent workup is dependent on the results of the initial prolactin assay. If plasma prolactin is elevated or if galactorrhea is present, radiography of the pituitary should be undertaken. When the plasma prolactin is normal in the anovulatory woman with estrogen absent, plasma gonadotropins should be measured. If the gonadotropin levels are elevated, the diagnosis is ovarian failure. If the gonadotropins are in the low or normal range, the diagnosis is either hypothalmic-pituitary disorder or anatomic defect of the outflow tract. As indicated previously, the diagnosis of outflow tract disorder is usually suspected or established on the basis of the history and physical findings. When the physical findings are not clear-cut, it is useful to administer cyclic estrogen plus progestogen (1.25 mg of oral conjugated estrogens per day for 3 weeks with 10 mg of medroxyprogesterone acetate added

for the last 5 to 7 days of estrogen treatment) followed by 10 days of observation. If no bleeding occurs, the diagnosis of Asherman's syndrome or other anatomic defect of the outflow tract is confirmed by hysterosalpingography or hysteroscopy. If withdrawal bleeding occurs following the estrogen-progestogen combination, the diagnosis of chronic anovulation with estrogen absent (functional hypothalamic amenorrhea) is suggested. Radiologic evaluations of the pituitary-hypothalamic areas may be indicated in the latter cases—irrespective of the prolactin level—because of the danger of overlooking a pituitary-hypothalamic tumor and because the diagnosis of functional hypothalamic amenorrhea is one of exclusion (see Chap. 321).

Infertility   Infertility, the failure to become pregnant after 1 year of unprotected intercourse, affects approximately 10 to 15 percent of couples and is one of the common complaints for which women seek gynecologic assistance. Male factors account for 40 percent of infertility problems (see Chaps. 44 and 330). In women, failure of ovulation accounts for 30 percent, pelvic factors such as tubal disease and endometriosis account for half, and a cervical factor is implicated in about one-tenth of infertility evaluations. In 10 to 20 percent of infertile women no etiology is found. An immunologic cause may explain a large fraction of infertility in these couples. Finally, infertility in women may be due to *luteal phase dysfunction* in which ovulation is assumed to occur but progesterone formation is insufficient to allow preparation of the endometrium for implantation; the disorder is believed to be due to inadequate FSH secretion or action and consequent inadequate estrogen formation by the dominant follicle during the follicular phase.

The first diagnostic step in evaluation of the infertile couple is to determine whether the man or woman is the infertile partner, ordinarily by first obtaining a semen analysis in the man (see Chap. 330) and demonstration of presumed ovulation in the woman. Documentation of ovulatory cycles is obtained by daily measurement of basal body temperatures throughout the month. Occasionally, accurate basal body temperature records are not obtained, and demonstration of elevated serum progesterone levels during the luteal phase may be used as evidence of ovulation. Dating of endometrium by histologic examination of a biopsy sample is also useful for establishing ovulation or luteal phase dysfunction.

If the infertility is associated with amenorrhea, then the workup is that described in Fig. 331-8. If anovulation due to polycystic ovarian disease is the basis for infertility, ovulation can be induced

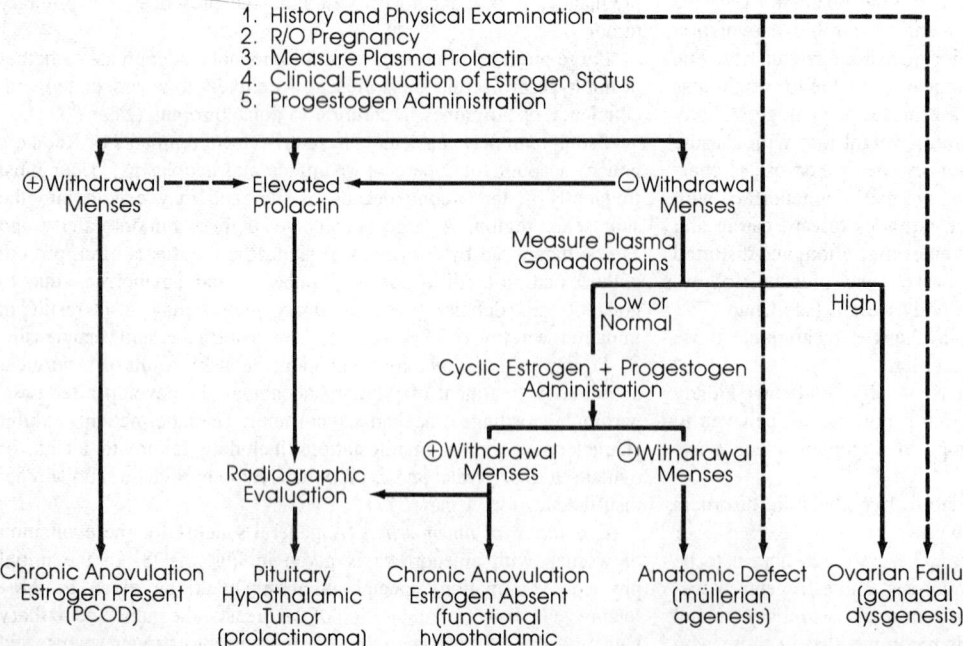

FIGURE 331-8 *Flow diagram for the evaluation of women with amenorrhea. The most common diagnosis for each category is shown in parenthesis. The dotted lines indicate that in some instances a correct diagnosis can be reached on the basis of history and physical exam alone.*

1. History and Physical Examination
2. R/O Pregnancy
3. Measure Plasma Prolactin
4. Clinical Evaluation of Estrogen Status
5. Progestogen Administration

⊕Withdrawal Menses ←→ Elevated Prolactin ← ⊖Withdrawal Menses

Measure Plasma Gonadotropins

Low or Normal   High

Cyclic Estrogen + Progestogen Administration

⊕Withdrawal Menses   ⊖Withdrawal Menses

Radiographic Evaluation

Chronic Anovulation Estrogen Present (PCOD) | Pituitary Hypothalamic Tumor (prolactinoma) | Chronic Anovulation Estrogen Absent (functional hypothalamic amenorrhea) | Anatomic Defect (müllerian agenesis) | Ovarian Failure (gonadal dysgenesis)

utilizing clomiphene, human menopausal gonadotropins, gonadorelin, or, on occasion, wedge resection of the ovaries. Bromocriptine is used to induce ovulation in cases of hyperprolactinemia. In the presence of prolactinomas the appropriate therapy prior to induction of ovulation remains controversial. Recommended therapies in this situation include observation, reinstitution of bromocriptine therapy, radiation therapy, or surgical resection of the tumor (see Chap. 321).

Hysterosalpingograms may be obtained to evaluate the fallopian tubes and uterine cavity. Further evaluation of tubal and ovarian disease is obtained by diagnostic laparoscopy and the demonstration of dye spillage from the fimbria after transcervical injection of dye during laparoscopy. Microsurgical repair of damaged or previously ligated fallopian tubes has resulted in an apparent increase in pregnancy rates. Removal of peritubular and fimbrial adhesions utilizing laser beam surgery is another treatment mode. Endometriosis can be diagnosed by laparoscopy, and treatment of endometriosis associated with infertility includes surgical resection of the endometrial implants or temporary gonadotropin suppression utilizing danazol (400 to 800 mg orally in divided doses for 4 to 6 months), LHRH analogues given by nasal spray or subcutaneous injection, or continuous low-dose oral contraceptive agents to promote regression of the implants.

The cervical factor in infertility is evaluated by study of cervical mucus at an appropriate time after coitus. The test is preferably performed just prior to ovulation (day 12 to 13) when cervical mucus is thin and stretches and provides information as to the penetration and survival of the sperm in the female genital tract. Treatment of infertility due to such abnormality is often unsuccessful.

When other treatment modalities are unsuccessful, in vitro fertilization and embryo transfer (IVF-ET) may be tried. Indications for the use of IVF-ET in infertile couples include tubal obstructive disease, cervical factors, endometriosis, oligospermia, and unexplained infertility. Multiple follicles are induced with clomiphene and/or hMG, and follicles are obtained by laparoscopy or transabdominal or transvaginal aspiration with ultrasound monitoring. After fertilization and cleavage, embryos are transferred to the uterine cavity. Although pregnancy rates vary, successful pregnancy has been reported in as high as 30 percent of cases after IVF-ET. A modification of IVF-ET, known as gamete-intrafallopian transfer (GIFT) in which a mixture of sperm and ova are introduced into the end of the fallopian tube at laparoscopy, has resulted in successful pregnancies.

Medical aspects of pregnancy The possibility of pregnancy should be considered in all women of reproductive age who are evaluated for medical illness or considered for surgery. Procedures such as x-ray exposure, drugs, and anesthetics may be harmful to the developing fetus, and a variety of medical problems may worsen during pregnancy, including hypertension; diseases of the heart, lungs, kidney, and liver; and metabolic and endocrine disorders. Indeed, all women who present with abnormal vaginal bleeding or amenorrhea during the reproductive years should be assumed to have a complication of pregnancy, such as incomplete abortion, ectopic pregnancy, or trophoblastic disease (hydatidiform mole or choriocarcinoma). Women who present with these complications of pregnancy often have histories of abdominal pain and vaginal bleeding and may have evidence of intraabdominal hemorrhage.

Choriocarcinoma is a particular problem because of its protean manifestations. Half of these malignancies follow pregnancies complicated by hydatidiform mole, and the remainder occur after spontaneous abortion, ectopic pregnancy, or normal deliveries. Patients may present with intraabdominal bleeding due to rupture of the uterus, liver, or ovary, with pulmonary manifestations (cough, hemoptysis, pleuritic pain, dyspnea, and respiratory failure), or with gastrointestinal symptoms, usually chronic blood loss or melena. In addition, patients can present with cerebral metastases or renal involvement. The diagnosis can be established by demonstrating an elevated level of the β subunit of hCG in plasma. Treatment and cure are possible with chemotherapeutic agents (actinomycin D and/ or methotrexate). (For manifestations of choriocarcinoma in men see Chap. 297.)

Ovarian tumors See Chap. 296.

TREATMENT

PROGESTOGENS The major use of progestogen is in conjunction with estrogen to ensure the full maturation of the endometrium, both in combination birth control pills and in the therapy of hypogonadal states. In certain circumstances, however, progestogen therapy is appropriate by itself—to induce a progestational effect on the estrogen-primed endometrium (diagnostic tests for the evaluation of amenorrhea), to inhibit pituitary gonadotropins (precocious puberty in girls, and the progestogen-only birth control pill), for prophylaxis to prevent hyperplasia in PCOD, and for palliation in endometrial and breast carcinoma or treatment of endometriosis. Even when a direct progestational effect is desired, the available oral drugs substitute a synthetic derivative for the naturally occurring hormone. Oral progestogens include medroxyprogesterone acetate, megestrol acetate, norethindrone, and norgestrel. Parenteral agents include progesterone in oil, medroxyprogesterone acetate suspension, and 17-hydroxyprogesterone caproate.

The most common undesirable side effect is breakthrough bleeding, which occurs when progestogens are used continuously. Other complications include nausea, vomiting, and hirsutism. Abnormal liver function is a side effect of those derivatives with alkyl substitution in the 17α position. Progestogens are contraindicated if pregnancy is known or suspected because of the risk of birth defects.

ESTROGENS Estrogenic drugs are used for three purposes—the treatment of gonadal failure, control of fertility, and in the management of dysfunctional uterine bleeding and carcinoma of the breast. (The use of estrogens in management of carcinoma of the breast is discussed in Chap. 295.) However, none of the presently available orally active or parenteral hormones replaces the pattern of concentration of estradiol characteristic of the normally cycling, premenopausal woman (Fig. 331-5). Estrogens that can be given by mouth are either nonsteroidal agents (such as diethylstilbestrol) that mimic the action of estradiol, estrogen conjugates that must be hydrolyzed before they become active (estrogen sulfates, predominantly estrone sulfate from pregnant mare's urine), or estrogen analogues that cannot be metabolized to estradiol (mestranol, quinestrol) (Fig. 331-9). Even when micronized estradiol is given orally, it is rapidly converted in the body to estrone. Because oral therapy neither replaces nor mimics the daily secretory pattern of the lost hormone, such therapy must be viewed as a pharmacologic substitution rather than a physiologic replacement. Likewise, the use of parenteral estrogens rarely mimics the physiologic situation. Parenteral preparations of conjugated estrogens, like the oral derivatives, are poor precursors of estradiol, and estradiol esters (estradiol benzoate and valerate) rarely cause plasma estradiol levels that mimic the normal monthly secretory pattern of the hormone. Transdermal estrogen results in constant levels of blood estrogen and is effective in the treatment of menopausal symptoms. The side effects of estrogen substitution differ at various times of life.

Hypoestrogenism In women with decreased estrogen production, whether due to disease of the ovaries (gonadal dysgenesis) or to hypogonadotropic hypogonadism, treatment with cyclic estrogens should be instituted at the time of expected puberty for development and maintenance of female secondary sexual characteristics and prevention of osteoporosis. The most commonly used medications are conjugated estrogens (0.625 to 1.25 mg per day by mouth) or ethinyl estradiol or its precursors (0.02 to 0.05 mg by mouth). The addition of medroxyprogesterone acetate (5 to 10 mg daily) is recommended by most physicians during the last several days of monthly estrogen treatment to prevent development of endometrial

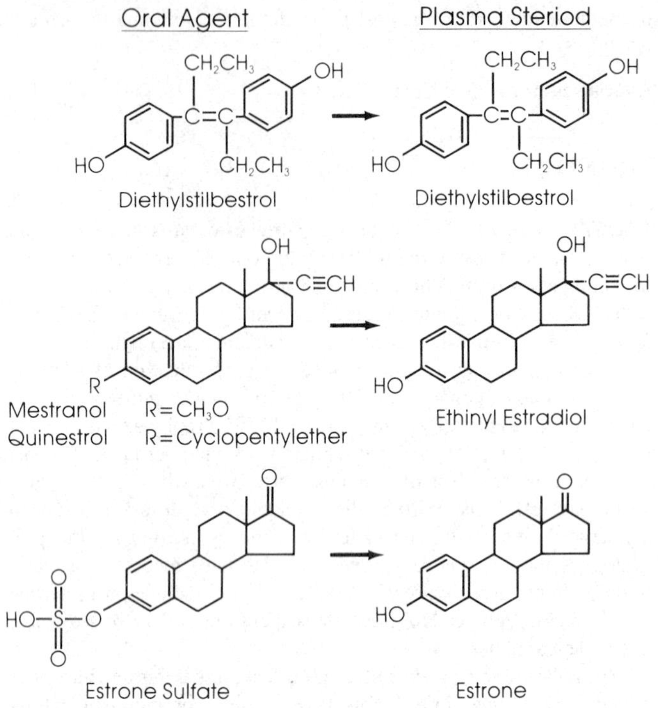

Oral Agent   Plasma Steriod

FIGURE 331-9   *The circulating forms of administered estrogenic drugs.*

hyperplasia during long-term estrogen treatment. Abnormal bleeding in women receiving estrogen replacement requires histologic evaluation of the endometrium. Such substitution therapy or the use of oral contraceptives (see below) may also be used for the purpose of suppressing pituitary gonadotropins, as in women with PCOD in whom the major therapeutic aim is suppression of ovarian androgen production prior to the time when fertility is desired.

Temporary administration of estrogens in larger quantities (up to two times the usual adult maintenance dose) may be necessary to induce full development of secondary sexual characteristics in girls and for the control of menopausal symptoms. Even larger doses of parenteral estrogens (10 mg of estradiol valerate or 25 mg of conjugated estrogen) in conjunction with progestogen may be required in some instances of dysfunctional uterine bleeding. Estrogen replacement (100 ng/kg) stimulates growth in women with gonadal dysgenesis, but at high doses (400 ng/kg) has no effect on growth. In addition to the potential long-term side effects of all estrogens (see below), these dosages may cause specific problems including nausea, vomiting, and edema.

Fertility control   Since the use of all contraceptive methods is associated with diverse side effects, an understanding of the use, methods of actions, and consequences of these agents is important to all physicians. Furthermore, since pregnancy may aggravate a variety of chronic illnesses, fertility control should be recommended in many patients.

To be effective, fertility control requires patient acceptance and compliance. The most widely utilized methods include (1) rhythm and withdrawal techniques; (2) barrier methods including the condom, jellies, foam, suppositories, and diaphragms; (3) intrauterine devices (IUD); (4) hormonal contraceptives; (5) sterilization; and (6) abortion.

The rhythm and withdrawal technique and the barrier methods are effective if used correctly and consistently but in actual practice result in high failure rates because of imperfect compliance. Nevertheless, these methods carry the lowest incidence of side effects, and the side effects, when produced, are minor except for local allergic reactions. Their use should be recommended when there is a relative or absolute contraindication to other therapy.

The most widely utilized nonsurgical methods of contraception, the IUD and birth control pills, are effective but associated with significant side effects.

IUD   The success rates of most IUDs are 95 to 98 percent. These devices are available in a variety of shapes and sizes, but the 7- or T-shaped devices cause minimal pain at insertion and are associated with low expulsion rates. Some IUDs contain copper, which enhances their effectiveness, and some contain slow-release progestational drugs, which makes replacement necessary at 1- to 3-year intervals. The IUD is believed to prevent pregnancy by the induction of a chronic inflammatory reaction in the endometrium, resulting in an unfavorable environment for the implantation of the blastocyst.

Once the IUD is inserted, it is necessary to check periodically to be certain that the device is in place. Both minor and serious side effects can occur. Intermenstrual spotting and increased bleeding and pain or cramps at the time of menses are frequent causes of discontinuation of the IUD. In addition, the device may be expelled spontaneously during a menstrual period without the subject being aware of its loss. The most serious side effect is pelvic infection, occasionally leading to the development of tuboovarian abscess and subsequent infertility. For this reason, use in nulligravida women is not advocated by many gynecologists. In addition, pregnancy with an IUD in place is more likely to be ectopic since intrauterine but not extrauterine pregnancies are inhibited. Because of the increased incidence of spontaneous and septic abortions when IUDs are in place, the device should be removed if pregnancy is detected. Any user who develops persistent, severe bleeding, lower abdominal pain, fever, or discharge should have the IUD removed.

ORAL CONTRACEPTIVES   Oral contraceptive agents have been used by over 200 million women worldwide and by 1 out of 4 women in the United States under the age of 45. These agents are popular because of ease of administration, low pregnancy rate (less than 1 percent), and a relatively low incidence of side effects.

The most widely utilized oral contraceptive pills are either combination tablets or biphasic or triphasic formulations. A list of oral contraceptives marketed in the United States is given in Table 331-3. Combination oral contraceptive tablets contain one of two synthetic estrogens (mestranol or ethinyl estradiol) and one of five synthetic progestogens (norethindrone, norethindrone acetate, norethynodrel, norgestrel, or ethynodiol diacetate). The combination or biphasic or triphasic tablets are taken for 21 consecutive days followed by 7 days' rest. Progestogen-only tablets are taken continuously on a daily basis. Presumably, the ideal contraceptive contains the lowest amount of steroid to minimize side effects but an amount that is at the same time sufficient to prevent pregnancy or breakthrough bleeding. The triphasic tablets containing 30 μg of estrogen and a progestogen come closest to this goal.

Oral contraceptives inhibit ovulation by suppressing FSH and LH secretion. As a consequence, the secretion of all ovarian steroids is also suppressed, including estrogen, progesterone, and androgen (Fig. 331-10). These agents also exert minor direct inhibitory effects on the reproductive tract, altering the cervical mucus and thereby decreasing sperm penetration and decreasing the motility and secretions of the fallopian tubes and uterus.

The death rates associated with oral contraceptives and other forms of birth control are summarized in Table 331-4. Up to age 40 the mortality rates in women using oral contraceptives and IUDs are lower than in women using no form of contraception (this difference is because of the increased risk of death associated with pregnancy). The decrease in death rate below age 40 is even more striking in nonsmokers than in smokers using contraceptives. In fact, the death rates in nonsmoking women age 15 to 24 who use oral agents are lower than those with other forms of fertility control. The increased death rates in women using rhythm or barrier techniques probably results from the higher failure rate and the consequent risk of pregnancy in such women. Oral contraceptive agents are not recommended for smoking women after age 35, all women after age 40, and women of all ages who are at increased risk for myocardial infarction.

Despite the overall safety of these agents, users are at risk for several serious side effects. In most retrospective and prospective studies an increased incidence has been found for *deep vein thrombosis* and *pulmonary embolism*. The relative increased risk varies from two- to twelvefold and is greater for women taking tablets containing more than 50 μg estrogen. The use of oral contraceptives is also associated with an increased risk of thromboembolism after surgery, and for this reason these agents should be discontinued at least 1 month prior to elective surgery. There is a 3- to 9-times increased risk for *thromboembolic stroke* and a twofold greater risk for *hemorrhagic stroke* in users of oral contraceptives. Therefore, the drugs should be discontinued in women who experience visual complaints or severe headaches. Smoking and age increase the risk for stroke as well as the frequency of death from complications of deep venous thrombosis, pulmonary emboli, and myocardial infarction.

A small rise in blood pressure while taking oral contraceptives is common, and 5 percent of women develop significant *hypertension* (blood pressure greater than 140/90) after 5 years of continuous use. Estrogens induce the synthesis of a variety of proteins by the liver including the renin substrate angiotensinogen. The resulting increased formation of angiotensin is believed to be involved in the development of hypertension. In most cases, blood pressure returns to normal when oral contraceptives are discontinued.

Serum lipids and lipoproteins are altered in women on oral contraceptives, the nature of the change depending on the specific components of the oral contraceptives. In general, estrogens increase serum high-density (HDL) and very low density lipoproteins (VLDL). Progestogens depress the concentration of HDL.

A few women taking oral contraceptives develop *impairment of glucose tolerance* as manifested by abnormal glucose levels and elevated plasma insulin after an oral glucose load, both of which usually return to normal after discontinuing the agents. Consequently, oral contraceptives are contraindicated in women with adult-onset diabetes. Because juvenile-onset diabetes may be associated with increased incidence of cardiovascular disease, it is also preferable to utilize other forms of contraception in these individuals.

Oral contraceptives should not be used by women with abnormal liver function tests or in women with acute or chronic liver disease. A rare complication linked to the long-term use of oral contraceptives is the development of peliosis hepatis, which can cause death due to

TABLE 331-3 Composition of oral contraceptives

Name	Estrogen	μg	Progestogen	mg
COMBINATION-TYPE				
Fixed type				
Estrogen content > 50 μg:				
Enovid E	Mestranol	100	Norethynodrel	2.5
Enovid 5	Mestranol	75	Norethynodrel	5.0
Ovulen	Mestranol	100	Ethynodiol diacetate	1.0
Norinyl 2	Mestranol	100	Norethindrone	2.0
Norinyl 1/80	Mestranol	80	Norethindrone	1.0
Ortho-Novum 2	Mestranol	100	Norethindrone	2.0
Ortho-Novum 1/80	Mestranol	80	Norethindrone	1.0
Estrogen content = 50 μg:				
Ortho-Novum 1/50	Mestranol	50	Norethindrone	1.0
Norinyl 1/50	Mestranol	50	Norethindrone	1.0
Ovcon 50	Ethinyl estradiol	50	Norethindrone	1.0
Ovral	Ethinyl estradiol	50	Norgestrel	0.5
Demulen	Ethinyl estradiol	50	Ethynodiol diacetate	1.0
Norlestrin 2.5/50	Ethinyl estradiol	50	Norethindrone acetate	2.5
Norlestrin 1/50	Ethinyl estradiol	50	Norethindrone acetate	1.0
Estrogen content <50 μg:				
Ortho-Novum 1/35	Ethinyl estradiol	35	Norethindrone	1.0
Norinyl 1 + 35	Ethinyl estradiol	35	Norethindrone	1.0
Modicon	Ethinyl estradiol	35	Norethindrone	0.5
Brevicon	Ethinyl estradiol	35	Norethindrone	0.5
Ovcon 35	Ethinyl estradiol	35	Norethindrone	0.4
Demulen 1/35	Ethinyl estradiol	35	Ethynodiol diacetate	1.0
Loestrin 1.5/30	Ethinyl estradiol	30	Norethindrone acetate	1.5
Loestrin 1/20	Ethinyl estradiol	20	Norethindrone acetate	1.0
Nordette	Ethinyl estradiol	30	Levonorgestrel	0.15
Lo-Ovral	Ethinyl estradiol	30	Norgestrel	0.3
Biphasic type				
Ortho-Novum 10/11	Ethinyl estradiol	35	Norethindrone	0.5
First 10 days	Ethinyl estradiol	35	Norethindrone	1.0
Next 11 days				
Triphasic type				
Ortho-Novum 7/7/7				
First 7 days	Ethinyl estradiol	35	Norethindrone	0.5
Second 7 days	Ethinyl estradiol	35	Norethindrone	0.75
Third 7 days	Ethinyl estradiol	35	Norethindrone	1.0
Tri-Norinyl				
First 7 days	Ethinyl estradiol	35	Norethindrone	0.5
Next 9 days	Ethinyl estradiol	35	Norethindrone	1.0
Next 5 days	Ethinyl estradiol	35	Norethindrone	0.5
Triphasil				
First 6 days	Ethinyl estradiol	30	Levonorgestrel	0.05
Second 5 days	Ethinyl estradiol	40	Levonorgestrel	0.075
Third 10 days	Ethinyl estradiol	30	Levonorgestrel	0.125
Tri-Levein				
First 6 days	Ethinyl estradiol	30	Levonorgestrel	0.05
Second 5 days	Ethinyl estradiol	40	Levonorgestrel	0.075
Third 10 days	Ethinyl estradiol	30	Levonorgestrel	0.125
PROGESTOGEN ONLY				
Micronor	None		Norethindrone	0.35
Nor Q.D.	None		Norethindrone	0.35
Ovrette	None		Norgestrel	0.075

Normal Cycle(•--•), n = 4   Oral Contraceptive Cycle (○----○), n = 4

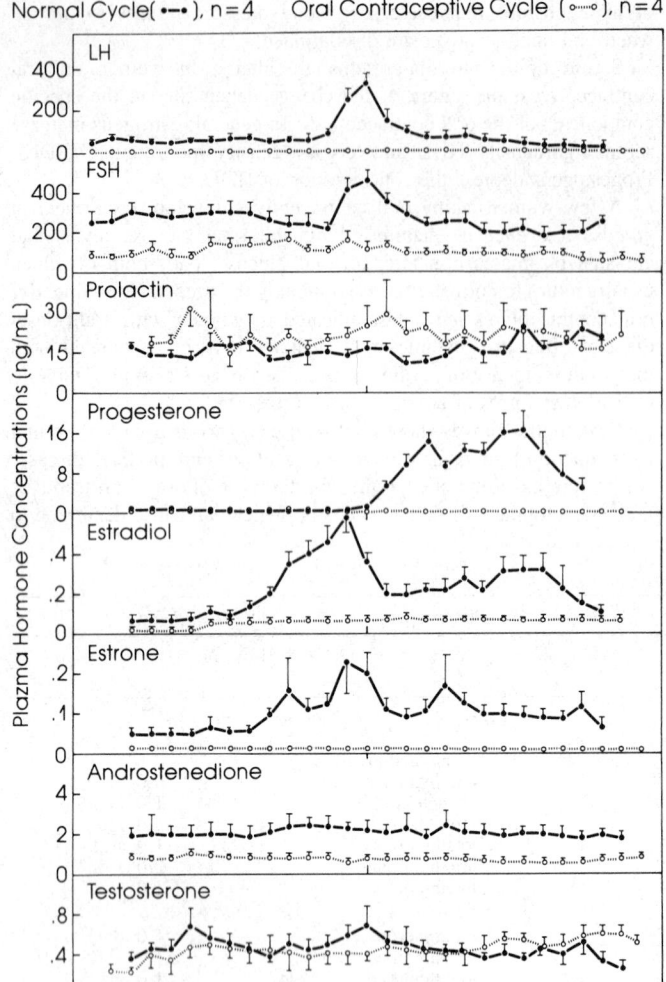

FIGURE 331-10 *The mechanism of action of the birth control tablet. Mean daily plasma hormone concentrations during the ovarian cycle are shown for four ovulating women and four women treated with combination-type oral contraceptives. Data for the normal ovarian cycle are presented in relationship to the day of the LH peak; day 1 of the contraceptive cycle corresponds to the first day of uterine bleeding. The values are the mean ± SE obtained from four women. (From BR Carr et al, 1979.)*

sudden rupture and hemorrhage of the liver. Cholestatic jaundice may occur in those women predisposed to the development of the syndrome of recurrent jaundice of pregnancy.

Oral contraceptives cause an increased concentration of cholesterol in the bile, which is probably the cause for the twofold increase in *cholelithiasis* and cholecystitis in women on oral contraceptives.

Estrogens induce elevation of a variety of proteins secreted by the liver including cortisol-binding globulin (CBG), testosterone-binding globulin (TeBG), and thyroxine-binding globulin (TBG). Consequently, various laboratory tests of adrenal and thyroid function may be altered and must be interpreted with caution (see Chaps. 320 and 324). Oral contraceptives also lower morning plasma ACTH levels, possibly due to an inhibitory effect on ACTH secretion or cortisol catabolism. Finally, serum prolactin levels are slightly elevated in women on oral contraceptives, but such treatment is not believed to play a role in the development of pituitary prolactinomas.

Other effects of oral contraceptive pills include minor dyspepsia, breast discomfort, weight gain, development of pigmentation of the face (chloasma), which is augmented by exposure to the sun, and a variety of psychological effects, such as depression and changes in libido. There is no convincing evidence that oral contraceptives are associated with an increased incidence of cancer of the uterus, cervix, or breast. In fact, oral contraceptives have many beneficial effects including control of dysmenorrhea and anovulatory bleeding, prevention of sexually transmitted diseases, and decreased incidence of endometrial and ovarian cancer.

The absolute contraindications to the use of oral contraceptives include previous thromboembolic disorders, cerebral vascular or coronary artery disease, known or suspected carcinoma of the breast or estrogen-dependent neoplasia, undiagnosed abnormal genital bleeding, or known or suspected pregnancy. Relative contraindications must be weighed against the risk/benefit ratio of the oral contraceptive pills and include hypertension, migraine headaches, diabetes mellitus, uterine leiomyomas, sickle cell anemia, hyperlipemia, and elective surgery.

OTHER STEROID CONTRACEPTIVES   Types of steroid contraception other than the conventional oral contraceptives include (1) postcoital contraception and (2) injectable steroids. Use of high-dose estrogen for 5 days during the fertile part of the cycle (the morning-after pill) is an effective method of contraception, but is associated with significant side effects, particularly nausea. Administration of progestogens by injection, implants, or vaginal rings is used infrequently in the United States.

Estrogen treatment of the menopause   The use of estrogens in postmenopausal women with osteoporosis is based on the belief that such therapy may relieve many of the disorders of the menopause and indeed of aging itself. In some parts of the United States by the mid-1970s as many as half of women in the menopausal age group used one or more forms of estrogen replacement for a median period of 5 years, accounting for more than 30 million prescriptions per year.

The menopause is not associated with a simple state of estrogen deprivation since some estrogens continue to be produced but is instead a state of altered estrogen metabolism; the predominant estrogen becomes estrone formed by extraglandular conversion of prehormone rather than estradiol secretion by the ovary. As is true for all estrogen therapy, the estrogen treatment of the menopause is actually a pharmacologic substitution of one or another estrogen analogue for the physiologic estradiol rather than a physiologic replacement of the missing steroid. Estrogens available for replace-

TABLE 331-4   Annual death rates associated with fertility control per 100,000 women

Contraceptive techniques	Age group					
	15–19	20–24	25–29	30–34	35–39	40–44
None (birth-related)	7.0	7.4	9.1	14.8	25.7	28.2
Oral contraceptives						
Smokers	2.4	3.6	6.8	13.7	51.4	117.6
Nonsmokers	0.5	0.7	1.1	2.1	14.1	32.0
IUD	1.3	1.1	1.3	1.3	1.9	2.1
Abortion	0.5	1.1	1.3	1.9	1.8	1.1
Barrier methods (birth-related)	1.5	1.4	1.0	0.8	1.3	7.6

SOURCE: *Adapted from HW Ory, Fam Plan Perspect 15:57, 1983.*

ment therapy include conjugated estrogens, estrogen substitutes (diethylstilbestrol), synthetic estrogen (ethinyl estradiol or derivatives), micronized estradiol, estrogen-containing vaginal creams, and estrogen-containing dermal patches. Regimens associated with low risk of complications include (1) cyclic estrogen therapy in the lowest effective dose for 21 to 25 days per month, and (2) cyclic estrogens plus the addition of progestogen during the last 10 days of estrogen therapy.

The most clear-cut benefit of estrogen therapy in the menopause is the relief of vasomotor instability (hot flashes) and of atrophy of the urogenital epithelium and skin. Estrogen therapy ameliorates these symptoms in the majority of cases. When estrogen therapy is designed to treat hot flashes alone, such therapy should be continued for only a few years since hot flashes tend to diminish after 3 to 4 years in untreated women.

Several lines of evidence indicate that routine estrogen therapy is beneficial in preventing the complications of menopausal osteoporosis, especially in high-risk women (i.e., thin white women). First, in women undergoing premature menopause the incidence and complication rates of osteoporosis are increased, and long-term estrogen replacement appears to be beneficial. Second, estrogen therapy has short-term positive effects on calcium balance and long-term beneficial effects on bone density. Third, in women given combination estrogen and calcium therapy, the incidence of fractures is decreased.

Of the potential side effects, the possibility of an increased risk of endometrial carcinoma is perhaps most worrisome. The relative risk of developing endometrial adenocarcinoma in estrogen users is between 6 and 8. The risk is increased with duration and dosage of estrogen but is decreased in women given combination estrogen-progestogen therapy.

Despite the large body of evidence linking endometrial carcinoma and estrogen use, two types of doubt have been raised about the clinical significance of the association. First, some epidemiologists have argued that the increased risk associated with estrogens has been exaggerated because of problems inherent in obtaining adequate controls in retrospective analyses. Second, in spite of an increased incidence of endometrial carcinoma in the United States, there was no concomitant increased mortality from this disease. Indeed the increased incidence apparently involves low-grade malignancies which may be difficult to distinguish histologically from various forms of hyperplasia. These forms of malignancy have little effect on life expectancy.

Apprehension concerning worsening of hypertension and thromboembolic disease appears to be due to reports of the effects of estrogen-progesterone oral contraceptive pills during the reproductive years and not to estrogen use in menopausal women. There is no documented evidence that low-dose estrogen therapy in the menopause enhances the development or the severity of thromboembolic disease, breast cancer, or hypertension. Low-dose estrogen treatment in the menopause does not appear to influence the development of atherosclerosis, myocardial infarction, or stroke. There is a slightly increased risk for the development of gallbladder disease with estrogen use in the menopause.

A reasonable approach to the use of estrogens in the menopause is as follows: (1) For long-term use, estrogens should be given in the minimal effective doses (0.625 mg conjugated estrogen or 0.01 to 0.02 mg ethinyl estradiol per day). Except when hot flashes preclude intermittent use, the agents should be prescribed for 25 days each month followed by a rest period. (For women with an intact uterus it is the practice in some clinics to give estrogens alone for 15 days, estrogen plus a daily progestogen for an additional 10 days, and nothing for a week.) (2) Such replacement therapy is indicated routinely in women undergoing premature menopause (surgically induced or spontaneous) at least until the age of normal menopause. (3) Estrogen therapy is also indicated routinely in women of all ages who have severe hot flashes or symptomatic atrophy of the urogenital epithelium. Hot flashes rarely persist for longer than 4 years, so that if given for this purpose the duration of therapy can be limited. (4)

In women who have had prior hysterectomy potential benefits of treatment appear to outweigh the dangers. Whether estrogens should be given routinely to all women with intact uteri is unsettled, but the authors prescribe it routinely in the absence of contraindications in hopes of ameliorating osteoporosis (in combination with calcium or fluoride). (5) Each woman receiving estrogens must be monitored indefinitely and frequently.

DRUGS TO INDUCE OVULATION   The most common treatment for ovulation induction in women with PCOD is *clomiphene*. This antiestrogen is believed to act by binding to estrogen receptors in the hypothalamus and allowing FSH to rise to stimulate follicular development and ultimately result in ovulation. Clomiphene therapy is usually begun in a dose of 50 mg by mouth daily for 5 days commencing on the fifth day of progestin-induced uterine bleeding. If ovulation does not occur, the dose may be increased to 100 or 150 mg per day. Such treatment results in ovulatory cycles in 60 percent of women with PCOD. Additional regimens include clomiphene in combination with human menopausal gonadotropins (hMG), estrogen, glucocorticoids, or human chorionic gonadotropin (hCG).

The most commonly used gonadotropins for induction of ovulation are hMG and hCG. These agents are indicated in women who fail to ovulate on clomiphene and in women with hypogonadotropic hypogonadism. The usual treatment regimen requires 1 to 3 ampuls of hMG per day over an 8- to 12-day period to achieve adequate follicular stimulation and growth, followed by a single injection of 10,000 units of hCG 12 to 24 h after the last injection of hMG. Ovulation is successful in 90 percent of women, and pregnancy rates exceed 50 to 60 percent. Measurement of daily estrogen levels and frequent evaluation of ovarian size by ultrasound are indicated to prevent ovarian hyperstimulation. Ovarian hyperstimulation syndrome results from excessive stimulation of ovarian follicles with resultant enlargement of the ovaries and may progress to the development of ascites, hypotension, and shock. Therapy using hMG and hCG also carries a 20 percent risk of multiple pregnancies.

Bromocriptine is a dopamine agonist that is effective in inducing ovulation in women with elevated prolactin levels. Treatment is instituted at a usual dosage of 2.5 mg by mouth two or three times a day. Treatment should be discontinued as soon as pregnancy is diagnosed. The management of prolactin-secreting pituitary tumors is discussed in Chap. 321.

Luteinizing hormone–releasing hormone (LHRH, gonadorelin) and analogues   Gonadorelin has been used successfully to induce ovulation in infertile women. The agent is infused subcutaneously or intravenously by a portable infusion pump which administers pulses at 90- to 120-min intervals for 10 to 20 days. After ovulation has occurred hCG is given to maintain corpus luteum function.

LHRH analogues that block ovulation have been used to treat a variety of gynecologic disorders; ovulation and ovarian steroidogenesis are inhibited due to down-regulation of LHRH receptors with a resultant decreased release of gonadotropins. Conditions in which these agents are under trial include fertility control, true precocious puberty, endometriosis, and uterine leiomyomas.

OTHER DISORDERS OF THE FEMALE REPRODUCTIVE TRACT

VULVA   Most disorders of the vulva are due to venereal disease, most commonly syphilis (painless chancre), condyloma acuminata (venereal warts), and herpes vulvitis (painful ulcers) (see Chap. 90). All other lesions of the vulva, particularly in older women, must be biopsied. Early biopsy of cancer of the vulva is mandatory, because when it becomes symptomatic (pruritus and bleeding), it has often progressed to an advanced stage.

VAGINA   Infections of the vagina usually present as vaginal discharge and pruritis. The most frequent organisms are *Trichomonas, Candida* *albicans,* and *Gardnerella vaginalis* (also see Chap. 90). The diagnosis is made by microscopic examination of the discharge, and appropriate therapy can be instituted utilizing vaginal or oral antibiotics.

Abnormalities of the vagina and cervix in female offspring of women given diethylstilbestrol during pregnancy include adenosis of the vagina as well as structural abnormalities of the vagina, cervix, and uterus; the risk of developing a rare form of vaginal cancer (adenocarcinoma, clear cell type) is increased (2 per 10,000 exposed women). Periodic examination of women at risk should commence at age 12 to 14, and reevaluation should be undertaken after any episode of abnormal bleeding.

CERVIX   Preinvasive lesions of the cervix (also known as cervical intraepithelial neoplasia) as well as invasive carcinoma of the cervix can be detected reliably by obtaining a Papanicolaou smear (Pap smear). Current recommendations by the American Cancer Society are that a Pap smear be obtained every 3 years after 2 negative Pap smears were obtained at yearly intervals in all women between the ages of 20 to 65 and in sexually active women below the age of 20. However, many gynecologists recommend yearly Pap smears especially in patients with more than one sexual partner.

UTERUS   Only 40 percent of endometrial adenocarcinoma is detected by Pap smears. In women at high risk for endometrial carcinoma (obesity, history of chronic anovulatory cycles, diabetes, hypertension, estrogen treatment), yearly endometrial sampling should be performed. Low-dose oral estrogen therapy rarely causes breakthrough or withdrawal bleeding in menopausal women. Therefore, irrespective of whether the patient is on estrogen therapy, occurrence of postmenopausal bleeding makes it mandatory to obtain a tissue diagnosis to exclude endometrial cancer either by endometrial sampling or by curettage.

One of the most common disorders of the uterus and the most frequent tumor of women (1 of 4 women affected) is the uterine leiomyoma, or fibroid tumor. Three-fourths of women with leiomyoma are asymptomatic, and the diagnosis is made on routine pelvic examination. When associated with excessive menstrual blood loss, excessive size or rapid growth, or significant pelvic pain (see Chap. 43), the preferred treatment is surgical removal by hysterectomy if there is no desire for further childbearing. In young women myomectomy may on occasion be indicated when infertility or repeated fetal wastage is a manifestation or where future childbearing is desired.

FALLOPIAN TUBES AND OVARIES   Infectious pelvic inflammatory disease is a common disorder of the fallopian tubes and usually becomes symptomatic after a menstrual period; the symptoms include fever, chills, abdominal pain, and vaginal discharge, and pelvic tenderness on physical examination is common. The initiating organism most often is *chlamydia trachomatis* or *Neisseria gonorrhoeae,* but tuboovarian abscess and sterility are probably caused by mixed aerobic and anaerobic superinfections and require wide-spectrum antibiotic treatment (see Chap. 91).

Endometriosis is a benign disorder characterized by the presence and proliferation of endometrial tissue (stroma and glands) outside the endometrial cavity. The clinical manifestations are variable. Endometriosis occurs most commonly between the ages of 30 to 40 and is found incidentally at the time of surgery in approximately one-fifth of all gynecologic operations. The fertility rate is significantly reduced in affected women. The disorder usually involves the posterior cul-de-sac or the ovaries and can give rise to ovarian enlargement (endometriomas), although it may also involve sites distant to the pelvis (lung, umbilicus). The most significant symptom is pelvic pain, characteristically dysmenorrhea (see Chap. 43). However, the frequency and degree of pelvic symptomatology correlate poorly with the extent of disease. Other symptoms include dyspareunia, pain with defecation, and infertility. The characteristic physical findings are multiple tender nodules palpable along the uterosacral ligament at the time of rectal-vaginal examination, a posteriorly fixed uterus, or

enlarged cystic ovaries. The diagnosis can only be confirmed by direct visualization, usually at diagnostic laparoscopy. Treatment depends on the degree of involvement and the desires of the patient and includes observation for mild disease with no associated infertility or pain, hormonal suppressive therapy (see infertility), conservative surgery if fertility is desired, or removal of the uterus, tubes, and ovaries in severe disease. Endometriosis is rarely found after the menopause.

Any adnexal mass that persists for more than 6 weeks or is larger than 6 cm must be evaluated. Although ovarian cysts and neoplasms compose the largest group of pelvic adnexal masses (see above), tumors of the fallopian tubes, uterus, gastrointestinal tract or urinary tract should also be considered. Sonography or radiographic evaluation is often helpful in identifying the nature of the adnexal mass prior to surgical exploration.

REFERENCES

CARR BR, GRIFFIN JD: Fertility control and its complications, in *Williams' Textbook of Endocrinology,* JD Wilson, DW Foster (eds). Philadelphia, Saunders, 1985, pp 452–475

—— et al: Plasma levels of adrenocorticotropin and cortisol in women receiving oral contraceptive steroid treatment. J Clin Endocrinol Metab 49:346, 1979

—— et al: Plasma lipoprotein regulation or progesterone biosynthesis by human corpus luteum tissue in organ culture. J Clin Endocrinol Metab 52:875, 1981

—— et al: The role of lipoproteins in the regulation of progesterone secretion by human corpus luteum. Fertil Steril 38:303, 1982

D'ARMIENTO M et al: McCune-Albright syndrome: Evidence for autonomous multiendocrine hyperfunction. J Pediatr 102:584, 1983

DiZEREGA GS, HODGEN GD: Folliculogenesis in the primate ovarian cycle. Endocrinol Rev 2:27, 1981

—— et al: The possible role for a follicular protein in the intraovarian regulation of steroidogenesis. Semin Reprod Endocrinol 1:309, 1983

DMOWSKI WP: Endocrine properties and clinical applications of danazol. Fertil Steril 31:237, 1979

ERICKSON GF et al: Functional studies of aromatase activity in human granulosa cells from normal and polycystic ovaries. J Clin Endocrinol Metab 49:514, 1979

FAIMAN C et al: Patterns of gonadotropins and gonadal steroids throughout life. Clin Obstet Gynaecol 3:467, 1976

FRASIER SD: *Pediatric Endocrinology.* New York, Grune & Stratton, 1980

FUTTERWEIT W: *Polycystic Ovarian Disease.* New York, Springer-Verlag, 1984

GEMZELL C, WANG CF: Outcome of pregnancy in women with pituitary adenoma. Fertil Steril 31:363, 1979

GLUCKMAN PD et al: The human fetal hypothalamus and pituitary gland, in *Maternal-Fetal Endocrinology,* D Tulchinksy, KJ Ryan (eds). Philadelphia, Saunders, 1980

GOLD JJ et al: *Gynecologic Endocrinology.* Hagerstown, Harper & Row, 1980

GOLDZIEHER JW: Polycystic ovarian disease. Fertil Steril 35:371, 1981

HAMMOND MG, TALBERT LM: *Infertility.* Chapel Hill, Health Sciences Consortium, 1981

HATCHER RA et al: *Contraceptive Technology 1980–1981.* New York, Irvington, 1980

JUDD HL et al: Estrogen replacement therapy: Indications and complications. Ann Intern Med 98:195, 1983

KAPLAN NM: Complications of the birth control pill, in *Update I: Harrison's Principles of Internal Medicine,* KJ Isselbacher et al (eds). New York, McGraw-Hill, 1981, p 57

KASE N, WEINGOLD A: Principles and practice of clinical gynecology. New York, Wiley, 1983

KELCH RP: Management of precocious puberty. N Engl J Med 312:1057, 1985

MISHELL DR JR, DAVAJAN V (eds): *Reproductive Endocrinology, Infertility, and Contraception.* Philadelphia, Davis, 1979

PIEPER DR et al: Ovarian gonadatropin-releasing hormone (GnRH) receptors: Characterization, distribution, and induction by GnRH. Endocrinology 108:1148, 1981

PRITCHARD JA et al: *William's Obstetrics.* New York, Appleton-Century-Crofts, 1985

RIGGS BL et al: Effect of the fluoride/calcium regimen on vertebral fracture occurrence in postmenopausal osteoporosis. N Engl J Med 306:446, 1982

ROMNEY SL et al: *Gynecology and Obstetrics: The Health Care of Women.* New York, McGraw-Hill, 1980

ROSS GT: Disorders of the ovary and female reproductive tract, in *Williams' Textbook of Endocrinology,* JD Wilson, DW Foster (eds). Philadelphia, Saunders, 1985, pp 206–258

ROSS JL et al: A preliminary study of the effect of estrogen dose on growth in Turner's syndrome. N Engl J Med 309:1104, 1983

SHEARMAN RP (ed): *Clinical Reproductive Endocrinology,* Edinburgh, Churchill Livingston, 1985

SCULLY RE: Ovarian tumors: A review. Am J Pathol 87:686, 1977

SITTERI PK, MACDONALD PC: Role of extraglandular estrogen in human endocrinology, in *Handbook of Physiology,* sec 7, *Endocrinology,* SR Geiger et al (eds). Washington, DC, American Physiological Society, 1973, p 615

SPEROFF L: Menopause. Semin Reprod Endocrinol 1:1, 1983

—— et al: The ovary, in *Endocrinology and Metabolism,* P Felig et al (eds). New York, McGraw-Hill, 1981, p 669

——— et al: *Clinical Gynecologic Endocrinology and Infertility*, 3d ed. Baltimore, Williams & Wilkins, 1983

STEINGOLD KA et al: Treatment of hot flashes with transdermal estradiol administration. J Clin Endocrinol Metab 61:627, 1985

STYNE DM, GRUMBACH MM: Puberty in the male and female: Its physiology and disorders, in *Reproductive Endocrinology*, SSC Yen, RB Jaffe (eds). Philadelphia, Saunders 1978 pp 189–240

WALLACH EE, KEMPERS RD: *Modern Trends in Infertility and Contraception Control*, vol 3. Baltimore, Williams & Wilkins, 1985

YEN SSC: Neuroendocrine regulation of the menstrual cycle. Hosp Prac 14:84, 1979

———: Clinical application of gonadotropin-releasing hormone and gonadotropin-releasing hormone analogs. Fertil Steril 39:257, 1983

———, JAFFE RB (eds): *Reproductive Endocrinology*, 2d ed. Philadelphia, Saunders, 1986

YING SY et al: Gonadocrinins: Peptides in ovarian follicular fluid stimulating the secretion of pituitary gonadotropins. Endocrinology 108:1206, 1981

332 ENDOCRINE DISORDERS OF THE BREAST

JEAN D. WILSON

Examination of the breasts is an important part of the physical examination. The breasts are the site of fatal and preventable disease in women and frequently provide clues to underlying systemic disease in both men and women. The internist frequently does not examine the male breast and in the evaluation of women is apt to refer this task to a gynecologist. It is the duty of every physician to distinguish the abnormal from the normal at the earliest possible stage and to call for assistance if there is any doubt. (For cancer of the breast see Chap. 295.)

ENDOCRINE CONTROL OF THE BREAST There is no histologic or functional difference in the breasts of boys and girls prior to the onset of puberty, but a profound sexual dimorphism in breast development ensues at the time of puberty. The endocrine control of female breast development is illustrated in Fig. 332-1. The development of the normal nonlactating female breast is dependent primarily upon the action of estradiol, which induces the growth, division, and elongation of the tubular duct system and maturation of the nipples. In men the administration of estrogen is equally effective in this regard. To produce true alveolar development at the ends of the ducts, however, the synergistic action of progesterone is required, a ratio of estrogen to progesterone of 1:20 to 1:100 being optimal. Once the anatomic development of the ducts and alveoli is complete, the continued action of estrogen and progesterone does not appear to be required for lactation itself.

The endocrine control of milk formation by the differentiated breast is complex, requiring in addition to appropriate priming by estrogen and progesterone specific lactogenic hormone and the permissive action of glucocorticoid, insulin, thyroxine, and in some species growth hormone. There are two lactogenic hormones. Human placental lactogen (hPL or chorionic somatomammotropin) is secreted in large amounts by the placenta during the latter phases of gestation and prepares the breast for milk production. It disappears from the fetal (and maternal) circulation shortly after termination of pregnancy. Prolactin, a peptide hormone synthesized in the pituitary (see Chap. 321), plays the critical role in the initiation and maintenance of normal as well as inappropriate lactation. The plasma level of prolactin rises during pregnancy; during late pregnancy and lactation 60 to 80 percent of the anterior pituitary may consist of prolactin-secreting cells.

Unlike most pituitary hormones, the predominant regulation of prolactin secretion is negative, i.e., under ordinary basal condition the hypothalamus secretes one or more inhibitory hormones, the most important being dopamine, which are delivered to the pituitary via the hypothalamic portal system and inhibit the release of prolactin into the blood (see Chap. 321). Most factors that influence prolactin release do so by affecting the synthesis or release of the inhibiting factors. Basal prolactin levels fall following delivery, but prolactin secretion is enhanced by stimulation of the breasts such as the act of nursing (the so-called sucking reflex), a phenomenon that is probably mediated by the reflex release of oxytocin. In the postgestational state the normal woman is capable of forming about a liter of milk per day containing 38 g fat, 70 g lactose, and 12 g protein. Normal lactation can be suppressed by the administration of estrogens or diethylstilbestrol, which inhibit milk production by direct effects on the breast, or by the administration of bromocriptine, which inhibits prolactin secretion by the pituitary. Alternatively, if a woman does not nurse or empty her breasts post partum, lactation usually ceases of its own accord in 1 to 2 weeks.

GALACTORRHEA Exactly what constitutes nonpuerperal or inappropriate lactation is not always clearly defined in the literature. According to the studies of Friedman and Goldfein, it is not possible to demonstrate any breast secretion whatsoever in normal, regularly menstruating nulligravid women, but breast secretions can be demonstrated in a fourth of normal women who have been pregnant in the past; thus, breast secretions may be of no clinical significance in these instances. Spontaneous leakage of milk from the breasts is usually of more concern than milk that must be expressed. A second problem is related to the composition of the breast secretions. When the secretion is milky or white, it is safe to assume that it contains casein and lactose and is in fact milk; however, when the secretion is brown or greenish in color, it rarely contains normal milk constituents and consequently may not result from an underlying

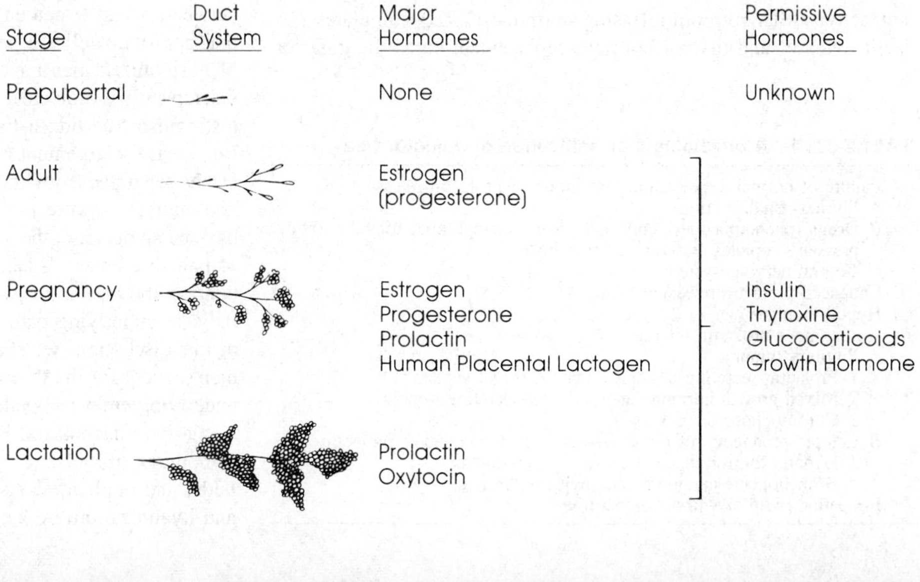

FIGURE 332-1 *Endocrine control of female breast development and function at various stages of life.*

Stage	Duct System	Major Hormones	Permissive Hormones
Prepubertal		None	Unknown
Adult		Estrogen (progesterone)	
Pregnancy		Estrogen Progesterone Prolactin Human Placental Lactogen	Insulin Thyroxine Glucocorticoids Growth Hormone
Lactation		Prolactin Oxytocin	

endocrinopathy. Furthermore, upon repeated sampling, the composition of milk carbohydrates and proteins may increase in a given individual from low, colostrum-like values to those typical of milk. Milky discharges must also be distinguished from blood or bloody secretions that may be present with neoplasms of the breast (see Chap. 295).

With these problems in mind galactorrhea can be defined as an inappropriate production of milk that is persistent or worrisome to the patient, recognizing that in some instances no underlying pathology will be demonstrated.

Since the action of a lactogenic hormone is a necessary requirement for the initiation of milk production, it is logical to consider galactorrhea as a manifestation of deranged prolactin physiology. However, as indicated above, a complex endocrinologic milieu is necessary for lactation, and in many instances in which prolactin is elevated both in women who have not been appropriately primed and in men, no production of milk takes place. As a consequence, hyperprolactinemia is more common than galactorrhea. Furthermore, although enhanced prolactin secretion is necessary for the initiation of milk formation, production can be maintained in the presence of minimally elevated or intermittently elevated prolactin levels so that basal plasma prolactin levels are not always elevated in patients with galactorrhea. For example, repeated stimulation of the nipples of women who have previously been pregnant can cause galactorrhea with minimal elevations of basal prolactin (the wet nurse phenomenon) similar to that in the normal nursing mother. Perhaps the strongest evidence that prolactin is always involved in galactorrhea is the fact that administration of bromocriptine, which suppresses plasma prolactin levels, causes a disappearance of galactorrhea even when the basal plasma prolactin levels are normal.

Differential diagnosis   It is thus appropriate to consider galactorrhea as the result of a failure of the normal hypothalamic inhibition of prolactin release, of enhanced prolactin-releasing factor, or of autonomous prolactin secretion by tumors (Table 332-1). Pituitary stalk section in humans results in a striking increase in prolactin secretion, as the result of the inhibition of the delivery of prolactin inhibitory factors to the pituitary. Likewise, many drugs that influence the central nervous system (including virtually all psychotropic agents, methyldopa, reserpine, and antiemetics) result in enhanced prolactin release, presumably by inhibiting synthesis or release of dopamine or other prolactin inhibitory factors. Estrogens enhance prolactin levels by an uncertain mechanism. Extrapituitary central nervous system diseases can cause galactorrhea, presumably by interfering with delivery of the inhibitory factors to the pituitary (central nervous system sarcoidosis, craniopharyngioma, pinealoma, encephalitis, meningitis, hydrocephalus, hypothalamic tumors).

The existence of a physiologic prolactin-releasing factor is still a matter of controversy, but in at least one pathologic state, primary hypothyroidism, galactorrhea results from enhanced prolactin-releasing activity. Thyrotropin-releasing hormone (TRH) stimulates prolactin release, and thyroid hormone replacement cures the galactorrhea.

TABLE 332-1 A physiologic classification of galactorrhea

I Failure of normal hypothalamic inhibition of prolactin release
  A Pituitary stalk section
  B Drugs (phenothiazines, butyrophenones, methyldopa, tricyclic antidepressants, opiates, reserpine, verapamil)
  C Central nervous system disease
II Enhanced prolactin-releasing factor
  Hypothyroidism
III Autonomous prolactin release
  A Pituitary tumors
    1 Prolactin-secreting tumors (Forbes-Albright syndrome)
    2 Mixed growth hormone and prolactin-secreting tumors
    3 Chromophobe adenomas
  B Ectopic production of human placental lactogen and/or prolactin
    1 Hydatidiform moles and chorionephitheliomas
    2 Bronchogenic carcinoma and hypernephroma
IV Idiopathic (with or without amenorrhea)

Enhanced prolactin release can also occur from pituitary or nonpituitary tumors. Three types of pituitary tumors (see Chap. 321) may be associated with galactorrhea: pure prolactin-secreting tumors (micro- or macroadenomas), mixed tumors that secrete both growth hormone and prolactin and result in acromegaly with galactorrhea, and some chromophobe adenomas. The latter may either secrete prolactin or interfere with the delivery of inhibitory factors to the pituitary. Prolactin can also be secreted on occasion by other malignancies such as bronchogenic carcinoma, and hydatidiform moles and choriocarcinomas may secrete placental lactogen.

The known etiologies account for only a part of the cases of galactorrhea. In four published series totaling more than 500 carefully studied patients, a pituitary tumor was identified in about one-fourth of the patients, other known causes could be identified in another fourth or fifth, and the remaining half fall into the unknown category. Many patients may prove ultimately to have prolactin-secreting pituitary tumors, some probably have subtle disorders of hypothalamic function, and in others a drug-related cause may have been missed, but the fact remains that no satisfactory diagnosis is reached in half or more of patients. When normal menses and galactorrhea coexist, the likelihood of establishing a diagnosis is poor.

Galactorrhea is unusual in men, even in the presence of profound elevations of plasma prolactin; when it does occur, it is usually upon the background of a feminizing state (see below).

Diagnostic evaluation   If hyperprolactinemia is present, the workup is fundamentally that of a pituitary tumor once drug causes and hypothyroidism are excluded (see Chap. 321). Even when a specific cause cannot be identified and a diagnosis of idiopathic galactorrhea is made by exclusion, it is necessary to remember that pituitary tumors may subsequently become manifest. The higher the prolactin values and the more persistent the galactorrhea, the greater the likelihood of such a development.

Treatment   The aim of treatment is to remove the source of the elevated prolactin, and resection of pituitary tumor, cessation of causative drugs, or correction of hypothyroidism is often followed by the disappearance of galactorrhea. Two other forms of therapy may have some usefulness. Breast binders can be effective in some patients with mild galactorrhea of unknown etiology, presumably by preventing stimulation of the nipple and the consequent perpetuation of lactation. Bromocriptine, which suppresses plasma prolactin, has been used to treat patients with idiopathic hyperprolactinemia as well as patients with prolactin-secreting tumors of the pituitary. This drug not only suppresses lactation but may also cause resumption of normal menstrual cycles (and even fertility) in patients in whom amenorrhea accompanies galactorrhea.

GYNECOMASTIA   A central issue in the evaluation of breast tissue in adult men is the separation of the normal from the abnormal. Whereas in autopsy data the incidence of active gynecomastia is between 5 and 9 percent, Nuttall and his colleagues have reported that approximately 40 percent of normal men and up to 70 percent of hospitalized men have palpable breast tissue. The reason for this discrepancy is not clear. On the one hand, it may be difficult to distinguish true breast tissue from masses of adipose tissue without true breast enlargement (lipomastia); in such cases true gynecomastia can be separated from lipomastia by mammography or by sonography. Alternatively, a true increase in the incidence of gynecomastia may have taken place, or the autopsy data may underestimate the frequency of palpable breast tissue. Regardless, we are left with major uncertainties; the finding of gynecomastia (in contrast to lipomastia) could indicate underlying pathology or a normal variant. For the purposes of this discussion, we shall assume that any palpable breast tissue in men (except for the three so-called physiologic states) may reflect an underlying endocrinopathy and deserves a limited evaluation.

Early gynecomastia is characterized by proliferation in the breast of both the fibroblastic stroma and the duct system, which elongates, buds, and duplicates. As gynecomastia persists, progressive fibrosis and hyalinization are associated with regression of epithelial proliferation. Eventually the number of ducts decreases. Resolution occurs by reduction in size and epithelial content with gradual disappearance of the ducts, leaving hyaline bands that eventually disappear.

Growth of the breast in men, as in women, is mediated by estrogen and results from disturbances of the normal ratio of active androgen to estrogen in plasma or within the breast itself. As described in Chap. 330 estradiol formation in the normal man occurs principally by the conversion of circulating androgens to estrogens in peripheral tissues; the normal ratio of production of testosterone to estradiol in adult men is approximately 100:1 (6 mg versus 45 μg), and the normal ratio of the two hormones in plasma is about 300:1. Feminization results when there is a significant decrease in this effective ratio, as the result of diminished testosterone production or action, enhanced estrogen formation, or both processes occurring simultaneously. The predominant manifestation of feminization in men is enlargement of the breasts.

Enlargement of the male breast can occur as a normal physiologic phenomenon at certain stages of life or as the result of a variety of pathologic conditions (Table 332-2).

Physiologic gynecomastia In the *newborn* transient enlargement of the breast results from the action of maternal and/or placental estrogens. The enlargement ordinarily disappears in a few weeks but may persist longer. *Adolescent* gynecomastia occurs in many boys at some time during puberty. The median age of onset is 14; it is often asymmetric, occasionally unilateral for a portion of its course, and frequently tender, and it regresses so that by age 20 only a small number of men have palpable vestiges of gynecomastia in one or both breasts. Although the origin of the excess estrogen has not been identified, the onset of gynecomastia correlates with transient elevations of plasma estradiol prior to the completion of puberty so that the androgen/estrogen ratio is altered. *Gynecomastia of aging* also occurs in otherwise healthy men. Forty percent or more of aged men have gynecomastia, as the result of true increase in frequency. A likely explanation is the elevation in plasma estrogen as the result of an increase with age in the conversion of androgens to estrogens in extraglandular tissues. Since abnormal liver function or drug therapy may be contributing causes to gynecomastia in such men, the significance of this finding in the aging man is uncertain.

Pathologic gynecomastia Pathologic gynecomastia can result from one of three basic mechanisms: deficiency in testosterone production or action (with or without a secondary increase in estrogen production), increase in estrogen production, or drugs (Table 332-2). Most of the individual disorders that cause primary and secondary testicular failure have been discussed in Chap. 330. The fact that a deficiency in testosterone production per se can cause gynecomastia is illustrated by the syndrome of congenital anorchia in which normal (or slightly low) estradiol production in the presence of profoundly decreased testosterone production results in florid gynecomastia. Such is the case in some patients with Klinefelter syndrome. In the inherited syndromes of androgen resistance, such as testicular feminization, deficient androgen action and increased testicular estrogen production are both present, although diminished androgen action is the more critical in inducing gynecomastia.

A primary increase in estrogen production can result from a variety of causes. Increased testicular estrogen secretion may result from elevations in plasma gonadotropins, for example, in cases of aberrant production of chorionic gonadotropin by testicular tumors or by bronchogenic carcinoma, from the ovarian elements in the gonads of men with true hermaphroditism, or as the result of direct secretion by testicular tumors (particularly interstitial cell and Sertoli cell tumors). Increased conversion of androgen to estrogens in peripheral tissues can either be due to increased availability of substrate for extraglandular estrogen formation or to increased amount of the enzymes of estrogen formation in peripheral tissues. Increased substrate availability for extraglandular conversion can result from increased production of androgens such as androstenedione (congenital adrenal hyperplasia, hyperthyroidism, and most feminizing adrenal

tumors) or because of diminished catabolism of androstenedione by the usual pathways (liver disease). Increased amount of extraglandular aromatase can occur as the result of a rare hereditary abnormality or in tumors of the liver or adrenal gland.

The ingestion of drugs can cause gynecomastia by several mechanisms. Many drugs either act directly as estrogens or cause an increase in plasma estrogen activity, for example, in men receiving diethylstilbestrol for prostatic carcinoma and in transsexuals in preparation for sex-change operations. Boys and young men are particularly sensitive to estrogen and can develop gynecomastia after the use of dermal ointments containing estrogen or after the ingestion of milk or meat from estrogen-treated animals. The gynecomastia of digitalis ingestion is usually attributed to an estrogen-like side effect of the drug, but in the experience of the author it is usually associated with abnormal liver function tests. A second mechanism by which drugs can induce gynecomastia is illustrated by gonadotropin, such as from human chorionic gonadotropin (hCG)–secreting tumors, which causes enhanced testicular secretion of estrogen. Other drugs cause gynecomastia by interfering with testosterone synthesis (ketoconazole and alkylating agents) and/or testosterone action, for instance by blocking the binding of androgen to its cytosol receptor protein in target tissues (spironolactone and cimetidine). Finally, drugs that cause gynecomastia by mechanisms which have not been defined include busulfan, ethionamide, isoniazid, methyldopa, tricyclic antidepressants, penicillamine, and diazepam, marijuana, and heroin. In some instances the feminization is due to effects of the drugs on liver function.

Diagnostic evaluation The evaluation of patients with gynecomastia should include the following procedures: (1) a careful drug history; (2) measurement and examination of the testes (if both are small, a chromosomal karyotype should be obtained; if they are asymmetric, an evaluation for testicular tumor should be instituted); (3) an evaluation of liver function; (4) an endocrine evaluation to include measurement of serum androstenedione or 24-h urinary 17-ketosteroids (usually elevated in feminizing adrenal states), measurement of plasma estradiol (helpful if elevated but usually normal), and measurement of plasma luteinizing hormone (LH) and testosterone. If LH is high and testosterone is low, the diagnosis is usually testicular

TABLE 332-2 Differential diagnosis of gynecomastia

PHYSIOLOGIC GYNECOMASTIA

Newborn
Adolescence
Aging

PATHOLOGIC GYNECOMASTIA

Deficient production or action of testosterone:
  Congenital anorchia
  Klinefelter syndrome
  Androgen resistance (testicular feminization and Reifenstein syndrome)
  Defects in testosterone synthesis
  Secondary testicular failure (viral orchitis, trauma, castration, neurologic and granulomatous diseases, renal failure)
Increased estrogen production:
  Estrogen secretion:
    True hermaphroditism
    Testicular tumors
    Carcinoma of the lung
Increased substrate for peripheral aromatase:
  Adrenal disease
  Liver disease
  Starvation
  Thyrotoxicosis
Increase in peripheral aromatase
Drugs:
  Estrogens (diethylstilbestrol, birth control pills, digitalis)
  Gonadotropins
  Inhibitors of testosterone synthesis and/or action (ketoconazole, alkylating agents, spironolactone, cimetidine)
  Unknown mechanisms (busulfan, ethionamide, isoniazid, methyldopa, tricyclic antidepressants, penicillamine, diazepam, marijuana, heroin)
Idiopathic

failure; if LH and testosterone are both low, the diagnosis is most likely increased primary estrogen production (for example, a Sertoli cell tumor of the testis); and if both LH and testosterone are elevated, the diagnosis is either an androgen-resistance state or a gonadotropin-secreting tumor.

Using these various tests a satisfactory diagnosis can be made in only half or fewer of the patients referred for gynecomastia. This implies either that the diagnostic techniques are not sufficiently refined to recognize mild disturbances, that many causes of gynecomastia are as yet undefined, that the causes may be transient and difficult to diagnose, or, as suggested by Nuttall, that gynecomastia may in some instances be normal rather than due to a pathologic state. Because of the problem of separating the normal from the pathologic, gynecomastia should probably be routinely worked up only if the drug history is negative, if the breast is tender (indicating rapid growth), or if the breast mass is larger than 4 cm in diameter. In other instances a decision to perform an endocrine evaluation depends on the clinical context. For example, all gynecomastia associated with signs of underandrogenization should be evaluated.

Treatment When the primary cause of the overestrogenization can be identified and corrected, the breast enlargement usually subsides promptly and eventually disappears. However, if the gynecomastia is of long duration (and fibrosis has replaced the original ductal hyperplasia), correction of the primary defect may not be followed by improvement. In such instances and when the primary cause cannot be corrected, surgery is the only effective therapy. Indications for surgery include several psychologic and/or cosmetic problems, continued growth, or a suspected malignancy. Although the relative risk of carcinoma of the breast is increased in men with gynecomastia, it is rare nevertheless. Prophylactic radiation of the breasts prior to the institution of diethylstilbestrol therapy is effective in preventing gynecomastia and has a low complication rate in elderly men. In rare patients who have painful gynecomastia and who are not candidates for other therapy, treatment with antiestrogens such as tamoxifen may be indicated.

REFERENCES

Galactorrhea

ADLER RA: The evaluation of galactorrhea. Am J Obstet Gynecol 127:569, 1977
CHOTINER HC et al: Lactose and casein content of nonpuerperal breast secretion. J Reprod Med 22:267, 1979
DAVAJAN V: The significance of galactorrhea in patients with normal menses, oligomenorrhea, and secondary amenorrhea. Am J Obstet Gynecol 130:894, 1978
FRANTZ AG, WILSON JD: Endocrine disorders of the breast, in Williams' Textbook of Endocrinology, 7th ed, JD Wilson, DW Foster (eds): Philadelphia, Saunders, 1985, pp 402–421
FRIEDMAN S, GOLDFEIN A: Breast secretions in normal women. Am J Obstet Gynecol 104:846, 1969
GOMEZ F et al: Nonpuerperal galactorrhea and hyperprolactinemia. Am J Med 62:648, 1977
KLEINBERG DL et al: Galactorrhea: A study of 235 cases, including 48 with pituitary tumors. N Engl J Med 296:589, 1977
KULSKI JK et al: Changes in the milk composition of nonpuerperal women. Am J Obstet Gynecol 139:597, 1981
PARKES D: Bromocriptine. N Engl J Med 301:873, 1979
TOLTS G: Prolactin: Physiology and pathology. Hosp Prac February 1980, p 85
TURKSOY RN et al: Diagnostic and therapeutic modalities in women with galactorrhea. Obstet Gynecol 56:323, 1980

Gynecomastia

ANDERSON JA, GROOM JB: Male breast at autopsy. Acta Pathol Microbiol Immunol Scand 90:191, 1982
CARLSON HE: Gynecomastia. N Engl J Med 303:795, 1980
CIMORA GA et al: Percutaneous oestrogen-induced gynecomastia: A case report. Br J Plast Surg 35:209, 1982
FRANTZ AG, WILSON JD: Endocrine disorders of the breast, in Williams' Textbook of Endocrinology, 7th ed, JD Wilson, DW Foster (eds). Philadelphia, Saunders, 1985, pp 402–421
GAGNON JD et al: Pre-estrogen breast irradiation for patients with carcinoma of the prostate: A critical review. J Urol 121:182, 1979
JEFFREYS DB: Painful gynecomastia treated with tamoxifen. Br Med J, April 1979, p 1119
NIEWOEHNER CV, NUTTAL FQ: Gynecomastia in a hospitalized male population. Am J Med 77:633, 1984
NUTTAL FQ: Gynecomastia as a physical finding in normal men. J Clin Endocrinol Metab 48:338, 1979
PORT A et al: Ketoconazole blocks testosterone synthesis. Arch Intern Med 142:2137, 1982
SATIANI B et al: Cancer of the male breast: A thirty-year experience. Am Surg 44:86, 1978

333 DISORDERS OF SEXUAL DIFFERENTIATION

JEAN D. WILSON / JAMES E. GRIFFIN III

Sexual differentiation is a sequential and ordered process. *Chromosomal sex,* which is established at the moment of fertilization, determines *gonadal sex,* and *gonadal sex* in turn causes the development of *phenotypic sex* in which the male or female urogenital tract is formed (Table 333-1). A disturbance during embryogenesis of any step in this developmental process may result in a disorder of sexual differentiation. Known causes of abnormalities in sexual development include environmental insults as in the ingestion of a virilizing drug during pregnancy, nonfamilial aberrations of the sex chromosomes as in 45,X gonadal dysgenesis, developmental birth defects of multifactorial etiology as in most cases of hypospadias, and hereditary disorders resulting from single gene mutations as in the testicular feminization syndrome.

Limitations of knowledge make it necessary to make empiric assignments as to the nature of the physiologic derangement in certain disorders. Nevertheless, a specific diagnosis can usually be made as the result of combined genetic, phenotypic, and chromosomal assessment. As a consequence appropriate gender assignment can be made, even in extreme instances of ambiguous genitalia, and tailoring of the phenotype can be undertaken when appropriate.

NORMAL SEXUAL DIFFERENTIATION

The first process in sexual differentiation is the establishment of chromosomal sex, the heterogametic sex (XY) being male and the homogametic sex (XX) female. The embryos of both sexes then develop in an identical fashion until approximately 40 days of gestation. The second phase of sexual differentiation is the conversion of the indifferent gonad into a testis or an ovary. The differentiation of the indifferent gonad into a testis is mediated by gene(s) on the Y chromosome, one of which is either identical to or closely linked to a gene that specifies the HY antigen. The final process, the translation of gonadal sex into phenotypic sex, is the direct consequence of the type of gonad formed and the endocrine secretions of the fetal gonads.

TABLE 333-1 Classification of disorders of sexual development in human beings

Disorders of chromosomal sex:
  Klinefelter syndrome
  XX male
  Gonadal dysgenesis
  Mixed gonadal dysgenesis
  True hermaphroditism
Disorders of gonadal sex:
  Pure gonadal dysgenesis
  Absent testis syndrome
Disorders of phenotypic sex:
  Female pseudohermaphroditism:
    Congenital adrenal hyperplasia
    Nonadrenal female pseudohermaphroditism
    Developmental disorders of müllerian ducts
  Male pseudohermaphroditism:
    Abnormalities in androgen synthesis
    Abnormalities in androgen action
    Persistent müllerian duct syndrome
    Development defects of male genitalia

The development of phenotypic sex results in the formation of the male and female urogenital tracts.

The internal genitalia are derived from the wolffian and müllerian ducts that exist side by side in early embryos of both sexes (Fig. 333-1A). In the male the wolffian ducts give rise to the epididymides, vasa deferentia, and seminal vesicles, and the müllerian ducts disappear. In the female the fallopian tubes, uterus, and upper vagina are derived from the müllerian ducts, and the wolffian ducts regress. The external genitalia and urethra in the two sexes develop from common anlage—the urogenital sinus and the genital tubercle, folds, and swellings (Fig. 333-1B). The urogenital sinus gives rise to the prostate and prostatic urethra in the male and to the urethra and a portion of the vagina in the female. The genital tubercle is the origin of the glans penis in the male and clitoris in the female. The urogenital swellings become the scrotum or the labia majora, and the genital folds develop into the labia minora or fuse to form the male urethra and the shaft of the penis.

In the absence of the testis, as in the normal female or in the male embryo castrated prior to the onset of phenotypic differentiation, the development of phenotypic sex proceeds along female lines. Thus, masculinization of the fetus is the positive result of action of hormones from the fetal gonad, whereas female development does not require the presence of a gonad. Development of the sexual phenotype normally conforms to the chromosomal sex. That is, chromosomal sex determines gonadal sex, and gonadal sex in turn controls phenotypic sex.

The formation of the male phenotype is vested in the action of three hormones. Two—müllerian-inhibiting substance and testosterone—are secretory products of the fetal testis. Müllerian-inhibiting substance is a protein hormone that acts to suppress the müllerian ducts and consequently prevents development of the uterus and fallopian tubes in the male. Testosterone acts directly to stimulate differentiation of the wolffian duct derivatives and is the precursor for the third fetal hormone, dihydrotestosterone (see Chap. 330).

FIGURE 333-1 *Normal sexual differentiation. A. Internal genitalia. B. External genitalia.*

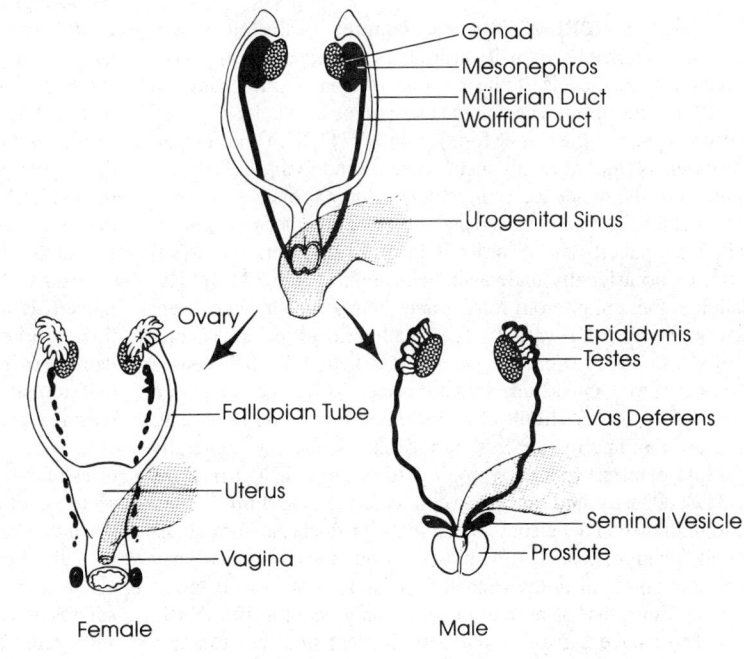

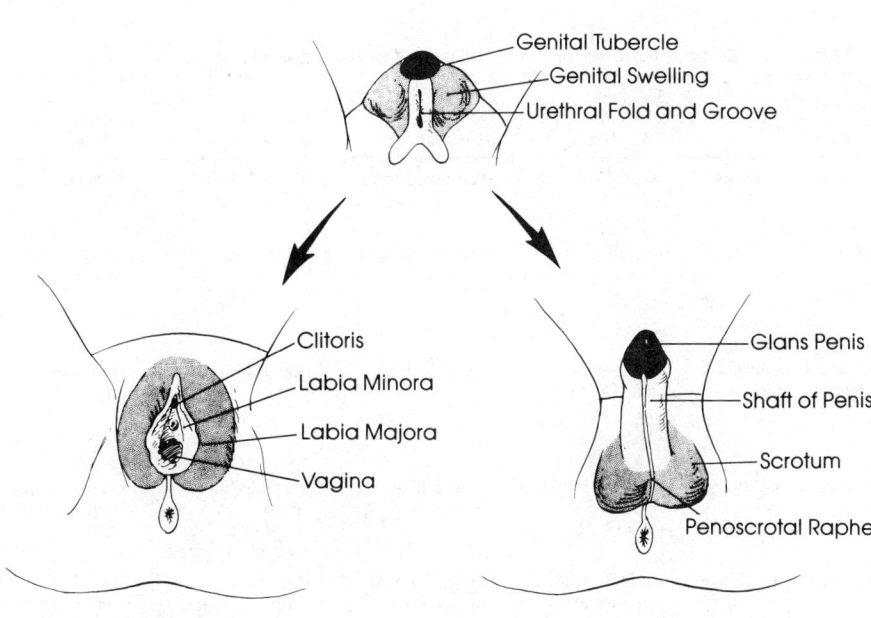

Dihydrotestosterone, which is formed from circulating testosterone, acts to induce formation of the male urethra and prostate and to cause formation of the penis and scrotum. Thus, testosterone and dihydro-testosterone function during fetal life to induce formation of the accessory organs of male reproduction by the same intracellular machinery by which they act in differentiated tissues (Chap. 330).

The secretion of testosterone by the fetal testis approaches a maximum by the eighth to tenth week of gestation, and formation of the sexual phenotypes is largely completed by the end of the first trimester. During the latter phases of gestation ovarian follicular development and maturation of the vagina occur in the female, and descent of the testes and growth of the external genitalia take place in the male.

DISORDERS OF CHROMOSOMAL SEX

Disorders of chromosomal sex (Table 333-2) occur when the number or structure of the X or Y chromosomes is abnormal (see Chap. 60).

KLINEFELTER SYNDROME Clinical features Klinefelter syndrome is characterized by small, firm testes, azoospermia, gynecomastia, and elevated levels of plasma gonadotropins in men with two or more X chromosomes. The common karyotype is either a 47,XXY chromosomal pattern (the classic form) or 46,XY/47,XXY mosaicism. The disorder is the most frequent major abnormality of sexual differentiation, the incidence being around 1 in 500 men.

Prepubertally, patients have small testes but otherwise appear normal. After puberty the disorder is manifest as infertility, gynecomastia, or occasionally underandrogenization (Table 333-3). Hyalinization of the seminiferous tubules and azoospermia are consistent features of the 47,XXY variety. The small, firm testes are characteristically less than 2.0 cm and always less than 3.5 cm in length (corresponding to 2 and 12 mL volume, respectively). The increased mean body height is the result of an increased lower body segment. Gynecomastia ordinarily appears during adolescence, is generally bilateral and painless, and may progress to become disfiguring (see Chap. 332). Obesity and varicose veins occur in one-third to one-half, and mild mental deficiency, social maladjustment, abnormalities of thyroid function, diabetes mellitus, and pulmonary disease may be more common than in the general population. The risk of breast cancer is 20 times that of normal men (but only about a fifth that in women). Most have a male psychosexual orientation and function sexually as normal men.

The mosaic variant comprises about 10 percent of the patients, as estimated by chromosomal karyotypes on peripheral blood leukocytes. The frequency of this variant may be underestimated since chromosomal mosaicism may be present only in the testes in subjects whose peripheral leukocyte karotype is normal. The mosaic form is usually not as severe as the 47,XXY variety, and the testes may be normal in size (Table 333-3). The endocrine abnormalities are also less severe, and gynecomastia and azoospermia are less common. Indeed, occasional patients with mosaicism may be fertile. In some the diagnosis may not even be suspected because of the minor degree of the physical abnormalities.

Approximately 30 additional karyotypic varieties of Klinefelter syndrome have been described, including those with uniform cell lines (such as XXYY, XXXY, and XXXXY) and a variety of mosaicisms of the X chromosome with or without associated structural abnormalities of the X. In general, the greater the degree of chromosomal abnormality (and in mosaic forms the more cell lines that are abnormal), the more severe the manifestations.

Pathophysiology The classic form is due to meiotic nondisjunction of the chromosomes during gametogenesis (Fig. 333-2). About 40 percent of the responsible meiotic nondisjunctions occur during spermatogenesis, and 60 percent occur during oogenesis. Advanced maternal age is a predisposing factor. The mosaic form is thought to result from chromosomal mitotic nondisjunction after fertilization of the zygote and can take place either in a 46,XY zygote (Fig. 333-2) or a 47,XXY zygote. The latter defect or double nondisjunction (meiotic and mitotic) may be the usual cause and thus explain why the mosaic form is less frequent than the classic disorder.

Plasma follicle-stimulating hormone (FSH) and luteinizing hormone (LH) are usually high; FSH shows the best discrimination, and little overlap occurs with normals, a consequence of the consistent damage to the seminiferous tubules. The plasma testosterone averages half normal, but the range of values overlaps the normal range. Mean plasma estradiol levels are elevated, the cause of which is not entirely clear. Early in the course, the testes may secrete increased amounts of estradiol in response to the elevated plasma LH, but the testicular secretion of estradiol (and testosterone) eventually declines. Elevated plasma estradiol late in the course is probably due to a combination of a decreased metabolic clearance rate and an increased rate of conversion of testosterone to estradiol in extraglandular tissues. The net result both early and late is a variable degree of insufficient androgenization and enhanced feminization. The feminization, including gynecomastia, depends on the ratio of circulating estrogen

TABLE 333-2 Clinical features of the disorders of chromosomal sex

Disorder	Common chromosomal complement	Gonadal development	External genitalia	Internal genitalia	Breast development	Comment
Klinefelter syndrome	47,XXY *or* 46,XY/47,XXY	Hyalinized testes	Normal male	Normal male	Gynecomastia	Most common disorder of sexual differentiation; tall stature.
XX male	46,XX	Hyalinized testes	Normal male	Normal male	Gynecomastia	Shorter than normal men; increased incidence of hypospadias. Similar to Klinefelter syndrome. May be familial.
Gonadal dysgenesis (Turner syndrome)	45,X *or* 46,XX/45,X	Streak gonads	Immature female	Hypoplastic female	Immature female	Short stature and multiple somatic abnormalities. May be 46,XX with structurally abnormal X chromosome.
Mixed gonadal dysgenesis	46,XY/45,X *or* 46,XY	Testis and streak gonad	Variable but almost always ambiguous; 60% reared as female	Uterus, vagina, and one fallopian tube	Usually male	Second most common cause of ambiguous genitalia in the newborn; tumors common.
True hermaphroditism	46,XX *or* 46,XY *or* mosaics	Testis and ovary or ovotestis	Variable but usually ambiguous; 60% reared as males	Usually a uterus and urogenital sinus; ducts correspond to gonad	Gynecomastia in 75%	May be familial.

TABLE 333-3 Characteristics of patients with classic versus mosaic Klinefelter syndrome*

	47,XXY, %	46,XY/47,XXY, %
Abnormal testicular histology	100	94†
Decreased length of testis	99	73†
Azoospermia	93	50†
Decreased testosterone	79	33
Decreased facial hair	77	64
Increased gonadotropins	75	33†
Decreased sexual function	68	56
Gynecomastia	55	33†
Decreased axillary hair	49	46
Decreased length of penis	41	21

* Table based on 519 XXY patients and 51 XY/XXY patients.
† Significantly different at p <.05 or better.
SOURCE: After Gordon et al.

to androgen (relative or absolute), and subjects with lower plasma testosterone and higher plasma estradiol levels are more likely to develop gynecomastia (see Chap. 332). The increase in plasma gonadotropins after the administration of luteinizing hormone–releasing hormone (LHRH) is exaggerated after the age of expected puberty, and the normal feedback inhibition of testosterone on pituitary LH secretion is diminished. Subjects with untreated Klinefelter syndrome may have "reactive pituitary abnormalities" in the form of enlarged or abnormal sella turcicas, presumably secondary to the persistent lack of gonadal feedback and hypertrophy of the gonadotrophes in response to stimulation by LHRH. It is not known whether actual adenoma formation occurs.

Management No method is available for reversing the infertility, and surgical removal is the only means for effective treatment of the gynecomastia. Some underandrogenized patients benefit from supplemental androgen, but such treatment may paradoxically worsen the gynecomastia, presumably by providing increased androgen substrate for the conversion to estrogens in the peripheral tissues. Androgen should be administered in the form of testosterone cypionate or testosterone enanthate. Following the administration of testosterone, plasma LH returns to normal only after several months, if at all.

XX MALE SYNDROME The incidence of a 46,XX karyotype in phenotypic males is approximately 1 in 20,000 to 24,000 male births. Affected individuals have absence of all female internal genitalia and male psychosexual identification. Indeed, the findings resemble those in the Klinefelter syndrome: the testes are small and firm (generally less than 2 cm), gynecomastia is frequent, the penis is normal to small in size, azoospermia and hyalinization of the seminiferous tubules are usual, mean plasma testosterone is low, plasma estradiol is elevated, and plasma gonadotropin levels are high. Affected individuals differ from typical Klinefelter patients only in that average height is less than in normal men, the incidence of mental deficiency is not increased, and the incidence of hypospadias is increased.

Four theories have been proposed to explain the pathogenesis of this disorder: (1) translocation of a portion of a Y chromosome to the X chromosome, (2) mosaicism for a Y chromosome in some cell lines or early loss of a Y chromosome, (3) mutation of an autosomal gene, or (4) deletion of genetic material on X chromosome that normally has a negative regulatory effect on testis development. Although some evidence has been marshalled to support each of these four possibilities in individual XX males, no unifying hypothesis can explain the disorder. While mosaicism appears to be unlikely in most cases, the other listed explanations remain possible. The etiology may be heterogeneous. The management of the disorder is similar to that of Klinefelter syndrome.

GONADAL DYSGENESIS (TURNER SYNDROME) Clinical features Gonadal dysgenesis is characterized by primary amenorrhea, sexual infantilism, short stature, multiple congenital anomalies, and bilateral streak gonads in phenotypic women with any of several defects of the X chromosome. This condition should be distinguished

from (1) mixed gonadal dysgenesis in which a unilateral testis and a contralateral streak gonad are present; (2) pure gonadal dysgenesis in which bilateral streak gonads are associated with a normal 46,XX or 46,XY karyotype, normal stature, and primary amenorrhea; and (3) the Noonan syndrome, an autosomal dominant disorder of males and females characterized by webbed neck, short stature, congenital heart disease, cubitus valgus, and other congenital defects despite normal karyotypes and normal gonads.

The incidence is estimated at 1 in 2500 newborn females. The diagnosis is either made at birth because of the associated anomalies or more frequently at puberty when amenorrhea and failure of sexual development are noted in conjunction with the associated anomalies. Gonadal dysgenesis is the most common cause of primary amenorrhea, accounting for a third of such patients. The external genitalia are unambiguously female but remain immature, and there is no breast development unless the patient is treated with exogenous estrogen. The internal genitalia consist of infantile fallopian tubes and uterus and bilateral streak gonads located in the broad ligaments. Primordial germ cells are present transiently during embryogenesis but disappear as the result of an accelerated rate of atresia (see Chap. 331). After the age of expected puberty these streaks lack identifiable follicles and ova but contain fibrous tissue that is indistinguishable from normal ovarian stroma.

The associated somatic anomalies primarily involve the skeleton and connective tissue. Lymphedema of the hands and feet, webbing of the neck, low hair line, redundant skin folds on the back of the neck, a shield-like chest with widely spaced nipples, and a low birth weight are features that suggest the diagnosis in infancy. In addition, the facies may be characterized by micrognathia, epicanthal folds, prominent low-set or deformed ears, a fishlike mouth, and ptosis. Short fourth metacarpals are present in half, and 10 to 20 percent have coarctation of the aorta. In adults the average height rarely exceeds 150 cm. Associated conditions include renal malformations, pigmented nevi, hypoplastic nails, tendency to keloid formation, perceptive hearing loss, unexplained hypertension, and autoimmune disorders. Frank hypothyroidism is present in 20 percent.

Pathophysiology About half have a 45,X karyotype, approximately one-fourth have mosaicism with no structural abnormality (46,XX/ 45,X), and the remainder have a structurally abnormal X chromosome with or without mosaicism (see Chap. 60). The 45,X variety may result from chromosome loss during gametogenesis in either parent or a mitotic error during one of the early cleavage divisions of the fertilized zygote (Fig. 333-2). Short stature and other somatic features result from loss of genetic material on the short arm of the X chromosome. Streak gonads result when genetic material is missing from either the long or short arm of the X. In individuals with mosaicism or with structural abnormalities of the X, phenotypes on average are intermediate in severity between that seen in the 45,X variety and the normal. In some patients with hypertrophy of the clitoris, there is an unidentified fragment of a chromosome present in addition to the X chromosome, assumed to be an abnormal Y. Rarely, familial transmission of gonadal dysgenesis can be the result of a balanced X-autosome translocation (see Chap. 60).

Assessment of sex chromatin was previously utilized as a means of screening for abnormalities of the X chromosome. Sex chromatin (the Barr body) in normal women is the result of inactivation of one of two X chromosomes, and women with a 45,X chromosome composition like normal men are said to be chromatin-negative. However, only about half of patients with gonadal dysgenesis (those with 45,X and those with the most extreme mosaicism and structural abnormalities) are chromatin-negative, and analysis of chromosomal karotype is necessary to establish the diagnosis and to identify the fraction with Y chromosomal elements and a high chance of developing malignancy in the streak gonads.

Sparse pubic and axillary hair develop at the time of expected puberty, the breasts remain infantile, and no menses occur. Serum FSH is elevated in infancy, falls during midchildhood to the normal range, and increases to castrate levels at the age of 9 or 10. At this time, serum LH is also elevated, and plasma estradiol levels are low (<10 pg/mL). Approximately 2 percent of 45,X subjects and 12 percent of mosaic subjects have sufficient residual follicles to allow some menstruation. Indeed, occasional pregnancy has been reported in minimally affected individuals; the reproductive life in such individuals is brief.

Management   At the anticipated time of puberty replacement therapy with estrogen should be instituted to induce maturation of the breasts, labia, vagina, uterus, and fallopian tubes (see Chap. 331). Linear growth and bone maturation rates are approximately doubled during the first year of treatment with estradiol, but the eventual height of patients rarely approaches the predicted height (see Chap. 331). Treatment with growth hormone has not been helpful.

Gonadal tumors are rare in 45,X patients but have occurred in several patients with mosaicism involving the Y chromosome; consequently, streak gonads should be removed in any patient with evidence of virilization or a Y-containing cell line.

MIXED GONADAL DYSGENESIS   Clinical features   Mixed gonadal dysgenesis is an entity in which phenotypic males or females have a testis on one side and streak gonad on the other. Most have 45,X/46,XY mosaicism, but the clinical entity is not confined to that chromosomal pattern. The incidence is unknown, but in most hospitals it is the second most common cause of ambiguous genitalia in the neonate after congenital adrenal hyperplasia.

About two-thirds are reared as females, and most phenotypic males are incompletely virilized at birth. The majority have ambiguous genitalia, including some degree of phallic enlargement, a urogenital sinus, and varying degrees of labioscrotal fusion. In most the testis is located intraabdominally; individuals with a testis in the inguinal or scrotal position are usually reared as males. A uterus, vagina, and at least one fallopian tube are almost invariably present.

The prepubertal testis appears relatively normal. The postpubertal testis contains abundant mature Leydig cells, but the seminiferous tubules lack germinal elements and contain only Sertoli cells. The streak gonad, a thin, pale, elongated structure located either in the broad ligament or along the pelvic wall, is composed of ovarian stroma. At puberty the testis secretes androgen, and virilization and phallic enlargement both occur. Feminization is rare; when it occurs, estrogen secretion from a gonadal tumor should be suspected.

Approximately a third exhibit the somatic features of 45,X gonadal dysgenesis, i.e., low posterior hairline, shield chest, multiple pigmented nevi, cubitus valgus, webbing of the neck, and short stature (height less than 150 cm).

Virtually all are chromatin-negative. In one series, two-thirds had the 45,X/46,XY karyotype, and in the remainder a 46,XY karyotype was present but mosaicism might have gone undetected or been limited to certain cell lines. The origin of 45,X/46,XY mosaicism is best explained by the loss of a Y chromosome during an early mitotic division of an XY zygote similar to the postulated loss of the X chromosome in the 46,XY/47,XXY mosaicism shown in Fig. 333-2.

Pathophysiology   It has been assumed that the 46,XY cell line stimulates testicular differentiation whereas the 45,X stem leads to the development of the contralateral streak gonad, but actual comparisons between karyotype and phenotypic expression have failed to substantiate such a relationship. Furthermore, no clear correlation has been found between the percentage of cells cultured from blood or skin containing 45,X or 46,XY and the degree of gonadal development or of somatic anomalies.

Both masculinization and müllerian duct regression in utero are incomplete. Since Leydig cell function is normal at puberty, inadequate virilization in utero may be the result of delayed development of a testis that is ultimately capable of normal Leydig cell function. Alternatively, the fetal testis may simply be incapable of synthesizing adequate amounts of müllerian-inhibiting substance and androgen.

Management   For the older child or adult in whom gender is fixed prior to diagnosis, the central issue in management is the possibility of tumor development in the gonads. The overall incidence of gonadal tumors is about 25 percent. Seminomas occur more frequently than gonadoblastomas, and the tumors may occur prior to puberty. The tumors occur most frequently in patients with a female phenotype who lack the somatic features typical of 45,X gonadal dysgenesis and are more common in intraabdominal testes than in the streak gonad. When the diagnosis is established in phenotypic females, early exploratory laparotomy and prophylactic gonadectomy should be undertaken both because gonadal tumors may occur in childhood and because the testis secretes androgen at puberty and thus causes virilization. Such subjects, like those with gonadal dysgenesis, are then given estrogen to induce and maintain feminization.

When the diagnosis is established in phenotypic males during late childhood or in adults the management is more complicated. Phenotypic males with mixed gonadal dysgenesis are infertile (no germinal elements are present in the testes) and also have a high risk of developing gonadal tumors. Which testes can be safely conserved? In general the following observations apply: (1) tumors develop in scrotal streak gonads but not in scrotal testes, (2) tumors that develop in intraabdominal testes are always associated with ipsilateral müllerian duct structures, and (3) tumors in streak gonads are always associated with tumors in the contralateral abdominal testis. Based on these observations, it is recommended that (1) all streak gonads should be removed, (2) scrotal testes should be preserved, and (3) intraabdominal testes should be excised unless they can be

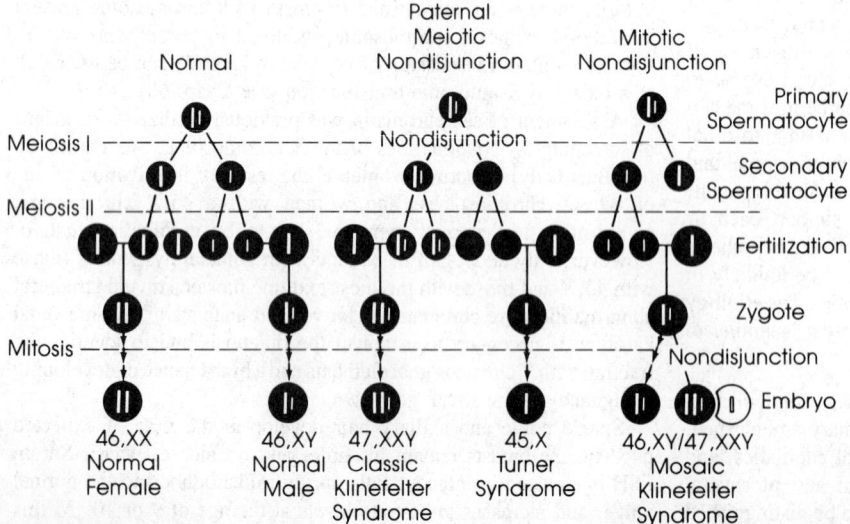

FIGURE 333-2 *Schema for normal spermatogenesis and fertilization showing effects of meiotic and mitotic nondisjunction leading to classic Klinefelter syndrome, Turner syndrome, and mosaic Klinefelter. The schema would be similar if the abnormal events took place during oogenesis.*

relocated in the scrotum and are not associated with ipsilateral müllerian duct structures. Decisions as to reconstructive surgery of the phallus depend upon the nature of the defect.

When the diagnosis is established in early infancy and the genitalia are ambiguous, gender assignment is usually female.Resection of the enlarged phallus and gonadectomy can then be accomplished in infancy, usually in one procedure. If the decision is for male gender assignment, the same criteria apply as to which testes should be removed in infants as in older males.

TRUE HERMAPHRODITISM Clinical features True hermaphroditism is a condition in which both an ovary and a testis or a gonad with histologic features of both (ovotestis) is present. To justify the diagnosis there must be histologic documentation of both types of gonadal epithelium, the presence of ovarian stroma without oocytes not being sufficient. The incidence is unknown, but more than 400 cases have been reported. Three categories are recognized: (1) one-fifth are bilateral—testicular and ovarian tissue (ovotestes) on each side, (2) two-fifths are unilateral—an ovotestis on one side and an ovary or a testis on the other, and (3) the remainder are lateral—a testis on one side and an ovary on the other.

The external genitalia display all gradations of the male-to-female spectrum. Two-thirds are sufficiently masculinized to be reared as males. However, less than one-tenth have normal male external genitalia; most have hypospadias, and more than half have incomplete labioscrotal fusion. Two-thirds of phenotypic females have an enlarged clitoris, and most have a urogenital sinus. Differentiation of the internal ducts usually corresponds to the adjacent gonad. Although an epididymis usually develops adjacent to a testis, development of the vas deferens is complete in only one-third. Of the patients with an ovotestis, three-fourths have an epididymis, two-thirds have a fallopian tube, one-tenth have a vas deferens, and one-tenth have both a vas deferens and a fallopian tube. A uterus is usually present although it may be hypoplastic or unicornuate. The ovary usually occupies the normal position, but the testis or ovotestis may be found at any level along the route of embryonic testicular descent, frequently associated with an inguinal hernia. Testicular tissue is present in the scrotum or the labioscrotal fold in one-third, in the inguinal canal in one-third, and in the abdominal area in one-third.

Variable feminization and virilization develop at puberty, three-fourths develop gynecomastia, and about half menstruate. In phenotypic men menstruation presents as cyclic hematuria. Ovulation occurs in approximately one-fourth and is more common than spermatogenesis. In men ovulation may present as testicular pain. Fertility has been reported in women following removal of an ovotestis and in a man who fathered two children. Congenital malformations of other systems are rare.

Pathophysiology About two-thirds of subjects have a 46,XX karyotype, a tenth have a 46,XY karyotype, and the remainder are chromosomal mosaics in which a Y cell line is present. The mechanism responsible for the gonadal development is unknown. Even if not demonstrable with conventional karyotyping methods, it is assumed that sufficient genetic material derived from the Y chromosome is present (as the result of translocation, nondisjunction, or mutation) to induce the development of testicular tissue. In rare instances multiple sibs with a 46,XX karyotype are affected, possibly the result of an autosomal recessive gene or a common translocation.

Because corpora lutea are present in the ovaries of more than one-fourth of subjects, it can be deduced that a female neuroendocrine axis is present and functions normally in such individuals. Feminization (gynecomastia and menstruation) is the result of secretion of estradiol by the ovarian tissue present. In masculinized patients secretion of androgen predominates over secretion of estrogen, and some produce sperm.

Management When the diagnosis is made in a newborn or early infant, gender assignment depends upon the anatomic findings. In older children and adults gonads and internal duct structures that are contradictory to the predominant phenotype (and the gender of rearing)

should be removed, and when necessary the external genitalia should be modified appropriately. Although gonadal tumors are rare in true hermaphroditism, a gonadoblastoma has been reported in an individual with an XY cell line. Consequently, the possibility of future tumor development must be taken into account when the decision regarding conservation of gonadal tissue is made.

DISORDERS OF GONADAL SEX

Disorders of gonadal sex result when chromosomal sex is normal, but for one of several reasons differentiation of the gonads is abnormal. Thus, chromosomal sex does not correspond to gonadal and phenotypic sex.

PURE GONADAL DYSGENESIS Clinical features Pure gonadal dysgenesis is a disorder in which phenotypic females with gonads and genitalia identical to those with gonadal dysgenesis (bilateral streaks, infantile uterus and fallopian tubes, and sexual infantilism) have normal height, few if any congenital anomalies, and either a normal 46,XX or 46,XY karyotype. This disorder is only about one-tenth as common as gonadal dysgenesis. On genetic grounds this can be considered a separate disorder from gonadal dysgenesis, but it cannot be distinguished clinically from those instances of gonadal dysgenesis associated with minimal somatic abnormalities. The height is normal or greater than normal, some subjects being over 170 cm. Estrogen deficiency varies from profound deficiency typical of 45,X gonadal dysgenesis to some breast development and appearance of menses that terminate in an early menopause. About 40 percent have some feminization. Axillary and pubic hair are scanty, and the internal genitalia consist of müllerian derivatives only.

Tumors may develop in the streak gonads, particularly dysgerminoma or gonadoblastoma in the 46,XY disorder. Such tumors are frequently heralded by the development of virilizing signs or a pelvic mass.

Pathophysiology Although chromosomal mosaicisms have been described under this nosology, the designation here is restricted to subjects with uniform 46,XX or 46,XY karyotypes. (Those with mosaicism are variants of gonadal dysgenesis or mixed gonadal dysgenesis as described above.) The rationale for this restricted definition is based upon the fact that both the XX and XY varieties can result from single gene mutations. Several sibships have been reported in which more than one individual is affected with the 46,XX type of the disorder, frequently the result of consanguineous matings, suggesting an autosomal recessive pattern of inheritance. Familial occurrence of the 46,XY variety has also been described; in some the mutation appears to be inherited in an X-linked recessive pattern, while in other families the occurrence is compatible with a male-limited autosomal recessive inheritance. In both the 46,XX and the 46,XY forms the mutation prevents differentiation of ovary or testis, respectively, by an uncertain mechanism; the development of the female phenotype is the consequence of the failure of gonadal development. As in all individuals with nonfunctional gonads, gonadotropin secretion is elevated and estrogen secretion is low.

Management The management of the estrogen deficiency is identical to that in gonadal dysgenesis, namely appropriate estrogen replacement therapy is initiated at the time of expected puberty and maintained in adult life (see Chap. 331). Because of the high frequency of gonadal tumors in the 46,XY variety, exploratory surgery and removal of the streak gonads should be undertaken once the diagnosis is made. The development of virilizing signs is indication for immediate surgery. The natural history of the gonadal tumors in this disorder is uncertain, but the prognosis after surgical removal is usually good.

THE ABSENT TESTES SYNDROME (ANORCHIA, TESTICULAR REGRESSION, GONADAL AGENESIS, AGONADISM) Clinical features A spectrum of phenotypes has been described in 46,XY males with absent or rudimentary testes but in whom unequivocal evidence exists that endocrine function of the testis (e.g., invariable müllerian duct regression and variable testosterone synthesis) was present at some time during embryonic life. This rare disorder can be distinguished from pure gonadal dysgenesis in which no evidence can be inferred for gonadal function during embryonic development. The disorder varies in its manifestations from complete failure of virilization through varying degrees of incomplete virilization of the external genitalia to otherwise normal males with bilateral anorchia.

The purest form is represented by 46,XY phenotypic females with absent testes, sexual infantilism, and absence of both müllerian duct derivatives and accessory organs of male reproduction. Such individuals differ from the 46,XY form of pure gonadal dysgenesis in that no gonadal remnant whatsoever can be identified, including no streak gonad, and in the absence of müllerian derivatives. Testicular failure must have occurred between the onset of formation of müllerian-inhibiting substance and the secretion of testosterone, that is, after development of the seminiferous tubules but before the onset of Leydig cell function.

In others the clinical features indicate that testicular failure occurred later in gestation, and these individuals may constitute problems in gender assignment. In some, failure of müllerian regression occurs to a greater extent than the failure of testosterone secretion, but none exhibit complete müllerian development. In those with more extensive virilization the external genitalia are phenotypically male, but rudimentary oviducts and vasa deferentia may coexist internally.

At the final extreme is the syndrome of bilateral anorchia in phenotypic men with absence of müllerian structures and gonads but male development of the wolffian system and external genitalia. Microphallus implies that failure of androgen-mediated growth occurred during late embryogenesis after anatomic development of the male urethra is complete. Persistent gynecomastia may or may not develop after the time of puberty.

Pathophysiology The pathogenesis is not understood. The testicular regression could be the result of mutant genes, teratogen, or trauma. Multiple instances of agonadism in the same family have been reported, some of whom have unilateral and others bilateral disease.

The quantitative dynamics of gonadal steroid production have been studied in only a few patients. In two phenotypic females who had primary amenorrhea, sexual infantilism, and no internal genital structures, androgen and estrogen kinetics were similar to those in gonadal dysgenesis; production rates of estrogen were low, and no glandular secretion of testosterone was found, confirming the functional as well as anatomic absence of the testes. In one phenotypic

male with bilateral anorchia testosterone and estrogen production was accounted for by peripheral conversion from plasma androstenedione. However, some subjects in whom no testes can be identified at laparotomy have blood testosterone values clearly above the castrate range, presumably derived from remnant testes.

Management The management of the two extremes is clearcut. Sexually infantile, phenotypic females should be treated like patients with gonadal dysgenesis, namely given adequate estrogen to ensure appropriate breast and female somatic development, and any coexisting vaginal agenesis should be treated by surgical or medical means. Likewise, phenotypic males with anorchia should be given adequate androgen replacement to allow normal male secondary sexual development. The cases with incomplete virilization or ambiguous development of the external genitalia are more complex and require individual assessment as to whether surgical therapy is appropriate in addition to hormonal therapy at the time of expected puberty.

DISORDERS OF PHENOTYPIC SEX

FEMALE PSEUDOHERMAPHRODITISM Congenital adrenal hyperplasia CLINICAL FEATURES The pathways by which glucocorticoids are synthesized in the adrenal gland and androgens are formed in the testis and adrenal are summarized in Fig. 333-3. Three enzymes are common to the formation of glucocorticoids and androgens (20,22-desmolase, 3β-hydroxysteroid dehydrogenase, and 17α-hydroxylase); deficiency of any of these enzymes results in deficiency of glucocorticoid and androgen synthesis and consequently in both congenital adrenal hyperplasia (due to enhanced ACTH levels) and defective virilization of the male embryo (male pseudohermaphroditism). Two enzymes are involved exclusively in androgen synthesis (17,20-desmolase and 17β-hydroxysteroid dehydrogenase); deficiency in either results in pure male pseudohermaphroditism with normal glucocorticoid synthesis. Deficiency of either of the terminal two enzymes of glucocorticoid synthesis (21-hydroxylase and 11β-hydroxylase) results in defective formation of hydrocortisone; the compensatory increase in ACTH secretion causes adrenal hyperplasia and a secondary increase in androgen formation that results in virilization in the female or precocious masculinization in the male.

The *adrenal insufficiency* in these disorders may produce equally severe and life-threatening problems in both sexes and is described

FIGURE 333-3 *Pathways of glucocorticoid and androgen synthesis.*

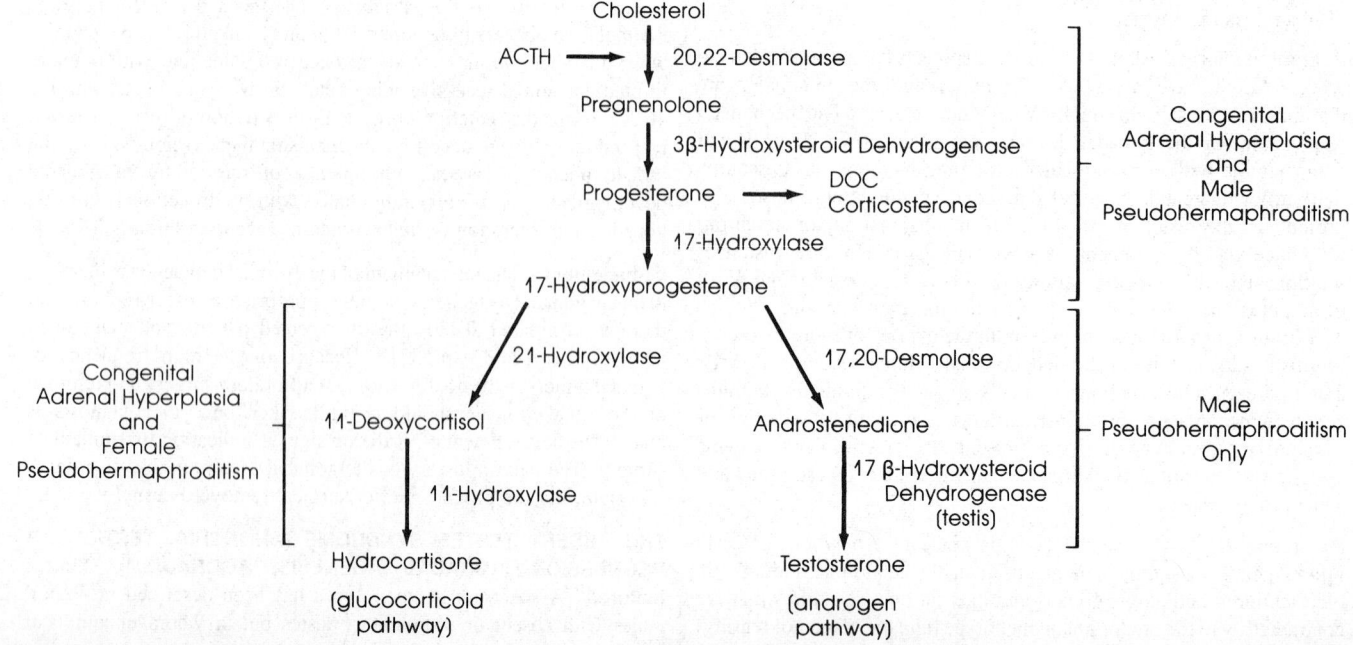

in detail in Chap. 325. The major features of the different forms of congenital adrenal hyperplasia are listed in Table 333-4. From the standpoint of *abnormal sexual development* it is helpful to consider separately those enzyme defects in steroidogenesis that result in female pseudohermaphroditism and those that cause male pseudohermaphroditism. (One disorder, 3β-hydroxysteroid dehydrogenase deficiency, can cause either male or female pseudohermaphroditism, but since the more common genital defect is incomplete virilization of the male, it will be discussed as an abnormality of male phenotypic differentiation.)

Congenital adrenal hyperplasia due to 21-hydroxylase deficiency is the most common cause of ambiguous genitalia in the newborn, with an incidence of between 1:5000 and 1:15,000 in Europe and the United States. Virilization is usually apparent at birth in the female and within the first 2 to 3 years of life in the male. Manifestations in females include hypertrophy of the clitoris associated with ventral binding (chordee), partial fusion of the labioscrotal folds, and variable virilization of the urethra. The internal female structures and ovaries remain unaltered, and the wolffian ducts regress normally, probably because the onset of adrenal function occurs relatively late in embryogenesis. The external appearance of affected females is similar to that of a male with bilateral cryptorchidism and hypospadias. The labioscrotal folds are bulbous and rugated and resemble a scrotum. Rarely the virilization is so severe that development of a complete male penile urethra and prostate results in errors in sex assignment at birth. Radiography following the injection of radiopaque dye into the external genital orifice is helpful in demonstrating the presence of a vagina, uterus, and sometimes even fallopian tubes. In a few cases virilization of the female is slight or absent at birth and becomes evident in later infancy, adolescence, or adulthood, presumably as the result of allelic variation of the mutant genes (the so-called late-onset or adult form of the disorder). The untreated female grows rapidly during the first year of life and has progressive virilization. At the time of expected puberty there is a failure of normal female sexual development and absence of menstruation. In both sexes rapid somatic maturation results in premature epiphyseal closure and a short adult height.

Since male phenotypic differentiation is normal, the condition is usually not recognized in the male at birth in the absence of overt adrenal insufficiency. However, early growth and maturation of the external genitalia, appearance of secondary sex characteristics, coarsening of the voice, frequent erections, and excessive muscular development are noticeable in the first few years of life. Virilization in the male can follow either of two patterns. Excessive adrenal androgens can inhibit gonadotropin production so that the testes remain infantile in size despite the acceleration of masculinization.

Such untreated adult men are capable of erection and ejaculation but have no spermatogenesis. Alternatively, adrenal androgen secretion can activate a premature maturation of the hypothalamic-pituitary axis and initiate a true precocious puberty including early maturation of spermatogenesis (see Chap. 330). The untreated male is also subject to the development of ACTH-dependent "tumors" of the testis composed of adrenal rest cells.

In 21-hydroxylase deficiency, which accounts for about 95 percent of congenital adrenal hyperplasia, there is a reduced activity of the 21-hydroxylase enzyme which leads to decreased production of hydrocortisone and consequently to increased release of ACTH, enlargement of the adrenal glands, and partial or complete compensation of the defect in the secretion of hydrocortisone. In about half the enzyme defect appears to be partial, and cortisol secretion is normal. This form is termed "simple virilizing" or "compensated." In the remainder there seems to be a more complete deficiency of the enzyme; the enlarged adrenal fails to produce adequate amounts of cortisol and aldosterone leading to severe salt wastage with anorexia, vomiting, volume depletion, and collapse within the first few weeks of life, the so-called salt-losing form of 21-hydroxylase deficiency. In all untreated patients overproduction of the cortisol precursors prior to the 21-hydroxylase step occurs, leading to increase in plasma progesterone and 17-hydroxyprogesterone. These act as weak aldosterone antagonists at the receptor level and in the compensated form result in greater than normal aldosterone production to maintain normal sodium balance.

Female pseudohermaphroditism may also occur in 11β-hydroxylase deficiency. In this disorder a block in hydroxylation at the 11 carbon results in the accumulation of 11-deoxycortisol and deoxycorticosterone (DOC), a potent salt-retaining hormone that causes hypertension rather than salt loss. The clinical features that stem from glucocorticoid deficiency and androgen excess are similar to those in 21-hydroxylase deficiency.

PATHOPHYSIOLOGY Both disorders are due to autosomal recessive mutations. The carrier frequency for 21-hydroxylase deficiency is about 1 in 50. At least three forms of 21-hydroxylase deficiency have been identified, all involving mutations of a gene on the sixth chromosome close to the HLA-B locus: the common type, which acts like an ordinary autosomal recessive enzyme mutation; a cryptic allele, which is clinically silent in homozygous form but which causes typical disease when present as a genetic compound with the common variety; and a late-onset variant. Carriers of the disorder (as well as homozygotes) within a given family can be identified on the basis of the HLA haplotype. In 11β-hydroxylase deficiency there is no known linkage of the mutation to the HLA system.

TABLE 333-4 Forms of congenital adrenal hyperplasia

Deficiency	Cortisol	Aldosterone	Degree of virilization of females	Failure of virilization in males	Dominant steroid secreted	Comment
21-Hydroxylase, partial (simple virilizing or compensated)	Normal	↑	+ + + +	0	17-Hydroxyprogesterone	Most common type (~95% of total); from one- to two-thirds salt losers
Severe (salt-losing)	↓	↓	+ + + +	0	17-Hydroxyprogesterone	
11β-Hydroxylase (hypertension)	↓	↓	+ + + +	0	11-Deoxycortisol and 11-deoxycorticosterone	Hypertension
3β-Hydroxysteroid dehydrogenase	0	0	+	+ + + +	Δ⁵-3β-OH compounds (dehydroepiandrosterone)	Probably second most common, usually salt loss
17α-Hydroxylase	↓	↓	0	+ + + +	Corticosterone and 11-deoxycorticosterone	No feminization of female, hypertension
20,22-Desmolase (lipoid adrenal hyperplasia)	0	0	0	+ + + +	Cholesterol(?)	Rare, usually salt loss

For discussion of the endocrine pathology see Chap. 325. In brief, excretion of ketosteroids is elevated, as is the excretion of the major metabolites that accumulate proximal to the enzymatic blocks. Plasma ACTH is elevated in untreated patients. In 21-hydroxylase deficiency, 17-hydroxyprogesterone accumulates in blood and is excreted predominantly as pregnanetriol. In 11-hydroxylase deficiency 11-deoxy-cortisol accumulates in blood and is excreted predominantly as tetrahydrocortexolone.

MANAGEMENT   Gender assignment should correspond to the chromosomal and gonadal sex, and appropriate surgical correction of the external genitalia should be undertaken as early as possible. This is of importance because appropriately treated men and women are capable of fertility. However, if the correct diagnosis is made late (after 3 years of age) gender assignment should be changed only after careful consideration of the psychosexual background.

Medical treatment with appropriate glucocorticoids prevents the consequences of hydrocortisone deficiency, arrests the rapid virilization, and prevents premature somatic advancement and epiphyseal maturation. The suppression of the abnormal steroid secretion results in cure of the hypertension in patients with 11β-hydroxylase deficiency and allows normal onset of menses and development of female secondary sex characteristics in both disorders. In males glucocorticoid therapy suppresses adrenal androgens and results in normal gonadotropin secretion, testicular development, and spermatogenesis. Measurements of plasma 17-hydroxyprogesterone, androstenedione, ACTH, and renin have all been used to assess adequacy of replacement therapy. In severe forms of 21-hydroxylase deficiency associated with salt loss or with elevated plasma renin activity treatment with mineralocorticoids is also indicated. In such patients the monitoring of plasma renin activity is useful for determining the adequacy of mineralocorticoid replacement.

Nonadrenal female pseudohermaphroditism   Nonadrenal causes of female pseudohermaphroditism are rare. In the past, the administration to pregnant women of progestational agents with androgenic side effects (such as 17α-ethinyl-19-nor-testosterone) to prevent abortion resulted in masculinization of female fetuses. Female pseudohermaphroditism may also occur in babies born to mothers who have virilizing tumors (e.g., arrhenoblastomas or luteomas of pregnancy) and, rarely, under circumstances in which no etiology can be determined.

Developmental disorders of müllerian ducts (congenital absence of the vagina, müllerian agenesis)   CLINICAL FEATURES   Congenital hypoplasia or absence of the vagina in combination with some form of abnormal or absent uterus (the Mayer-Rokitansky-Kuster-Hauser syndrome) is second only to gonadal dysgenesis as a cause of primary amenorrhea. Most patients are ascertained after the time of expected puberty because of failure to menstruate. The height and intelligence are normal, and the breasts, axillary and pubic hair, and habitus are feminine in character. The uterus may vary from almost normal, lacking only a conduit to the introitus, to the more characteristic rudimentary bicornuate cords with or without a lumen. In some patients cyclical abdominal pain indicates that sufficient functional endometrium is present to result in retrograde menstruation and/or hematometra.

About one-third have abnormal kidneys, most commonly agenesis or ectopy. Fused kidneys of the horseshoe type and solitary ectopic kidneys located in the pelvis also occur. Skeletal abnormalities are present in one-tenth; two-thirds involve the spine, and limb and rib abnormalities account for the remainder. Specific bone abnormalities include wedge vertebrae, fusions, rudimentary or asymmetric vertebral bodies, and supernumerary vertebrae. The Klippel-Feil syndrome (congenital fusion of the cervical spine, short neck, low posterior hairline, and painless limitation of cervical movement) is a frequent association.

PATHOPHYSIOLOGY   The karyotype is 46,XX. Most are believed to be sporadic in nature, but several instances of familial occurrence

have been described. The pattern of inheritance in most familial disease is consistent with a sex-limited autosomal dominant mutation. It is not known whether the sporadic cases represent new mutations of the type responsible for the familial disorder or are multifactorial in etiology. In the familial cases variable expressivity is common; some affected family members have skeletal or renal abnormalities only, while others have other abnormalities of müllerian derivatives such as a double uterus. Bilateral renal aplasia in stillborn infants is also commonly associated with absence of the uterus and vagina. Thus, the family histories should be probed for instances of isolated skeletal and renal abnormalities and for stillbirths that might result from congenital absence of both kidneys.

Documentation of ovulatory peaks of plasma LH and biphasic temperature curves during the cycle suggest that ovarian function is normal, and successful pregnancies have been reported following corrective vaginal surgery in patients who have normal uteri.

MANAGEMENT   Vaginal agenesis can be treated by surgical or nonsurgical means. Surgical repair generally utilizes a split-thickness skin graft around a solid rubber mold for the creation of an artificial vagina. Medical treatment consists of the repeated application of pressure against the vaginal dimple with a simple dilator to cause development of adequate vaginal depth. In view of the overall complication rate of around 5 to 10 percent in surgical series, medical treatment should be tried in most, and surgery should be reserved for patients in whom a well-formed uterus is present and the possibility of fertility exists. Continued coitus or instrumental dilatation is probably essential for maintaining the neovagina formed by either technique.

MALE PSEUDOHERMAPHRODITISM   Defective virilization of the male embryo (male pseudohermaphroditism) can result from defects in androgen synthesis, defects in androgen action, defects in müllerian duct regression, and uncertain causes. Four-fifths of male pseudohermaphrodites have normal androgen synthesis.

Abnormalities in androgen synthesis   CLINICAL FEATURES   Five enzymatic defects are known to result in defective testosterone synthesis (Fig. 330-3) and cause incomplete virilization of the male embryo during embryogenesis (Tables 330-4 and 330-5). Each of the enzymes catalyzes a step in the conversion of cholesterol to testosterone. Three (20,22-desmolase, 3β-hydroxysteroid dehydrogenase, and 17α-hydroxylase) are common to the synthesis of other adrenal hormones as well; consequently, their deficiency results in congenital adrenal hyperplasia (Table 333-4) as well as male pseudohermaphroditism. The other two (17,20-desmolase, and 17β-hydroxysteroid dehydrogenase) are unique to the pathway of androgen synthesis, and their deficiency results only in male pseudohermaphroditism. Since androgens are obligatory precursors of estrogens, it likewise follows that in all but the terminal defect (17β-hydroxysteroid dehydrogenase deficiency) synthesis of estrogen is also low in affected individuals of both sexes.

The adrenal dysfunction in the three relevant disorders is described in Chap. 325, and the present discussion concerns the abnormal sexual development. In 46,XY subjects there is usually no trace of uterus or fallopian tubes, indicating that the müllerian-inhibiting function of the testis takes place normally during embryogenesis. The masculinization of the wolffian ducts, urogenital sinus, and urogenital tubercle and the degree of virilization at puberty vary from almost normal to absent, and therefore, the clinical picture spans the range from phenotypic men with mild hypospadias to phenotypic women who prior to puberty resemble patients with complete testicular feminization. This extreme variability is the consequence of varying severity of the enzymatic defects in different patients and of varying effects of the steroids that accumulate proximal to the metabolic blocks in the different disorders. In patients with partial defects and in whom plasma testosterone is normal the diagnosis can only be made by measuring the steroids that accumulate proximal to the metabolic block in question.

20,22-Desmolase deficiency (lipoid adrenal hyperplasia) is a form of congenital adrenal hyperplasia in which virtually no urinary steroids (either 17-ketosteroids or 17-hydroxycorticoids) can be detected. The defect is prior to the formation of pregnenolone and is assumed to involve one or more of the enzymes of the 20,22-desmolase complex responsible for the conversion of cholesterol to pregnenolone. The syndrome is associated with salt wasting and profound adrenal insufficiency, and most affected individuals die during infancy. At autopsy the adrenals and testes are enlarged and infiltrated with lipid. Affected males are incompletely masculinized whereas affected female infants have normal genital development.

3β-Hydroxysteroid dehydrogenase deficiency is the second most common cause of congenital adrenal hyperplasia. In male infants it causes varying degrees of hypospadias or complete failure of masculinization associated with presence of a vagina. Female infants may be modestly virilized at birth due to the weak androgenic potency of dehydroepiandrosterone, the major steroid secreted. If the enzyme is absent in both the adrenal and testis, no urinary steroids contain a Δ^4-3-keto configuration, whereas in patients in whom the defect is partial or affects only the testis, the urine may contain normal or even elevated levels of Δ^4-3-ketosteroids. Most patients have marked salt wasting and profound adrenal insufficiency, and long-term survival in untreated cases occurs only in states of partial deficiency. Affected males may experience an otherwise normal male puberty except for profound gynecomastia. In these individuals a low-normal blood testosterone level is accompanied by elevated Δ^5 precursors. The enzyme in different tissues must be under complex control since deficiency of the enzyme in the testis may be less severe than in the adrenal and since enzyme activity in the liver may be normal in the face of profound deficiency in the adrenal and testis. Individuals with normal liver enzymes can be mistakenly identified as having 21-hydroxylase deficiency if urinary Δ^5-pregnenetriol is not documented to be greater than urinary pregnanetriol.

17α-Hydroxylase deficiency characteristically results in hypogonadism, absence of secondary sex characteristics, hypokalemic alkalosis, hypertension, and virtually undetectable hydrocortisone secretion in phenotypic women. The secretion of both corticosterone and desoxycorticosterone (DOC) by the adrenal is elevated, and urinary 17-ketosteroids are low. Aldosterone secretion is low, presumably as the result of high plasma DOC and depressed angiotensin levels, and returns to normal after suppressive doses of hydrocortisone are administered. In 46,XX subjects amenorrhea, absent sexual hair, and hypertension are common, but, since gonadal steroids are not required for female development during embryogenesis, the phenotype is that of a normal prepubertal woman. In males, however, the enzyme deficiency results in defective virilization that varies from complete male pseudohermaphroditism to ambiguous genitalia with perineoscrotal hypospadias. In males with partial enzyme deficiency pathologic gynecomastia may develop at puberty. Subjects with this disorder do not develop adrenal insufficiency, since the secretion of both corticosterone (a weak glucocorticoid) and DOC (a mineralocorticoid) is elevated. The hypertension and hypokalemia that are prominent features of the disorder (even in the neonatal period) remit after suppression of the DOC secretion by adequate glucocorticoid replacement.

17,20-Desmolase deficiency has been described in several families. Affected males have a 46,XY chromosome pattern, normal adrenocortical function, and a variable pattern of male pseudohermaphroditism. In the majority there is genital ambiguity at birth with some virilization at the time of expected puberty. However, two 46,XY patients have had a female phenotype and no virilization at the time of expected puberty. The disorder has been recognized in one 46,XX woman with sexual infantilism.

17β-Hydroxysteroid dehydrogenase deficiency involves the final step in androgen biosynthesis, reduction of the 17-keto group of androstenedione to form testosterone. This disorder is the most common of the enzymatic defects in testosterone synthesis. Affected 46,XY males usually have a female phenotype with a blind-ending vagina and absence of müllerian derivatives, but inguinal or abdominal testes and virilized wolffian duct structures are present. At the time of expected puberty, both virilization (with phallic enlargement and development of facial and body hair) and a variable degree of female breast development take place. In some untreated patients reversal of gender behavior from female to male occurs at puberty. Androgen and estrogen dynamics have not been elucidated in detail, but the 17-keto reduction of estrone to estradiol by the gonads is also low. 17β-Hydroxysteroid dehydrogenase is normally present in many tissues besides the gonads, and only the gonadal enzyme appears to be defective in this disorder. Plasma testosterone may be in the low-normal range, making it essential to document elevation in plasma androstenedione to make the diagnosis.

PATHOPHYSIOLOGY The available data for the 17α-hydroxylase and 3β-hydroxysteroid dehydrogenase defects are compatible with autosomal recessive inheritance. The limited family data for 17,20-desmolase deficiency and 17β-hydroxysteroid dehydrogenase deficiency are compatible either with autosomal recessive or X-linked recessive mutations, and insufficient data are available for the 20,22-desmolase defect to warrant any conclusions as to the pattern of inheritance.

The pattern of steroid secretion and excretion depends on the site of the various metabolic blocks (Fig. 333-3). In general, gonadotropin secretion is high, and as a consequence many individuals with incomplete defects are able to compensate so that the steady-state concentration of end products such as testosterone may be normal or almost normal.

In some cases of male pseudohermaphroditism testosterone formation is deficient for reasons other than a single enzyme defect in androgen synthesis. These include disorders in which Leydig cell agenesis (possibly due to absence of the LH receptor) or the secretion of a biologically inactive LH molecule has been thought to be the primary defect. In addition, as described above, a spectrum of defects in testicular development has been characterized, including familial XY gonadal dysgenesis, sporadic dysgenetic testes, and the absent testis syndrome in which deficient testosterone production is secondary to the underlying disorder of gonadal development.

MANAGEMENT Replacement therapy with glucocorticoids and in some instances mineralocorticoids is indicated in those disorders causing adrenal hyperplasia. The decision as to the management of the genital abnormalities depends upon the individual case. Fertility has not been reported, and its consideration does not enter into the decision of sex assignment. In genetic females there is no problem (except in diagnosis) in that affected individuals are raised appropriately as females, and suitable estrogen replacement is indicated at the time of expected puberty to promote development of normal female secondary sex characteristics. The decision as to whether affected newborn males with ambiguous genitalia should be raised as males or females depends upon the anatomic defect; in general the more severely affected should be raised as females, and corrective surgery of the genitalia and removal of the testes should be undertaken as early as possible. In subjects raised as females estrogen therapy is also indicated at the appropriate age to allow development of normal female secondary sex characteristics. In individuals raised as males, corrective surgery is indicated for any coexisting hypospadias, and careful monitoring of plasma androgens and estrogens should be undertaken at the time of expected puberty to determine whether long-term supplemental testosterone therapy is appropriate.

Abnormalities in androgen action Several disorders of male phenotypic development result from abnormalities of androgen action. The spectrum of phenotypes is illustrated in Fig. 333-4 and described in Table 333-5. In these disorders testosterone formation and müllerian regression are normal, but male development is impaired to a variable degree as a result of resistance to androgen action in the target cells.

5α-REDUCTASE DEFICIENCY This autosomal recessive form of male pseudohermaphroditism is characterized by (1) severe perineoscrotal

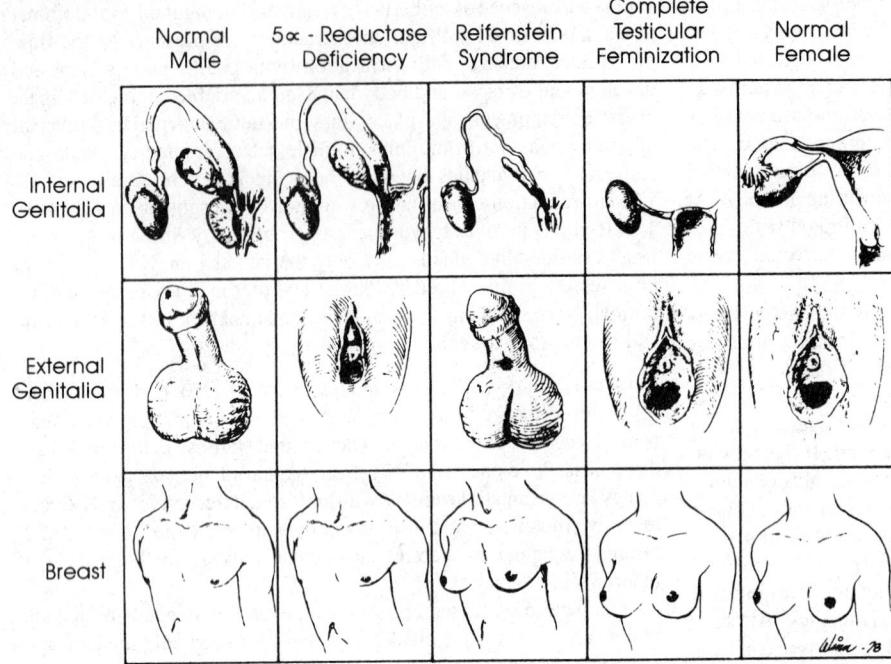

FIGURE 333-4 *Schema of the different appearance of the internal and external genitalia and breast development in androgen-resistance syndromes.*

hypospadias with a hooded prepuce, a ventral urethral groove, and opening of the urethra at the base of the phallus; (2) a blind vaginal pouch of variable size opening either into the urogenital sinus or onto the urethra immediately behind the urethral orifice; (3) well-developed testes with normal epididymides, vasa deferentia, and seminal vesicles, and termination of the ejaculatory ducts into the blind-ending vagina; (4) a female habitus without female breast development but with normal axillary and pubic hair; (5) the absence of female internal genitalia; (6) normal male plasma testosterone; and (7) masculinization to a variable degree at the time of puberty.

The fact that the defective virilization during embryogenesis is limited to the urogenital sinus and the anlage of the external genitalia provided insight into the nature of the fundamental abnormality. Testosterone, the androgen secreted by the fetal testis, is the intracellular mediator for differentiation of the wolffian duct into the epididymis, the vas deferens, and the seminal vesicle, whereas dihydrotestosterone mediates virilization of the urogenital sinus and the external genitalia. Consequently, in a male embryo with normal testosterone synthesis and normal androgen receptors a failure of dihydrotestosterone formation would be expected to result in the phenotype observed in this disorder, normal male wolffian duct derivatives with defective masculinization of the structures originating

TABLE 333-5   **Anatomic, genetic, and endocrine profile of hereditary male pseudohermaphroditism**

| Disorder | Inheritance | Phenotype | | | | |
		Müllerian ducts	Wolffian ducts	Spermatogenesis	Urogenital sinus	External genitalia
DEFECTS IN TESTOSTERONE SYNTHESIS						
Five enzyme deficiencies	Autosomal or X-linked recessive	Absent	Variable development	Normal or decreased	Variable from male to female	Generally female
DEFECTS IN ANDROGEN ACTION						
5α-Reductase deficiency	Autosomal recessive	Absent	Male	Normal or decreased	Female	Clitoromegaly
Receptor disorders: Complete testicular feminization	X-linked recessive	Absent	Absent	Absent	Female	Female
Incomplete testicular feminization	X-linked recessive	Absent	Male	Absent	Female	Clitoromegaly and posterior fusion
Reifenstein syndrome	X-linked	Absent	Variable development	Absent	Variable from male to female	Incomplete male development
Infertile male syndrome	Probably X-linked recessive	Absent	Male	Absent or decreased	Male	Male
Receptor-positive resistance	Uncertain	Absent	Variable	Absent or decreased	Variable	Female to male
DEFECTS IN MÜLLERIAN REGRESSION						
Persistent müllerian duct syndrome	Autosomal or X-linked recessive	Rudimentary uterus and fallopian tubes	Male	Normal	Male	Male

from the urogenital sinus, genital tubercle, and genital swellings. Since testosterone itself regulates LH secretion (see Chap. 330), plasma LH is usually only minimally elevated. As a result testosterone and estrogen production rates are those of normal men, and gynecomastia does not develop.

The fact that the 5α-reductase enzyme is deficient in this disorder was established by direct enzymatic assay in biopsied tissues and fibroblasts cultured from affected individuals. In most subjects the 5α-reductase is either profoundly deficient or functionally absent, and in others the enzyme protein is synthesized at a normal rate but is structurally abnormal. It is not clear why virilization at puberty appears to be more normal than the virilization that takes place during sexual differentiation.

RECEPTOR DISORDERS   Disorders of the androgen receptor may result in several distinct phenotypes. Despite differences in clinical presentation and molecular pathology these disorders are similar in regard to endocrinology, genetics, and basic pathophysiology. The major clinical features of the disorders will be considered first and followed by a discussion of the similar endocrinology and pathophysiology.

Clinical features. Complete testicular feminization is the most common form of male pseudohermaphroditism; estimates of frequency vary from 1 in 20,000 to 1 in 64,000 male births. It is the third most common cause of primary amenorrhea in phenotypic women after gonadal dysgenesis and congenital absence of the vagina. The features are characteristic. Namely, a woman is seen by the physician either because of inguinal hernia (prepubertal) or primary amenorrhea (postpubertal). The development of the breasts after puberty, the general habitus, and the distribution of body fat are female in character so that many patients have a truly feminine appearance. Axillary and pubic hair are absent or scanty, but slight vulval hair is usually present. Scalp hair is that of a normal woman, and facial hair is absent. The external genitalia are unambiguously female, and the clitoris is normal or small. The vagina is short and blind-ending and may be absent or rudimentary. All internal genitalia are absent except for undescended testes that contain normal Leydig cells and seminiferous tubules without spermatogenesis.

The testes may be located in the abdomen, along the course of the inguinal canal, or in the labia majora. Occasionally, remnants of müllerian or wolffian duct origin are present in the paratesticular fascia or in fibrous bands extending from the testis. Patients tend to be rather tall, bone age is normal, and intelligence is normal. The psychosexual development is unmistakably female in regard to behavior, outlook, and maternal instincts.

The major complication of undescended testes in this disorder as in other forms of cryptorchidism (Chap. 330) is the development of tumors. Since affected individuals undergo a normal pubertal growth spurt and feminize successfully at the time of expected puberty and since testicular tumors rarely develop until after puberty in patients with intraabdominal testes, it is usual to delay castration until after the time of expected puberty. Surgical intervention is indicated prepubertally if the testes are present in the inguinal region or the labia majora and result in discomfort or hernia formation. (If hernia repair is indicated prepubertally most physicians prefer to remove the testes at the same time so as to limit the number of operative procedures.) If the testes are removed prepubertally, estrogen therapy is required at the appropriate age to ensure normal growth and breast development. When castration is performed postpubertally menopausal symptoms and other evidences of estrogen withdrawal supervene, and suitable estrogen replacement is indicated (see Chap. 331).

Incomplete testicular feminization is about one-tenth as frequent as the complete form. In the incomplete disorder there is a minor virilization of the external genitalia (partial fusion of the labioscrotal folds and some degree of clitoromegaly), normal pubic hair, and some virilization as well as feminization at the time of expected puberty. The vagina is short and blind-ending, but in contrast to the complete form, the wolffian duct derivatives are often partially developed. The family history is usually uninformative, but in some instances multiple family members are affected in a pattern compatible with X-linkage. The management of patients with the complete and incomplete forms of testicular feminization differs. Since patients with the incomplete disorder virilize at the time of expected puberty, gonadectomy should be performed before the expected time of puberty in prepubertal patients with clitoromegaly or posterior labial fusion.

Reifenstein syndrome is the term applied to forms of incomplete male pseudohermaphroditism initially described by a number of eponyms (Reifenstein syndrome, Gilbert-Dreyfus syndrome, Lubs syndrome). Each of these phenotypes was originally assumed to be a distinct entity, but since families have now been described in which affected members exhibit variable manifestations that span the phenotypes described under these terms, these syndromes are now thought to constitute variable manifestations of a single mutation. The most common phenotype is a man with perineoscrotal hypospadias and gynecomastia, but the spectrum of defective virilization in such families ranges from men with azoospermia to phenotypic women with pseudovaginas. Axillary and pubic hair are normal, but chest and facial hair are minimal. Cryptorchidism is common, the testes are small, and azoospermia is present. Some have defects in wolffian duct derivatives such as absence or hypoplasia of the vas deferens. Since the psychological development in most is unequivocally male, the hypospadias and cryptorchidism should be corrected surgically. The only successful form of treatment of the gynecomastia is surgical removal.

The *infertile male syndrome* is the most common disorder of the androgen receptor and is not actually a form of male pseudohermaphroditism. Some such individuals are minimally affected subjects in families with Reifenstein syndrome with only azoospermia as a manifestation of the receptor abnormality. More commonly, the individuals present with male infertility and have negative family histories; indeed a disorder of the androgen receptor may be present in a fifth or more of men with idiopathic azoospermia. There is no treatment for the infertility in any of these disorders.

Pathophysiology. The karyotype is 46,XY, and the mutant gene is X-linked. The frequency of a positive family history varies from about two-thirds of patients with testicular feminization and Reifen-

Breast	Endocrine profile relative to normal male		
	Testosterone production	Estrogen production	LH
Usually male	Normal to decreased	Variable	High
Male	Normal	Normal	Normal or increased
Female	High	High	High
Female	High	High	High
Female	High	High	High
Usually male	Normal or high	Normal or high	Normal or high
Variable	Normal or high	Normal or high	Normal or high
Male	Normal	Normal	Normal

stein syndrome to only occasional patients with the infertile male syndrome. The patients with a negative family history are believed to be the result of new mutations.

Hormone dynamics are similar in all disorders of the androgen receptor. Plasma testosterone levels and rates of testosterone production by the testes are normal or higher than normal. The elevated rate of testosterone production is caused by the high mean plasma level of LH, which in turn is due to defective feedback regulation caused by resistance to the action of androgen at the hypothalamic-pituitary level. Elevated LH concentration is probably responsible also for the increased estrogen production by the testes (see Chap. 330). (In normal men most estrogen is derived from peripheral formation from circulating androgens, but when plasma LH is elevated the testes secrete significant amounts of estrogen into the circulation.) Thus, resistance to the feedback regulation of LH secretion by circulating androgen results in elevated plasma LH levels, and this in turn results in the enhanced secretion of both testosterone and estradiol by the testes. Gonadotropin levels rise even higher (and menopausal symptoms may develop) when the testes are removed, indicating that gonadotropin secretion is under partial regulatory control. Presumably, in the steady state and in the absence of an androgen effect, estrogen alone regulates LH secretion, a control that is purchased at the expense of an elevated plasma estrogen concentration for a male. The hormonal changes in the infertile male syndrome are similar to those in the other receptor disorders but less marked. Some men with this syndrome do not have an elevation of plasma LH or plasma testosterone.

Feminization in these disorders is the result of two interlocking phenomena. First, androgens and estrogens have antagonistic effects at the peripheral level, and virilization occurs in normal men when the ratio of androgen to estrogen is 100 to 1 or greater; in the absence of androgen action the cellular effect of estrogen is unopposed. Second, the production of estradiol is greater than that of the normal male (although less than that of the normal female). Variable degrees of androgen resistance coupled with variably enhanced estradiol production result in different degrees of defective virilization and enhanced feminization in the four clinical syndromes.

Each of these four syndromes is the result of an abnormality of the androgen receptor. Initially fibroblasts cultured from the skin of some subjects with complete testicular feminization were shown to have a near absence of high-affinity dihydrotestosterone binding. Subsequently, other individuals with complete testicular feminization as well as subjects with incomplete testicular feminization, Reifenstein syndrome, and the infertile male syndrome have been found to have either a decreased amount of an apparently normal receptor or a qualitatively abnormal androgen receptor.

Receptor-positive resistance. A category of androgen resistance that does not appear to involve either the 5α-reductase or the androgen receptor was first identified in a family with the syndrome of testicular feminization. Subsequent patients have been described with a variety of phenotypes ranging from incomplete testicular feminization to findings similar to those in the Reifenstein syndrome. The hormonal profile is similar to that seen in the receptor disorders. The site of the molecular abnormality in these patients is unclear. It could be due to defects of the androgen receptor too subtle to be detected by the usual assay. If the defect is truly distal to the receptor, there could be failure of generation of specific messenger RNA or an abnormality of RNA processing. Indeed, the disorder may represent a heterogeneous group of molecular abnormalities. Management depends on the phenotype.

Persistent müllerian duct syndrome

Men with this disorder have normal penile development but have in addition bilateral fallopian tubes, a uterus, and an upper vagina, and variable development of the vas deferens. The subjects commonly present with inguinal hernias which contain the uterus, and cryptorchidism is common. Most have uninformative family histories, but several pairs of siblings have been described in whom the condition must be inherited either as an autosomal recessive or an X-linked recessive mutation. Because the external genitalia are well developed and the patients masculinize normally at puberty, it is assumed that during the critical stage of embryonic sexual differentiation the fetal testes produced a normal amount of androgen. However, müllerian regression does not occur for one of three possible reasons: failure of the fetal testis to produce müllerian-inhibiting substance, poor timing of the release of müllerian-inhibiting substance, or failure of the tissues to respond to this hormone. To minimize the chance of tumor development and to maintain virilization, a primary or staged orchiopexy should be performed. Malignancy in the uterus or vagina has not been described, and because the vasa deferentia are closely associated with the broad ligaments, the uterus and vagina should be left in place to avoid disruption of the vasa deferentia during removal and consequently to preserve possible fertility.

Developmental defects of the male genitalia

HYPOSPADIAS Hypospadias is a congenital anomaly in which the urethra terminates in an abnormal position along the midline of the ventral surface of the penis at some site between the normal urethral meatus and the perineum. This malformation is often associated with some degree of ventral contraction and bowing of the penis (chordee). The disorder occurs in 0.5 to 0.8 percent of male births in the United States. It is common to categorize hypospadias as glandular (involving the glans penis), penile, or perineoscrotal. Since penile development is mediated by androgens, it is assumed that hypospadias results from some defect in earlier androgen formation or androgen action during embryogenesis. Indeed hypospadias occurs in most disorders of male sexual differentiation. A rare cause of hypospadias is maternal ingestion of progestational agents early in pregnancy. However, the known causes (single gene defects, chromosomal abnormalities, and maternal drug ingestion) at best can account for only about one-fourth of cases, and the etiology of most remains unknown. The management is surgical.

CRYPTORCHIDISM The normal descent of the testis is perhaps the most poorly understood portion of male sexual differentiation, both in regard to the nature of the forces that result in the movement and to the hormonal factors that regulate the process. In anatomic terms testicular descent can be divided into three phases: (1) transabdominal movement of the testis from its site of origin above the kidney to the inguinal ring, (2) formation of the opening in the inguinal canal (processus vaginalis) through which the testis exits the abdominal cavity, and (3) actual movement of the testis through the inguinal canal to its permanent site in the scrotum. This entire process occurs over a 6- to 7-month period during gestation, beginning at about the sixth week and not completed in some normal individuals until after birth. Whatever its involvement, androgen is probably not the sole hormone responsible for normal descent. Failure of any of the above anatomic events can be responsible for the failure of descent of one or both testes that occurs in 3 percent of full-term males and 30 percent of premature male infants. Cryptorchidism can be classified as intraabdominal, retractile (intermittently in the groin), obstructed (permanently in the groin), and high scrotal. Most are retractile and descend permanently by 6 weeks to 3 months of age so that the incidence of failure of descent in late teenagers is only 0.6 to 0.7 percent. It is this latter category that requires intervention.

The cryptorchid testis functions poorly after puberty, but the extent to which maldescent is the result of an abnormality of the testis or the cause of abnormal function is unknown. Two general theories have been advanced as to the etiology—inadequate intraabdominal pressure and deficient endocrine function of the testis either because of deficient testosterone synthesis or inadequate formation of müllerian-inhibiting substance. Indeed, hereditary defects that result in inadequate development of intraabdominal pressure or inadequate development of the testes themselves can cause cryptorchidism. As is true for hypospadias, however, the known causes of cryptorchidism constitute only a small fraction of the cases, and the etiology in most remains to be identified. Two complications of cryptorchidism are important; spermatogenesis cannot occur at the temperature of the abdominal cavity, and it is therefore necessary to correct the process as early as possible to allow possible fertility. However, the fact that infertility is common in men who have been treated for unilateral as well as bilateral cryptorchidism suggests that maldescent is usually the consequence rather than the cause of the testicular malfunction. There is also a greater frequency of malignancy in undescended testis, and all should be surgically corrected for this reason (see Chap. 297).

REFERENCES

DE LA CHAPELLE A: The etiology of maleness in XX men. Hum Genet 58:105, 1981

DONAHOE PK et al: Mixed gonadal dysgenesis, pathogenesis and management. J Pediatr Surg 14:287, 1979

EDMAN CD et al: Embryonic testicular regression: A clinical spectrum of XY agonadal individuals. Obstet Gynecol 49:208, 1977

GEORGE FW, WILSON JD: Sexual differentiation, in *Campbell's Textbook of Urology*, 5th ed, PC Walsh et al (eds). Philadelphia, Saunders, 1986, pp 1804–1818

GORDON DL et al: Pathologic testicular findings in Klinefelter's syndrome. 47,XXY vs 46,XY/47,XXY. Arch Intern Med 130:726, 1972

GRIFFIN JE et al: Congenital absence of the vagina. The Mayer-Rokitansky-Kuster-Hauser syndrome. Ann Intern Med 85:224, 1976

———, WILSON JD: Disorder of sexual differentiation, in *Campbell's Textbook of Urology*, 5th ed, PC Walsh et al (eds). Philadelphia, Saunders, 1986, pp 1819–1855

GRUMBACH MM, CONTE FA: Disorders of sexual differentiation, in *Williams' Textbook of Endocrinology*, 7th ed, JD Wilson, DW Foster (eds). Philadelphia, Saunders, 1985, pp 312–401

LEONARD JM et al: The classification of Klinefelter's syndrome, in *Genetic Mechanism of Sexual Development*, HL Vallet, IH Porter (eds). New York, Academic, 1979

McDONOUGH PG et al: Phenotypic and cytogenetic findings in eighty-two patients with ovarian failure-changing trends. Fertil Steril 28:638, 1977

NEW M et al: Congenital adrenal hyperplasia and related conditions, in *Metabolic Basis of Inherited Disease*, 5th ed, JB Stanbury et al (eds). New York, McGraw-Hill, 1983, pp 973–1000

SIMPSON JL: *Disorders of Sexual Differentiation*. New York, Academic, 1976, p 466

———: Gonadal dysgenesis and sex chromosome abnormalities: Phenotypic-karyotypic correlations, in *Genetic Mechanisms of Sexual Development*, HL Vallet, IH Porter (eds). New York, Academic, 1979

——— et al: XY gonadal dysgenesis: Genetic heterogeneity based upon clinical observations, H-Y antigen status and segregation analysis. Hum Genet 58:91, 1981

VAN NIEKERK WA: True hermaphroditism. Pediatr Adolesc Endocrinol 8:80, 1981

WILSON JD et al: The androgen resistance syndromes: 5α-Reductase deficiency, testicular feminization and related disorders, in *The Metabolic Basis of Inherited Disease*, 5th ed, JB Stanbury et al (eds). New York, McGraw-Hill, 1983, pp 1001–1026

ZAH W et al: Mixed gonadal dysgenesis. A case report and review of the world literature. Acta Endocrinol Suppl 197:3, 1975

334   DISORDERS AFFECTING MULTIPLE ENDOCRINE SYSTEMS

R. NEIL SCHIMKE

Multiple endocrine gland hyper- or hypofunction can result from mechanisms other than a primary abnormality in the hypothalamic-pituitary axis. While not common, certain of the conditions that affect multiple endocrine systems are inherited and thus have significance out of proportion to their frequency.

SYNDROMES WITH MULTISYSTEM HYPERFUNCTION

MULTIPLE ENDOCRINE NEOPLASIA, TYPE I (MEN I)   This disorder, also termed the *Wermer syndrome,* comprises tumors or hyperplasia of the parathyroids, pancreatic islet cells, pituitary, adrenal cortex, and thyroid. The clinical presentation is variable, depending on which of the potentially affected glands is hyperfunctioning at the time of diagnosis. About two-thirds of patients have adenomas of two or more endocrine systems, and one-fifth develop tumors of three or more systems.

The majority of affected subjects present with one of the following problems: (1) peptic ulcer and its complications, (2) hypoglycemia, (3) hypercalcemia and/or nephrocalcinosis, (4) complaints referable

to pituitary dysfunction such as headaches, visual field defects, and secondary amenorrhea, and (5) multiple lipomas of the skin. A minority (probably <10 percent) come to medical attention with acromegaly, Cushing's syndrome, nonfunctional thyroid adenomas, hyperthyroidism, hepatomegaly (due to metastatic liver disease), or flushing (associated with the carcinoid syndrome).

Parathyroid involvement in MEN I may be asymptomatic for prolonged periods, although most patients eventually show some signs of hyperparathyroidism. Tumors of the islet cells may elaborate excessive insulin or gastrin. Insulinomas cause hypoglycemia (Chap. 329), whereas excess gastrin secretion causes the Zollinger-Ellison syndrome with its multifocal or atypically located ulcers and massive hypersecretion of gastric acid. Symptoms may be identical with those of ordinary peptic ulcer, but there is a higher incidence of complications, including perforation, bleeding, and obstruction. Diarrhea is frequent, often with steatorrhea. Radiographic findings include giant gastric rugae, duodenal nodularity, ectopic ulcers in the esophagus, lower duodenum, and jejunum, and intestinal hyperperistalsis. Associated endocrine abnormalities consistent with the MEN syndrome are present in over one-quarter of patients with the Zollinger-Ellison syndrome and in half of the first-degree relatives of such patients. MEN I should be considered in a patient with the Zollinger-Ellison syndrome even when no other endocrine abnormalities are apparent.

Islet-cell tumors may also produce glucagon, vasoactive intestinal polypeptide (VIP), prostaglandins, adrenocorticotropic hormone (ACTH), parathyroid hormone, antidiuretic hormone (ADH), serotonin, somatostatin, calcitonin, and pancreatic polypeptide (also see Chap. 329). Glucagonomas cause hyperglycemia, weight loss, stomatitis, and a peculiar skin rash called *necrotizing migratory erythema*. VIP and prostaglandins have been implicated in the watery diarrhea (pancreatic cholera) syndrome sometimes seen in MEN I. Cushing's syndrome may be due to an adrenal adenoma or may occur as a consequence of ectopic ACTH production by an islet tumor or a thymic carcinoid. Some adrenal adenomas produce aldosterone or adrenal androgens. Involvement of the thyroid gland is uncommon in MEN I, but goiter, simple adenoma, and thyroiditis have all been reported. Other features of MEN I include small-intestinal and bronchial carcinoid tumors, schwannomas, thymomas, multiple lipomas, inclusion cysts, and cutaneous leiomyomas.

Patients with MEN I may develop symptoms at any age, but the condition presents rarely in childhood or after the age of 60. Affected individuals may demonstrate multiple endocrine system involvement simultaneously, or months to years may elapse between the discovery of one adenoma and the appearance of the next. Once the diagnosis is established, the patient must be surveyed periodically for appearance of new facets of the syndrome. By the same token, all first-degree relatives should be studied. A reasonable approach for screening relatives at risk is as follows: (1) review history for symptoms of peptic ulcer disease, hypoglycemia, renal calculi, lipomas, or hypopituitarism; (2) examine for multiple lipomas; (3) assay serum calcium, phosphorus, prolactin, and gastrin. Upper gastrointestinal series and sella turcica x-rays have proved of no value as screening tests. Serum pancreatic polypeptide determinations may be useful in centers where the assay is available.

The fundamental lesion in MEN I is unknown. Some have considered the basic abnormality to be in the islet cells with their extensive capability for hormone synthesis, attributing changes in the other glands to secondary effects of islet hormone hypersecretion. Others have classified MEN I as a neurocrestopathy implicating faulty differentiation or regulation of the embryonic neural crest, which is the anlage of at least part of the endocrine system. The endocrine components of the neural crest have been classified into a subsystem of APUD cells, so named because of their capacity for amine precursor uptake and decarboxylation. The evidence supporting the contention that all APUD cells are derived from neural crest is not strong; instead, cells of diverse origin probably develop similar characteristics; i.e., they represent a structural-functional convergence.

The pituitary and parathyroid tumors in MEN I are usually benign, but pancreatic tumors are frequently malignant. Surgical removal of the affected gland is the usual therapy, although standard radiation techniques may be employed for the pituitary tumors, and homergocryptine is useful in prolactinomas. Hyperparathyroidism may be due to a single adenoma, but diffuse hyperplasia of more than one gland is more common. In some centers selective venous catheterization with measurement of serum parathyroid hormone levels can be used to differentiate between those possibilities. Since new adenomas may arise in normal glands left after removal of an adenoma (and since second operations are difficult because of scar formation), some have advocated removal of all the parathyroid glands with transplantation of extirpated fragments into the thigh or forearm, where they can be easily removed should hyperparathyroidism recur. Successful transplantation obviates the need for long-term therapy of hypoparathyroidism. In hypergastrinemia due to islet-cell lesions, total gastrectomy has been used to prevent recurrent peptic ulcers, and in rare cases distant metastases have regressed after this procedure. Histamine-2-receptor antagonists are efficacious in controlling the hyperacidity and diarrhea seen with hypergastrinemia.

MULTIPLE ENDOCRINE NEOPLASIA, TYPE II (MEN II OR IIA)

MEN II, also known as the *Sipple syndrome,* consists of pheochromocytoma (frequently bilateral and occasionally extraadrenal), medullary thyroid carcinoma (MTC) and, in about half of the reported cases, parathyroid hyperplasia. MEN II can be related more directly to abnormal neural crest development than can MEN I, since both the adrenal medulla and the parafollicular or C cells of the thyroid originate in neural crest. However, there is no evidence that the parenchymal component of the parathyroid glands are so derived. The parafollicular cell elaborates calcitonin, the primary marker of medullary carcinoma of the thyroid. MTC is not common, comprising less than 10 percent of thyroid malignancies. At least 10 percent of MTC cases are familial, usually appearing as a component of MEN II or MEN III (see below). Medullary carcinoma may also occur in families without other associated endocrine dysfunction; this form is also transmitted as an autosomal dominant trait. MTC may present as a thyroidal mass or be clinically silent and undetectable by palpation or radioiodine scanning. The diagnosis is usually established by immunoassay of serum calcitonin, provided ectopic sites of calcitonin production can be excluded, e.g., breast, lung, and pancreatic islet-cell tumors. Occasionally, basal serum calcitonin levels are borderline in at-risk individuals, and measurement of plasma levels after calcium-pentagastrin infusion can be used to establish the diagnosis. MTC may on occasion secrete substances other than calcitonin, including ACTH, prolactin, serotonin, VIP, histamine, and various prostaglandins, resulting in a confusing array of symptoms.

The pheochromocytoma of MEN II may produce the classic signs of catecholamine excess as described in Chap. 326 or be asymptomatic. Approximately 7 percent of patients who present with pheochromocytomas also have MTC. Symptoms of hyperparathyroidism rarely bring the patient with MEN II to initial clinical attention.

Examination of cells from both the MTC and the pheochromocytoma components of MEN II using X-linked gene markers has led to the conclusion that the inherited defect produces multiple clones of abnormal cells; tumors then develop from a second mutation in the abnormal clone, accounting for the appearance of varying clinical patterns. Other tumors in MEN II include gliomas, glioblastomas, and meningiomas, all of which may be derived from the neural crest.

The age of the patient at the time of diagnosis varies from 2 to 67 years. C-Cell hyperplasia of the thyroid may precede development of malignancy by many years, making early screening studies for calcitonin elevation mandatory in all family members at risk. The only effective therapy for MTC is surgical removal of the entire thyroid, as the tumor is probably always multifocal in origin. Limited node dissection is often indicated since the cancer may progress slowly despite an aggressive histologic appearance, and prolonged survival is seen in patients with known metastatic disease. Serum calcitonin levels can be used to assess completeness of surgical

removal of the tumor and in concert with selective venous catheterization may be utilized to locate distant metastases that are surgically accessible. Neither standard radioiodine nor x-ray therapy is helpful in disseminated medullary thyroid cancer, and chemotherapy has been of limited value (see Chap. 324). The pheochromocytomas are usually benign and are also treated surgically. Unresectable malignant pheochromocytoma requires long-term sympathetic blockade. A new radiopharmaceutical, *meta*-iodobenzyl guanidine, shows promise as both a diagnostic and a therapeutic agent.

MULTIPLE ENDOCRINE NEOPLASIA, TYPE III (MEN III OR IIB)

MEN III also consists of medullary thyroid carcinoma and pheochromocytoma, but affected individuals have striking dysmorphic features such as neuromas of the conjunctival, labial, and buccal mucosa, the tongue, the larynx, and the gastrointestinal tract; hence the alternate designation of the condition as the *mucosal neuroma syndrome.* Other physical findings include enlarged corneal nerves, "blubbery" lips, soft-tissue prognathism, and a habitus resembling that seen in the Marfan syndrome with hypotonia, lax joints, kyphoscoliosis, genu valgus, and pes cavus. The patients may have café au lait spots or a diffuse lentiginous type of skin pigmentation along with cutaneous neuromas or neurofibromas. Megacolon may occur.

MEN III and MEN II appear to be distinct syndromes. For example, both parathyroid hyperplasia and production of hormones other than calcitonin by MTC are rare in MEN III. The mean survival of patients with MEN III is around 30 years compared with 60 years for those with MEN II, suggesting a more malignant course in the former disorder, although histologically the thyroid tumors appear to be identical. As with MEN II treatment of the medullary carcinoma is surgical. The unusual physical features of MEN III should immediately suggest the diagnosis of underlying thyroid malignancy. MTC has been documented in asymptomatic children with MEN III, and C-cell hyperplasia has been found at operation as early as 15 months of age. Clinically, the associated pheochromocytomas behave as expected (Chap. 326).

McCUNE-ALBRIGHT SYNDROME

This condition is characterized by the triad of polyostotic fibrous dysplasia, café au lait spots, and isosexual precocity, the latter occurring predominantly but not exclusively in females. The isosexual precocity may be hypothalamic in origin, but gonadotropin-independent ovarian function has been implicated in some cases (see Chap. 331). Cushing's syndrome, gigantism or acromegaly, and hyperprolactinemia may also occur in affected patients. The Cushing's syndrome may result from abnormal ACTH production or adrenal adenomas. Nodular toxic goiter and pheochromocytoma have also been reported. The bone lesion resembles that seen in hyperparathyroidism, and parathyroid hyperplasia has been described histologically but not clinically. The condition is usually sporadic, but pedigrees compatible with autosomal dominant inheritance have been seen. The cause of the condition is unknown (see Chap. 339).

SYNDROMES WITH MULTISYSTEM HYPOFUNCTION

POLYGLANDULAR DEFICIENCY SYNDROME (SCHMIDT SYNDROME)

(See also Chaps. 324 and 325) The prototype of a polyglandular deficiency state is the Schmidt syndrome, originally described as the presence of both Addison's disease and lymphocytic thyroiditis in a single patient. This syndrome has subsequently been expanded to include any combination of adrenal insufficiency, lymphocytic thyroiditis, hypoparathyroidism, and gonadal failure. Diabetes mellitus is a frequent accompaniment. The manifestations may be so extensive as to simulate panhypopituitarism; rarely, true pituitary deficiency has been described. The first evidence of endocrinopathy generally appears in adult life. The most significant laboratory feature, in addition to the low levels of circulating hormones, is the presence of antibodies to one or more endocrine glands. The antibodies may be directed against a clinically normal gland, but with time hypofunction usually supervenes. Additional evidence for an immune pathogenesis is provided by the increased frequency of antibodies to parietal cells of the stomach, with or without overt achlorhydria or pernicious anemia, and the presence of other disorders felt to have an autoimmune basis such as sprue, vitiligo, myasthenia gravis, pure red cell aplasia, and antibody-mediated immunoglobulin A deficiency. Hyperthyroidism may complicate the clinical picture.

The majority of affected individuals are female, and most cases are sporadic. A few reports have noted multiple affected family members, suggesting a genetic basis. Members of these families who show no endocrine disability frequently have serologic abnormalities indicative of a disturbance in immune function. Many of the component endocrine disorders in this syndrome are associated with the presence of certain HLA antigens, notably HLA-B8 and -Dw3 (in white populations). Other racial groups show different associations, e.g., hyperthyroidism with HLA-Bw35 in the Japanese. Because of this association it has been postulated that the basic lesion may reside in a mutation of an inherited immunologic mechanism. For example, a selective immunodeficient state might render an individual unduly susceptible to certain environmental antigens (e.g., viruses) that have a predilection for the endocrine system. Cell lysis or damage could result in release of intracellular contents and lead to development of autoantibodies. Such autoantibodies would not necessarily be pathogenic but could represent secondary phenomena, important as markers of potential clinical disease. Alternatively, the defect could reside in a genetically determined defect in suppressor T cells and with consequent inadequate suppression of antibody synthesis. The syndrome is probably etiologically heterogeneous, and several pathogenetic mechanisms may be operative. At present, treatment is confined to providing hormone replacement.

CANDIDIASIS-ENDOCRINOPATHY SYNDROME An autoimmune pathogenesis has also been invoked in the candidiasis-endocrinopathy syndrome. Features that differentiate this condition from the Schmidt syndrome include childhood onset and extensive mucocutaneous monilial infection that becomes evident shortly after birth. Hypoparathyroidism is common, and adrenal insufficiency may develop acutely. Diabetes is rare. Organ-specific antibodies against a variety of endocrine glands may be detected early, and pernicious anemia, sprue, chronic active hepatitis, and membranoproliferative glomerulonephritis have been seen. Defective cellular immunity to *Candida albicans* is present; some have more generalized anergy. A cause-and-effect relationship between the monilial infection and the endocrinopathy has not been established. The disorder has occurred in sibs, occasionally from consanguineous unions, and the disease may be inherited as an autosomal recessive trait. No association with the HLA system has been demonstrated, but affected individuals may have a deficiency of immunoglobulin A and hypergammaglobulinemia. Suppressor T-cell function may be defective, but the immune profile can be variable even in sibs. The fungal infection is usually refractory to conventional chemotherapeutic drugs, although partial remission has been reported with a combination of ketoconazole and transfer factor. Amelioration of the candidiasis in no way affects the endocrinopathy, and conventional replacement therapy is required.

LIPODYSTROPHIC SYNDROMES The lipodystrophic syndromes are described in Chap. 318. Insulin-resistant diabetes mellitus is common and may be associated with elevated growth hormone levels and with an increased incidence of polycystic disease of the ovaries, acromegaly, and Cushing's disease.

TABLE 334-1 Disorders with common polyglandular manifestations

Condition	Clinical feature	Type of endocrine involvement						Inheritance
		Hypothalamic-pituitary	Thyroid	Parathyroid	Pancreas	Adrenal	Gonads	
Ataxia-telangiectasia	Early ataxia Oculocutaneous telangiectasia Immunologic deficiency	?Variably decreased pituitary reserve			Diabetes mellitus	Cortical hypoplasia	Dysgenetic ovaries; gonadoblastomas later	Autosomal recessive
Pseudohypoparathyroidism	Short stature Short metacarpals and metatarsals Round facies Ectopic calcification	Variable deficiency of all pituitary hormones, including prolactin	Hypo- or hyperthyroidism	Elevated parathyroid hormone levels with either normo- or hypocalcemia	Diabetes mellitus		Ovarian failure	Probable X-linked dominant; heterogeneous
Myotonic dystrophy	Muscular dystrophy Premature baldness Mental retardation	Gonadotropin, growth hormone abnormalities, related to central integrative defect (?)	Hypothyroidism		Diabetes mellitus		Primary failure	Autosomal dominant
Noonan syndrome	Short stature Ptosis Webbed neck Pulmonary stenosis	Gonadotropin deficiency	Thyroiditis				Primary failure	Autosomal dominant
Fanconi syndrome	Short stature Bone marrow hypoplasia Abnormal skin pigmentation Radius malformations	Panhypopituitarism			Diabetes mellitus	Adrenal atrophy	Gonadal atrophy	Autosomal recessive
Werner syndrome	Premature aging of all organ systems Atrophic skin Cataracts Early osteoporosis		Papillary carcinoma		Diabetes mellitus		Gonadal atrophy	Autosomal recessive

DIABETES MELLITUS, DIABETES INSIPIDUS, AND OPTIC ATRO-PHY   This clinical triad has been noted in sibs and likely constitutes a rare autosomal recessive defect. Nerve deafness, usually mild, may also occur. The diabetes mellitus is of the early-onset insulin-dependent type. The diabetes insipidus usually appears prior to age 20. The varying manifestations are difficult to reconcile, and treatment requires replacement of the missing hormones.

OBESITY-HYPOGONADISM SYNDROMES   A number of seemingly discrete entities share obesity, generally with frank diabetes mellitus, and hypogonadism that may be either primary or secondary. The *Biedl-Bardet syndrome* features retinitis pigmentosa, polydactyly, mental retardation, and renal anomalies along with obesity, hypogonadotropic hypogonadism, and in some patients, diabetes mellitus. There is sufficient resemblance between this syndrome and the *Alström syndrome* (retinitis pigmentosa, nerve deafness, diabetes mellitus, and primary gonadal failure) to cause frequent diagnostic confusion. Both are autosomal recessive disorders. However, polydactyly and mental retardation do not occur in the Alström syndrome. A similar condition is the *Biemond syndrome* in which obesity, diabetes mellitus, secondary hypogonadism, and postaxial polydactyly are combined with iris colobomata rather than pigmentary retinopathy. Patients with the *Prader-Willi syndrome* (obesity, hypogonadism, hypotonia, mental retardation) also have diabetes mellitus of the maturity-onset type. A genetic basis has not been established for the Biemond or the Prader-Willi syndromes. A small deletion of chromosome 15 is present in some patients with the latter disorder.

CHROMOSOMAL DISORDERS WITH ENDOCRINE DEFICIENCY (See also Chaps. 60 and 333)   Patients with Turner syndrome have hypogonadism and an increased incidence of diabetes mellitus and thyroiditis, thought to be on an autoimmune basis. In the Klinefelter syndrome an increased frequency of diabetes mellitus may occur along with gonadal failure. In the Down syndrome hypogonadism is probably universal in males, and menstrual irregularities and early menopause are common in women; in addition, increased prevalences of lymphocytic thyroiditis and diabetes mellitus have been reported.

OTHER CONDITIONS WITH MULTISYSTEM MANIFESTATIONS   There are a number of other rare conditions in which involvement of more than one endocrine gland has been recorded often enough to constitute a significant facet of the syndrome. Some, like neurofibromatosis (von Recklinghausen's disease) and tuberous sclerosis, may show either hypo- or hyperfunction of endocrine glands because of interference with central regulatory mechanisms caused by the brain tumors characteristic of the diseases. By the same token, pheochromocytomas may occur in neurofibromatosis because the adrenal medulla is derived from the same embryonic source.

Table 334-1 lists some conditions in which disorders of multiple endocrine systems have been seen. It is noteworthy that both primary and secondary failures have been reported within the diagnostic confines of the same syndrome. For example, both gonadotropin deficiency and primary testicular atrophy have been documented in patients with the Noonan syndrome and in unaffected members of the same families. Whenever a clinical condition like diabetes mellitus occurs in such distinct entities as myotonic dystrophy and ataxia-telangiectasia, the molecular mechanisms underlying the disease are probably heterogeneous. A better understanding of the genetic defect would provide insight into the function of the endocrine system.

REFERENCES

FARID N, BEAR JC: The human major histocompatibility complex and endocrine disease. Endocr Rev 2:50, 1981

NEUFELD M et al: Two types of autoimmune Addison's disease associated with different polyglandular autoimmune syndromes. Medicine 60:355, 1981

RIMOIN DL, ROTTER JI: Genetic syndromes associated with diabetes mellitus and glucose intolerance, in *The Genetics of Diabetes Mellitus,* J Kobberling, R Tattersall (eds). New York, Academic, 1982, pp 149–181

SCHIMKE RN: Syndromes with multiple endocrine gland involvement. Prog Med Genet 3:143, 1979

————: Genetic aspects of multiple endocrine neoplasia. Ann Rev Med 35:25, 1984

YAMAGUCHI K et al: Multiple endocrine neoplasia type I. Clin Endocrinol Metab 9:261, 1980

335 CALCIUM, PHOSPHORUS, AND BONE METABOLISM: CALCIUM-REGULATING HORMONES

MICHAEL F. HOLICK / STEPHEN M. KRANE /
JOHN T. POTTS, JR.

BONE STRUCTURE AND METABOLISM (See also Chap. 337) Bone is a dynamic tissue, constantly remodeling itself throughout life. The skeleton is highly vascular and receives about 10 percent of the cardiac output. The arrangement of compact and cancellous bone provides a combination of strength and density suitable for mobility. In addition, bone provides calcium, magnesium, phosphorus, sodium, and other ions necessary for the support of homeostatic functions.

The properties of bone are a function of its extracellular components. The structure consists of a solid mineral phase in close association with an organic matrix of which 90 to 95 percent is type I collagen (see Chap. 319). The noncollagenous portion of the organic matrix contains proteins derived from serum (albumin and α_2-HS glycoproteins), an α-carboxyglutamic acid (GLA)–containing protein (called *bone GLA-protein* or *osteocalcin*), a glycoprotein called *osteonectin*, a bone proteoglycan, and other glycoproteins, phosphoproteins, and sialoproteins. Some of these proteins may function in initiating mineralization and in binding of the mineral phase to the matrix. The mineral phase is made up of calcium and phosphate, best characterized as a poorly crystalline hydroxyapatite, although the calcium/phosphate molar ratio is less than the 1.67 of hydroxyapatite [empiric formula, $Ca_{10}(PO_4)_6(OH)_2$]. In addition, other ions are present, predominantly in the surface layers. The mineral phase of bone is deposited in intimate relation to the collagen fibrils and is found largely in specific locations within the "holes" of the collagen fibrils that result from the manner in which the collagen molecules are packed. This architectural organization of mineral and matrix results in a two-phase material uniquely suited to withstand mechanical stresses. The formation and the localization of the inorganic phase are probably determined in part by the organic matrix.

Bone is formed by cells of mesenchymal origin that synthesize and secrete the organic matrix. Mineralization of the matrix, particularly in *osteons* (haversian systems), begins soon after it is secreted (primary mineralization) but is not completed until after several weeks (secondary mineralization). As an *osteoblast* secretes matrix which is then mineralized, this cell becomes surrounded by matrix and becomes an *osteocyte,* still connected with its blood supply through a series of canaliculi. Resorption of bone is carried out mainly by *osteoclasts*. Osteoclasts are multinucleated cells formed by fusion of precursor cells derived from a hematopoietic stem cell related to the mononuclear phagocyte series. Resorption of bone takes place in scalloped spaces (Howship's lacunae) where the osteoclasts are attached to the bone matrix through a ring of contractile proteins (clear zone) and form a specialized ruffled border. Mineral and matrix are removed in this space where the ruffled border is folded and is in contact with the bone. Proteins such as a proton pump ATPase are found in the ruffled border membrane, which contributes to the production of a unique acid environment in the enclosed extracellular compartment and results in solubilization of the mineral phase. Osteoblasts are involved in synthesis and secretion of most of the organic matrix and regulate the mineralization of the matrix. The alkaline phosphatase of bone is localized to the osteoblasts. The active principle that eventually results in formation of bone has been termed *bone morphogenetic protein.* Additional factors can stimulate growth and/or matrix synthesis by osteoblast-related cells (several bone-derived growth factors, somatomedins, transforming growth factor beta).

In the embryo and in the growing child, bone develops either by remodeling and replacing previously calcified cartilage (endochondral bone formation), or it is formed without a cartilage matrix (intramembranous bone formation). New bone, whether in embryos or infants or that formed in adults during repair, has a relatively high ratio of cells to matrix and is characterized by coarse fiber bundles of collagen that are interlaced and randomly dispersed (woven bone). In adults, the more mature bone is organized with fiber bundles regularly arranged in parallel or concentric sheets (lamellar bone). In long bones, the lamellar bone is deposited in a concentric arrangement around blood vessels and forms the haversian systems. Growth in length of bones is dependent upon proliferation of cartilage cells and on the endochondral sequence at the growth plate. Growth in width and thickness is accomplished by formation of bone at the periosteal surface and by resorption at the endosteal surface with the rate of formation exceeding that of resorption. In adults, after the epiphyses close, growth in length and endochondral bone formation cease, except for some activity in the cartilage cells beneath the articular surface. However, even in adults, remodeling of bone (remodeling of haversian systems as well as trabecular bone) continues through life, as can be shown by microradiographic studies utilizing radioisotopes or fluorescence of tetracyclines fixed in bone in regions of new mineralization. Quantitative histomorphometric techniques demonstrate that newly forming surfaces are characterized by smooth character, by uptake of tetracycline, and by relatively low mineral density. Actively forming surfaces are covered by active osteoblasts. The osteoid seam that results from the relative lag in mineralization of the newly formed organic matrix is normally no greater than about 12 μm. An index of the rate of bone formation can be obtained by examination of undemineralized sections of bone biopsies obtained from individuals who have received tetracycline for two periods separated by a drug-free interval. The distance between the fluorescent bands on the sections reflects the new bone formed. Resorption areas are characterized by their irregular configurations and the presence of osteoclasts (Fig. 335-1). Resorption precedes formation and is more intense, but it does not persist as long as formation. In adults, approximately 4 percent of the surface of trabecular bone (such as iliac crest) is involved in active resorption, whereas 10 to 15 percent of trabecular surfaces is covered with osteoid. Kinetic studies using isotopes such as radioactive calcium (^{47}Ca) provide estimates that as much as 18 percent of the total skeletal calcium may be deposited and removed each year. Thus, bone is an active metabolizing tissue, with its cells dependent upon an intact blood supply. The remodeling of bone occurs in a manner somehow related to the continuous mechanical stresses to which it is subjected. Bone also serves as an important reservoir of mineral ions, particularly calcium, which are critical for a variety of processes.

The response of bone to injuries, such as fractures, infection, interruption of blood supply, and to expanding lesions is relatively limited. Dead bone must be resorbed, and new bone must be formed, a process carried out in association with new blood vessels growing into the involved area. In injuries that disrupt the organization of the tissue, such as a fracture in which apposition of fragments is poor and motion exists at the fracture site, the osteoprogenitor stromal cells differentiate into cells with functional capacities other than those of osteoblasts, and repair is accompanied by formation of varying amounts of fibrous tissue and cartilage. When there is good apposition with fixation and little motion at the fracture site, repair occurs predominantly by formation of new bone without other scar tissue. Remodeling of this bone occurs along lines of force determined by mechanical stresses that are somehow translated into biologic response.

Expanding lesions in bone, such as tumors, induce resorption at the surface in contact with the tumor. A bowing deformity causes increased new bone formation at the concave surface and resorption at the convex surface, all seemingly designed to produce the strongest mechanical structure. Even in a disorder as architecturally disruptive as Paget's disease, remodeling is dictated by mechanical forces. Thus, the plasticity of bone is due to the response of cells interacting with each other and with the environment.

Mechanisms of bone formation and resorption   Bone formation is an orderly process in which inorganic mineral is deposited in relation to an organic matrix. The mineral phase is composed of calcium and phosphorus, and the concentration of these ions in the plasma and extracellular fluid influences the rate at which the mineral phase is formed. In vitro, mineralization can proceed, and crystals of hydroxyapatite can grow at concentrations of calcium and phosphorus similar to those in an ultrafiltrate of plasma. However, the concentration of these ions at the sites of mineralization is unknown, and the cells involved (osteoblasts, osteocytes) may somehow regulate the local

FIGURE 335-1 *Schematic representation of bone remodeling surfaces in trabecular bone. Most bone surfaces in adults are involved in neither formation nor resorption. Such surfaces are usually smooth, have no osteoid seam, and are covered either by no visible cells or by flattened cells. Active formation surfaces are smooth and covered by osteoblasts which have an osteoid seam (clear), normally no thicker than 12 μm. The calcification front is located at the junction of the osteoid seam and mineralized bone (stippled). Inactive forming surfaces are not covered by osteoblasts but by only a few flattened cells. Active resorbing surfaces are irregular or scalloped and contain multinucleated osteoclasts. The latter are not seen on inactive resorbing surfaces.*

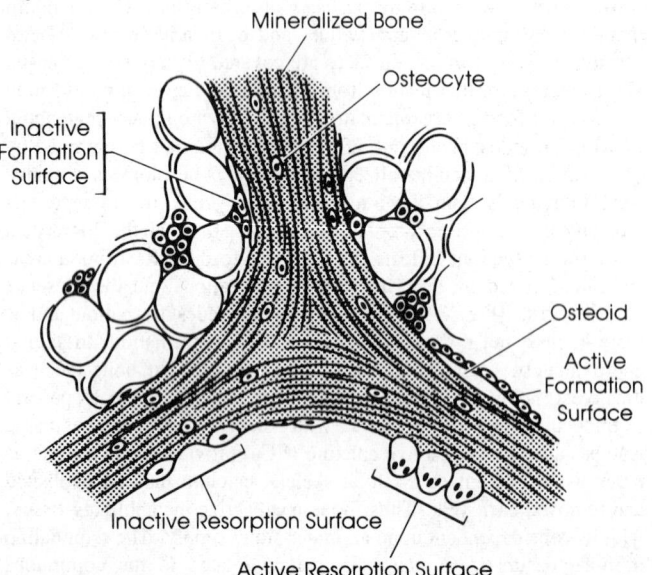

Mineralized Bone

Osteocyte

Inactive Formation Surface

Osteoid

Active Formation Surface

Inactive Resorption Surface

Active Resorption Surface

concentration of calcium, phosphorus, and other ions. Collagens from a variety of sources can catalyze the nucleation of a mineral phase of calcium and phosphorus from solutions of these ions, and the initial mineral phase is deposited in specific locations in the holes produced by the particular packing arrangement of the collagen molecules. The organization of collagen probably influences the amount and type of mineral phase formed in bone. There is one gene for each of the two α1 chains and the single α2 chain that make up type I collagen. The primary structures of type I collagen in skin and bone tissues are similar. There are differences, however, in posttranslational modifications of type I collagen such as hydroxylation, glycosylation, and the type, number, and distribution of intermolecular cross-links. In addition, the "holes" in the packing structure of the collagen are larger in normally mineralized collagen of bone and dentin than in unmineralized collagens such as tendon. The noncollagenous organic components such as the bone-GLA protein or osteonectin may also play a role in the formation of the mineral phase of bone. Alkaline phosphatase is a marker for osteoblasts, and cellular levels of this enzyme correlate with mineralization potential of osteoblasts. Although mineralization defects occur in individuals with decreased levels of alkaline phosphatase (hypophosphatasia), the function of alkaline phosphatase in the mineralization process is not completely understood. To explain how collagens from tissues that are normally not mineralized can catalyze nucleation of an inorganic phase from solutions similar to normal extracellular fluid, regulation of mineralization by inhibitory substances has been suggested. Inorganic pyrophosphate is a potent inhibitor of mineralization at concentrations below those necessary to bind calcium ions. Since alkaline phosphatase, present in osteoblasts and other cells, can catalyze the hydrolysis of inorganic pyrophosphate at neutral pH, this enzyme could regulate mineralization by controlling the concentrations of pyrophosphate. In addition, macromolecular inhibitors such as the proteoglycan aggregates may also influence the rate and extent of mineralization. In cartilage undergoing calcification, membrane-bound vesicles containing mineral are present outside the cells, and it has been suggested that this is the initial mineral phase.

In bone, the calcium phosphate solid phase at the inception of mineralization is brushite ($CaHPO_4 \cdot 2H_2O$). As mineralization progresses, the solid phase is a poorly crystalline hydroxyapatite with a relatively low (~ 1.2) calcium/phosphate molar ratio. With age and maturation, the degree of crystal perfection increases as does the calcium/phosphate ratio. Fluoride ions, when incorporated into the mineral phase, decrease the proportion of amorphous calcium phosphate and increase crystallinity.

There is a limit for the concentration of calcium and phosphorus ions in the extracellular fluid below which mineralization will not occur. A "solubility product" for bone mineral is difficult to calculate since the mineral phase itself is of variable composition and the true nature of species in solution governing this solubility product is not known. Nevertheless, when the concentrations of calcium and phosphorus in extracellular fluid are excessive, a mineral phase may be formed in areas that are not normally mineralized.

When bone is resorbed, calcium and phosphorus ions from the solid phase are released into the extracellular fluid, and the organic matrix is subsequently resorbed. It is not entirely clear how these processes occur. A decrease in pH, the presence of a chelating substance, and the operation of a cellular pump mechanism to shift the equilibrium between solids and solution may explain mineral release. The fact that bone resorption takes place in the region of the osteoclast adjacent to the bone surface, where the extracellular pH is low, lends support to the concept that this unique acid environment is required for solubilization of the bone mineral. Although osteoclasts are rich in tartrate-resistant acid phosphatase, a specific function for this enzyme has not been established. Whereas the activity of alkaline phosphatase in osteoblasts may be increased in serum when osteoblast number or function is increased, no such spillover from acid phosphatase is observed. The matrix is resorbed through the action of proteinases released by the osteoclasts. Matrix proteins in bone cannot be degraded, however, until the mineral phase is first removed. The rate of bone resorption is modulated by hormones such as parathyroid hormone and $1,25(OH)_2$ vitamin D and by local factors such as prostaglandins, heparin from mast cells, and various cytokines that augment the activity of osteoclasts already present or that enhance their differentiation from hematopoietic precursors. Some of these factors affect the osteoclast directly, and some act indirectly through effects on other cells such as osteoblasts or stromal fibroblasts. For example, parathyroid hormone receptors are present on osteoblasts but not on osteoclasts; therefore, parathyroid hormone effects on increasing bone resorption are mediated by the osteoblasts.

Interleukin 1, a monokine which increases bone resorption in vitro, also acts on the osteoclasts through osteoblasts or stromal fibroblasts. Interleukin 1 has been found to be an osteoclast-activating factor. Other such factors may be products of B or T lymphocytes. The bone-resorbing effects of ligands such as transforming growth factor alpha may in some bones be mediated through stimulation of prostaglandin synthesis and release. On the other hand, a major inhibitor of bone resorption, calcitonin, acts directly through receptors on osteoclasts. The cellular site of action of other inhibitors of bone resorption such as interferon gamma has not yet been elucidated.

CALCIUM METABOLISM   There is about 1 to 2 kg calcium in the average adult human body, of which over 98 percent is in the skeleton. The calcium of the mineral phase at the surface of the crystals is in equilibrium with ions of the extracellular fluid, but only a minor proportion of the total calcium (about 0.5 percent) is exchangeable. The calcium in the extracellular fluid is critical for a variety of functions, and it is remarkably constant. In normal adults, the range of plasma concentration is 8.8 to 10.4 mg/dL (2.2 to 2.6 mM). The calcium in plasma is in three forms: as free ions, bound to plasma proteins, and, to a small extent, as diffusible complexes. The concentration of free calcium ions influences neuromuscular irritability and other cellular functions and is subjected to tight hormonal control, especially through parathyroid hormone, as described below. The concentration of serum proteins is an important factor in determining the concentration of calcium ions; most of the protein binding is to albumin. One formula that approximates the amount of calcium bound to proteins is

% protein-bound Ca = 8 × albumin (g/dL)

$$+ \; 2 \; \times \; \text{globulin (g/dL)} \; + \; 3$$

Another correction is to subtract 1 mg/dL from the serum calcium concentration for every 1.0 g/dL serum albumin lower than 4.0 g/dL. Thus the concentration of ultrafiltrable calcium is usually about half the total calcium. In most laboratories only total calcium is determined, and knowledge of the concentration of proteins is essential to estimate concentration of calcium ions. Free ions can be measured with the use of calcium-specific electrodes.

The concentration of calcium ions in the extracellular fluid is kept constant by the interaction of processes that constantly feed calcium into and withdraw calcium from the extracellular fluid. Calcium enters the plasma via absorption from the intestinal tract and by resorption of ions from the bone mineral. Calcium leaves the extracellular fluid via secretion into the gastrointestinal tract, urinary excretion, deposition in bone mineral, and, to a minor extent, via losses in sweat. Resorption and formation are usually tightly coupled, approximately 0.5 mg calcium entering and leaving the skeleton daily (Fig. 335-2).

The average diet in the United States provides about 0.6 to 1 g calcium daily, mostly in the form of dairy products. However, in adults less than half of the calcium in the diet is absorbed. Calcium absorption increases during periods of rapid growth in children, in pregnancy, and in lactation and decreases with advancing age. If adequate vitamin D is available and vitamin D metabolism is normal, more dietary calcium is absorbed (adaptation). Most of the calcium is absorbed in the proximal small intestine, and the efficiency of absorption decreases in the more distal intestinal segments. Both

active transport and diffusion-limited absorption are involved; the former is more important in the upper, and the latter is more important in the lower, intestine. Both are influenced by vitamin D through the action of its metabolites. All forms of calcium in the diet may not be equally absorbed; even with defined salts, calcium as the chloride is probably absorbed more efficiently than that in other preparations.

Calcium is also secreted into the lumen of the gastrointestinal tract. When isotopes of radioactive calcium are administered intravenously, radioactivity appears in the feces, making possible calculations of *endogenous fecal calcium* (Fig. 335-2). Higher estimates of calcium losses in intestinal juices have been made by other approaches. Secretion of calcium into the intestinal lumen is constant and independent of absorption. If calcium availability in the diet is low (less than 500 mg per day), positive calcium balance requires an efficiency of absorption greater than 30 to 40 percent if intestinal uptake is sufficient to exceed losses via intestinal secretion and to match calcium losses through renal calcium excretion.

The urinary calcium excretion of normal adults on average calcium intakes ranges between 100 and 400 mg per day. When the dietary calcium is below 200 mg daily, urinary calcium excretion is usually less than 200 mg per day. However, in most normal individuals the level of dietary intake over a wide range has relatively little effect on the urinary excretion of calcium. Hence, in individuals on diets low in calcium, this relative inefficiency of renal calcium conservation leads to negative calcium balance unless calcium absorption is maximally efficient (Fig. 335-2).

FIGURE 335-2   *Calcium homeostasis. Schematic illustration of calcium content of extracellular fluid (ECF) and bone as well as of diet and feces; magnitude of calcium flux per day as calculated by various methods is shown at sites of transport in intestine, kidney, and bone. Ranges of values shown are approximate and chosen to illustrate certain points discussed in text. In intestine, absorption efficiency varies inversely with dietary calcium (chronic adaptation). This is reflected in typical quantities absorbed and excreted in feces; with 0.5-g intake, 50 percent absorption is depicted to occur (0.25 g), but at 1.5 g only 30 percent (0.5 g). Endogenous fecal calcium, the 0.1 to 0.2 g secreted into the intestinal lumen daily, is constant and does not vary with calcium intake or absorption. Quantities of calcium depicted as filtered, reabsorbed, and excreted at the kidney are chosen arbitrarily to indicate that at lower rates of filtration of calcium (expected at lower glomerular filtration rates), most is reabsorbed (e.g., 5.85 of 6 g), leading to urinary excretion of 150 mg; at higher rates of filtration (at high dietary calcium intake), slightly less is reabsorbed (e.g., 9.7 of 10 g), leading to a higher urinary excretion, 300 mg. In all situations, renal calcium reabsorption exceeds 95 percent of filtered load. Urinary calcium excretion is seen, therefore, to increase by only 150 mg despite a 1-g increase in dietary intake. In conditions of calcium balance, rates of calcium release from and uptake into bone are equal.*

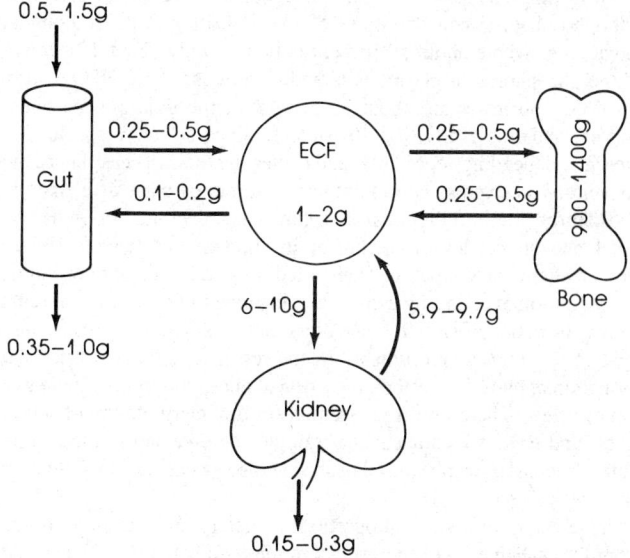

The amount of calcium in the urine is minute compared with that filtered through the glomerulus (about 6 to 10 g per day), but it is not certain whether some non-protein-bound, nonionic forms of calcium (e.g., calcium citrate) are cleared at rates considerably greater than others. The excretion of other electrolytes also affects the urinary excretion of calcium. For example, urinary calcium is usually proportional to urinary sodium; other ions, such as sulfate, also increase calcium excretion.

Maintenance of calcium balance (Fig. 335-2) is dependent upon the efficiency of intestinal absorption. Deficiency of parathyroid hormone or vitamin D, intestinal disease, or severe dietary calcium deprivation may provide challenges to calcium homeostasis that cannot be compensated adequately by renal calcium conservation, resulting in negative calcium balance. Increased bone resorption may protect against extracellular fluid calcium depletion even in states of chronic negative calcium balance but only at the expense of progressive osteopenia.

Pathophysiology Decrease in the concentration of free calcium ions in plasma results in increased neuromuscular irritability and the syndrome of tetany. This syndrome is characterized, when fully expressed by peripheral and perioral paresthesias, carpal spasm, pedal spasm, anxiety, seizures, bronchospasm, laryngospasm, Chvostek's, Trousseau's, and Erb's signs, and lengthening of the QT interval of the electrocardiogram. In infants tetany may be manifested only by irritability and lethargy. The level of calcium ions that determines which features of tetany will be manifested varies among individuals. The occurrence of tetany is also influenced by the concentration of other components of the extracellular fluid. For example, hypomagnesemia and alkalosis lower the threshold for tetany, whereas hypokalemia and acidosis raise the threshold.

Increases in total serum calcium are usually accompanied by increases in calcium ions and may be associated with manifestations including anorexia, nausea, vomiting, constipation, hypotonia, depression, and occasionally lethargy and coma. Persistent hypercalcemia, especially when accompanied by normal or elevated levels of serum phosphate, may result in deposition of a solid phase of calcium and phosphate in abnormal sites such as walls of blood vessels, connective tissue about the joints, gastric mucosa, cornea and renal parenchyma. Hypercalcemia per se alters renal function in addition to the pathologic effects of calcium-phosphate deposits in the lumen of renal tubules and in the interstitial areas of the kidney.

PHOSPHORUS METABOLISM Phosphorus is a major component of bone and is among the most abundant constituents of all tissues and in some form is involved in almost all metabolic processes. The total amount of phosphorus in the normal adult is about 1 kg, of which about 85 percent is in the skeleton.

In fasting plasma most of the phosphorus is present as inorganic orthophosphate in concentrations of 2.8 to 4.0 mg P/dL. In contrast to calcium, where about 50 percent is bound, only about 12 percent of the phosphorus in plasma is bound to proteins. Free HPO_4^{2-} and $NaHPO_4^-$ normally are about 75 percent of the total plasma phosphorus, and free $H_2PO_4^-$ is 10 percent. Since so many species are present, depending upon pH and other factors, it has been the convention to express concentrations in terms of mass of elemental phosphorus, i.e., milligrams phosphorus per deciliter, or molarity. Total phosphorus levels are higher in children and tend to rise in women after the menopause. There is a diurnal variation of phosphorus concentration even during a 24-h fast, mediated in part by the adrenal cortex. Ingestion of carbohydrate depresses serum phosphorus acutely by 1 to 1.5 mg/dL, presumably as the result of cellular uptake and formation of phosphate esters. Ingestion of phosphorus per se increases serum levels. Therefore, it is essential for the interpretation of serum levels and urinary clearances that samples be obtained in the fasting state. Decreases in plasma phosphorus also occur during induction of alkalosis.

Whereas only a small proportion of dietary calcium is absorbed from the intestine, phosphorus absorption is remarkably efficient. At low levels of dietary intake (less than 2 mg per kilogram of body weight per day) 80 to 90 percent of ingested phosphorus is absorbed. Even with the higher levels of intake (greater than 10 mg per kilogram of body weight per day) in the form of dairy products, cereals, eggs, and meat, absorption is about 70 percent. Hypophosphatemia due to deficient intestinal absorption is unusual except when excessive quantities of nonabsorbable antacids are consumed; the antacids bind phosphorus and prevent absorption from the intestinal lumen.

The major control of phosphorus economy is exerted at the level of the kidney. Phosphorus filtered through the glomerulus is largely reabsorbed in the proximal tubule (there is homeostatically important distal reabsorption as well) so that normally only about 10 to 15 percent of the filtered load is excreted. When filtered loads of phosphorus decrease, proximal tubular reabsorption increases. Conversely, when phosphorus loads are increased, tubular reabsorption decreases, and clearance rises. Thus, the urinary excretion of phosphorus normally reflects dietary intake, and conservation or elimination of excessive amounts of the ion depends upon adequate renal handling (Fig. 335-3). There is no good evidence for renal tubular phosphate secretion. Proximal reabsorption of phosphorus is dependent upon parallel sodium reabsorption, but whereas the sodium rejected by the proximal tubule may be reabsorbed distally, the rejected phosphorus is not. Therefore, the effects of volume expansion and decreased sodium reabsorption are to increase phosphorus clearance; similarly, diuretics such as acetazolamide, which act proximally, are phosphaturic parallel to the degree to which they are natriuretic.

Pathophysiology No direct symptoms result from hyperphosphatemia. However, when high levels are maintained for long periods, the driving force for mineralization is increased, and calcium phosphate may be deposited in abnormal sites. Severe, acute hypophosphatemia may or may not be accompanied by symptoms such as anorexia, dizziness, bone pain, proximal muscular weakness, and waddling gait. In severe hypophosphatemia (which may be aggravated, after hospitalization, by administration of nutrients to alcoholics or with therapy of diabetic ketoacidosis), elevations in serum creatine phosphokinase (CPK) suggest that rhabdomyolysis may be superimposed on myopathy. This sequence of events also occurs in experimental phosphate depletion in animals. Severe congestive cardiomyopathy has also been noted with chronic hypophosphatemia; restoration of phosphorus deficits leads to prompt reversal of the abnormalities. The bone pain and waddling gait are attributed to the osteomalacia which develops as a result of phosphate depletion. The muscular weakness may be due either to direct effects of hypophosphatemia on nerves and muscle or, in some instances, to the effects of hyperparathyroidism (either primary or secondary) which may have a role in the etiology of the hypophosphatemia. Defective growth in children may also be due to phosphate depletion. Hypophosphatemia results in decreased levels of 2,3-diphosphoglyceric acid and adenosine triphosphate (ATP) in erythrocytes which in turn alter the dissociation of oxyhemoglobin so that less oxygen is delivered in the periphery. Hemolytic anemia may be produced as the result of impairment of the ability of erythrocytes to deform in small vessels.

Negative phosphorus balance (Fig. 335-3) is rarely caused by inadequate phosphorus absorption in the intestine, and maintenance of normal phosphorus balance is dependent upon efficiency of renal excretion or conservation. In severe renal failure, hyperphosphatemia results from inadequate renal phosphorus clearance; heritable or acquired renal tubular defects may lead to hypophosphatemia due to inadequate renal conservation of phosphorus.

VITAMIN D

Vitamin D is a hormone, not a vitamin. With adequate exposure to sunlight, no dietary supplements are needed. The active principle of vitamin D is synthesized under metabolic control via successive hydroxylations in the liver and kidney and is transported through the blood to its target tissues (the small intestine and bone) to help maintain calcium homeostasis. Calcium and phosphate ions, parathyroid hormone, and possibly other peptide and steroid hormones play major roles directly or indirectly in the regulation of the renal metabolism of vitamin D. Analysis of hereditary and acquired defects in these metabolic processes have provided new insights into the pathophysiology of several disorders involving calcium, phosphorus, and bone metabolism. These discoveries have been the impetus for several advances, including the chemical synthesis of active vitamin D metabolites and analogues, the clinical use of $1\alpha,25$-dihydroxyvitamin D_3 [$1,25(OH)_2D_3$] in many vitamin D–resistant disorders, the development and application of assays for measuring vitamin D metabolites in blood to define suspected abnormalities in vitamin D metabolism, and a growing interest in developing more potent vitamin D analogues for clinical use.

PHOTOBIOGENESIS OF VITAMIN D   Vitamin D_3 is a derivative of 7-dehydrocholesterol (provitamin D_3), the immediate precursor of cholesterol. When skin is exposed to sunlight or certain artifical light

FIGURE 335-3 *Phosphate homeostasis. Schematic illustration of inorganic phosphorus content (termed here phosphate) in extracellular fluid (ECF) and bone as well as diet and feces; magnitude of phosphorus flux per day as estimated by various methods is shown at transport sites in intestine, kidney, and bone. Range of values shown illustrates special features of phosphorus metabolism discussed in text. Intestinal phosphorus absorption is highly efficient, 85 percent at a lower intake (0.5 g of a 0.6-g intake) and 70 percent at a higher intake (1.4 g of a 2.0-g intake). Estimates of magnitude of endogenous fecal phosphate are less well established than for calcium. Contribution of at least 0.15 g is estimated to be added to the nonabsorbed phosphorus to provide a total of 0.2 g fecal phosphorus at the low intake level. At high phosphorus dietary intakes, no correction for endogenous fecal phosphate is calculated. Higher quantities of phosphorus are excreted in urine at all levels of dietary intake than for corresponding intakes of calcium; quantities excreted match closely the quantities absorbed, thereby maintaining phosphorus balance (no correction in this illustration is made for endogenous fecal phosphorus). Note that renal phosphorus reabsorption, in contrast to high and relatively invariant renal calcium reabsorption, varies from a low of 75 percent of filtered load to greater than 85 percent. The compartment labeled ICF refers to intracellular phosphorus, both organic and inorganic; rapid shifts of phosphorus into cells (and corresponding, possibly slower, efflux of phosphorus from cells) contribute to changes in ECF phosphorus. These shifts between ECF and ICF and phosphorus release from and uptake by bone are equal in conditions of phosphorus balance.*

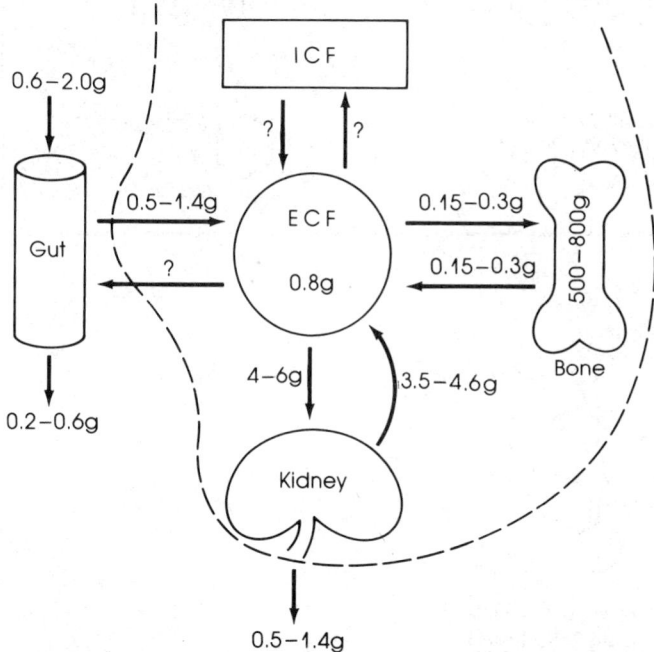

sources, the ultraviolet radiation enters the epidermis and causes a variety of photobiochemical events. Among them is the transformation of 7-dehydrocholesterol to vitamin D_3. Wavelengths between 290 and 315 nm are absorbed by the conjugated double bonds at C_5 and C_7 of 7-dehydrocholesterol that result in the fragmentation of the B ring between C_9 and C_{10} to yield a 9,10-secosterol (*seco* means "split"), previtamin D_3 (Fig. 335-4). Previtamin D_3 is biologically inert but is thermally labile and spontaneously undergoes a temperature-dependent molecular rearrangement of its conjugated triene system (three double bonds) to form the thermally stable 9,10-secosterol, vitamin D_3 (Fig. 335-4). At body temperature it takes approximately 3 days for previtamin D_3 to convert completely into vitamin D_3. Large changes in the temperature of the surface of the skin do not affect the rate of this conversion because the process occurs in the actively growing layers of the epidermis where the temperature is relatively constant; changes in the core body temperature also have little effect on this reaction. Once vitamin D_3 is synthesized, it is translocated from the epidermis into the circulation by the vitamin D–binding protein. Thus, vitamin D_3 is made in the skin from previtamin for days after a single sun exposure (Fig. 335-4). Although melanin in the skin competes with 7-dehydrocholesterol for ultraviolet photons and thus can limit the synthesis of previtamin D_3, the photochemical isomerization of previtamin D_3 to two biologically inert products (lumisterol$_3$ and tachysterol$_3$) appears to be more important in preventing excessive production of previtamin D_3 during prolonged exposure to the sun (Fig. 335-4).

Aging decreases the capacity of the skin to produce vitamin D_3; greater than twofold reduction occurs after the age of 70 years. Topical sunscreens reduce cutaneous vitamin D_3 production by absorbing the solar radiation that is responsible for vitamin D_3 synthesis in the skin. Other factors that affect the cutaneous synthesis of vitamin D_3 include altitude, geographical location, time of day, and area of exposure. When the entire body is exposed to sufficient sunlight to cause mild erythema, the increase in the blood vitamin D is equivalent to consuming an oral dose of 10,000 international units (1 IU = 0.025 μg) of vitamin D_3. Only when skin radiation is insufficient to produce the required quantities of vitamin D_3 is there a need for dietary supplementation to prevent skeletal mineralization defects. Fish liver oils, a natural source of vitamin D, were used widely for the treatment of rickets early in this century. Crystalline vitamin D_2 (Fig. 335-4) or vitamin D_3 is now added to milk and cereals. Such supplementations prevent rickets and osteomalacia. The National Research Council of the United States recommends an intake of 400 IU per day.

Once vitamin D enters the circulation, either by its absorption from the diet or through the skin, it is transported to the liver bound to a specific alpha$_1$ globulin (vitamin D–binding protein).

METABOLISM OF VITAMIN D   In the liver, vitamin D is metabolized to 25-hydroxyvitamin D [25(OH)D] by hepatic mitochondrial and/or microsomal enzyme(s) (Fig. 335-4). 25(OH)D is one of the major circulating metabolites of vitamin D, and its half-life is estimated to be about 21 days. The concentration of 25(OH)D and some of its metabolites in the serum is measured using competitive binding assays. The normal circulating concentration of 25(OH)D varies among different laboratories from 5 to 80 ng/mL. Individuals exposed to excessive sunlight may have concentrations of 25(OH)D up to 150 ng/mL without adverse effects on calcium metabolism. Assays that employ chromatographic separation prior to binding analysis often have a lower normal range, possibly because other vitamin D metabolites simulate 25(OH)D in this assay. The normal range, apparently independent of method, is lower in Great Britain than in the United States; in Great Britain dietary supplements of vitamin D are not routine, and exposure to sunlight is less than in most regions of the United States. The serum 25(OH)D levels routinely measured reflect both 25-hydroxyvitamin D_2 [25(OH)D_2] and 25-hydroxyvitamin D_3 [25(OH)D_3]. The ratio of these two 25-hydroxylated derivatives depends on the relative amounts of vitamins D_2 or D_3 present in the diet and the amount of previtamin D_3 produced by exposure to sunlight.

The hepatic 25-hydroxylation of vitamin D is regulated by a product feedback mechanism. This regulation, however, is not tight; an increase in dietary intake or endogenous production of vitamin D_3 is reflected by elevations in 25(OH)D concentration levels in the serum. The levels can rise to greater than 500 ng/mL when the intake of vitamin D is increased. Serum 25(OH)D concentration levels are reduced in severe chronic parenchymal and cholestatic liver disease (Table 335-1).

25(OH)D is not biologically active at physiologic levels in vivo but is active in vitro at high concentrations. Normally, after formation in the liver, 25(OH)D is bound by the high-affinity vitamin D–binding protein that is synthesized in the liver and transported to the kidney for an additional stereospecific hydroxylation on either C_1 or C_{24} (Fig. 335-4). The kidney plays a pivotal role in the metabolism of 25(OH)D to the biologically active metabolite. The renal mitochondrial 25(OH)D-1α-hydroxylase activity is enhanced by hypocalcemia so that the rate of conversion of 25(OH)D to 1,25(OH)$_2$D increases. However, hypocalcemia may not control this hydroxylation

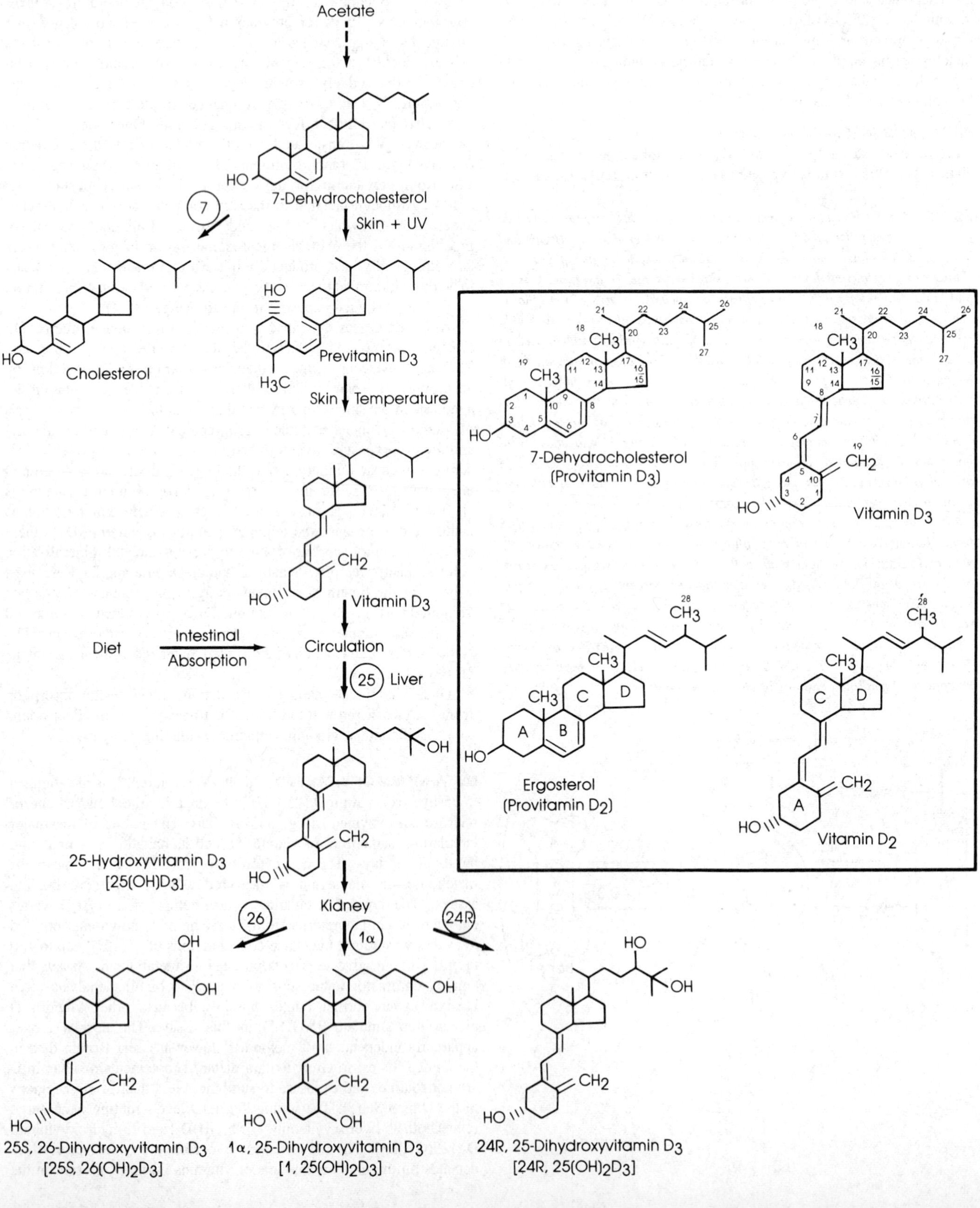

Acetate

7-Dehydrocholesterol

Cholesterol

Skin + UV

Previtamin D3

Skin / Temperature

Vitamin D3

Diet — Intestinal Absorption → Circulation

25 Liver

25-Hydroxyvitamin D3 [25(OH)D3]

Kidney

25S, 26-Dihydroxyvitamin D3 [25S, 26(OH)2D3]

1α, 25-Dihydroxyvitamin D3 [1, 25(OH)2D3]

24R, 25-Dihydroxyvitamin D3 [24R, 25(OH)2D3]

7-Dehydrocholesterol (Provitamin D3)

Vitamin D3

Ergosterol (Provitamin D2)

Vitamin D2

directly. Any decrease in the serum concentration of calcium below normal is a stimulus for increased secretion of parathyroid hormone. Parathyroid hormone acts physiologically as a tropic hormone to increase the synthesis of $1,25(OH)_2D$ in the renal proximal convoluted tubule. The mechanism by which parathyroid hormone exerts its influence on the renal metabolism of $25(OH)D$ is not established; however, the renal production of $1,25(OH)_2D$ correlates with the effects of parathyroid hormone in lowering circulating concentrations (and presumably renal intracellular concentrations) of phosphate. $1,25(OH)_2D$ also influences the renal metabolism of $25(OH)D$ by diminishing $25(OH)D-1\alpha$-hydroxylase activity and enhancing the metabolism of $24R,25$-dihydroxyvitamin D $[24,25(OH)_2D]$.

$24,25(OH)_2D$ is a circulating metabolite of $25(OH)D$ normally present in serum at a concentration of 0.5 to 5.0 ng/mL. $24,25(OH)_2D$ is also a substrate for renal $25(OH)D-1\alpha$-hydroxylase and is converted to $1\alpha,24R,25$-trihydroxyvitamin D $[1,24,25(OH)_3D]$. This trihydroxy metabolite is less potent than $1,25(OH)_2D$ in stimulating intestinal calcium transport; whether it has a physiologic role in maintaining calcium homeostasis is unclear. Cultured chondrocytes, skin fibroblasts, intestinal cells, and pituitary cells are among the cell types that also metabolize $25(OH)D$ to $24,25(OH)_2D$. $24,25(OH)_2D$ may play a role in the expression of vitamin D action, especially on the skeleton. There is no agreement, however, concerning the biologic importance of $24,25(OH)_2D$ per se as distinct from actions resulting from its conversion to $1,24,25(OH)_3D$.

The kidney also metabolizes $25(OH)D$ to $25S,26$-dihydroxyvitamin D $[25,26(OH)_2D]$. $25,26(OH)_2D$, like $24,25(OH)_2D$, is metabolized by the kidney to $1\alpha,25S,26$-trihydroxyvitamin D $[1,25,26(OH)_3D]$. $1,25,26(OH)_3D$ is less active than $1,25(OH)_2D$ in inducing intestinal calcium transport, and the physiologic function of this metabolite remains to be defined.

$1,25(OH)_2D$ is a substrate for the $25(OH)D-24R$-hydroxylase and is metabolized to $1,24,25(OH)_3D$, but this conversion is not believed to be important for the expression of biologic activity of $1,25(OH)_2D$.

FIGURE 335-4 *Photobiogenesis and. metabolic pathways for vitamin D production and metabolism. Circled letters and numbers denote specific enzymes:* (7) *= 7-dehydrocholesterol reductase;* (25) *= vitamin D-25-hydroxylase;* (1α) *= 25(OH)D-1α-hydroxylase;* (24R) *= 25(OH)D-24R-hydroxylase;* (26) *= 25(OH)D-26-hydroxylase. The insert denotes the basic $\Delta^{5,7}$-diene steroid structures for the precursors of vitamin D$_2$ (ergosterol) and vitamin D$_3$ (7-dehydrocholesterol) and the 9,10-secosteroid structures of vitamin D$_2$ (ergocalciferol) and vitamin D$_3$ (cholecalciferol). Historically, the subscripts for vitamin D are related to the order in which the compounds were isolated and characterized. What was originally called vitamin D$_1$ is a mixture of compounds, and the term is no longer used. The next two vitamin D compounds, vitamin D$_2$ and vitamin D$_3$, were isolated, respectively, from the irradiation products of ergosterol (a $\Delta^{5,7}$-diene steroid found primarily in plants) and 7-dehydrocholesterol (a $\Delta^{5,7}$-diene steroid precursor of cholesterol present in animal tissues, including humans). Vitamin D$_2$ and vitamin D$_3$ differ in their side chains; the side chain for vitamin D$_2$ contains a Δ^{22} and a C$_{24}$-methyl group. Even though vitamin D$_3$ is the only endogenous form of vitamin D in skin, both vitamins D$_2$ and D$_3$ are metabolized identically and have equivalent biologic potencies in most mammals; in the absence of subscript the term vitamin D may refer to either compound.*

In steroid nomenclature, substituents on the steroid ring skeleton that are spatially oriented below the plane of the molecule (drawn as a broken line) are called α substituents, and those substituents spatially oriented above the plane of the molecule (drawn as a solid line) are called β substituents. Because vitamin D is a structural derivative of a $\Delta^{5,7}$-diene steroid, by convention the numbering of the carbon atoms and the stereochemical designation of the functional groups remain the same as for the parent steroid. During the transformation $\Delta^{5,7}$-diene→previtamin D→vitamin D, the geometric position of ring A is altered, thereby changing the stereochemical orientation of its substituents; nonetheless, the original designation(s) of the hydroxyl function(s) on ring A of the steroid precursor are retained. The R,S notation, as in 24R,25-dihydroxy-vitamin D$_3$, specifies the spatial configuration of a substituent at an asymmetric carbon center.

More than twenty metabolites of vitamin D have been identified. All of the metabolites originate from $25(OH)D$ or $I,25(OH)_2D$. Most of the metabolites may be degradation products. Of particular interest is the metabolic sequence that results in the inactivation of $1,25(OH)_2D$ by the oxidative cleavage of the side chain between C_{23} and C_{24} to yield a biologically inert and water-soluble product, 1α-hydroxyvitamin D–23-carboxylic acid.

PHYSIOLOGY OF VITAMIN D $1,25(OH)_2D$, produced by the kidney and during pregnancy by the placenta, is the only known important metabolite of vitamin D; the potential roles of other metabolites have not been clarified. $1,25(OH)_2D$ bound to a vitamin D–binding protein is delivered to the intestine, where the free form is taken up by the cells and transported to a specific nuclear receptor protein. The interaction of $1,25(OH)_2D$ with its specific nuclear receptor results in the phosphorylation of the receptor complex, and subsequent interaction with the chromatin activates transcription of genes whose products stimulate calcium and phosphate transport from the small intestinal lumen into the circulation. Under physiologic conditions the action of $1,25(OH)_2D$ is believed to be synergistic with that of parathyroid hormone on bone resorption. However, effects on bone resorption of physiologic concentrations of $1,25(OH)_2D$ independent of parathyroid hormone are not established. $1,25(OH)_2D$ can, however, mobilize bone mineral independently at supraphysiologic levels by inducing differentiation of precursor mononuclear cells to osteoclasts. Whether $1,25(OH)_2D$ has direct effects on the renal handling of calcium and phosphorus is also uncertain.

Cytoplasmic receptors for $1,25(OH)_2D_3$ are present in bone, in renal tubular cells, and in tissues and cells that have not classically been recognized as target organs for this hormone, including skin, breast, pituitary gland, parathyroid glands, beta cells of the pancreatic islets, gonads, brain, skeletal muscle, circulating monocytes, and activated B and T lymphocytes. Although the physiologic role of $1,25(OH)_2D$ in these cells remains to be determined, $1,25(OH)_2D_3$ in vitro inhibits human fibroblast proliferation, stimulates terminal differentiation of human keratinocytes, induces monocytes to produce interleukin 1 and mature into macrophages and osteoclast-like cells, inhibits interleukin 2 production by T lymphocytes, and induces synthesis and secretion of thyroid-stimulating hormone (TSH) by pituitary cells. In addition, a variety of tumor cell lines including breast carinomas, melanomas, and promyeloblasts possess receptors for $1,25(OH)_2D$.

Cultured tumor cell lines that possess receptors for this hormone respond to the hormone by decreasing the rate of proliferation and by enhancing differentiation. For example, when malignant, receptor-positive human promyelocytic cells (HL-60) are exposed to $1,25(OH)_2D_3$, the cells mature into functioning macrophages within 1 week. Although the mechanism of $1,25(OH)_2D_3$ induction of maturation is unknown, $1,25(OH)_2D_3$ decreases the expression of c-*myc* oncogene coincident with decreasing replication. This effect, however, is not a lasting one; when the metabolite is removed from maturing HL-60 promyelocytes, the cells revert to their original malignant state, and expression of c-*myc* oncogene is no longer suppressed.

The importance of $1,25(OH)_2D$ in the regulation of differentiation and immunoregulation is unknown. Patients with vitamin D–dependent rickets type II who are unable to respond to physiologic concentrations of $1,25(OH)_2D_3$ (because of insufficient or defective receptors for this hormone) appear to have no demonstrable in vivo

TABLE 335-1   Serum concentrations of 25(OH)D in disorders of calcium, phosphorus, and bone metabolism

Disease states	Serum 25(OH)D
Vitamin D deficiency	↓
Intestinal malabsorption syndromes	↓
Liver disorders (chronic and severe)	↓
Nephrotic syndrome	↓
Osteopenia in the aged	N or ↓
Vitamin D intoxication	↑

NOTE: ↓ = *decreased*; N = *normal*; ↑ = *increased*.

defects in their cellular immune response. $1,25(OH)_2D_3$ may play a role in inducing differentiation of stem cells in the bone marrow to osteoclasts.

Most measurements of circulating $1,25(OH)_2D$ in humans in various physiologic or pathologic states utilize a receptor/competitive binding assay (Table 335-2). Serum concentrations of vitamin D and 25(OH)D vary with the seasons and with vitamin D intake. Serum concentrations of $1,25(OH)_2D$, however, appear to be unaltered by seasonal variation, by increases in dietary vitamin D, or by exposure to sunlight; as long as vitamin D supplies and circulating concentrations of 25(OH)D are sufficient, metabolic influences operate on the renal 25(OH)D-1α-hydroxylase to ensure a closely regulated circulating concentration of $1,25(OH)_2D$. The serum concentration of $1,25(OH)_2D$ ranges from 25 to 75 pg/mL. The serum half-life of $1,25(OH)_2D_3$ is from 3 to 6 h.

When the serum calcium falls below normal, secretion of parathyroid hormone is enhanced, resulting in increased production of $1,25(OH)_2D$. The principal physiologic regulation of the production of $1,25(OH)_2D$ appears to involve changes in serum calcium concentrations that result in reciprocal changes in secretion of parathyroid hormone, the latter controlling, possibly through actions on serum or tissue phosphorus concentrations, the rate of $1,25(OH)_2D$ production. Other factors that enhance $1,25(OH)_2D$ production in animals include estrogen, prolactin, and growth hormone. Humans adapt to increased calcium requirements during growth, pregnancy, and lactation by increasing the efficiency of intestinal calcium absorption, possibly by enhancing 25(OH)D-1α-hydroxylase activity. During the first two trimesters of pregnancy the concentrations of $1,25(OH)_2D$ increase proportional to increases in the concentrations of the vitamin D–binding protein; concentrations of free $1,25(OH)_2D$ do not change. During the last trimester when maximal mineralization of the fetal skeleton takes place, the increased demand for calcium is met by an increase in the free concentrations of $1,25(OH)_2D$, which in turn enhance maternal intestinal calcium absorption.

PATHOPHYSIOLOGY OF DISORDERS OF VITAMIN D NUTRITION AND METABOLISM

Hypovitaminosis D results from inadequate endogenous production of vitamin D_3 in the skin, insufficient dietary supplementation, and/or the inability of the small intestine to absorb adequate amounts of vitamin D from the diet. Disease states equivalent to hypovitaminosis D result from (1) effects of drugs that antagonize vitamin D action, (2) alterations in the metabolism of vitamin D, or (3) deficient or defective cellular receptors for vitamin D metabolites. Hypovitaminosis D results in (1) disturbances of mineral ion metabolism and secretion of parathyroid hormone and (2) mineralization defects in the skeleton (e.g., rickets in children, osteomalacia in adults). The changes in the skeleton are described in Chap. 337. With regard to calcium metabolism, lack of vitamin D action leads to deficient intestinal calcium absorption and to hypocalcemia. The latter stimulates compensatory secondary hyperparathyroidism; the increased secretion of parathyroid hormone, which enhances calcium release from bone and decreases calcium clearance by the kidney, tends to blunt the hypocalcemia. (Late in the course of untreated hypovitaminosis D, severe hypocalcemia develops.) Hypophosphatemia is more marked than hypocalcemia, especially in early stages of vitamin D deficiency. The efficiency of intestinal phosphate absorption, similar to that of calcium absorption, decreases with severe vitamin D deficiency. The increased secretion of parathyroid hormone, although partially effective in minimizing hypocalcemia, leads to urinary phosphate wasting through decreases in renal tubular reabsorption. This latter effect may be the most significant factor in causing hypophosphatemia. With an adequate glomerular filtration rate, the predominant changes in blood are severe hypophosphatemia, moderate or slightly low levels of calcium, and increased levels of parathyroid hormone. Blood levels of 25(OH)D are low (Table 335-1). As discussed in Chap. 337 defects in skeletal mineralization may accompany these disturbances in mineral ion metabolism.

Although the conversion of vitamin D to 25(OH)D is impaired in liver disease, there is no strong correlation between low serum 25(OH)D levels and osteopenia; multiple effects of the primary disease state seem to affect skeletal metabolism as well. There is a relation between chronic anticonvulsant therapy and the development of osteomalacia or rickets; mineralization defects are worse in patients on multiple drug therapy and where vitamin D intake or exposure to sunlight is inadequate. These drugs have multiple and complex effects on calcium metabolism. Phenobarbital induces hepatic microsomal enzymes, alters the kinetics of the vitamin D–25-hydroxylase and stimulates bile secretion, which results in decreased serum concentrations of vitamin D and 25(OH)D. Both phenytoin and phenobarbital influence calcium metabolism by inhibiting intestinal calcium transport and bone mineral mobilization, independent of effects of vitamin D metabolism.

Glucocorticoids in high doses cause disturbances in calcium metabolism and osteoporosis, but osteomalacia and rickets per se are not a consequence of glucocorticoid therapy. Actions of glucocorticoids on vitamin D–mediated calcium metabolism include a direct inhibitory effect of vitamin D–mediated intestinal calcium absorption and bone mineral mobilization and an enhancement of the sensitivity of $1,25(OH)_2D_3$ on bone cells either by stabilizing the $1,25(OH)_2D_3$ receptor or by increasing the affinity or number of receptors. Patients receiving glucocorticoids chronically may have depressed serum $1,25(OH)_2D$ concentrations; the mechanism(s) is unknown.

A genetic defect in the hepatic 25-hydroxylation of vitamin D has not been described. However, in one inherited disorder of calcium and bone metabolism renal production of $1,25(OH)_2D$ may be defective. In the syndrome of pseudovitamin D–deficient rickets (also known as vitamin D–dependent rickets, type I; see Chap. 337), low serum $1,25(OH)_2D$ concentrations and a normal therapeutic response to physiologic doses of $1,25(OH)_2D_3$ (calcitriol) (0.25 to 1.0 μg per day) have been attributed to an inherited deficiency in renal 25(OH)D-1α-hydroxylase activity. In addition, patients with a similar phenotype, pseudovitamin D–resistant rickets (vitamin D–dependent rickets, type II), appear to have a lack of (or defective) receptors for $1,25(OH)_2D$ rather than defective metabolism of the vitamin. Individuals with this defect have high serum $1,25(OH)_2D$ concentrations; therapeutic responses to high-dose vitamin D therapy are associated with a further increase in the serum $1,25(OH)_2D$ concentrations.

In patients with X-linked hypophosphatemic rickets, serum concentrations of $1,25(OH)_2D$ are normal or low. Since hypophosphatemia is a potent stimulus for the renal 25(OH)D-1α-hydroxylase,

TABLE 335-2   Serum concentrations of $1,25(OH)_2D$ in disorders of calcium, phosphorus, and bone metabolism

Disease states	Serum $1,25(OH)_2D$
Vitamin D deficiency	↓ *
Renal failure:	
GFR > (30 mL/min)/1.7 m²	↓ or N
GFR < (30 mL/min)/1.7 m²	↓
Hypoparathyroidism	↓ or N
Pseudohypoparathyroidism	↓ or N
Vitamin D–dependent rickets:	
Type I	↓ or N
Type II	↑ or N
X-linked vitamin D–resistant rickets	↓ or N
Tumor-induced osteomalacia	↓
Oncogenic hypercalcemia	↑
Some lymphomas	↑
Hyperparathyroidism	↑
Sarcoidosis, tuberculosis, silicosis	↑
Idiopathic hypercalciuria	N or ↑
Williams' syndrome	↑
Vitamin D intoxication	↓ or N

* *Serum $1,25(OH)_2D$ concentrations are normal or elevated in occasional patients with biopsy-proven osteomalacia and undetectable or low circulating concentrations of 25(OH)D. These patients also have secondary hyperparathyroidism, and they may represent a partially treated state; if a small amount of vitamin D is obtained from the diet or generated in the skin in these patients, the vitamin is efficiently converted to $1,25(OH)_2D$. The net effect is low or undetectable circulating concentrations of 25(OH)D along with normal or elevated concentrations of $1,25(OH)_2D$. However, in extreme vitamin D deficiency, circulating concentrations of $1,25(OH)_2D$ are low or undetectable.*

NOTE: ↓ = *decreased;* N = *normal;* ↑ = *increased;* GFR = *glomerular filtration rate.*

the serum 1,25(OH)$_2$D concentrations should be high. Thus, even a normal serum 1,25(OH)$_2$D concentration suggests a functional defect in the 25(OH)D-1α-hydroxylase system. In some cases, the combination of calcitriol and phosphate supplements offers a therapeutic advantage to phosphate therapy by itself (Chap. 337). In patients with mild to moderate chronic renal failure (glomerular filtration rate >30 mL/min) and decreased phosphate clearance, hyperphosphatemia and acidosis play important roles in suppressing the renal production of 1,25(OH)$_2$D despite high circulating concentrations of parathyroid hormone. As the destruction of the renal cortex progresses, the reserves of the 25(OH)D-1α-hydroxylase are depleted to a point at which the kidney is unable to produce sufficient quantities of 1,25(OH)$_2$D to maintain calcium homeostasis, even when serum phosphorus concentrations are normal. Under these circumstances replacement therapy with calcitriol is most beneficial (Chap. 337).

Patients with hypoparathyroidism and pseudohypoparathyroidism have lower than normal mean serum concentrations of 1,25(OH)$_2$D although individual values overlap with the normal range. In these hypocalcemic patients favorable response to small replacement doses of calcitriol (0.25 to 1.0 μg per day; see Chap. 336) occur even when the serum 25(OH)D concentrations are higher than normal. These observations are consistent with the concept that patients with hypoparathyroidism or pseudohypoparathyroidism due to absent or ineffective action of parathyroid hormone have defective function of renal 25(OH)D-1α-hydroxylase. It is not known to what extent serum 1,25(OH)$_2$D concentrations would be restored toward normal if the hyperphosphatemia were adequately controlled.

Patients with tumor-induced (oncogenous) osteomalacia have low serum phosphorus and 1,25(OH)$_2$D levels. These tumors presumably secrete a substance(s) that causes renal phosphorus wasting and inhibits the formation of 1,25(OH)$_2$D; after removal of the tumor the serum phosphorus and 1,25(OH)$_2$D levels return to normal.

In disease states equivalent to hypervitaminosis D such as sarcoidosis (and other chronic granulomatous disorders), lymphomas, idiopathic hypercalciuria, and Williams' syndrome there is an abnormality in the metabolism of 25(OH)D to 1,25(OH)$_2$D (Table 335-2). Hypercalcemia in sarcoidosis is associated with elevated circulating concentrations of 1,25(OH)$_2$D; sarcoid granulomas metabolize 25(OH)D to 1,25(OH)$_2$D in an unregulated manner, and pulmonary alveolar macrophages from patients with sarcoidosis synthesize 1,25(OH)$_2$D. In addition, normal pulmonary macrophages can be induced to metabolize 25(OH)D to 1,25(OH)$_2$D in vitro when exposed either to lipopolysaccharides from the cell wall of gram-negative bacteria or to gamma interferon. Most patients with tumor-induced hypercalcemia have low circulating concentrations of 1,25(OH)$_2$D (Table 335-2). The exceptions are patients with several types of lymphoma (including T-cell, mixed histiocytic-lymphocytic, and B-cell immunoblastic lymphomas) whose hypercalcemia is associated with elevated concentrations of 1,25(OH)$_2$D. In one report, surgical excision of a solitary splenic lymphoma resulted in rapid return of elevated serum 1,25(OH)$_2$D and calcium levels to normal suggesting that the lymphoma cells metabolize 25(OH)D to 1,25(OH)$_2$D in an unregulated manner. There is a direct association between elevated circulating concentrations of 1,25(OH)$_2$D in patients with primary hyperparathyrodisim, hypercalciuria, and renal stones. Similarly, in some instances of idiopathic hypercalciuria, intestinal calcium absorption is inappropriately increased. Approximately one-third of these patients have elevated circulating 1,25(OH)$_2$D. These findings are consistent with the hypothesis that excessive 1,25(OH)$_2$D production is responsible for the hyperabsorption of calcium by the small intestine. Infants with hypercalcemia associated with supravalvular aortic stenosis, mental retardation, and elfin facies (*Williams' syndrome*) also have elevated serum 1,25(OH)$_2$D concentrations. It is not clear whether the increased levels result from abnormal synthesis or degradation of 1,25(OH)$_2$D.

PHARMACOLOGY OF VITAMIN D AND ITS METABOLITES
A variety of over-the-counter vitamin preparations contain 400 IU of either vitamin D$_2$ or vitamin D$_3$. More potent forms of vitamin D (calciferol) are available in capsule and tablet form (50,000 IU) as well as in oil (500,000 IU/mL) and in oral solution 8000 IU/mL). A single oral dose of 50,000 IU of vitamin D$_2$ increases the circulating concentrations of vitamin D from less than 10 ng/mL to 50 to 100 ng/mL within 12 to 24 h; the plasma half-life is about 2 days. Serum concentrations of 25(OH)D and 1,25(OH)$_2$D are not changed. For treatment of vitamin D deficiency, 50,000 IU of vitamin D twice a week for several weeks raises the circulating concentration of 25(OH)D into the normal range; in the presence of secondary hyperparathyroidism the circulating concentrations of 1,25(OH)$_2$D increase to supranormal levels (up to 250 pg/mL). 25(OH)D$_3$ (calcifediol) is available in capsules containing either 20 or 50 μg. This drug may be useful in treating vitamin D deficiency [low 25(OH)D concentrations] in patients with severe liver dysfunction. Pharmacologic doses are used to treat disorders of 25(OH)D metabolism; in pharmacologic doses 25(OH)D$_3$ is believed to be effective through its interaction with the receptor for 1,25(OH)$_2$D. 1,25(OH)$_2$D$_3$ (calcitriol) is available in capsules containing 0.25 or 0.5 μg. Calcitriol is efficacious in therapy of a variety of calcium metabolic disorders (see Chap. 341). 1α-Hydroxyvitamin D$_3$ [1(OH)D$_3$] is also a potent 1,25(OH)$_2$D$_3$ agonist. The structure of this analogue is identical to that of the natural renal hormone with the exception that it lacks a C$_{25}$-OH (Fig. 335-5). In humans, this analogue is rapidly metabolized by the liver to 1,25(OH)$_2$D$_3$. This analogue is used in Europe and Japan.

When vitamin D is chemically manipulated to rotate the A ring through 180 degrees, the C$_3$-β-OH assumes a geometric position that mimics the C$_1$-α-OH (Fig. 335-5). These compounds, called pseudo-1α-hydroxyvitamin D analogues, include dihydrotachysterol and 5,6-*trans*-vitamin D$_3$. These analogues are less effective in stimulating intestinal calcium transport on a weight basis than either vitamin D or 1,25(OH)$_2$D$_3$. However, because the pseudo-1α-hydroxyvitamin D analogues do not require a renal 1α-hydroxylation to be active on intestinal calcium transport, they are 3 to 10 times more potent than vitamin D in disease states that adversely affect the renal 25(OH)D-1α-hydroxylase, such as hypoparathyroidism and chronic renal failure. These analogues are efficiently metabolized in the liver to the corresponding 25-hydroxy derivatives, which are the biologically active forms.

PARATHYROID HORMONE
Physiology The function of parathyroid hormone is to maintain extracellular fluid calcium concentration. The hormone acts directly on bone and kidney and indirectly on intestine through its effects on synthesis of 1,25(OH)$_2$D$_3$ to increase serum calcium; in turn, parathyroid hormone production is closely regulated by the concentration of serum ionized calcium. This feedback system is one of the most important homeostatic mechanisms for the close regulation of extracellular fluid calcium concentration. Any tendency toward hypocalcemia, as might be induced by calcium-deficient diets, is counteracted by an increased rate of secretion of parathyroid hormone. This in turn (1) acts to increase the rate of dissolution of bone mineral, thereby increasing the flow of calcium from bone into blood, (2) reduces the renal clearance of calcium, returning more of the calcium filtered at the glomerulus into extracellular fluid, and (3) increases the efficiency of calcium absorption in the intestine. The relative physiologic importance of these three actions of parathyroid hormone, stimulation of calcium transport in bone, kidney, and intestine, is not clear. Most evidence suggests that rapid changes in blood calcium are due to effects of the hormone on bone and, to a lesser extent, on renal calcium clearance; maintenance of calcium balance, on the other hand, is probably due to the effects of the hormone on 1,25(OH)$_2$D$_3$ levels and hence on the efficiency of intestinal calcium absorption. Evidence from calcium kinetic studies indicates that as much as 500 mg calcium is transferred between extracellular fluid and bone each day (a large amount in relation to the total extracellular fluid calcium pool), and parathyroid hormone has a major effect on this transfer. The action of the hormone tends to preserve calcium concentration in blood acutely at the cost of bone destruction and bone mineral release. However, the action

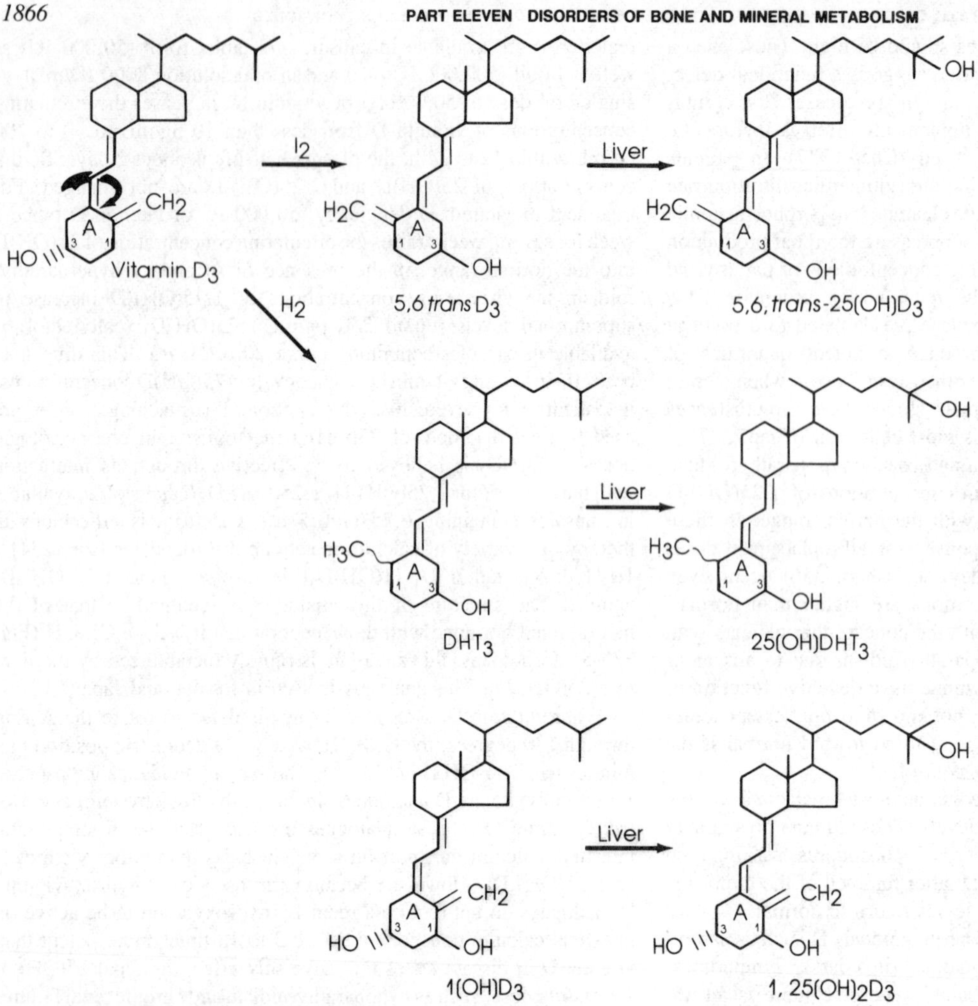

FIGURE 335-5 *When vitamin D is treated with I_2 or reduced with H_2, ring A of the vitamin D molecule rotates 180° to reorient spatially the 3β-OH in a pseudo-1α-OH position. These analogues, 5,6-trans-vitamin D_3 and dihydrotachysterol, (DHT_3), are called pseudo-1α-hydroxy analogues. $1(OH)D_3$ is a synthetic analogue of $1,25(OH)_2D_3$ that lacks a C_{25}-OH. $1(OH)D_3$, 5,6-trans-vitamin D_3, and DHT_3 all undergo a hepatic C_{25}-hydroxylation before they are biologically active.*

of parathyroid hormone on kidney to preserve calcium by increasing the reabsorption of filtered calcium may also be important in rapid regulation of blood calcium concentration.

Parathyroid hormone has a dual action on bone, the *calcium replacement* and the *bone remodeling* effects. There is an increased rate of release of calcium from bone into blood within minutes of the administration of parathyroid hormone, but a rapid efflux of calcium out of blood, presumably into bone cells, precedes the release of calcium. On the other hand, the more chronic effects of parathyroid hormone, mainly an increase in the number and activity of osteoclasts and a general increase in the remodeling of bone, are apparent only hours after the hormone is given. These latter actions, which involve increased protein synthesis, persist for hours after parathyroid hormone has been given. It is not clear whether the two effects of parathyroid action on bone represent a continuous spectrum with a common initiating biochemical event or whether they are separate actions. Only osteoblastic cells and not osteoclasts are believed to have receptors for parathyroid hormone.

Chemistry The complete amino acid sequences of the major forms of parathyroid hormone from cow, pig, rat, and human have been defined. The peptides consist of a single-chain structure composed of 84 amino acids. The molecules lack cysteine or cystine; the sequences of the three forms of the hormone are similar, as is illustrated in Fig. 335-6.

The structural requirements for the binding of the hormone to receptors and hence for its biologic activity have been defined. Synthetic fragments containing the amino-terminal sequence exert the known biologic actions of the hormone on mineral ion transport in kidney and bone and by stimulating the renal 25-hydroxyvitamin D-1α-hydroxylase also exert the capacity of the hormone to stimulate intestinal calcium absorption. Since osteoblasts and fibroblasts but not osteoclasts have receptors for parathyroid hormone, the effects

of parathyroid hormone on stimulating osteoclastic bone resorption are indirect.

Fragments shortened at the amino terminus lose binding affinity more slowly than capacity to stimulate biologic response. The peptide 7-34 is a competitive inhibitor of the binding of active hormone to receptors in vitro and serves as a competitive inhibitor of the renal responses to the hormone, including the increased excretion of cyclic AMP and the enhanced clearance of phosphate. Rapid mobilization of calcium from bone is also blocked in certain test systems in vivo.

Any fragment of parathyroid hormone, to be biologically active on bone and kidney, must consist of the continuous peptide sequence beginning with residue 2, valine, and extending as far as residue 26, lysine.

These observations are of particular interest because the biosynthesis and peripheral metabolism of parathyroid hormone are complex.

Biosynthesis, secretion, metabolism, and mode of action Several larger molecular forms have been identified in the biosynthetic sequence leading from gene transcription and translation to final packaging of the 84-amino acid peptide in secretory granules prior to secretion (Fig. 335-7). The earliest detected precursor form, termed *preproparathyroid hormone*, consists of 115 amino acids; this molecular form is converted to an intermediate form of 90 amino acids termed *proparathyroid hormone*. The details of intracellular regulation of biosynthesis are unknown. Parathyroid hormone shares, with other polypeptides and proteins destined for secretion from cells, this complex pattern of initial synthesis as a larger molecule which is then reduced in size by several cleavages prior to secretion. The hydrophobic regions of the preproparathyroid hormone are similar to preprotein-specific regions of other cell-secreted proteins and may serve a role in guiding transport of the polypeptide from sites of synthesis on polyribosomes through the cytoskeleton to secretory granules. The genes for bovine, rat, and human parathyroid hormone have been cloned, and their structures have been determined. There are considerable homologies in the gene structures as well as in the proteins from these two species.

Blood calcium concentration controls the secretion of parathyroid hormone, and the ionized fraction of blood calcium is the important determinant of hormone secretion. Hormone secretion increases steeply to a maximum value of fivefold above basal rates of secretion whenever calcium concentration falls from normal to the range of 7.5 to 8.0 mg/dL (measured as total calcium). Beta-adrenergic agonists such as epinephrine and histamine-2 agonists may also increase hormone secretion, but the physiologic significance of these secret-agogues is not established. Furthermore, drugs such as propranolol or cimetidine do not reproducibly decrease circulating parathyroid hormone levels.

Magnesium may influence hormone secretion in the same direction as calcium. It is unlikely that physiologic variations in magnesium concentration affect parathyroid secretion, but severe intracellular magnesium deficiency is associated with defective hormone secretion.

The hormone secreted in vivo from normal bovine and human parathyroid glands and from parathyroid adenomas is indistinguishable by immunologic criteria and by molecular size from the 84-amino acid peptide (molecular weight 9500) extracted from glands. However, much of the immunoreactive material found in the peripheral circulation of humans and animals (cow, dog) is smaller than the extracted or secreted hormone. The principal circulating fragments of immunoreactive hormone (approximate molecular weight 7000) lack a portion of the critical amino-terminal sequence required for biologic activity and, hence, are biologically inactive hormonal fragments.

Cleavage of the native peptide by an endopeptidase would be expected to result in formation of a second fragment, molecular weight 2000 to 3000, representing the amino-terminal, biologically active, portion of the hormone. There is uncertainty concerning the presence or absence of such a circulating amino-terminal fragment. It is also unclear (1) whether peripheral metabolism accounts for the circulating fragment(s) of hormone or whether fragments as well as intact hormone can also be secreted by the gland and (2) whether peripheral metabolism is a purely catabolic process concerned only with hormone destruction or whether the peripheral cleavage results in formation of a metabolically active amino-terminal fragment of parathyroid hormone. Present evidence suggests that the liver and kidney are the principal sites at which peripheral metabolism of hormone occurs. Cleavages in these organs may regulate the concentration of hormonally active polypeptides in the circulation (Fig. 335-5). Peripheral metabolism, in turn, may be affected by pathologic processes, such as renal failure or severe hepatic dysfunction.

The rate of clearance of the secreted 84-amino acid peptide from blood is more rapid than the rate of clearance of the smaller, biologically inactive fragment(s) that result from peripheral metabolism. Hence, measurements of parathyroid hormone in blood by most immunoassays provide only an overall index of parathyroid gland activity rather than a direct measure of biologically active hormone,

FIGURE 335-6

Model illustrating the sequence of human, cow, rat, and pig parathyroid hormone.

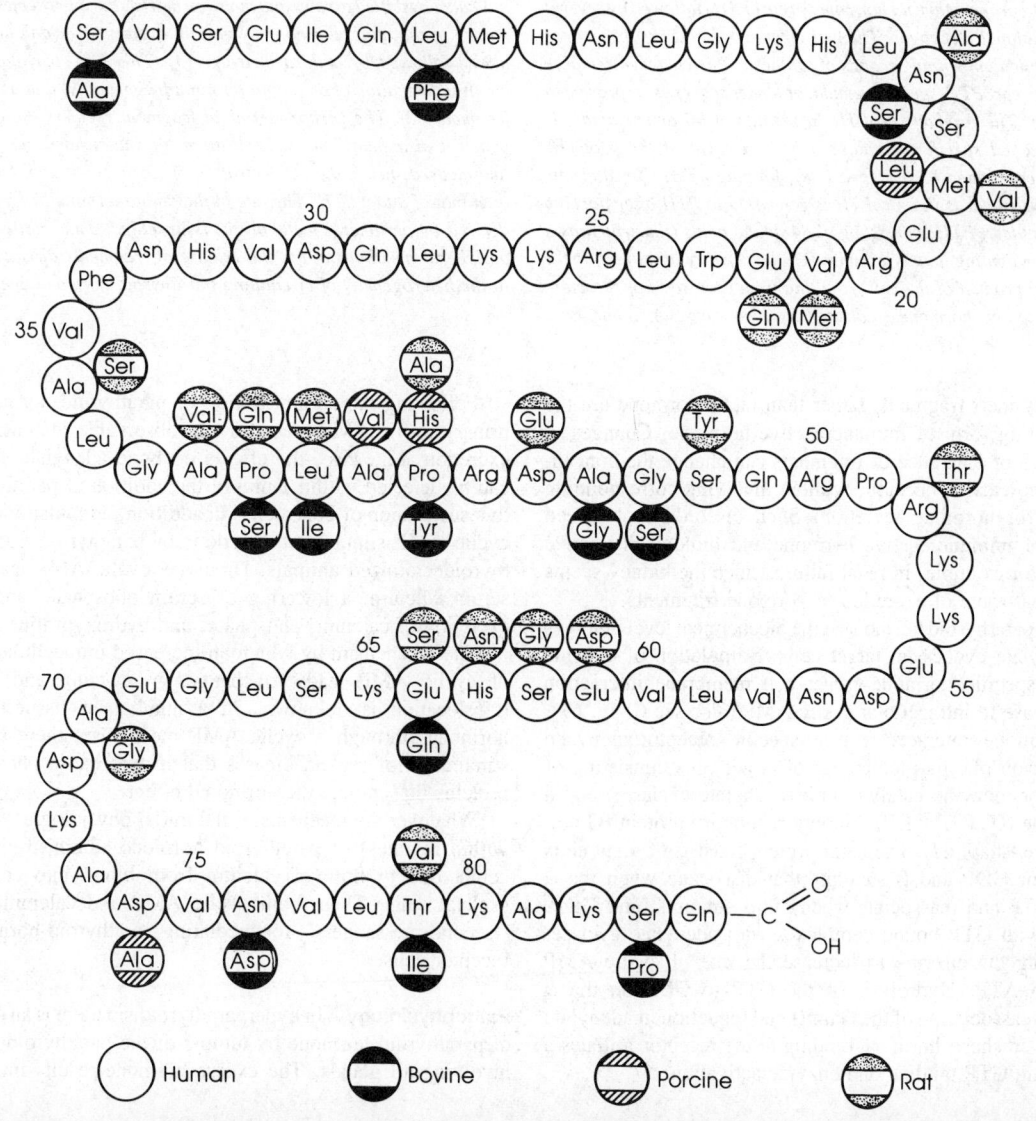

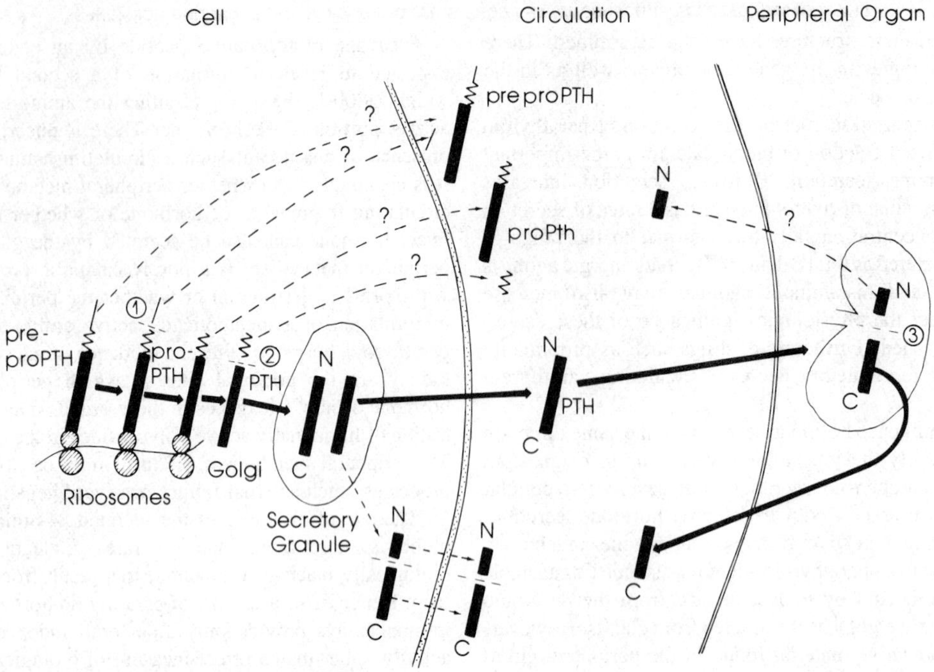

FIGURE 335-7 *Schematic model of the biosynthesis, secretion, and peripheral metabolism of parathyroid hormone, as well as contributions of these processes to the heterogeneity of circulating, immunoreactive parathyroid hormone (see text for details). Biosynthesis involves initial translation of parathyroid hormone–specific messenger RNA (mRNA) into a polypeptide of 115 amino acids, preproparathyroid hormone (preproPTH) followed by several specific posttranslational cleavages. The first cleavage (1) occurs on or near the endoplasmic reticulum within seconds of synthesis; this cleavage removes the 25-amino acid preproPTH-specific peptide, or leader sequence (represented by a straight line). The product, proPTH, a peptide of 90 amino acids, is converted by a second specific peptidase(s) with removal of the proPTH-specific peptide (represented by a jagged line), forming PTH. (An alternate possibility, not illustrated, is that proPTH is converted to PTH after packing into secretory granules.) PTH, consisting of 84 amino acids (illustrated as a heavy bar with N indicating amino terminus, C, the carboxy terminus), is the principal secretory product of the cell, resulting from exocytosis of secretory granules containing the hormone (indicated by heavy arrow). Some have reported that there is an alternate secretory pathway in which amino-terminal fragments (N) and carboxy-terminal fragments (C) of the molecule are formed by further proteolytic processing within the cell followed by release into the circulation (dotted arrows). Speculations concerning release of precursor forms, or fragments (not yet proved), from the cell into the circulation are indicated by dotted arrows and question marks. Peripheral metabolism involves uptake of the intact hormone by certain organs (liver and kidney being most likely) followed by a third cleavage (3). This last cleavage is presumed to result in formation of an amino-terminal fragment (N) and a carboxy-terminal fragment (C). The carboxy-terminal fragment reenters the circulation, from which it disappears more slowly than the intact hormone, and is taken up and cleaved; hence the concentration of carboxy-terminal fragment is higher than that of intact PTH. The fate of the amino-terminal fragment, presumably derived by peripheral metabolism, is unsettled. The relative contribution of peripheral metabolism and the release of fragments directly from the gland to the heterogeneity of circulating parathyroid hormone awaits clarification.*

since biologically inert fragments rather than intact hormone are the principal circulating form of immunoreactive hormone. Changes in rate of production or clearance of fragments can change the concentration of immunoreactive hormone without involving corresponding changes in rate of hormone secretion. Such discordance between concentrations of immunoreactive hormone and biologically active peptide occurs, for example, in renal failure, since the kidney seems to be the principal route of excretion of hormone fragments.

The action of parathyroid hormone at the biochemical level involves effects on adenylate cyclase in target cells. Stimulation of enzyme activity during specific hormone–target cell membrane interaction leads to an increase in intracellular cyclic AMP (also see Chap. 67). Parathyroid hormone interacts with a specific receptor/adenylate cyclase complex on plasma membranes of target cells consisting of hormone receptor, enzyme catalytic unit (adenylate cyclase), and a guanyl nucleotide (GTP or GDP)–binding regulatory protein (G unit or N protein) (see Chap. 67). The latter protein consists of α subunits that bind GTP or GDP and β subunits that dissociate when the α subunits bind GTP and reassociate when the α subunits bind GDP. The α subunit with GTP bound complexes with adenylate cyclase, thereby activating the enzyme to increase the rate of cyclic AMP production from ATP. Hydrolysis of the GTP to GDP on the α subunit leads to reassociation of the G units and reduction in adenylate cyclase activity. In short, hormone binding to the receptor initiates a cycle of α subunit/GTP binding and enzyme activation.

Following the administration of parathyroid hormone the rise in urinary cyclic AMP precedes any observable increase in phosphate excretion. Likewise, the effects on bone adenylate cyclase activity can be detected within 1 min of the addition of parathyroid hormone to a suspension of bone cells. In addition, administration of dibutyryl cyclic AMP simulates the actions of parathyroid hormone in parathyroidectomized animals. Dibutyryl cyclic AMP leads to a rise in serum calcium, a lowering of serum phosphate, and an increased excretion of calcium, phosphate, and hydroxyproline in urine.

The mechanism by which an increased intracellular concentration of cyclic AMP leads to changes in calcium and phosphate ion translocation is unknown. In a number of tissues responsive to hormones through a cyclic AMP mechanism there is evidence for stimulation of protein kinases that in turn cause phosphorylation of proteins that initiate the hormonal effect.

Whatever the mechanism, the initial physiologic effect (occurring within minutes) of parathyroid hormone administration is hypocalcemia due to flow of calcium from blood into cells, apparently skeletal cells. Thus, both cyclic AMP and calcium may serve as "second messengers" for mediating parathyroid hormone effects in receptor cells.

Pathophysiology In hyperparathyroidism there is an overproduction of parathyroid hormone by tumors of the parathyroid or hyperplasia involving all glands. The excess hormone results in hypercalcemia secondary to increased intestinal calcium absorption [increased synthesis of $1,25(OH)_2D_3$] and reduced renal calcium clearance. In many patients there is also increased bone resorption; bone turnover increases in all patients, with resorption exceeding formation in many. Individual patients respond to the excess hormone variably at intestinal, renal, and bone target sites; the factors influencing the variable response from patient to patient are not known (see Chap. 336).

Hypophosphatemia results from the actions of the excessive parathyroid hormone on renal tubular phosphate reabsorption. Hypophosphatemia in turn aggravates the hypercalcemia in part by increasing the synthesis of $1,25(OH)_2D_3$ and by increasing the sensitivity of the bone to resorption. The hypophosphatemia may also interfere with the normal mineralization of bone leading to a mixed picture of both increased resorption and deficient mineralization in adjacent skeletal sites.

Hypoparathyroidism causes hypocalcemia and hyperphosphatemia, a reversal of the response seen with hormone excess (see Chap. 336).

CALCITONIN (See also Chap. 334)   Calcitonin is the potent hypocalcemic, hypophosphatemic peptide hormone that, in many ways, acts as the physiologic antagonist to parathyroid hormone. Calcitonin reduces bone resorption and has opposing effects to parathyroid hormone on the kidney in that it increases renal calcium clearance. Calcitonin exerts its effects through stimulation of membrane-bound adenylate cyclase in receptor cells in kidney and bone. There is a variable hormonal responsiveness of renal tubular cells to calcitonin, parathyroid hormone, and vasopressin. In some portions of the nephron, cells respond to all three hormones, whereas in others the response is restricted to one or two. In bone, osteoclasts possess calcitonin receptors.

The thyroid gland is the major source of the hormone in mammalian species, and the cells involved in calcitonin synthesis arise from neural crest tissue. During embryogenesis these cells migrate into the ultimobranchial body. The latter body or gland arises from the last branchial pouch, hence the name _ultimobranchial body_. In submammalian vertebrates the ultimobranchial body remains as a discrete organ, anatomically separate from the thyroid gland. In mammals the ultimobranchial gland fuses with and is incorporated into the thyroid gland. Calcitonin is found in all vertebrate classes.

The naturally occurring calcitonins consist of a peptide chain of 32 amino acids. There is a considerable amount of variability in sequence among species. The entire chain of 32 amino acids appears to be required for biologic activity in the whole animal, although fragments function in in vitro systems. The factors that regulate the synthesis of calcitonin are not known. Calcitonin from salmon is 25 to 100 times more potent by weight in lowering serum calcium in animals than are other forms of calcitonin. For example, the salmon hormone is at least 10 times more potent in humans than human calcitonin. Slow turnover may explain in part the greater biologic potency of salmon calcitonin, but the hormone binds more strongly to receptor sites as well. Calcitonin is synthesized as a precursor molecule, the parent molecule being four times larger than calcitonin itself. Analysis of the sequence of the coding portions of the gene for rat calcitonin indicates that at least two peptides flank calcitonin from which they are separated by basic residues. It is likely (in analogy with the common precursor for ACTH and endorphin) that these peptides are released with calcitonin and have actions that, for example, might explain certain pathophysiologic features in syndromes associated with excess calcitonin production. There are two calcitonin genes, α and β, located on chromosome 11 in the general region of the beta globin and parathyroid hormone genes. The transcription of the calcitonin gene is complex. Two different messenger RNA molecules are transcribed from the α gene; one is translated into the precursor for calcitonin, and the other message is transcribed into an alternate product, calcitonin-gene-related peptide (CGRP). CGRP is synthesized wherever the calcitonin message is expressed, for example, in medullary carcinoma of the thyroid. The

β gene is transcribed into the messenger RNA for CGRP in the central nervous system in animals. CGRP may serve a neurotransmitter role; the expression of the β gene in human beings, as distinct from animals, has not been shown but is presumed to occur.

The secretion of calcitonin is under the direct control of blood calcium: an increase in calcium causes an increase and a decrease in calcium causes a decrease in calcitonin levels. Once secreted, calcitonin disappears rapidly from the circulation with a half-life of 2 to 15 min.

The concentration of calcitonin in the peripheral blood of normal humans is lower than in many other species. Basal and stimulated immunoreactive calcitonin levels are lower in women than in men and tend to decrease with age to a greater extent in women.

The physiologic role of calcitonin is incompletely understood. In animals calcitonin acts to lower both blood calcium and blood phosphate; the principal action is inhibition of bone resorption. The importance of calcitonin in increasing urinary calcium and phosphate clearance is synergistic with its effects on bone resorption. The actions of calcitonin on kidney and bone are in turn modulated by the regulation of calcitonin production by serum calcium. The view that calcitonin serves to protect against hypercalcemia is thus explained by the hypocalcemic effects of calcitonin triggered in response to hypercalcemia.

The role of calcitonin, if any, however, in normal adult humans is unknown. Changes in calcium and phosphate metabolism are not seen in humans despite extremes of variation in hormone production; there are no definite effects attributable to calcitonin deficiency (totally thyroidectomized patients replaced only with thyroxine) or excess (patients with the calcitonin-secreting tumor, medullary carcinoma of the thyroid). Patients with the latter disorder suffer multiple deleterious consequences of their malignancy (see Chap. 334), but no abnormalities in calcium or bone metabolism are recognized, perhaps because they become refractory to the skeletal effects of calcitonin.

Medical interest in calcitonin, therefore, at present is centered principally upon its use as a therapeutic agent and its usefulness, when deployed in radioimmunoassays, for detection of medullary carcinoma (Chap. 334). The use of calcitonin in the treatment of Paget's disease of bone is established (Chap. 338).

REFERENCES

ADAMS JS et al: Isolation and structural identification of 1,25-dihydroxyvitamin D_3 produced by cultured alveolar macrophages in sarcoidosis. J Clin Endocrinol Metab 60:960, 1985

AVIOLI LV, KRANE SM: _Metabolic Bone Disease._ New York, Academic, 1977 and 1978, vols I and II

BRINGHURST FR, POTTS JT JR: Calcium and phosphate distribution, turnover, and metabolic actions, in _Endocrinology,_ vol 2, LJ DeGroot (ed). New York, Grune & Stratton, 1979, p 551

BROADUS AE et al: The importance of circulating 1,25-dihydroxyvitamin D in the pathogenesis of hypercalcemia and renal stone-formation in primary hyperparathyroidism. N Engl J Med 302:421, 1981

BURGER EH et al: Osteoclast formation from mononuclear phagocytes: Role of bone-forming cells. J Cell Biol 99:1901, 1984

CENTRELLA M, CANALIS E: Local regulators of skeletal growth: A perspective. Endocrinol Rev 6:544, 1985

CHAMBERS TJ, DUNN CJ: Pharmacological control of osteoclastic motility. Calcif Tissue Int 35:566, 1983

DELUCA HF: The vitamin D system in the regulation of calcium and phosphorus metabolism. Nutr Rev 37:161, 1979

EIL C et al: A cellular defect in hereditary vitamin D-dependent rickets type II. Defective nuclear uptake of 1,25-dihydroxyvitamin D in culture skin fibroblasts. N Engl J Med 304:1588, 1981

FRAME B, POTTS JT JR: _Clinical Disorders of Bone and Mineral Metabolism._ Amsterdam Excerpta Medica, 1983

GRAY TK et al: Vitamin D and pregnancy: The maternal-fetal metabolism of vitamin D. Endocrinol Rev 2:264, 1981

KEUTMANN HT et al: Rat parathyroid hormone (1–34) fragments: Renal adenyl/cyclase activity and receptor binding properties in vitro. Endocrinology, 117:1230, 1985

KRANE SM, SCHILLER AL: Metabolic bone disease: Introduction and classification, in _Endocrinology,_ vol 2, LJ DeGroot (ed). New York, Grune & Stratton, 1979, p 839

MacLAUGHLIN J, HOLICK MF: Aging decreases the capacity of human skin to produce vitamin D_3. J Clin Invest 76:1536, 1985

NORMAN AW et al (eds): _Vitamin D: Chemical, Biochemical and Clinical Update_

(Proceedings 6th Workshop on Vitamin D, Merano, Italy). New York, de Gruyter 1985

PARFITT AM: The coupling of bone formation to bone resorption: A critical analysis of the concept and of its relevance to the pathogenesis of osteoporosis. Metab Bone Dis Relat Res 4:1, 1982

————: The cellular basis of bone remodeling: The quantum concept reexamined in light of recent advances in the cell biology of bone. Calcif Tissue Int 36:S37, 1984

POTTS JT JR et al: Parathyroid hormone: Chemistry, biosynthesis, and mode of action, in *Advances in Protein Chemistry,* CB Afinsen et al (eds). New York, Academic, 1982, vol 35

RAISZ LG, KREAM BE: Regulation of bone formation. N Engl J Med 309:29, 83, 1983

ROBEY PG, TERMINE JD: Human bone cells in vitro. Calcif Tissue Int 37:453, 1985

RODAN GA, MARTIN TJ: Role of osteoblasts in hormonal control of bone resorption—A hypothesis. Calcif Tissue Int 33:349, 1981

ROSENFELD MG et al: Production of a novel neuropeptide encoded by the calcitonin gene via tissue-specific RNA processing. Nature 304:129, 1983

ROSENTHAL N et al: Elevations in circulating 1,25-dihydroxyvitamin D in three patients with lymphoma-associated hypercalcemia. J Clin Endocrinol Metab 60:29, 1985

SCRIVER CR et al: Serum 1,25-dihydroxyvitamin D levels in normal subjects and in patients with hereditary rickets or bone disease. N Engl J Med 299:976, 1978

TALMAGE RV et al: *The Physiological Significance of Calcitonin in Bone and Mineral Research, Annual 1,* WA Peck (ed). Amsterdam, Excerpta Medica, 1983

URIST MR et al: Bone cell differentiation and growth factors. Science 220:680, 1983

336 DISEASES OF THE PARATHYROID GLAND AND OTHER HYPER- AND HYPOCALCEMIC DISORDERS

JOHN T. POTTS, JR.

HYPERCALCEMIA

Management of hypercalcemia is a particular problem when the patient is asymptomatic. The number of patients recognized with asymptomatic hypercalcemia has increased severalfold in the last two decades; the hypercalcemia is usually found after use of screening tests during annual physical examinations. If the patient is asymptomatic, does the hypercalcemia always require further evaluation? What are the most probable causes of hypercalcemia, and how can they be diagnosed? Can asymptomatic patients be followed, or is definitive therapy to eliminate the hypercalcemia the optimal medical management?

There is a consensus that whenever hypercalcemia is confirmed, a definitive diagnosis must be established. Although hyperparathyroidism, a frequent cause of asymptomatic hypercalcemia, is a chronic disorder in which manifestations, if any, may be expressed only over months or years, hypercalcemia can also be the earliest clue to the presence of malignancy, the second most common cause of hypercalcemia in the adult. In Table 336-1 the causes of hypercalcemia have been grouped into five categories based upon the pathophysiologic mechanism involved.

Before undertaking an evaluation of hypercalcemia it is essential to ensure that true hypercalcemia is actually present, not a false-positive laboratory test. Hypercalcemia is a chronic problem, and it is cost-effective to obtain several serum calcium measurements; these tests need not be in the fasting state. False-positive calcium tests are usually the result of inadvertent hemoconcentration during blood collection or elevation in serum proteins, particularly albumin. Measurement of ionized calcium in technically feasible, but there is no advantage, except in research applications, to measurement of ionized rather than total calcium.

All causes of hypercalcemia other than hyperparathyroidism and malignancy account for less than 10 percent of hypercalcemia. Hypercalcemia in an adult who is asymptomatic is usually due to primary hyperparathyroidism, but the problem of differentiating primary hyperparathyroidism from occult malignancy can occasionally present a problem in differential diagnosis. In most cases of malignancy-associated hypercalcemia the disease is not occult; rather, symptoms of the underlying malignancy bring the patient to the physician, and hypercalcemia is discovered during the workup. In patients with malignancy the interval between detection of hypercalcemia and death is often less then 6 months. Accordingly, if an asymptomatic individual has had hypercalcemia or some manifestation of hypercalcemia, such as kidney stones, for more than 1 or 2 years, it is unlikely that malignancy is the cause.

Hypercalcemia not due to hyperparathyroidism or malignancy can result from excessive vitamin D action, high bone turnover from any of several causes, or renal failure (Table 336-1). The sensitivity and specificity of various diagnostic tests for the differential diagnosis are not optimal. The radioimmunoassays for measurement of parathyroid hormone and $1\alpha,25$-dihydroxyvitamin D ($1,25(OH)_2D$), the active metabolite of vitamin D, are useful in distinguishing certain broad categories of disease associated with hypercalcemia, for example, primary hyperparathyroidism from malignancy-associated hypercalcemia. Dietary history and a history of ingestion of vitamins and drugs are often helpful in recognizing some of the less frequent causes. Except in malignancy-associated hypercalcemia, acute management of the hypercalcemia is usually easy to accomplish prior to the institution of definitive therapy. The type of treatment is based on the severity of the hypercalcemia and the nature of associated symptoms.

Hypercalcemia from any cause can result in fatigue, depression, mental confusion, anorexia, nausea, vomiting, constipation, reversible renal tubular defects, increased urination, alteration in the electrocardiogram (a short QT interval), and, in some patients, cardiac arrhythmias. There is a variable relation between the severity of hypercalcemia and the presence or absence of symptoms from one patient to the next. Generally, symptoms are more common at calcium levels above 11.5 or 12.0 mg/dL, but some patients, even at this level, are asymptomatic. When calcium exceeds 13 mg/dL, renal insufficiency and calcification in kidneys, skin, vessels, lungs, heart, and stomach may occur, particularly if blood phosphate levels are normal or elevated due to impaired renal function. Severe hypercalcemia, usually defined as 15 mg/dL or above, is a medical emergency. When serum calcium is 15 to 18 mg/dL or higher, coma and cardiac arrest can occur.

PARATHYROID-RELATED HYPERCALCEMIA   Primary hyperparathyroidism   NATURAL HISTORY AND INCIDENCE   Primary hyperparathyroidism is a generalized disorder of calcium, phosphate, and bone metabolism that results from an increased secretion of parathyroid hormone. The excessive concentration of circulating hormone usually leads to hypercalcemia and hypophosphatemia. There is great variation in the clinical presentation. Patients may present with multiple signs and symptoms, including recurrent nephrolithiasis, peptic ulcers, mental changes, and, less frequently, extensive bone resorption. However, with greater awareness of the disease and wider use of multiphasic screening tests, including blood calcium, the diagnosis is frequently made in patients who have no symptoms and minimal, if any, signs of the disease other than hypercalcemia and elevated

TABLE 336-1   Classification of causes of hypercalcemia

Parathyroid-related:	**Vitamin D-related**
1 Primary hyperparathyroidism	*1* Vitamin D intoxication
a Solitary adenomas	*2* ↑ $1,25(OH)_2D$; sarcoidosis
b Multiple endocrine neoplasia	and other granulomatous diseases
2 Lithium therapy	eases
3 Familial hypocalciuric hypercalcemia	*3* Idiopathic hypercalcemia of infancy
	fancy
Malignancy-related:	**Associated with high bone turnover:**
1 Solid tumor with metastases (breast)	*1* Hyperthyroidism
	2 Immobilization
2 Solid tumor with humoral mediation of hypercalcemia (lung, kidney)	*3* Thiazides
	4 Vitamin A intoxication
	Associated with renal failure:
3 Hematologic malignancies (multiple myeloma, lymphoma, leukemia)	*1* Severe secondary hyperparathyroidism
	2 Aluminum intoxication
	3 Milk alkali syndrome

levels of parathyroid hormone. If the frequency of diagnosis in referral centers reflects the incidence of the disease, hyperparathyroidism is more common than previously appreciated. In fact, the *incidence* of primary hyperparathyroidism may approximate *1 case per 1000 per year* in men over the age of 60, and *2 per 1000* in women 60 years of age older. This incidence is greater than earlier estimates of *1 case per 10,000 persons per year* which were based on evaluation of patients with symptoms, such as calcium-containing kidney stones. The clinical manifestations may be subtle, and the disease may have a benign course for many years or a full lifetime. Rarely, the disease seems to appear abruptly, and patients may exhibit severe complications, such as marked dehydration and coma, so-called hypercalcemic parathyroid crisis. The disease most commonly occurs in adults, with peak incidence between the third and fifth decades but it has been detected in young children and in the elderly.

ETIOLOGY AND PATHOLOGY   *Solitary adenomas*   Disease in a single gland occurs in approximately 85 percent (81 percent adenoma, 4 percent carcinoma), and hyperplasia of all glands is present in approximately 15 percent of cases (usually chief-cell hyperplasia). Rarely, adenomas are present in more than one gland with the other glands normal. The finding that either one gland only is abnormal or that all glands are abnormal is helpful to the surgeon in planning exploration of the neck. Resection of a single adenoma usually cures the disease.

Adenomas are most often located in the inferior parathyroid glands, but they are found in unusual locations in 6 to 10 percent of patients; such parathyroid adenomas may be located in the thymus, the thyroid, the pericardium, or behind the esophagus. Adenomas are usually 0.5 to 5 g in size, but may be as large as 10 to 20 g (normal glands are 25 mg in weight on average). Chief cells are predominant in both hyperplasia and adenoma. The adenoma is sometimes encapsulated by a rim of normal tissue. Chief-cell hyperplasia is especially common in familial cases of hyperparathyroidism and those that are part of the multiple endocrine neoplasia syndromes (see Chap. 334). Cells of a different histologic appearance such as oxyphil cells are occasionally present. The distinction between hyperplasia and adenoma can sometimes be difficult to establish. With hyperplasia the enlargement may be so asymmetric that some involved glands appear normal grossly. In this case, histologic examination reveals a uniform pattern of chief cells and disappearance of fat even in the absence of an increase in gland weight. Thus, microscopic examination of biopsy specimens of several glands is essential to interpret findings at surgery. When an adenoma is present, the other glands are normal and contain a normal distribution of all cell types (rather than only chief cells) and normal amounts of fat.

Parathyroid carcinoma is usually not aggressive in character. Long-term survival without recurrence is common if at initial operation the entire gland is removed without rupture of the capsule. Even recurrent parathyroid carcinoma is usually slow-growing with local spread in the neck, and surgical correction of recurrent disease may be feasible. Occasionally, parathyroid carcinoma is more aggressive in character with distant metastases (lung, liver, and bone) found at the time of initial operation. It may be difficult initially to decide if the primary tumor is carcinoma; increased numbers of mitotic figures and increased fibrosis of the gland stroma may precede invasive features. Hyperparathyroidism from a parathyroid carcinoma may be clinically indistinguishable from other forms of primary hyperparathyroidism; a potential clue to the diagnosis, however, is provided by the degree of calcium elevation. Calcium values of 14 to 15 mg/dL are frequent with carcinoma.

Multiple endocrine neoplasia   Hyperparathyroidism may occur in a familial pattern without other endocrinologic abnormality. More often, however, hereditary hyperparathyroidism is part of a multiglandular endocrinopathy (see Chap. 334). There are several distinct syndromes of multiple endocrine neoplasia (MEN). The type I disorder (MEN I, Wermer's syndrome) consists of hyperparathyroidism and tumors of the pituitary and pancreatic islet cells, often associated

with peptic ulcer and gastric hypersecretion (the Zollinger-Ellison syndrome). Another distinct constellation of endocrinologic abnormalities consists of hyperparathyroidism associated with pheochromocytoma and medullary carcinoma of the thyroid (MEN II). The pattern of inheritance is autosomal dominant. Tumors of the thyroid and adrenal medulla are not found in patients with MEN I, and pancreatic and pituitary tumors are not found in patients with MEN II. Since the different endocrine tumors can develop at widely separated intervals, hyperparathyroidism and the related endocrine disorders should be carefully and repeatedly searched for in kindreds afflicted with the MEN syndromes.

SIGNS AND SYMPTOMS   Half or more of patients with hyperparathyroidism are asymptomatic. These patients are either followed without therapy or are operated upon, eliminating the disease state. Specific signs or symptoms of hyperparathyroidism involve primarily the kidneys and the skeletal system. Kidney involvement, due either to deposition of calcium in the renal parenchyma or to recurrent nephrolithiasis, was present in 60 to 70 percent of patients prior to 1970. With the increased frequency of detection of asymptomatic individuals, the incidence of renal complications is lower.

Renal stones are usually composed of either calcium oxalate or calcium phosphate. Repeated episodes of nephrolithiasis or the formation of large calculi may lead to urinary tract obstruction and infection, and may result in loss of renal function. Nephrocalcinosis may also cause decreased renal function and phosphate retention. Nephrolithiasis and nephrocalcinosis rarely occur in the same patient.

The unique bone involvement in hyperparathyroidism is osteitis fibrosa cystica. Several decades ago, an incidence of osteitis fibrosa cystica of 10 to 25 percent or even higher was reported in patients with hyperparathyroidism. Histologically the pathognomonic features include a reduction in the number of trabeculae, an increase in the giant multinucleated osteoclasts in scalloped areas on the surface of the bone (Howship's lacunae), and a replacement of the normal cellular and marrow elements by fibrous tissues. Other bone changes include resorption of the phalangeal tufts and a replacement of the usually sharp cortical outline of the bone in the digits by an irregular outline (subperiosteal resorption). Loss of the lamina dura of the teeth is less specific. Tiny, "punched-out" lesions may be present in the skull, producing the so-called salt-and-pepper appearance.

At the present time osteitis fibrosa cystica is not common, even though there may be a long history of manifestations of the disease. The reduced frequency has not been explained. Other manifestations of bone disease, however, are still common. Histomorphometric analyses of biopsied bone reveal an abnormality in bone turnover in most patients, even in those who do not evidence progressive loss of net bone mass; in such patients, rate of bone formation and bone restoration may be increased but balanced. In many patients, however, who do not have symptomatic bone disease or osteitis fibrosa cystica, rates of formation and resorption are not balanced so that a progressive loss of bone mineral mass causes osteopenia, indicating the need for surgery. There are no pathognomonic criteria to separate unequivocally parathyroid-dependent osteopenia from "high-turnover" osteoporosis as occurs in patients who are not hyperparathyroid.

Improved techniques are now available for monitoring bone mineral density. Computer tomography of the spine provides reproducible quantitative estimates (within a few percent) of spinal bone density. Similar, highly reproducible quantitation is also possible by photon densitometry for measurement of cortical bone density in the extremities, and dual beam photometry can be used to estimate bone density in the spine. These techniques can provide an early indication of progressive osteopenia through serial measurements. In some patients surgery is recommended because of progressive loss of bone, with the presumption that the progressive osteopenia is parathyroid hormone–dependent and hence treatable by correction of the hyperparathyroidism. Some patients have been followed for periods of several years, on the other hand, without any evidence of loss of bone mass.

Hence, bone disease in association with primary hyperparathyroidism can be quite variable.

Symptoms attributable to the central nervous system, peripheral nerve and muscle function, the gastrointestinal tract, and the joints are the next most common manifestations of hyperparathyroidism after those attributable to the skeleton and the genitourinary tract. An awareness of the signs and symptoms of advanced disease may be the initial clue to diagnosis. In patients with serum calcium above 12 mg/dL, central nervous system manifestations and gastrointestinal disorders are more common; even more severe hypercalcemia may supervene in such patients with dehydration. It is not apparent why some patients with hyperparathyroidism have no symptoms, while others, with an equal degree of biochemical abnormality, develop symptomatic disease.

FIGURE 336-1 *The relation between blood calcium and iPTH in normal subjects (panel A) and subjects with 2° hyperparathyroidism (panel B). This is a model of secondary hyperparathyroidism associated with an increased mass of parathyroid tissue. The heavy line represents normal secretory patterns and the lighter line the exaggerated secretion (steeper slope) typical of secondary hyperparathyroidism [secretion represented as hormone concentration (PTH) plotted against blood calcium]. When calcium level in blood is raised or lowered by EDTA or calcium infusion, and multiple measurements of PTH and calcium are made, some portion of hormone secretion in normals or hyperparathyroid subjects is constant despite high calcium levels in blood (nonsuppressible secretion) and is higher in hyperparathyroidism. An elevation of blood calcium from low levels (8 mg/100 mL, X) to higher levels (9 mg/100 mL, ●) results in a reduction in PTH in both normal and hyperparathyroid individuals, but true involution of secondary hyperparathyroidism with improved treatment can be confirmed only by showing a return of the exaggerated response curve to a normal response.*

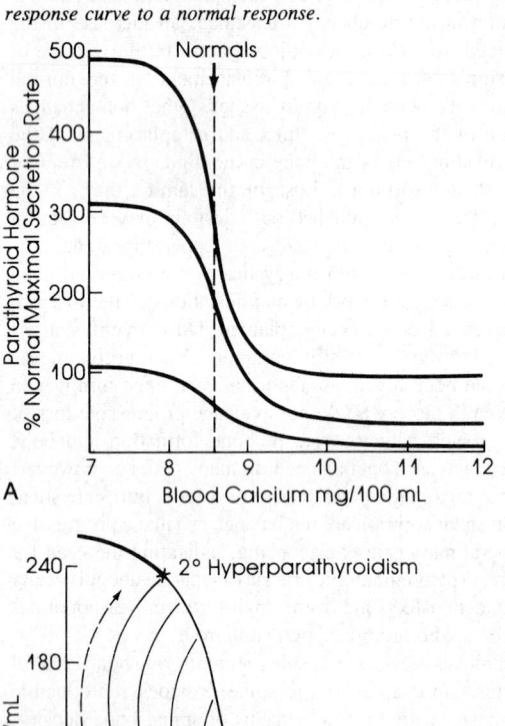

Central nervous system manifestations range from mild personality disturbance to severe psychiatric disorders to mental obtundation or coma. In some instances, multiple vague complaints can be mistaken for psychoneurosis. It must be emphasized, however, that mild depression, a common problem in the absence of hyperparathyroidism, cannot be the sole clinical criterion for parathyroid surgery.

Neuromuscular manifestations include proximal muscle weakness, easy fatigability, and atrophy of muscles. The electromyogram is abnormal, and muscle fibers atrophy without myopathic changes. The clinical signs may be so striking as to suggest a primary neuromuscular disorder. The distinguishing feature is the complete regression of neuromuscular disease after surgical correction of the hyperparathyroidism.

Gastrointestinal manifestations are sometimes subtle and include vague abdominal complaints and disorders of the stomach and pancreas. Duodenal ulcers occur more frequently than in the general population. In MEN I patients with hyperparathyroidism, duodenal ulcer is a result of the associated pancreatic tumors that secrete excessive quantities of gastrin (the Zollinger-Ellison syndrome). Pancreatitis has been reported in association with hyperparathyroidism, but the incidence and the mechanism are not established.

Chondrocalcinosis and pseudogout are said to be seen in sufficiently frequent association with hyperparathyroidism that screening of such patients is warranted. Occasionally, pseudogout is the initial manifestation.

DIAGNOSIS The diagnosis is made primarily on clinical grounds. The immunoassay for parathyroid hormone (PTH) is of value as a diagnostic test, but there are many problems in interpretation of assay results. Characteristically, immunoreactive PTH levels are frankly elevated or inappropriately normal for the degree of hypercalcemia (Fig. 336-1). Since hypercalcemia can be the presenting evidence for malignancy or other serious disease, a thorough evaluation of possible etiologies, including hyperparathyroidism, is indicated even in asymptomatic subjects. If the diagnosis of hyperparathyroidism is suspected after such an evaluation, a decision may be made to follow the patient for a time rather than recommend surgery.

Hypercalcemia is the most common manifestation, either sustained hypercalcemia or intermittent hypercalcemia. Careful consideration must be given to the justification for surgical exploration in the absence of hypercalcemia. So-called normocalcemic hyperparathyroidism, that is, patients with surgically proven hyperparathyroidism who have normal calcium but elevated values of immunoreactive PTH (iPTH), is rare in the absence of renal failure or gastrointestinal disease. If the patients have coexisting conditions that interfere with the calcium-elevating actions of PTH, such as chronic renal failure, severe malabsorption, or vitamin D deficiency, then the lack of calcium elevation need not argue against the presence of true hyperparathyroidism. Confusing situations can arise, however, in patients with recurrent kidney stones who are suspected of having hyperparathyroidism because of elevated iPTH levels but who have normal serum calcium. These patients may represent true normocalcemic hyperparathyroidism. In such situations where the symptoms call for an early definitive diagnosis, it may be useful to search for postabsorptive hypercalcemia (detectable in certain patients when fasting hypercalcemia is absent) or to use a provocative test with benzothiadiazides (see below).

Hypercalciuria is common in hyperparathyroidism. However, PTH actually reduces calcium clearance, and the daily excretion of calcium in urine is lower than in patients with equivalent degrees of hypercalcemia from nonparathyroid causes.

Serum phosphate is usually low but may be normal, especially if renal failure has developed. Hypophosphatemia is a less stringent diagnostic criterion than hypercalcemia for two reasons. One, phosphate levels are influenced by dietary intake, diurnal variations, and other factors; to be useful samples must be obtained in the morning under fasting conditions. Two, patients with severe hypercalcemia of all causes may have a low serum phosphate.

Other electrolyte abnormalities are not sufficiently specific to be of diagnostic value. Serum magnesium levels tend to be low, serum chloride and citrate are often elevated, and serum bicarbonate is reduced. The combination of elevated chloride and low phosphate (reflecting the acidosis and renal phosphate wasting, respectively) can be a diagnostic clue.

Blood alkaline phosphatase (of bone origin) and urinary hydroxyproline concentrations are elevated when bone involvement is significant. Renal involvement can be reflected by a decreased concentrating ability, by specific tubular defects such as renal tubular acidosis, or by frank renal failure with azotemia.

Assessing the response of serum calcium to glucocorticoid administration can be useful in differentiating the hypercalcemia of hyperparathyroidism from that associated with sarcoidosis, multiple myeloma, vitamin D intoxication, and some malignant diseases with osseous metastases. In these diseases, administration of hydrocortisone at 100 mg per day (or an equivalent dose of prednisone) for 10 days often results in a lowering of the serum calcium, whereas calcium does not usually decrease in hyperparathyroidism. Occasional falsepositive and false-negative results occur. The mechanism of the glucocorticoid effect in hypercalcemic states may reflect the physiologic antagonism between glucocorticoids and vitamin D action in vitamin D intoxication and sarcoidosis and the tumor-suppressive action of glucocorticoids in some forms of malignancy.

A variety of tests of parathyroid function are based on the known effects of the hormone on the renal handling of phosphate, namely PTH decreases tubular resorption of phosphate. Phosphate clearance is determined by standard techniques over 1- to 2-h periods. Normal phosphate clearance is 10.8 ± 2.7 mL/min; values 50 percent or more above this figure may occur in hyperparathyroidism. In normal subjects the tubular resorption of phosphate exceeds 85 percent; in hyperparathyroidism tubular resorption of phosphate may be as low as 50 to 60 percent.

Measurements of nephrogenous cyclic AMP are useful in diagnosis. The test requires timed urine collections and measurements of plasma and urinary cyclic AMP. The test is limited in applicability, not only by technical difficulties, but also by problems of specificity. For example, patients with the humoral hypercalcemia of malignancy may have elevated nephrogenous cyclic AMP values in the range seen in primary hyperparathyroidism. In other studies, nephrogenous cyclic AMP correlates poorly with the presence or absence of hypercalcemia, and urinary cyclic AMP levels may be elevated in some cancer patients, independent of whether skeletal metastases or hypercalcemia is present.

TREATMENT   *Medical treatment*   The medical treatment of hyperparathyroidism involves two separate issues. If hypercalcemia is severe and symptomatic, then the calcium must be lowered (the measures are described subsequently in the general section of the medical management of hypercalcemia of any cause). Hypercalcemia is not symptomatic in most patients with hyperparathyroidism, and it is usually not difficult to control the hypercalcemia. Simple hydration will suffice to lower the calcium concentration to values below 11.5 mg/dL. There have been some discussions in the past about whether chronic management of the hypercalcemia of hyperparathyroidism should be undertaken with oral phosphate therapy. Although the calcium concentration is lowered by phosphate in most patients, this is accompanied by an increase in iPTH levels in blood. It is unclear whether the increased PTH levels would cause more or less organ deterioration. There have been no systematic trials to evaluate effects of specific medical therapy for hypercalcemia.

Rather, the usual issue is to decide whether surgical intervention is required in a particular patient. If not, medical management consists of following the patient without specific therapy, but monitoring bone and renal function periodically to ensure that silent osseous and renal deterioration does not occur. If undesirable signs or symptoms occur, surgical intervention can then be recommended.

The natural history of the disease has been studied in several centers. Several hundred patients have been followed in attempts to afford a rational explanation for the benefits of surgery or the risks of medical observation. Large-scale randomized prospective clinical trials have not been undertaken, however. Rather, the long-term effects of hyperparathyroidism have been assessed in patients who do not have kidney stones, osteitis fibrosa cystica, or other clear-cut symptoms. Of principal concern is the possibility of progressive loss of bone density, a worrying problem in women who face the problem of age-dependent and estrogen-deficient bone loss in the absence of hyperparathyroidism. The concern is that such patients, even though asymptomatic, will suffer a degree of bone loss due to PTH excess that will lead to acceleration of symptomatic osteoporosis. No generalization can be made in this regard other than that some patients, followed with noninvasive techniques for measuring bone density, show no evidence of substantial bone loss. Others show bone loss that is progressive. The reproducibility of the available noninvasive techniques for assessing bone density is 1 to 2 percent, and if progressive bone loss becomes significant, for example, a loss of 10 percent of skeletal mass, most physicians recommend surgery to prevent further bone loss. Such decisions are arbitrary in that the loss of bone, particularly in an older patient, may not be due to the hyperparathyroidism, and bone loss may not cease once the patient is rendered euparathyroid. It is not that one can guarantee that parathyroidectomy will arrest progressive bone loss but rather that one cannot afford, except in a very elderly patient, to run the risk that persistent hyperthyroidism may accelerate skeletal disease.

There are no indexes that help in predicting whether bone loss will be progressive or whether skeletal mass will remain stable. Hence, if patients wish to avoid surgery, bone mass must be monitored systematically at intervals of 6 months to 1 year. Loss of renal function does not usually occur in the absence of kidney stones or infection.

No uniform recommendation can be made regarding medical (nonsurgical) management of patients with hyperparathyroidism. Decisions must be made in the light of the age of the patient and social and psychological factors. Most physicians believe it is appropriate to operate on young persons to avoid lifelong monitoring with time-consuming and expensive studies, particularly since surgical treatment is usually successful and does not carry a significant risk of mortality or morbidity. In patients over the age of 50 conservative evaluation without surgery is reasonable if the patient prefers and if progressive bone loss is not seen. The operation can be recommended in any patient in whom progressive bone loss is documented or in whom other symptoms of the disease appear, or if the stress of longterm follow-up is greater than the commitment to surgical "cure."

Surgical treatment   Parathyroid exploration should be undertaken only by an experienced surgeon with the help of an experienced pathologist. Certain clinical features help in predicting the pathology; for example, in familial cases, multiple abnormal glands are likely. However, some critical decisions regarding management can be made only during the operation. The examination of tissue removed at surgery by frozen section should direct the subsequent course of the operation. The usual procedure recommended by the author's colleagues is as follows: if an abnormal gland is identified, remove it and search for at least one additional gland. If the second gland is normal in size and normal histologically (frozen section), the hyperparathyroidism is likely due to a single adenoma, and exploration is stopped. Some surgeons have argued that several glands are usually involved and that subtotal parathyroidectomy is the procedure of choice. The risk of the former approach is lack of cure or early recurrence; the risk of the latter is hypoparathyroidism. It is our belief that single gland removal leads in most patients to long-term cure.

Hyperplasia involves even more difficult questions of surgical management. Once a diagnosis of hyperplasia has been established, it is necessary to identify all the glands. It usually is recommended that three glands be totally removed and that the fourth gland be partially excised; care should be taken to leave a good blood supply for the remaining gland. Some surgeons advocate transplantation of a portion of the removed, minced tissue into the muscles of the forearm to avoid late vascular failure of residual parathyroid tissue in the neck. When parathyroid carcinoma is encountered, the tissue should be widely excised; care must be taken to avoid rupture of the capsule to prevent local seeding of the tumor.

If no glandular abnormalities are found in the neck, the issue of further neck exploration must be decided. There are documented cases of five or six parathyroid glands and of unusual locations for adenomas. A variety of techniques have been developed to aid in the preoperative localization of the abnormal parathyroid tissue. The early techniques featured either selective intraarterial angiography or selective venous catheterization of the thyroid venous plexus and adjacent areas coupled with radioimmunoassay for PTH. The techniques were often successful, but the frequency of detection was too low in comparison with the rate of success of an experienced parathyroid surgeon in finding the abnormal tissue at the first operation to warrant the morbidity and complications of the procedures. Subsequently, noninvasive techniques were introduced, particularly ultrasound, computerized tomography of the neck and mediastinum, differential scanning after simultaneous radiothallium and technetium administration, and intraarterial digital angiography. These techniques, with the possible exception of ultrasonography, should be used only when the initial parathyroid exploration is unsuccessful.

Ultrasound is reported to detect abnormal parathyroid tissue in 60 to 70 percent of cases but is most useful for lesions in the vicinity of the thyroid and less successful for lesions in the anterior mediastinum. The technique may assist the surgeon even in the initial operation by directing the surgery to the side of the neck where the abnormal gland is located. Computerized tomography has a similar success rate and is more helpful in anterior mediastinal lesions. Caution is appropriate in that false-positives are encountered in the anterior mediastinum. Needle biopsy with radio immunoassay for PTH in aspirated tissue fluid can be coupled with computerized tomography prior to a second parathyroid exploration. The subtraction of the technetium image, which targets the thyroid, from the radiothallium image, which targets both thyroid and parathyroid, has led to successful preoperative localization in approximately half of patients undergoing a second exploration.

Several generalizations are warranted. Localization and removal of a single abnormal parathyroid gland at the first operation is usually successful, depending upon the experience of the surgeon (greater than 90 percent success for experienced surgeons). Preoperative localization techniques should be reserved for patients in whom initial exploration is unsuccessful. If a second exploration is indicated, ultrasound, computerized tomography, and thallium-technetium scanning should probably be combined with selective digital arteriography in one of the centers specializing in these techniques. At one center, there has been experience with angiographic ablation of mediastinal adenomas with reports of long-term cure using selective embolization or deliberate excessive injection of contrast material into the endarterial circulation feeding the parathyroid tumor. Such procedures and the continual intraoperative monitoring of urinary cyclic AMP as a marker for successful removal of abnormal parathyroid tissue may serve as adjuncts in the management of patients with unsuccessful initial operations.

A decline in serum calcium occurs within 24 h after successful surgery; usually blood calcium falls to low normal values for 3 to 5 days until the remaining parathyroid tissue resumes hormone secretion. Severe postoperative hypocalcemia is likely if osteitis cystica is present or if injury to the normal parathyroid glands occurs during surgery.

In general, patients with good renal and gastrointestinal function, who do not have symptomatic bone disease and a large deficit in bone mineral, have few problems with postoperative hypocalcemia. The extent of the postoperative hypocalcemia varies with the surgical approach. If all glands are biopsied, hypocalcemia may be more prolonged and may be transiently symptomatic. Symptomatic hypo-

calcemia is more likely to occur after second parathyroid explorations, when normal parathyroid tissue may have been removed at the unsuccessful initial operation and when the manipulation and/or biopsy of the remaining normal gland has been more extensive in the search for the missing adenoma. Patients with hyperparathyrodism have efficient intestinal calcium absorption due to the increased levels of $1,25(OH)_2D$ stimulated by parathyroid excess. Once hypocalcemia signifies successful surgery, patients can be put on a high calcium intake or be given oral calcium supplements. Despite manifestations of mild hypocalcemia, most patients do not require parenteral therapy and do not experience severe symptoms. If the serum calcium falls below 8 mg/dL, in particular if the phosphate level rises, the possibility of more extensive hypoparathyroidism must be considered. Coexistent hypomagnesemia should be checked for, as it interferes with PTH secretion, and causes a relative hypoparathyroidism. Parenteral calcium replacement at a low level should be instituted if symptomatic hypocalcemia supervenes, such as a general sense of anxiety and positive Chvostek and Trousseau signs coupled with serum calcium consistently below 8 mg/dL. For parenteral therapy, calcium (gluconate or chloride) solutions are prepared at a concentration of 1 mg/mL in 5% dextrose in water. The rate and duration of intravenous therapy are determined by the severity of the symptoms and the response of the serum calcium. A rate of infusion of 0.5 to 2 (mg/kg)/h or 30 to 100 mL/h of a 1-mg/mL solution usually suffices to relieve symptoms. Generally, parenteral therapy is required for only a few days. If symptoms become severe or if the need for parenteral calcium continues for more than 2 to 3 days, replacement therapy with vitamin D and/or oral calcium (2 to 4 g per day) should be started (see section on treatment of hypocalcemia). It is cost-effective to use calcitriol (doses of 0.5 to 1.0 μg per day) because of the rapidity of onset and rapidity of cessation of action in contrast to vitamin D per se (see below). A sudden rise in blood calcium after several months of vitamin D replacement may indicate restoration of parathyroid function to normal.

Magnesium deficiency may also complicate the postoperative course. Magnesium deficiency impairs the secretion of PTH, and, therefore, hypomagnesemia should be corrected whenever detected. Magnesium chloride is effective by mouth, but this compound is not widely available. Accordingly, repletion is usually parenteral. Only a fraction of body magnesium is present in extracellular fluid, but total-body magnesium deficiency is reflected by hypomagnesemia. Since the depressant effect of magnesium on central and peripheral nerve functions does not occur below 4 meq per liter (normal range, 1.5 to 2 meq per liter) parenteral replacement can be given rapidly. A cumulative dose as great as 1 to 2 meq per kilogram of body weight can be administered if severe hypomagnesemia is present; often, however, doses of 25 to 30 meq total are sufficient. The magnesium is given either as an intravenous infusion over 8 to 12 h or in divided doses intramuscularly (magnesium sulfate, USP).

Lithium therapy Lithium, employed in conventional doses for extended periods in the management of bipolar depression and other psychiatric disorders, causes hypercalcemia in approximately 10 percent of patients. The parathyroids appear to participate in mediation of the hypercalcemia. In some, elevated PTH levels have been documented; levels of vitamin D metabolites and of urinary cyclic AMP have not been reported. The hypercalcemia is dependent on continued lithium treatment, remitting and recurring when lithium is stopped and restarted, yet when the patients are explored, parathyroid adenomas are found. The histologic findings in the other parathyroids have not been described in the reported series.

The frequency with which hypercalcemia occurs is sufficiently high to make it unlikely that the association is fortuitous; a causal relationship is supported by the dependence of the hypercalcemia on the continuation of the lithium, but the presence of hypercalcemia does not correlate with plasma lithium level. Long-term follow-ups have not been reported; most patients are continued on lithium because of its importance in the management of psychiatric problems. These patients are presumably best managed according to the principles used in asymptomatic hypercalcemia, independent of lithium administration. If troubling symptoms or unfavorable signs, such as progressive bone demineralization or kidney stones, develop, it may be necessary to remove the abnormal parathyroid tissue so that the therapy can be continued.

Familial hypocalciuric hypercalcemia Familial hypocalciuric hypercalcemia (familial benign hypercalcemia, FHH) is transmitted as an autosomal dominant trait. Recognition of the disorder is important because affected individuals are frequently ascertained because of asymptomatic hypercalcemia; surgical exploration of the parathyroids is never indicated because it does not cure the disorder. It is, therefore, important to recognize such patients as differing from those with primary hyperparathyroidism.

The pathophysiology is not understood, and there is no single biochemical marker to distinguish these patients from patients with primary hyperparathyroidism. Nonetheless, the aggregate evidence serves to separate FHH from primary hyperparathyroidism. Few clinical signs or symptoms are present in patients with FHH. Unlike the MEN syndromes, other endocrine abnormalities are not present. The hypercalcemia may be detectable in the first decade of life, whereas hypercalcemia rarely occurs in the MEN syndrome patients under the age of 10 years. The iPTH values may be elevated in FHH, but the values are usually lower than in patients with primary hyperparathyroidism. Renal calcium reabsorption is high. The majority of patients with primary hyperparathyroidism have less than 99 percent calcium reabsorption, and most patients with FHH exceed 99 percent reabsorption. Serum magnesium levels are higher in FHH than in primary hyperparathyroidism.

Most patients are detected as a result of family screening after the diagnosis has been made in one member of the kindred. Unfortunately, the initial patient is frequently operated upon without reversal of the hypercalcemia. At operation, a moderate degree of hyperplasia of all parathyroid glands is seen. No patient has had reversal of hypercalcemia by surgery unless all of the parathyroid tissue is inadvertently removed, rendering the patient hypoparathyroid, a most undesirable result. The high renal calcium reabsorption and the prompt recurrence of excessive parathyroid secretion, as long as any parathyroid tissue remains, are consistent with some abnormality in the ratio of extracellular to intracellular calcium concentration or with some abnormal sensing mechanisms in cell membranes of parathyroid and renal tubular epithelium. The nature of this disorder and the proper long-term management are not clear. By no means is surgery to be advocated, nor is medical treatment needed to lower the calcium, in view of the lack of symptoms.

MALIGNANCY-RELATED HYPERCALCEMIA **Clinical syndromes and mechanisms of hypercalcemia** Hypercalcemia due to malignancy is common (as frequent as 10 to 15 percent in certain types of tumor such as lung carcinoma), often severe and difficult to manage, confusing as to etiology, and sometimes difficult to distinguish from primary hyperparathyroidism. Traditionally, hypercalemia in malignancy was thought to be due to a local invasion and destruction of bone by tumor cells or, in a minority of cases, to the elaboration by the malignant cells of humoral mediators of hypercalcemia.

Although the presence of malignancy is often clinically obvious, hypercalcemia can occasionally be due to an occult tumor. With occult malignancy, diagnosis and definitive treatment must be accomplished quickly if the patient is to be protected from the complications of the underlying malignancy.

Pseudohyperparathyroidism (humoral hypercalcemia of malignancy is the term used to define the syndrome of hypercalcemia in patients with malignancies, especially of lung and kidney, in which bone metastases are minimal or not detectable, the clinical picture resembles primary hyperparathyroidism (hypophosphatemia accompanies hypercalcemia), and cure or remission of the primary tumor

leads to disappearance of the hypercalcemia. Ectopic production by the tumor of PTH or material resembling PTH was initially felt to be the mechanism of the hypercalcemia, but the disease mechanisms are more complicated than simple ectopic production of PTH by the malignant tissue.

Investigations employing multiple diagnostic procedures, tests of serum and urinary mineral ion metabolism, hormone assays, and measurements of cyclic AMP excretion have clarified the issue in part. The level of iPTH is not elevated in most cases of hypercalcemia associated with malignancy, although most laboratories report detectable, rather than suppressed levels. If PTH were the mediator produced ectopically by tumor tissue, elevated levels of iPTH would be expected unless altered forms of hormone were secreted. On the other hand, if parathyroid function is normal and nonparathyroid-related humoral factors are responsible, undetectable iPTH levels would be expected. The low levels of iPTH may represent false-positive signals in the assay or altered forms of the hormone in the circulation.

Many patients with hypercalcemia and malignancy, generally of the type classified as pseudohyperparathyroidism, have elevated urinary nephrogenous cyclic AMP excretion, hypophosphatemia, and increased urinary phosphate clearance, findings compatible with the actions of a humoral agent that emulates PTH action. On the other hand, these same patients have barely detectable iPTH levels in multiple immunoassays, high, rather than low, renal calcium clearance, and low to normal levels of $1,25(OH)_2D$, suggesting mediation by humoral factors distinct from PTH.

The importance of skeletal metastases in the genesis of the hypercalcemia of malignancy has been reevaluated. The histologic character of the tumor is more important than the extent of skeletal metastases in predicting hypercalcemia. Small cell carcinoma (oat cell) and adenocarcinoma of lung, although the most common lung tumors associated with skeletal metastases, rarely cause hypercalcemia. By contrast, as many as 10 percent of patients with squamous cell carcinoma of the lung develop hypercalcemia. Histologic studies of bone in patients with squamous cell or epidermoid carcinoma of the lung, in sites invaded by tumor as well as areas remote from tumor invasion, reveal bone remodeling, including osteoclastic and osteoblastic activity. In contrast, minimal evidence of metabolic activation is seen despite extensive skeletal metastases of small cell (oat cell) carcinoma.

The cumulative findings suggest that agents other than PTH must be responsible for hypercalcemia and that only certain tumor types produce these factors. Two mechanisms of hypercalcemia are suspected. Some solid tumors associated with hypercalcemia, particularly squamous cell tumors and renal tumors, produce cellular growth factors that are believed to cause increased bone resorption and mediate the hypercalcemia through *systemic* actions on the skeleton as a whole, by stimulation of bone resorption. Substances produced by cells involved in the marrow response to hematologic malignancies resorb bone through *local* destruction and may be identical or analogous to some of the known lymphokines and cytokines.

Classification of the hypercalcemia of malignancy is arbitrary (Table 336-2). Multiple myeloma and other hematologic malignancies involving the bone marrow probably cause bone destruction and hypercalcemia through local mechanisms. Breast carcinoma also usually causes hypercalcemia through localized osteolytic destruction, probably mediated by locally secreted tumor products different from those involved in multiple myeloma or lymphoma. Finally, the category of pseudohyperparathyroidism (humoral mediation) can probably result from more than one distinctive mediator (Table 336-2).

In addition to the multiplicity of bone-resorbing factors elaborated by malignant cells in patients with hypercalcemia of malignancy, there is a variable synergism and antagonism between the bone-active agents secreted by the tumors. In the humoral hypercalcemia of malignancy, osteoclastic resorption is generalized, and there is an absence of an osteoblastic or bone-forming response to the surge of bone resorption, implying some inhibition of the normal coupling of formation and resorption. Cooperativity and anatagonism in the skeletal actions of cytokines may include blockade of cytokine-induced bone resorption by interferon, both of which may be produced by the same tumor cells. Thus, the interaction of more than one substance may determine whether hypercalcemia develops with a particular tumor rather than whether or not a particular factor is secreted.

Several distinctive hormones, hormone analogues, specific cytokines, and/or growth factors have been implicated through clinical assays or in vitro tests. In some lymphomas there is an increased blood level of $1,25(OH)_2D$. It is not clear whether the increased $1,25(OH)_2D$ is produced by stimulation of the renal 1α-hydroxylase or whether the metabolite is produced ectopically by lymphocytes. The principal interest in etiologic mechanisms in hematologic malignancies has focused on the production of bone-resorbing factors by activated normal lymphocytes and by myeloma and lymphoma cells. This factor(s), termed osteocyte activation factor (OAF), now appears to represent the biologic action of several different cytokines, including interleukin 1 and possibly lymphotoxin and tumor necrosis factor, two closely related cytokines.

In most instances, breast carcinoma is believed to cause hypercalcemia by local stimulation of osteoclasts directly by products secreted by the metastatic breast carcinoma cells and associated inflammatory cells. Breast carcinoma cells produce and secrete prostaglandins of the E series which are potent local stimulators of bone-resorbing cells.

More than one factor may be responsible for humorally mediated hypercalcemia in patients with solid tumors. Fractions partially purified from extracts of human tumors stimulate cyclic AMP production in in vitro assays, cause bone resorption in vitro, and induce hypercalcemia in nude mice. In other studies, extracts of tumors have given positive results in the cytochemical bioassay for PTH, and the cyclic AMP stimulation and cytochemical bioassay response given by these factors is blocked by a competitive inhibitor of PTH. On the other hand, the tumor extracts that act like PTH do not react with antiserum to the hormone, nor is their action blocked by neutralizing anti-PTH antibody. The active principle is believed, therefore, to be a substance with a distinct amino acid sequence that acts through the PTH receptor. The lack of identity with PTH probably explains the differences in the biologic actions of the tumor substance(s) and those of authentic PTH.

Another line of investigation points to the importance of cellular growth factors in the genesis of tumor hypercalcemia. Tumor-derived growth factors, believed to play a central role in maintaining the transformation and growth of tumor cells by acting as autocrine regulators, are also potent bone-resorbing agents in vitro. Among other actions, they stimulate production of prostaglandins of the PGE_2 type. Epidermal growth factor (EGF) and tumor-derived growth factor cause bone resorption in vitro, acting through the same receptor, and in some systems bone resorption by tumor extracts can be blocked by antibodies to the EGF receptor. Platelet-derived growth factor (PDGF), also a frequent product of tumors, also stimulates bone resorption in vitro. Further work is needed to clarify the role of the growth factors, cytokines, and PTH-like principles in the hypercalcemia of malignancy.

Diagnostic issues and treatment Ordinarily, the diagnosis of hypercalcemia secondary to tumor is not difficult to make because the tumor symptoms are prominent at the time the hypercalcemia is detected. Indeed, the hypercalcemia may be noted incidentally during the work-up of a patient with known malignancy. Patients with malignancy and hypercalcemia may have a coexistent parathyroid adenoma, some reports suggesting an incidence as high as 10 percent. Laboratory testing becomes critical when occult carcinoma is suspected. Levels of iPTH are not uniformly undetectable in tumor hypercalcemia, as would be expected with the mediation of the hypercalcemia due to a nonparathyroid agent (the hypercalcemia suppressing the normal parathyroid glands), but are lower than in patients with primary hyperparathyroidism.

Hypercalcemia in association with truly occult malignancy is rare. Clinical suspicion that malignancy is the cause of the hypercalcemia is heightened when weight loss, fatigue, muscle weakness, unexplained skin rash, symptoms associated with the paraneoplastic syndromes, or symptoms specific for a particular tumor are present. Tumors of the so-called squamous cell phenotype are most frequently associated with hypercalcemia, and the organs most frequently involved are the lung, kidney, and urogenital tract. X-ray examinations can focus on these areas. Bone scans with technetium-labeled diphosphonate are useful for detection of osteolytic metastases; the sensitivity is high, but it is of low specificity and must be confirmed by conventional x-rays to be certain that areas of increased uptake are due to osteolytic metastases per se. Bone marrow biopsies are helpful in patients with anemia or abnormal peripheral blood smears.

Treatment of the hypercalcemia of malignancy must be considered in the perspective of the history and presumed course of the individual patient. Control of the tumor is the principal objective, and reduction of tumor mass is usually also the key to satisfactory control of the hypercalcemia. If a patient has severe hypercalcemia, yet has an excellent chance for effective tumor therapy, treatment of the hypercalcemia should be vigorous. If hypercalcemia, on the other hand, is an accompaniment of the late stages of a tumor that is resistant to therapy, the treatment of the hypercalcemia should not be vigorous, as hypercalcemia can have a mild sedating effect. Standard therapies for hypercalcemia are applicable to patients with malignancy.

VITAMIN D–RELATED HYPERCALCEMIA Hypercalcemia related to abnormal vitamin D action can be due to *excessive ingestion* of vitamin D or *abnormal metabolism* of the vitamin. Abnormal metabolism of the vitamin is usually acquired in association with some widespread granulomatous disorder, but one rare hereditary form of vitamin D sensitivity in infants is associated with other developmental anomalies. As discussed in Chap. 337, vitamin D metabolism is carefully regulated, particularly the activity of the renal 1α-hydroxylase responsible for the production of $1,25(OH)_2D$. Many details of the regulation of 1α-hydroxylase remain unclarified, but the normal feedback suppression by $1,25(OH)_2D$ on the enzyme seems to work less well in infants than in adults and operates poorly, if at all, in ectopic sites, as distinct from the renal tubule.

There are difficulties in the clinical interpretation of assays for vitamin D metabolites, particularly at low levels of the metabolites. Nevertheless, with the above limitations in mind, a working model can be formulated for the pathophysiology of the several disorders associated with hypercalcemia and excessive vitamin D action.

Vitamin D intoxication The chronic ingestion of large doses of vitamin D, usually at least 50 to 100 times the normal physiologic requirement (doses in excess of 50,000 to 100,000 units per day) are required to produce hypercalcemia in normal individuals. In animals,

---

TABLE 336-2 Classification of tumor hypercalcemia

I Hematologic malignancies
  A Multiple myeloma, lymphomas:
    *OAF, lymphokines—*local bone destruction*
  B Certain lymphomas:
    * ↑ $1,25(OH)_2$—*systemic mediation*
II Solid tumors with *local bone destruction*
  A Breast carcinoma:
    Prostaglandin, E series
III Solid tumors, *humorally mediated bone resorption*
  A Lung (squamous cell)   *Tumor-derived growth factors
  B Kidney   (transforming growth factors);
  C Urogenital tract   adenyl cyclase stimulating factors
  D Other squamous cell tumors   (PTH-like); other humoral agents

* *Indicates a factor or hormone identified as present in human tumors, active on bone resorption in vitro, and putative etiologic agent in tumor hypercalcemia.*

vitamin D intoxication causes increased bone resorption and increased intestinal calcium absorption. In humans excessive vitamin D action leads to an increase in intestinal calcium absorption, but it is not known whether increased bone resorption occurs.

The immediate mechanism for the hypercalcemia is presumed to be an excessive production of $1,25(OH)_2D$ that occurs as a consequence of an increase in the substrate for the renal 1α-hydroxylase, namely, $25(OH)D$. $25(OH)D$ production is less tightly regulated than is the production of the active metabolite, $1,25(OH)_2D$. Hence, concentrations of $25(OH)D$ average 5 to 10 times above normal in patients on high-dose vitamin D, whether therapeutically, as in hypoparathyroidism, or accidentally, as in vitamin D intoxication. $25(OH)D$ has low biologic activity in intestine and bone. Hence, part of the excessive vitamin D action may be attributable to the high levels of $25(OH)D$ themselves, as well as supernormal levels of $1,25(OH)_2D$. Because of the infrequency of vitamin D intoxication, there have been few reports of the actual level of $1,25(OH)_2D$ in patients with vitamin D intoxication. Presumably, the presence of normal renal function and parathyroid reserve would lead to higher rates of formation of $1,25(OH)_2D$ than would occur in patients, for example, with impaired renal function or absence of PTH secretion in whom high doses of vitamin D may be given to counter calcium deficiency.

The diagnosis is substantiated by measurement of $25(OH)D$, confirming concentrations in excess of the upper limit of normal. Hypercalcemia is usually controlled by restriction of dietary calcium intake and appropriate attention to hydration. These measures, plus discontinuation of vitamin D, usually lead to satisfactory management, but vitamin D stores in fat may be substantial and vitamin D intoxication may persist for weeks after vitamin D ingestion is terminated. Such patients are sensitive to glucocorticoids, which in doses of 100 mg of hydrocortisone or its equivalent return calcium levels to normal over several days.

Sarcoidosis and other granulomatous diseases   Normal relations between $25(OH)D$ and the product, the active metabolite $1,25(OH)_2D$, are not maintained in patients with sarcoidosis and other granulomatous diseases. There is a positive correlation between $25(OH)D$ levels (reflecting vitamin D intake) and the circulating concentrations of $1,25(OH)_2D$ [normally, there is no increase in the active metabolite with increasing $25(OH)D$ levels]. In patients with sarcoidosis the site of synthesis of $1,25(OH)_2D$ is presumed to be in macrophages or other cells associated with the granulomatous deposits. Hypercalcemia has been reported in an anephric sarcoidosis patient in association with increased $1,25(OH)_2D$ levels. Macrophages obtained from granulomatous tissue form $1,25(OH)_2D$ at an increased rate when $25(OH)D$ is provided as substrate. Thus, the usual regulation of active metabolite production by calcium or PTH is circumvented in these patients, and high calcium intakes do not lead to a reduction in the blood levels of $1,25(OH)_2D$ in patients with sarcoidosis. Production of $1,25(OH)_2D$ was normal in one patient with sarcoidosis and hypoparathyroidism. Clearance of $1,25(OH)_2D$ from blood may be decreased as well.

Even normocalcemic patients with sarcoidosis have unregulated production of $1,25(OH)_2D$ in response to vitamin D loading. Exposure to sunlight, as in summer months, or administration of as little as 9000 units of vitamin D daily is followed by increased levels of the active metabolite. Treatment with moderate doses of steroids leads to a reversal, not only of the hypercalcemia as in other cases of excessive vitamin D actions such as vitamin D intoxication, but also to the reversal of the abnormal responsiveness of $1,25(OH)_2D$ levels to vitamin D challenge. Presumably, steroid administration causes multiple effects in the disease, and both excessive production of the metabolite and the responsiveness to it in target organs are blocked.

Variation in frequency of hypercalcemia in sarcoidosis (between 10 and 60 percent) is probably explained in part by the moderating influence of steroids used to control pulmonary complications and other manifestations of the granulomatous disease per se. Lytic lesions also occur in bone so that increased bone resorption could play a role in some cases. In most, however, hypercalcemia is directly related to an increased intestinal calcium absorption. Clinically, hypercalcemia is usually a manifestation of disseminated disease. Hence, pulmonary involvement is usual; chest x-ray may reveal a diffuse fibronodular infiltrate and/or prominent hilar adenopathy. Blood gamma globulin may also be elevated. The most useful diagnostic procedure is demonstration on noncaseating granulomas in liver or lymph node biopsy. The hypercalcemia of sarcoidosis can present a difficult problem in differential diagnosis, especially when many of the typical features of the disease are lacking (see Chap. 270).

Management of the hypercalcemia in these patients can be accomplished by avoiding excessive sunlight exposure and by limiting vitamin D and calcium intake; glucocorticoids in the equivalent of 100 mg of hydrocortisone per day or less are sufficient to control hypercalcemia when it occurs. Presumably, however, the abnormal sensitivity to vitamin D and abnormal regulation of $1,25(OH)_2D$ synthesis will persist as long as the disease is active. PTH levels are usually suppressed and $1,25(OH)_2D$ levels elevated, but primary hyperparathyroidism and sarcoidosis may occur in some patients.

Idiopathic hypercalcemia of infancy   This unusual disorder, sometimes referred to as Williams' syndrome, consists of multiple congenital developmental defects, including supravalvular aortic stenosis, mental retardation, and an elfin facies, in association with hypercalcemia due to abnormal sensitivity to vitamin D. The syndrome was first recognized in England after the introduction of vitamin D fortification of milk. Hypercalcemia develops with vitamin D intakes as small as 2000 to 4000 units per day. Levels of $1,25(OH)_2D$ are elevated, ranging from 150 to 500 pg/mL. The mechanism of the abnormal sensitivity to vitamin D and of the increased circulating levels of $1,25(OH)_2D$ is unclear. The children become hypercalcemic because of excessive intestinal calcium absorption. The abnormality in vitamin D metabolism and the increased sensitivity to vitamin D intake are not seen after the first year of life. Treatment is restriction of calcium intake. Occasionally, the hypercalcemia can be severe, and calcium values above 16 mg/dL are recorded. Treatment with glucocorticoids in the doses used for vitamin D intoxication or sarcoidosis, adjusted for body weight, rapidly reverses the hypercalcemia.

HYPERCALCEMIA ASSOCIATED WITH HIGH BONE TURNOVER

Hyperthyroidism   Mild elevation of serum calcium is common in patients with hyperthyroidism, and hypercalciuria is even more common. As many as 20 percent of patients show high normal or mildly elevated serum calcium concentrations. The hypercalcemia seems due to increased bone turnover with bone resorption exceeding bone formation; direct effects of thyroid hormone on the skeleton seem to be responsible. Severe calcium elevations are not typical, however, and the presence of such suggests a concomitant disease such as hyperparathyroidism. Indeed, patients with thyrotoxicosis are more sensitive to the hypercalcemic effects of PTH.

Usually, the hyperthyroidism is obvious, and the hypercalcemia is managed by specific therapy of the hyperthyroidism. Signs of hyperthyroidism may occasionally be occult, particularly in the elderly.

Immobilization   Immobilization in adults is rarely associated with hypercalcemia in the absence of an associated disease but may cause hypercalcemia in children and young adolescents, particularly after spinal cord injury and paraplegia or quadriplegia. Upon ambulation the hypercalcemia in children usually returns to normal spontaneously.

The mechanism appears to involve a disproportion between rates of bone formation and bone resorption that result from the sudden loss of weight bearing. Hypercalciuria and mobilization of skeletal calcium can be seen in normal volunteers subjected to extensive bed rest, although hypercalcemia does not usually occur. An underlying disease associated with high bone turnover, such as Paget's disease, may cause hypercalcemia with immobilization.

Thiazides   Administration of benzothiadiazines (thiazides) can cause hypercalcemia in patients with high rates of bone turnover, such as patients with hypoparathyroidism treated with high doses of vitamin D. Traditionally, thiazides are associated with aggravation of hypercalcemia in primary hyperparathyroidism and have been used as a provocative test to bring out hypercalcemia that is borderline in patients suspected of having hyperparathyroidism. However, the effect can be seen in other high bone turnover states as well. The mechanism of action of the drugs is complex, but the overall result seems to be to impose a challenge to calcium homeostasis by actions on renal calcium excretion, on bone-calcium turnover, and on the efficiency of parathyroid action per se. Thiazide administration to normal individuals causes a transient increase in blood calcium, usually within the normal range, which reverts to preexisting levels after a week or more of continued administration. If normal hormonal function and calcium and bone metabolism are present, homeostatic controls are reset to counteract the calcium-elevating effect of the thiazides. In the presence of hyperparathyroidism or increased bone turnover from another cause, homeostatic mechanisms cannot be reset. Thiazides are categorized as a cause of hypercalcemia in association with high bone turnover rather than parathyroid-related per se because thiazides aggravate but do not really cause hypercalcemia in primary hyperparathyroidism. The abnormal effects of the thiazide on calcium metabolism disappear within days of cessation of the drug.

Many aspects of the action of the thiazides in normal subjects and in patients with hyperparathyroidism remain unclear. Chronic thiazide administration leads to reduction in urinary calcium excretion. In hypoparathyroid patients the actions of the drug cannot be an augmentation of PTH's biologic actions. At the same time, the drug clearly augments PTH responsiveness of bone and renal tubule. The hypocalciuric effect of the drug appears to reflect the enhancement of proximal tubular resorption of sodium and calcium in response to sodium depletion and is more pronounced in subjects with parathyroid secretion, whether normal or increased. Nevertheless, the substantial hypocalciuric effect in hypoparathyroid patients on high-dose vitamin D and oral calcium replacement is the rationale for the use of thiazides as an adjunct to therapy in such patients.

Vitamin A intoxication   Vitamin A intoxication is a rare cause of hypercalcemia. Most vitamin A intoxication results from experiments with nutritional supplements. Calcium levels can be elevated into the 12 to 14 mg/dL range after the ingestion of 50,000 to 100,000 units of vitamin A daily (10 to 20 times the minimum daily requirement). The patients have typical features of severe hypercalcemia that include fatigue and anorexia. They also have severe muscle pain and sometimes diffuse bone pain. The excess vitamin A intake is presumed to increase bone resorption.

Diagnosis can be established by history and by confirmatory measurements of vitamin A levels in serum, which may be increased severalfold above normal. Occasionally, skeletal x-rays reveal periosteal calcifications, particularly in the hands. Withdrawal of the vitamin is usually associated with the prompt disappearance of the hypercalcemia and reversal of the skeletal changes. As in vitamin D intoxication, administration of 100 mg of hydrocortisone or its equivalent per day leads to a rapid return of the serum calcium to normal.

HYPERCALCEMIA ASSOCIATED WITH RENAL FAILURE   Severe secondary hyperparathyroidism
Secondary hyperparathyroidism is the state in which excessive production of PTH is due to partial resistance to the metabolic actions of the hormone. Parathyroid gland hyperplasia with resultant increased secretion of PTH occurs because resistance to the normal level of the hormone leads to hypocalcemia which, in turn, is a stimulus to enlargement of the parathyroid glands. This concept is based on animal and human studies, the former involving experimental renal failure with phosphate retention and the latter involving treatment of patients with diphosphonates which

acutely block skeletal resorptive response. Figure 336-1*A* and 1*B* illustrates the consequences of these changes. When the parathyroid secretory reserve is tested by deliberately lowering blood calcium, the extent of rise in PTH for each milligram of decrement of plasma calcium is greater with parathyroid hyperplasia than with the normal gland. There is, therefore, a higher concentration of hormone at any given level of calcium concentration. Since a portion of PTH secretion by each individual parathyroid cell is not suppressible by any degree of elevation of blood calcium concentration, larger glands (more cells) have a higher concentration of hormone output at the hypercalcemic end of the dose-response curve.

Secondary hyperparathyroidism occurs in patients with renal failure, osteomalacia (vitamin D deficiency), and pseudohypoparathyroidism (deficient response to PTH at the level of the receptor). The clinical manifestations of secondary hyperparathyroidism vary in these states. Hypocalcemia seems to be the common denominator of secondary hyperparathyroidism. Primary and secondary hyperparathyroidism can be distinguished by the autonomous nature of the growth of the parathyroid glands in primary hyperparathyroidism (presumably irreversible) and the adaptive increase in parathyroid gland size in secondary hyperparathyroidism (presumably reversible). In fact, reversal from an abnormal pattern of secretion, presumably accompanied by an involution of parathyroid gland mass to a normal pattern of function, has been shown following treatment with diphosphonate (Fig. 336-1*B*).

In progressive kidney disease, the initial tendency to hypocalcemia seems attributable to two causes: phosphate retention that develops because of the reduced renal capacity to excrete phosphate and reduced concentrations of $1,25(OH)_2D$ concomitant with progressive renal damage. The two disturbances reduce skeletal responsiveness to PTH. The deficient $1,25(OH)_2D$ also interferes with the absorption of calcium from the intestine, already impaired in uremia. The ultimate pathophysiologic consequences in chronic renal failure represent the divergent effects of stimuli that cause parathyroid gland hyperplasia and those that modify the hormonal responsiveness of the end organs—bone, gut, and residual renal tubules. Development of secondary hyperparathyroidism must be an imbalance between the rate of increased PTH secretion due to parathyroid hyperplasia versus a restoration of normal responsiveness to the peripheral action of the hormone. In a few patients with severe secondary hyperparathyroidism, hypercalcemia and hyperphosphatemia develop due to a sudden increase in bone resorption; parathyroid hypersecretion "overshoots" the degree of resistance to hormone action.

In addition to hypercalcemia and hyperphosphatemia, patients may develop bone pain, ectopic calcification, and pruritus. The bone disease in patients with secondary hyperparathyroidism and renal failure is usually termed *renal osteodystrophy*. Concomitant osteomalacia (vitamin D deficiency) and osteitis fibrosa cystica (excessive PTH action) may be seen. In fact, osteitis fibrosa cystica is now more common in untreated renal failure than in primary hyperparathyroidism.

Judicious medical therapy, which includes reduction of excessive blood phosphate by dietary phosphate restriction plus the use of nonabsorbable antacids and careful, selective addition of vitamin D metabolites in the form of 0.25 to 2.0 μg per day of calcitriol may reverse severe secondary hyperparathyroidism. Somewhat paradoxically, serum calcium and phosphate levels may return to normal despite the administration of increased amounts of the vitamin D metabolite and calcium supplements. As illustrated in Fig. 336-1*B*, involution of the parathyroids presumably occurs with reduction of increased cellular mass, and consequently the exaggerated secretory response returns to a normal rate of responsiveness. The level of PTH at any given level of blood calcium is now more appropriate, and excessive parathyroid action is reversed.

Aluminum intoxication   Aluminum intoxication occurs in patients on chronic dialysis; manifestations include acute dementia and unresponsive, severe osteomalacia. Bone pain, multiple nonhealing fractures, particularly of the ribs and pelvis, and a proximal myopathy may occur. Hypercalcemia occurs when attempts are made to treat these patients as in renal osteodystrophy and renal failure, namely, administration of vitamin D or calcitriol. Apparently, acute hypercalcemia develops with administration of vitamin D because of impaired skeletal responsiveness. Aluminum is present at the site of osteoid mineralization, and osteoblastic activity is minimal. Presumably, these patients are unable to incorporate the increased blood calcium into the skeleton. Prevention is accomplished by avoidance of aluminum excess in the dialysis regimen; treatment involves mobilizing aluminum through the use of the chelating agent deferoxamine. Aluminum is mobilized from bone and, being tightly bound to the chelating agent, can be removed via dialysis. After aluminum toxicity has been reversed, patients may show typical features of renal osteodystrophy and secondary hyperparathyroidism. They can then be managed like other patients with secondary hyperparathyroidism with renal disease. A failure to recognize the syndrome is associated with persistence of the disabling bone disease and a fatal course due to progressive fractures or to hypercalcemia inadvertently induced by treatment with vitamin D.

Milk-alkali syndrome   The milk-alkali syndrome can cause several clinical presentations—acute, subacute, and chronic—all of which feature hypercalcemia, alkalosis, and renal failure. The syndrome is due to an excessive ingestion of calcium and absorbable antacids such as milk or calcium carbonate. The disorder is less frequent since nonabsorbable antacids and H-2 receptor antagonists such as cimetidine and ranitidine became available for the treatment of peptic ulcer disease.

Individual susceptibility must be important in pathogenesis since many patients are treated with calcium carbonate without developing the syndrome. One important variable is the fractional calcium absorption as a function of calcium intake. Some individuals absorb a high fraction of calcium, even with intakes as high as 2 g and more of elemental calcium per day, instead of reducing calcium absorption with high intake, as occurs in most normal subjects. Resultant, mild hypercalcemia after meals in such patients may be the critical factor in the generation of alkalosis. Most individuals are resistant to the development of alkalosis after the ingestion of large quantities of non-calcium-containing alkali such as sodium bicarbonate. However, with the development of hypercalcemia, mild increased sodium excretion and some depletion of total body water occurs. This phenomenon and perhaps, additionally, some suppression of endogenous PTH secretion would lead to increased bicarbonate reabsorption. This bicarbonate retention then leads to alkalosis in the face of continued calcium carbonate ingestion. Alkalosis, per se, results in selective enhancement of calcium reabsorption in the distal nephron, thus aggravating the hypercalcemia. The cycle, mild hypercalcemia → bicarbonate retention → alkalosis → renal calcium retention → severe hypercalcemia, thus perpetuates and aggravates hypercalcemia and alkalosis as long as calcium and absorbable alkali are ingested.

Acute hypercalcemia and alkalosis within days of beginning calcium and alkali, *acute milk-alkali syndrome,* is manifested by weakness, myalgia, irritability, and apathy. The impairment of renal function, including reduced renal concentrating ability, tubular dysfunction, and hypercalcemia and alkalosis, reverses rapidly upon stopping the intake of calcium and alkali.

The far advanced milk-alkali syndrome, sometimes referred to as *Burnett's syndrome,* represents the results of long-standing calcium and alkali ingestion; severe hypercalcemia, irreversible renal failure, and phosphate retention may be accompanied by ectopic calcification. Some improvement may result when calcium and alkali ingestion is reduced, but prior to the availability of renal dialysis renal failure led to death. There is an intermediate or subacute form in which the renal failure is reversible over a period of weeks after withdrawal of excessive calcium and alkali intake.

DIFFERENTIAL DIAGNOSIS: SPECIAL TESTS   Differential diagnosis in hypercalcemic disorders is best achieved by using clinical

criteria (Fig. 336-2 and Table 336-3). While helpful, when several laboratory tests are applied simultaneously, they lack adequate sensitivity and/or specificity when considered individually. The points that deserve major emphasis in arriving at a correct diagnosis are the presence or absence of symptoms or signs and evidence of chronicity. If one discounts fatigue or depression, which is common in the population, patients with *asymptomatic hypercalcemia* have primary hyperparathyroidism in well over 90 percent of the instances; symptoms of malignancy are usually present when hypercalcemia is due to cancer. Disorders other than hyperparathyroidism and malignancy are estimated to cause no more than 10 percent of all cases of hypercalcemia, and some of the nonparathyroid causes are associated with manifestations such as renal failure, the signs or symptoms of which are evident on initial routine laboratory test screening.

Chronicity is the second most important clinical point. If hypercalcemia has been manifest for more than a year, malignancy can usually be excluded as the cause of hypercalcemia on clinical grounds alone. A striking feature of malignancy-associated hypercalcemia is the rapidity of the course, whereby signs and symptoms relatable to the underlying malignancy are evident within months of the first detection of hypercalcemia. Hyperparathyroidism is the likely diagnosis in patients with *chronic hypercalcemia.* Diseases other than hyperparathyroidism, such as sarcoidosis, are rare, alternative causes of chronic hypercalcemia. A careful *history* of dietary supplements and drug use will often readily reveal intoxication with vitamin D or A or the use of thiazides.

Although clinical considerations are helpful in arriving at the correct diagnosis of the cause of hypercalcemia, appropriate laboratory testing is essential for diagnosis. Theoretically, the radioimmunoassay for PTH should separate hyperparathyroidism from all other causes of hypercalcemia, those with hyperparathyroidism having elevated

FIGURE 336-2 *Schematic illustrating simultaneous measurements of immunoreactive parathyroid hormone (PTH RIA) and serum calcium in normal subjects (N), patients with tumor hypercalcemia (TH), hypoparathyroidism (HP), pseudohypoparathyroidism (PHP), chronic renal failure with secondary hyperparathyroidism [CRF (2° HPTH)], and primary hyperparathyroidism (1° HPTH). Enclosed areas indicate the range of values typical for each class of subject measured; note overlap of regions and interrupted scales (see text for details).*

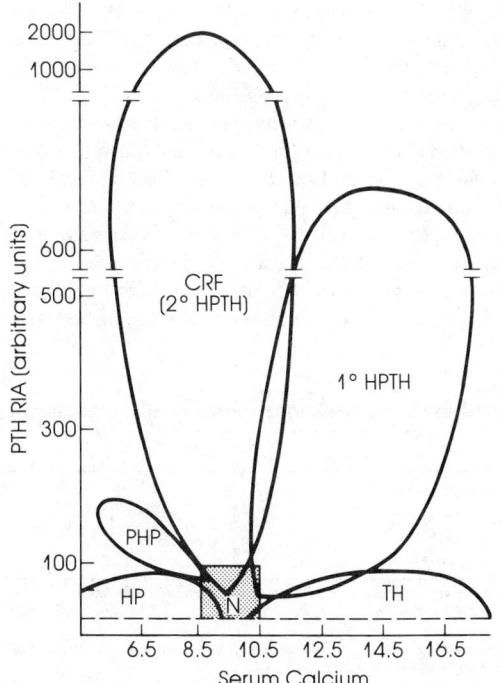

levels of iPTH despite hypercalcemia and patients with malignancy and the other causes of hypercalcemia (except those related to primary hyperparathyroidism, such as lithium-induced hypercalcemia and familial hypocalciuric hypercalcemia) having levels of hormone below normal or undetectable. 1,25(OH)$_2$D levels would be expected to be elevated in primary hyperparathyroidism as a secondary event and also increased in states of vitamin D intoxication, particularly sarcoidosis. In other disorders associated with hypercalcemia, concentrations of 1,25(OH)$_2$D would be expected to be low or, at the most, normal. Such clear distinctions in laboratory findings are not the rule in differential diagnosis of hypercalcemia, however.

Circulating iPTH is heterogeneous, as discussed in Chap. 335. Thus, what is measured may vary from one assay to another, depending on the region of the molecule recognized by different antiserums directed against the hormone. Furthermore, the concentration of PTH fragments may rise in the presence of renal failure, without implying a corresponding increase in the level of biologically active, intact hormone.

As illustrated in Fig. 336-2, the most useful clinical interpretation of PTH radioimmunoassays is achieved by covariant analysis [(iPTH) $\times$ (Ca^{2+})], plotting results of iPTH concentration in each patient against the simultaneously measured calcium concentration and then contrasting the individual test results with the results found in clinical correlation studies utilizing the particular immunoassay. A rectangular domain, in this type of plotting, includes the values found for many normal control individuals; the domain is bounded laterally by the upper and lower limits of serum calcium and vertically by the lower limit of assay detection, and the highest range of normal iPTH concentration.

Those patients with surgically documented hyperparathyroidism whose concentration of iPTH overlaps the upper limit of normal values can usually (especially with several repeated assays) be discerned as abnormal because iPTH level should be undetectable due to hypercalcemia if the parathyroids are normally responsive. Some overlap occurs between the values in patients with various types of hypercalcemia and much of the normal range. In some assays, more of an elevation of the PTH levels occurs in patients with tumor hypercalcemia than shown in Fig. 336-2.

Assays based on exclusive recognition of the amino terminal portion of the molecule obviate the difficulties inherent in detection of fragments. In general, however, all PTH radioimmunoassays must operate close to the limits of detectability to encompass all values found in normal subjects. Under these conditions, the assays are prone to interference by factors present in plasma, especially in renal failure and in malignancy. These problems appear to account for many false-positive and false-negative values. The assay for 1,25-(OH)$_2$D is also hampered by technical problems.

A certain fraction of surgically proven hyperparathyroid patients have PTH concentrations in the upper limit of normal (false-negative immunoassay results) (Fig. 336-2). Hormone concentration in patients with the hypercalcemia of malignancy is normal or even moderately increased in most assays (false-positives). Fortunately, the parathyroid radioimmunoassay values in malignancy are lower for the same degree of calcium elevation than in patients with hyperparathyroidism. Hence, the more severe the hypercalcemia, the more useful the parathyroid

immunoassay result in distinguishing between primary hyperparathyroidism and the hypercalcemia of malignancy. 1,25(OH)$_2$D levels are normal or low in these patients, as distinct from the elevated levels in most patients with primary hyperparathyroidism.

PTH levels are elevated in chronic renal failure, a part of which reflects accumulation of fragments secondary to renal failure rather than true parathyroid oversecretion and part of which is due to true secondary hyperparathyroidism. Patients with sarcoidosis have low or undetectable levels of iPTH. No systematic surveys have been reported concerning PTH radioimmunoassay results in many of the other non-parathyroid-related causes of hypercalcemia shown in Table 336-1, largely because of the infrequency with which the disorders are encountered.

In summary, iPTH values are elevated in >90 percent of parathyroid-related causes of hypercalcemia, normal or moderately elevated in malignancy-related hypercalcemia, increased to varying degrees (and therefore not usually helpful) in disorders associated with renal failure, and normal or undetectable in vitamin D–related and high bone turnover–related causes of hypercalcemia (although there is a paucity of data for these latter categories).

Measurements of nephrogenous cyclic AMP are of limited value in distinguishing the two major causes of hypercalcemia, primary hyperparathyroidism vs. malignancy. Elevation of nephrogenous cyclic AMP occurs in some patients with malignancy and in essentially all patients with primary hyperparathyroidism. Several other laboratory tests are of utility in confirming the diagnosis of particular disorders.

Table 336-3 summarizes laboratory findings among primary hyperparathyroidism, malignancies with local bone destruction (osteolytic metastases) and humorally related tumor hypercalcemia, or pseudo-hyperparathyroidism. It is evident by inspection of expected values for iPTH and 1,25(OH)$_2$D levels that laboratory testing may not be definitive in separating primary hyperparathyroidism from malignancy-related hypercalcemia. However, on the average, iPTH values are elevated in primary hyperparathyroidism and normal in malignancy-associated hypercalcemia; the same general tendency to separate groups is seen with measurements of 1,25(OH)$_2$D.

Some general recommendations can be made as to the differential diagnosis of hypercalcemia. If a specific disease traditionally associated with hypercalcemia (Table 336-1) is clinically evident, it is reasonable to assume that the disease is responsible for the hypercalcemia. The hypercalcemia can be managed initially by general measures, if necessary, and the suspected disease can be treated by specific measures. If the hypercalcemia disappears in response to specific therapy, as with surgery for hyperparathyroidism, for example, or after reduction of excessive intake of fat-soluble vitamins or alkali and calcium, as in the case of vitamin D intoxication or milk-alkali syndrome, respectively, then there is no need to search for other causes of hypercalcemia. If specific treatment does not lead to a reversal of the hypercalcemia, a search for an additional cause, such as primary hyperparathyroidism, must be undertaken. Signs suggestive of malignancy may be evident, and initial phases of evaluation will focus on arriving at a diagnosis of the malignancy.

When no clues are evident as to the diagnosis, either because the patient is asymptomatic or chronic illness obscures symptoms or

TABLE 336-3 Differential diagnosis of hypercalcemia: clinical criteria

Disease	Blood*			Urine†			
	Ca†	P$_i$	1,25(OH)$_2$D	iPTH	NcAMP	Ca†	TMP/GFR
Primary hyperparathyroidism	↑	↓	↑	↑ (↔)	↑	↔	↓
Malignancy-associated hypercalcemia:							
Humorally mediated (HHM)	↑↑	↓	↓,↔	↔,↓,(↑)	↑	↑↑	↓
Local destruction (osteolytic metastases)	↑	↔	↓,↔	↔,↓	↓	↑↑	↔

* *Symbols in parentheses refer to values rarely seen in the particular disease.*
† *Some report cyclic AMP values in malignancy vary greatly* ↑, ↓, ↔ *independent of systemic versus locally mediated bone resorption or even presence or absence of hypercalcemia.*
NOTE: *P$_i$ = inorganic phosphate; iPTH = immunoreactive parathyroid hormone; NcAMP = nephrogenous cyclic AMP; TMP = tubular maximal for phosphate reabsorption; GFR = gomerular filtration rate.*

signs that might provide a clue to the presence of malignancy, the following general approach can be used. If the patient is *asymptomatic* and if there is evidence by history of *chronicity* to the hypercalcemia, hyperparathyroidism is almost certainly the cause of the hypercalcemia. If iPTH levels on several occasions are elevated along with the typical features of hyperparathyroidism mentioned above, little other evaluation is necessary. Hyperparathyroidism is never confirmed until abnormal parathyroid tissue is surgically removed, correcting the hypercalcemia, but patients with asymptomatic hypercalcemia who have the presumptive diagnosis on the basis of elevated concentrations of iPTH can be followed, as described above, or recommended for surgery with reasonable confidence of cure. If in such patients there is a family history suggestive of other endocrine abnormality, more detailed screening for multiple endocrine neoplasia should be undertaken in the patient and family.

If the patient does not have clear-cut symptoms and there is only a short history or no clue to the duration of the hypercalcemia, *occult malignancy* must be considered with more care than if the hypercalcemia is known to be chronic. Even if the iPTH levels in such an asymptomatic patient are increased convincingly, it is probably useful to obtain values of 1,25(OH)$_2$D as well and follow the patient with the presumed diagnosis of primary hyperparathyroidism with less confidence.

If such patients have systemic symptoms and/or the iPTH levels are not elevated, then a thorough survey must be undertaken for malignancy, including chest x-ray, computerized tomography of chest and abdomen, and bone scan. Attention should also be paid to clues for underlying hematologic disorders such as anemia, increased plasma globulin, and abnormal serum immunoelectrophoresis; bone scans can be negative in patients with multiple myeloma. If no signs of a tumor are evident, the patient may have hyperparathyroidism with equivocal elevation in iPTH, and with time, the diagnosis of hyperparathyroidism may become more clear-cut.

Finally, if a patient is asymptomatic with chronic hypercalcemia but iPTH values are not elevated, it is useful to search for other chronic illnesses that cause hypercalcemia but may be atypical in presentation, such as occult sarcoidosis.

MEDICAL TREATMENT OF HYPERCALCEMIA The acute treatment of hypercalcemia is usually successful. The serum calcium concentration can be decreased by 3 to 9 mg/dL in 24 to 48 h in most patients, enough to relieve acute symptoms, prevent death from hypercalcemia crisis, and permit diagnostic evaluation. However the chronic medical management of hypercalcemia is usually unsatisfactory unless the underlying cause can be corrected because the available therapies are inconvenient or toxic.

Hypercalcemia develops because skeletal calcium release is excessive, intestinal calcium absorption is increased, or renal calcium excretion is inadequate. Understanding the particular pathogenesis helps guide therapy. For example, hypercalcemia in patients with osteolytic metastases or acute immobilization is primarily due to excessive skeletal calcium release and is, therefore, minimally affected by restriction of dietary calcium. On the other hand, patients with vitamin D hypersensitivity or vitamin D intoxication have excessive intestinal calcium absorption, and restriction of dietary calcium is beneficial. Decreased renal function or extracellular fluid depletion decreases urinary calcium excretion. If additional abnormalities, such as increased bone breakdown, are present, hypercalcemia will develop. This may happen, for example, when patients with resorptive bone disease become dehydrated. In such situations, rehydration may rapidly cure the hypercalcemia, even though excessive bone resorption and increased urinary calcium excretion continue.

Hydration, increased salt intake, mild and forced diuresis The first principle of treatment is to restore *normal hydration*. Many hypercalcemic patients are dehydrated because of vomiting, inanition, or hypercalcemia-induced defects in urinary concentrating ability. The resultant drop in glomerular filtration rate is accompanied by an additional decrease in renal tubular sodium and calcium clearance. Restoring a normal extracellular fluid volume corrects these abnormalities and increases urine calcium excretion by 100 to 300 mg (2.5 to 7.5 mmol) per day. Increasing urinary sodium excretion to 400 to 500 meq per day increases urinary calcium excretion even further than simple rehydration. Finally, after full benefits of simple rehydration have been achieved saline can be administered, or conventional doses of furosemide or ethacrynic acid can be given twice daily to depress the tubular reabsorptive mechanism for calcium (unless the diuretic is allowed to provoke dehydration). The combined use of these therapies can increase urinary calcium excretion to 400 mg per day or higher in most hypercalcemic patients. Since this is a substantial percentage of the exchangeable calcium pool, the serum calcium concentration usually falls 1 to 3 mg/dL (0.25 to 0.75 mmol per liter) within 24 h. The combination of fluids (by mouth), sodium, and furosemide or ethacrynic acid is also adaptable to chronic outpatient treatment, if necessary, using sodium chloride tablets. Precautions should be taken to prevent potassium and magnesium depletion during chronic therapy; calcium-containing renal calculi are a potential complication.

Under life-threatening circumstances, the above therapy can be pursued more aggressively, giving 6 liters of isotonic saline (900 meq sodium) daily plus furosemide in doses up to 100 mg every 1 to 2 h or ethacrynic acid in doses to 40 mg every 1 to 2 h. Urinary calcium excretion may exceed 1000 mg (25 mmol) per day, and the serum calcium may decrease by 4 mg/dL or more within 24 h. Severe potassium and magnesium depletion is inevitable unless replacements are given; pulmonary edema can be precipitated. The potential complications can be averted by careful monitoring of central venous pressure and plasma or urine electrolytes. A bladder catheter is usually necessary after the first day to allow the patient to sleep.

Plicamycin For the acute management of hypercalcemia plicamycin (mithramycin) which inhibits bone reabsorption, is a useful therapeutic agent. Plicamycin must be given intravenously, either as a bolus injection or by slow infusion. The usual dose is 25 μg per kilogram of body weight. Given once or twice a week, 10 μg/kg can be effective for chronic therapy in some patients; treatment should not be repeated until hypercalcemia recurs because the toxicity of the drug is dependent on the frequency of treatment and the total dosage.

Careful monitoring is needed if repeated doses are used. The major side effects are thrombocytopenia, hepatocellular necrosis with increased lactic acid dehydrogenase (LDH) and aspartate aminotransferase (AST) levels, and decreased levels of clotting factors with resultant epistaxis, bruising, hemorrhage, and bleeding gums. Azotemia, proteinuria, and hypocalcemia may occur. Hypophosphatemia and hypokalemia may also develop, as may nausea, vomiting, stomatitis, and facial swelling. Toxicity is rare when only one or two doses are used and can be minimized by repeating single doses only when hypercalcemia recurs. Toxic effects other than hemorrhage can usually be reversed by stopping the drug.

Other therapies Glucocorticoids increase urinary calcium excretion and decrease intestinal calcium absorption when given in pharmacologic doses (e.g., 40 to 200 mg prednisone daily in divided doses), but they also cause negative skeletal calcium balance. In normal subjects and in patients with primary hyperparathyroidism, glucocorticoids neither increase nor decrease the serum calcium concentration. In patients with hypercalcemia due to certain osteolytic malignancies, however, glucocorticoids may be effective as a result of antitumor effects. The malignancies in which hypercalcemia responds to glucocorticoid are usually hematologic malignancies such as multiple myeloma, leukemia, Hodgkin's disease, and other lymphomas; carcinoma of the breast may also respond, at least early in the course of the disease. Glucocorticoids are effective in treating hypercalcemia due to vitamin D intoxication or vitamin D hypersensitivity of sarcoidosis. The mechanism of action in the latter circumstances is unclear. In all the above situations, the hypocalcemic effect develops over several days, and the usual glucocorticoid dosage is 40 to 100 mg prednisone (or its equivalent) daily in four divided doses. The side effects of chronic glucocorticoid therapy may be acceptable in some circumstances.

The hormonal mediator of hypercalcemia secondary to malignancies that cause excessive bone breakdown without actually metastasizing to bone may be a prostaglandin of the E series in some patients. Since prostaglandin synthesis can be blocked by indomethacin or aspirin, these drugs sometimes correct the hypercalcemia in such patients. The analytical methods necessary to define prostaglandin excess are not widely available, and a therapeutic trial is the accepted diagnostic maneuver. Indomethacin, 25 mg every 6 h, or aspirin in sufficient doses to produce a serum salicylate level of 20 to 30 mg/dL generally lowers the serum calcium concentrations over several days if prostaglandin excess is the cause.

Hypercalcemia complicated by severe renal failure is difficult to manage; dialysis is often the treatment of choice. Peritoneal dialysis can remove 500 to 200 mg (12.5 to 50 mmol) of calcium in 24 to 48 h and lower the serum calcium concentration by 3 to 12 mg/dL (0.75 to 3.0 mmol per liter), if calcium-free dialysis fluid is used. Large quantities of phosphate are lost during dialysis, and serum inorganic phosphate concentrations usually fall, thus aggravating hypercalcemia. Therefore, the serum inorganic phosphate concentration should be measured after dialysis, and phosphate supplements should be added to the diet or to dialysis fluids if necessary.

Calcitonin decreases the skeletal release of calcium, phosphorus, and hydroxyproline within minutes of its intravenous injection. The subsequent changes in serum calcium and phosphorus depend upon the initial magnitude of skeletal resorption: subjects with the most rapid bone turnover show the greatest reduction in serum calcium concentration. Calcitonin also increases the renal clearance of calcium and phosphorus (and sodium). The most impressive results are seen in patients with hypercalcemia due to immobilization, thyrotoxicosis, or vitamin D intoxication, situations characterized by a high rate of bone turnover. Surprisingly, calcitonin is less effective than phosphate or plicamycin in patients with hypercalcemia due to malignancy or hyperparathyroidism, conditions in which bone turnover is also high. Escape from drug action occurs in patients and animals invariably after 12 to 24 h of high-dose therapy or after several days of continuous therapy with calcitonin. The mechanism of escape is unknown; there have been reports that coadministration of glucocorticoids and calcitonin prevents escape. This promising lead deserves further clinical evaluation since calcitonin would be advantageous due to its minimal toxicity. Calcitonin is effective by intravenous, intramuscular, or subcutaneous injection; doses used are 25 to 50 units every 6 to 8 h, usually in the form of salmon calcitonin.

Phosphate Patients with primary hyperparathyroidism are frequently hypophosphatemic, and hypercalcemia of other causes may also be complicated by hypophosphatemia. Hypophosphatemia decreases the rate of calcium uptake into bone, increases intestinal calcium absorption, and directly and indirectly stimulates bone breakdown. These effects aggravate hypercalcemia, and correcting hypophosphatemia lowers the serum calcium concentration. The usual treatment is 1 to 1.5 g of phosphate phosphorous per day for several days, given in four divided doses to minimize the chances of developing hyperphosphatemia. Such therapy has been administered for prolonged periods in selected patients. It is generally believed but not established that toxicity will not occur if the phosphate therapy is limited to restoring serum inorganic phosphate concentrations to normal rather than making them supranormal.

Raising the serum inorganic phosphate concentration above normal further decreases serum calcium levels. Intravenous phosphate is one of the most dramatically effective treatments available for severe hypercalcemia. A dose of 1500 mg phosphate phosphorus or more intravenously over 6 to 8 h leads to a prompt decrease in serum calcium of 2 to 10 mg/dL in patients with initially normal serum inorganic phosphate concentrations. However, this therapy should be employed only in extreme emergencies for two reason. First, fatal

hypocalcemia can be produced by excessive dosage; frequent serum calcium determinations are necessary if intravenous phosphate is administered. Second, unlike sodium chloride, sodium phosphate does not remove calcium from the body. In fact, urine calcium generally declines, and fecal calcium declines or remains the same. The decline in serum calcium reflects a redistribution of calcium within the body. There is a rapid efflux of calcium with no change in calcium influx to the circulation, findings indicative of precipitation of calcium phosphate salt. The calcium precipitates in bone, and metastatic calcification has also been reported in patients receiving oral or intravenous phosphate therapy for hypercalcemia. Indeed, hyperphosphatemia can cause metastatic calcification in normocalcemic animals. Thus, administration of intravenous phosphate is justifiable only as an emergency treatment.

Inorganic phosphate is commercially available for oral use in liquid, powder, and capsule form and as a liquid for intravenous use. It is important to calculate doses in terms of phosphate phosphorous (see Table 336-4).

Summary The various therapies for hypercalcemia are listed in Table 336-5. The choice depends upon the underlying disease, the severity of the hypercalcemia, the serum inorganic phosphate level, and the patient's renal, hepatic, and bone marrow function. Mild hypercalcemia (12 mg/dL or 3 mmol per liter) can usually be managed by hydration, sodium chloride, and small doses of furosemide or ethacrynic acid. Severe hypercalcemia (15 mg/dL or 3.75 mmol per liter) requires rapid correction. Aggressive sodium-calcium diuresis with large doses of furosemide and ethacrynic acid works rapidly but should only be undertaken if appropriate monitoring is available and cardiac function is adequate. Plicamycin is often the drug of choice, since it has the advantages of effectiveness and simplicity of use; the principal contraindication is its potential for toxicity. Renal, hepatic, or bone marrow disease may preclude its use.

Since continuation of intravenous therapy is usually impracticable and long-term use of plicamycin may increase chances of toxicity, there is a role for oral phosphate therapy for chronic management of hypercalcemia. Phosphate supplements should never be administered if hyperphosphatemia is present. Severe dietary calcium restriction should be employed if intestinal absorption is enhanced. Glucocorticoids and prostaglandin-synthesis inhibitors, even when effective in a particular disease, work slowly over several days and should not be relied upon as the sole treatment for life-threatening hypercalcemia. Dialysis should be reserved for hypercalcemia complicating acute or chronic renal failure.

The only satisfactory therapy for chronic use is a combination of dietary calcium restriction, administration of sodium chloride with or without furosemide and ethacrynic acid, and moderate-dose oral phosphate (the patient is kept normophosphatemic). The more effective remedies (plicamycin, glucocorticoids, high-dose oral phosphate) have significant toxicity when used chronically. There may be a role for calcitonin combined with glucocorticoids, but more experience is needed.

TABLE 336-4 Commercially available phosphate preparations

	1000 mg P	meq Na	meq K
Oral phosphate preparations:			
Neutraphos (1250-mg capsule)	4 caps	28.5	28.5
Neutraphos-K (1450-mg capsule)	4 caps	—	57
Phos-Tabs (860-mg tablet)	6 tabs	—	51
Fleets Phospho-Soda (liquid)	6.7 mL	40	—
Intravenous phosphate preparations:			
In-Phos	40 mL	65	8
Hyper-Phos-K	15 mL	—	50

SOURCE: *After Neer and Potts (with permission).*

TABLE 336-5 Summary of useful treatments for hypercalcemia

Therapy	Therapeutic details	Indications	Complications	Precautions
MOST GENERALLY USEFUL THERAPIES				
Hydration	2 liters or more	Universal	—	—
High salt intake	Achieve urine Na of 300 meq/day or more	Universal	Edema	—
Furosemide or ethacrynic acid	40–160 mg/day 50–200 mg/day	Universal	↓ K and ↓ Mg	Measure serum K and Mg
Forced diuresis	4–6 liters fluid IV/day containing 600–900 meq Na plus furosemide every 1-2 h, plus at least 60 meq K/day, plus at least 60 meq Mg/day	Universal	Pulmonary edema; ↓ K and ↓ Mg	Intensive monitoring, including venous pressure and serum Mg and K
Oral phosphate	250 mg P every 6 h PO	Universal if serum P < 3 mg/dL	Ectopic calcification	Keep serum P below 5–6 mg/dL
Mithramycin	10–25 µg/kg IV, repeat prn	Increased bone resorption	Liver; kidney; marrow toxicity	Monitor platelets CBC, BUN, SCOT
Prednisone or equivalent	5–15 mg every 6 h	Breast cancer, lymphomas, leukemias, multiple myeloma, vitamin D poisoning, sarcoidosis	Cushing's syndrome if chronic Rx	Alternate-day Rx for chronic use
SPECIAL THERAPIES FOR PARTICULAR USES				
IV phosphate	1500 mg P every 12 h until P 6 mg/dL	Severe hypercalcemia; diuresis or mithramycin contraindicated	Ectopic calcification: severe hypocalcemia	Monitor serum Ca and P closely
Calcitonin	2 units every 4 h subcutaneously	Adjunct when ↑ bone reabsorption; paralysis; immobilization	—	—
Indomethacin	25 mg every 6 h PO	Certain types of pseudo-hyperparathyroidism	Na retention: GI bleeding; headache	Careful clinical monitoring
Dialysis	Low-Ca bath	Acute renal failure	Multiple	Monitor serum P after dialysis

HYPOCALCEMIA

PATHOPHYSIOLOGY OF HYPOCALCEMIA: CLASSIFICATION BASED ON MECHANISM Chronic hypocalcemia is less common than hypercalcemia; causes include chronic renal failure, hereditary and acquired hypoparathyroidism, and hypomagnesemia. Critically ill patients may have *transient hypocalcemia* in association with disorders such as severe sepsis, burns, and acute renal failure or after extensive transfusions with citrated blood. In many instances, however, the hypocalcemia is more apparent than real. Although as many as half of patients in intensive care settings are reported to show calcium concentrations below 8.5 mg/dL, less than 10 percent have a reduction in ionized calcium. Often, hypoalbuminemia is the cause of the reduced total calcium concentration. In addition, however, alkalosis may tend to increase calcium binding to proteins, and in this setting direct measurements of ionized calcium should be made.

Medications such as protamine, heparin, and glucagon may cause transient hypocalcemia. These forms of hypocalcemia, apparent or real, are usually not associated with tetany and resolve with improvement in the overall medical condition. The transient hypocalcemia after repeated transfusions of citrated blood also usually resolves quickly.

Subacute hypocalcemia may also occur. Patients with acute *pancreatitis* have hypocalcemia which persists during the acute inflammation and varies in severity with the severity of the pancreatitis. The cause of the hypocalcemia in pancreatitis remains unclear. Parathyroid hormone (PTH) values may be low, normal, or elevated, and both resistance to PTH and impaired PTH secretion have been reported, leaving no clear view as to the principal mechanism. There are also occasional reports of a chronic low total blood calcium in elderly patients, with documented reduction in ionized calcium concentration but without obvious cause and with a paucity of symptoms of hypocalcemia.

Neuromuscular or neurologic symptoms are the most common manifestations of untreated chronic hypocalcemia. Patients may show muscle spasms, carpopedal spasm, facial grimacing, and in extreme cases, laryngeal spasm and convulsions. Respiratory arrest may occur. Increased intracranial pressure occurs in some patients with long-standing hypocalcemia, often in association with papilledema. Other chronic mental changes include irritability, depression, and psychosis. The QT interval on the electrocardiogram is prolonged, in contrast to its shortening with hypercalcemia. Arrhythmias are reported, and digitalis may be ineffective. Intestinal cramps and chronic malabsorption may occur. Chvostek's or Trousseau's signs can be used to confirm latent tetany.

The classification of hypocalcemia shown in Table 336-6 is based on the premise that PTH is responsible for minute-to-minute regulations of plasma calcium concentration within narrow limits and, therefore, that the occurrence of hypocalcemia must mean a failure of the homeostatic action of PTH. This can occur if PTH is simply absent due to hereditary or acquired gland failure, if the hormone is rendered ineffective by any of several mechanisms that interfere with its action at target organs, or if the action of the hormone to raise blood calcium is simply overwhelmed by the loss of calcium from the extracellular fluid at a rate faster than it can be replaced.

PTH ABSENT Hypoparathyroidism, whether hereditary or acquired, has a number of common components. Acute and chronic symptoms that result from untreated hypocalcemia are shared by the two disorders, although typically the onset of hereditary hypoparathyroidism is more gradual and although acquired hypoparathyroidism often does not cause abnormalities in the teeth. Traditionally, acquired hypoparathyroidism secondary to surgery in the neck was more common than hereditary hypoparathyroidism, but the frequency of surgically induced parathyroid failure has diminished with the recognition of the importance of parathyroid gland preservation and the use of nonsurgical approaches to treatment of hyperthyroidism. Basal ganglia calcification and extrapyramidal syndromes occur in both hereditary and acquired hypoparathyroidism but are more common and earlier in onset in hereditary hypoparathyroidism. Pseudohypoparathyroidism, an example of ineffective PTH action rather than a failure of parathyroid gland production, shares several features with hypoparathyroidism. Both disorders exhibit the extraosseus calcification and extrapyramidal syndromes, the latter including choreoathetoic movements and dystonia. Papilledema and raised intracranial pressure occur in both states, as do lenticular cataracts and chronic changes in fingernails and hair, the latter usually reversible with treatment of hypocalcemia. Certain skin manifestations, including alopecia and candidiasis, are seen exclusively in hereditary hypoparathyroidism.

Hypocalcemia associated with hypomagnesemia is associated both with deficient PTH release and impaired responsiveness to the hormone. Patients with hypocalcemia secondary to hypomagnesemia have absent or low levels of circulating iPTH, indicative of diminished hormone release despite maximum physiologic stimulus by hypocalcemia. Plasma PTH levels return to normal with correction of the hypomagnesemia. Thus, hypoparathyroidism, associated with low levels of PTH in blood, can be due to hereditary gland failure, acquired gland failure, or acute, but reversible, gland dysfunction (hypomagnesemia). Patients with acquired or hereditary hypoparathyroidism also have hyperphosphatemia and absent or very low levels of $1,25(OH)_2D$.

Hereditary hypoparathyroidism Hypoparathyroidism can occur as an isolated entity without other endocrine or dermatologic manifestations or, more typically, in association with other organ deficiencies, such as defective development of the thymus, adrenal insufficiency, and ovarian insufficiency.

One rare form of hypoparathyroidism due to congenital aplasia of the parathyroid glands is manifested shortly after birth. The hereditary patterns are unclear with no simple pattern established. A linkage between defective development of the thymus and the parathyroid glands is recognized in the *DiGeorge syndrome*, which is also associated with congenital cardiovascular and other developmental defects. Most patients die in early childhood.

Hypoparathyroidism can occur as part of a more complex autoimmune syndrome involving failure of the adrenals, the ovaries, and the parathyroids in association with recurrent mucocutaneous candidiasis, alopecia, vitiligo, and pernicious anemia (see Chap. 334). In many cases, antibodies to endocrine organs are present. The inheritance appears to be autosomal recessive, and some unaffected family members show antibodies to endocrine tissue without evidence of endocrine failure. The disorder is usually referred to as autoimmune polyglandular deficiency. There is a failure of cell-mediated immunity.

Hereditary hypoparathyroidism occurs also as an isolated entity. The disease is usually manifest in the first decade but may occur much later, including in adult life. The mechanism of inheritance is unclear.

Treatment of hereditary hypoparathyroidism is similar to that for acquired hypoparathyroidism and pseudohypoparathyroidism, although specific features of each disease lead to additional treatment

TABLE 336-6 Functionally based classification of hypocalcemia (excluding neonatal conditions)

I PTH absent
  A Hereditary hypoparathyroidism
  B Acquired hypoparathyroidism
  C Hypomagnesemia
II PTH ineffective
  A Chronic renal failure
  B Active vitamin D lacking
    1 ↓ dietary intake or sunlight
    2 Defective metabolism:
      Anticonvulsant therapy
      Vitamin D dependent rickets—type I
  C Active vitamin D ineffective
    1 Intestinal malabsorption
    2 Vitamin D–dependent rickets—type II
  D Pseudohypoparathyroidism
III PTH overwhelmed
  A Severe, acute hyperphosphatemia
    1 Tumor lysis
    2 Acute renal failure
    3 Rhabdomyolysis
  B Osteitis fibrosa after parathyroidectomy

considerations. Replacement therapy with vitamin D or the active metabolite $1,25(OH)_2D$ combined with a high oral calcium intake usually suffices to regulate blood calcium and phosphate levels satisfactorily. Care must be taken to avoid excessive urinary calcium excretion; oral calcium and vitamin D therapy restores the overall calcium-phosphate balance but does not reverse the lowered urinary calcium clearance typical of hypoparathyroidism. Kidney stones may form due to excessive urinary calcium excretion during vitamin D and calcium replacement therapy in hypoparathyroidism. Thiazide diuretics will lower urine calcium by as much as 100 mg per day in hypoparathyroid patients on vitamin D, and calcium replacement therapy has been adopted by many in the management of hypoparathyroid patients. The approach seems to be of benefit in preventing severe hypercalciuria and in improving the management of certain patients (see "Treatment" section below).

Acquired hypoparathyroidism Acquired, chronic hypoparathyroidism is usually the result of inadvertent surgical removal of all the parathyroid glands; in some instances, not all of the tissue is removed but the gland undergoes compromise of vascular supply secondary to fibrotic changes in the neck after surgery. Historically, the most frequent cause of acquired hypoparathyroidism was encountered in the surgical management of hyperthyroidism. Chronic hypoparathyroidism is now more often encountered following surgery for chief cell hyperplasia of the parathyroids where the surgeon, facing the dilemma of removing too little tissue and thus not curing the hyperparathyroidism, removes too much, with consequent hypoparathyroidism.

Parathyroid function is not totally absent in all patients with postsurgical hypoparathyroidism. Presumably, the persistence of some residual parathyroid activity reduces the amount of replacement therapy that is necessary, but therapy varies greatly from patient to patient irrespective of the type of hypoparathyroidism or the question of residual parathyroid activity.

There are other rare causes of acquired chronic hypoparathyroidism, such as radiation-induced damage subsequent to radioiodine therapy of hyperthyroidism or glandular damage in patients with hemochromatosis or with hemosiderosis after repeated blood transfusions. Other chronic infectious diseases, although they may involve one or more of the parathyroids, usually do not cause permanent hypoparathyroidism because all four glands are not usually involved.

Transient hypoparathyroidism is frequent following surgical exploration for hyperparathyroidism, particularly in patients in whom more than one exploration is required and in patients with multiple gland disease in which all glands must be identified and biopsied. Often, after a variable period of hypoparathyroidism, normal parathyroid function returns with hypertrophy of remaining tissue. Occasionally, recovery occurs months after surgery. The management of transient, postoperative hypoparathyroidism is discussed under the surgical treatment of hyperparathyroidism. The treatment of chronic, acquired hypoparathyroidism is similar to that used with idiopathic hypoparathyroidism—replacement with vitamin D and oral calcium.

Hypomagnesemia Hypomagnesemia, of a severe degree, is associated with severe hypocalcemia, and restoration of the total-body magnesium deficits leads to rapid reversal of the hypocalcemia. There are at least two separate causes, impaired secretion of PTH and reduced peripheral responsiveness to hormone action.

Hypomagnesemia is generally classified as primary or secondary; primary hypomagnesemia is due to hereditary defects in intestinal absorption or renal reabsorption of magnesium. Secondary hypomagnesemia, a more common condition, occurs on a nutritional basis or as a result of acquired intestinal or renal disorders. The most common causes of the secondary disorder are intestinal malabsorption syndromes, chronic alcoholism with poor nutritional intake, and parenteral nutrition in which magnesium replacement is omitted.

In experimental animals magnesium in extracellular fluid has effects similar to that of calcium on secretion of PTH; hypermagnesemia suppresses and hypomagnesemia stimulates PTH secretion.

Effects of magnesium on hormone secretion are normally of little physiologic significance, however, because the effects of calcium dominate. Greater change in magnesium than in calcium is needed to influence hormone secretion. Nonetheless, hypomagnesemia, if it influences hormone secretion at all, might be expected to increase hormone secretion. It is, therefore, surprising to find that severe hypomagnesemia is associated with blunted secretion of PTH. The explanation for the paradox is that severe, chronic hypomagnesemia is a marker of total-body magnesium deficiency; severe magnesium deficiency intereferes with normal secretory mechanisms and normal peripheral responses to PTH, both of which involve function of adenyl cyclase in glandular and target tissues. This chronic change, reduced intracellular stores, completely obscures any effects that might be brought about by acute changes in extracellular fluid magnesium in a magnesium-replete individual.

Severe hypocalcemia is often seen when serum magnesium is substantially below normal. Normal serum magnesium is 2 to 3 mg/dL or 1.5 to 2.5 meq per liter. In the majority of the cases in which hypomagnesemia is associated with hypocalcemia, serum magnesium has been below 0.8 meq per liter or 1.0 mg/dL.

Immunoreactive PTH (iPTH) levels are usually undetectable or inappropriately low despite the extreme stimulus of severe hypocalcemia. Even when iPTH levels are elevated, acute repletion of magnesium leads to a further increase in iPTH concentration. The overall data are interpreted to mean that PTH secretion is blunted in virtually all patients with severe hypomagnesemia; thus, absolute or relative acute hypoparathyroidism seems to be the rule in patients with hypocalcemia secondary to hypomagnesemia.

Diminished peripheral responsiveness to administered PTH can be shown in some patients with severe hypomagnesemia in addition to defects in hormone secretion. Some clinical reports document normal response in urinary phosphorus and urinary cyclic AMP excretion after administration of exogenous PTH to patients who are hypocalcemic and who have diminished PTH secretion. Both blunted PTH secretion and lack of renal response to administered PTH can occur in the same patient. Blunted skeletal responses have been claimed in many, but by no means all, patients studied with the hypomagnesemia-hypocalcemia syndrome. When acute magnesium repletion is undertaken, the restoration of PTH concentrations to normal or supranormal levels precedes by several days the restoration of serum calcium.

Overall, blunted PTH secretory response in hypomagnesemia is probably the more important cause of the hypocalcemia. The variable defect in peripheral responsiveness, particularly renal responses, may indicate that an even greater degree of magnesium deficiency is required to induce end organ resistance than for impairment of hormone secretion.

Several other features have been noted. The brisk response in hormone secretion following magnesium repletion, sometimes demonstrable within minutes of giving a large parenteral dose of magnesium, indicates that hormone biosynthesis is not impaired, only secretion. Serum phosphate levels are not elevated as they often are in patients with hypoparathyroidism, probably because phosphate deficiency is a frequent accompaniment of the nutritional deficiencies that cause hypomagnesemia. There have been a few reports of magnesium-wasting chronic renal disease; although magnesium is elevated in acute renal failure, increases in magnesium concentration are an infrequent accompaniment of chronic renal failure.

Repletion of magnesium is the cure of the condition, and attention must be given to restoring the intracellular deficiency which may be considerable. After intravenous magnesium, serum magnesium may return to the normal range, but unless replacement therapy is continued, it will rapidly fall to subnormal levels again. A sometimes useful indicator of restoration of magnesium deficiency is the urinary magnesium excretion; magnesium retention by the kidney is usually seen until magnesium deficiencies are repleted. Intracellular deficits can be as great as 100 meq or more, but in many of the reported cases parenteral administration of approximately 25 meq magnesium

seemed to reverse the signs of magnesium deficiency. Depending on the associated condition which caused the hypomagnesemia, treatment may have to be administered chronically to prevent recurrence.

PTH INEFFECTIVE PTH can be considered ineffective when the hormone's action to promote calcium absorption from the diet is interfered with because of a primary deficiency of vitamin D, because of a condition in which vitamin D is ineffective, or in chronic renal failure in which the calcium-elevating action of PTH is opposed by several different processes. With diverse pathophysiologic mechanisms, these conditions center around but are not limited to the unavailability of vitamin D as a cofactor for the hormone and are usually associated with mild hypomagnesemia. Typically, hypophosphatemia is more severe than hypocalcemia due to the increased secretion of PTH which, while ineffective to elevate blood calcium, still promotes renal phosphate excretion. Varying degrees of bone disease featuring impaired mineralization and/or frank osteomalacia are the more frequent and harmful consequences of chronic renal failure or inadequate or ineffective vitamin D action.

Pseudohypoparathyroidism, on the other hand, is distinct from the other disorders classified under ineffective PTH action. Pseudohypoparathyroidism resembles conditions in which there is a true absence of PTH synthesis and secretion and is manifested, in the untreated state, by severe hypocalcemia and hyperphosphatemia. The cause of the disease, however, is inadequate peripheral response to PTH involving any of several defects in the biochemical events involving hormone binding to the receptor, activation of guanyl nucleotide binding proteins, and stimulation of adenyl cyclase to increase intracellular cyclic AMP.

Chronic renal failure Severe abnormalities in mineral ion and bone metabolism occur in chronic renal failure. Even prior to the initiation of extensive programs of dialysis, however, improved medical management of chronic renal failure and/or a more indolent course of the renal disease allowed many patients to survive for a sufficiently long period that renal osteodystrophy, the mixed bone disease associated with renal failure, often became an important feature.

After the initiation of chronic dialysis programs, many of the impairments in mineral and bone metabolism became even more apparent. Now the roles of phosphate retention and impaired production of 1,25(OH)$_2$D are recognized as the principal factors responsible for inducing calcium deficiency, secondary hyperparathyroidism, and a picture of often severe bone disease. Less clearly, the uremic state appears to be associated with impairment of intestinal absorption by factors other than impairment in vitamin D metabolism. Nonetheless, replacement of physiologic levels of 1,25(OH)$_2$D usually leads to satisfactory calcium absorption, suggesting it is the lack of the vitamin D rather than intrinsic defects in intestinal cellular function that is the more important cause of the impaired mineral metabolism in chronic renal failure.

Hyperphosphatemia per se tends to lower blood calcium concentration by several actions; these include extraosseous deposition of calcium and phosphate, impaired sensitivity of the skeleton to the bone-resorbing action of PTH, reduced 1,25(OH)$_2$D production by surviving renal tissue, and reduction in calcium absorption due to trapping of calcium in insoluble form as calcium phosphate complexes. In animals prevention of hyperphosphatemia by dietary means can block the development of secondary hyperparathyroidism, emphasizing the importance of phosphate retention in the pathogenesis of secondary hyperparathyroidism and the associated disorders of mineral and bone metabolism. The low levels of 1,25(OH)$_2$D also play an important role, particularly in chronic renal failure.

Therapy of chronic renal failure (discussed elsewhere in this text) features careful medical management of patients prior to dialysis as well as careful adjustment of dialysis regimens once this becomes necessary. At various stages of the development of the renal failure, attention should be paid to restriction of phosphate in the diet, use of phosphate-binding antacids such as those based on aluminum hydroxide, provision of an adequate calcium intake by mouth, usually

1 to 2 g per day, and supplementation with calcitriol in doses from 0.25 to 1.0 μg per day. Each patient must be monitored closely. The aims of therapy are to restore a normal calcium balance to prevent osteomalacia and the development of secondary hyperparathyroidism. Renal osteodystrophy, as discussed above, is the principal disabling feature of chronic renal failure related to calcium metabolism. Reduction of hyperphosphatemia and restoration of normal intestinal calcium absorption by the use of supplemental calcitriol can lead to an improvement in blood calcium concentration and a concomitant reduction in secondary hyperparathyroidism.

Active vitamin D lacking   DEFICIENT DIETARY INTAKE AND/OR SUNLIGHT   Vitamin D deficiency is more common in the United States at the present time than previously recognized. Biopsies of bone in elderly patients with hip fracture and evaluation of patients with regard to concentrations of vitamin D metabolites, PTH, and mineral ions themselves have revealed that vitamin D deficiency may occur in as many as 25 percent of elderly patients, particularly in areas where there is little ambient sunlight. Concentrations of 25-(OH)D are at the lower limits of normal or well below normal in these patients. Quantitative histomorphometry on bone biopsy specimens reveals widened osteoid seams consistent with osteomalacia. Again, the bone disease is the serious problem. Hypocalcemia is modest in degree at best. PTH hypersecretion compensates for a tendency of the blood calcium level to fall but at the consequence of inducing renal phosphate wasting and a combined mineral ion abnormality that results in osteomalacia.

The genesis of the vitamin D deficiency is impaired intake of dairy products that are enriched with vitamin D, lack of vitamin supplementation in the elderly, and reduced sunlight exposure, particularly in winter in northern parts of the country.

Treatment involves the administration of vitamin D and provision of 1 to 1.5 g of calcium in the diet. Vitamin D supplementation should aim to provide several times the recommended daily requirement in younger people, which is probably a safe recommendation; 1000 to 2000 units of vitamin D per day would be satisfactory. Vitamin D is usually not available in multiple-dose forms. Hence, the administration of a capsule containing 50,000 units of vitamin D once monthly is safe in elderly patients who have osteomalacia. The increased awareness of the importance of calcium supplementation, particularly in women, even without supplementation of vitamin D, may lessen the frequency of this problem. It should be emphasized that severe hypocalcemia is rarely seen in the moderately severe vitamin D deficiency of the elderly but needs to be considered in the differential diagnosis of mild hypocalcemia.

DEFECTIVE VITAMIN D METABOLISM   *Anticonvulsant therapy*   Anticonvulsant therapy with any of several agents induces a state of acquired vitamin D deficiency by increasing the turnover of vitamin D into inactive compounds. The more marginal the degree of vitamin D intake in the diet, the more likely it is that anticonvulsant therapy will lead to abnormalities in mineral and bone metabolism. The syndrome in its extreme case involves severe rickets with bone fractures, hypocalcemia, and hypophosphatemia. Occasionally, a severe proximal myopathy is reported. More often, frank hypocalcemia is not detected, and mild osteomalacia is the only clinical symptom. In other patients on long-term anticonvulsant therapy, no symptoms or signs are present, but bone density is lower than normal and responds favorably to vitamin D supplementation.

Anticonvulsants stimulate the hepatic microsomal mixed-oxidase enzymes and hence increase the rate of clearance of vitamin D and its metabolites. Phenytoin also impairs intestinal calcium absorption independent of effects on vitamin D; the drug also has deleterious effects on bone cell function in vitro including inhibition of collagen synthesis. The syndrome can be reversed with adequate vitamin D supplementation.

Although $1,25(OH)_2D$ levels are lower for the degree of vitamin D intake in patients treated with chronic anticonvulsants than in the normal population, there is a great deal of variation. The greater

prevalence of the disorder in some European populations and in children in homes for the mentally retarded probably reflects the lower vitamin D intake of those groups. Restoration of bone mineral mass and reversal of hypocalcemia, when seen, can be accomplished with vitamin D replacement plus added oral calcium. Adjustments in dose are indicated depending on the age and body size of the patient, but approximately 50,000 units of vitamin D weekly plus 1 g of elemental calcium per day for several months are usually sufficient. Alternatively, administration of one 50,000-unit capsule of vitamin D once monthly may be preventative if the anticonvulsant therapy must be given chronically.

Vitamin D–dependent rickets type I   Rickets can be due to *resistance* to the *action* of vitamin D as well as to vitamin D deficiency. Vitamin D–dependent rickets type I, previously termed pseudo-vitamin D–dependent rickets, differs from vitamin D–resistant rickets in that it is less severe and in that the biochemical and radiographic abnormalities can be reversed with large doses of the vitamin.

Clinical features include hypocalcemia, often with tetany or convulsions, hypophosphatemia, secondary hyperparathyroidism, and osteomalacia, often associated with skeletal deformities and increased alkaline phosphatase. Doses of vitamin D or 25(OH)D, 100 to 1000 times above the usual amounts, are required to heal the bone disease, whereas physiologic amounts of calcitriol cure the disease. The disorder, an autosomal recessive trait, is due to a defect in conversion of $25(OH)D$ to $1,25(OH)_2D$. Plasma levels of $1,25(OH)_2D$ are low or undetectable even after administration of large doses of vitamin D or 25(OH). Response to high doses of vitamin D or 25(OH)D is probably due to direct actions of high levels of 25(OH)D. Treatment requires careful adjustment of calcitriol dose, particularly during growth periods.

ACTIVE VITAMIN D INEFFECTIVE   *Intestinal malabsorption*   Mild hypocalcemia, secondary hyperparathyroidism, severe hypophosphatemia, and a variety of nutritional deficiencies occur with gastrointestinal diseases. Hepatocellular dysfunction can lead to reduction in 25(OH)D levels, as in portal or biliary cirrhosis of the liver. Malabsorption of vitamin D and its metabolites, including calcitriol, may occur in a variety of intestinal diseases, hereditary or acquired. Hypocalcemia itself can lead to steatorrhea, due to deficient production of pancreatic enzymes and bile salts. Depending on the disorder, vitamin D or its metabolites can be administered parenterally, thereby guaranteeing adequate blood levels of active metabolites.

Vitamin D–dependent rickets type II   Pseudo-vitamin D–dependent rickets can be due to defective response as well as to defective production of $1,25(OH)_2D$. This disorder, vitamin D–dependent rickets type II, results from any of several types of end organ resistance to the active metabolite, including absence or qualitative defects of the cytosolic receptor protein for the hormone and postreceptor blocks in hormone action. The clinical features are similar to those with the type I disorder and include hypocalcemia, hypophosphatemia, secondary hyperparathyroidism, and rickets. Plasma levels of $1,25(OH)_2D$ are elevated at least three times above normal, in keeping with the refractoriness of the end organs. Severe alopecia totalis may commence early in life. Patients with this disorder usually require higher dose of vitamin D or vitamin D metabolites than in the type I disorder.

Pseudohypoparathyroidism   Pseudohypoparathyroidism (PHP) is a hereditary disorder characterized by symptoms and signs of hypoparathyroidism, typically in association with distinctive skeletal and developmental defects. The hypoparathyroidism is due to a deficient end organ response to PTH. Excessive secretion of PTH is the consequence of hyperplasia of the parathyroids, a response to the resistance to hormone action. The entity is actually a syndrome in which various individuals and kindreds exhibit different aberrancies in hormone-receptor complex response.

A working classification of the various forms of pseudohypoparathyroidism is given in Table 336-7. The classification scheme is based on the signs of ineffective parathyroid hormone action (low calcium and high phosphate), urinary cyclic AMP response to exogenous PTH, the presence or absence of Albright's hereditary osteodystrophy (AHO), and assays of the concentration of the G_s subunits of the adenylate cyclase enzyme (see Chap. 67). Using these criteria there are four types: pseudohypoparathyroidism (PHP) type I, subdivided into a and b categories; PHP-II; and pseudopseudohypoparathyroidism (PPHP). Individuals with PHP-I, the most common of the disorders, show a deficient response in urinary cyclic AMP following administration of exogenous parathyroid hormone. Pseudohypoparathyroidism type II refers to patients with hypocalcemia and hyperphosphatemia who have a normal urinary cyclic AMP response to PTH. These patients are assumed to have a defect in the response to PTH at a locus beyond that of cyclic AMP production. Patients with the PHP-I syndrome are divided into type a with reduced activity of the stimulatory G protein subunit (G_s) in in vitro assays and type b with normal amounts of G_s in erythrocytes. Subjects with PHP-Ia also have shortened metacarpals and metatarsals and the other features of Albright's hereditary osteodystrophy (AHO) syndrome and commonly show resistance to hormones in addition to PTH. Patients with PHP-Ib have a normal phenotype without the AHO syndrome and do not show resistance to any hormones other than parathyroid hormone. Fibroblasts cultured from the skin of some patients with PHP-Ib show a much reduced response of cyclic AMP accumulation to agents that stimulate adenylate cyclase such as prostaglandins, forskolin, and PTH, consistent with the presence of a defective receptor. A subset of these patients, however, have a normal response to cyclic AMP production in fibroblasts in vitro.

Patients with PPHP have typical features of the hereditary osteodystrophy syndrome despite normal serum calciums and normal response of urinary cyclic AMP to exogenous PTH. Some such individuals are first degree relatives of patients with PHP-Ia, and patients initially classified as having PPHP have subsequently developed mild hypocalcemia. Patients with PPHP on average have levels of G_s subunits that are half normal. These various features suggest that PPHP is a mild variant of PHP-Ia and illustrate the heterogeneity of the defect in PTH responsiveness. Further studies will be necessary to clarify the pathogenesis of these disorders.

Little is known about the pathophysiology of the skeletal defects. The AHO syndrome includes round facies, short stature, obesity, brachydactyly, and heterotopic calcification. Mental deficiency is frequent.

The mode of inheritance in these various disorders is uncertain and may itself be heterogeneous. In some families the disorder may be an X-linked dominant defect, whereas in others the disorder appears to result from an autosomal dominant mutation with variable expressivity.

The mineral deposits in ectopic sites may include true bone, whereas bone formation in ectopic sites never occurs in idiopathic hypoparathyroidism. Amorphous deposits of calcium and phosphate are found in the basal ganglia in about half of patients. The defects in metacarpal and metatarsal bones are sometimes accompanied by abnormal phalanges as well, possibly reflecting premature closing of the epiphyses. The typical findings are abnormally short fourth and fifth metacarpals and metatarsals. The defects are usually bilateral. Exostoses are frequent, as is radius curvus. Impairments in olfaction and taste and unusual dermatoglyphic abnormalities have been reported. There is little improvement in mental status even after adequate therapy with calcium and vitamin D.

The diagnosis can usually be made without difficulty. Positive family history for developmental defects and/or the presence of developmental defects characteristic of PHP-Ia, including brachydactyly, in association with the signs of hypoparathyroidism, low calcium, and high phosphate, essentially make the diagnosis on clinical grounds. On the other hand, patients with PHP-Ib or PHP-II do not have phenotypic abnormalities. In PHP-Ib, administration of exogenous parathyroid hormone can lead to detection of the blunted cyclic AMP response; such tests are usually used to confirm the diagnosis even in PHP-Ia. Low levels of G_s subunits in erythrocyte membranes can also distinguish patients with PHP-Ia from those with PHP-Ib. Patients in both categories have elevated serum PTH, particularly if they are hypocalcemic. The diagnosis of PHP-II is more complex, in that cyclic AMP responses in urine are, by definition, normal. Since vitamin D deficiency itself can result in dissociation between phosphaturic and urinary cyclic AMP responses to exogenous PTH, vitamin D deficiency must be excluded before diagnosis of PHP-II can be made. PHP-II is separated from hypoparathyroidism by finding of elevated PTH levels; this finding per se, however, does not distinguish between secretion of abnormal PTH and a post-cyclic AMP receptor defect. Some patients with the PHP-II phenotype may actually have hypoparathyroidism secondary to secretion of an abnormal, biologically inactive PTH.

Treatment of PHP and PPHP is similar to that of hypoparathyroidism, except that the dose of vitamin D and calcium is usually lower than that required in true hypoparathyroidism. Variations in individual responses make it necessary to establish the optimal therapeutic program for each patient, based on maintaining the appropriate blood calcium concentration and urinary calcium excretion.

PTH Overwhelmed Occasionally, loss of calcium from the extracellular fluid (ECF) is so severe that PTH cannot compensate. Such situations include severe, acute hyperphosphatemia, often in association with renal failure, and rapid loss of calcium from the ECF, as in acute pancreatitis. Severe hypocalcemia can occur quickly; PTH rises in response to hypocalcemia but does not return blood calcium to normal. The chance of hypoglycemia is enhanced when there is some degree of compromise of the target tissues, as when renal failure occurs.

Severe, acute hyperphosphatemia Severe hyperphosphatemia occurs in situations associated with extensive tissue damage or cell destruction. The combination of an increased release of phosphate from muscle and an impaired ability to excrete phosphorous secondary to the renal failure causes moderate to severe hyperphosphatemia. Calcium loss from the blood results in hypocalcemia of mild to moderate severity; hypocalcemia is usually reversed with tissue repair and restoration of renal function as phosphorus and creatinine values return to normal. There may even be a mild hypercalcemic period in the oliguric phase of recovery of renal function. This sequence, severe hypocalcemia followed by mild hypercalcemia, reflects widespread deposition of calcium in muscle with subsequent redistribution of some of the calcium to the ECF after restoration of phosphate levels to normal.

Other causes of hyperphosphatemia that lead to hypocalcemia include hypothermia, massive hepatic failure, and hematologic malignancies, either because of high cell turnover as part of the malignancy or because of cell destruction when chemotherapy is instituted.

TABLE 336-7 Classification of pseudohypoparathyroidism (PHP) and pseudopseudohypoparathyroidism (PPHP)

Type	Hypocalcemia, hyperphosphatemia	Response of Urinary cAMP to PTH	Serum PTH	G_s subunit deficiency	AHO	Resistance to hormones in addition to PTH
PHP-Ia	Yes	↓	↑	Yes	Yes	Yes
PHP-Ib	Yes	↓	↑	No	No	No
PHP-II	Yes	Normal	↑	No	No	No
PPHP	No	Normal	Normal	Yes	Yes	±

NOTE: ↓ = decreased; ↑ = increased; AHO = Albright's hereditary osteodystrophy.

Treatment is directed toward lowering of blood phosphate by the administration of phosphate-binding antacids or dialysis, often needed for the management of renal failure. Although calcium replacement may be necessary if hypocalcemia is severe and symptomatic, calcium administration during the hyperphosphatemic period may increase extraosseous cellular calcium deposition, thereby aggravating ultimate tissue damage. Although the levels of $1,25(OH)_2D$ may be low during the hyperphosphatemic phase and may return to normal during the oliguric phase of recovery, mineral ion imbalance per se seems to be the principal pathophysiologic mechanism.

Osteitis fibrosa after parathyroidectomy   Severe hypocalcemia after parathyroid surgery is less common now that osteitis fibrosa cystica is an infrequent manifestation of hyperparathyroidism. When osteitis fibrosa cystica is severe, however, bone mineral deficits can be large, and after parathyroidectomy, blood calcium levels can fall to the hypocalcemic range and remain depressed for days if calcium replacement is inadequate. The mechanism of the hypocalcemia is complex. Increased cellularity of bone in severe osteitis fibrosa cystica involves both osteoblastic and osteoclastic cells. High levels of PTH enhance bone-blood exchange, with resorption favored over formation; an abrupt decrease in PTH levels with surgery promotes bone formation. Calcium loss from blood is increased, and temporarily hyporesponsiveness of bone to the bone-resorbing actions of PTH hormone may add to the imbalance between bone resorption and bone formation. Treatment may require parenteral administration of calcium; addition of calcitriol and oral calcium supplementation may hasten the ability to withdraw parenteral calcium supplementation and/or reduce the amount needed.

DIFFERENTIAL DIAGNOSIS   Care must be taken to ensure that true hypocalcemia is present; in addition, acute transient hypocalcemia can be a manifestation of a variety of severe, acute illnesses as discussed above. *Chronic hypocalcemia*, however, can usually be ascribed to a few disorders associated with an absence of PTH or its ineffectiveness. Important clinical criteria include the duration of the illness, signs or symptoms of associated disorders, and the detection of features that suggest an hereditary abnormality in calcium and bone metabolism. A nutritional history can be helpful in detecting a low intake of vitamin D and calcium in the elderly, and a history of excessive alcohol intake can be the clue to magnesium deficiency.

Hypoparathyroidism and pseudohypoparathyroidism are life-long illnesses; hence, a recent onset of hypocalcemia in an adult will rarely prove to be due to hypoparathyroidism and is more likely due to nutritional deficiencies, renal failure, or intestinal disorders that result in vitamin D deficiency or ineffective vitamin D action. A history of seizure disorder raises the issue of anticonvulsive medication. Neck surgery, even in the past, can be associated with a delayed onset of postsurgical hypoparathyroidism. Developmental defects, particularly in childhood and adolescence may point to the diagnosis of pseudohypoparathyroidism. Rickets and a variety of neuromuscular syndromes and deformities may indicate ineffective vitamin D action, usually due in the United States to hereditary defects in vitamin D metabolism rather than to vitamin D deficiency.

A pattern of *low calcium* with *high phosphorus* in the absence of renal failure or massive tissue destruction almost invariably means hypoparathyroidism or pseudohypoparathyroidism. A *low calcium* with a *low phosphorus* points to absent or ineffective vitamin D, thereby rendering the action of PHT on calcium metabolism ineffective. The relative ineffectiveness of PTH in vitamin D deficiency, anticonvulsant therapy, gastrointestinal disorders, and hereditary defects in vitamin D metabolism leads to secondary hyperparathyroidism as a compensation. The relatively unopposed action of the excess PTH on renal tubule phosphate transport, less dependent on vitamin D sufficiency than calcium transport, accounts for renal phosphate wasting and hypophosphatemia.

Exceptions to these patterns may occur. Most forms of hypomagnesemia are due to long-standing nutritional deficiency, and, despite the fact that the hypocalcemia is due principally to an acute absence of PTH, phosphate levels are usually low rather than elevated as in

hypoparathyroidism. Chronic renal failure is often associated with hypocalcemia and hyperphosphatemia, despite secondary hyperparathyroidism.

Diagnosis is usually established by application of the PTH radioimmunoassay, tests for vitamin D metabolites, and measurements of the urinary cyclic AMP response to exogenous PTH. In hereditary and acquired hypoparathyroidism and severe hypomagnesemia, PTH is either undetectable or in the normal range. The latter finding may reflect in some instances a false-positive assay result, as in the case of tumor hypercalcemia, but the result in a hypocalcemic patient is supportive of hypoparathyroidism, as distinct from ineffective PTH action, in which even mild hypocalcemia is associated with clearly elevated PTH levels. Hence, a failure to detect elevated PTH levels establishes the diagnosis of hypoparathyroidism; elevated levels suggest the presence of secondary hyperparathyroidism as found in many of the situations in which the hormone is ineffective due to associated abnormalities in vitamin D action. Assays for $25(OH)D$ and $1,25(OH)_2D$ can be quite helpful. Low or low normal $25(OH)D$ indicates vitamin D deficiency due to lack of sunlight, inadequate vitamin D intake, or intestinal malabsorption. A low level of $1,25$-$(OH)_2D$ in the presence of elevated concentrations of PTH suggests ineffective PTH action, including chronic renal failure, severe vitamin D deficiency, vitamin D–dependent rickets type I, and pseudohypoparathyroidism. Recognition that mild hypocalcemia, rickets, and hypophosphatemia are due to chronic anticonvulsant therapy is made by history.

TREATMENT OF HYPOCALCEMIA   The chronic management of hypoparathyroidism or pseudohypoparathyroidism, chronic renal failure, and hereditary defects in vitamin D metabolism all feature the use of vitamin D or vitamin D metabolites and calcium supplementation. Vitamin D itself is the least expensive form of vitamin D replacement and is frequently used in the management of uncomplicated hypoparathyroidism and disorders associated with ineffective vitamin D action. When vitamin D is used prophylatically, as in the elderly or in those with chronic anticonvulsant therapy, there is a wider margin of safety than with the more potent metabolites. On the other hand, most of the conditions in which vitamin D is used for chronic management of hypocalcemia require the use of 50 to 100 times the daily replacement doses, because the formation of $1,25(OH)_2D$ is deficient. In such situations, vitamin D is no safer than the active metabolite because with high-dose vitamin D therapy, intoxication does occur. Calcitriol is more rapid in onset of action and also has a short biologic half-life; in high doses vitamin D is stored in body tissues and is cleared slowly.

One to five micrograms per day of vitamin D or calcifediol [25-$(OH)D_3$] and slightly lower doses of calcitriol (0.25 to 1.0 μg per day) are required to prevent rickets. In contrast, 500 to 3000 μg of vitamin D_2 or D_3 are typically required in hypoparathyroidism; doses of calcifediol are also high (several hundred micrograms per day) compared with doses required in euparathyroid individuals. The dose of calcitriol is unchanged in hypoparathyroidism since the defect is in hydroxylation by the 1α-hydroxylase.

The slightly greater therapeutic efficacy of calcifediol than vitamin D_3 in conditions in which the metabolism of the vitamin is impaired may be due to superior metabolic availability for the renal 1α-hydroxylase or to direct action directly by $25(OH)D$ at receptors in target tissues. Vitamin D is metabolized to a variety of compounds other than the principal product, $25(OH)D$. Calcifediol bypasses these alternate pathways and is directly available for metabolism to $1,25(OH)_2D$. In hypoparathyroidism and in hereditary defects in renal hydroxylase, the efficiency of formation of $1,25(OH)_2D$ from $25(OH)D$ is low, but some formation does occur with high substrate levels. Calcifediol has about 1 percent of the potency of calcitriol in in vivo and in vitro tests of vitamin D responsiveness.

Unless a loading dose is given, 2 to 4 weeks or even longer are required to achieve the maximum calcium replacement action of vitamin D or calcifediol; again, the onset of action of calcifediol is slightly more rapid. Calcitriol can be given for hypoparathyroidism at the same dose required for the prevention of rickets in euparathyroid individuals, 0.2 to 1.0 μg per day. Its onset of action is days rather than weeks. When vitamin D or calcifediol is withdrawn, weeks are required for the disappearance of the biologic effects but only a few days for calcitriol.

Patients with hypoparathyroidism should be given 2 to 3 g of elemental calcium by mouth each day. The two agents, vitamin D or vitamin D metabolites and oral calcium, can be varied independently. Higher doses of vitamin D or its metabolites increase the efficiency of intestinal calcium absorption; higher intakes of oral calcium permit adequate calcium assimilation despite a lower efficiency of intestinal calcium absorption. In the event of hypercalcemia during the treatment of chronic hypocalcemia, the withdrawal of the supplemental oral calcium is effective in lowering calcium within 24 h, even more rapidly than withdrawal of calcitriol. Most patients with hypoparathyroidism can be managed with high-dose vitamin D therapy combined with 2 to 3 g of oral calcium per day. If hypocalcemia alternates with episodes of hypercalcemia, then substitution of calcitriol will often make management easier.

The administration of thiazide diuretics in the usual antihypertensive doses to patients with hypoparathyroidism lowers urinary calcium excretion. This hypocalciuric effect allows the calcium and vitamin D supplementation to be reduced. The treatment also may protect against the development of kidney stones, a potential complication of the long-term management of hypoparathyroidism. If on dialysis, patients with chronic renal failure and hypocalcemia can have adjustments in dialysate calcium concentration as an alternative to vitamin D and calcium supplementation. The doses of vitamin D and calcium required for the management of pseudohypoparathyroidism are usually lower than those required for hypoparathyroidism, reflecting incomplete resistance to the action of PTH in pseudohypoparathyroidism. The acute treatment of hypomagnesemia is discussed above; the use of magnesium chloride by mouth may be sufficient to restore blood magnesium.

REFERENCES

AKITA Y et al: The stimulatory and inhibitory guanine nucleotide-binding proteins of adenylate cyclase in erythrocytes from patients with pseudohypoparathyroidism type 1. J Clin Endocrinol Metab 61:1012, 1985

BELL NH: Vitamin D endocrine system. J Clin Invest 76:1, 1985

DREZNER M et al: Pseudohypoparathyroidism type II: A possible defect in the reception of the cyclic AMP signal. N Engl J Med 289:1056, 1973

GARABEDIAN M et al: Elevated plasma 1,25-(OH)$_2$D concentrations in infants with hypercalcemia and elfin facies. N Engl J Med 312:948, 1985

HEUBI JE et al: Hypocalcemia and steatorrhea: Clues to etiology. Dig Dis Sci 28:124, 1983

KNOCHEL JP: Editorial: Serum calcium derangements in rhabdomyolysis. N Engl J Med 305:161, 1981

LEVINE MA et al: Activity of the stimulatory guanine nucleotide-binding protein is reduced in erythrocytes from patients with pseudohypoparathyroidism and pseudopseudohypoparathyroidism: Biochemical, endocrine, and genetic analysis of Albright's hereditary osteodystrophy in six kindreds. J Clin Endocrinol Metab 62:497, 1986

LIBERMAN UA et al: Resistance to 1,25-(OH)$_2$D. Association with heterogenous defects in cultured skin fibroblasts. J Clin Invest 71:192, 1983

MUNDY GR et al: Tumor products and the hypercalcemia of malignancy. J Clin Invest 76:391, 1985

—— et al: The hypercalcemia of cancer: Clinical implications and pathogenetic mechanisms. N Engl J Med 310:1718, 1984

NAGANT DE DEUXCHAISNES C et al: Dissociation of parathyroid hormone bioactivity and immunoreactivity in pseudohypoparathyroidism type I. J Clin Endocrinol Metab 53:1105, 1981

NEER RM, POTTS JT JR: Medical management of hypercalcemia and hyperparathyroidism, in Endocrinology, LJ DeGroot et al (eds). New York, Grune & Stratton, 1979, vol 2

NEUFELD M et al: Two types of autoimmune Addison's disease associated with different polyglandular autoimmune (PGA) syndromes. Medicine 60:355, 1981

ORWOLL ES: The milk-alkali syndrome: Current concepts. Ann Intern Med 97:242, 1982

RAO DS et al: Dissociation between effects of endogenous parathyroid hormone on adenosine 3'5'-monophosphate generation and phosphate reabsorption in hypocalcemia due to vitamin D depletion: An acquired disorder resembling pseudohypoparathyroidism type II. J Clin Endocrinol Metab 61:285, 1985

RUDE RK et al: Parathyroid hormone secretion in magnesium deficiency. J Clin Endcrinol Metab 47:800, 1978

SILVE C et al: Selective resistance to parathyroid hormone in cultured skin fibroblasts from patients with pseudohypoparathyroidism type Ib. J Clin Endocrinol Metab 62:640, 1986

ZALOGA GP, GHERNOW B: Stress-induced changes in calcium metabolism. Semin Respir Med 7:52, 1985

337 METABOLIC BONE DISEASE

STEPHEN M. KRANE / MICHAEL F. HOLICK

OSTEOPOROSIS

GENERAL CONSIDERATIONS *Osteoporosis* is the term used for diseases of diverse etiology that are characterized by a reduction in the mass of bone per unit volume to a level below that required for adequate mechanical support function. The reduction in mass is not accompanied by a significant reduction in the ratio of the mineral to the organic phase, nor by any known abnormality in the structure of the mineral or the organic matrix. Histologically, osteoporosis is characterized by a decrease in cortical thickness and in the number and size of the trabeculae of cancellous bone with normal width of the osteoid seams. Osteoporosis is the most common of the metabolic bone diseases (disorders in which all the skeleton is involved, presumably as a result of systemic factors acting on the skeleton) and is an important cause of morbidity in the elderly.

The remodeling of bone (its formation and resorption) is a continuous process. Any combination of changes in the rates of formation and resorption which results in bone resorption exceeding bone formation can cause a decrease in bone mass. In osteoporosis the bone mass *is* decreased, indicating that the rate of bone resorption must exceed that of bone formation. Osteoporosis is a heterogeneous disorder. In most series rates of bone formation are normal or low, although rates may be high in some patients, consistent with an absolute increase in bone resorption (high-turnover osteoporosis). For many years after closure of the epiphyses and after longitudinal growth has ceased, in normal individuals skeletal mass remains constant, and the rates of bone formation and resorption are relatively low and approximately equal. Resorption and formation of bone are normally tightly coupled. However, the rate of remodeling is not uniform throughout the skeleton after epiphyseal closure. Most of the bone surfaces are "inactive" and not involved at any given time either in formation or resorption. Active surfaces may be randomly distributed, but formation and resorption are locally coupled as units. Resorption areas are covered by osteoclasts if active; bone formation surfaces are characterized by the presence of osteoid seams and are covered by active osteoblasts. Resorption precedes formation and is probably more intense, but it does not last as long as formation. As a consequence, there are normally more sites of active formation than of resorption. Bone turnover is high when there are many units active and low when there are few. Unless formation compensates for resorption, bone mass decreases. After the age of 40 to 50 skeletal mass begins to decline, at a faster rate in women than in men, and at different rates in different parts of the skeleton. The loss has been documented in selected regions using techniques such as single- and dual-photon absorptiometry of the wrist, femoral neck, and spine, quantitative computerized tomography of the vertebral bodies of the lumbar spine, and neutron activation analysis. For example, the rate of loss is greater in the metacarpals, in the femoral neck, and in the vertebral bodies than in the midshaft of the femur, the tibia, and the skull. Over the succeeding three or four decades the total loss in skeletal mass may be 30 to 50 percent of that present at age 30 or 40. Kinetic studies (using radioactive isotopes of calcium and strontium) and quantitative microradiography (which includes both cortical and cancellous bone) indicate that in most older subjects the resorption rate is high, whereas the bone formation rate remains at a level similar to that of younger adults.

The fact that bone resorption is low in some osteoporotic subjects, especially in cancellous bone, is further evidence for the heterogeneity of the disorder and indicates that no single etiologic factor accounts for all cases. At some critical point if the difference between rates of formation and resorption is maintained, loss of bone substance may become so marked that the bone can no longer resist the normal mechanical forces to which it is subjected, and fracture results. Osteoporosis is then evident as a clinical problem. The level of reduction in bone mass sufficient to result in fractures after minimal trauma is variable. The strength of bones such as the vertebrae may depend upon additional factors such as adequacy of ligamentous support and the age-related changes in the intervertebral disks. The normal trabecular architecture is also disturbed. For example, the horizontal trabeculae of the vertebral bodies are preferentially lost in osteoporosis. Microfractures are also frequent.

In the process of remodeling of lamellar bone in adults, most of the net resorption occurs at the corticoendosteal surface. The abnormal remodeling in osteoporosis follows the same pattern; the bone loss includes cancellous bone, cortical bone at the endosteal surface, and intracortical bone, resulting in enlargement of the medullary cavity and thinning of the cortex. Since bone formation at the periosteum continues at a very slow rate, the diameter of the bone does not decrease, and the periosteal surface retains its smooth configuration. In addition, the cancellous bone also undergoes progressive resorption, with some trabeculae being resorbed at rates faster than others, particularly those vertebral trabeculae with horizontal orientation.

Although the loss of bone that accompanies advancing age is universal, it begins earlier and proceeds more rapidly in women than in men, and there is a trend toward acceleration of bone loss in the perimenopausal years in women. All of the reasons for this age-associated bone loss are not known, although several risk factors have been identified in those individuals whose bone loss is sufficient to predispose to fracture with minimal trauma. In general, white women have a greater risk than black women, and white men have a greater risk than black men. One explanation for these population differences is that the bone mass at skeletal maturity is one determinant of the bone mass at subsequent ages. Blacks tend to have a higher bone mass at maturity than whites. Osteoporotic subjects are frequently less muscular and have lower average body weight than their nonosteoporotic controls. Exercise may have a beneficial effect in maintaining bone mass. The facts that accelerated bone loss accompanies the menopause in some women and that premature osteoporosis occurs when bilateral oophorectomy is performed prior to the age of normal menopause suggest that estrogens play a major role in

preventing bone loss. Furthermore, osteoporotic women as a group may have an earlier menopause than age-matched nonosteoporotic women. Osteoporotic women also have a higher incidence of smoking; cigarette smoking might directly affect bone remodeling or have secondary effects on ovarian function. Dietary calcium intake and the efficiency of intestinal calcium absorption may also influence bone mass. Inability to synthesize normal amounts of $1\alpha,25$-dihydroxyvitamin D [$1,25(OH)_2D$] may play a role in the decreased calcium absorption, possibly because of decreased parathyroid hormone levels or impaired activity of the renal $25(OH)D$ 1α-hydroxylase.

A contributing role of the cytokines that alter either bone resorption or bone formation in the genesis of osteoporosis has yet to be established. Although osteoporosis is associated with Cushing's syndrome, there is no established role of adrenal steroids in the pathogenesis of the osteoporosis associated with the menopause or advancing age.

Another factor implicated in bone loss is the possibility that excessive acid intake, particularly in the form of high-protein diets, results in "dissolution" of bone in an attempt to buffer the extra acid. Prolonged use of heparin as an anticoagulant is also associated with osteoporosis, and heparin potentiates bone resorption in vitro. Patients with osteoporosis have increased numbers of mast cells, presumably capable of producing heparin, in their bone marrow. Circumscribed and diffuse areas of osteoporosis occur in patients with systemic mastocytosis.

As mentioned earlier, the remodeling of bone is responsive to mechanical forces of many types. The early response to immobilization in the normal skeleton is an increase in bone resorption while bone formation remains normal or is decreased; later there is a compensatory increase in bone formation. In osteoporosis, immobilization tends to aggravate the defect by increasing the gap between formation and resorption. It is, therefore, possible that a sedentary life in an individual with poor musculature reduces mechanical forces exerted on the skeleton and increases the tendency to bone loss.

CLASSIFICATION (See Table 337-1) In some instances osteoporosis is a well-defined feature of another disease such as Cushing's syndrome. A skeletal disorder that could also be considered osteoporosis (decreased bone mass with normal mineralization) is the major characteristic of certain heritable diseases of connective tissue such as forms of osteogenesis imperfecta (see Chap. 319). In most instances of osteoporosis, however, no other disease is apparent. This category of osteoporosis can be conveniently considered to comprise several forms. One form occurs in children or young adults of both sexes and with normal gonadal function. This form is frequently termed *idiopathic osteoporosis,* although most of the other forms are in fact also of unknown pathogenesis. So-called *type I osteoporosis* is found in a relatively small subset of postmenopausal women who are between 51 and 65 years of age and is characterized by an accelerated and disproportionate loss of trabecular bone as contrasted with cortical bone. In these individuals fractures of vertebral bodies and the distal forearm are the most common complications. Decreased parathyroid gland function in this group of individuals may be compensatory to increased bone resorption. So-called *type II osteoporosis* is found in a large proportion of women and men over the age of 75. Fractures of the femoral neck, proximal humerus, proximal tibia, and pelvis are most common in this group. These skeletal sites contain both cortical (compact) and trabecular bone. In these individuals circulating levels of parathyroid hormone tend to be higher than normal. Although both groups may have decreased mean circulating levels of $1,25(OH)_2D$ compared to age-matched controls, levels are often in the normal range.

GENERAL CLINICAL FEATURES Although osteoporosis is a generalized disorder of the skeleton, its major clinical manifestations result from fractures of the vertebrae, wrist, hip, humerus, and tibia, depending upon the pattern of the disease (type I or II osteoporosis) as described above. The most frequent symptoms that result from

TABLE 337-1 Classification of osteoporosis

I Common forms of osteoporosis of unknown cause unassociated with other disease
   A Idiopathic osteoporosis (juvenile and adult)
   B Type I osteoporosis
   C Type II osteoporosis
II Disorders or conditions in which osteoporosis is a common feature or pathogenesis partially understood
   A Hypogonadism
   B Hyperadrenocorticism
   C Thyrotoxicosis
   D Malabsorption
   E Scurvy
   F Calcium deficiency
   G Immobilization
   H Chronic heparin administration
   I Systemic mastocytosis
   J Adult hypophosphatasia
   K Associated with other metabolic bone diseases
III Osteoporosis as a feature of heritable disorders of connective tissue
   A Osteogenesis imperfecta
   B Homocystinuria due to cystathionine synthase deficiency
   C Ehlers-Danlos syndrome
   D Marfan's syndrome
IV Disorders in which osteoporosis is associated but pathogenesis not understood
   A Rheumatoid arthritis
   B Malnutrition
   C Alcoholism
   D Epilepsy
   E Diabetes
   F Chronic obstructive pulmonary disease
   G Menkes' syndrome

vertebral body fractures are pain in the back and deformity of the spine. Pain usually results from collapse of the vertebrae especially in the lower dorsal and upper lumbar regions, is typically acute in onset, and often radiates anteriorly around the flank into the abdomen. Such episodes frequently occur after sudden bending, lifting, or jumping movements which may seem to have been trivial; on some occasions they cannot be related to trauma. The pain may be increased even with slight movements such as turning in bed or by the Valsalva maneuver. Rest in bed in one position may relieve the pain temporarily, but it then may recur in spasms of variable duration. Radiation of pain down one leg is uncommon, and symptoms or signs of spinal cord compression are rare. The acute episodes of pain may also be accompanied by abdominal distention and ileus, thought to be due to retroperitoneal hemorrhage, but the use of narcotics at this stage also contributes to the ileus. Loss of appetite and apparent muscular weakness, which is probably due to fear of reproducing pain, may also be present. Episodes of pain usually subside after several days to a week, and by 4 to 6 weeks patients may be fully ambulatory and able to resume their normal activities. Although the acute pain may be minimal, many patients continue to have nagging, deep, dull, uncomfortable sensations localized to the area of fracture and brought about by straining or sudden changes in position. They may be unable to sit up in bed and have to arise by rolling over on their sides and then propping themselves up. Most patients have disappearance or marked diminution of pain between episodes of vertebral body collapse. Others never have acute episodes but complain of backache often made worse by standing or moving suddenly. Tenderness over involved areas of the spinous processes or rib cage is common. The collapse fractures of the vertebral bodies are usually anterior, producing a wedge-shaped deformity and contributing to loss in height. This is particularly common in the middorsal region where collapse may be unassociated with pain but result in a dorsal kyphosis and exaggerated cervical lordosis described as a "dowager's" or "widow's" hump. Postural slumping with increase in existing curves also contributes to the loss of height. Scoliosis is also common in women with osteoporosis. Generalized skeletal pain is uncommon, and between fractures most patients are free of pain. Although recurrent episodes of collapse fractures of vertebral bodies, increasing spine deformity, and loss of height are common in osteoporosis, the course of the disorder in any one subject is not predictable, and there may be intervals of several years between fractures.

RADIOLOGIC FEATURES   Prior to fracture and collapse the osteoporotic vertebral body shows a decrease in mineral density, an increase in prominence of vertical striations due to a relatively greater loss of the horizontally oriented trabeculae, and prominence of the end plates. The bodies may become increasingly biconcave because of weakening of the subchondral plates and expansion of the intervertebral disks, resulting in the so-called codfish vertebrae. When collapse occurs, most frequently in lower dorsal and upper lumbar spine, it usually produces a decrease in the anterior height of the vertebral body and irregularity in the anterior cortex (Fig. 337-1). Older compression fractures may show reactive changes and osteophytes about the anterior margins. Although the cortices of long bones may be thin because of excessive endosteal resorption, the outer margins are sharp in contrast to the typical effects of the subperiosteal resorption of hyperparathyroidism. Pseudofractures or Looser's zones are not present in osteoporosis in the absence of osteomalacia, but distinguishing osteoporosis from osteomalacia may be impossible on radiologic grounds alone. In the absence of fractures standard roentgenograms are insensitive indicators of bone loss since as much as 30 percent decrease in bone mass may not be appreciated. Other procedures are required to establish whether a given individual has a sufficient decrease in bone mass to be at risk for fracture. These include single- and dual-photon absorptiometry, quantitative computerized tomography, or neutron activation analysis of total-body calcium.

LABORATORY FINDINGS   The concentrations of calcium and inorganic phosphorus in the blood are usually normal in patients with osteoporosis; slight hyperphosphatemia is present in women who are past the menopause. The alkaline phosphatase in uncomplicated instances is normal, although slight increases may be seen after fractures. About 20 percent of postmenopausal women with osteoporosis have significant hypercalciuria. Urinary excretion of peptides containing hydroxyproline, an index of bone resorption, is usually normal or slightly increased.

DIFFERENTIAL DIAGNOSIS   Since decrease in skeletal mass is an age-associated finding, it is difficult to evaluate asymptomatic decreased bone density in older women, especially when unaccompanied by marked increase in biconcavity of vertebral bodies or fractures. In the presence of bone pain with or without fracture or deformity, it is important to establish the presence or absence of known causes of osteoporosis as listed in Table 337-1 and to be certain that osteoporosis in the broad sense is the correct diagnosis. Malignancies of various types, particularly *multiple myeloma, lymphoma, leukemia,* and *carcinomatosis,* may result in diffuse loss of bone, especially the trabecular bone of the vertebral column, even in the absence of hypercalcemia. The absence of anemia, elevated erythrocyte sedimentation rate, abnormal electrophoretic patterns of serum proteins, and Bence Jones proteinuria is helpful in eliminating the possibility of multiple myeloma. However, needle bone biopsy or marrow aspiration is frequently recommended in instances of severe osteoporosis with fractures. It is necessary to perform histomorphometry, usually on biopsies taken from the iliac crest, to quantitate bone mass and rule out osteomalacia, but the technique is not widely available.

Radiologic osteoporosis is common in patients with primary *hyperparathyroidism,* who may not have osteitis fibrosa (discrete lytic lesions of varying size and subperiosteal resorption) or elevation

FIGURE 337-1   *Lateral views of the lumbar spine of a 54-year-old man with idiopathic osteoporosis. A typical anterior compression fracture is indicated by the arrow.*

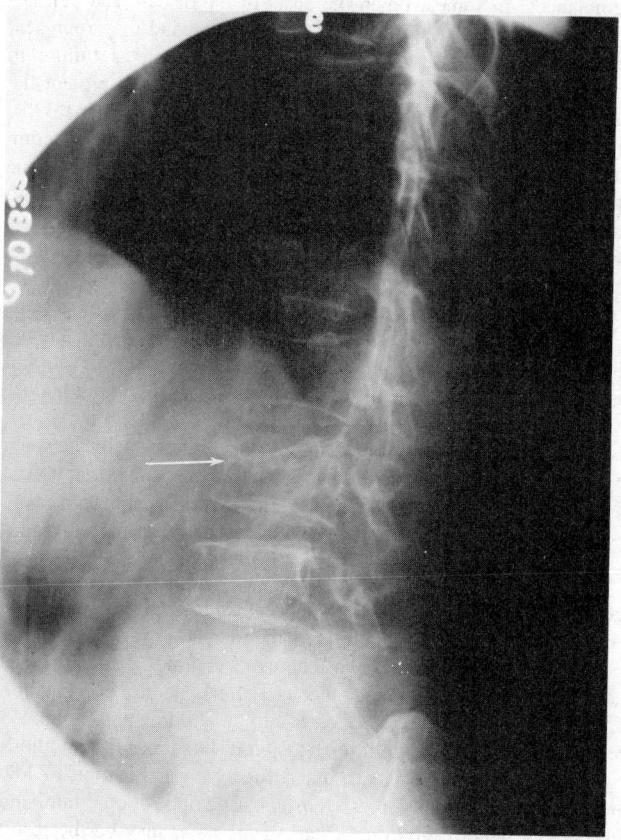

of serum alkaline phosphatase. Although hyperparathyroidism could accelerate osteoporosis and contribute to it, it is not clear that excessive secretion of parathyroid hormone is the sole cause of the bone disease, even in these cases, rather than an associated finding. Repeated determinations of fasting serum calcium and phosphorus levels are therefore necessary. An element of secondary hyperparathyroidism may be present in some elderly patients with type II osteoporosis and in others in whom there is impairment of renal function, inadequate oral calcium intake, or decrease of intestinal calcium absorption. Increased numbers of osteoclasts may be present in bone biopsy specimens from such patients.

Osteomalacia may mimic osteoporosis or coexist with it, yet specific radiologic signs of osteomalacia may not always be present. Although the presence of abnormalities such as low or undetectable circulating levels of 25-hydroxyvitamin D [25(OH)D] and/or hypophosphatemia would suggest the possibility of osteomalacia, these abnormalities too may be absent in some cases of osteomalacia, and bone biopsy may be essential for diagnosis, as discussed below. Since osteomalacia is more responsive to specific therapy than the usual case of osteoporosis, such diagnostic procedures are often warranted and provide, in addition, adequate specimens for examination for the presence of malignant cells.

In an occasional patient with *Paget's disease* the radiologic features may be almost purely lytic and be confused with osteoporosis. However, high alkaline phosphatase levels and moderately or markedly increased urinary excretion of hydroxyproline-containing peptides are clues to the presence of Paget's disease. Scanning procedures with bone-seeking isotopes are not helpful in differential diagnosis if fractures are present, because in any disease fractures demonstrate preferential uptake of isotope. However, in the absence of fracture, "hot spots" suggest presence of tumor or early Paget's disease, particularly if present in the appendicular skeleton.

IDIOPATHIC OSTEOPOROSIS   *Idiopathic osteoporosis* is the term used to describe the disorder in younger men or in premenopausal women in whom no other etiologic factor is detected. It is likely that these patients have a number of different disorders with superficial resemblances. In some women the onset of the disease and deterioration of bone appear to be related to pregnancy and may represent a transient failure in homeostatic mechanisms such as failure to increase circulating levels of $1,25(OH)_2D$ and hence to protect the maternal skeleton from the stresses of childbirth (see Chap. 335). Some patients with idiopathic osteoporosis have low levels of serum alkaline phosphatase, though not low enough to fulfill diagnostic criteria for *hypophosphatasia*. Estrogens are ineffective in therapy. Losses of calcium and phosphorus are probably excessive, and it is unwise to permit women with osteoporosis to breast-feed their infants since additional calcium losses via lactation are appreciable. Some patients have a disorder similar to mild forms of osteogenesis imperfecta, although such features as family history, blue scleras, and deafness are lacking. The course is variable; although recurrent episodes of fractures are characteristic, progressive deterioration does not occur in all patients, and in some the clinical problem is benign. Juvenile osteoporosis is a rare disorder with onset usually between the ages of 8 and 14 years and is characterized by the abrupt appearance of bone pain and fractures after minimal trauma. In many cases the disorder is self-limited, and recovery takes place spontaneously within 4 or 5 years.

GLUCOCORTICOID EXCESS   Glucocorticoid excess does not appear to be involved in osteoporosis of the idiopathic variety or in the type I or II disorder. However, osteoporosis commonly accompanies Cushing's syndrome, both endogenous and exogenous, and in some instances is rapidly progressive, especially in children and in women over the age of 50. The rapid progression of bone loss in conditions of glucocorticoid excess is accounted for by a combination of low rates of bone formation (depressed osteoblastic oppositional rate) and high rates of bone resorption. A part of the latter may be the result of glucocorticoid-induced secondary hyperparathyroidism, although

increases in circulating immunoreactive parathyroid hormone have not been found regularly using a variety of radioimmunoassays. Glucocorticoids, however, potentiate the effects of parathyroid hormone and $1,25(OH)_2D$ on isolated populations of bone cells. Glucocorticoids depress collagen synthesis in organs other than bone, as evidenced by delayed wound healing, thinning of the dermis, striae, and tendency to blue scleras. In some disorders in which glucocorticoids are administered in pharmacologic doses such as rheumatoid arthritis, a tendency to thin skin and osteoporosis is initially present, and the skeletal effects of the glucocorticoids may become particularly apparent. Even low dosages of glucocorticoids may accelerate bone loss in postmenopausal women with rheumatoid arthritis. Glucocorticoid excess also results in alteration in the metabolism of vitamin D; blood levels of 25(OH)D are normal or only slightly decreased, and blood levels of $1,25(OH)_2D$ are low in some patients, particularly in children. Part of the defect in calcium absorption is explainable by a vitamin D–dependent mechanism, but glucocorticoids also inhibit intestinal calcium absorption by a direct, vitamin D–independent action on the intestine. Osteomalacia is not observed histologically, despite possible abnormalities in vitamin D metabolism. Once osteoporosis develops in adults with Cushing's syndrome, the abnormality may persist indefinitely following alleviation of the glucocorticoid excess. In children, however, cure of the Cushing's syndrome may result in striking improvement in the appearance of the spine due to new endochondral bone formation around the less dense, older osteoporotic bone. This does not occur in adults since endochondral bone formation has ceased. Withdrawal of glucocorticoids or decrease of the dose by alternate-day schedule may be the only way to halt progression of the osteoporosis. Anabolic steroids are not effective in this regard. The defect in intestinal calcium absorption may be helped by administering vitamin D in doses of 50,000 IU two times weekly plus supplemental oral calcium of 1 to 1.5 g per day. The use of vitamin D metabolites such as 25(OH)D may be more effective. When large doses of vitamin D are used, it is important to monitor serum and urinary calcium and serum 25(OH)D levels at intervals of 2 to 4 months, especially if glucocorticoid dosages are lowered. In Cushing's syndrome, spontaneous, symptomless fractures may occur in bones such as ribs and pubic and ischial rami even in the absence of marked osteoporosis of the spine. These fractures often heal partially with an exuberant calcified callus surrounding a radiolucent zone of nonunion, which superficially resembles the pseudofractures of osteomalacia. If they appear in the thorax superimposed upon the lungs, they may be confused with nodules suggesting primary or metastatic tumor.

GONADAL DEFICIENCY   Estrogen lack is present in the postmenopausal woman with osteoporosis, and the administration of estrogen to such an individual reduces the negative calcium balance and decreases urinary hydroxyproline excretion as is consistent with a decrease in bone resorption. Estrogens are particularly useful in retarding the bone loss in women who have oophorectomy at an early age. Bone mass is also decreased in women athletes who are amenorrheic, such as marathon runners. Such women are particularly prone to tibial stress fractures. In patients of either sex castrated at an early age, the adult skeleton is smaller to begin with, and therefore age-related losses are more significant.

THYROTOXICOSIS   In many patients with hyperthyroidism, there is excessive bone resorption, occasionally marked in degree and far exceeding that in the usual patient with osteoporosis, associated with increased excretion of calcium and phosphorus in urine and feces. The excessive bone resorption is usually accompanied by a compensatory increase in bone formation. Parathyroid hormone secretion is decreased, and levels of $1,25(OH)_2D$ are normal or low. If the hyperthyroidism is of short duration, skeletal losses are inconsequential. However, in patients with chronic hyperthyroidism, especially in women after the menopause, this accelerated bone loss becomes clinically significant, and it is important to eliminate hyperthyroidism as a contributing cause of osteoporosis. Although typical osteitis fibrosa (resorption lacunae containing osteoclasts and a fibrous stroma) may be seen on biopsy, even in these cases the skeletal lesions have the appearance of osteoporosis when examined radiologically.

ACROMEGALY Hypercalciuria and overall net negative calcium balance occur in acromegaly, and occasionally osteoporosis is an associated finding. The panhypopituitarism secondary to a pituitary adenoma and the associated gonadal insufficiency may be factors in production of the osteoporosis. In adult animals growth hormone decreases endosteal resorption and stimulates bone formation, and it is therefore unlikely that excessive secretion of growth hormone in itself produces osteoporosis.

DIABETES MELLITUS Individuals with juvenile or adult-onset diabetes mellitus have a decreased bone mass. In some series the incidence of hip fractures has been increased, but studies of large groups of diabetic subjects have not revealed abnormal calcium metabolism or bone disease specifically attributable to the diabetes.

CALCIUM DEFICIENCY AND MALABSORPTION Although calcium deficiency may be a factor in some instances of osteoporosis, it cannot be the sole or major cause in idiopathic, senile, or postmenopausal osteoporosis. Osteoporosis is an associated finding in a significant number of cases of steatorrhea, prolonged obstructive jaundice, and lactose intolerance and in patients following gastrectomy. Other patients may have a specific defect in calcium absorption or a failure to adapt adequately to a low-calcium diet either by increasing the percentage of dietary calcium absorbed or by decreasing urinary calcium excretion. Presumably, vitamin D is adequate in these instances to prevent osteomalacia.

HERITABLE DISORDERS OF CONNECTIVE TISSUE In the strict sense, the bone disease of osteogenesis imperfecta is osteoporosis (see Chap. 319). *Osteogenesis imperfecta* is a heterogeneous disorder. The most common form is transmitted as an autosomal dominant trait and is associated with blue scleras and later with deafness. The bone disease in this form tends to be relatively mild, and the tendency toward fractures may decrease after puberty. Another form, which itself is likely autosomal recessive, is usually detected shortly after birth and is progressive with recurrent fractures of long bones and kyphoscoliosis. Sclerae are white, and deafness is uncommon. A lethal perinatal type (autosomal recessive) is also seen. The organization of the collagen in bone and skin is abnormal, and in some instances defects in the synthesis of type I collagen in bone and skin have been defined. It is possible that some cases of idiopathic osteoporosis represent unrecognized osteogenesis imperfecta. Osteoporosis also occurs in patients with *homocystinuria* due to cystathionine synthase deficiency, an autosomal recessive trait, associated with ectopia lentis, various deformities of the extremities, mental retardation, decreased pigmentation of hair and skin, and thromboembolism. The diagnosis is established by the finding of homocystine in urine. The osteoporosis may be due to the effect of homocysteine or other metabolites in interfering with the cross-linking of collagen.

THERAPY Before considering treatment of osteoporosis, it should be emphasized that one is dealing with a group of disorders rather than a single entity. Even in patients within the same category, e.g., those with idiopathic osteoporosis, the etiologies may be different. It is also difficult to predict the course of the disease in any patient, especially when seen initially because of pain and collapse-fracture. Many patients in the idiopathic, postmenopausal (type I), and senile (type II) groups have a few episodes of vertebral body collapse with symptom-free intervals of months or years but then go for many years without symptoms or further loss in height. Furthermore, the acute pain associated with vertebral body fracture tends to subside in a matter of weeks, and *any* treatment administered at that time might be considered efficacious. Therapy for this condition is far from ideal, despite claims to the contrary.

General measures Patients with acute pain secondary to fracture of vertebral bodies frequently require hospitalization with rest in bed in a position of maximum comfort, local heat, adequate analgesics, and avoidance of constipation. Use of traction or plaster jacket splints is not indicated. As soon as pain permits, the patient should attempt to move out of bed, slowly at first, perhaps with support of a walker or crutches. The patient should not become too fatigued when starting ambulation. Braces of various types are commonly employed, but their efficacy in preventing progression of spinal deformity has not been established. A well-made corset may provide support and comfort. Exercises to correct postural deformity and increase muscle tone are useful. Patients should be taught to avoid sudden painful movements such as jumping and how to lift and carry objects with minimal back strain. After the fractures have healed, a supervised exercise program which includes daily walking may be helpful in preventing further skeletal losses.

Estrogens and androgens The use of estrogens in postmenopausal women with osteoporosis causes a decrease in urinary calcium and hydroxyproline excretion, especially during the first few months of treatment (see Chap. 331). Estrogens decrease the rate of bone resorption, but bone formation does not increase and eventually usually decreases. Although still within the normal range, the mean level of circulating $1,25(OH)_2D$ is lower in osteoporotic subjects than in controls and is brought to the normal mean level by estrogen therapy. Thus, estrogens produce significant, although modest, calcium retention, decrease the difference between formation and resorption, and therefore tend to retard the progress of osteoporosis, but they are not capable of restoring skeletal mass. The magnitude of calcium retention also tends to decrease with continuous therapy. Therefore, it is not surprising that there is no change in radiologic features of the osteoporosis with such therapy. The major role of estrogens is in preventing osteoporosis in menopausal women rather than treating clinical disease already developed, although they may also be effective in the woman with mild or moderate disease within the first 5 to 6 years following cessation of ovarian function. Testosterone preparations are useful in treatment of osteoporotic men with gonadal deficiency, but there are no convincing reports of their efficacy in men with normal gonadal function. There is also no proven advantage to combinations of estrogens and androgens.

Calcium preparations Use of oral calcium preparations in doses of 1.0 to 1.5 g elemental calcium per day increases calcium retention in some osteoporotic subjects and decreases bone resorption. The elemental calcium content of available preparations varies, depending upon the accompanying anion and the composition (Table 337-2). However, as with the use of estrogens, this eventually results in decrease in bone formation and tends to arrest rather than "cure" the osteoporosis. Calcium preparations may be of greater use in patients with normal gonadal function and relatively mild disease. In patients with malabsorption, calcium may be effective in addition to vitamin D given orally in doses of 50,000 IU once weekly. The use of more active metabolites of vitamin D may prove more efficacious. Therapy with $1,25(OH)_2D$ (calcitriol), 0.25 μg daily, results in improved intestinal calcium absorption and suppression of bone resorption. Levels of serum calcium, $25(OH)D$, $1,25(OH)_2D$, and urinary calcium excretion should be monitored at intervals of several months to be certain that hypercalcemia and hypercalciuria do not result. Thiazide diuretics are useful in patients with high-turnover

TABLE 337-2 Elemental calcium content in various oral calcium preparations

Calcium preparation	Elemental calcium content per unit weight or volume
Calcium citrate	40 mg/300 mg
Calcium carbonate	400 mg/g
Calcium lactate	80 mg/600 mg
Calcium gluconate	40 mg/500 mg
Calcium carbonate + 5 μg vitamin D_2 (Os – Cal 250)	250 mg/tablet

osteoporosis associated with hypercalciuria and secondary hyperparathyroidism. In the absence of secondary hyperparathyroidism the thiazide diuretics lower urinary calcium excretion, suppress parathyroid gland function, inhibit synthesis of $1,25(OH)_2D$, and reduce intestinal calcium absorption.

Fluoride Fluoride ions are deposited in the skeleton where they become incorporated into the crystal lattice of hydroxyapatite, substituting for hydroxyl ions. This process results in a mineral phase of greater crystallinity. Fluoride ions in chronic high doses also increase new bone formation and produce a form of hyperostosis with dense bones, exostoses, neurologic complications due to bony overgrowth, and ligamentous calcification. Experimental treatment with fluoride has not resulted in uniformly satisfactory results, possibly because of variations in dosage of fluoride ion, retention of absorbed ion, and calcium intake while on fluoride. The stimulation of new bone formation, a desirable effect not seen with the other agents mentioned previously, unfortunately causes the production of bone that is poorly mineralized and also, presumably, structurally unsound. If the dose of fluoride ion is moderate (25 mg per day) and calcium supplements are given in doses of at least 1 g daily plus vitamin D, 50,000 IU twice weekly, considerable new bone may be produced associated with decreased incidence of fractures, particularly if combined with estrogen therapy. Significant toxicity is absent, although weight-bearing pain, especially in ankles and knees, may occur and disappears when fluoride is discontinued. It is likely that the use of fluoride to treat osteoporosis will soon be approved.

Other measures Although calcitonin therapy has been advocated, this therapy probably does not produce benefits greater than attained with supplemental calcium and vitamin D. Oral phosphates (greater than 1 g elemental phosphorus per day in divided doses) may decrease urinary calcium excretion and improve calcium tolerance in patients with marked hypercalciuria. However, phosphate is of no value in patients with postmenopausal osteoporosis who have normal levels of serum phosphorus.

RICKETS AND OSTEOMALACIA

The terms *rickets* and *osteomalacia* describe disorders in which mineralization of the organic matrix of the skeleton is defective (Table 337-3). In *rickets* the growing skeleton is involved; defective mineralization occurs not only in bone but also in the cartilaginous matrix of the growth plate. The term *osteomalacia* is usually reserved for the disorder of mineralization of the adult skeleton in which the epiphyseal growth plates are closed. A number of conditions result in rickets and/or osteomalacia such as inadequate dietary intake of vitamin D, inadequate exposure to ultraviolet radiation to form endogenous vitamin D, intestinal malabsorption of vitamin D, acquired and inherited disorders of vitamin D metabolism, inherited defects in the receptors for $1,25(OH)_2D$ in target tissues, chronic acidosis, renal tubular defects which produce hypophosphatemia or acidosis, and chronic administration of anticonvulsants. In the renal tubular disorders rickets and osteomalacia develop in the presence of normal intestinal function and are not cured by treatment with doses of vitamin D adequate to cure deficiency rickets. Thus the term *vitamin D–resistant* (or *–refractory*) *rickets* has been applied in these instances. Renal insufficiency, especially in children, is also associated with rickets or osteomalacia.

PATHOGENESIS AND HISTOPATHOLOGY For mineralization of skeletal tissues, sufficient calcium and phosphate must be present at the mineralization sites. Other conditions required for normal mineralization include intact metabolic and transport functions of osteoblasts and chondrocytes, adequate collagen matrix, possibly phosphorylation or other modifications of matrix components, and low concentrations of inhibitory substances such as proteoglycan aggregates or inorganic pyrophosphate. A specific function in the mineralization process for the γ-carboxyglutamic acid–containing proteins

synthesized by bone cells has not been demonstrated, although they bind calcium ions. In cartilage the initial mineral phase is in membrane-bound extracellular vesicles. If the osteoblast continues to produce matrix components which cannot be adequately mineralized, rickets and osteomalacia result. If calcification continues to be inadequate, the production of organic matrix (osteoid) also gradually decreases. In bone there will be an increase in the fraction of the forming surface covered by incompletely mineralized osteoid, an increase in osteoid volume and thickness (the latter normally less than 12 to 14 μm), and a decrease in the calcification or mineralization front. The latter is detected in undemineralized sections by the fluorescence of previously ingested tetracycline or by special stains. There is a marked

TABLE 337-3 Classification of rickets and osteomalacia

I Vitamin D deficiency
   A Dietary deficiency
   B Deficient endogenous synthesis
II Gastrointestinal
   A Small-intestinal diseases with malabsorption
   B Partial or total gastrectomy
   C Hepatobiliary disease
   D Chronic pancreatic insufficiency
III Disorders of vitamin D metabolism
   A Hereditary: pseudovitamin D deficiency or vitamin D dependency, types I and II
   B Acquired
     1 Anticonvulsants
     2 Chronic renal failure
IV Acidosis
   A Distal renal tubular acidosis (classic or type I)
   B Secondary forms of renal acidosis
   C Ureterosigmoidostomy
   D Drug-induced disease
     1 Chronic acetazolamide ingestion
     2 Chronic ammonium chloride ingestion
V Chronic renal failure
VI Phosphate depletion
   A Dietary: low phosphate intake plus ingestion of nonabsorbable antacids
   B Impaired renal tubular phosphate reabsorption
     1 Hereditary
       a X-linked hypophosphatemic rickets (vitamin D–resistant rickets)
       b Adult-onset vitamin D–resistant hypophosphatemic osteomalacia
     2 Acquired
       a Sporadic hypophosphatemic osteomalacia (phosphate diabetes)
       b Tumor-associated (oncogenous) rickets and osteomalacia
       c Neurofibromatosis
       d Fibrous dysplasia
VII Generalized renal tubular disorders (Fanconi's syndrome)
   A Primary renal
   B Associated with systemic metabolic abnormality
     1 Cystinosis
     2 Glycogenosis
     3 Lowe's syndrome
   C Systemic disorder with associated renal disease
     1 Hereditary
       a Inborn errors
         (1) Wilson's disease
         (2) Tyrosinemia
       b Neurofibromatosis
     2 Acquired
       a Multiple myeloma
       b Nephrotic syndrome
       c Transplanted kidney
     3 Intoxications
       a Cadmium
       b Lead
       c Outdated tetracycline
VIII Primary mineralization defects
   A Hereditary: hypophosphatasia
   B Acquired
     1 Diphosphonate (disodium etidronate) treatment
     2 Fluoride treatment
IX States of rapid bone formation with or without a relative defect in bone resorption
   A Postoperative hyperparathyroidism with osteitis fibrosa cystica
   B Osteopetrosis
X Defective matrix synthesis: fibrogenesis imperfecta ossium
XI Miscellaneous
   A Magnesium-dependent conditions
   B Axial osteomalacia
   C Parenteral alimentation
   D Aluminum intoxication

decrease in the rate of apposition of mineralized bone. A variety of methods are available to measure the thickness of the osteoid seams and the calcification front. In routine histologic sections stained with hematoxylin and eosin, the more heavily mineralized areas tend to appear violet or blue, whereas the osteoid seams appear pink. Subtle degrees of osteomalacia may not be appreciated with routine preparations, and undecalcified, thin sections (3 to 5 μm) stained, for example, with Goldner's trichrome method are necessary to establish its presence (Fig. 337-2). Rickets is also characterized by inadequate mineralization of the matrix of cartilage in the growing epiphyseal plate. Calcification in the interstitial regions of the hypertrophic zone is defective, the growth plate increases in thickness, the columns of cartilage cells (usually highly ordered) are disorganized, and there is a variable cupping of the epiphyses. The rachitic bones are often incapable of withstanding usual mechanical stresses and tend to undergo bowing deformities. If rickets is untreated, growth at the epiphyseal plates is slowed, and the eventual length of the long bones is diminished.

It has not been established whether vitamin D, through one of its metabolites, has a major direct effect on mineralization. Its primary roles after metabolic conversion to 25(OH)D and 1,25(OH)$_2$D are to regulate and enhance absorption of calcium ions from the intestinal lumen and, possibly, to enhance differentiation of stem cells to form osteoclasts. Insufficiency of the active metabolites of vitamin D leads to decreased intestinal absorption of calcium and decreased mobilization of calcium from bone, resulting in hypocalcemia. This stimulates increased synthesis and secretion of parathyroid hormone (PTH) and hyperplasia of the parathyroid glands. The increased circulating concentration of PTH tends to raise plasma calcium concentrations but also stimulates increased renal phosphate clearance, which, in turn, produces hypophosphatemia. When the concentration of phosphorus in the extracellular fluid falls below a critical level, mineralization cannot proceed normally. In severe vitamin D lack, normal levels of serum calcium cannot be maintained, and the driving force for mineralization is further decreased. The absence of some critical metabolite of vitamin D that acts directly on the skeleton may also play a role in the defective mineralization of rickets and osteomalacia.

Phosphate depletion alone can produce osteomalacia as in patients consuming large amounts of nonabsorbable antacids and in patients with excessive renal loss of phosphate due to decreased tubular reabsorption. Secondary hyperparathyroidism is usually not present in these patients. Hypophosphatemia per se produces mineralization defects despite its effect on increasing the activity of the renal 25(OH)D-1α-hydroxylase, but it cannot account for the osteomalacia in all the disorders listed in Table 337-3. In chronic renal failure, for example, plasma phosphate levels are not decreased and usually are increased. Similarly, plasma phosphorus levels are not depressed in infants and children with osteomalacia secondary to hypophosphatasia, a hereditary deficiency in alkaline phosphatase. Osteomalacia in some patients with chronic renal failure is associated with accumulation of aluminum in bone, and the aluminum probably plays a role in production of the mineralization defect.

CLINICAL FINDINGS The clinical manifestations of rickets are the result of skeletal deformities, susceptibility to fractures, weakness and hypotonia, and disturbances in growth. In extreme instances of vitamin D–deficiency rickets, hypocalcemia may be sufficient to produce tetany which, when severe, may be accompanied by laryngeal spasm and convulsive seizures.

In infants and young children features include listlessness, irritability, and often profound hypotonia and muscular weakness. As the disorder progresses, children become unable to walk without support. Abnormal parietal flattening and frontal bossing develop in the skull. The calvaria are softened (craniotabes), and widening of sutures may be evident. Prominence of the costochondral junctions is called the "rachitic rosary," and the indentation of the lower ribs at the site of attachment of the diaphragm is known as *Harrison's groove*. If untreated, progressive deformities of the pelvis and extremities result, with bowing particularly common in the tibia, femur, radius, and ulna. Fractures are frequent, dental eruption is often delayed, and enamel defects are common.

The presentation of osteomalacia in adults usually is not as dramatic as in infants and children. The skeletal deformities may be overlooked, and the features of the underlying disorder may dominate, as, for example, in the vitamin D loss associated with adult celiac disease. Symptoms, when they occur, include diffuse skeletal pain and bony tenderness. Pain may be especially prominent about the hips and result in an antalgic gait. Muscular weakness is also common, although it may be difficult to distinguish from hesitancy to move because of skeletal pain. Proximal weakness may mimic that of primary muscle disorders and contribute to the waddling gait. Pain and weakness may be sufficient to cause patients to be confined to bed and chair. Many factors, including the secondary hyperparathyroidism, contribute to the myopathy. Clinical improvement in the myopathy usually results from specific therapy such as vitamin D repletion in nutritional osteomalacia, phosphate replacement in renal hypophosphatemia, or correction of acidosis. Fractures of involved bones may occur with minimal trauma. When the ribs are involved, severe deformities may develop in the thoracic cage, and the collapse of vertebral bodies may produce loss of height.

RADIOLOGIC FEATURES Radiologic changes in the skeleton in rickets and osteomalacia reflect the pathologic changes. In rickets the alterations are most evident at the epiphyseal growth plate which is increased in thickness, cupped, and hazy at the metaphyseal border due to decreased calcification of the hypertrophic zone and inadequate mineralization of the primary spongiosa. The trabecular pattern of the metaphyses is abnormal, the cortices of the diaphyses may be thinned, and the shafts may be bowed.

In osteomalacia decrease in bone density is usually associated with loss of trabeculae and variable thinning of the cortices. The radiologic changes may be indistinguishable from those in osteoporosis. Trabecular patterns may be blurred, producing a homogeneous ground glass appearance. The specific finding that suggests osteomalacia is the presence of radiolucent bands ranging from a few millimeters to several centimeters in length, usually perpendicular to the surface of the bones. They are particularly common at the inner

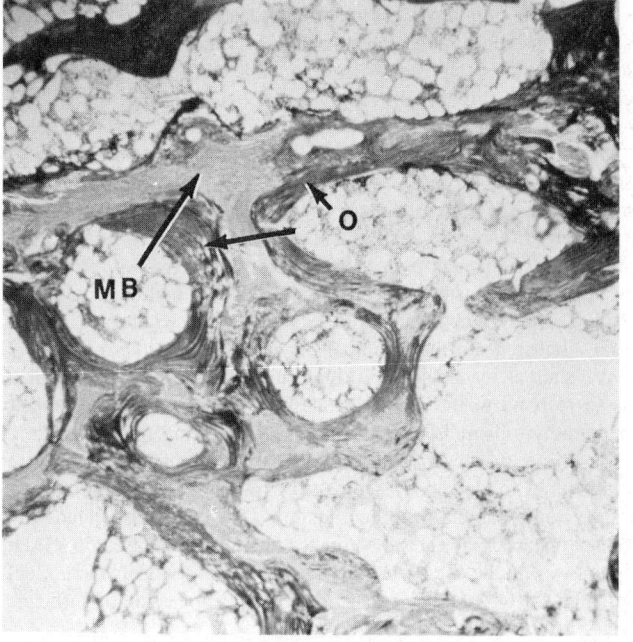

FIGURE 337-2 *Photomicrograph of an undemineralized section stained with Goldner method of an iliac crest bone biopsy from a 45-year-old man with chronic renal failure maintained on hemodialysis. Almost the entire surface is covered by osteoid (O) readily distinguished from mineralized bone (MB). The thickness of the osteoid seams exceeds 100 μm in several areas.*

aspects of the femur, especially near the femoral neck, in the pelvis, in the outer edge of the scapula, in the upper fibula, and in the metatarsals (Figs. 337-3 and 337-4). These radiolucent bands, called *pseudofractures* or *Looser's zones*, occur most often at sites where major arteries cross the bones, and are thought to be due to the mechanical stress of the pulsation of these vessels. Subperiosteal erosions along the diaphyseal cortices are sometimes seen in patients with secondary hyperparathyroidism.

Increased rather than decreased density of bones may be observed in patients with renal tubular disorders rather than with vitamin D deficiency and may produce a striking thickening of the cortices and trabeculae of spongy bone. Despite the increase in mass of bone per unit volume, the trabeculae are covered with thickened osteoid seams typical of osteomalacia. Similar findings may occur in patients with chronic renal failure. The reason for the hyperostosis is unknown; the bone is architecturally abnormal and subject to fracture with minimal trauma.

LABORATORY FINDINGS Changes in serum concentrations of calcium, inorganic phosphorus, 25(OH)D, and 1,25(OH)₂D vary with the different disorders (see Chap. 325). In vitamin D deficiency, whether due to dietary lack, inadequate sunlight exposure, or intestinal malabsorption, serum calcium levels are normal or low, whereas phosphorus and 25(OH)D levels are characteristically low, the latter usually < 5 ng/mL depending upon the assay. In contrast, levels of 1,25(OH)₂D may not be low due to secondary hyperparathyroidism (Table 327-2). In adults the lower limit of serum phosphorus concentration is around 2.8 mg/dL; in children the lower limit of normal is closer to 4.0 to 4.5 mg/dL. In *severe* vitamin D depletion, hypocalcemia may be sufficient to produce tetany. Mild acidosis and

FIGURE 337-3 *Radiographs of the scapula of a 58-year-old woman with phosphate diabetes. The presence of a pseudofracture or Looser's zone is indicated by the arrow.*

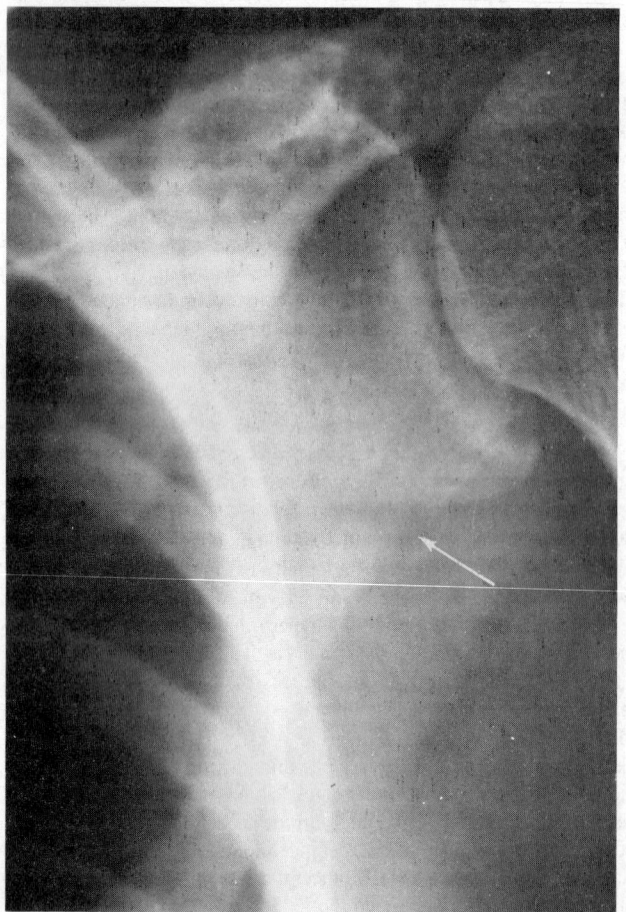

generalized aminoaciduria also result from secondary hyperparathyroidism. As a rule, patients with renal tubular disorders maintain normal serum calcium levels, while hypophosphatemia is characteristic. Other laboratory findings such as glucosuria, aminoaciduria, acidosis, and hypouricemia reflect variable degrees of disturbance of proximal tubular function or features of the underlying disease (e.g., low plasma ceruloplasmin in Wilson's disease or abnormalities of immunoglobulins in multiple myeloma). In chronic renal failure hyperphosphatemia and some degree of hypocalcemia are usually accompanied by normal 25(OH)D and low 1,25(OH)₂D levels. In nephrotic syndrome serum 25(OH)D levels can be low due primarily to urinary losses of protein-bound 25(OH)D. Serum phosphorus levels are also normal or elevated in hypophosphatasia. Increased excretion of hydroxyproline-containing peptides occurs in those conditions in which secondary hyperparathyroidism and excessive bone resorption are associated with the defect in mineralization. Alkaline phosphatase levels in plasma are usually elevated in rickets or osteomalacia, but typical and even severe osteomalacia, especially that due to renal tubular disorders, may be accompanied by normal or only borderline elevations. Levels may increase during the early phases of therapy.

DIETARY VITAMIN D DEFICIENCY AND INADEQUATE ENDOGENOUS SYNTHESIS Most foods unfortified with vitamin D contain insufficient amounts of the vitamin to prevent rickets in growing children or osteomalacia in adults living in temperate-zone cities. As discussed in Chap. 335, in the absence of supplements, vitamin D must be formed endogenously through the ultraviolet irradiation of precursor 7-dehydrocholesterol in the skin. Many factors decrease the formation of vitamin D₃ from its precursor: increased melanin pigmentation, hyperkeratosis, sunscreens, limited exposure of the body, short days of sunlight, oblique angle of ultraviolet irradiation, and factors in the atmosphere, such as smog, which prevent adequate penetration of ultraviolet radiation. Since fortification of dairy products and routine use of vitamin D supplements for infants have been in effect, deficiency rickets is unusual in the United States. Poor, dark-skinned infants living in crowded northern cities are most susceptible. However, osteomalacia due to vitamin D deficiency still occurs in adults, especially in elderly individuals who tend to remain indoors and whose dietary intake of vitamin D is inadequate (probably less than 70 to 100 IU per day) because of avoidance of milk due to lactose intolerance.

VITAMIN D LOSS AND INTESTINAL MALABSORPTION Osteomalacia may be seen in patients with intestinal malabsorption such as in adult celiac disease and regional enteritis. Prior to the discovery of gluten sensitivity in some of these cases, celiac disease was among the more common disorders underlying osteomalacia. Vitamin D absorption, which normally occurs via chylomicrons, is impaired in diseases causing steatorrhea where emulsification of fat is disturbed, such as chronic biliary obstruction. Patients with cholestatic liver disease or extrahepatic biliary obstruction may have low serum levels of 25(OH)D and osteomalacia, due not only to poor vitamin D absorption but also to decreased hepatic production of 25(OH)D and disruption of its enterohepatic circulation. Osteomalacia is less frequent in chronic pancreatic insufficiency. Patients who have had gastric surgery for peptic ulcer disease or gastric bypass for obesity may also develop osteomalacia, possibly due to malfunction of the proximal small bowel. Factors other than failure to absorb vitamin D may contribute to the osteomalacia in patients with small-bowel disease, such as inadequate absorbing surface and failure of intestinal cells to respond to the active metabolites of vitamin D. Secondary hyperparathyroidism is usually present in intestinal malabsorption, as it is in dietary lack of vitamin D and may be particularly severe in patients who develop osteomalacia following intestinal bypass surgery. Some patients who lack vitamin D, usually associated with intestinal malabsorption, have normal circulating levels of 1,25(OH)₂D, despite low or undetectable 25(OH)D. In these individuals the normal levels of 1,25(OH)₂D may be accounted for by ingestion of sufficient

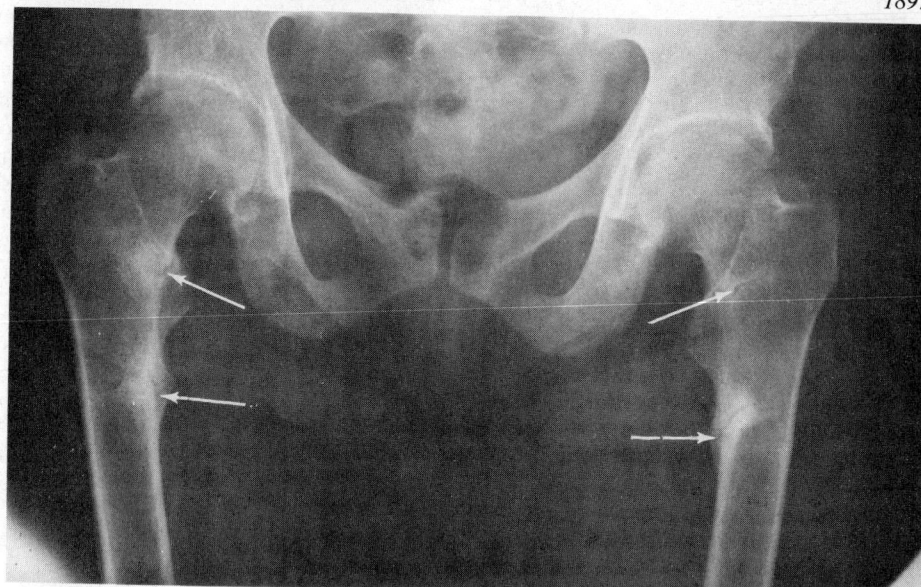

FIGURE 337-4 *Radiograph of the femurs of a 47-year-old woman with Fanconi's syndrome of adult onset. The presence of multiple pseudofractures is indicated by the arrows.*

vitamin D in hospital diets to produce substrate 25(OH)D for 1α-hydroxylation by the renal enzyme that is increased in activity due to secondary hyperparathyroidism. In other patients, circulating 1,25(OH)$_2$D levels may not reflect levels at critical target cells.

ABNORMAL METABOLISM OF VITAMIN D Serum 25(OH)D levels are reduced in some instances of parenchymal and obstructive liver disease, but these findings have not yet been correlated with quantitative histologic studies of bone. Patients consuming anticonvulsant drugs such as phenobarbital, phenytoin or carbamazepine may develop rickets or osteomalacia. For a given intake of vitamin D, patients receiving chronic anticonvulsant drugs have lower serum levels of calcium and 25(OH)D. Consumption of anticonvulsants may be especially important in individuals whose intake of vitamin D is marginal, who are nonambulatory and confined indoors, who have chronic recurrent infections, or in whom mild intestinal malfunction exists as in the postgastrectomy state. As discussed in Chap. 335 the anticonvulsant drugs have multiple actions on calcium homeostasis.

A syndrome superficially resembling vitamin D–resistant rickets has been termed *pseudovitamin D deficiency*. Because these patients respond to pharmacologic doses of vitamin D, this disease is also termed *vitamin D–dependent rickets* (also see Chap. 336). These patients have rickets or osteomalacia, a tendency to hypocalcemia but normal or only slightly depressed serum phosphorus levels, a response to moderate doses of vitamin D that is usually excellent and complete, and an autosomal recessive inheritance. No other renal tubular abnormalities are found. These patients also respond to small doses of 1,25(OH)$_2$D (calcitriol). Most patients have low serum 1,25(OH)$_2$D levels, suggesting a defect in the renal production of 1,25(OH)$_2$D; these have been classified as having vitamin D–dependent rickets, type I. Vitamin D–dependent rickets, type II, results from an impaired responsiveness of target tissues to 1,25(OH)$_2$D since skin fibroblasts cultured from most affected subjects have abnormalities in the amount or function of 1,25(OH)$_2$D receptors. In these subjects elevated serum 1,25(OH)$_2$D levels are elevated and increase further when large doses of vitamin D are administered.

Other individuals with rickets unresponsive to 25(OH)D (calcifediol) or calcitriol have low circulating levels of 24,25(OH)$_2$D and have return of serum calcium concentrations to normal when synthetic 24,25(OH)$_2$D is administered.

Osteomalacia may also occur in patients on long-term total parenteral nutrition. Some of these individuals have hypoparathyroidism but this cannot account for the osteomalacia. Serum levels of 25(OH)D are normal although levels of 1,25(OH)$_2$D may be low. Aluminum has been detected in increased amounts in plasma, urine,

and bone and may play a role in genesis of the osteomalacia similar to that postulated in patients with renal failure on chronic hemodialysis.

RENAL TUBULAR DISORDERS Rickets and osteomalacia occur in association with a variety of disorders of proximal renal tubular function. These disorders have in common increased renal clearance of inorganic phosphorus and hypophosphatemia with normal or near normal glomerular filtration rate. Increased phosphate clearance with resultant hypophosphatemia is usually an isolated defect with no other abnormalities except for increase in urinary glycine excretion (hyperglycinuria). X-linked hypophosphatemia (*phosphate diabetes* and *vitamin D–resistant rickets* are terms applied to these cases especially when the disorder presents in early childhood) is characterized by progressively severe skeletal deformities, dwarfism, and X-linked dominant inheritance. Many of these individuals have a unique disorder of tendons, ligaments, and joint capsules characterized by calcification or, more probably, ossification of insertions of tendons and ligaments and joint capsules. In some patients spontaneous remissions may be followed by recurrences in adult life associated, for example, with pregnancy and lactation. Serum levels of 25(OH)D are normal, and levels of 1,25(OH)$_2$D are in the low-normal range. The latter may be inappropriately low with respect to the hypophosphatemia (although the low levels of 1,25(OH)$_2$D do not account for the renal tubular defect in phosphate transport), and therefore high concentrations of 1,25(OH)$_2$D would be required to heal the osteomalacia. Similar mechanisms have been proposed to account for renal tubular and skeletal abnormalities. Combined therapy with calcitriol and inorganic phosphorus reverses the osteomalacia of trabecular bone surfaces and corrects the microscopic periosteocytic mineralization defects as well. Sporadic cases of hypophosphatemia have also been described in adults in whom family histories are negative and where proximal muscle weakness is a prominent feature. These patients also are best treated with a combination of calcitriol and inorganic phosphorus. As mentioned above, in most untreated patients with renal tubular disorders associated with rickets and osteomalacia, secondary hyperparathyroidism is not present.

In other patients the disorder in tubular function may be more widespread, involving (besides phosphorus) glucose, potassium, amino acids, and uric acid; the various combinations are termed the de Toni-Debré-Fanconi syndrome. The more complete renal tubular defects may occur sporadically or in families. In some instances the lesion is simply part of a more widespread disorder as in Wilson's disease and cystinosis. The acidosis of proximal tubular defects also plays a role in development of osteomalacia, possibly by altering metabolism of vitamin D or altering renal handling of calcium and phosphorus. In this regard osteomalacia has accompanied the hyperchloremic acidosis of ureterocolic anastomosis.

TUMOR-ASSOCIATED (ONCOGENOUS) OSTEOMALACIA Osteomalacia and hypophosphatemia with high renal phosphate clearance have been associated with a variety of mesenchymal tumors. The latter have included giant cell tumors (benign or malignant), reparative granulomas, hemangiomas, fibromas, and other mesenchymal neoplasms. A similar syndrome occurs in patients with prostatic carcinoma. In some instances, removal of the tumor resulted in return of renal phosphorus clearance to normal, rise in serum phosphorus levels, and healing of the osteomalacia (or the rickets in children). Serum $1,25(OH)_2D$ levels are low or undetectable, although chronic administration of sufficient calcitriol to raise circulating levels of this metabolite to normal does not alter renal phosphorus clearance or serum phosphorus concentrations. Some renal toxin released by the tumor may impair proximal tubular functions such as 1α-hydroxylation of 25(OH)D *and* phosphate transport; removal of the tumor results in a return of circulating levels of $1,25(OH)_2D$ and serum phosphorus levels to normal.

CHRONIC RENAL FAILURE Osteomalacia is common in patients with chronic renal failure; it often tends to be the predominant type of renal osteodystrophy in younger patients and is more frequent in those with the lower plasma levels of calcium and phosphorus. A component of secondary hyperparathyroidism and osteitis fibrosa almost always accompanies the defect in mineralization. The defect itself probably involves a decreased conversion of 25(OH)D to $1,25(OH)_2D$ either because of insufficient viable renal cortical tissue or the inhibitory effect of hyperphosphatemia on renal 25(OH)D-1α-hydroxylase activity. In addition, there may be a primary defect in intestinal calcium absorption. Part of the secondary hyperparathyroidism may also be due to decreased phosphate clearance and subsequent hyperphosphatemia. Under circumstances of near-normal plasma concentration of calcium and hyperphosphatemia, the presence of inhibitors probably accounts for the defective mineralization. In some patients the osteomalacia responds to large doses of vitamin D or dihydrotachysterol or to small doses of calcitriol or calcifediol. However, some patients with renal osteodystrophy do not respond to pharmacologic doses of vitamin D or improve when given small amounts of calcitriol. Accumulation of aluminum in the bone of some of these subjects accounts for the vitamin D–refractory osteomalacia. These individuals have deposits of aluminum at the mineralization fronts and decreased mineralization rates. They can be recognized by the extent to which the plasma aluminum levels are increased following a standard infusion of the chelating agent deferoxamine. Deferoxamine can mobilize aluminum from bone and other tissues and is effective therapy of the aluminum osteodystrophy. In some patients with renal osteodystrophy the total bone mass may be increased (osteosclerosis), resulting in increased density of bone. This is particularly evident in the spine, where a characteristic appearance is that of dense bone at the superior and inferior margins of the vertebral bodies with more radiolucent central portions ("rugger jersey sign"). Histologically, although there is more bone per unit area, each trabecula is covered by an abnormally wide osteoid seam.

HYPOPHOSPHATASIA Rickets is a feature of a deficiency of alkaline phosphatase in infants and children which is inherited as an autosomal recessive trait. The disorder that affects adults, however, is probably distinct from the infantile and childhood forms and is inherited as an autosomal dominant trait with variable expressivity. The precise defects are not known, although the fundamental abnormality relates to deficient circulating and tissue activity of the tissue nonspecific alkaline phosphatase isoenzyme. Despite the presence of osteomalacia serum phosphorus levels are not reduced. Phosphoryl ethanolamine is excreted in excessive amounts in the urine, and circulating levels of pyridoxal 5′-phosphate are elevated, although it is not clear how these findings are related to the inadequate skeletal mineralization. There is a direct correlation between plasma alkaline phosphatase and inorganic pyrophosphatase. Since patients with

hypophosphatasia are also deficient in pyrophosphatase, concentrations of inorganic pyrophosphate, a potent inhibitor of mineralization, may be too high to allow normal mineralization at formation sites. Elevated levels of inorganic pyrophosphate in this disorder could also account for the occurrence of arthropathy associated with chondrocalcinosis. Bone disease in adult hypophosphatasia may be due to a generalized defect in osteoblasts or other alkaline phosphatase–producing cells or to a qualitative defect in the alkaline phosphatase molecule.

OTHER DISORDERS ASSOCIATED WITH DEFECTIVE MINERALIZATION Disturbances in mineralization may be seen in patients consuming high doses of fluoride ion and in patients with Paget's disease treated with etidronate. Some decrease in mineralization of newly forming matrix, increase in surface covered by osteoid, and increase in the width of the osteoid seams occur in conditions that are not usually considered as osteomalacia except by these criteria. Biopsies in some of these conditions show a normal calcification front. Examples include patients with the osteitis fibrosa of hyperparathyroidism in the weeks to months following surgical cure. In these circumstances there is a temporary imbalance between the rate at which mineral is supplied to bone and the rate at which bone matrix is formed. Wide osteoid seams and hypophosphatemia are also seen in children with osteopetrosis in whom there is inadequate resorption of bone and calcified cartilage but active bone formation.

A condition that resembles osteomalacia and is associated with a coarsened, mottled bony trabecular pattern, pseudofractures, and bone pain but normal plasma levels of calcium and phosphorus is *fibrogenesis imperfecta ossium*. The bone has a distinctive histologic appearance, with wide osteoid seams and a distortion of the birefringent pattern of normal bone suggesting an abnormality in the collagen recently deposited. The nature of the abnormality is not known.

TREATMENT OF RICKETS AND OSTEOMALACIA In rickets and osteomalacia due to dietary absence of vitamin D or inadequate exposure to sunlight, vitamin D_2 (cholecalciferol) or vitamin D_3 (ergocalciferol) is given orally in doses of 2000 to 4000 IU (0.05 to 0.1 mg) daily for 6 to 12 weeks, followed by daily supplements of 200 to 400 IU, which are adequate to prevent the development of the disorder in otherwise normal subjects. In infants and children such treatment causes improvement in muscle tone and strength, increase in serum calcium and phosphorus, and fall in alkaline phosphatase levels after several weeks. Radiologic evidence of healing is first noted within weeks and may be complete by a few months. Calcium supplements and larger initial doses of vitamin D may be necessary in infants and children with tetany. In adults with nutritional osteomalacia healing of pseudofractures may be evident within 3 to 4 weeks after therapy with as little as 2000 IU (0.05 mg) vitamin D daily. Healing is complete usually by 6 months.

Patients with osteomalacia due to intestinal malabsorption do not respond to the relatively small doses of vitamin D that can cure osteomalacia due to dietary absence or inadequate sunlight. In the presence of active steatorrhea, daily oral doses of vitamin D of 50,000 to 100,000 IU (1.25 to 2.5 mg) and large doses of calcium (e.g., 15 g calcium lactate or 4 g calcium carbonate orally per day) may be required. In some instances oral vitamin D is ineffective, and the parenteral route is required (e.g., 10,000 IU intramuscularly per day). Another approach is the use of ultraviolet irradiation in addition to supplemental calcium. Small doses of calcitriol (0.5 to 1.0 μg daily) are usually effective in this form of osteomalacia. Inorganic phosphate therapy is not indicated either in deficiency or in intestinal malabsorption of the vitamins, since hypocalcemia will develop and intestinal calcium absorption will remain inadequate. In all patients in whom large doses of vitamin D are used, periodic monitoring of serum calcium and 25(OH)D levels is essential. Semiquantitative urinary calcium measurements alone are inadequate.

In patients on anticonvulsants, it is usually necessary to continue the drugs while adding supplemental vitamin D and monitoring levels of serum calcium and serum 25(OH)D until a therapeutic response (evidence of radiologic healing, improvement in symptoms) is obtained. Doses varying from 4000 to 40,000 IU daily have been recommended.

Treatment of rickets and osteomalacia in the presence of renal tubular disorders is more difficult. The X-linked form of hypophosphatemic osteomalacia is usually treated with large doses of vitamin D (from 50,000 to several hundred thousand IU or more daily). The use of dihydrotachysterol, a pseudo-$1\alpha(OH)D$ analogue, 0.2 to 0.6 mg, or calcitriol, 0.5 to 2.0 μg (see below) orally per day, in place of vitamin D has the advantage of shorter onset and duration of action and more consistent skeletal healing. With vitamin D therapy alone radiologic evidence of healing in many patients is incomplete; some hypophosphatemia persists, linear skeletal growth remains abnormally slow, and bony deformities continue to develop. In addition, hypercalcemia and its consequences are potential hazards. The addition of oral supplements of inorganic phosphate in divided doses of 1.0 to 3.6 g phosphorus daily has improved the clinical and radiologic response, allowed the use of smaller doses of vitamin D or calcitriol, and improved the rate of linear growth in many younger subjects. In some adults, therapy with inorganic phosphate alone abolishes muscle weakness and bone pain and produces radiologic and histologic healing. The addition of calcitriol improves calcium balance and helps decrease secondary hyperparathyroidism and maintain a sufficient level of serum phosphorus to permit complete healing. In some patients there may be temporary increase in bone pain and rise in serum alkaline phosphatase during the early phases of treatment. In the osteomalacia associated with the chronic acidosis of renal tubular disorders, the use of alkali may be of value in supplementing therapy with phosphate and calcitriol. In patients with ureterosigmoidostomy, oral sodium bicarbonate has reversed acidosis, improved serum phosphate level, and healed the bone disease; with maintenance doses of alkali, recurrence of symptoms has been prevented.

Patients with nephrotic syndrome and low serum 25(OH)D levels benefit from modest vitamin D supplementation. In chronic renal failure high doses of vitamin D, similar to those needed to treat osteomalacia of renal tubular disorders, are used. Dihydrotachysterol at doses of 0.2 to 1.0 mg daily is effective in treating hypocalcemia and osteodystrophy resulting from chronic renal failure. Calcitriol in small doses is equally effective in most cases of renal osteodystrophy. The recommended initial dose is 0.25 μg per day. If after 2 to 4 weeks on this dose the biochemical parameters are unaltered, the dose is increased by 0.25 μg per day every 2 to 4 weeks until a satisfactory clinical biochemical response (including elevation of serum calcium levels and decrease in PTH levels) is obtained. The usual dose is 0.5 to 1.0 μg per day. Because there are no regulatory mechanisms to control the biological responses to calcitriol, there is a high incidence of transient hypercalciuria and hypercalcemia, especially initially. Thus, serum calcium should be monitored frequently during the first 1 to 2 months of therapy and less frequently once a stable dose has been established. Since calcitriol has a short duration of action and is not stored in fat depots, hypercalcemia usually resolves in 2 to 7 days after the dose is discontinued or decreased. Phosphate supplements are, of course, contraindicated in the usual patient with chronic renal failure. Occasionally, however, hypophosphatemia may result from the excessive use of nonabsorbable antacids in addition to excessive removal of phosphate through hemodialysis.

In patients who have had rickets in childhood, the abnormal mechanical stress of severe deformities may contribute to the development of degenerative joint disease, particularly in hips and knees. Osteotomies at the proper time after healing may prevent this complication and more extensive arthroplasties later in life.

REFERENCES

Osteoporosis

AVIOLI LV: Osteoporosis: Pathogenesis and therapy, in *Metabolic Bone Disease*, LV Avioli, SM Krane (eds). New York, Academic, 1977, vol 1, p 307

ALOIA JF et al: Risk factors for postmenopausal osteoporosis. Am J Med 78:95, 1985

BROWN JP et al: Serum bone GLA-protein: A specific marker for bone formation in postmenopausal osteoporosis. Lancet 1:1091, 1984

CHRISTIANSEN C et al: Bone mass in postmenopausal women after withdrawal of oestrogen/gestagen replacement therapy. Lancet 1:459, 1981

DELMAS PD et al: Increase in serum bone γ-carboxyglutamic acid protein with aging in women. J Clin Invest 71:1316, 1983

DRINKWATER BL et al: Bone mineral content of amenorrheic and eumenorrheic athletes. N Engl J Med 311:277, 1984

Editorial: Fluoride and the treatment of osteoporosis. Lancet 1:547, 1984

Editorial: Risk factors in postmenopausal osteoporosis. Lancet 1:1370, 1985

GALLAGHER JC et al: Epidemiology of fractures of the proximal femur in Rochester, Minnesota. Clin Orthopaed Rel Res 150:163, 1980

GRUBER HE et al: Long-term calcitonin therapy in postmenopausal osteoporosis. Metabolism 33:295, 1984

HARRISON JE et al: Three-year changes in bone mineral mass of postmenopausal osteoporotic patients based on neutron activation analysis of the central third of the skeleton. J Clin Endocrinol Metab 52:751, 1981

HEATH H III: Athletic women, amenorrhea, and skeletal integrity (editorial). Ann Intern Med 102:258, 1985

HORSMAN A et al: The effect of estrogen dose on postmenopausal bone loss. N Engl J Med 309:1405, 1983

JENSEN J et al: Cigarette smoking, serum estrogens, and bone loss during hormone-replacement therapy early after menopause. N Engl J Med 313:973, 1985

KANIS JA: Treatment of osteoporotic fracture. Lancet 1:27, 1984

KLIBANSKI A et al: Decreased bone density in hyperprolactinemic women. N Engl J Med 303:1511, 1980

KRØLNER B et al: Physical exercise as prophylaxis against involutional vertebral bone loss: A controlled trial. Clin Sci Mol Med 64:541, 1983

LANE JM et al: Treatment of osteoporosis with sodium fluoride and calcium: Effects on vertebral fracture incidence and bone histomorphometry. Orthop Clin North Am 15:729, 1984

LINDSAY R et al: Prevention of spinal osteoporosis in oophorectomised women. Lancet 2:1151, 1980

NEED AG et al: 1,25-Dihydroxycalciferol and calcium therapy in osteoporosis with calcium malabsorption: Dose response relationship of calcium absorption and indices of bone turnover. Mineral Electrolyte Metab 11:35, 1985

PARFITT AM: Dietary risk factors for age-related bone loss and fractures. Lancet 2:1181, 1983

——— et al: Relationships between surface, volume, and thickness of iliac trabecular bone in aging and in osteoporosis: Implications for the microanatomic and cellular mechanisms of bone loss. J Clin Invest 72:1396, 1983

PROCKOP DJ: Mutations in collagen genes: Consequences for rare and common diseases. J Clin Invest 75:783, 1985

RECKER RR et al: Effect of estrogens and calcium carbonate on bone loss in postmenopausal women. Ann Intern Med 87:649, 1977

RIGGS BL, MELTON J III: Evidence for two distinct syndromes of involutional osteoporosis. Am J Med 75:899, 1983

——— et al: Effect of the fluoride/calcium regimen on vertebral fracture occurrence in postmenopausal osteoporosis: Comparison with conventional therapy. N Engl J Med 306:446, 1982

——— et al: Changes in bone mineral density of the proximal femur and spine with aging: Differences between the postmenopausal and senile osteoporosis syndromes. J Clin Invest 70:716, 1982

SAKHAEE K et al: Postmenopausal osteoporosis as a manifestation of renal hypercalciuria with secondary hyperparathyroidism. J Clin Endocrinol Metab 61:368, 1985

SEEMAN E et al: Risk factors for spinal osteoporosis in men. Am J Med 75:977, 1983

SILLENCE D: Osteogenesis imperfecta: An expanding panorama of variants. Clin Orthopaed Rel Res 159:11, 1981

SMITH R et al: Osteoporosis of pregnancy. Lancet 1:1178, 1985

SPENCER H et al: Chronic alcoholism: Frequently overlooked cause of osteoporosis in men. Am J Med 80:393, 1986

STEWART AF et al: Calcium homeostasis in immobilization: An example of resorptive hypercalciuria. N Engl J Med 306:1136, 1982

WAHNER HW et al: Assessment of bone mineral. J Nucl Med 25:1241, 1984

WEINSTEIN MC: Estrogen use in postmenopausal women—costs, risks, and benefits. N Engl J Med 303:308, 1980

Osteomalacia

CHARHON SA et al: Effects of parathyroidectomy on bone formation and mineralization in hemodialyzed patients. Kidney Int 27:426, 1984

FRAME B, PARFITT AM: Osteomalacia: Current concepts. Ann Intern Med 89:966, 1978

GODSALL JW et al: Vitamin D metabolism and bone histomorphometry in a patient with antacid-induced osteomalacia. Am J Med 77:747, 1984

GOLDRING SR, KRANE SM: Disorders of calcification: Osteomalacia and rickets, in *Endocrinology*, LJ DeGroot (ed). New York, Grune & Stratton, 1979, vol 2, p 853

HARRELL RM et al: Healing of bone disease in X-linked hypophosphatemic rickets/osteomalacia: Induction and maintenance with phosphorus and calcitriol. J Clin Invest 75:1858, 1985

HOCHBERG Z et al: 1,25-Dihydroxyvitamin D resistance, rickets, and alopecia. Am J Med 77:805, 1984

HODSMAN AB et al: Bone aluminum and histomorphometric features of renal osteodystrophy. J Clin Endocrinol Metab 54:439, 1982

——— et al: Vitamin D–resistant osteomalacia in hemodialysis patients lacking secondary hyperparathyroidism. Ann Intern Med 94:629, 1981

HOIKKA V et al: Carbamazepine and bone mineral metabolism. Acta Neurol Scand 70:77, 1984

KLEIN GL, COBURN JW: Metabolic bone disease associated with total parenteral nutrition. Adv Nutr Res 6:67, 1984

KUMAR R: Hepatic and intestinal osteodystrophy and the hepatobiliary metabolism of vitamin D. Ann Intern Med 98:662, 1983

LYLES KW et al: Hypophosphatemic osteomalacia: Association with prostatic carcinoma. Ann Intern Med 93:275, 1980

MANKIN HJ: Rickets, osteomalacia and renal osteodystrophy. J Bone Joint Surg (AM) 56A:101,352, 1974

MARIE PJ, GLORIEUX FH: Relation between hypomineralized periosteocytic lesions and bone mineralization in vitamin D–resistant rickets. Calcif Tissue Int 35:443, 1983

MILLINER DS et al: Use of deferoxamine infusion test in the diagnosis of aluminum-related osteodystrophy. Ann Intern Med 101:775, 1984

PARFITT AM et al: Metabolic bone disease with and without osteomalacia after intestinal bypass surgery: A bone histomorphometric study. Bone 6:211, 1985

PIKE JW et al: D₃-resistant fibroblasts have immunoassayable 1,25-dihydroxyvitamin D₃ receptors. Science 224:879, 1984

POLISSON RP et al: Calcification of entheses associated with X-linked hypophosphatemic osteomalacia. N Engl J Med 313:1, 1985

RYAN EA, REISS E: Oncogenous osteomalacia: Review of the world literature of 42 cases and report of two new cases. Am J Med 77:501, 1984

STEINBACH HL, NOETZLI M: Roentgen appearance of the skeleton in osteomalacia and rickets. Am J Roentgenol 91:955, 1964

SWEET RA et al: Vitamin D metabolite levels in oncogenic osteomalacia. Ann Intern Med 93:279, 1980

WHYTE MP et al: Markedly increased circulating pyridoxal-5′-phosphate levels in hypophosphatasia. J Clin Invest 76:752, 1985

—— et al: Adult hypophosphatasia with chondrocalcinosis and arthropathy: Variable penetrance of hypophosphatasemia in a large Oklahoma kindred. Am J Med 72:631, 1982

338   PAGET'S DISEASE OF BONE

STEPHEN M. KRANE

Paget's disease of bone (osteitis deformans) is usually focal, but occasionally it may be widespread. The initial event is excessive resorption of bone by cells such as osteoclasts, followed by the replacement of normal marrow by vascular, fibrous connective tissue. At some stage and to a variable degree, the resorbed bone is replaced by coarse-fibered, dense trabecular bone organized in haphazard fashion. The irregular and often rapid deposition of this new bone, to a great extent still lamellar, causes an increase in the number of prominent, irregular cement lines which gives the bone its characteristic "mosaic" pattern. Most lesions show evidence of both excessive resorption and the chaotic new bone formation.

INCIDENCE   The prevalence is difficult to determine since it is often asymptomatic and is frequently detected when roentgenograms are obtained for other reasons. On the basis of autopsy examination, the incidence has been estimated to be about 3 percent in individuals over the age of 40; there is increased likelihood of occurrence with increasing age. The incidence varies in different parts of the world. Figures based on radiological surveys indicate less than a 1 percent frequency in the adult population in the United States, Great Britain, and Australia. In India, Japan, the Middle East, and Scandinavia, the disease is rare.

ETIOLOGY   The etiology of Paget's disease is unknown. No convincing evidence of endocrine abnormality has been produced. Likewise, although pagetic bone can be exceedingly vascular, it has not been established that the vascular abnormality is primary. Some of the manifestations of the disease can be suppressed with the use of glucocorticoids, salicylates, and cytotoxic drugs, but there is not sufficient information to support the hypothesis that the fundamental lesion is inflammatory. Intranuclear inclusions have been found by electron microscopy in osteoclasts in pagetic bone but not in osteoclasts or any other cells in bone from normal persons or patients with various bone diseases with the exception of pyknodysostosis. Some of the inclusions are morphologically similar to nucleocapsids of viruses belonging to the measles group. Indirect immunofluorescence and immunoperoxidase studies support the suggestion that the inclusions are indeed measles virus nucleocapsids. Other evidence suggests that the inclusions are due to respiratory syncytial virus. In one area of England ownership of dogs is more common in pagetic subjects

than in controls, suggesting that a canine virus (for example, canine distemper) might be a primary infective agent. Thus, different viral agents might be responsible for Paget's disease in different instances.

PATHOPHYSIOLOGY   The characteristic feature is increased resorption of bone accompanied by an increase in bone formation, which is usually adequate to compensate. In the early phase bone resorption predominates (for example, in the variant, *osteoporosis circumscripta*), and the bones are exceedingly vascular. This has been termed the *osteoporotic, osteolytic,* or *destructive phase* of disease in which the external calcium balance may be negative. Commonly the excessive resorption is followed closely by formation of new pagetic bone. In this so-called mixed phase of the disease, the rate of bone formation is so geared to that of bone resorption that the magnitude of the increase in bone turnover is not reflected in the overall calcium balance.

As the activity decreases, a progressive decrease in resorptive rate may occur, eventually leading to the occurrence of hard, dense, less vascular bone (the so-called *osteoplastic* or *sclerotic* phase) and a positive external calcium balance. The rates of bone turnover may be increased enormously in patients with active Paget's disease, occasionally more than 20 times normal. Quantitative histomorphometry of pagetic bone biopsies confirms the extent of remodeling with findings of marked increase in resorption surfaces with deep scalloped lacunae containing giant osteoclasts with numerous nuclei. Resorption surfaces are also increased, and increased numbers of osteoblasts line the edges. The calcification rate is also increased. The normal hematopoietic marrow is replaced by a loose stroma which may be highly vascular. The magnitude of the increase in turnover varies with the extent as well as the activity of the disease. The increase correlates with the increased plasma levels of bone alkaline phosphatase, which are higher in Paget's disease than in any other condition with the exception of hereditary hyperphosphatasia. Although increased bone resorption enhances release of calcium and phosphate ions from bone, utilization of these ions for new bone formation and, presumably, feedback control of parathyroid hormone secretion usually maintain the concentration of calcium ions in the plasma at normal levels. The concentration of phosphate in the plasma is normal or slightly elevated. When marked imbalance between bone formation and resorption occurs in favor of resorption, as after prolonged immobilization or fractures, urinary calcium excretion may be increased, and rarely hypercalcemia may occur. If, on the other hand, bone formation exceeds resorption (relatively uncommon), circulating levels of parathyroid hormone may be increased. Resorption involves the organic phase of bone as well as the mineral phase. While the inorganic ions of the mineral phase are reutilized for bone formation, amino acids such as hydroxyproline and hydroxylysine are released during resorption of the collagen matrix of bone and are not reutilized for collagen biosynthesis. The urinary excretion of small peptides containing hydroxyproline is increased, reflecting the increased bone resorption. Peptides of about 1500 to 2000 mol wt containing hydroxyproline and other amino acids in proportions characteristic of collagen are also excreted in increased amounts in the urine and are correlated with increased bone formation. Other markers for increased matrix synthesis include elevated levels of osteocalcin (bone-GLA protein) (see Chap. 335) and procollagen extension fragments in plasma.

RADIOLOGIC CHANGES   The radiologic findings reflect the underlying pathology and the phase of the disease that predominates at the time of the examination. The pelvic bones are most commonly involved, followed by the femur, skull, tibia, lumbosacral spine, dorsal spine, clavicles, and ribs in that order; small bones are not as frequently diseased. The lytic phase of the disease may be overlooked except when it occurs in the skull as *osteoporosis circumscripta*, with areas of sharply demarcated radiolucency in the frontal, parietal, and occipital bones. In the long bones the lytic areas are usually first seen at one end, from which they progress toward the other end with a V-shaped advancing edge. The lesion may produce expansion of the cortex and exhibit other features which suggest malignancy. Usually the lytic area is followed by a zone of increased density, representing the new bone formation of the mixed phase of the disease. In general, the bone shows enlargement with irregularly widened cortex in a coarse, striated pattern and increased density, occasionally focal in distribution. Perpendicular lines of radiolucency (cortical infractions) are frequent and occur on the convex side of bowed long bones, particularly the femur and tibia. Transverse fractures may also occur, some initiated at the sites of these cortical infractions. The remodeling of the pagetic bone usually follows the lines of stress produced by muscle pull or gravity, accounting for the characteristic lateral bowing of the femur or anterior bowing of the tibia and the tendency for most of the dense bone to be deposited on the concave side of the bowed bone. In the skull, in the mixed stage, there is enlargement and thickening, especially of the outer table, with irregular areas of increased density, often spotty (Fig. 338-1). Basilar invagination is common with involvement of the base of the skull. The changes in the pelvis also consist of the combination of bone resorption and new bone formation and are frequently accompanied by a characteristic thickening of the pelvic brim. In the sclerotic phase of the disease, the bone may show uniform increase in density, often in the absence of striations. This is common in the facial bones but is occasionally seen as well in the vertebrae where a homogeneous, dense pattern gives an "ivory" appearance similar to that typical of Hodgkin's disease, although the involved vertebrae are not enlarged in Hodgkin's disease.

CLINICAL PICTURE The clinical presentation is variable and is a function of the extent of the disease, the particular bones involved, and the presence of associated complications. Many patients are asymptomatic. In these individuals the disorder is discovered during the course of radiologic examination of the pelvis or spine for an unrelated disease or complaint, or because of the finding of an elevated level of plasma alkaline phosphatase. Other individuals may gradually become aware of a swelling or deformity of a long bone or develop a disturbance in gait due to unequal length of and change in the distribution of mechanical forces in the lower extremities. Enlargement of the skull is often not noticed by the patients, or they may be aware of increasing hat size. Pain in the face and headache are initial complaints in some; backache and pain in the lower extremities are common. The pain is usually dull but may be shooting or knifelike. Back pain is most common in the lumbar region and may radiate into the buttocks or lower extremities. This pain is probably due to the pagetic process itself and to distortion of articular facets and secondary osteoarthritis. Pain in the lower extremities may be associated with the transverse cortical infractions along the convex lateral surface of the femur or the anterior surface of the tibia. Often the new lytic lesions detected on bone scan are the most painful. Pain may also be due to involvement of the hip joint resembling degenerative joint disease and characterized by narrowing of the joint space, bony lipping at the margin of the acetabulum, and deepening of the acetabulum. Angioid streaks may be present in the retina. Hearing loss is due to direct pagetic involvement of the ossicles of the inner ear or of bone in the region of the cochlea or to impingement on the eighth cranial nerve by pagetic bone narrowing the auditory foramen. More serious neurologic complications can result from overgrowth of pagetic bone at the base of the skull (platybasia) due to compression of the brainstem. Compression of the spinal cord with paraplegia has been observed, particularly with involvement of the middorsal spine. Pathologic fractures of vertebrae may also produce spinal cord lesions.

COMPLICATIONS Blood flow may be markedly increased in extremities involved with Paget's disease. There is proliferation of blood vessels in pagetic bone, but anatomic and functional studies have not confirmed the presence of arteriovenous fistulas. Although blood flow in the bone itself is increased, there is also cutaneous vasodilatation in the pagetic extremities, which accounts for the increased warmth noted clinically. When the disease is widespread, involving over one-third of the skeleton, the increased blood flow may be associated with *high cardiac output*. In the rare patient so-called high-output heart failure may result. However, heart disease in pagetic individuals is usually accounted for by the same conditions that occur in other patients of similar age. *Pathologic fracture* may occur in bones involved in the destructive phase of the disease. In the weight-bearing bones fractures are often incomplete, multiple, and on the convex side of the bone. They may occur spontaneously or follow only slight trauma; the lesions are painful but heal spontaneously with no major disability. More serious fractures may also occur. Complete fractures are often transverse as if the bone were snapped like a piece of chalk. Under these circumstances the fracture may upset the delicate balance between bone formation and resorption in favor of resorption. At this stage the imbalance may be reflected by increased urinary calcium excretion, and in rare instances the serum calcium level may rise to dangerous levels.

There is no characteristic level of urinary calcium excretion, although calcium excretion tends to be higher when the resorptive phase predominates. This may be a factor which accounts for the somewhat higher incidence of *urinary stone* in these patients, although many of the urinary calculi reported may be unrelated to the pagetic process. Secondary changes in the cartilage of the hip joint and in bones about the knees may result in articular symptoms. Hyperuricemia and gout commonly occur in men with Paget's disease, and calcific periarthritis may occur.

Sarcoma is the most dreaded complication. The incidence is probably no greater than 1 percent, although higher incidence has been noted in some series which include many patients with polyostotic involvement. The sarcomas most frequently arise in the femur, humerus, skull, face, and pelvis, and rarely in the vertebrae. In about 20 percent the tumors are multicentric. Histologically, they are usually osteosarcomas, although fibrosarcomas and chondrosarcomas have also been found. Increase in pain and swelling are the most common complaints that lead to recognition of the sarcomas. The level of alkaline phosphatase in the serum of patients with sarcomas usually reflects the activity and extent of the Paget's disease. In occasional patients an "explosive rise" of the phosphatase level may accompany the growth of the sarcoma, whereas in patients with limited Paget's disease, phosphatase levels may be only slightly elevated and give no clue to the development of the malignant lesion. The prognosis is poor following the development of sarcomas, and ablative surgery

FIGURE 338-1 *Lateral roentgenogram of the skull from a 58-year-old woman with Paget's disease of bone.*

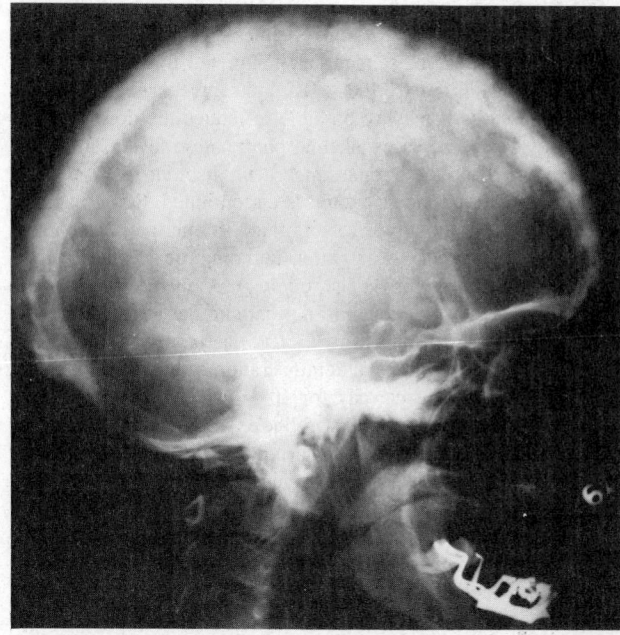

is rarely successful. Reparative granulomas closely resembling giant cell tumors may be locally destructive, but they do not metastasize.

THERAPY Most patients require no treatment, since the disease is localized and does not cause symptoms. Indications for therapy include persistent pain in involved bones, neural compression, rapidly progressive deformity resulting in disabling disturbance of posture and/or gait, high-output congestive heart failure, hypercalcemia, severe hypercalciuria with or without formation of renal stones, repeated fractures or nonunion in pagetic bone, and preparation for major orthopedic surgery. *Aspirin* is an effective analgesic, and if it can be tolerated in large enough doses (3.6 to 4.0 g per day) for months or years, disease activity may be suppressed, as shown by decreases in the level of plasma alkaline phosphatase and urinary hydroxyproline excretion. Nonsteroidal anti-inflammatory drugs such as *indomethacin,* 25 mg three or four times daily, may also relieve pain, especially in the presence of hip involvement. *Glucocorticoids* suppress the disease but only in large doses (greater than 60 mg prednisone per day) which are usually not tolerated and, therefore, are not recommended. It is of interest that the high cardiac output of some patients may be reduced significantly after only a few days of glucocorticoid treatment. Orthopedic procedures also have a role in the management of selected cases. Total hip replacement may be indicated in the patient with severe hip involvement, and osteotomy is useful to correct marked bowing deformities, particularly of the tibia. In patients with fractures or orthopedic procedures or in patients immobilized for any reason, urinary and serum calcium levels should be measured at intervals to anticipate the development of hypercalciuria and hypercalcemia. Early ambulation and adequate fluid intake are essential. Preparations of inorganic phosphate may reduce hypercalciuria under these circumstances (5 to 6 g neutral sodium phosphate daily in divided doses).

Several agents reduce the excessive bone resorption of Paget's disease and are of possible therapeutic value. Porcine, salmon, and human *calcitonins* have been administered subcutaneously for prolonged periods to pagetic patients, accompanied by a decrease in plasma alkaline phosphatase levels and in urinary hydroxyproline excretion. Treatment with calcitonin causes variable decrease in bone pain, improvement in neurologic symptoms, and decrease in elevated cardiac output. Some patients have not continued to respond to porcine and salmon calcitonins, possibly because of the development of neutralizing antibodies. These individuals usually continue to exhibit a satisfactory response to human calcitonin. In others in whom diminution in response is not associated with development of antibodies, the development of secondary hyperparathyroidism has been postulated, although this cannot account for resistance in all cases. The calcitonins are probably most useful in patients with pain corresponding to areas of pagetic involvement, not due to associated joint disease. The dose of salmon calcitonin (the form available in the United States) is 50 to 100 MRC units given subcutaneously daily. In some cases it may be possible to reduce the dose to three times weekly. In severe cases alkaline phosphatase levels, although reduced, do not reach the normal range. The disorder relapses after weeks or months when the calcitonin is discontinued. Some patients develop nausea, occasionally with vomiting, 30 min to several hours after injection. This may occur after initiating treatment or after months or years of therapy. The etiology is unknown, but the symptoms may be severe enough to discontinue the medication.

Cytotoxic drugs such as plicamycin and dactinomycin are potent agents in the disorder. Parenteral administration of plicamycin, 10 to 25 μg/kg of body weight per day for 10 to 14 days, has produced striking decrease in urinary hydroxyproline excretion with subsequent decreases in plasma alkaline phosphatase level and clinical improvement. The indexes of active disease again become abnormal within weeks to months following completion of plicamycin therapy. Maintenance therapy may be administered as a weekly intravenous bolus. With doses of less than 15 μg/kg of body weight per week toxicity is low despite potential risks.

Etidronate, a diphosphonate compound, given orally in doses up to 20 mg/kg of bodyweight per day has also been effective in reducing bone resorption in almost all and producing clinical improvement in some. In contrast to the calcitonins, etidronate often brings biochemical abnormalities to normal even in severe cases. Serum alkaline phosphatase and urinary hydroxyproline excretion remain decreased for several months after withdrawal of the drug and only gradually return to pretreatment levels. In doses of 20 mg/kg of body weight per day for periods of 6 months or longer mineralization of new bone may be inhibited and predispose to fracture. Some patients develop disabling pain over pagetic lesions within weeks or months of starting treatment that may be severe enough to warrant discontinuing the drug. Radiographs in some instances show an increase in bone lysis. This heals when the drug is stopped. It is therefore recommended that doses of 5 mg or occasionally 10 mg/kg of body weight per day be used for 6-month periods. Treatment could be reinstituted within 3 to 12 months if biochemical relapse occurs.

Other diphosphonate compounds such as the dichloromethylidene, 3-amino-1-hydroxypropylidine, aminohexane, or aminobutane derivatives have been introduced for therapy in Europe. Their onset is rapid and they do not inhibit mineralization. The use of these agents for brief periods (weeks) can cause remission that persists for months or even years. Although the diphosphonates and calcitonins act primarily to decrease bone resorption, the rate of new bone formation subsequently falls. As a result, the state of high bone turnover is shifted to a state of lower turnover, where rates of formation and resorption are still apparently geared to each other. In this lower turnover state, collagen fibers of the bone matrix are deposited in a more orderly fashion similar to normal bone.

REFERENCES

ALTMAN R, SINGER FR (eds.): Proceedings of the Kroc Foundation Conference on Paget's Disease of Bone, Arthritis Rheum 23:1073, 1980
BOYCE BF et al: Focal osteomalacia due to low-dose diphosphonate therapy in Paget's disease. Lancet 1:821, 1984
EVANS RA: Treatment of Paget's disease of bone. Med J Aust 1:159, 1983
HOSKING DJ: Paget's disease of bone. Br Med J 283:686, 1981
KRANE SM: Etidronate disodium in the treatment of Paget's disease of bone. Ann Intern Med 96:619, 1982
NAGANT DE DEUXCHAISNES C, KRANE SM: Paget's disease of bone: Clinical and metabolic observations. Medicine 43:233, 1964
O'DRISCOLL JB, ANDERSON DC: Past pets and Paget's disease. Lancet 2:919, 1985
SINGER FR et al: Paget's disease of bone, in *Metabolic Bone Disease*, vol 2, LV Avioli, SM Krane (eds). New York, Academic, 1978
———, MILLS BG: Evidence for a viral etiology of Paget's disease of bone. Clin Orthop 178:245, 1983
UPCHURCH KS et al: Giant cell reparative granuloma of Paget's disease of bone. A unique clinical entity. Ann Int Med 98:35, 1983
WALLACH S (ed): Paget's Disease. Clin Orthop 127:1, 1977
YATES AJP et al: Intravenous clodronate in the treatment and retreatment of Paget's disease of bone. Lancet 1:1474, 1985

339 HYPEROSTOSIS, NEOPLASMS, AND OTHER DISORDERS OF BONE AND CARTILAGE

STEPHEN M. KRANE / ALAN L. SCHILLER

HYPEROSTOSIS

A number of disease states have in common an increase in the mass of bone per unit volume (hyperostosis) (Table 339-1). Such increase in bone mass is detected radiologically as increased density of the bone, often associated with a variable disturbance in the architecture of the tissue. In the absence of quantitative histomorphometric data, it is usually not possible to distinguish between an increase in bone mass due to excessive formation of new bone or decreased resorption of bone already formed. When bone deposition is rapid, the new

TABLE 339-1   Causes of hyperostosis

1 Endocrine disorders
   a Primary hyperparathyroidism
   b Hypothyroidism
   c Acromegaly
2 Radiation osteitis
3 Chemical poisoning
   a Fluoride
   b Elemental phosphorus
   c Beryllium
   d Arsenic
   e Vitamin A intoxication
   f Lead
   g Bismuth
4 Osteomalacic disorders
   a Renal tubular osteomalacia (vitamin D resistance or phosphate diabetes)
   b Chronic renal glomerular failure
5 Osteosclerosis (localized) associated with chronic infection
6 Osteosclerotic phase of Paget's disease
7 Osteosclerosis associated with carcinomatous metastases, malignant lymphoma, and hematologic disorders (myeloproliferative disorders, sickle cell disease, leukemia, multiple myeloma, systemic mastocytosis)
8 Osteosclerosis of erythroblastosis fetalis
9 Osteopetrosis
   a Infantile (malignant, autosomal recessive form)
   b Adult (benign, dominant form)
   c Intermediate form with carbonic anhydrase II deficiency and renal tubular acidosis
10 Unclassified diseases
   a Pyknodysostosis
   b Osteomyelosclerosis
   c Hyperostosis corticalis generalisata
   d Hyperostosis generalisata with pachydermia
   e Hereditary hyperphosphatasia
   f Progressive diaphyseal dysplasia (osteopathia hyperostotica multiplex infantilis; Camurati-Engelmann disease)
   g Melorheostosis
   h Osteopoikilosis
   i Hyperostosis frontalis interna

bone may be of the woven type, but if the process is more chronic, true lamellar bone is formed. The additional bone may be located at the periosteum, within the compact bone of the cortex, or in the trabeculae of the cancellous regions. In the medullary area, the new bone is deposited on and between the trabeculae and encroaches upon the medullary spaces. Typical examples of such responses are seen in areas adjacent to tumors or in association with infection. In some diseases the increase in bone mass may be spotty, as in osteopoikilosis, whereas in others most of the skeleton may be involved, as in the malignant form of osteopetrosis in children. The increase in mass is usually not due to an excessive amount of mineral relative to matrix, except in disorders such as osteopetrosis where islands of calcified cartilage may persist. (The mineral density of calcified cartilage is greater than that of bone.) In some diseases such as the osteosclerosis of renal insufficiency, the bone mass and radiodensity may be increased, even though the new bone formed is poorly mineralized and contains widened osteoid seams.

Several of these conditions are discussed in more detail in other chapters, although some generalizations are pertinent. Bone that is denser than normal may be seen occasionally in the osteitis fibrosa associated with active hyperparathyroidism. When the hyperparathyroidism is successfully treated, the rate of bone resorption decreases abruptly out of proportion to the rate of bone formation; this imbalance may lead to the production of areas of bone density greater than in the surrounding skeleton, especially in the healing of brown tumors. In hypothyroidism, the rates of both bone formation and resorption may be decreased, but when the balance is in favor of formation bones are of increased density but normal architecture. Increased bone density also occurs in some instances of osteomalacia associated with disturbances in renal tubular function. The increased mass of bone occurs together with widened osteoid seams, as in chronic renal glomerular insufficiency. In the vertebral bodies the bone appears denser in transverse bands at the upper and lower margins, with a relatively radiolucent center. This "sandwich" appearance is similar to that seen in some patients with osteopetrosis and has been termed by the British the *rugger jersey sign.*

OSTEOPETROSIS   Osteopetrosis (marble bone disease) is clinically, biochemically, and genetically heterogeneous. The most severe form in infants can be ascribed to defects in differentiation and/or function of osteoclasts. Several different types of hereditary osteopetrosis which resemble the infantile human disease have been described in rodents, and in some the disorder can be cured by engraftment of hematopoietic cells from a normal donor. In humans infantile osteopetrosis is manifested in utero and progresses after birth with marked anemia, hepatosplenomegaly, hydrocephalus, cranial nerve involvement, and death, often due to infection. Some attempts to transplant bone marrow from normal donors to provide normal osteoclast precursor cells have been successful, and osteopetrotic bone has been repopulated with functioning osteoclasts of donor origin and radiologic and/or bone biopsy evidence of bone resorption. In some individuals with osteopetrosis, defects have also been recognized in peripheral blood monocyte function. In other cases of osteopetrosis, clinical improvement has been obtained using high doses of calcitriol.

The less fulminant adult form is inherited as an autosomal dominant trait, and the anemia is not as severe, neurologic abnormalities are not as frequent, and recurrent pathologic fractures are the main feature. Although most cases are in infants and children, many are discovered first in adult life when roentgenograms are obtained because of fractures or unrelated diseases. There is no particular predilection for either sex.

In kindreds where it has been associated with renal tubular acidosis and cerebral calcification, osteopetrosis is inherited as an autosomal recessive defect, is compatible with long survival, and is associated with a deficiency of one of the isoenzymes of carbonic anhydrase (carbonic anhydrase II). Disturbances in bone resorption may result from failure to secrete hydrogen ions at sites of bone resorption.

Both bone formation and resorption are depressed, particularly resorption. Islands of unresorbed calcified cartilage are frequently encased in bone. The defect in remodeling results in disorganization of bone structure with thickened cortices and lack of funnelization of metaphyses. Despite its increased density, the bone is abnormal mechanically and fractures readily. Osteomalacia or rickets is sometimes a component of the osteopetrosis in children (Fig. 339-1).

The histologic changes are reflected in the roentgenograms (Fig. 339-2), which reveal uniformly dense, sclerotic bone often without distinction between the cortical and cancellous regions. There is

FIGURE 339-1   *Lateral roentgenogram of the thorax of a 9-month-old boy with the "malignant" form of osteopetrosis. Note the uniform increase in mineral density of the vertebral bodies and the marked flaring of the ends of the ribs (arrows), indicative of rickets.*

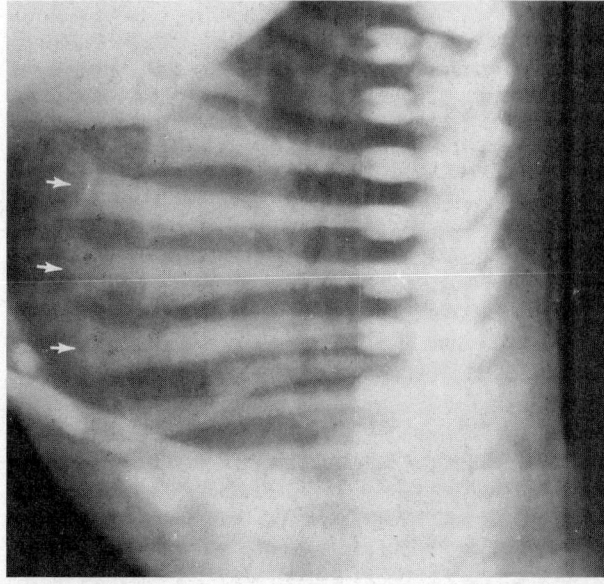

persistence of the primary spongiosa with central calcified cartilage cores surrounded by woven bone. Osteoclasts are often increased in number but apparently do not function properly. Osteoclasts may be morphologically normal or have loss of their ruffled borders suggesting that a spectrum of changes may occur. The variability may reflect heterogeneity in this syndrome, as in the osteopetrosis that occurs spontaneously in rodents. The long bones are usually involved, with increased density along the entire shaft. Foci of increased density may be seen in the epiphyses corresponding to regions of unresorbed calcified cartilage. The metaphyses have a characteristic clubbed or splayed appearance. Horizontal bandings of increased density alternating with zones of decreased density in the long bones and vertebrae suggest that the defect may be intermittent during periods of growth. The skull, pelvis, ribs, and other bones may also be involved. The phalanges and the distal humerus may appear normal when the disease is not severe.

Encroachment of bone upon the marrow cavity is associated with anemia of the myelophthisic type with foci of extramedullary hematopoiesis in liver, spleen, and lymph nodes and enlargement of these organs. In the malignant form of the disease the abundant osteoclasts may crowd out the hematopoietic marrow. Neurologic abnormalities are associated with encroachment on cranial nerves, which may result in optic atrophy, nystagmus, papilledema, exophthalmos, and impairment of extraocular motility. Facial paralysis and deafness are frequent; trigeminal lesions and anosmia have also been described. In infants with severe disease, macrocephaly, hydrocephalus, and convulsions may occur. Infections such as osteomyelitis are frequent in these children. Renal tubular acidosis is also a feature of the form of osteopetrosis associated with a deficiency in carbonic anhydrase II.

In the milder dominant osteopetrosis, about half of the patients have no symptoms, and the disorder is discovered incidentally on roentgenograms. Other such patients present because of fractures, bone pain, osteomyelitis, and cranial nerve palsies.

Fractures are a common complication even with trivial trauma.

FIGURE 339-2 *Roentgenogram of the spine and pelvis of a 55-year-old man with the more benign, dominant form of osteopetrosis.*

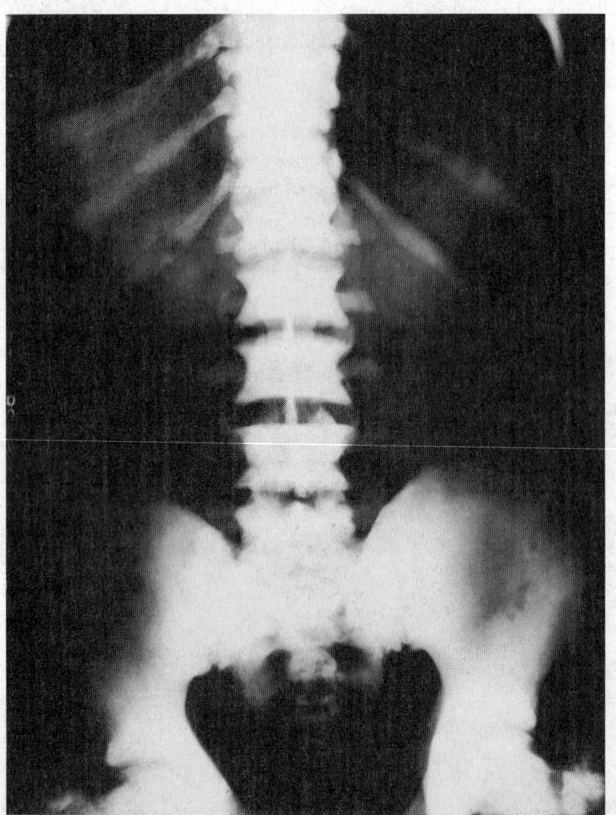

Healing of such fractures is usually satisfactory, although delayed union may occur. When the disease is manifested first in adult life, fractures may be the only clinical problem. Levels of calcium and alkaline phosphatase in the plasma are usually normal in adults, although in children hypophosphatemia and, occasionally, moderate hypocalcemia have been noted. Serum acid phosphatase levels are usually increased.

The skeletal defect is not the same in all forms of osteopetrosis, and within a clinical subtype genetic and biochemical heterogeneity is common. As mentioned, several children with severe osteopetrosis have received bone marrow transplants from HLA-identical siblings which resulted in histologic and radiologic increases in bone resorption, accompanied by improvement in anemia, vision, hearing, and growth and development. In one report, donor (male) nuclei were identified by Y-chromosome analysis in recipient (female) osteoclasts.

Unfortunately, it is not always possible to find appropriate donors for bone marrow transplantation, or patients may not be good candidates to receive transplants. Patients with the lethal forms have been treated with calcitriol. This therapy is associated with appearance of osteoclasts with normal ruffled borders and other evidence for increased bone resorption.

PYKNODYSOSTOSIS *Pyknodysostosis* resembles osteopetrosis but is usually a more benign condition not associated with hepatosplenomegaly, anemia, or cranial nerve involvement. In addition to a generalized increase in bone density, features include short stature, separated cranial sutures, hypoplasia of the mandible, persistence of deciduous teeth, and progressive acroosteolysis of the terminal phalanges. Life span is usually unaffected, and the patient usually presents because of frequent fractures. Pyknodysostosis is inherited as an autosomal recessive trait. In one case levels of plasma calcitonin were intermittently elevated, and the response of the plasma calcitonin to infusions of calcium and glucagon was exaggerated. The gene that causes this disorder may be located on the short arm of a small acrocentric chromosome.

OSTEOMYELOSCLEROSIS *Osteomyelosclerosis* is a disorder in which the marrow cells are replaced by diffuse fibroplasia, occasionally accompanied by osseous metaplasia. When the latter is prominent, increased skeletal density is seen on roentgenograms. In early stages woven bone may be found in intratrabecular locations whereas in more advanced stages woven bone is observed in the medulla. The disorder is probably a phase in the course of the myeloproliferative disorders and is characteristically accompanied by extramedullary hematopoiesis.

Hyperostosis corticalis generalisata (van Buchem's disease) is characterized by osteosclerosis of the skull (base and calvaria), lower jaw, clavicles, and ribs, and thickening of the diaphyseal cortices of the long and short bones. Alkaline phosphatase levels in the serum are elevated, and the disorder may be due to increased formation of bone of normal structure. The major manifestations are due to neural compression and consist of optic atrophy, facial paralysis, and perception deafness. In *hyperostosis generalisata with pachydermia* (Uehlinger), the sclerosis is due to increased formation of subperiosteal spongy bone and involves the epiphyses, metaphyses, and diaphyses. Pain, swelling of joints, and thickening of the skin of the lower arms are common.

HEREDITARY HYPERPHOSPHATASIA This disorder is characterized by severe structural deformities of the skeleton with increase in thickness of the calvaria, large homogeneous areas of increased density at the base of the skull, and widening and loss of normal architecture of the shafts and the epiphyses of the long and short bones. There is a failure to deposit normal bone, with haphazard orientation of lamellae suggesting active remodeling. Plasma alkaline phosphatase levels and urinary excretion of hydroxyproline peptides and other collagen degradation products are markedly increased. The disorder is apparently inherited as an autosomal recessive trait. Calcitonin therapy may be of value in some of these patients.

PROGRESSIVE DIAPHYSEAL DYSPLASIA A disorder in which a symmetric thickening and increased diameter of the diaphyses of long bones occurs, particularly in femurs, tibias, fibulas, radii, and ulnas, has been termed *progressive diaphyseal dysplasia* (Camurati-Engelmann disease). Pain over affected areas, fatigue, abnormal gait, and muscle wasting are the major manifestations. Serum alkaline phosphatase levels may be elevated and, on occasion, hypocalcemia and hyperphosphatemia may be found. Other abnormalities include anemia, leukopenia, and elevated erythrocyte sedimentation rate. Clinical and biochemical improvement may result from the use of glucocorticoids.

MELORHEOSTOSIS This rare condition usually begins in childhood and is characterized by areas of sclerosis in the bones of one limb. All segments of the bone may be involved, with sclerotic areas that have a "flowing" distribution. The involved limb is often extremely painful.

OSTEOPOIKILOSIS This benign disorder is usually discovered by chance and is not associated with symptoms. It is characterized by dense spots of trabecular bone less than a centimeter in diameter, usually of uniform density, that are located in the epiphyses and adjacent parts of the metaphyses. All bones may be involved except the skull, ribs, and vertebrae.

HYPEROSTOSIS FRONTALIS INTERNA *Hyperostosis frontalis interna* is an abnormality of the inner table of the frontal bones of the skull consisting of smooth, rounded enostoses covered by dura and projecting into the cranial cavity. These enostoses are usually less than 1 cm at their greatest diameter and usually do not extend posteriorly beyond the coronal suture. The abnormality is found almost exclusively in women, who are frequently obese, hirsute, and who have a variety of neuropsychiatric complaints (Morgagni-Stewart-Morel syndrome). However, hyperostosis frontalis interna also occurs in women with no obvious illness or particular associated disease. The finding in the skull may be a manifestation of a generalized metabolic disorder.

NEOPLASMS OF BONE

Primary neoplasms of the skeletal system reflect in their histology the cellular and extracellular components of the skeleton. However, it is not always possible to prove that a tumor arises from the same type of tissue that it produces. The precursor cells of bone tissue are probably derived from distinct cell lines in which the osteoclasts arise from hematopoietic cells and the osteoblasts arise from the stromal cell system. The primitive stromal cell could differentiate into chondroblasts and fibroblasts as well as osteoblasts. Neoplasms can arise from all these cell types. Each of these cells can produce its characteristic extracellular matrix, and neoplasms arising from them may thus be recognized. Primary neoplasms of bone can arise also from other hematopoietic, vascular, and neural elements.

PATHOPHYSIOLOGY Neoplasms in bone induce resorption of skeletal tissue. This bone resorption results from production by the tumor cells of factors that stimulate osteoclast function and/or recruitment and differentiation of the osteoclast hematopoietic precursor cells. Some of these factors are "parathyroid hormone–like" but immunologically and chemically different from the normal hormone. These factors, whose structures have not yet been elucidated, interact with the parathyroid hormone receptor or a similar receptor. Other resorption-inducing factors are related to transforming growth factors alpha and beta, platelet-derived growth factor, or interleukin 1. What has been termed "osteoclast-activating factor" includes interleukin 1 and other polypeptides produced by T lymphocytes. Prostaglandin production by some tumors may also mediate bone resorption. T lymphocytes infected with some viruses can metabolize circulating $25(OH)D$ to $1,25(OH)_2D$, which may also stimulate bone resorption. Tumors may also alter blood supply to bone by obstructing vessels or inducing angiogenesis. Tumors may also produce reaction in surrounding bone and alter the normal contour. The epiphyseal plate, articular cartilage, cortex, and periosteum of bone often offer a barrier to the spread of neoplastic tissue. Alteration of the contour of the cortex is not due to "expansion" but to remodeling of the bone in the area and formation of new bone with the new contour. Some tumors induce primarily an osteoblastic or sclerotic reaction in surrounding bone, which results in increased radiodensity. Primary neoplasms may be less radiopaque than surrounding bone or more radiopaque, depending upon the degree of calcification or ossification of the matrix and the density of the tissue. Bone tumors may be recognized because of (1) the presence of a mass in the soft tissues, (2) deformity of a bone, (3) pain and tenderness, or (4) pathologic fractures. Tumors of bone may also be detected incidentally on roentgenograms obtained for other reasons. Although it is usually possible to classify bone tumors as benign or malignant, prediction of the clinical outcome on histologic and radiologic criteria is not always possible.

The extent of the lesions should be defined by standard and computerized tomographic techniques and magnetic resonance imaging, if available. Lesions can also be assessed by bone scans utilizing ^{99m}Tc polyphosphonate. There are numerous pitfalls in the clinical diagnosis and interpretation of histologic features of tumors of bone. However, proper evaluation and selection of therapy require evaluation of both radiographic and histologic features. Management, therefore, requires cooperation of the orthopedist, oncologist, radiologist, radiotherapist, and pathologist.

BENIGN TUMORS The most common benign tumors are *osteochondromas* (exostoses) and *endochondromas* (which may be multiple in Ollier's disease), *benign giant cell tumors, unicameral bone cysts, osteoid osteomas,* and *nonossifying fibromas* (fibrous cortical defects). As a rule benign tumors are not painful except for osteoid osteomas, benign chondroblastomas, and benign chondromyxoidfibroma. The usual clinical problem is that of slowly progressing mass, pathologic fracture, or deformity. Treatment is usually accomplished by resection or curettage and bone grafting. When wide resection of tissue is necessary, insertion of metal and plastic prostheses or allograft transplantation may preserve limb function.

MALIGNANT TUMORS The most common malignant tumor of bone is multiple myeloma (see Chap. 258). Primary lymphoma may also arise locally in bone. Malignant tumors of nonhematopoietic origin include osteosarcomas, chondrosarcomas, fibrosarcomas, and Ewing's tumor. Giant cell tumors may be included here since they may metastasize and are locally destructive. *Osteogenic sarcomas* are presumed to arise from osteoprogenitor cells and have a wide variation in histopathology, with at least six histologic types. These tumors always contain woven bone at least in small foci, and may contain in addition cartilaginous and fibrous elements. They are most common in the second and third decades and are less common under the age of 10 and over the age of 40. When they occur in older individuals, some predisposing cause is usually present such as Paget's disease, prior exposure to ionizing radiation, or a bone infarct. In primary osteogenic sarcomas the lesions usually arise in the metaphyseal region of long bones, especially in the distal femur, proximal tibia, and proximal humerus. The most common symptoms are pain and swelling which may be present for weeks or months. The roentgenographic features of osteosarcomas depend upon the degree of bone destruction, the extent to which mineralized bone is formed by and within the tumor, and the type of reaction in the surrounding bone. Thus, the lesions may vary from purely lytic lesions to dense areas containing radiopaque lumps, clouds, or spicules of tumor bone in varying patterns of organization. Discontinuities may occur in the cortex surrounding the lesion. In other cases, hyperostotic periosteal reactions may involve grossly layered bone. If the tumor grows rapidly, it may destroy the cortex and penetrate the soft tissue surrounding the bone; it leaves only a cuff of periosteal new bone at the peripheral margin of the tumor, just at the point of penetration (Codman's triangle). High plasma alkaline phosphatase levels in those sarcomas that are predominantly osteogenic parallel the course of the tumor. When lesions are adequately treated by amputation, chemotherapy, or radiation, the level of alkaline phosphatase falls, and when metastases appear, the level rises again, often reaching values higher than those present initially. When values are initially high, the course is often rapidly fatal. Metastases occur primarily by the hematogenous route especially to the lung.

The prognosis of osteosarcoma was very poor prior to development of effective chemotherapy, with radiologic evidence of pulmonary metastases usually occurring within a year following surgical amputation that was potentially curative. The course varies with the type of tumor; for example, a "telangiectatic" variant has a very poor prognosis, unless treated with aggressive chemotherapy, whereas the less common low-grade intramedullary type has a better prognosis. In the typical intramedullary type of osteosarcoma, death occurs within 6 months from the onset of detectable pulmonary metastases, suggesting that the lesions in the lungs were present at the time of amputation or that cells were shed from the tumor during the operation.

Several chemotherapeutic programs are efficacious. The disease-free and overall survival rates of patients with nonmetastatic disease have increased from about 20 percent when the programs were first developed to 60 to 80 percent in 1985. Chemotherapeutic agents include high-dose methotrexate with leukovorum rescue, doxorubicin, cisplatin, and the combination of bleomycin, cyclophosphamide, and dactinomycin. Survival is also improved by resection of pulmonary metastases. Additional approaches include limb-sparing surgical resection and attempts to resect lesions such as pelvic osteosarcomas which were previously considered to be unresectable. Surgery of osteosarcomas, primarily amputation, still has an important place in therapy.

Chondrosarcomas are distinguishable from osteogenic sarcomas. In contrast to the latter, chondrosarcomas usually arise in adulthood and old age, with the peak incidence in the fourth, fifth, and sixth decades. Most are located in the pelvic girdle, ribs, and diaphyseal portions of the femur and humerus; distal portions of the extremities are involved rarely. Chondrosarcomas probably arise by malignant transformation in enchondromas and more rarely in the cartilaginous cap of osteochondromas. As a rule, chondrosarcomas are slow growing and slow to recur. Radiographically the lesions appear destructive, with mottled increases in radiodensity which reflect the variable degree of calcification of cartilaginous matrix and ossification. Radical excision is the treatment of choice. Histologic grading of the tumor can be valuable for predicting prognosis and determining appropriate surgical therapy.

Ewing's tumor This is a malignant sarcoma composed of small, round cells that occurs most frequently in the first three decades of life. Most are located in the long bones, although any bone may be involved. Ewing's sarcoma is highly malignant with a low incidence of cure by ablative surgery with or without radiation. However, combined radiation therapy and chemotherapy with doxorubicin, cyclophosphamide, vincristine, and dactinomycin improves survival of patients with Ewing's sarcoma, including some with metastatic disease.

TUMORS METASTATIC TO BONE The skeleton is a common site for metastases from carcinomas and occasionally even from sarcomas. Skeletal metastases may be silent or produce symptoms by the same mechanisms as primary tumors, i.e., pain, swelling, deformity, encroachment on hematopoietic tissue in the marrow, compression of spinal cord or nerve roots, and pathologic fractures. In addition, rapidly lytic skeletal metastases can result in hypercalcemia. The bones involved most commonly are the vertebrae, proximal femur, pelvis, ribs, sternum, and proximal humerus, in that order of frequency. The carcinomas that most frequently metastasize to bone arise in prostate, breast, lung, thyroid, kidney, and bladder. Malignant cells reach the skeleton via the bloodstream. Those that survive may

proliferate and distort the normal architecture, probably by production of substances that cause dissolution of both mineral phase and organic matrix.

Osteolysis most often results from modulation of osteoprogenitor cells to osteoclasts in the surrounding bone. Some mediators involved in induction of osteoclasts were described earlier in this section. Some carcinoma cells may also act directly to resorb bone. Carcinomatous metastases (which are usually predominantly osteolytic) arise from thyroid, kidney, and lower bowel. Other tumors induce *osteoblastic* response in which the new bone does not arise from the tumor itself, but is induced from normal skeletal cells by some product(s) of the tumor cells. The resulting lesion may be more dense than the surrounding tissue. Occasionally the increase in radiodensity is uniform, simulating osteosclerosis. Carcinoma of the prostate characteristically produces osteoblastic metastases. Carcinoma of the breast can cause both osteolytic and osteoblastic metastases. Malignant carcinoid tumors arising from the embryonic foregut and hindgut metastasize to bone with high frequency, producing an osteoblastic reaction. Hodgkin's disease in bone also produces an osteoblastic response both focal and diffuse. More malignant lymphomas in bone produce predominantly destructive lesions. As a rule, osteolytic metastases are the ones associated with hypercalcemia, hypercalciuria, and increased excretion of hydroxyproline-containing peptides (reflecting matrix destruction); they are usually associated with normal or only slightly increased levels of serum alkaline phosphatase. Osteoblastic metastases, on the other hand, may cause more marked elevations of serum alkaline phosphatase and may be associated with hypocalcemia. With some metastases (as in carcinoma of the breast) there may be phases in which osteolysis predominates (with hypercalciuria, hypercalcemia, and normal alkaline phosphatase levels) alternating with phases in which alkaline phosphatase levels rise and the skeletal lesions become more sclerotic.

Treatment of skeletal metastases is usually palliative. In slowly growing localized lesions (as in some instances of carcinoma of the thyroid or occasionally in carcinoma of the kidney), local radiation is useful to relieve pain or reduce compression of surrounding structures. Many patients with carcinomas of breast or prostate survive for years even after extensive skeletal metastases are recognized. Castration and estrogen therapy or receptor antagonists may slow the progress of the lesions in patients with metastatic prostatic carcinoma (see Chap. 298). When patients with mammary cancer are treated with estrogens or androgens, the character of the reaction to the metastases may temporarily shift from a predominantly osteoblastic to a lytic phase with resultant hypercalcemia (see Chap. 295). Plicamycin, which inhibits osteoclast function and is effective in treating hypercalcemia associated with malignant disease, may also be useful in palliation of osteolytic metastases. Etidronate, which has been used to decrease bone resorption in Paget's disease, also decreases the bone resorption secondary to malignant disease. The bone pain in patients with metastatic carcinoma may be relieved by the use of levodopa. Hypercalcemia in patients with malignant tumors is not due solely to skeletal metastases, although this is the most common cause. Production of circulating stimulators of osteoclast activity by extraosseous neoplasms is one cause of the humoral hypercalcemia of malignancy. Hypercalcemia per se, whether spontaneous or induced by therapy, may produce anorexia, polyuria, polydipsia, depression, and eventually coma. In addition, nephrocalcinosis can result from hypercalcemia, and death may result from renal insufficiency.

OTHER DISORDERS OF BONE AND CARTILAGE

FIBROUS DYSPLASIA (ALBRIGHT'S SYNDROME) This syndrome is characterized by osteitis fibrosa disseminata, areas of pigmentation, and endocrine dysfunction, with precocious puberty in females. The bony lesions, called *fibrous dysplasia,* may occur in the absence of the other features. The fundamental nature of the disorder is unknown; the disease does not appear to be heritable, although it has been

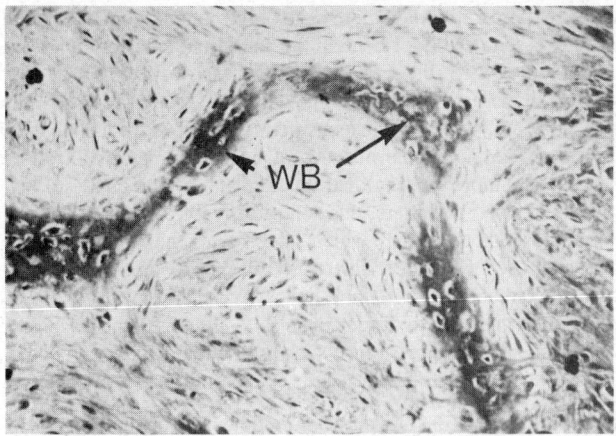

FIGURE 339-3 *Photomicrograph of the lesion of fibrous dysplasia. Note spicules of dark-staining woven bone (WB) surrounded by loose fibroblastic tissue.*

reported to affect monozygotic twins. The disease occurs with equal frequency in both sexes.

Incidence The disease may be divided into three main categories: (1) monostotic, (2) polyostotic, and (3) Albright's syndrome and its variants. The monostotic form is the most common. It can be asymptomatic or lead to a pathologic fracture. The majority of the lesions are in the ribs or in the craniofacial bones, especially the maxillas. Many other bones may be affected, however, such as metaphyseal or diaphyseal portions of the proximal femurs or tibias. Monostotic fibrous dysplasia is most often diagnosed between 20 and 30 years of age. There are usually no associated skin lesions. Approximately a quarter of the individuals with the polyostotic form have more than half the skeleton involved by disease. One side of the body may be affected, and the lesions may be distributed segmentally in a limb, particularly in the lower extremities. Craniofacial lesions are present in approximately half of patients with the polyostotic form. Whereas the monostotic form is usually detected in young adults, fractures and skeletal deformities occur in childhood in the polyostotic form; the disease is generally more severe and deforming with early clinical onset. Lesions, especially monostotic lesions, may become quiescent around the time of puberty and may worsen during pregnancy. Albright's syndrome is more common in females. Short stature is ascribed to premature closure of the epiphyses. The most frequent extraskeletal manifestations are the skin lesions.

Pathology All forms of fibrous dysplasia have an identical histologic appearance, although cartilage is more commonly involved in the polyostotic form. The marrow cavity is filled by gritty, gray-pink, rubbery tissue that replaces the normal cancellous bone. Often, the endosteal cortical surface is scalloped. Histologically, the lesions contain benign-appearing fibroblastic tissue arranged in a loose whorled pattern (Fig. 339-3). The grittiness is due to irregularly arranged woven bone spicules, most of which lack osteoblastic palisading or rimming, which are embedded in the fibrous tissue. These bone spicules may also have prominent cement lines. In approximately 10 percent of cases, islands of hyaline cartilage are present, and more rarely, myxoid tissue may predominate in young patients. Examination by polarized light and with the use of special stains indicates a contiguity of collagen fibers of the osseous and marrow tissue. In the polyostotic form cystic degeneration may be characterized by the presence of hemorrhage with hemosiderin-containing macrophages and osteoclast-type giant cells in the periphery of the cyst. Malignant degeneration into a sarcoma (osteosarcoma, chondrosarcoma, fibrosarcoma) occurs rarely, and in most instances these sarcomas arise in previously radiated lesions. Ossifying fibroma of long bones is a peculiar fibroosseous cortical lesion which may be a variant of fibrous dysplasia. It is most common in the tibial shaft

of teenagers. Although benign, the lesion has a tendency to recur if not adequately excised.

Radiologic changes The roentgenographic appearance of the lesions is that of a radiolucent area with a well-delineated, smooth or scalloped border, typically associated with focal thinning of the cortex of the bone (Fig. 339-4). Fibrous dysplasia and Paget's disease of bone are two disorders that can cause a bone to become larger than normal. The lesions of fibrous dysplasia are not usually cysts in the strict sense, since they are not fluid-filled cavities. They occasionally appear multiloculate. The so-called ground glass appearance reflects the content of the thin spicules of calcified, woven bone. Frequently, deformities are present such as coxa vara, shepherd's-crook deformity of the femur, bowing of the tibia, Harrison's grooves, and protrusio acetabuli. Involvement of facial bones, usually with lesions of increased radiodensity, may create a leonine appearance (leontiasis ossea) superficially resembling leprosy. Fibrous dysplasia of the temporal bones can cause progressive loss of hearing and obliteration of the external ear canal. Advanced skeletal age in females is correlated with sexual precocity but may also be seen in males without sexual precocity. The lesions tend to spare the epiphyseal regions before puberty, but in older individuals fibrous dysplasia may develop in the epiphyses. Occasionally, a focus of fibrous dysplasia may undergo cystic degeneration with an enormous distortion of the shape of the bone, and mimic the so-called aneurysmal bone cyst.

Clinical picture The clinical course is highly variable. Skeletal lesions are usually detected because of deformity or fractures. Symptoms ascribable to bone involvement are headache, seizures, cranial nerve abnormalities, hearing loss, narrowing of the external

FIGURE 339-4 *Roentgenogram of the upper extremity from a 33-year-old woman with fibrous dysplasia of bone. Typical lesions involve the entire humerus as well as the scapula and proximal ulna.*

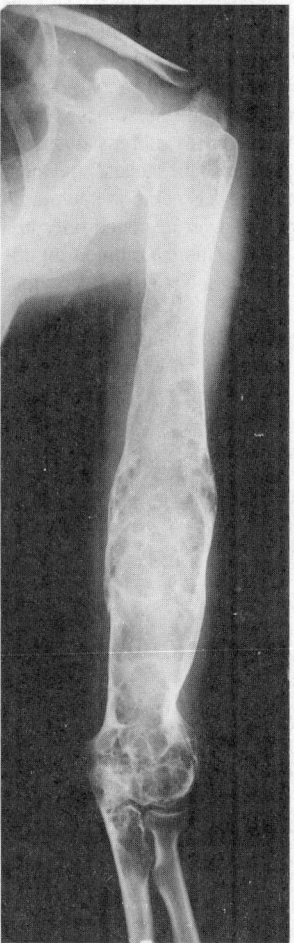

ear canal, or even spontaneous scalp hemorrhages if there is cranio-facial bone disease. In some females and even less commonly in males sexual precocity is the presenting complaint, occasionally before the appearance of skeletal symptoms. Serum calcium and phosphorus values are usually normal. In approximately one-third of patients levels of serum alkaline phosphatase may be elevated to high values, and urinary hydroxyproline excretion is often increased. In some subjects, high cardiac output similar to that in extensive Paget's disease may be found. In general, patients with extensive involvement have widespread disease when symptoms first appear, whereas when disease is mild at the onset extensive disease does not usually develop.

The cutaneous pigmentation in most patients with Albright's syndrome consists of isolated dark-brown to light-brown macules which tend to remain on one side of the midline (Fig. 339-5). The border is usually, although not always, irregular or jagged ("coast of Maine") in contrast to the smooth borders of the pigmented macules of neurofibromatosis ("coast of California"). As a rule there are fewer than six of the lesions, which range in size from 1 cm to those covering very large areas, particularly the back, buttocks, or sacral regions. When the lesions are present in the scalp, the overlying hair may be more deeply pigmented than that over the remainder of the scalp. Localized alopecia is associated with osteomas of the skin, and such lesions tend to have concordance with the skeletal lesions. The pigmentation tends to be on the same side as the skeletal lesions and actually overlie them.

The sexual precocity of unknown cause is found in females and rarely in males (see also Chaps. 330 and 331). Premature vaginal bleeding and development of axillary and pubic hair and of breasts are the main features. In the few ovaries that have been examined, no corpora lutea have been seen. The cause of the precocious sexuality is still not clear. In the few cases where measurements have been reported, the girls have high estrogen levels and low or undetectable gonadotropins. In one studied case gonadotropin levels did not respond to luteinizing hormone–releasing hormone (LHRH). Precocious sexuality is not limited to patients with cranial involvement, and the characteristic pigmented macules are usual but not invariable. Another endocrine abnormality with increased frequency is hyperthyroidism. Rarer associations include Cushing's syndrome, acromegaly, possibly hypogonadotropic hypogonadism, and soft tissue myxomas. Hypophosphatemic osteomalacia may also accompany fibrous dysplasia and resembles the disorder associated with other skeletal and non-skeletal tumors. As mentioned, sarcomatous degeneration may rarely occur in fibrous dysplasia. Sarcomatous changes are found only in a focus of preexisting fibrous dysplasia, are more common in the polyostotic forms, and have usually been associated with previous radiation of the lesions.

Although the lytic lesions of fibrous dysplasia resemble the brown tumors of hyperparathyroidism, the age of the patient, normal calcium levels, increased density of bone in the skull, and areas of cutaneous pigmentation identify the former condition. However, fibrous dysplasia and hyperparathyroidism may coexist. Neurofibromas may involve bone and produce cutaneous pigmentation as well as nodules in the skin. The pigmented macules of neurofibromatosis are more numerous and more widely distributed than in fibrous dysplasia, usually have smooth borders, and tend to involve areas such as the axillary folds. Other lesions which have roentgenographic features similar to those of isolated fibrous dysplasia are unicameral bone cysts, aneurysmal bone cysts, and nonossifying fibromas. Leontiasis ossea is most often due to fibrous dysplasia, although other disorders may also produce this appearance such as craniometaphyseal dysplasia, hyperphosphatasia, and, in adults, Paget's disease.

Treatment Fibrous dysplasia is not curable. The symptoms, however, can be managed using a variety of orthopedic procedures such as osteotomy, curettage, and bone grafting. Indications for such procedures include progressive deformity, nonunion of fractures, and pain unresponsive to conservative treatment. Calcitonin may be effective in treatment of widespread disease associated with bone pain and high serum alkaline phosphatase levels (see Chap. 338).

DYSPLASIAS AND CHONDRODYSTROPHIES A variety of diseases of bone and cartilage have been called *dystrophies* or *dysplasias*. The underlying defect is not usually known. It is possible that a biochemical lesion, such as the defect in the metabolism of the mucopolysaccharides in Hunter's and Hurler's syndromes, will also be found in a number of these disorders and permit more than a descriptive classification. However, a useful scheme has been proposed by Rubin based on the consideration of errors in modeling of bone and cartilage (Table 339-2). Other clinical and genetic features form the basis of a classification by Rimoin. Pathologic processes in the skeletal dysplasias may be expressed as a deficiency (hypoplasia) or excess (hyperplasia) in relation to normal development.

Spondyloepiphyseal dysplasia The spondyloepiphyseal dysplasias are disorders in which abnormalities of growth occur in various bones including the vertebrae, pelvis, carpal and tarsal bones, and the epiphyses of tubular bones. On the basis of roentgenographic findings, this group can be divided into (1) those with generalized platyspondyly, (2) those with multiple epiphyseal dysplasias, and (3) those with epiphysometaphyseal dysplasias. *Morquio's syndrome,* a mucopolysaccharidosis inherited as an autosomal recessive trait and associated with corneal opacities, dental defects, variable disturbances in intellect, and increased urinary excretion of keratosulfate, belongs in the first group. Other forms of spondyloepiphyseal dysplasias show no abnormality in mucopolysaccharide metabolism and are sometimes

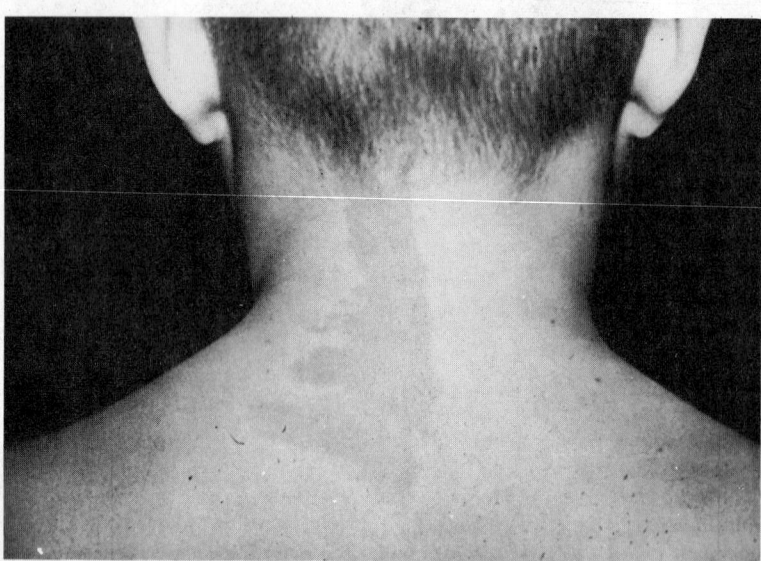

FIGURE 339-5 *Typical pigmented café au lait lesion of the skin in an 11-year-old boy with polyostotic fibrous dysplasia. The border has the jagged "coast of Maine" appearance that is characteristic of Albright's syndrome. Note that the lesion is limited to one side (left) of the body.*

TABLE 339-2 **Working classification of bone dysplasias**

I Epiphyseal dysplasias
  A Epiphyseal hypoplasias
    1 Failure of articular cartilage: spondyloepiphyseal dysplasia, congenita and tarda
    2 Failure of ossification of center: multiple epiphyseal dysplasia, congenita and tarda
  B Epiphyseal hyperplasia
    1 Excess of articular cartilage: dysplasia epiphysialis hemimelica
II Physeal (growth plate) dysplasias
  A Cartilage hypoplasias
    1 Failure of proliferating cartilage: achondroplasia, congenita and tarda
    2 Failure of hypertrophic cartilage: metaphyseal dysostosis, congenita and tarda
  B Cartilage hyperplasias
    1 Excess of proliferating cartilage: hyperchondroplasia
    2 Excess of hypertrophic cartilage: enchondromatosis
III Metaphyseal dysplasias
  A Metaphyseal hypoplasias
    1 Failure to form primary spongiosa: hypophosphatasia, congenita and tarda
    2 Failure to absorb primary spongiosa: osteopetrosis, congenita and tarda
    3 Failure to absorb secondary spongiosa: craniometaphyseal dysplasia, congenita and tarda
  B Metaphyseal hyperplasia
    1 Excessive spongiosa: familial exostosis
IV Diaphyseal dysplasias
  A Diaphyseal hypoplasias
    1 Failure of periosteal bone formation: osteogenesis imperfecta, congenita and tarda
    2 Failure of endosteal bone formation: idiopathic osteoporosis
  B Diaphyseal hyperplasias
    1 Excessive periosteal bone formation: Engelmann's disease
    2 Excessive periosteal bone formation: hyperphosphatasia

not recognized until late in childhood. Flat vertebral bodies are associated with other abnormalities in shape and alignment. The disordered development of the capital femoral epiphyses leads to irregularities in shape and flattening of the femoral heads and early onset of osteoarthritis of the hips.

Achondroplasia *Achondroplasia* is a physeal dysplasia in which dwarfism results from decrease in the proliferation of cartilage in the growth plate. This disorder is among the more common types of dwarfism and is inherited as an autosomal dominant trait. Histologic sections through the growth plate show a thin zone of cartilage cells with absence or abbreviation of the normal columnar arrangement and zone of provisional calcification, although endochondral ossification may not be completely disorganized. Formation of the primary spongiosa is reduced since there is often a transverse bar of bone sealing off the plate from further endochondral ossification. However, formation and maturation of the secondary ossification centers and articular cartilage are not disturbed. Appositional growth at the metaphysis continues, with resulting flare in this region of the bone; intramembranous bone formation at the periosteum is normal. The abnormal proliferation at the growth plate, leaving other areas relatively unaffected in the tubular bones, causes production of short bones that are proportionately thick. However, the length of the spine is almost always normal. The appearance of short limbs with a normal trunk is characteristically accompanied by a large head, saddlenose, and an exaggerated lumbar lordosis. The disease is usually recognized at birth. Those who survive the period of infancy usually have normal mental and sexual development, and life span may be normal. However, spinal deformity may lead to cord compression and nerve root encroachment, especially in those with kyphoscoliosis. Homozygous achondroplasia is a more serious disorder and a cause of neonatal death.

Enchondromatosis (dyschondroplasia, Ollier's disease) This is also a disorder affecting the growth plate in which the hypertrophic cartilage is not resorbed and ossified in a normal fashion. It results in masses of cartilage with disorderly arrangement of the chondrocytes showing variable proliferative and hypertrophic changes. These masses are located in the metaphyses in close association with the growth plate in very young patients but often are diaphyseal in teenagers and young adults. The disorder is usually recognized in childhood by the appearance of deformities or retardation in growth. The most common sites of involvement are the ends of long bones, usually in the region where rate of growth is most marked. The pelvis is often involved, but ribs, sternum, and skull are seldom affected. There is also a tendency toward unilateral involvement. Chondrosarcoma develops occasionally in the enchondromata. The association of enchondromatosis and cavernous hemangiomata in the soft tissues including the skin is known as Maffucci's syndrome.

Multiple exostoses (diaphyseal aclasis or osteochondromatosis) This is a disorder of the metaphysis, inherited as an autosomal dominant character, in which areas of the growth plate become displaced, presumably by growing through a defect in the perichondrium or so-called ring of Ranvier. The spongiosa forms within the mass as vessels invade the cartilage. Therefore, the diagnostic radiographic finding is the direct continuity of the mass to the marrow cavity of the parent bone with absence of underlying cortex. Usually the growth of these exostoses ceases when growth of the adjacent plate ceases. The lesions may be solitary or multiple and are usually located in the metaphyseal areas of long bones with the apex of the exostosis directed toward the diaphysis. Often the lesions produce no symptoms, but occasionally interference with the function of a joint or tendon or compression of nerves may result. Dwarfism may occur. The metacarpals may be shortened, resembling those seen in Albright's hereditary osteodystrophy. Multiple exostoses are sometimes seen in patients with pseudohypoparathyroidism.

An exostosis may suddenly begin to enlarge long after growth should have ceased, and rarely chondrosarcomas may develop from the cartilage cap of an exostosis. Pregnancy may stimulate growth of an exostosis that clinically may mimic malignancy. However, the lesion merely undergoes exuberant endochondral ossification and cartilage hyperplasia without malignant changes.

RELAPSING POLYCHONDRITIS See Chap. 278.

TIETZE'S SYNDROME (COSTOCHONDRAL SYNDROME) See Chap. 278.

REFERENCES

Hyperostosis

CANALIS E et al: Dynamic bone morphology and studies on the effects of serum on bone metabolism in vitro in a case of pycnodysostosis. Metab Bone Dis Rel Res 2:99, 1981

CHAN Y-L et al: Dialysis osteodystrophy: A study involving 94 patients. Medicine 64:296, 1985

COCCIA PF et al: Successful bone-marrow transplantation for infantile malignant osteopetrosis. N Engl J Med 302:701, 1980

———: Cells that resorb bone. N Engl J Med 310:456, 1984

COINDRE JM et al: Histomorphometric analysis of sclerotic bone from idiopathic myeloid metaplasia (nine cases). J Pathol 144:163, 1984

CRISP AJ, BRENTON DP: Engelmann's disease of bone—a systemic disorder? Ann Rheum Dis 41:183, 1982

ELMORE SM et al: Pycnodysostosis, with a familial chromosome anomaly. Am J Med 40:273, 1966

GENANT HK et al: Osteosclerosis in primary hyperparathyroidism. Am J Med 59:104, 1975

JACOBSON HG: Dense bone—too much bone: Radiological considerations and differential diagnosis. Part II. Skeletal Radiol 13:97, 1985

JAFFE HL: *Metabolic, Degenerative and Inflammatory Disease of Bones and Joints.* Philadelphia, Lea & Febiger, 1972

JOHNSON CC et al: Osteopetrosis: A clinical, genetic, metabolic and morphologic study of the dominantly inherited benign form. Medicine 47:149, 1968

KEY L et al: Treatment of congenital osteopetrosis with high-dose calcitriol. N Engl J Med 310:409, 1984

LORIA-CORTES R et al: Osteopetrosis in children: A report of 26 cases. J Pediatr 91:43, 1977

MANZKE E et al: Skeletal remodelling and bone-related hormones in two adults with increased bone mass. Metabolism 31:25, 1982

SHELDON J et al: Engelmann's disease (progressive diaphyseal dysplasia): A review and presentation of two cases with abnormal phosphate retention. Metab Bone Dis Rel Res 2:307, 1981

SLY WS et al: Carbonic anhydrase II deficiency in 12 families with the autosomal recessive syndrome of osteopetrosis with renal tubular acidosis and cerebral calcification. N Engl J Med 313:139, 1985

SMITH R et al: Clinical and biochemical studies in Engelmann's disease (progressive diphyseal dysplasia). Q J Med 46:273, 1977

SORELL M et al: Marrow transplantation for juvenile osteopetrosis. Am J Med 70:1280, 1981

THOMPSON RC JR et al: Hereditary hyperphosphatasia. Am J Med 47:209, 1969

VAN BUCHEM FSP et al: Hyperostosis corticalis generalisata. Am J Med 33:387, 1962

Neoplasms of Bone

CHARHON SA et al: Parathyroid function and vitamin D status in patients with bone metastases of prostatic origin. Mineral Electrolyte Metab 11:117, 1985

DOUGLAS DL et al: Effect of dichloromethylene diphosphonate in Paget's disease of bone and in hypercalcemia due to primary hyperparathyroidism or malignant disease. Lancet 1:1043, 1980

ETTINGER LJ et al: Adjuvant adriamycin and cisplatin in newly diagnosed, nonmetastatic osteosarcoma of the extremity. J Clin Oncol 4:353, 1986

FECHNER RE et al: A symposium on the pathology of bone tumors. Pathol Ann 19(Part 1):125, 1984

GOORIN AM et al: Osteosarcoma: Fifteen years later. N Engl J Med 313:165, 1985

HAN M-T et al: Aggressive thoracotomy for pulmonary metastatic osteogenic sarcoma in children and young adolescents. J Pediatr Surg 16:928, 1981

JAFFE HL: *Tumors and Tumorous Conditions of the Bones and Joints.* Philadelphia, Lea & Febiger, 1958

LICHTENSTEIN L: *Bone Tumors.* St. Louis, Mosby, 1972

MANKIN HJ: Current concepts. Advances in diagnosis and treatment of bone tumors. N Engl J Med 300:543, 1979

——— et al: Massive resection and allograft transplantation in the treatment of malignant bone tumors. N Engl J Med 294:1247, 1976

MINTON JP: The response of breast cancer patients with bone pain to L-dopa. Cancer 33:358, 1974

MOSELEY JE: *Bone Changes in Hematologic Disorders.* New York, Grune & Stratton, 1963

MUNDY GR et al: Tumor products and the hypercalcemia of malignancy. J Clin Invest 76:391, 1985

ROSEN G et al: Curability of Ewing's sarcoma and considerations for future therapeutic trials. Cancer 41:888, 1978

——— et al: Primary osteogenic sarcoma: The rationale for preoperative chemotherapy and delayed surgery. Cancer 43:2163, 1979

——— et al: Preoperative chemotherapy for osteogenic sarcoma: Selection of postoperative adjuvant chemotherapy based on the response of the primary tumor to preoperative chemotherapy. Cancer 49:1221, 1982

SCHILLER AL: Diagnosis of borderline cartilage lesions of bone. Semin Diag Pathol 2:42, 1985

SIRIS ES et al: Effects of dichloromethylene diphosphonate on skeletal mobilization of calcium in multiple myeloma. N Engl J Med 302:310, 1980

SUTOW WW et al: Survival after metastasis in osteosarcoma. Natl Cancer Inst Monogr 56:227, 1981

UNNI KK et al: Conditions that simulate primary neoplasms of bone. Pathol Ann 15(Part 1):91, 1980

YUNIS EJ, BARNES L: The histologic diversity of osteosarcoma. Pathol Ann 21(Part 1):121, 1986

Other Disorders of Bone and Cartilage

AKESON WH et al: *Symposium on Heritable Disorders of Connective Tissue.* St. Louis, Mosby, 1982

ALBRIGHT FA et al: Syndrome characterized by osteitis fibrosa disseminata, areas of pigmentation and endocrine dysfunction, with precocious puberty in females: Report of five cases. N Engl J Med 216:727, 1937

BENEDICT PH: Endocrine features in Albright's syndrome (fibrous dysplasia of bone). Metabolism 11:30, 1962

——— et al: Melanotic macules in Albright's syndrome and in neurofibromatosis. JAMA 205:618, 1968

DENT CE, GERTNER JM: Hypophosphatemic osteomalacia in fibrous dysplasia. Q J Med 45:411, 1976

GRABIAS SL, CAMPBELL CJ: Fibrous dysplasia. Orthoped Clin North Am 8:771, 1977

GRAF CJ, PERRET GE: Spontaneous recurrent hemorrhage as an unusual complication of fibrous dysplasia of the skull. J Neurosurg 52:570, 1980

HARRIS RI: Polyostotic fibrous dysplasia with acromegaly. Am J Med 78:539, 1985

HARRIS WH et al: The natural history of fibrous dysplasia: An orthopaedic, pathological and roentgenographic study. J Bone Joint Surg (Br) 44A:207, 1962

LICHTENSTEIN L: Polyostotic fibrous dysplasia. Arch Surg 36:874, 1938

NAGER GT et al: Fibrous dysplasia: A review of the disease and its manifestations in the temporal bone. Ann Otol Rhinol Laryngol 91(suppl 92):1, 1982

RIMOIN DL: The chondrodystrophies. Adv Hum Genet 5:1, 1975

RUBIN P: *Dynamic Classification of Bone Dysplasias.* Chicago, Year Book, 1964

SILLENCE DO et al: Neonatal dwarfism. Pediatr Clin North Am 25:431, 1978

STEENDIJK R: Metabolic bone disease in children, in *Metabolic Bone Disease,* LV Avioli, SM Krane (eds). New York, Academic, 1978, vol II, p 633

340　OSTEOMYELITIS

JAN V. HIRSCHMANN

DEFINITION　*Osteomyelitis* denotes infection of bone. While many types of microorganisms, including viruses and fungi, may cause osteomyelitis, it is usually bacterial in origin.

PATHOGENESIS　Organisms reach the bone to cause infection by one of three routes: (1) hematogenous spread, (2) extension from a contiguous site of infection, and (3) direct introduction of organisms into bone by trauma, including surgery.

Acute hematogenous osteomyelitis usually involves bone with rich, red marrow; in children the long bones, especially the femur and tibia, are most frequently affected. The infection begins in the metaphyseal sinusoidal veins, where sluggish blood flow and a paucity of phagocytes favor the growth of organisms. In adults acute hematogenous infection rarely involves the long bones, where adipose tissue has largely replaced the red marrow. Instead, hematogenous osteomyelitis most commonly occurs in the vertebrae, where cellular marrow and an abundant vascular supply exist. The organisms reach the spine directly through the nutrient branches of the posterior spinal artery or, probably less commonly, from retrograde flow through the valveless paravertebral venous plexus of Batson, which drains the vertebral bodies, body wall, and the pelvis. Infection usually begins in the vertebral body near the anterior longitudinal ligament and may spread to adjacent vertebrae by direct extension through the disk space or by a system of freely communicating venous channels. Because the disk in adults possesses no vascular supply, disk space infection in *hematogenous* infections is always secondary to osteomyelitis in an adjacent vertebra.

Osteomyelitis caused by extension from a contiguous site of infection may occur with soft tissue suppuration resulting from trauma, necrosis of a malignant tumor, radiation therapy, burns, pressure sores, or other causes. In patients with vascular insufficiency from diabetes mellitus or atherosclerosis, organisms commonly enter the soft tissues through a cutaneous ulcer, usually in the foot, causing cellulitis and subsequently osteomyelitis. Osteomyelitis of the skull bones may result from underlying sinus or dental infections.

Direct introduction of organisms into bone may occur with open fractures, the open surgical reduction of closed fractures, or penetrating trauma by bullets or other foreign bodies. Osteomyelitis may also occur from perioperative contamination of bone during surgery for nontraumatic orthopedic disorders. Most infections of joint prostheses arise in this way. Because the causative organisms, usually flora like *Staphylococcus epidermidis,* are often not very virulent, clinical manifestations may not appear for months after surgery.

PATHOLOGY　Pathologic findings during the acute phase include neutrophilic inflammation, edema, and vascular congestion. Because of the bone's rigidity, increased intramedullary pressure develops, compromising the blood supply and causing ischemia, cell death, and vascular thrombosis. After several days, the suppurative and ischemic injury may cause the bone to fragment into devitalized segments called *sequestra*. The inflammation spreads via the haversian and Volkmann canals to reach the periosteum, beneath which abscesses may form or through which the purulent material may penetrate to form soft tissue abscesses or sinus tracts.

With persistent infection, chronic inflammatory cells—lymphocytes, histiocytes, and plasma cells—may join the neutrophils. Fibroblastic proliferation and new bone formation also occur. Osteogenesis from the periosteum may surround the inflammation to form a bony envelope or *involucrum*. Occasionally, a dense fibrous capsule confines the infection to a localized area of suppuration, called *Brodie's abscess*. Rarely, exuberant osteogenesis may result in a sclerotic, nonpurulent osteomyelitis (Garré's sclerosing osteomyelitis).

MANIFESTATIONS Hematogenous osteomyelitis The bacteremia causing hematogenous osteomyelitis may be from a urinary infection, bacterial endocarditis, a distant soft tissue infection, or another location. Frequently, the original site is not apparent. Intravenous drug abusers, in whom *Pseudomonas aeruginosa* is the most common infecting organism, and patients receiving chronic hemodialysis are especially at risk for hematogenous osteomyelitis, presumably because of frequent bacteremias. Diabetes mellitus also seems to be a predisposing condition, perhaps because of impaired neutrophil function and frequent infections of the skin and urinary tract, sites from which bacteremias frequently originate.

Vertebral osteomyelitis may occasionally begin abruptly with back pain and systemic signs of infection, but usually the onset is insidious and the course gradually progressive. Persistent back pain, exacerbated by movement and commonly unrelieved by heat, analgesics, or bed rest, is the predominant symptom. Fever is usually minimal or absent. Physical examination typically reveals tenderness to percussion and palpation over the affected vertebrae, guarding and splinting on movement, and paravertebral muscle spasm.

Leukocytosis is usually absent, but the erythrocyte sedimentation rate is almost always increased. The earliest roentgenographic changes are erosion of the subchondral bony plate, narrowing of the intervertebral disk space, and involvement of the adjacent vertebra. Bony destruction follows, sometimes with loss of vertebral height, usually anteriorly. Anterior osteogenesis with coarse bony density and sclerosis may occur. Soft tissue densities, representing paravertebral abscesses, may lie adjacent to the vertebrae. The lumbar vertebrae are most frequently involved, the cervical vertebrae least. While roentgenographic changes may not develop for several weeks following infection, radionuclide scans with technetium pyrophosphate are positive early.

Complications of vertebral osteomyelitis include anterior extension to cause retropharyngeal abscesses, mediastinitis, empyema, pericarditis, subdiaphragmatic abscess, psoas muscle abscess, or peritonitis, depending upon the vertebrae involved. Posterior extension by pus (epidural abscess), bony fragments, or inflammatory tissue can cause spinal cord compression; if infection penetrates the dura to enter the subarachnoid space, meningitis results.

Acute hematogenous osteomyelitis occurring in sites other than the vertebrae is unusual in adults. When it does develop in such locations as the clavicle or the long bones of the extremities, its typical features are pain and evidence of soft tissue infection over the affected bone.

Hematogenous osteomyelitis acquired in childhood may present in adults as intermittent or persistent drainage from sinus tracts communicating with the involved bone—usually the femur, tibia, or humerus—or as a soft tissue infection overlying it. Signs of infection may recur after months or years of quiescence. Roentgenographic changes include bony destruction with radiolucent areas, radiopaque sequestra, and formation of an involucrum. A roentgenogram of contrast material injected into a sinus tract (sinogram) or computed tomography may help define the location and extent of involvement.

Posttraumatic osteomyelitis and osteomyelitis from a contiguous infection The clinical features of these forms of osteomyelitis are a varying combination of local pain, draining sinuses, and heat, swelling, tenderness, and erythema over the involved bone. Patients often are afebrile. Leukocytosis and an elevated erythrocyte sedimentation rate are present in a minority of patients. Radiographic changes are similar to those in chronic hematogenous osteomyelitis. With plates, nails, screws, pins, or prostheses there is frequently evidence of loosening of the appliance. Radionuclide scans with technetium pyrophosphate are nearly always positive. Since increased uptake in these scans depends in part on bone hyperemia, which may occur with adjacent inflammation alone, there may be difficulty in distinguishing early osteomyelitis from cellulitis or a subcutaneous abscess when the roentgenograms do not show bony destruction.

Infection of joint prostheses may become evident shortly after surgery, especially if the infecting organism is virulent. Erythema, warmth, and draining at the operative site are common findings. More frequently, the onset is later, with persistent pain and loosening of the prosthesis developing 3 to 12 months after surgery. Local signs of infection are typically absent, and the white cell count and erythrocyte sedimentation rate are often normal. Distinction from noninfectious mechanical loosening of the prosthesis can be very difficult and depends on isolation of an organism from the joint by arthrocentesis (although in up to 15 percent of infections the aspirate is sterile), or culture of material obtained at surgery.

DIAGNOSIS While radiographic or radionuclide studies may be helpful, definitive diagnosis requires isolation of the responsible organism. If blood cultures are negative (they usually are), patients with suspected vertebral osteomyelitis should undergo needle aspiration of the intervertebral disk space if it appears infected, percutaneous needle biopsy of the infected bone, or open bone biopsy at surgery. Although *Staphylococcus aureus* is the most common cause, aerobic gram-negative bacilli, typically arising from a previous or concurrent urinary infection, are also frequent. Moreover, pyogenic vertebral osteomyelitis is often impossible to differentiate from tuberculous or fungal vertebral osteomyelitis.

In patients with chronic hematogenous osteomyelitis, posttraumatic osteomyelitis, or osteomyelitis from a contiguous infection, the diagnosis is best established by careful cultures, both aerobic and anaerobic, of bone, tissue, or pus from a deep abscess obtained during surgery. These infections are often polymicrobial and sometimes include anaerobic bacteria; precise bacteriologic identification is necessary for appropriate antimicrobial therapy. Cultures of material obtained from draining sinuses are generally unreliable, even if only a single organism grows, because the tracts may become colonized by bacteria present on the skin surface but absent in the infected bone.

TREATMENT Bed rest and appropriate parenteral antimicrobial agents given for 4 to 6 weeks cure most cases of vertebral osteomyelitis.

The antibiotic(s) used in the treatment of osteomyelitis depend on the result of culture and sensitivity tests; the appropriate drugs are detailed in Chap. 88. In general, the first several weeks of therapy should be parenteral in order to achieve adequate levels of antibiotic in bony tissue. If no organisms are culturable, the choice of the antimicrobial must be based on cultures from other sites or, if these are negative, on the clinician's best estimate of the infecting pathogen. When staphylococcal infection is suspected, a penicillinase-resistant penicillin or a cephalosporin should be used.

External stabilization by traction or brace is indicated for an unstable cervical spine but is unnecessary for most patients with thoracic or lumbar osteomyelitis. Surgery is usually necessary only to drain paravertebral or spinal epidural abscesses. With successful therapy, bony bridging and spontaneous fusion of adjacent vertebral bodies occur, and the erythrocyte sedimentation rate returns to normal.

The main treatment of chronic hematogenous osteomyelitis, posttraumatic osteomyelitis, and osteomyelitis from a contiguous infection is surgery, with antimicrobial therapy an important adjunct. Antibiotics alone rarely cure these infections. The major surgical principles are thorough removal of all necrotic bone and tissue and the elimination of dead space. Rigid bone, unlike soft tissue, does not collapse around a site evacuated of pus; the resultant cavity provides an area for blood, debris, and organisms to collect. This dead space may be obliterated by (1) open packing of the wound, allowing the slow process of granulation to fill the defect, (2) packing the cavity with potentially viable grafts from cancellous bone, (3) transfer of a pedicle of skeletal muscle into the cavity, (4) skin grafting directly onto the granulating bone surface, or (5) constant irrigation to keep the cavity free of debris, followed by one of the methods mentioned above. These surgical measures are accompanied by appropriate parenteral antimicrobial therapy for 3 to 6 weeks. Since there are no controlled studies, the optimal choice and duration of antibiotics are unknown, but antimicrobial therapy is clearly doomed to failure unless the surgical debridement is thorough. Sometimes the location or extent of osteomyelitis makes surgical cure short of amputation impossible. In these patients, if amputation is not performed, treatment is given only for acute exacerbations, such as the formation of overlying soft tissue abscesses, where surgical drainage and a short course of antibiotics help control the acute manifestations.

Osteomyelitis associated with a prosthesis generally requires removal of the appliance, thorough debridement, and appropriate antimicrobial therapy. With either quiescent or low-grade infection, a new prosthesis may be implanted at the same operation as the removal of its predecessor; otherwise, the therapeutic choices are excision arthroplasty or replacement of the prosthesis later when the infection subsides.

Osteomyelitis associated with plates, screws, rods, or pins used for the open reduction of fractures also requires removal of the appliance, thorough debridement, and antimicrobial therapy if union of the fracture has occurred. In infected fractures with nonunion, the principles of treatment are the establishment of rigid bony stability and debridement of infected material to permit union to occur. Screws, plates, pins, and rods that have not loosened are left in place, and the wound is treated with open irrigation. If the hardware is loose and fails to provide rigid stability, it is removed, and stability is attained by other means, such as external fixation with pins above and below the fracture site. When the infection is controlled, bone grafts may be necessary for union to occur, but some fractures will unite without them.

In osteomyelitis associated with vascular insufficiency, cure is seldom possible without amputation. With single bone involvement removal of the infected bone may suffice. When many bones are affected, as is common in osteomyelitis of the feet in diabetics, a below-knee amputation is usually necessary.

REFERENCES

BONEAKDAR-POUR A, GAINES VD: The radiology of osteomyelitis. Orthop Clin North Am 14:21, 1983

BURRI C: *Posttraumatic Osteomyelitis.* Bern, Hans Huber, 1975

FITZGERALD RH, KELLY PJ (eds): Musculoskeletal sepsis. Orthop Clin North Am, July 1984

GRISTINA AG, KOLKIN J: Total joint replacement and sepsis. J Bone Joint Surg 65-A: 128, 1983

LEWIS RP et al: Bone infections involving anaerobic bacteria. Medicine 57:279, 1978

MACKOWIAK PA et al: Diagnostic value of sinus tract cultures in chronic osteomyelitis. JAMA 239:2772, 1978

SUGARMAN B et al: Osteomyelitis beneath pressure sores. Arch Intern Med 143:683, 1983

WALDVOGEL FA et al: Osteomyelitis: A review of clinical features, therapeutic considerations, and unusual aspects. N Engl J Med 282:198, 260, 316, 1970

———, VASEY H: Osteomyelitis: The past decade. N Engl J Med 303:360, 1980

section 1 Disorders of the central nervous system

341 DIAGNOSTIC METHODS IN NEUROLOGY

KEITH H. CHIAPPA / JOSEPH B. MARTIN / ROBERT R. YOUNG

The analysis and interpretation of data elicited by a careful history and examination may prove to be adequate for diagnosis in clinical neurology; special laboratory tests can then do no more than corroborate the initial impression. But more often the final conclusion of the nature of the disease is not reached by simple case study. The possibilities may be reduced to two or three, but the correct diagnosis cannot be determined. Under these conditions, one resorts to one or several of the laboratory tests outlined below.

It must be stressed that laboratory procedures should follow rather than precede clinical case study, except in emergencies when the disease threatens life and time does not allow detailed clinical observation. Laboratory procedures are but a part of the clinical method outlined in Chap. 10. Because many of the procedures are costly, time-consuming, and occasionally dangerous or painful, they should be undertaken only for the specific purpose of obtaining certain othewise unavailable data that can shed light on the clinical problem.

LUMBAR PUNCTURE AND EXAMINATION OF CEREBROSPINAL FLUID The information yielded by the examination of the cerebrospinal fluid (CSF) is often of crucial importance.

Indications for lumbar puncture Lumbar puncture is performed for the following reasons:

1 To obtain pressure measurements and to secure a sample of CSF for cellular, chemical, and bacteriologic examination.
2 To aid in therapy by the administration of spinal anesthetics and occasionally antibiotics or antitumor agents.
3 To inject air for air contrast myelography or, rarely, for pneumoencephalography; a radiopaque substance (Pantopaque) or a water-soluble contrast medium for myelography; or a radioactive substance [e.g., indium or radioactive iodinated serum albumin (RISA)] for the study of CSF dynamics and to aid in the diagnosis of hydrocephalus or CSF leak.

Lumbar puncture carries a risk if the CSF pressure is high (evidenced by headache and papilledema), for it increases the possibility of fatal cerebellar or tentorial herniation. In doubtful cases, it is wise first to obtain a computerized tomography (CT) or magnetic resonance imaging (MRI) scan to exclude a mass lesion before proceeding to perform a lumbar puncture. However, if it seems important in a given case of suspected increased intracranial pressure

to have the information yielded by CSF examination, the lumbar puncture may be performed with a fine-bore (no. 22 or 24 gauge) needle as the last part of the clinical study. (Note that if the pressure is over 400 mmHg, one should obtain the necessary sample of fluid, remove the needle, and then, according to the suspected clinical disease and patient's condition, administer a unit of urea or mannitol.) Dexamethasone (Decadron) should be started in a dose of 4 to 6 mg every 6 h in cases of tumor, cerebral trauma, hemorrhage, and certain types of encephalitis (acute hemorrhagic leukoencephalitis, herpes simplex encephalitis).

Cisternal puncture and lateral cervical puncture (C1–C2), although safe in the hands of the expert, are too hazardous to entrust to those without experience. The lumbar puncture is to be preferred except in obvious instances of spinal block requiring a sample of cisternal fluid or myelography above the lesions, or in rare instances where infection of the skin or subcutaneous tissue render needle penetration dangerous.

Experience teaches the importance of meticulous technique. Lumbar puncture should always be done under sterile conditions. If procaine is injected in and beneath the skin, the procedure should be painless. Failure to enter the lumbar subarachnoid space after two or three trials can usually be corrected by doing the puncture with patients in the sitting position and then assisting them to lie on their side for pressure measurements and fluid removal. The "dry tap" is more often due to an improperly placed needle than to a pathologic obliteration of subarachnoid space by compressive lesion of the spinal cord or chronic adhesive arachnoiditis. A bloody tap due to transfixation of a meningeal vessel may result in hopeless confusion of the diagnosis if it is falsely interpreted as indicating hemorrhage in the subarachnoid spaces and ventricles. Lumbar puncture should be undertaken with particular care in patients with thrombocytopenia or disorders of blood coagulation because serious hemorrhage into the extradural or intradural space may occur.

Examination procedures Once the lumbar puncture is successful, some or all of the following aspects of the CSF should be studied: (1) pressure and "dynamics"; (2) gross appearance of CSF including centrifugation, if blood is present, to examine the supernatant for xanthochromia; (3) number and type of cells and presence of microorganisms; (4) protein, sugar, and, in special instances, analysis of pigments; (5) exfoliative cytology using Millipore filters; (6) Wassermann reaction and appropriate serologic precipitation reactions; (7) protein immunoelectrophoresis for determination of gamma globulin levels, and other special biochemical tests (for NH_3, pH, CO_2, enzymes, etc.); and (8) bacteriologic cultures and virus isolation. See the appendix for normal values of CSF.

RADIOLOGIC EXAMINATION OF SKULL AND SPINE Plain x-rays of the skull or spinal column, according to the nature of the symptoms, constitute an indispensable part of the thorough study of traumatic,

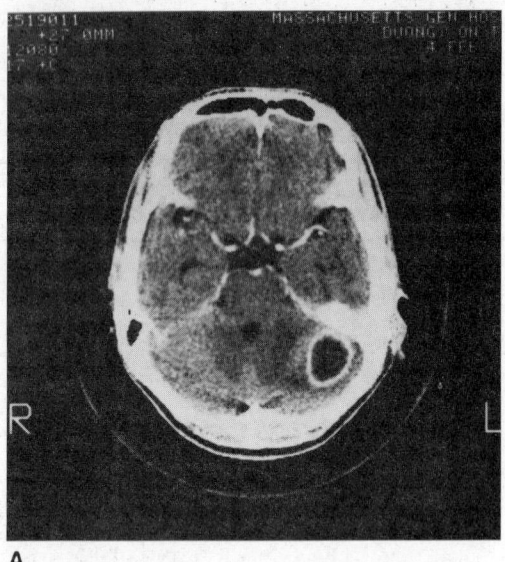

A

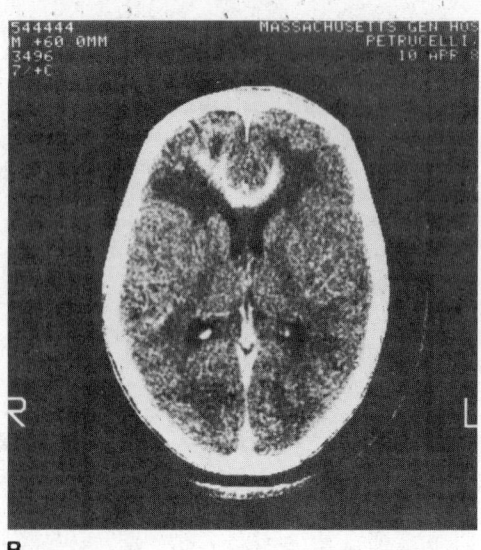

B

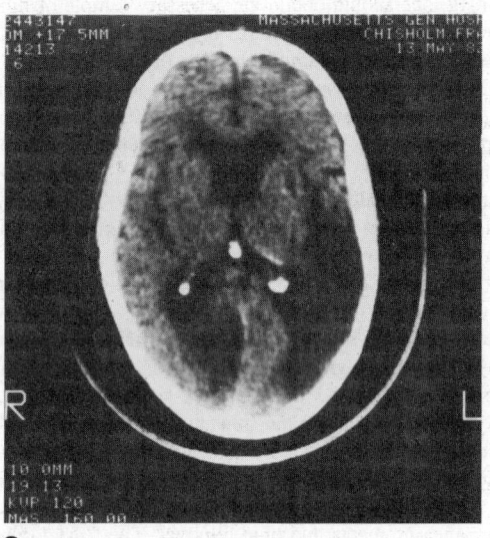

C

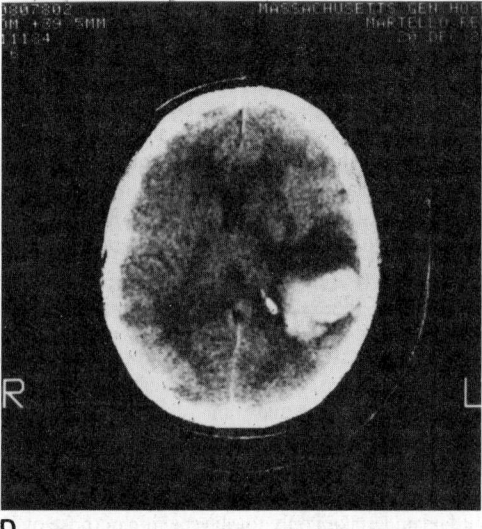

D

FIGURE 341-1 *Computerized tomography scans in disease. Frontal lobes above; right hemisphere to viewer's left. A. Left cerebellar abscess arising as a complication of mastoid sinus infection. Typical "ring" enhancement is evident in contrast-enhanced scan. B. Malignant astrocytoma infiltrating corpus callosum and bifrontal white matter. Edema surrounding tumor in frontal lobes is shown. C. Large cerebral infarcts, bilateral. Infarct on right is in distribution of posterior cerebral artery, that on left in distribution of middle cerebral artery. D. Intracerebral hematoma in left parietal lobe. Blood in hemorrhage is evident without administration of contrast media. E. Cerebral cortical atrophy in Alzheimer's disease.*

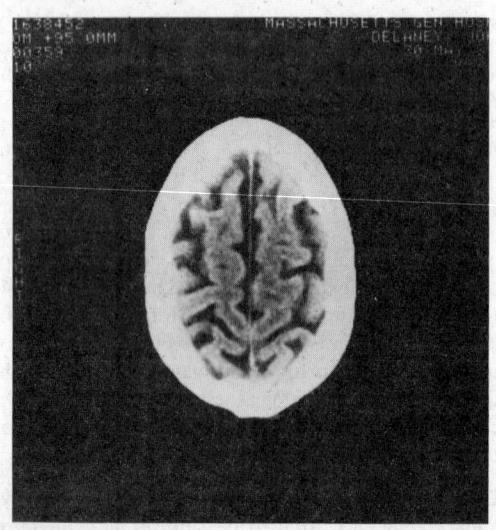

E

spondylitic, and neoplastic diseases but are of relatively little value in others. The procedure is relatively simple, and the findings are interpretable by most general radiologists. Space does not permit an illustration of such common findings as fractures, bone erosion, intracerebral calcifications, premature closure or separation of sutures, or alterations of skull configuration.

Of more specific value in neurology and neurosurgery are six special radiologic procedures which now permit the visualization of most parts of the brain and spinal cord and their vessels.

Computerized tomography (CT scan) This radiologic procedure, which computerizes the absorption offered by brain, CSF, and skull to more than thirty thousand 2- to 4-mm beams of x-ray and permits

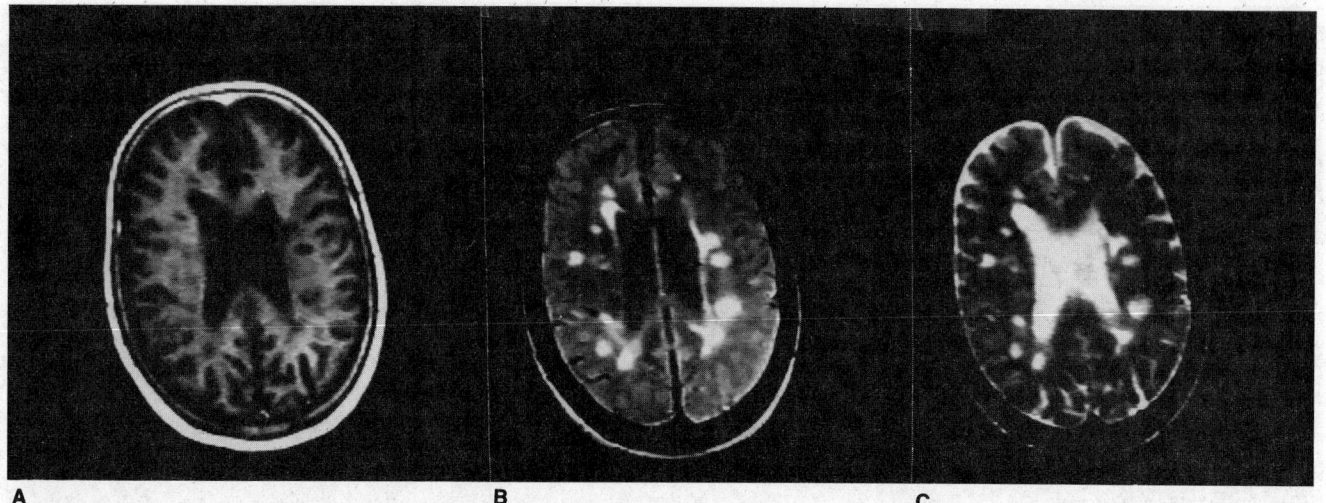

A   B   C

FIGURE 341-2 *Multiple sclerosis (MS) demonstrated by magnetic resonance imaging (MRI). Multiple foci of abnormally prolonged T1 and T2 relaxation times are evident in the white matter. In T1 MRI (A), MS plaques show decreased density. In T2 weighted images (B and C), plaques show increased signal intensity. A mild degree of brain atrophy is best noted in (C), where cerebrospinal fluid signal is brightest. Although the frequency, location, and distribution of such lesions in large numbers of patients with multiple sclerosis strongly suggest that the foci of abnormal relaxation may represent plaques, there has been a dearth of pathological confirmation. A. IR study: TR = 1500, TI = 450, TE = 20. B. SE study: TR = 2000, TE = 60. C. As in B, but TE = 120.*

visualization of the ventricles, subarachnoid space, and the major cisternal fissures and sulci in several horizontal planes (Fig. 341-1A to E), has become available in most medical centers and has replaced plain x-rays and most of the other contrast procedures such as pneumoencephalography and arteriography. It differentiates epidural, subdural, and intracerebral hemorrhages and deformities of the ventricular system from "mass" lesions, and demonstrates tumors, abscesses, granulomas [when done after an intravenous injection of meglumine diatrizoate (Renografin) or other contrast medium], as well as areas of brain edema and infarction, hydrocephalus, and brain atrophy. The simplicity of this noninvasive procedure, its low risk to patients with expanding lesions, and the low exposure to x-ray have virtually revolutionized diagnostic neurology and neurosurgery.

Magnetic resonance imaging The recent application of magnetic resonance imaging (MRI) has permitted the visualization of cerebral lesions not evident on CT scans (Figs. 341-2 to 341-4). MRI is noninvasive and does not involve exposure to ionizing radiation. The technique permits delineation of tissues without administration of contrast-enhancing agents, and because bone elicits no interference, it is particularly useful for visualizing structures at the brain-bone interface, i.e., in the posterior cranial fossa. MRI has already greatly improved neuroradiologic diagnostic abilities and promises, in the future, to permit measurement of brain metabolites by spectroscopic application. The high resolution of MRI in delineating white and gray matter has resulted in its widespread use in localizing lesions in the white matter, such as those caused by demyelination. Its use has been extended to visualize the spinal cord, which can be displayed in either sagittal or cross-sectional planes.

Angiography This has been developed over the last 30 years to the point where it is a relatively safe and extremely valuable method in the diagnosis of occluded arteries, aneurysms, and vascular malformations, tumors, abscesses, and intracranial hemorrhages. Its use has diminished greatly since the advent of CT and MRI scans. Following local anesthesia, a needle or cannula can be placed percutaneously

FIGURE 341-3 *MRI: Right carotid occlusion, with resultant right parieto-temporal infarction. T1-weighted inversion recovery study (IR), with repetition time of 1500 ms and inversion time of 450 ms (A) shows areas of prolonged T1 (dark) in the infarcted zones; in addition, small foci of prolonged relaxation times are also noted in the posterior frontal parietal and temporal areas of the coronae radiatae bilaterally. The T2-weighted studies (B and C) show the affected areas to also possess prolonged T2 characteristics (bright signals); the later echo (TE = 120 ms) shows some heterogeneity of signal, but it is undetermined whether the areas of longer T2 (brightest zones) represent infarct or edema. (Spin echo sequences: TR = 2000, TE = 60 in B and 120 in C.)*

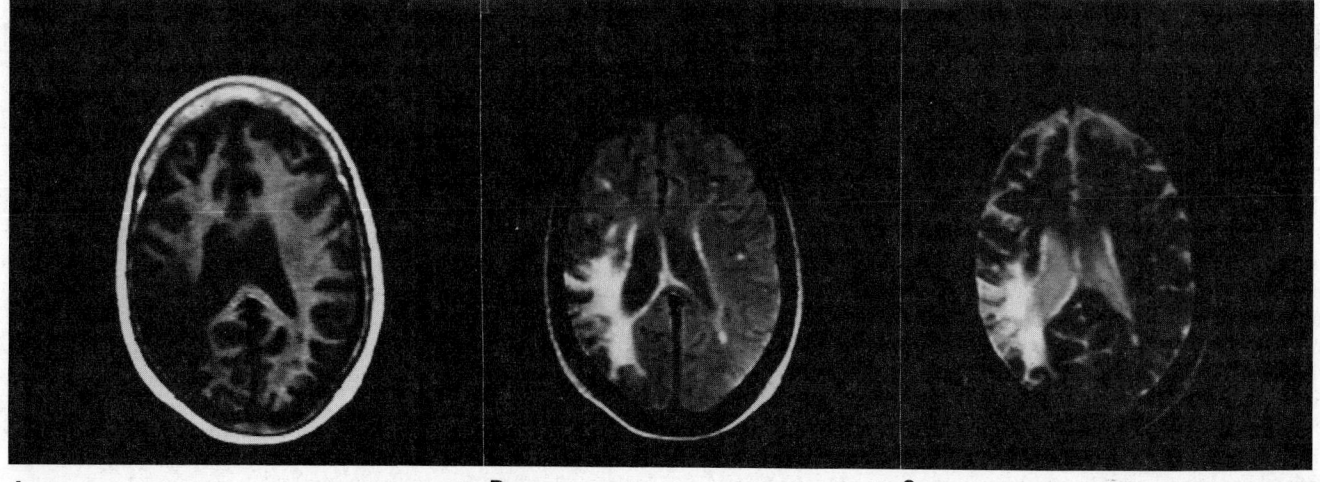

A   B   C

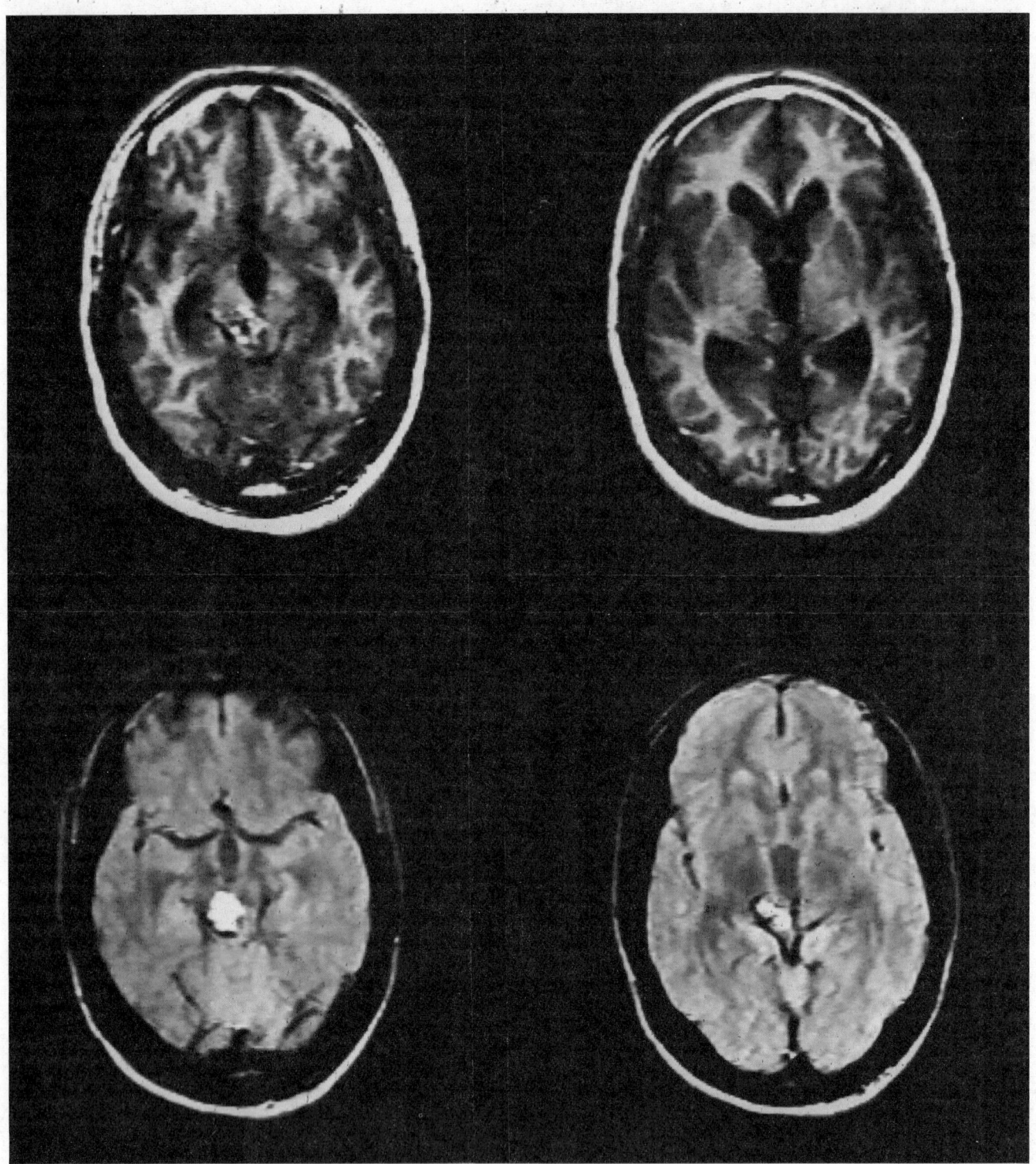

FIGURE 341-4 *Arteriovenous malformation. Thrombosed AVM involving the right posterior subthalamic and upper mesencephalic areas. Dark areas within the AVM on the IR study probably represent foci of abnormal brain with prolonged T1 rather than "flow void" effects; compare with the middle cerebral arteries. Bright zones on the IR study possess short T1; these areas also possess long T2 values; this combination is seen in subacute or chronic hemorrhages, in some fatty lesions, and metastases from melanoma. (Above: IR study, TR = 1500, TI-450, TE = 45; below: SE study, TR = 2000, TE = 60.)*

into the lumen of a brachial or femoral artery and a catheter can be introduced and threaded along the aorta to cannulate the major arteries in the cervical region. Radiopaque contrast media can be injected to visualize the arch of the aorta, the origins of carotid and vertebral systems and their extent through the neck into the cranial cavity, and when indicated, the spinal cord arteries. It is possible to show with clarity cerebral arteries down to about 0.1 mm lumen diameter under optimal conditions, as well as small veins of comparable size, vascular

abnormalities (angiomas, aneurysms), occluded arteries, delayed circulation from increased intracranial pressure as with masses or occlusion of dural sinuses and veins, displacement of vessels by mass lesions, or complete failure of intracranial vascular filling with cerebral death. *Digital subtraction venous angiography,* which requires pressure injection of contrast dye into a brachial vein, is commonly used as an alternative or adjunct to arterial angiography, particularly for initial study of the lumen diameters of the large extracranial arteries.

Pneumoencephalography and ventriculography Injection of air into the lumbar subarachnoid space with the patient in the sitting position permits visualization in considerable detail of the size and position of the ventricles, the subarachnoid space (upper spinal and cerebral), and, indirectly, the structures which lie between the ventricles and the meninges. This technique is now rarely used. Air myelography to demonstrate cavities within the spinal cord (syringomyelia) has now been largely replaced by injection of metrizamide. Ventriculography, accomplished by injection of air or contrast material directly into the lateral ventricles, is also largely of historic interest. CT scan and MRI have largely replaced both pneumoencephalography and ventriculography.

Iophendylate (pantopaque) myelography and ventriculography By injecting 5 to 15 mL iophendylate through a lumbar puncture needle and then tipping the patient on a tilt table, the entire spinal subarachnoid space and portions of the posterior cranial fossa may be visualized. The procedure is almost as harmless as the lumbar puncture, provided that the iophendylate is afterward removed through the needle. Ruptured lumbar and cervical disks and spinal cord tumors can be diagnosed accurately. Intraventricular injection of iophendylate is occasionally done to visualize the third and fourth ventricles and the aqueduct of Sylvius in tumors of the posterior fossa. Water-soluble contrast media (e.g., metrizamide) that are self-absorbing are now commonly used. Metrizamide injected in the lumbar CSF affords the additional advantage of assessing the subarachnoid space with a body CT scan. The body CT scan with or without metrizamide allows accurate visualization of the spinal canal and the spinal cord. It reveals tumors, ruptured disks, etc., that compress or displace the spinal canal and roots and also destructive lesions of the vertebrae. The latter may also be evident in bone scans.

Radioactive isotopes Radioactive isotopes, such as technetium (brain scan), are occasionally used for the visualization of tumors, inflammatory masses, viral encephalitis, and some vascular lesions such as "watershed" infarcts that are difficult to demonstrate otherwise. Since this is a simple, noninvasive procedure, the only limitation in its use is the expense. The more the lesion disrupts the blood-brain barrier, the more consistent its demonstration by these methods. Ultrasound can also be used to show displacement of central structures of the brain by a mass lesion.

POSITRON EMISSION TOMOGRAPHY Positron emission tomography (PET) is an experimental investigative technique currently available in only a few centers. The procedure involves the systemic administration of positron-emitting radionuclides of oxygen or ^{18}F 2-deoxyglucose (^{18}FDG) combined with computerized tomography. The latter permits three-dimensional localization of the disintegrating positrons with a tissue resolution of 0.5 to 1 cm. Administration of labeled O_2, CO_2, and ^{18}FDG provides regional quantitation of oxygen uptake, blood flow, and glucose utilization, respectively. Studies in patients with cerebrovascular diseases, seizure disorders, and degenerative conditions have been undertaken. In stroke, PET imaging is useful in acute studies to discriminate viable from nonviable tissue. In patients with seizure disorders interictal ^{18}FDG studies may show localized areas of decreased glucose metabolism in and around a seizure focus, with increased glucose metabolism evident during a seizure. Metabolic studies with ^{18}FDG have also shown decreased glucose uptake in the striatum in patients with Huntington's disease who have normal CT scans. Although these studies show great promise in the biochemical analysis of brain functions, the cost of the instrumentation and the technology required to produce isotopes will restrict PET scanning to major medical centers.

ELECTROMYOGRAPHY (EMG) This examination supplements the clinical study of patients with neurologic diseases which affect the neuromuscular apparatus or with primary or secondary diseases of the skeletal musculature. It is described in relation to muscle diseases (see Chap. 354). Newer EMG techniques ("central EMG") permit quantitative analysis of motor system function.

ELECTROENCEPHALOGRAPHY (EEG) The electroencephalographic examination is part of the clinical study of a patient suspected of having a cerebral disease; it is also used in the evaluation of the central nervous system (CNS) effects of many medical diseases.

In addition to the resting record, a number of so-called activating procedures are usually carried out.

1 The patient is requested to breathe deeply 20 times a minute for 3 min. The resulting alkalosis and cerebral vasoconstriction may activate characteristic seizure patterns or other abnormalities.

2 A powerful light (a stroboscope) is placed over the patient's face and flashed at frequencies from 1 to 20 per s with the patient's eyes opened and closed. The EEG may then show abnormal discharges in photosensitive patients.

3 The EEG is recorded after the patient is allowed to fall asleep naturally or following sedative drugs given by mouth or by vein. Procedures 1 and 2 are more commonly employed, but sleep is extremely helpful in bringing out abnormalities, especially where temporal lobe epilepsy and certain other seizures are concerned. Sleep deprivation the night prior to the study is a common adjunct to a sleep EEG.

Certain preparations are necessary if electroencephalography is to be most useful. The patient should not be sedated and should not have been for a long time without food, for both sedative drugs and relative hypoglycemia modify the normal EEG pattern. The same may be said of mental concentration, extreme nervousness, or drowsiness, all of which tend to suppress the normal alpha rhythm and increase muscle artifacts. When dealing with patients suspected of having epilepsy who are already being treated for it, most physicians prefer to record the first EEG while the patient continues to receive drugs.

Types of normal recordings The normal EEG in adults shows somewhat asymmetric 8- to 12-Hz, 50-μV sinusoidal *alpha* waves in both occipital and parietal regions. These waves wax and wane spontaneously and usually disappear promptly when patients open their eyes or fix their attention on something. Faster waves than 13 Hz of lower amplitude (10 to 20 μV), called *beta* waves, are also seen symmetrically in the frontal regions. Very slow waves (*delta* waves), sharp waves, or other unusual patterns are absent in a normal record. When normal subjects fall asleep, the rhythm slows symmetrically, and characteristic waveforms (vertex sharp waves and sleep spindles) appear; if the sleep is induced by barbiturates or benzodiazepines, an increase in the fast frequencies is seen and is considered to be normal (see Chap. 20). Excessive fast activity should raise the possibility that a patient is receiving one of these classes of compounds.

An occipital response to each flash may be seen in the normal EEG during stroboscopic stimulation and is called the evoked response, or, at faster repetition rates, photic "driving." The clinical utility of this evoked occipital response has increased the scope of electroencephalography in several ways: (1) one can be reasonably sure that a person with such a response can at least perceive light; (2) when this evoked response is absent on one side of the head but present on the other, there is physiologic evidence of a lesion interfering with normal transmission between the thalamus and the occipital lobe on this side; and (3) when the flashing light produces abnormal waves, there is evidence of increased excitability. Actual seizure patterns may be produced in the EEG if the activation procedure is continued (a "photoparoxysmal" response); if the sensitivity is still greater, frank myoclonic jerks of face or arms, or, rarely, major convulsions may occur. This finding is to be differentiated from the purely muscular response, also myoclonic, produced normally in contracting scalp muscles and often visible in routine EEGs (photomyoclonus).

Types of abnormal recordings The most pathologic finding of all is the disappearance of the EEG pattern and its replacement by "electrocerebral silence," which means that the electrical activity of the cortical mantle, measured at the scalp, is below 2 µV and probably absent. Acute intoxication with anesthetic levels of drugs, such as barbiturates, and extreme hypothermia (<70°F) can produce this sort of isoelectric EEG. However, in the absence of CNS depressants or extreme hypothermia, a record which is "flat" (except for artifacts) all over the head is almost always a result of cerebral hypoxia, ischemia, or widespread cortical destruction. Such a patient, without EEG activity, reflexes, spontaneous respiration, or muscular activity of any kind for 6 h or more, is said to be in "irreversible coma." The brain of such patients is largely necrotic. There is no chance for neurologic recovery, and the patient may be considered dead, despite the preservation of vegetative (cardiovascular) functions supported by mechanical means, such as respirators. There has been no exception to this statement in more than 900 patients examined at the Massachusetts General Hospital in the past 18 years.

Localized regions with absence of EEG activity may rarely be seen when there is a large area of infarction or an extensive surface tumor or clot lying between the cerebral cortex and the electrodes. The localization of this abnormality is precise, but of course the nature of the lesion cannot be ascertained by EEG. Most such lesions, however, are too small, relative to the recording arrangement, to be visible, and the EEG may then record abnormal waves arising from functional, though deranged, brain at the borders of the lesion. These abnormal waves are slower and of higher amplitude (50 to 350 µV) than normal. Those which are less than 4 Hz are called *delta* waves; those from 4 to 7 Hz are called *theta* waves; and the higher-voltage, faster waves are known as *spikes* or *sharp waves*. These fast and slow waves may be combined, and when a series of them suddenly interrupts relatively normal EEG patterns in a paroxysmal fashion, they are highly suggestive of epilepsy. The ones associated with *petit mal* (absence) spells are 3-Hz spike-and-wave complexes that characteristically appear in all leads of the EEG at the same time and disappear almost as suddenly at the end of the seizure.

Neurologic conditions with abnormal EEG   In the following groups of neurologic disorders, the EEG may be of considerable help in reaching the correct diagnosis.

EPILEPSY   All types of generalized epileptic seizures (grand mal and petit mal) are associated with some abnormality in the EEG, provided it is being recorded at the time. The EEG is also often abnormal during the more restricted types of seizure activity (complex partial, myoclonic, focal, and Jacksonian) (see Chap. 342). One exception is certain deep temporal lobe foci where the discharge fails to reach the scalp in sufficient amplitude to be seen against the background activity of the normal EEG, particularly if there is a strong alpha rhythm. A zygomatic or sphenoidal lead may localize an epileptic focus in the medial temporal lobe, but rarely does it provide the only EEG evidence of epileptic activity. Other exceptions in which, on occasion, no EEG abnormality may be recorded during a seizure include some of the patients with other focal seizures (sensory, Jacksonian, myoclonic, and epilepsia partialis continua). This fact presumably means that the neuronal discharge is too deep, discrete, fast, or asynchronous to be transmitted by volume conduction through the skull and recorded via the EEG electrode, which is some 2 cm from the cortex. The petit mal, certain myoclonic, and grand mal patterns correlate closely with the clinical seizure type and may be present in the interictal EEG. The artifact produced by motor activity during a "seizure" usually cannot be distinguished from brain electrical activity. The differentiation of psychogenic from true seizures requires careful inspection of the EEG at seizure onset where a typical pattern of fast frequency activity may be seen, or immediately following cessation of motor activity, when postictal slowing or suppression is the rule if consciousness has been affected. A normal alpha pattern postictally in an "unresponsive" patient suggests a psychogenic pseudoseizure.

A fact of importance is that between seizures as many as 20 percent of patients with petit mal and 40 percent with grand mal epilepsy show a normal EEG. Anticonvulsant therapy also tends to diminish the EEG abnormalities. The records of another 30 to 40 percent of epileptics, though abnormal between seizures, are nonspecifically so, and therefore the diagnosis of epilepsy can be made only by correct interpretation of the clinical data in relation to the EEG abnormality.

BRAIN TUMOR, ABSCESS, AND SUBDURAL HEMATOMA   Clinically significant intracranial space-occupying lesions are characteristically associated with abnormalities in the EEG, depending on their type and location, in some 90 percent of patients. In addition to diffuse changes, the classic abnormalities are focal or localized slow waves (usually delta), or, occasionally, seizure activity and decreased amplitude and synchronization of normal rhythms. As a rule, those lesions which expand more rapidly (abscess, some metastases, glioblastoma), especially when situated supratentorially, have the greatest frequency of EEG abnormalities (90 to 95 percent of the latter two and virtually 100 percent of abscesses). Slower growing tumors (astrocytomas) and particularly those outside the cerebral hemispheres (meningiomas, pituitary tumors) often produce no change in the EEG, though they may be very evident clinically. The EEG abnormality has the correct lateralization in as many as 75 to 90 percent of patients with supratentorial tumors or abscesses. The EEG may be focally abnormal at a time when a cerebral metastasis is not yet visible on a CT scan. A normal EEG and CT scan together almost exclude the presence of a supratentorial brain tumor or abscess. The EEG may be normal, however, in 20 to 25 percent of patients with infratentorial tumors.

CEREBROVASCULAR DISEASE   Both the diffuse and localized EEG changes produced by vascular lesions such as cerebral infarcts and intracranial hemorrhages depend on their location and size rather than their type. The EEG has been shown to be useful in the differential diagnosis of vascular hemiplegia. If the lesion responsible is in the internal carotid or a major cerebral artery, an area of decreased normal activity and excessive slowing is practically always seen acutely in the appropriate region. If the hemiplegia is due to small vessel disease, i.e., a lacunar infarction deep in the cerebrum or brainstem (Chap. 343), the EEG should be normal. Large hemispheral lesions associated with acutely depressed levels of consciousness also produce widespread, diffuse, slow-wave activity of a nonspecific type as is seen with stupor or coma from any cause. Resolution begins after a few days, cerebral edema subsides, and focal activity may then be seen (slow-wave activity or suppression of normal background rhythms). Smaller infarctions are associated with acute focal abnormalities which lateralize the lesion well but do not localize it precisely. In contrast with tumors, further resolution continues, and after 3 to 6 months roughly 50 percent of patients with cerebrovascular accidents have a normal EEG despite the persistence of clinical abnormalities. Under these circumstances the prognosis for further recovery is poor. Persistence of moderate- to high-voltage EEG abnormalities after this time period, particularly if spikes or sharp waves are present, suggests the presence of abnormally functioning tissue, which might be epileptogenic. The EEG may be of lateralizing value in acute subarachnoid hemorrhage, depending upon the extent to which the adjacent cerebrum is affected.

BRAIN INJURY   Cerebral contusion or laceration produces EEG changes similar to those described for cerebrovascular disease. Diffuse changes often give way to focal ones, especially if the lesions are on the lateral or superior surface of the brain, and these in turn usually disappear over a period of weeks or months unless seizures supervene. Sharp waves or spikes sometimes emerge as the focal slow-wave abnormality resolves. These or failure of the EEG to "normalize" usually precede the occurrence of posttraumatic epilepsy. Following head injury, therefore, serial EEGs may be of prognostic value as regards the prospect of epilepsy.

DISEASES WHICH CAUSE COMA AND STATES OF IMPAIRED CONSCIOUSNESS   The EEG is abnormal in almost all conditions in which there is some impairment of consciousness. With hypothyroidism the rhythms are normal in configuration but are usually slow.

In general, the more profound the change in consciousness, the more abnormal the EEG recording. In these latter situations slow waves (delta) are bilateral, are of high amplitude, and tend to be more conspicuous over the frontal regions. This pertains to such differing conditions as acute meningitis or encephalitis, severe disorders of blood gases, glucose, electrolyte and water balance, uremia, diabetic coma, liver coma, or impairment of consciousness accompanying the large cerebral lesions discussed above. In hepatic coma, the degree of abnormality in the EEG corresponds with the degree of confusion, stupor, or coma. Moreover, paroxysms of bilaterally synchronous large, sharp "triphasic waves" are characteristic, though they may also be seen with other metabolic encephalopathies associated with renal or pulmonary failure. Diffuse degenerative diseases (e.g., Alzheimer's disease) affecting the cerebral cortex are accompanied by relatively slight degrees of diffuse, slow-wave abnormality in the theta (4- to 7-Hz) range. Certain more rapidly progressive ones, such as subacute sclerosing panencephalitis (SSPE), Creutzfeldt-Jakob disease, and to a lesser extent the cerebral lipidoses, have, in addition, very characteristic, almost pathognomonic EEG changes consisting of recurring complex bursts of sharp and slow activity. A normal EEG in a patient who is apathetic, slow, depressed, or forgetful is a point in favor of the diagnosis of an affective disorder or schizophrenia.

An EEG may also assist the physician in caring for a comatose patient when the pertinent history is unavailable. It may point to such otherwise unexpected causes as hepatic encephalopathy (bilaterally synchronous triphasic waves), intoxication with barbiturates or benzodiazepines (excess fast activity), clinically inapparent continuous epileptic discharges, a large space-occupying lesion, or diffuse anoxia-ischemia ("burst-suppression" pattern with repetitive generalized complexes separated by periods with very little EEG).

OTHER DISEASES OF THE CEREBRUM There are many disorders of nervous function that cause little or no alteration in the EEG. Multiple sclerosis and other demyelinating diseases are examples, though as many as 50 percent of advanced cases will have an abnormal record. Delirium tremens, Wernicke-Korsakoff disease, and withdrawal seizures, despite the dramatic nature of the clinical picture, cause little or no changes in the EEG. Some degree of slowing usually accompanies confusional states which have been designated elsewhere as hypokinetic delirium. Interestingly, neuroses and psychoses, such as manic-depressive disorders or schizophrenia, abnormal states due to hallucinogenic drugs such as LSD, and the majority of cases of mental retardation are associated with no important modification of the normal record or with nonspecific abnormalities.

Special applications of the EEG Because the EEG provides information about the status and function of the cerebrum, it is useful as a monitor in the operating room to ensure the presence of a viable brain during the increasingly extensive procedures of modern cardiovascular surgery. EEG apparatus has long been available for indicating the level of anesthesia, and such simple equipment should eventually be used by the anesthetist to monitor both the cardiac and cerebral status of all patients during surgical anesthesia.

It is routine practice now for the EEG to be monitored continuously during carotid endarterectomies, a procedure performed in carefully selected patients suffering from stenotic or ulcerative carotid artery disease. Characteristic EEG changes (particularly marked voltage attenuation) signal the need for a temporary bypass shunt to maintain sufficient cerebral blood flow to preclude ischemic cerebral damage during surgery.

In the neurosurgical operating room the EEG can be recorded from exposed brain *(electrocorticogram)*, and seizure patterns can be localized more precisely than from the scalp so that resection of such physiologically abnormal tissue may be undertaken.

The routine EEG can be of value in the diagnosis of hysterical blindness. Similarly, a response evoked by noise during light sleep can be of help in confirming the presence of hearing in a patient who feigns total deafness. These responses may also be helpful in evaluating hearing and vision in infants.

EVOKED RESPONSES An *evoked response* (sometimes termed an *evoked potential*) is the record of electrical activity produced by groups of neurons within the cord, brainstem, thalamus, or cerebral hemispheres following stimulation of one or another sensory system by means of visual, auditory, or tactile input. The amplitude of these potentials, as recorded from the scalp using ordinary EEG electrodes, ranges from less than 0.5 to 20 μV. Because of their extremely small size, they can rarely be recognized on the ink-written EEG record with the background of ongoing EEG activity, which itself is usually 50 μV or more in amplitude. Therefore, special techniques, requiring simple computers, must be used to extract the evoked response waveform that one is interested in, from the continuous background EEG activity. These techniques are called "averaging" because the process involves repeating 100 to 1000 precisely timed stimuli and recording the electrical activity during a certain brief interval following each stimulus. The random ongoing EEG activity which, at any given point in time following the stimulus, is sometimes negative and at other times positive in polarity, tends to cancel out with sufficient repetition. The evoked response, on the other hand, is time-locked to the stimulus, and at a given time following the stimulus always has the same electrical sign as well as shape. The evoked response thus grows larger with repetition while the background averages out and becomes smaller. It is important to have special amplifiers, to apply the electrodes to the surface of the scalp with great care, and to time stimuli precisely with a minimum of accompanying electrical artifact. These evoked responses provide sensitive, objective extensions of the clinical neurologic examination of the related sensory system, but they are no more specific etiologically.

Visual evoked responses *Visual evoked responses* produced by a pattern shift (PSVER) have the longest history of clinical usefulness. During this test, patients are asked to watch an alternating black and white checkerboard pattern which is projected on a screen. When patients watch this pattern shift, it produces a characteristic waveform which can be recorded from the scalp over the posterior portion of the head. Under normal circumstances, this triphasic wave has a distinctive positive peak at 95 to 115 ms latency (usually called P100; see Fig. 341-5) from the time of pattern reversal. This latency, the duration of the response, and the amplitude of the peak are measured; the latency is the most important parameter clinically. Each eye is tested independently. A purely monocular abnormality indicates that the conduction defect is anterior to the chiasm.

Many disease processes affecting the optic nerve fibers in their intraocular, orbital, or intracranial portions produce abnormalities of this potential. Glaucoma, compression of the optic nerve, chiasm, or tract by various space-occupying lesions, and degenerative disease of this system often produce a reduction in amplitude and/or prolonged latency of the PSVER. If the visual system is sufficiently affected, no response may be recorded by stimulation of one or both eyes. In a general hospital setting, however, the most common cause of abnormality in this response is optic neuritis, frequently associated with multiple sclerosis. Demyelination of the optic nerve fibers, as a primary demyelinating disease or due to one of the lesions listed above, slows conduction in the nerve fibers so that the latency of the positive peak of the PSVER is prolonged (115 to 200 ms). In fact, almost all patients with optic neuritis, even after the visual acuity has returned to normal, continue to show distinct abnormalities in this PSVER at a time when detailed ophthalmologic evaluations reveal no abnormality. In multiple sclerosis, if the PSVER is normal, the neuroophthalmologic examination is always normal. We have found no exceptions to this rule in more than 200 patients. When the PSVER is abnormal, the visual fields, visual acuity, pupillary reactions, and optic fundus examination are normal in a considerable number of patients.

Approximately one-half of the patients with multiple sclerosis who have never had visual symptoms also show abnormalities, and this accounts for one of the most useful aspects of the test. If a patient presents with what appears to be the first episode of a neurologic illness in which the lesion is in the brainstem or spinal cord, a demonstration by means of an abnormal PSVER of another clinically unsuspected lesion in a different part of the central nervous system (the optic nerves) makes the diagnosis of multiple sclerosis more likely and may spare the patient certain neuroradiologic procedures.

Abnormalities in visual acuity have no effect on the PSVER unless the acuity is so poor that the patient cannot see the checkerboard pattern—patients with acuity of 20/200 or better are suitable for testing. The only other requirement is that the patient be cooperative enough to sit still for 20 min and watch the pattern. Infants and children can also be tested by using special techniques.

Brainstem auditory evoked responses   *Brainstem auditory evoked responses* (BAERs) are more difficult to obtain than PSVERs because BAERs are much smaller, of the order of 0.5 µV. These are produced by clicks transmitted to one of a patient's ears through earphones. The patient may be alert or comatose and need not be particularly cooperative except that excess movement or muscle artifact makes the response even more difficult to obtain. BAERs of essentially normal appearance can be recorded from infants and children. BAERs consist of a series of seven waves which appear within the first 10 ms after the click (Fig. 341-5). These (named I to VII) are considered to represent successive activation of the auditory nerve (I) and the brainstem auditory pathways (cochlear nucleus, II; superior olivary complex, III; lateral lemniscus, IV; inferior colliculus, V; and higher auditory centers, VI, VII). A lesion at or between any of these levels either obliterates or delays the appearance of waves from successively higher levels. Multiple sclerosis can, for example, also produce slow

conduction between any of the levels in this test. The same is true of other lesions affecting the brainstem, such as small vascular lesions, central pontine myelinolysis, hypoxic damage, and so on. The waves which arise from structures caudal to the lesion are perfectly normal in latency, whereas those arising from structures cranial to the lesion are either obliterated or delayed. This allows one to pinpoint quite accurately the level of the lesion within the brainstem auditory pathways and provides a very neat opportunity for correlation of clinical observations with neurophysiologic and occasionally pathologic data. This test is useful as a screening test for patients with acoustic neuromas (who always show an abnormality), for patients suspected of having multiple sclerosis, for comatose patients in whom the level of lesion within the central nervous system is not clear, and for other patients in whom documentation of brainstem lesions is important. Hearing loss can often be recognized in this test, since changes in the latency of the first (and, therefore, subsequent) waves are produced, and these must be taken into consideration in the evaluation of the results obtained. Interwave latencies, which are the parameters used to measure central conduction, are not affected by hearing loss or stimulus intensity. The test is also useful in screening high-risk infants for hearing defects.

Somatosensory evoked responses   *Somatosensory evoked responses* (SERs) are produced by small painless electrical stimuli administered to large sensory fibers in mixed nerves of the hand or leg. The afferent valley is recorded at many levels as it ascends the somatosensory pathways, and a series of waves can be recorded which reflect activity in peripheral nerve trunks, tracts in the spinal

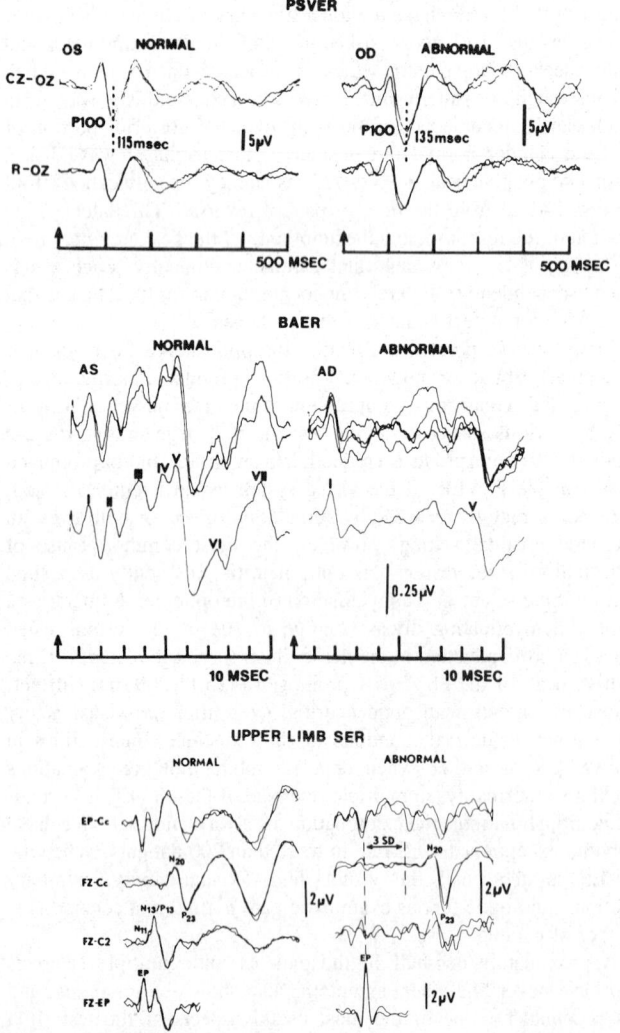

FIGURE 341-5   *Evoked responses (ER). PSVER. Pattern-shift visual ER recorded from a patient with multiple sclerosis showing a monocular latency abnormality. Latency of the occipital response (P100) following stimulation of the left eye (OS) was normal at 115 ms; right response (OD) was abnormal because the latency of the P100 peak was delayed at 135 ms. Relative positivity at G2 causes a downward trace deflection. Electrode locations; CZ = vertex, OZ = midline occipital, R = linked ears. [From EB Brooks, KH Chiappa, Clinical applications of evoked potentials, in Neurology, J Courjoun et al (eds), New York, Raven Press, 1982.]*

BAER. Brainstem auditory ERs from a patient with multiple sclerosis showing the marked asymmetry which can be present with monaural click stimulation. The responses following left ear (AS) stimulation are normal. The right ear (AD) responses are missing wave III (lower pons) and have a markedly abnormal I–V (cochlear nerve to midbrain) separation of 6.7 ms, evidence of a conduction defect in the pontine auditory tracts on the right. Left ear responses for superimposed trials (above) are produced by N = 1024 clicks each; in the right ear N = 2048 clicks each. The single trace below each is the grand average of the superimposed trials. Recording is from vertex to earlobe of stimulated ear; relative positivity at the vertex produces an upward trace deflection. (Reprinted from KH Chiappa et al, Ann Neurol 7:135, 1980.)

Upper limb SER. Short-latency somatosensory ERS produced by stimulation of the median nerve at the wrist. The left set of responses is from a normal subject; the right set is from a patient with multiple sclerosis who had no sensory symptoms or signs. In the patient, note preservation of the brachial plexus component (EP) and absence of cervical cord (N11) and lower medullary components (N13-P13). The latency of thalamocortical components (N20-P23) was prolonged markedly above the normal mean plus 3 standard deviations for the separation of N20 from the brachial plexus potential. Unilateral stimulation at 5 per second. Each trace is the averaged response to 1024 stimuli, with the superimposed trace a repetition following 1024 stimuli to demonstrate waveform consistency. Recording electrode locations: FZ = midfrontal, EP = Erb's point (supraclavicular), C2 = middle back of neck over C2 cervical vertebra, and Cc = scalp overlying sensoriparietal cortex contralateral to limb stimulated.

cord, gracile and cuneate nuclei, pontine and/or cerebellar structures, thalamus, thalamocortical radiations, and primary sensory fields of the cortex (see Fig. 341-5). Lesions of the pathways at any level affect the subsequent waves, thus providing localizing and confirmatory data in a similar fashion to the BAER.

Evoked responses can be used for a single evaluation of patients (looking for lesions in the various pathways discussed) or as a quantitative method for following a patient's course to document functional improvement or deterioration as time passes, following therapy, and so on. They also prove useful for on-line monitoring of function in optic nerve, brainstem, or spinal cord during neurosurgical procedures that involve manipulation of those structures. Since BAERs and SERs are unaffected by general anesthesia and high-dose barbiturates, they also can be used to follow CNS function in comatose patients. Longer latency auditory and somatosensory evoked responses have been studied for a number of years. These are largely cortically produced responses, dramatically affected by drowsiness, inattention, and other poorly controllable variables, and have not proved to be clinically useful. Neither have most visual evoked responses produced by stroboscopic flashes. They are very useful in evaluation of visual pathways in infants and young children who are not cooperative enough to watch the checkerboard pattern and in adults during surgery or when comatose. Under other circumstances, pattern-shift PSVERs afford a much more reliable and reproducible response.

PSYCHOMETRY, PERIMETRY, AUDIOMETRY, AND TESTS OF LABYRINTHINE FUNCTION These methods are of utility in quantitating and defining the nature of psychic or sensory deficits produced by disease of the nervous system. Limitations of space do not permit a description of them here. The precise indications for doing these tests are (1) to obtain confirmation of a functional disorder in particular parts of the nervous system and to ascertain its nature, and (2) to quantitate the disorder to determine, by subsequent examinations, the course of the underlying illness (see Chap. 23).

BIOCHEMICAL TESTS With advances in the biochemistry of metabolic diseases, a number of highly specific tests of serum, CSF, and circulating red and white blood cells have become available. These will be presented in relation to the metabolic diseases of which they are diagnostic.

REFERENCES

Buonanno FS et al: Applications of proton nuclear magnetic resonance imaging in neurology, in *Harrison's Principles of Internal Medicine, Update V,* RG Petersdorf et al (eds). New York, McGraw-Hill, 1984

Chiappa KH: *Evoked Potentials in Clinical Neurology.* New York, Raven Press, 1983

———, Ropper AH: Evoked potentials in clinical medicine. N Engl J Med 306:1136, 1982

Klass DW, Daly DD (eds): *Practice of Clinical Electroencephalography.* New York, Raven Press, 1981

Newton TH, Potts DG (eds): *Radiology of the Skull and Brain,* vol 3. St. Louis, Mosby, 1977

Niedermeyer E, Lopes da Silva F (eds): *Electroencephalography.* Baltimore, Urban & Schwarzenberg, 1982

Pykett IL: NMR imaging in medicine. Sci Am 246(5):78, 1982

Remond A: *Handbook of Electroencephalography and Clinical Neurophysiology,* vols 1–15. Amsterdam, Elsevier/North-Holland, 1976–1978

Spahlmann R: *EEG Primer.* Amsterdam, Elsevier/North-Holland, 1981

Stalberg E, Young RR (eds): *Clinical Neurophysiology.* London, Butterworths, 1981

Taveras J, Wood EH: *Diagnostic Neuroradiology,* 2d ed, *Golden's Diagnostic Radiology Series,* sec 1. Baltimore, Williams & Wilkins, 1976

Werner SS et al: *Atlas of Neonatal Electroencephalography.* New York, Raven Press, 1977

342 THE EPILEPSIES AND CONVULSIVE DISORDERS

MARC A. DICHTER

The *epilepsies* are a group of disorders characterized by chronic, recurrent, paroxysmal changes in neurologic function caused by abnormalities in the electrical activity of the brain. They are common neurologic disorders, estimated to affect between 0.5 and 2 percent of the population, and can occur at any age. Each episode of neurologic dysfunction is called a *seizure.* Seizures may be *convulsive* when they are accompanied by motor manifestations, or may be manifested by other changes in neurologic function (i.e., sensory, cognitive, emotional events). Epilepsy can be acquired as a result of neurologic injury or a structural brain lesion and can also occur as a part of many systemic medical diseases. Epilepsy also occurs in an *idiopathic* form in an individual with neither a history of neurologic insult nor other apparent neurologic dysfunction. Isolated, nonrecurrent seizures may occur in otherwise healthy individuals for a variety of reasons, and, under these circumstances, the individual is not said to have epilepsy.

CLASSIFICATION OF SEIZURES

The neurologic manifestations of epileptic seizures are varied, ranging from a brief lapse of attention to a prolonged loss of consciousness with abnormal motor activity. The proper classification of the kinds of seizures which an individual is experiencing is important for an appropriate diagnostic workup, prognostic evaluation, and selection of therapy. The classification of epileptic seizures provided in this chapter is based on the International Classification of Epileptic Seizures developed in 1969 and subsequently modified in 1981. It emphasizes the clinical seizure type and ictal (seizure-associated) and interictal (between seizures) electroencephalographic pattern (Table 342-1), whereas etiology, anatomic substrate, and pathways of spread are not major considerations. The older terminology of grand mal, petit mal, and psychomotor or temporal lobe epilepsy has been integrated into the current scheme.

The major underlying premise of this classification is that some seizures (partial or focal seizures) start in a localized area of brain (cortex) and either remain localized or secondarily generalize (that is, spread throughout the brain), whereas other seizures appear to be generalized from their earliest manifestation.

PARTIAL OR FOCAL SEIZURES Partial or focal seizures begin with the activation of neurons in one localized area of cortex. The

TABLE 342-1 Classification of epileptic seizures

1 Partial or focal seizures
  a Simple partial seizures (with motor, sensory, autonomic, or psychic signs)
  b Complex partial seizures (psychomotor or temporal lobe seizures)
  c Secondary generalized partial seizures
2 Primary generalized seizures
  a Tonic-clonic (grand mal)
  b Tonic
  c Absence (petit mal)
  d Atypical absence
  e Myoclonic
  f Atonic
  g Infantile spasms
3 Status epilepticus
  a Tonic-clonic status
  b Absence status
  c Epilepsia partialis continua
4 Recurrence patterns
  a Sporadic
  b Cyclic
  c Reflex (photomyoclonic, somatosensory, musicogenic, reading epilepsy)

specific clinical symptoms depend on the area of cortex involved and imply dysfunction in a localized area of cortex. The lesion may be due to birth injury, postnatal trauma, tumor, abscess, infarction, vascular malformation, or some other structural abnormality. The abnormal area of cortex underlying the seizure activity can be identified by the specific neurologic phenomena observed during the focal seizure. Partial seizures are classified as *simple* if there is no alteration of consciousness or awareness of the environment and *complex* if there is such a change.

Simple partial seizures   Simple partial seizures can occur with motor, sensory, autonomic, or psychic symptoms. A simple partial seizure with motor signs consists of recurrent contractions of the muscles of one part of the body (finger, hand, arm, face, etc.) without loss of consciousness. Each muscular contraction is caused by the discharge of neurons in the corresponding area of the contralateral motor cortex.

The muscle activity of a partial seizure (*ictus*) may remain confined to one area or may spread from the affected area to involve contiguous ipsilateral body parts (i.e., right thumb to right hand to right arm to right side of face). This "Jacksonian march," named after Hughlings Jackson who first described it, is caused by a demonstrable progression of epileptiform discharges in the contralateral motor cortex and may occur over seconds or minutes. The EEG manifestations of this form of seizure are often very striking and consist of regularly occurring spike discharges in the appropriate area of (frontal) motor cortex. Between seizures (interictal period) this region may give rise to irregular spike discharges in the EEG.

Simple partial seizures may have other behavioral manifestations if the seizure discharges occur in other cortical regions. Thus, sensory symptoms (paresthesias, vertiginous feelings, simple auditory or visual hallucinations) occur with epileptiform discharges in the contralateral sensory cortex, and autonomic and psychic symptoms [i.e., the sensation of having experienced something before (déjà vu), unwarranted sense of fear or anger, illusions, and even complex hallucinations] occur with discharges in temporal and frontal lobes.

Complex partial seizures (temporal lobe or psychomotor seizures)   Complex partial seizures are episodic changes in behavior in which an individual loses conscious contact with the environment. The onset of these seizures may consist of any of a variety of auras: an unusual smell (as of burning rubber), a feeling that the current experience has happened before (déjà vu), a sudden intense emotional feeling, a sensory illusion such as that of objects growing smaller (*micropsia*) or larger (*macropsia*), or a specifically formed sensory hallucination. Patients may come to recognize these as heralding their seizures, or the memory of the aura may be lost in the postictal amnesia which often occurs if the seizure becomes generalized. During complex partial seizures there may be a cessation of activity with some minor motor activity, such as lip smacking, swallowing, walking aimlessly, or picking at one's clothes (*automatisms*). Complex partial seizures may also be accompanied by the unconscious performance of highly skilled activities such as driving a car or playing complicated musical pieces. When the seizure ends, the individual is amnesic for events which took place during the seizure and may take minutes or hours to recover full consciousness.

Patients with complex partial seizures have EEGs which exhibit unilateral or bilateral spikes or slow wave discharges over temporal or frontotemporal regions both interictally and during seizures. Most of these seizures originate from epileptiform activity in the temporal lobes—especially the hippocampus or amygdala—or other parts of the limbic system, but others have been shown to originate from mesial parasagittal or orbital frontal regions. These seizures are also referred to as *temporal lobe epilepsy* and *psychomotor epilepsy* in older classification schemes.

Although often showing spike discharges or focal slowing during complex partial seizures, exceptionally the surface EEG may be normal. Nasopharyngeal or sphenoidal electrodes may record the abnormal discharges, but in some cases only depth electrodes in the amygdaloid nuclei or other limbic structures will show seizure discharges. The occasional discrepancy between surface and depth electrophysiologic events is a particularly difficult problem when trying to use the surface EEG to determine the nature of an abnormal behavior in an individual suspected of having complex partial seizures. (See "Differential Diagnosis of Seizures" below.)

Secondary generalization of partial seizures   Simple or complex partial seizures can progress to generalized seizures with loss of consciousness and often with convulsive motor activity. This may occur immediately or after many seconds or a minute or two. In addition, many patients with focal seizures have generalized seizures without an obvious initial focal component which are difficult to distinguish from primary generalized seizures. The presence of an aura or the observation of any focal feature (twitching of one extremity, aphasia, tonic eye deviation) at the onset of the generalized seizure or the presence of a postictal focal neurologic deficit (Todd's paralysis) is an important clue to a focal origin to the seizure.

PRIMARY GENERALIZED SEIZURES   Tonic-clonic (grand mal)   One of the most common kinds of epileptic paroxysms is the generalized tonic-clonic seizure. Some of these appear to be primary generalized seizures, and others are the result of secondary generalization from partial seizures. In either case, the seizures follow a common pattern. The primary generalized seizures usually start without warning, although some individuals sense a vague, nonspecific sense of the impending event. The onset is heralded by a sudden loss of consciousness, a *tonic* contraction of the muscles, a loss of postural control, and a cry produced by a forced expiration caused by contraction of the respiratory muscles. The individual falls to the floor in an opisthotonic posture, often sustaining injury, and remains rigid for many seconds. There may be cyanosis as respiration is inhibited. Soon a series of rhythmic contractions of all four limbs occurs. This *clonic* phase can last for a variable period of time and ends when the muscles relax. The individual remains unconscious and unarousable for a period of minutes or longer. There is usually a gradual return to consciousness and often a period of disorientation during recovery. The patient may even be combative if restrained. During the seizure, urinary or fecal incontinence and tongue biting may occur. Postictally there is amnesia for the seizure, and sometimes a retrograde amnesia as well. Headache and drowsiness are common sequelae, and the individual may not return to baseline functioning for days.

The EEG in patients with tonic-clonic seizures shows low-voltage fast (10 Hz or more) activity during the tonic phase, which converts gradually to slower, larger sharp waves throughout both hemispheres. During the clonic phase there are bursts of sharp waves associated with the rhythmic muscular contractions and slow waves coincident with the pauses. Often the excessive muscular activity of the seizure causes artifacts which interfere with ictal EEG recordings. Interictally, the EEG is usually abnormal with polyspike (or spike) and wave or occasionally sharp and slow wave discharges.

Tonic seizures   Tonic seizures are a less common form of primary generalized seizure which consist of the sudden occurrence of a rigid posturing of the limbs or torso, often with deviation of the head and eyes toward one side. They are not followed by a clonic phase and are often of shorter duration than tonic-clonic seizures.

Absence seizures (petit mal)   Pure absence seizures consist of the sudden cessation of ongoing conscious activity without convulsive muscular activity or loss of postural control. Such seizures may be so brief as to be inapparent. Usually they last for seconds or minutes. The brief lapses of consciousness or awareness may be accompanied by minor motor manifestations such as eyelid fluttering, small chewing movements of the mouth, or mild shaking of the hands. During longer absences, automatisms may occur which may be difficult to distinguish from complex partial seizures. At the end of the absence seizure, the patient regains awareness of the environment very quickly, and there is usually no period of postictal confusion.

Absence seizures almost always begin in young children (6 to 14 years of age) and rarely appear for the first time in adults. These brief seizures may occur hundreds or more times per day and go on for weeks or months before it is recognized that the child is having seizures. In fact, it is not uncommon for these to be first recognized when the child begins having problems with learning.

The EEG is pathognomonic in this form of seizure disorder. During the seizures there are 3-Hz spike-and-wave discharges which appear synchronously throughout all the leads. The EEG is usually normal during the interictal periods. Often the EEG demonstrates that the child is having more seizures than was thought from clinical observation alone.

Absence seizures usually occur in otherwise neurologically normal children. These seizures are usually sensitive to anticonvulsants (see below). Children with this condition often do quite well once it is treated. Approximately one-third outgrow the seizure disorder, one-third continue to have only absence seizures, and one-third have occasional concomitant generalized tonic-clonic seizures.

Absence seizures can be differentiated from absencelike attacks, which occasionally occur in complex partial seizures, by the lack of aura, immediate recovery from the absence, and typical 3-Hz spike-and-wave EEG pattern.

Atypical absence seizures Atypical absence seizures are similar to absence seizures but coexist with other forms of generalized seizures, such as tonic seizures, myoclonic seizures, or atonic seizures (see below). The EEG is more heterogeneous, containing spike-and-wave discharges at 2 or 4 Hz during the absence attacks and poorly developed background with spike or polyspike activity during interictal periods.

Atypical absence seizures commonly occur in children with some other form of underlying neurologic dysfunction and tend to be resistant to medication. In the most severe form of this disorder, the Lennox-Gastaut syndrome, children have several kinds of generalized seizures and often have intellectual impairment.

Myoclonic seizures Myoclonic seizures are sudden, brief, single or repetitive muscle contractions involving one body part or the entire body. In the latter case, the seizure is accompanied by a violent fall, without a loss of consciousness. Myoclonic seizures often coexist with other seizure types but may occur alone. The EEG shows polyspike-and-wave discharges or sharp and slow waves, both ictally and interictally. Although often idiopathic, myoclonic seizures occur as a major neurologic symptom in a variety of medical conditions including uremia, hepatic failure, Creutzfeldt-Jakob disease, subacute leukoencephalopathies, and a hereditary degenerative condition, Lafora body disease.

Atonic seizures Atonic seizures are brief losses of consciousness and postural tone not associated with tonic muscular contractions. The individual may simply drop to the floor without apparent cause. Atonic seizures usually occur in children and are often accompanied by other forms of seizures. The EEG contains polyspikes and slow waves. The "drop attacks" of atonic seizures need to be distinguished from cataplexy seen in narcolepsy (where the patient remains conscious), transient brainstem ischemia, or sudden rises in intracranial pressure.

Infantile spasms or hypsarrhythmia This form of primary generalized seizure occurs in infants between birth and approximately 12 months of age and consists of brief synchronous contractions of the neck, torso, and both arms (usually in flexion). Infantile spasms often occur in children with underlying neurologic diseases, such as anoxic encephalopathy or tuberous sclerosis, but can rarely occur in an otherwise apparently normal infant. The prognosis for children with this form of seizure disorder is grave, and approximately 90 percent develop mental retardation in addition to their seizures. The EEG is characterized by a very disorganized background, random high-voltage slow waves, spikes and burst suppression (hypsarrhythmia). The spasms and hypsarrhythmia tend to disappear over the first 3 to 5 years of life, only to be replaced by other forms of generalized seizures.

STATUS EPILEPTICUS Prolonged or repetitive seizures without a period of recovery between attacks can occur with all forms of seizures and is defined as *status epilepticus*. When tonic-clonic seizures are involved, this state can be life-threatening (see "Treatment of Seizures"). Absence status, on the other hand, may proceed for some time before it is recognized because the patient does not lose consciousness or have convulsive movements. Status epilepticus of partial seizures is called *epilepsia partialis continua* and may occur with partial motor, sensory, or visceral seizures. Complex partial seizures may also present as status epilepticus.

RECURRENCE PATTERNS All classes of recurrent seizures can occur sporadically or randomly, with no apparent triggering event, or can occur cyclically, i.e., in concert with the sleep-waking cycle or the menstrual cycle (*catamenial epilepsy*). Epileptic seizures can also occur as evoked reactions to a specific stimulus (*reflex epilepsy*), although this is relatively infrequent. Examples are seizures triggered by photic stimulation (*photomyoclonic or photoconvulsive epilepsy*), specific musical compositions (musicogenic epilepsy), tactile stimulation (somatosensory induced epilepsy), or reading (reading or language epilepsy). The latter usually consists of brief myoclonic jerks of the jaw, cheek, and tongue which occur during silent or oral reading and may progress to generalized tonic-clonic seizures.

PATHOPHYSIOLOGY OF EPILEPSY

Epileptic seizures can be induced in any normal human (or vertebrate) brain with a variety of different electrical or chemical stimuli. The ease and rapidity with which these seizures can occur, and the stereotyped nature of the seizures produced suggest that the normal brain, particularly the cerebral cortex, contains within its fine anatomic and physiologic structure a mechanism which is inherently unstable and which can be influenced in many different ways to produce a seizure. Thus, many kinds of metabolic abnormalities and anatomic lesions of brain can produce seizures, and conversely, there is no pathognomonic lesion of the epileptic brain.

The hallmark of the altered physiologic state of epilepsy is a rhythmic and repetitive hypersynchronous discharge of many neurons in a localized area of the brain. A reflection of this hypersynchronous discharge can be observed in the electroencephalogram (EEG). The EEG records the integrated electrical activity generated by synaptic potentials in neurons in the superficial layers of a localized area of cortex. Normally, the EEG records unsynchronized activity during periods when the mind is actively working, or mildly synchronized activity when the mind is in a restful state (i.e., alpha waves during relaxation with closed eyes) or during various stages of sleep. In the epileptic focus, neurons in a small area of the cortex are activated in an unusually synchronized manner, and this produces a larger, sharper waveform in the EEG—the *spike discharge*. If the neuronal hypersynchrony is large, a focal, simple seizure follows; if it spreads through the brain and lasts for seconds or minutes, a complex partial or generalized seizure (the *ictus*) will occur and the EEG can have a variety of appearances, depending on which areas of brain are involved and how the primary discharging areas project to the superficial cortex. During the seizure, the EEG may display low-voltage fast activity or high-voltage *spikes* or *spike-and-wave* discharges throughout both hemispheres.

During the interictal spike discharge, the neurons in the epileptic focus undergo a large membrane depolarization (the *depolarizing shift,* or DS) accompanied by action potential generation. After the DS, the neurons hyperpolarize and stop firing for several seconds. In areas around the discharging focus, the neurons are also inhibited but do not first have the large DS. Thus, it appears as if the epileptic discharge is limited to a localized area of cortex by a ring of inhibition around the focus and slightly delayed inhibition within the focus.

When the epileptic focus undergoes a transition from the isolated discharges to a seizure, the post-DS inhibition disappears and is replaced by a depolarizing potential. Neurons in contiguous areas and in synaptically connected distant areas are then recruited into the seizure and become activated. Local cortical circuits, long association pathways (including callosal), and subcortical pathways are all utilized for the spread of the discharges. Thus, a focal seizure can spread locally or generalize throughout the brain. Widely ramifying thalamocortical pathways are likely to be responsible for the rapid generalization of some forms of epilepsy, including absence seizures.

A number of metabolic events occur within the brain during the epileptic discharges which may contribute to the development of the focus, to the transition to seizures, or to postictal dysfunction. During the discharges, extracellular potassium concentration increases and extracellular calcium concentration decreases. Both of these changes have profound effects on neuronal excitability and neurotransmitter release and on neuronal metabolism. Neurotransmitters and neuropeptides are also released in unusually large amounts during seizure discharges. Some of these substances can have prolonged actions on central neurons and may be responsible for prolonged postictal phenomena such as Todd's paralysis. In addition to the ionic effects, seizures produce increases in cerebral blood flow to the primary involved areas, increases in glucose utilization, and alterations in oxidative metabolism and local pH. It is possible that these events are not just consequences of the seizures but actually contribute to the development of the seizure activity and that manipulation of such factors could become an effective means for controlling seizures.

There are many mechanisms by which seizures can develop in either normal or pathologic brains. One of the most common methods for producing epilepsy in experimental animals is to block inhibitory mechanisms. For example, agents which antagonize the inhibitory neurotransmitter γ-aminobutyric acid (GABA) are potent convulsants, both in animals and in human beings. A diminution of inhibition may also be involved in some forms of chronic focal epilepsy, as it has been demonstrated that inhibitory terminals on neurons in areas around cortical gliotic lesions are reduced. This reduction of inhibition may allow excess excitation to develop. It has been postulated that some forms of generalized epilepsy could also be due to an abnormality in the GABA-inhibitory system, but this has not yet been established. At least two antiepileptic drugs, including phenobarbital, and the benzodiazepines, can enhance GABA-mediated inhibition in the brain, and this effect is likely to contribute to their antiepileptic actions. Whether other antiepileptic drugs also enhance inhibition is not yet established.

Electrical stimulation is another mechanism by which seizures can easily be produced in a normal brain. At certain current strengths and stimulus frequencies seizure discharges are produced and become self-sustaining beyond the original stimulus. Generalized tonic-clonic seizures result. At lower stimulus parameters, seizure afterdischarges may not occur. However, if a stereotyped subthreshold stimulus is repeated at regular intervals (which may even be as infrequent as one stimulation per day), there is a gradual buildup of response until generalized seizures occur to the same stimulus which was originally subthreshold. Eventually spontaneous seizures may occur without any further electrical stimulation. This phenomenon has been called *kindling*. Its relationship to the pathophysiology of posttraumatic epilepsy or to the issue of whether the occurrence of seizures themselves tends to foster the continued development of a seizure focus in human beings has not been resolved.

THE CAUSES OF EPILEPSY

The likely etiology of a given seizure depends upon the age of the patient and the type of seizure (see Table 342-2). In young infants, anoxia or ischemia before or during birth; intracranial birth injury; metabolic disturbances, such as hypoglycemia, hypocalcemia, and hypomagnesemia; congenital malformations of the brain; and infec-

tions are the most common causes of seizures. In the young child, trauma and infections are common causes of epilepsy, although idiopathic seizures account for the majority of patients.

Genetic factors can influence the development of epilepsy and have also been shown to affect EEG patterns in general. Patients with primary generalized seizures, especially absence seizures, have a higher familial incidence of epilepsy than is found in the normal population, and relatives of such patients have higher incidences of dysrhythmic EEGs, even when they do not have seizures. The mode of inheritance of susceptibility to epilepsy appears complicated and probably represents multiple genes with variable penetrance. Even in the highest risk group, however, the chance of a sibling or a child of an individual with generalized seizures also having epilepsy is below 10 percent.

Young children also frequently (approximately 2 to 5 percent of the population) develop seizures with febrile illnesses. These febrile convulsions are short, generalized tonic-clonic convulsions which occur during the early phases of a febrile illness in children between the ages of 3 months and 5 years. Febrile seizures must be distinguished from seizures that are triggered by central nervous system infections which coincidentally produce fever (meningitis or encephalitis). There is minimal likelihood that the child will develop epilepsy or any neurologic impairment from the febrile convulsion if the seizure lasts less than 5 min, is generalized rather than focal, and is not associated with any interictal EEG abnormalities or abnormalities on neurologic exam. There may be a family history of febrile seizure. Febrile seizures of this kind are probably best treated with quick and relatively vigorous attempts to keep children from developing excessive fevers during various childhood illnesses but without specific antiepileptic medication. Some pediatricians prefer to maintain children susceptible to febrile convulsions on chronic phenobarbital medication. On the other hand, if the febrile convulsion is prolonged or focal or is associated with an abnormal EEG, or if the child has a neurologic abnormality, there is a significant risk of subsequent epilepsy. These children should be treated with chronic antiepileptic therapy. Intermittent antiepileptic medication given at the onset of a febrile illness is ineffective and should be avoided.

In adolescents and young adults, head trauma is a major cause of focal epilepsy. Epilepsy can be caused by any kind of serious head injury, with the likelihood of developing recurrent seizures being proportional to the extent of the damage. Injuries which either cause dural penetration or produce posttraumatic amnesia of more than 24-h duration may result in a 40 to 50 percent incidence of later epilepsy, while the incidence with closed head injuries with cerebral contusion varies from 5 to 25 percent. Brief concussive illnesses or nonpenetrating head injuries without loss of consciousness are not epileptigenic. Seizures which occur immediately or within the first

TABLE 342-2   The causes of seizures

Infant (0–2 years)	Paranatal hypoxia and ischemia
	Intracranial birth injury
	Acute infection
	Metabolic disturbances (hypoglycemia, hypocalcemia, hypomagnesemia, pyridoxine deficiency)
	Congenital malformation
	Genetic disorders
Child (2–12 years)	Idiopathic
	Acute infection
	Trauma
	Febrile convulsion
Adolescent (12–18 years)	Idiopathic
	Trauma
	Drug, alcohol withdrawal
	Arteriovenous malformations
Young adult (18–35 years)	Trauma
	Alcoholism
	Brain tumor
Older adult (over 35 years)	Brain tumor
	Cerebrovascular disease
	Metabolic disorders (uremia, hepatic failure, electrolyte abnormality, hypoglycemia)
	Alcoholism

24 h of injury are not associated with a poor prognosis, whereas seizures occurring after the first day and within the first 2 weeks indicate a high likelihood of posttraumatic epilepsy. Most recurring seizures develop by 2 years after the injury, although longer intervals may occur. Approximately 50 percent of patients with posttraumatic seizures spontaneously recover, 25 percent have medically controllable seizures, and 25 percent have seizures that are much more intractable to antiepileptic medication. The effectiveness of prophylactic anticonvulsant medication after head trauma still requires adequate documentation, although many physicians treat such patients (and other postoperative neurosurgical patients) with phenytoin or phenobarbital to attempt to prevent the development of posttraumatic seizures.

In the adolescent or young adult age group, generalized tonic-clonic seizures tend to be idiopathic or are associated with drug (especially barbiturate) or alcohol withdrawal. Arteriovenous malformations may present as focal seizures in this age group. Between ages 30 and 50, brain tumors become more common causes of seizures and may be present in 30 percent of patients with new focal seizures. In general, the incidence of seizures is higher with slowly growing brain tumors involving the cerebrum, such as meningiomas or low-grade gliomas, than with the more malignant types. However, seizures can occur in individuals with any kind of central nervous system mass lesion, including highly malignant metastatic tumors or completely benign vascular malformations.

Above age 50, cerebrovascular disease is the most common cause of focal or generalized seizures. Seizures can occur acutely in patients with an embolus, hemorrhage, or, more rarely, a thrombosis but more often as a late sequel to these lesions. Seizures can also result from "silent" cerebral infarctions in patients with no known cerebrovascular disease. Brain tumors, either primary or metastatic, also present with seizures in the older age group.

At any age, a variety of medical diseases can produce metabolic disturbances which may present as seizures. Uremia, hepatic failure, hypo- or hypercalcemia, hypo- and hyperglycemia, or hypo- and hypernatremia may be associated with myoclonic seizures or generalized tonic-clonic seizures.

EVALUATION OF THE PATIENT WITH A SEIZURE

Individuals with seizures present to physicians either in an emergency room setting during the acute attack or in an office setting days after the epileptic event. In the former case, the seizure may be the presenting symptom of a serious central nervous system disorder which requires immediate diagnosis and therapy. In the latter case, the seizure may be a symptom of a more chronic neurologic dysfunction and a different approach is warranted.

Initial emergency evaluation is directed toward ensuring adequate ventilation and perfusion and stopping the seizure (see "Treatment"). Once the patient is medically stable, the investigation is directed at determining the cause of the seizure. Often a careful history (either from the patient, if recovered, or from a friend or relative), a physical examination, and a few blood studies can provide the diagnosis.

A history suggesting a recent febrile illness accompanied by headaches, change in mental status, or confusion suggests an acute central nervous system (CNS) infection (either meningitis or encephalitis) and indicates the need for urgent examination of the cerebrospinal fluid. In this context, a complex partial seizure may be the presenting symptom of herpes simplex encephalitis. A history of headache and/or change in mental functioning preceding the seizure, coupled with either signs of increased intracranial pressure or a focal neurologic deficit suggests an underlying mass lesion (tumor, abscess, arteriovenous malformation) or a chronic subdural hematoma. Seizures with a clear focal onset or aura are especially worrisome in this regard. A computerized tomography (CT) scan should be performed for a more definitive diagnosis.

The general physical examination may provide important etiologic information. Gum hyperplasia is usually the result of chronic phenytoin therapy. Exacerbation of a chronic seizure disorder due to intercurrent infection, alcohol, or cessation of therapy is a common cause of patients presenting to an emergency room. Skin examination may reveal the port-wine facial stain of Sturge-Weber disease (with cerebral calcifications being detectable on skull x-ray), or the stigmata of tuberous sclerosis (adenoma sebaceum and shagreen patches) or neurofibromatosis (subcutaneous nodules, café au lait spots). Body or limb asymmetries may indicate hypotrophic somatic development contralateral to a congenital or infantile cerebral lesion.

The history or physical examination may also reveal evidence of chronic alcoholism. Heavy alcohol users commonly have seizures for any of several reasons—alcohol withdrawal *(rum fits)*, old cerebral contusion (from falls or fights), chronic subdural hematoma, or metabolic derangements of undernutrition and liver disease. Withdrawal seizures usually occur between 12 and 36 h after cessation of drinking and are brief, generalized tonic-clonic seizures. They occur singly or in a flurry of two or three. After the period of epileptic activity, the seizures do not have to be treated since they are usually self-limiting. Seizures in alcoholics which occur at other times should be treated, but this group of patients presents a particular challenge because of lack of compliance and metabolic problems which complicate drug therapy.

Routine blood studies will indicate if the seizure was caused by hypoglycemia, hypo- or hypernatremia, or hypo- or hypercalcemia. These biochemical abnormalities should be corrected and the cause determined. In addition, other less common causes of seizures which can be sought with the appropriate tests are thyrotoxicosis, acute intermittent porphyria, and lead or arsenic intoxication.

In the older patient, a seizure may indicate an acute cerebrovascular accident or may be a delayed effect of an old cerebral infarct (even a silent one). The manner in which further evaluation proceeds is dictated by the patient's age, cardiovascular status, and accompanying symptoms.

Generalized tonic-clonic seizures can occur in neurologically normal individuals after moderate sleep deprivation. Such seizures can be seen in individuals working double shifts, in college students around examination time, and in soldiers returning from short leaves of absence. After the first seizure, if all investigations are normal, such individuals do not require further treatment.

If the patient's history, physical examination, and blood chemistries are all normal after a seizure, it is likely that the seizure was *idiopathic* and was not caused by a serious underlying CNS lesion. However, tumors or other mass lesions may be entirely asymptomatic except for the seizure and further investigation of such cases is mandatory.

The EEG is important in relation to the differential diagnosis of the seizure, the determination of the cause of the seizure, and the proper classification of the seizure. When the diagnosis of a seizure is in doubt, as, for example, when trying to distinguish seizures from syncope, the presence of a paroxysmal EEG abnormality supports the diagnosis of epilepsy. For this purpose, special activation procedures (sleep recording, photic stimulation, or hyperventilation) or special EEG leads (nasopharyngeal, nasoethmoidal, sphenoidal) for recording from deep structures or prolonged monitoring even on an ambulatory basis, can be employed. The EEG can also reveal focal abnormalities (spikes, sharp waves, or focal slow waves) which would indicate the possibility of a focal neurologic lesion even if the seizure symptomatology appeared generalized from the outset.

The EEG is also used to help classify seizures. It can distinguish focal seizures with secondary generalization from primary generalized seizures and is especially useful in the differential diagnosis of brief lapses of consciousness. Absence seizures are always accompanied by bilateral spike-and-wave discharges, whereas complex partial seizures are accompanied by either focal paroxysmal spikes or slow waves or by a normal surface EEG. In cases of absence seizures, the EEG may reveal that the patient is having many more small seizures than was clinically apparent and may help in monitoring antiepileptic drug therapy.

Until very recently, lumbar puncture, skull x-rays, arteriography, and pneumoencephalography were important adjuncts to the evaluation of the seizure patient. Lumbar puncture is still employed in those situations where acute or chronic CNS infections or subarachnoid hemorrhage are suspected. CT scan and magnetic resonance imaging (MRI) can now provide more definite information about anatomic lesions than the older, invasive techniques. All adults with a new onset seizure disorder should have a diagnostic CT scan both without and with contrast enhancement. In initial studies are normal, continued difficulties with a focal seizure disorder warrant repeat evaluation at 6 to 12 months. MRI appears particularly useful early in the evaluation of a focal seizure disorder when it can demonstrate low-grade abnormalities better than the CT scan. Arteriograms are still performed if the suspicion of an arteriovenous malformation is high, even in the presence of a normal CT, or for the delineation of the vascular pattern in a lesion detected by noninvasive techniques.

DIFFERENTIAL DIAGNOSIS OF SEIZURES

SYNCOPE VERSUS SEIZURE   Sudden loss of consciousness, usually without convulsive movements, presents a common diagnostic problem in both children and adults (see Chap. 12). Faints are often preceded by a feeling of lightheadedness, of the room spinning, of a flush, and are often, but not always, precipitated by an environmental stimulus such as prolonged standing in a hot, crowded area, the sight of blood, a fright, etc. In older people, pure syncope is most often secondary to cardiovascular problems, such as Stokes-Adams attacks, tachyarrhythmias, or orthostatic hypotension, and these may occur with or without a warning. A clear focal onset of the event (i.e., abnormal smell, head turning, staring, etc.) favors seizure as the cause. In addition, convulsive muscular contractions, tongue biting, or incontinence commonly accompany seizures but are much less common with fainting spells. Occasionally vasovagal or other types of fainting episodes can be accompanied by either clonic movements or brief generalized tonic-clonic seizures. If the original loss of consciousness can be ascribed to a clearly nonepileptic cause (e.g., the patient was having blood drawn or a dental procedure at the time), it is not necessary to regard the episode as a manifestation of epilepsy, and antiepileptic drug therapy is not indicated.

When the origin of a syncopal episode is in doubt, the patient should undergo a complete cardiovascular evaluation and an EEG with sleep recording and, if available, a prolonged ambulatory EEG monitoring. If the EEG shows paroxysmal activity (which is often brought out by drowsiness and sleep onset), and the patient has no signs of cardiac arrhythmia with ECG monitoring or of valvular disease on echocardiogram, it is likely that the syncopal episode represented a seizure and the patient should be evaluated and treated accordingly.

TRANSIENT ISCHEMIC ATTACKS AND MIGRAINE   Transient ischemic attacks (TIAs) and migraine episodes can present as a transient alteration in neurologic function (usually without loss of consciousness) which may be confused diagnostically with focal seizures. Neurologic dysfunction due to ischemia (TIA or migraine) is often a negative symptom (i.e., loss of feeling, numbness, visual field deficit, paralysis), whereas deficits due to focal seizure activity are often positive (twitching, paresthesias, visual distortion, or hallucination), although this distinction is not absolute. Brief stereotyped episodes which conform to dysfunction in a single vascular territory in an individual with either known vascular disease, heart disease, or with risk factors for vascular disease (diabetes, hypertension) are more likely TIAs. However, since cerebral infarcts are a common cause of subsequent seizures in older patients, a paroxysmal EEG focus should be sought.

Classic migraine headaches with a visual aura, unilateral headache, and gastrointestinal upset are usually easy to distinguish from seizures. However, some migraine patients have only "migraine equivalents" such as a hemiparesis, numbness, or aphasia and may not have subsequent headache. These episodes, especially when they occur in older individuals, are hard to distinguish from TIAs, but may also represent focal seizures. The presence of loss of consciousness after some forms of vertebrobasilar migraine and the common occurrence of headaches after seizures makes this differential diagnosis more difficult. The slower development of neurologic dysfunction in migraine (often occurring over minutes) is the most helpful point. Nevertheless, occasionally such patients need to be investigated for all three problems with a CT scan, cerebral angiography, and specialized EEG procedures before a diagnosis can be made. In some cases, a therapeutic trial with antiepileptic drugs (which, interestingly, can prevent migraines as well as seizures in some patients) will be necessary for the final diagnosis.

PSYCHOMOTOR VARIANTS AND "HYSTERICAL" SEIZURES   As remarked above, patients with complex partial seizures often have bizarre behavioral manifestations of their seizures. These may consist of abrupt changes in personality, feelings of impending doom or of undirected fear, abnormal bodily sensations, episodic forgetfulness, or brief repetitive motor activities such as picking at one's clothes or stamping a foot. Many of these patients also have personality disorders, and a significant proportion have had psychiatric intervention. It is common, especially if these patients do not have tonic-clonic seizures or loss of consciousness and when these patients appear emotionally disturbed, for such episodes of psychomotor seizures to be called psychopathic fugues or hysterical seizures. This incorrect diagnosis is often reinforced by a "normal EEG" interictally, or even during one of the episodes. It must be emphasized that seizures can arise from foci deep in temporal lobe structures with *no* surface EEG manifestations. This has been repeatedly demonstrated with depth electrode recordings. Moreover, deep temporal seizures can be manifested only by the kinds of phenomena described above and may be free of the usual seizure phenomena of motor convulsions and loss of consciousness.

In a small number of cases, individuals present with seizurelike events which upon investigation turn out to be hysterical "pseudoseizures" or frank malingering. Often these individuals have had true seizures in the past or are acquainted with an individual with epilepsy. Such pseudoseizures can be quite difficult to distinguish from true seizures. Hysterical seizures are characterized by nonphysiologic events such as a progression of twitching from one hand to the other without spread to subjacent ipsilateral face or leg areas, twitching of all four extremities without loss of consciousness (or with surreptitious loss of consciousness), or careful attention to avoiding injury by moving away from a wall or bed edge while having motor convulsions. In addition, hysterical seizures, especially in adolescent girls, may have frankly sexual overtones, with pelvic thrusting or genital manipulation. While many forms of temporal lobe seizures can occur with normal surface EEGs, generalized tonic-clonic seizures always produce abnormal EEGs both during and after the seizure. Most generalized tonic-clonic seizures and many complex partial seizures of moderate duration are accompanied by rises in serum prolactin (during the immediate 30-min postictal period), whereas hysterical seizures are not. Although not an absolute distinguishing point, such measurements, especially if positive, can be very helpful in characterizing the origin of a given "spell."

TREATMENT OF SEIZURES

Treatment of the patient with a seizure disorder is directed at eliminating the cause of the seizures, suppressing the expression of the seizures, and dealing with the psychosocial consequences which may occur as a result of the neurologic dysfunction underlying the seizure disorder or from the presence of a chronic disability.

If the seizure disorder is a result of a metabolic disturbance, such as hypoglycemia or hypocalcemia, restoration of normal metabolic function is usually accompanied by cessation of the seizures. If the seizures are caused by a structural brain lesion, such as a brain tumor, arteriovenous malformation or cerebral cyst, removal of the offending lesion may eliminate the seizures. However, long-standing lesions, even nonprogressive ones, can result in gliosis and other denervation changes. These changes may lead to chronic epileptic foci which will not be eliminated by the subsequent removal of the original lesion. In such cases, surgical extirpation of the epileptic brain regions may be necessary for control of the epilepsy (see "Neurosurgical Treatment of Epilepsy" below).

There is a complex interrelationship between the limbic system and neuroendocrine function which may have significant implications for patients with epilepsy. Normal hormonal fluctuations may influence the frequency of seizures, and epilepsy can cause changes in neuroendocrine function. For example, some women will have a marked change in the pattern of their seizures during particular parts of the menstrual cycle (catamenial epilepsy), while others may have changes in seizure frequency in response to oral contraceptives or pregnancy. In general, estrogens tend to exacerbate seizures, while progesterones tend to be protective. On the other hand, some patients with epilepsy, especially complex partial seizures, may also have an associated reproductive endocrine dysfunction. Disorders in sexual interest, especially hyposexuality, are frequently observed. In addition, women may have polycystic ovary disease and men may have disturbances in potency. Some patients with these endocrine disorders have not had clinical seizures but have abnormal EEGs (often with temporal discharges). Whether the epilepsy causes the endocrine and/or behavioral dysfunction or whether the two conditions are separate manifestations of a common underlying neuropathologic process is not known. However, endocrine manipulation can sometimes be useful in controlling some forms of seizures, and antiepileptic medication may be a useful adjunct for treating some forms of endocrine dysfunction.

PHARMACOLOGIC CONTROL OF EPILEPSY The fundamental modality for the treatment of epilepsy is pharmacologic therapy. The goal is to protect the patient from having seizures without interfering with normal cognitive function (or, in the child, with development of normal intellectual function) and without producing harmful systemic side effects. If possible, the individual should be treated with the lowest possible dose of a single anticonvulsant medication. Precise knowledge of the kind of seizure the patient is having, the spectrum of action of the available anticonvulsant medications, and a few basic pharmacokinetic principles can result in the complete control of approximately 60 to 75 percent of patients with epilepsy. Many patients appear to be resistant to medications or develop unnecessary side effects because the medications chosen are not appropriate for the kind(s) of seizure or are not administered in the optimum doses.

The availability of serum levels of anticonvulsant drugs makes it possible to optimize dosage regimens for individual patients and to monitor drug compliance. Thus, patients can be placed on a medication and after a suitable equilibration period (usually several weeks, but at least five *half-lives*), the amount of medication in the serum can be determined and compared to standard *therapeutic ranges* established for each drug. Utilizing blood levels to adjust doses can compensate for individual patient variability in absorption or metabolism of drugs.

Many anticonvulsant drugs are bound by serum proteins, and it is the unbound, or *free,* drug which is in equilibrium with extracellular spaces within the brain; this level correlates best with seizure control. However, *total* drug is measured in the serum by conventional assays. Under most circumstances, this is adequate for determining if the anticonvulsant is in the therapeutic range. Occasionally, serum anticonvulsant levels will be high, yet the patient continues to have seizures without any pharmacologic side effects of the anticonvulsant. In these cases, it is possible that serum protein binding is higher than expected and that the patient is undermedicated in relation to the free drug available. "Free" levels can be determined by measurements of drug concentrations in saliva. Increase in dose may produce control

without any untoward side effects (despite a blood level above therapeutic range). Similarly, individuals with impaired liver or renal function may have low serum proteins or circulating "toxins" which reduce drug binding. In this case, toxicity may appear at unusually low serum levels because of a relatively higher free level of drug.

Intensive long-term EEG and video monitoring has demonstrated that careful characterization of seizures and selection of anticonvulsant drugs can significantly increase seizure control in many patients whose seizures had previously been considered intractable to conventional antiepileptic drugs. In fact, often these patients can have one or more of their multiple drugs removed while still achieving better control.

INDICATIONS FOR USE OF SPECIFIC DRUGS   Generalized tonic-clonic seizures (grand mal) There are three medications which are of proven value in this very common form of seizure—phenytoin (or diphenylhydantoin), phenobarbital (and other long-acting barbiturates), and carbamazepine (see Table 342-3). Most patients will be controlled by adequate doses of any one of these, although individual patients may respond better to one or another. The choice among them often relates to minimizing undesirable side effects. Phenytoin is probably the drug of choice producing effective control with no sedation and very little, if any, intellectual impairment. However, phenytoin does produce gum hyperplasia in some individuals and can produce mild hirsutism, which is especially unpleasant for young women. Prolonged use can produce coarsening of facial features. Phenytoin may produce lymphadenopathy and, in very high doses, may be toxic to the cerebellum. Carbamazepine is equally effective and does not have many of the side effects seen with phenytoin. Cognitive function appears as well or even better preserved than with phenytoin. However, carbamazepine can cause gastrointestinal upset and may cause bone marrow depression with mild to moderate falls in peripheral white count (3.5 to 4×10^3 per milliliter) which can occasionally become severe and which must be watched carefully. In addition, carbamazepine can produce hepatotoxicity. For these reasons, a complete blood count and liver function tests should be performed before starting carbamazepine and at 2-week intervals for a period after initiating therapy.

Phenobarbital is also effective against tonic-clonic seizures and has none of the side effects mentioned above. It can cause sedation and a dulling of intellect, however, especially early in its use, and this may lead to poor compliance. The sedation is dose-dependent and may limit the amount of drug which can be given to achieve complete control. However, if control can be achieved with nonsedative doses of phenobarbital, it may be the safest chronic regimen. Primidone is a barbiturate which is metabolized to phenobarbital and phenylethylmalonamide (PEMA) and may be more effective than phenobarbital alone because of its active metabolite. In children, the barbiturates can produce a state of hyperactivity and hyperirritability which will limit their usefulness.

In addition to their systemic side effects, all three classes of drugs have neurologic toxicities at higher doses. Nystagmus is common at therapeutic blood levels, but ataxia, dizziness, tremor, intellectual dulling, forgetfulness, confusion, and even stupor may occur with increasing blood concentrations. These are reversible when blood levels fall back to therapeutic levels.

Partial seizures, including complex partial seizures (temporal lobe epilepsy) The same drugs which are useful for tonic-clonic seizures are also effective for partial seizures. Although not definitely established, it may be that carbamazepine and phenytoin are slightly more effective than the barbiturates for these seizures. In general, complex partial seizures are difficult to control, and patients with these seizures often require more than one medication (i.e., carbamazepine and primidone or phenytoin and primidone or any one of the primary drugs and high doses of methsuximide) and may become candidates for neurosurgical intervention. These are the kinds of seizures for which many epilepsy centers are conducting trials of new antiepileptic drugs.

TABLE 342-3 Commonly used antiepileptic drugs

Generic name	Trade name	Principal uses	Dosage	Half-life
Phenytoin (diphenylhydantoin)	Dilantin	Tonic-clonic (grand mal) Focal Complex partial	300–400 mg/day (3–5 mg/kg—adult; 4–7 mg/kg—child)	24 h (with wide variation)
Carbamazepine	Tegretol	Tonic-clonic Focal Complex partial	600–1200 mg/day (20–30 mg/kg—child)	13–17 h
Phenobarbital	Luminol	Tonic-clonic Focal	60–200 mg/day (1–5 mg/kg—adult; 3–6 mg/kg—child)	90 h (shorter in children)
Primidone	Mysoline	Tonic-clonic Focal Complex partial	750–1000 mg/day (10–25 mg/kg)	Primidone—8 h PEMA—24–48 h Phenobarbital—90 h
Ethosuximide	Zarontin	Absence (petit mal)	750–1250 mg/day (20–40 mg/kg)	60 h (adult) 30 h (child)
Methsuximide	Celontin	Absence	600–1200 mg/day	
Clonazepam	Clonopin	Absence Atypical absence Myoclonic	1–12 mg/day (0.1–0.2 mg/kg)	24–48 h
Sodium valproate	Depakene	Absence Atypical sence (Tonic clonic)	750–1250 mg/day (30–60 mg/kg) 15 h	6–20 h
Trimethadione	Tridione	Absence Atypical absence (Use only with intractable seizures)	900–2100 mg/day (20–60 mg/kg)	6–13 days (for dimethadione)

Primary generalized absence seizures (petit mal, atypical petit mal)   These seizures respond to different classes of medications than either tonic-clonic or focal seizures. For simple absence, ethosuximide is the drug of choice. Side effects include gastrointestinal upset, behavior changes, dizziness, and lethargy, but are not often troublesome. For more difficult to control atypical absence seizures and for myoclonic seizures, valproic acid is the drug of choice. (It may also be useful in primary generalized tonic-clonic seizures.) Valproic acid can cause gastrointestinal irritation, bone marrow suppression (especially thrombocytopenia), hyperammonemia, and hepatic dysfunction (including rare instances of fatal progressive hepatic failure which appear to be idiosyncratic rather than dose-related). A complete blood count with platelet count and liver function tests should be performed before beginning therapy and at biweekly intervals after initiating therapy for a suitable period until the safety of the drug is established in the individual patient. Clonazepam (a benzodiazepine) can also be used for atypical absence and myoclonic seizures. It can cause drowsiness and irritability, but usually it does not cause other systemic side effects. Trimethadione was one of the first antiabsence drugs but is now rarely used because of its potential toxicity.

Approximately one-third of children who present with "pure" absence seizures also have tonic-clonic seizures at some later time. The question of whether these children should be treated prophylactically with an anti-tonic-clonic seizure medication has not been resolved. Since valproic acid has actions against both classes of seizures, its use has been increasing in children with absence. The concurrent use of phenobarbital with antiabsence drugs for this purpose should be avoided as it may interfere with therapy for the absence.

Status epilepticus   Generalized tonic-clonic status epilepticus is a life-threatening medical emergency, but overzealous and incautious treatment can produce more harm than good. Patients are in danger from hyperpyrexia and acidosis (from prolonged muscle activity) and less commonly, hypoxia or compromise of respiratory function.

Immediate treatment for status is protection of the airway, protection of the tongue (with a soft object, large enough not to be swallowed, between the clenched teeth), protection of the head, and then establishment of a secure parenteral (intravenous) access. A bolus of 50% glucose in water (after blood is drawn for analysis), even if hypoglycemia is not expected, may stop the seizures. All further intravenous medication should be given after preparation for respiratory and circulatory support is available.

Phenytoin, 500 to 1500 mg (13 to 18 mg/kg) in a slow intravenous "push" (not 5% dextrose in water—phenytoin precipitates in this low pH solution)—no faster than 50 mg/min—is one of the drugs of choice. It does not depress respiration but may produce mild AV block and, if given too rapidly, can cause a fall in blood pressure.

The benzodiazepines, diazepam 10 mg or lorazepam 4 mg (followed by another dose if necessary), are also effective in stopping status epilepticus when administered intravenously. However, these drugs may depress respiratory function (or even cause respiratory arrest), and measures for respiratory support should be available before they are administered. The use of a benzodiazepine after phenobarbital administration carries a particular risk. The benzodiazepines are short-acting drugs, and after they are administered, a second, longer-acting anticonvulsant such as phenytoin is usually required to prevent recurrence of seizures.

Phenobarbital, in a dose of 10 to 20 mg/kg (up to 1 g), divided into two to four doses at 30- to 60-min intervals, can also be administered for status epilepticus. Phenobarbital also causes respiratory depression and should not be used immediately after treatment with intravenous diazepam.

After stopping the seizures it is imperative to determine the cause of the status epilepticus in order to prevent its recurrence. In approximately two-thirds of adults the cause can be determined and is usually tumor, vascular disease, infection, cerebral damage, or precipitous withdrawal from alcohol or antiepileptic medication. In children, the incidence of idiopathic status is higher (approximately

Therapeutic range	% Protein-bound	Toxic effects		Drug interactions
		Neurologic	Systemic	
10–20 μg/ml	90	Ataxia Incoordination Confusion	Gum hyperplasia Lymphadenopathy Hirsutism Osteomalacia Skin rash Altered folate metabolism	Level increased by INH, dicumeral, sulfonamides Level decreased by carba- mazepine, phenobarbital Folate interferes with ef- fects
4–12 μg/ml	80	Ataxia Dizziness Diplopia Vertigo	Bone marrow suppression Gastrointestinal irritation Hepatotoxicity	Level decreased by pheno- barbital, phenytoin
10–50 μg/ml	40–60	Sedation Ataxia Confusion Dizziness	Skin rash	Level increased by val- proate, phenytoin
2–10 μg/ml	Small for primidone or PEMA	Same as phenobarbital	Same as phenobarbital	
40–100 μg/ml	Small	Ataxia Lethargy	Gastrointestinal irritation Skin rash Bone marrow suppression	
	Small	Ataxia Lethargy	Same as ethosuximide	
5–70 ng/ml	50	Ataxia Sedation Lethargy	Anorexia	May precipitate absence status if given with val- proic acid
50–100 μg/ml	80–94	Ataxia Sedation	Hepatotoxicity Bone marrow suppression Gastrointestinal irritation Weight gain Transient alopecia	May precipitate absence status if given with clona- zepam
700 μg/ml (for dime- thadione)	Small	Sedation Blurred vision	Skin rash Bone marrow suppression Nephrosis Hepatitis	

50 percent), and the remaining cases are divided between acute brain illnesses such as purulent meningitis, encephalitis, and dehydration with electrolyte disturbances, and chronic encephalopathies. Tonic-clonic status epilepticus is a dangerous condition; the mortality rate may be over 10 percent with another 10 to 30 percent of patients being left with permanent neurologic sequelae.

NEUROSURGICAL TREATMENT OF EPILEPSY If a structural lesion (i.e., tumor, cyst, abscess, etc.) is causing recurrent seizures, the removal of that lesion and nearby diseased brain will often eliminate the seizures or make them easier to control. Some patients, however, have uncontrollable seizures without a demonstrable structural lesion. These are often complex partial seizures with ictal and interictal EEG abnormalities emanating from one or both temporal lobes. Many surgical series have shown that if the epileptogenic lesion can be clearly localized to one temporal lobe, neurosurgical removal of that temporal lobe can result in significant improvement in 60 to 80 percent of the patients. Localization often depends on intensive EEG monitoring and even depth electrode recordings from the temporal lobes. In a high percentage of cases the removed temporal lobe can be shown to have microscopic pathology, such as *hippocampal* (or *Ammon's horn*) *sclerosis* (loss of pyramidal cells in the hippocampus), a hamartoma, or cortical ectopia.

Some individuals with complex partial seizures also develop a psychiatric illness characterized most often as a borderline personality with certain specific behavioral manifestations including hypergraphia, hyperreligiosity, lack of sense of humor, and disordered sexuality. The psychiatric aspects of this illness may result from the epilepsy or may be independently produced by the same underlying brain lesion which produces the epilepsy. The personality disorder may not significantly change after epilepsy surgery, even if the seizures are controlled.

TREATMENT OF A SINGLE SEIZURE Some individuals present with a single, brief generalized tonic-clonic seizure and, after complete evaluation, are found to have a normal EEG and no underlying cause for the seizure. Some of these individuals go on to have recurrent seizures, but an unknown proportion do not. The decision to treat such a patient with several years (at least) of antiepileptic medication must be made on an individual basis, considering the patient's lifestyle, risks from a sudden loss of consciousness, and feelings about medications.

CESSATION OF ANTIEPILEPTIC DRUG THERAPY Many patients with epilepsy require antiepileptic drug therapy for life. However, a large proportion of epileptic patients become seizure-free on appropriate medication, and approximately half of such patients can eventually stop their medications and remain seizure-free. The patient who has had no seizures for 4 years, who has had relatively few seizures before control was attained, who only required a single medication, who has a normal neurologic exam and no structural lesion causing the seizures, and who has a normal EEG at the end of the therapeutic period has the best chance of remaining seizure-free if medication is slowly tapered (over 3 to 6 months). An abnormal EEG is not a contraindication to discontinuing medication. When considering the discontinuance of antiepileptic therapy, the consequences of the recurrence of seizures must be carefully considered. One inopportune seizure in a previously well controlled patient who is not used to taking precautions may be a life-threatening event, or lead to loss of a driver's license or loss of employment. Nevertheless, since all medications carry some risk of toxicity and since medication compliance in a healthy individual is often variable, it is worth a careful trial of medication tapering in individuals who meet the above criteria and are willing to accept the risk.

EPILEPSY AND PREGNANCY Most women with epilepsy can undergo uneventful pregnancies and deliver healthy babies—even those taking anticonvulsant medications. During the pregnant state, however, body metabolism changes and close attention must be given to antiepileptic drug levels. Sometimes relatively high doses have to be given to ensure therapeutic levels. Most women who are well controlled before pregnancy will remain so during pregnancy and delivery. Women whose seizures are not under good control before becoming pregnant are at higher risk for having increased difficulties during the pregnancy.

One of the most serious complications of pregnancy, toxemia, often presents as a generalized tonic-clonic convulsion in the third trimester. This seizure is a symptom of a severe neurologic disturbance and is not a manifestation of epilepsy, nor is it more common in epileptic women. The toxemic state must be treated in order to control the seizures.

There is a two- to threefold higher incidence of fetal malformations in offspring of epileptic women, and this is likely due to a combination of the low incidence of medication-induced malformation and of genetic predisposition in this population. Among those malformations which do occur, a *fetal-hydantoin syndrome* consisting of cleft lip and palate, heart defects, digital hypoplasia, and nail dysplasia has been identified.

Although it would be ideal for women contemplating pregnancy to have their antiepileptic drugs discontinued, it is likely that for a large number of women this would result in recurrence of seizures which would, in the long run, be more harmful for both mother and baby. If patients meet the criteria for discontinuance of medication, this should be done with a suitable interval before pregnancy is to occur. Other patients should be tapered to a minimal effective dosage and, if possible, be maintained on only one medication. There are no clear data indicating differences in safety for phenobarbital, phenytoin, or carbamazepine when used alone. Less experience is available for valproate. Phenobarbital, primidone, or phenytoin can cause transient and reversible deficiency in vitamin K–dependent clotting factors in the neonate, and these should be promptly treated. Babies exposed to chronic barbiturates in utero are often transiently sluggish, hypotonic, jittery, and often show signs of barbiturate withdrawal. These babies should be considered at risk for neonatal problems and should be slowly withdrawn from barbiturates and closely observed in the nursery during the neonatal period.

DRIVING AND EPILEPSY Each state has its own regulations for determining when an individual with epilepsy can obtain a driver's license, and several states have laws about the physician's obligations in either reporting epileptic patients to the registry or informing the patients of their responsibilities to do so. In general, patients can drive after a seizure-free interval (on or off medications) which ranges from 6 months to 2 years. In some states there is no fixed interval, but the individual is required to have a physician's letter attesting to seizure control. It is the physician's responsibility to warn the epileptic patient of the risks of driving when seizures are not under control.

SOCIAL AND EDUCATIONAL REHABILITATION Most people with epilepsy attain adequate control of their seizures and are able to attend school, obtain employment, and live a relatively normal life. Children with epilepsy tend to have more problems in school than their peers, but every effort should be made to keep these children integrated into the mainstream of the educational process while supplying additional help in the form of academic tutoring or psychological counseling.

REFERENCES

AIRD R et al: *The Epilepsies: A Critical Review*. New York, Raven Press, 1984

BROWNE TR, FELDMAN RG (eds): *Epilepsy: Diagnosis and Management*. Boston, Little Brown, 1983

COMMISSION ON CLASSIFICATION AND TERMINOLOGY OF THE ILAE: Proposal for revised clinical classification of epileptic seizures. Epilepsia 22:489, 1981

EMERSON R et al: Stopping medication in children with epilepsy. N Engl J Med 304:1125, 1981

ENGEL J JR et al: Recent Developments in the Diagnosis and Therapy of Epilepsy. Ann Intern Med 97:584, 1982

LAIDLAW J, RICHENS A (eds): *A Textbook of Epilepsy*, 2d ed. London, Churchill Livingstone, 1982

LEPPIK IE: Drug treatment of epilepsy in *Current Therapy in Neurologic Disease*, RT Johnson (ed). Philadelphia, BC Decker Inc, 1986, pp 41–46

SOLOMON G et al: *Clinical Management of Seizures*. Philadelphia, Saunders, 1983

THURSTON J et al: Prognosis in childhood epilepsy. N Engl J Med 306:831, 1982

WOODBURY D et al (eds): *Antiepileptic Drugs*, 2d ed. New York, Raven Press, 1982

343 CEREBROVASCULAR DISEASES

J. PHILIP KISTLER / ALLAN H. ROPPER / JOSEPH B. MARTIN

Cerebrovascular disease is the third leading cause of death after heart disease and cancer in developed countries. More importantly, in adults, it is the most lethal and disabling of the neurologic diseases. It has an overall prevalence of 794 per 100,000. Five percent of the population over 65 has at one time in their lives had a stroke. In the United States it is estimated that more than 400,000 patients are discharged each year from hospitals after a stroke. The removal of these patients from the work force and the extended hospitalization they require make the economic impact of this disease one of the most devastating in medicine.

PATHOGENESIS OF STROKE Cerebrovascular disease implicates one or more of the blood vessels of the brain in a pathologic process. The process may be intrinsic to the vessel, as it is in atherosclerosis, lipohyalinosis, inflammation, amyloid formation, dissection (traumatic or spontaneous), developmental malformation, or aneurysmal dilatation; or the process may start at a remote site, as occurs when an embolus from the heart or extracranial circulation lodges in an intracranial vessel, or when decreased perfusion pressure or increased blood viscosity results in inadequate blood flow through a vessel. A vascular lesion tends to be silent until it causes critical narrowing with ischemia, or embolises, occludes, or ruptures. A *stroke* is defined as a neurologic injury occurring as a result of one of these pathologic processes. A thrombus, atheroma, or embolus may critically narrow or block a vessel and produce ischemia with infarction; or a vessel may rupture and give rise to intracerebral or subarachnoid hemorrhage. Other symptoms may occur secondary to vascular disease, such as pressure on cranial nerves from an aneurysm, vascular headache (migrainous or with arteritis or hypertension), or increased intracranial pressure accompanying a venous thrombosis.

CEREBRAL METABOLISM AND INFARCTION To function normally, the brain must receive a moment-to-moment supply of oxygenated blood, but even a reduced supply may suffice to forestall infarction for an indeterminate period. Cardiac arrest results in unconsciousness within 10 s; and in animal experiments, total cessation of blood flow produces irreversible cerebral infarction within 3 min. However, reduced flow allows the brain to remain ischemic but viable for prolonged periods before it either infarcts or recovers as flow returns toward normal. For example, patients who suffer cerebral embolism, or cerebral vasospasm following subarachnoid hemorrhage, often recover partially or completely. Such recovery suggests that focal areas of brain can remain functionless and ischemic for hours, even days, yet revive. This has led to the notion of an ischemic zone (penumbra or halo) that surrounds an infarct. The extent to which recovery can occur after ischemia remains uncertain. What is clear is that once brain cells become infarcted, cell membrane integrity is lost, the blood-brain barrier is disrupted, and mitochondrial high-energy phosphate metabolism ceases.

PATHOLOGY An infarcted brain is pale initially. Within hours to days, the gray matter, in particular, may become congested with engorged, dilated blood vessels and minute petechial hemorrhages (hemorrhagic infarction). The cause of such hemorrhagic infarction is uncertain, but is usually considered to result from an embolus blocking a major vessel, e.g., middle cerebral artery stem (Figs.

343-1 and 343-2) or one of its major branches; the embolus migrates, lyses, and disperses within hours, allowing recirculation into the infarcted area. The recirculation may cause the hemorrhagic infarction and possibly aggravate the subsequent edema formation after the blood-brain barrier has broken down. A primary intracerebral hemorrhage, on the other hand, damages the brain by disrupting tissue at the site of the hemorrhage and by compressing the surrounding tissue.

Once an ischemic stroke or intracerebral hemorrhage has occurred, or when transient spells of cerebral ischemia occur, the prelude to adequate therapy is a precise diagnosis. It must include definition of the character and location of the lesion, the vascular pathologic

process producing the symptoms, and knowledge of the anatomy of any spared collateral circulation to the ischemic area. The brain repairs itself only by forming fibrogliotic scar tissue at the site of an infarction or hemorrhage; therefore, therapeutic efforts can only be preventive. Such efforts should attempt to protect both the normal and ischemic brain from either initial or recurrent pathologic processes, as well as from the secondary effects of the stroke itself, e.g., brain compression from intracranial hemorrhage or edema. Broadly, such preventive therapy has three goals: to prevent stroke by reducing risk factors, thus attenuating the pathologic process; to prevent initial or recurrent stroke by removing the underlying pathologic process—for example, by performing a carotid endarterectomy; and to prevent

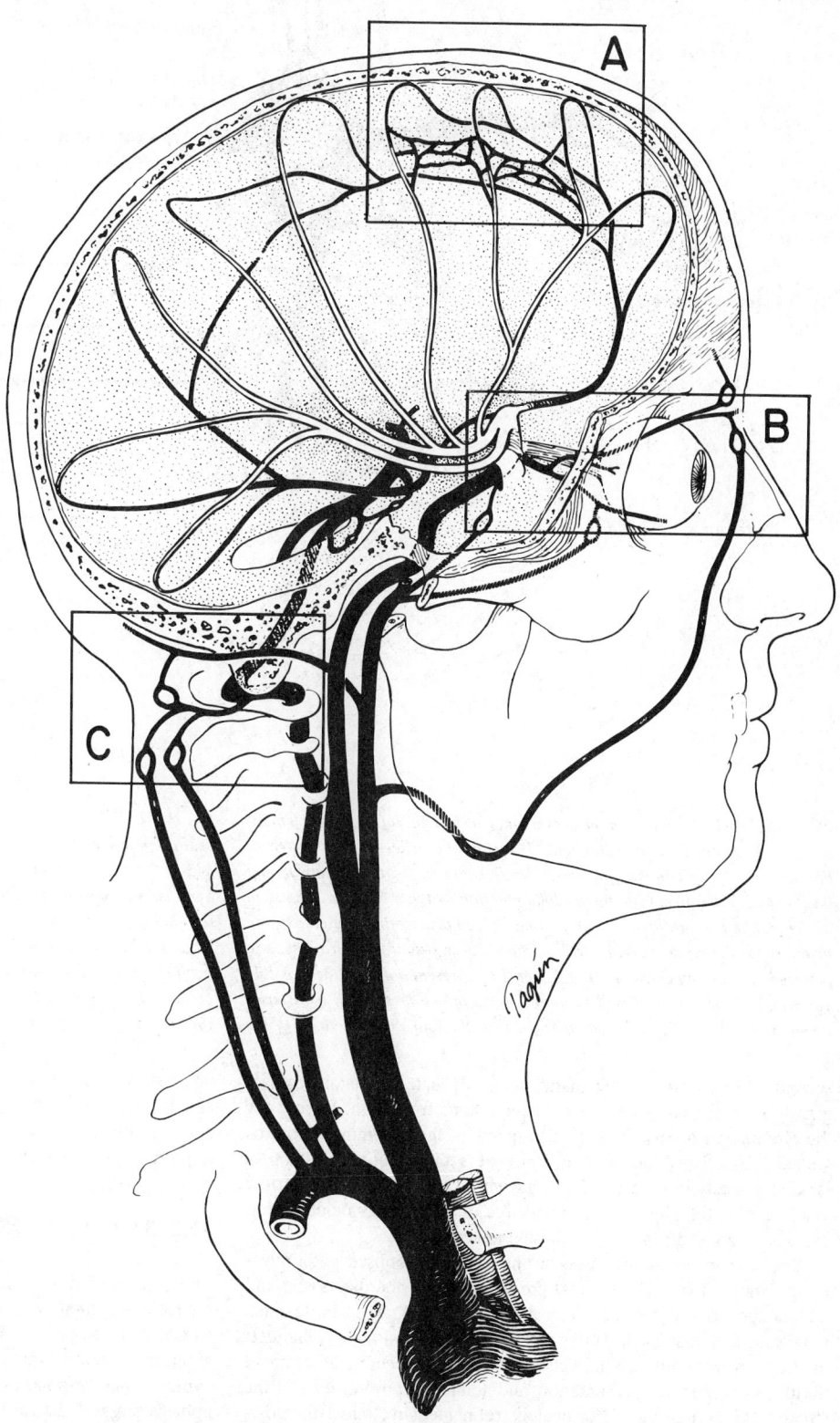

FIGURE 343-1 *Arrangement of the major arteries of the right side carrying blood from the heart to the brain. Also shown are vessels of collateral circulation that may modify the effects of cerebral ischemia (A,B,C). Not shown is the circle of Willis which also provides a source for collateral circulation. A. The anastomotic channels between the distal branches of the anterior and middle cerebral artery, termed borderzone or watershed anastomotic channels. Note that they also occur between the posterior and middle cerebral arteries and the anterior and posterior cerebral arteries. B. Anastomotic channels occurring through the orbit between branches of the external carotid artery and the ophthalamic branch of the internal carotid artery. C. Wholly extracranial anastomotic channels between the muscular branches of the ascending cervical arteries and muscular branches of the occipital artery that anastomose with the distal vertebral artery. Note that the occipital artery arises from the external carotid artery, thereby allowing reconstitution of flow in the vertebral from the carotid circulation. (Courtesy of C.M. Fisher, M.D.)*

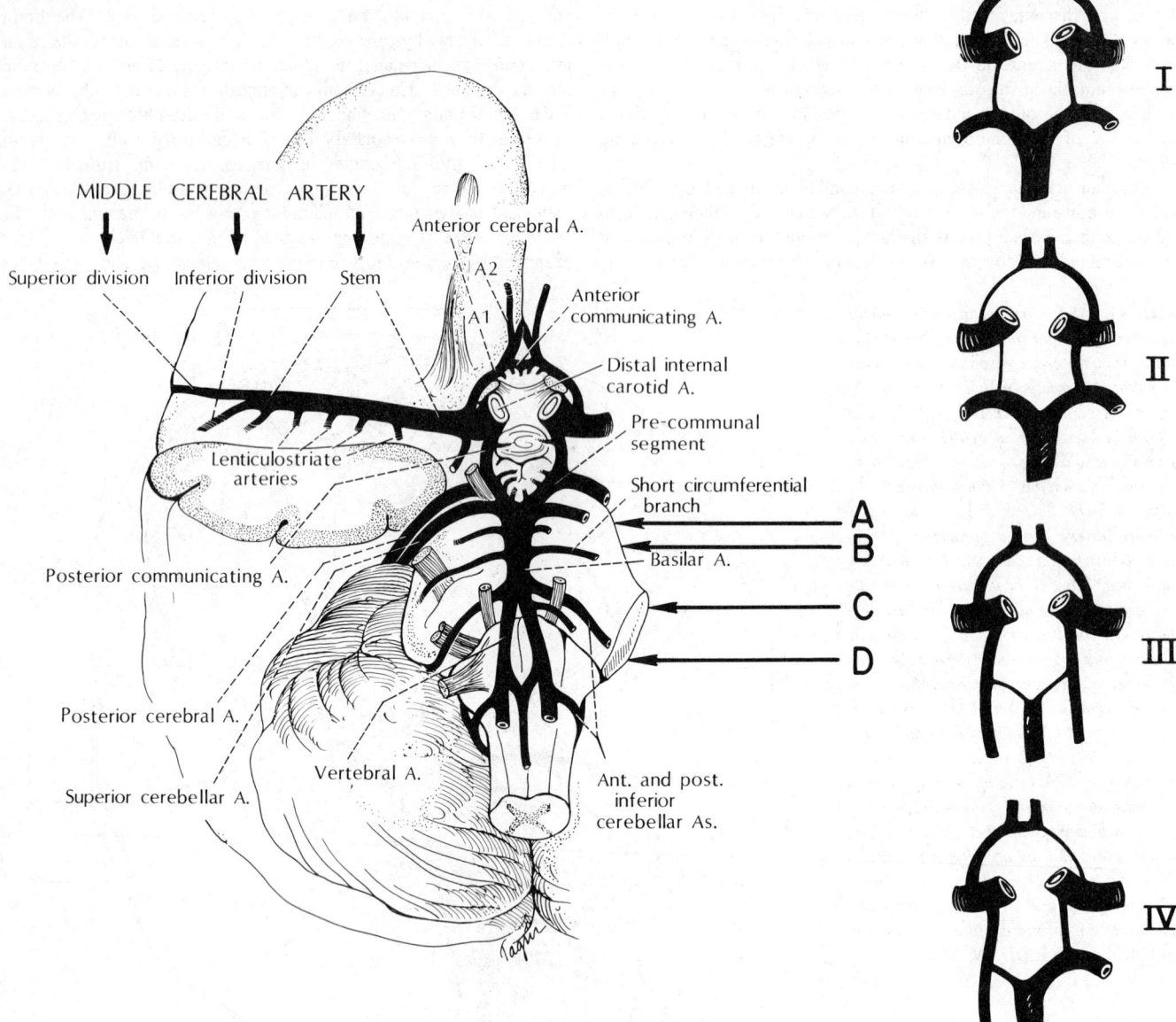

MIDDLE CEREBRAL ARTERY

Superior division Inferior division Stem

Anterior cerebral A.

A2
A1

Anterior communicating A.

Distal internal carotid A.

Pre-communal segment

Short circumferential branch

Lenticulostriate arteries

Basilar A.

A
B
C
D

Posterior communicating A.

Posterior cerebral A.

Superior cerebellar A.

Vertebral A.

Ant. and post. inferior cerebellar As.

I

II

III

IV

FIGURE 343-2 *Diagram of the brainstem, cerebellum, inferior right frontal lobe, and temporal lobe transected. Principal branches of the vertebral basilar arterial system are pictured. Small branches of the vertebral and basilar artery that penetrate the medulla and pons are not pictured. The stem of the middle cerebral artery with its small, deep penetrating lenticulostriate arteries and the circle of Willis with its small, deep penetrating branches are pictured. Roman numerals I, II, III, and IV represent some of the possible variations of the Circle of Willis due to atresia of one or more of its arterial components. A, B, C, and D arrows point to the four cross-sections of the brainstem diagrammed below (D = Fig. 343-7, A = Fig. 343-8, B = Fig. 343-9, C = Fig. 343-10). Although typical vascular syndromes of the pons and medulla have been designated by the shaded areas in Figs. 343-7 to 10, the shading is arbitrary. Great variability in infarct size and location occurs when the basilar or vertebral arteries, or one of their penetrating branches, occludes because of variation in arterial anatomic location and available collateral circulation. Thus the stroke syndromes produced are often atypical, incomplete, or merge with one another. (Courtesy of C.M. Fisher, M.D.)*

secondary brain damage by maintaining adequate perfusion to marginally ischemic areas and by reducing edema formation. Except for the elimination of risk factors, all aspects of therapy remain controversial. Established proof of efficacy of a therapeutic approach is lacking in many instances; hence, current therapy is largely empirical and based on the physician's knowledge of the risks associated with various diagnostic procedures and therapies.

Strokes can be classified according to their proposed pathophysiologic mechanism. The clinical presentation and the diagnostic and therapeutic options for each can then be defined. The single most important factor in establishing a precise pathophysiologic diagnosis of stroke or transient ischemic attack (TIA) is an accurate assessment of its initial clinical presentation and temporal profile, i.e., "the stroke or TIA syndrome." Fortunately, refinement in clinical diagnosis

and neuroradiologic techniques can now allow diagnosis of the type and location of strokes and their concomitant vascular lesions with considerable frequency and accuracy, making a more focused approach to therapy both possible and mandatory.

THE STROKE SYNDROME

The characteristics of the mode of onset, together with the specific neurologic symptoms and signs, suggest the lesion's location and its cause. In most cases, the abrupt, dramatic onset of focal neurologic symptoms stamps the process as a stroke, particularly when the symptoms correspond to a specific vascular territory: hemiparesis and aphasia suggest the middle cerebral artery territory of the dominant hemisphere; a sudden disturbance in a visual field suggests the territory of the posterior cerebral artery; or a pure motor hemiparesis suggests a small "lacunar" stroke in the internal capsule or basis pontis corresponding to the territory of the small penetrating branches of the middle cerebral or basilar arteries, respectively. The initial symptoms may be minimal or maximal at onset, or the deficit may fluctuate, improving or worsening in a stepwise manner. It is this temporal profile that first suggests whether a lesion is thrombotic, embolic, or hemorrhagic. For example, sudden deep coma can accompany either basilar artery embolism, subarachnoid hemorrhage, or hypertensive hemorrhage in the basis pontis. To define the nature of the lesion causing the coma, both the neurologic deficits found on examination and details of the subsequent neurologic course are needed. Frequently, the precise details of the early temporal course are difficult to delineate. The patient may not remember until prompted; or the location of a deficit may preclude awareness, as it does when anosognosia occurs in lesions of the nondominant hemisphere. Often the family is the best source of important historical details in cases of acute stroke or suspected transient cerebral ischemia.

The stroke syndrome, therefore, is recognized chiefly by its temporal profile and its characteristic pattern of symptoms and signs.

In hemorrhagic strokes, the location and size of the hemorrhage and its type (subarachnoid vs. intracerebral) determine the characteristic stroke syndrome. However, in ischemic stroke, the stroke syndrome is determined not only by the pathologic process and the size and location of the occluded vessel but also by the availability of collateral circulation. Often, there is sufficient collateral flow to prevent infarction or reduce the size of infarction significantly, altering the evolution of the stroke syndrome.

Collateral flow may be sufficient for a major arterial trunk to be entirely occluded without symptoms or visible damage to the brain parenchyma. In other cases, occlusion of major vessels may lead to softening throughout their entire arterial territory. Between these two extremes countless variations in the size, shape, and completeness of an infarct depend on the availability of collateral flow (Fig. 343-1). In addition, collateral flow depends on vascular anatomy, the speed of occlusion, and the level of the systemic blood pressure. These factors and possibly others such as altered physical state of

the blood (viscosity, polycythemia, abnormal red blood cells) may at times operate adversely to produce ischemia in the territory of partially occluded vessels.

The only vessels not subject to collateral flow are the small, deep penetrating vessels that arise from the stem of the middle cerebral arteries (lenticulostriate arteries), the distal vertebral arteries, the basilar artery, and the arteries of the circle of Willis (Figs. 343-2 and 343-3). They supply deep white and gray matter in the brainstem, thalamus, basal ganglia, and corona radiata. Occlusion of one of these small penetrating vessels, either by atherothrombotic or lipohyalinotic disease or embolism, produces a small "lacunar" infarction.

The terms *stroke in evolution* (also called *progressive stroke*) and *completed stroke* need special mention. Stroke in evolution refers to a neurologic deficit that progresses or fluctuates while the patient is under observation, whereas completed stroke implies that no further deterioration will occur. Several mechanisms have been attributed to stroke in evolution, among them progressive narrowing of an artery by thrombus, development of cerebral edema, thrombus propagation obliterating collateral branches to the ischemic brain, and systemic factors, e.g., arterial hypotension. Although these may have a role in some cases, it is more likely that fluctuating neurologic deficits are the result of emboli propagating, migrating, lysing, and dispersing, or are caused by recurrent artery-to-artery embolization, fluctuating collateral flow through the circle of Willis, through border zone anastomotic channels, or through orbital or cervical-vertebral collaterals (Figs. 343-1*A*, *B*, and *C*, and 343-2).

RISK FACTORS IN STROKE Certain types of cerebrovascular disease suggest themselves not only by their stroke syndromes but also by their association with risk factors. An atherothrombotic stroke often suggests that the patient has silent or symptomatic cardiovascular and peripheral vascular disease; conversely, severe atherothrombotic disease anywhere in the body suggests an atherothrombotic process as the cause of an ischemic stroke. Since atrial fibrillation, valvular heart disease, myocardial infarction, and bacterial endocarditis are sources of emboli, their presence suggests embolism as the diagnosis. Severe hypertension is invariably linked to small vessel lipohyalinotic

FIGURE 343-3 *Diagram of a cerebral hemisphere in coronal section, showing the territories of the major cerebral vessels. (Courtesy of C. M. Fisher, M.D.)*

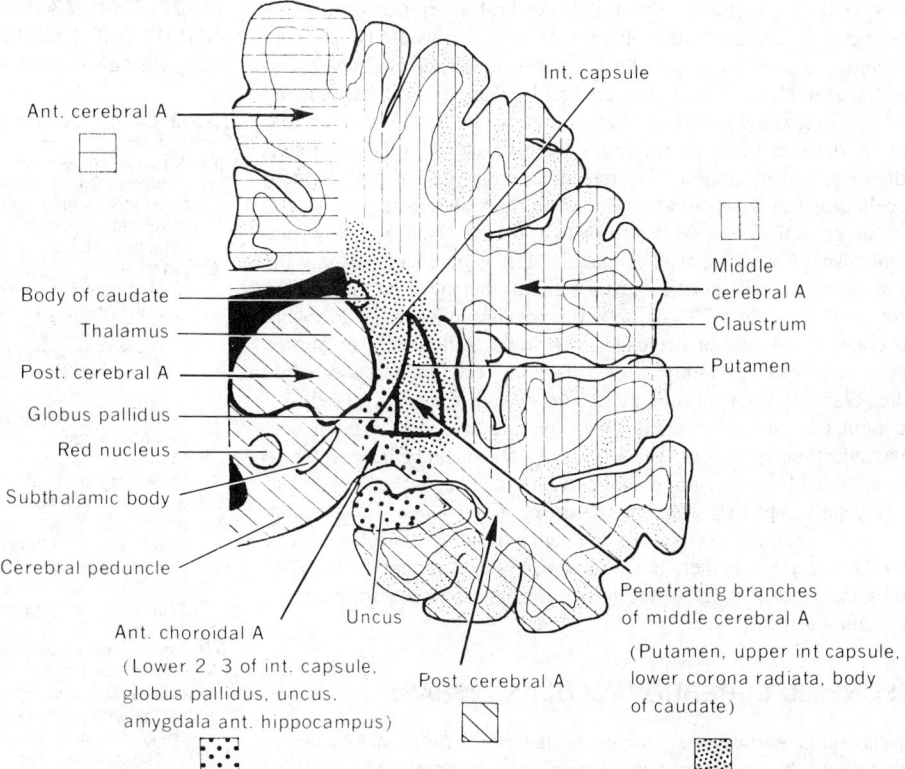

Ant. cerebral A

Int. capsule

Body of caudate
Thalamus
Post. cerebral A
Globus pallidus
Red nucleus
Subthalamic body

Cerebral peduncle

Middle cerebral A
Claustrum
Putamen

Uncus

Ant. choroidal A
(Lower 2/3 of int. capsule, globus pallidus, uncus, amygdala ant. hippocampus)

Post. cerebral A

Penetrating branches of middle cerebral A
(Putamen, upper int capsule, lower corona radiata, body of caudate)

disease, lacunar strokes, and the formation of atherothrombotic lesions at the carotid bifurcation, in the middle cerebral artery stem, and in the vertebral-basilar system. Hypertension also predisposes to deep intracerebral hemorrhages. Some argue that the advent of antihypertensive therapy is the principal factor accounting for the declining incidence of stroke. Smoking and familial hyperlipidemia, although less important than hypertension, are associated with an increased risk of atherothrombotic disease in general, and ischemic cerebrovascular disease in particular.

TIA SYNDROME

In the TIA syndrome, the character, duration, and repetitiveness of a transient neurologic dysfunction suggest its pathophysiologic cause; that is, the clinical symptoms and signs and the temporal profile of a TIA suggest the nature and location of the underlying arterial pathophysiology. The term *transient ischemic attack* has usually been applied to any sudden focal neurologic deficit that clears completely in less than 24 h. This definition is too broad, because it includes too many syndromes, some of which are not necessarily caused by ischemia, e.g., a focal epileptic manifestation or migraine attack with neurologic symptoms. Furthermore, ischemic symptoms that persist longer than an hour suggest that some of the tissue may have become infarcted.

The specific symptoms of a TIA point to the particular arterial territory involved [carotid, middle cerebral, vertebral-basilar, or small vessel penetrating artery (lacunar TIA)]. Furthermore, the duration, stereotypic nature, and frequency of repetitive spells suggest a pathophysiologic mechanism. For example, repetitive (up to 5 to 10 per day), short-lived (15 min or less), stereotypic spells of hand and arm weakness with or without speech difficulty suggest that proximal arterial narrowing or occlusion and inadequate collateral circulation have produced transient focal ischemia ("low flow") in the contralateral cortex. On the other hand, a single spell of speech difficulty with or without hand and arm and face weakness lasting 12 h suggests an embolic ischemic event probably with some degree of infarction in the left frontal lobe. A transient short-lived episode of pure motor hemiparesis—face, arm, leg, and foot—occurring *without* dysphasia or hemineglect suggests transient ischemia in the internal capsule, i.e., in the territory supplied by one of the small penetrating arteries arising from the stem of the middle cerebral artery (lenticulostriate arteries). Should a stroke evolve in this setting, it would be less than 1 cm in size, i.e., a lacune. Such a transient episode could be called a "lacunar TIA." TIA in the vertebral-basilar system, when it is the result of proximal basilar or bilateral, distal vertebral artery stenosis, often presents with short-lived, repetitive episodes of dizziness, diplopia, and dysarthria. The repetitive, short-lived nature of these spells suggests transient low flow rather than embolism.

In general, TIAs evolve from two causes: focal low flow and embolism. The mechanism of embolic TIA is obvious, and only the source needs to be considered in deciding therapy. The mechanism for focal "low-flow" TIAs, however, remains less certain. Probably a critically stenotic or occluded artery reduces flow in a focal area of normal brain. Certainly, poor collateral circulation to the ischemic area plays a prominent role, but factors such as viscosity, vessel wall compliance, and other unknown factors are needed to explain why the reduction is transient. These types of TIAs might be better referred to as true TIAs, i.e., not embolic events. Unlike stroke, TIAs clear completely, but they warn that a stroke may follow. Therefore, it becomes important to consider the pathophysiologic mechanisms of stroke and TIA together. In essence, a physician cannot treat a TIA, only the cause of it. TIA, like stroke, is a syndrome requiring a more specific diagnosis.

ISCHEMIC CEREBROVASCULAR DISEASE

Ischemic cerebrovascular disease results from arterial narrowing or thrombosis by a primary pathologic process or arterial occlusion by embolism. Most of this section will be devoted to cerebral thrombosis and its various pathologic causes. Cerebral embolism causes many of the same symptoms and signs as thrombosis. Where the symptomatology differs, it will be discussed in the section on cerebral embolism.

THROMBOSIS WITH ATHEROSCLEROSIS   Of the many causes of cerebral thrombosis listed in Table 343-1, thrombosis with atherosclerosis accounts for most cases. Atherosclerosis affects each of the extra- and intracranial arteries at specific locations. In general, atheromatous plaques tend to form at branchings and curves of large vessels, and thrombosis is likely to occur where plaque narrows the lumen most.

The details of the process which superimposes thrombosis on atherosclerosis are poorly understood (see Chap. 195). The atheromatous lesion itself lies between the intima and media of the vessel. It penetrates and disrupts the media. The plaque is composed of hyaline connective tissue, fibroblasts, macrophages, and smooth muscle cells. It is spotted with focal deposits of cholesterol crystals. Presumably, thrombosis forms when the underlying atherosclerotic formation fragments the endothelial lining of the vessel wall, establishing a nidus for platelet accumulation and mural thrombus formation. Occasionally, blood from the lumen dissects into an atheromatous plaque. This penetration may be the mechanism by which an ulcer crater forms and becomes a nidus for the production of a mural thrombus. Less often, hemorrhage into a plaque further narrows the lumen. The atheromatous narrowing of the lumen usually resembles an hourglass whose narrowest segment is only 1 to 2 mm long. A mural thrombus may form at this segment or proximal or distal to it. Thrombotic occlusion usually occurs when atheroma narrows the lumen to a point where distal blood flow is impeded.

It is difficult to predict the damage atherosclerotic thrombosis may cause to the brain. Available collateral flow, the speed of thrombotic occlusion, and the occurrence of embolism distal to the thrombosis may alter the clinical picture. Inevitably, the picture resulting from occlusion of a particular artery differs from one patient to another, and most syndromes are partial. The following descriptions apply to infarction and ischemia in specific arteries due to thrombosis, recognizing that similar clinical pictures may occur after embolism. Occasionally, hemorrhage within these vascular territories also may give rise to similar symptoms and signs.

ATHEROTHROMBOTIC DISEASE OF THE INTERNAL CAROTID ARTERY AND ITS BRANCHES   Pathophysiology   In the carotid artery system atherosclerosis and superimposed atherothrombosis that

TABLE 343-1   Causes of cerebral thrombosis

I Atherosclerosis
II Cerebral thrombophlebitis: secondary to infection of ear, paranasal sinus, face, etc.; with meningitis and subdural empyema; debilitating states, postpartum, postoperative; cardiac failure; hematologic disease (polycythemia, sickle cell disease), and of undetermined cause
III Arteritis
   A Meningovascular syphilis, arteritis secondary to pyogenic and tuberculous meningitis, rare types [typhus, schistosomiasis mansoni, malaria (?), trichinosis (?), mucormycosis, etc.]
   B Connective tissue diseases: polyarteritis (necrotizing, granulomatous, allergic, Wegener's), temporal arteritis, Takayasu's disease, granulomatous arteritis of aorta, lupus erythematosus
IV Hematologic disorders: polycythemia, sickle cell disease, thrombotic thrombocytopenic purpura, etc.
V Trauma to carotid
VI Dissecting aortic aneurysm
VII Systemic hypotension: "simple faint," acute blood loss, myocardial infarction, Stokes-Adams syndrome, traumatic and surgical shock, sensitive carotid sinus, severe postural hypotension
VIII Complications of arteriography
IX Migrainous aura with persistent deficit
X With tentorial, foramen magnum, and subfalcial herniation
XI Hypoxia
XII Miscellaneous: radioactive or x-ray radiation, lateral pressure of intracerebral hematoma, unexplained middle cerebral infarction in closed head injury, pressure of unruptured saccular aneurysm, mural thrombus in fusiform aneurysm, local dissection of carotid or middle cerebral artery, complication of contraceptive medication
XIII Undetermined cause as in childhood

lead to TIA or stroke most commonly occur at its origin and less often at the siphon (s-shaped portion of the internal carotid artery in the cavernous sinus) or at the proximal segment (stem) of the middle or anterior cerebral arteries. Rarely, it occurs at the origin of the common carotid artery. The natural history of atherosclerotic stenosis or ulcerated lesions at these locations that have not yet become symptomatic is unknown. Presumably, in most instances the disease is progressive.

INTERNAL CAROTID ARTERY ORIGIN Atherosclerosis in the proximal internal carotid artery is usually most severe in the first 2 cm and is located on the posterior wall; often it extends downward into the distal common carotid artery. Disease in this area is usually (50 to 80 percent of cases) heralded by a minor stroke or TIA caused by a "low-flow" hemodynamic crisis or embolism from the carotid artery to its intracranial branches. Clinical experience and pathologic examination suggest that emboli rather than low flow cause most strokes from carotid disease. Embolism from an atherosclerotic plaque at the origin of the internal carotid artery may cause TIAs, but when they are repetitive, short-lived, and stereotyped, a hemodynamic cause seems likely.

CEREBRAL ISCHEMIA CAUSED BY LOW FLOW Low arterial blood flow can cause cerebral infarction or TIA in the border zone or watershed areas where the cortical surface branches of the middle cerebral artery anastomose with the branches of the anterior and posterior cerebral artery (Fig. 343-1A). Two conditions contribute to this complication. First, blood pressure may be reduced distal to the carotid artery stenotic lesion if there is more than 80 percent reduction in carotid lumen diameter, or, equivalently, the residual lumen diameter is less than 1.5 to 2 mm. Second, impaired collateral circulation to the region may occur. Impairment generally results from an incomplete circle of Willis secondary to congenital atresia of the initial (A1) portion of the anterior cerebral artery or the anterior or posterior communicating arteries (Fig. 343-2B). Less often, impairment results from occlusion of either the contralateral carotid artery or the basilar artery—conditions that limit flow into the circle of Willis. Occasionally enough flow can be obtained through the external carotid ophthalmic collaterals (Fig. 343-1B) or cortical surface border zone collaterals (Fig. 343-1A) to ensure adequate flow or minimize the ischemic area, even if the circle of Willis is inadequate. It is this variation in collateral flow that is responsible for the variable location of low-flow stroke or TIA in the carotid territory.

Other explanations of the pathophysiology of low-flow TIAs have been given. It has been suggested that severely stenotic lesions at the carotid bifurcation may intermittently occlude the vessel due to spasm. On rare occasions, systemic hemodynamic factors, i.e., abnormal blood viscosity or arterial hypotension, may reduce flow to a critical level across a tightly stenotic lesion. Alternatively, regional circulation in the hemisphere may be altered to accommodate diminished carotid blood flow, and transient decompensation of this mechanism may cause TIAs. Other factors, including polycythemia vera, thrombocythemia, and cardiac arrhythmia, may rarely cause recurrent "low-flow"-type TIAs.

EMBOLISM When emboli arise from a stenotic or ulcerated atherosclerotic lesion at the origin of the internal carotid artery (*local embolism* or *artery-to-artery embolus*), symptoms usually relate to occlusion of the ophthalmic artery, the middle cerebral artery stem or one or more of its branches, or occasionally to the anterior cerebral artery or its branches. The size of an embolus determines which vessel is occluded. Small platelet emboli may occlude only the very distal vessels of the middle cerebral artery or ophthalmic artery, causing only transient monocular blindness (*amaurosis fugax*) or small asymptomatic infarctions in the cerebral arterial watershed. But larger emboli composed of platelet-fibrin clot may occlude the primary and secondary branches of the middle cerebral artery where discrete neurologic syndromes suggest the area involved. Some emboli are large enough to occlude the proximal "stem" of the middle cerebral artery, leading to devastating ischemia of the entire middle cerebral

territory (deep white matter, lenticular nuclei, and cortical surface). Other emboli large enough to occlude the middle cerebral stem may cause only deep infarction because collateral flow through the cortical surface is sufficient (Fig. 343-1A). Large emboli that occlude a major vessel may migrate or lyse and disperse. If this dispersion occurs early, the neurologic deficit may fluctuate or resolve.

In a few symptomatic patients, an ulcerated plaque may be the only lesion in the carotid bifurcation, but far more often there is a stenotic lesion with a residual luminal diameter of less than 2 mm. The incidence of large embolic strokes resulting from an ulcerated lesion alone is undetermined. It is probably low and mostly associated with large ulcers (4 mm or greater). *A nonstenotic or minor stenotic carotid lesion in conjunction with a stroke or a single prolonged TIA suggests the heart as the source of the embolus.* Atheromatous lesions at the origin of the great vessels in the aortic arch can also produce cerebral emboli that cause transient ischemia or infarction, but the incidence of this mechanism is also undetermined.

Internal carotid artery occlusion at its origin may be entirely asymptomatic if collateral circulation through the circle of Willis is adequate. On the other hand, if collateral circulation is inadequate, low flow may induce a stroke or TIA. In addition, a clot may propagate upward from the occlusion through the siphon to the origin of the middle or anterior arteries and cause a stroke. More often, a fresh embolus breaks off from the thrombotic material and lodges in the middle or anterior cerebral artery or one of its branches. Some authorities postulate that emboli can arise from the proximal stump of the internal carotid artery and travel through the external carotid collateral circulation to reach the intracranial internal carotid artery and its branches (Fig. 343-1B). This process is probably rare.

The cause of a delayed stroke—one occurring months after complete carotid occlusion—is often unclear, and the incidence has not been established. One study suggests it is as high as 5 percent per year. Yet that seems high by clinical experience. Most embolism from carotid occlusion occurs within the first year, although it can occur up to 2 years later. Strokes caused by low flow tend to occur earlier, usually within the first few weeks after carotid occlusion.

INTRACRANIAL INTERNAL CAROTID ARTERY The carotid siphon is less commonly involved with atherosclerosis than the proximal internal carotid. Lesions in the siphon can cause strokes and TIAs whose pathophysiologic and clinical features duplicate those discussed above. The natural history of siphon stenosis is undetermined. In general, one should not consider siphon stenosis as symptomatic until the atheromatous process has reduced the residual lumen to 1.5 mm or less. Only angiography can diagnose accurately carotid siphon stenosis distal to the ophthalmic artery. The effect of collateral flow around the circle of Willis undoubtedly influences the natural history of these lesions and their response to medical or surgical therapy.

MIDDLE CEREBRAL ARTERY Atheromatous lesions in the middle cerebral stem may cause ischemic symptoms either by narrowing the artery or occluding the origin of one or more of the lenticulostriate arteries supplying the deep white matter and basal ganglia. Symptomatic atheroma rarely occurs distal to the first bifurcation of the middle cerebral artery. Because the circle of Willis is proximal to the origin of the middle cerebral artery, collateral blood flow to the middle cerebral artery territory must arise from small cortical-surface border zones and anastomotic vessels of the anterior and posterior cerebral arteries. Existing evidence indicates that before infarction develops, TIAs in the middle cerebral artery territory usually warn of vessel narrowing prior to thrombotic occlusion. Symptoms resemble those due to low-flow hemodynamic TIAs occurring with a tightly stenotic lesion of the internal carotid artery. In contrast to the internal carotid artery, the middle cerebral stem or one or more of its major branches is usually occluded by embolus (artery-to-artery, cardiac, or unknown source).

ANTERIOR CEREBRAL ARTERY Atheromatous deposits in the proximal segment of the anterior cerebral artery rarely cause symptoms because the occlusion is circumvented by collateral circulation through the anterior communicating artery. However, if this source of collateral circulation is congenitally atretic or if the atheromatous lesion occurs more distally in the anterior cerebral artery, TIAs and stroke become more likely.

Clinical syndromes MIDDLE CEREBRAL ARTERY The cortical branches of the middle cerebral artery supply the lateral surface of the hemisphere except for (1) the frontal pole, (2) a strip along the superomedial border of the frontal lobe supplied by the anterior cerebral artery, and (3) the lowest temporal convolutions, which are in the territory of the posterior cerebral artery (Figs. 343-3 to 343-5).

The middle cerebral artery's area includes the cortex and white matter of the lateral and inferior aspects of the frontal lobe, the motor cortex (areas 4 and 6, the centers for contraversive eye movements, and in the dominant hemisphere the motor speech area of Broca), the cortex and white matter of the lateral parietal lobe (sensory cortex, angular and supramarginal convolutions), the lateral and superior parts of the temporal lobe, and the insula (Figs. 343-3 and 343-4). The penetrating branches of the middle cerebral artery supply the putamen, outer globus pallidus, the posterior limb of the internal capsule above the plane of the upper border of the globus pallidus, the adjacent part of the corona radiata, the body of the caudate

nucleus, and the superior and lateral portion of the head of the caudate nucleus (Fig. 343-3).

The middle cerebral territory is the region most frequently affected in embolic and thrombotic cerebrovascular disease. The entire artery may be occluded at its stem, blocking both penetrating branches to the deep white and gray matter as well as the major branches to the cortical surface. The classic picture of this lesion is contralateral hemiplegia and hemianesthesia. If the dominant hemisphere is involved, global or total sensorimotor aphasia also is present. If the nondominant hemisphere is affected, apractagnosia and anosognosia are added to the clinical syndrome (Fig. 343-4). While there may be dysarthria, dysphasia is absent.

Complete middle cerebral territory syndromes occur most often when an embolus occludes the stem of the artery. Effective cortical surface arterial collateral flow requires some time to develop (Figs. 343-1 and 343-4), but it is responsible for the development of partial syndromes when atherothrombosis occludes the stem of the middle cerebral artery. Partial middle cerebral territory syndromes also occur due to embolism. An embolus may enter the middle cerebral stem, progress distally, lodge in a distal branch, and lyse. Symptoms and signs then fluctuate accordingly (Fig. 343-4). Partial syndromes resulting from embolic occlusion of a single branch include hand or arm and hand weakness alone (brachial syndrome) or facial weakness

FIGURE 343-4 *Diagram of a cerebral hemisphere, lateral aspect, showing the branches and distribution of the middle cerebral artery and the principal regions of cerebral localization. Note the bifurcation of the middle cerebral artery into a superior and inferior division. (Courtesy of C.M. Fisher, M.D.)*

Signs and symptoms	*Structures involved*
Paralysis of the contralateral face, arm, and leg; sensory impairment over the contralateral face, arm, and leg (pinprick, cotton touch, vibration, position, two-point discrimination, stereognosis, tactile localization, barognosis, cutaneographia)	*Somatic motor area for face and arm and the fibers descending from the leg area to enter the corona radiata and corresponding somatic sensory system*
Motor aphasia	*Motor speech area of the dominant hemisphere*
Central aphasia word deafness, anomia, jargon speech, sensory agraphia, acalculia, alexia, finger agnosia, right-left confusion (the last four comprise the Gerstmann syndrome)	*Central, suprasylvian speech area and parietooccipital cortex of the dominant hemisphere*
Conduction aphasia	*Central speech area (parietal operculum)*
Apractognosia of the minor hemisphere (amorphosynthesis), anosognosia, hemiasomatognosia, unilateral neglect, agnosia for the left half of external space, dressing "apraxia," constructional "apraxia," distortion of visual coordinates, inaccurate localization in the half field, impaired ability to judge distance, upside-down reading, visual illusions (e.g., it may appear that another person walks through a table)	*Nondominant parietal lobe (area corresponding to speech area in dominant hemisphere); loss of topographic memory is usually due to a nondominant lesion, occasionally to a dominant one*
Homonymous hemianopsia (often homonymous inferior quadrantonopsia)	*Optic radiation deep to second temporal convolution*
Paralysis of conjugate gaze to the opposite side	*Frontal contraversive field or fibers projecting therefrom*

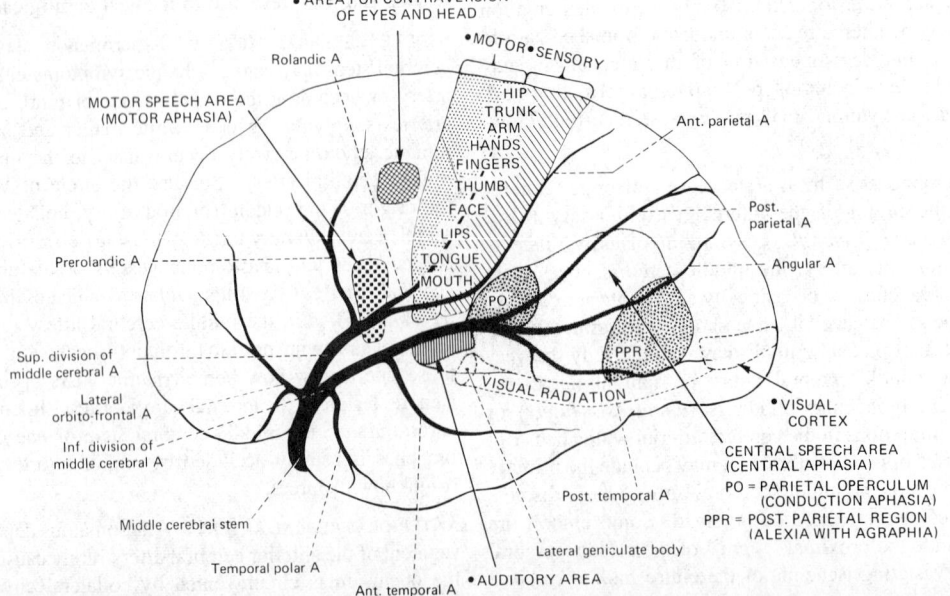

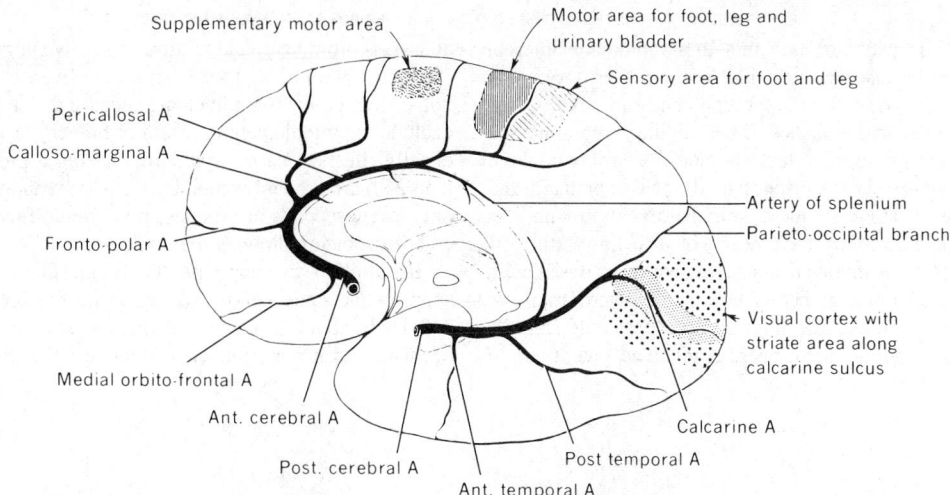

FIGURE 343-5 *Diagram of a cerebral hemisphere, medial aspect, showing the branches and distribution of the anterior cerebral artery and the principal regions of cerebral localization. (Courtesy of C.M. Fisher, M.D.)*

Signs and symptoms	Structures involved
Paralysis of opposite foot and leg	Motor leg area
A lesser degree of paresis of opposite arm	Involvement of arm area of cortex or fibers descending to corona radiata therefrom
Cortical sensory loss over toes, foot, and leg	Sensory area for foot and leg
Urinary incontinence	Sensorimotor area in paracentral lobule
Contralateral grasp reflex, sucking reflex, gegenhalten (paratonic rigidity)	Medial surface of the posterior frontal lobe (?) supplemental motor area
Abulia (akinetic mutism) slowness, delay, intermittent interruption, lack of spontaneity, whispering, motor inaction, reflex distraction to sights and sounds	Uncertain localization—probably cingulate gyrus and medial portion of parietal and temporal lobes
Impairment of gait and stance (gait apraxia)	Frontal cortex near leg motor area
Dyspraxia of left limbs, tactile aphasia in left limbs	Corpus callosum

with motor aphasia with or without arm weakness (frontal opercular syndrome). A combination of sensory disturbance, motor weakness, and motor aphasia suggests that the origin of the superior division branch has been embolized (Fig. 343-4). If receptive aphasia occurs without weakness, the inferior division of the middle cerebral artery is probably involved, for it supplies the posterior sensory part of the dominant hemisphere (Fig. 343-4). Sudden difficulty with hemineglect or spatial agnosia without weakness indicates that the inferior division of the middle cerebral artery in the nondominant hemisphere is involved.

ANTERIOR CEREBRAL ARTERY The anterior cerebral artery is divided into two segments: the precommunal (A1) circle of Willis, or stem segment, which connects the internal carotid artery to the anterior communicating artery, and the postcommunal (A2) segment beginning at the junction of the A1 segment and the anterior communicating artery (Fig. 343-2). The A2 segment of the anterior cerebral artery, through its cortical branches, supplies the anterior four-fifths of the medial part of the orbital surface of the frontal lobe, the frontal pole, a strip of the cortical surface along the superomedial border, and the anterior seven-eighths of the corpus callosum (Fig. 343-5). The A1 segment of the anterior cerebral artery, on the other hand, gives rise to many deep penetrating branches, which run chiefly to the anterior limb of the internal capsule, the anterior perforate substance, amygdala, anterior hypothalamus, and the inferior part of the head of the caudate nucleus (Fig. 343-3).

Infarction in the territory of the anterior cerebral artery is uncommon. Occlusion of the stem or A1 segment of the anterior cerebral artery proximal to the anterior communicating artery is usually well tolerated, since collateral flow is possible from the opposite side. The greatest disturbance occurs when both anterior cerebral arteries arise from a single anterior cerebral stem, occlusion of which then results in a devastating infarction of the anterior cerebral territory of both hemispheres. The clinical signs include bilateral pyramidal signs with paraplegia and profound mental symptoms due to bilateral frontal

lobe damage. The components of the typical syndrome resulting from occlusion of one anterior cerebral artery distal to the circle of Willis are indicated in the legend of Fig. 343-5.

ANTERIOR CHOROIDAL ARTERY This artery arises from the internal carotid artery and supplies the posterior limb of the internal capsule and the white matter posterolateral to it through which pass some of the geniculocalcarine fibers. This territory, however, is also supplied by penetrating vessels of the middle cerebral stem (lenticulostriate arteries), penetrating vessels of the posterior communicating artery, and the posterior choroidal artery. As a consequence, the complete clinical syndrome of contralateral hemiplegia, hemianesthesia (hypesthesia), and homonymous hemianopsia may not occur; instead syndromes with minimal deficits may be found. Indeed, cases of surgical occlusion of the artery for treatment of symptoms of Parkinson's disease have produced no deficit in some patients. Patients who initially have the full syndrome frequently recover in part or totally, presumably because of adequate collateral circulation.

INTERNAL CAROTID ARTERY The clinical picture of internal carotid occlusion varies depending upon whether the cause of ischemia is propagated thrombus, embolism, or low flow. Occlusion can be entirely asymptomatic. Less often an infarction is massive, involving the deep gray and white matter and cortical surface, as when an occlusive thrombus propagates up the internal carotid artery and projects into the middle cerebral stem and anterior cerebral arteries, or when a thrombotic fragment breaks off and embolizes the middle or anterior artery. Symptoms are identical to middle cerebral stem occlusion (see above). When both the anterior and middle cerebral arteries are involved, stupor is often seen in addition to the hemiplegia, hemianesthesia, and aphasia or anosognosia. When the posterior cerebral artery arises from the internal carotid artery (fetal posterior cerebral artery), it also may become occluded by the above processes and give rise to symptoms referable to its peripheral territory (Figs. 343-5 and 343-6).

No matter what the cause of ischemia in symptomatic internal carotid atherothrombotic disease, the middle cerebral territory alone is most often affected. Low-flow infarction tends to involve the territory of the distal cortical branches of the middle cerebral artery, giving rise to transient or stepwise hip, shoulder, or arm weakness. Ocasionally, transient ischemic episodes of dysphasia or hand and arm weakness occur, lasting 10 to 15 min before improving. As many as 5 to 10 episodes a day have been noted in this setting. If the dominant hemisphere is involved, transient aphasia or dyscalculia may occur. If the nondominant hemisphere is involved, transient hemineglect can ensue. When the inferior division of the middle cerebral artery in the dominant hemisphere is involved, fluent jargon aphasia is prominent, and written or oral language is incomprehensible (Wernicke's aphasia) (see Chap. 22). Even in artery-to-artery embolism symptoms often fluctuate because the embolus may not totally occlude the middle cerebral stem or branch, or it may lyse and move distally. In most cases, symptoms lasting a prolonged time but less than 24 h are probably embolic. But if a symptom is transient, lasting only a few seconds or minutes, it is often difficult to decide between embolism or low flow as the etiology.

In addition to supplying the brain, the internal carotid artery supplies the optic nerve and retina via the ophthalmic artery (Fig. 343-1). In about 25 percent of cases of symptomatic internal carotid occlusion, transient monocular blindness (TMB or amaurosis fugax)

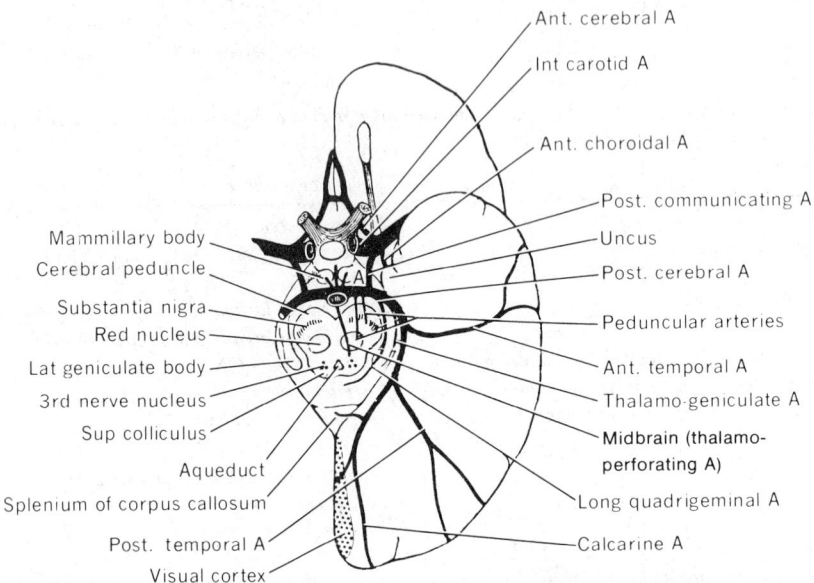

FIGURE 343-6 *Inferior aspect of the brain with the branches and distribution of the posterior cerebral artery and the principal anatomic structures shown. (Courtesy of C.M. Fisher, M.D.)*

Signs and symptoms	Structures involved
Peripheral territory (see also Fig. 343-5)	
Homonymous hemianopsia (often upper quadrantic)	Calcarine cortex or optic radiation nearby
Bilateral homonymous hemianopsia, cortical blindness, awareness or denial of blindness; tactile naming, achromatopsia (color blindness), failure to see to-and-fro movements, inability to perceive objects not centrally located, apraxia of ocular movements, inability to count or enumerate objects, tendency to run into things which the patient sees and tries to avoid	Bilateral occipital lobe with possibly the parietal lobe involved.
Verbal dyslexia without agraphia, color anomia	Dominant calcarine lesion and posterior part of corpus callosum
Memory defect	Hippocampal lesion bilaterally or on the dominant side only
Topographic disorientation and prosopagnosia	Usually with lesions of nondominant, calcarine, and lingual gyrus
Simultagnosia, hemivisual neglect	Dominant visual cortex, contralateral hemisphere
Unformed visual hallucinations, peduncular hallucinosis, metamorphopsia, teleopsia, illusory visual spread, irreminiscence, paliopsia, distortion of outlines, central photophobia	Calcarine cortex
Complex hallucinations	Usually nondominant hemisphere
Central territory	
Thalamic syndrome: sensory loss (all modalities), spontaneous pain and dysesthesias, choreoathetosis, intention tremor, spasms of hand, mild hemiparesis	Posteroventral nucleus of thalamus; involvement of the adjacent subthalamus body or its afferent tracts
Thalamoperforate syndrome: crossed cerebellar ataxia with ipsilateral third nerve palsy (Claude's syndrome)	Dentatothalamic tract and issuing third nerve
Weber's syndrome: third nerve palsy and contralateral hemiplegia	Third nerve and cerebral peduncle
Contralateral hemiplegia	Cerebral peduncle
Paralysis or paresis of vertical eye movement, skew deviation, sluggish pupillary responses to light, slight miosis and ptosis (retraction nystagmus and "tucking" of the eyelids may be associated)	Supranuclear fibers to third nerve, interstitial nucleus of Cajar nucleus of Darkschewitsch, and posterior commissure
Contralateral rhythmic, ataxic action tremor; rhythmic postural or "holding" tremor (rubral tremor)	Dentatothalamic tract (?)

occurs intermittently to warn of the onset. Describing the event, patients may say that a shade seemed to sweep up, down, or across the field of vision or that the periphery of vision faded away. They may also complain that their vision was blurred in that eye or that the upper or lower half of vision disappeared. In most cases, these symptoms last only a few minutes. Rarely, ophthalmic or central retinal artery occlusion develops at the time of stroke.

COMMON CAROTID ARTERY   All the neurologic symptoms and signs of internal carotid occlusion may also be present with occlusion of the common carotid artery. Both common carotid arteries may be occluded at their origin as in "pulseless disease" or the aortic arch syndrome (see Chap. 197). The following manifestations give a clue to this condition: absence of pulsation in carotid and radial arteries, faintness on arising from the horizontal position, recurrent loss of consciousness, headache, neck pain, transient blindness (unilateral or bilateral), dimness of vision with exercise, premature cataracts, retinal atrophy and pigmentation, atrophy of the iris, leukomas, peripapillary arteriovenous anastomoses, optic atrophy, and/or claudication of the jaw muscles. An incomplete aortic arch syndrome consisting of various combinations of carotid, subclavian, or innominate stenosis or occlusion is not uncommon (see below).

Laboratory evaluation   A variety of diagnostic techniques are available for evaluating patients with a carotid bruit, carotid-territory stroke, or TIA. Auscultation of a bruit over the bifurcation of the common carotid artery in the neck, or over the eye, and palpation of the arteries in the neck and over the face and forehead in conjunction with the compression of the preauricular artery (dynamic facial palpation) often provide suggestions about the presence and nature of disease at the bifurcation of the common and proximal internal carotid artery. High-pitched bruits that fade into diastole suggest a tightly stenotic lesion at the origin of the internal carotid. However, only trained experience can judge the duration and pitch of a bruit or assess subtle changes in pulse intensity during dynamic facial palpation. Therefore, several noninvasive tests have been developed to determine more reliably the severity and location of carotid atherothrombotic disease.

NONINVASIVE CAROTID TESTS   Ophthalmodynamometry, oculoplethysmography, and directional supraorbital Doppler examination indirectly assess pressure in the internal carotid artery. These tests are most helpful when the residual luminal diameter of the atheromatous lesion at the origin of the internal carotid artery is more than 2 mm and the tests are normal, or when the residual diameter is less than 1 mm and pressure distally is greatly reduced, rendering the tests abnormal.

Two types of noninvasive tests study the bifurcation of the common carotid artery directly. *Ultrasound techniques* include real-time B-mode ultrasound imaging and analysis of the Doppler-shift signal of the returning echo of flowing blood. Unfortunately, ultrasound imaging has limited resolution, because calcification in a plaque prevents penetration of the ultrasound beam, and a soft thrombus has approximately the same density as flowing blood. However, it reliably identifies atheromatous lesions at the common carotid bifurcation. Since blood flowing through an atherosclerotic stenotic lesion changes from laminar flow with uniform velocity to streamline flow with high velocity and then to turbulent flow with a broad range of velocities immediately distal to the stenosis, this change can be detected by continuous-wave (cw) or range-gated pulsed-Doppler techniques. It appears as a spectral broadening of the returning echoes of the Doppler-shift signal. Duplex ultrasound scanning combines B-mode images of the artery with range-gated pulsed-Doppler analysis of flowing blood at each point in the image. A second technique, *quantitative spectral phonoangiography*, analyzes the audible frequency-intensity components of the bruit of the turbulent blood flow. It estimates the residual luminal diameter of the internal carotid artery, and it differentiates between a bruit originating at the carotid bifurcation and one radiating from the base of the heart. External carotid artery bruits may, however, be mistaken for more serious

internal carotid artery sounds. This test tends to be most accurate when the bruit arises from a stenotic lesion with a residual luminal diameter between 0.9 and 2.5 mm. Therefore, it is most useful in the range of stenoses where other noninvasive tests are least accurate.

Experience suggests that an optimal set of noninvasive tests should include direct assessment of the bifurcation of the common carotid artery by duplex Doppler examination or B-mode ultrasound imaging combined with spectral analysis of the Doppler-shift signal. Quantitative phonoangiography should be used when a bruit is present. Oculoplethysmography is used in most laboratories to measure indirectly the pressure in the internal carotid artery and to assess more accurately the hemodynamic importance of the lesion. These tests help most in three clinical settings: assessing the bifurcation of the common carotid artery when an ischemic stroke or TIA of uncertain cause occurs in the territory fed by the internal carotid artery; following the progress of a known carotid stenosis; and evaluating an asymptomatic bruit. All noninvasive tests are subject to some error (10 percent in experienced hands). Furthermore, they cannot distinguish complete carotid occlusion from extremely tight stenosis at the origin of the internal carotid artery. Hence, they are less valuable when a patient who has had a minor stroke or TIA needs appropriate prompt therapy to prevent further stroke, in which case there is frequently no substitute for angiography. Most recently range-gated pulsed-Doppler analysis has been extended to examine the vertebral artery flow and flow in the large intracranial arteries, i.e., the middle cerebral stem, and anterior and posterior cerebral arteries. Efficacy of such analysis in documenting disturbed flow with constrictive lesions has yet to be demonstrated.

CEREBRAL ANGIOGRAPHY   Cerebral angiography performed by selective extracranial injection after transfemoral catheterization remains the most reliable method of assessing the cerebrovascular system. It can detect ulcerative lesions, severe stenosis, and formation of a mural thrombus at the carotid bifurcation, and it can visualize directly carotid artery dissections and atherothrombotic disease in the siphon and intracranial vessels. It can demonstrate collateral circulation around the circle of Willis and on the cortical surface and embolic occlusion of cerebral branch vessels. Although angiography cannot measure blood flow directly, it records certain features that indicate compromised flow in the internal carotid system. For example, the intracranial circulation may fill more slowly than the external carotid artery. Cerebral angiography, therefore, allows the physician to evaluate many of the factors that are relevant to an understanding of the pathophysiologic nature of the stroke.

However, the advantages of selective cerebral angiography must be seen in the context of its risks. According to various reviews, complications range from 1.3 to 12 percent. The risks that have attracted the most comment are aortic dissection and embolic stroke. Although some find angiography to be particularly risky for patients with a tightly stenotic lesion at the carotid bifurcation, others find it to be relatively safe in all settings if performed by experienced angiographers. Simply preventing dehydration and hypotension during and after angiography can often prevent cerebral ischemic complications. Patients with recurrent headaches or a history of migrainous phenomena have been given corticosteroids before angiography, but the medication's value in preventing ischemic complications has not been established. At times, the less risky technique of brachial artery injection offers as much relevant information as selective intracranial angiography from transfemoral catheterization.

INTRAVENOUS DIGITAL SUBTRACTION ANGIOGRAPHY   Intravenous digital subtraction angiography is a computer-reconstruction method developed to circumvent problems inherent in arterial catheterization. It demonstrates carotid occlusion or severe stenosis, but often leaves the degree of stenosis uncertain. It may miss a near occlusion with a threadlike lumen, and it fails to delineate adequately either intracranial arterial lesions or patterns of collateral blood flow. Digital subtraction angiography requires breath holding, cessation of swallowing, and a brisk cardiac output—all of which may be difficult for patients who have had a stroke. Furthermore, the large volume of contrast agent may precipitate angina, congestive heart failure, and renal failure. Arterial injection of the contrast agent used in digital angiography may offer some advantages over the intravenous method, but it has risks similar to those of conventional angiography. Usually, the local institutional experience will determine which technique is the safest for a particular patient.

CEREBRAL IMAGING   Methods that study the extent and location of infarcted brain tissue have all hinged on the development of computerized axial tomography (CT), positron-emission tomography, and magnetic resonance imaging. The latter two are currently in developmental phases. CT scanning provides an estimate of the extent and location of supratentorial cerebral infarction, including small 0.5-cm lacunar infarctions. In addition, it can detect surrounding edema, and less consistently, hemorrhagic infarction. CT, however, cannot differentiate early ischemic tissue from normal tissue, *nor can it detect most cerebral infarctions for at least 48 h.* Furthermore, when infarction occurs in the brainstem—i.e., in the vertebral or basilar territories—CT is less reliable because of bone and motion artifacts and the small size of many infarcts.

Xenon blood flow techniques and positron-emission tomography with use of labeled carbon dioxide and oxygen provide qualitative and quantitative tomographic assessment of cerebral blood flow. These methods are not in routine clinical use and are not used in guiding therapy. Proton magnetic resonance imaging (MRI) has been used to identify accurately the extent and location of infarcted tissue within hours of infarction. With the introduction of magnets of high-field strength (1.5 to 4 tesla), it may be possible to obtain in vivo a regional nuclear magnetic resonance spectrum of high-energy phosphate compounds and therefore to judge the viability of tissue. Once developed, this technology may permit moment-to-moment assessment of the response of brain tissue to therapy.

Therapy for carotid territory transient ischemic attacks   ANTICO-AGULANT THERAPY   When impending carotid or middle cerebral occlusion is suspected as the cause of a TIA, then acute anticoagulation with heparin is an option. Given the suggested pathophysiologic mechanism of stroke in this setting, a cogent argument can be made for such therapy. But in the absence of published proof of efficacy vs. hazard, it must be considered empirical.

The use of chronic anticoagulant therapy with sodium warfarin is even more controversial and problematic. Most studies of efficacy of chronic anticoagulant therapy to prevent stroke or to decrease TIAs are difficult to appraise for a number of reasons—e.g., lack of randomization, small number of patients, and lack of uniformity in the diagnosis of the cause of the TIA. In some studies, inclusion of TIAs not due to atheromatous disease of the internal carotid artery or inclusion of transient neurologic symptoms that were not related to ischemia have further complicated assessment of the results. Many believe that chronic anticoagulation therapy benefits patients with carotid-territory TIAs who are not candidates for surgery either for medical reasons or because the lesion is surgically inaccessible (carotid siphon or middle cerebral stem). Because of the often devastating effect of middle cerebral artery occlusions, anticoagulation is recommended when patients present with TIAs or minor strokes from a tightly stenotic lesion in the stem of the middle cerebral artery. To minimize the bleeding complications of warfarin sodium, the prothrombin time should generally not exceed $1\frac{1}{2}$ times control value. Contraindications to anticoagulant therapy have been well defined and include the presence of an actively bleeding ulcer, malignant hypertension, uremia, hepatic failure, or poor patient compliance. Relative contraindications are old age, systolic blood pressure above 190 mmHg, or a history of bleeding ulcer or bleeding diathesis. Heparin may be useful in the short term in stemming additional TIAs and preventing complete occlusion of a tightly stenotic lesion while the patient is awaiting angiography, surgery, or oral anticoagulation.

ANTIPLATELET THERAPY   Studies of the effect of antiplatelet agents on the natural histroy of TIAs and minor strokes can be criticized for the same reasons as the anticoagulation studies. Aspirin is the agent most widely investigated in the prevention of stroke. Eight randomized trials have considered either aspirin alone or aspirin in combination with another antiplatelet agent. The two largest have suggested that aspirin alone may be beneficial in preventing further TIAs and strokes in symptomatic patients. Another study, in which angiography was performed routinely, suggested that aspirin benefited patients who had TIAs associated with a lesion in the internal carotid artery but not those who had a single TIA and no carotid lesion—i.e., those thought to have emboli from the heart. In these studies, aspirin at best reduced the stroke risk over 3 years from approximately 19 to 12 percent, the latter risk being considerably higher than the risk of endarterectomy. Most physicians agree that aspirin may help, but it is not the treatment of choice for TIAs resulting from atherothrombotic disease of the internal carotid artery. It is often used when transient ischemic symptoms appear in association with tightly stenotic carotid siphon lesions or with minor degrees of stenosis at the origin of the internal carotid artery, carotid siphon, or stem of the middle cerebral artery.

There are theoretical reasons to avoid the excessive use of aspirin. Paradoxically, aspirin inhibits platelet formation of thromboxane A_2, a platelet-aggregating, vasoconstricting prostaglandin, but also inhibits the formation of prostacyclin, and antiaggregating, vasodilating prostaglandin derived from endothelial cells. Aspirin in low doses predominantly inhibits the production of thromboxane A_2; therefore, many physicians recommend aspirin in small doses of 300 mg or less per day.

Dipyridamole acts by inhibiting platelet phosphodiesterase, which is responsible for breakdown of cyclic adenosine monophosphate. The resulting elevation in platelet cyclic AMP level inhibits aggregation of platelets. However, there is no compelling clinical evidence to suggest that dipyridamole prevents recurrent TIAs or stroke in patients with symptomatic atherothrombotic cerebrovascular disease. Sulfinpyrazone inhibits the platelet-release reaction and interferes with platelet adhesion to subendothelial tissues. It does prolong platelet survival in patients with prosthetic heart valves. There is no evidence that proves that sulfinpyrazone or other antiplatelet agents such as clofibrate or ibuprofen have any benefit over aspirin alone in preventing TIAs or stroke.

CAROTID ENDARTERECTOMY   Carotid endarterectomy remains the usual therapy for TIAs caused by carotid stenosis. First introduced in 1954, the procedure has been associated with a morbidity ranging from 1 to 20 percent, depending on the patient population and the experience of the team of surgeons and physicians. Although many studies suggest that this procedure is effective in preventing additional TIAs or strokes, its value has yet to be confirmed by a well-designed, controlled, randomized clinical trial. *Unless the combined complication rate of angiography and surgery is less than 3 percent, performing surgery is likely to be more dangerous than no treatment.*

Patients with a tightly stenotic lesion in one carotid artery and either an occlusion of the contralateral carotid artery or an inadequate circle of Willis are at somewhat higher risk of intraoperative stroke during endarterectomy. However, intraoperative electroencephalographic monitoring can detect cerebral ischemia during the procedure and warn the surgeon to take steps to improve circulation.

Most patients who undergo endarterectomy have hypertensive arteriosclerotic cardiovascular disease and peripheral vascular disease. Active coronary diseases, such as unstable angina, recent myocardial infarction (within 6 months), or congestive heart failure, are contraindications to surgery. Severe hypertension is often corrected before surgery, but excessive lowering of the blood pressure should be avoided with tight carotid artery stenosis because it has been implicated in progression to total occlusion and stroke.

Stenosis can recur after surgery, although it seldom does. Poor surgical technique, excessive scar formation, and active arteriosclerotic disease have been implicated. Within the first year, the underlying pathologic process appears to be largely the proliferation of fibrous tissue; after the first year, of fibrous tissue and atherosclerosis. When restenosis gives rise to symptoms, surgery, although feasible, becomes more difficult technically.

Tandem lesions of the internal carotid artery—i.e., one at the carotid bifurcation and one at the carotid siphon—require special consideration. If the siphon stenosis has a residual luminal diameter of more than 2 mm and the lower carotid a diameter of less than 2 mm, then endarterectomy can be recommended. If the siphon narrowing is more severe, the value of endarterectomy is less certain. Anticoagulant or antiplatelet therapy may be preferable. But there is no consensus about the efficacy of either therapy in this setting.

EXTRACRANIAL/INTRACRANIAL BYPASS SURGERY Anastomosis of a superficial temporal branch of the external carotid artery to a cortical surface branch of the middle cerebral artery can provide collateral flow to the middle cerebral territory. Such surgery has been considered in patients with an occluded carotid artery or a tightly stenotic lesion of the carotid siphon or middle cerebral stem who present with recurrent TIAs or minor strokes. However, the results of a worldwide randomized study failed to prove greater efficacy of surgical compared to anticoagulation or antiplatelet therapy in these conditions.

Therapy for carotid territory stroke The severity of a recent stroke in the territory of the internal carotid artery is an important factor in the decision about therapy. If there is a complete hemiplegia, severe aphasia, or anosognosia, indicating involvement of the major portions of the middle cerebral territory, the prevention of additional strokes in that arterial distribution becomes less urgent. Instead, careful attention to maintenance of adequate blood pressure and prevention of delayed cerebral edema becomes important. There is little evidence to support the use of anticoagulant therapy once a ''completed'' or static major stroke deficit exists. However, if marked clinical improvement occurs during the first hours after onset or the deficit is small, some evidence suggests that short-term anticoagulation (heparin) prevents further damage, i.e., benefits ''stroke in evolution.'' Many authors now recommend that a fluctuating or progressing deficit be treated with heparin. Given the pathophysiologic mechanisms of carotid stroke, many physicians use short-term anticoagulation in a patient with a slight stroke from a recently occluded or tightly stenotic internal carotid artery, hoping to prevent a second, possibly more devastating, event. In such cases, small ischemic infarcts could become hemorrhagic but rarely do. For this reason, the timing and benefit of early heparinization remains controversial.

Even though no controlled studies exist, endarterectomy is recommended for patients with tightly stenotic internal carotid lesions who present with a minor stroke in the territory distal to the lesion. The risk of surgery in experienced hands may be as low as 2 percent if no medical contraindications exist. When the contralateral carotid artery is tightly stenotic or occluded, endarterectomy of the ipsilateral carotid artery has a higher morbidity. Comparison of the natural history of cases of symptomatic tight carotid stenosis with surgical results has not been made. Experience suggests that additional strokes develop in more than 3 percent of patients who are treated nonsurgically.

Hemorrhage into a cerebral infarct is an extremely rare event following internal carotid endarterectomy and probably is no more common than without surgery if postoperative hypertension is avoided. Nevertheless, after stroke, a 2- to 6-week delay of carotid endarterectomy has been recommended. Although it seems reasonable to allow patients to stabilize before surgery, undue delay can be disastrous. Early surgery, although controversial, may be preferable when the neurologic deficit is small or transient.

Surgery has also been performed in some cases of acute carotid artery occlusion, usually less than 8 h old, but the results are generally unsatisfactory when a major neurologic deficit is present. Hence, surgery should be reserved for patients with a mild neurologic deficit. For most patients with a mild to moderate stroke and demonstrated occlusion of the internal carotid artery, alternative therapies include the use of anticoagulants or antiplatelet agents or neither. Some physicians anticoagulate for 6 months in hopes of preventing embo-

lization of the propagated thrombus. Occasionally, endarterectomy of the external carotid artery or the contralateral stenotic internal carotid artery may be considered, depending on the findings of angiography and the nature of the recurrent clinical symptoms. The probable cause of an ischemic event determines the appropriate therapy. An embolism from an occluded carotid artery suggests the use of anticoagulation therapy, whereas recurrent symptoms suggestive of low flow in a hemisphere isolated from collateral sources of blood supply warrant consideration of surgery.

The appropriate therapy for stenosis of the carotid siphon or the middle cerebral stem associated with stroke or recurrent TIAs can be considered together. Because of the failure of external carotid/internal carotid (EC/IC) bypass surgery to reduce risks of ischemic stroke, antiplatelet therapy (aspirin) or anticoagulant therapy (sodium warfarin) is recommended in most cases. In the absence of randomized studies to indicate which is more efficacious, antiplatelet therapy is recommended initially for carotid siphon stenosis followed by anticoagulation if recurrent symptoms occur. Because of the potentially devastating effects of middle cerebral artery occlusion, anticoagulation with sodium warfarin is recommended for symptomatic middle cerebral stem stenosis. In cases where recurrent symptoms occur in spite of this therapy, lowering of the blood viscosity may be helpful. Often, with time, however, recurrent symptoms diminish despite the choice of treatment.

The unusual case of atherothrombotic stenosis or occlusion of the proximal anterior cerebral artery may cause intermittent symptoms involving the contralateral leg. Antiplatelet or anticoagulation therapy has been recommended, but no studies have documented the natural history of atherothrombotic disease at this location, and no surgical procedure protects the distal territory of the anterior cerebral artery from ischemia caused by proximal stenosis.

Although much attention has been directed toward the investigation of the opioid-like substance naloxone in the treatment of acute ischemic infarction, it has yet to be shown to be efficacious. Whole-blood viscosity reduction is a more promising innovative therapy for ischemic stroke. If the blood pressure remains constant, whole-blood viscosity reduction through lowering hematocrit and/or serum fibrinogen results in increased flow through a stenotic lesion. In theory, this form of therapy is expected to increase flow to the ischemic zone (penumbra) that lies between infarcted and normal brain. The size of the penumbra, however, is unknown for each individual stroke. The therapy has little risk.

ASYMPTOMATIC CAROTID BIFURCATION STENOSIS THAT CAUSES A BRUIT The natural history of a bruit caused by an atherosclerotic lesion of the carotid bifurcation that has not yet caused a TIA or stroke is unknown. The available studies have examined small populations and most failed to localize and quantitate the severity of the stenotic lesion. The studies of asymptomatic patients with cervical bruits who are about to undergo major surgical procedures have the same deficiencies. In most studies, patients with cervical bruits were found to be at increased risk of heart disease, stroke, and death. The strokes, however, did not necessarily occur in the vascular territory of the carotid bruit. Given these facts, there is little reason to operate on the carotid artery in patients with asymptomatic carotid stenosis, either routinely or before surgery.

However, patients with a tightly stenotic lesion at the origin of the internal carotid artery (1.5 mm or less) that reduces flow in the distal internal carotid artery may be at higher risk of thrombotic occlusion. Even though these patients have reduced flow in the distal internal carotid artery, they are asymptomatic because of adequate collateral flow across the anterior circle of Willis to the ipsilateral middle and anterior cerebral arteries. Stroke, therefore, should occur only by subsequent artery-to-artery embolism. The bruit associated with a tightly stenotic lesion at the origin of the internal carotid artery is high-pitched and prolonged, often fading into diastole. The bruit becomes fainter as the stenosis progresses and flow is further slowed, and finally disappears when occlusion is imminent. Noninvasive carotid testing that includes B-mode ultrasound imagery, Doppler analysis of flow immediately distal to the stenosis, quantitative spectral analysis of the bruit itself, and measurement of the oculo-systolic pressure by oculoplethysmography can identify these tightly stenotic lesions. In the absence of a randomized trial of the efficacy of endarterectomy vs. antiplatelet therapy for this type of lesion, the physician has an option for either. In most cases, antiplatelet therapy is recommended. Only when signs of progressive narrowing are documented and the residual lumen diameter is 1.5 mm or less is surgery considered an option at our institution. Surgical morbidity should be less than 2 percent. However, no evidence suggests that surgery is more efficacious than medical therapy, and a randomized trial is needed.

ATHEROTHROMBOTIC DISEASE OF THE VERTEBRAL-BASILAR–POSTERIOR CEREBRAL ARTERY SYSTEM
The two vertebral arteries join to form the basilar artery at the pontomedullary junction. The basilar artery divides into two posterior cerebral arteries in the interpeduncular fossa (Fig. 343-2). Each of these major arteries gives rise to large long and short circumferential branches and small deep penetrating branches that supply the cerebellum, medulla, pons, midbrain, subthalamus, thalamus, hippocampus, and medial temporal and occipital lobes. Atherosclerosis has a predilection for certain parts of the vertebral, basilar, and posterior cerebral arteries. Most frequently it occupies the origin of both vertebral arteries, the distal segments of both vertebral arteries, and the proximal basilar artery. In addition, atheroma tends to form at the origin of the major and minor branches of the vertebral, basilar, or posterior cerebral arteries. Predictably, atheromatous disease at each site carries its unique natural history, produces its own clinical syndromes, and has its own specific therapeutic implications.

POSTERIOR CEREBRAL ARTERY
Pathophysiology In 70 percent of cases, both posterior cerebral arteries come from the bifurcation of the top of the basilar artery; in 22 percent, one or the other comes from the ipsilateral internal carotid artery; in 8 percent, both come from the ipsilateral internal carotid artery (Fig. 343-2B). When the latter occurs, the posterior communicating arteries are large and become the origin of the posterior cerebral arteries; the precommunal segment (mesencephalic portion, A1 segment, or stem) of the true posterior cerebral artery is atretic (Fig. 343-2B).

Atheroma occurring at the top of the basilar artery or along the precommunal segment of the posterior cerebral artery may block or symptomatically narrow one or more of the small brainstem-penetrating branches (Figs. 343-2 and 343-6A). These important branches supply the middle portion of the cerebral peduncles, the ipsilateral substantia nigra, red nucleus, oculomotor nuclei, midbrain reticular formation, subthalamic nucleus of Luys, decussation of superior cerebellar peduncles, the medial longitudinal fasciculus, and the medial lemniscus. The artery of Percheron, i.e., the posterior thalamosubthalamoparamedial artery, is a single artery arising from either the right or the left medial precommunal (mesencephalic) segment of the posterior cerebral artery. It divides in the subthalamus to supply bilaterally the inferior medial and the anterior portions of the thalamus and subthalamus. The thalamic thalamogeniculate branches, also originating in the precommunal portion of the posterior cerebral artery, supply the dorsal, dorsomedial, anterior, and inferior thalamus and the medial geniculate body. These branches include the medial and lateral posterior choroidal arteries. The medial posterior choroidal artery supplies the superior dorsomedial and dorsal anterior thalamus and the medial geniculate body in addition to the tela choroidea of the third ventricle. The lateral posterior choroidal artery supplies the choroid plexus of the lateral ventricle. Both posterior choroidal arteries send branches that anastomose with branches of the anterior choroidal artery. But the other small branches of the precommunal segment of the posterior cerebral artery end without anastomosing.

Atheromas occurring in the posterior cerebral artery distal to the junction with the posterior communicating artery (Fig. 343–6B) may symptomatically occlude the small circumferential branches that course around the midbrain to supply the lateral part of the cerebral peduncles, medial lemniscus, tegmentum of the midbrain, superior colliculi, lateral geniculate body, and posterior lateral nucleus of the thalamus, choroid plexus, and hippocampus. On the rare occasions when atheromas occur more distally in the posterior cerebral artery (Fig. 343-6C), a symptomatic occlusion may produce ischemia and infarction in the medial inferior temporal lobe, parahippocampal and hippocampal gyri, and occipital lobe—including the calcarine cortex and the visual association areas 18 and 19.

Clinical syndromes The location of atheromatous disease in the posterior cerebral artery or at the origin of one of its branches and the degree of narrowing usually determine the onset, severity, and nature of the clinical syndrome. Other factors, including the collateral circulation via the posterior communicating artery or over the cortical surface and serum viscosity, play significant but less important roles. However, even when atheroma is present in the posterior cerebral artery, embolic occlusion of it or one of its branches is usually the mechanism responsible for the stroke. The pathologic anatomy of the posterior cerebral artery generates syndromes that divide into two groups: first, midbrain, subthalamic, and thalamic syndromes due to atheromatous narrowing or atherothrombotic or embolic occlusion of either the proximal precommunal segment of the posterior cerebral artery or the origin of its penetrating branches; second, those cortical syndromes due to atheromatous narrowing or atherothrombotic or embolic occlusion of the postcommunal segment of the posterior cerebral artery.

PROXIMAL PRECOMMUNAL SYNDROMES (THE CENTRAL TERRITORY) If the stem of the posterior cerebral artery is occluded, infarction occurs in the subthalamus and medial thalamus, extending either ipsilaterally or bilaterally, and in the ipsilateral cerebral peduncle and midbrain, producing concomitant signs (Fig. 343-6). Obviously, if the posterior communicating artery is not functional (i.e., atretic), the peripheral territory supplied by the postcommunal segment of the posterior cerebral artery will become symptomatic as well (Fig. 343-6). Unless the origin of the posterior cerebral artery is completely occluded, hemiplegia secondary to infarction of the cerebral peduncle rarely occurs. Partial proximal syndromes suggest but do not prove mesencephalic thalamic perforant branch occlusion. A superior syndrome, one including involvement of the red nucleus and/or dentatorubro-thalamo tract, can produce a gross contralateral ataxia. An inferior syndrome can produce a third nerve palsy and a contralateral ataxia (Claude's syndrome), or a third nerve palsy and a contralateral hemiplegia (Weber's syndrome). When the subthalamic nucleus of Luys is involved, contralateral hemiballismus may occur. Occlusion of the artery of Percheron produces paresis of upward gaze and drowsiness. It is often associated with abulia or a euphoric state giving way to abulia. CT scan and MRI may detect bilateral butterfly lesions in the subthalamus and medial inferior thalamus. Extensive infarction in the midbrain or subthalamus occurring with bilateral posterior cerebral stem occlusion is usually secondary to embolism. Deep coma, bilateral pyramidal signs, and "decerebrate rigidity" occur in this setting.

Atheromatous occlusion of the penetrating branches of the thalamic and thalamogeniculate group at their origin produces smaller thalamo and thalamocapsular lacunar syndromes. The *thalamic syndrome of Déjerine and Roussy* is the best known. Its main feature is contralateral hemisensory loss of both superficial sensation (pain and temperature) and deep sensation (touch and proprioception). Occasionally, it may affect only pain and temperature or vibration and joint position sense. Most often it affects face, arm, hand, trunk, leg, and foot; occasionally, only one extremity. Hyperpathia may occur; and after a few weeks or months, an agonizing, searing pain may develop in the affected areas. Patients describe it as tight, drawing, icy, and knifelike. It is devastatingly persistent and responds poorly to analgesics. Occasionally, anticonvulsants are beneficial. If the posterior limb of the internal capsule is involved, hemiparesis or hemiplegia may occur with the hemisensory syndrome. Other associated motor signs include hemiballismus, choreoathetosis, intention tremor, incoordination, and posturing of the hand and arm, particularly while walking.

POSTCOMMUNAL SYNDROMES (THE PERIPHERAL OR CORTICAL TERRITORY) (Figs. 343-6B and C) Infarction in the pulvinar of the thalamus may result from occlusion of a posterior thalamic thalamogeniculate penetrating branch of the postcommunal posterior cerebral artery. Occlusion in the peripheral posterior cerebral artery itself most often infarcts the cortical surface of the medial temporal and occipital lobe. Contralateral homonymous hemianopsia is the usual manifestation. If the visual association areas are spared and only the calcarine cortex is involved, the patient is acutely aware of visual defects. Occasionally, only the upper quadrant of the visual field is involved. Central vision may be spared if middle cerebral artery branches supply the tip of the occipital pole. Medial temporal lobe and hippocampal involvement may cause an acute disturbance in memory, particularly if it occurs in the dominant hemisphere, but the defect usually clears because memory has bilateral representation. If the dominant hemisphere is affected and the infarct extends laterally into the deep white matter involving the splenium of the corpus callosum, alexia without agraphia may occur. Visual agnosia for faces, objects, mathematical symbols, and colors and anomia with paraphasic errors (amnestic aphasia) may also occur in this setting even without callosal involvement. When the ipsilateral internal carotid is occluded, tight stenosis or occlusion of the ipsilateral posterior cerebral artery can reduce flow in the watershed territory between the posterior and middle cerebral arteries. Often, visual agnosia, visual neglect, and inability to enumerate objects in a contralateral visual field follow. Occlusion of the posterior cerebral artery can produce peduncular hallucinosis (visual hallucinations of brightly colored scenes and objects), but the exact location of the infarct remains uncertain.

Bilateral infarction in the distal posterior cerebral artery territory produces cortical blindness. The patient is often unaware that vision is gone and the pupil reacts normally to light. Even if the defect is complete on one or both sides, tiny islands of vision may persist; and the patient will report that vision fluctuates, as images are still captured in the preserved islands. Rarely, only peripheral vision is lost and central vision is spared; then the patient reports gun-barrel vision. Optic ataxia (inability to visually guide limb movements), ocular ataxia (inability to direct eyes to a precise point in the visual field), inability to enumerate objects in a picture or project meaning from a picture, and inability to avoid objects seen in one's path can occur with bilateral visual association area lesions. Such a constellation of symptoms has been termed Balint's syndrome. It is most often seen with bilateral infarctions, presumably secondary to low flow in the distal posterior and/or middle cerebral "watershed" territories as occurs in cardiac arrest cases. Finally, occlusion of the top of the basilar artery, most often due to embolism, can produce a clinical picture which includes any or all of the central or peripheral territory symptoms. Its hallmark is suddenness of onset and bilaterality of symptoms.

Laboratory evaluation Infarction in the peripheral territory of the posterior cerebral artery can be easily documented by CT scan. However, infarction in the central territory of the posterior cerebral artery, especially infarction secondary to occlusive disease of the penetrating branches of the posterior cerebral artery, is not reliably detected by CT scanning. MRI can detect infarctions greater than 0.5 cm in this area. Angiography remains the only certain method of documenting atheromatous disease or embolic disease of the posterior cerebral artery. No form of angiography, however, can detect occlusive disease in the small penetrating branches. Thus, the diagnosis rests mainly on clinical grounds corroborated by MRI.

Therapy When infarction occurs in the territory of the posterior cerebral artery, it is usually secondary to embolism from lower segments of the vertebral-basilar system or the heart. Anticoagulants to prevent further embolic events are appropriate. Atheromatous occlusion of the posterior cerebral artery, on the other hand, requires no special therapy. Transient ischemic symptoms in the territory of the posterior cerebral artery may result from atherothrombotic stenosis of its proximal portion or one of its penetrating branches (lacunar TIA). The natural history of such atheromatous disease is unknown. Thus, the efficacy of anticoagulants vs. antiplatelet therapy vs. no medication is still uncertain. In general, antiplatelet therapy seems safest in this setting.

VERTEBRAL AND POSTERIOR INFERIOR CEREBELLAR ARTERIES Pathophysiology The vertebral artery, which arises from the innominate artery on the right and the subclavian artery on the left, divides into four anatomic segments. The first segment extends from its origin to its entrance into the sixth or fifth transverse vertebral foramen. The second is the vertical segment through the C6 to the C2 vertebral foramen. The third is the horizontal segment through the transverse foramen, circling around the arch of the atlas to pierce the dura at the level of the foramen magnum. The fourth begins as it penetrates the dura and courses up to join the other vertebral artery to form the basilar artery. The fourth segment gives rise to small penetrating branches that supply the medial and lateral medulla and to a large branch, the posterior inferior cerebellar artery: the latter's proximal segments supply the lateral medulla; its distal branches, the inferior surface of the cerebellum. Anastomotic channels exist among the ascending cervical arteries, thyrocervical arteries, the occipital artery (branch of the external carotid artery), and the second segment of the vertebral artery (Fig. 343-1). In 10 percent of patients, one vertebral artery is too small (atretic) to contribute significant blood to the brainstem.

Atherothrombotic lesions have a predilection for the first and fourth segments of the vertebral artery. Although the atheromatous narrowing in the first segment (the origin) may be significant, it seldom produces brainstem ischemic strokes. Collateral flow from the contralateral vertebral artery or the ascending cervical and ascending thyrocervical or occipital arteries is usually sufficient (Fig. 343-1D). When one vertebral artery is atretic and atherothrombotic lesion threatens the origin of the other, the only avenues for collateral circulation are through the ascending cervical artery, the thyrocervical artery, and the occipital artery, or by retrograde flow down the basilar artery via the posterior communicating artery (Figs. 343-2 and 343-6). In this setting, low flow in the vertebral-basilar system exists and TIAs occur. In addition, incipient thrombosis in the distal basilar proximal vertebral system may occur. If the subclavian is blocked proximal to the origin of the vertebral artery, exercise of the left arm may draw blood from the vertebral-basilar system to the arm, sometimes causing symptoms of vertebral-basilar insufficiency, *subclavian steal*. It rarely leads to significant vertebral-basilar ischemia.

Atheroma in the fourth segment of the vertebral artery can occur proximal to the origin of the posterior inferior cerebral artery, at the origin of the posterior inferior cerebral artery or distal to it, and at the junction with the other vertebral artery to form the basilar artery. When it is proximal to the origin of the posterior inferior cerebral artery, a critical narrowing can threaten the lateral medulla and posterior inferior surface of the cerebellum.

Although atheromatous disease rarely narrows the second and third segments of the vertebral artery, they are subject to dissection lesions, fibromuscular dysplasia, and rare encroachment by osteophytic arthritic changes in the vertebral foramens.

Clinical syndromes Transient cerebral ischemic attacks resulting from vertebral artery insufficiency cause dizziness or vertigo, numbness of the ipsilateral face and contralateral limbs, diplopia, hoarseness, dysarthria, and dysphagia. Hemiparesis is exceedingly rare. These TIAs are usually short (up to 10 to 15 min) and repetitive (up to many times a day).

When infarction ensues, it most often affects the lateral medulla with or without the posterior inferior cerebellum (Wallenberg's syndrome). Its features are listed in Fig. 343-7. In 80 percent of the cases, the syndrome occurs after vertebral occlusion; in 20 percent, it results from posterior inferior cerebellar artery occlusion. Athero-thrombotic occlusion of the medullary penetrating branches of the vertebral or posterior inferior cerebellar artery results in partial syndromes of the ipsilateral lateral or medial medulla.

Rarely, a medial syndrome occurs in which the medullary pyramid becomes infarcted causing a contralateral hemiparesis of the arm and leg, sparing the face. If the medial lemniscus and emerging hypoglossal nerve fibers are involved, contralateral loss of joint position sense and ipsilateral tongue weakness occur.

Cerebellar infarction with edema formation can lead to sudden respiratory arrest due to raised intracranial pressure in the posterior fossa. Drowsiness, Babinski signs, dysarthria, and bifacial weakness may be absent or present only briefly before respiratory arrest ensues. Gait unsteadiness, dizziness, nausea, and vomiting may be the only early symptoms and signs and should arouse suspicion of this impending complication.

Laboratory evaluation When TIAs occur in the territory of the lateral medulla, it becomes important to determine the adequacy of blood flow in the distal vertebral artery and the posterior inferior

FIGURE 343-7 (Courtesy of C.M. Fisher, M.D.)

Signs and symptoms	Structures involved
1 Medial medullary syndrome (occlusion of vertebral artery or of branch of vertebral or lower basilar artery)	
On side of lesion:	
Paralysis with atrophy of half the tongue	Ipsilateral twelfth nerve
On side opposite lesion:	
Paralysis of arm and leg sparing face; impaired tactile and proprioceptive sense over half the body	Contralateral pyramidal tract and medial lemniscus
2 Lateral medullary syndrome (occlusion of any of five vessels may be responsible—vertebral, posterior inferior cerebellar superior, middle, or inferior lateral medullary arteries)	
On side of lesion:	
Pain, numbness, impaired sensation over half the face	Descending tract and nucleus fifth nerve
Ataxia of limbs, falling to side of lesion	Uncertain—restiform body, cerebellar hemisphere, cerebellar fibers, spinocerebellar tract (?)
Nystagmus, diplopia, oscillopsia, vertigo, nausea, vomiting	Vestibular nucleus
Horner's syndrome (miosis, ptosis, decreased sweating	Descending sympathetic tract
Dysphagia, hoarseness, paralysis of palate, paralysis of vocal cord, diminished gag reflex	Issuing fibers ninth and tenth nerves
Loss of taste	Nucleus and tractus solitarius
Numbness of ipsilateral arm, trunk, or leg	Cuneate and gracile nuclei
On side opposite lesion:	
Impaired pain and thermal sense over half the body, sometimes face	Spinothalamic tract
3 Total unilateral medullary syndrome (occlusion of vertebral artery): Combination of medial and lateral syndromes	
4 Lateral pontomedullary syndrome (occlusion of vertebral artery): Combination of lateral medullary and lateral inferior pontine syndromes	
5 Basilar artery syndrome (the syndrome of the lone vertebral artery is equivalent): A combination of the various brainstem syndromes plus those arising in the posterior cerebral artery distribution	
Bilateral long tract signs (sensory and motor; cerebellar and peripheral cranial nerve abnormalities)	Bilateral long tract; cerebellar and peripheral cranial nerves
Paralysis or weakness of all extremities, plus all bulbar musculature	Corticobulbar and corticospinal tracts bilaterally

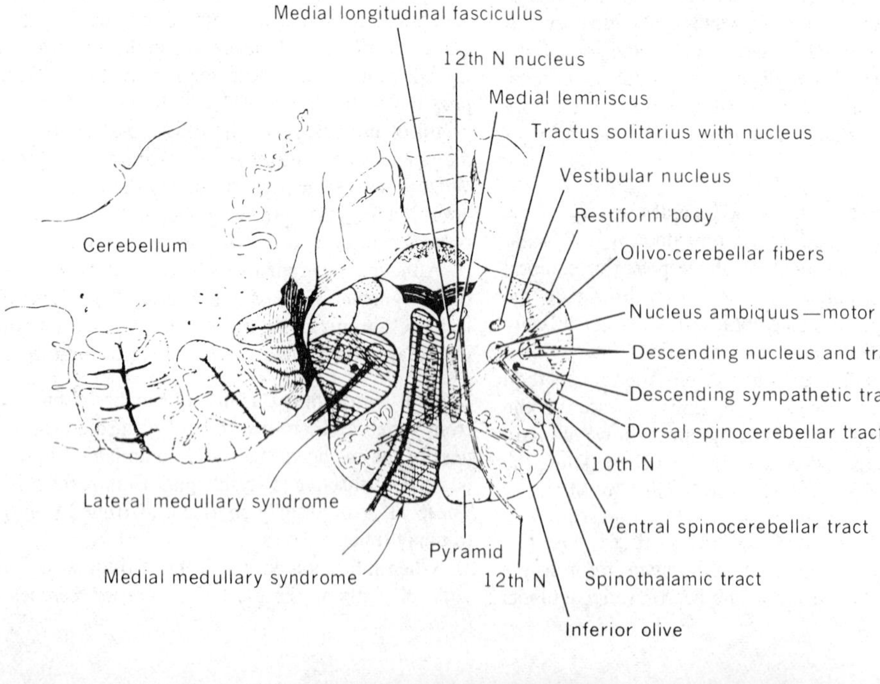

cerebellar artery. Angiography is therefore indicated. CT scanning may detect a large cerebellar infarction in the territory of the posterior inferior cerebellar artery. MRI can detect cerebellar infarction earlier and, with refinement in technique, may be able to detect lateral medullary infarction. Even now it has been able to image the fourth segment of the vertebral artery if it contains flowing blood. It is anticipated that with the further development of MRI technology it may be possible to image atherothrombotic material in the vertebral and basilar arteries and determine if they are patent or occluded, and supplant the need for angiography.

Therapy Four important therapeutic issues arise when dealing with a patient with ischemia or infarction in the territory of the vertebral or posterior inferior cerebellar artery. First, in vertebral or posterior inferior cerebellar artery occlusion, the posterior inferior cerebellum and sometimes the lateral medulla may be infarcted. The ensuing cerebellar edema can be treated with osmotic agents (mannitol), but surgical decompression may be necessary. Second, when the fourth segment of the vertebral artery becomes thrombosed, clot may propagate into the basilar artery or embolize up the basilar and lodge at the top or in one of its branches. Thus, in cases of lateral medullary infarction, symptoms or signs of basilar insufficiency may ensue. Acute anticoagulation with heparin is advocated in such cases. Some physicians argue for its prophylactic use in acute vertebral artery occlusion, although there is little support for chronic sodium warfarin anticoagulation. Third, when one vertebral artery is symptomatic with atheromatous disease and the contralateral vertebral is congenitally atretic or already occluded, basilar ischemia may ensue and proximal basilar thrombosis may develop. Acute anticoagulation with heparin followed by chronic sodium warfarin anticoagulation is recommended. Fourth, when the same circumstance occurs but the symptomatic vertebral atherothrombotic lesion lies immediately proximal to the posterior inferior cerebellar artery, occipital-to-posterior-inferior bypass grafting has been recommended. The efficacy of this surgery is unproven, and it should be considered only after anticoagulation therapy has failed.

BASILAR ARTERY Pathophysiology The basilar artery is formed by the union of the vertebral arteries at the pontomedullary junction. After coursing under the surface of the basis pontis, it ends in the interpeduncular fossa, where it bifurcates, forming the posterior cerebral arteries (Figs. 343-2 and 343-6). Branches of the basilar artery supply the basis pontis and superior cerebellum. The branches of the basilar divide into three groups: (1) paramedians, 7 to 10 in number, supply a wedge of pons on either side of the midline; (2) short circumferential branches, 5 to 7 in number, supply the lateral two-thirds of the pons and the middle and superior cerebellar peduncles; and (3) two bilateral long circumferential arteries (superior cerebellar and anterior/inferior cerebellar arteries) course around the pons to supply the cerebellar hemispheres.

Atheromatous lesions can occur anywhere along the basilar trunk, but are most often in the proximal basilar and distal vertebral segments. Typically, lesions occlude either the proximal basilar and one or both distal vertebral arteries. The clinical picture varies depending on the availability of retrograde collateral flow from the posterior communicating arteries.

Atherothrombosis occasionally occludes the top of the basilar artery; more often, an embolus from the heart or proximal vertebral or basilar segments occludes it. Such artery-to-artery emboli may also occlude one of the smaller basilar branches or one of the posterior cerebral arteries.

Clinical symptoms—basilar artery vs. basilar branch Because the brainstem contains so many different neuronal systems in close approximation, many clinical syndromes can emerge when it becomes ischemic. The most important symptom-producing systems include the corticospinal tracts, corticobulbar tracts, medial and superior cerebellar peduncles, spinothalamic tracts, and the cranial nerve nuclei. Figures 343-8 to 343-10 outline some of the vascular syndromes, including some which await clinicopathologic definition.

Unfortunately, the symptoms of transient ischemia or stroke in the territory of the basilar artery often do not indicate whether it is the basilar artery or one of its branches that is diseased, yet the difference has important implications for therapy. The complete picture of basilar insufficiency, however, is easy to recognize. A combination of bilateral long tract signs (sensory and motor) and signs of cranial nerve and cerebellar dysfunction suggest the diagnosis. A locked-in state of quadriplegia occurs with bilateral basis pontis infarction. Coma due to dysfunction of the reticular activating system and quadriplegia with cranial nerve signs suggest complete and devastating pontine and midbrain infarction. The goal, however, is to recognize impending basilar occlusion long before such a devastating infarction occurs. Thus a series of TIAs or a slowly progressive, fluctuating stepwise stroke becomes extremely significant when they herald an atherothrombotic occlusion of the distal vertebral or proximal basilar artery.

TRANSIENT ISCHEMIC ATTACKS   When transient ischemic spells herald occlusion of the proximal basilar, the medulla as well as the pons may be involved. Patients often say they are "dizzy"; when asked to describe what they mean, they may use the words "swimming," "swaying," "moving," "unsteady," or "light-headed." They may complain that the room is upside down or that the floor seems to move or come toward them. As such, dizziness is the most common symptom of transient basilar territory ischemia, but is usually associated with other symptoms before a basilar thrombosis produces an infarction (see Chap. 14). Thus, transient "dizziness" associated with diplopia, dysarthria, facial or circumoral numbness, and hemisensory symptoms indicates the presence of transient vertebral-basilar insufficiency. Usually, hemiparesis indicates the basilar artery is involved whether or not the vertebral is involved. Most often TIAs, whether due to impending occlusion of either the basilar artery or a basilar branch, are short-lived (5 to 30 min) and repetitive, occurring several times a day. The pattern suggests intermittent reduction of flow rather than recurrent embolism. In general, symptoms of basilar branch TIAs affect one side of the brainstem, whereas symptoms of basilar artery TIAs usually affect both sides.

STROKE   Atherothrombotic occlusion of the basilar artery with stroke usually causes bilateral brainstem signs. Sometimes, only gaze paresis or internuclear ophthalmoplegia associated with ipsilateral hemiparesis, i.e., a particular combination of cranial nerve and long tract (sensory and/or motor) deficits, signifies bilateral brainstem ischemia. More often, bilateral basis pontis signs coexist with unilateral or bilateral pontine tegmental signs.

When atherothrombotic occlusion of a basilar branch artery becomes symptomatic, it generates unilateral symptoms and signs involving motor, sensory, and cranial nerves. Occlusions of the long circumferential branches of the basilar artery produce specific clinical syndromes (see below and "Lacunar Disease").

SUPERIOR CEREBELLAR ARTERY   Occlusion of the superior cerebellar artery results in severe ipsilateral cerebellar ataxia (middle and/or superior cerebellar peduncles), nausea and vomiting, dysarthria, and contralateral loss of pain and temperature sensation over the extremities, body, and face (spino- and trigeminothalamic tract). Partial deafness, ataxic tremor of the ipsilateral upper extremity, Horner's syndrome, and palatal myoclonus may rarely occur. Partial syndromes occur frequently.

ANTERIOR INFERIOR CEREBELLAR ARTERY   Occlusion of the anterior inferior cerebellar artery produces variable degrees of infarction, because the size of this artery and the territory it supplies vary inversely with those of the posterior inferior cerebellar artery. The principal symptoms include ipsilateral deafness, facial weakness, true vertigo (whirling dizziness), nausea and vomiting, nystagmus, tinnitus and cerebellar ataxia, Horner's syndrome, and paresis of conjugate lateral gaze. The opposite side of the body loses pain and temperature sensation. An occlusion close to the origin of the artery may cause corticospinal tract signs.

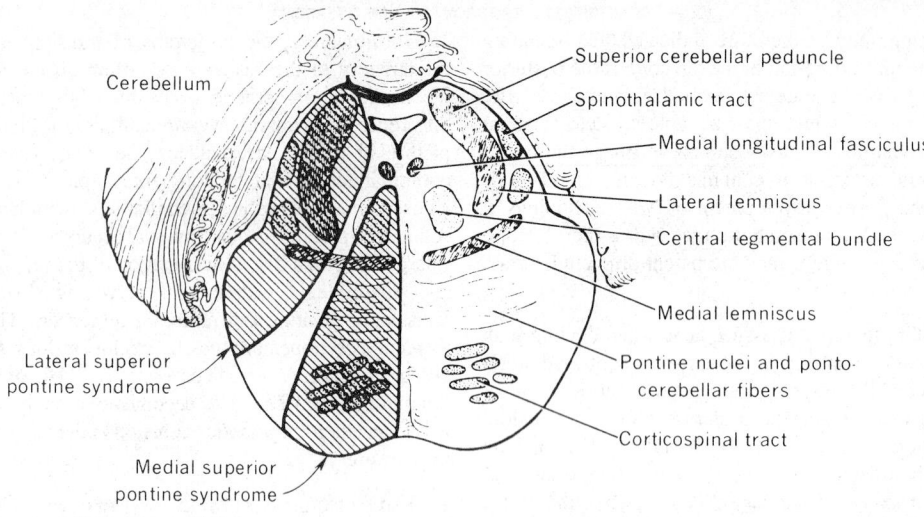

Cerebellum

Superior cerebellar peduncle
Spinothalamic tract
Medial longitudinal fasciculus
Lateral lemniscus
Central tegmental bundle
Medial lemniscus
Pontine nuclei and ponto-cerebellar fibers
Corticospinal tract

Lateral superior pontine syndrome

Medial superior pontine syndrome

FIGURE 343-8 *(Courtesy of C.M. Fisher, M.D.)*

Signs and symptoms	Structures involved
1 Medial superior pontine syndrome (paramedian branches of upper basilar artery)	
On side of lesion:	
Cerebellar ataxia (probably)	*Superior and/or middle cerebellar peduncle*
Internuclear ophthalmoplegia	*Media longitudinal fasciculus*
Myoclonic syndrome, palate, pharnyx, vocal cords, respiratory apparatus, face, oculomotor apparatus, etc.	*Localization uncertain—central tegmental bundle (?), dentate projection (?), inferior olivary nucleus (?)*
On side opposite lesion:	
Paralysis of face, arm, and leg	*Corticobulbar and corticospinal tract*
Rarely touch, vibration, and position are affected	*Medial lemniscus*
2 Lateral superior pontine syndrome (syndrome of superior cerebellar artery)	
On side of lesion:	
Ataxia of limbs and gait, falling to side of lesion	*Middle and superior cerebellar peduncles, superior surface of cerebellum, dentate nucleus*
Dizziness, nausea, vomiting; horizontal nystagmus	*Vestibular nucleus*
Paresis of conjugate gaze (ipsilateral)	*Pontine contralateral gaze*
Skew deviation	*Uncertain*
Miosis, ptosis, decreased sweating over face (Horner's syndrome)	*Descending sympathetic fibers*
Static tremor reported in one case	*Dentate nucleus (?), superior cerebellar peduncle (?)*
On side opposite lesion:	
Impaired pain and thermal sense on face, limbs, and trunk	*Spinothalamic tract*
Impaired touch, vibration, and position sense, more in leg than arm (there is a tendency to incongruity of pain and touch deficits)	*Medial lemniscus (lateral portion)*

Occlusion of one of the five to seven short circumferential branches of the basilar artery renders ischemic a specific area in the lateral two-thirds of the pons and/or middle or superior cerebellar peduncle, whereas occlusion of one of the seven to ten paramedian branches of the basilar artery renders ischemic a specific wedge-shaped area on either side of the medial pons (Figs. 343-8 to 343-10).

Many syndromes of brainstem lesions have been described and given eponyms, e.g., Weber, Claude, Benedict, Foville, Raymond-Cestan, Millard-Gubler. The pons contains so many neuronal structures that minor variations in the territory supplied by each arterial branch and variations in the overlap among vascular territories modify the clinical picture. For instance, dysarthria associated with a clumsy hand suggests a small basis pontis infarct. However, hemiparesis alone does not differentiate basis pontis ischemia from ischemia in the corticospinal tract above the tentorium, i.e., posterior limb of the internal capsule.

Hemiparesis coexisting with ipsilateral sensory loss suggests the stroke lies supratentorially. Dissociated sensory loss (pain and temperature only) over the face or half of the body suggests brainstem ischemia. On the other hand, sensory loss involving all modalities, i.e., pain and temperature as well as touch and joint position sense, suggests a lesion in the ventral posterior thalamus or in the deep parietal white matter and cortical surface adjacent to it. Findings indicative of cranial nerve dysfunction, i.e., deafness, peripheral seventh nerve weakness, sixth nerve weakness, or third nerve palsy, are extremely helpful in locating a segmental level of the pons or midbrain.

Laboratory evaluation Although CT scanning localizes most supratentorial strokes after 48 h, it is less reliable for detection and localization of stroke in the posterior fossa. Bone artifact often obscures details. Partial volume artifacts and plane restrictions further account for its poor resolution of infarcts in the brainstem. MRI eliminates many of these drawbacks. It reliably detects small (lacunar) infarcts in the basis pontis resulting from occlusion of paramedian basilar branches as well as larger infarcts resulting from disease of the larger basilar branches or the basilar artery itself. In addition, MRI can detect ischemic infarction earlier than CT scanning. On the other hand, CT scanning detects small pontine hematomas better than MRI and thus differentiates them from acute ischemic strokes. MRI is more sensitive for defining a pontine glioma or plaque of multiple sclerosis and can often differentiate them from infarction.

Only selective cerebral arteriography can document atherothrombotic disease of the basilar artery. Since arteriography entails potential morbidity and may precipitate the very stroke one is seeking to prevent, it must be recommended only when the information provided will assist in the management of the patient (see below). Occasionally, injection of angiographic dye in the posterior circulation precipitates a delirious state sometimes associated with cortical blindness. This state can last up to 24 to 48 h, and rarely several days. Arterial digital angiography may provide sufficient resolution to diagnose atheromatous narrowing at the distal vertebral and basilar arteries; intravenous digital angiography does not provide adequate resolution.

Therapy Suspected impending basilar occlusion causing transient or fluctuating symptoms should be treated with short-term anticoagulation with intravenous heparin, after a CT scan has excluded hemorrhage. Angiography is considered if the diagnosis is uncertain only after the patient's condition is stable. When basilar artery stenosis or occlusion is associated with minor or improving stroke, long-term anticoagulation with sodium warfarin is recommended. If, on the other hand, basilar branch disease is the cause, then the rationale for using sodium warfarin is uncertain. While embolism from the heart or atheroma in the distal vertebral system may occlude a penetrating basilar branch, this is unlikely. Therefore, chronic control of blood pressure and antiplatelet therapy are recommended as preventive measures in the management of small vessel basilar branch disease. Because of the long-term accumulative risk of anticoagulant therapy, it is generally reserved for larger vessel atherothrombotic disease, i.e. distal vertebral or proximal basilar disease.

LACUNAR DISEASE The term *lacunar disease* refers to atherothrombotic and lipohyalinotic occlusive disease of the penetrating branches of the circle of Willis, middle cerebral stem, and vertebral and basilar arteries.

Pathophysiology The middle cerebral artery stem, the arteries comprising the circle of Willis (A1 segment of the anterior cerebral artery, anterior and posterior communicating arteries, and precommunal segment of the posterior cerebral arteries), the basilar, and the vertebral arteries all give rise to 100- to 400-µm branches that penetrate the deep gray and white matter of the cerebrum or brainstem (Fig. 343-2). Each of these small branches can be thrombosed either by atherothrombotic disease at its origin (basilar or middle cerebral stem branch disease) or by the development of lipohyalinotic thickening of its wall more distally. When they become thrombosed, small (less than 2-cm) infarcts occur and are referred to as *lacunes*. Many may be as small as 3 to 4 mm. Hypertension is invariably a risk factor for such small vessel disease. These infarcts represent 10 percent of strokes.

Clinical syndromes The clinical picture resulting from lacunes are called lacunar syndromes. Often transient symptoms (lacunar TIAs) herald a lacunar infarct. Such TIAs may occur many times a day, but last only a few minutes. When infarction occurs, it may present with a sudden deficit or evolve in a progressive fashion over a few days. Recovery often begins within hours or days after the infarct, although in some cases significant disability persists. Recovery over weeks or months may be complete or result in minimal residual deficit.

Many neurologic or lacunar syndromes occur and many more await documentation. The most common syndromes are the following:

1 Pure motor hemiparesis from an infarct in the posterior limb of the internal capsule or basis pontis. Here, the face, arm, leg, foot, and toes are almost always involved. The weakness may be intermittent (TIA), progress in a stepwise manner, or appear abruptly. The weakness may progress to plegia, then commonly improve. In many cases, recovery is almost complete.

2 Pure hemisensory syndromes from a thalamic infarct.

FIGURE 343-9 *(Courtesy of C.M. Fisher, M.D.)*

Signs and symptoms	Structures involved
1 Medial midpontine syndrome (paramedian branch of midbasilar artery)	
On side of lesion:	
Ataxia of limbs and gait (more prominent in bilateral involvement	*Middle cerebellar peduncle*
On side opposite lesion:	
Paralysis of face, arm, and leg	*Corticobulbar and corticospinal tract*
Variable impaired touch and proprioception when lesion extends posteriorly	*Medial lemniscus*
2 Lateral midpontine syndrome (short circumferential artery)	
On side of lesion:	
Ataxia of limbs	*Middle cerebellar peduncle*
Paralysis of muscles of mastication	*Motor fibers or nucleus of fifth nerve*
Impaired sensation over side of face	*Sensory fibers or nucleus of fifth nerve*
On side opposite lesion:	
Impaired pain and thermal sense on limbs and trunk	*Spinothalamic tract*

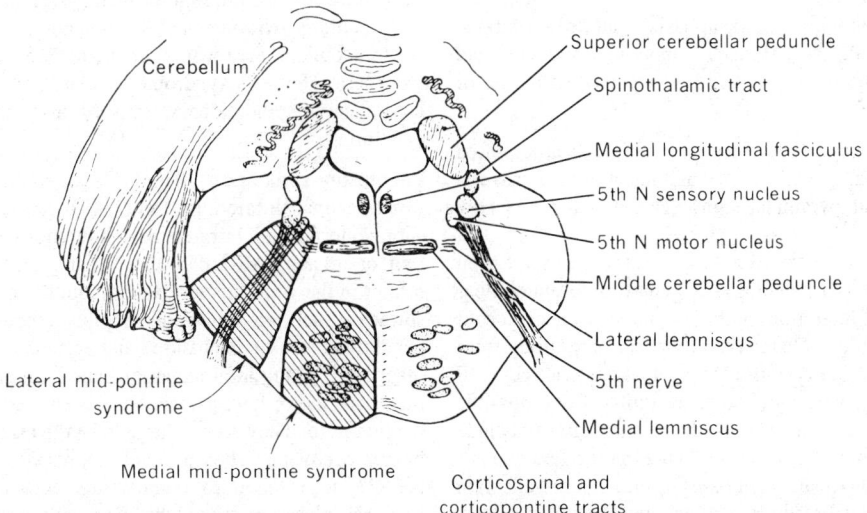

Cerebellum
Superior cerebellar peduncle
Spinothalamic tract
Medial longitudinal fasciculus
5th N sensory nucleus
5th N motor nucleus
Middle cerebellar peduncle
Lateral lemniscus
5th nerve
Medial lemniscus
Lateral mid-pontine syndrome
Medial mid-pontine syndrome
Corticospinal and corticopontine tracts

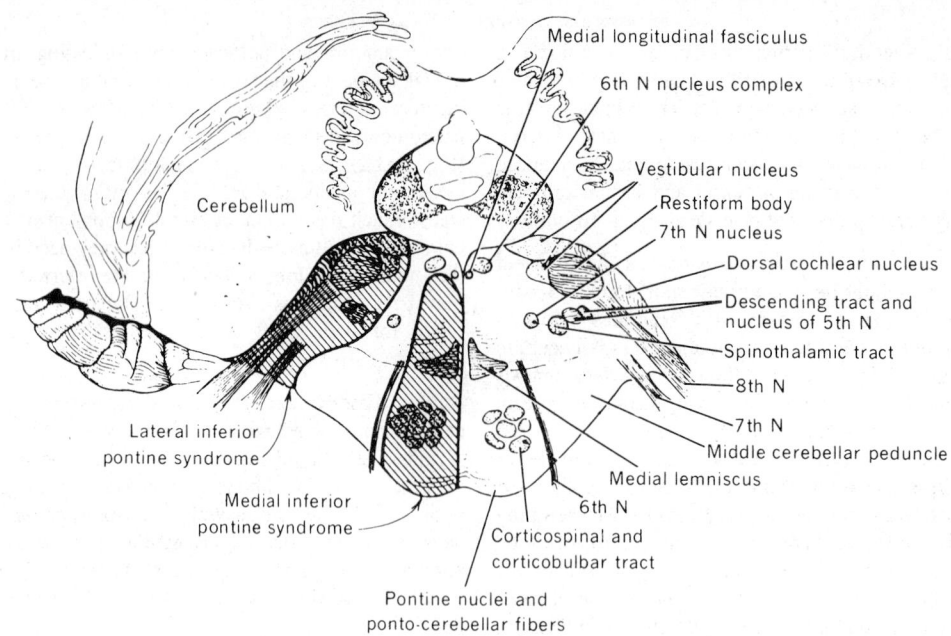

Medial longitudinal fasciculus
6th N nucleus complex
Vestibular nucleus
Restiform body
7th N nucleus
Dorsal cochlear nucleus
Descending tract and nucleus of 5th N
Spinothalamic tract
8th N
7th N
Middle cerebellar peduncle
Medial lemniscus
6th N
Corticospinal and corticobulbar tract
Pontine nuclei and ponto-cerebellar fibers
Medial inferior pontine syndrome
Lateral inferior pontine syndrome
Cerebellum

FIGURE 343-10 *(Courtesy of C.M. Fisher, M.D.)*

Signs and symptoms	Structures involved
1 Medial inferior pontine syndrome (occlusion of paramedian branch of basilar artery)	
On side of lesion:	
Paralysis of conjugate gaze to side of lesion (preservation of convergence)	*"Center" for conjugate lateral gaze*
Nystagmus	*Vestibular nucleus*
Ataxia of limbs and gait	*Middle cerebellar peduncle (?)*
Diplopia on lateral gaze	*Abducens nerve*
On side opposite lesion:	
Paralysis of face, arm, and leg	*Corticobulbar and corticospinal tract in lower pons*
Impaired tactile and proprioceptive sense over half of the body	*Medial lemniscus*
2 Lateral inferior pontine syndrome (occlusion of anterior inferior cerebellar artery)	
On side of lesion:	
Horizontal and vertical nystagmus, vertigo, nausea, vomiting, oscillopsia	*Vestibular nerve on nucleus*
Facial paralysis	*Seventh nerve*
Paralysis of conjugate gaze to side of lesion	*"Center" for conjugate lateral gaze*
Deafness, tinnitus	*Auditory nerve or cochlear nucleus*
Ataxia	*Middle cerebellar peduncle and cerebellar hemisphere*
Impaired sensation over face	*Descending tract and nucleus fifth nerve*
On side opposite lesion:	
Impaired pain and thermal sense over half the body (may include face)	*Spinothalamic tract*

3 True ataxic hemiparesis from a basis pontis infarct, and dysarthria with a clumsy hand or arm due to infarction in the basis pontis or the genu of the internal capsule.

4 Pure motor hemiparesis with "motor aphasia" due to thrombotic occlusion of a lenticulostriate branch supplying the genu and anterior limb of the internal capsule and adjacent white matter of the corona radiata.

Before the advent of hypertensive therapy, multiple lacunes often induced pseudobulbar palsy with emotional instability, a slowed abulic state, and bilateral pyramidal signs. This syndrome is now uncommon.

Other lacunar syndromes have been described that have not been correlated with actual arterial pathology. An anarthric pseudobulbar syndrome due to bilateral infarctions in the internal capsule can occur from disease in the lenticulostriate arteries. Syndromes resulting from occlusion of the penetrating arteries of the proximal posterior cerebral artery were discussed above. Syndromes resulting from possible occlusion of the penetrating arteries of the basilar artery include ipsilateral ataxia and crural (leg) paresis, pure motor hemiparesis with horizontal gaze palsy, and hemiparesis with a crossed sixth nerve palsy. Lower basilar branch syndromes include sudden inter-nuclear ophthalmoplegia, horizontal gaze palsy, and appendicular cerebellar ataxia. Syndromes resulting from possible vertebral branch occlusions include pure motor hemiparesis sparing the face involving the medullary pyramid, and those syndromes that involve the lateral pontomedullary area which may include vertigo, vomiting, facial weakness, Horner's syndrome, ipsilateral trigeminal numbness, and contralateral spinothalamic sensory loss (partial lateral medullary syndrome).

Laboratory evaluation The CT scan can document most supratentorial lacunar infarctions, and MRI successfully documents both supratentorial and infratentorial infarctions when the lacunes are 7 mm or greater. MRI can also reliably document whether a small infarct in the white matter extends into the gray matter of the cortical surface. Such an extension implies embolism rather than small penetrating vessel occlusion, and lacunar infarction should not be diagnosed. Many infarcts larger than 2 cm and associated with more than pure motor hemiparesis have been incorrectly called lacunes in the literature. They are too large to be the result of a single penetrating branch occlusion. They probably represent embolic infarction where the CT scan failed to demonstrate cortical surface involvement. Lacunar infarction should be diagnosed only when the size of the infarct is less than 2 cm and its location attributable to occlusion of a small penetrating branch of one of the major arteries at the base of the brain. Larger deep white matter infarcts in the territory of the middle cerebral artery are probably due to embolism. The electroencephalogram (EEG) is usually normal in contrast to cortical surface infarction. If the EEG is normal early after the onset of symptoms, it suggests the infarct is in the deep white matter.

Therapy The best therapy for small vessel disease is prevention, i.e., careful control of hypertension. However, during stroke evolution, a reduction in blood pressure may worsen the symptoms. Antihypertensive therapy is begun after the patient's symptoms become stable. The value of anticoagulant or antiplatelet agents to patients with lacunar TIAs and fluctuating stroke is unknown. Some suggest that thalamic lacunes secondary to lipohyalinosis may be associated with minor hemorrhage. Hemosiderin-laden macrophages are sometimes seen at autopsy in such infarctions. This condition precludes use of heparin. On the other hand, some patients with fluctuating hemiparesis from atherothrombotic disease of a basilar branch or of the middle cerebral stem lenticulostriate arteries may improve coincident with heparin administration. Lacunar stroke does not require long-term anticoagulant therapy; it requires, instead, careful control of hypertension to prevent progression of vascular disease.

OTHER CAUSES OF CEREBRAL INFARCTION Venous thrombosis Lateral or sagittal sinus thrombosis or thrombosis of small cortical veins occurs in relation to sepsis, intracranial infections (meningitis), or conditions associated with hypercoagulable states such as polycythemia, sickle cell anemia, or during pregnancy or administration of oral contraceptives. Venous thromboses may cause an increase in intracranial pressure, headaches, focal seizures, and focal neurologic signs. Massive cerebral infarction with secondary edema may be fatal.

Systemic hypotension Systemic hypotension from Stokes-Adams attacks or other causes may, on rare occasions, result in ischemia distal to a stenotic lesion. Usually infarction does not occur unless hypotension is prolonged, as it is in cardiac arrest. Infarction tends to occur in distal segments of the major intracranial arteries, i.e., the distal middle cerebral, anterior cerebral, or posterior cerebral territory, causing a border zone lesion between the middle and anterior or middle and posterior cerebral arteries (watershed infarction) (Fig. 343-1A). Here proximal weakness and distal parietal deficits suggest the diagnosis.

Dissection of the cervicocerebral arteries Dissection of the large extracranial arteries may cause cerebral infarction and is a frequent cause of stroke in children and young adults. The dissection divides the media of the vessel or separates the intima from the media. TIAs and infarction can occur when the vessel occludes or when dissection causes emboli. Trauma, either severe or trivial, accounts for a substantial proportion of cases. Spontaneous dissection also occurs in atheromatous lesions or as a complication of fibromuscular dysplasia, and in patients with homocystinuria or arteritis. Dissection of the internal carotid artery is the most common, but it may also occur in the vertebral and basilar arteries and in the stems of the middle and anterior cerebral arteries. Dissection of the internal carotid artery produces an oculosympathetic palsy (Horner's syndrome) in over half of the cases, and a self-audible bruit. Tenderness over the carotid bulb may be present. The above symptoms and signs and transient monocular blindness or TIAs often precede embolic or "low-flow" watershed carotid territory infarction; this leaves time for therapeutic intervention. However, the natural history of dissection lesions is so uncertain that proper management remains problematic. Therapeutic options for cervical carotid dissection include surgical exploration and removal of the dissection clot and intima with a Fogarty catheter or medical treatment with anticoagulation or antiplatelet agents. When the patient has only oculosympathetic palsy, TIAs, or a minor stroke, anticoagulation with heparin is preferable.

Surgical exploration is only considered for patients with increasingly severe TIAs or a mild stroke that is worsening. After the patient's symptoms have stabilized, anticoagulation with sodium warfarin is recommended for 6 months.

Patients with symptomatic vertebral, middle cerebral, or posterior cerebral artery dissection may also be managed in the acute phase with heparin and later with warfarin.

Fibromuscular dysplasia of the cervical vessels Fibromuscular dysplasia of the cervical vessels occurs mainly in young women. The carotid and/or vertebral arteries show multiple rings of segmental narrowing alternating with dilatation. Occlusion is usually incomplete. The process is often asymptomatic, but occasionally is associated with an audible bruit, TIAs, and stroke. Hypertension, if present, may be the result of renal artery stenosis. The cause and natural history of fibromuscular dysplasia is unknown (see Chap. 227). Caution should be used in attributing transient ischemic symptoms and/or embolic stroke to this disease when the residual lumen diameter of the narrowed portion of the artery is greater than 2 mm. Surgical dilatation of the cervical internal carotid artery is possible in symptomatic cases, but is associated with considerable morbidity. Anticoagulation may be more successful than surgery in patients with TIAs of increasing severity.

Arteritis Arteritis due to bacterial or syphilitic infection is no longer a common cause of cerebral thrombosis. The other arteritides are rare, yet any can cause cerebral thrombosis (see below and Chap. 269). *Necrotizing* or *granulomatous arteritis*, occurring alone or in association with generalized polyarteritis nodosa or Wegener's granulomatosis, involves the distal small branches (less than 1-mm diameter) of the main intracranial arteries and produces small ischemic infarcts in the brain, optic nerve, or spinal cord. The disease, although rare, is relentlessly progressive. In some cases, steroid therapy (prednisone, 40 to 60 mg per day) has been helpful, and recently, immunosuppressive drugs have been used with some success (see Chap. 269). *Idiopathic giant cell arteritis* involving the great vessels arising from the aortic arch (Takayasu's syndrome) may, on rare occasions, cause carotid or vertebral thrombosis. It is an infrequent cause of the aortic arch syndrome in the western hemisphere (see Chap. 195).

Temporal arteritis (cranial arteritis) (see Chap. 269) This is a relatively common affliction of elderly persons in which the external carotid system, particularly the temporal branches, is the site of a subacute granulomatous inflammation with an exudate of lymphocytes, monocytes, neutrophilic leukocytes, and giant cells. Usually the most severely affected parts of the artery become thrombosed. Headache or head pain is the chief complaint. Systemic manifestations include anorexia, loss of weight, malaise, and polymyalgia rheumatica. The inflammatory nature of the illness is indicated by some one or several of the following: fever, slight leukocytosis, increased erythrocyte sedimentation rate, and anemia. Occlusion of branches of the ophthalmic artery results in blindness in one or both eyes in over 25 percent of patients, and occasionally an ophthalmoplegia due to involvement of ocular nerves occurs. An arteritis of the aorta and its major branches, including carotid, subclavian, coronary, and femoral arteries, has been found at postmortem examination in some cases. Significant inflammatory involvement of intracranial arteries is rare, but strokes occur occasionally on the basis of occlusion of the internal carotid, middle cerebral, or vertebral arteries. The diagnosis depends on the finding of a tender thrombosed or thickened cranial artery and the demonstration of the lesion in a biopsy specimen. Corticosteroids bring striking subjective relief and often prevent blindness. Prednisone is most often used. It is generally started in large daily doses of 80 to 120 mg and is then tapered using the erythrocyte sedimentation rate as a guide.

Moya moya disease Moya moya disease is a poorly understood occlusive disease involving large intracranial arteries, especially the internal carotid artery and the stem of the middle and anterior cerebral artery. The lenticulostriate arteries develop a rich source of collateral flow around the middle cerebral occlusive lesion which, on cerebral angiography, gives the impression of a puff of smoke (*moya moya*). Other collaterals include transdural anastomosis between the cortical surface branches of the middle cerebral artery and the scalp arteries. This disease mainly occurs in the Oriental population, but should be suspected when TIAs or stroke occur in children or young adults. Its etiology is unknown. Few pathologic studies have been made; they suggest that hyalinotic fibrous-type material is associated with the arterial narrowing. Because of the occurrence of subarachnoid hemorrhage from rupture of the transdural anastomotic channels, anticoagulation is to be considered with caution in symptomatic cases. Extracranial/intracranial (EC/IC) bypass grafting has been recommended in some cases, but its efficacy is not established. The craniotomy needed for bypass grafting may disrupt the transdural anastomosis and theoretically could cause worsening of the deficit. In addition, EC/IC bypass grafting could precipitate proximal middle cerebral artery occlusion.

Oral contraceptive agents   Oral contraceptive agents have been associated with an increased incidence of stroke in young women (13.2/100,000 among women who take oral contraceptives compared to 2.8/100,000 among those who do not). In most cases, the suspected artery of involvement appears open on angiography; or if it appears occluded, it is found to be open later, a circumstance suggesting embolism as the primary cause of the stroke. The source of the embolus, however, is uncertain. The rare instances of pathologic examination found the affected arteries and the cardiac system normal. Migraine and cigarette smoking have been associated with such strokes in young women and suggest that a hypercoagulable state promotes thrombosis formation and embolization.

Polycythemia, thrombotic thrombocytopenic purpura, idiopathic thrombocytosis, hyperproteinemia, and sickle cell anemia   These diseases have been associated with ischemic infarction. Presumably, this is due to thrombosis formation with embolization in patients who because of these diseases have a hypercoagulable state (see Chaps. 279 and 280).

Binswanger's disease   Binswanger's disease (*chronic progressive subcortical encephalopathy*) is a rare condition in which the subcortical white matter (sparing the U fibers) becomes infarcted. The CT scan detects areas of periventricular low x-ray absorption. Lipohyalinosis invariably develops in the small arteries of the deep white matter, as it does in hypertension. Binswanger's disease may represent border zone ischemic infarction in the deep white and gray matter between the penetrating arteries of the circle of Willis and of the cortex. Unfortunately, the pathophysiologic basis of the disease, even its basic pathology, remains unknown. It is one of the causes of gait disability and abulia in the elderly.

CEREBRAL EMBOLISM Pathophysiology   Cerebral embolism is the most common cause of ischemic stroke; the heart, the most common source of embolic material. Artery-to-artery embolism, usually arising from an atherothrombotic lesion in either the carotid or vertebral-basilar system, occurs somewhat less frequently (see above). Other causes (Table 343-2) (thrombus in the pulmonary vein, fat emboli, tumor emboli, marantic air emboli, paradoxical emboli, and complications of neck or thoracic surgery) occur occasionally. Frequently, however, embolic cerebral infarction occurs without an obvious source.

"Unknown source" cerebral embolism poses one of the most perplexing problems in cerebrovascular disease. Granted, patients with an altered, heightened state of coagulation due to oral contraceptive agents, chronic illness, or metastatic tumor may develop sudden cerebral embolism. Sometimes physical diagnosis may not disclose a cardiac sound such as the opening snap of mitral stenosis or may miss an arrhythmia such as intermittent atrial fibrillation. Nevertheless, many patients, especially those in the second to fifth decade, suffer sudden embolic strokes that leave no clue to their etiology.

The size, site, and to some extent the pathologic nature of the fragment determines the size, location, and character of the ensuing infarct. Emboli large enough to occlude the stem of the middle cerebral artery (2 to 3 mm) lead to a large stroke, one that involves both deep gray and white matter as well as the cortical surface and its underlying white matter. A smaller stroke ensues if the embolus is small enough to occlude a small cortical surface branch or a small penetrating branch arising from the middle cerebral artery stem or basilar artery. Furthermore, embolic material composed of platelet fibrin clot characteristically has a tendency to migrate, lyse, and disperse, accounting for fluctuations in symptoms and, in some cases, complete recovery of the ischemic deficit. The location and size of an infarct also depends on the extent of any spared collateral circulation.

If collateral flow around the circle of Willis or through the other vertebral artery is sufficient, an embolic fragment lodging in the distal internal carotid artery, proximal A1 segment of the anterior cerebral artery, or distal vertebral artery may not result in brain ischemia or infarction. Similarly, emboli may block a cortical surface middle cerebral artery branch—or even the stem of the middle cerebral artery—and lead to no more than patchy infarction in the cortical surface or underlying white matter of the cerebral hemisphere if collateral flow occurs through the cortical surface border zone anastomotic channels from the anterior or posterior cerebral artery to the middle cerebral artery territory. The same holds true for cerebellar infarction. Because emboli migrate and lyse, recirculation into the infarcted brain often occurs. Here, bland infarcted tissue becomes laden with petechial hemorrhages 1 to 2 mm in size (hemorrhagic infarction). On rare occasions, petechial hemorrhages coalesce to form a significant hemorrhagic mass (hemorrhage into infarction). This is more likely to occur when the stem of the middle cerebral artery is occluded, and large areas of deep gray and white matter infarction develop before recirculation occurs. When the heart is the source of an embolus, it lodges in the middle cerebral artery 80 percent of the time, in the posterior cerebral artery 11 percent, and in the vertebral or basilar artery or their branches in the remainder.

Heart disease of many types may produce cerebral emboli. For conceptual purposes, they may be divided into arrhythmic and structural causes.

Cardiac arrhythmias of any type have been associated with symptomatic cerebral and systemic embolism. Of particular concern is the frequency of embolism associated with sick sinus syndrome and atrial fibrillation. The high incidence of cerebral embolism associated with atrial fibrillation in patients with rheumatic valvular disease is firmly established. In this setting it is accepted practice to institute chronic anticoagulation therapy with sodium warfarin to

TABLE 343-2   Causes of cerebral embolism

I Cardiac origin
  A Atrial fibrillation and other arrhythmias (with rheumatic, atherosclerotic, hypertensive, or congenital heart disease)
  B Myocardial infarction with mural thrombus
  C Acute and subacute bacterial endocarditis
  D Heart disease without arrhythmia or mural thrombus (mitral stenosis, etc.)
  E Complications of cardiac surgery
  F Valve prostheses
  G Nonbacterial thrombotic (marantic) endocardial vegetations
  H Paradoxical embolism with congenital heart disease
  I Trichinosis
II Noncardiac origin
  A Atherosclerosis of aorta and carotid arteries (mural thrombus, atheromatous material)
  B From sites of cerebral artery thrombosis (basilar, vertebral, middle cerebral)
  C Thrombus in pulmonary veins
  D Fat
  E Tumor
  F Air
  G Complications of neck and thoracic surgery
III Undetermined origin

prevent embolic events. Recently it has been documented that patients with atrial fibrillation, of whatever cause, are at increased risk of symptomatic embolization. Indeed, the incidence of cerebral embolism in patients with atrial fibrillation from nonvalvular causes is estimated to approach 4 to 7 percent per year, and in most cases, the initial stroke causes severe disability.

Mural thrombus formation with embolism occurs relatively frequently in patients with arteriosclerotic cardiovascular disease and myocardial infarction, whether or not papillary muscle dysfuntion, congestive heart failure, or a ventricular aneurysm is present.

SURGERY Intracardiac surgery and prosthetic valve surgery have an especially high risk of embolism. (Starr-Edwards and Bjork-Shiley valves have been particularly implicated in cerebral embolism.) Thoracic surgery (pulmonary vein embolism) and head-and-neck surgery (aortic or carotid artery-to-artery emboli) have an uncommon but definite association with cerebral embolism. Long bone fracture and thoracic surgery or angiography are associated with cerebral fat embolism and air embolism, both of which give rise to multiple areas of petechial hemorrhage. The principal complication of the use of artificial hearts is heart-to-brain embolism.

Congenital septal defects may give rise to paradoxical embolism. Material (thrombus, tumor, infective or fibrous marantic vegetation) accumulating on an endocardial surface, either valvular or chamber, may become displaced. Vegetations on the aortic and mitral valves from rheumatic or marantic endorcarditis are associated with systemic or cerebral emboli and can be diagnosed by a combination of history, physical examination, and laboratory tests. Typically flat vegetations under the mitral and, to a lesser extent, aortic valve leaflets have been noted in patients with systemic lupus erythematosus (Libman-Sacks vegetations). These may give rise to cerebral embolism, but more often are a nidus for bacterial endocarditis. The *vegetations of acute and subacute bacterial endocarditis* give rise to septic embolism (see Chap. 188). These emboli can cause large areas of infarction not different from noninfective embolic infarction if they occlude a major intracranial artery. Alternatively, they may be responsible for tiny septic infarcts with microscopic abscesses. Large brain abscesses, however, are not associated with embolization from subacute bacterial endocarditis. Mycotic aneurysms caused by septic embolism give rise to subarachnoid or intracerebral hemorrhage. The diagnosis of endocarditis should always be considered and ruled out when cerebral embolism is suspected.

Atrial myxoma results in tumor emboli arising from the endocardial surface. Here, physical signs of pulmonary hypertension or a high ESR and signs of systemic illness (fever, malaise) may help with the differential diagnosis. *Mitral valve prolapse* with mural thrombus formation has been associated with cerebral embolism, but insufficient data exist on the natural history of this abnormality to predict the incidence of recurrent embolism. It is presumably low. Echocardiography is valuable in establishing this diagnosis.

Clinical syndromes When embolism is the cause, the onset of the neurologic deficit is sudden and most often maximal. But the neurologic deficit may not be complete; and after its sudden onset, it may change significantly. In one instance, the deficit may wax and wane, lasting only a few minutes or hours then disappear, i.e., an embolic TIA. In another instance, a mild deficit may progress to complete major arterial territory infarction. In any case, the nature of the neurologic deficit corresponds to the location of the embolus in a specific territory either of the large extracerebral arteries or of the small penetrating arteries. The resulting deficits resemble those caused by either large vessel or small vessel disease. (See sections on atherothrombosis and lacunar stroke.) Obviously, the size of an embolus determines the size of the vessel it will occlude. Some neurologic syndromes strongly suggest embolism as their mechanism. In the middle cerebral artery territory these include (1) the frontal opercular syndrome, in which the face droops and severe aphasia and dysarthria are present; (2) the brachial or hand plegia syndrome, in which the entire arm and hand, the arm and hand from the elbow

down, or just the hand is paralyzed with or without cortical sensory abnormalities, depending on whether the sensory cortex is involved along with the motor cortex; (3) the syndrome of Broca's or Wernicke's aphasia alone, when the dominant hemisphere is involved; or (4) the syndrome of left visual neglect, when the nondominant parietal lobe is involved. A sudden hemianopic field defect fully realized by the patient suggests a posterior cerebral territory embolus, whereas a sudden foot incoordination or weakness suggests an anterior cerebral territory embolus. Sudden gait unsteadiness may suggest a cerebellar embolus. It is more difficult to determine whether an embolus or atherothrombotic or lipohyalinotic occlusion has caused a small vessel stroke. Most often it is one of the latter two. However, sudden sleepiness and an inability to look up, associated with bilateral ptosis, suggest embolus to the top of the basilar artery, specifically to the artery of Percheron (the small vessel supplying both sides of the medial subthalamus and thalamus arising from the top of the basilar artery).

Septic embolism with endocarditis or fat embolism often presents with nonfocal symptoms such as confusion, agitation, or delirium. Cardiac surgery may be associated with a particular neurologic syndrome in which the patient wakes slowly and when awake, thinks slowly, is disoriented, and possibly is agitated and combative. Poor memory is invariable and visual hallucinations are common. Most symptoms resolve within a week, but often a persistent visual perceptive deficit suggests a parietal occipital middle cerebral territory watershed infarct, presumably secondary to hypotension or multiple small emboli.

Seizures following cerebral infarction occur most often after embolic infarction and are not associated with deep white matter lacunar infarction. They are associated with supratentorial cortical surface infarction but never as the heralding event. Many cases of idiopathic epilepsy in the elderly are the result of silent cortical surface chronic infarction that can easily be treated with phenytoin.

Laboratory evaluation Before beginning anticoagulation therapy, a CT scan should be obtained to rule out the possibility of a small lobar hemorrhage masquerading as embolic stroke. Lumbar puncture is not necessary to detect red blood cells, unless dysarthria or clumsy hand syndrome or other posterior fossa syndromes suggest a small (possibly hemorrhagic) pontine infarct. Because of bone artifact, the CT scan may miss an occult hemorrhage masquerading as a small infarct in this area. Proton MRI can distinguish between acute vs. chronic hemorrhage vs. infarction and may be more reliable than CT in the early detection of infarction.

When a definitive diagnosis of cerebral artery embolism and its suspected arterial source is essential for management, cerebral angiography is justified. However, after 24 h, the embolus may have migrated, lysed, or dispersed, and evidence for embolism as the cause of an ischemic stroke becomes inferential. Intravenous digital subtraction angiography does not have adequate resolution to detect cerebral embolism.

Therapy Therapy of patients with embolic cerebral infarction consists of managing the stroke itself, in both the acute and chronic phases, and in prevention of further embolic strokes. When cerebral embolism is suspected, the immediate goal is to keep cerebral perfusion in the ischemic area as adequate as possible. The blood pressure should not be lowered even if hypertension is found unless it is malignant hypertension (see Chap. 196). If the blood pressure is low, raising it is a consideration. Caution is essential, however, for an excessive rise may aggravate edema formation. Once infarction becomes evident, edema seldom becomes problematic until the second or third day but can then remain for up to 10 days. Although there is some suggestion that recirculation in infarcted tissue due to lysis of the embolus contributes to the severity of edema formation, two rules governing the morbidity of the edema associated with cerebral embolism seem to apply. First, in instances of supratentorial embolic infarction, the larger the area of infarct, the more likely that edema formation will become a problem. Emboli that lodge in the middle cerebral artery stem are much more likely to cause symptomatic edema formation that could lead to coma and death from temporal lobe herniation than are emboli that lodge in a branch of the middle cerebral artery. Second, small amounts of edema formation in the cerebellum following embolic infarction, usually in the territory of the posterior inferior cerebellar artery (inferior cerebellum), can lead to an acute increase in intracranial pressure in the posterior fossa. The resulting compression of the brainstem may result in sudden coma and respiratory arrest requiring emergency surgical decompression. Water restriction and agents that raise the osmotic pressure should be considered early in both instances. Intravenous mannitol is most frequently used to raise the serum osmolality to 300 to 310 mosmol per liter; it is given as often as every 2 to 4 h. The acute management of artery-to-artery embolus, in either the carotid or vertebral territory, is discussed above (see Ischemic Cerebrovascular Disease).

The suspicion that fragments of clot from the heart or an unknown source are the embolic material raises the question of anticoagulation. Concern about developing hemorrhagic infarction and, more importantly, hemorrhage into infarction, makes timing of anticoagulation controversial. A conservative argument notes that reembolization seldom occurs in the first few days; therefore, anticoagulation can generally be delayed 3 to 4 days. However, another argument notes that serious hemorrhage into infarction is extremely rare and usually occurs in large infarcts involving the basal ganglia like those produced by middle cerebral stem emboli. Therefore, it may not be prudent to withhold anticoagulation for a few days unless the infarcted territory seems large. Certainly septic embolization contraindicates both immediate and delayed anticoagulation because of the threat of intracerebral or subarachnoid hemorrhage from mycotic aneurysm.

Except for marantic, septic, or tumor (myxoma) embolization, mural thrombus formation causes all cardiac embolization. It may be microscopic in the left atrial appendage, as in the case of atrial fibrillation, or large on the ventricular surface adjacent to an infarcted area, or it may occur in a ventricular aneurysm or on the mitral or aortic valve. Mural thrombus formation and embolization should be treated with chronic anticoagulation until the threat of reembolization is remote. In the setting of an acute myocardial infarction, 6 months of anticoagulation is considered sufficient; in the setting of chronic or intermittent atrial fibrillation, medication should be continued indefinitely. Although now rare, atrial fibrillation associated with rheumatic valvular disease indicates need for chronic lifelong anticoagulation even if embolization has not occurred. Patients with asymptomatic atrial fibrillation due to ischemic or other types of heart disease also have a higher incidence of cerebral embolism than age-matched controls. Here, however, controversy exists as to whether chronic anticoagulation is worth the risk. Most physicians agree that only a randomized, controlled study will settle the issue. When chronic anticoagulation is prescribed in any type of heart disease or cerebral embolism of unknown source, low-dose warfarin therapy is usually recommended. The prothrombin time should be no greater than $1\frac{1}{2}$ times the control, and all of the known contraindications to warfarin therapy apply (see Chap. 281). Finally, there are no reliable guidelines for the duration of anticoagulation therapy for patients with cerebral embolus of unknown source. But if the patient is under 50, anticoagulation for 6 months to 1 year seems appropriate.

INTRACRANIAL HEMORRHAGE

Although there are many causes of intracranial hemorrhage (Table 343-3), four are particularly common: hypertensive and lobar intracerebral hemorrhages, ruptured aneurysm (saccular), and ruptured arteriovenous malformation. Less common are hemorrhage associated with a bleeding disorder and rupture of a mycotic aneurysm. Rare causes include idiopathic brain purpura, brainstem (Duret) hemorrhages associated with brainstem torsion during uncal herniation, and small multifocal hemorrhages associated with hypertensive encephalopathy. These rarely simulate a stroke.

HYPTERTENSIVE INTRACEREBRAL HEMORRHAGE Pathophysiology Hypertensive hemorrhage typically occurs in four sites: (1) putamen and adjacent internal capsule, often extending into the central white matter (50 percent of cases), (2) thalamus, (3) pons, and (4) cerebellum. Hypertensive hemorrhage rarely originates in the central white matter. The vessel involved is generally one of the penetrating arteries arising from the middle cerebral artery stem, basilar artery, or circle of Willis, i.e., precisely the vessels involved with segmental lipohyalinosis as a consequence of hypertension.

The hemorrhage begins as a small oval mass, then spreads by dissection, growing in volume, displacing and compressing adjacent brain tissue. In these types of hemorrhage, rupture or seepage into the ventricular system almost always occurs, yet rupture from the white matter through the cortical surface gray matter is very rare. Only when the hemorrhage is small (1 to 2 cm) will it be confined to the central gray and white matter and not gain access to the CSF via the ventricular system. Large hemorrhages may compress the ventricular system and displace midline structures to the opposite side, leading to stupor, coma, and death.

Most hypertensive intracerebral hemorrhages develop in a few minutes, but some evolve over 30 to 60 min, and others, particularly those associated with anticoagulant therapy, evolve for as long as 24 to 48 h. In contrast to ruptured saccular aneurysm, once the bleeding stops, it generally does not start again. However, edema forms in the compressed tissue around the hemorrhage, leading to a greater mass effect and, in some cases, worsening the clinical status. Within 48 h, macrophages begin to phagocytize the hemorrhage at its outer surface. After 1 to 6 months, the hemorrhage mass is generally resolved to a slitlike orange cavity lined with astroglial scar tissue and hemosiderin-laden macrophages.

Clinical syndromes Although hyptertensive intracerebral hemorrhage may occur in anyone with hypertension, it is most common in those with sustained essential hypertension. Although not particularly associated with exertion, hypertensive intracerebral hemorrhage almost always occurs while the patient is awake. Unlike the sudden onset of embolism, these strokes evolve over a few minutes with the neurologic signs and symptoms dependent on the site and size of the extravasation.

The most common picture is that associated with a *putaminal hemorrhage*, in which the adjacent internal capsule is damaged. When these hemorrhages are large, the patient lapses within a few moments into a coma with hemiplegia. More often, however, the patient complains of something going awry within the head. In a few minutes the face sags on one side, speech becomes slurred or aphasic, the arm and leg gradually weaken, and the eyes tend to deviate away from the side of the paretic limbs. The history often documents that these events occurred gradually over a period of 5 to 30 min. This type of evolution is strongly suggestive of intracerebral bleeding.

TABLE 343-3 Causes of intracranial hemorrhage

I	Hypertensive intracerebral hemorrhage
II	Lobar hemorrhage of undetermined cause and intracerebral hemorrhage associated with congophilic angiopathy (analyzed)
III	Ruptured saccular aneurysm, giant aneurysm, or mycotic aneurysm
VI	Ruptured angioma
V	Hemorrhagic disorders: leukemia, aplastic anemia, thrombocytopenic purpura, liver disease, complication of anticoagulant therapy, hyperfibrinolysis, hypofibrinogenemia, hemophilia, Christmas disease
VI	Trauma, including posttraumatic apoplexy
VII	Hemorrhage into primary and secondary brain tissue
VIII	Hemorrhagic infarction, arterial or venous
IX	Inflammatory disease of the arteries and veins
X	Miscellaneous rare types: after vasopressor drugs, upon exertion, during arteriography, during painful urologic examination, as a late complication of early life carotid occlusion, complication of carotid-cavernous arteriovenous fistula, with anoxemia, migraine, teratomatous malformations (Acute inclusion body encephalitis produces xanthochromia and up to 2000 red blood cells or more in the cerebrospinal fluid; acute necrotizing hemorrhagic encephalopathy may be associated with up to 100 red blood cells in the cerebrospinal fluid; tularemia and snake venom poisoning may cause bloody cerebrospinal fluid.)

The paralysis worsens until the affected limbs become flaccid. Pinprick is then not appreciated, a Babinski sign appears, speaking becomes impossible (dominant hemisphere), and drowsiness gives way to stupor. In the worst cases, signs of upper brainstem compression appear. Coma ensues accompanied by deep, irregular, or intermittent respiration, a dilated and fixed ipsilateral pupil, bilateral Babinski signs, and decerebrate rigidity. When progressive deterioration occurs 12 to 72 h after the initial deficit, it is due to edema formation in adjacent brain rather than rerupture.

Thalamic hemorrhage of moderate size also produces a hemiplegia or hemiparesis from pressure on or dissection through the adjacent internal capsule. The sensory deficit is prominent and includes hemisensory abnormalities of pain and temperature as well as proprioception and touch. Dysphasia, often with preserved repeating aloud, may be present with lesions of the dominant side and apractagnosia with lesions of the nondominant. A homonymous field defect if present usually clears in a few days. Thalamic hemorrhage by virtue of its extension medially and inferiorly into the subthalamus causes a series of ocular disturbances, including paralysis of vertical gaze, forced deviation of the eyes downward, inequality of pupils with absence of light reaction, skew deviation with the eye opposite the hemorrhage being displaced downward and medially, ipsilateral ptosis and miosis, absence of convergence, an assortment of lateral gaze abnormalities (paresis or pseudoparesis of the sixth nerve), retraction nystagmus, and tucking in of the eyelids. Neck retraction may be present. Hemorrhage into the nondominant thalamus may produce mutism.

In *pontine hemorrhage,* deep coma usually ensues in a few minutes, and the clinical picture includes quadriplegia, prominent decerebrate rigidity, and small (1-mm) pupils that react to light. Reflex horizontal eye movements, evoked by head turning (doll's-head maneuver) or irrigation of the ears with cold water, are impaired (see Chap. 20). Hyperpnea, severe hypertension, and hyperhidrosis are common. Death usually occurs within a few hours, but there are rare exceptions where consciousness is retained and the clinical manifestations indicate a small lesion in the tegmentum of the pons, e.g., disturbances of lateral ocular movements, profound dysarthria, crossed sensory or motor disturbances, small pupils, cranial nerve palsies, and bilateral signs of pyramidal tract involvement.

Cerebellar hemorrhage usually develops over a period of several hours, and loss of consciousness at the onset is rare. Repeated vomiting with inability to walk or stand are the hallmarks of cerebellar hemorrhage. They occur early and must raise suspicion of the diagnosis to allow timely consideration of surgery. Occipital headache and vertigo are also prominent symptoms. There is a paresis of conjugate lateral gaze of the eyes to the side of the hemorrhage, forced deviation of the eyes to the opposite side, or an ipsilateral sixth nerve weakness. In the acute phase there may be little or no evidence of cerebellar disease, and only a minority of cases show nystagmus or cerebellar ataxia of the limbs. Other ocular signs include blepharospasm, involuntary closure of one eye, and skew deviation. Ocular bobbing, generally thought to be a sign of pontine disease, may be noted late when coma is present. Vertical eye movements remain, and small pupils continue to react until very late in the illness. A mild ipsilateral facial weakness and a diminished corneal reflex are common. Dysarthria and dysphagia may be prominent. Contralateral hemiplegia and contralateral facial weakness do not occur. Occasionally at the onset there is a quadriplegia with preservation of consciousness or a spastic paraparesis. The plantar reflexes are flexor early, extensor late. As the hours pass, and occasionally with unanticipated suddenness, the patient becomes stuporous, then comatose as a result of brainstem compression, at which point reversal of the syndrome, even by surgical therapy, is seldom successful.

Ocular signs are important in the localization of intracerebral hemorrhages. In putaminal hemorrhage, the eyes are deviated to the side opposite the paralysis; in thalamic hemorrhage, the eyes are deviated downward and the pupils may be unreactive; in pontine hemorrhage, the reflex lateral eye movements are impaired and the pupils tiny yet reactive; and in cerebellar hemorrhage, the eyes are deviated laterally (to the side opposite the lesion) in the absence of paralysis.

Headache is not an invariable finding associated with hypertensive intracerebral hemorrhage. It occurs in about half of the cases, while vomiting occurs in almost all cases. The patient need not be comatose, and if the hematoma is small, the patient may be fully alert even if the hemorrhage extends into the ventricular system. Seizures are uncommon, occurring in less than 10 percent of cases. In most instances, the correct diagnosis is suggested by the constellation of symptoms and signs. If, however, the patient is fully awake, confusion may exist between ischemic infarct and intracerebral hemorrhage. The CT scan allows precise differentiation and localization, especially with the more difficult small hemorrhages.

Laboratory evaluation The CT scan has revolutionized the diagnosis of intracerebral hemorrhage. It reliably detects all hemorrhages in the cerebral or cerebellar hemispheres of 1 cm or more in diameter if they are studied in the first 2 weeks. Because x-ray attenuation values of clotted blood diminish over time, intracranial hematoma may appear isodense after 2 weeks and may be missed if not associated with surrounding edema or mass effect. In some cases a rim of contrast-enhancing tissue appears after 2 to 4 weeks and may persist for months. Rarely, small pontine hemorrhages may not be identified because of motion and possibly bone artifact. MRI scans may prove more reliable than CT scanning for detecting either small pontine or medullary hematomas or hematomas in which the clot has become isodense. Here, however, precise pulse sequencing is required in order to differentiate acute hematomas, less than 3 days old, from chronic hematomas that are older than 3 days. The development of CT and MRI scanning minimizes the need for lumbar puncture except when a small pontine hemorrhage is in question. Such a hematoma could gain access to the cerebrospinal fluid without being visualized because of CT artifact. Lumbar puncture in a patient with intracerebral hemorrhage involves considerable risk, because it may aggravate temporal lobe herniation if the hematoma is large and located in a supratentorial area. However, when CT and MRI are not available, lumbar puncture may be necessary to establish the diagnosis if specific therapeutic measures are contemplated. When intracerebral hematoma occurs in the temporal lobe and appears near the sylvian cistern, rupture of an aneurysm at the bifurcation of the middle cerebral artery must be considered. Because of that and because temporal lobe swelling around the hematoma could occur and result in temporal lobe herniation, the etiology of the hemorrhage must be documented by angiography. Then, if temporal lobe edema threatens to cause herniation, it can be evacuated with knowledge that an aneurysm is or is not present. Angiography is also indicated if an intracerebral hematoma is not in one of the four classic locations for hypertensive hemorrhage, i.e., putamen, thalamus, pons, or cerebellum. Then surgically treatable arteriovenous malformations (AVM) may be responsible (see below). Angiography cannot completely exclude the possibility until the hematoma has been fully absorbed. A CT scan done without and with contrast may suggest that an AVM is the cause of intracerebral hematoma, but a negative result does not exclude this possibility. MRI may document an AVM once the hematoma resolves, for blood flowing in the malformation does not contribute to the MRI signal. The scan reveals the large vascular channels of an AVM as black. Chest x-ray and electrocardiogram often suggest cardiac hypertrophy secondary to chronic hypertension and provide a clue as to the etiology of the intracerebral hemorrhage.

The size of the hematoma, in many cases, determines the prognosis. Supratentorial hematomas greater than 5 cm in diameter have a guarded prognosis, and infratentorial pontine hematomas greater than 3 cm in size are almost invariably fatal. The formation of edema for up to a week after the intracerebral hemorrhage often worsens the prognosis. However, in intracerebral hematomas, the tissue surrounding the hematoma is displaced and compressed but not necessarily infarcted. Hence, after the resolution of the hematoma, considerable improvement can result, as the tissue regains its function. Careful management of the patient during the critical phase of the cerebral hematoma can lead to considerable recovery.

Therapy Surgical removal of the clot in the acute stage is rarely indicated. However, surgical evacuation of a supratentorial clot may prevent temporal lobe herniation in comatose patients who still have reflex eye movements. Surgical evacuation of acute cerebellar hemorrhage is usually the treatment of choice because it is often lifesaving and offers an excellent prognosis for recovery of function. If patients are alert without focal brainstem signs and if the cerebellar hematoma is small, the physician may elect against acute surgical removal. It must be remembered, however, that deterioration of the clinical state can be rapid. The option for acute surgery must always be available.

Mannitol and other osmotic agents reduce edema around an intracerebral hemorrhage. Steroids are of uncertain value in curtailing edema from intracerebral hematoma. Monitoring of the intracranial pressure may help to assess medical therapy. Both excessive hypo- and hypertension should be avoided. Dramatic reduction in blood pressure to "stop the hemorrhage" is not helpful, because most intracerebral hemorrhages have stopped bleeding by the time the patient is examined. Toxemia of pregnancy and malignant hypertension should be detected early and treated cautiously to avoid excessive or precipitous lowering of the blood pressure.

LOBAR INTRACEREBRAL HEMORRHAGE As control of hypertension in the general population improves, the relative proportion of hemorrhages outside the basal ganglia and thalamus increases. These "lobar hemorrhages" appear on CT scan as oval or circular clots in the subcortical white matter. The role of chronic hypertension in their genesis is controversial, but many occur without a history of increased blood pressure. A number of other underlying conditions are established in almost half the cases. The most common is arteriovenous malformation. Others are bleeding diathesis, often associated with warfarin administration; hemorrhages into tumor, often a melanoma; aneurysms of the circle of Willis that point upward and bleed into brain substance; and a large number whose causes remain undetermined even after extensive study including arteriography.

Among the latter, the most common is *amyloid angiopathy,* which can only be diagnosed at postmortem examination with demonstration that the vessels stain positive with Congo red. Amyloid is deposited in the walls of the cerebral arteries; the angiopathy is unassociated with amyloid deposition elsewhere in the body. The condition seems to account for many lobar hemorrhages among the elderly. Often patients suffer multiple hemorrhages, although months may elapse between occurrences.

Most lobar hemorrhages are small enough to cause a restricted clinical syndrome that simulates an embolus to a vessel supplying one lobe. Larger hemorrhages, associated with stupor or coma, cause larger deficits and affect two or more lobes. Most patients experience focal headaches: occipital hemorrhage afflicts the area around or over the ipsilateral eye; temporal hemorrhage, the area around or anterior to the ipsilateral ear; frontal hemorrhage, the forehead or diffusely in the frontal quadrant; and parietal hemorrhage, the temple region. At the onset, stiff neck or seizures are uncommon, but more than half the patients vomit or are drowsy. The neurologic syndrome appears suddenly, over one to several minutes, not instantaneously as it does in embolus. The clinical syndrome corresponds to the location of the hematoma: the major neurologic deficit of occipital hemorrhage is hemianopsia; of left temporal hemorrhage, aphasia and delirium; of parietal hemorrhage, thalamic-like hemisensory loss; of frontal hemorrhage, arm weakness. The region of hemorrhage adds other but less prominent signs to these.

Treatment depends upon the underlying condition. Angiography should be performed in most cases, but immediate angiography may not reveal a small vascular malformation. If a vascular malformation is still suspected, angiography should be performed again after 2 to 4 months, when the vessels adjacent to the clot may have decom-

pressed. In awake or drowsy patients, surgical evacuation offers little benefit over medical management with fluid restriction, corticosteroids, and small doses of an osmotic agent if necessary. But stuporous or comatose patients not responding rapidly to medical therapy for raised intracranial pressure should have the clot evacuated immediately.

SACCULAR ANEURYSM AND SUBARACHNOID HEMORRHAGE

Rupture of an intracranial saccular aneurysm is the most common cause of subarachnoid hemorrhage. In comparison, rupture of an intracranial arterial mycotic or myxomatous aneurysm is rare. Rupture of an arteriovenous malformation is the second most frequent cause of subarachnoid hemorrhage. Although autopsy studies estimate that 5 percent of the population harbor aneurysms, the incidence of ruptured saccular aneurysms is about 4/100,000 per year. It is a devastating disease; as many as 25 percent of patients die during the first day, and nearly half succumb in the first 3 months. Of those who survive, more than half are left with major neurologic deficits as a result of the initial hemorrhage or of a delayed complication, such as rerupture, symptomatic cerebral vasospasm, or hydrocephalus. More than half of those patients discharged home after neurosurgical treatment of the aneurysm never achieve the quality of life they enjoyed prior to the rupture. Given these alarming figures, it becomes evident that the major therapeutic emphasis should be placed on prevention, i.e., preventing the initial rupture and, if rupture occurs, preventing the direct complications that ensue.

Pathophysiology Saccular aneurysms occur at the bifurcations of the large arteries at the base of the brain and rupture into the subarachnoid space of the basal cisterns (Fig. 343-11). Mycotic aneurysms, on the other hand, occur at distal branch points of the middle, anterior, or posterior cerebral, vertebral, or basilar arteries. They rupture into the subarachnoid space over the cortical surface rather than into the basal cisterns. These differences determine the clinical features of saccular aneurysms, distinguishing them from mycotic aneurysms. The common sites of saccular aneurysms include the junction of the anterior communicating artery with the anterior cerebral artery, the junction of the posterior communicating artery and the internal carotid artery, the bifurcation of the middle cerebral artery, the top of the basilar artery, the junction of the basilar artery and the superior cerebellar artery or the anterior inferior cerebellar artery, or the junction of the vertebral artery and the posterior inferior cerebellar artery (Fig. 343-11). Approximately 85 percent of cases occur in the anterior circulation; 12 to 31 percent have multiple aneurysms; 9 to 19 percent have bilateral identical locations.

As an aneurysm develops, it often displays a neck with a dome. The length of the neck and the size of the dome vary greatly, factors that are important in planning microsurgical obliteration. The internal elastic lamina disappears at the base of the neck. The media thins, and connective tissue replaces smooth muscle cells. At the site of rupture, most often the dome, the wall thins to less than 0.3 mm, and the rent is often no more than 0.5 mm long.

It is not possible to determine which aneurysms are likely to rupture, but limited data suggest that size is an important variable and that those larger than 7 mm may warrant prophylactic microsurgical obliteration.

Clinical symptoms, evolution, and management PRODROMAL SYMPTOMS Prodromal symptoms may betray the location of an unruptured aneurysm and, at times, suggest progressive enlargement. The onset of a third nerve palsy, particularly when associated with pupillary dilation, loss of light reflex, and focal pain above and behind the eye, point to an expanding aneurysm at the junction of the posterior communicating artery and the internal carotid artery. In order for a third nerve palsy to occur, the aneurysm at the origin of the posterior communicating artery has to be 7 mm or greater and be expanding. Hence, prompt consideration of surgery is indicated. Sixth nerve palsy may indicate a cavernous sinus aneurysm, and visual field defects can occur with an expanding supraclinoid carotid

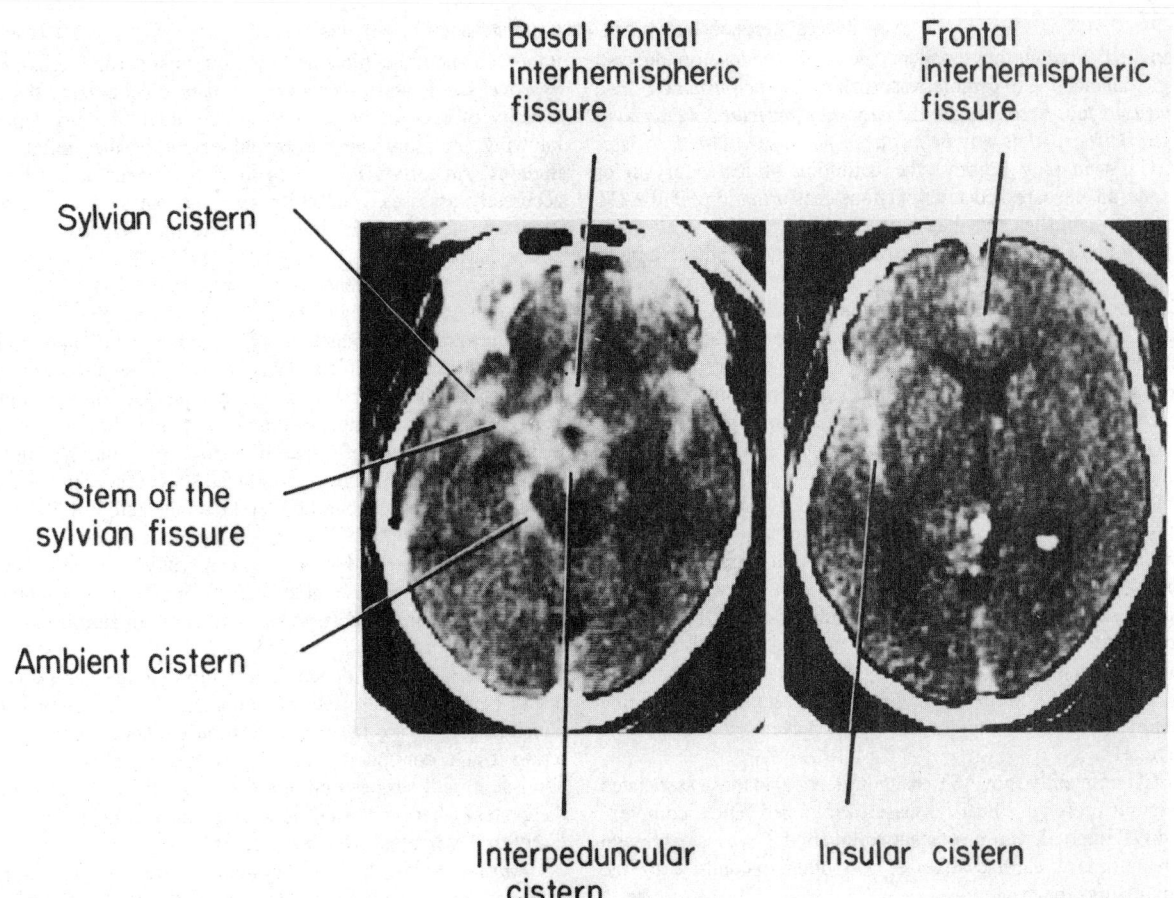

Sylvian cistern

Stem of the sylvian fissure

Ambient cistern

Basal frontal interhemispheric fissure

Frontal interhemispheric fissure

Interpeduncular cistern

Insular cistern

FIGURE 343-11 *Blood in the basal cisterns of the subarachnoid space. The main subarachnoid cisterns and fissures are labeled.*

aneurysm. Occipital and posterior cervical pain may signal a posterior/inferior cerebellar artery (PICA) or anterior/inferior cerebellar artery (AICA) aneurysm. Pain in or behind the eye and in the low temple can occur with an expanding middle cerebral aneurysm.

Whether an aneurysm can cause small, intermittent leakage of blood into the subarachnoid space is an unresolved issue. However, the importance of documenting the clinical correlates of the smallest aneurysmal rupture or leak is undeniable. Sudden unexplained headache at any location should rouse suspicion of subarachnoid hemorrhage and be investigated by a CT scan to look for blood in the basal cisterns. Often a small subarachnoid hemorrhage will not be detected by CT scan, necessitating a lumbar puncture to examine for subarachnoid blood.

INITIAL CLINICAL PRESENTATION: ACUTE MAJOR SUBARACHNOID HEMORRHAGE For the brief moment of aneurysmal rupture, when acute major subarachnoid hemorrhage occurs, intracranial pressure approaches the mean arterial pressure and cerebral perfusion pressure falls. This may account for the sudden transient loss of consciousness which occurs in 45 percent of cases. The sudden loss of consciousness may be preceded by a brief moment of excruciating headache, but most patients first complain of headache upon regaining consciousness. In 10 percent of cases, aneurysmal bleeding may be severe enough to cause loss of consciousness for several days. In about 45 percent of cases, severe headache, usually associated with exertion, but without loss of consciousness, occurs as the presenting complaint. The headache is often called by the patient "the worst headache of my life." Words like "explode" or "burst" may be used. Often it is described as "all over" or "in the back of the head and neck." Whatever the onset, vomiting is a prominent symptom, and vomiting with sudden headache should always raise the question of acute subarachnoid hemorrhage.

Although sudden severe headache in the absence of focal neurologic

symptoms is the hallmark of aneurysmal rupture, not infrequently neurologic deficits emerge. Unilateral third nerve palsy strongly suggests a posterior communicating artery aneurysm. Sixth nerve palsy is common but does not have great significance as a localizing sign, although it often corresponds to an infratentorial aneurysmal rupture. Anterior communicating artery aneurysms or a middle cerebral bifurcation aneurysm may rupture into the subdural space or into the basal cisterns of the subarachnoid space and form a clot that is large enough to produce a localized mass effect. The common deficits that result include hemiparesis, aphasia of the dominant hemisphere, anosognosia (hemineglect) of the nondominant hemisphere, memory loss, and abulia. An aneurysm, especially one located at the bifurcation of the middle cerebral artery, may rupture into the sylvian cistern, into the temporal lobe, or up into the frontal and parietal lobes. It may therefore present as a mass and be mistaken for an intracerebral hemorrhage. Cerebral edema often follows, resulting in progressive deterioration, sometimes requiring emergency surgical intervention.

Occasionally, acute unilateral hemispheric swelling and associated focal neurologic signs and stupor occur immediately following aneurysmal rupture. The reasons for such swelling are uncertain. The possibility exists that transient interruption of the cerebral circulation in a given arterial territory occurs, possibly secondary to acute vascular spasm of the stem of the artery. Often there is no adequate explanation for the initial neurologic deficits, and in most cases they gradually improve over a matter of days.

Careful documentation of the initial neurologic deficit, attempting to establish its cause, and closely following its course is of utmost importance for management of the patients and in timing the onset and evolution of delayed neurologic deficit.

INITIAL EVALUATION Over 75 percent of cases exhibit evidence of subarachnoid clot on a noncontrast CT scan if the scan is obtained within the first 48 h after aneurysmal rupture (Fig. 343–11). The extent and location of subarachnoid blood may help locate the aneurysm and identify the cause of the initial neurologic deficit. It may also help predict those patients destined to develop delayed neurologic deficits due to cerebral vasospasm. *A noncontrast CT scan should be done first because contrast may show arterial enhancement in the basal cisterns that may be mistaken for clotted blood.* A later contrast CT scan may improve the definition of an aneurysm or demonstrate an unsuspected arteriovenous malformation. If the CT scan neither establishes the diagnosis of subarachnoid hemorrhage nor demonstrates a mass lesion or obstructive hydrocephalus, a lumbar puncture should be done to establish the presence of subarachnoid blood. The only indication for lumbar puncture prior to CT scanning is if the CT scan is not available at the time of the suspected subarachnoid hemorrhage.

If the diagnosis of subarachnoid hemorrhage from ruptured saccular aneurysm has been firmly established, then angiography is delayed until the time of surgery. Cerebral angiography is usually planned immediately prior to surgery to localize and characterize the anatomy of the aneurysm and to document the presence or absence of focal cerebral vasospasm. If an arteriovenous malformation or mycotic aneurysm is suspected because of the presence of intraparenchymal blood or subarachnoid blood located over the hemisphere rather than in the basal cisterns, then angiography should be done without delay. Another indication for acute angiography is an intracerebral hematoma secondary to aneurysmal rupture which with cerebral edema formation may make emergency surgical evacuation necessary. Documenting the location and anatomy of the aneurysm before such surgery is imperative.

The ECG frequently shows ST changes identical to those associated with ischemic coronary heart disease. Prolonged QRS complex, increased QT interval, and prominent or inverted T waves, although suggesting primary cardiac disease, are often secondary to the intracranial hemorrhage.

Serum electrolytes are obtained because hyponatremia may develop secondary to inappropriate antidiuretic hormone (ADH) secretion with volume expansion or because of unknown factors that cause salt and water loss with subsequent volume depletion.

INITIAL MANAGEMENT   Following subarachnoid hemorrhage, a stuporous or comatose patient may have increased intracranial pressure. Care is required to maintain adequate cerebral perfusion pressure while avoiding excessive elevation of mean arterial pressure. Frequent arterial blood-gas determinations are helpful to assess alveolar ventilation. If hypercapnia exists, mechanically assisted ventilation is necessary. If a subdural or intracerebral hematoma mass is causing neurologic deterioration, its surgical removal and, if feasible, obliteration of the aneurysm become more compelling options.

Because of the threat of rebleeding, all patients are put on bed rest in a quiet, preferably darkened room and are given adequate bowel softeners to prevent constipation. Excessive sensory deprivation can lead to agitation, so the patient is permitted to read, listen to the radio, and visit with the family. If headache or neck pain is severe, mild sedation and analgesics are prescribed. Aspirin, an antiplatelet agent, is inappropriate, but acetaminophen or meperidine and phenobarbital or other sedatives may be used. Heavy sedation is avoided because it can obscure the assessment of initial or delayed neurologic deficits.

Seizures are uncommon at the onset of aneurysmal rupture. The quivering, jerking, and extensor posturing that usually accompany loss of consciousness are probably related to the sharp rise in intracranial pressure. However, phenytoin, 300 mg a day, or phenobarbital, 30 mg three times a day, are sometimes given as prophylactic therapy, since a grand mal seizure risks rerupture.

Steroids may help reduce the head-and-neck ache caused by the irritative effect of blood in the subarachnoid space, but there is no evidence to suggest they help in treatment of the cerebral edema that is sometimes seen in patients immediately after a subarachnoid hemorrhage.

DELAYED NEUROLOGIC DEFICITS   There are three major causes of delayed neurologic deficits (i.e., those following stabilization or

improvement of the initial neurologic symptoms and signs): *rerupture, hydrocephalus,* and *cerebral vasospasm.* Recognizing the onset and severity of each of these delayed neurologic deficits depends upon knowing precisely the cause and extent of the initial neurologic findings. An early CT scan (24 to 48 h after the hemorrhage) which accurately assesses ventricular size and the extent and location of subarachnoid blood is invaluable in the diagnosis of the three complications.

Rupture. The incidence of rerupture in the first 3 weeks following subarachnoid hemorrhage ranges from 10 to 30 percent. Because rerupture carries significant morbidity and mortality, numerous clinical investigations of the effects of antifibrinolytic agents have been carried out. Despite their widespread use, evidence of efficacy in preventing rebleeding is conflicting. Moreover, they may be associated with an increased incidence of ischemic stroke presumably from cerebral vasospasm. A prospective randomized study that correlates the extent and location of subarachnoid blood documented by CT scan with the incidence of rerupture and of symptomatic vasospasm is needed. Those patients destined to develop cerebral vasospasm severe enough to cause stroke because of the effect and location of blood in the basal cistern will probably do so whether or not antifibrinolytic agents are used.

Despite lack of evidence that antifibrinolytic therapy is unequivocally beneficial, the effect of rerupture is so devastating that many physicians advocate the use of epsilon aminocaproic acid, administering it as a continuous intravenous infusion of 30 g per day from admission until surgery, but not for longer than 3 weeks. In some of the centers where it is used, it is withheld in those patients who seem likely to develop severe symptomatic vasospasm.

Hydrocephalus. After aneurysmal rupture, communicating hydrocephalus with dilatation of the lateral, third, and fourth ventricles can occur at any time but usually between 4 and 20 days. There is no clinical or laboratory method to predict which patient is in jeopardy of developing hydrocephalus or how severe it might be. However, extensive subarachnoid blood in the ambient and suprasellar cisterns is ominous. Hydrocephalus may cause no detectable neurologic change or may lead to profound stupor developing over minutes to hours. Mild drowsiness, urinary incontinence, and inability to move the eyes above the mid position are associated with early, mild-to-moderate communicating hydrocephalus. Often, hydrocephalus is transient and requires no surgery; but if significant neurologic deterioration occurs, ventricular drainage or ventricular atrial shunting may be required. Knowledge of the precise site and location of the aneurysm is important before inserting a ventricular catheter.

Cerebral vasospasm. It is now clearly established that narrowing of the caliber of the arteries at the base of the brain following subarachnoid hemorrhage from ruptured saccular aneurysm (*cerebral vasospasm*) can lead to cerebral ischemia and infarction (*symptomatic cerebral vasospasm*).

Symptomatic cerebral vasospasm is the major cause of delayed morbidity or death, occurring in approximately 30 percent of patients. Most patients seem to improve or are stable during the period between the aneurysmal rupture and the onset of symptomatic vasospasm. Signs usually appear 4 to 14 days after the initial subarachnoid hemorrhage, peaking at 7 days. The new neurologic deficits are usually recognizable if the initial deficit and clinical course are clearly delineated. The new deficits correspond to ischemia in specific arterial territories, and the severity of vasospasm determines whether cerebral infarction will develop.

Cerebral vasospasm is a focal phenomenon related to the presence of blood in the cerebrospinal fluid, but why it occurs is not known. Laboratory studies have suggested that chemical substances such as serotonin, prostaglandins, and catecholamines can produce arterial narrowing. However, all these compounds break down rapidly in vivo, and only large amounts produce spasm in vitro. More sustained arterial vasospasm has been produced by experiments with incubated whole blood and erythrocyte breakdown products.

Clinical evidence suggests that the extent and location of clotted blood, seen on CT scans, in the basal cisterns and fissures of the subarachnoid space can be used to predict the incidence, location, and severity of cerebral vasospasm in patients after subarachnoid hemorrhage. In these studies, a high incidence of symptomatic cerebral vasospasm was found in patients whose early CT scans showed globular subarachnoid clots larger than 5 × 3 mm in the basal cisterns or layers of blood 1-mm thick or greater in the cerebral fissures. In addition, the location of the clot in the subarachnoid space as seen on CT scan correlated almost perfectly with the location of the spasm in the artery lying in the subarachnoid space. While these studies demonstrated that CT scans reliably predict the location and severity of vasospasm in the anterior and middle cerebral arteries, they provide less precision in the vertebral, basilar, or posterior cerebral arteries. The CT scan cannot reliably detect significant clot in the posterior fossa. Furthermore, for the prediction to be accurate, the CT scan should be obtained between 24 and 96 h following subarachnoid hemorrhage. Blood appearing on CT scan within the first hours following subarachnoid hemorrhage can disappear on a scan obtained after 24 h, presumably because it "washed away." With the further passage of time, x-ray attenuation values of clotted blood diminish so that its full extent and location may not be reliably detected after 96 h.

Because of the close relationship between the location of cerebral vasospasm and clotted blood surrounding the vessel, any hypothesis concerning the mechanism of vasospasm must take into account the prolonged effect of such a clot. The best current hypothesis suggests that a clot encases the artery; then after a few days spasmogenic hemoglobin breakdown products induce spasm. Once the vessel is in spasm, high-energy phosphate metabolism becomes impaired, due to the surrounding clot preventing cerebrospinal fluid from nourishing the vessels. (Vasa vasorum are not present in the vessels at the base of the brain or over the cortical surface.) This insulation may then prevent the artery from relaxing because that requires energy.

CLINICAL SYNDROMES OF SYMPTOMATIC CEREBRAL VASOSPASM   Clinically symptomatic severe cerebral vasospasm presents with symptoms referable to the specific arterial territories involved. For example, if the middle cerebral stem or its main branches are involved, contralateral hemiparesis and/or dysphasia (dominant hemisphere) or anosognosia or apractagnosia (nondominant hemisphere) may be present. But even severe vasospasm may not produce ischemic symptoms if sufficient collateral blood flow develops through border zone anastomotic channels (Fig. 343-1A). The ischemic symptoms of anterior cerebral territory involvement are an abulic state in which the patient lies quietly awake, eyes either open or closed, responsive to commands but with a delay. Such a patient may offer no spontaneous conversation but answer questions in short, whispered phrases. Food is chewed for a long time and often held between the cheek and the gum. Severe vasospasm of the posterior cerebral artery may produce homonymous field defects. Severe spasm of the basilar or vertebral arteries occasionally produces focal brainstem ischemia. All of these focal neurologic symptoms may develop over a few days or present abruptly, peaking within minutes to an hour.

If the entire middle cerebral artery territory becomes ischemic and infarcted, cerebral edema may ensue and cause a fatal rise in intracranial pressure. An early CT scan predicts this outcome when it demonstrates a large clot in the stem of the sylvian fissure and/or sylvian cistern and a second significant clot in the basal frontal interhemispheric fissure. Simultaneous clots in these areas correlate well with severe symptomatic spasm in the middle and anterior cerebral artery. In this setting, cortical surface collaterals over the cortical surface from the anterior cerebral artery fail to relieve ischemia in the middle cerebral artery territory.

Treatment   TREATMENT OF SYMPTOMATIC SEVERE CEREBRAL VASOSPASM   Therapeutic efforts to prevent or treat symptomatic cerebral vasospasm have been universally disappointing. Reserpine and kanamycin to reduce serum serotonin levels, isoproterenol or aminophylline to indirectly increase cyclic AMP, or nitroprusside to directly dilate the arteries have all failed.

The failure to find a satisfactory therapy for cerebral vasospasm has prompted a search for prophylactic measures to prevent or minimize its occurrence. In one study, treatment with the calcium channel–blocking agent nemodipine was reported to have beneficial effects, but patients in both the treated and untreated groups developed symptomatic vasospasm. Confirmation of this study and trials of other dilating agents are in progress. Because patients with symptomatic cerebral vasospasm have increased blood volume and many have cerebral edema, the small further rise in intracranial volume occurring with vasodilating agents may be detrimental. Therefore, vasodilating agents are not recommended once severe symptomatic vasospasm has become established.

The commonly accepted form of therapy for symptomatic cerebral vasospasm is to increase the cerebral perfusion pressure by increasing the mean arterial pressure through plasma volume expansion together with judicious use of pressor agents, ordinarily phenylephrine or dopamine. Dopamine is given in dosages of 3 to 6 μg/kg per minute. Therapy to raise the perfusion pressure has been associated with symptomatic improvement in some patients, but high arterial pressure entails the theoretical risk of rebleeding. This therapy requires information about the cerebral perfusion pressure and cardiac output, necessitating direct measurement of the central venous pressure, arterial pressure, and, in severe cases, the intracranial and pulmonary artery wedge pressure.

Severe edema formation in patients with symptomatic cerebral vasospasm may increase the intracranial pressure enough to reduce cerebral perfusion pressure sharply. This requires that the serum osmolality be raised with mannitol while maintaining an adequate intravascular volume and mean arterial pressure: 125 mL of 20% mannitol every 4 h is administered until the plasma osmolality is raised to between 300 to 310 mosmol per liter. As a last resort, barbituate coma has been used to reduce intracranial pressure. Although it is effective in lowering intracranial pressure in some patients, it has not been proven to have significant clinical benefit.

In conclusion, there is no proven, effective therapy for preventing or treating symptomatic cerebral vasospasm following subarachnoid hemorrhage. If further studies demonstrate that the CT scan reliably predicts those patients in jeopardy of developing cerebral vasospasm, early operation to remove the spasmogenic clot as well as the prophylactic use of vasodilators or prostaglandin agonists can be evaluated more accurately.

MEDICAL COMPLICATIONS OF SUBARACHNOID HEMORRHAGE   Complications following subarachnoid hemorrhage include thrombophlebitis with pulmonary embolism, perforated stress-induced duodenal ulcer, and ECG changes suggestive of myocardial infarction or ischemia. Subarachnoid hemorrhage causes overactivity of the sympathetic nervous system resulting in focal myofibrillar degeneration of the myocardium. Cardiac arrhythmias can develop. Beta-adrenergic blocking agents are useful but should be given cautiously, especially if an atrioventricular block is present. An additional complication is hyponatremia, occurring either from inappropriate ADH secretion or from secretion of a natriuretic hormone. Restriction of free water, while maintaining adequate intravascular volume, is the recommended treatment.

SURGICAL TREATMENT OF THE ANEURYSM   The advent of the operating microscope has made microsurgical obliteration of a ruptured aneurysm a safe and effective means of preventing disastrous rerupture. Most neurosurgeons delay surgery for at least 10 to 14 days. Operation is undertaken when the patient is clinically stable. Delayed surgery allows cerebral swelling from the initial rupture time to resolve, and minimizes the risk of symptomatic vasospasm in the postoperative period.

The wisdom of delaying surgery has been questioned, especially if the patient is neurologically intact. Surgery within the first 48 h eliminates the problem of rebleeding and can remove potentially spasmogenic clots from the basal cisterns, theoretically preventing vasospasm from occurring at that site. While it is technically possible to remove local clots and obliterate aneurysms early, some subarachnoid clots are too extensive for safe, complete removal. The timing of surgery should therefore be tailored to the individual patient. If a CT scan finds no threatening subarachnoid clot or if the location of a potentially dangerous clot permits its safe and effective removal, early surgery may be appropriate.

GIANT ANEURYSMS Giant aneurysms larger than 2 cm in diameter occur at the same sites as small aneurysms. The three most common locations are the intracranial internal carotid, middle cerebral bifurcation, and top of the basilar artery. Although they can rupture, they usually cause symptoms by compressing the brain as they expand. Edema formation in the compressed brain can be relentless and lead to major brain compression and death. This progression is particularly likely if a giant aneurysm occurs at the bifurcation of the middle cerebral artery. Surgical decompression remains the only adequate thereapy, but it is extremely difficult technically and entails a high morbidity in the presence of edema.

MYCOTIC ANEURYSMS When an aneurysm is located distal to the first bifurcation of the arteries of the circle of Willis, a mycotic aneurysm must be suspected. Bacterial endocarditis with embolization should be assumed and appropriate blood cultures taken. Because of their location more distal in the arterial tree (cerebellar hemisphere, cortical surface), they rarely leave significant amounts of clotted blood in the basal cisterns. Severe cerebral vasospasm almost never occurs. Mycotic aneurysms, however, are subject to rerupture. Although antibiotic therapy may decrease the threat of rebleeding, surgical obliteration remains the definitive treatment. It should be undertaken while the patient is receiving antibiotics for presumed or actual bacterial endocarditis.

OTHER CAUSES OF INTRACRANIAL HEMORRHAGE Arteriovenous malformation An angioma, or hemangioma, consists of a tangle of abnormal vessels forming an abnormal communication between the arterial and venous systems. In reality, it is an arteriovenous fistula that is a developmental abnormality where the constituent vessels enlarge and grow with the passage of time. Angiomas vary in size from a small blemish a few millimeters in diameter lying in the cortex or white matter to a huge mass of tortuous channels composing an arteriovenous shunt of sufficient magnitude to raise the cardiac output. Hypertrophic dilated arterial "feeders" approach the main lesion, disappear below the cortex, and break up into a network of thin-walled blood vessels which connect directly with draining veins. These often form huge, dilated, pulsating channels, carrying away arterial blood. The blood vessels forming the tangle interposed between arteries and veins are usually abnormally thin and do not have the normal structure of arteries or veins. Angiomas occur in all parts of the brain, brainstem, and spinal cord, but the larger ones are more frequently found in the posterior half of the hemispheres, commonly forming a wedge-shaped lesion extending from the cortex to the ventricular lining.

Angiomas predominate in males over females in a ratio of about 2:1. They may occur in more than one member of a family in the same or successive generations. Although the lesion is present from birth, the onset of complaints is most common between the ages of 10 and 30, but occasionally it is delayed as late as the fifties.

The chief clinical symptoms and signs are headache, seizures, and those associated with rupture or ischemia. When headache occurs, it may be hemicranial and throbbing or diffuse. It may mimic migraine. Occasionally it may be associated with hemiplegia and resemble hemiplegic migraines. Focal seizures that become generalized occur in about 30 percent of cases and are usually well managed with anticonvulsants. In half the cases, arteriovenous malformations herald their onset with intracerebral hemorrhage. In most of these cases, the hemorrhage is intraparenchymal to a greater extent than subarachnoid. Blood is usually not deposited in the basal cistern, and symptomatic cerebral vasospasm in the arteries in the cisterns rarely occurs. The threat of rerupture in the first 3 weeks is low so that there is no need to consider the use of antifibrinolytic agents. The

hemorrhage may be massive, leading to death acutely, or may be as small as 1 cm in diameter, leading to minor focal symptoms or no deficit. In either case, the hemorrhage mass may mask the arteriovenous malformation so completely that acute angiography cannot detect it. Hence, when arteriovenous malformation (AVM) is suspected, angiography is best postponed until the hematoma has completely resolved, i.e., after 2 to 4 months. Rarely, the angioma may be large enough to steal blood away from adjacent normal brain tissue, rendering the surrounding brain ischemic. This deprivation is most often seen when large AVMs in the middle cerebral–posterior cerebral system or middle cerebral–anterior cerebral system extend from the cortical surface to the ventricular system. Hydrocephalus may result when the vein of Galen is involved.

Large AVMs of the carotid–middle cerebral system may be associated with a systolic and diastolic bruit heard over the eye, forehead, or neck where a bounding, forceful carotid pulse may be perceived. At the time of rupture, the blood pressure may be normal and should suggest that an AVM, hemorrhage into a brain tumor, or a ruptured saccular aneurysm has occurred. Headache at the onset of AVM rupture is not as prominent or as common as it is with a ruptured saccular aneurysm. Vomiting, on the other hand, is common in any intracranial hemorrhage. Both MRI and contrast CT scan offer the opportunity to detect the channels of an arteriovenous malformation prior to rupture.

Although many AVMs eventually rupture, definitive surgical therapy is usually reserved until after the first rupture; the threat of rerupture is 3 percent per year thereafter. When surgery is not feasible because of the location and size of AVMs, other therapeutic options include artificial embolization and focused proton beam radiation.

Trauma Trauma may result in intracerebral (especially temporal lobe and inferior frontal) hematoma and infratentorial hematomas, subarachnoid bleeding, acute and chronic subdural hematoma formation, and acute epidural hematoma formation. It must be considered in any patient with an unexplained acute neurologic deficit (hemiparesis, stupor, or confusion), particularly if the strokelike deficit occurred in the context of a fall. CT scan and even angiography should be used without hesitation if such a diagnosis is suspected. Surgical intervention in these cases is often lifesaving. The diagnosis should not be missed. These entities and their distinction from spontaneous hemorrhage are discussed more fully in Chap. 344.

Hematologic disorders Intracerebral hemorrhage associated with hematologic disorders (leukemia, aplastic anemia, thrombocytopenic purpura) can occur at any intracranial site and may present as multiple intracerebral hemorrhages. Skin and mucous membrane bleeding is usually evident and offers a diagnostic clue. Intracerebral hemorrhage associated with anticoagulant therapy can occur at any location intracerebrally and may evolve slowly over 24 to 48 h. Fresh frozen plasma should be given immediately. When intracerebral hemorrhage is associated with aspirin, fresh platelet transfusions may be required to stop the oozing.

Brain tumors Hemorrhage into brain tumors may be the first manifestation of neoplasm. Choriocarcinoma, malignant melanoma, renal cell carcinoma, and bronchogenic carcinoma are among the most common metastatic tumors associated with intracerebral hemorrhage. Glioblastoma multiforme in adults and medulloblastoma in children are among the most common primary intracranial tumors that lead to intracerebral hemorrhage.

Other causes Occasionally hemorrhage of unknown origin occurs. This is most often associated with small angiomas or amyloid angiopathy. Primary intraventricular hemorrhage is rare. When it is suspected, it is usually secondary to a hemorrhage that begins intraparenchymally and dissects into the ventricular system immediately without leaving sign of intraparenchymal hemorrhage.

Hemorrhagic encephalitis consists of small petechial hemorrhages through the cerebral white matter. In this setting blood is not found in the spinal fluid, and this condition should not be confused with a stroke. Gram-negative sepsis is generally the cause. Herpes simplex encephalitis may also result in red blood cells in the CSF.

Brainstem hemorrhages occur with temporal lobe herniation when there is torsion of the brainstem. These occur as coma ensues and do not present as a stroke.

Inflammatory disease of the arteries and veins, especially polyarteritis nodosa and lupus erythematosus, can produce hemorrhage into the central nervous system. Most of the time it is associated with hypertension.

Other types of hemorrhage are noted (Table 343-3) and are self-explanatory. Hemorrhages into the spinal cord are usually the result of an arteriovenous malformation or metastatic tumor. Epidural spinal hemorrhage usually compresses the cord rapidly and should be diagnosed without hesitation if surgery is to effect the cure and prevent paraplegia (see Chap. 353).

HYPERTENSIVE ENCEPHALOPATHY (See Chap. 196)

This term refers to an acute syndrome in which severe hypertension is associated with headache, nausea, vomiting, convulsions, confusion, stupor, and coma. Focal or lateralizing neurologic signs, either transitory or lasting, may occur but are infrequent and always suggest some other form of vascular disease (hemorrhage, embolism, or atherosclerotic thrombosis). By the time neurologic manifestations appear, the hypertension has usually reached the malignant state, with retinal hemorrhages, exudates, papilledema (hypertensive retinopathy grade IV), and evidence of renal and cardiac disease. In many, but not all cases, the cerebrospinal fluid pressure and the protein values are both elevated, the latter sometimes to over 100 mg/dL. The hypertension may be essential or due to chronic renal disease, acute glomerulonephritis, acute toxemia of pregnancy, pheochromocytoma, Cushing's syndrome, or ACTH toxicity. Lowering of the blood pressure with hypotensive drugs may reverse the picture in a day or two. If the hypertension cannot be controlled, the outcome is fatal. Neuropathologic examination may reveal a rather normal-looking brain, but usually cerebral swelling and/or hemorrhages of various sizes from massive to petechial will be found. A cerebellar pressure cone reflects increased volume of brain tissue and increased pressure in the posterior fossa, and in some instances lumbar puncture may have precipitated a fatality. Microscopically there are, in addition to small hemorrhages, clusters of microglial cells, minute cerebral infarcts, and necrosis of arterioles.

The term *hypertensive encephalopathy* should be reserved for the above syndrome and not used to refer to chronic recurrent headaches, dizziness, epileptic seizures, recurrent TIAs, or small strokes which often occur in association with high blood pressure.

INFLAMMATORY DISEASES OF BRAIN ARTERIES

Inflammatory diseases of the vessels of the brain have been mentioned on several occasions in the preceding paragraphs, and here they are discussed briefly.

Meningovascular syphilis, formerly one of the most frequent causes of occlusive vascular disease in patients of all ages, has become a rarity since the introduction of penicillin therapy. Tuberculous meningitis, fungal meningitis, and the subacute forms of bacterial meningitis (*Haemophilus*, streptococcal, pneumococcal) may also be accompanied by vascular disorders of the occlusive type, in either the cerebral arteries or veins. Occasionally in tuberculous meningitis, a stroke may be the first clinical sign of meningitis; more often it develops after the meningeal symptoms are established.

Typhus, schistosomiasis mansoni, mucormycosis, malaria, and *trichinosis* are rare types of infective inflammatory diseases of the arteries and, unlike the above, are not secondary to meningeal inflammation. In typhus and other rickettsial diseases, capillary and arteriolar changes and perivascular inflammatory cells are found in the brain, and presumably they underlie the convulsions, acute psychoses, and coma which reflect the central nervous system involvement. They do not cause strokes, however. The internal carotid artery may be occluded in diabetic patients during orbital and cavernous sinus infections with mucormycosis. In trichinosis, the sudden onset of convulsions, aphasia, hemiplegia, and coma may either accompany or, as happens more often, follow the systemic and muscular symptoms. The cause of the cerebral symptoms has not been established. Parasites have been found in the brain; in one case, the cerebral lesions were produced by bland emboli arising in the heart and related to a severe myocarditis. Malaria of the malignant or falciparum variety is frequently attended by a clinical state known as cerebral malaria, in which convulsions, coma, and sometimes focal symptoms appear to be due to blockage of capillaries and precapillaries by masses of parasitized red blood corpuscles.

The *arteritides of obscure origin* include polyarteritis nodosa, disseminated lupus erythematosus, granulomatous arteritis, giant cell arteritis, temporal (cranial) arteritis, and rheumatic arteritis (see above and Chap. 269). In addition, herpes zoster and acquired immunodeficiency syndrome (AIDS) have been associated with cerebral arteritis.

Lupus erythematosus causes cerebral symptoms in over 50 percent of cases. Seizures and psychoses are common. Small cerebral infarcts lead to widespread focal deficits. Accompanying hypertension may precipitate hemorrhage or hypertensive encephalopathy, or endocarditis may cause cerebral embolism.

Thromboangiitis obliterans of cerebral vessels (Winiwarter-Buerger disease) has not been included in the foregoing list. Despite the large volume of literature on the subject, the pathology is so dubious that it does not merit further exposition. All the patients that have been well studied proved to have had either atherosclerosis of the carotid or cerebral arteries with "stasis thrombosis" of more distant cerebral branches. Buerger's disease of the legs has an equally uncertain status.

DIFFERENTIATION OF CEREBROVASCULAR DISEASE FROM OTHER NEUROLOGIC ILLNESSES

It has already been stated that the diagnosis of a vascular lesion rests solely on recognizing the stroke syndrome. Otherwise, the diagnosis always remains in doubt. Three useful criteria in the identification of stroke have already been emphasized: (1) the tempo of the clinical syndrome, (2) evidence of focal brain disease, and (3) the clinical setting. The temporal profile can usually be defined by means of a clear history of premonitory phenomena, the mode of the onset, and the evolution of the neurologic disturbance taken in relation to the medical status at the time of examination. If these data are lacking, the course may still be determined by extending the period of observation for a few more days or weeks. An inadequate history is probably the most frequent cause of diagnostic errors.

Few other neurologic illnesses mimic cerebrovascular disease. When the details of the history are missing, however, subdural hematoma, brain tumor, brain abscess, and senile dementia may lead to diagnostic difficulties.

REFERENCES

AUSMAN JI et al: Vertebrobasilar insufficiency: A review. Arch Neurol 42:803, 1985

BARNETT HJM: Heart in ischemic stroke: A changing emphasis. Neurol Clin 1:291, 1983

BOUGHNER DR, BARNETT HJM: The enigma of the risk of stroke in mitral valve prolapse. Stroke 16:175, 1985

BOUSSER MG et al: "AICLA" controlled trial of aspirin and dipyridamole in the secondary prevention of athero-thrombotic cerebral ischemia. Stroke 14:5, 1983

CANADIAN COOPERATIVE STUDY GROUP: A randomized trial of aspirin and sulfinpyrazone in threatened stroke. N Engl J Med 299:53, 1978

CAPLAN LR: "Top of the basilar" syndrome. Neurology 30:72, 1980

———: Vertebrobasilar disease: Time for a new strategy. Stroke 12:111, 1981

——— et al: Occlusive disease of the middle cerebral artery. Neurology 35:975, 1985

CEREBRAL EMBOLISM STUDY GROUP: Immediate anticoagulation of embolic stroke: Brain hemorrhage and management options. Stroke 15:779, 1984

DUNCAN GW et al: Concomitants of atherosclerotic carotid artery stenosis. Stroke 8:665, 1977

EC/IC BYPASS STUDY GROUP: Failure of extracranial-intracranial arterial bypass to reduce the risk of ischemic stroke: Results of an international randomized trial. N Engl J Med 313:1191, 1985

FISHER CM: Occlusion of the internal carotid artery. Arch Neurol Psychiatry 65:346, 1951

———: Occlusion of the carotid arteries: Further experiences. Arch Neurol Psychiatry 72:187, 1954

——— et al: Lateral medullary infarction: The pattern of vascular occlusion. J Neuropathol Exp Neurol 20:323, 1961

———: The arterial lesions underlying lacunes. Acta Neuropathol (Berl) 12:1, 1969

———: Cerebral ischemia: Less familiar types. Clin Neurosurg 18:267, 1971

———: Clinical syndromes in cerebral thrombosis, hypertensive hemorrhage, and ruptured saccular aneurysm. Clin Neurosurg 22:117, 1975

———: The natural history of carotid occlusion, in *Microneurosurgical Anastomoses for Cerebral Ischemia*, GM Austin (ed). Springfield, Ill, Charles C Thomas, 1976, pp 194–201

——— et al: Atherosclerosis of the carotid and vertebral arteries—extracranial and intracranial. J Neuropathol Exp Neurol 24:455, 1965

——— et al: Cerebral vasospasm with ruptured saccular aneurysm: The clinical manifestations. Neurosurg 1:245, 1977

——— et al: Spontaneous dissection of cervico-cerebral arteries. Can J Neurol Sci 5:9, 1978

——— et al: The correlation of cerebral vasospasm and the amount of subarachnoid blood detected by computerized cranial tomography after ruptured aneurysm. Neurosurg 6:1, 1980

———: Late-life migraine accompaniments as a cause of unexplained transient ischemic attacks. Can J Neurol Sci 7:9, 1980

———: Lacunar strokes and infarcts: A review. Neurology 32:871, 1982

GENTON E et al: Cerebral ischemia: The role of thrombosis and of antithrombotic therapy. Study group on antithrombotic therapy. Stroke 8:150, 1977

HINTON RC et al: Influence of etiology of atrial fibrillation on incidence of systemic embolism. Am J Cardiol 40:509, 1977

——— et al: Symptomatic middle cerebral artery stenosis. Ann Neurol 5:152, 1979

KISTLER JP: Cardiac embolic cerebrovascular disease. Primary Care 6:745, 1979

——— et al: The relation of cerebral vasospasm to the extent and location of subarachnoid blood visualized by CT scan: A prospective study. Neurol 33:424, 1983

——— et al: Vertebral basilar territory stroke. Delineation by proton nuclear magnetic resonance imaging. Stroke 15:417, 1984

——— et al: Therapy of ischemic cerebral vascular disease due to atherothrombosis. N Engl J Med 311:27, 100, 1984

MOHR JP: Valvular disease, cardiac arrest, systemic hypotension, and cardiac surgery, in *Handbook of Clinical Neurology*, GW Bruyn, PJ Vinken (eds). Amsterdam, North-Holland, 1978

——— et al: The Harvard Cooperative Stroke Registry: A prospective registry. Neurology 28:754, 1978

———: Lacunes. Stroke 13:3, 1982

ROPPER AH, DAVIS KR: Lobar cerebral hemorrhages: Acute clinical syndromes in 26 patients. Ann Neurol 8:141, 1980

TOOLE JF, YUSON CP: Transient ischemic attacks with normal arteriograms: Serious or benign prognosis. Ann Neurol 1:100, 1977

WILKINS RH: Natural history of intracranial vascular malformation: A review. Neurosurg 16:421, 1985

WOLF PA et al: Epidemiologic assessment of chronic atrial fibrillation and risk of stroke. Neurol 28:973, 1978

——— et al: Asymptomatic carotid bruit and risk of stroke: The Framingham study. JAMA 245:1442, 1981

344   TRAUMA OF THE HEAD AND SPINAL CORD

ALLAN H. ROPPER

Head injuries are frequent in industrialized countries, affecting many patients in the prime of life. To appreciate the medical and social magnitude of this problem it needs only to be recognized that almost 10 million Americans have head injuries yearly, about 20 percent serious enough to cause brain damage. Among men under 35 years old, accidents, usually motor vehicle collisions, are the chief cause of death, and over 70 percent of these involve head injury. Minor head injuries are so common that almost all physicians encounter patients requiring immediate care or suffering from various sequelae. Traumatic spinal cord injuries often occur in conjunction with head injury. The two are best considered together in the context of trauma to the nervous system.

In the last decade, declining mortality from head and spinal cord injuries can be attributed mainly to public health measures, such as use of seat belts and motorcycle helmets, and the development of ambulance systems with trained personnel. A systematic approach to the evaluation of patients with head and spine trauma, beginning at the scene of the accident, has improved outcome. An understanding of the pathologic lesions produced by trauma is essential for diagnosis and to provide a framework for management.

TYPES OF HEAD INJURIES

SKULL FRACTURES   A blow to the skull causes fractures if the elastic tolerance of the bone is exceeded. Significant intracranial lesions accompany two-thirds of skull fractures, and the presence of a skull fracture increases manyfold the chances of an underlying subdural or epidural hematoma. Consequently, fractures assume importance primarily as markers of the site and severity of injury. They also cause cranial nerve injuries and produce entry pathways to the cerebrospinal fluid (CSF) for bacteria (meningitis) and air (pneumocephalus), or for leakage of CSF. Fractures are classified as linear, basilar, compound, or depressed; linear fractures account for 80 percent of all skull fractures and are most often associated with subdural or epidural hematomas. Linear fractures usually extend from the point of impact toward the base of the skull.

Basilar skull fractures are often extensions of adjacent fractures over the convexity of the skull but may occur independently due to stresses on the floor of the middle cranial fossa or occiput. They are usually located parallel to the petrous bone or along the sphenoid bone toward the sella turcica and ethmoidal groove. Most are uncomplicated, but they may cause CSF leak, pneumocephalus, or cavernous-carotid fistula. Fractures of the basal skull bones are often accompanied by signs of hemotympanum (blood behind the tympanic membrane), delayed ecchymosis over the mastoid process (Battle's sign), or periorbital ecchymosis ("racoon sign"). Because routine x-ray examination can fail to disclose basilar fractures, they should be suspected in the presence of these clinical signs. Cerebrospinal fluid may also leak through the cribriform plate or the adjacent sinus and present as a watery discharge from the nose (CSF rhinorrhea). Persistence of rhinorrhea or recurrent meningitis is an indication for a surgical repair of torn dura underlying the fracture. The site of the leak is often difficult to determine, but metrizamide instillation into the CSF with subsequent computerized tomography (CT) scans, or radionuclide or fluorescein injection into the CSF followed by assessment of uptake by absorptive nasal pledgets, are useful diagnostic tests. The site of intermittent leaks is rarely delineated; most resolve spontaneously. Sellar fractures can also be radiologically occult, although they are sometimes associated with serious neuroendocrine dysfunction. Occasionally, fractures of the dorsum sella cause sixth or seventh nerve palsies or optic nerve damage. An air-fluid level in the sphenoid sinus suggests a fracture of the sellar floor.

About 20 percent of petrous bone fractures, usually along the long axis of the bone, are associated with facial palsy. Disruption of ear ossicles and CSF otorrhea are other complications. Transverse petrous fractures are less common, almost always damaging the cochlea or labyrinths and often the facial nerve. External bleeding from the ear can result from petrous bone fractures, though local laceration of the external canal from abrasions is more common. Frontal bone fractures are often depressed, involving the frontal and paranasal sinuses and the orbits; anosmia frequently follows if the olfactory filaments in the cribriform plate are disrupted.

Depressed skull fractures are often compound but are commonly asymptomatic, except for amnesia due to concussions, because the impact energy is dissipated in breaking the bone. Some cause brain contusions and focal neurologic signs appropriate to the underlying cortical area. Surgical repair and bone elevation with exploration of the dura is required in most cases. Delayed or incomplete debridement of the wound leads to a high incidence of infection. If the skin is lacerated over a skull fracture and the underlying meninges are torn, or if the fracture passes through the posterior wall of a nasal sinus, bacteria or air may enter the cranial cavity resulting in meningitis, abscess formation, or pneumocephalus.

CRANIAL NERVE INJURIES   Cranial nerves liable to injury with basilar skull fractures are the olfactory, optic, oculomotor, trochlear, and first and second branches of the trigeminal, facial, and auditory. Anosmia and an apparent loss of taste (actually a loss of perception of aromatic flavors, with elementary tastes retained) occurs in approximately 10 percent of serious head injuries, particularly with falls on the back of the head. This results from displacement of the brain and shearing of the olfactory nerve filaments. Recovery is usual with residual hyposmia, but if bilateral anosmia persists for several months, the prognosis is poor. Fractures of the sphenoid bone may bruise or transect the optic nerve, resulting in unilateral partial or complete blindness, and an unreactive pupil usually equal in size to the other side, with a preserved consensual light response. Partial optic nerve injuries from closed trauma result in blurring of vision, central or paracentral scotomas, or sector defects. Recovery of vision varies widely. Direct orbital injury may cause short-lived blurred vision for close objects because of reversible iridoplegia. Oculomotor nerve injury causes the globe to turn outward with loss of adduction and vertical movement and a fixed dilated pupil; vision is preserved. Diplopia only on looking down suggests trochlear nerve damage from fracture of the lesser sphenoid wing. It is not uncommon as an isolated problem from minor injury and may be delayed in appearance for several days. Patients report correction of the diplopia by tilting the head away from the affected eye. Direct facial nerve injury by a basal fracture is present immediately in 3 percent of severe injuries or may also be delayed 5 to 7 days. Petrous fractures, particularly the less common transverse type, are liable to produce this injury. Delayed facial palsy has a good prognosis; its mechanism is not known. Injury to the eighth cranial nerve with fractures of the petrous bone causes loss of hearing, vertigo, and nystagmus immediately after injury; the nystagmus is frequently positional. Deafness due to nerve injury must be distinguished from rupture of the eardrum, blood in the middle ear, or disruption of the ossicles from fracture through the middle ear. A high-tone hearing loss occurs with direct cochlear concussion.

CONCUSSION   Concussion refers to an immediate but transient loss of consciousness often described as dazed or "star-struck" and associated with a short period of amnesia. It typically occurs after blunt impact or deceleration of the frontal or occipital areas that creates sudden movement of the brain within the skull. In severe cases autonomic symptoms and signs such as facial pallor, bradycardia, faintness with mild hypotension, or sluggish pupillary reaction may occur, but most patients are neurologically normal. Higher primates are particularly susceptible to concussion; billy goats, rams, and woodpeckers, for example, can tolerate impact velocity and deceleration a hundred times greater than that experienced by humans. The mechanism of loss of consciousness in concussion is believed to be transient electrophysiologic dysfunction of the reticular activating system in the upper midbrain caused by rotation of the cerebral hemispheres on the relatively fixed brainstem. The mechanism of amnesia is not known. Gross and light microscopic changes in the brain are usually absent after concussion, but biochemical and ultrastructural changes such as mitochondrial ATP depletion and local disruption of the blood-brain barrier suggest that complex changes occur. The CT scan is normal, and there are usually no red blood cells in the CSF as occurs with more severe injuries.

Amnesia after concussion typically follows a few moments of unresponsiveness after impact. Rarely there is no loss of consciousness. The memory loss spans the time of, and moments before, mild impact injuries but may encompass previous weeks (rarely months) in more severe trauma. Any anterograde amnesia is usually brief and disappears rapidly in alert patients. The extent of retrograde amnesia has been suggested as a coarse measure of the severity of injury. Improvement usually occurs in an orderly progression from most distant to recent memories, with islands of amnesia occasionally remaining in severe cases. Hysterical posttraumatic amnesia is not uncommon. It should be suspected when abnormalities of behavior occur, such as a tendency to recount events that cannot be recalled on later testing, bizarre affect, a person forgetting his or her own name, disproportionate or selective memory loss, or exaggerated anterograde deficit in comparison to the degree of injury.

CONTUSION, BRAIN HEMORRHAGES, AND SHEARING LESIONS
Hemispheral lesions   Contusions on the surface of the brain and deeper hemorrhages result from mechanical forces that move the hemispheres relative to the skull. Deceleration of the brain against the inner skull causes contusions, either under a point of impact (coup lesion) or in the antipolar area (contrecoup lesion). Trauma sufficient to cause prolonged unconsciousness beyond concussion usually produces contusions varying from small superficial cortical petechiae to hemorrhagic and necrotic destruction of large portions of a hemisphere. Because the motion of the hemispheres brings them into contact with the prominences of the sphenoid and other frontal basal bones, blunt impact, as from an automobile dashboard, typically causes contusions on the orbital surfaces of the frontal lobes and the anterior and basal portions of the temporal lobes. The anterior corpus callosum may also be bruised from striking the falx. With lateral forces, as from the doorframe of a car, contusions occur on the convexity of the hemispheres.

Contusions are visible on CT scan, appearing early as smudged hyperlucencies from scattered cortical and subcortical blood and a mass that distorts adjacent structures, most prominently the lateral ventricles (Fig. 344-1*C*). After several hours the surrounding edematous tissue appears as a ring of lower density. Confluent, roughly spherical contusions can be distinguished from spontaneous cerebral hemorrhages because the former characteristically extend to the cortical surface. After a week some contusions have a surrounding ringlike contrast-enhancing density that may be mistaken for tumor or abscess. Glial and macrophage reactions begin within 2 days, years later resulting in scarred hemosiderin-stained depressions on the surface (*plaques jaune*) that are one source of posttraumatic epilepsy. Large single hemorrhages after minor trauma are found in patients with a bleeding diathesis or in the elderly, sometimes related to cerebrovascular amyloidosis.

The clinical signs produced by contusions vary with their location and size; most often a hemiparesis or gaze preference is seen, similar to a middle cerebral artery stroke. Bilateral large contusions produce coma with extensor posturing; when contusions are limited to the frontal lobes, an abulic-taciturn state or inappropriate jocularity and indifference occur. Contusions of the temporal lobes cause an aggressive combative syndrome, described below. With large contusions the secondary effect of progressive edema is the most threatening aspect of the injury. Coma and signs of secondary brainstem compression (pupillary enlargement) then dominate the examination. Seizures soon after trauma are rare with contusions, as indeed they are for several weeks after most acute head injuries.

Deep hemorrhages in the central white matter may result from confluent contusions in the depths of a sulcus. However, ganglionic, diencephalic, and other deep hematomas due to torsion or shearing forces in the brain often occur independently of surface damage. The areas around these hematomas may become edematous, resulting in enlargement of the affected region and progressively raised intracranial pressure.

Another type of white matter, or "shearing," lesion consists pathologically of widespread acute disruption of axons. Axonal shearing occurs at, or soon after, impact. The affected areas of white matter are replaced with glial proliferation over a period of several months. There are characteristically small areas of tissue disruption in the corpus callosum and dorsolateral pons. Widespread axonal shearing lesions in the deep white matter of both hemispheres may explain persistent coma or vegetative state, but hemorrhages in the midbrain and diencephalon are as often the cause. Shearing lesions are not usually visualized by CT scanning, but in severe cases small hemorrhages of the corpus callosum and centrum semiovale are seen.

On occasion head trauma causes diffuse brain swelling within a few hours after injury. Most instances are due to widespread contusion though CT scanning fails to reveal significant focal lesions or hemorrhage. The edema creates a mass effect with disastrous consequences. This problem is encountered in children and young adults who may develop a virtually instantaneous generalized edema probably due to microvascular disruption, hypertension, and greatly increased cerebral blood flow.

Deep cerebral hemorrhages may occur several days after severe injury. Sudden neurologic deterioration, often in already comatose patients, or a sustained and unexplained rise in intracranial pressure should prompt a CT scan to detect delayed hemorrhage.

Brainstem hemorrhages A syndrome with coma, midposition or larger pupils unreactive to light, and impaired or absent oculocephalic reflex eye movements results from small linear or oval-shaped hemorrhages in the high midbrain, visible on CT scan, though often delayed in appearance. Though extensor posturing occurs with stimulation, the limbs are otherwise flaccid. This clinical syndrome should be suspected even in the initial absence of a hemorrhage on CT scan. These acute midbrain hemorrhages may be the result of primary injury from rotational forces in the upper midbrain. They also occur from secondary compression of the brainstem by supratentorial hematomas and lateral tissue shifts or pressure from the adjacent temporal lobes. In pathologic material from severe, acutely fatal injuries, small linear and oval hemorrhages are found in the low thalamic and subthalamic regions and throughout the midline of the brainstem (termed *Duret hemorrhages*).

Residual symptoms and signs of primary or secondary brainstem hemorrhages or ischemic lesions include tremor, pupillary enlargement, eye movement abnormalities, or the "locked-in" syndrome (see Chap. 21). Midbrain or diencephalic hemorrhages are the only well-defined traumatic brainstem lesions responsible for coma. Most other cases of coma without fixed pupils and unexplained by CT scan

are probably due to diffuse axonal shearing injuries in the cerebral hemispheres.

SUBDURAL AND EPIDURAL HEMATOMAS In severe head injury, hemorrhages beneath the dura (subdural) or between the dura and skull (epidural) may be combined with contusions and other injuries, making it difficult to determine their relative contribution to the clinical state. However, subdural and epidural hematomas often occur as the primary lesion, each with a characteristic clinical and CT scan appearance. Because the mass effect of the hemorrhage and rise in intracranial pressure may be life-threatening, it is important to make an immediate diagnosis and carry out surgical evacuation.

Acute subdural hematoma Acute subdural hematomas become symptomatic in minutes to hours after injury. Up to one-third of patients have a lucid interval before coma supervenes, but the majority are drowsy or comatose from the moment of injury. Arousable patients complain of unilateral headache and frequently have a slightly enlarged pupil on that side. Stupor or coma with unilateral pupillary enlargement are the major signs in larger hematomas. Pupillary dilation is ipsilateral in most, but 5 to 10 percent are contralateral to the hematoma. Lateralizing signs such as a hemiparesis are helpful in only a few patients and may be ipsilateral to the clot. Acute seizures or isolated hemianopsias are uncommon. The CT scan shows the clot, allowing early evacuation (Fig. 344–1A). Angiography with oblique projections can also outline subdural hematomas and has been used if CT scanning is unavailable. In an acutely deteriorating patient with rapidly diminishing alertness and pupillary enlargement, burr holes or an emergency craniotomy are appropriate without prior radiographic confirmation of subdural hematoma. A subacute syndrome is seen in alcoholics and in the elderly, with drowsiness, headache, confusion, or mild hemiparesis occurring days to 2 weeks after injury.

FIGURE 344-1 *Computerized tomographic (CT) scans from patients with head trauma. A. Acute subdural hematomas with compression of adjacent brain tissue. B. Chronic subdural hematoma, less dense than brain tissue. C. Contusion–traumatic hemorrhage of the frontal and parietal lobes. D. Epidural hematoma in relation to a fracture and tearing of the middle meningeal artery. The lenticular shape of the hemorrhage is typical. E. Skull fractures in the path of a bullet trajectory. By manipulating the windows on the CT scan, fractures and radiodense objects are shown to advantage and appear similar to plain radiographs.*

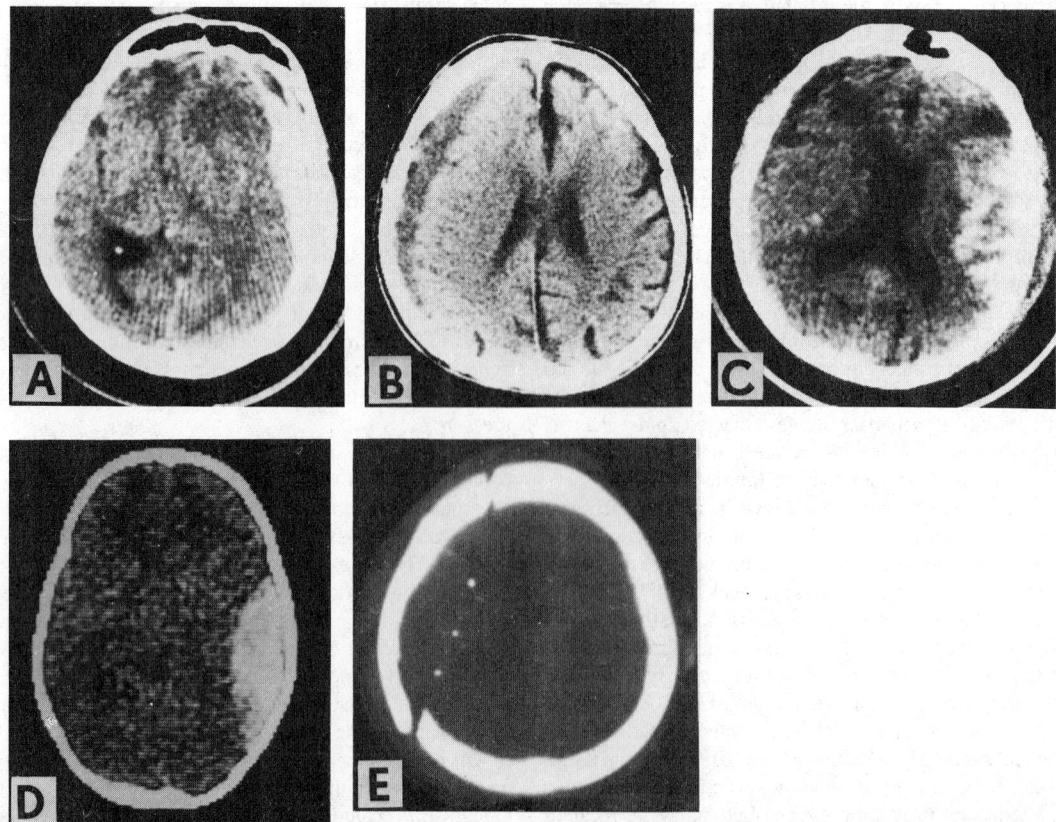

Direct trauma or surface contusions are not required for the formation of acute subdural hemorrhage; acceleration forces alone, as from whiplash, are adequate especially in the elderly. Most subdural hematomas are small crescentic collections over the hemispheral convexity, adjacent to variable degrees of surface hemorrhagic contusions. Larger clots are thought to be primarily venous in origin, though additional arterial bleeding sites are often found, and some appear to be exclusively arterial when explored surgically. Most are located over the frontotemporal region, less often in the inferior middle fossa or over the occipital poles. Less common instances of interhemispheric, posterior fossa, or bilateral convexity clots are difficult to diagnose clinically, although drowsiness and the signs expected for each region can be detected. Small subdural hematomas may be asymptomatic and usually do not require therapy.

Acute epidural hematoma Epidural hematomas evolve more rapidly and therefore can be more treacherous. They occur in 1 to 3 percent of all head injuries and in up to 10 percent of severe ones. They are less often associated with underlying cortical damage than subdural hematomas. The majority of patients are unconscious when first seen, often with associated injuries of subdural clot and contusion. A "lucid interval" of several minutes to hours before coma supervenes is said to be most characteristic of epidural hemorrhage, though it is not common and by no means the only cause of this temporal profile. The findings of drowsiness progressing to coma, pupillary enlargement, and focal hemispheral signs are similar in some respects to subdural hematoma, but occur more rapidly.

The location of epidural hematomas is explained by their origin from torn dural vessels, most commonly the middle meningeal artery. Epidural clots therefore overlie the lateral temporal convexity. The majority of patients have fractures of the squamous portion of the temporal bone, through the path of the torn vessel. Frontal, inferior temporal, or occipitoparietal epidural hematomas are less frequent, occurring when fractures disrupt branches of the middle meningeal artery. Dural laceration over the sagittal or lateral sinuses or rupture of small diploic veins can rarely cause venous epidural hemorrhages. Epidural hematomas strip the tightly attached dura from the inner table of the skull, producing a characteristic lenticular-shaped clot on CT scan (Fig. 344–1D). They may be relatively less frequent in the elderly because of the tighter attachment of dura to skull that occurs with aging. Posterior fossa epidural hematomas are rare and difficult to detect clinically; most result from surgery such as resection of an acoustic neuroma.

Chronic subdural hematoma In chronic subdural hematoma, a preceding traumatic cause is less often clear; 20 to 30 percent of patients fail to give a history of injury. Elderly patients or those with a bleeding diathesis seemingly form clots spontaneously. The causative injury may be trivial (striking the head against the branch of a tree, a sudden stop in a car with lurching forward, or striking the head during a fall or faint) and is often forgotten because it was remote in time. A period of weeks, or even months, follows when headaches (common but not invariable), slowed thinking, confusion, changes in personality, seizures, or a mild hemiparesis are the main findings. Fluctuation in the severity of the headache is typical, often with positional changes. Many chronic subdural hematomas are bilateral and give particularly misleading clinical syndromes. The initial clinical impression is often a stroke, brain tumor, drug intoxication, or a depressive, senile, or other type of dementia, the latter because disturbances of consciousness (drowsiness, inattentiveness, incoherence of thought) are more prominent than focal or lateralizing signs such as hemiparesis. Hemianesthesia or hemianopsia are seldom observed, probably because the anatomic structures subserving these functions are deep and not easily compressed. The diagnosis should be considered in dementias of apparently rapid onset, particularly if headache is present. The condition does not always progress. When it does, the patient may become comatose with fluctuations of alertness and pupillary dilation as occurs in acute subdural hematoma. Acute bleeding is superimposed on the chronic hematoma in these cases.

Occasionally patients present with "spells" of hemiparesis or aphasia typically lasting more than 10 min, indistinguishable from transient ischemic attack. Patients with undetected small bilateral subdural hematoma seem to tolerate surgery, anesthesia, and nervous system depressive drugs poorly, often remaining drowsy or confused for long periods postoperatively.

Skull x-rays are usually normal except for a shift of a calcified pineal body to one side or an occasional unexpected fracture. The CT scan without contrast infusion typically shows a low-density mass over the convexity of the hemisphere (Fig. 344–1B), but may show only a shift of the midline structures and compression of the lateral ventricles because the clot becomes isodense to adjacent brain after 2 to 6 weeks. Bilateral chronic hematomas are often missed because of the absence of lateral tissue shifts. A "hypernormal" CT scan with absent cortical sulci and small ventricles in an older patient should suggest the diagnosis of bilateral isodense hematomas. Contrast infusion demonstrates the chronic fibrous capsule in some cases. Radionuclide brain scans with anterior projections are often the most successful method of confirming the diagnosis. The CSF may be clear, bloody, or xanthochromic, depending on the presence or absence of recent or old contusion and subarachnoid hemorrhage, and the pressure is usually elevated. However, lumbar puncture is not recommended for diagnosis because of risk of worsening tissue shifts. Chronic subdural hematomas can gradually expand, and then behave clinically like a tumor. Treatment with corticosteroids alone is sufficient in some cases, but surgical evacuation is most often successful. Fibrous membranes (pseudomembranes) grow from the dura and encapsulate the region. Craniotomy and removal of the membranes is required if there is recurrent fluid accumulation. Small hematomas are largely resorbed, and only the organizing membranes remain, becoming calcified after many years.

PENETRATING INJURIES, COMPRESSIONS, AND LACERATIONS

Tangential scalp wounds from bullets can produce neurologic signs or delayed seizures due to small hemorrhages or contusions, even in the absence of missile penetration. Bullets entering the brain cause considerable damage because of tremendous kinetic energy. A cylindrical area of necrosis surrounds the bullet track. Injuries differ with varying projectiles; soft civilian bullets typically shatter on impact and leave a track of metallic fragments with disporportionately less parenchymal damage (Fig. 344–1E). Military bullets, because of high velocity and energy, disrupt tissue at great distances from the track and produce massive brain destruction.

Penetrating bullet injuries cause a rapid increase in intracranial pressure for several minutes followed by a drop depending on the volume of secondary hemorrhage and the degree of developing edema. Infection is a risk mainly from shell fragments, shrapnel, grenades, and mines, because such small projectiles carry surface bacteria and dirt into the brain. Nevertheless, most neurosurgeons administer systemic antibiotics prophylactically and perform local debridement in all types of penetrating injuries. Traumatic aneurysms can form due to disruption of vessel walls from the shock wave of the projectile; facial-orbital entrance wounds have the highest incidence. The aneurysms have an unpredictable course; most that rupture do so in the first month. The prognosis for survival after missile injuries is good if consciousness is preserved and poor if coma is present from the outset.

Other intracranial foreign bodies from knives, picks, studguns, or high-speed tool bits may be missed unless skull x-rays are taken after minor penetrating injuries. Surgical removal, debridement, and extensive exploration for hemorrhage and necrotic tissue is required. Simply removing a protruding object is not sufficient.

TRAUMATIC VASCULAR OCCLUSION AND DISSECTION Minor,
sometimes unnoticed, neck trauma can produce dissection (stripping of the intima or the media) of the internal carotid or vertebral arteries. Chiropractic neck manipulation accounts for some cases. Severe blunt trauma to the neck can initiate a dissection several centimeters above the origin of the internal carotid artery. In awake patients there is

usually local neck pain over the internal carotid artery, a Horner's syndrome, and headache over the ipsilateral anterior cranium. Some patients with carotid dissection subsequently have large middle cerebral artery strokes with hemiplegia, visual field and sensory deficits, and if the dominant hemisphere is affected, aphasia. In drowsy or comatose patients evidence of dissection or subsequent stroke is difficult to discern but is suggested by unexplained hemiplegia, unilateral miosis, or the appearance of cerebral infarction on CT scan. Angiography demonstrates either the typical "string sign" characterized by an elongated narrowed lumen extending over 5 to 10 cm, or complete occlusion of the carotid artery beginning several centimeters distal to the bifurcation, sometimes accompanied by a distal embolus in the middle cerebral artery. On rare occasion, basilar skull fractures cause carotid dissection beginning at the point of entry of the artery into the skull. Traumatic "false" aneurysms of the cervical carotid artery result from deep penetrating, and occasionally from nonpenetrating, blunt trauma of the neck. A pulsatile mass and bruit over the artery establish the diagnosis and mandate surgical repair. Traumatic vertebral artery dissection can produce vertigo, vomiting, suboccipital or supraorbital headache, and other signs of lateral medullary ischemia. These symptoms are frequently attributed to vestibular concussion. In drowsy or comatose patients the only indication of vertebral artery occlusion may be inferior cerebellar infarction on CT scan.

Intracranial vascular damage is rare except in penetrating injuries. High-velocity projectiles, as discussed above, disrupt vessel walls, leading to aneurysms of large vessels in the vicinity of the wound, usually a surface branch of the middle cerebral artery. Preexisting saccular aneurysms may rupture after basilar skull fractures, and this diagnosis should be considered if subarachnoid hemorrhage is profuse and inadequately explained by accompanying subdural blood on CT scan. Vasospasm from traumatic subarachnoid blood may be involved in the development of infarction after head injury.

Cavernous sinus arteriovenous fistulas are serious complications in patients surviving severe head injury. They are first evident as a self-audible bruit (many are also audible to the examiner), proptosis, conjunctival injection, or visual impairment. Angiography shows early filling of the cavernous sinus and its draining tributaries. The fistula generally enlarges, causing increasingly severe local changes around the eye and orbit and decreased chances of visual recovery. About 10 percent, mostly small fistulas, resolve spontaneously. Many surgical approaches have been tried including ligation of the carotid artery, direct obliteration of the fistula or cavernous sinus, and angiographic guided balloon embolization. A detachable balloon technique has proved successful in many cases. The inability to tolerate therapeutic carotid occlusion (because of an incomplete circle of Willis) can be remedied by a superficial temporal artery to middle cerebral artery anastomosis performed prior to correcting the fistula.

INTRACRANIAL PRESSURE AND CEREBRAL BLOOD FLOW

The pathophysiology of intracranial pressure (ICP) regulation and its relationship to cerebral blood flow (CBF), which is applicable to many pathologic processes including cerebral hemorrhage, encephalitis, and brain edema after stroke, is best understood in the context of head trauma. The components of the intracranial compartment are brain, CSF, and blood. Because the skull limits total intracranial content, the volume of these compartments is compromised by expanding lesions within the cranial cavity. The brain is virtually incompressible; therefore CSF and blood serve as the main buffers of increasing intracranial volume. The relationship between increments in intracranial volume and the associated rises in ICP, termed *compliance*, approximates an exponential function after the volume buffering capacity of CSF and blood are exceeded. ICP is normally between 2 and 12 torr. Raised ICP in the range 15 to 40 torr, while not harmful by itself, can rapidly result in secondary damage, either by precipitously decreasing global cerebral perfusion when ICP

exceeds blood pressure in the cranium, or by associated shifts of brain tissue that damage the thalamus and brainstem. The global damage from increased ICP is therefore ischemic in nature and related to the arithmetic difference between ICP and blood pressure in the major cerebral arteries. This difference is termed *cerebral perfusion pressure,* or CPP. Cerebral perfusion pressure below 40 to 60 torr is considered detrimental to nerve cells; therapy is therefore directed toward maintaining perfusion above this range. The rationale for keeping CPP even higher (i.e., bringing ICP below 15 to 20 torr) is to afford a margin of safety should transient increases in ICP occur. Physiologic changes or medications that increase blood pressure do not necessarily improve CPP because increased vascular pressures exacerbate brain edema in damaged areas and induce plateau waves (see below), resulting in further increases in ICP that ultimately lower perfusion.

The most important secondary complication of head injury is raised intracranial pressure arising from the added volume of contusions, hematomas, and the progressive edema surrounding them. A close relationship exists between clinical outcome and ICP in patients with closed head injury. At least 50 percent of patients who die as a result of head injury do so solely because of uncontrolled rises in ICP, and outcome is inversely related to the level of ICP after acute injury. Aggressive treatment of raised ICP in modern intensive care units is believed by many workers to improve survival after severe head injury. The role of direct monitoring of ICP to guide therapy is controversial.

Resting ICP, CPP, and compliance are spontaneously interrupted by rises in ICP termed *plateau waves*. They often are precipitated by iatrogenic maneuvers such as suctioning, physical therapy, excess fluid administration, or pain. Such plateau waves (lasting 1 to 10 min, and ranging from 25 to 60 torr) are most pronounced in patients with diminished intracranial compliance. They are best observed on continuous recordings of ICP. Plateau waves are probably due to a loss of cerebrovascular tone with a resultant increase in cerebral blood volume. Signs of apparent transtentorial herniation such as pupillary enlargement may occur after plateau waves (they more often do not), and occasionally brain death ensues. The proximate cause of deterioration is probably a reflex rise in blood pressure, part of the Cushing reflex (hypertension and bradycardia), greatly increasing intracranial blood volume and cerebral edema.

There is little consensus about the importance of alterations in cerebral blood flow caused by head injury. For several minutes to an hour after acute head injury, cerebral blood flow may increase in some patients although metabolic demands and oxygen consumption are diminished. Autoregulation, the ability of the cerebral vasculature to keep blood flow constant in response to decreased or increased perfusion pressure, is also impaired in damaged regions. The increased cerebral blood flow enhances already increased ICP by raising blood volume. The blood-brain barrier also becomes more permeable after head injury and may disappear in badly damaged regions, making edema formation more likely.

There is a complex relationship between raised ICP and clinical signs such as coma and pupillary enlargement that accompany supratentorial masses. ICP represents the accommodation of intracranial contents to additional mass; clinical signs are a parallel barometer of tissue shifts, particularly affecting structures around the tentorial opening. Raised ICP per se does not cause signs (including coma) until it reaches levels that preclude cerebral perfusion; it then causes global ischemia in a fashion similar to acute hypotension. Coma and other secondary signs resulting from tissue shifts in the region of the tentorial opening are described in Chap. 21. It has been our experience that horizontal midline shift at the level of the pineal body is most closely related to the level of consciousness with acute lesions.

Other secondary phenomena after severe head injury cause brain damage and alter outcome. Hypoxia, for example, is common from a number of causes, and when severe, is associated with a poorer outcome.

CLINICAL SYNDROMES AND TREATMENT OF HEAD INJURY

MINOR INJURY A fully alert and attentive patient presenting after head injury with one or more symptoms of headache, faintness, nausea, a single episode of emesis, difficulty with concentration, or slight blurring of vision has a good prognosis with little risk of subsequent deterioration. Focal signs of brain injury are absent. Such patients have sustained a concussion or have been dazed, and have a brief amnestic epoch surrounding the moment of impact. Occasionally vasovagal syncope occurs several minutes to an hour after the injury and causes concern. Constant generalized or frontal headache is common in the days following trauma; it is often throbbing or hemicranial in nature, like migraine. The majority of patients with a minor syndrome do not have a skull fracture on skull x-ray, or hemorrhage on CT scan. The decision to obtain these tests depends largely on the availability of CT scanning and clinical signs suggesting that the impact was severe (e.g., prolonged concussion, periorbital or mastoid hematoma, repeated vomiting, etc). Children and young adults are particularly prone to drowsiness, vomiting, and irritability, sometimes delayed for several hours after apparently minor injuries. After a period of observation for an hour or so, arrangements may be made for the patient to be accompanied home to be observed by family or friends.

Persistent severe headache and repeated vomiting in the context of normal alertness and no focal neurologic signs are usually benign, but CT scanning and/or skull x-rays should be obtained. Skull fractures increase the likelihood of a subdural or epidural hematoma. Patients with these exaggerated signs, even if they follow minor injury, deserve observation in the hospital for 24 h. Clinical judgment, the presence of associated noncranial injuries, the availability of others at home, and the examiner's certainty of a normal neurologic examination should guide the need for further surveillance.

INJURY OF INTERMEDIATE SEVERITY Patients who are not comatose but who have persistent confusion, behavioral changes, less than normal alertness, extreme dizziness, or focal neurologic signs such as hemiparesis should be admitted to the hospital and have a CT scan. The clinical syndromes most common in this group, in addition to postconcussive headache and dizziness, unsteadiness, photophobia, and vomiting of minor injury, include (1) delirium with a disinclination to be examined or moved, expletive speech, and resistance if disturbed, most often associated with anterior temporal lobe contusions; (2) a quiet, disinterested, slowed mental state (abulia) with dull facial appearance and slight irascibility if bothered, the patient lying quietly with eyes closed when undisturbed, sometimes with inappropriate jocularity (*witzelsucht*), seen with inferior and frontopolar frontal contusions (usually without grasp responses); (3) severe memory loss with poor retrograde and anterograde performance, headache, and photophobia, with medial temporal lobe contusions or diffuse injury; (4) a focal deficit such as aphasia or mild hemiparesis (hemianopsia is rare as an isolated posttraumatic finding), suggesting subdural hematoma or convexity contusion; (5) global confusion with inattention, poor performance on simple mental tasks, fluctuating or slightly erroneous orientation, associated with several types of injuries including the first two described above as well as medial frontal contusions and interhemispheric subdural hematoma; (6) repetitive vomiting, nystagmus, drowsiness, and unsteadiness, usually from a labyrinthine concussion but occasionally due to a posterior fossa subdural hematoma or vertebral artery dissection; (7) drowsiness alone or with muteness, often unassociated with significant CT scan abnormalities; and (8) diabetes insipidus with or without a frontal-temporal lobe syndrome, from damage to median eminence or pituitary stalk and adjacent medial cortex.

The syndromes of intermediate severity are usually preceded by brief loss of consciousness and many are associated with skull fractures. A CT scan is required to exclude surgically remediable subdural or epidural hematomas and to define areas of contusion that later enlarge with edema, or coalesce to form intraparenchymal hemorrhages. Paroxysmal or rhythmic EEG abnormalities, in contrast to acute convulsions, are common over the region of a large contusion. Many intermediate injuries are complicated by drug or alcohol intoxication making toxic screening important.

Close clinical observation in a well-staffed setting is advisable in order to detect increasing drowsiness, change in respiratory pattern or pupillary enlargement, and to ensure fluid restriction. Fully awake or slightly drowsy patients with small subdural hematomas may be treated with corticosteroids and fluid restriction; larger clots, especially with fluctuating or worsening alertness, require surgery. Epidural hematomas causing compression of adjacent brain should be evacuated in patients who have a good chance of recovery from other injuries. Free water intake must be limited, allowing serum osmolarity to rise spontaneously toward 290 to 305 mosmol per liter. Fever must be treated assiduously with antipyretics or a cooling blanket, and its source must be identified (usually aspiration). So-called central fever is rare. The routine, acute administration of phenytoin is controversial. About half of neurosurgeons advocate its use, particularly in children and young adults, in the belief that it may reduce the incidence of posttraumatic epilepsy. Corticosteriods may be useful if there is a contusion, hemorrhage, or edema on the CT scan; otherwise they complicate management and should be omitted. The possibility of associated cervical spine injuries should be considered in all patients with syndromes of intermediate severity. The neck should be immobilized, and adequate x-rays of the spine should be obtained.

The majority of patients with intermediate injury improve over 1 to 6 weeks. During the first week alertness, irascibility, memory, and mental performance fluctuate. Behavioral changes such as agitation are most evident at night and sometimes seem to be worsened by large doses of corticosteroids or CNS-depressant drugs. Haloperidol is useful when used sparingly. Subtle abnormalities of intellectual function particularly attention, spontaneity, and memory, tend to return to normal later, and frequently do so abruptly.

SEVERE HEAD INJURY AND COMA Patients who are stuporous or comatose from the outset require immediate neurologic attention and often, resuscitation. There is usually pupillary enlargement or asymmetry. Persistent unresponsiveness is a grave sign. After the patient is intubated and the blood pressure is stabilized, attention is given to life-threatening noncranial injuries, followed by a survey neurologic examination.

The possibility of cervical injuries should not be overlooked, and the cervical spine must be immobilized during the initial assessment. The depth of coma and the size of the pupils are most important. Most severely injured patients hyperventilate. Extensor limb posturing and bilateral Babinski signs, combined with apparently purposeful movements, are common. Asymmetry in limb posture, limb movement, or gaze perference suggest a subdural or epidural hematoma or a large contusion.

As soon as vital functions permit, the patient should be taken to a critical care unit; cervical spine x-rays and a CT scan are obtained. The finding of an epidural or subdural hematoma or large intracerebral hemorrhage are usually indications for surgery and intracranial decompression. In one large series the time between injury and evacuation of acute subdural hematomas was the major determinant of outcome. If such lesions are not present and the patient is still comatose and critically ill, attention is directed toward treating raised ICP. Patients with abnormal CT scans showing contusions, hemorrhages, or tissue shifts are the best candidates for ICP monitoring. Since the lumbar CSF pressure does not accurately reflect the intracranial pressure and may increase the risk of brain herniation, the practice in most head injury treatment centers is to use a subarachnoid screw device with a hollow bore, an epidural monitor, or a ventricular catheter to measure ICP. The pressure can be monitored continuously, disturbances in compliance and falling CPP can be identified, and appearance of plateau waves can be noted.

The treatment of raised ICP is best guided by direct measurement but may proceed on a presumptive basis using clinical status and CT scan as guides. All potentially exacerbating factors must be eliminated.

Hypoxia, hyperthermia, hypercarbia, awkward head positions, and high mean airway pressures from mechanical ventilation all increase cerebral blood volume and ICP. Many, but not all, patients will have lower ICPs when the head and trunk are elevated approximately 60° than when supine. Active management of raised ICP includes induced hypocarbia to an initial level of 28 to 33 torr P_{CO_2} and hyperosmolar dehydration with 20% mannitol (0.25 to 1 g/kg every 3 to 6 h), preferably using directly measured ICP as a guide. Otherwise, a serum osmolality of 305 to 315 mosmol per liter is desirable, as is ventricular or subarachnoid fluid drainage when it is possible.

Persistently raised ICP after inception of this conservative therapy generally indicates a poor outcome, but the addition of high-dose barbiturates may further lower ICP and salvage a small number of patients. In many instances there is a parallel reduction in ICP and blood pressure without resulting net improvement in cerebral perfusion. The beneficial effects of barbiturates, aside from their sedative and anticonvulsant activities, are not established, and they can cause disastrous hypotension. Further details of treatment of raised ICP are given in Chap. 21. Systolic blood pressure should be maintained above 100 torr by vasopressor agents, if necessary, but when pressors are required to support barbiturate use, there is usually little improvement in CPP. Mean blood pressure levels above 110 to 120 torr exaggerate brain edema and are associated with plateau waves; hypertension should be treated with diuretics and beta-adrenergic blocking agents. Fluid and electrolytes must be administered cautiously, and free water administration should be limited. Administration of phenytoin or phenobarbital to prevent seizures is recommended by many neurosurgeons. Cimetidine, 300 mg IV every 4 h, or hourly antacids by nasogastric tube to keep gastric pH above 3.5 is the usual prophylaxis to prevent gastrointestinal bleeding. The use of large doses of corticosteroids in severe head injury is controversial, but some patients appear to benefit, particularly those less severely injured. If the patient remains comatose, it is worthwhile to repeat the CT scan to exclude a delayed surface or intracerebral hemorrhage. Intensive care salvages some critically ill head-injured patients by concentrating efforts on simple treatments that avoid medical complications and preventable increases in ICP. Whether more assiduous control of ICP and CPP will produce better results remains to be proved.

ASSOCIATED DERANGEMENTS OCCURRING WITH SEVERE HEAD TRAUMA Injuries outside the cranium should be searched for at the outset, because they are likely to be forgotten if not initially noted. In particular, associated spinal, long bone, and abdominal injuries may cause delayed difficulties in management. However, medical complications dominate the intermediate-term intensive care of head trauma patients.

Fluids and electrolytes Over half of patients who persist in coma for 24 h after head injury develop abnormalities of electrolytes or fluid balance. Frequently these are a consequence of therapy, but the metabolic responses to head trauma are similar to those produced by trauma elsewhere and are important in planning treatment. Daily input-output records and body weights, when possible, are important in management. Water restriction and osmotic agents render most patients hyperosmolar and hypovolemic, requiring monitoring of serum osmolality and sodium concentrations. Diabetes insipidus should be suspected if urine output increases and urine specific gravity is low. Replacement of water losses suffices for mild cases, but vasopressin may be required in persistent cases. Serum osmolality above approximately 325 mosmol per liter should be avoided because of the associated decrease in cardiac output.

Aldosterone and antidiuretic hormone (ADH) secretion in response to stress favor sodium and free water retention, respectively. The latter usually predominates, leading to mild hypervolemic hyponatremia in untreated patients, but is obscured by concomitant administration of osmotic agents. Severe hyponatremia results from excessive ADH secretion, which may occur with raised ICP, basilar skull fractures, and after prolonged mechanical ventilation. Potassium is lost in head injury because of trauma-induced aldosterone hypersecretion, therapeutic osmotic diuresis, and corticosteroids. Because potassium is predominantly an intracellular ion, hypokalemia is frequently manifested as a hypochloremic alkalosis with normal or minimally depressed serum potassium and requires adequate replacement therapy with KCl.

Respiratory complications Some patients with head injuries have hypoxia acutely after injury without obvious pulmonary pathology. Aspiration pneumonia presents a great risk; acid burn injury from aspirated gastric contents, infection, and atelectasis may combine to produce the adult respiratory distress syndrome (ARDS) and severe arteriovenous shunting. ARDS can also occur due to disseminated intravascular coagulopathy, fat embolism, or rarely "neurogenic" pulmonary edema. Treatment is similar to other cases of ARDS with positive end-expiratory pressure (PEEP) to allow lowered inspired oxygen concentrations and to prevent further atelectasis. The effect of PEEP on ICP is complex, but PEEP should not be withheld if necessary for oxygenation.

Atelectasis is common in all poorly responsive patients and is treated with chest physical therapy and adequate ventilator tidal volumes. Pulmonary embolism is also a major threat to bedridden patients, and intermittent pneumatic calf compression or modest doses of subcutaneous heparin may be useful prophylaxis. The latter has not predisposed to intracerebral or gastrointestinal bleeding. Early recognition of deep leg vein thrombosis and aggressive treatment by occlusion of the inferior vena cava may prevent later emboli.

Gastrointestinal hemorrhage The majority of patients with severe head injuries develop gastric erosions, but only a few have clinically significant hemorrhages. Gastrointestinal bleeding usually occurs in the first days to 1 week. Unlike most patients in shock or with stress ulceration, head-trauma patients often have elevated gastric acidity. The synergistic effect of corticosteroids in causing upper tract hemorrhage has been questioned, but the incidence of viscus perforation, particularly of the cecum, is elevated. Prophylactic treatment with cimetidine or with frequent antacid administration to keep gastric pH high (above 3.5) reduces gastric hemorrhage in other stress states and is commonly used in head trauma.

Fat embolism Patients with severe long bone injuries are subject to widespread cerebral fat embolism. This complication is seen less often than previously, perhaps due to better fluid replacement. In the typical case, head injury is a minor part of the overall trauma; in a few, severe cranial injury masks the syndrome. Several days after the bone fractures, restlessness, delirium, or drowsiness progressing to coma in severe cases, seizures, generalized brain edema, and respiratory insufficiency develop. About half have retinal and conjunctival punctate hemorrhages or visible fat in retinal vessels. A petechial rash, prominent in the anterior axillary folds and supraclavicular fossae, diffuse interstitial infiltrates on the chest x-ray, fat in the urine, or renal failure occur in some patients. Severe reduction in arterial oxygen content is common from widespread lung injury (ARDS). Cerebral fat embolism causes cerebral purpura, mainly in the white matter, due to capillary occlusion by fat globules. There is evidence that cases recognized and treated early have a better prognosis. Massive doses of corticosteroids, reduction of ICP, and administration of positive-pressure ventilation with high end-expiratory pressures have been useful. Heparin or intravenous alcohol are no longer recommended.

Cardiovascular changes Acute head trauma may cause transient apnea and cardiac arrest. In the absence of overwhelming brain damage recovery from the arrest is the rule. Subsequently, raised ICP may cause systemic hypertension, either with the classically associated bradycardia (Cushing response) or, almost as frequently, with tachycardia. Cardiac arrhythmias are common, most notably sinus bradycardia, supraventricular tachycardias, nodal rhythm, and heart block. T-wave inversion and alterations in the ST segment may simulate subendocardial ischemia.

Neurogenic pulmonary edema is a form of ARDS in which the alveoli fill with fluid as they would in congestive heart failure but left ventricular end-diastolic pressure (measured by pulmonary capillary wedge pressure) is normal. A pulmonary vascular leak may be produced when a sudden shift of intravascular volume occurs from the systemic to pulmonary circulation as occurs transiently with suddenly raised ICP. Once the pulmonary vasculature has been damaged, an alveolar capillary leak may continue despite return of blood pressure to normal. The result is pulmonary edema with normal central venous and wedge pressures after the initial injury.

Hematologic complications A large number of patients demonstrate a mild coagulopathy, and 5 to 10 percent have various degrees of disseminated intravascular coagulation. A correlation may exist between the severity of injury and the level of increased fibrin degradation products in blood. The cause of the coagulopathy is thought to be the release of highly thromboplastic material into the systemic circulation from the damaged brain.

PROGNOSIS Extensive work by Jennet's group in Glasgow has provided data on the outcome in severe head injury (Table 344-1). Verbal output, eye opening, and the best motor response are important predictors of ultimate outcome. Eighty-five percent of patients with aggregate Glasgow Coma Scale scores of 3 or 4 die 24 h after injury. Yet a number of patients with a poor initial prognosis, including absent pupillary light responses, survive, suggesting that aggressive management is justified in virtually all patients. Patients below approximately 20 years of age, particularly children, may make remarkable recoveries after grave early neurologic signs.

Evoked potentials have prognostic value in head injury, and their accuracy probably exceeds clinical observations and ICP measurements. Somatosensory evoked potentials are the most useful, with bilaterally absent cortical potentials (with more caudal potentials present) are predictive of death or a vegetative state in 85 to 95 percent of patients. Prediction of a good functional outcome in the presence of normal or mildly abnormal tests is less certain.

SPINAL CORD TRAUMA

Approximately 10,000 patients a year in the United States, mostly young and otherwise healthy, become paraplegic or quadriplegic because of spinal cord injuries. There are an estimated 200,000 quadriplegics in the country. The majority of cord injuries in civilian life result from damage to the surrounding vertebral column, from fracture, dislocation, or both. Vertical compression with flexion is the main mechanism of injury in the thoracic cord, and hyperextension or flexion is the main cause of injury in the cervical cord. Preexisting spondylosis, a congenitally narrowed spinal canal, hypertrophied ligamentum flavum (see Chap. 353), or instability of the apophyseal joints of adjacent vertebrae from diseases such as rheumatoid arthritis, predispose to severe spinal cord damage after minor degrees of injury.

PATHOPHYSIOLOGY AND PATHOLOGY OF CORD INJURY Much damage to the spinal cord is due to secondary phenomena in the minutes and hours following injury. Even when a complete transverse myelopathy is evident immediately after impact, some secondary changes are avoidable, and the resultant damage may be reversible. The immediate injury causes pericapillary hemorrhages that coalesce and enlarge, particularly in the gray matter. Infarction of gray matter and early white matter edema are evident within 4 h of experimental blunt injury. Eight hours after injury there is global infarction at the injured level, and only at this point does necrosis of white matter and paralysis below the level of the lesion become irreversible. The necrosis and central hemorrhages enlarge to occupy one or two levels above, and below, the point of primary impact. Gliosis in these regions results in necrotic areas over several months and may cavitate causing a progressive syringomyelic syndrome.

The early phases of injury are associated with reduced regional blood flow from direct capillary damage and a more prolonged

TABLE 344-1 Glasgow Coma Scale for head injury

Eye opening (E):	
Spontaneous	4
To loud voice	3
To pain	2
Nil	1
Best motor response (M):	
Obeys	6
Localizes	5
Withdraws (flexion)	4
Abnormal flexion posturing	3
Extension posturing	2
Nil	1
Verbal response (V):	
Oriented	5
Confused, disoriented	4
Inappropriate words	3
Incomprehensible sounds	2
Nil	1

NOTE: *Coma score = E + M + V. Patients scoring 3 or 4 have an 85 percent chance of dying or remaining vegetative, while scores above 11 indicate 5 to 10 percent likelihood of death or vegetative state and 85 percent chance of moderate disability or good recovery. Intermediate scores correlate with proportional chances of patients recovering.*

secondary ischemia. A number of interventions including opiate antagonists, thyrotropin-releasing hormone, local cord cooling, dextran infusion, adrenergic blockade, corticosteroids, and hyperbaric oxygen are of uncertain clinical usefulness. More importantly, the critical factor for recoverable function is the time from injury to institution of therapy. Complete axonal disruption from the immediate trauma or secondary phenomena precludes recovery.

TYPES OF SPINAL CORD INJURY AND THEIR MANAGEMENT Any patient with severe head injury potentially has an associated instability of the spinal column. The care of such patients begins at the scene of the accident. The neck should be immobilized to prevent cord damage, and care should be taken during transport and during the physical and radiologic examinations to avoid neck extension or rotation and to prevent torsion-rotation of the thoracic spine. Blood pressure, respiratory status, and systemic injuries are attended to rapidly. Most patients can be intubated, if necessary, by blind nasotracheal technique without neck extension. High thoracic or cervical cord trauma regularly cause mild hypotension and bradycardia because of functional sympathectomy (often corroborated by bilateral ptosis and miosis—Horner's syndrome) that responds to infusion of crystalloid or colloid.

The neurologic examination in the awake patient focuses on neck or back pain, diminished limb power, a sensory level on the trunk, and deep tendon reflexes, usually absent below the level of an acute cord injury. Injuries above C5 cause quadriplegia and respiratory failure. At C5 and C6 the biceps are also weak, and at C4 and C5 the deltoid and supra- and infraspinatus are weak. C7 injuries cause weakness of the triceps, wrist extensors, and forearm pronators. Injuries at T1 and below cause paraplegia; the precise level can be determined from the level of sensory loss. Compression in the low thoracic and lumbar region causes a conus medullaris or cauda equina syndrome (see Chap. 353). Cauda equina injuries are usually incomplete, involving peripheral nerves rather than spinal cord, and therefore are surgically remediable for longer periods after injury than spinal cord compression. In a comatose patient absent reflexes should be sought in the legs, or in all the extremities, associated in the latter case with small pupils or paradoxical breathing from high cervical cord injury.

The next priority is to exclude a surgically remediable and potentially reversible cord compression due to dislocation of a vertebral body. Many traumatic myelopathies have no clearly associated fracture or dislocation. If x-rays suggest any aberration in the position of vertebrae, then reduction should be quickly undertaken. The role of myelography is controversial, but many neurosurgeons instill a few drops of Pantopaque into the spinal subarachnoid space to demonstrate a block to the flow of CSF. At present, examination by CT and magnetic resonance imaging scanning may be more useful. Decompression within 2 h of severe injury may lead to some recovery of cord function. With incomplete myelopathies, especially if the limbs are becoming progressively weaker, early decompression is strongly recommended, even many hours after injury. Surgical approaches to decompressing the spinal column depend upon the specific nature of the injury. In complete transverse myelopathies beyond 6 to 12 h in duration, decompressive laminectomies are usually unsuccessful in restoring function.

The concerns with spinal column fractures, with or without myelopathy, are threefold: (1) detection of vertebral dislocations causing cord compression, (2) instability caused by fractures that will lead to misalignment and cord compression in the future, and (3) the proper treatment of fractures through the pedicles, facets, or vertebral bodies. Some fractures heal with immobilizaton and time, usually 2 to 3 months; others require surgical fusion to ensure stability.

Atlantoaxial dislocations can cause immediate death from respiratory failure, an event that may occur with no neurologic signs. Rheumatoid arthritis predisposes to this injury. Atlantooccipital dislocations occur predominantly in children and are almost always fatal. "Jefferson's fractures" are burst fractures of the ring of the atlas resulting from a force descending on the vertex of the skull as in diving accidents; they are usually asymptomatic. "Hangman's fractures" are produced by hyperextension and longitudinal distraction of the upper cervical spine, as occurs with penal hanging or striking the chin on a steering wheel in head-on collisions. These are usually fractures through the pedicles of C2 with subluxation anteriorly of C2 on C3. Traction reduction and immobilization allow proper healing.

Hyperflexion dislocation of the cervical vertebrae commonly causes traumatic quadriplegia. Occasionally, a markedly displaced injury is unassociated with neurologic dysfunction, presenting only with neck pain. In most cases, however, minor subluxation is associated with a severe neurologic deficit. Ligamentous disruption presumably allows compression of the cord at the moment of impact, but the vertebral bodies return closer to their original stations afterward. Therefore, any degree of subluxation must be treated as potentially unstable.

Compression fractures of the cervical spine can cause neurologic damage if a bone fragment is driven backward (burst fracture) into the spinal cord. "Teardrop fractures" with crushing of a vertebral body, leaving a fragment of bone anteriorly, are usually associated with ligamentous disruption and spinal instability. Single compression fractures of the thoracic spine are usually stable because the thoracic cage provides support, but they may be associated with anterior cord compression and require decompression and stabilization with the insertion of metal rods.

Mild hyperextension injuries may cause only disruption of supporting ligamentous structures and be well tolerated. More severe injuries cause vertebral displacement and cord compression. The "central cord syndrome" is produced by brief compression of the cord and disruption of the central gray matter usually occurring in patients with an already narrow spinal canal, either congenitally or from cervical spondylosis. There is weakness of the arms, often with pinprick loss over the arms and shoulders, and relative sparing of leg power and sensation on the trunk and legs. Abnormality of bladder function is variable. The prognosis for recovery is good.

Thoracolumbar fractures are produced by impact in the high or midback, usually while the patient is bent over. Impingement on the spinal canal results in a complex combination of cauda equina and conus medullaris dysfunction. Pure lumbar fractures produce cauda equina compression. Myelography or CT scan allows precise localization, and surgical decompression is usually recommended, even with complete deficits, because the potential for recovery of peripheral nerves is great.

The subsequent care of patients with spinal cord injury is best undertaken in specialized centers. General principles of medical and urologic management are discussed in Chap. 353.

REFERENCES

ADAMS JH et al: Diffuse brain damage of the immediate impact type. Brain 100:489, 1977

BAKAY L, GLASSAUER FE: *Head Injury.* Boston, Little, Brown, 1980

BECKER DP et al: Outcome from severe head injury with early diagnosis and intensive management. J Neurosurg 47:491, 1977

DAVIS KR et al: Computed tomography in head trauma. Semin Roentgenol 12:53, 1977

JENNET B et al: Predicting outcome in individual patients after head injury. Lancet 1:1081, 1976

LANGFITT TW, GENARELLI TA: Can the outcome from head injury be improved? J Neurosurg 56:19, 1982

MARSHALL LF et al: The outcome with aggressive treatment in severe head injury. I: The significance of intracranial pressure monitoring. II: Acute and chronic barbiturate administration in the management of head injury. J Neurosurg 50:20, 1979

ROPPER AH et al (eds): *Neurological and Neurosurgical Intensive Care.* Baltimore, University Park Press, 1983

————, MILLER D: Acute traumatic midbrain hemorrhages. Ann Neurol 18:80, 1985

ROWBOTHAM GF: *Acute Injuries of the Head,* 4th ed. Baltimore, Williams & Wilkins, 1964

345 NEOPLASTIC DISEASES OF THE CENTRAL NERVOUS SYSTEM

FRED HOCHBERG / AMY PRUITT

Tumors of the brain, of its meningeal coverings, and of the spinal cord are estimated to cause the death of 90,000 patients in the United States each year. Of these tumors, more than three-quarters are metastases occurring in patients undergoing treatment for systemic cancer. Primary tumors arising within the meninges or the parenchyma of the brain or spinal cord are common at all ages of life. Brain neoplasms claim a disproportionate share of hospital beds, diagnostic tests, and other medical resources. One-fourth of the annual $4 billion cost for care of cancer patients in the United States is allocated to patients with neoplasms of the central nervous system (CNS).

Although the specialized care of such patients is usually delegated to the neurosurgeon, radiotherapist, or neurooncologist, with the advent of new imaging techniques the internist is increasingly involved in the initial diagnosis. Late in the course of the disease, such patients again may come under the care of a general physician. The proper care of patients with primary or metastatic tumors of the central nervous system requires a systematic approach that enables the physician to (1) distinguish tumor from other causes of neurologic dysfunction such as infection, metabolic derangement, pseudotumor cerebri, or subdural hematoma; (2) make proper use of sophisticated diagnostic techniques such as computerized tomography (CT) and magnetic resonance imaging (MRI) and of more invasive tests such as arteriography; (3) provide early therapy to control cerebral edema and seizure activity; (4) exclude systemic malignancy prior to referring the patient for a biopsy; and (5) recognize the medical complications of the tumor and of its therapy.

APPROACH TO THE PATIENT WITH CENTRAL NERVOUS SYSTEM TUMORS

CLASSIFICATION OF TUMORS   Tumors of the CNS may originate in the brain or spinal cord (primary tumors) or may spread from systemic sites of cancer (metastatic tumors). Both benign and malignant primary CNS tumors are capable of producing neurologic impairment. Primary tumors arise from glial cells (astrocytoma, oligodendroglioma, glioblastoma), ependymal cells (ependymoma), or supporting tissue (meningioma, schwannoma, papilloma of the choroid plexus). In childhood, tumors arise from more primitive cells (medulloblastoma, neuroblastoma, chordoma). Malignant astrocytoma or glioblastoma is the most common type of primary tumor in adults over age 20. A classification of intracranial tumors is given in Table 345-1.

CLINICAL MANIFESTATIONS OF INTRACRANIAL TUMOR Intracranial tumors may be located within the brain substance (intraaxial) or in close proximity to the brain (extraaxial). The latter produce symptoms by compression or infiltration of brain. Many of the symptoms caused by intracranial masses reflect tumor expansion within a fixed bony vault into space normally occupied by brain, blood, and cerebrospinal fluid (CSF). The nature and severity of these symptoms depend on the location of the tumor and the rate of its growth. Although brain tissue can accommodate the presence of slowly growing tumors, masses larger than 3 cm in diameter compress the brain, its blood supply, and CSF pathways. This compression is increased by peritumoral edema (vasogenic cerebral edema). Neurologic deterioration occurs as tumor infiltrates or displaces normal brain structures; as the tumor develops areas of hemorrhage, necrosis or cyst formation; or as the tumor obstructs the normal flow of CSF, producing hydrocephalus.

Papilledema, or choking of the optic nerve head, emerges in the setting of impaired retinal venous return or axoplasmic flow along the optic nerve. Increasing intracranial pressure caused by a mass in one hemisphere may displace the medial temporal lobe (uncus) through the tentorial notch. As the uncus is forced inferiorly (*uncal herniation*) the midbrain is displaced and the third cranial nerve is compressed. The clinical signs of a unilateral third-nerve palsy— fixed, dilated pupil followed shortly thereafter by depression of consciousness, dilation of the opposite pupil, and hemiparesis on the opposite side of the original pupillary abnormality—should alert the physician to uncal herniation. A mass located more centrally in the supratentorial region produces a less specific picture called *central herniation*. In this situation the patient develops depression of consciousness as supratentorial structures compress the diencephalon and upper midbrain. Cheyne-Stokes respiration develops, but there is preservation of pupillary activity until late in the course of the deterioration.

Cerebellar masses may cause the cerebellar tonsils to herniate into the foramen magnum. As the tonsils are pushed inferiorly, the medulla and portions of the cervical spinal cord are compressed or infarcted. Abnormalities of cardiovascular regulation ensue. The resulting bradycardia and hypertension are followed by irregularity or cessation of respiration. Posterior fossa lesions of small size may produce early hydrocephalus by obstruction of CSF flow at the level of the fourth ventricle or aqueduct of Sylvius.

Symptoms of intracranial tumor may develop in patients with previously diagnosed systemic cancer or in those not known to harbor a malignancy. Patients with intracranial tumor usually present with one or more of the following groups of symptoms: (1) headache with or without evidence of increased intracranial pressure; (2) progressive generalized decline in cognitive abilities or impairment of specific neurologic functions affecting speech and language, gait, or memory; (3) adult-onset seizures or increased frequency or severity of previously documented seizure activity; or (4) focal neurologic symptoms reflecting the particular anatomic site of the tumor, such as those caused by acoustic schwannoma (neuroma) in the cerebellopontine angle or by meningioma of the olfactory groove, sella, or parasellar areas.

Headache is the initial symptom in half of patients with brain tumors. Traction on the dura, blood vessels, or cranial nerves results from local compression, elevation of intracranial pressure, edema, or hydrocephalus. In most patients with supratentorial tumor, pain radiates to the side of the tumor mass, whereas patients with posterior fossa masses describe retroorbital, retroauricular, or occipital pain. Emesis, often without nausea, signals development of increased intracranial pressure and is especially common in patients with masses located beneath the tentorium.

Tumors of the frontal lobes may attain considerable size before symptoms develop, and then symptoms often are nonspecific. Subtle,

progressive disturbances of mentation, slowness of comprehension, loss of acuity in business affairs, memory disorders, or apathy, lethargy, and drowsiness may be reported. Spontaneity of thought and activity is lost. Incontinence of urine and disordered gait may be seen by family members. The development of a true dysphasia and/ or motor weakness signal progression of the tumor or its associated edema into motor cortex and speech areas of the frontoparietal region.

Masses in the temporal lobes are associated with personality changes which may resemble psychotic thought disorders. Various combinations of auditory hallucinations, abrupt shifts in mood, and altered sleep, appetite, and sexual functions are soon interspersed with complex partial seizures possibly accompanied by visual field defects in the superior quadrants contralateral to the tumor.

Disorders of communication and vision characterize parietooccipital masses. Receptive aphasia with contralateral hemianopsia characterizes left parietal tumors, while a combination of spatial disorientation, constructional apraxia, and left homonymous hemianopsia bespeaks right parietal tumors.

Tumors of the diencephalon often present with a combination of failure of pupillary constriction to light, failure of upward gaze, and neuroendocrine abnormalities. Hydrocephalus due to obstruction to CSF flow at the level of the third ventricle leads to headache. Syndromes suggesting tumors of diencephalon or posterior fossa origin are more fully discussed in the section of this chapter devoted to neoplasms of these regions.

Cerebellar and brainstem lesions lead to a combination of cranial nerve palsies and incoordination of limbs or gait with or without accompanying signs of hydrocephalus. (See Chap. 352 for discussion of cranial nerve symptoms and signs.)

Seizures occur as the initial symptom in 20 percent of patients with brain tumors. Patients with new onset of epilepsy after the age of 35 must be evaluated for brain tumor. Similar high-risk groups of new seizure patients include those with previously diagnosed systemic cancer, longstanding neurologic diseases (including such neuroectodermal disorders as von Recklinghausen's disease and tuberous sclerosis), or acute or atypical psychiatric disorders. A carefully obtained history may uncover "complex partial" (temporal lobe) seizures or personality changes that antedate the diagnosis by years. Occasionally, the first symptom simulates a transient ischemic attack with no residual deficit or discernible seizure, but more commonly the pattern of clinical seizures provides localizing information. Thus, the "Jacksonian march" of tonic-clonic seizure points to frontal tumors and a sensory march characterizes tumors of the sensory parietal cortex. Metastatic tumors, occupying the junction of gray and white matter, are more likely than are primary tumors to produce acute symptoms evolving in days to weeks. Even more rapid onset of symptoms reflects hemorrhage in tumors of lung, melanoma, renal cell, choriocarcinoma, or thyroid origins. In contrast, with the exception of malignant astrocytoma, primary brain tumors are unlikely to hemorrhage.

TABLE 345-1 Classification of intracranial tumors

Type of tumor	Percent of total
Glioma:	40
Glioblastoma	20
Astrocytoma grades I and II	10
Ependymoma	6
Medulloblastoma	2
Oligodendroglioma	1
Papilloma of choroid plexus	1
Metastases	23
Meningioma	17
Pituitary adenoma	5
Schwannoma	5
Lymphoma	3
Miscellaneous (congenital tumors, PNETs*)	7

* *Primitive neuroectodermal tumors.*

PHYSICAL EXAMINATION OF THE PATIENT WITH SUSPECTED CNS TUMORS

When the physician examines a brain tumor suspect who is not previously known to have a systemic cancer, the general examination should include (1) a survey of the skin for stigmata of neurocutaneous syndromes or melanoma, (2) a search for enlarged lymph nodes, (3) an examination of the abdomen for hepatic or splenic enlargement, (4) a rectal examination with stool guaiac test, (5) a breast examination in female patients, and (6) a cardiopulmonary examination.

The neurologic examination of the patient with suspected brain tumor should focus first on an evaluation of the mental status. The examiner should look for evidence of specific localizing cognitive deficits, such as dysphasia, dyspraxia, or memory loss, in addition to gleaning a sense of any personality change which has occurred. The patient is examined for increased intracranial pressure (papilledema or sixth cranial nerve paresis) and for other cranial nerve abnormalities. Asymmetries of strength, sensation, visual fields, and reflex activity should be sought. Attention should be paid to the constellation of signs suggestive of tumors in specific supratentorial, diencephalic or posterior fossa sites (see above). Combinations of cranial nerve abnormalities and corticospinal or lumbosacral radicular signs raise suspicion of leptomeningeal metastases (see below).

INVESTIGATION OF THE PATIENT WITH INTRACRANIAL TUMOR

Advances in neuroradiology have contributed greatly to the diagnosis and management of patients with suspected neoplastic disease of the central nervous system. A plan for appropriate diagnostic studies based on the initial CT or MRI scan results is outlined in Table 345-2. The language of neurooncology differs from that of medical oncology, familiar terms such as "benign," "malignant," and "metastasizing" taking on different connotations when the tumor involves the CNS. Benign and malignant tumors are not differentiated in the scheme of Table 345-2 because the initial clinical approach is identical. Although many primary CNS tumors exhibit characteristics classifiable as "benign" because they are well-differentiated histologically and grow slowly, they are, nevertheless, incurable. Tumors of identical histology may have very different prognoses, depending upon their location and amenability to resection. Secondary CNS tumors are malignant in the conventional sense, since they represent metastases and invade normal tissue. Both benign and malignant tumors may produce profound, irreversible neurologic impairment. Primary brain tumors, with rare exceptions, do not metastasize outside the CNS; however, virtually all primary brain tumors are capable of diffuse seeding to the leptomeninges. Thus, the approach to *all* intracranial tumors, summarized in Table 345-2, relies on the clinical history and physical examination and on information provided by CT scan and MRI.

The laboratory evaluation of intracranial tumors Contrast-enhanced CT scanning and MRI have now largely replaced the combination of skull x-ray, electroencephalogram, radionuclide brain scan, and arteriography as the principal tests for the evaluation of patients with suspected brain tumor. The universal use of CT and MRI is unlikely to be altered substantially by the introduction of other techniques such as computer-analyzed EEG, venous or arterial digital subtraction angiography, or brain scanning using radiolabeled monoclonal antibodies directed against specific tumor types.

CT SCAN Contrast-enhanced CT imaging delineates intracranial masses as small as 0.5 cm in diameter. Certain tumors whose density exceeds that of normal brain parenchyma, including meningioma, melanoma, and primary lymphoma, and tumors with spontaneous hemorrhage can be visualized without contrast enhancement. Reconstructions in coronal and sagittal planes and magnification of focal regions allow detection of 95 percent of intracranial masses and definition within 1 cm of the histologic border of the tumor. Tumors commonly appear as homogeneous or ring-enhancing masses surrounded by variable amounts of edema. Although not a substitute for biopsy diagnosis, the CT often correctly predicts the histology of the tumor (Fig. 345-1).

Initial CT studies may show no abnormality in meningeal carcinomatosis, small metastases, primary brain lymphoma, or some glial tumors; repeat CT scanning, utilizing single or double doses of contrast, 4 to 6 weeks later usually provides tumor detection. The clinician should be wary of attributing all CT scan masses to tumor, as ring-like enhancement may occur in abscesses, in recent cerebral infarctions, in the plaques of multiple sclerosis, and in certain vascular malformations with or without hemorrhage. Asymptomatic menin-

TABLE 345-2 Evaluation following CT or MRI scan of the patient with suspected neoplastic disease of the CNS

Clinical setting	Possible diagnoses	Pretreatment evaluation	Primary treatment	Secondary treatment
SOLITARY MASS ON CT OR MRI SCAN				
No known systemic cancer	Nonneoplastic disease Primary or secondary tumor Benign or malignant tumor	Metastatic evaluation Arteriogram Surgical opinion	Steroids Surgery	Radiation, chemotherapy as indicated Steroids as needed
Known systemic cancer	Radioresistant or radiosensitive tumor Unrelated tumor (second primary)	Double-dose contrast CT scan Metastatic evaluation Surgical opinion*	Steroids, radiation if radiosensitive tumor or active systemic disease found Steroids, surgery if radioresistant tumor or quiescent systemic disease found	Steroids as needed Postoperative radiation Steroids as needed
MULTIPLE MASSES ON CT OR MRI SCAN				
No prior known systemic cancer	Nonneoplastic disease Primary or secondary tumor	Metastatic evaluation	Steroids, radiation if systemic tumor identified Steroids, biopsy, radiation if no systemic tumor found	Steroids as needed Steroids as needed
Known systemic cancer	Metastases	None	Steroids, radiation	Steroids as needed
NEGATIVE† CT OR MRI SCAN				
No focal deficits on examination	Infection Metabolic abnormality	Lumbar puncture Exclude infection or metabolic problem	See text	——
Focal deficits on examination	Vascular disease Carcinomatous meningitis Seizure, paraneoplastic syndrome, complication of therapy	Lumbar puncture Follow-up CT 4–6 weeks	See text	——

* *Posterior fossa mass with hydrocephalus.*
† *Patient with cancer and neurologic signs.*

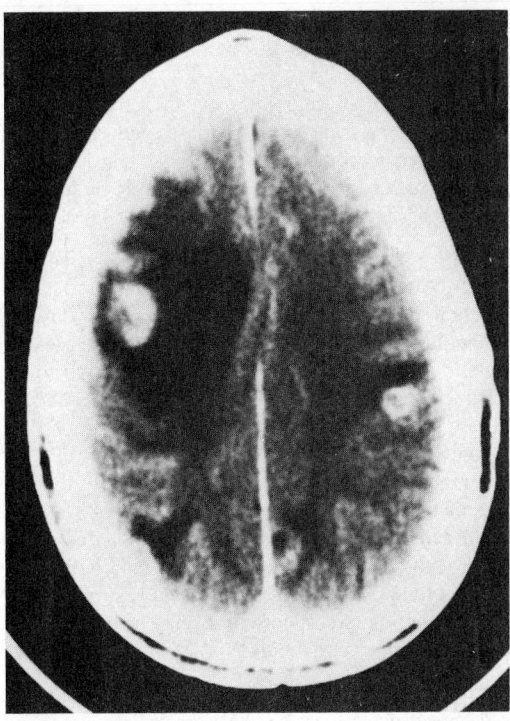

FIGURE 345-1 *Contrast-enhanced CT scan showing three metastatic brain tumors. Note extensive edema surrounding lesion in right frontal lobe with associated transfalcial herniation.*

giomas and aneurysms are often incidentally detected during the evaluation of a patient for intracranial mass.

Brainstem, cerebellar, and spinal cord masses can be defined further by combination of CT and subarachnoid administration of metrizamide. Because of the risk of seizures after instillation of metrizamide, patients should be treated prophylactically with phenobarbital.

MAGNETIC RESONANCE IMAGING Magnetic resonance imaging (MRI, nuclear magnetic resonance) delineates most metastatic and primary tumors and distinguishes surrounding edema (see Chap. 341). It is an important adjunct to CT, particularly for lesions located in close proximity to bone at the skull base. Tumors of the brainstem and spinal cord are also visualized, and advances in surface coil technology will reduce the need for contrast myelography. Recent observations show that MRI cannot at present distinguish radiation necrosis from recurrent tumor or edema secondary to chemotherapy from edema due to tumor growth. However, with intravenous gadolinium diethylenetriamine pentaacetic acid (DPTA) paramagnetic contrast, the MRI of the brain indicates defects in patterns quite similar to those observed with the use of organic iodides in CT. The combination of this paramagnetic agent and higher energy units may provide better separation of tumor from nontumor tissue.

ANGIOGRAPHY Transfemoral arteriography provides selective visualization of internal carotid and vertebral arteries and their branches. Vessels of malignant tumors are characterized by an angiographic "blush" with enlarged, early draining veins, features not seen in association with an intracerebral hemorrhage, infarction, or abscess. Preoperative neurosurgical planning is often aided by knowledge of the vascular anatomy. In some cases, sufficient detail is revealed after intravenous administration of contrast using digital subtraction angiography.

MANAGEMENT OF INTRACRANIAL TUMORS Surgery: biopsy and resection Surgical exploration allows tumor identification in patients with either solitary or multiple intracranial masses. Surgical exploration may be necessary to obtain a diagnosis in patients with multiple CT masses in whom a thorough systemic evaluation,

including hemogram, liver function studies, carcinoembryonic antigen, chest x-ray, sputum cytology, radionuclide bone and liver scans, and perhaps intravenous pyelography is unrewarding. Of patients with multiple CNS metastatic lesions, 20 percent have no evidence of systemic cancer.

Tumor biopsy is performed through an open craniotomy or with CT-guided stereotaxic techniques. The establishment of a diagnosis is important to determine prognosis and treatment. *Resection* is undertaken and may be curative for some primary tumors such as meningioma, ependymoma, oligodendroglioma, and low-grade astrocytoma (see below) in nondominant, frontal, anterior temporal, or occipital locations or in the ventricular system. *Partial resection* improves patient symptoms, often including better seizure control; by diminishing cerebral edema, it reduces dependence on corticosteroids. Although resection offers little to the patient with multiple intracranial lesions, it may be of value for solitary metastases. Resection of a *solitary tumor* in patients with known systemic cancer may be considered if: there is a greater than 2-year interval without known residual systemic malignancy; relief of specific symptoms such as hydrocephalus is required; the tumor is known to be radioresistant as in the case of melanoma, sarcoma, and renal or colonic carcinomas; symptomatic tumor recurs after radiation; and the patient's systemic disease is under good control and the cerebral tumor is the limiting factor in quality of survival. For selected patients, this approach offers survival free of neurologic disease of more than 1 year.

Acute treatment of intracranial tumors Clinical evidence of acute or subacute deterioration, such as stupor, focal neurologic signs, or evidence of transtentorial herniation, requires aggressive management. Treatment is directed to reducing cerebral edema, lowering intracranial pressure and reducing the risk of seizures. Treatment with daily doses of dexamethasone 30 to 60 mg or methylprednisolone 120 to 200 mg in four to six divided doses reduces cerebral edema and associated surgical morbidity. Corticosteroids may not control symptoms caused by obstruction of the ventricular system, and emergency ventricular drainage may be required. Anticonvulsant medications are usually prescribed for patients with seizures, though many physicians administer them prophylactically when intracranial tumor has been diagnosed.

SYSTEMIC CANCER AND THE CENTRAL NERVOUS SYSTEM

CEREBRAL METASTASES The most common CNS tumors are metastatic. The following section discusses the approach to patients who present with a CNS tumor where systemic cancer must be considered.

Pathogenesis and pathology Cerebral metastases occur in one-quarter of patients with systemic cancer. Spread to the calvarium, brain parenchyma, and subarachnoid space occurs through several mechanisms. *Hematogenous tumor embolism* from intermediate sites such as lung and liver is the most common mechanism in solid tumors of the breast and lung, and in melanoma. Spread into the spinal canal via the *perivertebral venous system* occurs with uterine, colonic, and prostatic tumors. *Direct extension* of tumors originating in the head and neck may occur through the base of the skull. *Paraspinal direct* infiltration may occur with lymphoma and with prostate and breast carcinomas. *Tumor passage into the eye* or through the choroid plexus to the brain and subarachnoid space occurs in lymphoma and leukemia.

Clinical manifestations Sixty percent of cerebral metastases occur in the setting of diagnosed systemic cancer. Cancers of lung in men and of breast in women account for the largest percentage, although melanoma is the tumor with highest likelihood of spread to the CNS. Of patients with a cerebral metastasis (most often arising in the lung) 20 percent develop neurologic symptoms before discovery of the primary malignancy. At some point after diagnosis of systemic cancer, 25 percent of patients with lung carcinoma, 6 to 20 percent of patients with breast carcinoma, and about 50 percent of those with melanoma (when this last tumor has already metastasized to a site outside the CNS) develop tumors in brain or spinal cord. Patients with recurrent sarcoma or ovarian or colorectal cancer who survive beyond 3 years after the original diagnosis face a heightened risk of neurologic involvement. These tumors rarely accounted for cerebral metastases in the past. In the majority of patients, cerebral metastases occur with systemic relapse (Table 345-3). An exception occurs in patients with lung cancer, where the CNS is frequently either the initial site of presentation or of first demonstrated recurrence in otherwise apparently well-controlled disease. As systemic treatment continues to improve survival, the incidence of CNS involvement can be expected to rise for virtually all tumors.

Diagnosis of cerebral metastases   More often than is the case with primary brain tumors, those of metastatic origin occur in a setting of seizure activity, increasingly severe head pain, and motor weakness. These difficulties often evolve in days to weeks. Contrast-enhanced CT scan is the procedure of choice for evaluating patients with known systemic cancer and new neurologic symptoms (Table 345-2). Tumors appear as multiple ring-enhancing lesions or solitary masses with equal frequency. Three categories of patients without neurologic symptoms or signs are initially evaluated by CT scanning. First, patients with lung carcinoma for whom attempted cure with pulmonary lobectomy is planned should have a CT scan preoperatively, since 5 percent of such patients will have clinically unsuspected cerebral metastases. Second, prophylactic brain radiation for small cell carcinoma of the lung should be preceded by a CT scan. Third, patients with widely disseminated cancer due to breast or testicular tumors, sarcoma, or melanoma who are about to receive systemic chemotherapy should have a CT scan to stage the disease.

Ten percent of patients with cancer develop neurologic difficulties in the absence of an intracranial mass on CT scan. Focal motor or cranial nerve symptoms, headache, or impaired intellectual performance may reflect cerebrovascular lesions known to be associated with systemic cancer, unwitnessed seizures, meningeal carcinomatosis, paraneoplastic syndromes, or complications of tumor therapy (Table 345-4).

Patients with systemic neoplasms can develop several types of cerebrovascular disease (see Graus et al.). Multiple cerebral infarctions are the most frequent in patients with solid tumors; those with lymphoma or leukemia may develop diffuse encephalopathic difficulties from infarcts due to disseminated intravascular coagulation or from hemorrhage in the setting of clotting abnormalities, or from thrombocytopenia.

Focal deficits in patients with negative CT scans may result from seizures due to undetectable metastatic disease or may be manifestations of meningeal carcinomatosis or paraneoplastic syndromes (see Chap. 304). Repeat CT scan in 4 to 6 weeks often discloses the tumor if present. A lumbar puncture with cytologic examination is mandatory in such patients both to exclude infection and to search for leptomeningeal tumor (see below). CSF pleocytosis with mild elevation of protein may be found with paraneoplastic disorders.

Treatment   The common assumption that brain metastases represent a uniform disease has been proved invalid. Therapeutic decisions must be based on the type, extent, and radiosensitivity of the primary tumor, the morbidity produced, and the number and location of metastases.

Patients with solitary lesions and little or no active systemic disease may require surgery, whereas for those with advanced, widespread systemic cancer, comfort is the prime consideration. Steroids may be used in such patients to maximize neurologic function and to reduce headache (see "Acute Treatment of Intracranial Tumors").

RADIATION THERAPY   After acute symptoms are treated, most patients with multiple cerebral metastases or unresectable solitary lesions receive radiation therapy. A common approach is palliative whole-brain radiation totaling about 30 Gy (3000 rad) given in 10 to 15 equal fractions. Three-quarters of patients improve clinically and by CT; over one-half are able to discontinue their steroid medication for a time. However, only 30 percent of patients who complete radiation therapy survive 6 months and fewer than 20 percent are alive at 1 year. Two-thirds of the latter patients die from recurrent systemic tumor and not from cerebral disease. Treatment is less effective in the elderly, in those with advanced systemic cancer, and in patients with radiation-resistant tumors such as melanoma and gastrointestinal and lung tumors. Reinstitution of corticosteroids may be useful when progressive neurologic deterioration recurs.

CHEMOTHERAPY   Systemic (intravenous or intraarterial) chemotherapy has been used with some success to treat cerebral metastases of lung (small cell), breast, and testicular origin. Anecdotal reports of brain metastases of breast origin responding to tamoxifen or other systemic chemotherapy have appeared.

LEPTOMENINGEAL METASTASES   Pathogenesis and pathology
Eight percent of patients with cancer develop diffuse infiltration of the meninges. The cranial and spinal nerve roots are usually affected. Tumors that commonly invade the meninges include non-Hodgkin's lymphoma, leukemia, melanoma, and adenocarcinoma of breast, lung, or gastrointestinal origin.

Clinical manifestations   The common symptoms are headache, alteration in mentation, cranial nerve abnormalities, and lumbosacral radiculopathies. Patients may also present with seizures. The CT scan usually is normal, but it may reveal enlarged ventricles and diffuse enhancement of the meninges over the cerebral hemispheres and at the base of the brain.

A lumbar puncture is required for diagnosis. Three-quarters of patients show a modest CSF mononuclear pleocytosis of 5 to 100 cells. Elevation of protein and lowered glucose content may occur, but demonstration of malignant cells is required to confirm the diagnosis. Repeat lumbar punctures may be necessary to obtain positive cytology. Myelography is often done in such patients because of back pain and radicular symptoms; it may disclose multiple small nodules on the nerve roots. Larger lesions can be detected and treated with radiation.

Treatment   Treatment of meningeal carcinomatosis usually requires a combination of cranial radiation and intrathecal administration of chemotherapeutic agents. Chemotherapy is given either into the lumbar subarachnoid space or (more effectively) into a reservoir

TABLE 345-3   Interval between diagnosis of cancer and occurrence of brain metastases

| Tumor | Patients with brain metastases, percent | | | Interval from diagnosis of primary tumor to diagnosis of brain metastasis |
	At diagnosis of primary	Sometime during course of tumor growth	At autopsy	
Lung tumor	10–15	22–30	15–30	90 after 3 months
Breast tumor	1	6–20	15–30	90 after 1 year
Melanoma	6	50	40–80	80 after 1 year
Renal tumor	4	11–13	8–20	90 after 1 year
Colorectal tumor	1	—	1	75 after 2 years
Sarcoma	1	36	—	90 after 1 year

SOURCE: *Weiss et al., Deutsch et al.*

connected to the lateral ventricle. Agents commonly used include methotrexate, triethylenethiophosphoramide (thio-TEPA), and cytosine arabinoside either alone or in combination.

About one-half of patients with breast carcinoma respond initially to these treatments, but the median survival is only 7 months. The prognosis is particularly grave for meningeal carcinomatosis of melanoma or lung tumor origin; few responses are seen. A much better prognosis is expected in patients with lymphoma or leukemia with control for 2 or more years being common. Treatment failures reflect tumor drug resistance, poor circulation of drug within the subarachnoid space, and complications arising from chemotherapy and radiation (see Table 345-4).

TOXIC EFFECTS OF CANCER TREATMENT Chemotherapy

Chronic corticosteroid therapy may induce insulin-dependent diabetes mellitus, myopathy, and aseptic necrosis of the hip and may predispose to thrombophlebitis. In the early stages the muscle changes reverse with steroid taper and intensive physical therapy. Administration of anticonvulsants is associated with cutaneous allergies. Anticonvulsant doses may need to be adjusted in patients receiving corticosteroids. Allergy to an anticonvulsant may be masked while the patient receives corticosteroids and revealed later when the steroid medication is tapered. Table 345-4 summarizes the neurologic toxicities of currently used *chemotherapeutic agents*.

Radiation therapy Radiation therapy may cause toxic effects on the CNS. Acute changes in mental status or exacerbation of previous symptoms and signs may develop within 1 to 2 weeks of its initiation. These effects are usually attributable to worsening cerebral edema and are best treated with increased doses of corticosteroids. Subacute changes that develop between 3 and 18 months after treatment are ascribed to radiation-induced demyelination and are unresponsive to steroids. These changes include the reappearance of previous neurologic impairment and the appearance of a mass which is indistinguishable from recurrent tumor on CT scan. Patients who have received spinal radiation may develop Lhermitte's phenomenon with tingling in the back and legs following flexion of the neck.

Between 18 and 60 months after radiation, still other less reversible changes occur. These include retarded growth rate and impaired intellectual development in children who have received more than 30 Gy (3000 rad) of whole-brain radiation. At doses above 50 Gy (5000 rad), adults may exhibit cortical atrophy, communicating hydrocephalus, and hypothalamic dysfunction with elevated prolactin levels and amenorrhea or impotence. Dementia resulting from these changes is irreversible and in the case of hydrocephalus is usually unimproved by ventricular shunting.

The peripheral nervous system can also be affected by radiation therapy. Localized dysfunction of the brachial or lumbosacral plexus may follow radiation in excess of 40 Gy (4000 rad), usually appearing more than 1 year after treatment (see Chap. 355). Unlike peripheral nerve problems due to tumor invasion, radiation plexopathy is commonly painless. Additional tests, including CT scan, may be necessary to distinguish tumor invasion from radiation toxicity. Corticosteroids may afford some benefit.

PRIMARY BRAIN TUMORS

In the following section, the most common primary brain tumors in adults are discussed by histologic type. Other tumors which occur in characteristic locations and whose presenting symptoms therefore reflect site rather than specific histology are then discussed by location. These include tumors located in the diencephalon-third ventricle, the posterior fossa, and the skull base.

MALIGNANT ASTROCYTOMA (GLIOBLASTOMA) Definition

Malignant astrocytoma or glioblastoma (also known as malignant glioma or grade 3 or 4 astrocytoma) and the less malignant anaplastic astrocytoma account for about one-quarter of the 5000 intracranial gliomas diagnosed yearly in the United States; 75 percent of gliomas

TABLE 345-4 Complications of chemotherapy

Neurologic problem	Drug(s)	Route
Encephalopathy	Steroids	PO/IM/IV
	L-Asparaginase	IV
	Procarbazine	PO/IV
	Nitrosoureas	PO/IV/IA/HDIV
	Cytosine arabinoside	HDIV
Leucoencephalopathy	Methotrexate	HDIV/IT
Cerebral edema	Cisplatin	IA
	Nitrosoureas	IA/HDIV
Optic nerve damage	Nitrosoureas	IA/HDIV
Cerebellar ataxia	5-Fluorouracil	IV
	Cytosine arabinoside	IT
Cranial neuropathy	Vincristine	IV
	Cisplatin*	IV/IA
Myelopathy/radiculopathy	Thio-TEPA	IT
	Methotrexate	HDIV/IT
	Cystosine arabinoside	HDIV/IT
Peripheral neuropathy	Vincristine†	IV
	Cisplatin	IV
Myopathy	Steroids	PO/IM/IV
	Vincristine	IV

* Ototoxicity and vestibular toxicity.
† Autonomic neuropathy may be seen as well.
NOTES: IA = intraarterial; IM = intramuscular; IV = intravenous; PO = per os; IT = intrathecal; HDIV = high dose intravenous.
SOURCE: Modified from Young.

in adults are of this category. Because of its profound and uniform morbidity, it contributes more to the cost of cancer on a per capita basis than does any other tumor. The patient, commonly stricken in the fifth decade of life, enters a cycle of repetitive hospitalizations and operations while experiencing the progressive complications associated with relatively ineffective treatments of radiation and chemotherapy.

Pathogenesis and pathology Epidemiologic studies offer few clues to the etiology of malignant astrocytoma. Some tumors arise in patients with longstanding seizure disorders or personality disorders resulting from temporal lobe dysfunction and in scars incurred from head trauma, suggesting that in certain instances the malignant cells emerge from a more benign glial proliferation. There are rare instances of malignant tumors occurring in families, suggesting a genetic propensity. At least four human viral oncogenes (*sis, myc, src, n-myc*) have been identified in cell lines derived from primary brain tumors. Small clusters of tumors have appeared in certain occupational settings, notably in the petroleum processing industry. The tumor has an appearance similar to that produced by a variety of viral agents inoculated into animals. Examined by the naked eye, normal brain is distorted and infiltrated by yellow tumor tissue containing areas of necrosis, cysts, and hemorrhage. Microscopic examination reveals a highly cellular composite of heterogeneous glial cells with elongated or rounded astrocytes whose processes stain for glial fibrillary acidic protein. Giant cells may be seen along with mitotic figures and the proliferation of small capillaries.

Clinical manifestations Patients commonly present with a subacute progressive neurologic deficit exhibiting either focal signs or personality changes. Prior mental changes or seizures may antedate tumor diagnosis by months to years. Clinical symptoms may occur abruptly with seizures or with sudden deficits secondary to tumor hemorrhage. The CT scan reveals a heterogeneous pattern of tumor enhancement interspersed with hypodense foci presumably corresponding to tumor necrosis and edema. Multiple tumors can occur but are uncommon. MRI scans often define more extensive tumor involvement than is indicated on the CT scan (Fig. 345-2).

Malignant astrocytoma can arise in the brainstem, cerebellum, or spinal cord in addition to the more common locations within the white matter of the cerebral hemispheres. The prognosis for any site, unfortunately, has not changed greatly in the last 20 years. Following treatment, less than 6 months of useful function can be expected for most patients before progression of symptoms signals recurrent tumor.

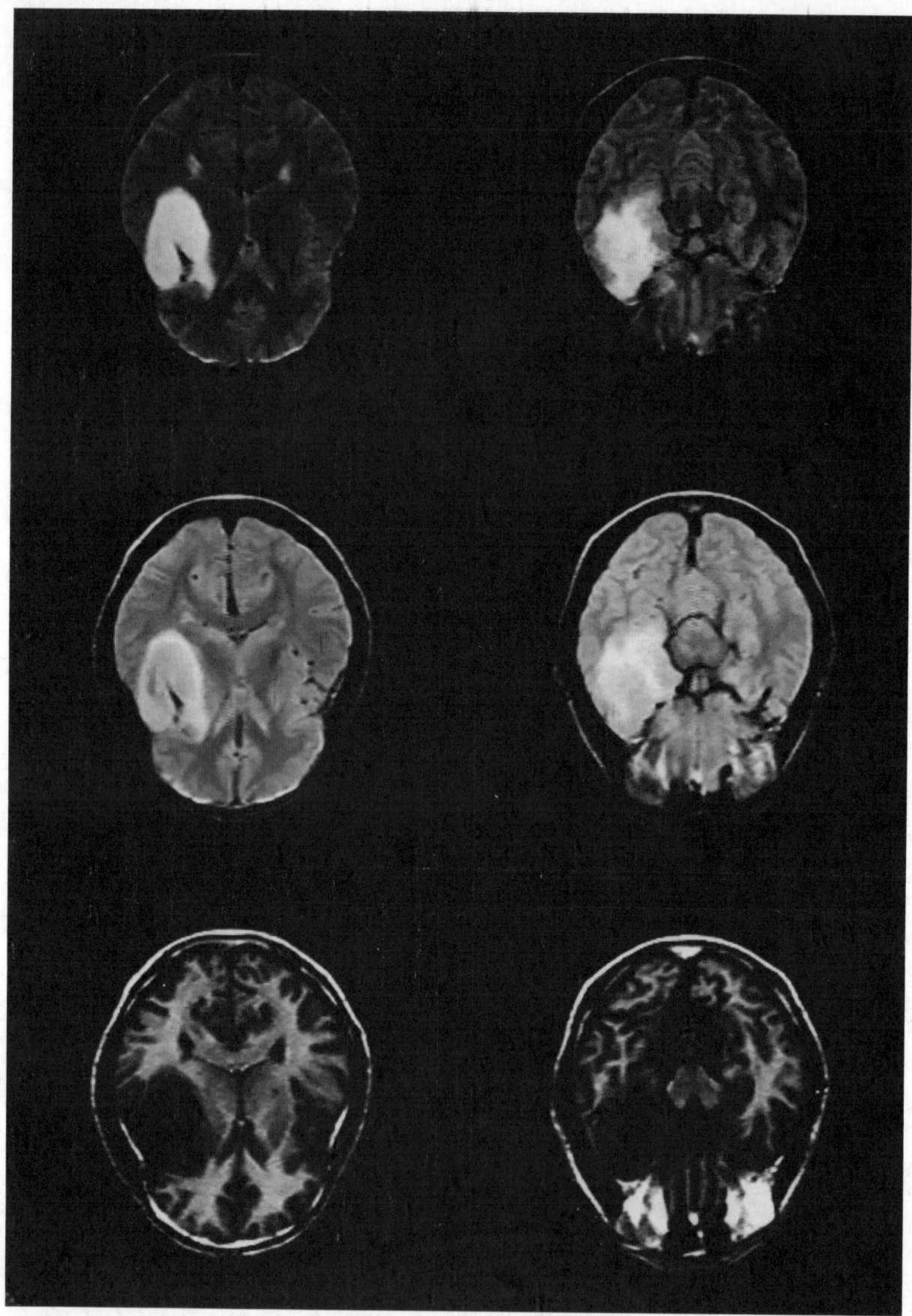

FIGURE 345-2 *MRI scans of glioblastoma multiforme. A large lesion is evident involving the anterior left temporal pole and operculum, with a central zone of markedly prolonged relaxation times (dark on IR sections, above, and bright on SE sections, below). This area is surrounded by a thin rim of moderately prolonged T1 (gray appearance) and T2 (brighter on earlier echo, middle row, and less bright on later echo, bottom row). It is thought, but not proven by histologic study, that the central area represents tumoral mass, with a greatly prolonged T2, surrounded by a thin rim of edema or compressed brain (moderately prolonged relaxation times). (Top row: IR study; TR = 1500, TI = 450, TE = 45 ms. Middle row: SE study; TR = 2000, TE = 60 ms. Bottom row: SE study; TR = 2000, TE = 120 ms.)*

Death results in 80 percent of patients from tumor recurrence within 6 to 12 months. Progressive neurologic deterioration is followed by stupor and coma. In patients who survive over 1 year, often young adults, CNS dissemination can occur to the meninges or the ventricular ependyma. Metastasis outside the CNS is extremely rare.

Treatment Confirmation of histology by biopsy should be performed in most patients; debulking of tumor is recommended if the tumor is located in an area that permits an extensive operation.

Therapeutic modalities are not highly effective. The average life expectancy of 17 weeks for untreated patients is improved by postoperative external beam radiation alone to 47 weeks and by radiation combined with chemotherapy to 62 weeks. A subgroup of young patients under age 50 obtains significant improvement in quality and duration of life. Such patients have a 20 percent 2-year survival after cranial radiation of 55 to 60 Gy (5500 to 6000 rad) combined with adjunctive chemotherapy with the nitrosoureas carmustine (BCNU) or lomustine (CCNU).

Efforts to improve prognosis for this malignancy include radiotherapy trials of implanted radiation sources (brachytherapy). Current chemotherapeutic trials are based on the localized nature of the tumor and of its recurrence and involve local arterial infusions of carmustine or cisplatin prior to radiation or at the time of tumor recurrence. Experimental approaches include the use of interferon or monoclonal antibodies.

ASTROCYTOMA Definition Low-grade astrocytomas occur throughout the brain and spinal cord. The subcortical white matter is the most common site in adults. In children and young adults astrocytomas arise in the optic nerves, cerebellum (cystic, juvenile, pilocytic astrocytoma), and brainstem (pontine glioma). These tumors are also associated with neurofibromatosis and tuberous sclerosis and are found in 20 percent of patients undergoing temporal lobectomy for control of chronic seizure disorders.

Pathogenesis and pathology The tumors are avascular without necrosis and contain homogeneous populations of well-differentiated astrocytes. In cerebellar locations and, less commonly, in supratentorial sites, the tumor may consist of a small nodule of astrocytes accompanied by a much larger cyst. Calcification is uncommon.

Clinical manifestations The tumors evolve slowly over several years, producing symptoms by displacement of normal brain or by invasion of white matter tracts. Optic nerve gliomas cause progressive, monocular or bitemporal visual field defects leading eventually to blindness and sometimes proptosis. Hypothalamic compression may cause endocrine dysfunction. Hydrocephalus is rare. In the brainstem, such tumors typically involve several cranial nerves (often the abducens, facial, and trigeminal) and later impinge on corticospinal fibers and medial lemniscal and spinothalamic tracts. These symptoms must be distinguished from those caused by multiple sclerosis, arteriovenous malformations, cysts of cysticercosis and echinococcal origin, and extramedullary tumors such as schwannomas or meningiomas. Cerebellar astrocytomas cause progressive incoordination and gait ataxia combined with abnormalities of eye movements. In supratentorial locations, these tumors may produce seizures before any focal abnormality appears on clinical examination or on CT scan.

The characteristic CT appearance is an indistinct mass which is hypodense with respect to surrounding brain and which exhibits little or no contrast enhancement or evidence of edema. MRI often demonstrates white matter abnormalities in patients with normal CT scans and is becoming the preferred procedure for early diagnosis and follow-up. A stable clinical course is common and repeat radiologic studies may show little change. In an extreme form this process of slow infiltration of white matter, known as *gliomatosis cerebri*, causes diffuse panhemispheric infiltration by atypical individual astrocytes without evidence of localized tumor. Malignant degeneration of astrocytomas is heralded by rapid progression of symptoms and signs, evidence of growth on CT, development of peritumoral edema, and contrast enhancement.

Treatment Surgical excision can be curative for some cerebellar, optic nerve, and lobar astrocytomas. Cyst drainage and partial resection are feasible for many. Biopsy should be obtained for supratentorial tumors but is less frequently considered for brainstem or spinal cord gliomas. Exceptions to the latter are tumors that have a cystic or extraaxial component. Postoperative radiation is recommended for incompletely resected tumors. Its role in the treatment of excised tumors is less clear. The timing of radiation therapy should be carefully weighed against the known long natural course of the astrocytoma, particularly those in supratentorial locations. Radiation is recommended when symptoms and signs progress or enlargement on CT or MRI is observed. Radiation may be safely delayed for several years in apparently totally resected tumors because of the accuracy of MRI and CT scans. The judicious use of corticosteroids during radiation or when symptoms recur improves function. The median life expectancy is 67 months for supratentorial tumors and 89 months for cerebellar tumors. Average survivals of 15 months after radiation are reported for patients with brainstem tumors. However, the 5-year survival is only 30 percent. Chemotherapy, currently under investigation for brainstem tumors, may offer some improvement in survival.

OLIGODENDROGLIOMA Definition This tumor of oligodendroglial origin may develop in isolation or may be mixed with other glial cells. An uncommon tumor, it represents less then 10 percent of all gliomas.

Pathology Microscopic examination discloses rounded cells containing darkly staining nuclei with poorly staining cytoplasm, the "fried egg" appearance. The tumor is prone to spontaneous hemorrhage.

Clinical manifestations Presentation is most commonly in the third or fourth decade and tumors are most frequently in the frontal lobes or within the ventricles. CT reveals a well-defined, low-attenuation mass with fine speckled calcium deposits and small cysts.

Treatment Although the oligodendroglioma is histologically "benign," resection is curative in only one-third of patients. The role of postoperative radiation is uncertain; it is recommended only for unresectable tumors or those with features suggesting malignant change, such as contrast enhancement or radiographically proven tumor growth. Prospective studies of postoperative radiation have not been performed. Chemotherapy is not effective. Approximately one-third of patients survive 5 years after diagnosis.

MENINGIOMA Definition Meningiomas account for 20 percent of brain tumors. They can arise in either the cranium or the spinal canal. They occur more frequently at all sites in women. They are commonly found as asymptomatic tumors at postmortem. When symptomatic they usually present in the fifth or sixth decades.

Pathogenesis and pathology Meningiomas arise from cells of the pia-arachnoid. Common sites include the midline along the falx cerebri and the lateral cerebral convexity, the olfactory groove and along the sphenoid ridge, the tuberculum sellae, foramen magnum, and tentorium of the cerebellum. They also arise on occasion within the ventricles, where on radiographic examination they are indistinguishable from a papilloma of the choroid plexus. Meningiomas may coexist with schwannomas in patients with the central form of neurofibromatosis. They occur more frequently in women with breast cancer; some meningiomas contain estrogen and progesterone receptors.

On the basis of microscopic characteristics, meningiomas are divided into seven categories: syncytial, transitional, fibroblastic, microcystic, psammomatous, angioblastic, and malignant meningiomas. Malignant tumors display mitoses, invade normal brain, and occasionally develop CNS and extraneural metastases. Angioblastic and malignant forms are more likely than the other types to recur.

Clinical manifestations The clinical presentation reflects the slow expansion of tumor in the characteristic locations within the skull and spine, with neurologic deficits evolving over many years. Tumors of the parasellar region produce a combination of second, third, fourth, fifth, and sixth cranial nerve deficits. Cerebellopontine tumors may produce a syndrome similar to that of acoustic schwannomas (see "Tumors of the Posterior Fossa" below). Early hearing loss is not a typical finding in meningioma. Parasagittal and frontal tumors may produce seizures or may be entirely asymptomatic, often growing to enormous size before they are discovered. Parasagittal lesions that attain sufficient size may cause spastic paraparesis and incontinence. Falx meningioma should be considered in the differential diagnosis of gait disorders in the middle-aged and elderly. In all locations, meningiomas must be distinguished from similar-appearing dural metastases from breast, prostate, and lung.

Treatment Tumor site, rather than histology, is the major determinant of outcome. Intraventricular or parasagittal tumors are usually resectable and recurrence is rare. Those in the olfactory groove, sphenoid ridge, and parasellar locations are more difficult to resect completely and are prone to recur. Tumors of the foramen magnum may be totally removed with microneurosurgical techniques (see "Spinal Tumors" below). Radiation is advocated for malignant meningiomas and for incompletely excised symptomatic tumors of other histologic subtypes.

PAPILLOMA OF THE CHOROID PLEXUS **Definition** Neoplasms derived from choroid plexus epithelium are rare, representing only 0.5 percent of all intracranial tumors.

Pathogenesis and pathology In children most such tumors occur in the lateral ventricles, whereas in adults the fourth ventricle is the most common site. The histologic structure resembles normal choroid plexus, with a connective tissue core covered by a single layer of cuboidal epithelium.

Clinical manifestations Very rare examples of malignant transformation have been described. Metastases to the leptomeninges may occur. The tumor may secrete excessive CSF leading to communicating hydrocephalus.

Treatment Surgery is the treatment of choice and is usually highly successful.

LIPOMA Lipoma can develop anywhere within the brain or spinal cord, though the corpus callosum is the most common location. The association of lipomas with partial or complete agenesis of this structure and with other dysplastic or hamartomatous anomalies such as ectopias, colloid cysts, and epidermoids supports the theory that they are the result of disorders of development. Intraspinal lipomas are most common in the thoracic region and are associated with spina bifida in one-third of cases. All lipomas can be easily demonstrated by MRI. The treatment of symptomatic cranial and spinal lipomas is excision.

DERMOID AND EPIDERMOID TUMOR **Definition** The distinction between dermoid tumors and epidermoids (true cholesteatomas) is often difficult. Both result from inclusion of ectodermal tissue at the time of closure of the neural groove and soon thereafter.

Pathology and pathogenesis Cholesteatomas are slowly growing tumors that most often afflict young adults, occurring commonly in lateral or midline locations within the skull, i.e., the cerebellopontine angle, the suprasellar region, the fourth ventricle, the pineal region, and over the hemispheres. No clear relationship has been established between cholesteatoma of the cerebellopontine angle and middle ear infection. Dermoid tumors, which are frequently cystic, occur largely in the posterior fossa or in the lumbosacral region. Rarely they are found in suprasellar or pineal regions.

Clinical manifestations Symptoms vary according to the location of these tumors, the general pattern being slow evolution of defects attributable to the specific area with seizures interspersed when the tumor occupies cortical regions.

Treatment Treatment of the cholesteatoma is total surgical removal of the tumor together with its capsule. Dermoid tumors similarly are curable if total surgical excision is possible.

PRIMARY LYMPHOMA OF THE CENTRAL NERVOUS SYSTEM **Definition** Primary lymphomas are now recognized to be relatively common in the CNS. Before 1972, fewer than 25 cases had been identified at the Massachusetts General Hospital over a 50-year period. Since 1977, 10 cases per year have been diagnosed. Primary lymphoma is distinguished from the more frequent secondary involvement of the meninges that occurs in patients with poorly differentiated non-Hodgkin's lymphomas.

Pathogenesis and pathology The tumor is uncommon in patients without immunologic compromise. It is usually seen in patients with mixed humoral and cellular immune deficits. Three such disorders are recognized: inherited disorders of immunity such as combined immunodeficiency disease, selective IgM deficiency, or selective IgA abnormalities seen with ataxia-telangiectasia and Wiskott-Aldrich syndrome; acquired immunodeficiency syndrome (AIDS); and therapeutic immunosuppression following organ transplantation or treatment of autoimmune disorders. The demonstration of Epstein-Barr virus (EBV) DNA within primary lymphoma and of elevated titers of anti-EBV antibodies in affected patients raises the possibility that this agent plays a role in the pathogenesis of this disease.

The tumor may be focal or multicentric in the subcortical white matter, the walls of the ventricles, or the subarachnoid space. Tumor cells are always found in a perivascular distribution. At biopsy, tumor cells are often indistinguishable from normal lymphocytes, leading to an erroneous early diagnosis of "encephalitis" or "nonspecific perivascular inflammation." The cells may be characterized as malignant by monoclonal antibodies to immunoglobulin surface proteins. The tumors contain cells defined histologically as diffuse histiocytic or poorly differentiated lymphocytes by the Rappaport system and as follicular center cells and small cleaved cells by the Lukes-Collins system (see Chaps. 293 and 294). Burkitt-type lymphomas are rarely reported.

Clinical manifestations A history of personality change, focal deficits, or seizures evolving over several weeks in an immunosuppressed patient should raise the suspicion of cerebral lymphoma. Obviously, in these circumstances infection must be excluded. The CT scan typically reveals multiple periventricular masses which enhance with contrast (Fig. 345-3). A characteristic feature, rarely observed with other types of intracranial tumor, is the marked reduction or disappearance of lesions after a few weeks of high-dose corticosteroid therapy (dexamethasone 6 to 10 mg four times daily). When both symptoms and CT abnormalities resolve after corticosteroids, remissions lasting several months are common, and steroids can be tapered. Spontaneous remissions without corticosteroid therapy have been described. The usual clinical course is recurrence after 4 to 6 months, with resistance to steroid administration. The tumor may seed the meninges in one-quarter of patients. Systemic lymphoma is found in less than 10 percent of patients and occurs late in the course of the disease. However uveitis or vitreitis may occur at the time of presentation or early in the evolution of the disease; when present, it is helpful in the initial diagnosis.

Treatment After biopsy or diagnosis by CSF cytology, the recommended treatment is corticosteroids and radiation. The median survival is 17 months. Increasingly used is chemotherapy before radiation and at recurrence of tumor. High-dose methotrexate administered parenterally at 3.5 gm/m^2 followed by citrovorum factor rescue has been demonstrated to achieve therapeutic drug levels in brain parenchyma and most importantly, in the CSF. When methotrexate is administered prior to radiation, there is a reduced risk of radiation-drug white matter damage.

TUMORS OF THE THIRD VENTRICLE AND PINEAL REGION Several categories of tumors occur in close proximity to the diencephalon,

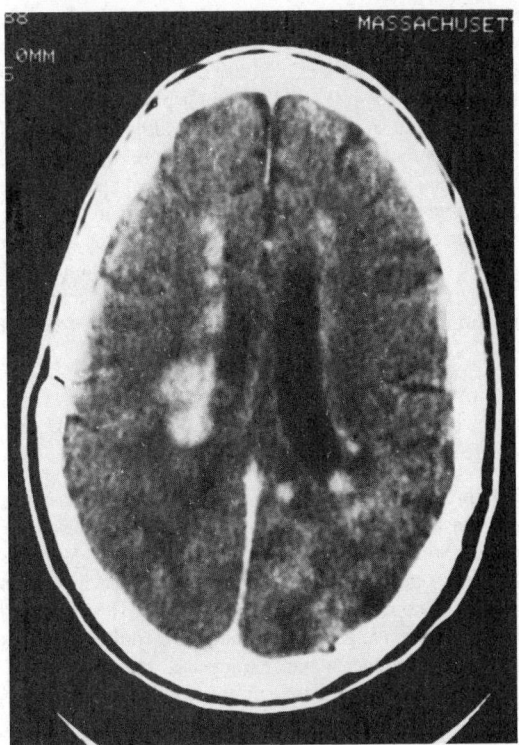

FIGURE 345-3 *Contrast-enhanced CT scan showing periventricular enhancement in a young man with primary CNS lymphoma. Note absence of surrounding edema.*

hypothalamus, and third ventricle; these are pituitary adenoma, craniopharyngioma, germ-cell neoplasms, pineal tumors, and glial, meningeal, or metastatic tumors.

Uncommon tumors of the pineal region include *astrocytomas, glioblastomas, meningiomas,* and *metastases.* Nonneoplastic masses occurring in this region include colloid cysts of the third ventricle (see "Colloid Cysts" below) and parasitic cysts (cysticercosis).

Pituitary adenomas These tumors are described in Chap. 321.

Craniopharyngiomas These tumors arise from remnants of Rathke's pouch, derived from the primitive stomatodeum. They are usually suprasellar in location and cause symptoms related to neuroendocrine dysfunction or visual compromise (see also Chap. 321).

Germ-cell tumors DEFINITION Germ-cell tumors, which account for half of all pineal region neoplasms, arise primarily during childhood or early adolescence and include germinoma, teratoma, embryonal carcinoma, endodermal sinus tumor, and choriocarcinoma.

CLINICAL MANIFESTATIONS The most common of these germ-cell tumors is the germinoma. It may occur in the pineal region or at the base of the hypothalamus. It occurs more frequently in males, who present with findings of diabetes insipidus and other neuroendocrine deficiencies, bitemporal visual field defects, paralysis of upward gaze (see Chap. 13), and sometimes hydrocephalus. The typical features of pineal masses occur more commonly with nongerminomatous germ-cell tumors. Findings include Parinaud's syndrome—a failure of upward gaze and pupillary dilatation with deficiencies in response to light. Rarely, other signs such as nystagmus retractorius or brainstem signs due to compression may occur. Diagnosis may be assisted by the finding of elevated serum and CSF levels of alphafetoprotein (AFP) and of human chorionic gonadotropin (hCG) in germinomas.

TREATMENT Germinomas are radiosensitive; up to 80 percent are cured by well-tolerated doses of radiation. Other histologic subtypes have poorer prognoses and recurrence is common, often with seeding of the cranial nerves and meninges. Recurrences sometimes respond

to drug treatment with etoposide, cisplatin, and doxorubicin, which are beneficial in testicular tumors of similar histology.

Pineoblastoma and pineocytoma These tumors account for 20 percent of growths in the pineal region.

PATHOGENESIS AND PATHOLOGY Pineoblastoma and pineocytoma arise from pineal organ cells. The pineoblastoma is a primitive malignant tumor of childhood and early adult life and is indistinguishable from primitive neuroectodermal tumors that arise elsewhere in the CNS. The tumor may contain astrocytic or neuronal elements. Recurrence is invariable and dissemination through the ventricular system and subarachnoid space is frequent.

TREATMENT Brain and neuraxis radiation are recommended, and chemotherapy as outlined above for germ-cell tumors has been successful in producing remissions in a few patients. The pineocytoma is a more slowly growing tumor which is often well-demarcated and resembles the normal structure of the pineal. Although histologically benign, it tends to recur, probably because of incomplete removal. It is resistant to radiation.

Colloid cysts PATHOGENESIS AND PATHOLOGY Colloid cysts arise within the anterior third ventricle and are considered to develop from the anlage of the paraphysis, a component of the third ventricle, or possibly from the ependyma itself. The cysts are well-encapsulated and consist of a layer of connective tissue covered with columnar ciliated cells. The cyst is filled with glycoproteinaceous material which stains with periodic acid Schiff (PAS).

CLINICAL MANIFESTATIONS Symptoms occur usually in adults and may be dramatic, with episodes of headache, weakness of the limbs, and loss of consciousness. These symptoms are attributed to intermittent acute hydrocephalus due to blockage of the foramen of Monro by the mobile cyst. Diagnosis cannot be made with certainty prior to operation; treatment is removal of the cyst.

TUMORS OF THE POSTERIOR FOSSA Tumors of the posterior fossa pose special problems in diagnosis and treatment. Rapidly growing tumors may cause obstructive hydrocephalus, and even small mass lesions in the posterior fossa may result in vomiting, lethargy, headache, and papilledema. Slowly growing tumors give rise to progressive signs which are recognized by rather specific syndromes. These include progressive unilateral hearing loss, facial weakness, pain or numbness, and a unilateral sixth nerve deficit occurring with tumors in the cerebellopontine angle. Gait ataxia and unilateral cerebellar signs occur with hemangioblastoma, medulloblastoma, or cystic astrocytoma of the cerebellum. Progressive diplopia, cranial nerve abnormalities, and crossed corticospinal tract and reflex abnormalities occur in brainstem glioma. Nuchal and occipital pain are common with all tumors of the posterior fossa. Corticospinal signs develop with further tumor enlargement and encroachment on the brainstem.

Acoustic schwannoma DEFINITION The acoustic schwannoma (synonymous with acoustic neuroma) is composed of myelin-forming Schwann cells that cover the acoustic nerve fibers. Schwann cells normally replace oligodendroglia as the nerve leaves the brain stem to enter the internal auditory meatus.

PATHOGENESIS AND PATHOLOGY Schwannomas are slow-growing masses that compress rather than invade normal tissue. When bilateral, they represent an inherited form of schwannoma which is diagnostic of "central" neurofibromatosis. Other CNS tumors associated with neurofibromatosis or von Recklinghausen's disease are schwannomas of spinal and other cranial nerves, intracranial and spinal meningiomas, gliomas, and ependymomas (see Chap. 351).

CLINICAL MANIFESTATIONS AND TREATMENT Early detection of acoustic schwannomas at a time of minimal hearing deficit and minimal facial motor difficulty is essential, as hearing may be spared by microneurosurgical intervention while the tumor is still restricted to the canal. Brainstem auditory-evoked responses, CT and MRI studies, and metrizamide cisternography have greatly enhanced the physician's ability to detect these tumors in their early stages.

Hemangioblastoma DEFINITION The cerebellar hemangioblastoma is an uncommon tumor which may be solitary but is frequently multiple. When the tumors are multiple, they are considered part of von Hippel-Lindau disease. This frequently familial syndrome typically consists of retinal, cerebellar, and spinal hemangioblastomas and visceral lesions, usually renal and/or pancreatic tumors or cysts. Polycythemia may be present.

PATHOGENESIS AND PATHOLOGY Hemangioblastomas are well-circumscribed and often cystic. The tumor may consist solely of a small nodule attached to the wall of a large cyst. The lesion is usually highly vascular and may be mistaken for an arteriovenous malformation. The microscopic appearance is one of numerous capillary vessels separated by sheets of clear cells with an abundance of intracytoplasmic vacuoles. The tumors are probably derived from capillary endothelial cells.

CLINICAL MANIFESTATIONS Dizziness, ataxia of gait or of the limbs, and symptoms of raised intracranial pressure are characteristic features of the cerebellar hemangioblastoma. The tumors may bleed spontaneously, resulting in a paroxysmal onset of headache and neurologic deficit.

TREATMENT Craniotomy with opening of the cerebellar cyst and excision of the mural tumor may be curative. Though the tumor is histologically benign, postoperative recurrences and the appearance of less operable spinal lesions worsen the prognosis. Patients with the von Hippel-Lindau syndrome should have periodic ophthalmologic evaluation for the appearance of retinal angiomas and general medical follow-up for early detection of renal tumors.

Ependymoma PATHOGENESIS AND PATHOLOGY These are glial tumors that occur chiefly in childhood and young adulthood, with a typical cranial location in the fourth ventricle. The tumor is composed of uniform ependymal cells surrounding a central lumen. Spinal ependymomas, which are more common, arise within the dura of the lumbar spine and represent more than half of spinal intramedullary gliomas. In this location, the prognosis is excellent.

TREATMENT Resection and radiation to the tumor site results in 5-year survival in excess of 80 percent for spinal cord lesions and between 30 percent and 50 percent for posterior fossa tumors. The role of chemotherapy in the treatment of local recurrences and of seeding within the subarachnoid space is not established.

PRIMITIVE NEUROECTODERMAL TUMORS (PNET) Several histologic varieties of tumor arise from primitive neuroectodermal tumors (PNET) which contain cells with a capacity to differentiate into medulloblasts, astrocytes, oligodendrocytes, ependyma, ganglion cells, or skeletal muscle. Some tumors have several cell types, but all PNETs share a propensity for local invasion, subarachnoid dissemination, and extraneural metastases. The initial evaluation should include CT scan and myelography with CSF cytology.

Medulloblastoma DEFINITION The *medulloblastoma* is the most common variety of PNET. It accounts for 25 percent of childhood brain tumors. However, one-fourth of medulloblastomas occur in patients over age 20.

PATHOGENESIS AND PATHOLOGY The tumor is usually located in the midline, in the inferior portion of the vermis of the cerebellum. It is composed of small, densely staining cells which elicit a brisk glial response. Invasion of the meninges, ventricles, and subarachnoid space is common.

CLINICAL MANIFESTATIONS The common presentation is occipital headache, vomiting, and trunkal ataxia. Hydrocephalus is frequent. With enlargement of the tumor other signs of brainstem compression emerge.

TREATMENT Resection of the tumor by resection is usually attempted, followed by radiation in doses of 45 to 50 Gy (4500 to 5000 rad) to the posterior fossa, together with 40 Gy (4000 rad) to the whole brain and 35 to 40 Gy (3500 to 4000 rad) to the spinal cord. Initial chemotherapy has not been shown to be effective, although it is used with some success in recurrent tumors. Nitrosourea, procarbazine, and vincristine combined with prednisone and intrathecal methotrexate are advocated. Five-year survival is nearly 75 percent in the most recently reported series. A pessimistic outlook exists for children under 3 years, those with large tumors, and those with subarachnoid spread. Metastases to lung, liver, vertebrae, and pelvis are reported. Some medulloblastomas may take on features reminiscent of neuroblastoma.

Neuroblastoma DEFINITION The neuroblastoma, a relatively common adrenal tumor, can rarely occur as a primary CNS tumor. Eighty percent of cases present during the first decade of life.

PATHOGENESIS AND PATHOLOGY Microscopically, neuroblastoma resembles medulloblastoma because of its dense small cells. Variations in pathology occur. Some tumors show differentiation to ganglion cells but do not have a better prognosis. The tumor can arise anywhere in the CNS but is most common in the posterior fossa. It resembles in its clinical behavior primitive glial tumors and the medulloblastoma, with neuraxis spread and occasional extraneural metastases. CT reveals a hypodense mass with dense, uniform enhancement after contrast administration, as well as variable hemorrhage and calcification.

TREATMENT Treatment of neuroblastoma consists of radical excision with postoperative radiation, though definitive evidence that radiation increases survival is lacking. Because of the frequency of local recurrence and CSF metastases, prophylactic spinal radiation may be justified. Chemotherapeutic trials have involved few patients and a variety of regimens. Long-term follow-up is incomplete, but with a greater than 30 percent 5-year survival, prognosis may be better than that of other primitive CNS tumors.

TUMORS OF THE SKULL BASE Tumors in this region produce characteristic clinical presentations which pose unique diagnostic difficulties even with advanced neuroradiologic procedures. Meningiomas, tumors of bone (including epidermoid and dermoid tumors and osteomas), chordomas, schwannomas (neurofibromas) of the cranial nerves, nasopharyngeal carcinoma, and metastases may all present with pain localized to the lower face, ear, or occiput and with involvement of one or more cranial nerves making exit from the skull. Metastases arise commonly from the lung, breast, nasopharynx, testicle, and prostate. Multiple myeloma and occasionally lymphoma may appear at this site. The mass may be palpable or may be visualized on polytomography, CT scan, or MRI; however, even a combination of all three studies may be negative. These studies usually differentiate successfully other erosive processes of the skull base, including fibrous dysplasia, Paget's disease, xanthomatosis, and osteitis fibrosa cystica. Enlargement of specific cranial nerve foramens may be the first evidence of schwannomas or of *glomus* tumors of the chromaffin cells in the jugular bulb. These last tumors invade temporal and occipital bone and produce hearing abnormalities and lower cranial nerve deficits.

Chordomas arise from remnants of the notochord. Of these, 60 percent are localized in the clivus, 30 percent in the sacral region, and the remaining 10 percent along the extent of the spine and skull base. They are highly invasive, expanding along the skull base and causing serial cranial nerve compression, sometimes with invasion of the nasopharynx. Up to one-third may metastasize via the subarachnoid space. A cauda equina syndrome (see "Spinal Tumors") results from sacral tumors. Clivus tumors may be difficult to visualize adequately on CT scan but are clearly delineated by MRI. Complete removal is rarely feasible and postoperative radiation therapy is recommended.

Metastases to the skull base are treated with radiation therapy. In the presence of characteristic patterns of pain and cranial nerve deficit, radiation may be considered to treat presumptive metastases in patients with known systemic malignancy even when radiographic examinations are inconclusive.

SPINAL TUMORS Pathogenesis and pathology Tumors of the spinal canal and of the cord are only one-quarter as common as are intracranial tumors. Spinal neoplasms arise from the same types of cells as their counterparts in the cerebrum. They are classified according to location as intramedullary (within the substance of the spinal cord), extramedullary (or intradural), and extradural. Some tumors, such as schwannomas, may be both extradural and intradural. The most frequent location for all types of spinal neoplasms is in the thoracic cord, presumably reflecting its greater total length. These tumors arise from cells of the spinal cord, nerve roots, meninges, vascular structures, or the vertebral column. Tumors of the spinal cord parenchyma are relatively infrequent compared to lesions arising outside the substance of the cord. In one large series, nerve sheath tumors (schwannomas) accounted for 29 percent of all spinal tumors, meningiomas for 25.5 percent, gliomas for 22 percent, and sarcomas for 12 percent. Metastatic lesions represent about 13 percent of all spinal tumors, but as with intracranial tumors, these figures reflect neurosurgical service statistics and metastases are likely underrepresented.

Clinical manifestations Any lesion that narrows the spinal canal sufficiently to encroach on neural structures can give rise to neurologic symptoms. Dysfunction may arise from direct compression of the spinal cord and its nerve roots or from interference with blood supply. The rapid growth of metastatic lesions leads to motor and sensory symptoms over a period of days to weeks, whereas slowly growing astrocytomas and ependymomas produce symptoms over a period of months to years.

Extramedullary tumors (both intradural and epidural) cause symptoms by compressing the spinal cord or nerve roots. The initial symptoms are usually focal back pain and paresthesias followed by sensory loss below the level of the pain, weakness, and bladder and bowel dysfunction. Intramedullary lesions usually extend over several spinal cord segments, and their symptoms and signs are more varied than those of extramedullary tumors. A common pattern is dissociated sensory loss, with pain and temperature sensation impairment in the segments of tumor origin and with sparing of posterior column sensory function. Later, as the tumor grows peripherally, spinothalamic tracts may be involved. Since, in the thoracic and cervical regions, the sacral pain and temperature fibers lie superficial to those fibers representing more rostral regions, the sacral segments may be spared. Atrophy in the appropriate segments due to anterior horn cell involvement may combine with corticospinal tract signs.

These clinical presentations are not diagnostic of spinal cord neoplasm. Transverse myelitis from multiple sclerosis or other causes can lead to rapid onset of spinal cord dysfunction associated with pain, paresthesias, and weakness (see Chap. 353). A similar syndrome can occur as a paraneoplastic process, resulting from a necrotic myelopathy (see Chap. 304). Syringomyelia can produce a chronic syndrome indistinguishable from that produced by intramedullary neoplasms. Other diseases that can lead to a progressive spinal cord syndrome include combined system degeneration due to vitamin B_{12} deficiency, amyotrophic lateral sclerosis, cervical spondylosis, arachnoiditis, vascular anomalies, meningeal carcinomatosis, and spinal stenosis due to a combination of degenerative disk disease and hypertrophy of the ligamentum flavum (see Chap. 353).

Additional specific clinical syndromes occur in two other locations within the spinal canal. *Foramen magnum tumors* may extend into the cervical region or rostrally into the posterior fossa. A combination of signs and symptoms referrable to lower cranial nerves, sensory loss in the distribution of the second cervical segment, posterior headache, and asymmetric sensory and motor involvement of the limbs leads to the suspicion of such a tumor, most commonly a meningioma. *Tumors of the conus medullaris or cauda equina* produce pain in the back, rectum, and/or both legs and may mimic lumbosacral disk disease. With tumor growth, muscle atrophy in the legs associated with sphincter dysfunction and reflex changes usually point to the correct site of involvement.

Diagnosis of spinal cord tumors Extradural metastastic spinal tumors cause changes in x-rays of the affected area in about 80 percent of cases. Lytic destructive lesions are the most common. Lymphomas less frequently show bony abnormalities. Radiographs aid in the diagnosis in only about 15 percent of primary spinal neoplasms, whether intradural or intramedullary in location. Findings include: changes in contour, separation of the pedicles, or enlargement of neural foramens which occur with schwannomas; proliferation of bone with meningiomas; and distortion of paraspinal tissues with masses that have grown into the spinal canal from extraneural sites. CT scans and MRI of the spine can demonstrate soft tissue masses encroaching on the canal and can visualize the bony structures; instillation of metrizamide is sometimes required to define the canal deformities of intraspinal tumor. When contrast medium flows into the cord, a diagnosis of syringomyelia may be established.

Magnetic resonance imaging (MRI) is now rapidly evolving as a useful diagnostic method for spinal cord tumor. Both intramedullary and extramedullary neoplasms are well seen with this technique and otherwise difficult to visualize regions such as the cervicomedullary junction are clearly evident. Meningeal carcinomatosis may also be suggested by MRI.

Myelography remains an important procedure for localizing and defining the level and extent of involvement. A small amount of contrast instilled at the beginning of the procedure can demonstrate whether a complete block is present; the rostral limit of the tumor can be defined by instillation of more dye through a lateral cervical puncture. Extramedullary lesions deform the contrast column on its outer surface, while intramedullary lesions widen the cord and displace the contrast laterally (see Chap. 353).

Cerebrospinal fluid removed at the time of myelography should be analyzed for cell count, protein content, and cytology. A specimen stained with Wright's stain should be analyzed and cells examined further after cytocentrifugation. The cell count is usually normal in spinal tumors unless there is meningeal tumor, but protein content is increased in virtually all cases of high-grade spinal cord block. The CSF glucose is usually normal unless there is meningeal tumor invasion.

Treatment Once the diagnosis of spinal cord tumor is established, rapid treatment is mandatory to maximize neurologic recovery. Extramedullary primary neoplasms are treated with microneurosurgery, and complete resection is usually possible. The most common intramedullary tumors, ependymomas and astrocytomas, usually can only be partially resected and are likely to recur. The role of radiation therapy for slowly growing tumors of this class is not well established; for high-grade astrocytomas a course of postoperative radiation is recommended. Corticosteroids may improve function temporarily. There is no established role for chemotherapy of spinal neoplasms.

EPIDURAL CANCER: THE PATIENT WITH CANCER AND BACK PAIN Spinal epidural cancer should be suspected in patients with back pain and known systemic malignancy even in the absence of neurologic signs. Progressive paraparesis with bladder dysfunction and development of a sensory deficit may be avoided by early intervention. High doses of steroids (up to 100 mg dexamethasone per day) are administered immediately and radiation therapy is usually recommended. The results of treatment in the large series of patients with epidural cancer reported by Gilbert has led to the conclusion that radiation therapy is as effective as surgery in the relief of symptoms. The clinical condition of the patient at the time of diagnosis is the most important factor in prognosis; only 3 percent of patients paraplegic at the time of treatment, regardless of type of therapy, regain ambulation. Reconsideration is being given to surgical decompression as a primary mode of treatment in patients with radioresistant malignancies such as melanoma and lung, prostatic, and colonic cancers and in the setting of paraparesis of recent onset.

PSEUDOTUMOR—BENIGN INTRACRANIAL HYPERTENSION

Symptoms of increased intracranial pressure may occur in the absence of demonstrable parenchymal or leptomeningeal tumor or hydrocephalus. However, little distinguishes the symptomatic presentation of true tumor from that of pseudotumor, which includes headache, papilledema, visual blurring and obscurations with enlargement of the blind spot, diplopia, nausea, and vomiting. Pseudotumor usually afflicts young, often obese women; it occurs most often in the absence of systemic cancer and focal neurologic difficulties. The marked increases in intracranial pressure may reflect impaired venous drainage within the brain or skull or may accompany the hormonal alterations of pregnancy, oral contraceptive use, or obesity. Less-common predisposing endocrinologic illnesses include both hypo- and hyperthyroidism, adrenal insufficiency, and both endogenous and exogenous excess of adrenocorticoids. A variety of drugs have been implicated, including supplemental Vitamin A, tetracycline, nalidixic acid, nitrofurantoin, and sulfa preparations. The diagnosis is confirmed by the exclusion of an intracranial mass lesion or meningeal cancer. In the presence of a normal or small ventricular system on CT scan, lumbar puncture carries no risk for brain herniation. Cerebrospinal fluid is invariably under increased pressure but is otherwise unremarkable. Treatment is aimed at prevention of visual deficits and lasting symptoms by reducing the CSF volume by repetitive lumbar punctures. The removal of an offending drug or metabolic cause will reverse symptoms within 1 week's time. Patients refractory to this may benefit from acetazolamide, furosemide, or short-term corticosteroid therapy. Lumboperitoneal shunting and surgical decompression are reserved for patients with progressive visual impairment who have failed medical therapy. The outlook for most patients is excellent—fully 80 percent respond to conservative therapy, but as many as 10 percent experience permanent or recurrent visual deficits.

REFERENCES

DEUTSCH M et al: Radiotherapy for intracranial metastases. Cancer 34:1607, 1974

GILBERT RW et al: Epidural spinal cord compression from metastatic tumor: Diagnosis and treatment. Ann Neurol 3:40, 1978

GRAUS F et al: Cerebrovascular complications in patients with cancer. Medicine (Baltimore) 64(1):16, 1985

HART R et al: Acoustic tumors: Atypical features and recent diagnostic tests. Neurology (NY) 33:211, 1983

HELLE TL et al: Primary lymphoma of the central nervous system: J Neurosurg 60:94, 1984

HOCHBERG FH et al: Central nervous system lymphoma related to Epstein-Barr virus. N Engl J Med 309:745, 1983

JENNINGS MT et al: Intracranial germ cell tumors: Natural history and pathogenesis. J Neurosurg 63:155, 1985

LAWS ER et al: Neurosurgical management of low grade astrocytomas of the cerebral hemispheres. J Neurosurg 61:665, 1984

SUNDAESAN N, GALICICH JH: Surgical treatment of brain metastases: Cancer 55:1382, 1985

WALKER MD (ed): Cancer Treatment and Research Series, Oncology of the Nervous System. WL McGuire, (series ed). Boston, Martinus Nijhoff, 1983

———— et al: Randomized comparison of radiation therapy and nitrosoureas for the treatment of malignant glioma of the brain. N Engl J Med 303:1323, 1980

WARA WM: Radiation therapy for brain tumors. Cancer 55:2291, 1985

WASSERSTROM WR: Diagnosis and treatment of leptomeningeal metastases from solid tumors. Cancer 49:759, 1982

WEISS L et al: Brain Metastases, Boston, Hall, 1980

YOUNG DP: Neurological complications of chemotherapy, in Neurological Complications of Therapy, A Silverstein (ed). Mount Kisco, NY, Futura Publishing Co, 1982, pp 57–113

346 PYOGENIC INFECTIONS OF THE CENTRAL NERVOUS SYSTEM

DONALD H. HARTER / ROBERT G. PETERSDORF

Pyogenic infections of the cranial contents originate in one of two ways, by hematogenous spread or by extension from surface structures, paranasal sinuses, osteomyelitic foci in the skull, penetrating cranial injuries, congenital sinus tracts, or following neurosurgical procedures.

ACUTE BACTERIAL MENINGITIS

DEFINITION Bacterial meningitis may be defined as an inflammation of the pia-arachnoid and the fluid residing in the space which it encloses and also that in the ventricles of the brain. Since the subarachnoid space is continuous around the brain, spinal cord, and the optic nerves, an infective agent (or tumor cells or blood) gaining entry to any one part of it may extend immediately to all of it, even its most remote recesses; therefore, meningitis is always *cerebrospinal*. It also reaches the ventricles, either directly or by reflux through the basal foramens of Magendie and Luschka.

PATHOLOGY The effect of bacteria or other organisms in the subarachnoid space is to cause an inflammatory reaction in the pia and arachnoid and in the cerebrospinal fluid (CSF); in pyogenic meningitis, pus accumulates in this space. The infective agent or its toxin, if allowed sufficient time to act, injures those structures which lie within the subarachnoid space (cranial and spinal roots) or ventricles (choroid plexuses) and adjacent to it (pial arteries and veins, underlying cerebral and cerebellar cortices, subpial white matter of the spinal cord, peripheral fibers of optic nerves, ependymal and subependymal tissues). In addition, purulent material may interfere with the flow of CSF from the ventricles or along the subarachnoid space over the brainstem, with resulting obstructive hydrocephalus. Although the outer arachnoidal membrane proves to be a remarkably effective barrier to the extension of infection, some reaction in the cranial subdural space and even in the inner surface of the dura and the spinal epidural space may occur. This happens more often in infants, approximately 15 percent of whom develop subdural effusions in response to meningitis, than in adults.

The most immediate clinical effects of acute subarachnoid suppuration, distinguishing it from infections in other parts of the body, are severe headache, vomiting, drowsiness, stupor, or coma, and, occasionally, convulsions. The one clinical sign of importance is stiffness of the neck (resistance to passive movement) on forward bending. Kernig's and Brudzinski's signs are of the same nature but less reliable.

ETIOLOGY The causes of bacterial meningitis vary with age as follows:

1 *Streptococcus pneumoniae* (see Chap. 93) causes 30 to 50 percent of cases in adults, 10 to 20 percent in children, and up to 5 percent of cases in infants.
2 *Neisseria meningitidis* (see Chap. 103) causes from 10 to 35 percent of cases in adults and from 25 to 40 percent in children up to age 15. It is a rare cause in infants.
3 *Haemophilus influenzae*, type B (see Chap. 109) is responsible for 40 to 60 percent of cases in children, but for only 1 to 3 percent in adults and for virtually none in infants.

Also important in the etiology of meningitis are *Staphylococcus aureus* and *Staph. epidermidis;* the latter accounts for 75 percent of infections associated with shunting procedures for hydrocephalus. Other causative organisms include group B streptococci, particularly in infants; anaerobic or microaerophilic streptococci and gram-negative bacilli, usually in association with brain abscess, epidural abscess, head trauma, neurosurgical procedures, or cranial thrombophlebitis; *Escherichia coli* and other Enterobacteriaceae such as *Klebsiella-Enterobacter, Proteus, Citrobacter, Pseudomonas,* and *Acinetobacter calcoaceticus,* usually as a consequence of head trauma, neurosurgical procedures, spinal anesthesia, lumbar puncture, or shunting procedures to relieve hydrocephalus. Heretofore, gram-negative bacilli were associated most often with neonatal meningitis, but the spectrum has shifted to adults with debilitating diseases and other predisposing causes. Almost one-fifth of bacterial meningitis cases occurring in persons 50 years of age or older are due to gram-negative enteric bacteria. The outcome in this group has been notoriously poor. Rare meningeal pathogens include *Salmonella, Shigella, Clostridium perfringens,* and *Neisseria gonorrhoeae.*

The changing etiology of bacterial meningitis is reflected by the appearance of *Listeria monocytogenes* as a major pathogen, particularly in elderly, debilitated patients or in those with immunosuppression secondary to transplantation, receiving therapy for cancer, or with connective tissue diseases. Alcoholism and high-dose steroids also appear to be predisposing factors. *Listeria* meningitis accounts for approximately 2 percent of all reported cases of bacterial meningitis in the United States. The mortality rate in the adult group with severe underlying disease is 70 percent.

EPIDEMIOLOGY AND CLINICAL SETTING The incidence of bacterial meningitis is between 4.6 and 10 cases per 100,000 persons per year. *H. influenzae* is the most frequent cause, followed by *N. meningitidis* and *S. pneumoniae.* About 70 percent of all cases occur in children under the age of 5. Pneumococcal, *H. influenzae,* and meningococcal infections have a worldwide distribution, tending to occur more often in males and during the fall, winter, and spring. *H. influenzae* meningitis is the most frequent meningeal infection in children between 2 months and 3 years of age. Meningococcal infections occur most often in children and adolescents, but they are also encountered throughout most of adult life with a sharp decline after age 50. Meningococcal meningitis differs from other forms of meningitis because it may occur in epidemics. Pneumococcal meningitis predominates in adults over 40 years of age.

A variety of factors apart from age predispose to the development of certain types of acute bacterial meningitis. Acute otitis media and mastoiditis occur in about 25 percent of patients with pneumococcal meningitis, and pneumonia occurs in another 25 percent. Recent head injury is recorded in 10 to 20 percent of patients with pneumococcal meningitis and may give rise to recurrent meningitis because of persistent cerebrospinal fluid rhinorrhea. Pneumococcal meningitis also occurs in patients with sickle cell disease, Hodgkin's disease, or multiple myeloma; in urban general hospitals many adults who develop pneumococcal infections suffer from chronic alcoholism. Immunoglobulin deficiency (whether congenital or acquired), splenectomy, and renal or bone marrow transplantation also predispose patients to pneumococcal infection. Adults who develop *H. influenzae* meningitis should be suspected of harboring an anatomic defect (dermal sinus tract, old skull fracture) or abnormality of immune defenses, diabetes mellitus, or alcoholism. Meningitis caused by *Staph. aureus* usually follows neurosurgical procedures or a penetrating cranial wound. This organism and *Staph. epidermidis* account for the majority of cerebral ventricular shunt infections and occasionally neonatal omphalitis and meningitis. Gram-negative bacillary infections also complicate neurosurgical operations and other nosocomial diseases; they are assuming progressively greater importance in meningitis in adults. Bacterial meningitis can also occur by extension from an abscess of the psoas muscle.

PATHOGENESIS The three common meningeal pathogens are invasive and depend upon antiphagocytic capsular or surface antigens for survival in the tissues of the infected host; all express their pathogenicity largely in the form of extracellular proliferation. All three are inhabitants of the nasopharynx in a significant part of the population. It is evident from the frequency with which the carrier state is detected that nasal colonization is not a sufficient explanation for infection of the meninges. The factors which predispose the colonized patient to bloodstream invasion, which is the usual route by which bacteria reach the meninges, are obscure but include antecedent viral infections of the upper respiratory passages or, as in the case of the pneumococcus, infections in the lung. Once bloodborne, the factors which lead to meningeal localization of bacteria are unknown, but it has been postulated that pneumococci, *H. influenzae,* and meningococci possess a unique predilection for the meninges. Other possibilities are that the entry of bacteria into the subarachnoid space is facilitated by disruption of the blood-CSF barrier by trauma, circulating endotoxin, or an initial viral infection of the meninges.

Avenues other than the bloodstream by which bacteria can gain access to the meninges include congenital neuroectodermal defects, craniotomy sites, diseases of the middle ear and paranasal sinuses, and cranial trauma, notably skull fractures. Occasionally brain abscesses may rupture into the subarachnoid space or ventricles, infecting the meninges. The isolation of anaerobic streptococci, *Bacteroides* spp., or *Actinomyces* or of a mixture of microorganisms in the CSF should suggest the possibility of a brain abscess occurring as an antecedent to meningitis.

SYMPTOMATOLOGY Fever, headache, seizures, vomiting, impairment of consciousness, and stiff neck and back are common to bacterial meningitis irrespective of its etiology. When the initial symptoms are pain in the neck or abdomen, a confusional state, or delirium, the diagnosis is much more difficult. Three patterns of onset have been documented. In approximately 25 percent of patients, meningitis has a fulminant onset and patients become seriously ill within 24 h, usually without antecedent respiratory tract infections. In over 50 percent, meningitis develops over 1 to 7 days and is associated with respiratory symptoms. Slightly less than 20 percent have meningeal symptoms after 1 to 3 weeks of respiratory symptoms.

In children, the onset is often nonspecific. Fever and vomiting are more frequent than headache. There is a higher incidence of seizures, and the error of misinterpreting seizures as febrile convulsions is greater. The classic signs of meningitis may often be minimal in elderly, debilitated patients where low-grade fever and changes in mental status may occur without headache or nuchal rigidity.

There are certain special clinical features that correlate with particular types of meningitis. Meningococcal meningitis should always be suspected in epidemics of meningitis; when the evolution is extremely rapid; when the onset is attended by a morbilliform, petechial, or purpuric skin eruption, larger ecchymoses, and lividity of skin of lower parts of the body; and if circulatory collapse has occurred. Since a rash accompanies approximately 50 percent of meningococcal infections, its presence should dictate immediate institution of therapy for a neisserial infection, even though similar rashes may be observed with echovirus type 9 meningitis and rarely with staphylococcal, *H. influenzae,* and streptococcal meningitis. Recurrent systemic infections should lead to the suspicion of complement deficiency. A family history of fulminant meningococcal disease in males in skipped generations suggests properdin deficiency. Pneumococcal meningitis is usually preceded by an infection in the lungs, ears, and sinuses, and the heart valves may be affected. In addition a pneumococcal etiology should be suspected in patients suffering from alcoholism, sickle cell disease, and basal skull fracture and following splenectomy or organ transplantation. *H. influenzae* meningitis usually follows upper respiratory and ear infections in young children.

The signs of meningeal irritation—stiff neck or positive Kernig's and Brudzinski's signs—may be absent in the very young, the very old, or the severely obtunded. Signs of focal cerebral disease, although seldom prominent, are more frequent in pneumococcal and influenzal meningitis and are associated with a comparatively poor prognosis. Seizures are encountered most often in infants with *H. influenzae* meningitis. In some instances they are caused by hypoglycemia or penicillin neurotoxicity, especially the latter if they are preceded by myoclonus of the face and extremities. Some of the more transitory focal cerebral signs may represent postictal phenomena (Todd's paralysis); stable, local, cerebral lesions are probably the result of vasculitis and occlusion of cerebral veins with infarction of cerebral tissue, or they may connote localization of pus as occurs in brain abscess or subdural empyema. Abnormalities involving the third, fourth, and sixth as well as other cranial nerves are particularly frequent with pneumococcal meningitis.

LABORATORY FINDINGS   The alterations of the cerebrospinal fluid are diagnostic. The *number of leukocytes* in the CSF ranges between 1000 and 100,000 per milliliter but averages between 5000 and 20,000. Cell counts above 50,000 per milliliter raise suspicion of the possibility of a brain abscess having ruptured into the ventricle (ventricular empyema). Neutrophilic leukocytes generally predominate, but an increasing proportion of mononuclear cells are found in the exudate as the infection continues, especially in partially treated meningitis. CSF lymphocytosis occurs in about one-third of bacterial meningitis patients with CSF cell counts of 1000 per milliliter or less. In the early stages careful cytologic examination may reveal some of the mononuclear cells to be myelocytes or young neutrophils. Later, as treatment takes effect, the proportions of lymphocytes, plasma cells, and histiocytes steadily increase.

The CSF *pressure* is so consistently elevated (above 180 mm-H_2O) that a normal or low pressure on the initial lumbar puncture in a case of suspected bacterial meningitis should raise the possibility that the needle was partially occluded or that the spinal arachnoid space was blocked.

The *protein levels* of CSF are higher than 45 mg/dL in 90 percent of cases, and most determinations fall in the range of 150 to 500 mg/dL.

The *sugar concentration* of CSF is depressed, usually to a level lower than 40 mg/dL or less than 40 percent of the blood sugar concentration (measured concomitantly), provided the latter is less than 250 mg/dL. However in atypical or "culture-negative cases," other conditions associated with a depressed CSF glucose should be considered. These include hypoglycemia from any cause, sarcoidosis of the central nervous system, meningeal carcinomatosis or gliomatosis, fungal or tuberculous meningitis, and subarachnoid hemorrhage. In acute cases of pyogenic meningitis, the CSF glucose concentration often approaches zero.

Gram stain of sedimented CSF permits identification of the causative agent in most cases of bacterial meningitis; it will be positive in about three-fourths of patients with untreated bacterial meningitis. Pneumococci and *H. influenzae* are identified more readily than are meningococci. Small numbers of gram-negative diplococci present within leukocytes may be indistinguishable from nuclear material which may also be gram-negative and of the same shape. In such cases a thin film of uncentrifuged CSF may lend itself more readily to morphologic interpretation than will a smear of sedimented CSF. The commonest errors in reading Gram-stained smears of CSF are misinterpretation of precipitated dye or debris as gram-positive cocci and confusion of pneumococci with *H. influenzae. Haemophilus* organisms may stain heavily at the poles so that they resemble gram-positive diplococci, and older pneumococci often lose their capacity to take a gram-positive stain. *Listeria monocytogenes* may be misidentified as a "diphtheroid" or hemolytic streptococcus in the microbiology laboratory. Staining with acridine orange and examination under a fluorescence microscope may demonstrate bacteria not observed with the Gram stain.

Cerebrospinal fluid cultures are positive in 70 to 80 percent of cases. When brain abscess is suspected, anaerobic cultures should be made, and meningococci should be cultured under 10% CO_2 (see Chap. 83). Partially treated meningitis poses a most difficult problem in diagnosis because cultures are often negative. The measurement of bacterial antigen in the CSF by latex agglutination tests or countercurrent immune electrophoresis (CIE) to determine the presence of a specific capsular polysaccharide associated with *H. influenzae* type B, *S. pneumoniae*, and meningococcal serogroups A, B, C, and Y has been helpful. It has limited value in *E. coli* and streptococcal group B infections. Latex agglutination appears the more sensitive of the two procedures. Detection of antigen in the serum or urine of bacterial meningitis patients is not a sensitive diagnostic method. The concentration of bacterial antigen diminishes as treatment progresses. Failure to detect antigen does not rule out bacterial meningitis.

The *Limulus* amebocyte gelation assay for endotoxin may be of diagnostic help, particularly in meningitis with trauma or following neurosurgery, where infection with *N. meningitidis* and *H. influenzae* (which also give a positive result) are uncommon causes. Measurements of the CSF C-reactive protein, lactic acid concentration, and lactic dehydrogenase (LDH) activity and isoenzyme pattern have been reported to be of help in differentiating bacterial from viral meningitis. The accuracy and usefulness of these tests are limited because elevated levels have been observed in a variety of conditions other than meningitis. Repeat CSF examination may provide an answer when the diagnosis is in question.

In addition to CSF cultures, *blood cultures* should always be obtained because they are positive in 40 to 60 percent of patients with *H. influenzae* and with meningococcal and pneumococcal meningitis and may provide the only definitive clue to the causative agent (if CSF cultures are negative). Routine cultures of the pharynx or external ear are as often misleading as helpful because pneumococci, *H. influenzae,* and meningococci are such common inhabitants of these locations. However, culture of pus from the middle ear or sinuses is often helpful.

The *blood leukocyte count* is generally elevated, and usually there is a shift to the left. Most patients with meningitis are sufficiently ill to require determination of blood urea nitrogen and serum electrolytes. These may be abnormal because of severe dehydration and may reveal inappropriate secretion of antidiuretic hormone (AVP) with resultant hyponatremia.

ROENTGENOGRAPHIC STUDIES   Patients with bacterial meningitis should have x-rays of the chest, skull, and sinuses as soon as possible after admission. Chest x-rays are particularly important because they may reveal a silent area of pneumonitis or abscess. Sinus and skull films may provide clues to the presence of cranial osteomyelitis, paranasal sinusitis, or skull fracture. Computerized tomography (CT scan) is usually not necessary in bacterial meningitis and is normal early in most infections. In severe cases there may be evidence of cerebritis, vascular occlusions, and encephalomalacia. Later in the course, CT will detect hydrocephalus, brain abscess, and subdural effusions or subdural empyema. If bacterial meningitis is suspected and the patient does not have papilledema or focal neurologic findings, lumbar puncture should not be delayed while waiting for a CT scan to be done.

COMPLICATIONS OF BACTERIAL MENINGITIS   The longer the duration of meningitis and the less effective the treatment, the greater the chances that complications and neurologic residua will develop. The cranial nerve palsies, usually third, sixth, seventh, and eighth nerves, which occur in some 10 to 20 percent of cases usually disappear within a few weeks. Approximately 10 percent of infants and children who have bacterial meningitis will be left with persistent unilateral or bilateral sensory hearing loss. The cochlea may be damaged by infection as it passes from the meninges along the cochlear duct. Deafness is especially frequent with pneumococcal and meningococcal meningitis. If focal and lateralizing neurologic signs last for some days or occur late in the course of meningitis, they are usually indicative of a vasculitis and cerebral infarction. Such lesions are most extensive in children with *H. influenzae* meningitis who are inadequately treated. If these lesions are extensive, they may leave the child retarded and epileptic. Persistent coma is more common in pneumococcal meningitis in adults. In infants or very young children with bacterial meningitis (particularly due to *H. influenzae*), prolonged alteration in state of consciousness or increased intracranial pressure (ICP) should raise the suspicion of obstructive hydrocephalus and subdural effusions.

DIFFERENTIAL DIAGNOSIS The diagnosis of bacterial meningitis is not difficult, providing a high index of suspicion is maintained. All febrile patients with lethargy, headache, or confusion of sudden onset, even if only low-grade fever is present, should be subjected to lumbar puncture. It is particularly important to consider meningitis in febrile, confused alcoholic patients. Too often the symptoms are mistakenly ascribed to inebriation, delirium tremens, or hepatic encephalopathy until the CSF reveals a meningitis.

Bacterial meningitis can be diagnosed definitively only by examination of the CSF. Viral meningoencephalitis and tuberculous, leptospiral, and fungal meningitides often enter into the differential diagnosis. Also to be considered are Behçet's syndrome, a disease characterized by recurrent oral and genital ulcers along with meningitis, and Mollaret's meningitis, which consists of recurrent episodes of fever, headache, and meningeal irritation accompanied by a leukocytosis in the CSF.

The diagnosis of other intracranial suppurative diseases is detailed below.

PROGNOSIS The case fatality rate for bacterial meningitis in the United States approximates 14 percent; it is highest for gram-negative and miscellaneous causes of meningitis. Of the three common forms of meningitis, pneumococcal meningitis is the most lethal. The triad of pneumococcal meningitis, pneumonia, and endocarditis has a particularly high fatality rate. The case fatality rate of *H. influenzae* or meningococcal meningitis has remained fixed at 5 to 15 percent for many years. Also in meningococcal infection, because of the fulminating nature of the disease and the often complicating adrenocortical necrosis (Waterhouse-Friderichsen syndrome), the mortality rate remains significant. Old age, infancy, abrupt onset, bacteremia, coma, seizures, and a variety of concomitant diseases including alcoholism, diabetes mellitus, multiple myeloma, and head trauma all worsen the prognosis.

It is often impossible to explain the death of the patient or at least to trace it to a single specific mechanism. Bacteremia with hypotension or brain swelling and bilateral temporal and/or cerebellar herniation are clearly implicated in the deaths of some patients during the initial 48 h. These events may occur in bacterial meningitis of any etiology; however, some observations suggest that they are more important in meningococcal infection. There is experimental evidence that acute centrally mediated respiratory failure (rather than circulatory collapse) is the major mechanism of early death. Deaths occurring later during the course of illness may be attributed to necrosis of brain tissue and respiratory failure, often consequent to aspiration pneumonia.

TREATMENT Antimicrobials Bacterial meningitis is a medical emergency; the rapid destruction of bacteria in the meninges and in the CSF is essential to survival. For this reason, bactericidal drugs should be used where possible. The following therapeutic regimens are recommended:

1 For adults with *pneumococcal* or *meningococcal meningitis*, penicillin G, 20 to 24 million units intravenously each day in four to six divided doses, is recommended; for children the dose of penicillin G should be 300,000 units per kilogram of body weight; and for neonates, up to one month of age, 150,000 to 200,000 units per kilogram of body weight. Chloramphenicol, 4 to 6 g given intravenously in divided doses, is an alternative treatment regimen in adults.

2 For children over 2 months of age with *H. influenzae* or uncomplicated meningitis of unknown etiology, ampicillin, 300 to 400 mg per kilogram of body weight intravenously in divided doses, plus chloramphenicol, 100 to 200 mg/kg per day intravenously, should be given. The reason for the use of two drugs is that 15 to 25 percent of *H. influenzae* isolates are resistant to ampicillin; a few strains of chloramphenicol-resistant *H. influenzae* have also been reported. In order to avoid interference between the two drugs, ampicillin should be given 30 min before chloramphenicol. Once the etiologic organism and its sensitivity have been determined, chloramphenicol can be discontinued if the organism is sensitive to ampicillin. In adults with *H. influenzae* meningitis, the doses of ampicillin (12 to 18 g daily) and chloramphenicol (4 to 6 g daily) are administered intravenously either as a constant infusion or in divided doses.

3 In adult patients with any of these types of bacterial meningitis who may be allergic to the penicillins, chloramphenicol in a dosage of 4 to 6 g per day intravenously may be used. The cephalosporins are questionable alternates for pneumococcal meningitis, and there have been some failures also in *H. influenzae* and meningococcal meningitis; hence, chloramphenicol is preferred in infections due to these organisms.

4 In community-acquired meningitis due to a gram-negative enteric bacillus, the organism is usually susceptible to third-generation cephalosporins; therapy should begin with either cefotaxime or moxalactam (2 g every 4 h). If gram-negative enteric meningitis is acquired in the hospital or follows head trauma or neurosurgery, *Pseudomonas aeruginosa* and *Acinetobacter calcoaceticus* are also likely pathogens and cefotaxime or moxalactam is given in combination with tobramycin intravenously (5 mg/kg daily) and intrathecally (8 to 10 mg daily). The antibiotic regimen can be modified when the bacterial species has been identified and its sensitivity to antimicrobials determined. Trimethoprim-sulfamethoxazole (TMP-SMX) may provide a useful alternative for gram-negative meningitis when the causative agent is resistant to cephalosporins such as cefotaxime.

5 Meningitis due to *Staphylococcus aureus* should be treated with a penicillinase-resistant penicillin rather than penicillin G because over 80 percent of isolates are penicillin-resistant. Nafcillin or oxacillin in daily doses of 12 to 18 g can be used alone or in combination with rifampin, 600 mg each day, in adult patients. Patients allergic to penicillin can be given vancomycin, 2.0 mg intravenously in divided doses.

6 When the etiology of meningitis is unknown, the drugs of choice are as follows: in adults, ampicillin 12 g per day in divided doses; in children, ampicillin 400 mg/kg and chloramphenicol 100 mg/kg over 24 h; and in neonates, ampicillin 100 to 200 mg/kg per day and an aminoglycoside, usually gentamicin (5 mg/kg per day), are recommended.

7 Foci of infection in the paranasal sinuses or mastoids, in an infected shunt, or in cranial osteomyelitis should be identified so that appropriate drainage may be carried out when the acute episode of meningitis has subsided.

8 In most patients bacterial meningitis need not be treated for longer than 10 days except when there is a persistent parameningeal focus of infection. Antibiotics should be administered in full doses parenterally (preferably intravenously) throughout the period of treatment. Treatment failures with several drugs, notably ampicillin, are attributable to oral or intramuscular administration, resulting in inadequate concentration in the CSF.

9 Repeated lumbar punctures are not necessary to follow the course of therapy as long as the patient is doing well. The CSF sugar may remain low for a number of days after cultures become negative and should occasion concern only if bacteria are present. Likewise, persistent but steadily diminishing mononuclear pleocytosis, following pyogenic meningitis, is the rule. CSF examination at the end of treatment for bacterial meningitis in patients who have recovered clinically is not useful because it may lead to unnecessary detention in the hospital or fail to identify patients who need further treatment.

Adrenocortical steroids The few controlled studies available have demonstrated that steroids exert no beneficial effects in pyogenic meningitis. These drugs should not be used except possibly in overwhelming meningococcal sepsis or as an adjunct to intravenous mannitol in severe cerebral edema.

Other forms of therapy Intrathecal administration of enzymes to lyse excessive subarachnoid cellular exudate which may be associated with spinal block or hydrocephalus in the subacute stages of bacterial meningitis is of no value. There is also no evidence to support the therapeutic efficacy of repeated drainage of CSF. In fact, increased CSF pressure in the acute phases of bacterial meningitis is largely a consequence of cerebral edema, and lumbar puncture may predispose to temporal lobe or cerebellar herniation and death. Mannitol and urea have been employed apparently successfully in some cases of severe brain swelling with unusually high initial CSF pressures (>400 mmH$_2$O). Either should be accompanied by dexamethasone in relatively high doses. An adequate but not excessive amount of parenteral fluids should be given, and phenytoin should be given to control seizures. In children care should be taken to avoid hyponatremia and water intoxication—a cause of brain swelling. Subdural effusions should be drained repeatedly by subdural taps; if they persist after the infection has subsided, surgical removal may become necessary.

RECURRENT MENINGITIS

Recurrent attacks of bacterial meningitis usually follow in the wake of trauma. The interval between the traumatic episode and the initial bout of posttraumatic meningitis may be as long as several years. *S. pneumoniae* is the usual bacterial pathogen. Often it proves to be one of the higher serologic types, reflecting the predominance of such strains in nasal carriers. *Cerebrospinal fluid rhinorrhea* is present in most of these patients but may be transient. The patient with recurrent meningitis of inapparent origin should always be suspected of having a fistulous connection between the nasal sinuses and the subarachnoid space. The fistula is usually traumatic (old basal skull fracture), and the site is the frontal or ethmoid sinuses or the cribriform plate. The rhinorrhea may be difficult to demonstrate except by injection of a radioactive tracer into the CSF and watching for its appearance in nasal secretions. Cerebrospinal fluid rhinorrhea may also be detected by measuring the glucose concentration of nasal secretions. The usual mucous secretions contain little glucose, but in CSF rhinorrhea the amount approximates that in CSF. The prognosis in recurrent meningitis is remarkably benign, and the mortality is much lower than in ordinary pneumococcal meningitis. Nevertheless, vaccination of these patients with pneumococcal vaccine is indicated, and long-term prophylactic chemotherapy with penicillin V should be considered. Treatment of recurrent meningitis is similar to that for first bouts. Attempts to demonstrate CSF rhinorrhea should be made only after the acute infection has subsided; if evidence of a fistula is found, surgical repair should be considered.

Other causes of recurrent meningitis include congenital bony abnormalities of the inner ear, congenital dermal sinus tract, and tumors at the base of the skull.

SUBDURAL EMPYEMA

DEFINITION Subdural empyema is a suppurative process in the cranial subdural space between the inner surface of the dura and the outer of the arachnoid. The proper term for this condition is not *abscess* but *empyema*, indicating suppuration in a preformed space. Subdural empyema accounts for approximately one-fifth of all localized intracranial infections. About three-fourths of cases are unilateral, and the remainder bilateral, usually in the parafalcial region.

ETIOLOGY The infection usually gains entry to the subdural space from the frontal or ethmoid sinuses or, less often, from the mastoid cells. These cases are termed *primary* subdural empyema. The subdural space may also become infected by extension of bacteria from a contiguous site of osteomyelitis or from a brain abscess. Septic thrombophlebitis and venous drainage of bacteria to the subdural space may be important in its development. Rarely has it been observed with bloodstream infections. Secondary subdural empyema usually follows neurosurgical drainage of a chronic subdural hematoma.

The bacterial flora in subdural empyema closely resembles that seen in chronic sinusitis and brain abscess; it may be polymicrobial.

Isolates in order of decreasing frequency include aerobic streptococci, staphylococci, microaerophilic and anaerobic streptococci, aerobic gram-negative rods, and other anaerobes.

PATHOLOGY A collection of subdural pus in quantities of a few milliliters to 100 to 200 mL lies over the cerebral hemisphere. It is often mistaken for meningitis. The arachnoid, when cleared of exudate, is cloudy, and thrombosis of meningeal veins may be seen. The underlying cerebral hemisphere is depressed, and in fatal cases there is often an ipsilateral temporal lobe pressure cone. Microscopic studies demonstrate various degrees of organization of the exudate on the inner surface of the dura and infiltration of the underlying pia with small numbers of neutrophilic leukocytes, lymphocytes, and mononuclear cells. There is superficial thrombophlebitis; the thrombi in cerebral veins appear to begin on the outer side (toward the empyema). The thrombosis extends to other dural sinuses, and the superficial layers of the cerebral cortex undergo ischemic necrosis, which probably accounts for the unilateral seizures and signs of disordered cerebral function.

SYMPTOMATOLOGY AND LABORATORY FINDINGS The usual history includes chronic sinusitis or otitis with a recent flare-up and evidence of local pain and increase in purulent nasal or aural discharge. The illness is severe and progressive. Generalized headache, fever, vomiting, and a depressed sensorium are the first indications of intracranial spread. They are followed within a few days by localizing signs including focal motor seizures, hemiplegia, hemianesthesia, and aphasia. Papilledema is present in one-half of the patients at the time of diagnosis. Stupor or coma develops rapidly as the cerebral symptoms progress. Fever is usually present, but the neck is not always stiff. There is a leukocytosis and increased erythrocyte sedimentation rate. Lumbar puncture poses a distinct risk because it may precipitate transtentorial herniation. It is generally contraindicated if the diagnosis of subdural empyema is suspected. When the CSF is examined, increased pressure, a raised white blood cell count in the range of 50 to 1000 per milliliter including both neutrophils and lymphocytes, elevated protein (75 to 300 mg/dL), and normal sugar values are the usual findings. Unless subdural empyema is complicated by bacterial meningitis, no bacteria can be recovered from the CSF. In the type of subdural empyema that follows drainage of a chronic subdural hematoma, the onset is more indolent, fever is lower, and there is usually a local wound infection.

DIAGNOSIS Skull films may show involvement of the sinus or mastoid. CT scanning is the method of choice for establishing the diagnosis and location of a subdural empyema. The usual CT scan appearance is a crescentic or elliptical hypodense area lying directly below the cranial vault or adjacent to the falx cerebri. After administration of contrast, the CT scan may demonstrate an intense line of enhancement between the subdural collection and cerebral cortex. False-negative CT scans have been reported. When there is question about the diagnosis after CT scanning, cerebral angiography may be required to define the lesion. In secondary empyemas, CT scan is invariably positive. Four conditions need to be distinguished clinically from subdural empyema: cerebral thrombophlebitis, brain abscess, viral encephalitis, and acute hemorrhagic encephalitis (see Chap. 347).

TREATMENT Drainage of pus is the single most important part of treatment. In particular, it is important to institute drainage early because delaying it sharply increases the mortality rate. Specimens of pus obtained at surgery should be transported to the laboratory in oxygen-free containers and cultured both aerobically and anaerobically. Appropriate empiric antibiotic therapy consists of 20 million units of penicillin per day plus chloramphenicol, 4 g per day, administered intravenously. Without such massive antimicrobial therapy and surgery, most patients will die, usually within 7 to 14 days, often while the unsuspecting physician and surgeon are waiting for better localization of an assumed cerebral abscess, the most commonly mistaken diagnosis. Antibiotic therapy can be made optimally when final culture and sensitivity results are available. It should be continued for 3 to 6 weeks. Drugs to reduce cerebral edema and to prevent seizures should be given. Mortality in subdural empyema is now between 10 and 20 percent. Long-term sequelae include seizures, hemiparesis, and dysphasia.

CRANIAL EXTRADURAL ABSCESS

This condition is almost invariably associated with osteomyelitis in a cranial bone which originates from an infection in the ear or paranasal sinuses. Pus and granulation tissue accumulate on the outer surface of the dura, separating it from the cranial bone. Symptomatically, the effects are those of a local inflammatory process: frontal or auricular pain, purulent discharge from the sinuses or ear, and fever and local tenderness. Unrelenting headache is a frequent complaint. Focal neurologic signs are uncommon. A cranial epidural abscess characteristically enlarges too slowly to cause sudden neurologic abnormalities. The CSF is usually clear and under normal pressure but may contain a few lymphocytes and neutrophils (20 to 100 per milliliter) and slightly raised protein concentration. CT scan is the diagnostic procedure of choice. False-negative scans have been reported; the diagnosis can then be made by contrast-enhanced CT scan or angiography. Treatment consists of prompt surgical drainage of the epidural space and appropriate systemic antibiotics. The primary sinusitis or mastoiditis, from which the extradural infection has arisen, may also require surgical drainage.

SPINAL EPIDURAL ABSCESS

This type of abscess possesses unique clinical features and constitutes an important neurologic and neurosurgical emergency. It is discussed in Chap. 353.

INTRACRANIAL THROMBOPHLEBITIS

The lateral, cavernous, and superior longitudinal sinuses are relatively uncommon sites of infection. Usually there is evidence that the intracranial process has extended from the middle ear and mastoid cells, the paranasal sinuses, and skin around the upper lip, nose, and eyes.

LATERAL SINUS THROMBOPHLEBITIS In lateral sinus thrombophlebitis, which usually follows otitis media and mastoiditis, the earache and mastoid tenderness are succeeded, after a period of days to a few weeks, by fever, headache, nausea, and vomiting due to increased ICP. There may be swelling over the mastoid region, distention of veins, and tenderness of the jugular vein in the neck. With jugular vein involvement, there may be neck pain and restriction of movement. Drowsiness and coma are common. Papilledema (unilateral in some patients) is seen in about one-half of cases. Convulsions occur, but focal neurologic findings are infrequent. Abducens nerve paralysis and trigeminal nerve involvement (Gradenigo's syndrome) are found when there is spread to the inferior petrosal sinus.

CAVERNOUS SINUS THROMBOPHLEBITIS In this condition, which is usually secondary to oculonasal infections, the clinical syndrome is one of orbital edema, chemosis, venous congestion, and evidence of palsy of the third, fourth, ophthalmic fifth, and sixth cranial nerves. Later spread through the circular sinus to the opposite cavernous sinus results in bilateral symptoms and signs. The posterior part of the cavernous sinus may be infected via the superior and inferior petrosal veins without the occurrence of orbital edema or ophthalmoplegia. The patient appears acutely ill with high fever, headache, nausea, and vomiting. There is eye pain and the orbits are tender to pressure. Chemosis, edema, and cyanosis of the upper face are present; the bulbs are proptosed. Sensorium may remain clear until late in the infection. Ophthalmoplegia, pupillary changes, retinal hemorrhages, papilledema, and sensory changes in the ophthalmic division of the trigeminal nerve may be present. The CSF is usually normal unless there is associated meningitis or subdural empyema. The only effective therapy in the fulminant variety, associated with thrombosis of the anterior portion of the sinus, has been antimicrobial therapy usually aimed at coagulase-positive staphylococci (see Chap. 94) and occasionally gram-negative pathogens as well. Anticoagulants have been used occasionally, but their value has not been proved. Cavernous sinus thrombosis must be differentiated from mucormycosis which may cause a similar clinical picture in uncontrolled diabetics or in immunosuppressed patients (see Chap. 147).

SUPERIOR LONGITUDINAL SINUS THROMBOPHLEBITIS The superior sagittal sinus may become infected by spread from the lateral or cavernous sinuses or by extension from the nasal cavities, from a focus of osteomyelitis, or from epidural or subdural infection. General signs include fever, headache, and papilledema. Edema of the forehead and anterior part of the scalp occur. The typical neurologic picture is one of unilateral convulsions and hemiplegia, first on one side of the body, then on the other, because of extension into the superior cerebral veins. The paralysis may be predominantly monoplegic and involve mainly the legs.

Cerebral angiography with particular attention to the late filling of venous sinuses is the most specific diagnostic test. Digital subtraction angiography has been useful in the diagnosis of sagittal sinus thrombosis. CT scans show normal or small ventricles, hemorrhages, low-density lesions, and a high-density lesion in the involved sinus. Postcontrast CT scan may demonstrate a filing defect in the involved sinus. Radionuclide dynamic and static scans may indicate termination of isotope activity in the midportion of the sinus.

All types of thrombophlebitis, especially those related to ear and paranasal sinus infection, may be complicated by other forms of intracranial suppuration including bacterial meningitis, subdural empyema, or brain abscess. The proper treatment of major sinus thrombosis due to infection is the systemic administration of appropriate antibiotics in high dosage and surgical drainage of infected bone and tissues. The initiating focus should be brought under control by surgery if necessary, once the patient's condition permits such a procedure. To operate on the primary focus before medical treatment is instituted is to court disaster. The better plan is to institute antibiotic therapy; surgery on the ears or sinuses should be decided upon only after the infection is controlled. In general, anticoagulants should be avoided because brain hemorrhage may be produced. Residual neurologic deficits are frequent, but the prognosis for recovery is good when optimal treatment is given early in the illness.

ASEPTIC THROMBOSIS OF INTRACRANIAL VENOUS SINUSES This may develop after sinus and ear infections and may lead to an obscure increase in intracranial pressure because of the occlusion of one lateral or superior sagittal sinus. The more common conditions which may be accompanied by aseptic thrombosis are postpartum and postoperative states, which are often characterized by thrombocytosis and hyperfibrinogenemia; use of oral contraceptive drugs; congenital heart disease and marasmus in infants; systemic cancer; Behçet's disease; sickle cell disease; primary or secondary polycythemia; disseminated intravascular coagulation; and cryofibrinogenemia.

MALIGNANT EXTERNAL OTITIS

This paracranial infection is found in elderly patients with diabetes mellitus. Beginning in the external auditory canal, it spreads from the outer ear to the soft tissues below the temporal bone and invades the parotid gland, temporomandibular joint, masseter muscle, and temporal bone. *Pseudomonas aeruginosa* is responsible for the infection. The high mortality rate (initially reported at 40 percent) led to the term *malignant* for the condition; the adjective *necrotizing* or *invasive* may be preferable.

Symptoms and signs include pain in the ear with or without a purulent discharge, swelling of the parotid gland, trismus, and paralysis of the sixth to twelfth cranial nerves. Death is usually due to the development of meningitis. CT scan findings include obliteration of the normal fat planes in the subtemporal area and patchy destruction of the bony cortex of the mastoid. Radionuclide scans using Tc 99m or Ga67 citrate are helpful in the initial identification of the disease and in following the course of the infection.

Prolonged intravenous administration of tobramycin and carbenicillin is used to treat the condition. Surgical debridement may also be indicated. Antibiotics should be given for 6 weeks or for at least 2 weeks after all symptoms have resolved; treatment for basilar skull involvement may need to last as long as 3 months.

BRAIN ABSCESS

PATHOGENESIS Most of the focal suppurative intracranial processes of this type are linked to chronic ear and sinus or pulmonary infections. The majority of brain abscesses are due to disease of the middle ear, mastoids, or paranasal sinuses. Infection spreads to the brain directly across bone and dura mater or through vascular channels by septic thrombophlebitis or arteritis.

With frontal or ethmoid sinusitis, the abscess forms in the frontal lobe; with middle ear or mastoid infection, the abscess localizes to the temporal lobe or cerebellum. Of the remaining cases, a small portion are due to contaminated penetrating wounds or postoperative infections; the rest are metastatic. Of these, about half are traceable to pleuropulmonary disease—usually bronchiectasis, empyema, lung abscess, or bronchopleural fistula. In the rest, the source of infection may be skin, bone, teeth, or heart. In about 10 percent of cases, the source cannot be ascertained. Brain abscess is seldom a consequence of bacterial meningitis. Brain abscess also occurs in patients whose immune systems are defective or suppressed. In these instances, nonbacterial causes such as fungi, protozoans, and helminths may be recovered from the abscess.

Brain abscess is particularly frequent in congenital heart disease with right-to-left shunts (e.g., tetralogy of Fallot) and may also complicate arteriovenous vascular abnormalities of the lung, as in cases of familial telangiectasia (Osler-Rendu-Weber syndrome). When brain abscess is associated with a right-to-left cardiac shunt, it is frequently single. With cranial trauma, the location of the abscess will depend on the site of the penetrating wound. In contrast to the otogenic and rhinogenic abscesses, abscesses of hematogenous origin are frequently multiple and may occur anywhere in the brain.

Bacterial endocarditis rarely gives rise to brain abscess. Instead, the picture is one of focal embolic encephalitis with or without signs of embolic vascular disease elsewhere (see Chap. 188). In subacute endocarditis the emboli are sterile and cause only infarction and mycotic aneurysms. The CSF may contain a small number of neutrophilic leukocytes, lymphocytes, and red blood cells; the protein level may be elevated, but cultures are sterile and sugar values remain normal. In acute bacterial endocarditis, miliary abscesses and purulent meningitis may develop. There may be infarcts and there may be subarachnoid or intracerebral hemorrhages secondary to rupture of a mycotic aneurysm. Rarely do the miliary abscesses progress to large ones. Rapidly evolving cerebral signs in endocarditis are nearly always caused by embolic infarction or hemorrhage.

ETIOLOGY (See Chap. 102) Streptococci, including *S. milleri* (a member of the viridans group), other viridans and nonhemolytic streptococci, enterococci, β-hemolytic streptococci, and peptostreptococci are the most commonly isolated group of microorganisms. Next in order of frequency are members of the *Bacteroides* group, Enterobacteriaceae (*Proteus, Escherichia coli, Klebsiella*) and *Staphylococcus aureus*. Pneumococci, meningococci, and *Haemophilus influenzae* rarely cause brain abscess. In addition to *Bacteroides* and anaerobic streptococci, anaerobic actinomyces, veillonellae, and fusobacteria have been isolated. Bacterial species vary with the site

of the abscess—staphylococcal abscesses are usually a consequence of penetrating head trauma or bacteremia; enteric organisms are almost always associated with ear infections; anaerobic streptococci are commonly metastatic from the lung. Two or more species of bacteria are often identified in a single abscess, and mixtures of aerobes and anaerobes may be found.

PATHOLOGY The location of brain abscess in decreasing order of frequency is in frontal, parietal, temporal, and occipital lobes, followed by cerebellum and basal ganglia. Abscesses rarely occur in the pituitary gland or brainstem. Localized inflammatory necrosis and edema, septic thrombosis of vessels, and aggregates of degenerating leukocytes (suppurative encephalitis) represent the early reaction of bacterial invasion of the brain. This is followed by encapsulation of the liquefied brain and of accumulated pus. the lesion becomes encapsulated by fibroblasts and newly formed vessels, and the capsule thickens over a period of weeks. The meninges adjacent to the abscess, especially near the point of entry of infection, are infiltrated by neurotrophils, lymphocytes, and plasma cells. Cerebral edema associated with the abscess and products of bacterial metabolism (such as aerobically produced gas) result in increased ICP. The evolution of cerebral abscess can be divided into four stages: early cerebritis (1 to 3 days), late cerebritis (4 to 9 days) early capsule formation (10 to 13 days) and late capsule formation (14 days and later).

CLINICAL MANIFESTATIONS Most patients have symptoms for less than 2 weeks. Characteristically the clinical presentation is more like that of an expanding intracranial mass lesion than an infectious process. In patients with chronic ear, sinus, or pulmonary infections, a recent reactivation of the infection usually precedes the onset of cerebral symptoms. In a number of patients, evidence of CNS invasion is acute, and headache, vomiting, increasing obtundation, seizures, and a variety of localizing neurologic signs appear within a few days. In other patients, bacterial invasion of the brain substance may be asymptomatic or may be attended only by a transitory focal neurologic disorder. Sometimes stiff neck accompanies generalized headache, suggesting the diagnosis of meningitis. Early symptoms may subside or appear to respond to antimicrobials. Within a week or two, recurrent headache, slowness in mentation, focal or generalized convulsions, and obvious signs of increased intracranial pressure provide evidence of a mass in the brain. At this stage, the symptoms of infection are not conspicuous. Fever is present in less than half of the patients. Symptoms are usually progressive in their intensity. The majority of patients will have altered consciousness with lethargy, irritability, confusion, or coma.

Hemiplegia is the most common focal finding. Seizures, either focal or generalized, occur in about one-third of patients; papilledema and neck stiffness are present in about one-quarter of patients.

Patients demonstrate focal neurologic signs related to location of the abscess as described below.

Frontal lobe abscess Headache, drowsiness, inattention, and general impairment of mental function are prominent. Hemiparesis with unilateral motor seizures and expressive aphasia are the most frequent neurologic signs.

Temporal lobe abscess Headache is usually on the side of the abscess and is localized to the frontotemporal region. If the abscess lies in the dominant hemisphere, there is aphasia and anomia (inability to name objects). A homonymous upper quadrantic field defect may also be demonstrable owing to interruption of the inferior portion of the optic radiation. This may be the only sign in abscess of the right temporal lobe. Contralateral motor or sensory defects in the limbs tend to be minimal, though weakness of the lower face is often observed.

Cerebellar abscess Headache in the postauricular or suboccipital region is usually the first symptom and may at first be ascribed to infection in the mastoid cells. Coarse nystagmus and gaze weakness to the side of the lesion and a cerebellar ataxia of the ipsilateral arm and leg are present in most patients. As a rule, the signs of increased ICP are more prominent than those of focal cerebral disease. Mild contralateral or bilateral pyramidal signs may provide evidence of ipsilateral brainstem compression.

DIAGNOSIS   The diagnosis of a brain abscess depends on (1) a demonstrated source of infection in the ears, sinuses, or lungs or the presence of a right-to-left cardiac shunt, (2) evidence of increased ICP, and (3) focal cerebral or cerebellar signs. Clues to the origin of the abscess are often present on initial evaluation. They include chronic ear disease with discharge, sinus infection, orbital cellulitis, pharyngitis, infected skin wound, and chest infection.

Lumbar puncture in suspected brain abscess is potentially dangerous, particularly when the ICP is obviously elevated, and the information to be derived is not specific enough to justify the risk. Routine x-rays of the skull may demonstrate gas in an abscess cavity. The electroencephalogram (EEG) is usually abnormal with focal changes.

The CT scan is the most valuable procedure for visualizing brain abscess(es). It also demonstrates ventricular distortion, surrounding edema of white matter, and the thickness of the capsule; it enables close follow-up of therapy. Injection of iodine-containing contrast material will enhance the selectivity of the CT scan and will permit the visualization of an abscess from the early stage of focal cerebritis to a densely encapsulated mass demonstrated as a ''ring'' that is sharply demarcated both internally and externally with a homogenous central area of decreased attenuation. Generally only a CT scan is required to make the diagnosis. Peripheral ring enhancement may also be found in tumor, cerebral infarction, resolving hematoma, radiation necrosis, and recent surgery; these conditions may enter into the differential diagnosis of the CT scan findings. Experience with magnetic resonance imaging (MRI) of brain abscess is limited, but no specific features identifying the infectious nature of the mass lesion have been described. If CT scanning is not available, radionuclide brain scan is a reliable method for localizing brain abscess. If both CT and radionuclide scans are negative, there is little likelihood of cerebral abscess. Scanning procedures have supplanted arteriography in most instances.

When the typical clinical picture is present and CT scan corroborates the presence of a mass lesion, the diagnosis is easy. If there is no source of infection and there are only signs and symptoms of a mass lesion, the diagnosis may be difficult. Sometimes only surgical exploration will settle the issue.

TREATMENT   During the stage of acute suppurative cerebritis, intracranial operation accomplishes little and probably causes only additional trauma and swelling of brain tissue. There is good evidence that many brain abscesses visible by CT scanning can be cured at this stage by the administration of adequate doses of antimicrobials. Since the bacteriologic diagnosis must be presumptive, the most widely used regimen for adults consists of 20 to 40 million units of penicillin G and 4 to 6 g of chloramphenicol, both drugs being given intravenously in divided doses. This choice of antimicrobial agents is based on the preponderance of anaerobic streptococci and *Bacteroides* that are usually isolated from brain abscess. Metronidazole (500 mg every 6 h) with cefotaxime (12 gm daily) is an alternative method of treatment. Treatment should be continued for 6 to 8 weeks, and if there is clinical improvement and recovery during the course of therapy, surgical intervention can be withheld.

Selection of specific antimicrobials requires recovery of the responsible microorganism(s). Pus from the abscess cavity can be obtained by needle puncture at the time of craniotomy or by CT-guided percutaneous stereotactic operation. The specimen should be sent to the laboratory for Gram stain and for routine and anaerobic bacteriologic cultures. Specimens must be handled in a way that will not kill fastidious bacteria. They cannot be kept for too long a time in too small a volume of material or in the presence of preoperatively administered inhibitory antimicrobials. Pus can be delivered to the laboratory in a capped sterile syringe from which all the air has been

removed. Once the infecting bacteria have been identified and their sensitivities determined, the appropriate antibiotic regimen can be chosen.

Serial CT scanning and prompt, aggressive antibiotic treatment has avoided surgical intervention in many cases. The instances for medical management include presence of multiple abscess, abscesses located in deep brain structures, concomitant meningitis or ependymitis, the presence of a ventricular shunt, and an underlying debilitating disease.

ICP monitoring is important in the management of brain abscess patients. Initial elevation of ICP and threatening temporal lobe or cerebellar herniation should be managed by the prompt intravenous injection of urea, mannitol, or dexamethasone. Persistence or progression of high ICP manifested by deepening coma mandates operation, regardless of the stage of the abscess. Likewise, clear-cut evidence of a mass lesion that is not improving with antimicrobial therapy is an indication for surgery. Gas-containing abscesses should be surgically excised. The usual methods of treatment are unroofing and drainage by aspiration. If the abscess is superficial and encapsulated, total excision is sometimes attempted; if deep, aspiration and the injection of antimicrobial agents into the abscess are the only possible treatment methods, and they may have to be repeated.

PROGNOSIS   With the availability of CT scanning, more effective antimicrobials, and ICP monitoring, abscesses have been treated earlier and more effectively. Mortality has fallen to approximately 10 percent. Neurologic abnormalities, particularly focal epilepsy, are sometimes troublesome sequelae to brain abscess surgery. Following successful treatment of cerebral abscess in patients with congenital heart disease, correction of the cardiac anomaly is indicated to prevent recurrence.

REFERENCES

ANON JB, MILLER GW: Malignant external otitis. South Med J 77:1541, 1984

BLAQUIÈRE RM: The computed tomographic appearances of intra- and extracerebral abscesses. Br J Radiol 56:171, 1983

CHERUBIN CE, ENG RHK: Experience with the use of cefotaxime in the treatment of bacterial meningitis. Am J Med 80:398, 1986

DURACK DT: Prevention of central nervous system infections in patients at risk. Am J Med 76(5A):231, 1984

FEIGIN RD, DODGE PR: Bacterial meningitis: Newer concepts of pathophysiology and neurologic sequelae. Pediatr Clin North Am 23:541, 1976

GARVEY G: Current concepts of bacterial infections of the central nervous system: Bacterial meningitis and bacterial brain abscess. J Neurosurg 59:735, 1983

GORDON JJ et al: Meningitis due to *Staphylococcus aureus*. Am J Med 78:965, 1985

GORSE GJ et al: Bacterial meningitis in the elderly. Arch Intern Med 144:1603, 1984

HARRISON MJG: The clinical presentation of intracranial abscess. Q J Med 204:461, 1982

KAUFMAN DM et al: Subdural empyema: Analysis of 17 recent cases and review of the literature. Medicine 54:485, 1975

LeFROCK JL et al: Gram-negative bacillary meningitis. Med Clin North Am 69:243, 1985

MARTON KI, GEAN AD: The spinal tap: A new look at an old test. Ann Intern Med 104:840, 1986

MAYHALL CG et al: Ventriculostomy-related infections: A prospective epidemiological study. N Engl J Med 310:553, 1984

POLLOCK SS et al: Infection of the central nervous system by *Listeria monocytogenes:* A review of 54 adult and juvenile cases. Q J Med 211:331, 1984

RAO KCVG et al: Computed tomographic findings in cerebral sinus and venous thrombosis. Radiology 140:391, 1981

SCHLECH WF III et al: Bacterial meningitis in the United States, 1978 through 1981: The national bacterial meningitis surveillance study. JAMA 253:1749, 1985

---

347   VIRAL DISEASES OF THE CENTRAL NERVOUS SYSTEM: ASEPTIC MENINGITIS AND ENCEPHALITIS

DONALD H. HARTER / ROBERT G. PETERSDORF

Viruses can affect the central nervous system (CNS) in a variety of ways. Although much is known about the nature and replication of viruses, the correlation between viral properties and the type of the neurologic disease produced is inadequate or incomplete. Viruses that differ widely in their morphology, chemical composition, and replication can provoke identical clinical and pathologic changes in the CNS.

It is helpful to consider the time between the patient's first exposure to the viral agent and the appearance of disease, that is, to distinguish between CNS infections of a "fast" or "slow" nature. In fast or acute viral disease, neurologic changes occur very shortly after the patient first becomes infected by the virus. The illness follows a course of one to several weeks. In slow viral disease, the neurologic changes appear months to years after viral invasion, are insidious in development, and progress slowly.

ACUTE VIRAL CNS DISEASE

GENERAL CONSIDERATIONS Most viral CNS infections are the end result of preceding infection in other tissues and organs. There is usually a phase of extraneural viral replication before the nervous system becomes involved. Acute viral CNS infections are classified according to the clinical findings presented by the patient or, more indirectly, by the part of the nervous system involved by the disease process. In these terms, acute viral CNS disease is defined as meningitis, encephalitis, or myelitis, depending on the patient's symptoms and signs and the location of the infection. It is often difficult, however, to arrive at a single satisfactory localization on the basis of clinical findings alone. This leads to the use of compound terms such as meningoencephalitis or encephalomyelitis to describe the disease. This manner of classification is less than satisfactory because it gives no clear idea about the virus causing the condition.

Viruses vary in size, morphology, chemical composition, and effect on the host. Their common characteristics include a genome, which is either RNA or DNA surrounded by a protective protein shell; the fact that they multiply only inside the cell; and the fact that the initial step in replication involves separation of the genome from

its protective shell. They are divided into two broad categories on the basis of their nucleic acid content and then into major families and genera (Table 347-1). Certain common properties of viruses are important determinants of the disease they produce. Herpesviruses have a tendency to remain latent in cells. Togaviruses and bunyaviruses are transmitted by insect vectors. Enteroviruses replicate in the gastrointestinal tract and are transmitted by the oral-fecal route. Myxoviruses contain a segmented genome which is prone to genetic recombination. Selection of the most effective methods of virus isolation depends in great measure on the virus's properties. Knowledge of a virus's biochemical composition is of help in determining whether antiviral therapy can be used. Understanding the biologic features of viruses within the major families and genera permits associations which are impossible when the location of the disease process is considered alone (see Chap. 128).

ASEPTIC OR VIRAL MENINGITIS **Etiology** The term *aseptic meningitis* designates a disease characterized by an acute onset, meningeal symptoms, fever, cerebrospinal fluid (CSF) pleocytosis, and bacteriologically sterile cultures. The illness has a relatively benign clinical course of short duration, and recovery is the rule. With the introduction of more refined methods of viral isolation and the use of new culture techniques to define other microorganisms, it has become clear that aseptic meningitis is a syndrome of multiple etiologies. When viral infection produces the syndrome, the condition should be referred to as viral meningitis.

Epidemiology Aseptic meningitis affects between 9000 and 12,000 persons in the United States every year. Although all ages are involved, more than 90 percent of the patients are under age 30. The peak incidence of aseptic meningitis is in the late summer. The majority of cases seen in the summer are due to picornaviruses other than polioviruses, such as the coxsackie- and echoviruses. Mumps meningitis occurs more often in the winter and late spring. Both sexes are affected equally by enteroviruses, but there is a 2:1 or 3:1 male predominance in the meningitis produced by mumps.

Clinical picture The symptoms and signs of viral meningitis are similar irrespective of the particular virus involved. The onset of illness is acute. There may be a prodromal "flulike" illness before the onset of meningitis, as in lymphocytic choriomeningitis. This biphasic pattern of illness also may be observed in young children with poliomyelitis or in illness due to other insect-borne viruses (see Chaps. 143 and 144). CNS involvement is manifested by an intense frontal or retroorbital headache. Malaise, nausea and vomiting, listlessness, and photophobia may be present. As a rule, there is little impairment of consciousness. The patient may be drowsy and slightly confused but is usually oriented and rational. Stupor and coma occur rarely. The temperature is usually elevated in the range of 38 to 40°C. There is neck stiffness on forward flexion. Kernig's and Brudzinski's signs are present in most cases but may be absent in patients with minimal meningeal irritation. Stiffness of the spine may be such that a child will sit with the head retracted and the arms extended posteriorly in the form of a tripod. Signs of focal damage to the central nervous system are rarely present. Occasionally, strabismus or diplopia, asymmetry of tendon reflexes, and an inconstant extensor plantar response may be found.

Clinical findings outside the nervous system may provide clues to the virus involved in the infection. Parotitis in association with viral meningitis suggests mumps. Skin rash has been a prominent feature of coxsackievirus or echovirus infections (see Chap. 139). Blotchy or punctate maculopapular rashes which involve the extremities and which occur chiefly in the summertime are commonly due to echovirus. Herpangina (large, painful vesicles in the posterior one-third of the oropharynx) are usually caused by coxsackieviruses. Sharp pains in the chest aggravated by deep respiration or coughing suggest the pleurodynia seen with Coxsackie B viruses.

Laboratory findings The lumbar CSF is usually under increased pressure and clear or slightly turbid in appearance. Slight turbidity

---

TABLE 347-1 Viruses of vertebrates

RNA-containing	DNA-containing
Picornavirus:*	Parvovirus:
Enterovirus*	Parvovirus
Cardiovirus	Dependovirus
Rhinovirus	Papovavirus:*
Aphthovirus	Papillomavirus
Calicivirus	Polyomavirus*
Reovirus:	Adenovirus:
Reovirus	Mastadenovirus
Orbivirus	Aviadenovirus
Rotavirus	Iridovirus
Togavirus:*	Herpesvirus:*
Alphavirus*	Alphaherpesvirus*
Flavivirus*	Betaherpesvirus*
Rubivirus*	Gammaherpesvirus*
Pestivirus	Poxvirus:
Orthomyxovirus:	Orthopoxvirus
Influenza virus	Parapoxvirus
Influenza C virus	Avipoxvirus
Paramyxovirus:*	Capripoxvirus
Paramyxovirus*	Leporipoxvirus
Morbillivirus*	Suipoxvirus
Pneumovirus	
Rhabdovirus:*	
Lyssavirus*	
Vesiculovirus	
Retrovirus:*	
Oncovirus	
Spumavirus	
Lentivirus*	
Bunyavirus:*	
Bunyavirus*	
Phlebovirus*	
Nairovirus	
Uukuvirus	
Arenavirus:*	
Coronavirus	

* *Virus families and groups of neurologic importance.*

can be demonstrated by holding a tube containing CSF to the light and agitating the fluid with a gentle finger tap. CSF usually contains 10 to 100 cells per cubic millimeter. At times, the cell count rises to levels of 3000 per cubic millimeter or greater. The cells are usually more than three-fourths lymphocytes or mononuclear cells. Polymorphonuclear cells may predominate in the early phases of aseptic meningitis. The CSF protein and sugar concentrations are usually normal. Isolated instances of depressed CSF sugar in patients with infections due to mumps or herpes simplex virus (HSV) have been reported but are rare. If the patient presents with a spinal fluid which contains less sugar than expected, meningitis due to bacteria, mycobacteria, or fungi should receive first attention. Oligoclonal IgG bands may be found in the CSF of patients with viral meningitis. In viral meningitis, Gram stain and india ink preparations fail to identify an organism; bacterial and fungal cultures are negative. Although certain viruses (such as mumps virus) can be recovered from CSF with relative ease, in most cases of viral meningitis, it is usually impossible to recover the responsible viral agent from the patient's CSF. The white cell count in the blood is usually normal, but leukopenia is present in about one-third of patients.

The specific viral diagnosis can usually be made by performing serologic tests on acute and convalescent serums and by attempting to isolate viruses from feces, urine, and throat washings. Attempts to isolate the agent from blood are usually unsuccessful.

Differential diagnosis The syndrome of viral or aseptic meningitis can be caused by a number of different infectious and noninfectious agents. The majority of cases of viral origin are due to picornaviruses, togaviruses, herpesviruses, paramyxoviruses, and arenaviruses. The list of nonviral infectious causes of the aseptic meningitis syndrome is extensive. It includes intracranial infections located near the meninges (otitis, mastoiditis, vertebral osteomyelitis); brain abscess; partially treated bacterial meningitis; and fungal, rickettsial, protozoan, or helminthic infections.

Also, there are a number of infrequently encountered neurologic diseases in which the CSF findings resemble viral meningitis. These include (1) Behçet's disease, characterized by uveitis, genital and oral ulcers, and focal neurologic abnormalities; (2) Vogt-Koyanagi and Harada's diseases, which combine uveitis, depigmentation of the hair and skin about the eyes, loss of eyelashes, and deafness; (3) Mollaret's meningitis; and (4) Lyme disease.

Noninfectious causes of the aseptic meningitis syndrome include the intrathecal introduction of drugs and agents for diagnostic tests and tumors in close proximity to the cerebral ventricles or that invade the subarachnoid space. Cytologic examination of cells in the CSF will distinguish neoplastic meningeal infiltration from viral meningitis. Systemic diseases such as sarcoidosis, disseminated lupus erythematosus, and infective endocarditis may be associated with aseptic meningitis.

Treatment The treatment of viral meningitis is symptomatic. Antiviral agents are not indicated in uncomplicated cases. Fever and other symptoms resolve in 3 to 5 days, and patients are usually entirely well within 2 weeks. CSF abnormalities are most pronounced from the fourth to sixth day, but the CSF white blood cell count may remain elevated for several weeks in patients who are otherwise asymptomatic. Initial therapy with antimicrobial agents may be appropriate if the initial elevation is not completely typical for viral infection. In most instances, patients recover from viral meningitis without sequelae. A limited number of patients may develop muscular weakness and other forms of motor disability. A very small number of patients may have recurrent attacks of viral meningitis; the multiple episodes are often due to different viruses.

Prognosis It is important to recognize that viral meningitis is an acute and self-limited illness and to realize that it may mimic life-threatening CNS infections which are potentially treatable. Most important to appreciate is the similarity between viral meningitis and partially treated bacterial meningitis, tuberculous meningitis, or fungal meningitis. If the CSF changes are not completely characteristic of

viral meningitis or if the patient's clinical response is atypical, it is important to perform repeated lumbar punctures and to reexamine the CSF within a relatively brief period of time, until the clinical picture becomes clear.

VIRAL ENCEPHALITIS Definition The term *encephalitis* is used when there is clinical and/or pathologic evidence of involvement of the cerebral hemispheres, brainstem, or cerebellum by the infectious process. It is customary to divide viral encephalitis into primary and postinfectious or parainfectious forms and to consider whether the disease is sporadic or epidemic. The *primary* form of the disease occurs when the encephalitis is the presenting form of the disease and is due to direct invasion and replication of virus within the CNS. The term *postinfectious* or *parainfectious* is used to describe an encephalitis which follows or occurs in combination with other viral illnesses or administration of certain vaccines. The cause of the encephalitis in such cases is believed to be a hypersensitivity reaction. The pathologic picture is typical of multifocal perivenous demyelination. The virus cannot be recovered from the CNS. If the inflammatory condition extends into the spinal cord, the term encephalomyelitis is used.

Clinical picture When encephalitis is the primary illness, such as with togaviruses and herpesviruses, there may be a minor illness consisting of such systemic symptoms as headache, myalgia, malaise, and upper respiratory symptoms. These nonspecific symptoms may occur several days before neurologic complaints and signs are recognized.

The onset of neurologic symptoms is abrupt. There is alteration in the patient's state of consciousness with lethargy, drowsiness, or stupor. The patient's behavior may be abnormal as a consequence of confusion, disorientation, and hallucinations. A convulsion or series of convulsions may occur at the start of the illness, and seizures may be the sole presenting symptom. The patient usually complains of headache, nausea, and vomiting. Fever is usually present, and there may be stiffening of the neck on forward bending. Focal neurologic abnormalities are found, depending on the portion of the nervous system involved by the inflammatory process. Involvement of the cerebral hemispheres may result in aphasia, signs of corticospinal and corticobulbar tract lesions, involuntary movements, ataxia, sensory defects, and loss of retentive memory.

Laboratory examinations General laboratory tests are usually of little help in the diagnosis of encephalitis. They may provide evidence of systemic disease, such as abnormal lymphocytes in infectious mononucleosis, cells in the urinary sediment with inclusions characteristic of cytomegalovirus infection, and elevated amylase and transaminase levels in mumps and certain picornavirus infections.

Lumbar puncture, followed by examination of the CSF, is the most important diagnostic test. The CSF is usually under normal or slightly elevated pressure, clear or slightly turbid, and contains an increased number of white cells (in the range of 50 to 500 per cubic millimeter), a slight-to-moderate elevation of protein content, and a normal glucose level. There may be a predominance of polymorphonuclear leukocytes in the early phase of the illness. The protein content will often rise as the total cell count diminishes. In HSV encephalitis, the CSF may be slightly bloody or xanthochromic and contain a significant number of red blood cells. This reflects the sometimes hemorrhagic nature of HSV encephalitis. Occasionally a viral encephalitis may exist without CSF abnormalities, which makes the diagnosis even more difficult.

The electroencephalogram (EEG) may be of diagnostic help in suspected encephalitis. Diffuse or bilateral abnormalities can be defined by the EEG in patients who present with focal or unilateral neurologic deficits. A number of EEG changes may be seen, but the most common pattern is a diffuse slow wave activity with disruption of normal rhythms, punctuated at times with periodic high-amplitude bursts and spike-and-wave complexes. Computerized tomography (CT), magnetic resonance imaging (MRI), and radionuclide scans may be helpful in demonstrating intracranial mass lesions or localized foci of infection about or within the brain. The cerebral cortex may be enhanced diffusely.

Diagnosis When presented with a patient with suspected viral encephalitis, it is important to exclude nonviral infections for which potential treatment is available. A number of conditions can mimic viral encephalitis (Table 347-2). It is imperative to consider these alternative causes when the patient is first evaluated. Once the diagnosis of primary viral encephalitis is secure, it is important to determine if the illness is occurring as part of an epidemic or as an isolated sporadic event. Knowledge of the seasonal, geographic, and age group occurrence of the disease can often furnish enough information to make an informed guess about the correct viral etiology. During the summer and early fall, togaviruses, bunyaviruses, and picornaviruses may prevail. Some of these viruses may produce milder disease than others; some, such as western equine and California encephalitis viruses, affect a predominantly young age group. In the winter, epidemic encephalitis is more often associated with paramyxovirus, varicella-zoster (V-Z), Epstein-Barr (EB), or rubella virus infection. HSV is responsible for more cases of nonepidemic sporadic encephalitis cases than any other virus.

The course of viral encephalitis is variable. It may be a short-lived, benign illness or a devastatingly severe one which leaves the patient with pronounced impairment of cerebral functions. Severe sequelae may be associated with certain viruses (HSV, eastern equine encephalitis, Japanese encephalitis, and St. Louis encephalitis). Other viruses cause milder disease (California encephalitis, western equine encephalitis). The acute phase of the disease usually lasts a few days to a week. Resolution can be abrupt or gradual. The disease may be complicated by a salt-wasting syndrome resulting from hypothalamic involvement and/or alterations in temperature or respiratory control centers owing to brainstem involvement. These events may occur rapidly and require prompt recognition and correction. Neurologic defects may continue to improve over a period of weeks to months.

In most instances of epidemic encephalitis, the viral diagnosis is made by serologic tests of acute and convalescent phase serums. Three major serologic tests are employed: complement-fixation, hemagglutination-inhibition, and neutralization. Because the serologic test is crucial for viral diagnosis, it is imperative to obtain an acute-phase serum as soon as the diagnosis of viral encephalitis is suspected. In vector-transmitted encephalitis which does not result in fatality, the blood is the most likely tissue source of viral isolation. Isolation of virus from blood is difficult, however, because viremia is usually brief and occurs before the onset of neurologic symptoms. In fatal cases, the virus can often be isolated from brain and spinal cord by inoculation of susceptible animals and tissue culture cells.

When HSV encephalitis is suspected, greater urgency is required

TABLE 347-2 Nonviral conditions mistaken for acute viral encephalitis

Infection:	
Bacterial	Early or imperfectly treated meningitis
	Brain abscess
	Parameningeal infections
	Illness due to mycobacteria, spirochetes, *Mycoplasma*
Fungi	*Cryptococcus, Coccidioides immitis, Histoplasma, Candida, Nocardia, Blastomyces*
Rickettsia	Rocky Mountain spotted fever
Protozoa	''Fresh water'' amebiasis, malaria, toxoplasmosis
Metazoa	Cysticercosis, trichinosis, and others
Intoxication	Salicylates, barbiturates, heavy metals, tick paralysis
Endocrine and metabolic disorders	Acute sodium, calcium, or carbohydrate imbalance; porphyria, pheochromocytoma
Systemic diseases	Sarcoidosis, hyperglobulinemia, collagen disease, neoplasms, endocarditis with embolization
Acute psychotic disorders	

SOURCE: *After Brown.*

in arriving at a viral diagnosis because there is a definite advantage in initiating antiviral therapy as quickly as possible (see Chap. 136). A number of patients with HSV encephalitis present with fever and neurologic findings compatible with a bilateral space-occupying lesion of the medial parts of the temporal and the orbital parts of the frontal lobes. A severe retentive memory defect is a frequent sequela. HSV can be best demonstrated in brain tissue obtained by biopsy. Examination of the tissue by light, electron, and immunofluorescence microscopy and inoculation of a brain homogenate into cell cultures and animals permit a specific diagnosis of HSV early in the course of the patient's illness. However, many neurologists object to biopsy as a diagnostic procedure because the risks and sequelae outweigh the dangers of treatment. Moreover, enhanced CT scans and radionuclide brain imaging often reveal the temporal lobe lesions which, when added to the clinical picture and a CSF pleocytosis, make the diagnosis fairly certain and permit treatment without brain biopsy.

Encephalitis may present as an infrequently encountered manifestation of a systemic disease such as measles, varicella, or neoplasia. When this is the case, the encephalitis occurs after the more characteristic features of the disease have become evident. Rarely, the systemic disease may appear after the diagnosis of encephalitis has been established.

UNUSUAL FORMS OF VIRAL ENCEPHALITIS   *Acute cerebellar ataxia* may be associated with a number of different viruses (picornaviruses, V-Z, and EB virus). The illness usually afflicts children between the ages of 1 and 5 years. The majority of patients have had a preceding mild infectious illness a week or so before the onset of neurologic signs. The onset of the illness is characteristically abrupt with prominent ataxia of the trunk and limbs. Complete recovery is the rule, but a permanent cerebellar deficit may ensue in patients when ataxia is profound in the early stages of the illness. In some instances of V-Z infection, the cerebellar lesions are of the parainfectious, demyelinating type (see Chap. 348).

Acute hemorrhagic leukoencephalitis is an infrequently encountered hyperacute disease of cerebral white matter which is often preceded by some form of systemic viral illness, most often an upper respiratory tract infection. The disease is marked by an acute onset, progressively deepening disturbance of consciousness, fever, seizures, and focal cortical abnormalities. Cerebral involvement is frequently unilateral. The course is rapid and usually fatal. There is a peripheral leukocytosis, and the CSF frequently contains mononuclear and polymorphonuclear leukocytes. The presence of mass effect or increased absorption coefficient on CT scan within the first 3 days of encephalitis should suggest this diagnosis. The cause of the disease is unknown. It has not been linked to infection by a specific virus or group of viruses and may well be allergic in nature. A virus has not been recovered from brain tissue. Treatment includes vigorous control of intracranial pressure and seizures and aggressive use of corticosteroids in high dosage (see Chap. 348).

Limbic encephalitis is a form of encephalitis localized to the temporal and frontal lobes—the limbic part of the brain. It is encountered as a remote effect of malignancy—most commonly carcinoma of the lung. A viral etiology has been suspected but never proved. Patients with limbic encephalitis have marked impairment of recent memory manifested by a confabulatory-amnestic state, and generalized seizures. The patient's CSF often contains a limited number of lymphocytes and mononuclear cells. The EEG is characterized by paroxysmal and/or slow waves over one or both temporal lobes. Pathologic changes are most pronounced in the hippocampal formation and amygdaloid nuclei. Encephalitis with predilection for the brainstem has also been reported as a remote effect of tumor.

Encephalitis lethargica (von Economo's disease) first occurred during and for about 10 years after World War I. A causative viral agent was never identified, but the clinical and pathologic features were those of a viral infection of the thalamus and midbrain. The disease was characterized by pronounced somnolence and ophthalmoplegia. A high proportion of survivors developed a parkinsonian syndrome months or years after the encephalitis. Sporadic case reports of patients with the clinical features of encephalitis lethargica appear even to the present time.

MYELITIS   Viral infection of the central nervous system may localize in the parenchyma of the spinal cord producing myelitis. Poliovirus infection with damage to spinal motor neurons is the prototype of a viral infection localized chiefly to the spinal cord. Vaccination has markedly reduced but not eliminated poliomyelitis because patients who have not been vaccinated remain susceptible. Progressive muscular weakness, fasciculations, and atrophy occur in some patients many years after an acute episode of poliomyelitis. The cause of this ''postpolio'' syndrome is still uncertain; it may be a recrudescence of viral activity.

Spinal paralytic disease has also been described with other enteroviruses (coxsackieviruses and echoviruses). The illness is characterized by an asymmetric flaccid paralysis of the limbs; it is usually less severe and has a higher rate of recovery from muscular weakness than poliomyelitis.

Other viruses have also been reported to affect the spinal cord directly. Herpesvirus infection in the genital and perineal region has been associated with paralysis of sphincter function, probably indicative of direct viral involvement of the sacral spinal cord. Myelitis due to V-Z virus (aside from the ganglionitis and unilateral poliomyelitis) is another very rare cause of a leukomyelitis resulting in bilateral weakness of the legs with occasional ankle clonus or extensor plantar responses. Sphincter disturbances are present in two-thirds of patients and a sensory level in about one-half of patients. The CSF contains from 25 to 125 cells per cubic millimeter; the protein content may be normal or elevated. Recovery of function is the rule.

There may also be delayed involvement of the white matter of the spinal cord following viral infection. This is a parainfectious demyelinative process that interrupts sensory and motor tracts at one level and is termed an acute transverse myelitis. It begins with the abrupt onset of bilateral weakness of the legs and concomitant involvement of ascending sensory pathways. Urinary bladder and bowel functions are usually disturbed early in the course of the illness. An exanthem or respiratory infection not uncommonly precedes neurologic symptoms. Acute myelitis in the absence of encephalitis has been described in association with measles, V-Z, echovirus, HSV, and infectious mononucleosis. It has also been observed after rabies and smallpox vaccination. Virus isolation from CSF has been unsuccessful. A small proportion of patients with acute transverse myelitis will later develop multiple sclerosis. Acute spinal epidural abscess should be considered and excluded in patients who present with an acute nontraumatic transverse spinal cord syndrome.

TREATMENT   Of the various viruses that cause acute encephalitis, HSV is the most responsive to antiviral chemotherapy. The drug of choice is acyclovir, given intravenously. Details of therapy are given in Chap. 136 and Table 136-1.

CNS DISEASES DUE TO SLOW VIRUS INFECTION

In slow virus infections, a protracted period, often on the order of months or years, passes between the introduction of the infectious agent and the appearance of clinical illness. Once neurologic disease is established, it may progress slowly over many months or years. The reasons why a certain virus will cause acute illness in one patient and slow infection in another are still largely unknown. Viruses causing slow infections do not appear to share any common features. No single virus property can be correlated with the slow virus disease process. The factors invoked to explain slow virus infections include (1) a defect in the composition of the virus; (2) a change in the virus's antigenicity; (3) an altered or defective host immune response; (4) a special property of the virus which permits it to remain latent or to become integrated in the host cell's genome; or (5) a yet incompletely understood and possibly unique method of replication. Slow virus CNS diseases affect the parenchyma of the cerebral

hemispheres and, in some instances, the cerebellum, brainstem, and spinal cord. These infections are not grouped by their topography, i.e., the part of the nervous system that they damage, or by their clinical presentation. Some slow viruses provoke a mild conventional inflammatory response during the time they are clinically silent; others are able to reside within cells for long periods without causing detectable cytopathic changes. The role of immunity in slow virus infection is largely unknown. Some slow virus infections occur in the presence of elevated levels of circulating antibodies; in others, there may be no detectable immune response.

Because infective agents causing some human slow CNS diseases have not been demonstrated to contain nucleic acid, the slow viral CNS infections are divided into those due to conventional viruses and those due to unconventional agents whose viral nature has not been fully established (Table 347-3). There are currently eight well-defined neurologic diseases caused by slow viruses. No consistently effective therapy is now available for any of them. Conventional viruses have been recovered from the CNS of patients with subacute sclerosing panencephalitis (SSPE), progressive multifocal leukoencephalopathy (PML), progressive rubella encephalitis, and persistent viral infection in immunodeficient patients. Each of these is based on an inflammatory reaction in the CNS. Kuru, Creutzfeldt-Jakob disease (CJD), and Gerstmann-Sträussler-Scheinker (GSS) disease share common neuropathologic features which are noninflammatory. They produce fine vacuolation of nervous tissue and hence are referred to as the subacute spongiform virus encephalopathies. Although these diseases have been shown to be of infectious etiology by the transmission of neurologic illness to higher primates, their causative agents remain incompletely characterized. They are classified as the slow virus infections due to unconventional agents.

The best studied of the unconventional transmissible agents is scrapie, a neurologic disease of sheep. The nature of the scrapie agent has not been defined. Concentrated and partially purified scrapie agent contains a sialoglycoprotein of 27,000 to 30,000 mol wt, designated PrP 27-30. Because of this association, the term *prion* was introduced as an operational name for the putative infectious agent. Prion is defined as a small proteinaceous infectious particle which is resistant to inactivation by most procedures that modify nucleic acids. PrP 27-30 is the product of a single gene; specific messenger RNA for PrP 27-30 is found in normal as well as infected tissues. Scrapie prion preparations aggregate into amyloid-like birefringent rods. In addition, filamentous structures, called scrapie-associated fibrils (SAF), have been found by electron microscopy of membrane fractions from scrapie-infected brain. These observations further testify to the unusual nature of the scrapie agent, but they do not fully exclude the possibility that the scrapie agent contains nucleic acid.

SUBACUTE SCLEROSING PANENCEPHALITIS (SSPE)   This progressive and ultimately fatal disease of children and adolescents had been suspected to be of viral origin since its initial description as inclusion body encephalitis. Measles virus or a virus very closely related to measles virus has been recovered from the brains of patients with the disease. The disorder may be considered to be a slow form of measles encephalitis (see Chap. 132).

SSPE occurs in patients between the ages of 4 and 20; 80 percent are under 11. The disease affects boys 3 to 10 times as frequently as girls. Mean annual incidence rates have fallen rapidly in the last two

TABLE 347-3   Slow virus diseases of the CNS

Conventional viruses	Subacute sclerosing panencephalitis (SSPE)
	Progressive multifocal leukoencephalopathy (PML)
	Progressive rubella encephalitis
	Persistent infection in immunodeficiency:
	Congenital or primary
	Acquired or induced
Unconventional viruslike agents	Kuru
	Creutzfeldt-Jakob disease (CJD)
	Gerstmann-Sträussler-Scheinker disease (GSS)

decades; the drop in incidence roughly parallels the decline in the number of measles cases diagnosed since the introduction of live attenuated measles vaccine. Most patients are from rural areas or small towns. Characteristically, they are entirely well until the disease begins. The onset of usually insidious mental deterioration, often expressed by a decline in the patient's schoolwork, is the presenting symptom. Incoordination, ataxia, and myoclonic jerks develop within a few months along with abnormalities of the pyramidal and extrapyramidal motor systems. Cortical blindness, papilledema, and optic atrophy may be present; focal chorioretinitis has been described. A few cases have occurred in association with infectious mononucleosis.

The patient becomes bedridden within 6 to 9 months. Death results from superimposed pulmonary or urinary tract infections or from decubiti. Signs of meningeal irritation are absent. The differential diagnosis includes cerebral storage diseases, nonstorage poliodystrophies, leukodystrophies, and demyelinating diseases of childhood.

The CSF gamma-globulin level, as determined by electrophoresis, quantitative immunochemical assay, or colloidal gold curve, is elevated, but the fluid is otherwise normal. The EEG typically shows a "burst suppression" pattern characterized by synchronous and symmetrical spike and high-voltage slow wave activity followed by electrical inactivity. Elevated levels of measles antibody are found in the serum and CSF. CT scan abnormalities correlate with the stage and duration of the disease. They include lateral ventricular dilatation, cortical atrophy, low parenchymal attenuation, and brainstem and cerebellar atrophy.

Pathologic findings include lymphocyte and mononuclear infiltrations about small cerebral arteries and veins, intranuclear and intracytoplasmic inclusions in neurons and glial cells, and varying degrees of destruction of medulated nerve fibers. The lesions occur in the cerebral gray and white matter, brainstem, and cerebellum.

Measles virus is the etiologic agent. Electron-microscopic studies show that the intranuclear inclusions in brain cells are composed of hollow tubular filaments resembling the internal nucleocapsid component of a paramyxovirus. Staining of brain tissue from patients with the disease demonstrates measles virus antigen in the inclusions. An agent serologically identical with measles virus and having the properties of measles virus has been recovered from brain by cocultivating cell cultures originating from brain tissue with established laboratory cell lines.

Attempts to transmit the disease to animals have met with variable results. Ferrets inoculated with suspensions of brain from patients with the disease develop a nonfatal neurologic disorder with EEG changes.

There is evidence that SSPE patients have clinical measles at an unusually early age, but SSPE appears many years after the patient's initial rubeola infection. A few reported cases may have been related to measles vaccination. The risk of SSPE following measles vaccination is far less, however, than the risk of encephalitis or SSPE following natural measles.

SSPE patients lack antibody to one of the measles virus proteins (the M or matrix protein) despite high titers of antibodies to the other viral proteins. Extracts of SSPE-infected brain lack significant quantities of M antigen. The M protein is a nonglycosylated protein localized to the inner surface of the viral membrane; it is important in the assembly of the virus particle at the cell surface. SSPE brain cells do not appear capable of synthesizing the M protein even in normal amounts. The molecular reasons for the absence of M polypeptide in terminal SSPE may involve decreased transcription and translation of M messenger RNA.

Isoprinosine[1] has been reported by some to affect the course of the disease favorably in an open therapeutic trial, but there is controversy about the drug's effectiveness. Other forms of treatment (including interferon and plasmapheresis) have been ineffective.

PROGRESSIVE MULTIFOCAL LEUKOENCEPHALOPATHY (PML)
This rare neurologic condition that usually occurs in patients who

[1] *This drug has not been approved by the Food and Drug Administration at the time of publication.*

have leukemia, malignant lymphoma, carcinomatosis, acquired immunodeficiency syndrome (AIDS), or a variety of other chronic disease processes, or who are involved with immunosuppressive therapy. The disease is consistently associated with disorders of cell-mediated immunity with which deficits in humoral antibody response may or may not coexist.

The disease affects adults of both sexes, and its duration from onset of symptoms to death is 1 to 6 or more months. The neurologic signs and symptoms reflect a diffuse, asymmetric involvement of the cerebral hemispheres. Hemiplegia, hemianopsia, aphasia or dysarthria, and organic mental changes are frequent; visual field abnormalities and complete or incomplete transverse myelitis may develop. Headache and convulsive seizures are rare, but EEG abnormalities consisting of diffuse or focal abnormalities are often present. Lesions in the white matter may be recognized on CT scans. MRI is helpful in demonstrating white matter destruction. CSF is normal. Specific diagnosis can be made by brain biopsy.

The pathologic changes consist of multiple areas of demyelination with little or no perivascular infiltration and abnormal mitotic figures in astrocytes. The presence of distinctive intranuclear inclusions in oligodendrocytes first suggested that the disease was of a viral etiology. Electron-microscopic observations show the intranuclear inclusion bodies to be composed of closely packed spheres, which have the physical dimensions and properties of the polyomavirus genus of the papovaviruses.

By employing tissue cultures derived from human fetal brain, it has been possible to recover a new human polyomavirus serotype (JC virus) from the brains of PML patients. Abundant virus particles are present in brain. Rapid identification of the virus in brain is possible using fluorescent antibody staining or electron-microscopic agglutination with monospecific hyperimmune rabbit serum. Serologic diagnosis using the patient's serum is unreliable. The virus has not been demonstrated in tissues other than brain; the disease has not been transmitted to animals. There are isolated reports of clinical remission with cytosine arabinoside, but no cures. Death usually occurs within 6 months of onset.

PML may result from the activation of a polyomavirus which has been latent in brain or other tissues since childhood infection. Alternatively, there may be certain individuals who fail to acquire immunity in childhood and have their first encounter with the virus when a disease which interferes with cell-mediated immunity develops. The demyelination which occurs may be related to virus-induced damage of oligodendroglia, cells which appear to be required for the normal maintenance of myelin.

PROGRESSIVE RUBELLA ENCEPHALITIS
A chronic progressive encephalitis developing in boys with the typical stigmata of the congenital rubella syndrome (Chap. 133) and sharing some of the features of SSPE was first described in 1974. Fewer than 20 patients have been reported.

The illness begins in the second decade and is characterized by dementia cerebellar ataxia, spasticity, and seizures. The CSF has an increased cell count, and the protein and IgG levels are elevated. High titers of antibody to rubella virus can be detected in both the serum and CSF. Rubella virus has been recovered from the brain by use of the cocultivation technique.

Unlike SSPE, patients with rubella panencephalitis have the stigmata of congenital rubella before the onset of progressive disease. Myoclonus is less constant, and the EEG does not show the burst suppression observed in SSPE. Histologic examination of the brain shows mineralization of old lesions and an inflammatory reaction, but not the inclusion bodies characteristically found in SSPE.

The clinical picture of progressive rubella encephalitis also resembles the rare case of juvenile paresis which may occur in patients with congenital syphilis. The immune status of patients with rubella encephalitis has not been fully defined, and the pathogenesis of the disease remains obscure.

PERSISTENT VIRAL DISEASE IN IMMUNODEFICIENT PATIENTS
Persistent or chronic neurologic infections of the nervous system may

occur in immunodeficient patients. The immunodeficiency state may be congenital (primary) or acquired. Enteroviruses may be recovered from the CSF of patients with primary agammaglobulinemia over a period of many years, during which time there is a persistent CSF pleocytosis. A chronic or subacute encephalitis has also been described in children with congenital hypogammaglobulinemia. A specific virus has not been associated with this disorder.

NEUROLOGIC CONDITIONS RELATED TO THE ACQUIRED IMMUNODEFICIENCY SYNDROME (AIDS) Involvement of the CNS in AIDS may produce complex clinical findings. Evidence is accumulating that the human immunodeficiency viruses (HIV) responsible for AIDS [human T-cell leukemia virus (HTLV III), lymphadenopathy-associated virus (LAV), or AIDS-associated retrovirus (ARV)] may produce a primary neurotropic disorder as well as furnish the immunologic compromise that permits other viruses to replicate in and damage nerve tissue.

The immunocompromised AIDS patient is susceptible to a variety of infectious agents that can attack the CNS. The most common viral agents that assert themselves belong to the herpesvirus and papovavirus groups, i.e., viruses that may remain latent until there is dysfunction of normal immunologic processes. The most commonly isolated viruses from these groups include herpes simplex virus (HSV), cytomegalovirus, and the PML agent (JC virus). Infection with these viruses in the AIDS patient can produce a variety of neurologic conditions—most notably atypical aseptic meningitis, acute or subacute encephalitis, PML, and viral myelitis. In addition to viral encephalitis and PML, the AIDS patient may also develop toxoplasma brain abscess and primary CNS lymphomas. Differentiation from PML is often difficult solely on the basis of CT scan and other laboratory tests. Because treatment for these conditions varies, it is often necessary to perform a brain biopsy and obtain a specimen of the cerebral lesion to make the correct diagnosis.

The AIDS patient may also develop a number of different conditions of the spinal cord. These include a vacuolar myelopathy that most severely affects the lateral and posterior columns of the thoracic cord, an acute viral myelitis usually due to HSV, and an ascending myelitis. AIDS can also affect peripheral nerves producing a neuropathy.

There is evidence that HTLV III can replicate in brain. Injection of brain suspension from AIDS patients into chimpanzees produced seroconversion in the animals; virus could be isolated from the chimpanzee's leukocytes. Seroconversion for anti-HTLV III has been associated with the appearance of acute encephalopathy in AIDS patients. HTLV III DNA and RNA have been found in the brains of both children and adults with AIDS, and HTLV III has been directly isolated from CSF and neural tissues of AIDS patients. HTLV III–specific IgG has been found to a higher measure in the CSF than in the blood in AIDS patients with neurologic symptoms, suggesting IgG synthesis within the CNS. The HTLV III agent has also been recovered from the spinal cord and sural nerve, suggesting that the AIDS myelopathy and peripheral neuropathy also may be caused by infection with this retrovirus.

AIDS dementia, a subacute dementia accompanied by motor system abnormalities, has been described in AIDS patients. This condition may well be a direct manifestation of HTLV III infection of the brain. The dementia is insidious in onset and progresses gradually. The early manifestations include an inability to recall, loss of capacity to concentrate, and difficulty in performing complex sequential tasks. There is slowing of verbal and motor responses; spontaneity and animation are reduced. The condition may be difficult to differentiate from depression. As the disease advances, there may be gait unsteadiness, leg weakness, impaired handwriting, and tremor. In the advanced stage, there is global cognitive impairment and pronounced psychomotor slowing. The CT scan may show cortical atrophy and enlargement of the ventricles. MRI demonstrates patchy multifocal areas of increased signal in the central white matter in T2 weighted images. The spinal fluid may contain mononuclear cells and have mildly elevated protein content.

The brains of patients with AIDS demonstrate moderate to marked cerebral atrophy and histologic changes involving the white matter and subcortical structures; the cortical gray matter is largely spared. The microscopic findings include multifocal perivascular rarefaction and focal vacuolation of the white matter with perivascular and parenchymal collections of macrophages and multinucleated giant cells. Neuronal loss is present only in the most severe cases.

There is no effective treatment for AIDS dementia.

KURU Kuru, or "trembling with fear," is a progressive and fatal neurologic disorder which occurs exclusively among natives of the New Guinea highland. The disease is rare and seems to be disappearing; its elucidation represented a major hallmark in microbiology.

Difficulty in walking is usually the first sign of kuru. This usually progresses from a minor disturbance in gait to marked ataxia with lurching and staggering. Eventually, ambulation becomes so incoordinated that patients are unable to walk independently or to use their limbs because of intention tremor. Patients display an inability to perform rapid alternating movements, hypotonia, and abnormal involuntary movements which take the form of myoclonus, athetosis, or chorea. Slurring of speech and convergent strabismus appear as the disease progresses. There are no abnormalities in the blood or CSF. Dementia develops in the later phases of the disease. The illness terminates fatally in 4 to 24 months, usually from decubitus ulcers or bronchopneumonia. Kuru was common in male and female children and in adult women, but rare in adult men. The incubation period may be longer than 20 years in older patients.

Pathologic changes are limited to the CNS and include widespread neuronal loss, intense astrocytosis and microglial proliferation, loss of myelinated fibers, and the presence of plaquelike bodies. Perivascular cuffing by lymphocytes and mononuclear cells is rarely present.

It was the close similarity between the neuropathologic and clinical findings found in kuru and in scrapie that suggested the possibility that kuru might be caused by a virus or some closely related infectious agent. The infectious origin of kuru was confirmed subsequently by the transfer of a kurulike syndrome in chimpanzees 10 to 82 months after intracerebral inoculation of suspensions of brain from human cases. Disease has also been produced in chimpanzees by inoculation of tissues other than brain. The clinical illness in chimpanzees appears 3 to 11 months after inoculation. The disease has also been successfully transmitted to a number of new world and old world monkeys as well as to other animals. The specific agent responsible for the disease has not been fully characterized.

Cannibalism is the probable mode of transmission of kuru. Native custom in New Guinea dictated that bone marrow, viscera, and brain be cooked and eaten. The agent may be introduced by conjunctival, nasal, or skin contamination during the practice of ritual cannibalism. The marked predilection of kuru for the adult female may be explained by the observation that cannibalism appears more prevalent among women and that males who practice cannibalism seldom eat the bodies of women. The recent influx of foreign settlers into the kuru area has led to increasing rejection of cannibalistic practices and this in turn may be responsible for the progressive decline in the number of cases of kuru since 1960. Oral feeding of kuru agent to squirrel monkeys has been reported to produce the disease.

CREUTZFELDT-JAKOB DISEASE (CJD) CJD is an invariably fatal degenerative disease of the CNS that afflicts persons between the ages of 55 to 75 years and presents as a rapidly evolving dementia with myoclonus. Unlike kuru, the disease is not geographically limited and has been reported from over 50 countries around the world. The annual incidence is about one case per million inhabitants in metropolitan areas. The majority of cases occur between the ages of 55 and 75, but patients as young as 16 and as old as 80 have been reported. The peak incidence is in the early 1960s.

Although CJD may have diverse clinical presentations, it usually begins with gradually progressive mental deterioration in the form of memory loss, mood changes, and errors in judgment. Disturbances of stance, gait, and motor control, visual disturbances, and dizziness and vertigo may be prominent in the early stages of the disease. Some patients complain of headache. The patient may experience distortions in the shape and appearance of objects. Higher cortical function deficits, such as aphasia or apraxia, may occur. Hallucinations, delusional ideas, and confusion may appear as the disease progresses. In certain patients, cerebeller signs and visual abnormalities may predominate and may be confused initially with cerebrovascular insufficiency. As the condition worsens, the patient becomes mute, stuporous, spastic, and rigid. Myoclonic jerks and other abnormal movements become more prominent as the disease progresses. Visual deterioration may advance to cortical blindness. Disturbances of oculomotor control and of the autonomic nervous system have been noted.

The disease progresses rapidly; the mean duration of illness is about 8 months, but about 5 to 10 percent of cases will have an illness lasting 2 years or more. The majority of patients die within 6 months, most often 2 to 3 months after the onset of their disease.

Only rarely has a second member of a family been affected. Fifteen percent of CJD patients have a family history of the disease consistent with an autosomal dominant transmission; the onset of the illness in familial cases is earlier than in sporadic cases. A family history of presenile dementia can be obtained in about 10 percent of CJD patients.

The EEG can often be helpful in making the correct diagnosis. During the early stages, it may only show mild, excessive generalized slowing more marked over one hemisphere or even focal. As the disease progresses, distinctive repetitive sharp waves with a characteristic interval of 0.5 to 1.0 s are seen. The sharp waves may first be unilateral, resembling periodic lateralized epileptiform discharges (PLEDS), but eventually they become bilateral and synchronous. In the final stages of the disease, all background EEG activity becomes progressively slower and of lower amplitude, sometimes with the persistence of period complexes. Repetitive sharp waves are also occasionally seen in the EEGs of patients with dementia due to other illnesses such as Alzheimer's disease or Binswanger's subcortical encephalopathy, but not with the regular rate that they are found in CJD patients. Serial EEG tracings are helpful in questionable cases.

A CT scan of the brain is usually normal, but sulcal widening, ventricular enlargement, and moderate cortical atrophy may be visualized. Rapid progressive atrophic changes on serial CT scans may suggest the diagnosis. MRI scanning demonstrates bilateral cortical atrophy without apparent white matter changes. Positron emission tomography (PET) has demonstrated temporal lobe hypometabolism with hemispheric asymmetry. The CSF is usually normal except for a slight elevation in the protein content. No immunologic response, either humoral or cellular, to the CJD agent has been demonstrated in the blood.

The cerebrum and cerebellum are affected predominantly. The brain may show cerebral atrophy. Microscopic examination demonstrates widespread status spongiosus, nerve cell loss, and intensive gliosis. Vacuoles are located within the neuropil, i.e., within axons, dendrites, and glial fibers. There is no inflammatory reaction.

Electron-microscopic observations in CJD have disclosed membrane fragments in vacuoles. Abnormal fibrils similar in appearance to the serum accelerator factor (SAF) have been observed in CJD brain fractions. The exact composition of these fibrils is unclear. CJD brains have been shown to contain protease-resistant proteins with molecular weights ranging from 10,000 to 50,000. These CJD proteins reacted with antibodies raised against the scrapie PrP 27-30. Immunological identification by Western blots provides a diagnostic adjunct to neuropathological examination and animal transmission experiments. Protein polymers from CJD brain exhibit the staining properties of amyloid. The SAF and protease-resistant proteins present in CJD brain resemble those observed in other naturally occurring and experimentally induced spongiform encephalopathies of humans and other animals. It is uncertain if they represent a form of the infectious agent or modified pathologic products.

Sixty percent of patients with kuru and CJD demonstrate an autoimmune antibody directed against 10-nm neurofilaments. The antibody usually appears late in the disease. It can occasionally be found in normal subjects. The significance of this antibody is unclear.

CJD may be mistaken for Alzheimer's disease with myoclonus. In this situation, the presence of cerebellar signs provides strong evidence against the possibility of Alzheimer's disease. At times, CJD can be confused with multi-infarct dementia, alcoholic or nutritional deficiency syndromes, or primary brain tumors. The hallmarks of the disorder (mental deterioration, multisystem neurologic signs, myoclonus, and typical EEG changes) evolving over a period of months in a middle-aged patient usually secures the diagnosis.

The CJD agent has been found in lymph nodes, liver, kidney, spleen, lung, cornea, and CSF of patients with the disorder. The way the disease is acquired naturally is unknown. Incubation periods as long as 20 years may occur in natural transmission. The higher incidence of CJD among Israelis of Libyan origin who eat sheep's eyeballs has led to speculation that the disease may be naturally transmitted by the ingestion of scrapie-infected meat. There is an unexpectedly high incidence of previous brain or eye operations among CJD patients. Human-to-human transmission has occurred by corneal transplantation, by the implantation of contaminated stereotactic electroencephalographic electrodes, and by the parenteral administration of growth hormone prepared from cadaveric human pituitary glands. Transmission of CJD has not been linked to blood transfusion.

There is no evidence of an increased risk among spouses, friends, and medical or nursing personnel caring for CJD patients. The patient's CSF and blood should be considered, however, as potential sources of infection. Precautions should be taken to avoid autoinoculation with needles, scalpels, or other instruments that have been contaminated by the patient's tissues. Maximum care should be taken to avoid accidental percutaneous exposure to blood, CSF, or tissue. Contaminated skin can be disinfected by a 5- to 10-min exposure to 1 N sodium hydroxide followed by extensive washing with water. Contaminated material should be steam-autoclaved for 1 h at a temperature of at least 132°C or immersed for 1 h in 1 N sodium hydroxide or a 10% sodium hypochlorite solution. More detailed guidelines for the handling of materials from patients with these disorders have been developed by the Centers for Disease Control. These should be applied to all patients who have evidence of rapid intellectual deterioration, particularly when it is associated with myoclonus.

There is no effective treatment for CJD. Claims that amantadine hydrochloride is effective have not been substantiated.

GERSTMANN-STRÄUSSLER-SCHEINKER (GSS) DISEASE GSS disease is a familial illness characterized by spinocerebellar ataxia with dementia and plaquelike deposits of amyloid in the brain. Inoculation of brain tissue from GSS disease produces spongiform encephalopathy in nonhuman primates. The usual onset of the disease is in the fifth decade. GSS disease follows a lengthy course, usually on the order of 2 to 10 years. Ataxia is prominent in the early phase of the illness; dementia follows later. The patient's symptoms and signs are reminiscent of olivopontocerebellar atrophy. Pathologic changes include spinocerebellar and corticospinal tract degeneration, extensive amyloid deposits, and spongiform degeneration. Like other human spongiform encephalopathies, there is no effective treatment for GSS disease.

There have been isolated reports that brain tissues for a restricted number of patients with familial Alzheimer's disease induced neurologic disease and spongiform changes in chimpanzees. Numerous other transmission attempts from patients with both familial and nonfamilial Alzheimer's disease have been negative. At present, there is no direct evidence to indicate that Alzheimer's disease is caused by a slow virus.

REFERENCES

BOCKMAN JM et al: Creutzfeldt-Jakob disease prion proteins in human brains. N Engl J Med 312:73, 1985

BROWN P: Acute viral encephalitis, in *Current Diagnosis 7*, RB Conn (ed). Philadelphia, Saunders, 1985, p 918

DYKEN PR: Subacute sclerosing panencephalitis. Current status. Neurol Clin 3:179, 1985

GAJDUSEK DC: Unconventional viruses and the origin and disappearance of kuru. Science 197:943, 1977

———: Unconventional viruses causing subacute spongiform encephalopathies, in *Virology*, BN Fields et al (eds). New York, Raven Press, 1985, p 1519

GRIFFITH JF, CH'IEN LT: Herpes simplex virus encephalitis. Diagnostic and treatment considerations. Med Clin North Am 67:991, 1983

HO DD, HIRSCH MS: Acute viral encephalitis. Med Clin North Am 69:415, 1985

——— et al: Isolation of HTLV-III from cerebrospinal fluid and neural tissues of patients with neurologic syndromes related to the acquired immunodeficiency syndrome. N Engl J Med 313:1493, 1985

HUDSON AJ et al: Gerstmann-Sträussler-Scheinker disease with coincidental familiar onset. Ann Neurol 14:670, 1983

KENNARD C, SWASH M: Acute viral encephalitis. Its diagnosis and outcome. Brain 104:129, 1981

LEVY RM et al: Neurological manifestations of the acquired immunodeficiency syndrome (AIDS). Experience at UCSF and review of the literature. J Neurosurg 62:475, 1985

PRICE RW et al: AIDS encephalopathy. Neurol Clin 4:285, 1986

RATZAN KR: Viral meningitis. Med Clin North Am 69:399, 1985

RICHARDSON EP: Progressive multifocal leukoencephalopathy. N Engl J Med 265:815, 1961

ROSENBERG RN et al: Precautions in handling tissues, fluids, and other contaminated materials from patients with documented or suspected Creutzfeldt-Jakob disease. Ann Neurol 19:75, 1986

WALKER DL: Progressive multifocal leukoencephalopathy, in *Handbook of Clinical Neurology*, JC Koetsier (ed). Amsterdam, Elsevier Science Publishers 1985, vol 3(47), p 503

WEIL ML et al: Chronic progressive panencephalitis due to rubella virus simulating subacute sclerosing panencephalitis. N Engl J Med 292:994, 1975

WILFERT CM et al: Persistent and fatal central-nervous-system echovirus infections in patients with agammaglobulinemia. N Engl J Med 296:1485, 1977

348 DEMYELINATING DISEASES

JACK P. ANTEL / BARRY G. W. ARNASON

The demyelinating diseases comprise a group of neurologic disorders important both because of the frequency with which they occur and the disability which they cause. Demyelinating diseases have in common the pathologic feature of focal or patchy destruction of myelin sheaths in the central nervous system accompanied by an inflammatory response. Some degree of axonal damage may occur as well, but demyelination always predominates. No cause has been determined for any of the demyelinating diseases. Current opinion holds that autoimmunity or viral infection is likely to be implicated in their pathogenesis.

Myelin loss occurs in other conditions as well, but in these others an inflammatory response is lacking. Included are genetically determined defects in myelin metabolism, exposure to toxins such as carbon monoxide, and opportunistic viral infection of oligodendrocytes (e.g., progressive multifocal leukoencephalopathy) against a background of immune incompetence. These entities, which are usually not classified as demyelinating diseases, are discussed in Chaps. 347 and 350.

Three demyelinating diseases can be distinguished on the basis of clinical history, examination, and pathologic findings: (1) multiple sclerosis, (2) acute disseminated encephalomyelitis (including postinfectious and postvaccinal encephalomyelitis), and (3) acute necrotizing hemorrhagic encephalomyelitis.

MULTIPLE SCLEROSIS

This disease usually presents in the form of recurrent attacks of focal or multifocal neurologic dysfunction, reflecting lesions within the central nervous system (CNS). Attacks occur, remit, and recur, seemingly randomly over many years. The disease begins most commonly in early adult life. The frequency of flare-ups is greatest during the first 3 to 4 years of disease, but a first attack, which may have been so mild as to escape medical attention and can barely be recalled, may not be followed by another attack for 10 to 20 years.

During typical episodes, symptoms worsen over a period of a few days to 2 to 3 weeks and then remit. Recovery is usually rapid over a period of weeks, although at times it may extend over several months. The extent of recovery varies markedly between patients and from one attack to the next in the same person. Remission may be complete, particularly after early attacks; often, however, remission is incomplete and as one attack follows another, a stepwise downward progression ensues with increasing permanent deficit.

In perhaps as many as one-third of cases the disease declares itself as a slowly but inexorably progressive illness. This is particularly likely to be the case if onset is after age 40. Although occasional patients die within the first few years of disease onset, most do not, and the average survival from multiple sclerosis (MS) is better than 30 years after onset of disease.

Multiple sclerosis is pleomorphic in its presentations. The clinical picture is determined by the location of foci of demyelination within the CNS. Classic features include impaired vision, nystagmus, dysarthria, decreased perception of vibration and position sense, ataxia and intention tremor, weakness or paralysis of one or more limbs, spasticity, and bladder problems.

Criteria which must be satisfied to establish a diagnosis of clinically definite MS include a reliable history of at least two episodes of neurologic deficit and objective clinical signs of lesions at more than one site within the CNS. Demonstration of a second lesion by laboratory tests (e.g., evoked potentials, computerized tomography, magnetic resonance imaging, or urologic studies), in concert with one objective clinical lesion, also fulfills the criteria. A finding of increased cerebrospinal fluid immunoglobulin with oligoclonal bands supports the diagnosis but will not substitute for the above criteria. Clinically probable MS is defined as either two attacks with clinical evidence of one lesion or one attack with clinical evidence of two lesions (or one clinical and one paraclinical lesion). Follow-up studies of probable MS patients indicate considerable diagnostic imprecision in this category. When signs pointing to damage of white matter tracts in optic nerves, brainstem, and spinal cord are present together and more than one attack is known to have occurred, a diagnosis of multiple sclerosis can be made with greater than 95 percent certainty. In the early years of the disease, when few relapses have occurred and fixed deficits are mild, the diagnosis may prove difficult, and single or multiple focal lesions due to other causes must be excluded.

PATHOLOGY Many scattered, discrete areas of demyelination, termed *plaques,* are the pathologic hallmark of multiple sclerosis. Macroscopically, plaques appear as gray-pink sharply defined areas which stand out against the surrounding white matter of the central nervous system. Lesions may extend into gray matter, although nerve cell bodies are seen to be preserved on microscopic examination. Plaques vary in size from a few millimeters to several centimeters; larger ones form by coalescence of smaller ones and by expansion of their margins. Plaques may be found anywhere in the white matter but typically occur in the paraventricular areas of the cerebrum and subpially, and within the brainstem and spinal cord. Their topography conforms to that of the venous drainage of the brain and spinal cord, and no particular anatomic structures are respected. The peripheral nervous system is not affected. The number of plaques found at autopsy invariably exceeds the number expected on the basis of physical signs. Many plaques, therefore, are clinically silent; this establishes that substantial impulse conduction occurs across regions of demyelination. In fact, autopsy studies indicate that 20 percent of multiple sclerosis cases are clinically silent during life.

The microscopic features of multiple sclerosis lesions depend on their age. Typically lesions of different ages and evidence of new activity about the margins of old lesions are encountered. Active multiple sclerosis lesions feature T-lymphocyte and monocyte-macrophage accumulations about venules and at plaque margins where myelin is being destroyed. The invasion of white matter by inflammatory cells is held responsible for the myelin breakdown. Macrophages (microglia) are believed to be the vectors of myelin breakdown.

They also function as scavengers of myelin debris; fat-laden macrophages may persist for months, perhaps for years, after the acute inflammatory response has subsided. Plasma cells accumulate within plaques and are usually found at or near their centers.

An astroglial response at or just beyond the margins of acutely demyelinating lesions is characteristic. In established, inactive plaques, a thick mat of fibrillary gliosis throughout the demyelinated regions is usual, and only a few residual perivascular macrophages are found. Oligodendrocyte number has been said to be normal or increased at the plaque margin. Yet, oligodendrocyte number is reduced within plaques, indicating that ultimately, this cell type is lost in multiple sclerosis. Indeed, damage to oligodendrocytes may be the primary event.

Only limited regeneration of myelin occurs in multiple sclerosis. The reason for this is unclear but may relate to loss of oligodendrocytes. At the pial margins of spinal cord plaques remyelination by peripheral nerve Schwann cells that have invaded the CNS may be encountered. Despite assiduous search, viral inclusions have not been detected in multiple sclerosis lesions. Mechanisms responsible for recovery from an MS attack are likely multiple. Resolution of edema, as documented by CT scan, and of inflammation may permit return of saltatory conduction along partially demyelinated axons (shadow plaque). Restoration of conduction, may also relate, in part, to insertion of K^+ channels along the length of denuded axonal segments rather than exclusively at the nodes of Ranvier as is the situation in myelinated nerve.

Axons within plaques tend to be spared, although in acute lesions frank necrosis with loss of axons sometimes occurs. At least 10 percent of multiple sclerosis plaques show marked axonal loss, and ultrastructural studies indicate that loss of axons may be more general than can be appreciated by routine histology. All gradations of pathologic change between the extremes described above are encountered.

The pathologic features of MS fail to account for the hour-to-hour and day-to-day waxings and wanings in function so characteristic of the disease. Conduction of impulses through demyelinated nerve is compromised and is further altered by transient changes in the internal milieu such as alterations in temperature and in electrolyte balance or by stress. Fever, or even minor increases in body temperature, such as may follow a hot bath or exercise, may cause a failure of conduction through demyelinated regions and lead to evanescent symptoms and signs. The mechanism of this axonal fatigability is unknown, but some type of conduction block is assumed to occur. It is important to distinguish transient fluctuations in symptomatology of the type just described from attacks of disease.

ETIOLOGY   The cause or causes of MS remain unknown. A role for immune-mediated or infectious factors has been proposed, but data to support these postulates are fragmentary and indirect.

Epidemiology   Epidemiologic studies have established several facts which will ultimately have to be incorporated into any coherent theory of the disease. Average age of onset of the first clinical episode of MS falls within the third and fourth decades. Females account for 60 percent of cases. For disease to begin in childhood or beyond the sixth decade is uncommon but not unknown.

In general, incidence in temperate climatic zones exceeds that in tropical zones; but variations within regions with similar climates do exist; hence the effect is not simply one of latitude or temperature. The incidence of MS in northern Europe, Canada, and the northern United States is approximately 10 new cases each year per 100,000 persons between the ages of 20 and 50. The incidence in Australia, New Zealand, and the southern United States is one-third to one-half of that; in Japan, elsewhere in the Orient, and in Africa MS is rare. Some epidemiologic evidence also suggests that persons migrating from high- to low-risk regions as children may be partially protected from MS. The data are consistent with the existence of an environmental factor, possibly a virus, and perhaps geographically restricted, that influences development of MS.

Genetic factors   The incidence of MS among American Indians and blacks is lower than among whites living in the same regions. This suggests that genetic factors also influence disease susceptibility. Blood relatives of MS patients (parents, siblings) have an eightfold increased risk of developing MS. This could reflect an interplay of several genetic factors, shared exposure to an environmental factor, or a combination of the two. A study of MS in identical twins has revealed concordance for MS to be markedly greater than for fraternal twins; concordance among identical twins exceeds 50 percent. Family studies have failed to reveal any predictable genetic pattern but do argue persuasively for a genetically determined predisposition to disease.

Certain histocompatibility antigens (HLA) are overrepresented in patients with MS. Among whites with the disease the HLA-B7 and -DW2 alleles occur with increased frequency. Most illnesses with which an HLA association has been shown are autoimmune or infectious in nature, a finding in keeping with current thought about the etiology of MS. Many American blacks with MS express the DW2 allele; this allele is rare in blacks in Africa, among whom MS is virtually unknown. It follows that an HLA-linked genetic factor which predisposes to MS exists, but inasmuch as the vast majority of persons bearing B7 or DW2 do not develop the disease, additional genetic or environmental factors must play a role. Paradoxically, siblings concordant for MS have concordance rates for HLA haplotypes little above those expected by chance. The HLA-B12 allele is less frequent in MS than in the population at large. This finding suggests that genetically determined protective factors may operate in MS.

Autoimmune factors   The lesions of MS are mimicked by those of experimental allergic encephalomyelitis (EAE), an autoimmune disease induced in animals by immunization with myelin. Lesions of EAE are demyelinating, perivenular, plaque-like, occur in chronic and recrudescent forms, and have an inflammatory infiltrate composed of lymphocytes, macrophages, and plasma cells. In EAE, T-lymphocyte sensitivity to a single antigen known as myelin basic protein can be shown to be the cause of the disease; yet in MS, sensitivity to myelin basic protein cannot be demonstrated. This indicates that should MS prove to be an autoimmune process, as the clinical and histologic parallels with EAE might suggest, the antigen is something other than myelin basic protein. Attempts to find any antigen to which only MS patients react have failed.

Attacks of MS are associated with changes in peripheral blood monocyte and lymphocyte properties. Reported changes include heightened prostaglandin secretion by macrophages (which may in turn influence lymphocyte properties), reduced suppressor cell function, an increased number of activated T cells as evidenced by expression of surface antigens characteristic of activated cells, heightened T cell–dependent in vitro immunoglobulin secretion, deficient interferon secretion, and possibly reduced natural killer (NK) cell function. Whether these changes relate to the etiology of MS is not known.

Within the cerebrospinal fluid (CSF), T-cell activation is apparent during active disease. Excessive IgG production within the CNS is characteristic of MS at all stages of disease; whether this reflects the presence of some stimulator of B cells in the brain in MS or is the result of a defect in immune regulation is not known. Viral infection of brain remains a possible cause of MS, despite the fact that all attempts to isolate, rescue, or ''passage'' a virus from MS brains or to visualize a virus within them have failed.

Precipitating factors   Various infections, injury, and even emotional upsets have been claimed to precipitate a first attack of MS. Evidence in support of these claims remains anecdotal and nonpersuasive. The probability that an attack of MS will occur during the first 6 months after pregnancy is greater than chance would predict, but this observation is counterbalanced by a decreased risk of an attack during the second and third trimesters of pregnancy. In established cases, trauma, including lumbar puncture, myelography, and surgery, has not been shown to relate to attacks or to progression of disability nor has emotional turmoil been shown to alter the tempo at which the disease evolves. Experience has also shown that vaccinations do not provoke attacks of MS.

CLINICAL MANIFESTATIONS The first attack of MS may declare itself as a single symptom or sign (45 percent) or as more than one (55 percent). Approximately 40 percent of MS patients will have an episode of optic neuritis, either as their first difficulty or at some point along the course of their disease. Optic neuritis presents as loss of vision, partial or total, usually in one eye, seldom in both, and is often associated with pain on movement of the eye. Macular vision tends to be most affected (central scotoma), but a wide range of field defects may occur. Disturbances of color perception sometimes provide an early indication of mild disease. Fewer than half of optic neuritis patients will show evidence of an inflamed optic nerve head (papillitis); most show no changes in the optic disc at the outset, indicating that the demyelinating lesion is developing some distance behind the nerve head (retrobulbar neuritis). Both forms of optic neuritis will be followed by optic nerve atrophy, detected as pallor of the optic disc.

It is important to recognize that most cases of optic neuritis occur as an isolated event. At most, 40 percent of individuals with optic neuritis subsequently go on to develop MS; unfortunately it is difficult to predict who will and who will not develop the disease, although presence of oligoclonal bands in the CSF is seemingly an unfavorable finding. Whether optic neuritis occurring alone and for unknown reasons constitutes a forme fruste of MS with but a single attack is not known. Approximately one-third of patients with optic neuritis recover completely, one-third partially, and one-third little or not at all. Visual evoked response testing reveals prolonged latencies of the evoked potential in the occipital cortex in more than 80 percent of established cases of MS; less than half of these can describe an antecedent optic neuritis. Clearly subclinical involvement of the optic pathways is common.

Symptoms and signs of neurologic dysfunction arising from brainstem, cerebellar, and spinal cord lesions are frequent in MS. Diplopia may occur either because the third, fourth, or sixth cranial nerve pathways are damaged along their course within the CNS or because an internuclear ophthalmoplegia (INO) has developed (see Chap. 13). An INO reflects involvement of the medial longitudinal fasciculus. The sign consists of an inability to adduct one eye on attempted lateral gaze together with full abduction of the other eye, which shows horizontal nystagmus. Bilateral INO in a young adult is virtually diagnostic of MS, although a few instances of bilateral INO in systemic lupus erythematosus are on record. Another clinical feature of brainstem involvement is either facial hypesthesia or tic douloureux (fifth cranial nerve). When tic douloureux occurs in a young adult, the possibility of underlying MS should be seriously entertained. Bell's palsy or hemifacial spasm (seventh cranial nerve), vertigo, vomiting, and nystagmus (vestibular connections of the eighth cranial nerve) are also frequent; less commonly there is complaint of deafness. Involvement of cerebellar connections or of spinocerebellar pathways results in ataxia which can affect speech (scanning), head or trunk (titubation), limbs (intention tremor), and stance and gait. Cerebellar ataxia may be combined with sensory ataxia due to involvement of the spinal cord.

Spinal cord lesions produce a myriad of motor and sensory problems. Corticospinal tract interruption results in the classical features of upper motor neuron dysfunction (weakness, spasticity, hyperreflexia, clonus, Babinski response, loss of abdominal skin reflexes). Posterior column lesions cause loss, or diminution, of joint-position and vibration senses as well as the frequently encountered complaints of tingling or tightness of the extremities and of bandlike sensations about the trunk. Less often pain and temperature sensations are lost or diminished, reflecting spinothalamic tract involvement. Partial lesions of sensory tracts or of the root entry zones of sensory nerves can produce painful dysesthesias as well as interruption of

reflex arcs. On occasion, spinal cord lesions will result in paroxysmal symptoms including tonic spasms which can be painful.

Symptoms of bladder dysfunction, including hesitancy, urgency, frequency, and incontinence, are common features of spinal cord involvement. Equally common is bowel dysfunction, particularly constipation. Males with MS, if questioned, often complain of sexual impotence; methods exist to distinguish physical from psychogenic causes. Patients with MS may experience an electric shock-like sensation on flexion of the neck, called Lhermitte's sign.

Severe spinal cord lesions can result in loss of function, sometimes total, below the level of the lesion; less complete lesions can result in the hemicord syndrome of Brown-Séquard (see Chap. 353). When either of these events occurs, it is referred to as a transverse myelitis. A single episode of transverse myelitis not followed by subsequent progression of disease may, as with an isolated episode of optic neuritis, represent a forme fruste of MS, although less than 10 percent of acute transverse myelitis cases develop MS. Again as with optic neuritis, approximately one-third of patients with transverse myelitis recover completely, one-third partially, and one-third not at all. It must be stressed that spinal cord involvement is the predominating feature in most advanced cases of MS.

Cerebral symptoms may occur in MS due to extensive involvement of subcortical and central white matter. With extensive lesions of brain, intellect may suffer, sometimes disastrously. By far the most frequent emotional feature of MS is depression. Euphoria, when it occurs, indicates widespread cerebral disease and is often associated with dementia and pseudobulbar palsy. Three to five percent of patients (twice the expected rate) will have one or more epileptic seizures, presumably because of extension of plaques into gray matter. Focal neurologic signs of cerebral origin, such as hemiparesis, homonymous hemianopsia, and dysphasia, while seen in MS, are rare.

Neuromyelitis optica and MS An ill-defined symptom complex known as Devic's syndrome, or neuromyelitis optica, is considered by some to be an entity distinguishable from MS. The complex is characterized by acute optic neuritis, usually bilateral, which is followed, or less frequently preceded, within hours to weeks by transverse myelitis. The cerebrospinal fluid may show a pleocytosis with polymorphonucler cells and a protein content that is higher than is usual for MS. Pathologic examination in fatal cases reveals more tissue destruction and cavitation than is expected in MS, although this may bespeak no more than the intensity of the process.

COURSE OF ILLNESS AND PROGNOSIS The clinical course of MS is unpredictable. In general, symptoms which appear acutely and those referable to sensory paths and the cranial nerves have a more favorable prognosis than those developing insidiously or involving motor and especially cerebellar function. According to McAlpine, 80 percent of patients who have a purely exacerbating and remitting disease have unrestricted function after 10 years. Of cases in which exacerbations and remissions are superimposed on a progressive tempo of evolution, 50 percent are disabled after 10 years. In cases that have a purely progressive course from the outset (in these the brunt of the disease usually falls on the spinal cord) long-term prognosis for ambulation is poor.

Rarely MS may be fulminant and fatal within weeks to months. Such cases, which are referred to as acute MS, show intense inflammatory responses within the plaques. Onset in such patients may be with headache, vomiting, delirium, convulsions, even coma, plus an array of signs indicating severe compromise of cortical, brainstem, optic nerve, and spinal cord function. Distinction from acute disseminated encephalomyelitis may be difficult in life; at autopsy the lesions are larger and more like those of MS.

DIFFERENTIAL DIAGNOSIS The diagnosis of MS becomes secure when signs referable to multiple lesions of CNS white matter have developed and remitted at different times. Particularly in the early phases of disease, the neurologic symptoms may suggest discrete dysfunction of the nervous system, and other causes of focal disease must be excluded. An excellent clinical rule is that MS should not be diagnosed when all the patient's symptoms and signs can be explained by a single lesion. A common aphorism is that MS presents with symptoms in one leg and signs in both.

Conditions to be excluded vary depending on the sites of the lesions. Abrupt monocular loss of vision may result from impaired vascular supply to the optic nerve, including embolic and thrombotic occlusion of the carotid, ophthalmic, or central retinal arteries, or as an accompaniment of migraine. When monocular visual loss is more gradual, compressive lesions affecting the optic nerve or an optic nerve glioma need to be considered.

In patients presenting with acute or progressive spinal cord disease, the presence of focal lesions affecting the cord and of degenerative-nutritional diseases which selectively affect spinal cord tracts should be considered (see Chaps. 349 and 353). Patients with progressive spastic paraplegia should be evaluated for the presence of intrathecal or extradural neoplasm and for cervical spondylosis. Such evaluation often requires a CT body scan, magnetic resonance imaging (MRI), or myelography. Hereditary ataxias can present as degeneration of multiple CNS tracts, with or without involvement of the peripheral nervous system. Degeneration of posterior columns and corticospinal and spinocerebellar tracts is common in these disorders. Hereditary ataxias are slowly progressive and feature stereotyped symmetric involvement as well as a family history consistent with autosomal dominant, or recessive, inheritance. Amyotrophic lateral sclerosis (ALS) usually presents with prominent lower motor neuron signs (atrophy, weakness, and fasciculations) in addition to pyramidal signs (spasticity, hyperreflexia) and without sensory abnormalities. Subacute combined degeneration of the cord can be excluded by symmetry of spinal symptoms and by a normal serum vitamin B_{12} level, a normal bone marrow, and a normal Schilling test.

When progressive brainstem dysfunction occurs, posterior fossa tumor as well as brainstem encephalitis should be excluded. Single cranial nerve palsies, particularly Bell's palsy, trigeminal sensory neuropathy, or tic douloureux may occur as part of the MS picture, but evidence of multifocal disease must be present before they can be ascribed to MS. When vertigo is the complaint and nystagmus is detected, inner ear disease should be considered as well as the possibility that barbiturates or phenytoin have been taken.

There are several multifocal and recrudescent diseases of the central nervous system which may mimic MS. Systemic lupus erythematosus and other vasculitides may cause scattered and recurring lesions within brain, brainstem, and spinal cord. Behçet's disease is characterized by recurrent episodes of focal brain disease, CSF pleocytosis, oral and genital ulcers, and uveitis. Other disorders to be excluded include meningovascular syphilis, cryptococcosis, toxoplasmosis, other chronic nervous system infections, and sarcoidosis.

When complaints are vague and findings minimal, a diagnosis of conversion reaction (hysteria) may come to mind. This diagnosis should always be made on the basis of positive criteria for hysteria and never as a "diagnosis by exclusion." Early in its course, MS is mislabeled as hysteria with distressing frequency. Patients with MS may develop superimposed hysterical phenomena adding to the complexity of the clinical syndrome.

A few patients present with pain as their principal symptom. Awareness of its occurrence in MS and careful attention to a thorough examination will usually clarify the diagnosis.

A firm diagnosis of MS should only be made when the evidence is unequivocal. Aside from the distress that such a diagnosis causes, it will serve to explain almost any subsequent neurologic event and may divert attention away from other possibly treatable diseases.

LABORATORY TESTS Although the diagnosis of MS continues to depend on its clinical features, laboratory aids have become increasingly useful as supports for the diagnosis. In the vast majority of patients with MS, one or more tests will be abnormal, although normal results do not rule out the diagnosis.

The CSF in MS patients typically reveals only a slight or no increase in cell number. Ninety percent of patients show fewer than 10 cells per cubic millimeter in their CSF; cell counts greater than 50 are rare. The cells in the CSF are predominantly T lymphocytes, although rare plasma cells may be found. Some correlation exists between the extent of pleocytosis and disease activity. Higher cell counts also are more typical in early stages of disease. Evidence that the lymphocytes in the CSF are activated not only during exacerbations of disease but also during seeming remission has been presented; this indicates that disease activity smolders at all times, even though neither the physician nor the patient may be able to detect changes. T-cell lines specifically reactive with various viral and nonviral antigens can be derived from the CSF of MS patients, again suggesting that a heterogeneous immune response is ongoing (see discussion of oligoclonal bands below). The CSF of 90 percent of patients contains less than 60 mg/dL of total protein; protein of greater than 100 mg/dL should raise questions about whether the diagnosis is correct.

The most characteristic CSF finding in MS is an increase in immunoglobulin G (IgG) which contrasts with relatively normal total protein and albumin concentrations. IgG levels are increased in 80 percent of MS patients; the increase is greatest in long-standing cases with severe neurologic deficits. Early in the disease, when the diagnosis is most in doubt, IgG values can be normal. IgG levels do not change in any meaningful way with relapses and remissions. Most of the IgG in the CSF is synthesized within the central nervous system. The increased IgG fraction in the CSF explains the first-zone abnormality of the colloidal gold curve, a test of historical interest.

When the CSF IgG from MS patients is subjected to electrophoresis or isoelectric focusing, it fractionates into a restricted number of bands (termed oligoclonal bands). Oligoclonal banding of IgG has also been found in the CSF in a number of acute and chronic central nervous system infections; in subacute sclerosing panencephalitis cases, these bands have been shown to be antibodies to the infective agent. In MS, the IgG bands have not been shown to be directed against any single viral or intrinsic brain antigen; more likely they represent a heterogeneous group of antibodies directed against many antigens. The number of bands in the CSF is greater in those with longer disease duration. It has also been suggested that high levels of IgG and many oligoclonal bands are associated with a severe course. The overall IgG shows further restrictions in its heterogeneity, with the IgG_1 being mainly of the $G1m_1$ allotype. Rare cases of MS without increased CSF IgG synthesis or oligoclonal bands have been documented at autopsy.

Within CSF, myelin debris as well as myelin basic protein appears during attacks of disease. Myelin basic protein levels can be measured by radioimmunoassay; the level seems to reflect the extent of myelin breakdown since levels also increase in other disorders associated with white matter breakdown such as stroke.

Conduction of nerve impulses along axons denuded of their myelin is slowed. Evoked response testing provides a sensitive means to detect slowed conduction of visual, auditory, or somatosensory impulses. Such tests employ repetitive sensory stimuli and utilize computer averaging techniques to record the electric responses evoked during the conduction of these stimuli along visual, auditory, or somatosensory afferent pathways. In normal subjects, the pattern of the evoked responses and time for conduction are highly predictable. One or more of the evoked response tests will reveal slowing of conduction in 80 percent of MS patients; in 30 to 40 percent of patients, abnormal evoked responses are detected without any clinical symptoms or signs in the involved pathway being apparent. Evoked response testing may confirm the presence of additional sites of disease in suspected cases with only a single clinically detectable lesion (see Chap. 341).

Computerized tomography (CT) of the brain may reveal low-density lesions within white matter, usually in a paraventricular or subcortical distribution. The incidence of such abnormalities discovered by CT scanning is reported to range from 10 to 50 percent and may reflect either active or chronic lesions as determined by pathologic criteria. Similar lesions may be noted in optic nerves and brainstem. At times, enhancement may be revealed by iodine infusion, particularly when coupled with use of high dosage of dye and delayed scanning. This finding indicates the presence of acute lesions and a disruption of the blood-brain barrier. Enhancement may disappear as the clinical symptoms resolve. Cortical atrophy with enlarged ventricles is also found in some patients.

Magnetic resonance imaging (MRI) provides an even more sensitive means to detect lesions corresponding to the low-density lesions found on CT scans. MRI scanning detects more lesions than CT scanning but fails to distinguish enhancing lesions with the sensitivity of the CT infusion scan.

Elevated CSF IgG, abnormal evoked responses, and lesions on CT scans and MRI provide useful adjuncts in evaluation of the patient with suspected MS; however, the clinical findings remain paramount in establishing the diagnosis.

TREATMENT OF MS No effective treatment for MS is known. Therapeutic efforts are directed toward (1) amelioration of the acute episode, (2) prevention of relapses, and (3) relief of symptoms.

In acute flare-ups of disease, glucocorticoid treatment may lessen the severity of symptoms and speed recovery; however, ultimate recovery is not improved by this drug nor is the extent of permanent disability altered. Glucocorticoids likely act chiefly via mechanisms other than modulation of the immune response. They may improve the ability of demyelinated nerve to conduct and reduce edema and inflammation within plaques. Usual regimens utilize either ACTH, to stimulate endogenous glucocorticoid synthesis, or prednisone. ACTH is preferred by many clinicians since the only controlled trials that demonstrated the efficacy of glucocorticoid therapy in flare-ups of MS and in acute optic neuritis were performed with this drug. ACTH is commonly given in a dose of 80 units daily intravenously for 3 to 7 days, followed by intramuscular injections in periodically decreasing doses over the next 2 to 3 weeks. Prednisone, 15 mg qid, is sometimes given rather than ACTH, again over 3 to 7 days with gradually tapering doses over the next 2 to 3 weeks. Since prednisone is taken by mouth, the treatment is simpler than with ACTH, and an admission to the hospital may sometimes be avoided. Use of long-term daily or alternate-day steroids is not advised.

Immunosuppressive agents such as azathioprine have been claimed to reduce the number of relapses in several series, but there is no consensus about the efficacy of this drug. Although the question of efficacy remains unresolved, the abnormal B-cell response seen in the blood in MS returns to normal levels with azathioprine treatment. Results from clinical trials with plasmapheresis and interferon have been equivocal. High-dose intravenous cyclophosphamide appears to transiently benefit a proportion of patients with the progressive form of MS. The above therapies and others including antithymocyte serum, total lymphoid irradiation, cyclosporine A, and copolymer I remain under active investigation.

Symptomatic treatment should address both the physical and psychological needs of patients. Patients should avoid excess fatigue and extremes of temperature and eat a balanced diet. Diets containing low levels of saturated fats have been advocated. The use of belladonna alkaloids and bethanechol chloride can help bladder dysfunction. Periodic checks for urinary tract infection should be performed. Bowel training can alleviate disorders of bowel function. Drugs available for the treatment of spasticity include diazepam, baclofen, and dantrolene sodium. Painful dysesthesias, facial twitching, tic douloureux, and tonic spasms may respond to carbamazepine or phenytoin. Occasionally trigeminal root injection is required to relieve tic douloureux (see Chap. 352).

ACUTE DISSEMINATED ENCEPHALOMYELITIS

Acute disseminated encephalomyelitis (ADEM) may be defined as a monophasic encephalitis or myelitis of abrupt onset characterized by symptoms and signs indicative of damage chiefly of the white matter of the brain or spinal cord. The process may be severe, and even fatal, or mild and evanescent. Pathologic features are those of innumerable minute foci of perivenular lymphocyte and mononuclear cell infiltration with demyelination. The topography of the demyelination corresponds to that of the inflammatory infiltrates. The condition most commonly follows vaccinations against rabies or smallpox or acute infectious illnesses, especially measles, but may occur without any obvious antecedent. The cause is uncertain but is believed by some to represent a hypersensitivity, perhaps to myelin basic protein, and to be the human counterpart of experimentally induced EAE.

ETIOLOGY The entity has been described after two types of vaccination: after rabies vaccination with the Semple vaccine, which contains brain tissue, now seldom used, and after vaccination against smallpox, now seldom performed.

Shortly after introduction of rabies vaccination by Pasteur, it became evident that neuroparalytic accidents could follow this procedure. After a course of injections a sudden encephalitic or myelitic catastrophe might occur coincident with hypersensitivity-type reactions at the sites of vaccine injection. The process clearly involved hypersensitivity to nervous system antigens. The incidence was variously reported as between 1 in 1000 and 1 in 5000 persons vaccinated. An identical syndrome has followed inoculation with noninfected brain material, indicating that killed rabies virus was not the cause; with the introduction of duck embryo killed rabies virus vaccine (which is free of myelinated nervous tissue), the condition has markedly decreased in incidence, although rare cases continue to be reported. Neuroparalytic accidents were most frequent in young adults, the peak age of occurrence corresponding to that of onset of MS.

Smallpox vaccination was also followed by an incidence of ADEM averaging perhaps 1 case per 5000 persons vaccinated but with marked differences between vaccination programs. The complication almost always occurred in conjunction with a primary take rather than a booster-type response. The encephalitis usually followed the peak of the vaccination response by a few days to a week or more but on occasion preceded it. The complication was unknown in children less than 2 years of age; in infants, smallpox vaccination was sometimes associated with an encephalopathy with brain swelling, i.e., toxic encephalopathy.

One case of measles in 1000 is followed by neurologic complications, which are often severe. The mortality rate averages 20 percent, and half the survivors are left with residual damage. The syndrome usually follows the rash by a few days. It bears no relationship to the severity of measles itself. Systemic lymphocyte sensitivity to myelin basic protein has been demonstrated in some patients. All attempts to isolate a virus have failed. Abnormal CSF and changes in the electroencephalogram are observed in perhaps half the children who contract measles, suggesting that subclinical neurologic involvement may be much more widespread than is usually appreciated. A subtle decline in performance and changes in behavior following measles may reflect this inapparent nervous system involvement. Measles vaccination has drastically reduced the frequency of this complication.

An identical clinical picture was seen formerly as a complication of smallpox and is still encountered during or following chickenpox and extremely rarely as a complication of rubella. Demyelinating encephalomyelitis is very rare in mumps; instead there is often a true viral meningitis. A clinical picture identical to postinfectious encephalomyelitis has been described after mycoplasma infections. Despite its striking association with measles, the occurrence of the same clinical picture after several different infections fits better with the postulate that the basic process involves hypersensitivity rather than a direct viral infection of the brain and spinal cord. All attempts to isolate a virus have failed.

CLINICAL MANIFESTATIONS The disease usually begins abruptly. Headache and delirium may give way to lethargy and coma. Coma has an ominous prognosis. Seizures at the onset or shortly thereafter are not infrequent. There may be stiffness of the neck, other signs of meningeal irritation, and fever. Focal signs may be engrafted on this picture, and spinal cord involvement with flaccid paralysis of all four limbs is particularly common. Monoparesis and hemiplegia are also seen. Tendon reflexes may be lost initially only to become hyperactive later; extensor plantar responses are the rule, and sphincter control is generally lost. Sensory loss is variable but may be extensive and severe. Brainstem involvement may be reflected by nystagmus, ocular palsies, and pupillary changes. Some cases may present as a purely spinal cord syndrome and in mild instances with minor signs such as a facial palsy. Chorea and athetosis are rare. Cerebellar signs may predominate, particularly in cases associated with chickenpox. Involvement of motor and sensory peripheral nerves can be documented clinically and electromyographically in some patients. The CSF almost always shows an increase in protein (50 to 100 mg/dL) and lymphocytes (10 to several hundred cells); rarely it is normal. The mortality is 20 percent, and perhaps half the survivors have residual deficits. Recurrences are almost unknown.

The diagnosis is not difficult if there is a history of rabies or smallpox vaccination or of measles. In cases without such a history, distinction from viral encephalitis may be difficult and at times not possible. Reye's syndrome (see Chap. 347) may be difficult to distinguish from acute disseminated encephalomyelitis. Vomiting at onset, a normal CSF, hyperammonemia, and raised intracranial pressure should suggest Reye's syndrome; frequent convulsions and focal signs argue against it. A distinction from acute MS may not be possible.

PREVENTION AND TREATMENT Since smallpox has been eradicated, there is no longer reason to vaccinate against it. Use of duck embryo and human diploid vaccine in rabies prophylaxis has almost eliminated neuroparalytic accidents, and measles vaccination has drastically reduced what used to be the largest group of postinfectious encephalomyelitides.

Administration of high doses of glucocorticoids every 4 to 6 h is the treatment of choice though controlled trials have not been carried out.

ACUTE NECROTIZING HEMORRHAGIC ENCEPHALOMYELITIS

Acute necrotizing hemorrhagic encephalomyelitis is a rare tissue-destructive disease of the CNS which occurs with explosive suddenness within a few days of an upper respiratory infection. The pathologic findings are distinctive. On sectioning the brain, much of the white matter of one or both hemispheres is seen to be destroyed almost to the point of liquefaction. The involved tissue is pink or yellowish-gray and flecked with multiple small hemorrhages. Sometimes similar changes are localized to the brainstem or spinal cord. On histologic examination the core lesion resembles that of acute disseminated encephalomyelitis in showing perivenular foci of demyelination, all of like age. As in acute disseminated encephalomyelitis lymphocytes and macrophages are present in the regions of myelin loss, but superimposed on and dominating the picture is an intense polymorphonuclear infiltrate, in keeping with the necrotizing nature of the process. The vessels themselves are partially necrotic; they may contain platelet or fibrin thrombi within their lumens and fibrin deposits beyond their walls. Multiple small hemorrhages at sites of vessel damage are an invariable feature as is a violent inflammatory reaction in the meninges. Large necrotic foci form by coalescence of smaller lesions in the hemispheres, brainstem, or spinal cord.

The clinical course of the illness resembles that of acute disseminated encephalomyelitis save for its apoplectiform onset and rapidity of progress, sometimes leading to death within 48 h. Neurologic signs are frequently unilateral, reflecting disease in one cerebral hemisphere, but may be bilateral. It is probable that certain patients showing an explosive myelitic illness are suffering from a necrotizing myelitis of similar type, but pathologic evidence in support of this

view has been difficult to obtain. The CSF examination discloses a more intense reaction than in other demyelinating diseases. Often a polymorphonuclear pleocytosis of up to 2000 cells and a considerable increase in amount of protein are detected. In cases of slower evolution the cell counts are lower and cells are mainly of the mononuclear type.

The etiology of this disease is not established; however, the entire clinical-pathologic entity bears a close resemblance to a hyperacute form of EAE which can be induced in animals by administration of endotoxin, pertussis vaccine, or its histamine sensitizing factor coincident with or shortly after injection of myelin in adjuvant. The lesions in this experimental disease can perhaps be considered as those of a Sanarelli-Schwartzman reaction within the brain superimposed on an acutely demyelinating process. Rarely a lesion like acute necrotizing hemorrhagic encephalomyelitis occurs in MS.

The differential diagnosis of this disorder includes acute encephalitis, particularly those types causing tissue necrosis (herpes simplex, arbovirus), acute bacterial cerebritis, septic embolic occlusion of an artery, thrombophlebitis, and suppurative brain abscess. The similarity of acute necrotizing hemorrhagic encephalomyelitis to acute disseminated encephaloymyelitis suggests that steroid therapy may be beneficial.

REFERENCES

Ebers GC, Paty D: HLA typing in multiple sclerosis sibling pairs. Lancet 1:88, 1982
Johnson RT et al: Measles encephalomyelitis: Clinical and immunological studies. N Engl J Med 310:137, 1984
McAlpine D et al: *Multiple Sclerosis: A Reappraisal.* London, Churchill Livingston, 1972
McFarlin DE, McFarland ME: Multiple sclerosis. N Engl J Med 307:1183 and 1246, 1982
Poser CM et al: *The Diagnosis of Multiple Sclerosis.* New York, Thieme-Stratton, 1984
Scheinberg L, Raine CS: *Multiple Sclerosis—Experimental and Clinical Aspects.* New York, Annals of The New York Academy of Sciences, 1984, vol 436
Waxman SG: Membranes, myelin, and the pathophysiology of multiple sclerosis. N Engl J Med 306:1529, 1982

349   NUTRITIONAL AND METABOLIC DISEASES OF THE NERVOUS SYSTEM

MAURICE VICTOR / JOSEPH B. MARTIN

Included under the title of this chapter is a large and diverse number of neurologic disorders which fall readily into two distinct types—acquired and inherited. In this chapter, emphasis will be on the *acquired* diseases, insofar as they are essentially disorders of adult life and a major source of concern to internist and neurologist alike. In fact, no other category of disease so clearly exemplifies the interdependence of these two medical disciplines. The *inherited* metabolic and nutritional diseases, on the other hand, are predominantly disorders of infancy and childhood, and are more appropriately considered in a textbook of pediatrics. However, a small proportion of the inherited diseases permit survival to adolescence or early adult life or may even have their onset during these periods. These latter instances, which need to be differentiated from certain degenerative and acquired metabolic diseases, are discussed here briefly and in other chapters of this book to which the reader will be referred.

DISEASES DUE TO NUTRITIONAL DEFICIENCY

The general aspects of deficiency disease have been presented in Chap. 76, which should be reviewed as an introduction to the discussion of deficiency diseases of the nervous system. The term *deficiency* will be used here in its strictest sense, to designate those diseases or syndromes which result from the *lack of an essential nutrient in the diet or from a conditioning factor which increases the need for that nutrient*. The neurologic diseases which belong in this category are the following:

1 Wernicke's disease and Korsakoff's psychosis
2 "Alcoholic" cerebellar degeneration
3 Nutritional polyneuropathy (neuropathic beriberi)
4 Pellagra
5 Deficiency amblyopia (nutritional optic neuropathy)
6 The syndrome of amblyopia, painful neuropathy, and orogenital dermatitis (Strachan's syndrome)
7 Subacute combined degeneration of the spinal cord (vitamin B_{12} deficiency)
8 Vitamin E deficiency

A number of general principles are applicable to all of the diseases under consideration. Of the known vitamin deficiencies, it is essentially those of the B group which are of importance in neurologic disease [vitamin E deficiency due to cholestasis is a rare cause of central nervous system (CNS) disease in young children]. Thiamine chloride, nicotinic acid, pyridoxine, pantothenic acid, and riboflavin all play a role in carbohydrate metabolism, upon which the CNS depends for its principal source of energy. These vitamins function as coenzymes in the Krebs tricarboxylic acid cycle; in addition, thiamine is involved in the hexose-monophosphate shunt. Vitamin B_{12} is required for the conversion of methylmalonyl to succinyl coenzyme A and for the conversion of homocystine to methionine.

Except for subacute combined degeneration of the spinal cord and other manifestations of vitamin B_{12} deficiency, it is not possible to relate the deficiency diseases in humans to the lack of one particular vitamin. For example, polyneuropathy may result from any one of several vitamin deficiencies [thiamine chloride (vitamin B_1), pyridoxine (vitamin B_6), pantothenic acid, and probably B_{12}]. Moreover, pellagra, beriberi, and Strachan's syndrome are probably related to a deficiency of several vitamins. These generalizations should not obscure the fact that certain manifestations of deficiency disease are related to the lack of a specific nutrient (e.g., the ocular signs of Wernicke's disease to a deficiency of thiamine).

In the western world the deficiency diseases of the nervous system are observed most often in the alcoholic population of large urban centers. Alcohol acts mainly by displacing food in the diet, but it also increases the demand for B vitamins, which are necessary to metabolize the carbohydrate furnished by alcohol itself, and it may impair the gastrointestinal absorption of vitamins. Dietary faddism, impaired absorption of dietary nutrients (as occurs in sprue or following plication of the stomach or resection of stomach and small bowel), and the use of certain drugs (e.g., isoniazid and hydralazine, which interfere with the enzymatic function of pyridoxine) account for a relatively small number of cases of deficiency disease.

Each of the deficiency diseases may occur in pure form and will be so described. More often they occur in various combinations. Stated in another way, it is usual for deficiency diseases to involve both the central and peripheral nervous systems, an attribute which they share with few other categories of disease. Also, the examination of patients with deficiency disease frequently discloses nonneurologic signs of malnutrition such as general wasting, lesions of the skin and mucous membranes, and circulatory abnormalities.

WERNICKE'S DISEASE OR ENCEPHALOPATHY In 1881, Carl Wernicke described an illness of acute onset characterized by mental disturbance, paralysis of eye movements, and ataxia of gait. Swelling of the optic discs and retinal hemorrhages were also said to be present. In all three of Wernicke's patients there was a progressive depression of the state of consciousness, leading to death, so that a fatal outcome was at one time thought to be a universal feature of this disease. Wernicke described focal vascular lesions, affecting the gray matter around the third and fourth ventricles and aqueduct of Sylvius. He regarded the disease as inflammatory in nature and suggested the

name *acute superior hemorrhagic polioencephalitis*. Since Wernicke's time, views regarding this disease have undergone considerable modification.

Symptoms and signs The most readily recognized abnormalities are the ocular motor signs, and it is difficult to make the diagnosis without them. The usual ocular abnormality is a weakness or paralysis of abduction (6th nerve palsy) which is invariably bilateral though rarely symmetric and is accompanied by horizontal diplopia, internal strabismus, and nystagmus. Three types of nystagmus may occur, conjugate horizontal or vertical gaze–evoked nystagmus being the most frequent. Rarely, one sees a primary position upbeat or downbeat nystagmus with oscillopsia. An asymmetric horizontal gaze–evoked nystagmus in the abducting eye is characteristic of internuclear ophthalmoplegia. The latter disorder may be present alone, but far more often a constellation of signs of disordered motility are present, including supranuclear paralysis of gaze. Horizontal gaze palsy, unilateral or bilateral, is more frequently seen than vertical gaze palsy. Rarely an isolated paralysis of downgaze occurs, or isolated paralysis of convergence or divergence. The vestibular responses to caloric stimulation are characteristically impaired. In advanced stages of the disease there may be complete loss of ocular movement, and the pupils, which ordinarily are spared, may become miotic and nonreacting. Ptosis and retinal hemorrhages are observed rarely. It is noteworthy that intravenous vitamin therapy in the early stages of the disease can result in dramatic recovery of the eye movement disorders although nystagmus may persist.

The *ataxia* affects stance and gait predominantly. It may be so severe initially that the patient is unable to stand or walk without support. With specific treatment the disorder of equilibrium improves, and the patient is left with a wide-based, uncertain gait. The mildest degree of ataxia is brought out only by heel-to-toe walking. In contrast to the gross disorder of locomotion, an intention (cerebellar) tremor of the limbs is relatively infrequent. The latter abnormality, when present, affects the legs more than the arms. Scanning speech is present only in isolated cases.

A derangement of mental function is found in about 90 percent of patients and takes one of several forms: (1) The most common is a *global confusional-apathetic state*, characterized by profound listlessness, inattentiveness, indifference to the surroundings, and disorientation. Unconsciousness or deep stupor as the initial abnormality is distinctly rare, but mild drowsiness is common. Spontaneous speech is minimal. Many questions directed to the patient go unanswered, or the patient may fall asleep while being questioned, a state from which he or she can be readily aroused, however. Whatever questions the patient answers betray disorientation in time and place, misidentification of those nearby and an inability to grasp the meaning of the illness or immediate situation. Many of the patient's remarks are irrational and show no consistency from one moment to another. Under these circumstances a more extensive evaluation of intellectual function is seldom possible. (2) Some patients, at the time they are first seen, already show a disproportionate disorder of retentive memory, i.e., Korsakoff's amnesic state (see Chap. 23 and later in this chapter). (3) A relatively small number of patients (less than 20 percent in our series) show the symptoms of alcohol withdrawal, either delirium tremens or a variant thereof.

The symptoms of Wernicke's disease may all appear simultaneously and rather acutely, but more often the ophthalmoplegia and/or ataxia precede the mental signs by a few days and sometimes by a week or more.

Wernicke's disease is usually associated with other nutritional disorders, both neurologic and nonneurologic. In more than 80 percent of patients, a *polyneuropathy* of varying degrees of severity is evident. Rarely, *amblyopia* or *spinal spastic ataxia* may be added to the clinical picture. Many patients in the chronic stage of the disease demonstrate impaired olfactory discrimination, a defect that is most likely related to the diencephalic lesions (see below).

Full-blown beriberi heart disease is rarely observed in association with Wernicke's disease, although indications of *disordered cardio-*

vascular function such as tachycardia, exertional dyspnea, postural hypotension, and minor ECG abnormalities are common. Occasionally patients may die suddenly, the mode of death suggesting "cardiovascular collapse." It has been shown that Wernicke's disease is characterized by a state of high cardiac output which is out of proportion to the oxygen consumption. This is probably due to an abnormal state of peripheral vasodilatation, which in turn may be related to thiamine deficiency. Postural hypertension and syncope are related to impaired function of the automatic nervous system, more specifically to a defect in sympathetic regulation.

Ancillary findings   Vestibular function, as measured by the response to standard caloric testing, is always impaired bilaterally and more or less symmetrically in the acute stages of Wernicke's disease (*vestibular paresis*). The cerebrospinal fluid (CSF) is normal or shows only a modest elevation of protein content; protein values above 100 mg/dL or a pleocytosis should always suggest the presence of a complicating illness. In untreated cases of Wernicke's disease, there is invariably an elevation of the *blood pyruvate,* and a marked reduction in the *blood transketolase* (a thiamine-dependent enzyme of the hexose monophosphate shunt). Diffuse slowing of the EEG, mild to moderate in degree, occurs in about one-half of the patients. On the other hand, total cerebral blood flow and cerebral oxygen and glucose consumption may be greatly reduced in the acute stages of the disease and may persist for several weeks after the institution of treatment.

Course of the illness   Death occurs in 15 to 20 percent of hospitalized patients and is usually due to a complicating infection (pneumonia, pulmonary tuberculosis, and septicemia being the most common) or to hepatic failure.

Patients who recover do so in a characteristic manner. Ocular palsies may *begin to improve* within hours after the administration of thiamine and practically always within several days. Failure of the patient to respond in this manner should raise doubts about the diagnosis of Wernicke's disease. Sixth nerve palsies, ptosis, and vertical gaze palsies recover completely, within a week or two in most cases, but gaze–evoked vertical nystagmus may occasionally persist for several months. Horizontal gaze palsies recover completely as a rule, but in more than half the patients a fine horizontal gaze–evoked nystagmus remains as a permanent sequela of the disease.

Ataxia improves somewhat more slowly than the ocular motor abnormalities. Approximately half the patients recover incompletely and are left with a slow, shuffling, wide-based gait and inability to walk tandem. The residual gait disturbance and horizontal nystagmus provide a means of identifying obscure and chronic cases of dementia as alcoholic-nutritional in origin. Vestibular function, as measured by caloric testing, improves at about the same rate as the ataxia of stance and gait, i.e., over a period of weeks or months, and recovery is usually but not always complete.

The symptoms of apathy, drowsiness, and confusion recede gradually, and as they do, the *defect in retentive memory and learning (Korsakoff's psychosis; see Chap. 23)* stands out more clearly. It is important to emphasize that in the alcoholic, nutritionally deficient patient Wernicke's disease and Korsakoff's psychosis are not separate diseases, but the changing ocular and ataxic signs and the transformation of the global confusion state into an amnesic syndrome are successive stages in the recovery of a single disease process. Stated in another way, Korsakoff's psychosis is the psychic component of Wernicke's disease. Hence the symptom complex should be called Wernicke's disease when the amnesic state is not evident and the Wernicke-Korsakoff syndrome when both the ocular-ataxic and amnesic symptoms can be recognized.

The outcome of Korsakoff's psychosis varies. Complete or almost complete recovery occurs in less than 20 percent of patients. In the remainder recovery is slow and incomplete. Depending on the severity of the residual symptoms, the patient may or may not be able to lead a supervised existence out of a hospital. The residual mental state is characterized by large gaps in memory, without confabulation, and

an inability of the patient to sort out events in their proper temporal sequence. This late stage of the disease, when the ocular and ataxic signs have receded or are not recognized, is often loosely referred to as "alcoholic deteriorated state" or "alcoholic dementia."

Pathologic changes   Postmortem examination of patients who die in the acute stages of Wernicke-Korsakoff disease discloses symmetrically placed lesions in the paraventricular regions of the thalamus and hypothalamus, the mamillary bodies, the periaqueductal region of the midbrain, the floor of the fourth ventricle, and the anterior-superior folia of the cerebellum, particularly of the vermis. Lesions are invariably found in the mamillary bodies and less consistently in the other areas. Microscopically, the principal change consists of varying degrees of necrosis of parenchymal structures. Many nerve cells and fibers are destroyed; others remain intact and are seen against a background of reactive glial elements, both astrocytes and microgliocytes. The blood vessels are prominent, owing to adventitial and endothelial proliferation. Hemorrhagic lesions are present in a small proportion of cases and usually give the appearance of being of recent origin. The oculomotor and vestibular nuclei are regularly involved, but to a lesser degree.

Clinical-pathologic correlations   The ocular motor signs are attributable to lesions in the brainstem affecting the abducens nuclei and eye movement centers in the pons and rostral midbrain (see Chap. 13). The lesions of the vestibular nuclei are probably responsible for the loss of caloric responses and gross abnormality of equilibrium that characterize the initial stage of the disease. The lack of significant destruction of nerve cells in these lesions accounts for the rapid improvement in oculomotor and vestibular function.

The persistent ataxia of stance and gait is related to the loss of neurons in the superior vermis of the cerebellum; extension of the lesion into the anterior parts of the anterior lobes accounts for the ataxia of individual movements of the legs. These cerebellar lesions are indistinguishable from those of so-called *alcoholic cerebellar degeneration* (see below).

The amnesic defect is related to lesions in the diencephalon, more specifically to those in the medial dorsal nuclei of the thalami. Lesions in the mamillary bodies are probably not critical in respect to memory function since they are found in patients with Wernicke's disease who had shown no disorder of memory during life.

Etiology and pathogenesis   Nutritional deficiency is now established as the causal factor. Wernicke's disease has been encountered in prisoners-of-war and in patients with wasting diseases of varied origin, i.e., circumstances in which alcohol played no part. The specific factor that is responsible for most, if not all, of the symptoms of the Wernicke-Korsakoff syndrome is a deficiency of thiamine. The marked sensitivity of the ocular abnormalities to the administration of thiamine accounts for their rapid abatement after the ingestion of a meal or two. The quality of prompt reversibility suggests that the ocular signs are due to a biochemical abnormality and not to irreversible structural changes. On the other hand, the slow and incomplete recovery of the memory defect suggests that this symptom is due to irreversible structural changes, presumably in the medial dorsal nuclei.

The selective vulnerability of certain periventricular regions to a deficiency of thiamine is not understood. McEntee and Mair have pointed out that the lesions lie in the monoamine-containing pathways and have presented evidence that 3-methoxy-4-hydroxyphenylglycol (MHPG), the primary brain metabolite of norepinephrine, is decreased in the CNS of patients with Korsakoff's psychosis; moreover, the administration of clonidine, an alpha$_2$ adrenergic agonist, seemed to improve the memory disorder in these patients. These authors theorized that damage to the ascending norepinephrine-containing neurons in the brainstem and diencephalon may be the basis for the amnesia.

The topography of the lesions caused by thiamine deficiency has been studied in rhesus monkeys. Witt and Goldman-Rakic found that the severity and number of brain nuclei affected are related to the duration and number of bouts of thiamine deficiency. Blass and Gibson have suggested that a genetically determined defect in transketolase may be operative in the pathogenesis of Wernicke's disease. They found that transketolase in cultural fibroblasts from patients with this disease bound thiamine pyrophosphate (TPP) less avidly than did the transketolase from control lines. This defect in transketolase would presumably be insignificant if the diet were adequate, but would be harmful if the diet were low in thiamine. These findings may explain why only a small proportion of alcoholics develop Wernicke-Korsakoff disease.

Treatment of the Wernicke-Korsakoff syndrome Wernicke's disease represents a medical emergency, and its recognition demands the immediate administration of thiamine. A delay of a few hours may be crucial in determining whether the patient with ocular and ataxic signs will be prevented from developing Korsakoff's psychosis and whether the patient with early Korsakoff's changes will be restored to a state of mental competency. Although 2 to 3 mg of thiamine may modify the ocular signs, much larger doses are needed to replenish the thiamine stores—50 mg intravenously and 50 mg intramuscularly, the latter dose being repeated each day until the patient resumes a normal diet. The other B vitamins may be given by mouth in the dosages outlined in Chap. 76. If the patient cannot or will not eat, parenteral feeding and administration of B vitamins become necessary.

A particular danger attends the treatment of the severely depleted alcoholic patient with intravenous glucose solutions. Such infusions may exhaust the patient's reserve of B vitamins and either precipitate Wernicke's disease in a previously unaffected patient or cause a rapid worsening of an early form of the disease. For this reason, B vitamins must be administered to all alcoholic patients requiring parenteral glucose. If there are signs of cardiac failure, rapid digitalization should be undertaken. Since these patients are confused and forgetful, they must be supervised continually, preferably on a medical ward.

A special problem in management arises when the patient recovers from the acute phase of the illness and the amnesic psychosis becomes prominent. The disposition of the patient to family, nursing home, or mental institution should be undertaken on the basis of the severity of the mental illness as well as the capacity of the family unit and social circumstances.

"ALCOHOLIC" CEREBELLAR DEGENERATION This is the term applied to a common, stereotyped, nonfamilial form of cerebellar ataxia which occurs on a background of prolonged ingestion of alcohol. Usually the symptoms evolve in subacute fashion, i.e., over several weeks or months, sometimes more rapidly. In some patients the symptoms are present in mild but stable form and worsen after an attack of pneumonia or delirium tremens.

The signs are those of cerebellar dysfunction, affecting stance and gait predominantly. The legs are involved more severely than the arms, and nystagmus and speech disturbances occur relatively infrequently. Once established, the signs change very little, although some improvement of gait may follow the cessation of drinking, due probably to improvement in general nutrition and recovery from an associated polyneuropathy.

The pathologic changes consist of degeneration of varying severity of all the neurocellular elements of the cerebellar cortex, particularly of the Purkinje cells, with a striking topographic restriction to the anterior and superior aspects of the vermis and adjacent parts of the anterior lobes of the cerebellum. The disorder of stance and gait is related to the lesion in the vermis, and the ataxia of the limbs to the involvement of the anterior lobes. A similar clinical-pathologic syndrome is observed occasionally in nutritionally depleted nonalcoholic patients.

NUTRITIONAL POLYNEUROPATHY (See also Chaps. 76 and 355) In the United States, nutritional polyneuropathy is essentially a disease of the alcoholic population. As mentioned above, it is present in more than 80 percent of patients with the Wernicke-Korsakoff syndrome, but it also occurs frequently as the only manifestation of deficiency disease. The peripheral neuropathy of alcoholics ("alcoholic polyneuropathy") does not differ in any fundamental way from that of beriberi. The clinical features of nutritional polyneuropathy and its identity with beriberi are discussed in Chaps. 76 and 355. A deficiency of thiamine chloride, pyridoxine, pantothenic acid, vitamin B_{12}, and perhaps folic acid has been demonstrated in individual cases to cause nutritional polyneuropathy. In the alcoholic patient it is usually not possible to incriminate any particular one of these vitamins.

Central nervous system toxicity to alcohol not associated with vitamin deficiency Alcohol-related brain lesions not attributable to nutritional deficiency or trauma are now recognized to occur. There is an increased incidence of hypertension in alcoholics and probably of strokes, both ischemic infarction and spontaneous subarachnoid hemorrhage. Alcoholics as a group also show dilatation of the lateral ventricles and widening of sulci on CT scanning compared to controls. The nature of these changes is obscure. They do not represent cerebral atrophy insofar as partial and sometimes complete reversal occur with sustained abstinence. The notion that alcohol can cause intellectual deterioration separate from effects due to nutritional deficiency is constantly reiterated in medical writings, but the entity of "alcoholic dementia" has never been established on the basis of clinical and neuropathologic studies. A syndrome of progressive myelopathy occurring in alcoholics has also been described clinically. Such patients show no evidence of nutritional deficiency (B_{12} or folic acid) or of liver disease (Sage et al.). The nature of the spinal cord disease is unknown, and a causal relationship to the toxic effects of alcohol remains to be established.

PELLAGRA This disease is described in Chap. 76. The comments here are concerned only with the neurologic manifestations, which in themselves are quite diverse. Pellagra is essentially an encephalopathy, although involvement of the spinal cord and peripheral nerves may occur. The early mental symptoms—insomnia, fatigue, anxiety, nervousness, irritability, and feelings of depression—may be mistaken for those of a psychiatric disorder. However, careful examination as the disease advances will reveal slowing and inefficiency of mental processes and impairment of memory. Pellagra may not only be the cause of psychiatric manifestations but occasionally may result from them because certain mental illnesses, including alcoholism, are accompanied by anorexia and dietary deficiency.

The spinal cord affection in pellagra has not been clearly delineated, perhaps because the mental state of the patients has precluded accurate testing. In general, there is evidence of both posterior and lateral column involvement, predominantly the former. Neuropathic signs are frequent and difficult to distinguish from other types of nutritional polyneuropathy. Other manifestations such as tremor, extrapyramidal rigidity, suck and grasp reflexes, and coma (referred to in the past as "nicotinic acid–deficiency encephalopathy") have indiscriminately been included in the pellagrous syndrome, as have various disorders of the special senses.

A *spastic paretic syndrome,* apart from the other symptoms and signs of pellagra, may be a rare manifestation of the deficiency. The chief clinical signs are spastic weakness of the legs with absent abdominal and increased tendon reflexes, clonus, and extensor plantar responses. These signs are usually accompanied by other manifestations of nutritional deficiency, such as Wernicke's disease, amblyopia, and peripheral neuropathy.

Pathologic features The distinctive neuropathologic changes in pellagra are most readily discerned in the large Betz cells of the motor cortex, although the same changes are seen to a lesser extent in the smaller pyramidal cells of the cerebral cortex and cells of the basal ganglia, cranial motor and dentate nuclei, and anterior horns of the spinal cord. The affected cells appear swollen and rounded with eccentric nuclei and loss of Nissl staining. This *central neuritis of pellagra,* as it is called, appears to represent a primary affection of the whole motor cell. The spinal cord lesions take the form of a symmetric degeneration of the dorsal columns, especially the fasciculus gracilis, and to a lesser extent of the corticospinal tracts. The posterior column degeneration is probably secondary to degeneration of specific dorsal root ganglion cells.

DEFICIENCY AMBLYOPIA (NUTRITIONAL OPTIC NEUROPATHY, TOBACCO-ALCOHOL AMBLYOPIA)

These terms refer to a characteristic form of visual impairment that complicates nutritional disease and is due to a lesion in the optic nerve, more or less confined to the zone of the papillomacular bundle. The cornea and other parts of the refractive mechanism are uninvolved, hence the term *amblyopia*.

The main symptoms are dimness or blurring of vision for near and distant objects and impairment of color vision which worsens progressively and insidiously for several days or weeks. In addition to a reduction in visual acuity, examination discloses the presence of bilateral and roughly symmetric central or centrocecal scotomas, which are larger for colored than for white test objects. Pallor of the temporal portion of the optic disc is observed in some cases. Untreated, this condition progresses to irreversible optic atrophy.

Deficiency amblyopia was a common occurrence during the second World War and the Korean War. Although this form of amblyopia had previously been described in association with beriberi (due to thiamine deficiency) and pellagra (due to niacin deficiency), the peak incidence among prisoners coincided with neither of these syndromes but with the syndrome of orogenital dermatitis and "burning feet" (see below, "Strachan's syndrome").

In the United States, most, if not all, of the cases of retrobulbar neuropathy attributed to the toxic effects of alcohol or tobacco—so-called tobacco-alcohol amblyopia—are of nutritional origin. Although optic neuropathy may occur as the only manifestation of vitamin deficiency, more often it is combined with other evidence of nutritional deficiency, such as peripheral neuropathy and the Wernicke-Korsakoff syndrome.

Although the nutritional origin of this type of amblyopia has been established, the specific vitamin deficiency can rarely be determined. Observations in both humans and experimental animals indicate that a deficiency of thiamine (vitamin B_1), vitamin B_{12}, or perhaps riboflavin may cause lesions in the optic nerves. Heavy smokers with vitamin B_{12} deficiency appear to be particularly vulnerable to optic neuropathy. Two causative mechanisms for the pathogenesis of tobacco amblyopia have been offered: (1) chronic cyanide (generated in tobacco smoke) poisoning; and (2) alterations of fatty acid metabolism resulting from derangement of proprionate metabolism in the central nervous system. The notion that cyanide or other substances in tobacco smoke have a toxic effect upon the optic nerves is not supported by experimental data. And, since fatty acids take part in the formation and preservation of myelin, it is conceivable that the biochemical consequences of vitamin B_{12} deficiency are sufficient in themselves to account for both ophthalmologic and neurologic involvement.

Treatment consists of the administration of a balanced diet, supplemented with B vitamins, and the interdiction of alcohol and smoking where this is a factor.

SYNDROME OF AMBLYOPIA, PAINFUL NEUROPATHY, AND OROGENITAL DERMATITIS (STRACHAN'S SYNDROME)

Beginning with the observations of Strachan, in 1888 and 1897, there have been many reports from diverse sources concerning a neurologic syndrome which is undoubtedly nutritional in origin but which cannot be forced into the boundaries of the classic deficiency diseases, beriberi and pellagra. Strachan attributed the disorder to malaria. Originally known as "Jamaican neuritis," the syndrome was soon recognized among the undernourished population of many other tropical countries. Large numbers of patients with this syndrome were observed also in the beseiged population of Madrid during the Spanish Civil War and later during World War II among prisoners of war in the Middle and Far East. In the United States, patients with this syndrome are found occasionally in the alcoholic population.

Strachan's syndrome is essentially a disorder of the peripheral and optic nerves. The peripheral nerve disorder is characterized mainly by sensory symptoms and signs (paresthesias and painful hyperesthesia of the feet, loss of superficial and deep sensation, and ataxia). On the other hand, foot drop and muscle weakness occur very rarely. A frequently associated disorder is failing vision, which may go on to complete blindness and pallor of the optic discs. Deafness and vertigo are rare additional complications, but in some outbreaks among prisoners of war these symptoms were so prominent as to earn the epithet "camp dizziness." In all these respects the syndrome differs from beriberi. Along with the neurologic signs there may be varying degrees of stomatoglossitis, corneal degeneration, and genital dermatitis. These mucocutaneous lesions are spoken of together as the *orogenital syndrome* and are quite distinct from the dermal changes of pellagra.

There have been only a few pathologic studies of this syndrome. Aside from the damage to the papillomacular bundle in the optic nerve, the most consistent abnormality has been a loss of myelinated fibers in posterior columns (fasciculus gracilis) of the spinal cord. This indicates a systematized degeneration of the central processes of the bipolar large sensory neurons of the lumbosacral spinal ganglia. The loss of pain and temperature sensation is thought due to an axonopathy. There are no reliable data concerning the specific vitamin deficiencies that cause this disease.

SUBACUTE COMBINED DEGENERATION (SCD) OF THE SPINAL CORD

(See Chap. 76)   This term designates the spinal cord disease that is due to vitamin B_{12} deficiency. The brain, optic nerves, and peripheral nerves may also be affected but far less often than the spinal cord. The neurologic manifestations of vitamin B_{12} deficiency and the hematologic ones (pernicious anemia) are distinctive insofar as they are caused not by a lack of vitamin B_{12} in the food but by an inability to transfer minute amounts of this nutrient across the intestinal mucosa—aptly characterized by Castle as "starvation in the midst of plenty." Such a nutritional disorder is referred to as a *conditioned deficiency*, since it depends upon the lack of an intrinsic factor in the gastric secretions (see Chap. 285). Rarely neurologic symptoms due to vitamin B_{12} deficiency occur in patients with disease of the distal small intestine (Crohn's disease, lymphoma) or after surgical resection.

Clinical manifestations   Neurologic symptoms are present in the majority of patients with vitamin B_{12} deficiency. The patient first notices general weakness and paresthesias, consisting of tingling, "pins-and-needles" feelings, or other vaguely described sensations in the distal parts of the limbs; the lower extremites may be involved before the upper ones or vice versa. The paresthesias tend to be constant, to progress steadily, and to be the source of much distress. As the illness progresses, the gait becomes unsteady, and movements of the limbs, especially the legs, become stiff and awkward.

Early in the course of the illness, when only paresthesias are present, there may be no objective signs. Later, the neurologic examination discloses a disorder of the posterior and lateral columns of the spinal cord, predominantly the former. Loss of vibration sense is by far the most consistent sign; it is more pronounced in the legs than in the arms, and frequently it extends over the trunk. Position sense is involved somewhat less frequently. The motor defects are usually limited to the legs and include loss of power, spasticity, changes in the tendon reflexes, clonus, and extensor plantar responses. At first the patellar and Achilles reflexes are found to be diminished as frequently as they are increased, and they may even be absent. With treatment, the reflexes may return to normal or become hyperactive. The gait at first is predominantly ataxic, later ataxic and spastic. If the disease remains untreated, an ataxic paraplegia with variable degrees of spasticity and contracture may develop.

A loss of superficial sensation below a segmental level on the trunk, implicating the spinothalamic tracts, occurs rarely, but such a finding should always suggest the possibility of some other disease of the spinal cord. More often the sensory defect takes the form of a blunting of tactile, painful, and thermal sensation over the distal segments of the lower limbs, implicating the peripheral nerves, but such findings are also uncommon.

The nervous system involvement in vitamin B_{12} deficiency is characteristically, though not perfectly, symmetric. A definite asymmetry of motor or sensory findings, maintained over a period of weeks or months, should always cast doubt on the diagnosis.

Mental signs are frequent, ranging from irritability, apathy, somnolence, suspiciousness, and emotional instability to a marked confusional or depressive psychosis, or even to intellectual deterioration. Optic neuropathy with impaired acuity and cecocentral scotoma has been reported with virtually all causes of vitamin B_{12} deficiency including postsurgical malabsorption syndrome and pernicious anemia. In all cases, variable improvement in acuity has occurred once systemic vitamin B_{12} has been administered. Pathologic studies in the setting of vitamin B_{12} deficiency optic neuropathy and subacute combined degeneration of the spinal cord have shown patchy demyelination of the optic nerves. If involvement of the optic nerve is severe, optic atrophy may occur. Although dementia and amblyopia are relatively uncommon occurrences, each may occasionally be the initial manifestation of the disease.

Pathology and pathogenesis The pathologic process takes the form of a diffuse, though uneven, degeneration of the white matter of the spinal cord and sometimes of the brain. At first there is swelling of myelin sheaths, characterized by separation of myelin lamellae and formation of intramyelinic vacuoles. This is followed by a coalescence of small foci of tissue destruction into larger ones, giving the tissue a vacuolated appearance. The myelin sheaths and the axis cylinders are both affected, the former perhaps earlier and to a greater extent than the latter. Astrocyte gliosis is minimal in the early lesions, but in the more chronic ones gliosis is pronounced. The changes begin in the posterior columns of the lower cervical and upper thoracic cord and spread from this region up and down the cord, as well as forward into the lateral columns. The lesions are not limited to specific systems of fibers within the posterior and lateral funiculi but are scattered irregularly through the white matter.

The *pathogenesis* of the nervous system lesions in vitamin B_{12} deficiency is not well understood. Impairment of DNA synthesis probably accounts for the hematologic abnormalities and the production of megaloblasts; however, since neurons do not divide, this mechanism cannot be invoked to explain the central nervous system changes. One of the better-understood functions of vitamin B_{12} is its role as a coenzyme in the methylmalonyl CoA mutase reaction. Impairment of this metabolic step may lead to the production of abnormal fatty acids, which are important building blocks of cell membranes and of myelin. Conceivably, this biochemical abnormality may in some way be responsible for the nervous system lesions.

Diagnosis and treatment The chief obstacle to early diagnosis is the lack of parallelism between the hematologic and neurologic signs. This is particularly true of patients who have received folic acid, which serves to maintain a hematologic remission for an indefinite period while the neurologic signs worsen, often to an irreversible stage. Under these circumstances the most reliable diagnostic procedures are the measurement of the serum B_{12} concentration and the two-stage Schilling test (see Chap. 285).

The treatment of the neurologic manifestations of vitamin B_{12} deficiency differs in no way from the treatment of the hematologic ones. Patients whose vitamin B_{12} stores have been depleted require large doses of cobalamin—1000 µg intramuscularly each day during hospitalization, then weekly for a month, and then monthly for the remainder of the patient's life.

The most important factor influencing the *response to treatment* is the duration of the neurologic disease. Recovery may be complete if therapy is instituted within a few weeks of the onset of symptoms. For this reason SCD and the other neurologic complications of vitamin

B_{12} deficiency represent medical emergencies. If symptoms have been present for longer than a month or two, only partial recovery can be expected, and in long-standing cases the best that can be expected is the arrest of progression of the symptoms.

Although many patients with vitamin B_{12} deficiency secondary to gastrointestinal disease also have folic acid deficiency, the contribution of the latter, if any, to neurologic symptoms and signs remains unsettled.

VITAMIN E DEFICIENCY Children or adults with chronic liver disease (biliary atresia) or malabsorption syndromes may present with neurologic dysfunction. The clinical features include dysarthria, cerebellar ataxia, diminution of vibration and position sense, sensory polyneuropathy, and absent deep tendon reflexes. Ophthalmoplegia occurs in some patients. Intellectual processes are usually preserved. Neuropathologic examination in two adults disclosed loss of large-diameter myelinated axons in the sural nerves with axonal degeneration. Nerve cell loss was evident in dorsal root ganglia with degeneration of the posterior columns and the cuneate and gracile nuclei. The condition shows improvement if treated early with vitamin E supplementation.

NEUROLOGIC SYNDROMES CAUSED BY HYPERVITAMINOSIS Acute toxicity with vitamin A causes symptoms of headache, dizziness, irritability, and drowsiness. Chronic hypervitaminosis A can give rise to chronic increased intracranial pressure (pseudotumor cerebri) (see Chap. 76).

Excess ingestion of pyridoxine in amounts in excess of 2 g daily can cause a sensory neuropathy characterized clinically by progressive ataxia, impairment of position and vibration sense, and loss of deep tendon reflexes. Motor strength is preserved. The syndrome is reversible with discontinuation of pyridoxine.

ACQUIRED (SECONDARY) METABOLIC DISEASES OF THE NERVOUS SYSTEM

In this important category of neurologic disease, a disturbance of cerebral function is usually consequent upon disease in some other organ system—heart (and circulation), lungs (and respiration), kidneys, liver, pancreas, and endocrine glands. Each of these visceral diseases affects the nervous system in a somewhat different way.

ANOXIC ISCHEMIC ENCEPHALOPATHY This common and often disastrous condition is caused by a lack of oxygen to the brain, resulting from hypotension or respiratory failure. Sometimes both are responsible, and one cannot say which predominates—hence, the ambiguous allusion in clinical records to "cardiorespiratory failure." The conditions which most often lead to anoxic/ischemic encephalopathy are (1) myocardial infarction; (2) cardiac arrest from whatever cause; (3) hemorrhage, with shock and circulatory collapse; in these situations vascular supply to the brain is compromised before respiration; (4) infective and traumatic shock; (5) suffocation (from drowning, strangulation, aspiration of vomitus or blood, compression of the trachea by hemorrhage or a surgical pack, or a foreign body in the trachea); (6) diseases which paralyze the muscles of respiration or compromise the central nervous system respiratory drive (trauma, vascular disease of the brain, epilepsy) with respiratory failure followed by cardiac failure; and (7) carbon monoxide (CO) poisoning, in which respiration fails first and then cardiovascular functions. Experimental studies support clinical observations that hypoxia alone may induce different clinicopathologic states than a combination of hypoxia and hypoperfusion (ischemia).

Clinical manifestations Mild degrees of hypoxia induce inattentiveness, impaired judgment, and motor incoordination but have no lasting effects. With severe hypoxia or anoxia, as occurs with cardiac arrest, consciousness is lost within seconds, but recovery will be complete if breathing, oxygenation of blood, and cardiac action are restored within 3 to 5 min. If anoxia persists beyond this time, there is serious and permanent injury to the brain, particularly to those parts in which the efficiency of circulation is marginal (globus pallidus, cerebellum, hippocampus, and the "borderzone regions" of the parietooccipital lobes). Clinically, it is difficult to judge the precise degree of hypoxia/ischemia since slight heart action or an imperceptible blood pressure may serve to maintain the circulation to some extent. Hence some individuals have made an excellent recovery after cerebral anoxia that allegedly lasted 8 to 10 min or longer. *An important clinical rule is that degrees of hypoxia which at no time abolish consciousness rarely if ever cause permanent damage to the nervous system.* P_{O_2} as low as 20 mmHg is well tolerated if it develops gradually and blood pressure is normal. Also, generally speaking, subjects who demonstrate intact brainstem function (as indicated by normal ciliospinal, oculovestibular, and pupillary light responses, and intact doll's-head eye movements) when the acute hypoxic event has terminated tend to have a better outlook for recovery of consciousness and perhaps all of their faculties. Conversely, absence of these reflex activities and the presence of pupils persistently fixed to light suggest a grave prognosis.

Extreme or sustained global ischemia causes brain death (see Chap. 21). Immediately after resuscitation from cardiorespiratory arrest, the signs may indicate brain death (dilated, unresponsive pupils, absent brainstem reflexes and respiration, and isoelectric EEG), yet full recovery may occur. However, persistence of the unresponsive state for more than an hour or two invariably carries a poor prognosis (see Chap. 21). The diagnosis of brain death must be made with caution because anesthesia, drug intoxication, and hypothermia may also cause deep coma, absent brainstem reflexes, and an isoelectric EEG, but permit recovery. Cases of brain death have been brought increasingly to public attention because of ethical and moral issues that surround the question of discontinuing supportive medical therapy (see Chap. 21). Issues of management are most difficult in the patient who has suffered severe but lesser degrees of cerebral anoxia.

Patients who suffer a severe degree of anoxic encephalopathy that falls short of causing "brain death" often stabilize breathing and heart action. Neurologic evaluation shows the patient to be profoundly comatose, with eyes slightly divergent and motionless but with reactive pupils, and flaccid or intensely rigid limbs, and diminished tendon reflexes. Within a few minutes after cardiac action and breathing have been restored, generalized convulsions and isolated or grouped twitches of muscles (myoclonus) may supervene. Decerebrate or decorticate postures may be present or occur upon pinching the limbs, and bilateral Babinski signs can be evoked. In the first 24 to 48 h death may terminate this state in a setting of rising temperature, deepening coma, and circulatory collapse. Or, with somewhat lesser degrees of injury, where the cerebral and cerebellar cortices are partly or completely destroyed but brainstem-spinal structures remain intact, the individual may survive in a state referred to as "irreversible coma" or "persistent vegetative state" (see Chap. 21). These patients remain mute, unresponsive, and unaware of their environment for weeks, months, or years. Criteria to predict accurately the outcome of this condition early in the comatose period have been developed (see Chap. 21). If intoxication can be excluded, the presence of fixed dilated pupils and paralysis of eye movement for 24 to 48 h, along with marked slowing of the EEG, usually signifies irreversible cerebral damage. Deep coma of this type, lasting more than a few days, is rarely attended by full recovery.

Patients with still lesser degrees of injury improve after a period of coma. Consciousness is regained, and then various degrees of confusion, visual agnosia, extrapyramidal rigidity, or movement disorder (action or intention myoclonus, choreoathetosis) become manifest. Some of these patients quickly pass through this acute hypoxic phase and proceed to make full recovery; others are left with permanent neurologic sequelae. The *posthypoxic syndromes* observed most frequently are (1) *persistent coma or stupor;* and, with lesser degrees of cerebral injury, (2) *dementia,* with or without extrapyram-

idal signs; (3) *visual agnosia;* (4) *parkinsonism;* (5) *choreoathetosis;* (6) *cerebellar ataxia;* (7) *intention or action myoclonus;* and (8) *Korsakoff's amnesic state. Seizures* may continue to be a problem, but are uncommon.

A relatively uncommon and unexplained phenomenon is *delayed postanoxic encephalopathy.* Initial improvement, which appears to be complete, is followed after a variable period of time (1 to 4 weeks in most cases) by a relapse, characterized by apathy, confusion, irritability, and occasionally agitation or mania. A few patients have recovered from this second episode, but in most of them there has been progression of the neurologic syndrome, with shuffling gait, diffuse rigidity and spasticity, coma, and death after 1 to 2 weeks. Postmortem examination of these patients has shown the major abnormality to be widespread cerebral demyelination. Exceptionally, there occurs yet another delayed syndrome, in which a period of hypoxia is followed by a slow, deteriorating state, affecting basal ganglia more than cerebral cortex and white matter and progressing for weeks to months until the patient is mute, rigid, and helpless.

The essential *mechanism* in hypoxic encephalopathy is a lack of oxygen and an arrest of all aerobic metabolic processes necessary to sustain the Krebs tricarboxylic cycle and the electron transport system. Lactic acid accumulates in the tissues. The pathophysiology of delayed progression is not understood.

Diagnosis   This depends on (1) the history of a hypoxic ischemic event and evidence of reduced oxygenation of arterial blood ($P_{O_2} < 40$ mmHg), CO intoxication (the latter is indicated by its spectroscopic band or cherry-red color of the skin for a few minutes to hours after the episode), blood pressures below 70 mmHg systolic, or cardiac arrest; and (2) as outlined above, the typical clinical sequence of events after a possible hypoxic/ischemic episode has terminated. Renal damage (anuria) and myocardial infarction may also have occurred and provide corroborative evidence of hypoxia.

Treatment   The treatment of anoxic encephalopathy is directed mainly at the prevention of a critical degree of hypoxic injury. After a clear airway is secured, artificial respiration, external thoracic cardiac massage, the use of a cardiac defibrillator or pacemaker, and open chest surgery all have their place, and every second counts in their prompt utilization. Once cardiac and pulmonary function are restored, there is no evidence that any pharmacologic treatment will benefit recovery. Barbiturates, corticosteroids, hypothermia, dimethylsulfoxide, and benzodiazepines have been given without proof of benefit. A small, unpredictable proportion of patients develop secondary complications of diffuse brain swelling after cardiac arrest; this condition is more common in children. This is detected by compression of lateral ventricles and cisterns on CT scan, or by very high lumbar CSF pressure. Treatment is detailed in Chap. 21. Seizures should be controlled by anticonvulsants. Posthypoxic myoclonus may respond to oral administration of 5-hydroxytryptophan.

HYPERCAPNIC ENCEPHALOPATHY   Chronic emphysema, chronic fibrosing lung disease, and in rare instances, an inadequacy of central respiratory drive lead to chronic respiratory acidosis, with an elevation of P_{CO_2} and a reduction in arterial P_{O_2}. Secondary polycythemia and cor pulmonale often accompany these diseases of the lungs, and pulmonary infection may be superimposed.

Clinical Manifestations   The clinical syndrome consequent upon hypercapnia (and hypoxia) comprises generalized or bilateral frontal or occipital headache, often intense and persistent for hours; papilledema; mental dullness, drowsiness, confusion, stupor, and coma; a fast-frequency action tremor and coarse twitching of all muscles, which are in a state of sustained contraction; and an ability to maintain a fixed posture or interruption of a voluntary movement because of brief lapses of sustained muscle contraction (asterixis). Intermittent drowsiness, indifference and inattention to the environment, reduction of psychomotor activity, imperception of the sequence of events, and forgetfulness constitute the more subtle manifestations of this syndrome.

In fully developed cases, the cerebrospinal fluid (CSF) is under increased pressure, P_{CO_2} may exceed 75 mmHg, and oxygen saturation of the arterial blood ranges from 85 to 40 percent. The EEG reveals slow activity, in the delta and theta range, sometimes bilaterally synchronous. The mechanism of the cerebral disorder is said to be CO_2 narcosis, but the biochemical details are not known. The danger of administering morphine or sedatives, which blunt the respiratory drive (already depressed by the CO_2 retention), or inhaled O_2, which removes the sole stimulus (low P_{O_2}) to the respiratory center, is now widely recognized.

Treatment   Forced ventilation with an intermittent positive-pressure respirator, treatment of heart failure with digitalis and diuretics, venesection to reduce the viscosity of the blood, and antibiotics to combat pulmonary infection are the most effective therapeutic measures. If stupor or coma persists, the arterial O_2 level should be rechecked; it may be critically reduced, and needs to be raised by controlled O_2 administration to a point (50 to 55 mmHg) where consciousness is improved but the stimulus to respiratory drive is not removed. Also, the pH of the CSF may be very low, in the range of 7.15 to 7.25. In CO_2 narcosis, correction of the acidosis of blood is easier than that of CSF, which tends to lag. Aminophylline administration is the initial treatment in chronic obstructive pulmonary disease because it improves both airway resistance and diaphragm contractility. Hypokalemia may complicate the rapid correction of CO_2 and pH abnormalities.

Differential diagnosis   Unlike pure hypoxic encephalopathy, hypercapnia rarely causes prolonged coma, and is not a cause of irreversible brain damage. Papilledema and asterixis (the latter is also characteristic of liver failure, uremia, and rarely other metabolic disorders) are important diagnostic features. The syndrome of hypercapnia is apt to be mistaken for brain tumor, a confusional psychosis of nondescript type, or a disease causing myoclonus or chorea. In the latter instance, it must be distinguished from a chronic extrapyramidal syndrome.

HYPOGLYCEMIC ENCEPHALOPATHY (See also Chaps. 327 and 329)   This condition is a relatively infrequent but important cause of episodic confusion, convulsions, coma, and sometimes focal neurologic signs, i.e., hemiparesis. The essential biochemical abnormality is a critical lowering of the blood glucose concentration to less than 25 to 30 mg/dL (lower in infants), which, if it lasts for many minutes leads to exhaustion of cerebral glucose reserve. As cerebral oxidation proceeds without exogenous glucose, the lipid and protein components of neurons are metabolized, and irreversible damage occurs. The severely hypoglycemic patient becomes deeply comatose before permanent damage occurs. Consequently prompt treatment is important.

Etiology   The most common causes of hypoglycemic encephalopathy are (1) the accidental or deliberate overdose of insulin or an oral antidiabetic agent, (2) an islet cell, insulin-secreting tumor of the pancreas, or retroperitoneal sarcoma, (3) rarely, a prolonged drinking spree associated with depletion of liver glycogen, (4) acute, nonicteric hepatic encephalopathy of childhood (Reye's syndrome), (5) glycogen storage disease in infancy, and (6) an idiopathic syndrome occurring in the neonatal period. In the past, hypoglycemic encephalopathy was a rather frequent complication of "insulin shock" therapy of schizophrenia. Postprandial and fasting hypoglycemia are never of sufficient duration or severity to damage the central nervous system.

Clinical manifestations   As the concentration of blood glucose decreases to about 30 mg/dL, the initial symptoms appear—nervousness, hunger, flushed facies, headache, palpitation, anxiety, sweating, and trembling—and these gradually give way to confusion, drowsiness, focal neurologic signs, and occasionally excitement or overactivity. In the next stage, forced sucking, grasping, motor restlessness, muscular spasms, and finally decerebrate rigidity occur, in that sequence. Myoclonic twitching and convulsions may develop in some

patients. Blood levels of approximately 10 mg/dL are associated with deep coma, dilatation of pupils, pallor, shallow respirations, bradycardia, and hypotonicity of limb musculature—the so-called medullary phase of hypoglycemia. If glucose is administered before the medullary phase is reached, the patient is restored to normalcy, retracing the aforementioned steps in reverse order with recovery within a few minutes. Once the medullary phase appears, and particularly if it persists for a time before the hypoglycemia is corrected, neurologic recovery is delayed for a period of days or weeks and may be incomplete.

A huge dose of insulin that produces severe hypoglycemia, even of relatively brief duration (30 to 60 min), is more dangerous than a series of less severe hypoglycemic episodes from smaller doses of insulin, possibly because the former impairs or exhausts essential enzymes. This condition cannot then be overcome by large quantities of glucose given intravenously.

Pathology   The major *neuropathologic effect* is on the cerebral cortex; nerve cells degenerate and are replaced by microgliocytes and astrocytes. The distribution of lesions is similar though not identical to that in hypoxic encephalopathy (the cerebellar cortex is relatively spared in hypoglycemic encephalopathy). The sequelae of the two disorders are also much alike.

Chronic episodes of hypoglycemia may give rise to two other syndromes, both relatively uncommon. One, termed *subacute hypoglycemia*, is characterized by drowsiness and lethargy, diminution in psychomotor activity, deterioration of social behavior, and confusion. Oral or intravenous glucose will immediately alleviate the symptoms. In the other, more *chronic syndrome*, there is gradual deterioration of intellectual function, raising the question of a presenile dementia, and in some reported instances there have been tremor, chorea, rigidity, cerebellar ataxia, and rarely signs of lower motor neuron involvement ("hypoglycemic amyotrophy"). These subacute and chronic forms of hypoglycemia have been observed with islet cell hypertrophy or tumor, carcinoma of the stomach, fibrous mesothelioma, carcinoma of the cecum, and hepatoma. An insulin-like substance is elaborated by these nonpancreatic tumors.

Differential diagnosis   The major clinical differences between hypoglycemia and hypoxia are in the clinical setting and mode of evolution of the neurologic disorder. Hypoglycemia usually disturbs cerebral function more slowly than hypoxia, over a period of 30 to 60 min rather than in a few seconds or minutes. The recovery phase and sequelae of the two conditions are much the same. *Recurrent hypoglycemia*, as occurs with an islet cell tumor, may masquerade for some time as an episodic confusional psychosis or convulsive illness, and diagnosis awaits a period of demonstrably low blood glucose or hyperinsulinism (see Chap. 329).

The correction of the hypoglycemia at the earliest moment is the obvious therapy. It is not known whether hypothermia or other measures will increase the safety period in hypoglycemia or alter the outcome.

HYPERGLYCEMIC COMA   Two hyperglycemic syndromes have been described, mainly in the diabetic: (1) hyperglycemia with ketoacidosis and (2) hyperosmolar nonketotic hyperglycemia. These are described in Chap. 327.

ACUTE HEPATIC ENCEPHALOPATHY   Chronic hepatic insufficiency with portacaval shunting of blood is often punctuated by episodes of stupor, coma, and other neurologic symptoms, a state referred to as hepatic coma or portal-systemic encephalopathy. Also, there are a number of hereditary hyperammonemic syndromes of infancy which may lead to episodic coma with or without seizures. A special type of nonicteric hepatic encephalopathy (Reye's syndrome) occurs in children, presenting as acute brain swelling, in conjunction with rapid enlargement of the liver, fine droplets of fat in hepatocytes, high serum glutamic oxaloacetic transaminase (SGOT) and other liver enzymes, and very high levels of serum ammonia (see Chap. 251).

Clinical features   The central feature of acute hepatic encephalopathy occurring in the adult is a derangement of consciousness, presenting first as mental confusion with increased or decreased psychomotor activity, followed by progressive drowsiness, stupor, and coma. The confusional state that occurs before coma intervenes is frequently combined with characteristic lapses of sustained muscle contraction (asterixis) and an EEG abnormality consisting of paroxysms of bilaterally synchronous delta waves, characteristically triphasic and prominent in the frontal regions which at first are interspersed with alpha activity and which later, as the coma deepens, displace all normal activity. A variable, fluctuating rigidity of the trunk and limbs, grimacing, suck and grasp reflexes, exaggeration or asymmetry of tendon reflexes, Babinski signs, and focal or generalized seizures round out the clinical picture.

The syndrome of acute hepatic encephalopathy usually evolves over a period of days to weeks and often terminates fatally. At times it does not advance beyond the stage of mild mental dulling and confusion with asterixis and EEG changes. This relatively mild form needs to be differentiated from other acute confusional psychoses and deliria. If the metabolic disorder persists for months and years, a mild dementia and a disorder of posture and movement may gradually appear (grimacing, tremor, dysarthria, ataxia of gait, choreoathetosis), and the condition must then be distinguished from the other dementing and extrapyramidal syndromes (see further on in this chapter).

Pathology and pathogenesis   The striking *neuropathologic finding* in patients who die in a state of hepatic coma is a diffuse increase in the number and size of the protoplasmic astrocytes (Alzheimer type II astrocytes) in the deep layers of the cerebral cortex and in the lenticular nuclei, with little or no visible alteration in the nerve cells or other parenchymal elements.

The *pathogenesis* of hepatic encephalopathy is not fully understood. The most plausible theory relates it to an abnormality of nitrogen metabolism, wherein ammonia or other amines, which are formed in the bowel by the action of urease-containing organisms on dietary protein and are carried to the liver in the portal circulation, fail to be converted into urea, either because of hepatocellular disease or portal-systemic shunting of blood, or both. As a result, these substances reach the systemic circulation, where they interfere with cerebral metabolism in some obscure way. Other theories of causation have related hepatic coma to the synergistic action of certain fatty acids and possibly methyl mercaptan with ammonia, or to the excess production of false neurotransmitters (e.g., octopamine), or to an increase in the inhibitory neurotransmitter γ-aminobutyric acid (GABA) (see Chap. 249). These and other theories have recently been reviewed by Victor (1986).

Treatment   Despite an incomplete understanding of the role of disordered nitrogen metabolism in the genesis of hepatic coma, an awareness of this relationship has provided the most effective means of treating this disorder: restriction of dietary protein; mechanical cleansing of the colon; oral administration of neomycin or kanamycin, which suppresses or eliminates urease-producing organisms in the bowel; and the use of lactulose, an inert sugar that acidifies the colonic contents. Should these measures not control the protein intolerance, surgical exclusion of the bowel may be undertaken, but this operation carries a high risk of mortality. More recent methods of treatment, the practicality of which remain to be established, include the use of keto analogues of essential amino acids (which theoretically should supply a nitrogen-free source of essential amino acids) and bromocriptine, a dopamine agonist which is thought to enhance dopaminergic transmission (see Chap. 249).

In acute hepatitis, delirious, confusional, and comatose states also occur, but their mechanisms are not understood. Blood ammonia levels are usually elevated, but of unclear significance, because of other associated metabolic abnormalities.

CHRONIC HEPATIC ENCEPHALOPATHY (ACQUIRED HEPATO-CEREBRAL DEGENERATION)   **Clinical manifestations**   Patients

who survive an episode or several episodes of hepatic coma are occasionally left with residual neurologic abnormalities, such as tremor of the head or arms, asterixis, grimacing, choreatic twitching of the limbs, dysarthria, ataxia of gait, or impairment of intellectual function, and these symptoms may worsen with repeated attacks of stupor and coma. In other patients with hepatic failure, these neurologic abnormalities become manifest in the absence of discrete episodes of hepatic coma. In either event, patients thus afflicted deteriorate neurologically over a period of months or years. As the condition evolves, a rather characteristic dysarthria, mild ataxia, wide-based, unsteady gait, and choreoathetosis, mainly of the face, neck, and shoulders, are joined in a common syndrome. Mental function is slowly altered—a simple dementia with lack of concern and indifference to the illness evolves. A coarse rhythmic tremor of the arms, appearing with certain sustained postures, mild corticospinal tract signs, and diffuse EEG abnormalities complete the clinical picture. Other less frequent signs are muscular rigidity, grasp reflexes, tremor in repose, nystagmus, asterixis, and action or intention myoclonus. Many of the neurologic abnormalities that occur as part of acute hepatic encephalopathy may also be observed in patients with chronic hepatocerebral degeneration, the only difference being that the abnormalities are evanescent in the former and irreversible in the latter.

The chronic cerebral symptoms, like the transient ones, may occur with all varieties of chronic liver disease. Portacaval shunts are always present; jaundice, ascites, and esophageal varices are manifest in most of the cases.

Pathology   Chronic hepatocerebral degeneration, like hepatic coma, is characterized by a widespread hyperplasia of protoplasmic astrocytes in the deep layers of the cerebral and cerebellar cortices as well as in the thalamic and lenticular nuclei and many other nuclear structures of the brainstem. In addition, in the chronic disease, medullated fibers and nerve cells are destroyed in the affected areas, and polymicrocavitation is prominent at the corticomedullary junction, in the striatum (particularly in the superior pole of the putamen), and in the cerebellar white matter. Protoplasmic astrocytic nuclei contain periodic acid Schiff (PAS)–positive glycogen granules. Nerve cells may appear swollen and chromatolyzed, accounting for the so-called Opalski cells. The similarity of the neuropathologic lesion in the familial (Wilson's) and acquired forms of liver disease suggests a common hepatogenesis.

UREMIC ENCEPHALOPATHY   Episodic confusion and stupor and other neurologic symptoms may accompany any form of severe renal disease. In addition, a number of neurologic syndromes complicate chronic hemodialysis and kidney transplantation. Chronic polyneuropathy, the most common neurologic complication of renal failure, is discussed in Chap. 355.

Acute uremic encephalopathy   The initial cerebral symptoms attributable to uremia consist of apathy, fatigue, inattentiveness, and irritability; later, confusion, disturbances of sensory perception, hallucinations, and stupor supervene. These later symptoms are practically always associated with twitching of the muscles and myoclonic jerks, and the patient may convulse. Similar twitch-convulsive phenomena occur in association with a variety of diseases, such as widespread neoplasia, delirium tremens, diabetes with necrotizing pyelonephritis, and lupus erythematosus, all when associated with renal failure. Elevated blood urea nitrogen is sometimes accompanied by subnormal serum calcium and magnesium levels.

The prognosis of uremic encephalopathy, if associated with irreversible and progressive renal disease, is poor and can only be managed with dialysis or renal transplantation. Convulsions, which occur in about one-third of cases, often preterminally, respond to relatively low plasma concentrations of phenytoin and phenobarbital.

The brains of patients with uremic encephalopathy and the twitch-convulsive syndrome show hyperplasia of protoplasmic astrocytes in some cases, but never to the degree observed in hepatic encephalopathy. Cerebral edema is notably absent. Restoration of renal function corrects the neurologic syndrome, attesting to a biochemical rather than a structural abnormality. Whether this is caused by the retention of organic acids, elevation of phosphate in the CSF, or by the action of other toxins has never been settled.

"Disequilibrium syndrome" and dialysis encephalopathy These terms refer to syndromes that commonly complicate hemodialysis or peritoneal dialysis. Under *disequilibrium syndrome* are included headaches, nausea, muscular cramps, nervous irritability, agitation, drowsiness, and convulsions. The headache develops in approximately 70 percent of patients, while the other symptoms are observed in 5 to 10 percent, usually in those undergoing rapid dialysis or in the early stages of a dialysis program. The symptoms tend to occur in the third to fourth hour of dialysis and last for several hours. Sometimes the symptoms appear 8 to 48 h after completing dialysis. Originally these symptoms were attributable to the rapid lowering of serum urea, leaving the brain with a higher concentration of urea than the serum and resulting in a shift of water into the brain to equalize the osmotic gradient ("reverse urea syndrome"). Now the condition is attributed to a shift of water into the brain, analogous to the volume expansion due to water intoxication and inappropriate secretion of antidiuretic hormone.

Dialysis encephalopathy or dialysis dementia is an unusual and now uncommon complication of chronic hemodialysis. It begins with stuttering and dysarthria, coupled with a predominantly motor aphasia, to which are added facial and generalized myoclonus, focal and generalized seizures, personality changes and psychotic episodes, intellectual decline, progressive aphasic disorder, and EEG abnormalities. The latter consist of bisynchronous predominantly frontal or multifocal bursts of slow wave discharges, associated with spikes and sharp waves. The CSF is usually normal. At first these symptoms are intermittent, occurring during or immediately after dialysis and lasting for only a few hours, but gradually they become more persistent and eventually permanent. Once established, the syndrome is usually steadily progressive over a 1- to 15-month period (average survival of 6 months in 42 cases analyzed by Lederman and Henry). A few patients have a waxing and waning course and survive for several years. In some patients the myoclonus and seizures subside for several months under the influence of clonazepam or diazepam.

The neuropathologic changes are subtle and consist of a mild microcavitation of the upper layers of the cerebral cortex. Although the changes are diffuse, the left (dominant) hemisphere is affected more than the right, and the left frontotemporal operculum more than other parts of the cortex (Winkelman). The predominant affection of the operculum would explain the striking disturbance of speech and language. Current concepts of the etiology center on the role of aluminum. Alfrey and his associates found that the cerebral gray matter of patients who died with dialysis encephalopathy contained a much greater amount of aluminum than analogous tissue from dialysis patients without encephalopathy. The aluminum is derived from both the dialysate and orally administered aluminum gels. These authors suggested that dialysis encephalopathy represents a form of aluminum intoxication, a view that is supported by the observations that (1) the frequency of dialysis dementia was related to the concentrations of aluminum in the dialysate, and (2) deionization of the water used in the dialysate prevented the occurrence of new cases. The possibility that other trace elements contribute to the syndrome has not been entirely excluded.

Kidney transplantation involves an increased risk of developing primary cerebral lymphoma, Wernicke's encephalopathy, and central pontine myelinolysis. Systemic fungal infections are found at autopsy in about 45 percent of patients who have had renal transplants and long periods of immunosuppressive treatment, and in about one-third of these patients there has been involvement of the central nervous system. *Cryptococcus, Listeria, Aspergillus, Candida, Nocardia,* and *Histoplasma* are the usual organisms. Other central nervous system infections that complicate transplantation are toxoplasmosis and cytomegalic inclusion disease.

ENCEPHALOPATHIES DUE TO ELECTROLYTE AND ENDOCRINE DISTURBANCES Brief reference to these important groups of metabolic encephalopathies is given here. More detailed accounts are found in the cross-referenced chapters.

Metabolic acidosis (arterial pH$<$7.30, $P_{CO_2}<$35, $HCO_3<$10 meq per liter) due to diabetes mellitus, renal failure, lactic acidosis, or poisoning with an acid substance produces a syndrome characterized by drowsiness, stupor, and coma with dry skin and Kussmaul breathing, described in Chap. 42. Extreme degrees of *hyperosmolality* of the blood may develop in the course of diabetes mellitus (blood glucose$>$400 mg/dL) and in *hypernatremic dehydration*, resulting in both instances in tremulousness, convulsions, and coma. In some instances the movement disorder resembles chorea or the myoclonic twitching of uremia. *Hypokalemia* is characterized by extreme muscular weakness associated with a stuporous-confusional state, and sometimes by striking changes in personality and behavior (see Chap. 42).

Hyponatremia, usually with water intoxication, is another cause of episodic coma, especially in infants. Among the many causes, the syndrome of inappropriate secretion of antidiuretic hormone (SIADH) is of special importance, since it commonly complicates neurologic diseases of many types—head trauma, bacterial meningitis and encephalitis, cerebral infarction and subarachnoid hemorrhage, neoplasm, and sometimes Guillain-Barré disease (see Chap. 323). The diagnosis of SIADH should be suspected in any critically ill neurologic or neurosurgical patient who excretes urine that is hypertonic relative to the plasma. As the hyponatremia develops, there is a decrease in alertness, which progresses through stages of confusion to coma, often with convulsions. Lack of recognition of this state may allow the serum Na^+ to fall to dangerously low levels, 100 meq per liter or lower. Treatment is described in Chap. 323. Replacement with intravenous NaCl in severe cases must be done cautiously because vigorous and rapid correction of severe hyponatremia has been incriminated in the pathogenesis of central pontine myelinolysis (CPM) and related brainstem, cerebellar, and cerebral syndromes (Laureno). Ayus and colleagues emphasize the risks of persistent severe hyponatremia and recommend the following therapeutic guidelines: serum Na^+ above 120 meq per liter does not require immediate correction. If Na^+ is $>$105 meq per liter, it can be safely corrected to a level of 125 to 130 meq per liter at a rate of administration of Na^+ of 2 meq per liter. If serum Na^+ is less than 105 meq per liter, it is corrected by 20 meq per liter at a rate of 2 meq per liter and then permitted to return slowly to normal.

In children more than adults, cholera being an exception, extremely *severe diarrhea* may be attended by an encephalopathy. Irritability, weakness, headache, seizures, stupor, and coma may develop over a period of 2 to 3 days and carry a grave prognosis unless promptly relieved. Presumably this is a metabolic encephalopathy due to loss of fluids and electrolytes and can be corrected by their replacement. In the more protracted illness of *typhoid fever,* approximately half the patients develop a delirium, and a small number will exhibit meningism and become comatose with twitching and seizures or spasticity and hyperactive reflexes, all of which are transitory.

In the *endocrine encephalopathies* the clinical phenomena are even more abstruse. Confusional states may be combined with agitation, hallucinations, delusions, anxiety, and depression. And the time course of the illness may be in terms of weeks and months, rather than days. Derangement of higher nervous function may follow the *administration of ACTH or corticosteroid agents,* and the same symptoms have been reported in *Cushing's disease* (see Chap. 325). The neurology of *thyrotoxicosis* has proved to be peculiarly elusive. Allusions to thyrotoxic psychosis are widely recorded in the medical literature; mental confusion, seizures, manic or depressive attacks, delusions, and chorea occur in various combinations with muscular weakness and atrophy, periodic paralysis, and myasthenia (see Chap. 324). Treatment of the hyperthyroidism gradually restores the patient to a normal mental state. *Myxedematous patients* may show slow mentation and depression, but only in a small proportion is there a major change in cerebral function, taking the form of drowsiness or extreme somnolence, inattentiveness, and apathy. These symptoms can be reversed within a few weeks by thyroid medication. The association of myxedema and cerebellar ataxia is well documented. The neuropathologic basis of this disorder remains unclear, as does the pathogenesis. In *hyperparathyroidism,* when the serum calcium levels reach 15 mg/dL or higher, the patient sinks into a quiet state of inattentiveness, lethargy, and confusion. Stupor, coma, and death may be caused by extreme degrees of hypercalcemia such as occur occasionally in cases of excessive vitamin D administration and metastatic tumors of the bones. Chronic *hypoparathyroidism,* either idiopathic or following thyroid or parathyroid resection may rarely give rise to intracranial calcifications and an extrapyramidal motor syndrome. *Addison's disease* (adrenal insufficiency) may be attended by episodic confusion, stupor, or coma, without special identifying features. Hypoglycemia, hypotension, and hyponatremia with diminished cerebral circulation are thought to be the underlying mechanisms, and measures which correct them appear to be beneficial.

The term *pancreatic encephalopathy* describes a syndrome of agitation and confusion, sometimes with hallucinations and clouding of consciousness, dysarthria, and changing rigidity of the limbs, in association with acute pancreatic disease. The status of this entity is uncertain. A uniform neuropathologic change has not been discerned. We agree with Pallis and Lewis who suggest that before such a diagnosis can be seriously entertained in a patient with acute pancreatitis, one should exclude delirium tremens, the cerebral effects of shock, renal or hepatic failure, hypoglycemia, diabetic acidosis, hyperosmolality, hypokalemia, hypo- or hypercalcemia, any one of which may complicate the underlying disease(s).

D-*Lactic acidosis* can cause encephalopathy in patients who undergo jejunoileostomy for treatment of morbid obesity. Up to 10 percent of such patients report episodes of confusion, ataxia, and slurred speech. D-Lactate, an isomer not normally found in the blood, is present in serum, urine, and stool in these patients. D-Lactate, a product of intestinal bacteria, causes encephalopathy by interfering with pyruvate metabolism. The symptoms are similar to those of thiamine deficiency. Diagnosis is dependent upon recognition of metabolic acidosis associated with hyperchloremia and measurement of elevated D-lactate (see Dahlquist; Cross).

HEREDITARY METABOLIC DISEASES OF LATE ONSET

Inherited metabolic disorders affecting amino acid metabolism (Chaps. 306 and 307), lysosomal enzyme functions (Chap. 316), and cerebral lipids (Chap. 316) are generally rare disorders that first are manifest during infancy or childhood. The salient features of these conditions are summarized in Chaps. 306, 307, and 316. In this chapter are described a small number of hereditary metabolic disorders which may have their onset in late adolescence and adulthood and which may present diagnostic problems because of the similarity of their clinical presentation to other more common acquired and degenerative diseases of the nervous system. Noteworthy attributes of these diseases are their chronicity and progressive nature.

METACHROMATIC LEUKODYSTROPHY (See Chap. 316)   Probably the most common member of this category is *adult metachromatic leukodystrophy (MLD).* While the majority of cases appear in early childhood, approximately 25 percent manifest their first symptoms beyond the twenty-first year of life. Cases among men have outnumbered those in women 2:1. The mode of inheritance is autosomal recessive in almost all instances. The onset is insidious and the course protracted, over 20 or more years.

Mental symptoms tend to dominate the clinical picture. Failing scholastic performance, forgetfulness, and irrationality occur early in the illness but may be obscured by peculiarities of personality, such as suspiciousness, delusional thinking, and bizarre actions. These latter qualities may raise the question of schizophrenia or immature

("borderline") personality development. Sooner or later a mild cerebellar ataxia presenting as awkwardness and falling, mild pyramidal signs, masked facies, and bizarre postures stamp the illness as neurologic. Eventually the patient's mental processes deteriorate to the point where he or she is totally helpless, demented, mute, incontinent of sphincteric control, and bedfast.

Specific diagnostic tests include (1) the demonstration of a diminished arylsulfatase A activity in white blood cells, serum, and urine, (2) increased excretion of sulfatides in urine, (3) slowed conduction velocity in nerves, and (4) deposits of metachromatic material in nerve biopsies.

No treatment is presently available.

ADRENOLEUKODYSTROPHY   In *adrenoleukodystrophy* either bronzing of the skin and Addison's disease or cerebral symptoms may be the initial manifestation. The cerebral lesions may present as a homonymous hemianopsia, cortical blindness, hemiparesis, aphasia, or dementia. Usually the signs are asymmetric at first and progress intermittently. A relatively pure polyneuropathic and myelopathic form has also been described. The diagnosis is usually settled by the finding of a low blood cortisol level in a male with cerebrospinal demyelinating disease, although recently a purely spinal type, taking the form of a progressive spastic paraparesis, has been described in the heterozygote (female carrier). Increased urinary concentration of C22-C26 fatty acids is diagnostic. Corticosteroid replacement therapy helps the Addison's disease but has no effect on the neurologic disorders. The latter progress intermittently over a few years, and usually the outcome is fatal.

ADULT LIPID STORAGE DISEASES G_{M2} *gangliosidosis* (hexosaminidase A deficiency) has been observed in young adults. Many are from non-Jewish families, and males and females in the same generation are equally affected. Generalized seizures may mark the beginning of a cerebral disorder that later is evidenced by alterations of behavior and intellectual decline. A progressive ataxia and mild signs of corticospinal disease, the combination of which interferes with independent locomotion, clarifies the diagnosis. The fundi and visual function are normal in most cases, but typical cherry-red macular spots are seen occasionally. The liver and spleen are normal or slightly enlarged. The CSF protein is normal. CT scans reveal a modest ventricular enlargement. A slowly developing dementia, cerebellar ataxia, polymyoclonus, and failing vision may characterize the clinical picture in some cases. In yet others, the presenting syndrome has consisted of prominent motor neuron involvement accompanied by muscle cramps, suggesting a diagnosis of spinal muscular atrophy or amyotrophic lateral sclerosis (see Chap. 350). G_{M2} ganglioside is shown to be increased by thin-layer chromatography of tissue obtained by cerebral biopsy. Membranous cytoplasmic bodies are visualized by electron microscopy of rectal, appendicular, and cortical neurons. Gaucher's and Niemann-Pick diseases are yet other storage diseases that may present in adult life.

Ceroid lipofuscinosis   The Kufs type of *ceroid lipofuscinosis* is another form of lipid storage disease that only becomes evident in adolescence or early adult life. Usually the disease begins with mental deterioration, followed by seizures, ataxia, increasing rigidity, athetotic posturing, and corticospinal signs. Skin and conjunctival biopsies (electron-microscopic examination) showed lipofuscin storage material in fibroblasts and endothelial cells.

LEIGH'S DISEASE   Some cases of Leigh's subacute necrotizing encephalomyelopathy only begin in adolescence, and take the form of a progressive polymyoclonus with seizures and cerebellar ataxia and relatively mild impairment of intellectual function.

SUMMARY   One should at least consider some of these rare forms of hereditary metabolic diseases whenever an adolescent or young adult becomes demented, shows a psychiatric syndrome with decline in cognitive functions, has seizures (especially with polymyoclonus), failing vision, and cerebellar ataxia in combination with corticospinal signs or a progressive polyneuropathy.

REFERENCES

ADAMS RD, FOLEY JM: The neurological disorder associated with liver disease of the nervous system. Proc Assoc Res Nerv Ment Dis 32:198, 1953

———, VICTOR M: *Principles of Neurology,* 3d ed. New York, McGraw-Hill, 1985

ALFREY AC et al: The dialysis encephalopathy syndrome: Possible aluminum intoxication. N Engl J Med 294:184, 1976

AYUS JC et al: Changing concepts in treatment of severe symptomatic hyponatremia. Am J Med 78:897, 1985

BLASS JP, GIBSON GE: Abnormality of a thiamine-requiring enzyme in patients with Wernicke-Korsakoff syndrome. N Engl J Med 297:1367, 1977

BRAIN RESUSCITATION CLINICAL TRIAL I STUDY GROUP. Randomized clinical study of thiopental loading in comatose survivors of cardiac arrest. N Engl J Med 314:397, 1986

CARDINALE GJ et al: Effect of methylmalonyl coenzyme A: A metabolite which accumulates in vitamin B_{12} deficiency on fatty acid synthesis. J Biol Chem 245:3771, 1970

CREMER GM et al: Myxedema and ataxia. Neurology 19:37, 1969

CROSS SA, CALLOWAY WC: D-Lactic acidosis and selected cerebellar ataxias. Mayo Clin Proc 59:202, 1984

DAHLQUIST NR et al: D-Lactic acidosis and encephalopathy after jejunoileostomy: Response to overfeeding and to fasting in humans. Mayo Clin Proc 59:141, 1984

FRASER CL, ARIEFF AI: Hepatic encephalopathy. N Engl J Med 313(14):865, 1985

HARDING AE et al: Spinocerebellar degeneration secondary to chronic intestinal malabsorption: A vitamin E deficiency syndrome. Ann Neurol 12:419, 1982

KLATSKY AL et al: Alcohol consumption and blood pressure. N Engl J Med 296:1194, 1977

KOLODNY EH, BOUSTANY RM: Storage diseases of the reticuloendothelial system, *Hematology of Infancy and Childhood,* 3d ed, D Nathan, F Oski (eds). Philadelphia, Saunders, 1986

LAURENO R: Central pontine myelinolysis following rapid correction of hyponatremia. Ann Neurol 13:232, 1983

LEDERMAN RS, HENRY CE: Progressive dialysis encephalopathy. Ann Neurol 4:199, 1978

McENTEE WJ, MAIR RG: Memory enhancement in Korsakoff's phychosis by clonidine: Further evidence for a nonadrenergic deficit. Ann Neurol 7:466, 1980

MARKS R, ROSE FC: *Hypoglycemia.* Oxford, Blackwell, 1965

MOSER HW et al: Adrenoleukodystrophy: Studies of the phenotype, genetics and biochemistry. John Hopkins Med J 147:217, 1980

NADEL AM, WILSON WP: Dialysis encephalopathy: A possible seizure disorder. Neurology 26:1130, 1976

O'HARE JA: Dialysis encephalopathy: Clinical, electroencephalographic, and interventional aspects. Medicine 62:129, 1983

PALLIS CA, LEWIS PD: *The Neurology of Gastrointestinal Disease.* Philadelphia, Saunders, 1974

PLUM F (ed): *Brain Dysfunction in Metabolic Disorders.* New York, Raven, 1974

———, POSNER JB: *Diagnosis of Stupor and Coma,* 3d ed. Philadelphia, Davis, 1980

POTTS AM: Tobacco amblyopia. Surv Ophthalmol 17:313, 1973

RASKIN NH, FISHMAN RA: Neurologic disorders in renal failure. N Engl J Med 294:143, 204, 1976

ROTHERMICH NO, VON HAAM E: Pancreatic encephalopathy. J Clin Endocrinol 1:872, 1941

SAGE JI et al: Alcoholic myelopathy without substantial liver disease. A syndrome of progressive dorsal and lateral column dysfunction. Arch Neurol 41:999, 1984

SCHAUMBURG HH et al: Sensory neuropathy from pyridoxine abuse. A new megavitamin syndrome. N Engl J Med 309:445, 1983

SHIMOJYO S et al: Cerebral blood flow and metabolism in the Wernicke-Korsakoff syndrome. J Clin Invest 46:849, 1967

VICTOR M: Polyneuropathy due to nutrional deficiency and alcoholism, in *Peripheral Neuropathy,* 2d ed, PJ Dyck et al (eds). Philadelphia, Saunders, 1984, pp 1899–1940

———: The neurologic complications of hepatic and gastrointestinal disease, in *Textbook of Neurology,* A Asbury et al (eds). Philadelphia, Saunders, 1986

———, ADAMS RD: On the etiology of the alcoholic neurologic diseases: With special reference to the role of nutrition. Am J Clin Nutr 9:379, 1961

——— et al: A restricted form of cerebellar degeneration occurring in alcoholic patients. Arch Neurol 1:577, 1959

——— et al: Deficiency amblyopia in the alcoholic patient: A clinicopathologic study. Arch Ophthalmol 64:1, 1960

——— et al: The acquired (nonwilsonian) type of chronic hepatocerebral degeneration. Medicine 44:345, 1965

——— et al: *The Wernicke-Korsakoff Syndrome. A Clinical and Pathological Study of 245 Patients, 82 with Postmortem Examinations.* Philadelphia, Davis, 1971

WILKINSON DS, PROCKOP LD: Hypoglycemia: Effects on the nervous system, in *Handbook of Clinical Neurology,* PJ Vinken, BW Bruyn (eds). Amsterdam, North-Holland, 1976, vol 27, pp 53–78

WINKELMAN MD, RICANATI ES: The neuropathology of dialysis encephalopathy. Hum Pathol (in press)

WITT ED, GOLDMAN-RAKIC PS: Intermittent thiamine deficiency in the rhesus monkey. I. Progression of neurological signs and neuranatomical lesions. Ann Neurol 13:376, 1983

350 DEGENERATIVE DISEASES OF THE NERVOUS SYSTEM

EDWARD P. RICHARDSON, JR. / M. FLINT BEAL / JOSEPH B. MARTIN

In classifying the diseases of the nervous system, it has long been customary to designate a group of them as *degenerative,* indicating that they are characterized by gradually evolving, relentlessly progressive neuronal death occurring for reasons that are still entirely unknown. The identification of these diseases depends upon careful, thoroughgoing exclusion of such possible causative factors as infections, metabolic derangements, and intoxications. Experience shows that a considerable proportion of the disorders that are classed as degenerative are associated with genetic predisposition, resulting in a pattern of dominant or recessive inheritance. Others, however, while not differing in any fundamental way from the hereditary disorders, occur only sporadically—as isolated instances in a given family.

Since by definition, classification of the degenerative diseases cannot be based upon any exact knowledge of their cause or pathogenesis, their subdivision into individual syndromes rests on descriptive criteria based largely upon pathologic anatomy but also taking into account clinical aspects. In practice, this group of diseases presents itself in the form of several clinical syndromes, the recognition of which can assist the clinician in arriving at a diagnosis. Apart from the individual differences that serve to allow distinction of one syndrome from another, there are some general attributes that typify the entire class of disorders under discussion.

GENERAL CONSIDERATIONS It is characteristic of the degenerative disorders that they begin insidiously and run a gradually progressive course that can extend over many years. As a rule, the course is more protracted than that of the hereditary metabolic diseases of the nervous system (see Chap. 349). The earliest changes may be so subtle that it often is impossible to assign any precise time of onset. At times the patient or the family may give a history suggesting an abrupt onset of disability—particularly when an injury or some other dramatic event in the patient's life has occurred, to which illness might conceivably be related. By careful questioning, it still may be possible to discern that the patient or family under these circumstances has suddenly become aware of a condition which had, in fact, already been present but had passed unnoticed.

The family history is of great importance, but denial of familial occurrence of a disorder cannot always be taken at face value. One reason is that patients or their relatives may be ashamed to disclose that a neurologic disease afflicts the family. Another is that the extent of the disease affecting other family members may be so slight that the patient or family may be unaware of its presence—as may occur, for instance, in the group of the hereditary ataxias. Moreover, small sibships in a family may prevent well-established hereditary diseases from being recognized. Familial occurrence, of course, does not always mean that a disease is hereditary; it may indicate instead that there has been a common exposure to an infective or toxic agent.

Another general aspect of the degenerative nervous system diseases is that their progressive course is in the long run uninfluenced by attempted therapeutic measures. Caring for a patient with an illness of this kind is often, therefore, an anguishing experience for all concerned. Yet symptoms can often be alleviated, sometimes remarkably so (as in Parkinson's disease), by wise and skillful management, and the physician's kindly interest may be of great help even when curative measures cannot be offered.

A noteworthy feature of this group of diseases is that the changes brought about by them tend to have a bilaterally symmetric distribution. This aspect alone may help to distinguish a disorder of this class from many other varieties of neurologic disease. It is true, nevertheless, that in the early stages, one side of the body, or one limb, may become involved in the presence of normal findings elsewhere. Sooner or later, though, despite the asymmetric beginning, the inherently bilateral nature of the process generally asserts itself.

It is a striking fact that many of the disorders classed as degenerative involve, almost selectively, particular anatomically or physiologically related systems of neurons while leaving others entirely intact. This is clearly exemplified in amyotrophic lateral sclerosis, in which the disease process is limited to cerebral and spinal motor neurons, and in some forms of progressive ataxia in which the Purkinje cells of the cerebellum are alone affected. In Friedreich's ataxia and some other syndromes, the disease process affects multiple neuronal systems.

In this respect these degenerative neuronal diseases resemble some disease processes of known cause, particularly intoxications, which likewise can result in similarly circumscribed effects on the nervous system. Diphtheria toxin, for example, produces selective breakdown of peripheral nerve myelin, triorthocresyl phosphate affects the corticospinal tracts in the spinal cord together with the peripheral nerves, and, as will be brought out later, the newly discovered neurotoxin 1-methyl-4-phenyl-1,2,5,6-tetrahydropyridine (MPTP) brings about localized nerve cell death in the substantia nigra. Selective involvement of particular neuronal systems is not, to be sure, characteristic of all of the degenerative diseases; some are characterized by pathologic changes that are diffuse and unselective. These exceptions nevertheless do not detract from the importance of affection of particular neuronal systems as a distinguishing feature of many of the diseases under discussion.

Typically, the pathologic process in the nervous system is one of slow involution of nerve cell bodies or their prolongations as nerve fibers, unaccompanied by any intense tissue reaction or cellular response, although the loss of neurons and fibers is accompanied by a reactive hyperplasia of fibrillary astrocytes (gliosis). The cerebrospinal fluid (CSF) thus shows little if any change—at most a slight elevation of protein, without abnormalities in specific proteins, cell count, or in other constituents. Moreover, since these diseases invariably result in tissue loss, rather than in new tissue formation, radiographic visualization of the brain, the ventricular system, or subarachnoid space shows either no change or an enlargement of the CSF compartments. These negative laboratory findings thus help to distinguish the degenerative disorders from the other large classes of progressive diseases of the nervous system—tumors and infections.

CLASSIFICATION   Since etiologic classification is impossible, subdivision of the degenerative diseases into individual syndromes rests on descriptive criteria based largely on pathologic anatomy, but to some extent on clinical aspects as well. In the terms used to designate many of these syndromes, the names of a number of distinguished neurologists and neuropathologists are commemorated. A useful way of keeping in mind the various disease states is to group them according to the outstanding clinical features that may be found in an actual case. The classification outlined in the following table (Table 350-1) and described below is based on such a plan.

SYNDROMES IN WHICH PROGRESSIVE DEMENTIA PREDOMINATES

In the disease entities about to be discussed, the clinical picture is dominated by gradual loss of intellectual capacities, i.e., by dementia. Other neurologic abnormalities, except in the terminal stages, are absent or relatively insignificant. (For further discussion of dementia, including its clinical evaluation, Chaps. 10, 11, and 23 should be consulted.)

ALZHEIMER'S DISEASE   Alzheimer's disease is perhaps the most important of all the degenerative diseases because of its frequent occurrence and devastating nature. It is the commonest cause of dementia in the elderly, with all that this implies in the way of distress for patients and families, and economic loss in the form

of the costs entailed in the long-term care of patients totally disabled by the disease. Historically, the term *Alzheimer's disease* was applied to progressive dementia coming on in late middle life but preceding the senile period, following the original description by Alois Alzheimer in 1907, in which the illness of a woman dying at the age of 55 was depicted clinically and pathologically. It became usual to classify cases of this kind under the heading of *presenile dementia*. Meanwhile, it became increasingly apparent that very old people dying with progressive mental deterioration, generally referred to as *senile dementia*, showed cerebral lesions that were identical to those found in cases of presenile dementia as described by Alzheimer. Consequently, to designate cases of this kind, the category of *senile dementia of the Alzheimer type* has been suggested. All evidence indicates that the disease process is the same, no matter what the age of occurrence may be. At the same time, it clearly is age-related. It is extremely uncommon in young people and rare in middle age; as age advances, however, it is increasingly frequent, such that its prevalence in persons over 80 years old is estimated at more than 20 percent (Ball, 1982). Advancing age is unmistakably a predisposing factor, and aging itself is accompanied by neuronal loss in the cerebral cortex, but it would be erroneous to consider Alzheimer's disease as the inevitable accompaniment of aging because, as general experience shows, there are many old people who remain mentally unimpaired to the end. Genetic predisposition to Alzheimer's disease does not emerge as a clear-cut pattern. In most instances, the disorder appears sporadically; there are well-documented familial cases, however,

TABLE 350-1   Clinical classification of the degenerative diseases of the nervous system

I Disorders characterized by progressive dementia in the absence of other prominent neurologic signs
   A Alzheimer's disease
   B Senile dementia of the Alzheimer type
   C Pick's disease (lobar atrophy)
II Syndromes combining progressive dementia with other prominent neurologic abnormalities
   A Mainly in adults
      1 Huntington's disease
      2 Multiple system atrophy combining dementia with ataxia and/or manifestations of Parkinson's disease
      3 Progressive supranuclear palsy (Steele-Richardson-Olszewski)
   B Mainly in children or young adults
      1 Hallervorden-Spatz disease
      2 Progressive familial myoclonic epilepsy
III Syndromes of gradually developing abnormalities of posture and movement
   A Paralysis agitans (Parkinson's disease)
   B Striatonigral degeneration
   C Progressive supranuclear palsy (see *II, A, 3* above)
   D Torsion dystonia (torsion spasm; dystonia musculorum deformans)
   E Spasmodic torticollis and other restricted dyskinesias
   F Familial tremor
   G Gilles de la Tourette syndrome
IV Syndromes of progressive ataxia
   A Cerebellar degenerations
      1 Cerebellar cortical degeneration
      2 Olivopontocerebellar atrophy (OPCA)
   B Spinocerebellar degenerations (Friedreich's ataxia and related disorders)
V Syndrome of central autonomic nervous system failure (Shy-Drager syndrome)
VI Syndromes of muscular weakness and wasting without sensory changes (motor neuron disease)
   A Amyotrophic lateral sclerosis
   B Spinal muscular atrophy
      1 Infantile spinal muscular atrophy (Werdnig-Hoffmann)
      2 Juvenile spinal muscular atrophy (Wohlfart-Kugelberg-Welander)
      3 Other forms of familial spinal muscular atrophy
   C Primary lateral sclerosis
   D Hereditary spastic paraplegia
VII Syndromes combining muscular weakness and wasting with sensory changes (progressive neural muscular atrophy; chronic familial polyneuropathies)
   A Peroneal muscular atrophy (Charcot-Marie-Tooth)
   B Hypertrophic interstitial polyneuropathy (Déjerine-Sottas)
   C Miscellaneous forms of chronic progressive neuropathy
VIII Syndromes of progressive visual loss
   A Pigmentary degeneration of the retina (retinitis pigmentosa)
   B Hereditary optic atrophy (Leber's disease)

some following an autosomal dominant pattern of inheritance. An exception to the statement that Alzheimer's disease is rare in young people occurs in the instance of Down's syndrome (trisomy 21), which leads to the development of the characteristic lesions of Alzheimer's disease in the majority of the patients after 30 years of age.

Pathology The outstanding pathologic feature is death and disappearance of nerve cells in the cerebral cortex. This leads ultimately to extensive convolutional atrophy, especially in the frontal and medial temporal regions. There is a corresponding enlargement of the ventricular system, but this is not extreme unless there is a concomitant hydrocephalus.

Two kinds of microscopic lesions are distinctive for the disease. The first, originally described by Alzheimer, consists of intracytoplasmic accumulations within neurons of a filamentous material in the form of loops, coils, or tangled masses—now often referred to as *Alzheimer neurofibrillary tangles*. The nature of these filaments is now under active investigation, because the neuropathologic evidence strongly suggests that these fibrillar masses are of major importance in bringing about the death of neurons. Electron microscopy shows them to be accumulations of paired helical filaments that clearly differ from the normal intracytoplasmic neurofilaments and tubules. Moreover, Rasool and Selkoe have produced evidence that the Alzheimer filaments differ antigenically from the normal neurofilaments. Apparently, therefore, these neurofibrillary tangles represent deposition of a pathologic substance rather than an overaccumulation of any normal cytoplasmic constituents. Neurofibrillary tangles tend to be most abundant, together with the most extreme degrees of neuronal loss, in the hippocampus and adjacent parts of the temporal lobe—structures that have been found to be of greatest importance in the faculty of retentive memory.

The other histopathologic change that characterizes Alzheimer's disease is the presence of intracortical foci of clustered thickened neuronal processes, both axons and dendrites (collectively referred to as *neurites*), generally in the form of an irregular ring surrounding a usually spherical deposit of amyloid fibrils. These lesions, which had already been recognized before Alzheimer's description of the neurofibrillary change, for many years were termed *senile plaques*. Recent elucidation of their structure has led to their currently being designated as *neuritic plaques*. The neuritic components of these plaques have been shown to contain paired helical filaments identical to those found in the perinuclear cytoplasm of the diseased neurons. The nature and origin of the amyloid component are being intensively studied. It is now evident that amyloid, identified by its staining reactions and ultrastructural features, is not a uniform substance; instead, its tinctorial and morphologic character depends upon a particular molecular spatial configuration (beta-pleated sheet fibrils) that can be brought about with various proteins, some of immunologic origin, some not. According to Glenner, the cerebral amyloid protein may be derived from an abnormal circulating protein (of as yet undetermined origin) which takes on the properties of amyloid as a result of the underlying pathologic process that is intrinsic to the disease. As far as can be determined, the earliest change in the development of the plaques is the production of the abnormal neurites; the amyloid deposition appears to be secondary.

There is another aspect to the problem of cerebral amyloidosis in Alzheimer's disease. In many, but not all, cases identical amyloid deposits may be found in the walls of small meningeal and intracortical arteries, and the question has arisen as to whether this cerebrovascular amyloidosis (often called *cerebral amyloid angiopathy* or *congophilic angiopathy* because of the characteristic staining of amyloid with the dye Congo red) has a close relationship, perhaps even causative (as suggested by Glenner), to plaque amyloidosis. At present, plaque amyloidosis and cerebrovascular amyloidosis are perhaps best considered as concomitant, or significantly interrelated, rather than interdependent; at any rate, experience shows that either one can be found in the brain independently of the other.

On the biochemical side, it is of interest that choline acetyltrans-

ferase, the key enzyme required for the synthesis of acetylcholine, is decreased in the cerebral cortex in Alzheimer's disease, as well as acetylcholinesterase. Recent studies have indicated that the major source of neocortical cholinergic innervation is a group of neurons situated in the basal part of the forebrain just beneath the corpus striatum—the nucleus basalis of Meynert. Careful pathoanatomic investigations have shown that in Alzheimer's disease, this nucleus is a site of major neuronal loss and of frequent Alzheimer neurofibrillary tangles. These studies suggest that impairment of cholinergic transmission may play a part in the clinical expression of the disease. However, attempted therapy with cholinomimetic agents has been largely unsuccessful. Less consistent reductions in cortical norepinephrine and serotonin appear to be caused by neuronal loss in the locus coeruleus and raphe nucleus, respectively. Loss of neurons in cerebral cortex is also associated with reduced cortical concentrations of somatostatin. Reduction in CSF concentrations of somatostatin is also reported.

It is to be hoped that the ongoing active investigations of the nature of these cerebral lesions will lead ultimately to an understanding of their causation. The remarkable discovery that one form of progressive dementia, Creutzfeldt-Jakob disease, is the result of infection with a transmissible virus-like agent has led to the question as to whether Alzheimer's disease and other neuronal degenerations might be due to a similar form of infectious agent. All attempts to transmit Alzheimer's disease have failed, however, so that currently an infective basis is thought unlikely. The fact, demonstrated by Perl and Brody, that neurofibrillary tangles contain aluminum is of interest, but its etiologic significance remains unclear.

Clinical manifestations The onset is insidious and subtle, with changes most noticeable first in memory for recent happenings and in other aspects of mental activity. Emotional disturbances such as depression, anxiety, or odd, unpredictable quirks of behavior, may be salient features in the early stages. Progression is usually slow and gradual, and unless other medical conditions supervene, it may smolder on for 10 or more years.

In the milder cases, including those of the senile period, the noteworthy features are those of simple dementia, as described in Chap. 23. More unusual disorders of thought and intellect, including aphasia, apraxic disturbances, and abnormalities of space perception, may be seen, especially in the presenile group. Exceptionally, and only in the advanced stages of the disease, extrapyramidal signs appear; the patient walks in a shuffling manner with short steps, and there is a generalized stiffness of the musculature with slowness and awkwardness of all movements. In some patients, sudden jerklike contractions of various muscles (myoclonus) may occur in the presence of otherwise typical Alzheimer's disease, but this is unusual and should immediately raise the suspicion of Creutzfeldt-Jakob disease (Chap. 347). Terminally the patient may become nearly decorticate, losing all ability to perceive, think, speak, or move. This is sometimes called "the late vegetative phase." Laboratory investigations, including the usual blood and CSF determinations, do not yield any conclusive or pertinent data. There is a diffuse slowing in the electroencephalogram in the more advanced stages of the disease. The enlargement of the ventricular system and subarachnoid space resulting from the diffuse brain atrophy can be demonstrated by computerized tomography (CT) scan and by magnetic resonance imaging (MRI). These imaging procedures, however, are not decisive for making the diagnosis, especially in the earlier stages, because the degree of cerebral atrophy demonstrated may be no more than that seen in patients of a similar age group who are functioning normally. During the course of the illness, occasional convulsive seizures may occur, but they are relatively rare and should raise suspicion of other diseases. Terminally, the patient dies from intercurrent disease, in a state of total helplessness. Institutional care is usually necessary long before the end.

Differential diagnosis The physician must be alert to the fact that what at first may appear to be dementia of the Alzheimer type, and hence be untreatable, may instead be mimicked by another disorder for which effective therapeutic measures are available. Evidence of space-occupying lesions, such as chronic subdural hematoma or slowly growing frontal neoplasms (for instance, meningioma or glioma) should be sought. CT and MRI scanning usually demonstrate mass lesions of these kinds, as well as an unsuspected hydrocephalus, which, when treated by a shunt procedure for ventricular decompression, may lead to dramatic improvement in the patient's state. Other treatable conditions producing a dementia-like state include metabolic derangements (as with liver disease), vitamin B_{12} (cyanocobalamin) deficiency, and hypothyroidism. Moreover, elderly people may be unusually susceptible to the sedative effects of medications, so that chronic drug intoxication may need to be considered. Cerebrovascular disease is not ordinarily a cause of uncomplicated dementia, but when, during study of a case, multiple small infarcts are disclosed on CT or MRI scanning, this poses a major problem in differential diagnosis and raises the possibility of multi-infarct dementia. Another disorder that can mimic dementia is depression, particularly in the elderly, in whom it may be all too easy to attribute deficits in thinking, motivation, and memory to an irreversible cerebral disease (see Chaps. 11 and 23). When due to depression—as may occur—these abnormalities may show a most gratifying response to appropriate treatment (see Chap. 360).

The evidence that cholinergic innervation may be impaired in Alzheimer's disease has led to attempts to correct the deficiency pharmacologically, much as is done in Parkinson's disease by giving L-dopa, but so far none of these has proved to be consistently effective.

Practical measures that may help in the management of cases of Alzheimer's disease are suggested in Chaps. 11 and 23, which are concerned with the delirious and demented patient.

PICK'S DISEASE (LOBAR ATROPHY)　This remarkable form of cerebral disease, which is characterized by the circumscription of the atrophy (lobar sclerosis), was first described by Arnold Pick at the turn of the century. In the differential diagnosis of dementia in the presenile period, it is often mentioned in the same breath with Alzheimer's disease. It is, however, an extremely rare condition as compared with diffuse cerebral atrophy of the Alzheimer type. Moreover, hereditary transmission (as a dominant trait) is more frequent in Pick's disease, and women are more frequently affected than men. The age distribution is similar in both of these varieties of progresive dementia.

Pathology　So striking are the gross pathologic changes in the brain that in typical cases the diagnosis can be made at a glance. Severe atrophy of the anterior portions of the frontal and temporal lobes occurs, and there is a curiously sharp line of demarcation between the atrophied portions and the remainder of the brain, which appears normal or nearly so. In some cases, the frontal atrophy is more prominent; in others, the temporal lobes are more severely involved; in general, both regions are affected. Rarely, the disorder has a predominantly unilateral localization—as in cases described originally by Pick. Characteristically, there likewise are atrophic changes in a number of subcortical structures: caudate nucleus, putamen, thalamus, and substantia nigra, and in the descending frontopontine fiber system. In the diseased regions, the local destruction of central and convolutional white matter may be out of proportion to the degree of loss of nerve cell bodies in corresponding areas of the cortex. In many cases (20 of 32 in the well-studied series of Tissot et al.), there are striking changes in nerve cells in the affected regions. These consist of fibrillary deposits within the cytoplasm—masses of straight fibrils, differing from the paired helical filaments of Alzheimer's disease. In some neurons, densely packed spherical aggregates (Pick bodies) can be seen with special staining techniques, such as silver-impregnation methods. In the other affected neurons, the fibrils are more widely dispersed, and the neuronal cytoplasm takes on a rounded, distended appearance, forming ballooned cells. Recent evidence suggests that despite the morphologic differences, these neuronal changes are biochemically related to those in Alzheimer's disease, as indicated by common antigenic properties. In the cases in which these cytopathologic changes are found, other pathologic features are identical to those seen in cases in which they are present: extreme neuronal loss and gliosis in the affected lobes and concomitant lobar atrophy of white matter. In rare instances of Alzheimer's disease, disproportionate atrophy of the frontal and temporal lobes may suggest Pick's disease, but in such cases the distinguishing feature is the presence of the characteristic plaques and neurofibrillary tangles, which are not found in Pick's disease.

Clinical manifestations　If Pick's disease has any distinctive clinical features, they consist of unusually severe signs of frontal lobe or temporal lobe dysfunction (see Chap. 24). Typical early manifestations are a general impoverishment of mental function, changes in behavior patterns, and a striking lack of insight. The later phases of the disease are characterized by loss of retentive memory (with temporal lobe involvement), loss of all language functions, and, when the frontal lobes are mainly affected, prominent grasp and sucking reflexes. In CT and MRI scans the shrinkage of the cortex and the low density of the white matter in the affected lobes may be diagnostic. Progression, as in Alzheimer's disease, is slow and relentless, the average duration being about 7 years. In the late stages, rigidity, dystonic postures, and perhaps tremor may be prominent features; these can be ascribed to extension of the disease process into the basal ganglia.

Differential diagnosis　The considerations already noted with regard to Alzheimer's disease apply to Pick's disease as well.

SYNDROMES COMBINING DEMENTIA WITH OTHER NEUROLOGIC SIGNS

HUNTINGTON'S DISEASE　This disorder, which is characterized by a combination of choreoathetotic movements and progressive dementia usually beginning in midadult life, is transmitted from generation to generation as an autosomal dominant disease. Recent genetic studies have shown that the determining gene is located on the short arm of chromosome 4. The classic description is that of George Huntington, who, together with his father and grandfather, both physicians, made clinical observations on familial cases living near their home on Long Island, New York. Huntington, writing in 1872, entitled his paper "On Chorea"; subsequently the disorder described by him came to be known as *Huntington's chorea*. The more general term used in this chapter—Huntington's disease—is preferable, since the disease state comprises more than abnormal movements, and the motor abnormalities often are more complex than would be implied by the unqualified term *chorea*.

Because of its distressing and incapacitating nature, and its implications for members of any family in which it appears (50 percent risk in all children of an affected parent), the disease has attracted attention in recent years and has been found to be considerably more frequent and widely distributed than once was thought. In virtually all cases that come to the notice of a physician, there is a family history of the disease, although very occasionally a new case may turn up as the result of an apparent genetic mutation; however, no proven case of a new mutation has occurred. An apparently negative family history may be obtained in a few cases of late onset, often classified as senile chorea, where family members have died of other causes before the disease became manifest.

Pathology　Distinctive for Huntington's disease is atrophy of the caudate nucleus, and, to a lesser extent, other structures of the basal ganglia (putamen and globus pallidus), out of proportion to any other changes in the brain. The degree of atrophy is directly related to the severity and duration of the disease. In the late stages, the caudate nucleus, which normally forms a convexly rounded eminence in the lateral wall of the lateral ventricle, takes on instead a flattened or concave appearance. As the result of the tissue loss, the ventricular system becomes correspondingly widened, especially the frontal horns. Along with these changes in the basal ganglia, there characteristically is diffuse gyral atrophy, most severe over the convex aspect of the brain.

The atrophy of the caudate nucleus and putamen is seen microscopically to be due to extensive loss of neurons, which stands out in contrast to the intactness of adjacent structures such as the nucleus accumbens septi, the nucleus basalis of Meynert (so strikingly involved in Alzheimer's disease), and the thalamus.

There are no morphologically distinctive or characteristic cytopathologic alterations in the neurons in Huntington's disease such as occur in Alzheimer's and some other diseases. Neurochemical studies have shown a striking decrease of γ-aminobutyric acid (GABA) and of its synthesizing enzyme, glutamic acid decarboxylase (GAD) in the caudate nucleus, putamen, globus pallidus, and pars reticulata of the substantia nigra, and some decrease also in choline acetyltransferase (CAT) in the caudate nucleus. The loss of GABA can be attributed to depletion of the abundant medium-sized *spiny* neurons within the striatum. Spiny neurons are characterized in Golgi studies by a large number of dendritic spines and have been shown to constitute the projection neurons of the striatum. They provide efferents to both the globus pallidus and substantia nigra. In contrast *aspiny* neurons, with few dendritic spines, are striatal interneurons with locally arborizing axons. In addition to GABA, other neurotransmitters contained within striatal spiny neurons, including substance P, enkephalins, and dynorphin, are similarly depleted in the striatum and its sites of projection.

Recent observations indicate that the peptide neurotransmitter somatostatin is relatively increased in the caudate nucleus and putamen in Huntington's disease, and cells identifiable as somatostatin neurons (*aspiny* neurons) are selectively preserved—in striking contrast to the loss of other neurons in the same regions. The pathophysiologic meaning of this sparing is not clear as yet; in any event, its occurrence further emphasizes the fact that in Huntington's disease, as well as in other neuronal-system degenerations, there is selective vulnerability of some neurons in a particular region and preservation of others. The nature of the resistance of particular neuronal groups is unknown but its investigation may provide clues to the underlying disease process. Another interesting point is that the disease informs us of the presence of a diversity of functions of seemingly identical-appearing small neurons in the striatum.

The progressive dementia of Huntington's disease is still not well characterized neuropathologically. It has generally been attributed to neuronal loss in the cerebral cortex, but we have had great difficulty in discerning abnormalities in the cortex in comparison with appropriately chosen control material. Recent biochemical studies, however, are consistent with a mild neuronal loss, particularly in frontal cortex. Further correlative biochemical and neuropathologic studies, using careful quantitative methods, will be needed to resolve this issue.

Clinical aspects The disorder has a prevalence in Europe and North America of 7 to 10 per 100,000 population. The movement disorder generally makes its appearance in early to middle adult years (average age of onset about 35 to 40 years). It is characteristic of the disease that younger patients, with onset of symptoms in the age group of 15 to 40 years, suffer a more severe form of the disorder than older patients, with onset in the 50s and 60s, and the neuropathologic changes in the brain are correspondingly more extensive and severe in the younger as compared with the older patients. There also is evidence that paternal transmission results in a more severe form of the disease than maternal transmission. Huntington's disease is occasionally manifest in childhood (even before the age of 4). Such cases are rare and tend to be characterized more by rigidity than by chorea and by other atypical features such as convulsive seizures and cerebellar ataxia (Westphal's variant).

The involuntary movements (bizarre grimacing, respiratory irregularity, faulty articulation of speech, and irregular, arrhythmic, unpatterned movements of the limbs, imparting to the gait a peculiar dancing quality) tend to be less quick and more athetoid than in

Sydenham's chorea (see Chap. 15). Some reported cases which on genealogic and pathologic grounds must be classified with Huntington's chorea have shown progressive rigidity rather than choreiform movements, even in the adult. As a general rule, dementia runs parallel with the motor disorder. Occasionally it may appear before or after chorea; very rarely it may be slight or lacking altogether. Neuropsychiatric manifestations of depression, erratic behavior, and emotional outbursts often seriously handicap the patient before dementia or the movement disorder are severe. The advance of the disease is slow. There is increasing disability because of both involuntary movements and mental changes, terminated after many years by death from intercurrent infection or, not rarely, by suicide.

Differential diagnosis There is no difficulty in the recognition of typical cases. The relatively late onset, the slowly progressive course, the prominent dementia, and lack of association with rheumatic fever help to exclude Sydenham's chorea. Patients with Parkinson's disease when overdosed with L-dopa may develop a widespread chorea or choreoathetosis, and this, combined with the early dementia that occurs in some patients, can reproduce the picture of Huntington's disease. Phenothiazine drugs may induce generalized chorea, unassociated with dementia, and the movement disorder may persist for months or years after the medication is discontinued (tardive dyskinesia). Finally, there is a form of self-limited chorea which, like other localized dyskinesias, may appear in older persons without identifiable cause. Hepatolenticular degeneration (Wilson's disease) and nonfamilial forms of hepatocerebral degeneration may display clinical abnormalities resembling those of Huntington's disease, but the specific changes characteristic of these disorders, including liver disease, corneal Kayser-Fleischer rings (in Wilson's disease), and the typical biochemical abnormalities, are absent in Huntington's disease (see Chap. 311). Choreoathetosis appearing during the second postnatal year and lasting throughout life is due to hypoxic birth injury or kernicterus. Sporadic cases of choreiform movements beginning in middle or late life may present a difficult problem in exact diagnosis. The occasional cases of violent choreiform movements produced by vascular lesions, classically in the subthalamic region, are characterized by sudden onset, unilateral distribution (hemiballismus), and a tendency to improve after a period of initial severity. A few cases of acute choreoathetosis have accompanied hyperthyroidism. Virus encephalitis may occasionally be associated with choreiform movements; acute development, fever, and pleocytosis in the CSF help in recognition of such cases. Hereditary acanthocytosis is a rare condition which can mimic Huntington's disease.

Treatment No form of treatment has as yet been devised that halts the relentless progression of this disease, and therapeutic attempts to alleviate the abnormal movements have generally been unsatisfactory. Dopamine receptor antagonists (butyrophenones or phenothiazines) may partially ameliorate the chorea, but the side effects characteristic of this class of drugs limit their use. The application of molecular genetic probes for presymptomatic and prenatal discovery of the gene is currently under evaluation.

MULTIPLE SYSTEM ATROPHY General experience has indicated that cases of multiple affection of neuronal systems may occur in which progressive dementia is combined with varying degrees of ataxia, dysarthria, and parkinsonian dyskinesia, depending upon the pattern of anatomic distribution of the pathologic changes. For cases of this kind, the general term *multiple system atrophy or degeneration* has been applied. In some, loss of neurons in the cerebellar cortex and in the pontine nuclei and inferior olivary nuclei results in the predominating picture of *olivopontocerebellar degeneration*, to be discussed below as one of the syndromes of progressive ataxia. These changes may be combined with similar neuronal loss in the substantia nigra (and in the striatum in striatonigral degeneration), resulting in parkinsonian features (discussed below under "Parkinson's Disease"). Pathologically, the disease process is characterized by death and disappearance of the affected cells and an accompanying reactive gliosis, without intracellular inclusions or other distinctive features. The cerebral cortex generally shows little discernible change, so that it may be difficult to ascribe a definite pathoanatomic basis for the dementia, which, for this reason, is sometimes designated as *subcortical*. Typically multiple system atrophy is a disorder of late adult life, occurring sporadically in some instances and genetically transmitted in others. Further details of individual syndromes are given in later sections.

PROGRESSIVE SUPRANUCLEAR PALSY (STEELE-RICHARDSON-OLSZEWSKI SYNDROME)

This disorder is discussed below among the syndromes characterized by gradually developing abnormalities of posture and movement. It is mentioned here because progressive dementia may accompany the other neurologic abnormalities, although it appears late in the course and generally is not severe.

HALLERVORDEN-SPATZ DISEASE

This unusual disorder, often affecting several siblings in a family in a manner suggesting an autosomal recessive trait, is associated with a rather variable clinical picture in which abnormalities of posture and muscle tone, involuntary movements, and progressive dementia predominate. Pathologically, there are characteristic abnormalities in the basal ganglia, suggesting a localized disorder of metabolism. The features of the condition were classically described in an affected family by Hallervorden and Spatz (1922).

Pathology   Distinctive for this condition is the accumulation of large amounts of pigmented material in the globus pallidus and pars reticulata of the substantia nigra, resulting in grossly visible brownish discoloration of these regions. Microscopically, there are irregular pigmented, ferruginous concretions and granules of varying brownish or greenish hues, depending on the stains used. Although much of this pigment contains iron, serum iron and ferritin are normal, and there is no systemic disorder of iron metabolism. There also is loss of nerve cell fibers. Another feature of the disease is the presence of focal swelling of axons, most probably in their terminal portions; this is especially pronounced in the regions affected by the pigmentary disorder, but typically can be found at all levels of the central nervous system, including the cerebral cortex. This neuroaxonal change may link the disease with childhood neuroaxonal dystrophy.

Clinical aspects   The disorder typically makes its appearance in childhood or adolescence, with abnormalities in muscle tone and movements, such as rigidity and choreoathetosis. Abnormal postures of the trunk characteristic of torsion spasm (dystonia) may be seen, or the clinical picture may be reminiscent of parkinsonism. Cerebellar ataxia is also present in some instances. Speech becomes indistinct, and there is progressive intellectual impairment. Eventually, the involuntary movements give way to increasing generalized rigidity, and death comes as a rule about 10 years after onset. A few cases of late onset have shown a parkinsonian syndrome.

Differential diagnosis   No feature of the clinical picture serves to distinguish this particular disorder from other conditions showing dementia with extrapyramidal motor abnormalities. Wilson's disease must be excluded by appropriate laboratory tests. The clearly progressive course sets this condition apart from clinically similar abnormalities resulting from accidents or illnesses at birth or in the neonatal period. It has lately been demonstrated that following intravenous injection of labeled ferrous citrate, there is a selective uptake of radioactive iron in the region of the basal ganglia; possibly a study of this kind would be helpful in diagnosis. In an advanced case, CT scanning may show extreme atrophy of the brain, especially including the structures of the basal ganglia, but the pigmented deposits do not show any increased radiographic density. In some cases there is lucency in the putamen and globus pallidus. At present no effective treatment is known. Treatment with a chelating agent, deferoxamine mesylate, has not shown definite benefit, and L-dopa and other antiparkinsonian medications, tryptophan, and megavitamin therapy have been of only temporary and questionable help.

PROGRESSIVE FAMILIAL MYOCLONIC EPILEPSY

There are several neurologic disorders that can result in a syndrome of convulsive seizures, myoclonic jerklike contractions of the musculature, and progressive dementia. Those most frequently encountered in practice are subacute sclerosing panencephalitis in children, adolescents, and young adults (Chap. 347), and subacute spongiform encephalopathy (Creutzfeldt-Jakob disease) in older adults (Chap. 347). The syndrome can also occur in some of the rare forms of metabolic familial disorders: neuraminidase deficiency associated with macular cherry-red spots (Chap. 316) and ceroid-lipofuscinosis (Chap. 318). When these and other disorders of known cause can be excluded from consideration, there remain some clinicopathologic entities which can appropriately be considered under the heading of the hereditary degenerative diseases. Several families presenting this syndrome have been carefully studied in northern Europe (Sweden and Finland), but there is no specific geographical distribution.

Lafora's disease   This variety of recessively inherited progressive myoclonic epilepsy is characterized by distinctive intracytoplasmic inclusions in cerebral neurons, called Lafora bodies following their original description by Gonzalo Lafora (1911). These have been found to be composed of polymers of glucose (polyglucosans) and thus indicate a disorder of carbohydrate metabolism, but the biochemical defect that leads to their accumulation is unknown. The Lafora bodies are widely distributed, but most numerous in the thalamus, substantia nigra, and dentate nucleus of the cerebellum. Subsequent to Lafora's reports, similar polysaccharide deposits have been found in myocardial and skeletal muscle fibers and in the liver, and it is now possible to establish the diagnosis in the presymptomatic phase by liver biopsy.

The disorder characteristically makes its appearance during childhood or adolescence in the form of recurrent seizures (generalized or restricted), or uncontrollable myoclonic jerks, or combinations of the two. With the passage of time, the myoclonic phenomena become increasingly severe, and there is deterioration of all intellectual functions. Death from intercurrent infection generally occurs before the age of 25. Anticonvulsive treatment may help in controlling the seizures, but there currently is no effective treatment for the underlying disease.

Other varieties of myoclonic epilepsy   When Lafora's disease and the metabolic and infective disorders mentioned above have been excluded, there remains a rather heterogeneous group of progressive neurologic illnesses having in common autosomal recessive inheritance, myoclonic phenomena, convulsive seizures, and mild dementia. Ataxia of stance, gait, and limb movements is a prominent feature in most cases—so much so that the term introduced by Ramsay Hunt, *dyssynergia cerebellaris myoclonica*, is often applied. In a few cases, including some of those originally described by Hunt, there is an overlap with Friedreich's ataxia, or with chronic sensorimotor neuropathies (see Chaps. 353 and 355). The neuropathologic changes in the few cases that have come to postmortem examination have varied from case to case. In some, atrophy of the dentate nucleus and its fiber projections has been prominent; in others, there has been loss of neurons, especially Purkinje cells, in the cerebellar cortex; in still others, changes have been confined to long-tract degeneration (posterior columns and spinocerebellar tracts) in the spinal cord; a few patients have had cortical, basal-ganglionic, or retinal lesions. Variations also occur in the age of onset and the rate of progression. Until more is known about the biochemistry and genetics of this group of disorders, no satisfactory classification is possible. For further details of these syndromes, general reference works on neurology, such as that of Adams and Victor, should be consulted.

Treatment with appropriate anticonvulsant medications has been helpful in some mild cases, but phenytoin is contraindicated. L-Tryptophan and carbidopa or valproic acid have ameliorated myoclonus in a few cases.

SYNDROMES OF ABNORMAL POSTURE, TREMOR, AND INVOLUNTARY MOVEMENT

PARALYSIS AGITANS (PARKINSON'S DISEASE) This is a common condition first named and described by James Parkinson in 1817. His remarkably complete account gives this definition:

Involuntary tremulous motion, with lessened muscular power, in parts not in action and even when supported; with a propensity to bend the trunk forward, and to pass from a walking to a running pace, the senses and intellects being uninjured.

Typically, paralysis agitans is a disorder of middle or late life, with very gradual progression and a prolonged course. Although it has been seen to occur in families (the estimated familial incidence is 1 to 2 percent), it usually is sporadic. It is well recognized, however, that the epidemic encephalitis of von Economo, which occurred in a worldwide distribution in the years following World War I, was followed by a syndrome clinically almost indistinguishable from paralysis agitans. It is usual in such instances to speak of postencephalitic parkinsonism, whereas the term *Parkinson's disease* should be reserved for true paralysis agitans of unknown cause. Paralysis agitans bears no consistent relation to any known disease process such as arteriosclerosis, trauma, or intoxication (except for MPTP, see below), although such conditions have often been invoked as etiologically significant and may at times produce somewhat similar clinical manifestations.

Pathology Despite the general medical familiarity with the condition and an extensive literature on the subject, it cannot be said that the pathologic changes of paralysis agitans are yet fully understood. The most regularly observed changes have been in the aggregates of melanin-containing nerve cells in the brainstem (substantia nigra, locus coeruleus), where there are varying degrees of nerve cell loss with reactive gliosis (most pronounced in the substantia nigra) along with distinctive eosinophilic intracytoplasmic inclusions (called Lewy bodies, after their description by F.H. Lewy in 1913). Similar changes are seen in the nucleus basalis of Meynert, to which reference is already made in the discussion of Alzheimer's disease. In the older literature, cell loss was also described in other structures of the basal ganglia, but these changes turn out not to be clearly different in nature or degree from what may be encountered in other patients of similar age without extrapyramidal motor disorders. Lesions in these same pigmented nuclei, but without Lewy bodies, characterize the pathologic findings in postencephalitic parkinsonism, in striatonigral degeneration, and in the Shy-Drager syndrome (discussed below).

Biochemical studies which show a decrease of dopamine in the caudate nucleus and putamen—an alteration consistently found in experimental ablation of the substantia nigra—emphasize the possibility that Parkinson's disease can be considered an example of neuronal system disease, involving mainly the nigrostriatal dopaminergic system.

Further confirmation of the importance of disease of the nigrostriatal dopaminergic system in Parkinson's disease comes from the accidental intoxication of drug users by self-injection with MPTP, which selectively destroys the pigmented (dopaminergic) neurons of the substantia nigra and produces the typical clinical manifestations of the disease. The pathologic features of MPTP-induced Parkinson's disease, however, differ from those of idiopathic cases in the absence of Lewy bodies and the lack of neuronal loss in the locus coeruleus. Although MPTP lesions do not exactly mimic those of idiopathic Parkinson's disease, the mechanism by which the drug kills substantia nigra neurons is under active investigation and may provide new insights about the pathogenesis of the idiopathic illness.

Clinical apsects In its fully developed form, this disorder cannot be mistaken for any other. The stooped posture, the stiffness and slowness of movement, the fixity of facial expression, and the rhythmic tremor of the limbs which subsides on active willed movement or complete relaxation are familiar to every clinician. Although symmetric in the later stages, the disorder typically begins asymmetrically, e.g., as a slight tremor of the fingers of one hand or in one leg. Also typical are more or less general hypokinesia and stiffness of the musculature so that even where tremor is inapparent, the disease may betray itself by a somewhat staring and immobile facial expression, a monotonous voice, a general slowness and diminution of all motor activity, and a curious lack of the little spontaneous movements of postural adjustment that are so characteristic of the normal individual. When tremor is minimal, patients often are able to alleviate it by relaxation or by movement or to hide it by keeping their hands in their pockets. The tremor is generally most pronounced in the hands but may involve the legs (and thus secondarily the trunk), lips, tongue, and neck muscles, and is easily seen in the eyelids when they are lightly closed. Its frequency is 4 to 5 per second, but another faster (action) tremor (7 to 8 per second) predominates in some patients. There is never total paralysis, although this is implied by the name of the disease; nevertheless, general enfeeblement of voluntary movement is characteristic of the fully developed disorder. Generally accompanying the stooped attitude is the typical festinating gait, whereby the patient, prevented by the abnormality of postural tone from making the appropriate reflex adjustments required for effective walking, progresses with quick shuffling steps at an accelerating pace as if to catch up with the body's center of gravity. Clinical examination of the tendon and plantar reflexes discloses no abnormalities. There are no sensory changes, although deep aching in joints and muscles is common. Eventually, patients may become so incapacitated by rigidity and tremor as to be helpless in caring for themselves. It has often been observed, however, that even severely disabled patients may, when excited or under great emotional stress, perform complex motor acts quickly and efficiently. Although the temporary alleviation under extreme provocation can never be long maintained, it is nevertheless true that the severity of the symptoms is considerably influenced by emotional factors, being aggravated by anxiety, tension, and unhappiness, and minimal when the patient is in a contented frame of mind. Despite the inherently progressive nature of the condition, much can be achieved with good medical management, and patients may continue for years to live effective, happy lives in spite of this affliction.

Although intellectual deterioration is not a consistent feature of early Parkinson's disease, dementia has been increasingly recognized to be a feature of advanced Parkinson's disease. It eventually afflicts up to one-third of all cases. The dementia is typically insidious in onset and may be heralded by disorientation at night. In advanced cases patients may suffer from vivid auditory and visual hallucinations often precipitated by levodopa therapy.

Differential diagnosis In typical cases, this is not difficult. The extrapyramidal syndromes associated with most diseases of known cause or established nature, such as cerebrovascular disease, cerebral hypoxia (including carbon monoxide asphyxia), or metallic poisoning, differ from paralysis agitans in a number of respects, such as atypical behavior or tremor, presence of signs of corticospinal tract deficit, or early onset of dementia. The differentiation from postencephalitic parkinsonism may be impossible; a clear history of an attack of epidemic encephalitis (prolonged somnolence, disturbance of consciousness, diplopia) and relatively early age of onset of the disorder and the presence of tics, localized spasms, and oculogyric crises may be the only clues to this diagnosis. A neurologic disorder similar to some degree to Parkinson's disease occurs with the prolonged administration of large amounts of reserpine and phenothiazine drugs, as the result of their blocking action on dopaminergic transmission. This drug-induced syndrome usually subsides on discontinuation or decrease in the dosage of the drug, but it may continue indefinitely in the syndrome of *tardive dyskinesia.* MPTP-induced parkinsonism persists because of the destructive effects of the drug on the nigral dopaminergic neurons. Parkinsonism very rarely is produced by cerebral neoplasms or other focal lesions, but then only when the nigrostriatal system has been largely destroyed, with relative sparing of the corticospinal projections.

Some Parkinson-like postural and motor abnormalities may be seen following the repeated blows to the head sustained by boxers— in the "punch drunk" syndrome, in which lesions of the substantia nigra are one of the neuropathologic components. In this condition, dementia, ataxia, dysarthria, and inappropriate behavior are prominent, and neuronal cell loss with neurofibrillary tangles is evident in cerebral coretex.

Multiple bilateral infarcts in the corticospinal pathways and central structures of the brain may induce a syndrome that in some ways resembles paralysis agitans (so-called arteriosclerotic parkinsonism), but careful clinical assessment of the history and findings, particularly the reflex status, serves to distinguish this disorder from true Parkinson's disease. Striatonigral degeneration is a rare syndrome which can be clinically indistinguishable from Parkinson's disease but which does not respond to dopaminergic agents (see below).

Treatment   Although there is no treatment that is known to halt or reverse the neuronal degeneration that presumably underlies Parkinson's disease, methods are now available which can bring about a considerable degree of relief from symptoms in many patients. An important part of any therapeutic program is the maintenance of optimum general health and neuromuscular efficiency by planned programs of exercise, activity, and rest; expert physical therapy may be of great help in achieving these ends. In addition, the patient often needs much emotional support in meeting the stress of the illness, in comprehending its nature, and in carrying on courageously in spite of it. Along with these general supportive measures, which are applicable to many chronic illnesses, patients generally require a carefully thought-out program of treatment specifically aimed at counteracting the pathophysiologic disorder that produces their disabilities.

The principles of medical treatment are those that have been presented by Growdon. According to his suggestions, the drug therapy should be adapted to the patient's needs, which vary with the stage of the disease and the predominant manifestation(s). Usually anticholinergic drugs are most effective in suppressing tremor at rest, and propranolol or primidone is best for action tremor. L-Dopa improves akinesia and postural imbalance; anticholinergic drugs have little effect on these two abnormalities.

The decision about whether to treat with a drug and the choice of drug(s) are influenced by the stage of the disease. The scale of Hoehn and Yahr is recommended:

Stage I: Unilateral involvement.

Stage II: Bilateral involvement but no postural abnormalities.

Stage III: Bilateral involvement with mild postural imbalance; the patient leads an independent life.

Stage IV: Bilateral involvement with postural instability; the patient requires substantial help.

Stage V: Severe, fully developed disease; the patient is restricted to bed and chair.

For patients with mild disease (stages I and II), no medication may be required, or only an anticholinergic drug, or amantadine (a dopamine agonist), or a combination of both. Levodopa is required for stages III, IV, and V. In each instance, one uses the lowest dose that gives satisfactory benefit; this decreases the chances of unwanted side effects such as dyskinesias, the on-off phenomenon, and mental confusion, as well as of loss of efficacy of the drug.

The anticholinergic drugs in use share the capacity to block muscarinic receptors and thereby to reduce cholinergic transmission. They are effective not only in relieving the rest tremor of mild Parkinson's disease but also may be combined with levodopa in the treatment of the severe forms of the disease. The anticholinergic drugs also reverse the dystonia and parkinsonian symptoms of neuroleptic drugs.

Currently available anticholinergic drugs are trihexyphenidyl,

benztropine, biperiden, and procyclidine. The usual dose of trihexyphenidyl is 1 to 2 mg qid. Benztropine has both anticholinergic and antihistaminic properties; the usual dose is 0.5 to 1.0 mg tid. The optimal dose of all these medications varies for each patient and often needs adjusting. Low doses of these drugs cause dry mouth but few if any other side effects. Larger doses should be given with caution for in the elderly they may cause confusion, visual and tactile hallucinations, narrow-angle glaucoma, and urinary retention. Anticholinergic drugs may exacerbate dementia and should be withdrawn when dementia becomes clinically evident.

Propranolol, a beta-adrenergic antagonist, is helpful in suppressing the fast-frequency action tremor in Parkinson's disease and in the hereditary tremor syndrome. The usual dose is 40 to 80 mg tid. In large doses, it may slow the heart rate and lower blood pressure, which are disadvantages in patients with a tendency to orthostatic hypotension. Metoprolol, a specific beta-adrenergic antagonist, is also effective and is safer in patients with suspected asthma. Primidone in a dose of 50 mg at bedtime has also been shown to be effective. If the tremor is not improved after 1 week, the dose can be increased up to 250 mg daily. Many clinicians now initiate therapy with this regimen.

Amantadine was found by accident to be helpful in Parkinson's disease. Its effect is achieved by its capacity to release stored dopamine from presynaptic terminals; thus it is efficacious in the earlier stages of the disease, before the majority of the dopaminergic neurons in the midbrain have degenerated. It tends to be especially beneficial for tremor. The usual dosage is 100 mg bid; larger doses may produce side effects such as skin changes (livido reticularis), ankle edema, and mental confusion. In some patients, the addition of amantadine to levodopa achieves better results then either medication alone.

Levodopa, which increases the dopamine levels in the striatum and restores neurotransmitter balance between dopamine and acetylcholine, improves akinesia and postural disorders (and sometimes rest tremor) in 75 percent of patients. Levodopa is now given in combination with a dopa-carboxylase inhibitor (carbidopa) which prevents destruction of levodopa in the bloodstream and peripheral tissues but does not pass the blood-brain barrier. This combination therefore makes it possible to achieve optimum effects with a smaller dosage of levodopa than would otherwise need to be used. In this way, some of the side effects of levodopa, particularly nausea and vomiting, can be greatly reduced. The combination (Sinemet) is available in ratios of 1:4 carbidopa to levodopa (25 mg/100 mg) or 1:10 (10/100, 25/250). A total dosage of levodopa from 300 to 2000 mg daily can be used; the relative amounts of carbidopa and levodopa, and the timing of the medications, should be adjusted according to the needs of the individual patient. Although levodopa now is the cornerstone of therapy, it can be combined with an anticholinergic drug, with amantandine, or with bromocriptine.

Bromocriptine is a dopamine agonist which acts directly upon dopamine receptors, unlike levodopa, which requires enzymatic transformation into dopamine within the brain. It has been found to be helpful in the treatment of Parkinson's disease, generally in combination with levodopa. When used alone, patients with mild early disease will often respond to doses of 15 to 30 mg daily. However, more advanced patients may need a dosage range of 50 to 100 mg daily. When given in combination with other drugs, smaller quantities should be used, beginning with 2.5 mg tid. Doses of bromocriptine ranging from 20 to 30 mg daily have been effective as an adjunct to levodopa therapy. Whether or not to use bromocriptine and the dosage are matters that must be decided on the basis of what seems best for an individual patient. The side effects are much the same as those with levodopa.

It must be said that although the modern treatment of Parkinson's disease is more successful than any that was available before the introduction of levodopa, including stereotactic surgery, there are still many problems. Underlying much of the difficulty undoubtedly is the fact that none of these therapeutic measures has an affect on the underlying disease process, which consists of neuronal degeneration. Ultimately a point seems to be reached where pharmacotherapy can no longer compensate for the loss. The major difficulties consist of fluctuations or sudden variations in the response to the drugs used (the on-off response), the development of weakness or immobility (akinesia), and dyskinesias, which increasingly become a problem as the years go by. The dyskinesias consist of choreiform or choreoathetotic movements, which in the late stages of the disease alternate with paralyzing akinesia depending upon a very narrow dosage variation (50 to 100 mg) of levodopa. Interference with absorption of levodopa may be partially responsible since continuous intravenous infusions of levodopa result in a stable clinical state. Loss of therapeutic efficacy also occurs: a single dose which at one time was effective for 5 to 6 h may last only an hour or so. Giving smaller amounts of medication more frequently is sometimes efficacious. In addition, agents acting directly on the postsynaptic receptor, such as bromocriptine, are sometimes more effective. It has recently been shown that temporary levodopa withdrawal, advocated as a method of dealing with the long-term complications of Parkinson's disease, carries some risk and does not result in improved efficacy of levodopa.

Progressive dementia, which eventually overtakes one-third to one-half of the patients in later years, may render them less tolerant to medication. Visual and tactile hallucinations are especially prominent in this group of patients.

As many as one-half of patients with Parkinson's disease have depressive symptoms. They should be treated along the lines suggested in Chap. 360.

The introduction of stereotaxic surgery, with the placement of precisely localized focal lesions in central structures in the brain—mainly the ventrolateral thalamus, or globus pallidus contralateral to the side of the major symptoms—was an important advance in the attempt to relieve the symptoms of Parkinson's disease. The success that has been achieved with levodopa has supplanted these procedures, which, although very beneficial in well-chosen cases, were not without risk and at times were followed by severe disability. Neurosurgical treatment of this kind can still be recommended for the very occasional patient who is relatively young and in good general health and who has a severe unilateral disabling or disfiguring tremor.

STRIATONIGRAL DEGENERATION This rare syndrome closely resembles Parkinson's disease clinically, but clearly differs from it pathologically. The classic clinicopathologic description is that of Adams, van Bogaert, and Vander Eecken, who encountered the disorder in four middle-aged patients with no family history of similar disease. Three of the patients showed the typical clinical picture of Parkinson's disease; orthostatic hypotension was observed in one of them, and cerebellar ataxia in another.

The principal neuronal cell loss in the striatum and substantia nigra. There is an association in some cases with a progressive ataxic disorder resembling olivopontocerebellar degeneration, and in others with degeneration of spinal cord neurons of the autonomic nervous system, similar to the Shy-Drager syndrome, in which postural hypotension is a major component (see below). The degree to which parkinsonian symptoms occur probably depends on the extent of the nigral lesions as balanced against those in the cerebellum and its connections. Cases of this kind represent examples of multiple system degeneration as described above.

The disorder characteristically occurs in late middle age. Treatment with anti-Parkinson's disease medications has usually not been successful. For measures which control hypotension see under "Shy-Drager Syndrome" (below and Chap. 12).

PROGRESSIVE SUPRANUCLEAR PALSY (STEELE-RICHARDSON-OLSZEWSKI SYNDROME) This disorder, first clearly described in 1963 by Richardson, Steele, and Olszewski, occurs in elderly individuals in approximately the same age period as paralysis agitans. Moreover, it is among the group of parkinsonian patients that most of the examples of this disease are to be found.

Pathology A loss of neurons and gliosis are found on postmortem examination in the tectum and tegmentum of the midbrain, the subthalamic nuclei of Luys, the vestibular nuclei, and to some extent the ocular nuclei. A characteristic finding is the presence of neurofibrillary tangles similar to those of Alzheimer's disease on light-microscopic examination, but differing from them on electron microscopy in that they are composed of straight rather than paired helical filaments. The cause of the disease is unknown. A slow virus has been suspected, but attempts to transfer it to monkeys by the intracerebral inoculation of brain tissue have failed.

Clinical manifestations The clinical features are quite distinctive: disturbances of balance and gait with unexpected falls; rigidity of the neck and other trunk muscles, resembling Parkinson's disease; "masking" of the face; reduction in the volume of the voice; extreme flexion or extension dystonia of the neck; and difficulty in looking down—all these are early symptoms and any one of them may first bring the patient to a physician. Ophthalmoplegia has been regarded as the cardinal clinical sign of the disease. Typically there is initial impairment of vertical saccadic movements and a loss of the fast component of optokinetic nystagmus usually affecting downward more than upward gaze. With progression of the disease horizontal eye movements are affected, with oculovestibular reflexes preserved. Symptoms progress over months and years, until the patient becomes virtually anarthric with total loss of voluntary control of eye movements, and severe cervical and truncal rigidity. Dementia is usually mild with forgetfulness, slowing of thought processes, apathy and impaired ability to manipulate acquired knowledge. There are no impairments of vision, hearing, somatic sensation, or voluntary power, and signs of corticospinal involvement are minimal or absent. The diagnosis should be considered whenever an elderly patient begins to fall repeatedly and inexplicably and has extrapyramidal symptoms with a rigid neck and paralysis of conjugate or vertical gaze.

Treatment Treatment has been unsuccessful. Relatively little benefit comes from the administration of the antiparkinsonian group of drugs, although they should be tried. Occasionally levodopa, or a combination of levodopa with an anticholinergic drug, has helped to diminish some of the symptoms.

NORMAL-PRESSURE HYDROCEPHALUS Normal-pressure hydrocephalus (NPH) is a syndrome of communicating hydrocephalus in which intracranial hypertension is either absent or not recognized. It is discussed here because of the common association of the condition with dementia and abnormalities of gait.

Pathology and pathophysiology Although it is recognized that delayed hydrocephalus can occur after meningitis, head injury, or subarachnoid hemorrhage, the majority of patients presenting with NPH give no history of such an illness. Studies of isotope cisternography indicate that NPH is a communicating hydrocephalus presumed to be due to partial obliteration of the subarachnoid space with defective CSF reabsorption through the arachnoid villi. Whether episodes of increased intracranial pressure occur during the course of the illnes is debated. Some patients monitored continuously show fluctuations in CSF pressure including so-called plateau waves.

Clinical manifestations Typically, the patient or family describe a subacute onset, over weeks, months, or sometimes years, of progressive intellectual deterioration accompanied by slowness and restriction of movements, particularly of gait. No single diagnostic gait disorder occurs (see description, Chap. 16). A broad-based stance with hesitant initiation of walking is common. In some patients ataxic features are present. Hyperreflexia in the legs and extensor plantar responses may be found. Urinary incontinence is noted in less than one-half of patients.

Differential diagnosis Parkinson's disease can be differentiated by its clinical features and the response to Sinemet. Bifrontal disease due to tumor (butterfly glioma), metastases, or cerebral infarction can be identified by CT or MRI. Multi-infarct dementia with gait disorder can be recognized by focal, often asymmetric, neurologic signs and by CT changes. Aqueductal stenosis may present occasionally in late adulthood with hydrocephalus, headaches, dementia, and incontinence. The CT or MRI usually will demonstrate an enlarged third ventricle with normal fourth ventricle.

Treatment   The diagnosis can be difficult because of the common association of ventricular enlargement and gait disorder in patients with degenerative brain conditions, particularly Alzheimer's disease. CSF pressure in NPH is usually in the normal range of 80 to 150 mmH$_2$O. Isotope cisternography demonstrating reflux into the ventricular system may be helpful in some cases. However, the finding of ventricular reflux has not proved to determine reliably which patients are likely to improve following a surgical shunt. Temporary benefit in the gait disorder after removal of 25 to 30 mL of CSF has been noted in some patients. When the history of dementia and gait disorder is subacute in onset and accompanied by considerable ventricular dilatation, surgical shunting is warranted. Ventricular-peritoneal shunting is the procedure most commonly performed. Between 40 and 70 percent of patients show benefit after surgery. The gait disorder tends to show a better response to shunting than the dementia (see Black et al. for review).

TORSION DYSTONIA (TORSION SPASM; DYSTONIA MUSCULORUM DEFORMANS)   This is a clinical term denoting a state characterized by nonrhythmic, relatively slow involuntary movements that produce abnormal, at times bizarre, postures of the limbs and trunk. Eventually these postures become more or less fixed. Underlying the clinical disorder may be any of several pathologic conditions, such as the lesions of neonatal hypoxia, Wilson's disease, the pigmented lesions of Hallervorden-Spatz disease (described above), GM$_1$ gangliosidosis, ataxia-telangiectasia, or kernicterus. There is, in addition, an important group of cases with a variable pattern of genetic transmission. Occasionally, a similar disorder occurs sporadically in late adult life. It is to these cases, both hereditary and sporadic, that the term *torsion dystonia* (torsion spasm, dystonia musculorum deformans) is correctly applied. In these conditions, the course tends to be progressive, and the cause and pathogenesis remain unknown.

Pathology   Few cases of dystonia musculorum deformans not due to one of the definable disease processes indicated above have been adequately studied neuropathologically. Reported results from these cases has led to uncertainty as to what the pathologic-anatomic basis of the clinical state might be, although it was generally assumed that the basal ganglia were diseased. A careful study by Zeman and Dyken which included comparison of the findings in patients with the disease with control material, failed to demonstrate any neuropathologic abnormality to which the clinical changes could reasonably be attributed. These negative findings, which are perhaps surprising, must not be interpreted as indicating that there is "no disease" in the brain, but rather that the pathologic state is not one that can be disclosed by the usual histopathologic techniques. It may well be that more careful quantitative assessments of certain populations of neurons and studies of the pathophysiology of neurotransmitters will result in further elucidation of this disease.

Clinical manifestations   The motor abnormalities are described in Chap. 15. In the early stages, the involuntary muscular contractions are intermittent and variable in location and severity, but typically interfere with motor performance by superimposing an unwanted posture upon parts in use. One leg may briefly be pulled into a flexed or extended position or one shoulder elevated. Later the lingual, pharyngeal, neck, and thoracic muscles participate, and grimacing may occur. These latter may also be the first and only signs of disease for several years. Progression may be relatively rapid in cases with onset during early childhood, but is slow in those beginning in late childhood or adult life. The end result is extreme disability, with grossly distorted postures of the trunk and contractures of the limbs.

Affection of face and tongue muscles results in faulty articulation of speech, which eventually becomes incomprehensible. The tendon and plantar reflexes are normal.

The most severe type, which occurs almost exclusively in Ashkenazi Jews, characteristically makes its appearance in childhood after a preceding period of normalcy. Typically it becomes first evident in the lower limbs and then evolves, sometimes relatively rapidly, into the generalized state of severe incapacity described above. The manner of genetic transmission—whether autosomal recessive or dominant with variable penetrance—is still not wholly settled. In the recognized autosomal dominant type, which occurs mainly in non-Jewish populations, the disorder comes on later (often in midadult life) and takes a milder form. It tends to appear first in the upper limbs and to remain more restricted in its extent than the early-onset variety, and progression is less relentless. The late-life sporadic cases are generally similar in character to those of the autosomal dominant form; here, the possibility of dominant transmission with incomplete penetrance cannot always be excluded.

FOCAL DYSTONIAS   In addition to the generalized dystonias noted above, there is a group of focal or segmental dystonias which appear sporadically in adult life. Their clearly involuntary nature, and lack of susceptibility to willed control by the patient, distinguish them from the common tics, habit spasms, and mannerisms described in Chap. 15. They have often been erroneously interpreted as manifestations of hysteria. If the muscle contraction is frequent and prolonged, aching pain accompanies it—for which the spasm may mistakenly be blamed.

The most frequent and familiar type of focal dystonia is *spasmodic torticollis*. This is a disorder of adults that afflicts women somewhat more frequently than men. It consists of an involuntary turning of the head to one side—intermittent at first, then gradually worsening to the point of being more or less continuous. In some cases, torticollis is the first manifestation of a generalized dystonia, but more usually it remains focal and segmental.

Another frequent focal dystonia of adults is exemplified by *writer's cramp*, in which the dystonic postures and movements occur only during the performance of specific acts, to the extent that carrying out the act in the usual way, such as writing with a pen or pencil, becomes impossible, while other motor activities using the same musculature are unimpaired. An analogous disorder sometimes afflicts musicians.

The combination of blepharospasm and oromandibular dystonia—*cranial dystonia*—is sometimes referred to as Meige's syndrome. When the throat and respiratory muscles are involved, this interferes with speech production, resulting in spastic dysarthria. The muscles of the neck are variably affected. It should be recalled that similar dystonic states (facial-cervical and more extreme dyskinesias) can result from the use of phenothiazine and similar drugs. This sometimes persists after discontinuation of the medication as *tardive dyskinesia*—a troublesome condition that may resist all forms of treatment.

Differential diagnosis   Hepatolenticular degeneration (Wilson's disease) should be seriously considered in any case presenting these motor symtoms and appropriate measures should be undertaken for its investigation (see Chap. 311). The progressive course, and possibly the family history, differentiate the degenerative group from the "symptomatic" dystonias resulting from infections or metabolic disorders occurring at birth or later. Hallervorden-Spatz disease, however, cannot be distinguished on clinical grounds alone. Rare instances of GM$_1$ gangliosidosis or other lipid storage diseases may begin in adult life with a dystonic syndrome, and drug-induced (tardive) dyskinesia must be considered in all cases of focal or generalized dystonia in adults, especially if they have or have had a psychiatric illness.

Treatment   This is extremely difficult and often unsatisfactory. In the generalized dystonias, pharmacotherapy should certainly be attempted and, in most patients, needs to be individualized. Marsden and Fahn, whose experience with this disorder is extensive, suggest beginning with an anticholinergic agent such as trihexyphenidyl or ethopropazine and very gradually increasing the dosage until either benefit ensues or intolerable side effects appear. They found that the response in children (who may be able to take as much as 80 mg per day of trihexyphenidyl) was better than in adults, who tolerated the high doses less well, generally because of mental disturbances. In their experience, the next best group of drugs for ameliorating dystonic spasms are the benzodiazepines (such as diazepam) which likewise are used in high dosage after a very gradual introduction and increase (up to 80 mg of diazepam daily). Again, children are more tolerant of the side effects (mainly drowsiness). A combination of anticholinergics and benzodiazepines may work out best. Other drugs—both dopaminergic agonists and antagonists—have been used, occasionally with success.

Stereotaxic surgical operations have been used in the past to treat generalized dystonias, with insufficient benefit to counterbalance the risks. Cervical cord stimulation, a less hazardous procedure, has helped some patients; referral to a neurosurgeon with experience in the technique should be considered when medical treatment has failed.

The symptoms of the focal dystonias, if not severe, may be more acceptable to the patient than prolonged trials with various drugs or surgical intervention. Biofeedback techniques are sometimes helpful. Denervative surgical procedures may at times be beneficial if only a very restricted group of muscles is involved (as in torticollis). Blepharospasm has recently been successfully treated temporarily with local injection of botulinum toxin into the orbicularis oculi muscles. Growdon suggests that neuroleptics (dopamine-antagonists) such as haloperidol or perphenazine may be useful in the treatment of focal dystonias. Here again, the program of management must be adapted to the individual patient's needs.

FAMILIAL TREMOR   One of the commonest hereditary disorders of the human nervous system is that which gives rise to a fast-frequency (6 to 8 per second) action tremor. This may appear at any age but more often during adolescence and adult years; once started, it lasts throughout life. The heredity is dominant. Probably all cases are not the same, for some patients have tremors of slower frequency, looking more like those of Parkinson's disease, but lacking the slowness of movement, rigidity, and flexed postures of that disorder. In patients of advanced age it is called *senile tremor*. Consumption of alcohol suppresses the fast-frequency forms, as does a beta-adrenergic blocking agent (propranolol) in doses of 20 to 40 mg three times daily. The slightly slower rhythmic action tremors with frequencies of approximately 6 per second do not consistently respond to propranolol or alcohol. Primidone 50 mg at bedtime has recently been found to be effective and has been advocated for use as initial therapy. If there is no response after 1 week the dose should be increased gradually up to 250 mg at bedtime. Usually the tremor is the only abnormality, but in a few patients a cerebellar ataxia or an extrapyramidal syndrome may appear years later. The pathologic basis is unknown.

GILLES DE LA TOURETTE SYDROME   This condition, of unknown cause and uncertain pathology, presents with multiple tics, associated with snorting, sniffing, and involuntary vocalizations. It begins in childhood, usually as isolated tics, which are at first difficult to distinguish from habit spasms. Progression occurs over years, and other behavioral findings appear; compulsive touching of others, repeating of words or phrases, and explosive utterance of obscenities (coprolalia). Careful attention to other members of the family has given evidence that the disease is hereditary, with the pattern of transmission uncertain, although autosomal recessive inheritance appears likely in some pedigrees.

The course of the illness is unpredictable. In some cases associated mild neurologic abnormalities are found with hyperactivity, disorders of attention, and abnormal psychologic tests. Dementia does not occur. In some patients the condition abates, in others it progresses, leading to serious disability. Treatment is only partially satisfactory.

Haloperidol has received the most clinical attention, but should be used only in severe cases, and in the smallest effective dosage: 0.25 to 0.5 mg daily. Clonidine has proved effective in some cases.

SYNDROMES OF SLOWLY DEVELOPING ATAXIA

These conditions are distinguished clinically by progressive unsteadiness in standing and walking, along with impaired coordination of the limbs. Pathologically, they are characterized by degeneration of the cerebellum and/or its related fiber systems, and thus constitute classic examples of the system diseases. Although sporadic instances occur, hereditary transmission is an outstanding feature in most cases; as a result, this group of disorders is often referred to as the *hereditary ataxias*. Their subdivision into more or less separate entities is largely arbitrary, with pathologic changes of varying distribution underlying clinically indistinguishable symptom complexes. As yet, not enough is known about the underlying basis for the pathophysiologic alterations for a more satisfactory classification to be established.

Attempts to establish a classification on a genetic basis, on the presumption that a defective gene expressed as a progressive ataxia would produce a distinctive clinicopathologic picture have not been successful. Instead, the phenotypic expression of the genetic abnormality commonly varies widely among affected members of an individual family. Because of these difficulties, the most that a clinician can do when confronted with a case is to exclude infective, toxic, metabolic, or neoplastic diseases for which there might be effective treatment, to search for evidence of genetic factors, and to assess the state of the patient as precisely as possible. There are now indications that some of the hereditary ataxic disorders may be associated with an identifiable biochemical abnormality though at present it is not possible to make use of this information in a way that would correct the abnormality and benefit the individual patient.

Nevertheless, if one takes a broad view of the whole group of hereditary ataxias, it turns out that there are certain clinicopathologic groupings that allow a very simplified descriptive classification. According to this principle, three main categories may be emphasized: (1) *cerebellar cortical degeneration*, (2) *olivopontocerebellar atrophy*, and (3) *spinocerebellar degenerations*, including *Friedreich's ataxia*.

CEREBELLAR CORTICAL DEGENERATION   In this disorder, the principal neuropathologic feature is loss of neurons (mainly of Purkinje cells) in the cerebellar cortex. Cases of this kind characteristically occur in late adult life. Although the condition can occur sporadically, in the majority it is inherited as an autosomal dominant trait.

Pathology   The loss of Purkinje cells tends to be most severe in the superior vermis and adjacent parts of the cerebellar cortex, but can be more extensive. The granule neurons are less affected. In long-standing cases, there is an associated atrophy of neurons in the olivary nuclei of the medulla, apparently representing a transsynaptic retrograde degeneration resulting from the loss of Purkinje cells, to which the olivocerebellar fibers project. In advanced cases atrophy of the cerebellar cortex can be readily demonstrated by CT scanning. In the purest forms of this disorder, as exemplified by the cases of late onset, slow progression, and dominant inheritance, other neuronal systems remain relatively intact.

Clinical manifestations   Incoordination first appears in the legs, resulting in abnormal stance and an unsteadiness of gait of a wavering, lurching character typical of cerebellar ataxia (see Chap. 16). This gait disturbance is a consequence of degenerative changes in the superior vermis of the cerebellum and adjacent parts of the cerebellar cortex. With more extensive cerebellar involvement, a disturbance in articulation and rhythm of speech occurs and the arms become ataxic. There may be nystagmus. The illness progresses gradually often extending over two or three decades, without appreciably curtailing the life span. Dementia tends not to be a feature of this circumscribed cerebellar atrophy of late life. However, cerebellar cortical degeneration with very similar features may occur as a component in many of the ataxic disorders.

In addition to this slowly evolving, relatively circumscribed form of cerebellar cortical degeneration, there is a subacutely developing diffuse cerebellar cortical degeneration that affects all parts of the cerebellar cortex indiscriminately, often in association with some inflammatory changes. This disorder occurs in the presence of malignant neoplastic diseases of various kinds and is referred to as *carcinomatous cerebellar degeneration* (see Chap. 304). It is now apparent that this is one of a number of interrelated neurologic degenerative syndromes that occur on the background of malignant disease but do not result from any direct effect of the neoplasm on the nervous system such as invasion or metastasis. These so-called paraneoplastic disorders are etiologically unclarified; an immunologic or viral attack on neural structures has been postulated, but never proven. Paraneoplastic cerebellar degeneration produces a striking clinicopathologic syndrome that tends to stand out as a particular entity (see Chap. 304).

OLIVOPONTOCEREBELLAR ATROPHY (OPCA) Grouped under this category are a number of similar disorders characterized by a combination of cerebellar cortical degeneration, atrophy of the inferior olivary nuclei secondary to this, and degeneration and disappearance of the neurons of the pontine nuclei and their fiber projections in the basis pontis and middle cerebellar peduncles. Konigsmark and Weiner distinguished five varieties on the basis of differences in the form of hereditary transmission and in the extent of other abnormalities both within and outside of the nervous system. Most instances of OPCA can now be considered to represent various forms of multiple system degeneration in which admixtures of parkinsonism, dementia, spasticity, choreoathetosis, retinal degeneration, myelopathy, and peripheral neuropathy may be encountered, sometimes obscuring the ataxic component. For present-day views of the classification of OPCA and the features of the various forms of disease brought under this heading, the monograph edited by Duvoisin and Plaitakis may be usefully consulted. The introduction of the new techniques of imaging—CT and MRI—now make it possible to visualize clearly the pontocerebellar lesions and some of the other atrophic changes in the central nervous system.

Autosomal dominant inheritance characterizes an important group of cases, and several families—most notably the Schut family, on which information extending over five generations has been obtained, and the families of Portuguese ancestry, mainly from the Azores, who manifest the various syndromes that have been brought together under the heading of Joseph's disease—have been extensively studied. These families illustrate with striking clarity the varied phenotypic expression of what seems to be a particular genetic abnormality.

Recessively transmitted OPCA has on the whole been less distinctly established than the dominant (or sporadic) forms, but of particular interest is a group of families with an autosomal recessive disorder and late-adult onset of neurologic symptoms, in whom the disease is characterized by multiple system degeneration, including a prominent OPCA component, and in which deficiency of glutamic acid dehydrogenase (GDH) has been demonstrated in leukocytes and cultured fibroblasts from affected family members (Plaitakis, in Duvoisin and Plaitakis monograph). Glutamate, among its other functions, acts as an excitatory neurotransmitter and is involved in the excitatory input to the Purkinje cells from the granule cells of the cerebellar cortex. In excess, this transmitter has neurotoxic effects, which might be the basis of the Purkinje cell degeneration that is so prominent in OPCA. These observations, and other biochemical leads that have opened up in connection with some of the dominant forms of OPCA, suggest a promising field of research that may give new etiologic and pathophysiologic insights into a wide group of neuronal degenerative diseases and may ultimately suggest avenues for therapeutic approach.

Pathology OPCA and the disorders related to it exemplify clearly the phenomenon of selective premature neuronal death, and of affection of particular, vulnerable neuronal systems with sparing of others. The distribution of neuronal lesions that characterizes OPCA as distinct from other neuronal system degenerations has already been indicated. The neuronal changes are in no way distinctive or specific in OPCA. Rather, it is the particular location of the neuronal loss that determines the clinicopathologic picture. Still not fully clarified in this group of disorders is what determines the dementia that so often accompanies them. It has been generally assumed that abnormalities occur in the cerebral cortex, but examination of the cortex in typical cases discloses insufficient pathology to account for the cognitive and behavioral alterations. On the other hand, the lesions of the cerebellum and related systems provide a reasonable explanation for the incoordination (ataxia) that is observed; the lesions in the basal ganglia and substantia nigra (equivalent to striatonigral degeneration) underlie the features of parkinsonism and of other postural and movement disorders that are so frequently seen as manifestations of OPCA; and involvement of the peripheral motor neurons, similar to what occurs in the motor neuron disease group to be discussed later, produces the severe muscular weakness and atrophy that may be encountered. The disturbances of ocular motility that typify some cases still are in need of further anatomic elucidation.

Clinical manifestations There is great clinical variation among cases of OPCA. Some present a picture of a relatively pure cerebellar ataxia indistinguishable from that seen in cases with atrophy of the cerebellar cortex (and secondarily of the inferior olivary nuclei) alone. Others are characterized by parkinsonian features. Superimposed is an evolving dementia. For accounts of these varied forms of clinical expression, general neurologic reference works and specialized monographs (such as that edited by Duvoisin and Plaitakis) should be consulted.

SPINOCEREBELLAR DEGENERATIONS (FRIEDREICH'S ATAXIA) This group of ataxic disorders is characterized by degeneration of long ascending and descending fiber systems in the spinal cord, including the spinocerebellar tracts, and concomitant degeneration of peripheral axons and myelin sheaths in the form of chronic peripheral neuronopathy.

The classic form of hereditary ataxia, first clearly depicted by Nikolaus Friedreich of Heidelberg in 1863, constitutes a relatively distinct symptom complex which generally runs true to form, although it overlaps other heredodegenerative syndromes, particularly other types of spinocerebellar atrophy. In some families, the disorder occurs with dominant inheritance; usually it is a recessive trait.

Pathology The principal changes are cell loss in the dorsal root ganglia and secondary degeneration in the posterior columns and spinocerebellar tracts of the cord and in the peripheral nerves. Degeneration is also evident in the corticospinal tracts in most cases. The cerebellum is variably affected. In addition to these neuropathologic changes there is in some cases a peculiar form of myocardial degeneration resulting in fiber loss and fibrosis. There are no other associated visceral lesions.

Clinical manifestations As with other progressive ataxias, the disorder first appears in the legs, affecting the individual during late childhood. The patient, previously healthy, begins to stagger and lurch in walking and is unsteady on standing. Clumsiness and cerebellar tremor of the hands and arms appear later along with dysarthria and abnormal rhythm (scanning) of speech. These symptoms result from changes in the dorsal root ganglia, the spinocerebellar tracts, and cerebellum; it is not easy to ascertain the relative contribution of lesions in each structure to the ataxia. The limbs, in addition to being ataxic, generally show considerable weakness. Examination usually discloses nystagmus and skeletal deformities: kyphoscoliosis, the basis of which is not certain, and a peculiar foreshortening of the feet (pes cavus) with cocking of the toes, best ascribed to atrophy and contractures of the musculature of the feet at a time when the bones of the feet are malleable. Typically, there is the unusual combination of total absence of tendon reflexes with extensor plantar reflexes (Babinski sign). This results from the presence of degeneration of the corticospinal tracts together with the involvement of peripheral sensory neurons that relay afferent signals from muscle spindles. Impairment of position and vibration sense in the extremities is prominent and, in some patients, sensation of pain, temperature, and light touch is diminished in a distal and roughly symmetric distribution consistent with an axononeuropathy affecting small nerve fibers. Mentation is usually preserved, though a few of the patients have been of low intelligence or have become demented late in the course of the disease. Survival beyond early adult life is rare, with death frequently the result of associated cardiomyopathy.

Occasionally very mild or fragmentary forms of the disorder (such as pes cavus and absent or hyperactive tendon reflexes) may be encountered with little if any disability or progression. Such abnormalities are most likely to be seen in other members of the family of a patient afflicted with the fully developed form of the disease. A related syndrome, the Roussy-Lévy syndrome, shows similarities to Friedreich's ataxia and to peroneal muscular atrophy. Mild ataxia, pes cavus, absent ankle and knee tendon jerks, and atrophy of lower leg muscles occur. In some well-documented cases the peripheral nerves show hypertrophy due to proliferation of Schwann cells (see Chap. 355). Chronic familial polyneuropathies are particularly difficult to distinguish since they also give rise to sensory ataxia, but signs of pyramidal tract disease are absent (see Chap. 355). Hereditary forms of cerebellar ataxia with corticospinal signs (hyperactive tendon reflexes) and sensory disturbances are also known to occur in the adolescent or adult. Familial spastic paraplegia with or without optic atrophy (Behr's syndrome) is another closely related disease. In the absence of a family history, and with atypical clinical findings, further diagnostic studies to exclude congenital malformation, spinal cord compression, foramen magnum tumor, and multiple sclerosis will be necessary.

No treatment is of proven value. Earlier reports of disturbed pyruvate metabolism have not been confirmed.

DIFFERENTIAL DIAGNOSIS OF THE ATAXIAS The slow but relentless progression in the absence of abnormalities in other parts of the nervous system and in the CSF distinguishes the hereditary group from other diseases and other forms of cerebellar ataxia such as may occur with hereditary metabolic diseases, or with neoplastic, infectious, or demyelinative disease, or with drug intoxications (e.g., phenytoin) or with hyperpyrexia. The degenerative disorders under discussion tend to develop slowly over many years in a setting of otherwise good general health, and in the absence of other neurologic symptoms and signs; this, together with the other clinical differences, distinguishes them from such hereditary metabolic diseases as juvenile Gaucher's disease, juvenile Niemann-Pick disease, and juvenile hexosaminidase deficiency and from alcoholic cerebellar ataxia or nutritional deficiency disease, with or without Wernicke-Korsakoff syndrome. Alcoholic cerebellar degeneration usually develops over a few days to weeks, and then may remain more or less unchanged for the remainder of the patient's life (Chap. 349).

In the cases associated with carcinoma, the tempo of evolution of the process is relatively rapid, with severe disability coming on within a period of months. Vertigo, diplopia, and nausea may be prominent. In an occasional patient, the neurologic symptoms have appeared before there was any obvious evidence of carcinoma. Opsoclonus (rapid side-to-side jerking of the eyes) and oscillopsia (movement back and forth of objects seen) may be conjoined. In contrast to the consistently normal CSF findings in the forms of cerebellar degeneration noted above, the CSF in paraneoplastic degeneration may show increased lymphocytes and protein.

TREATMENT No specific treatment is available for any of the progressive ataxias, although encouragement to remain active is beneficial to health in general. Gait training is of relatively little value in enabling patients to compensate for their disability. In cases where parkinsonian features are prominent, antiparkinsonian medications should be tried (see above), but the response in the group of

multiple system degenerations is generally unsatisfactory. Trauner has reported that baclofen in high dosage may help control involuntary movements in some cases of OPCA, but the ataxia is not benefited. Initial reports of benefit with thyrotropin-releasing hormone have not been confirmed.

IDIOPATHIC AUTONOMIC FAILURE (IDIOPATHIC ORTHOSTATIC HYPOTENSION, SHY-DRAGER SYNDROME)

Abnormalities of central autonomic nervous system functions manifest principally by failure to maintain blood pressure and by urinary incontinence are now recognized to be caused in some cases by a progressive degenerative disorder of the CNS that affects several systems; in some patients the peripheral nervous system is also involved (postganglionic sympathetic neurons). Bradbury and Eggleston in 1925 called attention to the combination of postural hypotension, incontinence, impotence, and abnormality of sweating (anhidrosis). Symptoms of central neurologic origin develop later in many of these patients consisting predominantly of extrapyramidal or cerebellar dysfunction.

PATHOGENESIS AND PATHOLOGY The cause of the disorder is unknown. In 1960 Shy and Drager described neuropathologic changes in the brainstem and basal ganglia, and subsequently others showed a prominent loss of neurons in central regions of the autonomic nervous system, affecting in particular the cells of the intermediolateral column of the thoracic spinal cord. Abnormalities have also been found in peripheral autonomic ganglia (cell loss). In the brainstem and basal ganglia there is widespread symmetric neuronal degeneration affecting the caudate nucleus, substantia nigra, locus coeruleus, olivary nuclei, dorsal vagal nuclei, and in some cases affecting the cerebellum. Cell loss is accompanied by gliosis; Lewy bodies typical of Parkinson's disease are present in some cases. For these reasons many neurologists consider the Shy-Drager syndrome to be a unique form of multisystem degeneration resembling but distinct from either Parkinson's disease or OPCA.

Clinical manifestations The onset is insidious, usually in the sixth or seventh decade. Men are more frequently affected than women. Disturbances of urinary bladder function, including hesitancy and incontinence, postural dizziness and syncope, impotence, and decreased sweating are the presenting manifestations. Later symptoms of extrapyramidal dysfunction resembling parkinsonism or cerebellar findings may emerge. The condition becomes severely disabling over the course of 5 to 7 years in most patients. The hallmark of the condition is postural hypotension, defined as a fall in blood pressure greater than 30/20 mmHg on standing upright from a supine position (see Chap. 12). Despite this fall in blood pressure there is usually a total failure of compensatory tachycardia, the pulse rate remaining unchanged. Autonomic signs of pupillary asymmetry, partial Horner's syndrome, or partial parasympathetic denervation occur in some patients. Anhidrosis is common and can be demonstrated by placing the individual in a warm room after application of a starch-iodine mixture to the skin. The parkinsonian manifestations may be identical to those of idiopathic parkinsonism, although in many patients rigidity and bradykinesia are more prominent than tremor. Cerebellar gait ataxia and mild limb ataxia may be evident. Other findings include laryngeal paralysis and sleep apnea.

Treatment The treatment is symptomatic. The postural hypotension is usually the most disabling initial symptom. Antigravity stockings to minimize pooling of venous blood in the legs are recommended. Pharmacologic agents are given to expand blood volume and to enhance vascular responsivity. Increased NaCl intake combined with fludrohydrocortisone 0.05 to 0.2 mg twice daily is usually beneficial (see Chap. 12). In severe cases, adrenergic drugs such as ephedrine, levodopa, or amphetamine may improve the disability. The parkinsonism symptoms often respond initially to Sinemet or bromocriptine, but later in the course most patients become refractory to these agents. Centrally acting alpha agonists (e.g., yohimbine or clonidine) may also be beneficial.

SYNDROMES OF MUSCULAR WEAKNESS AND WASTING WITHOUT SENSORY CHANGES: MOTOR NEURON DISEASE

AMYOTROPHIC LATERAL SCLEROSIS (ALS) ALS is the most frequently encountered form of progressive motor neuron disease, and it presents a clinical syndrome that is generally familiar to physicians who see patients with neurologic diseases. It is characteristically a disorder of late middle age. Most patients are older than 50 when they become aware of symptoms. The disease rarely develops before the third decade, and patients whose symptoms begin in the late teenage years often seem to have an inherited variant of the disorder. Men are more frequently affected than women. Because of its restriction to motor neurons of the central nervous system, ALS represents another prime example of a neuronal system disease. It occurs sporadically in most instances. Familial occurrence, with transmission as an autosomal dominant trait, is observed in about 10 percent of cases and differs in some clinical and pathologic aspects (Table 350-2).

Pathology The disease is characterized by progressive loss of motor neurons, both in the cerebral cortex and in the anterior horns of the spinal cord, together with their homologues in some motor nuclei of the brainstem. It typically affects both upper and lower motor neurons, although variants may predominantly involve only particular subsets of motor neurons, particularly early in the course of the illness. Thus, in bulbar palsy and spinal muscular atrophy (or progressive muscular atrophy) the lower motor neurons of brainstem and spinal cord, respectively, are most severely involved while pseudobulbar palsy and primary lateral sclerosis affect upper motor neurons innervating the brainstem and spinal cord. The loss of motor neurons is not accompanied by any distinctive or unique cytopathologic features. The affected cells undergo shrinkage, often with some excessive accumulation of the pigmented lipid (lipofuscin) that normally develops in these cells with advancing age, and they eventually disappear. Focal enlargement of proximal motor axons is frequently seen; ultrastructurally, these "spheroids" are composed of accumulations of neurofilaments. Beyond some astroglial proliferation, which is the inevitable accompaniment of all disintegrative processes in the central nervous system, the interstitial and supportive tissues and the macrophage system remain largely inactive, and there is no inflammation. The death of the peripheral motor neurons in the brainstem and spinal cord leads to denervation and consequent atrophy of the corresponding muscle fibers. Histochemical and electrophysiologic

TABLE 350-2 Categories of degenerative motor neuron diseases

I Amyotrophic lateral sclerosis
  A Spinal muscular atrophy
  B Bulbar palsy
  C Primary lateral sclerosis
  D Pseudobulbar palsy
II Heritable motor neuron diseases
  A Autosomal recessive spinal muscular atrophy (SMA)
    1 Type I: Werdnig-Hoffmann, acute
    2 Type II: Werdnig-Hoffmann, chronic
    3 Type III: Kugelberg-Welander
    4 Type IV: Adult onset
  B Familial amyotrophic lateral sclerosis
  C Familial ALS with dementia or Parkinson's disease (Guam)
  D Other
    1 Arthrogryposis multiplex congenita
    2 Progressive juvenile bulbar palsy (Fazio-Londe)
    3 Neuroaxonal dystrophy
III Associated with other degenerative disorders
  1 Olivopontocerebellar atrophies
  2 Peroneal muscular atrophy

evidence indicate that in the early phases of the illness denervated muscle can be reinnervated by sprouting of nearby distal motor nerve terminals, although reinnervation in this disease is considerably less extensive than in most other disorders affecting motor neurons (e.g., poliomyelitis, peripheral neuropathy). As denervation progresses, there is shrinkage of the musculature and a fiber atrophy that is readily recognized in muscle biopsies. It is this muscular atrophy that is designated by the term *amyotrophy,* which appears in the common name for the disease. The loss of motor neurons in the cortex results in disappearance of the long axons and their myelin sheaths that make up the corticospinal tracts, which travel via the internal capsule and extend through the brainstem, including the pyramids of the medulla oblongata, to the lateral (and a portion of the anterior) white matter columns of the spinal cord. The loss of fibers in the lateral columns, together with the fibrillary gliosis which imparts a particular firmness (sclerosis) to the affected tissues, makes up the lateral sclerosis component of the disease. The fact that the nerve fiber loss is more extensive in the distal parts of the affected tracts in the lower spinal cord rather than the more proximal parts, such as the internal capsule, suggests that the affected neurons first undergo disintegration at their distal terminals and the disease process proceeds in a centripetal direction until ultimately the parent cell body dies, a phenomenon referred to as "dying back." The disease clearly affects the large pyramidal neurons (Betz cells) of the motor cortex in the precentral gyrus, but in some cases the extent of degeneration in the long projection pathways provides evidence that many other neurons involved in voluntary movement, both in the cortex and in subcortical nuclei, are also affected.

A remarkable feature of the disease is the selectivity of neuronal cell death. The entire sensory apparatus, the regulatory mechanisms for the control and coordination of movement, and the components of the brain that are needed for intellect and thinking, remain intact. There is also some consistent selectivity in motor system involvement. The motor neurons required for ocular motility remain unaffected as do the parasympathetic neurons in the sacral spinal cord (the nucleus of Onufrowicz, or Onuf) which innervate the sphincters of the bowel and bladder.

Clinical manifestations The first evidence of the disease is manifest as insidiously developing asymmetric weakness, usually first apparent in one of the limbs. Fatigue and easy cramping of affected muscles can be prominent. The weakness is accompanied by visible wasting and atrophy of the muscles involved; particularly in the early stages of the disease, affected muscles may display focal twitchings—fasciculations—when not concealed by overlying adipose tissue. Virtually any muscle group may be the first to show signs of the disease, but as time passes, more and more muscles become involved until ultimately the disorder takes on a symmetric distribution in all regions, including the muscles of chewing, swallowing, and movements of the face and tongue. Early involvement of the muscles of respiration may lead to death before the disease is far advanced elsewhere; otherwise the disorder generally is terminated by pulmonary infection secondary to the profound generalized weakness.

The corticospinal component of the disease becomes apparent in the form of hyperactivity of the muscle-stretch reflexes (tendon jerks) and, often, spastic resistance to passive movements of the affected limbs. With corticospinal involvement the plantar reflex will be upgoing (the Babinski sign) until—as often occurs—lower motor neuron dysfunction in the legs advances sufficiently that extensor movement of the great toes is impossible. The disease process in the corticobulbar projections innervating the brainstem results in dysarthria and exaggeration of the motor expressions of emotion leading to involuntary weeping or laughter (so-called pseudobulbar affect), or strange admixtures of both. Ocular motility is spared, even when other brainstem functions are greatly impaired. Throughout the evolution of the disease, awareness and intellectual abilities typically remain intact. Dementia is not usually a component of ALS; when it occurs, it is due to the superimposition of another disease process.

The course is relentlessly progressive and leads ultimately to death, but the total duration of the illness is variable. In recent studies approximately 50 percent of patients can be expected to die within 3 to 5 years from the onset of the disease; some may live considerably longer. Very rarely, what seems to be ALS may become stabilized, or even regress to the point of recovery.

Differential diagnosis Because the underlying process in ALS is currently untreatable, it is imperative that potentially remediable causes of motor neuron dysfunction be excluded (see Table 350-3), particularly in atypical cases. Compression of the cervical cord or cervicomedullary junction from tumors in the cervical region or at the foramen magnum, or from cervical spondylosis with osteophytes projecting into the vertebral canal, can at times give rise to weakness, wasting, and fasciculations in the upper limbs and spasticity in the legs, thus closely resembling ALS. The absence of cranial nerve involvement may be helpful in differentiation, although some compressive lesions in the foramen magnum may implicate the twelfth cranial (hypoglossal) nerve, with resulting affection of the tongue. Absence of pain or of sensory changes, normal function of bowels and bladder, normal roentgenographic studies of the spine, and absence of changes in the composition or dynamics of the cerebrospinal fluid are all points in favor of ALS against spinal cord compression. Where doubt exists, CT scans and contrast myelography should be performed in order to visualize the cervical spinal cord.

Other treatable disorders that occasionally can mimic ALS are chronic lead poisoning and thyrotoxicosis. These may be suggested by the patient's social or occupational history or by unusual clinical features. When the family history is positive, inherited enzyme disorders such as hexosaminidase A or α-glucosidase deficiency must be excluded (see Chap. 349). These can readily be identified by appropriate laboratory tests. Benign fasciculations are occasionally a source of concern because on inspection they resemble the fascicular twitchings that accompany motor neuron degeneration. The absence of weakness or atrophy, and of denervation phenomena on electrophysiologic examination, excludes ALS or other serious neurologic disease. Poliomyelitis is now recognized to result in a delayed progressive deterioration of motor neurons which presents clinically with progressive weakness, atrophy, and fasciculations. Its cause is unknown but is thought to reflect prior sublethal injury to motor neurons by the poliovirus.

Treatment There is no treatment that has influence on the underlying pathologic process in any form of motor neuron disease. Modern rehabilitative measures, including mechanical aids of various kinds, can do much in helping patients to overcome the effects of their disabilities and often, with respiratory support, to survive longer than would otherwise have been the case. Recent observations (reviewed by Tandan and Bradley) suggest that intravenous (or intrathecal) infusions of thyrotropin-releasing hormone (TRH) result in transitory improvement of motor functions in some patients with ALS, for reasons that are not well understood. Whether TRH will have any long-term effect on the course of the disease is still unknown.

SPINAL MUSCULAR ATROPHY (SMA) In the varieties of motor neuron disease that are grouped under this heading, the peripheral motor neurons are affected without evidence of involvement of the corticospinal motor system (Table 350-2). In comparison with ALS, SMA in general occurs in a younger age group, runs a slower, more protracted course (except in the infantile form), and tends to be hereditary (usually autosomal recessive) rather than sporadic. The SMA group undoubtedly includes several distinct disease processes that differ from one another genetically and phenotypically.

Infantile SMA (Werdnig-Hoffmann disease) This rapidly fatal disorder is characterized by autosomal recessive transmission. Not infrequently, this severe form of infantile SMA (sometimes also referred to as SMA type I) is apparent even before birth, as indicated by decreased fetal movements in comparison with what normally would be expected. The afflicted infants are weak and floppy (hypotonic), though alert, and muscle-stretch reflexes are absent.

Weakness progresses relatively rapidly, and death ensues generally within the first year of life; rarely, the child survives to 3 years of age.

Neuropathologically, Werdnig-Hoffmann disease is characterized by extensive loss of the large motor neurons. Sections of the muscles show extreme degrees of denervation atrophy. During life, the diagnosis is made by electrophysiologic studies and by muscle biopsy, which shows the characteristic denervational pattern rather than an intrinsic myopathy or inflammatory disease of muscle. There is no effective treatment, but a family that has had an affected infant may be helped by genetic counseling.

There is another form of infantile muscular atrophy, also characterized by autosomal recessive inheritance, which appears to be distinct from Werdnig-Hoffmann disease in that the evolution is considerably slower, with survival into preadolescence or even into adult life. This disorder, which has been called *chronic childhood SMA*, or SMA type II, is considerably rarer than Werdnig-Hoffmann disease.

These motor neuron diseases can be distinguished from benign congenital hypotonia, which is nonprogressive form of myopathy, by electrophysiologic assessment and by muscle biopsy.

Juvenile SMA (Wohlfart-Kugelberg-Welander disease) This disorder, also referred to as SMA type III, manifests itself during late childhood and runs a slow, indolent course. Typically the muscles of the trunk and the proximal parts of the limb are earliest and most severely involved—a picture that closely resembles that of progressive muscular dystrophy, even to the presence of pseudohypertrophy of

TABLE 350-3 Etiology and investigation of secondary motor neuron disorders

Diagnostic categories	Investigations
I Structural lesions	
A Parasagittal or foramen magnum tumors	MRI/CT scan—head, spine including foramen magnum
B Cervical spondylosis	
C Chiari malformation or syrinx	MRI/CT scan or myelogram
D Spinal cord arteriovenous malformation	
II Infections	
A Bacterial—tetanus	CSF exam
B Viral—poliomyelitis, herpes zoster	Antibody titers
III Intoxications, physical agents	
A Toxins—lead, aluminum, other metals	24-h urine for lead, mercury arsenic, thallium, aluminum
B Drugs—strychnine, phenytoin, dapsone	
C Electric shock	
D X-irradiation	Serum lead and aluminum
IV Immunologic mechanisms	
A Plasma cell dyscrasias	Complete blood count, sedimentation rate
B Autoimmune polyradiculoneuropathy	Immunoprotein electrophoresis, Antinuclear antibody (ANA), cryoglobulins ($+/-$) bone marrow biopsy
V Paraneoplastic	
A Paracarcinomatous	
B Paralymphomatous; Hodgkin's	
VI Metabolic	
A Hypoglycemia	Fasting blood sugar (FBS)
B Hyperparathyroidism	Routine chemistries including calcium, magnesium, phosphate
C Hyperthroidism	Thyroid functions
D Vitamin B$_{12}$, Vitamin E deficiency	Vitamin B$_{12}$, folate, vitamin E levels
E Malabsorption	Stool fat (72-h; spot), carotene, prothrombin time (PT)
VII Hereditary biochemical disorders	
A Hexosaminidase A deficiency	Lysosomal enzyme screen
B α-Glucosidase deficiency (Pompe's)	
C Hyperlipidemia	Lipid electrophoresis
D Hyperglycinuria	Urine and serum amino acids
E Methylcrotonylglycinuria	CSF amino acids

the calf muscles in some cases. Electrophysiologic and biopsy evidence of denervation in the affected muscles serves to distinguish this disease from any of the myopathic syndromes.

Other genetically determined varieties of SMA In individual families, other syndromes characterized by SMA in varying patterns have been described. An infantile variety involving mainly the musculature innervated by the brainstem is referred to as the *Fazio-Londe syndrome*. In some juvenile cases, the distribution is distal, rather than proximal, as in the Wohlfart-Kugelberg-Welander variety. In addition, there is a slowly evolving adult form of SMA, sometimes called SMA type IV (Table 350-2). Depending upon the family, autosomal dominant, autosomal recessive, or X-linked recessive patterns of heredity may be discerned.

A component of SMA may also be found in some of the multiple system degenerations that have already been referred to, e.g., in Joseph's disease and in some of the syndromes characterized by olivopontocerebellar degeneration. Some of the recognized familial metabolic disorders also present a striking picture of progressive symmetric muscular weakness and atrophy, for instance, adult hexosaminidase A deficiency (the enzymopathy that results in Tay-Sachs disease in infancy) and adrenomyeloneuropathy. For details and more extensive discussions of these disorders, specialized monographs (such as that edited by Rowland), reviews (Tandan and Bradley), and general reference works on neurology (Adams and Victor) should be consulted.

Primary lateral sclerosis (PLS) It might be thought that this is a variant of ALS in which the amyotrophic component is lacking, but the few cases of this disorder that have been described have been encountered in remarkably pure form. It occurs as a sporadic disease of late life, affecting the same age group that is prone to develop ALS. The course may be similar to that of ALS with approximately 3 years from onset to death. Clinically, the illness is characterized by progressive spastic weakness of the limbs, preceded or followed by spastic dysarthria and dysphagia, indicative of corticobulbar tract involvement. Fasciculations, amyotrophy, and sensory changes are absent. On neuropathologic examination, there is selective loss of large pyramidal cells in the precentral gyrus and degeneration of the corticospinal and corticobulbar projections; the peripheral motor neurons and other neuronal systems are spared.

It may be necessary to consider PLS in the differential diagnosis of late-life progressive spastic paresis of the limbs, but obviously it is necessary, by appropriate studies of CSF and radiographic investigations, to exclude treatable disorders such as parasagittal intracranial tumors, neoplasms of the spinal cord, cervical spondylosis, or inflammatory diseases.

HEREDITARY SPASTIC PARAPLEGIA This is a very rare disorder which differs from PLS in several respects. Instead of occurring sporadically, it is characterized by genetic transmission—as an autosomal dominant trait in the majority of cases. Several families are on record in which it has appeared in many successive generations. It appears at a younger age, usually in the fourth decade and the course is very slowly progressive, to the extent that patients often live out a full life span. The condition is probably genetically heterogeneous; the group with onset in childhood or adolescence can be distinguished from those in whom the disease does not appear until the age of 35 years or older; as might be expected, there is considerable overlap between these groups. In a few families, a clinically indistinguishable disorder shows a pattern of autosomal recessive inheritance.

Pathology Neuropathologically, there is degeneration of the corticospinal (pyramidal) tracts, which appear almost normal at brainstem levels but become increasingly atrophic as they descend through the spinal cord. In addition, the ascending tracts in the posterior columns and the spinocerebellar tracts show some loss of fibers so that the picture resembles to some degree the findings in Friedreich's ataxia. In fact, some individual cases of what seems to be a fairly pure

spastic paraparesis may actually represent an incomplete form of Friedreich's ataxia. In such families spastic paraparesis is the outstanding phenotypic expression of Friedreich's ataxia.

Clinical manifestations As the name implies, the lower limbs are affected earliest and most severely. The major cause of disability is spasticity rather than weakness. There is concomitant exaggeration of the muscle stretch reflexes. Late in the course, urinary urgency and incontinence, and sometimes fecal incontinence, may occur; sexual potency tends to be preserved. In pure forms of the disorder, ataxia and amyotrophy are absent or minimal. In some patients, minor sensory changes (in the form of impaired vibration and position sense) may be observed in the late stages.

It is important in cases of otherwise unexplained progressive spastic paraparesis, despite a negative family history, to examine as many family members as possible. Members of a family with minimal degrees of the disease may be asymptomatic and unaware of its presence, even though they can be shown on examination to have spasticity and hyperreflexia.

SYNDROMES COMBINING MUSCULAR WEAKNESS AND WASTING WITH SENSORY CHANGES

PROGRESSIVE NEURAL MUSCULAR ATROPHY The degenerative disorders characterized by progressive weakness and wasting of skeletal muscles combined with sensory changes are usually chronic diseases of peripheral nerves, often occurring as hereditary conditions. Although clinical and pathologic subvarieties exist, there is no sharp dividing line between them, and they are best considered together under the designation given above, in which the term *neural* emphasizes the peripheral nerve affection. Chronic peripheral neuropathy is an associated disorder in some of the hereditary ataxias and is regularly encountered in the classic form of Friedreich's ataxia. It is also a component of adrenomyeloneuropathy and other leukodystrophies (see Chap. 316). In some cases of progressive neural muscular atrophy other genetically determined CNS diseases may occur such as progressive optic atrophy or pigmentary degeneration of the retina. The peripheral neuropathy begins distally and progresses in a centripetal fashion with the feet and legs first affected, and involvement of the hands and more proximal parts only after a considerable interval, usually several years.

The two most frequent forms of hereditary polyneuropathy, *peroneal muscular atrophy* (Charcot-Marie-Tooth disease) and *hypertrophic interstitial polyneuropathy* (Déjerine-Sottas disease), are described in Chap. 355. Brief reference is also made there to a rare condition known as *Refsum's disease*.

Although no specific treatment is available (except in Refsum's disease, as indicated in Chap. 355), patients whose disease is of slow progression and in whom conditions are otherwise favorable may be greatly helped by measures to ensure a stable walking surface, such as corrective shoes, braces to prevent foot drop, and even orthopedic procedures to stabilize the joints.

SYNDROMES OF PROGRESSIVE VISUAL LOSS Although the preceding discussion of the various hereditary progressive nervous system disorders categorized as degenerative has emphasized the intellectual, motor, and peripheral sensory derangements that result from these, many of these syndromes are accompanied by concomitant loss of the neural structures subserving vision. The hereditary ataxias, including Friedreich's, and hereditary spastic paraplegia stand out as examples. The pathologic changes, viewed broadly, take on two forms: selective degeneration of retinal ganglion cells with secondary optic atrophy, and a more diffuse degenerative process involving all retinal components, with subsequent migration of the melanin-containing cells of the pigment epithelium into the superficial retinal layers, resulting in the picture of *pigmentary degeneration of the retina* (formerly, but erroneously—since there is no inflammation—called retinitis pigmentosa). Occasionally, the peripheral visual system is the major, or only, site of disease resulting in progressive blindness without other neurologic defects. The major entities of this kind, including Leber's *hereditary optic atrophy,* are described in Chap. 352. A more complete review, with references to the pertinent literature, is given by Adams and Victor.

REFERENCES

General

ADAMS RD, VICTOR M: *Principles of Neurology,* 3d ed. New York, McGraw-Hill, 1985
——— et al: Striatonigral degeneration. J Neuropathol Exp Neurol 23:584, 1964
GILMAN S et al: *Disorders of the Cerebellum.* Philadelphia, Davis, 1981
Greenfield's Neuropathology, 4th ed, JH Adams et al (eds). New York, Wiley, 1984
MARSDEN CD, FAHN S (eds): *Movement Disorders.* London, Butterworth, 1982
ROSENBERG RN: *Neurogenetics: Principles and Practice.* New York, Raven, 1986

Alzheimer's disease

BALL MJ: Alzheimer's disease: A challenging enigma. Arch Pathol Lab Med 106:157, 1982
CANDY JM et al: Pathological changes in the nucleus of Meynert in Alzheimer's and Parkinson's diseases. J Neurol Sci 59:277, 1983
GLENNER GG: On causative theories in Alzheimer's disease. Human Pathol 16:433, 1985
HYMAN BT et al: Alzheimer's disease: Cell-specific pathology isolates the hippocampal formation. Science 225:1168, 1984
KATZMAN R: Alzheimer's disease. N Engl J Med 314:964, 1986
PERL DP, BRODY AR: Alzheimer's disease: X-ray spectrometric evidence of aluminum accumulation in neurofibrillary tangle-bearing neurons. Science 208:297, 1980
RASOOL CG, SELKOE DJ: Sharing of specific antigens by degenerating neurons in Pick's disease and Alzheimer's disease. N Engl J Med 312:700, 1985
WHITEHOUSE PJ et al: Alzheimer's disease and senile dementia: Loss of neurons in the basal forebrain. Science 215:1237, 1982

Huntington's disease

FERRANTE RJ et al: Selective sparing of a class of striatal neurons in Huntington's disease. Science 230:561, 1985
HAYDEN MR: *Huntington's Chorea.* Berlin, Springer-Verlag, 1981
MARTIN JB: Huntington's disease: New approaches to an old problem. Neurology 34:1059, 1984
VON SATTEL JP et al: Neuropathological classification of Huntington's disease. J Neuropathol Exp Neurol 44:559, 1985

Parkinson's disease

FAHN S et al (eds): *Recent Advances in Parkinson's Disease.* New York, Raven, 1986
GROWDON JH: Medical treatment of extrapyramidal diseases, in *Update III: Harrison's Principles of Internal Medicine,* KJ Isselbacher et al (eds). New York, McGraw-Hill, 1982
HOEHN MM, YAHR MD: Parkinsonism: Onset, progression and mortality. Neurology 17:427, 1967
LANGSTON JW et al: Chronic parkinsonism in humans due to a product of meperidine-analog synthesis. Science 219:979, 1983
MAYEUX R et al: Reappraisal of temporary levodopa withdrawal ("drug holiday") in Parkinson's disease. N Engl J Med 313:724, 1985
McGEER PL, McGEER EG: Amino acid neurotransmitters, in *Basic Neurochemistry,* GJ Siegel et al (eds). Boston, Little, Brown, 1981, pp 233–253
NUTT JG et al: The "on-off" phenomenon in Parkinson's disease: Relation to levodopa absorption and transport. N Engl J Med 310:438, 1984
SOURKES TL: Parkinson's disease and other disorders of the basal ganglia, in *Basic Neurochemistry,* GJ Siegel et al (eds). Boston, Little, Brown, 1981

Cerebellar degeneration

DUVOISIN RC, PLAITAKIS A (eds): *Advances in Neurology,* vol 41, *The Olivopontocerebellar Atrophies.* New York, Raven, 1984
KONIGSMARK BW, WEINER LP: The olivopontocerebellar atrophies: A review. Medicine 49:227, 1970
TRAUNER DA: Olivopontocerebellar atrophy with dementia, blindness, and chorea. Arch Neurol 42:757, 1985

Motor neuron disease

ROWLAND LP (ed): *Advances in Neurology,* vol 36, *Human Motor Neuron Diseases.* New York, Raven, 1982
TANDAN R, BRADLEY WG: Amyotrophic lateral sclerosis: Part 1, Clinical features, pathology, and ethical issues in management. Ann Neurol 18:271, 1985
———, ———: Amyotrophic lateral sclerosis: Part 2, Etiopathogenesis. Ann Neurol 18:419, 1985

Miscellaneous

BAUMANN RJ et al: Lafora disease: Liver histopathology in presymptomatic children. Ann Neurol 14:86, 1983
BEAL MF et al: Somatostatin: Alterations in the central nervous system in neurological diseases, in *Neuropeptides in Neurologic and Psychiatric Disease,* ARNMD vol 64, JB Martin, J Barchas (eds). New York, Raven, 1986, pp 25–258

BLACK PM et al: CSF shunts for dementia, incontinence and gait disturbance. Clin Neurosurg 32:632, 1985
BØGESEN S, GJERRIS F: The predictive value of conductance to outflow of CSF in normal pressure hydrocephalus. Brain 105:65, 1982
HARDING AE: Hereditary "pure" spastic paraplegia: A clinical and genetic study of 22 families. J Neurol Neurosurg Psychiatry 44:871, 1981
HENSON RA, URICH H: *Cancer and the Nervous System.* Blackwell Scientific, 1982
IIVANAINEN M, HIMBERG J-J: Valproate and clonazepam in the treatment of severe progressive myoclonus epilepsy. Arch Neurol 39:236, 1982
LOGIGIAN EL et al: Myoclonus epilepsy in two brothers: Clinical features and neuropathology of a unique syndrome. Brain (in press)
MUNOZ-GARCIA D, LUDWIN SK: Classic and generalized variants of Pick's disease: A clinicopathological, ultrastructural, and immunocytochemical study. Ann Neurol 16:467, 1984
O'BRIEN MD et al: Benign familial tremor treated with primidone. Br Med J 282:178, 1981
STEEL JC: Progressive supranuclear palsy. Brain 95:693, 1972
TISSOT R et al: *La Maladie de Pick.* Paris, Masson et Cie, 1975
ZEMAN W, DYKEN P: Dystonia musculorum deformans: Clinical, genetic and pathoanatomical studies. Psychiatr Neurol Neurochir 70:77, 1967

351 DEVELOPMENTAL AND CONGENITAL ABNORMALITIES OF THE NERVOUS SYSTEM

G. ROBERT DeLONG / RAYMOND D. ADAMS

This chapter discusses diseases traceable to insults or defects of development of the nervous system which have persisting effects into adult life, and which thus are likely to be of concern to the general physician and internist.

Specific diagnostic and therapeutic considerations arise in such developmental diseases—examples would be visceral tumors occurring in the neurocutaneous syndromes, or leukemia in Down's syndrome. A knowledge of these disorders is important to understanding the patient in the broader context of medical care: physical and mental limitations, ability to understand and comply with diagnostic and treatment programs, and genetic and familial issues. Finally, in the full cycle of life it is important for physicians caring for adults—especially for those who may become parents—to be aware of ways in which general medical disease and treatment, as well as genetic disorders, may affect the neurologic development of offspring.

Developmental abnormalities of the nervous system can conveniently be divided into those which are associated with recognizable somatic malformations, and those which are confined only to the nervous system (60 percent of all congenital malformations affect the nervous system). They may also be usefully classified as those determined by acquired or environmental factors, and those of genetic origin. In some cases, of course, there may be complicated interactions between genetic and environmental factors.

INFLUENCES ON NERVOUS SYSTEM DEVELOPMENT The effects of insults to brain during development are a complex function of the severity of the insult, its duration, the specific biologic impact of the insulting agent, and the precise stage in developmental time at which the insult is sustained. Environmental causes of developmental abnormalities of the nervous system are particularly important because they are potentially preventable.

Maternal toxins pose an important source of damage to developing brain and nerves. The fetal alcohol syndrome, an important cause of mental retardation, results from excessive exposure of the fetus to maternally ingested alcohol. Maternal exposure to other medications, especially anticonvulsants, may affect fetal brain development. Trimethadione produces severe fetal anomalies. Valproic acid has been implicated as causing spina bifida. Maternal use of phenytoin in the first months of pregnancy produces generally mild but identifiable effects on brain and somatic development. Isotretinoin, a preparation for acne, has been associated with congenital abnormalities of the brain. Organic mercury toxin in Minimata Bay, Japan, produced severe fetal brain abnormalities. Radiation and radiomimetic agents during the first trimester of pregnancy can produce microcephaly and mental retardation.

Maternal disease during gestation may damage the developing fetal brain. Examples include congenital infections (maternal rubella, toxoplasmosis, cytomegalic inclusion disease, syphilis, and herpes simplex); maternal diabetes; prolonged maternal hyperthermia causing anomalies of central nervous system development and microcephaly; severe maternal iodine deficiency causing endemic cretinism; and maternal hypoxia, shock, or carbon monoxide poisoning producing hypoxic-ischemic injury to fetal brain. Prolonged and severe fetal malnutrition, whether from placental insufficiency or maternal protein-calorie malnutrition, may permanently curtail brain and somatic growth and mental development. Isoimmunization by fetal Rh or ABO blood factors may result in erythroblastosis fetalis, hyperbilirubinemia, and kernicterus.

Diseases of the uteroplacental unit and of parturition are important causes of injury to the developing nervous system. The result is often hypoxic-ischemic insults of brain, either pre- or perinatally, resulting in impaired brain growth, ischemic necrosis, cerebral infarction, and porencephaly. Associated with this complex of insults is germinal matrix and intraventricular hemorrhage, seen in premature infants with respiratory distress and cardiovascular instability. These insults, depending on severity, result in sensory, mental, and motor deficits.

Genomic defects, whether point mutations or chromosomal anomalies, may profoundly affect central nervous system development. To review the hundreds of specific entities, often rare or even restricted to a single family, the reader is referred to a textbook on human genetics. Chromosomal abnormalities almost invariably impair brain development and function; they include some of the commonest and most important forms of mental retardation. Among these are Down's syndrome (caused by chromosome 21 trisomy or translocation); the fragile X syndrome, manifested by somatic signs (large ears, large testes), mental retardation, and language deficits (associated with a fragile site, revealed by culture in folate deficient media, on the X chromosome); Prader-Willi syndrome, characterized by hypotonia in infancy, pathologic obesity, and moderate psychomotor retardation (caused by a deletion on chromosome 15); and sex chromosome anomalies (XO, XXY, XYY, XXX, etc.), associated with mild or moderate somatic and mental aberrations. Genetic disorders affecting the nervous system are further discussed below, under neurocutaneous syndromes and mental retardation, and in the chapters on metabolic, hereditary, and degenerative diseases of the nervous system (Chaps. 349 and 350).

Neurodevelopmental abnormalities demonstrate complex and instructive interactions between genetic and environmental influences. Women with phenylketonuria invariably bear children with microcephaly and severe psychomotor retardation, not because of genetic transmission but because high maternal blood levels of phenylalanine are toxic to the developing fetal brain. In another example, offspring of mothers with myotonic dystrophy may suffer a double insult: They may inherit the autosomal dominant genetic trait, which may affect brain as well as muscle, and they may suffer perinatal asphyxia because of uterine dystocia that results in failure of normal progress of labor, caused by the maternal muscular dystrophy.

Spina bifida is an important example of a condition with interactive genetic and environmental determinants. Evidence for a genetic factor includes its high incidence in certain ethnic populations (especially in the United Kingdom where the incidence approximates 1 in 500 births) and a familial risk of recurrence of approximately 5 percent, many times higher than the population incidence. Data suggesting environmental factors include the decline in incidence (by about 50 percent) in both the United Kingdom and the United States in the past 40 years, and more recently, data implicating a nutritional factor. Controlled studies demonstrate a significant decrease in recurrence of spina bifida in offspring of women who received vitamin supplements, especially folic acid, during pregnancy.

Neurodevelopmental defects, primarily familial and genetic but also acquired, are being recognized in more subtle childhood developmental disorders which primarily affect intellect, language, behavior, and emotion. Examples include dyslexia, attention deficit disorder with hyperactivity, autism, and affective disease (major depression and manic depression).

Adult disorders of the nervous system that originate in early life may be classified under the following headings:

1 Congenital malformations of head, spine, and other structures, including dwarfism
2 Hereditary diseases which begin during childhood and persist throughout life, some progressing
3 Diseases which retard motor, speech, and intellectual development
4 Epilepsy

CONGENITAL MALFORMATIONS

MALFORMATIONS OF CRANIUM, SPINE, AND LIMBS Certain alterations in the size and shape of the head observed in the adult can be assumed to have had their origin prenatally or in early childhood. Beyond the first 4 to 5 years the brain approximates adult size, and the cranial sutures are so firmly closed that disease acquired later will have relatively little effect on the skull. Enlargement of the head is due either to *macrocephaly* with enlargement of brain (ventricles not enlarged significantly) or to *hydrocephalus*. Macrocephaly may be an incidental finding, often familial, in persons entirely normal neurologically, or it may be associated with neurologic disorders as in neurofibromatosis and the syndrome of cerebral gigantism (macrocephaly, tall stature, mental dullness, and seizures).

Microcephaly is related to lack of brain growth or to a destructive lesion of brain early in life. There are several rare forms of genetically determined microcephaly. In addition, microcephaly may result from chromosomal disorders, congenital infections, asphyxia, or any of the noxious insults detailed in the preceding section. In general, mental disability parallels the degree of microcephaly.

Unusual shape of head is usually caused by craniosynostosis. If the sagittal suture fuses too early, the head is long and narrow (scaphocephaly) with prominent brow and occiput; if the coronal suture closes prematurely, the head is wider than long (brachycephaly). Closure of all sutures produces a characteristic tower skull (turricephaly), shallow orbits, and bulging eyes. The last condition, if it is not recognized early and the suture lines excised, may prevent brain growth and raise intracranial pressure. Apert's syndrome (craniosynostosis with "mitten hands" or syndactyly) is associated often with enlarged ventricles and mental retardation. In achondroplasia true megalencephaly occurs, and disproportion between the base of the skull and the brain results in internal hydrocephalus in some cases.

Hydrocephalus of infancy and early childhood causes frontal bossing and variable degrees of cranial enlargement (usually over 60 cm, which is above the 97th percentile). In about 50 percent of cases the underlying condition is a congenital malformation, such as an Arnold-Chiari malformation, which is followed in frequency by meningeal fibrosis around the brainstem from subarachnoid or neonatal periventricular hemorrhage or meningitis, aqueductal stenosis, Dandy-Walker syndrome (cystic expansion of the fourth ventricle due to failure of foramens of Magendie and Luschka to open), or posterior fossa arachnoid cyst. Hydrocephalic states may arrest, only to present at a later age period with headache, spasticity, optic atrophy, and behavioral, emotional, and intellectual changes. Occult asymptomatic hydrocephalus may be destabilized in adulthood by seemingly minor head injury.

The main point to be remembered is that the cranial circumference is a valuable index of cerebral volume, and it reflects disease originating in the early period of life.

ABNORMALITIES OF THE SPINE A remarkable variety of lifelong neurologic syndromes are associated with abnormality of the vertebral column. Some of these, such as hemivertebra, platybasia, fusion of the atlas and occiput or of cervical vertebrae, or congenital dislocation of the atlas, are the consequence of a malformation of the spine itself, and the enclosed spinal cord may or may not be involved. Others, such as spina bifida occulta, spinal meningocele or myelomeningocele, or dysraphism, involve the whole neural tube, including spinal cord, investing meninges, vertebral bodies, and even the overlying skin and subcutaneous tissues. Finally there is a group of hereditary metabolic diseases that alter the spine progressively during childhood and adolescence (e.g., the mucopolysaccharidoses).

Primary malformations of vertebrae These are most frequent in the upper cervical region. The *Klippel-Feil deformity* consists of maldevelopment and fusion of two or more cervical vertebrae, resulting in a short neck of limited mobility. The hairline is low, often at the level of the first thoracic vertebra. There may or may not be associated neurologic symptoms or signs. The importance of the spinal deformity lies in its frequent association with other abnormalities, especially those of platybasia and syringomyelia, the symptoms of which may not become manifest until adolescence or adult life (see Chap. 353).

Deformity of the craniocervical junction or instability of the atlantoaxial joint may cause compression of the cervical spinal cord. Atlantoaxial dislocation may result from maldevelopment of the odontoid, seen with Down's syndrome, Morquio's syndrome, and spondyloepiphyseal dysplasia.

Platybasia and basilar impression This is a rare maldevelopment in which either the base of the skull is flattened or the occiput and upper cervical spine are invaginated into the posterior fossa. Often the foramen magnum itself is imperfectly developed, or the atlas and occiput are fused. Basilar impression may be caused by a group of diseases with biochemical and structural bony abnormalities of genetic origin. The conditions may be asymptomatic, but often there is "crowding," distortion, or compression of the spinal cord, medulla, and lower cranial and cervical spinal nerves. An acquired form of basilar impression occurs with rickets and Paget's disease. It is usually asymptomatic but sometimes involves the lower cranial nerves and may cause normal-pressure hydrocephalus.

The resulting clinical picture is variable. Symptoms may be present from early life or may begin in late childhood, adolescence, or even adult years. Early symptoms consist of "dizzy" or "weak" spells and downward nystagmus on tilting the head; evidences of increased intracranial pressure such as headache; occipital neuralgia; vomiting; transient paresthesias in the occipital region, neck, or arms; facial paresthesias, deafness, nasal voice, and dysphagia; cerebellar ataxia; and spastic weakness of the legs. The symptoms may first be intermittent and at any time in the course of the illness may be aggravated by straining, moving the head, or placing the head and neck in certain positions. Inspection alone provides a clue to diagnosis. The whole configuration of the head and neck is abnormal. The neck is short; the ears and hairline are low; the neck movements are obviously restricted; and the normal cervical lordosis is lost or greatly exaggerated, sometimes to the extent that the occiput lies almost on the upper dorsal spine and shoulders.

Platybasia and these related anomalies of the spine should be suspected in all cases presenting progressive cerebellar, brainstem, and cervical cord syndromes. Many of these cases have been misdiagnosed as multiple sclerosis or spinocerebellar degeneration. Others present a typical syringomyelic syndrome and have been so labeled. The clinical suspicion of platybasia and other spine anomalies can be confirmed by a true lateral roentgenogram of the skull.

Arnold-Chiari malformation This condition, in which the medulla and inferior-posterior portions of the cerebellar hemispheres project caudally through the foramen magnum, often to the level of the second cervical vertebra, is a common cause of hydrocephalus. It is often associated with a spinal myelomeningocele or meningocele, and usually there are deformities of the cervical spine and cervicooccipital junction. The symptoms of hydrocephalus dominate the clinical picture in infants. In milder cases, there may develop during adolescence or adult years any one of the several syndromes described above in the section "Platybasia and Basilar Impression." A second type of Arnold-Chiari malformation in patients who have no meningomyelocele is often associated with syringomyelia.

The treatment of platybasia and the Arnold-Chiari malformation has not been entirely satisfactory. If clinical progression is slight or uncertain, no treatment is warranted. If progression is certain and disability is increasing, upper cervical laminectomy and enlargement of the foramen magnum are indicated. Often this procedure halts the course of the illness or results in improvement. The surgical procedure must be done cautiously, however, for extensive manipulation of these structures may aggravate the symptoms or even cause death.

Malformations associated with a defect in closure of the neural arch These take the forms of craniorachischisis totalis, craniocele, spinal meningocele, meningomyelocele, spina bifida occulta, and sinus tracts. Since these conditions seldom figure in adult neurology, only some of the late complications are mentioned here.

Sinus tracts in lumbosacral or occipital regions are of importance, for at any age they may be sources of bacterial meningitis. They are often indicated by a small dimple in the skin or by a tuft of hair along the posterior surface of the body in the midline located high, above the buttocks. They may be associated with dermoid cysts at the central part of the tract. Evidence of such tracts should be sought in every instance of meningitis, especially when infection has recurred. The pilonidal sinus, which is found lower down, should not be included in this group.

There are, in addition, other congenital cysts (dermoids) and benign tumors (lipomas) which may produce progressive symptoms and signs by compressing the spinal cord or by implicating nerve roots. So-called tethering of the spinal cord is caused by a stout filum terminale exerting downward traction on the cord; the traction may cause ischemic injury to the conus medullaris and lower spinal segments. Diastematomyelia is a form of dysraphism characterized by a bony midline spur associated with partial duplication of the spinal cord at the same level; it may cause spinal symptoms by impingement on the cord.

Several clinical syndromes of delayed progressive disease (in the adolescent or adult) have been delineated in patients who have had an asymptomatic or symptomatic spina bifida, meningocele, or spinal dysraphism:

1 Progressive spastic weakness of some of the already weakened muscles of the legs.
2 An acute cauda equina syndrome following some unusual activity or incident, e.g., rowing, or a fall in a sitting position. The implicated sensory and motor roots are believed to be injured by sudden or repeated stretching. Weakness of bladder control, impotence (in the male), and numbness of feet and legs or footdrop compose the clinical syndrome.
3 Progressive cauda equina syndrome in the lumbosacral region.
4 Syringomyelia (see Chap. 353).

MALFORMATIONS OF THE EXTREMITIES These malformations include syndactylism, clinodactyly along with broad hand and transverse palmer (simian) line (common with Down's syndrome), club feet, and arthrogryposis multiplex. They are rarely of concern to internists.

DWARFISM IN RELATION TO NEUROLOGIC DISEASE It is noteworthy that the majority of mentally retarded individuals fall below normal in statural growth, and dwarfism is part of many special syndromes. Persons with Down's syndrome and with most of the other chromosomal abnormalities are examples, and there are others in which an inherited or acquired metabolic defect blights brain and skeletal growth (e.g., cretinism and mucupolysaccharidoses). Microcephaly characterizes many of the dwarfs with cerebral diseases.

The 30 or 40 neurologic syndromes with statural underdevelopment and neurologic disease are described and illustrated in the atlas of mental retardation by Holmes et al.

HEREDITARY DISEASES

THE PHAKOMATOSES   This is a unique group of diseases, usually hereditary, in which neurologic abnormalities are combined with congenital defects of skin, retina, and other organs. The terms *congenital ectodermal dysplasias, congenital neurocutaneous syndromes,* or *phakomatoses* (Greek *phakos,* "lentil," "mole," or "freckle") are used frequently to designate this general class of disorders. The major syndromes include neurofibromatosis, tuberous sclerosis, encephalotrigeminal syndrome, and rarely, ataxia telangiectasia, cerebelloretinal hemangioblastomatosis, and the Klippel-Trénaunay-Weber syndrome. Osler-Rendu-Weber disease, an autosomal dominant disease with vascular anomalies affecting skin, mucous membranes, and the gastrointestinal and genitourinary tracts, occasionally has angiomas in either spinal cord or brain, where they may produce bleeding (see Chap. 185). Cerebral abscess formation is another complication of this condition involving the central nervous system.

Neurofibromatosis (von Recklinghausen's disease)   This is an autosomal dominant disease, in which spots of increased skin pigmentation are combined with multiple neurofibromas. Its incidence is 1 per 3000; about 50 percent of cases are apparently sporadic. It has been characterized as a maldevelopment of cells of neural crest origin. The pigmented spots are irregular in shape with relatively even borders, vary in size from a few millimeters to several centimeters, and are of brownish coffee color (café au lait). They are most prominent over the trunk, in the axilla (axillary freckles), and about the pelvis. Similar lesions occur in individuals without neurofibromatosis, but in such instances they are generally smaller than 1.5 cm in diameter and fewer than five in number. The tumors arise from the neurilemmal sheath (Schwann cells) of the peripheral nerve. They are usually multiple and vary in size from minute lesions to large tumors several centimeters in diameter. The majority are smoothly rounded or lobulated, soft or firm, and can sometimes be seen or felt along the course of a peripheral nerve. Often they sink into the subcutaneous fat on gentle pressure. Like the pigmented lesions, the tumors are more frequent over the trunk than on the extremities. Both the pigmented areas, because of giant melanosomes in pigment epithelial cells, and also the tumors of nerve sheaths become increasingly apparent with age. Most of the tumors are asymptomatic; occasionally, if they attain a large size or occupy an unusual position, they may produce pressure upon contiguous structures. Tumors of the spinal nerve roots may compress the spinal cord and at the same time extend through the intervertebral foramens to form a large mass in the posterior mediastinum (dumbbell tumors). Acoustic neurinomas, usually bilateral in patients with neurofibromatosis, may produce deafness and other symptoms and signs of a cerebellopontine angle lesion (Chap. 345); this form apparently represents a distinct variant. Such patients almost always lack any peripheral neurocutaneous signs of neurofibromatosis. Other histopathologic types of tumor (meningioma, glioma) are encountered more often in neurofibromatosis than in the general population. Diffuse overgrowth of Schwann cells and fibroblasts may also occur, giving rise to plexiform neuromas. They may cause hideous deformities, often with overgrowth of underlying bone. Bone cysts may also form. Most of these associated tumors are rare in infancy and childhood, though glioma of the optic nerve and chiasm is an exception to the clinical rule. The latter condition should always be considered in the differential diagnosis of unilateral (rarely bilateral) blindness, proptosis, and extraocular muscle paralysis in childhood,

especially if there are signs of von Recklinghausen's disease. Diagnosis is evident by computed tomography (CT) scan. Pulsating exophthalmos resulting from congenital absence of part of the sphenoid bone is an infrequent but characteristic lesion of neurofibromatosis. Pheochromocytoma is a rare accompaniment of the disease. In about 5 to 10 percent of cases of neurofibromatosis one of the tumors will become sarcomatous.

Fibrous dysplasia, congenital vertebral anomalies, local gigantism of an extremity, subperiosteal bone cysts, and pseudoarthrosis of the tibia may be associated with neurofibromatosis. Scoliosis is a common skeletal deformity in children with this disease, so that neurofibromatosis must be added to the list of neurogenic and myogenic kyphoscolioses (the others are syringomyelia, Friedreich's ataxia, progressive muscular dystrophy, and poliomyelitis). Stenosis of the aqueduct of Sylvius with obstructive hydrocephalus is at times observed in neurofibromatosis. Also there may be a mild degree of mental retardation, related presumably to developmental abnormalities of the cerebral cortex. Spina bifida, hypospadias, glaucoma, and elephantiasis are occasionally seen. An association of vascular stenoses (renal, cerebral, or pulmonic) and neurofibromatosis has been recognized.

About one-third of cases of neurofibromatosis are discovered accidentally on routine examination, there being no complaints. Another third of these patients come seeking advice about the cosmetic aspects of the disease. The remainder have neurologic syndromes. Those with prominent neurologic signs may have few cutaneous lesions. There is no treatment for the disease other than excision of symptomatic tumors.

Tuberous sclerosis   This autosomal dominant disease is manifested by the clinical triad of convulsive seizures, mental deficiency, and adenoma sebaceum. The latter are fine, wart-like lesions distributed predominantly in a butterfly distribution over the cheeks, nose, and forehead. The individual adenomas vary in size from 0.1 to 1.0 cm and are elevated and pinkish or pinkish yellow in color. In addition, the skin over the lower part of the back may be thick, rough, and of yellowish color, like sharkskin or pigskin (shagreen patch). Actually the earliest lesions are ash-leaf-shaped hypopigmented spots ("white spots") over the trunk and limbs, which are seen most clearly under ultraviolet light (Wood's lamp). They are distinguishable on the basis of size, shape, and character from avascular nevi and vitiligo, and are highly diagnostic, often providing the earliest clue to the etiology of mental retardation or infantile epilepsy. The mental deficiency may be relatively stationary or progressive. The seizures are usually generalized but may be focal. Retinal tumors and other visible malformations may be conjoined.

Patients with the most advanced form of tuberous sclerosis are severely mentally retarded, but not all are so disabled. In general hospital clinics it is not unusual to see such patients with average intelligence and only seizures and a few skin lesions. Occasionally a focal cerebral syndrome will prove at biopsy to have a typical "tuber" or an associated glioma as its basis in a patient not known to have this disease. Family history is frequently unhelpful—approximately one-half of cases are sporadic, presumably due to mutation.

Pathologically, the lesions of the skin are fibromas and not true adenomas. Some are rather vascular and suggest telangiectasia. The brain lesions consist of areas of malformed cortex with extensive astrogliosis and a peculiar mixture of glioblasts and monster nerve cells. Calcification may or may not be present. Masses of subependymal glial tissue account for the nodules projecting into the walls of the ventricles that are often seen in computerized tomography. Most cases of rhabdomyoma of heart muscle are associated with tuberous sclerosis. Tumorous malformations may occur in the kidney, liver, adrenal glands, and pancreas.

The diagnosis is aided by CT scans. Calcified nodules occur, particularly in the temporal lobes and adjacent to the ventricles. If large, they may obstruct the foramen of Monro, causing a unilateral or bilateral hydrocephalus. The center of the nodule tends to be more densely radiopaque than the periphery. Hypodense areas may appear at the cortical junction with the white matter. The electroencephalogram is usually abnormal but without specific pattern. The cerebrospinal fluid may be normal; rarely, the total protein level is elevated.

Treatment is symptomatic, with excision of tumors as necessary. The prognosis for life beyond the third decade is poor. Death is usually due to seizures, associated tumors, or intercurrent diseases. Genetic counseling is an obligation of the physician.

Cerebelloretinal hemangioblastomatosis (von Hippel–Lindau syndrome)

As the name implies, the syndrome consists of vascular malformations of the retina and cerebellum. The retinal lesions are capillary angiomas, usually multiple, causing progressive loss of vision; the cerebellar lesion consists of a slowly growing hemangioblastoma, frequently multiple, with a large cystic component, lending itself to surgical removal; spinal and medullary hemangioblastomas also occur. The clinical symptoms and signs consist of progressive cerebellar ataxia, headache, and papilledema. Seldom is a vascular bruit audible over the head. Polycythemia, possibly related to the production of erythropoietin, has been observed in many cases and has in a few instances disappeared after excision of the tumor. The disease is transmitted as an autosomal dominant trait, but many cases are sporadic. Rarely do these tumors appear before adolescence. One should consider this diagnosis in all patients with a cerebellar tumor syndrome (see Chap. 345). Not all have a retinal lesion—the von Hippel part of the disease. The hemangioblastoma of the cerebellum is usually but one part of a constellation of abnormalities including angiomas and cysts of the liver, pancreas, and kidneys and tumors of the epididymis and kidney, the last named being the cause of death in some cases. Pheochromocytomas have been described in this and in other of the phakomatoses. Syringomyelia has been observed in a few cases, and if a careful search is made, a hemangioblastoma can often be found in relation to the syrinx at some level.

The cerebellar hemangioblastoma demands surgical treatment, and if the nodule of the tumor is found in the wall of the cyst and is excised, the results can be excellent; if the tumor cannot be operated on because of size or multiplicity, radiation may be tried. The retinal lesions, when small, can be arrested by photocoagulation.

Encephalotrigeminal syndrome (Sturge-Weber disease)

This disease consists of capillary or cavernous hemangiomas, within but not always limited to the cutaneous distribution of the trigeminal nerve unilaterally, and of a predominantly venous hemangioma of the leptomeninges over the occipital, parietal, or frontal lobe on the same side. The intracranial and cutaneous lesions may occur separately. The disease is usually sporadic; familial occurrence is exceptional.

Pathologically, the cortex subjacent to the abnormal meningeal vessels is progressively destroyed, owing probably to stagnation of blood flow and consequent hypoxia, and in some cases a band of calcium develops within the lesion. This band, following the convolutional pattern as it does, is responsible for the characteristic "railroad track" roentgenographic picture. Deeply situated arteriovenous malformations rarely coexist.

The first neurologic symptom is usually a focal seizure on the side opposite the skin lesion. Transient postictal (Todd's) paralysis or permanent paralysis may follow the seizure. Sensorimotor paralysis or permanent visual field defect, the most frequent findings, may be either of insidious onset with slow progression or apoplectic. Blindness in the eye on the side of the nevus is frequent and is nearly always due to glaucoma. Most patients with this malformation survive for many years, often with residual mental defects and hemiparesis.

The lesions are usually too extensive to be treated surgically, though hemispherectomy has been advised by some surgeons for intractable epilepsy. Anticonvulsant medication is indicated, but the seizures may be difficult to control.

Hemangioma of the trunk or upper or lower extremity may be associated with a spinal cord vascular malformation (Klippel-Trénaunay-Weber syndrome). The extremity may be hypertrophied. The cord lesion may bleed into or cause infarction in the nervous tissue, producing a spinal sensorimotor paralysis. Surgical exploration and decompression are seldom beneficial.

Ataxia telangiectasia

(see Chap. 256) This condition has attracted considerable interest because of theoretical implications of its apparent cause and pathogenesis. Inherited as a recessive trait, the disease is characterized neurologically by a progressive cerebellar ataxia, apraxia of ocular movement, and choreoathetosis beginning during the early years of life. Not all neurologists classify this condition as a phakomatosis because of its progressive nature and associated immunologic defects. Telangiectases of bulbar conjunctivas and skin, especially about the ears, neck, and in flexor creases at the elbows and knees, appear somewhat later in childhood or adolescence. Recurring pulmonary and sinus infections have been prominent in many cases, and a deficiency in the IgA globulins and a defect of delayed cellular hypersensitivity are found. The diagnosis can be supported by the finding of abnormal humoral and cell-mediated immunity and of raised levels of alpha fetoprotein and cytogenetic abnormalities. Fibroblasts and lymphocytes from patients with this disease have enhanced in vitro radiosensitivity, attributed to deficiencies in enzyme systems that repair DNA. The associated pathologic changes consist of an extensive loss of Purkinje cells of the cerebellum and possibly degeneration of the neurons in other parts of the basal ganglia. Dysplasia of the thymus has been well documented, and death usually occurs by the second or third decade of life from infection or a reticuloendothelial tumor.

Familial dysautonomia (Riley-Day syndrome)

This disease is characterized by autonomic instability (abnormal sweating, loss of vasomotor control, labile hypertension), impaired taste with absence of fungiform papillae, diminished pain and temperature sensation, hyporeflexia, episodic fever, vomiting attacks, lack of lacrimation (alacrima), and corneal anesthesia and ulceration. Familial dysautonomia is an autosomal recessive disease limited to Ashkenazi Jews.

The clinical manifestations become apparent soon after birth with difficulty in feeding (dysphagia) and motor functions which becomes increasingly evident in childhood. A few patients reach adult years, but the mortality rate is high because of recurrent pulmonary infections with inappropriate autonomic responses. Emotional instability presents a problem in most patients. Although intelligence has been within normal limits in some patients, in others it has been subnormal. Growth seems to be delayed for unclear reasons, and the natural tendency is to undernutrition and scoliosis. Neuropathic (Charcot) joints due to lack of pain and related injury have been reported.

Proof of the disturbance of the autonomic nervous system comes from special tests such as absence of skin flare after histamine and skin stroking (loss of axonal reflex), and hypersensitivity to both cholinergic and adrenergic agents. Nerve conduction velocities are decreased. Quantitative pathologic studies of peripheral and autonomic nervous systems have shown marked depletion of small-caliber axons in peripheral nerves (which could account for the deficit in pain and temperature appreciation) and decreased numbers of small neurons in the dorsal root ganglia, in sympathetic ganglia, and in the ciliary ganglia (which could account for some of the dysautonomic features). A primary enzymatic defect has not been demonstrated. Intermediolateral cell columns of the spinal cord are normal, as is the rest of the central nervous system.

In the differential diagnosis one must consider other forms of small-fiber polyneuropathy with analgesia and dysautonomia (including congenital indifference to pain and amyloidosis) (see Chap. 355), as well as the Shy-Drager syndrome (a degenerative disease of lateral horn cells and basal ganglia) (see Chap. 350).

Bethanechol may control vomiting attacks, increase tearing, and reduce the risk of pulmonary aspiration. Orthopedic measures are needed to stabilize neuropathic joints. Injury must be avoided and wounds treated carefully.

DISEASES THAT RETARD DEVELOPMENT

ABNORMALITIES OF MOTOR FUNCTION (CEREBRAL PALSY) In this category of neurologic defect a major disturbance of motor function, usually nonprogressive, has been present since infancy or childhood. The popular term for these conditions is *cerebral palsy*. Cerebral palsy may be used as a generic term defining a nonprogressive static disturbance of motor function, present from birth or early life, caused by a discrete encephaloclastic insult to the central nervous system during gestation, the perinatal period, or infancy. Most cases result from ischemic-hypoxic insults, but infection, hemorrhage, or trauma may occasionally have a similar outcome. Familial/genetic, metabolic, and degenerative diseases should be excluded from this classification.

Forms of cerebral palsy are designated according to the pattern of motor disturbance. Spastic diplegia (referring to spasticity in paired limbs but in practice referring to spasticity predominant in the legs) is the commonest form (accounting for 50 percent of cerebral palsy) and generally the mildest. Only about 8 percent of spastic diplegics are mentally retarded; most become ambulatory. The stiff, awkward movements of the legs, maintained in an extended, adducted posture, do not usually attract attention until several weeks or months after birth. Seizures occur in some cases, and it is not uncommon to observe a delay in all normal developmental sequences, especially those which depend on the motor system. Once walking is attempted, usually much later than in the normal child, the characteristic stance and gait become manifest. The legs are advanced stiffly in short steps, each describing an arc of a circle; adduction is often so strong as to lead to actual crossing (scissors gait), with lower legs slightly splayed out and the feet flexed and turned in, the heels not touching the ground. In the adolescent and adult, the legs tend to be short and small, but the muscles are not markedly atrophic. Passive manipulation of the limbs reveals marked spasticity in the extensors and adductors and also slight shortening of the calf muscles. The hands and arms may be affected only slightly, if at all; there may be awkwardness and stiffness of the fingers. In a few, pronounced weakness and spasticity are noted. Speech may be well-articulated or noticeably slurred, and in some instances the face is set in a spastic smile. The deep-tendon reflexes are exaggerated, those in the legs more so than those in the arms, and the plantar reflexes are extensor. Usually there is no disturbance of spincteric function, though delay in acquiring voluntary control is usual. Athetotic postures and movements of the face, tongue, and hands are present in some patients and may actually conceal the pyramidal weakness. Ataxic and hypotonic forms also exist.

The condition must be distinguished from familial types of spastic paraparesis, which are well-recognized clinical entities (Chap. 353).

Spastic quadriplegia, the term referring to spasticity of all four extremities (generally with legs more severely affected than arms) accounts for 30 percent of cerebral palsy; children so affected are generally markedly retarded and nonambulatory. Spastic hemiplegia accounts for 10 percent of cerebral palsy; it can be divided roughly into two groups: two-thirds to three-quarters have normal intelligence; one-third have seizures; and about one-quarter are mentally retarded. These two features tend to be correlated; i.e., patients with congenital hemiplegia with seizures have lower intelligence scores. Other forms of cerebral palsy together account for 10 percent. These include choreoathetotic, ataxic, dystonic, and atonic forms; these forms may be mixed, including features of spasticity and mental retardation. In patients with a combination of cerebral diplegia and ataxia, difficulty in standing and walking cannot be attributed to spasticity or paralysis. Incoordination, similar to that seen in cerebellar disease, and hypotonia are the principal findings. The motor defect may be so great that the individual is never able to sit or stand; the muscles are of normal size, and voluntary movements, though weak, are possible in all the limbs. In less severe cases, sitting, standing, and walking are merely delayed, and with advancing years cerebellar ataxia and tremor become manifest. Relative improvement may occur in later years.

The tendon reflexes are present, and the plantar reflexes are either flexor or extensor. Many of these patients suffer a severe degree of amentia and retardation of speech development. Pure choreoathetotic cerebral palsy may be associated with striking preservation of intelligence. At the opposite extreme, atonic cerebral palsy is uniformly accompanied by profound developmental deficit.

A rare condition, infantile quadriplegia without involvement of intellect or bulbar musculature, may result from a high cervical cord lesion. Although this may occasionally result from cysts, tumors, and other malformations, it is usually produced in the infant by a rupture of the cervical cord induced by traction during a difficult breech delivery. Similarly, in paraplegia, with weakness or paralysis limited to the legs, the lesion may be either a cerebral form of diplegia or a spinal one. Sphincteric disturbances and a definite loss of somatic sensation below a certain level on the trunk always favor a spinal localization. Congenital cysts including rare spinal arachnoid cysts, tumors, and diastematomyelia are more frequently the cause of paraplegia than of quadriplegia. An additional cause of infantile paraplegia is spinal infarction from thrombotic complications of umbilical artery catheterization.

The lesions associated with cerebral palsy are predominantly caused by ischemic-hypoxic insults to the immature brain because of asphyxia. Asphyxia has been estimated to occur antenatally in 50 percent of cases, intrapartum in 40 percent, and postpartum in 10 percent. Modern obstetric practice has reduced the incidence of perinatal asphyxia from 4 percent to 0.5 percent. The type of cerebral palsy which results depends on the pattern and severity of hypoxic-ischemic insult. Spastic diplegia probably results from ischemic-hypoxic necrotic lesions localized near the dorsolateral surfaces of the lateral ventricles, thought to be an end-arterial zone in preterm infants. More extensive ischemic-hypoxic insults produce extensive cystic destruction of central white matter of the hemispheres (deep lesion), a lesion associated with quadriplegia and mental deficiency. Hypoxic-ischemic insult in term infants tends to affect the parasagittal and parietooccipital cortex watershed zone, hippocampus, thalamus, and cerebellar hemispheres (superficial lesion). Congenital hemiplegia results from arterial occlusion in the middle cerebral artery territory (probably secondary to hypoxia and ischemia) resulting in a porencephalic lesion of the hemisphere, or from a more diffuse and partial hemispheral insult. Cohen and Duffner have shown that if a subsequent CT scan shows damage to the cerebral cortex, the likelihood of seizures and subnormal intelligence is increased.

Choreoathetotic cerebral palsy usually results from intrapartum asphyxia and hypoxia. It correlates with the pathologic finding of status marmoratus, a partial lesion of the basal ganglia characterized by neuronal loss, gliosis, and condensation of myelinating fibers.

Ataxic cerebral palsy is commonly associated with sclerotic lesions of the cerebellum. Other lesions of the cerebral hemispheres, as described above, may also be present.

Clinical pictures similar to those described above may result from postnatal disease states, including meningitis, herpes simplex encephalitis, seizures, trauma, subdural hematomas, or vascular insults. In the premature infant, ischemia followed by hyperperfusion may result in hemorrhage into the periventricular germinal matrix zones, lateral ventricles, and parenchyma of the hemispheres. This intraventricular hemorrhage (IVH), occurring in about 40 percent of premature infants with respiratory distress syndrome and requiring respiratory assistance, may result in hydrocephalus and delayed psychomotor development. Hypoxic-ischemic injury, independent of the hemorrhage, appears to play a role in the neurologic outcome of these infants.

Kernicterus is a special form of neonatal insult that can be considered with cerebral palsy. Its distinctive clinical picture includes choreoathetosis, deafness, failure of upward gaze, and sometimes mental retardation. The degree of involvement ranges from mild to severe. Either athetosis or ataxia may be present, and a few have also shown rigid limbs and a picture not too different from that of cerebral spastic diplegia with involuntary movements. The neuropathologic changes in these surviving patients consist of symmetrically distributed nerve-cell loss and gliosis in the subthalamic nucleus of Luys, the globus pallidus, thalamus, and oculomotor and cochlear nuclei. These lesions result from hyperbilirubinemia. In the newborn, unconjugated bilirubin can pass through the poorly developed blood-brain barrier into these central and brainstem nuclei, where it is directly toxic. Acidosis and hypoxia exacerbate the effect.

MENTAL RETARDATION Mentally retarded individuals pose special problems for physicians not only in childhood but also in adulthood. They are unable to give an adequate medical history; one must rely more on objective signs of disease than on subjective complaint. Often they cannot cooperate in diagnostic studies or independently manage treatment regimens. Then, too, the reactions of such patients to drugs and fever may be extreme and unpredictable. Recognition of the etiology of mental retardation also becomes important in genetic counseling for other members of the family.

Mental retardation poses a great challenge for the physician. Responsibilities may include the recognition and prevention of factors—both genetic and environmental—apt to cause mental retardation, diagnosis of mental retardation itself, genetic counseling, treatment of conditions causing mental retardation, treatment of intercurrent illnesses in the mentally retarded, advising about the social and educational management of the retarded, and treatment of behavioral disorders which may accompany mental deficiency. The task of differentiating mental retardation from deafness, from disorders of language or motor development, and from other medical illnesses falls largely to the pediatrician. Genetic counseling increasingly becomes the province of specialized geneticists. Neuropsychopharmacology may contribute greatly to the well-being of some mentally retarded persons with behavioral and emotional dyscontrol or with epilepsy.

The clinical manifestations of mental retardation are relatively easy to perceive. Dull or silly behavior and inability to give a sensible account of the medical problem constitute one useful datum. Slowness in motor development, inability to learn and poor school progress, lack of a concept of time or space, and inability to secure and hold a job or to perform more than the menial tasks of society are other useful indexes.

The differentiation of the various classes of mental retardation by clinical criteria is facilitated if the framework of reference in Table 351-1 is used. In spite of the wide spectrum of specific disease entities causing mental retardation, perhaps half of all mentally retarded persons cannot presently be classified in terms of specific etiology by clinical criteria. They probably represent the consequence of a wide variety of genetic and acquired insults impairing brain development. Many of the known noxious agents acting during gestation and early life have been described above. Many cases are familial, the patients coming from families in which other members are retarded or have important mental disorders, and the heritable factors may be polygenic. There also appears to be another group of disorders, due to single gene defects affecting only the brain, which have been poorly defined clinically and pathologically; included are several types of maldevelopment of the cerebral cortex. An important and varied group of X-linked recessive disorders causing mental retardation in males has recently come to medical attention. One subgroup of these affected males has physical stigmata including macroorchidism, prognathism, large ears, and dolichocephaly; an identifiable abnormality of the X chromosome, called the *fragile X*, appears when their cells are grown in folate-deficient media.

Within the spectrum of types of mental retardation, even within a group of persons of similar intelligence quotients (IQ), there are vast differences and contrasts in overall behavioral functioning. Some mentally retarded persons are pleasant and amiable and achieve a rather satisfactory social adjustment; this is especially true of simple mental retardates. At the opposite extreme is the ill-understood syndrome of autism, associated with varying degrees of retardation, in which the child or older person fails to manifest interpersonal social contact—including communicative language—and demonstrates a limited and bizarre interest primarily in inanimate objects (see ''Autism'' below). It is impossible to list all variations of mental retardation here, but the point should be made that all aspects of intellectual life and personality are touched in differing degrees. Many retarded individuals are dull, apathetic, and underactive. Others display an incessant hyperactivity, characterized by a very short attention span, a restless and inquisitive searching of the environment, and low frustration tolerance. They may be destructive or recklessly fearless, and may seem strangely impervious to injury. Some display a peculiar anhedonia and are indifferent to either punishment or reward. Improvement in these children can often be achieved by using amphetamines. Other aberrant types of behavior, such as violent aggressiveness and even self-mutilation, are not uncommon. Rhythmic rocking, rolling, head banging, and bouncing movements are features of the motor activities of some severely retarded persons and may be performed hour after hour without fatigue, often to the accompaniment of vocal ejaculations. Here the abnormality is not the appearance of rhythmic movements of the body, which are to be observed at one period in the development of many normal children, but their persistence and exaggeration.

It is apparent that the clinical and behavioral characteristics of

TABLE 351-1 Clinical classification of nonprogressive types of mental retardation

I Mental defect with associated developmental abnormalities in nonnervous structures
  A Those affecting cranioskeletal structures
    1 Microcephaly
    2 Macrocephaly
    3 Hydrocephalus (including myelomeningocele with Arnold-Chiari malformation and associated cerebral anomalies)
    4 Down's syndrome (mongolism)
    5 Cretinism (congenital hypothyroidism)
    6 Mucopolysaccharidoses (Hurler, Hunter, and Sanfilippo types)
    7 Acrocephalosyndactyly (craniosynostosis)
    8 Arthrogryposis multiplex congenita (some cases)
    9 Rare specific syndromes: e.g., Rubinstein-Taybi
    10 Dwarfism, short stature: Seckel's bird-headed dwarf, Cockayne-Neel dwarf, etc.
    11 Hypertelorism, median facial cleft syndromes, agenesis of corpus callosum
  B Those affecting nonskeletal structures
    1 Neurocutaneous syndromes; tuberous sclerosis, Sturge-Weber syndrome, neurofibromatosis
    2 Congenital rubella syndrome (deafness, blindness, congenital heart disease, small stature)
    3 Chromosomal disorders: Down's syndrome, some cases of Klinefelter's syndrome (XXY), Turner's (XO) syndrome (occasionally), fragile X syndrome
    4 Laurence-Moon-Biedl syndrome (retinitis pigmentosa, obesity, polydactyly)
    5 Eye disorders: toxoplasmosis (chorioretinitis), galactosemia (cataract), congenital rubella (chorioretinitis)
    6 Prader-Willi syndrome (obesity, hypogenitalism)
II Mental defect without developmental anomalies in nonnervous structures but with focal cerebral and other neurologic abnormalities
  A Cerebral spastic diplegia and quadriplegia
  B Cerebral hemiplegia, unilateral or bilateral
  C Congenital choreoathetosis or ataxia
    1 Kernicterus
    2 Status marmoratus
  D Congenital atonic diplegia
  E Posthypoglycemic, posttraumatic, postmeningitic, and postencephalitic states
  F Those associated with other neuromuscular abnormalities (muscular dystrophy, Friedreich's ataxia, etc.)
  G Cerebral degenerative diseases (lipidoses)
  H Lesch-Nyhan syndrome (choreoathetosis and self-mutilation)
III Mental defect without signs of other developmental abnormality or neurologic disorder (epilepsy may or may not be present)
  A Simple mental retardation, familial mental retardation
  B Some cases of encephaloclastic disease (hypoxia, hypoglycemia)
  C Infantile autism
  D Those associated with inborn errors of metabolism (phenylketonuria, other aminoacidurias, organic acidurias)
  E Congenital infections (some cases of congenital syphilis, cytomegalic inclusion disease)
  F Epileptic encephalopathies

individuals with retarded development cannot be adequately described by a single parameter, the IQ. There are many other factors which determine the social success of retarded children and which should give direction to their education and training. These include specific sensory or motor handicaps, such as blindness and deafness as well as athetosis or hemiplegia; specific language or speech deficits; behavioral disturbances, such as autism, aggressiveness, or hyperactivity; and the presence of seizures. Measures can be taken, including pharmacologic treatment, physical therapy, and behavior training, to help the handicapped person compensate for these deficiencies. These become primary considerations in functional diagnosis and in guiding the parents or guardians.

The least severely retarded individual (IQ of 50 to 70) grows and develops in many ways not different from normal ones, and he or she can be taught useful occupational skills. A few of these persons can work under careful supervision. All scholastic pursuits are relatively unsuccessful, and vocational training is of more value than other types of education.

Special varieties of mental retardation   Several of the special types of mental retardation are discussed in other chapters (see Chaps. 305, 306, 307, and 316). In the following sections are presented only those with special features likely to be seen in adults.

DOWN'S SYNDROME   This unique condition, although accounting for only about 1 percent of all mental defectives, accounts for nearly one-third of the admissions to state schools for the mentally retarded. The degree of mental retardation varies from mild to severe and is associated with a curious facial configuration and a dwarfed physical stature. Many stigmata of Down's syndrome can be recognized in the neonatal period. The head tends to be small and round, with sloping forehead. The ears are set low and are oval, with small lobules. The eyes slant slightly upward and outward owing to the presence of a medial epicanthal fold, which partly covers the angle of the palpebral fissure. The bridge of the nose is generally absent or poorly developed. The mouth tends to hang open, and the tongue is usually enlarged, heavily fissured, and protruding. Gray-white specks of depigmentation are seen in the iris (Brushfield's spots). The little fingers are often short and curved inward (clinodactyly), owing to a hypoplastic middle phalanx. The hands are broad and short, with a single transverse palmar crease. Lenticular opacities and congenital heart lesions (septal defects) are found in some cases. At birth these children are of average size, but at later periods of life they are characteristically small.

The brain shows a rather rounded shape which conforms to that of the skull, a subnormal weight, and a relatively simple convolutional pattern, with particular smallness of the frontal lobes and superior temporal convolutions.

The mortality rate is high in the first years of life, death usually being due to respiratory infections, cardiac disease, or leukemia. Of the patients who survive to adult life, many then suffer a premature form of Alzheimer's cerebral degeneration (onset in the majority before age 40).

Older mothers are more apt to have Down's syndrome babies than are young mothers. The mean age of the mother at the time of birth of these children is 37. Down's syndrome is caused by trisomy of chromosome 21 or translocation of parts of this chromosome. It is diagnosable in utero by amniocentesis.

CRETINISM AND CHILDHOOD HYPOTHYROIDISM   True endemic cretinism, along with endemic goiter, is an iodine deficiency disorder, occurring widely in remote areas of the world where severe iodine deficiency is not corrected. Cretins born of iodine-deficient mothers have irreversible deaf-mutism, mental retardation, and a spastic and rigid posture and gait.

This disorder is determined in utero by maternal iodine deficiency, which affects fetal brain development through a combination of failure of maternal provision of thyroxine to the fetus and failure of fetal

thyroxine production because of iodine deficiency. In the neurologic form, thyroid function may be normal by the time of birth, but neurologic deficits persist. In the myxedematous form, severe hypothyroidism persists after birth.

Sporadic cretinism occurs in infants suffering a congenital disorder of thyroid function. The latter occurs in about 1 in 4000 births. Symptoms of hypothyroidism may be evident at birth or later. If untreated, hypothyroidism impairs brain development causing mental retardation. This form may be detected by neonatal screening programs. With prompt treatment (within the first weeks of life), children with sporadic cretinism may develop normally, with virtually no permanent neurologic or intellectual impairment. If treatment is withheld or delayed, permanent mental retardation results.

Childhood hypothyroidism and myxedema resemble the adult forms of the diseases described in Chap. 324.

MUCOPOLYSACCHARIDOSES AND PHENYLKETONURIA (PHENYLPYRUVIC OLIGOPHRENIA)   These conditions are discussed in Chaps. 307 and 316.

AUTISM   Autism is a syndrome of pervasive developmental disorder of personality, characterized by failure of the young child to develop normal social interaction or communicative language and by a bizarre obsessiveness, preoccupation, perseveration, resistance to change, and stereotypic actions. Language, if it develops, is characterized by a pragmatic and semantic deficit. Islands of preserved or precocious function may be evident. Autism is now considered a disorder of brain development, though etiologies are unclear; evidence has been put forward of genetic determinants and also of gestational and perinatal risk factors. The autistic syndrome may probably result from any of several disparate disease processes.

CT scans or pneumoencephalograms have shown abnormalities in some cases, implicating the medial temporal regions or enlargement of lateral ventricles. A recent detailed histopathologic study of one case by Bauman and Kemper disclosed abnormalities of cell growth in hippocampus and amygdala bilaterally, and in neocerebellum. No consistent biochemical abnormality has been discovered. Electroencephalograms are nonspecific, although temporal lobe discharges are occasionally seen, and up to 30 percent of autistic children eventually manifest epilepsy. The ultimate prognosis depends largely on the child's IQ. Those high-functioning children who develop communicative language by age 5 and have a normal IQ may exhibit certain exceptional talents, as in mathematics, though they remain socially stiff and incompetent. Most autistic children prove to be retarded, and in adult life they retain the same characteristics. There is no effective treatment, though psychotropic medications may have useful benefits in some cases.

SIMPLE MENTAL RETARDATION   Although presented last, this category includes the great number of cases of defective mentality of indeterminate etiology in which neither somatic nor neurologic abnormality is exhibited. The degree of mental impairment tends to be mild (educable) or moderate (trainable). This group of retardates constitutes 25 percent of institutionalized individuals, and of course those who are in institutions represent only the more severely damaged individuals in our society. Their physical appearance is usually not strikingly abnormal, yet many of the aforementioned characteristics of the mentally retarded individual are to be observed. Seizures occur in a significant number, being several times more frequent than in a normal population. Within the limits of their intelligence, the success of these individuals in learning to look after themselves is often determined by how effectively their parents and teachers have inculcated or reinforced good work habits and stable personality traits. The brighter ones can profit to some extent from formal education. Those less well endowed may be trained to care for their personal wants and needs and may profit from special occupational training. Special schools and classes are of great help. Later in life, supervised work situations are possible solutions to their occupational needs.

EPILEPSY

The majority of adult patients with recurrent seizures acquire the tendency toward seizures during childhood. The seizures may represent the sequelae of disease processes which impinged on the brain in the distant past, or they may represent a familial genetic etiology. Seizures are generally much more common in childhood, and most childhood seizures disappear before adulthood. Certain types are peculiar to the earlier periods of life, depending on the occurrence of special diseases in these periods and the level of development of the nervous system. Others are identical in child and adult. The latter are discussed in Chaps. 12 and 342.

REFERENCES

Adams RD: Neurocutaneous diseases, in *Dermatology in General Medicine,* 3d ed, TB Fitzpatrick et al (eds). New York, McGraw-Hill, 1986

Bauman ML, Kemper TL: The brain in infantile autism: A histoanatomic case report. Neurology 34(suppl 1):275, 1984

Cohen MF, Duffner PK: Prognostic indicators in hemiparetic cerebral palsy. Ann Neurol 9:353, 1981

Cooper IS: *Involuntary Movement Disorders.* New York, Hoeber-Harper, 1969

Dobbing J (ed): *Prevention of Spina Bifida and Other Neural Tube Defects.* London, Academic, 1983

Greenberg AD: Atlantoaxial dislocations. Brain 91:655, 1968

Holmes LB et al: *Mental Retardation: An Atlas of Disease with Associated Physical Abnormalities.* New York, Macmillan, 1972

McCusick VA: *Mendelian Inheritance in Man,* 6th ed. Baltimore, Johns Hopkins, 1983

Myers RE: A unitary theory of causation of anoxic and hypoxic brain pathology. Adv Neurol 26:195, 1979

Riccardi VM: Von Recklinghausen neurofibromatosis. N Engl J Med 305:1617, 1981

Ritvo ER et al: Concordance for the syndrome of autism in 40 pairs of afflicted twins. Am J Psychiatry 142:1, Jan 1985

Rosenberg RN: *Neurogenetics: Principles and Practice.* Raven Press, New York, 1986

Salam M, Adams RD: Arnold-Chiari malformation, in *Handbook of Clinical Neurology.* Amsterdam, North-Holland, 1978

Swaiman KF, Wright FS: *The Practice of Pediatric Neurology,* 2d ed., St. Louis, Mosby, 1982, 2 vols

352   DISEASES OF THE CRANIAL NERVES

MAURICE VICTOR / JOSEPH B. MARTIN

The cranial nerves are susceptible to disorders that rarely affect the spinal peripheral nerves, and for this reason deserve to be considered separately. This chapter describes the principal syndromes of disordered function and the diseases that cause them. Cranial nerve disorders of taste and smell, vision and ocular movement, and vertigo and deafness are also discussed in Chaps. 13, 14, and 19.

OLFACTORY NERVE

SYNDROME OF ANOSMIA AND AGEUSIA AND RELATED DISORDERS OF OLFACTION (See Chap. 19)

OPTIC NERVE

SYNDROME OF TRANSIENT MONOCULAR BLINDNESS (AMAUROSIS FUGAX) (See also Chap. 343)

Definition   Amaurosis fugax is the name applied to an attack of transient, painless loss of vision in one eye. Frequently it is recurrent. (The term *amaurosis* refers to blindness from any cause, in distinction to *amblyopia,* which refers to a loss of vision from disease of structures other than the eye itself.)

Clinical manifestations   Amaurosis fugax is a common clinical symptom indicative of transient retinal ischemia, usually associated with ipsilateral internal carotid artery stenosis or to embolism of the retinal arteries. In some cases the basis for the symptom cannot be discerned.

Typically, the episode of blindness evolves swiftly, in a matter of 10 to 15 s, and is described as a shade that falls smoothly and painlessly over the field until the eye is completely blind. Or, a similar obliteration of the visual field may occur from below. The blindness lasts for a few seconds or minutes, sometimes longer, then clears slowly and uniformly, the patient's vision returning in the reverse direction from that in which it was lost. Sometimes there is only a generalized dimness of vision, rather than a complete loss, or only a segment of the visual field may be involved. Many patients who experience amaurosis fugax on the basis of carotid stenosis also have transient attacks of contralateral hemiparesis, but it is uncommon for the eye and ipsilateral cerebral hemisphere to be clinically involved simultaneously. This is presumably due to the fact that showers of microemboli occur and block pial-size hemispheral vessels without causing clinical symptoms or signs. An abnormal EEG immediately after an attack of amaurosis fugax may be found.

Differential diagnosis   The transient visual loss that accompanies migraine is of a different type. Often it begins with unformed flashes of light (photopsia) or dazzling zigzag lines (fortification spectra or terchopsia), which move across the visual field for several minutes, leaving scotomatous or hemianopic defects. The patient with migraine may complain of blindness in one eye, but examination usually shows the defects to be bilateral and homonymous, i.e., they occupy corresponding halves of both visual fields. The latter symptoms point to an origin in the visual cortex of one occipital lobe. In so-called vertebrobasilar migraine, in which the neurologic symptoms are referable to the territory of the basilar artery, the transient visual disturbances may occupy the whole of both visual fields.

Treatment   Amaurosis fugax is most commonly a manifestation of ipsilateral internal carotid artery disease. Attention should be directed to carotid bruits, and noninvasive tests for carotid blood flow and lumen diameter should be carried out in every case. The decision of when to proceed to angiography is discussed in Chap. 343. Definitive treatment is dependent upon the results of these investigations. In the absence of carotid disease investigations should be directed toward excluding another source of emboli (cardiac or aorta). Amaurosis fugax may herald occlusion of the central retinal artery or anterior ischemic optic neuropathy due to giant cell arteritis or to nonarteritic (arteriosclerotic) disease. The sedimentation rate is usually elevated in giant cell arteritis (Chap. 269).

SYNDROME OF RETROBULBAR OPTIC NEUROPATHY OR NEURITIS   **Definition**   This syndrome is characterized by the rapid development over hours or days of impaired vision in one or both eyes. In the latter case the eyes may be affected either simultaneously or sequentially. The visual loss in idiopathic cases (i.e., when other causes of optic nerve lesions have been ruled out) is the result of acute demyelination of optic nerve fibers.

Clinical manifestations   The most frequent setting is one in which a child, adolescent, or young adult notes a rapid diminution of vision in one eye (as though a veil or haze covered every object seen). The condition may progress to severe loss of vision (<20/100) within a few days but complete blindness is rare. The optic disc and retina may appear normal, but in some patients the optic disc is hyperemic and elevated with blurring of the disc margins (papillitis). Peripapillary hemorrhages are infrequently seen, and the veins are not engorged. *Papillitis* is distinguished from *papilledema* due to increased intracranial pressure by the acute and often marked reduction of visual acuity that accompanies the former. In retrobulbar neuropathy, characterized by a normal disc on initial examination, there is often pain on movement of the eye or on pressure on the globe. After a few days or weeks the other eye may become similarly involved, with loss, typically, of central vision but with some preservation of peripheral vision. The pupillary light reflex is impaired. In a high percentage of patients, no cause can be found, and after days or weeks there is spontaneous recovery of vision. In the majority of patients the visual acuity returns to normal or near normal within months of the attack. Sometimes a small central scotoma persists. The optic disc later becomes slightly pale due to atrophy, often most prominent in the temporal region. The CSF may be normal or may contain from 10 to 20 lymphocytes, and the protein content, particularly the gamma globulin portion, may be increased. Oligoclonal bands are found in some patients.

A considerable number of such patients (15 to 40 percent) will develop other symptoms and signs consistent with multiple sclerosis within 10 to 15 years, and even more will do so if the patients are observed for longer periods (see Chap. 348). Less is known about children with retrobulbar neuropathy, but the prognosis for them is considerably better than that for adults. Multiple sclerosis is the most common cause of a *unilateral retrobulbar neuritis*. Bilateral optic neuritis may occur a few days or weeks in advance of an attack of transverse myelitis. This combination is called neuromyelitis optica or Devic's disease (Chap. 348). Other causes of unilateral optic neuropathy include postinfectious or disseminated encephalomyelitis, posterior uveitis (sometimes with reticulum cell sarcoma), vascular lesions of the optic nerve, tumors (glioma of optic nerve, von Recklinghausen's neurofibromatosis, meningioma, metastatic carcinoma), and fungus infections.

Differential diagnosis   *Anterior ischemic optic neuropathy (AION)* is a condition caused by interruption of blood supply to the optic nerve secondary to atherosclerotic or inflammatory disease of the ophthalmic artery or its branches. It presents clinically as acute, painless, visual loss in one eye, usually accompanied by an altitudinal visual field defect. In severe cases visual loss is complete and permanent. The fundus shows a pale swollen optic disc surrounded by splinter-shaped peripapillary hemorrhages. Occasionally only a section of the disc is pale and swollen. The macula and the retina are normal (see Fig. A4-6).

Investigations are directed toward excluding temporal arteritis (see Chap. 269). Rarely, microemboli can cause occlusion of the posterior ciliary arteries and AION; for example, following open heart or coronary artery bypass surgery.

Central retinal artery occlusion (CRAO) also presents with sudden blindness. In this entity the optic disc initially appears normal. The retina is infarcted and appears pale with accentuation of the macular cherry-red spot (see Fig. A4-2).

Treatment   Acute optic neuropathy due to demyelination usually resolves without specific treatment. Severe visual loss is commonly treated with prednisone 40 to 80 mg daily in divided doses for 7 to 10 days with gradual tapering over a few days. Some physicians recommend ACTH treatment. Neither form of treatment has been proven to be more beneficial than no treatment.

TOXIC-NUTRITIONAL OPTIC NEUROPATHY   Simultaneous impairment of vision in the two eyes, with central or centrocecal scotomas, occurring over a period of days or weeks, is usually due to a toxic or nutritional disorder rather than to a demyelinative process (see Chap. 349). Impairment of vision due to *methyl alcohol intoxication* is abrupt in onset and is characterized by large symmetric central scotomas, as well as by symptoms of systemic disease and acidosis (see Chap. 171). Here the lesion is in the optic nerve and the outer segments of the retina, the rods, and cones. Treatment is directed mainly to correction of the acidosis. Other drugs with proven but less devastating toxic effects on the optic nerve include chloramphenicol, ethambutol, isoniazid, streptomycin, sulfonamides, digitalis, ergot, disulfiram, and heavy metals.

Degenerative diseases may affect the retina or the optic nerves, taking the form of optic atrophy. There are several types of hereditary

optic atrophy, the most frequent being the Leber type, which is sex-linked, occurring in males (see Chap. 350). An autosomal dominant form of congenital or early infantile optic atrophy and optic atrophy with diabetes mellitus and deafness are described. Senile macular degeneration and various forms of retinitis pigmentosa may cause visual loss (see Chap. 13).

SYNDROME OF BITEMPORAL HEMIANOPSIA   This type of visual disorder is usually related to suprasellar extension of a pituitary adenoma (often with an enlarged sella), but may also be due to a craniopharyngioma, saccular aneurysm of the circle of Willis, meningioma of the tuberculum sellae (normal sella or thickened tuberculum by radiography), and rarely sarcoidosis, metastatic carcinoma, and Hand-Schüller-Christian disease (see Chap. 321). The lesion involves the decussating nasal fibers from each retina.

SYNDROMES OF HOMONYMOUS HEMIANOPSIA (See Chap. 13)

SYNDROME OF VISUAL AGNOSIA (See Chap. 24)

OCULOMOTOR, TROCHLEAR, AND ABDUCENS NERVES

SYNDROME OF OPHTHALMOPLEGIA   The acute development of a sixth or third nerve palsy on one side is a relatively common occurrence in the adult, the former being about twice as common as the latter. An isolated sixth nerve palsy frequently proves to be due to diabetes mellitus, neoplasm, or increased intracranial pressure. Involvement of the third, fourth, and sixth cranial nerves may occur with lesions affecting their nuclei or fibers of exit in the pons or mesencephalon, or in the course of the nerves through the subarachnoid space, the cavernous sinus, and the superior orbital fissure. Different syndromes occur with lesions at each of these sites (Table 352-1). Pontine glioma in children and metastatic tumor from the nasopharynx in adults may cause isolated sixth nerve lesions. Tumor at the base of the brain (primary, metastatic, meningeal carcinomatosis) is an important cause of isolated third nerve palsies. Other causes of sixth and third nerve palsies are trauma, ischemic infarction of nerve, and aneurysms of the circle of Willis. An acute palsy of the fourth nerve is relatively uncommon; usually it is due to trauma. In all cases of isolated ocular motor paralysis, exophthalmic ophthalmoplegia (Graves' disease) and myasthenia gravis must be ruled out. In third nerve lesions due to compression by aneurysm, tumor, or temporal lobe herniation, enlargement of the pupil is an early sign because of the peripheral location of the pupilloconstrictor fibers. Infarction of the third nerve, associated with pain in or around the eye, as occurs in diabetes mellitus or, rarely, in cranial arteritis, usually spares the pupil. In cases of undetermined cause, continued observation is essential to confirm recovery or to prompt reinvestigation.

Rarely, children or adults may have one or more attacks of ocular palsy in conjunction with an otherwise typical migraine (*migrainous ophthalmoplegia*). The muscles innervated by the oculomotor nerve, less often by the abducens nerve, are affected. Presumably, intense vascular spasm affecting the nutrient artery to the nerve causes transitory ischemia. Arteriograms, done after the onset of the palsy, usually reveal no abnormality. Recovery is the rule.

Combined unilateral ocular palsies of painful type (Tolosa-Hunt syndrome) is most often indicative of parasellar granuloma. An acute onset of unilateral or bilateral ophthalmoplegia and drowsiness occurs in pituitary apoplexy. Visual loss and signs of chiasmal compression may be associated. The slow development of a complete ophthalmoplegia on one side is most often due to an enlarging aneurysm (it may also be of acute onset), tumor, or inflammatory process in the cavernous sinus or at the superior orbital foramen. This is known as the *syndrome of Foix* (see Table 352-1). Such a syndrome frequently presents first with affection of the sixth nerve.

Gaze palsies or mixed ophthalmoplegia and gaze palsies, due usually to vascular, demyelinative, or neoplastic processes in the brainstem, are discussed in Chap. 13.

TRIGEMINAL NERVE

The trigeminal nerve supplies sensation to the skin of the face and half of the vertex of the skull and motor innervation to the masseter and pterygoid masticatory muscles.

SYNDROME OF PAROXYSMAL FACIAL PAIN (TRIGEMINAL NEURALGIA, TIC DOULOUREUX)

Definition The most striking disorder of the trigeminal nerve is tic douloureux, a condition consisting of excruciating paroxysms of pain in the lips, gums, cheek, or chin, and, very rarely, in the distribution of the ophthalmic division of the fifth nerve. The disorder occurs almost exclusively in middle-aged and elderly persons. The pain seldom lasts more than a few seconds or a minute or two but may be so intense that the patient winces, hence the term *tic*. The paroxysms recur frequently, both day and night, for several weeks at a time. Another characteristic feature is the initiation of pain by obvious stimuli applied to certain areas on the face, lips, or tongue (the so-called trigger zones) or by movement of these parts. Sensory loss cannot be demonstrated. In studying the relations between stimuli applied to the trigger zone and the paroxysm of pain, it is found that the adequate stimulus for precipitating an attack is a tactile one and possibly tickle, rather than a noxious or thermal stimulus. Usually a spatial and temporal summation of impulses is necessary to trigger an attack, which is followed by a refractory period of up to 2 or 3 min.

The diagnosis of this disorder rests upon these strict clinical criteria, and the condition must be distinguished from other forms of facial and cephalic neuralgia and pain arising from diseases of the jaw, teeth, or sinuses. Tic douloureux is usually without assignable cause; occasionally it is a manifestation of multiple sclerosis when it appears in younger adults and may be bilateral. Very rarely it may occur with herpes zoster or a tumor. To a degree that remains

uncertain and controversial, pain of tic douloureux may be caused by a redundant or torturous artery in the posterior fossa, causing an irritative lesion of the nerve or its root. Usually, however, space-occupying lesions, such as aneurysms, neurofibromas, or meningiomas affecting the nerve, produce a loss of sensation (trigeminal neuropathy).

Treatment The initial treatment of tic douloureux is pharmacologic. Carbamazepine is the drug of choice and is effective initially in 75 percent of patients. Unfortunately, up to one-third cannot tolerate the drug in the doses required to alleviate pain. Carbamazepine should be started gradually, 100 mg with food, as a single dose, and increased to 200 mg qid. Doses greater than 1200 to 1600 mg provide no additional benefit.

If drug treatment fails, surgical therapy should be offered. The two primary operations are gangliolysis and suboccipital craniectomy with decompression of the trigeminal nerve. Gangliolysis is a minor surgical procedure performed by transcutaneous injection, usually under local anesthesia. Glycerol or alcohol injection or radiofrequency lesions have been widely used. Glycerol injections have proved beneficial in many patients, but onset of effect is slow and pain may recur. Radiofrequency lesions abolish pain in 80 percent of cases for 1 year and 60 percent for 5 years. The procedure results in partial numbness of the face and carries a risk of corneal denervation with secondary keratitis when used for first division trigeminal neuralgia.

Suboccipital craniectomy is a major procedure requiring about 1 week of hospitalization. It has an 80 percent efficacy but is accompanied by a 5 percent major complication rate. Not all patients operated upon have a demonstrated vascular or other compression lesion of the trigeminal nerve. The most troublesome complication of all surgical treatments is the development of anesthesia dolorosa or denervation hypersensitivity. This condition responds poorly to treatment. Tricyclic antidepressants or phenothiazines are usually given with only partial success in alleviating the discomfort.

TRIGEMINAL NEUROPATHY A variety of rare causes of trigeminal neuropathy in addition to those mentioned above may be found. Most present with sensory loss on the face or with weakness of the jaw muscles. Deviation of the jaw on opening indicates weakness of the pterygoids of the side to which the jaw deviates. Tumors of the middle cranial fossa (meningiomas), of the trigeminal nerve (schwannomas), or of the base of the skull (metastatic) may cause a combination of motor and sensory signs. Lesions in the cavernous sinus can affect the first and second divisions of the trigeminal nerve, and lesions of the superior orbital fissure can affect the ophthalmic first division. The accompanying corneal anesthesia increases the risk of ulceration (neurokeratitis).

Anesthesia and analgesia of the face have been reported after treatment with stilbamidine (formerly used in the treatment of kala azar and multiple myeloma). Pain and itching may occur during recovery. Rarely, an idiopathic form of trigeminal neuropathy is observed. It is characterized by feelings of numbness and paresthesias, sometimes bilaterally, and loss of sensation but without weakness of the jaw. Recovery is the rule, but the symptoms may be troublesome for many months, or even years. Leprosy may involve the trigeminal nerves.

Tonic spasm of the masticatory muscles, known as *trismus*, is symptomatic of tetanus. It may also occur as an idiosyncratic reaction in patients treated with phenothiazine drugs; lesser degrees may be associated with disease of the pharynx, temporomaxillary joint, teeth, and gums.

FACIAL NERVE

SYNDROMES OF FACIAL PALSY AND FACIAL SPASM The seventh cranial nerve supplies all the muscles concerned with facial expression. The sensory component is small (the nervus intermedius of Wrisberg); it conveys taste sensation from the anterior two-thirds of the tongue and probably cutaneous impulses from the anterior

TABLE 352-1 Cranial nerve syndromes

Site	Cranial nerves involved	Eponymic syndrome	Usual cause
Sphenoid fissure (superior orbital)	III, IV, first division V, VI	Foix	Invasive tumors of sphenoid bone, aneurysms
Lateral wall of cavernous sinus	III, IV, first division V, VI, often with proptosis	Foix Tolosa-Hunt	Aneurysms or thrombosis of cavernous sinus, invasive tumors from sinuses and sella turcica, sometimes benign granuloma responsive to steroids
Retrosphenoid space	II, III, IV, V, VI	Jacod	Large tumors of middle cranial fossa
Apex of petrous bone	V, VI	Gradenigo	Petrositis, tumors of petrous bone
Internal auditory meatus	VII, VIII		Tumors of petrous bone (dermoids, etc.), infectious processes, acoustic neuroma
Pontocerebellar angle	V, VII, VIII, and sometimes IX		Acoustic neuroma, meningioma
Jugular foramen	IX, X, XI	Vernet	Tumors and aneurysms
Posterior latero-condylar space	IX, X, XI, XII	Collet-Sicard	Tumors of parotid gland, carotid body, and metastatic tumor
Posterior retro-parotid space	IX, X, XI, XII and Horner syndrome	Villaret Mackenzie Tapia	Tumors of parotid gland, carotid body, metastatic tumor, lymph node tumors, tuberculous adenitis

wall of the external auditory canal. The motor nucleus of the seventh nerve lies anterior and lateral to the abducens nucleus. After leaving the pons the seventh nerve enters the internal auditory meatus with the acoustic nerve. The nerve continues its course through the middle ear to exit from the skull via the stylomastoid foramen. It then passes through the parotid gland and subdivides to supply the facial muscles.

A complete interruption of the facial nerve at the stylomastoid foramen paralyzes all muscles of facial expression. The corner of the mouth droops, the creases and skin folds are effaced, the forehead is unfurrowed, and the eyelids will not close. Upon attempted closure of the lids, the eye on the paralyzed side is seen to roll upward (Bell's phenomenon). The lower lid sags also, and the punctum falls away from the conjunctiva, permitting tears to spill over the cheek. Food collects between the teeth and lips, and saliva may dribble from the corner of the mouth. The patient complains of a heaviness or numbness in the face, but no sensory loss is demonstrable and taste is intact.

If the lesion is in the middle ear portion, taste is lost over the anterior two-thirds of the tongue on the same side. If the nerve to the stapedius is interrupted, there is hyperacusis (painful sensitivity to loud sounds). Lesions in the internal auditory meatus may also affect the adjacent auditory and vestibular nerves, causing deafness, tinnitus, or dizziness. Intrapontine lesions that paralyze the face usually affect the abducens nucleus and often the corticospinal and sensory tracts.

If the peripheral facial paralysis has existed for some time and recovery of motor function has begun but is incomplete, a kind of contracture (actually a continuous diffuse contraction) of facial muscles may appear (hemifacial spasm). The palpebral fissure becomes narrowed and the nasolabial fold deepens. With the passage of time, the face and even the tip of the nose become pulled to the unaffected side. Attempts to move one group of facial muscles result in contraction of all of them (associated movements, or *synkinesis*). Facial spasms may develop and persist indefinitely, being initiated by every facial movement (see below). Anomalous regeneration of the seventh nerve fibers may result in other curious disorders. If fibers originally connected with the orbicularis oculi come to innervate the orbicularis oris, closure of the lids may cause a retraction of the mouth; or if fibers originally connected with muscles of the face later innervate the lacrimal gland, anomalous tearing (crocodile tears) may occur with any activity of the facial muscles, such as eating. Yet another unusual facial synkinesia is one in which jaw opening causes a closure of the eyelids on the side of the facial palsy (jaw-winking).

BELL'S PALSY   Definition   The most common form of facial paralysis is idiopathic, i.e., *Bell's palsy*. The incidence rate of this disorder is about 23 per 100,000 annually, or about 1 in 60 or 70 persons in a lifetime. The pathogenesis of the paralysis is unknown. The few autopsied cases of this disease have shown only nondescript changes in the facial nerve and not inflammatory changes, as is commonly presumed.

Clinical manifestations   The onset of Bell's palsy is fairly abrupt, maximum weakness being attained by 48 h as a general rule. Pain behind the ear may precede the paralysis for a day or two. Occasionally taste sensation is lost, and hyperacusis may be present. In some cases there is mild CSF pleocytosis. Fully 80 percent of patients recover within a few weeks or months. Electromyographic evidence of denervation after 10 days indicates that there has been axonal degeneration and that there will be a long delay before regeneration occurs, and that it may be incomplete. Electromyography may be of value in distinguishing a temporary conduction defect from a pathologic interruption in the continuity of nerve fibers. The presence of incomplete paralysis in the first week is the most favorable prognostic sign.

Treatment   Protection of the eye during sleep, massage of the weakened muscles, and a splint to prevent drooping of the lower part of the face are the measures generally employed in the management of such cases. A course of prednisone beginning with 60 to 80 mg daily during the first 5 days and then tapered over the next 5 days

may be beneficial. Unroofing of the facial nerve in the facial canal has been suggested, but there is no evidence that this measure is helpful, and it may be harmful.

Differential diagnosis   There are many other causes of facial palsy. Tumors which invade the temporal bone (carotid body, cholesteatoma, dermoid) may produce a facial palsy, but the onset is insidious and the course progressive. The *Ramsay Hunt syndrome*, presumably due to herpes zoster of the geniculate ganglion, consists of a severe facial palsy associated with a vesicular eruption in the pharynx, external auditory canal, and other parts of the cranial integument; often the eighth cranial nerve is affected as well. Acoustic neuromas frequently involve the facial nerve by local compression (see Chap. 345). Infarcts and tumors are the common pontine lesions which may interrupt the facial nerve fibers. Bilateral facial paralysis (facial diplegia) occurs in acute inflammatory polyradiculoneuritis (Guillain-Barré disease) and in a variety of sarcoidosis known as *uveoparotid fever (Heerfordt's syndrome)*. The *Melkersson-Rosenthal syndrome* consists of a rarely encountered triad of recurrent facial paralysis, recurrent—and eventually permanent—facial (particularly labial) edema, and less constantly, plication of the tongue. Many causes of this syndrome have been suggested, but none has been established. Leprosy frequently involves the facial nerve.

A puzzling disorder is the *facial hemiatrophy of Romberg*. It occurs mainly in females and is characterized by a disappearance of fat in the dermal and subcutaneous tissues on one side of the face. It usually begins in adolescence or early adult years and is slowly progressive. In its advanced form the face is gaunt and the skin is thin, wrinkled, and rather brown. The facial hair may turn white and fall out, and the sebaceous glands become atrophic. The muscles and bones are not involved as a rule. Sometimes the atrophy becomes bilateral. The condition is a form of lipodystrophy, and the localization within a dermatome suggests a disorder of some neural trophic factor of unknown nature. The treatment is transplantation of skin and subcutaneous fat by a plastic surgeon.

The facial muscles on one side may be affected by irregular clonic contractions of varying degree (*hemifacial spasm*). This condition may represent a transient or permanent sequela to a Bell's palsy but may also appear de novo, as a benign phenomenon in adults. Hemifacial spasm may also be due to an irritative lesion of the facial nerve (e.g., an acoustic neuroma, an aberrant artery which compresses the nerve and is relieved by surgery, or a basilar artery aneurysm). However, in the most common form of hemifacial spasm, the cause and pathology are unknown. A fine fibrillary activity of the facial muscles (*facial myokymia*) may be caused by a plaque of multiple sclerosis. An involuntary recurrent spasm of both eyelids (*blepharospasm*) may occur in elderly persons as an isolated phenomenon or with varying degrees of spasm of the facial muscles. Relaxant and sedative drugs are of little help, although in many patients this disorder subsides spontaneously. In very severe and persistent cases, an effective treatment has been differential facial nerve section of selected branches of the nerve or nerve decompression (from vessels) intracranially. More recently, cases have been successfully treated by local injection of botulinum toxin into the eyelids.

Abnormalities of taste are discussed in Chap. 19.

All these forms of nuclear or peripheral facial palsy must be distinguished from the supranuclear type. In the latter the frontalis and orbicularis oculi muscles are involved less than those of the lower part of the face, since the upper facial muscles are innervated by corticobulbar pathways from both motor cortices, whereas the lower facial muscles are innervated only by the opposite hemisphere. In supranuclear lesions there may be a dissociation of emotional and voluntary facial movements, and often some degree of paralysis of the arm and leg or an aphasia (in dominant hemisphere lesions) is conjoined.

VESTIBULAR NERVE

The eighth cranial nerve has two components, vestibular and auditory. Symptoms and signs of involvement of the vestibular portion are discussed in Chap. 14 and in this section. The auditory nerve and its disorders are discussed in Chap. 19.

SYNDROME OF BENIGN RECURRENT VERTIGO Ménière's syndrome DEFINITION AND CLINICAL MANIFESTATIONS Ménière's disease, or Ménière's syndrome, is the name applied to recurrent vertigo accompanied by tinnitus and deafness. The latter symptoms may be absent during the initial attack(s) of vertigo, but they invariably appear as the disease progresses and are increased in severity during an acute attack. With milder forms of the syndrome the patient may complain more of head discomfort, slight instability, and difficulty in concentration than of vertigo and may be considered to be anxious or depressed. Provided that deafness is not complete, the recruitment phenomenon can be demonstrated (see Chap. 19).

Ménière's disease has its onset most frequently in the fifth decade of life, though younger adults and the elderly are not spared. The pathologic changes are said to consist of a dilatation of the endolymphatic system which leads to a degeneration of the delicate vestibular and cochlear hair cells. The relation of these pathologic changes to the paroxysmal disorder of labyrinthine function is unknown.

TREATMENT During an acute attack, rest in bed is the most effective treatment, since the patient can usually find a position in which vertigo is minimal. Dimenhydrinate, cyclizine, or meclizine in doses of 25 to 50 mg tid is useful in the more protracted cases. A low-salt diet is still used in treatment, but its value is difficult to judge. Mild sedative drugs may help the anxious patient between attacks. Usually the deafness is unilateral and progressive, and when it is complete, the vertiginous attacks cease. However, the course is variable, and if the attacks persist in a severe manner, permanent relief can be obtained by surgical destruction of the labyrinth or section of the vestibular portion of the eighth nerve intracranially.

Benign positional vertigo Another disorder of labyrinthine function is characterized by the occurrence of paroxysmal vertigo and nystagmus with the assumption of certain critical positions of the head. This is the positional vertigo of Bárány, of the so-called benign paroxysmal type (see Chap. 14). In refractory cases, in which attacks continue, vestibular exercises, as outlined by Lee, may be beneficial.

Differential diagnosis of vertigo There are many other causes of acute vertigo, such as purulent labyrinthitis complicating meningitis, serous labyrinthitis due to infection of the middle ear, "toxic labyrinthitis" due to drug intoxication (e.g., with alcohol, quinine, streptomycin, gentamicin, and other antibiotics), motion sickness, trauma, and hemorrhage into the internal ear. In these instances the attacks of vertigo tend to last longer than in the recurrent form, but in other respects the symptoms are similar. Streptomycin or gentamicin may damage the fine hair cells of the vestibular end organs and cause a permanent disorder of equilibrium (as well as hearing), especially in older patients.

There has been described a dramatic clinical syndrome, characterized by the abrupt onset of severe vertigo, nausea, and vomiting, without tinnitus or hearing loss. The vertigo persists for several days or weeks, and labyrinthine function is permanently ablated on one side. Occlusion of the labyrinthine division of the internal auditory artery would logically explain this syndrome, but pathologic or angiographic confirmation of this hypothesis has so far not been obtained.

Vertigo of vestibular nerve origin may occur with diseases that involve the nerve in the petrous bone or the cerebellopontine angle. Except that it is less severe and is less frequently paroxysmal, it has many of the characteristics of labyrinthine vertigo. The adjacent auditory division of the eighth cranial nerve may also be affected, which explains the frequent association of vertigo with tinnitus and deafness. The function of the eighth cranial nerve may be disturbed by tumors of the lateral recess (especially acoustic neuroma), less frequently by meningeal inflammation in this region and rarely, by an abnormal vessel which compresses the nerve.

Vestibular neuronitis and *benign recurrent vertigo* are the names that have been applied to a clinical syndrome which occurs mainly in middle-aged and young adults (sometimes in children) and is characterized by the abrupt onset of vertigo, nausea, and vomiting, without impairment of hearing. The attacks are brief and leave the patient for some days with a mild positional vertigo. They may occur only once or recur in varying degrees of severity. The cause is unknown. The medical treatment is the same as for Ménière's disease.

A particular variety of paroxysmal vertigo affects children. The attacks occur in a setting of good health and are of sudden onset and brief duration. Pallor, sweating, and immobility are prominent manifestations, and occasionally vomiting and nystagmus occur. No relation to posture or movement of the head has been observed. The attacks are recurrent but tend to cease spontaneously after a period of several months or years. The outstanding abnormal finding is demonstrated by caloric testing, which shows impairment or loss of vestibular function, bilateral or unilateral, frequently persisting after the attacks have ceased; cochlear function is unimpaired, however. The pathologic basis of this disorder has not been determined.

Cogan has described a peculiar syndrome in young adults, in which an interstitial keratitis is associated with vertigo, tinnitus, nystagmus, and rapidly progressive deafness. The prognosis for life and vision is good, but the deafness is usually permanent. The cause or pathogenesis of this disease is not understood, although several patients have later developed aortitis and a vasculitis that resembles periarteritis nodosa.

GLOSSOPHARYNGEAL NERVE

SYNDROME OF GLOSSOPHARYNGEAL NEURALGIA Glossopharyngeal neuralgia resembles trigeminal neuralgia in many respects. The pain is intense and paroxysmal; it originates in the throat, approximately in the tonsillar fossa. In some cases the pain is localized in the ear or may radiate from the throat to the ear, because of implication of the tympanic branch of the glossopharyngeal nerve (Jacobson's nerve). Spasms of pain may be initiated by swallowing. There is no demonstrable sensory or motor deficit. Cardiac symptoms of bradycardia with hypotension are reported. A trial of carbamazepine or phenytoin is the recommended therapy, but if this is unsuccessful, division of the glossopharyngeal nerve near the medulla is the definitive treatment.

Very rarely, herpes zoster may involve the glossopharyngeal nerve. Glossopharyngeal neuropathy in conjunction with vagus and accessory nerve palsies may occur due to a tumor or aneurysm in the posterior fossa or in the jugular foramen. Hoarseness due to vocal cord paralysis, some difficulty in swallowing, deviation of the soft palate to the intact side, anesthesia of the posterior wall of the pharynx, and weakness of the upper part of the trapezius and sternocleidomastoid muscles make up the syndrome (see Table 352-1, jugular foramen syndrome).

VAGUS NERVE

SYNDROME OF DYSPHAGIA AND DYSPHONIA Complete interruption of the intracranial portion of one vagus nerve results in a characteristic paralysis. The soft palate droops ipsilaterally and does not rise in phonation. There is loss of the gag reflex on the affected side, as well as the "curtain movement" of the lateral wall of the pharynx, whereby the faucial pillars move medially as the palate rises in saying "ah." The voice is hoarse, slightly nasal, and the vocal cord lies immobile in the cadaveric position, i.e., midway between abduction and adduction. There may also be a loss of sensibility at the external auditory meatus and back of the pinna. Usually no change in visceral function can be demonstrated.

Complete interruption of both vagi is said to be incompatible with life, and this is probably true if the nuclei are involved in the medulla by poliomyelitis or some other disease. However, in the cervical region, both vagi have been blocked with procaine (Novocain) for the treatment of intractable asthma, without mishap. The pharyngeal branches of both vagi may be affected in diphtheria; the voice has a nasal quality, and regurgitation of liquids through the nose occurs during the act of swallowing.

The vagus nerve may be implicated at the meningeal level by neoplastic and infectious processes and within the medulla by tumors and vascular lesions, e.g., the lateral medullary syndrome of Wallenberg, and by motor neuron disease. This nerve may be involved by the inflammatory lesion of herpes zoster. Polymyositis and dermatomyositis, which cause hoarseness and dysphagia by direct involvement of laryngeal and pharyngeal muscles, may be confused with diseases of the vagus nerves. Also dysphagia is a symptom in some patients with myotonic dystrophy (see Chap. 32 for discussion of nonneurologic forms of dysphagia).

The recurrent laryngeal nerves, especially the left, are most often damaged as a result of intrathoracic disease. Aneurysm of the aortic arch, an enlarged left atrium, and tumors of the mediastinum and bronchi are much more frequent causes of an isolated vocal cord palsy than are intracranial disorders.

When confronted with a case of laryngeal palsy, the physician must attempt to determine the site of the lesion. If it is intramedullary, there are usually other signs, such as ipsilateral cerebellar dysfunction, loss of pain and temperature sensation over the ipsilateral face and contralateral arm and leg, and an ipsilateral Horner's syndrome. If the lesion is extramedullary, the glossopharyngeal and spinal accessory nerves are frequently involved (see discussion of the jugular foramen syndrome above). If it is extracranial in the posterior laterocondylar or retroparotid space, there may be a combination of ninth, tenth, eleventh, and twelfth cranial nerve palsies and a Horner's syndrome. Combinations of these lower cranial nerve palsies have a variety of eponymic designations, listed in Table 352-1. If there is no sensory loss over the palate and pharynx and no palatal weakness or dysphagia, the lesion is below the origin of the pharyngeal branches, which leave the vagus nerve high in the cervical region; the usual site of disease is then the mediastinum.

HYPOGLOSSAL NERVE

The twelfth cranial nerve supplies the ipsilateral muscles of the tongue. Lesions affecting the motor nucleus may occur in the brainstem (tumor, poliomyelitis, or motor neuron disease) during the course of the nerve in the posterior fossa, or in the hypoglossal canal. Isolated lesions of unknown cause can occur. Atrophy and fasciculation of the tongue develop weeks to months after interruption of the nerve.

MULTIPLE CRANIAL NERVE PALSIES

Several cranial nerves may be affected by the same disease process. In this situation, the main clinical problem is to determine whether the lesion lies within the brainstem or outside of it. Lesions that lie on the surface of the brainstem are featured by involvement of adjacent cranial nerves (often occurring in succession) and late and rather slight involvement of the long sensory and motor pathways and segmental structures lying within the brainstem. The opposite is true of intramedullary, intrapontine, and intramesencephalic lesions. The extramedullary lesion is more likely to cause bone erosion or enlargement of the foramens of exit of cranial nerves. The intramedullary lesion involving cranial nerves often produces a crossed sensory or motor paralysis (cranial nerve signs on one side of the body and tract signs on the opposite side).

Involvement of multiple cranial nerves outside the brainstem is frequently the result of trauma (sudden onset), localized infections such as herpes zoster (acute onset), granulomatous disease such as Wegener's granulomatosis (subacute onset), Behçet's disease, or tumors and enlarging saccular aneurysms (chronic development). Of the tumors, neurofibromas, meningiomas, chordomas, cholesteato-

mas, carcinomas, and sarcomas have all been observed to implicate a succession of lower cranial nerves. Owing to their anatomic relationships, the multiple cranial nerve palsies form a number of distinctive syndromes, listed in Table 352-1. Sarcoidosis has been found to be the cause of some cases of multiple cranial neuropathy, and chronic glandular tuberculosis (scrofula) the cause of a few others. Malignant granuloma of the nasopharynx may also affect mutilple cranial nerves, as do nasopharyngeal tumors, platybasia, and basilar invagination of the skull, and the Arnold-Chiari malformation that becomes evident in adult life. A purely motor disorder without atrophy always raises the question of myasthenia gravis (see Chap. 358). Guillain-Barré syndrome commonly affects the facial nerves bilaterally (facial diplegia). In the Miller Fisher variant of the Guillain-Barré syndrome oculomotor paresis occurs with ataxia and areflexia in the limbs. Wernicke's encephalopathy can cause a severe ophthalmoplegia combined with brainstem signs (see Chap. 349).

A benign idiopathic form of multiple cranial nerve involvement on one or both sides of the face is occasionally seen. The disease may recur over a period of years with variable degrees of recovery between attacks. The condition is called *polyneuritis cranialis multiplex*.

REFERENCES

ADAMS RD, VICTOR M: *Principles of Neurology*, 3d ed. New York, McGraw-Hill, 1985
ALEXANDER GE, MOSES H: Carbamazepine for hemifacial spasm. Neurology 32:286, 1982
BRODAL A: The cranial nerves, in *Neurological Anatomy in Relation to Clinical Medicine*, 3d ed. New York, Oxford, 1980, chap 7, pp 448–577
BROWNSTONE PK et al: Bilateral superior laryngeal neuralgia. Arch Neurol 37:525, 1980
COGAN DG: *Neurology of the Ocular Muscles*, 2d ed. Springfield, Ill, Charles C Thomas, 1956
————: *Neurology of the Visual System*. Springfield, Ill, Charles C Thomas, 1966
DURELLI L et al: The Melkersson-Rosenthal syndrome: A case with increased CNS IgG synthesis. Ann Neurol 18:623, 1985
EISEN A, BERTRAND G: Isolated accessory nerve palsy of spontaneous origin: A clinical and electromyographic study. Arch Neurol 27:496, 1972
GLASER JS: Heredofamilial disorders of the optic nerve, in *Genetic and Metabolic Eye Diseases*, MF Goldberg (ed). Boston, Little, Brown, 1974
————: *Neuro-ophthalmology*. Hagerstown, Harper & Row, 1978
GROVES J: Bell's (idiopathic) facial palsy, in *Scientific Foundations of Otolaryngology*, R Hinchcliffe, D Harrison (eds). London, Heinemann, 1976, pp 446–459
HAUSER WA et al: Incidence and prognosis of Bell's palsy in the population of Rochester, Minnesota. Mayo Clin Proc 46:258, 1971
KARNES WE: Diseases of the seventh cranial nerve, in *Peripheral Neuropathy*, 2d ed, PJ Dyck et al (eds). Philadelphia, Saunders, 1984, chap 55, pp 1266–1299
KAYE AH, ADAMS CBT: Hemifacial spasm: A long-term follow-up of patients treated by posterior fossa surgery and nerve wrapping. J Neurol Neurosurg Psychiatry 44:1100, 1981
LIEBOLD JE: Drugs having a toxic effect on the optic nerve. Intern Ophthalmol Clin 11:137, 1970
LOESER J: Trigeminal and glossopharyngeal neuralgia, in *Current Therapy in Neurologic Disease*, RT Johnson (ed). Philadelphia, BC Decker, 1985/1986, pp 86–89
ZEE D: Vertigo, in *Current Therapy in Neurologic Disease*, RT Johnson (ed). Philadelphia, BC Decker 1985/86, pp 8–13

353 DISEASES OF THE SPINAL CORD

ALLAN H. ROPPER / JOSEPH B. MARTIN

Diseases of the spinal cord are frequently devastating, causing permanent and severe neurologic disability. Small lesions can produce quadriplegia, paraplegia, and sensory deficits far beyond the damage they would inflict elsewhere in the nervous system because the spinal cord contains, in a small cross-sectional area, almost the entire motor output and sensory input systems. Many diseases, particularly extrinsic cord compression, are reversible, making acute spinal cord lesions among the most critical of neurologic emergencies.

The spinal cord is organized in a stereotyped fashion, innervating the limbs and trunk segmentally through 31 pairs of spinal nerves, making anatomic diagnosis relatively straightforward. A sensory level, paraplegia, or other typical syndromes usually permit recognition of a spinal cord process. Full assessment of cord disease requires a careful examination supplemented by laboratory tests, including magnetic resonance imaging (MRI), computerized tomography (CT) scanning, often myelography, analysis of cerebrospinal fluid (CSF), and somatosensory evoked responses. Most deficiencies in evaluating patients with signs of spinal cord disease result from cursory physical examination or inadequate x-rays. Computerized tomography and MRI are replacing conventional myelography because of their ease of performance and better resolution; MRI gives particularly valuable information about intrinsic cord structure.

SPINAL COLUMN AND SPINAL CORD ANATOMY RELEVANT TO CLINICAL SIGNS The spinal cord is organized in a uniform somatotopic fashion throughout its length giving rise to easily identifiable syndromes (see Chaps. 3, 15, and 18). The longitudinal location of lesions is established by the uppermost level of sensory and motor dysfunction. However, the relationship between the vertebral bodies of the spinal column (or their surface markers, the vertebral spines) and the cord segments that underline them complicates anatomic interpretation of signs of spinal cord diseases. Spinal cord syndromes are described according to the spinal cord segment affected rather than the surrounding vertebrae. During embryologic development the growth of the cord lags behind that of the spinal column, so that the cord ends behind the first lumbar vertebral body and nerve roots must take an increasingly oblique downward course to exit near their targets in the limbs or viscera. A useful rule is that the cervical roots (except C8) exit from neural foramina above their respective vertebral bodies, while thoracic and lumbar roots exit below each body. The upper cervical cord segments lie behind the same numbered vertebral body, whereas the lower cervical segments are located one above each corresponding vertebral body, the upper thoracic cord two segments higher, and the lower thoracic cord three segments higher. The lumbar and sacral cord segments, the latter forming the conus medullaris, are located behind the ninth thoracic to first lumbar vertebrae. In judging encroachment by various extrinsic masses, particularly spondylosis, careful measurement of the sagittal diameters of the spinal canal is important; they are normally 16 to 22 mm in the cervical and thoracic spine, 15 to 23 mm from L1 to L3, and 16 to 27 mm below.

CLINICAL SYNDROMES OF SPINAL CORD DISEASE The principal clinical signs of spinal cord damage are loss of sensation below a circumferential horizontal line on the trunk, a "sensory level," and weakness in the extremities innervated by the descending corticospinal fibers. Sensory symptoms, particularly paresthesias, may begin in the feet (or in one foot) and ascend, giving the impression early on of a polyneuropathy before a static sensory level is apparent. Lesions that disrupt descending corticospinal and bulbospinal tracts at a single cord level cause paraplegia or quadriplegia, with the characteristics of increased muscle tone, exaggerated deep tendon reflexes, and Babinski signs. A careful examination often also elicits segmental signs such as a band of altered sensation at the rostral extent of the sensory level (hyperalgesia or hyperpathia), and flaccidity, atrophy, or isolated diminished deep tendon reflexes. The sensory level and segmental signs are approximate indicators of the location of a transverse lesion. Midline back pain is often an accurate localizing sign, particularly in the thoracic region, where interscapular pain may be the first sign of cord compression. Radicular pain that marks the primary site of a more laterally placed spinal lesion may also occur. Pain from lower cord (conus medullaris) lesions is often referred to the low back.

Early in the course of an acute transverse lesion there may be flaccidity of the limbs rather than spasticity, due to so-called spinal shock. This state may last for several weeks and be mistaken for extensive segmental damage, but the reflexes later become increased. Brief clonic or myoclonic limb movements often precede paralysis in acute transverse lesions, particularly those due to infarction. Autonomic dysfunction, mainly urinary retention, is another promi-

nent sign in transverse spinal lesions and should call attention to cord disease if it occurs in conjunction with spasticity or a sensory level.

Much is made of the clinical distinction between intramedullary (within the cord) and extramedullary compressive lesions, but most rules are approximations, not distinguishing dependably one from the other. Features said to favor extramedullary lesions include radicular pain; a Brown-Séquard hemicord syndrome (see below); lower motor neuron signs in one or two segments, often asymmetric; early corticospinal signs; marked sacral sensory loss; and early, prominent CSF abnormalities. On the other hand, poorly localized burning pain, dissociated loss of pain sensation with sparing of joint position sensation, sparing of sensation in the perineal and sacral areas, late and less prominent corticospinal signs, and normal or minimally altered CSF generally favor an intramedullary lesion. "Sacral sparing" refers to the preservation of pinprick and temperature sensation in the sacral dermatomes, usually S3 to S5 with rostral areas up to the sensory level affected. This is usually a dependable sign of intrinsic cord disease damaging the innermost fibers of the spinothalamic tracts while sparing those placed more laterally which subserve sacral sensation. The *Brown-Séquard syndrome* is an eponym given to a hemicord syndrome consisting of ipsilateral mono- or hemiplegia, accompanied by joint position and vibration sense loss, associated with contralateral pain and temperature (spinothalamic) sensory loss. The segmental level for pain and temperature loss is sometimes one or two levels below the anatomic lesion, a result of the course of sensory fibers which ascend and cross to the opposite spinothalamic tract after synapsing in the dorsal horn. Segmental signs, such as radicular pain, muscle atrophy, or decreased tendon reflexes when they occur, are often unilateral.

Lesions limited to, or primarily occurring within, the central portion of the cord preferentially damage gray matter neurons and segmental tracts crossing at that level. Traumatic contusion, developmental syringomyelia, tumors, and vascular lesions in the territory of the anterior spinal artery are the most common lesions localized to the central cord. In the cervical cord, the central cord syndrome gives arm weakness out of proportion to leg weakness, and a "dissociated" sensory loss signifying analgesia (loss of pin sensation)—in a cape distribution over the shoulders and lower neck—without anesthesia (loss of touch sensation) or pallanesthesia (loss of vibration sense).

Lesions located in the region of the first lumbar vertebral body or below compress the spinal nerves of the cauda equina and cause a flaccid, areflexic, asymmetric paraparesis usually accompanied by bladder and bowel dysfunction. A sensory level is found in a saddle distribution up to L1, corresponding to the roots carried in the cauda equina. The Achilles and patellar reflexes are diminished or absent. Pain is common and projected to the perineum or thighs. With conus medullaris lesions pain is less prominent than in cauda equina lesions, and bladder and prominent bowel symptoms occur earlier; only the Achilles reflex is diminished. Compressive lesions may involve both the cauda and conus causing a combined syndrome of lower motor neuron signs and some hyperflexia or a Babinski sign.

The classic syndrome of the foramen magnum is weakness of the shoulder and arm followed by weakness of the ipsilateral leg, then contralateral leg, and finally, contralateral arm. Masses in this region sometimes produce suboccipital pain spreading to the neck and shoulders. A Horner's syndrome is another clue to a high cervical cord lesion; it does not occur with lesions below T2. A few diseases are capable of producing sudden "strokelike" myelopathy without preceding symptoms. They include epidural hemorrhage, hematomyelia, cord infarction, nucleus pulposus embolism, and compression by spinal subluxation.

SPINAL CORD COMPRESSION Tumors of the spinal cord Tumors in the spinal canal may be primary or metastatic, and are classified as extradural ("epidural") or intradural, and the latter as intra- or extramedullary (see Chap. 345). The majority are epidural arising from metastases to the adjacent spinal column. Neoplasms originating in the prostate, breast, and lung, and lymphoma and plasm cell dyscrasias are particularly common, though virtually every malignant tumor has been reported to cause metastatic epidural cord compression. The initial symptom in epidural compression is usually local back pain, often worse in the recumbent position, and causing the patient to awaken at night. Radiating radicular pain exacerbated by coughing, sneezing, or straining may be an accompaniment. Pain and local tenderness often precede other symptoms by many weeks. Neurologic signs commonly evolve over several days to a few weeks. The cord syndrome begins with progressive weakness, eventually acquiring all the hallmarks of a transverse myelopathy with paraparesis and a sensory level. A plain radiograph may show lytic or blastic changes, or a compression fracture at the level appropriate to the cord syndrome; radionuclide bone scans are more frequently positive. CT scan, MRI, or myelography remain the optimal way of demonstrating cord compression. A horizontally and symmetrically widened and flattened cord from extrinsic compression is seen at the margins of the subarachnoid block, and the adjacent vertebral body is usually abnormal (Fig. 353-1).

In the past, emergency laminectomies were considered necessary to treat extrinsic cord compression, but recent treatment with high-dose corticosteroids and rapid, fractionated radiation therapy has been as successful. Outcome is most closely related to the tumor type and its radiosensitivity. Paraparesis frequently improves within 48 h of the administration of corticosteroids. Some incomplete or early transverse cord syndromes may still be better treated surgically, but each case must be analyzed individually taking into account the radiosensitivity of the tumor, distribution of other metastases, and the patient's general medical condition. Whichever therapy is chosen, it is wise to proceed quickly and use corticosteroids as soon as the diagnosis of cord compression is suspected.

Intradural, extramedullary tumors are a less frequent cause of spinal cord compression and evolve more slowly than extradural lesions. Meningiomas and neurofibromas are most common; hemangiopericytomas and other tumors of meningeal origin are rare.

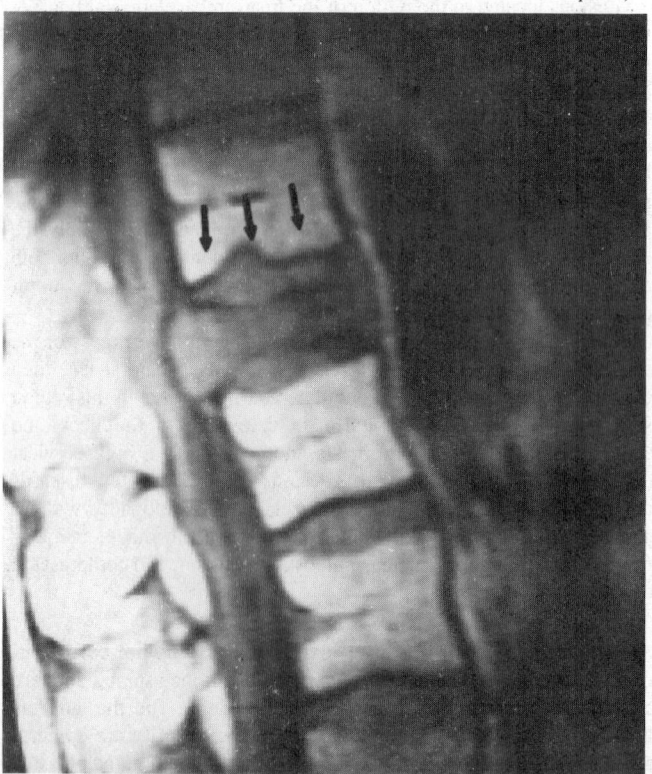

FIGURE 353-1 *Sagittal section MRI showing compression deformity of the T12 vertebral body from metastatic adenocarcinoma (below arrows), and compression and displacement of the spinal cord. (Courtesy of Greg Shoukimas, M.D., Department of Radiology, Massachusetts General Hospital.)*

Symptoms usually begin with radicular sensory changes and an asymmetric syndrome. The CT and myelogram have a typical appearance with dislocation of the cord to one side and outline of the tumor within the subarachnoid space. Primary intramedullary tumors of the spinal cord are discussed in Chap. 345.

Neoplastic compressive myelopathies of all types initially cause minimal elevation of CSF protein, but with complete block of the subarachnoid space CSF protein concentration rises to the 100 to 1000 mg/dL range due to impediment of CSF circulation from the caudal sac to the intracranial subarachnoid space. There are usually few or no cells, cytology for malignant cells is often negative, and CSF glucose concentration remains normal unless there is accompanying widespread carcinomatous meningitis (see Chap. 345).

Epidural abscess   This is a treacherous lesion, often misdiagnosed at first (see Chap. 346). The predisposing clinical settings are furunculosis of the back or scalp, bacteremia, or minor back injury. The condition can occur as a complication of operation or lumbar puncture. Spinal osteomyelitis acts as the nidus for the abscess formation which subsequently enlarges to compress the cord. The osteomyelitis is usually small and not often evident on plain radiographs. For several days to 2 weeks there may be only unexplained fever and mild spinal ache with local tenderness; later, radicular pain occurs. As the abscess expands, it rapidly causes cord compression with a transverse and usually complete transection syndrome. The proper treatment is rapid decompression by laminectomy and drainage, followed by appropriate antibiotics determined from culture of the purulent material. Incomplete drainage is not uncommon resulting in a chronic granulomatous and fibrous reaction that may be sterilized with antibiotics but continues to act as a compressing mass. Tuberculous pyogenic abscess formation, more common in the past, still occurs in developing countries.

Spinal epidural hemorrhage and hematomyelia   An acute transverse myelopathy evolving over minutes or hours accompanied by severe pain may be produced by hemorrhage into the spinal cord (hematomyelia), subarachnoid, or epidural space. Although these may originate from an arteriovenous malformation, or from hemorrhage into a tumor during anticoagulation with warfarin, more commonly they are spontaneous. Those in an epidural location may occur in the setting of minor trauma, lumbar puncture, warfarin anticoagulation, or secondary to hematologic disorders. Back pain, with associated radicular pain, can precede weakness by several minutes to hours, and be so severe that patients may be perceived to act in a peculiar, exaggerated fashion. Lumbar epidural hematoma results in loss of both knee and ankle reflexes, whereas retroperitoneal hematomas usually cause only absence of the knee reflexes. A myelogram defines the mass; computerized tomography is sometimes normal because the clot cannot be distinguished from adjacent bone. Subdural and subarachnoid clots are particularly painful and may occur spontaneously or under circumstances similar to those causing epidural hemorrhages. The CSF with epidural hemorrhage is usually clear or contains a few red blood cells; in subarachnoid or subdural hemorrhage the CSF is grossly bloody at first and later becomes discolored to a deep yellow-brown characteristic of blood pigments present in the CSF. There may be, in addition, a pleocytosis and lowered CSF glucose, giving the impression of bacterial meningitis.

Acute disk protrusion   Lumbar disk herniation, a common disorder, is discussed in Chap. 7. Thoracic or cervical disk protrusion is less often a cause of spinal cord compression, usually occurring after direct trauma to the spinal column. Degeneration of cervical disk spaces with adjacent osteoarthritic hypertrophy causes a subacute spondylitic-compressive myelopathy in the cervical region, discussed below. Embolism from nucleus pulposus material causing acute spinal cord infarction is also described below.

Other unusual compressive lesions   Patients with iatrogenic or primary Cushing's syndrome have a tendency to form increased epidural fat tissue that rarely can reach a size large enough to compress the thoracic cord. Extramedullary hematopoiesis has caused cord compression in a number of hematologic diseases. Eroding aortic aneurysms, echinococcal or other parasitic cysts, gummas, lymphomatoid-granulomatosis, mucopolysaccharidoses, and other rare lesions can also compress the cord.

Arthritic diseases of the spine occur in two clinical forms: a lumbar or cauda equina compression from ankylosing spondylitis, or cervical cord compression from destruction of the cervical apophyseal or atlantoaxial joints in rheumatoid arthritis. Spinal complications arising as one component of severe generalized joint disease in rheumatoid arthritis are often overlooked. Forward subluxation of cervical vertebral bodies, or of the atlas on the axis, can cause a devastating, even fatal, acute cord compression after minor trauma such as whiplash, or it may present as a chronic compressive myelopathy similar to cervical spondylosis. Separation of the odontoid process from the axis may narrow the upper spinal canal compressing the cervicomedullary junction, particularly in flexion movements.

NONCOMPRESSIVE NEOPLASTIC MYELOPATHIES Intramedullary metastasis, paracarcinomatous myelopathy, and radiation myelopathy

In the context of known cancer most myelopathies are compressive. However, when radiologic studies fail to show a block, there is often difficulty distinguishing between several less common entities: intramedullary metastasis, paracarcinomatous myelopathy, and radiation myelopathy. In a patient with known metastatic cancer and a progressive myelopathy shown to be noncompressive by myelography, CT scan, or MRI, intramedullary metastasis is the most likely diagnosis; paraneoplastic myelopathy is rarer (see Chap. 304). Back pain is the most common initial symptom with intramedullary metastasis, though it is not invariable, followed by progressive spastic paraparesis and less often paresthesias. Dissociated sensory loss or sacral sparing, though more characteristic of intrinsic than extrinsic compression, is uncommon, and asymmetric paraparesis and incomplete sensory loss is the rule. Myelography, CT scan, or MRI show a swollen cord without extrinsic compression; in almost half of patients CT or myelography are normal; MRI is more successful in outlining a metastatic mass or primary intramedullary tumor (Fig. 353-2). Intramedullary metastases usually arise from bronchogenic carcinoma and less often from breast cancer and other solid tumors (see Chap. 304). Metastatic melanoma, an uncommon cause of extrinsic cord compression, more often presents as an intramedullary mass. The pathology of the metastasis is usually a single eccentrically placed nodule that seeds hematogenously. Radiation therapy may be helpful in appropriate circumstances.

Carcinomatous meningitis, a common form of CNS invasion in malignancy, does not cause a myelopathy unless there is extensive subpial infiltration from adjacent roots causing nodules with secondary compression or infiltration of the cord. An incomplete, painless cauda equina syndrome can result from carcinomatous root infiltration (see Chap. 345). Headache is common, and repeated CSF examinations eventually reveal malignant cells, an elevated protein, and, in some cases, reduced CSF glucose concentration.

A progressive necrotic myelopathy associated with a paucity of inflammation can occur as a remote effect of cancer, usually with solid tumors. The myelogram and CSF are normal or there may be slightly elevated protein. A subacute progressive spastic paraparesis evolves over days or weeks, usually asymmetrically, with distal paresthesias ascending to establish a sensory level, and late bladder dysfunction. Several adjacent segments of cord are involved.

Radiation produces a delayed subacute progressive myelopathy due to microvascular hyalinization and vascular occlusion (see Chap. 345). It frequently presents a differential diagnostic problem when the cord lies within radiation portals used to treat other structures such as the mediastinal lymph nodes. Differentiation from paracarcinomatous myelopathy or intramedullary metastasis is difficult except by circumstantial history of prior radiation.

INFLAMMATORY MYELOPATHIES Acute myelitis, transverse myelitis, and necrotic myelopathy

These are a group of related diseases marked by intrinsic inflammation of the cord and a clinical syndrome evolving over several days to 2 or 3 weeks. There may be a transverse or virtually complete spinal syndrome (transverse myelitis) or incomplete variants such as a posterior column myelopathy with ascending paresthesias and a sensory level for vibration; ascending, predominantly spinothalamic findings; or a Brown-Séquard syndrome with leg paresis and contralateral spinothalamic-type sensory changes. Many cases follow a viral illness. The most common presenting findings in transverse myelitis are back pain; progressive paraparesis; and asymmetric ascending paresthesias in the legs, later affecting the hands if the disease progresses, creating confusion with Guillain-Barré syndrome. Radiologic studies are necessary to exclude a compressive lesion. The CSF contains 5 to 50 lymphocytes per cubic millimeter in most patients; occasionally more than 200 cells per cubic millimeter are found, and, rarely, polymorphonuclear cells predominate. The inflammatory process is most common in the mid and low thoracic regions, but any level of the cord may be affected. A chronic progressive cervical myelitis has been described, predominantly in older women, and is believed to be a form of multiple sclerosis (see Chap. 348).

In some cases necrosis is profound and may progress intermittently for several months to involve contiguous portions of the cord, reducing much of it to a thin gliotic ribbon. The term *progressive necrotic myelopathy* has been given to this condition. Exceptional cases of necrotic myelopathy progress to involve virtually the entire cord (necrotic panmyelopathy). When a transverse necrotic lesion occurs before or shortly after optic neuritis, it has been termed Devic's disease or neuromyelitis optica. All of these processes appear to be related to, and many are variants of, multiple sclerosis. Systemic lupus erythematosis and other autoimmune disorders have been associated with myelitis. The postinfectious demyelinating disorders are usually monophasic and only rarely recur, though fluctuation of symptoms related to a single level of the cord is common (see Chap. 347).

FIGURE 353-2 *Sagittal MRI showing intrinsic fusiform enlargement of the cervical spinal cord from an intramedullary tumor. The tumor displays a low-density signal (arrows). (Courtesy of Greg Shoukimas, M.D., Department of Radiology, Massachusetts General Hospital.)*

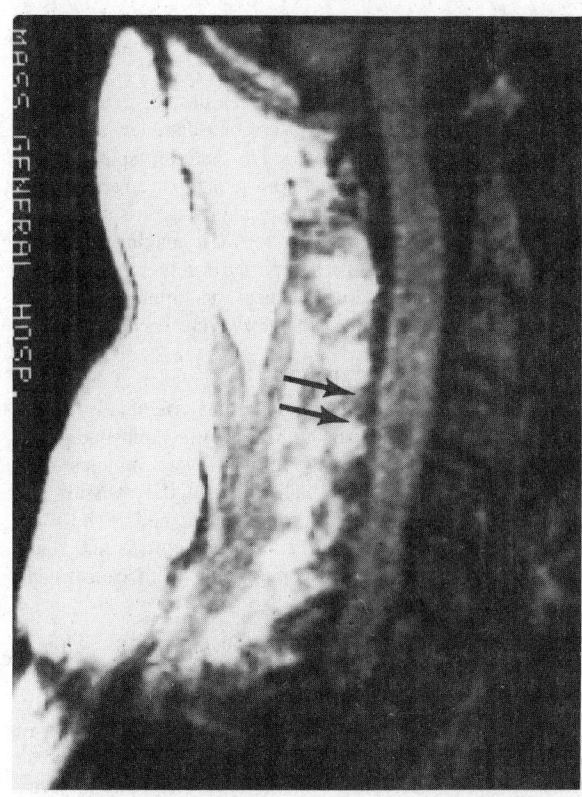

Infectious myelopathy   Direct viral infection of the cord produces specific types of myelitis. In the past, the most common form was poliomyelitis. Herpes zoster, preceded by radicular symptoms, is presently the most common cause of viral myelitis. The pathologic process is not restricted to the gray matter as is polio. Lymphocytes are always found in the CSF. Intramedullary cord abscesses caused by bacteria or mycobacteria arising in the context of systemic infection have been reported. Chronic meningitic lesions due to syphilis may produce a secondary subpial myelitis and radiculitis that evolve slowly (see below). An intense granulomatous, necrotic, and inflammatory myelitis is peculiar to infestation by *Schistosoma mansoni*, caused by a local response to tissue-digesting enzymes produced by ova from the parasite.

Toxic myelopathy   A toxic noninflammatory myelopathy, sometimes with optic atrophy, has been reported, mainly in Japan, and linked to ingestion of iodochlorhydroxyquinoline. Most patients have recovered, but many have persistent paresthesias.

Arachnoiditis   This is a nonspecific term referring to inflammation, scarring, and fibrous thickening of the arachnoid membrane capable of compressing nerve roots or rarely the spinal cord. It is usually a postoperative complication or results from instillation of radiographic dye, antibiotics, or noxious chemicals into the subarachnoid space. The CSF contains many cells and an elevated protein concentration soon after the inciting event, but the inflammation then subsides. There may be slight fever in acute cases. Bilateral asymmetric radicular limb pain is the most prominent feature, with additional signs of root compression, such as reflex loss. Back pain and radicular symptoms are attributed to lumbar arachnoiditis, perhaps more often than justified; nor is arachnoiditis often responsible for cord compression (see Chap. 7). Treatment is controversial; laminectomy has led to improvement in some patients. Multiple meningeal cul-de-sacs, or arachnoid cysts, along nerve roots, occur as a congenital process that may produce severe radicular pain in midadulthood when the cysts enlarge and distort or exert traction on spinal nerve roots or ganglia.

SPINAL CORD INFARCTION   Because the anterior or posterior spinal arteries are not usually involved by atherosclerosis, and only occasionally are affected by angiitis or emboli, most infarctions of the spinal cord are due to ischemia due to distant vascular occlusions. Aortic thrombosis or dissection causes cord infarction by interrupting the entire radicular and direct arterial supply to the anterior and posterior spinal arteries. The infarction typically occurs in a vascular watershed region of the thoracic cord between the large tributary to the spine arising from the aorta, the artery of Adamkiewicz below, and the anterior spinal artery above. The anterior spinal artery syndrome usually appears abruptly, like a stroke, or emerges postoperatively if the proximal aorta has been clamped. In some cases, however, symptoms progress over 24 to 72 h making diagnosis difficult. Spinal infarction has been reported rarely with systemic arteritis, immune reactions of serum sickness, and after intravascular contrast injection, heralded in the latter by severe back pain at the time of injection.

Cord infarction caused by microscopic fragments of herniated nucleus pulposus may occur after minor trauma, frequently during athletics. There is sharp local pain followed by a rapid paraplegia and a transverse cord syndrome evolving over several minutes to an hour. Pulposus tissue is found in small intramedullary vessels and often within the marrow of the adjacent vertebral body. The route from the disk space to marrow and thence to the cord is uncertain. This entity should be suspected in young adults with catastrophic transverse cord syndromes.

VASCULAR MALFORMATION OF THE SPINAL CORD   Arteriovenous malformations (AVM) of the spinal cord are among the most difficult lesions to detect because of their great clinical variability. They may simulate multiple sclerosis, transverse myelitis, spinal cord stroke, or neoplastic compression. AVMs are most often found in the low thoracic or lumbar cord in middle-aged men. The majority begin with an incomplete progressive cord syndrome that may advance subacutely or episodically, like multiple sclerosis, producing bilateral corticospinal, spinothalamic, and posterior column symptoms and signs in any combination. Almost all patients are paraparetic and unable to walk within several years. About one-third have an abrupt syndrome with a single acute transverse myelopathy from bleeding, which simulates acute myelitis; others present with several acute exacerbations. About half have back or radicular pain, a few have a claudication syndrome similar to lumbar canal stenosis, and rare patients describe an acute onset with severe, localized back pain. Fluctuation of pain or neurologic signs with exercise, posture, or menses is helpful in suspecting the diagnosis. Bruits over the lesion are rare but should be sought at rest and after exercise. Most patients have mild elevation of CSF protein and a few show CSF pleocytosis. Bleeding into the cord or CSF may occur. Myelography or CT shows a lesion in 75 to 90 percent of cases if the dorsal subarachnoid space is examined by placing the patient in the supine position. The anatomic details of most AVMs can be demonstrated with selective spinal angiography, a procedure requiring experience for safe performance and completeness.

The pathogenesis of the myelopathy caused by AVMs (that have not bled) is incompletely understood, but appears to be a necrotic noninflammatory process consistent with ischemia. A dorsal AVM with a prominent progressive intramedullary syndrome has been reported with necrotic myelopathy. Since any necrotic process within the cord may give rise to neovascularization and thick-walled vessels, the pathologic basis of this vascular malformation remains controversial.

CHRONIC MYELOPATHIES   Spondylosis   This is a general term for several related degenerative changes of the spine giving rise to compression of the cervical cord and adjacent roots. The cervical form is primarily a disease of older patients, affecting men more often than women, and consisting of a combination of (1) narrowing of intervetebral disk spaces with nucleus pulposus herniation or annulus bulging, (2) osteophytic spur formation on the dorsal aspect of the vertebral bodies, (3) partial subluxation of vertebrae, and (4) hypertrophy of the dorsal spinal ligament and dorsolateral facet articulations (see Chap. 7). The bony changes are reactive in nature, but there is no true arthritis. The most important feature causing spinal cord symptoms and signs is a "spondylitic bar" formed by osteophytes arising from the dorsal surfaces of adjacent vertebral bodies resulting in a horizontal compression of the ventral cord (Fig. 353-3*A* and *B*). Extension of the bar laterally accompanied by articulatory hypertrophic changes or encroachment on the neural foramina often causes additional radicular symptoms. The sagittal diameter of the spinal canal may be narrowed further by actual disk protrusion, or by hypertrophy or buckling of the dorsal spinal ligament, particularly during neck extension. Though the radiographic findings of spondylosis are common in the elderly, only a few patients develop myelopathy or radiculopathy, often dependent upon a congenitally narrow canal.

Neck and shoulder pain with stiffness are early symptoms; pressure on nerve roots is associated with radicular arm pain, most often in a C5 or C6 distribution. Compression of the cervical cord produces a slowly progressive spastic paraparesis, at times asymmetric, and often accompanied by paresthesias in the feet and hands. Vibratory sense is substantially diminished in the legs in most patients, and occasionally there is a sensory level for vibration on the upper thorax. Coughing or straining often produces leg weakness or radiating arm or shoulder pain. Dermatomal sensory loss in the arms, atrophy of intrinsic hand muscles, increased deep tendon reflexes in the legs, and asymmetric Babinski signs are common. Urinary urgency or incontinence do not occur unless the process is well-advanced. The reflexes in the arms are often diminished at some level, notably the biceps, corresponding to C5–C6 cord compression or root involvement. Either radicular, myelopathic, or combined signs may predominate. The diagnosis should be considered in cases of progressive cervical myelopathy, paresthesias of feet or hands, or wasting of the hands. Spondylosis is also one of the most common causes of gait difficulty in the elderly often causing an unexplained increase in leg reflexes or Babinski signs.

Plain radiographs demonstrate spondylitic bars, intervertebral narrowing and subluxations, reversal of the normal cervical spine curvature, and reduction of the sagittal diameter of the canal to less than 11 mm, or to 7 mm with neck extension (Fig. 353-3A). The CSF is usually normal or shows a slightly elevated protein concentration. Somatosensory evoked potentials can be very helpful by demonstrating normal conduction in peripheral large sensory fibers and a delay in central conduction in the mid or high cervical cord.

Cervical spondylosis is both an under- and overdiagnosed disease. Many patient with intrinsic cord processes, particularly amyotrophic lateral sclerosis, multiple sclerosis, and subacute combined degeneration, have had cervical laminectomies in the belief that spondylosis was responsible. Often there is temporary improvement suggesting that there was an element of spondylolytic compression, but the underlying intrinsic myelopathy soon progresses. On the other hand, mild progressive gait disorder with sensory symptoms in the feet and hands caused by cervical spondylosis may be incorrectly attributed to peripheral neuropathy.

Rest and cervical immobilization with a soft collar are helpful in minor cases, traction may be helpful in others, but an operation is advisable if there are advanced symptoms of gait difficulty, severe hand weakness, or bladder difficulty, or if there is a virtually complete myelographic or CT spinal block.

Lumbar stenosis (also discussed in Chap. 7) is an intermittent and chronic compression of the cauda equina usually based on congenital narrowing of the lumbar spinal canal, which is further compromised by disk protrusion or spondylitic changes. Exercise brings about an aching pain in the buttocks, thighs, and calves, frequently sciatic in distribution, ceasing with rest and thereby simulating vascular-induced claudication. During the peak of pain, deep tendon reflexes and sensation may be reduced as compared to the resting state, and vascular studies are normal. Lumbar stenosis and cervical spondylosis commonly occur together, the former probably explaining occasional lower extremity fasciculations in cervical spondylosis.

Degenerative and inherited myelopathies The prototype of the inherited disorders causing spinal cord syndromes is Friedreich's ataxia, a progressive, recessively inherited, leg and truncal ataxia of late childhood onset. Intention tremor, clumsiness of the arms, and, later dysarthria occur. Kyphoscoliosis and pes cavus are common. Areflexia, Babinski signs, and severely impaired vibratory and joint position sense loss are found on examination. Fragmentary or milder forms of the illness occur and overlap with other syndromes including spastic paraparesis (Strümpell-Lorrain form), cerebellar cortical degeneration with ataxia, and olivopontocerebellar atrophy.

Amyotrophic lateral sclerosis (motor neuron disease) must be considered in patients presenting with symmetric spastic paraparesis without sensory findings. It causes a pure motor syndrome with combined corticospinal, corticobulbar, and anterior horn cell involvement. Clinical or electromyographic evidence of muscle fasciculations and denervation indicating motor neuron degeneration confirms the diagnosis (see Chaps. 350 and 354).

Subacute combined degeneration due to vitamin B₁₂ deficiency This treatable myelopathy causes a progressive spastic and ataxic paraparesis and neuropathy, usually with prominent distal paresthesias of the feet and hands. It should be considered in cases simulating cervical spondylosis, late-onset degenerative myelopathies, and symmetric late-onset spinal multiple sclerosis. The disease can also involve the peripheral and optic nerves, and the brain. The diagnosis is confirmed by low B_{12} serum concentration and a positive Schilling test. This entity and related nutritional degenerations are discussed in Chap. 349. Whether folate or vitamin E deficiencies can produce a similar syndrome is controversial. Rarely, multiple sclerosis and B_{12} deficiency myelopathy are found in the same patient.

Syringomyelia Syringomyelia is a progressive myelopathy characterized pathologically by cavitation of the central spinal cord. It is often idiopathic or developmental (see Chap. 351) but may result from trauma, primary intramedullary tumors, extrinsic compression with central cord necrosis, arachnoiditis, hematomyelia, or necrotic myelitis. The developmental type usually begins in the midcervical cord and extends upward to the medulla or downward as low as the lumbar cord. It commonly takes an eccentric position often causing unilateral long tract signs or reflex asymmetries. Many cases occur in association with craniovertebral abnormalities, most commonly the Arnold-Chiari malformation, but also including myelomeningocele, basilar skull impression (platybasia), atresia of the foramen of Magendie, or Dandy-Walker cysts (see Chap. 351).

The cardinal clinical signs of syringomyelia correspond to a central high cervical cord syndrome and depend on the extent of the syrinx and associated abnormalities such as the Arnold-Chiari malformation.

FIGURE 353-3 *A. Lateral x-ray of the cervical spine showing spondylitic "bar" formation from the junction of adjacent osteophytes at C6–C7 (arrow). B. Horizontal CT section at C6 from patient shown in A, after instillation of water-soluable dye into the subarachnoid space. A spur of the bony osteophyte compresses and distorts the spinal cord (arrows).*

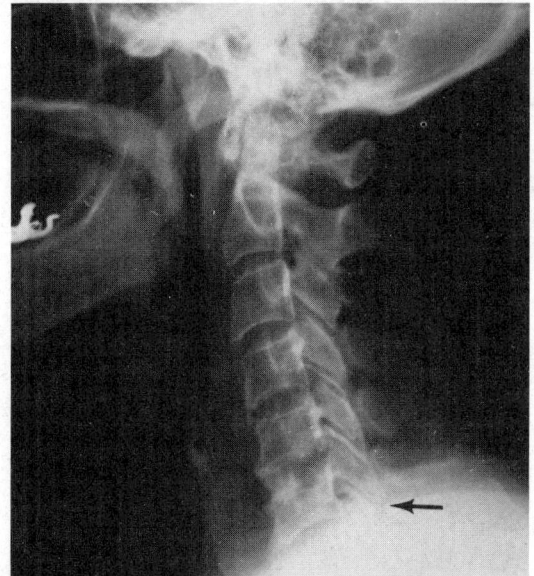

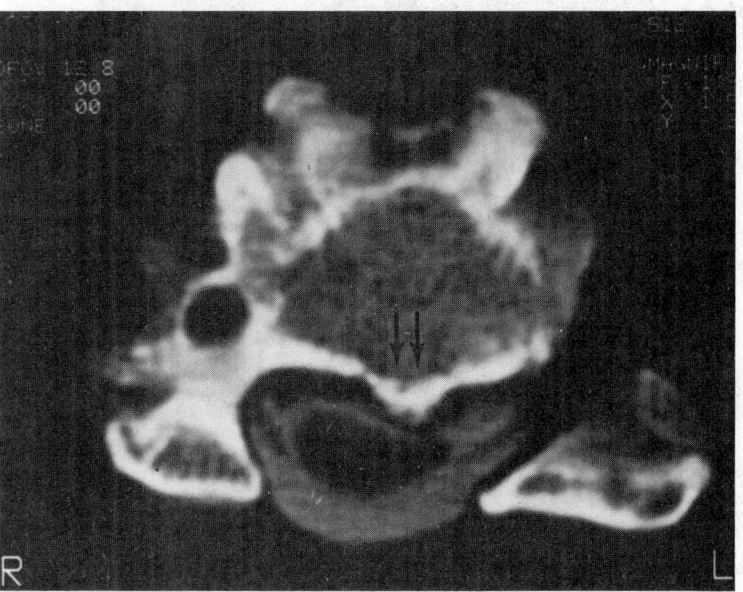

The classic presentation is (1) sensory loss, usually of a dissociated type (loss of pain and temperature and preservation of touch and vibration senses), which is "suspended" over the nape of the neck, shoulders, and upper arms (cape distribution), and eventually extends to the hands, (2) wasting of muscles in the lower neck, shoulders, arms, and hands, with asymmetric or absent reflexes, and (3) high thoracic kyphoscoliosis. The majority begin asymmetrically with unilateral sensory loss. A number of patients develop loss of pin sensation on the face attributed to damage to the descending tract of the trigeminal nerve in the upper cervical cord. Cough-induced headache and neck pain are common with associated Arnold-Chiari malformations.

Symptoms in idiopathic cases begin in adolescence or early adulthood, progress irregularly, and frequently arrest for several years. A few patients escape major disability, but over half become wheelchair-bound. Analgesia leads to injuries, burns, and trophic ulcers in the fingertips. Charcot joints in the shoulders, elbows, or knees are common in advanced cases. Prominent lower extremity weakness or hyperreflexia suggest an associated abnormality at the craniovertebral junction. Syringobulbia results from extension of the cavity into the medulla, or rarely the pons, usually occupying the lateral medullary tegmentum. Palatal and vocal cord paralysis, dysarthria, nystagmus, episodic dizziness, tongue weakness, and Horner's syndrome may occur.

Slow enlargement of the cavity may create a narrowing or complete block of the subarachnoid space. The cavity is separate from the central canal but usually communicates with it. The diagnosis can be made dependably from the clinical features, confirmed by finding an enlarged cervical cord on myelography or on delayed CT images several hours after subarachnoid instillation of metrizamide or another water-soluble contrast material (Fig. 353-4A). Syrinx cavities are shown to greatest advantage by magnetic resonance imaging (MRI) (Fig. 353-4B). The cervicomedullary junction should be examined for associated developmental abnormalities.

Therapy is directed at decompressing the cavity to prevent progression of damage and decompressing the spinal canal if the cord is distended. Laminectomies and suboccipital decompression are advisable when an Arnold-Chiari malformation accompanies an enlarged cervical cord.

Tabes dorsalis Tabes and meningovascular syphilis of the spinal cord are presently rare but at one time had to be considered in the differential diagnosis of most spinal cord syndromes. The most common symptoms of tabes are characteristic fleeting and repetitive, lancinating pains occurring mostly in the legs, less commonly in the back, thorax, abdomen, arms, and face. Severe gait and leg ataxia due to loss of position sense occurs in half of patients. Paresthesias, bladder disturbances, and acute abdominal pain with vomiting (visceral crisis) occur in 15 to 30 percent. The cardinal signs of tabes are loss of reflexes in the legs, impaired position and vibratory sense, Romberg's sign, and bilateral abnormalities of the pupils, Argyll Robertson pupils that fail to constrict to light but react with accommodation.

Traumatic spinal cord lesions and compression of the cord secondary to orthopedic disorders are discussed in the chapter on cranial and spinal injury (Chap. 344).

GENERAL CARE OF THE PATIENT WITH ACUTE PARAPLEGIA OR QUADRIPLEGIA Protection from secondary damage to the urinary tract is a high priority in the acute stages of paraplegia. The bladder is areflexic, retains urine, and the patient is unaware of bladder distention, making damage to the detrusor muscle form overdistention possible. Urologic rehabilitation requires bladder drainage and avoidance of urinary infection. This is best accomplished by intermittent catheterization by trained personnel. Continuous closed system urinary drainage, which is associated with a higher infection rate than intermittent catheterization, or suprapubic drainage are alternatives. Patients with acute lesions, especially those causing spinal shock, frequently need special cardiovascular care because of paroxysmal hypertension or hypotension often requiring fluids to correct volume aberrations. Ileus and gastric stress ulcers are other potential acute medical problems in patients with complete transverse cord lesions. Cimetidine and ranitidine may be useful in these circumstances.

High cervical cord lesions cause varying degrees of mechanical respiratory failure requiring artificial ventilation. In cases of incomplete respiratory failure with forced vital capacities of 10 to 20 mL/kg, chest physical therapy is useful, and a negative pressure cuirass may be used to alleviate atelectasis and fatigue, particularly if the major lesion is below C4. With severe respiratory failure, tracheal

FIGURE 353-4 *A. Horizontal CT section 1 h after subarachnoid instillation of water-soluble contrast medium showing the cervical spinal cord surrounded by contrast and dye in a large intramedullary syrinx cavity (arrow). B. Sagittal MRI of same patient shown in A showing the syrinx cavity and enlargement of the spinal cord (arrows). (Courtesy of Greg Shoukimas, M.D., Department of Radiology, Massachusetts General Hospital.)*

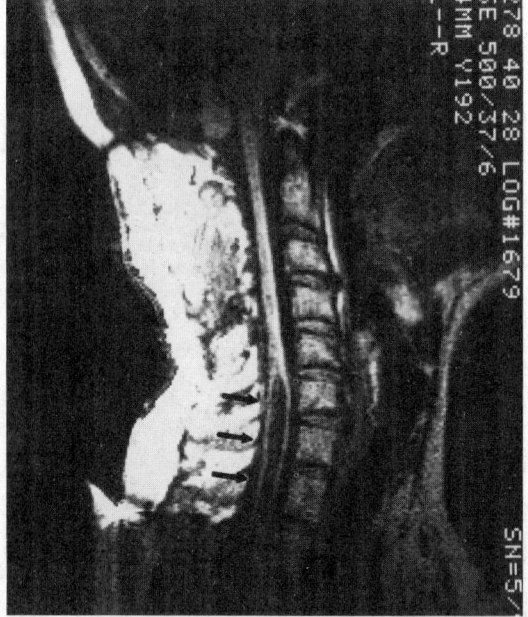

intubation (performed over an endoscope if the spine is unstable), followed by tracheostomy, provides tracheal access for ventilation and suctioning. A promising new technique is phrenic nerve pacing in patients with lesions at C5 or above.

As clinical signs stabilize, attention should be directed to the psychological state of the patient and the development of a rehabilitation plan framed by realistic expectations. An aggressive program is often remarkably successful with younger and middle-aged patients allowing return to home and a productive lifestyle.

Chronic nursing care problems can be handled by patients with varying degrees of assistance. The major issues are related to immobilization: skin breakdown over pressure points, urinary sepsis, and autonomic instability, and the potential for pulmonary embolism. Early care includes frequent repositioning, application of skin emollients and soft bed coverings. Specialized beds turn the patient or distribute body weight evenly rather than predominantly on bony prominences. If the sacral cord segments are undamaged, then a large degree of automatic voiding can be entrained. Patients initially void reflexly between catheterizations and later learn to induce voiding with various maneuvers. If residual urinary volumes lead to infection, surgical procedures or an indwelling catheter may be necessary. Bowel regimens and disimpaction are necessary in most patients to ensure at least biweekly evacuation and avoid colonic distention or obstruction.

Severe hypertension and bradycardia occur in response to noxious superficial stimuli, bladder or bowel distention, or surgery, particularly in patients with cervical and high thoracic cord lesions. Flushing and diaphoresis above the level of the lesion may accompany the hypertension. The mechanism of this dysautonomia is not well understood. A potent antihypertensive agent may be necessary, particularly during surgery, but beta-blocking drugs should probably be avoided. Some patients become severely bradycardic with tracheal suctioning; this can be prevented with small doses of atropine. Pulmonary embolism due to immobilization is a grave early risk occurring in approximately one-third of patients after acute cord trauma.

Detailed aspects of the physical therapy, rehabilitation, and orthotics related to severe spinal cord diseases may be found in specialized texts. The orthopedic stabilization of the spine in relation to cord trauma is discussed in Chap. 344.

REFERENCES

ADAMS CBT, LOGUE V: Studies in cervical spondylitic myelopathy. Brain 94:579, 1971

AMINOFF MJ, LOGUE V: Clinical features of spinal vascular malformations. Brain 97:197, 1974

AULD AW et al: Metastatic spinal epidural tumors: An analysis of 50 cases. Arch Neurol 15:100, 1966

BAKER AS et al: Spinal epidural abcess. N Engl J Med 293:463, 1975

BARNETT HJM et al: *Syringomyelia*. Philadelphia, Saunders, 1973

BRAIN WR et al: The neurological manifestations of cervical spondylosis. Brain 75:188, 1952

EDELSON R et al: Intramedullary spinal cord metastasis. Neurology 22:1222, 1972

GILBERT et al: Epidural cord compression from metastatic tumor: Diagnosis and treatment. Ann Neurol 3:40, 1978

GREENBERG HS et al: Epidural spinal cord compression from metastatic tumor: Results with a new treatment protocol. Ann Neurol 8:361, 1980

HARDY AG, ROSSIER AB: *Spinal Cord Injuries: Orthopedic and Neurological Aspects*. Stuttgart, Thieme, 1975

LOGUE V: Angiomas of the spinal cord: Review of the pathogenesis, clinical features, and results of surgery. J Neurol Neurosurg Psychiatr 42:1, 1979

————, EDWARDS MR: Syringomyelia and its surgical treatment. J Neurol Neurosurg Psychiatr 44:273, 1981

McILROY WJ, RICHARDSON JC: Syringomyelia: A clinical review of 75 cases. J Can Med Assoc 93:731, 1965

ROPPER AH, POSKANZER DC: Prognosis of acute and subacute transverse myelopathy based on early signs and symptoms. Ann Neurol 4:51, 1978

ROSSIER AB et al: Posttraumatic cervical syringomyelia. Brain 108:439, 1985

SRIGLEY et al: Spinal cord infarction secondary to intervertebral disc embolism. Ann Neurol 9:296, 1981

section 2 Diseases of nerve and muscle

354 APPROACH TO THE PATIENT WITH NEUROMUSCULAR DISEASE

ROBERT C. GRIGGS / WALTER G. BRADLEY / BHAGWAN T. SHAHANI

The neuromuscular diseases are disorders of the *motor unit* and of the sensory and autonomic peripheral nerves. Each motor unit consists of (1) the *motor neuron* cell body, located in either the anterior horn (for muscles innervated by the spinal cord) or a cranial nerve nucleus (for ocular, facial, and bulbar musculature); (2) *the axon* of the motor neuron in the peripheral nerve; (3) the *neuromuscular junction*; and (4) the *muscle fibers* innervated by the motor neuron. The sensory peripheral nerves comprise (1) the *sensory neuron* cell body in the posterior root ganglion; (2) the *central axon* passing to the spinal cord in the posterior root; (3) the *distal* axon in the peripheral nerve; and (4) the *sensory nerve terminal* in skin, muscle, joint capsule, etc. The autonomic nerves are divided into *sympathetic* and *parasympathetic* nerves. The sympathetic preganglionic fibers arise from cell bodies in the intermediolateral column of the spinal cord and enter the sympathetic ganglia, from whence postganglionic fibers arise to innervate blood vessels or viscera. The parasympathetic preganglionic neurons lie in the brainstem and sacral spinal cord, and axons terminate in the viscera, which contain the postganglionic neurons and their nerve terminals.

The major symptoms of diseases of the motor unit are muscle weakness, fatigue, cramps, pain, or stiffness. Symptoms of peripheral nerve disease include, in addition, decreased sensation (hypesthesia or hypalgesia), abnormal sensations (paresthesias), or painful sensations (dysesthesias) (see Chap. 18). Symptoms of autonomic nervous system disease include postural dizziness, abnormal cardiac, visceral, and ocular function, and changes in sweating.

CLINICAL ASSESSMENT

History and physical examination will lead to a diagnosis in a majority of patients with neuromuscular disease. Failure to arrive at a diagnostic impression before routine and sophisticated laboratory studies are done often leads to diagnostic inaccuracy and confusion. Few of the biochemical, histologic, and electrodiagnostic studies used to evaluate patients with neuromuscular disease are pathognomonic, since nerve and muscle can respond in only a limited number of ways to disease processes.

CLINICAL HISTORY **Weakness and fatigue** (see Chap. 15) The patient with weakness, particularly of gradual onset, may not recognize it; this emphasizes the useful axiom that "signs of muscle weakness precede symptoms of weakness." Words such as numbness, deadness, tiredness, or fatigue may be used by a patient unfamiliar with what is taking place. On the other hand, some complaints of "weakness" result from systemic rather than neuromuscular disease. In such patients, strength is often normal or only mildly reduced, since the complaint is usually loss of stamina and endurance. The patient with fatigue should be asked to distinguish between true weakness and the less specific symptoms of lassitude and asthenia. If the patient is unable to perform a normal activity, true weakness is suggested. Objective evidence of weakness is established if symptoms exceed the bounds of normal variation (e.g., double vision, drooping eye lids, difficulty in swallowing, or aspiration of food or liquids into the airway) as opposed to the more subjective complaints of inability to lift, carry, or push an object.

The time course and severity of weakness must be quantitated by questions concerning alterations in functional abilities: for the legs, difficulty in rising from a chair or commode, rising from a squatting position, or climbing and descending stairs and a history of frequent tripping, stumbling, or falling; for the trunk, difficulty in sitting up in bed; or for the arms, difficulty in washing the hair, opening jars, fastening buttons, or raising objects onto a shelf.

Abnormalities of sensation (see Chaps. 18 and 355) Sensory symptoms suggest peripheral nerve disease although, as with weakness, sensory abnormalities can occur with disease at any level of the nervous system. The characteristics and localization of sensory symptoms in the various peripheral nerve syndromes and diseases are discussed in Chap. 18. In contradistinction to weakness, it is axiomatic that "sensory symptoms precede objective sensory signs."

Muscle pain (see Chap. 17) Muscle aches and pains may suggest inflammatory or metabolic muscle disease but are far more common in bone, joint, and nerve disease. Persistent muscle pain with normal strength usually results from a cause other than myopathy. Intermittent muscle pain, on the other hand, particularly when precipitated by exercise, suggests a substrate utilization defect such as a glycogen or lipid storage myopathy or the purine nucleotide cycle disorder, myoadenylate deaminase deficiency. It is important to determine if other factors, such as fasting, precipitate pain and then to inquire about associated findings such as dark urine, which may indicate myoglobinuria.

Autonomic dysfunction The most common complaint is of "dizziness," or "blackouts," which prove to be precipitated by standing up. Loss of male potency, explosive diarrhea, cyclic diarrhea-constipation or partial urinary retention may also occur.

PHYSICAL EXAMINATION **Strength testing** Reliable testing of strength requires that the examiner have an adequate frame of reference for normal strength and that the patient be motivated and able to cooperate with testing. As with history taking, it is helpful to quantitate the ability to perform tasks of daily living. The legs are particularly easy to test by observing the following: walking on heels and toes; rising from a chair, noting whether there is a need to use the arms; rising from a squat; and stepping up onto a chair. It is useful to examine the legs for a *knee extension lag*, the inability to fully extend the leg against gravity. This sign is an indication of quadriceps weakness; patients with even a minor extension lag almost invariably report frequent tripping and falling. Trunk and neck muscles can be tested by having the patient sit up; extending the head over the edge of an examining table is a sensitive method of detecting neck weakness. The arms are not as easily evaluated with function testing; inspection of shoulders for scapular winging as the arms are elevated and observation of the patient lifting the arms above the head test shoulder girdle function. Hand strength can be judged by determination of the degree of difficulty in extraction of two fingers

from the grip of the patient and by the ability of the patient to blanch the knuckles when making a tight fist. When the lesion affects a specific region, e.g., the brachial plexus or the ulnar nerve, it is essential to test each individual muscle of the arm or hand.

Formal muscle testing, assigning a numeric grade to muscle strength, is usually based on the MRC (Medical Research Council of Great Britain) 0 to 5 scale:

5 — normal
4 — able to oppose gravity plus resistance
3 — able to move fully against gravity but not resistance
2 — able to move when gravity is eliminated
1 — trace movement
0 — no movement

Other scales expand the ratings to 10, allowing for greater precision in the ranges of 3 to 5 (or 6 to 10).

An important distinction to be made with any scale is whether a muscle is indeed *weaker than might be expected,* with allowances for age, male-female differences, inactivity, or generalized illness. If there is a limited time for the testing of muscle strength, the assessment of function is likely to be of more value than formal muscle testing.

Muscle bulk Muscle atrophy and hypertrophy are often difficult to recognize because of wide variation among normal persons. The problem is accentuated in young children and in obese patients because of overlying adipose tissue. Atrophy is easier to appreciate when asymmetric. Muscle enlargement or hypertrophy is a normal accompaniment of physical training. It is occasionally a sign of disease in patients with long-standing spasticity or myotonic disorders. So-called pseudohypertrophy, in which the muscles become enlarged by replacement with connective tissue or fat, may be prominent in certain of the muscular dystrophies but is also seen with spinal muscular atrophy and other denervating conditions. Actual hypertrophy of muscle fibers may also be present in these patients. Muscle enlargement may also be caused by infiltration with substances such as amyloid or by parasitic infestation (e.g., cysticercosis).

LOCALIZED ENLARGEMENT OF MUSCLE Focal muscle swelling may be due to inflammatory infiltrates, calcium deposits, or tendon rupture. Preservation of some parts of a muscle, while other parts atrophy, may occur in spinal muscular atrophy and some forms of muscular dystrophy, giving an appearance of a focal swelling during muscle contraction. Single or multiple muscle masses in a patient without weakness may indicate a neoplastic process. Other causes of muscle enlargement include focal myositis, sarcoidosis, ectopic ossification, and tendon rupture.

Pathologic fatigue Patients with disorders of neuromuscular transmission such as myasthenia gravis can usually be shown on examination to fatigue. Sustained upward gaze produces gradual ptosis of the eyelids (curtain sign); eye movements become disconjugate on sustained horizontal gaze; the voice may become hoarse, slurred, or nasal with prolonged speech; a smile may rapidly become a sneer when the patient cannot maintain facial muscle activity. The inability of the patient to sustain limb activity is less easily quantitated since patients who are weak from any cause may have decreased endurance.

Sensory testing Patients with peripheral neuropathy usually have sensory loss. The distribution of sensory disturbance as well as the modalities affected are often of diagnostic importance (see Chaps. 18 and 355).

Autonomic testing A fall of systolic blood pressure of more than 20 mmHg from lying to standing indicates impaired autonomic control of peripheral blood vessels. A greater fall often occurs with exercise in the erect position. The pulse rate does not increase normally in response to this hypotension if there is an autonomic neuropathy. Similarly, there is no slowing of the heart rate following a sustained Valsalva maneuver.

TABLE 354-1 Presenting clinical features of the neuromuscular diseases

Site of involvement	Anterior horn cell	Peripheral nerve	Neuromuscular junction	Muscle
Example	Spinal muscular atrophy	Nutritional neuropathy	Myasthenia gravis	Polymyositis
Distribution of weakness	Asymmetric limb or bulbar	Symmetric distal	Extraocular, bulbar, proximal limb	Symmetric proximal limb, bulbar
Atrophy	Marked and early	Moderate	None	Slight
Sensory involvement	None	Paresthesias, hypesthesia	None	Aching
Characteristic features	Fasciculations, cramps, tremor		Diurnal fluctuation	
Reflexes	Variable	Decreased out of proportion to weakness	Normal	Parallel strength

Other findings Myotonia, fasciculations, myokymia, and other spontaneous activity (Chap. 17) should be looked for. Certain disorders such as myotonic dystrophy and facioscapulohumeral dystrophy have distinctive and virtually pathognomonic facial features. Less characteristic but significant facial weakness is found in other myopathies and in myasthenia gravis. Joint contractures, particularly of the Achilles tendons and the hips, and scoliosis may indicate that weakness is of long duration.

DIFFERENTIAL DIAGNOSIS The portion of the motor unit involved by a disease process is usually evident from clinical findings (Table 354-1). Motor neuron diseases (Chap. 350) are suggested in the patient whose weakness is accompanied by prominent atrophy, fasciculations, and lack of sensory involvement. The reflexes may be depressed if anterior horn cell disease alone is present and may be pathologically increased if there is coexistent upper motor neuron disease, as in amyotrophic lateral sclerosis. Peripheral neuropathy (Chap. 355) is suggested by the findings of distal weakness associated with sensory loss. Patients with peripheral neuropathy usually have depressed tendon reflexes; preservation of reflexes combined with significant weakness suggests another cause for the dysfunction. Neuromuscular junction disorders (Chap. 358) come to mind if ocular and bulbar weakness is prominent, particularly if there is *diurnal variation*, with the patient becoming weaker as the day progresses. Pathologic fatigue can usually be demonstrated. Reflexes are preserved in most neuromuscular junction disorders, particularly myasthenia gravis.

Myopathy versus other neuromuscular disease Clinical features which suggest myopathy in contrast to other motor unit diseases include a proximal distribution of weakness, relative preservation or increase of muscle bulk, and the preservation of reflexes. Table 354-2 presents a classification of primary muscle diseases. Many patients with muscle symptoms, however, have disorders that do not fit into this classification because evaluation discloses disease in another portion of the motor unit or in another system (see Chap. 15). For example, a patient with a denervation produced by nerve root damage from a lumbar disk protrusion may have muscle cramps, pain, and weakness in muscles innervated by those nerve roots. Furthermore, fatigue, weakness, and pain are common accompaniments of derangements of cardiac, hematologic, gastrointestinal, pulmonary, renal, or hepatic function. The expectation of strength and endurance in such patients is diminished since the patient is acutely or chronically ill. Despite complaints of weakness and fatigue and the finding of atrophy, patients with pulmonary or cardiac disease are rarely mistaken for those with primary muscle disease.

Proximal weakness, although characteristic of most myopathies, can also occur in acute or chronic inflammatory polyneuropathy, in neuromuscular junction disorders, and in anterior horn cell diseases. Many disorders are termed "myopathies" solely on the basis of proximal weakness, including the weakness associated with hyperthyroidism, corticosteroid administration, and hyperparathyroidism. However, the underlying pathophysiology of these muscle disorders has not been defined.

Acute generalized weakness Weakness developing over the course of less than an hour is usually caused by a metabolic or toxic disorder affecting either the neuromuscular junction or the muscle. A sudden alteration in circulating potassium, calcium, sodium, magnesium, or phosphate may result in partial or complete paralysis of muscle. Acute failure of neuromuscular junction transmission may occur with botulism and other toxins, hypermagnesemia, and with aminoglycoside antibiotics and other medications. Weakness developing over the course of 24 h may occur in electrolyte, metabolic, and toxic disorders; in periodic paralysis (Chap. 359); and in acute inflammatory myopathies, particularly those related to viral and parasitic infection (Chap. 356) and certain acute polyneuropathies (Chap. 355). Occasionally, patients with more chronic disorders first realize that they are weak when the insidious progression of their weakness produces an abrupt change in function.

Subacute weakness Weakness developing over days is more common in peripheral nerve or neuromuscular junction diseases than in muscle or anterior horn cell disease. Acute inflammatory polyneuropathy (Guillain-Barré syndrome) and porphyric, diphtheritic, and toxic neuropathies are of subacute onset. Myasthenia gravis and other neuromuscular junction diseases must also be considered in the differential diagnosis. Subacute weakness can occur in severe polymyositis and dermatomyositis. Weakness from endocrine disorders and certain muscle toxins (Table 354-2) may also develop subacutely (Chap. 357). Of the anterior horn cell disorders only infections with poliomyelitis and other viruses evolve subacutely.

Slowly progressive weakness *Slowly progressive proximal weakness* evolving over weeks to months may be caused by polymyositis or dermatomyositis or by an unsuspected endocrinopathy. When the course has extended for a year or more, however, one of the muscular dystrophies, spinal muscular atrophy, or a neuromuscular junction

TABLE 354-2 Classification of primary muscle diseases

I Hereditary
   A Muscular dystrophy (Chap. 357): Duchenne, myotonic, facioscapulohumeral, limb-girdle, oculopharyngeal, scapuloperoneal, congenital, distal, ocular
   B Congenital myopathies (Chap. 357): Central core, nemaline, centronuclear, fiber-type disproportion
   C Metabolic myopathies (Chap. 357):
      1 Glycogen: Deficiencies of phosphorylase, phosphofructokinase, phosphoglyceromutase, acid maltase, others
      2 Lipid: Defective synthesis or transport of carnitine; deficiency of carnitine palmityl transferase
      3 Purine nucleotide cycle: Deficiency of myoadenylate deaminase
   D Myotonia (Chap. 357); Congenita, paramyotonia
   E Periodic paralysis (Chaps. 17 and 359): Hypokalemic, hyperkalemic
II Inflammatory (Chap. 356)
   A Collagen disease: Systemic lupus erythematosus, rheumatoid arthritis, scleroderma, mixed-connective tissue
   B Sarcoidosis, carcinoid, neoplastic disease
   C Infections: Numerous, especially viral (influenza B), protozoal (toxoplasmosis), parasitic (trichinosis)
   D Idiopathic: Polymyositis, dermatomyositis
III Endocrine and metabolic (Chap. 357)
   A Electrolyte abnormalities: Calcium, phosphate, magnesium, sodium, potassium
   B Endocrine abnormalities: Hypo- and hyperfunction of thyroid, adrenal, parathyroid, pituitary
IV Toxic (Chap. 357): Alcohol, opiates, pentazocine, clofibrate, others
V Tumors and masses: Primary and metastatic neoplasms, infection, sarcoidosis, myositis ossificans, calcinosis, muscle rupture and hemorrhage

defect such as myasthenia gravis may be present. Neuropathies are seldom proximal, the major exceptions being acute and chronic inflammatory polyneuropathy, porphyric neuropathy, and diabetic proximal mononeuropathy. *Slowly progressive distal weakness* is more characteristic of anterior horn cell or peripheral nerve disorders than of disorders of muscle or the neuromuscular junction. The only commonly encountered distal myopathy is myotonic dystrophy. Less common disorders such as distal muscular dystrophy, nemaline and centronuclear myopathies (see Chap. 357), and a variant of polymyositis known as *inclusion body myositis* may present with distal weakness (Chap. 356). Prominent distal lower limb weakness is also present in the facioscapulohumeral and scapuloperoneal muscular dystrophies, but more proximal involvement is invariably also present in such patients. *Slowly progressive bulbar weakness* is more typical of anterior horn cell or neuromuscular junction disorders than of myopathies. Bulbar weakness (difficulty in speaking, coughing, and swallowing) occurs commonly in motor neuron disease (especially amyotrophic lateral sclerosis) and neuromuscular junction disorders. It is also seen in oculopharyngeal dystrophy, myotonic dystrophy, and polymyositis or dermatomyositis. *Ocular muscle weakness and ptosis* do not occur in motor neuron disease and are uncommon in peripheral neuropathy. Ophthalmoparesis is typical of myasthenia gravis and may occur in myotonic and oculopharyngeal dystrophies. Weakness limited to or predominantly of an ocular location (*progressive external ophthalmoplegia*) occurs in disorders such as the Kearns-Sayre syndrome (Chap. 357).

LABORATORY ASSESSMENT

Patients with impaired strength merit thorough diagnostic study. Hematologic, renal, and hepatic function and serum electrolytes should be evaluated. In many instances thyroid, adrenal, and other endocrine studies may be indicated. Other useful diagnostic tests are the serum creatine kinase test, nerve conduction studies, electromyography, and in many instances muscle biopsy. Nerve conduction studies should be obtained when the history and examination suggest peripheral neuropathy. Nerve biopsy is a more specialized technique with a relatively small number of specific indications (see Chap. 355). Repetitive stimulation of nerve with recording from muscle should be obtained when a neuromuscular junction defect is suspected. In requesting each diagnostic test it is important to consider what information is being sought in order to prevent the accumulation of misleading data. For example, creatine kinase may be elevated after minor muscle trauma such as that caused by electromyography. Electromyography and muscle biopsy obtained from a muscle affected by past nerve root disease (e.g., from a herniated disk) may show neuropathic abnormalities unrelated to a new disease process. Muscle biopsy from a muscle that has been recently injured, even by the minor trauma of an injection or electromyogram, may mislead the unwary into a diagnosis of myositis.

If a patient complains of weakness and fatigue but is not found on examination to have weakness, the indications for diagnostic studies are less definite. Depending on other clinical assessment, complaints of long duration and severity usually warrant diagnostic evaluation. When the history is suggestive of a metabolic myopathy (Chap. 357) further metabolic testing may be indicated.

ANATOMIC AND PHYSIOLOGIC BASIS OF HISTOPATHOLOGY AND ELECTROPHYSIOLOGY

The motor unit is the final common pathway for motor activity of the nervous system, and muscle is the final effector of the motor unit. All movement, posture, and reflex activity result from integrated discharge of large numbers of motor units by spinal and supraspinal mechanisms. The strength of a muscle contraction depends upon the number of motor units recruited, the frequency of motor unit discharge,

the speed of contraction of muscle fibers in the motor unit, and the nature of the motor unit (whether fatigue-resistant or fatigue-prone). The number of motor units varies greatly between muscles, ranging from approximately 100 in the intrinsic muscles of the hands to several thousand in leg muscles. The number of muscle fibers per motor unit varies between as few as 10 in the extraocular muscles to nearly 2000 in leg muscles such as the gastrocnemius. The number of muscle fibers per muscle varies nearly a thousandfold, from 1000 in extraocular muscles to over 1 million in large leg muscles. An understanding of the organization of motor units and their patterns of firing is important in the interpretation of clinical and laboratory findings in normal and diseased muscle. The muscle fibers of the motor unit are dispersed randomly within a muscle, and fibers innervated by the same anterior horn cell are generally not contiguous.

Motor units differ both in size and in the biochemical and physiologic properties of their muscle fibers. On the basis of these properties, muscle fibers are subdivided into two types. The ATPase stain identifies two major types of fibers: type I fibers that stain lightly and type II fibers, which appear dark. This differentiation of histologic type is often useful in the interpretation of muscle pathology, since certain muscle diseases are characterized by preferential abnormalities of a single fiber type. Type II fibers are diminished in many congenital myopathies, whereas in myotonic dystrophy, type I fibers are often atrophic.

All muscle fibers within a motor unit are probably of identical histochemical type. Cross-innervation experiments in animals in which all of the muscle fibers of certain muscles are of the same histochemical type (as opposed to human muscle, where the fibers are dispersed in a random pattern throughout the muscle) have shown that muscle fibers change their histochemical, biochemical, and physiologic properties in response to changing innervation. The basis for the neurogenic control of muscle fiber characteristics is probably related to the characteristics of the firing pattern, since experimental chronic electric stimulation of nerves can change the biochemical and physiologic properties of muscle. A similar change in muscle fiber type in man can be induced by endurance exercise training, where an increase in type I (aerobic) muscle fibers is observed.

The physiologic characterization of the muscle fibers relate importantly to the exercise capacity of muscle. Motor units with type I, slow-twitch muscle fibers are designed for continuous and prolonged activity, since their energy supply for ATP generation is derived from substrate metabolism through the oxidative pathways of mitochondria. The muscle fibers of these motor units are activated (*recruited*) by small, low-threshold, slowly conducting motor neurons which are activated by low intensity exertion. Higher-intensity effort, such as the lifting of a heavy weight, recruits larger, higher-threshold, more rapidly conducting motor neurons which innervate type II muscle fibers.

The physiologic properties of motor units and their response to voluntary contraction are such that there is a stereotyped pattern of recruitment for each muscle with an orderly sequence of activation of muscle units. Certain motor units are activated only with intense activity. This fact underlies in part the ability of muscles to gain size and strength with repeated heavy exertion. An increase in the myofibril content of muscle fibers and possibly a small increase in the number of muscle fibers occurs with repeated heavy exertion. The lack of activation of some motor units except with vigorous training may underlie the weakness common in many sedentary persons and explain the response to physical therapeutic maneuvers in such patients.

As muscles relax, the cessation of firing of individual motor units occurs in a groupwise fashion so that a patient exerting an inadequate effort owing to functional weakness (e.g., malingering), lack of motivation, or pain will frequently have a ratchet-like or "give-way" quality on muscle testing which permits the distinction between true and feigned weakness.

ELECTROMYOGRAPHY   The measurement of electric activity arising from muscle fibers is usually performed by inserting a needle electrode percutaneously into muscle. The electric activity from this electrode is then displayed on a cathode-ray oscilloscope and can be made audible by inserting a loudspeaker into the circuit.

Skeletal muscles are numerous and often large. As a result, electrode studies provide only an average picture of the electric activity of muscle. Since many neuromuscular diseases are restricted to selected muscles, normal electric activity in one area does not exclude the possibility of pathologic phenomena close by. Accurate physiologic analysis requires that fine concentric needle electrodes be placed within carefully selected muscles so as to register the activity of only a small number of motor units and muscle fibers in those muscles.

The action potential As an electric impulse travels from the center toward either end of the muscle fiber, current flows outward through the normally polarized region of the muscle membrane (sarcolemma) toward the depolarized zone (Fig. 354-1). The recording electrode initially becomes slightly positive relative to the reference electrode. When the depolarized region moves under the recording electrode, a negative deflection occurs. As the active region moves away from the electrode, the membrane under the electrode slowly becomes repolarized. The net result is a *triphasic action potential* recorded on the oscilloscope (Fig. 354-1).

Recording of motor unit activity Triphasic action potentials result from the activity of single muscle fibers. In normal muscle, excitation is initiated by motor nerves supplying many muscle fibers so that all muscle fibers of one motor unit are activated by one impulse from the motor neuron. The number of muscle fibers in a single motor unit varies, and muscle fibers differ in diameter, length, and shape and in spatial orientation with regard to the electromyogram (EMG) electrode. Muscle fibers of one motor unit are not clustered tightly together but are dispersed in a region of the muscle, interspersed with fibers of adjacent motor units. Therefore, muscle activation produces complex motor unit potentials, resulting from the summation of individual action potentials.

The normal electromyogram Normal muscle is electrically silent when at rest. Once *insertional activity,* produced by the trauma of placing the needle, has died down, electrodes record no action potentials. When a muscle is voluntarily contracted, action potentials appear; with increasing strength of contraction, second or third units are recruited. As the contraction becomes stronger, action potentials of more and larger motor units appear, until with full contraction, a disorderly array of action potentials varying at rates of up to 20 to 50 Hz appears. Individual motor unit potentials can no longer be distinguished, and a *complete recruitment (interference) pattern* is produced. In disease of the central or peripheral nervous system, the recruitment pattern produced by maximal voluntary effort is reduced because fewer motor units are activated with voluntary effort. In patients with muscle disease, the recruitment pattern with maximal effort remains complete; however, the peak-to-peak amplitude of the recruitment pattern is reduced. *A complete recruitment pattern of reduced amplitude in a weak muscle is one of the most characteristic EMG findings in muscle disease.*

The abnormal electromyogram Findings of pathologic significance include (1) the occurrence of spontaneous activity during relaxation (fibrillations, positive sharp waves, and fasciculations); (2) abnormalities in the amplitude, duration, and shape of single motor unit potentials; (3) decrease in the number of motor units which can be recruited; (4) demonstration of myotonia, coupling (tetany), bizzare repetitive potentials, or the occurrence of electric silence during shortening of the muscle (contracture).

SPONTANEOUS ACTIVITY DURING COMPLETE RELAXATION Persistent insertional activity occurs in myotonic disorders, in polymyositis, and in denervated muscles. Spontaneous activity of part of or an entire motor unit is called a *fasciculation,* and spontaneous activity of single muscle fiber is called a *fibrillation.* Fibrillations appear with destruction of the motor neuron or its axon and in muscle diseases where a portion of a muscle fiber is separated from its innervated portions by segmental necrosis. When a motor neuron is destroyed by disease or when its axon is severed, the distal part of the axon degenerates over a period of several days. Muscle fibers formerly innervated by the branches of the dead axon are disconnected from the nervous system. The chemosensitive region of the sarcolemma at the motor end plate spreads after denervation to involve the entire surface of the muscle fiber. This, together with the lowered resting membrane potential of denervated muscle fibers, results in the development of spontaneous activity in denervated muscle fibers 7 to 25 days after the death of the axon (depending upon the distance of the denervated muscle fibers from the site of the lesion). This spontaneous activity is similar to that found in the sinoatrial node of the heart; that is, each fiber contracts at its own rate without relation to the activity of adjacent fibers. The denervated muscle has a random conglomeration of brief, triphasic fibrillation potentials and diphasic *positive sharp waves.* Fibrillation and positive sharp wave activity continue until muscle fibers are reinnervated by the outgrowth of new axons, either from the proximal end of the damaged nerve or from nearby healthy nerve fibers, or until the muscle fibers are replaced over a period of months or years by connective tissue. *Fasciculations* are the involuntary single contractions of a part of or an entire motor unit. Since a large number of muscle fibers contract together, visible dimpling or twitching of the skin occurs, though ordinarily not enough power is exerted to move a joint. The form of the accompanying EMG potential, like that of an ordinary motor unit, is relatively constant for any one fasciculating unit. It usually has three to five phases (polyphasic), a duration of 5 to 15 ms, and an amplitude of several hundred microvolts. In the *benign fasciculations* seen in many normal subjects, the same unit tends to contract at a regular rate, which indicates a rhythmic activation of muscle fibers innervated by a particular axon. The EMG appearance of benign fasciculations is

FIGURE 354-1 *The triphasic muscle action potential. The shaded area represents the zone of the action potential, which is negative to all other points on the fiber surface. It is shown at three points in its course (from left to right) along the fiber. At each point, the correspondingly lettered portion of the triphasic muscle action potential displayed on the cathode ray oscilloscope (CRO) reflects the potential difference between the active (vertical arrow) and reference (Ref.) electrodes. Polarity in this and subsequent figures is negative upward as depicted. The time calibration is on the CRO screen. (For further details see text.)*

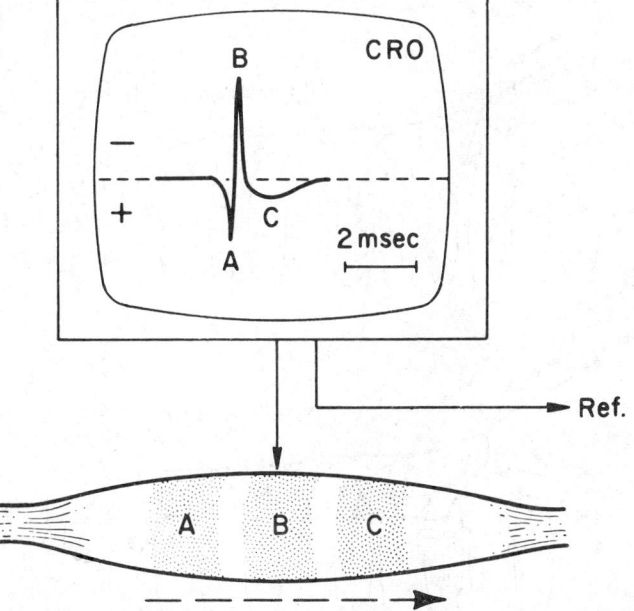

similar to that of normal motor unit potentials, and their rate of firing is usually faster than that of fasciculations indicative of disease.

The fasciculations seen with slowly progressive disease of the anterior horn cells, such as amyotrophic lateral sclerosis and progressive spinal muscular atrophy, are numerous, of relatively prolonged duration, and of high amplitude. Such fasciculations also occur with compressive nerve root lesions, in some motor neuropathies, and early in the course of acute inflammatory polyneuropathy. With nerve root lesions such as those caused by a herniated nucleus pulposus (ruptured disk), large numbers of axons may be affected, producing prominent fasciculations. In these cases the damaged neuron seems to be ''irritated'' by the disease process, fires repetitively, and in doing so, produces activity in muscle fibers innervated by it. Fasciculations may also follow traumatic peripheral nerve lesions, giving way to fibrillations upon death of the axon. Fasciculations in the calves and hands occur in many normal persons.

ABNORMALITIES IN MOTOR UNIT POTENTIALS   Motor unit potentials may show abnormalities in *amplitude, number, duration,* and *shape.*
Increased amplitude   Early in the course of denervation, motor units with functional connection to the spinal cord remain normal, but the

FIGURE 354-2 *Motor unit potentials. The shaded muscle fibers are functional members of one motor unit; the axon, which enters from the upper left, branches terminally to innervate the appropriate muscle fibers. The motor unit action potential produced by each motor unit is seen in the upper right; its duration is measured between the two small vertical lines. The normal-appearing but unshaded fibers belong to other motor units. A. The normal situation, with five muscle fibers in the active unit. B. In this myopathic unit, only two fibers remain active; the other three (shrunken) have been affected by a muscle disease. C. Four fibers which belonged to other motor units and had been denervated have now been reinnervated by terminal axon sprouting from the healthy motor unit. Both the motor unit and its action potential are now larger than normal. Note that only under these abnormal circumstances do fibers in the same unit lie next to one another.*

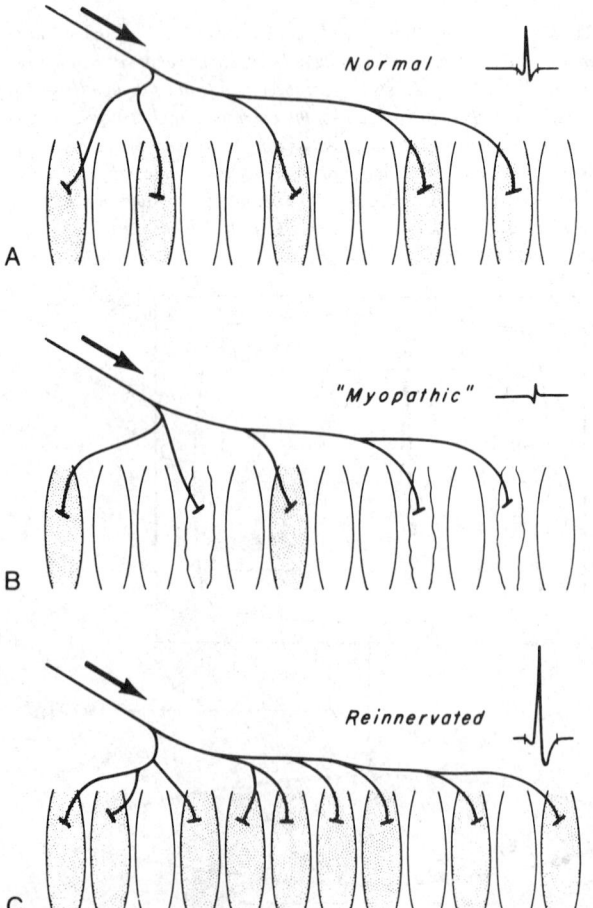

number of motor unit potentials appearing during contraction is reduced. In time, the remaining motor unit potentials may increase in amplitude to as much as two to three times normal, become longer in duration, and become polyphasic (more than 4 phases). Such large potentials (greater than 5 mV) arise from motor units (Fig. 354-2C) that contain an increased number of muscle fibers distributed through an enlarged territory within the muscle. These enlarged motor units arise when new nerve twigs sprout from undamaged axons and reinnervate previously denervated fibers, adding them to their own motor units. These reinnervated units may produce polyphasic and prolonged action potentials, a finding pathognomonic of reinnervation. These units must be differentiated from the polyphasic potentials of normal duration that occur in normal muscles, particularly in the end-plate zone, and brief polyphasic potentials seen with muscle disease.

Reduced amplitude and duration   Diseases such as polymyositis, the muscular dystrophies, and other myopathies that destroy scattered fibers within a motor unit (Fig. 354-2B), reduce the population of fibers per motor unit. When such a unit is activated, its potential is of lower amplitude and shorter duration than normal and may appear polyphasic since individual muscle fiber potentials are visible. When most of the muscle fibers within a motor unit are affected, the action potentials may be difficult to differentiate from fibrillation, and when destruction of all fibers is completed, electric activity ceases. The small, brief action potentials cause characteristic high-pitched crackling sounds from the loudspeaker.

In myasthenia gravis and other disorders where the transmission of impulses fails progressively at one neuromuscular junction after another, the EMG potential of that unit may be normal at first and become more myopathic as fatigue develops. Action potentials from weak muscles in myasthenia gravis are therefore proportionately myopathic. As shown in Fig. 354-2B, motor unit potentials appear equally ''myopathic'' whether the disease process directly affects single muscle fibers within the unit, as in a muscular dystrophy, or disturbs neuromuscular transmission at single junctions, as in myasthenia gravis.

Decrease in the number of motor units   Diseases that reduce the number of lower motor neurons or motor axons within the peripheral nerve decrease the number of motor units which can be recruited in affected muscles. The number of motor units available for activation in denervated muscles varies in proportion to the strength of maximum voluntary contraction, and the action potential appears no longer as a complete recruitment (interference) pattern but rather as a *single unit pattern* or *mixed pattern* with maximum voluntary effort.

Decrease in number of muscle fibers   In muscle diseases such as muscular dystrophy or other myopathies, where individual muscle fibers are affected, there is little or no reduction in the number of motor units available for recruitment even though each unit has fewer muscle fibers than normal. Maximum voluntary effort produces a normal full recruitment pattern despite marked weakness. Because fewer muscle fibers are active, however, the amplitude of the pattern is reduced from normal. *A full recruitment pattern of less than normal amplitude, in the face of significant clinical weakness, is the hallmark of a so-called myopathic EMG.*

Variation in the shape of action potentials   In certain neuromuscular junction disorders, such as myasthenia gravis and Lambert-Eaton syndrome, there is abnormal variation in the shape and amplitude of single motor unit potentials with sustained voluntary activity. This variation of motor unit potentials results from an intermittent block of conduction at individual neuromuscular junctions.

Other abnormalities   In *myotonia*, the sarcolemmal membrane is irritable, and repeated muscle depolarization and contraction occur despite voluntary attempts at relaxation (Chap. 17). Such patterns occur in myotonia congenita, myotonic dystrophy, and hyperkalemic periodic paralysis. On EMG, myotonia causes high-frequency repetitive discharges which wax and wane in amplitude and frequency, producing a ''dive bomber'' or ''motorcycle'' sound on the loud speaker. Myotonia occurs with percussion or movement of the needle electrode or following voluntary contraction of the muscle. Motor unit potentials appear normal but are not followed by the silence which normally occurs on relaxation. Instead there is a burst of rapid activity which may take as long as several minutes to subside. Some of the potentials of this prolonged discharge have the duration, amplitude, and form of single-fiber activity, while others have characteristics of motor unit potentials.

Bizarre, repetitive high-frequency discharges without waxing and waning are seen in hypothyroidism and other disorders affecting peripheral nerve or muscle. High-frequency *coupling* of action potentials into doublets, triplets, or higher multiples of single units occurs in tetany and hemifacial spasm and indicates instability in repolarization of the nerve fiber. Electric silence characterizes *contracture*, as in McArdle's disease or malignant hyperthermia.

Single-fiber EMG and macro EMG In addition to conventional EMG with concentric needle electrodes, specialized techniques permit the recording of the EMG of single muscle fibers or of the entire motor unit (macro EMG). Single fiber techniques, by recording *jitter*, can measure accurately, within microseconds, the performance of individual neuromuscular junctions. Characteristic quantitative abnormalities are found in patients with myasthenia gravis and other disorders of neuromuscular transmission. Single-fiber EMG studies are also used to calculate *fiber density*, the number of single muscle fiber action potentials belonging to one motor unit within the recording area of the single-fiber EMG electrode (approximately 200 μm). Fiber density values are increased after denervation-reinnervation processes.

Macro EMG techniques measure all fibers belonging to a motor unit and allow estimation of true motor unit size. The amplitude and area of macro EMG motor unit potentials is increased in reinnervation and decreased in primary muscle diseases that cause reduction in the number of muscle fibers per motor unit.

NERVE CONDUCTION STUDIES Stimulation of the larger peripheral motor and sensory nerves permits the recording of their action potentials and provides objective quantitative data of *latency* and *conduction velocity*. The technique is performed by stimulating the nerve with surface electrodes placed on the skin over the nerve. The resulting *compound action potential* is recorded by electrodes—over the nerve proximally in the case of large sensory fibers; over the muscle distally in the case of motor fibers in a mixed motor-sensory nerve (Fig. 354-3). The conduction time from the most distal stimulating electrode, measured in milliseconds from the stimulus artifact to the onset of the response, is termed the *distal* or *peripheral* latency. If a second stimulus is applied to a mixed nerve, more proximally (or if recording electrodes are placed more proximally in the case of sensory fibers), a new and longer conduction time can be measured. When the distance (in millimeters) between the two sites of stimulation of motor fibers or recording of sensory fibers is divided by the difference in conduction times (in milliseconds), a *maximal conduction velocity* (in meters per second) is obtained. It describes the velocity of propagation of the action potentials in the largest and fastest nerve fibers. These velocities in normal subjects vary roughly from 40 or 45 m/s, depending upon which nerve is studied, to 75 or 80 m/s. Values are lower in newborn infants (approximately half of the adult values) and reach the adult range by 3 to 4 years of age. Normal values also exist for peripheral latencies from the most distal site on various mixed nerves to the appropriate muscles. When one stimulates the median nerve at the wrist, for example, the latency for conduction through the carpal tunnel to the abductor pollis brevis muscle is usually less than 4.5 ms in normal subjects. Tables of similar normal values have been compiled for conduction velocity and distal latencies that vary with the distance. It is important to maintain normal body temperature during nerve conduction studies because subnormal temperatures cause slower conduction velocity. Nerve conduction velocity is related to fiber diameter and to the degree of demyelination. Unmyelinated and small-diameter fibers have slower conduction velocities than large-diameter, myelinated

fibers. Fibers with segmental demyelination have decreased conduction velocities. When motor fibers in the mixed peripheral nerve are stimulated and when each nerve fiber is in functional continuity with its many muscle fibers, the large *compound muscle action potential* arising from many firing muscle fibers can be recorded from skin electrodes over the muscle. Sensory action potentials, recorded from nerve fibers themselves, lack the "amplification" provided by muscle fibers; hence, more electronic amplification is required. In abnormal nerves, sensory potentials may be small or absent, and sensory conduction measurements may be impossible to record. In contrast, reliable measurement of motor conduction velocities is usually possible even though only one functional nerve fiber remains intact.

Nerve conduction velocity measurements reflect the status of the best surviving nerve fibers and, if even a few fibers are unaffected by the disease process, may be normal despite extensive nerve degeneration. After incomplete transection of nerve by a sharp object, the maximum motor conduction velocity may be normal in the few remaining fibers although the muscle involved is almost totally paralyzed. The axon is the primary site of pathology in alcoholic, nutritional, uremic, and diabetic neuropathy. The axons which remain intact conduct impulses normally, so that when the larger fibers are affected, the remaining smaller-diameter fibers, which normally conduct more slowly, account for a slightly slower maximum motor conduction velocity.

Nerve conduction velocity in many neuropathies is often normal or only slightly below normal. Ordinary nerve conduction studies

FIGURE 354-3 *Measurement of nerve conduction velocity. The median nerve is stimulated through the skin at the wrist (1) or in the antecubital fossa (2), and the resultant compound muscle action potential is recorded as the potential difference between a surface electrode over the thenar eminence (vertical arrow) and a reference electrode (Ref.) more distally. Sweep 1' on the cathode ray oscilloscope (CRO) depicts the stimulus artifact (moment of stimulation at 1) followed by the muscle potential. The distal latency is the time A' on the CRO sweep (3.0 ms, for example) which corresponds to conduction over distance A in the hand. The same is true for sweep 2', where stimulation is at point 2 and the time from artifact to response is A' + B'. The maximal motor conduction velocity from point 2 to point 1 is obtained by dividing distance B by time B'.*

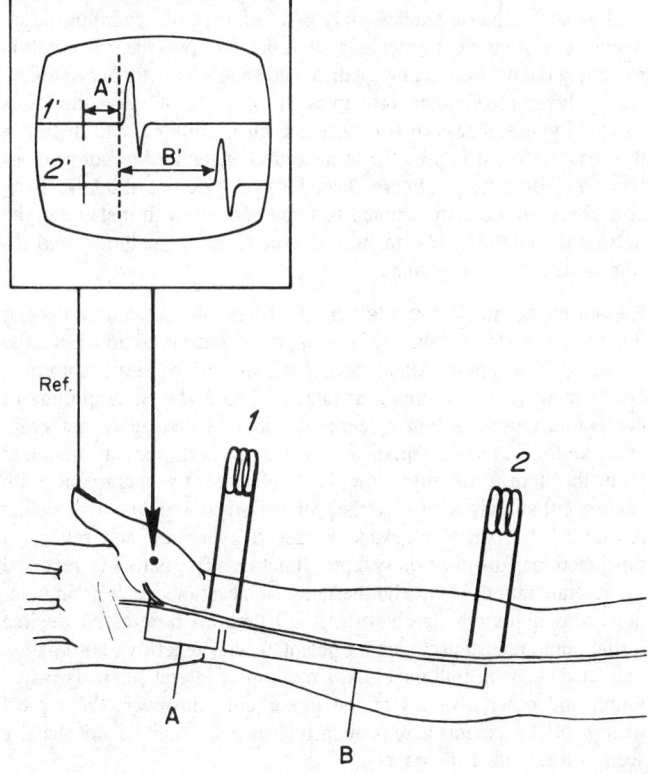

can usually, therefore, be used to document the presence of neuropathy only by comparison of recorded values with those from an adequate control group of the same age and sex.

Although many diseases of peripheral nerves do not cause reduction in nerve conduction velocity, disorders such as acute idiopathic polyneuropathy (Guillain-Barré syndrome), diphtheria, metachromatic leukodystrophy, and the hypertrophic neuropathies cause slowed velocities because they affect Schwann cells primarily and produce segmental demyelination. Focal compressions of nerve, as in entrapment syndromes, produce localized slowing of conduction because of narrowing of axons and demyelination at the site of compression. The demonstration of such localized slowing of conduction is useful in confirming nerve entrapment. A comparison of the peripheral (terminal) latency of one median nerve with the other median nerve or with an ulnar nerve may provide evidence for compression of the median nerve in the carpal tunnel. Normal conduction times do not, however, exclude an entrapment syndrome.

Other techniques for evaluation of nerve conduction Methods for study of conduction in more proximal segments of nerve include measurements of latencies for *F responses, H reflexes,* and *blink reflexes.* These techniques determine conduction velocity in nerves going from the periphery (of a limb or the face) to the central nervous system (spinal cord or brainstem) and back again. The *F response* measures the time required for a stimulus applied to the axon of an alpha motor neuron to pass antidromically to the anterior horn of the spinal cord and then to return orthodromically down the same axon. The *H reflex* measures the time required for orthodromic conduction up the nerve via group IA sensory fibers, through the spinal monosynaptic connection with the alpha motor neuron, and then orthodromically down the motor axon. Thus, conduction along proximal sensory and motor nerves and spinal roots can be measured. The application of these techniques to the measurement of proximal nerve conduction has increased the likelihood of recognition of abnormal conduction velocity in patients with peripheral neuropathy to 80 to 90 percent. The *blink reflexes* measure conduction in branches of the trigeminal and facial nerves. The blink reflex evoked by electric stimulation of the supraorbital branches of the trigeminal nerve permits localization of lesions in the distribution of facial or trigeminal nerves.

The nerve conduction studies described above, conventional as well as late-response studies, only give information regarding large-diameter fast-conducting axons and do not provide information regarding conduction in intermediate and small-diameter nerve fibers. By applying physiologic principles of collision of nerve impulses evoked by stimulation to two different sites (proximal and distal) in the same nerve, it is possible to measure conduction in motor axons with small diameters. Abnormal conduction velocities of intermediate size fibers can be demonstrated in some patients with metabolic and nutritional neuropathies in whom conventional methods and F-response studies are normal.

Repetitive stimulation tests In disorders of the neuromuscular junction, the size of the initial compound muscle action potential produced by a supramaximal electric stimulus to the nerve is normal; however, after a few stimuli at rates of 2 to 3 Hz the amplitude of compound muscle action potential declines; it then increases again after the fourth or fifth stimulus. This pattern of decrement, maximal with the fourth or fifth stimulus, followed by increment with subsequent stimuli is characteristic of myasthenia gravis. This defect resembles the partial blockade produced by curare and reflects a postjunctional disorder of synaptic function. The defect is reversed by administration of anticholinesterase medications such as intravenous edrophonium hydrochloride (5 to 10 mg). A progressive decline in the compound muscle action potential with repetitive stimulation may also occur in poliomyelitis, amyotrophic lateral sclerosis, myotonia, and other diseases of the motor unit; however, the typical pattern of decrement-increment in myasthenia gravis is not usually seen in these other disorders.

In the Lambert-Eaton (myasthenic) syndrome, repetitive stimulation causes a facilitation of transmission. Rapid stimulation of nerve (20 to 30 Hz) results in a progressive increase in muscle action potentials, which are small or virtually absent at the first stimulus, to a nearly normal amplitude. This facilitation response is not affected by anticholinesterase drugs but may be reversed by guanidine hydrochloride (10 to 30 mg/kg per day in divided doses). The neuromuscular transmission defect of this "reversed" myasthenic syndrome is prejunctional and is the result of a defective release of acetylcholine; a similar defect results from botulinum toxin or from the paralysis produced by the aminoglycoside antibiotics (see Chap. 358).

EMG IN DISORDERS OF THE CENTRAL NERVOUS SYSTEM The application of EMG and nerve conduction studies to evaluation of function of the central nervous system is termed *central EMG.* Since the motor unit is the final common path for all nerve impulses controlling skeletal muscles, the disorders of motor control produced by lesions of the central nervous system result in abnormal discharge patterns of motor neurons that can be documented by electrophysiologic techniques. For example, surface EMG recordings from pairs of antagonistic muscles, analysis of single motor unit recruitment patterns, and microneurographic studies are useful in evaluating different types of tremor, including rest tremor of Parkinson's disease, essential familial tremor, and physiologic tremor. Cerebellar ataxia can usually be separated from other tremors and from sensory ataxia. Asterixis can be distinguished from tremor, and different types of myoclonus can be documented. Studies of proprioceptive and exteroceptive reflexes are helpful in the differential diagnosis of movement disorders and in differentiating spasticity from other types of rigidity. Studies of the H reflex and F responses provide information regarding the excitability of the motor neuron pool. The effect of vibration on the H reflex has been used to evaluate presynaptic inhibition in different neurologic disorders. Silent-period studies have been used to evaluate function of proprioceptive input from muscle spindles. Mismatching of information from muscle spindles and joint receptors can result in an apparent "cerebellar" ataxia in patients with acute inflammatory polyneuropathy (Fisher syndrome) due to a lesion in the peripheral nervous system. EMG recordings and blink reflexes are useful in documenting clinically inapparent lesions of the brainstem in multiple sclerosis and in localizing early compressive lesions of trigeminal and facial nerves produced by small posterior fossa tumors.

HISTOPATHOLOGY OF MUSCLE AND NERVE *Muscle biopsy* is useful in (1) distinguishing between neurogenic and myopathic processes; (2) recognizing specific disorders of muscle such as muscular dystrophy or the congenital myopathies; (3) identifying specific metabolic defects of muscle by histochemical or biochemical techniques; and (4) diagnosing diseases of connective tissue and blood vessels, such as polyarteritis nodosa, and infections such as trichinosis or toxoplasmosis.

Muscle biopsy is performed under local anesthesia. In children and in adults with chronic conditions, an adequate specimen can often be obtained by needle biopsy. Open biopsy may be necessary to diagnose focal, patchy processes such as myositis or vasculitis. In all instances the muscle chosen for sampling must be appropriate for the condition suspected, and the specimen must be handled by a laboratory skilled in the evaluation of muscle. If the biopsy is taken from a muscle that has recently been traumatized by an EMG needle or that has been affected by a preexisting disease (e.g., coincidental nerve root compression), misleading information will be obtained.

Normal muscle histology Transverse sections of normal muscle show large numbers of muscle fibers grouped into areas (or fascicles) by connective tissue septa (perimysium), which may contain nerve bundles and blood vessels. The individual muscle fibers lie surrounded by thin collagen sheaths (endomysium) and by capillaries. The range of muscle fiber diameter is 40 to 80 μm in adult limb muscles, and the distribution of diameters is unimodal. Each fiber consists of myofibrils surrounded by and interspersed with cytoplasm containing glycogen, mitochondria, and sarcotubular systems. The muscle fiber is surrounded by a plasmalemma (sarcolemma) and a basal lamina. Multiple muscle nuclei are present in each fiber (which is a syncitium) and are almost all restricted to the subsarcolemmal region. A few stem cells or satellite cells are located between the basal lamina and the plasmalemma of the muscle fiber, and these provide the major source of myoblasts for regeneration of damaged muscle fibers. The histochemical separation of fibers into types I and II has been described above.

Muscle has a relatively limited number of pathologic reactions.

DENERVATION, REINNERVATION A denervated muscle fiber undergoes atrophy, and in the initial stages myofibrils are lost to a greater degree than is sarcoplasm containing the mitochondria, so that muscle fibers appear "super dark" with stains for oxidative enzymes (Fig. 354-4). Such denervated fibers are squeezed by adjacent innervated fibers and therefore become angulated and atrophic. In the initial stages of denervation, because of the overlap of many motor units in the same area, denervated atrophic fibers are distributed randomly throughout the muscle. Remaining motor axons sprout to reinnervate such fibers, eventually producing fiber type grouping (Fig. 354-2C). With subsequent death of such enlarged motor units, grouped fiber atrophy occurs. The typical appearance of a denervated and reinnervated muscle is shown in Fig. 354-4. The fiber diameter distribution in chronically denervated and reinnervated muscle is bimodal, with the atrophic denervated fibers making up one population and the normal size (or hypertrophied) innervated fibers making up the other population. It is generally difficult to make a specific diagnosis or determine a specific etiology from the muscle biopsy in cases of muscle denervation and reinnervation.

MUSCLE FIBER NECROSIS AND REGENERATION Damage of the sarcolemma of the muscle fiber allows entry of calcium at the high extracellular concentration into the low-calcium environment of the sarcoplasm. Calcium entry activates a neutral protease, thereby initiating proteolysis. Calcium also poisons mitochondrial function and causes cell death. Invading macrophages phagocytose the muscle fibers. Satellite cells, which provide the basis for regeneration of muscle fibers, are spared in most of the processes that damage muscles. They proliferate and fuse to produce multinuclear myotubes leading to regeneration of the muscle fiber. Characteristically, regenerating fibers are small, are basophilic owing to an increased concentration of RNA, and have large vesicular internal nuclei. The distribution of muscle fiber diameters in a typical chronic myopathy is broad and unimodal—very different from the bimodal diameter distribution of denervated and reinnervated muscle.

Muscle fiber necrosis and regeneration are common responses to damage, including damage caused by trauma, Duchenne's dystrophy, polymyositis, and dermatomyositis. Eventually, if the necrosis is sufficiently chronic, regeneration may fail, causing progressive loss of muscle fibers and replacement with fat and fibrous tissue. A chronic myopathy, Duchenne's dystrophy, is illustrated in Fig. 354-5. Differences in the extent and tempo of these processes allow histologic distinction between the muscular dystrophies, inflammatory myopathies, and acute rhabdomyolysis.

STRUCTURAL CHANGES IN MUSCLE FIBERS Degeneration of muscle fibers without frank necrosis produces structural alteration of individual muscle fibers; disorganization of myofibrils and sarcoplasm produces target fibers (Fig. 354-4), ringbinden (appearance of a portion of a fiber wrapped around another), central cores, cytoid bodies, and nemaline bodies. In one condition the fibers resemble

FIGURE 354-4 *A. Normal skeletal muscle biopsy stained for myosin ATPase (pH 9.4). Type I fibers are light, type II dark. B. Chronic denervation-reinnervation showing fiber type grouping. (Myosin ATPase, pH 9.4.) C. Chronic denervation-reinnervation in amyotrophic lateral sclerosis, prepa-* *ration stained for mitochondrial enzyme, NADH-TR. There are groups of reinnervated type II fibers (light) and of denervated angulated atrophic fibers, many of them "superdark" and showing target fiber changes. D. Type II fiber atrophy. (Myosin ATPase, pH 9.4.)*

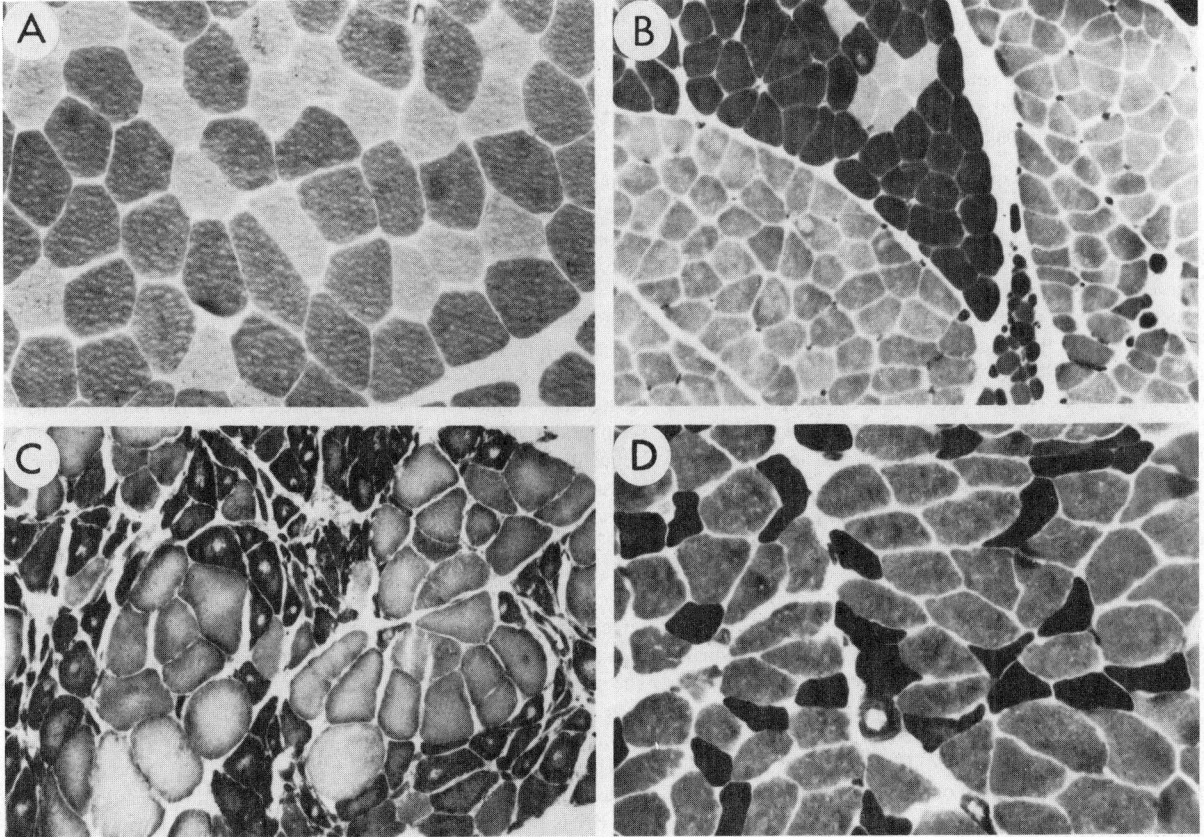

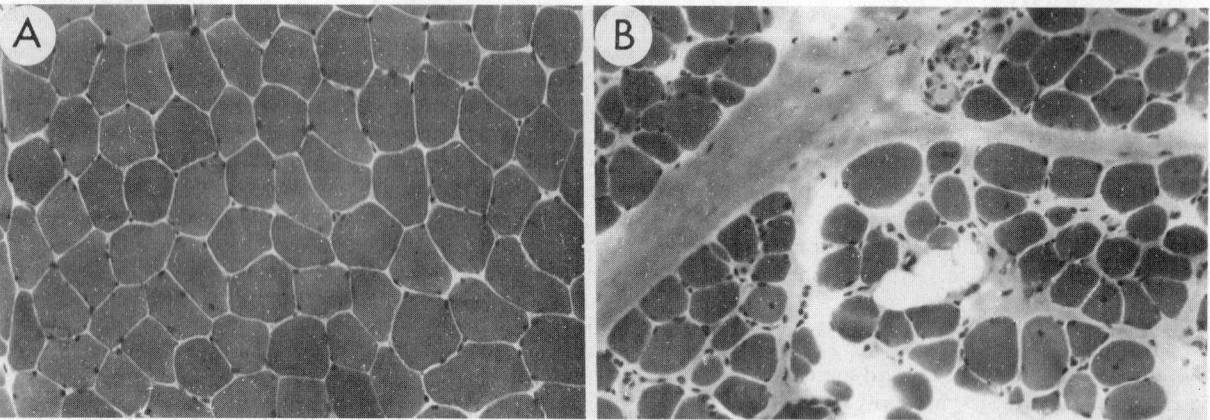

FIGURE 354-5 *A. Normal muscle (Hematoxylin-eosin.) B. Duchenne's muscular dystrophy, showing hypertrophy and atrophy of fibers, fiber degeneration, loss of fibers and fibrosis. (Hematoxylin-eosin.)*

myotubes (centronuclear myopathy). In others, abnormal mitochondria suggest an abnormality of mitochondrial biochemistry, while the presence of vacuoles suggests a disturbance of glycogen or lipid metabolism. Rimmed vacuoles (accumulations of degenerating phospholipid material between myofibrils) occur particularly in oculopharyngeal muscular dystrophy and inclusion body myositis.

INFLAMMATORY CHANGES Perivascular and interstitial inflammatory cell infiltration with lymphocytes is characteristic of polymyositis and dermatomyositis. Necrosis and regeneration of muscle fibers are also present. In some instances, atrophy of the fibers located on the periphery of muscle fasciculi (perifascicular atrophy) is prominent and can be an indicator of inflammatory myopathy, even though a focus of inflammation is not present in the muscle taken at biopsy. Muscle biopsy may show vasculitis in patients with collagen diseases or granulomas in patients with sarcoidosis.

CHANGES SPECIFIC TO FIBER TYPE Pathologic changes may be restricted to one fiber type in the muscle. The most common such condition is type II fiber atrophy (Fig. 354-4), which occurs in a wide range of disorders that limit activity such as disuse, muscle pain, joint pain, and upper motor neuronal dysfunction. Atrophy of type I fibers is less frequent and occurs in myotonic dystrophy, rheumatoid arthritis, and some congenital myopathies.

NERVE BIOPSY *Nerve biopsy* is more difficult and more traumatic than muscle biopsy and is useful in a limited number of specific circumstances (see Chap. 355). The sural nerve in the leg or the superficial radial nerve at the wrist are the usual biopsy sites. Both are sensory nerves and may show no changes in pure motor neuropathies. The procedure is performed under local anesthesia, and specimens are obtained for light and electron microscopy and for teasing of individual nerve fibers. Nerve biopsy aids in (1) distinguishing between segmental demyelination and axonal degeneration; (2) identification of inflammatory neuropathies; and (3) establishing specific diagnoses such as amyloidosis, sarcoidosis, leprosy, and several metabolic neuropathies. Full evaluation of the nerve biopsy requires the facilities of a laboratory with special interest and experience in peripheral nerve disease. There are two basic pathologic processes seen in nerve biopsies.

Light microscopic examination of biopsied nerves is of limited value, showing only gross changes such as vasculitis, inflammation, infiltration by granuloma or amyloid, loss of axons, and axonal degeneration. More information is obtained by electron microscopy and studies of single, teased nerve fibers. Some diseases affect specific fiber types; large myelinated fibers are affected in Friedreich's ataxia and unmyelinated fibers in familial amyloidosis. Quantitative morphometry (measurement of the number of fibers and the distribution of their diameters) is of additional help.

SEGMENTAL DEMYELINATION Diseases may attack either myelin or the Schwann cell, causing the myelin sheath to undergo degeneration but leaving the axon essentially unchanged. Healing of this segmental demyelination proceeds through a phase of abnormally thin myelin sheaths, which may eventually return to normal thickness. However, even after apparent recovery of segmental demyelination, single, teased nerve fiber studies demonstrate short and variable lengths of the internodes (distance between the nodes of Ranvier). If this process is progressive, "onion-bulb" formation occurs with thinly remyelinated fibers lying at the center of concentric lamellae of redundant Schwann cell cytoplasm.

AXON DEGENERATION Death of the nerve cell body or section of the axon at any level will lead to degeneration of the distal parts of the axon with secondary degeneration of the myelin sheath. If the nerve cell body remains intact proximally there is attempted axonal regeneration with sprouting. Such nerve sprouts (clusters) are characteristic of an axonal, degenerating and regenerating neuropathy.

Axonal degeneration is most common in toxic, inherited, traumatic, and ischemic diseases. Segmental demyelination may occur in the inherited and autoimmune inflammatory disorders; in the latter condition inflammatory cell infiltration may be seen. A mixed picture of axonal degeneration and segmental demyelination, together with a vasculopathy, is characteristic of diabetes mellitus. Some specific pathologic changes may indicate the probable etiology of a neuropathy. The deposition of IgM on the myelin-associated glycoprotein of myelin in IgM gammopathies can be detected by immunofluorescence techniques and leads to an increase in myelin periodicity in the nerve. Amyloid fibrils are present in nerve in amyloid neuropathy. Specific inclusions may be seen in the Schwann cells in metachromatic leukodystrophy and adrenomyeloleukodystrophy.

BIOCHEMICAL EVALUATION Certain enzymes that occur in high concentrations in the sarcoplasm of muscle may leak into blood and serve as an indicator of muscle damage. Creatine kinase (CK) is the most sensitive and specific. While the CK level is usually normal in peripheral neuropathies and neuromuscular junction disorders, it is frequently mildly elevated in spinal muscular atrophy, amyotrophic lateral sclerosis, and other motor neuron disorders. Serum aspartate aminotransferase (AST, SGOT), alanine aminotransferase (ALT, SGPT), lactic dehydrogenase (LDH), and aldolase levels may be elevated in the serum of a patient with active muscle destruction. Since several of these enzymes are determined during routine office screening, it is not uncommon for a patient with muscle disease to be first identified by an unexpected elevation in one of these enzymes. The reason for the disproportionate increase in CK level is not entirely clear. For evaluating a patient with neuromuscular disease, only the CK need be studied.

Three isoenzymes of CK occur—MM, MB, and BB. MM predominates in skeletal muscle, MB occurs mainly in cardiac muscle, and BB is mainly in brain. Elevations of CK-MB level are used to indicate the presence of myocardial damage. CK level elevation caused by acute muscle injury is usually due to the MM isozyme. However, in patients with long-standing muscular diseases, in athletes, and in others who have a chronic elevation in CK level, the proportion of MB in skeletal muscle rises and in consequence the proportion of CK-MB in blood is elevated. A greater than tenfold elevation of CK level usually indicates the presence of muscle destruction. Lesser elevations of CK level can occur in many neuromuscular diseases as well as from minor muscle trauma, such as that after electromyography, in psychotic or alcoholic patients, in hypothyroidism or hypoparathyroidism, in individuals with muscle hypertrophy, and in the carrier state of certain genetic myopathies. Strenuous exercise or muscle trauma can elevate the level of CK in normal individuals. This elevation occurs 6 h or more following exercise.

Muscle composition and mass Computerized tomography and magnetic resonance imaging can differentiate between muscle fibers, fat, and connective tissue and may show distinctive differences between muscular dystrophy and other forms of muscle disease. The high cost, the limitations in terms of the number of cross sections of a limb that can be examined, and the nonspecificity of the findings suggest that the role of these techniques is limited. Estimations of total muscle mass are of some importance in metabolic studies. A simple decline in muscle mass without weakness is indicative of a process other than a neuromuscular disease, for example, aging, neoplasm, malnutrition, or renal or hepatic disease. The 24-h urine creatinine excretion is the most widely available technique used to estimate muscle mass; creatinine excretion is decreased in patients with wasting from any cause. Patients with wasting neuromuscular diseases have decreased serum creatinine levels, with values as low as 0.2 to 0.5 mg/dL. In patients with muscle wasting this reduction results in a disproportionately low serum creatinine level despite impaired renal function; patients with active muscle destruction have a correspondingly *increased* serum creatinine level.

Metabolic and endocrine studies Hypo- and hyperkalemia, hypernatremia, hypo- and hypercalcemia, hypophosphatemia, and hypermagnesemia can all cause severe, usually acute, weakness. Serum potassium levels are labile and subject to rapid shifts induced by acidosis or alkalosis. The intracellular concentration of potassium is high, so that hemolysis during blood collection may spuriously elevate the potassium level. Acute muscle damage producing rhabdomyolysis may produce a true hyperkalemia. Such elevations in serum potassium are not greater than 0.1 meq per liter, however, unless the serum is stained with hemoglobin, as occurs with hemolysis, or the urine with myoglobin, as in the case of rhabdomyolysis. Chronic endocrine disorders, either hypo- or hyperfunction of thyroid, adrenal, or parathyroid glands, may cause weakness. Thyroid and parathyroid disorders may cause muscle weakness in the absence of other clinical evidence of endocrinopathy. Rheumatoid arthritis, systemic lupus erythematosus, scleroderma, and the polymyalgia rheumatica syndrome may present with or be complicated by muscle weakness. Tests for these diseases are usually indicated in the evaluation of unexplained muscle pain and weakness. The weakness in most of these disorders is related to disuse atrophy and joint pain; muscle inflammation and evidence of muscle destruction are relatively uncommon.

Exercise testing (see Chap. 357) Patients with substrate utilization defects characteristically have decreased exercise tolerance and muscle pain and weakness during or following exercise. Most defects in the enzymatic pathways of glycolysis result in the failure of muscle to generate adenosine triphosphate (ATP) from glycogen and a diminished or absent production of lactic acid. Patients with these disorders can be evaluated with a forearm exercise test evaluating the level of venous lactic acid. Patients with disturbance of fatty acid metabolism (such as carnitine palmityl tranferase deficiency, in which long-chain fatty acids cannot be transferred into mitochondria for beta oxidation) generate lactic acid normally. Patients with myoadenylate deaminase deficiency generate lactate in normal or increased amounts but fail to produce ammonia in the exercise test (Chap. 357). Measurement of other muscle metabolites and specific enzymes can define the cause of the disorder.

Myoglobinuria Acute muscle destruction, *rhabdomyolysis* associated with myoglobinuria, occurs with acute toxic, metabolic, infectious, and traumatic muscle damage (Chap. 356). The molecular weight of myoglobin is lower than that of hemoglobin so that the urine rather than the serum changes color in extensive rhabdomyolysis. Lesser degrees of myoglobinuria can cause positive urine tests for blood in the absence of urinary erythrocytes. Confirmatory testing for myoglobin is possible with a specific immunoassay.

GENERAL THERAPEUTIC CONSIDERATIONS Cardiac disease Most disorders of skeletal muscle also involve cardiac muscle. Clinical cardiac dysfunction is relatively uncommon, perhaps because the limited exercise capacity of the patient with weakness decreases demand on cardiac performance. Relatively specific electrocardiographic abnormalities occur in Duchenne's dystrophy and infantile acid maltase deficiency. Cardiac conduction disorders including complete heart block occur in patients with myotonic dystrophy. An electrocardiogram should be obtained in all patients with neuromuscular disease, particularly in patients with myopathies.

Respiratory disease Diminished pulmonary function in patients with acute or chronic neuromuscular disease may progress to ventilatory failure. The earliest manifestation of respiratory muscle weakness is a decrease in maximum expiratory and inspiratory pressures. Diaphragmatic weakness, in particular, may be significant in patients with neuromuscular disease; diaphragmatic function should be evaluated by examining pulmonary function both while the patient is supine and sitting. The patient with diaphragmatic weakness has a greater impairment of pulmonary function in the supine position than in the erect position, as well as having paradoxical abdominal movements. Patients with chronic respiratory failure may be maintained with home respiratory support.

Physical therapy Physical therapy is of greatest value in patients with muscle weakness when joint contractures are developing and when enforced immobility, such as due to an injury, results in decreased activity. Exercises may increase strength in muscles weakened by disease just as it does in normal persons, but there is little convincing evidence that exercise improves functional abilities. On the other hand, therapeutic standing in patients with marginal leg and trunk function has considerable psychological benefit and may help to preserve bone mineralization and cardiovascular reflexes.

Dietary modification Dietary restriction is often necessary in patients with muscle weakness since caloric expenditure is decreased because of immobility and loss of muscle mass. Development of obesity further compromises already reduced mobility, worsens pulmonary function, and may depress ventilatory drive. Unless there is specific evidence for malabsorption of vitamin B_{12} or vitamin E, neither these nor any other vitamin has a specific role in the treatment of neuromuscular disease. Certain vitamins are hazardous in excessive doses, including vitamins B_6, A, and D (see Chaps. 76 and 336).

Bracing In patients with distal leg weakness, particularly of foot dorsiflexion, ankle-foot orthoses can restore gait to nearly normal. With more proximal weakness, however, leg braces diminish mobility and are of value only in enabling patients who are unable to walk to perform therapeutic standing. In most adults, even this use of braces is impractical because such standing in braces usually requires assistance.

Scoliosis Spinal deformity may complicate neuromuscular diseases that occur before puberty. Duchenne's dystrophy, spinal muscular atrophy, and congenital myopathies are particularly liable to this complication. Once full long-bone growth has been achieved, many of these patients have surgical correction of the scoliosis. Severely impaired pulmonary function is a contraindication to such therapy, and patients with limited life expectancy should probably be spared the pain and risks of the procedure.

Genetic evaluation and counseling (see also Chap. 357)   Management of the patient with hereditary muscle disease should include family pedigree analysis and genetic counseling. The family history may initially be negative in many patients with autosomal dominant diseases such as Charcot-Marie-Tooth disease, myotonic dystrophy, and facioscapulohumeral dystrophy because of the variable expressivity of the disorders. The availability of chromosomal markers for linkage analysis has made carrier detection, antenatal diagnosis, and early diagnosis of disease feasible in several hereditary neuromuscular diseases (e.g., in Duchenne's and myotonic dystrophy). The availability of therapy for disorders such as periodic paralysis, myotonia, and certain metabolic myopathies and of preventive measures in disorders such as malignant hyperthermia provides a strong impetus for early diagnosis. History is inadequate for family evaluation. Physical examination of, or inspection of photographs of, family members may provide clues to the characteristic facial or other features of the disorder and will often identify mildly afflicted individuals.

REFERENCES

BRADLEY WG: *Disorders of Peripheral Nerves.* Oxford, Blackwell, 1974

BROOKE MH: *A Clinician's View of Neuromuscular Disease,* 2d ed, Baltimore, Williams and Wilkins, 1986

BUCHTHAL F, SIMPSON JA (eds): *Handbook of Electroencephalography and Clinical Neurophysiology,* vol 16: *Electromyography,* Part A: *Nervous and Muscular Evoked Potentials;* Part B: *Neuromuscular Disease.* Amsterdam, Elsevier, 1973

CARPENTER S, KARPATI G: *Pathology of Skeletal Muscle.* New York, Churchill Livingston, 1984

DYCK PJ et al (eds): *Peripheral Neuropathy.* Philadelphia, Saunders, 1984

ENGEL AG, BANKER BQ (eds): *Myology.* New York, McGraw-Hill, 1986

KIMURA J: *Electrodiagnosis in Diseases of Nerve and Muscle: Principles and Practice,* Philadelphia, Davis, 1983

LANG H, WURZBURG U: Creatine kinase, an enzyme of many forms. Clin Chem 28:1439, 1982

SHAHANI BT: *Electromyography in Central Nervous System Disorders: Central Electromyography.* Boston, Butterworth, 1984

SCHAUMBURG HH et al: *Disorders of Peripheral Nerves.* Philadelphia, Davis, 1983

---

355   DISEASES OF THE PERIPHERAL NERVOUS SYSTEM

ARTHUR K. ASBURY

Peripheral neuropathy is a general term indicating a disorder of peripheral nerve of any cause; therefore, the knowledge that a peripheral neuropathy is present in a particular patient should instigate a search for its basis.

The basic processes affecting nerve and muscle and the approach to diseases of nerve and muscle are fully set forth in Chap. 354. The first purpose here is to build upon that base by providing an overview of the wide array of peripheral neuropathies which afflict humans. Disorders of peripheral nerve exhibit such a bewildering and complex set of manifestations that it is difficult for the physician to know where to begin and how to proceed. Therefore the second purpose here is to develop a logical approach and assessment scheme (summarized in Fig. 355-1) which will guide the examiner to correct diagnoses and management decisions.

GENERAL DESCRIPTION OF NEUROPATHIC SYNDROMES   The prototypical picture of polyneuropathy occurs with acquired toxic or metabolic neuropathic states. From a symptom standpoint, the first noticeable features tend to be sensory and consist of tingling, prickling,

burning, or bandlike dysesthesias in the balls of the feet or tips of the toes, or in a general distribution over the soles. Symmetry of symptoms and findings in a distal graded fashion is the rule, but occasionally dysesthesias appear in one foot a brief time before the other or may be more pronounced in one foot. Some care and judgment must be exercised here to avoid confusion with mononeuropathy multiplex. If the polyneuropathy remains mild, no objective motor or sensory signs may be detectable.

With progression, a definite pansensory loss is usually found over both feet, ankle jerks will be lost, and a weakness of dorsiflexion of the toes, best demonstrated in the great toe, may be present. In some instances, the process begins with weakness in the feet, usually dorsiflexion of the toes and feet without subjective sensory symptoms. As worsening occurs, sensory loss moves centripetally in a graded "stocking" fashion, and the patient may complain that the feet have a numb or "wooden" feeling or may say "I feel as though I'm walking on stumps." Patients experience difficulty walking on their heels during examination and their feet may slap while walking. Later, the knee jerk reflex disappears and foot drop becomes more apparent. By the time sensory disturbance has reached the upper shin, dysesthesias are generally noticed in the tips of the fingers. The degree of spontaneous pain varies, but is often considerable. Light stimuli to hypesthetic areas, once perceived, may be experienced as extremely uncomfortable (hyperpathia). Unsteadiness of gait may be out of proportion to muscle weakness because of proprioceptive loss.

Worsening proceeds in a centripetal, symmetrically graded manner with muscle atrophy, pansensory loss, and areflexia and with motor weakness that is usually greater in the extensor muscles than in corresponding flexor groups. When the sensory disturbance reaches mid thigh, generally a tent-shaped area of hypesthesia on the lower abdomen may be demonstrated. This will grow broader, and the apex will extend rostrally toward the sternum as the neuropathy worsens. By this time, patients generally cannot stand or walk or hold objects in their hands.

In the most extreme cases, ventilatory capacity may be impaired along with sphincteric function. Hypesthesia at the crown of the scalp may be present and spreads radially into both the trigeminal and C2 distribution. In considering this entire sequence of events, it becomes apparent that nerve fibers are affected according to length of axon without regard to root or nerve trunk distribution—hence, the aptness of the term "stocking-glove" to describe the pattern of sensory deficit. In general, the motor deficit is also graded, distal, and symmetric.

Variations on the general sequence outlined above are manifold. They include the rate of evolution of symptoms; fluctuations in the course; the eventual degree of severity; the presence or absence of positive motor and sensory symptoms; the symmetry of features and their distribution in terms of proximal versus distal, arms versus legs, and motor versus sensory; the relative proportion of dysfunction attributable to large fiber deficit and to small fiber deficit; and the determination, mainly by electrodiagnostic examination, of axonal versus demyelinating processes.

ASSESSMENT AND DIAGNOSIS OF NEUROPATHY   Taking the first step   Clues to the diagnosis of specific peripheral neuropathies often lie in unnoted or readily forgotten events occurring weeks or months prior to the onset of symptoms. Inquiry should be made about recent viral illnesses; other systemic symptoms; institution of new medications; potentially toxic exposures to solvents, pesticides, or heavy metals; the occurrence of similar symptoms in family members or coworkers; habits concerning alcohol; and the presence of known preexisting medical disorders. It is also useful to ask patients if they would otherwise feel well if free of their neuropathic symptoms, to obtain an idea of the presence or absence of an underlying systemic illness.

It is important to learn how symptoms first appeared. Even with distal polyneuropathies, symptoms may appear in the sole of one foot a few days or a week before the other, but usually the patient will

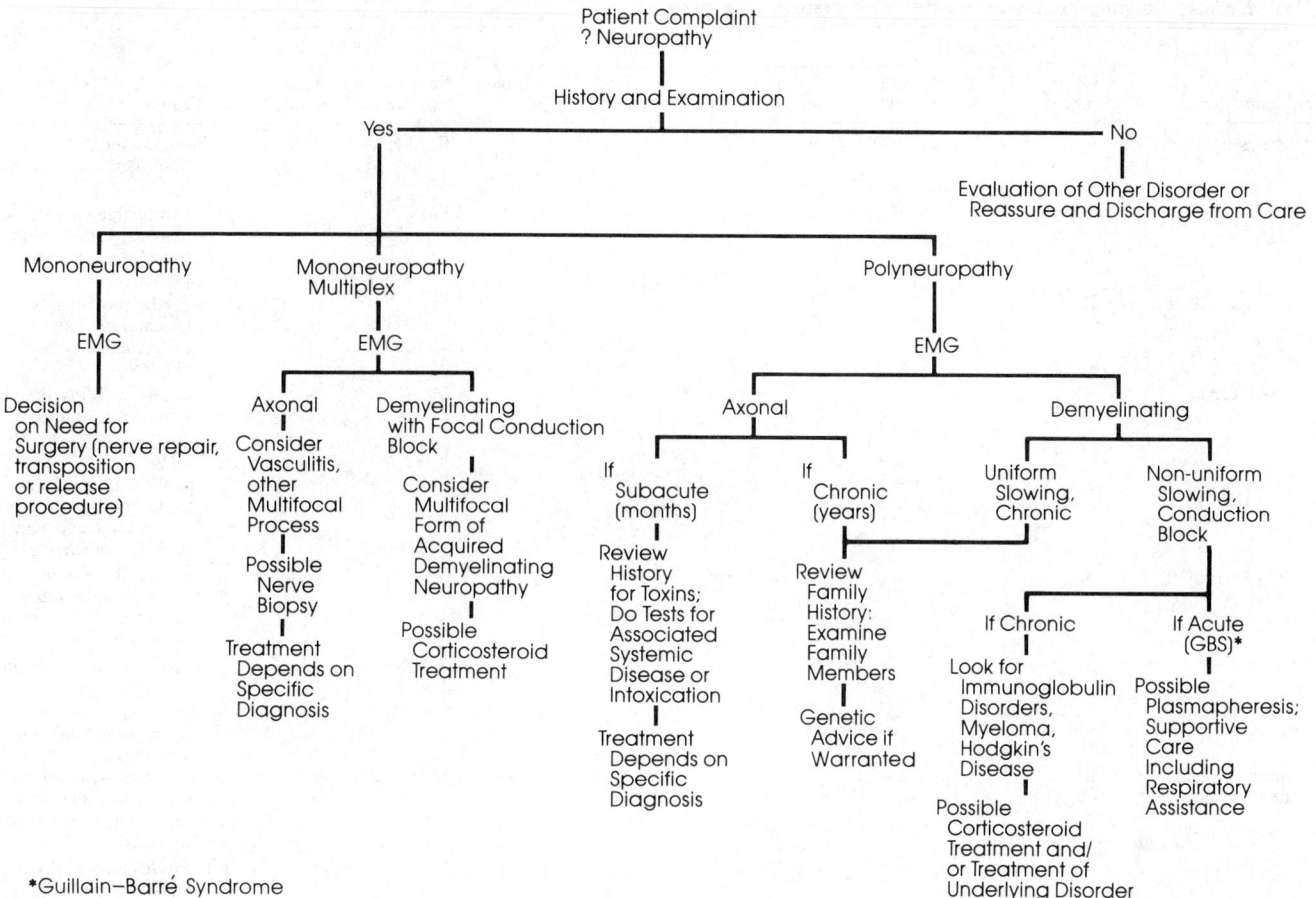

FIGURE 355-1 *Flowchart approach to the evaluation of peripheral neuropathies. (After Asbury, 1983.)*

describe a distal graded disturbance that moves evenly and symmetrically in centripetal fashion. Tingling dysesthesias will appear in the fingertips only when similar symptoms have reached the level of the knees. It is most important to determine whether symptoms first appeared in the distribution of individual digital nerves involving only one-half of a digit at a time and then gradually spread to become coalescent. This pattern of onset raises strong suspicions of a multifocal process (mononeuropathy multiplex) such as might be encountered with a systemic vasculitis or cryoglobulinemia.

The evolution of neuropathy ranges from rapid worsening over a few days to an indolent process extending many years. Polyneuropathies with a slowly progressive course lasting more than 5 years are most likely to be genetically determined, particularly if the major manifestations are distal atrophy and weakness with few or no positive sensory symptoms. Exceptions are diabetic polyneuropathy and paraproteinemic neuropathies in which the progression may be insidious over 5 to 10 years. Axonal degenerations of toxic or metabolic origin tend to evolve over several weeks to a year or more, and the rate of progression of demyelinating neuropathies is highly variable, ranging from a few days in Guillain-Barré syndrome to many years in others.

Major fluctuations in the course of neuropathy bring to mind two possibilities: (1) relapsing forms of neuropathy, or (2) repeated toxic exposures. A slow fluctuation in symptoms taking place over weeks or months (reflecting changes in the activity of neuropathy) should not be confused with day-to-day variation or diurnal undulation of symptoms. The latter are common to all neuropthic disorders. An example is carpal tunnel syndrome in which dysesthesias may be prominent at night but absent during the day.

In polyneuropathies, the findings can be expected to be quite symmetric on both sides of the body. If only one foot slaps when the patient walks, the process is not symmetric and the possibility of a multifocal process is raised. In addition, in acquired symmetric polyneuropathies, the muscles of extension and abduction tend to be weakened to a greater extent than the muscles of flexion and adduction.

Hence, a weakness in lower legs often affects the peronei and anterior tibial muscles, with attendant foot drop, more than the gastrocnemius group or foot inverters. In most polyneuropathies the legs are more severely affected than the arms and the distal muscles more than the proximal ones. There are exceptions to this rule, as in lead neuropathy, in which manifestations of bilateral wrist drop may predominate, and occasionally in porphyric neuropathy, in which arms may be more affected than legs and proximal muscles more than distal.

Palpation of the nerve trunk to detect enlargement is a frequently forgotten part of the neurological examination. In mononeuropathies, the entire course of the nerve trunk in question should be explored manually for focal thickening; the presence of neurofibroma, point tenderness, or Tinel's phenomenon (generation of a tingling sensation in the sensory territory of the nerve by tapping along the course of the nerve trunk); and elicitation of pain by putting the nerve trunk on stretch. In leprous neuritis, fusiform thickening of nerve trunks is frequent, and beading of nerve trunks may be encountered in amyloid polyneuropathy. Certain genetically determined neuropathies of the hypertrophic variety may be attended by uniform thickening of all nerve trunks, often to the caliber of a clothes line or larger.

Most neuropathies involve nerve fibers of all sizes, but on occasion selective damage restricted to large or to small fibers predominates. In a polyneuropathy affecting mainly small fibers, diminished pinprick and temperature sensation, often with burning painful dysesthesias, may predominate along with autonomic dysfunction but with relative sparing of motor power, balance, and tendon jerks. Selected cases of amyloid and distal diabetic polyneuropathies fall into this category. In contrast, large-fiber polyneuropathy is characterized by areflexia, imbalance, relatively minor cutaneous sensory deficit, and variable but often severe motor dysfunction.

In addition to taking a history and doing a physical examination that bears in mind the emphases described above, certain other measures can be undertaken routinely in the evaluation of a patient

TABLE 355-1 Polyneuropathy associated with systemic diseases

Systemic disease	Occurrence*	Axonal†			Demyelinating†			Sensory vs. motor‡	Autonomic†	Comment
		Acute	Subacute	Chronic	Acute	Subacute	Chronic			
Diabetes mellitus	C	—	±	+	—	±	+	S, SM, rarely M	± to +	Mixed axonal-demyelination often seen; see Table 355-4
Uremia	S	±	+	+	—	—	—	SM	±	Controllable with proper dialysis; curable with successful renal transplant
Porphyria (3 types)	R	+	±	—	—	—	—	M	± to +	May be proximal > distal and may have atypical proximal sensory deficits
Hypoglycemia	R	±	+	±	—	—	—	M	—	Usually with insulinoma; arms often > legs; ? anterior horn cells affected
Vitamin deficiency, exclude B₁₂	S	—	+	+	—	—	—	SM	±	Involves at least thiamine, pyridoxine, folate, pantothenic acid; probably others
Vitamin B₁₂ deficiency	S	—	±	+	—	—	—	S	—	Peripheral nerve involvement variable; often overshadowed by myelopathy
Chronic liver disease	S	—	—	—	—	—	+	S or SM	—	Usually mild or subclinical
Primary biliary cirrhosis	R	—	±	+	—	—	—	S	—	Epineurial and subperineurial xanthomatous deposits
Primary systemic amyloidosis	R	—	±	+	—	—	—	SM	+	Also seen with amyloidosis associated with myeloma or macroglobulinemia
Hypothyroidism	R	—	—	—	—	±	+	S	—	May respond to thyroid replacement
Chronic obstructive lung disease	R	—	±	+	—	—	—	S or SM	—	Few reports; a questionable entity
Acromegaly	R	—	—	+	—	—	—	S	—	Carpal tunnel syndrome also frequent
Malabsorption (sprue, celiac disease)	S	—	±	+	—	—	—	S or SM	±	Basis for neuropathy unclear; deficiency suspected
Carcinoma (sensory)	R	—	+	+	—	—	—	Pure S	—	Carcinomatous sensory neuropathy; due to gangliitic neuronopathy; mostly breast carcinoma; paraneoplastic; relatively rare

with neuropathy. Electrodiagnostic examination is a key procedure in all patients. For patients with polyneuropathy or mononeuropathy multiplex, standard tests should include a complete blood count and erythrocyte sedimentation rate, urinalysis, chest x-ray, postprandial blood glucose, and serum protein electrophoresis. Further tests should be dictated by the formulation arrived at via the combined history and physical and electrodiagnostic examination (see Fig. 355-1).

Taking the next step The next step is electrodiagnostic examination. It is not generally possible to make the distinction between axonal versus demyelinating disorders on clinical examination alone, and it is in this category that electrodiagnostic analysis is particularly useful. Electrodiagnostic features of demyelination are slowing of nerve conduction velocity (NCV), dispersion of evoked compound action potentials (CAPs), conduction block (major decrease in amplitude of muscle CAP upon proximal stimulation of its nerve as compared to distal stimulation), and marked prolongation of distal latencies. In contrast, axonal neuropathies are characterized by a reduction in amplitude of evoked CAPs with relative preservation of NCV. The distinction between a primarily demyelinating neuropathy from one which is primarily axonal is crucial because of the differing approaches to diagnosis and management. If in a particular instance of progressive polyneuropathy or subacute or chronic evolution the electrodiagnostic findings are those of an axonopathy, a long list of metabolic states and exogenous toxins come into consideration (see Tables 355-1 and 355-2). If the course is protracted over several years, it raises the likelihood of the neuronal (axonal) form of peroneal muscular atrophy (HMSN-II); family members must be examined and additional attention given to the family history.

Alternatively, if the electrodiagnostic findings are more indicative of primary demyelination of nerve, the approach is entirely different. The possibilities then include acquired demyelinating neuropathy, thought to be immunologically mediated, and genetically determined neuropathies, some of which are marked by uniform and drastic slowing of nerve conduction velocities.

With these considerations in hand, a flowchart can be constructed (Fig. 355-1) which summarizes the clinical and electrodiagnostic approach to the evaluation and management of a neuropathic disorder. Using this scheme, the clinician determines for each patient the tempo, distribution, severity, and functional impairment, and other features previously discussed, making a clinical judgment as to whether the problem represents a mononeuropathy, a mononeuropathy multiplex, or a polyneuropathy. Often this distinction is obvious. With the sum of clinical and electrodiagnostic information in hand,

TABLE 355-1 Polyneuropathy associated with systemic diseases (*continued*)

Systemic disease	Occurrence*	Axonal† Acute	Axonal† Subacute	Axonal† Chronic	Demyelinating† Acute	Demyelinating† Subacute	Demyelinating† Chronic	Sensory vs. motor‡	Autonomic†	Comment
Carcinoma (sensorimotor)	S	—	+	+	—	—	—	SM	±	Sensorimotor axonal neuropathy; mostly with lung carcinoma; more common than pure sensory, but still infrequent
Carcinoma (late)	C	—	+	+	—	—	—	S>M	±	Mild, late axonal neuropathy, probably related to weight loss and wasting
Carcinoma (demyelinating)	S	—	—	—	+	+	±	SM	—	Acute or relapsing demyelinating neuropathy sometimes seen with carcinoma
Lymphoma including Hodgkin's	S	—	+	+	+	+	±	See above	±	Same as carcinomatous types, although pure sensory type is even rarer
Polycythemia vera	R	—	±	+	—	—	—	S	—	Also many CNS manifestations; often shooting pains in limbs
Multiple myeloma lytic type	S	—	±	+	—	—	—	S, M, or SM	±	Symptomatic neuropathy uncommon, subclinical neuropathy frequent
Multiple myeloma§: osteosclerotic or solitary plasmacytoma	S	—	—	±	—	±	+	SM	—	Although may show severe slowing of nerve conduction velocity recent work suggests this is secondary demyelination
Benign monoclonal gammopathy:	S									
IgA		—	±	+	—	—	—	SM	—	IgMκ (or occasionally IgMλ) may bind to myelin-associated glycoprotein or glycolipids
IgG		—	±	+	—	—	—	SM	—	
IgM		—	—	—	—	±	+	SM	—	
Macroglobulinemia	R	—	—	±	—	—	+	SM	—	Usually but not always axonal
Cryoglobulinemia	R	—	±	+	—	—	—	SM	—	May be mononeuropathy multiplex in presentation

* *R = rare; S = sometimes; C = common.*
† *± = sometimes; + = usual.*
‡ *S = sensory; M = motor; SM = sensorimotor.*
§ *Some cases associated with POEMS syndrome (see text).*

the differential diagnostic possibilities and management options will have been narrowed to only a few. The remainder of this chapter deals with the details of this formulation.

Electrodiagnosis As seen in Fig. 355-1, electrodiagnosis is a key part of the evaluation of any neuropathy. See Chap. 354 for details of technique and interpretation. For example, electrodiagnosis helps one to be certain about the presence or absence of a sensory deficit when this is not clear by clinical examination alone. It provides information about the distribution of subclinical findings, thus sharpening the diagnostic focus. A listing of the general questions which may be posed by the clinician to the electrodiagnostician includes

1 The distinction between disorders primary to nerve or to muscle.
2 The distinction between root involvement and more distal nerve trunk involvement.
3 The distinction between generalized polyneuropathic processes and widespread multifocal nerve trunk affection.
4 The distinction between upper and lower motor neuron weakness.
5 The distinction, in a given generalized polyneuropathic process, between a primary demyelinating neuropathy and axonal degeneration.
6 The assessment, in both primary axonal and demyelinating neuropathies, of many factors bearing on the nature, activity, and likely prognosis of the neuropathy.
7 The assessment, in mononeuropathies, of the site of the lesion and its major effect on nerve fibers, especially the distinction

between demyelinating conduction block and wallerian degeneration.
8 The characterization of disorders of the neuromuscular junction.
9 The identification, often in muscle of normal bulk and strength, of chronic partial denervation, fasciculations, and myotonia.
10 The analysis of cramp, and its distinction from physiologic contracture.

Nerve biopsy The sural nerve at the ankle is the preferred site for cutaneous nerve biopsy. There are only a few indications to employ this invasive technique. The main one is in asymmetric and multifocal neuropathic disorders producing a clinical picture of mononeuropathy multiplex, the basis of which is still unclear after other laboratory investigations are complete. Diagnostic considerations include vasculitis, amyloidosis, leprosy, and occasionally sarcoidosis. Nerve biopsy is also helpful when one or more cutaneous nerves are palpably enlarged. Another clinical application is in establishing the diagnosis in some genetically determined pediatric disorders such as metachromatic leukodystrophy, Krabbe's disease, giant axonal neuropathy, and infantile neuroaxonal dystrophy. In all of these recessively inherited diseases, both the central nervous system (CNS) and the peripheral nervous system (PNS) are affected.

There is a tendency to carry out sural nerve biopsy in distal symmetric polyneuropathies of subacute or chronic evolution. This practice is discouraged because it is a low-yield measure. Nerve biopsy in this situation is only useful as part of an approved research

TABLE 355-2 Polyneuropathy associated with drugs or environmental toxins

	Axonal* Acute	Axonal* Subacute	Axonal* Chronic	Demyelinating* Acute	Demyelinating* Subacute	Demyelinating* Chronic	Sensory vs. motor†	Auto-nomic*	CNS*	Comment
DRUGS										
Amiodarone (antiar-rhythmic)	—	—	+	—	—	+	SM	—	—	Dose-dependent neuropathy, reversible by decreasing dose; lysosomal dense body accumulation
Aurothioglucose (anti-rheumatic)	±	±	—	+	+	—	SM	—	—	Idiosyncratic reaction, ? immune-mediated
cis-Platinum (antineoplastic)	—	+	+	—	—	—	S	—	—	Severe sensory neuropathy, ? neuronopathy; also ototoxicity; dose-related
Dapsone (dermatologic including leprosy)	—	±	+	—	—	—	M	—	—	Dose-related pure motor neuropathy
Disulfiram (antialcohol)	±	+	+	—	—	—	SM	—	±	Usually occurs after months of treatment
Hydralazine (antihypertensive)	—	±	+	—	—	—	S>M	—	—	A pyridoxine antagonist; only rarely neurotoxic
Isoniazid	—	±	+	—	—	—	SM	±	—	A pyridoxine antagonist; neurotoxic in slow acetylators
Metronidazole (antiprotozoal	—	—	±	—	—	—	S	—	+	Dose-related central-peripheral distal axonopathy
Misonidazole (radiosensitizer)	—	±	+	—	—	—	S	—	+	Neurotoxicity is the limiting factor
Perhexilene (antiar-rhythmic)	—	—	±	—	—	+	SM	±	—	Dose-related neuropathy; lysosomal dense body accumulation
Phenytoin (anticonvulsant)	—	—	+	—	—	—	S>M	—	—	Large-fiber neuropathy, mild, after 20–30 years of phenytoin use
Thalidomide (anti-leprous)	—	—	+	—	—	—	S>M	±	+	Red skin and brittle nails; also teratogenic; recovery from neuropathy poor
Vincristine (antineoplastic)	—	+	+	—	—	—	S>M	—	—	Mild sensory neuropathy is nearly universal, hands>feet; motor signs should prompt cessation of treatment

protocol when the biopsy will provide crucial information not otherwise obtainable.

POLYNEUROPATHY Although this term connotes a widespread symmetric process, usually distal and graded, polyneuropathies present a high degree of diversity because of the extreme variability of tempo, severity, mix of sensory and motor features, and presence or absence of positive symptoms. The patient with a fulminant, severely dysesthetic sensory neuropathy and alopecia who is in the early phases of thallium intoxication bears little similarity to the patient with a 40-year history of insidiously progressive clumsiness of gait whose findings are foot drop, lower leg atrophy, pes cavus, and minimal asymptomatic distal sensory deficit (i.e., peroneal muscular atrophy, either type I or II; see Table 355-3). These two patients fall near opposite ends of the spectrum of polyneuropathy.

The classification of peripheral neuropathies has become increasingly complex as the capacity to discriminate new subgroups and identify new associations with toxins and systemic disorders improves. Further, our grasp of the pathophysiologic basis for the clinical phenomena observed in neuropathy has increased rapidly (see Chap. 354). But these advances are primarily descriptive, little or no progress has been made in illuminating the fundamental pathogenetic events in nervous tissue which eventuate in any one of the polyneuropathies.

The important features of each major grouping of polyneuropathies are summarized below and key aspects of specific polyneuropathies may be found in Tables 355-1 to 355-4.

Acute axonal polyneuropathy In this setting the term acute means evolution over days, making these neuropathies relatively uncommon.

Included are porphyric neuropathy and massive intoxications, often suicidal or homicidal in intent. For example, an individual receiving a large dose of arsenic (e.g., 100 mg of arsenous oxide) will become violently ill in a few hours with vomiting, diarrhea, and circulatory collapse. In 1 to 3 days serious renal and liver failure will ensue, and between 14 and 21 days polyneuropathy will appear, often as the systemic disorder abates. Progression occurs for 2 or 3 weeks, but following a plateau, recovery requires months.

Subacute axonal polyneuropathy Subacute, meaning to evolve in weeks, characterizes many instances of toxic and metabolic polyneuropathy, but perhaps even more of these are chronic in evolution (months). Scanning the appropriate columns in Tables 355-1 and 355-2 provides many possibilities. Management in almost all instances involves removing from contact the offending agent or treating the associated systemic order.

Chronic axonal polyneuropathy This category includes many more types of polyneuropathy, in part because the term chronic subsumes neuropathies which have progressed over a period as short as 6 months to as long as 60 years. As a rough approximation, a slow worsening for more than 5 years, an absence of positive symptoms, mainly motor deficit, and an absence of systemic disorder all favor a genetically determined neuropathy. Although these are mostly autosomal dominant in inheritance pattern, recessively inherited and X-linked varieties also occur, including a form phenotypically resembling dominantly inherited peroneal muscular atrophy (HMSN-II) and also adrenomyeloneuropathy (see Table 355-3). To complete the picture, an array of rare autosomal recessive neuropathies occur in childhood.

TABLE 355-2 Polyneuropathy associated with drugs or environmental toxins (*continued*)

	Axonal*			Demyelinating*			Sensory vs. motor†	Auto-nomic*	CNS*	Comment
	Acute	Subacute	Chronic	Acute	Subacute	Chronic				
Nitrofurantoin (urinary antiseptic)	—	±	+	—	—	—	SM	—	—	Generally total dose-related; presence of renal failure may enhance toxicity
TOXINS										
Acrylamide (flocculant; grouting agent)	—	±	+	—	—	—	S>M	±	+	Large-fiber neuropathy; sensory ataxia
Arsenic (herbicide; insecticide)	±	+	+	—	—	—	SM	±	±	Skin changes and Mees' lines in nails; if acute intoxication, many systemic effects
Buckthorn (toxic berry)	—	—	—	+	+	—	SM	—	—	Only occurs where berries grow; may mimic GBS
Carbon disulfide, CS₂ (industrial)	—	—	+	—	—	+	SM	—	+	Neurofilamentous accumulation in axons; demyelinating features are secondary
Diphtheria	—	—	—	+	+	—	SM	—	—	Clinically very rare now; can be confused with GBS
Dimethylamino propionitrile (industrial)	—	—	+	—	—	—	S>M	+	—	Small-fiber neuropathy with prominent bladder symptoms and impotence in males
γ-Diketone hexacarbons (solvents)	—	±	+	—	—	+	SM	±	+	Same features as CS₂; these solvents now in restricted use
Inorganic lead	—	—	+	—	—	—	M>S	—	±	Selective motor neuropathy with prominent wrist drop
Organophosphates	—	±	+	—	—	—	SM	—	+	Brain and spinal cord are also affected, the latter irreversibly
Thallium (rat poison)	—	+	+	—	—	—	SM	—	+	Also alopecia, Mees' lines in nails; ? selective damage to neural mitochondria
Pyridoxine (vitamin)	—	±	+	—	—	—	S	—	—	Occurs with megadose intake; >1 g per day

* ± = *sometimes,* + = *usual.*
† *S = sensory; M = motor; SM = sensorimotor.*

Acute demyelinating polyneuropathy For all practical purposes, this category is synonymous with Guillain-Barré syndrome (GBS). This acute, frequently severe and fulminant polyneuropathy occurs at a rate of one case per million population per month, or approximately 3500 cases per year in the United States and Canada. In over two-thirds, a viral infection, either clinically overt or evidenced by serum titer rise, precedes the onset of neuropathy by 1 to 3 weeks. Herpes infections [cytomegalovirus, Epstein-Barr virus (EBV)] account for a large proportion of virus-triggered cases. Another 5 to 10 percent of cases occur within 1 to 4 weeks of a surgical procedure. GBS occurs on a background of lymphoma, including Hodgkin's disease, and in lupus erythematosus more frequently than can be attributed to chance alone. Although the weight of evidence suggests that GBS is immune-mediated, the immunopathogenesis remains obscure. In 1976 to 1977, a flurry of some 500 cases followed in the wake of the national swine flu vaccination program in the United States. This exceeded by severalfold the baseline incidence expected in this period among the vaccines. The epidemiologic features of this outbreak resembled a point-source epidemic with an ''incubation'' period of 1 to 6 weeks.

The clinical features of GBS typically include areflexic motor paralysis with mild sensory disturbance coupled with an acellular rise of total protein in the cerebrospinal fluid by the end of the first week of symptoms. Most patients with GBS require hospitalization, and about one-fourth will need ventilatory assistance at some point during the illness. The prognosis is good; approximately 85 percent of patients make a complete or nearly complete recovery. The mortality rate is 3 to 4 percent. Management is generally supportive care, but plasmapheresis also has a role. A large, multicenter, controlled trial in North America has demonstrated a beneficial effect of plasmapheresis, especially when initiated in the first 2 weeks of illness. In contrast, corticosteroid treatment is generally not considered to be effective.

Other acute demyelinating polyneuropathies are rare and include buckthorn berry intoxication and diphtheritic polyneuritis (see Table 355-2).

Subacute demyelinating polyneuropathy Neuropathies in this category are heterogeneous in origin, although all are acquired. Most common is a relapsing and remitting neuropathy which has many clinical features in common with GBS, but differs from GBS in tempo, course, and absence of discernible triggering events. Previously mentioned toxins (buckthorn berry, diphtheria toxin, aurothioglucose) may also induce a picture of widespread subacute demyelination of peripheral nerves (see Table 355-2).

Chronic demyelinating polyneuropathy Although more common than the subacute neuropathies, chronic polyneuropathy with demyelinating features encompasses a wide diversity of disorders, including hereditary neuropathies, inflammatory neuropathies, and other acquired neuropathies associated with diabetes mellitus, dysproteinemias, other metabolic states, and some chronic intoxications. To complicate matters, many of these disorders present an electrodiagnostic picture of mixed axonal-demyelinative findings. Frequently it is difficult to determine which process, axonal degeneration or demyelination is the primary event. Aspects of many of these

TABLE 355-3 Genetically determined neuropathies

Genetic disorder	Inheritance pattern	Age of onset	Basic process	Other features*	Other systems involved	Metabolic defect	Comment
Peroneal muscular atrophy (HMSN-I)†	Dominant	Decades 2–3	Demyelinating	Hypertrophic change with onion bulb formation; marked ↓ NCV	Some families—Duffy locus linkage	Unknown	Pes cavus, congenital hip problems, motor deficit predominates
Peroneal muscular atrophy (HMSN-II)*	Dominant	Decades 3–5	Axonal	Marked ↓ NAP; NCV sl. decreased	—	Unknown	Same as HSMN-I
Hereditary amyloid neuropathies	Dominant	Decades 3–4	Axonal	Small fiber involvement; endoneurial amyloid deposition	Some families—cornea	Prealbumin is major protein of amyloid fibril	Dysautonomia may be prominent
Hereditary sensory neuropathy (HSN-I)	Dominant	Decades 1–3	Neuronopathic	DRG neurons selectively involved	Sensorineural deafness, some families	Unknown	Frequent distal mutilation—hands and feet
Porphyric neuropathy	Dominant	Adult life	Axonal	Neuropathy part of attacks; may be recurrent	Widespread cellular abnormality	Enzyme defects in porphyrin pathway	Acute intermittent porphyria, variegate porphyria, and erythropoietic porphyria
Hereditary liability to pressure palsy	Dominant	Decades 2–3	? Demyelinating	Tomaculous changes in myelin	—	Unknown	Ulnar, peroneal, and brachial plexus involvement particularly
Fabry's disease	X-linked	Young males	Neuronopathic	Sensory neuronopathy, small DRG neurons	Kidney, skin, lung	Accumulation of ceramide-trihexoside	Neuropathy painful; often die of renal failure
Peroneal muscular atrophy (Phillips et al., 1985)	X-linked	Infancy to 2d decade	Axonal or demyelinating	Heterozygote females may have symptoms		Unknown	Localizes to long arm of X chromosome
Adrenomyeloneuropathy	X-linked	Young males	? Axonal	Mild neuropathy, spastic paraparesis, baldness, hypogonadism	Adrenal cortex, cerebral white matter, spinal cord	Accumulation of very long chain fatty acids	Phenotypic variant of adrenoleukodystrophy; dietary therapy possible
Hereditary sensory neuropathy (HSN-II)	Recessive	Decades 1–3	Neuronopathic	DRG neurons selectively involved	—	Unknown	May be less severe than HSN-I

neuropathies are included in Tables 355-1 to 355-3 and in the sections below.

SPECIAL CATEGORIES OF NEUROPATHY Hereditary neuropathies The major characteristics of this highly variegated group of disorders are summarized in Table 355-3. With the exception of the porphyric neuropathies, the onset of neuropathic dysfunction is insidious and progression is indolent over years or decades. Most of these diseases are quite rare with the striking exception of the dominantly inherited peroneal muscular atrophies (HMSN-I and HMSN-II; see Table 355-3). In peroneal muscular atrophy, phenotypic expression is often variable, so that affected family members of a propositus may have no symptoms and minimal neurologic findings but (in HMSN-I) may still show severe reduction of nerve conduction velocity.

Neuropathies with inflammation Acquired inflammatory demyelinating neuropathies fall into two major groups, the acute form called Guillain-Barré syndrome (GBS) and more chronic forms. The entire group of acquired inflammatory demyelinating neuropathies constitutes a significant proportion of all cases of polyneuropathy and shares a distinctive clinical, electrophysiologic, and pathologic pattern. The diagnosis rests upon recognition of the clinical pattern and of other features, including elevated cerebrospinal fluid protein level, electrophysiologic changes (marked slowing of conduction velocities, delayed late responses, prolonged distal latencies, dispersion of evoked responses, and frequent evidence of conduction block), and pathologic changes of low-grade inflammation and demyelination-remyelination of peripheral nerves. The course of GBS is acute and monophasic, whereas the more chronic forms pursue either a slowly progressive or a relapsing course. Cases with an intermediate course occur frequently enough to blur the diagnostic delimitation of GBS from the more chronic types of acquired inflammatory demyelinating neuropathy.

Pathogenetically, this group of inflammatory neuropathies is generally agreed to be immune-mediated, but the specific antigens involved and the crucial events of the immune response and why it is activated are uncertain.

Management of chronic, acquired inflammatory neuropathies involves a judicious mix of corticosteroid therapy, other immunosuppressants, and plasmapheresis. These powerful agents are used only if the disorder is severe enough to threaten walking.

Diabetic neuropathies Classifications of the neuropathies of diabetes are found in Table 355-4. Although this provides a satisfactory frame of reference, the limitations inherent in classifying diabetic neuropathies should be understood. The most serious limitation is that most patients will not fit neatly into any single category, but rather will have overlapping clinical features of several. For instance, many diabetics with distal, primarily sensory polyneuropathy also can be shown to have autonomic dysfunction, usually in the form of vasomotor disturbance in the limbs and abnormalities of sweating. Similarly, patients who develop a proximal motor syndrome may have dysautonomic features (including sexual impotence in males) and some degree of distal sensory polyneuropathy. To compound matters, such patients appear at risk to develop a cranial mononeuropathy.

TABLE 355-3 Genetically determined neuropathies (continued)

Genetic disorder	Inheritance pattern	Age of onset	Basic process	Other features*	Other systems involved	Metabolic defect	Comment
Déjerine-Sottas neuropathy (HMSN-III)	Recessive	1st decade	Demyelinating	Hypertrophic change with onion bulb formation	May be mentally retarded	Unknown	Marked nerve trunk enlargement
Refsum's disease	Recessive	1st or 2d decade	Demyelinating	Hypertrophic change with onion bulb formation	Retinitis pigmentosa, ichthyosis, sensorineural deafness	Defect in α-oxidation of β-methylated fatty acids	Low phytanate diet, plasmapheresis therapy
Ataxia-telangiectasia	Recessive	Decade 1 or 2	Axonal	Neuropathy moderate	Cell nuclear aneuploidy, skin and scleral telangiectasia, cerebellar atrophy, immunopathy	Basic defect unknown	High incidence of early neoplasia
Abetalipoproteinemia	Recessive	Decade 1 or 2	Neuronopathic	Large DRG neurons	Retinitis pigmentosa, acanthocytosis of red blood cells	Absence of all lipoprotein-containing apo B	Proprioceptive disturbance marked, minimal small fiber deficit
Giant axonal neuropathy	Recessive	1st decade	Axonal	Massive segmented accumulation of neurofilaments in axons	Slowly progressive encephalopathy with Rosenthal fibers	Generalized disorder of 10-nm filaments	Intermediate filament masses in other cell types
Metachromatic leukodystrophy	Recessive	1st decade	Demyelinating	Schwannopathy with cerebroside accumulation	Cerebral white matter disease predominates	Defect of arylsulfatase A	Infantile, juvenile, and adult onset forms
Globoid cell leukodystrophy	Recessive	1st decade	Demyelinating	Schwannopathy with galactocerebroside accumulation	Cerebral white matter disease predominates	Defect of β-glactosidase	Characteristic clefts in Schwann cell cytoplasm
Friedreich's ataxia	Recessive	1st decade	Axonal	Spinocerebellar and corticospinal tracts involved; also 1° sensory neuron	Cardiomyopathy; usual cause of death	Controversial	Ataxia is both sensory and cerebellar

* *DRG, dorsal root ganglia; NAP, nerve action potential; sl, slightly; HMSN, hereditary motor-sensory neuropathy; HSN, hereditary sensory neuropathy.*
† *Both forms are also collectively referred to as Charcot-Marie-Tooth neuropathy.*

Classifying the diabetic neuropathies does not reveal any knowledge of the basis or pathogenesis of the neuropathic lesion. Rather, attempts at classification represent an educated guess at identifying the apparent anatomic sites of disorder and the critical clinical features. Pain is a frequent feature of diabetic neuropathies (see Table 355-4) but is variable in incidence and degree and is subjective in nature. The term diabetic amyotrophy should be avoided because of its ambiguity.

Diabetic neuropathies tend to occur in the setting of long-standing hyperglycemia (decades) whether insulin-dependent or not. By far the most common neuropathies related to diabetes are the diffuse sensory and autonomic types (categories 1 and 2 under "Symmetric" in Table 355-4). Sensory and autonomic polyneuropathy, chronic and indolent in evolution, may first be noticed in the third or fourth decade in patients with juvenile-onset diabetes but tends to occur after age 50 in patients with adult-onset diabetes. Focal and multifocal types of neuropathy are less common but quite dramatic (categories 1, 2, and 3 under "Asymmetric" in Table 355-4). They rarely occur before the age of 45 and are usually subacute or acute in onset. Cranial mononeuropathies refer to isolated sixth or third nerve palsies. The latter spares the pupil in three-fourths of cases, and some local pain or headache occurs in one-half. Truncal, or thoracoabdominal, neuropathy is painful, involves one or more intercostal or lumbar nerves unilaterally, and frequently coexists with the asymmetric proximal motor neuropathy. Femoral and obturator nerve innervated muscles (quadriceps femoris, iliopsoas, adductor magnus) and loss of knee jerk on that side are the most evident features of asymmetric proximal motor neuropathy. Sensory deficit is minor, but pain in the hip and anterior thigh may predominate. Common to all of these multifocal and focal neuropathies is the strong likelihood for subsi-

dence of pain within weeks to a year and partial or complete recovery of function. The same is true of symmetric proximal motor neuropathy (category 3 under "Symmetric" in Table 355-4).

Focal and multifocal diabetic neuropathies are considered to be ischemic in origin, but the basis for symmetric polyneuropathies is thought to involve abnormality of nerve metabolism as well as the possibility of ischemia.

Management of diabetic neuropathies is directed toward optimal control of hyperglycemia and symptomatic pain suppression. Entrapment neuropathies are frequently amenable to surgical decompression procedures.

Neuropathies with dysproteinemia An association between polyneuropathy and both multiple myeloma and macroglobulinemia has been recognized for many years. With commonly encountered multiple myeloma (MM) having either lytic or diffuse osteoporotic bone

TABLE 355-4 Classification of diabetic neuropathies

A Symmetric
  1 Distal, primarily sensory polyneuropathy
    a Mainly large fibers affected
    b Mixed*
    c Mainly small fibers affected*
  2 Autonomic neuropathy
  3 Chronically evolving proximal motor neuropathy*†
B Asymmetric
  1 Acute or subacute proximal motor neuropathy*†
  2 Cranial mononeuropathy†
  3 Truncal neuropathy*†
  4 Entrapment neuropathy in the limbs

* *Often painful.*
† *Recovery, partial or complete, is likely.*

lesions, clinically overt polyneuropathy is relatively infrequent, occurring in approximately 5 percent of patients. These neuropathies are sensorimotor, may be severe, and generally do not reverse with successful suppression of the myeloma. In most cases, electrodiagnostic and pathologic features are consistent with a process of axonal degeneration.

In contrast, myeloma with osteosclerotic features, although representing only 3 percent of all myelomas, is associated with a polyneuropathy in almost one-half of cases. These neuropathies, which may also occur with solitary plasmacytoma, seem to be different from these linked to MM in that they (1) often respond to radiation or removal of the primary lesion, (2) are more frequently demyelinating in character, (3) are associated with different monoclonal proteins and light chains (almost all lambda as opposed to mostly kappa in MM), and (4) frequently occur in association with other systemic findings. These include skin thickening, hyperpigmentation, hypertrichosis, organomegaly, endocrinopathy, anasarca, papilledema, and clubbing of fingers. (POEMS syndrome: *p*olyneuropathy, *o*rganomegaly, *e*ndocrinopathy, *m* protein, and *s*kin changes.) A great deal of attention has been paid to this curious syndrome in Japan where it is prevalent, but the underlying mechanism remains unknown.

Benign monoclonal gammopathy with an IgM serum spike, and usually with kappa light chains, is described in association with demyelinating polyneuropathy that often follows a protracted course and indolent progression. In about one-quarter of cases, the monoclonal serum protein binds to normal human peripheral myelin, specifically to myelin-associated glycoprotein. Immunocytochemical studies show binding of IgM to nerve obtained at biopsy or autopsy of these patients, but in a pattern different from that seen following incubation of sections of nerve with the IgM serum. Incubated nerves show uniform staining of the entire expanse of compact myelin sheath, but in vivo deposited IgM can be demonstrated to localize more selectively, probably at sites of myelin splitting, the latter being a phenomenon which occurs characteristically in most dysglobulinemic neuropathies. Whether the IgM bound to nerve in vivo plays a role in damaging nerve is unresolved.

Autonomic neuropathy   The autonomic nervous system regulates the visceral organs and vegetative functions. Many pharmacologic agents modify specific autonomic functions, but autonomic neuropathy (dysautonomia) with structural changes in pre- and postganglionic neurons can also occur. Usually autonomic neuropathy is a manifestation of a more generalized polyneuropathy also affecting somatic peripheral nervous function, as in diabetic neuropathy, GBS, and alcoholic polyneuropathy, but occasionally syndromes of pure pandysautonomia are encountered. Symptoms of dysautonomia are mainly negative (i.e., loss of function) and include postural hypotension with faintness or syncope, anhidrosis, hypothermia, bladder atony, obstipation, dry mouth and dry eyes from failure of salivary and lachrymal glands to secrete, blurring of vision from lack of pupillary and ciliary regulation, and sexual impotence in males. Positive phenomena (hyperfunction) may also occur and include episodic hypertension, diarrhea, hyperhidrosis, and either tachycardia or bradycardia.

Miscellaneous causes of neuropathy   Ischemia of nerve severe enough to produce clinical symptoms has as its basis the widespread compromise of blood flow in the vasa nervorum. Typically, this is the result of small-vessel disease involving the vasa nervorum directly, as occurs with vasculitis, rather than large-vessel disease, such as atherosclerosis. Clinically, widespread disease of the vasa nervorum produces mononeuropathy multiplex, which electrodiagnostically has the features of a patchy axonal process.

Cold exerts deleterious effects on peripheral nerve directly without an intermediate step of ischemia being necessary. Cold injury to nerve occurs after prolonged exposure, usually of a limb, to moderately low temperatures, as with immersion of the feet in seawater; actual freezing of tissue is not required. Axonal degeneration of myelinated fibers is the pathologic expression of cold injury. Frequently limbs affected by cold injury to nerve show sensory deficit and dysesthesias, cutaneous vasomotor instability, pain, and marked sensitivity to minimal cold exposure, which persist for many years. The pathophysiology of these phenomena is uncertain.

TROPHIC CHANGES IN SEVERE NEUROPATHY   The array of observable changes in completely denervated muscle, bone, and skin, including hair and nails, is well known, if incompletely understood. It is unclear what portion of the changes is due purely to denervation versus that caused by disuse, immobility, lack of weight bearing, and particularly recurrent, unnoticed, painless trauma. Considerable evidence favors the view that ulceration of skin, poor healing, tissue resorption, neurogenic arthropathy, and mutilation are the result of repeated heedless injury to insensitive parts. This sequence of events is avoidable with proper attention to and care of the insensitive parts by both patient and physician.

RECOVERY FROM NEUROPATHY   In contrast to axons in the central nervous system, peripheral nerve fibers have an excellent capability to regenerate under proper circumstances. The process of regeneration following axonal degeneration may take from 2 months to more than a year, depending on the severity of the neuropathy and the length of regeneration required. Whether regeneration takes place depends upon the subsidence of the initial basis for neuropathy. This could be removal from contact with a neurotoxic substance or correction of an abnormal metabolic state. A deficit secondary to demyelination may recover rapidly since intact axons may remyelinate in just a few weeks. For example, a patient with GBS, in whom demyelination but no secondary axonal degeneration has occurred, may recover to normal strength from bedfastness and paralysis of arms and legs in as little as 3 to 4 weeks.

MONONEUROPATHY MULTIPLEX (MULTIFOCAL NEUROPATHY) This term means simultaneous or sequential involvement of individual noncontiguous nerve trunks, either partially or completely, evolving over days to years. Since the disease process underlying mononeuropathy multiplex involves peripheral nerves in a multifocal and random fashion, there is a tendency, as worsening occurs, for the neurologic deficit to become less patchy and multifocal and more confluent and symmetric. Some patients present initially with a distal symmetric neuropathy. Attention to the pattern of early symptoms is therefore important in making the judgment that a particular neuropathy is indeed a mononeuropathy multiplex.

Once that issue is settled, the next question is whether the process is primarily axonal or demyelinating. Almost one-third of all adults with the clinical syndrome of mononeuropathy multiplex have a clearcut picture of a demyelinating disorder usually with multiple foci of persistent conduction block by electrodiagnostic examination. More intensive study of this subgroup suggests that the multifocal demyelinating neuropathy represents part of the spectrum of chronic acquired demyelinating neuropathy, also known as chronic inflammatory demyelinating polyradiculoneuropathy (CIDP). Management of this multifocal subgroup is the same as for CIDP.

The remaining two-thirds of patients with mononeuropathy multiplex have a picture by electrodiagnostic examination of axonal involvement that is heterogeneously distributed. Although ischemia would be suspected as the basis for neuropathy in these patients, only about one-half can be shown to have a process, usually vasculitis, affecting the vasa nervorum. The others remain undiagnosed even on follow-up, and the basis for their mononeuropathy multiplex is uncertain. Management in this group is conservative, but the management of those with proven vasculitis of vasa nervorum is the same as treatment for systemic vasculitis (see Chap. 269).

In individuals in whom vasculitic change in vasa nervorum can be demonstrated, any one of a large number of underlying disorders may be responsible. The primary vasculitides of the polyarteritis nodosa group constitute the most frequent basis, followed closely by the vasculitis syndrome occurring in the course of other connective tissue disorders. In descending order of frequency, the latter are rheumatoid arthritis, systemic lupus erythematosus, and mixed connective tissue disease. Other rarer causes of mononeuropathy multiplex due to nerve ischemia from occlusion of vasa nervorum include mixed cryoglobulinemia, Sjögren's syndrome, Wegener's granulomatosis, progressive systemic sclerosis, Churg-Strauss allergic granulomatosis, and hypersensitivity angiitides. Management of the neuropathy in each instance is predicated upon the appropriate treatment of the responsible disease.

Mononeuropathy multiplex syndrome may also be seen as a manifestation of leprosy, sarcoidosis, certain types of amyloidosis, hypereosinophilia syndrome, cryoglobulinemia, and multifocal types of diabetic neuropathy.

MONONEUROPATHY Mononeuropathy means focal involvement of a single nerve trunk and therefore implies a local causation. Direct trauma, compression, and entrapment are the usual causes. Ulnar neuropathies, due to lesions either at the ulnar groove or in the cubital tunnel, and median neuropathy due to compression in the carpal tunnel constitute the great majority of mononeuropathies encountered in clinical practice. In the absence of a history of trauma to the nerve trunk, factors favoring conservative management include sudden onset, no motor deficit, few or no sensory findings even though pain and sensory symptoms might be present, and no evidence of axonal degeneration by electrodiagnostic criteria. Factors favoring surgical intervention include chronicity and worsening neurologic deficit on examination, particularly if motor, and electrodiagnostic evidence that the lesion has produced a degree of Wallerian degeneration.

Ulnar nerve This nerve is derived from the eighth cervical and first thoracic roots. It innervates the ulnar flexor of the wrist, the inner half of the deep finger flexors, the adductors and abductors of the fingers, the adductor of the thumb, the two medial lumbricals, and the muscles of the hypothenar eminence. It is the sensory nerve to the fifth and ulnar half of the fourth fingers and the ulnar border of the hand. Complete ulnar paralysis results in a characteristic claw-hand deformity owing to wasting of the small hand muscles and hyperextension of the fingers at the metacarpophalangeal joints and flexion at the interphalangeal joints. The flexion deformity is most pronounced in the fourth and fifth fingers. Sensory loss occurs over the fifth finger, the ulnar aspect of the fourth finger, and the ulnar border of the palm. The ulnar nerve is most commonly injured at the elbow because of fracture or dislocation involving the joint. Delayed ulnar palsy may occur many years after an injury to the elbow joint which has resulted in a cubitus valgus deformity of the joint. Because of the deformity, the nerve is stretched in its course over the ulnar condyle. The superficial location of the nerve at the elbow makes it a common site of pressure palsy. The ulnar nerve may also become entrapped just distal to the elbow in the cubital tunnel formed by the aponeurotic arch linking the two heads of the flexor carpi ulnaris. Prolonged pressure on the base of the palm may result in damage to the deep palmar branch of the ulnar nerve, causing weakness of the small hand muscles but no sensory loss.

Median nerve This nerve is derived from the sixth cervical to the first thoracic root and is formed by the union of two heads from the medial and lateral cords of the brachial plexus. It innervates the pronators of the forearm, long finger flexors, and abductor and opponens muscles of the thumb and is a sensory nerve to the palmar aspect of the hand. Complete median nerve paralysis results in wasting of the affected muscles and inability to pronate the forearm, weakness of wrist flexion, paralysis of flexion of the index finger and terminal phalanx of the thumb, weakness of flexion of the remaining fingers, weakness of abduction and opposition of the thumb, and sensory impairment over the radial two-thirds of the palmar aspect of the hand and over the distal phalanges of the dorsum of the index and third fingers. The nerve may be injured in the axilla by shoulder dislocation and in any part of its course by laceration, stab, or gunshot wounds. The wrist is the most common site of external injury,

particularly in association with Colles' fractures of the wrist. Compression of the nerve at the wrist (carpal tunnel syndrome) may be secondary to prolonged occupational pressure, tenosynovitis with arthritis, or local infiltration, for example, by a thickening of connective tissue and deposit of amyloid with multiple myeloma or one of the mucopolysaccharides. Other systemic diseases associated with an increased incidence of carpal tunnel syndrome are acromegaly, hypothyroidism, rheumatoid arthritis, and diabetes mellitus. The treatment of carpal tunnel syndrome is surgical section of the carpal ligament. Incomplete lesions of the median nerve between the axilla and wrist may result in causalgia (a particularly severe type of burning pain; see Chap. 3).

Radial nerve This nerve is derived from the fifth to eighth cervical roots and is the termination of the posterior cord of the brachial plexus. It innervates the triceps muscle and the supinator and extensor muscles of the forearm and hand. Complete radial paralysis results in the inability to extend the elbow, paralysis of supination of the forearm, and complete wrist and finger drop. Sensation is impaired over the posterior aspect of the forearm and a small area over the radial aspect of the dorsum of the hand. The nerve may be injured in the axilla, for example, in "crutch" palsy, but most common trauma occurs in the midarm where the nerve winds around the humerus. Common types of injury at this site are fractures and pressure palsies incurred during sleep, or during coma in association with intoxications.

Musculocutaneous nerve This nerve is derived from the fifth and sixth cervical roots and is a branch of the lateral cord of the brachial plexus. It innervates the biceps and brachialis anticus muscles. Lesions of the nerve result in weakness of elbow flexion. It is rarely injured alone.

Axillary nerve This nerve arises from the posterior cord of the brachial plexus and supplies the teres minor and deltoid muscles. It may be involved in injuries resulting from fractures of the neck of the humerus, serum neuritis, or brachial neuritis. The anatomic localization depends on the recognition of paralysis of abduction of the arm, wasting of the deltoid, and a patch of impaired sensation over the outer aspect of the shoulder.

Suprascapular nerve This nerve is derived from the fifth and sixth cervical roots and supplies the supra- and infrasinatus muscles. Lesions may be diagnosed by the presence of weakness of abduction and external rotation of the arm and atrophy of the supra- and infraspinatus muscles. The nerve may be injured by blows on the top of the shoulder, fracture dislocations of the shoulder joint, or by entrapment in the suprascapular notch.

Long thoracic nerve This nerve is derived from the fifth, sixth, and seventh cervical roots and supplies the serratus magnus muscle. Paralysis of the serratus magnus muscle results in an inability to raise the arm over the head from a forward position, and there is winging of the medial border of the scapula on pushing forward against resistance. It is injured most commonly by pressure on the shoulder, from either a sudden blow or prolonged pressure from carrying heavy weights. It is also involved at times in diabetic patients and as a manifestation of brachial and serum neuritides.

Brachial plexus Brachial plexus lesions, which are usually unilateral, are relatively common and readily distinguishable on clinical grounds from upper limb mononeuropathies. The usual causes are direct trauma to the plexus, stretch injury, cervical rib or bands, infiltration or compression by malignancy, brachial neuritis (neuralgic amyotrophy), and damage due to therapeutic radiation. As an approximation, injury to the upper plexus, which arises from C5 to C6 roots, results from particular types of trauma (arm jerked downward), brachial neuritis, and radiation damage. The muscles affected are the biceps, deltoid, brachialis anticus, supinator longus, supra- and infraspinatus, and the rhomboids. The arm hangs at the side, internally rotated, with the elbow extended. The forearm is pronated. Hand motion is unaffected. The prognosis for spontaneous recovery is generally good, especially in cases of birth injury.

Findings localizing to the lower plexus, which arises from C8 to T1 roots, are likely to be due to malignant infiltration, other types of trauma (arm jerked upward), and cervical rib or bands. There is paralysis and wasting of the small muscles of the hand and a characteristic claw-hand deformity. Sensory loss is limited to the ulnar border of the hand and inner side of the forearm, and there may be an associated paralysis of the cervical sympathetic nerve with Horner's syndrome (ptosis and meiosis) if the first thoracic motor root is involved. Involvement of the brachial plexus by malignancy is more likely to present with pain, Horner's syndrome, and a subacute course, whereas radiation damage to the brachial plexus is more likely to result in paresthesias without pain, indolent progression, and more prominent electrodiagnostic findings.

Lesions of the cords of the brachial plexus   The lateral and medial cords are most commonly affected. Dislocation of the head of the humerus, pressure of the cervical ribs, and stab wounds are the most frequent causes. Injury to the lateral cord results in paralysis of the biceps and coracobrachialis muscles and all muscles supplied by the median nerve except the intrinsic hand muscles. There is some loss of sensation over the radial aspects of the forearm. Involvement of the medial cord, as may occur in compression by a cervical rib, results in paralysis of the muscles supplied by the ulnar nerve together with the median-innervated intrinsic muscles of the hand and sensory loss over the ulnar aspect of the hand and forearm. Sternum-splitting operations may compress the lower brachial plexus by displacement of the clavicle. Usually it is the medial cord of the brachial plexus that is affected.

Lumbosacral plexus lesions   The lumbosacral plexus is subject to a number of disease processes, mostly secondary. Disease of the upper plexus produces a unilateral weakness in the flexion and adduction of the hip, extension of the knee, and sensory loss over the anterior thigh and leg; those of the lower plexus cause a weakness of the posterior thigh, leg, and foot muscles with the loss of sensation over the fifth lumbar and first and second sacral roots. The diseases that affect the plexus are carcinoma of the cervix and prostate, retroperitoneal tumors, iliopsoas hemorrhages from a ruptured aneurysm or hemophilia, lumbosacral plexitis, abdominal and thoracolumbar operations, and diabetes mellitus.

Lateral femoral cutaneous nerve   This nerve is derived from the second and third lumbar roots. It is a sensory nerve supplying the lateral aspect of the thigh. The nerve enters the thigh beneath the lateral end of the inguinal ligament and then enters the fascia lata, where it may become constricted. Compression of the nerve results in uncomfortable paresthesias in its cutaneous distribution and in sensory impairment. The condition is called *meralgia paresthetica*. The definitive treatment is surgical, usually decompression of the nerve at the inguinal ligament, but this is seldom necessary.

Obturator nerve   This nerve is derived from the second, third, and fourth lumbar roots. It supplies the adductor muscles of the thigh, and injury to the nerve results in almost complete paralysis of adduction of the thigh. The nerve is most frequently injured during the course of a difficult labor and also as a result of dislocation of the hip or an obturator hernia. It may be affected in diabetes, polyarteritis nodosa, osteitis pubis, and retroperitoneal and pelvic malignant tumors.

Femoral nerve   This nerve is derived from the second, third, and fourth lumbar roots. It supplies the iliopsoas muscles (hip flexion) and the quadriceps femoris muscles (knee extension) and conveys cutaneous sensation from the anterior thigh and medial side of the lower leg (saphenous nerve). Following injury to the nerve, there is paralysis of extension of the knee, with wasting of the quadriceps muscle and also some weakness of hip flexion. The knee jerk is abolished. The nerve may be involved in fractures and dislocation of the hip, in fractures of the pelvis, and in attempts to catheterize the femoral artery. It may be affected in diabetes, in polyarteritis nodosa, and in retroperitoneal, pelvic, or abdominal lesions such as a tumor, psoas abscess, or retroperitoneal hemorrhage. Because the femoral artery may also be severed, wounds in the femoral triangle may be fatal.

Sciatic nerve   This nerve is derived from the fourth and fifth lumbar and first and second sacral roots. It provides the motor innervation of the hamstring muscles and all those below the knee; it carries sensory impulses from the posterior aspect of the thigh and posterior and lateral aspects of the leg and entire sole. In complete sciatic paralysis, the knee cannot be flexed and all muscles below the knee are paralyzed. The sciatic nerve is commonly injured in fractures of the pelvis or femur, in gunshot wounds of the buttock and thigh, by lying or sitting insensate and compressing the nerve in the lower buttock area, and by inadvertent intraneural injections. It may also be involved by pelvic tumors and in both diabetes mellitus and polyarteritis nodosa. Cryptogenic forms also occur and are actually more frequent than those with an identifiable cause. A ruptured lumbar disk often simulates sciatic neuropathy. Incomplete lesions of the sciatic nerve occasionally result in causalgia.

Common peroneal nerve   This nerve is one of the terminal divisions of the sciatic nerve in the popliteal fossa. It supplies the dorsiflexors of the foot and toes, the everters of the foot, and sensation to the dorsum of the foot and lateral aspect of the lower half of the leg. These functions are lost with lesions which completely interrupt the nerve. Pressure or sleep palsy is one of the most frequent types of injury, the compression being of that part of the nerve which passes over the head of the fibula. It is also commonly involved by fractures involving the upper end of the fibula and in diabetic neuropathy, polyarteritis nodosa, and operations on the knee.

Tibial nerve   This nerve is the other of the two terminal divisions of the sciatic nerve in the popliteal fossa. It supplies all the calf muscles and the flexors of the foot. Complete paralysis of the nerve results in a calcaneovalgus deformity of the foot, which no longer can be plantar-flexed. There is loss of sensation over the plantar aspect of the foot.

OTHER FOCAL NEUROPATHIES   Peripheral nerve tumors   These are mostly benign and can arise on any nerve trunk or twig. Although peripheral nerve tumors occur anywhere in the body including the spinal roots and cauda equina, many are subcutaneous in location and present as a soft swelling, sometimes with a purplish discoloration of the skin. Two major categories of peripheral nerve tumors are recognized: neurilemmoma (Schwannoma) and neurofibroma. Neurilemmomas are usually solitary and grow within the nerve sheath, rendering the tumor relatively easy to dissect free. In contrast, neurofibromas tend to be multiple, grow within the endoneurial substance, rendering them difficult to dissect, may undergo malignant changes, and are the hallmark of von Recklinghausen's neurofibromatosis. This disease is characterized by an autosomal dominant inheritance pattern, any number of neurofibromas from one to thousands, five or more café au lait–pigmented skin lesions greater than 1.5 cm (80 percent of patients), axillary freckles (93 percent of patients), and an increased incidence of seizure disorder and mental retardation (see Chap. 351).

Herpes zoster   This is a sensory neuritis of viral cause characterized by acute inflammation of one or more dorsal root ganglia, due to varicella-zoster virus infection. Lancinating pain and hyperalgesia over the skin surface supplied by affected roots occur for 3 to 4 days, followed by the appearance of herpetic eruption in the same segment characterized by painful raised blisters on reddened bases. If the inflammatory process spreads to involve adjacent motor roots of anterior horns of the cord, segmental motor weakness and wasting appear. Paralysis of the oculomotor nerves may occur in conjunction with ophthalmic division involvement of the trigeminal ganglion (ophthalmoplegic zoster). Facial paralysis may occur with involvement of the geniculate ganglion and herpetic eruption on the ipsilateral tympanic membrane or external ear canal (Ramsay Hunt syndrome).

Leprous neuritis This is a major worldwide cause of neuropathy. *Mycobacterium lerae* organisms readily invade Schwann cells in cutaneous nerve twigs, particularly those associated with unmyelinated nerve fibers. Two major forms of leprous neuritis are recognized, tuberculoid and lepromatous, which actually represent the far ends of a spectrum of disease, the middle of which is called dimorphous leprosy (patchy and multifocal involvement of skin and nerve). Tuberculoid (high-resistance) leprosy is restricted to a single patch of hypesthetic or anesthetic skin in any location. The skin patch is frequently thickened, reddened, or hypopigmented. If a superficially placed nerve trunk, typically a cutaneous nerve, courses just beneath the area of affected skin, it may be engulfed in the inflammatory reaction, resulting in an associated mononeuropathy. Such a nerve may be palpably enlarged and beaded. Lepromatous (low-resistance) leprosy is marked by immunologic tolerance and widespread skin thickening, cutaneous anesthesia, and anhidrosis, sparing only the warmest parts of the body, notably the axilla, groin, and beneath the scalp hair. Motor signs (focal weakness and atrophy) result from damage to mixed nerves lying close to the skin, particularly the median, ulnar, peroneal, and facial nerves.

Bell's palsy This is due to inflammation of the facial nerve in the facial canal, the basis for which remains obscure. Edema may play a part leading to compression of nerve fibers, with resulting acute unilateral paralysis of facial muscles (see Chap. 352).

Sarcoidosis This may involve single or multiple peripheral nerves, producing asymmetric mononeuritis or polyneuritis. Unilateral or bilateral facial paralysis is common in association with parotitis and uveitis (Heerfordt's syndrome).

Polyneuritis cranialis This is a relapsing and remitting mononeuropathy multiplex restricted to cranial nerves. It is usually associated with indolent tuberculous cervical adenitis (scrofula) or sarcoidosis. Treatment of the underlying condition will halt the cranial nerve palsies.

Acknowledgment

Portions of this section also appear in substantially the same form in Asbury AK: Diseases of peripheral nerve, in *Diseases of the Nervous System*, AK Asbury, GM McKhann, WI McDonald (eds), by arrangement with the publishers, Philadelphia, Saunders, 1986, and London, Heinemann, 1986.

REFERENCES

ASBURY AK: New aspects of disease of the peripheral nervous system, in *Harrison's Textbook of Internal Medicine, Update IV.* McGraw-Hill, New York, 1983, 211–229
———, GILLIATT RW: *Peripheral Nerve Disorders: A Practical Approach.* London, Butterworth, 1984
——— et al: Criteria for diagnosis of Guillian-Barré syndrome. Ann Neurol 3:565, 1978
DAWSON DM et al: *Entrapment Neuropathies.* Boston, Little, Brown, 1983
DYCK PJ et al (eds): *Peripheral Neuropathy,* 2d ed. Philadelphia, Saunders, 1984
LAYZER RB: *Neuromuscular Manifestations of Systemic Disease,* vol 25: *Contemporary Neurology Series.* Philadelphia, Davis, 1984
SCHAUMBURG HH et al: *Disorders of Peripheral Nerves,* vol 24: *Contemporary Neurology Series.* Philadelphia, Davis, 1983
SPENCER PS, SCHAUMBURG HH (eds): *Experimental and Clinical Neurotoxicology.* Baltimore, Williams & Wilkins, 1980
SUMNER AJ (ed): *The Physiology of Peripheral Nerve Disease.* Philadelphia, Saunders, 1980

356 DERMATOMYOSITIS AND POLYMYOSITIS

WALTER G. BRADLEY

Dermatomyositis and polymyositis are conditions of unknown etiology in which the skeletal muscle is damaged by a nonsuppurative inflammatory process dominated by lymphocytic infiltration. The term *polymyositis* is applied when the condition spares the skin and the term *dermatomyositis* when polymyositis is associated with a characteristic skin rash. One-third of cases are associated with various connective tissue disorders, such as rheumatoid arthritis, lupus erythematosus, mixed connective tissue disorder, and scleroderma and one-tenth with a malignancy.

ETIOLOGY The cause of these diseases is unknown. The two main theories are that the diseases are due to a viral infection of the skeletal muscle or to an autoimmune disorder (Chap. 269). Experimental viral myositis can be induced in animals by Coxsackie virus. A mild inflammatory myopathy can occur with influenza. The numerous electron-microscope observations of virus-like particles in muscle fibers in dermatomyositis or polymyositis have not been confirmed by virus isolation, rising titers of antiviral antibodies have not been demonstrated, and the disease has not been passed into animals by injection of extracts of affected muscles. One-third of cases have elevated serum antibodies to toxoplasma, but the disease does not generally respond to therapy against toxoplasmosis. A disease resembling polymyositis has been reported in laboratory animals injected with sterile muscle extracts together with Freund's adjuvant (experimental allergic myositis). Circulating lymphocytes reactive against skeletal muscle antigens and the lymphocytic infiltration of affected muscles suggest the presence of cell-mediated immunity. A small proportion of patients have deposition of immunoglobulins on intramuscular blood vessels, suggesting that circulating antibodies may play some role in the disease. The close association of polymyositis and diseases of connective tissue favors the notion of a common autoimmune etiology or pathogenesis. In older patients dermatomyositis is frequently associated with a malignancy. Thus dermatomyositis-polymyositis is a syndrome which probably has a number of different causes.

CLASSIFICATION The classification of the dermatomyositis-polymyositis group which is most widely used is given in Table 356-1. This classification is not based on known differences in etiology and has a number of drawbacks, as noted below. Other uncommon associations of polymyositis are sarcoidosis, giant cell myositis with thymoma, and myositis in systemic infections due to viruses or toxoplasma. A focal infective myositis due to streptococcal or staphylococcal infection is mostly seen in the tropics. Focal nodular myositis is a variant of polymyositis where focal areas of myositis cause hot, often painful, multifocal muscle masses. Inclusion body myositis is an inflammatory myopathy with characteristic clinical and pathologic features (see below).

INCIDENCE Current estimates that the annual incidence of the inflammatory myopathies is about five per million of the population are probably too low.

TABLE 356-1 Classification of polymyositis-dermatomyositis

Group I:	Primary idiopathic polymyositis
Group II:	Primary idiopathic dermatomyositis
Group III:	Dermatomyositis (or polymyositis) associated with neoplasia
Group IV:	Childhood dermatomyositis (or polymyositis) associated with vasculitis
Group V:	Polymyositis (or dermatomyositis) with associated collagen-vascular disease

SOURCE: *Classification suggested by Bohan et al.*

CLINICAL MANIFESTATIONS Group I: Primary idiopathic polymyositis This group comprises about one-third of all cases of inflammatory myopathy. It is insidiously progressive over weeks, months, or even years. Rarely the disease is acute, producing severe muscle weakness in a matter of days. The disease may develop at any age and in either sex. Females outnumber males two to one.

The patients first become aware of weakness of the proximal limb muscles, especially the hips and thighs, and find difficulty in arising from the squatting or kneeling position and in climbing or descending stairs. When shoulder girdle muscles are involved, placing an object on a high shelf or combing the hair becomes difficult. Occasionally the disease is more restricted, affecting only the neck, the shoulder, or the quadriceps muscles. Pain of an aching type in the buttocks, thighs, and calves is experienced in about 10 percent of the cases, and tenderness on palpation in another 20 percent. Early symptoms of dysphagia and weakness of extensor muscles of the neck in a patient with a chronic myopathy suggest the diagnosis of polymyositis.

When the patient is first seen, there may be weakness of the muscles of the trunk, the upper and lower limb girdles, the upper arms and thighs, the posterior and anterior neck, and the pharynx. Ocular muscles are almost never affected except in a rare association with myasthenia gravis. The distal muscles are spared in about 75 percent of cases. Muscle atrophy, contractures, and diminished tendon reflexes are rare in early myositis and never as pronounced as in muscular dystrophies and denervating conditions. When the reflexes are disproportionately reduced, carcinoma with polymyositis and polyneuropathy or the Lambert-Eaton syndrome should be considered. Occasionally, the reflexes may be paradoxically brisk in dermatomyositis-polymyositis, perhaps due to irritation of muscle spindle receptors by the inflammation.

At presentation about 25 percent of patients have dysphagia, about 5 percent have significant respiratory impairment, and 5 percent are unable to walk. Dysphagia is due to involvement of striated muscles of the pharynx and upper esophagus. At some time in the course of the disease cardiac abnormalities are observed in about 30 percent of cases; these include ECG changes, arrhythmias, and heart failure secondary to myocarditis. About half of the fatal cases have pathologic evidence of cardiac disease with necrosis of myocardial fibers, usually with only modest inflammatory reaction. The frequency of myocardial infarction may be increased in those treated for long periods with corticosteroids. In a few cases there is dyspnea due to pulmonary fibrosis. Arthralgia, Raynaud's phenomenon, and rarely low-grade fever may also be present.

Group II: Primary idiopathic dermatomyositis This group comprises about one-quarter of all cases of myositis. The skin changes may precede or follow the muscle syndrome and include a localized or diffuse erythema, maculopapular eruption, scaling eczematoid dermatitis, or rarely an exfoliative dermatitis. The classic lilac-colored (heliotrope) rash is on the eyelids, bridge of the nose, cheeks (butterfly distribution), forehead, chest, elbows, knees and knuckles, and around the nailbeds. Itching may be troublesome in some cases. The skin lesions may be subtle and easily overlooked. Periorbital edema is frequent, particularly in acute cases. The skin lesions may occasionally ulcerate. Subcutaneous calcification may occur, especially in children.

The typical rash and myositis allow a diagnosis of dermatomyositis, and such cases may be placed in this category (group II, Table 356-1) if idiopathic and into groups III, IV, and V if there are other features, namely malignancy, vasculitis in children, and an established collagen-vascular disease. About 40 percent of all patients with myositis have dermatomyositis. Most patients over the age of 60 with dermatomyositis have an underlying malignancy.

Group III: Polymyositis or dermatomyositis with neoplasia This syndrome, which comprises about 8 percent of all cases of myositis, is categorized separately, although muscle and skin changes are indistinguishable from those in the other groups. The malignancy may antedate or postdate the onset of the myositis by up to 2 years. The incidence of this paraneoplastic syndrome is higher in patients with dermatomyositis over the age of 55; therefore, in such patients the search for an underlying malignancy is mandatory. The most common malignancies are lung, ovary, breast, gastrointestinal tract, and myeloproliferative disorders. The myositis is a paraneoplastic syndrome, the cause of which may lie in an altered immune status or an occult viral infection of the muscle.

Group IV: Childhood polymyositis and dermatomyositis associated with vasculitis This group comprises about 7 percent of all cases of myositis. Inflammatory myopathy in childhood is frequently associated with skin involvement and clinical or pathologic evidence of vasculitis in skin, muscles, gastrointestinal tract, and other organs. There are degeneration and loss of capillaries in a perifascicular distribution in the skeletal muscles; often necrotizing lesions of the skin; and ischemic infarction of kidneys, gastrointestinal tract, and rarely brain. Consequently, authors of some reports on series of cases have reported mortality rates of up to one-third in childhood dermatomyositis, though most have found that the prognosis is better than it is in adult dermatomyositis-polymyositis. One limitation of the classification of Bohan et al is that it is not clear whether or not all cases of childhood myositis should be included in group IV. Subcutaneous calcification is frequently present in the childhood form of dermatomyositis.

Group V: Polymyositis or dermatomyositis with an associated connective tissue disorder This "overlap group" comprises about one-fifth of all cases of myositis. Rheumatoid arthritis, scleroderma, mixed connective tissue disease, and lupus erythematosus are the most common associated conditions; polyarteritis nodosa and rheumatic fever are more rarely associated. Criteria for placement in the overlap group combine the demonstration of the appropriate clinical and laboratory abnormalities required for the diagnosis of the connective tissue disorder together with clinical and laboratory evidence of myositis. The diagnosis of myositis is often difficult in patients with connective tissue disorders producing arthritis, since this may often produce muscle weakness with type II fiber atrophy. Moreover, perivascular inflammatory foci are common in muscle in connective tissue disorders. Demonstration of increased serum creatine kinase (CK), electromyography (EMG), and muscle biopsy are often required to make this diagnosis. Though patients in this overlap group respond to corticosteroid therapy, the prognosis for recovery of function is poorer than it is in pure dermatomyositis-polymyositis. Dysphagia in group V patients with scleroderma is often due to involvement of the smooth muscle of the distal third of the esophagus.

Other disorders associated with myositis SARCOIDOSIS AND POLYMYOSITIS The skeletal muscle contains noncaseating granulomas with Langhans-type multinuclear giant cells in at least one-quarter of patients with sarcoidosis. Symptomatic polymyositis is, however, uncommon. Regenerating multinuclear myoblasts resemble Langhans' giant cells, which has led to misdiagnosis in many of the cases reported in the literature to have "sarcoid myositis." A giant cell or granulomatous polymyositis, sometimes associated with myasthenia gravis, has been recorded in patients with thymomas.

FOCAL NODULAR MYOSITIS A syndrome of acutely developing and painful focal inflammatory nodules, sometimes occurring sequentially in different muscles, has been termed *focal nodular myositis*. The pathologic appearance and response to therapy are similar to those in generalized polymyositis. The differential diagnosis includes, when single, a muscle tumor (sarcoma or rhabdomyosarcoma) and, when multiple, muscle infarcts such as can occur in polyarteritis nodosa.

INFECTIOUS POLYMYOSITIS Rare cases of polymyositis have clearcut evidence of being due to known pathogens such as toxoplasmosis (Chap. 157) and Coxsackie virus infection (Chap 139). Antibody screening will suggest the diagnosis in such cases. Trichinosis may be confused with idiopathic polymyositis, particularly if the history of raw pork ingestion is not obtained. The symptoms of trichinosis are variable and depend upon the parasitic load. Low-grade fever, muscle pain of variable degree, conjunctival and periorbital edema, and fatigue are frequent. Weakness is generally mild. Heavy infestation is often associated with central nervous system symptoms of delirium, coma, or focal neurologic deficit. The frequent myocardial involvement is manifested by tachycardia and ECG changes. The diagnosis is made by the history of ingestion of undercooked pork, marked eosinophilia, sensitivity to intradermal *Trichina* antigen, and the appearance of serum antibodies to *Trichina* during the course of the disease. Occasionally the diagnosis is not recognized until a muscle is biopsied. Pyomyositis, a suppurative inflammation of muscle due to staphylococcus or streptococcus, is mainly seen in the tropics. The presentation is that of a diffuse abscess of the muscle.

INCLUSION BODY MYOSITIS The clinical features of this condition are similar to those of chronic idiopathic polymyositis, except that distal muscle involvement is more frequent. Muscle biopsy shows interstitial and perivascular inflammatory infiltration, necrosis, and regeneration of muscle fibers, but in addition there are "rimmed vacuoles" in the fibers. Electron microscopy reveals paramyxovirus-like filaments in the nuclei and sarcoplasm. A recent study suggests these are mumps virus. This disorder responds poorly to immunosuppressive therapy, and the prognosis is poor.

LABORATORY FINDINGS In all forms of polymyositis there may be elevated serum levels of the enzymes present in skeletal muscle, such as CK, aldolase, serum glutamic oxaloacetic transaminase (SGOT), lactic acid dehydrogenase (LDH), and serum glutamic pyruvate transaminase (SGPT). The degree of rise decreases from the first to the last in this series of enzymes, and the pattern is the reverse of that seen in liver disease. Tests for circulating rheumatoid factor and antinuclear antibodies are positive in less than one-half of the cases. Myoglobin can be found in the urine when muscle destruction is acute and extensive; rarely, acute polymyositis causes the full syndrome of rhabdomyolysis and myoglobinuria. The erythrocyte sedimentation rate is elevated in about two-thirds of cases. Most other hematologic indices are normal. In about 40 percent of cases the electromyogram reveals a markedly increased insertional activity (muscle irritability), together with the typical myopathic triad of motor unit action potentials which are of low amplitude, are polyphasic, and have an abnormally early recruitment. In a further 40 percent of the patients only myopathic changes are present. The ECG is abnormal in about 5 to 10 percent of the cases at presentation. The muscle biopsy should be taken from two clinically affected muscles, and muscles recently used for EMG or intramuscular injection must be avoided. In about two-thirds of cases, the biopsies will demonstrate the typical pathologic changes of myositis. Since the lesions have a patchy distribution, it is recommended that skip serial sections of all the specimens be studied. Despite this, about 10 percent of cases have a normal muscle biopsy.

Skeletal muscle pathology The principal changes in muscle consist of infiltrates of inflammatory cells (lymphocytes, macrophages, plasma cells, and rare eosinophils and neutrophils) and destruction of muscle fibers with a phagocytic reaction. Perivascular (usually perivenular) inflammatory cell infiltration is the hallmark of polymyositis. Interstitial inflammatory cell infiltration is also a prominent feature of the disease, but lesser degrees of it may be seen in other conditions as a secondary reaction (e.g., in facioscapulohumeral and Becker's muscular dystrophy). Evidence of muscle fiber degeneration and regeneration is almost invariably present. Many of the residual muscle fibers are small, with increased numbers of sarcolemmal nuclei. Either the degeneration of muscle fibers or the infiltration of inflammatory cells may predominate in any given biopsy specimen. Perifascicular atrophy of muscle fibers, type II muscle fiber atrophy, and muscle infarcts may also be found.

DIAGNOSIS Patients with dermatomyositis with the characteristic skin rash, muscle weakness, and evidence of muscle damage by EMG and elevation of serum CK may not require a muscle biopsy to confirm the diagnosis. In the case of idiopathic polymyositis,

however, a firm diagnosis must be based on the presence of a typical clinical picture, a typical EMG, elevation of serum CK, and a diagnostic muscle biopsy. All four criteria are required to be certain of the diagnosis, since inflammatory changes may occasionally occur in other myopathies (e.g., facioscapulohumeral muscular dystrophy) and in other connective tissue disorders without clear muscle weakness. However, in less than one-third of cases of polymyositis are *all* these criteria satisfied. It may be particularly difficult to obtain a diagnostic muscle biopsy because of the patchy nature of the disease. Thus, a therapeutic trial of corticosteroids should be given when full investigation of a patient with significant disability leaves a diagnosis of "possible polymyositis," usually because of a nondiagnostic muscle biopsy.

DIFFERENTIAL DIAGNOSIS The clinical picture of skin rash and proximal or diffuse muscle weakness has few causes other than dermatomyositis. However, proximal muscle weakness without skin involvement can be due to many conditions other than polymyositis and necessitates detailed investigation to establish the correct diagnosis.

Subacute or chronic progressive muscle weakness This may be due to denervating conditions such as the spinal muscular atrophies or amyotrophic lateral sclerosis. Upper motor neuron signs in the latter in addition to the muscle weakness aid in the diagnosis. The muscular dystrophies, such as those of Duchenne and Becker and the limb-girdle and facioscapulohumeral types, may appear similar to polymyositis (Chap. 357). However, the muscular dystrophies usually develop more slowly, rarely present after the age of 30, usually involve the pharyngeal and posterior neck muscles only in their later course, and have a pattern of muscle involvement which is selective, involving some muscles such as the biceps and brachioradialis early in the course of the disease, and sparing others, such as the deltoid. Nevertheless, in rare patients it may be difficult, even with a muscle biopsy, to distinguish chronic polymyositis from a rapidly advancing muscular dystrophy. This is particularly true of facioscapulohumeral muscular dystrophy, where interstitial inflammatory cell infiltration is commonly found early in the disease. Such doubtful cases should always be given an adequate trial of corticosteroid therapy. Dystrophia myotonica produces a characteristic facies with ptosis, facial myopathy, temporalis muscle wasting, and grip myotonia (Chap. 357). Some of the metabolic myopathies, including glycogen storage disease due to myophosphorylase deficiency and the lipid storage diseases due to carnitine and carnitine palmityltransferase deficiency, produce exertional cramps, rhabdomyolysis, and muscle weakness; diagnosis rests upon biochemical studies of the muscle biopsy (Chap. 357). Glycogen storage disease due to acid maltase deficiency also requires muscle biopsy for diagnosis. The endocrine myopathies such as those due to hypercorticosteroidism and hyper- and hypothyroidism require the appropriate laboratory investigations for diagnosis. Toxic myopathies (e.g., those due to aminocaproic acid or emetine) have a different pathology from polymyositis and require a careful drug history for diagnosis. Muscle wasting in patients with an underlying neoplasm may be true polymyositis, but it can be due to a protein-wasting state (cachexia), a paraneoplastic neuropathy, or type II fiber atrophy.

Muscle weakness with marked exercise-induced fatigue Fatigue without much muscle wasting may be due to the neuromuscular junction disorders, myasthenia gravis, or the Lambert-Eaton syndrome. Repetitive nerve stimulation studies aid in the diagnosis of these conditions (Chap. 358).

Acute muscle weakness This may be caused by an acute neuropathy such as that due to the Guillain-Barré syndrome or a neurotoxin. When combined with painful muscle cramps, rhabdomyolysis, and myoglobinuria, it may be due to known metabolic disorders including some of the glycogen storage diseases such as myophosphorylase deficiency (McArdle's disease), carnitine palmityltransferase deficiency, and myoadenylate deaminase deficiency. Acute viral infections may cause a similar syndrome. In other cases investigation reveals no etiology, and these may be due to a true acute autoimmune polymyositis or to an as yet undiscovered metabolic defect.

Pain on movement and muscle tenderness   Patients with muscle pain and little or no weakness may be thought to be neurotic or hysterical. A number of conditions including *polymyalgia rheumatica* (Chap. 269) and arthritic disorders of adjacent joints enter into the differential diagnosis of polymyositis. The muscle biopsy either is normal or discloses type II fiber atrophy, but in polymyalgia rheumatica the temporal artery biopsy may show giant cell arteritis (Chap. 269). *Fibrositis* and *fibromyalgia* are syndromes which frequently enter into the differential diagnosis of polymyositis. Patients complain of focal or diffuse muscle tenderness, aching, and weakness, which is sometimes poorly separated from joint pain. In other patients there may be minor signs of a collagen-vascular disorder, such as an increased erythrocyte sedimentation rate, antinuclear antibody (ANA), or rheumatoid factor, and occasionally there is slight elevation of the serum CK. The muscle biopsy occasionally shows a few interstitial inflammatory cells. Where there is a focal "trigger point," biopsy may show inflammatory infiltration of the connective tissue. Rarely does this syndrome develop into frank polymyositis, and the prognosis is therefore more benign than that of polymyositis (see below). Many such patients show some response to nonsteroidal anti-inflammatory agents, though most continue to have indolent complaints.

TREATMENT   Corticosteroids in high dosage are the accepted treatment for severe dermatomyositis-polymyositis, though there is no controlled trial to prove their effectiveness. The best results are obtained from the use of prednisone, starting at a dose of 1 to 2 mg per kilogram of body weight per day (60 to 100 mg per day for adults). Improvement may begin within 1 to 4 weeks, though in some patients treatment may need to be continued for 3 months before improvement occurs. When there is significant improvement in the weakness, the dose may be reduced every 4 weeks by 5 mg per day. Repeated manual muscle testing and serum CK determinations should be performed to ensure that the myositis does not relapse. At about 40 mg per day, the schedule is changed gradually to 80 mg every other day in order to reduce the incidence of corticosteroid side effects. Children and patients with acute to subacute dermatomyositis-polymyositis tend to improve more rapidly than those with chronic polymyositis. If the dose is reduced too rapidly, or to too low a level, relapse will occur, necessitating return to high dosage. Prednisone therapy may have to be continued for several years, but an attempt should be made every year to withdraw the therapy from patients who are clinically stable in order to determine if the disease is still active.

Cytotoxic drugs should be tried when the disease is severe, when the response to corticosteroids is inadequate, or when relapses are frequent. Azathioprine (2.5 to 3.5 mg per kilogram of body weight per day in divided doses) is the most commonly used cytotoxic drug in this disease. Cyclophosphamide and methotrexate have also been used with benefit. The aim of cytotoxic therapy is to lower the total lymphocyte count to about 750 per cubic millimeter, while maintaining the hemoglobin level above 12 g/dL, the total white cell count above 3000 per cubic millimeter, and the platelet count above 125,000 per cubic millimeter. Weekly blood counts are required to monitor the cytotoxic drug therapy. The combined use of prednisone and a cytotoxic drug usually allows a lower dose of prednisone to be used. Bed rest has been recommended in the acute phase of the disease but is harmful in the long term. Physiotherapy and rehabilitative devices are important in the long-term treatment of patients with dermatomyositis-polymyositis.

Elderly patients, particularly those with dermatomyositis, should be investigated at yearly intervals for a malignancy. If a malignant lesion is found, it should be treated, since the muscle weakness may disappear if the neoplasm is eradicated. However, a response to corticosteroids can usually be obtained even in patients with polymyositis associated with a malignancy.

The serum CK activity is useful for following patients during reduction of immunosuppressant therapy, since a rise in level generally indicates an incipient clinical relapse. However it cannot be used to indicate initial response in patients being treated with prednisone for dermatomyositis-polymyositis, since this drug lowers the serum CK activity in a way which is not fully understood, but which is not related to the suppression of muscle inflammation.

Side effects of high-dose corticosteroid therapy (Chap. 325) are relatively common in patients treated for polymyositis, and these may limit therapy. When patients who have been stable on a static dose of prednisone develop increasing muscle weakness, this may be due to either a relapse of the myositis or to corticosteroid myopathy. An EMG, serum CK measurement, and rarely muscle biopsy may help in differentiating these two conditions if the changes of myositis are present. However, often the only way to separate them is to reduce the dose of prednisone slowly; if corticosteroid myopathy is the cause of the weakness, it will improve; if a relapse of the myositis is responsible, the weakness will increase.

Side effects of cytotoxic drugs include marrow suppression, alopecia, gastrointestinal tract disorders, damage to the testes and ovaries (including potential genetic damage), and disorders of chronic immunosuppression.

PROGNOSIS   The overall mortality rate of individuals with dermatomyositis-polymyositis is about four times that of the general population; death is due usually to pulmonary, renal, and cardiac complications. Females and blacks have a worse prognosis. Nevertheless, the 5-year survival rate is about 75 percent overall, and is better than this in children. The majority of patients improve with therapy. Many patients make a full functional recovery, though some weakness of the shoulders and hips, usually not disabling, remains at the conclusion of treatment. Relapse may occur at any time. Corticosteroids should not be discontinued too soon, for the relapse which may follow is often more difficult to treat than the original presentation. About one-half of the patients with this disease recover and can discontinue therapy within 5 years after the onset of the symptoms; about 20 percent still have active disease requiring continued therapy. The remaining 30 percent have inactive disease but residual muscle weakness.

REFERENCES

Bohan A et al: A computer-assisted analysis of 153 patients with polymyositis and dermatomyositis. Medicine 56:225, 1977

Bradley WG: Inflammatory diseases of muscle, in *Textbook of Rheumatology*, 2nd ed., WN Kelley et al (eds). Philadelphia, Saunders, 1984, chap 79

Carpenter S, Karpati G: *Pathology of Skeletal Muscle*. New York, Churchill Livingstone, 1984, pp 515–592

Curie S.: Inflammatory myopathies, Part I: Polymyositis and related disorders, in *Disorders of Voluntary Muscle*, 4th ed., JN Walton (ed). London, Churchill Livingstone, 1981, chap 15

DeVere R, Bradley WG: Polymyositis: Its presentation, mortality, and morbidity. Brain 98:637, 1975

Engel AG, Banker BQ (eds): *Myology*. New York, McGraw-Hill, 1986

Mastaglia FL, Ojeda VJ: Inflammatory myopathies. Ann Neurol 17:215, 317, 1985

---

357   MUSCULAR DYSTROPHY AND OTHER CHRONIC MYOPATHIES

JERRY R. MENDELL / ROBERT C. GRIGGS

Most myopathies (see Table 354-2) including the hereditary, inflammatory, endocrine, metabolic, and toxic disorders can result in chronic weakness. The approach to differential diagnosis of these disorders is summarized in Chap. 354.

HEREDITARY MYOPATHIES

MUSCULAR DYSTROPHIES *Muscular dystrophy* refers to a group of disorders that have little in common except for their name and the fact that they are inherited. Each type of muscular dystrophy has unique phenotypic and genetic differences (Table 357-1).

Duchenne's muscular dystrophy   This disorder was first described by Edward Meryon (1852) but the disease bears the name of the French neurologist Duchenne. Duchenne dystrophy is an X-linked recessive disorder affecting males almost exclusively. Estimates of incidence range from 13 to 33 per 100,000 live-born males. In one-third or more of cases the family history is negative, suggesting that many are due to new mutations.

Careful studies of rare females with the Duchenne phenotype have provided information about the localization of the Duchenne gene on the chromosome. Translocations and deletions have been consistently found on the short arm of the X chromosome at the Xp21 site. Confirmation of a close proximity of the Duchenne locus to the Xp21 site has been accomplished through genetic linkage studies employing restriction endonucleases. The further development of a specific DNA probe will permit identification of fetuses at risk and provide a direct and definitive carrier detection test. Heterozygous female carriers of the trait often manifest some features of the disease, but current methods of detection using the serum levels of creatine kinase (CK), pyruvate kinase, and lactic dehydrogenase or other methods fail to identify half of such carriers.

Clinical manifestations usually begin at 3 to 5 years of age. The boys fall frequently and have difficulty keeping up with their friends when playing. Running, jumping, and hopping are invariably abnormal. Motor milestones may be delayed even before age 2, but if there is no family history the diagnosis is often not suspected.

By age 5 muscle weakness is obvious by manual muscle testing or by observing the inability to run, jump, or hop. On getting up from the floor the patient must use his hands to climb up himself (Gowers' maneuver). In younger children the calf muscles are usually enlarged from muscle hypertrophy; later, calf enlargement is appropriately called *pseudohypertrophy* since muscle is replaced by fat and connective tissue.

Contractures of heel cords and iliotibial bands become apparent by age 7 to 8, when toe walking is associated with a lordotic posture. Loss of muscle strength is progressive with predilection for proximal limb muscles and the neck flexors; leg involvement is more severe than arm involvement. Between ages 8 and 10 walking usually requires the use of braces; joint contractures and limitation of hip flexion and knee, elbow, and wrist extension are made worse by prolonged sitting. By age 12 most patients are confined to a wheelchair. Contractures become fixed and a progressive scoliosis often develops which may be associated with considerable discomfort. The chest deformity associated with scoliosis further impairs pulmonary function which is already diminished by the muscle weakness. By age 14 to 18 patients may develop serious, even fatal, pulmonary infections. Other causes of death include aspiration of food and acute gastric dilatation.

A cardiac cause of death is uncommon despite the existence of a cardiomyopathy in almost all patients. Congestive heart failure seldom occurs except with severe stress such as pneumonia. Cardiac arrhythmias are rare. The typical ECG shows an increased net RS in lead V_1; deep narrow Q waves in the lateral precordial leads; and RSR′ or polyphasic R waves in V_1.

TABLE 357-1   Progressive muscular dystrophies

Type	Usual inheritance	Clinical features	Other organ systems involved
Duchenne's (pseudohypertrophic)	X-linked recessive	Onset by age 5 Progressive weakness of girdle muscles Inability to walk after age 12 Kyphoscoliosis Respiratory failure in second to third decade	Cardiomyopathy Mental impairment
Becker's (benign pseudohypertrophic)	X-linked recessive	Onset in early to late childhood Slowly progressive weakness of girdle muscles Ability to walk after age 5 Respiratory failure after fourth decade	Cardiomyopathy
Myotonic	Autosomal dominant	Onset any decade Slowly progressive weakness of eyelids, face, neck, distal limb muscles Myotonia	Cardiac conduction defects Mental impairment Cataracts Frontal baldness Gonadal atrophy
Facioscapulohumeral	Autosomal dominant	Onset second to fourth decade Slowly progressive face, shoulder girdle, foot dorsiflexion weakness	Hypertension
Limb-girdle (may include several disorders)	Autosomal recessive	Onset early childhood to adult Slowly progressive weakness of shoulder and hip girdle muscles	Cardiomyopathy
Oculopharyngeal	Autosomal dominant (French-Canadian or Hispanic background)	Onset fifth to sixth decade Slowly progressive weakness of extraocular, eyelid, face, and pharyngeal muscles Cricopharyngeal achalasia	
Less well-characterized forms of muscular dystrophies: Congenital (may include several disorders)	Autosomal recessive	Onset at birth Hypotonia, contractures and delayed milestones Early respiratory failure in some; others have static course	
Distal (may include several disorders)	Autosomal recessive	Onset second to third decade Slowly progressive weakness of legs beginning with foot drop	
Scapuloperoneal (may include several disorders)	Autosomal dominant	Onset third to fifth decade Progressive shoulder girdle and foot dorsiflexor weakness	Cardiomyopathy

Intellectual impairment is common in Duchenne's dystrophy. One-third of patients have intelligence quotients below 75 and the mean is estimated at 85. The intellectual impairment is not the result of weakness since verbal skills are impaired before weakness is severe; its basis is not known. In contrast to the muscle disease, intellectual impairment is nonprogressive.

Laboratory confirmation includes assessment of serum CK level, which is invariably elevated twentyfold and may be as high as 100 times normal. The levels are abnormal at birth, making it possible to diagnose an affected boy early in life. Serum CK activity remains high until late in the disease, when levels decline because of inactivity and loss of muscle mass.

Myopathy can be demonstrated by electromyography (EMG). The muscle biopsy shows muscle fibers of varying size as well as small groups of necrotic and regenerating fibers. Connective tissue and fat replaces lost muscle fibers.

Becker's muscular dystrophy   This less severe form of X-linked recessive muscular dystrophy was described by Becker and Keiner in 1955. It is often called the benign form of pseudohypertrophic muscular dystrophy. The presentation is similar to that of Duchenne's dystrophy except that the time course is slow. The incidence of Becker's dystrophy is approximately one-tenth that of the Duchenne type. The condition is not usually recognized before age 5 and walking continues well beyond age 15, sometimes into the fourth decade. Calf muscle enlargement is prominent. Death from complications similar to those of Duchenne's dystrophy may occur after age 40.

The fact that the Becker and Duchenne genes are at or near the same locus on the X chromosome suggests that the disorders may be allelic. Carrier detection methods are identical for Duchenne's and Becker's dystrophies, and both suffer the same shortcomings. Unlike Duchenne's dystrophy, Becker patients reach child-bearing age; while none of their sons will be affected, the daughters of the Becker patient will all be carriers.

Laboratory confirmation of Becker's dystrophy is the same as that for Duchenne's dystrophy in that high serum CK levels are present early in the course and then gradually decline. The EMG and muscle biopsy changes are similar to those of Duchenne's dystrophy.

Facioscapulohumeral muscular dystrophy   This slowly progressive, relatively mild disorder is usually inherited as an autosomal dominant disorder, affecting males and females equally. It is extremely variable in severity and may start at any age, commonly in the third or fourth decade. Patients may, however, remain asymptomatic throughout life. As the name implies, there is characteristic weakness of facial, shoulder girdle, and proximal arm muscles. Scapular winging and sloping shoulders reflect weakness of the serratus anterior, trapezius, and rhomboid muscles; later, the biceps and triceps muscles are affected; the deltoid muscles are usually relatively spared. Facial involvement often produces a lifelong inability to whistle, an expressionless face, and a sullen appearance. Foot drop may occur early in the disease from peroneal and anterior tibial muscle weakness. Leg weakness may eventually progress to loss of ambulation.

Other systems are usually unaffected in facioscapulohumeral dystrophy. Cardiac disease and respiratory compromise are rare, and their occurrence usually suggests a coincidental illness. Patients frequently appear to have exophthalmos but thyroid function is normal; a mild but labile hypertension is common. Intellectual function is intact and life span is often normal.

Diagnostic studies may be unnecessary in typical cases, particularly when a family history is present. CK level may be normal or slightly elevated; EMG and muscle biopsy tend to have mixed features of myopathy and neuropathy and may be misleading. No specific treatment is available; ankle-foot orthoses are occasionally helpful for foot drop. Scapular stabilization procedures improve scapular winging but may not improve function.

Limb-girdle dystrophy   This term encompasses more than one disorder, and since inheritance is usually by autosomal recessive transmission, cases are often sporadic. Proximal muscle weakness may begin in either the legs or the arms but usually progresses to all extremities. Weakness may begin before age 5 or as late as the third decade and may be associated with pseudohypertrophy of calves and other muscles. Ambulation continues for over 20 years after the disease first appears. In some patients cardiac involvement results in congestive heart failure or arrhythmias; occasional patients may present with a cardiomyopathy. Respiratory failure ensues after 30 or more years of disease. Intellectual function remains normal. Diagnosis requires the exclusion of inflammatory and metabolic myopathies as well as the phenotypically similar spinal muscular atrophies. The serum CK level is elevated in limb-girdle dystrophy although the values are usually lower than in Duchenne's and Becker's dystrophies; the EMG pattern is that of a myopathy. The muscle biopsy shows active myopathy but is not specific.

Myotonic dystrophy   This autosomal dominant disorder affects muscle and numerous other tissues. The incidence is estimated to be 1 per 10,000 and may be higher since many cases escape recognition. Associated features include intellectual impairment, hypersomnia, cardiac disease, cataracts, gonadal atrophy, respiratory failure, and gastrointestinal disease. Weakness initially involves eyelid, temporalis, facial, and neck flexor muscles, as well as the distal extremity muscles. Myotonia is demonstrable in hand grip or by percussion of the tongue, the wrist extensors, or the thenar eminence. Disease onset is usually in the second and third decade, but affected individuals may remain free of signs or symptoms throughout life. A severe form of the disease, *congenital myotonic dystrophy,* occurs in some infants of affected mothers and is characterized by severe facial and bulbar weakness; neonatal respiratory insufficiency may occur but is usually self-limited. Affected infants are frequently intellectually impaired.

Diagnosis is often self-evident because of the distinctive facial appearance; the characteristic pattern of weakness and the abnormalities cause the typical narrow, "hatchet" face; premature frontal balding is frequent. The presence of distal weakness and myotonia confirm the diagnosis. Laboratory studies are often unnecessary and may be misleading. The CK activity is normal or slightly elevated. EMG of distal hand muscles usually shows myotonia and myopathic features. Muscle biopsy often shows distinctive type I fiber atrophy; severely involved muscles may have a characteristic appearance including ring fibers, sarcoplasmic masses, and numerous central nuclei.

Cardiac involvement most commonly affects the conduction system; first-degree heart block is present in a majority, and complete heart block may require pacemaker implantation. Since sudden death may occur, patients must be monitored carefully for conduction disturbances, though precise criteria for the timing of pacemaker implantation are lacking. Tachyarrhythmias and congestive failure are less frequent. Respiratory muscle weakness may be severe even in patients with minor limb weakness. Impaired ventilatory drive and hypersensitivity to the depressant effects of small doses of opiates and sedatives may result in sudden ventilatory failure, particularly in the pre- or postoperative setting. Sleep apnea may occur on both a central and peripheral basis (Chap. 215). Chronic hypoxia may lead to cor pulmonale and is the usual cause of heart failure.

Myotonia is seldom disabling enough to require treatment; phenytoin is the therapy of choice since the other antimyotonia agents, quinine and procainamide, may worsen cardiac conduction.

Myotonic dystrophy is transmitted by a mutant gene on chromosome 19 which is linked to the genes for secretor substance, the Lutheran blood group, peptidase D, and the third component of complement. Early disease detection and antenatal diagnosis are now possible in selected families using linkage techniques. Furthermore, prior to the onset of symptoms affected family members can frequently be identified by clinical and EMG evaluation for myotonia and by slit-lamp examination for the characteristic posterior subcapsular cataracts.

Myotonia congenita This disorder occurs in autosomal dominant (Thomsen) and autosomal recessive forms (Chap. 17). Patients with the autosomal recessive form may develop slight weakness; patients with the dominant form do not develop weakness. Myotonia can be markedly alleviated by antimyotonia agents including quinine, procainamide, phenytoin, or acetazolamide. These patients have no cardiac involvement.

Oculopharyngeal dystrophy The term *progressive external ophthalmoplegia* describes disorders characterized by slowly progressive ptosis and limitation of eye movements with the sparing of pupil and accommodation muscles. Patients usually do not complain of diplopia, in contrast to conditions with a more acute onset of ocular muscle weakness. *Oculopharyngeal dystrophy* is an autosomal dominant disorder in which ophthalmoplegia appears in the fifth or sixth decade. Many patients are of French-Canadian or Hispanic ancestry. Pharyngeal weakness leads to cricopharyngeal achalasia, progressive difficulty in swallowing, and frequent, often asymptomatic, aspiration. Severe malnutrition may develop but can be alleviated by surgical correction of cricopharyngeal achalasia.

Additional types of *ocular myopathies* are associated with mitochondrial abnormalities in muscle (see discussion of metabolic myopathies below).

Congenital muscular dystrophy This rare disorder may represent more than one disease. The usual picture is infantile hypotonia and muscle wasting associated with joint contractures of limbs. Serum CK level is usually elevated and the muscle biopsy shows features typical of muscular dystrophy. The condition is relatively nonprogressive, but many patients are not able to walk. Respiratory failure may occur in the first or second decade. Hypomyelination of the deep white matter of the brain can be detected in some cases by computerized tomography (CT), but it has no known clinical manifestations.

Distal muscular dystrophy This rare disorder has at least three separate variants. The most frequent is an autosomal recessive or sporadic disorder that presents with distal leg weakness in the second or third decade. Slow progression to more proximal muscles occurs. The CK level is markedly elevated. Other distinct forms of a distal myopathy include an autosomal dominant Scandinavian form (Welander) which begins in the hands, and a late-onset (fourth to fifth decade) autosomal dominant disorder that begins in the legs and in which cardiomyopathy is frequent.

Scapuloperoneal dystrophy Several forms of neuromuscular disease cause foot drop and winging of the scapulas. An autosomal dominant form presents in the third to fifth decade and is variable in its progression; respiratory failure is uncommon, but cardiomyopathy may occur. An X-linked recessive form (Emery-Dreifuss) begins in early childhood and is associated with prominent joint contractures and cardiac conduction disorders. Certain cases of facioscapulohumeral dystrophy may lack facial weakness and resemble scapuloperoneal dystrophy.

CONGENITAL MYOPATHIES These rare disorders are distinguished from muscular dystrophies by the presence of specific histochemical and structural abnormalities in muscle. A nonprogressive course is common but not invariable. The typical infant has hypotonia and delayed motor milestones. Pectus excavatum, kyphoscoliosis, hip dislocation, and pes cavus are common. The diagnosis is important, since the long-term prognosis and management differ from that of the muscular dystrophies.

Four major forms of congenital myopathies have been described: central core disease, nemaline (rod) myopathy, myotubular (centronuclear) myopathy and congenital fiber-type disproportion.

Central core disease This disease, the first congenital myopathy described, was identified by Shy and Magee in 1956. The disorder is inherited as an autosomal dominant disorder but sporadic cases also occur. In infancy hypotonia and delayed motor milestones are

typical, but the diagnosis may come to attention in an adult with muscle weakness or skeletal abnormalities.

Short, slender stature and skeletal abnormalities including congenital hip dislocation, scoliosis, pes cavus, and pectus excavatum are characteristic. Weakness of the muscles of the face and limbs, particularly the legs, is mild. The muscle biopsy is diagnostic; it shows fibers with single or multiple central or eccentric discrete zones (cores) devoid of oxidative enzymes. Other laboratory studies are less helpful since the serum CK and the EMG may be normal. Patients with this disorder may be predisposed to develop malignant hyperthermia (Chap. 8).

Nemaline myopathy This disorder, also called rod myopathy, was described by Shy and colleagues in 1963. Inheritance is usually as an autosomal dominant trait but it may be recessive or sporadic. Infantile hypotonia is frequent, and death may occur from respiratory failure. The skeletal abnormalities are striking; they include a long face, high arched palate, and slender musculature. Kyphoscoliosis, pectus excavatum, and pes cavus may be present. Muscle weakness affects the face, palate, and limb muscles. The prognosis is variable, with some patients progressing to wheelchair confinement or respiratory failure while in others the disease does not progress.

Muscle histology shows clusters of small rod or nemaline (threadlike) bodies for which the condition was named. Rods, derived from Z-band material, are usually found in type I fibers, and the muscle often shows type I predominance. The serum CK level may be normal or mildly elevated, and the EMG usually shows myopathy.

Myotubular myopathy This disorder was described by Spiro, Shy, and Gonatas in 1966. The histologic abnormality in myotubular myopathy resembles the embryonic or developmental myotube stage of a muscle fiber. Others have preferred to call the disease *centronuclear myopathy*, arguing that the fibers are not embryonic. The condition is usually sporadic, but inheritance may be as an autosomal dominant, recessive, or X-linked recessive trait. Infantile hypotonia and weakness are common and may cause death. Presentations at an older age include features similar to nemaline myopathy with a long narrow face, pes cavus, and scoliosis. Muscle bulk is reduced, and proximal and distal weakness is of varying severity. The feature that separates these patients from those with other congenital myopathies is the presence of external ophthalmoplegia. The course may or may not be progressive.

Serum CK activity is normal or slightly elevated. The EMG is usually abnormal with excessively recruited small motor unit potentials associated with fibrillations and positive sharp potentials. Muscle biopsy shows muscle fibers with rows of central nuclei often surrounded by a perinuclear clear zone. Type I fibers may be preferentially affected and may be atrophic.

Congenital fiber-type disproportion Clinical features of this disorder include hypotonia, weakness, delayed milestones, and skeletal deformities similar to those of other congenital myopathies. The diagnosis is established by the muscle biopsy which shows an increased number of small type I fibers and normal or hypertrophied type II fibers. The pathogenesis is poorly understood. The prognosis is generally good, with most patients showing improvement with age although some residual motor impairment commonly persists; occasional patients may have progressive weakness.

DISORDERS OF MUSCLE ENERGY METABOLISM Skeletal muscle utilizes two principal sources of energy—fatty acids and glucose. Abnormalities in either glucose or lipid utilization can be associated with distinct clinical features. The more dramatic feature is an acute muscle pain syndrome which can evolve into severe rhabdomyolysis and myoglobinuria. The other is progressive muscle weakness simulating muscular dystrophy. The explanation for the different clinical syndromes is often unknown.

Glycogen storage and glycolytic defects There are four disorders of glycogen metabolism (types II, III, IV, and V) and four disorders of glycolysis (types VII, IX, X, and XI) associated with significant skeletal muscle manifestations (also see Chap. 313).

ACID MALTASE DEFICIENCY (TYPE II GLYCOGENOSIS)   Acid maltase is a lysosomal enzyme, an acid hydrolase, having α-1,4- and α-1,6-glucosidase activity which breaks down glycogen to glucose; however, the enzyme has no well-defined role in carbohydrate metabolism. Three clinical forms of acid maltase deficiency are each inherited as autosomal recessive traits. The biochemical basis for the different clinical presentations is not understood.

In infancy, acid maltase deficiency has features of a generalized glycogenosis. No abnormalities are noted at birth, but shortly thereafter severe muscle weakness, cardiomegaly, hepatomegaly, and tongue enlargement develop. Glycogen accumulation in motor neurons of the spinal cord and brainstem contribute to the muscle weakness. Death usually occurs by 1 year of age.

In children and adults, the picture resembles muscular dystrophy. The childhood form is associated with delayed developmental milestones, proximal limb muscle weakness, and calf enlargement and may progress to respiratory failure and death before the end of the second decade. Cardiac involvement may be present, but hepatomegaly and macroglossia are infrequent.

The adult form begins in the third or fourth decade and may be misdiagnosed as limb-girdle dystrophy or polymyositis. Respiratory failure from diaphragmatic weakness may be the initial manifestation of the disease. The heart, liver, and tongue are not involved. The diagnosis is suggested by muscle biopsy which shows vacuoles containing glycogen and the lysosomal enzyme, acid phosphatase. By electron miscroscopy, membrane-bound and free tissue glycogen are found. Definitive diagnosis is established by muscle biochemistry. Acid maltase activity is also reduced in the urine. Serum CK level may be as high as ten times normal. EMG distinguishes acid maltase deficiency from muscular dystrophy by the occurrence of bizarre high-frequency and myotonic discharges accompanying short-duration motor unit potentials, fibrillations, and positive sharp potentials.

DEBRANCHER ENZYME DEFICIENCY (TYPE III GLYCOGENOSIS)   Muscle weakness is uncommon in debrancher enzyme deficiency. This mild disease of childhood is dominated by hepatomegaly, growth retardation, and hypoglycemia. These findings usually diminish or disappear after puberty, and muscle weakness and wasting associated with decreased exercise tolerance may develop. Diagnosis is suggested by a failure of lactic acid level to rise following exercise of the forearm. The serum CK level is elevated. EMG shows myopathy which may be accompanied by membrane irritability with myotonic discharges. Muscle biopsy shows a vacuolar myopathy with increased glycogen. Definitive diagnosis requires muscle biochemistry.

BRANCHER ENZYME DEFICIENCY (TYPE IV GLYCOGENOSIS)   Brancher enzyme deficiency is a severe fatal disorder of infancy in which skeletal muscle manifestations are relatively minor in the face of the chronic liver failure. The muscle hypotonia and wasting may, however, suggest the possibility of a primary muscle disease or spinal muscular atrophy.

MUSCLE PHOSPHORYLASE DEFICIENCY (TYPE V GLYCOGENOSIS)   Exercise intolerance is the dominant feature of muscle phosphorylase deficiency, first described in 1951 by McArdle. The disorder, usually inherited as an autosomal recessive trait, has an unexplained predilection for males. Painful muscle cramps and fatigue after intense exercise such as running or lifting heavy objects usually develops after adolescence. Early infantile and late onset variants have been described. Many patients report a ''second wind'' phenomenon if they rest briefly or slow down during exercise, which allows them to continue an activity for a longer period of time. Overexertion may lead to rhabdomyolysis and myoglobinuria, and renal failure can result. Persistent weakness and wasting of muscle is rare, and examination of the patient between attacks is usually normal. Other organs are not affected.

Serum CK levels fluctuate widely and may be elevated even during symptom-free periods. The forearm exercise test shows no rise in lactic acid. The EMG is often normal except when taken following an episode of rhabdomyolysis. Muscle biopsy often shows subsarcolemmal blebs containing glycogen. Muscle phosphorylase deficiency can be recognized by a histochemical stain and confirmed by biochemistry. Patients can remain moderately active once they establish their limitations. Dietary supplementation with either glucose or fructose has not alleviated symptoms.

PHOSPHOFRUCTOKINASE DEFICIENCY (TYPE VII GLYCOGENOSIS)   This disorder resembles muscle phosphorylase deficiency and is also an autosomal recessive trait with a male predominance. The precipitating events and the laboratory features also resemble phosphorylase deficiency. A histochemical stain for phosphofructokinase (PFK) can demonstrate the deficiency. Definitive diagnosis requires biochemical analysis of muscle enzymes. Some patients with PFK deficiency have mild hemolysis, increased reticulocyte count, and elevated bilirubin because of a deficiency of a PFK subunit shared by muscle and red blood cells.

NEW GLYCOLYTIC ENZYME DEFICIENCY SYNDROMES   Since 1981 deficiencies of three additional glycolytic enzymes have been identified: phosphoglycerate kinase (PGK) deficiency (type IX), phosphoglycerate mutase (PGAM) deficiency (type X) and lactate dehydrogenase deficiency (LDH) (XI). The clinical pictures of the three are similar. In each, episodic myoglobinuria and myalgias precipitated by intense exercise begin in childhood or adolescence. Autosomal recessive inheritance is probable in each disorder. Serum CK level may be elevated during and between episodes. In PGAM and LDH deficiencies, the rise in lactic acid following forearm exercise is lower than normal. PGK deficiency shows no rise in lactate and closely resembles muscle phosphorylase and PFK deficiencies. The muscle histology is unremarkable in these disorders with little evidence of glycogen storage. Diagnosis requires muscle biochemistry.

Disorders of lipid metabolism   Lipid is an important muscle energy source during rest and prolonged, moderately intense exercise (Fig. 357-1).

CARNITINE DEFICIENCY   Carnitine deficiency occurs in myopathic and systemic forms.

Myopathic carnitine deficiency is associated with generalized muscle weakness, usually beginning in childhood. The clinical features overlap with muscular dystrophy and polymyositis. Most cases are sporadic, but the inheritance pattern is thought to be autosomal recessive. Cardiomyopathy may be present. Serum CK level is mildly elevated, and the EMG shows myopathy. The muscle biopsy shows striking lipid accumulation. Serum carnitine is normal. The cause for decreased muscle carnitine is not understood. A defect of transport into muscle has been postulated. Some patients respond to oral carnitine supplements; this should be tried in all cases. Other patients have responded to prednisone for unknown reasons. A diet substituting medium-chain for long-chain triglycerides has been helpful in some cases. Rare patients have also responded to riboflavin.

Systemic carnitine deficiency, an autosomal recessive disease of infancy and early childhood, is characterized by progressive weakness and episodes of hepatic encephalopathy with nausea, vomiting, confusion, coma, and early death. The low *serum* carnitine level distinguishes this condition from the myopathic form. No single cause has been identified to explain the low serum carnitine level. Decreased synthesis explains some cases while increased urinary excretion is seen in others. Serum CK level may be slightly elevated. The muscle biopsy shows lipid storage. In some cases the liver, heart, and kidney also show increased lipid. Treatment with oral carnitine supplements or corticosteroids has helped some but not all patients.

CARNITINE PALMITYLTRANSFERASE DEFICIENCY   Deficiency of carnitine palmityltransferase (CPT) presents with recurrent myoglobinuria. It is not known if CPT I or CPT II activities are selectively deficient; the deficiency apparently results from disordered regulatory properties of an abnormal enzyme. Rhabdomyolysis may follow prolonged exercise such as soccer, football, or a long hike, but at times no precipitating cause can be found. Initial symptoms often commence in childhood. In contrast to defects in glycolysis where muscle cramps follow short intense bursts of exercise, limiting the amount of exercise and protecting the patient, in CPT deficiency muscle pain does not occur until the limits of energy utilization have been exceeded and muscle breakdown has begun. Episodes of rhabdomyolysis may produce severe weakness, and some patients require ventilatory assistance. In contrast to carnitine deficiency, strength is normal between attacks and the muscle biopsy does not show lipid accumulation. The diagnosis requires direct measurement of muscle CPT. Treatment consists of increasing carbohydrate intake before exercise or of substituting medium-chain for long-chain triglycerides in the diet. Neither has been entirely satisfactory.

Myoadenylate deaminase deficiency The enzyme adenylate deaminase converts 5'-adenosine monophosphate (5'-AMP) to inosine monophosphate (IMP) with liberation of ammonia and may play a role in regulating adenosine triphosphate (ATP) levels in muscle. In 1978 a group of patients with myalgias and exercise intolerance were found to be deficient in the muscle isoenzyme, myoadenylate deaminase. The deficiency, however, occurs in as many as 1 percent of the population and can be detected by histochemical staining of muscle tissue as well as by biochemical analysis. Muscle ammonia production is decreased following forearm exercise. Since the original description, a less consistent clinical picture has emerged. Patients with other neuromuscular disorders including anterior horn cell disease, muscular dystrophy, and myasthenia gravis occasionally have the same enzyme deficiency. The full clinical significance of myoadenylate deaminase deficiency is not established.

Mitochondrial myopathies A heterogeneous group of disorders is characterized by abnormal mitochondria in "ragged-red fibers," named for their appearance in the trichrome stain of biopsied muscle. The *Kearns-Sayre syndrome* is a sporadic disorder beginning in childhood in which progressive external ophthalmoplegia is accompanied by cardiac conduction defects that often culminate in complete heart block. Retinal degeneration, short stature, and gonadal defects

also occur. A familial disorder with progressive external ophthalmoplegia and proximal weakness may be difficult to distinguish from the Kearns-Sayre syndrome. Another disorder recently assigned the acronym *MERRF syndrome,* because of its myolonic epilepsy and ragged-red fibers, presents between the first and fifth decades with generalized seizures, myoclonus, dementia, hearing loss, and ataxia. A third disorder, the *MELAS syndrome*, is a slowly progressive disease characterized by mitochondrial myopathy, encephalopathy, lactic acidosis, stroke-like episodes including alternating hemiparesis, hemianopsia or cortical blindness, and focal or generalized seizures. The cause of the mitochondrial myopathies is unknown but there is evidence that familial cases may be transmitted by mitochondrial as opposed to chromosomal DNA.

INFLAMMATORY MYOPATHIES

Polymyositis and dermatomyositis (Chap. 356) develop slowly over the course of months. The presence of a characteristic skin rash usually makes the diagnosis of dermatomyositis straightforward. Chronic polymyositis, with slowly progressive proximal weakness, may be impossible to separate on clinical grounds from sporadic cases of limb-girdle dystrophy. Even with detailed EMG and biopsy studies it may prove difficult to establish the diagnosis of polymyositis with confidence. A subgroup of subacute or chronic inflammatory myopathy has been identified and is termed *inclusion body myositis* because of distinctive cytoplasmic membranous inclusions and nuclear inclusions consisting of abnormal filaments. Inclusion body myositis does not respond to corticosteroid therapy. Chronic myositis may also occur with all of the collagen-vascular diseases and with sarcoidosis.

ENDOCRINE AND METABOLIC MYOPATHIES

Many endocrine disorders cause weakness. Muscle fatigue is more common than true weakness. The cause of weakness in these disorders is not well-defined. It is not even clear that weakness results from

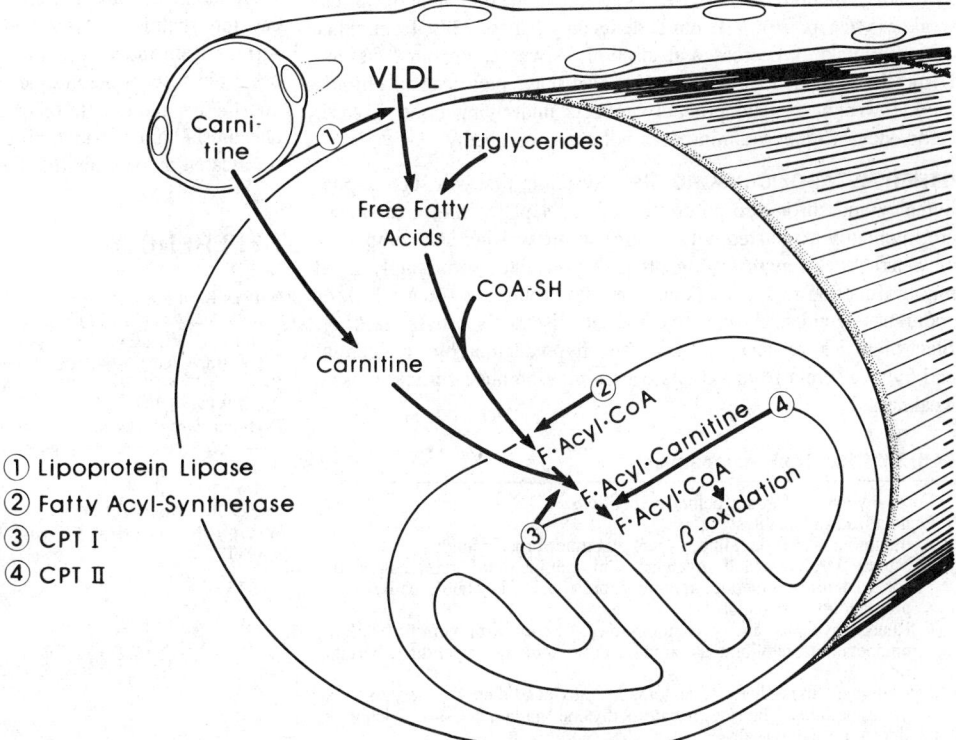

FIGURE 357-1 *Free fatty acids for muscle energy are derived from triglycerides stored in muscle and from circulating very low density lipoproteins (VLDL) which are broken down by endothelial lipoprotein lipase (1) in the capillary. Carnitine, an essential substrate for lipid metabolism, is made in the liver and transported to muscle. In muscle, free fatty acids combine with coenzyme A (CoA SH) through the action of fatty acylsynthetase (2) found in the outer mitochondrial membrane forming fatty acylcoenzyme A (F acyl CoA). Transport through inner mitochondrial membrane requires transfer to carnitine by carnitine palmityltransferase I (CPT I) bound to the outer surface of the inner mitochondrial membrane (3). Inside the mitochondrion, fatty acylcarnitine (F acyl carnitine) is regenerated by CPT II (4) bound to the inner surface of the inner mitochondrial membrane. The fatty acylcoenzyme A then proceeds to beta oxidation.*

① Lipoprotein Lipase
② Fatty Acyl-Synthetase
③ CPT I
④ CPT II

disease of muscle as opposed to another part of the motor unit since the CK level is often normal and the muscle histology is characterized by atrophy rather than by destruction of muscle fibers. Nearly all respond to appropriate endocrine management.

THYROID DISORDERS (See Chap. 324) *Hyperthyroidism* may occasionally present as muscle weakness, and the majority of patients are weak. *Hypothyroidism* commonly presents with muscle weakness and pain. The serum CK is often elevated and levels as high as 100 times normal may occur even with minimal clinical evidence of muscle disease. Adult patients may have muscle hypertrophy with cramps (Hoffmann's syndrome) and in children with cretinism a distinctive myopathy with muscle hypertrophy may occur (Kocher-Debré-Sémélaigne syndrome).

PARATHYROID DISORDERS (See Chap. 336) *Hyperparathyroidism* is often associated with muscle weakness and atrophy and may be accompanied by ''muscle'' pain which is probably from associated bone disease. *Hyperreflexia* is characteristic. *Hypoparathyroidism* frequently presents with neurologic involvement. The neuromuscular manifestations are usually those of tetany, but since the serum CK level is often elevated such patients are occasionally considered to have polymyositis. Hyporeflexia or areflexia is usually present despite the presence of Chvostek's and Trousseau's signs.

ADRENAL DISORDERS (See Chap. 325) Endogenous elevations of corticosteroids may produce severe muscle weakness and wasting. Adrenal insufficiency is frequently associated with lassitude and weakness although there is usually little objective reduction in strength.

PITUITARY DISORDERS (See Chap. 321) Acromegaly is occasionally associated with muscle enlargement. Myopathic weakness may occur, but weakness usually results from associated endocrine abnormalities or from neuropathy. The weakness of panhypopituitarism is probably due to coexisting adrenal or thyroid insufficiency.

DIABETES (See Chap. 327) Proximal weakness in the patient with diabetes is usually the result of neuropathy. The finding of evidence on EMG or biopsy for myopathy or of a markedly elevated serum CK level usually suggests coincidental illness.

VITAMIN DEFICIENCY Severe malabsorption, particularly when it occurs in early childhood, may lead to a vitamin E deficiency myopathy. Vitamin E otherwise has no role in the treatment of muscle weakness (Chap. 76). Vitamin D deficiency (Chap. 337), from either decrease intake or decreased absorption, as well as impaired vitamin D metabolism such as occurs in renal disease may lead to chronic muscle weakness; pain probably reflects underlying bone disease. Deficiency of other vitamins does not cause myopathy.

OTHER METABOLIC DISORDERS Systemic illnesses such as malignancy and chronic respiratory, cardiac, hepatic, and renal failure are frequently associated with severe muscle wasting and complaints of weakness. Strength testing often demonstrates surprisingly good muscle function in such patients, and the problem is often a lack of endurance. Evidence for active muscle disease is usually lacking. Electrolyte disturbances such as chronic hypokalemia, hypercalcemia, and hypocalcemia from various causes may produce chronic muscle weakness.

TABLE 357-2 Toxic myopathies

I Focal myopathies: Pentazocine, meperidine
II Generalized myopathies
   A Inflammatory: Cimetidine, D-penicillamine, procainamide
   B Muscle weakness and myalgias: Chloroquine, clofibrate, colchicine, corticosteroids, emetine, ε-aminocaproic acid, labetalol, perhexilene, propranolol, vincristine
   C Rhabdomyolysis and myoglobinuria: Alcohol, azathioprine, heroin, amphetamine, clofibrate, ε-aminocaproic acid, phencyclidine, barbiturates
   D Malignant hyperthermia: Halothane, ethylene, diethyl ether, methoxylflurane, ethyl chloride, trichloroethylene, gallamine, succinylcholine, lidocaine, mepivacaine

TOXIC MYOPATHIES

A classification of toxic myopathies is shown in Table 357-2. Drugs and chemicals may produce focal or generalized damage of skeletal muscle.

The most common cause of focal damage is the injection of narcotic analgesics. Two agents in particular, pentazocine and meperidine, may cause a severe fibrotic reaction in muscle. Common injection sites include deltoid, triceps, gluteus maximus and quadriceps muscles. The muscles become indurated and hard and may have local abscess formation. Cutaneous ulcerations and depressions may occur. Severe joint contractions may develop.

Other drugs may induce generalized muscle weakness, particularly affecting the proximal muscles. In most cases the exact mechanism of drug toxicity is poorly understood. D-Penicillamine induces a condition simulating the clinical and pathologic picture of dermatomyositis and polymyositis. A similar condition has been reported with cimetidine. Procainamide may cause myositis as part of a systemic lupus-like reaction. After many months of treatment, chloroquine produces a distinctive vacuolar myopathy that may involve the heart. Clofibrate is associated with muscle pain and weakness either shortly after the start or following several months of treatment. Serum CK elevation may be the only clofibrate-induced abnormality. Emetine hydrochloride (used for treatment of amebiasis), ε-aminocaproic acid (an antifibrolytic agent), and perhexilene (used for angina pectoris) have all been observed to cause weakness and muscle fiber necrosis following several weeks of therapy.

Drug-induced myopathy accompanied by proximal weakness occurs with corticosteroid therapy. Those fluorinated in the 9α-position, such as triamcinolone, dexamethasone, and betamethasone, are most likely to cause weakness, but chronic administration of all corticosteroids including prednisone also causes weakness. Divided-dose as opposed to single-morning-dose therapy produces more severe weakness. A single-dose, alternate-day regimen has the greatest muscle-sparing effect (Chap. 325). The clinical diagnosis of steroid-induced muscle weakness can be difficult if the medication is being used to treat an underlying inflammatory myopathy. The presence of a normal serum CK level, minimal or no changes of myopathy on EMG, and type II muscle fiber atrophy on biopsy are helpful in suggesting corticosteroid-induced weakness.

In some instances toxic myopathy may be more catastrophic, causing rhabdomyolysis and myoglobinuria (Chap. 376). A very serious drug-induced condition, *malignant hyperthermia* (Chap. 8), occurs in susceptible individuals following exposure to certain general anesthetics and depolarizing muscle relaxants (Table 357-2). In local anesthesia, amides including lidocaine and mepivacaine have been implicated as precipitating agents.

REFERENCES

BAKKER et al: Prenatal diagnosis and carrier detection of Duchenne muscular dystrophy with closely linked RFLPs. Lancet 1:655, 1985
BENDER AN: Congenital myopathies, in *Handbook of Clinical Neurology*, PJ Vinken, GW Bruyn (eds). New York, North-Holland, 1979, vol 41
BROOKE MH: *A Clinician's View of Neuromuscular Disease*, 2d ed. Baltimore, Williams and Wilkins, 1985
DiMAURO S et al: Disorders of lipid metabolism in muscle. Muscle Nerve 3:369, 1980
————: Mitochondrial myopathies. Ann Neurol 17:521, 1985
ENGEL AG et al: The spectrum and diagnosis of acid maltase deficiency. Neurology (NY) 2:395, 1973
GRIGGS RC, MOXLEY RT (eds): Metabolic Myopathies. Semin Neurol, 3:225, 1983
WALTON JN, MASTALGIA FL (eds): The Muscular Dystrophies. Br Med Bull 36:105, 1980

358 MYASTHENIA GRAVIS AND OTHER DISORDERS OF NEUROMUSCULAR TRANSMISSION

ANDREW G. ENGEL

Disorders of neuromuscular transmission are genetic or acquired diseases associated with abnormal weakness and fatigability on exertion. In each disorder the generation of an end-plate potential that is of sufficient amplitude to trigger a propagated muscle fiber action potential is compromised by one or more specific mechanisms. Table 358-1 shows a classification of currently recognized disorders of neuromuscular transmission.

MYASTHENIA GRAVIS

DEFINITION Myasthenia gravis (MG) is an acquired autoimmune disorder associated with acetylcholine receptor (AChR) deficiency at the motor end plate. The number of acetylcholine (ACh) quanta released from the nerve terminal by a nerve impulse and the probability of quantal release are normal, but the lack of available receptors to bind ACh reduces the amplitude of the end-plate potential. The response to single ACh quanta released from the nerve terminal during rest, the miniature end-plate potential, is also reduced. The disease involves the external ocular muscles selectively or is generalized. The symptoms are improved by rest and anticholinesterase drugs. Circulating AChR antibodies are present in 80 to 90 percent of the cases, and immune complexes (IgG and complement components) are deposited on the postsynaptic membrane of the motor end plate.

CLINICAL FEATURES The incidence of the disease is 2 to 5 per year per million and its prevalance is 13 to 64 per million. The ratio of female to male patients is 6:4. The disease may present at any age, but the incidence in females peaks in the third decade and in males in the sixth or seventh decade.

The symptoms may fluctuate from hour to hour, day to day, or over longer periods. They are provoked or worsened by exertion, exposure to extremes of temperature, viral or other infections, menses, and excitement. Ocular muscle involvement is usually bilateral, asymmetric, and typically is associated with ptosis and diplopia. Weakness of other muscles innervated by cranial nerves results in loss of facial expression, everted lips, a smile that resembles a snarl, jaw drop, nasal regurgitation of liquids, choking on foods and secretions, and a slurred, hypernasal speech of a reduced volume. Abnormal fatigability of the limb muscles causes difficulty in combing the hair, lifting objects repeatedly, climbing stairs, walking, or running. Depending on the severity of the disease, dyspnea appears on moderate or mild exertion or is present even at rest. The abnormal fatigability can be demonstrated by asking the patient to look up without closing the eyes for 1 min, count loudly from 1 to 100, hold the arms abducted to the horizontal position for 1 min, or perform repeated deep knee bends. The deep tendon reflexes are normally active even in weak muscles. Atrophy of masseter, temporal, facial, or tongue muscles, and less often of other muscles, occurs in about 15 percent of the patients.

The natural history of the disease During the first month after the onset, the symptoms are purely ocular in 40 percent of patients, generalized in 40 percent, involve only the extremities in 10 percent, and involve only the bulbar or bulbar and eye muscles in 10 percent. With progression from mild to more severe disease the weakness spreads from ocular to facial to lower bulbar muscles and then to torso and limb muscles, but this sequence may vary. Proximal limb muscles are more affected than distal ones, but in the most advanced cases the weakness is universal. By the end of the first year, the ocular muscles are affected in nearly all patients. The symptoms remain ocular in only 16 percent. In nearly 90 percent of those patients in whom the disease becomes generalized, this occurs within the first year. Progression is most rapid within the first 3 years, and more than half of the deaths stemming from the disease occur in that period. Spontaneous remissions lasting from weeks to years can occur, but long spontaneous remissions are uncommon and most remissions occur during the first 3 years.

Two-thirds of MG patients have thymic hyperplasia, and 10 to 15 percent have thymoma. A few with thymoma also develop myocarditis and/or giant cell myositis. In about 10 percent the MG is associated with another autoimmune disease, such as hyperthyroidism, polymyositis, systemic lupus erythematosus, Sjögren's syndrome, rheumatoid arthritis, ulcerative colitis, pemphigus, sarcoidosis, pernicious anemia, and Lambert-Eaton myasthenic syndrome.

Clinical types of myasthenia gravis A classification proposed by Osserman, based on the distribution and severity of symptoms, is as follows:

Group 1, ocular symptoms
Group 2A, mild generalized symptoms
Group 2B, moderately severe generalized symptoms
Group 3, acute fulminating symptoms
Group 4, late severe symptoms

An alternative classification is related to thymoma and age of onset:

Type 1, *MG with thymoma:* The disease is usually severe and the AChR antibody level is high. There is no association either with sex or HLA antigen.
Type 2, *no thymoma, onset before age 40:* The AChR antibody level is intermediate. There is female preponderance and an increased association with HLA-A1, HLA-B8, and HLA-DRw3 antigens (HLA-B12 in Japan).
Type 3, *no thymoma, onset after age 40:* The AChR antibody level tends to be low. There is male preponderance, and increased association with HLA-A3, HLA-B7, and HLA-DRw2 antigens (HLA-A10 in Japan).

Striated-muscle antibodies are found in 90 percent, 5 percent, and 45 percent in the three types, respectively. The association with other autoimmune disease is highest in type 3 and lowest in type 1.

Transient neonatal myasthenia gravis Circulating AChR antibodies can be detected in most infants born to myasthenic mothers, but only 12 percent of infants develop myasthenic symptoms. The disease usually presents during the first few hours of life and its mean duration is 18 days. The principal findings are feeding difficulty, generalized weakness, respiratory difficulty, feeble cry, facial weakness, and ptosis. There is no relation between the severity of symptoms in the mother and the infant. The disease is caused by the passive transfer of AChR antibodies or the adoptive transfer of immunocytes from mother to infant, or perhaps fetal AChR damaged by maternal antibodies triggers a transient immune response in the infant.

TABLE 358-1 Classification of disorders of neuromuscular transmission

Autoimmune:
    Myasthenia gravis
    Lambert-Eaton syndrome
Congenital:
    Familial infantile myasthenia*
    End-plate acetylcholinesterase deficiency†
    Slow-channel syndrome‡
    End-plate acetylcholine receptor deficiency*
Toxic:
    Botulism
    Drug-induced disorders

* *Autosomal recessive inheritance*
† *Autosomal or X-linked recessive inheritance*
‡ *Autosomal dominant inheritance*

IMMUNOPATHOGENESIS The autoimmune character of MG and the pathogenic role of AChR antibodies has been established by several measures. These include (1) the demonstration that animals immunized with AChR develop a syndrome which in many respects resembles human MG; (2) the detection of circulating AChR antibodies in most patients; (3) the passive transfer with IgG of several features of the disease from human to mouse; (4) the localization of immune complexes on the postsynaptic membrane; and (5) the beneficial effects of plasmapheresis. That AChR deficiency occurs at the end plate in MG was established by autoradiographic, ultrastructural, and radiochemical studies in which α-bungarotoxin, a molecule that binds with high affinity to AChR, was used to quantitate end-plate AChR. Further, the AChR decrease in myasthenic muscles can be correlated with the decrease of the miniature end-plate potential amplitude.

Antibodies bound to end-plate AChR induce AChR deficiency by two major mechanisms—complement attack and modulation. Complement fixation and activation of the lytic phase of the complement reaction sequence causes focal destruction of the junctional folds and loss of AChR into the synaptic space. Modulation is the accelerated internalization and destruction of AChRs cross-linked by antibody. AChR depletion occurs if synthesis and membrane insertion of new AChR cannot keep up with the loss of AChR. Further, lysis of the junctional folds by complement reduces the membrane surface available for insertion of new AChR and enhances the subsequent AChR depletion by both modulation and complement. Some AChR antibodies may also interfere with AChR function by blocking the binding of ACh to AChR. Blocking antibodies account for only a minor fraction of all AChR antibodies.

The frequent thymus gland abnormalities and the beneficial effects of thymectomy implicate the thymus in the pathogenesis of MG. It has been postulated that lymphocyte sensitization to AChR occurs in the thymus and that antigen-specific T-helper cells are subsequently exported from the gland to other antibody-producing sites.

DIAGNOSIS This is based on the characteristic history, physical examination, anticholinesterase tests, and laboratory studies. The latter include electromyographic studies, serologic tests, and, in selected cases, in vitro microelectrode studies of neuromuscular transmission and ultrastructural and cytochemical studies of the end plate.

Anticholinesterase tests Edrophonium given intravenously acts within a few seconds and its effects last for a few minutes. An amount of 0.1 to 0.2 mL out of 10 mg/mL is injected intravenously over 15 s. If there is no response in 30 s, 0.8 to 0.9 mL of the drug is injected. The evaluation of the response requires objective assessment of one or more signs such as degree of ptosis, range of ocular movements, and the force of the hand grip. Possible side effects of the drug include fasciculations, flushing, lacrimation, abdominal cramps, nausea, vomiting, and diarrhea. The drug must be given cautiously to patients with cardiac disease, for it may cause sinus bradycardia, atrioventricular block, and rarely cardiac arrest. Atropine is used to reverse toxicity. Intramuscular neostigmine, 0.5 to 1.0 mg, acts maximally in about 30 min and its effects last up to 2 h allowing a more leisurely evaluation of changes in clinical status.

Electromyography In MG supramaximal stimulation of a motor nerve at 2 to 3 Hz results in a 10 percent or greater decrement of the amplitude of the evoked compound muscle action potential from the first to the fifth response. The test is positive in nearly all patients provided that two or more distal and two or more proximal muscles are examined. The decrement is caused by a normally occurring decrease in the number of quanta released from the nerve terminal, and hence in the amplitude of the end-plate potential, at the beginning of low-frequency stimulation. In MG, the end-plate potential amplitude is already reduced by the AChR deficiency, and the additional decrease during stimulation results in blocking of transmission at an increasing number of end plates. The transmission defect improves for a few seconds after a 15- to 30-s period of maximal voluntary

contraction and becomes worse a few minutes later. These phenomena also reflect normally occurring presynaptic mechanisms that increase or decrease the quantal content of the end-plate potential and hence the safety margin of neuromuscular transmission. Single-fiber electromyography compares the timing of action potentials between pairs of closely adjacent muscle fibers in the same motor unit. In MG the low amplitude and prolonged rise time of the end-plate potentials cause abnormally long interpotential intervals and intermittent blocking of action potential generation at some fibers.

Serologic tests The AChR antibody test is positive in nearly all patients with moderately severe or acute severe MG, in 80 percent with mild generalized MG, in 50 percent with ocular MG, but in only 25 percent of those in remission. The antibody titer correlates only loosely with disease severity in a series of patients, but in individual patients a greater than 50 percent decrease in titer for more than 12 months is nearly always associated with sustained clinical improvement. Striated-muscle antibodies also occur in MG patients. Their role in MG remains unknown, but their association with thymoma is clinically relevant.

Other diagnostic studies Immune complexes can be localized at the MG end plate in cryostat sections even when circulating AChR antibodies cannot be detected. The technically easiest and most convenient way to confirm the suspected diagnosis is by C3 localization. To date, immune complexes have not been demonstrated by light microscopy at the end plate in other neuromuscular diseases. In vitro electrophysiologic studies of neuromuscular transmission can distinguish between atypical cases of MG, the Lambert-Eaton myasthenic syndrome, and some of the congenital myasthenic syndromes.

DIFFERENTIAL DIAGNOSIS This includes consideration of neurasthenia, oculopharyngeal dystrophy, the progressive external ophthalmoplegias with or without associated weakness of other cranial or limb muscles, intracranial mass-lesions compressing cranial nerves, drug-induced myasthenic syndromes, and other disorders of neuromuscular transmission (Table 358-1). Neurasthenia is recognized by giving way on muscle testing and by the lack of objective clinical and laboratory findings. In those myopathies involving the ocular muscles the weakness does not fluctuate, diplopia is seldom a symptom, the muscle biopsy may show distinct morphologic abnormalities, and pharmacologic and laboratory tests for MG are negative. Drug-induced and other myasthenic syndromes are considered in subsequent sections.

TREATMENT Anticholinesterases, alternate-day prednisone treatment, azathioprine, thymectomy, and plasmapheresis are currently used forms of therapy for MG.

Anticholinesterases are useful in all clinical forms of the disease. Pyridostigmine bromide (60-mg tablets) acts for 3 to 4 h and neostigmine bromide (15-mg tablets) for 2 to 3 h. Because pyridostigmine bromide acts longer and has fewer muscarinic side effects than does neostigmine bromide, it is the more widely used drug. One-half to four tablets of pyridostigmine bromide are given every 4 h in the daytime. Pyridostigmine bromide is also available in 180-mg "timespan" tablets for use at bedtime and as a syrup for children and patients requiring nasogastric feeding. If the muscarinic side effects are significant, these can be treated with 0.4 to 0.6 mg atropine given orally two to three times daily. Postoperatively or in critically ill patients, intramuscularly injectable pyridostigmine bromide (dose = 1/30 of oral dose) and neostigmine methyl sulfate (dose = 1/15 of oral dose) can be used.

Progressive weakness with increasing amounts of anticholinesterases usually signals the onset of a myasthenic or cholinergic crisis. Cholinergic crises are associated with muscarinic effects such as abdominal cramps, nausea, vomiting, diarrhea, miosis, lacrimation, increased bronchial secretions, diaphoresis, and bradycardia. The crisis is myasthenic rather than cholinergic if muscarinic effects are not conspicuous and if 2 mg of edrophonium given intravenously improves rather than worsens the weakness. In practice, however, the two types of crises are difficult to distinguish, and overmedication of a myasthenic crisis can convert it into a cholinergic crisis. Therefore, patients with increasing difficulty with respiration, feeding, or handling secretions and not responding to relatively high doses of anticholinesterases are best treated by drug withdrawal, tracheal intubation or tracheostomy, support with a respirator, and intravenous feeding. Refractoriness to drug therapy usually disappears after a few days.

In patients with generalized disease not responding adequately to modest doses of anticholinesterases, other forms of therapy must be employed. Thymectomy increases the remission rate and improves the clinical course of MG. Although controlled clinical studies of thymectomy according to age, sex, and severity of disease have never been carried out, there is general agreement that the best response occurs in young women with hyperplastic thymus glands and high antibody titer. Thymoma represents an absolute indication for thymectomy because the tumor is often locally invasive. Chest x-rays combined with linear tomography detect most thymomas. Computerized tomography of the mediastinum is a sensitive screening test, but may also yield false-positive results.

Alternate-day prednisone treatment induces remission or significantly improves the disease in more than half of the patients. The treatment is relatively safe provided that the usual precautions for patients taking corticosteroid therapy are instituted. With an average dose of 70 mg on alternate days, the average time for significant improvement is 5 months. After the improvement reaches a plateau the dose must be lowered over several months to establish the minimum maintenance dose.

Azathioprine in doses of 150 to 200 mg per day also induces remissions or significantly improves the disease in more than half of patients, but some responding patients have also received concurrent prednisone treatment or have had thymectomy. The minimum time for improvement is 3 months. Surveillance to detect side effects (pancytopenia, leukopenia, serious infection, and hepatocellular injury) must be maintained during therapy.

Plasmapheresis is indicated in severe generalized or fulminating MG refractory to other forms of treatment. Daily exchanges of 2 liters of plasma result in objective improvement and lower the AChR antibody titer in a few days. However, plasmapheresis itself does not confer greater long-term protection than do immunosuppressants alone.

LAMBERT-EATON MYASTHENIC SYNDROME

This is an acquired autoimmune disease associated with a reduced probability of quantal release from the nerve terminal by nerve impulse. Presynaptic ACh stores and the postsynaptic response to ACh quanta are normal.

The male/female ratio is close to 1:1. Carcinoma is present in 72 percent of males and 32 percent of females, but is uncommon under age 40. More than 80 percent of the tumors are small cell carcinomas of the lung. The syndrome may present up to 3 years before the tumor can be detected. In one-third of the patients the syndrome is nonneoplastic and occurs at any age.

Patients have weakness and fatigability of proximal limb and torso muscles with relative sparing of extraocular and bulbar muscles. The lower limbs are more severely involved than the upper ones. On maximal voluntary contraction, the force produced by a weak muscle increases for a few seconds and then again decreases. The tendon reflexes are hypoactive or absent in most patients. Autonomic manifestations (dry mouth, impotence, decreased sweating, orthostatic hypotension, or altered pupillary reflexes) occur in one-half of the patients.

On electromyography, the amplitude of the compound muscle action potential evoked by a single nerve stimulus from rested muscle is abnormally small. Repetitive stimulation at 2 Hz induces a further decrement, but stimulation at frequencies higher than 10 Hz or

voluntary exercise for a brief period markedly facilitates the response so that the evoked potential attains normal amplitude.

Freeze fracture electron microscopy reveals a paucity and disorganization of presynaptic membrane active zones and active zone particles. These particles are topographically related to quantal release and are thought to be the voltage-sensitive calcium channels of the presynaptic membrane. The reduced quantal release by nerve impulse is attributed to reduced ingress of calcium into the nerve terminal.

Evidence for the autoimmune origin of the syndrome rests on its responsiveness to immunosuppressants and plasmapheresis, association of nonneoplastic cases with other autoimmune disorders and organ-specific autoantibodies, and the passive transfer of the electrophysiologic and morphologic features of the disease from human to mouse with IgG. The presynaptic membrane active zone particles are direct or indirect targets of the pathogenic autoantibodies.

Anticholinesterases have only a slight beneficial effect. Guanidine hydrochloride (10 mg/kg per day) or 3,4-diaminopyridine (1 mg/kg per day) increase quantal release from the nerve terminal and relieve the symptoms. However, the former drug has severe toxic side effects and the latter is not yet available in clinical practice. Optimal treatment of nonneoplastic cases consists of modest doses of alternate-day prednisone and 2 mg/kg per day of azathioprine.

CONGENITAL MYASTHENIC SYNDROMES

FAMILIAL INFANTILE MYASTHENIA This is an autosomal recessive disorder characterized by fluctuating ophthalmoparesis since birth, feeding difficulty during early infancy, weakness after exercise, and attacks of apnea precipitated by crying, vomiting, or fever. The symptoms tend to improve with age. A decremental electromyographic response is present in muscles weak when examined. Weakness can be induced in some, but not all, muscles by exercise or repetitive stimulation at 10 Hz for a few minutes. In contrast to autoimmune MG, the postsynaptic region is intact and there is no AChR deficiency. The miniature end-plate potential amplitude is normal in rested muscle but decreases to abnormally low values after 10-Hz stimulation for a few minutes. This suggests a presynaptic defect in ACh resynthesis or in ACh packaging into synaptic vesicles. Weakness, when present, responds to small or modest doses of anticholinesterases. Parenteral anticholinesterase therapy is indicated in crises. Parents of young patients must be taught to use a hand-assisted ventilatory device and to inject appropriate doses of neostigmine intramuscularly during crises.

CONGENITAL END-PLATE ACETYLCHOLINESTERASE DEFICIENCY Sporadic cases of the disorder, occurring only in males, have been observed to date. Weakness and a decremental electromyographic response are present in all voluntary muscles from birth. The symptoms are refractory to anticholinesterases and cause severe disability. The basic abnormality is total absence of acetylcholinesterase from the end-plate. ACh-AChR interaction and the duration of the end-plate potential are prolonged, so that a single stimulus applied to a motor nerve evokes two or more compound muscle action potentials. The motor nerve terminals are abnormally small and contain a reduced number of releasable ACh quanta. Smallness of the nerve terminals is not as constant as, and is probably secondary to, the enzyme deficiency. AChR is preserved or reduced at the end-plate. The AChR loss, if present, is caused by degenerative changes in the junctional folds, which can be accounted for by the ACh excess, but this itself is mild because ACh release is also reduced. The safety margin of neuromuscular transmission is compromised by lack of releasable ACh quanta and by AChR deficiency.

SLOW-CHANNEL SYNDROME This is an autosomal dominant disorder with high penetrance and variable expressivity. It presents in infancy or later life with selective weakness, fatigability, and atrophy of cervical, shoulder girdle, and forearm muscles. There is variable involvement of extraocular, other cranial, trunkal, or limb muscles.

The tendon reflexes are normal or hypoactive. Anticholinesterases are usually ineffective. A decremental electromyographic response appears in clinically affected muscles. The basic abnormality is an abnormally slow closure of the AChR ion channel. This prolongs the duration of the end-plate potential, causes a stimulus-linked repetitive compound action potential in all muscles, and allows abnormal accumulation of calcium in the postsynaptic region. The calcium excess results in destruction of the junctional folds, loss of AChR, and myopathic changes near the end plates. The safety margin of neuromuscular transmission is compromised by the AChR deficiency.

CONGENITAL END-PLATE AChR DEFICIENCY   This is an autosomal recessive disorder that presents during infancy. The symptoms and electrophysiologic abnormalities resemble those in autoimmune MG and respond to anticholinesterases. Circulating AChR antibodies are absent and no immune complexes are found at the end plate. The cause of the AChR deficiency has not been established. It could stem from decreased synthesis, impaired membrane insertion, or accelerated degradation of AChR or from abnormal ACh-AChR interaction.

BOTULISM

Botulinum toxin, described in Chap. 100, interferes with the mechanism by which calcium facilitates the release of ACh quanta from the nerve terminal. *Food botulism in adults* follows the ingestion of food that already contains the toxin. The food originally contained *Clostridium botulinum* spores that had germinated into toxin-producing bacilli. *Food botulism in infants* is caused by ingestion of food that contains viable bacilli that produce toxin in the intestine. The contaminated food usually remains unidentified. *Wound botulism* occurs after open injuries that allow the growth of anaerobic bacilli in devitalized tissues.

In adults, the illness may begin with nausea, vomiting, diarrhea, abdominal cramps, and a dry, painful throat. Blurred vision, loss of accommodation, and dilated pupils can occur at this stage. The external ocular and other cranial muscles are affected early, and in severe cases this progresses to generalized paralysis. The deep tendon reflexes may or may not be preserved, and there may be a slight response to anticholinesterases. In infants, the syndrome is associated with constipation, hypotonia, multiple cranial nerve palsies, descending muscle weakness, and sudden apnea or progressive respiratory failure.

The electromyographic findings resemble those in the Lambert-Eaton syndrome but may not be present early in the disease and may occur in one but not another extremity. The diagnosis is confirmed by detection of the toxin in serum and/or feces. The paralysis improves with the gradual elimination of the toxin, and with guanidine or 3,4-aminopyridine. Respiratory support may be needed.

DRUG-INDUCED MYASTHENIC SYNDROMES

These are uncommon in clinical practice. Tetracycline, polymyxin and aminoglycoside antibiotics, antiarrhythmic agents (procainamide, quinidine), β-adrenergic blockers (propranolol, timolol), phenothiazines, lithium, trimethaphan, methoxyflurane, and magnesium, given parenterally or in cathartics, reduce the safety margin of neuromuscular transmission. However, overt myasthenic symptoms do not usually appear unless an overdose of the drug is administered or the renal or hepatic elimination of the drug is impaired. The same drugs also can potentiate neuromuscular blocking agents used during surgical procedures and both may worsen or unmask preexisting disorders of neuromuscular transmission. Treatment of these syndromes is reviewed by Swift.

Poisoning with insecticides containing long-acting anticholinesterases causes ACh accumulation at central, muscarinic, and nicotinic cholinergic synapses. The intoxication is associated with alterations in sensorium, severe muscarinic effects, and muscle weakness from desensitization of AChR at the neuromuscular junction. Therapy consists of respiratory support, large doses of atropine (2 to 4 mg intramuscularly, repeated as necessary), and pralidoxime (1 g intravenously, repeated in 20 min if necessary).

Penicillamine induces autoimmune MG in a small proportion of patients who receive the drug for another autoimmune disease. The MG gradually disappears when the drug is discontinued.

REFERENCES

Engel AG: Myasthenia gravis and myasthenic syndromes. Ann Neurol 16:519, 1984

Grob D et al: The natural course of myasthenia gravis and effect of therapeutic measures. Ann NY Acad Sci 377:652, 1981

Lambert EH, Elmqvist D: Quantal components of end-plate potentials in the myasthenic syndrome. Ann NY Acad Sci 183:183, 1971

Lang B et al: Autoimmune etiology for myasthenic (Eaton-Lambert) syndrome. Lancet 2:224, 1981

Lewis GE Jr (ed): *Biomedical Aspects of Botulism.* New York, Academic, 1981

Lindstrom J et al: Antibody to acetylcholine receptor in myasthenia gravis. Neurology 26:1054, 1976

Swift TR: Disorders of neuromuscular transmission other than myasthenia gravis. Muscle Nerve 4:344, 1981

359   PERIODIC PARALYSIS

ROBERT C. GRIGGS

Disorders that cause patients of normal strength to become weak intermittently are not common. In contrast, the complaint of intermittent weakness is frequently encountered. The evaluation of such symptoms is challenging because the examination is often normal between attacks and because reliance on history is crucial for diagnosis. This chapter considers the primary periodic paralyses. Other disorders that cause episodic weakness are considered elsewhere (see Chap. 17).

All primary periodic paralyses have some features in common. In most patients the disorders are inherited as autosomal dominant traits. Symptoms usually begin early in life and rarely commence after age 25. Attacks typically follow rest or sleep and almost never occur in the midst of vigorous activity, although antecedent exercise frequently provokes weakness. Patients remain alert during the attacks. Early in the course of these disorders interattack strength is normal, but after years of attacks progressive weakness may develop. All forms of periodic paralysis are amenable to treatment, and progressive weakness can be prevented and even reversed.

Diagnosis is based upon patient history and confirmed by appropriate evaluation of serum electrolytes during attacks and on evaluating the response of strength to provocative testing with glucose, insulin, potassium, and cold.

HYPOKALEMIC PERIODIC PARALYSIS   This disorder occurs as an autosomal dominant condition in two-thirds of cases and as sporadic cases in one-third. Males are more frequently and more severely affected. Attacks of weakness characteristically begin in adolescence but may commence in the first decade. Onset after age 25 is rare; the new onset of episodic paralysis in older individuals is almost never due to periodic paralysis.

Attack frequency varies from daily to yearly. Attacks last from 3 to 4 h to as long as a day or more. Meals high in carbohydrate or high in sodium may provoke attacks. Paralysis involves limb muscles, usually proximal more than distal; rarely ocular, bulbar, or respiratory muscles are weakened, and bulbar and respiratory involvement may prove fatal. Reflexes become hypoactive, and cardiac arrhythmias may occur during attacks. Patients may develop persistent proximal weakness after years of attacks. Examination during attack-free intervals is otherwise normal except for the frequent presence of eyelid myotonia.

Diagnosis is established by demonstrating a low serum potassium during a paralytic attack and by excluding secondary causes of hypokalemia (Chap. 17). Electrocardiograms during attacks show characteristic features of hypokalemia. Electromyography is not helpful in diagnosis, but muscle biopsy often shows the presence of single or multiple centrally placed vacuoles. Patients whose attacks are so infrequent as to preclude the study of a spontaneous attack require provocative testing with glucose and insulin administration. Such tests are potentially hazardous, and patients must be carefully monitored during their performance. Since these disorders are rare such testing is most appropriately carried out in referral centers.

Pathogenesis The pathogenesis of paralytic attacks is incompletely understood. Patients with hypokalemic periodic paralysis do not have a decrease in total body potassium. There is no increased excretion of potassium in the urine before or during attacks, but there is excessive flux of potassium from blood into muscle, possibly owing to an abnormality of muscle membrane that causes muscle to become electrically inexcitable. Muscle from these patients is abnormally sensitive to the effect of insulin on potassium uptake; the significance of this increased sensitivity is not known since weakness is often severe at levels of serum potassium that do not affect normal individuals. Moreover, attacks may occur when insulin levels are low. Therefore, factors other than hypokalemia per se are important in the induction of weakness.

Treatment ACUTE ATTACKS The acute paralysis improves following the administration of potassium salts. Oral KCl (0.2 to 0.4 meq/kg) should be given to patients with severe weakness and repeated at 15 to 30 min intervals depending on the response of the electrocardiogram, serum potassium, and muscle strength. Milder attacks usually resolve spontaneously; resolution of weakness is hastened by exercising affected muscles. When patients are unable to swallow or are vomiting, intravenous therapy may be necessary. Small, repeated bolus therapy with KCl (0.1 meq/kg) may be administered over 5 to 10 min with careful monitoring of the electrocardiogram and serum potassium. If potassium is administered as a dilute solution (20 to 40 meq per liter) in 5% glucose or in physiologic saline solution, serum potassium may decline, and weakness may worsen. Mannitol is the preferred vehicle for administering intravenous potassium in such situations, since it facilitates rapid return of serum potassium to normal and avoids the hazard of lowering of serum potassium as may occur when glucose or saline solution are given.

PREVENTION OF ATTACKS The goal of therapy is the elimination of attacks, which also prevents interattack weakness and may improve interattack weakness after it has developed. Prior to availability of effective means of attack prevention, chronic progressive interattack weakness frequently caused serious disability. Prophylactic administration of potassium salts, even in large dosage, does not prevent attacks but acetazolamide (125 to 1000 mg per day in divided dosage) abolishes attacks in the majority of cases. The mechanism of action of acetazolamide is not fully understood, but it may block the flux of potassium from serum into muscle. The metabolic acidosis that it produces may underlie its beneficial effect. Paradoxically, acetazolamide lowers serum potassium through kaliuresis; to achieve an adequate response in some patients it may be necessary to give supplementary potassium along with acetazolamide and to avoid high-carbohydrate meals. Chronic acetazolamide treatment may be associated with renal calculi, and patients should be monitored for this complication. In occasional patients attacks may not respond to or may even be worsened by acetazolamide. In such patients triamterene (25 to 100 mg per day or spironolactone 25 to 100 mg per day) may prevent attacks.

THYROTOXIC PERIODIC PARALYSIS Attacks of hypokalemic periodic paralysis can occur in subjects with thyrotoxicosis, most commonly in young Latin American or oriental men where up to 10 percent of thyrotoxic patients may have periodic paralysis. In many patients thyrotoxicosis has also been overlooked for many months; periodic paralysis has also occurred with T_3-toxicosis and with exogenous thyroid hormone administration. The usual age of onset of the disorder is that of thyrotoxicosis; otherwise the clinical features resemble familial hypokalemic periodic paralysis. Acute attacks respond to potassium administration. Treatment of underlying thyrotoxicosis abolishes attacks, and β-adrenergic blocking agents reduce the frequency and severity of attacks while measures to control thyrotoxicosis are being instituted. Acetazolamide is not helpful in preventing attacks.

HYPERKALEMIC PERIODIC PARALYSIS This disorder differs from hypokalemic periodic paralysis in that attacks are usually brief (1 to 2 h or less) and more frequent; clinical or electromyographic myotonia is often demonstrable. Attacks are usually precipitated by fasting or by rest following exercise. The disease onset is usually at an earlier age than is the case for hypokalemic periodic paralysis, and attacks or myotonia may be evident in the first year of life. The disorder is usually transmitted as an autosomal dominant defect; rare sporadic cases occur.

The name "hyperkalemic" is misleading, since patients are often normokalemic during attacks. It is the fact that attacks are *precipitated by potassium administration* that best defines the disorder. "Potassium-sensitive" periodic paralysis is probably preferable terminology. Moreover, the serum potassium is often slightly elevated when patients are not having attacks of weakness. Attacks are characterized by limb weakness predominantly, though cranial and respiratory muscle involvement may occur. Cardiac arrythmias occur occasionally. Paresthesias and muscle pain are present during many attacks, and Chvostek's sign is often present during attacks.

Diagnosis is suggested by a modest elevation of serum potassium during attacks in nearly half of patients; at times, however, the serum potassium is normal or even low. Intravenous glucose-insulin loading does not precipitate weakness but potassium-loading tests (0.05 to 0.15 g/kg) will provoke weakness in such patients. Myotonia may be increased. Potassium-loading tests are potentially hazardous and are contraindicated in patients with renal disease and diabetes. Random serum potassium measurements may suggest the diagnosis, since potassium elevations are frequent during attack-free intervals. Electromyographic evidence of myotonia and the finding of vacuoles on muscle biopsy provide supporting data.

Pathogenesis Hyperkalemia during attacks of hyperkalemic periodic paralysis seldom reaches levels that would be expected to produce paralysis. Furthermore, serum potassium may remain within the normal range. Factors other than hyperkalemia are clearly important in the pathogenesis of attacks. An abnormality of the sarcolemma may cause spontaneous depolarization of the muscle cell and lead both to myotonia and to paralysis. A decreased activity of the sodium-potassium pump may be involved in the spontaneous depolarization.

Treatment Attacks of weakness are seldom severe enough to require emergency treatment and are never fatal. Oral glucose or other carbohydrate hastens recovery. Since interattack weakness may develop after repeated attacks, prophylactic treatment is usually indicated. Remarkably, acetazolamide (125 to 1000 mg per day), the treatment of choice for hypokalemic periodic paralysis, was first found to be beneficial for hyperkalemic periodic paralysis, possibly because of its kaliopenic effect. Thiazide diuretics (e.g., chlorothiazide, 250 to 1000 mg per day) are usually more effective and have fewer side effects.

NORMOKALEMIC PERIODIC PARALYSIS Most subjects with periodic paralysis in whom potassium is normal during attacks behave like those with typical "hyperkalemic" periodic paralysis, since they are similarly sensitive to potassium administration. In fact, the so-called hyperkalemic and normokalemic forms of this disorder may be one entity.

Rarely, patients with episodic normokalemic paralysis are not potassium sensitive, but they usually show evidence of muscle destruction or other features suggesting that they should not be classified with the primary periodic paralyses.

PARAMYOTONIA WITH PERIODIC PARALYSIS Attacks of paralysis may occur in the paramyotonias, either provoked by cold or spontaneously. Paramyotonia congenita is characterized by paradoxical myotonia (i.e., myotonia worsening with activity), cold provocation, spontaneous attacks, and a family history compatible with an autosomal dominant defect. The cold provocation of weakness distinguishes this disease from other periodic paralyses. A therapeutically useful subclassification of the paramyotonias has been proposed as follows: (1) paramyotonia congenita, in which spontaneous attacks of weakness are associated with a lowering of serum potassium and in which measures that decrease serum potassium provoke weakness; and (2) paralysis periodica paramyotonica, in which spontaneous attacks may be associated with hyperkalemia and may be provoked by oral potassium administration. This potassium sensitivity has led in the past to the incorrect classification of this disorder as a variant of hyperkalemic or normokalemic periodic paralysis.

Diagnosis depends upon the provocation of weakness with cold. Glucose and insulin loading and potassium challenges aid in the subclassification of the disorder and provide assistance in the choice of medication for treatment.

Pathogenesis The two types of paramyotonia probably have different etiologies. In paramyotonia congenita cooling of muscle results in an abnormal depolarization, leading first to myotonia and then to inexcitability. Sodium and potassium conductance become abnormal with cooling of muscle. An abnormality of sodium channels may account for this alteration in conductance.

Treatment Spontaneous attacks of periodic paralysis in paramyotonia congenita are relatively infrequent. Many patients do not require prophylactic treatment for prevention. In the case of paramyotonia congenita, patients with severe and frequent attacks of weakness may respond to spironolactone, and subjects with paralysis periodica paramyotonica may respond to acetazolamide or thiazides. Acetazolamide may provoke weakness in paramyotonia congenita, whereas myotonia in paramyotonia congenita may improve with either acetazolamide or tocainide; the latter may work by blocking abnormal sodium channels.

REFERENCES

GRIGGS RC et al: Intravenous treatment of hypokalemic periodic paralysis. Arch Neurol 40:539, 1983

MARTIN AR, LEVINSON SR: Contribution of the Na$^+$-K$^+$ pump to membrane potential in familial periodic paralysis. Muscle Nerve 8:359, 1985

RESNICK JS et al: Acetazolamide prophylaxis in hypokalemic periodic paralysis. N Engl J Med 278:582, 1968

RIGGS JE et al: The diagnosis and treatment of the periodic paralyses. Clin Neuropharmacol 4:123, 1979

PART THIRTEEN PSYCHIATRY

section 1 Psychiatric disorders

360 MAJOR AFFECTIVE DISORDERS

LEWIS L. JUDD / LEIGHTON Y. HUEY

For centuries it has been recognized that extremes in mood are inherent in the human condition, but distinguishing mood alterations that are pathologic from those that are not has been an elusive problem until recently. The realization that major mental disorders are psychobiologic phenomena resulting from abnormal brain mechanisms together with the development of a more empirically based diagnostic classification scheme has now made it possible for clinicians to distinguish consistently between abnormal mood states and the normal evanescent changes in feeling tones that are a part of everyday life.

Recent surveys indicate that 5 to 6 percent of the adult population in this country is suffering from clinically significant mood or affective disorders. The major affective disorders are a heterogenous group of mental disorders characterized by extreme exaggerations and disturbances of mood and affect which also affect cognitive and psychomotor functions. There is a marked tendency to periodicity and recurrence throughout the patient's lifetime, in which diagnosable affective episodes appear and remit and are followed by symptom-free periods (euthymia) lasting weeks, months, or years. The two most prevalent and important diagnostic syndromes among the major affective disorders are *major depression* and the *bipolar disorders*.

To reduce diagnostic heterogeneity, the major affective disorders are divided into those depressed patients with a history of manic episodes (bipolar) and those who manifest episodes of depression only (unipolar). The *unipolar-bipolar* distinction is a useful dichotomization in regard to clinical characteristics, life course, and treatment. Evidence continues to accumulate indicating that unipolar and bipolar depressions are, in all likelihood, psychobiologically different but very closely related disorders. An additional diagnostic dichotomization which has also been helpful in reducing heterogeneity among those disorders is the *primary-secondary* distinction. The rationale behind this is that affective disorders occurring in a pure form are likely to be more similar than affective disorders which coexist with other psychiatric or medical conditions. A major affective disorder is *primary* when the affective episode (manic or depressive) is the first-appearing psychiatric illness in a patient's lifetime and is not associated with other psychiatric or medical illnesses. Conversely, an affective disorder is classified as *secondary* when it appears in conjunction with other psychiatric or medical conditions. For example, depressive episodes can be observed in conjunction with virtually every mental disorder, for example, schizophrenia, alcoholism, dementia, and personality disorders. Affective disorders can also be associated with medical diseases and occur during treatment with commonly prescribed medications. The diseases associated with depressive disorders include the following: endocrinopathies (Cushing's disease, hyper- or hypothyroidism), collagen diseases (systemic lupus erythematosus), cardiovascular diseases (congestive heart failure, myocardial infarction), neurologic diseases (multiple sclerosis), infections (hepatitis, influenza), malignancies (pancreatic adenocarcinoma), metabolic disorders (porphyria), and vitamin deficiencies (vitamin B_1 deficiency, nicotinic acid deficiency). In addition, the chronic administration of the following medications can also precipitate an affective episode: corticosteroids, alpha-methyldopa, propranolol, benzodiazepines, reserpine derivatives, and L-dopa. It should be noted, however, that even though an affective episode may be classified as being secondary, it can be the most important and compelling aspect of a patient's clinical picture requiring immediate and specific therapeutic intervention (see also Chap. 11).

A conceptual overview of the major affective disorders is presented in Table 360-1. In this classification the relationships and interaction of the unipolar-bipolar and primary-secondary dichotomizations are clearly demonstrated.

DIAGNOSTIC CATEGORIES OF AFFECTIVE DISORDERS The diagnosis of a clinically significant affective episode is based upon the criteria contained in the third edition of the Diagnostic and Statistical Manual (DSM-III). This method of diagnostic classification has been developed and approved by the American Psychiatric Association and is the standard diagnostic system in use in this country today. There are two general types of affective episodes which manifest in patients: major depressive episodes and manic episodes. The diagnostic criteria for *major depressive episodes* and *manic episodes* are included in Tables 360-2 and 360-3. Most experienced clinicians require that the dysphoric mood or the euphoric, expansive, or irritable mood be persistently present for at least 1 week before these two diagnoses are considered.

Major depression The diagnosis of major depression is made when the patient presents with the necessary signs and symptoms of a major depressive episode (see Table 360-2). The diagnostic category of major depression represents the unipolar form of the major affective disorders, in which patients manifest only the single pole of affect, that of depression. The diagnosis of *recurrent major depression* is made when major depressive episodes are repeated throughout a patient's lifetime and is synonymous with the term *recurrent unipolar depression*. Following the first episode, between 50 and 80 percent of patients will have at least one more major depressive episode. Approximately 10 to 15 percent will have a subsequent manic episode, at which point the patient is then reclassified as having a bipolar disorder. Major depression is approximately twice as common in

TABLE 360-1 Major affective disorders

Primary affective disorder:
    Unipolar depression (major depressive episodes only)
    Bipolar depression (manic and major depressive episodes)
Secondary affective disorder:
    Disorder occurring with medical diseases
    Disorder secondary to medications
    Disorder occurring with other mental disorders

TABLE 360-2 Diagnostic criteria for a major depressive episode

A Dysphoric mood or loss of interest or pleasure in all or almost all usual activities and pastimes. The dysphoric mood is characterized by symptoms such as the following: patient is depressed, sad, blue, hopeless, low, down in the dumps, irritable. The mood disturbance must be prominent and relatively persistent but is not necessarily the most dominant symptom and does not include momentary shifts from one dysphoric mood to another dysphoric mood (e.g., anxiety to depression to anger) such as are seen in states of acute psychotic turmoil

B At least four of the following symptoms have each been present nearly every day for a period of at least 2 weeks:
  1 Poor appetite or significant weight loss (when not dieting) or increased appetite or significant weight gain
  2 Insomnia or hypersomnia
  3 Psychomotor agitation or retardation (not merely subjective feelings of restlessness or being slowed down)
  4 Loss of interest or pleasure in usual activities or decrease in sexual drive (not limited to a period when delusional or hallucinating)
  5 Loss of energy; fatigue
  6 Feelings of worthlessness, self-reproach, or excessive or inappropriate guilt (may be delusional)
  7 Complaints or evidence of diminished ability to think or concentrate, such as slowed thinking or indecisiveness (not associated with marked loosening of associations or incoherence)
  8 Recurrent thoughts of death, suicidal ideation, desire to be dead, or suicide attempt

women as men. The point prevalence in the adult population ranges from 4.5 to 9.3 percent for women and 3.2 percent for men. The peak onset for first episodes in women is from 35 to 45 years; it decreases with age until 55, when the risk increases. The risk for younger men is lower but appears to increase steadily with age. Most natural-course studies indicate that unipolar patients average two to three major depressive episodes during their lifetimes, although some patients have only single episodes and others have many more. The average duration of an untreated depressive episode is 8 to 9 months with a range of 5 to 13 months. There is no established relationship between risk for major depression and socioeconomic class, race, education, or occupation.

Not all clinically significant depressive phenomena present as classic major depressions. The diagnostic categories of *dysthymic disorder* and *atypical depression* are clinical manifestations of depression without the full features of a major affective disorder. There is a high degree of heterogeneity and overlap between these two diagnostic categories. Patients who have some of the signs and symptoms of a depressive episode and who feel chronically dysphoric but do not meet full criteria for major depression are categorized here. Continued research has gradually identified a more homogeneous patient population with atypical features. Patients with atypical depression may have initial insomnia rather than early morning awakening and often may be hypersomniac. Their mood is frequently worse in the evening rather than the morning, and they also complain of a generalized dysphoria combined with fatigue, low energy, irritability, tension, and anxiety. Rather than being unreactive to environmental changes, as is usually seen in major depressive episodes, they often can be temporarily cheered up by specific

TABLE 360-3 Diagnostic criteria for a manic episode

A One or more distinct periods with a predominantly elevated, expansive, or irritable mood. The elevated or irritable mood must be a prominent part of the illness and relatively persistent, although it may alternate or intermingle with depressive mood

B Duration of at least 1 week (or any duration if hospitalization is necessary), during which, for most of the time, at least three of the following symptoms have persisted (four if the mood is only irritable) and have been present to a significant degree:
  1 Increase in activity (socially or at work) or physical restlessness
  2 More talkativeness than usual or pressure to keep talking
  3 Flight of ideas or subjective experience that thoughts are racing
  4 Inflated self-esteem (grandiosity, which may be delusional)
  5 Decreased need for sleep
  6 Distractibility (attention too easily drawn to unimportant or irrelevant external stimuli)
  7 Excessive involvement in activities that have a high potential for painful consequences which is not recognized (buying sprees, sexual indiscretions, foolish business investments, reckless driving)

environmental changes. Further, they are often not anorexic and may be hyperphagic and crave carbohydrates. Some experts have suggested that patients with atypical depression should be classified in a new diagnostic category entitled *mood reactive depression.*

Bipolar disorders Bipolar disorders are diagnosed using the criteria for both manic and major depressive episodes. In this category of major affective disorder, both the affective poles of mania and depression are present. Bipolar disorders are diagnosed as bipolar disorder, manic, if the current episode meets criteria for a manic episode and as bipolar disorder, depressed, if the episode meets criteria for a major depressive episode. Bipolar patients who have more rapid cycling, with manic and depressive episodes alternating every few days or weeks, are classified as bipolar disorder, mixed. Bipolar depression is more frequent in women than men in a ratio ranging from 1.2:1 to 2:1. Men have significantly more manic than depressive episodes, whereas women have significantly more depressive than manic episodes. The age of risk for bipolar disorder extends from as early as 6 or 7 years to over 65, but the peak age of onset in both men and women for the first attack is in the early thirties, with a mean age of onset of 32.5 years. About two-thirds of first episodes are manic and 60 percent of these patients will have a predominantly manic course, while the remaining 25 to 30 percent manifest primarily depressive episodes. Most natural-course studies of untreated bipolar patients generally agree that they will average nine diagnosable affective episodes during their lifetimes (range 1 to more than 20). The pattern is that the cycle length, which is measured from the onset of one episode to the onset of the next, will decrease and the number of episodes will increase over time. For example, in untreated bipolar patients the time between the first and second episode averages from 3.5 to 4 years, between the second and third episodes about 2 years, and between episodes three and four somewhere between 12 and 18 months. Episode duration is from 4 to 13 months, and the average is about 8.5 months. Attempts have been made to categorize affective episodes in the bipolar patient based on how often the episodes occur in juxtaposition to those of opposite polarity. The vast majority of episodes are uniphasic, i.e., a manic or depressive episode is preceded by a symptom-free period; however, approximately 10 or 15 percent are biphasic with a depressive episode more often preceding the manic.

There is a small but distinct group of bipolar patients who manifest very *rapid cycling* patterns (bipolar disorder, mixed). The rapid cycler is a patient who presents with more than four or five episodes in 1 year, but there are patients who have considerably more episodes and there are case reports of patients cycling every 24 h. The rapid-cycling bipolar patient has eight times the number of affective episodes in his or her lifetime in comparison to slow cyclers. Eighty percent of rapid cyclers are women, and the appearance of rapid cycling is sometimes related to impaired thyroid function. Although it is still controversial, there is evidence that rapid cycling may be induced by a course of tricyclic antidepressants and can only be effectively controlled after the patient is euthyroid and removed from tricyclics.

The life-long intensity of illness in bipolar disorder, even among the slow cyclers, is much more extreme than it is in unipolar disorder. Bipolar patients have significantly more episodes of illness, more hospitalizations, and spend more total time in the hospital during their lifetimes.

ETIOLOGY AND PATHOPHYSIOLOGY OF THE MAJOR AFFECTIVE DISORDERS Considerable progress has been made in identifying and characterizing the etiologic factors in major affective disorders, but a comprehensive and detailed understanding of the etiology of these disorders has yet to be achieved. Tremendous advances in knowledge during the past 20 years have provided excellent leads for focused scientific inquiry into the causes of these disorders; these leads, in turn, have led to the development of very specific and effective treatments. Like many other human diseases, the affective disorders are the result of interactions between the patient's genetic makeup and the environment. Evidence continues to mount that significant genetic factors are involved in these disorders, but the genetic components do not appear to be so overwhelming that the disorder is manifested without any environmental challenges. In general, the causality of a major affective episode can effectively be conceptualized by using an interactional model of two intersecting continua both with progressive intensities. One involves the patient's inherited constitutional predisposition to develop affective episodes; this interacts with the second continuum of the environmental stresses and life events to which the patient is exposed. Thus, there are those individuals with very high genetic predispositions for affective psychopathology in whom the disorder will be manifested seemingly without identifiable precipitating events. In contrast, there are patients with lower genetic predisposition in whom the disorder is manifested only when the patient is exposed to more serious precipitating life events and cumulative life stresses.

Genetic factors Data derived from virtually every methodologic strategy in human genetics strongly suggest significant genetic influences in the major affective disorders, but as yet the mode of genetic transmission has not been established. The degree of genetic expression varies considerably from patient to patient and in some patients marked and predictable genetic factors are present; in others genetic expression appears to be significantly less influential. The *twin studies* have been one of the major research strategies used by psychiatric geneticists to attempt to quantify genetic loading in various psychiatric diseases. Twin studies in affective disorders have reported concordance rates among monozygotic (MZ) twins ranging from 33.3 to 75 percent, with an average of 65 percent. In contrast, the concordance rates for dizygotic (DZ) twins range from 9 to 23 percent, averaging 15 percent. The difference in concordance rates between MZ and DZ twins strongly suggests inherited genetic vulnerability. Further, there is evidence that even the polarity of the disorder may be genetically controlled, since there is an 80 percent concordance for bipolar and 59 percent concordance for unipolar disorders in MZ twins. In an attempt to separate the ''nature'' and ''nurture'' contributions to the development of affective disorders, the *adoption study* strategy has also been used. Unfortunately, because of methodologic problems and the paucity of subjects studied, no definitive answers are available. There is, however, a trend indicating that adoptees with affective disorders have a greater incidence of affective illness in their biologic parents than in their adopted parents. A large number of *family studies* have been conducted in the affective disorders. The standard paradigm is to make independent and blind diagnoses in the first-degree relatives of affective disorder patients, anticipating that if genetic components are present, the consanguineous relatives will manifest an increased risk for affective illness. First-degree relatives of bipolar patients have a morbidity risk for bipolar disorder ranging from 2.8 to 17.7 percent and a risk of 0 to 22.4 percent for unipolar depression. The first-degree relatives of unipolar patients have a risk of 6.4 to 17 percent for unipolar depression and of 0.3 to 29 percent for bipolar disorder. Thus, bipolar patients have both unipolar and bipolar disorders among their blood relatives, whereas unipolar patients have increased incidence for unipolar, but not bipolar, disorders in their relatives. Modern studies of *genetic transmission* combine careful family pedigree studies with molecular genetics in an attempt to identify the linkage between the specific gene markers and manifestation of major affective disorder in an afflicted or informative family. At present, no clear dominant or recessive inheritance pattern has been identified. It appears that genetic heterogeneity is present, which suggests a multiple threshold model in order to account for the varying degrees of genetic variability in the affective disorders. Genetic marker surveys in informative families have been conducted, including studies which have used genetically regulated markers that are etiologically significant in affective illness, such as the concentrations of dopamine β-hydroxylase, monoamine oxidase A, monoamine oxidase B, and lithium red blood cell (RBC)/plasma ratio. No marker has yet been found which segregates to the presence of affective disorder. There is however, a small subgroup of bipolar patients who do manifest a linkage of protan-deutan (red-green) color blindness and the Xg blood group with the presence of bipolar disorder. Unfortunately this very interesting genetic linkage pattern has not been present in other families similarly afflicted with major affective disorder.

In summary, the genetic studies strongly indicate the inheritance of a vulnerability to affective illness, but the genetic expression is heterogeneous and the degree of vulnerability varies significantly. There is evidence that the genetic factors are stronger in bipolar disorder than in unipolar depression. There are currently several large-scale surveys combining molecular and pedigree methodologies which are either in progress or in the final stages of implementation, and it is possible that the gene(s) coding for affective disorders will be identified and cloned in the foreseeable future.

Neurotransmitter systems The most consistent search for etiologic mechanisms in the affective disorders has involved studies of the various neurotransmitter systems in the brain. The original *biogenic amine hypothesis* focused primarily on the central nervous system (CNS) neurotransmitters norepinephrine, serotonin, and dopamine, attributing depression and mania, respectively, to the deficiency or excess of these neurotransmitters at important synaptic sites in the brain. This hypothesis has stimulated and directed research in the field for many years, and data consistent with the hypothesis continue to emerge. Urinary and cerebrospinal fluid (CSF) studies of norepinephrine, its metabolite 3-methoxy-4-hydroxyphenylethyleneglycol (MHPG), and the catalytic enzyme dopamine β-hydroxylase have been consistently reported as being increased or decreased in the predictable direction during depressed and manic episodes. More recently, increases in norepinephrine have been described in both mania and depression. Alterations in serotonin and its metabolites have also been identified in patients during depressive episodes. In addition, 5-hydroxyindole acetic acid (5HIAA), a serotonin metabolite, has been found to be reduced in the CSF of depressed patients who make frequent and aggressive suicide attempts. Deficits in other neurotransmitters such as dopamine and gamma-aminobutyric acid (GABA) have also been identified in some patients with major depression. Finally, another neurotransmitter hypothesis which has directed research in the affective disorders is the *cholinergic hypothesis,* which postulates increased central cholinergic tone in depression, decreased cholinergic tone in mania, and an imbalance between the cholinergic and adrenergic neurotransmitter systems as being a central pathophysiologic mechanism in affective disorders.

Within the last 5 years, there has been a shift of research focus from the neurotransmitter biosynthetic, storage, and release mechanisms in the presynaptic neuron to the study of receptors on postsynaptic neurons. There is growing evidence that postsynaptic receptor kinetics and activity are predictibly and consistently altered during affective episodes and by the psychotropic medications known to ameliorate these disorders. Future research in the pathophysiology of the affective disorders will be concentrated on the role of *postsynaptic receptor systems* and the cascade of intraneuronal biochemical events in the postsynaptic neuron which follow the binding of the neurotransmitter to the receptor.

In summary, there is a general agreement in the large number of studies which have been conducted to date that the relative paucity of a neurotransmitter or the inactivation or down-regulation of postsynaptic receptors has often been correlated with depressive episodes, but the reciprocal changes which one would predict have not been consistently identified in manic episodes.

Environmental factors There is little systematic data available indicating what role environmental stresses and untoward life events play or what types of stressors might be etiologically significant in the development of major affective episodes. Attempts have been made, for example, to relate early childhood loss and parental separation as predisposing factors for the future development of an affective illness, but the data are inconsistent. In general, studies have shown an overall temporal relationship between stressful and negative life events and the subsequent appearance of affective episodes. Research attempting to characterize qualitative differences in the impact of life stress have been disappointing, although serious life events such as the death of a child or a spouse, job loss, marked changes in social status, and even severe assaults on self-esteem have been linked to affective episodes. While the relationship between environmental stresses and the appearance of affective episodes has not always been demonstrated, generally speaking most experts agree that a single severe or multiple severe adverse events in life can interact with the constitutional predisposition of a patient and result in the triggering of an affective episode.

In further support of the influence of environmental events are the studies which have been conducted in higher primates. In these studies, phenomena which resemble or are analogous to the depressive states in humans are seen in monkeys following both mother/infant and peer separation paradigms. Furthermore, the monkey's "despair" response to the separation paradigms can be predictably enhanced by drugs known to specifically alter central concentrations and metabolism of various relevant CNS neurotransmitters (e.g., norepinephrine, dopamine).

Biologic rhythms   The marked tendency of major affective disorders to periodic manifestation and possibly to seasonal variations has stimulated hypotheses which suggest that the dysregulation of biologic rhythms may be centrally involved in the pathophysiology of affective disorders. There are reports of dysynchronization of circadian rhythms in some bipolar patients in which these patients manifested both rapid free-running circadian rhythms (e.g., 23- versus 24-hour rhythms) and a phase delay in their rhythms. There is also a specific subgroup of patients with major depression in which the depressive episodes are manifested seasonally during the wintertime. These patients, while residing in more northern latitudes, experience major depressive episodes during the winter when days are significantly shorter and periods of darkness more prolonged; they do not experience depression of this type when residing in latitudes where the environmental light/dark cycle is not as extreme.

BIOLOGIC CORRELATES AND LABORATORY STUDIES   **Neurohormonal correlates**   For a number of years probes into the pathophysiologic mechanisms of the affective disorders have used various neurohormones whose secretion is regulated by one or more of the CNS neurotransmitters. One consistent finding from these studies has been that a significant subpopulation of patients with major depression hypersecrete cortisol and have abnormal cortisol circadian secretion patterns. In addition, even though it is now somewhat controversial, the *dexamethasone suppression test (DST)* has been useful in both diagnosis and monitoring of treatment. The standard DST used in psychiatry involves the administration of 1 mg of dexamethasone at 2300 hours with subsequent cortisol determinations at 1600 and 2300 hours the following day. The nonsuppression of cortisol is an abnormal or positive response (>5 µg/dL cortisol concentration in the 1600 or 2300 sample). Initial studies reported that up to 50 percent of patients with serious major depression were nonsuppressors on the DST. Further investigations indicate that DST nonsuppression is most likely a state marker, which is positive during the depressive episode but returns to normal after successful resolution of the episode. False positives on the DST can occur in patients with alcoholism, malnutrition, obesity, pregnancy, major physical illnesses, and in patients over 65 years and this has eroded the usefulness of the test. In addition, more recently a number of studies have appeared in the literature reporting a much smaller percentage of DST nonsuppressors associated with major depressive episodes and an increased percentage in many other psychiatric illnesses. The range of DST nonsuppression among depressed patients has now been reported as low as 10 to 15 percent to as high as 50 percent. While the status of this diagnostic marker is still controversial, it is useful in monitoring treatment efficacy in DST-positive depressives, since the DST response reverts to normal when the episode remits.

Other neuroendocrine markers have also been explored, but none

as widely as the DST. In major depression, between 25 and 30 percent of patients respond to thyrotropin releasing hormone (TRH) with blunted *thyroid stimulating hormone (TSH)* responses. TSH blunting is not specific to depressive episodes and the use of this test for diagnostic purposes has been abandoned. Small subgroups of depressed patients have manifested blunted *growth hormone* responses to the following challenge agents: clonidine, amphetamine, L-dopa, 5-hydroxytryptophan, and hypoglycemia (insulin tolerance test). Even though 15 to 25 percent of depressed patients have blunted growth hormone responses, it has not proved to be diagnostically useful. More recently, blunted *prolactin* responses to both TRH and opiate alkaloid challenges have also been reported in subpopulations of depressed patients; while these findings may be of interest in terms of pathophysiologic mechanisms, they are not useful diagnostically.

Sleep studies   The disruption of sleep patterns is present in virtually every patient with major affective disorder, and polysomnographic studies of sleep in these patients have proved to be of interest. In 25 to 45 percent of cases of major depression there is a significantly shortened time period between the onset of sleep and the appearance of the first rapid eye movement (REM) (i.e., decreased REM latency). In addition, the density of the REM epoch, measured by the number of eye movements, is increased, there is a tendency for the REM epoch to be increased in duration, and there is a shift of REM activity to an earlier part of the night. These findings from all-night EEG sleep recordings have remained among the most consistent biologic markers for major depression, although they lack specificity, since short REM latency has also been reported in anorexia nervosa, obsessive-compulsive disorders, schizoaffective schizophrenia, and narcolepsy.

Neurotransmitter metabolites   The neurotransmitter hypotheses of affective disorders have stimulated a number of studies correlating biogenic amine metabolites with manic and depressive episodes. The data are inconsistent and have not been useful either diagnostically or therapeutically. The one possible exception is MHPG, a metabolite of norepinephrine. Some workers have reported low MHPG excretion as predicting a positive therapeutic response to the antidepressants imipramine, desipramine, etc., and high MHPG excretion as predicting a response to amitriptyline, nortriptyline, etc. While these data are of interest and with further study may result in the identification of biochemical subtypes in major depression, these findings have not been consistently replicated in other laboratories.

TREATMENT OF THE MAJOR AFFECTIVE DISORDERS   Important advances have been made in the treatment of the major affective disorders, and the majority of these patients can now be treated with a high degree of specificity and success. The most important discoveries have been in the development of potent psychotropic medications for both major depression and the bipolar disorders. The central therapeutic tools in the treatment of the major affective disorders are the antidepressants and lithium. The use of these psychotropic medications is covered in much greater detail in Chap. 364.

Because major affective disorders have strong tendencies for recurrence, an important aspect of the patient's treatment is the comprehensive education of patients and their families about the disorder. It should be emphasized to the patient that these are psychobiologic disorders which involve altered biochemical states in the brain, and that episodes can be triggered by adverse events and stresses in the environment but may occur spontaneously as well. Each patient should be urged to become an expert on his or her own disorder, concentrating on how it manifests and what early signs and symptoms may herald an impending manic or depressive episode. The patient and the family must be urged to take on the responsibility for the early recognition of the impending episode, since the earlier a patient presents for treatment, the easier it is to remediate the episode. The absolute necessity of medication compliance must be emphasized, and the patient must understand thoroughly the need to take the medications as prescribed and to be aware of side effects and of the potential medical sequelae from the medications.

The counseling and therapeutic techniques the physician uses in dealing with patients who are suffering acute manic or depressed episodes are simple and relatively straightforward. During the acute phase of these episodes, patients respond better to short (10 to 20 min) visits one to three times per week. During these visits the general focus is on monitoring the medication and side effects, but it is also essential that the physician be very reassuring and supportive to the patient. Because patients are functioning essentially in an altered state secondary to the depressive or manic episode, the treatment must be sustained by the physician's optimism and knowledge that with time these episodes can be treated if the right medication and dose are prescribed. Virtually all the mood-stabilizing and -ameliorating psychotropic medications have a significant delay between the time the patient begins the medication and the time of achieving full therapeutic benefits. It is during this time that supportive reassurance and encouragement from the physician is particularly important in sustaining the patient in treatment.

There are approximately 25,000 suicides a year in this country, and clinical surveys have indicated that approximately 30 percent of these patients have major affective disorders. Suicidal ideation is one of the important symptoms which accompany major depression, in both bipolar and unipolar disorders; considerations of suicidal lethality are significant components of the management of these patients. Although it is not possible to distinguish precisely between patients who will attempt suicide and those who will not, there are some factors which should be considered. Generally speaking, many experts agree that patients who have given detailed thought to the method of suicide, who have concomitant alcoholism, and who are socially isolated with few (if any) social supports, in addition to elderly males and patients with terminal medical illnesses, have a greater potential risk for suicide. On the other hand, all of the characteristics lack true specificity in the assessment of suicidal risk.

Once the acute depressive or manic episode is under control, the switch from supportive to more insight-oriented psychotherapy is a useful adjunct to the pharmacotherapy. Recent studies have established that the combination of psychotherapy with pharmacotherapy is significantly better than either of these two modalities alone. There is also evidence that specific types of psychotherapy (e.g., cognitive therapy) can be successfully used in the treatment of mild to moderate depressive disorders, but learning to become a competent psychotherapist requires considerable effort and time to achieve results comparable to that of the relatively simple administration of an antidepressant. It is, therefore, recommended that the nonpsychiatric physician rely primarily on the antidepressants or lithium (depending upon the disorder being treated) in combination with educational and supportive psychotherapeutic approaches in the management of patients with major affective disorders (see Chap. 364).

REFERENCES

BALDESSARINI RJ: Biological hypotheses in psychiatry, in *Chemotherapy in Psychiatry*. Cambridge, Mass, Harvard, 1985, pp 9–12

———: *Biomedical Aspects of Depression*. Washington, DC, APA Press, 1982, pp 1–83

CLAYTON PJ, BARRETT JE (eds): *Treatment of Depression: Old Controversies and New Approaches*. Raven, New York, 1983

Diagnostic and Statistical Manual of Mental Disorders (3d ed). American Psychiatric Association, Washington, DC, 1980

KLERMAN GL: History and development of modern concepts of affective illness, in *Neurobiology of Mood Disorders*, RM Post, RC Ballenger (eds). Baltimore, Williams & Wilkins, 1984, pp 1–19

MARTIN JB, REICHLIN S: *Clinical Neuroendocrinology*, 2d ed. Davis, Philadelphia, 1987

POST RM, BALLENGER JC (eds): *Neurobiology of Mood Disorders*. Williams & Wilkins, Baltimore, 1984, vol 1

ROBINS LN et al: Lifetime prevalence of specific psychiatric disorders in three sites. Arch Gen Psychiat 41:949, 1984

361 ANXIETY DISORDERS

KAREN THATCHER BRITTON / S. CRAIG RISCH / J. CHRISTIAN GILLIN

Anxiety is a common emotion and as such is often a normal response to the vicissitudes of life. In its mild forms, anxiety may be adaptive. A little anxiety, for example, helps a student prepare for examinations. In its extreme forms, however, anxiety is incapacitating or terrifying. High anxiety may cause the same student to lose concentration, memory, or even his or her voice.

Physicians observe anxiety most commonly in patients experiencing an acute external stress. Although short-term treatment with antianxiety or sedative drugs, such as benzodiazepines, has a place in the management of such patients, physicians often can offer more help by their presence, reassurances, and attitude. Anxiety states often resolve spontaneously with time, although clinicians should be aware that acute stress can lead to chronic anxiety or posttraumatic stress disorder.

The word *anxiety* has more precise diagnostic meaning in psychiatry. It refers to both *paroxysmal* and *persistent* psychological feelings (dread, irritability, ruminations) and physiologic changes (dyspnea, sweating, insomnia, trembling) which endure over time and impair normal functioning. These are often chronic disorders in which symptoms persist in the absence of obvious contemporaneous external stresses or in which the degree of symptoms seems out of proportion to the degree of external stress. Anxiety disorders were formerly lumped together under the term "anxiety neurosis." It is now recognized that a number of relatively distinct clinical syndromes exist under the general rubric of anxiety disorders, as reflected in the diagnostic criteria in the third edition of the Diagnostic and Statistical Manual (DSM-III) (Table 361-1).

PANIC DISORDER Definition The cardinal feature of panic disorder is the sudden, unexpected, and often overwhelming feeling of terror and apprehension accompanied by somatic symptoms in multiple organ systems such as dyspnea, palpitations, and faintness. The symptoms and signs of panic disorder are similar to those occurring during intense physical exertion or in a life-threatening situation.

Incidence and epidemiology Panic disorder is estimated to occur in 1 to 2 percent of the population, with women outnumbering men two to one. The most frequent age of onset of panic attack is the late teen years and early twenties. Panic disorders tend to be familial, and both panic disorder and affective disorder often coexist in the same family. If an individual has a diagnosed panic disorder, up to 18 percent of first-degree relatives also will have panic disorder. Furthermore, twin studies demonstrate a greater incidence in monozygotic twins, suggesting that panic anxiety may have a genetic basis.

Clinical features A typical panic attack often begins abruptly and without warning while a patient is involved in a relatively nonthreatening and nonstressful activity, like entering a store, driving a car, or sitting at a desk working. The patient becomes flushed, lightheaded, and sweaty and is overwhelmed by feelings of terror, apprehension, and impending doom. Dyspnea may occur with a subjective sense of choking or smothering, and palpitations or chest pain are often so

TABLE 361-1 Classification of anxiety disorders

Anxiety states:
  Panic disorder
  Generalized anxiety disorder
  Obsessive-compulsive disorder
  Posttraumatic stress disorder
Phobic disorders:
  Agoraphobia (with and without panic attacks)
  Social phobia
  Simple phobia

severe that patients believe they are having a heart attack or are dying. The symptoms of panic attacks usually peak in less than 10 min and resolve in 20 to 30 min. Most patients experiencing their first panic attack obtain help, sometimes going to a doctor's office or emergency room, but the fear has usually subsided by this time. Fatigue or exhaustion frequently follows a panic attack, and the patient may sleep.

The DSM-III criteria for diagnosis of panic disorder are listed in Table 361-2.

Complications After repeated panic attacks, most patients develop some degree of anticipatory anxiety and try to avoid those situations that have been paired with panic attacks in the past. Some patients develop *agoraphobia*—an irrational fear of being alone or in public places. Without effective treatment, the course of panic attacks and agoraphobia leads to an increasingly restricted life-style marked by preoccupation with avoiding those situations that might trigger an attack. Cases of severe panic disorder with agoraphobia may result in patients remaining house-bound for one or more decades, convinced that leaving the house will induce an attack.

Other complications of panic disorder include major depressive syndrome, higher death rates from both suicide and cardiovascular disease, and drug and alcohol dependency. Losses from unemployment and health care costs are estimated to exceed $100 million a year.

Laboratory findings Lactate infusions precipitate panic attacks in vulnerable individuals, although at present this is only used as a test in research paradigms. One study employing positron emission tomography demonstrated a decreased rate of blood flow in the left parahippocampus during panic attacks.

Differential diagnosis Many patients with panic disorder complain of chest pain, cardiac extrasystoles, and palpitations. The diagnostic challenge is to differentiate anxiety with cardiovascular symptoms from the organic diseases it mimics. Because there may be an increased prevalence of mitral valve prolapse in patients with panic disorder this condition should be investigated; however, in the vast majority of patients wtih panic disorder, no significant cardiac pathology is ever found.

Other diagnostic possibilities include both hyperthyroidism and hypothyroidism, a catecholamine-secreting pheochromocytoma, complex partial seizures, and hypoglycemia. Drug ingestions (amphetamine, cocaine, caffeine, sympathomimetic nasal decongestants) and drug withdrawal (alcohol, barbiturates, opiates, minor tranquilizers) may produce symptoms that simulate panic attacks.

Etiology and pathophysiology The etiology of panic disorders is uncertain and involves an interplay of multiple psychological and biologic determinants.

PSYCHOLOGICAL FACTORS In the psychodynamic model, anxiety is considered to be a response to the threatened emergence into consciousness of painful, unacceptable thoughts, impulses, or desires,

TABLE 361-2 Diagnosis of panic disorder

A At least three panic attacks within a 3-week period in circumstances other than during marked physical exertion or in a life-threatening situation. The attacks are not precipitated only by exposure to a circumscribed phobic stimulus
B Panic attacks are manifested by discrete periods of apprehension or fear, and at least four of the following symptoms appear during each attack:
    1 Dyspnea
    2 Palpitations
    3 Chest pain or discomfort
    4 Choking or smothering sensations
    5 Dizziness, vertigo, or unsteady feelings
    6 Feelings of unreality
    7 Paresthesias (tingling in hands and feet)
    8 Hot and cold flashes
    9 Sweating
    10 Faintness
    11 Trembling or shaking
    12 Fear of dying, going crazy, or doing something uncontrolled during an attack

i.e., psychological conflicts from the past and present. The anxiety response is an attempt to mobilize and ward off danger to the self.

PHYSIOLOGIC FACTORS Clinical and experimental evidence point to the involvement of noradrenergic neurons, particularly those projecting rostrally from the locus coeruleus in the upper brainstem, in the pathophysiology of panic disorder. Three lines of evidence suggest that hyperactivity of noradrenergic pathways may play a role in the pathogenesis of panic. First, the clinical manifestations of panic attacks are similar to those induced by sudden, massive stimulation of beta-adrenergic receptors. Second, isoproterenol hydrochloride, a beta agonist, and yohimbine, an alpha-adrenergic receptor antagonist that increases noradrenergic function, produce signs and symptoms that mimic panic attacks. Third, clinical studies support a role for noradrenergic beta blockers, such as propranolol, in successful treatment of pathologic anxiety.

Another avenue of investigation is based on the finding that infusions of sodium lactate into patients with a history of panic disorder often provoke a panic attack indistinguishable from a spontaneous one. Normal subjects without a history of panic disorder are unaffected. In addition, patients whose panic attacks are controlled by antidepressants are protected against lactate-induced panic attacks. Although the mechanism of lactate's effect is unclear, the findings appear to have diagnostic usefulness and provide a good model of anxiety for further clinical investigation.

Overall, the evidence suggests that the main contribution to panic disorder may be a genetic vulnerability to a biologic disease state. Over time, panic attacks may become associated with environmental events that by themselves are able to elicit symptoms. The particular constellation of environmental stimuli that precipitate panic attack may be influenced by past experience or particular psychological conflicts. A full understanding of the etiology of anxiety probably will require knowledge of a combination of genetic, biologic, and psychological factors.

Treatment A comprehensive treatment program combines both pharmacologic and psychotherapeutic approaches. The first step is to block the attacks pharmacologically, usually with tricyclic antidepressants or monoamine oxidase inhibitors (see Chap. 364). These drugs have 80 to 90 percent effectiveness in the treatment and prevention of spontaneous panic attacks. New antianxiety medications such as alprazolam given in high dose are as effective as antidepressants, have fewer side effects, and work within 1 or 2 days. Other benzodiazepines have not proved efficacious. Antidepressant medication may take 4 to 6 weeks before being effective. Beta blockers, e.g., propranolol or atenolol, may block the peripheral manifestations of the panic attacks but have proved ineffective in preventing the psychic fear or panic and may also predispose to or worsen depressive symptomatology. Clonidine may also block panic manifestations, but its efficacy is usually only transient. Relapse is common on discontinuance of pharmacotherapy.

For some patients with panic disorder, particularly those with debilitating agoraphobia, psychotherapy is indicated. The exact form of psychotherapy needed is controversial, but approaches that seek to understand the anxiety and encourage the patient to confront the feared situations are the most effective.

GENERALIZED ANXIETY DISORDER Definition Unlike patients with panic disorders whose symptoms come on suddenly, patients with generalized anxiety disorder experience persistent diffuse anxiety, without the specific symptoms that characterize phobic disorders, panic disorders, or obsessive-compulsive disorders. Although the symptoms and signs of anxiety vary from individual to individual, common signs are motor tension, autonomic hyperactivity, apprehensive expectation, and vigilance. Patients with generalized anxiety disorder do not report acute fluctuations in anxiety level and autonomic arousal characteristic of panic disorder.

Incidence and epidemiology The prevalence of generalized anxiety disorder has been estimated at 2 to 3 percent, but precise epidemiologic

TABLE 361-3 Diagnosis of generalized anxiety disorder

A Generalized, persistent anxiety is manifested by symptoms from three of the following four categories:
  1 Motor tension: shakiness, jitteriness, jumpiness, trembling, tension, muscle aches, fatigability, inability to relax, eyelid twitch, furrowed brow, strained face, restlessness, easy startle
  2 Autonomic hyperactivity: sweating, heart pounding or racing, cold and clammy hands, dry mouth, dizziness, light-headednesss, paresthesias (tingling in hands or feet), upset stomach, hot or cold spells, frequent urination, diarrhea, discomfort in the pit of the stomach, lump in the throat, flushing, pallor, high resting pulse and respiration rate
  3 Apprehensive expectation: anxiety, worry, fear, rumination, and anticipation of misfortune to self or others
  4 Vigilance and scanning: hyperattentiveness resulting in distractibility, difficulty in concentrating, insomnia, feeling "on edge," irritability, impatience.
B The anxious mood has been continuous for at least 1 month
C Patient is at least 18 years of age

---

data are lacking because of variations in definition and case acquisition. In patients who seek professional help for anxiety, women outnumber men by two to one. There is no evidence to support the popular belief that anxiety is related to the stresses of modern society. In contrast to panic disorder, studies showing a familial or genetic basis for generalized anxiety disorder are inconclusive.

The diagnostic criteria for generalized anxiety disorder are listed in Table 361-3.

Complications In contrast to panic disorder, generalized anxiety disorder has a more chronic course and favorable outcome. However, the symptoms are persistent and can lead to secondary depression and alcohol and drug abuse, especially of benzodiazepines.

Differential diagnosis Symptoms and signs resembling anxiety may occur with a number of medical disorders including coronary artery disease, thyroid disease, and drug intoxication or withdrawal. Anxiety may be present in other psychiatric disorders such as depression, schizophrenia, and organic mental states. Diagnosis of these conditions is essential, since the treatment of them is different from that of the anxiety disorders. Because patients with generalized anxiety may abuse alcohol or antianxiety medications to reduce or block anxiety, a careful history of drug use is important. Although the overall degree of psychosocial or occupational impairment is generally less than that noted for the other anxiety disorders, chronic anxiety is an uncomfortable emotion that can restrict a person's ability to enjoy a normal life.

Etiology and pathophysiology One approach to understanding the etiology of anxiety has been to delineate the mechanisms by which antianxiety drugs exert their therapeutic effects. High affinity, stereospecific receptors for benzodiazepines have been discovered which appear to be coupled to the receptor for the inhibitory neurotransmitter gamma-aminobutyric acid (GABA). Considerable evidence supports the hypothesis that the anxiolytic actions of the benzodiazepines are mediated through this receptor.

These findings have several implications. First, the characterization of a benzodiazepine receptor complex implies the existence of a natural (endogenous) ligand for the receptor. Conceivably, the levels of this substance might correlate with individual differences in anxiety or emotionality or tolerance to stress. Second, pharmacologic antagonists of this receptor block the effects of benzodiazepines and may induce anxiety, a finding which implicates these mechanisms in pathologic anxiety. Third, new *anxiolytic* compounds that influence benzodiazepine receptor binding are being discovered that have fewer and potentially less serious side effects. The possibility exists that *anxiogenic* substances may also be found in the brain. Though major questions remain to be answered, these advances have opened new avenues for understanding the origins and management of anxiety.

Treatment Because feelings of anxiety are normal human emotions with adaptive value, a decision must be made before any treatment or medication is considered concerning whether or not the manifestations of anxiety are within the normal range. There is no justification

for the use of anxiolytic drugs in anxiety if it is considered to be within the normal limits of human experience.

Once a decision is made to treat, consideration should be given first to modalities of nonpharmacologic intervention, including supportive or intensive psychotherapy. These approaches may modify maladaptive life-styles, cognition, and avoidance behaviors. Behavior therapy aims at teaching the patient practical means to reduce anxiety and includes techniques like relaxation training, biofeedback, and desensitization. These techniques are of at least temporary benefit for many people.

When generalized anxiety is severe enough to warrant treatment with drugs, benzodiazepines are the agents of choice. In many patients, short courses of anxiolytic drugs (5 to 7 days) are effective, following which the drug should be discontinued. Patients should be warned about the possibility of dependence with long-term use, and the physician should make regular assessments of the need for continuation of medications.

POSTTRAUMATIC STRESS DISORDER Definition Acute and chronic psychological distress following traumatic events have long been recognized. The diagnostic criteria for posttraumatic stress disorders (PTSD), according to DSM-III, are listed in Table 361-4.

PTSD is classified as either acute or chronic (or delayed). In the former, onset of symptoms begin within 6 months of the trauma, or the duration of the symptoms persist less than 6 months. In the latter, symptoms persist more than 6 months (chronic) or start more than 6 months after the trauma (delayed).

Etiology Whether or not PTSD develops appears to depend upon the nature of the trauma, the characteristics of the individual, and the context in which these events take place. The trauma can be anticipated or not, acute or chronic, constant or repetitive, due to natural events (e.g., an earthquake) or malevolence (e.g., rape, child abuse, torture). PTSD can develop in individuals who were apparently healthy, successful, and well-adjusted prior to the traumatic experiences. Among the factors which influence the development of PTSD are (1) the extent to which the individual's life-space is affected, (2) the duration of the impact, (3) the extent to which the individual perceives human malevolence behind the traumatic event (e.g., a fire attributed to arson will probably be more traumatic than one attributed to lightning), and (4) social isolation.

Epidemiology It is difficult to gauge the extent of PTSD following a traumatic event because the studies that have been done have often followed subjects for only a short period of time, and the nature of the events is often so situation-specific. About 15 percent or more of the civilian population may experience mental distress severe enough to require treatment following a major natural disaster. For example,

TABLE 361-4 Diagnosis of posttraumatic stress disorder

A Existence of a recognizable stressor that would evoke significant symptoms of distress in almost everyone
B Reexperiencing of the trauma as evidenced by at least one of the following:
  1 Recurrent and intrusive recollections of the event
  2 Recurrent dreams of the event
  3 Sudden acting or feeling as if the traumatic event were recurring, because of an association with an environmental or ideational stimulus
C Numbing of responsiveness to or reduced involvement with the external world, beginning some time after the trauma, as shown by at least one of the following:
  1 Markedly diminished interest in one or more significant activities
  2 Feeling of detachment or estrangement from others
  3 Constricted affect
D Presence of at least two of the following symptoms that were not present before the trauma:
  1 Hyperalertness or exaggerated startle response
  2 Sleep disturbance
  3 Guilt about surviving when others have not, or about behavior required for survival
  4 Memory impairment or trouble concentrating
  5 Avoidance of activities that arouse recollection of the traumatic event
  6 Intensification of symptoms by exposure to events that symbolize or resemble the traumatic event

in a study that followed survivors of a shipboard fire for $3\frac{1}{2}$ to $4\frac{1}{2}$ years, one-third were found to be unable to return to sea because of psychological symptoms. Following extreme prolonged harsh conditions such as combat, prisoner-of-war camps, or Nazi death camps, a higher incidence of both acute and delayed PTSD is likely. Some evidence, based on follow-up of World War II veterans 20 years after the war, indicates an increasing incidence of new patients seeking psychiatric care for war-associated symptoms. The vicissitudes of normal aging may unmask a latent traumatic stress disorder.

Complications   Anxiety, depression, alcoholism, drug abuse, impaired marital and occupational activities, and perhaps increased physical morbidity and mortality have been blamed on various forms of PTSD.

Differential Diagnosis   In adjustment disorder, symptoms such as reexperiencing the trauma are absent. Other considerations include major depressive disorder, generalized anxiety disorder, phobic disorder, organic mental disorders, and other conditions such as "compensation neurosis" and "postconcussion syndrome."

Prophylaxis   Military experience suggests that PTSD can be prevented partially if soldiers are taught that a degree of fear and anxiety are normal concomitants of battle rather than signs of cowardice or mental illness. Furthermore, the development of chronic PTSD can often be prevented if the soldier with acute PTSD is seen close to the battle front under the principles of immediate treatment, expectancy of return to normal duties, and brevity of treatment contact.

Treatment   The treatment goals of PTSD are reduction of target symptoms, prevention of chronic disability, and occupational and social rehabilitation. An important therapeutic issue is the extent to which the victim of acute PTSD should be allowed to leave the traumatic situation, to regress, and to enjoy the secondary gains of the patient role. The caretakers' unthinking natural sympathy, nurturing instincts, admiration, and, indeed, gratitude (for example, in the case of soldiers who are protecting the homeland) may be as detrimental as an unreasonably cynical, suspicious distrust of someone who is seen as trying to get attention and avoid responsibilities or hoping to collect money from the consequences of the traumatic experience. Successful treatment involves a combination of psychosocial support systems, psychotherapy, behavioral and conditioning techniques, and medications. Group therapy with others who have shared similar experiences may be beneficial.

OBSESSIVE-COMPULSIVE DISORDER Definition   The major characteristics are recurrent *obsessions* (persistent intrusive thoughts) and *compulsions* (intrusive behaviors) which the patient experiences as involuntary, senseless, or repugnant. The DSM-III diagnostic criteria for obsessive-compulsive disorder are listed in Table 361-5.

Common obsessions include thoughts of violence (e.g., killing a loved one), obsessive slowness, fears of germs or contamination, and doubt (e.g., a priest who worries excessively that he had not said his

TABLE 361-5   Diagnosis of obsessive-compulsive disorder

A   Either obsessions or compulsions are present:
   1   Obsessions: Recurrent, persistent ideas, thoughts, images, or impulses that are ego-dystonic, i.e., they are not experienced as voluntarily produced, but rather as thoughts that invade consciousness and are experienced as senseless or repugnant. Attempts are made to ignore or suppress them.
   2   Compulsions: Repetitive and seemingly purposeful behaviors that are performed according to certain rules or in a stereotyped fashion. The behavior is not an end in itself but is designed to produce or prevent some future event or situation. However, either the activity is not connected in a realistic way with what it is designed to produce or prevent or it may be clearly excessive. The act is performed with a sense of subjective compulsion coupled with a desire to resist the compulsion (at least initially). The individual generally recognizes the senselessness of the behavior (this may not be true for young children) and does not derive pleasure from carrying out the activity, although it provides a release of tension.
B   The obsessions or compulsions are a significant source of distress to the individual or interfere with social or role functioning.

prayers properly). Examples of compulsions include repeated checking to be assured that something was done properly, hand washing, extreme neatness, and counting rituals, as in numbering steps while walking.

Obsessions and compulsions do not invariably coexist in the same individual. The relationship of the obsessive-compulsive disorder to obsessive or compulsive characterologic traits remains controversial.

Etiology and pathophysiology   The etiology of the obsessive-compulsive state is uncertain, but it can be viewed from psychodynamic, psychosocial, and biologic perspectives. Obsessions and compulsions often seem to symbolize unconscious wishes, impulses, and fears and to reflect dynamic adaptations to unwanted aggressive or sexual urges. Biologic factors are suggested by reports of an increased incidence of obsessive compulsive disorder in monozygotic twins and first-degree relatives of probands, of biologic markers associated with the disorder, and of favorable response to certain tricyclic antidepressants and monoamine oxidase inhibitors.

Epidemiology   The lifetime prevalence of obsessive compulsive disorder, based upon interviews of the general population 18 years and older, varies between 1.9 and 3.0 percent. The prevalence tends to be slightly higher in females than males but does not vary significantly by race, education, or urbanization of area of residence.

Clinical manifestations   These disorders usually begin in adolescence or young adulthood, with about 65 percent of cases beginning before age 25. They are rarely seen in children. Clear precipitants are reported in up to 60 percent of cases. Long term prognosis appears to be variable. Some patients (perhaps 10 percent) show a chronic, unremitting course; some show periods of complete remission; the majority show an episodic course with periods of incomplete remission.

Complications   Depression is probably the most common secondary problem but anxiety, avoidant behavior, alcoholism, abuse of sleeping pills and tranquilizers, and impairment of social, marital, and occupational life can be marked.

Laboratory findings   No pathognomonic pathologic or laboratory abnormalities have been found.

Differential diagnosis   Repetitive self-destructive behaviors, such as gambling, drinking, drug abuse, and overeating, should not be diagnosed as "obsessive-compulsive" disorder since the individual normally derives pleasure from the activity. Stereotyped behavior is also common in schizophrenia, Tourette's syndrome, and depression.

Treatment   Controlled studies have shown that both behaviorally oriented psychotherapy and psychopharmacology can be helpful in these disorders. Compulsions and rituals probably respond more than do obsessions and ruminations to behavior therapy. The tricyclic antidepressant drugs and monoamine oxidase inhibitors are relatively effective but require chronic administration. In severe unresponsive cases of obsessional-compulsive disorder cingulotomy or modified frontal leukotomy is reported to be helpful.

PHOBIC DISORDERS   Phobic disorders comprise a group of disorders having in common persistently recurring, irrational severe anxiety of specific objects, activities, or situations with secondary avoidance behavior of the phobic stimulus. Phobias are relatively commonplace, and the diagnosis of a phobic disorder is made only when fear or avoidance behavior is a significant source of distress to the individual or interferes with social or occupational functioning.

The phobic disorders listed in DSM-III include three separate disorders—agoraphobia, social phobia and simple phobia.

Agoraphobia   DEFINITION   Agoraphobia, the fear of being alone or in public places (see Table 361-6), may occur rarely in the absence of panic disorder, but it is almost invariably preceded by that condition.

Social phobias   DEFINITION   Social phobias are persistent irrational fears and the need to avoid any situation where one might be exposed

TABLE 361-6 Diagnosis of agoraphobia

A The individual has marked fear of and thus avoids being alone or being in public places from which escape might be difficult or help not available in case of sudden incapacitation, e.g., crowds, tunnels, bridges, public transportation.
B There is increasing constriction of normal activities until the fear or avoidance behavior dominates the individual's life.

to scrutiny by others and potentially be embarrassed or humiliated. Even the possibility of such a situation evokes anticipatory anxiety. The individual is aware that this fear is excessive. Common examples are excessive fear of public speaking and anxiety induced by eating in restaurants or by any public performance. The resulting anxiety may actually impair performance and thereby potentiate the phobic disorder.

EPIDEMIOLOGY AND PATHOGENESIS Social phobias are relatively rare, and there is no evidence for a genetic or familial transmission. Social phobias presumably arise from stressful life events occurring during early development. The disorder usually begins in late childhood or early adolescence and tends to be chronic and to wax and wane in severity.

COMPLICATIONS Complications are rare and the disorder is not often incapacitating; it may lead to sedative or hypnotic drug and alcohol abuse and addiction, and to problems in professional advancement.

TREATMENT Treatment of social phobia is primarily behavioral, with use of such techniques as relaxation therapy, systematic desensitization, and related techniques. Pharmacotherapy with beta blockers, i.e., propranolol or atenolol and/or alprazolam, may also be helpful.

Simple phobia DEFINITION Simple phobias are persistent irrational fears and avoidance of specific objects or situations.

CLINICAL FEATURES The individual experiences significant distress when confronted with the phobic stimulus or even the possibility of confrontation with the phobic stimulus and also recognizes this fear and anxiety as irrational and excessive. When confronted with the phobic stimulus the individual may experience symptoms identical to those of panic attacks. Common examples include fear of heights (acrophobia), fear of closed spaces (claustrophobia), and fear of animals. Fear of the possibility of exposure to the phobic stimulus will often cause the individual to attempt to elicit significant information, e.g., if the party or restaurant is at the top of a high-rise building; if they have a dog.

Age of onset is variable, but the disorder often begins in childhood. Simple phobias that begin in childhood may disappear without treatment, but may persist into adulthood. Although phobias are relatively common in the general population, they rarely result in significant impairment and individuals rarely seek treatment. Simple phobias are more common in women. Treatment, if required, is behavioral using relaxation therapy and systematic desensitization.

REFERENCES

CHARNEY DS et al: Noradrenense function in panic anxiety. Arch Gen Psychiat 41:75, 1984

LECKMAN JF et al: Panic disorder and major depression, alcoholism, panic, and phobic disorders in families of depressed patients with panic disorder. Arch Gen Psychiat 40:1055, 1983

LIEBOWITZ MR et al: Lactate provocation of anxiety attacks. Arch Gen Psychiat 41:764, 1984

ROSENBAUM JF: Current concepts in psychiatry. The drug treatment of anxiety. N Engl J Med 306:401, 1982

ROTH M: Agoraphobia, panic disorder and generalized anxiety disorder: Some implications of recent advances. Psychiat Dev 2:31, 1984

TALLMAN JF et al: Receptors for the age of anxiety. Pharmacology of the benzodiazepines. Science 207:274, 1984

362 SCHIZOPHRENIC DISORDERS

DAVID L. BRAFF

Schizophrenic disorders are serious mental illnesses that have a duration of 6 months or more and cause significant social, vocational, and personal disability and suffering. The schizophrenic patient often appears to be bizarre, inappropriate, and mentally impaired. Despite its stereotypic presentation, perhaps no other psychiatric disorder has proved as vexing and difficult to define, identify, and treat.

Schizophrenia has a lifetime prevalence rate of about 1 percent across all cultures. In the United States alone there are perhaps 2 million affected individuals who often become ill in their late teenage years and in the third decade of life. Poor outcome frequently leads to extensive disability, and schizophrenia accounts for a staggering estimated $20 billion per year of lost productivity. Most patients with schizophrenic disorders also cause major perturbations for family and social support systems, adding to the economic losses and the toll of human misery.

DEFINITION AND CLINICAL MANIFESTATIONS In 1919, Emil Kraepelin first made the distinction between dementia praecox, a psychotic illness with progressive deterioration, and manic depressive psychosis. Kraepelin's emphasis on deteriorating outcome was a new thrust in the largely descriptive nineteenth century psychiatric literature. Kraepelin noted, however, that about 13 percent of patients with dementia praecox did not have an inevitably deteriorating outcome, and this favorable outcome has significantly increased owing to the development and use of antipsychotic medications. Eugen Bleuler concentrated on the putative underlying psychological splitting of personality functions in his classic paper on the "group of schizophrenias." Bleuler's emphasis was on the "four As" of schizophrenia: *a*utism, flattened *a*ffect, loose *a*ssociations, and *am*bivalence. Other authors have focused on specific symptoms of schizophrenia, such as the sense of being influenced by others and feelings of being controlled by outside forces. To date, research has yet to identify specific and inevitably pathognomonic signs or symptoms of the schizophrenic disorders.

According to the third edition of the Diagnostic and Statistical Manual of the American Psychiatric Association (DSM-III), after the first and most central criterion of psychotic symptoms is met (see Table 362-1), the schizophrenic individual must show deterioration from a previous level of functioning in such areas as work, social relations, and self-care. Finally, continuous signs of the illness should be present for 6 months at some point during the individual's life with some signs of illness at the time of diagnosis. There may be prodromal, active, and/or residual phases of the illness that are not always clearly demarcated. Prodromal or residual symptoms are quite characteristic of the schizophrenic illness and may consist of isolation; marked psychosocial impairment; peculiar behavior; impaired personal

TABLE 362-1 Diagnosis of schizophrenia disorders

A Presence of certain psychotic symptoms during the active phase of the illness before the patient is 45 years old
B Psychotic features must last at least 6 months and include at least one of the following:
1 Bizarre delusions
2 Somatic, grandiose, religious, nihilistic or other delusions without persecutory or jealous content
3 Delusions with persecutory or jealous content
4 Delusions with persecutory or jealous content if accompanied by hallucinations
5 Auditory hallucinations in which a voice maintains a running commentary or two or more voices converse
6 Auditory hallucinations on several occasions with content of more than one or two words
7 Incoherence, marked loosening of associations, markedly illogical thinking, or poverty of speech content associated with either blunted or inappropriate affect, delusions, hallucinations, or catatonic or other grossly disorganized behavior

hygiene and grooming; blunted, flat, or inappropriate affect; digressive, vague, over-elaborate, circumstantial, or metaphorical speech; odd or bizarre ideation or magical thinking; and unusual perceptual experiences.

The DSM-III lists four major types of schizophrenic disorders: *disorganized, catatonic, paranoid,* and *undifferentiated.* This emphasis on subtypes carries forward Bleuler's notion of the "group of schizophrenias." There is moderate support for a paranoid/nonparanoid dichotomy as being important in schizophrenia. In an attempt to reduce diagnostic heterogeneity, Crow (1980) and other researchers have identified "type I" schizophrenic patients with a predominance of "positive" symptoms (e.g., hallucinations, paranoid ideation), normal cerebral ventricular size, and symptoms that respond to the hypothesized dopaminergic-blocking effects of antipsychotic drugs. In contrast, "type II" schizophrenic patients seem similar to Kraepelin's dementia praecox patients. Type II patients show a predominance of "negative" symptoms (e.g., anhedonia, social withdrawal, asociality), neuropsychological impairment, and possibly increased cerebral ventricular volume; they do not respond well to antipsychotic medications.

DIFFERENTIAL DIAGNOSIS Schizophrenic patients have no unique or pathognomonic signs and symptoms; at times, this makes the diagnosis difficult. DSM-III separates psychotic illnesses by a durational criterion into *brief reactive psychoses* lasting 2 weeks or less, *schizophreniform* disorders lasting between 2 weeks and 6 months, and *schizophrenic disorders* lasting more than 6 months. While these distinctions are practical and heuristic, the scientific basis for such a durational criterion is poorly documented. In addition, an acute manic patient may be difficult to distinguish from the schizophrenic patient, especially on a cross-sectional as opposed to longitudinal basis. To complicate matters further, the initial clinical appearance of a patient intoxicated with phencyclidine (PCP) or amphetamines may also be indistinguishable from that of the schizophrenic patient. It appears then that many functional and organic states may lead to a final common pathway of psychotic symptoms. The diagnosis can only be established reliably by a broad-based multifactorial approach utilizing neurobiologic data (e.g., toxicologic screens, genetic history) and psychosocial data (e.g., premorbid adjustment status) obtained both acutely and over time. Despite these problems, the DSM-III criteria for schizophrenic disorders have undergone extensive and successful field trials for reliability and validity. In general, clinicians using the DSM-III criteria can accurately and consistently diagnose schizophrenia.

PREDISPOSING, PRECIPITATING, AND SUSTAINING FACTORS IN SCHIZOPHRENIA Factors that contribute to the development of schizophrenia can be analyzed in terms of predisposing, precipitating, and sustaining factors. These factors may be anlayzed in terms of neuroanatomic and biochemical factors and neurophysiologic, psychophysiologic, intrapsychic, interpersonal, social, and socioeconomic factors. In a complex, multifactorial disorder such as schizophrenia, these neurobiologic and psychosocial factors should be seen as interactive rather than as competing or mutually exclusive. This approach is analogous to comprehensive analyses of diabetes mellitus or hypertension, which also have contributions based on genetics, receptor physiology, and physiologic, familial, psychosocial, and a myriad of other conceptually diverse factors. Within this context, predisposing factors are limited to etiologic variables, precipitating factors are related to pathophysiology, and sustaining factors are linked to outcome variables.

Etiology (predisposing factors) GENETIC FACTORS It is clear from twin, family, and adoptive studies that schizophrenia has a significant genetic basis. Monozygotic twins have roughly a 65 percent or greater concordance rate for schizophrenia, whereas dizygotic twins have a 12 percent concordance rate. Other family studies show that the morbid risk for developing schizophrenia is 5 to 10 percent if one parent is schizophrenic. This figure rises to 46 percent or more if both parents are schizophrenics. Second-degree relatives of schizophrenics run a 2 to 4 percent risk of developing the illness compared to a risk of 1 to 2 percent in the general population.

Adoption studies reveal that these risk factors are largely genetically linked and are not primarily due to the "schizophrenogenic" psychosocial environment of certain families. Still, these figures are fraught with methodologic complexities. For example, reflecting the probable complex mode of inheritance, 89 percent of schizophrenics do not have a parent who is schizophrenic. Eighty-one percent of schizophrenics do not have either a schizophrenic sibling or parent. The appropriate model with which to explain these figures is complex and may include a weighted polygenic model or other sophisticated interpretations of genetic theory.

The *stress-diathesis model* hypothesizes that there is a vulnerability which is inherited in schizophrenia-prone individuals. These vulnerable individuals are at high risk for developing schizophrenia under certain stressful circumstances. Studies of high-risk children with one or two schizophrenic parents indicate that such children may have a significantly increased incidence of morbidity in utero, at birth, and in the perinatal period. In addition, these infants and children may have psychophysiologic lability, attentional dysfunction, and specific motor disturbances. A number of human and animal studies suggest that such labile attentional mechanisms may result partly or largely from instabilities and increased activity of the mesolimbic dopaminergic system that has significant connections to the frontal cortex. The literature on neurophysiologically labile and vulnerable children seems to tie the genetic, dopaminergic, and attentional dysfunction hypotheses together. According to the stress-diathesis model, a host of stressful factors may precipitate a psychotic state in a high-risk individual. These factors include intoxication with PCP or amphetamines as well as more nonspecific factors such as medical illnesses with concomitant general stress. Further, specific hallucinogens such as lysergic acid diethylamide (LSD) may precipitate a psychotic episode that is ultimately indistinguishable from a schizophrenic disorder. Lastly, there have been a number of hypotheses that a viral vector may be important as an etiologic agent in at least some cases of schizophrenic disorders.

PSYCHOSOCIAL FACTORS There are many psychosocial hypotheses concerning creation of a predisposition or vulnerability to developing schizophrenia. Empirical support for most of these hypotheses is variable and far from definitive.

In the vulnerable individual, schizophrenia is seen as having its onset in a critical developmental period. The teenager may attempt to leave home and separate from family members for school or work reasons. The onset is often, but not invariably, insidious. In terms of psychosocial approaches to schizophrenia, there is felt to be a developmental or intrapsychic deficit in the vulnerable individual. Once set into motion, the psychosis passes through a series of stages leading to the final common pathway of a psychotic state.

Despite much theorizing, there is no inevitable schizophrenia-prone personality type, although at least a small but significant percentage of schizoid, paranoid, and schizotypal personality-disordered individuals do seem to be vulnerable to developing schizophrenic disorders. In the 1960s, a more family-systems-oriented view emerged. An example of this approach is the hypothesis of Bateson and coworkers who analyzed the formal communications patterns in "schizophrenogenic" families. In this view, communications content is less important than the frequently conflicting and self-contradictory form of communications style of schizophrenic patients' families. It remains unclear whether these familial factors are a cause or a result of having a schizophrenic child in the family. As the importance of biologic factors in schizophrenia have become clearer, family psychosocial factors have been seen more as secondary or epiphenomenal factors.

Psychosocial researchers have also examined the importance of socioeconomic factors in schizophrenia. Lower socioeconomic status correlates with a higher incidence of schizophrenia. There are two possible interpretations of these data. First, there may be a "social drift'' of vulnerable individuals to lower socioeconomic status. The second hypothesis is more etiologic—socioeconomic stresses may precipitate schizophrenic episodes, especially in vulnerable individuals.

Pathophysiology (precipitating factors) NEUROTRANSMITTERS AND NEUROPEPTIDES A number of neurobiologic factors have been correlated with schizophrenic episodes. Which neurobiologic systems underlie the acute psychotic symptoms? Currently, the predominant neurotransmitter hypothesis explaining the pathophysiology of schizophrenic disorders involves dopaminergic overactivity. Evidence supporting the *dopamine hypothesis* comes from several sources. First, the potency of all antipsychotic medications can be roughly predicted by their dopaminergic-blocking capacity. Second, mesolimbic dopamine plays a role in attentional mechanisms and stimulus filtering. When stimulus-filtering mechanisms break down, there is a collapse of the information-processing capacity of the individual, with resulting sensory inundation, cognitive fragmentation, and symptoms of thought disorder. Despite this support, the dopamine theory of schizophrenia is fraught with complexities when compared with the catecholamine theory of the affective disorders. Affective disorders hypothetically (and oversimplistically) reflect a decrease in norepinephrine tone in hypothalamic nuclei leading to a final common pathway of neurovegetative symptoms. In schizophrenia, there seems to be increased dopamine tone in mesolimbic-frontal cortical pathways leading to a final common pathway of cognitive fragmentation, thought disorder, and clinical impairment, but the impairment and the clinical symptoms are quite complex and highly variable. In this framework, affective disorders may be seen as impinging on the diencephalic "core" of the brain, whereas schizophrenia is conceptualized as a disorder of the mesolimbic-frontal cortical mantle. It is doubtful if any "one neurotransmitter" theory of any psychiatric disorder can reflect the interactive complexity of various neurobiologic and psychosocial systems, although such theories may be heuristically useful.

The hypothesis of dopamine overactivity in schizophrenia is generally characterized as a static theory. In reality, dopamine tone is related in a dynamic and variable manner to gamma-aminobutyric acid, serotonin, and other neurotransmitters that are functionally arrayed in important brain systems. Longer-term correlates of schizophrenia may also involve alterations of neuropeptides with their longer latency and response effects on behavior. At an electrophysiologic level, it has been hypothesized that the initial disturbance in schizophrenia is an aberrant temporal lobe focus that perturbs the homeostasis of the dopamine system. All of these theories are receiving critical experimental scrutiny.

NEUROPATHOLOGIC CHANGES The use of computerized tomography (CT) and magnetic resonance imaging (MRI) has been widely employed in studies of schizophrenic patients. Initial reports indicated that a minority of schizophrenic patients had abnormally increased ventricular brain ratios, reflecting increased ventricular fluid volume associated with brain atrophy. Subsequent studies have been less dramatic but the presence of increased ventricular brain ratios, mostly in type II schizophrenic patients, has supported the type I–type II dichotomy and stimulated further interest in "Kraepelinian" schizophrenia. It is quite possible that these type II patients have a disorder that is distinct and associated with poor medication response and poor clinical outcome. Positron emission tomography (PET) data reveal patterns of decreased frontal lobe activity in schizophrenia (hypofrontality) that seem important, especially in view of the close relationship of dopamine activity and frontal lobe function. Future PET studies utilizing new ligands will undoubtedly add to the knowledge of dopamine and other neurotransmitters in the schizophrenic disorders.

PSYCHOPHYSIOLOGY AND INFORMATION PROCESSING Important insights into the pathophysiology of schizophrenia have also been generated by psychophysiologic and information-processing studies. Individuals at high risk for developing schizophrenia and patients with a schizophrenic disorder are frequently psychophysiologically labile and vulnerable to being inundated by stimuli. The proposed mechanism for such vulnerability is an impairment in an individual's ability to screen out irrelevant stimuli and an associated inability to habituate to externally and internally generated cues. Ultimately, this dysfunction, which has been linked to dopamine overactivity in humans and animals, leads to an information-processing overload. The affected person becomes inundated with stimuli and displays cognitive fragmentation and thought disorder. Using attentional tasks, skin conductance habituation, and other measures, investigators have increasingly underscored the importance of these dysfunctions in the schizophrenic disorders.

Treatment and outcome (sustaining factors) NEUROBIOLOGIC FACTORS Five-year follow-up studies show that 60 percent of schizophrenic individuals have social recovery and half of those are employed. Thirty percent are handicapped and 10 percent remain hospitalized. This pattern of outcome seems still to be generally accurate. Which factors determine the outcome of the schizophrenic disorders are not clear. It is commonly stated that the outcome of schizophrenia is better when disorientation, affective symptoms, and acute onset are present. The outcome of schizophrenic disorders is thought to be poorer when the patient is well-oriented and has fewer affective symptoms and when the onset is insidious.

The outcome of schizophrenic disorders has been greatly improved by the use of potent and efficacious antipsychotic medications, such as the phenothiazines (see Chap. 364). Studies indicate that antipsychotic medications (often expressed in terms of chlorpromazine equivalents) act selectively against specific target symptoms that are similar to the "positive" symptoms of type I schizophrenia, which include hallucinations and psychotic agitation. In contrast to these responsive target symptoms, antipsychotic medications may not necessarily improve "negative" symptoms such as anhedonia and social withdrawal. The primary treatment modalities for the acute schizophrenic disorders are antipsychotic medication along with psychosocial therapies. The typical schizophrenic patient usually requires at least the equivalent of 600 to 800 mg per day of chlorpromazine, although higher doses are sometimes necessary. Maintenance doses of antipsychotic medications are often required to prevent relapse.

Antipsychotic medications alter dopaminergic-cholinergic balance in nigrostriatal structures (via dopamine blockade) so that acute extrapyramidal side effects are induced (e.g. dystonia, motor restlessness). These side effects can be treated with anticholinergic medications that restore dopaminergic-cholinergic balance. Aliphatic phenothiazines (such as chlorpromazine) with inherent anticholinergic properties cause fewer extrapyramidal side effects but induce more anticholinergic side effects, such as hypotension or blurred vision. Additionally, blood dyscrasias, liver toxicity, and other idiosyncratic reactions can occur. Also, the long-term use of antipsychotic medications may induce tardive dyskinesia, a long-lasting and potentially disabling motor syndrome (see Chaps. 15 and 364).

PSYCHOSOCIAL FACTORS The outcome of schizophrenic patients can be divided into the semiindependent axes of symptoms, rehospitalization, social function, and vocational function. It is possible to treat the specific psychotic symptoms of a schizophrenic individual (affecting the symptomatic axis of outcome), but the patient may be left with major psychosocial deficits (the social axis of outcome). Antipsychotic medications should thus be combined with sensitive psychosocial management including, where appropriate, individual psychotherapy, family counseling, and vocational rehabilitation in order to maximize therapeutic outcome and to restore the patient to the premorbid level of adjustment. For example, returning an acutely treated schizophrenic patient to a home filled with anger and turmoil (the so-called high-expressed-emotion family) without the benefit of family therapy is poor psychosocial management and may lead to relapse and poor outcome. Family counseling is often a critical determinant of therapeutic outcome in the schizophrenic disorders.

Antipsychotic medication alone cannot reverse years of psychosocial deficits and poor premorbid adjustment. Consequently, a large part of the therapeutic variance in outcome is accounted for by psychosocial factors. The range of outcome for schizophrenic patients is broad, and the clinician should use a broad multifactorial therapeutic approach.

REFERENCES

BATESON G et al: Towards a theory of schizophrenia. Behav Sci 1:251, 1956

BLEULER E: *Dementia Praecox or the Group of Schizophrenias*, J Zinkin (trans). New York, International Universities Press, 1950

BRAFF DL: Attention, information processing, and habituation in psychiatric disorders. *Psychiatry, III*. Philadelphia, Lippincott, 1985

BROWN GW et al: Influence of family life on the course of schizophrenic disorders: A replication. Br J Psychiatry 11:241, 1972

CARLSON G, GOODWIN F: The stages of mania. Arch Gen Psychiatry 28:221, 1973

CROW TJ: Molecular pathology of schizophrenia: More than one disease process? Br Med J 280:66, 1980

DOCHERTY JP et al: Stages of onset of schizophrenic psychosis. Am J Psychiatry 135:420, 1978

GOTTESMAN II, SHIELDS J: *Schizophrenia: The Epigenetic Puzzle*. New York, Cambridge, 1982

KRAEPELIN E: *Dementia Praecox*, RM Barclay (trans). Edinburgh, ES Livingstone Ltd, 1919

ROSENBAUM CP: *The Meaning of Madness*. New York, Science House, 1970

ROSENTHAL D, KETY S: *The Transmission of Schizophrenia*. New York, Pergamon, 1968

SNYDER SH: Dopamine receptors, neuroleptics, and schizophrenia. Am J Psychiatry 138:460, 1981

Special issue: Negative symptoms in schizophrenia. Schizophr Bull 11, 1985

STRAUSS JS, CARPENTER WT: *Schizophrenia*. New York, Plenum Medical Book Company, 1981

SWERDLOW NR, BRAFF DL, et al: Central dopamine hyperactivity in rats mimics abnormal sensory gating of the acoustic startle response in schizophrenics. Biol Psychiatry 21:23, 1986

WALKER E et al: Environmental factors related to schizophrenia in psychophysiologically labile high-risk males. J Abnorm Psychol 90:313, 1981

ZUBIN J, SPRING B: Vulnerability: A new view of schizophrenia. J Abnorm Psychol 86:103, 1977

363　PERSONALITY DISORDERS

IGOR GRANT

Personality denotes characteristic ways of thinking, feeling, behaving, and reacting to the environment. When this "psychological signature" strikes a useful balance between consistency and adaptive flexibility, we speak of personality *traits*. A personality *disorder* is said to exist when a person chronically uses certain mechanisms of coping in an inappropriate, stereotyped, and maladaptive fashion.

DIAGNOSIS OF PERSONALITY DISORDERS　The *Diagnositc and Statistical Manual* of the American Psychiatric Association (DSM-III) recognizes 11 distinctive personality disorders. These are grouped into three thematic clusters. *Paranoid, schizoid,* and *schizotypal* personality disorders are characterized by oddness or eccentricity. *Histrionic, narcissistic, antisocial,* and *borderline* personality disorders share a dramatic presentation along with self-centeredness, emotionality, and erratic behavior. Anxiety and fear underlie *avoidant, dependent, compulsive,* and *passive-aggressive* personalities.

The DSM-III diagnostic classification scheme stipulates specific inclusion and exclusion criteria for diagnosis of each disorder. Since the number of criteria for individual disorders ranges from 3 to 24, the descriptions in this chapter are highlights rather than complete expositions. The reader is referred to the DSM-III for the detailed listing of the necessary signs and symptoms required to make the diagnosis of the various personality disorders.

Paranoid personality disorder　People with this disorder are suspicious and hypersensitive to perceived slights and injuries. They are hypervigilant to the possibility that someone might trick or harm them and tend to be guarded and secretive and to blame others. They may be jealous and concerned with hidden meanings. They tend to exaggerate difficulties and to take offense and become hostile easily. Their affective range is limited, and they are often perceived as cold, unemotional, and humorless.

Schizoid personality disorder　Schizoid individuals are loners who seem to have little need for others. They appear emotionally cold and aloof and indifferent to praise and criticism; they lack close friendships, and may be social recluses.

In earlier nomenclatures eccentric thinking was sometimes added to the schizoid picture. DSM-III, however, has split off a second category, schizotypal, to describe persons whose principal difficulties are cognitive rather than interpersonal.

Schizotypal personality disorder　Schizotypal persons share with schizophrenics certain eccentricities of thinking, perception, speech, and interpersonal interaction; however, the degree and pervasiveness of such "schizophrenic-like" symptomatology is not sufficient to meet diagnostic criteria for schizophrenia. Odd speech (e.g., vague, circumstantial, metaphorical), ideas of reference (inappropriately inferring that neutral events have some special relevance to the person), magical thinking, and suspiciousness can be prominent. Many schizotypal persons are also socially isolated, and this can lead to confusion with schizoid personality.

Borderline personality disorder　Borderline persons have been described as having "stable instability," characterized by chronic difficulty in regulating mood and interpersonal attachments and in maintaining a consistent self-image. Borderline persons can manifest impulsive behavior, some of it self-damaging (e.g., self-mutilation, suicidal behavior). Their mood is unpredictable. Some have brief outbursts of anger, irritability, sadness, and fear. Others suffer from a chronic emptiness. Despite having chaotic interpersonal relationships punctuated by intense love and hate, borderline persons generally are intolerant of being alone. The defense mechanism of "splitting" (regarding persons and events either as "all good" or "all bad") can be prominent.

Histrionic personality disorder　People with a histrionic personality have seemingly intense but actually superficial relationships. They present in a dramatic, engaging, but self-centered fashion. There is an exaggerated expression of emotions, attention seeking, craving for excitement, and a tendency to overreact. While superficially warm and charming, histrionic persons are generally perceived as shallow, inconsiderate, self-indulgent, vain, demanding, dependent, and manipulative. Some make frequent suicidal threats or attempts.

Narcissistic personality disorder　The narcissistic person has an inflated sense of self-importance, and may be preoccupied with being unique, powerful, and gifted. The patient exaggerates his or her talents and contributions, seeks admiration, and uses others to achieve a better position, while being indifferent to their feelings and needs. A rejection can produce excessive rage, inferiority, shame, or humiliation. The narcissistic person has difficulty seeing others in a realistic light, tending either to overidealize or devalue them.

Antisocial personality disorder　Antisocial behavior is characterized by unconcern with the rules and expectations of society and repeated violation of the rights of others. The diagnosis is limited to adults (persons under 18 with antisocial features are classified as having conduct disorder) and requires a history of antisocial behaviors which have their onset before age 15. Such behaviors include truancy, delinquency, running away from home, lying, precocious sexuality, troubles with the law, and alcohol or drug abuse. Beyond such historical considerations, the antisocial diagnosis requires current evidence of certain deviant behaviors which include irresponsibility in work, as a parent, in financial matters, and in personal behavior (e.g., recklessness, driving while intoxicated). Additionally, antisocial persons will usually commit multiple illegal acts, lie and deceive, manifest an inability to maintain a long-term attachment to a sexual partner, and exhibit irritability and agressiveness. Alcohol or other substance abuse is common.

Avoidant personality disorder People who are inappropriately concerned with rejection or humiliation, and for this reason avoid close ties with others, are classified as having an avoidant personality disorder. Despite being withdrawn, they give evidence for wishing that they did have intimate relations with others. In contrast with the narcissistic individual, the avoidant person tends to manifest low self-esteem and a tendency to exaggerate his or her shortcomings.

Dependent personality disorder Dependent people allow others to assume responsibility for major aspects of their life and decision making. Because they see themselves as helpless or inept, they are willing to subordinate their needs and wishes to those of others in order to avoid taking personal responsibility.

Passive-aggressive personality disorder Passive-aggressive people resent responsibility, either social or work-related. Rather than expressing their opposition directly, they tend to procrastinate, dawdle, behave stubbornly, work inefficiently, and "forget." As a consequence, they fail to achieve their potential.

Compulsive personality disorder This disorder, which is equivalent to the term *obsessive-compulsive personality*, describes people who tend to be preoccupied with rules, procedures, and detail. They are often stubbornly insistent on certain things being done a particular way, yet at other times may become indecisive to the point of ineffectiveness. Compulsives tend to value their work and possessions more than their interpersonal relationships. They have difficulties expressing warm and tender feelings toward others and are sometimes seen as stiff, cold, and awkward.

Atypical, mixed, or other personality disorder This residual DSM-III category accommodates personality disturbances that do not fit neatly into any of the categories listed above. The most commonly used is *mixed personality disorder*, which indicates that an individual's behavior fulfills the criteria for more than one personality disorder, e.g., passive-aggressive and dependent. *Atypical personality disorder* is used when a personality disorder is suspected but there is not sufficient information to make a clear classification. *Other personality disorder* indicates presence of a personality disturbance not specifically included in *DSM-III*, e.g., masochistic, impulsive, or immature personality (which are concepts from other diagnostic schemes). One increasingly recognized disorder is *adult attention deficit disorder (ADD)*, a residual form of childhood ADD (hyperkinesis). As adults, such individuals continue to have problems in attending and manifest labile mood, explosive temper, impulsivity, stress intolerance, and inability to complete tasks. They may also manifest a paradoxical (calming) reaction to central nervous system (CNS) stimulants.

RELIABILITY OF PERSONALITY DISORDER DIAGNOSES Despite continued research efforts to improve interclinician agreement through specification of diagnostic criteria, reliability is problematic for most personality disorder diagnoses. While trained clinicians tend to agree whether or not some form of personality disorder is present, this reliability breaks down when specific diagnoses are attempted. Best agreement is reported for antisocial and paranoid personality disorders.

DIFFERENTIAL DIAGNOSIS Major mental disorders In its early phases, *schizophrenia* can be mistaken for schizoid, schizotypal, paranoid, and borderline personality disorders. *Affective disorders* can mimic some features of borderline, histrionic, and compulsive personality disorders. *Anxiety disorders* can share features with compulsive, histrionic, and avoidant personalities. *Alcohol and substance abuse disorders* may need to be differentiated from antisocial, borderline, and histrionic personalities. *Paranoid disorders* can sometimes be difficult to differentiate from paranoid, schizotypal, and borderline personalities. Differential diagnostic points are that the major mental disorders tend to have a definite time of onset, that the symptomatology is more severe and causes greater disturbance

in everyday functioning, and that specific diagnostic features will be present that transcend the criteria for personality disorders.

Additional personality disorders DSM-III criteria for personality disorders sometimes overlap. "Schizophrenic-like" phenomena, including eccentricity and psychotic experiences, can form part of the picture of paranoid, schizoid, schizotypal, and borderline personalities. Dramatic presentation, emotional outbursts, and erratic behavior can lead to confusion among antisocial, borderline, narcissistic, and histrionic personalities. Impulsivity is found in antisocial, borderline, and histrionic personalities; while anxiety and fearfulness can be part of avoidant, passive-aggressive, dependent, and compulsive behavior.

Medical conditions Medical and neurologic conditions can mimic personality disorders. For example, persons with complex partial seizures with foci in the left temporal lobe can present with excessive orderliness, religiosity, and "viscosity" which might be confused with compulsive personality. Alternatively, they can develop paranoid features or fuzzy thinking suggestive of paranoid or schizotypal personality. Rigid, orderly, and ritualistic behavior mirroring compulsive personality can be part of a dementing process or a sequel of head injury, while irritability, dysregulation of affect, and inappropriate interpersonal behavior in such patients can be confused with borderline personality. Beyond these specific examples, virtually any disease affecting the brain can cause behavioral change suggestive of a personality disorder. The key differential points are that there is a relatively sudden onset and that there are neuropsychological changes indicative of compromised brain function.

ETIOLOGY AND PATHOPHYSIOLOGY It was commonly held that the personality disorders reflected the warping effect of adverse early social environment. Now there is mounting evidence that personality is, in great measure, biologically determined. Both genetic and constitutional (i.e., intrauterine and early physical developmental) factors may be important.

Genetic factors Although not all personality disorders have been examined, for the majority there is a severalfold increase in concordance between monozygotic twins compared with dizygotic twins.

Some of the most careful work has been with antisocial personality. Here it is noted that prevalence among men is three- to fourfold higher than in women, and that first-degree relatives of persons diagnosed as antisocial show increased prevalence of antisocial personality, alcoholism, and somatization disorder (Briquet's syndrome). The latter is characterized by intractable multiorgan system complaints in women who often have a histrionic personality. The association of these two disorders in the same pedigrees has led to suggestions that Briquet's syndrome and antisocial disorder are expressions in women and men of a common biogenetic substrate.

The operation of genetic factors in antisocial personality is further demonstrated by the finding that biologic offspring of antisocial and alcoholic parents have a higher risk of developing antisocial personality disorder even if they are raised by adoptive parents who do not have any antisocial traits. The converse has also been demonstrated: children adopted by antisocial parents tend not to develop antisocial disorder themselves unless they have antisocial personality or alcoholism in their blood relatives.

The XYY chromosomal abnormality was once thought to be related to antisocial personality disorder. More recent studies indicate that although XYY might be overrepresented in certain prison populations, the vast majority of XYY men are not antisocial.

The schizotypal, borderline, and schizoid diagnoses evolved orginally from the notion that there ought to be a "preclinical" form of schizophrenia characterized by lesser severity or fewer numbers of the cognitive and interpersonal symptons of that disorder. Thus, the schizotypal personality might, theoretically, embody earlier forms of the disturbance in thinking, perception, and attention that occur in schizophrenia; whereas the schizoid personality would represent the interpersonal awkwardness inherent in that disorder. Genetic studies have confirmed that there is some increase in schizotypal (but not schizoid) personality in relatives of diagnosed schizophrenics.

The borderline personality is genetically heterogeneous. Up to 50 percent of borderline patients have a family history of affective disorder. Borderline disorder itself, as well as other personality disorders, are also more common in first-degree relatives of borderline patients, but schizophrenia is not consistently related.

There is increased schizophrenia in the families of patients with paranoid personality. For compulsive disorder, twin studies indicate increased concordance for obsessional traits in monozygotic versus dizygotic twins. There is also some evidence that orderliness and rigidity run in families.

The other personality disorders have not been studied carefully from a biogenetic standpoint.

Constitutional factors   Although there is good evidence that infants are born with certain temperamental characteristics (e.g., high versus low activity level; long versus short attention span), there is little evidence that these temperamental characteristics persist into adolescence. Infant temperament does not appear to predict later personality disorder with the exception that the "difficult child" (irritable, hard to console, irregular rhythms) tends to exhibit more behavioral disturbances. Low intelligence quotient and poor physical health as a child have been noted more frequently in the histories of persons with personality disorders.

Neurophysiologic and neuroendocrine correlates   Several neurophysiologic and biochemical changes may be associated with personality disorders. Abnormal slow waves and spikes have been reported in the EEGs of antisocial persons. For borderline patients, patterns suggestive of periodic limbic epileptiform discharges have sometimes been noted.

Some observers suggest that a common neurophysiologic feature of both antisocial and hysterical disorders is reduced cortical arousal to cortical stimulation, secondary to increased inhibition from lower brain regions. This may be coupled with motor disinhibition in antisocial persons and autonomic disinhibition in hysterics.

The schizotypal personality disorder has been associated with disturbance in smooth pursuit eye movement (SPEM). Since many schizophrenics are also poor trackers, it may be that schizotypals share with schizophrenics decreased neural effectiveness in "centering." Some schizophrenics and schizotypals have lowered platelet monoamine oxidase (MAO) levels. It has been suggested that lowered MAO activity could be related to inefficient degradation of certain biologically active amines, leading to accumulation of substance with psychotomimetic properties.

Cortisol escape from dexamethasone suppression and shortened rapid eye movement (REM) latency (REM latency is the time between falling asleep and first REM episode) are associated with affective disorder. Both phenomena have also been observed in borderline and obsessive-compulsive personalities, suggesting a link among the affective, borderline, and obsessive-compulsive disorders.

There are no specific data on biologic correlates of the other personality disorders.

Environmental factors   Early social environment has proved to be an inconsistent predictor of late personality disorder. For example, one study found that 30 percent of men with personality disorders who were investigated reported lack of maternal warmth as children, but so did 24 percent of controls. Multiple problems in the early environment were found in 16 percent of personality-disordered men and 10 percent of those without disorders. Being abused as a child is associated with violence in later life.

The relative weakness of both temperamental and environmental factors as predictors of future personality disorder has led to a "goodness of fit" hypothesis. This theory suggests that later behavioral disorders are more likely when there is a severe mismatch between a child's temperament and childrearing practices and environmental circumstances.

EPIDEMIOLOGY   The prevalence of personality disorders ranges from 5 to 23 percent. Antisocial personality is diagnosed more commonly in men than women, whereas borderline and histrionic personalities are diagnosed more commonly in women.

There is increased prevalence of personality disorder in inner cities, prisons, and areas of social disintegration. Personality disorders are three times as common in the lowest social classes as compared to the highest. These sociodemographic patterns are particularly striking for antisocial personality disorder.

NATURAL HISTORY AND PROGNOSIS   Compared to controls, a disproportionate number of persons with personality disorders are found to have emotional problems as children. The prevalence of most personality disorders declines with age, the peak being in the age group 20 to 29. This trend is especially prominent for antisocial personality disorder. It is possible that slowly evolving maturational processes during adulthood account for these age effects.

Although only about 20 percent of persons with personality disorders seek psychiatric treatment, the majority evidence long-standing difficulties in maintaining stable employment, marriages, and friendships.

With regard to psychiatric complications, about one-third of persons with personality disorders have significant depression or anxiety. Alcohol abuse is related to personality disorder, with the association being particularly striking for men, whose rate of alcohol problems approaches 50 percent.

TREATMENT   Persons with personality disorders generally do not recognize the inner source of their difficulties. They tend to blame others and their environment and make those around them feel badly. Only 20 percent of persons with personality disorders actually seek psychiatric treatment.

Treatment usually consists of psychotherapy in some form. In some specific instances psychopharmacology has been used. Success has been claimed for various types of psychotherapy. Individual, group, couples, and family treatments all have been employed. Despite differences in techniques and orientations, most psychotherapists emphasize the importance (and initial difficulty) of establishing a trusting relationship. The goals tend to be to identify inner sources of maladaptive behavior. From a psychodynamic standpoint this means that the painful feelings which are being avoided need to be identified and their causes traced. Cognitive-behavioral therapists will try to identify the faulty assumptions, lack of foresight regarding consequences of behavior, and ineffectiveness of the existing coping repertoire, with an eye to teaching more useful behavior.

As a broad generalization patients with "dramatic" presentations (borderline, antisocial, histrionic, narcissistic) tend to require a more intrusive, confrontative, limit-setting posture by the therapist. More specifically, antisocial personality probably cannot be treated in an outpatient setting and requires a containing enviroment (e.g., prison, inpatient unit). In such a setting groups emphasizing mutual interdependence and confrontation appear to produce some success. Regarding the treatment of borderline persons, psychiatrists are divided as to whether a supportive "here and now" versus intensive exploration work best. In either instance, treatment is often punctuated by prolonged periods in which the patient expresses negative feelings toward the therapist, makes suicide attempts, or undergoes psychotic decompensation requiring hospitalization.

In contrast to this more intrusive posture, patients whose personalities fit into the "fearful" and "odd" clusters may benefit from a more gentle, accepting, and clarifying approach.

Psychotherapy tends to be a long-term enterprise, lasting many years. Therapists can expect to feel frustrated, angry, helpless, and inadequate at times. Clinical reports of major improvements are many, but controlled outcome studies are practically nonexistent. This reflects continuing problems in achieving reliable diagnoses and in general methodologic issues in outcome research, especially in prospective studies spanning many years.

There is increasing evidence that psychopharmacologic intervention may be helpful for some of the personality diagnoses. Borderline patients, particularly those with coexisting mood disorder, have benefited from tricyclic antidepressants and MAO inhibitors. Other groups of borderline patients in whom mood dysregulation and impulsiveness are prominent have responded to lithium. Still others with explosive outbursts have benefited from carbamazepine. A few such patients have had EEG abnormalities suggestive of epileptic foci in limbic structures. Both borderline and schizotypal patients undergoing cognitive disorganization can improve with low doses of neuroleptic drugs.

Persons with compulsive personality disorder who have obsessional ruminations may benefit from the tricyclic clomipramine (unavailable in the United States). Clomipramine may have specific antiruminative effects which go beyond its antidepressive activity. The utility of other antidepressants for this disorder has not been established, although the MAO inhibitors show promise in compulsives who also experience anxiety or panic attacks.

Methylphenidate may improve inattention and reduce motor overactivity, affective lability, and impulsivity in persons whose personality difficulties are related to adult attention deficit disorder.

REFERENCES

AMERICAN PSYCHIATRIC ASSOCIATION: *Diagnostic and Statistical Manual of Mental Disorders*, 3d edition. Washington, DC, APA Press, 1980

DRAKE RE, VAILLANT GE: A validity study of Axis II of DSM-III. Am J Psychiatry, 142:555, 1985

FROSCH JP: The psychosocial treatment of personality disorders, in *Current Perspectives on Personality Disorders*, JP Frosch (ed). Washington, DC, APA Press, 1983, pp 96–112

GRANT I: *Behavioral Disorders: Understanding Clinical Psychopathology*, New York, Spectrum, 1979

GUNDERSON JG: DSM-III diagnoses of personality disorders, in *Current Perspectives on Personality Disorders*, JP Frosch (ed). Washington, DC, APA Press, 1983, pp 20–39

LIEBOWITZ MR: Psychopharmacological intervention in personality disorders, *Current Perspectives on Personality Disorders*, JP Frosch (ed). Washington DC, APA Press, 1983, pp 68–93

LION JR: *Personality Disorders: Diagnosis and Management (Revised for DSM-III)*, 2d ed. Baltimore, Williams, & Wilkins, 1981

MILLON T: *Disorders of Personality, DSM-III, Axis II*, New York, Wiley, 1981

SIEVER LJ et al: Biogenetic factors in personalities, in *Current Perspectives on Personality Disorders*, JP Frosch (ed). Washington, DC, APA Press, 1983, pp 42–65

WALDINGER RJ: *Psychiatry for Medical Students*. Washington, DC, APA Press, 1984

WENDER PH et al: A controlled study in the treatment of attention deficit disorder, residual type, in adults. Am J Psychiatry, 142:547, 1985

364 THE THERAPEUTIC USE OF PSYCHOTROPIC MEDICATIONS

LEWIS L. JUDD

Perhaps no other area of pharmacology has experienced the rapid development that has occurred in psychopharmacology during the past two decades. An almost bewildering array of specific and effective psychotropic agents are currently available, with new medications appearing with great frequency. This chapter presents an overview of the major classes of psychopharmacologic drugs to provide the reader with a pragmatic understanding of these potent medications. The most clinically meaningful classification schema is based upon the therapeutic use in patients, as follows: antidepressant medications, lithium and other mood stabilizing medications, anxiolytic or antianxiety medications, and antipsychotic or neuroleptic medications.

ANTIDEPRESSANT MEDICATIONS The successful search for new and better antidepressant medications has resulted in the two generations of antidepressants that are currently available. The first-generation antidepressants include the tricyclic (TCA) and the monoamine oxidase (MAO) inhibitor antidepressants. To date, no newly developed drug has greater efficacy than the antidepressants in these two major classes. The MAO inhibitors are clinically effective and recently have experienced a resurgence in clinical use, but the problems of drug-drug and drug-food interactions have made these the second-line medications in the treatment of depressive disorders. In contrast, the TCAs imipramine and amitriptyline have emerged as the standards for antidepressant efficacy.

No antidepressant is ideal, and all currently available drugs have at least one of the following undesirable characteristics: delayed onset of therapeutic action (7 to 28 days), significant anticholinergic side effects, sedation, cardiotoxicity, weight gain, the possible induction of manic episodes in patients with bipolar disorders, or other equally problematic side effects. Therefore, the developmental goal of the second-generation antidepressants has been to increase efficacy and eliminate side effects, but the search has not met with notable success.

Mechanisms of action The primary brain mechanism originally hypothesized for the TCA antidepressants was the capacity to increase synaptic concentrations of central nervous system (CNS) monoaminergic neurotransmitter substances (e.g., norepinephrine, serotonin, and dopamine) by blocking their reuptake by presynaptic monoaminergic neurons. While this is still valid, the focus now is on the regulation of postsynaptic receptor activity in monoaminergic neurons, and down-regulation of neurotransmitter receptors has been identified with the antidepressant effect. Most of the proven antidepressants fit the mechanisms hypothesized, but some newer antidepressants do not. At present, therefore, there is a great deal of information available about how antidepressants may ameliorate the pathophysiologic mechanisms of depressive disorders, but no precise central mechanism(s) has been identified by which all drugs with antidepressant properties work.

Clinical conditions in which antidepressant medications are used Antidepressants are very effective in treatment of major depression (Chap. 360) but do not affect the vicissitudes of mood inherent in normal human behavior nor do they make unhappy people into happy ones. Chronic low-grade depression or dysthymic disorders (neurotic depression) do not respond well to antidepressants, but patients with major depression are very likely to respond. Antidepressants are not often prescribed for patients who become temporarily depressed over difficult and stressful life situations (situational depression).

There is, however, growing evidence that antidepressants are effective in the treatment of some anxiety disorders (Chap. 361). TCA and the MAO inhibitor antidepressants are the drugs of choice for agoraphobia, simple phobias, and panic disorder. Patients with phobic or panic disorders have concomitant anxiety about the recurrence of these attacks; this "anticipatory" anxiety may not respond to antidepressants but often requires treatment with antianxiety medication. There may also be a potentially broader role for the antidepressants in the management of pure anxiety disorders, but this requires further study.

Clinical use of the antidepressants Table 364-1 lists the more commonly used first-generation antidepressants and the oral doses needed for therapeutic efficacy in the typical patient. Currently imipramine and amitriptyline are the standards for antidepressant potency. Amitriptyline is more sedative while imipramine is more energizing. Because of the undesirable side effects observed in these original TCAs, during the past decade there has been a gradual shift among experienced clinical psychopharmacologists to the secondary tricyclic amines of desipramine and nortriptyline. The advantage of desipramine is that it has relatively fewer anticholinergic side effects, and nortriptyline appears to have a clearer relationship between plasma levels and clinical efficacy.

Before antidepressants are prescribed, a patient's physical health must be evaluated by a physical examination and the patient should show normal values on baseline complete blood count (CBC), urinalysis, liver function tests, and (if over 45 years) an electrocardiogram (ECG). Patients are started on low doses in a twice daily regimen for 1 day (e.g., 25 mg desipramine bid) and checked for idiosyncratic reactions (e.g., postural hypotension). The dose is then raised quickly over a few days to that needed for a full therapeutic response. The minimum daily dose for clinical response is the low figure in the ranges listed in Table 364-1, but often higher doses are needed. Physicians inexperienced in psychopharmacology should not exceed the upper dosage limits listed in the table. From 7 to 28 days are required for a full therapeutic effect to be present. Changes in the depressive symptoms are often noted by friends and family before the patient reports feeling subjectively better. A therapeutic trial of an antidepressant requires at least 28 days at the upper end of the dose range. Patients are maintained on antidepressants for approximately 8 months after the depressive symptoms disappear. Medications can be given in a single dose an hour before bedtime once an appropriate dose for a given patient has been established. The advantages of this procedure are improved medication compliance; that the sedative side effects induce sleep in depressed patients, who are often insomniac; and that the troublesome side effects occur while the patient is asleep. Some patients cannot tolerate the single bedtime dose, and in these patients a daytime twice daily or three times daily schedule is necessary.

Plasma levels of the tricyclic antidepressants are routinely available, but unfortunately the relationship of plasma levels to clinical response has been inconsistent. Linear relationships between plasma levels and therapeutic response exist for imipramine, desipramine and amitriptyline, while nortriptyline may have a curvilinear plasma level–response relationship, implying a therapeutic window. Plasma levels may be useful in treatment-resistant patients to evaluate compliance and to see if the dose is sufficient to maintain concentrations above the threshold necessary for response (e.g., imipramine > 180 ng/mL; desipramine > 125 ng/mL; amitriptyline > 95 ng/mL; and nortriptyline 60 to 140 ng/mL).

After a number of months of treatment with antidepressants, it is recommended that the drug be withdrawn gradually over a 3- to 4-week period rather than that it be stopped suddenly. Should depressive symptoms reemerge, restoration of the antidepressant treatment is necessary for several more months, and then the withdrawal attempt can be repeated.

Side effects and interactions with other drugs　Listed in Table 364-2 are some of the more common side effects from the tricyclic antidepressants; they include dry mouth, sedation, a fine tremor of the hands, and mild constipation. More serious are the effects on the cardiovascular system, where tachycardia and postural hypotension are the most common. The TCAs, especially imipramine, have a quinidine-like action, can induce cardiac arrhythmias, and have been associated with sudden death in a few patients (see section below on overdose). Patients with preexisting cardiac illness, especially those with heart block, should be treated cautiously with the TCAs, or drugs with milder cardiac effects should be considered. The most bothersome symptoms are from the anticholinergic effects; while rarely serious, they do cause discomfort and compliance problems.

Some preexisting medical conditions increase the risk of using TCAs in certain depressed patients. Tricyclics can produce tachycardia, which may push some patients from asymptomatic congestive failure into symptomatic heart failure. TCAs lower the seizure threshold and should be used cautiously in patients with seizures. The anticholinergic effects preclude TCAs in patients with glaucoma, and men with mild to moderate prostatic hypertrophy can develop urinary retention. Finally, the use of tricyclic antidepressants in patients with bipolar disorders may act to shorten the cycle length between affective episodes and may induce an acute manic episode in some patients.

The tricyclics, especially amitriptyline, imipramine, and doxepin, potentiate the effects of other CNS-depressant medications (e.g., ethanol, benzodiazepines) and patients should be cautioned about ethanol use while on antidepressants. Patients should either not drink or reduce their usual ethanol dose by one-half during tricyclic treatment. Other drug interactions include the potentiation of other anticholinergic agents (e.g., antihistamines, antiparkinsonian agents), which can result in severe constipation, urinary retention, and even paralytic ileus. This combination in the elderly can produce a serious anticholinergic blockade (e.g., paralytic ileus, fecal impaction) and not uncommonly has been the cause of frank delirium and confusional states in geriatric patients. Therefore this combination should be used with caution in the elderly.

Despite the problems, the risk/benefit ratio is overwhelmingly in favor of the antidepressants, and literally hundreds of thousands of patients have been treated with these compounds safely and effectively.

The newer antidepressant medications　The development of new antidepressant medications has proceeded rapidly and many second-generation drugs are now available. Table 364-3 lists the more prominent second-generation drugs for which some evidence of antidepressant efficacy exists. Unfortunately, many of the clinical trials in which these drugs were studied are sufficiently flawed that the antidepressant potency of the new antidepressants has not been fully established. How these drugs will fare over time under more rigorous scrutiny is unknown. An example of the unforeseen problems which arise when promising new drugs are given broader exposure is the experience with zimelidine. This relatively selective serotonin uptake blocker was originally reported to be an effective antidepressant

TABLE 364-1　Commonly used first-generation antidepressants

Antidepressant	Daily oral therapeutic dose range, mg
Tricyclic derivatives:	
Amitriptyline (Elavil, etc.)	150–300
Nortriptyline (Aventyl, etc.)	50–150
Imipramine (Tofranil, etc.)	150–300
Desipramine (Norpramin)	150–250
Doxepin (Sinequan, etc.)	150–300
Monoamine oxidase inhibitors:	
Phenelzine (Nardil)	45–90
Tranylcypromine (Parnate)	10–30
Isocarboxazid (Marplan)	10–30

TABLE 364-2　More common side effects of tricyclic antidepressants

Anticholinergic (atropine-like) responses:
　Dry mouth*
　Nausea and vomiting*
　Constipation
　Urinary retention
　Blurred vision (mydriasis and cycloplegia)
Cardiovascular effects:
　Postural hypotension*
　Tachycardia
　Cardiotoxic side effects—can induce an arrhythmia
Obstructive jaundice—more rare—is reversible when drug is removed
Drowsiness and sleepiness—may want to avoid driving a car until this diminshes*
Fine rapid tremor*
Dizziness, ataxia
Hematologic effects:
　Leukopenia

* Side effects seen most commonly

TABLE 364-3　Selected second-generation antidepressants

Antidepressant	Daily oral therapeutic dose range, mg
Tricyclic derivatives:	
Trimipramine (Surmontil)	100–250
Amoxapine (Asendin)	150–300
Tetracyclic derivatives:	
Mianserin (Bolvidon)	50–150
Maprotiline (Ludiomil)	150–300
Derivatives of other chemical classes:	
Trazodone (Desyrel)	100–600
Alprazolam (Xanax)	0.75–4

with milder anticholinergic side effects. With increased study it has been associated with Guillain-Barré syndrome in several patients and has now been withdrawn pending further investigation. This new generation of psychotropic medications is promising and may eventually lead to drugs that offer additional benefits.

One of the first of the new medications developed is *trimipramine*, a tricyclic derivative. It has proved to be similar in its antidepressant potency and clinical spectrum to imipramine and amitriptyline. It is quite sedative and may actually have specific anxiolytic characteristics. The potential advantage of this drug is that patients may report fewer anticholinergic symptoms, even though the drug has anticholinergic properties.

Amoxapine is also a tricyclic derivative with clinical efficacy equal to that of the original antidepressants. It has been claimed that this compound may have earlier onset of action (within the first week), although its clinical efficacy at the endpoint of treatment is identical to that of the original TCAs. This compound has the interesting feature that one of its metabolites (7-hydroxyamoxapine) is a neuroleptic which has been associated with the unwanted side effects seen with the antipsychotic drugs (e.g., extrapyramidal syndrome). Other side effects from amoxapine appear to be similar to those of the original tricyclics although a disproportionate number of seizures was found in some retrospective studies. It is claimed, but not yet established, that it is less cardiotoxic.

Clomipramine, a tricyclic antidepressant commonly used in Europe and Canada but not approved for use in the United States, has been shown in controlled studies to be an effective drug in the treatment of depression and to be perhaps uniquely effective in obsessive-compulsive disorders.

Mianserin is a tetracyclic derivative, but there are very few placebo-controlled studies in the United States establishing its antidepressant efficacy. There is one unpublished controlled study indicating that it is similar in its antidepressant effects to amitriptyline, but many of the studies involving mianserin have been open studies which are of dubious value in assessing its therapeutic spectrum and potency. The advantage of this drug is that it has virtually no anticholinergic side effects and little if any cardiotoxicity, but it does produce considerable sedation.

Maprotiline is also a tetracyclic derivative which is equal in antidepressant potency to the original tricyclics. It is reported to have fewer anticholinergic side effects. Originally it was offered as a promising drug for use in patients with cardiovascular problems, but this has not been established and it is not recommended for this purpose. Initially it was also felt to have less effect on the seizure threshold but it has now been reported to have caused grand mal seizures in several patients. Moreover, its use has been associated with more than the expected incidence of blood dyscrasias.

Nomifensine, a potentially interesting antidepressant related to a nonanalgesic opiate derivative, has now been withdrawn from the market worldwide because of serious hypersensitivity reactions.

Trazodone is a triazolopyridine derivative and is the first of its type to be used as an antidepressant. There is considerable controversy whether or not this drug has the same antidepressant efficacy and spectrum as the original tricyclics. The advantage of this drug is that it has few if any anticholinergic side effects. It is reported to be a potentially useful drug in patients with cardiac illness, but this has not been established. The major problems with trazodone include an unacceptable level of sedation and increased risk of priapism.

Alprazolam, a benzodiazepine derivative with proven anxiolytic efficacy, has been reported to be an effective antidepressant. It has not been established that it is as potent as the original TCAs in the treatment of major depressive disorders. It is likely to have a place in the treatment of mixed anxiety and depressive syndromes, and it has the added advantage of a more rapid onset. It has no anticholinergic effects but does cause sedation and lethargy. Since it is a benzodiazepine, withdrawal symptoms may appear after prolonged use in high dose. This is a promising new drug, which may herald the development of other benzodiazepines with antidepressant properties.

Bupropion initially appeared to be a promising antidepressant, but its tendency to cause seizures in some patients has resulted in its removal from the market for further study.

Clinical management of tricyclic overdosage Antidepressants are the fourth most common cause of drug overdose seen in emergency departments in the United States and the third most frequent cause of drug-related death (after alcohol-drug combinations and heroin). Of the antidepressants, tricyclics were the primary cause of death. In the California study (Callaham and Kassel) the annual incidence of fatal tricyclic overdose was 1.3 per 100,000 of population. More than two-thirds were women. Amitriptyline, desipramine, and nortriptyline were the most frequently implicated.

The first 6 h after an overdose of a tricyclic antidepressant are crucial. CNS depression and seizures, respiratory arrest, and cardiovascular arrhythmias are the principal causes of death. ECG changes showing QRS prolongation are early signs of toxicity, and ventricular fibrillation is a common complication. ECG changes are a more sensitive measure for monitoring patients than are blood levels of the drug.

LITHIUM AND OTHER MOOD-NORMALIZING MEDICATIONS The most important psychotropic medication in this group is lithium. Although lithium possesses some antidepressant properties, it is not, strictly speaking, an antidepressant. Lithium's effectiveness in the treatment of patients with bipolar disorders (see Chap. 360) and other disorders of mood has revolutionized the practice of psychiatry. Since lithium's approval by the FDA in 1969, there has been an explosion of basic and clinical research focused on its pharmacologic mechanisms and clinical use.

Mechanism of action of lithium Considerable progress has been made in advancing our understanding of its clinical use, but the underlying mechanism by which lithium works is largely unknown. Lithium exerts effects on the brain's monoaminergic neurotransmitter concentrations at the synapse, and there is agreement that, in part, this mediates its clinical effects. Lithium has strong effects on biologic membranes, and this has been offered as an additional mechanism of action in the CNS. Lithium is unique since it both attenuates the frenetic agitation of mania and controls depression in bipolar disorders. However, the central mechanisms by which lithium exerts its clinical effects on extremes of mood are not fully understood.

Conditions in which lithium is used Lithium is the drug of choice of acute manic/hypomanic episodes and for the prevention of recurrent episodes of mania and depression in bipolar depression. Although evidence exists that lithium is a low-grade antidepressant, especially in depressions seen in bipolar disorders, it is not a drug of choice for depression per se. Lithium may also be an effective agent in the prophylaxis of recurrent unipolar depressive disorders. It has been successfully used in conjunction with neuroleptics in schizoaffective schizophrenia; there may be a subpopulation of schizophrenics responsive to lithium, although most workers feel that lithium responders are atypical bipolar patients and not schizophrenics. Finally, there are reports that lithium may be useful in alcoholism; while this is of interest, it has not been established.

Clinical use of lithium Lithium is a very safe drug with an excellent risk/benefit ratio when it is used knowledgeably. The only genuine contraindication to lithium's use is seriously compromised renal function. The following baseline studies should be obtained before prescribing lithium: CBC, routine urinalysis with a concentration test, total thyroxine (T_4), serum creatinine, electrolytes, and (for those over 40) an ECG.

Serum lithium levels peak 1 to 3 h after an oral dose, and the biologic half-life is 24 h, but this varies with age. Elderly patients frequently have a drug half-life over 30 h (requiring lower doses) and adolescent patients less than 20 h (requiring higher doses). Lithium is monitored by serum levels, which are most informative approximately 10 h after the last dose. Therapeutic efficacy in acute mania is achieved at levels between 0.8 and 1.5 meq per liter. There is rarely a necessity for patients to be treated at serum levels above 1.5 meq per liter. Lithium is always administered orally, and the oral dose range is from 600 mg to 3000 mg qd. A general rule of thumb equates a 0.2 meq per liter rise in serum level with each additional 300-mg tablet of lithium. Unless sustained release tablets are used, lithium is usually administered in a two or three times daily regimen, allowing for smooth, sustained 24-h serum levels. There is a 7- to 10-day delay between starting lithium and achieving full therapeutic effects, which often necessitates the addition of antipsychotic medications during the early phase of treating a manic patient. Patients during acute manic episodes often tolerate relatively higher doses of lithium, but once the manic episode remits it is necessary to quickly reduce the dose to prevent toxicity. When an isolated acute manic/hypomanic episode is being treated, it is common practice to maintain the patient on lithium for 6 to 8 months following symptom disappearance. The drug is tapered gradually over 3 to 4 weeks.

Because of medical complications, clinicians have become increasingly conservative about long-term maintenance on lithium unless it is clearly justified. Generally, for maintenance therapy, the patient should have had a total of three diagnosed and treated episodes of mania and/or depression, with two of the episodes occurring within a 2-year period and the next episode during the following 2 years. In other words, the clinician should be convinced that the patient is experiencing frequent, serious, and disruptive episodes. The current maintenance strategy is to seek the lowest possible serum levels that will prevent relapse. Previously, higher serum levels were used, but now maintenance levels range from 0.4 to 1.0 meq per liter with recent evidence indicating that the relapse rate is significantly increased only when serum levels fall below 0.4 meq per liter.

Lithium's excretion rate is very stable within each patient; as a result patients can be maintained on the same dose day in and day out, with relative certainty that stable levels are present. Patients during maintenance are seen every 3 to 6 months, and serum lithium, sodium, potassium, T_4, TSH, and creatinine are monitored along with urinalysis with a concentration test. The lithium excretion pattern is altered by conditions which change sodium concentrations, and patients on thiazide diuretics or low-salt diets should be monitored more frequently.

Side effects and interactions with other drugs Lithium's side effects are listed in a continuum ranging from those seen relatively commonly to those which indicate lithium toxicity (see Table 364-4). Many of these are minor side effects, which appear early and disappear as time passes, but some may persist throughout treatment. As a general rule the rapid escalation of serum levels often induces side effects, especially those involving the gastrointestinal tract, and therefore smoother, more gradual serum lithium increases are desirable.

Usually the first signs of lithium toxicity are increases in the deep tendon reflexes and muscle fasciculations. Unusual degrees of sedation and cognitive disruption also may herald lithium toxicity. Lithium toxicity mimics barbiturate intoxication, and when death occurs it is secondary to respiratory depression and its complications. The treatment involves good supportive care and excellent hydration; and since lithium's half-life is 24 h, this treatment sustains the patient while awaiting the kidney's elimination of lithium at the predictable rate. Various methods have been tried to improve the treatment of lithium toxicity, such as increasing lithium excretion by aminophylline or alkalinizing the urine, but all have been disappointing. For life-threatening cases, the last resort is renal dialysis, but toxicity rarely progresses to the point where this intervention is needed.

Lithium's interactions with other drugs primarily involve its reciprocal relationship with the sodium ion. Diuretics, which increase sodium excretion, can increase lithium toxicity. There have also been reports that combined neuroleptic and lithium therapy has resulted in a reversible neurotoxicity in a small number of middle-aged and older patients. Clinical observations indicate that this combination is safe and effective provided that the antipsychotic drug and lithium are used in low to moderate doses and are carefully monitored, and that the combination treatment is discontinued as soon as the lithium effect is sufficiently present for the patient to be managed without it.

Medical sequelae of lithium's use Several medical complications can develop during lithium treatment. Because of its effect on adenylate cyclase activity, lithium inhibits the secretory function of the thyroid gland; nontoxic goiters and hypothyroidism can develop, which can be readily corrected during lithium therapy by thyroid supplement. Lithium may induce the following ECG changes especially in older patients: T-wave depression, sinus node dysfunctions, and very rarely sinoatrial block and ventricular irritability.

The most important sequelae are the renal complications. About 25 percent of patients develop some degree of antidiuretic hormone–resistant nephrogenic diabetes insipidus with polyuria and polydipsia. The lithium inhibition of adenylate cyclase activity is responsible for the disruption of renal tubular transport. These symptoms are usually completely reversible by lithium withdrawal and often can be ameliorated by reduction in serum level. The most economic and accurate method of monitoring changes in renal function during lithium treatment is by the urine concentration test and serum creatinine level. Urine concentration levels below a specific gravity of 1.025 indicate an early renal effect, and a creatinine clearance test should be obtained. If creatinine clearance is abnormal, the patient's clinical condition is reevaluated and termination of the lithium treatment should be considered. There have been reports of renal focal necrosis and interstitial fibrosis in a few long-term lithium patients, and there is evidence, by biopsy, for an increased basal rate of renal pathology among patients with affective disorders. Nonetheless, this nonspecific renal lesion does appear with a higher degree of frequency in patients receiving long-term lithium. Therefore, many experienced clinicians do not maintain patients on lithium for more than 5 years without a drug-free trial.

Evidence has emerged linking the more serious renal complications to increased episodes of lithium toxicity and possibly to prolonged combined use of lithium and neuroleptics. While good clinical practice

TABLE 364-4 Common lithium side effects

Severity	Side effect
SIDE EFFECTS COMMONLY SEEN	
Very mild	Thirst
	Nausea (particularly during first few days of treatment)
	Fine tremor of hands
Mild to moderate	Anorexia
	Vomiting
	Diarrhea
	"Upset stomach" or "abdominal pain"
	Polydipsia and/or polyuria
	Muscular weakness and fatigue
SIDE EFFECTS INDICATING TOXICITY	
	Muscle hyperirritability with twitching, muscle fasciculation, or chronic movements
	Sedation, sluggishness, languidness, drowsiness, giddiness
	Coarse tremor
	Ataxia
Moderate to severe	Hypertonic muscles
	Hyperactive deep tendon reflexes
	Hyperextension of arms and legs with grunts and gasping
	Chorea, athetotic movements
	Impairment of consciousness
	Somnolence, confusion, stupor
	Seizures
	Transient focal neurologic signs
	Dysarthria
	Cranial nerve signs
Very severe	Coma
	Complications of coma
	Death

should obviate lithium toxicity, it may be equally important to avoid extremes of high and low serum lithium levels during the day. Despite these concerns, lithium remains one of the most important and effective psychotropic agents with an excellent risk/benefit ratio.

Carbamazepine and other mood-stabilizing medications The anticonvulsant *carbamazepine* has, in controlled trials, been used successfully in the treatment of manic and, to a lesser extent, depressive episodes in bipolar patients. There is also growing evidence that a significant number of bipolar patients who do not respond to lithium benefit from carbamazepine treatment, and that the combination of lithium and carbamazepine may be therapeutically additive. The drug regimen for bipolar disorders is initated beginning with 200 mg bid administered orally increasing to 600 to 1600 mg daily in divided doses with the therapeutic blood levels ranging from 8 to 12 mg/dL. Carbamazepine is not a completely benign drug; side effects include nausea, blurred vision, and ataxia, and more importantly there have been cases of aplastic anemia reported. Patients treated with carbamazepine must be monitored for renal, liver, and bone marrow functions during the time they are on the medication. There are also reports of reversible CNS toxicity when this drug is combined with lithium, therefore patients on this combination should be monitored carefully. *Valproic acid,* the drug of choice in certain seizure disorders, has also been reported to prevent recurrence of manic episodes in a small number of bipolar patients. The development of this new class of psychotropic compounds is very promising and may herald the future development of a new and useful group of medications.

ANTIANXIETY OR ANXIOLYTIC MEDICATIONS The development of the benzodiazepines has been a great advance in the pharmacologic management of anxiety. They have also replaced barbiturates as the sedative-hypnotic drugs of choice. The benzodiazepines, unlike the barbiturates, are not complete CNS depressants and even at high doses are rarely associated with lethal respiratory depression or vasomotor collapse. True addiction to benzodiazepine compounds is also very rare. In addition, depending upon the drug, benzodiazepines possess anticonvulsant and muscle relaxant properties as well.

Mechanisms of action There is growing evidence that gamma-aminobutyric acid (GABA), an inhibitory amino acid neurotransmitter, may play a central role in the brain mechanism(s) of anxiety. Benzodiazepines selectively, but indirectly, enhance GABA neurotransmission, possibly by increasing neuronal receptor sensitivity to GABA. Also, a close interaction has been described between GABA and benzodiazepine receptor binding, which involves the neuronal chloride ionophore channel. Despite these observations, the specific mechanism by which benzodiazepines mediate their clinical effects is not completely understood.

Clinical conditions in which anxiolytic medications are used The antianxiety medications are most effective in the management of relatively short-lived reactive states of tension and anxiety and are the drugs of choice in the treatment of generalized anxiety disorders (see Chap. 361). The anxiolytic benzodiazepines are useful in treating panic disorders but are not the drugs of choice, although alprazolam at higher doses (4 to 10 mg) can block panic attacks. Rather, it is the TCA and MAO inhibitor antidepressants which are the drugs of choice to suppress symptoms of panic disorder (see Chap. 361). However, the anxiolytics may have a role in the treatment of anticipatory anxiety, which is almost always present in patients with panic disorders. Sometimes, both a TCA and a benzodiazepine anxiolytic may be necessary in the treatment of panic disorder. The anxiolytics are also useful in the treatment of anxiety symptoms that accompany phobic disorders.

Clinical use of the antianxiety medications Clinically the benzodiazepines are divided on the basis of their use as either primarily anxiolytics or sedative-hypnotics. The more commonly prescribed drugs are listed in Table 364-5 along with the usual oral dose ranges. The pharmacokinetic characteristics of many of the benzodiazepines are complicated by long drug elimination half-lives and the metabolic conversion of parent compounds to active metabolites (see Table 364-5). Diazepam is converted to the active metabolite desmethyldiazepam (nordiazepam) which, in turn, can be hydroxylated to yield oxazepam, also a potent benzodiazepine. This metabolic pathway extends the activity half-life of diazepam threefold. The hypnotic flurazepam is converted to its active metabolite N-1-desalkylflurazepam, whose half-life is more than 48 h; hence, repetitive daily doses given in excess of a week or two can result in the accumulation of the active metabolites of the drug. Prazepam has metabolic compounds identical to those of diazepam and has a similar drug elimination half-life. Oxazepam and lorazepam, both of which undergo glucuronide conjugation, have no active metabolites and therefore have the advantage of a shorter half-life. The benzodiazepines temazepam, triazolam, and alprazolam also have the advantage of shorter half-lives and to date, no long-acting active metabolites have been identified.

Diazepam has been the standard against which all anxiolytic drugs are measured, and no other anxiolytics have demonstrated better antianxiety potency. The newly developed benzodiazepines appear equally effective and have eliminated certain of the undesirable side effects. Specifically, lorazepam, oxazepam, and alprazolam are without active metabolites and cumulative effects of daytime sedation are less noticeable.

Treatment regimens usually last 4 weeks or less and medications are prescribed continually for 7 to 10 days followed by a 2- to 3-day drug holiday; then this sequence is repeated. This helps avoids the development of tolerance to the anxiolytic effects. The shorter-acting medications (lorazepam, alprazolam, etc.) are prescribed in a three or four times daily regimen, and the longer-acting drugs (diazepam, etc.) are given in a single dose or a twice daily regimen. For example, it is common practice to prescribe one dose of diazepam at bedtime, since it will both promote sleep and reduce anxiety levels during the following day.

In prescribing the anxiolytic benzodiazepines clinicians should avoid the possibility of habituating patients to chronic benzodiazepine use. One of the earliest signs is the development of tolerance, where the patient repeatedly requests escalations in drug dose. Since benzodiazepines do produce mild euphoria and a sense of well-being, anxious patients often want to preserve this feeling and request additional medication. On the other hand, clinical surveys of prescription practices have shown that clinicans are aware of the problems of benzodiazepine habituation and sometimes respond by being too cautious and by unnecessarily undertreating patients. The use of the drug holiday treatment regimen described above and the physician's resistance to repetitively increasing dosage will help to minimize the problem of drug habituation.

In addition to its role as an anxiolytic, diazepam is also the drug of choice in this class for muscle relaxation and for the treatment of alcohol withdrawal syndromes. It is the benzodiazepine of choice for intractable seizures. Oxazepam, because of the nonaccumulation of active metabolites, is a good choice for anxiolysis in the elderly.

TABLE 364-5 More commonly used benzodiazepines

Benzodiazepines	Daily oral dose range, mg	Half-life, h*
Anxiolytics:		
Chlordiazepoxide (Librium)	20–100†	7–28*
Diazepam (Valium)	5–40†	20–90*
Lorazepam (Ativan)	1–10‡	10–12
Oxazepam (Serax)	30–120‡	3–20
Prazepam (Centrax)	20–60†	40–70*
Alprazolam (Xanax)	0.75–10.0‡	12–15
Sedative-hypnotics:		
Flurazepam (Dalmane)	15–30§	24–100*
Temazepam (Restoril)	30§	8–10
Triazolam (Halcion)	0.5–1.0§	2–5

* *Indicates long-acting active metabolites.*
† *Prescribed in a daily or twice daily regimen.*
‡ *Prescribed in a three or four times daily regimen.*
§ *Prescribed in a daily or bedtime regimen.*

Side effects and interactions with other drugs The most important adverse effect of the benzodiazepines is the discomfort caused by the withdrawal syndrome, which can occur after chronic treatment. While there is very little risk of physiologic dependence on these drugs when used appropriately, the withdrawal symptoms do contribute to the development of psychological habituation. Between 40 and 50 percent of patients develop minor withdrawal symptoms after cessation of chronic benzodiazepine treatment. Symptoms include muscle aches, agitation, restlessness, insomnia, and generalized anxious dysphoria. In some patients more serious CNS withdrawal symptoms may appear, including confusional and delirium states and, more rarely, grand mal seizures. Rebound anxiety can also be seen in patients with anxiety disorders but is less prevalent when benzodiazepines with long-acting metabolites are used and less frequent if the drug is gradually discontinued. Risk for withdrawal increases with the length of the treatment and is reported with much greater frequency (e.g., more than 90 percent) among patients who have been treated for 1 year or more. Withdrawal symptoms occur within the first 24 to 48 h after cessation of drug use in the short-acting benzodiazepines, but in those benzodiazepines with long-acting metabolites (e.g., diazepam, chlordiazepoxide), the withdrawal symptoms can occur 4 to 6 days and even longer after drug cessation. With the usual recommended dosage regimens and the gradual withdrawal technique (e.g., over 3 to 4 weeks), the appearance of a withdrawal syndrome in patients can be minimized significantly. While there is little true addiction potential, patients should be on these medications for only as long as necessary.

The most common minor side effects are daytime sedation, mild cognitive impairment, motor clumsiness and, with some drugs, specific memory decrements (e.g., lorazepam). Another rare but troublesome side effect from some benzodiazepines is paradoxical emotional responses, primarily manifested as aggressive and impulsive behavior.

Unlike barbiturates, the benzodiazepines do not noticeably induce hepatic microsomal enzyme activity and therefore do not affect the metabolism of other medications. Their primary interaction with other drugs is their additive effects with other CNS depressants. The cross-tolerance with ethanol has made the benzodiazepines ideal medications for the treatment of alcohol withdrawal syndromes. Patients should be cautioned that ethanol is potentiated by benzodiazepines and this combination ought to be avoided.

The newer anxiolytic medications It has been established that certain beta-adrenergic blocking agents, such as *propranolol,* can dampen the peripheral physiologic symptoms of anxiety. Initially, it was felt that these drugs might be better nonsedative anxiolytic compounds, but this has not held up in controlled studies. While propranolol does attenuate somatic manifestations of anxiety (e.g., palpitations, tremor), it appears to have lesser effects on the psychological components (e.g., intense fearfulness). Although propranolol has been used in the treatment of severe cases of fear of public speaking and in musicians (oral dose 40 to 320 mg qd), it is not a comprehensively effective anxiolytic. It is possible that with additional study other peripheral blocking agents may prove to be more effective.

A new class of anxiolytic drugs, the azaspirodecanediones, has been developed. One of the first compounds studied clinically is *buspirone.* It has little structural similarity to other anxiolytics or even to other psychotropics. It is not anticonvulsant, does not interact with the putative benzodiazepine receptor, is not cross-tolerant to other CNS depressants, and no abstinence syndrome has yet been described. In several controlled trials it has proved to be an effective anxiolytic with relatively less sedation and decrements in psychomotor performance. To date it has not been extensively studied and it is possible that efficacy problems and as yet unidentified side effects may be associated with its use.

In addition to their efficacy in panic and phobic disorders, there are controlled studies reporting that *tricyclic antidepressants* are anxiolytics as effective as the benzodiazepines in generalized anxiety disorders. It is possible that continued investigations will identify a broader role for TCAs in the treatment of the full spectrum of anxiety disorders.

ANTIPSYCHOTIC OR NEUROLEPTIC MEDICATIONS The antipsychotics have the capacity to sedate, tranquilize, blunt emotional expression, attenuate aggressive and impulsive behavior, and cause disinterest in the environment and lack of initiative. Unique features of the drugs are that higher intellectual functions are left relatively intact and yet they act to specifically ameliorate the agitation and bizarre behavior and thinking of psychotic patients. Unfortunately no antipsychotic medication currently available even approaches what an ideal drug in this group should be. Virtually all have prominent anticholinergic side effects and produce a wide variety of dystonias and extrapyramidal symptoms. Of greater concern is the fact that these agents cause tardive dyskinesia (see Chap. 15), a seriously disabling movement disorder that is often irreversible. Nonetheless, the antipsychotics, primarily used in schizophrenia, have reduced enormously the patient populations in mental hospitals and have allowed for maintenance in the community of chronic mentally ill patients who before the advent of neuroleptics would have been lifelong residents of hospitals.

Mechanism of action of the antipsychotics With few exceptions, antipsychotics have notable effects on the brain's dopaminergic neurotransmitter system. Specifically, antipsychotics antagonize the effects of the neurotransmitter dopamine in the basal ganglia and in the limbic portions of the forebrain. Since one of the central characteristics of neuroleptics is their capacity to block dopaminergic neurotransmission, this has led researchers to postulate that abnormalities in the CNS dopaminergic neurotransmitter systems are one of the central underlying pathophysiologic mechanisms in the etiology of schizophrenia. While specific aspects of the brain mechanism(s) by which the antipsychotics mediate their effects have been well-established, the full and detailed understanding of how these drugs actually work is not yet available.

Clinical conditions in which the antipsychotic medications are used Because the risk of tardive dyskinesia is significant, antipsychotics should only be used when necessary and in those conditions for which they are the drug of choice. Antipsychotics are drugs of choice in the treatment of schizophrenic disorders (see Chap. 362), in combination with lithium for acute manic episodes (see Chap. 360), and in combination with antidepressants for psychotic and agitated depressions. They are also used in Tourette's syndrome and Huntington's disease. There is a relatively narrow spectrum of mental disorders for which the antipsychotics should be used, although these disorders, in terms of sheer numbers of patients, make up a significant majority of patients with serious and chronic mental illness.

Clinical use of the antipsychotics The more commonly used antipsychotics from each of the pharmacologic classes and their average daily oral doses are given in Table 364-6. Chlorpromazine, one of the first drugs of this class developed, is the prototype antipsychotic drug and is the potency standard for the others. Dose equivalency for the antipsychotics is calculated on a ratio of the effect of that particular drug compared to the effect of 100 mg of chlorpromazine. For example, 5 mg of trifluoperazine or 2 mg of haloperidol is equivalent in potency to 100 mg of chlorpromazine. Using this ratio as a reference point, acutely psychotic patients usually require an accumulated dose of 500 to 800 mg orally of a chlorpromazine equivalent during the first 24 to 36 h. Following control of the acute agitation, the oral dose is increased over the next week to the chlorpromazine equivalent of between 600 and 1500 mg a day in divided doses. It is uncommon for therapeutic benefits to be measurably increased by exceeding the daily dose equivalent of 1500 mg of chlorpromazine, although it may be necessary to go to two and three times this level in some patients.

Schizophrenia is a chronic disorder and patients need long-term maintenance on antipsychotics to prevent relapse. In controlled studies as many as 60 percent of schizophrenics relapse within 6 months

TABLE 364-6   Some of the more commonly used antipsychotic medications

	Average daily oral dose range, mg	Potency ratio compared to 100 mg of chlorpromazine
Phenothiazines:		
Aliphatics:		
Chlorpromazine (Thorazine)	400–800	1:1
Piperazines:		
Fluphenazine (Pro-lixin)	4–20	1:50
Fluphenazine enan-thate or decanoate	25–100*	
Perphenazine (Trila-fon)	8–32	1:10
Trifluoperazine (Ste-lazine)	6–20	1:20
Piperidines:		
Thioridazone (Mel-laril)	200–600	1:1 (approx)
Butyrophenones:		
Haloperidol (Haldol)	8–32	1:50
Thioxanthenes:		
Chlorprothixene (Tar-actan)	400–800	1:1
Thiothixene (Navane)	15–30	1:25
Oxoindoles:		
Molindone (Moban, Li-done)	40–200	1:10
Dibenzoxazepines:		
Loxapine (Loxitane, Daxolin)	60–100	1:10

* Intramuscular injection, long acting, every 1–3 weeks

after discontinuing drug therapy. Patients are maintained on the lowest dose possible that will prevent reemergence of symptoms. This is usually in the range of 20 percent of the peak dose level needed to ameliorate the acute phase of the psychotic symptoms. Compliance is difficult to achieve in this chronically disordered group of patients, and it is often therapeutically advantageous for the clinician to use parenteral long-acting fluphenazine enanthate or decanoate, which can be administered by injection every week or two. Previously it was recommended that drug holidays be used, but this has not prevented tardive dyskinesia and there are few if any advantages to this technique, which is now rarely used.

Side effects and interactions with other drugs   Initially patients are sedated, lethargic, and drowsy, but within days they develop tolerance to these effects. All of the antipsychotics have anticholinergic action, which may produce dry mouth, cycloplegia, postural hypotension, constipation, and urinary retention. Obstructive jaundice, retinal pigmentation, lenticular opacities, skin pigmentation and hypersensitivity to sunlight, and male impotence are also side effects seen with antipsychotics.

It is the extrapyramidal side effects that are the most bothersome. During the first five days of treatment patients may develop acute muscular dystonic reactions but the extrapyramidal Parkinson-like syndrome is the most common. Both the dystonias and the parkinsonism respond well to antiparkinsonian medications (benztropine mesylate, 1 to 2 mg bid or tid; trihexyphenidyl, 2 to 5 mg bid or tid, etc.). Another common side effect is akathisia, a motor restlessness in which patients feel compelled to move their extremities and to move about. It is not uncommon to mistake akathisia for psychotic agitation and increase the antipsychotic dose, exacerbating the problem. Akathisia may respond to antiparkinsonian agents but more often requires decreasing the dose of the antipsychotic. It is rarely necessary to continue antiparkinsonian drug treatment beyond the first 3 months of antipsychotic maintenance.

The most serious side effect of the antipsychotics is *tardive dyskinesia*, which has been seen with virtually every neuroleptic. The specter of tardive dyskinesia has altered the risk/benefit ratio of the antipsychotics so that exposure to these drugs should be reserved for those disorders in which these compounds are clearly the drugs of choice. Usually the symptoms of tardive dyskinesia appear late and consist of involuntary, repetitive movements of the lips, tongue (tongue thrusting, lip smacking, etc.) and not infrequently, of the extremities and trunk. Patients over 60 and those with preexisting CNS pathology are at a higher risk for this disorder, but no other risk factors have been identified. Further, no method of prevention or effective treatment for this frequently irreversible disorder has been developed. Mild to moderate tardive dyskinesia has been found in 10 to 20 percent of chronically hospitalized schizophrenics.

The *malignant neuroleptic syndrome*, a rare complication of neuroleptic drugs, is discussed in Chap. 8.

Newer antipsychotic drugs   The newer antipsychotic drugs offer, at best, only slight improvements in the side effect profile over the older drugs and achieve little or no improvement in clinical effectiveness. Two of the more promising new antipsychotics are *clozapine* and *sulpiride*, but they are not routinely available in the United States. Each has a different molecular structure from the other neuroleptics, which may herald the development of new classes of safer and better antipsychotics.

REFERENCES

APPLETON WS, DAVIS JM: *Practical Clinical Psychopharmacology*, 2d ed. Baltimore, Williams & Wilkins, 1980

BALDESSARINI RJ: *Chemotherapy in Psychiatry*. Cambridge, Mass., Harvard, 1985, pp 1–354

BOEHNERT MT, LOVEJOY FH JR: Value of the QRS duration versus the serum drug level in predicting seizures and ventricular arrhythmias after an acute overdose of tricyclic antidepressants. N Engl J Med 313:474, 1985

CALLAHAM M, KASSEL D: Epidemiology of fatal tricyclic antidepressant ingestion: Implications for management. Ann Emerg Med 14:1, 1985

CLARK WG, DEL GUIDICE J (eds): *Principles of Psychopharmacology*, 2d ed. New York, Academic, 1978

COOPER TB et al (eds): *Lithium: Controversies and Unresolved Issues*, Amsterdam, Excerpta Medica, 1979

GILMAN AG, GOODMAN LS (eds): *The Pharmacological Basis of Therapeutics*, 7th ed. New York, MacMillan, 1985

GUZÉ BH, BAXTER LR JR: Current concepts: Malignant neuroleptic syndrome. N Engl J Med 313:163, 1985

HANESTON PD: *Drug Interactions*, 3d ed. Philadelphia, Lea & Febiger, 1975

HIPPUIS H, WINOKUR G (eds): Part 2, clinical psychopharmacology, in *Psychopharmacology 1*. Amsterdam, Excerpta Medica, 1983

HOLLISTER, LE: *Clinical Pharmacology of Psychotherapeutic Drugs*. New York, Churchill Livingston, 1978

IVERSON LL, SNYDER SS (eds): *Handbook of Psychopharmacology*. New York, Plenum, 1977

JARVIK ME: *Psychopharmacology in the Practice of Medicine*. New York, Appleton-Century-Crofts, 1977

KLEIN DF et al: *Diagnosis and Drug Treatment of Psychiatric Disorders: Adults and Children*, 2d ed. Baltimore, Williams & Wilkins, 1980

POST RM, BALLENGER JC (eds): Neurobiology of mood disorders, in *Frontiers of Clinical Neuroscience*. Baltimore, Williams & Wilkins, 1984, vol 1

SHADER RI: *Psychiatric Complications of Medical Drugs*. New York, Raven Press, 1972

365 ALCOHOL AND ALCOHOLISM

MARC A. SCHUCKIT

Ninety percent of people drink alcohol, 40 to 50 percent of men have temporary alcohol-induced problems, and 10 percent of men and 3 to 5 percent of women develop pervasive and persistent alcohol-related problems (alcoholism). Even light drinking may adversely interact with other medications, temporary heavier drinking can exacerbate most medical illnesses, and alcoholism can masquerade as many different medical disorders and psychiatric syndromes. The following sections describe the pharmacology and clinical effects of alcohol and identify circumstances where drinking may cause a major medical or psychiatric problem or exacerbate a preexisting disorder. While these comments apply to the hypothetical "average" person, there is considerable individual variability depending on genetic vulnerability, concomitant drug use and prior unrelated pathology or disease.

PHARMACOLOGY OF ETHANOL: ABSORPTION AND METABOLISM Ethanol is a weakly charged molecule that moves easily through cell membranes, rapidly equilibrating between blood and tissues. The effects of drinking depend in part on the amount of ethanol consumed per unit of body weight; the level of alcohol in the blood is expressed as milligrams or grams of ethanol per deciliter (e.g., 100 mg/dL or 0.1000 g/dL). In round figures, 12 oz of beer, 4 oz of nonfortified wine, and 1.5 oz (a shot) of 80-proof beverage each contain approximately 10 g of ethanol; 1 pint of 86-proof beverage contains approximately 160 g and 1 liter of wine contains approximately 80 g of ethanol. Congeners found in alcohol beverages may contribute to body damage with heavy drinking; these include low-molecular-weight alcohols (e.g. methanol and butanol), aldehydes, esters, histamine, phenols, tannins, iron, lead, and cobalt.

Ethanol is a central nervous system (CNS) depressant that decreases activity of neurons, although some behavioral stimulation is observed at low blood levels. This drug has cross-tolerance and shares a similar pattern of behavioral problems with other brain depressants, including the benzodiazepines, barbiturates, and other sedatives and hypnotics. Alcohol is absorbed from mucus membranes of the mouth and esophagus (in very small amounts), from the stomach and large bowel (in modest amounts), and from the proximal portion of the small intestine (the major site). The rate of absorption *increases* with rapid gastric emptying; the absence of proteins, fats, or carbohydrates (which interfere with absorption); the absence of congeners; dilution to a modest percentage of ethanol (maximum absorption is seen at about 20 percent by volume); and carbonation (champagne).

Between 2 percent (at low blood alcohol concentrations) and about 10 percent (at high blood alcohol concentrations) of ethanol is excreted directly through the lungs, urine, or sweat, but the greater part is metabolized to acetaldehyde in the liver. At least two metabolic routes, each with different optimal concentrations of ethanol (K_m), result in the metabolism of approximately one drink per hour. The *first* and clinically most important pathway occurs in the cell cytosol via alcohol dehydrogenase (ADH) with a K_m of about 2 mmol. This reaction produces acetaldehyde which is then rapidly destroyed by aldehyde dehydrogenase (ALDH) in the cytosol and mitochondria. Each of these steps requires nicotinamide adenine dinucleotide (NAD) as a cofactor, and it is the increased ratio of the reduced cofactor

(NADH) to NAD (NADH:NAD) that is responsible for many of the metabolic derangements observed after drinking. *Second*, microsomes of the smooth endoplasmic reticulum (the microsomal ethanol-oxidizing system or MEOS) with a K_m of about 10 mmol may be responsible for 10 percent or more of ethanol oxidation at high blood alcohol concentrations. Increased activity of this system can be induced after repeated exposure to ethanol.

All pathways result in the production of acetaldehyde, which is oxidized to acetate. The clinical significance of acetaldehyde is not known, but accumulation in liver, brain, or other body tissues may cause organ damage.

BEHAVIORAL EFFECTS, TOLERANCE, AND DEPENDENCE The behavioral and physiologic effects of any drug depend upon the dose, its rate of increase in plasma, the concomitance of other drugs or medical problems, and the past experience with the agent. With alcohol, one must also consider whether observation is during rising (where the effects are more intense) or falling blood alcohol levels.

Even though "legal intoxication" requires a blood alcohol concentration of at least 80 to 100 mg/dL (0.1 g/dL), behavioral, psychomotor, and cognitive changes are seen at levels as low as 20 to 30 mg/dL (i.e., after one to two drinks). Narcosis or deep sleep is induced in many people at twice the legal intoxication level, and even in the absence of concomitant medications, death can occur with levels between 300 and 400 mg/dL. Ethanol, either alone or in combination with agents such as benzodiazepines, is probably responsible for more toxic overdose deaths than any other agent.

The mechanisms of action of ethanol on nervous tissues are not fully understood because even modest doses simultaneously change many neurotransmitters and increase the fluidity of neuronal cell membranes. After repeated exposure to the drug, the body compensates in at least three ways to tolerate higher ethanol levels. *First,* after 1 to 2 weeks of daily drinking the liver can increase the metabolic rate of ethanol in humans by as much as 30 percent; i.e., there is *metabolic or pharmacokinetic tolerance,* an adaptation that disappears almost as rapidly as it develops. *Second,* cellular or *pharmacodynamic tolerance* probably occurs through complex neurochemical adaptations or changes in cell membranes with subsequent altered ion flow—changes that may contribute to physical dependence. *Third,* even at the same blood alcohol concentrations and neuronal adaptation, organisms can learn to adapt behavior and to function better than expected under drug influence (*behavioral tolerance*). For example, practicing driving while intoxicated might result in a psychomotor performance which (*while still impaired*) is better than that observed before practice.

Once the cells have adapted to chronic ethanol exposure, the structural or biochemical changes may not return to normal for several weeks or more. In the face of these adaptations, the neurons require ethanol to function optimally; i.e., the person is physically addicted or drug-dependent. This physical condition is distinct from psychological dependence, a poorly defined concept indicating that the person is psychologically uncomfortable without the drug.

NUTRITIONAL FACTORS One gram of ethanol has approximately 7.1 kcal, and a drink contains between 70 and 100 kcal from ethanol and other carbohydrates. Therefore, 8 to 10 drinks can yield over 1000 kcal per day, but these are "empty" of nutrients such as minerals, proteins, and vitamins.

Any vitamin absorbed through the small intestine by active transport or stored in the liver can be deficient in alcoholics. These include folate (folacin or folic acid), pyridoxine (B$_6$), thiamine (vitamin B$_1$), nicotinic acid or niacin (B$_3$), and vitamin A. Thiamine deficiency causes Wernicke's and Korsakoff's syndromes (see Chap. 349).

Low blood potassium, magnesium, calcium, zinc, and phosphorous can occur as a consequence of dietary deficiency and acid-base imbalances during excess alcohol ingestion or withdrawal. Hypokalemia can lead to periodic muscle paralysis and areflexia. Deficiencies in magnesium can add to a clouded sensorium and other neurologic symptoms; hypocalcemia can cause tetany and weakness; low levels of zinc are speculated to contribute to gonadal dysfunction, anorexia, problems with wound healing, and immune deficiencies; and low phosphate levels can contribute to myocardial failure, brain dysfunction, weakness of muscles (including those of respiration), and white blood cell and platelet dysfunction.

An ethanol load in a fasting, healthy individual is likely to produce transient hypoglycemia within 6 to 36 h, secondary to the acute actions of ethanol on gluconeogenesis. This impairment is exacerbated by poor diet and by liver and pancreatic disease. As a result, glucose intolerance may be marked until the alcoholic has been abstinent for 2 to 4 weeks. Alcohol ketoacidosis, probably reflecting a decrease in fatty acid oxidation coupled with poor diet or recurrent vomiting, should not be misdiagnosed as diabetic ketosis. With the former, patients show an increase in serum ketones along with a mild increase in glucose but a large anion gap, a mild to moderate increase in serum lactate, and a β-hydroxybutyrate/lactate ratio of between 2:1 and 9:1 (with normal being 1:1).

THE EFFECTS OF ETHANOL ON BODY SYSTEMS

This overview of acute and chronic effects of alcohol on body systems outlines signs and symptoms that can aid in the recognition of the hidden alcoholic. It emphasizes the interactions between drinking and medications and the effects of alcohol on chronic medical conditions.

CENTRAL NERVOUS SYSTEM In addition to acute behavioral effects, an evening of heavy drinking can result in an alcoholic "*blackout*," i.e., an episode of forgetting all or part of what occurred during drinking. This problem is experienced by 30 to 40 percent of men in their late teens and early 20s, most of whom do not go on to develop more serious and pervasive alcohol-related problems. Even after only a few drinks, alcohol acutely decreases *sleep* latency (helping people to fall asleep) and depresses rapid eye movement (REM) sleep early in the night, sometimes followed by later REM rebound associated with bad dreams. The consequence is to "fragment" sleep, causing a more rapid than normal alternation between sleep stages and a deficiency in deep sleep.

Chronic intake of high doses of ethanol can cause *peripheral neuropathy* in 5 to 15 percent of alcoholics (see Chaps. 349 and 355). This syndrome probably results from both thiamine deficiency and direct effects of ethanol and/or acetaldehyde. Patients complain of bilateral limb numbness, tingling, and parasthesias, more pronounced distally than proximally. Although these symptoms can be incapacitating, more often the pain and numbness are mild to moderate in severity. The treatment is abstinence and thiamine supplementation.

Wernicke's and Korsakoff's syndromes are important problems in alcoholics (see Chap. 349). Thiamine deficiency is the major cause in vulnerable individuals (possibly interacting with a genetic transketolase deficiency). Classically, patients with Korsakoff's syndrome present with profound anterograde and retrograde amnesia along with possible impairment in visuospatial, abstract, and conceptual reasoning but with a normal intelligence quotient (IQ). In general, the level of recent memory loss is out of proportion to the global level of cognitive impairment. While most patients demonstrate an acute onset of Korsakoff's syndrome in association with the neurologic stigmata seen with Wernicke's syndrome (e.g., sixth nerve palsy and ataxia), some individuals may have a more gradual development of symptoms probably secondary to repeated bouts of thiamine deficiency. Wer-

nicke's syndrome responds rapidly to oral thiamine replacement of 50 to 100 mg followed by 50 to 100 mg per day. However, only one-quarter of Korsakoff's patients are likely to achieve full recovery, one-half experience partial recovery, and one-quarter show no improvement with thiamine even after many months of supplementation.

About 1 percent of alcoholics with long histories of associated malnutrition develop *cerebellar degeneration,* a syndrome of progressive unsteady stance and gait often accompanied by mild nystagmus (see Chap. 349). Cerebellar atrophy is seen on computerized tomography (CT) scans but the cerebrospinal fluid is usually normal. While ethanol or acetaldehyde might contribute to the problem, the major cause is probably nutritional, and identical symptoms can be seen with some forms of severe malnutrition alone. Treatment consists of abstinence and multiple vitamin supplementation.

Alcoholics can show severe *cognitive* problems and impairment in recent and remote memory for weeks to months after an alcoholic binge. Cortical functioning (e.g., psychomotor performance and short-term memory) tends to improve with abstinence, but long-term memory problems, perhaps reflecting subcortical damage, may persist. Increased size of the brain ventricles and cerebral sulci are seen in up to 50 percent of chronic alcoholics. These changes are partially reversible, returning toward normal after a year or more of abstinence. Permanent CNS impairment (*alcoholic dementia*) may supervene. Up to 20 percent of chronically demented patients may have had prior alcoholism. There is no single alcoholic dementia syndrome; rather, this label is used to describe patients who have apparently irreversible cognitive changes (possibly from diverse causes) in the midst of chronic alcoholism (see also Chap. 349).

Finally, to borrow a phrase from the past, alcohol could be termed "the great mimicker" because almost every psychiatric syndrome can be seen during heavy drinking or subsequent withdrawal. This includes intense *sadness* lasting for days to weeks in the midst of heavy drinking, severe *anxiety* during alcoholic withdrawal and remaining for many months after cessation of drinking, *psychoses* during the severe form of the alcohol abstinence syndrome, and auditory *hallucinations* and/or *paranoid delusions* in the absence of any obvious signs of withdrawal—a state called alcoholic hallucinosis or alcoholic paranoia. Whatever the cause, the treatment of alcohol-induced psychopathology includes abstinence and supportive care, with the likelihood of full recovery within several days or weeks. Another alcohol-related psychiatric syndrome is *pathologic intoxication* or alcohol idiosyncratic intoxication, a state of severe agitation, confusion, and violence lasting minutes to hours which is seen after a very low dose of ethanol (e.g., one to two drinks) and for which the individual is amnestic. This extremely rare phenomenon, seen almost exclusively in individuals with severe preexisting brain damage, is sometimes invoked erroneously for the purposes of legal defense.

THE GASTROINTESTINAL SYSTEM Esophagus and stomach Acute alcoholic intake can result in inflammation of the esophagus (possibly secondary to reflux of gastric contents) and stomach (resulting from damage to the gastric mucosal barrier). Esophagitis can cause epigastric distress, and gastritis, the most frequent cause of gastrointestinal bleeding in heavy drinkers, can present with anorexia and abdominal pain. Chronic heavy drinking, if associated with violent vomiting, can produce a longitudinal tear in the mucosa at the gastroesophageal junction—a Mallory-Weiss lesion. Although many gastrointestinal problems are reversible, two complications of chronic alcoholism, esophageal varices secondary to cirrhosis-induced portal hypertension and atrophy of gastric cells, may be irreversible (see Chaps. 234 and 236).

Small bowel The greater part of the ethanol is absorbed from the proximal small bowel, where it may interfere with absorption of B vitamins and other nutrients. Acutely, ethanol can cause hemorrhagic lesions of the duodenal villi and diarrhea secondary to increased small-bowel motility and decreased water and electrolyte absorption.

Chronic alcoholism can contribute to diarrhea through its effects on the pancreas (see Chaps. 237 and 255).

Pancreas Alcoholics commonly develop acute or chronic pancreatitis (see Chap. 255).

Liver Ethanol absorbed from the small bowel is carried directly to the liver, where it becomes the preferred fuel; NADH accumulates and oxygen utilization escalates, gluconeogenesis is impaired (with a resulting fall in the amount of glucose produced from glycogen), lactate production increases, and there is a decreased oxidation of fatty acids in the citric cycle with an increase in fat accumulation within liver cells. In the healthy individual taking no medications these changes are reversible, but with repeated exposure to ethanol more severe changes in liver functioning are likely to occur. These include, in overlapping stages, fatty accumulation, alcohol-induced hepatitis, and cirrhosis (see Chap. 249).

Increased cancer risk Cancer is the second leading cause of death in alcoholics (after cardiovascular disease), who have a rate of carcinoma 10 times higher than that expected in the general population. The sites with the greatest increase over expected rates include the head and neck, esophagus, cardia of the stomach, liver, and pancreas.

HEMATOPOIETIC SYSTEM Ethanol exerts multiple reversible acute and chronic effects on all blood cells. Alcohol alters acutely the production of red blood cells (RBC), which reaches clinical significance after days to weeks of heavy drinking. The most common finding is an increase in RBC size (mean corpuscular volume, MCV) with a mild anemia. If this is accompanied by folic acid deficiency, there can also be hypersegmented neutrophils, reticulocytopenia, and hyperplastic bone marrow. Other forms of anemia, including sideroblastic changes, can occur concomitantly, especially in the presence of severe malnutrition.

Chronic heavy drinking can also decrease production of most white blood cells (WBC), decrease granulocyte mobility and adherence, and impair the delayed hypersensitivity response to new antigens (with a possible false-negative tuberculin skin test). While the changes in WBCs themselves are usually temporary, they may contribute to the risk of infections, liver damage, and perhaps to the increased risk of cancers in alcoholics. Alcohol can also cause toxic granulocytosis.

Many alcoholics present with mild thrombocytopenia (rarely associated with hemorrhage) due to a decrease in platelet survival and altered function; hypersplenism may occur as a complication of cirrhosis. Alcohol may decrease platelet aggregation and inhibit release of thromboxane A_2. These problems usually return toward normal within a week of abstinence.

CARDIOVASCULAR SYSTEM Modest doses of alcohol can have both deleterious and beneficial effects in individuals with normal cardiovascular status who take no medications. Ethanol decreases myocardial contractility and causes peripheral vasodilatation resulting in a mild drop in blood pressure and a compensatory increased heart rate and cardiac output. Exercise-induced increases in cardiac oxygen consumption are higher after alcohol. On the other hand, one to two drinks per day over long periods may decrease the risk of cardiovascular death, perhaps through an increase in high density lipoprotein cholesterol (HDL) or changes in clotting mechanisms.

Although ethanol in low doses causes a mild acute drop in blood pressure, the consumption of three or more drinks per day results in a dose-dependent increase in blood pressure which returns to normal within weeks of abstinence. Chronic heavy drinking can cause cardiomyopathy with symptoms ranging from unexplained arrhythmias in the presence of left ventricular impairment to heart failure with dilatation of all four heart chambers and hypocontractility of heart muscle. Mural thrombi can form in the left atrium or ventricle, while heart enlargement exceeding 25 percent can cause mitral regurgitation. Finally, there is an association between cerebrovascular accidents and alcoholism, especially within 24 h of heavy drinking. Atrial or ventricular arrhythmias, especially paroxysmal tachycardia,

can also occur after a binge in individuals showing no other evidence of heart-disease—a syndrome known as the "holiday heart."

GENITOURINARY SYSTEM CHANGES, SEXUAL FUNCTIONING, AND FETAL DEVELOPMENT Acutely, modest ethanol doses (e.g., blood alcohol concentrations of 100 mg/dL or even less) increase sexual drive in men. However, modest ethanol doses may simultaneously decrease erectile capacity. Even in the absence of liver impairment, a significant minority of chronic alcoholic men may show irreversible testicular atrophy with concomitant shrinkage of the seminiferous tubules and loss of sperm cells (see Chap. 330).

The repeated administration of ethanol to women can result in amenorrhea, a decrease in ovarian size, an absence of corpora lutea with associated infertility, and spontaneous abortions. Heavy drinking during pregnancy results in the rapid placental transfer of both ethanol and acetaldehyde, which may have serious consequences for fetal development. The *fetal alcohol syndrome* can include a mixture of any of the following: facial changes with epicanthal eye folds, poorly formed concha, and small teeth with faulty enamel; cardiac atrial or ventricular septal defects; an aberrant palmar crease and limitation in joint movement; and microcephaly with mental retardation. More severe syndromes occur with heavy and persistent drinking, although the specific amount of ethanol and/or specific time of vulnerability during pregnancy have not been defined. Considering the possibility that one to two drinks per day might increase the risk for mild aspects of this syndrome, it is advisable for pregnant women to abstain completely.

OTHER EFFECTS OF ETHANOL Heavy drinking can produce an acute *alcoholic myopathy* characterized by painful and swollen muscles, high levels of serum creatine phosphokinase (CK), and rarely myoglobinemia and myoglobinuria. Effects on the *skeletal system* include alterations in calcium metabolism with an increased risk for fractures and osteonecrosis of the femoral head. *Hormonal* changes include an increase in cortisol levels, which can remain elevated during heavy drinking; inhibition of vasopressin secretion at rising blood alcohol concentrations and the opposite at falling blood alcohol concentrations, with the final result that most alcoholics are likely to be slightly overhydrated; a modest decrease in serum thyroxine (T_4); and a more marked decrease in serum triiodothyronine (T_3). After weeks of abstinence, T_4 and T_3 levels usually return to normal.

ALCOHOLISM

Because many drinkers occasionally imbibe to excess, temporary alcohol-related pathology is common in nonalcoholics. The time of heaviest drinking is usually the late teens to the late twenties when between one-third and one-half of male drinkers experience some isolated (although potentially dangerous) alcohol-related social, occupational, or driving difficulty. These include alcohol-related blackouts, a single drunk driving arrest, arguments with friends, and so on. This prevalent alcohol-related morbidity, however, is temporary and a separate problem from alcoholism. The following sections describe diagnostic criteria for alcoholism, offer suggestions for identifying the usual (i.e., middle-class) alcoholic in everyday medical practice, review evidence that alcoholism is a biologic and genetically influenced disorder, and offer advice on confrontation, detoxification, and rehabilitation of alcoholics.

DEFINITIONS AND EPIDEMIOLOGY The original version of the Third Diagnostic and Statistical Manual of the American Psychiatric Association (DSM-III) divides alcoholism into alcohol abuse and alcohol dependence, but this distinction may not be clinically relevant. *Alcohol abuse* indicates psychological dependence, i.e., the need for alcohol for adequate functioning, along with occasional heavy consumption, and continuation of drinking despite social or occupational problems. *Alcohol dependence* encompasses similar impairment *along* *with* evidence of increased ethanol tolerance or physical signs on withdrawal from alcohol.

A modified approach to a definition of alcoholism is easier to apply in clinical settings. The diagnosis of *alcoholism* is made when an individual ignores the early warning signs that alcohol is causing problems in marriage and goes on to an alcohol-related marital separation or divorce; *or* when alcohol-related problems on the job actually result in the patient being fired or laid off; *or* when there are two or more arrests related to alcohol; *or* when there is physical evidence that alcohol has harmed health (e.g., cardiomyopathy, cirrhosis, alcoholic hepatitis), including signs of alcoholic withdrawal.

It is important to distinguish between *primary and secondary alcoholism*. For example, serious alcohol-related problems occurring during the course of mania or a preexisting antisocial personality disorder (i.e., secondary alcoholism) might be symptomatic of the primary diagnosis, and the course is likely to be that of the primary disorder, not alcoholism. The information on alcoholism offered in this chapter is relevant for *primary alcoholism*. This diagnosis applies to the majority of alcoholics (70 to 80 percent) who develop major life problems from alcohol *before* they fulfill criteria for any other major psychiatric illness.

Using this or similar criteria, the lifetime risk for primary alcoholism in most western countries is about 10 percent for men and 3 to 5 percent for women. Alcoholism is seen in all races, ethnic groups, and socioeconomic strata and, therefore, the average alcoholic (just as the average person) is a blue-collar or white-collar worker or housewife. The homeless or skid row alcoholic represents only 5 percent or less of alcoholics.

GENETICS OF ALCOHOLISM There is strong evidence that alcoholism is a multifactorial disorder in which biologic and genetic factors interact. The importance of genetic factors in alcoholism is supported by family, twin, and adoption studies. Close relatives of primary alcoholics have an approximate fourfold increased risk for the disorder but are not significantly more vulnerable for other psychiatric illnesses. The probability that the familial nature of the problem is in part a consequence of genetic factors is supported by twin research, where the risk for the identical twin of an alcoholic is about 60 percent while the concordance rate for fraternal twins is only about 30 percent. Finally, adoption studies reveal that the fourfold increased risk for children of alcoholics is true even if they were adopted away at birth and raised without knowledge of the problems of their biologic parents.

The evidence supporting genetic influences in alcoholism has stimulated numerous studies of children of alcoholics. The goal is to identify possible trait markers of a vulnerability toward the disorder before alcoholism appears. For example, some studies suggest that these children become significantly less intoxicated at a given blood alcohol concentration than do controls, even before alcoholism develops. After modest alcohol doses, the sons of alcoholics report less intense subjective feelings of intoxication, show less alcohol-related impairment in cognitive and psychomotor tests, and have less intense changes in prolactin and cortisol secretion than do controls. However, after heavy alcohol intake the differences between the two groups are less marked. These data may indicate that men at high future risk for alcoholism may be less able than controls to tell when they are beginning to become intoxicated. Taken as a whole these data underscore the probability that alcoholism is biologically influenced and not related to a lack of "moral fiber." It is not surprising that the average alcoholic may continue to work, has a family, and may be difficult to identify if the physician persists with old stereotypes.

NATURAL HISTORY For the "average" alcoholic, the age of first drink and first minor problems (e.g., an argument with a friend while drunk or an alcoholic blackout) are similar to those in the general population. However, by the mid to late twenties, most men and women moderate their drinking (perhaps learning from minor problems), whereas difficulties for alcoholics are likely to escalate, with the first major life problem from alcohol appearing in the late twenties to early forties. Once established, the course of alcoholism is likely to be one of exacerbations and remissions; the alcoholic becomes frightened when a problem develops and abstains for a period of days to months before experimenting with controlled drinking; this step almost inevitably results in escalation of drinking and problems. The course is not hopeless because a fifth or more achieve permanent abstinence without formal treatment or aid from self-help groups such as Alcoholics Anonymous (AA). However, should the alcoholic continue to drink, the life span is shortened by an average of 15 years with the leading causes of death, in decreasing order, being heart disease, cancer, accidents, and suicide.

IDENTIFICATION AND CONFRONTATION OF THE ALCOHOLIC
The physician should recognize that any patient may have alcoholism and must therefore pay attention to physical findings and laboratory tests that are likely to be abnormal in the alcoholic. These include a high normal or slightly elevated MCV, γ-glutamyl transferase (GGT) (35 to 40 or more units), serum uric acid (greater than 7 mg/dL), and triglycerides (180 mg/dL or more). Mild and fluctuating levels of hypertension (e.g., 140/95), repeated infections such as pneumonia, and otherwise unexplained cardiac arrhythmias all suggest that the patient might be an alcoholic. Certain specific clinical findings also should raise suspicions, including cancer of the head and neck, esophagus, or cardia of the stomach as well as cirrhosis, unexplained hepatitis, pancreatitis, bilateral parotid gland swelling, and peripheral neuropathy.

Once the likelihood of alcoholism is established, only a few moments are needed to gather the history of alcohol-related life problems. The patient *and spouse* should be asked about patterns of accidents, marital difficulties, problems on the job, and driving-related difficulties, after which the role played by alcohol should be identified. All physicians should be able to take the time needed to gather such information. In addition, a simple 25-item form to be answered by the patient, the Michigan Alcohol Screening Test (MAST), or the CAGE questionnaire (see Ewing) are available to aid in identifying the alcoholic.

After an alcoholic is identified, he or she should be confronted with the diagnosis. The presenting complaint can be used as an entrée to the alcohol problem. For instance, the patient complaining of insomnia or hypertension could be told that these are clinically important symptoms and that laboratory tests and physical findings indicate that alcohol appears to have contributed to the complaints and is increasing the risk for further medical and psychological problems. The physician should share information about the course of alcoholism and explore possible avenues of attacking the problem.

The process of confrontation is rarely accomplished in one session. It is helpful to let patients know that they are responsible for their own actions and that the decision to quit drinking rests with them. For the person who refuses to stop drinking at the first confrontation, a logical step is to "keep the door open," establishing future meetings so that help is available as problems escalate. In the meantime the family may benefit from counseling or referral to self-help group such as Alanon (the Alcoholics Anonymous group for family members) and Alateen (for teenage children of alcoholics).

Those patients who refuse to stop but who want to "cut down" should be reminded that the average alcoholic successfully cuts back scores of times but that sooner or later drinking again escalates. The patient who refuses to stop might be offered a guideline of drinking no more than two drinks (4 oz of wine, 12 oz of beer, or 1.5 oz of 80-proof beverage amounts to one drink) in any 24-h period, but it is very unlikely that this will be effective for an extended period of time. This is another way of keeping the door open in the hope that the patient will return as drinking escalates.

TREATMENT OF THE ALCOHOL-RELATED WITHDRAWAL SYNDROME The clinical syndrome In the presence of ethanol-induced cellular tolerance, any sudden decrease in ethanol may lead to symptoms of withdrawal from the CNS-depressant effects. As with most syndromes, most patients do not develop every symptom and the usual clinical picture is mild. Features include a tremor of the hands (shakes or jitters); autonomic nervous sytem dysfunction such as mild increases in pulse, respiratory rate, and body temperature; insomnia, possibly accompanied by bad dreams; feelings of generalized anxiety or panic attacks; and gastrointestinal upset. Symptoms begin within 5 to 10 h of decreasing ethanol intake (addicted patients are likely to awaken in the morning with some signs of withdrawal), peak in intensity on day two or three, and disappear by day four or five. Anxiety, insomnia, and mild levels of autonomic dysfunction may persist for 6 months or more. These continuing phenomena may contribute to the tendency to return to drinking.

About 5 percent of alcoholics show evidence of severe withdrawal symptoms. These include a state of confusion sometimes accompanied by visual, tactile, or auditory hallucinations. These psychotic symptoms are likely to disappear as the mental state becomes clearer over a period of several days and are distinct from the chronic alcoholic auditory hallucinosis with a clear sensorium described earlier in this chapter. A small percentage of alcoholics also demonstrate one or two generalized seizures ("rum fits"), usually within 48 h of stopping drinking. These are rarely focal in nature (unless there is underlying neuropathology) and electroencephalographic abnormalities are mild and usually return to normal within several days. There is no evidence that withdrawal seizures represent "latent" epilepsy.

The diagnosis of delirium tremens (DTs) is made when the course progresses beyond the usual symptoms of withdrawal to include confusion (with associated delusions and hallucinations), severe agitation, and generalized seizures. The likelihood of developing severe withdrawal symptoms increases with concomitant infections or medical problems, a prior history of withdrawal seizures or DTs, and higher quantity and frequency of drinking. Most periods of severe withdrawal begin and end abruptly, rarely lasting longer than 3 to 5 days. The mortality risk is less than 5 percent but increases with preexisting medical illnesses or organ system failure.

Treatment of withdrawal The *first* and most important step is to perform a *thorough* physical examination in all alcoholics who are considering stopping drinking and in those patients who might be undergoing withdrawal. It is necessary to evaluate organ systems likely to be impaired by heavy drinking, including searching for evidence of liver failure, gastrointestinal bleeding, cardiac arrhythmia, and glucose or electrolyte imbalance.

The *second* step in treating withdrawal is to give patients adequate nutrition and rest. All patients should be administered multiple B vitamins, including 50 to 100 mg of thiamine daily for a week or more. Most patients enter withdrawal with normal levels of body water or mild levels of overhydration, and intravenous fluids should be avoided unless there is evidence of hypotension or a history of recent excessive bleeding, vomiting, or diarrhea. Usually medications can be administered orally.

The *third* step in treatment is to recognize the symptoms due to CNS dysfunctions caused by removal of the brain-depressant effect of ethanol. Symptoms can be alleviated by administering another CNS depressant and gradually decreasing the levels of the drug over a 3- to 5-day period. While many CNS depressants are effective, the *benzodiazepines* have the highest margin of safety and are, therefore, the preferred class of drugs in the treatment of alcohol withdrawal. Benzodiazepines with short half-lives (see Chap. 364) are especially useful for patients with serious liver impairment or evidence of preexisting encephalopathy or brain damage. On the other hand, short half-life benzodiazepines, e.g., oxazepam or lorazepam, result in rapidly changing drug blood levels; administration every 4 h is required to avoid abrupt fluctuations in blood levels that may increase the risk for seizures. Therefore, most clinicians use drugs with longer half-lives, like diazepam or chlordiazepoxide. The goal is to administer sufficient drug on day one to alleviate most of the symptoms of withdrawal and then to decrease the dose by 20 percent on successive days over a period of 3 to 5 days. The dose is increased if signs of withdrawal escalate, and the medication is withheld if the patient is

sleeping or shows signs of increasing orthostatic hypotension. The average patient requires 25 to 50 mg of chlordiazepoxide or 10 mg of diazepam given orally every 4 to 6 h on the first day.

The most effective treatment of more *severe withdrawal* including delirium tremens remains controversial. Most clinicians use benzodiazepines, but despite as much as 300 mg or more per day of chlordiazepoxide the patient may still remain awake and agitated. Since it is probable that the confused, agitated state will persist for 3 to 5 days regardless of the pharmacologic intervention used, drugs are given to control behavior rather than to change the course of the syndrome. Antipsychotic medications like thioridazine or haloperidol have no place in the treatment of mild withdrawal symptoms and should only be used for treatment of psychotic patients with delusions and hallucinations.

The generalized seizures or "rum fits" rarely require aggressive pharmacologic intervention beyond that given to the usual patient undergoing withdrawal, i.e., adequate doses of benzodiazepines. There is little evidence that phenytoin is effective in drug withdrawal seizures, and the risk of seizures usually has passed by the time effective drug levels are reached. The rare patient with status epilepticus can be treated initially with intravenous diazepam. If anticonvulsants are used for alcohol withdrawal seizures, they should be stopped within 5 to 7 days unless a cause for a persisting seizure disorder is documented.

While alcohol withdrawal is usually treated in a hospital, efforts at reducing health care costs have resulted in experimentation with outpatient detoxification for alcoholics with mild abstinence syndromes. This is appropriate for patients in good physical condition who demonstrate mild signs of withdrawal despite low blood alcohol concentrations and for those without prior history of DTs or withdrawal seizures. Such individuals still require careful physical examination, evaluation of blood tests, treatment with vitamin supplementation, and appropriate doses of benzodiazepines. The latter are given *in a 1- to 2-day supply* to be administered to the patient by a spouse four times a day. Patients are asked to *return daily* for evaluation of vital signs, and the patient's family or friends are told to bring him or her to the emergency room if signs and symptoms of withdrawal escalate.

THE TREATMENT OR REHABILITATION OF ALCOHOLICS After completing alcoholic rehabilitation, 60 percent or more of middle-class alcoholics maintain abstinence for at least a year, many for a lifetime. There is no single best way to rehabilitate the alcoholic, and therapeutic approaches center on general supports which meet commonsense guidelines. Considering the lack of evidence for superiority of any specific treatment type, it is best to keep interventions as simple, safe, and inexpensive as possible.

Maneuvers in rehabilitation fall into two general categories. *First* are attempts to help the alcoholic achieve and maintain a high level of motivation toward abstinence. This includes educating the patient about alcoholism, educating family and/or friends to stop protecting the alcoholic from the problems caused by alcohol, and the use of disulfiram to help the physically healthy alcoholic avoid returning to drinking on the spur of the moment. The *second* series of maneuvers help the patient to readjust to life without alcohol and to reestablish a functional life-style through personal counseling, vocational rehabilitation, family support, and sexual counseling.

There is no convincing evidence that inpatient rehabilitation is more effective for the average primary alcoholic than is outpatient care. The decision to hospitalize can be made if (1) the patient has medical problems that are difficult to treat outside a hospital; (2) depression, confusion, or psychosis interfere with outpatient care; (3) the patient has such a severe life crisis that it is difficult to get his or her attention as an outpatient; (4) outpatient treatment has failed; or (5) the patient lives too far from the treatment center. If inpatient care is needed, free-standing treatment programs, units that are divisions of general hospitals, and those in psychiatric hospitals are equally effective. The characteristics of the patient predict outcome more than any specific attribute of the program.

Whether the treatment begins in an inpatient or an outpatient setting, subsequent contact should be maintained for a minimum of 6 months after abstinence is achieved. Counseling with an individual physician or through groups focuses on day-to-day living—emphasizing areas of improved functioning in the absence of alcohol (i.e., why it is a good idea to continue to abstain) and helping the patient to deal with free time without alcohol, develop a nondrinking peer group, and handle stresses on the job without alcohol.

The physician serves an important role in identifying the alcoholic, treating medical or psychiatric syndromes associated with alcoholism, carrying out detoxification, referring to rehabilitation programs, and counseling alcoholics in an inpatient or outpatient setting. The physician must also regulate drug treatment during alcoholism rehabilitation. Once acute detoxification is complete (an average of 3 to 5 days), there is *no place* for hypnotics or antianxiety drugs in the treatment of most alcoholics. The patient has already demonstrated an inability to moderate the use of one brain depressant, alcohol, and is at considerable risk for abusing sleeping pills or tranquilizers. Anxiety and insomnia can be treated with behavior modification such as relaxation training, meditation, and exercise or through increased activity in hobbies or religion.

One medication which has been used in alcohol rehabilitation is disulfiram. This drug inhibits aldehyde dehydrogenase, causing very high levels of acetaldehyde to accumulate after alcohol is consumed. The height and timing of the acetaldehyde level (usually peaking $\frac{1}{2}$ h after drinking) depend upon the dose of ethanol and its rate of intake. The disulfiram-ethanol reaction includes tremor, hypertension or hypotension, nausea and possibly severe vomiting, and diarrhea. Disulfiram must not be given to persons for whom such a reaction could be dangerous, including patients with portal hypertension, diabetes mellitus, heart disease, or a history of stroke. For healthy individuals for whom no contraindication for disulfiram exists, patients can be given 250 mg per day, with instructions to take the medication at the same time daily, preferably in the presence of someone else, so that there can be no "forgetting" to take the drug. There are no data about how long disulfiram should be continued, but many experienced physicians suggest giving the drug for a period of 6 to 12 months. All drugs have their dangers, and the physician is advised to read carefully about disulfiram and be fully aware of the potential, although rare, serious adverse reactions that can occur. Many physicians experienced in the treatment of alcoholics now aovid its use entirely or prescribe it for only short periods of time. Patients should be warned of the dangers of taking disulfiram and should sign a form acknowledging that mixing disulfiram with ethanol can result in a lethal reaction.

Finally, an inexpensive, readily available, and dedicated additional support for all alcoholics is available in almost every community. Alcoholics Anonymous (AA) is a self-help group of recovering alcoholics (men and women who have stopped drinking, perhaps many years ago) which offers an effective model showing that abstinence can be achieved, provides a sober peer group, and makes crisis intervention available when the drive to drink escalates. No matter what type of rehabilitation program is planned, the alcoholic should be offered the option of joining Alcoholics Anonymous.

REFERENCES

ADAMS KM, GRANT I: Failure of nonlinear models of drinking history variables to predict neuropsychological performance in alcoholics. Am J Psychiatry 141:663, 1984

ALTURA BM (ed): Alcohol, stroke, hypertension, and the heart. Proceedings of the Symposium of the American Medical Society on Alcoholism, April 13, 1984. Alc: Clin Exp Res 1:319, 1984

BLASS JP, GIBSON GE: Abnormality of a thiamine-requiring enzyme in patients with Wernicke-Korsakoff syndrome. N Engl J Med 297:1367, 1977

BRANDT J et al: Cognitive loss and recovery in long-term alcohol abusers. Arch Gen Psychiat 40:435, 1983

CICERO TJ: Neuroendocrinological effects of alcohol. Ann Rev Med 32:123, 1981

DEYKIN D, JANSON P: Ethanol potentiation of aspirin-induced prolongation of the bleeding time. N Engl J Med 306:852, 1982

DREYFUS PM: Diseases of the nervous system in chronic alcoholics, in *The Biology of Alcoholism*, B Kissin, H Begleiter (eds). New York, Plenum, 1974, vol 3 p 265

EWING JA: Detecting alcoholism. JAMA 252:1905, 1984

FRANK D, RAICHT RF: Alcohol-induced liver disease. Alc: Clin Exp Res 9:66, 1985

GEOKAS MC: Ethanol, the liver, and the gastrointestinal tract. Ann Intern Med 95:198, 1981

GOLDSTEIN DB: *Pharmacology of Alcohol*. New York, Oxford University Press, 1983

GOODWIN DW, GUZE SB: *Psychiatric Diagnosis*, 2nd ed. New York, Oxford University Press, 1979

GREENSPON AJ, SCHAAL SF: The "holiday heart": Electrophysiologic studies of alcohol effects in alcoholics. Ann Intern Med 98:135, 1983

HAGLUND RMJ, SCHUCKIT MA: The epidemiology of alcoholism, in *Alcoholism: Development, Consequences, and Intervention*, N Estes et al (eds). St. Louis, Mosby, 1981

LIEBER C: *Metabolic Aspects of Alcoholism*. Lancaster, England, MTP Press, 1977

————: To drink (moderately) or not to drink? N Engl J Med 310:846, 1984

LISHMAN WA: Cerebral disorder in alcoholism: Syndromes of impairment. Brain 104:1, 1981

MEAGHER RC et al: Suppression of hematopoietic-progenitor-cell proliferation by ethanol and acetaldehyde. N Engl J Med 307:845, 1982

MELLO NK, BREE MP: Alcohol self-administration disrupts reproductive function in female macaque monkeys. Science 221:677, 1983

MENDELSON JH, MELLO NK: Biologic concomitants of alcoholism. N Engl J Med 301:912, 1979

POTTER JF, BEEVERS DG: Pressor effect of alcohol in hypertension. Lancet: 1:119, 1984

SCHUCKIT MA: Genetic and clinical implications of alcoholism and affective disorder. Am J Psychiatry 143:140, 1986

————: *Drug and Alcohol Abuse: A Clinical Guide to Diagnosis and Treatment*, 2d ed. New York, Plenum, 1984

————: Studies of populations at high risk for alcoholism. Psychiatr Dev 3:31, 1985

————: Genetics and the risk for alcoholism. JAMA 254:2614, 1985

SELLERS EM, KALANT H: Alcohol intoxication and withdrawal. N Engl J Med 294:757, 1976

STREISSGUTH AP, LANDESMAN-DWYER S: Teratogenic effects of alcohol in humans and laboratory animals. Science 209:353, 1980

VAILLANT GE: *The Natural History of Alcoholism*. Cambridge, Mass., Harvard, 1983

VAN THIEL DH: Gastrointestinal and hepatic manifestations of chronic alcoholism. Gastroenterology 81:594, 1981

VICTOR M et al: *The Wernicke-Korsakoff Syndrome*. Philadelphia, Davis, 1971

366 OPIOID DRUG USE

MARC A. SCHUCKIT / DAVID S. SEGAL

The principal effects of the opioids (opiate-like drugs) are a significant damping of pain perception along with modest levels of sedation and euphoria. Tolerance to any one drug is likely to generalize to the others (i.e., cross-tolerance is likely) and all share a similar pattern of drug-related problems. Each of these substances is capable of producing physical addiction (and thus they all have some legal restrictions), and the abstinence syndrome from any one of the substances can be treated with administration of any of the others.

PHARMACOLOGY The prototypic opiates, morphine and codeine (3-methoxymorphine), are taken directly from the milky juice of the poppy, *Papaver somniferum*. The semisynthetic drugs produced from the morphine or thebane molecules include hydromorphone, codeine, diacetylmorphine (heroin), and oxycodone. The purely synthetic opioids, sharing many of the basic properties of opium and morphine, include meperidine, propoxyphene, diphenoxylate, methadone, and pentazocine. Despite claims to the contrary, all of these substances (including almost all prescription analgesics) are capable of producing euphoria as well as psychological and physical dependence when taken in high enough doses over prolonged periods of time.

The opioids interact with opiate receptors throughout the body including the central nervous system (CNS). Endogenous opioid peptides (i.e., enkephalins, endorphins, and dynorphin) have been identified. These appear to be natural ligands for opiate receptors and possess many of the same pharmacologic properties as the opiate alkaloids. Substances capable of antagonizing some actions of both the endogenous and exogenous opioids include nalorphine, levallorphan, cyclazocine and pentazocine, each of which have mixed agonist and antagonist properties, as well as naloxone and naltrexone, which are pure opiate antagonists. Mixed agonist-antagonist drugs, for example pentazocine, if administered to a patient addicted to other narcotics may precipitate opiate withdrawal symptoms.

Opiate tolerance, dependence, and withdrawal are considered to be related phenomena with common underlying mechanisms. A number of neurochemical systems and psychological processes are implicated in these effects which emerge with chronic administration of morphine or related opiates. Among the possible biochemical mechanisms, the endogenous opioid system has received the most attention. The results of this research to date have been somewhat disappointing; there is little consistent evidence for changes in opioid receptors or in the levels of endogenous opioid peptides corresponding to the development of tolerance and dependence. The discrepant findings may reflect methodologic differences as well as the complexity introduced by the apparent multiplicity of the opioid systems and the difficulties in accurately measuring indices of the activity of these peptides (i.e., turnover and biosynthesis). Other biochemical systems that might contribute to the development of tolerance and dependence include changes in intracellular modulators such as adenyl nucleotides, calcium and related substances, as well as alterations in neurotransmitters, including acetylcholine, serotonin, and the catecholamines, norepinephrine and dopamine. Evidence also implicates environmental and learning factors. For example, clinical observations suggest that classic conditioning plays a role in maintaining dependence in at least some addicts and that conditioning extinction procedures may be useful when integrated into a comprehensive treatment program for opioid addiction. Further research into these phenomena and efforts to elucidate neurochemical mechanisms could significantly facilitate the development of more effective approaches to treatment and prevention.

All of the opioid drugs are easily absorbed from the gastrointestinal (GI) system, the lungs, and the muscles. The most rapid and pronounced effects occur following intravenous administration, and the least intense actions are seen after absorption from the digestive tract, at least in part because some of the oral drug is metabolized before it passes into the general circulation. Most of the metabolism of opiates occurs in the liver, primarily through conjugation with glucuronic acid, and only small amounts are excreted directly in the urine or feces. The plasma half-lives of these drugs range from 2.5 to 3 h for morphine to more than 22 h for methadone and even longer for methadyl acetate.

Street heroin typically contains only 5 to 10 percent of the opiate. The remainder consists of materials such as lactose and fruit sugars, quinine, powdered milk, phenacetin, caffeine, antipyrine, and strychnine which are used to "cut" the drug and increase the margin of profit.

THE ACUTE AND CHRONIC EFFECTS OF OPIOID DRUGS ON BODY SYSTEMS With the exception of overdose conditions and changes associated with physical addiction, most opiate actions are relatively benign and rapidly reversible.

Effects on body systems Acute changes in the *GI system* are the result of decreased GI motility with resulting constipation and anorexia. Chronic GI problems in opiate addicts typically occur as a consequence of impaired liver function resulting from concomitant administration of other drugs and from the development of hepatitis B from shared "dirty" needles.

The direct effects on opiate receptors in the *CNS* can result in nausea and vomiting (medulla), decreased pain perception (spinal cord, thalamus, and periaqueductal grey region), euphoria (limbic system), and sedation (reticular activating system and striatum). The adulterants added to street drugs may contribute to some of the more permanent nervous system damage, including peripheral neuropathy, amblyopia, myelopathy, and leucoencephalopathy, while use of contaminated needles can produce abscesses in the CNS. Acute opiate administration results in decreases in luteinizing hormone (LH), with a subsequent decrease in testosterone which might contribute to the decreased sex drive reported by most opiate addicts. Other hormonal changes include a decrease in the release of thyrotropin as well as increases in prolactin and possibly in growth hormone (see Chap. 321).

Acute changes in the *respiratory system* include respiratory depression, which results from a decreased response of the brainstem to carbon dioxide tension, a component of the drug overdose syndrome described below. At even low drug doses, this effect can be clinically significant in individuals with compromised lung activity. *Cardiovascular* changes tend to be relatively mild with no direct opiate effect on heart rhythm or myocardial contractility, but there is a potential problem from orthostatic hypotension, probably secondary to dilatation of peripheral vessels. Bacterial infections of both the lungs and heart valves can occur from contaminated needles.

The toxic reaction or overdose syndrome High doses of opiates taken intentionally (in a suicide attempt) or by the street user who has misjudged the potency of the injected substance can result in a toxic reaction or overdose syndrome with a potentially lethal consequence. The typical syndrome, which occurs immediately with intravenous (IV) overdose, includes shallow respirations of two to four per minute, pupillary miosis (with mydriasis once brain anoxia develops), bradycardia, a decrease in body temperature, and a general absence of responsiveness to external stimulation. If this medical emergency is not treated rapidly, symptoms can progress to cyanosis, and death can ensue from respiratory depression and cardiorespiratory arrest. Postmortem examination reveals few specific changes except for diffuse cerebral edema. An "allergic-like" reaction to adulterants can also occur and is characterized by decreased alertness, a frothy pulmonary edema, and an elevation in the blood eosinophil count.

The preferred treatment for the typical opiate overdose is the narcotic antagonist naloxone, given in an initial dose of 0.4 mg (1 mL) or 0.01 mg/kg intramuscularly (IM) or IV, which can be repeated in 3 to 10 min if no response occurs. Because the effects of this drug diminish within 2 to 3 h, it is important to monitor the individual for at least 24 h after a heroin overdose and 72 h after an overdose of longer-acting drugs such as methadone. Patients who are also physically addicted to an opioid are likely to experience a precipitous onset of an abstinence syndrome within 2 to 8 h after administration of the opioid antagonist, but aggressive treatment of this syndrome is not appropriate until all vital signs are relatively stable.

As with any drug overdose, treatment of either the typical or the "allergic" type of opiate toxic reaction often requires support of vital signs until the body detoxifies the substance. Patients may require a respirator (especially one using oxygen and positive pressure breathing for the "allergic" type of overdose), IV fluids perhaps accompanied by pressor agents to support blood pressure, and gastric lavage to remove any remaining drug, with care taken to use a cuffed endotracheal tube to prevent aspiration if the patient is not alert. Cardiac arrhythmias and/or convulsions, especially likely to be seen with codeine, propoxyphene, or meperidine, also need to be treated.

THE OPIATE ABUSER The medical abuser Two groups of individuals are at high risk for abusing analgesics. First, evidence suggests that a majority of people with *chronic pain syndromes* (e.g., back, joint, and muscle disorders) may misuse their prescribed drugs at various times. If physical dependence is established, abstinence syndromes can then intensify the pain, promoting continued drug intake. A few precautions can help the physician to avoid contributing to physical dependence in chronic pain patients, particularly those who have demonstrated a propensity to misuse opioids: (1) the goal is to minimize the debilitating effects of pain with the understanding that discomfort may not be completely eliminated; (2) all possible efforts must be taken to reinforce the need for the patient to become actively involved in and committed to improvement; (3) analgesic medication should be only one component of treatment and limited to oral administration of the least potent analgesic required to take the "edge off" the pain (e.g., propoxyphene); all such drugs should be coordinated through one physician; (4) behavior modification techniques can include muscle relaxation and meditation, while carefully selected exercises can help increase function and decrease pain; (5) nonmedicinal approaches including electrical transcutaneous neurostimulation for muscle and joint disease can be applied (see also Chap. 3).

The second group at high risk are *physicians, nurses, and pharmacists,* primarily because of their easy access to substances of abuse. Physicians may begin to use opiates to help them sleep or to reduce stress or physical aches and pains. A family history of substance abuse (including alcoholism) probably helps to identify the physician at exceptionally high risk. Because of the growing awareness of these problems, impaired physician programs have been established in many hospitals and by most state medical societies. These groups attempt to identify and aid substance-impaired physicians, giving them peer support and education so as to achieve abstinence before problems escalate to the point of licensure revocation. In general, doctors are advised to never prescribe opiates for themselves or for members of their family—physicians deserve the same level of care and protection from future problems as their patients.

The street abuser Some opiate addicts satisfy criteria for the antisocial personality disorder as evidenced by serious antisocial problems beginning prior to age 15 and before the first major life problem from drugs (see Chap. 363). However, the majority of opiate addicts have a relatively high level of premorbid functioning. The usual street abuser begins using opiates occasionally, often after experimenting with tobacco, then alcohol, then marijuana, and then brain depressants or stimulants. Occasional opiate use, or "chipping," might continue for some time, and some individuals probably never escalate their intake to the point of developing serious problems. Another pattern of temporary or intermittent abuse is represented by the experiences of Vietnam soldiers, most of whom had little or no prior experience with opiates and who found themselves in a situation of high stress and readily available drugs. Under these circumstances, as many as one-half tried opiates and, although many became physically addicted, those who had not misused drugs before Vietnam tended to return to drug-free status when back in their home communities.

Once persistent opiate use is established, the outcome is often extremely serious. At least 25 percent of such opiate abusers are likely to die within 10 to 20 years of active abuse, with death from suicide, homicide, accidents, and infectious diseases such as tuberculosis or serum hepatitis. As many as 50 percent of male and 25 percent of female addicts turn to alcohol when their primary drug is not available, and many of these people meet the criteria for secondary alcohol abuse. The prevalence of alcohol misuse is higher in drug treatment dropouts than in those who stay with therapy, and abuse is more likely in individuals with a history of alcohol problems before they developed opiate-related difficulties.

PHYSICAL ADDICTION AND THE OPIATE ABSTINENCE SYNDROME   The symptoms of withdrawal   The time to onset as well as the intensity and duration of the acute abstinence syndrome are influenced by a number of factors including the drugs' half-life, its dose, and the chronicity of administration. The withdrawal symptoms tend to be opposite to the acute effects of the drug and include nausea and diarrhea, coughing, lacrimation, rhinorrhea, profuse sweating, twitching muscles, and piloerection or "goose bumps"; mild elevations in body temperature, respiratory rate, and blood pressure are also observed. In addition, sensations of diffuse body pain, insomnia, and yawning occur with intense drug craving. Drugs with a short half-life, such as morphine or heroin, cause symptoms typically within 8 to 16 h of the last dose (thus, many addicts awake in mild withdrawal every morning); peak effects are apparent within 36 to 72 h after discontinuation of the drug, and the acute syndrome disappears within 5 to 8 days. However, a protracted abstinence phase of mild symptoms (e.g., slight changes in pupillary size, autonomic dysfunction, changes in sleep pattern) may persist for 6 or more months.

Treatment of the withdrawal syndrome   Patients *must* receive a thorough physical examination which includes an assessment of liver and neurologic function as well as identification of local and systemic infections, especially abscesses. Proper nutrition and rest must be initiated as soon as possible.

Effective treatment of withdrawal, however, also requires readministration of sufficient opiate medication on day one to decrease symptoms, followed by a more gradual withdrawal of the drug, usually over 5 to 10 days. Any opiate will work (they all have some level of cross-tolerance) but for ease of administration many physicians prefer to use a long-acting drug like methadone. In estimating the first day's dose from the patient's history, 1 mg of methadone is approximately equivalent to 3 mg of morphine, 1 mg of heroin, or 20 mg of meperidine. Most patients require between 10 and 25 mg of methadone orally given twice on day one, with higher doses given if prominent symptoms of withdrawal are not damped. After several days of a stabilized drug dose, the opiate is then decreased by 10 to 20 percent of the original day's dose each day.

Most states have restrictions on the prescription of opiates to addicts, and in the absence of special permits, detoxification with opiates is usually limited to 1 month or less. One relatively successful nonopiate approach to the treatment of withdrawal is the use of the alpha$_2$-adrenergic agonist, clonidine, used in part to decrease sympathetic nervous system overactivity. Given at doses of approximately 5 μg/kg (up to 0.3 mg given two to four times a day), clonidine causes most patients undergoing opiate withdrawal to experience a decrease in autonomic nervous system dysfunction. Opiates, however, are more effective in relieving discomfort and pain, and clonidine is often not well tolerated because it produces high levels of sedation and orthostatic hypotension. Therefore, under most circumstances opiates are the treatment of choice.

A special case of opiate withdrawal is seen in the newborn, passively addicted by the mother's drug misuse during pregnancy. Some level of addiction develops in 50 to 90 percent of children of heroin-dependent mothers, and the withdrawal syndrome carries a mortality of between 3 and 30 percent if not treated when prominent signs are apparent. In distinction to street addicts, as few as 25 percent of infants of methadone-maintenance-addicted mothers show clinically relevant withdrawal symptoms. The syndrome consists of irritability, crying, a tremor (in 80 percent), increased reflexes, increased respiratory rate, diarrhea, hyperactivity (in 60 percent), vomiting (40 percent), and sneezing/yawning/hiccuping (in 30 percent). The child usually has a low birth weight but may be otherwise unremarkable until the second day, when symptoms are likely to begin.

The treatment follows the same general steps used in the treatment of the physically addicted adult. The child must be carefully evaluated to rule out medical problems such as hypoglycemia, hypocalcemia, infections, and trauma; general supports in a warm, quiet environment and regulation of electrolytes and glucose are also required. The infant with moderate to severe symptoms can be treated with any of the following: paregoric (0.2 mL orally every 3 to 4 h); methadone, (0.1 to 0.5 mg/kg per day); phenobarbital (8 mg/kg per day); or diazepam (1 to 2 mg/kg every 8 h). Medication should be given in decreasing levels for 10 to 20 days. It is also possible to treat the addicted infants of mothers on methadone maintenance by having them breast feed while the mothers continue to take methadone.

REHABILITATION OF OPIATE ADDICTS   Despite some differences in demographics, the same general rules for rehabilitation apply to the opiate abuser and to the alcoholic. The basic strategy includes beginning detoxification and general family support. It is also important to establish realistic patient goals and a program of counseling and education to increase motivation toward abstinence. A long-term commitment to rebuilding a life-style without the substance is essential for preventing recidivism.

Identifying and confronting the patient   The first step in treatment requires identification of the opiate abuser—an especially difficult problem with the middle-class street abuser and the medical patient or physician with an iatrogenic addiction. An important step is to gather a clinical history which includes the patterns of opiate usage, information regarding the possible existence of an antisocial personality disorder, or a history of chronic pain. Blood and urine screens can be used to identify opiates in patients in whom misuse is suspected, and clinicians should search for physical stigmata of misuse (e.g., needle marks). One potentially important diagnostic procedure (which should be used carefully because it can precipitate an intense withdrawal) is the opiate antagonist challenge. A 0.4 mg dose of naloxone is given subcutaneously or slowly IV over a 5-min period, and the patient is observed for signs of withdrawal over the next several hours. This challenge test should only be carried out in the presence of a physician and it is important to be prepared to begin treating withdrawal if needed.

After identifying the opiate addict, the next step is confrontation. The need for active treatment of the abstinence syndrome can be presented, and the availability of help in establishing a drug-free life-style can be emphasized. The final decision, of course, rests with the patient.

Rehabilitation Most rehabilitation approaches have common elements. Patients are educated about their responsibility for improving their lives and *motivation for abstinence* is increased by providing information about the medical and psychological problems that can be expected if addiction continues. Patients and families are helped to *establish an opiate-free life-style* by being educated about dealing with chronic pain and developing realistic vocational planning (e.g., this applies to pharmacists, physicians, and nurses). The addict should also be encouraged to establish a drug-free peer group and to participate in self-help groups such as Narcotics Anonymous (NA). Much of this advice and counseling can be given by the physician, but many clinicians refer patients to more formal drug programs, including methadone maintenance clinics, programs using narcotic antagonists, and therapeutic communities. Long-term follow-up of treated patients shows that approximately one-third of addicts are completely drug free in the year before the follow-up interview, and that a total of 60 percent are off opiates, although some may be abusing other substances. Individuals who stay in methadone maintenance or in therapeutic communities show significant decreases in police and social problems and increases in job functioning. In general, the best prognosis for rehabilitation is for those who are employed, who have higher levels of school completion, and who remain in treatment for at least 2 months.

METHADONE MAINTENANCE Methadone and methadyl acetate maintenance should only be used along with education and counseling. It is important to note that drug maintenance is not aimed at "curing" opiate addiction; rather it provides a substitute drug that is legally accessible. The goal is to help the addict who has failed in drug-free programs to improve functioning within the family and job, to decrease legal problems, and to improve health.

Methadone is a long-acting opiate that possesses almost all the physiologic properties of heroin. The addict who has been carefully screened to rule out prior psychiatric disorders may be maintained on a relatively low dose (e.g., 30 to 40 mg per day); a higher dosage schedule (100 to 120 mg per day) can also be used and may be more effective in blocking heroin-induced euphoria. Although the results are not definite, there is some evidence that the higher methadone doses may result in greater retention in treatment and consequently lower levels of arrest and readdiction to street drugs. Methadone is administered in an oral liquid given once a day at the program center, with weekend portions taken by the patient at home. The longer acting analogues, such as methadyl acetate, can be given in lower doses (e.g., 20 to 30 mg) two or three times a week, with levels increased to as high as 80 mg three times a week if needed.

After a period of maintenance (usually 6 months to 1 year or longer), the clinician should work closely with the patient to regulate the rate of drug decrease (by about 5 percent per week). The British have used heroin maintenance with similar goals and following similar guidelines as those used for methadone. There is no evidence that heroin maintenance has any advantages over methadone maintenance, but the heroin approach does add the risk that the drug will be sold on the streets.

OPIATE ANTAGONISTS The opiate antagonists (e.g., naloxone) compete with heroin and other opiates for opioid receptors, reducing the effects of the opiate agonists. Administered over long periods of time in order to block the "high" produced if the patient takes opiates, these drugs can be useful as part of an overall treatment approach which includes counseling and support. Cyclazocine was the first antagonist tested, but its blockade of receptors is incomplete and the level of side effects (including a drunken feeling) are unacceptable. Naloxone is an excellent narcotic antagonist with no agonistic properties, but it has such a short period of action (2 to 3 h) that it is of little use in rehabilitation. The most widely used antagonist in rehabilitation is naltrexone, which is effective for about 24 h with few side effects. An amount of 50 mg of naltrexone per day will block 15 mg of heroin for 24 h, and higher doses (125 to 150 mg) are capable of blocking the effects of 25 mg of IV heroin for up to 3 days. Naltrexone is free of agonist properties, there are no known withdrawal symptoms when the medication is stopped, and side effects tend to be mild. Patients started on this antagonist should be free of opiates for a minimum of 5 days. In addition they must be given a thorough physical examination and should be challenged with 0.4 or 0.8 mg of the shorter-acting naloxone to be certain that they are able to tolerate the long-acting antagonist. Following this procedure, a test dose of 10 mg of naltrexone can be given, with the expectation that any withdrawal symptoms will be seen in $\frac{1}{2}$ to 2 h. Over the next 10 days, the daily dose should be increased to about 100 mg on Mondays and Wednesdays and 150 mg on Fridays. Unfortunately, despite the apparent advantages of this treatment approach, patients demonstrate great resistance to continuing care. In one study, only about 60 percent of the patients completed 6 days of naltrexone induction, and only 10 percent remained in the program at the end of 6 months.

DRUG-FREE PROGRAMS Most existing half-way houses and recovery centers for the opiate abuser utilize the therapeutic community (TC) approach. This is an exception to the general preference for short-term inpatient rehabilitation, as care lasts up to a year while the addict is taken out of the street culture and given a new life within the group. In this structure members, including addict leaders, frequently confront participants in an attempt to help them gain insights into more successful life-styles for coping with problems.

REFERENCES

CHARNEY DS et al: The clinical use of clonidine in abrupt withdrawal from methadone. Arch Gen Psychiat 38:1273, 1981

CROUGHAN JL et al: Alcoholism and alcohol dependence in narcotic addicts: A prospective study with a five-year follow-up. Am J Drug Alcohol Abuse 8:85, 1981

CROWLEY T et al: Naltrexone-induced dysphoria in former opioid addicts. Am J Psychiatry 142:1081, 1985

GREENSTEIN RA et al: Naltrexone: A short-term treatment of opiate dependence. Am J Drug Alcohol Abuse 8:291, 1981

HARTNOLL RL et al: Evaluation of heroin maintenance in controlled trial. Arch Gen Psychiat 37:877, 1980

JAFFE JH, MARTIN WR: Opiate analgesics and antagonists, in *The Pharmacological Basis of Therapeutics,* AG Gilman et al (eds). New York, Macmillan, 1980, pp 494–534

JASINSKI D et al: Clonidine in morphine withdrawal. Arch Gen Psychiat 42:1063, 1985

KLEBER HK, RIORDAN CE: The treatment of narcotic withdrawal: A historical review. J Clin Psychiatry 43:30 1982

McCUE JD: The effects of stress on physicians and their medical practice. N Engl J Med 306:458, 1982

MIRIN SM et al: Opiate use and sexual function. Am J Psychiatry 137:909, 1980

O'BRIEN CP, WOODY GE: Long-term consequences of opiate dependence. N Engl J Med 304:1098, 1981

O'BRIEN CP et al: Classical conditioning is opiate dependence, in *Problems of Drug Dependence,* LS Harris (ed). NIDA Research, Monograph 49, pp 35–46. Washington, DC, US Government Printing Office, 1984

OLIVERIO A et al: Psychobiology of opioids. Int Rev Neurobiol 25:277, 1984

REDMOND DE JR, KRYSTAL JH: Multiple mechanisms of withdrawal from opioid drugs. Annu Rev Neurosci 7:443, 1984

Rounsaville BJ et al: Identifying alcoholism in treated opiate addicts. Am J Psychiatry 140:764, 1983

Schuckit MA: *Drug and Alcohol Abuse: A Clinical Guide to Diagnosis and Treatment*, 2d ed. New York, Plenum, 1984

Simon E: Recent studies on opioid receptors: Heterogeneity and isolation, in *Problems of Drug Dependence*, LS Harris (ed). NIDA Research Monograph 49, pp 5–13. Washington, DC, US Government Printing Office, 1984

Simpson DD et al: Six-year follow-up of opioid addicts after admission to treatment. Arch Gen Psychiat 39:1318, 1982

Vaillant GE: A 20-year follow-up of New York narcotic addicts. Arch Gen Psychiat 29:237, 1973

Wallot H, Lambert J: Characteristics of physician addicts. Am J Drug Alcohol Abuse 10:53, 1984

367 COMMONLY ABUSED DRUGS

JACK H. MENDELSON / NANCY K. MELLO

Drug abuse in America appears to be an increasing public health problem. In 1984, the largest and most comprehensive survey of noninstitutionalized persons in the United States (the National Institute of Mental Health's Epidemiologic Catchment Area Surveys) showed that drug abuse and dependence was the third most frequently reported psychiatric disorder by men aged 18 to 65. Among young women (aged 18 to 24), drug abuse was the second most frequent psychiatric disorder. The initiation and continuation of drug abuse is determined by a complex interaction of the pharmacologic properties and relative availability of each drug, the personality and expectancy of the user, and the environmental context in which the drug is used. Over the years, drugs of choice have changed; marijuana superceded heroin as the focus of drug abuse concern during the 1970s while expensive "boutique" drugs such as cocaine have achieved extraordinary popularity and widespread abuse during the 1980s.

Polydrug abuse, the concurrent use of several drugs with different pharmacologic effects, is increasingly common among individuals from all socioeconomic strata. Sometimes the goal is to attenuate one drug effect with another, e.g., alcohol is used to modulate the cocaine "high," sometimes one drug is used to enhance the effects of another, as with benzodiazepines and methadone. Toxic drug interactions associated with polydrug abuse are likely to further increase the health impact of drug abuse. This chapter discusses marijuana, cocaine, two hallucinogens (PCP and LSD), and polydrug abuse.

MARIJUANA AND CANNABIS COMPOUNDS *Cannabis sativa* contains over 400 compounds in addition to the psychoactive substance, delta-9-tetrahydrocannabinol (THC). Marijuana cigarettes are prepared from the leaves and flowering tops of the plant, and a typical marijuana cigarette contains 0.5 to 1 g of plant material. Although the usual THC concentration varies between 5 and 20 mg, concentrations as high as 100 mg per cigarette have been detected. Hashish is prepared from concentrated resin of *Cannabis sativa* and contains a THC concentration of between 8 to 12 percent by weight. "Hash oil," a lipid-soluble plant extract, may contain a THC concentration of 25 to 60 percent, and it may be added to marijuana or hashish to enhance their THC concentration. Smoking is the most common mode of marijuana or hashish self-administration. During pyrolysis, over 150 compounds in addition to the THC are released in the smoke. Although most of these compounds do not have psychoactive properties, they do have potential physiologic effects.

THC is quickly absorbed from the lungs into blood and is then rapidly sequestered in tissues. It is metabolized primarily in the liver where it is converted to 11-hydroxy-THC, a psychoactive compound, and more than 20 other metabolites. Most THC metabolites are excreted through the feces at a rate of clearance that is relatively slow in comparison to that of most other psychoactive drugs.

Prevalance of marijuana use A 1983 National Household Survey on Drug Abuse indicated that 64 percent of young adults (aged 18 to 25) stated that they used marijuana. This represents a 59 percent increase in marijuana use over a decade; in 1972, a similar survey found that only 5 percent of young adults had tried the drug. The rate of increase in marijuana use by males appeared to have stabilized by 1985 but marijuana use among women continues to increase. A recent detailed evaluation of social and behavioral concomitants of marijuana use (published in 1984) found that young marijuana users also reported significant use of other psychoactive substances and are likely to become polydrug abusers. Survey data also report that although adolescents and young adults are aware of the potential health hazards of marijuana use, this information does not effectively deter use by many individuals.

Acute and chronic marijuana intoxication Acute intoxication from marijuana and cannabis compounds is related to both THC dose and route of administration. THC is absorbed more rapidly from marijuana smoking than from orally ingested cannabis compounds. The most frequent form of acute intoxication consists of a subjective perception of relaxation and mild euphoria resembling mild to moderate alcohol intoxication. This condition is usually accompanied by some impairment in thinking, concentration, and perceptual and psychomotor functions. Higher doses of cannabis may produce behavioral effects analogous to severe alcohol intoxication. Although the effects of acute marijuana intoxication are relatively benign in normal users, the drug can precipitate severe emotional disorders in individuals who have antecedent psychotic or neurotic problems. As with other psychoactive compounds both set (user's expectancy) and setting (environmental context) are important determinants of the type and severity of behavioral intoxication.

As is true of alcoholics, *chronic* marijuana abusers may lose interest in common socially desirable goals and devote progressively more time to drug acquisition and use. However, it should be emphasized that THC does not cause a specific and unique "amotivational syndrome." The range of symptoms sometimes attributed to marijuana use are difficult to distinguish from mild depression and the maturational dysfunctions often associated with protracted adolescence. Chronic use of marijuana has also been reported to increase the probability of exacerbation of psychotic symptoms in individuals with a past history of schizophrenia.

Physical effects of marijuana Conjunctival injection and tachycardia are the most frequent immediate physical concomitants of smoking marijuana. Tolerance for marijuana-induced tachycardia develops rapidly among regular users; angina may be precipitated by marijuana smoking in persons with a history of coronary insufficiency. Exercise-induced angina may be increased after marijuana use to a greater extent than after tobacco cigarette smoking. Patients with cardiac disease should be strongly advised not to smoke marijuana or use cannabis compounds.

Significant decrements in pulmonary vital capacity have been found in regular daily marijuana smokers. Because marijuana smoking typically involves deep inhalation and prolonged retention of marijuana smoke, marijuana smokers may develop pulmonary disease such as chronic bronchial irritation. Impairment of single-breath carbon monoxide diffusion capacity (DL_{CO}) is greater in persons who smoke both marijuana and tobacco than in tobacco smokers. At present, there is no direct evidence that marijuana smoking induces lung cancer that is comparable to the well-documented association between tobacco smoking and lung cancer, although it should be emphasized that heavy marijuana use among Americans may be of too brief duration for detection of this problem.

Although marijuana has also been associated with adverse effects on a number of other systems, many of these studies await replication and confirmation. For example, the reported correlation between marijuana use and decreased testosterone levels in males has not been confirmed. Decreased sperm count and motility and abnormalities of morphology of spermatozoa following marijuana use have also been reported. Administration of high doses of marijuana to female rhesus monkeys has revealed significant marijuana-induced suppression of pituitary gonadotrophins and gonadal steroids. Carefully conducted prospective studies demonstrated a significant correlation between impaired fetal growth and development and heavy marijuana use during pregnancy. Marijuana also has been implicated in derangements of the immune response system, in chromosomal abnormalities, and in inhibition of DNA, RNA, and protein synthesis, but these findings have not been confirmed or related to any specific physiologic effect of marijuana in humans. One report of cannabis-induced brain atrophy in young adults has not been confirmed in studies of computerized tomography with young men who had documented histories of heavy marijuana smoking.

Tolerance and physical dependence   Habitual marijuana users rapidly develop tolerance to the psychoactive effects of marijuana, often smoking more frequently and trying to secure more potent cannabis compounds. Tolerance for physiologic effects of marijuana develops at different rates; e.g. tolerance for marijuana-induced tachycardia develops rapidly, but tolerance for marijuana-induced conjunctival injection develops more slowly. Tolerance to both behavioral and physiologic effects of marijuana decreases rapidly upon cessation of marijuana use.

Mild to moderate withdrawal signs and symptoms have been reported in chronic cannabis users, with severity of symptoms related to dosage and duration of use. These include tremor, sweating, nausea, vomiting, diarrhea, irritability, anorexia, and sleep disturbances. Withdrawal signs and symptoms observed in chronic marijuana users are usually relatively mild in comparision to those observed with heavy opiate or alcohol users and rarely require medical or pharmacologic intervention. Somewhat more severe and protracted abstinence syndromes may occur after sustained use of high potency cannabis compounds for long periods.

COCAINE   Cocaine is a stimulant and a local anesthetic with potent vasoconstrictor properties. Leaves of the coca plant (*Erythroxylon coca*) contain 1 to 1.5 percent cocaine. The drug is marketed illicitly in the form of a white crystalline powder, usually adulterated with lactose or glucose to 50 percent purity. Frequently cocaine is adulterated with other local anesthetics such as lidocaine, procaine, and tetracaine. Cocaine's biologic effects result from alteration and blockade of cellular membrane transport, particularly prevention of the reuptake of biogenic amines, an effect shared with the tricyclic antidepressants.

Prevalence of cocaine use   Cocaine is expensive in comparison to most other illicit drugs and has attained the reputation of a "status" drug in western industrialized societies. The actual extent of illicit cocaine use is unknown, but there is evidence of a recent escalation in the United States. The Drug Abuse Warning Network (DAWN) reported that emergency room mentions of cocaine abuse increased by 75 percent from 1981 through the fourth quarter of 1983. During the first quarter of 1984, approximately 2000 cocaine mentions were reported, a number equal to all the cocaine mentions for the full year of 1978. A National Household Survey conducted in 1982 revealed that 21.6 million persons had tried cocaine at least once, a dramatic increase from the 5.4 million who reported at least one use of cocaine during 1974. The most prevalent pattern of use in America appears to be occasional, sporadic intake of relatively low doses of cocaine.

Acute and chronic cocaine intoxication   The most common mode of cocaine self-administration is by inhalation or "snorting," where the drug is rapidly absorbed from the nasal mucosa and produces a brief, dose-related stimulation and enhancement of mood. Cardiac rate and blood pressure also increase in a dose-related manner. An increase in body temperature usually occurs following cocaine administration, and high doses of cocaine may induce lethal pyrexia or hypertension. Because cocaine inhibits reuptake of catecholamines at adrenergic nerve endings, the drug potentiates sympathetic nervous system activity. During recent years smoking of coca paste (a product produced by extracting cocaine preparations with flammable solvents) has become increasingly popular. Administration of the drug via

intravenous injection also occurs more frequently. Cocaine has a short plasma half-life of approximately 1 h. In humans, cocaine is primarily metabolized by plasma esterases, and cocaine metabolites are excreted in urine. The very short duration of euphorigenic effects of cocaine observed in chronic abusers is probably due to both acute and chronic tolerance. Frequent self-administration of the drug (2 to 3 times per hour) is often reported by chronic cocaine abusers. Modulation of both the cocaine "high" and the abrupt dysphoric disappearance of cocaine's effects with alcohol is often reported.

The prevalent assumption that cocaine use is relatively safe is challenged by reports of death from respiratory depression, cardiac arrhythmias, and convulsions after cocaine snorting and intravenous administration. Severe pulmonary disease may develop in individuals who smoke coca paste; this is attributed both to the direct effects of cocaine and to residual solvent contaminants in the smoked material. Numerous clinical reports, dating from the late nineteenth century, strongly suggest that protracted cocaine abuse may induce paranoid ideation and visual and auditory hallucinations, a state which resembles alcoholic hallucinosis. Psychological dependence upon cocaine, as manifested by inability to abstain from frequent compulsive use, has also been reported. Although occurrence of withdrawal syndromes involving psychomotor agitation and autonomic hyperactivity remains controversial, severe depression ("crashing") may be a concomitant of drug withdrawal.

Treatment of cocaine intoxication and abuse   Treatment of cocaine overdose is a medical emergency which involves resuscitation in an intensive care unit. Cocaine toxicity produces hypertension, tachycardia, tonic-clonic seizures, dyspnea, and ventricular arrhythmias. Intravenous diazepam in doses up to 0.5 mg/kg administered over an 8-h period has been shown to be effective for control of seizures. The systemic concomitants of a hypermetabolic state produced by cocaine toxicity with concurrent ventricular arrhythmias have been managed successfully by administration of 0.5 to 1.0 mg of propranolol intravenously. Since many instances of cocaine-related mortality have also been associated with concomitant use of other illicit drugs (particularly heroin), the physician must be prepared to institute effective emergency treatment for multiple drug toxicity.

Treatment of chronic cocaine abuse requires combined efforts by family physicians, psychiatrists, and psychosocial care providers. Early abstinence from cocaine use is often complicated by symptoms of depression and guilt, insomnia, and anorexia, which may be as severe as those observed in major affective disorders. Individual and group psychotherapy, family therapy, and peer group assistance programs are often useful for inducing prolonged remission from drug use. Preliminary reports suggest that both lithium treatment and tricyclic antidepressant medication may be of value for the long-term treatment of cocaine abuse, even when affective disorder or depression are not present. In fact, depressive illness does not appear to be a frequent antecedent of cocaine abuse.

LYSERGIC ACID DIETHYLAMIDE (LSD)   The serendipitous discovery of psychedelic effects of LSD in 1947 culminated in an epidemic of LSD abuse during the 1960s. Imposition of stringent legal and regulatory constraints on the manufacture and distribution of LSD (classified as a Schedule I substance by the FDA), as well as public recognition that psychedelic experiences induced by LSD were a health hazard, has resulted in a significant reduction in LSD abuse. During 1984, relatively few instances of LSD abuse were reported, but the drug still retains some popularity among adolescents and young adults.

LSD is a very potent drug; oral doses as low as 20 μg may induce profound psychological and physiologic effects. Tachycardia, hypertension, pupillary dilation, tremor, and hyperpyrexia occur within minutes following LSD in oral doses of 0.5 to 2 μg/kg. A variety of bizarre and often conflicting perceptual and mood changes, including visual illusions, synesthesias, and extreme lability of mood states, occur within one-half hour after LSD intake. The action of LSD can persist for 12 to 18 h even though the half-life of the drug is only 3 h.

Tolerance develops rapidly for LSD-induced changes in psychological function when the drug is used one or more times per day over a course of 4 days or more. Abrupt abstinence following continued use does not produce withdrawal signs or symptoms. To date there have been no clinical reports of death caused by the direct effects of LSD.

The most frequent acute medical emergency associated with LSD use is panic episodes which may persist up to 24 h ("the bad trip"). Management of this problem is best accomplished by supportive reassurance ("talking down") and, if necessary, administration of small doses of anxiolytic drugs. Adverse consequences of chronic LSD use include enhanced risk for schizophreniform psychosis and derangements in memory function, problem solving, and abstract thinking. Treatment of these disorders is best carried out in specialized psychiatric facilities.

PHENCYCLIDINE (PCP) Phencyclidine, a cyclohexylamine derivative, is widely used in veterinary medicine to briefly immobilize large animals and is sometimes described as a *dissociative anesthetic*. PCP is easily synthesized and is abused, primarily by young people and polydrug users. The true extent of PCP abuse is unknown, but recent national surveys indicate an increase in frequency of use.

Phencyclidine is taken orally, by smoking, or by intravenous injection. It is also used as an adulterant in illicit sales of THC, LSD, amphetamine, or cocaine. The most common street preparation, "angel dust," is a white granular powder which contains 50 to 100 percent of the drug. Low doses (5 mg) produce agitation, excitement, impaired motor coordination, dysarthria, and analgesia. Users may have horizontal or vertical nystagmus, flushing, diaphoresis, and hyperacusis. Behavioral changes include distortions of body image, disorganization of thinking, and feelings of estrangement. Higher doses of PCP (5 to 10 mg) may produce hypersalivation, vomiting, myoclonus, fever, stupor, or coma. PCP doses of 10 mg or more cause convulsions, opisthotonus, and decerebrate posturing which may be followed by prolonged coma.

The diagnosis of PCP overdose is difficult because the patient's initial symptoms may suggest an acute schizophrenic reaction. Confirmation of PCP use is possible by determination of PCP levels in serum or urine. PCP analysis is currently available at most toxicologic centers. Large quantities of PCP remain in urine for 1 to 5 days following high-dosage PCP intake.

PCP overdose requires prompt life support measures including treatment of coma, convulsions, and respiratory depression in a hospital intensive care unit (see Chap. 21). There is no specific antidote or antagonist for PCP. PCP excretion from the body can be enhanced by acidification of urine and gastric lavage (see Chap. 171). Death from PCP overdose may occur as a consequence of some combination of pharyngeal hypersecretion, hyperthermia, respiratory depression, severe hypertension, seizures, hypertensive encephalopathy, and intracerebral hemorrhage.

Acute psychosis associated with PCP use should be considered a psychiatric emergency since patients may be at high risk for suicide or extreme violence toward others. *Phenothiazines should not be used for treatment of acute PCP psychosis because these drugs potentiate PCP's anticholinergic effects.* Haloperidol (5 mg intramuscularly) has been administered on an hourly basis to induce suppression of psychotic behavior. PCP, like LSD and mescaline, produces vasospasm of cerebral arteries at relatively low doses. Chronic PCP use has been shown to induce insomnia, anorexia, severe social and behavioral changes, and, in some cases, chronic schizophrenia.

POLYDRUG ABUSE Although drug abusers often report a preference for a particular drug, such as alcohol or opiates, the concurrent use of other drugs is common. Multiple drug use often involves substances which may have different pharmacologic effects from the preferred drug. Concurrent use of such dissimilar compounds as stimulants and opiates or stimulants and alcohol is not unusual. The diversity of reported drug use combinations suggests that achieving some perceptible change in state, rather than any particular direction of change (stimulation or sedation), may be the primary reinforcer in polydrug use and abuse.

A practical determinant of polydrug use patterns is the relative availability and cost of the drugs. There are many examples of situationally determined drug use patterns, including the fact that soldiers who became dependent on heroin in Vietnam seldom continued heroin use after separation from military service. However, a significant number of Vietnam heroin addicts abused alcohol and became alcohol-dependent when they returned to the United States. Alcohol abuse, with its attendant medical complications, is one of the most serious problems encountered in former heroin addicts participating in methadone maintenance programs.

The physician must recognize that perpetuation of polydrug abuse and drug dependence is not necessarily a symptom of an underlying emotional disorder. Neither alleviation of anxiety nor reduction of depression accounts for initiation and perpetuation of polydrug abuse. Severe depression and anxiety are as frequently the consequences of polydrug abuse as they are the antecedents. There is also evidence that some of the most adverse consequences of drug use may be reinforcing and contribute to the continuation of polydrug abuse.

Adequate treatment of polydrug abuse, as well as other forms of drug abuse, requires innovative and eclectic programs of intervention. The first step in successful treatment is detoxification, a process which may be difficult because the patient has abused several drugs with different pharmacologic actions (e.g. alcohol, opiates, and cocaine). Since patients may not recall or may deny simultaneous multiple drug use, diagnostic evaluation should always include urinalysis for qualitative detection of psychoactive substances and their metabolites. Treatment of polydrug abuse requires hospitalization or inpatient residential care during detoxification and the initial phase of drug abstinence. When possible, specialized facilities for the care and treatment of chemically dependent persons should be used. Outpatient detoxification of polydrug abuse patients is likely to be ineffective and may be dangerous.

As in the treatment of alcohol abuse, no single therapeutic modality has been shown to be uniquely effective in inducing remission. Polydrug abuse is a chronic disorder with an unpredictable pattern of remission and recrudescence. Therapeutic management of chronic disorders such as cardiac or neoplastic disease should serve as a model for helping the person with polydrug abuse problems. Even temporary remissions with attendant physical, social, and psychological improvements are preferable to the continuation or progressive acceleration of polydrug abuse and its related adverse medical and interpersonal consequences. In polydrug abuse, as in most chronic disorders, definitive "cures" rarely occur. The concerned physician should continue to assist polydrug abuse patients throughout the cyclic oscillations of this complex behavior disorder, recognizing that resumption of drug use may be the rule rather than the exception.

REFERENCES

ABEL EL: *Marihuana: The First Twelve Thousand Years*, New York, Plenum, 1980

BERNSTEIN JG: Medical consequences of marihuana use, in *Advances in Substance Abuse, Behavioral and Biological Research*, NK Mello (ed). Greenwich, JAI Press, 1980, vol 1, pp 255–258

DOMINO EF (ed): *PCP (Phencyclidine): Historical and Current Perspectives.* Ann Arbor, NPP Books, 1981

GRABOWSKI J (ed): *Cocaine: Pharmacology, Effects, and Treatment of Abuse*, NIDA Research Monograph 50, DHEW Publication (ADM) 84–1325. Washington DC, US Government Printing Office, 1984

JAFFE JH: Drug addiction and drug abuse, in *The Pharmocological Basis of Therapeutics*, 4th ed, AG Gilman et al (eds). New York, Macmillan, 1980, pp 535–584

KANDEL D: Marihuana users in young adulthood. Arch Gen Psychiat 41:200, 1984

MELLO NK: A behavioral analysis of the reinforcing properties of alcohol and other drugs in man, in *The Pathogenesis of Alcoholism, Biological Factors*, B Kissin and H Begleiter (eds). New York, Plenum, 1983, vol 7, pp 133–198

MENDELSON JH: Chronic effects of cannabis on human brain function and behavior, in *Cannabis and Health Hazards. Proceedings of an ARF/WHO Scientific Meeting on Adverse Health and Behavioral Consequences of Cannabis Use*, KO Fehr and H

Kalant (eds). Toronto, Alcohol and Drug Addiction Research Foundation, 1983, pp 475–500

MENDELSON JH, MELLO NK (eds): *The Diagnosis and Treatment of Alcoholism,* 2d ed. New York, McGraw-Hill, 1985

PETERSEN RC, STILLMAN RD (eds): *Phencyclidine (PCP) Abuse: An Appraisal,* NIDA Research Monograph 21, DHEW Publication (ADM) 78–728. Washington, DC, US Government Printing Office, 1978

VAN DYKE C, BYCK R: Cocaine use in man, in *Advances in Substance Abuse, Behavioral and Biological Research*, NK Mello (ed). Greenwich, JAI Press, 1983, vol 3, pp 1–24

APPENDIX LABORATORY VALUES OF CLINICAL IMPORTANCE

INTRODUCTORY COMMENTS

Since *Principles of Internal Medicine* is a textbook used internationally, in preparing the Appendix the editors have taken into account the fact that the system of international units (SI, système international d'unités) has been adopted by many laboratories. To this end, where possible and appropriate, common laboratory values are expressed in terms of both traditional units and SI units. *Values in SI units appear in brackets* after values in traditional units. The use of SI units in medicine was endorsed by the Thirtieth World Health Assembly (May 1977) with the purpose of implementing an international language of measurement.[1] The SI *base* units, SI *derived* units, other units of measurement referred to in this Appendix, and SI prefixes are listed in Tables A-1 to A-3. These and other tables of laboratory values are to be found at the end of the Appendix.

ASCITIC FLUID

See Table 39-1, page 190.

BODY FLUIDS AND OTHER MASS DATA

Body fluid, total volume: 50 percent (in obese) to 70 percent (lean) of body weight
  Intracellular: 30 to 40 percent of body weight
  Extracellular: 20 to 30 percent of body weight
Blood:
  Total volume:
    Males: 69 mL per kilogram of body weight
    Females: 65 mL per kilogram of body weight
  Plasma volume:
    Males: 39 mL per kilogram of body weight
    Females: 40 mL per kilogram of body weight
  Red blood cell volume:
    Males: 30 mL per kilogram of body weight (1.15 to 1.21 liters per square meter of body surface area)
    Females: 25 mL per kilogram of body weight (0.95 to 1.00 liters per square meter of body surface area)

$$meq/liter = \frac{mg/dL \times 10 \times valence}{atomic\ weight}$$

$$mg/dL = \frac{meq/liter \times atomic\ weight}{10 \times valence}$$

CEREBROSPINAL FLUID[2]

Osmolarity   292–297 mosmol per liter

---

[1] *The SI for the Health Professions, Geneva, World Health Organization, 1977.*

[2] *Since cerebrospinal fluid concentrations are equilibrium values, measurement of blood plasma obtained at the same time is recommended.*

Electrolytes:

Sodium	137–145 meq per liter
Potassium	2.7–3.9 meq per liter
Calcium	2.1–3.0 meq per liter
Magnesium	2.0–2.5 meq per liter
Phosphorus	1.2–2.0 mg/dL
Chloride	116–122 meq per liter
Bicarbonate	20–24 meq per liter
P_{CO_2}	45–49 mmHg
pH	7.31–7.34
Glucose	40–70 mg/dL
Lactate	10–20 mg/dL
Pyruvate	0.078–0.081 meq per liter
Lactate/pyruvate ratio	26.0
Total protein:	20–45 mg/dL
Prealbumin	2–6%
Albumin	56–75%
Alpha$_1$ globulin	2–7%
Alpha$_2$ globulin	4–12%
Beta globulin	8–16%
Gamma globulin	3–12%
IgG	1.0–1.4 mg/dL
IgA	0.1–0.3 mg/dL
IgM	0.01–0.12 mg/dL
IgG synthesis rate	(−) 9.9 to (+) 3.3 mg per day
Ammonia	25–80 µg/dL
Urea	4.4–4.8 mmol per liter
Creatinine	0.5–1.9 mg/dL
Uric acid	0.23–0.27 mg/dL
Putrescine	130–230 pmol/mL
Spermidine	110–190 pmol/mL
Cyclic AMP	3–30 nmol per liter
HVA (homovanillic acid)	35–85 µg/mL
5-HIAA (5-OH indoleacetic acid)	0.03–0.05 µg/mL
MHPG (3-methoxy-4-hydroxy-phenylethyleneglycol)	13.0–17.0 mg/dL
Myelin basic protein	<4 ng/mL
CSF pressure	50–180 mmH$_2$O
CSF volume (adult)	100–160 mL
Leukocytes:	
Total	<4 per cubic millimeter
Differential:	
Lymphocytes	60–70%
Monocytes	30–50%
Neutrophils	1–3%

CHEMICAL CONSTITUENTS OF BLOOD

See also "Function Tests," especially "Metabolic and Endocrine."

Acetoacetate, plasma: <1.0 mg/dL [<0.1 mmol per liter]
Albumin, serum: 3.5 to 5.5 g/dL [35 to 55 g per liter]
Aldolase: 0 to 8 units per liter [0 to 130 nmol/s per liter]
Alpha$_1$ antitrypsin, serum: 85–213 mg/dL [0.85–2.13 g per liter]

α-Amino nitrogen, plasma: 3.0 to 5.5 mg/dL [2.1 to 3.9 mmol per liter]

Alpha fetoprotein (adult), serum: <30 mg/mL

Aminotransferases, serum:

Aspartate (AST, SGOT): 10 to 40 Karmen units per milliliter; 6 to 18 units per liter [100 to 300 μmol/s per liter]

Alanine (ALT, SGPT): 10 to 40 Karmen units per milliliter; 3 to 26 units per liter [50 to 430 μmol/s per liter]

Ammonia, whole blood, venous: 80 to 110 μg/dL [47 to 65 μmol per liter]

Amylase, serum: 60 to 180 Somogyi units per deciliters; 0.8 to 3.2 units per liter [13 to 53 nmol/s per liter]

Arterial blood gases:

[HCO_3^-]: 21 to 28 meq per liter [21 to 28 mmol per liter]

P_{CO_2}: 35 to 45 mmHg [4.7 to 6.0 kPa]

pH: 7.38 to 7.44

P_{O_2}: 80 to 100 mmHg [11 to 13 kPa]

Ascorbic acid (vitamin C), serum: 0.4 to 1.0 mg/dL [23 to 57 μmol per liter]

Leukocytes: 25 to 40 mg/dL [1420 to 2270 μmol per liter]

Barbiturates, serum: nondetectable

Phenobarbital, "potentially fatal" level (Schreiner): approximately 9 mg/dL [390 μmol per liter]

Most short-acting barbiturates: 3.5 mg/dL [150 μmol per liter]

Base, total, serum: 145 to 155 meq per liter [145 to 155 mmol per liter]

β-Hydroxybutyrate, plasma: <3mg/dL [<0.3 mmol per liter]

Bilirubin, total, serum (Malloy-Evelyn): 0.3 to 1.0 mg/dL [5.1 to 17 μmol per liter]

Direct, serum: 0.1 to 0.3 mg/dL [1.7 to 5.1 μmol per liter]

Indirect, serum: 0.2 to 0.7 mg/dL [3.4 to 12 μmol per liter]

Bromides, serum: nondetectable

Toxic levels: >17 meq per liter; 150 mg/dL [17 mmol per liter]

Bromsulphalein, BSP (5 mg per kilogram of body weight, intravenously): 5 percent or less retention after 45 min

C-reactive protein, serum: 7–820 μg/dL

Calciferols (vitamin D), plasma:

1,25-dihydroxyvitamin D [1,25(OH)₂D]. 20 to 60 pg/mL [48 to 144 nmol per liter]

25-hydroxyvitamin D [25(OH)D]. 8 to 42 ng/mL [20 to 100 μmol per liter]

Calcium, ionized: 2.3 to 2.8 meq per liter; 4.5 to 5.6 mg/dL [1.1 to 1.4 mmol per liter]

Calcium, plasma: 4.5 to 5.5 meq per liter; 9 to 10.5 mg/dL [2.2 to 2.6 mmol per liter]

Carbon dioxide-combining power, serum (sea level): 21 to 28 meq per liter; 50 to 65 volume percent [21 to 28 mmol per liter]

Carbon dioxide content, plasma (sea level): 21 to 30 meq per liter; 50 to 70 volume percent [21 to 30 mmol per liter]

Carbon dioxide tension, arterial blood (sea level): 35 to 45 mmHg [4.7 to 6.0 kPa]

Carbon monoxide content, blood: nondetectable symptoms with over 20 percent saturation of hemoglobin

Carcinoembryonic antigen (CEA): 0 to 2.5 ng/mL (in healthy nonsmokers) [0 to 2.5 μg per liter]

Carotenoids, serum: 50 to 300 μg/dL [0.9 to 5.6 μmol per liter]

Ceruloplasmin, serum: 27 to 37 mg/dL [1.8 to 2.5 μmol per liter]

Chlorides, serum (as Cl⁻): 98 to 106 meq per liter [98 to 106 mmol per liter]

Cholesterol: see Table A-4

Complement, serum:

Total hemolytic (CH₅₀): 150 to 250 units per milliliter

C3: 55 to 120 mg/dL [0.55 to 1.20 g per liter]

C4: 20 to 50 mg/dL [0.20 to 0.50 g per liter]

Copper, serum (mean ± 1 SD): 114 ± 14 μg/dL [17.9 μmol per liter]

Creatine phosphokinase, serum (total):

Females: 10 to 70 units per millimeter [0.17 to 1.18 mmol/s per liter]

Males: 25 to 90 units per milliliter [0.42 to 1.51 mmol/s per liter]

Isoenzymes, serum: fraction 2 (MB) <5 percent of total

Creatinine, serum: <1.5 mg/dL [<133 μmol per liter]

Digoxin serum:

Therapeutic level: 1.2 ± 4 ng/mL [1.54 ± 0.5 nmol per liter]

Toxic level: >2.4 ng/mL [>3.2 nmol per liter]

Ethanol, blood:

Mild to moderate intoxication: 80 to 200 mg/dL [17 to 43 mmol per liter]

Marked intoxication: 250 to 400 mg/dL [54 to 87 mmol per liter]

Severe intoxication: >400 mg/dL [>87 mmol per liter]

Fatty acids, free (nonesterified), plasma: <18 mg/dL [<0.7 mmol per liter]

Ferritin, serum: 15 to 200 ng/mL [15 to 200 μg per liter]

Fibrinogen, plasma: see "Platelets and Coagulation"

Fibrinogen split products: see "Platelets and Coagulation"

Folic acid, serum: 6 to 15 ng/mL [14 to 34 nmol per liter]

Folic acid, red cell: 150 to 450 ng per milliliter of cells [340 to 1020 nmol per liter cells]

γ-Glutamyl transferase (transpeptidase), serum: 4 to 60 units per liter [0.07 to 1.00 μmol/s per liter]

Gastrin, serum: 40 to 200 pg/mL [40 to 200 ng per liter]

Globulins, serum: 2.0 to 3.0 g/dL [20 to 30 g per liter]

Glucose (fasting), plasma:

Normal: 75 to 115 mg/dL [4.2 to 6.4 mmol per liter]

Diabetes mellitus: >140 mg/dL (on more than one occasion) [>7.8 mmol per liter]

Glucose, 2 h postprandial, plasma:

Normal: <140 mg/dL [<7.8 mmol per liter]

Impaired glucose tolerance: 140 to 200 mg/dL [7.8 to 11.1 mmol per liter]

Diabetes mellitus: >200 mg/dL [>11.1 mmol per liter] (on more than one occasion)

Hemoglobin, blood (sea level):

Males: 14 to 18 g/dL [8.7 to 11.2 mmol per liter]

Females: 12 to 16 g/dL [7.4 to 9.9 mmol per liter]

Hemoglobin A₁c: up to 6 perrcent of total hemoglobin

Immunoglobulins, serum:

IgA: 90 to 325 mg/dL [0.9 to 3.2 g per liter]

IgD: 0 to 8 mg/dL [0 to 0.08 g per liter]

IgE: <0.025 mg/dL [<0.00025 g per liter]

IgG: 800 to 1500 mg/dL [8.0 to 15.0 g per liter]

IgM: 45 to 150 mg/dL [0.45 to 1.5 g per liter]

Iron, serum:

Males and females (mean ± 1 SD): 105 ± 35 μg/dL [19 ± 6 μmol per liter]

Iron-binding capacity, serum (mean ± 1 SD): 305 ± 32 μg/dL [55 ± 6 μmol per liter]

Saturation: 20 to 45 percent

Ketones, total: 0.5 to 1.5 mg/dL [5.0 to 15.0 mg per liter]

Lactate dehydrogenase, serum:

200 to 450 units per milliliter (Wrobleski)

60 to 100 units per milliliter (Wacker)

25 to 100 units per liter [0.4 to 1.7 μmol/s per liter]

Lactic dehydrogenase isoenzymes, serum (agarose):

Fraction 1 (% of total): 14–26

Fraction 2: 29–39

Fraction 3: 20–26

Fraction 4: 8–16

Fraction 5: 6–16

Lactate, venous plasma: 5 to 15 mg/dL [0.6 to 1.7 mmol per liter]

Lead, serum: <20 μg/dL [<1.0 μmol per liter]

Lipase, serum: 1.5 units (Cherry-Crandall)

Lipids: see Table A-4

Lipids, triglyceride, serum: see Table A-4

Lipoprotein: see Table A-4

Lithium, serum:

Therapeutic concentration: 0.6 to 1.2 mmol per liter

Toxic concentration: >2 mmol per liter [>2 mmol per liter]

Magnesium, serum: 1.3 to 2.1 meq per liter; 2 to 3 mg/dL [0.8 to 1.3 mmol per liter]

Nitrogen, nonprotein, serum: 15 to 35 mg/dL [0.15 to 0.35 g per liter]

5'-Nucleotidase, serum: 0.3 to 2.6 Bodansky units per deciliter [27 to 233 nmol/s per liter]

Osmolality, plasma: 285 to 295 mosmol per kilogram of serum water

Oxygen content:
    Arterial blood (sea level): 17 to 21 volume percent
    Venous blood, arm (sea level): 10 to 16 volume percent

Oxygen percent saturation (sea level):
    Arterial blood: 97 percent [0.97 mol/mol]
    Venous blood, arm: 60 to 85 percent [0.60 to 0.85 mol/mol]

Oxygen tension, blood: 80 to 100 mmHg ob11 to 13 kPa]

pH, blood: 7.38 to 7.44

Phenytoin, plasma:
    Therapeutic level: 10 to 20 μg/mL [40 to 79 μmol per liter]
    Toxic level: >30 μg/mL [>119 μmol per liter]

Phosphatase, acid, serum:
    Bessey-Lowry method: 0.10 to 0.63 units [28 to 175 nmol/s per liter]
    Bodansky method: 0.5 to 2.0 units
    Fishmann-Lerner (tartrate sensitive): <0.6 units per deciliter (up to 0.15 units per deciliter)
    Gutman method: 0.5 to 2.0 units
    International units: 0.2 to 1.8 [3 to 30 nmol/s per liter]
    King-Armstrong method: 1.0 to 5.0 units

Phosphatase, alkaline, serum:
    Bessey-Lowry method: 0.8 to 2.3 units (3.4 to 9 units[3])
    Bodansky method: 2.0 to 4.5 units (3.0 to 13.0 units[3]) [0.18 to 0.40 nmol/s per liter]
    Gutman method: 2.0 to 4.5 units (3.0 to 13.0 units[3])
    International units: 21 to 91 per liter at 37°C [0.4 to 1.5 μmol/s per liter]
    King-Armstrong method: 4.0 to 13.0 units (10.0 to 20.0 units[3])

Phospholipids, serum: 150 to 250 mg/dL (as lecithin) [48 to 81 mmol per liter]

Phosphorus, inorganic, serum: 1 to 1.5 meq per liter; 3 to 4.5 mg/dL [1.0 to 1.4 mmol per liter]

Potassium, serum: 3.5 to 5.0 meq per liter [3.5 to 5.0 mmol per liter]

Proteins, total, serum: 5.5 to 8.0 g/dL [55 to 80 g per liter]

Protein fractions, serum:
    Albumin: 3.5 to 5.5 g/dL (50 to 60 percent) [35 to 55 g per liter]
    Globulin: 2.0 to 3.5 g/dL (40 to 50 percent) [20 to 35 g per liter]
    Alpha$_1$: 0.2 to 0.4 g/dL (4.2 to 7.2 percent) [2 to 4 g per liter]
    Alpha$_2$: 0.5 to 0.9 g/dL (6.8 to 12 percent) [5 to 9 g per liter]
    Beta: 0.6 to 1.1 g/dL (9.3 to 15 percent) [6 to 11 g per liter]
    Gamma: 0.7 to 1.7 g/dL (13 to 23 percent) [7 to 17 g per liter]

Pyruvate, venous, plasma: 0.5 to 1.5 mg/dL [0.06 to 0.17 mmol per liter]

Quinidine, serum:
    Therapeutic range: 1.5 to 3 μg/mL [4.6 to 9.2 μmol per liter]
    Toxic range: 5 to 6 μg/mL [15.4 to 18.5 μmol per liter]

Salicylate, plasma: 0 mmol per liter
    Therapeutic range: 20 to 25 mg/dL [1.4 to 1.8 mmol per liter]
    Toxic range: >30 mg/dL [2.2 mmol per liter]

Sodium, serum: 136 to 145 meq per liter [136 to 145 mmol per liter]

Steroids: see "Metabolic and Endocrine" under "Function Tests"

Transaminase, serum glutamic oxaloacetic (SGOT, AST): 10 to 40 Karmen units per milliliter; 6 to 18 units per liter [100 to 300 μmol/s per liter]

Transaminase, serum glutamic pyruvic (SGPT, ALT): see Aminotransferases, serum

Transferase, γ-glutamyl, serum: 4 to 60 units per liter [0.07 to 1.00 μmol/s per liter]

Triglycerides: see Table A-4

Urea nitrogen, serum: 10 to 20 mg/dL [3.6 to 7.1 mmol per liter]

Uric acid, serum:
    Men: 2.5 to 8.0 mg/dL [0.15 to 0.48 mmol per liter]
    Women: 1.5 to 6.0 mg/dL [0.09 to 0.36 mmol per liter]

Vitamin A, serum: 20 to 100 μg/dL [0.7 to 3.5 μmol per liter]

Vitamin B$_{12}$, serum: 200 to 600 pg/mL [148 to 443 pmol per liter]

Zinc, serum (mean ± 1 SD): 120 ± 20 μg/dL [18 ± 3 μmol per liter]

FUNCTION TESTS

Circulation

Arteriovenous oxygen difference: 30 to 50 mL per liter

Cardiac output (Fick): 2.5 to 3.6 liters per square meter of body surface area per minute

Contractility indexes:
    Maximum left ventricular dp/dt: 1650 ± 300 mmHg/s
    Maximum $(dp/dt)/p$: 44 ± 8.4 s^{-1}
    $(dp/dt)/DP$ at DP = 40 mmHg: 37.6 ± 12.2 s^{-1} (DP = diastolic press.)
    Mean normalized systolic ejection rate (angiography): 3.32 ± 0.84 end-diastolic volumes per second
    Mean velocity of circumferential fiber shortening (angiography) 1.66 ± 0.42 circumferences per second

Ejection fraction, stroke volume/end-diastolic volume (SV/EDV):
    Normal range: 0.55 to 0.78; average: 0.67

End-diastolic volume: 75 ± 15 mL/m^2

End-systolic volume: 25 ± 8 mL/m^2

Left ventricular work:
    Stroke work index: 30 to 110 (g·m)/m^2
    Left ventricular minute work index: 1.8 to 6.6 [(kg·m)/m^2]/min
    Oxygen consumption index: 110 to 150 mL per liter

Pressures, intracardiac and intraarterial: see Table A-5

Pulmonary vascular resistance: 20 to 120 (dyn·s)/cm^5 [2 to 12 kPa·s per liter]

Systemic vascular resistance: 770 to 1500 (dyn·s)/cm^5 [77 to 150 kPa·s per liter]

Systolic time intervals: see Table A-6

Gastrointestinal   See also "Stool."

Absorption tests:
    D-Xylose absorption test: After an overnight fast, 25 g xylose is given in aqueous solution by mouth. Urine collected for the following 5 h should contain 5 to 8 g [33 to 53 mmol] (or >20 percent of ingested dose). Serum xylose should be 25 to 40 mg per 100 mL 1 h after the oral dose [1.7 to 2.7 mmol per liter].
    Vitamin A absorption test: A fasting blood specimen is obtained and 200,000 units of vitamin A in oil is given by mouth. Serum vitamin A levels should rise to twice fasting level in 3 to 5 h.

Bentiromide test (pancreatic function): 500 mg bentiromide (chymex) orally; p-aminobenzoic acid (PABA) measured in plasma and/or urine
    Plasma: >3.6 (±1.1) μg/mL at 90 min
    Urine: >50 percent recovered as PABA in 6 h

Gastric juice:
    Volume:
        24 h: 2 to 3 liters
        Nocturnal: 600 to 700 mL
        Basal, fasting: 30 to 70 mL/h
    Reaction:
        As pH: 1.6 to 1.8
        Titratable acidity of fasting juice: 15 to 35 meq/h [4 to 10 μmol/s]
    Acid output:
        Basal:
            Females (mean ± 1 SD): 2.0 ± 1.8 meq/h [0.6 ± 0.5 μmol/s]
            Males (mean ± 1 SD): 3.0 ± 2.0 meq/h [0.8 ± 0.6 μmol/s]

---

[3] *Values in parentheses are those found in children.*

Maximal [after subcutaneous histamine acid phosphate 0.004 mg/kg and preceded by 50 mg promethazine (Phenergan); or after betazole (Histalog) 1.7 mg/kg or pentagastrin 6μg/mg]:

Females (mean ± 1 SD): 16 ± 5 meq/h [4.4 ± 1.4 μmol/s]
Males (mean ± 1 SD): 23 ± 5 meq/h [6.4 ± 1.4 μmol/s]
Basal acid output/maximal acid output ratio: 0.6 or less

Gastrin, serum: 40 to 200 pg/mL [40 to 200 ng per liter]

Secretin test (pancreatic exocrine function): 1 unit per kilogram of body weight, intravenously

Volume (pancreatic juice): >2.0 mL/kg in 80 min
Bicarbonate concentration: >80 meq per liter [>80 mmol per liter]
Bicarbonate output: >10 meq in 30 min [>10 mmol in 30 min]

Metabolic and endocrine

ACTH, plasma, 8 A.M.: <80 pg/mL [<80 ng per liter]

Adrenal cortex function tests: see Chap. 325

Adrenal medulla function tests: see Chap. 326

Adrenal steroids, plasma:

Aldosterone, 8 A.M.: <8.5 ng/dL [<0.24 nmol per liter] (patient supine, 100 meq Na and 60 to 100 meq K intake)

Cortisol:
8 A.M.: 5 to 25 μg/dL [138 to 691 nmol per liter]
4 P.M.: 3 to 12 μg/dL [82 to 331 nmol per liter]

Dehydroepiandrosterone (DHEA): 0.2 to 0.9 μg/dL [7 to 31 nmol per liter]

Dehydroepiandrosterone sulfate (DHEA sulfate): 50 to 250 μg/dL [1.3 to 6.5 μmol per liter]

11-Deoxycortisol (compound S): <1 μg/dL [<30 nmol per liter]

17-Hydroxyprogesterone:
Women: follicular phase, 20 to 100 ng/dL [0.6 to 3 nmol per liter]; luteal phase, 50 to 350 ng/dL [1.5 to 10.6 nmol per liter]
Men: 6 to 300 ng/dL [1.8 to 9.0 nmol per liter]

Adrenal steroids, secretion rates:
Aldosterone: 50 to 250 μg per day [138 to 690 nmol per day]
Cortisol: 8 to 24 mg per day [22 to 69 μmol per day]

Adrenal steroids, urinary excretion:
Aldosterone: 5 to 19 μg per day [14 to 53 nmol per day]
Cortisol, free: 20 to 100 μg per day [54 to 276 nmol per day]
17-Hydroxycorticosteroids: 2 to 10 mg per day [5.4 to 28 μmol per day]
17-Ketosteroids:
Men: 7 to 25 mg per day [24 to 88 μmol per day]
Women: 4 to 15 mg per day [14 to 52 μmol per day]

Angiotensin II, plasma, 8 A.M.: 10 to 30 pg/mL [10 to 30 nmol per liter]

Arginine vasopressin (AVP), plasma:
Random fluid intake: 1 to 3 pg/mL [1 to 3 ng per liter]
Fluid deprivation, 18 to 24 h: 6 to 12 pg/mL [6 to 12 ng per liter]

Calcitonin, plasma: <50 pg/mL [<50 ng per liter]

Catecholamines, urinary excretion:
Free catecholamines: <100 μg per day [<590 nmol per day]
Epinephrine: <50 μg per day [295 nmol per day]
Metanephrines: <1.3 mg per day [<6.2 μmol per day]
Vanillylmandelic acid (VMA): <8 mg per day [<40 μmol per day]

Gastrin, plasma: <120 pg/mL [<120 ng per liter]

Glucagon, plasma: 50 to 100 pg/mL [14 to 29 pmol per liter]

Gonadal function tests: see Chaps. 330 and 331

Gonadal steroids, plasma:
Androstenedione:
Women: 110 to 190 ng/dL [3.9 to 6.6 nmol per liter]
Men: 80 to 130 ng/dL [2.9 to 4.6 mmol per liter]
Estradiol:
Women: 20 to 60 pg/mL [0.07 to 0.22 nmol per liter], higher at ovulation
Men: <50 pg/mL [<0.18 nmol per liter]

Progesterone:
Men, prepubertal girls, preovulatory women, and postmenopausal women: <2 ng/mL [<6 nmol per liter]
Women, luteal, peak: >5 ng/mL [>16 nmol per liter]
Testosterone:
Women: <100 ng/dL [<3.5 nmol per liter]
Men: 300 to 1000 ng/dL [10 to 35 nmol per liter]
Prepubertal boys and girls: 5 to 20 ng/dL [0.17 to 0.7 nmol per liter]

Gonadotropins, plasma:
Women, mature, premenopausal, except at ovulation:
FSH: 5 to 20 mU/mL [5 to 20 U per liter]
LH: 5 to 25 mU/mL [5 to 25 U per liter]
Ovulatory surge:
FSH: 12 to 30 mU/mL [12 to 30 U per liter]
LH: 25 to 100 mU/mL [25 to 100 U per liter]
Postmenopausal women:
FSH: >50 mU/mL [>50 U per liter]
LH: >50 mU/mL [>50 U per liter]
Men, mature:
FSH: 5 to 20 mU/mL [5 to 20 U per liter]
LH: 5 to 20 mU/mL [5 to 20 U per liter]
Children of both sexes, prepubertal:
FSH: <5 mU/mL [<5 U per liter]
LH: <5 mU/mL [<5 U per liter]

Growth hormone, after 100 g glucose by mouth: <5 ng/dL [<50 ng per liter]

Human chorionic gonadotropin, β subunit (β-hCG), plasma:
Men and nonpregnant women: <3 mIU/mL [<3 IU per liter]

Insulin, serum or plasma, fasting: 6 to 26 μU/mL [43 to 186 pmol per liter]

Insulin-like growth factor I (somatomedin C, IGF-1/SM C): see Chap. 322

Oxytocin, plasma:
Men and preovulatory women: 0.5 to 2 μU/mL [2 to 4 mU per liter]
Lactating women: 5 to 10 μU/mL [5 to 10 mU per liter]

Pancreatic islet function tests: Chap. 327

Parathyroid function tests: see Chap. 336

Pituitary function tests: see Chaps. 321 to 323

Pregnancy tests: see Chap. 331

Prolactin, serum: 2 to 15 ng/mL [2 to 15 μg per liter]

Renin-angiotensin function tests: see Chap. 325

Semen analysis: see Chap. 330

Thyroid function tests:
Dynamic tests of thyroid function: see Chap. 324
Radioactive iodine uptake, 24 h: 5 to 30 percent (range varies in different areas due to variations in iodine intake)
Resin T_3 uptake: 25 to 35 percent (varies among laboratories; for calculation of indexes of resin T_3 uptake, see Chap. 324)
Reverse triiodothyronine (rT_3), plasma: 10 to 40 ng/dL [0.15 to 0.61 nmol per liter]
Thyroid-stimulating hormone (TSH): <5 μU/mL [<5 mU per liter]
Thyroxine (T_4), serum radioimmunoassay: 5 to 12 μg/dL [64 to 154 nmol per liter]
Triiodothyronine (T_3), plasma: 70 to 190 ng/dL [1.1 to 2.9 nmol per liter]

Pulmonary See Tables A-9 and A-10.

Arterial blood gas measurements in normal subjects (sea level):
P_{CO_2}, seated (mean ± 1 SD): 38.0 ± 2.9 mmHg (no change with age) [5.0 kPa]
P_{O_2}:
Seated (mean ± 1 SD): (104.2 ± 0.27 mmHg) × age in years [13.8 kPa]
Supine (mean ± 1 SD): (103.5 ± 0.42 mmHg) × age in years [13.8 kPa]

Renal

Clearances (corrected to 1.72 m² body surface area):
  Measures of glomerular filtration rate:
    Inulin clearance (C1):
      Males (mean ± 1 SD): 124 ± 25.8 mL/min [2.1 ± 0.4 mL/s]
      Females (mean ± 1 SD): 119 ± 12.8 mL/min [2.0 ± 0.2 mL/s]
      Endogenous creatinine clearance: 91 to 130 mL/min [1.5 to 2.2 mL/s]
      Urea: 60 to 100 mL/min [1.0 to 1.7 mL/s]
  Measures of effective renal plasma flow and tubular function:
    p-Aminohippuric acid clearance (Cl$_{PAH}$):
      Males (mean ± 1 SD): 654 ± 163 mL/min [10.9 ± 2.7 mL/s]
      Females (mean ± 1 SD): 594 ± 102 mL/min [9.9 ± 1.7 mL/s]
Concentration and dilution test:
  Specific gravity of urine:
    After 12-h fluid restriction: 1.025 or more
    After 12-h deliberate water intake: 1.003 or less
Phenosulfonphthalein:
  After intravenous injection:
    Excretion in urine in 15 min: 25 percent or more
    Excretion in urine in 2 h: 55 to 75 percent
Protein excretion, urine: <150 mg in 24 h [<0.15 g per day]
  Males: 0 to 60 mg in 24 h [0 to 0.06 g per day]
  Females: 0 to 90 mg in 24 h [0 to 0.09 g per day]
Specific gravity, maximal range: 1.002 to 1.028
Tubular reabsorption, phosphorus: 79 to 94 percent of filtered load

HEMATOLOGIC EXAMINATIONS

See also "Chemical Constituents of Blood."

Bone marrow See Table A-11.

Erythrocytes and hemoglobin See also Table A-12.

Carboxyhemoglobin:
  Nonsmoker: 0 to 2.3 percent
  Smoker: 2.1 to 4.2 percent
Erythrocyte "life span":
  Normal survival: 120 days
  Chromium-labeled, half-life ($t_{\frac{1}{2}}$): 28 days
  Glucose 6-phosphate dehydrogenase: 12.1 ± 2 IU/gHb (WHO)
Ham's test (acid serum): negative
Haptoglobin, serum (mean ± 2 SD): 128 ± 15 mg/dL [1.3 ± 0.2 g per liter]
Heinz body stain: negative
Hemoglobin, plasma: 1 to 5 mg/dL [0.03 to 0.05 g per liter]
Hemoglobin A$_2$ (HbA$_2$): 1.5 to 3.5 percent
Hemoglobin, fetal (HbF): <2 percent
Hemoglobin H prep: negative
Methemoglobin: <1.7 percent
Nitroblue tetrazolium (chronic granulomatous disease): normal
Osmotic fragility:
  Slight hemolysis: 0.45 to 0.39 percent
  Complete hemolysis: 0.33 to 0.30 percent
Plasma iron turnover: 20 to 42 mg per 24 h [0.47 mg/kg]
Protoporphyrin, free erythrocyte (FEP): 16 to 36 μg per deciliter of red blood cells [0.28 to 0.64 μmol per liter]
Red cell distribution width (Coulter): 13 ± 1.5 percent
Sedimentation rate:
  Westergren, <50 years of age:
    Males: 0 to 15 mm/h
    Females: 0 to 20 mm/h
  Westergren, >50 years of age:
    Males: 0 to 20 mm/h
    Females: 0 to 30 mm/h
  Wintrobe:
    Males: 0 to 9 mm/h
    Females: 0 to 20 mm/h
Sucrose hemolysis: negative

Leukocytes See Table A-13.

Platelets and coagulation

Alpha$_2$ antiplasmin: 70 to 130 percent
Antithrombin III: 80 to 120 percent
Bleeding time:
  Ivy method, 5-mm wound: <9 min
  Duke method: <4 min
  Simplate: <7 min
Clot retraction, qualitative: apparent in 60 min, complete <24 h, usually <6 h
Euglobulin lysis time: >2 h
Factor II: 60 to 100 percent
Factor V: 60 to 100 percent
Factor VII: 60 to 100 percent
Factor IX: 60 to 100 percent
Factor X: 60 to 100 percent
Factor XI: 60 to 100 percent
Factor XII: 60 to 100 percent
Factor XIII: clot stable in urea
Fibrinogen: 200 to 400 mg/dL
Fibrin split products: <10 μg/mL
Plasminogen: 2.4 to 4.4 CTA U/mL
Protein C (antigenic assay): 58 to 148 percent
Protein S (antigenic assay): 58 to 148 percent
Partial thromboplastin time (activated PTT): comparable to control
Prothrombin time (quick one-stage): control ± 1 s
Protamine paracoagulation (3P) test: negative
Platelets: 130,000 to 400,000 per cubic millimeter
Thrombin time: control ± 3 s
von Willebrand's antigen: 60 to 150 percent

Miscellaneous

Leukocyte alkaline phosphatase (LAP): 13 to 100
Lysozyme (muramidase), serum: 5 to 25 μg/dL
Lysozyme, urine: <2 μg/mL
Schilling test: excretion in urine of orally administered radioactive vitamin B$_{12}$: 7 to 40 percent
Viscosity, plasma: 1.7 to 2.1
Viscosity, serum: 1.4 to 1.8

STOOL

Bulk:
  Wet weight: <197.5 (115 ± 41) g per day
  Dry weight: <66.4 (34 ± 16) g per day
Alpha$_1$ antitrypsin: 0.98 (± 0.17) mg per gram of dry weight stool
Coproporphyrin: 400 to 1000 μg in 24 h [610 to 1500 nmol per day]
Fat (on diet containing at least 50 g fat): <6.0 (4.0 ± 1.5) g per day when measured on a 3-day (or longer) collection
  Percent of dry weight: <30.4 (13.3 ± 8.07)
  Coefficient of fat absorption: >95 percent
Fatty acid:
  Free: 1 to 10 percent of dry matter
  Combined as soap: 0.5 to 12 percent of dry matter
Nitrogen: <1.7 (1.4 ± 0.2) g per day
Protein content: minimal
Urobilinogen: 40 to 280 mg in 24 h [67 to 470 μmol per day]
Water: approximately 65 percent

URINE

See also "Metabolic and Endocrine" under "Function Tests."

Acidity, titratable: 20 to 40 meq in 24 h [20 to 40 mmol per day]

α-Amino nitrogen: 0.4 to 1.0 g in 24 h [28 to 71 mmol per day]

Ammonia: 30 to 50 meq in 24 h [30 to 50 mmol per day]

Amylase: 35 to 260 Somogyi units per hour

Amylase/creatinine clearance ratio [(Cl$_{am}$/Cl$_{cr}$) × 100]: 1 to 5

Bentiromide (pancreatic function): 50 percent excreted in 6 h as *p*-amino benzoic acid (PABA) after 500 mg oral bentiromide

Calcium (10 meq or 200-mg calcium diet): <7.5 meq in 24 h; <150 mg in 24 h [<3.8 mmol per day]

Catecholamines: <100 μg in 24 h

Copper: 0 to 25 μg in 24 h [0 to 0.4 μmol per day]

Coproporphyrins (types I and III): 100 to 300 μg in 24 h [150 to 460 nmol per day]

Creatine, as creatinine:

    Adult males: <50 mg in 24 h [<0.38 mmol per day]

    Adult females: <100 mg in 24 h [<0.76 mmol per day]

Creatinine: 1.0 to 1.6 g in 24 h [8.8 to 14 mmol per day]

Glucose, true (oxidase method): 50 to 300 mg in 24 h [0.3 to 1.7 mmol per day]

5-Hydroxyindoleacetic acid (5-HIAA): 2 to 9 mg in 24 h [10 to 47 μmol per day]

Ketones, total (mean ± 1 SD): 50.5 ± 30.7 mg in 24 h

Lactic dehydrogenase: 560 to 2050 units in 8-h urine

Lead: <0.08 μg/mL; <120 μg in 24 h [0.39 μmol per liter]

Protein: <150 mg in 24 h [<0.05 g per day]

Porphobilinogen: none

Potassium: 25 to 100 meq in 24 h (varies with intake) [25 to 100 mmol per day]

Sodium: 100 to 260 meq in 24 h (varies with intake) [100 to 260 mmol per day]

Urobilinogen: 1 to 3.5 mg in 24 h [1.7 to 5.9 μmol per day]

Vanillylmandelic acid (VMA): <8 mg per day [<40 μmol per day]

D-Xylose excretion: 5 to 8 g within 5 h after oral dose of 25 g [33 to 53 mmol in 5 h]

TABLE A-1 SI and other units

Quantity	Name of unit	Symbol for unit	Derivation of units
SI BASE UNITS			
Length	meter	m	
Mass	kilogram	kg	
Time	second	s	
Thermodynamic temperature	Kelvin	K	
Amount of substance	mole	mol	
SI DERIVED UNITS			
Force	newton	N	$(m·kg)/s^2$
Pressure	pascal	Pa	$N·m^2$
Work, energy	joule	J	N·m
Celsius temperature	degree Celsius	°C	K
OTHER UNITS RETAINED FOR USE			
Time	minute	min	
	hour	h	
	day	d	
Volume	liter	L	

TABLE A-2 Radiation derived units

Quantity	Old unit	SI unit	Name for SI unit (and abbreviation)	Conversion
Activity	curie (Ci)	Disintegrations per second (dps)	becquerel (Bq)	$1 Ci = 3.7 × 10^{10} Bq$; 1 mCi = 37 mBq; 1 μCi = 0.037 MBq or 37 GBq; $1 Bq = 2.703 × 10^{-11} Ci$
Absorbed dose	rad	joule per kilogram (J/kg)	gray (Gy)	1 Gy = 100 rad; 1 rad = 0.01 Gy; $1 mrad = 10^{-3} cGy$
Exposure	roentgen (R)	coulomb per kilogram (C/kg)	—	1 C/kg = 3876 R; $1 R = 2.58 × 10^{-4} C/kg$; 1 mR = 258 pC/kg
Dose equivalent	rem	joule per kilogam (J/kg)	sievert (Sv)	1 Sv = 100 rem; 1 rem = 0.01 Sv; 1 mrem = 10 μSv

TABLE A-3 SI prefixes and their symbols

Factor	Prefix	Symbol for prefix
10^9	giga	G
10^6	mega	M
10^3	kilo	k
10^2	hecto	h
10^1	deka	da
10^{-1}	deci	d
10^{-2}	centi	c
10^{-3}	milli	m
10^{-6}	micro	μ
10^{-9}	nano	n
10^{-12}	pico	p
10^{-15}	femto	f
10^{-18}	alto	a

TABLE A-4 Plasma lipid concentration in normal subjects*

Age	Total plasma cholesterol, mg/dL Men	Women	Plasma LDL-cholesterol, mg/dL Men	Women	Plasma HDL-cholesterol, mg/dL Men	Women	Plasma triglyceride, mg/dL Men	Women
19	113–197	120–203	62–130	59–137	30–63	35–74	37–148	39–132
29	133–244	130–229	70–165	71–164	31–63	37–83	46–249	40–172
39	146–270	141–245	81–189	75–172	29–62	34–82	54–321	41–194
49	158–276	152–268	98–202	79–186	30–64	34–87	58–327	47–228
59	156–276	169–294	88–203	89–210	28–71	37–91	58–286	56–257
69	158–274	171–297	98–210	92–221	30–78	35–98	57–267	60–241
70+	151–270	167–288	80–186	96–206	31–75	33–92	58–258	60–235

* 5th and 95th percentiles not ideal ranges for white men and women; data are too fragmentary to ascertain whether these values apply to other groups.
SOURCE: *The Lipid Research Clinics Population Studies Data Book, vol 1, The Prevalence Study, NIH Publication No 80-1529, Bethesda, National Institutes of Health, July 1980.*

TABLE A-5 Hemodynamic values

Pressures (mmHg):
Systemic arterial:
  Peak systolic/end-diastolic   100–140/60–90
  Mean   70–105
Left ventricle:
  Peak systolic/end-diastolic   100–140/3–12
Left atrium (or pulmonary capillary wedge):
  Mean   2–12
  a wave   3–10
  v wave   3–15
Pulmonary artery:
  Peak systolic/end-diastolic   15–30/4–14
  Mean   9–17
Right ventricle:
  Peak systolic/end-diastolic   15–30/2–7
Right atrium:
  Mean   2–6
  a wave   2–8
  v wave   2–7
Resistances [(dyn·s)/cm⁵]:
Systemic vascular resistance   700–1600
Total pulmonary resistance   100–300
Pulmonary vascular resistance   20–130
Flows:
Cardiac index (liters per minute per square meter)   2.4–3.8
Stroke index (milliliters per beat per square meter)   30–65
Oxygen consumption (liters per minute per square meter)   110–150
Arteriovenous oxygen difference (milliliters per liter)   30–50

TABLE A-7 Normal values of echocardiographic measurements in adults*

	Range, cm	Mean, cm	Number of subjects
Age (years)	13 to 54	26	134
Body surface area (m²)	1.45 to 2.22	1.8	130
RVD—flat	0.7 to 2.3	1.5	84
RVD—left lateral	0.9 to 2.6	1.7	83
LVID—flat	3.7 to 5.6	4.7	82
LVID—left lateral	3.5 to 5.7	4.7	81
Posterior LV wall thickness	0.6 to 1.1	0.9	137
Posterior LV wall amplitude	0.9 to 1.4	1.2	48
IVS wall thickness	0.6 to 1.1	0.9	137
Mid IVS amplitude	0.3 to 0.8	0.5	10
Apical IVS amplitude	0.5 to 1.2	0.7	38
Left atrial dimension	1.9 to 4.0	2.9	133
Aortic root dimension	2.0 to 3.7	2.7	121
Aortic cusps' separation	1.5 to 2.6	1.9	93
Percentage of fractional shortening†	34 to 44%	36%	20
Mean rate of circumferential shortening (Vcf)‡, or mean normalized shortening velocity	1.02 to 1.94 circ/s	1.3 circ/s	38

* *RVD = right ventricular dimension; LVID = left ventricular internal dimension; d = end diastole; s = end systole; LV = left ventricle; IVS = interventricular septum.*

† $\dfrac{\text{LVIDd} - \text{LVIDs}}{\text{LVIDd}}$

‡ $\dfrac{\text{LVIDd} - \text{LVIDs}}{\text{LVIDd} \times \text{ejection time}}$

SOURCE: *From H Feigenbaum, Echocardiography, in Heart Disease—A Textbook of Cardiovascular Medicine, E Braunwald (ed), Philadelphia, Saunders, 1980.*

TABLE A-6 Systolic time intervals in normal individuals (in milliseconds)

Regression equation	SD of index
QS₂ (M) = −2.1 HR + 546	14
QS₂ (F) = −2.0 HR + 549	14
PEP (M) = −0.4 HR + 131	13
PEP (F) = −0.4 HR + 133	11
LVET (M) = −1.7 HR + 413	10
LVET (F) = −1.6 HR + 418	10

NOTE: *QS_2 = total electromechanical systole, PEP = preejection phase, LVET = left ventricular ejection time, HR = heart rate, M = male, F = female, SD = standard deviation of the systolic time interval index. Systolic ejection period = 220–320 ms per beat; diastolic filling period = 380–500 ms per beat.*
SOURCE: *AM Weissler, CL Garrard, Mod Concepts Cardiovasc Dis 40:1, 1971.*

TABLE A-8 Amplitude of Q, R, S, and T waves in scalar electrocardiogram of 100 normal adults*

	I	II	III	aV$_R$	aV$_L$	aV$_F$	V$_1$	V$_5$	V$_6$
Patients with Q wave	38%	41%	50%	—	38%	40%	0%	60%	75%
Q amplitude:									
Mean	0.4	0.6	0.9	—	0.4	0.7	0	0.3	0.3
Range	0 to 0.10	0 to 1.6	0 to 2.3	—	0 to 1.1	0 to 1.7	0	0 to 1.8	0 to 1.8
R amplitude:									
Mean	5.6	8.9	4.5	1.3	3.4	6.0	1.9	12.6	10.2
Range	1.0 to 10.0	2.0 to 16.9	1.0 to 12.1	0 to 2.9	0 to 8.2	0 to 13.8	1.0 to 6.0	7.0 to 21.0	5.0 to 18.0
S amplitude:									
Mean	2.0	2.1	2.4	7.0	2.6	—	8.0	2.5	1.3
Range	0 to 5.0	0 to 3.7	0 to 6.4	2.2 to 11.8	0 to 5.8	—	3.0 to 13.0	0 to 5.0	0 to 2.0
T amplitude:									
Mean	1.9	2.3	1.0		0.3	1.7	1.0	3.3	1.0
Range	1.0 to 3.0	1.0 to 4.0	−2.0 to 2.0		−1.0 to 2.0	0 to 4.0	−2.0 to 2.0	2.0 to 7.0	1.0 to 4.0

* *Values of Q, R, S, and T amplitudes are in millimeters (1 mm = 0.1 mv).*
SOURCE: *From J D Cooksey et al, Clinical Vectorcardiography and Electrocardiography, 2d ed, Chicago, Year Book Medical Publishers, 1977. Used by permission.*

TABLE A-9 Summary of values useful in pulmonary physiology

	Symbol	Typical values Men	Women
PULMONARY MECHANICS			
Spirometry—volume-time curves:			
Forced vital capacity	FVC	$\geq$4.0 liters	$\geq$3.0 liters
Forced expiratory volume in 1 s	FEV_1	>3.0 liters	>2.0 liters
FEV_1/FVC	$FEV_1\%$	>60%	>70%
Maximal midexpiratory flow	MMF (FEF 25–27)	>2.0 liters per second	>1.6 liters per second
Maximal expiratory flow rate	MEFR (FEF 200–1200)	>3.5 liters per second	>3.0 liters per second
Spirometry—flow-volume curves:			
Maximal expiratory flow at 50% of expired vital capacity	$\dot{V}_{max}$ 50 (FEF 50%)	>2.5 liters per second	>2.0 liters per second
Maximal expiratory flow at 75% of expired vital capacity	$\dot{V}_{max}$ 75 (FEF 75%)	>1.5 liters per second	>1.0 liters per second
Resistance to airflow:			
Pulmonary resistance	RL (R_L)	<3.0 cmH_2O/s per liter	
Airway resistance	Raw	<2.5 cmH_2O/s per liter	
Specific conductance	SGaw	>0.13 cmH_2O/s	
Pulmonary compliance:			
Static recoil pressure at total lung capacity	Pst TLC	25 $\pm$ 5 cmH_2O	
Compliance of lungs (static)	CL	0.2 L/cmH_2O	
Compliance of lungs and thorax	C(L + T)	0.1 L/cmH_2O	
Dynamic compliance of 20 breaths per minute	C dyn 20	0.25 $\pm$ 0.05 liters per cmH_2O	
Maximal static respiratory pressures:			
Maximal inspiratory pressure	MIP	> 90 cmH_2O	> 50 cmH_2O
Maximal expiratory pressure	MEP	>150 cmH_2O	>120 cmH_2O
LUNG VOLUMES			
Total lung capacity	TLC	6–7 liters	5–6 liters
Functional residual capacity	FRC	2–3 liters	2–3 liters
Residual volume	RV	1–2 liters	1–2 liters
Inspiratory capacity	IC	2–4 liters	2–4 liters
Expiratory reserve volume	ERV	1–2 liters	1–2 liters
Vital capacity	VC	4–5 liters	3–4 liters
GAS EXCHANGE (SEA LEVEL)			
Arterial O_2 tension	Pa_{O_2}	95 $\pm$ 5 mmHg	
Arterial CO_2 tension	Pa_{CO_2}	40 $\pm$ 2 mmHg	
Arterial O_2 saturation	Sa_{O_2}	97 $\pm$ 2%	
Arterial blood pH	pH	7.40 $\pm$ 0.02	
Arterial bicarbonate	HCO_3^-	24 + 2 meq per liter	
Base excess	BE	0 $\pm$ 2 meq per liter	
Diffusing capacity for carbon monoxide (single breath)	DL_{CO}	25 mL CO/min/mmHg	
Dead space volume	V_D	50 $\pm$ 25 mL	
Physiologic dead space: dead space-tidal volume ratio (rest)	V_D/V_T	$\leq$35% V_T	
(exercise)		$\leq$20% V_T	
Alveolar-arterial difference for O_2	A-a D_{O_2}	$\leq$20 mmHg	

TABLE A-10 Prediction equations for spirometric tests, lung volumes, and gas exchange in adults

Variable	Sex	Age (A)	Height (H)	Weight (W)	Constant (C)	Standard deviation (SD)
PULMONARY MECHANICS						
Spirometry—volume-time curves* (H in inches):						
FVC	M	−0.025	+0.148	—	−4.241	0.74
	F	−0.024	+0.115	—	−2.852	0.52
FEV_1	M	−0.032	+0.092	—	−1.260	0.55
	F	−0.025	+0.089	—	−1.932	0.47
MEFR	M	−0.047	+0.109	—	+2.010	1.66
(FEF 200–1200)	F	−0.036	+0.145	—	−2.532	1.19
MMF	M	−0.045	+0.047	—	+2.513	1.12
(FEF 25–75)	F	−0.030	+0.060	—	+0.551	0.80
Spirometry—flow-volume curves† (H in centimeters):						
$\dot{V}_{max}$ 50	M	−0.015	+0.069	—	−5.400	1.422
(FEF 50%)	F	−0.013	+0.035	—	−0.444	1.22
$\dot{V}_{max}$ 75	M	−0.012	+0.044	—	−4.143	1.026
(FEF 75%)	F	−0.014	—	—	+3.042	0.936
Lung volumes‡ (H in meters; W in kilograms):						
TLC	M	—	+6.92	−0.017	−4.30	0.67
	F	−0.015	+6.71	—	−5.77	0.48
FRC	M	+0.015	+5.30	−0.037	−3.89	0.56
	F	—	+5.13	−0.028	−4.50	0.41
RV	M	+0.022	+1.98	−0.015	−1.54	0.38
	F	+0.007	+2.68	—	−3.42	0.32
VC	M	−0.020	+4.81	—	−2.81	0.50
	F	−0.022	+4.04	—	−2.35	0.40
Gas exchange§ (H in meters; W in kilograms):						
DL_{CO}	M	−0.20	+32.5	—	−17.6	5.1
	F	−0.16	+21.2	—	−2.66	3.6

NOTE: Answer = (A × age) + (H × height) + (W × weight) + C ± 2 SD. Example: The normal value and lower limit for the FEV_1 are sought in a man, age 40 years, height 183 cm, and weight 91 kg. The following equation gives the normal value:

FEV_1 = (−0.032 × 40) + (0.092 × 72) + (−1.260) = 4.08 liters

The lower limit of normal:

4.08 − (2 × SD) = 4.08 − (2 × 0.55) = 2.98 liters

Only 2.5% of a normal population will fall below this value (2 SD below the mean).

For other abbreviations, see Table A-9.

* Morris et al, Am Rev Respir Dis 103:57, 1971.
† Knudson et al, Am Rev Respir Dis 113:587, 1976.
‡ Grimby G, Söderholm B, Acta Med Scand 173:199, 1963.
§ Coates, JE, Lung Function and Application in Medicine, Davis, 1965.

TABLE A-11 Differential nucleated cell counts of bone marrow

	Normal, mean%*	Range, %†
Myeloid:	56.7	
Neutrophilic series:	53.6	
Myeloblast	0.9	0.2–1.5
Promyelocyte	3.3	2.1–4.1
Myelocyte	12.7	8.2–15.7
Metamyelocyte	15.9	9.6–24.6
Band	12.4	9.5–15.3
Segmented		
Eosinophilic series	3.1	1.2–5.3
Basophilic series	<0.1	0–0.2
Erythroid:	25.6	
Pronormoblasts	0.6	0.2–1.3
Basophilic normoblasts	1.4	0.5–2.4
Polychromatophilic normo-blasts	21.6	17.9–29.2
Orthochromatic normoblasts	2.0	0.4–4.6
Megakaryocytes	<0.1	
Lymphoreticular:	17.8	
Lymphocytes	16.2	11.1–23.2
Plasma cells	2.3	0.4–3.9
Reticulum cells	0.3	0–0.9

* *Frm MM Wintrobe et al, Clinical Hematology, 8th ed, Philadelphia, Lea & Febiger, 1981.*
† *Range observed in 12 healthy men.*

TABLE A-12 Erythrocytes and hemoglobin: Normal values at various ages

Age	Red blood cell count,* millions/mm³	Hemoglobin,* g/dL	Vol. packed RBCs,* mL/dL	Corpuscular values			
				MCV, fl	MCH, pg	MCHC, g/dL	MCD, μm
Days 1–13	5.1 ± 1.0	19.5 ± 5.0	54.0 ± 10.0	106–98	38–33	36–34	8.6
Days 14–60	4.7 ± 0.9	14.0 ± 3.3	42.0 ± 7.0	90	30	33	8.1
3 months to 10 years	4.5 ± 0.7	12.2 ± 2.3	36.0 ± 5.0	80	27	34	7.7
11–15 years	4.8	13.4	39.0	82	28	34	
Adults:							
Females	4.8 ± 0.6	14.0 ± 2.0	42.0 ± 5.0	90 ± 7	29 ± 2	34 ± 2	7.5 ± 0.3
Males	5.4 ± 0.9	16.0 ± 2.0	47.0 ± 5.0	90 ± 7	29 ± 2	34 ± 2	7.5 ± 0.3

* *The range of values represents almost the extremes of observed variations (93 percent or more) at sea level. The blood values of healthy persons should fall well within these mean ± SD figures.*
NOTE: *MCV = mean corpuscular volume, MCH = mean corpuscular hemoglobin, MCHC = mean corpuscular hemoglobin concentration, MCD = mean corpuscular diameter.*
SOURCE: *MM Wintrobe et al, Clinical Hematology, 8th ed, Philadelphia, Lea & Febiger, 1981.*

TABLE A-13 Normal leukocyte count, differential count, and hemoglobin concentration at various ages

Age	Leukocytes, total	Neutrophils			Eosinophils	Basophils	Lympho-cytes	Monocytes	Hemoglo-bin, g/dL blood
		Total	Band	Segmented					
12 mo	11.4(6.0–17.5)	3.5(1.5–8.5)	0.35	3.2	0.3(0.05–0.7)	0.05(0–0.20)	7.0(4.0–10.5)	0.55(0.05–1.1)	11.6(9.0–14.6)
		_31_	_3.1_	_28_	_0.4_	_0.4_	_61_	_4.8_	
4 yr	9.1(5.5–15.5)	3.8(1.5–8.5)	0.27(0–1.0)	3.5(1.5–7.5)	0.25(0.02–0.65)	0.05(0–0.20)	4.5(2.0–8.0)	0.45(0–0.8)	12.6(9.6–15.5)
		_42_	_3.0_	_39_	_2.8_	_0.6_	_50_	_5.0_	
6 yr	4.3(1.5–8.0)	0.25(0–1.0)	4.0(1.5–7.0)	4.0(1.5–7.0)	0.23(0–0.65)	0.05(0–0.20)	3.5(1.5–7.0)	0.40(0–0.8)	12.7(10.0–15.5)
		_51_	_3.0_	_48_	_2.7_	_0.6_	_42_	_4.7_	
10 yr	8.1(4.5–13.5)	4.4(1.8–8.0)	0.24(0–1.0)	4.2(1.8–7.0)	0.20(0–0.60)	0.04(0–0.20)	3.1(1.5–6.5)	0.35(0–0.8)	13.0(10.7–15.5)
		_54_	_3.0_	_51_	_2.4_	_0.5_	_38_	_4.3_	
21 yr	7.4(4.5–11.0)	4.4(1.8–7.7)	0.22(0–0.7)	4.2(1.8–7.0)	0.20(0–0.45)	0.04(0–0.20)	2.5(1.0–4.8)	0.30(0–0.8)	♂15.8 (14.0–18.0)
		_59_	_3.0_	_56_	_2.7_	_0.5_	_34_	_4.0_	♀13.9 (11.5–16.0)

NOTE: *Values are expressed as "cells × 10³/μL." The numbers underlined are percentages.*
SOURCE: *WJ Williams et al (eds), Hematology, 3d ed, New York, McGraw-Hill, New York, 1983. By permission.*

INDEX

INDEX

(Page numbers in **boldface** indicate major discussions.)

Antigens:
Epstein-Barr, 700, 702
gonococcal, 577
H, 1483, 1484
hepatitis, 1325–27, 1331–32
histocompatibility, **337–42.** *See also* HLA system.
I and i, 1484
influenza, 672–73
Kell, 1485
Kidd, 1485
Lewis (Le), 1484
Lutheran, 1485
lymph node function and, 273
lymphocyte differentiation, 1386
microbial, 460–61
oncofetal, 431
pneumonitis, hypersensitivity, 1065, 1066
PPD, 626, **630**
renal disease and, 1170–73
Rh, 1485
serologic tests and. *See* Serology.
shifts of, influenza and, 673
streptococcal, 544
sunlight and, 257–58
T, 661
T cells and, 329, 330
tuberculosis, 626, 630
variant surface glycoprotein (VSG), of trypanosomes, 772
viral, 666
capsid (VCA), 700, 702
western blotting of, 298
Xgᵃ, 1486
Antiglobulin test, 1508
transfusion reaction and, 1488
Antihemophilic factor. *See* Coagulation factor VIII.
Antihistamines:
allergic rhinitis and, 1413–14
anaphylaxis and, 1410
poisoning by, 842
urticaria/angioedema and, 1412
Antihyaluronidase, streptococcal disease and, 953, 954
Antihypertensive agents, 1031–36
antagonists of, 350
Anti-inflammatory agents, 13
back pain and, 42
gout and, 1629
nonsteroidal, 15. *See also* Acetaminophen; Aspirin; Indomethacin; Phenylbutazone; *etc.*
gastritis from, 1257
osteoarthritis and, 1458
platelet defects induced by, 1474
renal disease induced by, 1199
rheumatoid arthritis and, 1427
SLE and, 1422
steroid, 1773. *See also* Corticosteroids; Glucocorticoids; Prednisone.
Antilymphocyte globulin, renal transplantation and, 1168
Antimicrobials, **485–501.** *See also specific agents.*
abscesses and, 480, 488–89
acne vulgaris and, 236
antagonism of, 490
approach to use of, 458
bactericidal titers and, 491
colitis associated with, **564–65,** 567, 1284–85
combinations of, **489–90**
compromised host and, 469
concentrations of, 486, 487
failure of therapy with, 501
foreign bodies and, 489
fractional dosage of, 347
genetic factors and, 488
half-life of, 486, 487
hepatic function and, 488

Antimicrobials:
host factors affecting, 487–89
identification of pathogen and, 485
intravenous, 491
meningitis and, 488
minimal inhibitory concentration, 487–488
minimal microbicidal concentration, 487
monitoring of, 491
pelvic inflammatory disease and, 523
pH influence on, 489
pharmacology of, 486
photosensitizing, 259
pregnancy and, 487, 488
prophylactic, **531–33.** *See also* Chemoprophylaxis.
endocarditis and, 973–74
gonorrhea and, 582
H. influenzae and, 604–5
long-term, 531, 532
meningococcal infections and, 576
rheumatic fever and, 955
scrub typhus and, 755
short-term, 532
single-drug, 531
surgery and, 531–32
susceptible hosts and, 532–33
tuberculosis and, 632
urinary tract infections and, 1193
wound infections and, 471
renal function and, 487–88
resistance to, 489
Corynebacterium, 553
gonorrhea, 578, 581
H. influenzae, 602, 604
pneumococcal, 536
staphylococcal, 539
tuberculosis, 632
route of administration of, 490–91
selection factors, 485
septic shock and, 477
site of infection and, 488–89
susceptibility of pathogen to, 485–87
synergism, 489, **490**
tabulation of data on individual agents, 486
therapeutic trials of, fever and, 56
volume of distribution of, 487
Antimonials, leishmaniasis and, 786, 787
Antimony dust, 1072
Antimuscarinic poisoning, 842
Antinuclear antibodies. *See* Antibodies, antinuclear.
Antiparasitic agents, 770–71
Antiplatelet agents, stroke and, 1940, 1941
Antipsychotic agents, **2104–5**
schizophrenia and, 2095
Antipyretics, 50–51
pyrogens and, 45
Antiserum. *See* Antitoxin; Immunoglobulins.
Antisocial behavior, 2096–97, 2098
Antistreptolysin O test, 544
rheumatic fever and, 953, 954
Antistreptozyme test, 953–54
Antithrombin, 268–69
deficiency, **1481**
schema of reactions involving, 270
Antithymocyte globulin:
graft-vs.-host disease and, 1540
serum sickness from, 1416, 1417
Antithyroid therapy, 1745–46
pregnancy and, 1747
thyrotoxic crisis and, 1749
Antitoxin:
botulinus, 563
diphtheria, 530–31, 553, 554
gas gangrene, 567
tetanus, 560, 561
Antitrypsin:
emphysema and, 1088
gene replacement therapy and, 309
hepatic lesions and, 1355

Antitrypsin:
panniculitis and, 1679
prenatal analysis for, 303
protein loss and, 1275–76
Antivenin (antivenom), 531, 833, 834
fish envenomation and, 837
Antiviral agents, **667–72**
Anton's syndrome, 63, 74
Anton test, 554
Antrectomy, peptic ulcer and, 1248
consequences of, 1248, 1249
Antrum, gastric:
eosinophilia and, 1260
fibroid polyp of, 1260
gastrin secretion by, 1239, 1252
gastritis and, 1258
ulcer of, 1246
vagotomy and, 1248
Antrypol, 789
Anuria, 192
acute renal failure and, 1151
hyperkalemia and, 207
obstruction and, 1216
Anus:
bleeding from, 181. *See also* Rectum, bleeding from.
cancer of, chemotherapy for, 442
Crohn's disease and, 1281
defecation and, 177
donovanosis of, 609, 610
fissures and fistulas, 1302
hemorrhoids and, 1301–2
herpetic lesions of, 516, 694
homosexuality and lesions of, 516, 517
inflammation of, 1302
lymphogranuloma venereum of, 762, 763
pruritus of, enterobiasis and, 816
sphincter tone, 219
streptococcal infection, 548
warts of, 734
Anxiety, **2089–93**
approach to patient with, 60
carcinoid and, 62
chest pain and, 20
classification, 2089
definition, 2089
dream, 113
drug therapy for, 2099, **2103–4**
dyspnea and, 143
examination for, 61
faintness and, 67
generalized, 2090–91
hyperventilation and, 143, 1134
palpitation and, 22–23
panic disorder, 2089–90
posttraumatic, 2091–92
symptoms, 62
thyrotoxicosis and, 1745
Aorta, **1037–40**
aneurysms, **1037–38**
abdominal, 1037–38
ascending, 1038
descending, 1038
hypertension and, 1038
sinus of Valsalva, 945–46
syphilitic, 643, 1038
arteriosclerosis, **1039–40**
obliterans, 1041, 1042
atherosclerosis, 1016, 1017
coarctation, **948**
hypertension and, 1027
reverse, 1040
connective tissue of, 1681
coronary artery bypass graft with, 981
counterpulsation devices, 991
dissection, **1038–39**
pain from, 19, 1039
femoral bypass graft with, 1040
inflammation. *See* Aortitis.
pulse of, 865

Pyridoxine (vitamin B₆), **413–14**
  biochemistry and action, 413–14
  deficiency, 386, **414**
  diseases responsive to, 414
  food groups and, 400
  glycol poisoning and, 845
  hyperoxaluria and, 1618
  neuropathy from, 2063
  parenteral, 407
  requirements, 385, 414
  sideroblastic anemia and, 1498
  structure, 411
  toxicity, 417
Pyrimethamine:
  malaria and, 782, 783
    prophylaxis of, 784
  toxoplasmosis and, 793, 796
Pyrimidine, genetic code and, 285
Pyrimidine-5′-nucleotidase, 1518
Pyrogens, **44–45**
  streptococcal, 544
Pyrophosphate:
  AMP and, cyclic, 371, 372
  bone mineralization and, 1858
  deposition disease (pseudogout), **1458–60**
  gout and, 1626
  infarct scintigraphy and, 887
  osteomalacia and, 1898
  synovial, 1455
Pyropoikilocytosis, hereditary, 1515
Pyrosis, 172, 1231
Pyrroloporphyria, 1640–41
Pyruvate:
  excess, 1798
  lactic acidosis and, 1798
Pyruvate carboxylase deficiency, 1802
Pyruvate kinase deficiency, 1516–17
Pyrvinium pamoate, enterobiasis and, 816
Pyuria:
  cystitis and, 1191
  etiology, 1190
  pyelonephritis and, 1192
  renal abscess and, 484
  sterile, 1142
    gonococcal infection and, 578
  toxic nephropathy and, 1197
  urethritis and, 1192
    chlamydial, 760
  in women, 509, 511

Q fever, 748, 749, **756–57,** 1078
Q wave, 873, 877
QRS complex, 873, 875–76. *See also* Electro-
    cardiography.
  intrinsicoid deflection, 875
  vector concept and, 874
QS complex, 873
QT interval, 873
QT syndrome, 934
Quadrantectomy, breast, 1570
Quadrantopia, homonymous, 74
Quadriplegia, 83
  basilar occlusion and, 1945
  management of, 2046–47
  spastic, 2032
  spinal injuries and, 1967, 1968
Quality of life, 3
  clinical reasoning and, 11
Quartz dust, 1070
Queensland tick typhus, 748, **756**
Quellung reaction, 533
Quinacrine, giardiasis and, 506, 801
Quincke's pulse, 967
Quinestrol, 1831, 1832
Quinidine:
  digitalis and, 350, 911
  dosage and metabolism, 937
  electrophysiologic effects, 928–29
  malaria and, 782–83
  plasma levels, 352

Quinidine:
  programmed stimulation and, 936
  sudden death prevention and, 160
  toxicity, 929
Quinine, malaria and, 782, 783
Quinolones, **500–1**
Quinsy, 481, 1112

R binder, gastric, 1499
R wave, 873
Rabbit fever, 613
Rabies, **712–15**
  diagnosis, 713
  etiology and epidemiology, 712
  immune globulin, 531, 714–15
  immunization, **714–15**
    encephalomyelitis from, 1999
  pathogenesis, 712–13
  treatment, 713–15
Rabson-Mendenhall syndrome, 1796
Radial nerve, 2067
  biopsy, 2056
Radiation:
  heat, 43
  immunosuppression by, bone marrow trans-
    plantation and, 1537, 1538
  injury, 445–46
    brain damage, 1973
    cancer induction, 445, 1567
    chromosomal damage, 319
    esophagitis, 1237
    infertility, 1581, 1814
    leukemia induction, 1541
    malabsorption, 1271–72
    myelopathy, 2043
    myocarditis, 1004
    nephritis, 1200
    neurotoxic, 1973
    thyroiditis, 1746
  solar. *See* Sunlight.
  therapeutic. *See* Radiotherapy.
  ultraviolet. *See* Ultraviolet light.
  units of, *Appendix 6*
Radicular pain, 34
Radiculomyeloencephalitis, 814–15
Radiculopathy:
  diabetic, 1792
  facet syndrome, 38
  multiple spondylitis caudal, 38
Radioallergosorbent technique, 1413
Radiofibrinogen test, 1105
Radiography. *See* Angiography; Roentgenogra-
    phy.
Radioimmunoassay, 460
  gastrin, 1251
  gonadotropin, 1810, 1824
  immune complexes and, 1416
  parathyroid hormone, 1867–68, 1872, **1879–
    80**
  testosterone, 1810
  thyroid hormone, 1736–37
Radioimmunosorbent test, allergic rhinitis and,
    1413
Radioisotopes:
  erythrocyte, 1507–8
  iodine:
    for prostate cancer, 1584
    thyroid ablation with, 1745, 1746, 1751
    thyroid uptake of, 1736
    for toxic goiter, 1748
  iron, 1490, 1495
  myelosuppressive, 1530, 1531
  phosphorus, polycythemia vera and, 1530,
    1531
Radionuclide studies:
  bone metastases and, 1583
  brain, 1917
  cardiac, **886–87,** 978
    infarct, 887, 984
    perfusion, 887

Radionuclide studies:
  shunts and, 886–87
  ventricular performance, 886
  fever of unknown origin and, 56
  gallbladder, 1360, 1361
  gastrointestinal hemorrhage, 1291, 1292
  hepatic, 1319
  pheochromocytoma and, 1777–78
  PIPIDA, 1228
  protein-losing enteropathy and, 1275
  pulmonary, 1058
    embolism and, 1108
    interstitial disease and, 1098
    sarcoidosis and, 1449
  thyroid gland, 1738, 1751, 1752
  venography, 1045
Radiotherapy, **440–41**
  astrocytoma, 1975
  brain, 1972
    toxic effects of, 1973
  breast cancer, 441, 1570, 1571–72
  complications, 445–46. *See also* Radiation in-
    jury.
  dosage, 440, 445
  dose-response relationship, 438, 439
  equipment for, 440
  esophageal cancer, 1237
  Hodgkin's disease, 1559–60
  hyperthermia and, 441
  kilovoltage, supervoltage, and megavoltage,
    440
  leukemia, 1545
  lung cancer, 1120–21, 1122
  lymphocytic lymphoma, 1564
  medulloblastoma, 1978
  metastases and, 444
  midline granuloma, 1453
  multimodal therapy and, 444, 445
  mycosis fungoides, 1594–95
  neurotoxicity of, 1973
  pituitary, **1712**
    acromegaly and, 1705
    Cushing's syndrome and, 1764
    prolactinoma and, 1700, 1712
  polycythemia vera and, 1530, 1531
  pregnancy and, 446
  prostate cancer, 1584
  renal transplantation and, 1168
  sensitizers to, 440–41
  vs. surgery, 441
  surgery combined with, 444
  testicular cancer, 1579–80
Radium therapy of cancer, 440
Raeder's paratrigeminal syndrome, 32
Raffinose, flatulence and, 173, 180
Raji cell assay, 1416
Rales:
  heart failure and, 908
  interstitial lung disease and, 1098
  respiratory distress and, 1135
Ramsay Hunt syndrome, 690, 2038
Ranitidine:
  drug metabolism inhibited by, 350
  gastrinoma and, 1252
  peptic ulcer and, 1245, 1246
  structure of, 1244
Raphe magnus, pain and, 14
Raphe nuclei, cerebellar projections of, 92
Rash, **240–44**. *See also* Erythema.
  angioimmunoblastic lymphadenopathy and,
    1565
  arbovirus infection, 721–23
  arthritis and, 1465
  Boston, 686
  boutonneuse fever, 756
  caterpillar, 836
  chickenpox, 690, 691
  course of, 241–42
  dengue fever, 722
  dermatomyositis, 2070